D0131464

# ORIGINS

# ORIGINS

## A SHORT
## ETYMOLOGICAL DICTIONARY
## OF MODERN ENGLISH

*by*

## ERIC PARTRIDGE

GREENWICH HOUSE
*Distributed by Crown Publishers, Inc.*
NEW YORK

Copyright © MCMLVIII, MCMLIX, MCMLXI, MCMLXVI by Eric Partridge
All rights reserved.

This 1983 edition is published by Greenwich House, a division of Arlington House, Inc.,
distributed by Crown Publishers, Inc., 225 Park Avenue South, New York, New York
10003, by arrangement with Macmillan Publishing Company

Manufactured in the United States of America

This edition for sale only in the United States;
its territories and possessions and the Philippine Republic.

ISBN: 0-517-414252

l  k  j  i

*piam in memoriam*

CECIL ARTHUR FRANKLIN
a kindly and generous man
and a remarkable publisher

Philologists who chase
A panting syllable through time and space,
Start it at home, and hunt it in the dark,
To Gaul, to Greece, and into Noah's Ark.
Cowper, *Retirement*

# CONTENTS

# FOREWORD

PROFESSOR W. W. SKEAT'S large and small etymological dictionaries were last revised in 1910; Ernest Weekley's *Concise Etymological Dictionary* and Ferdinand Holthausen's *Etymologisches Wörterbuch der englischen Sprache*, both excellent in their way, treat words so briefly and ignore ramifications so wholeheartedly that it was easy to plan a work entirely different—a remark that applies equally to Skeat's *Concise* and, for relationships, almost as much to his larger book.

'Exigencies of space'—not always a myth, nor always a mere excuse for laziness —preclude a large vocabulary. The number of entries in *Origins* is comparatively small, even for an etymological dictionary, but the system I have devised has enabled me, with the aid of cross-references, not only to cover a very much wider field than might have seemed possible but also, and especially, to treat all important words much more comprehensively and thoroughly. I have concentrated upon civilization rather than upon science and technology; dialect and cant have been ignored; slang is represented only by a very few outstanding examples (e.g., *phoney*).

On the other hand, I have included a certain number of words not usually found in a small British etymological dictionary: words that, little known in Britain, form part of the common currency of Standard English as it is spoken and written in the United States of America, Canada, South Africa, Australia, New Zealand, India and Pakistan.

One class of words has deliberately been treated very meagrely: such exotics as do not fall into the classification 'Americanisms'—'Australianisms'—etc. It does not much help the searcher to be told that *llama* has been adopted—that is, accepted unchanged—from Quechuan, or *okapi* from Bambulan (Mbuba); only a little more does it help him to learn that *cassowary* has been adapted from Malayan *kasuari*. For Amerindian, Australian aboriginal, Maori, Hindi and similar words, I have, wherever possible, avoided the baldness and inadequacy of such entries as '*kangaroo*. Australian aboriginal word' or '*pakeha*. Maori for a white man'.

In a book of this size a certain number of abbreviations is unavoidable. These abbreviations will not impede the easy flow of the consecutive English I hold to be indispensable in a book designed for the use of the general intelligent public as well as for that of the erudite. Nor, I hope, will scholars and students find readability a defect; after all, a work is not necessarily the more scholarly for being written in philological shorthand. Where, however, the conventions of lexicography make for clarity and simplicity, I have followed most of these conventions: and where either extremely brief etymologies or multiple cognates and complex histories occur, I have employed a brevity hardly less austere than compact. This combination of consecutiveness and terseness should prevent the treatment from becoming too deadly monotonous.

Warmest thanks are due, both to Professor John W. Clark, of the University of Minnesota, for help in choosing terms important in the United States of America, yet little known in Britain and the British Dominions, and to Professor D. Winton Thomas for occasional help in Semitic origins.

ERIC PARTRIDGE

*Postscript to the second edition.* I have to thank Professors John W. Clark, Norman Davis, Simeon Potter, for some valuable notifications and corrections.

*Postscript to the third edition.* I owe much to Professors John W. Clark, Norman Davis, Simeon Potter and especially R. M. Wilson; and something to Mr R. W. Burchfield (by salutary indirection)—Dr A. J. R. Green—Professor Mario Pei—Mr Stephen Potter—and Mr T. Skaug of Oslo. All these gentlemen have been most generous: I can only hope that the third edition approaches their ideals a little more closely than did the first: it leaves me a shade less dissatisfied than I was.

*Postscript to the fourth edition.* In addition to several correspondents telling me of this or that printers' error, I have to thank especially Professor Ralph W. V. Elliott of the University of Adelaide, for both corrections and suggestions; Professor Yoshio Terasawa (of Tokyo City University), whose corrections largely duplicate Professor Elliott's; also Dr Nicola Cerri, Jr, of Maryland. It is difficult to thank at all adequately all the persons concerned, but I can at least assure them that I am most grateful.

# HOW TO USE THIS DICTIONARY

An etymological dictionary supplies neither pronunciations nor definitions. Here, pronunciation is indicated only where it affects the origin or the development of a word; and definitions only where, in little-known words, they are necessary to an understanding of the problem. Wherever the meaning of a word has notably changed, the sense-transformation is explained, as, for instance, in *knave*, *marshal*, *phoney*, adjectival *rum*: here we enter the domain of semantics, the science of meanings, for semantics will sometimes resolve an otherwise insoluble problem.

If the reader intends to use this book extensively and even if he intends merely to consult it occasionally, he will spare himself much time and trouble if he previously familiarizes himself with the list of abbreviations immediately preceding the dictionary proper.

If he wishes to be in a position to understand words in their fullest implications and subtleties, in their nuances and most delicate modifications, he will do well to study the list of suffixes and then the little less important list of prefixes; lists that are themselves etymological. By the way, the prefixes and suffixes are my own idea; the list of compound-forming elements (this list, too, is etymological), that of an eminent and humane, practical yet imaginative French philologist, the late M. Albert Dauzat. Like his, my list is confined to learnèd elements: where he omits such elements as, in the fact, are self-contained French words, I omit such elements as are English words recorded in the dictionary itself. My list, however, is more than twice as long as his and, in treatment, much more spacious, for *Origins* differs considerably from the *Dictionnaire étymologique de la langue française*.

This list of compound-forming elements will enable inquirers to ascertain the etymology of most of the innumerable learnèd words—scientific and technical, philosophical and psychological, economic and sociological, linguistic and literary —missing from the dictionary; these are specialist terms. Take, for example, *Calyptorhynchus*, a genus of dark-coloured cockatoos: such a word has no right to appear in an etymological dictionary and no privilege to appear in any 'straight' dictionary other than one of the Universal Stores class. Yet the list of elements will reveal that the word is compounded of *calypto-*, meaning 'covered', hence 'hidden', and *-rhynchus*, 'beak'.

Having assimilated the table of abbreviations and the lists of Prefixes, Suffixes, Elements, inquirers will find consultation easy and reading unimpeded. The cross-references will present no difficulty, for if one word is to be sought at another, as for instance *erg* at *work*, and if the latter entry be at all long, the long entry is divided into numbered paragraphs.

'See WORK' would mean 'See that word in the Dictionary'. If the dictionary contains any such references as 'See *para-*'—'See *-ace*'—'See *calypto-*', the application is clearly to *para-* in Prefixes, *-ace* in Suffixes, *calypto-* in Elements. If the reference happens to be double, as in 'See PSEUDO and *pseudo-*', the application would be to the former in the dictionary and to the latter in Elements.

All words belonging to alphabets other than 'English'—to Greek, Russian, Egyptian, for instance—have been transliterated. The transliteration of Greek words, in particular, has been more exact than in several dictionaries one might, but does not, name. I have, for $\chi$, preferred *kh* to *ch*, and represented $\gamma\gamma$ as *ng*, $\gamma\kappa$ as *nk*, $\gamma\xi$ as *nx*, $\gamma\chi$ as *nkh*. In pre-Medieval Latin words I have retained *i* and *u*, as in *Iulius*, ML *Julius*, and *uinum*, ML *vinum*, for reasons too obvious to be enumerated. Long Greek and Latin vowels have been shown as long. I have, however, omitted that over the final *-ī* of Latin passives and deponents.

# ABBREVIATIONS[1]

*(including those for the most frequently cited authorities)*

| | | | |
|---|---|---|---|
| A or Am | American (U.S.A.) | b/f | back-formation (from) |
| abbr | abbreviation of; abbreviated (to) | Bio | Biology, biological |
| abl | ablative | Boisacq | Emile Boisacq, *Dictionnaire étymolo-* |
| acc | accusative (or objective) case | | *gique de la langue grecque*, 4th ed., |
| A.D. | *Anno Domini*, in the year of (our) | | 1950 |
| | Lord | Bot | Botany, botanical |
| adj | adjective, adjectival | Br | Breton |
| adv | adverb, adverbial | Bu | Bantu |
| AE | American English | Buck | Carl Darling Buck, *A Dictionary of* |
| Aer | Aeronautics, aeronautical | | *Selected Synonyms in the Principal* |
| AF | Anglo-French | | *European Languages*, 1949 |
| Afr | Afrikaans | Byz Gr | Byzantine Greek |
| AIr | Anglo-Irish | | |
| Akk | Akkadian | C | Celtic |
| AL | Anglo-Latin (= Medieval Latin as | c | *circa*, about (in dates) |
| | used in Britain) | C16, 17 | 16th (etc.) Century; CC16–17, 16th– |
| Alb | Albanian | | 17th Centuries |
| Alg | Algonquin | CA | Central America(n) |
| Am | American | Can | Canadian |
| Amerind | American Indian | Cat | Catalan |
| AmF | American French | caus | causative |
| An | Anatomy, anatomical | cf | *confer*, compare! |
| anl | analogous, analogously, analogy | c/f | combining-form; pl: c/ff |
| app | apparently | c/f e | compound-forming element |
| approx | approximately | Ch | Chinese |
| Ar | Arabic | Chem | Chemistry, chemical |
| Aram | Aramaic | Clark | John W. Clark (private communica- |
| Arch | Architecture, architectural | | tion) |
| Arm | Armenian | Class | Classical (Greek, Latin) |
| AS | Anglo-Saxon | coll | colloquial, -ism, -ly |
| ASp | American Spanish | comb | combination, combiner |
| Ass | Assyrian | comp | comparative |
| Astr | Astronomy, astronomical | cond | conditional (mood) |
| aug | augmentative | conj | conjunction, conjunctive |
| Aus | Australia, Australian | conjug | conjugation |
| Av | Avestic (or Zend) | conn | connotation |
| | | cons | consonant, consonantal |
| B | British | contr | contracted, contraction |
| Bab | Babylonian, Babylonish | Cor | Cornish |
| Bact | Bacteriology, bacteriological | corresp | corresponding |
| Baker | Sidney J. Baker, *The Australian* | cpd | compound |
| | *Language*, 1945 | Craigie | Sir William Craigie, *A Dictionary of* |
| B & W | O. Bloch and W. von Wartburg, | | *the Older Scottish Tongue*, 1931– |
| | *Dictionnaire étymologique de la* | Cz | Czechoslovak |
| | *langue française*, 2nd ed., 1950 | | |
| B.C. | Before Christ | D | Dutch |
| BE | British English | Da | Danish |

[1] Except for A.D. and B.C., and for *e.g.*, *f.a.e.*, *i.e.*, *o.o.o.*, *q.v.* and *s.f.*, the very modern practice of using as few points (periods, full stops) as possible has been followed. In philology, OHG, MLG, ONF, etc.—not O.H.G., etc.—have long been usual; I have merely extended the practice to, e.g., *n* for noun.

| | |
|---|---|
| DAE | *A Dictionary of American English*, edited by W. A. Craigie and J. R. Hulbert, 1936–44 |
| DAF | R. Grandsaignes d'Hauterive, *Dictionnaire d'ancien français*, 1947 |
| dat | dative |
| Dauzat | Albert Dauzat, *Dictionnaire étymologique de la langue française*, edition of 1947 |
| dial | dialect, -al, -ally |
| Dict | (this) dictionary; dict (pl dictt), any dictionary |
| dim | diminutive |
| E | English |
| E & M | A. Ernout and A. Meillet, *Dictionnaire étymologique de la langue latine*, 3rd ed., 1951 |
| Eccl | Ecclesiastics, ecclesiastic(al) |
| ED | Early Modern Dutch |
| EDD | Joseph Wright, *The English Dialect Dictionary*, 1896–1905 |
| EE | Early Modern English ⎫ 1500– |
| EF | Early Modern French ⎭ 1700 |
| Eg | Egyptian |
| EgAr | Egyptian Arabic |
| e.g. | *exempli gratia*, for example |
| EI | East Indian, East Indies |
| Ekwall | B. O. E. Ekwall, *The Concise Oxford Dictionary of English Place-Names*, 4th ed., 1958 |
| El | Electricity |
| Enci It | *Enciclopedia Italiana* |
| Eng | Engineering |
| Ent | Entomology, entomological |
| esp | especially |
| etc. | et cetera |
| etym | etymology, etymological(ly) |
| euphem | euphemism, euphemistic(ally) |
| EW | Ernest Weekley, *Concise Etymological Dictionary*, 2nd ed., 1952 |
| Ex | example; Exx: examples |
| extn | extension |
| F | French |
| f | feminine |
| f.a.e. | for anterior etymology |
| f/e | folk-etymology or -etymological(ly) |
| Feist | Sigmund Feist, *Vergleichendes Wörterbuch der gotischen Sprache*, 3rd ed., 1939 |
| fig | figurative(ly) |
| Fin | Finnish |
| Fl | Flemish |
| fl | flourished (lived) |
| foll | following |
| fpl | feminine plural |
| freq | frequentative |
| Fris | Frisian |
| fs | feminine singular |
| FU | Finno-Ugric |
| G | German |

| | |
|---|---|
| Ga | Gaelic |
| Gaul | Gaulish |
| gen | genitive (possessive case) |
| Geog | Geography, geographical |
| Geol | Geology, geological |
| Geom | Geometry, geometrical |
| Gmc | Germanic |
| Go | Gothic |
| Gr | Greek |
| Gram; gram | Grammar; grammatical |
| H | Hebrew |
| Ham | Hamitic |
| Hell | Hellenistic |
| Her | Heraldry, heraldic |
| HG | High German |
| Hi | Hindi |
| Hind | Hindustani |
| hist | historic(al) |
| Hit | Hittite |
| Hofmann | J. B. Hofmann, *Etymologisches Wörterbuch des Griechischen*, 1950 |
| Holthausen | Ferdinand Holthausen, *Wörterbuch des Altwestnordischen*, 1948 |
| Holthausen[1] | F. Holthausen, *Altfriesisches Wörterbuch*, 1925 |
| Holthausen[2] | F. Holthausen, *Etymologisches Wörterbuch der englischen Sprache*, 3rd ed. |
| Hung or Hu | Hungarian |
| ibid | *ibidem*, in the same place |
| Ice | Icelandic |
| Ich | Ichthyology |
| id | *idem*, the same; identical |
| IE | Indo-European |
| i.e. | *id est*, that is |
| illit | illiterate, illiterately |
| imm | immediately |
| imp | imperative (mood) |
| impf | imperfect (tense) |
| inch | inchoative |
| incl | included, including, inclusion |
| ind | indicative (mood) |
| inf | infinitive (mood), infinitival |
| instr | instrument, instrumental |
| int | intensive, intensively |
| interj | interjection, interjective(ly) |
| Ir | Irish |
| irreg | irregular, irregularly |
| It | Italian |
| J or Jap | Japanese |
| Jav | Javanese |
| joc | jocular(ly) |
| Kluge | Kluge-Götze, *Etymologisches Wörterbuch der deutschen Sprache*, 14th ed., 1948 |
| L | Latin |

| | | | |
|---|---|---|---|
| L & S | Liddell and Scott, *A Greek-English Lexicon*, in H. Stuart Jones's recension, 1925–40 | neu | neuter; neupl: neuter plural; neus: neuter singular |
| l.c. | *locus citatus*, the passage (or book) quoted | NL | New Latin, especially Modern Scientific Latin |
| Lett | Lettish (Latvian) | nom | nominative (subjective case) |
| LG | Low German | Nor | Norwegian |
| LGr | Late Greek | NT | (The) New Testament |
| LH | Late Hebrew | NZ | New Zealand |
| lit | literal, literally | O | Old |
| Lith | Lithuanian | OB | Old Bulgarian (=Old Church Slavic) |
| LL | Late Latin (c A.D. 180–600) | | |
| loc | locative (case) | OBr | Old Breton |
| | | obs | obsolete |
| | | obsol | obsolescent |
| m | masculine | OC | Old Celtic |
| MacLennan | Malcolm MacLennan, *A Dictionary of the Gaelic Language*, 1925 | occ | occasional, occasionally |
| | | OE | Old English |
| Mal | Malayan | OED | *The Oxford English Dictionary* |
| Malvezin | Pierre Malvezin, *Dictionnaire des racines celtiques*, 2nd ed., 1924 | OF | Old French |
| | | OFris | Old Frisian |
| Malvezin[1] | P. Malvezin, *Dictionnaire complétif du latin*, 1925 | OGmc | Old Germanic |
| | | OHG | Old High German |
| MAr | Medieval Arabic | OIr | Old Irish |
| Math | Mathematics, mathematical | OIt | Old Italian (Middle Ages) |
| Mathews | Mitford M. Mathews, *A Dictionary of Americanisms*, 1951 | OL | Old Latin |
| | | OLG | Old Low German |
| MBr | Medieval Breton | ON | Old Norse |
| MD | Medieval Dutch | ONF | Old Northern French |
| mdfn | modification | o.o.o. | of obscure origin |
| ME | Middle English | OP | Old Prussian |
| Med | Medicine, medical | OPer | Old Persian |
| Medit | Mediterranean | opp | opposite (adj, n): opposed to |
| Mencken | H. L. Mencken, *The American Language*, 4th ed., 1936; *Supplement One*, 1945, and *Two*, 1948 | OProv | Old Provençal |
| | | orig | original, originally |
| | | Orn | Ornithology, ornithological |
| Met | meteorology, -ological | OS | Old Saxon |
| MF | Medieval French (CC13–15) | o/s | oblique stem |
| MGr | Medieval Greek | OSl | Old Slavic |
| MHG | Middle High German | OSp | Old Spanish |
| Min | Mineralogy, mineralogical | OSw | Old Swedish |
| MIr | Middle Irish | OT | (The) Old Testament |
| mispron: | mispronounced, mispronunciation | OW | Old Welsh |
| ML | Medieval Latin | | |
| MLG | Middle Low German | P | Eric Partridge, *A Dictionary of Slang and Unconventional English*, 4th ed., 1950 |
| Mod, mod: | modern, as in Mod E, Modern English | | |
| Morris | E. E. Morris, *Austral English*, 1898 | P[1] | E.P., *A Dictionary of the Underworld*, 1950 |
| mpl | masculine plural | | |
| ms | masculine singular | P[2] | E.P., *Name into Word*, 2nd ed., 1950 |
| MSc | Middle Scots | | |
| Mus | Music, musical | P[3] | E.P., *Here, There and Everywhere*, 2nd ed., 1950 |
| MW | Middle Welsh | | |
| Myth | Mythology, mythological | P[4] | E.P., *From Sanskrit to Brazil*, 1952 |
| Mx | Manx | pa | participial adjective |
| | | Pal | Palaeography, palaeographical |
| N | north, northern | para | paragraph |
| n | noun | PC | Primitive Celtic |
| NA | North America, N American | pej | pejorative, -ly |
| naut | nautical | Per | Persian |
| Nav | the (Royal) Navy, naval; navigation(al) | perh | perhaps |
| | | Pettman: | C. Pettman, *Africanderisms*, 1913 |
| neg | negative, negatively | PGmc | Primitive Germanic |

| | | | |
|---|---|---|---|
| PGr | Primitive Greek | s.f. | *sub finem*, near the end |
| Pharm | Pharmacy, pharmaceutical | sing | singular; in the singular |
| Phil | Philosophy, philosophical | Skeat | W. W. Skeat, *An Etymological Dictionary of the English Language*, 4th ed., 1910 |
| phon | phonetic, phonetically, phonetics | | |
| Phys | Physics | | |
| Physio | Physiology, physiologica | Skt | Sanskrit |
| PL | Primitive Latin | Sl | Slavonic |
| pl | plural | sl | slang |
| PlN | place-name | Slov | Slovene |
| PN | personal name | Sophocles | E. A. Sophocles, *Greek Lexicon of the Roman and Byzantine Periods* (146 B.C.–A.D. 1100), ed. of 1893 |
| Pol | Polish | | |
| Poly | Polynesian | | |
| pop | popular (speech) | Souter | A. Souter, *A Glossary of Later Latin*, 1949 |
| Port | Portuguese | | |
| pos | positive | Sp | Spanish |
| pp | past participle | spec | specialized |
| pps | past-participial stem | subj | subjunctive |
| Prati | Angelico Prati, *Vocabolario etimologico italiano*, 1951 | sup | superlative |
| | | Surg | surgery, surgical |
| prec | preceding | Sw | Swedish |
| prep | preposition(al) | syn | synonym; synonymous |
| pres inf | present infinitive | | |
| presp | present participle | T | Technics, Technology; technical, technological; technicality |
| presp o/s | present-participial oblique stem | | |
| prob | probable, probably | taut | tautological(ly), tautology |
| pron | pronounced (as), pronunciation | tech | (a) technical (term) |
| prop | properly, strictly | Theo | Theology, theological |
| Prov | Provençal | Tokh | Tokharian |
| Psy | Psychology, psychological | Topo | Topography, topographical |
| Psychi | Psychiatry, psychiatrical | Torp: | Alf Torp, *Nynorsk Etymologisk Ordbok*, 1919 |
| pt | past tense (preterite) | | |
| | | trans | translated, translation |
| q.v. | *quod vide*, which see! (Plural references: qq.v.) | Tregear | Edward Tregear, *The Maori-Polynesian Comparative Dictionary*, 1891 |
| | | trld; trln | transliterated; transliteration |
| | | Tu | Turkish |
| R | Romance (language or languages) | | |
| r | root | ult | ultimate, ultimately |
| redup | reduplication | usu | usually |
| ref | reference; in or with reference to | | |
| reg | regular(ly) | v | verb |
| resp | respective, respectively | var | variant |
| Rom | Romany | Ve | Vedic |
| Ru | Russian | vi | verb intransitive |
| Rum | Rumanian | viz | to wit |
| | | VL | Vulgar (or Low) Latin |
| S | south, southern | vn | verbal noun |
| s | stem | vr | verb reflexive |
| SAE | Standard American English | vt | verb transitive |
| SAfr | South Africa, S. African | | |
| SAm | South America, S. American | W | Welsh |
| Santamaria | F. J. Santamaria, *Diccionario de Americanismos*, 1942 | Walde | A. Walde and J. B. Hofmann, *Lateinisches etymologisches Wörterbuch*, 3rd ed., 1938–56 |
| Sc | Scots, Scottish | | |
| sc | *scite*, understand! or supply! | Walshe | M. O'C. Walshe, *A Concise German Etymological Dictionary*, 1952 |
| Scan | Scandinavian | | |
| Sci | Science, scientific | Webster | *Webster's New International Dictionary*, 2nd ed., 1934, impressions of 1945 and later |
| SciL | Scientific Latin | | |
| SE | Standard English | | |
| Sem | Semitic | Whitehall | Harold Whitehall in *Webster's New World Dictionary*, College Edition, 1953 |
| sem | semantics, semantic(ally) | | |
| sep | separate, separately (treated) | | |

WI      West Indian, West Indies

Y & B      H. Yule and A. C. Burnell, *Hobson-Jobson*, revised by W. Crooke, 1903

Zoo      Zoology, zoological

\* before a word indicates a presumed word, or form of a word, or sense

= equal(s); is, or are, equivalent to; equivalent to

+ (in compounds and blends) and

† died; e.g., '† 1792'—died in 1792

# A

**a**, indefinite article. See ONE.

**aback.** See BACK.

**abaft.** See AFT, para 2.

**abandon** comes, in ME, from OF *abandoner* (whence *abandonement*, whence E *abandonment*), itself from the n *abandon*, arising from the phrase (*mettre* or *laisser*) *a bandon*, in(to) the power (of someone): *a*, Mod *à*, from L *ad*, to+*bandon* (cf Norman *banon*), power or authority, from *ban*, a sovereign's proclamation within his jurisdiction. Cf BAN.

**abase**: late ME *abeese*, *abasse*: OF *abaissier* (F *abaisser*): *a*, to+*baissier*, to lower, from VL *\*bassiāre*, from *bassus*, low: cf the adj BASE. *Abasement*: prompted by F *abaissement*, but from *abase*+suffix *-ment*.

**abash**: ME *abashen*, earlier *abaisshen*, earliest *abaissen*: OF *esbair*, *esbahir* (F *ébahir*), to astound: formed either of *es*, from L *ex*, out (of)+*bah!* (astonishment)+inf suffix *-ir*, hence lit 'to get a *bah* out of someone', or, more prob, of *es*+*baer* (Mod *bayer*), to bay, influenced by *baïf*, astounded (B & W): cf 'to BAY'. *Abashment*: OF *esbahissement*, from *esbahir*, influenced by *abaissier* (see ABASE). Cf ABEYANCE.

**abate**; **abatement.** See BATE. (Cf *debate*, *combat*, *rebate*.) Cf the 2nd BAT, para 3.

**abattoir.** See BATE. Cf the 2nd BAT, para 3.

**abbé, abbot, abbess; abbey, abbacy.**
The descent is from Aramaic *abbā*, father, thus: post-Class Gr ἀββᾶ (*abba*), indeclinable; ἀββᾶς, *abbas* (gen *abbados*), 'reverend father', abbot:

I. LL *Abba*, 'God the Father'; LL *abbās* (gen *abbātis*), abbot: LL acc *abbātem*, OF *abet*, *abe*, F *abbé*: LL o/s *abbāt-*, OE *abbad*, *abbod*—whence E *abbot*:

II. LL *abbātissa* (from *abbāt-*, o/s of LL *abbās*)— OF *abaesse*, *abbesse*—whence E *abbess*:

III. ML *abbātia* (same origin), monastery, convent, headed by an abbot or an abbess, hence an abbot's office or dignity—whence E *abbacy*; and, from the basic LL sense, OF *abaie*, *abeie* (F *abbaye*), whence E *abbey*; the derivative ML adj *abbātialis* yields *abbatial*.

**abbreviate.** See ADDENDA TO DICTIONARY.

**abdicate, abdication.** See DICT, para 8.

**abdomen; abdominal.**
L *abdōmen*, o.o.o., perh derives from *abdere* (*ab*+*dare*), to put away, aside, at a distance, hence to cover or hide. The basic sense of *dare*, to give, has been lost in the cpds, which take on that of the IE r *\*dhe-*, to place. *Abdominal*: *abdomin-*, o/s of *abdōmen*+adj suffix *-al*. Cf the element *abdomino-*.

**abduct, abduction, abductor.** See DUKE, para 6.

**aberrant, aberration.** See ERR, para 2.

**abet, abettor.** See BAIT.

**abeyance** is an AF word deriving from MF-EF *abeance*, expectation, from MF-EF *abeer*: *a* (mod *à*), to+*baer*, *beer*, to gape (at): cf ABASH and esp BAY, v. Basic idea: hope deferred, pointless expectation.

**abhor, abhorrence, abhorrent.** See HEARSE, para 7.

**abide.** See BIDE, para 2.

**ability.** See HABIT, para 5.

**abject, abjection**: f.a.e. JET.—Imm from L *abiectus* (ML *abj-*), pp of *abi(i)cere*, to throw away, and from the derivative *abiectio*, o/s *abiection-* (ML *abj-*).

**abjure, abjurement** or **abjuration.** Cf CONJURE, but see JURY, n, para 4.

**ablation, ablative.** See the 1st TOLL, para 6.

**ablaut.** See LOUD, para 3.

**ablaze**: *on*, in+BLAZE.

**able; ability.** See HABIT, para 5.

**abluent, ablution.** See LAVA, para 9.

**abnegate, abnegation.** See NEGATE, para 2.

**abnormal, abnormality.** See NORM, para 3.

**Abo, abo.** See ORIGIN, para 6.

**aboard.** See BOARD.

**abode.** See BIDE, para 3.

**abolish, abolishment, abolition** (-ism, -ist): 1st, via *abolissant*, pres p, or (*nous*) *abolissons*, we abolish, from late MF-F *abolir*, to abolish—cf *perish* from F *périr*—from L *abolēre*, to destroy, to abolish, perh ex *abolescere*, to perish (*ab*, away, (hence) not+*alescere*, to nourish, cf ALIMENT); 2nd either=*abolish*+suffix *-ment* or, more prob, derives from F *abolissement*; 3rd, *abolition* (whence *abolitionism*, *abolitionist*: cf the suffixes *-ism*, *-ist*): adopted from late MF-F, which took it from *abolitiōnem*, the acc of L *abolitiō*, itself from *abolitus*, pp of *abolēre*.

**abominable; abominate, abomination.** See OMEN, para 2.

**aboriginal, aborigine.** See ORIGIN, para 6.

**abort, abortion, abortive.** See ORIGIN, para 4.

**abound.** See UNDA, para 4.

**about**: ME *aboute*, earlier *abouten*, earliest *abuten*: OE *ābūtan*, for *onbūtan*, on the outside of:

1

*on+būtan*, outside, itself contracting *be*, by+*ūtan*, outside, itself deriving from *ūt*, out: cf therefore ON, BY, OUT. Adv from prep. Cf:

**above**: ME *above*, earlier *aboven*: late OE *abufan*: *a*, on+*bufan*, above, itself contracting *be*, by+*ufan*, above: cf therefore ON, BY, OVER. Prep very soon from adv. Cf. prec.

**abracadabra**: o.o.o., it is explained either (in B & W) as the LL transcription of Gr ἀβϱαcάδαβϱα (*abrasadabra*, where *c*=*s* but was read as *k*), the whole being an elaboration of LL (Church Fathers') *Abraxas*, for Basilides the Gnostic's *'Aβϱασάξ*, *Abrasax*, the Lord of Heaven—'The numerical value of this figment is 365, the number of days in the year' (Sophocles)—found on amulets; or else (in Webster) as L *abracadabra* from Aram *abhadda kĕdābrah*, 'Disappear (O sickness) as this word'—*abracadabra* written as a diagram resting finally on the initial *a*.

**abrade, abrasion, abrasive**. See RASE, para 1.

**abrasax, abraxas**. A charm, an amulet. See ABRACADABRA.

**abreast**. See BREAST.

**abridge, abridgement**.

The latter comes from MF-EF *abregement*, from OF-MF *abregier* (F *abréger*), from ML *abbreviāre*, from L *abbreuiāre*: *ab*-, either the assimilation (to *b*) of *ad*, to, or, more prob, *ab*, from, in nuance 'off'+*breuiāre*, to shorten, from *breuis*, short: cf BRIEF. OF *abregier* yields ME *abregen*, whence 'to *abridge*'.

**abroad**. See BROAD.

**abrogate, abrogation, abrogator**. See ROGATION, para 3.

**abrupt, abruption, abruptness**. See RUPTURE, para 3.

**abscess**: L *abscessus*, a departure, a gathering (esp of bad matter), an abscess. See CEDE.

**abscissa, abscind, abscission**. See the 2nd SHED, para 4.

**abscond**. See RECONDITE, para 1.

**absence; absent**. See ESSE, para 5.

**absinthe** (occ AE **absinth**): EF-F *absinthe*: reshaped from OF-EF *absince*: L *absinthium*: Gr *apsinthion*, wormwood, from OPer. The v *absinthiate*, to treat or impregnate with wormwood, comes from the LL pa *absinthiātus*, flavoured with wormwood.

**absolute, absolution, absolve**. See LOSE, para 5.

**absonant**. See SONABLE, para 5.

**absorb; absorbent (absorbency); absorption; absorptive.**

'To *absorb*' comes (perh via MF-F *absorber*) from L *absorbēre*: *ab*, away+*sorbēre* (s *sorb*-), to suck in or up, akin to Gr *rhophein* (s *rhoph*-) to swallow—cf Ionic *rhuphein*; to Lith *suŕbti* (s *surb*-), to suck, *srĕbti*, to sip, lap up; to MIr *srub*, snout (esp a pig's), and Ga *srubadh*, to suck, and *sruab*, to drink with smacking lips.

*Absorbent* (whence, via suffix -*cy*, *absorbency*): *absorbent*-, o/s of L *absorbens*, presp of *absorbēre*.

*Absorption*: *absorption*-, o/s of L *absorptiō*, formed from *absorpt*-, the s of *absorptus*, pp of

*absorbēre*; *absorpt*- yields also *absorptive* (cf suffix -*ive*), as if from ML *\*absorptivus*.

**abstain, abstainer**. See TENABLE, para 5.

**abstemious**: L *abstēmius*: *abs*, var of *ab*, (away) from+the r (*tem*-) of *tēmētum*, potent liquor, perh akin to Skt *tāmyati* (s *tam*-), he is dazed or dumbfounded.

**abstention; abstinence, abstinent**. See TENABLE, para 5.

**abstergent, abstersion**. See TERSE, para 2.

**abstract, abstraction, abstractive**. See TRACT, para 10.

**abstruse**. See THRUST, para 2.

**absurd, absurdity**. See SURD, para 3.

**abundance, abundant**. See UNDA, para 4.

**abuse**, n and v; **abusive**. See USE, para 9.

**abut, abutment, abuttal**. See BUTT, to push or strike with the head.

**abysm, abysmal; abyss, abyssal.**

Both adjj simply tack the suffix -*al* to the nn; *abysm* derives from OF-MF *abisme* (F *abîme*), LL *\*abismus* (by influence of suffix -*ismus*, cf. -*ism*), from LL *abyssus* (whence E *abyss*), bottomless gulf or pit, itself from Gr *abussos*, bottomless: *a*-, not+*bussos*, bottom or depth, akin to *buthos*, bottom (of the sea), itself prob akin to *bathos*, depth, and *bathus*, deep, qq.v. at BATHOS.

**acacia**: L *acacia*: Gr *akakia*, very prob from Egyptian, the name being orig applied to a thorny Egyptian tree or shrub: cf Gr *akakalis*, the seed(s) of the Egyptian tamarisk, with influence from the IE r *ak*-, sharp, (hence) thorny. (Boisacq.) Chem *acacetin* and *acacin*=acacia+*acetin* (cf ACID) and *acacia*+Chem suffix -*in*.

**Academe, academy, academic(al), academician, academicism** or **academism.**

The development is natural and easy: the Gr hero *Akadēmos* (L *Acadēmus*), orig *Hekadēmos*, gave his name to *Akadēmeia* (orig a f adj), orig *Hekadēmeia*, that gymnasium in a suburb of Athens where Plato taught, hence (*akadēmeia*) a place of superior learning, the L form *acadēmia* yielding, via F *académie*, the E *academy* and the now literary *academe*; the Gr adj *Akadēmeikos*, hence *akadēmeikos*, became L *acadēmicus*, became alike F *académique* and E *academic* (adj, hence also n), with elaboration *academical* (adj suffix -*al*). *Academism*=*academy*+-*ism*; *academicism*= *academic*+-*ism*. *Academician* derives from F *académicien*, which=L *acadēmic(us)*+suffix -*ien* (cf the suffix -*ian*).

**acajou**. See CASHEW.

**acanth, acanthus, acanthine; acantha**; cf the element **acantho-**.

*Acanth* anglicizes *acanthus*, the L trln (whence the adj *acanthīnus*, whence E *acanthine*) of Gr *akanthos*, a herb with spiny flowers, itself from *akantha*, a thorn or prickle (Webster): ? perhaps rather *akantha* from *akanthos*, lit 'spine flower': *akē*, a point+*anthos*, a flower. Cf ACUTE.

**acariform; acaroid**. See element *acari*-, *acaro*-.

**acaulous**. See CAUL.

**accede**, whence **accedence** (suffix -*ence*); **access;**

**accessary,** from **accessory; accessible; accession:** resp, L *accēdere* (supine *accessum,* s *access-*), to move towards, to approach, *ad,* to+*cēdere* (s *ced-*), to move, cf CEDE; *access,* L *accessus,* from *accedere; accessary,* an *-ary* (as in *necessary*) var of *accessory* (adj, hence n), itself from ML *accessōrius,* from *accessus; accessible,* from LL *accessibilis,* approachable, from *accedere*—cf the suffix *-ible; accession,* from *accession-,* o/s of L *accessiō,* an approach, from the pp (*accessus*) of *accedere.*
Cf CONCEDE, PRECEDE, RECEDE; PROCEED, SUCCEED; ABSCESS.

**accelerate, acceleration, accelerative, accelerator;** f.a.e.: CELERITY. Imm from L *accelerātus,* pp of *accelerāre,* to cause to go faster; EF-F *accélération* and EF-F *accélérateur,* both from EF-F *accélérer* (from L *accelerāre*); the 3rd term, anl from 'to *accelerate*'.

**accent** (n, hence v); **accentor, accentual; accentuate,** whence **accentuator; accentuation.**
The effective origin resides in L *canere* (s *can-*), to sing: cf CANTO. Resp, *accent,* adopted from MF-F, from L *accentus* (*ad,* to+*cantus,* a singing, a song), from *canere; accentor,* adopted from L (*ad*+*cantor,* a singer, from *canere*); *accentual*= *accent*+*-ual* (cf the *-ual* of *gradual* in relation to *arade*); *accentuate,* ML *accentuātus,* pp of *accentuāre,* from *accentus; accentuation,* adopted from EF-F, from *accentuātiōn-,* o/s of ML *accentuātiō,* from *accentuāre.*

**accept, acceptable, acceptance, acceptant; acceptation—acception; acceptive, acceptor.**
Here we have two groups: first, the derivatives, via F, from L *acceptāre* (s *accept-*), the freq of *accipere,* to receive, whence, via the pp *acceptus* or its s *accept-,* the second group, *accipere* (s *accip-*) being an *ad-* (to) cpd of *capere* (s *cap-*), to take: cf CAPABILITY. Thus, I: *accept,* MF-F *accepter,* L *acceptāre; acceptable,* adopted from OF-F, from LL *acceptābilis,* from *acceptare*—cf the suffix *-able; acceptability,* prob direct from LL *acceptābilitās* (gen *-itatis*); *acceptance,* adopted from OF (*accept-,* s of *accepter*+suffix *-ance*); *acceptant,* prob via F, from *acceptant-,* o/s of *acceptans,* presp of *acceptāre; acceptation,* perh via MF-F, from LL *acceptātiō,* o/s *acceptātiōn-.* Group II: *acception,* perh via late EF-F, from *acceptiōn-,* o/s of L *acceptiō,* an accepting, acceptance, formed (abstract *-iō,* gen *-iōnis*) upon *accept-,* s of *acceptus* (as above), whence also *acceptor,* adopted by E; *acceptive* (cf the suffix *-ive*), as if from ML *\*acceptivus.* Cf CAPABILITY, para 7.

**access, accessary, accessible, accession, accessory.** See ACCEDE.

**accidence** (obs), **accidency;** gram **accidence; accident,** adj and n; **accidental; accidented.**
L *accidere* (*ad,* to+*cadere,* to fall: cf CADENCE and CHANCE), to befall, to happen, has presp *accidens,* o/s *accident-,* whence the rare adj *accident,* now usu *accidental* (MF-F *accidentel,* from ML *accidentālis*); whence also the n *accidentia,* chance, a chance, whence the obs syn E *accidence* and the extant *accidency* (cf suffix *-cy*).

The gram *accidence* stands for *accidents,* pl of *accident,* something that *happens* to a word, a special sense of *accident,* a chance event, from the OF-F n *accident,* from the L presp (as above). *Accidented,* uneven of surface, owes much to the syn F *accidenté.*
Cf CADENCE, para 7.

**accidia, accidie; acedia.**
The 2nd is the obs form (adopted from OF) of the 1st, itself from ML *accidia,* a faulty shape— influenced by L *accidere,* to happen—of LL *acēdia,* trln of Gr *akēdia,* lit 'a not-caring' (privative *a-,* not+*kēdos,* care, anxiety); LL *acēdia* accounts for E *acedia,* apathy, (eccl) sloth. Gr *kēdos* is akin to HATE, q.v.

**acclaim, acclamation, acclamatory.** See CLAIM, para 4.

**acclimate, acclimation, acclimatize, acclimatization.** See CLIME, para 5.

**acclinal, acclinate.** See CLIME, para 7.

**acclivitous, acclivity, acclivous.** See CLIVUS, para 2.

**accolade:** adopted from EF-F: It *accollata* (s *accol-*), itself from *accollare* (s *accol-*), to embrace: from L *ad,* to+*collum* (r *col-*), neck: cf COLLAR.

**accommodate, accommodation.** See MODAL, para 14.

**accompany; accompaniment, accompanist.** See PANTRY, para 9.

**accomplice.** See *complice* at PLY, para 21:

**accomplish,** adj **accomplished; accomplishment.** See PLENARY, para 7.

**accompt:** an old form of ACCOUNT.

**accord,** n and v; **accordable; accordance, accordancy; accordant; according; accordion.**
All except the last come from OF *acorder,* from LL *accordāre, ac-* for *ad,* to+*cord-,* the o/s of *cor* (gen *cordis*), heart: cf CORDIAL and HEART. Thus: the n *accord,* ME *ac(c)ord* or *acorde,* from OF *acord(e),* from *acorder,* whence, via ME *ac(c)orden,* 'to *accord*', whence the pa *according,* whence the advv *according, accordingly; accordant,* however, derives from ME *acordant,* adopted from the OF *acordant,* presp of *acorder,* whence also both OF *acordable* (cf suffix *-able*), whence E *accordable,* and OF *acordance,* whence E *accordance,* with var *accordancy.* The musical *accordion* consists of It *accord-,* the s of *accordare,* to play in tune+the *-ion* of, e.g., *clarion* and *melodion.*

**accost.** See COAST, para 3.

**accouchement.** See COUCH.

**account,** n and v; **accountable; accountancy; accountant; accounting.** See the 2nd COUNT, para 5.

**accouter** (AE), **accoutre; accouterment** (AE), **accoutrement.** See SEW, para 6.

**accredit, accredited.** See CREDENCE, para 7.

**accrescence, accretion, accrete.** See CRESCENT, para 3.

**accrual, accrue.** See CRESCENT, para 4.

**accumbent, accumbency.** See HIVE, para 8.

**accumulate, accumulation,** etc. See CUMULATE, para 2.

accuracy, accurate. See CURE, para 3.

accursed. See CURSE.

accuse; accusable, accusal, accusant, accusation, accusative, accusatorial, accusatory. See CAUSE, para 5.

accustom. See CUSTOM.

ace, n hence v: ME *as*, OF-F *as*, L *ās*, a unit of the duodecimal system, hence a monetary standard and, later, a copper coin: perh an Etruscan word. Semantically, what serves as a standard is (or is regarded as) the best: hence the card-game sense: hence the sporting, hence again the aeronautical sense.

acedia. See ACCIDIA.

acerb. See ACRID and cf ACUTE.

acescent, acetate, acetic, acetylene. See ACID, 2nd para.

ache, n and v: (to) *ache* derives from ME *aken* (cf the obs spelling *ake*) OE *acan*, o.o.o.—but perh akin to Gr *akē* (s *ak-*), a sharp point, and L *acēre*, to be sharp: cf ACUTE. Whitehall postulates the IE etym *agos*, fault, guilt, and adduces MD *akel*, shame, and LG *äken*, to smart. But, ult, the two IE rr *ag-* and *ak-*, may have been id.

achieve; achievement—heraldic hatchment.

The 3rd either corrupts the 2nd, influenced by F *hachement*, an ornament in heraldry, or (EW) comes direct from F *hachement*, an inferior form of *acesmement*, from OF *acesmer*, to adorn, itself o.o.o.; the 2nd derives from MF-F *achèvement* (cf the suffix *-ment*), from OF-F *achever*, to bring to a head, to conclude: *a* (Mod *à*), to+*chef*, head: cf CHIEF; and the 1st derives from ME *acheven*, from the OF-F *achever*.

acid, adj hence n; acidic; acidific, acidify; acidity; acidulate, acidulous; acescence, acescent; acetate; acetic, acetous; acetylene.

The adj *acid* comes, perh via EF-F, from L *acidus* (s *acid-*, r *ac-*: cf *torrid* from L *torrēre*, s *tor-*); the derivative n *acid* yields the subsidiary adj *acidic* (cf the suffix *-ic*). The derivative L n *aciditās* yields, perh via EF-F *acidité*, the E *acidity* (cf *-ity*). The dim L adj *acidulus* accounts for *acidulous*, whence *acidulate*: *acidul*(ous)+the v suffix *-ate*. *Acidific, acidify*: *acid*+*ific* and *-fy*; the latter has derivative *acidification*.

*Acescence*=*acescent*+*-ce*; *acescent* comes, perh via F, from L *acescent-*, o/s of *acescens*, presp of *acescere*, to become or turn sour, the inch of *acēre*, to be sharp, hence sour. *Acetate* comes from L *acētum*, vinegar, itself from *acēre*, akin to *acer*, sharp; and *acētum* gives us the adjj *acetic* (acid) and *acetose* or *acetous* (cf *-ose* and *-ous*). In Chem, both L *acētum* and E *acetic* possess numerous derivatives: here we need mention only *acetylene*: *acetyl* (*acet-*+Chem *-yl*)+Chem *-ene* (as in *benzene*). Cf the element *aceti-* or *aceto-*.

F.a.e.: ACUTE.

acknowledge, acknowledgement. See CAN, para 6.

acme: Gr *akmē*, a point, the topmost point, the prime: IE r, *ak-*. Adj: *acmic* (for *acmeīc*). F.a.e., ACUTE, s.f.

acne: SciL perh from Gr *akhnē*, a particle,

hence chaff: s *akhn-*, prob r *akh-*; cf Gr *akhuron* (s *akhur-*, prob r *akh-*), straw.

acolyte: ME *acolyt, acolite*: ML *acolitus*, earlier *acolithus*: LL *acolūthus*, acolyte: Gr *akolouthos* (adj hence n), attendant: *a-*, with+*keleuthos* (r *kel-*), a path—cf L *callis*.

aconite (plant, hence an extract), whence the adj aconitic (unless direct from Gr *akonītikos*) and the Chem aconitine: L *aconitum*, Gr *akonīton*, o.o.o.— but perh suggested by *akonīti*, the adv of the adj *akonitos*, without dust (*a-*, not+*konis*, dust), i.e. without the dust of the arena, hence of combat or struggle (L & S; Hofmann): it affords cardiac relief.

acorn: ME *akern*, OE *aecern*, var *aecren*, akin to ON *akarn*, forest-tree fruit, and Go *akran*, fruit, itself prob from Go *akrs*, a field, akin to L *ager*, a field: f.a.e., see ACRE, the basic meaning of *acorn* being 'fruit (or produce) of the field'. The Mod E spelling is folk-etymological for *oak* (OE *āc*)+*corn*.

acoustic, acoustics; catacoustics; dysacousia or -acousis.

The n *acoustics* derives from the adj *acoustic*, much as *ethics* from *ethic*: and *acoustic* descends, perh via F *acoustique*, from Gr *akoustikos*, aural, from *akouein* (s *akou-*), to hear, itself akin to HEAR. *Catacoustics*=*cat-*, for prefix *cata*+*acoustics*; *dysacousia* or *-acousis*=*dys-*, bad(ly)+*acousia*, Sci L for Gr *akousis* (whence *-acousis*), a hearing.

acquaint; acquaintance.

The latter derives from ME *aqueyntance*, from OF-EF *acointance*, from OF-EF *acointier*, from LL *accognitāre*: *ac-* for *ad-*, to+*cognitus*, known, from *cognoscere*, to know (a person), itself=*co-*, with+*gnoscere*, the old form of *noscere*, to know: cf *cognition* and *quaint*: f.a.e., CAN. OF-EF *acointier* becomes ME *acointen*, later *aqueynten*, becomes 'to *acquaint*'.

acquest. See QUERY, para 7, s.f.

acquiesce; acquiescence, acquiescent. See QUIET, para 5.

acquire, acquirement; acquisition, acquisitive. See QUERY, para 7.

acquit; acquitment, acquittal, acquittance. See QUIET, para 6.

acre, whence collective acreage (suffix *-age*): ME *aker*, OE *aecer*, akin to ON *akr* (cf Da *ager*)— OHG *achar* (cf G *Acker*)—OS *akkar*—Go *akrs*— all meaning 'a field'; to L *ager*, a field; Gr *agros*, a field; Skt *ájras*, a plain. IE r: *agr-*. Basic sense, prob 'pasture' or 'pasture land'—cf L *agere*, to lead or drive flocks or herds. Cf ACORN and PILGRIM.

acrid, acridity; acrimonious, acrimony; acerb, acerbity.

*Acridity* (suffix *-ity*) derives from *acrid*, which app blends *acr-*, the o/s of L *acer*, sharp, with *acid-*, the s of L *acidus*. *Acrimonious* comes from ML *ācrimoniōsus*, the adj of L *ācrimoniā*, sharpness, bitterness, from *acer*; *ācrimoniā* yields *acrimony* perh via F *acrimonie*. *Acerbity* goes, perh via MF-F *acerbité*, back to L *acerbitās*, bitterness, itself from *acerbus*, bitter (whence OF-F *acerbe*, whence E *acerb*), a modification of *acer*, itself from an IE r *\*ac-* (*ak-*), a point, pointed, to be pointed—cf Gr *akē*, a point, and *akōn*, a javelin. But, f.a.e., see ACUTE. (Cf ACID.)

**acrobat; acrophobia; acropolis; acrostic.**

For *acro-*, from Gr *akros*, at the farthest point (usu upwards), see Elements. The cpds have originated thus:

*acrobat*, via F *acrobate* (n), either from the Gr adj *akrobatos*, walking a-tiptoe, hence walking aloft, from *akrobatein*, to walk a-tiptoe, or, more prob, from Gr *akrobatēs*, an acrobat, from *akrobatein*, the element *bat-* deriving from *bainein* (s *bain-*), to walk; the adj *acrobatic* comes from Gr *akrobatikos*;

*acrophobia*, a dread of high places: a SciL formation: cf PHOBIA;

*acropolis*, the citadel—lit 'highest (part) of a city', esp in Greece: cf POLICE, para 4; adj, *acropolitan*;

*acroscopic*. Cf the element *-scope*;

*acrostic*: L *acrostichis*, Gr *akrostikhis*, lit 'extreme line', i.e. at the beginning or the end of a verse-line (Gr *stikhos*, order, verse: cf the element *-stich*).

**across.** See CROSS, n.

**acrostic.** See ACROBAT, s.f., and, for 2nd element, the 3rd STY, para 2, s.f.

**act,** n and v; **acta; action; active, activate, activism, activity; actor, actress; actual, actualism, actuality; actuary; actuate, actuation.** Prefix-cpds: **enact, enactive, enactment, enactor, enactory; exact** (adj and v), **exacting, exaction, exactitude, exactor; inaction, inactive; react, reactance, reactant, reaction, reactionary, reactive, reactor; redact, redaction, redactor; transact, transaction, transactional, transactor.** Cognate group: AGENT, q.v. also f.a.e.

I. *Act* and its simple derivatives:

*act*, n: perh via MF-F *acte*, from L *actum*, a thing done (pl *acta*, adopted by E for 'proceedings, transactions'), orig the neu of *actus*, pp of *agere*, to (drive, hence) do, but also partly from L *actus* (gen *actūs*), a doing, an action. The v *act* comes from the L pp *actus*, but has been influenced by the n *act*.

*action*: via MF-F *action* from L *actiō*, o/s *actiōn-*, formed on *actus*, pp of *agere*+the suffix *-io* (o/s *-ion-*), whence E *-ion*; *actionable* comes from ML *actionābilis*, subject to an action at law.

*active*: perh via *active*, the f of OF-F *actif*; from ML *activus*, L *actiuus*: pp s *act-*+*-iuus* (cf the E suffix *-ive*). Subsidiaries: *activity*, prob via late MF-F *activité*, from ML *activitās*; *activate* (whence *activation*, *activator*), from *active*+v suffix *-ate*; *activism*=*active*+suffix *-ism*.

*actor* (cf MF-F *acteur*): L *actor*, one who does things, esp in a purposeful way: pp s *act-*+agential suffix *-or* (cf E *-or*); whence, via *\*actoress*, derives *actress*—perh influenced by F *actrice* and even by the ML *actrix* (*pars*).

*actual* (whence *actualism*, *actualist*, *actuality*— perh influenced by LL *actuāliter*, practically): ME

from OF *actuel*, from LL *actuālis*, from *actus*, a doing, an act.

*actuary*, whence *actuarial*: L *actuārius*, shorthand writer, bank clerk, from the n *actus*, influenced by the pl n *acta*.

*actuate*: from ML *actuātus*, pp of *actuāre*, to put into action, from n *actus*; *actuation*, from ML *actuātiō*, o/s *actuātiōn-*, from *actuātus*.

II. Prefix-cpds from L *actum* (or *actus*, n) or from E *act*, n and v:

*enact*, to make into act or law, to perform legislatively: prefix *en-*+*act*; perh influenced by the AL freq *inactitare* and the rural L *inigere* (pp *inactus*), to drive (stock); hence, *enactment* (suffix *-ment*)—*enaction*, *enactive*, *enactor*, *enactory*.

*exact*, adj: L *exactus*, precise, orig the pp of *exigere*, (lit, to drive out) to enforce, to demand, to complete; *exactus* yields the F *exactitude* (*-itude*), adopted by E. Cf:

*exact*, v: from L *exactus*, pp of *exigere*; derivative L *exactiō*, o/s *exactiōn-*, yields, perh via OF, *exaction*; *exactive*, from LL *exactiuus*; *exactor*, from L; *exacting* (adj), from 'to *exact*'.

*inaction*: *in-*, not+E *action*; *inactive* (whence *inactivity*), prob *in-*+*active*, but perh from ML *inactivus*, negligent.

*react*: prob *re-*, back, again+*act*, v, but cf the medieval schoolmen's L *reagere*, pp *reactus*, and, for *reaction*, their *reactiō*, o/s *reactiōn-*; *reactionary* (adj hence n), from *reaction*; as *reactance*=*react*+suffix *-ance*, so *reactant*=*react*+*-ant*; *reactive*, *reactor*=*react*+*-ive*, *-or*.

*redact*: L *redactus*, pp of *redigere*, to bring back, (hence) to reduce; *redaction*, from LL *redactiō*, o/s *redactiōn-*; *redactor*=*redact*+*-or*.

*transact*: L *transactus*, pp of *transigere*, to drive across, (hence) to 'put through' or achieve; derivative L *transactiō*, o/s *tranlsactiōn-*, yields *transaction*, whence *transactiona*; *transactor*, adopted from L.

III. All the prec words, whether single or prefixed, come from the L pp s *act-* of *agere*, to drive, to do; the *ag-*, complementaries—*agent*, *reagent*, etc.—will be found at AGENT, q.v. also f.a.e.

**acuity.** See ACUTE.

**acumen; acuminate, acumination; acuminous.**

*Acumen*, sharpness of mind, shrewdness, comes direct from L and represents *acū-*, the s of *acuere*, to sharpen+the suffix *-men*; the derivative LL *acūmināre*, to sharpen, has pp *acūminātus*, whence both 'to *acuminate*' and the adj *acuminate*, tapering to a point; *acuminous*=*acumin-* (o/s of L *acūmen*) +adj suffix *-ous*. Cf ACUTE.

**acushla**, AIr for 'darling': Ir *a*, the voc *O*+Ir *cuisle*, vein, pulse (of the heart): cf AIr *cushlamochree* (or *-machree*), for Ir *cuisle mo chroidhe*, vein of my heart; cf also the F *O, mon cœur!* and the sl *heart throb* (darling).

**acute—cute, cutie—acuteness; acuate—aculeate —acutate; acuity.**

*Acuteness* merely adds the abstract *-ness* to *acute* (whence *cute*, whence the Am sl *cutie*): *acute* comes from L *acūtus*, orig the pp of *acuere*, to sharpen.

Akin to *acútus* is L *acus*, a needle, s *acu-*, whence *acuate* (pa *-ate*), sharp-pointed; the L dim *acúleus* has subsidiary *acúleátus*, whence *aculeate*, possessing a sting or a sharp point. The LL *acútáre*, to sharpen, from *acútus*, has pp *acútátus*, whence *acutate*, slightly sharpened. The ML *acúitás* (*acú-+itás*, cf E *-ity*), prob an avoidance of *acútitás*, becomes late MF-F *acuité* and E *acuity*.

Cf ACANTH, ACID, ACME, ACRID, ACROBAT, ACUMEN. The IE r *ac-*, *ak*, occurs not only in Gr *aké*, a point, in L *acus* and *acútus*, in L *acer*, sharp, keen (edge, mind), in L *acidus* and *aciés*, a sharp edge, but also in Gr *akis*, a point, *akón*, a javelin, *akaina*, a point, a spur, and *akanos*, a thistle, and notably in Skt *asanis*, a cutting edge, a sharp weapon, and *ásris*, edge, (sharp) corner; cf also Oscan *akrid*, sharply, keenly, bitterly—and even L *occa*, a harrow, and *ocris*, a very uneven mountain, Umbrian *ocar*, a mountain, Ir *ochar*, a wedge, and many OC words. Also akin are EAGER and EDGE; L *acer*, thinly 'disguised' in *eager*, shows clearly in *exacerbate*.

**adage:** adopted from F, from L *adagium*, app composed of *ad*, to+the r of *aió*, I say—cf *prodigy*. '*Aió* representsan ancient *ag-yo*' (E & M).

**Adam.** The H *Ádám* usu has preceding article, 'the *adam*', which means either 'the made (or, created) one', the man (cf Assyrian *adamu*, to make or produce), or 'one of earth', from H *adamah*, earth—cf *Genesis*, ii, 7, 'God formed man of the dust of the ground'. *Adam's ale:* the poor fellow had only water to drink. *Adam's apple:* the forbidden fruit of the tree of knowledge got stuck, they say, in his throat (EW).

**adamant, adamantine; diamond, diamantiferous, diamantine.**

*Adamant*, adopted from OF, comes, via L *adamas*, o/s *adamant-*, from Gr *adamas* (gen *adamantos*), the hardest metal: *a-*, not+n from *daman* (s *dam-*), to tame: f.a.e., see TAME. The adj *adamantine* goes, via EF-F *adamantin* and L *adamantinus*, back to Gr *adamantinos*. Now, L *adamas* had, in ML—perh influenced by Gr *diaphanés*, transparent—the var *diamas*, o/s *diamant-*, which entered OF as *diamant*, which became ME *diamaunt*, later *diamaund*, whence Mod *diamond*: L *adamas*, the hardest metal, merges into ML *diamas*, the very hard diamond. *Diamantiferous*: F *diamant*+connective *-i-*+element *-ferous* (cf the element *-fer*). *Diamantine*: from F *diamantin*, f *-ine*.

**adapt,** whence **adaptable, adaption, adaptive, adaptor; adaptation.**

*Adapt:* MF-F *adapter*: L *adaptáre*—*ad*, to+ *aptáre*, to fit, from *aptus*, fit, suitable: see APT. *Adaptation:* adopted from EF-F, from ML *adaptátió*, o/s *adaptátión-*; *adaptat-*, s of *adaptátus* (pp of *adaptáre*)+*-ió*, abstract suffix.

**add; addend, addendum (pl addenda); addition** (whence **additional**)—**additament**—**additive.**

*Add* comes from L *addere* (s *add-*), which, combining *ad*, to+*dare*, to place, to give (*dó*, I place, I give), means 'to place beside', hence 'to add'. The

L vn *addendum*, thing to be added, is anglicized in the Math *addend*. *Addit-*, the s of *additus*, pp of *addere*, accounts for (1) *additio*, o/s *addition-*, whence, via MF, the E *addition*; (2) *additámentum*, whence E *additament*; (3) *additíuus*, ML *additivus*, whence E *additive*.

**adder,** snake, derives from ME *addre*, from *a naddre* apprehended as *an addre*; ME *naddre* or *neddere* derives from OE *náédre*, akin to the syn OS *nádra*, OHG *nátara*, Go *nadrs*, ON *nathr*—to OIr *nathir*, adder, snake—and (perh the origin of *nathir*) L *natrix*, water snake, the sense perh influenced by L *natáre*, to swim. (For the formative process, see 'Articled Nouns' in P⁴.)

**addict; addiction.** See DICT, para 7.

**addition, additament, additional, additive.** See ADD.

**addle,** v, derives from the adj *addle*, empty, confused, muddled, itself from the now dial n *addle*, (liquid) filth, OE *adela*, akin to OSw *-adel*, urine, and MLG *adele*, liquid manure.

**address.** See REX, para 9.

**adduce,** whence **adducible; adduction.** See DUKE, para 6.

**adenoids; adenoid, adenoidal.**

*Adenoids* is strictly the pl of n *adenoid* (whence *adenoidal*: adj suffix *-al*), itself from adj *adenoid*, Gr *adenoeidés*, glandular: *adén*, a gland: cf the element *-aden* and the suffix *-oid*.

**adept,** n hence adj; whence **adeptness.**

The n *adept* comes from L *adeptus* (*artem*), one 'that has attained to (an art)', pp of *adipisci*, to attain to: *ad*, to+*apisci*, to obtain, from *apere*, to tie, pp *aptus*: cf therefore APT.

**adequacy, adequate.** See EQUAL, para 7.

**adhere; adherence, adherent; adhesion, adhesive.**

*Adhere* comes, prob through MF-F *adhérer*, from L *adhaerére* (s *adhaer-*), to be attached (to): *ad*, to+*haerére*, to be attached, remain fixed: f.a.e., HESITATE; cf COHERE and INHERE. The presp *adhaerens*, o/s *adhaerent-*, yields, prob via MF-F *adhérent*, the E *adherent*; derivative ML *adhaerentia* yields, prob via MF-F *adhérence*, the E *adherence*. The s *adhaes-* of pp *adhaesus* leads to *adhaesió*, o/s *adhaesión-*, whence, perh via late MF-F *adhésion*, E *adhesion*; *adhesive* arises in F *adhésif*, f *adhésive*: *adhésion*+*-if*, f *-ive*.

**adhibit, adhibition.** See HABIT, para 11.

**adieu:** OF *adieu*, for *a Dieu*, in full *je vous recommande a* (F *à*) *Dieu*, I commend you to God, spoken to a departing guest or traveller; OF *a Dieu*=LL *ad Deum*. Cf DEITY.

**adipose,** whence **adiposity** (suffix *-ity*). See the element *adipo-*.

**adjacence** or **adjacency, adjacent:** ML *adjacentia*, from ML *adjacent-* (whence E *adjacent*), L *adiacent-*, o/s of *adiacens*, presp of *adiacére*, to lie (*iacére*) towards or by (*ad*, to, towards); *iacére*, lit 'to be in the state of some person or thing cast or thrown (down)', derives from *iacére*, to cast or throw. (E & M.) For *iacére*, c/f *-icere*, cf the *-ject* of *abject, deject, inject, object, project, reject, subject*, and:

**adjective:** ML *adjectīvum* (LL *adiectīuum*), elliptical for *adjectivum verbum*, added word (cf the Gr *ἐπίθετον*, q.v. at EPITHET); neu of ML *adjectīvus*, L *adiectīuus*, tending to add or increase, from *adicere*, to cast (*-icere*) towards (*ad*) or beside, (often merely) to add. Cf prec; f.a.e., see JET.

**adjoin**, whence the pa **adjoining**; **adjunct** (adj hence n), **adjunction**, **adjunctive**. See JOIN, resp para 17 and para 14.

**adjourn**; **adjournment.** See DIANA, para 11.

**adjudge**; **adjudicate, adjudication, adjudicator.** See DICT, para 18.

**adjunct, adjunction.** See JOIN, para 14.

**adjure**; **adjuration, adjuratory.** See JURY, n, para 4.

**adjust**; **adjustment.** See JURY, n, para 7.

**adjutant, adjutancy.**

The latter is for *adjutantcy* (suffix *-cy*): and *adjutant* comes from *adjutant-*, the o/s of ML *adjutans*, L *adiutans*, presp of *adiutāre*, freq of *adiuuāre* (*ad*+ *iuuāre*, to help): cf AID. The *adjutant* (*bird, crane, stork*) stands about like an adjutant.

**administer**; **administrate, administration,** etc. See MINOR, para 13.

**admirable.** See MIRACLE, para 4.

**admiral, Admiralty; amir, emir.**

*Emir* is an E var of *amir* (or *ameer*), from Ar *amīr*, a commander, as in *amīr-al-bahr*, commander of the sea, an admiral: the frequency of *amir-al* in various combinations explains the EF-F *amiral*, MF *amirail*, OF *amiralt*, the *d* of the MF-EF var *admiral* intruding from *admirable*; ME adopted both forms, the *-d-* form prevailing; ME *amiral*, however, here derives from ML *amirālis*. The MF *amiralte* (F *amirauté*) leads to E *Admiralty*.

**admire**, hence **admirer**; **admiration, admirative.** See MIRACLE, para 4.

**admissible, admission, admissive; admit,** whence **admittance** (suffix *-ance*). See MISSION, para 7.

**admix, admixture.** See MIX, para 9.

**admonish,** hence **admonishment** (suffix *-ment*); **admonition, admonitor, admonitory.** See MIND, para 18.

**adnate.** See NATIVE, para 9.

**ado.** See DO, para 2, s.f.

**adobe:** adopted from Sp, from *adobar*, to plaster, from ML *adobāre*, to adorn, the *a-* being prob L *ad*, used intensively, and *dobāre* being prob akin to MF-F *dauber*, to plaster. See DAUB.

**adolescence; adolescent.** See OLD, para 5.

**Adonis:** Gr *Adōnis* (deriving from Phoenician *adōn*, lord, and prob akin to Babylonian *Tammūz*), an exceedingly handsome youth, beloved of Aphrodite.

**adopt, adoption, adoptive:** resp from MF-F *adopter*, L *adoptāre* (s *adopt-*)—*ad*, to+ *optāre*, to choose: cf OPT; perh via MF-F, from L *adoptiō*, o/s *adoptiōn-*; perh via OF-F *adoptif*, f *adoptive*, from ML *adoptīvus*, L *adoptīuus*.

**adore,** whence **adorer; adorable, adoration.** See ORATION, para 5.

**adorn; adornment.** See ORDER, para 9.

**adrift.** See DRIVE, para 1, s.f.

**adroit.** See REX, para 7.

**adscititious.** See SCIENCE, para 4.

**adscript, adscription.** See SCRIBE, para 9.

**adsignification.** See SIGN, para 11.

**adsum.** See ESSE, para 6.

**adulate, adulation, adulator, adulatory:** L *adūlātus* (s *adūlāt-*), pp of *adūlāri*, to flatter, orig of a dog wagging its tail (cf Skt *vāla*, tail) as it approaches; *adulation*, perh via OF-MF *adulacion* (MF-F *adulation*), from L *adūlātiō*, o/s *adūlātiōn-*; *adulator*, adopted—cf the MF-F *adulateur*—from LL *adūlator*; *adulatory*, L *adūlātōrius*—cf the adj suffix *-ory*.

**adult.** See OLD, para 5. Cf ADOLESCENT.

**adulterate, adulterant; adulteration, adulterator; adulterine; adulterer, adulteress, adulterous, adultery.**

The L *adulterāre* (for *\*adalterāre: ad*, to+v from *alter*, other; hence, different), to alter, (hence) to corrupt, (hence) to seduce a woman, (hence) to commit adultery, has presp *adulterans-*, o/s *adulterant-*, whence the adj and n *adulterant*, and pp *adulterātus*, whence the E adj and v *adulterate*; the derivative *adulterātiō*, o/s *adulterātiōn-*, yields *adulteration*; the equally derivative *adulterātor*, a counterfeiter, has been form-adopted, sense-adapted into E.

*Adulterine* (*-ine*, adj suffix), L *adulterīnus*, prob from *adulter-*, the s of *adulterāre*, rather than from L *adulter*, an adulterer, itself from *adult-*, the r of *adulterāre*; but E *adulterer* derives, by suffix *-er*, from the obs E *adulter*, to corrupt (a woman), to commit adultery, and *adulteress*, by suffix *-ess*, from the obs E *adulter*, an adulterer. *Adultery:* from L *adulterium* (*adulter*āre+suffix *-ium*); *adulterous:* prob from *adultery*+suffix *-ous*, but perh from the obs E n *adulter*+*-ous*. Cf ALTER.

**adumbrant, adumbrate, adumbration, adumbrative.** See UMBRA, para 6.

**advance, advancement.** See the 1st VAN, para 3.

**advantage** (n and v), **advantageous; disadvantage, disadvantageous.**

1. With intrusive *d* as in ADVANCE, the n *advantage* comes, via ME *avantage, avauntage*, from OF-F *avantage*, which=the suffix *-age* attached to *avant*, before, from L *ab ante*; the v *advantage* comes from MF-F *avantager* (from the n). *Advantageous:* late MF-F *avantageux*, f *avantageuse*. Cf the 1st VAN, para 3.

2. *Disadvantage:* ME *disavauntage:* MF *desavantage* (EF-F *dés*), whence both the EF-F v *désavantager*, whence 'to *disadvantage*', and the EF-F adj *désavantageux*, f *désavantageuse*, whence E *disadvantageous*.

**advection, advectitious.** See VIA, para 12.

**advene, advenience; advent, adventitious.** See VENUE, para 3.

**adventure, adventurous.** See VENUE, para 4.

**adverb, adverbial.** See VERB, para 7.

**adversary, adversative; adverse, adversity; advert —advertise, advertisement.** See VERSE, para 15.

advice; advise, advisable, advisement, adviser, advisory. See VIDE, para 13.

advocate, whence advocacy; advocation. See VOCABLE, para 10.

advowson. See VOCABLE, para 10.

advolution. See VOLUBLE, para 4.

adze: ME *adese, adse, adsse, adis,* an adze: OE *adesa,* an axe or a hatchet: perh akin to AXE (OE *acas, aex, eax*)—cf the extremely relevant Go *aqizi,* an axe.

aegis: L: Gr *aigis,* shield of Zeus: perh from Gr *aix* (gen *aigos*), a goat, many primitive shields being goatskin-covered.

aeon. See AGE, para 5.

aer, aerate, aerial. See AIR.

aerobatics; aeronaut. See the element *aero-.* For aeroplane, see PLANE, para 3.

aery, n. See EYRIE.

aesthete, aesthetic, aesthetics; anaesthesia, anaesthetic, anaesthetist: AE spellings esthete, etc.

1. *Aesthete,* from Gr *aisthētēs,* a (keen) perceiver; *aesthetic,* Gr *aisthētikos,* sensory, sensitive; hence *aesthetics*—cf *ethics* and adj *ethic.* The Gr words derive from *aisthanomai,* I perceive, aorist inf *aisthesthai,* akin to Gr *aiō,* L *audio,* I hear.

2. *Anaesthesia:* Gr *anaisthēsia,* lack of feeling— *an-,* not+a c/f var of *aisthēsis,* feeling; *anaesthetic* (adj, hence n), an -*ic* elaboration from Gr *anaisthētos,* devoid of feeling; *anaesthetist,* one who administers, and *anaesthetize,* to administer, an anaesthetic, represent *anaesthet*ic+suffixes *-ist* and *-ize.*

aestival. See the element *estivo-.*

afar. See FAR.

affable, affability. See FABLE, para 3.

affair: ME *affere,* earlier *afere:* OF-MF *afaire* (MF-F *affaire*), from *a* (F *à,* L *ad*), to+*faire,* to do, from L *facere:* cf ADO and, for *faire,* FACT. Cf also:

affect, n and v (whence the adj affected); affectation; affective;—affection, affectionate.

The effective origin of all these words is L *afficere,* to do to, set oneself to: *ad,* to+-*ficere,* c/f of *facere,* to do, make: cf FACT. *Afficere* has pp *affectus* (s *affect-*), whence (as, e.g., of a disease) *affect,* to attack. From that pp s *affect-* derive: the freq *affectāre,* to aim at, whence late MF-F *affecter* and, perh independently, E 'to *affect*'— the n *affect,* however, comes from L *affectus* (gen -*tūs*), a disposition, from the pp s *affect-* (from *afficere*); *affectātiō* (imm from *affectāre*), o/s *affectātiōn-,* whence F, hence E *affectation; affectiō,* o/s *affectiōn-,* whence OF-F, hence E, *affection*—cf *affectionate,* an -*ate* (adj) derivative from F *affectionné,* pp of *affectionner,* from F *affection.* But *affective* (suffix -*ive*) derives from late MF-F *affectif,* f *affective,* of, by, for affect, from ML *affectīvus;* hence the Psy *affectivity* (suffix -*ity*).

affiance. See FAITH, para 10.

affidavit. See FAITH, para 9.

affiliate, affiliation. See FILIAL, para 1.

affinity. See FINAL, para 7.

affirm; affirmance, affirmation, affirmative, affirmatory. See FIRM, para 4.

affix, affixation. See FIX, para 3.

afflatus. See FLATUS, para 3.

afflict; affliction, afflictive.

Prob, like the obs adj *afflict,* afflicted, 'to *afflict*' comes from L *afflictus,* pp of *affligere,* to deject: *ad,* to-*fligere,* to strike: cf CONFLICT, INFLICT—and PROFLIGATE. The L pp s *afflict-* yields both *afflictiō,* o/s *afflictiōn-,* whence, via F, *affliction,* and ML *afflictivus,* whence, prob via MF-F *afflictif,* f *afflictive,* the E *afflictive* (-*ive*).

affluence, affluent, afflux. See FLUENT, para 5.

afford: ME *aforthen:* OE *geforthian,* int of *forthian* (s *forth-*), to further, (hence) to accomplish, to afford: f.a.e., FORTH.

afforest, afforestation. See FOREST.

affray, n and v—fray (n); afraid.

The n *fray,* combat, is short for *affray;* the obs v *fray* derives from the short n. *Affray,* fight, tumult, ME *af(f)rai,* comes from OF *esfrei* (F *effroi*), from *esfreer,* to disquiet, to frighten, (lit) to put out of (OF *es,* from L *ex*) peace (Gmc root for 'peace'— cf OHG *fridu,* peace); OF *esfreer, effreer,* yields ME *af(f)raien,* whence E 'to *affray*'; the ME pp *af(f)rayed,* later *affraide,* frightened, has become E *afraid.*

affright. See FRIGHT.

affront, n and v. See FRONT, para 5.

afoot. See FOOT, para 2.

afore: ME *afore,* earlier *aforn:* OE *on oran, aetforan,* in or at the front. Cf FORE.

afraid. See AFFRAY, s.f.

afresh. See FRESH, para 2.

Africa; African, adj hence n; Afric; Afrikaans.

L *Afer,* gen *Afri,* African, has derivatives *africus,* f *africa,* as in *terra africa,* land of the Africans, whence *Africa; Africānus* (imm from *Africa*), whence *African; africus,* whence the archaic *Afric,* African or an African, or even Africa. *Afrikaans* is SAfr D, from D *Afrikaan:* cf D *Afrikaner,* whence, after *Hollander* and prob *Englander,* comes *Afrikander,* a born white South African of either (and esp) D or Huguenot origin.

But *Afer* may derive from L *Africa,* Gr *Aphriké,* both from a Phoenician name for 'land of Carthage'; the name extended only after a millennium to the entire continent.

aft—abaft; after, adv, hence adv and prep.

1. *Aft:* OE *aeftan,* behind—cf Go *afta,* properly *aftra,* behind, and *aftana,* from behind, both advv, and OS (*at*)*aftan;* IE r, *\*aft-.* an elaboration of *\*af-;* var *\*ap,* as in ON (merely scribal) and Hit.

2. *Abaft: a-,* on+ME *baft,* itself from OE *beaeftan*—*be,* by+*aeftan* (as above).

3. Prob akin to *aft* is the adv *after:* OE *aefter,* after, behind, akin to Go *aftaro,* from behind, behind, backwards, OHG *aftara* and ON *aptra,* behind—and, more remotely, Gr *apōtero,* farther off. The suffix -*ter,* in E also -*ther,* was orig comp: *after* is the comp of *of,* off (see OF). The prep *after* derives from the adv; the adj *after,* OE *aeftera,* from OE *aefter.*

4. Two simple derivatives merit a note: *aftermost* (opp *foremost*), ME *aftermest*, earlier *eftemest*, from OE *aeftemest*—cf Go *aftumist*, the last, *aeftemest* being orig the sup of *of*, off (cf OF); and *afterward*, OE *aefterweard*, *aeftanweard*, (adj) behind, the form *afterwards* being orig the gen *aefterweardes*.

5. The cpds are mostly self-explanatory. Thus: *afterbirth*, *afterglow*, *afterlife*, *afternoon*, *afterthought*. *Aftermath*=*after*+*math*, a mowing, OE *maēth*: cf MOW (grass).

**aftermath.** See AFT, para 5, and cf MOW, para 2.

**afterward, afterwards.** See AFT, para 4; cf the suffix *-ward*.

**again; against;—gainsay.**

*Gainsay:* ME *geinseien* (or *ageinseien*), to say (cf SAY) against, to contradict: *gain-*, ME *gein-*, derives from OE *gegn-* or *gēan-*, again, against, akin to ON *gagn-*. *Against:* ME *agens*, *ageynes*: OE *ongegn*, *ongēanes*, the *-s* being a gen ending (OE *-es*) and the *t*, as in *amidst* and *whilst*, intrusive. *Ongēanes* is the gen of *ongēan*, which, with its varr *ongegn* and the worn-down *agēn*, yields ME *agen*, *agayn*, *agein*, whence the E *aga n*. The OE *ongēan* and *ongegn* reveal their origin as *on*, on (or in)+*\*gagn* or *\*gegn*, straight: cf OHG *ingagan*, *ingegin*, OS *angegin*, again, against, and ON *gegn* (or *gagn*), against, from *gegn*, straight.

**agaric:** L *agaricum:* Gr *agarikon*, perh the neu of adj *Agarikos*, of *Agaria* in Eastern Europe.

**agate:** adopted from F, from L *achates* (cf G *Achat*), from Gr *akhatēs*, itself from Gr *Akhatēs*, the Sicilian river where agate was earliest found.

**agathology.** See the element *agatho-*.

**age; coëval—medieval (or -aeval); eternal (and sempiternal), eterne, eternity; aeon or eon; ay or aye,** always; perh EVER, q.v. separately.

1. There are three IE sub-families represented: Germanic, Latin, Greek. In the first we have *ay*, *aye*, always: ME *ai*, earlier *ei*, from ON *ei*, intimately akin to OE *ā*, *āwa*, always—cf OFris *ā*, OS *ēo*, *eo*, *io*, Go *aiw*, always: and *aiws*, an age, and OHG *es*, always: f.a.e., see para 6.

2. ML *aevum*, L *aeuum* (earlier *aeuom*; s *aeu-*), an age, a lifetime, appears in *coëval* (formerly *coaeval*), adj hence n, an *-al* formation from ML *coaevus* (prefix *co-*+*aevum*), contemporary, and in *medieval*, *mediaeval* (*medius*, middle+*aevum*+*-al*), and in *primeval* (earlier *primaeval*), an *-al* formation from ML *primaevus*, L *primaeuus* (*primus*, first+*aeuum*); less clearly in E *age*, OF *aage*, VL *\*aetāticum*, from L *aetātem*, acc of *aetās*, a contraction of *aeuitās* (ML *aevitās*), from *aeuum*.

3. *Aet-*, the o/s of L *aetās*, recurs in *aeternus* (adj suffix *-ernus*), whence the literary *eterne*; *aeternus* has the derivative LL var *aeternālis* (*aet-*+*ernus*+*-ālis*), whence, via OF-MF *eternel* (EF-F *é-*) the E *eternal*, and the derivative LL n *aeternitās*, whence, via OF-MF *eternité* (EF-F *é-*), the E *eternity*. But *eternize* goes no further back than EF-F *éterniser*, from EF *éterne*.

4. *Sempiternal* comes from ML *sempiternālis*, from L *sempiternus* (whence the rare *sempitern*), a contraction of *semperaeternus*—*semper*, always.

5. AE *eon*, E *aeon* (adopted from L), comes from Gr *aiōn* (s *ai-*), lifetime, age, intimately akin to PL *aeuom*; Gr *aiōnios*, eternal, yields *aeonian* (adj suffix *-an*). Cf Gr *aiei* (s *ai-*), always.

6. Gr *aiōn* app derives from PGr *aiwōn*, s *aiw-*: cf the L r *aeu-*, OHG *ēwa*, a long time, eternity, and Go *aiw* (always). Cf further the Skt *āyus*, Av *āyu*, life, with s *ay-*: cf ON *ei* (always). Clearly the IE r is *\*aiu-* (or *\*aiw-*), with var *\*aeu-* (*\*aew-*), basic sense 'duration'—usu 'long time' and often 'limitless time, eternity'.

**agency; agenda.** See:

**agent, agency, agential; agenda.**

*Agenda*, things to be done, has been adopted from the neupl of *agendus*, gerundive of *agere*, to drive or lead, hence to act or do. The pp *actus* leads into the ACT group. The presp *agens*, gen *agentis*, o/s *agent-*, yields the obs adj *agent* and (ML *agens*) the n *agent*, whence the adj *agential* (suffix *-ial*); yields also the ML *agentia*, whence the E *agency*.

*Agere* (s *ag-*) is akin to Gr *agein* (s *ag-*), to lead or drive—cf the ON *aka* (s *ak-*), to drive, Arm *acem* (s *ac-*), I lead, OIr ad-*aig*, he leads or rushes towards, and Skt *ájati* (s *aj-*), he goes or drives. IE r, *\*ag-*; perh akin to the r of WORK.

**agglomerate; agglomerant, agglomeration, agglomerative.**

L *agglomerāre* (*ad*, to+*glomerāre*, to make a ball of) has presp *agglomerans*, o/s *agglomerant-*, whence the n *agglomerant*; the pp *agglomerātus* yields both 'to *agglomerate*' and adj *agglomerate*, whence n *agglomerate*. Derivative *agglomerātiō*, o/s *agglomerātiōn-*, leads to *agglomeratton*; but *agglomerative* is an E *-ive* formation upon the L pp s *agglomerat-*.

Cf CONGLOMERATE and, f.a.e., CLAM.

**agglutinate,** adj and v; **agglutination, agglutinative:** whether adj or v, *agglutinate* comes from L *agglutinātus* (s *agglutin-*), pp of *agglutināre*, to stick, orig to glue, to something: *ad*, to+*glutināre*, to glue: f.a.e., GLUE. On *agglutinat-* have arisen *agglutination* and *agglutinative*, via EF-F *agglutination* and *agglutinatif*.

**aggradation.** See GRADE, para 6.

**aggrandize, aggrandizement.** See GRAND, para 1.

**aggravate, aggravation.** See GRAVE, adj, para 3, s f.

**aggregate,** adj (hence n) and v; **aggregation, aggregative.** See GREGAL, para 4.

**aggress,** v; **aggression, aggressive, aggressor.** See GRADE, para 6.

**aggrieved.** See GRAVE, adj, para 4.

**aghast.** See GHOST, para 2.

**agile, agility.**

L *agilitās*, o/s *agilitāt-*, which became MF-F *agilité*, whence E *agility* (*-lty*), derives from L *agilis*, nimble (*ag-*+adj suffix *-ilis*, cf E *-ile*), itself from *agere* (s *ag-*), to drive or lead—f.a.e., AGENT.

**agio:** F *agio* or *agiot* (whence *agiotage*, adopted

by E): It *aggio* (or *agio*), ease, convenience, obs var *asio*, prob from OF *aise*: f.a.e., EASE.

**agist, agistment, agistor**: OF *agister* (s *agist-*), from *a* (F *à*), to+*gister*, to provide lodging, from *giste*, (a) lodging, ult from ML *jacēre*, L *iacēre*, to lie (stretched out): cf ADJACENT. *Agister* yields both OF *agistement*, whence E *agistment*, and AF *agistour*, whence E *agistor*.

**agitate; agitation, agitative, agitator.**

L *agitāre* (freq of *agere*, to drive), to set moving, has pp *agitātus*, whence 'to agitate'. The pp s *agitāt-* has derivatives *agitātiō*, o/s *agitātiōn-*, whence F, whence E, *agitation*; *agitātor*, adopted by E; and LL *agitātiuus*, ML *agitātivus*, whence the adj *agitative*. Cf AGENT and COGITATE.

**agnail.** See NAIL, para 2.

**agnate.** See NATIVE, para 9.

**agnomen.** See NAME, para 4.

**agnostic**, whence **agnosticism.** See the 2nd GNOME, para 5.

**ago**: ME *ago*, *agoon*, *agon*, pp of *agon*, to go away, OE *āgān*, to go away, pass by: *ā-*, off+*gān*, to go.

**agog**; earlier, *on gog*: MF *en gogues*, lively, merry—cf EF-F *être en goguette(s)*, to be on the spree, and EF-F *goguenard*, mockingly playful. The MF *gogue* is prob echoic; but perh, by false division, from It *agognare*, to be eager, to long, itself akin to:

**agony; agonist, agonistic, agonize; antagonist (antagonistic, antagonism)** and **protagonist.**

The Gr *agōnia*, a contest—from *agōn*, a sports gathering (from *agein*, s *ag-*, to drive, lead, hence to celebrate: cf AGENT), derivatively an athletic contest—became applied also to a non-physical striving, agony, and has passed through LL *agōnia* and MF-F *agonie* to E *agony*. Three Gr derivatives have influenced E: *agōnistēs*, a contestant, LL *agōnista*, E *agonist*, esp in Physio; the subsidiary adj *agōnistikos*, LL *agōnisticus*, E *agonistic*; and *agōnizesthai*, LL *agōnizāre*, (perh via EF-F *agoniser*) E *agonize*.

The two principal Gr cpds are *antagōnia*, obs E *antagony*, *antagōnizesthai*, to struggle against, whence *antagonize*—(from the v) *antagōnisma*, whence *antagonism*—and *antagōnistēs* (*anti-*, against+*agōnizesthai*) LL *antagōnista*, E *antagonist*, whence *antagonistic*; and *prōtagōnistēs* (*prōtos*, first +*agōnistēs*), whence *protagonist*, orig 'the actor taking the leading part', hence the chief spokesman, the champion of a cause.

**agora.** See ALLEGORY and the element *agora-*.

**agouara** and **agouti**: SAm animals, with SAm names: the former, from Tupi via Port; the latter, from Guarani via Sp.

**agrarian; agriculture, -cultural, -culturist; agronomy.**

The base is L *ager*, o/s *agr-*, gen *agri*, a field; in *agronomy*, from Gr *agronomos*, manager of public lands, it is *agros*, a field, the 2nd element coming from *nemein* (s *nem-*), to distribute, (hence) to manage. The IE r is *\*agro-*, an uncultivated field—

cf Av *ajras*—perh akin to the IE *\*ag-* seen in *agere*, to drive: cf AGENT.

*Agrarian*: L *agrārius*, adj of *ager*; *agriculture*: via F from L *agricultūra*, (lit) cultivation (cf *cultivate* at CULT) of the field; hence *agricultural* (*-al*, adj) and *agriculturist* (*-ist*).

**agree, agreeable, agreement**—**disagree**, etc.; **maugre.**

The L *grātum*, strictly the neu of *grātus*, pleasant, is prob akin to Skt *gūrtás*, celebrated, and said to be of religious origin; it becomes OF-MF *gre* (MF-F *gré*), pleasure, will, whence OF-MF *agreer* (*a*, F *à*, to), to please, whence ME *agreen*, whence 'to agree'; the derivative OF-MF *agreable*, later *agréable*, yields *agreeable*, and late MF-F *agrément* yields *agreement*. Cf DISAGREE, from MF-F *désagréer* (*dés-*, OF *des-*, L *dis-*, from)—*disagreeable*, from MF-F *désagréable*—*disagreement*, from EF-F *désagrément*. The archaic *maugre*, despite, comes from OF *maugre*, MF *maugré*, EF-F *malgré*, (lit) ill-will, hence a prep 'in *despite* of'.

**agricultural, agriculture.** See AGRARIAN.

**agriology.** See the element *agrio-*.

**agronomy.** See AGRARIAN.

**ague**: OF (fievre) *ague*: ML (febris) *acūta*, acute fever: f.a.e., ACUTE. Adj: *aguish* (suffix *-ish*).

**ahead.** See HEAD, para 3.

**ahem!** See the 3rd HEM.

**ahoy!**=interjective *a*+interjection *hoy!*—cf *ho* and D *hui!* With *ahoy!* cf F *ohé!*

**aid**, n and v; **aidance, aidant; aide-de-camp.**

*Aid*, n: OF-F *aide*—as in *aide-de-camp*, 'aid of camp' or camp assistant, hence a civil-life adjutant —from OF-F *aider*, to help, whence 'to aid', from ML *adjutāre*, L *adiutāre*, freq of *adiuuāre*, to help, from *ad*, to+*iuuāre*, to give pleasure to, (hence) to help; *iuuāre*, s *iuv-*, is akin to *iucundus* (s *iu-*+ suffix *-cundus*, as in *fecundus*—cf FECUND); the IE r is app *\*iu-*, to please.

*Aidance, aidant*: adopted from OF, the former deriving from the latter (*aidant*, presp of *aider*).

**ail**, whence (via suffix *-ment*) **ailment**: ME *ailen*, earlier *eilen*, from OE *eglan*, to pain, (? orig) to trouble, akin to Go us-*agljan*, to distress, and *agls* (neu s *agl*), disgraceful. Prob akin to ILL.

**aileron.** See AISLE, para 2.

**aim**, v hence n: ME *amen*, *aimen*, *eimen*, to estimate, (hence) to aim (at): OF *aesmer* (*a*, to+ *esmer*, to estimate): L *aestimāre*, to estimate, or a LL *\*adaestimāre*: f.a.e., see ESTEEM.

**air**, n hence v; **airy;**—**aerate, aerial, acrification; aria; aero-**, see Elements.

*Air* comes, via ME *aire* (or *eir*) and OF *air*, from L *āerem*, acc of *āēr*, air, from Gr *aēr*, haze, mist, (later) air, akin to *aētēs*, (strong) wind, and Aeolic *auēr*, Attic *aura*, cool breeze or fresh air, and *aēmi*, I breathe hard, for *\*awēmi*—cf Skt *vāti*, it blows, and Go *waian*, to blow. Hence *airy* (adj suffix *-y*).

'To *aerate*' (whence *aeration*)=L *aer*+v suffix *-ate*; *aerial*=*āerius* (Gr *aérios*)+adj *-al*; *aerification*, from *aerify*, itself=*āeri-*, L c/f+-*fy* (see Elements). Mus *aria*: It *aria*: L *āera*, var acc of *āēr*.

**aisle**: ME *ile* or *ele*: OF-MF *ele* (late MF-F *aile*), wing, (hence) wing of a building: L *āla*, point of articulation, (hence) armpit and wing, akin to L *axilla*, armpit, dim of *axis* (see AXIS), and to OHG *ahsla*, OE *eaxl*, (articulation of) the shoulder. Mod *aisle* shows the influence of *isle* and, for sense, *alley*.

2. L *āla* has adj *ālaris*, whence *alar*; and F *aile* has dim *aileron*, adopted by E.

**ajar**, occ on the jar, derives from ME *on charr*: *charr*, from OE *cerr*, a turn. *Ajar* denotes (a door) 'on the turn'.

**akimbo. See** KINK.

**akin. See** KIN.

**alabaster**: OE *alabastre*, adopted from OF (var *albastre*, F *albâtre*): L *alabaster*: Gr *alabastros*, prop *alabastos*, perh from an Egyptian town where first treated industrially (cf P²).

**alack(a day)!** Prob *ah! lack!*; ME *lak*, loss—cf LACK.

**alacrity; alacritous.**

The adj represents *alacrity* + suffix *-ous*. *Alacrity* comes from L *alacritās*, o/s *alacritāt-*, abs n (cf suffix *-ity*) from *alacer* (gen *alacri*), lively. The s *alac-* derives app from IE r *al-*, var *ul-*, to go, as in L *ambulare* (s *ambul-*), to walk; cf AMBULATE. But perh rather from L *āla* + *acer*, lit 'wing-keen'.

**Aladdin**: European form of *Aladin*, from Ar *'Alā-ad-dīn* (*ad-* for *al*, the), 'the height of religion'.

**alar. See** AISLE, para 2, and cf the element *ali-*.

**alarm**, n—hence v, hence also **alarum** (rolled *r*) and **alarmist** (suffix *-ist*)—derives from ME, from MF, *alarme*, from It *all'arme!*, 'To arms!': f.a.e., ARM. Cf ALERT.

**alas! See** LATE, para 4.

**alb**; ? **Alban, alban**; **albescent**; **albino**; ? **Albion**; **albugo**; **album**; **albumen, albumin**—**albuminous**; **aubade.**

1. The base is L *albus* (s *alb-*), white, akin to Gr *alphos* (s *alph-*), a white leprosy, and *alphiton*, barley flour, and significantly OHG *albiz*, a swan; IE r, *albh-*, occ var *alph-*.

2. The Eccl vestment *alb* is white, from ML *alba* (*vestis*, white garment), f of *albus*. Whereas the Chem *alban* certainly derives from *albus*, the PN *Alban* may be of independent C origin. *Albescent* comes from *albescent-*, o/s of *albescens*, presp of *albescere*, inch of *albāre*, to whiten, from *albus*; *album* is prop the neu s of *albus*—from the blank white pages; *albugo*, coming direct from L, means lit 'whiteness'—*albus* + suffix *-ūgō*; L-become-E *albumen*, white of egg, derives (suffix *-men*) from *albus*, and *albumin* is a Chem alteration, and *albuminous* (*albumin-*, o/s of *albumen* + suffix *-ous*) the adj of either. *Albino* is Port for 'whitish', from *albo*, white, from *albus*.

3. F *aubade*, a song at *aube* or dawn, represents *aube* + n suffix *-ade*: and *aube* derives from VL *alba* (as later in OPr and in Sp), n from the f of *albus* and prob elliptical for *alba lux*, the pale 'white light' of dawn.

4. *Albion*, adopted from L for 'England', derives from OC; *alb-*, white, occurs in C as in other IE languages; and the name may genuinely refer to

'the white cliffs of Dover' (and other parts of Britain).

**albatross**: with *b* folk-etymologically substituted (for *c*) from L *albus*, white, *albatross* truly comes from E *alcatras*, orig pelican, then frigate bird: Port *alcatraz*, cormorant, albatross, from Port *alcatraz*, bucket: Ar *al-qādūs*, lit 'the (*al*) water jar or vessel', *qādūs* deriving perh from Gr *kados* (itself from Phoenician or else from H *kad*), but prob direct from H *kad*, water jar, bucket. 'Basic idea: water carrier' (Webster).

**albeit**, (even) though: ME *al be it*, 'all (though) it be'.

**albert**, watch-chain: Prince *Albert*, Queen Victoria's consort.

**albescent, albino** (both para 2); **Albion** (para 4); **albugo, album, albumen, albumin** (all para 2). See ALB.

**alcanet; alcanna. See** HENNA.

**alchemist, alchemy. See** CHEMICAL, para 2.

**alcohol**, whence the sl **alky** and the adj, hence **n**, **alcoholic.**

*Alcohol* comes direct from ML, which adapted it from Ar *al-kuḥl*, 'the (*al*) powder (*kuḥl*: whence E *kohl*)' for painting the eyelids. For *al*, cf:

**alcove**: EF-F *alcôve*: Sp (and Port) *alcoba*: Ar *al-qubbah*, the arch or vault, hence a small-recessed room, usu with a couch. (Cf 'Articled Nouns' in P⁴.)

**alder**: ME *alder*, earlier *aller*: OE *aler, alor*, akin to ON *elrir, ölr*, OHG *elira*—Lith *alksnis*—Pol *olcha*—L *alnus*—and prob E ELM. IE r, *al-*, var *el-*.

**alderman. See** OLD, para 4.

**ale**; **alegar**; **alum—aluminium, aluminium**; **aluminous.**

*Alegar* blends *ale* and vine*gar*: and *ale* derives from OE *alu*, var *ealu*, akin to ON *öl*, ale, and OSl *olŭ*, beer—and also to L *alūmen* (alum), whence, via OF-MF *alum* (EF-F *alun*), the ME and F *alum*, which tastes astringent; 'basic idea: bitter' (Webster). L *alūmen*, o/s *alumin-*, yields the Chem *alumina*, whence *aluminium* (Sci suffix *-ium*) and AE *aluminum*, both with adj *aluminous*, prompted by L *alūminōsus*, the adj of *alūmen*, perh akin, incidentally, to Gr *aludoimon* or *aludimon*, prop the neu s of *aludoimos*, bitter.

**alembic**: ME, from MF, *alambic*: Ar *al-inbiq*, the still; *al*, the + *inbiq*, from Gr *ambix* (o.o.o.), cap of a still. Hence, by aphesis, the archaic *'mbec(k)*.

**alert**, adj hence n, hence v: F *alerte*, EF *a* (F *a*) *l'erte*, on the watch: It *all'erta*, (standing) in a look-out, e.g. on a watch-tower: It *all'* = *alla* = *a* (L *ad*) *la*, at or in the + *erta*, a look-out, orig the f of adj *erto*, steep, from *erto*, elevated—the pp of *ergere*, from L *ērigere*, to raise: cf ERECT. Orig a call to arms: cf ALARM. (P⁴: 'Articled Nouns'.)

**alethiology; alethoscope. See** the element *aletho-*.

**aleurometer. See** the element *aleuro-*.

**Alexander — Alexandria — Alexandrian—Alexandrine, alexandrine; sawney.**

*Alexander*, 'protector of men', L *Alexander*, comes from Gr *Alexandros* (*alexein*, to protect +

*andros*, gen of *anēr*, a man); the f *Alexandra*, from It *Alessandra*; from Alexander the Great, the derivative city-name *Alexandria*, whence *Alexandrian*—L *Alexander* has adj *Alexandrīnus*, whence *Alexandrine*, whence, via MF-F *alexandrin*, the *alexandrines* of verse, from MF heroic poems about Alexander the Great. (Cf P².)—E *Alexander*, a favourite given name in Scotland, has pet-form *Sandy*, occ corrupted to *Sawney*—not the origin of B dial *sawney*, foolish, idle (fellow), cf ZANY.

**alfalfa** (lucerne): adopted from Sp, earlier *alfalfez*, from Ar *al-fiṣfiṣah* or *-façfaçah*, the best sort of fodder.

**algae**, pl of L *alga* (s *alg*), seaweed: perh *alga* is akin to *algēre* (s *alg-*), to be cold. Cf *algid*, cold, from L *algidus*, itself from *algēre*.

**algebra**, whence **algebraic**, **algebraist**: adopted from either It or ML *algebra*, from Ar *al-jabr*, elliptical for *al-jabr w-al-muqūbalah*, 'the reduction and the comparison' by equations: *al*, the+n from *jabara* (triconsonantal r: *jbr*), to bind together. *Al-jabr*, the reduction (lit, reparation), became, in Math, understood as 'the reduction of arithmetic to a better form'. (B & W.)

**algid.** See ALGAE.

**alias; alibi:** L *alias*, otherwise, esp otherwise called; L *alibi*, elsewhere: both from *alius*, other. Cf:

**alien**, adj hence n; **alienage; alienate, alienation; alienist.**

L *alius*, other (adj), another (pron)—f.a.e., ELSE —has derivative *aliēnus*, of, belonging to, another, whence: *alien*, via OF-EF *alien*; *alienage* (suffix *age*), from F *aliénage*; *alienate*, from L *aliēnātus*, pp of *aliēnāre*, to estrange, from *aliēnus*; *alienation*, MF *alienation* (EF-F *alié-*), L *aliēnātiō* (acc *aliēnātiōnem*), from *aliēnāre*; *alienist*, from F *aliéniste* (*alien+-iste*, E *-ist*). Cf ALIAS.

**aliferous, aligerous, aliform.** See the element *alī-*.

**alight**, adj: either *a-*, on+*light*, fire, or the pp of ME *alihten*, to set aflame, OE *ālīhtan* (*a*, on+*līhtan*, *lyhtan*, to shine: cf LIGHT, v).

**alight**, v, to descend. See LEVER, para 11.

**align, alignment.** See LINE, para 6.

**alike.** See LIKE, para 4.

**aliment; alimentary; alimentation.**

*Aliment*, adopted from OF-F, comes from L *alimentum*, food, lit 'what nourishes', from *alere* (s *al-*), to nourish, a v with numerous IE cognates: f.a.e., OLD. *Alimentum* has adj *alimentārius*, whence E *alimentary*, and LL v *alimentāre*, whence ML *alimentātiō*, o/s *alimentātiōn-*, whence E *alimentation*, sustenance. Cf:

**alimony:** L *alimōnia*, sustenance, from *alere*, to nourish. Cf prec.

**aliped; alitrunk.** See the element *ali-*.

**alive.** See LIFE, para 2.

**alkali:** ME *alkaly* or *alc-*: MF *alcali*: Ar *al-qilī*, the ashes (of saltwort). Hence the adj, whence the n, *alkaloid*: *alkali*+suffix *-oid*.

**alkanna.** See HENNA.

**all**, adj—hence adv and n; **albeit—almighty— almost—also—although; withal.**

1. *All* derives, via ME *al*, pl *alle*, from OE *all*, *eall*, pl *alle*, *ealle*: akin to OFris (and OS) *all*, OHG *al* (G *all*), Go *alls*, ON *allr*—? to Cor *ōl* and OIr *uile*, *ule*, Ga *uile*, OC *\*oljos*—Lith *alvíenas*, each one—Oscan *allo*—perh the rare L *allers*, learned (? 'gifted with *all* knowledge'); IE r, perh *\*al-*. (Feist.)

2. *Albeit*: sep entry; *almighty* (adj hence n), OE *ealmihtig*, 'all, i.e. entirely, mighty'; *almost*, OE *ealmǣst, aelmǣst*, all—i.e., quite—(the) most; *also*, ME *al so*, OE *ealswā*, *aelswā*, *alswā*, from *eal* (etc.)+*swā*, so, lit therefore 'quite so'—cf OFris *al-sa*; *although*=all+ON *thōh*.

3. *Withal* merely= *with all*, ME *with all* or *with alle*.

**Allah:** Ar *Allāh*, conflation of *al-ilāh*, the god, *the* god, God. Cf Hit *ilu*, god or goddess, Aram *alāhā* (cf Syriac *allāhā*), Biblical Aram *'elāh*, H *'elōah*; the Sem r is *il-*, var *el-*, and it occurs in, e.g., *Elijah* and *Elisha*.

**allantoic.** See the element *allanto-*.

**allay**, (obs) to lay aside, to quieten, hence **allayment** (suffix *-ment*): ME *alaien*, earlier *al eggen*, to lay down, humble, end: OE *ālecgan*, from *ā-*, out+ *lecgan*, to lay (see LAY, v): Go *us-lagjan*, OHG *ar-leggēn*.

**allegation:** adopted from OF, from IL *allegātiō* o/s *allegātiōn-*, from *allegāre* (pp *alegātus*), to, send a message: *ad*, to+*legāre*, to send, to commission: f.a.e., see LEGATE. Sense-influenced by:

**allege.** See LITIGANT, para 2.

**allegiance:** ME *alegeaunce*: a- to+OF *ligeance*, from *lige*, *liege*: f.a.e., LIEGE. Sense-influenced by L *ligāre*, to bind.

**allegory; allegoric(al), allegorism, allegorist, allegorize.**

The Gr *allēgoria*, *allos*, other (cf ELSE)+a n deriving from, or akin to, *agoreuein*, to speak in the *agora* (s *agor-*) or assembly (from *agein*, s *ag-*, to drive or lead), became L *allēgoria*, whence F *allégorie* and E *allegory*, 'a speaking otherwise'. The derivative Gr adj *allēgorikos* yields, via LL *allēgoricus*, the F *allégorique* and E *allegoric*, whence the elaboration *allegorical*. LGr *allēgorizein* became LL *allēgorizāre* became F *allégoriser*, whence E *allegorize*, whence *allegorization*. *Allegorism, allegorist*=*allegory*+the suffixes *-ism*, *-ist*; the latter perh came from LL *allegoristes*, itself from LGr *allēgoristēs*.

**allegro.** See ALACRITY, para 2.

**alleluia** (hallelujah): LL *allēlūia*: Gr *allēlouia*: H *hallēlū-yāh*, praise ye Jah (Jehovah).

**allergic, allergy.** See ENERGETIC, para 3.

**alleviate, alleviation, alleviative, alleviator.** See LEVER, para 7.

**alley:** ME *aley*: OF *alee* (F *allée*), a going, (hence) a passage, from *aler*, to go: L *ambulāre*, to walk. 'The abnormal reduction of *ambulāre* must have happened in military orders, thus *\*allate* for imp *ambulate*, "March!" '; this sense of *ambulāre* occurs in LL. (B & W.) Cf AMBLE.

**Allhallows.** See HOLY, para 3.

**alliance; ally,** v hence n. See LIGAMENT, para 5.

**alligator.** See LEG, para 3.

**alliterate; alliteration, alliterative.** See LETTER, para 6.

**allocate; allocation;** ML *allocātus*, pp of *allocāre*, to put into its place, to apportion: L *ad*, to+ *locāre*, to place, from *locus*, a place: f.a.e., LOCAL. Hence ML *allocātiō*, o/s *allocātiōn-*, whence *allocation*. Cf ALLOW.

**allochromatic; allomorph; allopathy.** See the element *allo-*.

**allot, allotment.** See LOT, para 3.

**allow,** whence (? via F *allouable*) **allowable; allowance.**

*Allow* comes, via ME *alouen* and OF-EF *alouer*, to place, to assign, from L *allocāre*: cf ALLOCATE and, f.a.e., LOCAL: sense-confused with OF *alouer*, to laud, to approve (L *allaudāre*, to belaud). OF *alouer*, to place, has derivative *alouance*, whence *allowance*, n hence v.

**alloy,** n and v; **alloyage.**

*Alloy*, n, comes from MF-F *aloi*, from OF *aloier*, earlier *aleier* (var *alier*), to bind, to combine, from L *alligāre*: cf ALLIANCE and, f.a.e., LIGAMENT. OF *aloier* became F *aloyer*, whence 'to alloy' and F *aloyage*, whence E *alloyage* (suffix *-age*).

**allude; allusion, allusive.** Cf *collusion, delude, elude, illusion, prelude*—but see LUDICROUS, para 3.

**allure.** See LURE, para 2.

**alluvial; alluvion; alluvium.** See LAVA, para 9.

**ally.** See LIGAMENT, para 5.

**almanac:** ME *almenak*: ML *almanachus* or *almanach*: either from Byz Gr *almenikhiaka*, calendars, pl of *almenikhiakon* (ἀλμενιχιακόν), itself from Ar, or direct from the Moorish Ar *al-manākh*, the calendar: Ar *al*, the+*manākh*, weather, orig a place (connoted by prefix *ma-*) where camels kneel (*nākha*, to kneel)—hence, a camp—hence, a settlement—hence, (settled) weather: *al-manākh*, '(that which records) the weather (one may expect)'.

**almighty.** See ALL, para 2.

**almond:** ME *almande*: OF *alemande* (MF-F *amande*): Late VL *amandula* (cf Rum *mandula*, var of *migdala*): L *amygdala*: Gr *anugdalē*, perh from Asia Minor—if not the Orient—but cf H *magdī'ēl* (or *meged'ēl*), 'precious gift from God', and OProv *amela*.

**almoner.** See ALMS.

**almost.** See ALL, para 2.

**alms,** whence **almsdeed** (act—cf DEED—of charity) and **almshouse; almoner, almonry;— eleemosynary,** adj hence n.

*Alms:* ME *almes*, earlier *almesse*: OE *aelmysse*: LL *el(e)ēmosyna*: LGr *eleēmosunē*, compassion, alms, from Gr *elaēmōn*, merciful, from *eleos*, compassion (o.o.o.). LL *el(e)ēmosyna* acquired, in ML, the adj *el(e)ēmosynārius*, whence E *eleemosynary*; also prob via VL *alemosina*, it yielded OF *almosne*, whence the agent *almosnier, aumosnier*, whence ME *aumener*, whence E *almoner*; and OF *almosne* yielded *aumosnerie*, whence E *almonry*.

**aloe** (adj *aloetic*): L *aloë*: LGr *aloē*: H *alōth*,

aloe (cf *'ahālīm*, aloe wood). The var *aloes* comes, via F *aloès*, from LL *aloës* (orig the gen of *aloë*), var of *aloë*. *Aloetic* app derives from F *aloétique*, a learned formation, as if from ML *\*aloeticus* or LGr *\*aloētikos*.

**aloft.** See the 2nd LIFT, para 1, s.f.

**alone.** See ONE, para 10.

**along.** See LONG, para 2.

**aloof.** See LUFF, para 2.

**aloud:** *a-*, on (connoting manner)+LOUD; cf obsol *alow*.

**alp,** whence the **Alps; alpenstock; alpine:** from L *Alpes* (cf the LGr *Alpeis*), the Alps, whence the adj *alpīnus*, whence *Alpine, alpine* (cf EF-F *alpin*); *alpenhorn* and *alpenstock* are borrowings from G (*Alpen*, pl of *Alpe*). L *Alpes* is app of C origin; several authorities (e.g. Walshe) think it prob non-IE, but cf the C *\*alp*, high mountain (Ir *ailp* or *alpa*, a protuberance, a high mountain)—perh a var of the C *\*alb*, (to be) white, akin to L *albus*, Sabine *alpus*, Gr *alphos* (cf ALB); perh cf Hit *alpas*, a cloud. Only the high mountains tend to be white.

**alpaca** is cloth made from hair of the *alpaca* (a SAm llama): Sp *alpaca*: Quechua *alpaca*, perh from Quechua *paco*, red.

**alpenstock.** See ALP; cf STAKE, para 6.

**alphabet:** perh adopted from late MF-F: LL *alphabētum*: LGr *alphabētos*, from the 1st two letters of Gr alphabet, A, B, *alpha, bēta* (cf H *beth*). *Alpha* (akin to H *āleph*) occurs also in *alpha and omega*, the beginning and the end, *omega* (ω) being the last letter: cf *Revelations*, i, 8.

**alpine.** See ALP.

**already; alright.** Simply *all ready* and *all right*.

**Alsace; Alsatia,** whence **Alsatian:** ML *Alsatia*, from OHG *Elisaz* (G *Elsass*), whence *Alsace*, the much-contested marches between France and Germany, hence, in C17–early C18 London, a sanctuary for debtors and criminals. The quadruped *Alsatian* is elliptical for *Alsatian wolf dog* (German sheepdog).

**also.** See ALL.

**altar; altarist.** The latter comes, prob via F *altariste*, from LL *altarista*, from LL *altāre* (usu of a Christian altar and as pl *altāria*), whence, via OE and ME, the E *altar* (cf the OF *alter*); the connexion with L *altus*, high, is prob f/e—but then so perh also is that with L *ōra*, a pagan altar.

**alter,** whence **alterable** (cf the MF-F *altérable*); **alterant; alteration; alterative,** adj hence n.

*Alter:* MF-F *altérer*: LL *alterāre*, to change, from *alter*, the other (of two)—orig a comp of, or at the least akin to, *alius*, other, (pron) another: f.a.e., see ELSE. *Alterāre* (s *alter-*) has presp *alterans*, o/s *alterant-*, whence the E adj (hence n) *alterant*; and pp *alterātus*, s *alterāt-*, on which arose both the LL *alterātiō*, o/s *alterātiōn-*, whence, prob via MF-F *altération*, the E *alteration*, and the ML *alterātivus*, whence *alterative*. Cf ALTERNATE and:

**altercate, altercation.**

The L *altercāri*, to be at variance, esp heatedly, derives from *alter*, other (see prec), and has pp *altercātus*, whence 'to *altercate*', and subsidiary n *altercātiō*, o/s *altercātiōn-*, whence MF-F, hence E, *altercation*.

**alternate**, adj (whence n) and v; **alternant**, adj hence n; **alternation; alternative**, adj hence n; **alternator**.

The adj and v *alternate* both come from L *alternātus*, pp of *alternāre*, from *alternus* (suffix *-nus*), from *alter* (see ALTER); *alternus* yields the rare *altern*. *Alternāre* has presp *alternans*, o/s *alternant-*, whence *alternant*, whence the irreg formed *alternacy*; and on the pp *alternātus* (s *alternāt-*) arose both the L *alternātiō*, o/s *alternātiōn-*, whence *alternation*, and the ML *alternātivus*, whence the adj *alternative*. *Alternator* is an E formation.

**although.** See ALL, para 2.

**altitude; alto, altissimo;** cf the element *alti-*.

L *altus* (s *alt-*), high, was orig the pp of *alere*, to nourish: f.a.e., OLD. Its derivative *altitūdō* yields E *altitude*, and the It form *alto* has, with its sup *altissimo*, been adopted, by Mus, everywhere—so has its cpd *contralto* (prefix *contra*, against), the lowest female voice.

**altogether:** ME *altogedere*, from *al*, all+*togedere*. See ALL and TOGETHER.

**altruism, altruist, altruistic.**

*Altruism:* F *altruisme*, (with L *l*) from *autrui*, other persons, itself deriving, under the influence of *lui*, he, from *autre*, another, from L *alter*, other: f.a.e., ALTER. *Altruistic* comes (by *-ic*) from the F adj *altruiste*, which prob suggested the E n *altruist·*

**alum; alumina, aluminium,** etc. See ALE.

**alveolar:** the adj corresp to the element *alveoli-*.

**always.** See VIA, para 6.

**am,** OE *am* and *eom*, comes, like *is* and *are* and '(thou) *art*', from an IE r *es-*, to exist: f.a.e., ESSENCE.

**amain.** See MAIN.

**amalgam; amalgamate, amalgamation, amalgamative, amalgamator.**

*Amalgam:* late MF-F *amalgame*: late ML *amalgama*: Ar *al-malgham*: Ar *al*, the+Gr *malagma*, an emollient, from *malassein*, to soften, from *malakos*, soft, IE r perh *mal-*. *Amalgam*+v suffix *-ate* yields 'to *amalgamate*', whence *amalgamation* (suffix *-ion*, cf *-ation*)—*amalgamative* (*-ive*) —*amalgamator* (agential *-or*).

**amanuensis.** See MANUAL.

**amass,** whence (suffix *-ment*) **amassment:** OF-F *amasser: a* (F *à*), L *ad*, towards, to+*masser*, to assemble, from the n *masse* (see MASS).

**amateur,** n hence adj and **amateurism; amative; amatory; amorist, amorous,** *amour*—**enamour,** AE **enamor,** and **paramour**—**inamorata, inamorato;**—**amicable, amiable (amiability); amity; inimical; enemy.**

The chain is this:

IE r *am-*, to love: cf Gr *adamnein* (*ad-*, Phrygian int prefix+*am-*+infix *-n-*+inf suffix *-ein*);

I: L *amāre* (s *am-*), to love; whence

1, *amator*, a lover, whence MF-F, hence E, *amateur*—cf the suffix *-ator*;

2, *amatōrius*, whence *amatory*—cf the suffixes *-atory* and *-ory*;

3, ML *amatīvus*, worthy of love—but in E, tending to love.

II: L *amor* (s *am-*), love, prob imm from *amāre*; personified as *Amor*; hence the OF-F *amour*, sense-adapted by E to 'love affair'; whence

1, LL *amorōsus*, full of (passionate) love, whence OF *amorous* (F *amoureux*), whence E *amorous*;

2, *amorist*, an E formation (suffix *-ist*) from *amor*;

3, the prefix cpds *enamour*, AE *enamor*, from OF-MF *enamorer*, EF-F *enamourer* (*en*, in+*amour* +inf suffix *-er*), and *inamorata* (f), *inamorato* (m), a person in love or a person loved, from It *innamorata, innamorato*, f and m of the pp of *innamorare*, to enamour; and *paramour*, ME *par amur, par amour, paramur*, (C14 onwards) *paramour*, from OF *par amour*, orig adv, by (or with) love.

III: —*amīcus*, friend, whence

1, LL *amīcābilis*, whence E *amicable* and OF-EF *amiable*, whence, influenced by OF-MF *amable*, MF-F *aimable* (L *amābilis*, from *amāre*), the E *amīable*, whence *amiability*;

2, VL *amicitās*, acc *amīcitātem*, whence OF-MF *amistié* or *-té* (EF-F *amitié*), whence E *amity*;

3, the opp *inimīcus* (for *inamīcus*), an enemy, whence OF *enemi*, whence E *enemy*; with derivatives LL *inimīcālis*, whence *inimical*, hostile, and VL *inimīcitās* (o/s *inimīcitāt-*), whence OF *enemistié*, whence ME *enemyte*, whence *enmity*.

**amaze, amazement.** See MAZE.

**Amazon, amazon.**

An *amazon*, or proficiently bellicose or merely tall, strong woman, derives from *Amazon*: L *Amazon*; Gr *Amazōn*, member of a race of mythical (?) female warriors: perh privative *a-*+*mazos*, breast+presp suffix *-ōn*, with *mazos* akin to *madan*, to be moist, IE r *mad-*, to drip: from removal of right breast to facilitate archery; prob, however, from Iranian, esp OPer, *hamazan-*, a warrior, as Boisacq holds.

The river *Amazon*, Sp *Rio Amazonas*, takes its name from some riverine women that impressed the early explorers.

**ambassador, ambassadorial.** See EMBASSY.

**amber: ambergris.**

*Ambergris* half-anglicizes the F *ambre gris*, grey amber (cf GRAY). *Amber* itself came into ME from OF-F *ambre*, from Ar '*anbar* (ambergris).

**ambidextrous, ambidexterity:** the latter, prompted by **dexterity,** derives by suffix *-ity* from the former, which anglicizes the rare *ambidexter*, adopted from ML: *ambi-*, both+*dexter* (manus), right hand: 'having two right hands'. Cf AMBIGUITY.

**ambience, ambient.** See AMBIT.

**ambiguity, ambiguous.**

The former comes, via MF-F *ambiguité*, from L *ambiguitās*, o/s *ambiguitāt-*, from *ambiguus*, whence E *ambiguous* (suffix *-ous*): and *ambiguus* derives from *ambigere*, to drive, hence to go—L *agere* (f.a.e.: AGENT)—on both sides—L *ambo*, both, c/f *ambi-* (Elements). Cf:

**ambit; ambition, ambitious; ambience, ambient.**

Resp, *ambit*: L *ambitus*, a circuit, from *ambīre*, to go around or about—cf the element *ambi-* and, for the r *it-*, ISSUE; *ambition*, perh via MF-F, from L *ambitiō* (o/s *ambitiōn-*), a going about, esp for votes; *ambitious*—perh via MF-F *ambitieux*, f *ambitieuse*—from L *ambitiōsus*, adj corresp to *ambitiō*; *ambience*—perh via F *ambiance*—from *ambient*+abstract suffix *-ce*; *ambient*, perh via EF-F *ambiant*, from L *ambient-*, o/s of *ambiens*, presp of *ambīre*—cf the LL *ambienter*, ambitiously.

**ambivalence, -valent.** See VALUE, para 11.

**amble, n and v—preamble—?** ramble, v hence n and rambler; ambulance, ambulant—ambulate, ambulation, ambulatory; circumambulate, circumambulation; perambulate, perambulation, perambulator; alley (sep).

1. *Amble*, n, adopted from OF-F: from OF *ambler*, whence, at the ME stage, 'to amble': perh via OProv *amblar*: from LL *ambulāre*, to amble, from L *ambulāre*, to go about, take a turn, make a tour, (hence) to walk: *amb-*, for *ambi-*, (lit) on both sides, (hence) about, around+*al-*, to go+inf suffix *-āre*. The r *ul-*, like *al-* (see ALACRITY), is a var of IE r *\*el-*, to go; perh cf Gr *alaomai* (s *al-*), I wander, and *elaunō* (s *elaun*, r *el-*), I drive—and certainly cf L *exul*, one who goes out (from his homeland)—and W *el*, let him go!

2. *Ambulāre* has presp *ambulans*, o/s *ambulant-*, whence the E adj *ambulant*, also in F; the F *hôpital ambulant*, a field hospital, yields F, hence E, *ambulance*. The pp *ambulātus* accounts for 'to ambulate', and the subsidiary *ambulātiō*, o/s *ambulātiōn-*, becomes E *ambulation*; *ambulator* comes direct from L, *ambulatory*—perh via late MF-F *ambulatoire*—from L *ambulatōrius*.

3. The rare 'to *preamble*', lit 'to walk before' (cf the prefix *pre-*), comes from LL *praeambulāre*, whence the LL adj *praeambulus*, whence the ML n *praeambulum*, whence MF-F *préambule*, whence E *preamble*.

4. L *perambulāre*, to walk *per* or through, has pp *perambulātus*, whence 'to *perambulate*', to walk, hence to travel, over; the derivative LL *perambulātiō*, o/s *permabulātiōn-*, yields *perambulation*; *perambulator* is an E formation (cf agential *-or*): the baby-carriage sense is derivative.

5. LL *circumambulāre*, to walk *circum* or around, has pp *circumambulātus*, whence 'to *circumambulate*', whence E has analogously derived *circumambulation*, etc.

6. Now, 'to *ramble*', whence 'a *ramble*' and *rambler* (person, later a rose), is usu described as 'o.o.o.': but ME *ramblen* could, after *amble*, have come from VL *\*rambulāre*, for LL *reambulāre*, an inferior var of L *redambulāre*, to walk back, esp from an excursion.

7. Cf sep ALLEY.

**ambrosia, ambrosial:** L, from Gr, *ambrosia*, from *ambrotos*, immortal: *am-*, euphonic for *an-*, not+ *brotos*, mortal: cf MORTAL and MURDER. *Ambrosial*: E *ambrosia*+adj suffix *-al*; or an *-al* adaptation of L *ambrosius* (Gr *ambrosios*).

**ambulance; ambulant; ambulate.** See AMBLE, para 2.

**ambuscade, n hence v; ambush, n and v.**

*Ambuscade* comes from late MF-F *embuscade*, from MF-F *embusquer*, to ambush, from OF *embuscher*, *embuschier* (influenced by It *imboscare*), whence the n *embusche* (later *embûche*), whence E 'an *ambush*'; whence also, via ME *embuschen*, the E 'to *ambush*'. *Embuscher, embuschier*, lit 'to take to the woods'= *em-*, in(to)+*busche*: f.a.e., BUSH.

**ameliorate, ameliorant, ameliorate, amelioration, amelorative.** See MELIORABLE, para 1.

**amen:** LL *āmēn*: Aram Gr *amēn*: H *āmēn*, Truly, or thus be it.

**amenable.** See MINATORY, para 6.

**amend, amendment, amends; amende honorable.** See MENDICANT, para 4.

**amenity:** late MF-F *aménité*: L *amoenitās*, o/s *amoenitāt-*: *amoenus*, pleasant: perh orig 'lovable', from *amare* (s *am-*). to love.

**amentia.** See MIND, para 11.

**America,** whence **American** (cf *-an*, adj): as if (*terra*) *America*, 'Amerigo's Land', from *Americus* (*Vespucius*)—L form of It *Amerigo* (Vespucci)— apprehended as adj: Amerigo Vespucci may or may not have discovered the mainland of America late in C15; certainly his writings (early C16) publicized it.

With *Americanism* cf *Anglicism*, which prompted it.

**amethyst, amethystine; mead.**

*Amethyst*: ME *ametist*: OF-MF *ametiste* (EF-F *améthyste*): L *amethystus*: Gr *amethustos*, amethyst, orig a remedy against intoxication, this precious stone being fabled to possess that virtue: *a-*, not+*-methustos*, app a blend of *methusos* and *methustas*, drunken, from *methuein*, to be tipsy, from *methu*, an intoxicating drink, closely akin to Skt *madhu*, honey, mead (made from honey); akin also to OSl *medu*, OP *meddo*, honey; to OIr *mid*, W *med*, Cor *medhu*, mead, *mēdh*, *medd*, mead; and to OFris *mede*, OGH *metu*, OE *meodu*, ME *mede*, E *mead* (the drink). The IE etymon is *\*medhu*, honey, from adj *\*medhus*, sweet, ult akin to Gr *meli*, L *mel*, honey. The word is prob Medit: cf, in Sem, the tri-consonantal r *mtq*, 'sweet' or 'sweetness' (hence perh 'honey'), as in H *māthōq*, sweet, sweetness, and the rare *metheq*, sweetness— Ugaritic *mṭq*, sweet—Akkadian *matqū*, sweet, *mutqū*, sweetness, *muttāqū*, sweet food, perh honey —Ar *matqā*, sweetness—Ethiopic *metūq*, sweet, *metqat*, sweetness. (With thanks to Professor D. W. Thomas.) Perhaps related, in Ham, are Eg *k(h)ebi*, wild honey, and *retchem-t*, anything sweet. The Medit r is app *\*madk-*, var *\*medk-*; and in Sem the r *mtq* bears also the related meaning 'to suck'.

2. *Amethystine*: L *amethystīnus*: Gr *amethustinos*, from *amethustos*.

amiable and amicable. See AMATEUR, III, 1.

amid, amidst. See MEDIAL, para 13.

amir. See ADMIRAL.

amiss, adv hence adj: *a-*, on *+miss*, n: 'on the miss', i.e. astray.

amity. See AMATEUR, III, 2.

ammonia, ammoniac, ammonium: the 3rd comes, by Chem suffix *-ium*, from the 1st; the 1st is adopted from LL *ammōnia*, itself app, by suffix *-ia*, from Gr *ammōn*; E *ammoniac* is elliptical for *sal ammoniac*, with *ammoniac* an adj, adopted from the C16–18 F adj *ammoniac*, itself deriving from ML *ammoniacus*, adj of L *ammoniacum*, from Gr *ammōniakon*, already used as n for the salt (*ammonia*) and the gum (*ammoniac*), from Gr *Ammōn* (Jupiter Ammon), from Eg *Ámen*, lit 'the *Hidden* (One)': both of these products were gathered from the vicinity of Ammon's temple, the salt from camels' dung, the gum from plants.

ammunition. See MUNIMENT.

amnesia, amnesiac. See MIND, para 8.

amnesty. See MIND, para 8.

amoeba: SciL, from Gr *amoibē*, a change, from *ameibein* (s *ameib*-), to change: *a-* is app int, or merely formative: with *meib*-, cf the *mig-* of L *migrāre*, q.v. at MIGRATE.

amok and, mostly AE, amuck: Malay *amok*, furious—esp, homicidally maniac: perh akin, ult, to L *amens*, mad, (lit) out of one's mind: *a-*, (away) from+*mens*, mind (cf MIND).

among, amongst: ME *among*, ME *amonges* (later *amongist*): OE *on*, in+*gemang*, a crowd, (orig) a mingling, from *gemengan*, to mingle—cf MINGLE and MONGREL.

amoral, amorality. See MORAL, para 4.

amorist; amorous. See AMATEUR, II, 1 and 2.

amorphous. See MORPHEUS, para 3.

amortize, -zation, -zement. See MORTAL.

amotion. See MOVE, para 9.

amount, v hence n: OF *amonter*, to increase, (lit) to ascend: *amont*, upwards: L *ad montem*, to the mountain: f.a.e., MOUNT.

amour. See AMATEUR, II.

ampère, now usu ampere: from André *Ampère* (1775–1836), F physicist.

ampersand: '*and' per se 'and*', written '& per se and': & by itself (makes) and.

amphibian, amphibious: the former (-*an* for -*ous*) from the latter, itself from Gr *amphibios*, living (cf the element *bio-*) on both sides (element *amphi-*).

ample; amplify, amplitude.

*Ample*, adopted from OF-F, comes from L *amplus*, perh akin to L *ampla*, var of *ansa*, a handle; 'basic idea: holding' (Webster). *Amplus* has notable derivatives (1) *amplificāre*, whence late MF-F *amplifier*, whence 'to *amplify*', with subsidiary *amplificātiō*, o/s *amplificātiōn*, whence—perh imm from MF-F—the E *amplification*, and (2) *amplitūdō*, whence, via MF-F, the E *amplitude*.

amputate; amputation; amputative. See the 2nd COUNT, para 3.

amuck. See AMOK.

amulet comes—cf EF-F *amulette*—from L *amulētum*, o.o.o. Perh cf Eg *amiasta*, amulet; Ancient Egypt was famous—and had many names —for its amulets.

amuse; amusement. See MUSE, para 2.

an, indefinite article. See ONE, para 8.

ana, memorable or odd sayings: from L -*ana*, neu pl of adjj in -*ānus*, pertaining to, as in *Americana* and in *Johnsoniana* (connective -*i*-), the sayings, the *ana*, of Dr Johnson.

anachronism, whence anachronistic: perh via F *anachronisme*, from Gr *anakhronismos*, itself from *anakhronizein*, to refer wrongly (lit, backwards: Gr *ana*-) in time (Gr *khronos*: cf CHRONICLE).

anaconda is prob either a Singhalese (Webster) or (OED) a Singhalese and Tamil word; Enci It, however, says that it originates in Surinam (Dutch Guiana). If Singhalese or Tamil, it app (OED) means 'the crusher' or 'the killer'—or, says Skeat, 'lightning stem'.

anaemia, anaemic; also, in AE, anemia, anemic: *añaemia*, SciL from Gr *anaimia*, blood-deficiency: *an*-, var of *a*-, not+*haima*, blood. Hence *anaemic* (-*ic*, and adj suffix)—perh prompted by Gr *anaimos*. Cf the element *haemo*-.

anaesthesia, anaesthetic, anaesthetist. See AESTHETE, 2nd para.

anagram. See GRAMMAR, para 3.

anal. See ANNULAR.

analecta, analectic. See LEGEND, para 24.

analogy; analogic(al), analogism, analogist, analogize, analogous, analogue. See LEGEND, para 24.

analysis; analyst, analytic, analyse. See LOSE, para 10.

anapaest: L *anapaestus*, trln of Gr (*daktulos*) *anapaistos*, ᴗᴗ–, (a dactyl: –ᴗᴗ) reversed, lit struck (*paistos*, pp of *paiein*, to strike) back (*ana*). Adj, *anapaestic*: via L, from Gr *anapaistikos*.

anarchy; anarch, anarchic, anarchism, anarchist.

The Gr *anarkhos* (*an*-, not+*arkhos*, ruler: f.a.e., the element *arch*-) becomes E *anarch*, of which *anarchist* (suffix -*ist*) is a needless elaboration; moreover, Gr *anarkhos* has derivative *anarkhia*, whence, prob via MF-F *anarchie*, the E *anarchy*, with needless var *anarchism* (-*ism*). *Anarchic*, with -*al* elaboration *anarchical*, either anglicizes EF-F *anarchique* or=*anarch*+ adj suffix -*ic*.

anathema: L, from Gr *anathema*, a thing devoted, esp to evil, hence a curse: from *anatithenai*, to dedicate: *ana*, up+*tithenai*, to place or put—cf THESIS.

anatomical, anatomist, anatomize, anatomy. See TOME, para 4.

ancestor, whence (suffix -*ess*) ancestress; ancestral, ancestry.

L *antecedere*, to go (*cēdere*: cf CEDE) before (*ante*), has derivative *antecessor*, a goer before, whence OF *ancestre*, ME *ancestre*, Mod *ancestor*. OF-MF *ancestre* has derivative *ancesserie*, whence, anl, E *ancestry*. *Ancestral*, if not prompted by MF *ancestrel*, is a contr of *ancestor*+-*al* (adj).

anchor, n and v

The v, if not direct from the n, comes from OF-F *ancrer* (from n *ancre*, from L); the n, ME *anker*, OE *ancor*, comes from L *ancora*, *anchora*, itself from Gr *ankura*, r *ank-*, akin to E *angle*, r *ang-*: f.a.e., the n ANGLE. Although from *anchor*, v (+suffix *-age*), *anchorage* was perh suggested by F *ancrage*.

**anchoret** or **anchorite** (influence of agential *-ite*): EF-F *anachorète*: L *anachōrēta*: Gr *anakhōrētēs*, from *anakhōrein*, to retire: *ana*, back+*khōrein*, to give place, from *khōros*, a place: cf the 1st element *choro-*.

**anchovy**: Sp *anchova*, var of *anchoa*, either from Basque *anchua*, itself from *antzua*, sterile, dry (Webster), or from Gr *aphuē*, some small fish, via VL *apyia*, from L *aphya*, *apua*—cf the It *acciuga* and, for the infix *-n-*, the Port *enchova* (B & W): those rude, virile illiterates, the many-countried Mediterranean sailors, reshaped *aphua* to their needs.

**ancient** (adj hence n), whence **ancientry** (suffix *-ry*): ME *auncien*: OF-F *ancien*, irreg from VL *\*antianus*, from VL *\*antius*, from *ante* (prep) or *antea* (adv), before—cf the prefix *ante-*. The *-t* may owe something to OF-F *ancienneté*, ancientry.

**ancillary**: LL *ancillāris*, from L *ancilla*, hand-maiden, f of *anculus* (o.o.o.).

**and**: OE *and*, *end*, akin to OFris *and* or *anda*, and *end*, *enda*, *ende*—cf also OS *ande* or *endi*, OHG *anti*, *enti*, *inti*, *unti* or *unta* (G *und*)—perh ON *enn*, even, also, and esp Skt *átha*, then, also, and. The IE r could be *\*and-* or *\*end-*, varr *\*ant-* or *\*ent-*; but I suspect that the *-n-* is simply a nasalization and that the IE r is *\*at-* or *\*et-*: cf Skt *átha* and perh *ati*, beyond—Gr *eti*, moreover, still—L *et*, and—perh Go *ith*, and, and *id-*, again—Gaul *itic*, and—perh OIr *acus*, Ga *agus*, and.

**andante** (Mus), moderately yet fluently slow: It presp of *andare*, to go: o.o.o.; ? an IE r *\*and-*, to go—cf Hit *anda*, *andan*, to go (to a person, to a place), app only in the taut *anda pai-* and *andan pai-*.

**andiron**: influenced by *iron*: ME *aundiren* (or *-yrne*): OF *andier*, prob from Gaul *andero*, young bull, *\*andera*, heifer—cf Ir *ainder*, young woman, and W, Cor, Br *anner*, heifer. 'Andirons often have, at their extremities, an animal's head' (B & W, at *landier*).

**androgynous**, etc. See the elements *andro-* and *-gyn*.

**anecdote**; **anecdotal**, **anecdotist**; **anecdotage**. *Anecdote* comes, via F, from Gr *anekdotos*, un-published—*an-*, not+*ekdotos*, published, from *ekdidōnai*, to publish, (lit) give out: *ek*, out+*didōnai*, to give: f.a.e., *date* (time). But between F *anecdote* and Gr *anekdotos* there intervened Procopius's gossipy memoirs of his day (C7), *Anekdota* (n from the neupl of the adj *anekdotos*), 'Things Unpub-lished'. (B & W.) The derivatives arise thus: *anecdot*(e)+*-al*; *anecdot*(e)+*-ist*; *anec*dote+*dot-age*.

**anemia**. See ANAEMIA.

**anemone**: L *anemone*: Gr *anemōnē*, from *anemos*, wind: cf the element *anemo-*.

**anent**. See ADDENDA.

**anesthesia**, **anesthetic**. See AESTHETE.

**aneurism**, better **aneurysm**: Gr *aneurusma*, an opening: *ana*, back, up+*eurus*, broad, wide+suffix.

**anew**. See NOVA, para 8.

**angel**, **angelic**, **Angelica**, **angelica**.

Whereas the 3rd arises in ML, from L *angelicus*, and the 4th is elliptical for L *herba angelica* ('angelic' because reputedly curative), the 2nd, imm from MF-F *angélique*, comes—via LL *angelicus*—from Gr *angelikos*, the adj of *angelos* (ἄγγελος), a messenger, hence, in LGr, a divine messenger, an angel, whence, via LL *angelus* and OF *angele*, the E *angel*. With *angelos*, cf the Gr *angaros*, a Persian courier, itself of Iranian origin, and Skt *aṅgiras*, a divinity.

2. Note the cpds (1) *archangel*, perh via OF *archangel*, from LL *archangelus*, from Gr *arkhan-gelos* (cf the element *arch-*), with adj *arkhangelikos*, whence, via ML *archangelicus*, the E *archangelic*; (2) *evangel*, ME from OF *evangile*, ML *evangelium*, LL *euangelium*, Gr *euangelion*, glad tidings, from *euangelos*, bringing good news (Gr adv *eu*, well), with adj *euangelikos*, whence, via LL *euangelicus*, ML *ev-*, MF-F *évangélique*, the E *evangelic*, whence *evangelical*—with agent *euangestlis*, whence, via LL *euangelista*, ML *ev-*, OF *evangeliste*, the E *evangelist*—and v *euangelizesthai* (s *euangeliz-*), to bring, announce, good news, whence, via LL *euangelizāre*, ML *ev-*, MF *evangeliser*, the E *evangelize*, *evangelism* being an E formation (*evangel*+*-ism*); (3) Los *Angeles*, Sp for '(the convent of) the angels'.

**anger** (n and v)—hence **angry** (for *angery*): ME *angre*: ON *angr*, sorrow, distress, whence *angra*, to grieve or distress, whence 'to *anger*': akin to ANGINA, ANGUISH, ANXIOUS.

**angina**: L *angina*, quinsy: Gr *ankhonē*. Akin to ANGER and QUINSY.

**angle** (1): n (a corner): adopted from OF, from L *angulus* (r *ang-*), corner, angle, akin to Gr *ankulos* (r *ank-*), bent, from *ankos* (s *ank-*), a bend. Hence, *triangle*, *quadrangle*, etc., and, via L *angu-lāris* and perh EF-F *angulaire*, the adjj *angular*, *triangular*, etc. Cf ANCHOR and:

**angle** (2): n (a fish-hook): OE *angel* or *angul*, akin to OHG *angul*, *ango*, and ON *öngull*—to L *uncus*, a hook, cf Gr *onkos*, an arrow-barb, and *onkē*, a corner—esp Skt *aṅka*, a hook—but also, ult, to prec. Hence, to *angle* or fish, whence *angler*.

**Anglia**, **Anglian**; **Anglican**; **Anglicize**, etc. See ENGLAND.

**Anglo-Saxon**. See SAXON, para 3.

**angostura**. See ANGUISH.

**angry**. See ANGER.

**anguish**, n and v; **angostura**.

1. The latter derives from the *angostura* bark of a SAm tree (Sp *angostura*): from *Angostura*, built on the *narrows* of the Orinoco: Sp *angostura*, a strait, narrows: from L *angustus*, narrow, from *angere* (s *ang-*), to constrict, akin to L *angulus*, a corner—cf 1st and 2nd ANGLE.

2. L *angustus* has derivative *angustia*, narrow-

ness, (hence) distress, whence OF *anguisse* (F and OF *angoisse*), whence ME *anguise*, later *anguishe*, E *anguish*. 'To *anguish*' comes from the OF *angoissier*, OF-F *angoisser* (either from *angoisse* or from LL *angustiare*, *angustare*, to compress, to afflict). Cf ANXIOUS.

**angular.** See 2nd ANGLE.

**angulate.** See the element *angulato-*.

**aniline** derives, by Chem -*ine*, from *anil*, a dye from the WI shrub *anil*: EF-F, from Port, *anil*: Ar *al-nil*, the (*al*) indigo plant: Skt *nīlī*, indigo, from *nīla*, dark blue, whence also Per *nīl*, blue, whence the dim *nīlak*, bluish, whence Ar *laylak*, Sp *lilac*, whence, via EF, the E *lilac*.

**animadversion, animadvert.**

The former comes from ML *animadversiōn-*, o/s of *animadversiō*, L -*uersiō*, from *animaduersus*, pp of *animaduertere*, for *animumaduertere*, lit 'to turn (*uertere*) the mind· (*animus*—cf next) to (*ad*)': cf *advert* at VERSION.

**animal,** n and adj (whence **animality, animalize**): **animate** (adj and v)—**inanimate**—**animation; animism, animistic: animus, animosity—equanimity; longanimity; magnanimous, magnanimity; pusillanimous, pusillanimity; unanimous, unanimity.**

1. L *animus* (s *anim*-), mind, spirit, is a parallel to *anima* (s *anim*-), spirit, soul. Strictly, *animus* is the thinking principle opp both *corpus*, body, and *anima*, soul: and *anima* (hence, ult, *animus*) is orig 'breath of air', hence breath of life, hence the soul, whether of the living or of the dead. *Anima* is perh the most echoic of all words: *a-ni-ma*: *a-*, a slow in-breathing+-*ni-*, (a moment of) relaxed breathing+-*ma*, a strong out-breathing: cf, echoically and sem, L *flātus* and *spiritus*—Gr *atmos*—Skt *ānilas*, *ātman*, breath—and even 'a *breath*' and 'to *breathe*'.

2. *Animus*, adopted by E, has gradually assumed the sense 'feeling of hostility'; the L adj *animōsus* has derivative *animōsitās*, o/s *animōsitāt-*, whence, via MF-F *animosité*, the E *animosity* (cf suffix -*ity*).

3. *Animus* recurs in *animadversion*, q.v. sep; *equanimity*, *magnanimous*, *unanimous*, contain a blend, sem and phon alike, of both *animus* and *anima*.

4. *Anima* issues in the v *animāre* (*anim-*+inf suffix -*āre*), to endow with breath, hence with life, to put life into, with pp *animātus*, whence both the adj *animate* and the v 'to *animate*'; whence also the L *animātiō*, o/s *animātiōn-*, hence E *animation*, and the agential *animātor*, adopted by E. *Anima* leads also to E *animism* (*anima*+-*ism*) and *animist* (cf -*is*), whence *animistic* (cf -*ic* and -*istic*).

5. Prefix derivatives of *anima*, *animāre*, etc., include *exanimāre*, to deprive of breath, pp *exanimātus*, whence E *exanimate*, and LL *inanimātus* (*in*, not+*animātus*, alive), whence *inanimate*. 'To *reanimate*' and *reanimation* are E formations: *re-*, again+*animate*, *animation*.

6. Certain true L cpds of *anima* and *animus*, or of both, result in E words:

*aequanimus*, from *aequo animo ferre*, to bear with an equal, hence even, mind—hence the E *equani-*

*mous*; derivative *aequanimitās*, o/s *aequanimitāt-*, yields (prob via EF *équanimité*) *equanimity*;

LL *longanimis*, long-minded, i.e. patient, has derivative *longanimitās*, o/s *longanimitāt-*, whence, prob via MF-F *longanimité*, the E *longanimity*;

*magnanimus*, great-minded, (esp) generous, yields *magnanimous*, and its derivative *magnanimitās*, o/s *magnanimitāt-*, yields—prob via MF-F *magnanimité*—*magnanimity*; its opposite

LL *pusillanimis*, perh from *pusillo animo*, with very little (*pusillus*) courage (a special sense of *animus*), gives us *pusillanimous*, mean-spirited, (usu) cowardly, and its derivative *pusillanimitās*, o/s -*animitāt-*, gives—prob via MF-F *pusillanimité* —*pusillanimity*;

*unanimus* (*unus*, one), which produces E *unanimous* (and F *unanime*), has derivative *unanimitās*, o/s *unanimitāt-*, whence MF-F *unanimité*, whence E *unanimity*.

7. Also from L *anima* comes the L adj *animālis*, breathing, animate, whence the E adj *animal*; *animālis* has neu *animāle*, whence the n *animal*, a breathing thing, i.e. an *animal*. The E formations are simple: *animalism*=*animal*, n+suffix -*ism*; *animality*=*animal*, adj+-*ity*; *animalize* (whence *animalization*)=*animal*, adj+-*ize*. *Animality* (cf LL *animālitās*) and *animalize* may owe something to F *animalité* and *animaliser*.

8. L *animal* has dim *animalaculum*, whence, perh via EF-F, *animalcule*.

**aniseed**=*anise seed* (cf SEED); *anise* comes, through ME *anys* and MF-F *anis*, from L *anisum*, var *anethum*, from Gr *anison*, var *anēthon*, anise, app a loan-word.

**ankle:** ME *ancle*, perh from ON *ökla* (cf OFris *ankel* or *onkel*, *anklēu* or *onklēu*); the earlier ME form *anclowe* derives from OE *anclēo*, *anclēow* akin to OHG *anchlāo* (early Mod HG *Enkel*) and prob to Skt *aṅga*, limb.

**Ann,** F *Anne*, It from L *Anna*: Gr *Anna*: H *Ḥannāh*, grace, whence E *Hannah*. The dim *Nanny* accounts for *nanny* (goat) and perh for *nanny*, children's nurse, although the latter may be childish for *nursie*, mother's reference to nurse— cf the F *nounou*.

**anna,** small Indian coin: Hi *ānā*.

**annalist; annals.** See ANNUAL, para 2.

**anneal:** ME *anelen*: OE *anǣlan*: *an*, on+-*ǣlan*, to kindle, bake.

**annex, annexation, annexion.** See the 2nd NET, para 8.

**annihilate, annihilation.** See FILAMENT, para 12.

**anniversary.** See ANNUAL, para 5.

**annotate, annotation, annotator.** See NOTABLE, para 7.

**announce, announcement, announcer.** See NUNCIO, para 3.

**annoy, annoyance.** See ODIOUS, para 6.

**annual, annuity** (whence **annuitant**); **annals, annalist; anniversary; biennial, triennial; centenary, centennial; millennium, millenary, millennial; perennial; superannuate, superannuation;** cf SOLEMN.

1. The source of all these words is L *annus* (s

*ann-*, r *an-*), a year, akin to the *-en-* of Gr *dienos* (*di-*, two+*-en-*+formative *-o-*+nom *-s*), of two years, Skt *atati*, it passes—to Go *athnam* (dat pl), once, and *ata-athni*, (lapse of) a year—perh also Oscan *akenei*, in a year, and Umbrian *acnu* (acc pl), years. Basic sense: 'passing of a year's period'. (E & M.)

2. The following L derivatives result in E words: *annuālis*, MF-F hence ME *annuel*, E *annual* (*-al*, adj);

ML *annuitās* (o/s *annuitāt-*), MF-F *annuité*, E *annuity* (*-ity*)—whence *annuitant* (cf *-ant*, n);

*annālis*, annual, whence (*libri*) *annāles*, chronicles (year by year), whence E *annals* and late MF-F *annales*, whence EF-F *annaliste*, whence E *annalist* (*-ist*).

3. L numerical cpds relevant to E include: *biennālis*, from *biennium*, a period of two years (cf *bis*, twice, and prefix *bi-*): hence E *biennial*; *triennial* comes analogously from L *triennium*, a period of three years; *quadrennial*, four-yearly, from L *quadriennium*, period of four years; *quinquennial* from L *quinquennis*, five-yearly; *millennium* Mod L (from *mille*, a thousand), adopted by E; *milleni*, a thousand each, has LL derivative *millenārius*, whence E *millenary*; *millennial* derives from *millennium* on analogy of *biennial*, etc., as also does *centennial* from L *centum*, a hundred; but *centenary*, n, comes from LL *centenārium*, a century, from L *centenārius*, of a century, whence the E adj *centenary*.

4. One L prep cpd is relevant: *perennis*, lasting *through* the year, whence—cf *biennial*, *centennial*, etc.—*perennial*, adj hence n. Cf the E formation *superannuate*: L *super*, above+ L *annus*, a year+ suvffix *-ate*; hence *superannuation*.

5. There remains L *anniuersārius*, ML *-versārius*, returning, each year, with a particular day of the year: from *anni versus*, the turning of the year (*uersus*, ML *versus*, from *uertere*, *vertere*, to turn—cf VERSE): whence E *anniversary*, adj hence n, perh via the OF-F adj and n *anniversaire*.

**annul**, whence **annulment**. See NULL, para 1.

**annular**, ring-shaped: L *annulāris*, from *annulus*, a ring, better *anulus*, orig the dim of *anus*, (perh cf OI *āune*, *āinne*), a ring, adopted by E in its physio sense, with adj **anal**. *Annulus* leads to the E dim *annulet* (cf *-let*); cf OF-F *annelet*.

**annunciation**. See NUNCIO, para 3.

**anode**. See ODOGRAPH (heading).

**anodyne**, adj and n: ML *anodynus*, adj: LL *anodynos*: Gr *anodunos*, pain-free or -stilling: *an-*, not+*odunē*, pain. The E n comes from ML *anodynum*, itself from Gr *anodunon*, orig the neu s of the adj.

**anoint, anointment**. See UNCTION, para 4.

**anomalous, anomaly**. See the element *anomalo-*.

**anon**, adv. See ONE, para 9.

**anon.**: short for **anonymous; anonym, anonymity**. See NAME, para 3.

**anormal**. See NORM, para 3.

**another**. See OTHER.

**answer**, n and v (whence **answerable**). See SWEAR, para 2.

**ant**: ME *ante*, earlier *amete* or *emete* (cf the archaic *emmet*): OE *ǣmete*, akin to OHG *āmeiza* (G *Ameise*)—*ā-*, off+*meizan*, to cut (cf G *Meissel*, a chisel)—and to Go *maitan*, ON *meita*, to cut. Lit, therefore, 'the cutter-off, gnawer' (Walshe).

**antagonism, antagonist**. See AGONY, 2nd para.

**Antarctic**. See ARCTIC.

**antecedent**, whence **antecedence** and **antecedency**: MF-F *antécédent*: L *antecedent-*, o/s of *antecedens*, presp of *antecedere*, to go (*cēdere*: cf CEDE) before (*ante*: cf prefix *ante-*).

**antechamber**. See CHAMBER.

**antedate**. See DATE (in time).

**antediluvian**, adj hence n: before (*ante*) the Flood (ML *Dilūvium*, L *dilūuium*: cf DELUGE).

**antelope**: OF *antelop*: ML *antalopus*, earlier *anthalopus*: MGr *antholops* (gen *antholopos*), o.o.o.

**antenna** (pl *antennae*). See the element *antenni-*.

**antepone, anteposition**. See POSE, para 4.

**anterior**, earlier: LL word, a comp adj from *ante*, before—cf POSTERIOR and the element *antero-*.

**antevenient**. See VENUE, para 7.

**anteversion**. See VERSE, para 15.

**anthem; antiphon.**

Both of these words come from Gr *antiphōna*, neu pl of *antiphōnon*, an antiphon or anthem, itself orig the neu s of the adj *antiphōnos*, sound-returning (*anti*, over against+*phōnē*, a voice, a sound: cf *-phone*): Gr *antiphōna* became LL *antiphōna* (f sing) became E *antiphon*—cf E *antiphonary* (suffix *-ary*, n) from the derivative ML *antiphonārium*, and *antiphonal* from E *antiphon*; Gr *antiphōna* became also LL *antefana* (var of LL *antiphōna*), which became OE *antefen*, *antefn*, became ME *antefne*, later *antem*, whence, under Gr influence, the E *anthem*.

**anther**. See para 2 of:

**anthology**, whence **anthological, -logist, -logize**: Gr *anthologia*, from the adj *anthologos*, flowergathering: *anthos*, a flower, akin to Skt *ándhas-*, a herb, and prob to OIr *ainder*, a girl, and OBr *enderic*, MBr *annoer*, a young bull; IE r, perh *\*andh-* (or *\*and-*), var *\*endh-* (or *end-*); +*-logos*, -gathering, from *legein*, to gather—cf LOGIC and LEGEND.

2. *Anther*: EF-F *anthère*: L *anthēra*, medicine concocted from flowers: Gr *anthēros*, flowery, from *anthos*, flower.

3. Cf *polyanthus*, SciL from Gr *poluanthos*, rich (cf the element *poly-*) in flowers: it has a manyflowered umbel.

**anthracite**, whence **anthracitic** (*-ic*, adj); **anthrax**: L *anthracites*, bloodstone: Gr *anthrakitēs*, from *anthrax*, coal, charcoal, carbuncle, whence, via L *anthrax*, the E *anthrax*. With Gr *anthrax*, perhaps cf the Arm *ant'el*, a glowing coal; *anthrax*, however, could contract *\*antherax*, from *anthos*, a flower.

**anthropoid; anthropology, anthropomorphic, anthropophagy.**

1. The Gr *anthrōpos*, a human being (cf the element *anthropo-*), akin to *anēr* (gen *andros*), a man, has several Gr derivatives relevant to E. . Note:

*anthrōpoeidēs*, resembling a human being— hence *anthropoid*;

*anthrōpomorphos*, of human form (*morphē*, form, shape: cf MORPHEUS)—hence *anthropomorphous*, whence *anthropomorphism* (*-ism*) with adj *anthropomorphic*;

*anthrōpophagia*, cannibalism—hence *anthropophagy* (cf the element *-phaga*).

2. Of the numerous other cpds, one stands out: *anthropology* (whence *anthropological* and *anthropologist*): element *anthropo-*+element *-logy*, q.v. at *-logia*: perh imm from EF-F *anthropologie*.

antibiotic. See VIVA, para 11, s.f.

antic, adj hence n; antique (adj and n), antiquity —antiquary (adj hence n), antiquarian: antiquate, antiquated.

1. The n *antic*, a caper, derives from the adj *antic*, grotesque: It *antico*, ancient: L *antiquus*, ancient, (lit) former, from *ante*, before, (lit) over against: the suffix *-quus* may be id with that in *propinquus*, near. Cf the prefix *ante-*, akin to prefix *anti-*.

2. The E n *antique* has been adopted from the F n *antique*, itself from the MF-F adj *antique* (itself from L *antiquus*), whence the E adj.

3. L *antiquus* has several derivatives relevant to E:

*antiquitās*, o/s *antiquitāt-*, OF-F *antiquité*, E *antiquity* (suffix *-ity*);

*antiquārius* (adj), loving the ancient, hence a n: whence the E rare adj and the n *antiquary* (cf EF-F *antiquaire*), whence the adj (hence n) *antiquarian* (suffix *-an*, adj);

*antiquāre*, L 'to throw back, reject, abrogate', LL 'to cause to fall into oblivion', pp *antiquātus*, whence 'to *antiquate*', to render old or ancient, (hence) to render obsolete, whence the pa *antiquated*.

anticipate, anticipation, anticipative, anticipator, anticipatory.

The 5th derives, by adj suffix *-y*, from the 4th, itself adopted from L; the 3rd=L *anticipāt-*+suffix *-ive*; the 2nd, if not direct from MF-F, comes from L *anticipātiōn-*, the o/s of *anticipātiō*, itself from *anticipātus* (s *anticipāt-*), pp of L *anticipāre*, to forestall: *ante*, before+a derivative from *capere*, to take, 'to take beforehand'. The L presp *anticipans*, o/s *anticipant-*, yields the adj, hence n, *anticipant*.—Cf CAPABILITY, para 4.

anticlimax. See CLIMAX.

antidote, whence antidotal: L *antidotum*: Gr *antidoton* (pharmakon), 'the (medicine) given against': orig the neu of *antidotos*, given against: *anti*, against+*dotos*, given, pp of *didonai*, to give: cf DOSE.

antimacassar. See MACASSAR.

antimilitarism. See MILITANT, para 3.

antimony, whence antimonial, antimonic, antimonious: ML *antimonium*, perh Ar *al-uthmud* or

*-ithmid*; *al* being the Ar 'the', and *-ithmid* prob borrowed from Gr *stimmi* (var *stibi*, whence L *stibium*, adopted by Chem), itself app a borrowing of popular Eg *stim*, hieratic Eg *stm* (Hofmann).

antinomy, whence antinomian, antinomic: L, from Gr, *antinomia*: *anti*, against+*nom*os, law+abstract suffix *-ia*; *nomos* (s *nom-*) derives from *nemein* (s *nem*), to distribute. Cf NOMAD.

antipathetic, antipathy. See PATHIC, para 2.

antiphon. See ANTHEM.

antiphrasis, antiphrastic. See PHRASE, para 2.

antipodes, whence antipodal, antipodean. See FOOT, para 24.

antipope. See FATHER, para 18.

antiquarian, antiquary; antiquated; antique, antiquity. See ANTIC, paras 2–3.

anti-Semite, -Semitic, -Semitism. See SEMITE.

antisepsis, antiseptic. See SEPSIS.

antistrophe, antistrophic. See STRAP, para 3.

antithesis, antithetic. Cf SYNTHESIS, SYNTHETIC, and see THESIS, para 6.

antler. See OCULAR, para 6.

antonym (whence *antonymous*). See NAME, para 3.

antral, adj of antrum. See the element *antro-*.

anus. See ANNULAR and cf the element *ano-* (2).

anvil derives, through ME *anvelt*, earlier *anfelt*, from OE *anfealt* (var *anfilte*), akin to OHG *anafalz* and MD *aenvilt*, *aenvelt*, *aenbilt*, *aenbelt*, *ambelt*, and perh (Webster) to L *pellere*, to strike.

anxiety; anxious: the former comes from L *anxietāt-*, o/s of *anxietās*, abstract n from *anxius* (? for *ang-s-ius*, *-s-* being euphonic), itself from *angere* (s *ang-*), to cause pain: cf ANGER. *Anxius* yields E *anxious*.

any. See ONE, para 14.

Anzac: a member of the Australian and New Zealand Army Corps.

aorist. See HORIZON, para 2.

aorta, aortic, See the element *aorto-*.

ap-, in surnames. See FILIAL, para 3.

apache, a Parisian professional criminal: *Apache*, a member of an Amerindian tribe (esp Arizona, Texas, New Mexico): Zuni (N.M. Indians') *ápuchu*, enemy.

apanage, appanage. See PANTRY, para 10.

apart; apartment. See PART, para 17.

apathy, whence apathetic, derives, perh via EF-F *apathie*, from L *apathia*: Gr *apatheia*: privative *a-*+*pathos*+abstract suffix *-eia*. Cf SYMPATHY and see PATHIC.

ape, n hence v: OE *apa*, akin to ON *api* and OHG *affo* (G *Affe*): 'an early Teutonic loan word, perhaps from Celtic' (Webster)—but from which C language, if indeed from any? Cf OSl *opica* and Cz *opice* (Walshe). Perh rather cf Eg *aāfi*, a hideous man—and *gafi*, *gef*, an ape. If, however, *ape* be 'the imitator', then a C origin is not impossible: Ga *atharrais*, a mimic, prop *ath-*, an int prefix++*aithris*, mimicry, to mimic, and EIr *aithrisim*, I re-tell, and Mx *arrish*, mimicry, a mimic.

aperient; aperitive; aperture, whence apertural; ? April.

1. The L *aperīre* (s *aper-*), to open, (hence) to uncover, discover, is the complement of *operīre*, to shut, to cover—cf COVER. The IE r is therefore *\*uer-*: cf Lith *at-veriu*, I open, and *už-veriu*, I shut; cognates exist also in OSl and Skt. (E & M.)

2. *Aperīre* has presp *aperiens*, o/s *aperient-*, whence *aperient*, adj hence n; and derivative n *apertūra* (whence, E *aperture*), built upon the pp *apertus*, whence, via OF, the archaic adj *apert*; the LL *apertīuus* (ML *apertīvus*) perh suggested F *apéritif*, adj and n, whence E *aperitive*.

3. The ancient grammarians may have correctly derived L *Aprīlis*—whence *April*—from *\*Aperīlis*, from *aperīre*: Aprilis comes in the middle of the European spring, the month in which buds open. But Walde proposes that, April being the second month of the year, *Aprīlis* derives from IE *\*apero*, the later, akin to Skt *áparas*, later, following; and E & M support Benveniste's derivation from Etruscan *apru*, itself borrowed from Gr *Aphrō*, pet-form of *Aphroditē*, April being, in Medit countries, when young people's fancy turns to love. The third theory is the most convincing.

**apert.** See PERT.

**apex,** pl **apices; apical:** L *apex* (s *ap-*), summit, esp of something small, e.g. of a cap: perh from *apere* (s *ap-*), to attach. *Apical*=*apic-*, o/s of L *apex*+adj *-al*.

**aphelion.** See SOLAR, para 6.

**aphid, Aphis.** See the element *aphidi-*.

**aphorism, aphoristic.**

The latter comes from Gr *aphoristikos*, adj of *aphorismos*, a definition, hence a pithy saying, from *aphorizein*, to define: *aph-*, for *apo*, from+ *horizein*, to separate: f.a.e., HORIZON. Gr *aphorismos* became LL-ML *aphorismus* became MF-F *aphorisme* became E *aphorism*.

**aphrodisiac; Aphrodite:** Gr *aphrodisiakos*, of sexual love, from *Aphroditē*, perh 'descendant (*-itē*) of the foam (*aphros*)', with euphonic or formative *-d-*. With *aphros* (whence *aphrite*, a pearly calcite), cf Skt *abhrás*, cloudy weather.

**apiary; apiculture.**

L *apis* (s *ap-*), a bee, has c/f *api-*, as in *apiculture* (cf CULT), and derivatives *apiānus*, whence *apian*, and *apiārium*, whence *apiary*. Cf the element *api-* and perh BEE (*b* for *p*; aphesis).

**apical.** See APEX.

**apiece.** See PIECE.

**aplomb:** EF-F *aplomb*, uprightness, exact poise: F *à plomb*, adv, with plummet: *plomb*, lead, plummet: f.a.e., PLUMB.

**apocalypse, apocalyptic.**

The latter comes from Gr *apokaluptikos*, the adj of *apokalupsis*, whence, via LL *apocalypsis*, the E *apocalypse*: and Gr *apokalupsis* derives from *apokaluptein*, to uncover, to reveal: *apo*, from+ *kaluptein*, to cover, the origin of Gr *Kalupsō*, whence E *Calypso*, whence perh the WI *calypso*. Ult Gr r, *kal-*; IE r, *\*kel-*, cf L *celāre*, to hide.

**apocope.** See the element *-copate*.

**Apocrypha,** whence (adj *-al*) **apocryphal:** *apocrypha*, neu pl of LL *apocryphus*: Gr *apokru-*

*phos*, hidden (hence, spurious), from *apokruptein*, to hide away: *apo*, from+*kruptein*, to hide: cf *cryptic* at CRYPT.

**apodeictic.** See DICT, para 23.

**apogee:** (perh via EF-F *apogée*) L *apogaeum*, trln of Gr *apogaion*, prop the neu s of adj *apogaios*, (situated) up from (*apo*) the earth *gaia*, var *gē*—cf GEOGRAPHY.

**Apollo,** adopted from L, comes from Gr *Apollōn*, earlier *Apellōn*, perh from IE r *\*apel-*, to excite, promote, procreate: 'The Exciter or Generator', Apollo being the god of sun and light: cf, sem, the Skt epithet *savitá*, applied to a sun god. (Boisacq.)

**apologia, apology; apologist, apologize; apologetic, apologetics; apologue.** See LEGEND, para 25.

**apophthegm,** adj **apophthegmatic:** Gr *apophthegma*, something uttered, lit 'spoken out': *apo*, off, from+a derivative from *phthengesthai*, to speak—cf *diphthong*; hence *apophthegmatikos*, whence *apophthegmatic*.

**apoplectic; apoplexy.**

The adj comes, perh via F, from LL *apoplēcticus*, itself from Gr *apoplēktikos*, adj of *apoplēxia*, whence, via LL *apoplēxia* and MF-F *apoplexie* (adopted by ME), the E *apoplexy*: and Gr *apoplēxia* derives from *apoplēssein*, to strike cripplingly: *apo*, from+*plēssein*, to strike: f.a.e., PLAGUE.

**apostacy** or **-sy; apostate:** Gr *apostēnai*, to stand (*stēnai*: cf STAND) off (*apo*) has two notable derivatives: *apostasia*, adopted by LL, whence, perh through MF, the ME *apostasie*, E *apostasy*, var *apostacy*; and the agent *apostatēs*, whence L *apostata*, whence MF (later *apostat*), hence ME hence E, *apostate*.

**apostil.** See POSTERIOR, para 3.

**apostle; apostolate; apostolic.** See STALL, para 15.

**apostrophe, apostrophize.** See STRAP, para 3.

**apothecary.** See THESIS, para 7.

**apotheosis,** whence **apotheosize:** via LL from Gr *apotheōsis*, from *apotheoun*, to deify (*theos*, a god: cf THEISM): *apo-* connotes '(up) from mankind'.

**appal, appall.** See PALE, para 2.

**appanage.** See PANTRY, para 10.

**apparatus:** adopted from L (gen *-ūs*), from *apparāt-*, s of *apparātus*, pp of *apparāre*, to prepare: *ap-* for *ad*, to+*parāre*, to make ready, s *par-*, app akin to *parere* (s *par-*), to bring forth (a child): the sem link is clear and strong. Cf:

**apparel** and **v.**

Then n comes, through ME *aparail*, from OF *aparail*, *apareil* (F *appareil*), itself from OF *apareillier* (F *appareiller*), to prepare, whence 'to *apparel*': and *apareillier* comes from VL *\*appariculāre*, a freq from L *apparāre*—cf prec.

**apparent, apparition.** See APPEAR.

**appeach, appeachment.** See FOOT, para 13.

**appeal.** See the 2nd PULSE, para 6.

**appear, appearance; apparent, apparition, apparitor.**

*Appearance* comes, through ME *aparaunce*, *apparence*, and OF *aparance*, from L *apparentia*, from *apparent-* (whence E *apparent*), o/s of *apparens*, presp of *apparēre*, whence OF *aparoir* (note *ils aperent*, they appear) and ME *aperen*, *apperen*, whence the E *appear*. On *apparit-*, s of *apparitus*, pp of *apparēre*, arose both *apparitiō*, o/s *apparitiōn-*, whence, via OF-F, the E *apparition*, an appearance, esp a ghostly appearance, a spectre; and *apparitor*, adopted by E law. *Apparēre*=*ap*- for *ad*, to+*parēre* (s *par*), to be visible, to appear, prob akin to Gr *pəparein* (s *par*-), to display, *pe*- being app an int prefix.

**appease, appeasement.** The latter represents OF-F *apaisement*, itself from *apaiser*, to pacify, quieten, OF *apaisier*, OF-F *apaiser* (*a*, to+*pais*, peace+*-er*, inf suffix), whence, via ME *apaisen, apesen*, the E *appease*. Cf PEACE.

**appellant, appellate, appellation.** See the 2nd PULSE, para 6.

**append, appendage, appendant; appendix, appendicitis.** See PEND, para 13.

**apperceive, apperception.** See PERCEIVE.

**appertain.** See PERTAIN, para 3.

**appetency, appetent, appetite.** See PETITION, para 3.

**applaud, applause.** See PLAUDIT, para 2.

**apple:** ME *appel, eppel*: OE *aeppel, aepl*, akin to OFris *appel*, OS *appul*, OHG *apful* (MHG-G *apfel*); to ON *eple, epli*; to OIr *aball*, MIr *uball*, *ubull*, OW *aballen*, Ga *ubhal*, Cor *aval*(*l*) or *avell*, Br *aval*, Manx *ooyl*; to OSl *ablŭko* (or *jablŭko*) and Lith *obuolas*; prob also to L *Abella* (*malifera*, rich in apples: Virgil) in Campania. Indeed, *Abella* may well constitute the origin of this European word. The var *Auella*, ML *Avella* (the sole modern form), accounts for the E adj *avellan*, from L *auellana*, ML *av-*, the filbert, elliptical for *nux auellana*, nut of Abella.

**appliance; applicable; applicant; applicate; application, applicative, applicator, applicatory; appliqué; apply,** whence the adj **applied.** See PLY, paras 7–8.

**appoint, appointment.** See PUNGENT, para 21.

**apport.** See the 3rd PORT, para 3.

**apportion, apportionment.** See PART, para 23.

**appose, apposite, apposition.** See POSE, para 4; for *appose*, see also para 14.

**appraise,** whence **appraiser** (agential *-er*); **appraisal, appraisement.** See PRICE, para 3.

**appreciate, appreciation, appreciative, appreciator.** See PRICE, para 5.

**apprehend; apprehensible, apprehension, apprehensive.** See PREHEND, para 5.

**apprentice, apprenticeship.** See PREHEND, para 6.

**appressed, appressorium.** See the 2nd PRESS, para 4.

**apprise,** to inform: MF-EF *apprise*, f of *appris*, pp of OF-F *apprendre*, to learn, to teach, from L *apprehendere*, to grasp: f.a.e., PREHEND.

**apprize,** to price or value. See PRICE, para 2.

**approach,** v hence n and—prob suggested by late MF-F *approchable*—**approachable:** ME *ap*(*p*)*rochen*: OF-MF *aprochier* (MF-F *approcher*): LL *appropiāre*: *ap*- for *ad*, to+L *propiāre*, to come

near, itself from *prope* (adv and prep), near, near to, perh an elaboration of *pro*, forwards, akin to the syn Gr *pro* and Skt *pra-*. Cf REPROACH.

**approbation, approbatory.** See PROVE, para 7.

**appropriate,** adj and v; **appropriation, appropriative, appropriator.** See PROPER, para 3.

**approve** (1), to make use of, to profit by. See IMPROVE, para 3.

**approve** (2), to authenticate, (hence) to sanction, to favour; **approval.** See PROVE, para 7.

**approximate** (adj, v)—**approximation.** See PROPINQUITY, para 3.

**appulse, appulsion.** See the 2nd PULSE, para 7.

**appurtenance, appurtenant.** See PERTAIN.

**apricot:** F *abricot*: Cat *abercoc*, earlier *albercoc*: like the Sp and Port words, from Sp Ar *al-barqouq*: MAr *al-burquq* (cf Per *barquq*): L (Pliny) *praecoquum*, orig the neu of *praecoquus*, var of *praecox*, early ripe (f.a.e., PRECOCIOUS). The Ar word came from L via Gr which had carried the L word to Syria: LGr *praikokion* (Byz Gr *berikokkion*: note *p* to *b*) merely transliterates L *praecoquum*, lit 'cooked beforehand', prob an example of folketymology: the apricot ripens before the similarly coloured peach. (B & W; Sophocles.)

**April.** See APERIENT, para 3.

**apron.** See MAP, para 3.

**apropos:** F *à propos*, to the purpose: f.a.e., PURPOSE.

**apse, pl apsides:** L *apsis*: Gr *apsis*, better *hapsis*, from *haptein*, to fasten. Perh cf HASP. The adj is *apsidal*.

**apt,** whence **aptness** (suffix *-ness*); **aptitude**— **attitude, attitudinal** (*-al*, adj), **attitudinize** (*-ize*); **inept, ineptitude.** Cf sep ADAPT, ADEPT, COPULA.

1. L *aptus*, 'fastened', hence 'well fastened' hence 'well fitted (for)', was orig the pp of *apere*, to tie or fasten, akin to Skt *āpta*, fit, very suitable, and *āpnoti*, he reaches, attains, obtains, and to Ve *ắpa*, he has attained or obtained, and *ắpat*, he attained or obtained. The Hit *ēpmi*, I take, and *ēpzi*, he takes, and *appanzi*, they take, suggest IE r *ap-*, var *ep-*, or vice versa.

2. L *aptus* yields E *apt*; its LL abstract derivative *aptitūdō* yields, via MF-F, *aptitude* (cf *-itude*), adj *aptitudinal*, from *aptitūdin-*, the o/s of *aptitūdō*.

3. The opp of *aptus* is *ineptus* (*in-*, not), whence, perh via MF-F *inepte*, the E *inept*; from the LL derivative *ineptitūdō* comes *ineptitude*.

4. LL *aptitūdō*, gen *aptitūdinis*, became It *attitudine* became EF-F *attitude*, adopted by E; the adj *attitudinal* and the v *attitudinize* have arisen by analogy with other L *-itudo, -itudin*-formations.

**aqua** (pura); **aquamarine; aquarelle; aquarium,** adj **aquarian; aquatic; aquatint; aqueduct; aqueous;** cf the elements *aqui-, aquo-*; Scandinavia; **eau (de Nil), ewer; ea, eagre, osier; usquebaugh**—**whisk(e)y;** ? akin to WATER.

1. L *aqua*, water, is akin to Go *ahwa*, river, OS and OHG *aha*, river, and OHG *ouwa*, watery meadow, ON *āēger*, sea; perh to Skt *ắpas*; perh even to Gr *hudōr* and therefore to E WATER. The

IE r was prob *akw-. L aqua occurs undisguised
in aquamarine, from L aqua marina, sea water,
hence a dullish green-blue; in aquaplane; in aqua-
vitae, water of life, hence brandy; also in aqua pura,
pure or fresh water, and aqua regia, royal water,
hence its Chem use.

2. L derivatives relevant to E include:
aquārium, orig the neu of the adj aquārius, of or
for water; adopted by E, aquarium has adj aquarian
(suffix -an);
aquāticus, of water, whence, prob via MF-F
aquatique, the E aquatic;
aquaeductus, lit 'a leading, a duct, of water',
whence EF (EF-F var aqueduc) aqueduct, adopted
by E;
*aqueus, whence aqueous; L aquōsus, whence
the rare aquose.

3. Aquatint—cf F aqua-tinta—comes from It
acqua (L aqua) tinta (f of tinto, dyed).

4. L aqua became F eau (as in eau-de-vie, water
of life, hence brandy: L aqua vitae, as above)—OF
eaue, ewe, eve, eive. The var eve had derivative
eviere, whence AF ewer, whence E ewer (cf suffix
-er), a wide-mouthed pitcher.

5. Akin to L aqua is the C r av-, au-, water or
watercourse whence *ausarios, whence ML
ausāria, osier-bed, and OF *ausier, whence OF-F
osier (OF-MF var osiere), whence E osier, willow,
a plant that grows near water.

6. A fully formed C word akin to, prob deriving
from the C r au-, is the Ga and Ir uisge, OIr uisce,
usce, water: hence the E whisk(ey), influenced by
uisgebeatha, water of life, hence whisky, the AIr
usquebaugh. (Cf aquavita and eau-de-vie above.)

7. There are also two noteworthy 'Anglo-
Saxon' relatives: the dial ea, water, a stream, from
OE ēa (cf OFris ē or ā), and eagre, a bore (tidal
wave) in a river, app from ēa+gār, a spear, eagre
being lit 'a spear(-thrust) of water'—cf, however,
ON ǣgir, sea, god of the sea.

8. The Gmc form (para 1) appears, slightly disguised, in Scandinauia, ML Scandinavia, where the
first element is a Gmc form of ON Skāney, a
region of S Sweden: cf ISLAND. Nevertheless, I
tentatively propose '(land of) climbing waters'
(waterfalls and fiords)—L scandere, to climb.

aquiline. See EAGLE.

**Arab; street arab; arabesque; Arabia (Araby),
Arabian; Arabic; Arabis; Arabist; Mozarab, Mozarabic.**

1. The Ar 'Arab, whence Gr Araps, L Arabs, then
Arabus, whence L, hence E, Arabia (unless L
Arabia represents Gr Arabia), whence the F Arabie
(whence poetic E Araby),—the Ar 'Arab may
signify 'nomad(s)'; perh akin to H 'arābāh, steppe,
'Arab nevertheless prob derives from the Ass pl
Arabu (or Aribi), itself perh 'Men of the Master
Race' (cf Ass arbob, a man of high position).

2. E Arab comes, via EF-F Arabe, from L
Arabus; and street arab, an outcast, esp boy, arises
from the numerous Arab vendors in E Medit ports.

3. The Gr adj Arabikos (from Araps), L Arabicus,
MF arabic (EF-F arabique), yields E Arabic, adj,

hence n; whence, with -ian for -ic, Arabian, adj
hence n. The It arabesco (adj, hence n), from Arabo
(L Arabus), an Arab, became EF-F arabesque,
adopted by E: Arabic art delighted in intricate
patterns and floral designs. F arabiste became E
Arabist.

4. The rock cress arabis prob means 'Arabian
(plant)'—from the Gr adj Arabis, Arabian—
because it grows in dry places.

5. Mozarab (or Mazarab), whence Mozarabic,
represents Sp Mózarabe, from Ar musta'rib, a
would-be Arab.

arable: (perh via MF-F, from) L arābilis, from
arāre (s ar-), to plough.

arachnid, arachnoid. See the element arachno-.

Aramaean and Aramaic anglicize (adj suffixes
-an, -ic) L Aramaeus: Gr Aramaios: Aram, H
Arām, 'signifying perhaps Highland, a name given
to Syria and upper Mesopotamia' (Webster).

arbalest. See ARC, para 4, and BALL, n.

**arbiter; arbitrage, arbitral, arbitrament; arbi-
trary; arbitrate, arbitration, arbitrative, arbitrator.**

1. The starting-point for the group rests in L
arbiter, witness, arbitrator, judge, hence master (cf
arbiter elegantiarum, a judge of elegancies, hence
an authority on good taste), itself o.o.o: cf the
Umbrian arputrati, by arbitrage; Webster proposes ar- for ad, to+the r of baetere, betere, bitere
(s baet-, bet-, bit-), to go—cf Gr bainein, whence the
c/f -batēs (s bat-), one who goes.

2. L derivatives of arbiter relevant to E include:
LL arbitrālis, adj, whence, perh via MF-F, the E
arbitral (suffix -al);
LL arbitrārius, whence arbitrary (suffix -ary, adj),
cf MF-F arbitraire;
arbitrāri, to make a decision, pp arbitrātus,
whence 'to arbitrate'; hence:
LL arbitrātiō, a decision, o/s arbitrātiōn-,
whence, prob via MF, the E arbitration;
LL arbitrātor, f arbitrātrix, likewise built upon
arbitrāt-, the s of the pp arbitrātus: both adopted
by E.

3. From F words not of imm L origin have
come:
arbitrage (suffix -age), adopted from MF-F, from
F arbitre: cf the rare ML arbitrāgium;
arbitrament (cf -ment), adapted from MF-EF
arbitrement: cf the rare ML arbitrāmentum.

4. Thoroughly E are:
arbitrable, from the clumsier, more logical
arbitratable, from arbitrate;
arbitrational, from E arbitration;
arbitrative, which=arbitrate+suffix -ive; as if
from ML *arbitrātivus.

**arbor** (1), a tree, cf ARBOR DAY; **arboreal,
arboreous, arborous; arborescence, arborescent;
arboret, arboretum; arboricole** (element -cole);
**arboriculture** (cf the element arbori-); **arborize,
arborization; arbuscule; arbustum.**

1. L arbos (gen arboris) or arbor (gen arboris),
a tree, has s arb-; the word is o.o.o; perh cf the syn
Ga craobh and MIr cráeb or cróeb. L arbor occurs
as E in Arbor Day, a felicitous A custom and

festival, and in the tree named *arbor vitae* (ML *vita*, L *uita*), lit 'the tree of life'.

2. L derivatives affecting E include:

*arboreus*, whence *arboreous*; cf *arboreal*, with *-al* substituted for *-ous*; and LL *arborōsus*, whence *arborous*;

*arborescere* (*arbor*+*-escere*, inch suffix), to become a tree, with presp *arborescens*, o/s *arborescent-*, whence the adj *arborescent*, whence *arborescence* (*arborescent*+*-ce*);

*arborētum*, a tree-plantation, e.g., an orchard; adopted by E, with special sense 'botanical garden consisting of trees and shrubs';

*arbuscula* (LL *arbusculus*), a little tree, whence E *arbuscule*, with adj *arbuscular* (suffix *-ar*).

*arbustum*, a copse or thicket, adopted by E; orig the neu of the adj *arbustus*, planted with trees.

3. The few E formations include: *arboret*, a shrub or small tree (L *arbor*+dim suffix *-et*); *arborize* (L *arbor*+suffix *-ize*), whence *arborization*; *arboreal* (as above), var *arboral*, and *arboraceous*, as if from L *\*arboraceus*.

4. L *arbūtus*, adopted by E, may represent *arb-utus* and therefore be akin to *arbor*.

**arbor** (2) or **arbour**: ME *herber*, a herb-garden: OF-F *herbier*: L *herbārium*: *herba*, grass, herb+ suffix *-ārium*: f.a.e., HERB.

**arbutus.** See 1st ARBOR, last para.

**arc** (n hence v), **arcual, arcuate, arcuation; arcade; arch,** n and v (whence **arched**), **archer, archery; arbalest;** akin to sep ARROW.

1. The effective origin lies in L *arcus*, something bent or curved (hence the shape), hence a bow for shooting, and a rainbow: akin to OE *earh* (see ARROW) and perh to Gr *arkus* (s *ark-*), a snare, a net.

2. *Arcus* became OF-F *arc*, adopted by E. Its presumed derivative, the VL *\*arca*, became OF-F *arche*, whence E *arch*; OF *arche* had the derivative v *archier*, whence 'to arch'.

3. VL *\*arca* may, through Prov *arcada*, have yielded EF-F *arcade*, whence E *arcade*; prob, however, F *arcade* merely adapts It *arcata*, lit 'the space of a bow shot', from *arcare*, to use a bow, from *arco*, a bow, from L *arcus*.

4. Certain L derivatives of *arcus* concern E: *arcuāre*, to bow (v.t.), has pp *arcuātus*, whence E *arcuate*, bow-shaped: on its s *arcuāt-* arose *arcuātiō*, o/s *arcuātiōn-*, whence E *arcuation*;

LL *arcaballista* or *arcu-*, a military machine for throwing arrows (cf BALL), whence OF *arcbaleste*, eased to *arbaleste*, whence, perh via late OE, the ME *arbelaste*, whence *arbalest*; the agent *arbalester* comes, via OF-EF *arbalestier*, from L *arcuballistārius*, the operator;

LL *arcārius*, var of *arcuārius*, a bowman, became OF *archier*, OF-F *archer*, whence ME and E *archer*; OF *archer* had derivative *archerie*, whence E *archery*.

5. *Arcual*, of an arc, represents L *arcus*+suffix *-al*.

**arcade.** See prec, para 3.

**Arcadia, Arcady; Arcadian.** *Arcadian* derives,

less from the L adj *Arcadius* than from E *Arcadia*, adopted from L, itself a trln of Gr *Arkadia*, that hilly region of Ancient Greece which was famed for bucolic bliss: from *Arkas*, an Arcadian, o/s *Arkad-* (pl *Arkades*), itself o.o.o. *Arcady* represents F *Arcadie*.

**arcana**, pl of **arcanum; arcanal, arcane.** See ARK, para 2.

**arch,** adj: from such cpds as *archknave* and *-rogue*. Cf the element *arch-*.

**arch,** n and v. See ARC, para 2.

**archaeology** (arche-); **archaeologic(al), archaeologist.**

The 3rd=*archaeology*+suffix *-ist*; the 2nd comes from Gr *arkhaiologikos*, the adj of *arkhaiologia*, LL *archaeologia* (whence EF-F *archéologie* and AE *archeology*, E *archaeology*), knowledge (cf the element *-logia*) of the *arkhaios* or ancient. Cf the element *archaeo-* and:

**archaic, archaism, archaist, archaize:** resp, via LL *archaicus* from Gr *arkhaikos*, old-fashioned, a phon and sem extn of *arkhaios*, ancient (cf prec), from *arkhē*, a beginning; *archaism* (cf the late EF-F *archaïsme*) via LL *archaismos*, from Gr *arkhaismos*, from *arkhaios*; *archaist*, from *archaic* +*-ist*; its adj *ar,chaistic*(*-ic*); *archaize*, from Gr *arkhaizein*.

**archangel.** See ANGEL, para 2.

**archbishop, archbishopric:** the latter derives from OE *arcebiscoprīce* (cf suffix *-ric*), from OE *arcebiscop* or *-bisceop* (whence *archbishop*), itself from LL *archiepiscopus*, Gr *arkhiepiskopos*, lit 'the chief overseer'. Cf the element *arch-* and BISHOP; also cf:

**archdeacon:** OE *arcedīacon*: LL *archidiaconus*: Gr *arkhidiakonos*. Cf prec—the element *arch-*— and **deacon.**

**archduchess, -duke.** See DUKE, para 4.

**archer, archery.** See ARC, para 4.

**archetype,** whence (*-al*, adj) *archetypal*. See the element *-type*.

**archipelago,** whence the adj **archipelagic** (*ic*): It *arcipelago*, lit 'chief sea': element *arcih-*+L *pelagus* from Gr *pelagos*, sea, whence *pelagios*, of the sea, L *pelagius*, E *pelagian*; the syn *pelagic* represents L *pelagicus*, from *pelagus*. With Gr *pelagos* (s and r *pelag-*), cf Gr *plax*, surface of the sea, a plain: IE r, *\*pela-*, flat, to be flat, to stretch.

**architect, architecture** (whence **architectural**); **architectonic,** whence **architectonics.** See TECHNIC, para 5.

**architrave.** See TAVERN, para 4.

**archive,** whence **archival** (*-al*); **archivist.**

The 3rd represents ML *archīvista*, from ML *archīvum*, LL *archīuum*, a record-office, var of *archīum*, a transliteration of Gr *arkheion*, government house, from *arkhē*, a beginning, the first place, the government. E *archive* prob comes from ML *archīvum*; *archives* (collective n), prob from late MF-F (*les*) *archives*, from Gr (*ta*) *arkheia*, archives, via ML *archīva*, pl of *archīvum*.

**arctic,** adj hence n **Arctic; Arcturus; Antarctic.**

*Arctic* comes from MF-F *arctique*, from L *arcticus*, from Gr *arktikos*, adj of *arktos*, a bear, akin to Skt *ŕkṣas*, L *ursus*, OIr *art*: perh 'the storer' (of honey); cf Skt *rákṣas-*, a storing, a store. (Hofmann.) Gr *arktos* signified also the northern constellation so called: *Ursa*, The Bear: cf L *Arcturus*, from Gr *Arktouros*, the Bear Guard (*ouros*, guard). The n *Antarctic* derives from the adj *antarctic*, from MF-F *antarctique*, from L *antarcticus*, from Gr *antarktikos*: *anti*, opposite+ *arktikos*: opposite the north pole or the arctic circle.

**arcual; arcuate, arcuation.** See ARC, resp paras 5 and 4.

**Ardennes, ardennite.** See ARDUOUS.

**ardent,** whence **ardency** (*ardent*+suffix -*cy*); AE **ardor,** E **ardour; arid, aridity; arson,** whence **arsonist** (-*ist*); perh ASHES, q.v. The base, phonetic and semantic alike, is L *arēre* (s *ar-*), to be dry, akin to Skt *ásas*, ashes—Gr *azein* (s *az-*), to dry— Tokh A *ásar*, dry—Arm *azazem*, I dry—OHG *asca*, Go *azgō*, ashes. (E & M.) The IE r is perh *ā-*, to be dry, to be hot: cf Hit *a-a-ri*, an extn of Hit *ā-*, to be hot, and perh Hit *Agniš*, the Fire-God.

2. Deriving from *arēre*, the following L words affect E:

*aridus* (occ *ardus*), dried up, parched, whence *arid*, the derivative *ariditās*, o/s *ariditāt-*, yielding *aridity*;

*ardēre* (s *ard-*, r *ar-*), to be on fire, with presp *ardens*, o/s *ardent-*, whence, via OF *ardant* and ME *ardaunt*, the E *ardent*;

*ardor* (akin to and prob deriving from *ardēre*), orig '(extreme) dryness', hence 'a burning heat', leads to OF *ardor* or *ardour*, whence ME *ardure* or *ardeur*, whence E *ardour*, *ardor*.

3. *Ardēre* became OF *ardre*, pp *ars*, whence the n *arson*, adopted by E: cf the suffix -*on*.

**arduous; Ardennes.**

*Arduous* comes from L *arduus*, high, steep, hence difficult and strenuous; akin to OIr *ard*, high, and perh to Skt *ūrdhvás*, upright, and to Gr *ardis*, a point: IE r, *ard*. Gaul *Arduenna*, name of a mountain, is at least akin to the mountainous *Ardennes* (pl), whence the min *ardennite*.

**are,** n. See AREA.

**are,** v: Northumbrian OE *aron*, we, you, they are: akin to ON *eru*, they are: cf ART, v, and AM.

**area; are,** n.; **areola.** The F *are* (100 square metres) derives from L *ārea*, a piece—usu broad— of level ground, a courtyard, a threshing floor; the dim *āreola* has likewise been adopted by E; the L adj *āreālis* becomes E *areal*. With *area*, o.o.o., perh cf Hit *arás*, a granary, esp if 'threshing floor' be the orig sense of L *ārea*.

**arena; arenaceous; arenose** (whence **arenosity**).

A gladiatorial ring, later a bull-ring, *arena* consists of sand or a sanded surface: L *arēna*, sand, hence a sandy, usu enclosed, space, is a var of early *harēna*, itself with var *hasena*, found also in Sabine: app o.o.o., although Hit *korăiz* (dat *karaitti*), sand, may be relevant; IE r, ? *khar-*. The derivative adjj *arēnăceus*, *arēnōsus*, yield *arenaceous* (suffix -*aceous*) and *arenose* (-*ose*).

**argent,** n hence adj; **argenteous, argentine** (ad hence n)—**Argentina; argil;** cf ARGUE.

The L *argentum*, silver, becomes OF *argent*, adopted by E; its derivative adj *argenteus* yields *argenteous*; *argentine* (adj -*ine*), however, represents OF-F *argentin*, from *argent*. *Argentina* is app elliptical for Sp (*tierra*) *argentina*, silvery land, from the country's wonderful rivers (esp Rio de la Plata, river of silver) and lakes. Now, L *argentum* is akin to Gr *arguros*, silver, from *argos*, *argēs*, white—cf Skt *rajatá-*, white, hence silver, and OIr *argat*, silver; *argos* has another derivative, *argilla*, adopted by L, whence OF-F *argile*, whence E *argil*, (white or potter's) clay.

**argon:** Gr *argon*, neu of *argos*, inactive: *a-*, not+ *ergon*, work (cf ERG).

**Argonaut.** See NAUTIC, para 3, s.f.

**argosy:** EE *ragusye*: app from It (*nave*) *ragusea*, orig 'ship of *Ragusa*'—sailing from that port.

**argue,** whence **arguable** and **arguer; argufy** and **argy-bargy; argument, argumental, argumentation, argumentative; argute.**

1. *Argue*, ME *arguen*, comes from OF-F *arguer*, from L *argutāre* (or -*āri*), freq of *arguere*, to clarify, akin to L *argentum*, silver: see ARGENT. Certain L derivatives affect E:

*argumentum*, proof, argument, becomes OF-F *argument*, adopted by E; its derivative LL adj *argumentālis* yields *argumental*;

another derivative, *argumentāri*, to demonstrate or argue, has derivative *argumentātiō*, o/s *argumentātiōn-*, whence, prob via MF-F, *argumentation*;

LL *argumentātiuus*, ML -*ivus*, yields *argumentative*;

*argūtus*, pp of *arguere*, hence adj 'clear; hence shrewd, subtle', yields *argute*.

2. E formations include the coll and dial *argufy* either *argue*+element -*fy* or *argument*+-*fy*, and the mostly dial *argy-bargy*, a rhyming redup of *argue*.

**aria.** See AIR.

**arid, aridity.** See ARDENT, para 2.

**aright.** See REX, para 3.

**arise,** pt **arose,** pp **arisen.** See RAISE, para 2.

**aristocracy, aristocrat, aristocratic:** resp Gr *aristokratia*, *aristokratēs*, *aristokratikos*, all via L and then MF-F: cf the elements *aristo-* and -*crat*. Cf *Aristophanes*, ? 'he who shows (things) best', and *Aristotle*, ? 'he who fulfils the best'.

**arithmetic,** whence **arithmetical** and **arithmetician:** L *arithmētica*; Gr *arithmētikē* (*tekhnē*), from *arithmētikos*, numerical, from *arithmein*, to number, from *arithmos*, (a) number: akin to OHG and OIr *rīm*, number; IE r, *ari-* or *ri-*, to arrange, esp in numbers.

2. *Logarithm*, whence *logarithmic*, derives from SciL *logarithmus*: Gr *logos*, account, proportion+ *arithmos*: cf LGr *logariasmos*, a calculation.

**ark: arcane, arcanum; coerce, coercion, coercive; exercise,** n and v.; **exercitant, exercitation.**

1. All these terms ramify from L *arcēre* (s *arc-*), to contain or maintain, hence to maintain at a distance, to keep or ward off: prob akin to Gr *arkein*

(s *ark-*), to keep off, and perh to Arm *argelum* (s *argel-*, r ? *arg-*), I prevent.

2. Relevant L derivatives of *arcēre* are *arca*, basket, box, coffer, whence OE *arc* (or *earc*), whence *ark*; *arcānus* (from *arca*), boxed, closed, hence secret, whence *arcane*; neu *arcānum*, become n and adopted by E, occurs mostly in pl *arcāna*.

3. Relevant L prefix cpds of *arcēre*:

*coercēre* (*co-*, *con-*, together), to contain, hence to refrain, whence 'to *coerce*'; its derivative *coerciō* (for *coercitiō*), o/s *coerciōn-*, gives us *coercion*; but *coercive*=*coerce*+*-ive*;

*exercēre* (*ex*, out of), to drive out, pursue, hence to keep (someone) moving, hence to practise, to exercise, whence the n *exercitium*, exercise, MF-F *exercice*, ME and E *exercise*, whence 'to *exercise*';

*exercitāre* (freq of *exercēre*), to practise or exercise diligently, with presp *exercitans*, o/s *exercitant-*, whence, via F, the n *exercitant*, and with derivative n *exercitātiō*, o/s *exercitātiōn-*, whence, prob via OF-EF, *exercitation*.

**arm** (1), weapon. See ARMS.

**arm** (2), upper limb: OE *arm*, *earm*: akin to OFris *arm*, *erm*—OHG *aram*—Go *arms*—ON *armr*; to OP *irmo*; to L *armus* (s *arm-*), shoulder, arm—and to Skt *īrmas*, arm; perh also to Hit *āra*, something right or fitting: IE r, prob *ar-*, var *er-*, with *-m-* as a formative. Perh akin to ARMS.

2. The derivatives are obvious—e.g., *armlet*, (lit) little arm; *armpit* (*arm*+*pit*, a hollow).

**arm** (3 and 4), v—answering to prec and to **arms**.

**armada**; **armadillo**. See ARMS.

**Armageddon**: LL *Armagedon*: L Gr *Armagedōn*, *Harmagedōn*, the H *har*, mountain of *Megiddo*. See *Revelations*, xvi, 16, and *Judges*, v, 19.

**Armenia**, **Armenian**. See ERMINE.

**armor**, **armour**. See para 2 of:

**arms**; **army**.

The base rests on L *arma*, neu pl used as a collective, whence OF-F *armes*, hence ME *armes*, whence *arms*; the s is a b/f. *Arma* may well, as Bréal suggested, derive from *armāre* (next para), itself from *armus*, the arm (see the 2nd ARM): he compares *pugna*, a fight, from *pugnāre*, to fight, itself from *pugnus*, fist.

2. *Arma* has the foll cognates and derivatives relevant to E:

*armāre*, to equip with arms, whence, via OF-F *armer*, the E 'to *arm*'; OF-F *armer* has derivative OF-MF *desarmer* (EF-F *dés-*), whence ME *desarmen*, whence 'to *disarm*';

(from *armāre* comes) *armāmentum*, whence, like MF-F *armement*, the E *armament*;

*armātūra* (likewise from *armāre*), whence the MF-F and E *armature*; it yields also OF *armeüre*, MF-F *armure*, whence ME *armure*, whence E *armour*, AE *armor*.

3. *Armoury*, AE *armory*, app derives from E *armo(u)r*; there has been confusion with EF-F *armoiries*, coats of arms, MF *armoieries*, from OF-MF *armoier*, to paint (coats of) arms, from OF

*armes* (cf para 1). Either adopted from EF-F or formed anl from *armory* comes *armorial*.

4. F in origin are: *army*, from MF-F *armée*, from *armer*, from L *armāre* (para 2 above);

*armo(u)rer*, from ME *armurer*, from MF-F *armurier*, from MF-F *armure*;

*armistice*, adopted from late EF-F which, after F *solstice*, coined it from L *armi-*, c/f of *arma*+ *-stitium*, n c/f of *stāre*, to stand: a standing (still) of *arms*.

5. Sp intervention occurs in:

*armada*, adopted from Sp from L *armāta*, prob elliptical for *classis armāta*, an armed fleet, where *armāta* is the fs of *armātus*, pp of *armāre*;

*armadillo*, a plated mammal: adopted from Sp— dim of *armado*, armed, pp of *armar*, to arm, itself from L *armāre*.

**aroma**, **aromatic**.

The latter descends, via LL *arōmaticus* and F *aromatique*, from Gr *arōmatikos*, adj of *arōma*, itself o.o.o., but perh, as Hofman proposes, from Gr *arōmenai*, to plough (L *arāre*), presumably from the smell of good earth upturned. Gr *arōma*, adopted by LL, yields E *aroma* and F *arome*.

**around**. See ROLL, para 22.

**arouse**. See RAISE, para 2.

**arrack**. See the 7th RACK.

**arraign**, **arraignment**. See REASON, para 8.

**arrange**, **arrangement**. See RANGE, para 5.

**arrant**: var of *errant*, q.v. at ERR.

**arras**: for and from *Arras tapestry*: first made in NE France, land occupied formerly by the L *Atrebates* (L Gr *Atrebatoi* or *-tioi*).

**array**, n and v, whence **arrayal** (n suffix *-al*) and **arrayment** (*-ment*)—cf RAIMENT; DISARRAY, n, v; CURRY, v.

1. The n *array*, ME *arrai* or *arai*, comes from OF *arrei* or *ar(r)oi*, arrangement, dress, itself from *areer*, to arrange (*areie*, he arranges), whence, via ME *araien*, the E 'to *array*': and OF *areer* comes from VL *arrēdāre*, to arrange—*ad*, to+a s of Gmc origin, cf Go *garaiths*, set in order, arranged: f.a.e., READY.

2. OF *areer* has derivative n *areement* or *araiement*, whence the E *arrayment*, meaning both an arraying and raiment; indeed, *raiment*, garments, is aphetic for *arraiment*, an early var of *arrayment*.

3. OF *areer* has derivative MF v *desarreier*, influential in the forming of E 'to *disarray*', whence app the n *disarray*—cf F *désarroi*.

4. With 'to *array*' cf 'to *curry*', to dress—esp to comb—a horse's coat: ME *curreien*: OF *correer* (var *conreer*), to curry (a horse), special sense of *correer*, to arrange or prepare: *cor-*, or L *con-*, with, together (often merely int)+OF *rei* (var *roi*), order, arrangement, of Gmc origin (see para 1, s.f.).

**arrear**, **arrears**. See the first REAR, para 1.

**arrect**. See REX, para 26.

**arrest**, n, v; **arrestation**, **arrestive**, **arrestment**.

*Arrest*, n, passes through ME *arest* from OF *arest* (F *arrêt*), itself from the v *arester* (VL *arrestāre*: *ad*, to+*restāre*, to stop or remain:

f.a.e., REST, remainder)—whence, via ME *aresten*, the E 'to *arrest*', whence the pa *arresting*. OF *arester* has derivatives MF *arestaison*, whence, influenced by L *restare* and the many nn in *-ation*, the EF-F, hence the E, *arrestation*, and MF-EF *arestement*, whence E *arrestment*; the MF *arestif*, tardy, may have form-suggested E *arrestive*, fixative.

arrière-pensée. See PEND, para 11.

arrive; arrival; arrivé, arriviste. See RIVER, para 3.

arrogance, arrogant; arrogate, arrogation, arrogative. See ROGATION, para 4.

arrow, n—hence v, and adj arrowy: ME *arewe*: OE *arwe* or *earh*, akin to ON *ör*, gen *örvar*, and Go *arhwazna* (Gmc s *\*arhwo-*): also to L *arcus* (a bow), q.v. at ARC. Of the cpd *arrowroot*, Webster remarks that 'the Indians are said to have used the roots to neutralize the venom of poisoned arrows'.

arroyo, a watercourse, a (dry) gully formed by water: adopted from Sp, which has thus reshaped ML *arrogium* (akin to L *arrugia*, gallery of a mine, a canal), itself from L *riuus* (ML *rivus*), watercourse, brook.

arse: OE *ears* or *aers*, akin to the syn OFris *ers*, OHG *ars* (Mod *Arsch*), ON *ars*—and to Hit *arraš*, Gr *orrhos*, the behind. IE r, *\*ars-*, varr *\*ers-*, *\*ors-*.

arsenal: perh via ML *arsenal* (cf EF-F *arsenal*, MF *archenal*), var of *arsena*: It *arsenale, arzenale*, dockyard (as orig in E): Old Venetian *arzaná*: prob via MGr *arsēnalēs*: Ar (*dār*) *al šinā'ah*, maritime arsenal, lit '(court or house) of manufacture'.

arsenic: MF-F *arsenic*: L *arsenicum, arrhenicum*: L Gr *arsenikon*, Gr *arrhenikon*, yellow orpiment, itself—via Sem channels (esp Syriac *zarnīg*)—from OPer: cf Skt *hiranya*, Av *zaranya*, gold. Adj *arsenious*; derivative *arsine* (chem suffix *-ine*)

arson. See ARDENT, para 3.

art (1), n; artful, artless, arty; artifice, artificer, artificial, artificiality; artisan; artist, artiste, artistic, artistry; cf theelement *arti-*;—inert, inertia, inertial. Cf sep ARM and ARTICLE.

1. L *ars*, as in *ars poetica*, the poetic art, has o/s *art-*, acc *artem*, whence, via OF-F, the E *art*: and *ars*, a way of being or of acting, hence a skill, hence talent, has r *ar-*; indeed, the IE r itself is *\*ar-* or *\*er-*; L prefers the former, as in *armus* (cf ARM), and *artus*, a joint, hence a limb (cf ARTICLE).

2. The purely E derivatives include *artful, artless, arty*: cf the adj suffixes *-ful, -less, -y*.

3. The main L derivatives relevant to E are:

*iners*, unskilful (*in-*, not+*ars*), hence inactive, lazy, inert, has o/s *inert-*, whence E *inert*, with derivative *inertia*, adopted by E, which coins the adj *inertial* (*-al*);

*artifex*, artificer, artist, derives from *artem facere* and generates *artificium*, whence MF-F *artifice*, adopted by E, with own derivative *artificer*; *artificium* has adj *artificiālis*, technical, merely technical, artificial, whence E *artificial* (cf the MF-F *artificiel*), with own derivative *artificiality*.

4. It intervention accounts for E *artisan*, an adoption from EF-F; F *artisan* comes from It *artigiano*, from *arte*, itself from L *ars*, o/s *art-*.

5. Predominantly F in formation is *artist*, from MF-F *artiste* (adopted by E for an artist of theatre, ballet, music-hall), from F *art*; F *artiste* has adj *artistique*, whence E *artistic*; but *artistry* represents E *artist*+suffix *-ry*.

art (2), v (ME *eart, art*): an inflexion of AM, q.v.

artery, arterial.

The adj represents the MF *artérial* (soon *artériel*), from MF-F *artère*, from L *artēria*, windpipe, artery (from Gr *artēria*), whence E *artery*; *artēria* is app akin to, perh derived from, *artaō*, I suspend. Cf the element *arterio-*.

artesian: F *artésien*, adj from L *Artesium*, F *Artois*, F district where this type of well was first made.

artful. See ART, para 2.

arthritic, arthritis. See the element *arthro-*.

artichoke: northern dial It *articiocco* (cf Sp *alcarchofa*, significant var of *alcachofa*): Ar *al-khurshūf*, where *al* is the Ar 'the'. (Cf 'Articled Nouns' in P².)

article, n hence v; articulant; articular; articulate (adj and v)—articulacy; articulation, articulative, articulatory.

L *artus*, a joint (cf the element *arthro-*), has dim *articulus*, an articulation or joint, hence a precise moment (e.g., *in articulo mortis*, in the article of death) or a precise part, a division, an *article* (via MF-F *article*). L derivatives affecting E include *articulāre*, to divide into joints or precise parts, to utter distinctly; the presp *articulans*, o/s *articulant-*, yields the E n *articulant*; the pp *articulātus* (s *articulāt-*) yields both the adj *articulate*, whence *articulacy* (*articulate*+*-cy*: cf *accuracy* from *accurate*), and the v 'to *articulate*'; derivative from *articulat-* are *articulātiō*, o/s *articulātiōn-*, whence late MF-F *articulation*, adopted by E, and ML *articulātor*, adopted by E, and the E formations *articulative* and *articulatory*. ML *articularis* (from *articulus*) accounts for *articular*—cf the EF-F *articulaire*.

artifact. See FACT, para 2; cf ART.

artifice, artificial, artificiality. See ART, para 3.

artillery, whence artillerist (suffix *-ist*): ME *artilrie*: MF-F *artillerie*, from OF-MF *artiller*, to equip, deriving—? influenced by OF *art*, skill—from *atillier*, to arrange, to equip, app of Gmc origin—cf OHG *ziarī* (G *Zier*) and OE *tir* (E *tire*; cf ATTIRE), ornament.

artisan. See ART, para 4.

artist, artistic, artistry. See ART, para 5.

artless; arty. See ART, para 2.

arum (lily): perh via EF-F: from L *arum*: Gr *arōn*.

Aryan: Skt *ārya*, noble, à noble, an Aryan: akin to the syn Av *airya* and OPer.*ariya* (whence Per *Īrān*, Iran), and also to PN element *ario-* in C and Gmc—e.g., in *Ariovistus*.

as, adv (whence conj and pro): ME *as*, earlier *als, alse, also*, earliest *al swa*: OE *alswā, ealswā*, *eal swā*, all so, all thus, (hence) quite so, quite as: akin, both to G *als*, as, than, from MHG *als*, earlier *alse*, earliest *alsō*, usu 'as if', from OHG *alsō*; and to OFris *al-sa* and its contrr *asa*, *ase*, esp *as*. For E *also*, see ALL, para 2.

**asbestos**, whence adj **asbestine** (suffix *-ine*): L *asbestos* (n): Gr *asbestos*, inextinguishable: *a-*, not+pp of *sbennunai*, to extinguish, with many prob, but no certain, IE cognates.

**ascend; ascendency (-ancy), ascendent (-ant); ascension** (whence ascensional), **ascensive; ascent.— descend; descendence (-ance), descendent (-ant); descension, descensional, descensive; descent:** cf **condescend, condescendence, condescension, condescensive.—transcend, transcendence** or **-ency, transcendent** (adj hence n), **transcendental,** whence **transcendentalism; transcension.—scan, scansion.** —Intimately akin: **scandal, scandalize, scandalous** and the parallel **slander** (n, v), **slanderer, slanderous;** also **scale,** a ladder.

1. L *scandere*, to climb, hence to scan (verse), 'in reference to the movements of the foot raised and lowered to mark the metre' (E & M), yields 'to *scan*' (verse), hence the sense 'to examine'—look at carefully—hence (orig as a careless misuse) to look at hastily. The pp *scansus* has s *scans-*, whence *scansiō*, o/s *scansiōn-*, whence E *scansion* (of verse). *Scandere* consists of r *scan-*+formative *-d-*+inf suffix *-ere*: cf the Skt *skan*, he leapt, and *skándati*, he leaps, and such C forms as MIr *scendim*, I leap, OIr *sescaind*, he leapt, and W *cy-chwynnu*, to rise or climb.

2. Cf also Gr *skandalon*, a stumbling block, whence LL *scandalum*, OF-F *scandale* and ME *scandle*—both operative in E *scandal*. *Skandalon* has derivative *skandalizein*, whence LL *scandali-zāre*, leading to OF-F *scandaliser* and E *scandalize*; but *scandalous* comes from MF-F *scandaleux*, f *scandaleuse*, from *scandale*.

3. LL *scandalum* yields not only the var OF *escandele*, MF *escandle*, whence *scandal*, but also that additional var, the MF-F *esclandre*, whence, with deviation of sense, ME *sclaundre*, whence E *slander*; OF *esclandre* has derivatives MF-EF *esclandrer*, whence 'to *slander*', whence a *slanderer*, and EF adj *esclandrux*, f *esclandreuse*, perh concerned in the formation of E *slanderous* (more prob merely *slander*, n+suffix *-ous*).

4. L *scandere* (s *scand-*, r *scan-*) has an important derivative not imm obvious: from *\*scand-slā*: *scāla*, a ladder, is that by which one *scandit* or climbs. 'To *scale*' or climb derives from the n. And L *scāla* becomes It *scala*, whence the v *scalare*, whence *scalata*, a mounting by ladders, whence late MF-F *escalade*, adopted by E, whence 'to *escalade*' (cf EF-F *escalader*, whence the agential trade-name *Escalator*, whence any *escalator*.

5. L *scandere* is hardly less influential in its prefix cpds *ascendere—dēscendere*, whence *condēscendere* —*transcendere*. (*Conscendere* and *inscendere* became learnèd, long obs' E *conscend*, *inscend*; and *escendere* has lacked issue.)

6. *Ascendere*, which represents *as-* for *ad*, to+

*-scendere*, c/f of *scandere*, became E *ascend*, whence *ascender*. *Ascendere* has presp *ascendens*, o/s *ascendent-*, which became E *ascendent*, adj, and, via MF-F, *ascendant*, n, whence the nn *ascendence, -ance*, or *-ency, -ancy*. The pp *ascensus*, s *ascens-*, has derivative *ascensiō*, o/s *ascensiōn-*, whence, via OF, *ascension* and, as an E formation, *ascensive* (*-ive*). *Ascent* imitates *descent*.

7. *Descent* was adopted from MF *descent* (soon *descente*), from OF-F *descendre*, after such formations as *vente*, sale, from *vendre*, to sell. *Descendre*, which yields 'to *descend*' (whence *descender*), comes from L *dēscendere* (*dē*, down from+ *-scendere*). The L presp *dēscendens*, o/s *dēscendent-* yields adj *descendent* and, via MF-F n *descendant*, whence the nn *descendence, -ance*. On the L pp s *dēscens-*—arises *dēscensiō*, o/s *dēscensiōn-*, whence, via MF-EF, *descension* and the E formation *descensive*.

8. *Dēscendere* has subsidiary LL *condēscendere*, whence, prob via OF, 'to *condescend*'; the derivative *condēscensiō*, o/s *condēscensiōn-*, yields *condescension*; but the now mostly legal *condescendence* shows the influence of EF-F *condescendance*. A ML derivative, *condēscensivus*, accounts for *condescensive*.

9. L *transcendere*, to raise oneself beyond, became 'to *transcend*'; the L presp *transcendens*, o/s *transcendent-*, became *transcendent*, and the ML derivative *transcendentia* became *transcendence*, occ elaborated to *transcendency*. The n *transcendent* gained, esp in Phil, its own adj *transcendental*, whence *trasncendentalism*. The rare *transcension* comes from LL *transcensiō*, o/s *transcensiōn-*.

**ascertain.** See CERTAIN, para 5.

**ascetic** (adj hence n), whence **asceticism** (suffix *-ism*): Gr *askētikos*, self-denying in the cause of gymnastics, from *askēsis*, exercise, practice, from *askein* (s *ask-*), to practise gymnastics: o.o.o.

**ascribe, ascription.** See SCRIBE.

**aseptic.** See SEPTIC.

**ash** (1). See ASHES.

**ash** (2), tree: ME *asch, esch*: OE *aesc*, akin to OHG *asc*, MHG *asch, esche* (G *Asch*baum, *Esche*) and ON *askr*, also to Arm *haçi*, ash, to Lith *uosis*, ash, OB *jasene*, to OIr *uinnius*, ash, to L *ornus* (for *\*osinus*), mountain ash, to Gr *oxua, oxuē*, beech, and perh to Eg *āsh*, cedar. IE r: *\*ask-* or *\*esk-* or *\*osk-*. Adj *ashen*, C14 onwards=*ash*+adj suffix *-en*.

**ashamed.** See SHAME, para 2.

**ashen.** See ASH (2) and next.

**ashes:** ME *asche*: OE *asce, aesce*, occ *axe*, akin to OHG *asca* (MHG *asche*), Go *azgō*, ON *aska*, prob also to Skt *ásas*, ashes; the s is a b/f. The IE r is perh *\*as-* or *\*az-*. Adj *ashen*, a late formation: *ash*+*-en*.

**ashore.** See SHORE.

**Asia; Asian, Asianic, Asiatic; Eurasia.**

*Eurasia* blends *Eur*ope and *Asia*: and *Asia*= L from Gr *Asia*, o.o.o., but perh from Ass *Asu*, the East—as opp to *Ereb*, the West (*Europe*); note also that 'the Polynesians hailed from a legendary Atia, perhaps our Asia' (Erle Wilson, private letter of 14 Dec. 1952). But more prob the Gr *Asia*, Ionic *Asiē*, represents Gr *Asioi+-ia*, region; and *Asioi*, s *Asi-*, r *As-*, app derives from Ch *Yueh-chi*, the name of a great nomadic people inhabiting central Asia. (Cf W.W. Tarn, *The Greeks in Bactria and India*, 1938, at pp 284–5.) Gr *Asia* has derivatives *Asianos*, whence L *Asianus*, whence *Asian*, whence *Asianic*, and *Asiatikos*, L *Asiaticus*, (F *asiatique* and) E *Asiatic*, adj hence n.

**aside.** See SIDE.

**asinine.** See ASS.

**ask**, whence vn **asking**: ME *asken*, *axien*: OE *āscian*, *ācsian*, akin to OFris *āskia*, OS *ēscōn*, OHG *eiscōn*, ON *oeskia*; to OSl *iskati* (s *isk-*), to seek (cf Lith *ieškoti*); to Skt *iččháti*, he seeks: IE r, *\*isk-*, var *\*eisk-*, *\*esk-*.

**askance**, obliquely: o.o.o: perh from It *a scancio*, earlier *a schiancio*, obliquely, cf It *cansare*, to turn aside, from L *campsāre*, akin to Gr *kampsos*, crooked; IE r, *\*kamp-*.

**Askari.** See LASCAR, s.f.

**askew**: *a-*, on+*skew*, on the slant: see SKEW.

**aslant.** See SLANT.

**asleep.** See SLEEP.

**aslope.** See SLEEVE, para 5.

**asp** (1). See ASPEN.

**asp** (2), **aspic**, a small poisonous snake: *asp*, app short for *aspic*, adopted from MF-F, which has allowed F *piqu*er, to sting, to influence L *aspis*, itself adopted from Gr: Gr *aspis* (ἀσπίς) is o.o.o, but cf both H *ṣepa* a basilisk, and, much more prob, Eg *ḥefat*, an asp.

**asparagus**: adopted from L, from Gr *asparagos* or *aspharagos*, orig a shoot or sprout, akin to Av *sparegha*, a sprout: *asparagos* could represent *a-* for *ana*, up+*spargān*, to swell. (Boisacq).

**aspect.** See SPECTACLE, para 6.

**aspen**=*aspen* (*tree*), adj of obsol *asp* (this tree): OE *aesp*, var *aeps*, akin to OHG *aspa*, MHG *aspe*, G *Espe*, ON *ösp*, Lett *apsa*, OSl *osina* (for *\*opsina*). IE r: *\*aps-*.

**asperge, aspergillum.** See SPARSE, para 3.

**asperity; asperate**, adj and v.

L *asper* (s *asp-*: o.o.o.), rough, has derivatives *asperāre*, to roughen, pp *asperātus*, whence both adj and v *asperate*, and *asperitās*, o/s *asperitāt-*, whence *asperity*. The cpd *exasperāre* has pp *exasperātus*, whence 'to *exasperate*' and the obsol adj *exasperate*; the derivative *exasperātiō*, o/s *exasperātiōn-*, produces *exasperation*.

**asperse, aspersion, aspersive, aspersorium.** See SPARSE, para 3.

**asphalt**: (perh via OF-F *asphalte*, from) LL *asphaltus*: Gr *asphaltos*, perh akin to *asphalēs*, secure (*a-*, not+derivative from *sphallein*, s *sphall-*, r *sphal-*, to cause to fall).

**asphodel.** See DAFFODIL.

**asphyxia**, whence (suffix *-al*) the adj **asphyxial** and, anl, **asphyxiate** and **asphyxiation**. Gr *asphuxia*, a ceasing (*a-*, not) to throb (*sphuzein*, s *sphuz-*).

**aspic** (1), serpent. See 2nd ASP.

**aspic** (2), meat jelly: adopted from F, where it represents a fig use of the prec, 'by a comparison of the jelly's various colours with those of the serpent' (B & W).

**aspidistra**: SciL, usu explained as from Gr *aspis*, shield+*astron*, star, or, more precisely, *aspid-*, the o/s+*astra*, the pl, *\*aspidastra* becoming *aspidistra*. Perh rather from, or at the least prompted by, LL *aspidisca*, an ornament that, on a Jewish priest's vestments, was shaped like the boss of a shield (Souter).

**aspirant, aspirate, aspiration, aspirator, aspiratory; aspire.** See SPIRIT, para 7.

**asportation.** See the 3rd PORT, para 3.

**asquint.** See SQUINT.

**ass; asinine**: ME *asse*: OE *assa*: OIr *assan*: L *asinus*, adj *asinīnus*, whence E *asinine*. With *asinus* cf Gr *onos* and esp Sumerian *ansŭ*, *ansĕ*. The IE r is app *\*-ons-*, var *\*ans-*, with metathesis in L *asinus*.

2. The dim *asellus*, f *asella* (for *\*asinellus*, *-ella*), became the G *Esel* and esp the MD *esel*, D *ezel*, (little) donkey, hence, because a 'beast of burden', an artist's *easel*.

**assail, assailant.** See SALLY, para 9.

**assassin; assassinate, assassination.**

*Assassination* derives from 'to *assassinate*', itself from ML *assassinātus*, pp of *assassināre*, from ML pl *assassini*, assassins, whence, by b/f, the It sing *assassino*, whence EF-F, whence E, *assassin*: and ML *assassini* represents Ar *ḥashshāshīn*, drinkers of *hashīsh*, hemp (lit, herb). The Mohammedan order of Assassins, founded c1090, flourished during the Crusades; its members got drunk o hashish before they went out to slay Christians.

**assault.** See SALLY, para 10.

**assay**, n and v. See ESSAY.

**assemble; assemblage, assembly.** See SAME, para 11.

**assent** (n and v), **assentaneous, assentation.** See SENSE, para 14.

**assert, assertion, assertive.** See SERIES, para 7.

**assess, assessment, assessor.** See SIT, para 11.

**assets.** See SAD, para 7.

**asseverate, asseveration, asseverative.** See SEVERE, para 2.

**assident; assiduity**, etc. See SIT, para 10.

**assign, assignation, assignment, assignee,** etc See SIGN, para 12.

**assimilate, assimilation,** etc. See SAME, para 6.

**assist, assistance, assistant** (adj hence n), **assistive.** See SIST, para 2.

**assize(s).** See SIT, para 12.

**associate**, adj (hence n) and v; **association, associative; assoiable.**

The last is adopted from F, from MF-F *associer*, from L *associāre*: *ad*, to+*soci*us, a companion+inf suffix *-āre*: f.a.e., SOCIAL. *Associāre* has pp *associātus*, whence both *associate*, adj, and 'to *associate*'; built upon the s *associāt-* are both ML *associātiō*, o/s *associātiōn-*, whence, perh via MF-F, *association*, whence the adj *associational*, and the E formation *associative* (*-ive*, adj).

**assonance, assonant, assonate.** See SONABLE, para 5.

**assort, assortment.** See SERIES, para 6.

**assuage, assuagement, assuasive.** See SUAVE, para 5.

**assume, assumpsit, assumption, assumptive.** See SUMPTION, para 2.

**assurance; assure.** See CURE, para 10.

**Assyrian.** See SYRIA, para 2.

**astatics** is the neg (Gr *a-*, not) of STATIC.

**aster, asterisk, asterism, asteroid, astral; astro-labe, astrology, astronomy.** See STAR, paras 5–7.

**astern.** See the 2nd STEER, para 3.

**asthma:** Gr *asthma*, perh from *aenai*, to breathe hard, hence difficultly; Gr adj *asthmatikos*, whence, via L *asthmaticus* and perh EF-F *asthmatique*, the E *asthmatic*.

**astigmatic, astigmatism.** See STICK (heading).

**astir.** See STIR.

**astonied.** See THUNDER, para 7.

**astonish, astonishment.** See THUNDER, para 6.

**astony.** See THUNDER, para 7.

**astound.** See THUNDER, para 7.

**astrakhan:** *Astrakhan* (S Central Russia), where the wool was first obtained.

**astral.** See STAR, para 6.

**astray.** See STRATUM, para 8, s.f.

**astrict, astriction.** See the 2nd STRAIN, para 5.

**astride.** See STRIDE.

**astringe, astringency, astringent.** See the 2nd STRAIN, para 5.

**astrolabe; astrology; astronomy.** See STAR, para 7.

**astute,** whence **astuteness** (suffix *-ness*); **astucious, astucity.**

*Astute* comes from L *astūtus*, itself from *astus*, skill, craft, cunning, perh (cf var *astu*) from Gr ἄστυ, a city, for *Ϝαστυ, *wastu*, akin to Skt *vắstu*, a dwelling: sem, 'characteristic of "city slickers"'. The derivative L *astūtia* suggested late MF-F *astucieux*, f *astucieuse*, whence *astucious*; the EF *astuc*, astute, prob resulted in *\*astucité*, whence *astucity*.

**asunder:** OE *on sundran*, lit on (or onto) a position apart: f.a.e., SUNDER.

**asylum:** L trln of Gr *asulon*, a sanctuary, from *asulos*, inviolable: *a-*, not+*sulon*, right of seizure, cf *sulein*, to plunder, o.o.o.

**asymmetrical, asymmetry.** See SYMMETRY.

**asymptote** (Math): Gr *assumptōtos*, not falling together: *a-*, not+*sum-*, c/f of *sun*, with+derivative from *piptein*, to fall: cf SYMPTOM.

**asyndeton:** L trln of Gr *asundeton*, orig neu of *asundetos*, not (*a-*) bound together (*sundetos*); cf *syndetic*, Gr *sundetikos*, from *sundein*, to bind together: *sun*+*dein*, to bind.

**at:** OE *aet*, akin to OFris *et* (occ *at*), Go and OS *at*, OHG *az*, ON *at*—and L *ad*, q.v. in Prefixes.

**atavism, atavist, atavistic:** the 3rd, by *-ic*, from the 2nd; the 2nd, by *-ist*, from the 1st, and the 1st, by *-ism*, from ML *atavus*, L *atauus*, ancestor—a development from L *auus* (ML *avus*), a grand-father, s *au-*: akin to Arm *haw*, grandfather, and OP *awis*, OIr *aue*, maternal uncle: cf UNCLE.

**atheism, atheist, atheistic.** See THEISM, para 2.

**Athena, Athene; Athenaeum, athenaeum; Athenian, Athens; Attic, attic.**

Gr *Athēnai* (cf Gr *Thēbai*, E *Thebes*) became F *Athènes* became E *Athens*; the adj *Athēnaios* became *Athenian* (*-ian* substituted for *-aios*), and its neu *Athēnaion* was used as n for 'the temple of *Athēne* or *Athēna*'—which shows that *Athens* means '*Athena*'s city'; *Athēna* appears to be pre-Hellenic (? Mycenaean): ? 'The Protectress'. Gr *Athēnaion* became L *Athēnaeum*, but with predominant meaning 'a school of rhetoric, philosophy jurisprudence' at Rome—hence, the London *Athenaeum* and the generic *athenaeum*, a literary association or club.

2. App deriving from *Athēna*, *-nē*, is *Attika*, L *Attica*, E *Attica*, the region and state, the land of Athene, the adj being *Attikos*, L *Atticus*, E *Attic*, connoting a refined elegance and purity of taste and style (as in *Attic salt*, delicate wit: *sal Atticum*) whence, from Attic architecture, the F *attique* (Attic), whence E *attic*.

**athirst.** See THIRST.

**athlete; athletic,** whence both **athleticism** (*-ism*) and **athletics** (*-ics*, q.v. at suffix *-ic*).

*Athletic*, L *athlēticus*, Gr *athlētikos*, answers to *athlete*, L *athlēta*, Gr *athlētēs* (agential *-ēs*), from *athlein*, to compete for a prize in the public games, from *athlos*, a contest (physical), itself perh from *athlon*, Hom *aethlon*, a prize: if *aethlon*, *-os*, represents an earlier *\*awethlon*, *-os*, it may be akin to Skt *vắyati*, he exhausts himself, with IE r *\*aue* (Boisacq).

**athwart.** See THWART.

**Atlanta, Atlantic, Atlantis; Atlas, atlas.**

The 1st is a SciL derivative suggested by *Atlantic*, L *Atlanticus*, Gr *Atlantikos*, the adj of *Atlas*, pl *Atlantes* and o/s *Atlant-*; in Gr Myth, *Atlas* was that Titan who, forced to uphold the heavens and esp the Earth, much later became Mt Atlas in NW Africa: from pictures of Earth apprehended as a globe upheld by the Titan came *atlas*, a collection of maps. *Atlantis* lay in the Atlantic, out from Mt Atlas. See TOLERATE, *Atlas* 'the Upholder' deriving from Gr *tlēnai*, to uphold, bear.

**atmosphere,** whence **atmospheric** (*ic*, adj): *atmo-*, c/f of Gr *atmos*, breath, hence vapour+Gr *sphaira*, a sphere: see the element *atmo-* and word SPHERE.

**atoll:** *atolu* in Maldivan, the basically Malayan language (of the Maldives, coral islands SW of India) with Dravidian and Ar admixtures.

**atom, atomic, atomize, atomy.** See TOME, para 5.

**atonal, atonality.** See TEND, para 29, s.f.

**atone,** whence **atonement.** See ONE, para 11.

**atonic, atony.** See TEND, para 29, s.f.

**atrabiliar.** See ATROCIOUS, s.f.

**atrium.** See the element *atrio-*.

**atrocious, atrocity.**

The latter comes, through MF-F *atrocité*, from

L *ātrōcitas*, itself an *-itās* (E *-ity*) derivative from *ātrŏx* (o/s *ātrōc-*), cruel, whence both MF-F *atroce* and E *atrocious* (cf suffix *-ious*): cf L *ferox*, F *féroce*, E *ferocious*. Orig 'black of aspect', hence 'terrible', hence 'cruel', *atrox* extends *atr-*, the o/s of *ater*, black, preserved for E in *atrabiliar* (cf EF-F *atrabilaire*, var *-iaire*), hypochondriacal, var of *atrabilarious*, ML *atrabilārius*: *atra*, f of *ater*, black+*bili*s (see BILE)+adj suffix *-ārius* (E-*arious*)

**atrophy**, whence **atrophic** (*-ic*, adj) and **atrophied** (*-ed*, pp). See TROPHIC, para 2.

**attaboy** (whence, anl, **attagirl**): approbatory or incitant '*At's* (dial for *That's*) *the boy!*

**attach, attaché, attachment.** See TACH, para 2.

**attack.** See TACH, para 3.

**attain,** whence **attainable** and **attainment** (suffix *-ment*); **attainder, attaint** (n and v), **attainture.** See TACT, para 11.

**attainder.** See TACT, para 11.

**attainment.** See TACT, para 11.

**attaint.** See TACT, para 11.

**attar, ottar, otto:** all from Per '*aṭar*, itself from Ar '*iṭr*, perfume, esp from rose petals.

**attemper, attemperate.** See TEMPER.

**attempt.** See TEMPT, para 3.

**attend, attendance, attendant** (adj hence n); **attention, attentive.** See TEND, para 7.

**attenuant, attenuate, attenuation.** See TEND, para 25.

**attest, attestation, attestative, attestor.** See TESTAMENT, para 7.

**Attic; attic.** See ATHENA, para 2.

**attinge, attingent.** See TACT, para 10.

**attire,** n and v (whence **attirement**; suffix *-ment*).
The n derives from ME *atir*, adopted from OF-MF *atir*, equipment, whence prob the OF-EF v *atirier*, hence ME *atiren*, E 'to *attire*': f.a.e., TIER. The archaic *tire*, furniture, apparel, headdress, derives from ME *tir*, aphetic for *atir*; and the archaic v *tire*, to dress (e.g., the hair), is aphetic for 'to *attire*'. The *tire* (needlessly *tyre*) of a vehicular wheel is 'so called as being an attire or covering for a wheel' (Webster).

**attitude.** See APT, para 4.

**attorn; attorney.** See TURN, para 4.

**attract, attractant, attraction, attractive.** See TRACT, para 11.

**attribute, attribution, attributive.** See TRIBUTE, para 5.

**attrite, attrition, attritus.** See THROW, para 8.

**attune.** See TUNE.

**aubade.** See ALB, para 3.

**auburn:** ME *auburne*, fair (-haired, -complexioned): MF *auborne*, OF *alborne*: ML *alburnus*, rather white, from *albus*, white: f.a.e., ALB.

**auction,** n hence v (whence **auctioneer**). See AUGMENT, para 2.

**audacious, audacity.**
The adj comes from late MF-F *audacieux*, f *audacieuse*, from MF-F *audace* (audacity), from L *audācia*, from *audāx*, from *audēre* (s *aud-*), to desire to, hence to dare to, itself a modification of *auēre*, to desire strongly to—akin to *auidus*, whence

AVID, q.v. *Audacity=audāc-*, o/s of *audāx*,+*ity-*, as if from L *\*audācitās*—cf ML *audāciter*, audaciously.

**audible** (whence **audibility**)—**inaudible** (-ility); **audience, audient; audile; audit** (n hence v)—**audition—auditor—auditorium — auditory.— Exaudi. — obedience, obedient, obediential, obedientiary—obeisance, obeisant—obey; disobedience, disobedient, disobey.**

1. All these words come-, as adoptions of or as derivatives, whether direct or through F, from L *audīre* (s *aud-*), to hear, akin to the syn Gr *aiein* (s *ai-*), presumably for *\*awein* (s *aw-*), and to Skt *āvis*, OSl *avé*, evidently. The IE r is *\*au-*, L *aud*rei being clearly an extension.

2. *Audīre* has the foll simple derivatives relevant to E:

L *audībilis*, hearable, whence *audible*, whence *audibility* (suffix *-i y*), the neg ML *inaudībilis* yielding *inaudible*, whence *inaudibility*;

presp *audiens*, o/s *audient-*, whence *audient*; hence L *audientia*, whence F, whence E, *audience*;

pp *audītus*, s *audīt-*, whence (1) the n *audītus* (gen *-ūs*), a hearing, whence E *audit*, whence 'to audit'—(2) LL *audītiō*, o/s *audītiōn-*, whence, prob via MF-F, the E *audition*, whence the very mod 'to audition'—(3) *audītor*, a hearer, LL investigator in a lawsuit, whence AF *auditour* (MF-F *auditeur*), whence E *auditor*, with accountancy sense influenced by *audit*—(4) adj *audītōrius*, whence *auditory*, the neu *audītōrium* becoming n and yielding both *auditorium* and (n) *auditory*.

3. *Audile=aud-+*adj suffix *-ile*; anl with *tactile*.

4. Derivative *exaudīre* occurs in E only as Eccl *Exaudi*, conn 'Hear, O hear!'

5. But the irreg formed *oboedīre—ob* (see prefix *ob-*)+*audīre*—later *obedīre*, to obey, accounts for *obedient*, OF-MF *obedient*, L *obedient-*, o/s of *obediens*, presp of *obedīre*—for *obedience*, adopted from OF-MF (EF-F *obé-*), from L *ob*(*o*)*edientia*, from the presp—for *obediential*, ML *obedientiālis*, adj of *obedientia*—and Eccl *obedientiary*, ML *obedientiārius*. Cf *inobedience, inobedient*, perh adopted from F, but prob direct from LL *inoboediens*, presp, and derivative *inoboedientia*.

6. F influence is even clearer in:
*obey*, ME *obeyen*, OF-MF *obeir* (EF-F *obéir*), L *obedīre*;
*obeisance*, (orig) obedience, a deep bowing, MF *obeissance* (EF-F *obé-*), from the MF presp *obeissant*, whence E *obeisant*.

7. Cf *disobey*, MF *desobeir—des-* for L *dis-* (prefix *dis-*)+*obeir*; *disobedience, disobedient*, are adopted from MF formations consisting of OF *des+*OF *obedience*, OF *obedient*, as above.

**auger:** *a nauger*, misapprehended, in ME, as *an auger*: OE *nafugār*, lit a nave-borer: cpd of *nafu* nave of wheel+*gār*, a spear.

**aught.** See NAUGHT, para 2.

**augment,** n, v; **augmentation, augmentative.— auction,** n hence v, whence **auctioneer** (suffix *-eer*): **augur,** n, v; **augural, augury.—august; August, Augustan; Augustine.—author,** whence **authorial;**

authoritarian, authoritative, authority, authorize (whence authorization).—auxiliary, adj hence n.—inaugurate, inauguration.

1. L *augēre* (s *aug-*), to enlarge, increase; IE r, prob *au-*, with *g* (etc.) as extension. Cognates: syn Go *aukan*, OFris *āka* (v and n), ON *auka* (v) and *auki* (n), OHG *ouhhōn*, OE *ēacan* (see sep *eke*, v); Lith *augti*, to grow, and *áukštas*, high; Gr *auxein* (s *aux-*=*auks-*), to increase; Skt *ukṣati*, he grows, and *ojas*, strength. Cf sep WAX.

2. *Augēre* has pp *auctus*, on which arose both *auctiō*, (lit) an increasing, (but always) a public sale, with o/s *auctiōn-*, whence E *auction*, and *auctor*, lit an increaser, hence a founder, an auctioneer, an author: indeed, *auctor* became OF *autor* (F *auteur*) became ME *autour*, later *authour*, E *author*. The derivative L *auctoritās* (acc *auctoritātem*), which corresponded to *auctor* in all its senses, led to OF *auctoritei*, *-iteit*, later *autorité*, whence ME *autorite*, E *authority* (*-ity*); and derivative late ML *auctorizāre* became OF-F *autoriser* became late ME *autorize* became E *authorize*. Authoritarian, authoritative represent authority+ suffixes *-arian*, *-ative*.

3. The inf *augēre* has derivative *augmentum*, an increase, whence F, then E, *augment*. *Augmentum* itself has derivative LL *augmentāre*, whence MF-F *augmenter*, whence 'to *augment*'; on the pp *augmentātus* were built both the LL n *augmentātiō*, o/s *augmentātiōn-*, whence, prob via MF-F, the E *augmentation*, and the F *augmentatif*, f *-ive*, whence E *augmentative*.

4. Less obvious than the *aug-*, *auct-* derivatives are those from L *augur*, *augustus*, *auxilium*. The last perh=s *aug-*+connective or formative *s-*+*ilium* (*-um*, neu nom and acc) and prop means 'an increase of forces, a reinforcement'—hence, assistance, help, with adj *auxiliāris*, whence *auxiliary* (cf EF-F *auxiliaire*).

5. Lit, an *augur* (formerly derived usu from L *auis*, a bird: cf *auspice*) means 'one who predicts an increase, hence success' (later, any issue to an undertaking): *aug-*, s of *augēre*+*-ur*, prob a var of agential *-or*. *Augur* has derivatives:

*augurālis*, whence EF-F and E *augural*, of an augur, (hence) ominous;

*augurium*, a (favourable) presage or prediction, whence, prob via OF-MF *augurie*, the E *augury*;

*auguro* (*-or*), inf *augurāre* (*-āri*) to make an augury, to augur, to predict, whence 'to *augur*'; the pp *augurātus*, whence the obs *augurate*, to augur, leads to LL *augurātiō*, o/s *augurātiōn-*, whence the obs *auguration*; hence:

*inaugurāre* (*in-*, in, into+*augurāre*), to augur, esp before an important undertaking, hence to destine, give a start to, to consecrate, with pp *inaugurātus*, whence 'to *inaugurate*'; the derivative n *inaugurātiō*, o/s *-ātiōn-*, yields *inauguration*; the adj *inaugural* was adopted from F (*inaugurer*+*-al*, anl with *augural*).

6. L *augustus*, whence E *august*, signified orig either 'consecrated by the augurs' or 'undertaken under favourable auguries'; it was in 27 B.C.

applied to Octavius Caesar: and the first *Augustus* bestowed his title upon the month *Augustus*, our *August*. *Augustus*, the PN, had two adjj: *Augustānus*, whence E *Augustan*, transferred to any period similar to that of Caesar Augustus; and *Augustīnus*, which became a PN, whence (St) *Augustine* or *Augustin*, which by shortening became *Austin* (*canons*, *friars*).

augur, augury. See prec, para 5.

august; Augustan. See AUGMENT, para 6.

auk, whence auklet (dim suffix *-let*). See HALCYON, para 2.

auld: Sc form of OLD.

aunt: OF *ante*: L *amita*, father's sister, akin to L *\*amma*, nursery word for 'mother' (cf MAMA).

aura. See SOAR, para 2.

aural. Adj of prec; also the Med adj for 'ear': cf EAR.

aureate; aureole; auri-, auro-: see Elements; oriole; loriot.

*Aureate* comes from L *aureātus*, gilded, golden, from *aureus*, golden, from *aurum*, gold; *aureus* has dim *aureolus*, whence ML *aureola*, elliptical for *aureola corona*, a crown of gold, hence a halo; *aureolus*, used as n, became OF *oriol*, whence, via Sci L *oriolus*, the E *oriole*; and OF *oriol* became (suffix *-ot* for suffix *-ol*) OF *oriot*, and *l'oriot*, apprehended as one word *loriot*, became MF-F, hence E, *loriot*; the bird was so named from its bright-yellow plumage.—Perhcf AURORA.

auricle, auricular. See EAR.

aurochs. See OX, para 3.

aurora (whence the adj auroral), the reddish-golden dawn-light, personified as Aurora, the Roman goddess of dawn; aurora australis, a. borealis, the austral or Southern lights, the boreal or Northern lights. Adopted from L, *aurora* perh derives from *aurum*, gold; many scholars relate it to EAST. The IE r is prob *\*au-*, extended, in L, as *aur-*.

auscultate, auscultation. See EAR.

auspice, auspicial, auspicious; auspicate.

L *auspex* is one who, for omens, examines (*specere*, *spicere*—a *spec-*, *spic-*, to see) the flight of birds (*auis*, ML *avis*, s *au-*, a bird)—for the elements, see AVIARY and SPY; *auspex* has derivatives *auspicium*, whence MF-F, hence E, *auspice*, an omen so obtained, hence any, usu a favourable, omen, and *auspicāre* or *-āri*, to take an augury, with pp *auspicātus*, whence 'to *auspicate*'. Both the lit *auspicial* (*-ial*) and the fig *auspicious* (*-ious*) are of E formation.

austere, austerity.

The latter comes, via MF-F *austérité*, from L *austēritās*, o/s *austēritāt-*, a derivative of *austērus*, rough, harsh, from Gr *austēros*, itself from *auein*, to parch: cf SEAR. *Austērus*, via MF *austere* (F *austère*), yields *austere*.

Austin (friars, etc.). See AUGMENT, last para, s.f.

austral; Australia, whence Australian, adj hence n also.

L *austrālis*, whence E *austral*, derives from the o.o.o *auster*, the south wind, hence the south,

Either the L *Terra Austrālis*, southern land, has prompted *Australia*, anl with the numerous *-ia* lands; or, as Enci It impressively implies, *Australia* is 'erudite' f/e from '*Austrialia* del Espirito Santo', as, in honour of an *Austrian* prince (cf next), the Port navigator Pedro De Queiros named, in 1606, the largest of the New Hebrides; the name was confused with L *austrālis* and, much later, transferred to Australia. The s *Aussie* represents both *Aus*tralia and, usu, *Aus*tralian.

**Austria,** whence **Austrian,** adj hence also n; **austrium.**

The 3rd=*Austri*a+the Chem (element) suffix *-ium*: and *Austria* is the L form (A.D. 996) of the medieval Gmc *Ostarrichi* or *Osterriche*, MHG *Osterriche*, G *Osterreich*, 'Eastern Kingdom' (Enci It): cf EAST and REX.

**authentic; authenticate; authenticity.**

The 3rd derives, by suffix *-ity*, from *authentic*, ME *autentike*, adopted from OF (later *autentique*, F *authentique*)—from LL *authenticus*, from Gr *authentikos*, adj of *authentēs*, one who acts on his own authority, a chief: *auth-*, for *aut-* for *auto-* (q.v. in Elements)+*-hentēs*, a c/f o.o.o. Gr *authentēs*, by the way, became Mod Gr *aphentēs*, became Tu *efendi* became E *Effendi*, a title of respect. LL *authenticus* had derivative ML *authenticāre*, pp *authenticātus*, whence 'to *authenticate*', whence *authentication*.

2. The Gr *aut(o)-*, *auth-*, is the c/f of *autos*, self, (adj) same; *autos* represents *au-*+theme *to-*+nom suffix *-s*; and *au-* derives, app, from *\*asu-*, akin to Skt *ásus*, life, esp of the soul (Boisacq).

**authigenic.** See *auto-* in Elements.

**author, authoritative, authority, authorize.** See AUGMENT, para 2.

**autobiography, autobiographical autobiographer:** *auto-* (see AUTHENTIC, para 2)+*biography*, etc.: lit, 'self life-story'.

**autochthon, autochthonous.** See HOMO, para 3.

**autocracy, autocrat, autocratic:** resp Gr *autokrateia*—(via F, from) Gr *autokratēs*—the *-ic* adj of *autocrat*: *auto-*, for *autos*, self+*krateia*, power, from *kratus*, powerful. See the elements *auto-* (cf AUTHENTIC, para 2) and *-crat*.

**auto-da-fé.** See FAITH, para 3.

**autograph,** n hence adj and v; **autographic; autography.**

The 2nd and 3rd are anl formations—cf BIOGRAPHY; the 1st comes from L *autographum*, orig the neu of *autographus*, written (cf GRAPH) with one's own (*auto-*: cf AUTHENTIC, para 2) hand, from Gr *autographos*.

**automat, automatic, automatism, automaton** (pl **automata**). See MIND, para 9.

**automobile:** F *automobile*, adj then also n: *auto-*, self (cf AUTHENTIC, para 2)+*mobile*.

**autonomous,** Sci **autonomic; autonomy.** See NIMBLE, para 8.

**autopsy,** whence (suffix *-ic*) **autopsic; autoptic.** See OPTIC, para 3.

**autumn, autumnal.**

The latter—perh imm from OF-F *automnal*—represents L *autumnālis*, adj of *autumnus*, whence, via OF *autompne* or *automn* (F *automne*), the E *autumn*: and L *autumnus* is o.o.o., perh Etruscan, although the old L explanation by *augēre*, to increase, may, after all, be correct, autumn being the season when the crops' increase is yielded at the harvest. Conceivably *autumnus* represents PL *\*uertumnus*, from *uertere*, ML *vertere*, to turn, (later) to convert, autumn being the season of change from warmth to cold. This *\*uertumnus* was perh altered to avoid confusion with the Etruscan *Uertumnus*, god of the seasons.

**auxiliary.** See AUGMENT, para 4.

**avail,** v whence n; derivatively **available,** whence **availability.** See VALUE, para 12.

**avalanche.** See VALE, para 3.

**avant-garde.** See the 1st VAN, para 1.

**avarice, avaricious:** the latter comes from MF-F *avaricieux*, f *avaricieuse*, from OF-F *avarice*, whence E *avarice*: and OF *avarice* comes from ML *avāritia*, L *auāritia*, from *avārus*, *auārus*, from *avēre* (*auēre*), to covet: f.a.e., AVID.

**avast** (esp *heaving*): perh either Port *abasta*, it is enough, or the term being nautical, D *houd vast*, hold fast! (EW): the former is phon preferable.

**avatar:** Skt *avatāra*: from *ava*, down+*tarati*, he crosses over.

**avenge, avengement, avenger, avengeress.** See DICT, para 21.

**avenue.** See VENUE, para 6.

**aver** (1), n. See HABIT, para 12.

**aver** (2), v; **averment.** See VERACIOUS, para 4.

**avera, average,** feudal services. See OPERA, para 7.

**average,** n hence adj and v: app form-influenced by ME *average*, a feudal service (work), but strictly from F *avarie*, damage to a ship or its cargo, (hence) port dues: It *avaria*: Ar '*awārīyah* (pl), goods damaged by sea water, from the sing '*awār*, damage. E sense-development: 'tariff on goods': 'mean tariff': 'a mean': Mod 'average'.

**averment.** See VERACIOUS, para 4.

**averse, aversion, aversive; avert.** See VERSE, para 15.

**aviary,** whence **aviarist; avian.—aviation, aviator, aviatorial.**

Here the key is L *auis* (s *au-*), ML *avis*, a bird: cf Arm *haw*, Gr *oiōnos*, large bird, and *aietos* (? for *\*awietos*), eagle (*the* bird), and Vedic *ves* (pl *vayas*), Av *vayō* (pl), and Skt *vi*, bird: IE r, *\*aw-*.

2. L *auis* has derivative adj *auiārius*, of a bird, whence (orig, neu s adj) *auiārium* (ML *av-*), whence E *aviary*. The adj *avian*=ML *av-*+*-ian*.

3. F derivatives from ML *avis* include *aviation*, adopted by E, and *aviateur* (orig a flying machine), adapted as *aviator*. The adj *aviatorial*=*aviat*ion+ *-orial*.

**avid, avidity.**

The latter comes, via late MF-F *avidité*, from ML *aviditās*, L *auiditās*, derivative from *auidus*, ML *avidus*, whence, via MF-F *avide*, the E *avid*: and L *auidus* derives from *auēre*, to be desirous.

(hence) greedy, itself with several not irrefutable C cognates. Cf AUDACIOUS and AVARICIOUS.

**aviso.** See VIDE, para 13.

**avocado**: Sp *aguacate* or *ahuacate*: Nahuatl (Aztec) *ahuacatl* or, esp, *auacatl*: perh, as Webster suggests, the form *avocado* owes something to Sp *bocado*, a delicacy.

**avocation.** See VOCABLE, para 10.

**avoid**, whence **avoidable** and **avoidance.** See VACANT, para 7.

**avoirdupois**: ME *avoir de pois*, earlier *aver de peis*: OF-MF *aveir de peis*, goods of weight: OF-MF *aveir*, F *avoir*, goods, property, from OF *aveir* (F *avoir*), to have—*de*, of—*peis*, later *pois* (F *poids*), weight, from *pensum*: f.a.e., POISE.

**avouch.** See VOCABLE, para 8.

**avow**, to acknowledge, to declare; **avowal.** See VOCABLE, para 10.

**avulse, avulsion.** See VELLICATE, para 3.

**avuncular.** See UNCLE, para 2.

**await.** See VIGOR, para 11.

**awake, awaken.** See VIGOR, para 11.

**award**, n and v. See WARD.

**aware, awareness.** See WARY, para 2 and heading.

**away.** See VIA, para 6.

**awe**, n hence v; **(aweful) awful, awesome.**

The adjj merely represent *awe*, n+adj suffixes *-ful* (cf FULL) and *-some* (cf SAME). The n *awe* (ME *aghe*) comes from ON *agi*, akin to OHG *agison*, to frighten, Go *agis*, fear, and *ōg*, I am afraid, OIr *-ágor*, I fear, and, more remotely, Gr *akhos*, distress, pain.

With coll *awful*, cf *dreadful, shocking, terrible.*

**awkward**, whence **awkwardness** (suffix *-ness*): ME *awkwarde*, awkward, (but usu) awkwardly: ON *öfugr*, turning the wrong way+the E suffix *-ward*, conn 'direction'.

**awl** comes, through ME *aule* or *alle*, from OE *awel* or *al* (or *ael*), akin to OHG *āla*, MHG *āle*, G *Ahle*, and ON *alr*—cf Lith *yla* and, remotely, Skt *ārā*. The Gmc r is *\*ǣlō*; the IE r, prob *\*ēlā*. (Walshe.)

**awn**, a bristle at end of spikelet of barley or oats: ME *awne* or *agune*: ON *ögn*, pl *agnir*, akin to Go *ahana*, OHG *agana* (G *Ahne*), chaff. Perh ult akin to IE r *\*ak-*, a point.

**awning**: o.o.o.; perh, with Webster, cf F *auvent* (OF *auvan*) and Pr *anvan*, or, with B & W (apropos *auvent*), the OProv *amban*, a (sort of) parapet or gallery in fortification, and Langue d'Oc *embans*, awning of a shop, from Gaul *\*andebanno-*: *ande*, aug prefix (C r *\*and*, up against)+*banno-*, animal's horn (Langue d'Oc *bano*), 'bulls' horns having been employed by the Gauls as a totem protecting the house'.

**awry.** See WRATH, para 4, s.f.

**ax** (AE), **axe**, n hence v: OE *eax, aex*, also *acas*: akin to OFris *axa*, OHG *acchus* (MHG *ackes* or *axt*, G *Axt*), OS *acus* or *accus*, Go *aqizi*, ON *öx*; also to L *ascia*, hoe, pick, and Gr *axinē*, axe.

IE r, prob *\*aks-*: perh, therefore, akin to, or even extended from, IE r *\*ak-*, a point.

**axial; axil, axilla, axillary.** See AXIS.

**axiom, axiomatic.**

The latter comes from Gr *axiōmatikos*, adj of *axiōma*, a worthy thought, from *axioun*, to think worthy, from *axios*, worthy, akin to Gr *agein* (s *ag-*), to drive, (also) to weigh so much: *axios* represents *\*agtios*, 'that draws or pulls by its weight, pulls its own weight' (Boisacq). *Axiom* derives from EF-F *axiome*, from L-from-Gr *axiōma*.

**axis, axial, axil, axilla, axillary; axle, axletree.**

1. The L *axis* (s *ax-*), adopted by E, has E adj *axial* (*ax-*+*-ial*) and dim *axilla*, armpit, adopted by Sci and also anglicized as *axil*, with adj *axillary*, from F *axillaire* (s *axill-*+adj suffix *-aire*). Now, *axis*, which means either *axis* or—the orig sense—axle, is akin to Gr *axōn* (? for *\*aksōn*), axle, and Skt *akṣas*, also to OP *assis* and Lith *ašis*, and to OHG *ahsa*.

2. Also cognate is OE *eax*, axis, axle, surviving in dial *axtree*. Note that E *axle* derives from the first element of ME *axeltre* (whence *axletree*), itself from ON *öxultrē*, where (*-trē* answers to E TREE and) *öxul* is akin to OE *eaxl*, OFris *axle* or *axele*, OHG and OS *ahsla*, all meaning axle, and, ult, to L *axilla*, armpit.

3. The IE r is presumably *\*aks-*. Cf AISLE.

**ay**, usu **aye**, always; **ay** or **aye**, yes. The latter, by many said to be o.o.o., prob derives from the former: cf, sem, such terms as *certainly*, the Am coll *sure*, *right*, as emphatic synn of *yes*. *Aye, ay*, always, constantly, derives from ME *ai* or *ei*, itself from ON *ei*, akin to OE *ā*, always, Go *aiw* (prob the acc of *aiws*, an age) and OHG *io* or *eo* (MHG *ie*: G *je*, ever—cf *ja*, yes): IE adv, ult from the IE n exemplified in Go *aiws*, OHG *ēwa*, L *aeuum* (ML *aevum*), Gr *aiōn*, an age, and in Skt *āyus*, life: cf AGE, para 6.

**azalea** Sci L: Gr *azalea*, f of *azaleos*, dry, from *aza*, dryness, akin to *azein* (s *az-*), to parch: cf Cz *ozditi*, to dry, Go *azgō*, ash, Skt *ásas*, dust, ashes—and to L *arēre* (cf ARID).

**azimuth.** See ZENITH, para 2.

**azote**, nitrogen (incapable of maintaining life): F: b/f from Gr *a-*, not+*zōtikos* (*zoē*, life), life-maintaining, whence perh imm the adj *azotic*, unless from the F derivative *azotique*.

**Aztec**, n (inhabitant) hence adj hence n (language): Sp *Azteca*, an Aztec: from Aztec *Aztlan*, 'Land or region or place of the Herons' or 'White Land', less prob 'Seacoast'.

**azure**, n hence adj: ME *azure, asur*: OF-F *azur*, OF *asur* (with *l-* lost, as if the article 'the'): Ar *lāzaward*: Per *lāzhuward*, lapis lazuli, hence the colour; Ar *lāzaward* also became ML *lazulus*, whence (*lapis*, stone) *lazuli* (prop gen).

**azygous**: Gr *azugos*, unyoked, pl *azugoi*, unpaired: *a-*, not+*zugon*, a yoke: f.a.e., YOKE.

# B

baa, like *bow-wow*, is an echoic rural and nursery word.

**Baal; Bel; Beelzebub.**
Akk *bel*=Phoen *ba'al*, owner, lord, whence H *Ba'al*, any of numerous ancient Semitic gods; *Beelzebub*=Gr *Beelzeboub*=H *Ba'al zĕbūb*, Lord of Flies, (later) a powerful associate of Satan's.

**baas.** See BOSS.

**babble; bibble-babble.**
The latter merely reduplicates the former: and *babble*, n, derives from 'to *babble*', arising in early ME as an echo-word akin to G *babbeln*, ON *babba*, LL *babulus*, a babbler. Cf, sem, PRATTLE and, phon and sem, BARBARIAN and:

**babe; baby,** whence babyish (suffix *-ish*, adj): ME *babe* or *bab*; ME *baby* or *babi*, prob dim: akin to MHG *bābe*, mother, *buobe*, boy (G *Bube*); LL *babulus*, a babbler or prattler; Gr *babazein* (s *babaz-*, r *bab-*), to prattle; Skt *barbaras*, (given to) stammering, with var *balbalā-* in *balbalākaroti*, he stammers. Cf BABBLE and BARBARIAN.

**babel, Babel; Bab el Mandeb, Babylon.**
Generic *babel* comes from 'the tower of *Babel*' (see *Genesis*, xi, 9): H *Bābel*: Ass-Bab *Bābilu*, Gate of God (cf ALLAH), which, becoming Gr *Babulōn*, passed into L, hence E, as *Babylon*; cf *Bab el Mandeb*, Gate of Tears.

**baboo.** See BABU.

**baboon:** ME *baboyne* (or *babewyn*): MF *babuin* (F *babouin*): from *babine*, lip, 'the baboon having prominent lips' (B & W), influenced by the cognate MF *baboue*, a grimace.

**babu,** often anglicized **baboo:** Hi *bābū*, a Hindu title of respect, hence a Hindu gentleman, whence *babu English* (pej).

**baby, babyish.** See BABE.

**Babylon.** See BABEL.

**baccalaureate:** F *baccalauréat*: ML *baccalaureātus*, from *baccalaureus*, a 'joking alteration—after *bacca lauri*, "laurel bay"—of ML *baccalarius*, bachelor' (B & W): cf BACHELOR.

**baccarat:** adopted from F, var *baccara*, o.o.o.: ? from the F town of *Baccarat* (Meurthe-et-Moselle) famous for its glassware.

**bacchanal, Bacchanalia, bacchanalian; Bacchae; bacchant, bacchantic; Bacchic, bacchic; Bacchus.**
The L *Bacchus* transliterates *Bakis*, the Lydian origin of Gr *Bakkhos* (Βάκχος), syn of predominant *Dionusos*: derivatives include *Bankhai*, whence L *Bacchae*, female companions of this God of Wine;

L *bacchanālis*, adj ('of Bacchus'), hence n ('devotee'), whence the E n *bacchanal*, with adj *bacchanalian*, influenced by L *Bacchanālia* (orig the neupl of *bacchanālis*), the festival of Bacchus; L *bacchāri*, to celebrate that festival, with presp *bacchans*, o/s *bacchant-*, whence E *bacchant*, f *bacchante* (from F), with adj *bacchantic*, perh influenced by *Bacchic* (L *Bacchicus*), of Bacchus or his festival, whence *bacchic*, drunken.

**baccy:** coll for **tobacco.**

**bachelor:** ME *bachelor*: OF-MF *bacheler* (MF-F *bachelier*), a young gentleman aspiring to knighthood, hence young man: ML *\*baccalāris*, usu *baccalārius*, a tenant farmer, perh of C origin: cf OIr *bachlach*, a shepherd, from *bachall*, from L *baculum*, a staff, but also—of Gaul-Roman stock—the OProv *bacalar*, young man (B & W).

**bacillus.** See the element *bacilli-*. The adj *bacillary*=E *bacill*(us)+*-ary*.

**back,** adv. See para 5 of:

**back,** n, hence adj and v; **aback; backward(s); backblocks — backbone — backfire — backgammon —background—backside—backwater.**
*Back:* OE *baec*, akin to ON (and OS) *bak*, back, and to OHG *bach*, back, and *baccho* or *bahho*, haunch, ham; cf BACON. Earlier etym, obscure.

2. Of the many cpds, note *backblocks*, from blocks of land in the *back* (remote) areas—*backbone* (cf BONE)—*backfire* (*back*, adv+FIRE), n hence v—*backgammon*, prob from *back*, adv+*gammon*, a game, 'because the men are often set *back*' (Webster)—*background* (GROUND), ground at back—*backside*, the part (e.g., of the body) at the back—*backwater*, lit water turned back, hence remote, cf *backwoods*.

3. The adj *backward* derives from the adv *backward*, var of *backwards*, towards the back: cf TOWARDS.

4. The derivative 'to *back*' has agent *backer* and vn *backing*.

5. The adv *aback*—whence, by aphesis, the adv *back*—represents the ME *abak*, earlier *on bak*, from OE *on baec*, on or at (the) back.

**backgammon.** See para 2 of prec.

**backsheesh,** coll **backshee.** See BAKSHEESH.

**bacon,** whence the surname *Bacon*, with derivative adj (whence n) *Baconian*: ME, from OF-MF *bacon*: (perh via OProv *bacon*, from) ML *bacon*em acc of *baco*: OHG *bac(c)ho* or *bahhō*, haunch, ham (buttocks and rear part of thigh), hence flitch of

bacon: from OHG *bach*, the back: cf BACK.
(Walshe.)

**bacteria**, whence (suffix *-al*) **bacterial**; **bacterio-logy**. See the element *-bacter*.

**bad** (adj hence n), whence adv **badly** (suffix *-ly*)
and **badness** (*-ness*): ME *bad*, earlier *badde*: perh
(Webster) from OE *baeddel*, a hermaphrodite, cf
OE *baedling*, an effeminate; but ? rather from C
*\*bados* (well attested in derivatives), with var
*\*badtos*, whence *\*bassos* (cf the LL *bassus*, squat,
short, low), the r being *\*bad*, to be wide or open,
the basic idea of the adj being 'wide-open (to all
influence, esp the worst)'. (Cf Malvezin at BAD².)

**bade**. See BID.

**badge; badger.**

*Badge:* ME and EE *bage* or *bagge*, o.o.o. Hence,
prob (OED; Webster), in ref to the white mark
(*badge*) on its brow, that burrowing quadruped the
*badger*, EE *bageard*: EE *bage*+suffix *-ard*, in-fluenced by the agential *-er*: cf, sem, F *blaireau*
(B & W).

**badinage**: adopted from EF-F: f.a.e., the 5th
BAY, para 2.

**baffle**, whence the pa **baffling**: Sc *bauchill, bachill,
bauchle*, to disgrace publicly, to ridicule, prob from
Sc *bauch*, ineffective, inferior, prob from ON *bagr*,
clumsy, or ON *bāgr*, uncomfortable, in difficulties.
(Craigie.)

**bag**, n hence v; **baggage**; direct from *bag*:
**bagman, bagpipe, baggy.**

*Baggage* derives from MF-F *bagage*, itself
(collective suffix *-age*) from OF-EF *bague*, a bundle,
akin to ON *baggi*, a packet, whence, via ME *bagge*,
the E *bag*.

**bagatelle**: EF-F *bagatelle*: It *bagatella*, app the
dim of *baca*, a berry: L *baca*, perh (E & M) akin
to *Bacchus*.

**bail** (1), surety: MF-F *bail*, from OF-MF *baillier*,
MF-F *bailler* (whence 'to *bail*'), to deliver, give,
from L *baiulāre*, to carry a burden, from *baiulus,
baiiulus*, a burden-carrier: 'from *Baiiae*?' ask E &
M; *Bai(i)ae* was a favourite seaside resort of the
ancient Romans. Perh rather akin to BEAR, v.

2. L *bai(i)ulus* yields LL *bai(i)uluus*, ML *bai(i)ul-vus*, whence OF-EF *baillif* (F *bailli*) custodian,
hence magistrate, adopted by ME, whence E
*bailiff*, Sc *bailie*, whence *bailiwick*, which cpds
*baili(e)* or *baili(ff)*, and *wick*, a hamlet or village,
OE *wic* (L *uicus*, cf VICINITY).

**bail** (2), a bucket, hence 'to bail' (water out of,
e.g., a boat): late MF-F *baille*, a bucket: VL
*\*bai(i)ula*, f of *bai(i)ulus*, as in prec.

**bail** (3), an outer defence: partly from MF-F
*bail*: L *bai(i)ulus*, as in precc, and partly from L
*baculum*, a staff. The ME *bail* has, prob via the var
*bayle*, the further var *baily*, whence E *bailey*, occ
*baily*, a castle's outer wall, later a castle-prison,
finally a prison—cf 'the Old *Bailey*', London's
central criminal court.

2. The MF-F *bail* had the dial sense 'crosspiece':
hence the cricket sense of E *bail*.

3. Akin to 'crosspiece' is the sense 'a pole, a
bar' hence 'to *bail*', to confine, e.g., cattle, hence

prob the Aus (orig, bushrangers') *bail up*, to stop
and rob wayfarers.

**bailey**, See the 3rd BAIL.

**bailie, bailiff**. See 1st BAIL, para 2.

**bailiwick**. See 1st BAIL, para 2.

**bait; abet, abetment, abettor; bet.**

1. 'To *bet*' derives from 'a *bet*': and *bet*, n, app
derives from ME *abet*, an abetting, from OF *abet*,
from *abeter*, to excite or instigate, from *a*, to+
OF-MF *beter*, to bait, of Gmc origin: and OF
*abeter* yields ME *abetten*, whence 'to *abet*', to
incite or, at the least, countenance; *abet*, assisted
by AF *abetement*, leads to *abetment* (suffix *-ment*),
and, assisted by AF *abettour*, to *abettor*.

2. The OF-MF *beter* mentioned above is akin to
OHG *beizēn*, OE *bǣtan*, ON *beita*, to cause to bite;
*beita* became ME *beytan* or *baiten*, whence E 'to
*bait*', to incite (a dog) to bite, (hence) to harass an
animal by setting dogs on to it, (later) to feed, e.g.,
a horse, esp on the road. From 'to *bait*' and ON
*beita*, pasture, food, comes *bait*, food serving as
allurement, hence any allurement or temptation.

3. Cf BITE, whose OGmc forms have the causs
mentioned above.

**bake, baker, bakery; batch.**

*Bakery* derives, with suffix *-ery*, from 'to *bake*';
*baker*, however, derives from OE *baecere*, itself
from OE *bacan*, to roast or bake, akin to ON
*baka*, OHG *bahhan* (MHG and G *backen*), Gmc r
*bak-*, var *bōk-*; IE r, *\*bhag-*, var *\*bhōg-*, as in Gr
*phōgein* (s *phōg-*), to roast. (Walshe.) OE *bacan*
directly leads to E 'to *bake*'.

2. OE *bacan* also yields ME *bach* or *bache*,
whence *batch*, a baking, the loaves of a baking,
hence anything else used in, or produced at, one
operation.

**baksheesh, bakshish**; often anglicized to **back-sheesh**: via Ar, from Per *bakhshīsh*, from *bakshīdan*,
to give, akin to Skt *bhajati*, he allots.

**balance**, n hence v: ME *balance*, adopted from
OF: L *bilancem*, acc of *bilanx* (o/s *bilanc-*), adj
(having two plates or scales), hence n (a balance,
or pair of scales): *bi-*, twice+*lanx* (gen *lancis*), a
plate, esp of a pair of scales. *Lanx* is app of Medit
stock: cf the Gr *lekos*, a plate, and *lekanē*, a basin;
perh akin to the IE r *\*lek-*, to bend or curve.

**balcony**: It *balcone*, aug of *balco*, a scaffold,
from OHG *balcho*, a beam, akin to OE *balca*, a
ridge; f.a.e., the n BALK.

**bald**, whence **baldly** (*-ly*, adv) and **baldness**
(*-ness*): ME *balled*, akin to Da *baeldet*, bald, Go
*bala*, a whitefaced horse, Gr *phalios* (r *phal-*), white
or clear(-shining): IE r, *\*bhel-*, to gleam, esp to
gleam whitely.

**baldric**. See BELT.

**bale** (1), malign evil, torment: OE *balu*, akin to
OFris *balu-*, OS, OHG *balu*, ON *böl*, evil (adj)—cf
Go *balweins*, pain.

**bale** (2). See the 1st BALL.

**balk**, n, loosely **baulk**: OE *balca*, a ridge, whence
the sense 'unploughed ridge between furrows',
whence both 'beam, rafter' and 'hindrance' (as in
*ba(u)lk*): akin to ON *bālkr*, a partition, and *bjalki*,

a beam—OFris, *balka*, OHG *balcho*, OS *balko*,
a beam—L *fulcīre* (s *fulc-*), to prop: cf BOLE and
FULCRUM, also BLOCK.

2. 'To *ba*(*u*)*lk*', to avoid, to check or baffle,
(v.i.) to stop or swerve (whence *balky*), derives
from *balk*, either as 'a ridge between furrows' or as
'a beam'.

**ball** (1), a sphere: ME *bal* or *balle*: ON *bolle*,
akin to OHG *balla*, whence, via MF *bale* (MF-F
*balle*), the ME and E *bale*, a large bundle, close-
pressed and packaged. Cf BALLOON and BOWL (2).

**ball** (2), obs 'a dance', hence 'an assembly for
dancing': OF-F *bal*, from OF-MF *baler*, MF-EF
*baller*, to dance: LL *ballāre*: Gr *ballein* (syn with
its extension *ballizein*), to dance, akin to Skt
*balbalīti*, he whirls about: IE r, *\*bal-*.

2. LL *ballāre* became OProv *balar*, whence
*balada*, a dancing song, whence MF *balade* (EF-F
*ballade*), ME *balade*, E *ballad*.

3. LL *ballāre* passed into It, with derivative
*ballo*, a dance, dim *balletto*, whence, soon sense-
adapted, the EF-F, hence E, *ballet*.

**ballad** .See prec, para 2.

**ballast**, n hence v: MD-LG *ballast*: Da *barlast*
*bar*, bare + *last*, load, esp cargo.

**ballet.** See the 2nd BALL, para 3.

**ballistic**, explosively hurled, whence **ballistics**
(cf *-ics*), the science of projectiles in motion,
whence **ballistician** (after *statistician*): L *ballista*, a
stone-throwing military engine, from Gr *ballein*,
to throw; cf the syn LGr *balistra*.

**ballock.** See the 2nd BUTT.

**balloon**, n hence v; **ballot**, n and v: former, EF-F
*ballon*, It *ballone*, aug of *balla*, a ball, of Gmc
origin (cf the 1st BALL); latter, It *ballotta*, dim of
*balla*, the E v deriving from It *ballotare*, from
*ballotta*.

**bally**, coll euphemism for expletive *bloody*, owes
something to the boisterous village of *Ballyhooly*
(County Cork), whence perh AE coll *ballyhoo*,
noisy preliminary publicity, whence AE *hooey*,
bunkum.

**balm, balsam; balsamic, balmy; embalm.**

*Balm*, whence *balmy*, derives, through ME
*baume* or *basme*, from OF-EF *basme*, MF *bausme*,
MF-F *baume*, from L *balsamum* (whence E *balsam*,
whence *balsamic*): Gr *balsamon*, app of Sem origin
—cf H *bāsām*; perhaps cf Eg *m'aām*. *Embalm*, ME
*enbaumen*, comes from OF-MF *embasmer*, later
*embaumer*: *em-*, for *en*, in(to) + *baume* + inf suffix
*-er*; and *embalmer* owes something to EF-F
*embaumeur*.

**baloney.** See BOLONEY.

**baluster, balustrade; banister.**

The 3rd is *baluster* corrupted: and *baluster*
anglicizes EF-F *balustre*, from It *balaustro* (whence
*balaustrata*, for (? *via*) *balaustrata*, a way set with
balusters: hence EF-F *balustrade*, adopted by E);
*balaustro* derives from It *balaustra*, the flower of
the wild pomegranate, itself—via L *balaustium*—
from Gr *balaustion*; the sense-transition refers to
the shape-resemblance.

**bamboo**: (? via D or Port) from Mal *bambu*.

**bamboozle**: o.o.o. Probably this is an arbitrary
redup of *baffle*, approximately equivalent in sense,
perh form-blended with the echoic Gr *bamba-
luzein* (s *bambaluz-*), to chatter with cold, to
stammer, and perh prompted by BANTER.

**ban, n, v, and banns; banish and bandit; banal.**

1. *Banns* or *bans*, a proclamation enabling an
objection to be made to a marriage, is merely a pl
derivative of 'a *ban*': and *ban*, ME *ban*, derives
from ME *bannen*, to summon, interdict, curse, but
also from OF *ban*, from LL *bannum*, akin to OFris,
OS, OHG, ON *bann*, a public prohibition. ME
*bannen* derives from OE *bannan*, to summon by
proclamation, akin to OFris *banna*, OHG *bannan*,
ON *hanna*, and prob to Gr *phanai*, to say, and Skt
*bhánati*, he speaks: IE r, *\*bhā-*, to speak.

2. The LL *bannum*, proclamation, has v *bannīre*,
whence MF *banir* (EF-F *bannir*), whence, via 'ils
*banissent*' and '*banissant*', the ME *banishen*, E 'to
*banish*'; *banishment*, influenced by MF *banissement*,
proclamation of a ban, effectively derives from 'to
*banish*' (suffix *-ment*). B & W hold *bannir* to be,
ult, independent of *ban*; the confusion must have
happened very early indeed.

3. LL *bannīre* had var *bandīre*, whence It *bandire*,
to banish, with pp *bandito*, which became n, 'an
outlaw', whence, perh via late EF-F *bandit*, the
E *bandit*. B & W, however, postulate the origin of
It *bandire* to be Go *bandwjan*, to give a signal. The
older view seems the more prob.

4. The OF *ban*, an edict, has adj *banal* (1293),
'of or for obligatory feudal service', hence 'merely
obligatory; perfunctory', hence (1778) 'commonplace, trite' (B & W), adopted, mid-C19, by E;
the derivative *banalité* became E *banality*.

5. Cf 'a*ban*don' and 'contra*ban*d'—and perh
FAME.

**banal, -ity.** See prec, para 4.

**banana**: Sp and Port *banana*: Taino (WI) *banana*,
akin to Arawak *prattana*, therefore to E *plantain*,
a kind of banana, from Sp *plantano*, *prattana*
having var *platena* and several WI cognates.

**banco.** See BANK, para 2.

**band, n hence v; bandage; bandanna; bandeau;
bandoleer.—bond, n hence v.**

1. F.a.e.: see BIND and cf BEND, v.

2. The n *band*, ME *band*, comes from ON *band*,
akin to OHG *bant*, Go *bandi*, Skt *bandha*. In sense
'strip' it comes from MF-F *bande*, OF *bende*, of
Gmc origin; in sense 'group of associates' it comes,
via MF-F *bande*, from It *banda*, itself of Gmc origin.

3. *Bandage*, adopted from EF-F, derives from F
*bande*; so does the even more Gallic *bandeau*, a
narrow band; cf *bandoleer*, F *bandoulière*, Sp
*bandolera*, from *banda*, of Gmc origin.

4. *Bandanna*, however, goes much further back:
the Hi *bāndhnū*, a dyeing process in which the tied
parts of the cloth remain uncoloured: cf BIND.

5. *Bond*, ME *bond*, is a mere var of *band*, a
fastening. In *bond*(*s*)*man*, *bondswoman*, the origin is
different: ON *bōndi*, for *būandi*, from *būa*, to dwell.

**bandicoot**, Aus nuance deriving from: Telugu
(India) *pandi-kokku*, (lit) pig rat.

**bandit.** See BAN, para 3.
**bandoleer.** See BAND, para 3.
**bandore.** See MANDOLIN.
**bandy,** adj, n, v: *bandy* (e.g., legs) comes from F *bandé*, bent, from OF-F *bander*, to bend (esp a bow), whence also *bandy*, a game similar to hockey, though orig a form of tennis: cf 'to *bandy*', to beat (a ball) to and fro, hence to hit or toss from one to another, hence to exchange (pleasantries), from OF-F *bander*, of Gmc origin: cf BAND and BIND.

**bane,** a deadly agent, hence fatal mischief or harm, hence ruin: OE *bana*, murderer, akin to OFris *bana*, Os and OHG *bano*, murderer, and OHG *bana*, murder, and to ON *bani*, murderer, murder, death, and ult to Av *banta*, ill, harm. Adj *baneful* (cf -*ful*).

**bang,** v hence n and adv: ON *banga*, to hammer: echoic. Cf BUNGLE.

**bangle,** ornamental bracelet: Hi *bangṛe*, bracelet, bangle: -*le*, perh from 'circ*le*'.

**banish, banishment.** See BAN, para 2.

**banister.** See baluster.

**banjo.** See MANDOLIN.

**bank,** n hence v; **banker, bankrupt, embankment; banco (bunco), banquet; bench.**

1. *Bank*, a sloped mound, whence 'to *embank*', whence *embankment* (suffix -*ment*), via ME *banke*, is of Scan origin (the ON *bakki*) and akin to *bench*, ME *benk*, OE *benc*, of Gmc origin, cf ON *bekkr* and OFris and OS *bank*. The monetary *bank*, orig a paying counter, comes, via late MF-F *banque*, from It *banca*, a counter, orig a bench, of Gmc origin and clearly akin to BENCH; the derivative 'to *bank*' (money) yields *banker* (-*er*); the adj and v *bankrupt* derive from the n, orig bankruptcy, hence a person in bankruptcy: late MF-F *banqueroute*; It *banca rotta*, broken bank, *rotta* representing L *rupta*, f of *ruptus*, pp of *rumpere*, to break (cf RUPTURE).

2. It *banca* has var *banco*, orig a bench, hence a bank (money), with a special sense in baccarat: hence AE *bunko* or *bunco*, a monetary swindle.

3. It *banco* has dim *banchetto*, which passed into MF-F as *banquet*, feast, adopted by E: the trestled bench became 'the festive board', whence the food and wine upon it, whence the occasion.

**banner,** n hence adj and v; **banneret.**

The latter, ME *baneret*, comes from MF *baneret* (EF-F *banneret*), a dim of OF-MF *baniere* (EF-F *bannière*), the origin of E *banner*: from LL *baneria*, for *banderia*, from *bandum*, a banner: Go *bandwa* (or -*wō*), a sign, akin to ON *benda*, to give a sign; IE r, *\*bhen-*, cf Gr *phainō* (s *phain-*), I indicate.

**bannock.** See BUN.

**banns.** See BAN.

**banquet.** See BANK, para 3.

**banshee.** See SHEE.

**bantam:** from *Bantam*, the very small fowl coming from Bantam, in Java.

**banter,** v hence n: to ridicule playfully: o.o.o. Perh from the obs Sp *bandear*, to cross from one to another.

**Bantu:** *ba-*, plural prefix + *ntu*, a person: 'The Persons' (*the* persons).

**banyan** (tree): via Hi from Skt *vaṇij*, merchant: its wide-spread branches afford a market-place for native traders.

**baptism, baptismal; Baptist, baptistery; baptize.**

The effectual origin lies in Gr *baptizein*, a modified form of *baptein* (s *bapt-*, r *bap-*), to dip in water, akin to ON *hafa*, to dive. *Baptizein* passes through LL *baptizāre* to OF-F *baptiser*, whence 'to *baptize*'; its derivative *baptisma*, adopted by LL, became OF *baptesme* (F *baptême*), whence the E *baptism*; OF-F *baptismal* (from LL *baptisma*) is adopted by E; the Gr agent *baptistēs* passes through LL *baptista* and OF *baptiste* to E *baptist*, now only in John the *Baptist* and the *Baptist* sect, and the derivative *baptistērion*, LL *baptistērium*, OF-MF *baptisterie*, became *baptist(e)ry*, the font recess of a church.

**bar,** n and v; **barrack,** n; **barrage, barricade; barrier; barrister.—embarrass, embarrassment; embargo.**

1. 'To *bar*', ME *barren*, represents OF-F *barrer*, from OF-F *barre*, a usu flat, long piece of wood or metal, serving as support or leverage or esp obstruction: from LL *barra*, o.o.o but perh of C origin: the C r *\*bar(s)*, an eminence, appears in Br *barr*, mountain top, tree top, hence branch (esp as *barri*), bar (*bar*), cf Ir and W *bar(r)*, and W *bar*, branch, mountain top, Manx *barr*, a bar, and Cor *baar*, n, and *bara*, v, (to) bar, and Cor *bar*, a branch; cf also Ga *barra*, a bar, a spike, and *barrach*, the top branches of trees; the sense 'branch' certainly could, as Cor shows, lead to the sense of F *barre*, E *bar*.

2. *Barrack*, orig a temporary hut for soldiers, became the modern *barracks*: late MF-F *baraque*, a hut: It *baracca*: Sp *barraca*, prob from Sp *barra*, itself from LL *barra* (as above).

3. *Barrage* (military) derives from F *tir de barrage*, obstructive fire; OF-F *barrage*, which has, moreover, been adopted by E, esp in engineering, derives from OF-F *barrer*, to close the way to, from *barre* (para 1).

4. *Barricade*, v, comes from the EF-F v *barricader*, itself from the EF-F n *barricade* (adopted by E): It *barricata*, from *barricare*, from *barra* (from LL *barra*), a bar.

5. *Barrier*, ME *barrere*, represents MF *barriere* (EF-F *barrière*), from *barre*.

6. *Bar*, in its special sense 'the entire body of advocates or barristers', derives from the *utter* (outer) *bar* formerly, in E Inns of Court, separating the benchers from the students, who, when duly called to participate in debates, became *utter barristers* (cf *be called to the bar*), finally *barristers*; and *barrister*, earlier *barraster* or -*ester*, consists of E *bar* (rather than F *barre*, the equivalent F term being *barreau*) + formative *r* + a suffix app connoting 'a stander (at)', from Gr *histasthai* (vi), to stand, the -*ister* form being prob influenced by, e.g., *chorister*.

7. *Embarrassment* represents EF *embarrassement*,

itself from EF-F *embarrasser*, whence 'to *embarrass*': and *embarrasser* comes from Sp *embarazar* or perh It *imbarazzare*, lit 'to [put] a *bar* (LL *barra*) into (L *in*)'.

8. *Embargo*, Sp word, perh comes into E via EF-F; it derives from Sp *embargar*, to issue an edict against: VL *\*imbarricāre*: L *in-*, in(to)+LL *barra*.

**barb** (1), horse: EF-F *barbe*: It *barbero* (L *barbarus*), a horse of Barbary (N Africa). Cf, therefore, BARBARIAN.

**barb** (2), beard (obs) and backward projection; **barbate, barbel, barber; beard,** n hence v; **halberd.**

1. *Halberd*, via It and F, comes from MHG *helmbarte*, an axe to split a helm (cf HELMET), a beard-shaped axe.

2. *Barb* (F *barbe*, L *barba*), a beard, hence a beard-like projection, hence the backward projection of arrow or fish-hook, has derivative 'to *barb*', to furnish with barbs: cf *barbate*, bearded, L *barbātus*, from *barba*, which has LL dim *barbellus*, whence, via MF-F, the E *barbel*. *Barba*, moreover, has a VL derivative *barbātor* (agential *-ātor*), whence MF *barbeor*, EF-F *barbier*, and ME *barbour*, EE-E *barber*.

3. Now, *beard* derives from OE *beard*, akin to OFris *berd*, OS *bard*, OHG *bart*; PGmc *\*barth-*(?), IE *\*bhardh-*: cf OSl *brada*, Lith *barzdà*, L *barba*. (Walshe.)

**barbarian** (adj and n), **barbaric, barbarism, barbarity, barbarize, barbarous; Barbary, Berber;** cf 1st BARB.

1. The effectual base consists of Gr *barbaros*, non-Greek, also n, esp in pl *barbaroi*: *hoi barbaroi*, the non-Greeks, are lit 'the Unintelligibles, The Stammerers': cf the Skt adj *barbaras*, stammering: orig echoic, as also is the stammering redup in *Tatar* (loosely *Tartar*). Cf BABBLE and BABE.

2. Gr *barbaros* becomes L *barbarus*, whence E *barbarous*, whence (abstract suffix *-ity*) *barbarity* and *barbarian* (*-ian* for *-ous*), n and—cf F *barbarien* —adj. The secondary Gr adj *barbarikos*—answering to *hoi barbaroi*—becomes L *barbaricus* becomes E *barbaric*. *Barbaros* has two other derivatives affecting E: *barbarizein*, to behave or speak like a barbarian, (vt) to mistreat barbarously, whence obs F *barbariser* and E *barbarize* (*-ize*); and *barbarismos*, use of a foreign or misuse of one's own language, the qualities of a barbarian, whence MF-F *barbarisme* and, perh independently, E *barbarism*.

3. L coined *barbaria*, 'barbarianness', hence foreign lands, hence, in ML, Saracen lands, esp *Barbaria*, whence MF-F *barbarie, Barbarie*, whence E *Barbary*, North Africa from the western borders of Egypt to the Atlantic coast. The inhabitants, called *barbari* by the Latin settlers and their descendants, were, by the conquering Arabs, named, collectively, *al-Barbar*; *Berberi*, prob a ML reshaping of the Ar pron of L *barbari*, yields E *Berbers*, soon applied to the Arabs themselves. (Enci It.).

**barbate.** See 2nd BARB, para 2.

**barbecue** (the entertainment from the animal roasted whole, from the raised platform serving as open-air kitchen): Sp *barbacoa*, a raised frame or platform: Taino (WI) *barbacoa*.

**barbel.** See 2nd BARB, para 2.

**barber.** See 2nd BARB, para 2.

**bard:** C in origin: cf Ir and Ga *bard*, Br *barz*, a poet, and OIr *bard*, an inferior poet. (LL *bardi*, LGr *bardoi*, the Gaulish bards: from C.)

**bare,** adj and v; **barefoot** (OE *baerfōt*, cf OFris *berfōt*).

*Bare*, adj: ME *bar*: OE *baer*, akin to OHG and OS *bar* and, in cpds, OFris *ber-*; also to ON *berr*. The v derives from OE *barian*, from the adj. The Sl languages show the var *bās-* or *bos-*; IE r, prob *\*bhos-*. (Walshe.)

**bargain,** n (hence adj) and v.

The n derives from ME *bargayn*, from OF-MF *bargaigne* or *-gagne*, a market, from OF-EF *bargaignier*, whence, via ME *bargaynen*, the E 'to *bargain*': and OF-EF *bargaignier*, to buy and sell in the market-place, to chaffer, higgle, comes from LL *barcaniāre* (o.o.o): perh cf OHG *borgēn*, to spare, hence, as in G, to borrow, and OProv *barganhar*, to bargain.

**barge,** n, hence—from slow, heavy motion—v: adopted by ME from OF, from L *\*barica*: cf LL *barca*: see 3rd BARK. *Bargee=barge*, n+suffix *-ee*, irreg for *-er*.

**baritone.** See the element *-bar*.

**bark** (1), of tree; hence v: from ON *börkr*; cf Skt *bhūrja*, birch-bark.

**bark** (2), of dog: n, perh from v, but cf OE *beorc*, *bearce*; 'to *bark*', ME *berken*, OE *beorcan*, akin to ON *berkja*, to bark, and *barkliga*, like a bark, and also to Lith *burgèti*, to growl: echoic. (Holthausen.)

**bark** (3), a small sailing ship: MF-F *barque*, often so in E: OProv *barca*: LL *barca*, prob for *\*bārica*: from L *bāris*, a barge: Gr *baris*, an Egyptian barge: from Eg—cf Coptic *barī* and perh Eg *bák*, a barge, orig a hawk-boat, from *bak*, a hawk.

2. *Barkentine, barquentine* app=*bark, barque*+ brigantine.

3. The cpds come from F: *debark*, EF-F *débarquer*; *disembark*, EF-F *désembarquer*; *debarkment*, EF-F *débarquement*; *disembarkment*, EF-F *désembarquement*; *disembarcation*, however, is formed after E *embarcation*;—*embark*, EF-F *embarquer*; *embarkment*, EF-F *embarquement*; *embarcation* (now usu *embarkation*), adopted from F, itself from Sp *embarcación*. (B & W.)

**barley:** ME *barly*, earlier *barlich*: OE *baerlīc*, orig 'barley-like': *bere*, barley+*līc*, like. With OE *bere*, cf ON *barr*, barley, Go *barizeins*, made of barley, and several Sl cognates. Cf BARN and perh:

**barm:** ME *berme*: OE *beorma*, akin to LG *barme*, G *Bärme*, Alb *brum*, and perh to L *fermentum*, yeast—cf FERMENT.

**barn:** ME *bern*: OE *bern*, orig *berern*: OE *bere*, barley (see BARLEY)+*ern* (*aern*), a closed place: a barley, hence grain, place (shed).

**barometer:** a meter or measure of atmospheric

heaviness (hence pressure): see *baro-* at the element *-bar*. Adj: *barometric*.

**baron: baronet** (whence **baronetcy**: suffix *-cy*); **barony**.

A *baronet* is a little (dim suffix *-et*) baron; *barony*, ME from OF-MF *baronie* (EF-F *baronnie*), from *baron*: and OF *baron*, which yields ME hence E *baron*, is the acc of *ber* (cf OProv *bar*), orig a free man, a warrior, later a high-ranking feudal officer: usu said to be Gmc (Frankish *\*baro*: B & W), but perh from the C r *\*bars*, eminence, whence *\*barron*, whence *baron*, eminent man, later a feudal baron (Malvezin).

**baroque**, (orig) irregularly shaped: adopted from EF-F: from Port *barroco*, an irregular pearl: prob Ar, for cf Port and Sp *aljofar*, a (usu small) pearl irregularly shaped, from Ar *al-cháuhar*.

**barouche**. See ROLL, para 15.

**barque, barquentine**. See the 3rd BARK, paras 1, 2.

**barrack, n.; barracks**. See BAR, para 2.

**barrack**, Aus v: perh Aborigine *borah*, derision. (Cf P² for a var proposal.)

**barracuda**: Sp *barracuda*, perh from Valencian *barraco*, a large, protrusive tooth.

**barrage**. See BAR, para 3.

**barrator, barratry**. See BARTER, para 2.

**barrel**: ME *barel*: OF-F *baril*, very doubtfully from either OF *barre*, a bar, or Frankish *\*bera*, to carry: cf OProv *barril* and It *barile*. Dauzat, citing the late C9 OF *barriclos*, derives it from VL *\*barriculus*, o.o.o. Malvezin implies a dim derivative from the C r *\*bar*, liquid (cf *\*mar*, liquid, akin to L *mare*, sea).

**barren**, adj hence n: ME *barain, barein*: OF *brehaing*, f *brehaigne* or *baraigne* or *baraine*, elliptical for *terre brehaigne* (*baraigne, baraine*), barren land: perh (Webster) from L *barbarus* in sense 'uncultivated', but prob from nearer home. In short, I propose a Br origin, the Br form of *brehaing, brehaigne*, being *breheign* or *brehagn*: perh 'Brehn (land)', the Br name of *Brittany* (F *Bretagne*) being *Breigh* or *Bréh*: the coast lands are rocky and sterile.

**barricade**. See BAR, para 4.

**barrier**. See BAR, para 5.

**barrister**. See BAR, para 6.

**barrow** (1), a mound: ME *beoruh* and *bergh*: OE *beorg, beorh*, mound, mountain, akin to OFris *berch*, OFris and OHG-G *berg*, mountain: cf 'iceberg' (see ICE). Cf also BOROUGH and BURY.

**barrow** (2), as in *wheelbarrow*: ME *barow, barewe*: from OE *bearwe*, wheelbarrow: cf BEAR, v, and BIER.

**barse** See BASS, n.

**barter** (v hence n) comes, via ME *bartren*, from OF-MF *barater, bareter*, to cheat, e.g. in exchanging goods, (rarely) to exchange: either from Gr *prattein* (s *prat-*), to do, to deal, to practise tricks, or from C—cf Ir *brath*, trickery, treachery, Ga *brath*, to betray, OIr *mrath*, betrayal.

2. OF *barater* has the MF derivative *barateor*, deceiver, whence ME *baratour*, whence E *barrator*,

one guilty of *barratry*: and *barratry* comes from MF-F *baraterie*, deception, hence, in late C17, marine fraud by a ship's master, from *barater*, itself from *barat*, deception, trickery, o.o.o. but perh from C *bar*, din, brawl (DAF).

**basal**. See BASE, n.

**basalt**: perh via EF-F *basalte*: L *basaltes*, a hard, dark Abyssinian marble: of African origin; perh cf Eg *bekhen*, basalt, and *baa kam*, black basalt.

**base**, adj; **bass** (voice); **abase, debase**, with nn in *-ment*.

1. E *base* derives from ME *bas, bass*: OF *bas, basse*: LL *bassus*, squat, low, ? of Oscan origin. Hence *baseness* (suffix *-ness*).

2. The *bass* (voice)=*base*, adj, influenced by It *basso* and perh EF-F *basse*.

3. *Abase*, ME *abasse*, comes from OF-MF *abaissier* (MF-F *abaisser*), VL *\*adbassiāre*: *ad*, to + *bassi-*, c/f of *bassus*, low + inf suffix *-āre*; and *debase*=*de*, down from + *base*, v, anl with *abase*.

**base**, n hence v; **basal, basic; basis; basement** (prob the v + suffix *-ment*).

Whereas *basal*=E *base* + adj *-al*, *basic*=*base* + *ic*; *base*, adopted from OF-F, comes from L, from Gr, *basis*, a stepping, a step, a stepping-stone, a pedestal, a base, from *bainein*, to step or go, akin to L *uenīre* and E COME; E *basis* comes straight from L *basis*.

**bash**, v hence n: echoic: cf CLASH, CRASH, PASH, SLASH, SMASH.

**bashaw**. See CHECK, para 4.

**bashful**: from obs *bash* (ME *baschen*), aphetic for *abash*; suffix *-ful*.

**basic**. See BASE, n.

**basil**, aromatic herb; **basilica**, a 'royal' building, a noble church; **basilisk**, a fabled serpent.

The base is Gr *basileus*, a king: o.o.o: perh *basi-* (from *bainein*, to step or go) + Ionic *\*leus* (for *lēos*), people, hence 'guide of the people'. It affects E in the foll words: *Basil*, from L *Basilius*, Gr *Basileios*, The Kingly, from *basileus*; *basil*, OF *basile*, ML *basilicum*, from Gr *basilikon*, prop the neu of *basilikos*, royal, from *basileus*, basil having sovereign qualities; *basilica*, adopted from L, from Gr *basilikē*, elliptical for *basilikē oikia*, royal dwelling, or perh *b. stoa*, royal (roofed) colonnade; *basilisk* (suffix *-isk*), L *basiliscus*, Gr *basiliskos* 'little king'—reputedly its breath was fatal, its hissing expulsive.

**basin**: ME *bacin*, adopted from OF-MF *bacin* (MF-F *bassin*): VL *\*baccīnum* (cf LL *bacchinon*), (? dim) from L *bacca*, a water vessel: o.o.o, but perh from the C r *\*bac*, liquid, as in F *bac*, vat or tank, dim *baquet*, bucket.

**basioscopic**. See the element *-scope*.

**basis**. See BASE, n.

**bask**, to sunbathe: contr of ON *bathask*, to bathe oneself: *batha*, to bathe (cf BATHE) + reflexive *sk*.

**basket**: ME *basket*: o.o.o: the L poet Martial says that L *bascauda* is a C word; cf Cor *bascauda*, usu *basced*; W *basgawd*; Manx *bascad*.

**Basque, basque, basquine; Biscay, Biscayan.**

The *basque* of a garment=the F *basque*, earlier *baste*, from It and OProv *basta*, from *bastir(e)*, to build (with dress material), the form *basque* being influenced by F *basque*, adj of F *Basque*, a Basque (Dauzat); *basquine*, adopted from F, comes from Sp *basquina*, from the adj *basco*, better *vasco*, Basque. The N Sp province *Vizcaya*, F *Biscaye*, whence E '(bay of) *Biscay*', has adj *Biscayan* (F *biscaïen*). The F *Basque*, a Basque, comes prob from the Sp adj and n *Vascón*, itself from ML *Vascōnes*, L *Uascōnes*, the Basques.

**bas-relief.** See LEVER, para 9.

**bass,** adj hence n, ref voice: see BASE, adj, para 2.

**bass,** n, the European perch: deviation from *barse*, OE *bears* or *baers*, akin to MHG *bars*, the fish, and G *barsch*, D *bars*, rough: therefore prob cf BRISTLE.

**bass,** n, fibre. See:

**bast,** woody fibre: OE *baest*, akin to OHG, ON *bast*, and perh to L *fascia*; the form *bass* is a corruption. The OHG *bast* accounts, via OF *bastir*, ME *basten*, for *baste*, to sew.

**bastard,** adopted from OF *bastard* (F *bâtard*): orig the (legitimate) son of a noble and his concubine: prob, with pej suffix *-ard*, from OF *fils* (and *fille*) *de bast*, where *bast* app derives from PGmc *\*bansti*, a granary, a barn, cf the syn Go *bansts*: 'barn son', 'barn daughter'. (B & W.) Dauzat prefers to interpret *bast* as OF *bast*, F *bat*, a packsaddle: 'son, or daughter, begotten on a packsaddle', after the fashion among muleteers.

**baste** (1), to sew loosely. See BAST.

**baste** (2), to moisten (roasting meat) with melted butter or fat: from C16 *baast*, pp, whence C16–17 *bast* and C16–20 *baste*: app from OF *basser*, to moisten slightly, from *bassiner*, to moisten, from *bassin*, a basin (contents usu liquid)—cf BASIN.

**baste** (3), to thrash: ON *beysta*, to beat: cf BEAT.

**bastille:** MF-F *bastille*, a small fortress, hence a fortress prison, esp *la Bastille de Paris*: MF *bastide*: OProv *bastida*, from *bastir*, to build, itself of disputed etym. Cf:

**bastion,** adopted from F, comes from It *bastione*, aug of *bastia*, bastion, from *bastire*, to build, perh (B & W) from Frankish *\*bastjan*, cf OHG *bestēn*, to lace, and MHG *bast*, G *Bast*, inner bark of lime-tree, cf BAST. With It *bastire*, cf OF and OProv *bastir*: both may (Webster) rather come from VL *\*bastīre*, to build, var of VL *\*bastāre*, (? LL-)ML *bastāre*, to suffice, (? orig) to carry, itself from Gr *bastazein* (s *bastaz-*, r *bast-*), to carry. But the Gmc origin (supported also by Dauzat, Prati, EW) seems preferable, for, as B & W remark, the ancient Gmc peoples often built the walls of their dwellings with bark, or similar materials, plaited or interwoven. Cf prec.

**baston.** See 2nd BAT, para 2.

**bat,** 1 (flying): corruption of ME *bakke*, cf Da *backe*, Sw *backa*: app from ON *blaka*, to flutter: 'the flutterer'.

**bat,** 2, n hence v (to strike as with a bat, hence to cudgel): ME *batte*: OE *batt*, prob akin to MF-F

*batte*, a thing with which one beats, from OF-MF *batre*, MF-F *battre*, to beat: LL *battere*: L *battuere*, app from C r *\*bat-*, to strike: ult, prob echoic.

2. The simple cognates include:

*baston*, adopted from OF-MF, whence also the EF-F *bâton*, adopted by E: from LL *bastum*, staff, stick, prob of C origin;

*batten*, a long, narrowish, shallow strip of sawn timber: from EF-F *bâton*;

*batter*, to strike repeatedly: ME *hateren*, OF-MF *batre*, MF-F *battre*, to strike (cf para 1);

*batter*, culinary n; ME *batere*, from ME *bateren*, to beat;

*battery*, act of striking repeatedly, as in *assault and battery*, hence apparatus, esp military: late OF-F *batterie*, from *battre*: cf, sep, *battalion* at BATTLE;

*battue:* adopted from EF-F, orig the f of *battre*, pp of *battre*, to beat.

3. Prefix-cpds include:

*abate:* OF-MF *abatre* (EF-F *abattre*), cf next;

*abatement*, MF (EF-F *abattement*), from *abatre*;

*abattoir* (often pl *abattoirs*), slaughterhouse: F: from *abattre*, to fell, ML *abattere*, ad, to+LL *battere* (as in para 1);

*combat*, n: EF-F, from OF-F *combattre*, whence to *combat*': VL-ML *com battere*: *com*, from *cum*, with+LL *battere*; *combatant*, n from adj from F *combattant*, presp of *combattre*; *combative*, from *combat*, (v)+suffix *-ive*;

*debate*, n: MF-F *débat*, from OF-F *débattre* (OF *debatre*), whence 'to *debate*': *debatre*, to beat severely= *de-*, int L *dē-*, from *dē*, down from+ *batre* (cf para 1), perh suggested by Petronius's *debattuere*;

*rebate:* MF-F *rabat*, from OF-F *rabattre* (OF *rabatre*), whence 'to *rebate*', perh influenced by the MF-F var *rebattre*; MF-F *rabat* has the doublet derivative *rabbet* (in carpentry).

**batch.** See BAKE, para 2.

**bate:** aphetic for *abate*, to reduce.

**bath,** n hence v; *bathe*, v hence n.

*Bath* derives from OE *baeth*, akin to ON and OS *bath*, G *Bad*, MHG *bat*, OHG *bad*, from OHG *bāien*, to foment, and to OE *bathian* (cf ON *batha*), whence ME *bathien*, whence 'to *bathe*'. Cf BASK.

**bathos,** adj **bathetic** (after *pathetic*): Gr *bathos*, depth: cf the element *batho-* (*bathy-*).

**bâton, baton.** See the 2nd BAT, para 2.

**battalion.** See BATTLE.

**battels.** See 2nd BATTEN.

**batten** (1), strip of sawn timber. See 2nd BAT, para 2.

**batten** (2), to thrive, esp to grow fat: ON *batna*, to grow better: cf BETTER. University of Oxford *battels* is prob akin—cf the obs *battle*, freq of *batten*.

**batter,** culinary n; *batter*, to strike often. See the 2nd BAT, para 2.

**battery.** See 2nd BAT, para 2.

**battle; battalion.**

'To *battle*' comes, via ME *batailen*, from OF *bataillier* (MF-F *batailler*), from *bataille*, a battle, whence, via ME *batayle*, the E n **battle**: and OF *bataille* comes from LL *battālia*, from L *battuālia*, from L *battuere*, to strike, prob orig echoic: cf the 2nd BAT. LL *battālia* became It *battaglia*, with aug *battaglione*, whence EF-F *bataillon*, whence, influenced by *battle*, the E *battalion*.

**battue.** See 2nd BAT, para 2.

**bauble.** See BEAU, para 3.

**baulk.** See BALK.

**bawbees,** money: pl of *bawbee*, a Sc copper coin: the Laird of Sille*bawby*, mintmaster c1540. (Cf Sc *siller*, silver, a prob element in the pun.)

**bawd, bawdry, bawdy:** ME *baude*: MF *baud(e)*, OF *balt, bald*, bold in all senses, derived from OHG *bald*, bold: cf therefore BOLD. *Bawdy*=*bawd*+adj suffix -*y*; *bawdry*=ME *baudery*=MF *bauderie*, OF *balderie*, merriness, boldness=*baud*+abstract-n suffix -*erie* (E -*ery*). EW, however, makes *bawd* aphetic for *ribaud*, ribald, *bawdry* for *ribaudry*, ribaldry. (Cf RIBALD.) But Webster's etym is supported by EF *baud*, hunting term for a running dog: C14 *baut*, f *baude*: C12 *balt*: OHG *bald*. (Dauzat.)

**bawl:** either from ML *baulāre*, to bark, which= *bau-*, echoic (cf E '*bow*-wow')+euphonic *l*+-*āre*; or from the echoic Icelandic *baula*, (of cows) to low, itself from ON *baula*, a cow.

**bay** (1), adj: OF-F *bai*: L *badius*, bay, brown, akin to Ir and OIr *buide*, Manx *buigh*, yellow; Pr C *bodios*, yellow, yellowish brown.

**bay** (2), n, marine inlet: ME *baye*: MF-F *baie*: prob via OSp *bahia*, certainly from LL *baia*, o.o.o., perh (B & W) from L *Baiiae* (from Gr *Baíai*, *Baíai*), favourite seaside resort of ancient Romans.

**bay** (3), n in Arch: ME *bay*, influenced by prec: OF *baee*, a gap or opening, from OF *baer, beer*, to be gaping or open: VL *batāre* (C8), to yawn.

**bay** (4), n, a (laurel) berry, hence laurel tree: OF-F *baie*: L *bāca*, var *bacca*, perh akin to L *Bacchus*, q.v. at BACCHANAL. Cf BACHELOR.

**bay** (5), v and n (hounds): to *bay*, ME *bayen*, OF *bayer, baier*, aphetic for OF-EF *abayer* (EF-F *aboyer*): VL *adbatāre*: *ad*, to, at+VL *batāre*, to yawn: cf the 3rd BAY. The n *bay*, a deep, loud bark, derives from the v; but in *at bay*, orig of a stag F *aux abois*, exposed 'to the barks' of the dogs encircling it at chase's end, *abois* is the pl of *aboi*, a bark(ing), OF-MF *abay, abai*, ME *abay*, apprehended as *a*, at+*bay*, a bark(ing).

2. VL *batāre*, to yawn, yields OProv *badar*, to yawn or gape, whence late MF-F *badin*, a simpleton, hence (C18 onwards)—from actors playing the fool—a joker, whence EF-F *badiner*, to play the fool, to joke, whence, in C16, *badinage*, playful banter, adopted by E.

**bayonet:** F (1575) *baïonnette*: manufactured first at Bayonne in Southern France.

**bayou,** AE: AmF, of Amerind origin—cf Choctaw *bayúk*, a minor river or the branch of a delta.

**bazaar:** via EF-F and Port from Per *bāzār*, a public market or a street of shops.

**bazooka** derives prob from a sound-and-shape-resemblance to radio comedian Bob Burns's *bazooka*, a raucous trombone-like sound-contraption (Webster); *bazooka* comically alters *bazoo*, var of *kazoo* (o.o.o.), a rough musical instrument with catgut sounding in a tube hummed or blown upon.

**be,** presp (hence vn) **being,** pp **been** (ME *ben* or *bin*).

*Be* derives from ME *been*, var *beon*, OE *bēon*: cf OE *bíom*, OHG *bim* (G *bin*), OIr *biu*, I am, OSl *byti*, to become or be, esp Skt *bhávati*, he is, *bhūtas*, been, become; IE r, prob *bheu-*, with natural offshoots *bhe-* and *bhu-*; simple developments occur in, e.g., Gr *phunai* (r *phu-*), to be born, to be, and L *fui*, I have been. Cf ARE, IS, WAS.

**beach:** o.o.o.: perh cf the C r *bac-*, liquid: ? 'the wet place' (cf Br *bag*, a boat).

**beacon,** n hence v; **beck** (v, hence n)—**beckon.**

'To *beckon*' derives, via ME *beknen, bekenen*, from OE *bēacnian, bȳcnian*, from *bēacen*, a sign: and *bēacen*, var *bēcen*, becomes ME *bekene* becomes *beacon*. OE *bēacen, bēcen*, is akin to the syn OFris *bēken* or *bāken*, OS *bōkan*, OHG *bouhhan*, MHG *bouchen*: IE s, *bhaug-*; IE r, *bha-*, to shine. (Walshe.) 'To *beckon*' yields 'to *beck*', perh via the vn *beckoning*, 'a *beck*' or nod.

**bead,** n hence v; **beadsman, bedesman.**

*Bedesman, beadsman*, is a *beads man*, one who prays for, e.g., his benefactor: and *bead*, a very small globular body, derives from a *bead* in a rosary, from *bead, bede*, a prayer: ME *bede*, a prayer, hence a prayer bead: OE *bed* (or *gebed*), a prayer, lit an *asking* from God, hence already a prayer bead: akin to OE *biddan*, OHG-MHG-G *bitten*, to ask, G *Gebet*, a prayer, OHG *gibet*, Go *bidjan*. Cf BID.

**beadle:** ME, from OF-EF *bedel* (F *bédeau*): cf OE *bydel*, OHG *betil*: ult from the r of BID.

**beagle:** ME *begle*: perh from MF *bee gueule*, open throat (for *bee-*, cf the 5th BAY; with *gueule*, cf GULLET), hence a vociferous person.

**beak,** n, v; **beaked, beaky.**

*Beaky* derives from *beak*, n; 'to *beak*', whence the pa *beaked*, from MF-F *bequer*, from OF-F *bec*, a beak, whence ME *bec*, E *beak*: and OF *bec* comes from LL *beccus*, from the C r *bec* (or *beic*), a point, PrC *beccos*, a beak (Malvezin): cf Br *beg*.

**beaker:** ME *biker*: ON *bikarr*: LL *becārium*, for L *bacārium*, from *bac(c)a*, a water vessel: cf BASIN and PITCHER. Cf also the 1st PECK.

**beam,** n hence v; **boom,** a long pole—**bumboat**—nautical **bum(p)kin.**

1. A *beam* of wood, hence of light (cf the sem development of RADIUS), derives from OE *bēam*, already bearing both of these senses, also that of tree: akin to OFris *bām*, OHG *boum* (G *Baum*), OS *bōm*, a tree, and perh to Gr *phuma*, a growth; IE r, ? *bheu-* or, better, *bhou-*.

2. The corresponding D word is *boom*, whence the nautical E *boom*; cf *bumboat*, prob from LG *bumboot*, parallel to MLG *būmschip*, D *boomschip*: a boat hewn from a tree-trunk. The D and Flemish

dim *boomken*, little tree, accounts for nautical E *boomkin, bumkin, bumpkin*. The other *bumpkin*, a rural lout, app comes, however, from D *bommekijn*, a small cask.

**bean**: ME *bene* (or *ben*): OE *bēan*, akin to OFris *bāne*, OHG *bōna* (G *Bohne*), ON *baun*: perh akin also to OSl *bobŭ* (Ru *bob*) and OPrus *babo*, and therefore to L *faba*; IE r, ? *bhab-*, with nasalization in the Gmc languages.

**bear**, n: ME *bere*: OE *bera*, akin to the syn OHG *bero* (MHG *ber*, G *Bär*), MD *bare, bere*, D *beer*, OFris and OS *bern-* in cpds, ON *björn* and 'shebear' *bera*, Skt *bhalla*, and also to Lith *béras*, brown: 'the *brown* animal'; cf, therefore, *Bruin* at BROWN (G *braun*) and, sem, BEAVER. IE r, prob *bhar-*: (the Skt *bhalla* app=*bharla*), with var *bher-*.

**bear**, v (agent **bearer**; vn **bearing**): ME *beren*: OE *beran*, akin to OFris *bera*, ON *bera*, OHG *beran* (cf *giberan*, G *gebären*, give birth to), Go *bairan*; IE r *bher-*, as in Skt *bhárāme*, I carry, cf Gr *pherō* and L *fero*, and several C and Sl cognates.

2. The pt is *bore*, formerly *bare*; the pp is *born* (come into existence), var *borne* (carried), a differentiation that arose only in late C18. For *bore, born, borne*, see the magistral note at *bear* (v) in OED.

3. Cf BERTH and BIRTH; BIER; BURDEN; and 2nd BARROW.

**beard**. See the 2nd BARB, para 3.

**beast**, whence **beastly** (adj *-ly*): ME *beest*, earlier *best*, earliest *beste*: OF-MF *beste* (EF-F *bête*): VL *besta*: L *bēstia* (o.o.o.), with derivative LL adj *bēstiālis*, whence *bestial*, and L adj *bēstiārius*, whence ML *bēstiārium*, whence OF-F *bestiaire*, E *bestiary*, a book about beasts; *bestiality* derives from MF-F *bestialité*, from ML *bēstiālitās* (from *bēstiālis*).

**beat**, v hence n: ME *beaten* or *beten*: OE *bēatan*, akin to ON *bauta* or *beysta* (cf the 3rd BASTE) or esp *beyta*, and OHG *bōzan*, perh also to L *fustis*, a club; IE r, perh *bhaud-*.

**beatific, beatify; beatitude; Beatrix**.

The L *beātus*, blest, orig the pp of *beāre*, to bless, o.o.o., has derivatives *beātitūdō*, whence MF-F *béatitude*, whence E *beatitude*; *beātificus*, blestmaking (cf the element *-fic*), whence *beatific* (cf EF-F *béatifique*); *beātrix*, she who renders happy, whence the PN *Beatrix*.

**beau; beau ideal, beau monde; beauteous, beautiful, beautify, beauty.—belladonna; belle, belleslettres; bauble; bibelot; 'bo'.—embellish, embellishment**.

1. The effective origin lies in L *bellus*, handsome, a specialized dim of *bonus*, good. The derivative It *bello* has f *bella*, as in *belladonna*, for *bella donna*, pretty lady, euphemistic for the very poisonous plant. The corresp F derivative is OF-F *heau*, as in E *beau ideal*, misapprehension of F *le beau idéal*, ideal beauty, and *beau monde*, F *le beau monde*, the world of fashion. The F derivative *beau* (pl *beaux*), a fop, has become E *beau*, a social escort; hence prob the AE *bo*, as term of address (cf

HOBO). OF-F *beau*, adj, has derivative OF-F *beauté*, whence *beauty*, whence *beauteous* (*-ous*) and *beautiful* (*-ful*) and *beautify* (element *-fy*, to make).

2. The F adj, hence n, *beau* has f *belle*, pl *belles*; adopted by E in the n *belle* (e.g., *of the ball*), a popular beauty, and in *belles-lettres*, fine literature having aesthetic value, orig the humanities. Agent: *belle-lettrist*; adj: *belle-lettristic*, often abbr *belle tristic*.

3. The prevocalic m of the F adj *beau* is *bel*, reduplicated in OF *belbel*, a plaything, whence OF-MF *baubel* (or *babel*), whence E *bauble*. Cf *bibelot*: MF-F *bibelot*, from OF *beubelot*, *-et* (cf OF-MF *babelet*), etc, from OF *beubelot, -et* (cf OF-MF *babelet*), a small jewel, a trinket, from OF *belbel*: *beu-* (for *bel-*)+*-bel*+dim suffix *-ot*.

4. F has a derivative OF v, *embellir*: *em-*, for *en-*, in (used int)+*bel-*+euphonic *-l-*+inf suffix *-ir*: whence, via such forms as 'embellissant' (presp) and 'ils *embellissent*', they beautify, the ME *em belisen, -belisshen*, E 'to *embellish*', whence, prompted by MF-F *embellissement*, the n *embellishment* (suffix *-ment*).

**beaver** (1), the rodent amphibian: ME *bever*: OE *beofor*, akin to OHG *bibar* (G *Biber*) and ON *biórr* and Av *bawra*: cf also Skt *babhrúś*, brown: like the BEAR, the beaver is named from its brown colour, and indeed *beaver*, like *bear*, is ult akin to BROWN.

**beaver** (2), covering, in medieval armour, the lower face: ME *baviere*, OF *baviere*, orig a bib, from *bave*, saliva, prob echoic.

**because**. See CAUSE, para 2.

**beche-la-mar** or **beach-la-mar**, Western Pacific pidgin English: from fishers' distortion of F *bêche-de-mer*, 'sea caterpillar'—trepang.

**beck** (1), small brook: ME *bek*: prob from OE *becc* or *bece*, a brook, but perh from ON *bekkr*, itself intimately akin to OHG *bach* or *bah* (G *Bach*), OS *beki*; ? cf the OSl *begati* (r *beg-*), to run, and, less imm, the MIr *búal*, as Walshe and Webster resp suggest; but ? rather the C r *bac-*, liquid.

**beck** (2) nod. See BEACON.

**beckon**. See BEACON.

**become**: ME *bicumen, becumen*: OE *becuman*, i.e., to come beside, near, to (by): akin to Go *biqiman*, OHG *biqueman*, to come upon. What *comes to* one is often suitable; it *becomes* one, hence the adj *becoming*.

**bed**, n and v, with many cpds, all obvious.

'To *bed*' derives from OE *beddian*, itself from OE *bed, bedd*, a bed, akin to the syn OFris (and OS) *bedd*, OHG *betti*, MHG *bette*, G *Bett*, Go *badi*, and to ON *bedr*, a mattress, a feather-bed: C etymon, *bed*; IE r, *bhod-*, and a var *bhed-*, with basic meaning 'dug-out' or 'hollow', cf L *fodere*, to dig (see FOSSIL), and W *bedd*, a grave. (Walshe.)

**bede, bedesman**. See BEAD.

**bedizen**. See STAFF, heading and para 3.

**bedlam**: from *Bedlam*, ME *Bedlem*, earlier

*Bethlem*, Bethlehem: H *Bēth-!eḥem*, the house of food, *bēth* (house) occurring in many H-derived words, e.g. *bethel* and *bethesda*. Late ME *bedlem*, EE *Bedlam*, denoted the London hospital of St Mary of *Bethlehem*, used from c1400 for lunatics: hence, in EE, a lunatic: then a lunatic asylum: finally, fig, a madhouse, or the confusion and noise associated with one.

**bedraggled.** See *draggle* at DRAW.

**bee**, with numerous cpds, all self-evident, and with sense, as in 'sewing *bee*' and 'spelling *bee*', deriving from the humming of bees: OE *bēo*, akin to OHG *bīa* (whence OHG *bini*, MHG *bine*, G *Biene*)—ON *bȳ*—OIr *bech*, Ga *beach*—Lith *bītis*; IE r, *\*bhi*; for basic idea, ? cf the PC *\*bic-*, *\*bek-*, little (Ga *beag*, OIr *becc*).

**beech**, adj **beechen** (OE *bēcen*); **book**, n, hence v and numerous cpds, all obvious; **buck**, **lye**; **buckwheat**.

1. The *beech* tree derives from ME *beche*, from OE *bēce*, akin to OFris *bōk*, OE (and OS) *bōc bōk*, OHG *buohha* (G *Buche*), ON *bōk*, beech— OSl *bŭzŭ*, elm—L *fāgus*, beech—Gr *phēgos*, edible oak; IE r, *\*bhāg-*.

2. The OE var *bōc*, *bōk*, became ME *bok*, *book*, became E *book*, with cognates as above: add OHG *buoh*, MHG *buoch*, G *Buch*, a book, and Go *bōka*, letter of alphabet, pl *bōkōs*, documents, (potential) books (cf L *literae*, q.v. at LETTER), orig 'beechwood sticks on which runes were carved' (Walshe). The 'written document' sense occurs already in OE.

3. The *beech* is also known as *buck*: intimately akin is *buck*, lye (cf G *Bauche*, LG *Buke*), lye being orig 'made from beech ashes' (Webster). *Buckwheat* (*buck*, beech+WHEAT) is akin to G *Buchweizen*, but was prob suggested by D *boekweit*.

**beef**, pl **beeves**; hence **beefy** (adj *-y*) and, e.g., **beefwood** (red like raw beef).

Orig an ox or cow or bull, hence—except in rural *beeves*, (so many) head of cattle—the flesh: ME *beef*, earlier *befe*, earliest *boef*: OF *boef* or *buef* (F *bœuf*): ML *bovem* (L *bouem*), acc of *bōs*, an ox: f.a.e., COW. The *Beefeaters* of the Tower of London formerly received a handsome allowance of beef.

**Beelzebub.** See BAAL.

**been.** See BE.

**beer**, hence adj **beery** (adj: *-y*): ME *ber*, var *beor*: OE *bēor*, akin to OFris *biār*, OHG *bior* (MHG *bier*, G *Bier*), ON *bjōrr*, perh also to ON *bygg*, barley, malt of (usu) barley being the source of beer.

**beet**: OE *bēte*: L *bēta*, akin to L *blitum*, which, designating similar plants, is a trln of Gr *bliton* (o.o.o.).

**beetle** (1) 'the little biter': ME *bityl* or *bittle*: OE *bitela*, from *bītan*, q.v. at BITE. In *beetle-browed*, ME *bitelbrowed*, *beetle* app derives from ME *bitel*, projecting, (? orig) sharp, therefore from *bitan*; hence, e.g., '*beetling* cliffs'.

**beetle** (2), a tool: OE *bētel* or *bītel*, ? 'little beater': cf BEAT.

**befall.** See FALL.

**before**: ME *beforen*: OE *beforan*, which=*be-*, by+*foran*, before (adv): f.a.e., FORE.

**befriend.** See FRIEND, heading.

**beg**; **beggar** (**beggarly**, **beggary**); **Beghard**; **Beguine**, **biggin**.

'To *beg*' derives from ME *beggen*, from AF *begger*, from MF *begard*, *begart*, prob from MD *beggaert*, a beggar. *Beggar* comes, via ME *begger*, *beggar*, from the same source; E *beggar* has adj *beggarly* (adj *-ly*), and ME *begger* has abstract n *beggerie*, whence E *beggary* (cf suffix *-ery*).

2. MF *begard*, *begart*, became ML *begardus*, *beghardus*, whence the eccl *Beghard*; it had also the MF-F derivative *béguine*, whence the eccl *Beguines*, female counterparts of the Beghards. F *béguine* had the MF-F derivative *béguin*, 'hood': whence the E *biggin*, coif.

**beget.** See GET, para 2.

**beggar**, **beggarly**, **beggary**. See BEG.

**begin**, pt **began**, pp **begun**: OE *beginnan*, akin to OFris *biginna*, OHG (and OS) *biginnan*: *bi-*, for *be-*, prefix, here int+*-ginnan*, to start (something). Cf the obs *gin*, short for *begin*.

**begone!** Be gone!

**begonia**, orig a tropical flowering plant: C17 coinage from M *Bégon*, Governor of Santo Domingo.

**begrudge**: a *be-* int from GRUDGE.

**beguile.** See VICTIM, heading—cf para 3.

**behalf** (*of*), *in* or *on*: ME *on-bihalve*, in the name of: *on*, on, in+*half*.

**behave**, whence **behaviour** (abstract suffix *-our*): prefix *be-*+HAVE, q.v. at para 4.

**behead**, **beheadal**. See HEAD, para 2.

**behest**: ME *bihest(e)*: OE *behǣs*, a promise, from *behātan*, to vow or promise: *be-*+*hātan*, to command. The shorter *hest* derives from OE *hǣs*, a command, from *hātan*.

**behind**, adv hence adj, prep, n: OE *behindan* (*be-*+*hindan*: see HIND, adj).

**behold**; **beholden**, pp hence adj. See HOLD, v, para 3.

**behoove**, now usu **behove**; (obsol) **behoof**.

'To *beho(o)ve*' has passed through ME *bihoven*, *behoven*, from OE *behōfian*, to need, from *behōf*, advantage (*be-*+derivative from root of HEAVE): and, via ME *to bihove*, to (hence for) the use of, OE *behōf* yields E *behoof*.

**beige.** See BOMBAST, para 3.

**being.** See BE.

**Bel.** See BAAL.

**belabo(u)r.** See LABOR, para 3, s.f.

**belay** (nautical): the syn D *beleggen* (*be-*, as in E+*leggen*, to lay). Hence *belaying pin*.

**belch**, v hence n: OE *bealcian*, akin to *belly*, q.v. at BELLOWS.

**beleaguer.** See the 2nd LIE, para 4.

**belfry**: ME *berfray*, a movable siege-tower: OF *berfrei* (or *berfroi*, whence MF-F *beffroi*): MHG *bërcvrit*, from OHG *bergfrid*, lit that which guards (G *bergen*) peace (G *Friede*: cf FREE).

**Belgian**, adj hence n (*Belg-*+*-ian*); *Belgic* (L

*Belgicus*); **Belgium,** adopted from L, itself from *Belgae* (s *Belg-*), the ancient Belgians: cf Gr *Belgai*: o.o.o.: prob C *\*belg-*, var of *\*balg-*, to be large: 'the big fellows' (Malvezin).

**belie** (orig, to tell lies about): ME *bilien* or *bilyen*: OE *belēogan*: cf the int prefix *be-* and LIE (speak falsely).

**belief; believe,** whence **believer.** See the 1st LEAVE, para 3.

**belike.** See LIKE, para 4.

**belittle, belittlement.** See LITTLE, para 2.

**bell:** OE *belle*, cf MHG *belle*: f.a.e., BELLOW. 'To *bell*' (of stags), OE *bellan*, is of the same Gmc origin.

**belle: belles-lettres.** See BEAU, para 2, and cf LETTER, para 1, s.f.

**bellicose.** See the element *belli-*.

**belligerence:** from *belligerent*, adj hence n: see the elements *belli-* and *-ger*.

**bellow,** to roar, hence n: ME *belwen*: OE *bylgan*, akin to OE *bellan*, to bellow, OHG *bellan*, MHG and G *bellen*, to bark, Lith *balhsas*, voice, and esp Skt *bhasaṭi*, he barks: IE s, *\*bhel-*, with a var *\*bhol-*; IE r,*\*bhe-*, with a var*\*bho-* (clearly echoic). Cf BELCH and BELL.

**bellows; belly,** n hence v.

The n *bellows* derives, through ME *below*, earlier *bely* (whence *belly*), meaning either 'bellows' or 'belly', from OE *belig*, *belg*, bag, hence bellows and belly—which, basically, are bags; *bellows*, obviously, was orig a pl. The OE word *belig*, *belg*, is akin to ON *belgr*, bag, bellows; to Go *balgs*, a wineskin; to OHG (and G) *balg*, a hide or skin, hence a bellows: and to several C words. The IE r is app *\*ɔhal-* or *bhel-*; the s, *\*bhalg-* or *\*bhelg-*. Cf. BELCH, BOLSTER, BUDGET.

**belong:** ME *belongen*: prefix *be-*+obs *longen*, to belong, from OE *gelang*, dependent, belonging. Hence the vn *belongings*, things belonging to a person.

**below,** adv hence prep: *be-*, by+LOW.

**belt,** n hence v; **baldric.**

*Belt*, OE *belt*, comes, as do ON *belti* and OHG *balz*, from L *balteus* (s *balte-*, r *balt-*), itself o.o.o.— ? Etruscan. Less directly from *balteus* comes *baldric*, from ME *baudrik*, *baudry*, from MF *baudrei*, OF *baldrei*.

**bemire.** See MIRE.

**bemoan.** See the 4th MEAN, para 2, s.f.

**bemuse.** See MUSE.

**bench.** See BANK.

**bend** (1), n: a bending: from 'to *bend*', q.v. at BEND (3).

**bend** (2), n: a band: OE *bend*. Cf BAND, para 2.

**bend** (3), v: pt and pp (whence the n) **bend.** 'To *bend*' derives from OE *bendan*, akin to ON *benda*, to bend, to bind, MHG *benden*, to bend, and OE *bindan*, to bind: f.a.e., BIND.

**beneath.** See NETHER, para 2.

**benedict, benediction, benedictory.** See DICT, para 7.

**benefaction, benefactor** (whence **benefactress**): L *benefactiōn-*, o/s of LL *benefactiō*, from *bene-*

*facere*, to do good to (someone): *bene*, well+ *facere*, to make or do. *Benefactor*, adopted from LL=*benefact-* (s of the pp *benefactus*)+agential *-or*. Cf BENEFIT and:

**benefice; beneficence, beneficent; beneficial, beneficiary** (adj hence n): resp, adopted from MF *benefice* (EF-F *béné-*), from L *beneficium*, from the adj *beneficus*, well-doing, whence the rare E *benefic*; *beneficence*, perh via F, from L *beneficentia*, from *beneficus*; *beneficent*, anl with other *-ficent* agents; *beneficial*, perh via MF-F, from L *beneficiālis*, from *beneficium*; *beneficiary* (cf EF-F *bénéficiaire*), L *beneficiārius*, from *beneficium*. L *bene-*, well, from *bonus*, good+*-ficere*, a cf of *facere*, to make or do: cf FACT and:

**benefit,** n hence v: ME *benefet*, euphonious for ME *benfet*, with which 'Gallic' form cf the OF-F *bienfait*: L *benefactum*, neu n from *benefactus*, pp of *benefacere*: cf BENEFACTION.

**benevolence, benevolent.** See VOLITION, para 2.

**benign,** whence **benignant,** whence **benignancy; benignity.**

*Benign*, ME *benigne*, adopted from OF-MF, descends from L *benignus*, short for *benigenus*, well-born, good-natured, *bene*, well+*-genus*, adj c/f from *genus*, q.v. at GENERAL. *Benignity*=OF-MF *benignite* (EF-F *bénignité*)=L *benignitāt-*, o/s of *benignitās*, an *-itas* abstract-n derivative from *benignus*.

**benison.** See DICT, para 7.

**bent,** tendency. See 3rd BEND.

**bent** (2), reed-like grass, or a stalk of such grass, whence the adj *benty*: OE *beonot-*, only in place-names, but akin to OHG *binuz* (G *Binse*), OS *binut*, rush: o.o.o., but perh C.

**benumb:** ME *binomen*, pp of *benimen*, OE *beniman*, to take away: prefix *be-*+*niman*, to take: f.a.e., NUMB.

**benzene, benzine:** Chem *-ene*, *-ine* derivatives from *benzoin*, earlier *benjoin*, EF-F *ben oin*, blending Sp *benjue* and Port *beijoim*: It *benzoi*, for *lobenzoi* (with *lo-* apprehended as *lo*, the): Ar *lubān jāwi*, frankincense of Java (Sumatra). *Benzol* =*benz*(ene)+*-ol*, oil.

**bequeath,** whence **bequeathal** (n *-al*); **bequest.** See QUOTH, paras 2–3.

**Berber.** See BARBARIAN, s.f.

**bereave, bereavement.** See ROB, para 3.

**beret:** F *béret*, occ *beret*: Old Gascon *berret*: LL *birrettum*, a capped hood, dim of LL *birrum*, *birrus*, a cloak, itself app of C origin: cf Br *bèr* and OIr *berr*, short. E *biretta* loosely merges It *berr etta* and its source, the LL *birrettum*. Cf BURNOUS.

**berg,** short for *iceberg*, of Scan origin: cf Sw *isberg*: 'mountain of ice': cf ICE and G and OHG *berg*, MHG *berc*, mountain, ON *biarg*, a (great) rock, Go *baírgahei*, mountain range, OE *beorh*, a tumulus, therefore the 1st BARROW.

**berry:** ME *berie*: OE *berie* (or *berīge*), akin to OHG (and OS) *beri*, MHG *ber*, G *Beere*, and ON *ber*, 'perh of Caucasian origin or from "Japhetic" (pre-IE) stratum in Gmc' (Walshe). Holthausen suggests basic meaning 'red' and a C origin: cf

MIr *basc*, red, and perh Manx (? ex E *berries*) *berrish*.

**berth**, n hence v; **birth**: both, from the r of BEAR, to carry; *birth*, ME *burth*, ? from ON *burthr*. Cf the n-suffix *-th*, as, e.g., in *stealth* from 'to *steal*'.

**beryl**: adopted, by ME, from MF *beryl* (OF *beril*, EF-F *béryl*): L *beryllus*: Gr *bērullos*: Skt *vaiḍūrya*, prob via Prakrit *velūriya* (Webster). Hence *beryllium*: *beryl*+euphonic *l*+chem *-ium*.

**beseech**, pt **besought**. See SEEK, para 2.

**beseem**. See SAFE, para 18, s.f.

**beside**, **besides**, adv hence prep: the latter (ME) is orig the gen of the former; the former derives from ME *biside*: prefix *be-*+SIDE.

**besiege**. See SIT, para 3, s.f.

**besmirch**. See SMIRCH (heading).

**besom**: ME *besum*, earlier *besme*: OE *besma*, akin to OHG *besamo*, MHG *besme*, G *Besen*; IE r, *bhes-*. The orig sense 'broom' plant leads naturally to the domestic broom.

**besotted**. See SOT (heading).

**bespeak**: pt **bespoke**; pp **bespoke**, whence the adj (*bespoke* tailors), now **bespoken**: ME *bispeken*, a modernizing of OE *besprecan*, to talk about: cf the G *besprechen* and, f.a.e., SPEAK.

**best**; **better**: resp OE *best*, for *betst*, *betest*, akin to ON *beztr*, OHG *bezzist* (MHG and G *best*), Go *batists*; ME *betere*, *bettre* (adv *bet*), from OE *betera* (adv *bet*), akin to ON *betri* (adv *betr*), OHG *bezziro* (MHG *bezzer*, G *besser*), with adv *baz*, Go *batiza*. 'No certain cognates outside Gmc' (Walshe); cf BOOT, advantage.

**bestial**; **bestiary**. See BEAST.

**bestir** (OE *bestyrian*): prefix *be-*+STIR.

**bestow** (prefix *be-*+STOW) derives from ME *bistowen*.

**bestride**, OE *bestrīdan*, consists of prefix *be-*+STRIDE, v.

**bet**, n and v. See BAIT.

**betel**, the nut of the *betel* palm of India and Malaya, was brought to Europe by the Portuguese voyagers, deriving it either from Tamil *veṭṭilei* or, rather more prob, Malayan *veṭṭila*, both presumably from the syn Skt *vīṭi*.

**bethink** (OE *bethencan*): *be-*+THINK.

**Bethlehem**. See BEDLAM.

**betide** and **betimes**. See TIDE, para 3.

**betoken**=int prefix *be*,+TOKEN.

**betray**, whence **betrayal**. See TRADITION, para 4 and heading.

**betroth**, **betrothal**. See *troth* at TRUE.

**better**, whence, by suffix *-ment*, **betterment**. See BEST.

**betty**, thieves' short crowbar: from *Betty*, pet-form of *Elizabeth*: cf the syn *jemmy* or *jimmy*.

**between**: ME *bytwene*, var *bitweonen*: OE *betwēonan* (or *-num*): *be-*, by+a form from the root of TWO.

**betwixt**. See TWO, para 10.

**bevel** app comes from a lost OF form (? dim *baivel*) of F *béveau* (var *biveau*), itself prob from OF *baïf*, open-mouthed: cf ABEYANCE. (Dauzat.)

**bever**; **beverage**. Orig 'a drink(ing)', now dial and coll 'a snack', *bever*=ME *beivre*, a drink from OF-MF *beivre*, to drink, whence also, OF-MF *bevrage*, anglicized as *beverage*: f.a.e., BIBULOUS. With *bever* cf that other L *bibere* derivative, *bubby* (now low), a woman's breast: cf the rustic LL *ubuppa*, 'teat, feeding-bottle' (Souter). Cf:

**bevy**: ? orig 'a drinking company': AF *bevee*, a hunting n of assembly, o.o.o., but cf OF-MF *bevee* (from OF-MF *beivre*, to drink), a drink or drinking. Cf prec.

**beware**. See WARY, para 2.

**bewilder**, **bewilderment**. See WILD, para 4 and heading.

**bewitch**. See VICTIM, heading, and cf para 2.

**bewray**. See WRAY, s.f.

**beyond**. See YON.

**bezant**. See BYZANTINE.

**bezique**: F *bésigue* (occ *bésy*): o.o.o., say Dauzat and B & W; EW adduces the two-centuries earlier form *basseque* and compares the still earlier It card-game *bazzica*, which Prati derives from the echoic It *bazzicare*, to frequent or resort to.

**bias**, n hence v: F (*en* or *de*) *biais*, (on or from) a bias: app from OProv *biais*, from Gr *epikarsios* (oblique), 'which would have penetrated by the Greek colonies of the Provençal coast, through a form *(e)bigassius*' (B & W). Gr *epikarsios* derives from *epi*, upon+*karsion*, side or flank; with *karsion* and its adj *karsios*, cf OP *kērscha* (or *kerscha*), over the top of.

**bib**, n and v (whence **bibber**). See BIBULOUS.

**bibble-babble**. See BABBLE.

**bibelot**. See BEAU, para 3.

**Bible**, whence **Biblical**: OF-F *bible*: LL *biblia* (neu pl): Gr *ta biblia*, the little books, pl of *biblion*, dim of *biblos*, (inner rind of) papyrus, hence a book, from the Phoenician city *Bublos* (*Byblos*), 'whence papyrus wàs exported' (Webster).

**bibulous**: **bib**, n and v (whence **bibber**). 'A *bib*' derives from 'to *bib*': a bib *drinks* a child's slopped-over beverage. 'To *bib*' or drink comes from L *bibere*, s *bib-*, whence the adj *bibulus*, whence E *bibulous*. App *bibo* (I drink) represents *pibo*, the *p* being assimilated to the interior *b*: cf Skt *pibati*, he drinks, and L *potus*, (of one) who has drunk. Cf also the C r *pib-*, often shortened to *pi-*: cf Gr *pinein* (s *pin-*, r *pi-*), to drink. The IE r, therefore, is *pi-*, var *po-*, with extensions *pib-*, *pin-*, *pob-*, *pon* (cf Lesbian Gr *pōnō-*, s *pōn-*), *pot-*.

**biceps**. See CHIEF, para 2.

**bicker**: ME *bikeren*, to skirmish: o.o.o., but cf OHG *bicchan*, to hack or stab, perh influenced by OF-F *piquer*, to peck (F *bequer*); *bec* is also a C r. Cf, therefore, BEAK.

**bicycle**. See CYCLE, para 1.

**bid**, v (pt **bade**, **bid**, pp **bidden**) hence n: ME *bidden*, to beg, ask, pray (cf BEAD): OE *biddan*, akin to OFris *bidda* (cf ON *bithja*), OS *biddian*, OHG (and G) *bitten*, Go *bidjan*: IE r, prob *bheidh-*, cf Gr *peithein* (s *peith-*), to persuade, for *pheithein*. Cf also BIDE.

2. The one notable cpd, apart from *unbidden* (prefix *un-*), is *forbid*, pt *forbid* or *-bade*, pp *forbidden*: ME *forbeden*: OE *forbēodan* (cf the privative *for-*), akin to ON *forbjōtha* and G *verbieten*. Cf also:

bide; abide—abode (n).

1. 'To *bide*' derives, through ME *biden*, from OE *bīdan* (s *bīd-*), akin to ON *bīda*, *bītha*, Go *beidan*, OFris *bidia*, OHG *bītan*; cf also L *fīdo* (s *fīd-*), I trust, and Gr *peithomai*, I follow; IE r, *bheid-*; cf BID.

2. *Abide* derives from OE *ābīdan* (*a-*+*bīdan*), akin to Go *usbeidan*, to expect; from the transitional ME *abiden* comes the ME n *abood*, whence *abode*.

**bident.** See TOOTH, para 11.

**biennial.** See ANNUAL, para 2.

**bier:** ME *beere*, earlier *baere*: OE *bāēr*, akin perh to OFris *bare*, certainly to OHG *bāra* (G *Bahre*) and ON *barar*; cf also Gr *pheretron* (from *pherein*, to bear, s *pher-*); the r of *bier* is that of 'to *bear*', and the IE r is that in Skt *bharás*, a burden.

**bifurcate, bifurcation.** See FORK.

**big,** whence **bigger** (*big*+orthographic *g*+*-er*) and **biggest** (*big*+*g*+sup *-est*): ME *big*, earlier *bigge*, akin to Nor *bugge*, an important man ('big fellow')—cf E BUG (big insect) and, ult, L *buccae*, (puffed) cheeks, the basic idea being 'puffed up, swollen' (Webster). The L word may be of C origin —cf E BEAK (L *beccus*); the C root would be *buc* (Malvezin).

**bigamist, bigamous, bigamy.** See MONOGAMIST, para 2.

**biggin,** coif. See BEG, s.f.

**bight.** See BOW, to bend.

**bigot, bigotry.** See GOD, para 6.

**bike.** See CYCLE, para 1.

**bile, biliary, bilious.**

*Bile*, adopted from EF-F, comes from L *bīlis* (s *bīl-*), app of C origin: cf the Cor *bistel*, Br *bestl*, W *bustl*; not in Ir, W, Manx. *Biliary*=F *biliaire*, from *bile*; *bilious*=F *bilieuse*, f of EF-F *bilieux*, itself from LL *biliōsus*, from *bilis*.

**bilge** is short for *bilge water*, gathered in a ship's *bilge*, a thinning of BULGE.

**bilingual:** L *bilinguis*; after LINGUAL.

**bilious.** See BILE.

**bilk:** a thinning or reduction of BALK.

**bill** (1), beak, whence 'to *bill* (and coo)': ME *bile* or *bille*: OE *bile*, prob akin to:

**bill** (2), weapon (broadsword), then a staff bladetipped): ME *bil*: OE *bil* or *bill*, akin to OHG *bill*, pickaxe, and *bīhal*, axe, OS *bil*, sword, ON *bīldr*, axe, also to OSl *biti*, to strike; IE s, perh *bithl-*, r perh *bith-*. Cf prec.

**bill** (3), a written document: ME *bill* or *bille*: AF *bille*, AL *billa*: ML *bulla*, document, (earlier) seal: L *bulla*, (orig) air bubble: cf 'papal BULL'.

**billabong,** a river's anabranch or 'dead-end' off-channel: adopted from Aus Aboriginal. The 1st element, *billa-*, water, occurs singly in 'billy can', water can, esp a kettle: cf Henry Lawson's famous short stories, *While the Billy Boils*, 1897.

**billet** (1) a note: ME, from MF, *billette*, thinning of OF-MF *bullette*, dim of *bulle*: ML *bulla*, document: see the 3rd BILL. MF *billette* has derivative late MF-F *billet*, as in *billet doux*, love-letter or *-note*.

**billet** (2), a small piece of (e.g. fire)wood: ME *billette*: MF *billete*, dim of OF-F *bille*, a (small round) log: ML *billia*, log, branch, trunk: cf OIr *bile*, large or old or sacred tree, Ir *bile*, tree, Ga *bile*, large tree, Br *bilh*, *bill*, tree trunk; C r, *bil-*, to be solid (and strong).

**billiards:** EF-F *billard:* MF *billart* (cf the suffix *-ard*), a staff, hence a cue, from *bille*, a log: see prec. For the F *-ll-*, cf:

**billion:** EF-F F *bis*, twice+F mi*llion* (see MILLION).

**billow:** ON *bylgja*, akin to *belly*, q.v. at BELLOWS.

**billy,** (policeman's) club, cf the 2nd BILLET; kettle, see BILLABONG.

**biltong,** dried meat: Afr: cpd of D *bil*, a buttock (rump-drawn)+ D *tong*, tongue (appearance).

**bin:** ME *binne*: OE *binne* or *binn*, manger, bin: perh C (many, though peripheral, cognates in Webster).

**binary:** L *bīnārius*: *bīni*, two by two+adj suffix *-ārius* (E *-ary*): L r *bi-*, ult akin to E *two*.

**bind,** pt and pp **bound; binder, bindery.** vn **binding; bund—bundle.**

1. 'To *bind*', with derivative agent *binder* (*-er*), vn *binding* (*-ing*) and trade-n *bindery* (*-ery*), derives from OE *bindan* (pp *bunden*), akin to OFris (and ON) *binda*, OS and Go *bindan*, OGH *bintan* (MHG *binden*), and to Skt *badhnáti*, later *bandhati*, he binds; IE r *bhendh-*. (Walshe.)

2. The G-adoption *bund*, MHG *bunt*, comes from MHG *binden* (see para 1). G *Bund* has dim *Bundel*, with cognate MD *bundel* (var *bondel*), whence ME *bundel*, whence E *bundle* (basically, things fastened together), whence 'to *bundle*'; akin to the MD form is the OE *byndele*, a binding, from OE *bindan* (para 1).

3. Cf BAND and BEND and (at BAND, para 5) BOND and:

**bine,** a dial var, mostly in cpds, of *bind*, esp in *woodbine*, from OE *wudubind*.

**binnacle.** See HABIT, para 13.

**binocular.** See OCULAR.

**binomial.** See NIMBLE, para 8.

**biographer; biographic(al); biography:** resp *biography*+agential *-er*; *biography*+*ic*(al); Gr *biographia*, element *bio-*, life+*-graphia*, a writing, from *graphein*, to write: f.a.e., GRAPH.

**biology** (element *bio-*, life+element *-logy*, q.v. at *-loger*) yields *biological* (*-ical*: cf *logical* at LOGIC) and *biologist* (*-ist*: cf *theologist*). Cf:

**bion,** Bio's physical individual: Gr *biōn*, presp of *bioun* (s *bi-*), to live: cf the element *bio-* and VIVA, paras 9 and 14.

**biotic.** See VIVA, para 11.

**bipartite.** See PART, para 4.

**biped.** See FOOT, para 20.

**biplane.** See PLANE, para 3.

**birch,** n hence v: ME *birche* (or *birk*): OE *birce, bierce, beorc,* akin to OHG *birka, birihha,* MHG *birke, birche,* G *Birke,* to ON *björk,* to several Sl words, and to Skt *bhūrja;* IE etymon, prob *\*bherja;* perh 'the bright tree', for BRIGHT is a cognate. Adj: *birchen* (C15 onwards).

**bird,** with many cpds, all obvious: by metathesis from ME *brid,* bird or young bird, from OE *brid* or *bridd,* a young bird: ? a 'nursling'—from OE *brēdan,* to cherish or keep warm.

**biretta.** See BERET and cf BURNOUS.

**birth.** See BERTH.

**biscuit:** EF-F *biscuit*: OF-MF *bescuit*: It *biscotto*: L *bis,* twice + It *cotto* (pp of *cuocere*), cf L *coctus,* pp of *coquere,* to cook: 'twice cooked' (baked hard).

**bishop, archbishop—bishopric, archbishopric; episcopal, archiepiscopal—episcopate.**

*Bishop* derives, via ME *bischop,* earlier *biscop* or *bisceop,* from OE *bisceop, biscop,* itself from LL *episcopus,* superintendent, (later) bishop, from the Gr *episkopos* (prefix *epi-,* on or over + *skopos,* inspector, cf the E SCOPE), a superintendent; *archbishop,* from OE *arcebisceop* (*-biscop*), from LL *archiepiscopus,* from Gr *arkhiepiskopos* (*arkhi-,* chief). The adjj derive from LL and ML *episcopālis, archiepiscopal* being anl; *episcopate* comes from LL *episcopātus, archiepiscopate* being anl; *episcopacy = episcopate* + the suffix *-cy,* much as *accuracy* derives from *accurate. Archbishopric* derives from OE *arcebiscoprīce;* its prototype *bishopric,* from OE *bisceoprīce* (*bisceop* + *rīce,* kingdom—cf the element *-ric*).

**bismuth:** adopted from G, var of *Wismut:* o.o.o.: MLG *wesemot,* perh from 'the first bismuth-mine (1440) at St Georgen in der *Wiesen*'; the 2nd element app comes from OHG *muotōn,* to demand, sc 'permission to open a mine'. (*Walshe.*) For *v* (*w*) *-b* mutation, cf:

**bison:** late MF-F, from L, *bison:* prob from LGr *bisōn,* itself perh from the Thracian *bisontes,* wild oxen (cf ML *bissonus,* wild ox): orig a European wild ox (the urus), hence the A bison. Rather than from Gr and Thracian, the L *bison* may have a Gmc origin: cf OHG *wisant,* OE *wisend:* ? orig Balto-Slavic.

**bit** (n); **bite,** pt bit, pp bitten.—**bitter, bitterness.** —Cf BAIT and BEETLE.

1. *Bit,* a bite (obs), hence a horse's bit, derives, through ME *byt, bite,* etc., from OE *bite,* a bite or biting, akin to ON *bit* and to—prob from—OE *bītan,* to bite; *bit,* a morsel, derives, through ME *bite,* from OE *bita,* akin to, prob from, OE *bītan,* to bite: a morsel is a portion bitten off at one attempt.

2. 'To *bite*', whence 'a *bite*', derives, through ME *biten,* from OE *bītan,* akin to OFris (and ON) *bīta,* OS *bītan,* OHG *bīzan, bīzzan* (G *beissen*), Go *beitan*—and Skt *bhedati,* he cleaves; IE r, perh *\*bheid-.*

3. *Bitter,* OE *bittor, biter,* is akin to OS *bittar,* OHG *bittar* (MHG and G *bitter*), ON *bitr,* Go *báitrs:* and prob to OE *bītan,* to bite, although, as

Walshe proposes, it may rather be akin to L *foedus,* disgusting, itself o.o.o. *Bitterness* derives from OE *biternys,* from the adj.

**bitch:** ME *bicche:* OE *bicce,* akin to ON *bikkja,* bitch, and *grey-baka,* (int) bitch; to G *Petze* (? from E); perh to F *biche,* OF *bische,* dial form of OF *bisse,* prob (B & W) from VL *\*bistia,* from L *bēstia,* beast. Perh cf the Skt *bhagas,* genitals. 'To *bitch*' is akin to 'to BOTCH'.

**bite.** See BIT, para 2.

**bitter, bitterness.** See BIT, para 3.

**bittern:** ME *bitoure* or *botor:* OF *butor:* doubtfully from VL *\*butitaurus:* the app echoic L *būtiō* (s *būti-,* r *būt-*), a bittern + *taurus,* a bull, introduced for echoic reasons. The ME word was perh influenced by *ern(e),* the (sea) eagle.

**bitumen:** L *bitūmen,* either of Osco-Umbrian or (E & M) of C origin—perh cf the Ga *bigh-thalmhuinn* and certainly cf the C r *\*beit-,* to be thick or viscous (Malvezin).

**bivouac.** See VIGOR, para 11, s.f.

**bizarre:** EF-F *bizarre:* It *bizzarro,* capricious: Sp *bizarro,* brave, prob from Basque *bizar,* a beard, whence the Sp senses 'energetic'—'manly'— 'brave'.

**blab, blabber.** *Blab,* a telltale, derives from ME *blabbe,* akin to ME *blaberen,* to blab, which is echoic. *Blabber,* v hence n, is a freq: cf 'to *blubber*', equally echoic.

**black** (adj hence n and v), with many obvious cpds; **blacken.**

1. 'To *blacken*' derives, by v suffix *-en,* from adj *black;* and *black,* adj, ME *blak,* derives from OE *blaec,* akin to OHG *blah* and ON *blakkr* and, further off, the L *flagrāre* (s *flagr-,* r *flag-*), Gr *phlegein* (s, r *phleg-*), to burn; IE r, *\*bhleg-;* basic idea, ? 'to burn with black smoke' or 'to burn black with smoke'.

2. Of cpds not too obvious, note *blackguard,* orig one of the kitchen menials in a great house, and *blacksmith,* from the dark metals he handles.

**blackmail.** See the 3rd MAIL, para 2.

**bladder** derives from OE *blǣd(d)re,* blister, bladder, akin to OHG *blāt(t)ara,* MHG *blātere,* G *Blatter,* and ON *blathra:* akin to OE *blāwan,* to blow. Cf

**blade:** ME *blad:* OE *blaed,* leaf, hence blade of an oar, akin to OHG-MHG *blat* (G *Blatt*) and ON *blad, blat(h)*—and OE *blāwan,* to blow. Cf prec, BLAIN, the 1st BLOW, (in)FLATE.

**blah,** pretentious nonsense or verbiage: *blah!,* term of contempt: ? blend of *bleat* + *bah.*

**blain,** obsol except in *chilblain* (chill + *blain*): ME *blein, bleyn:* OE *blēgen,* with cognates in at least two Scan languages; akin to *bloat* and ult to 'to *blow*'.

**blame,** v (whence *blamable:* cf EF-F *blâmable*) and n (whence *blameless*); **blaspheme, blasphemous, blasphemy.**

1. *Blame,* n, comes, in ME, from OF-MF *blasme* (EF-F *blâme*), from OF-MF *blasmer* (EF-F *blâmer*), to blame, whence, via ME *blamen,* the E 'to *blame*': and OF *blasmer* comes from LL *blas-*

*phēmăre*, to BLASPHEME, to blame, from L *blas-phēmāre*, to blaspheme, from Gr *blasphēmein* to speak ill of, from the adj *blasphēmos*, evil-speaking, *-phemos* from *phanai*, to speak, with 1st element (*blas-*) perh akin to Gr *meleos*, futile, itself with C and Skt cognates.

2. LL *blasphēmāre* yields OF *blasfemer*, whence ME *blasfemen*; whence, classically reshaped, E 'to *blaspheme*'; *blasphemous*=L *blasphēmus*=Gr *blasphēmos* (as above); and *blasphemy* is a similar reshaping of ME *blasfemie*, adopted from OF-MF, from L *blasphēmia*, Gr *blasphēmia*, from—abstract suffix *-ia*—*blasphēmos*.

**blanch** (1), in hunting: a var of BLENCH.

**blanch** (2), to render, or become, white or pale: ME *blaunchen* or *blanchen*: OF-F *blanchir*, from OF-F *blanc*, f *blanche*, white: f.a.e., BLANK.

**bland; blandish**, whence (suffix *-ment*) **blandishment**.

'To *blandish*' comes, through ME *blaundisen*, from OF-EF *blandir* (presp *blandiss*ant), from L *blandīri*, to flatter, from *blandus*, (flatteringly) mild, whence the E *bland*. L *blandus*, s *bland-*, is o.o.o.—? echoic.

**blank**, adj hence n: ME *blank*, *blonc*, *blaunc*: influenced by OF-F *blanc*, f *blanche* (cf E BLANCH), but perh from OE *blanca*, akin to OHG *blanc*, bright (G *blank*) and therefore also to ON *blakkr*, a white horse; app the OF word comes from the OHG

**blare**, v hence n: ME *blaren*, var *bloren*, to weep, akin to G *plärren*, to bleat: echoic.

**blasé**: pp (as adj) of EF-F *blaser*, to weary (someone) with strong liquor: D *blasen*, to cause to swell: 'bloated with liquor'. (B & W.)

**blaspheme, blasphemous, blasphemy**. See BLAME, para 2.

**blast**, n hence v: OE *blǣst*, a blowing, a gust (or a breeze) of wind, akin to OHG *blāst* and ON *blāstr*, and to the OE *blāwan*, to blow, OHG *blāsan* (G *blasen*) and *blāian*, ON *blasa*, OFris *blā*; the Gmc r is therefore *bla-*, the IE r *\*bhla-*, with varr *\*bhle-*, *\*bhlo-*, cf the L *flō*, I blow, *flāre*, to blow, *flātus*, blown; ult echoic. Cf BLAZE, 2nd BLOW, BLUSH, BLUSTER.

**blat, blate, bleat; blatant; blather.**

1. The first two are varr of 'to bleat' (whence the n), ME *bleten*, OE *blǣtan*, akin to G *blöken*; echoic. The adj *blatant* (whence *blatancy*; suffix *-cy*) app derives from Spenser's 'the *Blatant* (or *Blattant*) Beast', a bellowing monster, perh suggested by L *blaterāre* (s *blater-*, r *blat-*), to babble, whence the mainly dial E *blatter*, to prate.

2. *Blather*, n, comes from ON *blathr*, nonsense; 'to *blather*', from ON *blathra*, to talk nonsense, two intimately related ON words that, clearly echoic, are obviously akin to OE *blǣtan* and L *blaterare*. *Blether* is a Sc var.

**blaze**, effusion of light (and heat or flame): ME *blase*: OE *blaese* or *blase*, akin to OE *blas*, white or whitish, and G *blass*, pale, MHG and OHG *blas*, whitish, with a white forehead, the MLG var *blase* leading to E *blaze*, a white mark on the face, usu

the forehead, of (domestic) quadrupeds; cf the ON *bles*, in both senses; perh, ult, of OSl origin or, at the least, akin to OB *bĕlyj*, white (Walshe). 'To *blaze*', to burn brightly and vigorously, derives from the prec n, as, from its latter sense, does 'to *blaze*', to mark with a white spot or patch.

2. A *blazer* (jacket) is so named because it glows. A *blazon*, whence directly the v (cf, however, the MF-F *blasonner*), comes, via ME *blasoun*, from OF-F *blason*, a shield (with coat of arms), prob of Gmc origin and akin to *blaze*.

**blazon.** See prec, para 2.

**bleach**, v hence n; 'bleachers'.—**bleak.**—**blight**, n hence v.

1. 'To *bleach*' or whiten derives, through ME *blechen*, from OE *blǣcan*, itself from *blāc*, *blǣce*, pale: cf ON *bleikja*, MHG *blīchen*, G *bleichen*, and the adjj ON *bleikr*, OHG *bleih*, MHG-G *bleich*: IE r, ? *\*bhla-*, *\*bhlei-*.

2. 'Bleachers' are wooden seats that, exposed to the weather, turn paler and paler, season after season.

3. *Bleak* is of Scan origin: cf ON *bleikr*, pale, white.

4. And *blight* app comes from the same Gmc r as *bleach*.

**blear** (v hence n), **blear** (adj), **bleary**; **blur** (v hence n), **blurry.**

'To *blear*', render dim and watery, derives from ME *bleren*, cf LG *bleer-oged*, blear-eyed; the ME adj *blere*, whence E *blear*, is cognate, cf G *Bleor*, eye-soreness; o.o.o. *Bleary*=*blear*, n+adj suffix *-y*. *Blurry*=*blur*, n+euphonic r+*-y*; 'to *blur*' is app of same obscure r as 'to *blear*'

**bleat.** See BLAT.

**bleb.** See BLOB.

**bleed; blood.**

'To *bleed*': ME *bleden*: OE *blēdan*, derived from the OE *blōd*, ME *blod*, E *blood*: cf OFris *blēda*. With OE *blōd*, cf. ON *blōth*, Go *blōth*, OFris and OS *blōt*, OHG *bluot*, G *Blut*, perh akin to *Blume*, a flower, with basic idea 'florid' (Webster); IE r, perh *\*blodh-*. Cf BLESS.

**blemish**, v hence n: ME *blemishen*, earlier *blemissen*: from OF-MF *blesmir* (F *blêmir*), to fade or cause to fade, in such parts as *blesmissant*, *blesmissent*: either from the r occurring in OHG *blas*, G *blass*, pale (cf BLAZE, para 1), or from OScan *blami*, pale blue (cf G *blau*, E *blue*).

**blench** (1), to pale: a var of the 2nd BLANCH, to turn pale.

**blench** (2), with var **blanch**, in, e.g., hunting, to turn aside (vt and vi): ME *blenchen*, to divert, to deceive: OE *blencan*, to deceive, akin to ON *blekkja*, to impose upon: perh, as Webster proposes, a caus of *blink*, to make (someone) wink, hence to deceive. 'To *blink*', vi as well as vt, ME *blinken*, *blenken*, is akin to G *blinken*, to gleam or shine; ME *blinken* is prob only app a nasalization of OE *blēcan*, to gleam. The n *blink* occurs already in ME. Derivatives from the v: *blinkard* (*-ard*) and *blinker(s)*.

**blend**, to mix, hence n; obs **blend**, to dazzle or

blind; **blind,** adj, hence n and v; **blunder,** v hence n.

1. If we set out from the predominant meaning —'to render dark, (hence) to confuse'—the dark is light enough, and the path becomes clear: 'to *blend*' (mingle) comes, through ME *blenden,* from ON *blanda,* akin to OFris *blenda,* OHG *blentēn.* MHG-G *blenden,* to blind, esp to OE *blendan,* to dazzle or blind (hence the EE *blend,* to blind), and to OHG *blantan,* to mix (Go *blandan*); akin to the OE, whence the E, adj *blind* (ON *blindr,* OFris and OS *blind,* Go *blinds,* OHG-MHG *blint,* G *blind*); akin also to ON *blunda,* to close one's eyes in sleep, itself akin to ME *blunderen,* to confuse, (v.i) to move clumsily, to blunder, hence the E 'to *blunder*'. With all three OE-ME originals, cf the Lith *blandus.* dusky, (of soup) thick, and *blandytis,* to lower the eyes, and the Orkneys *bland,* buttermilk diluted with water, from ON *blanda,* hot whey similarly diluted. (Notably Walshe.)

2. *Blende,* as in *pitchblende,* is G (from *blenden,* to blind, to deceive): so named, either from its brilliance or from its deceptive lack of lead.

3. The IE r is prob *b(h)lend-* or *bhlendr-.*

**bless,** whence the pa **blessed, blest,** and the vn **blessing**: ME *blessen,* earlier *bletsen, bledsen*: OE *blētsian, blēdsian, bloedsian,* to sanctify or consecrate with *blood,* q.v. at *bleed*: by rendering holy, to render happy. (For sem, see esp OED.)

**blether.** See BLAT.

**blight.** See BLEACH, para 4.

**Blighty:** Pl N from Hobson-Jobson adj *blighty*: Hind *bilātī* (foreign, hence European, esp E), var of *wilāyatī,* adj of *wilāyat,* country, esp if foreign, itself from Ar *wilāyat,* a province, hence a country, from Ar *wāli,* governor (of a province): cf Tu *vilāyet,* from Ar *wilāyat.*

**blimp,** a small, non-rigid airship, hence a flabby, pompous (old) reactionary: coined ? in 1915, by Horace Shortt: prob a blend of *bloody+limp* (adj).

**blind.** See BLEND, para 1.

**blink, blinkers.** See the 2nd BLENCH.

**bliss,** whence **blissful; blithe.**

*Bliss* derives, through ME *blis, blisse,* from OE *bliss,* an 'eased' var of *blīths,* itself from OE *blīthe,* whence E *blithe*: cf OFris *blīth*-ship, 'blitheship', joy—Go *bleiths,* kind—ON *blīthr,* gentle—OHG *blīdi,* kind, blithe; IE etymon, *bhleitio,* extension of r *bhlei,* to shine.

**blister,** n hence v: ME *blister* or *blester,* either from MD *bluyster* or from OF *blestre,* itself from ON *blāstr,* a swelling, (orig) a BLAST—cf, sem, '*puff* of wind' and '*eyes puffed* up'.

**blithe.** See BLISS.

**blitz,** n hence v; **Blitzkrieg.**

The former shortens the latter, which, in G, means 'lightning war'. G *Blitz,* lightning (MHG *blicze*), is akin to G *Blick,* a glance (MHG, OHG *blic,* a flash, lightning); the IE s is *bhleg-,* perh cf *bhlei-,* to shine (see BLISS, s.f.). G *Krieg,* war, derives from OHG *krēg,* obstinacy.

**blizzard** is a suffix *-ard* derivative and sense-adaptation of *blizz,* a storm, itself app a thinning of

*blaze,* a bright flame, the hiss of rain being likened to that of a blazing fire.

**bloat,** to cause to swell, hence to cure (fish), whence *bloater,* a large cured herring: OE *blātian*: cf BLAIN and the Gr *phloidaō* (s *phloida-,* r *phloid-*), I let swell; IE s, *bhleid-,* r *bhlei-.*

**blob,** blister or bubble, hence a small drop or lump: from dial, where the syn *blob* or *blab* is clearly echoic, with intimate cognate *blub,* to become puffed, as with weeping, hence to weep noisily, with the freq derivative *blubber,* (orig) to bubble, hence weep noisily; *blubber,* (whale's) fat, derives from *blubber,* a large marine nettle, from *blubber,* foam or a bubble, from *blubber,* to bubble.

**block,** n and v; **blockade,** n hence v; **blockhead, blockhouse.**

*Blockhead*= *block+* HEAD; *blockhouse*=*block* *+*HOUSE, and is prob imitative of G *Blockhaus* (cf MD *blochuus*). *Blockade* is a suffix *-ade* derivative of 'to *block*': cf the It *bloccata.* 'To *block*' comes from late MF-F *bloquer,* itself from MF-F *bloc,* whence, via ME *blok,* E 'a *block*': and MF-F *bloc* derives from MD *blok,* a felled tree-trunk, akin to MHG, from OHG, *bloc,* a block: prob cf BALK.

**blond** (m), **blonde** (f): adj hence nn: adopted from F. The OF-F *blond* (cf OProv *blon,* It *biondo*) is dubiously of Gmc origin, although cf the OE *blonden*-feax, grey-haired, where *blonden* derives from OE *blondan, blendan,* to mix: cf the basic meaning of BLEND.

**blood.** See BLEED. Note the derivatives *bloodless* (OE *blōdlēas*) and *bloody* (OE *blōdig*); the latter, used by sl as an int, results naturally from the violence and viscosity of blood.

**bloom,** n hence v; **blossom,** n and v.

1. A *bloom,* ME *blome,* comes from ON *blōm,* var *blōmi,* akin to OFris *blōma,* Go *b ōma,* OHG *bluomo* (G *Blume*), OS *blōmo*—and to OE *blōma,* a lump or heavy mass, whence the metallurgical E *bloom.*

2. 'To *blossom*' derives from OE *biōstmian,* itself from OE *blōstm* or *blōstma* (with further var *blōsma*), a flower, whence E *blossom*: and the OE words are akin to MHG *blossem* and ON *blōmstr.* *Blossom* is therefore, in its early Gmc forms, an extension of *bloom*: f.a.e., the 1st BLOW—cf 'Every flower that *blows*'.

**blot,** n, v (whence *blotter*); **blotch,** n hence v.

1. 'To *blot* ' comes from MF *blotter,* to stain or blot, from MF *blotte, bloutte, bloute,* from OF *bloste* or *blostre,* a clod or a mound of earth, a blister, of Gmc origin: cf BLISTER.—The *blot* in backgammon app derives from Scan *blot(t),* naked, hence exposed.

2. Akin to MF *bloute* is MF *bloche,* a clod of earth, whence the E n *blotch.*

**blouse,** adopted from F (recorded 1798), is o.o.o; but since, as Dauzat sagely remarks, the primitive form was prob *belouse,* the word is perh C and ult akin to L *follis,* a pair of bellows, later an air-filled pillow or cushion: cf the phon kinship of C *bel,* a leaf (as in *beliu*), to L *folium,* a leaf.

**blow** (1), to bloom or blossom: ME *blowen*: OE

*blōwan*, to blossom, akin to the syn OS *blōjan*, OHG *bluoen* (for *\*bluojan*), MHG *blüejen*, G *blühen*, OFris *blōia*, to several C words and, further back, to L *florēre* (s *flor-*), to 'bloom' or flourish. The IE r is app *\*bhlo-*. Cf BLADE and BLOOM.

**blow** (2), of air: to move swiftly and strongly: ME *blowen*, earlier *blowen*: OE *blāwan*, (of wind) to blow: akin to OFris *blā* and OHG *blāhan*, *blāen* (for *\*blājan*), MHG *blāējen*, G *blähen*, and prob to L *flāre*, to blow, *flō*, I blow: ult echoic, cf BLAST.

**blow** (3), forcible stroke with fist or instrument: ME *blowe*, *blow*, akin to OHG *bliuwan*, MHG *bliuwen*, G *bläuen*, Go *bliggwan* (=*bliwwan*), to thrash: prob echoic.

**blowze**, whence **blowzy**. *Blowze*, a ruddy-faced woman, (later) a slattern, app derives from the same r as BLUSH.

**blub; blubber.** See BLOB.

**blucher**, a half-boot: from General *Blucher*, of Waterloo fame. Cf *wellington*, a high boot, loose-topped, from the Duke of *Wellington*.

**bludgeon**, n hence v (whence **bludgeoner**, whence Aus s **bludge**), is o.o.o. EW proposes that, influenced by *blood* (? rather *blow*, a heavy stroke), it comes from OF *bougeon*, dim of OF *bouge* (var *bolge*), a club, prob id with OF-F *bouge*, the concave or swollen part of an object, itself prob, as Dauzat mentions, akin to—if not, indeed, from—OF-F *bouge*, OF-MF *bolge*, a leather bag, from L *bulga*, itself prob of C origin, with several modern C cognates.

**blue**, adj, hence n and v: ME *bleu* (var *blew*), adopted from MF: OF *blau*, *blo*, *bloe*: of Gmc origin: cf OFris *blāu*, OHG (and OS) *blāo* (G *blau*), and—not itself the source of *blue*—OE *blāw* or *blāēw*. 'Orig. meaning "bright"; cognate with Lat. *flavus* [better *flāuus*, s *flāu*-] "yellow" ' (Walshe).

**bluff** (1), adj hence n.
A *bluff* or high, steep river or seaside bank, derives from the adj, 'broad- and flat-fronted; rising high and steep; hence, abrupt, unceremonious, roughly good-natured': and the adj is app of LG origin—cf MLG *blaff*, smooth, and MD *blaf*, flat, broad, flat and broad, and *blaffaert*, a broad-faced person.

**bluff** (2), v hence n: like prec, of LG origin: prob from D ver*bluffen*, to baffle (*ver-*, int prefix), cf LG *bluffen*, to frighten: prob orig echoic.

**blunder.** See BLEND, where cf *blind*.

**blunderbuss.** See THUNDER, para 2.

**blunt**, occurring since early ME: adj hence v: perh. akin to early G. *pluntsch* blunted, depressed, clumsy, and to Lith *beldēti* to knock, beat' Webster); perh (OED) of ON origin—cf ON *blunda*, to doze, and *blundr*, a dozing, themselves prob akin to ON *blanda*, to mix, (hence) confuse, and the adj *blindr*, blind: cf therefore BLEND.

**blur**, v hence n. See BLEAR.

**blurb** was coined in 1907 by Frank Gelett Burgess, who dubbed a 'lovely' appearing in a comic book-jacket designed by him: 'Miss Blinda *Blurb*'. (Mencken, Sup I.) Perh it is a blend of '*bloody* ab*surd*', Burgess knowing colloquial (British) English very well and often writing for British periodicals.

**blurt** is echoic. EW adduces the Sc *blirt*, a sudden weeping.

**blush**, v hence n: ME *bluschen*, to be (or turn or shine) red: OE *blyscan*, to shine, esp red, to be red, from *blysca*, a flame, a torch (clearly akin to BLAZE), and *āblyscan* (int *a-*), to blush: cf ON *blys*, a torch. Cf also:

**bluster**, v hence n: prob from LG *blustern*, (of weather) to storm, hence to bluster: ult akin to BLAZE and to the 2nd BLOW.

**'bo':** see BEAU.

**boa** (constrictor). The huge A snake derives from L *boa*, a water snake, answering to Gr *hudra* (E HYDRA). Perh L *boa* comes from the idea of cattle (*boues*, ML *boves*) coming to drink at stream or pool. (Cf BOVINE.)

**boar:** ? ME *bor*, which has the var *bar*: OE *bār*, akin to OHG *bēr*, G dial *bär*, syn with MHG *eber* (G *Eber*), OHG *ebur*, and OS *evur*: since the dissyllabic form corresponds to L *aper* and since OE *bār* is syn with OE *eofor* (cf the basic meaning of ON *iöforr*, a prince), the Gmc s is app, as Walshe proposes, *\*ebhuraz*, presumably with r *\*ebhur-*; the IE r is perh *\*abher-*, var *\*ebher-*.

**board** (1), n (plank) hence v: ME-OE *bord*, akin to ON *borth*, plank, and Go *fōtubaúrd*, footstool, also to OE *bred*, OHG-MHG *bret* (G *Brett*), a board or plank: basic idea, 'to cut' (Webster).

**board** (2), n (side of ship; border) hence v: OE *bord*, border, akin to OFris (and OS) *bord* and OHG *bort* (G *Bord*) and ON *barth*, *borth*: basic idea 'something that projects' (Webster); like Walshe, however, I think that (1) and (2) are cognates.

**boast**, v hence n: ME *bosten* or *boosten* (n *bost* or *boost*): perh akin to OHG *bōsi*, worthless, slanderous (MHG *boese*; G *böse*, evil), itself o.o.o.

**boat**, n hence v: ME *boot*, var *bat*: OE *bāt*, akin to ON *beit*, *beitr* and G *Boot* (modern only). Perh OE *bāt* comes from ON *beit(r)*, itself from ON *bita*, to split (up): cf, sem, 'dug-out' (boat).— For *boatswain*, see SWAIN, para 2.

**bob**, n (bunch or cluster, esp if pendent, as in *bobtail*; knob; ball of a pendulum; short, jerky motion) and v (to strike severely; then, strike lightly; to move (vt, vi) shortly and jerkily): ME *bob*, *bobbe*, bunch, and *boben*, *bobben*, to strike: prob echoic, but just possibly C: cf Ga *bad*, Br *bod*, tuft, bunch, cluster. 'To *bob*' has freq *bobble*.

**bob** (sl for a shilling). See ROBERT, para 2, s.f.

**bobbin:** EF-F *bobine*, from *bobiner*, to wind, itself o.o.o., but prob echoic (see, e.g., B & W at *bobard*)—cf the 1st BOB.

**bobble.** See the 1st BOB, s.f.

**bobby**, a policeman. See ROBERT, para 2.

**bobolink; bobwhite:** *Bob Lincoln*; *Bob White*: from the bird-calls or -notes.

**bock:** F *bock*: G *Bockbier*: Bavarian *Etmbock*: G *Einbecker*, for *einbecker Bier*, beer made at Einbeck in Germany. (Walshe.)

**bode**, to announce or foretell, (later) to portend (ill), hence the now obs n **bode**, whence the adj **bodeful** (*-ful*); **forebode**, whence adj and n **foreboding**.

1. 'To *bode*' derives, via ME *bodien*, from OE *bodian*, to announce, from *boda*, a messenger, itself from the same r as *bēodan*, to command (cf, therefore, BID); OE *bodian* is akin to OFris *bodia*, to summon.

2. 'To *forebode*'=to *bode*, tell or announce, *fore*, in advance.

**bodice; bodily.** See BODY.

**bodkin**: ME *boydekyn, boidekin, boitequin*, a dagger: o.o.o. EW proposes AF *\*boitekin*, dim of F *boîte* (earlier *boiste*), a box, and, sem, compares TWEEZERS; no less tentatively I suggest that the first element (the *-kin* is prob dim) comes from IE r *\*bhod-*, var *\*bhed-*, issuing in L as *fod-*, as in *fodere*, to dig, and in C as *\*bod-* (with var *\*bed-*), as in W *bedd*, a tomb, and several F dial terms in *bod-* (Malvezin); there are Sl cognates, both ancient and modern.

**body**, n hence v; **embody, embodiment; bodice; bodily.**

*Embodiment*=*embody*+*-ment*; *embody* (with var *imbody*)=*em-*, for *en-*, in+*body*. *Bodily*, adj hence adv, represents *body*+*-ly*; *bodice*, orig 'corset', is merely a graphic and phon alteration of *bodies*, much as the OF, whence E, *corset* lit means 'little body'. The v *body* derives from the n: and the n, through ME *bodi*, derives from OE *bodig*, akin to OHG *botah*, perh akin to OHG *botahha* (G *Bottich*), tub, vat, cask: sem cf 'tubby' persons. In *anybody, nobody, somebody* we see the 'person' sense of *body*: cf the combatant Services' use of *bodies*.

**Boer.** See BOOR.

**bog**, n hence v and the adj **boggy**: Ga and Ir *bog*, damp, miry, OIr *bocc* (cf *bocaim*, I soak), Ir *bogach*, Ga *bogalach, bogainn*, a bog or marsh: orig, prob echoic.

**bogey** (or **bogy**), **bogle**, goblin, bugbear; **boggle.** 'To *boggle*', start or shy in alarm, (hence) to hesitate, derives from *boggle*, var of *bogle*, app the dim of *bog* (var of *bug*, ME *bugge*, a bugbear), whence also *bog(e)y*: and *bug*, whence *bugbear* (see BEAR, n), has cognates in G and is ult akin to PUCK.

**bogie**: var of prec.—*bogie*, in transport, is an E dial word, o.o.o.

**bogle.** See BOGEY.

**bogus**, adj hence n: ? short, as Webster proposes, for dial (SW England) *tankerabogus*, var *tantarabogus*, a goblin, where *-bogus* clearly refers to *bog*, or *bog(e)y*, a goblin, and the first elements are fanciful; *bog* or *bog(e)y* has perh been influenced by *hocus-pocus*.

**bogy.** See BOGEY.

**bohemia**, n hence adj: *Bohemian*, a native of *Bohemia*, fig a romantic land (picturesque scenery, gypsies): the sense '(poor and) unconventional artist or writer' springs from the tremendous success of Henry Murger's stories entitled *Scènes*

*de la vie de Bohème*, 1849, and of the play, *La vie de Bohème*, 1851. *Bohemia*, G *Böhmen*, derives from L *Boii*, a C people that emigrated, c400 B.C., from Gaul.

**boil**, v hence n ('come to the boil') and agential **boiler** and vn **boiling**: ME *boilen*: OF-MF *boillir* (EF-F *bouillir*): L *bullire*, var of *bullāre*, from *bulla*, a bubble: cf 'ebullition'. A *boil* or inflamed swelling has been influenced by *boil*; it derives from the obs syn *bile*, OE *byl*, itself akin to L *bulla*.

2. The cpd *parboil*, ME *parboilen*, comes from OF *parboillir*, itself from LL *perbullire*, to boil well (*per-* being here an int).

**boisterous**: ME *boistous*, prob influenced by BLUSTER (orig, to wander blindly): Webster aptly compares the MD adj *bijster*, running wild: the MD varr *bister, bestier* do rather suggest an origin at least partly echoic.

**bold**, whence (suffix *-ness*) **boldness**: ME *bold*, earlier *bald*: OE *bald, beald*, akin to OHG (and OS) *bald* and ON *ballr*, and to Go *balthei*, boldness, and *balthaba*, boldly; perh ult to the v BLOW; Feist proposes an IE etymon *\*balths*, swollen.

**bole** (1), tree-trunk, came into ME from ON *bolr*, akin to MHG and MLG *bole* (G *Bohle*), a plank. Kluge proposes a Frankish *\*bolo-*; Holthausen a kinship with the n BOWL. Hence ME *bolroysche, bulrysche*, whence E *bulrush* (*rush*, a plant).

**bole** (2), friable clay: L *bōlus*, clay, lump of clay, lump: Gr *bolos*, a clod (i.e., lump) of earth, perh akin to L *bulla*, a bubble. The med *bolus* is the L word *bōlus*.

**bolero**, short jacket, derives from the Sp dance named *bolero*, itself app from *bola*, a ball: f.a.e., BOWL, a ball.

**boloney**, occ **baloney**: *Bologna* sausage, all sausages being gastronomic inferiors.

**bolster**: OE *bolster*, akin to OHG *bolstar*, MHG (and G) *polster*, ON *bōlstr*: cf OHG *belgan*, to swell (see BELLY).

**bolt** (1), a shaft or arrow: OE *bolt*, akin to ON *bolti*, OHG and MHG *bolz*, MLG *bolte*, G *Bolzen*. The Gmc words come perh from L *catapulta*, influenced by MHG *boln*, to throw. (Walshe.) Hence 'to *bolt*', orig to start forth like a bolt or arrow.

**bolt** (2), to sift: ME *boulten, bulten*: MF-OF *buleter* (MF-F *bluter*): MD *biutelen*, rather than MHG *biuteln*, to sift—perh cf G *Beutel*, MHG *biutel*, OHG *būtil*, a bag, a purse, hence a boltingcloth (B & W), known, tech, as a *boultel*, from OF *buletel*.

**bolus.** See the 2nd BOLE.

**bomb**, n hence v (whence **bomber**); **bombard**, n and v; **bombardier, bombardment.**

'To *bombard*' comes from EF-F *bombarder*, itself from MF-F *bombarde*, a heavy projectile-firer, whence the obs E n *bombard*; *bombardier* is adopted from late MF-F (*bombard*er+agential *-ier*); *bombardment* (suffix *-ment*) merely adapts F *bombardement* (from *bombarder*); and the E n *bomb* represents EF-F *bombe*, from It *bomba*, bombsl ell, from L *bombus*, a dull, heavy noise, from Gr *bombos*, itself echoic: cf echoic BOOM.

bombast, whence bombastic; bombazine (or -sine); beige.

1. *Bombast* comes from MF *bombace*, cotton, hence padding: LL *bombāc-*, o/s of *bombāx*, a fusion (? confusion) of LL *bambāx*, cotton, and post-Classical *bombyx*, silk, silkworm, themselves from Gr *bambax*, cotton, and *bombux*, silk worm or cocoon, hence silk, both perh from Per—cf Pahlavi *pambak*, cotton (Webster).

2. *Bombasine*, *-zine*=MF-F *bombasin*, either from It *bambagino*, modification of It *bambagia*, cotton, from LL *bambax*, or, more prob, from LL *bombasinum*, alteration of *bombycinum*, a fabric of cotton or of silk, orig the neu s of *bombycinus*, adj of L *bombyx* (as above).

3. *Beige*, n hence adj, is adopted from MF-F, which, perh by aphesis, takes it from It *bambagia* (as in para 2); EW, more prob, proposes *beige*, F dial form of OF-EF *bis* (f *bise*), yellowish grey, and compares It *bigio*, grey; *bis* is o.o.o.

bon, F adj (f *bonne*), as in *bon mot* (cf MOTTO) and *bon vivant* (cf VIVACIOUS), and, disguised, in *debonair* (OF *de bon aire*, of good stock)=the L *bonus* (f *bona*), good: cf BONNY.

bonanza: Sp, fair weather, hence prosperity: from *bono*, good, early form of *bueno*: f.a.e., BONNY.

bonbon: F: nursery redup of bon.

bond, a band or fastening: see BAND, last para.

bondage: ML *bondagium* (with *-agium*, cf the suffix *-age*): ME *bond(e)*, a serf: OE *bonda*, a servant, orig a householder, esp a hus*band*: ON *bōndi*, for *būandi*, lit 'a person dwelling', from ON *būa*, to dwell.

bondsman, bondswoman. See BAND, last para.

bone, n hence v; bonfire.

A *bonfire* was orig a fire of bones, ME *bonefire*: and *bone* derives, via ME *bon*, *ban* (also *bane*), from OE *bān*, akin to OFris (and OS) *bēn*, OHG *bein*, bone, MHG *bein*, bone, leg, G *Bein*, leg, ON *bein*, bone, leg. Adj: *bony*, for *boney*.

bonnet: ME, from MF, *bonet*, var *bonnet*: late ML *boneta*, *bonetta*, *bonet(t)um*: by aphesis, from ML *abonnis*, a cap, o.o.o. but perh Gmc (B & W).

bonny; bonus.

*Bonny* derives, prob influenced by *joly* (*jolly*), from ME *bonie*, itself from F *bon*, f *bonne*, from L *bonus*, good, which, sense-adapted, becomes the commercial E *bonus*: and L *bonus* is app for *\*duenus* (IE *\*dwenos*), the r being *\*duen-*, Gr *\*dun-* (as in *dun*amis, power): basic idea, 'health, energy, strength'.

bony. See BONE, s.f.

boob is short for booby, from Sp *bobo*, stupid, ltself from L *balbus* (adj), stammering, the stammerer appearing stupid: and *balbus* is echoic (cf BARBARIAN).

boodle; caboodle. The latter prob=either *kit and boodle* (Webster) or int prefix *ker-+boodle*; *boodle* itself appears to represent either MD-D *boedel*, property, or MD *budel*, ED *buydel*, D *buidel*,

MLG *būdel*, a purse, the latter being, sem, the more likely.

book. See BEECH, para 2.

boom (1), a long pole: see BEAM, para 2.

boom (2), echoic v hence n, including the stock-market sense: cf ME *bommen*, to hum; the noise has become deeper.

boomerang, n hence v, is an Australian Aboriginal word.

boon, adj: F *bon*: L *bonus*, good: f.a.e., BONNY.

boon, n: ME *bone*: ON *bōn*, a petition: a petition granted constitutes a favour or advantage, a sense influenced—cf prec—by F *bon*, good.

boor, boorish; Boer; the Bowery.

*Boor*, whence *boorish*, comes from D *boer*, a farmer, hence a country lout, for earlier *geboer*, cf LG *gebur*, OHG *gibūro*, OE *gebūr*, a countryman, from *ge-*, together+*būr*, a dwelling (cf the 2nd BOWER). The D farmers in SAfr, hence all Dutchmen there, became known as *Boers*. The *Bowery* district of New York City represents D *bouwerij*, from *bouwer*, farmer, akin to *boer*.

boost, v hence n and the agent booster: Scots dial *boost*, to purposefully drive or push, itself o.o.o., but very prob echoic.

boot (1) amends, remedy, profit, whence bootless: ME *bot* or *bote*: OE *bōt*, akin to OFris *bōte*, OS and Go *bōta*, OHG *buoza*, MHG *buoze*, G *Busse*: akin to BETTER.

boot (2), footwear: ME *bote*: OF *bote* (F *botte*): o.o.o., but prob formed from the same r as F *bot*—in *pied bot*, a club-foot, akin to *bot*, a toad, a squat creature—in the sense 'heavy shoe or boot' (B & W). *Bootee* is diminutive: cf the suffix *-ee*.

2. A *bootlegger* is the agent of 'to *bootleg*', orig to carry on the person, usu in a *bootleg*, liquor that is illicit.

bootlegger. See prec, s.f.

bootless. See the 1st BOOT.

booty; freebooter.

1. *Booty* comes from MF-F *butin*, plunder, from MF-F *butiner*, to take as plunder: of LG origin, cf MD (and MLG) *buten*, to take booty, and esp MLG *bute*, MHG *biute*, MD *buyt*, D *buit*, booty, akin to ON *byte*; ME *bote*, E BOOT, profit, has intervened.

2. *Freebooter*=D *vrijbuiter*, whence also the G *Freibeuter*: *vrij*, free+*buit*, booty+agential *-er*.

3. Spaniards reshaped E *freebooter* to *flibustero*, which became *filibustero*, which Englishmen turned into *filibuster*, whence the AE 'to *filibuster*'.

booze or bouse, v hence n and boozer, boozy: ME *bousen*: MD *bousen*, *busen*, to drink intoxicants, akin to MLG *busen*, to carouse: ult akin to BOAST.

bora. See BOREAL.

borax, adj boracic. See the element *boro-*.

bordel. See BROTHEL.

border, n hence v (whence borderer): ME, from MF-F *bordure*—from OF-F *border*, to border or edge—from OF-F *bord*, a border or edge: f.a.e., the 2nd BOARD.

bore (1), pt of 'to BEAR'.

**bore** (2), auger, n hence v; whence **boredom.**

The tool derives from OE *bor*, whence both *bora*, a hole, orig one made by boring, the source of E *bore*, including finally the sense 'ennui' (cf the F *Quelle scie!*), now usu expressed by *boredom*; 'he who bores' derives rather from OE *bor*. 'To *bore*' has, in all its senses, passed through ME *borien* from OE *borian*, from OE *bor*, the tool. Akin are, e.g., ON *bora*, a hole made by boring, and the vv ON *bora*, OHG *borōn* (G *bohren*), to pierce, esp with a bore or auger, themselves akin to L *forāre* (s *for-*), to bore, and Gr *pharan* (s *phar-*), to plough, lit to make a long hole in the earth; IE r, *\*bhar-*, varr *\*bher-* and *\*bhor-*, to pierce. Cf the metathetic Arm *brem*, I hollow or dig.

**bore** (3), a tidal wave: ON *bāra*, akin to MD *bāre*: prob source, ON *bera* (cf MD *baren, beren*), to carry, q.v. at 'to BEAR'.

**boreal, borean, hyperboreal, -borean; Boreas, bora.**

*Borean* and *Hyperborean* are varr of E *boreal* (L *boreālis*) and *Hyperboreal*, adj and n (L *hyperboreus*, Gr *huperboreos*: ? 'beyond'—cf prefix *hyper*—'the mountains'), *Hyperboreans* being mythical inhabitants of the extreme north. The base is L, from Gr, *Boreās*, God of the North Wind, the North Wind itself, whence It *borea*, with dial var *bora*, a strong wind blowing over the N Adriatic; Gr *boreās* perh means 'wind from the mountains', cf the OSl *gora* and Skt *giris*, mountain. (Hofmann.)

**born, borne.** See BEAR, v, para 2.

**borough, burgh, burg, burgess, burgher, burgomaster; bourgeois; burrow;** (in place-names) **-bury,** and 'to **bury**'; **burglar.**

1. *Borough* derives, through ME *burgh* (whence E *burgh*, whence, in turn, *burgher*; perh, however, from D) or *burw* or *boru*, from OE *burh* or *burg* (whence E *burg*), akin to OFris *burg*, a castle— OHG *burg*, fortified place, esp a citadel, hence a city or town, MHG *burc*, G *Burg*, a castle—Go *baúrgs*, city—ON *borg*, wall, hence fortified place or castle: prob akin to OE *beorgan*, to shelter, defend, preserve, cf OHG *bergan*, G *bergen*, to bring to safety; Gmc s, *\*berg-*, IE s *\*bherg-* (Walshe).

2. Whereas *burgomaster* prob comes from D *burgemeester*, 'city master' (cf OFris *burga-mâstere* and G *Bürgemeister* and *Bürgermeister*), *burgess* comes, through ME *burgeis*, from OF-MF *burgeis*, itself from OF-MF *burc*, either from MHG *burc*, as above, or from ML *burgus*, itself from OHG *burg*. OF-MF *burc* became EF (and F) *bourg*, whence the adj (hence n) *bourgeois*, whence *bourgeoisie*, both adopted by E.

3. A *burrow* or animal's made hole in the ground—whence 'to *burrow*'—was prob, orig, a var of *borough*, and is certainly akin to it.

4. *Bury*, a manor (house), derives from OE *byrig* (dat of *burh*); it survives only in place-names, whether independently in *Bury* or in cpds, as in Canter*bury* and Shrews*bury*.

5. 'To *bury*' derives, through ME *burien* or *berien*, from OE *byrgan*, akin to OE *beorgan*, to

shelter or preserve (para 1, s.f.). The ME forms had derivatives *buryel, beriel*: whence *burial*.

6. The ML *burgus*, a fortified place (esp town)— see para 2—has a derivative agent *burgātor*, with varr *burglātor, burgulātor*, with *-l-* perh suggested (Webster) by that of L *latrō*, a thief: *burgulātor* looks suspiciously like a var of *\*burgilātor*, for *\*burgilātrō*, a city thief: a *burglar* is an essentially urban malefactor. *Burgle* is a b/f; *burglary* merely adds n-suffix *-y*.

7. Cf also HARBO(U)R and:

**borrow:** ME *borwen*: OE *borgian*, from *borh* or *borg*, a pledge: akin to OFris *borgia* (var *burgia*), OHG *borgēn* (orig 'to spare', later 'to borrow'), G *borgen*, to borrow or to lend, ON *borga*, to stand surety: also to OE *beorgan*, to protect, to preserve, and G *burgen*, to stand surety: cf, therefore, BOROUGH. The n *borrow* derives from OE *borh, borg*.

**boscage.** See BUSH, para 1.

**bosh** (coll), nonsense: adopted from Tu *bosh* empty, useless, worthless.

**bosky.** See BUSH, para 1.

**bosom,** whence the adj **bosomy:** OE *bōsm*: akin to OFris *bōsem*, OS *bōsm*, OHG *buosam*, MHG *buosem*, G *Busen*: o.o.o., but prob (Webster) cf Skt *bhastrā*, bellows, and *bhasman*, blowing.

**boss** (1), protuberance; **emboss.**

'To *emboss*' comes from OF *embocer*: *em-*, for *en-*, in(to)+*bocer* (var *bocier*), whence, via ME *bocien*, the E 'to *boss*' or ornament with bosses: and *bocier, bocer* derives from OF *boce*, itself of Gmc origin—cf OHG *bōzan*, MHG *bōzen*, to knock, strike—*boss* (ME *bose*, earlier *boce*) being ult akin to BEAT.

**boss** (2), overseer, master, hence 'to **boss**': D *baas*, master, MD *baes*, uncle, prob akin to OHG *basa*, aunt, MHG-G *base*, female cousin.

**bossy:** the adj of **boss** (1) and (2).

**bosun.** See SWAIN, para 2.

**botanic(al), botanist, botanize, botany.**

*Botanical* merely elaborates, with suffix *-al*, the adj *botanic*, from the EF-F adj *botanique*, itself —via LL *botanicus*—from Gr *botanikos*, concerning plants, from *botanē*, a herb, a plant, (orig) pasture, from *boskein*, to graze. *Botanist* (*-ist*) comes from late EF-F *botaniste*, 'to *botanize*' from F *botaniser*. *Botany* is usu said to come from the EF-F n *botanique* (Webster), from Gr *botanikē*, prop the f of the adj *botanikos*, or (OED) from the E *botanic*, but perh it rather comes—prob via F *\*botanie* (cf the C16 *botanomantie*, divination with plants)—from LGr *botania*, herbs (collectively).

**botch,** to mend (roughly), hence to bungle, whence the n **botch,** a bungling: ME *bocchen*, app from MD *botsen, butsen*, to mend, to patch: ? orig echoic.

**both:** ME *bothe*, earlier *bathe*: ON *bāthir* ( where *-ir* is a suffix or other mdfn): cf OE *bā*, Go *bai*, and OHG *bēde*, OHG-G *beide* OFris *bēthe* OS *bēthia*; cf also the 2nd syllable of L *ambō* Gr *amphō*, Skt *ubhā*.

**bother** See PUT, para 2.

**bottle,** n hence v; **butler—butt,** a cask—**buttery.**

1. *Bottle* passes through ME *botel*, earlier *botelle*, from OF-F *bouteille*, from *buticula*, var of popular Early ML *butticula*, dim of LL *buttis*, vase, cask, prob of C origin, r \**but-*, var of \**bot-*, swollen, round, whence EF *botte*, a cask (Malvezin), and Ga *buideal*, OIr *buidel*, cask. 'To *bottle*' was perh prompted by OF *bouteiller*.

2. LL *buttis* yields also Prov *bota*, var *bouto*, whence EF (and F) *botte*, var *boute*, cask, whence E *butt*, a (large) cask. *Buttis* has derivative ML adj *buttārius*, set in charge of the wine-vessels, whence (?) *botāria*, a place for casks, whence MF *boterie*, a place for bottles, whence ME *botery*, E *buttery*, a store-room for liquors, hence for provisions.

3. OF *bouteille* has derivative OF-EF agent *botillier* (later *bouteillier*), bottle- (or cup-) bearer, whence ME *boteler*, later *buteler*, wine-servant, whence E *butler*. *Butlery* descends from OF-F *bouteillerie*, from *bouteille*.

**bottom, bottomless, bottomry.** See the 1st FOUND, para 6.

**botulism.** See element *botuli-*.

**boudoir:** F: from MF-F *bouder* (to pout), expressive of the grimace: a room to which a woman can retire, not only to pout. Perh ult akin to *pout* (*p* for *b*, *t* for *d*).

**bough:** ME *bogh*: OE *bōg, bōh*, akin to ON *bōgr*, shoulder, (hence) bow of ship—OHG *buog*, MHG *buoc*, G *Bug*—Skt *bāhu*, arm; IE r, ? \**bhagh-*, var \**bhogh-*. Cf the 2nd BOW.

**bought.** See BUY.

**boulder:** of Scan origin: cf Sw *bullersten*, a large (lit, noisy) stone in a stream, and *bullra*, to roar (Nor *buldra*, Da *buldre*); cf Nor *bulder*, a rumble, a roar: clearly echoic.

**boulevard.** See BULWARK.

**boultel.** See the 2nd BOLT, s.f.

**bounce,** v hence n: ME *bunsen*, perh akin to LG *bunsen*, D *bonzen*, themselves possibly akin to OF-F *bondir*, to leap, cf the 4th BOUND.

**bound** (1), adj: 'prepared, ready' (obs), 'intending to go, going', as in 'homeward-*bound*': pp of ME *bounen*, to prepare, from *boun*, ready, from ON *būinn*, pp of *būa*, to dwell (cf BOWER, room).

**bound** (2), adj: 'compelled; morally obliged': pp of **bind,** to tie.

**bound** (3), n: 'landmark; limit, boundary', hence 'to bound, set limits to': ME *bounde* or *bunne*: OF-MF *bonde* or *bone, bonne*, or *bodne*: ML *bodina, butina*, a territorial boundary, perh of C origin (r \**but-*).

**bound** (4), to leap suddenly, hence the n: OF-F *bondir*, to rebound, then simply to leap, orig to resound: VL \**bombitare*, to hum, from L *bombus*, a buzzing: f.a.e., BOMB. The social *bounder* is to be compared with '*jumped*-up' and *bounce*, impudence.

**boundary:** a blend of 3rd BOUND+ML *bonnārium* (s *bon-*+euphonic *-n-*+*-ārium*), a well-defined piece of land; with the E n-suffix *-ary* substituted for L *-ārium*.

**bounder** (socially). See the 4th BOUND, s.f.

**bounteous, bountiful, bounty.**

Whereas *bountiful*=*bounty-full*, *bounteous* derives from ME *bountevous*, which tacks *-ous* to altered *bontive*, f of OF-MF *bontif*, the adj of *bonté*, whence E *bounty*; *bonté* represents *bonitātem*, the acc of *bonitās*, itself an *-itās* (E *-ity*) derivative from *bonus*, good: cf BONNY.

**bouquet,** nosegay, hence its smell, hence the smell of wine: F: OF-MF *boschet*, dim (*-et*) of *bois*, a wood, from ML *boscus*: f.a.e., BUSH.

**bourbon** is elliptical for *Bourbon whisky*, manufactured orig in *Bourbon* County, Kentucky: the *Bourbon* dynasty of France: a seigniory (and its castle) in central France: *Borvon* (var *Bormon*), God of Warm Springs, a sort of Gaulish Apollo: C \**borvo*, r \**borv-*, var of \**berv-*, to be hot (cf L *feruēre*, ML *fervēre*, s *ferv-*), hence boiling, hence bubbling, as hot springs do.

**bourdon.** See the 2nd BURDEN.

**bourgeois,** adj & n. See BOROUGH, para 2.—The printers'-type *bourgeois*=*Bourgeois* type, after a F type-founder.

**bourgeon.** See BURLY.

**bourn, bourne** (1), a brook; Sc var, **burn:** ME *burne, borne*: OE *burna*, metathesis of *brunna*, akin to OFris *burna*, spring, well, OHG *brunno*, MHG *brunne*, spring, well, G *Brunnen*, well, and *Born*, fountain, OS *brunno*, Go *brunna*, spring, well, ON *brunnr*: all of which, further, are prob akin, both to OHG *brennen*, to set fire to, G *brennen*, to burn, OE *bernan, birnan* (see BURN, v), and to the Ir *brenn-*, to gush forth. Cf also FERVENT.

**bourn, bourne** (2), a limit, a goal: F *borne*, OF *bourne*, var of OF *bodne*, var *bonne*: ML *bodina*: f.a.e., the 3rd BOUND.

**Bourse.** See PURSE, para 2.

**bouse.** See BOOZE.

**bout,** a circuit (obs), a going and returning (a turn), a contest, an attack of, e.g., fever: a sense-adapted var of obsol *bought*, a bend, app a ME derivative from LG *bucht*, akin to E *bight*, q.v. at BOW, to bend.

**bovine:** ML *bovīnus*, LL *bouīnus* (s *bouīn-*, r *bou-*), the adj of *bōs* (gen *bouis*, ML *bovis*), ox, cow: cf BUCOLIC and, f.a.e., COW.

**bow** (1), an arc, hence a bow for arrows, whence **bowyer** (cf suffix *-yer*): ME *bowe*, earlier *boge*: OE *boga*, akin to OFris *boga*, OHG *boge*, MHG *boge*, G *Bogen*, ON *bogi*: a bow is bent, cf therefore *bow*, to bend (3rd BOW).

**bow** (2), of ship: ON *bōgr*: akin to BOUGH, q.v. Cf BOWSPRIT.

**bow** (3), to bend or curve, hence 'a **bow**' or inclination of one's head: ME *bowen*, earlier *bogen*, earliest *bugen*: OE *būgan* (r *bū-*), akin to OS *bugan*, Go *biugan*, OHG *biogan*, MGH and G *biegen*, to bend, ON *bogin-n*, bent, *beygia*, to bend, and remotely yet importantly Skt *bhujáti*, he bends; IE r, perh \**bheug(h)-*, to bend. Cf also the intimately cognate OHG *bougen*, G *beugen*, to bow.

**bowdlerize:** from Thomas *Bowdler*, who in 1818 issued an expurgated edition of Shakespeare.

**bowel; embowel; disembowel, disembowelment.**

*Bowel,* ME *bouel(e),* comes from OF-MF *boel,* LL *botellus,* an intestine, from the shape of L *botellus,* a small sausage, dim of *botulus,* a sausage —cf *botulism* at the element *botuli-.* To *embowel* =*em-,* for *en-* (L *in-*), in, into+*bowel*; hence *disembowel* (prefix *dis-*), whence *disembowelment* (*-ment*).

**bower** (1), in cards: G *Bauer,* (lit) a peasant, from the figure occ depicting a knave: MHG *gebūre*; OHG *gibūro,* orig a fellow-villager: *ge-,* together+ agent of *bouen* (OHG *būan*), to cultivate, akin to Go *bauan,* to dwell. Cf:

**bower** (2), a cottage, a room, (much later) an arbour: ME *bour,* earlier *bur,* a dwelling, a room: OE *būr,* a dwelling, from *būan,* to dwell, to cultivate, akin to OHG *būan,* ON *būa,* to dwell, to cultivate: Gmc r, ? *bū-,* akin to E BE. Cf prec and BYRE. Derivatives: 'to *embower*' and *bowery,* q.v. sep at BOOR.

**bowl** (1), a concave vessel: ME *bolle*: OE *bolla,* akin to OFris *bolla,* OHG *bolla,* MHG *bolle,* a round vessel, G *Bolle,* a bulb, esp an onion—to ON *bolli*—also to L *follis,* bag, bellows. Perh cf:

**bowl** (2), a ball, whether solid or hollow, for rolling or throwing, hence 'to bowl'. the cricketing **bowler,** the game of *bowls*: MF-F *boule*: because it is round, like L *bulla,* a bubble: cf BULL, an edict. Some etymologists, e.g. B & W and Walshe, suppose *bowl* (1) and (2) to be, ult, of one origin: cf BALL, a sphere.

**bowler** (1). See prec.

**bowler** (2), hat: from the hatters named *Bowler.* EW.)

**bowls,** game of. See the 2nd BOWL.

**bowsprit.** See SPROUT, para 2.

**box** (1), tree (whence tautologically **boxwood**), derivatively a wooden case: OE *box*: L *buxus*: Gr *puxos,* app of Medit origin: cf the Eg *petsu-t,* a box, and perh the Maltese *bùx* (tree).

**box** (2), v (whence **boxer**), derives from *box,* a buffet, now usu a cuff on the ear: o.o.o., but prob, like BUFFET, orig echoic.

**boy:** ME *boi*: perh akin to EFris *boi,* a young gentleman, MHG *buobe,* boy, scoundrel, G *Bube,* boy, itself akin to ON *bofi,* a rogue, and MD (and D) *boef,* a scoundrel: cf the sem of KNAVE.

**boycott,** v hence n: Captain *Boycott,* a land agent obstructed and ostracized, 1880, by the natives of County Mayo in Ireland.

**brace,** n and v (whence the pa **bracing**); **embrace,** v hencen; **bracelet**; perh, in part, the 3rd BRAKE, q.v.

1. 'To *embrace*' comes from OF *embracer,* which, an int, combines the prefix *em-* with altered *bracier,* to embrace, which leads to the E v *brace,* with its easily detectable sense-developments: and OF-MF *bracier* derives from OF-MF *brace,* an embrace, (lit) the two arms, L *brachia,* the arms (outstretched), pl of *brachium,* arm, from Gr *brakhion,* arm, usu the upper arm, from *brakhus,* short—cf the element *brachy-.*

2. *Bracelet,* worn on the wrist, is adopted from OF-F, where it is the dim (*-et*) of OF-MF *bracel,*

armlet, itself from *brachiāle,* armlet or bracelet, var of LL *brachiālis* (var *-cch-*), prob orig the adj of, and certainly from, *brachium.*

3. Cf BRASSARD (with BRASSIÈRE).

**bracken,** a large, coarse fern, often collectively: ME *braken,* of Scan origin: cf Sw *braken,* fern: clearly akin to the 1st BRAKE.

**bracket,** n hence v: EF-F *braguette,* codpiece: dim of EF-F *brague,* a mortising, influenced by EF-F *bragues,* breeches: L *brācae,* breeches, pl of the much less used *brāca,* adopted from Gaulish, with r *brāc-,* to encircle, to gird on (e.g., a sword with its supporting belt).

**brackish** is an *-ish* modification of the now only dial *brack,* salty, from D *brak,* MD *brac,* bitter, salty, perh akin to BRINE.

**brad, bradawl.**

The latter (see AWL) serves to make holes for brads (small, thick nails): and *brad,* ME *brod,* comes from ON *broddr,* any pointed piece of hard metal, akin to OE *brord,* a spire of grass (OHG *brort*) and MIr *brot,* a thorn or a spike. C BROIDER.

**brae.** See BRAID, para 4.

**brag,** v hence n; hence the merely app Sp-It *braggadocio,* after Spenser's *Braggadocio* in *The Faerie Queene*: ME *braggen*: cf EF *braguer,* perh from the root of BRAY. *Braguer* has the derivative EF adj *bragart,* boastful, whence E *braggart.*

**Brahma,** anglicized form of Skt *Brahman,* the Hindu god, from *brahman,* prayer, divine essence; *Brahman,* one of the priestly caste, is derivative, with var *Brahmin.*

**braid,** v hence n: to jerk, then to weave or plait: ME *braiden, breiden,* OE *bregdan,* to move back and forth, to weave: akin to OS *bregdan,* OFris *breida,* OHG *brettan,* ON *bregtha,* of identical or closely allied meanings: IE, ? *bregh-.*

2. OE *bregdan* has prefix (*up-*) cpd *upbregdan,* ME *upbreiden,* E *upbraid,* (lit) to twist up (cf 'twist a sense'), hence to reproach, accuse.

3. OFris *breida* has var *brīda,* intimately related to OE *brīdel,* ME *bridel,* E *bridle,* cf OHG *brittil,* MHG *bridel*: many ancient bridles were plaited. 'To *bridle*' (fig sense from horse's head bridle-upheld) derives from OE *brīdlian,* from *brīdel.*

4. Also akin to *braid* is Sc and N dial *brae,* slope or bank: ME *brai, bra*: prob akin to ON *brā,* eyelash, and OE *brāēw,* eyelid, OS and OHG *brāwa,* eyelash, eyelid, G *Braue,* OFris *brē,* eyebrow.

**braille** characters for the blind: invented, 1829, by Louis *Braille,* himself blind.

**brain,** n (hence v), whence adj **brainy** (*-y*): OE *bragen, braegen,* influenced by OFris *brein* and MD *brein* (varr *bragen, bregen*): Gr *brekhma,* varr *bregma, bregmos, brekhmos* (s *brekhm-,* r *brekh-*), the upper part of the head; IE r, ? *bregh-*; r *bhregh-* might also account for G (*Ge*)*hirn,* OHG *hirni,* ON *hiarni,* brain, for *hirn,* etc., may well be metathetic for *hrin-.*

**braise.** See the 2nd BRAZE.

**brake** (1), fern, came into ME from, it seems, Scan sources—cf BRACKEN.

brake (2), thicket, first in ME, is app of LG origin: cf MLG *brake*, bushes, perh orig either 'broken branches' (OED) or 'the growth on rough broken ground, from the root of E BREAK, v' (Webster). Cf:

brake (3), mechanical, n hence v: ME: from LG *brake*, a flax-breaking instrument: from r of the E v BREAK, q.v. Cf prec.

bramble: ME *brembil*: OE *brembel, braembel,* varr of *brēmel,* akin to OHG *brāmal:* cf BROOM.

bran: ME *bran,* earlier *bren:* OF-MF *bren* (F *bran*), prob of C origin, with r *bren-,* to break: cf Br *brenn,* and Ga and Ir *bran,* bran, chaff; and notably Ir *branar* (or -*air*), the loose surface of a field *broken up* by grubbing.

branch, n hence v: ME *braunche:* OF-F *branche:* LL *branca,* a paw (and its claws), a claw, from a proximate resemblance: o.o.o., but perh (E & M) connected with L *brachium,* the (fore)arm, presumably by nasalization; perh rather from the C r *branc,* a nasalized var of *brac,* to break, a paw being a 'broken off' part of the body (Malvezin)— cf Br *brank,* a branch.

brand, n hence v: piece of wood partly burnt, hence torch and, from charring, a recognizable mark, and, from the flashing of the blade, a sword: OE *brand,* akin to OFris *brand,* OHG *brant* (G *Brand*), all meaning both torch and (blade of sword): further, akin to the old Gmc forms of E BURN, q.v. Cf BRANDY.

2. 'To *brandish*' comes, via ME *braundisen,* from OF-F *brandir* in such forms as presp *brandissant* and esp 'ils *brandissent*', they brandish, from the idea of waving something as if it were a sword (OF *brand:* from Gmc, prob the OFris *brand*).

3. *Brand goose* (cf Sw *brandgos*) becomes *brant goose* becomes *brant:* a goose with head, neck and upper shoulders so dark as to look 'burnt black'; for *brant,* cf the *brannt-* of G *Brannt*wein. *Brant* has var *brent.*

brandish. See BRAND, para 2.

brandy: earlier *brandywine:* D *brandewijn,* lit 'distilled wine': *branden,* to burn, hence to distil+*wijn,* wine: cf the G *Branntwein.*

brant. See BRAND, para 3.

brash, boldly impudent, impudently tactless, is usu explained as a sense-development from *brash,* (of timber) brittle, lifeless, itself app from *brash,* debris, app from OF-F *brèche,* a breach: all very 'iffy'. Perh it is rather a blend, either of *bold+rash,* or of *brassy+rash.*

brasier. See the 2nd BRAZE.

brass, n hence adj and v; braze; brazen.

'To *braze*', make or cover or adorn with brass, drives from OE *braesian,* from *braes,* brass, whence, via ME *bras* (var *bres*), the E *brass:* f.a.e., FERROUS. The adj is *brassy* (-*y*). *Brăzen,* adj, derives, via ME *brasen,* from OE *braesen,* adj of *braes,* brass; 'to *brazen*', usu *brazen* (it) *out,* derives from the adj *brazen,* perh influenced by the derivative sense 'impudent' of *brassy.* A *brazier,* cr worker in brass, derives from ME *brasiere,* from ME *bras.*

brassard; brassière (whence the sl bra, already by 1953 become commercial j).

*Brassard,* arm badge, derives from *brassard, brassart,* armour for upper arm: EF-F *brassard,* from *bras,* arm, from L *brachium:* f.a.e., BRACE. *Brassière* is adopted from MF-F, where orig it meant some kind of arm-guard, the modern senses (C16 onwards) being prob euphemistic. Cf the suffixes -*ard* and -*ier.*

brat, child (usu pej): from ME (now—except in dial—obs) *brat,* a coarse garment: OE *bratt,* a covering, e.g. mantle, of C origin: cf OIr *brat(t),* cloth, cloak, Ga *brat,* a covering, mantle, W *brat,* clout, rag, Manx *breid,* cloak: OC *brattos,* ? var *brettos.* The sem transition is afforded by child's clout or perh bib.

bravado. See:

brave, adj hence n and v; bravery; bravado; bravo!; bravura; braw.

1. *Bravado* is a well-meant E attempt at Sp: but the Sp word happens to be *bravada* (now -*ata*), a boast; *bravura,* however, happens to be a mere sense-adaptation (cf the C16 Sc *bravetie,* display, elegance) of It *bravura,* high spirit; *bravo,* a daring villain, hence a hired assassin, is likewise It, as also is *bravo!,* m, the f usu being *brava!*—cf the E *good girl!* The It *bravo,* wild, savage, fierce, (later) daring, became MF-F *brave,* adopted by E, whence the n; 'to *brave*' comes from EF-F *braver,* from F *brave;* cf *bravery* from EF *braverie* from F *brave.* The It adj *bravo* is perh a conflated reshaping of L *barbarus,* q.v. at BARBARIAN, but Prati suggests that it rather comes from L *prāuus,* ML *prāvus,* crooked (Skt *pravas, púrvas*), crooked, hence perverse, vicious.

2. *Braw,* fine, splendid, derives from OSc *brawf,* brave, app from MF-F *brave.* Cf the OProv *brau,* (of bulls) wild, savage, occurring in late ML as *brāvis,* a young ox or bull.

braw. See prec para.

brawl, v, hence n and agent brawler, pa and vn brawling: ME *braulen,* to quarrel (noisily), *brallen,* to weep noisily, make a noise: perh cf LG *brallen,* D *brallen,* to boast, but rather cf OProv *braulhar,* to brawl, from the r present in BRAY (1).

brawn: OF *braon,* fleshy part, muscle, piece of flesh, fat of thigh, of Gmc origin: cf OHG *brāto,* tender meat, flesh, ON *brāth,* flesh, raw meat, MHG *brāte* and G *Braten,* a roast. Adj: *brawny.*

bray (1), to utter a cry like an ass's, loud and harsh: ME *brayen:* OF-MF *braire,* to cry aloud (F, to bray), perh of C origin: cf Ga *braigh,* to crackle, *brag* (and *braghadh*), noise, explosion, OIr *braigim,* I break wind, and possibly Cor *begy,* to bray: prob akin to BRAG and ult to L *fragor* (s *frag-*), a crashing noise, by denasalization from *frangere,* to break: IE r, ? *brag(h).* Therefore akin, ult, to:

bray (2), to pound, to grind or rub small: ME *brayen:* MF *breier* (F *broyer*), from West G *brekan* (cf OE *brecan*): f.a.e., BREAK. Cf prec.

braze (1), to hard-solder: F *braser,* var *braiser,* from OF-F *braise* (at first written *breze*), embers, live coals: PGmc *brasa*, preserved in Sw *brasa*, fire, burning log—cf OProv *brasa* and early It *brascia, bracia, bragia*, It *brace*. Derivatives: 'to *braise*', now only in cookery, from OF-F *braiser*; *brasier* or *brazier*, from OF-F *brasier*.

2. OF-F *braise*, live coals, has OF-MF derivative *bresil* (EF-F *brésil*), whence, or from cognate Port and Sp *brasil*, the ME *brasil*, whence E *brazil*, the hard *red* wood usu called *brazilwood*; hence, ult, *Brazil*. (See P².)

**braze** (2); **brazen**. See BRASS.

**brazier**. See BRASS, s.f., and 1st BRAZE, s.f.

**brazil; Brazil**. See the 1st BRAZE, para 2.

**breach**. See BREAK, para 2.

**bread**: OE *brēad*; akin to OFris *brād*, OS *brōd*, OHG-MHG *brōt*, G *Brot*, MD *brot* or *broot*, D *brood*, ON *brauth* (cf BROTH); cf also Gr *broutos, brutos* (or *-on*), fermented liquor, beer; the basic idea is that of fermentation—cf L *feruēre* (ML *fervēre*), to seethe (see FERVENT) and the E BREW.

**breadth**. See BROAD, para 2.

**break**, v, hence n and also **breaker** (*-er*), **breakage** (*-age*); pt **broke**, pp **broken**;—**breach**, n hence v.

1. The n *break*, ME *brek, breke*, derives from ME *breken*, whence 'to *break*', from OE *brecan*, akin to OFris *breka*, OHG *brehhan*, MHG (and G) *brechen*, OS *brecan, brekan*, Go *brikan*, MD (and D) *breken*; cf the nasalized L *frangere*, pt *frēgi*, and the Skt element *-bhraj-*, breaking forth: IE r, prob *bhreg(h)-*, app echoic. Cf BRICK and perh BROOK.

2. A *breach* comes, through ME *breche*, from OF-MF *breche* (F *brèche*), itself from OHG *brecha*, a fracture—cf the syn OE *brice, bryce*, from the pres tense of *brecan*.

**bream**, a fish: ME *brem, breme*: OF-MF *bresme* (F *brême*), var of OF *braisme*: Frankish *brahsima* —cf OHG *brahsema*, OS *bressemo*, MD *brasem* (also D), *bressem, breesem*.

**breast**, n hence v: ME *brest*, earlier *breost*: OE *brēost*, intimately akin to OS *breōst, briōst*, OFris *briāst*, ON *briōst*, less closely to OHG-G *brust* and Go *brusts* (pl). The varr OFris *borst, burst*, and MD *borst* (also D), *burst, berst, barst*, could easily mislead: cf rather (with Webster) the MHG *briustern*, to swell, and the OIr *bru*, belly, also OIr *briunne*, the chest, EIr and Ga *brollach*, bosom, chest, and Br *bruch, brusk, bresk*, the chest: IE s, *bhreus-*, to swell (Walshe), a merely phonetic extension of *bhreu-*. Cf BRISKET.

**breath**, n, whence **breathless** (suffix *-less*), **breathe**, v.

'To *breathe*' derives from ME *brethen*, from the ME n *breth*, earlier *breath*, from OE *brāeth, brēth*, breath, odour, akin to OHG *brādam*, vapour, breath, MHG *brādem*, G *Brodem* (fumes): comparison with OE *āēthm*, OHG *ātam, atum* vapour (G *Atem*), and with Gr *atmos*, vapour, suggests (EW) that *br-* is the vestige of a lost prefix (? int *ber-*); for *āēthm*, etc., cf the atmo- of ATMOSPHERE. Cf also BREED.

**bred**. See BREED.

**breech, breeches**.

The former is partly a b/f from the latter: the latter derives, through ME *brech*, from OE *brēc*, breeches, the pl of *brōc*, breech, breeches, akin to OFris *brōk*, OHG *bruoh*, MHG *bruoch*, G *Bruch*, ON *brōk*: cf also L (from Gaul) *brācae*, sing *brāca*.

**breed**, pt and pp **bred; brood**.

'A *breed*' derives from 'to *breed*': ME *breden*: OE *brēdan*, to nourish (and cherish), to keep warm, akin to OHG *bruotēn*, G *brüten*, and OE *brōd*, ME *brod*, E *brood* (whence 'to *brood*'), akin to MHG *bruot*, G *Brut*, akin to G *bruhen*, to scald, orig 'to hatch out by warmth' (Walshe). The basic idea is 'a warming', prob orig by breathing upon— certainly cf BREATH and 1st BROIL.

**breeze**, n hence v: F *brise* (C16 onwards), perh an expressive alteration of OF-F *bise*, from Frankish *bīsa*—cf OHG *bīsa*, OProv *bīza*: prob echoic, cf L *susurrus*.

**brent**. See BRAND, para 3.

**brer; brethren**. See FRATER, para 7 (*brer*) and heading.

**Breton**. See BRITISH.

**breve, brevet, breviary, brevity**. See BRIEF, paras 1 (*breve* only) and 2.

**brew**, v hence n; **brewery; brewster**, a -*ster* var of **brewer** (*brew*, v+*-er*).

A *brewery* represents *brew*, v+*-ery*: and 'to *brew*' passes through ME *brewen* from OE *brēowan*, akin to OFris *briūwa*, OHG *briuwan*, MHG *brūwen*, G *brauen*, ON *brugga*; also to the OFris n *broute* and to the *-frū-* of L *defrūtum*, must boiled down: IE r, *bhrū-*. (Walshe.) Cf BROTH and BREAD, the basic idea being 'fermentation'.

**briar**. See BRIER.

**bribe**, n hence v; **bribery**.

The ME *brybery*, roguery, whence E *bribery*, is akin to MF *brimberie*, beggary (*brimb*er, to beg+ *-erie*, E *-ery*), from MF *brimbe*, a nasalized var of MF-F *bribe*, a worthless trifle, hence a scrap one begs; *brimbe*, or *bribe*, is o.o.o., but prob echoic.

**brick**, n hence v: OF-F *brique*: MD *bricke*, a brick—akin to E BREAK.

**bride, bridal**.

The adj *bridal*=*bride*+adj suffix *-al*; the n *bridal* (ME *bridale, brudale*: OE *brȳdealo*) is lit 'bride-ale', served at the marriage feast. The OE *brȳd*, whence E *bride*, is akin to OFris *breid*, OHG-MHG *brūt*, G *Braut*, ON *brūthr*—and Go *brūths*, daughter-in-law; IE r,? *brūd-*. For *bridegroom*, see HOMO, para 14.

**bridge**, n hence v: ME *brig(ge)* or *brug(ge)*: OE *brycg* or *bricg*, akin to OFris *bregge* (occ *brigge*), OS *bruggia*, OHG *brucca* or *brücka*, MHG *brucke*, G *Brücke*, bridge, ON *bryggia*, pier, app an extension of *brū*, bridge (Da *bro*), Gaul *brīva*, bridge. Webster poses the basic meaning as 'beam'; Walshe says, 'The original meaning was apparently "brow" (from the shape). Cf *Braue*' (OHG *brāwa*, cf ON *bra*, E BROW) and he cites an OB word signifying both 'bridge' and 'brow': whereas the Gmc s is app *brug-*, the Gmc r—as the ON words tend to show—is *bru-*, with 'brow' the more likely sense. Cf *Bristol*, OE *bryggstōw* or *Bricgstōw*, 'Bridge Place'.

**Bridget.** See BRIGADE, para 2.

**bridle.** See BRAID, para 3.

**brief**, adj and n; **breve, brevet, breviary, brevity**; — **abbreviate** (sep entry), **abridge** (sep).

1. The n *breve* comes, legal from ML *breve*, a summary, a letter, musical from It *breve*, other senses from F *brève*, all from L *breue*, neu of *breuis* (ML *brevis*, neu *breve*), short; ML *breve*, letter (prob suggested by LL *breuis*, a summary), became OF-MF, whence ME, *bref*, whence—influenced by the E adj—the E n *brief*. The adj *brief* derives, prob via ME *bref*, from OF-MF *brief* (var of *bref*), from ML *brevis*, L *breuis*, s *breu-*, akin to the syn Gr *brakhus*, s *brakh-*.

2. *Breviary* comes from MF-F *bréviaire*, from ML *breviārium*, a summary, from the LL adj *breuiārius*, abridged, an extn of L *breuis*; *brevet* is adopted from MF-F *brevet*, earliest *brievet*, app a dim from ML *brevis* (L *breuis*); *brevity* perh comes rather from *brevitāt-*, o/s of ML *brevitās*, L *breuitās*, an *-itas* or abstract derivative from *breuis*, than from the equally derivative late MF-F *brièveté*.

**brier**, occ **briar**, is a sense-adapted derivative from OF-F *bruyère*, heather, heath (F *-ère* corresponding to L *-āria*, cf the suffix *-ārium*): VL *brucāria*: VL *brūcus*, heather: C *brūko*, r *bruk-* or *bruc-*, perh a var of *brac-* or *brec-*, to break: cf EIr *fráech, frōech*, bristles, Ga *fraoch*, heath, heather, W *grug*, heath, Br *brug, bruig*, heath, heather, Cor *grig*, heather, Manx *freouch*, heath. Cf BRISTLE and BRUSH, also BRISK and BRUSQUE. But *brier*, thornbush, comes from OE *brēr* or *brāēr*, perh independent of *brier*, the tree (or white) heath, from which pipes are made.

**brig.** See para 3 of:

**brigade, brigadier; brigand, brigandage; brigantine; brigue.**

1. *Brigadier*, adopted from EF-F, is an agent from MF-F *brigade* (cf the suffix *-ade*), likewise adopted by E: from It *brigata*, from *brigare*, to quarrel or fight, from *briga*, strife, whence MF-F, hence obs E, *brigue*, quarrel, intrigue: It *briga* is of C origin—cf OIr *brīg*, Ga *brīgh*, substance, importance, power, W *bri*, authority, Br *bri*, (formerly) dignity, (now) respect, Manx *bree*, substance, importance. The C r is *brig-*, var of *berg-*, an eminence, hence eminence (Malvezin), the OC n being *brīga* or, in cpds, *brigo-*.

2. It *brigare*, to fight, has presp *brigante*, which, as n, became MF-F *brigand*, duly adopted by E, as was the late MF-F derivative *brigandage*. Cf the Br and W *brigant*, a robber, and prob cf the *Brigantes*, a powerful tribe or people of ancient Ireland and N Britain, and *Brigid, Brigit* (whence *Bridget*), their patron goddess, akin to Skt *bṛhati*, lofty, hence powerful.

3. The It n *brigante* has a dim derivative *brigantina*, orig a pirate ship, whence MF-F *brigantin*, whence F and E *brigantine*, often abbr as *brig*.

**bright, brighten, brightness.**

Whereas 'to *brighten*'=*bright*+v suffix *-en*, *brightness* (*-ness*) derives from the OE *beorhtnes*, from OE *beorht*, var *bryht*, whence, via ME *briht*, comes E *bright*: cf OHG *bëraht*, MHG *bīrht*, OS *berht*, Go *bairhts*, ON *bjartr*, with cognates in C and Sl; IE r, *bherek-*, basic idea 'to become white (and bright)': cf Skt *bhrāśatē*, it shines. (Walshe.) Cf BIRCH.

**brigue.** See brigade.

**brilliance** (suffix *-ce*) derives from the adj *brilliant*, from F *brillant*, presp (whence the F n *brillant*, whence the E n *brilliant*) of *briller*, to sparkle or shine: It *brillare*, o.o.o., but (B & W) prob from L *beryllus* (cf BERYL): to shine like a beryl, although (Prati) it may simply be, like It *prillare*, imitative.

**brim**, edge, brink, hence.v (esp *brim over*): ME *brim*, earlier *brimme*, akin to MHG *brem* (G *Brame*) and ON *barmr*; *brim* could be a shortened metathesis of *barmr*.

**brimstone.** See ADDENDA TO DICTIONARY.

**brindled**, whence **brindle**, is a dim of **brinded**, ME *brended*, streaked: *brended* is a form of *branded*—see BRAND.

**brine**, whence the adj **briny** (for *briney*), derives from OE *brȳne*, akin to MD *brīne* and one or two Sl and Skt words: basic idea, 'bitter' (?).

**bring**, pt and pa **brought**: ME *bringen*: OE *bringan*, akin to OFris *bringa*, varr *brenga, branga*, OS *brengian*, OHG *bringan*, MHG (and G) *bringen*, Go *briggan* (pron *bringan*): perh cf W 'he-*brwng*', to bring, and Cor 'he*brency* (*-ky*)' or hem*bryncy* (*-ky*), to lead.

**brink**, edge (esp at top): ME *brink* or *brenk*, app of Scan origin, akin to MD *brinc*, MLG *brink*, brim, shore: a nasalization of OGmc *brik-*, var of *brek-*, to BREAK—cf ON *brekka*, a slope, and Go *brikan*, to break.

**briny.** See BRINE.

**brisk**, whence **brisken** and **briskness**: perh a thinning of *brusque*, q.v. at para 2.

**brisket**: ME *brusket*, perh influenced by the Da syn *bryske*: ult akin to BREAST.

**bristle**, n hence v: ME *brustel* (var *brostle*), app a dim (*-el, -le*) and metathesis of OE *byrst*, akin to OHG *burst*, MHG *borst*, G *Borste*, OS *bursta*, ON *burst*—and Skt *bhṛṣṭis*, point, edge. Cf BROOM and BUR.

**Bristol.** See BRIDGE, s.f. *Bristol milk*, a fine sherry, was so named because, as smooth as milk, it was—and is—landed in Bristol.

**Britain, Britannia, Britannic; British; Briton; Brythonic; Brittany, Breton.**

*Britannic* comes from L *Britannicus*, the adj of *Britannia*, the Roman name for Britain; *Britain* comes from ME *Bretayne* (or *-eyne*), from OF *Bretaigne*, whence also *Brittany*—cf *Breoton* (or *-en*), *Bryten*, from an OGmc *Brituna*. *British* derives from OE *Brettisc* or *Bryttisc*, from *Bret*, usu in the pl *Brettas* or *Bryttas*, Britons; *Briton*, from OF *Breton*—whence obviously F *Breton*—from L *Brittōn-*, o/s of L *Brittō* (var *Brītō*), a

Briton. The transference of the F name for Brittany and Bretons to Britain and Britons points to a C origin: cf *Brythonic*, the adj of *Brython*, a collective pl for the British Celts, *Brython* being W and deriving from the OC name (? *\*Britto*, pl *\*Brittones*) that yields alike the OE *Bryttas* (and its adj *Bryttisc*) and the L *Brit(t)ō*. Important is the Gr name (c300 B.C.) *Prētanikai nēsoi*, British isles; the s of *Pretanikai* (adj suffix *-ikos*, cf E *-ic*) is *Pretan-*; the name answers to Ir *cruithin*, Picts, MIr *cruthen*, a Pict—cf OGa *cruithneach*, a Briton, for, as the late R. G. Collingwood remarks in *Roman Britain* (2nd ed., 1937), 'It can hardly be doubted . . . that the inhabitants of these islands . . . were called Pretani or Priteni'; *Pretani*, he says, must be identical with 'the old Welsh Priten, the "P" [Celtic] form, of which the corresponding "Q"-form is Cruithin, the name by which many Irish writers refer to the Picts';—*Picti* is a L translation;—it was, he points out, prob Caesar who, for *Pretani* and *Pretania* (Latinized forms of the C words), substituted *Britanni* and *Britannia*. The basic meaning of the name could be, as for W *Brython* it app is, 'the tumultuous, hence warriors'.

**brittle** derives from ME *britel* (var *brutel*), from OE *brēotan*, to break, akin to ON *brjōta*, to break, and OHG *brōdi*, fragile: the OE *brēot-* has 'thinned' to *brit-* and the *-le* is an adj suffix (cf L *fragilis* from *frangere*), the sense being 'easily broken, essentially breakable'.

**broach** (n and v) and **brooch; brocade,** n hence v; **brochure; broker, brokerage.**

1. *Brooch* (F *broche*) is historically identical with the similarly pronounced *broach*: *broach* (n) comes, through ME *broche*, from OF-F *broche*, from L of C origin; OF *broche* has derivative OF-F *brocher*, to stitch, whence E 'to *broach*'; the basic meaning is 'pointed head' of weapon or tool.

2. *Brocade*, a fabric with raised design, comes from Sp *brocado*, prob from ML *brocāre*, to prick, hence to figure (a textile), itself of same C origin as *broach*.

3. *Brochure* is F: from *brocher*, to stitch.

4. *Broker* derives from ME *brocour*, from ONF *brokeor* (OF *brocheor*), from ONF *brokier*, to broach: orig a broacher of wine casks, hence a retailer of wine.

5. The C r appears to have been *\*broc-*, a point (Malvezin).

**broad,** whence **broadness** (*-ness*); **broaden; abroad; breadth.**

1. *Abroad*=*a-*, on, in+*broad*: and *broad*, ME *brod*, earlier *brad*, derives from OE *brād*, akin to OFris (and OS) *brēd*, OHG-G *breit*, MD *breet* (D *breed*), ON *breithr*, Go *braiths* (neu *braid*): o.o.o.: IE r, ? *\*brādh-*, var *\*brēdh-*. 'To *broaden*' derives (suffix *-en*) from *broad*—cf OE *brāēdan*, OFris *brēda*, OS *brēdian*, ON *breitha*.

2. *Breadth* derives, through ME *bredethe*, earlier *brede* or *breede*, from OE *brāēdu*, from *brād*: cf OHG *breiti*, G *Breite*, from *breit*, and OFris *brēde*, from *brēd*.

**Brobdingnagian** is the adj of *Brobdingnag* (incorrectly *Brobdignag*), Swift's land of giants in *Gulliver's Travels* (1726). Contrast LILLIPUTIAN. (See P[3] for an essay on Swift's neologisms.)

**brocade.** See BROACH, para 2.

**brochure.** See BROACH, para 3.

**brock** (badger): OE *broc*, lit 'the speckled (beast)': cf Ir (and Ga) *breac*, OIr *brec*, variegated, freckled, piebald, and W *brech*, *brych*, Br *breac'h*, variegated-brown, and EIr *brocc*, Ir and Ga *broc*, Cor *brōch*, *brogh*, a badger; cf also W *brych*, a brindled brown.

**brogue** (1), stout shoe: an Irishism: Ir *brōg*, EIr *brōc*, a shoe, a hoof, prob from ON *brōk*, hose; cf, therefore, BREECHES.

**brogue** (2), a dial pron, esp the Ir pron of E: Ir *barrōg*, a hold or bond, e.g. on the tongue, hence a defective pron, hence the E sense: a mdfn of Ir *barra*, a bar, a hindrance: cf, therefore, BAR.

**broider, broidery; embroider, embroidery.**

*Embroidery* derives from 'to *embroider*' and *broidery*; *embroider*=*em-*, here merely int+*broider*; *broider* comes perh rather from OProv *broidar*, than from MF-F *broder* (OF *brosder*), prob from Frankish *\*brozdōn*: cf ON *broddr*, a spike, and therefore BRAD. F *broder* has derivative MF-F *broderie*, which prompted E *broidery* (suffix *-ery*).

**broil** (1), to char (by burning), hence cookery sense; ME *broilen*: OF *bruillir*, from—though perh influenced by OF *boillir*, to boil—OF *bruir*, to burn, from OGmc *bruëjen* (G *brühen*, to warm up): cf E BREED.

**broil** (2), to confuse, to entangle; hence n; **embroil, embroilment.**

1. 'To *broil*' comes from EF-F *brouiller*, MF *broueillier*, prob (B & W) from *brou*, mud, mire, influenced by such vv as *mouiller* and *souiller*; its MF-F prefix (*em-*, in) derivative *embrouiller* produces E *embroil*; the subsidiary EF-F *embrouillement* prob produces E *embroilment*, which may, however, derive, by suffix *-ment*, from *embroil*.

2. *Imbroglio*, an adoption from It, derives from It *imbrogliare*, cpd of *brogliare*, itself from the OProv form corresp to the OF v.

**broke; broken.** See BREAK.

**broker.** See BROACH, para 4.

**brolly.** See UMBRELLA.

**bromide**=*brom*ine+chem *-ide*; *bromine*=F *brom*e+the chem *-ine* of *chlorine*; and F *brome* comes from Gr *brōmos*, bad smell: see the element *brom(o)-*.

**bronchial; bronchitic, bronchitis:** Gr *bronkhos*, windpipe, s *bronkh-*, anglicized as *bronch-*+adj *-ial*; +*-itic*, adj of *-itis*, denoting disease or constitutional weakness: see the element *bronch(o)-*.

**bronco** (superior to **broncho**), a half-wild, smallish horse: elliptically from Sp *bronco*, wild, perh from L *broncus* (*bronchus*), var of *brochus*, *broccus*, (adj) projecting, hence (too) prominent, app of C origin (*\*broc-*, a sharp point).

**bronze,** n hence adj and v: adopted from EF-F: It *bronzo*: ML *bronzium* (var *brundium*): o.o.o.: perh Per *birindj*, for the alloy came to Europe from the East (B & W).

**brooch.** See BROACH.

**brood,** n, v (cf '*broody* hen'). See BREED.

**brook** (1), n: OE *brōc*; akin to OHG *bruoh*, MHG *bruoch*, G *Bruch*, LG *brōk*, a marsh, and D *broek*, MD *broec, broeke, brouc*, marshy ground: prob from the r of E BREAK, G *brechen*; a breach in a river bank causes a swamp. (Walshe.)

**brook** (2), v, to enjoy possession of, (hence) to make use of, (hence) to endure: ME *brucen, broken* (etc.), to use, to enjoy: OE *brūcan*, to enjoy, akin to OHG *bruhhan*, MHG *brūchen*, G *brauchen*, to use, to need, OFris *bruka*, OS *brūcan*, Go *brūkjan*, to use; distantly akin to L *frui*, to enjoy the use of, for *\*frugui*, cf *frūx*, fruit (for *\*frūgs*); Gmc r, *\*bhrūk-*; IE r, *\*bhrug(h)-*. (Walshe.)

**broom,** a shrub, hence a besom (orig a bundle of twigs): ME *brom, brome*: OE *brōm*: akin to G *Brombeere*, blackberry, OHG *brāmo*, brier, D *brem*, MD *brem, breme, bremme*: akin to BRISTLE (f.a.e.) and BUR.

**broth** comes straight down from OE: akin to MIr em*bruthe*, broth, and *bruith*, to boil, perh also OIr *broth*, corn (cf 'corn whisky'), Cor *brōs*, broth, W *broch*, froth, Manx *brott* (cf Ga *brot*), broth, and *broit*, boiled—to OHG-G *brōt*, ON *brauth*, bread, G *brodeln*, to bubble—L de*frūt*um, must boiled down (*de-*)—Gr *brut*on, a fermented beer: cf, therefore, BREW.

**brothel:** ME *brothel, brethel*, a whore, (but also and earlier) any vile person good for nothing, from *brothen*, pp of *brēothan*, to destroy, to go to ruin: *brothel house*, 'vile persons' house', displaced *bordel*, adopted from F *bordel*, dim from OF *borde*, a hut, from Gmc *\*bord* (see the 1st BOARD).

**brother,** old pl brethren (ME *bretheren*); brother-hood; brotherly (*brother*+adj *-ly*); brer (Brer Rabbit). See FRATER, para 6—and para 1.

**brougham** commemorates Lord *Brougham* (1778–1868).

**brought.** See BRING.

**brow:** ME *browe*, earlier *bruwe*: OE *brū*, akin to ON *brūn*, OIr,*forbru* (acc pl), OSl *brŭvĕ*, Skt *bhrū*. (The G *Braue* is unrelated.)

**brown** (adj hence n), **brownie; Bruin; brunette, burnet; burnish,** v hence n; **prunella.**

1. A *brownie* or good-natured goblin (whence *Brownie*, a Girl Guide of 8–11) is so named from its tawny colour: *brown*+dim *-ie*: the Ga *bruinidh* (pron *broony*) is merely a rough trln of *brownie*. *Brown*, ME *broun*, earlier *brun*, derives from OE *brūn*, akin to OFris, OS, OHG, MHG *brūn* (G *braun*); to ON *brūnn*; perh to Gr *phrunē*, a toad; certainly to the Skt redup ba*bhrūš*, brown (hence, a beaver): IE r, *\*bhru-*; cf the var *ber-* in BEAR, n.

2. *Bruin* the bear derives from D *bruin*, brown, so named from his colour: cf BEAR, n.

3. *Brunette* (adj hence n)=the f of OF-F *brunet*, dim of OF-F *brun* (f *brune*), brown, from OHG *brun*. The derivative MF n *brunete* has metathesis *burnete*, whence ME-E *burnet*, a brown woollen fabric, hence several brown-hued plants.

4. 'To *burnish*' comes, via ME *burnischen*, earlier *burnissen*, from OF-MF *burnir*, metathesis of OF-F *brunir*, to render *brun* or brown, hence, to polish: cf MHG *briunen*, to render brown, to polish; *burnishment*='to *burnish*'+suffix *-ment*.

5. The old med term *prunella*, thrush (the disease), angina, is a Sci L var of *brunella*, Mod L dim of ML *brunus*, brown, from MHG *brūn* (para 1); *brunella* was suggested by G *Bräune*, quinsy (lit, brownness). The plant *Prunella* was formerly supposed to cure quinsy. But *prunella*, a sloe-coloured woollen fabric, comes from F *prunelle*, dim of PRUNE (a plum), q.v.

**browse.** 'To *browse*' comes from MF *brouster* (OF *bruster*; F *brouter*), from MF *broust* (OF *brost*), a sprout, a shoot, of Gmc origin: cf OS *brustian*, to sprout: basic meaning, 'to swell' (IE *\*bhreus-*), therefore cf BREAST. *Browse*, young shoots, hence such fodder, prob comes from MF *broust*; but *browse*, an act of browsing, clearly derives from 'to *browse*'.

**Bruin.** See BROWN, para 2.

**bruise,** v hence n and the agential **bruiser.** 'To *bruise*' derives, through ME *brusen* (var *brisen*), from OE *brȳsan*, to bruise, influenced by OF-MF *bruisier*, to break into small pieces, to shiver, of C origin: cf MIr *brúim*, I crush, smash, bruise, Ga *brooth* (pron *broo*), to bruise, Cor *brew*, (pp) bruised; the C r is prob *\*brug-*, I break.

**bruit,** n hence v: adopted from OF-F *bruit*, from the v *bruire*: VL *\*brūgere*, itself either from C *\*brug-*, to make a noise, or from L *rūgīre*, to roar+VL *\*bragere*, to cry out (cf 1st BRAY).

**brunette.** See BROWN, para 3.

**brunt,** a blow (hence its force), an assault (hence its impact or shock): ME *brunt* is app akin to OE *brūnetha*, heat, ON *bruni*, a torch, therefore cf BRAND.

**brush** (1), n and v.

*Brush*, a čleaning device, ME *brusshe*, comes from OF-MF *broisse* (F *brosse*), perh of Gmc origin: cf OHG *bursta* (MHG *borst*, G *Borste*), a bristle, ult akin to Skt *bhṛštiš*, a point. 'To *brush*', ME *bruschen, brusshen*, derives from the ME n. Cf, however, the more prob origin in:

**brush** (2), lopped branches of trees, hence **brushwood.** ME *brusche*: OF *broche, broce, brouce* (etc.) —cf MF-F *brosse, broussaille*—perh from the r occurring in F *bruyère*, heather, q.v. at BRIER. The OF n has derivative MF-F *brosser*, orig to dash through brushwood or underbrush, whence ME *bruschen*, to rush, whence 'to *brush* (usu *off*)', to hurry off; hence, *brush*, a skirmish. B & W derive both OF nn from the one source, with primary sense 'brush(wood)', secondary 'a *brush* or cleaning device'; the earliest brushes being made, not of bristles but of leaves and twigs; they derive *broce*, etc., from VL *\*bruscia*, a collection of shoots, from *bruscum*, woody excrescence on a maple tree, a post-Classical L word of app C origin, prob from the r of BROWSE.

**brusque, brusquerie; brisk, brisken, briskness.**

1. *Brusquerie*, EF-F, derives (cf the E suffix *-ery*) from MF-F *brusque*: and F *brusque* comes from It *brusco*, rough (of manner), abrupt, from L

*bruscum* or *bruscus*, the plant named butcher's-broom (very rough). 'It seems that there has been a confusion between *bruscum* (*brustum*) and *rūscus* (*rūstum*) [holly] and perh also *\*brūcus*' (E & M)—cf BRIER.

2. *Brisk*, whence *brisken* (v suffix *-en*) and *briskness* (*-ness*), is perh a thinned form of *brusque*, but prob of C origin: cf EIr *brisc*, Ga *brisg*, brittle, fragile, and Br *bresk*, brittle, (also) brusque: *\*brec-*, *\*breg-*, and *\*bric-*, *\*brig-*, are app thinned forms of C *\*brac-*, *\*brag-* (and *\*brad-*), to break, akin to the *\*frag-* of L *frangere* (nasalized; cf *frēgi*, I have broken).

**brutal**, whence **brutality** and **brutalize**; **brute**, adj hence n.

*Brutal*, unless from LL *brutālis*, = *brute* + adj *-al*; *brute* comes from MF *brute*, later differentiated as *brut*, m, and *brute*, f from L *brūtus*, f *brūta*, heavy, stupid, unreasoning, as in 'the *brute* creation', prob of Oscan origin: cf Lett *grūts*, L *grauis* (s *grau-*), heavy; IE r, app *\*b(h)ru-*, var *\*g(h)ru-*, prob cf Skt *gurús*, heavy, and perh the syn Gr *barus*.

**bryology**. See the element *bryo-*, whence also **bryony**.

**Brythonic**. See BRITAIN.

**bubby**. See BEVER.

**bubble**, n and v; adj, hence n, **bubbly;—burble**.

*Burble*, to speak confusedly and pointlessly, imperfectly blends *bubble* and *gurgle*. A *bubble* derives from ME *bobel*, or *boble*, akin to MD *bobbel* (also D) and *bubbel* and Sw *bubbla*; to *bubble* derives from late ME *buble*, *bobel*, akin to MLG *bubbeln*, MHG *brodelen*. The *-le* (*-el*) is freq; the r, prob echoic.

**buccan; buccaneer.**

A *buccan*, or grid for grilling or drying meat, comes from EF-F *boucan*, from SAmerind *bocan*, a grill for either smoking or drying meat; the derivative EF-F v *boucaner* yields 'to *buccan*', grill (meat) thus; and *boucaner* has late EF-F agent *boucanier*, one who does this, whence E *buccaneer* (cf suffix *-eer*), applied first to F settlers in Haiti, then to the Caribbean pirates, who subsisted largely upon buccan.

**buck** (1), beech. See BEECH, para 3.

**buck** (2), lye. See BEECH, para 3.

**buck** (3), male deer: ME *buk, bucke*: OE *buc, bucca*, a he-goat, app of C origin: cf OIr *bocc*, Ga *boc*, he-goat, roe-buck, Cor *bŏc(k)*, *bocca* (etc.), W *boch*, Br *bouc'h*, he-goat; the OC word would be *\*buccos*, lit '(the beast) that flees', from *\*buc-*, to flee, answering to L *fug-* in *fugere*. Cf:

**buck** (4), Am sl for a dollar: o.o.o., but prob from *buck*, a counter used in poker (whence *pass the buck*: Mathews), this counter usu being, at least orig, a *buck*-knife, a knife made with a handle of *buck*-horn.

**buck** (5), to leap abruptly, plungingly: from BUCK (3), the lit sense being 'to leap like a buck', cf Ga *boc*.

**buckaroo**. See VACCENIC (heading).

**buck mate, buck Negro**, etc. *Buck* is here an adj from BUCK (3).

**bucket**: ME *bucket*: AF *buket*, *buquet*, a dim from OE *būc*, a pitcher, any (water-) vessel, the belly, akin to OFris *būk*, OHG *būh*, MHG *buch*, G *Bauch*, belly, and ON *būkr*, belly, body: Gmc r, *\*būk-*; IE r, *\*bhug-*. (Walshe.)

**buckeye** is a plant with a seed like a buck's eye.

**buckle** (1), n and v; **buckler.**

A *buckler*, or shield with boss, ME *bocler*, comes from OF *boucler* (MF-F *bouclier*), itself from OF-MF *bocle*, MF-F *boucle*, the boss of a shield, whence, via ME *bocle*, the E *buckle*, with sense-adaptation; also from OF-MF *bocle* comes ME *boclen*, whence 'to *buckle*'. Now, OF *bocle* derives from L *buccula*, little cheek (or mouth), dim of *bucca*, a cheek, a shield's boss, a boss or knob resembling a cheek; *bucca* is prob C.

**buckle** (2), to bend more or less permanently: either from late MF-F *boucler* (from the n *boucle*— see prec), esp in the sense '(of a wall) to bulge', as OED holds, or, as a freq (*-le*), from MD *bucken* (var *bocken*; D *bukken*), to bow (vi), akin to the 3rd BOW, as Webster prefers, and so do I.

**buckler**. See 1st BUCKLE.

**buckram**: ME *bukeram*, *buckram* (later *bokeram*): OF-EF *boquerant*; prop *bo(u)queran* (? adj as n), cf Sp *bucarán* and It *bucherame*: Per *Bukhārā*, *Bukhara*, E usu *Bokhara*, where this fine linen was orig manufactured. *Bukhārā* was app so named from the ancient Buddhist monastery—Skt *vihāra* —situated nearby; through the Turco-Mongolian form *bukhar*. (Enci It.)

**buckwheat**. See BEECH, para 3.

**bucolic**: L *būcolicus*: Gr *boukolikos*, orig 'of a *boukolos* or cowherd', from *bous*, an ox (cf BOVINE and, f.a.e., COW); the 2nd element = *\*kolos*, akin to L *colere* (s *col-*), to cultivate—here, one who tends cows, not crops. (Hofmann.)

**bud** (n hence v) derives from ME *budden*, akin to MD *bote*, *botte*, D *bot*, a bud—to MHG *butzen* (s *but-*), to swell—perh also MLG *budel*, a purse (G *Beutel*): basic idea, 'a swelling': IE r, *\*bhu-*, to swell.

**Buddha**, whence **Buddhism** and **Buddhist**: Skt *buddha*, awakened, hence aware, hence enlightened, of same r as *bodhati*, he awakes, hence becomes aware, hence understands.

**budge**, to move slightly, hence n: OF-F *bouger*, to stir: VL *\*bullicāre*, vi, to boil and bubble: L *bullīre*, to boil, from *bulla*, a bubble: cf BOIL.

**budgerigar** is an Aus aboriginal word.

**budget**, n hence v. See BULGE.

**buff** (1), a superior leather, derives from obs *buff*, earlier *buffe*, a buffalo, the first buff having been prepared from buffalo hide: f.a.e., BUFFALO. Hence, 'to *buff*', polish with a buff.

**buff** (2), a buffet: OF *buffe*: f.a.e., BUFFET. 'To *buff*' or strike: OF *buffer*, from *buffe*.

**buffalo**: It *buffalo*, var of *bufalo* (cf Port *búfalo*): L *būfalus*, var of *būbalus*: Gr *boubalos*, orig 'N African antelope', later 'buffalo', from *bous*, ox (cf BOVINE and, f.a.e., COW), *boubalos* being orig an adj 'of, for, like an ox' (cf L *būbulus*), and ult, though remotely, akin to Skt *gavalas*, wild buffalo (Boisacq).

**buffer.** See:

**buffet** (1) derives, through ME, from MF *buffet*, a slap, dim of OF-EF *buffe*, a blow: prob echoic (cf PUFF). 'To *buffet*', ME *buffeten*, derives from MF *buffeter*, from *buffet*. E *buffer* derives from either of the two vv BUFF, qq.v.; the sense 'fellow', usu 'old *buffer*', derives prob from *buff*, to strike, but perh from cant *buffer*, a dog—cf the fig use of *dog*.

**buffet** (2), a sideboard, now often one set with food: adopted from OF-F: usu, by E philologists, said to be o.o.o., but B & W mention that OF *buffet*, like OProv *bufet*, denotes both 'a sort of table' and, earlier, 'a box (on the ear)', and add, 'Perhaps the word became the designation of a piece of furniture because the latter was, orig, furnished with a board that one could lower'—(presumably) with a smart tap or with the sound of a slap.

**buffoon, buffoonery.**

The latter, deriving (by suffix *-ery*) from the former, was prompted by EF-F *bouffonnerie*, itself from EF-F *bouffon*, whence E *buffoon*: and F *bouffon* comes from It *buffone*, prob from *buffa*, a rough joke, a fooling-about, a jape, but perh from the intimately cognate *buffare*, to play the fool, to puff out one's cheeks: echoic (cf PUFF). The operatic *buffo* merely shortens *buffone* (Prati).

**bug**, goblin; **bugbear.** See BOGEY.—As coll for 'insect', a 'creepy-crawly' form of life, it derives from the basic sense 'goblin'.

**bugger, buggery; Bulgar** (n), **Bulgaria** (Byz Gr *Boulgaria*), whence **Bulgarian**, adj hence n.

*Buggery* comes from MF-EF *bougrerie*, (MF) heresy, (EF) sodomy, from MF-F *bougre* (OF *bogre*), whence E *bugger*; or so the dictt tell us. I prefer to derive *buggery* from MD *buggerie*, and *bugger* from MD *bugger*. The OF *bogre*, MF-F *bougre*, and MD *bugger* derive, the former from ML *Bulgarus*, a Bulgar, hence a heretic and, by lay slander, a sodomite, the latter from the 'eased' ML forms *Bugarus* (s *Bugar-*) and esp *Bugerus* (s *Buger-*): by b/f from C6 LL *Bulgari*, the Bulgars (Tatars, settling in what became *Bulgaria*): from C5 Byz Gr *Boulgaroi*, Bulgars, a name akin to the river *Volga*, itself perh a confusion of Tatar *Ethil* or *Itil* and Gr *Rha*. (Enci It.)

**buggy**, a light carriage: 'o.o.o.' is the usual verdict; but perh *buggy* is simply *bogey* influenced by *bug*, insect, from the 'spidery' appearance of its framework.

**bugle** (1), musical instrument, whence **bugler**: OF-MF *bugle*: L *būculus*, a young ox, dim of *bos*, an ox (cf BOVINE and, f.a.e., COW): orig 'buffalo', then 'hunter's horn', used orig in the hunting of buffaloes.

**bugle** (2), plant, whence **bugleweed**: MF-F *bugle*; LL *bugula* (var *bugillo*): o.o.o., but perh of same origin as (1)—cf the plant *bugloss*, lit 'ox's tongue'.

**build** (pt, pp **built**): a compromise between the two predominant ME forms *bulden, bilden*: OE

*byldan*, from *bold* (var *botl*), a house, akin to OFris *bold*, house, and *-belda*, to build, to ON *bōl*, farm, farmhouse, abode, and to OSw *bol, bole*, dwelling, house: prob from the OGmc r present in ON *būa*, to dwell. Derivatives: *builder, building*.

**bulb**, with adjj **bulbar** (*bulb+-ar*) and **bulbous** (L *bulbōsus*): L *bulbus*: Gr *bolbos*, app a redup of r *bol-*, akin to the *bul-* of L *bulla*, a bubble. Cf the 1st BULL.

**Bulgar, Bulgarian,** etc. See BUGGER.

**bulge**, n hence v and pa **bulging**, and adj **bulgy; budget**, n hence v and the adj **budgetary** (*-ary*).

*Budget*, a wallet (or sack), hence its contents, esp if monetary, comes from OF *bougette*, a small bag, a wallet, dim of OF *boge, bouge*, from L *bulga*, a leather bag, of Gaul origin: cf the Ga *bolg*, bag, belly, and *bolgach*, bulging, bulgy—the EIr *bolg*, bag—Manx *bolg*, belly—perh Cor *bolitho*, a large belly—certainly Br *bolc'h*, a pod, and W *bol*, bag, belly, bulge: C r, *\*bolg-*, var of *\*balg-, \*balc-*, to swell, to be large (Malvezin). OF *boge* or *bouge* has var *boulge*, whence ME-E *bulge*.

**bulk** (1), n hence v and the adj **bulky**: ME *bulke, bolke*: ON *bulki*, cargo (cf 'to break *bulk*'), heap, akin to ON *böllr*, a ball, a globe: basic idea, 'to swell', therefore cf BALL (1) and BOLD.

**bulk** (2), as in *bulkhead*, is akin to—almost a var of—BALK.

**bull** (1), a seal, hence a papal letter sealed with a bulla, derives from ME *bulle*, from ML *bulla*, seal, hence document, from L *bulla*, air bubble, hence seal: *bulla*, prob imitative, is either echoic, like BUBBLE or, as E & M hold, pictorial for a round protuberance, like Gr *bolthos*, onion, bulb, and E BULB.

2. L, hence It, *bulla*, leads to the It dim *bulletta*, which acquires its own dim *bullettino*, whence EF-F, hence E, *bulletin*. Cf the 3rd BILL.

**bull** (2), male corresp to **cow**; whence **bulldog, bulldoze, bullfrog, bull(-)headed, bull's-eye,** etc.

*Bull* derives from ME *bule* from OE *bula*, bull, with extension *bulloc*, whence *bullock*; akin to ON *boli*, MD and MLG *bulle*, bull; to OSw *bulin*, swollen; to OIr *ball*, ? Mx *bwoid*, penis; perh also to OHG *ballo*, MHG *balle*, a ball (sphere), L *follis* (s *fol-*), bellows, and Gr *phallos* (s *phal-*), penis (cf PHALLIC): the basic idea and the IE r are 'to swell', IE *\*bhel-*.

**bullet** represents a blending of MF-F *boulet*, cannon ball, and EF-F *boulette*, a small ball, dimm of MF-F *boule*, ball (sphere), from L *bulla*, q.v. at 1st BULL.

**bulletin.** See 1st BULL, para 2.

**bullion**: a C15 loan from MD *bulioen*, varr *bolioen* and esp *billioen*: MF-F *billon*, an ingot, a modification of OF-F *bille*, a round stick: f.a.e., the 2nd BILLET.

**bullock.** See the 2nd BULL.

**bully** (1), meat: F *bouilli*, boiled beef, *boullli* being prop the pp of *bouillir*, to BOIL.

**bully** (2), orig 'good or dear fellow' (whence the adj *bully*, excellent), then a blusterous browbeater: D *boel*, brother, friend, lover, MD *boele*: MHG *buole*, relative, friend (G *Buhle*, paramour): prob cf Lett *bāleninš*, little brother: o.o.o.; sense-influenced by 2nd BULL. (Walshe.)

**bulrush.** See 1st BOLE.

**bulwark; boulevard.**

Both words, the former directly, the latter through EF-F, come from MLG *bolwerk* (cf MD *bolwerc, bollewerc*, D *bolwerk*), lit 'stem-work': f.a.e., the 1st BOLE and WORK.

**bum** (1), n and v: echoic: a var of the 2nd BOOM. This may form the origin of:

**bum** (2), the behind: see prec; perh, however, the ME *bom* comes from D dial *bom*, for D *bodem*, the behind (cf BOTTOM).

**bum** (3), n and v: a *bum* or tramp shortens the syn G *Bummler*, from *bummeln*, to loaf, to wander, whence 'to bum'; *bum*, worthless, derives from the n.

**bumble,** n and v. The n derives from *bumble*, v, ME *bumblen*, prob a freq of *bum*, to hum: cf the 2nd BOOM.

**bumblebee.** See HUMBLEBEE.

**bumboat.** See BEAM, para 2. Cf:

**bumkin** (nautical). See BEAM, para 2.

**bump** (v hence n and the agent **bumper**): echoic (sound upon impact): cf the equally echoic *thump*, v and n. Adj: *bumpy*.

**bumpkin,** (1) a spar, (2) a rural lout. See BEAM, s.f.

**bumptious,** obtusely pert: *bump*+presump*tious* (illiterate for *presumptuous*).

**bun,** formerly often *bunn*: the shape of the round, raised, sweetened bread-confection leads to *bun* of hair: and the edible *bun* derives from ME *bunne*, var *bonne*, prob of C origin: cf Ga *bonnach*, var *bannach*, Sc *bannock*, also MF *buigne*, F *beignet*, a fritter: the basic idea is app 'a swelling', hence a 'swollen' confection.

**bunch,** n hence v and the adj **bunchy; bunk** (bed, esp nautical).

The common idea is 'pile, heap', e.g. of bed-clothes; *bunk* is a doublet of *bunch*, ME *bunche*, but comes direct from the Scan origin of *bunche*: OSw *bunke* or ON *bunki*, heap, pile; the former also denotes 'boarding', a sense formative in *bunk*.

**buncombe,** insincere speech—hence insincere talk, hence nonsense; in C20 usu **bunkum**, whence, by abbr, **bunk**: *Buncombe*, that county in North Carolina which was represented (1819–21) by Felix Walker; persisting in a long-winded speech, he said that his electors expected him to 'make a speech for Buncombe'. (Webster.)

**bund,** association; **bundle.** See BIND, para 2.

**bung,** n hence v: MD *bunge* (var *bonge*, as in D): MHG *bunde*: MF-F *bonde*, of C origin: cf OIr *bond*, Ir and Ga *bonn*, W *bon*, base, sole of foot— Mx *bong*, bung—and perh Cor *bēn*, base.

**bungalow:** Hindi *bangla*, Bengali: elliptical for '(house, characteristic) of Bengal'.

**bungle** is app of Scan origin: cf OSw *bunga*, to strike (cf BANG), and *bangla*, to work inefficiently: ? a phonetic blend, with sense predominantly from *bangla*.

**bunk** (1), nautical bed. See BUNCH.

**bunk** (2), nonsense. See BUNCOMBE.

**bunker,** a large bin or chest, hence a small sand-pit (hence, in golf): Sc *bunker*, var *bunkart*, a bench, a chest serving as seat: akin to BENCH.

**bunkum.** See BUNCOMBE.

**bunny,** pet-name for a rabbit, is a dim of Sc and N dial *bun*, rabbit, itself from *bun*, rabbit's tail, of C origin: cf Ga and EIr *bun*, stump, and derivative Ga *bunabhas*, buttock; OC *\*bonu-* (MacLennan).

**bunt** (1), middle part of net or sail; hence **bunt-line** (cf LINE), a special rope: cf MHG *bunt* (G *Bund*), and esp MD *bont*, a bundle.

**bunt** (2), to butt, hence n: o.o.o.; app echoic and perh influenced by Sc and N dial *bunt*, tail of rabbit or hare, var of *bun* (as at BUNNY), from butting with one's rear: cf SHUNT.

**bunting,** occ **buntine,** flags collectively, derives from *bunting*, that thin woollen material from which flags are made: ME *bontin*, to sift (whence E dial *bunt*, to sift), this material having perh been used for sifting meal.

**buntline.** See the 1st BUNT.

**bunyip** is an adoption from an Aus aboriginal language.

**buoy,** n hence v; **buoyant, buoyancy.**

*Buoyancy*=*buoyant*+suffix *-cy*; *buoyant* derives from *buoy*, v, as if from a F presp; a *buoy* comes from MD *boeie*, from OF-MF *boie, buie*, a chain, hence—because held by a chain—a buoy, of Gmc origin: cf OHG *bouhhan*, MHG *bouchen*, OS *bōkan*, OFris *bāken*, E BEACON, q.v.

**bur** or **burr**, prickly cone, etc., of plant: ME *burre, borre*, burdock (itself=*bur*+ the *dock* plant): OSw *borra*, burdock, thistle. Cf the 2nd BURR.

**burble.** See BUBBLE.

**burden** (1), n hence v and the adj **burdensome** (suffix *-some*); **burthen,** survival of a ME spelling, along with late ME *burden* and early *birthen*, from OE *byrthen*, akin to Go *baúrthei*, OHG *burdi*, MHG-G *bürde*: from the r of 'to BEAR' (OE *beran*).

**burden** (2), in music: influenced by prec, but from ME *burdoun*: MF-F *bourdon*, the bass in music: ML *burdō*, bumblebee, o/s *burdōn-*, of echoic origin.

**burdock.** See BUR.

**bureau; bureaucrat, -cratic, -cracy; burlesque,** adj hence n and v.

*Burlesque*, adopted from EF-F, comes from It *burlesco*, adj of *burla*, jest, joke, mockery, ? from VL *\*burrula*, a flock of wool, dim of LL *burra*, shaggy garment, (orig) coarse hair, perh elliptical for *lana burra*, from *burrus*, ruddy, from the syn Gr *purros*, from *pur*, fire (cf FIRE). Now, LL *burra* has app a VL var *\*būra*, whence OF-F *bure*, with OF-MF dim *burel* (suffix *-el*), woollen fabric, adopted by E (now obs), whence OF-F *bureau*, a coarse woollen cloth, used for covering tables; hence, a desk; hence, an office; whence E *bureau*, (mostly) office. The F word has three notable derivatives: *bureaucrate*, whence E *bureaucrat* (cf the element *-crat*, as in ARISTOCRAT); *bureaucratie*, whence *bureaucracy*; and *bureaucratique*, whence *bureaucratic*.

**burg.** See BOROUGH.

**burgeon.** See BURLY.

**burgess; burgh, burgher.** See BOROUGH.

**burglar, burglary; burgle.** See BOROUGH, para 6.

**burgomaster.** See BOROUGH, para 2.

**Burgundy**, the wine, comes from this ancient province of France, from ML *Burgundia*, from L *Burgundii*, an ancient Gmc tribe, a var of *Burgundiōnes*, earlier *Burgodiōnes*, which suggests the same Gmc origin as that of *burg*, q.v. at BOROUGH; *Burgundiōnes* may have prompted the n *Burgundian*; the adj *Burgundian* derives rather from *Burgundia*. The F form *Bourgignons* led to the head-armour called *burgonet*.

**burial.** See *bury* at BOROUGH (para 5).

**burlesque.** See BUREAU.

**burly**, whence **burliness; burgeon**, n hence v (perh from the OF-F v), with F var **bourgeon.**

A *burgeon*, bud, derives from ME *burgen*, earlier *burjon*, adopted from OF-MF *burjon* (F *bourgeon*), prob of Gmc origin: cf esp OHG *burjan*, to raise, itself akin to OHG *burlih*, lofty, excellent, OE *borlīce*, excellently, eminently, whence prob ME *borlich*, late ME *burly*, taken over by E. OGmc forms are clearly akin to Go *baíran*, to carry—usually one raises before one carries—and therefore to E 'to BEAR'.

**burn** (1), a brook. See the 1st BOURN.

**burn** (2), to be, to cause to be, on fire, v hence n: pt **burned**, pp **burnt.**

'To *burn*' derives from ME *bernen* (var *brennen*), vt, confused with ME *beornen* or *birnen*, vi, themselves from OE *baernan* or *bernan*, vt, and *beornan*, vi: cf the merely app metathetic varr in the OGmc cognates, e.g. OFris *barna*, *berna*, esp *burna*, OS and OHG *brennian*, vt, OHG *brinnan*, vi, Go *brannjan*, vt, and *brinnan*, vi, ON *brenna*, vt, and *brinna*, vi: perh akin to the Ir r *brenn-*, to gush forth; cf also Skt *bhurati*, it quivers or flickers. Cf BRAND.

**burnet.** See BROWN, para 3.

**burnish.** See BROWN, para 4.

**burnous**, occ **burnoose**: F *burnous*, with EF varr *bernus*, *bernous*, *barnusse*: Ar *burnus*: Gr *burros*, var of *birros* (L *birrus*), a kind of cloak. Both F *beret* and It *biretta* come from the same IE r. Cf BERET.

**burp** (of a child) is, like **gurk**, varr **gherk**, **ghurk** (of an adult), purely and excellently echoic.

**burr** (1), of plant. See BUR.

**burr** (2), of speech: n hence v: of same origin as prec: *bur* of plant, hence numerous mechanical devices (usu *burr*), hence the noise made by several of them, hence that rough or whirring-hum pron, the trilled *r*; Webster, however, derives the final sense from a '*bur* in the throat' (cf, sem, 'frog in the throat').

**burro** comes straight from Sp, which 'shortens' it from *borrico*, ass, itself from LL *burricus*, *buricus*, *bur(r)ichus*, a small or inferior horse, a pony, a nag, perh (E & M) from Tacitus's *Buri* (Gr *Bouroi*), a German tribe: 'the *Buric* beast'.

Malvezin, however, derives it from Gaul *burs* (or *bors*), var of *bars*, height, (whence) physical strength: 'the *strong* beast': cf EIr *borr*, puffed (up), proud, Ir *borr*, proud, strong, Ga *borr*, pride, words derived by MacLennan from OC *\*borsos*, strong.

**burrow**, n, v. See BOROUGH, para 3.

**bursar, bursary.** See PURSE, para 2.

**burst**, n, v. As 'injury, damage', the n derives from OE *byrst*, loss, failure, crash, akin to OHG *brust* and, of course, to OE *berstan*, whence, via ME *bersten* (var *bresten*), the E 'to *burst*'. Akin to OE *berstan* (impf pl *burston*) are, e.g., OFris *bersta*, to burst, break, also to fail; OHG *brestan*, MHG *bresten* and *bersten*, G *bersten*; OS *brestan*; MD *bersten* (also D), *barsten*, *borsten*; ON *bresta*; OIr *brissim*, I break. The OGmc *barst-*, *berst-*, *borst-* forms are metatheses for *brast-*, *brest-* forms; and the IE r is app *\*bhrest-*, with varr *\*bhrast-*, *\*bhrost-*. Cf G *brechen*, E 'to BREAK'.

**bury.** See BOROUGH, paras 5–6.

**bus** shortens *omnibus*, 'a carriage that is *for all*' (L *omnibus*).

**busby**: o.o.o.: ? from a PN (manufacturer or first notable wearer).

**bush**, a (thick) shrub, hence a thicket, hence an uncleared piece of country, hence, in Aus, the outback; **boscage, bosky.**

1. *Boscage*, ME *boskage*, comes from OF-MF *boscage*, *boschage*, a grove, from ML *boscus*, whose It shape *bosco* has dim *boschetto*, whence EF-F *bosquet*, adopted by E with var *bosket*, a thicket, whence, by abbr, the syn *bosk*, whence the adj *bosky*, bushy, wooded.

2. ML *boscus* prob originated both OHG *busc* (MHG and G *busch*) and MD *busch* (var *bussche* and, as in D, *bosch*); ME *busch* (var *busk*), whence E *bush*, prob comes from the MD *busch* rather than from OHG or MHG. Now, the ML *boscus* either derives from or is very intimately related to Gr *boskē*, pasture (as Walshe proposes), cf *boskein* (s *bosk-*), to graze (vt).

**bushel**: ME *buschel*, *boischel*: OF-MF (presumed) and OProv *boissel*, dim (-*el*) of OF-MF (presumed) and EF (recorded) *boisse*, a grain-measure, of C origin: cf Ga *bas*, occ *bois*, palm of hand, concave side of a club, OIr *bass* (dat *boiss*), Mx *bass*, palm of hand: OC etymon *\*bostā*. (B & W; MacLennan.)

**business.** See BUSY.

**busk** (1) of corset: var (It *busco*) of BUST, n.

**busk** (2), to seek, hence to seek to provide entertainment, whence *busker*, singer (etc.) in public-house or to a theatre queue: EF-F *busquer*, to seek: Sp *buscare*, to search (the woods): ? ult a parallel to BUSH.

**busk** (3). See BUSTLE.

**buskin**: app a slovened borrowing of MD *hroseken* (o.o.o.), a small shoe, perh via MF *brosequin*.

**bust** (1), n: EF-F *buste*: It *busto*: ? L *bustum*, a tomb (orig, a—usu, shaped—log of wood): from the busts often set over tombs (B & W).

**bust** (2) n and v: coll and dial form of BURST. Hence the AE *buster*, gay fellow, hence merely voc.

**bustard** blends OF *bistarde*, a bustard, prob (DAF) for *\*vistarde*, from ML *avis* (L *auis*) *tarda*, lit 'slow bird'+the MF doublet *oustarde* (F *outarde*), from L *auis* (ML *avis*) *tarda*, prob (B & W) via Gaul L *\*austarda*. This kind of tautology does occur.

**bustle**, v hence n. 'To *bustle*' derives from EE *buskle*, a freq (*-le*) of the obs *busk*, to make oneself ready, itself, via ME *busken*, from ON *būask*, vr from *būa*, to prepare, (orig) to dwell: cf the 2nd BOWER. From a person *bustling* (moving fussily) along, derives the *bustle* worn beneath a woman's skirt.

**busy**, whence the v 'to *busy*', the adv **busily** (*-ly*), the n **business** (*-ness*), derives from ME *busi*, var *bisi*, from OE *bysig*, var *bisig*, akin to MD *besech*, *besich*, D *bezig*, LG *besig*, o.o.o: Cf OFris *bisgia*, to use, and OE *bysgian*, *bisgian*, to occupy or employ: IEr, *\*bes-*, var *\*bis-*, perh orig echoic.

2. Hence *pidgin* (further corrupted to *pigeon*), elliptical for *pidgin English*, a Chinese-coast and China Sea lingua franca, *pidgin* being a Ch attempt at *business*. Cf 'That's not my *pigeon*', not my business nor my concern.

**but**, conj, is elliptical for *but that*, lit 'without, (hence) except for, that', and therefore derives from the prep *but*, itself deriving, via ME *bute*, earlier *buten*, earliest *butan*, outside (of), without, except, from OE *būtan* (cf OFris *būta*), on the outside of, outside, without, except, orig an adv, outside, besides: *be-*, by+*ūtan*, outwards, without, itself an extension of the adv *ūt*, from the interior to or towards the exterior: therefore see BY, prep, and OUT.

**butcher**, n hence v; **butchery**.

The latter, orig a slaughterhouse, derives from ME *bocherie*, shambles, from OF-MF *bocherie*, MF-F *boucherie*, slaughterhouse, from OF-MF *bouchier*, var *bochier* (MF-F *boucher*), perh (Webster) from ML *buc*- in *bucida*, *bucola*, a cattle-slayer, from Gr *bouthytēs*, a sacrificer of oxen (Gr *bous*, L *bōs*, an ox: cf BOVINE); Dauzat and B & W prefer to derive OF-MF *bouchier*, MF-F *boucher*, 'vendor of goat-flesh', from OF-F *bouc*, he-goat, itself from Gaul *\*bucco-*: cf OIr *bocc*, he-goat, and see the 3rd BUCK.

**butler**. See BOTTLE, para 3.

**butt** (1), a cask. See BOTTLE, para 2.

**butt** (2), the thicker end, e.g. a buttock, stump, handle: ME *but*, *butte*, where the *but*- is prob that of OE *buttuc*, end, end-piece, whence ME *buttoke*, rump, whence E *buttock*, the *-uc* being app the dim suffix OE *-uc*, E *-ock*, cf OE *bealluc*, E *ballock*, a testicle (? orig a bull's), now vulgar—cf the 1st BALL (and the s, ? coll, *balls*, testicles). Even in ME and indeed in OF, there has been a certain confusion, caused by F *but*, goal, and *bout*, end, of Gmc origin: cf BUTTE.

**butt** (3), to thrust at, to push, esp with head or horns or rump: ME *butten*: OF-MF *boter* (MF-F *bouter*), to strike, to push, of Gmc origin: cf MD

*boten*, and esp ON *bauta*, to strike. The word has been influenced by the 2nd BUTT. A *butt* with the head drives from the v BUTT. Cf BUTTON.

**butte**, a lone, steep-sided hill: MF-F *butte*, var of MF-F *but*, goal, boundary: akin to the 2nd BUTT.

**butter**, n, whence the adj—not the n—**buttery** and the v 'to *butter*': ME *butter*, earlier *butere*: OE *butere* or, in cpds, *buttor*-: L *butyrum*: Gr *bouturon*, butter: *bous*, cow (cf BOVINE)+*turos*, cheese, cf the element *tyro-*. (The OGmc and Scythian etymologies are unconvincing.)

2. The *butterfly*, OE *buterflēge*, *buttor-flēoge*, was prob so named because a common species is yellow: 'the yellow flier'.

**buttery**, n. See BOTTLE, para 2, s.f.

**buttock**. See the 2nd BUTT.

**button**, n and v. The n derives from ME *bouton*: OF-MF *boton* (F *bouton*), orig a bud, very soon the 'bud' of a garment, a button: from OF-MF *boter* (F *bouter*), orig to strike, thrust, push, then to bud: f.a.e., the 3rd BUTT. 'To *button*' comes, via ME *botonen*, from OF-MF *botoner*, from *boton*. Cf:

**buttress**, n hence v: ME *butrasse*, earlier *boterace*: the OF-MF *boterez*, *bouterez*, adj 'projecting', then n 'projecting structure': from *boter*, later *bouter*, to thrust: cf prec and, f.a.e., the 3rd BUTT.

**buxom**: ME *buxum*, earlier *buhsum*, obedient, (lit) pliable: OE *\*būhsum*: the suffix OE *-sum*, E *-some*, attached to the r of OE *būgan*, to bow, to bend: cf the G *biegsam*, pliant, manageable, from *biegen*, to bend, MHG *biegen*, OHG *biogan*, akin to Go *biugan*, OS *būgan*: f.a.e., the 3rd BOW.

**buy**, pt and pp **bought** (late OE-early ME pt, *bohte*; pp, *boht*). 'To *buy*', whence the coll n, as in 'a good *buy*', derives from ME *buggen*, *biggen*, from OE *bycgan*, akin to Go *bugjan* and OS *buggean*; Gmc r, *\*bug-*.

**buzz**, v hence n, is purely echoic.

**buzzard**: ME, from OF-F, *busard* (suffix *-ard*): from OF-F *buse*: L *būtiōnem* or *būteōnem*, acc of *būtiō* or *būteō*, s *būt-*, r perh *bū-*, as in *būbō* (gen *būbōnis*), an owl, *būbō* being a redup of echoic *bū-*.

**by**, prep hence adv hence adj, with var **bye**, whence the n (something that goes *by* or to the side): ME *bi*: OE *bī*, by the side of, near—by, of, from—after, according to: akin to OFris and OS *bī* (or *bĭ*), *be*, OHG (and MHG) *bī*, G *bei*, Go *bi* (around, about; by), MD *bie*, D *bij*; OHG *bī* is ult identical with OHG *umbi*, cf the *amb-* (? for *\*ambi*) of L *ambīre*, to go around, make a circular tour of, and Gr *amphi* (for *\*amphi*), around, about: the IE etymon would be *\*ambhi*, var *\*umbhi*, often, perh even at that stage, shortened to *\*bhi* (Walshe). Cf the un-nasalized form in Skt *abhi*, about, around, and *abhi-tas*, on both sides, and such C cognates as OIr *imb-* and W *ambi-*, around; cf also G *um*, around, for. Clearly, therefore, this OGmc *bĭ*, E *by*, is ult identical with the prefix *be-*.

**bye**. See prec.

**bygone** is merely 'gone by, hence past'.

byre, cowshed, cow-house: OE *bȳre*, mdfn of
OE *būr*, a dwelling: f.a.e., the 2nd BOWER.

byword. See VERB, para 1, s.f.

Byzantine, Byzantium: bezant or besant.

*Bezant*, a gold coin issued by Byzantium
throughout the CC6–15, derives from ME *besant*,
*besaunt*, from OF-MF *besan*, var of OF-F *besant*,

L *bȳzantium*, elliptical for *aes bȳzantium* or
'*Byzantine* coin', from *Bȳzantius*, adj of *Bȳzantium*,
from Gr *Buzantion*, 'The Close-Pressed (City)',
compactly built, akin to Gr *buzēn* (adv), close-
pressed, itself akin to *buzein* (s *buz-*), to be frequent.
The L adj *Bȳzantīnus* yields E *Byzantine*, whence
*Byzantinism* (-*ism*).

# C

**cab, cabby, cabriolet.**

1. The 2nd pet-forms '*cab*-driver'; *cab* shortens *cabriolet*; *cabriolet*, adopted from F, is a dim of EF-F *cabriole*, a leap, a caper, var of *capriole*: prob from *cabrioler*, var of *caprioler*, from It *capriolare*, to leap like a goat, to caper, from *capriolo*, roebuck, from L *capreolus*, roebuck, orig a wild goat, from *caper*, he-goat, *capra*, she goat, perh akin to Gr *kapros*, a wild boar, and to ON *hafr*, OE *haefer*, he-goat. The IE r may have been *\*khap-*, varr *\*kap-* or *\*kep-*. The *cabriolet* was so named (1755) from 'the leaps made by these light vehicles' (B & W).

2. The EF-F *capriole*, n, was adopted by C17 E; the v *caprioler* was adapted as 'to *capriole*': these two E words yielded resp 'a *caper*' and 'to *caper*'.

3. *Capricious* comes from EF-F *capricieux*, f *capricieuse*, adj, from EF-F *caprice*, itself from It *capriccio*, a horripilation, then a shivering, a shudder, finally (sense-influenced by It *capro*, a goat) a whim: but *capriccio* does not derive from *capro*; it derives from It *capo*, head (from L *caput*), perh rather from its pl *capora+riccio*, hedgehog (L *ericius*); the basic idea (Webster) being that of a head with hair 'standing on end', like a hedgehog's spines.

**cabal, n and v; cabala, occ cabbala.**

'To *cabal*' comes from EF-F *cabaler*, itself from EF-F *cabale*, whence E *cabal*, n: and *cabale* derives from ML *cabala*, var *cabbala*, a trln of H *qabbālāh*, received, hence traditional, lore, from *qābal*, to receive (? ult akin to L *capere*, s *cap-*). The sense-development of the F and E *cabale*, *cabal*, is '(secret) tradition, secret, secret machinations, secret meeting, secret meeters, an intriguing group'. The adj *cabalistic* derives from EF-F *cabalistique*.

**caballero.** See CAVALCADE, para 2.

**cabaret** is adopted from MF-F: MD *cabaret*, varr *caberet*, a vocalized form of MD *cabret*, itself a denasalized form of MD *cambret*: either from Old Picard *camberete*, dim (cf the suffix *-et*) of Picard *cambre*, chamber, large room, F *chambre* (f.a.e., CHAMBER), as B & W propose, or from Ar *khamārāt*, a place of refreshment, as Dauzat suggests.

**cabbage:** ME *cabage*, earlier *caboche*: by shape-resemblance from Old Picard *caboche*, head, var of OF-MF *caboce*: OF-MF *boce* (MF-F *bosse*),

a swelling (f.a.e.: BOSS, protuberance), with prefix *ca-*, perh suggested by L *caput*, head.

**cabby.** See CAB.

**cabin,** n hence v: ME *cabane*: MF-F *cabane*: OProv *cabana*: LL *capanna*, perh a metathesis for LL *cannapa*, hemp, influenced by *capere*, to take (E & M), but prob of C origin: cf Ir *caban*, W *cabban* (and *cab*), hut, and Mx *cabbane* (and *cab*), with var *bwane*, contr of *bo-ane*, a stall for oxen, perh by f/e. In C, *cab-* has var *cap-*; both mean orig 'to take', hence 'to contain', and are therefore akin to L *capere* (s *cap-*): *cabin* prob has orig sense 'container', perh via the presp form. For the F *cabine* (except for 'ship's *cabin*' sense, borrowed from E *cabin*), see:

**cabinet** has at least three different etymologies: OED and EW preferring to make it a dim of E *cabin*; Webster and Dauzat deriving it from F *cabinet*, early var *gabinet*, an adaptation of It *gabinetto*, already a piece of furniture, dim of *gabbia*, a cage or a basket, from ML *cavea*, L *cauea*, var *cauia*, prob not from L *cauus*, ML *cavus*, hollow; B & W postulating an *-et* dim—F *cabinet* being orig a small, intimate room—of F *cabine* (1364), orig cant for a gaming-house, a word 'born in the underworld of the rich Flemish cities', with r o.o.o., though just possibly from, or akin to, the r of MD *gabben* (s *gab-*), to mock.

**cable,** n hence v.

*Cable* (message) is short for *cablegram*, sent by electric *cable*, orig, as still naut, a thick, long, strong rope: MF-F *câble*: OProv (? rather ONF) *cable*: ML *caplum*, contr of ML *capulum*, some kind of cord, prob from *capere* (s *cap-*), to take. MF-F *câble*, however, could have come from MHG *kabel*; certainly both the OF and the MHG words could derive from Ar *ḥabl*, a rope (Walshe).

**caboodle.** See BOODLE.

**caboose,** a cook's galley, hence railroad sense: prob either MLG *kabūse* or, better, MD *cabuse*, *cabuus*, o.o.o.; but perh a var of MD *kookhuis*, cookhouse, galley.

**cabriolet.** See CAB.

**cacao.** See COCOA.

**cache,** n hence v; **cachet.**

*Cache*=EF-F *cache*, a hiding-place, from MF-F *cacher*, to hide or conceal: Gallo-Roman *\*coactitare* (S) and *\*coacticare* (N), to compress, hence, because, by forcing something into a small space, one renders it less noticeable, to conceal:

L *coactāre*, to compress: *coactus*, pp of *cogere* (for *co-agere*, to drive together), to force: cf COGENT. From the 'compress' sense of F *cacher* derives late MF-F *cachet*, adopted by E: 'seal of a letter' (very distinctive), hence 'distinctive quality'.

**cacique.** See SHEIK, para 2.

**cack,** v hence n. (Cf the element -*cace*.) The word is not only IE, as attested by L *cacō*, Gr *kakkáō*, OIr *caccaim*, I defecate, Ru *kakal'*, to defecate, and other terms, incl the corresp nn (e.g., Gr *kakkē*); but prob Medit: cf Hit *sakkar*, *zakkar*, excrement, and Eg *ḥaḥa*, a foul excretion, and *kai-t*, excrement. The Eg *kai-t*, with -*t* merely indicating the f gender, suggests that the IE (and other) vv are redupp of a Medit r *\*ka-*, itself clearly echoic.

**cackle,** v hence n: ME *cakelen*, adopted from MD *cakelen* (var *kekelen*; D *kakelen*): ult echoic. Cf GAGGLE and GIGGLE.

**cacoëthes scribendi.** See SCRIBE, para 8, s.f.

**cacophony:** Gr *kakophōnia*, lit 'bad sound': cf the elements *caco-* and *phon-*.

**cactus:** L *cactus*: (Sicilian) Gr *kaktos*, a prickly plant, esp a cardoon: usu said to be o.o.o., but prob adapted from Eg *qatcha*, thorns, thornbush.

**cad,** whence **caddish** (*cad*+euphonic *d*+adj suffix -*ish*); **cadet, caddie** (or -*y*).

The 4th merely represents the E pron of the F original of *cadet*: late MF-F *cadet*, younger son, (hence) young officer, derives from Gascon *capdet*, a chief, from Prov *capdel*, itself from LL *capitellum*, the top, dim of L *caput*, head: f.a.e., CHIEF. Cf, sem, the sl 'the *heads*' and 'the big white *chief*'. *Cad* merely shortens *cadet*; orig *cad* was an unbooked, hence inferior, passenger, occupying an inferior seat on coach or primitive omnibus.

**cadaver, cadaveric, cadaverous.**

The 2nd (cf the F *cadavérique*) is an E var (suffix -*ic*) of the 3rd (cf the EF-F *cadavéreux*), itself from ML *cadāverōsus* (suffix -*ōsus*), L *cadāuerōsus*, the adj of ML *cadāver* (adopted by E), L *cadāuer*, which has s *cadāu-*, r *cad-*: the r, in short, of *cadere*, to fall: f.a.e., CADENCE.

**caddis, occ caddice.**

Both the *caddis* or anglers' artificial fly and the *caddis fly* (and *caddis worm*) derive from *caddis*, *caddice*, floss silk, cotton wool, worsted yarn, esp ribbon, itself from EE *caddis*, lint, from ME *cadace, cadas* (cf late MSc *cadas, caddas*), from MF *cadas, cadaz*; the sense 'heavy woollen twill' used in Scotland derives from MF *cadis* (1352), a kind of serge made in the S of France, from OProv *cadis*, var *cadiz*, prob connected with Sp *Cadiz*; the form *cadis* is app the F prototype. (Craigie; Dauzat and B & W.) But the 'heavy woollen twill' sense perh represents a different word, and the 'floss silk' or 'lint' sense may, as EW proposes, derive from OF *cadarce*, from OProv *cadarz*, aphetically from Gr *akathartos*, uncleansed, *a-*, not+*kathartos*, pp of *kathairein*, to cleanse (f.a.e. CATHARSIS).

**caddie** (golf). See CAD.

**caddy** (1), var of prec.

**caddy** (2), for tea: earlier *catty*: Malay *kaṭṭi*, *kātī* a solid, hence a lump used as a weight.

**cadence, cadent, cadenza; cadaver** (sep); **caducity, caducous; cascade; case, casual; chance, chancy; chute; parachute.**—**accidence, accident, accidental; coincide, coincidence, coincident(al); decadence, decadent, decay; deciduous;—escheat;—incidence, incident. incidental; occasion, occasional; occident, occidental;—recidivism, recidivist, recidivous.**

1. *Cadence*, with var *cadency* (-*y*, n), is adopted from late MF-F, which thus adapts It *cadenza*, itself taken over, internationally, by Music: and It *cadenza* derives from ML *cadentia*, a falling, e.g. of dice, an offshoot from *cadent-* (whence the E adj *cadent*), the o/s of L *cadens*, presp of *cadere*, to fall. Now *cadere* has s *cad-*, akin to Skt *çad-*, to fall, to the *kad-* of Gr *kekadonto*, they have yielded (fallen to opponents), and prob to EIr, Cor, Ga *càs* (*kàs*), case, predicament: cf *case* in next para.

2. The pp *cāsus* has s *cās-*, whence the n *cāsus* (gen *cāsūs*), fall, accident, happening, whence MF-F *cas*, whence ME *cas*, later *case*. The L n *cāsus* has derivative LL adj *cāsuālis*, whence MF-F *casuel* and E *casual*; *casualty*, contr of *casuality*, comes from ML *cāsuālitās*, gen -*itātis*; (see esp B & W) derivative EF-F *casuiste*, imm from Sp *casuista*, comes from ML *cāsus*, a case of conscience, with subsidiary *casuistique*, whence E *casuistic(al)*; *casuistry* is an E formation.

3. L *cadere* also has adj *cadūcus*, falling, hence tending to fall, whence E *caducous*; the derivative LL *cadūcitās*, o/s *cadūcitāt-*, became, perh via late MF-F *caducité*, the E *caducity*.

4. L *cadere* issues, through its *cas-* form, into a VL *\*casicāre*, to fall because nothing impedes, whence It *cascare*, with derivative *cascata* (*d'acqua*), whence EF-F, hence E, *cascade*, whence 'to *cascade*'.

5. 'To *chance*' derives from 'a *chance*', whence also *chancy*: and *chance*, n, ME *cheance*, represents OF-MF *cheance*, from ML *cadentia* (see para 1).

6. L *cadere* becomes OF-MF *cheoir* (MF-F *choir*), whence, from the f pp *cheoite* (as n), influenced by *chu*, pp of *choir*, derives MF-F *chute*, orig a fall, adopted by E, which has also adopted the F derivative *parachute* (prefix *para-*).

7. L *cadere* has numerous prefix cpds; some have entered E, the most important being these, mostly based upon *cid-*, the c/f of *cadere*:

*accidence*, for *accidents*; *accident*, adj hence n (whence *accidental*), L *accident-*, o/s of *accidens*, presp of *accidere*, to happen: *ac-* for *ad*, to;

*coincidence* eases *coincident+ce*; *coincident*, adj hence n (whence *coincidental*), ML *coincident-*, o/s of *coincidens*, presp of *coincidere*, to fall in with or together, to occupy the same space: *co-+incidere* (see below);

*decadence*: MF-F *décadence*: ML *dēcadentia*, a falling away (L *dē*, away from), hence deterioration, an abstract n consisting of -*ia* tacked onto *\*dēcadent-* (whence E *decadent*, adj hence n), o/s of *dēcadens, presp of *dēcadere; influenced by cadentia;

decay, v (whence the pa decayed) hence n: ONF decaër (OF decheeir): ML *dēcadere: dē, (down) away from + cadere;

deciduous: L dēciduus, adj from dēcidere, to fall off: dē + cid- + inf -ere; the L neu pl dēcidua, adopted by An, has adj decidual (-al);

escheat, whence 'to escheat' and escheatage (-age), escheator deriving prob from AF eschetour: ME, from MF, eschete, var eschĕoit(e), from escheoir (F échoir): VL *excadere, to fall out for, hence to the lot of: ex, out + cadere;

incidence: via F incidence, from LL incidentia (neupl), circumstances; incident, adj hence n (whence incidental), derives, prob via MF-F, from incident-, o/s of incidens, presp of incidere, to fall upon: in, into, onto;

occasion, n hence v and the adj occasional: via OF-F from occāsiōn-, o/s of L occāsiō, from occās-, the s of occāsus, pp of occidere (oc- for prefix ob-), to fall, go down, esp of sun or stars; cf:

occident, (adj and) n: where the sun sets, hence the west: OF-F occident: L occident-, o/s of occidens, presp of occidere: the OF n arose imm from the L n occidens, elliptical for sol occidens, the setting sun; the derivative L adj occidentālis passed through MF-F to become E occidental, whence the n Occidental, opp Oriental;

recidivism (-ism) and recidivist (-ist), an habitual criminal, derive from recidivous, tending to fall back (re-): ML recidivus, L recidiuus, from recidere, to fall back.

cadet. See CAD.

cadge, to carry (as a burden), hence to hawk, hence to sponge: b/f from cadger, hawker, hence sponger, itself from cadge, a wicker basket, from F cage (see CAGE); codger, dial and coll, is prob a var.

cadmia, cadmium.
The latter derives, by Chem suffix -ium, from the former, an adoption of L cadmia, calamine (calamine, ML calamina, a distorted derivative of cadmia), from Gr kadmeia ('so named because found near Thebes, the city of Cadmus': B & W), n from f of adj kadmeios, of the myth Kadmos, slayer of a dragon whose teeth became warriors—whence Cadmean victory.

caducity, caducous. See CADENCE, para 3.

Caesar, Caesarean; Kaiser—Czar, Tsar;—caesura, whence caesural; the -cide and -cise cpds are treated sep;—sherry.

1. L caedere (s caed-), to cut, esp to cut off, has pp caesus, s caes-, whence caesūra, a cutting-off, hence a part cut off, a division, break, stop, adopted by E metric: cf Skt khidáti, he tears, s khid-.

2. Perh f/e, but prob correct, is the old L explanation of Caesar: caesus matris utero, cut from his mother's womb, one who, caesa matre nascitur, is born after his mother has been cut open; thus reputedly born, Julius Caesar accounts

for Caesarean (L Caesarianus) in Caesarean section or operation.

3. The title Kaiser particularizes kaiser, an emperor: G Kaiser, MHG kaiser, OHG keisar, akin to Go kaisar, OE cāsere, OB cĕsarb: L Caesar.

4. L Caesar, in becoming Go kaisar, led to OSl cēsari, whence Ru tsesar', later tsar', whence Tsar, with frequent var Czar. A Czar's son was tsarevich, whence E Czarevich; a daughter, tsarevna, E Czarevna; wife, tsaritsa, but G Czarin, whence, by blend, E Czarina.

5. Julius Caesar gave his name to Caesaris (urbs), Caesar's City: whence Sp Xeres (now Jerez), whence EE sherris, which, apprehended as a pl, produces the b/f sherry, '(wine of) Xeres'.

café, cafeteria, caffein(e). See COFFEE.

cag. See KEG.

cage, n hence v: OF-F cage: ML cavea, L cauea, a cavity, hence a cage: from cauus, hollow: f.a.e., CAVE. Hence perh the adj cagey, wary, from birds shy of capture.

cairn; cairngorm.
The latter is lit 'azure of a cairn': Ga gorm, azure + cairn, of a cairn, gen of carn, a heap, esp a rounded heap of stones over, or to the memory of, the dead: of C origin: cf the syn Ir (and EIr), Cor, W, Br, Mx carn (karn): perh an extension of OC car-, var of *bar(s), an eminence.

caisson. See 2nd CASE, para 4.

caitiff. See captivus, in para 3 of CAPABILITY.

cajole, cajolery.
The latter comes from F cajolerie, an -erie (E -ery) derivative of cajoler, whence 'to cajole'; EF-F cajoler, orig 'to babble like a jay in a cage'. from the syn EF gaioler, from Picard gaiole, a cage, from ML caveola dim of cavea, L cauea, a cage: f.a.e., CAVE. (B & W.)

cake, n, whence 'to cake' and the adj cak(e)y.
The ME cake derives from ON kaka, akin to MLG kōke, MD coeke, coec, coke (D koek), MHG kuoche, OHG kuocho (G Kuchen); the D koek has dim koekje, whence E, esp AE, cookie, cooky. The exact connexion with 'to COOK', G kochen, is obscure.

calabash: EF-F calebasse, earlier EF calabasse, either (Webster), by l for r, from Prov carbasse, perh from Ar qar 'ah yābisah, a dry gourd, or more prob (B & W) from Sp calabaza, from Cat carabasa (or -baça), perh from the syn Ar qar 'ah, with obscure suffix or 2nd element. EW derives the F word from Sp calabaza; the latter, from Per kharbuz, a melon.

calaboose (AE), jail: Sp calabozo, dungeon, akin to—? from—Galician cabouco, from caber, L capere, to take, to contain.

calamine. See CADMIA.

calamitous, calamity.
The adj comes, via late MF-F calamiteux, f -iteuse, from L calamitōsus, from calamitās, o/s calamitāt-, whence, via MF-F calamité, the E calamity (-ity): and calamitās, presumably from an adj, is akin prob to the -colum- of L incolumis,

unharmed, perh to Gr *kolobos* and *klambos*, mutilated, and perh to Gr *kēdein* (s *kēd-*), to afflict, *kēdos*, affliction, anxiety, and Skt *kadanan*, destruction (cf the syn L *clādēs*).

**calcareous; calcine; calcium.**

The 1st comes from L *calcareus*, the adj of *calx*, lime, o/s *calc-*, whence the Sci L *calcium* and the MF-F *calciner*, whence 'to *calcine*': f.a.e., CHALK. Cf the element *calcareo-* and:

**calculable, calculate, calculation, calculator, calculatory, calculus; incalculable.**

*Incalculable: in-*, not+*calculable; calculable*, perh from F, as if from LL *\*calculābilis*, from LL *calculāre*, to reckon, which has pp *calculātus*, whence 'to *calculate*'. On the L pp s *calculāt-* arose LL *calculātiō*, a reckoning, with o/s *calculātiōn-*, whence E *calculation*, and the LL agent *calculātor* and the ML adj *calculātōrius*, whence *calculatory*. Now *calculāre* derives from L *calculus*, dim of *calx* (gen *calcis*) or limestone: f.a.e., CHALK. *Calculus*, pebble, hence (a round) one used in voting or in gambling, hence a children's counter used in reckoning.

**caldron or cauldron:** ME, from ONF, *caudron*, mdfn of ONF *caudiere* (OF *chaudiere*): VL and LL *caldāria*, n from L adj *caldārius*, warming, for warming: *caldus*, warm: *calēre*, to be warm: f.a.e., CALORIC; cf CAUDLE.

2. F *chaudière*, caldron, results in *chowder*, a stew cooked in one.

**Caledonia,** whence **Caledonian,** adj hence n: L name (Lucan, Tacitus) for Scotland (cf Gr *Kalēdonia*, adj *Kalēdonios*), adj *Caledonius*: of C origin: cf W *cel*, OIr *ceil*, a concealing (? cf L *celāre*, to conceal, s *cel-*), a shelter, and W *celydd*, a woody shelter; cf also Mx *keyll*, Ga *coille*, OIr *caill*, Cor *coid*, Br *koed*, a wood or forest; perh the *-keld* of Sc *Dunkeld*; OC *\*kaldet*. The 'concealment' origin is doubtful; the 'forest', attractive.

**calendar, calends; intercalary, intercalate, intercalation.**

1. *Calendar*: ME *calender* (or *k-*): L *calendārium*, an account book, a book showing interest: *calendae* (or *k-*), calends, the first day of the Roman month, because such days were proclaimed: from *calāre*, to proclaim. *Calendae* yields OE *calend*, a month, and ME *kalendes*, a month, (but also) *calends*, whence E *calends*, *kalends*. (F.a.e., CLAIM.)

2. L *calāre* has cpd *intercalāre*, to call between, to proclaim (a day) among (*inter*) the orig days of a month, whence, from the pp *intercalātus*, the E 'to *intercalate*'; on the pp s *intercalāt-* arose *intercalātiō*, o/s *intercalātiōn-*, whence E *intercalation*. *Intercalary*, however, comes from L *intercalārius*, an *-ārius* (E *-ary*) adj on *intercal-*, the inf s.

**calender.** See CYLINDER, para 2.

**calf,** pl **calves; v, calve.**

1. The *calf* of the leg comes from ON *kālfi*, akin to ON *kālfr*, a quadruped calf, itself akin to OE *cealf*, whence the quadruped *calf*. OE *cealf* is akin also to OHG (and G) *kalb*, Go *kalbō*, ON *kālfr*.

That the basic idea in IE is app 'a swelling of the body' is supported by Gaul *galba*, a fat man, and Skt *gárbhas*, womb. The Gmc r is *\*kalbh-*; the IE r, *\*gwolbh-*, with var *\*gwalbh-*: cf Ga *calpa*, OIr *colpa*, calf of the leg.

2. 'To *calve*' derives from OE *cealfian* (s *cealf-*), from the OE n.

**caliber** (AE) or **calibre; calibrate, calibration.**— **caliper** or **calliper.**

*Cal(l)iper*, usu pl *cal(l)ipers*, an instrument, is a form-corruption and sense-change of *caliber*, var of *calibre*, the diameter of a projectile, hence of the bore of the weapon discharging it: and *calibre* has come from late MF-F *calibre* (cf It *calibro*, obs *calibra*), itself from Ar *qālib*, a form, or mould (cf Tu *kalyb*), from *qalaba*, to turn over, hence to form or mould. The derivative It v *calibrare* has pp *calibrato*, whence 'to *calibrate*', whence, anl with other *-ation* nn, *calibration*.

**calico:** orig imported, via EF-F *calicot*, from *Calicut*, on the Malabar coast of India.

**California,** whence **Californian,** adj hence n: perh (Enci It) a Sp reshaping—*California* occurs first in a Sp romance of c1500—of that imaginary land *Califerne* (o.o.o.) which appears in the *Chanson de Roland*.

**caliper.** See CALIBER.

**calisthenics.** See CALLISTHENICS.

**calk** (1), of horse's shoe: perh from L *calcar* (s *calc-*), a spur. Cf:

**calk** (2), occ **calque,** to trace or copy: EF-F *calquer*, to trace: It *calcare*, to trace, (orig) 'to trample: L *calcāre* (s *calc-*), to trample, from *calx*, a spur, orig a heel. Cf:

**calk** (3) or **caulk,** to prevent a ship from leaking by driving tarred oakum into seams: ME *cauken*: ONF *caukier*: L *calcāre*, to trample: L *calx*, a heel, o.o.o. Cf prec.

**call,** v hence n; derivatively, **caller, calling** (cf, sem, VOCATION).

'To *call*': ME *callen*: OE *ceallian*, akin to OHG *callōn* (or *k-*), ON *kalla*, to call, MD *callen*, to talk, also to OIr *gall*, a swan, W *galw*, to call, Ga *glaodh*, a call, to call, MIr *gloed*, a call, Br *galu*, called, *galùein*, to call, Cor *galow*, n, and *galu*, *galua*, *galwy*, v, and prob to OSl *glasiti* (*gla-* for *gal-*), to speak, call out, and *glasŭ*, a voice. The relationship to L *calāre* (s *cal-*) is obscure, as is that of L *calāre* to L *clamāre* (cf CLAIM); both, however, are extremely probable.

**calligraphy,** beautiful writing; **callipygian,** fair-buttocked; **callisthenics,** var **calisthenics,** bodily exercise to promote health and grace. For *calli-*, see that element; for *-graphy*, Gr *-graphia*, writing, see element *-graph*; *-pygian*, from Gr *pugē*, buttocks; Gr *sthenos*, strength.

**calliper.** See CALIBRE.

**callosity, callous, callus.**

L *callus* (var *callum*), indurated skin, adopted by E, is akin to OIr *calath*, hard, W *caled*, Cor *calés*, *calas*, *calys*, Br *kalet*, W *caleden*, hardness, a callus, and remotely to Skt *kina*, callosity; its adj *callōsus* yields E *callous* and its derivative abstract n *callōsitās*, o/s *callōsitāt-*, yields, prob via EF-F *callosité*, the E *callosity*.

**callow** (whence **callowness**): ME *calewe*, earlier *calu*: OE *calu*, featherless, bald, akin to OFris *kale*, baldness, *kalia*, to deprive of hair or feathers —to OHG *kalo*, MHG *kal*, G *kahl*, bald—prob to OB *golŭ*, naked—perh to L *caluus* (ML *calvus*), bald, thence to Skt *khalaṭis*, bald.

**callus.** See CALLOSITY.

**calm**, n hence v; **calm**, adj, whence the superfluous **calmness**; **calmative**, adj hence n.

The adj *calm* derives from MF-F *calme* (adj from n), from It *calmo*, adj, from *calma*, n, from LL *cauma*, warmth, heat, from Gr *kauma*, a burning heat, the heat of the day, when beasts are at rest, winds fallen, the fields quiet—cf OProv *cauma*, heat—from *kaiein* (s *kai-*), to burn, for *\*kawein* (s *kaw-*); IE r, *\*kau-* (*kaw-*) or *\*kēu-*: cf CAUSTIC. The n *calm* derives, via ME and MF-F *calme*, from the It n *calma*, whence the v *calmare*, whence MF-F *calmer*, whence 'to *calm*'. *Calmative* imitates *palliative* and *sedative*.

**calomel**: element *calo-*, beautiful (Gr *kalo-*)+Gr *melas*, black: cf the occ F *calomelas*: a white resultant of a black mixture.

**caloric, calorie** (var **calory**), **calorific; nonchalance, nonchalant.**

1. *Caloric*=F *calorique*, from L *calor*, heat, from *calēre*, to be hot, s *cal-*; IE r, *\*kal-* (var *\*kel-*), var *\*kla-* (or *\*kle-*)—cf OHG *lawer*, ON *hlāer*, lukewarm. (Cf CALDRON, CAUDLE, CHAFE, CHAUFFEUR.) *Calory* anglicizes *calorie*, adopted from F, which derives it from L *calor*. *Calorific*= F *calorifique*=L *calorificus*, heat-making, cf the element *-fic*, from L *facere*, to make.

2. *Nonchalance*, adopted from OF-F, derives from F *nonchalant*, likewise adopted by E: *non*, not+*chalant*, presp of OF-MF *chaloir*, to care (vi), from L *calēre*, to be hot, hence desirous, hence concerned.

**calotte.** See CAUL.

**caltrop** varies **caltrap**, ME *calketrappe*, ONF *kauketrape*: lit, a *trap* for the *calk* or heel.

**calumet**, Red Indians' ceremonial pipe: EF-F dim (suffix *-et*) of L *calamus*, a reed, from Gr *kalamos*: f.a.e., HAULM.

**calumniate, calumniation, calumniator; calumnious, calumny.**

L *calumnia*, whence MF-F *calomnie* and E *calumny*, derives from *\*calumnus* (pa), from *caluāri* (or *-āre*), to trick or deceive; IE r, *\*kal-*, var of *\*kel-*. *Calumnia* has adj *calumniōsus*, whence MF-F *calomnieux* and E *calumnious*, and v *calumniāri*, to slander, with pp *calumniātus*, whence 'to *calumniate*', and with LL agent *calumniātor*, adopted by E, and with LL abstract *calumniātiō*, o/s *calumniātiōn-*, whence E *calumniation*.

**Calvary**: ML *calvāria*, LL *caluāria*, a bare skull, from *caluus*, bald: cf CALLOW, s.f. The LL *Caluāria* renders Gr *Kranion* (cf CRANIUM), which in turn renders Aram *gŭlgŭlthā*, place of skulls, from H *gulgōleth*, a skull. (*Golgotha* is a LL adoption of Gr *golgotha*, from *gŭlgŭlthā*.) Cf *Luke*, xxii, 33, and *Matthew*, xxvii, 33.

**calve.** See CALF, para 2.

**calx.** See CALCAREOUS.

**Calypso, calypso.** See APOCALYPSE.

**calyx**: L *calyx*: Gr *kalux*, akin to Gr *kulix*, L *calix*, a cup, and to Skt *kalásás*, a cup, and *kalikā*, a bud: IE s, *\*kalik-*, *\*kolik-*, *\*kulik-*, with r *\*kul-*, varr *\*kol-*, *\*kal-*: possibly, however, Gr *kalux* and L *calix* are of different origins. Cf CHALICE.

**cam**, as in **camshaft** (cf SHAFT), derives from D *kam*, MD *cam*, a comb: f.a.e., COMB.

**camaraderie.** See CAMERA, para 2

**camas**, usu **camass**, also **quamash**, an edible-bulbed lily of West NA: Chinook Jargon *kámass*, a bulb: Nootka *chamas*, pleasant-tasting, sweet. (DAE.)

**camber**: OF-MF *cambre*, curved, bent, a Norman or Picard form of OF-MF *chambre*, convex, from L *camur* or *camurus*, varr *camer*, *camerus*, perh a loan-word: cf Hit *kam*, *gam*, down, convexity having a downward curve; or L *camer*, *-ur*, s *cam-*, might be a nasalized mdfn of Eg *khab*, to bend, or *khab*, a crescent.

**cambial, cambium.** See CHANGE, para 2.

**Cambria(n).** See CYMRIC.

**cambric**: earlier *camerike*; blending F *Cambra* and Fl *Kamerik*, the Fl-become-F city where the fabric was orig made.

**Cambridge**—the latinized *Cantabrigia* yields *Cantabrigian*, usu abbr *Cantab*—was orig 'Roman fort on the Granta', later 'bridge over the Granta' (whence *Cam*): C8, *Grantacaestir*; C11, *Cantebruge*; C15, *Cambrugge*. (Ekwall.)

**came.** See COME.

**camel**: ME, OE *camel*: L *camēlus*: Gr *kamēlos*: of Sem origin—cf H (and Phoen) *gāmāl* and Ar *gaml*, *jamal*. But surely the source might rather have been the Eg *kamál*, *kamali*, with var *gemr*? The obs *camelopard* (see (PARD)=L *camēlopardus*, altered from *camēlopardalis*: Gr *kamēlopárdalis*.

**camellia** is Sc L, from Georg *Kamel* or *Camelli*, the Jesuit reputed to have brought it, c1700, from the East to Europe; thus: *kamel* (with *c* for *k*)+euphonic *l*+suffix *-ia*.

**camelopard.** See CAMEL.

**camera** and in **camera**; **Camorra**; **comrade** (whence **comradeship**) and **chum** and **camaraderie**; **camber** (sep).—**chamber**, n hence v; **chamberlain**; **chamber-pot.**

1. *In camera*, in secret, is L, lit 'in chamber' or private room. The L *camera*, var *camara* (whence perh, by dial var, *camorra*), orig 'vaulted roof, a vault', came, in LL, to mean '(large) room', esp if at all private; it derives from Gr *kamárā*; IE r *kam-*, curved, bent, crooked—cf Skt *kmarati*, (it) is crooked, and Av *kamarā*, a girdle; cf also the sep CAMBER.

2. L *camera*, *-ara*, was adopted by Sp in sense 'chamber'; Sp *camara* had derivative *camarada*, chamber-fellowship, (hence) chamber fellow, whence EF-F *camarade*, whence both *camaraderie*, adopted by E, and the E *comrade*; and a slurring

of 'chamber fellow' produces chum, whence 'to chum'.

3. L camera became OF-F chambre, whence E chamber; the 'bedroom utensil' sense derives from chamber-pot (EF-F pot de chambre). In chamberlain, -lain = the suffix -ling, but the entire word comes from OF chamberlenc, from Frankish *kamerling—cf OHG chamarling, the stem representing OHG chamara, from L camara, camera.

4. Cf CHIMNEY.

camisade, camise, camisole. See CHEMISE, para 2.

camomile. See HOMO, para 4.

camouflage, n hence v: F: by suffix -age from camoufler, to disguise, orig a cant word: It camuffare, to disguise, to deceive, itself orig cant, perh (Prati) via It *camuffo from ML camuzzum, a sort of cloth—used as a mask.

camp, n and v (whence camper, camping), and campus; decamp, decampment; encamp, encampment; scamp (rogue) and scamper.—campaign, n hence v (whence campaigner); champaign and champagne; champignon; champion, n hence adj and v.

1. The source of all these terms is the L campus (s camp-), a field, app o.o.o.—prob a survival from an ancient Italic language (B & W); a remotely possible cognate is the Hit kanza, grass, cereal. 'To camp' comes from EF-F camper, itself from either Picard or Prov camp, from It campo, from campus, itself surviving in AE for college, or university, grounds.

2. Decampment anglicizes F décampement, by suffix -ment from EF-F décamper, whence 'to decamp': dé- (L dis-), from+(F) camp+inf -er.

3. Encampment derives, by -ment, from 'to encamp': en-, in+camp, v.

4. A scamp, highwayman, hence rogue, derives from dial scamp, to roam, itself from scamper, to run hastily or speedily: It scampare (L ex, out of, away from+campus in its frequent sense, 'field of battle'), to escape, orig—it seems—from a battlefield (Prati).

5. L campus has LL adj campānius (var -āneus), whence Campānia, the flat or flattish country about Naples, whence ML campānia, flat country, whence EF-F, from ONF, campagne, such country, hence a war fought in it or a period spent in it, hence in any country, by an army; hence E campaign (orig, flat country).

6. Campaign has the doublet champaign, a plain: ME champayne: OF-MF champaigne: ML campānia. OF-MF champaigne has MF var champagne, whence Champagne, the F province, whence champagne, the scintillant wine made there.

7. The champignon or field-mushroom is adopted from MF-F, which derives it, with a fresh suffix, from the MF champegneul, either from LL campāneus, OF campegneus, or, less prob, from VL *campāniolus, of the campi or fields, (hence) growing in the fields.

8. Champion: ME, from OF-F, champion (earliest, campiun), either, as Webster, from LL-ML campiō, o/s campiōn-, orig a warrior (cf It campione), or, as B & W, from W Gmc *kampjo, warrior, from *kamp, borrowed by G mercenaries from L campus.

campaign. See prec, para 5.

campanology. See the element campani-.

camphor. See element campho-.

campus. See CAMP, para 1.

can, n, whence 'to can', put into cans: ME, from OE, canne: akin to OHG channa, kanne, MHG and G kanne, OS kanna, ON kanna, and prob to MIr gann, Cor canna (kanna): IE s, perh *gandhn- (Holthausen). The LL canna, a drinking vessel, prob lays a false trail.

can, pt could; con; couth, uncouth—kith; cunning; keen; ken, kenning; know, knowledge.—See sep ACQUAINT(ANCE) and QUAINT; AGNOSTIC; COGNITION, COGNIZANT, CONNOISSEUR; GNOME, with GNOMON, GNOSIS, etc.; IGNORANT, with IGNORE, etc.; INCOGNITO; NARRATE, etc.; NOTE, etc.; RECOGNIZE, with RECOGNITION, RECONNAISSANCE, etc.

1. Could, influenced, as to l, by would (and should), derives from ME coude, earlier couthe, earliest cuthe, from OE cūthe, pt of cunnan (ME cannen, connen), with the importantly operative Ic cann (or can), ME I can, I know, hence know how (to), hence be able: with OE cunnan, to know (etc.), cf OE -cennan, to make known, ME kennen, to make known, to teach, but also, influenced by ON kenna, to know, whence E 'to ken', to make known (obs), to discern, to know, hence a kenning (cf OFris kanninge, kenninge); OE cunnan is also akin to OFris kunna and kenna, to OHG kunnan, MHG kunnen, G können, to be able, and to OHG -kennēn, MHG and G kennen; to Go kunnan, to know, and -kannjan, to make known; to ON kunna, to know, and kenna, to make known, to know; ken is, in short, a caus of can (in orig sense 'to know').

2. Prob akin to can, OE cunnan, to know, is OE cēne, daring, daringly shrewd, wise, hence sharp, whence ME kene, bold, sharp, whence E keen. The OE cēne is akin to OHG kuoni, MHG küene, G kühn, keen, and ON kōenn, experienced, wise.

3. Orig the presp of OE cunnan, to know (how), to be able, is cunning, which has become a simple adjective. Compare the obsol couth, known (cf L nōtus), familiar, orig the pp of cunnan; we know it better in the form uncouth (OE uncūth), orig unknown, therefore strange—hence unknowing, therefore ignorant. OE cūth, known, had derivative cȳth, cȳththe, native land (one's known land) —whence ME cuththe, kith—whence E kith, (obs) knowledge, hence (obs) familiar land or district, hence neighbours, friends, hence, by confusion, relatives, as in 'kith and kin'.

4. OE cunnan, to know, be able, yields, through its ME var connen, to know (and to be able), the E 'to con', whence conner and conning.

5. Akin to all the prec words, esp to can, to know (how), be able, is 'to know', ME knowen, earlier knawen, from OE cnāwan (s cnāw-): cf OHG -knāan or -chnāan, to know, and ON knā,

can, perh for *knēga; cf also Tokh knān, to know, OIr gnāth, known, Skt janati, he knows. (Holthausen.)

6. The n knowledge, ME knowledge, earlier knowleche, perh comes from the v: ME knawlechen, knowlechen, knowlegen, to admit, confess, prob, as OED proposes, from ME cnaw, confession, acknowledgement; the -legen, -ledge is o.o.o. Hence acknowledge, which=ac- for ad, to+'to knowledge'; with derivative acknowledgement.

7. F.a.e.: NOTE.

Canada, whence Canadian (adj hence n), derives from 'an erroneous interpretation of the Amerindian word canada or canata, 'huts, hovels', which the earliest explorers took for a placename' (Enci It).

canaille. See CANINE, para 3.

canal, whence (by suffix -ize) canalize; channel, n hence v.

From L canna, a reed (f.a.e., CANE), derives L canālis, water-pipe, large ditch, canal, whence both OF-F canal, whence E canal, and OF chanel, reshaped, after canal, to chenal, the E channel deriving, however, from the older form.

canary, the Canaries.

The L insula Canāria, one of the Canary Islands, was so named from its large canes or dogs (f.a.e., CANINE); the derivative Sp adj canario became n, with senses 'Canary wine' and 'Canary bird', the latter yielding EF-F canari or canarie, whence E canary.

canasta, orig an Argentinian card-game: Sp canasta, a basket, from canasto, large basket, an 'eased' form of the earlier canastro, from L canistrum (f.a.e., CANE). Two packs or decks are used—a 'basketful'.

cancel (v hence n), cancellation; chancel, chancellery, chancellor, chancery.—incarcerate, incarceration.

1. The L carcer, a prison, has var carcar: it is therefore a redup of r car-. Cf the Gr karkaron, karkaros, and Skt karkaṭas, crayfish (hard-shelled). Clearly the IE r *kar- means hard, and it occurs, unreduplicated, in E HARD; clearly, also, we must ult relate both these words to CANCER, the r-n alternation being entirely characteristic of the IE languages.

2. For E, the only important direct impact of carcer results from the prefix-cpd incarcerāre, to put into prison, with pp incarcerātus, whence 'to incarcerate'; the derivative LL incarcerātiō, o/s incarcerātiōn-, yields incarceration.

3. The IE s *karkr- becomes *kankr-, seen in L cancer, a lattice, pl cancri, with dim cancelli, (cross-)bars, a trellis or lattice, whence cancellāre, to cover with a trellis or make like a lattice, hence to bar, or cross, out, whence MF-(archaic)F canceller, whence E 'to cancel'. Cancellation prob comes from ML cancellātiō, o/s cancellātiōn-.

4. L cancelli, bars, lattice, became OF chancel, adopted by E: the chancel of a church was orig enclosed with lattices. L cancellārius, from cancelli (which encircled a seat of judgement or

other similar authority), became OF-F chancelier, which became ME chanceler, which, influenced by agential -or, became E chancellor. OF chancelier had OF-F derivative chancellerie, whence E chancellery, with contracted doublet chancery.

cancer, whence cancerous; cf the element cancero-. Cancer, the malignant growth, derives from L cancer, a crab, akin to Gr karkinos, Skt karkaṭa, a crab; f.a.e., CANCEL, para 1. L cancer becomes late MF-F chancre, adopted by E in Med sense.

2. The var canker, orig a corroding ulcer, represents ONF cancre (L cancer), adopted by ME, with anglicized var canker.

candelabrum. See candle in para 3 of:

candid, candour; candidate, candidature; incandescence, incandescent. — candle, candelabrum; chandelier.—incendiary, incense (n and v).— sandalwood.

1. Candour, AE candor, comes, the former through F, the latter direct from L candor, itself from candēre (s cand-), to glow white, akin to Gr kandaros (s kandar-, r kand-), a live coal, and Skt candrás (s cand-), shining, shining-white, with cognates in C—e.g., W cann, white, and Br kann, full moon, and kannein, to blanch. Also from candēre is candidus, brilliantly white, whence, perh via F candide, the E candid. Candidus has derivative candidātus, as if from *candidāre, to garment in white; as n, candidātus signifies and indeed produces candidate: those who sought Roman office wore a white toga.

2. Candēre has inch candescere, with presp candescens, o/s candescent-, whence E candescent, less usu than incandescent, from presp of incandescere, to become warm, in- being int; incandescence = incandescent + the suffix -ce, much as candidacy = candidate + -cy; candidature = candidate + suffix -ure.

3. Candēre has a prefix-cpd of some importance: incendere, to set fire to, with pp incensus, whence OF-F encenser, whence E 'to incense'; the derivative L n incensus (gen incensūs) yields OF-F encens, adopted by ME, whence incense, material for producing a perfume. Incendere has adj incendiārius, whence E incendiary (cf the suffix -ary); the L adj used as n produces the E noun incendiary.

4. Skt candrás, shining (as in para 1), is akin to Skt candana, sandalwood, with derivative or, rather, cognate L Gr sandalon, santalon, whence ML sandalum, santalum, whence EF sandal (MF sandalle), EF-F santal, whence E sandal, with explanatory wood added in sandalwood: a fragrant, insect-routing wood.

5. Less remote is candle: ME, from OE, candel: L candēla, a candle, from candēre. Candēla has derivative candēlābrum, adopted by E, usu in the L pl candēlābra; candēlābrum becomes OF chandelabre, whence OF-F chandelier, adopted by E. L candēla becomes OF chandoile, a candle, whence MF-F chandelle, whence MF-F chandelier, one who sells candles, whence the contracted E chandler, who orig sold mainly ship's candles.

**candle.** See prec, last para.

**candy** is elliptical for *sugar candy*, a 'translation' of MF-F *sucre candi*, itself from It *zucchero candi*, where *candi* represents Ar *qandī*, adj of *qand*, cane sugar, from Skt *khaṇḍa*, broken sugar. The MF-F *candi* has the EF-F v *candir*, whence E 'to *candy*'.

**cane,** n hence v; **caramel.** *Caramel*, adopted from late EF-F, comes from OF *calemele*: ML *calamella* (*-mellus*), var of *cannamella* (etc.), sugar cane: L *canna*, reed, cane+*mel*, honey (f.a.e., MELLIFLUOUS).

2. L *canna* passes through OProv *cana* to become MF *cane*, MF-F *canne*, whence ME *canne* or *cane*: and L *canna*=Gr *kanna*, usu said to be of Sem origin (cf H *qāneh* and Ar *qanāh*), but perh rather from Eg *ganu* (varr *gen* and *kenn*), a reed, a more likely origin also than the Sumerian-Akkadian *gin* proposed by Hofmann. Cf CANISTER, CANNON, CANYON.

**canine, canaille; kennel.**—**cynic** (adj hence n), whence **cynical** and **cynicism; cynosure;** cf the element *cyno-*; **hound** (n hence v), **dachshund.**

1. Here we have the Gmc (*hound, hund*), the L (*canis*), the Gr (*kuōn*) shapes of an IE word represented in Skt by *śván* (gen *súnas*) and in Ve by *śuván-*; the IE s was prob *kuon-* or *kwon-*, or *kuan-* or *kwan-*, with shorter form *kun-*, the r being perh *ku-*: cf OIr *cū*, gen *con*, and Tokh A *ku*, both meaning 'dog'.

2. First the Gmc: *dachshund*= *Dachs*, a badger+ *Hund*, a dog. G *Hund*, OHG *hunt*, is intimately akin to E *hound*, OE *hund*, itself akin to OFris (and OS) *hund*, Go *hunds*, ON *hundr*.

3. Then the L: *canis*, prob for *quanis* (IE *kuan-*+*-is*), has adj *canīnus*, whence E *canine* (cf the adj suffix *-ine*). From L *canis* derives It *cane*, whence *canaglia*, a pack of dogs, whence the late MF-F *canaille*, the rabble, partly adopted by E. *Canis* has also a derivative *canile*, a kennel, whence ONF *kenil* and MF-F *chenil*, whence ME *kenel*, whence E *kennel*.

4. The Gr *kuōn*, gen *kunos* (o/s *kun-*), has adj *kunikos*, whence L *cynicus*, applied to the *Cynics*, a philosophical school (lit 'the snarlers'), whence MF-F (modern sense: C17) *cynique*, whence E *cynic*, used also as n, with consequent extension of the adj to *cynical*; *cynicism* is an E formation (*cynic*, adj+the suffix *-ism*); *cynosure*, app borrowed from EF-F, derives from L *Cynosura* (a constellation), from Gr *kunosoura*, lit 'dog's tail'—cf the element *-ure*.

**canister:** L *canistrum*, a basket woven of reeds: prob Gr *kanistron*, from *kanna*, a reed: f.a.e., CANE.

**canker.** See CANCER, para 2.

**cannabis.** See CANVAS.

**cannery**=*can*, n+euphonic *n*+suffix *-ery*.

**cannibal,** n hence adj and **cannibalism** (*-ism*), whence, or from *cannibal*, **cannibalistic; Carib,** whence the adjj **Cariban** (*-an*) and **Caribbean** (*-ean*).

The *Caribs*, an Amerindian race of northern S Am and the West Indies, were anthropophagous:

in Cuba, Columbus heard the form *caniba*: the Cariban name, *calina* or *galibi* (lit, strong men), became Sp *canibal* (var *caribal*), a cannibal, whence E *cannibal*.

**cannon, canon, cañon** or **canyon.**

L *canna*, a reed (f.a.e., CANE), became It *canna* with aug *cannone*, a large reed, esp a large tube, whence MF-F *canon*, whence E *cannon*; became also Sp *caña*, whence *caño*, a tube, whence *cañon*, a (large) tube, a hollow, whence a *cañon* or deep valley, high-sided, duly Englished as *canyon*. Derivative It *cannonata* prompted EF-F *canonade*, whence, anl, the E *cannonade*.

2. Akin to Gr *kanna* (the origin of L *canna*) is Gr *kanōn*, a rod, hence a rule, whence L *canon*, a rule, whence OE *canon*, a moral rule, whence E *canon*, a rule, esp a code. The L *canon*, a rule, (LL) a list, has adj *canonicus* (perh direct from the Gr adj *kanonikos*), named on the list of a large church's staff, whence, in LL, a clergyman, whence the ONF *canoine*, whence ME *canoun*, whence E *canon*, officer of the Church. In ML, *canonicus* has the mdfn *canonicālis*, whence E *canonical*, whence the pl n *canonicals*. 'To *canonize*' comes from ML *canonizāre*, perh via MF-F *canoniser*.

**canny,** shrewd, careful: *can*, to know+orthographic *n*+adj *-y*: f.a.e., CAN, v, where cf *cunning*.

**canoe:** EE *canoa*, adopted from Sp: Taino *canoa* and (Antilles') Carib *canaoa, canaeua*.

**canon,** a rule, and officer of the Church. See CANNON, para 2.

**cañon.** See CANNON, para 1.

**canonical, canonize.** See CANNON, para 2.

**canopy,** n hence v: EF-F *canapé*: ML *canapeum*, a canopy: L *canopeum*, a curtain, e.g. one over a bed: Gr *kōnōpeion*, a mosquito-net: orig the neu of *kōnōpeios*, the adj of *kōnōps*, mosquito, gnat: *kōn-* became *kan-*, perh (Hofmann) under the influence of the Ancient Eg city *Canōpus*. *Kōnōps* itself is app a loan-word: perh cf Eg *khenus, khnemes*, gnat, mosquito.

**cant** (1), an angle, a tilt, an inclined plane: ONF *cant*, edge, angle, prob via MD: L *cantus*, var of *kanthus*, an iron band around a carriage wheel, a metal tire: Gr *kanthos*, felly of a wheel (from L), orig the corner of the eye: perh of Gaul origin, but prob from IE s *kanth-*, extension of *kam-*, curved, bent (see CAMERA). Hence: 'to *cant*'.

2. Akin is 'to *decant*' (whence a *decanter*): F *décanter*: ML *decanthāre*, to pour from the *canthus* or edge (the lip) of a vessel.

3. L *cantus*, edge (etc.), has derivative OProv *canton*, orig a corner, hence a mountainous district: adopted by MF-F, hence by E; 'to *canton*' prob comes from the MF-F *cantonner*, to divide into parts, hence into districts, with derivative *cantonnement*, whence E *cantonment*.

4. ONF *cant*, edge, angle, has dim *cantel*, corner, side, adopted by ME, whence E *cantle*.

**cant** (2), n hence adj and v, whence **canter and canting,** adj and n: the singing, whining utterance of certain preachers and, from much earlier, of beggars: L *cantus* (gen *cantūs*), chanting, singing, perh via ONF *cant*: akin to *cantāre* (s *cant-*), to sing or chant, orig an int of *canere* (s *can-*), to sing or chant: f.a.e., HEN.

2. It, from L, *cantare* has pp *cantato*, with f *cantata*, adopted by E, elliptical for 'musica *cantata*': '*sung* music'.

3. L *cantus* became OF-F *chant*, adopted by E; *cantāre* became OF-F *chanter*, whence E 'to *chant*'.

**Cantab.** See CAMBRIDGE.

**cantata.** See para 2 of the 2nd CANT.

**canteen:** late EF-F *cantine*, a case for bottles, a store (and café) for enlisted men: It *cantina*, a cellar, 'prob derived from *canto*, "corner", apprehended as "reserve" ' (B & W): therefore from L *cantus*, q.v. at the 1st CANT.

**canter** (1). See the 2nd CANT.

**canter** (2), n hence v: from '*Canter*bury gallop', a slow and easy gallop, adopted by pilgrims riding to the shrine of Thomas à Becket at Canterbury (England).

**cantharides,** made from the **cantharis** (pl *cantharides*), blister beetle or Spanish fly; L, from Gr *kantharis*, o.o.o.

**canticle:** L *canticulum*, dim of *canticum*, a song, from *canere*, to sing: f.a.e., HEN; cf the 2nd CANT.

**cantilever:** ? *cant*, an (external) angle, cf the 1st CANT+euphonic *i*, for 'easement'+LEVER.

**canting.** See the 2nd CANT.

**cantle.** See 1st CANT, para 4.

**canto:** It, from L *cantus*, a song: cf 2nd CANT and, f.a.e., see HEN.

**canton; cantonment.** See 1st CANT, para 3.

**canvas,** n, and **canvass,** v; **cannabis.**

The 3rd is adopted from L, where it means 'hemp' (indeed, see HEMP): its derivative VL *\*cannabaceus,* hempen, yields ONF-F *canevas,* adopted by ME, whence E *canvas,* whence 'to *canvas*', differentiated as *canvass*, to toss in a *canvas* sheet, hence to castigate, hence to examine severely, hence to solicit for votes: Webster compares OF *canabasser*, to sift through canvas, hence to sift thoroughly, hence to examine thoroughly. But F *canevas* could blend Picard *canavach* and OF *cheneves* (orig 'made of hemp'), a derivative of OF *chaneve*, itself from L *cannabis*, as B & W hold.

**canyon.** See CANNON, para 1, s.f.

**cap,** n hence v; **cape** (garment); **cope, coping stone; chapel.**

1. *Cap*, a simple head-covering, derives, via ME *cappe*, from OE *caeppe*, cap, cape, from LL *cappa*, perh from *caput*, head (E & M). L *cappa* becomes OProv *capa*, whence late MF-F, hence E, *cape*. *Cappa* has ML var *capa*, a long cape, whence ME, hence E, *cope*, with derivative sense 'arch' or 'vault', whence '*coping* stone'.

2. *Cappa* has dim VL *\*cappella*, a short cloak, later a reliquary or a sacred vessel, then a chapel, whence OF-MF, hence ME, *chapele*, whence EF-F *chapelle* and E *chapel*. (Webster.) B & W, however, after deriving OF *chapele* from VL *\*cappella*, explain the 'chapel' sense by the fact that 'it served

at first to designate the place where they kept the cape (*chape*) of St Martin of Tours—a cape venerated by the first kings of France'. But note that OF *chapele* more prob derives from ML *capella*, a chapel, whence ML *capellānus*, a chaplain. Whatever the VL or the LL form may have been, the ML word for 'chapel' is *capella*, not *cappella*.

3. Cf CHAPERON, CHAPLAIN, CHAPLET.

**capability, capable.**

1. The former, anl with *able, ability*, derives from the latter: and the latter comes, prob through MF-F *capable,* from LL *capābilis,* capacious, (then) capable, itself from *capere* (s *cap*-), to take in one's hands, to contain, to take: IE r, *\*kap*-, varr *\*kep*- and *\*kŏp*- or *\*kŏp*-.

2. On the s *cap*- arises the adj *capāx,* able to hold or contain, hence spacious, with o/s *capāc*-, whence, by suffix *-ious*, the E adj *capacious*; the derivative *capācitās,* o/s *capācitāt*-, becomes MF-F *capacité* becomes E *capacity,* whence *capacitate*, usu in the neg *incapacitate*, anl with other *-ate* vv; *incapacity* renders EF-F *incapacité*.

3. On the s *capt*- of the pp *captus* arise: *captiō*, a taking, o/s *captiōn*-, whence, partly by confusion with *caput*, head, the E *caption*; hence *captiōsus*, whence E *captious*; *captīuus*, ML *captīvus*, whence ONF *caitif*, whence ME *caitif*, whence E *caitiff* (adj hence n), and F *captif* and E *captive*; the derivative *captīuitās*, ML *captīvitās*, o/s *captīvitāt*-, yielding E *captivity*, and the derivative LL *captiuāre*, ML *-vāre*, with pp *captīvātus*, yielding 'to *captivate*';

LL *captor*, a taker, hence a capturer, adopted by E;

*captūra*, whence MF-F *capture*, adopted by E, whence 'to *capture*'.

4. V cpds in *-āre* include:

*anticipāre*, to take (*capere*) before (*ante*) the proper or usual time, with pp *anticipātus*, whence 'to *anticipate*'; the derivative *anticipātiō*, o/s *anticipātiōn*-, yields *anticipation*; *anticipative* and *anticipatory* are E adj formations in *-ive, -ory*;

*occupāre* (*oc*- for *ob*-): OF-F *occuper*: ME *occupien*: E 'to *occupy*', whence *occupier*; *occupant* (whence *occupancy*) comes, perh via F *occupant*, from L *occupant*-, o/s of the presp *occupans*; on the pp *occupātus* (s *occupāt*-) arises *occupātiō*, o/s *occupātiōn*-, whence, via OF-F, the E *occupation*, with adj *occupational*;

*participāre*, from *particeps* (see para 8), has pp *participātus*, whence 'to *participate*'; on the pp s *participāt*- arises LL *participātiō*, o/s *participātiōn*-, whence, via MF-F, the E *participation*; the presp *participans* has o/s *participant*-, whence the E adj, hence n, *participant*; LL *participātor*, adopted by E; whereas *participative, -atory*, are E formations, *participable* represents the LL *participābilis*;

*recuperāre*, to get back, to recover, has pp *recuperātus*, whence 'to *recuperate*'; the derivative *recuperātiō*, o/s *recuperātiōn*-, yields *recuperation*; *recuperātiuus*, ML *-īvus*, becomes *recuperative*;

*recuperātor* is adopted by E; *recuperatōrius* becomes *recuperatory*.

5. Also from *recuperāre* comes, via OF *recovrer*, ME *recoveren*, the E 'to *recover*'; *recovery* is prob *recover*+n suffix -*y*, although cf the OF *recovree* (from *recovrer*).

6. The freq *captāre*, to catch, has pp *captātus*, with derivative *captātiō*, o/s *captātiōn*-, whence, via EF-F, the E *captation*; legal *ad captandum*=L *ad captandum vulgus*, for the purpose of winning over the crowd by appealing to sentiment. Cf the sep entry CATCH, where also. CHASE, to pursue.

7. Cpd vv in -*cipere* (s *cip*-), the true c/f of *capere*, have considerably influenced E:

*accipere*, to take to (L *ad*) oneself, hence to receive: see the sep ACCEPT;

*concipere*, to take together (L *con*), to contain, to gather, notably *concipere semina*, (of a woman) to gather the male seed, to conceive; from the derivative n *conceptus* (gen -*ūs*) derives E *concept*, whence the adj *conceptual*; from the derivative *conceptiō*, o/s *conceptiōn*-, derives, via OF-F, the E *conception*; *conceit* (n hence v, whence the pa *conceited*) prob comes from the L n *conceptus*, but perh stands to *conceive* as *deceit* to *deceive*; 'to *conceive*' derives either from OF *conceivre* (F *concevoir*), esp from 'ils *conceivent*', they conceive, or, more prob, from the var *conceveir*, itself from L *concipere*, pp *conceptus*; *conceivable*=*conceive*+ *able*, or it represents EF-F *concevable*; *inconceivable*=*in*-, not+*conceive*+-*able*, or it represents EF-F *inconceivable*; *preconceive* (whence *preconceivable*)=*pre*-, before+*conceive*; *preconception*=*pre*-+*conception*;

*dēcipere*, to take by causing game to fall (*dē*, down from) into a trap, hence to capture by ruse, hence to trick, hence to betray; *dēcipere* becomes OF *deceivre*, *deceveir* (F *décevoir*), whence E 'to *deceive*', whence *deceiver*; on the pp *dēceptus* (s *dēcept*-) arises LL *dēceptiō*, o/s *dēceptiōn*-, whence, via OF-F, the E *deception*; *deceptive* either represents F *déceptive*, f of *déceptif*, prob from *déception*, or comes, perh via F, from LL *dēceptīuus*, ML -*īvus*; *deceptious* comes from MF *deceptieux*, f *deceptieuse*, from LL *dēceptiōsus*; *deceit* (whence *deceitful*), ME *deceite*, adopted from OF, comes from LL *dēceptus* (gen -*ūs*), fraud, deception;

*excipere*, to take separately (*ex*, out of, the general), has pp *exceptus*, whence both the E prep *except* and the L v *exceptāre*, whence F *excepter*, whence E 'to *except*'; *exception* (whence the adj *exceptional*) comes, via AF *excepcioun*, from the derivative L n *exceptiō*, o/s *exceptiōn*-; *exceptive* prob derives from LL *exceptīuus* (cf LL *exceptīuue*, by way of an exception);

*incipere*, to undertake (lit, take in), hence to begin, has pp *inceptus*, with derivative *inceptiō*, o/s *inceptiōn*-, whence E *inception*, and the freq *inceptāre*, whence 'to *incept*', and the agent *inceptor*, adopted by E, and the LL adj *inceptīuus* (ML -*īvus*), whence E *inceptive*;

*intercipere*, to take from among, i.e. to intercept,

has pp *interceptus*, whence, perh via EF-F, 'to *intercept*'; derivative *interceptiō*, o/s *interceptiōn*-, yields, perh via EF-F, *interception*; *interceptive* is an E formation, prob after *receptive*; *interceptor* is adopted from L;

*percipere*, to take (something) through (something else), hence to perceive, has pp *perceptus*, neu *perceptum*, whence the Psy *percept*; on the pp s *percept*- arise both LL *perceptibilis*, whence MF-F, hence E, *perceptible* (cf E from MF-F *imperceptible*, from ML *imperceptibilis*), and L *perceptiō*, o/s *perceptiōn*-, whence, perh via F, *perception*; *perceptive* is an E formation, prob on *receptive*; 'to *perceive*' comes from OF *perceveir* (esp 'ils *perceivent*', they perceive), var of *parceivre*, from *percipere*;

*praecipere*, to take in advance, hence to recommend or prescribe, has pp *praeceptus*, neu *praeceptum*, used also as n, whence OF-MF, whence E, *precept*; on the pp s *praecept*- arise *praeceptiō*, o/s -*ceptiōn*-, whence E *preception*—the agent *praeceptor*, whence E *preceptor*—the adj *praeceptīuus* (ML -*īvus*), whence E *preceptive*;

*recipere*, to gather, to take something offered, has pp *receptus*, whence the n *recepta*, elliptical for *pecunia recepta*, money received, whence OF *recepte*, eased to *recete* (F *recette*), whence ME *receite*, whence, influenced by the L, the E *receipt*, whence 'to *receipt*'; on the pp s *recept*- arise LL *receptibilis*, whence E *receptible*—*receptiō*, o/s *receptiōn*-, whence, prob via OF-F, the E *reception*, whence *receptionist* (-*ist*)—ML *receptīvus*, whence E *receptive*—and the int *receptāre*, whence *receptāculum*, whence—prob via MF-F—the E *receptacle*; 'to *receive*', whence (perh by F example) *receivable* and *receiver*, comes from OF *receivre*, esp 'ils *receivent*', they receive, from *recipere*;

*suscipere*, to take from underneath (*sub*), hence to undertake, has pp *susceptus*, neu *susceptum*, whence the Bio n *suscept* (cf the El *susceptance*, suffix -*ance*); on the pp s *suscept*- arise LL *susceptibilis*, neg *insusceptibilis*, whence E *susceptible*, neg *insusceptible*, and derivative ML *susceptibilitās*, o/s -*itāt*-, whence E *susceptibility*—and *susceptiō*, o/s *susceptiōn*-, whence E *susception*.

8. L *capere* has an agential c/f -*ceps*, which occurs, relevantly to E, in:

*forceps*, tongs, pincers, for *\*formiceps* or *\*formuceps*, lit 'a hot-taker, a taker of what is hot': L -*formus* (s *form*-), hot (akin to WARM)+-*ceps*; adopted by E;

*manceps*, a taker-in-hand, i.e. one who takes something, lit in his hand (L *manus*: see MANUAL), in order to possess or re-possess it: o/s *mancip*-, seen in *mancipāre*, pp *mancipātus*, whence 'to *mancipate*', to transfer (a slave) by selling, with subsidiary *mancipātiō*, o/s *mancipātiōn*-, whence E *mancipation*; commoner is the prefix cpd *ēmancipāre*, pp *ēmancipātus*, whence 'to *emancipate*', with subsidiary *ēmancipātiō*, o/s *ēmancipātiōn*-, whence E *emancipation*, and LL *ēmancipātor*, adopted by E; *emancipatory* and *emancipist* are E formations;

*municeps* (where *muni-* represents *munia*, official duties: f.a.e., MEAN, adj), inhabitant of a free town, with derivative adj *municipālis*, whence EF-F and E *municipal*; *municipality* comes from F *municipalité*, derived anl from L *municipālis*;

*particeps*, 'who takes his part of' (*pars*, a portion, o/s *part-*: f.a.e., PART), has the derivative Gram term *participium*, whence OF *participle*, adopted by E; the L adj *participiālis* yields E *participial*;

*princeps*, a prince=*primus*, first (f.a.e., PRIME)+ *-ceps*, taker, \**primceps* becoming *princeps*, whence OF-F *prince*, adopted by E (whence *princely*), the derivative MF-F *princesse* being adapted to *princess*; the derivatives are important—*principālis* (*princip-*, o/s of *princeps*+*-ālis*, E *-al*, adj suffix), whence the E adj hence n *principal*, the subsidiary LL *principālitās*, princeliness, pre-eminence, yielding, via MF *principalité*, the E *principality*—*principātus* (gen *-atūs*), a prince's power or domain, whence E *principate*—*principium*, where the emphasis lies upon the 1st element, whence MF-F *principe*, whence, influenced by OF *principel*, princely, hence principal, the E *principle*, whence the v *principle*, mostly in the pa *unprincipled*.

9. Cf HEAVE.

**capacious, capacity.** See prec, para 2.

**cap-a-pie.** See FOOT, para 15.

**caparison.** The v comes from EF-F *caparaçonner*, from late MF-F *caparaçon* (whence the E n), itself from Prov and ult akin to:

**cape** (1), a garment. See CAP.

**cape** (2), a headland: MF-F, from It *capo*, head: L *caput*: f.a.e., CAPITAL.

**caper**, (1), n and v. See CAB, para 2.

**caper** (2), a shrub, with buds and berries used in sauces: late MF-F *câpre*: It *cappero*: L *capparis*, trln of Gr *kapparis*, prob of Medit stock.

**capillary**, adj ('hair-like') hence n, hence also **capillarity**: L *capillāris*, from *capillus*, the hair of the head: o.o.o.: ? *ca*put, head+*pilus*, hair (Jules Bloch). Cf the element *capilli-*.

2. *Dishevelled* is the pa of *dishevel*, to loosen or disarray (one's hair), from MF *descheveler*, from VL \**discapillāre*: *dis-*, apart from+*capillus*.

**capital**, adj hence n, whence also **capitalism, capitalist, capitalize; capitation; capitulate, capitulation.**

The adj *capital* is adopted from OF-F *capital*: L *capitālis*, of the head, concerning loss of head, from *caput*, the head, o/s *capit-* (f.a.e., CHIEF); the n *capital* is adopted from EF-F. *Capitation* derives from LL *capitātiōn-*, o/s of *capitātiō*, a poll tax, from *capit-*; 'to *capitulate*', from ML *capitulātus*, pp of *capitulāre*, to number, hence to distinguish, by heads or chapters, with derivative *capitulātiō*, o/s *capitulātiōn-*, whence, via EF-F, the E *capitulation*, with E-formed adj *capitulatory*. The cpd LL *recapitulāre*, to number again, has pp *recapitulātus*, whence 'to *recapitulate*', and subsidiary *recapitulātiō*, o/s *-ātiōn-*, whence, perh via MF-F, the E *recapitulation*.

**capon**, a castrated cock or male chicken: OE

*capun*: L *capon-*, o/s of *capō*, akin to Gr *koptein*, to cut: cf COMMA.

**caprice, capricious.** See CAB, para 3.

**Capricorn.** See the element *capri-*.

**capsize**: earlier *capacise*, o.o.o.: prob cf F *chavirer*, to capsize, from Prov *capvira*, to turn (F *virer*) the head (L *cap*ut) downwards, as B & W have shown.

**capstan**: MF-F, from OProv, *cabestan*: Prov *cabestran*, orig the presp of a v deriving from Prov *cabestre*, halter, (later) a pulley cord: L *capistrum*, a snaffle, (later) a halter, a strong cord: o.o.o., but prob deriving from L *capere* (s *cap-*), to hold, to take—unless it comes from L *caput* (s *cap-*), head. (B & W; E & M.)

**capsule.** See the 2nd CASE, para 2.

**captain** (hence v), whence **captaincy** (suffix *-cy*): ME *capitain*: MF-F *capitaine*: LL *capitāneus*, adj from L *caput*, head, o/s *capit-*: f.a.e., CHIEF.

**captation.** See CAPABILITY, para 6.

**caption; captious.** See CAPABILITY, para 3.

**captivate; captive.** See CAPABILITY, para 3.

**captor; capture,** n and v. See CAPABILITY, para 3.

**car; career,** n hence v; **carriage, carry; charge; chariot.**

1. *Car*, a chariot, later a vehicle, derives from ME, from ONF, *carre*, from LL *carra* (L *carrus*): of C origin: cf Br *kar(r)*, chariot, carriage, Cor *car*, chariot, and *carios*, cart, carriage, Ga and OIr *carr*, dray, sledge, W *car*, chariot, dray, sledge: OC \**carsos* (\**karsos*), from \**cars*, to run: cf *current* at COURSE.

2. *Career* represents EF-F *carrière*, highway, (race)course, hence a running, from OProv *carriera*, deriving from ML (*via*) *carrāria*, a road for vehicles, itself from L *carrus*; with the ML adj *carrārius*, cf the LL adj *carrāricus*.

3. *Carriage* derives from ONF *cariage*, a carrying, from *carier*, to carry in a vehicle, whence 'to *carry*', whence *carrier*: and ONF *carier* (cf the OF-F *charrier*, from *char*) derives from ONF *car*, itself from L *carrus*.

4. *Charge*, n, adopted from OF-F, comes from OF-MF *chargier*, to load, whence 'to *charge*', orig to load, hence to place, upon someone, a load other than of weight: and OF-MF *chargier* (EF-F *charger*) represents VL \**carricāre*, from *carrus*, a waggon, (earlier) chariot. A *charger*, whether a large platter or a cavalry or ceremonial horse, carries a weight: ME *chargeour*: MF *chargeor*, from *chargier*. *Discharge*, n, derives from 'to *discharge*': ME *dischargen*, earlier *des-*: OF-MF *deschargier*: VL \**discarricāre*: *dis-*, away or apart from (i.e. riddance)+\**carricāre*. *Surcharge*, adopted from late MF-F, derives from OF-MF *surchargier*, EF-F *surcharger* (*sur*=L *super*, over), whence 'to *surcharge*'.

5. *Chariot* itself, adopted from MF-EF *chariot*, *chariote*, is a dim of OF-F *char*, itself from L *carrus*; hence the v 'to *chariot*', whence a *charioteer*.

6. Cf CARGO and CARK.

**caracul.** See KARAKUL.

**caramel.** See CANE.

**carapace:** late EF-F *carapace*: Sp *carapacho*, o.o.o.: ? L *caro*, flesh (akin to Gr *keirein*, to cut) +Gr *pakhus*, thick (cf *pachyderm* at element *dachy-*).

**carat:** MF-F *carat*: alchemists' ML *carratus*: (like It *carato*, from) Ar *qīrāt*, bean, weight of four grains, carat: Gr *keration*, a little *keras* or horn (f.a.e.: CEREBRAL), a carab bean, a carat.

**caravan; caravanserai,** anglicized as **caravansary.**

*Caravanserai* is EF-F *caravansérai* (now *-sérail*): Per *kārwānsarāi*, cpd of *kārwān*, caravan+*sarāī*, palace, (large) inn, the form *-seraī* being due to Tu *serāī*, derived from Per *sarāī*. *Kārwān*, a company of travellers, esp merchants or pilgrims, whence the mod sense 'covered vehicle', became MF *carvane*, later *caravane*, whence E *caravan*, which, drastically lopped, yields *van*, a light waggon, (later) a large covered vehicle.

**carbide.** See the element *carbo-*.

**carbine; carabineer** (or **-ier**).

The latter is EF-F *carabinier*, from EF-F *carabine*, a carbine, whence E *carbine*: *carabine* derives from EF-F *carabin*, a carabineer, itself from EF *escarrabin*, vocalized form of *scarrabin*, a bearer of plague-stricken corpses, prob (Webster) orig a carrion beetle, from *scarabée*, a beetle, itself from L *scarabaeus*, a dung-beetle, from the syn Gr *skarabeios*, itself app a mdfn of *karabos*, any horned beetle or prickly crustacean: perh cf the 1st CRAB; perh also cf the Eg *kheprer*, a dung-beetle.

**carbon:** F *carbone* (cf OF-F *charbon*, coal): from L *carbō*, coal, o/s *carbōn-*: perh ult akin to HEARTH. Adj: *carbonic*.

**carbuncle,** orig a *red*-hued precious stone: ONF *carbuncle*: L *carbunculus*, a little piece of *carbō* (see prec) or coal, later the precious stone and the tumour. Adj: *carbuncular*.

**carburettor** (**-etor, -etter**) is the agent *-or, -er,* of *carburet*, to combine (something) with carbon; cf the suffix *-et*, a *carburet* being a carbide.

**carcase** or **carcass:** EF-F *carcasse*: MF *charcois*, *carcois*: perh from MF-F *carquois*, a quiver for arrows, influenced by *chair*, flesh (B & W).

**card** (1), a tool used in cloth-making: MF-F *carde*, head of a thistle, hence the tool: Prov *carda*, from *cardar*, to card, whence MF-F *carder*, whence E 'to card'. The Prov *cardar* derives from VL *\*caritāre*, itself app a blend of L *cārere* (s *car-*), to card+*cardu(u)s*, a thistle.

**card** (2), made of paper; **carte blanche; cartel; carton** and **cartoon** (n, hence v and **cartoonist**); **cartography,** whence anl **-grapher, -graphic(al); cartridge; cartulary;—chart,** n hence v; **Magna C(h)arta; charter,** n hence v; **Chartist; chartulary; —écarté.**

1. *Card* anglicizes MF-F *carte*: L *carta*, var of *charta*: Gr *khartēs*, a leaf of papyrus, a writing: o.o.o., but prob of Hamitic origin—cf Eg *tche-t*, papyrus, and *tchamaa*, (a roll of) papyrus, a document.

2. *Carte blanche*, complete freedom, comes from EF-F *donner carte blanche*, lit 'to give a blank sheet of paper'.

3. *Cartel*, orig a letter of challenge, much later an agreement between opponents: EF-F *cartel*: It *cartello*, dim of *carta*: L *c(h)arta*.

4. *Carton* is adopted, *cartoon* adapted, from EF-F *carton*: It *cartone*, aug of *carta* (L *carta*, as in para 1).

5. *Cartography* owes something to F *cartographie*, lit map-drawing: cf the elements *carto-* and *-graph*.

6. *Cartridge*: earlier *cartrage*, a slovening of F *cartouche*, EF *cartuche*: It *cartuccia*, a suffix (*uccia*, cf *-accia*, E *-ace*) derivative of *carta*, paper: L *c(h)arta*. Many sorts of cartridge are wrapped in pasteboard; hence *cartridge paper*.

7. *Cartulary* is a var of *chartulary*, from ML *chartulārium*, an *-ārium* derivative from L *chartula*, dim of *charta*, paper; the sense 'archivist' comes from LL *chartulārius*, an adj used as n.

8. *Charter*, a written legal instrument, represents MF-F *charte* (pron *char-te*), a charter, but orig a map, from L *charta*; OF-F *charte*, map, accounts for E *chart*, a map, esp nautical, hence a graphic presentation of, e.g., statistics. The *Chartists*, promulgators and adherents of *Chartism*, are so named from *The People's Charter*, formulated in 1838.

9. The F card game *écarté* was orig the pp of EF-F *écarter*, (at cards) to put aside, to discard: lit, to take a card out (*é-*). 'To *discard*' itself derives from late MF-EF *descarter* (cf the It *scartare*): *des-*, L *dis-* (prefix)+*carte*, a playing card+*inf* suffix *-er*; hence the n *discard*.

**cardiac.** See CORDIAL, para 3.

**cardinal,** adj and n. The n, adopted from MF-F, comes, as does the It *cardinale*, from ML *'cardinālis* (adj as n) ecclesiae Romanae': and the E adj, likewise adopted from MF-F, comes from L *cardinālis*, adj of *cardō* (o/s *cardin-*), a hinge, a pivot: cf, sem, 'key man'. L *cardō*, s *card-*, is o.o.o.: cf, however, Skt *kūrdati* (s *kurd-*), he leaps, and the perh metathetic Gr *kradē* (s *krad-*), a waving, hence turning, tree-branch, a tree-top, itself akin to Gr *kordax*, a quivering twig (etc.) at branch's end, and perh to ON *hrata*, to oscillate, quiver. (Boisacq.)

**care** (n and v), **careful, careless** (whence **carelessness**); **chary; cur; garrulous, garrulity.**

1. 'To *care*' derives from OE *cearian* (s *cear-*), itself from OE *cearu* (s *cear-*), var *caru* (s *car-*), grief, sorrow, akin to syn OS *kara*—to Go *kara*, OHG *chara*, a lament, OHG *karrōn, kerran*, to cry—to L *garrīre* (s *gar-*), to chatter—to Gr *gērus* (s *gēr-*), Doric *gārus* (s *gar-*), voice—to Ga *gàir*, EIr *gáir*, a (loud) laugh, a many-voicèd clamour, OIr *gairim*, I cry (out), cf W *garm* (s *gar-*), Cor *garm*, a cry or call or shout, Br *garm*, a cry or weeping, OC *\*gar-*, to cry. The IE r *\*gar-*, to cry (out), is clearly echoic: cf Tokh A, B, *kar, ker*, to laugh.

2. *Careful*=OE *cearful*; *careless*=OE *cearlēas* (cf *-less*).

3. OE *cearu* has adj *cearig*, whence E *chary*.

4. Akin to OE *cearu* are OE *ceorian*, to murmur, complain, ON *kurra*, to grumble, and MLG *kurren*, to growl; the latter perh yields ME *curre*, E *cur*, orig any dog, lit 'growler'. The adj is *currish* (*cur*+orthographic *-r-*+*ish*, adj).

5. L *garrīre*, to talk, esp to chatter, has derivative adj *garrulus*, whence E *garrulous*: from *garrulus* derives LL *garrulitās*, o/s *garrulitāt-*, whence, prob via EF *garrulité*, the E *garrulity*.

**career**, to incline (a ship) well over to one side, in order to cleanse it, hence (vi) to lurch, hence to go fast and lurchingly: EF *cariner*, EF-F *caréner*, from MF-EF *carine*, MF-F *carène*, a ship's keel: It *carena*: L *carīna*, orig a nut's shell, s *carīn-*, r *car-*: akin to Gr *karuon*, a nut, s *karu-*, r *kar-*: IE r, *\*kar-*, hard (cf HARD itself).

**career.** See CAR, para 2.

**careful, careless.** See CARE, para 2.

**caress.** See CHERISH, para 2, and cf CHARITABLE.

**caret**, the sign ∧ : 'there is lacking': L *caret*, from *carēre*, to be lacking, perh (E & M) akin to L *castus*.

**cargo**: Sp *cargo*, a load, from *cargar*, to load: VL *\*carricāre*: therefore cf CAR, esp para 4. *Supercargo*, earlier *supracargo*, is a reshaping of Sp *sobre cargo*, lit a load over (*sobre*, L *super*) the normal.

**Carib, Cariban, Caribbean.** See CANNIBAL.

**caribou**: EF-F (Can F): of Alg origin: cf Micmac *khalibu*, *kalibu*, the pawer, the pawing beast (Webster).

**caricature**, n hence v and the *-ist* agent **caricaturist**: F *caricature*: as a painting term from It *caricatura*, from *caricare*, to (over-)load: VL *\*carricāre*: cf, therefore, CAR and CARGO.

**caries.** See CARRION.

**carillon.** See QUADRA, para 9, s.f.

**cark**, n, derives from 'to cark': ONF *carquier*: cf OF-MF *chargier*, EF-F *charger*, to load: cf, therefore, CAR, esp para 4. Sem, 'to load (someone) with care'.

**carl** or **carle**, a fellow. See CHURL.

**carmine; crimson**, n hence v. *Carmine*: OF-F *carmin*=ML *carminium*: Ar *qirmiz*, kermes+L *minium* (Iberian in origin), vermilion. Now, Ar *qirmiz* also becomes EF-F *kermès*, whence E *kermes*, an insect yielding a purplish colouring matter. Ar *qirmiz*—from Skt *kṛmi*, insect or worm (akin to Per *kirm* and Lith *kermis*, and to L *uermis*, s *uerm-*, worm),—further becomes the Sp *cremesín*, whence E *crimson*. In the tortuous peregrinations of the Arabic word, the Byz Gr *khermezi* has app intervened. (B & W.) Cf WORM.

**carnage; carnal (carnality) and charnel; carnate and incarnate, carnation and incarnation (and reincarnation) and incarnadine.—carnify, carnification, carnival; Carnivora, carnivore, carnivorism, carnivorous.**

1. The full cpds first:

*carnification* derives, anl, from *carnify*, to make or become flesh, from L *carnificāre*: *carni-*, c/f of

L *carō* (gen *carnis*), flesh+*-ficāre*, a c/f of *facere*, to make (cf FACT);

*carnival*: either EF *carneval*, EF-F *carnaval*, or its source, the It *carnevale*: not from It *Carne*, *vale !*, O flesh, farewell (sheer f/e), but prob either from ML *carnelevamen*, a taking-away of flesh, or, by contr, from the Milanese trans thereof—*carnelevale*; perh, however, simply It *carne*+*-vale*, a false-division adj suffix—cf *manovale* from *mano*: therefore '(the festival) of flesh'. (Hoare; Prati; Tommaseo & Bellini.) Orig, the festival before the fasting of Lent;

*Carnivora*, the flesh-eating quadrupeds: Sci L, from the neu pl of L *carniuŏrus*, ML *-vŏrus*, flesh-eating (cf VORACIOUS), whence the E adj *carnivorous* and the EF-F adj, whence n, *carnivore*, adopted, as n, by E; *carnivorism*=*carnivor*ous+the suffix *-ism*.

2. The prefix-cpds include:

*incarnadine*, adj whence v, comes from EF-F *incarnadin*, from It dial *incarnadino*, for *incarnatino*, dim of *incarnato*, itself from LL *incarnātus*; cf

*incarnate*, adj whence v: LL *incarnātus*, pp of *incarnāre*, to invest with flesh (*in-*, in); the derivative *incarnātiō*, o/s *incarnātiōn-*, becomes OF-F, whence E, *incarnation*;

*reincarnate* (adj and v), *reincarnation*: by prefix *re-*, again, anl with *incarnate* and *incarnation*.

3. Next, *carnate* and *carnation*. The former, now rare, derives from L *carnātus*; the latter (late MF *carnacion*, EF-F *carnation*), a becoming-flesh, from LL *carnātiō*, o/s *carnātiōn-*. The flower *carnation* derives from the sense 'flesh tints': F painting term, from lit OF *carnacion*.

4. Only two much-used simple L derivatives of *carō* remain: LL *carnālis*, fleshly, with its derivative *carnālitās*, o/s *carnālitāt-*, issuing resp into E *carnal* and E *carnality*; and LL *carnāticum*, animals' flesh, whence Prov *carnatge*, whence EF-F *carnage*, adopted by E in sense 'a mass or collection of animals' or men's carcasses', the mod sense deriving, through F, from It *carnaggio*, from *carnāticum*.

5. LL *carnālis* had the ML derivative *carnāle* (orig the neu of the adj), a burial place, whence OF-F *charnel*, adopted by E, often in the form *charnel house*.

6. L *carō* (s *car-*), orig a piece of flesh, part of a carcass, is akin to Umbrian *karu*, a part or portion, and *kartu*, distribution; to Gr *keirō* (s *keir-*), I cut, future *kerō* (s *ker-*); and to Hit *karss-*, 'to cut off': basic idea 'a piece of flesh cut off', orig in sacrifices. Cf CUIRASS.

**carol**, n and v. 'To *carol*', orig to dance a carol, then to sing and dance one, then merely to sing one, comes from OF-MF *caroler*, whence the OF-MF n *carol*, whence the E n *carol*; OF-MF *caroler*, prob from L *choraula*, a flute-player accompanying a choral dance, earlier *choraules*, from Gr *khoraulēs*, itself from *khoros*, a dance+*aulein*, to play a flute, from *aulos*, a flute: the 1st element is allied to CHOIR.

**Caroline.** See CHURL.

carotid (artery, supposed by Ancient Greeks to cause drowsiness): Gr *karōtídes*, carotid arteries: from *karos*, torpor, drowsiness, from *karousthai*, to feel heavy-headed, from *kara*, the head, s *kar-*; cf the *cer-* of L *cerebrum*.

carousal is an *-al* (n) derivative from 'a *carouse*', whence 'to *carouse*' (cf EF *carousser*): and the n *carouse* comes fron EF *carrouse*, earlier EF *carous*: G *garaus*, thoroughly (*gar*) out (*aus*), all out, as in *garaus trinken*, to drink it all.

carp (1), a fresh-water fish: MF-F *carpe*: Prov *carpa*: ML *carpa*, app of Gmc origin: cf OHG *karpo*, var *charpfo*, MHG *karpfe*, G *Karpfen*, and ON *karfi*, themselves o.o.o.

carp (2): ME *carpen*, to talk: ON *karpa*, to boast. In its passage to E, *carp* was influenced by L *carpere* (s *carp-*), to gather or pluck, (hence) to slander (cf 'ex*cerpt*').

carpal. See CARPUS.

carpel: SciL *carpellum*, a dim from Gr *karpos*, fruit.

carpenter (n hence v), carpentry.

The latter (cf the suffix *-ry*) derives from ONF *carpenterie*, from ONF *carpentier*, whence the E *carpenter* (cf agential *-er*): and ONF *carpentier* (OF-F *charpentier*) derives from LL 'artifex *carpentārius*', a waggon- or carriage-maker, from *carpentum*, waggon, carriage, of the same C origin as CAR.

carpet: OF-MF *carpite*: perh via It *carpita* (sing); certainly from ML *carpita*, var *carpeta* (pl), woolly cloths. from L *carpere* (s *carp-*), to pluck, e.g. wool: f.a.e., HARVEST.

carpus, wrist, with derivative adj (hence n) carpal: SciL: Gr *karpos*, wrist: f.a.e., WHORL.

carriage, carrier. See CAR, para 3.

carrion, n hence adj; crone; caries.

1. ME *carion*, earlier *caroine*, comes from ONF *caroigne*, *carogne*, carrion, from VL *carōnia*, var of *cariōnia*, from L *cariēs*, decay (adopted by Sci E), perh akin to Gr *kēr*, death. *Cariēs* has adj *cariōsus*, whence E *carious*.

2. ONF *carogne* becomes ED *karonje*, carcass, old ewe, whence, in its contr form *kronje*, derives E *crone*, a withered, usu poorish or poor, old woman, dial an old ewe.

carrot, whence the adj carroty: MF-F *carotte*: LL *carōta*: Gr *karōton*, perh from *\*karos*, var of *kara*, the head: cf, sem, Gr *kephalōton*, garlic, from *kephalē*, head. (Boisacq.)

carry. See CAR, para 3.

cart, n hence v (whence carter); cradle, n hence v.

1. *Cart* derives, by metathesis, from OE *craet*; prob orig made of wickerwork, the cart has a name app akin to MD *cratte*, a woven mat or hamper, therefore to *cradle*, from OE *cradel* or *cradol*, itself akin to OHG *kratte*, a basket, and perh to Skt *grantha* (nasalized form), a knot.

2. *Crate*, by some derived from L *crātis*, wickerwork, a hurdle, might equally come from MD *cratte*, a basket.

carte blanche. See the 2nd CARD, para 2.

cartel. See the 2nd CARD, para 3.

cartilage, adopted from F, comes from L *cartilāgō*, akin to L *crātis*, wickerwork; derivative LL *cartilāginōsus* yields *cartilaginous*. Cf *crate* at CART, para 2.

cartography, etc. See the 2nd CARD, para 5.

carton. See 2nd CARD, para 4.

cartoon, cartoonist. See 2nd CARD, para 4.

cartridge. See 2nd CARD, para 6.

cartulary. See 2nd CARD, para 7.

carve, pt carved, pp carven, vn carving.

*Carve* derives from OE *ceorfan*, to cut, (hence) to carve, with several Gmc cognates: cf also the Gr *graphein* (s *graph-*), to write, q.v. at GRAPH (cf 1st GRAFT).

cascade. See CADENCE, para 4.

case (1), occurrence, legal cause. See CADENCE, para 2.

case (2), a box, hence v (usu encase: prefix *en-*) in); casement; caisson; capsule; chase (jewellery, and enchase; chassis; sash (of window).

1. *Case*, ME *cass*, ONF *casse*, goes back to L *capsa*, box, chest, case, itself from *capere* (s *cap-*: f.a.e., CAPABILITY), to hold, contain, take.

2. The L form is visible in E *capsule*, adopted from EF-F, from L *capsula*, a little box, dim of *capsa*; the E adj is *capsular*—cf the adj suffix *-ar*.

3. *Casement* derives, by aphesis, from MF *encassement* (var of MF-EF *enchassement*, from MF-F *enchasser*: cf para 5), a frame, and in Mod E it is elliptical for *casement window*.

4. *Caisson*, orig a chest for explosives, comes straight from EF-F, which thus adapts It *cassone*, aug of *cassa*, from L *capsa*.

5. 'To *chase*' jewellery is aphetic for 'to *enchase*', from MF-F *enchâsser*, which=*en*, in+OF-F *châsse*, a box for relics+inf suffix *-er*: and *châsse*, whence the E n *chase*, setting of a gem, (later) a groove, derives—? influenced by It *cassa*—from L *capsa*.

6. The OF-F *châsse* yields OF-F *châssis*, a frame, whence E *chassis*; F *châssis* perh (Webster) derives rather from OF *chassiz*, from VL *\*capsiceum*, from LL *capsum*, from L *capsa*.

7. E *sash* (of window) is app a b/f from *sashes*, earlier *shashes*, earliest *shasses*, trln of F *châssis*, a sing misapprehended as pl. *Sash*, a scarf, a band, a wide belt, etc., is an entirely different word, deriving from Ar *shāsh*, a long band of fine material worn as a turban.

8. Cf CASH.

caseic, casein. See CHEESE, para 2.

casement. See the 2nd CASE, para 3.

caseous. See CHEESE, para 2.

cash, n hence v; cashier, n.

*Cash*, orig a money-box, comes, either through EF-F *casse* or through It *cassa* (or via EF-F *casse*, from It *cassa*), from L *capsa*, a box: cf the 2nd CASE. L *capsa* became, prob via a VL derivative, the Prov *caissa*, whence EF-F *caisse* (MF *quecce*), with EF-F agent *caissier*, whence, via D *kassier*, the E *cashier*.

cashew derives, either aphetically from EF-F *acajou* (adopted by E in differentiated sense), from Port *acaju*, or direct from the Port aphetic var *caju*; the Port *acaju* represents the Tupi (S Am) *acajú*, the tree concerned.

**cashier** (1), n. See CASH, s.f.

**cashier** (2), v: C16 *casseir, casseer*: MD-ED *casseeren, casseren* (D *kasseeren*): OF-F *casser* (cf Prov *cassar*): LL *cassāre*, to annul, to destroy, from *cassus*, empty, vain, prob from *carēre*, to lack. (Not from *quassāre*, freq of *quatere*, to shake.)

**cashmere** is elliptical for *Cashmere shawl*, a shawl made in Kashmir (India); hence, the goat's wool used therefor.

**casino**, adopted from It (orig, country house, summerhouse), is the dim of *casa*, a house, from L *casa*, a hut, a lowly cottage, o.o.o.: perh of C origin, ? *cadsa*, from *cad-*, var of *cap-*, to cover —cf the F Alpine dial *case*, jacket. The It *casino* yields also the card-game *cassino*. Cf CASSOCK.

**cask** and **casque** (helmet) both come from Sp *casco*, orig a potsherd, then a skull, a helmet, a cask: from *cascar*, to break, from L *quassāre*, to break, orig to shake vigorously and continuously, a freq and int of *quatere*, to shake, o.o.o. Cf QUASH.

**casket**: MF-F *cassette*: It *cassetta*, dim of *cassa*, from L *capsa*, a box: cf the 2nd CASE.

**casque.** See CASK.

**cassava**: F *cassave*: Sp *cazabe*: Taino (extinct Caribbean Amerind language) *casavi*, maniocflour.

**casserole**: EF-F *casserole*, saucepan: extn of MF-F *casse* (now a ladle, a scoop): OProv *cassa*: VL *cattia*, saucepan, trowel: Gr *kuathion*, dim of *kuathos*, a cup. (B & W; Dauzat.)

**cassia**: L *cassia*: Gr *kassia*, var of *kasia*: either from H *qĕtsī'āh*, from *qātsa*, to strip off the bark (Webster), or, more prob, from Eg *khasit, khesait*.

**cassino.** See CASINO.

**cassock; chasuble.**

The latter, adopted from OF-F, arises in LL *casubla*, hooded garment, alteration of LL *casula*, hooded cape, prob a fig use of LL *casula*, a small hut, from *casa*, hut: f.a.e., CASINO. The r of *casubla* is *cas-*: perh from it arose the It *casacca*, whence MF-F *casaque*, whence E *cassock*, the long, close-fitting eccl garment. Certainly the E word comes from the F, but the MF-F *casaque* (cf the EF var *casaquin*), orig a tunic, more prob (as B & W propose) comes from Per *kazagand*, a kind of jacket.

**cassowary**: Mal *kasavārī, kasuārī*, prob via the C17 naturalists' Sci L *casoaris, casuaris*, dat *casoari, casuari*. The mod Sci L *casuarius* has adj *casuarinus*, f *casuarina*: the tree *casuarina* is elliptical for *arbor casuarina*, 'cassowary tree', its twigs resembling a cassowary's feathers.

**cast** (v, hence n **cast** and the vn **casting**); **castaway.**

*Castaway* merely='a person *cast away*'. 'To *cast*' derives, via ME *casten*, from ON *kasta*, to throw, prob akin to L *gestāre* (s *gest-*), orig a freq of *gerere*, to carry, and formed from the s (*gest-*) of its pp *gestus*: therefore cf JEST.

**castanet.** See CHESTNUT.

**caste**—chaste, chastity; castigate, castigation—chasten, chastise, chastisement;--incest, incestuous.

1. *Caste*, orig a race or stock of men, comes from Port *casta*, (strictly, unmixed) race, from L (gens) *casta*, f of *castus*, 'conforming to religious rules and rites', hence—by fusion with *castus*, lacking, deprived, from *carēre*, to lack—'exempt, free or pure' of some fault, esp sexual, hence 'virtuous, sexually chaste'. The orig *castus* is akin to Skt *çiṣṭás*, well educated, well trained.

2. L *castus*, chaste, yields OF-F *chaste*, adopted by E; the derivative L *castitās*, o/s *castitāt-*, becomes OF-F *chasteté*, whence E *chastity*.

3. The orig *castus* has cpd *castigāre*, lit to drive (*agere*), hence to render, chaste, hence to correct, to reprimand, or punish, with pp *castigātus*, whence 'to *castigate*'. On the pp s *castigāt-* arise *castigātiō*, o/s *castigātiōn-*, whence *castigation*, and *castigātōrius*, punitive, whence *castigatory*.

4. L *castigāre* becomes OF-MF *chastier* (F *châtier*), whence ME *chastien*, later *chasten*, whence E 'to *chasten*', with pa *chastening* and pa *chastened*. The ME *chastien* acquired, by anl with other *-ise* (or *-ize*) vv, the var *chastisen*, whence E 'to *chastise*', whence *chastisement* (suffix *-ment*).

5. L *castus* has the opp *incestus*, soiled, impure (*in-*, not+*castus*), becoming specialized as 'incestuous', whence the nn *incestum, incestus* (gen *-ūs*)—source of E *incest*—whence the adj *incestuōsus*, whence E *incestuous*.

**castellan.** See CASTLE, para 4.
**castellated, castellation.** See CASTLE, para 5.
**caster.** See the 2nd CASTOR.
**castigate, castigation.** See CASTE, para 3.

**castle,** n hence v; **castellated, castellation; château, chatelaine; castral, castrametation; -caster, -cester, -chester.**—Akin to CASTRATE, treated sep.

1. The basic word is L *castrum*, an entrenched or fortified place, mostly in pl *castra*, a strongly entrenched, hence a fortified, camp; whence the E adj *castral*. The cpd *castrametāri*, to measure off (*metāri*) a camp, has derivative *castrametātiō*, o/s *-metātiōn*, whence, through F, the E *castrametation*, camp-surveying.

2. *Castrum, castra*, have the Pl N derivatives *-caster*, as in *Doncaster*—*-cester*, as in *Worcester*—*-chester*, as in *Chester* and *Manchester*. Cf Elements.

3. L *castrum* has dim *castellum*, fortified camp, fortress, whence ONF and OE *castel*, whence, esp from the ONF (C14 onwards) sense 'castle', ME *castel*, whence E *castle*.

4. L *castellum* ult becomes F *château* (for *chasteau*), adopted by E. Moreover, *castellum* has adj, hence n, *castellānus*, whence ONF *castelain*, whence obsol E *castellan*, a castle's governor or warden; whence also OF-MF *chastelain*, EF-F *châtelain*, with f *châtelaine*, a castellan's wife, a castle's mistress, whence E *chatelaine*, mistress of a large house, whence, from the keys she formerly handled, an ornamental hook, etc., for keys.

5. *Castellum* has, in ML, the derivative *castel-*

*lāre*, to build as or like a castle, with pp *castellātus*, whence the E v *castellate* and the pa *castellated* and the anl n *castellation*.

**castor** (1), a rodent: OF-F, from L, *castor*, a beaver: Gr *kastōr*, from *Kastōr*, twin of Pollux. The secretion *castor* (whence *castor oil*) derives from ML *castoreum*, rendering Gr *kastorion*, neu sing of adj *kastorios*, of the *kastōr* or beaver. That secretion was used in maladies of the womb: and *Kastor* was a noted preserver of women. (Boïsacq.)

**castor** (2), as in the castor of a chair- or bed-leg: earlier *caster* (still occ used), from *cast*, to throw, to turn (in packing, e.g., furniture).

**castor oil.** See the 1st CASTOR.

**castral; castrametation.** See CASTLE, para 1.

**castrate, adj, n, v; castration.**

The Bot adj *castrate* and the v 'to *castrate*' come from L *castrātus*, pp of *castrāre*, to castrate; the n *castrate*, castrated person, eunuch, has the same origin, but reaches E prob via It *castrato* (applied to operatic singers) and F *castrat*; on the pp s *castrāt*- arises the n *castrātiō*, o/s *castrātiōn*-, whence, prob via F, the E *castration*. The L *castrāre*, s *castr*-, derives from PL *kastrom* (*kas*-, r+-*ro*-, a formative+-*m*, suffix of neu n), 'that which serves to cut', whence L *castrum*, (lit) a cutting off, (hence) a place cut off, hence an entrenchment, hence a place trench-fortified, hence a fortified camp: cf CASTLE. With *castrum*, cf the Skt *çastrám*, a cutting instrument, and, with the L r *cas*-, cf the Skt *çásati*, he cuts; prob cf also the Gr *keazō* (s *keaz*-, elongation of *\*kaz*-), I split or cleave. The IE r would be *\*kez*-, var *\*kaz*-. (E & M.)

**casual, casualty.** See CADENCE, para 2.

**casuarina.** See CASSOWARY.

**casuist, casuistry.** See CADENCE, para 2.

**cat; catbird, catfish, catgut, catkin, catsup, cat-tail; cat's-claw, -cradle, -ear, -eye, -paw, -tail; caterpillar, caterwaul; catty.—kitten, kitling, kitty, kit.**

1. ME *cat* derives partly from OE *cat, catt, catte*, partly from ONF *cat*: LL *cattus*, f *catta*, s *catt*-, r *cat*-: either of C origin, cf Gaul *\*kattos* (s *\*katt*-), PN *Cattos*, derived by Malvezin from r *\*cat*-, to flee, cf also Ga and OIr *cat*, Mx *cat* or *cayt*, W *cath*, Br *cas, caz* (*kaz*) and earlier *kad*, Cor *câth* (*kâth*) or *cât* (*kât*); or, less prob, but as E & M suggest, African—but the closest word afforded by Eg is *àmàit* or *màit*, cat. The other cognates, e.g. OHG *kazza*, ON *köttr*, cat, Serb *kotiti* (r *kot*-), to whelp, Ru *kot*, tomcat, merely serve to indicate that the C origin is at least possible.

2. *Catbird*: one of its calls resembles a cat's mew;
*catfish:* with teeth, barbels—and ferocity—resembling a cat's;
*catgut:* folklore; made usu from the intestines of sheep;
*catkin: cat*+dim suffix -*kin*: it resembles a cat's tail;
*catnip:* cats enjoy it;
*cat-tail* (*cattail*): a plant with furry spikes;

*cat's-claw:* a shrub with hooked tendrils;
*cat's cradle:* strings so arranged as to form a small cradle—fit for a cat;
*cat's-ear:* a plant with leaves not unlike a cat's ear;
*cat's-eye:* a gem emitting reflections, as does a cat's eye;
*cat's-paw:* a light wind ruffling the water much as it would ripple to a cat's paw; as 'dupe' it arises from the fable of a monkey using a cat's paw to pull chestnuts out of a fire;
*cat's-tail:* any of several plants that resemble one.

3. The adj of *cat* is *catty*: *cat*+euphonic *t*+adj suffix -*y*.

4. Two not entirely obvious cpds of *cat* are:
*caterpillar:* ONF *cate plue*, var *catepelose*: LL *catta pilosa*, (lit) hairy cat;
*caterwaul:* either from MD *kater*, tomcat+D *wauwelen*, to tattle, cf LG dial *katterwaulen*, to caterwaul, or for *catawail*, an easing of *cat-wail*, to wail like a cat.

5. *Kitling*, a kitten, derives from ON *ketlingr*, dim of *köttr*, cat—or of its E-derived var *ketta*. *Kit* is short for *kitten*: and *kitten* derives from ME *kitoun*, itself (the -*i*- influenced by the 1st -*i*- of *kitling*) from ONF *caton*, dim of ONF *cat*, cat; its adj is *kittenish* and its pet-form is *kitty*.

**catachresis:** adopted from L: Gr *katakhrēsis*, a misuse, from *katakhrēsthai*: *kata*-, against (see Prefixes)+*khrēsthai*, to use. The Gr adj *katakhrēstikos* yields E *catachrestic*.

**cataclysm,** whence the adj *cataclysmic*: EF-F *cataclysme*: LL *cataclysmus*, the Biblical Flood: Gr *kataklusmos*, from *katakluzein*, to inundate: *kata*-, down+*kluzein*, to wash.

**catacomb:** MF-F *catacombe*: It *catacomba*: LL *catacumba*, prob a hybrid, either of Gr *kata*, down+L *tumba*, tomb, or of Gr *kata*+*cumbere* (s *cumb*-), to lie down, to be abed, sense-influenced by *tumba*.

**catacoustics.** See ACOUSTIC.

**catafalque.** See SCAFFOLD.

**catalepsy, cataleptic.** See EPILEPSY, para 2, and cf the element -*lepsia*.

**catalogue,** n hence v (whence **cataloguer**): MF-F: LL *catalogus*: Gr *katalogos*, a list, (lit) a counting up, from *katalegein*: *kata*-, down+*legein*, to say, to count (cf LOGIC).

**catalpa,** an A tree: SciL, from Creek (Amerind) *kutuhlpa*, lit 'wingèd head', ref its flowers. (Mathews.)

**catalyse, catalysis, catalyst, catalytic.** See LOSE, para 11.

**catamenia.** See MEASURE, para 2.

**catamount**=*cat* of (*a*) *mount*, cat of the mountain(s). Also *catamountain*.

**catapult:** MF-F *catapulte*: L *catapulta*: G *katapaltēs* or -*peltēs*: *kata*, down+*pallein* (s *pall*-, r *pal*-), to hurl.

**cataract,** perh via EF-F *cataracte*: L *cataracta*, earlier *catarractes*: Gr *kataraktēs*, an easing of *katarrhaktēs*, a waterfall, either from *katarassein*, to dash down (*kata*, down+*arassein*, to smite), or from *katarrhēgnunai*, to break down (*kata*+*rhēgnunai*, to break). A *cataract* in the eye comes from the same Gr word.

**catarrh.** See RHEUM, para 3.

**catastrophe, catastrophic.** See STRAP, para 3.

**catawba:** Choctaw *Katápa*, '(a tribe) *separated* (from other Siouan tribes)'. Mathews.

**catch,** v hence n (whence adj **catchy**); **chase,** to pursue, a pursuit; **purchase,** v and n.

1. 'To *catch*', ME *cachen*, derives from ONF *cachier* (cf OF *chacier*, whence F *chasser*), from VL \**captiāre*, for L *captāre*, int of *capere*, to take: f.a.e., CAPABILITY; cf HEAVE.

2. VL \**captiāre* becomes OF-MF *chacier* (EF-F *chasser*), whence ME *chacen*, later *chasen*, whence 'to *chase*' or pursue; the derivative OF-MF n *chace* (EF-F *chasse*) becomes ME *chace*, later *chase*, continuing in E.

3. OF *chacier* has the OF-MF cpd *porchacier*, var *purchacier*, to chase eagerly (*por-, per-*=L *per*, through, used int): hence ME *porchacen*, later *purchasen*, whence 'to *purchase*', to chase and catch, hence to attain or obtain, esp with money. The OF-MF v has derivative n *porchace, pourchace*, etc., which becomes *porchas, pourchas, purchas*, etc., whence E *purchase*.

**catechism, catechist, catechize.**

'To *catechize*' comes—perh via MF-F *catéchiser*—from LL *catechizāre*, from LGr *katēkhizein*, var of Gr *katēkhein*, to instruct, (lit) to sound through or over: *kata*, down, used int+*ēkhein*, to sound, from *ēkhē*, a sound, itself echoic. *Katēkhein* has (1) agent \**katēkhistēs*, an instructor, (later) esp in religious knowledge, whence LL *catechista*, whence E *catechist* (ct EF-F *catéchiste*), and (2) abstract-n derivative *katēkhismos*, whence LL *catechismus*, whence MF-F *catéchisme* and, perh imm from F, the E *catechism*. Cf ECHO.

**categoric(al),** adj hence (longer form) n; **category,** whence **categorist** and **categorize** (whence **categorization**).

*Categorical* is an E elaboration of *categoric* (cf EF-F *catégorique*), from LL *catēgoricus*, trln of Gr *katēgorikos*, the adj of *katēgoria*, whence LL *catēgoria*, whence E *category* (cf EF-F *catégorie*); and *katēgoria* derives from *katēgorein*, to accuse, (but also) to affirm or predicate: *kata*, against, also merely int+(the r of) *agoreuein*, to harangue, (but also) to assert, from *agora*, an assembly: ult from *agein*, to drive, (hence) to do: cf ACT and AGENT.

**catena, catenary, catenate (catenation).** See CHAIN, para 1.

**cater,** v (whence **caterer**), derives from *cater*, obs for 'caterer': ME *catour*, caterer, (*lit*) purchaser, aphetic for *acatour*, purchaser: AF, from ONF, *acatour* (cf OF *achateor, acateor*, the former yielding EF-F *acheteur*): VL \**accaptātor*, purchaser (cf ML *acaptātiō*, a purchasing), from VL presumed, through ML factual, *accaptāre*, to

purchase, buy: *ad*, to+*captāre*, int of *capere*, to take.

**caterpillar.** See CAT, para 4.

**caterwaul.** See CAT, para 4.

**catgut.** See CAT, para 2.

**catharsis:** Gr *katharsis*, a cleansing, a purification, deriving from *kathairein* (s *kathair-, kathar-*), to cleanse, from *katharos*, pure, (lit) utterly clean, spotless: o.o.o.; perh akin to L *castus* (cf CASTE). *Kathairein* has derivative adj *kathartikos*, whence E *cathartic*, whence the Med n, meaning 'a purgative'.

**cathedral,** adj and n: resp LL-ML *cathedrālis* (adj of *cathedra*) and ML *cathedrālis* (ecclesia), church with a bishop's *cathedra* or chair: f.a.e., CHAIR, where see *cathedratic*.

**cathode:** Gr *kathodos*, a way (*hodos*) down (*kata*).

**catholic,** adj, whence **Catholic,** adj, whence *Catholic*, n; **Catholicism** (cf EF-F *catholicisme*), from *Catholic*, adj; and **catholicity** (cf EF-F *catholicité*), from *catholic*, both by anl.

Orig and strictly, *catholic* means 'general, world-wide', and comes, perh through MF-F *catholique*, from L *catholicus*, itself from Gr *katholikos*, general, universal: adj from Gr *kath holou*, concerning (*kath'* for *kata*, down, concerning) the whole (*holos*, adj: akin to SAFE).

**catkin.** See CAT, para 2.

**catnip.** See CAT, para 2.

**cat's-paw.** See CAT, para 2.

**cattle; chattel;** resp property in general, then of live stock (quadrupeds), finally the domesticated bovines; and personal property, esp movable goods.

The words are doublets, thus: *cattle*, from ME *catel*; *chattel*, from the ME var *chatel*; *catel*, from ONF *catel*, but *chatel* from OF-EF *chatel*; both from L *capitāle*, n from the neus of the adj *capitālis*, chief, (lit) concerning the *caput* or head: cf CAPITAL and, f.a.e., CHIEF.

**catty.** See CAT.

**Caucasian,** adj hence n; **Caucasus.**

The adj derives from Gr *Kaukasia*, the region (*-ia*), itself from *Kaukasos*, Mt Caucasus, whence, via L, *Caucasus*: of Caucasian origin.

**caucus:** perh of Amerind origin, prob Alg—cf Virginian *caucauasu*, an elder of the tribe, a counsellor (Webster); but more prob (Mathews, after the *Century*) from ML *caucus*—cf LL *caucum*—from LGr *kaukos*, a drinking-vessel.

**cauda,** adj **caudal.** See CODA.

**caudle,** a warm medicinal drink: ONF *caudel*, by metathesis from L *calidus*, warm: cf CALDRON, see CALORIC.

**caul,** a membrane; **calotte.** *Caul*: late MF-F *cale*, b/f from MF-F *calotte*, a skullcap: Prov *calota, callotta*: Gr *kaluptra*, a covering, from *kaluptein*, to cover, conceal: akin to HELL; cf APOCALYPSE. B & W, however, derive *calotte*, presumably as a dim, from *cale*, which, for them, is aphetic for *écale*, shell, husk, pod, from Frankish \**skala*—cf the Go *skalja*, a tile.

**cauldron.** See CALDRON.

**cauliflower**: reshaped after the element *cauli-* and the E *flower*: earlier *coly-flory*: EF-F *chou-fleuri* (soon *chou-fleur*), lit 'flowery cabbage': L *caulis* (s *caul-*), a stalk, intimately akin to Gr *kaulos*+L *flos*, a flower, o/s *flor-*.

**caulk.** See CALK.

**cause, causal** (whence **causality**), **causation, causative, causidical; because; accuse, accusation, accusative, accusatory; excuse** (n and v), **excusable, excusal, excusatory, excusive; inexcusable; recuse, recusancy, recusant** (adj hence n), **recusation;**—kickshaw.—Cf, remotely, HEW.

1. 'To *cause*' derives from MF-F *causer*, itself from the OF-F n *cause*, from L *causa*, cause, origination. *Causa* acquired in law the special sense 'lawsuit', cf *causidical* and *accuse*: o.o.o.: 'Would it be a loan-word?' (E & M). The PL *kaussa* suggests a loan from Eg *khe-t*, cause, perh via *\*khetsa*, *\*khessa*, *\*khassa*.

2. *Because* is elliptical for '*because* (earlier *by cause*) that'.

3. L *causa* has simple derivatives LL *causālis*, whence E *causal*; LL *causātiō*, o/s *causātiōn-*, whence *causation*; and LL *causātiuus*, ML *-ivus*, whence, prob via F, the E *causative*.

4. The cpd adj *causidicālis*, cause-saying, hence -pleading, whence E *causidical*, has 2nd element deriving from *dicere* (s *dic-*), to say.

5. The relevant prefix-cpd vv are *accusāre*, to bring a lawsuit against (*ad*, to), *excusāre* and *recusāre*. *Accusāre*, via OF-MF *acuser* (EF-F *accuser*) and ME *acusen*, yields 'to *accuse*', whence *accuser*; derivative *accusābilis* leads, perh via EF-F, to *accusable*; *accusātiō*, o/s *accusātiōn-*, to *accusation*, prob imm from MF-F; *accusātiuus*, ML *-ivus*, to *accusative* (adj hence n), perh via F; *accusatōrius* to *accusatory* and, by elaboration, *accusatorial*.

6. L *excusāre*, to take out of (*ex*) a lawsuit (*causa*), to absolve of blame, becomes OF-F *excuser*, whence ME *excusen*, whence 'to *excuse*'; an *excuse*, adopted from MF-F, derives from OF *excuser*. The derivative LL *excūsabilis* becomes, prob via MF-F, *excusable*; *excusal*, *excusative*= 'to *excuse*'+n suffix *-al*, adj suffix *-ative*.

7. LL *inexcūsabilis* gives us *inexcusable*.

8. L *recusāre* becomes, via MF *recuser* (F *ré-*), the legal *recuse*; the presp *recusans*, o/s *recusant-*, yields *recusant*, whence *recusancy* (*t*, dropped for ease); the derivative *recusātiō*, o/s *recusātiōn-*, yields legal EF-F and E *recusation*.

9. The Shakespearean *kickshaw*, a toy, a delicacy, represents EF-F *quelque chose*, something: *quelque*, from L *quālis* (as in *quality*); *chose*, from L *causa*, cause, (hence) thing.

**causeway; causey.** The former is f/e for the latter, which, ME *cauci*, comes from ONF *caucie*, from LL (*uia*) *calciāta*, from *calciāre*, to make a road, either (by paving with lime) from L *calx*, lime, or (by treading firm) from L *calx*, heel.

**causidical.** See CAUSE, para 4, and DICT, para 11.

**caustic** (adj and n), whence **causticity** and **causticize; holocaust; cauter, cauterize** (whence **cauterization**), **cautery.**

1. The n *caustic* represents L *causticum*, elliptical for *causticum medicamentum*, *causticum* being orig the neus of *causticus*, from Gr *kaustikos*, from *kaiein* (s *kai-*), to burn, akin to *kausos*, a burning fever; IE r *\*kēu-*, *\*keu-*, var *\*kau-*.

2. *Holocaust* comes, prob via OF-F *holocauste*, from LL *holocaustum*, from LGr *holokauston*, prop the neus of Gr *holokaustos*, burnt whole: *holo-* (see Elements)+*kaustos*, burnt, pp of *kaiein*.

3. 'To *cauterize*' comes from LL *cauterizāre*, from Gr *kautēriazein*, itself from *kautērion*, a branding iron, from *kaiein*; *kautērion* becomes L *cautērium*, whence both the E *cautery*, branding iron, now usu a curative branding, and, via MF-F *cautère*, the E *cauter*, the instrument.

4. Cf INK.

**caution** (n hence v), **cautionary** (adj hence n), **cautious; incautious; precaution** (n and v), **precautionary; cavey.**

1. The base is L *cauēre*, ML *cavēre*, to be on guard (against, lest), to take great care, with ML imp *cave*, whence the sl *Cavey!*, and with the subj *caveat*, let him beware, whence the E legal n *caveat*. Having s and r *cau-*, *cauēre* is perh akin to Gr *koeō*, I understand or notice, and Skt *ākuvate*, he intends, *ākūtis*, intention, and esp *kavís*, prudent, observant; perh also to OS *skawōn*, OFris *skāwia*, OHG *scouwōn*, to notice, observe, and therefore to E SHOW. (E & M.)

2. *Cauēre* has derivative *cautus*, on guard, wary, prudent, whence *cautious*, influenced by *caution*, which comes, prob via MF-F *caution*, a security, from L *cautiōn-*, o/s of *cautiō*, built upon the adj s *caut-*; 'to *caution*', although prob influenced by MF-F *cautionner*, derives from the E n *caution*, whence also *cautionary* (adj suffix *-ary*).

3. L *cautus* has opp *incautus*, whence, after E *cautious*, the E *incautious*; *incaution*, however,=*in-*, not+*caution*.

4. L *cauēre* has prefix-cpd *praecauēre*, whence, in LL, *praecautiō*, o/s *praecautiōn-*, whence, prob via EF-F *précaution*, the E *precaution*; 'to *precaution*' owes something to late EF-F *précautionner* (from the n); *precautionary* derives, after *cautionary*, from the n *precaution*.

**cavalcade; cavalier** (n hence adj); **cavalla; cavalry—chivalry, chivalric, chivalrous; caballero.**

1. The imm base is L *caballus*, a horse, esp a working horse or a gelding, perh from the rare Gr *kaballēs*: Hofmann proposes, for the Gr word, a Balkan origin (? Illyrian); Boisacq thinks *kaballēs* a borrowing from some language of NE Europe and adduces the OSl *kobyla*, a mare; E & M, after mentioning the Gr word and the Balkan possibility, lean towards C, as does Malvezin. The C origin (cf CAR) seems the most prob: cf the Gaul PN *Caballos*, Br *caval*, Cor *cevil* (or *k-*), also *keffyl*, W *ceffyl*, Mx *cabbyl*, Ga and Ir (and EIr) *capall*. The C r would be *\*cab-*, to run, to flee, with var *\*cap-*, as in L *caper*, a he-goat (see CAB, para 2).

2. *Caballus* has LL agent *caballārius*, a horseman, whence both the Sp *caballero*, a knight, a gentleman, and the It *cavaliere*, whence late MF-F *cavalier*, adopted by E, a well-born mounted soldier (cf, sem, the L *eques*), whence the *Cavaliers* (cf L *Equites*).

3. The LL *caballa*, a mare (the f of *caballus*), adopted by Sp, became, in Port, *cavalla*, a fish with an equine head, adopted by AE

4. *Caballus* has a LL derivative *caballicāre*, to ride a horse, whence It *cavalcare*, whence the n *cavalcata*, whence MF-F *cavalcade*, adopted by E; cf the suffix *-ade*.

5. *Caballus* has a LL adj *caballāris*, on horseback, whence, via its neupl *caballāria*, the ML *cavallāria*, a military ceremony of inauguration, with a differentiated var, *cavalleria*, horse soldiers, cavalry, adopted by It, whence the EF-F *cavalerie*, whence E *cavalry*.

6. *Caballus* itself became OF-F *cheval*, whence the OF-F agent *chevalier*, horseman, later a knight; its OF-F derivative *chevalerie* yields the E *chivalry* (cf suffixes *-ry*, *-ery*), with E-formed adj *chivalric* and F-formed adj *chivalrous* (OF-EF *chevaleros*, *-ereus*, *-erus*). The late MF-F *chevaleresque* (from It *cavalleresco*, influenced by F *chevalier*) blends with the E *chivalry* to produce the absurd E *chivalresque*.

cave, n hence v; cavern, cavernous; cavity;—concave, concavity; excavate, excavation, excavator;—decoy, n hence v; gabion (cf the sep CAGE); gaol, jail (n hence v), gaoler, jailer (*-or*).

1. *Decoy* (n)=D *de kooi*, the enclosure for trapping wildfowl, D *de* being apprehended as part of the word; *kooi* comes from ML *cavea*, L *cauea*, from L *cauus*, ML *cavus*, hollow. ML *cavea* becomes It *gabbia*, with aug *gabbione*, a large cage, (hence) a gabion, whence EF-F *gabion*, adopted by E.

2. E *gaol* (now often *jail*) and AE *jail* derive from ME *gail*, *gayhol*, *jaile*: OF-MF *jaiole* (whence EF-F *geôle*): ONF *gaiole*: ML *caveola*, VL *caueola*, dim of L *cauea*, as above. *Gaoler*, *jailer*, later *jailor*, derive from ME *gailer*, *jailer*: MF *jaiolier* (EF-F *geôlier*): ONF *gaiolier*, from ONF *gaiole*.

3. L *cauus* has two notable prefix-cpds: (1) *concauus*, ML *-cavus*, whence MF-F *concave*, adopted by E; 'to *concave*' represents ML *concavāre* (L *-cauāre*); *concavity* represents ML *concavitās* (LL *-cauitās*), prob through MF-F *concavité*; and (2) *excauāre*, ML *-cavāre*, to hollow out, with ML pp *excauātus*, whence E 'to *excavate*'; the derivative *excauātiō*, ML *excavātiō*, has o/s *excavātiōn-*, whence E *excavation*; *excavator* is an E formation, prob after *navigator*.

4. L *cauus* has LL derivative *cauitās*, ML *cavitās*, o/s *cavitāt-*, whence, via MF-F *cavité*, the E *cavity*.

5. *Cauus* also yields—perh, for the suffix, after *cisterna* and *laterna*, *lanterna*—*cauerna*, ML *caverna*, whence, via OF-F *caverne*, the E *cavern*, whence the rare 'to *cavern*'; and *cauerna* has adj

*cauernōsus*, ML *cavernōsus*, whence, perh via *caverneuse*, the f of MF-F *caverneux*, the E *cavernous*.

6. The r is *cau-*, with var *cou-*, as in the early var *couus*, for PL **couos*, hollow; prob akin are MIr *cūa*, Gr *koilos*, hollow, Gr *kuar*, a hollow; perh ult akin is HOLE.

caveat; Cavey! See CAUTION, para 1.

caviar, occ caviare: EF-F *caviar* (earliest as *cavyaire*): It *caviaro* (now *caviale*): Tu *khāvyār* (modern *havyàr*).

cavil, v hence n and the agent caviller; cavillation.

*Cavillation*, a cavilling, a (legal) quibble, derives, perh via MF-EF, from *cavillātiōn-*, the o/s of L *cauillātiō* (ML *cav-*), itself built on *cauillāt-*, the pps of *cauillāri*, to banter, to censure, from *cauilla*, mockery, perh—by dissimilation—from *caluāri*, to deceive (cf CALUMNIATE). *Cauillāri* becomes MF-EF *caviller*, whence 'to *cavil*'.

cavity. See CAVE, para 4.

cavort. See *curvet* at CURVE.

caw, v hence n: echoic: the cries of crows, rooks, ravens, etc.

cay. See the 2nd KEY.

cayenne pepper: Tupi *kyinha*: from the Tupi version of the island of *Cayenne*, off F Guiana, rather than of *Cayenne*, the capital of F Guiana. *Guiana* and *Cayenne* (F shape) are the same word.

cayman: Sp *caimán*: of Caribbean Amerind origin—cf Galibi *cayman* and Cariban *acagouman*.

cayuse, an Indian pony, prop one bred by the *Cayuse* tribe of the NW U.S.A.: o.o.o.

cease, v and n; ceaseless, unceasing.

*Ceaseless*=*cease*, n+suffix *-less* (cf LESS); *unceasing*=*un-*, not+*ceasing*, presp of 'to *cease*'. The n *cease* comes from OF *ces* (F *cesse*), itself from OF-F *cesser*, to cease, whence ME *cessen*, later *cesen*, whence 'to *cease*': and OF-F *cesser* derives from L *cessāre*, to cease, prop a freq of *cēdere*, to go, walk, hence esp to retire, hence to halt, hence to cease: f.a.e., CEDE. *Cessāre*, pp *cessātus*, has derivative n *cessātiō*, o/s *cessātiōn-*, whence, via MF-F, the E *cessation*. LL has presp used as adj, *incessans* (*in-*+*cessans*, presp of *cessare*), o/s *incessant-*, whence, via EF-F, the E *incessant*, unceasing, whence *incessancy* (abstract suffix *-cy*).

cedar: ME, from OF-MF, *cedre* (F *cèdre*): L *cedrus*: Gr *kedros*, cedar, juniper, akin to Lith *kadagys*, juniper: L *cedrus* is prob akin, ult, to L *citrus*, q.v. at CITRON. The adj is *cedarn*.

cede, cedent, cession; abscess (sep); accede (sep), with access, accession; antecede (sep), with antecedent; ancestor (sep); cease (sep); concede, concession, concessionaire, concessionary, concessive; decedent—decease, n hence v; exceed, exceeding, excess (n hence adj), excessive; intercede, intercession, intercessor, intercessory; necessary (sep), with necessity, etc.; precede, precedence, precedent (adj and n), precess, precession (whence precessional); proceed, proceeding (n)—procedure, procedural—process (n hence v)—procession (n hence v), processional, processionary, processive; recede,

**recess** (n hence v), **recession** (whence **recessional**), **recessive**; **secede, seceder, secession** (whence **secessional, secessionist**), **succeed**—**succedent**—**success, successful, succession, successive, successor.**— Prob akin to Gr *hodos*, (high)way, journey, as, e.g., in EPISODE and METHOD.

1. *Cede* comes, prob via EF-F *céder*, from L *cēdere* (s *cēd-*), to go, hence to go back, hence to halt, give way (cf CEASE): perh akin to L *cadere* (s *cad-*), to fall; to Gr *hodos*; to Skt *utsad-*, to step aside, (hence) to disappear; perh also to L *sedēre* (s *sed-*), hence to E SIT.

2. The presp *cedens*, o/s *cedent-*, yields the legal E *cedent*, assignor of property; the pp *cessus* has s *cess-*, whence the n *cessiō*, o/s *cessiōn-*, whence, via MF-F, the E *cession*.

3. Most of the L prefix-cpds of *cēdere* have affected E, thus:

*abscedere*, to depart: see ABSCESS;

*accedere*, to approach: see ACCEDE;

*antecedere*, whence *antecessor*: see ANTECEDENT and ANCESTOR.

4. The remaining relevant L prefix-cpds are *concedere, dēcedere, excedere, intercedere, praecedere, prōcedere, recedere, sēcedere, succedere*.

5. *Concedere*, to retire, yield position (to), concede, whence, perh via MF-F, 'to *concede*'; on the pp *concessus* arise *concessiō*, o/s *concessiōn-*, whence, perh via MF-F, the E *concession*, with adjj *concessional, concessionary*; *concessionaire*, holder of a concession, anglicizes EF-F *concessionnaire*; *concessive* represents LL *concessīuus*, ML *-cessīvus*.

6. *Dēcedere*, to depart, (hence) to die, has presp *dēcedens*, o/s *dēcedent-*, whence the legal E n *decedent*; its derivative n *dēcessus* (gen *-ūs*) becomes OF-MF *deces* (EF-F *déces*), adopted by ME, whence *decease*, whence 'to *decease*'.

7. *Excedere*, to go out from, to pass beyond (lit, hence fig), becomes MF *exceder* (EF-F *excéder*), whence 'to *exceed*', whence the pa *exceeding*; the derivative *excessus* (gen *-ūs*), an extravagance, becomes MF *exces* (EF-F *excès*), whence E *excess*; *excessive* comes from the ML *excessīvus*, immodest, perh via F *excessive*, the f of MF-F *excessif*.

8. *Intercedere*, to intervene, yields 'to *intercede*'; on *intercess-*, the s of the pp *intercessus*, arise *intercessiō*, o/s *intercessiōn-*, whence, perh via MF-F, the E *intercession*, and *intercessor*, adopted by E (cf the MF-F *intercesseur*), and the ML *intercessōrius*, whence E *intercessory*.

9. *Praecedere*, to walk or march at the head, to precede, yields, perh via MF-F, 'to *precede*'; the presp *praecedens*, o/s *praecedent-*, becomes, prob via MF-F *précédent*, the E adj *precedent*, whence (or from the F derivative n) 'a *precedent*', whence *precedence*, the *t* being omitted for ease before the suffix *-ce*; on *praecess-*, the s of the pp *praecessus*, arise LL *praecessiō*, o/s *praecessiōn-*, whence E *precession*, whence, by b/f, 'to *precess*'. *Predecessor* comes, via ME *predecessour* and MF-F *prédéces-*

*seur*, from LL *praedēcessor*, which = *prae*, before + *dēcessor*, withdrawer (cf para 6).

10. L *prōcedere* (*prō-*, forwards), to advance, to progress, becomes MF-F *procéder*, whence ME *proceden*, whence 'to *proceed*', whence, from the presp, the n *proceeding(s)*; *procedure* represents MF-F *procédure*, from MF-F *procéder*, the F adj *procédural* yielding E *procedural*. The derivative L n *processus* (gen *-ūs*) becomes MF *proces* (EF-F *procès*), adopted by E, whence *process*, whence 'to *process*'; the derivative EF-F adj *processif*, f *processive*, perh suggested the E *processive*. The derivative L n *processiō*, o/s *processiōn-*, becomes OF-F *procession*, adopted by E; whereas *processional*, adj, represents late MF-F *processionnel*, early also *-al*, the n comes from ML *processiōnāle*, prop the neu of the rare ML adj *processiōnālis* (whence the F adj), a commoner adj being ML *processiōnārius*, whence E *processionary*.

11. L *recedere*, to march back, to retreat, yields 'to *recede*'; the derivative n *recessus* (gen *-ūs*) yields *recess*, whence 'to *recess*'; the derivative LL *recessiō*, o/s *recessiōn-*, yields *recession*; *recessive* is an E formation.

12. *Sēcedere*, to go *sē-* or aside, leads to *secede*, whence *seceder*; the derivative *sēcessiō*, o/s *sēcessiōn-*, to *secession*.

13. *Succedere*, to go under, hence to follow or succeed, hence to be successful, leads, perh via OF-MF *succeder* (EF-F *succéder*), to *succeed*; the presp *succedens*, o/s *succedent-*, accounts for the adj and n *succedent*. The derivative n *successus* (gen *-ūs*) becomes E *success*, whence *successful* and *successless*: derivative LL *successiō*, o/s *successiōn-*, becomes, perh via late OF-F, the E *succession*; the ML adj *\*successīvus*, deduced from ML adv *successīve*, yields *successive*; L *successor*, built, like the prec, on *success-*, the s of the pp *successus*, becomes, prob via OF-F, the ME *successour*, whence E *successor*.

14. In short, the *-ceed* forms indicate F intervention; the *-cede* forms come direct from L *-cedere*.

**cedilla** is adopted from Sp: dim of Gr ζ (*zēta*), i.e. *z*, 'formerly written after the *c* to indicate the sibilant value' (Webster). But is Sp *cedilla* perh not rather the dim of Sp 'letra *Ce*', letter *C*?

**ceil**, v; **ceiling**; **celestial,** adj hence n.

1. *Ceiling* is vn from *ceil*, to overlay, to roof (a room), app from OF-F *ciel*, sky, canopy, from L *caelum* (s *cael-*), sky, canopy or arched covering, o.o.o., but perh akin to *celāre* (s *cel-*), to hide, with basic sense 'a covering', or even to *caedere* (s *caed-*), to cut, to cut up, to divide by cutting up: ? *caelum* for *\*caedlum*, the sky being regarded as 'cut up' into regions.

2. *Caelum* has adj *caelestis*, whence OF *celestiel*, whence E *celestial*; *Celestial*, obsol for 'a Chinese', derives from '*Celestial* Dynasty'—a kingdom ruled by a heaven-appointed dynasty. The OF-F equivalent adj *céleste* accounts for the colour *celeste*, sky-blue.

**celandine.** See YELL, para 3.

celebrate, celebrated; celebrant; celebration, celebrative, celebratory; celebrity.

The base is L *celeber*, frequented, hence famous: o.o.o.; perh akin to Gr *kelomai* (s and r *kel*-), I push or excite, perh also to Gr *kellō* (s *kell*-, r *kel*-), I accost. Its derivative *celebritās*, o/s *celebritāt*-, yields E *celebrity* (cf MF-F *célébrité*). But the most influential derivative is *celebrāre*, to frequent, hence to celebrate. Its presp *celebrans*, o/s *celebrant*-, yields *celebrant*; its pp *celebrātus* yields 'to celebrate', whence the pa *celebrated*, and on the pps *celebrāt*- arise *celebrātiō*, o/s *celebrātiōn*-, whence, prob via OF-F, *celebration*, and the agent *celebrātor*, adopted by E, and the E formations *celebrative* (-*ive*, cf -*ative*) and *celebratory* (-*ory*, adj—cf -*atory*).

celerity: (perh through MF-F *célérité*, from) *celeritāt*-, o/s of L *celeritās*, from *celer*, swift, prompt; r *cel*-, therefore cf Gr *kelēs* (r *kel*-), a racehorse.

celery: late EF-F *céleri*: It dial *selīeri*, var of It *seleni*: L *selīnum*: LGr *sélīnon*, celery: Gr *sélīnon*, parsley: o.o.o.: but perh from IE r *\*suel*-, shortened to *\*sel*-, a var of *\*uel*-, to roll (up), to wind. The Ancient Greeks used parsley for garlands. (Boisacq.)

celestial. See CEIL, para 2.

celibacy, celibate.

The former = *celibate* + abstract suffix -*cy*: and *celibate* comes from L *caelibātus*, an -*atus* adj from *caelebs*, itself adj, meaning 'single, unmarried': o.o.o., but perh akin to Skt *kévalas*, alone, private.

cell; cellar, cellarer, cellarage; cellule, adj cellular; celluloid; cellulose. See HALL, paras 11–12.

'cellist, 'cello. See FIDDLE, para 5, s.f.

Celt, Celtic. The latter comes from the L adj *Celticus*, influenced by Gr *Keltikos* but deriving from L *Celta*, whence, prob through F *Celte*, the E *Celt*; *Celta* is a b/f from the pl *Celtae*, itself from Gr *Keltai*, earlier *Keltoi*; perh akin to L *celsus*, high, but prob of C origin, with r *\*cel*-, to rise or mount. If, however, it does belong to the *celsus* group, it must be aligned with HILL.

celt, an archaeological chisel, often of flint: LL *celtis*, perh of C origin: cf MIr *celtair*, a stake, and W *cellt*, flint, flint stone.

cement, n (whence the adj cemental)—hence v (whence cementation).

*Cement*, ME *ciment*, comes from MF-F *ciment*: L *caementum*, marble chips used for making mortar: for *\*caedimentum*, an easing of *\*caedmentum*, from *caedere*, to cut, to cut down, s *caed*-: cf the -*cise* of CONCISE and PRECISE, the -*cide* of DECIDE; IE r, perh *\*kād*-, *\*kēd*-.

cemetery: cf OF *cimitere*, MF *cimetiere*, EF-F *cimetière*, both the OF and the E coming from LL *coemētērium*, itself from Gr *koimētērion*, lit 'resting- or sleeping-place', hence 'burial place', from *koiman* (s *koim*-: cf COMA), to put to sleep: akin ult to CITY.

cenotaph. See the 2nd *ceno*- in Elements. Lit 'empty tomb'. The EF-F *cénotaphe* was formed by

the most prolific, the most brilliant, of all F wordmakers: Rabelais (cf RABELAISIAN).

censer is aphetic for incenser: OF-MF *encensier*, from OF-F *encens*, incense: cf para 3 of CANDID.

censor (n hence v), censorious, censorship; censure, n and v; census, adj censual.

1. *Censorious* represents L *censōrius*, the adj of *censor*, which E has adopted; E *censor* has derivative *censorship* (suffix -*ship*). L *censor* is the agent of *censēre* (s *cens*-), to declare formally, hence to describe officially, to evaluate, to tax: akin to Skt *sámsati* (*çámsati*), he recites or announces, with s *çaṃs*-, r perh *\*cam*- for *\*can*-, to chant, q.v. at the 2nd CANT. *Censēre* has also the derivatives *censūra*, evaluation, judgement, hence a condemning, whence, via MF-F, the E *censure*, and MF-F *censure* has derivative EF-F *censurer*, whence 'to censure'; *census* (gen -*ūs*), the act of taking a census, adopted by E; *censual* stands for L *censuālis*, adj of *census*.

2. The prefix-cpd *recensēre*, to estimate afresh, to review, hence to revise, whence, perh via MF-F *recenser*, the E *recense*, to revise (a text); the derivative *recensiō*, o/s *recensiōn*-, becomes, perh via F, the E *recension*.

cent, orig 100, hence the 100th part of a dollar, etc.: F *cent*: L *centum*, 100: f.a.e., HUNDRED.

centaur. See the element *centauro*-.

centenarian, n from adj from centenary, q.v. at ANNUAL, para 3.

center. See CENTRE.

centigrade, centigramme, centilitre, centimetre, etc. See the element *centi*-, denoting 100, and, of course, the 2nd element (-*grade*, etc.).

centipede: obs F *centipède*: L *centipeda*, 100-footed (*pes*, o/s *ped*-, a foot: cf PEDAL).

central. See para 1 of:

centre, AE center, adj central; centri-, as in *centrifugal*—see FUGITIVE, para 5; centric, whence centricity.—concenter, concentrate, concentrated, concentration; concentric; eccentric (adj hence n), eccentricity.

1. *Centre*, *center*, derives from MF-F *centre*: L *centrum*: Gr *kentron*, any sharp point (from *kentein*, to prick, s *kent*-, IE r *\*kent*-, to prick), hence any point, hence a geom centre L *centrum* has adj *centrālis*, whence EF-F and E *central*; *centric* was form-suggested by Gr *kentrikos*, of a cardinal point.

2. The derivative LL *centrātus*, situated about a centre, leads to E 'to concentrate', whence the pa *concentrated* and, by anl (cf the F *concentration*), the n *concentration*. MF-F *centre* has derivative EF-F *concentrer*, whence 'to concentre or concenter'.

3. The ML derivative *concentricus* becomes MF-F *concentrique* and, perh independently, E *concentric*, whence *concentricity*.

4. The ML derivative *excentricus*, out from (*ex*-) the centre, away from the centre, from Gr *ekkentros*, becomes MF-F *excentrique* and, thereby, E *eccentric*; subsidiary ML *excentricitas*, o/s *excentricitat*-, becomes late EF-F *excentricité* and

E *eccentricity* (perh, however, by anl from *eccentric*).

**centurion, century.**

*Centurion*, perh adopted from OF-F, comes from *centuriōn-*, the o/s of L *centuriō*, the leader of 100 soldiers, from or intimately akin to L *centūria*, a company of 100 soldiers, from *centum*, 100: cf CENT and, f.a.e., HUNDRED. From meaning '100 soldiers', *century* came to denote any sequence of 100, but esp of 100 years.

**cephalic**, of the head: (perh via F *céphalique*, from) LL *cephalicus*, trln of Gr *kephalikos*, adj of *kephale*, the head: cf the element *cephalo-*.

**ceramic**, adj, whence **ceramics**, n. See HEARTH, s.f.

**Cerberus**, a Gr mythical hound: L *Cerberus*: Gr *Kerberos*, akin to Skt *Karbarás*, one of Yama the Lord of the Netherworld's two dogs: prob echoic.

**cere.** See CEREMENT.

**cereal**, n from adj: L *Cereālis*, belonging to *Ceres*, goddess of agriculture, esp of grain crops: akin to *creāre*, to create.

**cerebral, cerebration, cerebrum, cerebellum.**

The 4th is the dim of the 3rd; L *cerebrum*, the brain, leads to the EF-F adj *cérébral*, whence E *cerebral*; *cerebration*, mental activity, is suggested by *cerebrate*, to think actively, itself formed by anl. Ult akin to Gr *kara*, head; IE r, prob *\*kar-* or *\*ker-*, hard.

**cerement; cerecloth; cere,** n and v.

*Cerement*=EF-F *cirement* (obs), from OF-F *cirer*, to wax+suffix *-ment*: from OF-F *cire*, wax, from L *cēra*, akin to Gr *kēros*. *Cēra* has derivative *cērāre*, whence F *cirer*, whence E 'to cere', to treat with wax; F *cire*, wax, becomes the E n *cere*; *cerecloth* (cf CLOTH) stands for *cered cloth*.

**ceremony; ceremonial**, adj hence n; **ceremonious.**

*Ceremony*: ME *cerimonie, ceremoin*: MF *cerimonie, ceremonie* (EF-F *céré-*): L *caerimōnia*, a cult, pl *caeremōniae*, ritual observances: o.o.o: perh Etruscan (E & M), but prob akin to L *cūra* (see CURE). Its LL adjj *caerimōniālis* and *caerimōniōsus* become, the latter perh via MF-F, the E *ceremonial* and *ceremonious*.

**Ceres.** See CEREAL.

**cerise.** See CHERRY.

**cern**, to decide, is rare singly: see the cpds CONCERN and DISCERN. Cf:

**certain, certainty; certify, certificate, certification, certificatory; certiorari; certitude;**—**ascertain,** whence (suffix *-ment*) **ascertainment; incertitude; uncertain, uncertainty**—**incertain.**—Akin to L-derived con*cern*, dis*cern*, dis*creet*, dis*crete*, dis*crimi*nate, *crime*, ex*crement*; to Gr-derived *crisis* and *critic*; to Gmc-derived *riddle* (a sieve): see sep.

1. The L base is *cernere* (s *cern-*), to pass through a sieve, hence to distinguish or discern, hence to decide, akin to Gr *krinein* (s *krin-*), to separate, to decide: IE r, *\*krei-*, to separate, occ shortened to *\*kre-* and often enlarged to *\*krein-*. The pp of *cernere* is *crētus*, of which the adj *certus* may be a metathesis; orig 'decided, fixed, appointed', it soon became also 'decided, determined, sure'.

2. *Certus* passes through a derivative VL *\*certānus* into late OF-F as *certain*, adopted by ME and confirmed by E; OF-F *certain* has derivative MF-EF *certaineté*, whence E *certainty*.

3. L *certus* has several LL and ML derivatives relevant to E:

LL *certificāre* (c/f *certi-+-ficāre*, a c/f of *facere*, to make), to establish (one) in faith, to define, ML to make certain, whence, via MF-F *certifier*, the E *certify*; the pp *certificātus* has influenced 'to *certificate*'; 'a *certificate*' derives, via MF-F *certificat*, from ML *certificātum*, prop the neus of the pp; *certificative* is an E formation (*-ive*, adj); *certificatory* derives from ML *certificātōrius*;

LL *certiorāre*, to inform (legally), from *certiorem facere*, to make (someone) more sure, *certior* being the comp of *certus*; the passive *certiorāri*, as an E legal term for a Chancery writ, is short for *certiorāri volumus*, we wish to be certainly informed, hence to be certified;

LL *certitūdō*, a state of certainty, becomes, perh via MF-F, the E *certitude*.

4. LL *incertitūdō* becomes, prob via late MF-F, the E *incertitude*. The obs *incertain*, adopted from MF-F, derives, by way of VL *\*incertānus*, from L *incertus*, uncertain: and *uncertain* itself=*un-*, not+ E *certain*; hence *uncertainty* instead of the obs *incertainty* (from EF).

5. *Ascertain* derives from MF *ascertainer, acertener*: OF-MF *a*, to+MF *certainer* (*certain*+inf *-er*): cf para 2.

**cervical**, of the neck: adj *-al* tacked to *cervic-*, the o/s of ML *cervix*, L *ceruix*, the neck, perh akin to L *cerebrum*, the brain. Cf the element *cervici-, cervico-*.

**cessation.** See CEASE.

**cession.** See CEDE, para 2.

**cesspit**, suggested by cesspool.

For the 2nd element, see PIT (hole) and POOL; *cess* derives either from *cess*, a peat bog, o.o.o. (but, sem, cf sl *bog*, a privy), or from It *cesso*, a privy, aphetically from L *sēcessus*, a place of retirement, a privy, or, the earliest (C16) form being *cesperalle*, a corruption of obs *suspiral*, from OF-MF *suspiral*, MF *souspirail* (EF-F *soupirail*), from OF-MF *s(o)uspirer* (EF-F *soupirer*), to sigh, from L *suspirāre*, to sigh, to breathe. (Resp, E.P.; OED, Webster; EW.)

**Ceylon**, hence adj (whence n) **Ceylonese** (suffix *-ese*); **Singhalese** or **Sinhalese** or **Cingalese**, adj hence n.

*Sinhalese* (etc.)=national *-ese* tacked onto *Sinhala*, the Aryan conquerors (C5 A.D.), hence the native population: and *Sinhala* derives from Skt *Simhala* (? from *simha*, a lion), the conquerors' name for the island. It is, however, from *Silān* (pron *see-lahń*), the Hi name, that, via F *Ceylan*, we get *Ceylon*.

**cha.** See TEA, para 2.

**chafe**, v hence n: ME *chaufen*, to warm or heat: OF-MF *chaufer* (EF-F *chauffer*): VL *\*calefāre*, contr of L *calefacere*, to make (*facere*) warm (*calēre*, to be warm): cf CALDRON and, f.a.e., CALORIC. Hence *chafing-dish* or *-pan*—cf DISH and PAN.

2. F *chauffer*, to warm, has late EF-F agent *chauffeur*, lit and orig a stoker.

chaff (1), n, husks of grain, straw cut fine; chaffinch.

The bird *chaffinch* is a FINCH addicted to *chaff*: and *chaff* derives from OE *ceaf*, akin to G *Kaff*, MHG *kaf*, and D *kaf*, MD *caf*, very prob akin to OHG *cheva*, MHG *këve*, a husk. (Kluge.)

chaff (2), to make fun of, hence n: from CHAFE, phonetically and graphically influenced by *chaff*(1), perh in its derivative use as a v (*chaff*, to mix with chaff, to cut for straw).

chafing-dish, -pan. See CHAFE, s.f.

chagrin (1), anxiety, grief, vexation: adopted from EF-F. The F n *chagrin* derives imm from the MF-F adj *chagrin*, whence also the late MF-F v *chagriner*, whence E 'to *chagrin*'. The adj *chagrin* is, say B & W, o.o.o.: perh of Gmc origin, for cf OHG-G *gram*, irritated, hostile, OE *gram*, OS *gram*, ON *gramr*, angry, all akin to OE-E *grim*, OFris and OS *grimm*, OHG-MHG *grim*, G *grimm*, ON *grimmr*, fierce: cf GRIM, para 6. Indeed, OHG *gram* would account for OF-MF *graim*, *grain*, grieved, and this OF-MF *grain* would, with the int prefix *cha-* (as in 'se *cha*mailler', to quarrel noisily), account for the MF-F adj *chagrin*, as Dauzat proposes. With *cha-*, var *ca-*, cf the E *ker-*, as in *kerwallop*.

chagrin (2), untanned leather, usu spelt shagreen: EF *sagrin*, F *chagrin*: Tu *şāghri*. The *-n* is prob due to that of OF-F *grain*; the change from *sa-* to *cha-*, prob to the 1st *chagrin*. (Dauzat.)

chain, n and v; enchain; catena, catenarian, catenary, adj and n; catenate, catenation—concatenate, concatenation.

1. The starting-point is L *catēna*, a chain, o.o.o.: perh of Etruscan origin, with final syllable (? rather suffix) the same as that in the rare L *sacēna*, o.o.o.; perh akin to L *cassis*, a net, and *cassis*, a helmet. The following derivatives concern E:

*catēnārius*, adj, whence *catenary* (suffix *-ary*) and *catenarian*;

*catēnātus*, enchained, whence *catenate*, adj and v; *catēnātiō*, o/s *catēnātiōn-*, whence *catenation*; LL *catēnula*, a little chain, whence, anl, the adj *catenulate*.

2. LL has the prefix-cpd *concatēnāre*, to chain together, with pp *concatēnātus*, whence 'to *concatenate*', with subsidiary *concatēnātiō*, o/s *concatēnātiōn-*, whence *concatenation*.

3. L *catēna* becomes OF-MF *chaeine* (EF-F *chaîne*), whence ME *chayne* (or *cheyne*), whence E *chain*, whence 'to *chain*'.

4. 'To *enchain*' derives from OF-F *enchaîner*, from OF *en*, in, to+OF *chaener* (from L *catēnāre*); derivative MF-F *enchaînement* leads to E *enchainment*.

chair, n hence v; chaise (longue) and chay; (ex) cathedra, cathedral (adj and n), cathedratic; element *-hedral*, *-hedron*, q.v. sep.

1. Gr *hedra*, a seat (cf Gr *hezesthai*, to sit, and, ult, E SIT), combines with *kata*, down (cf the prefix *cata-*), to form *kathedra*, a backed, four-legged, often two-armed seat, whence L *cathedra*, LL bishop's chair, ML professor's chair, hence dignity, as in 'to speak *ex cathedra*', as from—or as if from—a professor's chair, hence with authority. L *cathedra* has LL-ML adj *cathedrālis*—see sep CATHEDRAL; and the secondary ML adj *cathedrāticus*, whence E legal *cathedratic*.

2. L *cathedra* becomes OF-MF *chaiere* (whence F *chaire*, a pulpit), which becomes ME *chaiere* (var *chaere*), whence E *chair*.

3. OF-MF *chaiere* has Central F (MF) var *chaeze*, whence EF-F *chaise*, partly adopted by E in its specialized 'carriage' sense; *chay* is a b/f from E *chaise* apprehended as pl.

chaise. See prec. para 3.

chalcedony. See element *chalcedo-*.

chalet is adopted from F, which adopts it in C18 from Swiss *chalet*, dim (cf the suffix *-et*) of *\*cala*, a shelter, prob from a pre-L Medit tongue. (B & W.) 'The original sense must have been "shelter of stone": from r *\*cal-*, stone [as in *caillou*, a pebble]': Dauzat. Cf CHALK.

chalice: ME *chalis*: Central MF *chalice* (cf OF-MF *calice*): L *calix* (o/s *calic-*), a cup, akin to L *calyx*: f.a.e., CALYX.

chalk derives from OE *cealc*, itself from L *calx* (o/s *calc-*), stone, chalk, from Gr *khalix*, pebble, limestone, with IE r *\*khal-*, varr *\*khel-* and *\*khil-*, often weakened to *\*kal-*, etc.; cf CHALET, s.f. The adj is *chalky*.

challenge, n—and v, whence the pa challenging and the agent challenger.

'To *challenge*', ME *chalengen*, to claim, to accuse, comes from the syn OF-EF *chalengier*, var *chalongier*, from L *calumniāri*, to accuse falsely: f.a.e., CALUMNIATE. From OF *chalengier* derives OF *chalenge*, a claim, an accusation, adopted by ME, whence E *challenge*.

chamber; chamberlain. See CAMERA, para 3.

chameleon. See HOMO, para 4.

chamfer, n hence v: alteration of F *chanfrein*, earlier *chanfraint*, from *chanfraindre*, a cpd of OF-F *chant*, edge (cf the 1st CANT)+*fraindre*, to break, from L *frangere* (cf FRACTION).

chammy. See:

chamois, whence, by eased pron, chammy or shammy (chamois leather): OF-F *chamois*: LL *camōx*, acc *camōcem*: of Alpine origin.

champ, to bite vigorously and noisily: earlier, also *cham*, prob echoic—cf JAM, to squeeze.

champagne. See CAMP, para 6.

champaign. See CAMP, para 6.

champignon. See CAMP, para 7.

champion. See CAMP, para 8.

chance, n and v. See CADENCE, para 5.

chancel, chancellery, chancellor; chancery. See CANCEL, para 4.

chancre, whence the adj chancrous. See CANCER, para 1, s.f.

chancy. See CADENCE, para 5.

**chandelier.** See CANDID, last para.

**chandler.** See CANDID, final sentence.

**change** (n and v), **changeable; changeless, changer; exchange** (n, v), **exchangeable; interchange,** etc.; **cambium,** adj **cambial; gambit.**

1. The LL *cambiāre*, to change, esp to exchange, is app of C origin, prob Gaul: cf OIr *camm* or *camb*, Ir *cam*—Ga, W, Mx *cam*—OBr *camb*, Br *kam*—all meaning 'bent, crooked'; cf Cor *camma*, (? by metathesis) *cabmy*, to bend; and perh cf MIr *cimb*, tribute, EIr *càin*, statute, Ga *càin*, tribute, Ir *gaimbīn*, interest (on money), whence the AIr *'gombeen* man', money-lender. Malvezin poses PC *\*camb*, to bend, *\*cambos*, bent, with basic idea 'to turn'.

2. LL *cambiāre* has derivative n *cambium*, exchange, adopted by E and sense-adapted by Bot; *cambium* has adj *cambiālis*, whence E *cambial*.

3. *Cambiāre* becomes OF-F *changer*, whence 'to change'; and OF-F *changer* has derivative OF-F n *change*, adopted by ME, and derivative OF-F adj *changeable*, likewise adopted. *Changeless* is an E formation, but *changer* derives from OF-F *changeur*.

4. *Exchange*, n, ME *eschange* (or *-chaunge*), derives from MF-EF *exchange*, itself from MF-EF v *eschangier*, from VL *\*excambiāre* (*ex*, out of + *cambiāre*); and OF *eschangier* yields 'to exchange', whence *exchangeable*.

5. *Interchangeable* has at least been suggested by the MF-EF *entrechangeable*, from MF-EF *entrechangier* (*entre*, L *inter*, between), whence, via ME *entrechangen*, the E 'to *interchange*'; MF-EF *entrechangier* has derivative MF-EF n *entrechange*, which duly becomes E *interchange*.

6. Akin to OF-F *change*, an exchange, but presumably from It *cambio* (from *cambiare*, from LL *cambiāre*), is Prov *cambi*, an exchange, which becomes F *gambit*, adopted by E, esp for an opening 'exchange' at chess, whence the general sense 'opening move'.

**channel.** See CANAL.

**chant,** n and v. See the 2nd CANT, para 3.

**chanticleer:** ME *Chaunticlere* or *Chauntecler*: MF *Chantecler*, the cock in the C13 *Roman de Renart*, a medieval epic about beasts: *il chante cler*, he sings clearly. Cf CLEAR and the 2nd CANT.

**chantier.** See GANTRY, para 1.

**chaos, chaotic; chasm, chasmal, chasmic, chasmy; gas** (n whence v), with obvious cpds **gasbag, gasoline** (or **-ene**), **gasometer,** etc.—with adjj **gaseous** and **gassy**—and v **gasify.**

1. *Gas*, 'invented' early in C17 by chemist Van Helmont, was suggested by L *chaos* or its Gr source, *khaos*: 'Halitum illud gas vocavi, non longa a chao veterum'—as Van Helmont himself states. (B & W.) *Gaseous*=*gas*+adj suffix *eous*; *gassy*=*gas*+euphonic *s*+adj *-y*; *gasify*, which= *gas*, n+combiner *-i-*+-*fy*, to make, perh owes something to F *gazéifier*.

2. Intimately akin to Gr *khaos* is Gr *khasma*, a gaping abyss, a vast cleft in the earth: whence L *chasma*, adopted by Med for excessive yawning:

whence E *chasm*, with its adjj formed with *-al, -ic, -y*.

3. Of Gr *khasma*, as of Gr *khaos*, the r is *kha-*; the IE r is app *\*kha-* or *\*khe-*, with varr *\*gha-* or *\*ghe-*, often in extended forms *\*khau-* or *\*ghau-*, etc., with basic meaning 'to gape', hence 'empty space', as in Gr *khaos*, which, from being 'the atmosphere' and 'unformed matter', becomes 'vast chasm', etc. Gr *khaos* becomes L *chaos*, whence MF-F and E *chaos*. The adj *chaotic*, of E formation, is anl with, e.g., *erotic* and *hypnotic*.

**chap** (1), a blain, derives from 'to *chap*', ME *chappen*, to chop, (later) to cause to crack or split, with pa *chapped*, as in '*chapped* hands': f.a.e., CHOP, to cut (wood).

**chap** (2), coll for 'a fellow, a man', is short for *chapman*, a trader or dealer, later an itinerant dealer, from OE *cēapman*, lit 'trade (or market) man': f.a.e., CHEAP. Orig, *chapbooks* were sold by chapmen.

**chap** (3). See CHOP, jaw.

**chaparral,** a dense thicket, orig of evergreen oaks, is adopted from Sp, which derives it, by n-suffix *-al*, from Sp *chaparro*, an evergreen oak, from syn *chaparra*, itself from Biscayan dial *zabarra*, an evergreen oak, the dim of Biscayan *abarra*, an oak.

**chapbook.** See the 2nd CHAP, s.f.

**chapel.** See CAP, para 2.

**chaperon,** often (esp of a woman) anglicized as **chaperone,** is adopted from OF-F *chaperon*, orig a (males' and females') hood covering the Middle Age'd head and neck, then, as protection, an escort to a (young) woman: from OF-F *chape*, a mantle, a cap, from LL *cappa*: f.a.e., CAP. 'To *chaperon(e)*', although prob deriving from the E n, owes something to the OF-F *chaperonner*, itself from F *chaperon*. Cf:

**chaplain:** OF-F *chapelain*: either the ML *capelānus*, one who officiates in a *capella* or chapel, or OF-MF *chapele* (EF-F *chapelle*), a chapel (itself from ML *capella*)+suffix *-ain* (L *-ānus*): f.a.e., CAP, esp para 2. Cf prec and:

**chaplet,** a garland, orig and prop for the head, represents OF-F *chapelet*, dim of OF *chapel*, hat or garland, itself a dim of OF-F *chape*, a mantle or a churchman's cope, from LL *cappa*: f.a.e., CAP. Cf CHAPERON and CHAPLAIN.

**chapman.** See the 2nd CHAP.

**chaps** (of face). See CHOP, jaw.—In AE, *chaps* is a coll shortening of Mexican Sp *chaparajos* (or *-ejos*), or *chaparreras*, cowboys' leather separate trouser-legs, worn over ordinary trousers, so called 'because they protect the legs against chaparros or chaparrals' (Santamaria)—i.e., against dense thickets or thorny shrubs. Cf CHAPARRAL above.

**chapter:** ME, from MF-F, *chapitre*, OF *chapitle*: L *capitulum*, title at *head* of a section, hence the section itself: dim of L *caput*, head, o/s *capit-*: cf CAPITAL and, f.a.e., CHIEF. From the reading of a chapter, esp of the Bible, at the beginning of all formal meetings of persons in religious orders, comes *chapter*, a body of, e.g., canons of a cathedral.

char (1), n.

1. Short for *charwoman*, one who does the *chars*, rare for *chares* or *chores*. *Char*, then, is a var of *chare*, a single or odd, esp household, job, earlier a turn of work, earliest a turn or recurrence: ME *char*, earlier *cherre*: OE *cerr, cyrr*, a turn, occasion, esp of work, from *cerran, cyrran*, to turn, whence 'to *chare*'.

2. *Chare*, both n and v, has var *chore*, orig mainly AE, but now, esp as n, predominant everywhere—except in *charwoman*.

char (2), to reduce to charcoal, (hence also) to burn superficially: b/f from *charcoal*, lit '(wood) *turned* to *coal*', the 1st element being that of CHAR (1) in its orig sense 'to turn', hence 'to convert'.

char (3), sl. See TEA, para 2.

character, n hence v; characteristic, adj hence n; characterize, whence characterization.

1. A *character*, a sign, a brand or stamp, hence a graphic symbol, hence an attribute, comes, through ME *caracter* and MF *caractere* (F *-ère*), from L *character*, trln of Gr *kharaktēr*, a marking instrument, hence a symbol, from *kharassein* (? for *kharaksein*), to sharpen, hence to cut into grooves, hence to engrave, r *kharak-*; IE r, *\*khar-*, var *\*kher-*, or *\*ghar-*, var *\*gher-*, to scratch, to cut: cf Lith *žerti, žeriù* (r *žer-*), to scratch or scrape, and the freq *žarstýti*, to scratch often: perh cf the Hit r *kar-*, to cut (often in extension *kars-*): perh of Medit pre-Gr stock, for cf Eg *kha*, to carve or engrave, perh also the synn *kheti* and *qeḥqeḥ*.

2. Gr *kharaktēr* has derivatives the adj *kharaktēristikos* (an extension of *kharaktērikos*, whence the obsol *characterical*), whence E *characteristic*— *kharaktērizein*, to engrave, to characterize, whence 'to *characterize*' (*-ize*)—whence *kharaktērismos*, whence E *characterism* (*-ism*), representation by symbols.

charade, adopted from F, derives from Prov *charrado*, conversation, (later) charade, from *charra*, to chatter or gossip: echoic—cf the syn It *ciarlare*, to chatter.

charcoal. See the 2nd CHAR.

chare, n and v. See 1st CHAR.

charge, n and v; charger. See CAR, para 4.

chariot. See CAR, para 5.

charitable; charity; sep cherish.

1. *Charitable*, adopted from OF-F, derives from OF-F *charité* (whence E *charity*), from L *caritās*, o/s *caritāt-*, itself from *carus*, beloved, dear, akin to Skt *cárus*, lovable, and to several words in the C and Sl languages; IE r, *\*kar-* .

2. On the Gmc side, cf *whore*, n hence v (cf ON *hōra*), hence also the adj *whorish*; *whoredom* (cf *-dom*), ME *hordom*, comes from ON *hordomr*. The n *whore*, ME *hore*, OE *hōre*, comes from ON *hōra*, akin to OHG *huora* (G *Hure*), and to Go *hōrs*, adulterer.

charlatan, charlatanry.

The latter derives from EF-F *charlatanerie* (cf It *ciarlataneria*), an *-erie* (E *-ery, -ry*) derivative of

EF-F *charlatan*, itself from It *ciarlatano*, prob an easement—? influenced by *ciarlare*, to chatter—of *ciarratano*, var of *cerratano*, charlatan, orig an inhabitant of the village of *Cerreto*, near Spoleto in Umbria; there long existed the intermediate sense 'vendor of medicines and salves, *cum* dentist, *cum* juggler, plying his trade in the streets', the first such cheapjacks (etc.) coming from Cerreto. (B & W; Prati.)

Charles. See CHURL.

charm, n and v, whence charmer (cf EF-F *charmeur*, MF *charmeor*) and charming (cf F *charmant*).

'To *charm*' derives from OF-F *charmer*, (orig) to enchant with magic, to bewitch, hence to attract strongly, itself (prob not, as in B & W, from LL *carmināre*, to sing, to sing and play, but) from OF-F *charme*, orig a magical formula, incantation, (later) attraction, attractiveness, itself from L *carmen*, chant, esp a magical incantation, app for *\*canmen* (suffix *-men*), from *canere* (s *can-*), to sing. 'A *charm*' derives from the OF n.—Cf the 2nd CANT and, on Gmc side, HEN.

charnel. See CARNAGE, para 5.

charqui. See JERKEE.

chart, n and v. See the 2nd CARD, para 8.

charter, n hence v. See 2nd CARD, para 8.

Chartism, Chartist. See id, ibid.

chartulary. See id, para 7.

charwoman. See the 1st CHAR.

chary. See CARE, para 2.

chase (1), n and v, in jewellery. See the 2nd CASE, para 5.

chase (2), v and n: to pursue, a pursuit. See CATCH, para 2.

chasm. See CHAOS, para 2.

chassis. See the 2nd CASE, para 6.

chaste. See CASTE, para 2.

chasten. See id, ibid.

chastise, chastisement. See id, para 4.

chastity. See id, para 2.

chasuble. See CASSOCK.

chat, orig to chatter, derives from the v chatter, whence the n *chatter*; *chat*, n, derives from 'to *chat*'; chatterbox=one who is a box of *chatter*; chit-chat is a redup of *chat*, n. 'To *chatter*' (whence *chatterer*), ME *chateren*, is echoic.

château; chatelaine. See CASTLE, para 4.

chattel. See CATTLE.

chatter. See CHAT.

chauffeur. See CHAFE, para 2.

chauvinism, exaggerated patriotism, derives from F *chauvinisme* (suffix *-isme*, E *-ism*), from F *chauvin*, orig a naïvely enthusiastic celebrator and eulogist of Napoleon Bonaparte, esp as soldier, a type popularized by draughtsman Charlet and then, in 1831, by the playwright brothers Cogniard: an *-in* derivative of OF-F *chauve*, bald, the Napoleonic veterans tending, by the late 1820's, to be bald; there may also, in the fact as in legend, have been a Nicolas Chauvin (of Rochefort), so demonstratively Napoleonist as to be ridiculed by his comrades.

chaw, chawbacon. See CHEW.

chay. See CHAIR, para 3.

cheap (adj and n), cheapen, cheapness; cheapjack, Cheapside; sep chap, chapman.

A *cheapjack* is a *Jack*, fellow, dealing—usu itinerantly—in cheap goods; *Cheapside*, orig an open square, later a street, where, in London, there are many shops, in short a *cheap* or market. *Cheapness*=*cheap*, adj+the suffix *-ness*; *cheapen*= obs 'to *cheap*', to buy, trade (in)+v suffix *-en*, and *cheap*, v, derives from ME *cheapien*, from OE *cēapian*, to trade, to buy, to sell, itself from OE *cēap*, a sale or a bargain, a price, deriving, like OHG *koupo*, a trader, from L *caupō*, a huckster, an innkeeper, perh akin to L *cūpa*, a vat. The OE n *cēap* becomes the now obs *cheap*, a bargain(ing), a trading, hence (extant in PlNn) a market.

cheat, n hence v and further agent cheater and cheatery (suffix *-ery*): aphetic for *escheat* (q.v. at CADENCE, para 7) in specific sense 'act of confiscation'.

check, n hence v; checkers (or chequers), checkmate; cheque, chequered (or checkered); chess; exchequer; shah, pasha—and satrap.

1. 'To *check*', orig at chess, results naturally from the chess term *check*, an interj, warning one's opponent that he is in a dangerous position, whence flow all the other 'hindrance' senses, incl that of the banking *cheque* (F influence), AE *check*: and a *check*, ME *chek*, is aphetic for OF-MF *eschec*, var of *eschac* which comes, via Ar, from Per *shāh*, king—whence obviously the title *Shāh*, E *Shah*—akin to Skt *kṣáyati*, he possesses, controls, rules, and *kṣatra*, power, rule; cf also Gr *ktáomai*, I acquire, *ktēma*, anything acquired, a possession; IE r, *\*khe-* or *\*khei-*, varr *\*kha-*, *\*khai-*, to acquire.

2. *Checkmate* (n, whence v), ME *chek mate*, derives from OF-MF *eschec (et) mat*, itself from Ar *al-shāh māt*, the king is dead (cf MATE, v). *Checkers*, *chequers* is the pl of *checker*, *chequer*, orig a square on a chessboard, hence an alternating black and white (element of a) pattern: MF *eschequier* (OF *eschaquier*), chessboard, from OF-MF *eschec* (OF *eschac*): hence 'to *checker*, *chequer*', whence the pa *checkered*, *chequered*. *Eschequier* becomes ME *escheker*, orig a chessboard, whence—chess being, by etym, a royal game, a kingly matter—the *Exchequer* or royal, (later) governmental, treasury.

3. *Checkers*, the game of draughts, is doubly derivative; *chess*, however, comes, through ME *ches*, from OF-MF *esches*, the acc pl of *eschec* (para 1): cf F *échecs*, chess, prop the pl of *échec* (from *eschec*).

4. Per *shāh* becomes Tu *pāshā*, whence the anglicized title *Pasha*; both the merely graphic E var *pacha* and the phonetic Tu var *bāshā*, in its E form *bashaw*, are obsol.

5. Somewhat remotely akin is *satrap*: perh via MF-F *satrape*: L *satrapes*: Gr *satrapēs*: OPer *shathrapāvan*, satrap (governor of a province), lit 'protector of the (royal) power': 1st element akin

to Skt *kṣatra*, power, dominion (cf para 1), 2nd element to Skt *pātē*, he protects: cf FUR.

Cheddar is short for the very common *Cheddar cheese*, made orig at *Cheddar* in Somersetshire, England: OE *Ceoder*, akin to OE *cēod*, a pouch, in ref either to Cheddar *Gorge* or to the caverns.

cheek, n, hence the coll n (impudence) and v (speak impudently to)—cf the coll uses of *lip* and *jaw*—and the coll adj cheeky (impudent): ME *cheke*, *cheoke*: OE *cēace*, *cēoce*, akin to MD *cake*, D *kaak*, o.o.o.

cheep. See CHIRP.

cheer, n hence v and the adjj cheerful (*-ful*) and cheerless (*-less*) and cheery (*-y*); cheerio and cheero.

Prob *cheero!*=(good) *cheer*+hello; *cheerio!*= *cheery* (times)+hello; in both, however, the *-o* is perh the brisk, coll *-o* occurring in 'all-aliveo' or an 'eased' form of *ho!*, cf *bung-ho!*, good cheer, as a toast. The sem development is: 'face'—'expression of face'—'glad or happy expression'—the mood 'gaiety' or 'gladness' accompanying or causing that expression—the cause of the gaiety, esp 'good food and drink (*good cheer*), entertainment, kindly encouragement or consolation, etc.'—'a shout expressing joy or warm approval'. *Cheer* derives from ME *chere*, face, welcome, adopted from MF *chere* (OF *chiere*), face (later *chère*): LL *cara*: Gr *kara*, head, face, akin to Gr *kephalē*, head, and L *cerebrum*, brain—cf CEREBRAL.

cheese, whence cheesemonger (see MONGER); 'cheesed off';—caseic, casein, caseous.

1. *Cheese* derives, through ME *chese*, from OE *cēse* (var *cȳse*), itself—like G *Käse*, OHG *kāsi*— from L *cāseus* (s *case-*, r *cas-*): f.a.e., WHEY.

2. L *cāseus* yields caseic (s *case-*+*-ic*, adjj)— casein (*case-*+Chem *-in*)—caseous (*case-*+*-ous*); cf the element *casei-*, *caseo-*.

cheetah; chintz; chit (document, note).

All three spring from Skt *citra* (*chitra*), marked, spotted, variegated, brightly marked, for it yields (1) Hi *cītā*, that spotted quadruped the *cheetah*; (2) Hi *chīnt*, E *chint*, pl *chints*, altered to *chintz*, orig a stained or painted calico imported by Europe from India, now a printed, often glazed, cotton cloth; (3) Hi *ciṭṭha* (Mahratti *chittī*), E *chitty*, shortened to *chit* (black ink on white paper).

chef; chef-d'œuvre. See CHIEF, para 6.

chemical, chemism, chemist, chemistry; alchemic, alchemical, alchemist, alchemistic, alchemy.—For found, foundry, and fuse, fusion, etc., see FOUND, to melt.

1. The base is Gr *kheō-*, I pour, let flow, (later) smelt (metals), cast (statues), IE r *\*gheu-* (*\*kheu-*), to pour, with extension *\*gheud-* (*\*kheud-*), nasalized in L *fundere*, to pour, hence to shape by melting, whence E 'to *found*' (see FOUND, to melt); whereas the Gr past s (in aorist and pp) is *khu-*, as in *khuma*, a fluid, and *khumos*, a juice, the L past s is *fu-*, as in pp *fūsus*, whence E 'to *fuse*' (see FOUND, to melt).

2. Gr *khumos*, juice of a plant, has derivative *khumeia*, an infusion, often, in LGr, in form *khēmeia*, the extracting of medicinal juices (and,

later, their mixing), whence the Ar *al-kīmiyā'*
(where *al* is prop the article 'the'), whence ML
*alchimia*, whence MF *alquimie, -quemie*, with varr
*alkimie* and *alkemie*, whence E *alchemy*. The ML
*alchimia* has adj *alchimicus*, whence E *alchemic*,
with elaboration *alchemical*, and agent *alchymista*,
whence MF *alquemiste* (EF-F *alchimiste*), whence
E *alchemist*, the adj *alchemistic* coming from ML
*alchymisticus*.

3. *Alchemic(al)* leads, by aphesis, to the obs
*chemic* and its surviving extn *chemical*, with perh
some impulse from the LGr adj *khēmeutikos*;
*alchemist* likewise leads to *chemist,* whence prob
(though cf the obs *alchemistry*, syn of *alchemy*)
*chemistry*; *chemism (-ism)* app blends E *chem*istry
and F chim*isme*.

**chemise, camisade, camise, camisole; 'shimmy'.**
1. The last is a sl, then coll, 'familiarization' of
the first: cf *chemmy* for the game *chemin*-de-fer.
*Chemise*, adopted from OF-F, comes from LL
*camīsa*, var *camīsia*, a shirt, itself prob either
through C from Gmc *\*kamītya* (cf OHG *hemidi*,
G *Hemd*); or from C (whence the OHG ?), cf Ir
*caimis*, OIr *caimmse*, W *camse*, Cor *cams*, tunic,
smock, shirt, shift, priest's alb (cf Br *kamps*), with
PC r *\*cam-*, to cover (the body), as Malvezin proposes; or, most prob, from LGr *kamision*, var
*kamason*, a kind of outer garment, ? a smock: all,
however, from an IE r *\*kam-*, usu in extended form *\*kamas-, kamis-*: cf (Walshe) the Skt
*śámulyám*, a woollen shirt. (The Ar *qmits*, cited by
Sophocles, is presumably a borrowing.)

2. LL *camīsia* becomes It *camicia*, with dim
*camiciola*, whence EF-F *camisole* (by B & W,
however, derived from OPr *camisola*, dim of
OProv *camisa, camiza*, from LL *camīsa*), adopted
by E; It *camicia* has derivative *camiciata*, from obs
*incamiciata*, a night attack by soldiers wearing
shirts as means of recognition, hence Prov *\*camisade*, whence EF-F *camisade*, adopted by E for 'a
night attack'. But E *camise*, smock, tunic, has,
from LL *camīsia*, perh passed through the derivative Ar *qamīṣ*.

3. Cf SHAME, para 1, s.f.
**chemist, chemistry.** See CHEMICAL, para 3.
**cheque.** See CHECK, para 1.
**chequered.** See CHECK, para 2.
**cherish, cherishment; caress (n and v), caressing**
(adj and n), **caressive**; cf **charitable** (sep).
1. *Cherishment* comes, by suffix *-ment*, straight
from *cherish*, from OF-MF *cherir* (esp in such
forms as *cherissant, cherissons, cherissent*), from
*cher*, from L *cārus*, dear to one: f.a.e.,
CHARITABLE.
2. A *caress* derives from EF-F *caresse*, itself
from the late MF-F v *caresser*, whence 'to caress':
and F *caresser* derives from It *carezzare*, from
*caro*, from L *cārus*. *Caressing, caressive*, derive by
*-ing* (adj) and *-ive* from 'to caress'.
**cheroot:** Tamil *curuṭṭu*, the written form of
*śuruṭṭu*, cigar, orig a curl, from *śuruḷ*, a curl.
**cherry; cerise.**
The latter, 'cherry-colour(ed)', derives from OF-F

*cerise*, a cherry, from VL *\*ceresia*, from Gr *kerasia*,
var of *kerasion*, a cherry, from Gr *kerasos*, a
cherry tree, prob a loan-word (? Phrygian) from
Asia Minor (Hofmann); and *cherry*, ME *chery*, the
fruit, derives from ONF *cherise*, app mistaken for
a pl, from VL *\*ceresia*. The Gr *kerasos* is prob akin
to Gr *kranos*, cornel tree. The place *Kerasos* in
Pontus (Asia Minor) might have given its name to
the tree and its fruit; the reverse is more likely.
**cherub**, pl **cherubim** (*-im*, H pl): H *kĕrūbh*.
Hence **cheru**b**ic** (*-ic*, adj).
**chervil:** OE *cerfille*: L *caerefolium*, shrewd f/e
for *chaerephyllum*, trln of Gr *khairephullon*, cpd of
*khairein* (s *khair-*), to rejoice+*phullon*, a leaf (cf L
*folium*, E *folio*), an aromatic herb culinarily
desirable.
**chess.** See CHECK, para 3.
**chest.** See CIST, para 2.
**Chester.** See CASTLE, para 2.
**chestnut** and **'chestnut'; castanet.**
1. 'Chestnut', an old joke or story, prob comes
from roasted chestnuts eaten at the glossipy fireside;
*chestnut*, earlier *chesten nut*, derves from ME
*chesten*, earlier *chesteine*, earliest *chasteine*, from
OF-MF *chastaigne* (EF-F *châtaigne*), from L
*castanea*, trln of Gr *kastanea*, var of *kastanon*, a
chestnut; prob a loan-word from Asia Minor (cf
CHERRY): cf Arm *kaskeni*, chestnut tree, from
*kask*, a chestnut.
2. L *castanea* has derivative *castanētum*, chestnut grove (cf the suffix *-etum*), which has influenced
Sp *castañeta*, a paired percussion instrument named
from its resemblance to a pair of chestnuts, from
*castaña*, a chestnut, from L *castanea*; *castañeta*
becomes EF-F *castagnette* becomes E *castanet*.
**chevalier.** See CAVALCADE, para 6.
**chevaux-de-frise.** See FRISIAN, para 2.
**chevron:** OF-F *chevron*, orig a after, then, from
rafter-like bands on a blazon, a small galloon worn
as a badge of rank: an *-on* derivative from OF-MF
*chevre* (F *chèvre*), from L *capra*, a she-goat (f.a.e.,
CAB, para 3), the *-on* being partly due to that of
OProv *cabrion*, from *\*capriōnem*, acc of VL
*\*capriō*, from L *capra*. (B & W.)
**chevy**, coll **chivy**, usu **chivvy**, to pursue, hence
(coll) to harass or tease, derives from *chevy* (coll
*chivvy*), a chase or pursuit, earlier a hunting cry,
from the EE ballad of *Chevy Chase*—for *Cheviot
Chase*, in the *Cheviot* Hills of the English-Scottish
border.
**chew**, v hence n; **chaw** (v hence n), **chawbacon.**
*Chaw* is a var of *chew*; *chawbacon*, a rustic,
from this habit. 'To *chew*' descends from OE
*cēowan*, akin to the syn OHG *kiuwan*, MD *keuwen*
or *couwen*, D *kauwen*, and prob to L *gingīua*, the
gum.
**chiaroscuro.** It *chiaro*, clear+*oscuro*, obscure.
**chiasmus:** Gr *khiasmos*, a setting crosswise, from
*khiazein*, to mark with a *khi*: χ.
**chic**, n hence adj: F, orig painters' sl: either
short for EF-F *chicane* or id with C17–18 *chic*,
legal trickery. *Chicane* derives from Villon's
*chicaner*, to quibble, app from MLG-G *schicken*

(cf ON *skikka*), to arrange, in nuance 'to arrange to one's advantage'. (B & W.) The E *chicanery* represents late MF-F *chicanerie*, from *chicaner*.

Chicago city: *Chicago* river: Amerind, perh Ojibwa *she-kag-ong*, 'wild-onion place' (Ency. Brit.).

chicane, chicanery. See CHIC.

chick. See CHICKEN.

chick pea. See CICERO, para 3.

chickadee (NAm bird): from its note.

chicken; chick, chickweed.

*Chick* is app a b/f from *chicken*: and *chicken* derives from OE *cicen* or *cycen*, akin to the rare MHG *küchelîn* (G *Küchlein*, *Kücken*), to MD *cuken*, *kieken* (D *kieken*, *kuiken*), and to ON *kiuklingr*—also to COCK (bird). *Chickweed* (cf WEED) has foliage and seeds enjoyed by birds (Webster).

chickpea. See CICERO, para 3.

chickweed. See CHICKEN.

chicory; succory. *Chicory* represents MF-F *chicorée*, by metathesis for MF *cichorée*: ML *cichorea*: L *cichoreum* (or *-ium*): Gr *kikhora*, *kikhoreia*, *kikhōrē*: o.o.o.

2. ML *cchorea* became MD *sūkerie* and MLG *suckerie*: whence EE *sycory* (var *cicoree*), whence E *succory*.

chide: OE *cīdan* (s *cīd-*), o.o.o.; perh related to the *-cīdere* (s *-cīd-*) of L *occīdere*, to slay (not to *occidere*, to succumb).

chief, n hence adj, and chieftain; chef, chef-d'œuvre; kerchief, handkerchief; mischief, mischievous.—achieve (etc.), cad, cadet, cape (headland), capital, captain, cattle, chapter, all treated scp. biceps; decapitate, decapitation; occipital, occiput; precipice, precipitance, precipitant, precipitate (adj, hence n and v), precipitation, precipitator, precipitous.—head (behead, etc.): sep.

1. L *caput* (orig *kaput*; LL *capus*, gen *capi*), the head, has s *cap-* and is akin to Skt *kapālam*, skull, and to OE *hēafod*, akin to OE *hafud*, ON *höfuth*, OHG *houbit* (G *Haupt*), Go *haubith*: the IE s, therefore, would prob be *\*khaph-*, with varr *\*khab-* and *\*khap-*. If L *capere* (s *cap-*) be akin (then cf HEAVE), the basic idea would be 'vessel' (Webster).

2. The L derivatives affecting E are *biceps*, *dēcapitāre*, *occiput*, *praeceps* (whence *praecipitāre*), *sinciput*. *Biceps*, two-headed, becomes the An n *biceps*, a two-headed (i.e., -origined) muscle. *Occiput* (*ob-*+*caput*), adopted by An, has o/s *occipit-*, whence the ML adj *occipitālis*, whence E *occipital*; likewise *sinciput* (*semi*, half+*caput*), adopted by An, acquires E adj *sincipital*.

3. LL *dēcapitāre* (*de-*, off from+o/s *capit-*+inf suffix), to behead, has pp *dēcapitātus*, whence 'to *decapitate*', and ML derivative n *dēcapitātiō-*, o/s *dēcapitātiōn-*, whence E *decapitation*.

4. *Praeceps* (*prae-*, before+c/f of *caput*), with head before, headlong, has o/s *praecipit-*, whence *praecipitium* (b/f from the neupl *praecipitia* of the adj), whence EF-F *précipice*, whence E *precipice*. The F n has obs adj *précipiteux*, f *-euse*, whence E

*precipitous*. Also on the adj o/s *praecipit-* arises the v *praecipitāre*, with presp *praecipitans*, o/s *praecipitant-*, whence the adj *precipitant*, whence (suffix *-cy*) *precipitancy*; with pp *praecipitātus*, whence the adj (whence the n and the v) *precipitate*; with subsidiaries *praecipitātiō*, o/s *praecipitātiōn-*, whence, perh via F, the E *precipitation*, and LL agential *praecipitātor*, whence *precipitator*; *precipitative* is an E formation: *precipitat*ion+*-ive*, adj.

5. Through F have come *chef*, *chief*, *kerchief*, *mischief*, with their subsidiaries.

6. OF-F *chef*, orig 'the head', later 'person at the head', is adopted in the forms *chef*, elliptical for *chef de cuisine*, and in *chef-d'œuvre*, 'master(piece) of work', masterpiece.

7. OF *chef* has var *chief*, adopted by ME and, in the sense 'person at the head' (of, e.g., a clan), surviving in E *chieftain*; ME *cheftayne*, earlier *chevetayn*, derives from OF-MF *chevetain*, from ML *capitānus* (var *-āneus*): cf CAPTAIN.

8. *Kerchief*, ME *coverchef*, derives from OF-F *couvrechef*, lit a cover-head (cf COVER). *Handkerchief* simply adds HAND.

9. *Mischief*, ME *meschef*, misfortune, ill result, derives from OF-EF *meschef*, *meschief*, from OF-MF *meschever*, to fare badly, be unfortunate: *mes-* (cf E *mis-*) from L *minus*, less+*chef*, *chief*, head. OF *meschef* has, in AF, the adj *meschevous*, unfortunate, (hence) causing misfortune, whence E *mischievous*.

chigger (or jigger) anglicizes chigoe (cf F *chique*), of WI Amerind origin.

chilblain. See BLAIN.

child, pl children; childe; Childermas; childhood; childish.

*Child* derives from OE *cild* (pl *cildru*), akin to Go *kilthei*, womb, and Skt *jaṭhara*, belly, (hence) womb. The late ME-EE sense 'well-born youth' survives in the archaic spelling *childe*, e.g. *Childe Harold*. OE *cild* has OE derivatives *cildisc*, whence *childish* (*-ish*, adj); *cildamaesse*, whence *Childermas* (2nd MASS), Holy Innocents' Day; *cildhād*, whence *childhood* (*-hood*).

chili, varr chilli, chile; Sp *chili*, *chile*: Nahuatl (Aztec) *chilli*.

chill, n hence adj (also chilly) and v: ME *chele*: OE *cele* (*cyle*), intimately akin to OE *calan*, to be cold: cf COOL and, f.a.e., COLD.

chilli. See CHILI.—chilly. See CHILL.

chimaera. See CHIMERA.

chime, n hence v; cymbal.

*Chime*, ME *chime*, earlier *chimbe*, orig a cymbal, derives from OF-MF *chimble*, *cimble*, *cimbe*: L *cymbalum*: Gr *kumbalon*, a cymbal, from *kumbē*, *kumbos*, anything hollow, esp a hollow vessel, akin to Skt *humbha*, a pot, and, on the Gmc side, HUMP. L *cymbalum* issues into OE as *cymbal*, retained by E: cf the OF var *cymbale*, retained by F. IE r: *\*kumb-*, to be curved.

chimera, formerly chimaera; chimeric, now often chimerical. See HIBERNACLE, para 3.

chimney: ME *chimenee*: OF-F *cheminée*, orig a

room with a fireplace: LL *camīnāta*, from L *camīnus*, oven, furnace, hearth, trln of Gr *kaminos*, furnace, kiln, flue for heating a room—akin to *kamara*, a vault (cf CAMERA).

chimpanzee, coll chimp, represents Kongo (Bu tribe, S of the Congo) dial *chimpenzi*.

chin, n hence v: OE *cin*, chin: cf OHG *chinni*, chin, jaw (G *Kinn*, chin)—OFris *zin-*, OS *kinni*, Go *kinnus*, cheek, jaw—ON *kinn*, cheek; cf also L *gena*, cheek, Gr *genus*, lower jaw, and *geneion*, chin, and Skt *hánus*, jaw; and, for sense-kinship, the cognate OIr *gin*, Cor *genau*, mouth. IE r, perh *khan-*, varr *khen-*, *khin-*. (Cf Gr *gnathos*, jaw: perh for *genathos*.)

china is short for *chinaware*, i.e. *China ware*, ware of China: *China*, from the *Ch'in* dynasty (255-206 B.C.). A native is a *Chinese*, from the adj *Chinese* (*China*+*-ese*); from the n *Chinese* illiterately apprehended as pl only, comes the coll *Chinee*.

chinchilla, adopted from Sp, comes from Quechua *sinchi*, strong+*-lla*, dim suffix (Webster): 'strong little (animal)'.

chine, backbone. See SHIN, para 3.

Chinee; Chinese. See CHINA.

chink (1), a crack, app derives from obs *chine*, a fissure, itself from OE *cinu*—cf OE *cīnan*, to crack (open), to gape, to burst, Go *keinan*; IE r, *kei-*, *ki-*, to split or crack open. (Walshe.)

chink (2), n and v, (to make) a short, sharp, tinny sound; echoic; cf JINGLE. The sl *chink*, a prison, derives from the jangling of fetters and great keys.

Chinook Indian, hence his speech, hence the trade-jargon of NW U.S.A. and S.W. Canada: *Tsinúk*, the Chinook tribe's name bestowed by adjacent Chehalis tribe. The wind so named blows from the Chinook lands.

chinquapin, occ chinkapin, (edible nut of) the dwarf chestnut of NA: of Alg origin—cf Virginian *chechinkamin*. The lit meaning is prob 'great nut' —cf Delaware *chinqua*, large+(with *p* for *m*) Alg *min*, fruit, nut, seed. (Mathews.)

chintz. See CHEETAH.

chip, v hence n (whence sl chippy, a carpenter): OE *cippian*, akin to MHG *kippen*, to strike, G *kippen*, to pare or clip, and prob to ON *kippa*, to snatch.

chipmunk, ground squirrel: eased from earlier *chitmunk*: of Alg origin.

chippy, carpenter. See CHIP.

chirograph, chirology, chiromancy. See the element *-cheiria*.

chiropodist, chiropody: *chiro-*, hand, hence manual care of +*pod-*, o/s of Gr *pous*, foot. Cf the elements *-cheiria* and *-pod*.

chiropractic, adj of *chiropraxis*: element *chiro-*, q.v. at *-cheiria*+*praxis*, q.v. at PRACTICE.

chirp, v hence n: (? freq) chirrup, v hence n: echoic, as in the phon and sem var *cheep*, v hence n.

chirurgeon, chirurgic(al). See SURGEON, s.f.

chisel, n hence v (whence chisel(l)er): ONF *chisel* (OF-MF *cisel*, MF-F *ciseau*): VL *cisellus*, on anl

of *martellus*: L *caesellus*, instrument serving to *caedere* (pp *caesus*, s *case-*) or cut: cf 'concise'. The sl v *chisel*, to cheat, derives from 'cutting too close'.

chit (1), orig a cub or a whelp, hence a child: app, as in E dial *chit*, a cat, a thinning of OF-F *chat*, a cat, sense-influenced by *kitten*, ME *kitoun*.

chit (2), document, note. See CHEETAH.

chit-chat. See CHAT.

chitterling, usu pl chitterlings, smaller intestines of esp pigs: akin to G *Kutteln*, tripe, MHG *kutel*, gut, Go *qithus*, belly, stomach, and esp OE *cwith*, womb, of which it is app a distorted dim.

chivalric, chivalrous, chivalry. See CAVALCADE, para 6.

chloral, chloride, chlorine (whence chlorinate); chloroform, chlorophyll.

*Chloral*=*chlor*ine+*al*cohol; *chloride*=*chlor*ine+ Chem suffix *-ide*; *chlorine*=*chlor*os, from Gr *khlōros*, pale-green (ult akin to YELLOW)+Chem suffix *-ine*; *chloroform*, see element *chloro-*; *chlorophyll*, see elements *chloro-* and *-phyll*.

chock, a block or wedge, usu of wood, prob derives from ONF *choque*, identical with OF *çoche* (whence F *souche*), stump, log: Gaul *tsukka*, akin to OHG *stoc* (G *Stock*) and therefore to E STOCK. Hence *chockfull*, with f/e var *chokefull*.

chocolate: EF *chocolate* (F *chocolat*): Sp *chocolate*: Aztec *chocólatl*.

choice, n hence adj; choose, pt chose, pp chosen.

*Choice* derives from ME *chois*, adopted from OF-MF *chois* (EF-F *choix*), from OF-F *choisir*, orig to perceive, then to choose, from Go *kausjan*, var *kiusan*, to test or examine, to taste, akin to OHG *kiosan*, MHG *kiesen*, OS *kiosan*, ON *kjōsa*, and esp OE *cēosan*, whence ME *chesen* or *chosen*, the E 'to *choose*': all akin to L *gustāre*, Gr *geuesthai*, to taste, and to Skt *jósati*, *juṣaté*, he enjoys. IE r, *keus-*, to taste.

choir or quire; choral, chorister, chorus; chorography, see element *choro-*; Terpsichore, whence Terpsichorean;—carol, sep.

1. *Terpsichore*, Gr *Terpsikhorē*, Muse of the Dance and of Choral Song, blends *terpsis*, joy, enjoyment, with *khoros*, a dancing-place, hence a dance, dancing, with song accompaniment: and *khoros* is either akin to Gr *khortos*, an enclosed place, a courtyard (cf COURT), or, less prob, a 'thinning' of Gr *khōros*, a place, a district, with specialized sense. The L trln is *chorus*, adopted by E and F, with adj *choral*, from ML *chorālis* (L *chorus*+adj suffix *-alis*); *chorister*, for earlier *chorist*, shows the influence of MF-F *choriste* and its source the ML *chorista*. *Chorus* has, in order, the senses 'choral dance'—'choir'—'burden of a song'.

2. *Choir*, ME *quer* (whence the archaic var *quire*), comes from MF *cuer* (EF-F *choeur*, cf G *Chor*), from L *chorus*.

choke, v, whence n and the agent choker and adj chok(e)y.

'To *choke*', derivative as vi, has come, through ME *choken*, var *cheken*, by aphesis from OE *ācĕocian*, to suffocate (someone): prob the int prefix *a-*+a v formed from the Gmc r occurring in ON *kok*, gullet, mouth—perhaps cf also OE *cēace*, MD *cake* (D *kaak*), MLG *kāke*, all meaning both 'jaw' and 'cheek'.

**choler, choleric; cholera.**
E *cholera* derives its form from L *cholera*, a bilious disease, but its meaning from Gr *kholera* (whence the L word), itself prob from either Gr *kholē*, bile, or Gr *kholos*, gall, or from both: f.a.e., Med GALL. L *cholera* became MF *colere*, whence ME *coler*, whence E *choler*, the bile, supposed by medieval physicians to be the source of irritability; the adj *choleric* derives from MF *colerique* (EF-F *colé-*), L *cholericus*, on anl of Gr *kholerikos* but from L *cholera*.

**choose.** See CHOICE.

**chop** (1), jaw; var **chap**: app from ME *chappen*, to chop: therefore cf:

**chop** (2), v hence n (e.g., a mutton chop): to cut with repeated blows of esp an axe: ME *choppen*, var *chappen*, prob from MD *cappen* (D and LG *kappen*), app influenced, as EW points out, by Picard *choper*, var of OF-MF *coper* (EF-F *couper*), to cut.—Hence the agent *chopper* and the adj (of sea) *choppy*.

**chop** (3), v hence n: to barter, to exchange whether for money or in kind: ME *chapien*, var of *cheapien*, to trade: f.a.e., CHEAP.

**chop** (4), n hence v: a seal, its impression, hence a licence or permit: Hind *chāp*, a brand, imprint, stamp.

**chop-chop.** See CHOPSTICK.

**chopper; choppy.** See the 2nd CHOP, s.f.

**chopstick**: pidgin version of Ch name, which means lit 'the speedy ones'—cf *chop-chop*, a pidgin mispron of the Cantonese version of a Pekinese word for 'promptly' or 'speedily'. (Y & B.)

**choral.** See CHOIR.

**chord** (1), thin rope, string. See CORD.

**chord** (2), in music. See the element *-chord*.

**chore.** See the 1st CHAR, para 2.

**chorister.** See CHOIR.

**chorography**: via L from Gr *khōrographia*, description of a district, regional geography. See elements *choro-* (place, district) and *-graph*.

**chortle** was coined, 1872, by Lewis Carroll: a blend of *chuckle*+*snort*.

**chorus.** See CHOIR.

**chose, chosen.** See CHOICE.

**chough**: ME *choughe*, var *kowe*: OE *cēo*, akin to OHG *kāha* and MD *cauwe*, D *kauw*: ? echoic.

**chow**, sl for 'food', is also, as *Chow*, a breed of dog orig Ch: short for *chowchow*, a dish of mixed preserves orig Ch: elliptical for pidgin adj *chow-chow*, mixed, of unknown Ch origin.

**chowder.** See C/DRON, para 2.

**chrism**, archaic **chrisom; chrismal; chrismation; chrismatory.**—**Christ; christen; Christian, Christianity; Christmas; criss-cross.**—**cream, creamy; cretin, cretinism, cretinous.**

1. *Chrism*, consecrated oil, hence consecration and a consecratory, e.g. baptismal, garment (var

*chrisom*), derives, through ME *crisme*, from OE *crisma*, itself from LL *chrisma*, trln of Gr *khrisma*, an anointing, an oil used therefor, from *khriein* (s *khri-*), to rub, to anoint, akin to Skt *gharṣati*, he rubs or grinds, e.g. oil from seeds; IE r, *\*ghrei-* or *ghri-*, to rub; akin to GRIND. LL *chrisma* has LL adj *chrismālis*, whence E *chrismal*, the neu *chrismāle*, used as n, becoming the E n *chrismal*; the ML *chrismātiō*, o/s *chrismātiōn-*, yields *chrismation*; the ML *chrismatōrium*, prop the neus of the adj *chrismatōrius* (whence the E adj), yields the n *chrismatory*.

2. Gr *khriein* has pp *khristos*, whence the LGr *Khristos*, The Anointed (One), whence LL *Christus*, whence E *Christ*. A follower of· Christ is LGr *khristianos*, n then adj—LL *christiānus*, adj then n —E *Christian*, almost simultaneously (early in C16) n and adj, displacing ME and OE *cristen*, a Christian, itself from LL *christiānus*. This OE *cristen* has two notable derivatives, the v *crīstnian*, to make a Christian of, whence ME *cristnian*, later, *cristnen*, whence E 'to *christen*' (whence *christening*, adj and n), and *crīstendōm* (cf the suffix *-dom*), whence *Christendom*, orig syn with *Christianity*, itself from LL *christiānitās* (o/s *christiānitāt-*): *christiānus*, adj+abstract suffix *-itās* (E *-ity*). *Christianize* represents LL *christiānizāre*, from LGr *khristianizein*. *Christmas*, however, merely blends *Christ*+religious MASS: a C16 reshaping of ME *Cristes maesse*, later ME *cristmaesse*, *-masse*, etc.

3. The not imm obvious *criss-cross* (n hence adj and v) 'eases' the earlier *Christcross*: X for Gr χ (*khi*), the *Ch* of *Christ*.

4. LL *chrisma* becomes OF *cresme*, becomes ME *creme* becomes E *cream*, obs for 'chrism'; note, however, that the precise OF *cresme*, var *craime*, yielding E *cream* of milk (F *crème*), has been blended with LL (C6: VL) *crama*, cream, of Gaul origin (? akin to W *cram*, *cramen*, incrustation)— perh rather vice-versa. Hence 'to *cream*' and the adj *creamy*; *creamery* owes something to F *crèmerie*.

5. LL *christiānus* becomes OF-MF *chrestien* (EF-F *chrétien*), which, in the diall of Valois and Savoy, becomes *cretin*, a congenital idiot (of the Alps), whence F *crétin*, whence E *cretin*; derivative F *crétinisme* becomes E *cretinism*; *cretinous* is, however, of E formation. F dial *cretin* 'was at first used in pity, only later pej' (B & W).

**Christ, christen, Christian**, etc. See prec, para 2.

**chromatic, chrome**, whence the Sci L **chromium** (suffix *-ium*). See the element *-chroia*.

**chronic; chronicle, chronicler; crony; synchronize, synchronization; chronometer**, etc., see the element *chrono-*.

1. The base rests on Gr *khronos* (s *khron-*), time, age: IE r, *\*gher-*, to wear out, with n sense 'time'. The Gr adj is *khronikos*, L trln *chronicus*, whence, prob via MF-F *chronique*, the E *chronic*, of time, esp taking or lasting a long time, with Med sense already recorded in LL. The Gr neupl is *khronika*, whence the L f sing *chronica*, a register or account of events, whence MF *cronique* (later *chronique*),

whence, as if a dim, the ME *cronicle*, Renaissance-shaped to *chronicle*, whence 'to *chronicle*', whence *chronicler*.

2. The Gr v answering to *khronos* is *khronizein*, with cpd *sunkhronizein* (*sun*, with, together, simultaneously), whence 'to *synchronize*', whence *synchronization*; the corresp Gr adj is *sunkhronos*, LL trln *synchronus*, whence E *synchronous*.

3. Gr *khronos* has another adj: *khronios*, whence E *chrony*, now *crony*, orig a university contemporary, hence an intimate friend.

**chrysalis**, adopted from L, comes from Gr *khrusallis*, from *khrusos*, gold (Sem origin). Cf the element *chrys*(*o*)- and:

**chrysanthemum**, lit 'the golden flower'. See element *anth-*.

**chthonian.** See HOMO, para 3.

**chub**, a squat fish: ME *chubbe*, o.o.o.; but, in dial, *chub* means 'log of wood'—therefore cf Nor *kubbe*, Sw *kubb*, a log, and Nor *kubben*, stumpy (EDD). Hence the adj *chubby*.

**chuck** (1), to make a clucking noise, is echoic; perh influenced by *chick*, which has certainly influenced dial *chuck*, a hen. 'To *chuck*' has freq 'to *chuckle*', whence the n *chuckle*.

**chuck** (2), to tap (e.g., under the chin), to toss, to throw, hence the n *chuck*: perh from *chuck*, a dial var of *chock* or block of wood, whence the various SE (esp tech) senses; the sl *chuck*, food, has been influenced by the 1st CHUCK.

**chuckle.** See the 1st CHUCK, s.f.

**chug**, redup **chug-chug**: echoic.

**chum.** See CAMERA, para 2, s.f. Hence the n and adj **chummy**.

**chump**, orig a block of wood, hence coll (cf *blockhead*) a dolt or stupid fellow, and sl head: perh *chunk*+*lump*, as EW suggests.

**chunk**, log, stump, hence a fair-sized piece, hence also a stumpy person or quadruped; whence, influenced by the 2nd CHUCK, the AE *chunk*, to throw; whence also the adj *chunky*, squat.

**church**, n hence v; cpds self-explanatory by the 2nd element, as **churchman, churchwarden, churchyard; kirk; kermess** or **kermis; Kyrie eleison, kyrin(e).**

1. The effectual base of all these words is Gr *kurios*, a master, lord, king, from *kuros*, power, s *kur-*, akin to Skt *śuras*, powerful, bold, a hero; perh (Hofmann) the Gr word derives from a Gr *\*kuros* (s *kur-*), powerful; the IE s would be *\*keur-*, the IE r *\*keu-* or *\*keua*, strong, to be strong: cf Ir *caur*, hero, and Cor *caur*, W *cawr*, giant; perh of Medit stock, for cf Eg *khu-t*, power.

2. *Church*, ME *chirche*, derives from OE *circe*, *cyrice*, itself, like OHG *kirihha* (G *Kirche*) and ON *kirkia*, *kirkja*, from LGr *kurikon*, for Gr *kuriakon*, (house) of the Lord, from *kurios*, lord. (Walshe.)

3. The Sc *kirk* app owes something to ON *kirkia* (*-ja*).

4. *Kermis*, var *kermess*, a semi-religious outdoor festival, derives from D *kermis*, MD *kermisse*, for *kercmis*, *kercmesse*, lit 'Church mass'.

5. The eccl *Kyrie eleison* is the LL trln of LGr

*Kurie eleeson*, Lord, have mercy (upon us); the 2nd element occurs in E ALMS.

6. The Chem *kyrine*, *kyrin*, represents Gr *kur*os, power, validity+the Chem suffix *-ine* or *-in*: a substance held to be 'a basic protein nucleus' (Webster).

**churl, churlish; carl, Carl, Charles.** The hist *carl*, peasant, serf, bondman, etc., derives from ON *karl*, a man, a freeman; the PN *Carl* derives from G *Karl*; both are akin to OE *ceorl*, man, lowest-ranked freeman, whence ME *cheorl* (*cherl*), whence *churl*, (now usu) a boor, with adj *churlish*, from OE *ceorlisc*. *Charles*, adopted from F, comes from MHG *karl*, a freeman. The ML form *Carolus* derives from G *Karl*; the adj is *Caroline*—cf *Carolina*, f dim from *Carolus*.

**churn**, n and v. See GRAIN, para 10.

**chute.** See CADENCE, para 6.

**chutney**, occ **chutnee**: Hi *catnī* (pron *chahtnēē*), ? from *cāṭnā*, to lick.

**chyle; chyme.** See the 2nd FOUND, para 16.

**cicada, cicala.**

The latter is the It (and ML-VL) derivative of L *cicāda*, itself echoic: cf the equally echoic Gr syn *tettix*.

**cicatrice, cicatrix, cicatrize.**

The first comes either from L *cicātrīcula*, a small scar, dim of *cicātrīx*, a scar, or by b/f from *cicātrīces*, pl of *cicātrīx*, or, most prob, from MF-F *cicatrice*, suggested by *cicātrīc-*, the o/s of *cicātrīx*; *cicatrize* derives, perh vi a MF-F *cicatriser*, from ML *cicātrīzāre*, var of LL*cicātrīcāre* (from *cicatrix*, o.o.o.).

**Cicero, Ciceronian, cicerone; chich; chick(-pea).**

1. The L *cicer*, a chick-pea, has s *cic-* and is akin to OP *keckers*, pea, s *keck-*, and Arm *sisern* (? s *sis-*), chick-pea. (E & M.)

2. The derivative ML *cicerō*, chick-pea, suggests that the PN *Cicerō* may derive from *cicer*; *Cicerō* has adj *cicerōniānus*, whence *Ciceronian*; the It form *Cicerone* (cf the F *Cicéron*) has derivative *cicerone*, a guide: *Cicero* and *ciceroni* (It pl; E, *cicerones*) alike are talkative.

3. The obs *chich*, chick-pea, derives from MF-F *chiche*, elliptical for *pois chiche*, earlier *ciche*, from L *cicer*; the extant E term is *chick-pea*, by f/e from the earlier *ciche pease*.

**cider**, rare var **cyder**, derives, via ME *sidre*, from MF *sidre*, OF *cisdre* (EF-F *cidre*), from VL *\*cisera*, from LL *sicera*, an intoxicant, from LGr (Septuagint) *sikera*, borrowed from H *shekar* (whence *shikkor*, tipsy, whence E sl *shicker*).

**cigar; cigarette.**

The latter, adopted from F *cigarette* (earliest *cigaret*), is the dim of F *cigare*, earlier *cigarro*, adopted from Sp *cigarro*, itself o.o.o., but perh (Webster) from Maya *sik'ar*, to puff, inch of *sik'eh*, to smoke, from *sik'*, tobacco.

**ciliary; cilium; supercilious; seel.**

1. The falconry term *seel*, to close (the eyes), ME *silen*, comes from OF-MF *siller*, var of OF-F *ciller*, from OF-F *cil*, eyelash, from L *cilium* (pl *cilia*), eyelid, r *cil-*, akin to Gr *kalia*, hut, barn,

shrine; the IE r would be *khel-, to hide, whence *kel-, as in L celāre, to hide, OIr celim, I hide, and in *hel-, becoming E HELL and OHG hulla, envelope. The adj ciliary=L cili(um)+E -ary; the adj ciliate derives from L ciliātus.

2. L cilium has cpd supercilium, eyebrow (super, above), hence pride, with adj superciliōsus, whence E supercilious, addicted to raising the eyebrows. The Sci adj superciliary is anl to ciliary.

cinch, n hence v; cingle; cinct, cincture; enceinte, adj and n; precinct; succint; surcingle; shingles (disease).

1. Cinch, a strong, esp if tight, girth, hence a firm, tight grip (hence prob also the card-game cinch), hence something easy to do, derives from the Sp cincha, from L cingere (s cing-), to gird, to encircle, app akin to Skt kañcate, he binds, kāñcī, a belt or girdle, and Lith kinkýti, to harness (a beast).

2. Cingere has pp cinctus (s cinct-), whence E cinct, girdled, girt, surrounded; the derivative L cinctūra, a girdle, becomes cincture (cf the F ceinture).

3. Cingere has three cpds relevant to E: incingere, to gird about (int in-); praecingere, to gird from in front (prae, before), hence to surround; succingere, to gird from below, to tuck up. Incingere has pp incinctus, LL incincta, pregnant, whence F enceinte (m enceint), adopted by E; the n enceinte, likewise adopted from MF-F, is prob elliptical for place, or forteresse, enceinte, where enceinte is the f of the pp of enceindre (L incingere). Cf:

4. Praecingere has pp praecinctus, whence the ML, praecinctum, an enclosure, esp of a church, whence E precinct, now usu precincts, immediate environs of a cathedral, hence a legally determined district.

5. Succingere has pp succinctus, tucked-up, held tightly in place, hence compressed: whence the E succinct.

6. Surcingle derives from MF surcengle: sur, from L super, over, above+OF-MF cengle, from L cingulum, a girdle (cing-, s of cingere+suffix -ulum). OF-MF cengle (later sangle) yields E cingle, a girth.

7. L cingulum has ML derivative cingulus, an acute skin disease, girdle-area'd: whence E shingles.

cinchona. See QUININE, para 2.

cinct, cincture. See CINCH, para 2.

cinder, sinter; Cinderella; cinerary, cinereous; incinerate, incineration, incinerator.

1. Sinter, dross of iron, is adopted from G (OHG sintar): and it answers to OE sinder, dross, slag, akin to ON sindr, dross, OSl sedra. OE sinder yields E cinder, with sense, esp in pl cinders, influenced by that of the independent F cendres, ashes.

2. OF-F cendres has derivative Cendrillon of Perrault's fairy tale (1697): whence sem, though phon from E cinder, the E Cinderella (-ella, f dim suffix).

3. F cendres, sing cendre, derives from LL cendra, var cindra, from LL cinus, gen cineris, from L cinis (gen cineris), ashes, a dead coal; with its

s and r cin- cf Gr kon-, s of konis, dust; IE r, *ken-, varr *kin-, *kon-.

4. L cinis, o/s ciner-, has derivative adjj cinereus, whence E cinereous, and cinerārius, whence E cinerary.

5. The derivative ML incinerāre, to reduce to ashes, has pp incinerātus, whence 'to incinerate'; its derivative incinerātiō, o/s incinerātiōn-, yields, perh via MF-F incinération, the E incineration; incinerator, one who, hence that which, incinerates, is an E formation (incinerate+agential -or).

cinema, cinematic; cinematograph, -grapher, -graphic, -graphy.

1. Cinema, with Grecized adj cinematic, is short for cinematograph, a motion picture: kinēmato,-c/f of Gr kinēma, motion, from kinein (s kin-), to move, whence kinēsis, movement, and its adj kinētikos, whence resp the Sci kinesis and kinetic: f.a.e., CITE.

2. Cinematograph has agent -grapher, adj -graphic, abstract n -graphy: cf -grapher, etc., at GRAPH.

cinerary, cinereous. See CINDER, para 4.

cingle. See CINCH, para 6.

cinnamon derives, perh via MF-F cinnamone, from L cinnamon, from Gr kinnamon, trln of H qinnāmōn, perh ult Malayan (Hofmann).

cinquain, cinque, Cinque Ports.

Cinquain, adopted from EF (cf quatrain), derives from OF-F cinq, five, whence cinque, as in Cinque Ports, the (orig) five charter ports of Kent and Sussex. F cinq derives from VL cīnque, from L quīnque, to which E FIVE is ult akin.

cion. See SCION.

cipher (n hence v), occ cypher; zero; decipher (v), whence decipherer and decipherment.

'To decipher' (influenced by the MF-F déchiffrer) =prefix de-, from+cipher: and the n cipher derives from MF-EF cifre, zero, itself from Ar ṣifr, empty, hence zero; and zero represents EF-F zéro, from It zero, a conflation of the earlier zefiro, a violent attempt at the Ar ṣifr. The sense 'a secret writing' comes from Commynes's use (1486) of F chiffre, which derives from It, from ML, cifra, from the Ar word. (See esp B & W at chiffre and zéro.)

circa. See para 2 of:

circle, n and v; encircle, encirclement; circlet; circuit (n hence v), circuitous, qq.v. sep; circular, circularize; circulate, circulation, circulatory; circum and circa; circus;—search, n, v (whence pa and vn searching), searchlight; research, n, v (whence researcher); recherché.

1. The firm base upholding all these words is the L circus, a circle, hence—circus 'circle' being displaced by the dim circulus—a circus in the modern sense, whence both the MF-F cirque and the E circus: and L circus, s circ-, is akin to Gr kirkos, s kirk-, a ring; akin also to L curuus, ML curvus, curved—cf, therefore, CURVE. The IE r of Gr kirkos, L circus, is *kirk- or *kerk-; of the two groups combined, *ker-, var *kir-.

2. L circus, circle, yields the adv-prep circum,

in a circle, around, orig the acc sing (cf the prefix *circum*); and *circa* (cf *extra*, *supra*, etc.), around, becomes 'about', esp of dates.

3. The dim *circulus* becomes OF-F, whence ME, *cercle*, whence, by L influence, E *circle*; ME *cercle* has derivative v *cerclen*, whence, by L influence, 'to *circle*'. 'To *encircle*', whence *encirclement* (suffix *-ment*; cf the F *encerclement*)=prefix *en-*, in+ *circle*: cf the OF-F *encercler*. *Circlet*=*circle*+dim suffix *-et*.

4. *Circulus*, s *circul-*, has two notable L derivatives:

*circulāris*, whence E *circular* (adj suffix *-ar*, L *-aris*), whence 'to *circularize*' (cf F *circulariser*), whence *circularization*; on the L s *circulār-* arose ML *circulāritās*, gen *-itātis*, whence E *circularity*;

*circulāri*, vi and vt, to gather—to put—into a circle, has pp *circulātus*, whence 'to *circulate*'; derivative *circulātiō*, o/s *circulātiōn-*, yields, perh via MF-F, the E *circulation*; derivative *circulātor* is adopted by E, its adj *circulātōrius* becoming *circulatory*.

5. From L *circum*, *circa* (para 2 above), rather than from L *circus*, derives the LL *circāre*, to go around, (hence) go about, whence OF-MF *cercher* (EF-F *chercher*), whence ME *cerchen*, later *serchen*, whence 'to *search*', whence *searcher* (cf EF-F *chercheur*) and 'a *search*'—cf the OF-MF n *cerche* from the v *cercher*. *Searchlight* is an obvious, though important, cpd with LIGHT.

6. OF *cercher* has the OF-MF cpd *recercher*, whence 'to *research*', whence the n *research*, unless it comes from the EF-F *recherche*, itself from *rechercher*, the EF-F development of *recercher*; and *rechercher* has pp *recherché*, sought after, hence, as adj, particularly elegant, hence also far-fetched.

circuit, n hence v; circuitous.

*Circuit*, adopted from MF-F, comes from L *circuitus*, itself from *circuīre*, to go around or about, a contr of *circumīre*: *circum*, around (f.a.e., CIRCLE, para 1)+*īre*, to go, supine *itum* (cf ISSUE). The derivative ML adj *circuitōsus* yields E *circuitous*.

circular; circulate, circulation, etc. See CIRCLE, para 4.

circumcise, -ision; (sep *circumduce*, q.v. at DUKE, para 6); circumference; circumflex; circumlocution, -locutory; circumnavigate, -navigation; circumscribe, -scription; circumspect, -spection; circumstance, -stantial; circumvent, -vention.

1. For *circum-*, see both CIRCLE, para 2, and the entry in Prefixes.

2. *Circumcise*: L *circumcīsus*, pp of *circumcīdere*, to cut around, hence to circumcise; derivative L *circumcīsiō*, o/s *circumcīsiōn-*, yields E *circumcision*.

*Circumference*: L *circumferentia*; *circumferential* (cf *deferential*)=*circum*+*-ferent-*+adj suffix *-ial*: cf also *differential*.

*Circumflex*. See FLEX, para 5.

*Circumlocution*: LL *circumlocūtiōn-*, o/s of *circumlocūtiō*, a talking around and about, from LL *circumloqui*, pp *-locūtus*, to talk thus: cf LOCUTION, LOQUACIOUS. Hence the adj *circum-*

*locutory*: cf LL *locūtōrium*, a conversation-room.

*Circumnavigate*: ML *circumnavigātus*, pp of *circumnavigāre*, L *-nauigāre*, to sail around; hence *circumnavigation*, *-navigator*, on *navigation*, *navigator*.

*Circumpose*, *circumposition*. See POSE, para 5.

*Circumscribe*. See SCRIBE, para 10.

*Circumspect*: L *circumspectus*, pp of *circumspicere*, to look around and about; the derivative *circumspectiō*, o/s *-spectiōn-*, yields *circumspection*. Cf SPECTACLE, para 7.

*Circumstance*. See STAND, para 22.

*Circumvent*, *circumvention*. See VENUE, para 8.

*Circumvolute*, *circumvolution*; *circumvolve*. See VOLUBLE, para 4.

circus. See CIRCLE, para 1.

cirrus (Met): L *cirrus*, a curl or ringlet: o.o.o.; perh (E & M) cf the syn Gr *kikinnos*, ? for *kirkinnos*, with *kirk-* as in Gr *kirkos*, a ring, q.v. at CIRCLE, para 1, s.f.

cisco, a Great Lakes fish: var of *sisco*, itself short for *siscowet*: Can F *ciscoette*: Ojibway *pemitewiskawet*, (lit) oily-fleshed fish. (Mathews.)

cist, cyst, kist; cistern; cf element *cysto-*; chest.

1. *Kist* is the Sc form, *cyst* a misspelling of E *cist*, box, chest, from L *cista*, basket, chest, from Gr *kistē*, s *kist-*, basket: perh of OIr *ciss*, *cess*, basket, ain*chis*, bread basket: IE r, *kis-*, extension *kist-*. The derivative *cisterna* has the Etruscan suffix *-erna*; hence OF-MF, whence ME, *cisterne*, hence E *cistern*.

2. In OE, the L *cista* became *cist* or *cyst* or *cest*: whence ME *chist* or *chest*; the latter prevailed in E. The *chest* of an animal's, esp a human's, body encloses the lungs, as if in a box.

3. The spelling *cyst* is prop applied, in Med and Bot, to a sac or a sac-like spore: and it represents Sci L *cystis*, trln of Gr *kustis*, bladder, sac, s *kust-*, akin to Skt *kuṣṭhas*, the lumbar cavity, and *kōṣṭha-*, entrails, and perh, after all, to Gr *kistē*, as in para 1. If this latter kinship be real, IE *kis-*, *kos-*, *kus-*, are extensions of an ult r *ku-*, with varr *ke-*, *ki-*, *ko-*. (Perh cf C**T.)

cit (mid C17–mid C19): short for citizen.

citadel: late MF-F *citadelle*: It *cittadella*, dim of *cittàde*, city: ML *cīvitàs*, L *cīuitàs*, gen *cīutātis*: f.a.e., CITY. A 'little' or nuclea' 'city': a fortress within a city.

cite, citation, citatory; exciter excitable, excitant, excitation, excitatory, excitement; incite, incitant, incitation, incitement; recite, recital, recitation, recitative, reciter; resuscitate, resuscitation, resuscitative; suscitate; SOLICIT (etc.), sep; kinetic, sep at CINEMA.

1. The effective base is L *ciēre* (s *ci-*), to set in motion, akin to Gr *kiein* (s *ki-*), whence *kinein* (s *kin-*, r *ki-*), to move. *Ciēre* has pp *citus*, whence the adj *citus*, quick, prompt, s *cit-*. *Citus* has derivative *citāre*, to cause to come quickly, to convoke or summon, (later) to set moving, to stir up. *Citāre* becomes MF-F *citer*, whence 'to *cite*', to summon, to adduce or quote; the derivative n *citātiō*, o/s

*citātiōn-*, yields, prob via MF-F, the E *citation*, and the adj *citatōrius* yields *citatory*.

2. *Citāre* has the following relevant prefix-cpds: *excitāre, incitāre, recitāre, suscitāre* and its subsidiary *resuscitāre*.

3. *Excitāre*, to summon forth (*ex*), hence to provoke or excite, whence, through OF-F *exciter*, the E 'to *excite*'; its LL derivative *excitābilis* becomes E *excitable*, whence, on anl of *ableability, excitability*; presp *excitans*, o/s *excitant-*, becomes E *excitant*, adj hence n; derivative *excitātiō*, o/s *excitātiōn-*, becomes MF-F *excitation*, adopted by E; *excitatory* perh derives from ML *\*excitatōrius*; *excitement=excite+-ment*.

4. *Incitāre*, to move, hence thrust, forward, yields MF-F *inciter*, whence 'to *incite*'; presp *incitans*, o/s *incitant-*, yields adj *incitant*; derivative n *incitātiō*, o/s *incitātiōn-*, yields—perh via MF-F—*incitation*; for *incitement*, cf *excitement*.

5. *Recitāre*, to repeat names of defendants, hence to read loudly, gives us, perh via OF-F *réciter*, 'to *recite*', whence *recital* (*-al*, n suffix of action); derivative *recitātiō*, o/s *recitātiōn-*, gives, perh via MF-F *récitation*, the E *recitation*; *recitative* comes from It *recitativo* (adj, whence n), itself prompted by the ML *recitative*, by name, expressly; *reciter= recite+-er*.

6. *Suscitāre* (*sus-* for *sub*, under), to raise, has pp *suscitātus*, whence 'to *suscitate*', now obsol; its *re-* 'again' cpd *resuscitāre*, to raise again, hence to restore or revive, has pp *resuscitātus*, whence 'to *resuscitate*'. The derivative LL *resuscitātiō*, o/s *resuscitātiōn-*, accounts for E *resuscitation*; *resuscitative* is an E formation (cf *-ive*, adj); LL *resuscitātor*, adopted by E.

**citified.** See CITY, para 1.

**citizen, -ry, -ship.**

The two longer words derive, by suffixes *-ry* and *-ship*, from *citizen*, ME *citezein* (var *citesein*), itself —influenced prob by *denizen*—from OF-MF *citeien, citeain*, from OF-F *cité*, city, from ML *cīvitās*, o/s *cīvitāt-*, a city state: f.a.e., CITY.

**citron, citrus; citrange; citric, citrous, citrate.**

*Citrange* blends *citr*us+*orange*; *citrate=citr*us+ Chem suffix *-ate*; *citric=citr*on (or *citr*us)+adj suffix *-ic*; *citrous* derives from L *citrōsus*, adj of *citrus*. *Citron*, adopted from MF-F, is either an alteration of L *citrus* or from LGr *kitron*, itself from L *citrus*, citron tree, cedar, akin to, rather than from, Gr *kedros*, cedar, (earlier) juniper: cf CEDAR. Both L *citrus* and Gr *kedros* are prob of Medit stock: perh cf Eg *seb* or *seb-t*, cedar.

**city;** sep **citadel** and **citizen; citify; civic, civicism, civics; civil, civilian, civility, civilize** and **civilization; hide** of land; akin ult to *Siva, Shiva* (Skt *śiva*, friendly, hence dear to one) and to sep HOME.

1. *Citify*, to render urban, esp *citified*, excessively urban, represents *city+i* for *y+-fy*, to make or render.

2. *City* itself comes, through ME *cite*, from OF-F *cité*, a contr from ML *cīvitātem*, acc of *cīvitās*, L *cīuitās*, city-state, prop an aggregation of *cīues*, pl of *cīuis* (ML *cīvis*), a citizen, s *cīu-*, r *cī-*,

akin to the *kei-* of Gr *keitai*, he lies down, is recumbent, and (Hofmann) prob to the *ke-* of the syn Hit *keta*; IE s *\*kei-*, r *\*kei-*, to lie down, issuing, as above, in Gr and L, and as *\*hei-, \*hi-*, in PGmc—cf OHG-MHG-G *heim*, house, home, and *hīwo*, husband; also OE *hīgan, hīwan* (pl), household, and *hīd*, short for *hīgid*, family (cf syn *hīred*), whence *hide*, an old land-measure, orig sufficient to maintain a family; and Go *haims*, village; and ON *heimr*, village. Prob cf HOME.

3. L *cīuis*, citizen, has adjj *cīuicus*, ML *cīvicus*, whence E *civic*, whence—cf *ethics* from adj *ethic* —the n *civics*, and, soon predominating, *cīuīlis*, ML *cīvīlis*, whence, prob via MF-F, the E *civil*, of a citizen, hence of a good citizen, hence well-mannered and well-moral'd, whence the n, hence the adj, *civilian* (*-ian*, n); the derivative L *cīuīlitās*, sense of citizenship, LL affability, ML *cīvīlitās*, o/s *cīvīlitāt-*, yields, very prob via MF *civileté*, EF-F *civilité*, E *civility*. The MF-F *civil* has derivative EF-F *civiliser*, whence 'to *civilise* or *-ize*', whence *civilisation* (F influence) or *-ization*.

**civet**, the substance, and its source, the **zibet** (var **zibeth**) or civet cat, both derive from It *zibetto*, from ML *zibethum*, from Ar *zabād*, musk.

**civic, civics.** See CITY, para 3.

**civil, civility, civilize (-ization).** See CITY, para 3.

**clack**, v hence n: echoic: cf MF-F *claquer*, to clap, whence MF-F *claque*, a body of hired applauders. For echoism, cf SMACK and CLATTER and CLANG.

**clad**, adj (clothed, arrayed), derives from the pp of OE *clǣthan*, to clothe.

**claim** (n and v), **claimant; acclaim** (v hence n), **acclamation; conclamation; declaim, declamation, declamatory; disclaim, -er; exclaim, exclamation, exclamatory; proclaim, proclamation; reclaim, reclamation.**—**clamant, clamo(u)r, clamorous.**

1. The n *claim* derives from OF-MF *claim, claime*, itself from OF-EF *clamer* (il *claime*, he calls), from L *clamāre*, to call (out), to cry out, s *clam-*; 'to *claim*', ME *claimen*, derives from OF-EF *clamer*. L *clamāre* is akin to *calāre*, to summon, s *cal-*, and *clārus*, loud, clear, s *clar-*, cf DECLARE; akin also to Gr *kalētōr*, a herald, and *kalein*, to call or summon; IE r *\*kal-*, var *\*kla-*, with extensions *\*klam-, \*klar-*.

2. *Claimant*, deriving from 'to *claim*', has perh been influenced by OF-EF *clamant*, presp of *clamer*; the E *clamant*, however, derives from L *clamant-*, o/s of *clamans*, presp of *clamāre*; and *clamāre* has derivative *clamor*, a shouting, a din, whence, via OF-MF *clamor, clamour, clamur* (cf the EF-F *clameur*), the E *clamour*, with AE *clamor* reverting to L; 'to *clamo(u)r*' follows from the n; the ML adj *clamorōsus* yields E *clamorous*.

3. L *clamāre* has, relevant to E, these prefix-cpds: *acclamāre, conclamāre, dēclamāre, exclamāre, prōclamāre, reclamāre*; only erudite or rare terms issue from *inclamāre* and *succlamāre*.

4. *Acclamāre*, to cry out to (*ad*), to address noisily, yields 'to *acclaim*', whence the modern n

*acclaim—acclamation* (L *acclamātiō*, o/s *-clamātiōn-*) is, however, customary.

5. *Conclamāre*, to cry out, whether altogether or vigorously, has presp *conclamans*, o/s *conclamant-*, whence the E adj *conclamant*, rarer than the E n *conclamation*, from *conclamatiōn-*, o/s of L *conclamātiō*.

6. *Dēclamāre*, to call noisily, hence to declaim, yields EF-F *déclamer*, whence E *declaim*; the derivative *dēclamātiō*, o/s *dēclamātiōn-*, mostly in rhetoric, and *dēclamatōrius*, yield—perh via F— E *declamation* and *declamatory*.

7. *Exclamāre*, to call out, either loudly or suddenly, leads to MF-F *exclamer* and, perh thence, E *exclaim*; derivative *exclamātiō*, o/s *exclamātiōn-*, leads, perh via MF-F, to *exclamation*; *exclamatory* imitates *declamatory*.

8. *Prōclamāre*, to call openly, plead noisily, becomes ME *proclamen*, whence, anl, 'to *proclaim*'; derivative *prōclamātiō* yields *proclamation*; for *proclamatory*, cf *exclamatory*.

9. *Reclamāre*, to cry back at, to appeal to, becomes MF-F *reclamer* (il *reclaime*), whence ME *reclamen*, *reclaimen*, whence 'to *reclaim*'; derivative *reclamātiō* yields *reclamation*.

10. 'To *disclaim*' derives, anl, from AF *desclamer* (F *des-*, from L *dis-*, apart): and this *desclamer*, used as n, yields *disclaimer*, a denial; *disclamation* and *disclamatory* are 'reversions' to imaginary L words.

**clairvoyance**, EF-F b/f from MF-F **clairvoyant**, clear-seeing: OF-F *clair*, cf E CLEAR; *voyant*, presp of OF-F *voir*, to see, cf CLARIFY.

**clam: clamshell.**

The shellfish *clam* is short for *clamshell* (cf SHELL), the 1st element being *clam*, a clamp, from OE *clamm*, a bond or fetter, akin to CLAMP; cf MHG *klamm*, constriction, and *klamere* (G *Klammer*), a fetter; Gmc r, *\*klam-*, IE r *\*glam-*, *\*glem-*, *\*glom-*. (Walshe.) Cf CONGLOMERATE.

**clamant.** See CLAIM, para 2.

**clamber:** ME *clambren*; akin to, prob an echoic mdfn of, CLIMB.

**clammy** app derives from OE *clām*, clay, influenced by OE *clamm*, a fetter, q.v. at CLAM.

**clamor, clamour; clamorous.** See CLAIM, para 2.

**clamp**, n hence v: a holding or binding device: MD *clampe* (D *klamp*, as also in LG): akin to CLAM: prob echoic. Hence the tool *clamper*.

**clan, clannish.** See the 2nd PLANT, para 6.

**clandestine.** See HALL, para 13.

**clang, clango(u)r.** See LAUGH, para 2.

**clank**, n hence v, prob comes from MD *clanc* (D *klank*), itself echoic. Cf prec and also CLINK.

**clannish.** See the 2nd PLANT, para 6.

**clap**, v hence n: ME *clappen*: OE *clappan*, to clap, (*claeppan*) to throb: akin to ON *klappa*, to clap: echoic. Cf:

**clapboard:** f/e for obs *clapbolt*, itself from LG *Klappholt*: echoic G *klappen*, to fit noisily together, bang to (cf prec)+G *Holz*, wood.

**claque.** See CLACK.

**claret** is elliptical for OF-MF 'vin *clairet* (extant),

*cleret'*, light red wine, the adj being the dim of OF-MF *cler*, clear—cf the F *clairet* and see CLEAR.

**clarify:** OF-F *clarifier*: LL *clārificāre*, to render (*-ficāre* for *facere*) glorious, lit clear (*clārus*): cf the elements *clari-* and *-fy*.

**clarinet:** F *clarinette*, dim (cf suffix *-ette*) of EF-F *clarine*, a musical bell, orig the f of the old adj *clarin*, from L *clārus*, clear-toned: f.a.e., CLEAR. Cf the next three entries.

**clarion**, ME *clarioun*, modifies MF *claron* (EF-F *clairon*), from ML *clāriō*, o/s *clāriōn-*, from *clārus* (cf prec): f.a.e., CLEAR.

**clarisonous.** See element *-sonance* and cf prec.

**clarity:** perh through EF *clarité* (EF-F *clarté*): from L *clāritās* (o/s *clāritāt-*), abstract n from *clārus*: f.a.e., CLEAR.

**clash**, v hence n: echoic, cf BASH, CRASH, SMASH, SPLASH.

**clasp**, v hence n: ME *claspen*, metathesis of *clapsen*, freq of *clap* in its sense 'to fit noisily together': akin to CLIP.

**class**, n hence v (cf F *classer*); **classic**, adj (elaboration **classical**)—hence n; **classicism**, **classicist**; **classify**, **classification**, **classificatory**, **classifier**; **déclassé.**

1. The n *class* derives from MF-F *classe*, from L *classis*, prob orig a summons, hence a summoned collection of persons, a group liable to be summoned: perh for *\*calassis*, from *calāre*, to call, hence to summon, itself perh akin to CALL; cf CLAIM.

2. The adj *classicus*, applied in gen to the civic classes of the Roman people and esp to the 1st class, the *classici*, cre ated by Servius Tullius (C6 B.C.), came, in the term *scriptores classici*, to mean 'writers of the first rank', the *classics*: hence both the E adj and the E n, also the EF-F *classique*; whence *classicism* (suffix *-ism*) and *classicist* (*-ist*).

3. 'To *classify*'=L *classi*s+element *-fy*, to make; hence the agent *classifier* and the abstract *classification* (? borrowed from F); *classificatory* prob= *classifica*tion+adj *-ory*.

4. *Déclassé*, adopted from F, is prop the pp of *déclasser*, remove from a specified class.

**clatter**, v hence n; perh a b/f from OE *clatrung*, a rattle, but prob from MD *clateren*, to rattle, to clatter, cf the D var *kletteren*, to clatter: echoic: cf BATTER and SPATTER.

**clause**, whence **clausal** (*-al*, adj), is adopted from MF-F: ML *clausa*, perh elliptical for *sententia clausa*, lit a thought closed, and prob suggested by the syn L *clausula*, the *close* of a rhetorical period, *clausa* being app the f of *clausus*, pp of *claudere*, to shut, hence to end. Cf CLEF.

**claustral.** Cf *cloistral* at CLOISTER.

**claustrophobia:** SciL cpd of L *claustr*um, a confined space (see CLOISTER)+comb *-o-*+*-phobia*, fear, q.v. in Elements.

**clave.** See 1st and 2nd CLEAVE.

**clavicle**, collarbone: EF-F *clavicule*: ML *clavicula*, L *clauicula*, little key, dim of *clauis*, a key. The r *clau-*, to close, occurs also in the closely related *clauus*, ML *clavus*, a nail, and *claudere*, to close (cf CLAUSE).

**claw**. 'To *claw*' derives from OE *clawan*, itself from OE *clawu* (var of *clēa*), whence E 'a *claw*': akin to G *Klaue*, OHG *klāwa*, MHG *klā*, *klāwe*, OFris *klāwe*, *klē*, ON *klō*, and prob to CLEW.

**clay**, whence adj **clayey** (*-ey*), derives from OE *clǣg*, akin to MD *clei*, D *klei*, OFris *klāi*, OHG *klīwa*, G *Kleie*, bran: basic idea, 'stickiness': f.a.e., GLUE; cf the 1st CLEAVE.

**clean**, adj, adv, v (whence **cleaner**, n); adj **cleanly**; **cleanness**; **cleanse**.

*Clean*, v, derives from *clean*, adj, which derives, via ME *clene*, from OE *clǣne*, whence OE adv *clǣne*, whence *clean*, adv. *Clǣne*, adj, has OE derivatives *clǣnnes*, whence *cleanness*; secondary adj *clǣnlīc*, whence adj *cleanly*; derivative secondary adv *clǣnlīce*, whence *cleanly*; and v *clǣnsian*, whence 'to *cleanse*'. The OE adj *clǣne* is akin to OFris *klēne*, small, narrow, OHG *kleini*, pure, elegant, neat, MHG *kleine*, elegant, hence small, G *klein*, small; sem cf the E FINE, adj. (Walshe.)

**clear**, adj, hence adv, n, v; **clearance** (suffix *-ance*) and **clearness** (*-ness*) from the adj.

*Clear* derives, via ME *cleer*, earlier *cler*, from OF-MF *cler* (F *clair*), itself from L *clārus*, clear in sound, hence to sight: akin to *clamāre*, to cry out. The L r is *clā*-, with extnn *clam*-, *clar*-: and *clā*- is perh a metathesis of *cal*-, as in *calāre* (s *cal*-), to summon. Cf CALL and CLAIM.

**clearstory**. See CLERESTORY.

**cleat**, n hence v: ME *cleete* or *clete*: OE *clēat*, akin to MD *cloot*, D *kloot*, a ball, and to CLEW.

**cleavage** derives from the 2nd CLEAVE.

**cleave** (1), to adhere, pt **cleaved**, archaic **clave** and **clove**, pp **cleaved**: ME *clevien*, *cleovien*, *clivien*, *cliven*: OE *cleofian*, *clifian*, akin to OHG *klebēn* (vi), MHG and G *kleben*, OHG *klīban*, OS *klibōn*, prob also to ON *klifa*, to repeat again and again ('*stick* to a subject'), and, more remotely, L *glūs*, Gr *glia*, glue; cf, therefore, CLAY and GLUE—and CLIFF.

**cleave** (2), to forcibly part (e.g., by splitting) or divide or pierce, pt **cleaved**, **cleft**, **clove**, archaic **clave**, and pp **cleaved**, **cleft**, **cloven**: ME *cleven*, earlier *cleoven*: OE *clēofan*, akin to OHG and OS *klioban*, MHG and G *klieben*, and ON *kliūfa* (*kljūfa*), to split, and OHG *kluft*, tongs (a *split* instrument), G *Kluft*, a chasm (gap), akin to the OFris *kleft* and the E n *cleft* (ME *clift*)—cf the pp *cleft* used as adj; akin also to Gr *gluphein* (s *gluph*-), to carve, q.v. at element glypto-. A butcher's *cleaver* (instrumental *-er*) derives from the v.

**cleaver**. See prec, at end.

**cleek**, in golf, derives from the mainly Sc *cleek*, to seize, ME *cleken* or *clechen*—akin to CLUTCH.

**clef**, in music, is adopted from OF-F, which takes it from ML *clāvis*, L *clāuis*, a key, which serves to CLOSE a door.

**cleft**, adj and n. See 2nd CLEAVE.

**clematis**. See the element *-clema*.

**clemency**, **clement**, **Clement**, **Clementina**, **Clementine**; **inclemency**, **inclement**.

*Clementina* is It, *Clementine* adapts F *Clémentine*, feminines deriving from L *Clemens*, PN from *clēmēns*, gentle of character, whether moral or physical, perh from *\*clināre* (s *clin*-), to bend (vi, vt), well attested in cpds. L *clēmēns* has o/s *clēment*-, whence both the E *clement* (cf the MF-F *clément*) and the L *clēmentia*, whence E *clemency*.

The L opposites *inclēmens*, *inclēmentia* result in E *inclement*, *inclemency*.

**clench**, v hence n; **clinch**, v (whence **clincher**) hence n.

Both *clench* and its thinned var *clinch* derive, via ME *clenchen*, from OE *-clencan*, to hold fast, akin to OHG *klenkēn* and MD *clinken*, D *klinken* —and to CLING.

**clerestory** varies *clearstory*, i.e. 'clear storey': it rises clear of the other roofs of the building.

**clergy**, whence **clergyman**; **cleric**, **clerical** (whence **clericalism**); **clerk** (n hence v), **clerkly**.

1. *Clerkly* = *clerk* + adj *-ly*. *Clerk* comes, via OF-F *clerc* and OE *clerc*, *cleric*, both from LL *clēricus*, a priest, from LGr *klērikos*, belonging to the clergy, from *klēros*, a piece of wood used in drawing lots, hence lot, allotment, hence, an allotment of priests, hence, in LGr, the clergy; s *klēr*-, akin to OIr *claar*, Ga *clār*, W *claur*, a plank; OC *\*klār*-; IE r, *\*klār*-.

2. E *cleric*, n, derives from the OE var *cleric* and the LL *clēricus* alike; the derivative LL adj *clēricālis* yields E *clerical*. *Clergy* derives from ME *clergie*, adopted from OF-F, where it = *clerc* + suffix *-ie*, the c being changed to g. (F *clergé*: OF *clergie*: LL *clēricātus* (gen *-ūs*), priestly office or life.)

**clerk**. See para 1 of prec.

**clever**, whence **cleverness** (suffix *-ness*): prob from ME *cliver*, dexterous, skilled, expert, prob either from OE *clibbor*, adhesive, or from ME *clīven*, OE *clīfan*, to adhere—cf the 1st CLEAVE. EW, however, suggests ME *cliver*, from OE *clifer*, a claw, with sem parallel in *handy*, dexterous, q.v. at HAND.

**clew** or **clue** (whence **clueless**), n hence v, derives, through ME *clewe* or *clue*, from OE *clēowe*, *cleowen*, *cliwen*, ball, skein, akin to syn OHG *kliuwa* (*chliuwa*, *chliwa*), and MD *cluwen*, also *cluwe*, D *kluwen*; akin also to Skt *glāuš*, ball. Cf, therefore, CLAW, CLEAT, CLOD. A ball of thread was, in Ancient Gr myth and fact, used for finding one's way out of a labyrinth: hence, a means of discovery, hence a discovery that assists in the solution of a crime.

**cliché**, adopted from F, was orig the pp of the echoic *clicher*, to stereotype. Therefore cf:

**click**, n and v; **clique**.

*Click* is echoic; with 'to *click*', cf the OF *cliquer*, to make a noise, akin to *claquer*, to clap (see CLACK). This OF *cliquer* has derivative MF-F *clique*, a resounding blow, later a noisy band of persons (cf *claque* at CLACK), whence a closely knit circle, adopted by E.

client; clientèle, whence AE clientele. See LOUD, para 4.

cliff, whence cliffy: OE *clif*, akin to OS and ON *klif*, and to ON *klifa*, to climb, to which a nasalized cognate occurs in CLIMB. Cf the 1st CLEAVE.

climacter, climacteric; climate; climax. See CLIME.

climb, v hence n, derives from OE *climban*, akin to OHG *chlimban* (*klimban*), MHG and G *klimmen*, and, without nasal (*n*), ON *klifa*; prob akin to the 1st CLEAVE, for climbing is a progress marked by continual *sticking* (holding tight).

clime, climate, climatic; climacter, climacteric; climax, n hence v;—acclimate, acclimation and acclimatize, acclimatization.— -cline, see Elements; clinic, clinical; acclinal, acclinate; decline (v, n), declination (and declension), declinatory, declinature; incline (v, n), inclinable, inclination, inclinatory, and disinclined, disinclination; recline, reclinate, reclination; syncline, synclinal;—enclitic;— L-derived subsidiaries acclivity (-itous), declivity (-itous), proclivity, all treated sep at CLIVUS.— Gmc-derived LEAN, v, treated sep.

1. *Clime* represents L *clima* (s *clim*-), gen *climatis*, o/s *climat*-, from Gr *klima* (s *klim*), gen *klimatos*, o/s *klimat*-, inclination, esp an earth-point's obliquity in relation to the sun or the imagined inclination or slope of the earth towards the North Pole, hence a region on the earth's surface, hence that region's weather. Gr *klima* derives from Gr *klinein*, s *klin*-, to slope: IE r, *\*klei-*: cognates in Gr, L, Skt, C, Sl.

2. L *climat*- yields OF-F *climat*, whence E *climate*, whence the adj *climatic* (*ic*).

3. Gr *klinein*, to slope, has also the derivative *klimax*, a ladder ('it *leans aslant*': L & S), hence, in LGr, a rhetorical climax; hence L, whence E, *climax*, with adj *climactic*, as if from Gr *\*klimaktikos*. *Klimax* has subsidiary *klimakter*, round or rung of a ladder, hence an important step or stage, whence L *climacter*, adopted by E; *klimakter* has adj *klimakterikos*, proceeding by steps or stages, whence L *climactericus*, whence E adj hence n *climacteric*, esp in its Med sense, whence adj *climacterical*.

4. *Klinein* has yet another relevant derivative: *kline*, a couch, a bed, with adj *klinikos*, whence L *clinicus*, whence E *clinic*, adj whence n, with subsidiary adj *clinical* (*-al*).

5. OF-F *climat* has derivative v *acclimater*, which = *a* for *à*, from L *ad*, to+euphonic *-c-*+*climat*+ inf suffix *-er*; hence 'to *acclimate*'; E *acclimation* is adopted from F. But E has coined 'to *acclimatize*'. whence *acclimatization*.

6. Gr *klinein* leads to L *clinare*, hardly found outside its compounds and their cognates: *acclinare*, *declinare*, *inclinare*, *reclinare*. Note that the Geol n *syncline*, whence the adj *synclinal*, represents the Gr *sunklinein*, to slope together (so as to meet): *sun*, with+*klinein*. Possibly, however, *syncline* is a b/f from *synclinal*, itself anl to *acclinal*, as in:

7. L *acclinare*, to lean towards (*ad*) or against,

has pp *acclinatus*, whence the adj *acclinate*, somewhat oddly meaning 'sloping upwards'; the Geol adj *acclinal*, (of a stratum) 'leaning upon another' = L *acclin*is+E *-al*.

8. L *declinare* (vt and vi), to turn oneself away (*de*), to remove oneself (hence to fall, to fail, to deteriorate), to avoid, yields OF-MF *decliner*, whence ME *declinen*, whence 'to *decline*'; 'a *decline*' adapts EF-F *déclin* (OF-MF *de*-), from *décliner* (OF-MF *decliner*). *Declinare* has two relevant derivatives:

ML *declinatorius*, tending to refuse, whence *declinatory*, perh via MF-F *déclinatoire*;

*declinatio*, o/s *declination*-, yields *declination*, perh via MF-F *declinacion*, whence EF-F *déclinaison*, whence E *declension*, a 'decline from the nominative'; *declinature* is anl with *curvature*, *signature*, etc.

9. 'An *incline*' (cf the OF-F *enclin*) derives from 'to *incline*', itself, through ME *inclinen* (var *enclinen*), from OF-MF *incliner* (var *encliner*): L *inclinare* (vt, vi), to lean, or cause to lean, inwards. *Inclinable* was adopted from MF-EF, as was *inclination*, from L *inclinationem* (o/s *inclination*-), acc of *inclinatio*, an inclining, hysical then emotional, in fact an inclination; *inclinator* and *inclinatory* seem to be E formations.

10. The adj *disinclined* and *disinclination* are likewise E formations: cf the prefix *dis*-.

11. L *reclinare*, to lean back, (LL) to rest, yields MF-EF *recliner* and E 'to' *recline*; the pp *reclinatus* yields the Bot *reclinate*, bent backwards; LL *reclinatio*, a leaning back, has o/s *reclination*-, whence E *reclination*.

12. LL has the adj *encliticus*, whence in the same grammatical sense, the E *enclitic*; but *encliticus* is a mere trln of Gr *enklitikos*, deriving from Gr *enklinein*, to incline: cf, in para 9, the influence of Gr *en*, in, upon the OF var forms.

clinch. See CLENCH.

cling: OE *clingan*, to adhere, akin to G *Klüngel* (s *klüng*-), a ball of thread, OHG *klungilin* (? dim of OHG *klunga*), and to OE *-clencan*, q.v. at CLENCH.

clinic, clinical. See CLIME, para 4.

clink (v, hence n), ME *clinken*, app derives from MD *clinken*: echoic: cf CLANK. The sl *clink*, a prison, prob derives from the clink of chains. MD *clinken*, D *klinken*, has derivative *klinchaerd*, a brick so hard that, struck, it rings: hence the E *clinker*, kind of brick, stony matter. *Clinker*, a fast mover (esp ship), derives from 'to *clink*' in its secondary sense, 'to move quickly or suddenly'. *Clinker-built* comes from *clinker*, var of *clincher* (from 'to *clinch*').

clinology; clinometer. Cf the element *clino*-.

Clio. See LOUD, para 5.

clip (1), to cut (off), hence n; hence also clipper (it cuts through air or waves) and the vn clipping. 'To *clip*', ME *clippen*, comes from ON *klippa*, *klyppa*, to cut, to shear: prob echoic.

clip (2), to embrace, hence n; hence also clippers, clip hooks.

This v *clip* derives, through ME *clippen*, *cluppen*,

from OE *clyppan*, akin to OFris *kleppa*, *klippa*, to embrace, OHG *chláftra*, MHG *kláfter*, width of the outstretched arms, whence G *Klafter*, a fathom, and Lith *glóbiu* (s *glob-*), I embrace, and L *globus*, globe, and *glēba*, clod: cf, therefore, GLEBE, GLOBE, also CLASP.

**clique.** See CLICK.

**clivus** (in An); **acclivity, acclivitous**—accclivous; **declivity, declivitous**—declivous; **proclivity, pro**clivitous—proclivous.

1. ML *clīvus*, L *clīuus*, a slope, hence a hill, has s *clīu-*, r *clī-*, as in *clīnāre* (s *clīn-*, r *clī-*), to which *clīuus* is intimately akin: f.a.e., CLIME, para 1.

2. ML *acclīvis*, L *acclīuis* (*ac*, for *ad*, to+*clīuis*, adj form of *clīuus*), var *acclīuus*, ML *-ivus*, yields the E adj *acclivous*; derivative *acclīvitās*, o/s *acclīuitāt-*, ML *acclīvitāt-*, yields *acclivity*, whence adj *acclivitous*.

3. ML *dēclīvis*, L *dēclīuis*, accounts for E *de*clivous; derivative ML *dēclīvitās*, L *dēclīuitās*, o/s *dēclīuitāt-*, ML *dēclīvitāt-*, accounts for *declivity*, whence *declivitous*: cf prefix *de-*, down from.

4. L *prōclīuis*, var *prōclīuus*, ML *-īvis*, *-īvus*, gives us *proclivous*, inclined *pro* or forward, esp obliquely forward; derivative *prōclīuitās*, ML *prōclīvitās*, o/s *prōclīvitāt-*, gives *proclivity*, whence *proclivitous*.

**cloaca, cloacal; clyster.**

*Cloacal* represents L *cloācālis*, adj of *cloāca*, a sewer, a privy, from *\*cloāre*, var of rare *cluere* (s *clu-*), to cleanse, akin to Gr *kluzein* (s *kluz-*, r *klu-*), to wash, to cleanse with water, with derivative *klustēr*, a cleansing injection of water, whence L *clyster*, whence, ? through MF-F *clystère*, the E *clyster*, with subsidiary, now obsol, sense 'enema'.

**cloak,** n hence v: ME *cloke*: OF-MF *cloke* for *cloque*, var of *cloche*, cloak, from OF-F *cloche*, a bell, because of a 'filled' cloak's bell-shape: from ML *clocca*, *cloca*, bell: f.a.e., CLOCK.

**cloche,** an airtight utensil in cooking, a tight, bell-shaped hat: adopted from F: f.a.e., prec. Cf:

**clock,** n hence v: ME *clok* or *clokke*: MD *clocke* (cf D *klok*, clock, bell): either from OF-MF *cloque*, which has var *cloche* (the F form), or from ML *clocca* (C7), var *cloca*, a bell, of C origin: the EIr *cloc*, bell, was 'brought to the Continent by the Irish monks' (B & W); cf Ga *clag*, W *cloch*, Cor *clōch*, *clōgh*, bell. Prob echoic.

**clod; clot** (n hence v). The former derives from ME *clodde*, a later form of ME *clot*, a clod, from OE *clot* or *clott*, the modern differentiation between 'clod of earth' and 'clot of blood' being a natural development. With OE *clot*(*t*), clod, cf G *Klotz*, a block, and MHG *kloz*, block, earlier a lump; cf also CLOUD.

**clog,** orig a block of wood, a short, thick log, whence a heavy shoe and also an impediment; hence the v. From ME *clogge*, block of wood, stump: o.o.o.: perh cf CLOD.

**cloister** (n hence v), **cloistral**—claustral—cf the element *claustro-*.

*Cloister* derives from ME *cloistere*, adapted from OF-EF *cloistre* (whence EF-F *cloître*), a blend of the OF-MF *clostre* with OF-EF *cloison*, an enclosure, whence, incidentally, *cloisonné*; OF-MF *clostre* derives from L *claustrum*, a means of closing, later an enclosure, from *claudere*, to close, pp *clausus*: f.a.e., CLOSE. *Claustrum* had LL adj *claustrālis*, acting as a barrier, whence *claustral*, which, 'blended' with *cloister*, explains *cloistral*.

**close** (adv from adj; n; v); **closet,** n hence v; **closure;**—**disclose, disclosure; enclose, enclosure.**

1. The adj *close*, ME *clos*, derives from OF *clos*, from L *clausus* (s *claus-*), pp of *claudere*, to close or shut, s *claud-*, r *clåu-*, as in *clauis*, a key, and *clåuus*, a nail: cf CLAVICLE and CLAUSE: cf also Gr *kleis*, a bolt or a key (? PGr *klåwis*), and *kleiein* (s *klei-*), to close; OIr *clo*, nail; and, with the IE int prefix *s-*, the G *schliessen*, to close, to lock, OHG *sliogan* (pron *slioyan*), MLG *slüten*, OFris *slūta*, to close; and several Sl cognates in *kl-*.

2. The n *close*, ME from OF-F *clos*, comes from L *clausum*, an enclosure, prop the neu of *clausus*, pp of *claudere*, to close. *Close*, conclusion, derives from 'to *close*'.

3. The v *close*, to shut, derives from ME *closen*: inf suffix *-en* attached to *clos-*, the pp s (cf para 1, 1st sentence) of OF-F *clore*, to close, from L *claudere*.

4. *Closet* is the MF-EF *closet*, a small enclosure, hence a small room, dim (cf *-et*) of the n *clos* (as in para 2).

5. *Closure*, adopted from OF-MF, comes from LL *clausūra*, itself consisting of *claus-* (pp s of *claudere*)+suffix *-ūra* (E *-ure*).

6. *Disclosure*, imitating *closure*, derives from 'to *disclose*', ME *disclosen*, earlier *desclosen*, from the pres-ind s of OF-MF *desclore*, from L *disclaudere* (cf prefix *dis-*), to open that which has been closed.

7. *Enclosure* comes *l*from OF-MF, from the *enclos-* s of OF-F *enclore*, to shut in, from VL *\*includere*, from L *incūdere*; the F s *enclos-* has prompted 'to *enclose*', strictly *en-*, in+'to *close*': cf INCLUDE.

**clot.** See CLOD.

**cloth,** pl **cloths,** kinds of cloth, and **clothes,** garments; **clothe.**

'To *clothe*', ME *clothen*, earlier *clathen*, derives from OE *cláthian*, *clǽthan*, itself from OE *cláth*, cloth in general, a garment in particular, whence ME *clath*, cloth, garment, later *cloth*, retained by E: akin to OFris *kláth*, *klēth*, ON *klǽethi*, MHG *kleit* (G *Kleid*), dress, garment: f.a.e., perh cf OE *clīth*, plaster. (Walshe.)

**clothes.** See prec.

**cloud,** n hence v: ME *cloud*, earlier *clud*, rock, hill(ock), cloud: OE *clūd*, rock, hill(ock): basic idea, mass—cf CLOD and its derivative *clot*. Hence *cloudless* (suffix *-less*) and *cloudy* (*-y*, adj). Cf:

**clout.** 'To *clout*', ME *clouten*, earlier *clutien*, derives from OE *clūt*, a patch, a small cloth or piece of metal, akin to ON *klūtr*, kerchief, Fris *klūt*, a lump, and E *clot*, q.v. at CLOD. The 'to strike' sense of *clout* derives from the 'patch clumsily' sense; 'to *clout*' orig meant 'to cover or bandage or patch with a (piece of) cloth'.

**clove**, as used in cooking: ME *clow*: MF-F *'clou de girofle'*, lit 'nail of clove', hence 'clove': L *clāuus* (ML *clāvus*), nail: f.a.e., CLOSE.

**clove**, pt. See 1st and 2nd CLEAVE.

**cloven**, pp. See 2nd CLEAVE.

**clover** derives, through ME *clover*, earlier *claver*, from OE *clāfre* or *clǣfre*, akin to MLG *klever* and MD *claver*, *-ere*, D *klaver*: app the r *cla-*+an obscure element *-fre* (MD *-vere*, MLG *-ver*), because the G *Klee*, clover, MLG *klē*, has OHG form *chlēo*, s *chlē-*. (Walshe.)

**clown**, n hence v. Orig (C16) a farm worker, hence a boor, hence—boors seeming funny to townsmen—a funny fellow, a buffoon, a jester, *clown* is o.o.o.: cf, however, the NFris *klönne*, clown, Icelandic *klunni*, clumsy boor, and D *kloen*, hoyden, from *kluwen*, a clew: basic idea, 'lump—lumpish'.

**cloy** (whence the pa **cloying**) shortens the obs *accloy*, orig to drive-in a nail, hence to stop up, choke up, esp to excess, hence to glut or satiate: from OF-MF *encloer* (cf the F derivative *enclouer*: *en*+*clou*+*-er*), itself from ML *inclāuāre*: *in*+*clāu*us, a nail+inf *-āre*. Cf 1st CLOVE.

**club** (n hence v), heavy weapon of wood, usu with bulbous or *knobbed* striking end, hence a knob, hence a bunch, hence a group, orig forcibly associated: ME *clubbe*: ON *klubba*, var *klumba*: akin to CLUMP.

**cluck**, v hence n: OE *cloccian*, akin to MHG *klucken* or *glucken*, LG *klukken*, G *glucken*, MD *clocken*, D *klokken*: echoic.

**clue**. See CLEW.

**clump**, an unshaped mass, a lump, hence a cluster, hence also a heavy blow (cf CLOUT); whence the v.

*Clump* app comes from MLG *klumpe*, var *klompe*, akin to OE *clympre*, (heavy) piece of metal, and ON *clumba*, a club, and MLG *klumpe*, a clog, G *Klumpen*, a lump, a clump, MD *clompe* or *clomp*, D *klomp*, also G *Klampe*, a clamp: OGmc s, **klamp*-, var **klump*-; IE s, **glemb*-, var **glomb*-; IE r, **gleb*-, var **glob*-, as in L *glēba*, a sod (see GLEBE), and *globus* (see GLOBE).

**clumsy**, whence **clumsiness** (suffix *-ness*), derives from ME *clumsed* (pa from pp), benumbed, from *clumsen*, to be or become numb: intimately akin to Sw dial *clumsig*, numb with cold, (hence) clumsy; also akin to CLAM.

**cluster**, n hence v: OE *cluster*, akin to OE *clot(t)*, q.v. at CLOD.

**clutch** (cletch, clitch).

The n *clutch*, a grasp or a grasping, a claw (usu pl *clutches*), derives from 'to *clutch*', to grasp, seize, hold tightly, ME *cluchen*, var *clicchen* (whence the dial *clitch*), from OE *clyccean*, akin to *cling*. But a *clutch* of eggs, or brood of chicks, varies *cletch*, itself a dial derivative from the mainly Sc *cleck*, to hatch, from ON *klekja*, cf Nor *'klekke* (ut)'.

**clutter**, n and v: var of *clotter* (n from v): a *-ter* freq of 'to *clot*': cf *pat*, *patter*, *spat*, *spatter*: f.a.e., CLOD.

**clyster**. See CLOACA, s.f.

**coach**, n hence v, derives from EF-F *coche*, from G *Kutsche*, either from Hung *kocsi*, 'of *Kocs*', i.e. '(carriage) of Kocs', the Hung town where, supposedly, coaches were first manufactured, or from Cz *cotchi*, '(carriage) of *Kosice*' in Czechoslovakia, where, supposedly, coaches were first manufactured (B & W). Perhaps, however, both EF-F *coche* and G *Kutsche* derive from ML *cocha*, varr *coccha*, *cocca*, *cogga*, *cogo*, a barge or passenger boat or merchant ship, according to the region. Du Fresne's Du Cange defines *cogo* as 'a kind of ship, which the English call *cogs*, the French *coquets*' (rare dim form). The ME *cogge* is usu said to come, perhaps via MLG *kogge* or MD *kogghe*, from ON *kuggi*, var *kuggr*. But the OF *coque* or *cogue* or predominantly *coche* might rather (DAF) come from L *cōdica* (*nāuis*), a ship, esp a barge, made from *cōdex*, better *caudex*, a tree-trunk. The transition from sea- to land-conveyance is far from impossible: cf the AE use of 'to *ship*'.

**coadjutator** needlessly lengthens *coadjutor*: ML *coadjūtor*, LL *coadiūtor*, a fellow-helper: *co-*, together+*adiūtor*, helper (cf ADJUTANT).

**coagulate, coagulation.**

The latter comes, perh via MF-F, from L *coagulātiōn-*, o/s of *coagulātiō*, itself formed upon *coagulāt-*, the s of *coagulātus*, pp of *coagulāre*, prob from *coagulum*, something that causes coagulation, from *coac*tus, pp of *cogere*, to drive (hence, force) together, to coagulate: *co-*, together+*agere*, to drive: cf COGENT (f.a.e., ACT).

**coal**, n hence v: ME *cole*, earlier *col*: OE *col*, akin to OHG *kol*, *kolo*, charcoal, MHG *kol*, G *Kohle*, coal, MD *cole*, charcoal, coal, OFris (and MLG) *kole* and ON *kol*, (wood-)charcoal, the sense also in OE, the mineral sense hardly antedating C13: cf OIr *gual*, charcoal, prob from **goulo*; perh akin to the *jual-* of Skt *jualati* (*jvalati*), it burns (Holthausen).

2. ME *col* has derivative *colier*, whence E *collier*, whence—influenced by the obs *coalery—colliery* (*-y*, n).

3. *Collie*, a large, black-and-white sheepdog, prob derives from *coaly*, coal-black; app influenced by *collier*.

**coaming**, a raised frame, whether at floor (orig, deck) or at ceiling level, to prevent water from entering: o.o.o.: but cf Nor luke*karm*, a coaming; Nor *karm*, a frame, has perh been blended with E 'incoming (water)', the sense being 'a (protective) framing'.

**coarse**, whence, by v suffix *-en*, 'to **coarsen**': C15, *cors*, *corse*; C16-17, usu *course*: app from the n *course*, the general run of things (as in 'of *course*'), hence common (cf *common* in its subsidiary sense 'vulgar, coarse').

**coast** (n and v), **coastal**; **costal**, **intercostal**; **accost**; **costard**—**costermonger**; **cutlet**.

'To *coast*' derives both from ME *costen*, earlier *costien*, from MF *coster*, *costier*, and from *costeien*, from OF-MF *costoier* (later *côtoyer*), from OF-MF *coste* (F *côte*), a coast, whence ME *cost*, whence E *coast* (n). OF-MF *coste* derives from L *costa*, a rib, hence side (of the body), hence coast, prob akin to OSl *kostĭ*, a bone, and perh also L *os*, bone, Skt *ásthi*; a *k*- prefix (as in *caper*, goat) being presumed and possible (B & W).

2. The E *coastal* (*coast*, n+adj -*al*) was perh suggested by L *costālis*, whence the Med adj *costal* and its cpd *intercostal* (*inter*-, between).

3. *Accost* (v hence n), lit to come to (*ad*) the *costa* or side of a person or a land, comes from OF-F *accoster*, from It, from LL, *accostare*.

4. *Costard*, an apple with prominent ribs or angles, is app 'a *ribbed* apple', from OF-MF *coste*, rib+suffix -*ard*, connoting largeness. The obs *costardmonger*, apple-seller (cf MONGER), became eased to *costermonger*.

5. *Cutlet* is a f/e adaptation of syn MF-F *côtelette*, lit a small rib, dim of *côte*, a rib, OF *coste* (see para 1).

**coat**, n hence v (whence vn **coating**), ME *cote*, derives from OF-MF *cote*, OF-F var *cotte*, a tunic, of Gmc origin: cf OHG *chozza*, *kozzo*, a coarse cloak, MHG *kotze*, G *Kotze*, a coat of rough material: prob from Frankish *\*kotta*, whence the ML *cotta* and the OF-F *cotte*. (Kluge.) Cf COTILLON.

**coax**, whence the pa and vn **coaxing**, seems to derive from the obs *cokes*, var *cox*, a fool, esp a dupe, itself o.o.o., but perh, as EW has proposed, from F *cocasse*, ridiculous (recorded in E in 1546): cf *hoax* from *hocus*. *Cocasse* is a var of OF-EF *coquard*, foolish, vain, from *coq* (cf COCK).

**cob**, a lump or heavy piece, hence nut, stone of fruit, cob of corn, a short, stocky horse, etc., derives from ME *cob*, earlier *cobbe*, app of Scan and LG origin, with basic idea 'something plump, esp if round': cf D *kobbe*, var *kob*, Fris *kobbe*, var *kub*, a seagull, ON (and Ice) *kobbi*, a seal, and, in cpds, -*kubbi*, a block or stump: akin also, therefore, to CUB.

**cobalt; kobold; cove** (Geog).

1. *Cobalt*, a G word, derives—because miners used to find the metal dangerous to work, the ore being arsenical—from G *Kobold*, goblin, gnome, likewise adopted by E, often with spelling *cobold*: and *Kobold*, MHG *kobolt*, familiar spirit, prob derives from OHG *\*kobwalto*, a household spirit (lit, power, ruler): cf, sem, the OE *cofgodu*, household gods, OE *cofa*, a room+*godu*, gods, and, etym, the G *Koben*, MHG *kobe*, a hovel+*walten*, to rule or control, E WIELD. (Walshe.)

2. OE *cofa*, a room, akin to ON *kofi*, cell, hut, yields *cove*, (Sc) a rock-hollow, (E) a small, esp if sheltered, inlet (e.g., bay); the Arch sense owes something to both of the others.

**cobber** (Aus), sl now coll for 'comrade, mate, chum': Yiddish *chaber* (pron *khah'ber*), comrade.

**cobble** (1), a cobblestone (also a piece of waste metal), hence to pave with cobblestones: dim of COB, a lump.

**cobble** (2), to make, or to mend, roughly; to patch or patch up: o.o.o.; prob, however, from ME *\*cobelen*, a freq of *cob*, to strike or thump,

itself akin to COB. Agent *cobbler* (ME *cobelere*), a boot-and-shoe mender, hence a clumsy worker.

**cobbler.** See prec, s.f.

**cobold.** See COBALT.

**cobra**: elliptical for Port *cobra de capello*, hooded serpent, *cobra* deriving from VL *\*colobra*, from L *colubra*, itself o.o.o. but prob Eg.

**cobweb**, lit spider-web: ME *coppeweb*: obs *cop*, a spider, ME *coppe*, OE -*coppe*+WEB.

**cocaine** is a Chem -*ine* derivative of *coca*, a SAm shrub with medicinal leaves. A Sp word (earlier, *cuca*), adopted from Quechua or Aymara (var *cuca*).

**coccal** is the adj of **coccus**, a Bact cell (c/f element -*coccic*, *cocco*-): Gr *kokkos*, a grain, a seed; akin to *kikkos*, the sheath containing the seeds of a pomegranate: exotics. Cf COCO and COCOON.

**coccyx.** Akin to CUCKOO.

**cochineal** adapts EF-F *cochenille*, itself from Sp *cochinilla*, cochineal, orig a wood louse: the dried bodies of this parasite, in the specific form of the cochineal insect, yield a valuable dye. *Cochinilla* is the dim of Sp *cochina*, a sow, m *cochino*, akin to F *cochon*: 'prob formed from the cries uttered by those who call pigs to the trough' (B & W), perh akin to LL *cuciōnes*, better *cutiōnes*, wood lice, sing *cutiō*, from *cutis*, skin ('thick-skinned creature': E & M).

**cochlea** (whence **cochlear**: cf adj suffix -*ar*): L for 'snail' or 'snail's shell': Gr *kokhlias*, snail, from *kokhlos*, shellfish having a spiral covering, akin to *konkhē* (χόγχη), mussel: f.a.e., CONCH.

**cock** (bird; faucet; penis), hence prob the v 'to cock'; **cocker** (spaniel); coll adj **cocky; cockchafer, cock-eyed, cockhorse, cockpit, cockspur, cocksure, cocktail; cockscomb, coxcomb;—coquet, coquetry.**

1. Certain derivatives of *cock*, the male of the common domestic fowl, include *cocker* (agential -*er*), lit a fighter; and *cocky*, as confident as a cock; and the foll—and many other—cpds:

*cockchafer: cock*, either used fig in ref to size, or euphem for *cack*, dung+*chafer* (OE *ceafor*, akin to OHG *chevar*, MHG *kever*, G *Käfer*, prob 'the gnawer', for cf MHG *kiven*, to gnaw: Walshe);

*cockpit*, a *pit* for cockfights, hence a district, or a country, noted for much past fighting;

*cockscomb: a cock's comb*, occ corrupted to *coxcomb*, a badge that, resembling a cock's comb, was worn by jesters in their caps, hence the cap, hence the wearer, hence a fool or a vain, silly fellow, a fop, with derivative *coxcombry* (suffix-*ry*);

*cockspur: a cock's spur*, or plants with features resembling one;

*cocksure*: as confident as a cock;

*cocktail*, any creature with tail resembling a cock's, hence (?) a lively, cheerful, basically spirituous drink.

2. Prob from 'a *cock*' derives 'to *cock*', ME *cocken*, (obs) to fight, to strut, prob from the brisk, confident movements of a cock's head; prob from a cock's upright posture when it is crowing, come the senses (vi) to turn up, stick up, and (vt) to set

upright, tip upwards, e.g. a firearm's hammer, a hat's brim.

3. Derivatives of 'to *cock*' include:

*cock-eyed*, squinting, hence crooked, from *cock-eye*, a squinting eye: *cock*, to tip up+EYE;

*cockhorse:* anything, esp a rocking *horse*, that a child rides astride, i.e. with legs *cocked* or turned up.

4. The *cock* of a gun and *cock*, a faucet, derive quite naturally from a fancied resemblance to the bird or its head or its comb.

5. The sense-development of the n seems to be: male bird; faucet or tap, and then, very soon, a cocking mechanism; finally, prob from the 'faucet' sense, the true C18–20 SE word for·'penis'.

6. The n *cock* derives from OE *cocc* (predominant form), akin to the rare ON *kokr*, to OSl *kokotŭ*, to OF-F *coq*, to LL *coccus*, app deriving from L *coco coco*, the cock's cry, LL var *cucurru*—cf the syn Skt *kukkuṭa*.

7. OF-F *coq* has the derivative late MF-F adj *coquet*, as vain and swaggering as a cock, f *coquette*, both soon nn; *coquet* has derivative EF-F *coqueter*, whence 'to *coquet*'; *coqueter* has derivative EF-F *coquetterie*, whence E *coquetry*. Cf COCKADE.

(hay)**cock**, n hence v: prob from ON *kökkr*, lump, whence also Nor *kok* (cf Da *kok*), heap—cf Sw *koka*, clod.

**cockade**: EF-F *cocarde*, perh elliptical for *chose cocarde*, vain thing, from OF-EF *cocard, coquard*, vain, from OF-F *coq*, cock: cf para 7 of 1st COCK.

**cockatoo**: Aus sl **cocky**, small farmer, from *cockatoo* (*squatter* or *farmer*). The bird *cockatoo* derives perh from D *kaketoe*, but prob from Port *cacatua*, itself from Mal *kakatūwa*, prob echoic, but perh a cpd of *kaka*', brother, sister+*tuwa*, old, from the scoldings to be expected from elder brothers and sisters.

**cockatrice**, fabulous serpent: MF *cocatris*, influenced by OF-F *coq* (the bird *cock*) but deriving either from LL \**calcatrix*, female treader, from *calcāre*, to tread, from *calx*, heel (f.a.e., CALCAREOUS), or, far more prob, by f/e alteration from MF *cocadrile*, var of OF-EF *cocodril(l)e*, metathesis of L *crocodīlus*.

**cockboat**, a small boat: ME *cokbote, cogbote*, f/e for ME *cogge*, q.v. in latter half of COACH.

**cockchafer**. See 1st COCK, para 1.

**cocker** (spaniel). See 1st COCK, para 1.

**cock(-)eyed**. See 1st COCK, para 3.

**cockhorse**. See 1st COCK, para 3.

**cockle** (1), darnel, corn cockle, etc.: OE *coccel*.

**cockle** (2), a bivalvular mollusc: ME *cockille*: MF *cokille*, later *coquille*, a shell: L *conchylium*: Gr *konkhulion*, dim of *konkhulē*, mdfn of *konkhē*, a (large) shell: f.a.e., CONCH. In *warm the cockles of one's heart*, cockle is app an anglicizing of COCHLEA, itself akin to CONCH.

**Cockney**: ME *coknay*, earlier *cokenay* (or -*ey*): milksop (Chaucer), then townsman, then (c 1600) Londoner: perh by aphesis from some MF dial form corresp to EF-F *acoquiné*, pampered, lit rascally, from *a-*, L *ad*, to+*coquin*, beggar, rogue+

inf -*er*, OF-F *coquin* being prob a pej derivative (cf *coquard*, vain, foolish, and *coquet*) of *coq*, q.v. at 1st COCK, though perh from MLG *kak*, a pillory: thus EW and, after him, Webster and, in part, B & W. The OED, however, derives ME *cokeney, -ay*, from *coken*, of cocks+*ey, ay*, an egg, lit a cock's egg: 'cocks' eggs', cf G *Hahneneier*, are, in E folklore, small or misshapen eggs: the phrase is applied to milksops, very soon after being applied to eggs (easily broken, soft-shelled). The former etymology would seem to be the more convincing, even though the latter is the better attested.

**cockpit**. See 1st COCK, para 1.

**cockroach** is a f/e adaptation of Sp *cucaracha*, an aug derivative of *cuco*, an insect, perh from L *cucus*, a daw.

**cockspur**. See 1st COCK, para 1.

**cocksure**. See 1st COCK, para 1.

**cocktail**. See 1st COCK, para 1.

**cocky**, adj. See 1st COCK, para 1.

**cocky**, n. See COCKATOO.

**coco**, whence **coconut** (wrongly **cocoanut**): Port and Sp *coco*: L *coccum, coccus*, kernel, fruitstone: Gr *kokkos*, a grain, a seed. Cf COCCAL and COCOON.

**cocoa**, a Sp word influenced by prec, derives from Sp *cacao*, itself from Nahuatl or Aztec *cacahuatl*, the seed of the cacao tree.

**coconut**. See COCO.

**cocoon**: EF-F *cocon*: Prov *coucoun*, cocoon, (earlier) egg-shell, from *coco*, a shell, from L *coccum*, excrescence on a plant, kernel: f.a.e., COCO.

**cod** (fish) is o.o.o.: ? suggested by *cod*, the enclosed part of a fishing net, itself identical with *cod*, a small bag, a pouch, hence a pod or husk (as in *peasecod*), from OE *codd*, a small bag, akin to ON *koddi*, pillow, and MD *codde*, testicle (whence the E dial and obsol sl *cods*, testicles), also to OE *cēod, cēoda*, OHG *kiot*, LG *küdel*, a sack. The sl *cod*, fellow, fool, and 'to *cod*' or hoax, prob belong here.

**coda** (Mus), adopted from It, comes from L *cōda*, a var of *cauda*, a tail, whence the erudite E (and F) adj *caudal*, as also the E Sci adj *caudate*.

2. L *cauda, cōda*, has a far more notable derivative, the E *coward*, thus: *coward* (whence *cowardly*: -*ly*, adj): OF-F *couard*, a coward, orig cowardly, lit 'with tail between legs', from OF *coe*, tail+pej suffix -*ard*: *coe* deriving from L *cōda*. (The L word, usu said to be o.o.o., is prob (Webster) akin to Lith *kuodas*, a tuft.) *Cowardice*, ME *cowardise*, derives from OF-F *couardise*, from *couard*.

**coddle**, to cook, esp boil, slowly, hence to pamper, app derives either from CAUDLE or from its ONF source.

**code**, n hence v (whence **decode** and **encode**); **codify**; **codex**—**codicil**, **codicillary**.

1. The last comes from L *cōdicillāris* (-*ārius*), of a *codicil*, itself from L *cōdicillus*, tablet, hence memorandum, hence a legal codicil, dim of L *cōdex*, a book in manuscript, hence, in E, an ancient manuscript, but, in L, a writing tablet,

consisting of a wax-smeared board for writing (whence 'book'), earliest a tree-trunk or a shrub-stem, with var *caudex* (cf the *cŏda-cauda* var), perh (E & M) akin to L *cŏda*, tail; only very improb akin to L *cŭdere*, beat, and E HEW.

2. L *cŏdex* becomes MF-F *code*, adopted by E; the F *code* has derivative *codifier*, whence app 'to *codify*', whence, or from F, *codification*.

**codger.** See CADGE.

**codicil; codify.** See CODE, paras 1 and 2 resp.

**codlin** or **codling**, a kind of apple, whence **codlin(g) moth**, was orig a hard-cored cooking apple: F *cœur-de-lion*, lion's heart, (hence) hard *core*.

**coeliac.** See the element *-coele*.

**coerce, coercion, coercive.** See ARK, para 3.

**coeval.** See AGE, para 2.

**coffee**, whence **coffee-bean, -house**, etc.; **café, cafeteria, caffein(e)**.

E *coffee*, like the EF-F *café*, coffee, hence a place where they sell it, comes from It *caffè*: Tu *qahveh* (*kahvé*): Ar *qahwah*, wine, but also coffee. F *café* has derivative *caféine* (Chem *-ine*), anglicized to *caffeine* (or *-in*). Tu *kahvé*, *cahvé*, also becomes Sp *café*, whence the AmSp *cafeteria*, coffee shop, whence AE, whence E, *cafeteria*, a self-service café.

**coffer; coffin.**

The Gr *kophinos* (s *kophin-*), a basket, perh of Medit stock (? cf Eg *kareḥtà* and *qar*, basket), becomes LL *cophinus*, whence, on the one hand, MF-F *cofin*, whence ME *coffin*, basket, container, whence E *coffin* in its modern sense, and, on the other hand, the M F *cofre*, MF-F *coffre*, whence ME *coffre*, *cofer*, which, linked, yield E *coffer*.

**cog**, an Arch and miners' securing device, prob derives from *cock*, to secure (e.g., make ready a fire-arm), from the 1st COCK, q.v. at para 2.

**cogency** derives, by suffix *-cy*, from *cogent*, itself from *cogent-*, o/s of *cogens*, presp of L *cogere*, to force, (lit) drive (*agere*) together (*co-*): cf COAGULATE and, f.a.e., ACT.

**cogitate, cogitation, cogitative, cogitator; excogitate, excogitation, excogitative, excogitator.**

1. *Agere* (s *ag-*), to drive (see ACT), has the int-freq derivative *agitāre* (see AGITATE), which, in turn, has derivative *co-agitāre*, whence L *cōgitāre*, to set astir in one's mind, to think actively about. The pp *cōgitātus* yields 'to *cogitate*'; its derivative *cōgitātiō*, o/s *cōgitātiōn-*, E *cogitation*, perh via F; LL *cōgitātiuus*, ML *-ivus*, whence, perh via F, *cogitative*; *cōgitātor*, adopted by E.

2. *Cōgitāre* has subsidiary *excōgitāre*, to thoroughly think out, to ponder deeply: the pp *excōgitātus* yields 'to *excogitate*'; the derivative *excōgitātiō* (o/s *-ātiōn-*), *excogitation*; *excogitative* and *excogitator* are E formations.

**cognac** is adopted from F: made at *Cognac* in the department of Charente.

**cognate, cognation.** See NATIVE, para 9.

**cognition, cognitive, cognizable, cognizance, cognizant, cognize; connoisseur;—recognition, recognitive, recognizable, recognizance, recognizant, recognize; reconnaissance.**

1. The effective base (f.a.e.: CAN) rests upon L *cognōscere*, to know, to learn about, a cpd of *co-*, together+*gnōscere*, early form of *nōscere*, to know (cf NOTION). The pp *cognitus*, preserved in the neu-become-n *cognitum*, an object of knowledge, has derivative *cognitiō*, o/s *cognitiōn-*, whence E *cognition*; on the pp s *cognit-*, *cognitive* (*-ive*) arises. *Cognize*, whence *cognizable*, is prob a b/f from *cognizance*, ME *conisaunce*, earlier *conoissance*, adopted from OF-MF, itself from OF-MF *conoistre*, from L *cognōscere*; the adj *cognizant* prob represents OF-MF *conoissant*, presp of *conoistre*.

2. *Connoisseur* is adopted from F (now *connaisseur*): OF-MF *conoisseor*, from *conoistre*.

3. *Recognize* (whence *recognizable*), to *cognize* or know again (*re-*), owes its sense to L *recognōscere*, whence OF-MF *reconoistre*, with presp *reconoissant*, whence, in part, the E *recognizant* and, wholly, the OF-MF *reconoissance*, *reconissance*, whence ME *reconissaunce*, whence E *recognizance*; the OF *reconoissance* becomes F *reconnaissance*, adopted by military E.

4. L *recognōscere* has pp *recognitus*, s *recognit-*, whence the n *recognitiō*, o/s *recognitiōn-*, whence, perh via F, the E *recognition*; for *recognitive*, cf *cognitive*.

**cognomen.** See NAME, para 4.

**cohabit, cohabitation.** See HABIT, para 10.

**cohere, coherence, coherent, cohesion.**

L *cohaerēre* (s *cohaer-*), to stick (*haerēre*) together (*co-*), yields 'to *cohere*'; its presp *cohaerens*, o/s *cohaerent-*, yields—perh via EF-F *cohérent*—the adj *coherent*, and the derivative *cohaerentia*—perh via EF-F *cohérence*—*coherence*. The pp *cohaesus* (s *cohaes-*) has subsidiary *\*cohaesiō*, o/s *\*cohaesiōn-* (cf the real *adhaesiō*, *adhaesiōn-*), F *cohésion*, E *cohesion*; cf *cohesive* (? after *adhesive*). Cf ADHERE and INHERE and, f.a.e., HESITATE.

**cohibit, cohibition.** See HABIT, para 11.

**cohort:** MF-F *cohorte*: L *cohort-* (acc *cohortem*), o/s of *cohors*, a farm enclosure, hence division of an army camp, hence the appropriate number of soldiers, hence a subdivision of the Legion: a contraction of *\*cohortus*, lit an enclosure (*hortus*, later a garden) together (*co-*): f.a.e., HORTiculture.

**coif**, n, hence v; **coiffeur, coiffure.**

Both the 2nd and the 3rd, adopted from F, derive from MF-F *coiffer*, to dress (someone's) hair, itself from OF-MF *coife* or *coiffe*, whence, via ME *coyfe*, the E *coif*, n, the v deriving from *coiffer*: and OF-F *coif(f)e* comes from LL *cofia*, var *cofea*, earlier *cuphia*, head-dress, cap, by psilosis from Gr *skuphion* (s *skuph-*), skull, mdfn of *skuphos*, a cup: shape-resemblance.

**coign.** See COIN.

**coil.** See LEGEND, para 6.

**coin**, n and v (whence **coiner, coining**), **coinage; coign; quoin;—cuneiform.**

'To *coin*' derives from OF-MF *coignier*, whence *coignaige* (*-aige*=F *-age*, E *-age*), whence E *coinage*: and OF-MF *coignier* (later *cogner*) derives from OF-EF *coing*, an angle or a corner—whence

E *coign*— a wedge—a metal stamp, later a piece of metal certified by the assay-master, who signified his approval by stamping it; in tin-mining, he weighed the tin and then 'chiselled a small piece from the corner (coign) of each block of tin and assayed it for quality before stamping it' (W. G. Hoskins, *Devon*, 1954): OF-EF *coing* became EF-F *coin*, adopted by E, with var *quoin*, specialized in Arch as 'a solid exterior angle'. Now, OF-EF *coing* derives from L *cuneus*, wedge, whence a wedge-shaped or triangular coin, with s *cun-*, r perh *\*cu-*, cf L *culex*, a gnat, and Skt *śúlas*, a sharp tool. From *cuneus*: *cuneiform*, wedge-shaped.

**coincidence, coincident, coincidental.** See CADENCE, para 7.

**coit; coition:** L *coitum*, supine of *coīre*, to go together; derivative L *coitiō*, o/s *coitiōn-*: f.a.e., ISSUE.

**coke:** ? ME *coke*, for *colke*, core, perh influenced by ME *cole*, coal: the 'core', because it is the residue of coal after it has been 'destructively distilled': Webster, who adduces Sw *kalk*, pith, and Gr *gelgis* (s *gelg-*), clove of garlic. The EDD offers E dial *colk(e)* or *coke*, core or pith, and adduces OFris *kolk*, a hole (id in MLG): cf E dial *kelk*, any *hollow*-stalked plant.

**col; collar, collarbone.**
1. *Col*, a pass that, in a mountain chain, separates two adjacent peaks, is adopted from OF-F: L *collum*, neck, s *col-*: cf OFris, Go, OHG, ON *hals*, and OE *heals*: IE r, perh *\*kol-*, to turn.
2. L *collum* has adj *collāris*, whence the n *collāre* (prob elliptical for *collāre uinculum*, neck-bond), whence OF-MF *colier*, *coler*, whence ME *coler*, *coller*, whence E *collar*, with cpd *collarbone* (cf BONE); 'to *collar*' derives from the n.

**colander**, often phon spelt **cullender**, app comes either from It *colino*, strainer, sieve, from It *colare*, to strain or filter, from syn L *cōlāre*, itself from L *cōlum*, a filter, a sieve (cf L *cōlātōrium*, ML *cōlātor*, whence Sp *colador*, a sieve), or, less prob, from L (lanx) *cōlanda*, (a dish) to be strained or sieved, hence for straining.

**cold,** adj, hence n and v (OE *cealdian*) and, by suffix *-ness*, **coldness.**
The adj *cold*, ME *cold*, earlier *cald*, derives from OE *cald*, var *ceald*, akin to OFris and OS *kald*, OHG-G *kalt*, Go *kalds*, ON *kaldr*; more remotely to L *gelidus*, very cold, and *gelū*, frost, severe cold; IE r, *\*gal-*, with var *\*gel-*. Cf CHILL and COOL and GELID, JELLY, GLACIER.

**cole,** the plants rape and kale; **coleslaw; colewort** (cf WORT); **kale.**
1. *Cole*, ME *col*, derives from OE *cāl*, *cāwel*, *cawl*, intimately akin to ON *kāl*: L *caulis* (s *caul-*), a stalk, akin to Gr *kaulos* (s *kaul-*). The AE *coleslaw*, cabbage salad, represents D *kool sla*, *kool* being MD *cole*, identical with the E word.
2. *Kale* is the N form: Sc *kale* or *cale* or *kail*.

**colic; colon** (in An).
*Colic* derives from MF-F *colique*: L *colica*, n from the f of the adj *colicus*, sick with colic, from

Gr *kolikos*, adj of *kolon*, (part of) the large intestine, whence, of course, L *colon*, the colon, adopted by E. The Gr *kolon* has cognates in Arm and Lith. E *colic* has dial and coll redup *collywobbles*, stomach-ache.

**collaborate, collaboration, collaborator.** See LABOR, s.f.

**collapse.** See LABOR, para 2.

**collar; collarbone.** See COL, para 2.

**collate, collation.** See the 1st TOLL, para 6. Note that the E *collation* is lit a bringing together, hence a comparison of, e.g., manuscripts, hence a meal, orig a 'light evening meal in monastery, after the reading aloud of *collations*, or Lives of the Fathers' (EW).

**collateral.** See LATERAL, para 2.

**collation,** meal. See COLLATE.

**colleague.** See LEGAL, para 7.

**collect, collection, collective, collector.** See LEGEND, para 6.

**colleen:** Ir *cailín*, dim of *caile* (id in Ga), girl, EIr *cale*. Cf the suffix *-een*.

**college, collegiate.** See LEGAL, para 7.

**collide; collision.** See LESION, para 3.

**collie.** See COAL, para 3.

**collier, colliery.** See COAL, para 2.

**collimate, collimation, collimator.** See LINE, para 5.

**collineate, collineation.** See LINE, para 5.

**collision.** See LESION, para 3.

**collocate, collocation, collocative.** See *locate* at LOCAL.

**collocution, collocutor.** See LOQUACIOUS, para 3.

**collodion; colloid,** adj hence n, with adj **colloidal.** Both come from Gr *kollōdēs*, like glue: *kolla*, glue+*-ōdēs*, -like, from *eidos*, form: cf the suffixes *-ion* and *-oid*.

**colloquial, colloquy.** See LOQUACIOUS, para 3.

**collude, collusion, collusive.** See LUDICROUS, para 4.

**colluvial, colluvies.** See LAVA, para 9.

**collywobbles.** See COLIC, s.f.

**Cologne.** See *colony* at COLONIAL.

**colon** (1), large intestine. See COLIC.

**colon** (2), in punctuation; whence **semicolon.** This 2nd *colon* has come, through L *colon*, from Gr *kōlon*, limb, member, hence member (clause) of a sentence.

**colonel,** whence **colonelcy,** comes, like earlier *coronel*, straight from EF: It *colonnello*, from *colonna*, a column (cf COLUMN) of soldiers.

**colonial,** adj hence n; **colonist; colonize**— **colonization; colony.**
*Colonial* is adopted from F: its source the MF-F *colonie* derives, like E *colony* (perh with F intervention), from L *colōnia* (whence *Cologne*), an *-ia* derivative of *colōnus*, a settler, orig a farmer, from *colere*, to cultivate: cf CULT. *Colonist* and *colonize* (whence *colonization*) are E *-ist*, *-ize* formations from either or both of E *colony* and L *colōnia*.

**colonnade.** See COLUMN, para 2.

**colony.** See COLONIAL.

**colophon:** LL: Gr *kolophōn*, summit, (hence)

finishing stroke or touch: s *koloph-*, r *kol-*, akin to the *col-* of L *collis*, hill: f.a.e., HILL.

**color, colour,** derives not by adoption from L *color* (s *col-*) but through OF *color*, var *colour* (cf the assimilated F *couleur*): and L *color* is very prob akin to L *celāre* (s *cel-*), to conceal, as, e.g., varnish does. The derivative *colorāre*, to colour—E 'to colour' derives from OF-F *colorer*—has subsidiary *colorātiō*, o/s *colorātiōn-*, whence late MF-F and E *coloration*; L *colorābilis* yields *colo(u)rable*. *Coloratura*—orig, ML—is imported from Italy.

2. L *colorāre* becomes Sp *colorare*, with pp *colorado*, used also as adj for 'reddish', hence Rio *Colorado* and, derivatively, the State of *Colorado*.

3. 'To *discolo(u)r*', ME *descolouren*, comes from OF-MF *descolorer*: *des-* for *dis-*+*colorer* from L *colorāre*; *discoloration* blends 'to *discolo(u)r*'+ *coloration*.

**Colorado.** See prec, para 2.

**colossal, colossus; Colosseum, Coliseum.**

The 4th is a var of the 3rd, itself orig the neu of L *colosseus*, huge, from *colossus*, a huge statue, trln of Gr *kolossos*; *colosseus* became (EF-F and) E *colossal*. The Gr *kolossos* is prob akin to Gr *kolophōn*, q.v. at COLOPHON: in form, cf Gr *Molosso s*, E *molossus*, a metrical foot of three long syllables.

**colour.** See COLOR.

**colt:** ME *colt*, young horse—ass—camel: OE *colt*, young ass or camel: mainly Scan: ult akin to CHILD. Hence *coltish*.

**colter, coulter:** ME *colter*, *culter*: OE *culter*: L *culter*, any cutter, esp ploughshare and knife: o.o.o.

**columbine:** (perh via MF-EF *colombine*, but certainly from) LL *columbīna*, from *columbīnus*, of or like a *columba* or dove: 'from the fancied resemblance of its inverted flower to a group of five pigeons' (Webster). With L *columba*, cf Gr *kolumbos*, the little grebe, 'both birds having been named from their colour' (Boisacq): cf *kelainos*, sombre. The IE r, therefore, would be *\*kel-*, var *\*kol-*, sombre.

**column, columnar, columnist, columniation; colonnade;** sep **colonel.**

1. A *columnist* (suffix *-ist*) writes literary or journalistic columns: and *column* derives from L *columna*, an Arch column, akin to L *columen*, a summit (cf CULMINATE and, f.a.e., HILL); its LL adj *columnāris* yields E *columnar* (*-ar*, adj). The Arch *columniation* is oddly formed from L *columnātus*, supported with columns.

2. *Columna* becomes It *colonna*, whence *colonnata*, whence F *colonnade*, adopted by E; cf the suffix *-ade*.

**coma** (1): Gr *kōma*, lethargy, (lit) profound sleep, intimately akin to *kōmainō*, I sleep profoundly, s *kōmain-*, r *kōm-*, and *koimaō*, I lull to sleep. On the o/s *komat-* is formed the E adj *comatose* (suffix *-ose*).

**coma** (2), nebulous mass, blur of light. See COMET, last sentence.

**comb,** n hence v: OE *camb*, akin to OHG *kamb*

(G *Kamm*) and ON *kambr*: more remotely, to Gr *gomphos, gomphios*, molar tooth, and Skt *jámbhas*, tusk: IE r, *\*gambh-*, var *\*gombh-*, tooth.

**combat, combatant, combative.** See 2nd BAT, para 3.

**combe.** See COOMB.

**combine,** v hence n; **combination, combinative.**

The 3rd is an E formation (*-ive*), suggested by the 2nd, which, perh via MF-EF, comes from *combīnātiōn-*, the o/s of LL *combīnātiō-*, itself from LL *combīnāre*, whence, perh via MF-F *combiner*, the E 'to *combine*', whence 'a *combine*': *com-*, together+*bini*, two at a time, from *bis*, twice: cf BINARY.

**combustible, combustion.**

Adopted from MF-F, *combustible* suggests a LL *\*combustibilis*, formed—like LL *combustiō*, o/s *combustiōn-*, whence OF-F, hence E, *combustion*— from *combust-* (cf the obs E adj *combust*, burnt up), the s of *combustus*, pp of *combūrere*, virtually a blend of *co-urere*, to burn together or simultaneously+*ambūrere*, to burn on both sides. L *ūrere*, to burn, has s *ūr-* and prob r *ū-*: cf Gr *heuō*, Skt *óṣāmi*, I burn, and, for the pp *ustus*, Skt *uṣṭá*, burnt.

**come,** pt **came,** pp **come,** presp (and vn) **coming;** sep **become; income, incoming; oncome, oncoming; outcome;** obvious cpds, **come-back,** etc.

1. The etym constellation of *come* is too vast to be conveniently grouped. But cf such Latin cognates as ad*vene*, con*vene*, inter*vene*—ad*vent*, con*vent*, e*vent*, in*vent*, pre*vent*—con*vention*, in*vention*, pre*vention*, sub*vention*, with such adjj as con*ventional*, pre*ventive*; such F 'intermediaries' as ad*venture*, a*venue* (and *venue*), par*venu*, re*venue*— pro*venance*; and such Gr cognates as acro*bat* and the n *base*: all recorded sep in this dict.

2. 'To *come*' derives, through ME *comen*, earlier *cumen*, from OE *cuman*, s *cum-*: akin to OFris *kuma, koma*, OS *cuman* or *k-*, Go *qiman*, OHG *queman*, MHG *komen*, G *kommen*, MD *comen*, *commen*, D *komen*, ON *koma*: Gmc *\*kwem-*, IE *\*gwem-* or *\*guem-*: cf L *uenīre* (ML *venīre*), s *uen-*, for *\*guemīre*; cf Gr *bainein*, to go, s *bain-*; cf also Skt *gámāmi*, I go.

3. The principal prefix-cpds are:

*become*, treated sep;

*income*, n (cf REVENUE), app derives from obs 'to *income*' (OE *incuman*);

*oncome*, n, mainly Sc: ME *on-come, on-kume*; *oncoming*, adj, from presp of obs *oncome*, vi, ME *on-comen, on-kumen*;

*outcome*, n, prob from obs *outcome*, vi, ult from OE *ūtcymen*, for *ūtan-cumen*.

**comedy, comedian, comédienne, comedic.** See ODE, para 3.

**comely,** whence **comeliness** (*-ness*): ME *comlich* or *comeliche*, earlier *cumlich*: OE *cȳmlīc*, by *-līc* (E *-like*) from *cȳme*, pretty, beautiful, fine, tender, delicate: akin to OHG *chūmo*, MHG *kūme*, weakly (adv), and MHG *kūm*, weak, and OHG *chūma*, sorrow, and G *kaum*, scarcely. (Walshe.)

**comestible.** See EDIBLE, para 2.

comet, whence adjj cometary (cf F cométaire) and
cometic, derives, like OF-F comète, from L comtēa,
var of comētes, trln of Gr komētēs, (lit) the long-
haired, elliptical for astēr komētēs, long-haired
star, from koman, to wear one's hair long, from
komē, hair, itself o.o.o.; komē becomes L coma,
adopted by E Astr and Bot.

comfit. See CONFECTION, para 2.

comfort, comfortable. See FORCE, para 7.

comfrey. See SOLID, para 7, s. f.

comic(al). See ODE, para 4.

comity: L cōmitās, courtesy, o/s cōmitāt-, from
cōmis, affable, courteous, earlier cosmis, perh from
IE r *smei, to smile, to laugh (cf SMILE), with co-
(for con-, from cum, with) used as an int prefix.
(E & M.)

comma: L comma, clause, (later) comma: Gr
komma, clause, ? for *koptma, from koptein, to
cut off: s *kopt-, r kop-: IE r *kap-, varr *kep- and
*kop-: cf Alb kep, I cut or dress stone. Cf CAPON.

command (n and v), commandant, commandeer,
commander. commandery, commandment. See
MANUAL, para 22.

commemorable, commemorate, commemoration,
commemorative, commmemorator. See MEMORY,
para 6.

commence, commencement; recommence, recommencement.

Recommencement, adopted from EF-F, derives,
by suffix -ment, from OF-F recommencer: re-,
again+commencer. And OF-F commencer—
whence OF-F commencement, adopted by E—is
OF comencer, whence ME comencer, whence 'to
commence'; OF comencer derives from VL
*cominitiāre, an int (com-, with, together) of
initiāre (orig 'to initiate' someone into esp a
religion, then, from C5), 'to begin': f.a.e.,
INITIAL.

commend, commendation, commendatory. See
MANUAL, para 24.

commensurable, commensurate. See MEASURE,
para 6.

comment, n, v; commentary; commentate, commentation, commentator. See MIND, para 15.

commerce, commercial. See MARKET, para 4.

commère. See FATHER, para 3.

commination, comminatory. See MINATORY,
para 2.

comminute, comminution. See MINOR, para 7.

commiserate, commiseration, commiserative. See
MISER, para 2.

commissar, commissariat, commissary; commission (n hence v), commissionaire, commissioner.
See MISSION, para 8.

commissure. See MISSION, para 8.

commit; committee. See MISSION, para 8.

commix. See MIX, para 9.

commodate, commodation. See MODAL, para 14.

commode, commodious, commodity. See MODAL,
para 11.

commodore: earlier commandore: prob D kom-
mandeur: certainly OF-F conmandeur, from the v
commander: cf command, q.v. at MANUAL, para 22.

common, adj (with neg uncommon), hence nn
common (land held in common) and commons (the
Commons; food eaten in common); commonalty;
commoner; commonness; such cpds, all easily
derivable, as commonplace (n hence adj), commonsense, commonweal and commonwealth.—commune (cf the adj communal) and 'to commune';
communicable, communicant, communicate, communication, communicative (neg in-), communicatory; communion, Communion; communiqué;
communist (adj communistic), community; sep
MEAN, held in common, to be consulted f.a.e.

1. Common, adj, blends as it were the two predominant ME forms, commun and comon: OF-MF
comun, OF-F commun: L commūnis. Commonness
merely attaches the suffix -ness; commonalty
anglicizes, in the ME period, the MF communalté
(F communauté), which attaches -té; for -ité, to F
communal (see para 3); commoner, perh suggested
by OF-MF communier, one who holds something
in common.

2. Cpds worth a remark include:

commonplace, imitative—cf F lieu commun—
of L locus commūnis, itself prompted by Gr topos
koinos;

commonsense, earlier common sense: cf the F le
sens commun and see SENSE, para 2;

commonweal, earlier common weal: archaic form
of commonwealth, orig merely common wealth,
public welfare: cf VOLITION, para 17.

3. The L origin appears very clearly in:

communal, adopted from OF-F, from LL com-
mūnālis, mdfn of L commūnis;

commune, n, deriving from 'to commune', itself
from OF-MF communer, to render available to all,
to share, from the adj commun;

communicable, adopted from MF-F, from LL
commūnicābilis;

communicant, from L commūnicant-, o/s of
commūnicans, presp of commūnicāre, to impart
(news, knowledge), hence, in LL, to take Communion, from *commūnicus, mdfn of commūnis;

communicate, v, from commūnicātus, pp of
commūnicāre;

communication, prob via MF-F, from L com-
mūnicātiō, o/s commūnicātiōn-, from commūnicāre;

communicative: prob via MF-F communicative,
f of communicatif, from ML commūnicātīvus, LL
commūnicātiuus;

communicatory, from LL commūnicātōrius;

communion, perh via OF-F, from L commūniō,
o/s commūniōn-; Communion is a sharing with
God;

communiqué, n from the pp of MF-F com-
muniquer, to communicate;

communism, from F communisme, and communist, from F communiste;

community, from OF-MF communeté, com-
munité, from L commūnitās (o/s commūnitāt-),
from commūnis.

4. The prefix cpds are two:

LL incommūnicābilis, whence E (and EF-F)
incommunicable;

LL *excommūnicāre*, to exclude from the Eucharist, with pp *excommūnicātus* (used also as n), whence the E 'to *excommunicate*' and the pa and n *excommunicate*; derivative LL *excommūnicātiō*, o/s *excommūnicātiōn-*, explains *excommunication*; derivative LL *excommūnicator* is adopted by E.

5. L *commūnis=com-*, with+*mun*us, an official occupation (with secondary sense 'present one gives'—cf REMUNERATE)+*-is*, adj suffix. Basic idea of *munus* is 'exchange': see MEAN, held in common.

commotion; commove. See MOVE, para 10.

commune, n and v. See COMMON, para 3.

communicate, communication, communicative. See COMMON, para 3.

communion, Communion. See COMMON, para 3.

communism, communist, etc. See COMMON, para 3.

commutable, commutation, commutative, commutator, commute, commuter. See MUTABLE, para 5.

compact, compaction. See PACT, para 3.

companion, n hence v; companionway; companionable, companionate, companionship; company. See PANTRY, para 8.

compare (v hence n), comparable, comparative, comparator, comparison. See PAIR, para 9.

compart, compartition, compartment. See PART, para 18.

compass, n and v. See PACE, para 5.

compassion, compassionate (adj and v); compatible, compatibility. See PATIENCE, para 7.

compatriot. See FATHER, para 15, s.f.

compeer. See PAIR, para 5.

compel, compellation. See the 2nd PULSE, para 8.

compendent, compendious, compendium. See PEND, para 14.

compensable, compensate, compensation, compensative, compensator, compensatory. See PEND, para 15.

compère. See FATHER, para 3.

compete, competence, competent; competition, competitive, competitor. See PETITION, para 4.

compilation derives, prob via MF-F, from L *compīlātiō* (o/s *compīlātiōn-*), itself from *compīlāre*, to press together, hence to gather together, hence to compile: *com-*, together+*pīlāre* (s *pīl-*), to press. Derivative MF-F *compiler* leads to E *compile*. L *pīlāre* derives from *pīla*, pillar: f.a.e., PILE, pillar.

complacence (or complacency), complacent. See PLEASE, para 9.

complain, complainant, complaint. See the 2nd PLAIN, para 3.

complaisance, complaisant. See PLEASE, para 9.

complanate, complanation. See PLANE, para 9.

complement (n hence v), complemental, complementary. See PLENARY, para 9.

complete, completion. See PLENARY, para 8.

complex, adj and n; complexion; complexity. See PLY, para 20.

compliance, compliant. See COMPLY.

complicant, complicate, complication. See PLY, para 9.

complice, complicity. See PLY, para 21.

compliment (n and v), complimentary. See PLENARY, para 10.

complin (AE), compline. See PLENARY, para 11.

complot. See PLANE, para 23.

comply; compliant, compliance. 'To *comply*' derives from It *complire*, to compliment, orig to complete, from Sp *complir*, *cumplir*: cf COMPLIMENT. *Compliance=compliant+-ce*; *compliant*, on anl of *pliant*.

component. See POSE, para 6.

comport, comportment. See the 3rd PORT, para 4.

compose, whence pa composed and agent composer; composite, adj hence n; composition; compositor; compost and compote; composure. See POSE, para 6.

compound (1), an enclosure: Mal *campuñ*, influenced by the n in:

compound (2), to combine, to mix, whence adj and n compound and agent compounder and pa and vn compounding. See POSE, para 6, s.f.

comprehend, comprehensible, comprehension, comprehensive. See PREHEND, para 7.

compress, compression, compressor. See the 2nd PRESS, para 5.

comprise, occ comprize. See PREHEND, para 9.

compromise, n hence v; compromissary; compromit. See MISSION, para 20.

comptroller. See ROLL, para 7, s.f.

compulsion, compulsive, compulsory. See the 2nd PULSE, para 8.

compunction. See PUNGENT, para 19.

computation, compute. See the 2nd COUNT, para 2.

comrade. See CAMERA, para 2.

Comus. See ODE, para 3.

con, to learn by reading. See CAN, para 4.

concatenate, concatenation. See CHAIN, para 2.

concave, concavity. See CAVE, para 3.

conceal, concealment. The latter comes from MF *concelement*, a *-ment* formation from OF-MF *conceler* (*il conceile*, he conceals), whence 'to *conceal*', and *conceler* derives from L *concelāre*, an int (*con-*) of *celāre*, to hide, s *cel-*: f.a.e., HILL.

concede. See CEDE, para 5.

conceit. See CAPABILITY, para 7, at *concipere*.

conceivable, conceive. See CAPABILITY, para 7, at *concipere*.

concenter, concentrate, concentration. See CENTRE, para 2.

concentric. See CENTRE, para 3.

concept, conception. See CAPABILITY, para 7.

concern, v, whence n, the pa concerned, the prep concerning, and concernment (by suffix *-ment*). 'To *concern*' derives from MF-F *concerner*, itself from ML *concernere*, to regard, (hence) to concern, a development, from LL *concernere*, to mix, to mingle together, formed upon Gr *συγκρίνω*, *sunkrīnō*, I combine, compare, decide, and falsely referred to *cernere*, to pass through a sieve. (E & M.)

concert, n, v (whence pa concerted), concertina; disconcert, pa disconcerted, disconcertion,

1. 'To *disconcert*' derives from obs F *disconcerter* (*dis*+*concerter*); hence *disconcertion*.

2. 'To *concert*': EF-F *concerter*, perh from EF-F n *concert* but prob from It *concertare*, to act together, to agree; L *concertāre*, to contend, to be rivals: *con-* with+*certāre*, to strive, from *certus*, decided, determined, hence sure, certain: f.a.e., CERTAIN. The It *concertare* has derivative *concerto*, agreement, later a musical concert; hence the F *concert*, active agreement, a concert, adopted by E.

3. Prob on the anl of other musical instruments: *concertina* from *concert*: perh, however, suggested by It *concertino*, a brief concert, a concerted piece of music, dim of *concerto*.

**concession, concessive.** See CEDE, para 5.

**conch,** whence **conchoid** (-oid); cf the element *concho-*.

*Conch* derives from L *concha*, trln of Gr *konkhē* (κόγχη), perh orig echoic: akin to Skt *śaṇhkás*, conch, shell.

**conciliate, conciliation, conciliator, conciliatory; reconcile, reconciliation, reconciliatory.**

1. 'To *reconcile*' comes, perh via OF-F, from L *reconciliāre*, to bring together again, to reunite: *re-*+*conciliāre*. Derivative L *reconciliātiō*, o/s *reconciliātiōn-*, leads, perh via MF-F, to E *reconciliation*; *reconciliatory*=*re-*+*conciliatory*.

2. L *conciliāre* (f.a.e., COUNCIL) has pp *conciliātus* whence 'to *conciliate*'; derivative L *conciliātiō*, o/s *conciliātiōn-*, explains MF-F and E *conciliation*; L *conciliātor*, adopted by E (cf MF-F *concilateur*), prob suggested the E adj *conciliatory*.

**concise, concision.** The former (cf EF-F *concis*) represents L *concīsus*, cut off short, orig the pp of *concīdere*, to cut into pieces: *con-*, used int+ *caedere*, to cut: cf CAESAR, para 1. Derivative L *concīsiō*, o/s *concīsiōn-*, becomes—perh via late MF-F—*concision*.

**conclamant: conclamation.** See CLAIM, para 5.

**conclave:** MF-F: ML *conclāve*, L *conclāue*, orig the neu of *\*conclāuis*, 'with (*con-*) a key (*clāuis*)': a key-lockable (room): f.a.e., CLAVICLE. Cf:

**conclude, conclusion, conclusive.**

'To *conclude*' derives from L *conclūdere*, int (*con-*) of *claudere*, to close: cf CLAUSE and CLAVICLE. On *conclūs-*, s of the pp *conclūsus*, arise:

*conclūsiō*, o/s *conclūsiōn-*, whence, perh via MF-F, the E *conclusion*;

LL *conclūsiuus*, ML *-ivus*, whence E *conclusive*.

**concoct, concoction.** Cf *decoct* and see COOK, para 2.

**concomitant.** See 1st COUNT (nobleman), para 4.

**concord, concordance, concordant.**

*Concordance*, adopted from OF-F, comes from LL *concordantia*, an agreeing, (general) agreement, formed upon *concordant-* (whence, via F, the E adj *concordant*), o/s of *concordans*, presp of *concordāre*, to be in agreement, from adj *concors* (*con-*, with+*cors*, gen *cordis*, heart), agreeing. L *concors*, o/s *concord-*, has derivative *concordia*,

whence, via OF-F *concorde*, the E n *concord*. Cf CORDIAL, f.a.e.

**concourse.** See COURSE, para 2.

**concrete, concretion.** See CRESCENT, para 5.

**concubine; concubinage.** See HIVE, para 5 and heading.

**concupiscence, concupiscent, concupiscible.**

The 2nd derives from L *concupiscent-*, o/s of *concupiscens*, presp of *concupiscere*, inch of *concupere*, to desire ardently: *con-*+*cupere*, to desire: cf *cupidity* at COVET; on *concupiscent-* arises the LL *concupiscentia*, whence, prob via MF-F, the E *concupiscence*; *concupiscible* derives, prob via MF-F, from LL *concupiscibilis*: *concupisc*ere+ *-ibilis* (E *-ible*).

**concur, concurrence, concurrent.** See COURSE, para 10.

**concuss, concussion.**

'To *concuss*' represents L *concussus*, pp of *concutere*, to shake (*quatere*) violently (*con-* used int): f.a.e., QUASH. Derivative L *concussiō*, o/s *concussiōn-*, explains *concussion*.

**condemn, condemnation, condemnatory.** See DAMN.

**condense,** whence pa **condensed; condensation.** The n derives, perh via MF-F, from LL *condensātiō*, o/s *condensātiōn-*, from L *condensāre* (int *con-*+*densāre*, to thicken: f.a.e., DENSE), whence, via MF-F *condenser*, 'to *condense*'.

**condescend, condescension.** See ASCEND, para 8.

**condiction.** See DICT, para 7 (at *condicere*).

**condign,** well-deserved: MF-EF *condigne*: L *condignus*, very (int *con-*) worthy (*dignus*: f.a.e., DIGNITY).

**condiment** derives, through MF-F, from L *condīmentum*, a spice, from *condīre*, to pickle.

**condition, conditional, conditionate.** See DICT, para 10.

**condole, condolence.** See DOLOR, para 2.

**condominium.** See *dominium* in DOMESTIC, para 5.

**condonation, condone.** See DONATION, para 2.

**condor:** Sp *cóndor*: Quechuan *condor*.

**condottiere.** See DUKE, para 8.

**conduce, conducive.** See DUKE, para 6. Cf:

**conduct, conductance, conduction, conductive** (whence **-ivity**), **conductor.** See DUKE, para 6.

**conduit.** See DUKE, para 9.

**cone,** n hence v; **conic** (whence **conics**) and **conical; conifer,** adj **coniferous.**

1. The geom *cone* derives from the *cone* of a tree, esp of a pine: L *cōnus*: Gr *kōnos*, s *kōn-* (=IE *\*kō-*+*n* infix). The Gr adj *kōnikos* becomes EF-F *conique* and E *conic*, with extension *conical*.

2. The L cpd adj *cōnifer*, cone-bearing (cf element *-fer*), is adopted by E as a n, with consequent adj *coniferous* (cf *-ferous* at *-fer*).

**confabulate, confabulation.** See FABLE, para 1.

**confection, confectioner, confectionery; comfit; confetti.**

1. L *conficere*, to prepare (int *con-*+*facere*, to make: f.a.e., FACT), has pp *confectus*, whence the rare E v *confect*; derivative L *confectiō*, o/s *con-*

*fection-*, becomes, via OF-F, the E *confection*, whence *confectioner* and *confectionery* (*-ery*): cf para 3.

2. L *conficere* becomes OF-F *confire*, pp *confit*, with its n use borrowed by E in form *comfit*. *Conficere* has in VL the cpd *disconficere*, whence OF *desconfire*, pp *desconfit*, whence the E 'to *discomfit*'; OF *desconfire* has derivative *desconfiture*, whence E *discomfiture*.

3. L *conficere* becomes It *confire*, pp *confetto*, used also as n, with pl *confetti*, adopted by E, orig in It sense 'confections, sweetmeats'.

**confederacy, confederate, confederation.** See FEDERAL, para 2.

**confer, conference, conferment.**

The 3rd=the 1st+*-ment*; the 2nd derives, via late MF-F *conférence*, from ML *conferentia*, formed from the o/s of the presp of *conferre*, to bring together, to consult: *con-*+*ferre*, to bear, bring: f.a.e., FERRY. *Conferre* yields 'to *confer*'.

**confess, confession, confessional** (adj, n), **confessor.**

'To *confess*' derives, via OF-F, from LL *confessāre*, from L *confess-*, s of *confessus*, pp of *confitēri*, to confess, int (*con-*) of *fatēri*, to confess, akin to *fāri*, to speak: cf PROFESS. *Confession* derives, via OF-F, from L *confessiō*, o/s *confessiōn-*; the derivative ML adj *confessiōnālis* yields E *confessional* (adj), and its subsidiary n *confessiōnāle* becomes EF-F *confessional*, adopted by E. LL *confessor*, adopted by OF (whence the F *confesseur*), passes into E.

**confetti.** See CONFECTION, para 3.

**confide, confidence, confident; confidant, confidante.** See FAITH, para 12.

**configuration.** See FIGURE, para 5.

**confine** (n and v), **confinement.**

The 2nd, adopted from EF-F (obs), derives by suffix *-ment* from MF-F *confiner*, to border upon, to hold within limits, whence 'to *confine*'; MF-F *confiner* derives from *OF-MF *confines* (later *confins*), whence, indeed, the E *confines*, whence, by b/f, the sing *confine*; and MF *confines* represents LL *confines*, limits, borders, from the L adj *confinis*, limiting, bordering: int *con-*+*finis*, end, esp in pl *fines*, borders: f.a.e., FINAL.

**confirm, confirmation, confirmative** and **confirmatory.**

The last is an E formation: *-ory* attached to *confirmat-* as in *confirmative*, from LL *confirmātiuus* (ML *-ivus*); *confirmation* derives, prob via MF-F, from L *confirmātiōn-*, o/s of *confirmātiō*, itself from L *confirmātus*, pp of *confirmāre* (int *con-*+*firmāre*, to strengthen, from *firmus*, firm, solid: see FIRM), to strengthen, later to confirm, whence, via OF-EF *confermer*, MF-F *confirmer* and ME *confermen, -firmen*, the E 'to *confirm*'.

**confiscate** (adj and v), **confiscation, confiscator, confiscatory.**

The last is an E formation; *confiscator* is sense-adapted from L *confiscātor*, a treasurer; *confiscation* derives, via MF-F, from L *confiscātiōn-*, o/s of *confiscātiō* (lit, a treasuring), from *confiscāre*, to

safeguard in a special basket or *fiscus*: see FISCAL. *Confiscāre*, esp in sense 'to appropriate for the treasury', has pp *confiscātus*, whence 'to *confiscate*'.

**conflagration.** See FLAGRANT, para 2.

**conflate, conflation.** See FLATUS, para 4.

**conflict, n, v; confliction; conflictive** and **conflictory.**

The two adjj are of E formation from *conflict-*, the s of L *conflictus*, pp of *conflīgere*, to strike or clash (*flīgere*) together, to conflict: cf AFFLICT and INFLICT. L *conflictus* yields E 'to *conflict*'; the derivative LL n *conflictus* (gen *-ūs*) yields 'a *conflict*'; the abstract *conflictiō*, o/s *conflictiōn-*, becomes *confliction*.

**confluence, -ent.** See FLUENT, para 6.

**conform, conformation, conformity.** See FORM, para 4.

**confound.** See the 2nd FOUND, para 5.

**confront, confrontation.** See FRONT, para 5.

**Confucius:** L form, earlier *Confutius*, of Pekinese *K'ung fu-tzu,* 'K'ungmaster', K'ung the philosopher: *K'ung* was his family name. Hence the adj *Confucian*. (Enci It.)

**confuse, confusion.** See the 2nd FOUND, para 5.

**confute; confutation, confutative.**

The 3rd=*confute*+*-ative*; the 2nd derives from *confutātiōn-*, o/s of L *confutātiō*, from *confutāre*, whence, perh via EF-F (obsol), the E 'to *confute*'; int *con-*+*futāre*, to fell, to abase, perh an int or a freq, or both, of *fundere* (see the 2nd FOUND): cf REFUTE.

**congeal, congealment, congelation.**

The 3rd derives, perh via MF-F *congélation*, from L *congelātiō*, o/s *congelātiōn-*, from *congelāre*, to freeze (*gelāre*: cf JELLY) hard (int *con-*); the 2nd='to *congeal*'+*-ment*; 'to *congeal*' derives from MF-F *congeler*, from *congelāre*.

**congener.** See GENERAL, para 20. Cf:

**congenial,** whence **congeniality.** See GENERAL, para 20. Cf:

**congenital.** See GENERAL, para 20.

**conger:** ME *congre*, var *cungre*: MF-F *congre*: L *conger*, var *gonger*, and, in LL and glossaries, *congrus, gongrus*: Gr *gongros* (γόγγρος), the L *con-* being due to the frequency of *con-* in L words: akin to Gr *gongulos* (γογγύλος), round or rounded.

**congeries.** See GERUND, para 8.

**congest,** mostly as pa **congested; congestion; congestive.** See GERUND, para 9.

**conglomerate,** adj (whence n and v); **conglomeration.**

The latter—cf AGGLOMERATION—derives from *conglomerātiōn-*, o/s of *conglomerātiō*, formed from *conglomerātus*, pp of *conglomerāre*, to roll together (*con-*) as if into a ball (*glomus*). Cf CLAM.

**congratulate, congratulation, congratulatory.** See GRACE, para 11.

**congregate,** adj hence v; **congregation,** with adj **congregational.** See GREGAL, para 5.

**congress; congressional.** See GRADE, para 7.

**congruence** (or **congruency**), **congruent, congruity, congruous; incongruence, incongruent, incongruity, incongruous.**

1. *Incongruous* comes from L *incongruus*; *incongruence* from L *incongruentia*, formed from *incongruent-*, o/s of L *incongruens*; *incongruity*, perh via EF-F *incongruité*, from LL *incongruitās*, o/s *incongruitāt-*.

2. These neg (*in-*) L forms may be referred to:

L *congruus*, whence E *congruous*: from L *congruere*, to come together (*con-*), to coincide, to be harmonious: *con-*+formative *g* (cf *ingruere*, to rush into)+*ruere*, to rush, itself akin to *ruīna*, a (down)fall, ruin: f.a.e., RUIN;

L *congruentia*, whence E *congruence* and var *congruency*;

L *congruens*, o/s *congruent-*, whence E *congruent*;

LL *congruitās*, harmony, whence, perh via late MF-F *congruité*, the E *congruity*.

**conic(al), conics, conifer(ous).** See CONE.

**conject, conjective; conjecture** (n, v), **conjectural.**

*Conjective* adds adj *-ive* to the obs v *conject*, from ML *conjectāre*, LL *coniectāre*, an int of *coniicere* (pp *coni(i)ectus*), to throw (*con-*), hence to conjecture, *-iicere* being a c/f of *iacere*, to throw: f.a.e., JACULATE. *Conjecture*, n, derives, perh via F, from ML *conjectūra*, LL *coniectūra*, from the pp s *coniect-*; the v *conjecture* perh derives either from the E n or from MF-F *conjecturer* (from F *conjecture*), but, most prob, from the LL *coniectūrāre*, to conjecture, s *coniectūr-*, ML *conjectūr-*; the adj *conjectural*, however, comes—perh via EF-F— from ML *conjectūrālis*, L *coniectūrālis*.

**conjoin, conjoint.** See JOIN, para 17. Cf:

**conjugal, conjugant, conjugate** (adj, n, v), **conjugation, conjugative; conjunct, conjunction, conjunctive** (adj hence n), **conjunctivitis, conjuncture.** See JOIN, resp para 13 and para 14.

**conjuration; conjure,** whence **conjuror,** var **conjurer,** and **conjury** (now usu **conjuring**). See JURY, para 4.

**connate, connatural.** See NATIVE, para 9.

**connect,** whence **connector** or **-er; connection** or **connexion; connective** (whence **connectivity**). See the 2nd NET, para 9.

**connivance, connive.**

L *conniuere*, better *coniuere* (or *-ere*), ML *conivere*, to shut, esp the eyes (to), *con-* used int+a cognate of *nictāre*, to wink: whence 'to *connive*'. (Cf OE *hnǣgan*, Go *hneiwan*, OFris *hnīga*, OS and OHG *hnīgan*, to bend; IE r, perh *kneigh-*, to lean upon.) *Connivance*, earlier *connivence*, derives either from EF-F *connivence* or its source, ML *con(n)iventia*, LL *coniuentia*.

**connoisseur.** See COGNITION, para 2.

**connotation, connote:** cf *denote*, but see NOTABLE, para 8.

**connubial.** See LYMPH, para 5.

**conquer** (whence pa **conquering**), **conqueror, conquest; Conquistador.** See QUERY, para 8.

**consanguineous, consanguinity.** See SANGUINARY, para 4.

**conscience, conscientious, conscionable** and **unconscionable; conscious, consciousness.** See SCIENCE, para 5.

**conscribe, conscript, conscription.** See SCRIBE, para 11.

**consecrate** (whence pa **consecrated**), **consecration, consecratory.** See SACRAMENT, para 15.

**consecution, consecutive.** See SEQUENCE, para 8.

**consension, consensus.** See SENSE, para 15.

**consent,** n, v; **consentaneous; consentience, consentient; consentive.** See SENSE, para 15.

**consequence, consequent.** See SEQUENCE, para 8.

**consertal.** See SERIES, para 8.

**conserve,** n, v; **conservancy; conservation; conservatism, conservative** (adj hence n); **conservator, conservatory** and **conservatoire.**

1. The base is ML *servāre*, L *seruāre*, to keep safe or well, to preserve, s *serv-* (ML) or *seru-* (L), with prob r *ser-*; perh akin to L *seruus*, *guardian, slave, and prob akin to L *seruīre*, to serve: cf the other cpds OBSERVE, PRESERVE, RESERVE.

2. ML *conservāre*, L *conseruāre*, int (*con-*) of *seruāre*, becomes OF-F *conserver* becomes 'to *conserve*'; OF *conserver* has derivative MF-F n *conserve*, adopted by E. The L presp *conseruans*, o/s *conseruant-*, ML *conservant-*, yields the adj *conservant*; the derivative LL *conseruantia*, ML *conservantia*, yields *conservancy*. The pp *conseruātus*, s *conseruāt-*, ML *conservāt-*, appears in

L *conseruātiō*, o/s *conseruātiōn-*, ML *conservātiōn-*, whence, very prob via MF-F, the E *conservation*;

LL *conseruātiuus*, ML *conservātivus*, yields, perh via F, the E *conservative*, whence *conservatism*;

L *conseruātor*, ML *conservātor*, is adopted by E;

LL *conseruātōrius*, ML *conservatōrius*, yields the adj *conservatory*, the E n coming from the ML neu *conservatōrium* used as n, whence also the F *conservatoire*.

**consider, considerable, considerate, consideration;** neg: **inconsiderable, inconsiderate, inconsideration.**

1. *Inconsiderable* derives from LL *inconsiderābilis*, hard to understand; *inconsiderate*, from L *inconsiderātus*; *inconsideration*, from LL *inconsiderātiō*, o/s *inconsiderātiōn-*. In all, *in-* is 'not'.

2. 'To *consider*' derives from OF-F *considérer*, from L *consīderāre*, to examine carefully, prob orig a term in augury and therefore deriving from *sīdus* (o/s *sīder-*), mostly in pl *sīdera*, the stars: if the s be *sīd-*, the r *sī-*, the word is perh Medit: cf Eg *siu*. *Consīderāre* has derivatives:

LL *consīderābilis*, whence both EF-F *considérable* and E *considerable*;

L *consīderātus*, pp used as adj for 'carefully examined', hence *homo consīderātus*, one who thus considers others, whence E *considerate*;

its derivative *consīderātiō*, o/s *consīderātiōn-*, whence, prob via OF-F, the E *consideration*.

3. Likewise from *sīdus* (adjj *sīdereus, sīderālis*, whence the blended E *sidereal*) comes L *dēsīderāre*, to cease to view, hence to regret the absence of, with pp *dēsīderātus*, whence 'to *desiderate*'; neu *dēsīderātum*, pl *dēsīderāta*, used as n, are adopted by E; derivative *dēsīderātiō*, o/s *dēsīderātiōn-*

becomes E *desideration*; and LL *dēsiderātiuus*, ML
*-ivus*, becomes E *desiderative*, used also as n.

consign, consignation, consignee, consignment,
consignor. Cf DESIGN, INSIGNIA, RESIGN—but
see SIGN, para 13.

consignification, consignify. See SIGN, para 13,
s.f.

consist; consistence (or -ency), consistent; consistory. See SIST, par 3. ′

consolation, consolatory, console (v). See SOLACE.

console, n. See *consolidate* at SOLID, para 6.

consolidate, consolidation, etc. See SOLID, para 6.

consols. See *consolidate* at SOLID, para 6, s.f.

consommé. See SUM, para 6.

consonance, consonant. See SONABLE, para 5.

consort, consortion, consortium. See SERIES,
para 6.

consound. See SOLID, para 7.

conspectus. See SPECTACLE, para 8.

conspicuity, conspicuous. See SPECTACLE, para 8.

conspiracy, conspiration, conspirator, conspiratorial, conspire. See SPIRIT, para 8.

conspue. See the 2nd SPIT, para 3, s.f.

constable, constabulary (adj hence n).

*Constable*, the same in ME, derives from earlier
ME *conestable*, adopted from OF-MF (OF var
*cunestables*),which adapts it from LL *comes stabuli*,
the officer in charge of the Emperor's stable, later
the head of the household army: lit, count of the
stable. Derivative ML *constabulārius*, of, by, for
a constable, yields the E *constabulary*; the predominant adj is now *constabular*. Cf COUNT (the
person) and STABLE.

constancy, constant. See STAND, para 22.

constat; constate. See STAND, para 22.

constellate, constellation; constellatory. See
STAR, para 4.

consternate, consternation. See STRATUM, para 6.

constipate, constipation.

The latter comes, perh via MF-F, from *con-
stipātiōn-*, o/s of LL *constipātiō*, a crowding, or
being crowded, together, itself deriving from L
*constipāre*, to press, or crowd, together: int *con-*+
*stipāre*, to press, esp to surround or enclose
narrowly: f.a.e., COSTIVE. *Constipate* derives from
L *constipātus*, pp of *constipāre*.

constituency, constituent, constitute, constitution,
constitutional, constitutive. See STAND, para 22, s.f.

constrain, constraint. See the 2nd STRAIN, para 7.

constrict, constriction, constrictive, constrictor;
constringent. See the 2nd STRAIN, para 6.

construct, adj (whence n) and v; construction,
whence constructional (-al, adj); constructive; constructor;—construe, v hence n. See STRUCTURE,
para 6.

consubstantial, consubstantiality. See STAND,
para 35.

consul, consular, consulate; proconsul, proconsular.

The last represents L *prōconsulāris*, from L *prō-
consul*, adopted by E—as is the simple *consul*, prob
orig 'one who is consulted': see next. *Consul* has
adj *consulāris*, whence E *consular*, and n *consulatus*

(gen *-ūs*), office, hence the offices, of a consul,
whence E *consulate*.

consult, consultant, consultation, consultative,
consultatory, consultor (or -er).

The last, adopted from L, is built upon *consult-*,
s of *consultus*, pp of *consulere*, to consult; but it is
the derivative *consultāre*, to consult, which is concerned in the other E words, for 'to *consult*'
derives, via MF-F *consulter*, therefrom; *consultant*
*=consultant-*, o/s of the presp *consultans*; *consultation* derives, perh via MF-F, from *consultā-
tiōn-*, o/s of the derivative *consultātiō*; *consultative*
derives, perh via EF-F *consultatif*, from LL *con-
sultātiuus*, ML *-ivus*, and *consultatory* from *\*con-
sultatōrius*. See COUNSEL, f.a.e.

consume, whence consumer. See SUMPTION,
para 3.

consummate, consummation, consummative, consummatory; consummator. See SUM, para 5.

consumption, consumptive. See SUMPTION, para
3.

contact (n and v), contactor; contagion, contagious. Cf *intact*; see TACT, paras 13 and (*contagion*) 14.

contain, whence container; contents; content
(adj, n, v), contentment and discontent (n, v);
continence, continent (adj, whence n), continental;
incontinence, incontinent; countenance (n, whence
v).

1. All these words come from L *continēre*, to
hold (*tenēre*) together (*con-*), to hold within, to
contain, to retain: f.a.e., TENABLE.

2. *Continēre* has presp *continens*, o/s *continent-*,
whence the E adj *continent*, whence, influenced by
L *terra continens* (source of the F *terre continente*),
the n *continent*, with adj *continental*; derivative L
*continentia* leads to OF-F *continence*, adopted by
E; neg L *incontinentia* yields *incontinence*, and *in-
continens* yields *incontinent*.

3. ML exhibits *continentia* in the secondary sense
'demeanour', which takes in OF the distinct form
*contenance*, adopted by ME, with later var *cou-
tenance*, surviving into E. (B & W, however, derive
OF *contenance* from OF *contenir*.)

4. *Continēre* has pp *contentus*, neu *contentum*,
which, used as n, yields E *content*, 'that which is
contained', usu pl *contents*. *Content*, state of quiet
satisfaction, app derives from the adj *content*,
quietly pleased or satisfied or happy, adopted from
MF-F *content*, from L *contentus*; the OF *content*
has derivative MF-F v *contenter*, whence 'to
*content*', which, in turn, has derivative late MF-F
n *contentement*, duly adapted by E as *contentment*.

5. *Discontent*, adj, n, v, and *discontentment* are
E *dis-* formations.

6. The OF-F *contenir* becomes ME *contenen*, var
*conteinen*, whence 'to *contain*'.

contaminable, contaminate, archaic adj and living
v; contamination; contaminative; contaminator. See
TACT, para 14.

contango. See TACT, para 12, s.f.

contemn. See CONTEMPT, para 1.

contemplable, contemplant. contemplate, contemplation, contemplative, contemplator, contemplatory. See TEMPER, para 15.

contemporaneous, contemporary (adj, hence n). See TEMPER, para 11.

contempt, contemptible, contemptuous; contemn, whence contemner or -or.—Perh akin: contumacy, contumacious, and contumely, contumelious.

1. *Contemptuous* is an E *-uous* formation from *contempt*, which derives, perh via EF, from L *contemptus* (gen *-ūs*), itself from *contemnere*, to slight or despise, whence, prob via EF *contemner*, the E 'to *contemn*'; the pp s *contempt-* (pp *contemptus*) has further derivative LL *contemptībilis*, whence MF-EF, hence E, *contemptible*. *Contemnere* is an int (*con-*) of the syn rare *temnere*, which has s *temn-* and is perh akin to Gr *temnein* (s *temn-*), to cut: sem cf *cutting*.

2. Perh akin to L *contemnere* is L *contumax*, o/s *contumac-*, whence, by suffix *-ious*, the E *contum cious*; *contumax* has derivative *contumācia*, whence E *contumacy*.

3. Also perh akin to L *contemnere* is L *contumēlia*, a slight, an insult, whence EF *contumelie*, whence E *contumely*; the derivative L adj *contumēliōsus* becomes E *contumelious*. Benveniste attaches *contumēlia* to *tumēre* (s *tum-*: see TUMID), to be puffed up, e.g. with insolence.

contend, whence contender. Cf *intend*—but see TEND, para 8.

content. See CONTAIN, para 4.

contention, contentious. See TEND, para 8.

contest, contestable, contestant, contestation. See TESTAMENT, para 8.

context, contextual; contexture. See TECHNIC, para 13.

contiguity, contiguous. See TACT, para 15.

continence, continent, continental. See CONTAIN, para 2.

contingency, contingent (adj, hence n.) See TACT, para 12.

continual, continuance, continuation, continuity, continuous; continue; continuum; and discontinuance, discontinuation, discontinuity, discontinuous, discontinue.

1. 'To *discontinue*' derives from MF-F *discontinuer*; *discontinuance* is AF (from the v), *discontinuation* is adopted from MF-F, and *discontinuity=dis+continuity*. *Dis-* implies a breaking-off, a ceasing.

2. The *con-* terms likewise come, with one exception, from, or imitate, or are present also in F: *continual*, ME *continuel*, OF-F *continuel*, comes from L *continuus*; *continuance* is adopted from OF; *continuation* derives, via MF-F, from L *continuātiōn-*, o/s of *continuātiō*, from the v *continuāre*, itself from *continuus*; *continuity*, via MF-F, from L *continuitās* (o/s *continuitāt-*), from *continuus*; *continuous*, however, comes straight from L *continuus*, whose neu *continuum* supplies a n to modern Physics; 'to *continue*' passes through OF-F *continuer* on its journey from L *continuāre*. The 'active principle' of L *continuus* springs from its source or, at the least, its influential cognate, *continēre*, to

hold together, (almost) to ensure the continuance of: cf, therefore, *continent* at CONTAIN, para 2, and for the basic idea 'holding on', see TENABLE.

contort, contortion. See TORT, para 7.

contour. See TURN, para 5.

contraband: EF-F *contrebande*: It *contrabbando* (or perh its Sp 'imitator', *contrabando*): *contra* (orig L), against + *bando*, edict: cf BAN, edict.

contract; contractile; contraction; contractor; contractual. See TRACT, para 12.

contradict, contradiction, contradictory. See DICT, para 7.

contralto, like so many terms in Mus, comes straight from It: *contra alto*: cf *alto* at ALTITUDE.

contraponend; contrapose, contraposition. See POSE, para 7.

contraption, a contrivance, perh blends *contrivance* + *adaptation*.

contrary (adj hence n), whence contrariness; contrariety.

The 3rd comes, via ME *contrariete* and OF *contrarieté*, from LL *contrārietās*, itself from L *contrārius* (from *contra*, against), whence, via OF-MF hence ME *contrarie*, the E *contrary*.

contrast, n, derives from EF-F *contraste*, orig a contest, from It *contrasto*, itself from *contrastare*, whence, via EF-F *contraster*, the E 'to *contrast*': and It *contrastare*, to be opposed to, is the LL *\*contrāstāre*, from L *contra stāre*, to stand (*stāre*: f.a.e., STATE, cf STAND) against (*contra*).

contravene, contravention. See VENUE, para 12.

contrectation. See TRACT, para 12, s.f.

contribute, contribution, contributor, contributory. See TRIBUTE, para 6.

contrite, contrition. See THROW, para 8.

contrivance, contrive. See TROUBADOUR, para 3.

control (n, v), controller. See ROLL, para 7.

controversial (whence controversialist); controversy; controvert. See VERSE, para 15.

contumacious, contumacy. See CONTEMPT, para 2.

contumelious, contumely. See CONTEMPT, para 3.

contund. See PIERCE, para 2.

conturbation. See TURBID, para 5.

contuse, contusion. See PIERCE, para 2.

conundrum: orig Oxford University sl: of mock-L type: EW compares the later *panjandrum* (Gr *pan-*, all + mock-L ending). Dial *con(n)undrums*, one's belongings or odds-and-ends, is borrowed from the sl term. Perh suggested by L *conuoluulus*, ML *convolvulus*, a caterpillar that wraps itself in a leaf, a bind-weed (the convolvulus), from L *conuoluere*, ML *convolvere*, to roll (*uoluere, volvere*: cf *involve*) around (*con-* used int); the ending might have been influenced by Triv*andrum*, a famous, ancient city of India. But most prob a punning, mock-L var of QUANDARY, itself of academic origin.

conurbation. See URBAN, para 1.

convalesce, convalescence, convalescent. See VALUE, para 13.

convection, convector. See VIA, para 12.

convene, convenance; convenience (n and v), conveniency, convenient, and their negg; convent and its adj **conventual; conventicle; convention, conventional, conventionalize;— coven** (or **-in**); **covenant** (n hence v), **covenanter.**

1. The n *inconvenience,* whence 'to *inconvenience',* takes its form from LL *inconuenientia,* disagreement, its sense as neg of *convenience; inconvenient* derives from *inconuenient-,* ML *-venient-,* o/s of *inconueniens,* neg of *conueniens,* accordant (para 3).

2. The effectual origin of all these terms is L *conuenīre,* ML *convenīre,* to come (*uenīre,* s *uen-*) together (*con-*), to unite, whence, via OF-F *convenir,* the E 'to *convene',* orig vi: f.a.e., COME.

3. The L derivatives relevant to E include: presp-become-adj *conueniens,* o/s *conuenient-,* ML *convenient-,* whence E *convenient*;

its derivative *conuenientia,* ML *convenientia,* whence E *convenience* (with rare derivative v) and *conveniency*; the Gallicism *convenance* derives from F *convenir*;

*conuentiō,* ML *conventiō,* o/s *convention-,* whence, perh via MF-F, E *convention*; its LL adj *conuentiōnālis,* ML *conv-,* yields *conventional,* whence *conventionalism* (*-ism*)—*conventionalist* (*-ist*)—*conventionalize* (*-ize*);

*conuentus,* a meeting, ML *conventus* (gen *-ūs*), a convent, whence E *convent*; its ML adj *conventuālis* yields *conventual,* of a convent; its dim *conuenticulum,* ML *conv-,* yields *conventicle.*

For paras 1–3, cf VENUE, paras 9–10.

4. *Coven,* var *covin* or *covine,* derives either from OF-MF *covin,* var *covine,* or from OProv *coven,* itself prob from It *covento,* from ML *coventus,* contr form of *conventus,* L *conuentus*; the E word is now applied only to an assembly of witches.

5. The contr L *couenīre,* ML *covenīre,* becomes OF-MF *covenir,* presp *covenant,* used also as n 'an agreement between persons or esp parties'— and, as this n, adopted by E; its derivative v has agent *covenanter.* Cf VENUE, para 11.

**converge, convergence, convergent.** See the 3rd VERGE, para 2.

**converse, conversion; conversance, conversant; conversation, conversational.** See VERSE, para 13.

**convert,** n, v. See VERSE, para 14.

**convex, convexity.** See VIA, para 12.

**convey, conveyance** (n, hence v—whence conveyancer, **-ancing**), **conveyor.** See VIA, para 15.

**convict** (n, v), **conviction, convictive; convince,** whence pa **convincing.** See VICTOR, para 5.

**convivial, -ity; convivium.** See VIVA, para 6.

**convocation; convoke.** See VOCABLE, para 10.

**convolute, convolution; convolve.** See VOLUBLE, para 4.

**convolvulus.** See VOLUBLE, para 2—and cf CONUNDRUM.

**convoy.** See VIA, para 15.

**convulse; convulsant, convulsion, convulsionary, convulsive.** See VELLICATE, para 5.

**cony** or **coney,** rabbit (skin or fur): MF-EF *conil* or *connil*: L *cuniculus,* app of OSp stock.

**coo** is echoic: cf the cow's *moo,* the owl's *toowittoowoo.* Cf:

**cooee** or **cooey:** Aus echoic.

**cook** (n, whence directly the v); **cookery** (C14 *cokerie*).

1. The latter merely attaches *-ery,* connoting 'trade of', to *cook,* n. A *cook* derives from OE *cōc,* itself from L *cocus,* var of *coquus,* a cook, from *coquere* (s *coqu-*), to cook: Italic r, ? \**kokw-,* var of \**kekw-,* itself akin to \**pekw-,* as seen in Gr *pessein,* to cook, with var \**pakw-,* as seen in Skt *pácāmi,* I cook (cf the syn Alb *pjek*); IE r, \**pekw-,* with var \**pokw-.*

2. Two L derivatives concern E: *concoquere,* lit to cook together (*con-*), hence to cook entirely, with pp *concoctus,* whence 'to *concoct',* and derivative *concoctiō,* o/s *concoctiōn-,* whence E *concoction*; and *dēcoquere,* to reduce (*dē-,* down from) by cooking, with pp *dēcoctus,* whence 'to *decoct',* and derivative *dēcoctiō,* o/s *dēcoctiōn-,* whence, perh via MF-F *décoction,* E *decoction.*

**cookie** or **cooky** (small cake). See CAKE.

**cool,** adj, n, v; **coolant, cooler, coolness, coolth.** The last derives by suffix *-th* (as in *warmth*) from the adj *cool,* whence also *coolness* (*-ness*); *coolant* attaches suffix *-ant* (n) to the adj *cool*; the n *cool* derives from the adj; 'to *cool'* descends from OE *cōlian,* from the OE adj *cōl,* whence E *cool.* OE *cōl* is akin to OHG *kuoli,* MHG *küele,* G *kühl,* cool, and ON *koela,* to cool—also to CHILL and COLD.

**coolie,** occ **cooly:** Hind *qūlī,* a native (usu unskilled) hired labourer: cf Tamil *kūli,* hire (n), hired labourer or servant. EW, however, proposes derivation from *Kulī,* var *Koli,* the name of a native tribe of *Guzerat* (*Gujarat*) in India, the word having been so used, in Port, in C16.

**coolth.** See COOL.

**cooly.** See COOLIE.

**coomb** or **combe,** a narrow—or a short, steep—valley, derives from OE *cumb,* of C origin: cf OIr *comm, cumm,* a hollow, a coomb, Ir *com,* a hollow (cf Ga *com,* the chest)—Cor *cūm,* small valley, W *cwm,* coomb—Mx *coan, couan,* coomb—Br *kom(m),* a trough; cf also ML *comba,* var of *cumba,* curvature, declivity. Malvezin postulates C \**comb,* var of \**camb,* to curve or bend; C *cūm,* therefore, is basically a curved hollow.

**coon,** with adj **coony; raccoon** or **racoon.**

*Coon,* the quadruped, hence the fur, merely shortens *raccoon*; from its predominant grey, black-marked, comes the A sl *coon,* a Negro. *Rac(c)oon* is of Alg origin: Webster compares Virginian *ärä'kun,* raccoon, from *ärä'kunĕm,* 'he scratches with his hands' (feet).

**coop** (n hence v), **cooper.** See HIVE, para 2.

**co-operate, co-operation, co-operative.** See OPERA, para 4.

**co-opt, co-optation.** See OPINE, para 3.

**co-ordinate, -ordination:** *co-,* with + *ordinate,* q.v. at ORDER, para 4, s.f.

**coot,** a black, rather duck-like bird: ME *cote* or *coote*: cf D *koet,* MD *coet* or *cuut*: ? echoic.

**cop** (1), n, head, top, hence a heap or pile (cf the Afr *kopje,* hillock, dim of D *kop,* hill): ME *cop* or *coppe,* head, top; OE *cop* or *copp,* top, summit: akin to G *Koppe,* summit, and OFris *kopp,* G

*Kopf*, head, either from Gmc *\*kuppa* head, or from LL *coppa, cuppa*—cf CUP.

**cop** (2), v, to catch or capture (sl and dial), whence A sl *cop*, a policeman, E sl *cop*, a capture, and E sl *copper*, policeman: prob OF-MF *caper*, to seize, catch, capture: L *capere* (s *cap*-), to take, to catch: f.a.e., CAPABILITY.

**cope** (1), n. See CAP.

**cope** (2), v (to deal adequately with): ME *coupen*: OF *couper, colper*, to hit, strike, from *coup*, a blow, (powerful) stroke, an extant form adopted by E (cf *coup de grâce*), with OF var *colp*: VL *\*colpus*, contr of VL *\*colapus*, from LL *colaphus*, a kick, a cuff or punch: Gr *kolaphos*, a cuff (e.g., on the ear): IE r, prob *\*kola*-, to strike resoundingly.

**cope** (3), to pare. See COPPICE.

**coper**, (horse) dealer, derives from E dial *cope*, to barter, ME *copen*: MD *copen*: akin to CHEAP.

**coping stone.** See CAP, para 2.

**copious.** See COPY, para 1, s.f.

**copper** (1), the metal: OE *coper* (or *-or*): L *cuprum* (adj *cupreus*: E *cupreous*), a coll form of *Cyprium*, elliptical for *Cyprium aes*, Cyprian copper: Gr *Kuprios*, of *Kupros* or Cyprus, anciently renowned for its copper mines. *Cyprian*=L *Cypri*us+E suffix *-an*; *Cypriot(e)* is a F formation.

**copper** (2), policeman. See the 2nd COP.

**coppice** and its contr form **copse**: OF *copeiz*, from *coper* (whence the tech *cope*, to pare), var *couper*, to cut: VL *\*cuppāre*, to behead, from VL *\*cuppum*, skull, from LL *cuppa*: cf CUP and also COUPON.

**copra**: Port (and Sp) *copra*: Mal *koppara*: Hind *khoprā*: perh akin to, or even deriving from, Skt *kharpara*, skull.

**coprological.** See element *copro*-.

**copse.** See COPPICE.

**Copt, Coptic.** See EGYPT, para 6.

**copula, copulate, copulation, copulative, copulatory; couple,** n and v (whence **coupling,** n, and **coupler**)—**couplet.**

1. *Copula* is L for 'a bond': for *\*co-apula*: *co*-, together+a derivative from *apere* (s *ap*-), to bind. L *copula* has derivative *copulāre*, to bind (together), to unite, with pp *copulātus*, whence 'to *copulate*'. On the pps *copulāt*- arise *copulātiō*, o/s *copulātiōn*-, whence, perh via MF-F, the E *copulation*, and the LL adj *copulātiuus*, ML *-ivus*, whence *copulative*, and syn LL *copulatōrius*, whence *copulatory*.

2. L *copula* becomes OF-F *couple* (OF-MF varr *cople, cuple*), adopted by E, soon with predominant sense 'two linked persons'; 'to *couple*' derives from OF-F *coupler* (OF-MF varr *copler, cupler*), itself from L *copulāre*. OF-F *couple* has the MF-F dim *couplet*, adopted by E, esp in versification.

**copy** (n and v); **copious; copyist; copyright.**

1. *Copyright* is the exclusive right to copy; *copyist* merely attaches the agential *-ist* to the v *copy*; 'to *copy*' derives, via MF-F *copier*, from ML *cōpiāre*, from ML *cōpia*, a transcript, from L *cōpia*, abundant supply, (large) number: *co*-, together+*\*opia*, from *ops* (gen *opis*), abundance, hence power, wealth, akin to Skt *apnas*, property,

and—clearly operative—L *opus*, work (cf OPERATE). ML *cōpia* becomes OF-F *copie*, whence the E n *copy*; and the L adj *cōpiōsus*, abundant, becomes E *copious*.

2. L *ops* has adj *opulentus* (for the suffix cf fraud*ulentus*: E & M), abundant, rich, whence MF-F, hence E, *opulent*; derivative L *opulentia* yields EF-F and E *opulence*.

**coquet, coquetry, coquette.** See 1st COCK, para 1.

**coracle**: W *corwgl*, coracle, mdfn of *corwg*, trunk, anything round, e.g. a coracle: akin to EIr (and Ga) *curach*, coracle: OC *\*kuruko*- (MacLennan).

**coral, coralline.**

The adj derives from LL *corallīnus*, coral-pink, from *corallum*, var *coralium*, from Gr *korallion*, perh of Sem origin—cf the H *gōrāl*, pebble; L *corallum* becomes OF-EF *coral* (EF-F *corail*), adopted by E.

**corbel; cormorant.** The Arch *corbel*, orig a raven, comes from F: dim (*-el*) of OF *corb*, raven, from ML *corvus*, L *coruus*, prob echoic. L *coruus* (ML *corvus*) *marīnus*, raven of the sea, becomes OF *cormareng* (for *corb marenc*), whence F *cormoran* and E *cormorant*.

**cord,** thin rope or stout string, hence 'to **cord**'; syn **chord; cordon,** n hence v; **corduroy.**

1. *Chord*, cord, derives from L *chorda*, catgut, hence cord, trln of Gr *khordē*, ult akin to YARN. L *chorda* becomes OF *corde*, whence E *cord*; OF-F *corde* has the OF-F aug *cordon*, ornamental cord.

2. Perh from F *\*corde de roi*, king's cord, derives E *corduroy*, which may, however, be a contr of the earlier fabric *colourderoy* (F *couleur de roi*, king's colour), 'the purple'—but in mid C17, a bright tawny. (EW.)

**cordial** (adj hence n), whence **cordiality; misericord;** sep **accord, concord, discord, record; cardiac;** sep **core** (of fruit); **courage, courageous**—**discourage, discouragement,** and **encourage, encouragement;** ult akin to HEART (f.a.e.); cf Hit *karza*, illuminatingly peripheral to Gr *kardia* and to E *heart*.

1. L *cor*, heart, gen *cordis*, has ML adj *cordiālis*, of the heart, intimate, whence, perh via MF-F, the E *cordial*; *cordiality* prob derives from the late MF-F *cordialité*, itself either from MF-F *cordial* or from ML *cordiālitās*, o/s *cordiālitāt*-.

2. The cpd *misericordia* derives, via OF-F *miséricorde*, from the L cpd *misericordia*, compassion: from *misericors*, o/s *misericord*-: *misereri*, to feel pity (from *miser*, wretched)+*cord*-, o/s of *cor*, heart+abstract suffix *-ia*.

3. Intimately akin to L *cor*, o/s *cord*-, is Gr *kardia* (f.a.e., HEART), which has adj *kardiakos*, whence L *cardiacus*, whence, perh via MF-F *cardiaque*, the E *cardiac*.

4. L *cor* becomes OF-MF *cuer*, whence *curage*, var *corage*, whence ME *corage*, whence E *courage*, whence the adj *courageous*—cf the OF-MF *corajus*, F *courageux*, f *courageuse*.

5. OF-MF *corage* has derivatives MF *descoragier*, whence 'to *discourage*', with subsidiary MF

*desco(u)ragement*, whence E *discouragement*; and
MF *enco(u)rager*, whence 'to *encourage*', with subsidiary MF *enco(u)ragement*, whence E *encouragement*.

**cordite**: by Chem *-ite*, after dynam*ite*: from
CORD.

**cordon**. See CORD, para 1, s.f.

**corduroy**. See CORD, para 2.

**cordwainer**: ME *cordwainer*: MF *cordoanier*,
worker (*-ier*) in *cordoan*, Cordovan leather: OProv
*cordoan*, a re-shaping of Sp *cordobán*, n from Ar
adj-become-n *cortobanī*, 'of Cordoba'; it was the
Arabs who founded the leather industry of
Cordoba. (B & W.)

**core** (of fruit), whence 'to *core*': ME *core*:
prob from L *cor*, heart; cf CORDIAL and, f.a.e.,
HEART.

**Corinthian**. See CURRANT.

**cork**, n hence v: Sp *alcorque*: Ar *al*, the, *corque*,
cork-oak, prob from L *quercus*, oak, akin to FIR.

**cormorant**. See CORBEL.

**corn** (1), grain: OE *corn*, akin to OFris, OHG,
OS, ON *korn* and Go *kaúrn*, and to L *grānum* (cf
Olr *grān*); Gmc r, *\*kurna-*; general European r,
perh *\*gran-*; IE r, perh *\*grnom-* (Walshe). Cf
GRAIN.—For *corncrake*, see CROAK, para 2.

**corn** (2), on foot. See HORN, para 2.

**cornea**, **corneous**. See HORN, para 2.

**corner**. See HORN, para 3.

**cornet**. See HORN, para 4.

**cornice**, adopted from EF after being adopted
from It, comes by contr from L *coronis*, trln of Gr
*korōnis*, mdfn of *korōnē*: f.a.e., CROWN.

**cornicle**. See HORN, para 4.

**Cornish**, **Cornwall**. The adj=*Corn*wall+*-ish*;
the n derives from OE *Cornweallas*, the Headland
Welsh: C *corn* (akin to L *cornu*, horn), a horn, a
headland; cf WALES, WELSH. The Cor name is
*Cerneu* or *Cernow* (or *K—*), cf the Br *Kerneu*, (the)
Headland.

**cornucopia**. See HORN, para 5.

**cornute**. See HORN, para 5.

**corolla**, **corollary**; **corona**, **coronal** (adj hence n);
**coronary**; **coronated**, **coronation**; **coroner**; **coronet**;
**crown**, n and v.

1. The pedestal is L *corōna*, a crown; the foundation, Gr *korōnē*, a circle or ring, s *korōn-*,
prob from *korōnos*, curved; with r *korō-*, cf the
*curu-* of L *curuus* (ML *curvus*), curved; basic idea,
to curve.

2. L *corōna* has adjj *corōnālis*, whence E *coronal*,
and *corōnārius*, whence *coronary*; and dim *corolla*,
adopted by E, with adj *\*corollārius*, whence the n
*corollārium*, whence the E *corollary*; and derivative
v *corōnāre*, with pp *corōnātus*, whence the rare 'to
*coronate*', surviving mostly in the Bot and Zoo pa
*coronated*; on *corōnāt-*, s of *corōnātus*, arises LL
*corōnātiō*, o/s *corōnātiōn-*, whence, perh via MF-
EF, the E *coronation*.

3. L *corōna* becomes OF-MF *corone*, whence the
AF agent *coroneor*, *coronere*, adapted by E: a
*coroner* represents the Crown. The rural *crowner*
is a dial alteration. OF-MF *corone* has MF-EF dim

*coronete*, whence E *coronet*, a little crown: cf the
suffix *-et*.

4. OF-MF *corone*, var *corune* (cf the F *couronne*),
becomes ME *corune*, later *croun*, whence *crown*;
'to *crown*', ME *crounen*, earlier *corunen*, derives
from OF-MF *coroner*, from L *corōnāre*.

**coronation**. See prec, para 2, s.f.

**coroner**. See COROLLA, para 3.

**coronet**. See COROLLA, para 3.

**corporal**, adj and n; **corporate** (adj, rare v)—
**corporation**—**corporative**, and **incorporate** (adj, v),
**incorporation**, **incorporator**; **corporeal** (whence **corporeality**) and **incorporeal**, and **corporeity**; **corps**,
**corpse**; **corpulence**, **corpulent**; **corpus**; **corpuscle**,
**corpuscular**; **corsage**; **corse**; **corselet** or **corslet**;
**corset**.

1. The effective origin, the L *corpus* (adopted by
E for 'body of a man's work'), has s and r *corp-*,
with IE r *\*korp-*, with potent var *\*kerp-*: cf the Av
*kehrpem*, form, body, and perh the OP *kērmens*,
body. (E & M.)

2. L *corpus* has o/s *corpor-*, on which arises
*corpōrālis*, of the body, whence, prob via OF
*corporal*, the E adj *corporal*. The Eccl n *corporal* (a
Communion cloth) derives from ML *corporāle*,
prop the neu of *corpōrālis*; but the Army *corporal*,
although form-influenced by the E adj, represents
EF *corporal*, a f/e var of EF-F *caporal*, from It
*caporale*, from *capo*, a chief, orig the head, from L
*caput* (f.a.e., CHIEF).

3. Also on the L o/s *corpor-* arise:
*corporāre*, orig to slay, then to furnish a body
and, in passive, to take bodily shape, with pp
*corporātus*, whence the E adj *corporate* and the
rare v 'to *corporate*';

LL *corporātiō* (*corporāt*us+suffix *-iō*), incorporation, o/s *corporātiōn-*, whence E *corporation*;

LL *corporātiuus* (*-iuus*, ML *-ivus*, E *-ive*), whence,
E *corporative*;

L *corporeus*, whence the ML *corporeitās*, o/s
*corporeitāt-*, whence E *corporeity*; *corporeal*, however, derives from LL *corporeālis*.

4. *Incorporeal* derives from L *incorporeus*, influenced by LL *incorporālis*;

*incorporate*, adj and v, derives from LL *in-
corporātus*, pp of *incorporāre*, to incarnate—an int
of *corporāre* in its passive sense;

*incorporation* derives from LL *incorporātiō*, o/s
*incorporātiōn-*;

*incorporative* and *incorporator* are E formations.

5. On the r *corp-* arise:
LL *corpulentus*, well-bodied, hence stout, whence,
prob via late MF-F, the E *corpulent*;

its LL derivative *corpulentia*, LL bodily nature,
ML stoutness, becomes E *corpulency* and, via
MF-F, *corpulence*;

*corpusculum*, lit 'little body', therefore a dim of
*corpus*, whence the E *corpuscle*, with adj *corpuscular*, perh from F *corpusculaire*.

6. Imm from F, come:
OF-F *corsage*, a woman's bust, later the waist of
a woman's dress, last a flower, or a bouquet, worn

at waist or, as now, on bust, from OF-MF *cors*,
body+suffix *-age*;

corslet, earlier *corselet*, adopted from OF-F
*corselet*, dim (*elet*) of Of *cors*;

corset, a MF-F dim (*-et*) of *cors*: orig, surcoat,
basque, bodice, etc.

7. Also from F, come:
corse, archaic spelling of *corpse*: OF-MF *cors*;
corpse: ME *corps*, earlier *cors*, adopted from
OF-MF: from L *corpus*;
corps, adopted from F, with a sense-differentiation present already in Classical L: EF-F *corps*,
earlier *cors*, as above.

corps. See prec, para 7.

corpse. See CORPORAL, para 7.

corpulence, corpulent. See CORPORAL, para 5.

corpus. See CORPORAL, para 1.

corpuscle, corpuscular. See CORPORAL, para 5,
s.f.

corral: Sp *corral*, a yard, esp for cattle, from
*corro*, a ring, from *correr*, to run: L *currere*: f.a.e.,
COURSE. The Port *curral*, cattle pen, becomes D
*kraal*, enclosure, village in S Afr, a native village.

correct (whence correctness), correction (adj
correctional), correctitude, corrective, corrector. See
REX, para 27.

correlate, correlation, correlative. See RELATE,
para 2.

correption. See RAPT, para 11.

correspond, whence the pa corresponding; correspondence, correspondent (adj hence n).

'To *correspond*' derives from ML *correspondēre*:
*cor-*, for *con-*, used int+*re*+*spondēre*, to engage
oneself to (do something): cf RESPOND. The
ML pp *correspondens*, o/s *correspondent-*, yields E
correspondent, whence *correspondence* (cf the
MF-F *correspondance*).

corridor, adopted from EF-F: OIt *corridore*,
from *correr*, to run: L *currere*: f.a.e., COURSE.

corrigible. See REX, para 27.

corrival. See RIVER, para 10.

corroborate, corroboration, corroborative, corro-
borator, corroboratory; corroborant. See ROBUST,
para 5.

corroboree is adopted from the Aus aborigines.

corrode, corrodent; corrosible, corrosion, corrosive. See RAT, para 3.

corrugate, whence the pa corrugated; corrugation. See RAG, para 4, s.f.

corrupt, corruptible, corruption. See RUPTURE,
para 4.

corsage. See CORPORAL, para 6.

corsair: MF-F *corsaire*, earlier *corsar*: OProv
*corsari*: It *corsaro*: ML *cursārius*, adj become n:
L *currere*, to run: f.a.e., COURSE. (B & W.)

corse. See CORPORAL, para 7.

corset. See CORPORAL, para 6.

corslet. See CORPORAL, para 6.

cortege. See COURT, para 3.

cortex, cortical.

The adj *cortical* merely tacks *-al* to *cortic-*, o/s
of L *cortex*, bark, akin to Sl *kora*, bark, and perh
to L *corium*, leather; IE r, perh *ker-*, var *kor-*, to

cut, bark being easily cut—or separable—from the
trunk. Cf CUIRASS.

corundum: Tamil *kurundam*, from Skt *kuruvinda*,
a ruby—a red, crystallized form of corundum.

coruscate, coruscation. L *coruscāre* (orig, prob
echoic), to sparkle, has pp *coruscātus*, whence 'to
*coruscate*'; derivative LL *coruscātiō*, o/s *coruscā-
tiōn-*, becomes E *coruscation*.

corvée. See ROGATION, para 5.

cosh, n hence v: akin to, indeed prob from,
QUASH, to shatter, to crush.

cosher. See KOSHER.

cosine. See SINE, para 1.

cosmetic, adj hence n (usu, pl cosmetics). See:

cosmic, occ elaborated to cosmical (*-al*, adj);
cosmos—cf the element *cosmo-*, as in *cosmology*
and esp in cosmopolite (*-itan*) and cosmopolis;
macrocosm and microcosm;—cosmetic, adj, whence
n.

1. For the *cosmo-* cpds, see the element *cosmo-*;
for *cosmopolis*, *cosmopolitan*, etc., see POLICE,
para 6.

2. The source of all these terms, the Gr *kosmos*
(prob for *\*konsmos*), order of harmony, hence the
world, has s *kosm-*, perh akin to L *censēre*, s *cens-*,
to think, to order, the IE r being *\*kens-*, var
*\*kons-*, to speak or announce authoritatively
(Boisacq).

3. Gr *kosmos* has adj *kosmikos*, whence L
*cosmicus*, whence E *cosmic*.

4. The Gr s *kosm-* recurs, in its L form *cosm*(os),
in *macrocosm* and *microcosm*: MF-F *macrocosme*,
as opp MF-F *microcosme*: Gr *makros*, long, big,
and *mikros*, small: the latter, LL *microcosmus*, Gr
*mikros kosmos*.

5. Derivative Gr *kosmētikos* (from the 'order,
harmony' sense of *kosmos*), skilled in adorning,
yields EF-F *cosmétique* and E *cosmetic*, whence the
n use, esp in *cosmetics*.

Cossack: Ru *kozak*, var *kazak*: Tu *quzaq*
(*kazák*), var *quzāq*, an adventurer. Cf the EF-F
*Cosaque*.

cosset, v, derives from *cosset*, a pet lamb: ? OE
*cotsǣta*, cottager, lit a 'cot (cottage) sitter'—cf
SIT.

cost, n and v; costly. See STAND, para 22.

costal. See COAST, para 2.

costard. See COAST, para 4.

costermonger. See COAST, para 4.

costive, whence costiveness (*-ness*): MF *costivé*,
*costevé* (orig, pp): L *constipātus*, constipated, orig
the pp of *constipāre*, to cram: *con-*, together+
*stipāre*, to press: *stipāre* (s *stip-*) is akin to Gr
*stiphros*, crammed (together), compact, and OE
*stīf* (see STIFF).

costly. See COST.

costume, n hence v; costumier.

The latter, adopted from F, derives from the F
v *costumer*, itself from F *costume*, C19–20, a suit of
clothes, a dress, earlier 'truth of usage, clothes,
etc., reproduced in works of art' (B & W): from It
*costume*, dress, (earlier) custom: LL *\*costūmen*: L
*consuētūdō*, custom, from *consuēscere*, to accustom,

to become accustomed: *con-*, used int+*suēscere*, to become accustomed (to): *suēscere* (s *suēsc-*) is orig the inch of a Lucretian *suere* (s *su-*), itself from *sui*, of or for oneself—cf SUICIDE.

**cosy.** See COZY.

**cot** and **cote; cottage, cottager; cotter** or **cottar** —**cottier;**—**coterie.**

1. *Cote*, cottage, hence as in *dovecote*, is a var of the syn *cot*, ME *cot* or *cote*, OE *cot* or *cote*, hut, akin to MD *kote*, LG *Kot* or *Kote*, ON *kot*, hut (ML *cota, cotta*: from OE or ME); perh of C origin (? *\*cut*, to hide, to cover, with var *\*cot*) —cf EIr *coite*, Ga *coit*, W *cwt*, hut, cottage, and, basically, Br *kut*, hide-and-seek, *kuza*, to hide, MBr *cud*ennec, obscure, and Cor *cudhe*, to hide, and *cüth*, hidden, secret; Malvezin adduces an OF (and F dial) *cute*, dark place, hut, and proposes kinship with Gr *keuthein*, to hide, which is akin to Skt *kuharam*, a hole, and has IE r *\*keu-* (*\*ku-*).

2. *Cottar* or *cotter*, influenced by Ga *coitear*, derives app from ML *cottārius* or *cotārius*, var *coterius*, from *cota, cotta* (para 1). *Cottier*, now only hist, adapts MF *cotier*, from OF *\*cote*, hut, deduced from the OF-MF syn *cotin*, itself from OE *cot*.

3. *Cottage*, ME *cotage*, rather adds suffix *-age* to ME *cot* than comes from AF *cotage* (from OF *\*cote*)—note that ML *cotāgium*, pl *cotāgia*, antedates ME *cotage*; agential *-er* attached to *cottage* accounts for *cottager*.

4. OF *\*cote* has derivative MF-EF adj *cotier*, whence (f *-erie*, E *-ery*) *coterie*, in C14–16 an 'association of peasants holding in common the lands of a lord' (B & W), hence, mid C17 onwards, a set or circle of persons.

**cotillon,** AE **cotillion**: elliptical for F *danse avec le cotillon*: late MF-F *cotillon*, petticoat, dim of *cote*, OF-EF var of OF-F *cotte*, tunic, here in sense 'woman's dress or robe': f.a.e., COAT.

**cottage, cottager.** See COT, para 3.

**cottar, cotter; cottier.** See COT, para 2.

**cotton**—n hence adjj **cotton** and **(-y) cottony** and 'to cotton'—derives from ME *coton*, adopted from OF-F, which takes it from Sp *cotón*, a re-shaping of Ar *quṭun*, var *quṭn*, cotton. Cf Eg '*khet en* shen', lit '*khet* or plant [usu, tree, shrub]+*en* or of+ *\*shen* or hair', the 'hair plant' being prob the shrub that is the cotton plant: cf Eg *shenti*, (?) a hairy plant, and Eg *shent*, cloth, tunic, prob both of cotton. The A *cottontail*, wood rabbit, has a tail with white-tufted under side, and the A *cottonwood* a cottony hair-tuft investing the seeds (Webster).

**couch** (grass). See VIVA, para 8.

**couch** (2), a form of bed, and 'to couch'; **couchant; accouchement, accoucheur.**

*Accoucheur*, f *accoucheuse*, obstetrician, f midwife, adopted from EF-F, derive from OF-F *accoucher*, orig to put to bed, then go to bed: *a*, for *à*, to (L *ad*)+*coucher*; *accoucher* has also the OF-F derivative *accouchement*, a delivery, partly adopted by E. OF-F *coucher* derives from L 'se *collocāre*', to put oneself to bed, from *collocāre*, to

put to bed, orig to place firmly, an int (*con-*) of *locāre*, to place: f.a.e., LOCAL. *Coucher* has presp *couchant* and pp *couché*, both occurring in E Her; it has the OF-F derivative n *couche*, a person's horizontal outstretching, then the place one does this: whence E *couch*. 'To *couch*' derives from OF-F 'se *coucher*', to go to bed.

**cough,** v hence n: ME *coughen* or *coghen*, intimately related to OE *cohhetan*, to cough, app an int of *\*cohhan*, to gasp—cf MHG *kūchen*, to breathe, to blow, G *keuchen*, to gasp or pant, MHG *kīchen*, to breathe heavily, MD *cochen*, var *cuchen*, D *kuchen*, to cough: clearly echoic.

**could.** See CAN, para 1.

**coulter.** See COLTER.

**council, councillor** (AE **councilor**).

The latter derives by agential *-or* from the former; prob with influence from *counsellor* (see next entry). A *council* derives from ME *counceil*, adapted from OF-MF *cuncile*, var *concile*, themselves from L *concilium*, a calling together, hence an assembly, esp if deliberative: *con-*, together+ *calāre*, to call, summon; cf the formation of:

**counsel,** n and v; **counsellor** (AE **counselor**).

The 2nd derives, through ME *counseiller* and OF-MF *conseillier*, from L *consiliārius*, ? from *consiliāri*, to deliberate, give counsel, itself from *consilium*, a place of deliberation or counsel, hence the deliberation or counsel, akin to—indeed, prob from—*consulere*, to gather for deliberation, to consult (an assembly), to deliberate: *con-*, together +the r of a simple v app lost, but perh akin to L *censēre*, to be of the opinion, to state or give an opinion. L *consiliāri* becomes OF-F *conseiller*, whence ME *conseillen*, whence, influenced by the ME n, 'to *counsel*'; and L *consilium* becomes OF-MF *cunseil*, OF-F *conseil*, whence ME *counseil* (var *conseil*), whence E *counsel*. There has been some confusion between this and the prec word.

**count** (1), a nobleman; **county; concomitant; viscount.**

1. All stem from L *comes*, a companion, orig on the march: contr of *\*comites*: *com-*, with+*it-*, from the supine s (*it-*) of *īre*, to go+*-es*, agential suffix. *Comes* has o/s *comit-*.

2. From the acc *comitem* derives the OF-MF *conte* (F *comte*) or *cunte*, whence E *count*; derivative OF-MF *contesse* yields *countess*; derivative OF-MF *conté* or *cunté* yields E *county*, orig the estate of a count or an earl; the territorial division *county* has been influenced by L *comitātus*, orig a body of well-born men, hence their status, their (district, etc., of) authority, a *comes* having, in C4, become a personage employed at court— a companion to the Emperor.

3. L *comes* has the ML cpd *vicecomes*, whence OF-MF *visconte* (F *vicomte*), whence ME *vicounte*, whence E *viscount*, whence *viscountess* (cf F *vicomtesse*)—with OF *vis-* restored (silent *s*).

4. *Comes*, o/s *comit-*, has derivative v *comitāre*, to accompany, with cpd *concomitāre* (*con-* used int); the presp *concomitans* has o/s *concomitant-*, whence the E adj, hence n, *concomitant*; the

derivative ML *concomitantia* yields *concomitance*.

**count** (2), n and v, enumeration, to compute; **counter** (token), **countless**; **account** (n and v), **accountant**, **accountancy**; **recount**, **recountal**;— **putation**, **putative**; **amputate**, **amputation**; **compute**, **computation**, **computative**; **depute**, **deputation**, **deputy**; **dispute**, **disputant**, **disputation**, **disputatious**; **impute**, **imputable**, **imputation**, **imputative**; **repute**, **reputable**, **reputation**.

1. The base is L *putāre*, (*a*) to prune, (*b*) to purify, to correct (an account)—hence, to count or calculate: perhaps there were two separate rr, with the latter (to purify, esp to count) deriving from the L *putus*, pure, esp (of money) unalloyed: prob akin to Skt *pūtás*, purified. (E & M.) Cf PAVE, para 1.

2. *Putāre*, to reckon, has pp *putātus*, s *putāt-*, whence *putātiō*, o/s *putātiōn-*, whence E *putation*, a supposing; whence also LL *putātīuus*, ML *putātīvus*, whence *putative*, supposed or reputed.

3. *Putāre* has the following cpds relevant to E: *amputāre*, to prune (or cut) around (*am-* for *ambi-*, on both sides), pp *amputātus*, whence 'to *amputate*'; derivative *amputātiō*, o/s *amputātiōn-*, yields *amputation*, perh imm from EF-F; *amputative* is an E formation in *-ive*; *computāre*, to count (int *con-*), whence 'to *compute*'; on *computāt-*, s of pp *computātus*, arise *computābilis*, whence *computable*—*computātiō*, o/s *computātiōn-*, whence *computation*—and *computātor*, adopted by E; *computative* is an E formation; *dēputāre*, to cut downwards (*dē-*), to esteem, LL to allot; whence 'to *depute*', perh via MF-F *députer*, pp *député*, whence E *deputy*, whence (!) 'to *deputize*'; LL *dēputātiō*, o/s *dēputātiōn-*, yields MF-F *députation* and *deputation*; LL *dēputātīuus*, ML *-īvus*, yields *deputative*; *disputāre*, to think about contentiously, becomes OF-MF *des-* and MF-F *disputer*, whence ME *des-* or *disputen*, whence 'to *dispute*', whence 'a *dispute*' (cf EF-F *dispute*); on *disputāt-*, s of pp *disputātus*, arise *disputātiō*, o/s *disputātiōn-*, whence *disputation*—LL *disputātīuus*, ML *-īvus*, whence *disputative*—LL *disputātor*, adopted by E; *disputatious*, however, derives from *disputation*; *disputant* derives from L *disputant-*, o/s of presp *disputans*; *imputāre*, to put into (*im-* for *in-*) the reckoning, hence to charge or impute, becomes OF *emputer*, MF-F *imputer*, whence 'to *impute*'; derivative ML *imputābilis* yields *imputable*—LL *imputātiō*, o/s *imputātiōn-*, yields, prob via late MF-F, *imputation* —LL *imputātīuus*, ML *-īvus*, *imputative*; *reputāre*, to reckon or examine accounts again and again, to think over, LL to credit to, whence MF-F *réputer*, whence 'to *repute*', whence both *repute*, n, and *reputed*, pa, and—perh via MF—*reputable*; derivative LL *reputātiō*, o/s *reputātiōn-*, yields—prob via late MF-F *réputation*—*reputation*.

4. L *computāre* has, via F, important issue in E, thus: 'to *count*', ME *counten*, a 'blend' of OF-MF *cunter* and *conter*, L *computāre*; *count*, a reckoning, ME *counte*, OF-MF *cunte* and *conte*, LL *computus*

(gen *-ūs*), a reckoning, from *computāre*; *countable*. OF-MF *cuntable*, *contable*, from *cunter*, *conter*; *counter*, a reckoning device, ME *contour*, OF-MF *cuntouer*, *contouer*, ML *computātōrium*, counting-house. *Countless* derives from *count*, n.

5. An *account*, deriving from ME *acount*, earlier *acunt*, *acont*, comes from OF-MF *acunter*, *aconter* (*a*, F *à*, to+*cunter*, *conter*), whence ME *acounten*, E 'to *account*', whence *accountable*; *accountancy* derives, by *-cy*, from *accountant*, OF-MF *acuntant*, *acontant*, presp of *acunter*, *aconter*.

6. A *re-count* (*recount*) derives from 'to *re-count*' (*recount*)', count again, orig identical with 'to *recount*', to relate, OF-MF *reconter* (*re-*, again+ *conter*, as in para 4), whence F *raconter*, to relate, and *recompter*, to count again: cf the differentiation of OF-MF *conter*, to count, to tell, into F *conter*, to tell, and F *compter*, to count; *recountal*= *recount*, v+the n suffix *-al*.

**countable**. See 2nd COUNT, para 4.

**countenance**, n, v. See CONTAIN, para 3.

**counter** (1), adv hence adj: F *contre*: L *contra*, against.

**counter** (2), a reckoning device. See 2nd COUNT, para 4. The 'shop *counter*' (display table) derives from the board, hence the table, on which money is counted. *Counter*, the opposite, an effectual reply, derives from **counter** (1).

**counter** (3), v: partly from **counter** (1), esp as used in cpds, and partly from **encounter**.

**counterfeit**, adj, hence n and v: a 'blend' of OF-MF *contrefet* and MF-F *contrefait*, orig pp of *contrefaire*, to counterfeit, lit to make against the law: cf the 1st COUNTER and OF-F *faire*, to make, from L *facere*, q.v. at FACT.

**countermand**, n, derives either from F *contremande* (from the F v) or from 'to *countermand*', itself from OF-F *contremander*: *contre* (L *contra*, against)+*mander*, L *mandāre*, to command (cf COMMAND).

**countermine**: *counter* (1)+MINE, v.

**counterpane** is a blend of the obs *counter*point, coverlet (MF-EF *contrepointe*), and *pane*, coverlet (see PANE).

**counterpart**: 1st COUNTER+PART.

**counterpoint**. See PUNGENT, para 23.

**counterpoise**, n, v. See PEND, para 9.

**counterscarp**. See SCARP, s.f.

**countersign**, n, comes from EF *contresigne*, from the source of 'to *countersign*': EF-F *contresigner*, a cpd of *signer*: f.a.e., SIGN.

**countervail**. See VALUE, para 14.

**countess**. See 1st COUNT, para 2.

**countless**. See 2nd COUNT, para 4, s.f.

**country** (whence **countrified**): ME *cuntree* or *contree* (or *contre*): OF-F *contrée*: ML *contrāta*, elliptical for *contrāta regiō* or *c. terra*, region or land set over against (*contra*) another, hence distinct from it.

**county**. See 1st COUNT, para 2.

**coup**. See the 2nd COPE.

**couple**. See COPULA, para 2.

**couplet**. See COPULA, para 2, s.f.

**coupon**, adopted from OF-F, derives from OF-F *couper*, to cut: f.a.e., COPPICE.

**courage, courageous.** See CORDIAL, para 4.

**courier.** See para 5 of:

**course**, n hence v (whence **courser**, influenced by OF-F *coursier*); **concourse, discourse, recourse; courier; cursive; cursory; current** (adj and n), **currency; curricle, curriculum;** sep **corral** (incl **kraal**)—**corridor**—**corsair**—and **coarse; hussar; scour**, to run.—Cpds in the L mode: **concurrence, concurrent, concursus; decurrent, decursive; discursion, discursive, discursus; excurrent, excursion (excursionist), excursive, excursus; incur, incurrent** (whence **incurrence**), **incursion; occur, occurrence, occurrent; precurrent, precursal, precursive, precursor, precursory; procurrent, procursive; recur, recurrent** (whence **recurrence**), **recursion, recursive; succour** (AE **succor**), **succo(u)rer, succursal** (adj and n); **transcurrent.**

1. A *course* derives from F *cours* (OF-MF *curs*, *cors*), course of, e.g., streams or stars, itself from L *cursus* (gen -*ūs*), a running, a place for running, from *curs-*, s of *cursus*, pp of *currere* (v *cur-*), to run, with influence from MF-F *course*, a running, a race, itself from It *corsa*, from It *correre*, to run, from L *currere*, which is of C and Gmc stock: cf the C CAR and the Gmc HORSE; IE r perh *\*khar-*, with varr *\*khor-*, *\*khur-*.

2. *Concourse*: MF-F *concours*: L *concursus*, from *concurrere*, to run together (*con-*).

3. *Discourse*, v, derives from *discourse*, n: EF-F *discours*: L *discursus*, from *discurrere*, to discourse, lit to run to and fro (*dis-*, separative).

4. *Recourse:* MF-F *recours*: L *recursus*, from *recurrere*, to run back (*re-*).

5. *Courier:* MF-F *courrier*: It *corriere*, from *correre*, to run, from L *currere*.

6. L *currere* has the folllowing simple derivatives (from *curs-*, s of pp *cursus*) relevant to E:

ML adj *cursīvus*, running, flowing, whence *cursive*;

L *cursor*, runner, adopted by E Math;

L *cursōrius*, whence *cursory*.

7. *Currere* has presp *currens*, o/s *current-*, whence, prob partly via OF-MF, the adj *current*; the n *current* derives perh from the E adj *current*, but prob from the OF presp-become-n *curant* (or *corant*), from OF *corre*, to run, from L *currere*; derivative ML *currentia* yields *currency*.

8. L *currere* has derivative *currus* (gen -*ūs*), car, with dim *curriculum*, a chariot, a racecourse, a race, a running, hence a general course, adopted by E; its LL adj *curriculāris*, of a carriage, becomes E *curricular*, of a course; and the 'carriage' sense of *curriculum* becomes E *curricle*, a two-wheeled chaise.

9. The E *hussar* derives from Hung *huszár*, freebooter, from Serbian *husar*, *huzar*, from Byz Gr *koursōrios*, adj-become-n from *koursōr*, a skirmisher, from L *cursor*, runner; ML *cursārius*, pirate (cf CORSAIR), has prob intervened.

10. The L cpds of *currere*, to run, appear in easily recognizable dress in the remaining E words:

*concurrere*, to run together, has presp *concurrens*, o/s *concurrent-*, whence *concurrent*; derivative *concurrentia* yields *concurrence*; on *concurs-*, s of the pp *concursus*, arise *concursiō*, o/s *concursiōn-*, whence *concursion*, and *concursus* (gen -*ūs*), adopted by E;

*dēcurrere*, to descend at a run, to run down, has presp *dēcurrens*, o/s *dēcurrent-*, whence *decurrent*; *decursive* is an E formation upon the pp *dēcursus*;

*discurrere*, to run to and fro, has pp *discursus*, s *discurs-*, on which arise *discursiō*, o/s *discursiōn-*, whence *discursion*—ML *discursīvus*, whence *discursive*—*discursus* (gen -*ūs*), adopted by learnèd E;

*excurrere*, to run out, has presp *excurrens*, o/s *excurrent-*, whence *excurrent*, and pp *excursus*, s *excurs-*, whence LL *excursiō*, o/s *excursiōn-*, whence *excursion* (whence *excursionist*: -*ist*)—and *excursus* (gen -*ūs*), adopted by learnèd E; *excursive* is an E formation;

*incurrere*, to run onto or against, whence 'to *incur*', has presp *incurrens*, o/s *incurrent-*, whence *incurrent*, and pp *incursus*, s *incurs-*, whence *incursiō*, o/s *incursiōn-*, whence *incursion*; *incursive* is an E formation;

*occurrere*, to run in front of, present oneself to, whence 'to *occur*', has presp *occurrens*, o/s *occurrent-*, whence *occurrent*; derivative ML *occurrentia* yields *occurrence*;

*percurrere*, to run through, has presp *percurrens*, o/s *percurrent-*, whence the adj *percurrent*;

*praecurrere*, to run ahead, to precede, has presp *praecurrens*, o/s -*current-*, whence *precurrent-*, and pp *praecursus*, o/s *praecurs-*, whence *praecursor*, forerunner, anglicized as *precursor*, with adjj *precursal*, *precursive*, *precursory* (L *praecursōrius*);

*prōcurrere*, to run forward, has presp *prōcurrens*, whence *procurrent*; *procursive* is an E formation;

*recurrere*, to return at the run, to run back, also to run again, whence 'to *recur*', has presp *recurrens*, o/s *recurrent-*, whence *recurrent*, whence (after *occurrence*) *recurrence*, and pp *recursus*, s *recurs-*, whence *recursiō*, o/s *recursiōn-*, whence *recursion*; *recursive* is an E formation;

*succurrere*, to run under or towards, hence run to the help of, whence OF-MF *sucurre* or *soucourre*, ME *socouren*, E 'to *succo(u)r*'; the n *succo(u)r* comes, via ME or OF-MF from ML *succursus* (gen -*ūs*), built on *succurs-*, s of the pp *succursus*, as in the late EF-F adj *succursal*, auxiliary, adopted by E, along with derivative n *succursal* or *succursale*, auxiliary institution, a branch (of business);

*transcurrere*, to run across or beyond, has presp *transcurrens*, o/s *transcurrent-*, whence the adj *transcurrent*.

11. 'To *scour*' or run swiftly or rovingly, app simple is prob cpd, for it seems to come, by aphesis, from OF-EF *escourre*, var of *escorre*, to run forth, from L *excurrere* (as in prec para).

**court**, n (whence **courtly**) and adj and v; **courteous; courtesan; courtesy, curtsy** (n hence v), **courtier; curtain.**

1. A *court* or area enclosed by buildings, hence all the other senses, derives from ME *court*, *curt*,

*cort*, from the same forms in OF, *cort* being the clearest derivative from L *cort-*, o/s of *cors*, a contr of *cohors*, o/s *cohort-*: *co-*, for *con-*, with+ s and r id with those of *hortus*, a garden: f.a.e., HORTICULTURE. 'To *court*' has perh been influenced by F *courtiser*.

2. *Courteous* derives through ME *courteous*, rare var of *corteis*, from OF-MF *corteis, curteis*, adj of *cort, curt*, court; *courtesan* from F *courtisane*, a court mistress, f of late MF-F *courtisan*, a courtier, from It *cortigiano*, orig the adj of *corte*, court, from the L word; *courtesy*, through ME, from OF-MF *curteisie, cortoisie*, etc., from the adj *curteis*, etc.; *curtsy* (or *-cy*), contr of *curtesy*, var of *courtesy*. *Courtier* derives from *court*: by agential *-ier*.

3. It *corte*, court, has a derivative *corteggio*, whence EF-F *cortège*, whence E *cortege*.

4. On *cort-*, o/s of *cors* (as in para 1), arises the LL *cortīna*, which, orig a cauldron, takes the sense 'curtain' under the influence of L *aulaeum* or *aulaea* (Gr *aulaia*, from *aulē*, court), a tapestry, hence a curtain, tapestries being characteristic of courts; ? at first, a tapestried screen in front of a fire. LL *cortīna*, occ var *curtīna*, becomes OF-MF *cortine, curtine*, ME *cortine, curtin*, E *curtain*:

cousin, cousinage, cousinly, coz.

*Coz* is an EE pet-form of *cousin* (whence *cousinly*: *-ly*, adj); *cousin*, adopted from F *cousin*, OF-MF *cosin* (var *cusin*), derives from ML *cosīnus*, contr of L *consobrīnus*, a mother's sister's child: *con-*, with+*sobrīnus*, f *sobrīna*, hence used as n for male or female cousin on the mother's side, from *soror*, sister, prob for *sosor*: f.a.e., SISTER. *Soror* has ML derivative *sororitās*, whence *sorority*, sisterhood; *sororal*, sisterly, is an E and F formation, balancing *fraternal* (*-nel*). *Cousinage* (*-age*) is adopted from OF-F. Cf COZEN.

couvade. See HIVE, para 6.

cove (1), small inlet. See COBALT, para 2.

cove (2), a fellow: sl: Rom *covo*, that man.

coven. See CONVENE, para 4.

covenant (n, v), covenanter. See CONVENE, para 5, and cf VENUE, para 11.

cover, v hence n and, by suffix *-age* (cf *acreage*), coverage; coverlet; covert (adj and n) and coverture.

1. The last, adopted from OF-MF, derives from OF-MF *covert*, covered, hence hidden—whence both the E n *covert* and the E adj *covert*—orig the pp of *covrir* (F *couvrir*), to cover, E 'to *cover*': L *cooperīre*, int (*co-* for *con-*) of *operīre*, to shut, to cover, to keep hidden. *Operīre*, like its opp *aperīre*, to open, is multifariously explained by E & M and by Walde, both on the basis of an assumed *uerīre*, which must then have a sense it would need an Aquinas to adequately postulate: perhaps *aperīre* is fundamental, its opp *operīre* explicable as *ob*, against+*aperīre*, with *obaperīre* becoming *operīre*.

2. A *coverlet*, ME *covrelyte*, derives from MF *covrelit* (Mod *couvre-lit*), lit and factually bedcover; *lit*, bed, derives from L *lectus*—cf the 2nd LIE, para 13.

3. The cpds *discover, re-cover, uncover* are easy:

ME *discoveren*, OF-MF *descovrir* (F *découvrir*), LL *discooperīre*; *re-*, again+'to *cover*', contrasted with *recover*, get back; *uncover*, *un-*, active 'not'+ 'to *cover*'. *Discoverer* and *discovery*=*discover*+ agent *-er*, *discover* and n *-y*.

covet, covetous.

The latter derives from OF-MF *coveitos*, from OF-MF *coveitier*, whence 'to *covet*': and OF-MF *coveitier* derives from VL *cupidietāre*, from VL *cupidietās*, an alteration of L *cupiditās*, from *cupere*, to desire: cf CUPID. (B & W.)

covey. See HIVE, para 6.

covin. See CONVENE, para 4.

cow, female to 'bull' (cattle): ME *cou*, earlier *cu*: OE *cū*, pl *cȳ*, whence *kyen*, whence *kine*. The OE *cū* is akin to OFris *kū*, OHG *chuo*, MHG *kuo*, G *Kuh*, OS *kō*, MD *couwe*, usu *coe*, D *koe*, and ON *kýr*; to L *bōs*, Gr *bous*; to Skt *gāus*—cf the Lett *guovs*: Gmc r, *kwō-*; IE r, *gwōw-*. (Walshe.) The cpds of *cow* present no difficulty; note *cowslip*, OE *cūslyppe* (lit cow's droppings).

cow (2), to daunt or overawe: ON *kūga*, to oppress.

coward, cowardice, cowardly. See CODA, para 2.

cower. See GYRATE, para 4.

cowl, n hence v: ME *coule, couele*: OE *cuhle, cugele*: L *cuculla*, var of *cucullus*, cap, cape, prob of C origin: C *cucullos*, s *cucul-*, redup from C *cuc-*, to cover: cf Br *kougoul*, Cor *cugol*, cape. (Malzevin and Malzevin[1].)

cowslip. See 1st COW, s.f.; cf SLEEVE, para 4.

cox. Short for COXSWAIN.

coxa. See HEEL, para 2.

coxcomb. See 1st COCK, para 1.

coxswain. See SWAIN, para 2.

coy. See QUIET, para 3.

coyote: ASp *coyote*: Nahuatl *coyotl*.

coz. See COUSIN.

cozen, obsol 'to cheat': EF-F *cousiner*, to cheat, lit to treat as if a cousin: from OF-F *cousin* (cf COUSIN).

cozy, occ cosy, esp as n in 'tea *cosy*': Sc *cozie, cosie*, of Scan origin—cf, perh indeed from, Nor *koselig*, snug, from *kose sig*, to make oneself comfortable. (EW.)

crab apple: cf Sw *krabäpple*: perh from:—

crab, a crustacean: OE *crabba*, akin to ON *krabbi*, LG *krabbe*, G *Krebs*, OHG *chrebiz*, whence MF *crevice* (F *écrevisse*), whence ME *crevis*, whence, by f/e, the E *crayfish*.

2. Hence both *crabbed*, morose, peevish, and *crabby*.

crack, v hence n: ME *cracken, craken*, to crack, crash, break, also to boast: OE *cracian*, to crack, akin to OHG *chrahhōn*, MHG-G *krachen*, to crack or crash; also to Skt *gárjati*, he rustles or rumbles or roars: clearly echoic; cf CRASH.

2. The freq (or dim) of 'to *crack*' is 'to *crackle*', whence *crackling*, adj and n: cf *cracknel*, a brittle biscuit, from MF-F *craquelin*, from MD *crakelinc* (D *krakeling*), from MD *craken* (D *kraken*), to crack.

cracknel. See para 2 of prec.

**cradle.** See CART.

**craft,** whence **craftsman; crafty.** The adj *crafty* derives from OE *craeftig* (adj *-ig*, E *-y*), from OE *craeft*, strength, skill (hence cunning), art: akin to OFris *kraft* or *kreft*, OS *kraft*, OHG-G *kraft*, MD *craft* or *cracht*, D *kracht*, ON *kraftr*, strength, cf ON *kraefr*, strong: perh akin to ON *krefia*, to demand, E CRAVE. (Walshe.)

**crag,** whence **craggy:** C, perh with basic idea 'to hang suspended': cf EIr *crec*; Ir *craig* or, as also in Ga, *creag*; W *craig*, pl *creigiau*; Mx *creg*; Br *karreg*, pl *kerreg*; Cor *clegar*.

**crake.** See CROAK, para 2.

**cram,** v hence n; hence also **crammer:** OE *crammian*, akin to ON *kremja*, to squeeze, and prob to L *gremium* (s *grem-*), an armful (hence the lap), and Skt *grāmas* (s *grām-*), group of persons. Perh cf:

**cramp,** n hence v. Both the mechanical and the Med sense come, the latter via OF *crampe*, from MD *crampe* or *cramp*, cramp iron, a painful contraction of muscles: akin to OHG *krampfs*, MHG *krampf*, MLG *krampe*, G *Krampf*, convulsion, cramp. The E n perh derives rather from the E adj *cramp*, contracted, confined, strait, itself prob from OHG *kramph*, crooked, akin to ON *krappr* (for *krampr*), squeezed in; perh cf **crimp.** If the r is *cram-*, *cramp* is akin to CRAM. (Walshe.)

**cranberry:** LG *kranbere:* cf CRANE and BERRY.

**crane,** long-necked bird, hence, from the instrument's long neck, the machine used for lifting heavy weights: OE *cran*, allied to late MHG *kran*, *krane*, the bird, G *Kran*, the machine, cf OHG *kranuh*, MHG *kranech*, G *Kranich*, the bird; allied also to W and Cor *garan* and Gr *geranos* (s *geran-*): ult from 'the bird's call *gru*, from which L *grūs* [cf F *grue*] is more directly derived' (Walshe). Hence 'to *crane*'. Gr *geranos*, crane (bird), has derivative *geranion*, whence L *geranium*, adopted by E, with syn *crane's-bill*, 'from the long slender beak of the carpels' (Webster).

**cranial** is the adj (*crani-+-al*) of **cranium,** s *crani-*, r *cran-*: ML *cranium*: LL *cranion*, bald head: Gr *kranion*, skull, s *krani-*, r *kran-*, akin to Gr *kara*, head: cf CEREBRAL.

**crank** (1), adj: bent, distorted, shaky: partly from next, partly from MD *cranc*, D *krank*, weak (OE *cranc*, tender, brittle; MHG *kranc*, weak, G *krank*, ill).

**crank** (2), n hence v: something bent or crooked, esp as a mechanical device, hence a crotchety person: OE *cranc*. Cf CRINGE.

**cranky,** (dial) ill, twisted or disordered, derives from prec, influenced by 1st CRANK.

**cranny:** E dim (*-y*) from OF *cran*, var *cren*, from OF-EF *crener*, to (cut with a) notch, either from VL *crena*, a notch, o.o.o., or from Gaul *crināre*, akin to OIr ar-a-*chrinnim*, I disappear (B & W). *Crena*, by the way, yields the OF-MF, from OProv, dim *crenel*, embrasure in a battlement, lit an indention, adopted by E; derivative OF-F

*créneler*, to indent, leads, anl, to E *crenellate*, or *crenellated*, and to *crenellation*.

**crape.** See CRISP, para 2.

**crappie.** Am freshwater fish, derives either from F dial *crape* or from LG *Krape*, of approx the same meaning.

**craps,** Am game played with two dice, is merely a sense-changed F *craps*, a game of dice, earlier *crabs*, from E *crabs*, a two-aces throw, the lowest throw, at hazard. Cf CRAB.

**crash** (1), a heavy, coarse linen: app of Ru origin, for cf Ru *krush*enina, coloured linen.

**crash** (2), v hence n: ME *craschen*, ult echoic— cf G *krachen*, to crash, and therefore cf CRACK.

**crass, crassitude, crassness.**

1. The 3rd derives (suffix *-ness*) from the 1st; *crassitude* derives from L *crassitūdō*, itself by suffix *-itūdō* from the adj *crassus*, thick, fat, gross, s *crass-*, r *cras-*, prob akin to Skt *kṛtsna*, entire.

2. From L *crassus*, via the VL derivative n *crassia*, derives OF-MF *craisse*, with varr OF-F *graisse* and MF *gresse*, whence ME *grese* (var *grece*), whence E *grease*; hence, perh influenced by late MF-F *graisser*, 'to grease', and hence also *greasy*; the v has agent *greaser*.

**crate.** See CART, para 2.

**crater,** orig a drinking vessel, hence a volcano's crater (cf EF-F *cratère*), descends, via L *crater*, from Gr *kratēr*, from *kerannunai*, to mix, esp wine with water: s *keran-*, IE r *ker-*.

**cravat:** EF-F *cravate*, a neckcloth worn by a *Croate*, is a var of F *Croate*, from G *Kroate*; *Cravate* prob derives imm from the G dial form *Krawat*. (B & W.)

**crave,** whence the vn **craving:** OE *crafian*, to demand, akin to syn ON *krefja* (or *-ia*): cf CRAFT.

**craven,** adj hence n: ME *cravant*, adopted from OF-MF *cravant* (OF-F *crevant*), prop the presp of *craver, crever*: L *crepant-*, o/s of *crepans*, presp of *crepāre*, to crack, crackle, rattle, applied esp to wood and fabrics, and later, fig, to persons: s *crep-*: prob akin to Skt *kṛpate*, he laments; certainly the word belongs to the considerable echoic group in cr- (*kr-*).

**craw,** a bird's crop, an animal's stomach: ME *crawe*: akin to OFris *kraga*, OHG *krago*, neck, MHG *krage*, neck, collar, G *Kragen*, collar; perh also to Gr *bronkhos*, windpipe. (Walshe.)

**crawfish** is the predominant AE form of *crayfish*, q.v. at 2nd CRAB, para 1, s.f.

**crawl,** v hence n and the agent **crawler:** ON *krafla*, to scrabble with one's hands, Sw *kräla*, to crawl, MHG *krabelen*, G *krabbeln*, to crawl: Gmc r, prob *krabh-*. (Walshe.)

**crayfish.** See the 2nd CRAB, para 1, s.f.

**crayon,** adopted from EF-F, derives, by dim *-on*, from MF-F *craie*, from L *crēta*, chalk, adj *crētāceus*, whence E *cretaceous*, chalky.

**craze,** v hence n, the pa **crazed,** the adj **crazy:** ME *crazen, crasen*, to break: echoic: cf Sw *krasa*, to break; akin to CRASH: cf, sem, *cracked*, insane, from CRACK. Note that EF-F *éraser*, EF var *ac(c)raser*, derives from the E v.

**creak,** v hence n and the adj **creaky:** ME *creken,* to croak: f.a.e., CROAK.

**cream, creamery, creamy.** See CHRISM, para 4.

**creance.** See CREDENCE, para 6.

**crease,** n hence v; **crest,** n hence v.

*Crease* is an easing of *creast,* an obs var of *crest*: OF-MF *creste* (EF-F *crête*): L *crista,* a cock's comb, a bird's tuft (if on the head): o.o.o.; but perh cf ON *krista,* to shake or cause to tremble. Derivatives: *crested, crestfallen* (from cock-fighting), *crestless* (*-less*).

**crease** (2). See KRIS.

**create, creation, creative, creator, creature; procreate, procreation, procreative, procreator; (re-create) recreate, recreation, recreative.**

1. L *creāre* (s *cre*-), to produce, cause to grow, was orig a rustic term, clearly allied to *crēscere,* to grow, hence to come into existence; *crēscere* prob began as an inch of *creāre;* cf L *Cerēs* (q.v. at CEREAL)—Arm *serem,* I engender—Lit *šérti,* to nourish. (E & M.)

2. *Creāre* has pp *creātus,* whence 'to create'; derivative *creātiō,* o/s *creātiōn-,* yields *creation; creative* is an E formation (*creat-,* s of the pp+ *-ive*); *creātor,* adopted by E; LL *creātūra,* a creating, hence a (living) thing created, whence, prob via OF, the E *creature.*

3. *Prōcreāre,* to engender, where *prō*-, forward, forth, emphasizes the physical acts of conception and birth, has pp *prōcreātus,* whence 'to *procreate*'; derivative *prōcreātiō,* o/s *prōcreātiōn-,* leads to *procreation;* whereas *procreative* is an E formation, *procreator* is adopted from L.

4. *Recreāre,* to cause to grow again, to give new life to, hence to revitalize or refresh, has pp *recreātus,* whence *re-create,* to produce again, and *recreate,* to refresh; derivative *recreātiō,* o/s *recreātiōn-,* leads, through MF-F, to *recreation,* with adj *recreational;* derivative LL *recreātor* is adopted by E; *recreative* is of E formation.

5. Somewhat less obvious is *Creole*: late EF-F *créole,* earlier EF *criole*: Sp *criollo*: Port *crioulo,* from *criar,* to nourish or rear, from L *creāre,* to breed. The obscure Port suffix *-oulo* prob answers to the L dim *-ulus,* a Creole being, as it were, a *by-product* of certain racial and sociological conditions.

**crèche,** adopted from MF-F, derives from Frankish *\*kripja,* akin to G *Krippe,* MHG *krippe,* OHG *krippa* or *kripia,* and to E **crib** (manger, child's cot).

**credence, credent, credential** (adj hence n, esp **credentials**); **credenda; credible, credibility, credit** (n and v), **creditable, creditor; credo; credulity, credulous;**—**accredit, accreditation, accredited; discredit** (v hence n), **discreditable; incredible, incredibility; incredulous, incredulity;**—**creed, creedal** (**ism**); **creance, creant**—**recreant** (adj hence n), **recreancy; miscreant.**

1. The base is formed by L *crēdō,* I trust or believe, whence the *Credo* or Christian confession of faith, whence *credo,* any professed belief, with inf *crēdere* and s *crēd*-; IE r *\*kred*-, as in L, with

var *\*kret*-, as in C (cf OIr *cretim,* but W *credaf,* I believe), and with an alternative *\*krad*-, *\*krat*-, somewhat obscured in Skt.

2. *Crēdere* has presp *crēdens,* o/s *crēdent*-, whence *credent;* derivative ML *crēdentia* yields *credence* and also the adj, hence n, *credential.* L *crēdenda,* things to be believed, hence doctrines, is adopted by Theo.

3. Two simple L derivatives of *crēd*-, s of *crēdere,* are relevant to E:

*crēdibilis,* believable, whence *credible;* its derivative *crēdibilitās,* yields o/s *crēdibilitāt-, credibility;* the negg *incrēdibilis* and *incrēdibilitās* become *incredible, incredibility;*

*crēdulus,* tending to believe, and its derivative *crēdulitās,* o/s *crēdulitāt-,* become *credulous* and *credulity;* the negg *incrēdulus, incrēdulitās,* become *incredulous, incredulity.*

4. *Crēdere* has pp *crēditus,* neu *crēditum* apprehended as n, whence the It n *credito,* commercial credit, whence EF-F *crédit,* whence E *credit;* but late MF-F *crédit,* trust, reputation, comes direct from L *crēditum* and fathers the E *credit,* reputation. (B & W.) *Credit,* reputation, has derivative *creditable.* The v 'to *credit*' prob derives from the n; at least, that is the general view. It perh comes, however, from LL *crēditāre,* to believe.

5. The pp s *credit-* has derivative *crēditor,* lit believer, whence, perh aided by MF-F *crēditeur,* the E *creditor.*

6. Other notable E derivatives from simple *crēdere* are *creed* and *creance,* the former deriving from ME *crede,* OE *crēda,* from L *crēdō,* I believe (cf para 1), and the latter from OF *creance,* from ML *crēdentia* (cf para 2); adj *creant,* believing, is extant in *recreant,* cowardly, whence the n, coward, from OF-MF, orig the presp of *recreire* (var *recroire*), to go back on one's faith, to surrender, from ML (*se*) *recrēdere; re*-, back+*crēdere;* derivative is *recreancy* (*recreant*+*-cy*). Cf *miscreant*: OF-MF *mescreant*: *mes*- (cf the prefix *mis*-)+*creant,* presp of *creire,* to believe (L *crēdere*).

7. Two F prefix-cpds of *credere* are relevant to E:

EF-F *accréditer* (*a,* to+*crédit*+inf *-er*), whence 'to *accredit*', whence the pa *accredited* and, anl, *accreditation;*

EF-F *discréditer,* whence 'to *discredit*', whence the n *discredit* and, after *creditable,* the adj *discreditable.* The EF-F *discréditer* owes something to LL *discrēdere,* to disbelieve.

**creed.** See prec, para 6.

**creek,** small inlet, (AE, Aus, NZ) a brook or rivulet: ME *creke, crike*: ON *-kriki,* in cpds; cf MD *creke,* D *kreek,* inlet. Basic idea: a *bend* in the coastline.

**creel,** fisherman's basket or trap: OF-MF *\*creïl,* for *greïl, greïle,* from a dim (? *\*crāticula*) of L *crātis,* wickerwork: cf *crate* at CART.

**creep,** v hence n (whence *creepy*) and the agent **creeper:** ME *crepen,* earlier, *creopen*: OE *crēopan,* s *crēop*-, akin to MD *crupen.* D *kruipen,* and ON *krjŭpa*, to creep; perh also to Gr *grupos*, curved, bent; basic idea, perh 'to walk with back bent'— so as to keep out of sight. Cf CRIPPLE.

**creese.** See KRIS.

**cremate, cremation, crematory** (adj and n).

'To *cremate*' derives from L *cremātus*, pp of *cremāre*, to burn esp corpses, s *crem-*: perh akin to HEARTH. Derivative *cremātiō*, o/s *cremātiōn-*, yields *cremation*; LL *cremātor* is adopted by E; but *crematorium* is Sci L, and *crematory* its E derivative.

**crenel, crenellate(d), crenellation.** See CRANNY, s.f.

**Creole.** See CREATE, para 5.

**creosol** = *creos-* (short for *creoso-*), c/f of *creosote* + *-ol*, oil (f.a.e., OIL); and **creosote** = *creo-*, Gr *kreo-*, c/f of *kreas* (gen *kreōs*), flesh + *-sote*, from the pp of *sōzein*, to preserve.

**crêpe.** Cf *crape* at CRISP, para 2.

**crepitant, crepitate, crepitation.**

L *crepitāre*, to crackle, is a freq of *crepāre*, to crack (f.a.e., CREVASSE); its presp *crepitans*, o/s *crepitant-*, yields the adj *crepitant*, crackling; its pp *crepitātus* yields 'to *crepitate*'; LL derivative *crepitātiō*, o/s *crepitātiōn-*, yields *crepitation*.

**crepuscular** is the adj (*-ar*) of *crepuscule*, var *crepuscle*, twilight, from L *crepusculum*, from *creper*, dusky, perh of Sabine origin.

**crescendo.** See para 1, s.f., of:

**crescent,** adj and n; **crescive; crescendo; crew;** cpds: **accrescence, accrescent, accrete** (adj and v), **accretion, accretionary, accretive—accrue, accrual;** **concresce, concrescence, concrescible,** sep **concrete** and **concretion; decrease,** n and v (whence pa **decreasing),** and **decrement; excrescence** (or **-ency), excrescent, excrescential; increase,** n and v (whence **increaser** and pa **increasing),** and **increment, incremental,** and **increscence, increscent;** **recrescence, recrescent—recruit,** n and v (whence **recruiter), recruital** and **recruitment—'rooky'.**

1. L *crēscere*, (vi) to grow, is akin to *creāre*, to produce: f.a.e., CREATE, para 1. Its presp *crēscens*, o/s *crēscent-*, whence the E adj, as in 'the *crescent* moon', whence the n *crescent* in several of its senses; but *crescent*, the waxing moon, whence the Byzantine, later the Tu, national emblem, appears to come, via ME *cressant*, from OF-MF *creissant*, orig the presp of *creistre* (F *croître*), itself from *crēscere*. The adj *crescentic* derives from the n *crescent*; *crescive* = L *crēsc-*, s of *crēscere* + *-ive*, adj. *Crescendo*, adv and adj, hence n, is adopted from It *crescendo*, gerundive of *crescere*, to grow, from L *crēscere*.

2. Not immediately recognizable as from *crēscere* is the E *crew*: MF *creüe* (F *crû*), growth, increase, hence reinforcement, soon applied to persons: from the pp, perh via *force creüe*, of *creistre*, to grow (para 1).

3. Several L prefix-cpds affect E, the first being *accrēscere* (*ad-* + *crēscere*), to increase itself, hence come to add itself, with presp *accrēscens*, o/s *accrēscent-*, whence the E adj *accrescent*; the LL derivative *accrēscentia* becomes E *accrescence*,

a continuous growing, hence an accretion; pp *accrētus* (s *accrēt-*) yields the adj and v *accrete*, grow(n) together; the derivative L *accrētiō*, o/s *accrētiōn-*, yields *accretion*, with its own abj *accretionary*; *accretive* is an E formation.

4. *Accrual* = 'to *accrue*' + *-al*, n; and 'to *accrue*' derives from the obs n *accrue*, an increase or accession: F *accrue*: MF *acreüe*, from the f of the pp (*acreu*) of OF-MF *acreistre*: L *accrēscere*.

5. L *concrēscere*, to grow together, hence to become congealed or condensed, yields 'to *concresce*' or coalesce; presp *concrēscens*, o/s *concrēscent-*, yields the adj *concrescent*, and derivative L *concrēscentia* yields *concrescence*; *concrescible* is an E formation. The pp *concrētus* yields both the adj, whence the n, *concrete* and the v 'to *concrete*'; derivative *concrētiō*, o/s *concrētiōn-*, yields *concretion*, which develops its own adj *concretionary*.

6. L *dēcrēscere*, to grow down (*de-*), hence to grow or become less, has the LL var *discrēscere*: hence OF-MF *decreistre*, *descreistre*: ME *decrecen*, *discresen*: E 'to *decrease*'; the n *decrease* derives, via ME *decrees*, from OF-MF *decreis* (var *descreis*), from the OF v. The derivative L n *dēcrēmentum* becomes E *decrement*.

7. L *excrēscere*, to grow out from, to form excrescences, has presp *excrēscens*, o/s *excrēscent-*, whence the E adj *excrescent*; the L neu pl *excrēscentia*, used as n ('excrescences'), becomes, in ML, apprehended as f sing, whence the OF-MF *excressance* (F *excroissance*, a re-shaping) and the E *excrescence*, var *excrescency*, with its particular adj *excrescential*.

8. L *incrēscere* (*in-* used int), to grow larger, becomes OF *encreistre*, whence ME *encresen*, later *incresen*, whence 'to *increase*'; the n *increase* derives from ME *encres* or *encrese*, app from the *en-* form of the ME v. The presp *incrēscens*, o/s *incrēscent-*, whence the adj *increscent*, waxing, with n *increscence*. Derivative L *incrēmentum* (cf *dēcrēmentum* in para 6) yields E *increment*, with its own adj *incremental*.

9. L *recrēscere*, to grow again (vi), has presp *recrēscens*, o/s *recrēscent-*, whence *recrescent*, whence *recrescence*, a new growth (*recrescent* + *-ce*). *Recrēscere* becomes OF \**recreistre*, var of *recroistre*, with pp *recreü*, whence the EF-F n *recrue*, with var *recrute*, whence both the E n *recruit*, lit a reinforcement, and the late EF-F v *recruter*, whence E 'to *recruit*'. Whereas *recruitment* was prompted by F *recrutement*, *recruital* is an E formation (*recruit*, v + n suffix *-al*).

10. Army sl *rooky* derives from the n *recruit*, via \**rekroot*, by contr and metathesis, with dim *-y* attached to *rook-*.

**cress:** ME *cres(se)* or *kers(e)*: OE *cresse* or *caerse*, *cerse*: akin to MD *kerse*, D *kers*, and OHG *chresso*, *chressa*, MHG (and G) *kresse*, perh from OHG *kresōn*, to creep or crawl. (Walshe.)

**crest; crestfallen.** See CREASE.

**cretaceous.** See CRAYON.

**cretin, cretinism, cretinous.** See CHRISM, para 5.

**cretonne,** adopted from F, derives from *Creton*, a Normandy village, renowned, since C16, for the fabrics manufactured there. (B & W.)

**crevasse, crevice.**

Sense-differentiated into 'large or deep crack or fissure' and 'crack or fissure', *crevasse* and *crevice* come resp from EF-F *crevasse*, OF-MF *crevace*, from *crever*, to crack open, to burst, from L *crepāre* (s *crep-*, IE s *\*krep-*, IE r *\*kra-* or *kre-*, cf CRACK, CRASH, Gr *krazō*, I croak, bawl, scream), and from ME *crevice*, var *crevace*, from OF-MF *crevace*.

**crew.** See CRESCENT, para 2.

**crib,** a manger, whence the other senses, whence also 'to *crib*' or confine, whence, not very clearly, the sense 'to pilfer, to plagiarize', whence, by suffix *-age*, the game of *cribbage*, with 2nd *b* euphonic: OE *cribb*, a manger: akin to OFris *kribbe*, OHG *kripia, krippa*, MHG (and G) *krippe*, OS *krippja*, MD *cribbe* (D *krib*) or *crebbe*; cf also MLG *krebe*, a basket, and even OHG (and G) *korb*, L *corbis* (s *corb-*), basket.

**crick** in the neck, hence v: o.o.o., but prob a thinned CREAK. Cf:

**cricket** (1), chirping insect: ME *criket*: OF-F *criquet*: MD *crīkel*, akin to CREAK: in short, echoic.

**cricket** (2), game: EF-F *criquet,* a goal stake at bowls: MD *cricke*, a staff or stick: akin to CRUTCH and to CROOK and OF-F *croc*, a hook. (Orig there were only two stumps, with a top cross-bar.)

**crier,** as in *town crier.* See CRY.

**crime, criminal, criminality, criminology** (whence **criminologist), criminate, crimination, criminatory, criminous; incriminate, incrimination, incriminator, incriminatory; recriminate, recrimination, recriminatory.**

1. *Crime,* adopted from OF-F, derives from L *crīmen,* \*that which serves to sift (hence, to decide), decision, esp a legal one, hence an accusation, finally the object of the accusation—the misdeed itself, the crime: for \**cernīmen* (cf *regīmen* from *regere,* s *reg-*), from *cernere*, to sift: f.a.e., CERTAIN, para 1.

2. L *crīmen* has o/s *crīmin-*, on which arise:

LL *crīminālis*, of, by, for an accusation, hence also of (a) crime, whence, perh via OF-F *criminel,* the E adj *criminal,* whence the n *criminal*; from the ML derivative *crīminālitās*, o/s *crīminālitāt-*, derives—perh via EF-F *criminalité—criminality*; *crīmināre* (or *-āri*), to accuse, has pp *crīminātus,* whence 'to *criminate*', now mostly in the two cpds (paras 4, 5); on the pp s *crīmināt-* arise *crīminātiō,* o/s *crīminātiōn-*, whence *crimination*, and the agent *crīminātor,* accuser, adopted—though seldom used—by E; *criminatory* is an E formation; *crīminōsus,* whence *criminous,* guilty.

3. On *crīmin-* is built *criminology* (cf the elements *-ology* and, at *-loger, -logy*), whence *criminological* and *criminologist*.

4. The LL cpd *incrīmināre* (*in-*, into, against) has pp *incrīminātus,* whence 'to *incriminate*'; its LL derivative *incrīminātiō,* o/s *incrīminātiōn-*, yields

*incrimination*; both *incriminator* and *incriminatory* are E formations, prompted by *criminator* and *criminatory.*

5. The ML cpd *recrīmināre* (*re-*, again, back at), to make a counter charge, has pp *recrīminātus,* whence 'to *recriminate*'; the derivative *recrīminātiō,* o/s *recrīminātiōn-*, becomes *recrimination*; *recriminator, recriminatory* (var *recriminative*) are E formations.

**crimp,** v hence adj and n, including the 'decoy' v and n: MD and LG *crimpen*, MD *crempen*: akin to, perh—in Middle Gmc—a thinned form of, CRAMP, q.v.

**crimson.** See CARMINE.

**cringe,** whence pa **cringing; cringle; crinkle** (v hence n), **crinkly.**

'To *cringe*', ME *crengen,* is a form- and sense-adaptation of OE *cringan,* var *crincan,* to yield, and is akin to MD *cringen, crengen,* D *krengen,* to turn, and MD *cring,* var *crinc,* D *kring,* a circle: cf the 2nd CRANK.

2. MD *cring* has dim *cringel,* a spiral, whence the naut E *cringle.* Allied is *crinkle,* a freq of *cringe*; the derivative n has adj *crinkly.*

**crinkle, crinkly.** See para 2 of prec.

**crinoline** is adopted from F, itself from It *crinolino*; It *crino* (L *crinis,* s *crin-*, hair)+It *lino* (Gr *linon,* flax, hence linen).

**cripes!:** euphem for (by) *Christ!*

**cripple,** n hence v: ME *cripel, crepel, crupel*: OE *crypel,* akin to OFris *kreppel,* MD *crepel, creupel, crupel,* D *kreupel,* MHG-G *krüppel,* and prob to OE *crēopan* (see CREEP).

**crisis, critic, critical, criticism, criticize, critique; criticaster; criterion.**

1. *Crisis* is the L trln of Gr *krisis,* a sifting, from *krinein*, to sift: f.a.e., CERTAIN, para 1. Cf DISCERN (and DISCREET) and SECRET.

2. Gr *krisis* has adj *kritikos,* able to discern—judge—discuss, whence a critic, whence L *criticus,* whence E *critic,* whence adj *critical (-al)* and the n *criticism* and v *criticize*; Med *critical* goes back to LL *criticus,* in grave condition, and ML *criticāre,* to be extremely ill. On s *krit-*, Gr has raised also *kritērion,* a judgement, whence, perh aided by LL *critērium,* the E *criterion,* a standard or means of judgement. *Criticaster* is an E formation (*critic+* pej suffix *-aster*), after *poetaster. Hypercritical, hypercriticize, hypercritic* were perh suggested by the EF-F *hypercritique.* The EF-F, hence E, *critique,* a criticism, represents Gr *kritikē* (*tekhnē*), the critical art.

**crisp,** adj hence n (whence adj **crispy**) and also **crispness** (*-ness*); 'to **crisp**'.

1. The adj *crisp,* already in OE, derives from L *crispus,* (of hair) curly, curling, hence quivering, undulatory: metathetic for \**kripsos*, of C origin: cf Ga and EIr *crith,* to quiver, and W *crych,* curly; C r, \**krit-*, to tremble. 'To *crisp*' derives, perh via F *crisper,* from L *crispāre,* to curl, to quiver; the L pp *crispātus* yields the adj *crispate*; F *crisper* has derivative *crispation,* adopted by E.

2. F *crisper* was OF *cresper,* from the adj *crespe*

(L *crispus*), curly, whence *crêpe*, (f) a sort of pastry (c13), (m) a fabric (c14), adopted by E, with anglicized spelling *crape*.

**criss-cross.** See CHRISM, para 3.

**criterion.** See CRISIS, para 2.

**critic, critical, criticaster, criticism, criticize, critique.** See CRISIS, para 2.

**croak,** v, hence agent **croaker** and vn **croaking;** from n **croak** (from the v), the adj **croaky.**

1 To *croak*' derives from the r of the OE syn *crācettan*: cf CROW: ult echoic.

2. Akin also is the bird *crake*, with cpd *corncrake*, frequenter of grain fields: ME *crake*, orig a crow, a rook, prob from ON *krāka*, a crow: ult echoic.

3. Cf CREAK.

**croceous.** See CROCUS.

**crochet.** See CROOK, para 2.

**crock** (1), a piece of earthenware; **crockery.**

The latter=*crock*+suffix *-ery*: and *crock* derives from OE *croc*, var *crocca*, akin to ON *krukka*; also to OHG *krōg, kruog*, MHG *kruoc*, G *Krug*, a pitcher, and syn OE *krog*: beyond OGmc, o.o.o. Cf. CRUET.

**crock** (2), an old or barren ewe, an old or decrepit horse, hence, coll, a broken-down person, prob influenced by the secondary, i.e. 'potsherd', meaning of CROCK (1): cf Fris and LG *krakke*, an old, decrepit horse, hence man: prob akin to CRACK. The v 'to *crock*', to disable or to become disabled, owes something to each *crock* n.

**crocket.** See CROOK, para 2.

**crocodile,** whence the adj **crocodilian:** EF-F *crocodile*: L *crocodīlus*: Gr *krokodīlos* (later *krokodeīlos*), lizard, esp 'the lizard of the Nile' (sem, cf ALLIGATOR): dissimilation of *\*krokodrīlos*, worm of the stone: *krokē*, a pebble, c/f *kroko-*+ *drīlos*, a worm: 'lizards sun themselves on smooth stones' (Boisacq). Cf COCKATRICE.

**crocus, croceous.**

The latter derives from L *croceus*, adj of *crocus*, trln of Gr *krokos*, saffron, of Sem origin: cf the syn H *karkōm*. (Hofmann.) Cf the element *croceo-*.

**Croesus,** as rich as: L trln of Gr *Ḳroisos*, a fabulously wealthy king of ancient Lydia.

**croft,** whence *crofter*, derives from OE *croft, a* (small) enclosed field, esp one with a cottage: akin to MD *croft*, D *kroft*, field, hillock, and perh to E CREEP, with basic idea 'a curving'. (Webster.)

**crone.** See CARRION, para 2.

**cronk.** See the 2nd CROOK.

**crony.** See CHRONIC, para 3.

**crook,** n and v (whence the adj **crooked); crookback.**

1. The latter=the now obs adj *crook*, crooked+ BACK; 'to *crook*' derives from ME *croken*, from ME *crok*, whence a *crook*, even in its criminological sense: and ME *krok* derives from ON *krōkr*, a hook, (basically) a bend, akin to OF-F *croc*, a hook, from Frankish *\*krōk*.

2. OF-F *croc* has OF-F dim *crochet*, a (small) hook, whence E *crochet*, knitting done with long,

hooked needle, whence 'to *crochet*', perh influenced by late MF-F *crocheter*; OF-F *crochet* yields also ME *crochet*, whence E *crotchet*, a curl or *crocket* (ONF *croquet*, from OF *crochet*), a small hook, hence a whim, esp if unreasonable, whence the adj *crotchety*; the Mus *crotchet* also derives from OF-F *crochet*.

3. A direct dim of OF *croc* is MF *croche*, a hook, whence E *crotch*, a fork, esp that of the body;

4. From ONF *croquet* derives the game of *croquet*, orig applied to a hooked stick used in the game.

5. Akin to ON *krōkr* and OF-F *croc* is OE *crycc*, whence ME *crucche*, whence E *crutch*, a lame or ill person's supporting staff, with a propping crosspiece; the basic sense 'hook', hence 'fork', accounts for *crutch*, the fork of the human body. With OE *crycc*, cf also OHG *chrucchia*, MHG *kruche*, G *Krüche*.

6. From the Gmc r of *crutch* and *crook* derives ML *crucca*, a crutch, with var *croccia*, whence OF-MF *croce*, MF-F *crosse*, whence MF *crocier* or *crossier*, staff-bearer, whence E *crozier* or *crosier*, the bearer of a bishop's crook (pastoral staff), whence the bishop's crook itself. The F *la crosse*, the hooked stick, i.e. the crozier, lends its name to *lacrosse*, the game played orig by the NA Indians, esp those of Canada.

7. OF-F *croc*, a hook, has MF derivative *crochir*, to become hooked-like or bent, whence ME *cruchen*, later *crouchen*, whence E 'to *crouch*', whence 'a *crouch*' and the agent *croucher*.

8. OF-F *croc* has the derivative cpd v MF *encrochier*, EF *encrocher*, to fasten to (*en*, into) a hook, hence seize, also to perch, whence E 'to *encroach*', whence *encroachment* (suffix *-ment*).

9. Akin is CRICKET.

**crook** (2), Aus sl for 'ill', owes its form to E *crook*, esp in its personal meanings, but its sense mainly to G *krank*, ill (MHG *kranc*, weak), whence the likewise Aus sl syn **cronk.**

**croon,** v hence n and the agent **crooner:** MD *cronen* (D *kreunen*), to whimper or groan: perh cf GROAN; certainly ult echoic.

**crop,** n hence v (whence *cropper* in farming); **croup,** a quadruped's hinderpart, **croupier, crupper.**

1. A *crop* derives from ME *crop* or *croppe*, a bird's craw, a plant's top, a harvest, from OE *crop* or *cropp*, craw, top, an ear of corn: akin to ON *kroppr*, trunk of body, MD *crop*, D *krop*, craw, and OHG-G *kropf*, crop, hump; basic idea, (a) swelling, a hump.

2. The Gmc *\*croppa*, Frankish *\*kruppa*, yields OF *croupe*, whence ME *croupe*, E *croup*; OF-F *croupe* has derivative EF-F *croupier*, orig one who rides, on the horse's croup, behind the guiding horseman, hence an assistant at a gaming table.

3. OF *croupe* has var *crope* (the earlier form), whence OF-MF *cropiere* (F *croupière*), whence ME *cropere*, whence E *crupper*, a leather strap passing under a horse's tail.

4. P Gmc *\*croppa*, Longobard *crüp(p)a*, becomes It *gruppo*, a cluster, a group, whence EF-F *groupe*,

whence E *group*, whence, aided by late EF-F *grouper*, the E 'to *group*', whence the vn *grouping*. (B & W.)

**croquet.** See CROOK, para 3.

**crosier.** See CROOK, para 6.

**cross,** n hence adj ('not parallel; athwart; lit and fig, contrary'): **crossbow, crosspatch, cross-staff, crosstree, crossword,** and other obvious cpds; **crux, crucial, cruciate, crucible, crucifix, crucifixion, crucify; crusade** (n, v), **crusader; cruise** (n, v), **cruiser; cruciform; excruciate, excruciation.**

1. The keyword is the L *crux*, o/s *cruc-*, a perpendicular supporting a horizontal beam, hence, in LL, the Cross upon which Christ was suspended: o.o.o., but app Punic (Carthaginian); Webster suggests kinship with the n RUNG.

2. From the derivative sense 'torture' comes *crux*, a problem, the decisive point. The L adj *crucius* becomes EF-F *crucial*, adopted by E; the likewise derivative *cruciāre*, to crucify, has pp *cruciātus*, whence the E adj *cruciate*, cross-shaped; the subsidiary LL *cruciātiō*, o/s *cruciātiōn-*, yields *cruciation*. The ML *crucibulum* (*cruci-*, c/f of *crux*+suffix *-ibulum*), a light burning before the Cross, hence a hanging lamp, hence an earthenware pot for the melting of metals, becomes E *crucible*.

3. LL *crucifer*, he who or that which bears (cf the element *-fer*) a cross, has E adj *cruciferous*. LL *crucifigere*, to torture on a cross, to crucify, has pp *crucifixus*, hence n 'the crucified Christ', hence a representation thereof, hence loosely the Cross, adopted by E; derivative LL *crucifixiō*, being attached to a cross, o/s *crucifixiōn-*, yields *crucifixion*; *crucifigere* itself becomes OF-F *crucifier*, whence 'to *crucify*'. *Cruciform*=of the *form* of a cross.

4. The prefix-cpd *excruciāre*, to torture thoroughly (*ex-* used int), has pp *excruciātus*, whence 'to *excruciate*', whence the pa *excruciating*; derivative LL *excruciātiō*, o/s *excruciātiōn-*, yields *excruciation*.

5. L *crux* becomes Sp *cruz*, whence *cruzada*, whence E *crusade* (suffix *-ade*), from the Cross marked upon the soldiers' breastplates or shields: cf the It *crociata* and late MF-F *croisade*; hence crusader and 'to *crusade*'.

6. L *crux* becomes MD *cruse, cruyse*, D *kruis*, whence *crusen* (*crucen*), D *kruisen*, to move, esp to sail, crosswise, hence 'to *cruise*', whence *cruiser* and 'a *cruise*'.

7. L *crux* becomes OF-MF *crois* (F *croix*), adopted by ME, and OIr *cros*, whence ON *kross*, whence late OE *cros*, extant in ME: ME *crois*, sem, and ME *cros*, both sem and phon, yield E *cross*, whence 'to *cross*'.

8. The adj *cross-country* derives from 'a run made *across country*'.

**crotch.** See CROOK, para 3.

**crotchet, crotchety.** See CROOK, para 2.

**crouch.** See CROOK, para 7.

**croup** (1), of body. See CROP, para 2.

**croup** (2), an affection of the throat: from the

now only dial 'to *croup*', to cry or speak hoarsely, to croak: echoic. Adjj: *croupous* (Med), *croupy*.

**croupier.** See CROP, para 2.

**crow** (1), the bird: OE *crāwe*, akin to OHG *krā* (also MHG), *krāha, krāja, krāwa*, G *Krähe*, and to 'to *crow*': echoic. Such cpdd as *crow'sfoot* are self-explanatory.

**crow** (2), to utter the cock's cry, or one like it: OE *crāwan*, akin to OHG *krāen*, MHG *kraejen*, G *krähen*: 'orig must have denoted the sound made by crows, but early applied to the cock' (Walshe): cf Lith *grōjù*, I croak, *groti*, to croak. Hence *crow*, a crowing sound; *crow*, a bar of iron, hence *crowbar*, so named because orig beaked.

**crowbar.** See prec, s.f.

**crowd,** v hence n: ME *crouden*, earlier *cruden*: OE *crūdan*, akin to *creōdan*, to press, to push hard, and to MD *crūden* to push or shove. Prob from OE *crūdan* is ME *crud* (var *crod*), whence, by metathesis, ME *curd* (with adj *curdy*), adopted by E, whence 'to *curd*', whence the freq 'to *curdle*', whence the pa *curdled*.

**crown,** n and v. See COROLLA, para 4.

**crowner, coroner.** See COROLLA, para 3.

**crozier.** See CROOK, para 6.

**crucial, cruciate.** See CROSS, para 2.

**crucible.** See CROSS, para 2.

**cruciferous.** See CROSS, para 3.

**crucifix, crucifixion, crucify.** See CROSS, para 3.

**crude, crudity; recrudescence, recrudescent; cruel, cruelty.**

1. *Crudity* derives from *crūditāt-*, o/s of L *crūditās*, rawness, undigested matter, cruelty, from *crūdus*, bloody-handed or -minded, cruel, with secondary sense 'raw'. Its s *crūd-* is an extension of of r *crū-*, seen in *crūor* (s *crū-*), bloody flesh, hence predominantly a pool of blood, coagulated blood; akin to Gr *kreas* (for *\*krewas*), flesh, and Skt *kravis*, raw meat.

2. From *crūdus*, bleeding, derives *crūdescere*, to bleed, with cpd *recrūdescere*, to bleed again, hence to break out afresh, with presp *recrūdescens*, o/s *recrūdescent-*, whence the E adj *recrudescent*; hence *recrudescence*.

3. Also from r *crū-*, with s *crūd-* (cf *fidelis* from *fides*) derives L *crūdēlis*, delighting in blood, hence cruel, whence OF *cruel*, adopted by E; derivative L *crūdēlitās*, o/s *crūdēlitāt-*, becomes OF *cruelte*, whence E *cruelty*.

**cruet** is an AF dim of OF-MF *crue*, var *cruie*, from Frankish *\*krūka*, akin to MHG *krūche* (cf the MF-F *cruche*), also to OHG *krōg, kruog* (G *Krug*), a pitcher—cf, therefore, the 1st CROCK.

**cruise, cruiser.** See CROSS, para 6.

**cruller,** a small cake, cut into rings or twists: lit, 'curler': MD *crullen*, D *krullen*, to curl: cf CURL.

**crumb,** n hence v; also from the n, **crumby** (whence the sl **crummy**, lousy); **crumble,** whence—influenced by *crumby*—**crumbly.**

'To *crumble*' is a freq of 'to *crumb*' or break into crumbs: cf the G *krumeln*, (vi) to crumble away, orig to crumb, from *Krume*, a crumb, MHG (and MLG) *krūme*, akin to OE *crūma, crŭme*, and ON *krumr*, and, further off, the L *grūmus* (s *grūm-*), a small heap.

'crummy': see prec.

crump (1), dial for 'bent, crooked' and 'a hunchback'; derivative v 'to *crump*', to curl up, with freq crumple, (of fabrics) to cause to wrinkle, to become wrinkled, whence 'a *crumple*' and the pa *crumpled*. The adj *crump* has always, in E, been *crump*, with OE var *crumb*: akin to OFris *krumb*, OHG *krumb*, MHG *krump*, G *krumm*.

crump (2), to crunch, to make a dull, heavy thud, hence n: echoic.

crumpet: ME *crompid cake*: OE *crompeht*, a flat, thin cake, from the OE adj *crompeht*, full of wrinkles or crumples: perh of C origin, for cf W *crempog*, pancake, crumpet, and *crammwyth*, pancakes—Br *krampoez, krampoe'ch*, pancake, or a flat, thin cake—Cor *crampethen, -pedhan, -podhan, -pothan*, pancake.

crumple. See 1st CRUMP.

crunch, v hence n and the adj crunchy: earlier *craunch*: echoic. Cf SCRUNCH.

crupper. See CROP, para 3.

crural. See the element *cruro-*.

crusade, crusader. See CROSS, para 5.

cruse, jar, pot: MD *cruese*, varr *croese* and *crose*: of Gmc orgin—cf the MF-F *cruche* and E CRUET.

crush, v hence n and crusher and pa crushing: ME *cruschen*: OF-MF *cruisir*, var of OF-EF *croissir, croissier*, to gnash, crack, crash, break, from P Gmc *\*krostian*—cf Go *kriustan*, to gnash. Echoic; cf CRASH.

crust, n hence v and the adj crusty; crustacean (adj hence n), crustaceous, crustose; crustate, crustation;—incrust or encrust, incrustation.

1. The keyword is L *crusta*, a hard, wrinkled covering, hence a crust on bread or cake; the IE r is app *\*kru-*, hard, coagulated: cf Gr *kruos* (s *kru-*), extreme cold, and *crustallos*, ice or CRYSTAL, with cognates in Gmc, C, Sl.

2. L *crusta* has adj *crustōsus*, whence E *crustose*, and derivative v *crustāre*, to incrust, with pp *crustātus*, whence the adj, and the obs v, *crustate*, whence *crustation*.

3. The cpd *incrustāre* yields 'to *incrust*', perh via learned EF-F *incruster*; the v 'to *encrust*', whence *encrustment*, presumably comes from MF *encrouster*; the L pp *incrustātus* accounts for the adj *incrustate* and, anl, for EF-F, hence E, *incrustation*.

4. From L *crusta*, Sci L coins the adj *crustaceus*, whence both E *crustaceous* (suffix *-aceous*) and E *crustacean*; cf the Zoo *Crustacea*, lobsters, barnacles, crabs, shrimps, etc.

crutch. See CROOK, para 5.

crux. See CROSS, para 1.

cry. The n derives from OF-F *cri*, a cry, from the source of 'to *cry*': OF-F *crier*, to cry out, call out, itself from L *quirītāre* (s *quirīt-*), to wail, orig to implore the *Quirītēs* or Roman citizens, sing *quiris*, s *quir-*, perh akin to L *uir*, ML *vir*, a man

(cf VIRILE). Derivative agent, *crier*; derivative vn and pa, *crying*.

crypt, cryptic.

*Cryptic* derives from *crypticus*, the LL trln of Gr *kruptikos*, hidden, secret, from *kruptos*, hidden, pp of *kruptein*, to hide, s *krupt-*; IE r, perh *\*krubh-*, to hide. Gr *kruptos*, hidden, has derivative n, *kruptē*, perh elliptical for *kruptē oikēsis*, a hidden room. Cf APOCRYPHAL and GROTTO.

cryptogam, cryptogamous. See MONOGAMIST, para 2.

cryptogram. See the element *crypto-*.

crystal, n hence adj; crystalline; crystallize (*crystal*+euphonic *l*+*-ize*), whence crystallization; crystallography (see the element *crystallo-*).

*Crystalline* derives from L *crystallinus*, trln of Gr *krustallinos*, adj of Gr *krustallos*, ice, crystal, from *kruos*, frost: cf CRUST, para 1. From *crustallos* derives L *crystallum*, whence, perh via OF-F *cristal*, the E *crystal*.

cub, n hence adj and v: the young of canine and feline quadrupeds, orig of the fox: C16, *cubbe*: o.o.o. The OED tentatively compares the rare OIr *cuib*, a dog; EW more firmly the Nor *kubbe*, *kub*, a block or stump, the basic idea being shapelessness.

cubbyhole: *cubby*, a snug, confined space, from *cub*, a pen or stall, a bin or cupboard, from MD *cubbe*, a stall, a cattle-shed: cf COVE, a nook.

cube, n hence v; cubic, adj, whence cubicity and the extended adj cubical. See HIVE, para 10.

cubicle, cubicular. See HIVE, para 7.

cubism, cubist. See HIVE, para 10, s.f.

cubit. See HIVE, para 9.

cuckold. See:

cuckoo, adj cuculine; cuckold (n hence v), cuckoldry.

1. *Cuckoo* derives from EF-F *coucou* (OF-EF *cocu*, MF *cucu*), itself from L *cucūlus*: echoic, with many IE cognates. Either from the cuckoo's habit of laying eggs in another bird's nest, or from the female's never remaining long with the same male, L *cucūlus* has transferred sense of 'adulterous lover', whence, in F (sem as differentiated *cocu*), that of 'betrayed husband'; from the F var *cucu* derives MF *cucuault*, whence ME *cocold* (etc.), whence E 'a *cuckold*', whence *cuckoldry* (suffix *-ry* for *-ery*).

2. From L *cucūlus* comes the erudite adj *cuculine*.

cucumber compromises between ME *cucumer* and ME *cocumber*: prob via MF *coucombre*, *cocombre* and OProv *cogombre*, from L *cucumis*, o/s *cucumer-*, akin to syn Gr *kukuon*: of Medit stock; with the syn Gr *sikuon, sikuos*, cf H *quissu'a* (Hofmann) and prob Eg *ashep*.

cud: OE *cudu*, with varr *cwudu, cwidu*: the latter yields the chewable QUID of tobacco. Akin to BITUMEN.

cuddle, v hence n: perh a freq of the now only dial *cull*, var of the now dial *coll*, to hug or fondle (ult from L *collum*, neck: cf COLLAR); prob a var of CODDLE.

cudgel (n hence v), ME *cuggel*, derives from OE *cycgel*, akin to MHG-G *kugel*, a ball, itself prob a var of MHG *kiule*, *kule*, G *Keule*, a cudgel; prob cf also COG. (Walshe.)

cue, certainly as 'tail-like plait' and 'tapering rod' (as in billiards) and prob as 'last word(s) or act, gesture, in an actor's speech', hence 'warning, hint', comes from OF-F *queue*, tail, (derivatively) end, itself from L *cŏda*, var of *cauda*, tail: f.a.e., CODA. F *queue*, tail, hence a file of persons, esp if waiting, has been adopted by E, with derivative v 'to *queue*'.

cuff, a blow, derives from 'to *cuff*', to strike flat-handedly, late ME *cuffe*, perh from ME *cuffe*, E *cuff*, a glove, a mitten, later that part of a glove which covers the wrist, later an ornamental wrist-band, then the sleeve-part covering the wrist; the ME var *coffe* suggests derivation from the s of COIF, 'as if a mitten or cuff were a cap for the hand' (Webster). Note that MF-F *coiffer*, to dress the hair, has the MF var *coueffer*, whence perh (EW) the ME *cuffe*, *coffe*, to buffet: cf, sem, the coll *dress down*, to beat, reprimand.

cuggermugger. See HUGGERMUGGER.

cuirass: MF-F *cuirasse*, a breastplate, orig of leather, either from It *corazza* (via the L adj *coriāceus*, from L *corium*, leather, hide) or, by *-asse* (E *-ass*), from OF-F *cuir*, leather, L *corium*, s *cori-*, r *cor-*, akin to Gr *khor-*, r of *khorion*, intestinal membrane, and ult to IE *ker-*, to cut, as in Gr *keirein* (s *keir-*), to cut: cf SHEAR, and also CARNAGE,final para,and CORTEX. MFF *cuirasse* has EF-F agent *cuirassier*, a cavalryman with a cuirass.

2. L *corium* has LL derivative *excoriāre* (*ex*, out from, off+s *cori-*+inf suffix *-āre*), to take the hide off, to flay (lit and fig), with pp *excoriātus*, whence 'to excoriate'; derivative ML *excoriātiō*, o/s *excoriātiōn-*, yields *excoriation*.

cuisine. See KITCHEN.

culinary: L *culīnārius*, adj of *culīna*, kitchen: f.a.e., KILN.

cull. See LEGEND, para 6, s.f.

culm, a stalk: L *culmus* (s *culm-*), stem, stalk: akin to E *haulm*, ME *halm*, OE *healm*, itself akin to Gr *kalamos*, a reed: IE r *khal-*, with extension *khalm-* issuing in L and in Gmc.

culminate, culmination; culminant.

L *culmināre*, to come to a peak, derives from *culmen*, upper part, summit, app a contr of the syn *columen*, akin to *columna* (cf COLUMN) and to *collis*, a hill. The pp *culminātus* yields 'to culminate', whence, anl, *culmination*; presp *culminans*, o/s *culminant-*, yields the adj *culminant*.

culpable, whence culpability; culprit; exculpable, exculpate, exculpation, exculpatory; inculpate, inculpation, inculpatory.

1. L *culpa*, (act of) negligence, a fault (as in *mea culpa*, my fault), earlier *colpa*, has s *colp-*, r perh *col-*. Derivative *culpāre*, to blame, has derivative *culpābilis*, whence *culpable*. Culprit= OF-MF *cul(pable) prit*, var of *cul prist*; *prist* is a var of OF-MF *prest* (F *prêt*), ready (to prove it), from LL *praestus*.

2. The LL cpd *inculpāre*, to impute something to (*in*) somebody, to blame, has pp *inculpātus*, whence 'to inculpate'; derivative LL *inculpātiō*, accusation, o/s *inculpātiōn-*, yields *inculpation*; *inculpatory* is an E formation. *Inculpable*, blameless, derives from LL *inculpābilis*: in-, not+ *culpābilis*.

3. ML *exculpātiō*, o/s *exculpātiōn-*, whence E *exculpation*, suggests a ML *exculpāre*, to clear of fault or guilt, with pp *exculpātus*, whence 'to exculpate', with subsidiary *exculpatory*.

cult; cultivable, cultivate, cultivation, cultivator; culture (G Kultur), cultural, culturist; cf the element *-cole*; sep COLONIAL (etc.).

1. The starting-point is L *colere* (s *col-*), to till or cultivate; IE r, *kwel-*, to move around (a place); akin, therefore, to WHEEL. Its pp is *cultus*, whence the n *cultus*, gen *-ūs*, a cultivating, hence active care, hence the religious sense, whence, perh via EF-F *culte*, the E *cult*; whence also *cultūra*, orig a tilling, cultivation (soon fig), whence, prob via MF-F *culture*, the E *culture*, whence *cultural* (*-al*, adj) and, esp in cpds, *culturist* (*-ist*).

2. The pp *cultus* has subsidiary LL adj *cultiuus*, attested in *cultiua*, elliptical for *cultiua terra*, cultivated land, whence the ML *cultivāre*, to cultivate (lit, then fig), with pp *cultivātus*, whence 'to cultivate'. ML *cultivāre* becomes late OF-F *cultiver*, with derivatives *cultivable* and *cultivation* adopted by E; MF-F *cultivateur* becomes E *cultivator*.

culvert: o.o.o.; perh from EF *coulere*, *coulouere* (F *couloir*), a channel, from OF-F *couler*, to flow, itself from L *colāre*, to filter, from *cŏlum*, a filter, prob influenced by OF-F *couvert*, f *couverte*, covered (over).

cumber, v hence n; from the n, both *cumbersome* (*-some*) and *cumbrous* (for *cumberous*: suffix *-ous*).

'To *cumber*', ME *cumbren*, var of *combren*, is aphetic for late ME *encomber*, from OF-F *encombrer*, to obstruct: *en*, in (used int)+*combre*, an abatis (felled trees used in fortification)+inf suffix *-er*. Late ME *encomber* becomes E 'to encumber'; the E *encumbrance* (suffix *-ance*) derives from OF-MF *encombrance* from *encombrer*.

cumin. See KÜMMEL.

cummerbund: Hind *kamarband*: (via Ar) from Per *kamar*, loins+Per *band*, a band or bondage.

cumquat. See KUMQUAT.

cumulate (adj and v), cumulation, cumulative; cumulus; accumulate (adj and v), accumulation, accumulative, accumulator.

1. L *cumulus*, a heap (whence the E Met sense), then an excessive heap, then a surplus, has s *cumul-*, with prob IE r *cum-*; cf L *tumulus*, a mound. Its derivative *cumulāre*, to heap up, has pp *cumulātus*, whence 'to cumulate'; derivative LL *cumulātiō*, o/s *cumulātiōn-*, yields *cumulation*; *cumulative* is of E formation.

2. The cpd *accumulāre*, to put heap to (*ad*) heap, has pp *accumulātus*, whence 'to accumulate'. Derivative *accumulātiō*, o/s *accumulātiōn-*, yields

*accumulation*, and derivative *accumulātor* is adopted by E; *accumulative* is an E formation.

**cuneiform**, wedge-shaped. See the elements *cunei-* (of a wedge) and *-form* from FORM.

**cunning**. See CAN, para 3, both adj and n deriving from the presp of OE *cunnan*, to know.

**cunt**: ME *cunte* (occ *counte*), recorded once in OE: OFris *kunte*, akin to ON *kunta*, MLG-LG *kunte*, D *kunte*, MD *conte*; also to MF (and F) *con*, OF varr *cun*, *cunne*: like It *conno*, from L *cunnus*, s *cun-*. The presence of *t* in the Gmc has long puzzled the etymologists: even Walther von Wartburg aligns the Gmc *kunta*, *kunte*, with the L *cunnus* only under the aegis of a question-mark; for *cunnus*, E & M adduce the syn Gr *kusthos* and the Per *kun*, the posterior, but they omit to cite the Hit *kun*, tail; for *kusthos*, Hofmann proposes an orig *\*kuzdhos*, with extended r *\*kus-* or *\*keus-* and with true IE r *\*ku-* or *\*keu-*, to hide or conceal, and he adduces L *cutis*, skin, which has s *cut-*, extension of r *\*cu-*, *\*ku-*, the skin being a coverer.

But is it not probable that the word is of common Medit stock? Eg offers *qefen-t*, vagina, vulva, akin to the *n*-lacking Eg *ka-t*, vagina, vulva, mother, women collectively. There are also several Sem cognates. The basic idea is prob 'essential femineity'.

**cup**, n hence v; **cupboard**; **cupola**, **cupule**.

A *cup*, ME *cupp* or *cuppe*, derives from OE *cuppe*, itself from LL *cuppa*, cup, from L *cūpa*, a tub or a cask: akin to Gr *kupē*, ship, hut, hole, and Skt *kupas*, hole, well. L *cūpa* has dim *cūpula*, small cask, a small burial-place, a tomb, whence the Bot *cupule* (suffix *-ule*); L *cūpula* becomes It *cupola*, adopted by E. A *cupboard* was orig a shelf (BOARD) for *cups* and dishes.

**Cupid**, the god of Love; **cupidity**.

*Cupid*=L *Cupidō*, from *cupidō*, desire (of love), from *cupidus*, desirous, from *cupere*, to desire, s *cup-*: o.o.o.; perh an int of *capere*, to take: to long to take. *Cupidus* has derivative *cupiditās*, o/s *cupiditāt-*, whence, via MF-F *cupidité*, the E *cupidity*. Cf COVET.

**cupola**. See CUP.

**cupreous**. See the 1st COPPER.

**cupule**. See CUP.

**cur**. See CARE, para 5.

**curate**; **curator**. See CURE, para 1.

**curb** (1), AE n. See *kerb* at CURVE. Therefore cf:

**curb** (2), E n: a restraining strap or chain, a restraint or check or hindrance, whence 'to curb' or restrain. This n *curb* derives from OF-F *courbe*, a curve, hence a curved instrument or device: from OF-F *courbe*, curved, bent, crooked: from ML *curvus*, L *curuus*, curved, bent: f.a.e., CURVE.

**curd**; **curdle**. See CROWD.

**cure**, n and v; **curable**, **incurable**; **curative**; **curator**, **curate**, **curé**; **curious** (**incurious**), **curiosity**; —**accurate**, **accuracy**; **procure**, **procurable**, **procuration**, **procurator** (and **proctor**, with adj **proctorial**), **procurer**, **procuress**; **proxy**; **scour**, to cleanse; **secure** (adj, hence v), **security**, and **insecure**,

insecurity; **sure**, **surety**—**assure**, **assurance**—**ensure**—**insure**, **insurable**, **insurance**.

1. L *cūra*, anxiety, care, medical care, hence a medical cure, is o.o.o. It becomes OF-F, hence ME, *cure*. 'To cure' derives from OF *curer*, from L *cūrāre*, to take care of, from *cūra*. *Cūrāre* has the foll derivatives relevant to E:

*cūrābilis*, whence *curable;* from its LL neg *incūrābilis* derives *incurable*

pp *cūrātus* becomes the ML n for 'one charged with the cure of souls', whence E *curate*, whence *curacy* (*curate*+*-cy*); MF-F *curé* also comes from this ML n;

derivative *cūrātiō*, o/s *cūrātiōn-*, yields *curation*; agent *cūrātor*, adopted by E.

(*Curative* is from F *curatif*, *-ive*.)

2. Irreg formed from *cūra* is the adj *cūriōsus*, anxious about, hence inquisitive, whence E *curious*; its derivative *cūriōsitās*, o/s *cūriōsitāt-*, yields OF-MF *curiosete* (EF-F *curiosité*), adopted by ME, whence E *curiosity*; the neg L *incūriōsus* yields *incurious*. From *curiosity*, by abbr, derives *curio*.

3. The foll prefix-cpds affect E:

*accūrāre*, to give care to (*ad*), be careful about, with pp *accūrātus*, whence the adj *accurate*, whence *accuracy* (*accurate*+*-cy*)

LL *excūrāre*, to clean off, whence OF-MF *escurer*, whence, by aphesis, MD *schuren*, whence E 'to *scour*', to rub hard, to cleanse by rubbing hard;

*prōcūrāre*, to occupy oneself with (*prō*, for), hence to provide oneself with, becomes OF *procurer*, whence 'to *procure*', whence *procurable*, *procurer*, *procuress*; on *prōcūrāt-*, the s of the pp *prōcūrātus*, arise *prōcūrātiō*, o/s *prōcūrātiōn-*, whence, prob via MF-F, *procuration*, and *prōcūrātor*, adopted by E, and LL *prōcūrātōrius*, whence *procuratory*.

4. L *prōcūrātor* became OF-MF *procuratour* (EF-F *procurateur*), whence, by contr, the ME *procutour*, later *proketour*, whence E *proctor*, with several obvious derivatives.

5. L *prōcūrātiō* has, in ML, a needless syn: *prōcūrātia*, var *procuracia*, whence ME *procuracie*, whence E *procuracy*. Now ME *procuracie* has the ME contr *prokecie*, a doing business through an agent or a substitute, hence that agent or substitute: whence 'a *proxy*', used derivatively as adj and v.

6. There remains, held over from para 3, the L prefix-cpd *sēcūrus*: the privative prefix *sē-*, without+*-cūrus*, from *cura*: 'without anxiety or care': whence the adj *secure*. L *sēcūrus* has derivative *sēcūritās*, o/s *sēcūritāt-*, whence *security*. The ML *\*insēcūrus* and *insēcūritās* yield *insecure*, *insecurity*.

7. L *sēcūrus* becomes OF *seür*, later *sur* (F *sûr*), whence ME *seur*, *sur*, later *sure*; derivative OF *seurté* becomes ME *seurte* becomes E *surety*. *Unsure*, therefore, is an E formation.

8. OF *seür* has an AF derivative *enseurer*, whence 'to *ensure*'.

9. Late ME *sure* has derivative *ensuren*, perh by confusion between AF *enseurer* and ME *assuren* (see next para): whence 'to *insure*', with derivatives the abstract *insurance* (cf *assurance*) and the agent *insurer*, as well as the adj *insurable*.

10. L *sēcūrus* has LL derivative *assēcūrāre* (as-for *ad-*, to, used int), to render safe or secure, whence OF-MF *aseürer*, whence 'to assure'; derivative OF-MF *aseürance* becomes ME *assur-aunce* becomes E *assurance*; 'to *assure*' has agent *assurer* and pa *assured*.

**curé.** See prec, para 1.

**curfew.** See FOCAL, para 5.

**curio, curiosity, curious.** See CURE, para 2.

**curl**, v hence n (whence the adj **curly**): ME *curlen*, by metathesis from *krul*, curly, akin to MD *krul*, MHG *krol*, curly, MD *crulle* or *crolle* or *crol*, a curl, MD *crullen* or *crollen*, to curl, D *krul*, a curl, *krullen*, to curl: perh ult akin to ROLL and ROUND.

**curlew:** MF *corlieu* or *courlieu* (C13), EF-F *courlis*: echoic (cf Picard dial *corlu*). B & W.

**curling**, the Scottish game, is played with *curling stones*: from CURL.

**curmudgeon**, whence **curmudgeonly** (-*ly*, adj): o.o.o.: perh akin to the echoic Sc *curmurring*, a low rumbling or murmuring (*cur-mur*), a source of grumbling, ? cf the Shetlands and Orkney dial *curmullyit*, a dark, ill-favoured fellow. (E.D.D.) Derivation from F *coeur méchant*, ill-tempered heart, is 'erudite' f/e.

**currant:** elliptically from AF raisins de *Corauntz*, grapes of Corinth (F *Corinthe*: L *Corinthus*: Gr *Korinthos*), the Gr city of *Corinth* being prob the orig centre of exportation. *Corinth* has adj, hence n, *Corinthian*, licentious, a rake, the ancient city being noted for luxury and licence.

**currency, current.** See COURSE, para 7.

**curricle; curriculum.** See COURSE, para 8.

**currier.** From 2nd CURRY.

**curry** (1), n (hence v): orig a condiment: Tamil *kari*.

**curry** (2), v, esp 'to *curry* a horse, to *curry* leather', whence *currier*, a dresser of tanned leather. See ARRAY, para 4.

**curse**, n and v; **accurse**, whence the pa **accursed**.

'To *accurse*' derives from ME *acursien*, *a-* used int+*cursien*, to curse, whence 'to *curse*': ME *cursien* derives from OE *cursian*, itself from late OE *curs*, whence 'a *curse*'. The OE word is o.o.o.: perh from ML *cursus*, a COURSE or series of prayers (esp prayers of imprecation), from LL *cursus*, the order of a church service; cf, however, OIr *cūrsagim*, I chide, with r *cūrs-*, akin to the syn OIr *cairigim*, (cf Ga *coirich*), I blame or chide. EW suggests that OE *curs* derives from ONF *curuz*, from OF *coroz*, anger, from OF-MF *corocier*, to anger, from VL *\*corruptiāre*, from L *corruptus*, pp of *corrumpere* (cf CORRUPT): a likelier origin.

**cursive; cursory.** See COURSE, para 6.

**curt**, whence **curtness**; **curtail**, whence **curtail-ment**.

1. *Curt* (cf the OF-F *court*, short) derives from

L *curtus*, cut off, cut short, prob the pp of a lost v from the IE r *\*ker-*, to cut. OF-F *court* has derivative MF *courtault* (EF-F *courtaud*), whence the obs E *curtal*, having a short tail, hence wearing a short frock: whence, f/e-influenced by TAIL, the v *curtail*, to shorten.

2. Prob from L *curtus* derives OE *cyrtel*, whence ME *curtle*, later *kirtle*, extant in E, now usu a woman's short skirt.

**curtain.** See COURT, para 4.

**curtsey, curtsy.** See COURT, para 2.

**curve**, n, derives from *curve*, adj, which derives from ML *curvus* (L *curuus*), curved, bent, whence ML *curvāre*, L *curuāre*, to bend, to curve, pp *curuātus*, ML *curvātus*, whence the adj *curvate*; derivative *curuātiō*, o/s *curuātiōn-*, ML *-vātiōn-*, yields *curvation*; derivative *curuatūra*, ML *-vatūra*, yields *curvature*.

2. ML *curvus* has It dim *corvetta*, whence EE *corvetto*, whence the n *curvet* (made with arched back); 'to *curvet*' derives from It *corvettare*, from It *corvetta*.

**cushion**, n hence v: ME *cusshyn*, *cuisshin*: OF *cussin* (C12), *coissin* (C12–16), *coussin* (as still): Gallo-Roman *\*coxīnus*, from L *coxa*, the thigh, 'cushions being orig intended for chairs and forms' (B & W).

**cushy** (sl): Hind *khush*, pleasant, influenced by Hind *khushi*, pleasure: Per *khūsh*, pleasant.

**cusp:** L *cuspis* (r *cus-*), a pointed end, e.g. of a spear: o.o.o.

**cuspidor.** See the 2nd SPIT, para 5.

**cuss**, sl for 'a fellow', is short for *customer* (q.v. at CUSTOM); 'to *cuss*' is an AE coll form of CURSE; the pp *cussed* has derivative *cussedness*, contrari-ness.

**custard:** by metathesis from ME *crustade*, a crusted pie: MF *croustade*, from OF-MF *crouste*, a crust: f.a.e., CRUST.

**custodian**=*custody* (*y* becomes *i*)+n suffix -*an*; and *custody* derives from L *custōdia*, a guarding, by -*ia* from *custōd-*, o/s of *custōs* (s *cust-*), a guard, perh akin to Gr *keuthein* (s *keuth-*), to hide, *keusō* (s *keus-*), I shall hide, and Skt *kuharam*, a hole, and therefore to HIDE. (Hofmann.)

**custom, customary, customer; accustom.**

'To *accustom*': OF *acustumer*, var of *acostumer*: *a-*, L *ad*, to+*custume*, var of *costume*+inf -*er*: f.a.e., COSTUME. OF *custume* and its var *costume* are adopted by ME: whence E *custom*. The deriva-tive OF adj *costumier* (C12; as n, C14), somehow blending with LL *consuētūdinārius*, usual, yields E *customary*—and also, as n from adj, the doublet *customer*, orig a toll-gatherer, influenced by the syn ML *custūmārius*. *Customs*, customary dues, is merely the pl of *custom* in its obsol sense 'a duty expected by ruler or government'.

**cut**, v, hence adj and n, derives from ME *cute*, *cutte*, *cutten*, varr *ketten* and *kitten*, and is o.o.o.: EW's conjecture that it derives from OF-MF *escurter* (F *écourter*), to shorten, to dock, from L *curtus*, cut off, cut short (see CURT), is not to be sneered off, for, as he remarks, '*cutty* (*pipe, sark*) corresponds exactly to F *écourté'*. Hence the pa *cutting* and the agent *cutter* (the boat cuts through the water).

**cute** is prop *'cute*, aphetic for *acute*.

**cuticle**: L *cuticula*, dim of *cutis* (s *cut-*), skin, ult skin to the E n HIDE.

**cutlass**: EF-F *coutelas*, prob a reshaping of It *coltellaccio*, itself from L *cultellus*, a little knife, dim of *culter*, a knife: see COLTER. Cf:

**cutler, cutlery.**

The former derives from OF-F *coutelier* (cf *couteau*, a knife): LL *cultellārius*, knife-maker, from *cultellus* (see CUTLASS); the latter from MF-F *coutellerie*, itself from *couteau*.

**cutlet.** See COAST, para 5.

**cutter.** See CUT, s.f.

**cuttlefish** has 2nd element *fish*, and 1st element *cuttle*, (influenced by CUT, but deriving from) ME *cotul*, earlier *codull*, OE *cudele*, akin to COD.

**cutty pipe; cutty sark.** See CUT. A *sark*, shirt or *chemise*, derives from OE *serc* or *serce*, akin to ON *serkr*.

**cyanide** tacks Chem *-ide* to *cyan-*, s of *cyanic* (acid), itself from Gr *kuanos*. Cf the element *cyano-*.

**cybernetics.** See GOVERN, para 3.

**cyclamen** is adopted, perh via the id MF-F, from L, which thus adapts Gr *kuklaminon* (or *-nos*).

**cycle,** n hence v; **bicycle, tricycle; cyclic,** with elaboration **cyclical**—cf **encyclical; cyclone, cyclonic; Cyclops** (see the element *-ope*), with adj **Cyclopean;** for **cyclo-** cpds in general, see the element *cyclo-*.

1. E *cycle* derives, perh via EF-F *cycle*, from L *cyclus*, trln of Gr *kuklos*, ring, circle, hence a circular movement in time, hence also a wheel, whence *bicycle* (n hence v), *bi-*, two, and *tricycle*, *tri-*, three; the coll *bike* derives from the wrong division *bic-ycle*. Gr *kuklos*, s *kukl-*, has r *kuk-*, the IE r being *\*kuk-* or *\*kak-*: cf Skt *čakráš*, Tokh A *kukal*, Tokh B *kokale*, a wheel, all ult akin to WHEEL. (Hofmann.)

2. Gr *kuklos* has adj *kuklikos*, whence L *cyclicus*,

whence EF-F *cyclique* and E *cyclic*; the prefix-cpd *encyclical*, adj hence n, tacks *-al* to the adj *encyclic*, LL *encyclicus*, LGr *enkuklikos* (ἐγκυκλικός): *en*, in+*kuklikos*: 'circular (letter)'.

3. Irreg from Gr *kuklos*, a circle, or more prob from Gr *kukloōn* (presp of *kukloō*, I go round, I encircle), contr to *kuklōn*, is the E *cyclone*, whence the adj *cyclonic*.

**cyder.** See CIDER.

**cygnet**: E dim, in *-et*, from MF-F *cygne*, OF *cisne*, a swan: VL *cicinus*: L *cycnus*: Gr *kuknos*, prob akin to Skt *śakunas*, a large bird, perh orig a large white bird, from Skt *śucis*, white, shining-white, brilliant—cf Skt *śōcati*, to shine. (Boisacq.)

**cylinder, cylindrical; calender,** n and v.

1. *Cylinder* derives from MF-F *cylindre*, L *cylindrus*, Gr *kulindros*, from *kulindein*, to roll, akin to Skt *kuṇḍám*, a round container, a round hole, and *kuṇḍalám*, a circle; IE r, app *\*kel-*, to bend, to curve. *Cylindrical* is an *-al* elaboration of the obsol *cylindric*, via Sci L *cylindricus* from Gr *kulindrikos*, adj of *kulindros*.

2. 'To *calender*' (cloth) derives from MF-F *calandrer*, as the E n does from MF-F *calandre*, app from ML *calendra*, itself obscurely from Gr *kulindros*. (Cf B & W at *calandre*.)

**cymbal.** See CHIME.

**cyme**: L *cyma*, young cabbage-sprout: Gr *kuma*, orig anything swollen: cf CAVE.

**Cymric,** adj hence n; **Cambria,** whence **Cambrian.**

*Cymric* adds adj suffix *-ic* to the *Cymr-* of W *Cymry*, the Welsh, and *Cymru*, Wales: *Cymry* is the pl of *Cymro*, from *cymro*, a compatriot (*com*, with+*brog*, land). *Cambria* is the ML name for Wales: from W *Cymru*.

**cynic, cynical, cynicism.** See CANINE, para 4.

**cynosure.** See CANINE, s.f.

**cypher.** See CIPHER.

**Cyprian, Cypriot.** See COPPER.

**cyst.** See CIST, para 3; cf the element *cysto-*.

**cytology.** See the element *cyto-*.

**czar.** See CAESAR, para 4.

# D

dab. n and v; dabble, dabbler, dabster; dap (n and (v—dabchick;—dib (n, v), dibble (n, v)—dibbler.

1. 'To dab', ME dabben, prob derives from MD dabben, app echoic. From the basic sense 'to strike smartly and lightly' (vt, hence vi) come the answering n and the sense 'a flat, or flattish, mass of, e.g., butter' and the coll sense 'somebody very smart at'; dabster is derivative (cf the suffix -ster); and dabble is a freq of 'to dab', with agent dabbler.

2. Dap, to gently drop a bait upon the water, is a var of 'to dab'; from the sense 'to dip into water' comes dapchick, soon dabchick.

3. 'To dab' has the obs thinned form dib, with freq dibble, whence the n dibble and the agent dibbler; dib, n, as counter or token, and as pl dibs, a children's game, played with knucklebones or pebbles, hence sl for 'money', app derives from 'to dib' or dab lightly.

dace (fish): ME darce, darse: OF dars (F dard): LL darsus, of Gaul origin.

dachshund. See CANINE, para 2.

dactyl, dactylic; date (fruit).

The adj dactylic comes, via L dactylicus, from Gr daktulikos, the adj of daktulos, a finger, hence the metric foot —◡◡, L dactylus, E dactyl: perh for *datkulos, o.o.o., but perh Sem, the Gr daktulos, a date (fruit) being very prob Sem and certainly, via L dactylus, yielding, either via OProv datil or via It dattero, the OF date (MF-F datte), whence the E date (fruit), the transition from 'finger' to 'date fruit' arising from the fruit's long, narrow form (B & W). Nevertheless, I suspect that the Gr daktulos, date fruit, is Sem and that daktulos, s daktul-, has r *dak-, akin to the deik- (cf Hind dekho, look!) of deiknumi, I show, point out, the finger being the orig pointer.

dad, whence pet-form daddy; dada, dadda; grandad (grand dad).

Dad is the usu E form (cf the Ir daid and Cor, Br, W tad); dada is the form that corresponds most closely with L tata, Gr tata or tetta, Skt tatas, familiar (prob orig childish) forms of L pater, Gr patēr, Skt pitṛ; cf also Ru táta; f.a.e., FATHER.

daddle. See DAWDLE.

dado is adopted from It: from L datum, a die, prop the neu of datus, given (pp of dare, to give): cf DATE (2). The Arch dado was at first the die-shaped part of a pedestal.

daemon. See DEMON.

daffodil: D de affodil, the affodil or asphodel:

EF-F asphodèle (cf MF afrodille): L asphodelus (whence E asphodel), trln of Gr asphodelos, itself o.o.o.

daft; deft. whence deftness.

Deft, ME defte, is a doublet of daft, the latter deriving from ME dafte, var defte: ME dafte, defte, 'stupid' as well as 'meek', derive from OE gedaefte, gentle or mild, akin to OE gedafen (s -dafen) or gedēfe (s -dēfe), suitable, fitting, due, akin to Go gadaban, to be suitable to or fit for, and gadob, gadof, suitable, fitting, and ON dafna, to grow strong: perh akin to FORGE. Whereas daft specializes as 'stupid', deft specializes as 'adroit': cf, sem, SOFT.

dagger: MF-F dague: OProv, or perh It, daga: ML daggerius, daggarius, daggarium, earlier dagga: o.o.o., but prob of C origin—cf the syn OIr daigean: OC *dag, a (sharp) point.

Dago, orig a Spaniard, derives from Diego, the Sp equivalent of James.

daguerreotype=Daguerre (F inventor, c1838) +comb -o-+TYPE.

dahlia: Dahl (a Sw botanist)+flower-name suffix -ia.

daily. See DAWN, s.f.

daimon. See DEMON.

dainty, adj, derives from the n: see DECENCY, para 8.

dairy: ME deierie, an -ery derivative from ME deie or daie, a maid: OE dāēge, kneader of OE dāh (see DOUGH): cf Gr deigan, to knead.

dais. See DISH, para 3.

daisy: ME daiseie: OE daeges ēage, 'day's eye', with ref to the flower's yellow disk.

dale comes from the OE dael, akin to OE—whence E—dell, which, a valley so much smaller than a dale, suggests that OE dell is a mutation of OE dael. With dell, cf OFris and MD del, delle, and OHG tellia; with dale, cf OS and Go dal, OHG tal (G Thal), ON dalr, and, more remotely, Gr tholos (s thol-), a rotunda.

2. Through LG and D daler, from G thaler (now Taler), a coin worth 3 marks, short for Joachimsthaler, made, 1519 onwards, at Joachimst(h)al, St Joachim's Valley, in Bohemia, comes the dollar, E and, much later, AE. Cf OPHTHALMIA.

dalliance comes, by suffix -ance, from 'to dally', itself from OF dalier, o.o.o., but perh a var of OF deslier (vi), to rejoice, enjoy oneself: des- used int+ lie (contr form), joyous, from L laetus, joyous+

inf -er. DAF has OF *daillier*, syn of *deslier*, yet declares it o.o.o.

2. *Dally* has the redup *dilly-dally*.

**Dalmatian** (dog); **Dalmatic, dalmatic.**

The former is the E adj (-*an*) for 'of *Dalmatia*'; *Dalmatic* represents the syn L *Dalmaticus*, whence, via L *Dalmatica uestis*, Dalmatian garment, Eccl LL *dalmatica*, derives the OF-F *dalmatique*, whence E *dalmatic*, a priestly vestment, made orig of white wool from Dalmatia (B & W).

**dam** (1), a quadruped's mother. See DAME.

**dam** (2), (water confined by) a barrier: app taken by ME, either from the syn OFris *damm*, or from MD *dam*, var *damm*, akin to MHG *tam* and OE *fordemman* (*for-*, private+*demman*), to stop up: notably cf the syn ON *dammr*; IE r, perh *dab-ma* (Walshe). Hence 'to *dam*'.

**damage**, n: ME, from OF-MF, *damage*: suffix -*age* tacked onto OF *dam*, from L *damnum*, damages, a fine or penalty: f.a.e., DAMN. OF-MF *damage* has the OF-MF derivative *damagier*, whence 'to *damage*'.

**damascene**, v, from adj **Damascene; damask; damson.**

Damascus, an ancient Syrian cultural and industrial city, famed for its silks and its steel, is L *Damascus*, Gr *Damaskos*, perh cf the H *Dammeseq* (the Ar *Dimashq*) and esp *Dumashqa* in the Letters of Tel-el-Amarna. The L adj is *Damascēnus*, whence E *Damascene*, applied esp to swords marked in a peculiar way (*damascened, damascene*). The L *Damascus* becomes It *Damasco*, whence *damasco*, a figured fabric, whence E *damask*; and L *Damascēnum* (*prūnum*) becomes *damascēnum* (mostly in pl *damascēna*), whence ME *damasin*, plum of Damascus, whence E *damson*.

dame, adopted by ME, with var *dam* (extant in E), from OF, derives from L *domina*, f of *dominus*, master, lord: cf DOMINIE and, f.a.e., DOMESTIC. *Madam* anglicizes F *madame*: *ma dame*, my lady: cf the It *madonna*.

**damn** (n hence v), **damnable, damnation, damnatory, damnify** (whence **damnification**), **damnous; condemn, condemnation, condemnatory; indemnify** (whence **indemnification, indemnificatory**) and **indemnity;—darn** (it)! and **darned;—sep damage.**

1. *Darn it!* and *darned* are eupheum for *Damn it* and *damned*.

2. 'To *damn*', ME *damnen*, OF-F *damner*, comes from L *damnāre*, to fine, penalize, condemn, from *damnum*, damage, loss, expense, hence, in Law, monetary fine for material loss, hence a penalty, perh akin to Gr *dapanē*, expense, and *daptō*, I share, hence to Skt *dāpayatē*, he shares; IE r, perh *da-* or *dai-*, to share, with extension *dap-*. (Hofmann.)

3. *Damnum* has adj *damnōsus*, whence the legal *damnous*, injurious. The v *damnāre* has pp *damnātus*, s *damnāt-*, whence both the n *damnātiō*, o/s *damnātiōn-*, whence, prob via OF-F, *damnation*, and the adj *damnātōrius*, whence *damnatory*; *damnāre* itself, s *damn-*, has LL derivative *damnābilis*, worthy of a penalty, whence late OF-F,

hence E, *damnable*, and the cpd adj *damnificus* damage-causing, whence LL *damnificāre*, to injure or fine, whence EF *damnifier*, whence 'to *damnify*', the LL derivative *damnificātiō*, o/s *damnificātiōn-*, becoming *damnification*.

4. *Damnāre* has the prefix-cpd *condemnāre*, whence OF-EF *condemner*, whence 'to *condemn*'; derivative *condemnātiō*, o/s *condemnātiōn-*, yields, prob via MF-EF, the E *condemnation*; *condemnatory* is an E anl formation, perh prompted by L *condemnātor*, a condemner.

5. The adj prefix-cpd *indemnis*, unharmed (*in-*, not), s *indemn-*, has LL derivative *indemnitās*, a not being hurt, acc *indemnitātem*, whence MF-F *indemnité*, whence E *indemnity*; 'to *indemnify*'= L *indemn-*+connective -*i*-+-*fy*, to make.

**damozel.** See DAMSEL.

**damp**, n hence adj (whence **dampness**) and v **damp** (whence **damper**) and v **dampen** (whence **dampener**): MD (and MLG) *damp*, vapour, very closely akin to ON *dampi*, dust, and to OHG-MHG *damph*, G *Dampf*, steam, and to DUMP, despondency, and DIM—cf MHG *dimpfen*, to steam. (Walshe.)

**damsel** and archaic **damozel**: ME *damesel*, earlier *damaisele, dameisele*: OF *dameisele*, var *damoisele* (influencing *damozel*), a gentlewoman: VL *domini-cella*, dim of L *domina* (cf DAME), f of *dominus*, master, lord: f.a.e. DOMESTIC. The MF-F *demoiselle*, young lady, whence EF-F *mademoiselle* (*ma*, f of *mon*, my), derives from OF-MF *damoisele*.

**damson.** See DAMASCENE, s.f.

**Dan** (title: cf *Don*). See DOMESTIC, para 6.

**dance**, n and v (whence **dancer, dancing**).

A *dance*, ME *daunce*, derives from OF *dance*, var *danse* (as in F), itself from the v *dancier*, var *danser* (as in F), app of Gmc origin—cf OHG *dansōn*, to stretch out (here, one's limbs), cf E THIN; B & W, however, propose a Frankish *dintjan*, (vi) to move here and there, as in the syn D *deinzen*; cf DANDLE. The OF v yields ME *dauncen* or *daunsen*, whence 'to *dance*'.

**dancetté.** See TOOTH, para 4, s.f.

**dandelion.** See TOOTH, para 10; sem cf DAISY.

**dandle.** See GONDOLA, para 2.

**dandruff** app blends E dial *dander* (var *dan*), scurf+ON *hrufa*, scab; the former is o.o.o., the latter akin to OHG *hruf* and MD *rove*, scurf.

**dandy**, n, whence the coll adj **dandy** and the literary adj **dandiacal.**

*Dandy*, a fop, is o.o.o.: perh from *Dandy*, a pet-form of *Andrew*, esp as the term was first used on the Scottish border and St Andrew is the patron saint of Scotland; perh, however, as a b/f from Sc and North Country *dander*, to saunter, a word used by Scott: sem cf the F *flâneur*.

**Dane, Danish; Danegeld, Danelaw.**

*Dane* derives from Da *Daner*, Danes, from ON *Danir*, akin to LL *Dani*. (The OE form is *Dene*.) *Danish*=*Dane*+adj -*ish*. *Danegeld* was a tribute (with OE *geld*, cf YIELD) paid to the Danish invaders of England; *Danelaw* derives from or was, at least, suggested by OE *Dena lagu*, 'law of the

Danes', NE England under the law of the Danes. *Denmark* is Da *Danmark*, the territory of the Danes: cf MARK.

**danger, dangerous; endanger.**

1. *Danger*, ME *daunger*, later *danger*, dominion, jurisdiction, (later) difficulty, danger, derives from MF-F *danger*, earlier *dangier*, earliest *dongier*, orig a lord's jurisdiction or power, itself from VL *domniārium*, power, esp a lord's power, from L *dominus*, master, lord: cf DOMINIE and, f.a.e., DOMESTIC.

2. *Dangerous*—in ME 'haughty (like a master), hence difficult, dangerous'—derives from MF *dangeros* (F *dangereux*), from OF *danger, dangier*.

3. The cpd *endanger* = (to put) *en-*, in + *danger*.

**dangle**, whence the pa **dangling**: of Scan origin (cognates in *-ang*, and *-ing-*): app the freq of a v akin to DING; cf the redup *dingle-dangle*.

**dank**, adj hence n, akin to DAMP, is of Scan origin (cognates in *-ank* and *-unk*).

**dap.** See DAB, para 2.

**daphne**, shrub or its flower, derives—via L—from the Gr nymph *Daphnē*, changed into the *daphnē* or laurel tree whence she gets her name, itself of Medit origin.

**dapper**, orig 'brave': MD-D *dapper*, nimble, strong, akin to OHG *tapfar*, MHG *tapfer*, heavy, weighty, G *tapfer*, brave, and ON *dapr*, heavy-hearted: with Sl cognates; IE r, perh *tab-*, prob echoic.

**dapple**, n hence v and the pa **dappled**, app meant orig 'a small splash', hence 'blot' or 'spot', for its source, the ON *depill*, a spot, hence a dog with spots above the eyes, derives from ON *dapi*, a pool, and is presumably a dim thereof.

**dare**, v hence n and the pa and vn **daring; der-ring-do.**

1. 'To *dare*' comes from ME *I dar*, earlier *I dear*, I dare, from OE *ic dear*, the inf being *durran* (s *dur-*): akin to OS *gidar*, inf *gidurran*, and Go *gadars*, inf *gadaúrsan*, where *gi-, ga-* are varr of the OE prefix *ge-*; to OHG *tar*, inf *turran* (MHG *turren*), and OFris inf *dūra*; to Gr *tharsein*, *tharrein* (r *thar-*), to be courageous; to Skt *dharšati*, he dares; to several Sl words, e.g. Lith *drasus*, *dresus*, bold; IE r, *dhars-*, *dhers-*, to be courageous, to dare.

2. App *derring-do*, audacious action, audacity, is a contr of *daring* [to] *do*; perh rather was Chaucer's *durring don* (daring to do) supposed by Spenser, who coined *derring-do*, to mean 'bold, chivalrous action', and his misapprehension, perpetuated, has fathered a word. (EW.)

**dark**, adj hence n, hence also *darkness* (*-ness*) and 'to **darken**' (*-en*, v suffix); **darkling**, in the dark.

The last = *dark*, adj + *-ling*, adv; and the adj *dark*, ME *darke*, earlier *derk(e)*, earliest *dearc*, comes from OE *dearc* (OE *deorc*): cf OHG *tarchanjan*, to hide, render obscure; to Lith *darga*, dull, rainy weather; and to several C words, e.g. OIr *dorche*, darkness, and *derg*, dark-red—Ga *dorch*, W *duog*, Mx *dorragh(e)y*, dark, obscure.

**darling.** See DEAR, para 4.

**darn** (1), to mend (e.g., stockings), with early var *dern*: Channel Islands F *darner, derner*, to darn, to patch: NF *darne*, a piece: Br *darn*, a piece: akin to syn W and Cor *darn*, the C r being *dar-*, to split or divide, cut or tear; but akin also to Skt *dērna*, torn.

**darn** (2), in *darn* (*it*)! and *darned*. See DAMN, para 1.

**darnel.** See NEGRO, para 8.

**dart** (n hence v): OF-MF *dart* (MF-F *dard*): like the OProv *dart* and the OHG *tart* (javelin, dart), it derives from Frankish *daroth*—cf OE *daroth*, *darath*, dagger, and ON *darrathr*, dart.

**dash**, v hence n and the pa **dashing**, the agent **dasher**, and the adj **dashy** (*-y*): ME *daschen*: of echoic Scan origin. For *-ash*, cf *clash, crash, flash, gnash, lash, mash, pash, smash, thrash*, etc.

**dastard**, whence **dastardly; daze** (v hence n), whence the freq 'to **dazzle**', whence the n.

'To *daze*', ME *dasen*, comes from the r *dasa-* of ON *dasask*, to grow weary and exhausted. From the ON pp *dasathr*, weary and exhausted, prob comes the E n *dastard*.

**data** is the pl of L *datum*, orig the neu of *datus*, pp of *dare*, to give (cf *dat*, he gives), akin to Skt *dádati*, he gives, with cognates in Gr and Sl: cf DONATE. *Date* in chronology derives, prob via MF-F *date*, from the ML n *data* (var *datum*), used in this sense, orig for *littera data*, letter given, *data* being the 'first word of the formula indicating the date on which an act [or document] had been drawn up' (B & W). 'To *date*' comes from MF-F *dater* (from the n).

2. On the pps *dat-* arises L *datīuus*, ML *datīvus*, suitable for giving, whence the F *datif* and the E *dative*, adj hence n.

**date** (1), fruit. See DACTYL.

**date** (2) in time. See DATA, para 1.

**dative.** See DATA, para 2.

**daub** (v hence n and agent **dauber**): ME *dauben*, to smear: MF-F *dauber*, to plaster, prob not from L *dēalbāre*, to whiten (*dē-* used int + *albus*, white + inf suffix *-āre*), as so often stated, but, as B & W propose, by aphesis (in a dial) from OF-F *adouber* as influenced by Sp *adobar*, to plaster (cf ADOBE).

**daughter** (whence **daughterly**): ME *doughter*, earlier *doghter*, earliest *dohter*: OE *dohter, dohtor*, akin to OFris and MD-D *dochter*, G *Tochter*, MHG-OHG *tohter*, OS *dohtar*, Go *dauhtar*; to ON *dóttir*; to certain Sl, but not to C nor to L, words; to Gr *thugatēr*; and notably to Skt *duhitā*: IE prototype, perh *dhugter*. Cf the distribution of and varr in BROTHER.

**daunt.** v hence obsol n (whence **dauntless**), derives, via ME *daunten*, from OF *danter*, var of OF-MF *donter* (EF-F *dompter*): L *domitāre*, int of *domāre*, to tame: cf DOMESTIC and TAME.

**Dauphin.** See DELPHINIUM.

**davenport**, a small writing-desk, and, in AE, a large well-upholstered sofa, derive prob from an E cabinet-maker and from an Am furniture-maker. (See P² but cf EW.)

**David; davit; Davy Jones('s locker).**

*Davit*, a naut crane, from OF *daviot* or *daviet*,

from *Daviot, Daviet*, dim of *David*, perh (EW) an 'allusion to David being let down from a window (1 *Samuel*, xix, 12)'. *David* is the H *Dāwid* or *Dāwīd*, beloved. The *Davy* of *Davy Jones*, the malevolent spirit of the sea, as in *gone*, or *sent*, *to Davy Jones's locker*, drowned, prob arises from *Jonah*, ii, 5; the prophet *Jonah* of Jonah and the Whale, 'formerly called *Jonas*, being made into *Jones* and supplied with a fitting Welsh Christian name' (EW), St David being the patron saint of Wales—cf sem DANDY. (Webster has a far too erudite, far too un-British explanation of this orig and predominantly British term.)

**daw**, a jackdaw, ME *dawe*, is akin to OHG *taha*, MHG *tahe*: ? echoic.

**dawdle**, v (hence n), whence **dawdler**, is akin to the dial *daddle*, to toddle, app a freq of the C16–17 SE, then dial, *dade*, to walk unsteadily, (vt) to support with leading strings, itself o.o.o., but prob echoic.

**dawn**, v (the n from the v), derives from **dawning**, daybreak, itself of Scan origin: cf Da, Nor, Sw *dagning*, an *-ing* n from ON *daga*, to become day, akin to OE *dagian* (late ME *dawen*), to become *daeg* or day.

2. Now, OE *daeg* survives as *day* (ME *dai*) and is akin to ON *dagr*, OS *dag*, Go *dags*, OHG (and G) *tag*, O Fris *dei*, the basic Gmc idea being 'hot period' of the 24-hours cycle, for cf such remoter cognates as Skt *nidāgha*, heat, summer, and *dáhati*, it burns, and Lith *dãgas*, harvest-time, and *dègti*, to burn; IE r, *\*dhagh*- (Gmc r *\*dag*-), varr *\*dhegh*- and *\*dhogh*-. (Walshe.) The cpds are self-explanatory. The adj *daily*, whence the adv, derives from OE *daeglīc* (*daeg*+*-līc*. E *-like*), cf OFris *degelik*.

**day**. See prec, para 2.

**daze**. See DASTARD.

**dazzle**. See DASTARD.

**deacon; diaconal, diaconate.**

1. *Deacon*, ME *deken*, derives from OE *dīacon*: LL *diaconus*, trln of Gr *diakonos* (Ionic *diēkonos*), a servant, in LGr a minister of the church: *dia*-, thoroughly, in all things+*enkonéō* (ἐγκονέω), I am active in service+*-os*, m n-suffix; *enkonéō* consists of *en*-, in, used int+*konéō*, I hasten, lit I raise dust (*konis*).

2. LL *diaconus* has adj *diaconālis*, whence E *diaconal*, and 'office of' n *diaconātus* (gen *-ūs*), whence *diaconate*.

**dead**, adj hence n ('the dead') and adv; hence also **deaden** (*-en*, v); **deadly;—death, deathly— deathful, deathless;**—to **die**, whence vn and pa **dying** (neg **undying**);—perh akin to sep FATIGUE.

1. *Deadly* comes from OE *dēadlīc*, dead-like, subject to death, (later) causing death, from OE *dēad*, whence, via ME *deed, ded, dead*, the E *dead*; OE *dēad* is akin to OFris *dād*, OS *dōd*, OHG-MHG *tōt*, G *tot*, Go *dauths*, ON *dauthr*; app *dēad* was orig the pp of a lost OE v for 'to die' (see para 3). With *dead*, phon cf DEAF.

2. Also from this lost v comes OE *dēath*, whence E *death*; derivative OE *dēathlīc*, death-like, subject

to death, (later) causing death, yields E *deathly*; *deathful* (*-ful*) and *deathless* (*-less*) are post-ME formations. OE *dēath* is akin to ON *dauthi*, Go *dauthus*, OS *dōth*, OHG *tōd* (G *Tod*).

3. 'To *die*', ME *dien*, earlier *deyen*, comes from ON *deyja*, akin to Go *diwan*, OS *doian*, OHG *touwēn*, to die, and to OFris *dēia*, to cause to die, to kill; cf also OIr *duine*, man (subject to death: a mortal) and prob L *fūnus*, q.v. at FUNERAL. (Walshe.)

**deaf** (adj, hence n 'the d.'), whence **deafen** (*-en*, v) and **deafness** (*-ness*), comes from OE *dēaf*, akin to Go *daufs* and ON *daufr*, also to OFris *dāf*, OS *dōf*, OHG *toub*, G *taub*, deaf, and, less nearly, to Gr *tuphlos* (s *tuphl*-, r *tuph*-), blind, perh a dissimilation of *\*thuphlos*; IE r, *\*dheubh*-, to be or render misty or obscure; of the Gmc words, the basic meaning is perh 'dull, stupid'—cf the perh cognate DUMB.

**deal**, a part or share; 'to *deal*' or share, hence to do business, whence 'a *deal*' or piece of business; also from the v: **dealer** and the pa and vn **dealing**.

1. 'To *deal*', ME *delen*, earlier *daelen*, derives from OE *dǣlan*, to divide, to distribute or share out, from *dǣl*, a part, hence a share, akin to OFris (and OS) *dēl*, OHG-G *teil*, Go *dails*, ON *deild*, with cognates in Sl. With the OE v, cf OFris *dēla*, OS *dēlian*, Go *dailjan*, ON *deilja*. The IE r is *\*dhāi*-, var of *dāi*-, to cut into parts, hence to divide into parts. (Whitehall.)

2. OE *dǣel* has a cpd *ordǣel* (with var *ordāl*), a judgement, lit a dealing out, this *or*- (perh cf ORT) being influenced by G *ur*- and *er*- (cf the Go *us*-); cf MD *ordeel*, D *oordeel*, and OHG-G *urteil*, judgement, a judge's sentence against the prisoner. 'The various kinds of mediaeval ordeal (by fire, water, combat) were regarded as judgements of God' (Walshe).

**deal** (2), a board of pine or fir wood, derives from MD *dele* (D *deel*), plank, perh reinforced by MLG *dele*, intimately akin to MHG *dile*, OHG *dil*, board (G *Diele*, plank), ON *thili*, plank, OE *thille*, board or plank, whence E *thill*, either of the two shafts of a vehicle drawn by one horse. The OE *thille* has cognate *thel*, plank, perh ult akin to L *tellus* (s *tel*-), earth, IE r *\*tel*-.

**dean**, whence **deanery; doyen**.

L *decem*, 10 (f.a.e., TEN), has LL derivative *decānus*, leader or chief of ten persons, which becomes OF *deien* (cf OProv *degan*), whence both the F *doyen*, partly adopted by E, and the ME *deene, dene*, whence *dean*.

**dean** (2). Cf *dene*, see DEN.

**dear** (adj hence n), whence **dearness; endear,** whence **endearing** and **endearment; dearth; darling.**

1. *Dear*, highly esteemed, hence precious, highly priced, derives, through ME *dere*, earlier *deore*, from OE *dēore*, var *dīere*, akin to OHG *tiuri*, MHG *tiure*, G *teuer*, OS *diuri*, ON *dȳrr*.

2. 'To *endear*'=*en*, in, to+*dear*, used as v: to render dear to.

3. ME *dere* has derivative *derthe*, dearness, hence scarcity, hence famine: whence E *dearth*.

4. OE *dēore* has derivative *dēorling* (*-ling*, connoting a possessor of the quality implied by the adj): whence ME *derling*, E *darling*.

**death, deathly.** See DEAD, para 2.

**debar.** See DISBAR and, f.a.e., BAR.

**debark.** See the 3rd BARK, para 3.

**debase, debasement.** See BASE, adj, para 3.

**debate.** See 2nd BAT, para 3.

**debauch** (n and v); from the v: **debaucher, debauchery.**

The n *debauch* anglicizes EF-F *débauche*, itself from the MF-F *débaucher*, orig to entice away from one's work, whence 'to *debauch*': and F *débaucher* derives from OF *desbochier*, to quit one's work, to be idle: *des-*, L *dis-*, apart from+ *-boschier*, for *\*baucher*, from *bauch* (earlier *balc*, later *bau*), a beam, from Frankish *\*balc* (cf BALK): the semantic development, as detailed by B & W, is clear enough.

**debenture.** See DEBT, para 2.

**debilitant, debilitate, debilitation, debility.**

L *dēbilis*, physically weak, infirm, appears to consist of *dē*, away from+r *bil-*+adj suffix *-ilis*, with *bil-* answering to Skt *bálam* (s *bal-*), strength, to Gr *belteros* (r *bel-*), better, and to OIr *ad-bal* (r *bal-*), strong. *Dēbilis* has derivatives *dēbilitās*, weakness, whence, perh via MF-F *débilité*, the E *debility*, and *dēbilitāre*, to render weak, with presp *dēbilitans*, o/s *ilitant-*, *dēb*whence E adj, whence n, *debilitant*—with pp *dēbilitātus*, whence 'to *debilitate*—and with a pp-derivative *dēbilitātiō*, o/s *dēbilitātiōn-*, whence *debilitation*.

**debit.** See DEBT, para 3.

**debonair:** ME *debonaire*: OF *de bon aire* (F *débonnaire*), of good stock or race, where *aire*, bird's nest, usu area, derives from L *area*: f.a.e., AREA.

**deboshed** is a C18–19 Society form of *debauched* (see **debauch**).

**debouch,** to emerge, flow out: EF-F *déboucher*: *dé-* for *de-*, (down) from+*bouche*, mouth (L *bucca*, mouth cheek)+inf suffix *- er*. The n *debouchment* anglicizes F *débouchement* (suffix *-ment*). Cf *disembogue*, to flow (into a lake, the sea): Sp *desembocar*: *des-*, L *dis-*+*embocar*, to put into the mouth: *em-* for *en-* in+*boc*a, mouth (L *bucca*)+ inf *-ar*.

**debris:** EF-F *débris*, from MF *debrisier*: *de-*, down from+*brisier*, *briser*, to break, from early ML *brisāre*, of Gaulish origin—cf OIr *brissim*, I break, Ga *bris*, to break, Cor *brewy*, to shatter; cf also BRUISE.

**debt, debtor; debenture; debit; indebted;—devoir; —due,** adj hence n; **duty; endeavour** (AE **endeavor**), v hence n.

1. The base, L *dēbēre*, to owe, is a contr of *\*dēhabēre*, to have or possess (*habēre*: cf HABIT) by holding it from (*dē*) someone (E & M).

2. From *dēbentur*, (moneys) are owed, therefore due, comes the commercial share known as a *debenture*, usu in pl *debentures*.

3. The pp *dēbitus* has neu *dēbitum*, soon used as n, whence the E *debit*, whence 'to *debit*'; VL app

substituted *dēbita*, either f sing from neu pl or simply elliptical for *pecunia dēbita*, money owed, for *dēbitum*, and thus accounts for OF *dette*, adopted by ME, with E then reviving the *b* of the L word. On *dēbit-*, s of pp *dēbitus*, arises the agent *dēbitor*, whence, influenced by OF-F *dette*, the OF *detor* (*detur, detour*), whence ME *dettour, dettur*, whence ME *dettour, dettur*, whence, with L *b* restored, the E *debtor*.

4. OF-F *dette* has the late OF-F cpd *endetter*, to put or bring into (*en*) debt (*dette*), with pp *endetté*, whence ME *endetted*, whence the E *indebted*, as if harping back to L *\*indēbitus*.

5. L *dēbēre* becomes OF-F *devoir*, soon also a n, partly adopted by E in 'pay one's *devoirs*' or social duties.

6. OF-F *devoir*, to owe, has OF-MF pp *deü* (F *dû*), whence the E adj *due*, owed, therefore to be paid or otherwise performed; its neg is *undue* (*un-*, not) with derivative sense 'excessive'. Prob from *deü* comes AF *dueté*, as if ult from L *\*dēbitās*, o/s *\*dēbitāt-*: whence E *duty*, due conduct, hence any service (etc.) required by ruler or state. (With AF *dueté*, however, cf OProv *deuta, deute*, debt, the former prob from VL *dēbita*, the latter from L *dēbitum*.)

7. F *devoir*, to owe, was OF *deveir*, whence the n *dever, devor*, duty, whence, via *se mettre en devor*, to put oneself in duty, to make it one's duty, the ME *endever* or *endevor* (*en*, in), to strive, whence 'to *endeavour*'.

**debut,** n hence v: EF-F *début*, beginning (of a career): from EF-F *débuter*: *de*, from+*but*, mark (in game or sport)+inf suffix *-er*; MF-F *but* prob derives from Frankish *\*but*, stump or block of wood. (B & W.)

**decade,** whence the adj *decadal*: MF-F *décade*: L *decad-*, o/s of *decas* (s *dec-*), a set or group of *decem* (s *dec-*) or ten: Gr *dekas*, o/s *dekad-*: f.a.e., TEN.

**decadence, decadent.** See CADENCE, para 7.

**decamp.** See CAMP, para 2.

**decant, decanter.** See 1st CANT, para 2.

**decapitate, decapitation.** See CHIEF, para 3.

**decathlon** is an athletic contest (see ATHLETE) of ten events (Gr *deka*, L trln *deca*).

**decay.** See CADENCE, para 7.

**decease.** See CEASE, para 6.

**decedent.** See CEASE, para 6.

**deceit.** See CAPABILITY, para 7, s.f.

**deceive.** See CAPABILITY, para 7.

**December; decimal** (adj hence n), **decimate, decimation; decuman; decuple, decuplet; dicker; dime.**

1. *December*, with suffix as in *September, October, November*, derives from L *decem*, 10 (f.a.e., TEN), it being the 10th month in the ancient Roman year. L *decem* has adj *decimus* (whence the PN *Decimus*, lit the tenth-born), whence ML *decimālis*, whence E *decimal*—whence also LL *decimāre*, to take 1 in 10, whether as punishment (e.g., 1 soldier in 10, for mutiny) or, later, as tithe, with pp *decimātus*, whence 'to *decimate*', with sub-

sidiary LL *decimātiō*, o/s *decimātiōn-*, whence *decimation*.

2. L *decem* has also adj *decumānus*, of the tenth, one in ten, whence E *decuman* (esp wave); also on the *decu-* var, *decuplus*, tenfold, whence E *decuple*, whence, after *couplet* and *triplet*, a *decuplet* or set of ten musical notes.

3. L *decima* (*pars*), tenth (part), becomes OF *disme*, *dime* (F *dîme*), whence E *dime*, a tenth part (cf *tithe*), hence the Am coin of 10 cents (one-tenth of a dollar).

4. L *decem* has derivative *decuria*, a division, part, group of ten: whence MLG *deker*, G *Decker*, whence E *dicker*, a set of 10 hides, etc., whence prob AE *dicker*, a bartering, whence 'to *dicker*' or barter, (later) to haggle.

decency, decent—indecency, indecent; décor, decorate, decoration, decorative, decorator; decorous, decorum;—deign; indignant, indignation; dignified, dignitary, dignity; disdain; dainty; all akin to DOGMA, q.v. sep.

1. *Decency* comes from L *decentia*, formed upon *decent-* (whence the E *decent*), the o/s of *decens*, presp of *decēre*, esp *decet*, it is fitting or seemly; the opposites *indecentia*, *indecens*, o/s *indecent-*, yield *indency*, *indecent*. L *decēre*, s *dec-*, is akin to Gr *dokein*, s *dok-*, to seem (good), and Skt *daśas-yati*, he seeks to please, he is gracious

2. Very intimately akin to *decet*, s *dec-*, are L *decor* and its virtual syn *decus*, o/s *decor-*, ornament, thing of beauty, whence the v *decorāre*, with pp *decorātus*, whence 'to decorate', whence *decorative* (*-ive*, adj); *decoration* comes from *decorātiōn-*, o/s of LL *decorātiō*, formed upon *decorāt-*, s of the pp; *decorātor* is adopted from ML. L *decorāre* becomes MF-F *décorer*, whence *décor*, adopted by E.

3. L *decor* has adj *decōrus*, whence E *decorous*; the L neu *decōrum*, used as n, is adopted by E. The L opp *indecōrum* (*in-*, not), likewise adopted by E, is the neu of the adj *indecōrus*, with LL var *indecōrōsus*, whence perh—though more prob from the former—the E *indecorous*.

4. Also akin to *decet*, it is seemly, is the adj *dignus*, fitting, worthy, with derivative *dignitās*, merit, dignity (in various senses), whence OF-MF *dignité* (extant), *digneté*, whence ME *dignite* (*dignete*), whence *dignity*. *Dignus* has LL cpd *dignificāre*, to render worthy: *digni-*, c/f+-*ficāre* (var of *-ficere*), a c/f of *facere*, to make; whence EF *dignifier*, whence 'to *dignify*', whence *dignified*. The F *dignitaire*, whence E *dignitary*, comes more prob from F *dignité* than from L *dignitās*. *Condign*, although passing through F, almost embalms L *condignus*, thoroughly worthy (*con* used int+ *dignus*), hence the predominant E sense, thoroughly deserved, as in '*condign* punishment'.

5. The L neg *indignitās*, o/s *indignitāt-*, yields late MF-F *indignité*, whence E *indignity*; it derives from *indignus*, unworthy, whence LL *indignāri*, to be angry with (as at some unworthy act), with presp *indignans*, o/s *indignant-*, whence E *indignant*; on *indignāt-*, s of the pp *indignātus*, arises LL

*indignātiō*, o/s *indignātiōn-*, whence, prob via OF-F, the E *indignation*.

6. Less imm obvious a derivative is 'to *deign*', ME *deinen*, *deignen*, from OF-MF *deignier* (F *daigner*): LL *dignāri* (*dignāre*), to deem worthy, from *dignus*.

7. LL *dēdignāri* (*-āre*), to think unworthy, becomes VL *disdignāre*, whence OF-MF *desdeignier*, whence ME *desdainen*, *disdainen*, whence 'to *disdain*'. OF-MF *desdeignier* has derivative OF-MF n *desdeign*, *desdain*, whence ME *desdeyn*, *disdayn*, whence *disdain*, whence *disdainful*.

8. L *dignitās* has acc *dignitātem*, whence OF-MF *deintié*, var *daintié*, whence ME-E *dainty*, n, whence *dainty*, adj.

**deception, deceptive.** See CAPABILITY, para 7.

**decide,** whence pa **decided** (neg **undecided**); **decision, decisive**—**indecision, indecisive**.

1. 'To *decide*' comes from MF-F *décider*: L *dēcīdere*, to cut (*-cīdere*, c/f of *caedere*) thoroughly (*dē-*, down, used int), hence to decide; *caedere*, s *caed-*, is perh akin to Skt *khidati*, he tears. Cf CONCISE.

2. *Dēcīdere* has pp *dēcīsus*, s *dēcīs-*, whence both the L *dēcīsiō*, o/s *dēcīsiōn-*, whence, prob via MF-F *décision*, the E *decision*, and the ML *dēcīsivus*, whence MF-F *décisif* and E *decisive*.

3. *Indecision* derives from EF-F *indécision* (*in-*, not); *indecisive*=*in-*, not+*decisive*, but perh owes something to the ML adv *indēcīsim*, without the lawsuit being decided.

**deciduous.** See CADENCE, para 7.

**decimal, decimate, decimation.** See DECEMBER, para 1.

**decipher, -er, -ment.** See CIPHER.

**decision, decisive.** See DECIDE, para 2.

**deck,** n, derives from MD *dec* (D *dek*), from *decken* (D *dekken*), to cover: f.a.e., THATCH.

**declaim, declamation, declamatory.** See CLAIM, para 6.

**declare; declarant, declaration, declarative, declaratory, declarer.**

'To *declare*', whence *declarer*, comes, via MF *declarer*, from L *dēclārāre*, to make very clear: *dē-*, used int+*clārāre*, to make clear, from *clārus*, clear: f.a.e., CLEAR. L *dēclārāre* has presp *dēclārans*, o/s *dēclārant-*, whence E *declarant*; on *dēclārāt-*, s of the pp *dēclārātus*, arise *dēclārātiō*, o/s *dēclārā-tiōn-*, whence, prob via OF-F, the E *declaration*, and LL *dēclārātiuus*, LL *dēclārātivus*, whence E *declarative*. *Declaratory* is either an E formation (*-ory*, adj) or a derivative of EF-F *déclaratoire*.

**déclassé.** See CLASS, para 4.

**declension.** See CLIME, para 8.

**decline; declination.** See CLIME, para 8.

**declivitous, declivity.** See CLIVUS, para 3.

**decoct, decoction.** See COOK, para 2.

**decode.** See CODE.

**decollation, décolleté.** See COL.

**decompose, decomposition.** See COMPOSE, para 5.

**décor, decorate, decoration, decorative, decorator.** See DECENCY, para 2.

**decorous, decorum.** See DECENCY, para 3.

**decoy.** See CAVE, para 1.

**decrease,** n and v. See CRESCENT, para 6.

**decree,** n hence v; **decretal.**

The adj *decretal* comes from LL *dēcrētālis,* of a decree, from L *dēcrētum,* whence OF-MF *decret, decré,* whence ME *decre,* whence E *decree*: and *dēcrētum* is prop the neu of *dēcrētus,* pp of *dēcernere,* to decide: *dē,* from+*cernere,* to sift, hence to decide: cf CRISIS.

**decrement.** See CRESCENT, para 6, s.f.

**decrepit, decrepitude.**

*Decrepit* anglicizes MF-F *décrépit*: L *dēcrepitus,* perh from *dē-,* used int+*crepāre* (s *crep*-), (vi) to crack or split or tear noisily: echoic; cf all the other echoic words (Skt, Gr, L, Gmc) in *cr-, kr-.* Whereas the ML derivative *dēcrepitūdō* yields MF-F *décrépitude* and, perh independently, E *decrepitude,* the LL derivative *crepitātiō,* o/s *crepitātiōn-,* yields *crepitation*: *crepitātiō* is built upon the freq *crepitāre,* to crackle, pp *crepitātus,* whence 'to *crepitate*'; the presp *crepitans,* o/s *crepitant-,* yields the E adj *crepitant.* Cf CRAVEN.

**decretal.** See DECREE.

**decry,** whence decrial (-*al,* n): F *décrier,* MF *descrier: des-,* L *dis-*+*crier,* q.v. at CRY.

**decuman.** See DECEMBER, para 2.

**decumbency, decumbent.** See HIVE, para 8.

**decuple, decuplet.** See DECEMBER, para 2.

**decurrent, decursive.** See COURSE, para 10.

**dedicate, dedication, dedicator** (and **dedicatee**), **dedicatory.** See DICT, para 8, at *dedicare.*

**deduce, deduction, deductive.** See DUKE, para 6 at *deducere.*

**deed.** See DO, para 2.

**deem, deemster.** See DOOM, para 2.

**deep, deepen; depth.**

1. *Deep,* adj, has derivatives *deep,* n (the adv comes from OE *dēope,* from the OE adj), and *deepen* (-*en,* v): and the adj *deep,* ME *dep,* earlier *deop,* derives from OE *dēop,* akin to OFris *diāp,* OS *diop,* Go *diups,* MD *diep, diepe,* D *diep,* OHG *tiof, tiuf,* MHG-G *tief,* ON *diōpr, djūpr*; prob to W *dwfn, dofn,* OIr *domain,* OC *\*dubnos,* var of *\*dubos* (or* *doubos*), r *\*dub-*; cf Lith *dubùs.* (Walshe.) Cf also DIP and DIVE.

2. Much as *width* from *wide, breadth* from *broad, length* from *long,* so *depth* from *deep.*

**deer; reindeer.**

The latter comes from ON *hreindȳri* (*hreinn,* reindeer+*dȳr,* deer): and ON *dȳr* is akin to the source of E *deer,* viz.: OE *dēor, dīor,* beast, ME *deor,* later *der,* beast, later *deer.* OE *dēor* (*dīor*) is akin to OFris *diār,* OHG *tior,* MHG-G *tier,* Go *dius,* all '(wild) beast': perh cf, sem, E *animal* from L *anima,* breath, soul—the Gr *theos,* a god, being possibly related to *deer* in its orig sense '(wild) animal': the breather, (*theos*) the animator.

**deface, defacement.** See FACE.

**defalcate, defalcation, defalcator.**

L *dēfalcāre,* to cut off (*dē*-) with a sickle (*falx,* o/s *falc-*), hence to deduct, has pp *dēfalcātus,* whence 'to *defalcate*'; late derivative *dēfalcātiō,*

o/s *dēfalcātiōn-,* yields *defalcation*; *defalcator* is an E formation in agential -*or.* Perh cf FALCON.

**defamation, defame.** See FAME.

**default.** See FAULT.

**defeat,** n (whence **defeatism**: -*ism*) and v.

'A *defeat*'—influenced by MF-F *défaite*—derives from 'to *defeat*', and 'to *defeat*' derives from ME *defet,* dejected, depressed, from OF-MF *desfait,* undone, pp of *desfaire,* from VL *\*disfacer* (*dis-,* apart+*facere,* to do or make: cf FACT).

**defecate, defecation.** See FAECAL.

**defect, defection, defective.**

LL *dēfectīuus,* ML -*īvus,* whence E *defective,* and L *dēfectiō,* o/s *dēfectiōn-,* whence *defection,* and L *dēfectus* (gen -*ūs*), whence *defect,* are all built upon *dēfect-,* the s of *dēfectus,* pp of *dēficere,* to fail or be wanting: *dē-,* from+*-ficere,* c/f of *facere,* to make or do: f.a.e., FACT.

**defence,** AE **defense; defend, defendant; defensible, defensive.** See FEND.

**defenestration.** See PENATES, para 4.

**defer** (1), to postpone. See DIFFER, para 1.

**defer** (2), to yield (vi), to refer (vt) to; **deference, deferent, deferential.**

*Deferential* is the adj (*t* for *c*+suffix -*ial*) of *deference,* itself from MF-F *déférence,* from MF-F *déférent,* from L *dēferent-* (whence E *deferent,* adj hence n), o/s of *dēferens,* presp of *dēferre,* to bring (*ferre*) down (*dē*): cf INFER, PREFER, PROFFER, REFER: f.a.e., 'to BEAR'. *Dēferre* becomes MF-F *déférer,* whence 'to *defer*'.

**defiance, defiant.** See DEFY.

**deficiency, deficient.** L *dēficere,* to be wanting (see DEFECT), has presp *dēficiens,* o/s *dēficient-,* whence E *deficient*; derivative LL *dēficientia* yields *deficiency.*

**defile** (1), to befoul, to sully or pollute, blends the obs *file,* to foul, with the true origin: ME *defoulen* (contaminated var, *defoilen*): OF *defouler* (*de-,* down+*fouler,* to trample, akin to L *fullō,* a cloth fuller, see 'to FULL'). Hence, by suffix -*ment,* the n *defilement.*

**defile** (2), to march in a file, comes from EF-F *défiler*; the pp *défilé,* used as n (EF-F), becomes EE *defilee,* whence E *defile*; f.a.e., FILE, a rank or row.

**defilement.** See the 1st DEFILE, s.f.

**define, definite, definition, definitive.**

*Definitive* comes, via OF-F, from L *dēfinitīuus,* ML -*īvus*; *definition,* via OF-F, from L *dēfinitiō,* acc *dēfinitiōnem*; both the L words being formed upon *dēfinīt-,* s of *dēfinītus* (whence E *definite*), pp of *dēfinīre,* to limit (*dē-,* from+*finis,* a boundary, hence an end): *dēfinīre* becomes OF-MF *definir* (EF-F *dé-*), var *defenir,* whence 'to *define*': f.a.e., FINAL.

**deflate, deflation** (whence **deflationary**).

'To *deflate*' comes from L *dēflātus,* pp of *dēflāre,* lit to let the breath out of: cf INFLATE and, f.a.e., 'to BLOW'. *Deflation* is an E formation on anl of *inflation.*

**deflect, deflection** (-**flexion**), **deflector.** See FLEX.

**defloration, deflorescence, deflower.** See FLORA.

deform, deformation, deformity. See FORM.

defraud. See FRAUD.

defray (whence defrayal) comes from F *défrayer* (C14), an int (*de-*) of *frayer* (C13), itself from *\*frait, \*fret*, deduced from the C13 *fres, frais*; *\*frait*, var *\*fret*, derives from L *fractum*, a thing broken or infringed, from *fractus*, pp of *frangere*, to break: the earliest sense was 'damage caused by breaking something' (B & W). Dauzat holds that *fractum* was blended with—or, at the least, influenced by—ML *fredus, fredum, fridus*, a fine for breakages, war indemnity, from Frankish *\*fridu* (OHG *fridu*, MHG *fride*, G *Friede*, OS *frithu*, OFris *fretho*), peace.

deft. See DAFT.

defunct. See FUNCTION.

defy; defiance, defiant.

*Defiance* derives from OF-MF *desfiance*, app from *desfiant*, presp of *desfier*, orig to renounce a sworn faith, hence, to remove one's confidence from, to provoke or defy: *des-*, for L *dis-*, apart+ OF-F *fier*, to entrust to, to trust in, from VL *\*fidāre*, to entrust, from L *fidēs*, faith: cf FIDELITY and, f.a.e., FAITH. OF-MF *desfiant* becomes F *défiant*, whence E *defiant*; and OF-MF *desfier* yields 'to *defy*'.

degeneracy, degenerate (adj, v), degeneration, degenerative. See GENERAL, para 8.

deglutinate, deglutination. See GLUE.

degradation, degrade. See GRADE, para 8.

degree. See GRADE, para 9.

degression. See GRADE, para 8.

degust, degustation. See GUST, para 2.

dehisce, dehiscent. See YAWN, para 3.

dehydrated, dehydration. See HYDRO and cf the element *hydro-*.

deictic. See DICT, para 23.

deify, deific, deification; deicide; deism, deist; deity.

Of all, the base is L *deus*, a god, LL God: and *deus*, akin to L *diuus* (ML *divus*: cf DIVINE) and Gr *dios*, godlike, akin also to L *diēs*, Skt *dyaús*, day (Skt, also sky): f.a.e., DIANA. L *deus*, a god, has LL*i* derivative *deitās*, acc *deitātem*, whence OF *dete*, adopted by ME, whence E *deity* (cf the EF-F *déité*); the EF derivatives *déisme, déiste*, become E *deism, deist*. The LL cpd adj *deificus*, god-making (*facere*, to make), becomes E *deific*; subsidiary LL *deificāre* (pp *deificātus*) becomes MF-F *déifier* becomes 'to *deify*'; from LL *deificātiō* come late MF-F *déification* and E *deification*; *deicide* comes from LL *deicīda*, God-slayer, suggested by L *homicīda*, a man-slayer.

deign. See DECENCY, para 6.

deism, deist; deity. See DEIFY.

deject, whence pa dejected; dejection; dejectory.

'To *deject*' comes from ML *dējectus* (L *dēiectus*), pp of L *dēiicere*, to throw (*-iicere*, c/f of *iacere*) down (*dē-*): cf ABJECT, CONJECT; INJECT, OBJECT, PROJECT, REJECT, SUBJECT, and, f.a.e., JET. On *dēiect-*, s of *dēiectus*, arises *dēiectiō*, o/s *dēiectiōn-*, whence, via ML, the E *dejection*; but *dejectory* (cf TRAJECTORY) is an E formation.

delated, elation, delator. See the 1st TOLL, para 6.

delay, n v. See LANGUID, para 10.

delectable, delectation. See DELICACY, para 7.

delegacy, delegate, adj, n, v; delegation. See LEGAL, para 6.

delete, deletion, deletory; delible, indelible (whence indelibility).

L *dēlēre* (s *dēl-*), to efface, to destroy, app (E & M) confuses *dēlināre* (s *dēlin-*), to smear or anoint (cf the 1st LIME), and *\*dēolēre*, syn of *abolēre*, to destroy, to efface: cf ABOLISH. *Dēlēre* has the foll derivatives relevant to E:

*dēlēbilis*, whence *delible*, its neg *indēlēbilis* yielding *indelible*;

*dēlētiō*, o/s *dēlētiōn-*, whence *deletion*. *Deletory*, however, is an E formation (*delet-*, from the L pp *dēlētus*+adj suffix *-ory*).

deleterious. ML *dēlētērius*, noxious (cf LL *dēlētērion*, a poison): Gr *dēlētērios*, from *dēleisthai*, to harm, akin to Lett *delit*, to torture; IE r, *dĕl-*, to cut, hence to harm by cutting.

delf or delft; Delft. See DELVE, para 2.

deliberate (adj, v), deliberation, deliberative. See LEVEL, para 4.

delible. See DELETE.

delicacy, delicate, delicatessen; delicious; delight (n, v), delightful; dilettante; delectable, delectation; —elicit, elicitation, elicitory;—lace (n, v) and enlace; lash (to bind); lassoo; latch, latchet.

1. The clue to this app tangle is very simple: L *laqueus*, a noose or snare, a cord, a lace, akin to *lax* (o/s *lac-*), deceit, trickery, seduction: o.o.o.

2. *Laqueus* becomes OF-MF *laz* (F *lacs*), whence ME *las*, a cord, a snare, whence E *lace*, (obs) noose, snare, net, (extant) cord, string, lace—whether of a shoe or of an openwork fabric; 'to *lace*' comes from OF-MF *lacier* (F *lacer*), from L *laqueāre*, to noose, to take in a *laqueus* or snare. 'To *enlace*' (whence, by suffix *-ment*, the n *enlacement*, perh adopted from OF-F) derives from OF-MF *enlacier* (*en L in*, in); a cpd of *lacier*.

3. OF-MF *lacier* has dial var *lachier*, whence 'to *lash*' or bind with cord or rope.

4. *Lachier* has derivative n *lache*, a tie or fastening, whence, via ME *lacche*, E *latch*, anything that fastens; the *latch* of a door (whence *latch-key*) or in a knitting machine derives from ME *lacche*, which is prob the same word but might owe something to ME *lacchen*, to seize, from OE *laeccan*, whence certainly 'to *latch*', to seize, to catch, to receive, extant in dial ('*latch* milk in a pail'); 'to *latch*' a door obviously derives from the n. *Latchet*, loop or thong, derives from ME *lachet*, adopted from MF *lachet*, a dial var of MF-F *lacet*, itself an *-et* dim of OF *laz* (as in para 2).

5. L *laqueus* becomes Sp *lazo*, whence E *lasso*, whence 'to *lasso*'.

6. Intimately akin to *laqueus* is *lacere* (s *lac-*), to entice—cf *lax* in para 1. *Lacere* has cpd *ēlicere*, to draw out by trickery, to wheedle from (*ē, ex*, out of) someone; the pp *ēlicitus* yields 'to *elicit*', whence the E formations *elicitation* (by anl with other *-ation* nn) and *elicitory* (*-ory*, adj).

7. *Lacere* has int-freq *lactāre*, with cpd *dēlectāre*, to draw clear of, to draw out from, to seduce, hence to charm or delight; pp *dēlectātus* yields 'to *delectate*', and subsidiary *dēlectātiō*, o/s *dēlectātiōn-*, yields OF and (? hence) E *delectation*; *dēlectābilis* yields, perh via OF, the E *delectable*.

8. L *dēlectāre* becomes OF-MF *deleitier*, MF *deliter*, whence ME *deliten*, whence—perh influenced by LIGHT, illumination—'to *delight*'; the n *delight* derives from ME *delit*, adopted from OF-MF, from the OF v; *delightful* (*-ful*) is an E formation from n *delight*. Moreover, *dēlectāre* becomes It *dilettare*, with presp *dilettante*, which, used as n, is adopted by E.

9. L *lacere*, to snare, has, in addition to *ēlicere* (para 6), the cpd *dēlicere*, to turn aside by trickery or seduction, with derivative pl n *dēliciae*, (means of) enticement, (sources of) delight, with adj *dēliciōsus*, whence, via OF-MF *delicieus*, the ME-E *delicious*.

10. Akin to *dēliciae* is *dēlicātus* (unless for *dēlicitus*, pp of *dēlicere*), grateful to the senses, enticing, voluptuous, whence—cf the F *délicat*—the E *delicate* (adj, hence n), whence *delicacy* (*delicate+-cy*): cf *accuracy* from *accurate*). Late MF-F *délicat* has EF-F derivative *délicatesse*, delicacy, whence—perh influenced by G *essen*, to eat—G *delicatessen*, adopted by E.

**delimit, delimitation.** See LIMIT, para 3.

**delineate, delineation, delineator.** See LINE, para 4.

**delinquency, delinquent.** See LEND, para 6.

**deliquescence, deliquescent.** See LIQUEFY, para 6.

**deliration, delirious, delirium.** See LEARN, para 3.

**deliver, deliverance, deliverer, delivery.** See LIBERAL, para 4.

**dell,** a small valley. See DALE.

**delphinium; dolphin; Dauphin.**

1. The third, orig bestowed in C12 on the Count of Vienne, prob as a nickname, became, in C14, the title of the eldest son of the successive Kings of France: F *dauphin*, earlier *daufin*, the fish dolphin: OProv *dalfin*: VL *dalfinus* (early C8), var *dalphinus*: L *delphinus*: Gr *delphis*, o/s *delphin-* (gen *delphinos*), from *delphus*, uterus, womb. The flower *delphinium* (Sci L) is 'so named from the shape of the nectary' (Webster).

2. OF *daufin* has var *daulphin*, whence ME *dolphyn*, whence E *dolphin*.

**delta,** whence the adj **deltaic; deltoid.**

The third (adj, whence n) represents Gr *deltoeidēs*, delta-shaped (cf IDOL and the suffix *-oid*): and *delta*, adopted from Gr, is the name of the capital letter *Δ*, the E *D*; Gr *δ*, *Δ*, comes from Phoenician. The form *Δ* gives its name to the marshy tract at Nile's mouth, hence to any other such tract.

**delude; delusion, delusive, delusory.** See LUDICROUS, para 5.

**deluge.** See LAVA, para 9.

**delusion, delusive, etc.** See LUDICROUS, para 5.

**delve; delf; Delft.**

1. *Delve*, to dig, derives from OE *delfan* (s *delf-*):

akin to OHG pi-*tëlpan*, to bury, and MHG *tëlben*, to dig—to OS bi*delban*, to bury—to MD *delven*, to dig, to bury, D *delven*, to dig - esp to OFris *delva*, to dig—and perh to several words in Sl; IE r, *\*dhelbh-*. (Walshe.)

2. OE *delfan* has derivative n *delf*, a digging, preserved in rural E for 'pond' or 'ditch': cf the D town of *Delft*, earlier *Delf*, named from MD *delf*, a canal; hence *delft* or *delf*, from *Delf(t) ware*.

**demagogue, demagogic, demagogy.**

The adj *demagogic* comes from Gr *dēmagōgikos*, adj of *dēmagōgos*, a leader (*agōgos*, adj, leading, from *agein*, to lead: cf AGENT) of the *dēmos* or people (cf DEMOCRACY and the element *demo-*). *Demagogy*=Gr *dēmagōgia*, leadership of the people: *dēmo-*+a derivative, in *-ia*, from *agōgē*, guidance.

**demand.** See MANUAL, para 23.

**demarcation, demarcate.** See MARK, para 9.

**demean** oneself, to lower oneself, perh comes from *de-*, down from, used int, and *mean* in sense 'common, base', rather than from '*demean* oneself', to behave, carry oneself well or ill, q.v. at MINATORY, para 6.

**demented, dementia.** See MIND, para 11.

**demerit.** See MERIT, para 2.

**demerse, demersion.** See MERGE, para 2.

**demesne.** See DOMESTIC, para 5, s.f.

**Demeter.** See MATER, para 2.

**demijohn:** f/e for late EF-F *dame-jeanne*, dame Jeanne, Lady Jane: either a witticism in the same order as F dial *christine* and *jacqueline* (B & W) and perh as E *jeroboam* and *rehoboam*, or, in F, a jocular comparison of fat, wicker-dressed bottle to fat, overdressed lady (EW). Dauzat derives F *dame-jeanne* from Prov *damajano*, itself perh from Prov *demeg*, a half, reshaped by f/e; his is the most ingenious, perh the best, explanation.

**demilune.** See the 3rd LIGHT, para 11.

**demilitarize.** See MILITANT, para 3, s.f.

**demise,** n hence v; **demission.** See MISSION, para 9.

**demobilize, -ization.** See MOVE, para 6.

**democracy, democrat, democratic.**

1. *Democrat* derives from EF-F *démocrate*, b/f from MF-F *démocratie* (whence E *democracy*), itself from LL *dēmocratia*, from Gr *dēmokratia*: *dēmo-*, c/f of *dēmos*, the people+*-kratia*, from *kratos*, power. *Democratic*: MF-F *démocratique*: ML *dēmocraticus*: Gr *dēmokratikos*, adj of *dēmokratia*. Gr *dēmos* perh derives from *daiomai*, I divide, akin to OIr *dām*, troop, company, and Skt *dati*, to distribute. (Cf DEMON.)

2. *Dēmos* appears in three relevant prefix-cpds: *endemic*, Gr *endēmos*, *-dēmios*, with *en-*, in; *epidemic* (adj hence n), Gr *epidēmios*, with *epi-*, upon, hence among; *pandemic*, Gr *pandēmos*, *-dēmios*, with *pan-*, all-, throughout.

**démodé.** See MODE, para 2.

**demoiselle.** See DAMSEL.

**demolish; demolition.** See the 3rd MOLE, para 3.

**demon (daemon, daimon), demoniac, demonic; demonology.**

E *demon*, a spirit, esp 'one's good angel', now usu *daimon*, comes, via LL *daemon*, from Gr *daimōn* (δαίμων), a protective spirit, a divinity, perh from *daiomai*, I distribute, a divinity being a distributor of fate: cf DEAL, para 1. But *demon*, an evil spirit, seems to have come from LL *daemonium*, from Gr *daimonion*, neu of *daimonios*, adj of *daimōn*. The adjj *demoniac* and *demonic* represent LL *daemoniācus* (from *daemon*) and LL *daemonicus* (from Gr *daimonikos*). *Demonism* and *demonology* are F formations: element *demon(o)-*+suffix *-ism* and element *-logy*.

**demonetize.** See MIND, para 21.

**demonstrable, demonstrate, demonstration, demonstrative,** etc. Cf *remonstrate*, but see MONSTER, para 4.

**demoralize, demoralization.** See MORAL, para 4.

**demos.** See DEMOCRACY. The adj is *demotic* (Gr *dēmōtikos*).

**demote.** See MOVE, para 11.

**dempster.** See DOOM, para 2.

**demur (n, v), demurrage.**

1. *Demur*, n, derives from OF-MF *demor* or *demore*, itself from OF-MF *demorer*, var *demurer*, whence 'to *demur*': and OF-MF *demorer*, etc., derives from L *dēmorāri*, int (*dē-*) of *morāri*, to delay (vt, vi), from *mora*, a delay or pause or postponement: o.o.o. OF-MF *demorer* has derivative OF-MF *demorage*, whence E *demurrage*. The legal *demurrer* comes from the AF v *demurer* used as n.

2. L *morāri*, to delay, has derivative adj *moratōrius*, whence E *moratory*; *moratorium* is the L neu of that adj used, although not in L, as n.

**demure.** See MATURE, para 5.

**demurrage, demurrer.** See DEMUR, para 1.

**demy.** See the element *demi-*.

**den; dene,** var dean, valley.

A beast's *den* comes from OE *denn*, intimately akin to OE *denu, dene*, a valley, whence E *dene*, and to MLG *denne*, a hollow, a beast's den, and OFris *dene*, down (adv).

**denationalize.** See NATIVE, para 10.

**denature.** See NATIVE, para 9.

**denegate, denegation.** See NEGATE, para 3.

**dengue** fever: a WI Sp reshaping (after Sp *dengue*, prudery) of Swahili *kidinga* popo, dengue fever.

**denial.** See NEGATE, para 3.

**denigrate, denigration.** See NEGRO, para 8.

**denim** is elliptical for F serge *de Nîmes*, Nîmes serge, first made in that city.

**denizen:** easement of OF-MF *denzein*, var of *deinzein*, adj hence n, (one) living *deinz* or within (city or state): *deinz* represents L *dē intus*, from within, with *intus* deriving from L *in*, in; *-ein*, F *-ain*, E *-an*, connotes 'of'. Opp FOREIGN.

**Denmark.** See DANE, s.f.

**denominate, denomination, denominator.** See NAME, para 9.

**denotation, denote.** See NOTABLE, para 9.

**dénouement** (AE *de-*). See NET, para on *nodus*.

**denounce.** See NUNCIO, para 4.

**dense, densen, density; condense** (whence **condensed, condenser)** and **condensation.**

*Dense* comes, via MF-F, from L *densus*, close-set, crowded, a nasal cognate of Gr *dasus*, (of hair) thick; *densen*=*dense*+v-suffix *-en*; *density*= F *densité*, from L *densitās* (o/s *densitāt-*), from *densus*. The derivative L v *densāre* has cpd *condensāre*, whence MF-F *condenser*, whence 'to *condense*'; subsidiary LL *condensātiō*, o/s *condensātiōn-*, accounts for MF-F and E *condensation*.

**dent** (1), a blow, a small depression. See DINT.

**dent** (2), a toothlike notch. See TOOTH, para 3.

**dental, dentary, dentate, dentellate, dentelle, dentelure, denticle, denticulate, dentifrice, dentin(e), dentist** (whence **dentistry), dentition, denture.** See TOOTH, paras 4–6.

**denude; denudant, denudation.** See NAKED, para 3.

**denumerate,** etc. See NUMBER.

**denunciation, denunciative,** etc. See NUNCIO, para 4.

**deny, denial.** See NEGATE, para 3.

**deodar:** Hind *deodar*: Skt *devadāru*, 'gods' timber'—an IE cedar. (Cf DIVINE.)

**deodorant, deodorize:** that which removes, to remove (connoted by *de-*), a bad smell (ODOR).

**depart, department** (with adj in *-al*), **departure.** See PART, para 19.

**depend, dependable; dependant, dependent** (cf **dependence, dependency).** See PEND, para 16.

**depict, depiction.** See PAINT, para 3.

**depilatory.** See PILE, hair.

**deplete, depletion, depletive, depletory.** See PLENARY, para 12.

**deplore,** whence **deplorable,** prompted by late MF-F *déplorable*; **deploration.**

1. The 3rd comes, prob via F *déploration*, from L *dēplōrātiō*, o/s *dēplōrātiōn-*, built upon *dēplōrāt-*, s of *dēplōrātus*, pp of *dēplōrāre*, to bewail or lament, a cpd of *plōrāre*, to wail, s *plor-*, app orig echoic.

2. *Plōrāre* has also the cpd *implōrāre*, to wail *in* or *to*, hence to appeal, in piteous manner, to, whence 'to *implore*'; derivative *implōrātiō*, o/s *implōrātiōn-*, yields *imploration*.

**deploy, deployment.** See PLY, para 11.

**depone, deponent.** See POSE, para 8.

**depopulate, depopulation.** See PEOPLE, para 4.

**deport, deportation, deportment.** See the 3rd PORT, para 5.

**depose, deposit, deposition, depositor, depository.** See POSE, para 8.

**depôt,** AE **depot.** See POSE, para 8, s.f.

**deprave,** whence pa **depraved; depravation, depravity.**

The last, influenced by obs *pravity* (ML *prāvitās*, L *prāuitās*, from *prāuus*), comes from 'to *deprave*'; *depravation*, from L *dēprāuātiō*, ML *-prāvātiō*, o/s *-prāvātiōn-*, from *prāuus*; *deprave*, from MF-F *dépraver*, from ML *dēprāvāre*, L *-prāuāre*: *dē-*, used int+*prāuus* (ML *prāvus*), crooked, perverse, itself o.o.o.

deprecate, deprecation, deprecative, deprecatory. Cf *imprecation* (etc.) and see PRAY, para 4.

depreciate, depreciation, depreciative, depreciator, depreciatory. See PRICE, para 6.

depredation. See PREY, para 2.

depress, depressant, depression, depressive, depressor. See the 2nd PRESS, para 6.

deprivation, deprive. See PRIVATE, para 5.

depth. See DEEP, para 2.

depurant, depurate, depurative. See PURE, para 7.

deputation, depute, deputize, deputy. See the 2nd COUNT, para 3.

deracinate, déraciné. See RADICAL, para 7.

deraign. See REASON, para 9.

derange, derangement. See RANGE, para 5.

derby (hat): *Derby hat*: perh because worn by those famous sportsmen, the Earls of *Derby*. OScan *diurby*, a *by*, or homestead, with deer or a deer-park (Ekwall).

derelict, dereliction. See LEND, para 5.

deride, derision, derisive, derisory. See RISIBLE, para 3.

derive, whence derivable; derivate, derivation, derivative (adj hence n). See RIVER, para 10.

dermatitis is an *-itis* or disease of the *dermis* or skin: cf suffix *-itis* and the element *-derm*.

derogate, derogation, derogatory. See ROGATION, para 6.

derrick, hoisting device, comes from the early C17 E hangman, Thomas *Derrick*, app from D *Dierryk*, contr of *Diederik*, akin to LL *Theodericus*, var *-doricus*, prob of Go origin (cf DUTCH): *thiuda-reiks*, people's king.

derring-do. See DARE, para 2.

dervish: Tu *dervish*: Per *darvish*, poor, (hence n) a beggar, esp a begging religious. Sem cf FAKIR.

descant, n, is ONF *descant* (cf MF-EF *deschant*), from ML *discantus* (gen *-ūs*): *dis-+cantus*, a singing, a melody, from *canere*, to sing: f.a.e., HEN. 'To *discant*' derives prob from the E n.

descend, descent, etc. See ASCEND, para 7.

describe, description, descriptive. See SCRIBE, para 12.

descrive. See SCRIBE, para 12, s.f.

descry, catch sight of, derives, in ME, from MF *descrier*, to cry down, proclaim: cf DECRY and, f.a.e., see CRY. The ME word, influenced by late ME *discerne*, to distinguish, was orig applied to shouting one's discovery of an enemy, of game, and (cf EXPLORE) of land.

desecrate, desecration. See SACRAMENT, para 16.

desert (1), often in pl deserts, merit, merits. See SERVE, para 6.

desert (2), arid wasteland; also v; deserter, desertion. See SERIES, para 9.

deserve. See SERVE, para 6.

desiccate; desiccant; desiccation, desiccative, desiccator, desiccatory.

L *dēsiccāre*, to dry up, is an int (*dē*) of *siccāre*, to dry, from *siccus* (s *sic-*), dry, akin to Gr *iskhnos* (s *iskhn-*, r *iskh-*, of which *\*sikh-* is a metathesis), dry, dried up, and perh to Skt *hikus*, dry. Its presp *dēsiccans*, o/s *dēsiccant-*, yields the E adj hence n

desiccant; pp *dēsiccātus* yields both the adj and the v *desiccate*. On *dēsiccāt-*, s of *dēsiccātus*, are built: LL *dēsiccātiō*, o/s *dēsiccātiōn-*, E *desiccation*; LL *dēsiccātīuus*, ML *-īvus*, E adj hence n *desiccative*, the simple L adj *siccātīuus*, ML *-īvus*, yielding E *siccative*, adj hence n; LL *dēsiccātor*, adopted by E; and LL adj *dēsiccātōrius*, whence E *desiccatory*.

desiderata, desiderate, desideration, desiderative. See CONSIDERATE, para 3, and cf DESIRE.

design, n and v; designate, designation. Cf *assign*, *consign*, *resign*: see SIGN, para 14.

desire, n and v; desirable; desirous.

*Desire*, n, comes from OF-MF *desir*, itself from OF-MF *desirer*, whence 'to *desire*': and *desirer* comes from L *dēsiderāre*, (orig in augury) to cease to see, regret the absence of, hence to seek, to desire: *dē-*, (away) from+*sidus*, a star, o/s *sider-+* inf suffix *-āre*; *dēsiderāre* was prob suggested by *considerāre*. Derivative *dēsiderābilis* becomes OF-MF *desirable*, adopted by E; LL *dēsiderōsus* becomes OF-MF *desiros*, whence E *desirous*.

desist, whence desistance. See SIST, para 4.

desk. See DISH, para 2.

desmoid. See the element *desmidio-*.

desolate, adj and v; desolation. See SOLE, para 4.

despair, v hence n; desperado; desperate, desperation; esperance, Esperanto; perh prosper, prosperity, prosperous.

1. The basic word is L *spēs*, (a) hope: o.o.o.; prob IE r, *\*spe-*, with cognates in Sl, Baltic, Gmc. Primitive o/s: app *\*sper-*.

2. Derivative L *spērāre*, to hope, becomes OF *esperer*, presp *esperant*, whence the n *esperance* (F *espérance*), adopted by E; *Esperanto* ('the hopeful artificial language') adds an It-Sp ending to *esper-*.

3. L *spērāre* has cpd *dēspērāre*, to lose (*dē-*, down from) hope, which becomes OF-MF *desperer* (note *il despeire*, he loses hope), whence ME *despeiren*, *despayren*, whence 'to despair', whence the n *despair*, prompted by OF-MF *despoir* (from *desperer*). In Sp, L *desperare* becomes OSp *desperar*, with pp *desperado*, whence the Sp n *desperado*, a desperate man, hence a desperate criminal. L *dēspērāre* has pp *dēspērātus*, whence the E adj *desperate*; subsidiary L *dēspērātiō*, o/s *dēspērātiōn-*, yields, prob via OF-MF, the E *desperation*.

4. The ancient derivation of the L adj *prosper*, arriving opportunely, faring well, from *\*prō spēre*, conforming to, answering, one's hope, is, despite much opposition, at least plausible; the kinship with Skt *sphirás*, abundant, rich, is possible (E & M)—but why then *pro-*? The L adj *prosper* accounts for the PN *Prosper*; its derivative var *prosperus* accounts for E *prosperous*—derivative *prosperitās* (o/s *prosperitāt-*), via OF-F *prosperité* accounts for E *prosperity*; its derivative *prosperāre*, perh via OF-F *prospérer*, accounts for 'to prosper'.

despatch. See PACT, para 5.

desperado. See DESPAIR, para 3.

desperate, desperation. See DESPAIR, para 3.

despicable. See SPECTACLE, para 10.

despise, despisable. See SPECTACLE, para 9.

despite, despiteful. See SPECTACLE, para 9.

DESPOIL 149 DETHRONE

**despoil, despoliation.** See SPOIL, para 3.

**despond,** v hence the obs n; **despondency, despondent.**

1. *dēspondēre*, to promise (*spondēre*) away (*dē-*, down or away from, used int): *spondēre*, to solemnly undertake or engage to, hence to promise, has s *spond-*, akin to Gr *spondē*, a drink-offering, hence, libations being made on the occasion, a solemn truce, and its v *spendein* (s *spend-*), to make a drink-offering, hence to make a treaty, and to Hit *šipand-*, var *špand-*, to pour a libation.

2. *Spondēre* has two notable cpds: *dēspondēre* and *respondēre*. The former, to separate oneself formally from (*dē-*), hence to abandon, to lose, yields 'to *despond*'; presp *dēspondens*, o/s *dēspondent-*, yields E *despondent*, whence *despondency*.

3. *Respondēre*, to undertake in return (*re-*), to perform one's part in a solemn engagement, yields, prob via OF-MF *respondre*, 'to *respond*'; MF *respondance* (formed from the F presp) explains *respondence*, var *-cy*. The L presp *respondens*, o/s *respondent-*, explains E adj, whence n, *respondent*. The ML subsidiary *correspondēre* (*cor-*, for *con-*, with) becomes MF-F *correspondre* and, prob independently, E *correspond*, whence (cf the MF-F *correspondant*) *correspondent* (adj hence n)—whence, in turn (cf MF-F *correspondance*), *correspondence* *Corresponsion* and *corresponsive* answer to *responsion*, from L *responsiō*, o/s *responsiōn-*, whence E (and F) *responsion*, and *responsive*, from ML *responsīvus*, LL *responsīuus*, answering. *Respondēre* has, one perceives, the pp *responsus* (s *respons-*), with neu *responsum* used as n, whence, prob via OF-MF *response*, var of *respons*, the E *response*. *Responsibility* derives, by anl, from *responsible*, adopted from MF (cf the F *responsable*), perh altered from ML *responsābilis*.

4. The simple *spondēre* has, of course, pp *sponsus*, f *sponsa*, used as nn ('the promised'), whence OF-MF *espos*, var *espous*, f *espouse*, whence both the F *époux*, f *épouse*, and the common-gendered E *spouse*, husband or wife; derivative OF-MF *esposer*, MF *espouser*, yields 'to *espouse*'. The L terms have derivative v *sponsāre*, to betroth, whence OF *espousailles*, whence E *espousal*, a betrothal—or a wedding— ceremony, whence the aphetic *spousal(s)*.

5. The pps *spons-* has a further derivative, the agent *sponsor*, a guarantor, hence a responsible person; adopted by E.

6. The Gr *spondē*, a drink-offering (as in para 1), has adj *spondeios*; whence the elliptical n *spondeios* (*pous*), a metre (– –) favoured, for its solemnity, at libations: hence L *spondeus*, whence MF-F *spondée*, whence E *spondee*; the derivative Gr prosodic adj *spondeiakos*, L *spondiacus*, *spondaicus*, (EF-F *spondaïque* and) E *spondaic*.

**despot, despotic, despotism.**

Gr *despotēs*, for *demspota*, akin to Skt *dámpatis*, lord of the house (cf L *domus*, house, and *potis*, able), becomes MF-F *despote*, whence E *despot*; the Gr adj *despotikos* becomes MF-F *despotique*, whence E *despotic*; Gr *despoteia* becomes, with new suffix, EF-F *despotisme*, whence E *despotism*. Cf DOMESTIC, para 1.

**dessert.** See SERVE, para 7.

**destinate, destination, destine, destiny; predestinate, predestination, predestine,** and, anl with other *-arian* adjj (hence nn), **predestinarian.**

1. *Predestinate*, adj and v, comes from L *praedēstinātus*, pp of *praedēstināre*, to determine, or to doom, in advance (*prae-*); subsidiary LL *praedēstinātiō*, o/s *-dēstinātiōn-*, yields—perh via OF-F—*predestination*; 'to *predestine*', however, comes, like OF-F *prédestiner*, straight from *praedēstināre*.

2. *Dēstināre*, to determine, arrange definitely, is a cpd (int *dē*) of *stanāre* (s *stan-*), to fix, a nasal mdfn of *stāre*, to stand (cf STATE); the pp *dēstinātus* yields the obs adj and the v *destinate*; subsidiary *dēstinātiō* (*dēstināt-+-iō*), o/s *dēstinātiōn-*, yields—perh via OF-F—the E *destination*; OF-F *destiner* (L *dēstināre*) accounts for 'to *destine*'; the OF-F derivative n *destinée* (f of pp *destiné*), becomes ME *destine*, *desteny*, whence *destiny*.

**destitute** (adj hence v), **destitution.** See STAND, para 23.

**destroy, destroyer; destruction, destructive, destructor.** See STRUCTURE, para 4.

**desuetude:** EF-F *désuétude*: L *dēsuētūdō*, from *dēsuēscere*, to fall out of use: *dē-*, away from+ *suēscere*, to grow accustomed, from the adj *suus*, one's own: cf, therefore, CUSTOM.

**desultor, desultory.** Cf *exult*, *insult*, *result*, but see SALLY, para 11.

**detach,** whence the pa **detached; detachment.** See TACH, para 4.

**detail.** See the 2nd TAIL, para 5.

**detain, detainer; detention, detentive.**

L *dētinēre*, to hold (*tenēre*) from (*dē-*) one's wish or business—f.a.e., TENANT—becomes OF *detenir*, whence 'to *detain*' and AF *detener*, whence the legal *detainer*. The L pp *dētentus*, s *dētent-*, has LL derivative *dētentiō*, o/s *dētentiōn-*, whence E *detention*, whence, by anl, the adj *detentive* (cf *retentive* at RETAIN).

**detect, detection, detective** (adj hence n), **detector.** See TECHNIC, para 9.

**detent, détente.** See TEND, para 9.

**detention, detentive.** See DETAIN.

**deter.** See TERROR, para 1.

**detergent.** See TERSE, para 2.

**deteriorate, deterioration, deteriorative.**

The 3rd is an E anl formation (*-ive*, adj); the 2nd derives from *dēteriorātiōn-*, o/s of LL *dēteriorātiō*, degeneration; the 1st, from *dēteriorātus*, pp of LL *dēteriorāre*, from L *dēterior*, worse, a comp of *dēter*, bad, from *dē*, down from.

**determinable, determination; determine, determined;** etc. See TERM, para 5.

**deterrent,** whence **deterrence.** See TERROR, para 1.

**detersion, detersive.** See TERSE, para 2.

**detest, detestable, detestation.** See TESTAMENT, para 9.

**dethrone,** etc. See THRONE.

detonate, detonation, detonator. See THUNDER, para 5.

detorsion. See TORT, para 8.

detour. See TOUR, para 6.

detract, detraction, detractor, detractory. See TRACT, para 13.

detriment, detrimental. See THROW, para 8.

detrition, detritus. See THROW, para 8.

detrude, detrusion. See THRUST, para 3.

deuce, deuced. See DUO, para 4.

Deuteronomy. See the element deutero-.

devaluate, devaluation. See VALUE, para 15.

devastate, devastation, devastator, devastavit. See VACANT, para 17.

develop or develope, whence developable, developer; development, whence developmental, developmentary (adj suffixes -al, -ary);—envelop, envelope, envelopment.

1. Envelope derives from MF-F enveloppe, itself from envelopper, OF-MF enveloper, whence 'to envelop': and OF-MF enveloper is an alteration of OF envoloper: en-, in+OF-MF voloper, to wrap up, to envelop, either from ML volvere, L voluere, to roll, esp into a spiral or a ball, or (B & W), influenced by volvere, from ML faluppa, mostly in pl faluppae, chaff, a bale of corn, o.o.o., or, more prob, from Celtic *volup-, extn (Malvezin) of PC *vol-, to turn, akin to ML vol-, L uol-, as in L uoluere, ML volvere: OF-MF voloper is a var of OF voluper and there is even the MF var veloper: with OF voluper, cf the OF volu, from ML volūtum, neu of volūtus, L uolūtus, pp of uoluere. Also from OF-F envelop(p)er derives MF-F enveloppement, whence E envelopment (suffix -ment).

2. Deriving from the same r as OF-MF enveloper, and prompted by that word, is OF-MF developer, F développer, whence 'to develop', whence (suggested by late MF-F développement) development.

devest. See VEST, para 3.

deviate, deviation, deviator, devious. See VIA, para 15.

device, whence deviceful (-ful for full), comes from ME devis, intention, invention: OF-F devis, intention, wish, plan, from OF-F deviser, to direct or regulate, to distribute: VL *divīsāre, to distribute, divide, from ML divīsus, L diuīsus, pp of diuīdere: f.a.e., DIVIDE. OF-F deviser yields 'to devise', (obs) to divide or distribute, hence to invent, to plan, hence, in Law, to give by will.

devil (n hence v), with obvious animal and plant cpds (devil fish, devil's bit, etc.) and one less obvious (devil's advocate) and with derivatives devilish (-ish, adj) and devilry (-ry for -ery); diabolic (whence diabolical: -al, adj), diabolism, diabolist.

1. A devil's advocate—trans of ML advocātus diaboli—is a Catholic official charged with pointing out flaws in the character of a person to be either beatified or canonized; hence, one who quibbles for the sake of truth; hence, loosely, one who, for argument's sake, champions the worse or weaker cause.

2. Devil, OE dēofol (var -ful), comes from LL diabolus, trln of Gr diabolos (LGr Diabolos, Satan), the slanderer, from diaballein, to slander, lit to throw (ballein) across (dia); with the Gr r bal-, cf Skt gal- in galati, it trickles, and, for E, ballistic.

3. The Gr adj is diabolikos (for bol-, a var of bal-, cf metabolism): LL diabolicus: MF-F diabolique: E diabolic. On s diabol- arise the E formations diabolism (-ism) and diabolist (-ist); the game diabolo represents It diabolo, devil (LL diabolus).

devious. Cf deviate; see VIA.

devirginate. See VIRGIN, para 3.

devise, legal n from legal v. See DEVICE, s.f.

devoid. See VACANT, para 8.

devoir. See DEBT, para 5.

devolute, devolution. See VOLUBLE, para 4.

devolve. See VOLUBLE, para 4.

Devonian is the adj (-ian) of Devon; devonite an -ite derivative of Mt Devon in Missouri; and Devon is short for Devonshire, OE Defenscīr, Defnascīr, the SHIRE of the Defenas or Defnas, an OE re-shaping cf C Dumnonii (cf C Dumnonia, the territory), perh 'sons of the god, or goddess, Dumnŭ'.

devote (pa devoted), devotee, devotion. See VOTAL, para 5.

devour. See VORACIOUS, para 2.

devout. See VOTAL, para 5.

dew, n, whence 'to dew'; dewberry; dewlap; dewy.

The last=dew+adj -y; dewberry is an obvious cpd; dewlap, ME dewlappe, is a LAP, or fold, that tends to moistness, cf the 1st LAP, para 2; and dew itself, OE dēaw, is akin to the syn OFris dāw, OHG-MHG tou, G Tau, ON dögg—to Gr theō, I run—and to Skt dhávati, it runs or flows, and dhāutis, spring (of water).

dexter, dexterity, dexterous (now usu contr to dextrous); dextral, dextrin; dextrose.

The last two are Chem derivatives, in -in and -ose, from dextr-, c/f of the first; dextral=dextr-+ adj -al; dexterous=dexter+-ous; dexterity comes, perh via EF-F dextérité, from L dexteritās, an -itās derivative of the L adj dexter: and L dexter, of or situated on the right, to the right, is the complement of L sinister, of or situated on the left, to the left, with derivative dextra or dextera, the right hand (cf sinistra, the left hand); the right hand being normally the stronger and defter, L dexteritās and dexter, E dexterity and dexterous, gain the further and now predominant sense of manual skill: cf ADROIT. As in L sinister, the ending -ter connotes situation or direction: cf the Gr adjj dexiteros, aristeros, right, left (of a pair); for the r dex-, cf the syn Gr dexios, Skt dákṣinas (Av dašina-), OSl desnŭ, Lith dēšinas, OIr dess, Go taishwa, OHG zeso; cf also OSl desnica and OHG zesara or zeswa, right hand, and Gaul Dexiva or Dexsiva, Goddess of Fortune. The IE r is therefore *deks-, right (adj), hence right hand, and is prob a reduction of IE *dekos (cf L decus), that which is fitting, hence favourable, good: the right hand and the right side are those which are fitting on solemn occasions (esp in augury), hence in ethics and in matters rather more trivial. (Boisacq. esp; E & M.)

**diabetes, diabetic.**

The latter—cf the EF-F *diabétique* -attaches adj suffix *-ic* to *diabet-*, s of LL *diabētes*, Gr *diabētēs*, lit 'a passer through', from *diabainein*, to walk or go (*bainein*) through (*dia*): the disease is characterized by a constant and excessive passage of urine.

**diabolic(al), diabolism, diabolist, diabolo.** See DEVIL, para 3.

**diaconal, diaconate.** See DEACON, para 2.

**diadem:** OF-MF *diademe* (EF-F *diadème*): L *diadēma*: Gr *diadēma*, from *diadein*, to bind about or around: *dia*, through, across + *dein*, to bind (cf Gr *hupodēma*, ὑπόδημα, a sandal), akin to Skt *dyáti*, he binds; IE r, *\*dei-*, to bind.

**diaeresis.** See SERUM, para 4.

**diagnosis, diagnostic, diagnostician.** See the 2nd GNOME, para 5.

**diagonal,** adj hence n; L *diagōnālis*: Gr *diagōnios*, passing through or across (*dia*) something from angle (*gōnia*) to angle, akin to Gr *gonu*, knee.

**diagram**—whence, by anl (cf *anagram—anagrammatic*), **diagrammatic**—comes from L, from Gr, *diagramma*, itself from *diagraphein*, to write (*graphein*) across (*dia*), hence to mark out with lines: cf GRAPH.

**dial,** showing the time of day: late ML *diāle*, dial of a clock, prop the neu of ML *diālis* (s *diāl-*), adj of L *diēs*, day: f.a.e., DIANA.

**dialect, dialectal; dialectic, dialectical, dialectician.** See LEGEND, para 26.

**dialogue.** See LEGEND, para 27.

**diamantiferous.** See DIAMOND.

**diameter.** See MEASURE, para 7.

**diamond** (n hence v): ME *diamaund*, earlier *diamaunt*: OF-F *diamant*: ML *diamant*·, o/s of *diamas*: an aphetic corruption (? suggested or aided by Gr *diaphanēs*, transparent) of L *adamas* (gen *adamant*is), the hardest iron, (later) diamond, from Gr *adamas*, the hardest metal, (later) diamond: cf ADAMANT.

**Diana** (whence **Dian**); **diva, divine, divination, divinity;** sep **deify, deism, deist, deity, deus;** sep **deodar;** sep **dial; dies—diary—dismal—diurnal** (adj hence n) and **journal** (adj hence n), **journalese, journalism, journalist—journey** (n hence v), with obvious cpds, **journeyman, journeywork,** etc.— **adjourn, adjournment** and **sojourn** (n and v), **sojournment; hodiernal; meridian; quotidian; Jupiter, Jove, jovial; joss; Zeus, Dyaus; Tuesday.** —Cf the 2nd DIET.

1. L *Diāna* is either an *-āna* (m *-ānus*) derivative of L *dīus*, the oldest adjective of *deus*, a god, or a contraction of L *diuiāna*, itself a shadowy derivative of *dius*; *diva*, a prima donna, is the f of lt *divo*, divine, from the L var *dīuus*, ML *dīvus*; L *dīuīnus*, an *-īnus* derivative of *dīuus*, becomes ML *dīvīnus*, of or by or for a god, the gods, also inspired by them, whence MF-F *divin*, OF-MF *devin*, both adopted by ME with later form *divine*,

extant in E, whence, prob, the n, the v appearing to derive from ME *divinen*, var *devinen*, from OF-F *deviner*, from ML *dīvīnāre*, L *dīuīnāre*, from the 'god-inspired' sense of *dīuīnus*, whose 'of or for a god' sense yields *dīuīnitās*, the quality or power of a god, ML *dīvīnitās*, whence OF-MF *devinité*, MF-F *divinité*, whence ME *devinite*, var *divinite*, whence E divinity. L *dīuīnāre* has derivative *dīuīnātio*, acc *dīuīnātiōn*em, ML *div-*, whence EF-F, whence E, *divination*.

2. The base of those words, as of the sep treated DEIFY (where also *deity*), is the L *deus*: and L *deus* stems from an IE *\*deiwo*, whereas the very closely linked L *diēs*, day, a day, and *Iuppiter* stem from IE *\*dieu-* or *\*dei-*: cf Skt *devas*, a god, and the syn OP *deywis* or *deiwas*, ON *tīvar* (pl), OIr and Ga *dia*, OW *duu*, W *duw*, Cor *deu, dew*, OC *\*dewos* or *\*divos*. The derivative L adj *dīus* means three different but very closely related things: divine; of the sky; luminous: 'The luminous day and the sky are confused with the god' (E & M). In part, L *dīus* imitates the Gr adj *dios*, of a god, of the gods, divine: and *dios* (for *\*diuios* or *\*diwos* ?) is akin to Skt *divyas, diviyas*, celestial.

3. The Gr adj *dios* may have derived almost imperceptibly from Gr *Dios*, the gen of *Zeus* (for *\*Diwos* ?); in Boeotian and Laconian Gr, *Zeus* (Ζεύς) is *Deus* (Δεύς); cf Skt *dyáús*, the sky, day, heaven (IE *diēus*, sky, bright day), whence *Dyáús*, Heaven, also elliptical for *Dyaus-pitr*, Father of Heaven, Gr *Zeus patēr*, voc *Zeu pater*, which prob suggested the L *Iupiter, Iuppiter*, ML *Jup(p)iter*, whence E *Jupiter*; note, too, the form of the syn L *Diespiter*. With Gr *Zeus*, *Deus*, and L *deus*, cf also Hit *sius* (contr of *siunas*), a god, and the syn OHG *Zīo*, ON *Tȳr*, OE *Tīw*, the *God* of War; OE *Tīw* has cpd *Tīwesdaeg* (whence E *Tuesday*), the War-God's day, akin to OFris *Tīesdei*, OHG *Zīestac*, ON *Tȳrsdagr, Tȳsdagr*.

4. In L, *Iupiter* has gen *Iovis* (PL *Diouis*), used also as nom: ML *Jovis*, whence E *Jove*. Derivative LL adj *Iouiālis*, ML *Joviālis*, yields F, whence E, *jovial*.

5. L *deus* becomes Port *deos*, whence the Pidgin *joss*, a Chinese domestic divinity, whence sl *joss*, luck.

6. As we have seen, L *deus* has a very close cognate: *diēs*, daylight, day, duration of a day. *Diēs* was refashioned from the acc *diem*, itself app modelled upon Ve *dyắm*, var *diyắm* (cf Homeric Gr *Zēn*). The link between 'light (of day), day' and 'the sky', on the one hand, and 'god', on the other, is a double link: sem in the fact that the luminous sky (the source of daylight) and daylight were apprehended as divine forces and manifestations, also a god is 'the shining one'; phon in the IE r *\*dei-*, to shine, be luminous. This *\*dei-* appears in C, usu shortened to *di-*, as in OIr *dië* and Br *deiz*, day (cf the OW *diu*, a god), OIr *in-diu*, today; it appears also in Arm *tiv*, day, and, of course, in L *diēs*.

7. *Diēs* occurs, disguised, in the adj *dismal*; but then, this adj derives from the n *dismal*, a period of

(L) *dies mali*, bad or unlucky days, OF *dis mal*, whence ME *dismale*.

8. Clearer is the origin of *diary*: L *diārium* (esp in pl *diāria*), ration for a day, a daily record; with the form *diārium*, cf that of L *diālis*, daily (see DIAL), both deriving from *diēs*. Also deriving from *dies* is the adj *diurnus*, complementary to and prompted by *nocturnus*, of the *nox* or night; its extn *diurnālis*, daily, esp in ref to *diurnum*, a journal (from *acta diurna*, things done daily—and recorded), comes the E adj *diurnal*, daily, whence the n *diurnal*, a daybook or diary, later a newspaper.

9. Now, L *diurnālis* becomes the OF-EF adj *journal*, which, used by EF-F as n, is adopted by E for a newspaper—a modern *diurnal*. F *journal*, newspaper, has derivative *journalisme*, whence E *journalism*, and *journaliste*, whence E *journalist*. *Journalese* is an E formation (orig coll) in *-ese*, after *Johnsonese*.

10. The L adj *diurnus* has neu *diurnum*, turned by LL into a n meaning a day', whence VL *\*diurnāta*, a day's work or travel, whence OF-MF *journee* (F *journée*), whence E *journey*; with OF-MF *journee* (OF *jornee*), cf OProv *jornada* and It *giornata*—note, however, that these three words more prob derive from the contemporaneous words for 'day'—OF-MF and OProv *jorn* (later F *jour*) and It *giorno*, themselves all from LL *diurnum*, a day.

11. OF-MF *jorn* has two cpds relevant to E: *ajorner* and *sojorner*. MF *ajorner*, var *ajurner*, whence ME *ajornen*, whence 'to *adjourn*', derives from ML *adjurnāre*, LL *adiurnāre*; *ad*, to+*diur*nus +inf *-āre*. The MF derivative *adjournement* becomes E *adjournment*. OF *sojorner*, OF-MF *sejorner* (whence F *séjourner*), whence ME *sojornen*, *sojournen*, whence 'to *sojourn*', derives from VL *\*subdiurnāre*: *sub*, under, hence a little after+ *diur*nus+*-āre*. OF *sojorner* has derivatives *sojorn* (and *sojor*, *sejor*), whence the E n *sojourn*, and *sojornement*, whence *sojournment*.

12. Three L cpds of *diēs* remain: *hodiernus*, *meridiānus*, *quotidiānus*. *Hodiernus*, s *hodiern-*, yields E *hodiernal* (*-al* substituted for *-ous*), of this day, and it represents an *-ernus* adj derivative from *hodiē* (adv), today: (*in*) *hoc diē*, on this day: cf Skt *adya*.

13. *Meridiānus*, whence OF-MF, whence ME, *meridien*, whence E *meridian* (adj, whence n), derives from *meridiēs*, noon (from adv *meridiē*, at noon, a dissimilation of *\*mediei diē*), for OL *medidiēs*, middle day, from adj *medius* (s *medi-*, r *med-*), middle.

14. *Quotidiānus*, later *cottidiānus*, whence OF-MF *cotidian*, *cotidien* (later *quo-*), both adopted by ME, whence E *quotidian* (adj hence n), derives from the adv *quotidiē*, daily: *quotus*, in what number, adj from adv *quot*, how many+*diēs*. (Cf QUOTA.)

**diapason**, adopted from L, comes from Gr *d apasōn*, formed of the 2nd and 3rd elements of ἡ διὰ πασῶν χορδῶν συμφονία, *hē dia pasōn*

*khordōn sumphonia*, the through-all-chords symphony, i.e. the concord of all notes—in short, the octave. Cf the prefix *dia-* and PAN.

**diaper**, orig a rich, later a cloth or linen, textile fabric, hence a table napkin, now—esp in AE—a baby's napkin (breech-cloth), derives from ME, from MF, *diapre*, OF-MF *diaspre*, from ML *diasprum*, var of *diasprus*, trln of LGr-MGr *diaspros*, pure white (cf Gr *dialeukos*): *dia*, through, hence thoroughly+LGr-MGr *aspros*, white, from G *aspros*, rough (cf the LGr *aspron*, white of egg), akin to L *asper* (cf ASPERITY). From *diaper* in the sense 'figured design' (orig on the textile) comes 'to *diaper*', perh from EF-F *diaprer*, OF-MF *diasprer*, from OF-MF *diaspre*; hence the pa *diapered*.

**diaphanous**. See the element *-phane*.

**diaphragm**: MF-F *diaphragme*: LL, from Gr, *diaphragma*, the muscle separating thorax from abdomen, (lit) a barrier or partition, from *diaphragnunai*, to fence (*phragnunai*, to fence) thoroughly (*dia-*): f.a.e., FARCE. Adj: *diaphragmatic*, from F *diaphragmatique*, an *-ique* (L *-icus*, Gr *-ikos*) learned adj from Gr *diaphragmat-*, o/s of *diaphragma*.

**diarist** is an E *-ist* derivative from *diary*, q.v. at DIANA, para 8.

**diarrhoea** (AE *-rrhea*). See RHEUM, para 3.

**Diaspora**. See the element *-spora*, 2nd para.

**diastole**. See STALL, para 13.

**diathesis**. See THESIS, para 8.

**diatom, diatomous**. See TOME, para 6.

**diatonic** comes, via F and LL, from Gr *diatonikos*, adj of *to diatonon*, the diatonic scale, prop the neu of *diatonos*, stretched, extended, from *diateinein*, to stretch out; prefix *dia-*, through+ *teinein* (s *tein-*) to stretch: cf TONE.

**diatribe**. See THROW, para 11.

**dibble, dibbler**. See DAB, para 3.

**dibs**, game, (sl) money. See DAB, para 3.

**dice** (n hence v). See 1st DIE.

**dichotomy**, adj **dichotomous**.

The former derives from Gr *dikhotomia*, an *-ia* derivative of *dikhotomos*, whence, via LL *dichotomos*, the E *dichotomous*, cut (*-tomos*: cf TOME) in two (*dikho-*: cf the element *dicho-*).

**dickens!, what the**, What the devil!: *Dickens*, for *\*Diccons* for *Diccon's* or *Dickon's* (son), *Diccon* being an extn of *Dick*, pet-form of *Richard*, itself adopted from F, of Gmc origin—cf OHG *Richhart* (cf RICH and HARD).

**dicker**. See DECEMBER, para 4.

**dickey**, var of **dicky**, any of several—either inside or inferior—articles of clothing: perh from *D dek*, a covering: f.a.e., DECK. Hence the coll adj *dick(e)y*, inferior, weak, shaky.

**dict**, cf **dicta, dictum; dictate, dictation, dictator** (whence **dictatorship**: suffix *-ship*), **dictatorial; diction** and **dictionary**; cf the element *dicto-*; **dight; digit; ditto; ditty**. Latin prefix-cpds: **abdicate, abdication; addict** (adj, n, v), **addiction; benedict, benediction, benedictive, benedictory,** cf **benison**— and **malediction, maledictory,** cf **malison; causi-**

dical; condition (n, v), conditional (whence **uncon-ditional**), conditionate; contradict, contradiction, contradictory; dedicate, dedication, dedicatory; edict (whence adj edictal); fatidic(al); index (pl indices), indicate, indication, indicative, indicator; indict (whence indictable), indiction, indictive, indictment—cf indite, inditement; interdict (n, v), interdiction, interdictive, interdictor, interdictory; judex, judge (n, v), judgement—cf misjudge, misjudgement—judicable, judicative, judicator, judicatory (adj, n), judicature, judicial, judiciary, judicious—cf adjudge, adjudicate, adjudication, adjudicative, adjudicator—cf also juridic(al), juris-diction, jurisdictive; predicable, predicament (whence adj predicamental), predicant, predicate (adj, n, v), predication, predicative, predicator, predicatory—cf preach, preacher, preachment; predict, prediction, predictive; vendetta; vengeable, vengeance, vengeful —avenge, avenger—revenge (n, v), revengeable, revengeful; verdict; veridical; vindex, vindicable, vindicate, vindication, vindicative (and, of course, vindictive), vindicator, vindicatory.—Greek cog-nates: deictic, apodeictic, epideictic; paradigm, paradigmatic; remotely cf TEACH.

1. Obs *dict*, a saying, comes from L *dictum* (pl *dicta*), prop the neu of *dictus* (s dict-), pp of *dicere* (s *dic*-), to say: OL *deicere* (s *deic*-) is akin to Gr *deiknunai*, to show (r *deik*-); to Skt *diśati*, he points out or shows (pp *diṣṭás*, shown: cf *dictus*); to Go ga-*teihan*, to show, tell, proclaim (*ga*-, int prefix; r *teih*-), and OHG *zeigōn* (G *zeigen*: s *zeig*-), to show, int of OHG *zīhan* (r *zīh*-), G *zeihen*, to accuse; and prob to Hit *tek*-kusmu, to show or prove. The IE r is *deik*-, var *deig*-, with shorter forms *dīk*-, *dīg*-, to point to, to show; the sem relation between pointing to, hence showing, and telling, hence merely saying, hardly needs to be laboured.

2. The neu pp *dictum* used as n becomes It *ditto* (var *detto*), adopted by E: lit, the said, hence the aforesaid, thing.

3. Not from pp *dictus* but prob from the IE var r *dig*- comes L *digitus*, s digit-, whence E *digit*: ? orig 'the pointer', hence a toe or, usu, finger. Derivative adj *digitālis* yields *digital*; derivative *digitāre* has pp *digitātus*, which, used as adj (having fingers), yields the E adj *digitate*; cf *prestidigitation* and *prestidigitator*, the former adopted from F, the latter adapted from F *prestidigitateur*, learned cpds with 1st element the F *preste*, nimble, from It *presto* (as in *hey presto!*) from late VL *praestus*, ready at hand.

4. On L *dict*-, s of pp *dictus*, is formed L *dictiō*, saying, a saying, a word, o/s *dictiōn*-, whence OF-F and E *diction*, now usu a manner of speaking. On o/s *dictiōn*- is formed the -*ārius* (E -*ary*) adj *dictiōnārius*, whence, for *d. liber*, the ML *dictiōn-ārius*, later *dictiōnārium*, a book of words, whence E *dictionary*.

5. L *dīcere* has int and freq *dictāre*, to say loudly, to say often (so as to be easily reported), later to compose, with pp *dictātus*, whence 'to dictate'; the neu *dictātum*, used as n, becomes both the E n *dictate* and, via OF-MF *ditié*, var

*dité*, the ME *dite*, E *ditty*, orig a composition. On the pps *dictāt*- arise LL *dictātiō*, o/s *dictātiōn*-, whence E *dictation*, and, with changed senses, the agent *dictātor*, adopted by E, with adj *dictātōrius*, whence (with -*al* for -*ous*) *dictatorial*, and the office *dictātūra*, whence *dictature*. *Dictāre*, to say often, hence to order, yields OE *dihtan*, to dictate, order, dispose, whence ME *dihten*, whence the obs 'to *dight*', extant in its pp *dight*, furnished, clad.

6. Such derivatives of L *dīcere*, to say, as *dīcāre* (durative and int), to say solemnly, to proclaim, and *dīciō*, a word or a formula of command, and the elements -*dex* and -*dīcus*, both connoting an agent, occur, as to E, only in cpds: e.g., *abdīcāre* (see para 8); *condīciō* (para 10); *index*, *iudex*, *uindex* (paras 13, 15, 19, resp) and their derivatives *indīcāre*, *iudīcāre*, *uindīcāre* (paras 14, 15–18, 20–21, resp); *causidīcus* . . . *ueridīcus* (para 11).

7. Of *dīcere*, the L prefix-cpds affecting E are these:

*addīcere*, to adjudge or accord, with pp *addictus*, whence the obs adj, the n, the v *addict*; derivative *addictiō*, o/s *addictiōn*-, becomes *addiction*;

*benedīcere*, to say 'well' (*bene*) to, i.e. to bless, with imp *benedīcite*, Bless ye!, whence E *benedicite*, a blessing, and with pp *benedictus*, whence the PN *Benedict* (anglicized as *Benedick*) and the adj, hence n, *benedict*, blest, a married man; derivative LL *benedictiō*, o/s *benedictiōn*-, becomes directly the E *benediction* and indirectly, via OF *beneiçun*, *beneïson*, and ME *beneysoun*, *benesoun*, the E *benison*; ML *\*benedictōrius* accounts for E *bene-dictory*; cf *maledīcere* below;

*condīcere* (int *con*-), to conclude (an arrange-ment), has derivative *condiciō*, whence the legal *condiction*—cf *condition* in para 10;

*contradīcere*, to speak *contra*, or against, with pp *contradictus*, whence 'to *contradict*'; derivative *contradictiō*, o/s *contradictiōn*-, whence via OF-F, the E *contradiction*; and LL *contradictōrius*, whence E *contradictory*, adj whence n;

*ēdīcere* (*ē*-, out), to say out, to proclaim (e.g., a law), with pp *ēdictus*, with neu *ēdictum* used as n, whence E *edict*;

*indīcere*, to proclaim (a war) or impose (a tribute), has pp *indictus*, s indict-, whence both *indictiō*, o/s *indictiōn*-, whence E *indiction*, pro-clamation, edict, and *indictīuus*, ML -*īvus*, whence E *indictive*; but that pp merely form-influences 'to *indict*', to accuse, which (pron *indite*) derives from ME *enditen*, to write down, to accuse, whence clearly 'to *indite*', to (compose and) write; ME *enditen* comes from OF *enditer*, to indicate, to write; *en*, from L *in*, in(to), against+*dictāre*, to dictate, to proclaim; and derivative ME *enditement* becomes, under the same influence, *indictment* (pron *inditement*)—*inditement* being now rare;

*interdīcere*, to legally interpose, to prohibit, has pp *interdictus*—whence 'to *interdict*'—with neu *interdictum* used as n, whence the E n *interdict* (perh, however, from LL *interdictus*, gen -*ūs*), both v and n experiencing OF intermediation in *entre*-; derivative LL *interdictiō* o/s *interdictiōn*-, becomes *interdiction*, itself suggesting *interdictive*; LL *interdictor* is adopted, LL *interdictōrius* adapted, by E;

*maledīcere*, to speak ill of, to curse, with pp *maledictus*, s *maledict-*, whence *maledictiō*, o/s *maledictiōn-*, whence directly the E *malediction* and indirectly, via OF *maleïçon*, the E *malison*—cf *benison* at *benedīcere* above; *maledictory* is an anl E formation;

*praedīcere*, to foretell, has pp *praedictus*, whence 'to predict'; derivative *praedictiō*, o/s *praedictiōn-*, becomes *prediction*, as derivative *praedictīuus*, ML *-īvus*, becomes *predictive*;

*ualedīcere* (ML *vale-*): for *valediction, valedictory*, see VALUE, para 21.

8. L *dīcāre*, to proclaim, has three prefix-cpds:

*abdīcāre* (*ab*, from), to refuse to recognize, and *se abdīcāre*, to renounce, with pp *abdīcātus*, whence 'to abdicate'; derivative *abdīcātiō*, o/s *abdīcātiōn-*, yields *abdication*; LL *abdīcātīuus*, ML *-īvus*, yields *abdicative*; ML *abdīcātor* is adopted;

*dēdīcāre* (*dē-* used int), to consecrate to the gods, to declare solemnly, has pp *dēdīcātus*, whence the obsol adj and the v *dedicate*; derivative *dēdīcātiō*, o/s *dēdīcātiōn-*, becomes, prob via OF, the E *dedication*; *dēdīcātīuus*, ML *-īvus*, becomes *dedicative*, mostly displaced by *dedicatory* (*-ory*, adj), itself suggested by *dedicator* (adopted from L);

*praedīcāre* (*prae*, before), to proclaim, LL to preach, has presp *praedīcans*, o/s *praedīcant-*, whence the E adj, hence n, *predicant*; pp *praedicātus* yields adj and v *predicate*, and its neu *praedīcātum*, used as n, the n *predicate*; derivative *praedīcātiō*, o/s *praedīcātiōn-*, becomes OF, whence E, *predication*; *praedīcātīuus*, ML *-īvus*, becomes *predicative*; *praedīcātor* becomes *predicator*; LL *praedīcātōrius* becomes *predicatory*. Moreover, *praedīcābilis* yields *predicable*, and LL *praedīcāmentum*, something predicated, hence a quality, hence a condition or a circumstance, esp if unpleasant, yields *predicament*.

9. L *praedīcāre*, to proclaim, to preach, becomes OF-MF *preechier* or *prechier* (the F *prêcher*): ME *prechen*: 'to preach'; *preacher* comes from MF *preecheor*, deriving from the OF v but suggested by L *praedīcātor*; *preachment*, from MF *preechement*, from the v.

For *indīcāre*, see para 14.

10. L *dīciō*, a word or formula of command, has a notable prefix-cpd: *condiciō*, a formula of agreement between two persons (*con*, with, together), o/s *condiciōn-*: OF *condicion*, adopted by late ME, whence E *condition*; F *condition* has derivative *conditionner*, whence 'to *condition*', whence the pa *conditioned*. LL *condiciōnālis* becomes OF *condicionel*, whence, influenced by ML *condītiōnālis*, the E *conditional* (with neg *unconditional*). Derivative ML *condītiōnāre* (perh influencing F *conditionner*) has pp *condītiōnātus*, whence the adj and v *conditionate*.

11. The c/f e *-dīcus*, connoting an agent or, as adj, an agential quality, occurs in the foll words relevant to E:

*causidīcus*, a pleader in a law court, with adj *causidīcālis*, whence E *causidical*;

*fātidīcus* (adj), telling of FATE: E *fatidic*, now usu *fatidical* (*-al*);

*iuridīcus*, ML *juridīcus*, of or by or for (legal) justice, whence E *juridic*, now usu *juridical*; *iurisdictiō*, o/s *iurisdictiōn-*, ML *juris-*, whence, perh via MF-EF, the E *jurisdiction*;

*uēridīcus* (adj), telling the truth (L *uērum*, ML *vērum*): E *veridic*, now usu *veridical*; cf the ML *vēredictum* or *vēridictum*, often contr to *vērdictum*, whence the E *verdict*, L-remade from ME *verdit* (OF *veirdit*, from *vērdictum*).

12. Thus we reach the cpds in *-dex* (akin to OL *dix*, as in *dicis causa*, because of the formula, (hence) in a manner of speaking), connoting an agent or an instrument: *index, iudex, uindex*, prob for *\*indix*, etc., influenced by *artifex*, etc.

13. L *index*, o/s *indic-*, is lit a 'pointer at or to' (*in*, in, into, against), whence esp 'forefinger', whence the senses 'table of contents' (now 'alphabetical list of contents') and 'catalogue of books', as in the Catholic *Index Expurgatorius* (of books with suspect passages) and *Index Librorum Prohibitorum* (of books entirely forbidden to the laity).

14. Serving as the v answering to L *index* is L *indīcāre*, which perh rather= *in*, into, at+ *dicāre*, to proclaim. Its pp *indīcātus* yields 'to *indicate*'; on the pps *indīcāt-* arise *indīcātiō*, o/s *indīcātiōn-*, whence, perh via F, the E *indication*—LL *indīcātīuus*, ML *-īvus*, whence *indicative*—and LL *indīcātor*, adopted by E.

15. L *iūdex*, ML *jūdex*, is 'he who points to or shows the law' (L *ius*, r *iu-*). Retained in certain legal terms, *iūdex* has s *iūdic-*, ML *judic-*, and becomes OF(-F) *juge*, adopted by ME, whence E *judge*; 'to *judge*' derives from ME *jugen*, from OF *jugier*, from ML *jūdicāre*, L *iūdicāre* (s *iūdic-*), itself from *iūdex*. ML *jūdicamentum* (L suffix *-mentum*, cf E *-ment*) yields OF *jugement*, adopted by ME, whence E *judgement*. 'To *misjudge*' and *misjudgement* are E *mis-* cpds of the simple words.

16. L *iūdicāre* has several derivatives affecting E:

LL *iūdicābilis*, whence *judicable*;

pp *iūdicātus*, whence, via ML, the rare E 'to *judicate*';

LL *iūdicātor*, whence, via ML, the E *judicator*, whence *judicatorial* (suffix *-ial*);

LL *iūdicātōrius*, whence the adj *judicatory*; the neu *iūdicātorium*, used as n, becomes the n *judicatory*;

ML *jūdicātūra*, office or profession of judge, yields *judicature*.

17. L *iūdex*, ML *jūdex*, has the derivative *iūdicium*, with adjj *iūdiciālis* and *iūdiciārius*, whence, via ML, the E *judicial* and *judiciary*, adj whence n; *judicious* (neg *injudicious*), however, derives from F *judicieux*, f *judicieuse*, from ML *jūdicium*; *judicative* is an E formation in *-ive*.

18. The L cpd *adiūdīcāre*, ML *adjūdīcāre*, int (*ad-*) of *iūdicāre*, leads to the foll E words:

adjudge, ME *ajugen*, OF *ajugier* (ML *adjŭdīcāre*); adjudicate, from ML *adjŭdīcātus*, the pp (s *adjŭdīcāt-*);

adjudication, from ML *adjŭdīcātiōn-*, o/s of *adjŭdīcātiō*, LL *adiūdīcātiō*, from the pps;

adiudicative, adjudicator, adjudicature, anl E formations on the simple words.

18a. A more important prefix-cpd of *iūdīcāre* is *praeiūdīcāre*, to judge *prae* or beforehand, which, via ML *praejūdīcāre*, becomes F *préjuger*, whence 'to prejudge'; derivative F *préjugement* becomes E prejudgement. The L pp *praeiūdīcātus*, ML *-jūd-*, yields the adj and obsol v prejudicate; derivative LL *praeiūdīcātiō*, o/s *-ātiōn*, yields prejudication. Moreover, *iūdīcium* (para 17) has LL cpd *praeiūdīcium*, lit a legal judgement made beforehand, whence OF *prejudice*, adopted by E; derivative F *préjudicier* (? influenced by Tertullian's LL) accounts for 'to prejudice'. Derivative LL *praeiūdīciālis*, of a previous judgement, becomes legal prejudicial, decided prior to a hearing before a judge; the sense 'hurtful' app derives from OF *prejudicial* and is influenced by the non-legal senses of the F and E n *prejudice*. But already in LL does 'hurtful' appear; esp in Tertullian's use of *praeiūdīcāre* for 'to do harm to', which follows, with complete sem naturalness, from the L 'pre-judge' sense. (Souter.)

19. Completing the L words in *-dex* is *uindex* (o/s *uindic-*), ML *vindex*, he who guarantees, stands surety for, (hence) proves the innocence of, avenges. It has obscure 1st element: he who points to—what? Perhaps for **uimdex*, he who shows the *uis* (ML *vis*) or violence done to his client; E & M (rightly, I think) prefer the 1st element to be a lost L cognate of OHG *wini*, friend, one who 'belongs' to the family, cf OIr *fine*, relationship, clan, tribe, Ga *fine*, tribe, OC *venjá* (cf the Cor *vensy*, to vindicate).

20. L *uindex* has derivative v *uindīcāre*, with senses answering exactly to those of the n. Its pp *uindīcātus*, ML *vindīcātus*, yields 'to vindicate'; on the pps *uindīcāt-* arise *uindīcātiō*, o/s *uindīcātiōn-*, whence E *vindication*—ML *vindīcātīvus*, tending or designed to vindicate, whence *vindicative*, whence (influenced by L *uindīcāta*, restitution of or to liberty, (later) punishment, itself, by contr, from *uindīcāre*) vindictive, disposed to, or aiming at, revenge, whence vindictiveness (*-ness*); LL *uindīcātor*, ML *vindīcātor*, adopted by E. Vindicable is as if from ML **vindīcābilis*; vindicatory as if from ML **vindīcātorius*. Revindicate, revindication answer to ML *revindīcātus*, pp of *revindīcāre*, and **revindīcātiō*, o/s **revindīcātiōn-*.

21. *Uindīcāre*, ML *vindīcāre*, passes through F with these results for E:

OF *venchier* and *vengier*, F *venger*, whence obs 'to venge'. The OF-F vv have derivatives MF-EF *vengeable*, adopted by E—OF-F *vengeance*, adopted by E—OF-MF *vengement*, adopted by E, now obs—OF-MF *vengeor* (F *vengeur*), whence E *venger*, avenger, and OF-MF *vengeresse*, whence obs E *vengeress*; but *vengeful* is an E formation;

OF-MF *avengier* (a-, L *ad-*, to, app used int), to take or exact retribution for (someone), whence 'to avenge', whence *avengeful* and *avenger*, *avengeress*, on anl of the simple words; hence OF *avengement*, adopted by E;

OF-MF *revengier* (re-, L *re-*, back, again) has varr *revenchier* and esp *revencher*, soon usu *revancher*, OF to avenge, EF-F to revenge—hence the E 'to revenge', whence *revengeable* and *revenger*; MF-F *revancher* has derivative EF n *revanche*, whence the E n revenge, whence *revengeful*.

22. L *uindicta*, ML *vindicta*, in sense 'revenge', becomes It *vendetta*, adopted by E, in sense 'blood feud'.

23. Gr *deiknunai* (r *deik-*), to show—see para 1—has derivative *deiktikos*, serving to point out or show, demonstrative, whence the erudite E *deictic*. The cpd *apodeiknunai* (apo-, away from, from, of), to point out, has derivative *apodeiktikos*, whence E *apodeictic*, the derivative L *apodicticus* accounting for the var *apodictic*; the cpd *epideiknunai*, to show forth (cf the prefix *epi-*), has derivative *epideiktikos*, whence *epideictic*; and the cpd *paradeiknunai*, to show *para* or by the side of, esp as an example, aas derivative *paradeigma*, whence LL *paradīgma*, an example (in grammar or in rhetoric), whence EF-F *paradigme*, whence E *paradigm*, a patterned or diagrammatic table of examples, with adj *paradigmatic* (Gr *paradeigmatikos*).

diction; dictionary. See prec, para 4.

dictum. See DICT, para 1.

didactic (whence didactician and didacticism): Gr *didaktikos*, from *didaskein*, to teach: f.a.e., DOCILE.

diddle, to cheat or hoax, is prob a b/f from Jeremy *Diddler*, a resourceful sponger in James Kenney's *Raising the Wind*, 1803: and *Diddler* prob derives from E dial *diddle*, 'to busy oneself with trifles' (EDD), prob akin to the app echoic E dial *diddle*, to jog up and down, to dance about, a thinned form of *daddle* (to totter, to toddle), q.v. at DAWDLE.

die (1), n; pl dies—but, as cubes employed in gambling, dice.

A *die* or gambling cube, later a shaping tool, the mould used, a perforated block, etc., derives from ME *dee*: OF *de* (F *dé*), a gambling die: L *datum*, a piece or 'man' in games, prop the neu of *datus*, pp of *dare*, to give, to cast or throw: f.a.e., DATA.

die (2), v. See DEAD, para 3.

Diesel is elliptical for *Diesel engine*, invented in 1900 by Rudolf *Diesel* (1858–1913) of Munich.

diet (1), n whence v; dietary, adj hence n; dietetic, adj whence n dietectics; dietician (loosely dietetian).

The last=diet, n+physician; the 3rd comes from LL *diaetēticus*, trln of Gr *diaitētikos*, adj of *diaita*, manner of living; the 2nd from LL *diaetārius* (adj used as n), a house-steward; and diet from Gr *diaita*, through L *diaeta*, MF *diete* (F *diète*), ME *diete*. Gr *diaita* is app a *di-* (for *dia*, through) prefix-cpd from *aisa* (αἶσα), a god's dispensation, a share—esp at a meal; *aisa* is akin to Gr *oitos* (οῖτος), lot, luck: cf the Av *aēta-*, the lot that befalls: IE *\*oitos*, a share (Boisacq).

**diet** (2), (obs) a day's journey, (Sc) a sessions day, (general and extant) a formal, esp governing, assembly: ML *diēta*, a day's journey: an *-eta* derivative of *diē*s, a day: f.a.e., DIANA, para 6.

**differ; difference, different**, with negg **indifference, indifferent; differential; differentiate** (whence **differentiator**), **differentiation;—defer**, to delay, postpone, whence, by suffix *-ment*, **deferment.**

1. The last derives from ME *differen*, to delay, from MF *differer*, this being also the imm origin of 'to *differ*': L *differre*, to carry (*ferre*) from one side or another, to disperse, (by a time extension) to put aside (*di-* for *dis-*) for later, to postpone, and, as *se differre*, to carry oneself from one side or another, hence to be different: f.a.e. *ferre*, see FERTILE.

2. The presp *differens* has o/s *different-*, whence E *different* (and MF-F *différent*); on that o/s *different-* was coined *differentia*, whence OF-MF *différence*, adopted by E, whence both 'to *difference*' and the adj (hence n) *differential*, prob suggested by It *differenziale* (cf Sp *diferencial*); 'to *differentiate*' recalls It *differenziato*, pp of *differenziare*; *differentiation* recalls It *differenziazione* (from the v).

**difficult**, app a b/f of **difficulty**, was perh suggested by EF-F *difficultueux*, the adj of MF-F *difficulté*, whence E *difficulty*: and *difficulté* comes from L *difficultās*, o/s *difficultāt-*, the n of *difficilis* (*di-*, for *dis-*, apart, not), the opp of *facilis*: f.a.e., FACILE.

**diffidence, diffident.** See FAITH.

**diffraction.** See FRACTION.

**diffuse** (adj and v), **diffusion.** See FUSE, to melt.

**dig** (pt and pp **dug** or **digged**), whence n **dig** and agent **digger** and vn **digging(s); dike** or **dyke; ditch,** n and v (whence **ditcher); vandyke** (beard).

'To *dig*' comes, through ME *diggen*, from MF *diguer*, to excavate, from MF *digue*, earlier *dike*, from MD *dijc* (D *dijk*), akin to OFris *dīka*, to dig, and *dīk*, a dike, itself akin to the syn ON *dīki* and esp OE *dīc*, ME *dīc*, var *dike*, adopted by E, with var *dyke*; ME has the further var *dich*, whence E *ditch*; all these E words have cognates in OLG, MLG, MHG—perh (Walshe) cf also the Gr *tiphos*, stagnant water. A *vandyke* (pointed, very trim) is elliptical for *Vandyke* beard, characteristic of men painted by *Vandyke*, better *Van Dyck*, '(He) of the dyke'.

The Australian voc *digger* and the PN *Digger* come from the *gold-diggers* of the 1850's-60's; the Californian *gold-diggers* have originated *gold-digger*, a mercenary female.

**digest,** n and v; **digestible; digestion, digestive.** See GERUND, para 10.

**Digger, digger.** See DIG, s.f.

**dight.** See DICT, para 5, s.f.

**digit, digital, digitate.** See DICT, para 3. The drug *digitalis* derives from *Digitales*, a genus of herbs

with flowers having a *finger*-shaped (L *digitālis*) corolla.

**dignified, dignitary, dignity.** See DECENCY, para 4.

**digraph** is a double (*di-*) writing (*graph*): two letters, usu vowels, with one sound.

**digress, digression, digressive.** See GRADE, para 10.

**dihedral,** adj hence n, is lit 'two (*di-*) seated' (Gr *hedra*, a seat)—cf *cathedral* at CHAIR.

**dike.** See DIG.

**dilaceration.** See LACERATE.

**dilapidate, dilapidation.** See LAPIDARY, para 3.

**dilatant, dilatation, dilate, dilation, dilator.** See LATERAL, para 4.

**dilatory.** See the 1st TOLL, para 6.

**dilemma,** adopted from LL, comes from Gr *dilēmma*, a double (*di-*) *lēmma* or assumption, hence, in logic, an ambiguous proposition; Gr *lēmma*, (lit) anything received, derives from the r of *lambanein*, to take, akin to Skt *lambhate*, he takes. The adj *dilemmatic* is formed anl (*-atic, -ic*) from the Gr gen *dilēmma*tos.

**dilettante.** See DELICACY, para 8, s.f.

**diligence, diligent.** See LEGEND, para 7.

**dilly,** a tree. See SAPODILLA.

**dilly(-)bag.** See DITTY BAG, s.f.

**dilly-dally.** See DALLIANCE, para 2.

**dilute, dilution; diluvial, diluvium;** also **diluent.** See LAVA, para 9.

**dim,** adj hence v (whence the n **dimmer); dimness.**

The latter derives from OE *dimnes* (with *-nes* cf *-ness*), itself from OE *dim*, var *dimme*, whence E *dim*: akin to OFris *dimm*, dim, ON *dimmr*, dim, sombre, dark, OHG *timber*, sombre—perh also the *ten-* of L *tenebrae*, darkness, the *them-* of Gr *themeros*, august, and the *dam-* of G *dämmerung*, twilight (cf OHG *dem*ar, darkness).

**dime.** See DECEMBER, para 3.

**dimension.** See MEASURE, para 7.

**diminish** (whence pa **diminished**), with *-ment* derivative **diminishment; diminuendo; diminution, diminutive** (adj hence n).

1. 'To *diminish*' blends the now obsol *minish* and the obs *diminue*, from MF-F *diminuer*, from L *diminuere*, earlier and better *dēminuere* (*dē*, down from+*minuere*, to lessen); *minish* has passed through OF and ML from L *minūtus*, very small, orig the pp of *minuere*: cf MINUTE, small, and, f.a.e., MINOR.

2. *Diminūt-*, s of *diminūtus* (earlier *dēminūtus*), pp of *diminuere*, accounts both for L *diminūtiō* (earlier *dē-*), o/s *diminūtiōn-*, whence, via MF-EF, *diminution*, and for *diminūtīuus* (earlier *dē-*), ML *-īvus*, whence—prob via MF-F *diminutif*, f *-ive*—the E adj *diminutive*.

3. In It, L *diminuere* remains unchanged; its gerund *diminuendo*, with diminishing volume, has been adopted by music.

**dimity,** a corded cotton fabric: It *dimiti*, pl of *dimito*: Gr *dimitos*, double-threaded, hence, as n, dimity: *di-*, twice+*mitos*, a warp-thread, s *mit-*, prob akin to Hit *mitis*, thread, string (Hofmann).

dimmer, n. See DIM.

dimorphic, dimorphism, dimorphous. See MORPHEUS, para 3.

dimple, n (whence dimply: -y, adj), hence v (whence pa dimpled): ME dympull, prob akin to MHG tümpfel, G Tümpel, pool, OHG tumphilo, whirlpool, and, if that be so, perh also to E DIP, dimples being likened to ripples.

din, v, derives from OE dynnan, var of dynian, itself prob from—certainly very intimately related to—OE dyn, dyne, (as still) a loud, confused, discordant noise: with the OE v, cf the syn ON dynja, OS dunian, MHG tünen, also Skt dhuni, roaring (cf dhunáyati, it roars): ult echoic.

2. 'To dun' a debtor may be a 'thickened' var of 'to din': to din it into his ears that he owes this money.

dine (whence diner and dining) and dinner; déjeuner; jejune.

1. Dinner, ME diner, represents the OF-MF disner (F diner), to dine, used as n: and disner— whence ME dinen, whence 'to dine'—orig means 'to breakfast', hence the speculative derivation from VL *disiēiūnāre, *disjējūnāre, to break one's fast: dis-, apart, connoting cessation+L ieiūnāre, to fast, itself from the adj ieiūnus, ML jējūnus, fasting, hence hungry, hence dry, thin, weak, whence the E jejune. Ieiūnus is prob akin to L ientāre (s ient-), with redup var ieientāre (s ieient-), to make one's first meal of the day: iē-, ML jē-, therefore, merely constitutes an int-by-redup: ient- remains o.o.o.

2. From VL *disiēiūnāre, disjējūnāre, later *disjūnāre, comes OF-F desjeuner, to breakfast, whence F déjeuner, used also as n, orig breakfast, now lunch (breakfast being le petit déjeuner). According to the *disjējūnāre theory, F déjeuner and diner are doublets. But, whatever the origin of déjeuner, diner or rather OF-MF disner (whence both 'to dine' and dinner) may rather come from the C r *dei, to be luminous, whence *diies, contr to *dies, whence Br deiz, day, perh even the L diēs (cf DIANA, para 6). 'By a shortening to dis, we have diner, for the old disner, to take the meal of the day, of midday, disner coming from an earlier derivative *disnos or *disna, but not from the VL *disjūnāre for L disjējūnāre, given by Darmesteter.' Malvezin's theory is not to be lightly dismissed. (He does not deny the disjējūnāre-déjeuner etymology.)

ding, to strike or hurl. See DINT.

ding-dong: no less imitative than (say) the L tintinnabulum, a bell.

dinghy: Bengalese dingi, dim of dinga, a boat: ? from Skt dru, wood (cf the Gr drus, s dru-, the oak).

dingo (Aus) is an aboriginal word.

dingy. See DUNG.

dinner. See DINE.

Dinornis and dinosaur. See the element dino- and cf DIRE; for the latter, cf also SAURIA, para 2.

dint, n hence v, with var dent; ding, to strike or hurl.

Dint, n, derives from ME dint, var of dunt (retained in Sc), from OE dynt, akin to syn ON dyntr, var dyttr; to Lith dundëti, to knock, and to Alb gdhende, to beat: ult echoic. 'To ding' comes, through ME dingen, var of dengen, from ON dengja, to beat or hammer, akin to OHG tangol, a hammer, OHG *tingan, to strike, G dengeln, to beat or hammer. (Kluge.)

diocesan, diocese.

Diocesan represents MF-F diocésain, adj of OF-F diocèse, which, like E diocese (ME diocise), derives from OF diocise: L dioecēsis: Gr dioikēsis, housekeeping, hence administration, hence a province, LGr a diocese; from dioikein, to keep house: dia, through, thoroughly+oikein, to keep house: from oikos, a house: f.a.e., ECONOMY.

diorama. See the element -orama.

dip, v (hence n), whence dipper.

1. 'To dip' comes, through ME dippen, var of duppen, from OE dyppan, akin to syn ON deypa and to OFris dēpa, Go daupjan, OS dōpian, to baptize.

2. The last two are akin to MD dopen, D doopen, to dip, whence the n doop, a dipping, a sauce, any viscous liquid, whence the E dope, whence 'to dope', to treat with dope (in any of its senses).

3. Cf also DEEP and DIVE.—The IE r is *dheub-.

diphtheria, Sci L: F diphthérie: Gr diphthera (var dipsara), a prepared hide or a piece of leather, used by F for a membrane: akin to Gr depsein, to tan, orig, as also the basic var dephein, to soften by kneading, itself o.o.o.

diphthong. See PHONE, para 5.

diploma; diplomacy, diplomat, diplomatic, diplomatist.

Adopted from L, diploma is simply the Gr diplōma, a paper folded double, from diploun, to double, from diploos, twofold, var diplasios: f.a.e., DOUBLE. L diploma has (modern) adj diplomaticus, whence F diplomatique, whence E diplomatic; by b/f, diplomatique yields diplomate, whence E diplomat; diplomate has derivatives diplomatie, whence E diplomacy (-cy), and diplomatiste, a student of diplomatics, whence the needless E diplomatist, a diplomat.

dipper. See DIP.

dipsomania, dipsomaniac. See MIND, para 4.

dire: L dirus, of bad augury, sinister, hateful, s dir-, perh akin to the s dein- of Gr deinos, terrible, and to Skt dvéṣṭi, he hates—cf also Gr deidō (s deid-, r dei-), I fear.

direct; direction (whence directional), directive, director (whence directorate, directorial, directorship), directory. See REX, para 28.

direption. See RAPT, para 11.

dirge. See REX, para 29.

dirigent, dirigible. See REX, para 28.

dirt, whence dirty, adj (whence the v): by metathesis from ME drit, from ON drit, excrement, from the v drīta, akin to OFris drīta, OE drītan, to MLG dret, n, and driten, v, cf OHG trīzan, to MD drite, n, and D dryten, v, and to several Sl vv. (Holthausen).

**disable** (whence the pa **disabled**), **disability**. See HABIT, para 5.

**disabuse.** See USE, para 9.

**disadvantage, disadvantageous.** See ADVANTAGE, para 2.

**disaffect, -ed, -ion:** *dis-* anl formations from AFFECT, etc.

**disagree, disagreeable, disagreement:** resp OF-F *désagréer*, MF-F *désagréable*, EF-F *désagrément*: *des-* (L *dis-*) derivatives from *agréer, agréable, agrément*: cf AGREE.

**disallow**—whence (after *allow-allowance*) **disallowance**—comes from MF-EF *desalouer*, to disapprove. Cf ALLOW.

**disappear** (prefix *dis-*), whence **disappearance** (*-ance*), derives from APPEAR.

**disappoint, disappointment.** See PUNGENT, para 22.

**disapprobation, disapprove** (whence **disapproval**). See PROVE, para 7.

**disarm,** whence, after *armament*, **disarmament.** See ARMS, para 2.

**disarray.** See ARRAY, para 3.

**disaster, disastrous.** See STAR, para 8.

**disavow** (whence **disavowal:** *-al*, n): MF-F *désavouer*: cf AVOW.

**disband** (whence **disbandment:** suffix *-ment*): EF (se) *desbander*: *des-* for L *dis-*, apart+*bande* (see BAND), a company+inf *-er*.

**disbar,** to expel from the Bar; **debar,** to prevent, as with a bar: OF-MF *desbarer*; its derivative *débarrer*: *des-*, L *dis-*, apart+OF-F *barre*, q.v. at BAR.

**disbelief, disbelieve,** are merely the *dis-* (not) 'answers' to belief, believe.

**disburse, disbursement.** See PURSE, para 2.

**disc.** See DISH.

**discard.** See the 2nd CARD, para 9.

**discern, discernible, discernment.**

The 3rd, if not from EF-F *discernement*, comes straight from the 1st, which represents MF-F *discerner*, L *discernere*, to distinguish (*cernere*) apart (*dis-*), to make out with the eye: f.a.e., CERTAIN; cf DISCREET. *Discernible* comes perh via F *discernable* from LL *discernibilis*.

**discharge.** See CAR, para 4.

**disciple; discipline, disciplinarian, disciplinary.**

*Disciple,* adopted by ME from OF-F, derives— like OE *discipul*—from L *discipulus*, itself from *discere* (s *disc-*), to learn, akin to *docēre* (s *doc-*), to teach, q.v. at DOCILE. *Discipulus* has derivative *disciplīna*, education, military education and training, discipline, whence, via OF-F, the E *discipline*. *Disciplīna* has derivatives LL *disciplīnāre*, to teach or train, whence 'to *discipline*', with derivative *disciplīnābilis*, whence *disciplinable*; ML *disciplīnārius*, whence, with *-an* substituted for *-ous*, the adj *disciplinarian*, whence the n, and, directly (cf the F *disciplinaire*), *disciplinary*.

**disclaim, disclaimer; disclamation.** See CLAIM, para 10.

**disclose, disclosure.** See CLOSE, para 6.

**discoid.** See DISH.

**discoloration, discolo(u)r.** See COLOR, para 3.

**discomfit, discomfiture.** See CONFECTION, para 2.

**discomfort,** n and v. See COMFORT, para 1.

**discommode.** See COMMODIOUS, para 3.

**discompose, discomposure.** See COMPOSE, para 6.

**disconcert, disconcertion.** See CONCERT, para 3.

**disconnect, disconnection:** anl 'answers' to connect (connection).

**disconsolate.** See SOLACE.

**discontent.** See CONTAIN, para 7.

**discontinuance, discontinue, discontinuity.** See CONTINUAL, para 1.

**discord, discordance, discordant.**

The 3rd comes from OF-MF *descordant* (whence OF-MF *descordance*, whence EF-F and E *discordance*), presp of *descorder* (whence obsol E 'to *discord*'), from L *discordāre*, from the adj *discors*, o/s *discord-*: *dis-*, apart+*cord-*, o/s of *cor*, heart (f.a.e., CORDIAL)+inf *-āre*; the OF-MF *descorder* has the derivative OF-MF n *descort*, MF-EF *descorde*, EF-F *discorde*, the latter adapted by E.

**discount,** n, comes from EF *descompte*, itself from MF *descompter*, from which, in its var *desconter*, comes 'to *discount*': cf the 2nd COUNT.

**discountenance:** EF *descontenancer*: *des-*, L *dis-*+*contenance* (cf *countenance* at CONTAIN)+inf *-er*.

**discourage, discouragement.** See CORDIAL, para 5.

**discourse.** See COURSE, para 3.

**discourteous, discourtesy:** opp *courteous, courtesy*, qq.v at COURT.

**discover, discovery.** See COVER, para 2.

**discredit, discreditable.** See CREDENCE, para 7.

**discreet, discrete, discretion.**

Whereas *discrete*, clearly separate, derives straight from L *discrētus*, *discreet* passes through OF-F *discret*; *discretion*, adopted from OF-MF, comes from L *discrētiō* (o/s *discrētiōn-*), separation, discernment, from *discrēt-*, the s of *discrētus*, the pp of *discernere*, q.v. at DISCERN. *Indiscreet, indiscretion* derive from MF-F *indiscret, indiscrétion*.

**discrepancy, discrepant.**

The former, perh adapted from MF-EF *discrepance*, comes from L *discrepantia*, formed from *discrepant-* (whence the E adj *discrepant*), the o/s of *discrepans*, presp of *discrepāre*, to sound out of tune: *dis-*+*crepāre* (s *crep-*), to rattle (cf CREAK).

**discrete; discretion.** See DISCREET.

**discriminant** (adj hence n); **discriminate** (adj and v), **discrimination, discriminator, discriminative** and **discriminatory.**

The last two are E anl formations (*-ive, -ory*, adjj) from 'to *discriminate*', which, like the adj *discriminate*, derives from the pp (LL adj) *discrīminātus* of *discrīmināre*, to distinguish, from *discrīmen*, a sifting-out, division, distinction, from *discernere*, q.v. at DISCERN. The presp *discrīminans* has o/s *discrīminant-*, whence the E adj *discriminant*. On L *discrīmināt-*, s of *discrīminātus*, arose both the LL *discrīminātiō*, o/s *discrīminātiōn-*, whence E *discrimination*, and LL *discrīminātor*, adopted by E. *Indiscriminate*=*in*-, not+*discriminate*, adj.

**disculpate** (whence, by anl, **disculpation**): ML *disculpātus*, pp of *disculpāre*, to excuse (connoted by *dis*-) from *culpa* or blame: f.a.e., CULPABLE.

**discursive, discursus.** See COURSE, para 10 (at *discurrere*).

**discus.** See DISH.

**discuss, discussion, discussive.**

The 3rd is an E -*ive* formation from 'to *discuss*', itself from L *discussus*, pp of *discutere*, to strike (*quatere*, also to shake) apart (*dis*-), in LL to discuss: for *quatere*, see QUASH. Derivative *discussiō*, o/s *discussiōn*-, becomes OF-F, whence E *discussion*.

**disdain, disdainful.** See DECENCY, para 7.

**disease,** n and v (whence pa **diseased**). See EASE.

**disembark.** See the 3rd BARK, para 3.

**disembogue.** See DEBOUCH, s.f.

**disembowel:** *dis*-, apart+*embowel* (*em*- for *en*-, in+BOWEL).

**disenchant**=*dis*-, apart+*enchant*, q.v. at CHANT.

**disengage.** See ENGAGE.

**disert.** See SERIES, para 11.

**disfavo(u)r.** See FAVOR.

**disfigure, disfigurement.** See FIGURE.

**disfranchise.** Cf *franchise* at FRANK.

**disgorge.** See GORGE, para 2.

**disgrace.** See GRACE, para 3.

**disgruntle** (esp in pa **disgruntled**)—whence **disgruntlement** (-*ment*)—combines *dis*-, apart+(now only dial) *gruntle*, to grunt often, to complain, a freq of GRUNT.

**disguise.** See GUISE in ADDENDA TO DICTIONARY.

**disgust.** See GUST, para 3.

**dish** (n hence v); **disk; disc, discus, discoid; desk; dais.**

1. *Dish* comes from OE *disc*, a plate, from L *discus*, dish, disk, quoit (sense adopted by E), whence both *disc* and *disk*: and L *discus* represents Gr *diskos* (s *disk*-), platter, quoit, from *dikein* (s *dik*-), to throw, IE r *dik*-, to throw. *Diskos* has derivative *diskoeidēs*, quoit-like (or -shaped), whence E *discoid*.

2. L *discus*, with LL sense 'table', becomes It *desco* (cf OProv *desc*), table, board, desk, whence ML *desca*, whence ME *deske*, E *desk*.

3. L *discus* also becomes OF-MF *deis*, table (EF-F *dais*, canopy), whence ME *deis*, table, (later) dais, whence E *dais*.

**disharmonious, disharmony.** See HARMONY, para 3.

**disherit.** See HEIR.

**dishevelled.** See CAPILLARY, para 2.

**dishonest, dishonesty.** See HONEST, s.f.

**dishono(u)r.** See HONOR, para 3.

**disillusion, -ment.** See ILLUSION.

**disinclination, disinclined.** See CLIME, para 10.

**disinfect, disinfectant, disinfection.** See INFECT, para 2.

**disinherit.** See HEIR, para 4, s.f.

**disintegrate, disintegration.** See INTEGER.

**disinter.** Cf *inter*, see TERRA.

**disinterest.** See INTEREST.

**disjoint, -ure; disjunct, -ion, -ive.** See JOIN, resp paras 17 and 14.

**disk.** See DISH.

**dislike.** See LIKE, para 4.

**dislocate, dislocation.** See LOCAL.

**dislodge.** See LODGE, para 2.

**disloyal, disloyalty.** See LEGAL, para 3, s.f.

**dismal.** See DIANA, para 7.

**dismantle.** See MANTLE.

**dismay.** See the 2nd MAY, para 3.

**dismember, -ment.** See MEMBER, para 2.

**dismiss, -al,** etc. See MISSION, para 10.

**dismount.** See MINATORY, para 10.

**disobedience, disobedient, disobey.** See AUDIBLE, para 7.

**disobligation, disoblige.** See LIGAMENT, para 8.

**disorder, disorderly.** See ORDER, para 3.

**disorganize, disorganization.** See ORGAN, para 4.

**disorient, disorientate, -ation.** See ORIENT, para 3.

**disown.** See OWN.

**disparage, -ment.** See PAIR, para 7.

**disparate:** L *disparātus*, pp of *disparāre*, to separate: *dis*-, apart+*parāre*, to make ready. Cf PREPARE.

**disparity.** Cf the L *par*, equal and see PAIR, para 3, s.f.

**dispassionate.** See PATIENCE.

**dispatch, despatch.** See PACT, para 5.

**dispel.** See the 2nd PULSE, para 9.

**dispend, dispendious.** See PEND, para 17.

**dispensable, dispensary, dispensation, dispensatory, dispense, dispenser.** See PEND, para 19.

**dispersal, disperse, dispersi n.** See SPARSE, para 4.

**dispirited.** See SPIRIT.

**displace, -ment.** See PLANE, para 14.

**displacency.** See PLEASE, para 10.

**display.** See PLY, para 10.

**displease, displeasure.** See PLEASE, para 8.

**dispone, disponent.** See POSE, para 9.

**disport.** Cf *sport*, see the 3rd PORT, para 6.

**disposal, dispose, disposition.** See POSE, para 9.

**dispossess.** See POSSESS, para 2.

**dispraise.** See PRICE, para 3.

**disproof.** See PROVE, para 8.

**disproportion, disproportionate.** See PART, para 25.

**disprove.** See PROVE, para 8.

**disputable, disputant, disputation, dispute.** See the 2nd COUNT, para 3.

**disqualification, disqualify.** See QUALE (heading).

**disquiet.** See QUIET, para 7.

**disquisition.** Cf *inquisition* and *requisition*; see QUERY, para 9.

**disregard.** Cf *regard* at WARD.

**disrobe.** See ROBE, para 2.

**disrupt, disruption, disruptive.** See RUPTURE, para 5.

**dissatisfaction, dissatisfy** (whence pa **dissatisfied**). See SAD, para 6, s.f.

**dissect, dissection.** See the 2nd SAW, para 10.

**dissemble, dissembler.** See SAME, para 12.

disseminate, dissemination. See the 2nd SAW, para 3.

dissension, dissent (v hence n), dissenter; dissentient, dissentious. See SENSE, para 16.

dissert, dissertate, dissertation. See SERIES, para 10.

disservice. See SERVE, para 8.

dissever. See PARE, para 9.

dissidence, dissident. See SIT, para 13.

dissimilar, -ity. See SAME, para 5, s.f.

dissimilate, dissimilation. See SAME, para 6.

dissimilitude. See SAME, para 6.

dissipate, whence pa dissipated; dissipation, dissipative, dissipator.

L dissipāre, to throw on this side and that, to disperse, scatter, consists of dis-, apart, and *sipāre, var *supāre, to throw, akin to OSl rasypati, to scatter, Skt kṣipáti, he throws, and also, prob, Lith supù, sùpti, to rock (a cradle). Dissipāre has pp dissipātus, whence 'to dissipate'; derivative LL dissipātiō, o/s dissipātiōn-, yields— perh via MF-F—dissipation, and LL dissipātor is adopted; dissipative is an E anl formation in -ive.

dissociate, dissociation, etc. See SOCIABLE.

dissoluble, dissolute, dissolution; dissolve. See LOSE, para 6.

dissonance, dissonant, dissonous. See SONABLE, para 5.

dissuade, dissuasion, dissuasive. Cf persuade; see SUAVE, para 4.

dissyllable, -syllabic. See SYLLABLE, para 3.

distaff. See STAFF, para 2.

distain. See STAIN, para 1.

distal. See STAND, para 24, s.f.

distance (n hence v), distant. See STAND, para 24.

distaste, distasteful. Cf taste; see TACT, para 9.

distemper. See TEMPER, para 5.

distend, distention. See TEND, para 10.

distich. See the 3rd STY, para 2.

distil(l), distillation, distiller, distillery. See the 3rd STILL.

distinct, distinction, distinctive, distinguish. See STICK, para 6.

distort, distortion. See TORT, para 8.

distract, distraction. See TRACT, para 14.

distrain, distraint. See the 2nd STRAIN, para 8.

distrait; distraught. Cf distract; see TRACT, para 14.

distress. Cf stress; see the 2nd STRAIN, para 9.

distribute, distribution, distributive, distributor. See TRIBUTE, para 7.

district. Cf strict and see the 2nd STRAIN, para 9.

distrust. See TRUE, para 4, s.f.

disturb, -ance. Cf perturb(-ation); see TURBID, para 5.

disunion, disunite. See ONE, para 3.

disuse. See USE, para 9.

disutility. See USE, para 9.

ditch. See DIG.

dither, n and v: of E dial origin, app echoic: cf the dial diddle at DIDDLE, s.f.

dithyrambic: L dithyrambicus, trln of Gr

dithurambikos, adj of dithurambos, an epithet of, hence lyric poetry honouring, Bacchus, whence, via L, the E dithyramb. The o.o.o. dithurambos is perh for *dithriambos: di-, doubly, hence intensely +thriambos, a Bacchic hymn, itself perh for *triambos, a choral dance in triple (tri-) time, with an *-ambos identical with that of IAMBIC: Boisacq thinks dithurambos to be a loan-word, but whence? Perh cf the Hit dingirmes, gods, a god.

ditto. See DICT, para 2.

ditty. See DICT, para 5.

ditty (bag or box): prob from obs dutty, a coarse brown calico, itself prob from Hi dhot, a loincloth; improb from Aus dilly bag, itself taut from Queensland aborigines' dilli, a bag made of rushes. (EW.) See also MODAL, para 12.

diuretic. See URINE, para 7.

diurnal. See DIANA, para 8, s.f.

diva. See DIANA, para 1.

divagate, divagation. See VAGABOND, para 4.

divan, diwan; douane, douanier.

The 1st=Tu divān, the 2nd the earlier Ar from Per diwan, a many-leaved, hence an account, book, derivatively a governing deliberative body; the sense 'large, low, unbacked couch' has app come to E, through EF-F, from Eg Ar, where earliest recorded: among Persians and Arabs, cushions serve as seats. Ar dīwan has the further sense 'customs office or house', whence OIt doana (It dogana), whence MF-F douane, whence the EF-F agent douanier.

divaricate, divarication. See VACILLATE, para 8.

dive, v (hence n)—whence diver—comes from ME diven, var duven: OE dūfan (vi), dȳfan (vt), to sink: akin to ON dūfa, dȳfa, to dive or dip, MLG düven—and to E DIP.

diverge, divergence, divergent. See the 3rd VERGE, para 3.

divers (adj), diverse, diversify, diversion, diversity. See VERSE, para 15.

divert, divertisement. See VERSE, para 15.

divest, divestment. See VEST, para 3.

divide (v hence n), whence divider; dividend; divisible (indivisible), division, divisor.—individual (adj hence n), individualism, individualist, individuality, individualize.

1. The last four terms derive from the adj individual, yet owe something to the corresp F terms. Individual (cf the EF-F individuel) comes from ML indiviuālis, an -ālis (E -al) mdfn of L indiuiduus (ML -viduus), indivisible: in-, not+ diuiduus, divisible, from diuidere, ML -videre, to separate, disjoin, to divide, itself app di- for dis-, apart+*uidere, to deprive, perh akin to uiduus (ML viduus), deprived, hence as n, uiduus, a widower, and uidua, a widow (f.a.e.: WIDOW).

2. The ML dividere becomes ME dividen (var de-), whence 'to divide'. Derivative dividendum (L diui-), something to be divided, yields, perh via EF-F dividende, the E dividend.

3. On diuīs-, ML divīs-, s of pp diuīsus, ML divīsus, arise diuīsiō, o/s diuīsiōn-, ML divīsiōn-, whence, via OF-F, the E division; LL diuīsibilis,

ML *divī-*, yields MF-F, whence E, *divisible*, the neg *indivisible* deriving from the ML form of LL *indiuīsibilis*; L *diuīsor*, ML *divīsor*, is adopted by E.

**divination; divine** (adj, n, v); **divinity.** See DIANA, para 1.

**divisible, division, divisor.** See DIVIDE, para 3.

**divorce, divorcée.**

'To *divorce*' comes from MF *divorcer*; *divorcée*, adj used as n, is the f of the F pp *divorcé*. MF-F *divorcer* derives from MF-F *divorce*, adopted by E: ML *divortium*, L *diuortium*, from *diuortere*, var of *diuertere*, to turn (*uertere*) apart (*di-* for *dis-*), to divert, to divorce: f.a.e., VERSATILE.

**divulgate, divulgation, divulge, divulgence.** See VULGAR.

**divulse, divulsion.** See VELLICATE, para 6.

**diwan.** See DIVAN.

**dixey, dixie, dixy:** Hind *degcī* (var *degcā*), a pot or kettle, prob lit 'receptacle'—cf Gr *dekomai* (s *dek-*), Att *dekhomai* (s *dekh-*), I receive, with IE r *\*dek-*.

**dizen.** See STAFF, para 3.

**dizziness, dizzy.**

The former derives from OE *dysigness* (suffix *-ness*), folly, itself from OE *dysig*, foolish, whence ME *dusi, disi*, foolish, whence *dizzy*, giddy: akin to OFris *dusia*, to be or feel dizzy, OHG *dusīg*, *tusīg*, MHG *dusec*, foolish, LG *duselig*, silly, MD *duiselen, duselen*, D *dulzelen*, to be or become dizzy; akin also to OE *dwāes*, foolish, and to G *Tor*, a fool, MHG *tōre*, fool, deaf person; Gmc r *\*dus-*, var *\*dauz*. (Walshe.)

**do**, pt **did**, pp **done**, presp **doing** used also as vn; **undo; deed—indeed; doff, don, dup.**

1. 'To *undo*' comes from OE *undōn* (*un+dōn*, to do, put). *Doff=do off*, do—put—off; *don=do on*, do—put—on, complementary to *doff*; and the now dial *dup=do up*, put up (the latch), i.e. to open.

2. The adv *indeed=in deed*, in (proved) fact: and *deed* comes from OE *dēd, dāed* (cf OFris *dēd, dēde*, OS *dād*, OHG *tāt*, ON *dāth*), intimately akin to OE *dōn*, to perform, (often narrowed to) to place or put, whence, through ME *don*, later *do*, the E 'to *do*': cf *to-do*, fuss, from 'something *to do*', to be done, and *ado*, contr of ME (N form) *at do*, to do, '(something) to be done', and, sem, *affair* (F *à faire*).

3. OE *dōn* is akin to OFris *dūa*, to do, to make, OS *duan*, MD *doen* (extant), *doon, donne, don, duen*, OHG-MHG *tuon*, G *tun*, to do, and, less closely, OSl *dēti*, to put or place, Lith *dēt*, to lay eggs, Gr ti*thēm*i, Skt dá*dhām*i, I place, set, establish, L *fēci* (*fē-* for *\*dhē-*), I have made, Skt *dai-* or *te-*, to place or put, Tokh A *tā-*, to lay; IE r *\*dhē-*, to put, place, set, lay. Cf the sep epi*thet* and *theme*.

**Dobbin.** See ROBERT, para 4.

**docile, docility; doctor** (n hence v), **doctoral, doctorate; doctrine, doctrinal, doctrinaire—indoctrinate, indoctrination; document** (n hence v), **documentary** (adj hence n), **documentation; sep didactic, disciple, discipline.**

1. *Docility* has come, via late MF-F *docilité*, from

L *docilitās*, acc *docilitātem*, from *docilis*, teachable, willing to be taught—whence, via late MF-F, the E *docile*—itself from *docēre* (s *doc-*), to teach, akin to L *discere* (s *disc-*), to learn, and Gr di*daske*in (s *didask-*, redup of r *\*dask-*), to teach, and perh Gr *dokeō* (s *dok-*), I believe; IE r, *\*dek-*, with varr *\*dak-* and esp *\*dok-*.

2. *Docēre* has pp *doctus* (used also as adj for 'erudite'), with s *doct-*, upon which arise:

*doctor*, a teacher, hence a learned person, esp in medicine—adopted by E, with derivative adj *doctoral* (*-al*); derivative ML *doctorātus* (gen *-ūs*) yields E *doctorate* and EF-F *doctorat*;

*doctrīna* (perh imm from *doctor*), whence, via OF-F, the E *doctrine*; the derivative LL adj *doctrīnālis* yields OF-F, whence E, *doctrinal*; OF-F *doctrine* has MF-F adj *doctrinaire*, adopted by E as adj (merely theoretical, yet dogmatic) and n; 'to *indoctrinate*' and *indoctrination* derive resp from *in-*, used int+ML *doctrīnāre*, to teach or instruct (itself from *doctrīna*), and from int *in-*+ derivative *doctrīnātiō*, o/s *doctrīnātiōn-*, the former perh suggested by OF-F *endoctriner*;

OL *documen*, whence L *documentum*, a teaching or lesson, whence OF-F *document*, used in modern sense only since ca 1800 and duly adopted by E; derivative F *documentaire* becomes E *documentary*; derivative LL *documentāre*, to warn, has subsidiary ML *documentātiō* (o/s *documentātiōn-*), a warning, form-adopted in E and F *documentation* but, in the modern sense, reasonably derivable from E and F *document*.

**dock** (1), a weed: OE *docce*, akin to G *Dockenblatter* (G *Blatt*, OHG *blat*, a leaf), and prob to:

**dock** (2), the stump or solid part of an animal's tail: ME *dok*, akin to OFris *dōk*, a bundle, and MLG *docke*. Hence 'to *dock*', to curtail.

**dock** (3), a natural, then an artificial, inlet or hollow for receiving vessels under repair: MD (and MLG) *docke*, Sw *docka* (1698): ? from a late VL *\*ductia*, from *dūcere*, to lead, as Kluge proposes. Hence, of a ship, vi and vt 'to *dock*', whence *docker*.

**dock** (4), in law-court: Flem *dok* or *docke*, an enclosure, cage, hutch: ? akin to prec.

**docket**, n hence v, is often declared to be o.o.o.; EW, however, derives it, via the earlier *doggette*, a summary, an abridgement, from EIt *doghetta*, (Her) bendlet, a dim of *doga*, a cask-stave (o.o.o.).

**doctor, doctorate.** See DOCILE, para 2.

**doctrinaire, doctrinal, doctrine.** See DOCILE, para 2 at *doctrina*.

**document, -ary, -ation.** See DOCILE, para 2 at *documen*.

**dodder** (leafless, *yellow*-stemmed, parasitic plant): ME *doder*: akin to MLG *doder* or *dodder*, MHG *toter* (OHG *totoro*), G *Dotter*, yolk of egg: perh akin to E *dot* (1).

**dodge**, v (whence **dodger**) hence n (whence **dodgy**, evasive, tricky, whence sl 'dangerous'): perh (EW) akin to MHG *tucken*, G *ducken* (obs *docken*), to duck (down), to bow, to dodge, orig a freq of *tauchen*, to dive: cf therefore DUCK.

**dodo**: Port *dodó*, *doudo*, (a) silly (bird), cf the Sp *dido*: a heavy, flightless, now extinct bird, hence a person blissfully and entirely unaware of change in the world about him.

**doe**: ME *dou*, *do*: OE *dā*, perh of C origin: cf OIr *dam*, ox, Cor *da*, fallow deer; cf also Gr *damalēs*, young steer, and *damalis*, *damalē*, heifer; perh ult akin to L *domō*, I subdue, E TAME, the C r being *\*dom-*, to tame.

**doff.** See DO, para 1.

**dog** (n hence v and the adj **doggy**): late OE *docga*: o.o.o., but prob echoic: cf the cant *bufe* and *buffer* (Sc cant *bugher*) and the mastiff's *woof!* *woof!* 'To lie *doggo*': from a dog pretending to be asleep, with familiar suffix *-o*. The adj *dogged* refers to bulldogs and mastiffs.

**doge.** See DUKE, para 3.

**doggerel**: ME *dogerel*: prob, as EW suggests with several convincing parallels in G, D, Prov, E itself, from L *doga*, a cask-stave.

**doggo.** See DOG.

**doggone** (it)!: AE euphem for *God damn* (it)!

**dogie** (AE), motherless calf in a range herd, (esp of cattle) an inferior animal: o.o.o.: perh a blend of *dobie* (later-recorded in this sense)+*doggie*, pet-form of DOG.

**dogma, dogmatic** (whence the n **dogmatics**—cf *apologetics* from *apologetic*), **dogmatism, dogmatist, dogmatize; doxology, paradox, orthodox** and **heterodox, orthodoxy, heterodoxy.**

1. *Dogma*, adopted from L, is the Gr *dogma* (o/s *dogmat-*), from *dokein*, to believe (*dokei*, it seems), with s *dok-*, IE r *\*dek-*, as in L *decet*, it seems good or is fitting, becoming. The Gr adj *dogmatikos* becomes LL *dogmaticus*, whence E *dogmatic*; derivative Gr *dogmatismos*, LL *dogmatismus*, becomes E *dogmatism*; Gr *dogmatistēs*, LL *dogmatistes*, becomes *dogmatist*; Gr *dogmatizein* becomes LL *dogmatizāre*, whence MF-F *dogmatiser* and E *dogmatize*.

2. Gr *dokein* has the further derivative n *doxa* (for *\*doksa*), opinion, praise, glory, with cpd adj *doxologos* (cf LOGIC), praising (esp, in L Gr, God), whence the n *doxologia*, adopted by ML, whence E *doxology*.

3. From *doxa* derive the cpd adjj *heterodoxos*, of another (*heteros*) opinion, esp in religion, whence E *heterodox*, whence—after *orthodoxy*—*heterodoxy*; and *orthodoxos*, of right (*orthos*) or true opinion, whence LL *orthodoxus*, whence E *orthodox*, Gr derivative *orthodoxia* yielding *orthodoxy*; and *paradoxos*, contrary-thinking, with neu *paradoxon* used as n, whence (late MF-F *paradoxe*, hence prob) E *paradox*, with adjj *paradoxal* (L *paradoxus*: *-al* substituted for *-ous*) and *paradoxical* (*-ical*).

**doily**: Doily, a C17 draper in the Strand, London. (Prob anglicized from F surname *Doillet*.)

**doit.** See WHITTLE, para 3.

**doldrums.** See DULL.

**dole**, a share. See 1st DEAL, para 2.

**dole** (2), grief (obs), whence **doleful.** Cf con*dole*; see DOLOR.

**Doll**, whence **doll; Dolly**, whence **dolly.**

*Doll* is a pet-form of *Dorothy*, the E shape of *Dorothea*, from L Gr *Dōrothea*, gift (*dōron*) of God (*Theos*: cf THEISM). *Dolly* is a further familiarization, prop a dim, of *Doll*; its adj is *dolly*.

**dollar.** See DALE, para 2.

**dolmen; menhir.** *Dolmen*, adopted from F, consists of Br *tol*, var of *taol*, a table+*men*, var of *mean* or *maen*, a stone; *menhir*, likewise adopted from F, consists of Br *men*+*hir*, long; and these etymologies truly describe.

**dolor** (AE) or **dolour; dolorous; Dolores.**—**dole**, grief, whence **doleful; condole, condolence.**

1. *Dolo(u)r* derives from OF-MF *dolor*, varr *dolour*, *dolur*, from L *dolor*, pain, grief, from *dolēre*, to suffer; the derivative LL adj *dolorōsus* yields *dolorous*. *Dolēre* becomes E 'to dole', now dial; the n *dole* comes from MF-F *dol*, itself, via VL *dolus*, from L *dolēre*. *Dolores* derives from Sp *Maria de los Dolores* (as in L, the pl of *dolor*), Mary of the Sorrows.

2. *Dolēre* has the LL cpd *condolēre*, to suffer, hence to grieve, with (*con*), whence 'to condole', whence—cf the late MF-F *condoléance*—*condolence*.

**dolphin.** See DELPHINIUM, para 2.

**dolt**, whence **doltish** (*-ish*, adj), perh derives from ME *dold*, var *dult*, pp of *dullen*, to DULL.

**Dom** (title: cf *Dan* and *Don*). See DOMESTIC, para 6.

**dome.** See para 1 of DOMESTIC.

**Domesday Book.** See DOOM, para 1, s.f.

**domestic, domesticate, domesticity; dome; domicile, domiciliary; domain, demesne; dominant, dominate, domination**—whence **predominant, predominate, predomination; domineer; dominical, Dominican, dominie, domino, Dominus; dominion** (and **condominium); Dom, Don, Dan; Domina, Donna, Dona, dame; sep dam; sep demoiselle** (and **mademoiselle), damozel, damsel**—**madame, madam, Madonna; sep danger** (**endanger), dangerous; sep daunt, dauntless; perh cf** *indomitable*, q.v. at TAME; certainly cf DESPOT.

1. *Dome* comes from L *domus* (s *dom-*), a house; the IE r is app *\*dem-*, with varr *\*dam-* and *\*dom-*: cf Gr *domos* and Skt *dámas*, house, and perh Gr *demein* (s *dem-*), to build; cf also Gr *despotēs* (for *demspotēs*).

2. L *domus* has adj *domesticus* (cf *rusticus* from *rus*), whence MF-F *domestique* and, perh via F, the E *domestic*; derivative LL *domesticitās* yields *domesticity* (cf the late EF-F *domesticité*); the *domesticus*-derivative ML *domesticāre*, to reside in, has pp *domesticātus*, whence 'to domesticate', whence *domestication*.

3. *Domus* has mdfn *domicilium* ('more abstract than *domus*': E & M)—whence MF-F, hence E, *domicile*, whence, perh prompted by EF-F *domicilier*, 'to domicile'; the derivative ML adj *domiciliārius* yields both *domiciliar* and *domiciliary*.

4. The master of the *domus* or house is naturally *dominus*; the mistress, *domina*. LL *Dominus* is the Lord God: *the* lord. The voc *domine* becomes Sc and E *dominie*, schoolmaster, and the dat or abl *domino* becomes the F, hence E, *domino*, a kind of monastic hood, hence a hooded masquerade costume with a small mask, hence a small mask, hence a piece in the game of *dominoes*, perh ref the black spots. The adj *dominicus* leads to the PN *Dominic*; its LL extn *dominicālis* produces *dominical*, the further extn ML *Dominicānus*, from *Dominicus* the founder, explains the adj hence n *Dominican*.

5. On the s *domin-* arise also:
*domināri*, to be master of, to dominate, with presp *dominans*, o/s *dominant-*, whence—perh via OF-F—the E *dominant*, adj hence, esp in Mus, n; hence *dominance*, as if from *\*dominantia*;

its pp *dominātus*, s *domināt-*, yields 'to *dominate*'; the derivative *domināti̅ō*, o/s *domināti̅ōn-*, yields— perh via OF—the E *domination*;

(the ML cpd *praedominium*, supreme power, may have suggested the E formations *predominant, -dominate, -domination*;)

*domināri* becomes OF-F *dominer* becomes D *domineren*, whence 'to *domineer*';

*dominium*, right of property (orig the master's), survives in Law; cf its modern cpd *condominium*, joint rights over a territory; in ML, *dominium* becomes *domini̅ō*, o/s *domini̅ōn-*, whence, prob via F, the E *dominion*; L *dominium*, however, becomes MF-F *domaine*, whence E *domain*—contrast *demesne*, adopted from AF (*s* silent) *demesne*, for OF-MF *demeine*, from L *dominicus* (as in para 4), —but both of these F words were influenced by ML *domānium*.

6. L *dominus* becomes Sp *don* (whence, ult, the coll academic sense) and Port *dom*; *domina* becomes It *donna*, whence *madonna*, my lady, *Madonna*, Our Lady, and Sp *doña* and *dueña* (whence E *duenna*, orig the Queen of Spain's chief lady-in-waiting). In OF-MF, *dominus* takes the form *danz* (nom) or *dan* (acc), adopted by ME, the latter form surviving in archaic *Dan* (Chaucer).

**domicile.** See prec, para 3.
**dominate, domination**, etc. See DOMESTIC, para 5.
**dominie.** See DOMESTIC, para 4.
**dominion.** See DOMESTIC, para 5.
**domino.** See DOMESTIC, para 4.
**don, n.** See DOMESTIC, para 6.
**don, v.** See DO, para 1; cf ON, para 2.
**donate, donation, donative, donator, donatory; condonation, condone; pardon (n and v), pardonable, pardoner.**

1. L *dare*, to give, *do*, I give (cf DATA), has derivative *donum* (s *don-*), a gift, whence *donāre* (s *don-*), to make a gift of, with pp *donātus*, whence 'to *donate*'. On the pps *donāt-* arise:

*donāti̅ō*, a giving, o/s *donāti̅ōn-*, whence, prob via MF-F, the E *donation*;

*donāti̅uus*, adj, ML *-i̅vus*, whence the E adj *donative*; hence the LL n *donāti̅uum*, ML *-i̅vum*, whence the E n *donative*;

*donātor* (*-or*), adopted by E, becomes also the MF *doneor*, whence E *donor*;

ML *donātōrius*, adj, whence the E legal n *donatory*.

2. The cpd *condonāre* (int *con-*, lit 'together'), to give up or remit (e.g., a sin), to forgive, yields 'to *condone*'; derivative *condonāti̅ō*, o/s *condonāti̅ōn-*, yields *condonation*.

3. LL *perdonāre* (int *per-*, lit 'through') becomes OF-MF *pardoner*, whence 'to *pardon*'; the OF-F n *pardon* (from *pardoner*) is adopted by E; *pardonable* derives either from 'to *pardon*' or from OF-F *pardonnable*; MF *pardonier* (from *pardoner*) yields the medieval *pardoner*.

**donjon.** See DUNG.
**Don Juan.** See JOHN, para 1.
**donkey:** ? *dun* (*-*coloured)+dim *-key* (cf mon*key*); ? a nickname (*Dominic* or *Dunc*an) like the syn *cuddy, dicky, neddy*. (EW.) Unrecorded before Grose, 1785, it might possibly derive from that egregious ass, *Don Quixote*, Cervantes's book having appeared in Shelton's translation in 1612–20, revised by John Stevens in 1700; in Motteux's (1710–12), 8th edition, 1749, and revised by Ozell, 1766; in Jarvis's, 1742, 4th edition, 1766, and in Smollett's in 1755, 5th edition, 1782. Don Quixote was, in short, familiar to the C18.

**donna** (whence the Aus sl *donah*). See DOMESTIC, para 6.
**donor.** See DONATE, para 1.
**doom,** n hence v; **doomsday—Doomsday**, or **Domesday, Book; deem, deemster** and **dempster.**

1. The ancestral OE *dōm*, a law or decree, hence justice, a verdict, is akin to OFris (and OS) *dōm*, Go *dōms*, OHG *tuom*, ON *dōmr*, and perh to Gr *themis*, law, s *them-*, itself perh akin, ult, to *histēmi*, I set upright, L *stāre*, to stand, with IE r *\*sta-*, to stand; others, however, relate OE *dōm* to OE *dōn*, to do. The OE *dōmes daeg*, day of judgement, yields *doomsday*, as in *Doomsday* Book, with var *Domesday* Book.

2. Intimately akin to OE *dōm* is OE *dēman*, whence ME *demen*, to judge, hence often to condemn, whence 'to *deem*', in the same senses (now obs), hence to have an opinion about, to believe or to suppose. ME *demen*, s *dem-*, has a *-ster* derivative *demester*, whence *deemster*, a judge, the var *dempster* deriving from the ME var *demster* (later *dempster*): cf the now rare EE var *doomster*.

**doon,** var of the n *dun*: see TOWN.
**door; indoors, outdoors,** with derivative adjj in *-door.*

*Indoors*=*in* (sense of *within*) *doors*, inside the house; *outdoors*=*out* (in archaic sense of *out of*) *doors*, outside the house. *Door* itself comes, through ME *dore* (var *dure*), from OE *dor* (var *duru*): akin to OFris *dore*, var *dure*, OS *dora*, var *duru*, OHG *turi*, MHG *tür*, G *Tür* or *Türe* (intimately akin to G *Tor*, MHG-OHG *tor*, gate, cf the syn Go *daúr*), ON *dyrr*; akin also to OSl *dvĭri*, Lith *dùrys*—to OIr *dorus*, Br and W *dor* (from *\*dora*), C r *\*dor-*—to L *foris* (*f* from *dh*),

pl *fores*—to Gr *thura* – to Skt *dvār*, pl *dvāres*; IE r,
*\*dhur-*, with var *\*dhwer-*. Cf FOREIGN (where also
*forensic* and *forum*).

**dope,** whence the adj **dopey** or **dopy,** lethargic.
See DIP, para 2.

**Doric:** L *Doricus*: Gr *Dōrikos*, adj of *Dōrios*, a
Doric Greek.

**dormant, dormer, dormitive, dormitory** (whence
the coll **dorm); dormouse.**

1. The L *dormīre* (s *dorm-*), to sleep, has r *\*dor-*,
a var of IE r *\*der-*; the *-m* of *dormīre* represents
*-em*, a fundamental suffix connoting present time:
akin to OSl *dremati*, Gr *darthanein* (formed upon
the aorist e*darthen*, Homeric e*drathon*), to sleep,
and Skt *drấyati* (Ve *drāti*), he sleeps.

2. On *dormit-*, the s of the pp *dormitus*, arise
both the L *dormitōrius*, of or for sleeping, with neu
*dormitōrium* used (LL-ML) as n, whence the E
*dormitory*, and, by anl, the E formation *dormitive*
(perh via F *dormitif*), soporific.

3. *Dormīre* becomes OF *dormir*, with presp
*dormant*, whence the E adj *dormant*; *dormitōrium*
becomes OF *dormeor*, whence E *dormer*, orig a
bedroom or a dormitory, then a bedroom window,
then elliptically a *dormer* (window).

4. OF-F *dormir* has agent *dormeur* (C14), f
*dormeuse*, whence perh, by f/e, the E *dormouse*,
which, however, could=F dormir+E *mouse* or,
more prob, E dial *dorm* (from F *dormir*), to sleep
or doze+*mouse*. Cf, sem, the syn MD *slaepmuus*
or *-muys*.

**dormy** or **dormie** (in golf): ? F *dormi*, asleep,
hence, in the game, safely asleep: pp of *dormir*,
q.v. in para 3 of prec.

**dorsal; doss;** cf the element *dorsi-*.

1. *Dorsal* comes, prob via MF-F, from L
*dorsālis*, the adj of *dorsum*, the back, s *dors-*; perh
for *\*dēorsum*, short for *\*dēuorsum*, var of
*\*dēuersum*, with prefix *dē-*, down+*uers*, as in
*uersus*, pp of *uertere*, to turn, s *uert-*, r *\*uer-* or
*\*wer*, to turn. *Dorsum* becomes OF-F *dos*, whence
prob the sl *doss*, a bed, whence 'to *doss*'.

2. Also from OF *dos* comes MF-F *dossier*, a
bundle of papers concerning a certain, usu suspect,
person; so named from being described on the
back.

3. 'To *endorse* or *indorse*' represents, the latter
ML *indorsāre*, to put on (in) the back (*dorsum*),
and the former a blend of the ML word+OF-F
*endosser* (ME *endossen*), itself=*en*, in+*dos*, back
+euphonic *s*+inf *-er*. Hence *endorsement*.

4. But *parados* is adopted from F: *para-*, against
+*dos*, the back: the complement to *parapet*, which,
likewise adopted from EF-F (whence so many E
military terms, esp of fortification), comes from
It *parapetto*: *parare*, to protect+*petto*, the breast
(L *pectus*).

**dory** (fish): F *doré*, gilded, pp of OF-F *dorer*,
itself from LL *dēaurāre*: int *dē-*+*aurāre*, to gild,
from *aurum*, gold: f.a.e., AUREATE.

**dose,** n hence v (whence, in turn, **dosage:** suffix
*-age*): late MF-F *dose*: ML *dosis*, adopted from
Gr: lit 'action of giving (sc medicine)', from

*didonai*, to give, redup of r *\*don-*, to give (cf L
*donāre*).

**doss.** See DORSAL, para 1, s.f.

**dossier.** See DORSAL, para 2.

**dot** (1), a small piece, a small point, whence the
v 'to **dot**' and prob, as dim, **dottle,** residue of
(tobacco and) ash in a pipe bowl: OE *dott*: akin to
OE *dyttan*, to stop up, to plug; cf also OHG *tutta*,
nipple, and D *tot*, knot.

**dot** (2), woman's marriage-portion, is adopted
from MF-F: L *dot-*, o/s of *dos*, a gift, esp a *dot*:
from *do-*, r of *donum*, itself from *dare*, to give:
f.a.e., DATA.

**dotage** derives, by suffix *-age*, from 'to **dote**', to
act foolishly, to be foolish, whence 'to *dote*
(up)on': ME *doten*, var *dotien*, akin to MD *doten*,
to doze, to become childish, and MHG *tūzen*, to
be or keep still.

**dottle.** See the 1st DOT.

**douane, douanier.** See DIVAN, s.f.

**double,** adj (whence n) and v; **doublet; doubloon.**
See PLY, para 23.

**double-entendre.** See TEND, para 12.

**doubt** (n and v), **doubtful; redoubtable; dubitable
(indubitable), dubiety, dubious.**

1. *Doubtful*=doubt, n+*-ful*: and *doubt*, n,
comes, via ME *doute* (var *dute*), from OF-F *doute*,
itself from OF-F *douter* (OF var *duter*), to doubt,
from L *dubitāre*; OF-F *douter* (*duter*) becomes ME
*douten* (*duten*), whence 'to *doubt*'.

2. L *dubitāre* is a freq of the rare *dubāre*, to be
in two minds, prob from an adj *\*dubus* (*duo*, two+
formative *-b-*+nom *-us*). Derivative *dubitābilis*
and its neg *indubitābilis* yield E *dubitable*,
*indubitable*.

3. *\*Dubus*, of two minds, in doubt, survives in
the L var *dubius*, whence *dubium*, doubt, with its
own adj *dubiōsus*, whence E *dubious*; the derivative
LL *dubietās*, o/s *dubietāt-*, leads to *dubiety*.

4. *Redoubtable* derives from ME *redoutable*,
adopted from OF-F; the OF word derives from
OF-F *redouter*, var of *redoubter*, from ML
*redubitāre*, to fear ('doubt back at'), a *re-* cpd of
L *dubitāre*. The E *redoubt*, to dread, is obs.

**douce; douceur.** See DULCET.

**douche,** n (whence the v), adopted from EF-F,
comes from syn It *doccia*, from *docciare*, to pour,
from *doccia*, waterpipe, from *doccione*, conduit,
from L *ductiōn-*, o/s of *ductiō*, a leading or con-
ducting, from *ductus*, pp of *dūcere*, to lead: f.a.e.,
DUKE.

**dough** (whence the adj **doughy); duff,** as in *plum
duff*.

1. Both *dough* and *duff* come from ME *dogh*,
from OE *dāh*, *dāg*, akin to OHG(-G) *teig*, Go
*daigs* (cf *deigan*, to knead, to shape), ON *deig*:
IE r, *\*dheig-*, cf the Gr *teikhos*, a wall, *thinganein*,
to handle (s *thingan-*; r *thing-*, with *n* infix), and
Skt *dehmi*, I smear, and L *fingere* (with *n* infix), to
form. Cf therefore FEIGN.

2. The coll *doughboy*, an A infantryman, combines *dough*+*boy*: he formerly had to eat so much
doughy food.

**doughty**: ME *douhhti, dohti, duhti*: late OE *dohtig*, earlier *dyhtig*, akin to MHG *tühtec*, G *tüchtig*, fit, capable; also to OE *dugan*, OFris *duga*, OHG *tugan* (G *taugen*), Go *dugan*, ON *duga*, to be of use—fit, strong—capable, and app also to Gr *teukhein* (s *teukh-*), to make ready. IE r, *dheugh-*.

**dour.** See DURABLE, para 2. (Cf *douce* at DULCET.)

**douse, dowse**, the former usu for 'to strike, lower hastily, extinguish', the latter (whence **dowser** and **dowsing rod**) for 'to strike, hence to find, water by using the divining rod', a much later sense following naturally from 'to strike': ? from LG—cf the archaic *doesen*, to strike, as EW suggests.

**dove**—hence **dovetail**, n (anything shaped like a dove's tail), hence v—derives from ME *dove*, earlier *douve, duve*, OE *dūfe*, of Gmc origin: cf OS *dūba, duve*, Go *-dubo*, OHG *tūba*, MHG *tūbe*, G *Taube*; ON *dúfa*, prob also to OIr *dub*, Ir *dubh*, dark-coloured, and perh to DEAF.

**dowager; dower, dowry; endow, endowment.**

1. *Dowager* comes from late MF *douagiere*, agent from MF *doage, douage*, woman's marriage-portion, itself from MF-F *douer*, OF *doer*, to make a gift of, esp as a marriage-portion, from L *dotāre*, from *dos*, marriage-portion, o/s *dot-*: cf the 2nd DOT. *Dotāre* has the ML derivative *dotārium*, whence MF *douaire*, whence both E *dower* (n whence v) and obs E *dowery*, whence *dowry*.

2. MF-F *douer* has MF cpd *endouer* (*en-* for L *in*, in, into), whence 'to *endow*'; *endowment* (suffix *-ment*) is adopted from AF *endow(e)ment*, MF *endouement*.

**dowdy**: adj (*-y*) from EE *dowd*, an ill-dressed or slovenly woman: ME *doude*: o.o.o.—perh cf DEED.

**dower.** See DOWAGER.

**down** (1), adv (whence the adj and prep, whence, in turn, the v) and n; **dune.**

The adv *down* is aphetic for *adown*, ME *adun, adune*, representing OE *of dūne*, from off the *dūn* or hill, whence, through ME *dun*, later *doun*, the E *down*, orig hill, esp a hillock of sand, later an upland (cf *South Down*): and OE *dūn* is akin to MD and MLG *dune*—whence, via MF-F, the E *dune*—and perh to Skt *dhan*van, seashore, dry land.

**down** (2), soft, fluffy feathers, hence soft, short hair: ME *downe*, earlier *doun*: ON *dūnn*: prob cf DUSK and perh cf DUST. Hence *downy* (adj *-y*).

**downright.** See REX, para 3.

**dowry.** See DOWAGER.

**dowse, dowser, dowsing rod.** See DOUSE.

**doxology.** See DOGMA, para 2.

**doyen.** See DEAN.

**doze**, v hence n: of Scan origin: perh ult from ON *dusa*, to doze, itself prob akin to OFris *dusia*, to be or feel dizzy, and therefore to DIZZY.

**dozen**, whence **dozenth**, comes, via ME *dosein(e)*, from OF-MF *doseine* (EF-F *douzaine*): *douze*, 12+suffix *-aine*, E *-ain, -en*: OF-F *douze* deriving from L *duodecim*, 12: *duo*, 2+*decem*, 10. *Duodecim*

has adj *duodecimus*, whence (*in*) *duodecimo*, lit 'in twelfth'; whence also *duodecimal*, influenced by *decimal* (cf DECEMBER, para 1).

**drab**, a dull brownish or yellowish woollen cloth, hence the adj ('so coloured; monotonously dull') and perh the n *drab*, a slatternly, or a loose, woman: OF-F *drap*, cloth: LL *drappus*, o.o.o.—but perh (Malvezin) for OC *drappos*, a thing broken, torn, divided, hence a piece (esp of cloth) from *drap*, to break: cf W *drab*, a piece cut off or torn off, and *drabio*, to cut into pieces; E & M cf such PNN as *Drappo, Drappus, Draponus*.

2. OF-F *drap* has MF-F derivative *draper*, whence 'to *drape*': and this E v and that F n confusedly combine to form 'a *drape*'. The MF-F *draper* has two important MF-F derivatives: the agent *drapier*, whence the AF *draper*, adopted by E, and the collective *draperie*, (manufacture of, trade in) cloth or woollens in general, whence E *drapery*.

3. LL *drappus* becomes besides OF-F *drap*, the It *drappo* and, notably for E, the Sp *trapo*, both meaning 'a rag': from a confusion of the OF, It, Sp words with the MF derivative *drapure*, an ornamented cloth-covering for a horse, come ME *trappe* and *trappure*, trappings, whence ME *trappen*, to caparison, whence the syn obsol E 'to *trap*', with vn *trapping*, an ornamental horse-cloth, now usu pl *trappings*, esp in senses 'gay clothes and ornaments; mere outward signs'; from *trapping* influenced by obsol 'to *trap*' comes, by b/f, the obs *trap*, usu pl *traps*, an ornamental horse-cloth, whence the coll E *traps*, personal belongings.

**drachm.** See DRAM.

**draff.** See DRIVEL.

**draft.** See DRAW, para 4.

**drag.** See DRAW, para 5.

**draggle.** See DRAW, para 5.

**dragon**, with many cpds, based upon similar-ities real or fancied; **dragoon** (n hence v); **drake**, battle standard, cannon; **rankle.**

1. *Dragon*, adopted from OF-F, comes from L *dracō* (o/s *dracōn-*), itself from Gr *drakōn* (gen *drakontos*; s *drak-*), dragon, huge serpent, so named because of its quick-glancing, terrible eyes: cf the Gr *drakein* (s *drak-*), *derkesthai* (s *derk-*), to glance or look, and *drakos*, eye—cf the syn OIr *derc*; IE r, *derk-*, with metathesis *drek-*, var *drak-*, to look or glance.

2. The L acc *dracōn*em yields OF-F *dragon*, whence, in late C16, 'cavalryman'—whence the E *dragoon*—from fighting under the *dragon* (C13 onwards) or battle standard, from L *dracō*'s LL sense 'military standard like a serpent' (Souter): cf the syn E *drake*, which, however, derives from OE *draca*, dragon, from L *dracō*.

3. *Dracō* has dim *dracunculus* (cf *homunculus* from *homo*), a little dragon or serpent, which takes, in ML, the derivative senses, a fiery sore, an abscess, an ulcer, adopted in the derivative OF-MF *draoncle*, whence, by aphesis, MF *raoncle*, contr to *rancle*, whence *rancler* (OF-MF *draoncler*),

to fester, hence to fester in the mind, whence 'to *rankle*', whence 'a *rankle*, a *rankling*'.

4. Gr *drakōn*, a dragon, has dim *drakontion*, with derivative sense 'adderwort, snakeroot', whence the Ar *tarkhun*, which becomes Sp *taragona* whence the E *tarragon*, a herb allied to wormwood and used for seasoning.

**drain** (v hence n), whence, by suffix *-age*, **drainage**: OE *drēhnian*, var *drēahnian*, to drain: akin to DRY.

**drake** (1). See DRAGON, para 2, s.f.

**drake** (2), male duck; **sheldrake**.

The latter is lit 'variegated drake': E dial *sheld*, akin to—? from—MD *schillede*, variegated. *Drake*, ME *drake*, is of Gmc origin: perh by aphesis from MLG *andrake*, cf MHG *antrach*, *antreche*, OHG *antrahho* 'for **ant-trahho** "duck-drake" ' (Walshe).

**dram; drachm.**

The former derives from OF *drame*: L *drachma*, whence MF-F *drachme* and E *drachm*: Gr *drakhmē*, lit a grasping, hence a handful: from *drassesthai*, to grasp. ? for **drak(h)sesthai**: Gr **drakh-**, metathetic var of IE r **dergh-**, to grasp. From the sense 'measure' derives that of 'liquid measure'.

**drama, dramatic, dramatist, dramatize, drama-turgy—melodrama, melodramatic; drastic.**

1. *Drama*, adopted from LL, is the Gr *drama* (s *dram-*, r *dra-*), from *dran*, to do, act, make, akin to Lith *daraũ*, *darýti*, to do or make. Gr *drama* has adj *dramatikos*, whence LL *dramaticus*, whence E *dramatic*; the learned F derivatives from F *drame* (from LL *drama*) include *dramatiser*, *dramatiste*, *dramaturgie* (from the Gr *dramatourgia*, itself from *dramatourgos*, a worker—cf ERG—in drama, a dramatist): whence E *dramatize*, *dramatist*, *dramaturgy*.

2. Gr *dran*, to do, has adj *drastikos*, whence E *drastic*.

3. Another learned F formation is *mélodrame*, whence E *melodrama*, whence by anl the E *melodramatic*: Gr *melos*, a song+*drama*.

**drape, draper, drapery.** See DRAB, para 2.

**drastic.** See DRAMA, para 2.

**drat** (it)!: euphem for God *rot it*!

**draught, draughtsman.** See DRAW, para 4.

**Dravidian** and **Dravidic** are the adjj (hence nn) of *Dravida*, (a native of) Southern India: Skt *Drāviḍa*, from *drameḷa* or *damiḷa*, and therefore akin to *Tamil*.

**draw** (v—with pt **drew**; hence n), whence **drawer**(s), **drawing**, **drawing-room**, (pp as adj) **drawn**, and prob **drawl** (v hence n); **withdraw**, **withdrawal**, **withdrawn**;—**draft** (n hence v), **draftsman**—**draught**, **draughts**, **draughtsman**, **draughty**; **drag** (v hence n), **draggle**, **bedraggled**; **dray** (n hence v), **drayage**; **dredge** (n hence v), whence **dredger** and **dredging**.

1. 'To *draw*', to pull, haul, drag, bear or carry along, hence to change the shape of, hence to represent in line, etc., derives from ME *drawen*, earlier *drahen* (etc.), itself from OE *dragan*: akin

to OFris *draga*, usu *drega*, OS *dragan*, Go *dragan*, OHG *tragan*, MHG-G *tragen*, to carry, and ON *draga*, to drag; perh also to L *trahere*, to draw, pull, drag, pp *tractus*—see sep TRACE, TRACK, TREK; perh even to Gr *trekhein* (s *trekh-*), to run.

2. *Drawing-room* is aphetic for *withdrawing-room*, from *withdraw* (*with*, against, hence back), to draw back (vi, vt), take back, go back; whence *withdrawal* (*-al*, n), act of withdrawing.

3. *Drawl* app=to *draw*+(often with freq or dim force) suffix *-l* for *-el* or *-le*: to draw out slowly.

4. *Draft*, the predominantly AE spelling of E *draught*, is however virtually obligatory for the v: ME *draught* (now pron *draft*), earlier *draht*: from OE *dragan*, to draw, pull, etc. For the game, *draughts* predominates; the atmospheric *draught*, AE *draft*, is an in- or out-drawing of air, with adj in *-y*.

5. 'To *drag*', ME *draggen*, comes prob from the syn ON *draga* but perh, by a dial deviation, from OE *dragan*; the freq is *draggle*, to drag so as to soil with mud or moisture, and it has cpds *draggle-tail*, a slatternly woman, and the int *bedraggle*, mostly in the pa *bedraggled*.

6. *Dray*, OE *draege*, a dragnet, from OE *dragan*, was, in late ME-early EE, a sledge; hence *drayage* (suffix *-age*).

7. *Dredge*, from the r of draw, prob derives from MD *dregge*, a dredge, from MD *dregen*, to carry, akin to OFris *drega* (as in para 1).

**dread**, v hence n (cf OFris *dred*), whence **dreadful** and **dreadless**.

*Dreadnought* is a *dread-nought* (nothing): and 'to *dread*' comes from ME *dreden*, aphetic for *adreden*, from OE *ādrǣdan*, worn-down var of *andrǣdan*, akin to OS *andrādan*, to frighten, and OHG *intrātan*, to dread; the division, therefore, of the OE *ondrǣdan* is prob *ond-rǣdan*, where *ond-* is a var of *and-*, akin to OFris *and-*, OS *and(e)-*, Go *and-*, OHG *ant-* (var *int-*), in, on, against.

**dream**, n hence v; from n, **dreamless**, **dreamy**; from v, **dreamer**, **dreaming**.

A *dream*, ME *dream*, earlier *dreme*, prob from OE *drēam*, joy, music, and certainly akin to ON *draumr*, OHG-MHG *troum*, G *Traum*, MD *droem*, *drome*, *droom* (as in D), OS *drōm*, and esp OFris *drām*, all meaning 'dream'; the last also means '(shout of) joy'.

**drear**, adj, is a b/f from **dreary**, ME *dreri*, earlier *dreori*, from OE *drēorig*, sad, (orig) bloody, deriving in *-ig* from OE *drēor*, blood, gore, akin to OHG *trūren*, MHG *trūren*, G *trauern*, to mourn, and to OE *drēosan*, Go *driusan*, to fall, and OE *drūsian*, to sink, therefore ult to E DROP. (Walshe.)

**dredge, dredger.** See DRAW, para 7.

**dree.** See DRUDGE.

**dreg**, usu pl **dregs**: ME *dreg*: ON *dregg*: akin to OP *dragios* (cf DROSS).

**drench**, n, derives from OE *drenc*, itself from OE *drencan*, to supply with drink, to *drench*; OE *drencan* is the caus of OE *drincan*, to drink: f.a.e., DRINK.

**dress, dressage, dressing.** See REX, para 8.

**drib; dribble.** See DRIP, para 1.
**dried; drier, driest; drily.** See DRY, para 1.
**drift, drifter.** See DRIVE, para 1.

**drill** (1), a heavy linen or cotton fabric: b/f of EE *drilling*, with E suffix *-ing* for G suffix *-ich*: G *Drillich*, OHG *drilīh*, with G *drei* for L *tri-*: L *trilix*, three-threaded (fabric): *tri-* from *tres*, 3+-*lix*, from *licium*, a warp-thread.

**drill** (2), to pierce, bore, to exercise soldiers (*et al.*), hence—cf MD *dril*, *drille*—the n (instrument; military exercise, perh also the farming implement): MD *drilen*, MD-D *drillen*, to pierce or bore, to drill (soldiers): akin to MHG *drillen*, to turn; cf also the F *vrille*, a gimlet, app by blending the earlier *veïlle* with *virer*, to turn (cf VEER).

**drill** (3), the farming implement: perh from *drill*, to cause to trickle, hence to sow seeds thus, itself perh from *trill*, vt to turn or twirl, vi to trickle, ME *trillen*, to turn about or around, to roll, of Scan origin but akin to OF-F *virer*, OProv *virar*, to turn, from ML *virāre*, LL *uirāre*, from L *uibrāre*, (vt and vi) to whirl; f.a.e., VIBRATE.

**drink,** n, derives from 'to **drink**', pt **drank**, pp **drunk** (OE *druncen*) and (now only pa) **drunken** (OE *druncen*); from v: **drinker, drinking**; from pa **drunk: drunkard** (pej suffix *-ard*); sep **drench**; akin to *drunken*: **drown**, whence vn **drowning**.
1. 'To **drink**' comes from OE *drincan*: cf OS *drincan*, OFris *drinka*, OHG *trinchan*, MHG-G *trinken*, also Go *drigkan* and ON *drekka*: 'not found outside of Gmc' (Walshe).
2. 'To **drown**' derives from ME *drounen* or *drunen*: cf OE *druncnian*, to be drowned, to become drunk, and ON *drukna*, to be drowned.

**drip** (v hence n), hence also the vn **dripping**); **drib** (v hence n), **dribble** (v hence n); **drop** (n and v); **droop** (v hence n).
1. 'To **dribble**' is the freq (suffix *-le*) of 'to *drib*', mdfn of 'to *drip*': and 'to *drip*' derives from OE *drȳpan*, akin to syn MD *drupen*, D *druipen*, and MLG *druppen*.
2. OE *dryppan* is perh a mutated form (and sense) of OE *dropian*, *droppan*, whence ME *droppen*, whence 'to *drop*', whence several of the modern senses of *drop*, n; the n *drop* has come through ME *drope* from OE *dropa*: akin to the nn OS *dropo*, ON *dropi*, OFris *dropta*, OHG *tropfo*, and to vv OE *drēopan*, OFris *driāpa*, OS *driopan*, OHG *triofan*, MHG-G *triefen*, ON *drjūpa*, to drip or trickle; also app to OIr *drucht* (for *drupt*), dewdrop, dew. Orig *drop* was only a globule of liquid, esp water, as it *falls*, hence 'to *fall*', vi to fall in drops, vt to cause to, or let, fall in liquid globules.
3. ON *drjūpa* is very intimately akin to the partly syn ON *drūpa*, to droop, whence, through ME *dr(o)upen*, comes 'to *droop*'.

**drive** (whence the n—and the agent **driver**), pt **drove**, pp and pa **driven**; **drift** (n hence v)—**adrift**; **drove**, n, whence the v, whence **drover**.
1. 'To **drive**' comes from the OE *drīfan*, akin to OFris *drīva*, Go *dreifan* (-*ban*), OS *drīban*, OHG *trīban*, MHG *trīben*, G *treiben*, ON *drīfa*. Derivative is the ME n *drift*, lit a driving or a being driven

(persons, quadrupeds, snow), influenced by OFris, ON, MD *drift*, cf MHG *trift*; for the formation of *drift*, cf *gift* (*give*)—*rift* (*rive*)—*shrift* (*shrive*)—*thrift* (*thrive*). *Adrift*=*a*- for *on*+the n *drift*.
2. OE *drīfan* has derivative n *drāf*, things but esp cattle collected for driving, hence being driven: whence *drove*.

**drivel,** to slaver, hence to talk like a congenital idiot, hence as a fool; whence, by contr (? dial), 'to **drool**', whence the AE n; **draff.**
'To *drivel*' comes, through ME *drevelen*, var *dravelen*, from OE *dreflian*, which is perh a freq; cf OE *draef*, ME *draf*, which, becoming E *draff*, refuse or lees or dregs, is akin to ON *draf* and MD-D *draf*, also to OHG *trebir*, MHG-G *treber*—perh cf G *trübe*, dull, sad, and Gr *trephein* (s *treph*-), to curdle.

**drizzle** (v hence n): app a freq of ME *dresen*, to fall, from OE *drēsian*. Cf DREAR.

**droit.** See REX, para 6.

**droll** (adj and n) and **drollery.**
The latter=EF-F *drôlerie*, from the n *drôle*, earlier *drolle*: MD *drolle, drol*, a jolly little fellow, a wag, cf MD *droelen* (*drulen*, etc.), to play.

**'drome.** See the element *-drome*.

**dromedary.** See the element *-drome*.

**drone,** the male (honey-)bee, larger and fatter than the worker—hence a sluggard—derives, through ME *drane*, from OE *drān*, akin to OS *drān* and OHG *treno*, MHG *trene*, MLG *trone* (whence G *Drohne*), LG *dron*; cf also the syn Laconian Gr *thrōnax* and Gr *tenthrēnē* (redup), wasp. 'To *drone*', hum loudly and monotonously, blends the form of the n *drone* and the form and, in part, the sense of MD *dronen* (D *dreunen*), to roar—cf Go *drunjus*, a loud sound; cf also Skt *dhrániti* (r *dhran*-), it resounds, and perh Gr *thrēnos*, lamentation. (Walshe.)

**drool.** See DRIVEL.

**droop.** See DRIP, para 2.

**drop.** See DRIP, para 3.

**dropsy,** whence **dropsical** (*-ical*); **hydropsy.**
*Dropsy*, ME *dropsie* or *dropesie*, is aphetic for ME *ydropesie*, from OF *idropisie* (later *hydropisie*), from L *hydropisis*, from Gr *hudrōpisis*, extn of *hudrōps*, dropsy, from *hudōr*, water: cf *Hydra* and, f.a.e., WATER.

**dross:** OE *dros*, filth, esp lees, dregs, akin to OE *drosna* (pl), dregs, and ult to *dreg*. Hence the adj **drossy.**

**drought, drouth.** See DRY, para 2.

**drove, drover.** See DRIVE, para 2.

**drown.** See DRINK, para 2.

**drowse,** v, hence n and adj **drowsy** (*-y*): OE *drūsian*, var *drūsan*, to sink (cf DREAR), become sluggish, akin to OE *drēosan*, to fall.

**drub,** to cudgel, orig to bastinado, is perh 'to dry-rub' but prob from Ar *ḍarb*, a beating, or rather by metathesis from *durb*, (?) a mispron of Tu *darbè, darba*, a stroke or blow, from Ar *daraba*, to strike or beat.

**drudge,** v, hence as n, hence, by suffix *-ery*, **drudgery,** derives from ME *druggen*, perh akin to

# DRUG

—or even derived from—OE *drēogan*, to work (hard, physically), hence to suffer, endure.

2. Certainly from OE *drēogan* comes 'to dree', as in *dree one's weird*, to endure one's ill fortune (ME *wirde*, OE *wyrd*, akin to OE *weorthan*, to become).

**drug, druggist.** See DRY, para 3.

**drugget.** See DRY, para 4.

**druid**—whence **druidess** and **druidic(al)** and **druidism**—comes from MF-F *druide*, by b/f from L *druidae, druides*, druids, of C origin: cf EIr *drui* (gen *druad*), Ga *draoi, draidh*, W *derwydd*, Br *drouiz* (pl *drouized*), Cor *druw*, Mx *druï*, a druid, OC *\*drúis, \*druidos*. These C words are prob independent, yet they could, because of the traditional association of *druids* with oaks, be akin either to Gr *drus*, tree, esp the oak, s *dru-* (see DRYAD), or to the C words for 'tree; oak' cf Cor *dâr* or *derven* (pl *derow*), W *derven*, pl *derw*, Ga *daragh* (or *-ach*), Mx *darrag(h)*, oak. If, however, Ga *druidh*, W *derwydd*, is a cpd (Ga *\*druvides*, OC *\*druvida* or *-vidos*), it=C *\*dru-*, to be strong or vigorous+C *\*uid* or *\*vid*, to see (L *uidēre*, ML *vidēre*), to get to know, to know, a druid then being 'a *very learned* man': with *\*dru*, cf OW *drut*, W *drud*, strong, violent, audacious, Cor *dru*, precious, Br *dru*, abundant.

The druids could have been 'the tree-knowers': cf the derivation of *true* (cf *soothsayers*) from *tree* (cf Skt *drumas*, tree, with Gr *drus*, tree, oak).

**drum** (n hence v, whence **drummer**). See the 2nd TRUMP, para 5.

**drunk, drunken; drunkard.** See DRINK, para 1.

**dry, drier, driest; drily;** obvious **dryasdust; dryness;** sep **drain; drought, drouth; drug** (n hence v), **druggist.**

1. The adj (whence the n) *dry* comes, via ME *dry* or *drie*, from OE *drȳge*, akin to MD *droge, druge* (cf MD *drogen*, to dry) and the syn OHG *trucchan*, MHG *trucken* and, as in G, *trocken*, and ON *draugr*, dry wood, a dry log: 'no cognates outside Gmc' (Walshe). 'To *dry*' comes from OE *drȳgan*, from the adj. E *dry* (adj) has derivatives *dryly* (*-ly*, adv), now usu *drily*, and *dryness* (*-ness*).

2. OE *dryge* has a cognate *drūgian* (cf *drȳgan*), to dry, with derivative n *drūgath*, whence ME *droughth* (whence archaic *drouth*) and *droght*, which, combined, yield *drought*, whence *droughty*.

3. The n *drug*, ME *drogge*, derives from MF-F *drogue*, from MLG '*droge* vate', dry casks or packing-cases, the 'dry' being 'wrongly taken to be a designation of the contents' (Webster): cf MD *droge, droege, druge* (etc.), dry. Derivative EF-F *droguiste* influences the formation of *druggist*.

4. MF-F *drogue* has EF-F dim *droguet*, with spec sense 'cheap woollen stuff', whence the E *drugget*: casks and packing-cases were cheap as compared with the contents.

**dryad.** See TREE, para 2.

**dual,** whence **dualism, -ist, -ity.** See DUO, para 1.

**dub:** OE *dubbian*, to dub a knight: a Gmc r *\*dub-* (as in Frankish *\*dubban*), to strike; at the conclusion of the ceremony, the recipient has app always been tapped (esp with sword) on the shoulder: prob echoic. Hence the vn *dubbing*.

**dubiety, dubious, dubitable.** See DOUBT, paras 2–3.

**Dublin** (whence **Dubliner**): Ir *dubh linne*: 'Black Pool' (cf the E *Blackpool*).

**ducal; ducat; duchess, duchy.** See DUKE, paras 3 and (DUCAT) 8.

**duck** (1), the bird: ME *duk*, var *doke*: OE *dūce*, at the least akin to and prob, as 'the diver', from the r of a Gmc v for 'to dive': cf ME *duken, douken*, to dive—whence 'to *duck*', orig to dive—and syn OHG *-tūhhan* (cpds only), MHG *tūchen*, G *tauchen*, and OFris *dūka*, D *duiken*, MD *duken, duycken*.

**duck** (2), a linen, canvas-like fabric: MD *doec, doeke* (cf D *doek*), *douc, duec*, cloth or canvas: akin to OFris and OS *dok*, OHG *tuoh*, MHG *tuoch*, G *Tuch*, and ON *dukr*, cloth—and perh Skt *dhvajám*, a banner.

**duck** (3), v. See 1st DUCK.

**duct, ductile, duction.** See DUKE, para 5.

**dud** (1), adj, derives from *dud*, n, one who is a failure, app substituted for coll AE *dub*, an awkward performer, perh from E dial *dub*, blunt (of point), dull.

**dud** (2), garment: ME *dudde*, prob akin to ON *dūtha*, to swathe, cf EFris be*dud*eln, to clothe. Usu in pl *duds*, one's clothes.

**dude** (AE), a dandy: perh (EW) G dial *dude*, a fool.

**dudgeon,** in (high): C16 *take in* usu (*great* or *high*) *dudgeon*: o.o.o.: EW proposes derivation from It *aduggiare*, to overshadow, from *uggia*, a shadow (? a dial var of *ombra*, from L *umbra*, cf LL *umbrātiō*, a shadowing) and cfs 'to take *umbrage*': perh rather from MF *prendre en* (sc *mauvaise*) *duison* or *duiçon*, to take in (bad) instruction, or perh by a false division ('to digest badly') of MF-EF *enduison*, digestion, from *enduire*, to digest; a rare C17 var is en*dugine*, which certainly suggests a F origin.

**due,** adj hence n. See DEBT, para 6.

**duel.** See DUO, para 2.

**duenna.** See DOMESTIC, para 6.

**duet.** See DUO, para 3.

**duff** (pudding). See DOUGH.

**duffel** (a D word) was orig made at *Duffel*, near Antwerp.

**dugong:** Mal (and Jav) *duyun*: with unjustified *g* for *y*.

**duke, duchess, duchy**—cf archduke, etc.; **ducal, ducat; dux; duct** (Med **ductus**), **ductile, duction; -duce, -ducent, -ducible, -ducive, -duct, -duction, -ductive, -ductor** in: **abduce, abduct, abduction, abductor; adduce, adducent, adducible, adduct, adduction, adductive, adductor; circumduce, circumduct, circumduction; conduce, conducent, conducible, conducive, conduct** (n and v), **conductance, conduction, conductive** (whence **conductivity**), **conductor; deduce, deducible, deduct, deduction, deductive; educe, educt, eduction, eductive, eductor; induce** (whence **inducement**), **inducible, induct, inductance,**

induction, inductive, inductor; introduce (whence introducer), introduction, introductory; produce (whence producer), productible, product, productile, production, productive (whence productivity—after activity), cf reproduce, reproduction, etc.; reduce (whence reducer), reducible, reduction, reductive, reductor; seduce (whence seducement and seducer and seductive), seduction (whence seductionist), seductress; subduce, subduction; traduce (whence traducer), traduction;—educable, educand, educate, education (whence educational, educationist), educative, educator;—via It: condottiere and dogal (dogate, doge) and ducat and Duce and ridotto;—prefix-cpds via F: conduit, sep douche (partly It), endue, redoubt (n); subdue (whence, by n-suffix -al, subdual).

1. L dux, leader, hence chief, stands for *ducs (*duks), s duc-, from dūcere (s dūc-), draw to oneself, draw on or along, to lead, conduct; IE s *duk-, var *deuk-, to lead. The Gmc var of the IE r is seen in OE tēon, to draw (pull, drag), cf Go tiuhan, and OE heretoga (here, army), an army leader—cf G Herzog, duke, orig an army (Heer) leader, OHG herizogo, MHG herzoge, akin to and syn with the OE cpd and to OFris hertoga, OS heretogo, ON hertoge; with OE tēon, cf G ziehen.

2. The E derivatives and cognates of OE tēon are treated sep: see, e.g., 'to TOW' and 'to TUG'—TAUT—TEAM and TEEM—TOY—TIE.

3. L dux becomes It duce, as in Il Duce, The Leader Mussolini; Venetian doge, chief magistrate, with derivatives dogale, whence E dogal, of a doge, and dogato, whence dogate (cf -ate, n), the office or rank of a doge; Sp duque; OF ducs (nom), duc (acc), whence F duc; OF duc becoming ME duc, later duke, adopted by E. The OF duc(s) has derivatives OF-F duchesse, whence E duchess, and—rather than from LL ducātus (gen -ūs)—OF duchee, later duché, whence E duchy, and—rather than direct from LL ducālis (duc-, o/s of dux, adj-suffix -alis) —OF-F ducal, adopted by E. (For ducat, see para 8.)

4. OF duc(s) has late MF-F cpd archiduc, with derivatives archiducal, archiduché, archiduchesse, which prompted the E archduke, archduchess, etc.

5. L dūcere has pp ductus, s duct-, on which arise the n ductus (gen -ūs), a leading, that which leads, a canal or channel, whence E duct (whence ductless), and the adj ductilis, whence, prob via EF-F, the E ductile (whence ductility), and the n ductiō, o/s ductiōn-, whence duction, and the agent ductor, adopted by E.

6. L dūcere has numerous prefix-cpds, which originate E vv in -duce and, from the pp ductus, several in -duct; the presp ducens, o/s ducent-, leads to adjj in -ducent; (?) ducibilis, able to lead—or be led, occurs in adjj in -ducible; most adjj in -ducive lack forebears in -ductīuus, ML -ducīvus; for nn in -duction, -ductor, cf the prec para. The relevant L prefix-cpd vv are these:

abdūcere, to lead ab or away, whence 'to abduce'; presp abdūcens, o/s abdūcent-, whence the adj abducent; pp abductus, whence 'to abduct'; deriva-tive LL abductiō, o/s abductiōn-, whence abduction; abductor (cf F abducteur) is an anl agent-in-or formation;

addūcere, to draw to oneself, to bring ad or to, whence 'to adduce'; with presp addūcens, o/s addūcent-, whence the adj adducent; anl adducible; pp adductus, whence 'to adduct'; LL adductiō, o/s adductiōn-, whence adduction; anl adductive; agent adductor, adopted by E;

circumdūcere, to lead circum or around, whence 'to circumduce'; pp circumductus, whence 'to circumduct', and derivative circumductiō, o/s circumductiōn-, whence circumduction;

condūcere, to bring con- or together, to lead together (in a party), hence favourably, whence 'to conduce'; presp condūcens, o/s condūcent-, whence conducent; condūcibilis, whence conducible; anl conducive; pp conductus, whence 'to conduct' (whence conductance), with derivative n conductus, gen -ūs, whence the E n conduct, with E hybrid misconduct (n and v); derivative conductiō, o/s conductiōn-, whence conduction; anl conductive (cf deductive, inductive); LL conductor, adopted by E;

dēdūcere, to draw dē or down, to lead away, bring from or out, whence 'to deduce'; anl deducible; pp dēductus, whence 'to deduct'; derivative dēductiō, o/s dēductiōn-, whence deduction-; likewise derivative LL dēductīuus, ML -īvus (esp in Logic), whence deductive;

ēdūcere, to lead ē or out, bring forth, hence to rear, whence 'to educe'; pp ēductus, neu ēductum, which, used as n, yields educt; derivative ēductiō, o/s ēductiōn-, whence eduction; anl eductive; derivative LL agent ēductor, adopted by E in mechanical sense;

indūcere, to lead to or (in-) into, (later) to persuade, whence 'to induce'; anl inducible; pp inductus, whence 'to induct' (whence inductance—c, conductance); derivative inductiō, o/s inductiōn-whence induction; derivative LL inductīuus, ML -īvus, whence inductive; derivative agent inductor, adopted by E;

introdūcere, to bring intro or within (house or circle), whence 'to introduce'; derivative introductiō, o/s introductiōn-, whence, prob via F, introduction; anl introductive; LL introductōrius, whence introductory;

prōdūcere, to lead or bring prō or forward, hence to beget, produce, whence 'to produce'; presp prōdūcens, o/s prōdūcent-, whence producent; anl producible; pp prōductus, neu prōductum, whence the E n product; derivative LL prōductilis, prōductīuus (ML -īvus), whence E productile, productive; derivative LL prōductiō, o/s prōductiōn-, whence, prob via MF-F, production; E reproduce (whence reproducer), reproduction, reproductive, were prompted by F reproduïre, reproduction, reproductif (f -ive);

redūcere, to lead or bring re or back, (later) to diminish, whence 'to reduce'; presp redūcens, o/s redūcent-, whence reducent; anl reducible; reductiō (as in L r. ad absurdum), o/s reductiōn-, whence *reduction*; anl *reductive*; but E *reductor*=*reduct*ion +agential *-or*;

*sēdūcere*, to lead *sē* or aside, hence to mislead, hence seduce, whence E *seduce*; LL *sēdūcibilis*, whence *seducible*; pp *sēductus*, s *sēduct-*, whence LL *sēductibilis*, whence *seductible*; derivative *sēductiō*, o/s *sēduction-*, whence—perh via OF-F *séduction*— E *seduction*; anl *seductive*; anl *seductress*, perh suggested by LL *sēductrix*;

*subdūcere*, to draw from below, to lead *sub* or under, whence 'to *subduce*'; derivative *subductiō*, o/s *subduction-*, whence *subduction*; cf 'to *subdue*', para 9, s.f.;

*trādūcere* (for *\*transdūcere*), to lead *trans* or across, hence to transfer, translate, to disgrace, etc.; whence 'to *traduce*', (esp) to slander; derivative *trāductiō* (from pp *trāductus*), o/s *trāduction-*, whence—perh via EF-F—the E *traduction*.

7. L *dūcere*, to lead, has durative *dūcāre*, used only in cpds, esp *ēdūcāre*, to rear (a child), hence to educate; its gerundive *ēdūcandus*, fit to be reared, yields the E n *educand*, a student; *educable* is an anl formation, as if from L *\*ēdūcābilis*; pp *ēdūcātus* yields 'to *educate*'; derivative *ēdūcātiō*, o/s *ēdūcā-tiōn-*, yields *education*; *educative* and *educatory* are anl in *-ive, -or*; derivative *ēdūcātor* is adopted by E.

8. Through It come *condottiere*, from L *con-ductor*; *doge* (etc.) and *Duce*, as in para 3; sep *douche*; *ducat*, adopted from late OF, from It *ducato*, a coin bearing the effigy of a *duca* or duke, ult from L *dux*; *ridotto* (in fortification), either from ML *reductus* (gen *-ūs*), from *reduct-*, s of L *reductus*, pp of *redūcere*, or from It *ridurre*—see next para.

9. From F come:

*conduit*, taken by ME (*conduyte, condyte*, etc.) from OF-F *conduit*, from L *conductus* (gen *-ūs*)— cf para 6 at *condūcere*; sep DOUCHE (F from It);

*endue*, influenced by OF *enduire*, to lead into (*en*, L *in*) but strictly from L *induere* (s *indu-*: *in*, onto+r *du-*, to put, as in *exuere*, to put off), which has direct derivative 'to *indue*';

*redoubt*, from EF *redoute* (earlier *ridotte*), from It *ridotta* (now *ridotto*), f of *ridotto*, pp of *ridurre*, to lead back, itself from L *redūcere* (as in para 6);

*subdue*, ME *soduen*, from OF-MF *soduire*, *souduire*, *sousduire*, to draw or lead away, from L *subdūcere* (para 6, where cf the E doublet 'to *seduce*'), to draw from below.

**dulcet; dulcify; dulcimer; dolce** (far niente); **douce, douceur; edulcorate.**

1. *Dulcet* is a refashioning, after the L, of ME from OF-F *doucet*, dim of *douz*, from L *dulcis*, sweet (of taste, hence of disposition), perh akin to Gr *glukus* (see GLYCERIN); *dulcify*=*dulci-*, L c/f+element *-fy*, to make; *dulcimer* comes from OF *doulcemer*, alteration of *doulcemele*: *doulce*, from *dulcis*+*mele* from Gr *melos*, song (cf the element *melo-*); *dolce* is the It shape of *dulcis*; Sc *douce*= F *douce*, f of *doux* (OF *douz*), and *douceur*, adopted from OF-F, derives from F *doux*.

2. L *dulcis* has LL derivative *dulcor*, whence ML

*ēdulcorāre*, in *ē-*+*dulcorāre*, to sweeten; pp *ēdul-corātus* yields 'to *edulcorate*'.

**dull** (adj whence v), whence **dul(l)ness** and **dullard** (pej suffix *-ard*); **doldrums**; cf sep DWELL.

*Doldrums* is the pl of *doldrum*; app (EW) it blends and 'corrupts' *dull*+tantrum. *Dull*, ME *dul*, is akin to—perh from—OE *dol*, foolish: cf OHG-MHG *tol*, foolish (G *toll*, mad), OFris *doll*, *dull*, mad, and Go *dwals*, foolish.

**dumb** (whence **dumbness**), **dumbbell**; **dummy** (adj, whence n, v).

*Dumbbell* is orig a muted bell; and *dummy* is an easement of *dumby*, with pej sense from dumbness apprehended as stupidity. *Dumb* is OE *dumb*, akin to OFris and OS *dumb*, OHG *tumb*, dumb, stupid, G *dumm*, stupid, whence A sl *dumb*, stupid; Go *dumbs*, ON *dumbr*, dumb; perh akin to DEAF and to Gr *tuphlos*, blind.

**dump** (1), usu *the dumps*, low spirits: MD *domp*, a haze, akin to G *dumpf*, dull-sounding, (of air) close and damp, and *Dampf*, steam, therefore to E DAMP.

**dump** (2), shapeless piece, whence the n **dump-ling** (*-ling*, dim n suffix) and the adj **dumpy**, is akin to, perh derived from, the next; the senses 'a thump, temporary store, sawmill yard, (sl) shabby house, (sl) any inhabited place' prob belong to the same word.

**dump** (3), to let fall, unload, (vi) to fall heavily, whence **dumpage, dumper, dumping**: ME *dumpen*, to fall heavily, to cause to fall (heavily), to care-lessly throw down: of Scan origin, orig echoic: cf Nor *dumpa*, Da *dumpe*, to fall suddenly or heavily, but esp ON *dumpa*, to strike, esp to thump.

**dumpling.** See 2nd DUMP.

**dumpy.** See 2nd DUMP.

**dun** (1), adj; **dunlin.**

The latter, for *dunling*, consists of *dun*, brown+ n-suffix *-ling*: and *dun*=OE *dunn*, prob of C origin; cf OIr *donn*, brown, dark, syn Ga *donn* (comp *duinne*) and W *dwn*, OC *\*donnos*, var *\*dunnos* (? for *dubnos*), dark.

**dun** (2), n, fortified place. See TOWN.

**dun** (3), v, to importune a debtor, whence he who does this. See DIN, para 2.

**dunce:** ironically from 'a *Duns* man', a student or disciple of the great medieval schoolman, *Duns* Scotus.

**dune.** See DOWN. (Adj *dunal*.)

**dung** (n whence v), with adj **dungy** (*-y*); **dungeon**, predominantly an underground prison in a castle, and **donjon; dingy.**

The last is app a thinning of *dungy*. *Dungeon*= ME *dongeon*, var *donjoun*: OF-F *donjon*, itself adopted, in the F sense, by E: perh of Gmc origin —cf ON *dyngja*, an underground working-place covered with dung. Now, *dung*—the same in OE --is akin to OFris *dung*, G *Dung*, MHG *tunge*, OHG *tunga*, dung; in the OHG form *tunc* and sense 'underground chamber covered with dung' (cf ON *dyngja*), cf the syn OS *dung*; perh akin to Lith *dengti*, to cover, as with a roof (Webster); Walshe, however, notes that G *Dung*, therefore E *dung*, could be akin to Gr τάφος (*taphos*, s *taph-*), a grave, on the assumption of an IE form *\*dhenghuos*, varr *\*dhonghuos*, *\*dhunghuos*. B & W, like Dauzat and EW, dissociate OF-F *donjon*, lit 'master tower of a château' or 'the lord's tower', from *dung* and derive it from VL *\*dominiōnem*, acc of *\*dominiō*, itself from *dominus*, master of the house (cf DOMESTIC, para 4). In all, it seems best to separate E *dung* from OF-F *donjon* (whence, of course, E *dungeon*) and to accept the VL origin of *donjon*.

**dungaree.** Hi *dungrī* (a coarse cotton fabric).

**dunk.** See DYE, s.f.

**dunlin.** See 1st DUN.

**dunnage.** The sense 'personal effects' derives from the naut sense 'loose materials (brushwood, wood, mats, netting, ropes, etc.) on the bottom of a hold or among goods to protect cargo': o.o.o.: the *-age* is the semi-collective, semi-agential or -instrumental *-age* of other nn (e.g., *cordage*) with that suffix; therefore the word prob=*dun*+ euphonic *n*+*-age*. What, then, is *dun-*? The ref is, I think, to *dun*, greyish-brown, the colour of the materials used for the protection of cargo. Since, however, the E word is unrecorded before the 1620's, it may well derive from D or LG, like so many other naut terms of the period: OED neatly adduces the LG *dunne twige*, brushwood; cf MD *dunne* (D *dun*) and MHG *dünne* (G *dünn*), thin, and, of course, THIN itself. The early varr *dennage*, *dinnage*, *donnage* cause one to glance at MD *denne*, a ship's deck, and *dennen*, to load, and *dennenhout*, a ship's hold.

**duo** (cf the element *duo-*); **dual, duality; duel; duet; duodenum** (see the element *duodeno-*); **deuce**; sep **duodecimo** and **dozen** (where see both); sep **double**, where also see *duple* (etc.). For the Gmc cognates, see TWO, where also *twain*, *twelve*, *twenty*, *twice*, *twin*, *twine*, and such less obvious derivatives as *tweed*, *twig*, *twill*, *twist*, *between* and *betwixt*.

1. L *duo*, 2, is intimately akin to Gr *duo*, with IE etymon *\*duwo*: f.a.e., TWO. Its adj is *duālis* (s *duāl-*), whence E *dual*; the LL derivative *duālitās*, o/s *duālitāt-*, yields *duality*; *dualism* and *dualist* (whence *dualistic*) are E formations in *-ism*, *-ist*.

2. The L *duellum*, war, is the earliest form of *bellum*, which was by the ancients declared to be etym a struggle, battle, war between *duo*, or two, parties: although E & M and others assert the *duo* origin of *duellum* to be merest f/e, the ancients may, after all, have been right. Certainly L *duellum*, often used even in L for a fight between two persons, becomes It *duello* and EF-F *duel*, adopted by E.

3. L *duo* survives in It, where, as n, it gains the sense 'duet': with resulting dim *duetto*, duet, whence E *duet*.

4. L *duo* has m acc *duos*, whence OF *deus*, F *deux*, whence E *deuce* (C15–16 *deux*, C16 *deuis*, *dewse*, C16–17 *deuse*, *dewse*), the 2-pipped side of a die, a cast of 2, a 2-spotted card. (OED.) Hence prob the senses 'bad luck, the Devil', whence the adj *deuced*, devilish.

**duologue.** See LEGEND, para 28.

**dup.** See DO, para 1.

**dupe** (n and v), **dupery; hoopoe.**

1. *Dupery* comes from late EF-F *duperie*, itself from EF-F *duper*, to trick, whence E 'to *dupe*'; F *duper* comes from late MF-F *dupe*, whence the E n *dupe*; F *dupe* derives from MF (orig, underworld) *duppe*, a gamester's victim, app from *d'uppe*, of—hence like—an *uppe*, F *huppe*, hoopoe, a stupid-looking bird.

2. E *hoopoe* derives from EE *hoop*, *houpe*; F *huppe* (Gmc *h-*), OF-MF *uppe*: VL *\*ūpupa*: L *ūpupa*, from its cry: cf for the form, L *ulula*, the screech-owl (cf ULULATE), and, for both the form and the sense, Gr *apaphos* (? alteration of *\*epaphos*), syn and prob a derivative of Gr *epops* (gen *epopos*), hoopoe.

**duple, duplex, duplicate, duplicity.** See PLY, para 22.

**durable, durability; durance; duration, durative** (adj, hence n); **duress**; obs v **dure**—cf **endure** (whence pa **enduring**), **endurance**; obs adj **dure**—cf **dour; indurate** (whence pa **indurated**), **induration, indurative; obdurate**, whence **obduracy** (for *\*obduratecy*: cf *accuracy* from *accurate*); **perdurable, perdurance, perdure.**—L terms: **dura mater**, with adj **dural; duramen; durum** (wheat).

1. L *dūrus*, hard, has s *dūr-*, perh a dissimilation of IE *\*drur-*, cf Skt *dāruṇás*, rough, strong, Lith *drútas*, strong, solid, Ir *dron*, OIr *tromm*, Ga *trom*, solid, OIr *trén*, Ga *treun*, strong, W *tren*, strenuous, and Argive Gr *droón* (neu=*iskhuron*), strong.

2. *Dūrus* becomes OF-F *dur*, whence obs E *dure*, severe, and prob the Sc *dour*.

3. *Dūrus* has L derivative *dūrāre* (vi, vt), to harden, with cpd *indūrāre* (int *in-*), to harden (vt), with pp *indūrātus*, whence both the adj *indurate*, hardened, and 'to *indurate*' or harden; derivative LL *indūrātiō*, o/s *indūrātiōn-*, yields *induration*; *indurative* is an anl E formation. Cf *endure* in para 9.

4. Derivative LL *obdūrāre* (int *ob-*), to harden (vt), has pp *obdūrātus*, whence the E adj *obdurate*, obstinate (cf LL *obdūrus*); derivative LL *obdūrātiō* perh suggested *obduracy*.

5. By most modern etymologists, L *dūrāre* (vi), to last, is usu dissociated from *dūrāre* (vt, vi), to harden, and by them related to that IE r *\*dū-*, connoting a long time, which occurs in L *dūdum*, formerly, long since, and perh in L *dum*, while: but does not *dūrāre*, to last, ensue very naturally from *dūrāre*, to harden, used intransitively? 'To harden, to become or be hard, therefore to be strong and firm, therefore time-resisting, to last long in time'—can there be a more natural sense-development?

6. *Dūrāre* (s *dūr-*), to last, becomes the obs *dure*, to last, (vt) to endure; derivative *dūrābilis* becomes OF-F *durable*, adopted by E; subsidiary *dūrābilitās* becomes EF-F *durabilité* and, prob from F, the E *durability*; the presp *dūrans*, o/s *dūrant-*, shapes the

OF presp *durant*, whence OF *durance* (suffix *-ce*), duration, whence E *durance*, with subsidiary sense 'imprisonment' (so long in the enduring)—cf *duress* in para 8; derivative *dūrātiō* (from *dūrāt-*, s of the pp *dūrātus*), o/s *dūrātiōn-*, passes through MF-EF to become the E *duration*; *durative* (*-ive*, adj) is an anl E formation.

7. *Dūrāre*, to last, has cpd *perdūrāre*, to last *per* or throughout, for a very long time, whence the obsol 'to *perdure*'; derivative LL *perdūrābilis* becomes MF-EF *perdurable*, adopted by E; adopted from MF is *perdurance*.

8. Other L derivatives of *dūrus* concern E:

*dūra mater* (lit 'hard mother'), adopted from ML physiology;

*dūramen* hardness, a ligneous vine-branch, adopted by Bot for heartwood;

*dūritia*, hardness, whence OF-MF *durece*, EF-F *duresse*, hardship, whence E *duress*;

*dūrum* (*wheat*) is, lit and factually, hard wheat, *dūrum* being prop the neu of *dūrus*: cf L *dūrum*, elliptical for *dūrum lignum*.

9. L *indūrāre*, to harden (cf para 3), becomes VL 'to tolerate' and LL (Eccl) 'to harden one's heart against', both senses persisting in OF-F *endurer*, which further contains something of *durer*, to last: hence E 'to *endure*', to last or persist, (vt) to sustain, successfully undergo; whence—unless from MF *endurance*—then *endurance*.

**durian**, a hard-rinded East Indian fruit, is adopted from Mal: from Mal *duri*, a thorn.

**durum.** See DURABLE, para 8.

**dusk**, adj whence n (with its own adj **dusky**), comes, through ME *dosc*, *deosc*, later *dusc*, from OE *dox*, *dosc*, akin to L *fuscus* (s *fusc-*), sombre, dark—cf Skt *dhūsara*, dust-coloured, and therefore:

**dust**, whence 'to *dust*' (whence **duster** and the vn **dusting**) and the adj **dusty** (cf OE *dȳstig*): OS *dūst*, akin to OLG and ON *dust*, dust, and OHG *tunist*, MHG *tunst*, a storm, G *Dunst*, vapour, MD *dust*, *dunst*, D *duist*, meal dust; cf also Skt *dhūsara*, dust-coloured, and *dhvǫsati*, is scattered, and Hit *tuhhwis*, smoke, vapour: 'primary notion "that which is blown in a cloud" ' (Walshe). Cf DUSK.

**Dutch**, adj hence n; **Teutonic**.

1. *Dutch* comes from MD *dutsch*, *duutsch*, *duutsc*, of Holland, (more generally) Germanic (cf D *duitsch*, German)—akin to G *deutsch*, German, and MGH *tiutsch*, *tiusch*, OHG *diutisc*, the German language, lit the popular language as opp Latin, from OHG *diot*, *diota*, a people or nation, akin to OFris *thiäde*, OS *thiōd*, *thiode*, Go *thiuda*, OE *thēod*, ON *thiōd*, *thjōth*, OIr *tūath*, Cor *tūs*, *tǔz*, *dūs*, *dūz*, OC *\*teuts*, and Lith *tauta*, a people, and the Gmc (? rather the Celtic) tribe the *Teutones*, also OP *tauto*, W *tūd*, land, Ga *tuath*, the country, country people, and Lith *Tauta*, Germany; perh also Hit *tuzzias*, army. The IE r is prob *\*teut-*, a people, the people.

2. L *Teutones*, var *Teutoni*, app of Gmc origin ('*the* people'), yields the b/f *Teuton*; the L adj is *Teutonicus*, whence *Teutonic*.

3. The numerous pej expressions containing *Dutch* (*Dutch courage—uncle—*etc.) result, orig, from the D-E trade, hence other, rivalry of C17–18.

**duty.** See DEBT, para 6.

**dux.** See DUKE, para 1.

**dwarf** (whence **dwarfish**: *-ish*, adj): ME *dwarf*, earlier *dwerf*, earliest *dwergh*: OE *dweorg*, *dweorh*: akin to the syn OFris *dwerch*, OS *dwerg*, OHG *twerg* (G *Zwerg*), ON *dvergr*; perh cf Skt *dhváras*, a demon, a phantom.

**dwell**, whence **dweller** and **dwelling**, comes from OE *dwellan*, to wander, to linger, to tarry, akin to OE *dwalian*, OFris *dwalia*, to wander, be in error, OE *dwala*, error, OFris *dwalinge*, OE *dwolung*, doubt, and ON *dvelja*, to linger, delay, tarry; also to DULL.

**dwindle** (whence pa and vn **dwindling**): freq (*-le*) or dim of obs *dwine*, to pine: ME *dwinen*, to waste away: OE *dwīnan*, akin to ON *dvīna*, to dwindle, LG and MD *dwinen*, to vanish.

**dyad**, a pair, a couple: cf the element *dy-* and the suffix *-ad* (as in *triad*).

**dye**, n and v (whence pa and vn **dyeing** and the agent **dyer**).

'To *dye*' comes, through ME *dyen*, earlier *deyen*, from OE *dēagan*, *dēagian*, itself from OE *dēag*, var *dēah*, a dye, a colour, whence E 'a *dye*': o.o.o., but perh akin to the *ti-* of L *tingō*, I steep in water, hence dye, s *ting-*, perh a nasal form of IE r *\*tig-*, extn of *\*ti-*, to colour or dye: cf the syn Gr *tengō* (τέγγω) and OHG *thunkōn*, *dunkōn*, MHG *dunken*, G *tunken*, to dip (something) in water, whence AE *dunk*, to dip (esp bread into milk, coffee, soup).

**dying.** See DEAD, para 3.

**dyke.** See DIG.

**dynamic**, adj (whence **dynamics**); **dynamism**; **dynamite** (n whence v); **dynamo** (cf the element *dynamo-*); **dynast, dynastic, dynasty**; **dyne**.

1. The effective r is grounded in Gr *dunasthai*, to be able, have strength, s *dun-*, r either *\*dun-* or more prob *\*du-*, to have the strength (to), be able (to) perh ult akin to E DO, ? 'have the strength to do, and then perform it': cf Hit *dù*, to make.

2. *Dunami*, I am able, has derivative *dunamis* (? for *\*dunis*: *dun-+-i+-s*), ability to do, (hence) power, with derivative adj *dunamikos*, whence F *dynamique*, whence E *dynamic*; the learned F formation *dynamisme* yields *dynamism*; *dynamite*, created, 1866, by Sw physicist Nobel, from Gr *dunamis*, power; *dynamo*, elliptical for *dynamo-electric machine*.

3. F *dyne*, from LL *dynamis*, from Gr *dunamis*, is adopted by E 'for unit of force'.

4. Gr *dunasthai*, to have strength, hence power, hence great power, has derivative *dunastēs* (s *dunast-*), whence L *dynastes*, whence late MF-F *dynaste* and E *dynast*, a ruler; subsidiary Gr *dunastikos* yields F *dynastique* and E *dynastic*; and subsidiary Gr *dunasteia* becomes LL *dynastia*) whence EF-F *dynastie* and (perh from the F word, E *dynasty*.

**dysacousia.** See ACOUSTIC.

**dysentery, dysenteric; enteric, enteritis.**

The 1st derives, via MF-F, from L *dysenteria*, trln of Gr *dusenteria*; *dus-*, ill-, badly+*-enteria*, from *entera*, intestines, pl of *enteron*, from *entos*, within, from *en*, in; derivative adj *dusenterikos*, L *dysentericus*, MF-F *dysentérique*, E *dysenteric*. E *enteric*, n=*enteric fever*, from Gr *enterikos*, adj of *entera*; and *enteritis*=*entera*+suffix *-itis*.

**dyslogistic, dyslogy.** See LEGEND, para 30.

**dyspepsia, dyspeptic.** See the element *-pepsia*.

# E

---

**each** comes, through ME *eche*, earlier *elc* and esp *aelc*, from OE *āēlc*, a contr of *ā-gelīc*, ever like (cf LIKE): akin to OFris *ellik, elk*, OHG *eo-gilīh*, orig 'always alike', hence 'each, every', MHG *ieglīch*, G *jeglich*: Cf also AYE, always.

**eager,** adj: ME *egre*, sharp, spirited, keenly desirous: OF-F *aigre*: VL *\*ācrus*: L *ācer*, f *ācris*, neu *ācre*, s and r *ac-*; akin to Gr *akros* (r *ak-*), highest, which connotes the idea of a sharp point at the top. Cf ACID—and also EDGE.

2. OF-F *aigre* has the MF-F cpd *vinaigre* (*vin*, wine: cf WINE), whence ME *vinegre*, whence E *vinegar*.

**eagle** derives, through ME *egle*, adopted from OF-MF *egle*, var of OF-F *aigle*, itself—perh via OProv *aigla*—from L *aquila*, which has adj *aquilīnus*, whence E *aquiline*, applied esp to a nose like an eagle's. F *aigle* has derivative MF-F *aiglette*, whence E *eaglet*.

**eagre,** a tidal flood, etc. See AQUA, para 7.

**ear** (1), the organ of hearing: OE *ēare*: cf OFris *āre*, OS and OHG *ōra* (G *Ohr*), MD *ore* (D *oor*), ON *eyra*; cf also L *auris*; Go *ausō*, Lith *ausis*, Lett *ausu, aušu*, ear, and Av *usi*, both ears; OSl *ucho*, ear, *uši*, both ears; Gr *oûs*, Doric *ōs*; OIr *āu* or *ō*. IE r is therefore *\*au*, varr *\*ou* and *\*ō*, with extn *\*aus-* (also *\*ous*), var *\*aur-*.

**ear** (2), a cereal's fruiting spike: OE *ēar* (var *aehher*): akin to OFris *ār*, OS *ahar*, OHG *ahir, ehir*, MHG *eher* (G *Ähre*), Go *ahs*, ON *ax*, and, further off, the L *acus*, chaff, and *agna* (for *\*acna, \*akna*), ear of a cereal. Hence 'to *ear*', put forth ears.

**earl, earldom.**
*Earl*, ME *erl* or *eorl*, derives from OE *eorl*, a man, esp a nobleman, akin to OS and OHG *erl*, boy, man, and ON *jarl*, nobleman. The OE cpd *eorl-dōm*, an earl's territory or jurisdiction (cf the suffix *-dom* and the word DOOM), becomes *earldom*. —Perh it is related to CHURL.

**early,** adj, ME *earlich*, is very closely akin to the ME adv *erliche*, later *erli*, whence the E adv *early*: and ME *erliche* derives from OE *āērlīce*: *āer*, sooner +*-līce*, whence adv-suffix *-ly*. Cf ERE.

**earmark,** n whence v, is orig a domestic animal's identification-*mark* (a slitting, a notching) on the *ear*.

**earn, earning** (pa and vn, usu in pl).
The latter, as n, derives from OE *earnung*, from OE *earnian*, whence 'to *earn*': akin to OHG *arnōn*,

to harvest, and OHG *aran* (syn with the intimately related OHG *arnōd*, G *Ernte*, MHG *ernede*, pl, a harvest), Go *asans*, a harvest, OP *assanis*, harvest-season, autumn; prob also to ON *önn*, working season, and perh L *annus* (r *an-*), year. (Walshe.)

**earnest,** adj. See EARNEST (3), s.f.

**earnest** (2), a pledge: ME *ernes*: app by a scribal error from OF-MF *erres* (pl)—cf the refashioned EF-F *arrhes*—from (Law) L *arra*, for *arrha*, short for *arrhabō*, a pledge, from Gr *arrhabōn*, certainly of Sem origin—prob from H *'ērābōn*.

**earnest** (3), a close, grave attention or purpose: OE *eornest, eornost*: akin to OHG *ernust*, MHG *ernest*, G *Ernst* (seriousness), but also to OE *eornes*, with var *eornest*, a combat or duel, to Go *arniba*, firmly, safely, and to Av *arenu*, a contest or combat.
The adj *earnest* derives from OE *eorneste, eornoste*, itself from the n: cf OFris *ernst*, OHG *ernust*.

**earning(s).** See EARN.

**earth** (n hence v); **earthen, earthenware; earthly; earthy:** such obvious cpds as **earthborn, -bound, -quake, -work, -worm.**

1. *Earth*, ME *erthe* and earlier *eorthe*, derives from OE *eorthe*, akin to OFris *erthe* (var *irthe*), OS *ertha*, Go *airtha*, OHG *erda* (MHG-G *erde*), the OE varr *eord(e), eard*, MD *aerd, aert, ard, art*, ON *jörth, iörth*. That the r is *er-* appears from OHG *ero* and Gr *era*, earth, and Gr *eraze*, to earth: cf such C words as OIr *-ert* (in cpds), EIr *úr*, Ga *ùir*, Cor *aor*, the OC prototype being prob *\*urā*. But the distribution is still wider: cf Arm *erkir*, Akk *erṣetu, irṣetum*, and perh Eg *àakhut*, earth.

2. The derivative adjj are *earthen* (*-en*), with cpd *earthenware* (cf WARE)—*earthly*, from OE *eorthlīc* —*earthy* (*-y*).

3. The only important prefix cpd is 'to *unearth*'.

**earwig:** OE *ēarwicga*: OE *ēar*, the ear+*wicga*, beetle or worm: folklore has it that this insect creeps into the human ear. For the elements, cf EAR and VETCH.

**ease,** n (whence **easeful**) and v; **easement; easy.**
1. *Easy* comes from MF-F *aisié*, prop the pp of *aisier*, whence 'to *ease*': and MF *aisier*, OF *aaisier*, derives from OF-F *aise*, whence, in ME, the n *ease*. Now, OF-F *aise*, comfort, elbow-room, derives from VL *adiacēs*, var of VL *adiacens*, a, or the, neighbourhood, n from L *adiacens*, presp of

174

*adiacēre*, to be situated near: f.a.e., ADJACENT. The obsol *easement* (suffix *-ment*)=OF-MF *aisement*, from the OF v; *easiness* (*-ness*) derives from *easy*.

2. The chief cpds are *unease*, n, whence *uneasy* (*-y*, adj); the n *disease*, ME *disese*, earlier *desese*, from MF *desaise* (*des-*, L *dis-*), and the v *disease*, ME *disesen*, from MF *desa(a)isier*, from *desaise*; *malaise*, adopted from OF-F (OF-F *mal*, badly).

**easel.** See ASS, para 2.

**east** (n hence adj and v); **easterly, eastern, eastward.**

1. The n *east* derives from OE *ēast*, also in cpds an adj—cf OE *ēastan*, from the east, also as adj: akin to OHG *ōstan*, MHG *ōsten*, G *Osten*, and OHG *ōstar*, in (or to) the east, and *ōstana* (OE *ēastan*, ON *austan*), from the east; ON *austr*; Lith *aušra*, dawn, and the syn L *aurōra* (for *ausōsa*), Homeric Gr *ēōs*, Attic *heōs*, Aeolic *auōs*, Skt *ušás* (cf *ucchati*, it dawns, (lit) shines). The Gmc r is *aust-*; the IE r, *aus-*, itself perh an extn of *au-*; basic idea, 'the shining'. Cf EASTER.

2. *East* has adj *easter* (now only dial), whence adj and adv *easterly* (*-ly*); OE *ēast* has adj *ēasterne*, whence *eastern*; also from *east*, n, comes *eastward*, adv and adj (cf the suffix *-ward*).

**Easter,** whence *Eastertide* (*tide*, time: cf TIDE), derives from OE *ēastre* (pl *ēastron*), from OE *Eastre*, var *Eostra*, the old Gmc goddess of Spring: after dull Winter, Spring comes as 'the shining (season)': akin to OHG *ōstarūn* (cf the OE var *ēastrun*), MHG *ōsteren*, G *Ostern* (pl), and to Skt *usra*, dawn: since dawn comes in the east, the kinship of *Easter* with *east* is prob.

**easterly, eastern, eastward.** See EAST, para 2.

**easy.** See EASE.

**eat;** pt eat (*ĕt*) and ate; pp eaten.

'To *eat*' derives, through ME *eten*, from OE *etan*, akin to OS *etan*, Go *itan* (cf OFris *īta*), OHG *ezzan*, MHG *ezzen*, G *essen*, ON *eta*; also to Ga *ith*, to eat, OIr *ithim*, I eat, and Mx *ee* (n), eating; to L *edere*, to eat, Gr *edein*, to eat—both with s *ed-*; to Skt *ádmi* and Lith *edmi*, I eat, and Hit *et-*, *at-*, *ez-*, *az-*, to eat, and *adai*, he eats. The OGmc r is *et-*; the IE r, *ed-*. (Walshe). Cf EDIBLE.

**eaves** (orig sing): ME *evese* (pl *eveses*): OE *efes*, brink or brim, hence eaves: akin to OHG *obisa*, *obasa*, porch, and OHG *obana*, from above, G *oben* (adv), above: cf, therefore, OVER.

**eavesdrop.** See OVER, para 3.

**ebb** n and v. 'To *ebb*' derives from OE *ebbian*, itself from the source of the n *ebb*: OE *ebba*, akin to OFris *ebba*, OS *ebbia*, MD-D *ebbe* (v *ebben*), and perh to the Go adj *ibuks*, turned backwards, backward, with IE r *ibh-*, to turn.

**ebon, ebony, ebonite.**

The 3rd=*ebony*+chem *-ite*; the 2nd is prob the n use of *ebony*, the *-y* adj of the n *ebon*, the wood ebony; the 1st (n, then adj) comes, via OF *ebaine*, MF *ebene* (F *ébène*), from L *ebenus*, the tree (*ebenum*, the wood), from Gr *ebenos*, itself from Eg *hebin* (varr *hebni*, *habni*)—cf the syn *iban*.

**Ebriety, ebriosity, ebrious; inebriety—inebriate inebriation; sobriety, sober.**

1. The adj *ebrious*, tipsy, derives from L *ēbrius*, prob coming either from *ē*, out of+*bria*, a winejar, and therefore applied to one who has emptied the jar or cup, or from *ē*, out of+the r of *ferre*, to bear, carry—cf, sem, L *ēlātus*, E *elate*.

2. L *ēbrius* has derivatives *ēbrietās*, o/s *ēbrietāt-*, whence MF-F *ébriété*, whence E *ebriety*, intoxication, and *ēbriōsus*, whence *ēbriōsitās*, o/s *ēbriōsitāt-*, whence E *ebriosity*, habitual intoxication, and LL *ēbriāre*, to render drunk, with pp *ēbriātus*, whence *ebriate*, intoxicated.

3. *Ebriare* has int *inēbriāre*, with pp *inēbriātus*, whence both the adj (hence the n) and the v *inebriate*; derivative LL *inēbriātiō*, o/s *inēbriātiōn-*, yields *inebriation*.

4. The opp of L *ēbrius* is *sōbrius*, who has not (yet) drunk from the wine-jar, hence who does not drink wine: either *so-* for privative *sē-*, apart from, without+an adj from *bria*, wine-jar, or *so-*+*ēbrius*, *soebrius* being eased to *sōbrius*. *Sōbrius* becomes OF-F *sobre*, adopted by ME, whence E *sober*, whence 'to *sober*'; derivative *sōbrietās*, o/s *sōbrietāt-*, yields, perh via OF-F *sobriété*, the E *sobriety*.

**ebullience** derives from **ebullient**, itself from L *ēbullient-*, o/s of *ēbulliens*, presp of *ēbullīre*, to bubble- or boil-up: *ē*, out+*bullīre* (s *bull-*), to boil (see BOIL); on *ēbullit-*, s of pp *ēbullitus*, rises *ēbullitiō*, o/s *ēbullitiōn-*, whence, prob via MF-F, the E *ebullition*.

**écarté.** See the 2nd CARD, para 9.

**eccentric, eccentricity.** See CENTRE, para 4.

**ecclesia, ecclesiarch, ecclesiast, Ecclesiastes, ecclesiastic(al), ecclesiasticism, ecclesiology.**

1. LL *ecclēsia*, assembly of people, esp of Christians, congregation, (*E-*) the Church, a church, derives from Gr *ekklēsia*, a political assembly of citizens, (app for *ekklētia*, but cf *klēsis*, a summoning) from *ekklētos*, called out, the pp of *ekkalein*; *kalein*, to call, or summon by crier+*ek-*, out: *kaleō*, I name by calling, call by name, has r *kal-*, var *kel-*, to call, summon: cf CLAMOR and (of cattle) 'to LOW'.

2. The chief derivatives are:

*ecclesiarch:* LL *ecclēsia*+*archo*s, for Gr *arkhos* a ruler;

*ecclesiast:* perh via the OF-MF adj *écclesiaste*: either from LL *ecclēsiastēs* or from Gr *ekklēsiastēs*, a preacher; the Biblical *Ecclesiastes* is a specialization;

*ecclesiastic* (whence the *-al* extn *ecclesiastical*), adj hence n: perh via MF-F *ecclésiastique*, from: LL *ecclēsiasticus*: Gr *ekklēsiastikos*, adj of *ekklēsia*; hence *ecclesiasticism* (*-ism*);

*ecclesiology: ecclesio-*, c/f of *ecclēsia*+*-logy* (element): hence *ecclesiologist* (cf *-logist* at the element *-logia*).

**echelon:** OF-F *échelon*, aug of *échelle*, a ladder: an initial *-e* vocalization of L *scāla*: f.a.e., SCALE.

**echo** (n hence v), **echoic, echoism; sough** (n hence v).

*Sough*, ME *swough* or *swogh*, a sound, derives from OE *swōgan*, to sound, akin to OS *swōgan*, to rustle, and Go gas*wōgjan* (int *ga*-), to sigh—and to Gr *ekhos*, sound, noise, itself intimately related to Gr *ēkhō*, sound, esp an echo, whence, via L *echo*, the E *echo*. With both *sough* and *echo*, cf the Lith *svagiù*, I echo: all, ult, are echoic. And *echoic* itself derives either from E *echo* or, more prob, from the LL adj *echōicus*; *echoism*=E *echo*+ suffix *-ism*.

**eclair**, prop **éclair**, is adopted from OF-F *éclair*: lit, a flash of lightning, *éclair* came, in C19, to designate a pastry, so named because 'eaten in a flash'. (Dauzat.)

**éclat.** See SLATE.

**eclectic, eclecticism.** See LEGEND.

**eclipse**, n hence—? influenced by MF-F *éclipser* —v; **ecliptic**, adj and n.

An *eclipse*, adopted from OF-F, derives from L *eclipsis*, trln of Gr *ekleipsis*, lit an omission, an abandonment, from *ekleipein*, to leave (*leipein*) out (*ek*), to abandon: f.a.e., LEND. The derivative Gr adj *ekleiptikos* becomes L *eclipticus*, whence E *ecliptic* (cf F *écliptique*); *ekleiptikos*, used as n, leads to the Astr n *ecliptic*.

**eclogue.** See LEGEND, para 29.

**ecology**: element *eco-* (connoting 'environment') +*-logy*, q.v. at the element *-logia*.

**economic**, adj, whence **economics; economical; economist, economize, economy; ecumenical; sep diocese; parish, parishioner; parochial**, whence **parochialism.**

1. The base of all these words is Gr *oikos*, a dwelling place, esp a house, app for *\*woikos*, having r *\*woik-* and being therefore akin to L *uīcus*, ML *vīcus*, and so to E *village* and *vicinity*, treated at VICINAGE (f.a.e.). For the simple word, cf the element *eco-*.

2. *Oikos* occurs in the notable cpd *oikonomos*, steward, with 2nd element *-nomos*, from *nemein*, to distribute (cf the element *nomo-*): whence *oiko-nomia*, household management, whence, via L *oeconomia* and perh MF-F *économie*, the E *economy*. The derivative Gr adj *oikonomikos* becomes L *oeconomicus*, whence, perh via MF-F, the E *economic*, with extn *economical* having special sense 'thrifty'. MF-F *économie* has derivatives *économiste* and *économiser*: whence E *economist*, *economize*.

3. Gr *oikos* has derivative *oikein*, to live in (a house), to inhabit, with pp *oikoumenos*, whence *oikoumenē* (*gē*), the inhabited world, with its own adj *oikoumenikos*, LL *oecūmenicus*, E *ecumenic*, usu in extn *ecumenical*, world-wide, esp concerning the Church as a whole.

4. *Oikos* has the prefix-derivative adj *paroikos*, dwelling *para* or beside, whence *paroikia*, a sojourning, LGr a diocese, whence LL *paroecia* (with var *parrocia*), whence OF-F *paroisse*, whence ME-E *parish*; the OF-F derivative adj *paroissien* becomes ME *parishen* and then adds agential *-er* to form *parishioner*.

5. LL *paroecia* has the further var *parochia*, with

adj *parochiālis*, whence ONF *parochial*, adopted by E: lit 'of a parish', hence 'confined to a parish', hence 'narrow-minded'.

**écossaise.** See SCOT, para 4.

**ecstasy, ecstatic** (adj hence n); Gallic varr **extasy, extatic.** See STAND, para 7.

**ectoplasm.** See PLASM, para 2.

**Ecuador.** See EQUAL.

**ecumenical.** See ECONOMIC, para 3.

**eczema** is Sci L, from Gr *ekzema*: *ek*, out+ *zema*, a fermentation, a boiling, from *zein*, to boil: f.a.e., YEAST. On the o/s *ekzemat-* arise the E adjj *eczematoid* (*-oid*) and *eczematous* (*-ous*).

**edacious, edacity.** See EDIBLE.

**eddy** (n hence v): ME *ydy*: ? ON *itha*, from *ith-*, back, again (OE and OS *ed-*, OFris *et-*, Go *id-*, OHG *et(a)-*, *it(a)-*), ult akin to L *et*, and, Gr *eti*, moreover, again, and Skt *ati*, beyond.

**edelweiss**: G *Edelweiss*, '(a flower) nobly white': *edel*, noble+*weiss*, white: cf WHITE, para 7.

**Eden** (whence adj **Edenic**) is adopted from LL, which takes it from H *'edēn*, delight, hence a place of delight, the latter deducible from H *gan 'edēn*, garden of delight (hence the Vulgate's *paradisus uoluptātis*).

**edentate**, toothless. See TOOTH, para 7.

**edge**, whence the adj **edgy** and also the v 'to **edge**', whence **edger, edging.**

An *edge*, ME *eg* or *egge*, derives from OE *ecg*, akin to OFris *egg*, OS *eggia*, OHG *ekka*, MHG-G *ecke*, ON *egg*; also to L *aciēs*, edge, hence a sword, and *ācer*, sharp (cf EAGER), Gr *akē, akis*, a point, and *oxus*, sharp, and Skt *aśri*, edge.

**edible** (whence **edibility**); **edacious, edacity.**

1. *Edible* derives from LL *edibilis*, eatable, from *edere*, to eat, o/s *ed-*: f.a.e., EAT. *Edere* has derivative adj *edāx*, voracious, with o/s *edāc-*, whence E *edacious* (*-ious*), and with derivative *edācitās*, o/s *edācitāt-*, whence E *edacity*.

2. *Edere* has two prefix-cpds relevant to E: *comedere*, to eat *com-* or entirely, and *obedere*. *Comedere* has pp *comēsus*, whence agent *comestor*, whence LL adj *comestibilis*, whence MF-F *comestible*, suitable for eating, hence the E n 'suitable food', usu in pl *comestibles*.

3. *Obedere* occurs only in pp *obēsus*, gnawed (prefix *ob-*), hence adj 'emaciated, thin' (very rare), whence, ironically, fat, whence E *obese*; derivative LL *obēsitās*, o/s *obēsitāt-*, yields E *obesity*.

**edict.** See DICT, para 7 at *edicere*.

**edification, edificatory, edifice, edificial, edify** (whence pa **edifying**).

'To *edify*', orig to build, hence to improve (character), derives, through ME *edifien*, from OE-MF *edifier* (F *é-*), from L *aedificāre*, for *aedem facere*, to make a house: *aedēs*, orig a hearth, akin to Gr *aithein*, s *aith-*, to burn, and OIr *āed*, a fire; for *facere*, see FACT. On the pp *aedificātus*, s *aedificāt-*, arises *aedificātiō*, o/s *aedificātiōn-*, whence, perh via OF-F, the E *edification*, whence, anl, the adj *edificatory* (*-ory*); on the inf s *aedific-* arises *aedificium*, a building, whence, via OF-F, the E *edifice*; the adj *edificial* comes from the derivative L *aedificiālis.*—Cf OAST.

**edit, edition, editor** (whence **editorial,** adj hence n).

'To *edit*' comes from L *ēditus,* pp of *ēdere,* to give (*dare*), hence put, *ē* or out, to publish: f.a.e., temporal DATE. On the pps *ēdit-* are formed both *ēditiō,* a publishing, o/s *ēditiōn-,* whence, prob via MF-F, the E *edition,* and *ēditor,* a putter forth, hence a publisher, adopted by E, esp for a newspaper or a textual editor.

**educable, educand, educate, education, educator,** etc. See DUKE, para 7.

**educe, eduction,** etc. See DUKE, para 6 at *ēducere.*

**edulcorate.** See DULCET, para 2.

**Edward,** whence the *-ian* adj (hence n) **Edwardian,** derives from OE *Ēadweard* or *-ward,* an OE *weard* or defender of *ēad* or property.

**eel:** OE *āel:* akin to OHG-MHG *āl,* G *Aal,* and ON *āll:* perh akin to Gr *elaion,* olive oil, because of its slipperiness; IE r, *el-.* (Walshe.)

**eerie, eery,** orig timid, hence that which causes timidity, esp in a ghostly way: Sc: from OE *earg* or *earh,* timid, akin to OFris *erg,* bad, OHG *arg,* MHG *arc,* cowardly, ON *argr,* timid.

**efface, effacement.** See FACE, para 5.

**effect** (n hence v), **effective** (adj hence n), **effector, effectual; efficacious, efficacity; efficiency, efficient; ineffective, ineffectual.**

1. The last two merely tack-on the neg prefix *in-.*

2. 'An *effect*', adopted from MF-EF (cf the modern *effet*), derives from L *effectus* (gen *-ūs*), from *effect-,* s of the pp of *efficere,* to bring about: *ē,* out+c/f of *facere,* to do or make: f.a.e., FACT. On *effect-* arise:

LL *effectīuus,* ML *effectīvus,* whence—perh via MF-F *effectif,* f *effective*—the E *effective;*

*effector* (agential *-or*), adopted by E. But *effectual* derives from ML *\*effectuālis* (deducible from the ML adv *effectuāliter*), built upon the n *effectus.*

3. *Efficere* has derivative adj *efficāx,* o/s *efficāc-,* whence *efficacious* (*-ious*); whereas subsidiary *efficācitās,* o/s *efficācitāt-,* yields *efficacity,* subsidiary LL *efficācia* yields *efficacy.*

4. *Efficere* has presp *efficiens,* o/s *efficient-,* whence, prob via MF-F, the E adj *efficient;* derivative L *efficientia* yields *efficiency.*

**effeminacy, effeminate.** See FEMALE, para 1.

**effendi.** See AUTHENTIC, para 1.

**effervesce; effervescence** (or *-cy*); **effervescent.** See FERVENT, para 1.

**effete:** L *effētus,* that has brought forth young and is therefore exhausted: cf FETUS, paras 1, 2.

**efficacious, efficacy.** See EFFECT, para 3.

**efficiency, efficient.** See EFFECT, para 4.

**effigy** (whence the adj **effigial**): MF-F *effigie:* L *effigiēs,* a de-nasalized derivative of *effingere,* to shape (*fingere*) forth (*e,* out): f.a.e., FEIGN.

**efflorescence, efflorescent.** See FLORA, para 14.

**effluence, effluent.** See FLUENT, para 7.

**effluvium.** See FLUENT, para 7.

**efflux.** See FLUENT, para 7.

**effort, effortless.** See FORCE, para 8.

**effraction.** See FRACTION, para 6.

**effrontery.** See FRONT, para 5, s.f.

**effulgence, effulgent.** See FLAGRANT, para 4.

**effuse** (adj, v), **effusion, effusive.** Cf *diffuse* and see the 2nd FOUND, para 7.

**egalitarian.** See EQUAL, para 4.

**egest, egestible, egestion.** See GERUND, para 12.

**egg** (1), n, derives, not from OE *āeg* (whence ME *ei, ey*) but from ON *egg,* akin to OE *āeg,* OHG-G *ei,* Crimean Go *ada,* OSl *aje* (var *jaje*); also to L *ouum* (ML *ovum*), Gr *-ōion;* IE r, *\*ouĭ-.*

2. The 2nd element in *kidney,* ME *kidenei,* is ME *ei;* the 1st is o.o.o.

**egg** (2), to urge or incite: ME *eggen:* ON *eggja,* (lit) to put an *egg,* or edge, on: cf EDGE.

**eglantine:** EF-F *églantine,* orig the f, taken as n, of the EF *aiglantin,* adj of OF-MF *aiglent:* VL *\*aculentum,* from L *aculeus,* a prickle, from *acus,* a needle, akin to *ācer,* q.v. at EAGER. (B & F.)

**ego, egoism, egoist, egoistic; egotism, egotist, egotistic; egocentric; egolatrous; egomania, egomaniac** (adj, hence n, whence **egomaniacal**).—**I** (pronoun).

1. The pronoun *I,* ME *i,* earlier *ich,* earliest *ic,* derives from OE *ic:* akin to OFris, OS, Go, D *ik* (MD *ic*), OHG *ih* (MHG-G *ich*), ON *ek, ik,* the Gmc etymon being *\*ika,* unstressed form of *\*eka;* the IE etymon is *\*ego,* var *\*egom,* as in L *egŏ* and Gr *egō* (dial var *egōn*); cf the IE varr occurring in Skt *ahám* (OPer *adam,* Av *azem*)—in OLith *eš* (Lith *aš*), OP *es,* usu *as,* Lett *es*—Arm *es;* Hit has both *ug-* and *ŭk,* later *ammuk.* Note also that the syn Eg *uȧ* suggests that the word is Medit.

2. L *ego,* adopted by E Phil and Psy, has the foll derivatives and cpds:

*egoism,* F *égoïsme:* L *ego+-isme,* E *-ism;*

*egoist,* F *égoïste;* L *ego+-iste,* E *-ist;* whence *egoistic* (*-ic*);

*egotism:* L *ego+-t-,* as in despotism+*-ism;*

*egotist:* a blend of *egotism+egoist;* whence *egotistic* (cf *egoistic*), with extn *ego istical* (*-al,* adj);

*egocentric:* L *ego+centric,* q.v. at CENTER; whence *egocentricity* (*-ity*);

*egolatrous:* L *ego+*the *-latrous* of *ido atrous;*

*egomania:* Sci L: L *ego+*the Med c/f *-mania* (cf MANIA), whence *egomaniac* (cf *maniac* at MANIA).

**egregious.** See GREGAL, para 6.

**egress.** See GRADE, para 11.

**egret.** See HERON.

**Egypt, Egyptian** (adj hence n), **Egyptology** (*Egypt+*connective *-o-+-logy,* q.v. at the element *-logia*); **Gypsy, Gipsy**—cf **gyp** or **gip,** to cheat; **Gitano.**—**Copt, Coptic** (adj hence n).

1. *Egypt* derives, via F *Égypte,* from L *Aegyptus,* itself from Gr *Aiguptos,* not 'the land of the *aigupios* or vulture' but (Enci It) app from Bab *Ḥikuptah,* the very ancient city of Memphis—cf the Eg *Àtur,* as in *Àtur-meh,* Lower Egypt, and *Àtur-res,* Upper Egypt.

2. Gr *Aiguptos* has adj *Aiguptios,* whence L

*Aigyptius*, whence F *égyptien*, whence ME *Egypcian*, *Egipcian* (adj and n), the former yielding E *Egyptian*.

3. ME *Egipcian*, *Egypcian* (both with var *-ien*) have the C16 aphetic derivatives, resp *gipcyan*, *gyptian*, the former yielding *gipsy* (or *Gipsy*), the latter *gypsy* (or *Gypsy*), the *gi-* form being the commoner. Gypsies, coming from India, sojourned long in Egypt, hence their early name *Egipcian*, *Egypcian*, C16-17 *Egyptian*.

4. 'To *gip* or *gyp*', to cheat, derives from *gip* or *gyp*, a swindler, very prob from *gipsy*, *gypsy*.

5. L *Aegyptus*, Egypt, became Sp *Egipto*, whence *Egiptano*, an Egyptian, whence *gitano*, a Gipsy, pl *gitanos*.

6. Gr *Aiguptios*, an Egyptian, became Coptic *Guptios*, with var *Kuptios*, whence Ar *Quft*, *Qibt*, the Copts, whence learned L *Cophtus*, *Coptus*, the latter yielding both E *Copt* and learned L *Copticus*, whence E *Coptic*; the Coptic language derives (early A.D.) from Egyptian.

**eider** (also **eider duck**) comes from Ice *aēthr*, pron *aithr*—cf Skt *ātíš*, water bird; **eiderdown**, via G *Eiderdaune*, from Ice *aēthardūnn*—cf DOWN, soft hair or feathers. (Walshe.)

**eidetic**; **eidolon.** See IDEA, para **3**.

**eight, eighteen, eighty.**

*Eight* derives from OE *eahta*, akin to OFris *achta*, OS *ahto*, OHG *ahto*, MHG *ahte*, G *acht*, Go *ahtau*, ON *ātta*: Gmc etymon, *\*ahta* or *\*ahtau*; IE etymon, *\*oktō* or *\*oktou*: cf OIr *ocht*, L *octō*, Gr *oktō*, also Skt *asta*: cf OCTAVE. *Eighteen*=OE *eahtatýne* or *-tēne* (cf TEN); *eighty*=OE *eahtatig* (for *-tig*, cf TEN).

**eigre.** See NATIVE, para 11.

**Eire.** See IRISH, para 1.

**eisegesis, eisegete, eisegetic.** See SEEK, para 8.

**either,** adj hence pron and conj and adv: ME *either*, earlier *aither*: OE *aēgther*, contr of *aēghwaether*, var *āhwaeder*, each: akin to OFris *aider*, *eider*, contr of *ahwedder* (cf var *āuder*), OHG *iowedar*, *iohwedar*, contr of *ēogihweder*, *eigowedar*, MHG *ieder*, contr of *ieweder*, G *jeder*: orig, each of two. The elements are OE *ā* (E AYE, always) and *hwaether* (E WHETHER).

**ejaculate, ejaculation, ejaculative, ejaculator; ejaculatory; eject, ejection, ejective, ejectment, ejector.**

1. L *ēiaculāri* (ML *ej-*), to throw out, derives from L *ē*, out+*iaculāri*, to throw, from *iaculum*, dart, javelin, from *iacere* (s *iac-*), to throw. The pp *ēiaculātus*, ML *ējaculātus*, yields 'to *ejaculate*'; on the pps *ēiaculāt-* arise the E formations *ejaculation*, etc., on anl of the *eject-* words.

2. 'To *eject*' derives from ML *ējectus*, L *eiectus*, pp of *ēicere*, to throw out: *ē*, out+c/f of *iacere*, to throw. On the pps *ēiect-* arises *ēiectiō*, o/s *ēiectiōn-* (ML *ēj-*), whence E *ejection*. The other *eject-* words are E anl formations, with suffixes *-ive*, *-ment*, agential *-or*.

3. Cf JET.

**eke,** adv, conj: OE *ēac*; akin to OFris *āk*, OS *ōc*, OHG *ouh*, MHG *ouch*, G *auch*, ON *auk*, also, and

Go *auk*, but, moreover; also to L *autem*, but, Gr *auge*, *aute*, again, Skt *u*, and, but.

2. But Go *auk* is akin to Go *aukan*, to increase, therefore to syn OE *ýcan*, *ēcan*, OFris *āka*, OS *ōkian*, OHG *ouhhōn*, ON *auka*; also to L *augēre* (s *aug-*) and Gr *auxein* (s *aux-*, for *\*auks-*). OE *ēcan* (var *ýcan*) becomes ME *echen*, dial *eken*, whence E 'to *eke*' or increase.

**elaborate** (adj, v), **elaboration**, etc. See LABOR, para 6.

**elaidic, elaidin.** See OIL, para 6.

**élan.** See LANCE, para 5.

**eland.** See ELK, para 2.

**elapse.** See LABOR, para 2.

**elastic,** adj (hence n), whence **elasticity**: Sci L *elasticus*: Gr *elastikos*, propulsive, springy, from *elaunō* (s *elaun-*), I drive, extn of syn *elaō* (PGr *\*elami*); akin to Arm *elanem*, I come, or go, forth, and perh to L *alacer*, lively; IE r, *\*ela-*, to push or drive. (Boisacq.)

2. *Elaunō* has agent *elatēr*, a driver, adopted, as *elater*, by Bot and Zoo.

**elate** (adj, v), **elation, elative.**

*Elate* derives from L *ēlātus*, pp of *efferre*, to carry out or away, to lift up, *ē*, out+*ferre*, to bear or carry. On s *elat-* arises *ēlātiō*, o/s *ēlātiōn-*, whence, perh via EF, the E *elation*; *elative* is an E anl formation.

**elater.** See ELASTIC, para 2.

**elation.** See ELATE.

**elbow** (n hence v). See ELL.

**eld, elder** (adj), **eldest.** See OLD, paras 2-3.

**elder** (tree): ME *eldre*, *eller*: OE *ellern*, *ellen*: with Flemish and LG cognates (e.g., MLG *ellern*); perh akin to ALDER and therefore to ELM.

**El Dorado** is Sp for 'the Gilded', hence 'the Golden Land, Land of Gold': Sp *dorar*, to gild.

**eldrich** or **eldritch**, eery (orig Sc, with wholly Sc var *elphrish*): earlier *elrish*; from ELF.

**elect** (adj, v), **election, elective, elector, electoral, electorate.** See LEGEND, para 8.

**electric,** whence **electrical** and **electricity** and **electrify** (*electric+-fy*); **electrocute,** whence **electrocution; electron**; such obvious cpds (with c/f *electro-*) as **electrode, electrolysis, electromagnetic, electromotive, electroscope, electrotype.**

1. *Electric* derives from Sci L *electricus*, produced (by friction) from amber, adj of L *electrum*, amber, trln of Gr *ēlektron* (whence E *electron*), orig the neu of adj *ēlektros*, gleaming, shining, brilliant, akin to syn *ēlektōr*, which, used as n, denotes the sun ('the shiner'): o.o.o., but prob cf Skt *ulkā́*, a meteor.

2. *Electrocute*=c/f *electro-*+the *-cute* (from L *secūtus*, pp of *sequi*, to follow) of *execute*.

**electuary.** See LICK, para 4.

**eleemosynary**: ML *eleēmosynārius*, adj of *eleēmosyna*: f.a.e., ALMS.

**elegance, elegant.** See LEGEND, para 10.

**elegy,** adj **elegiac.**

The adj comes, perh via late MF-F *élégiaque*, from LL *elegiacus*, trln of Gr *elegeiakos*, adj of *elegeia*, whence, via L *elegia* and, prob via late

MF-F *élégie*, the E *elegy*: and Gr *elegeia* is elliptical for *elegeia ōidē*, mournful song, from *elegeios*, elegiac, from *elegos*, a song of mourning, accompanied on the flute: o.o.o.: perh akin to LEGEND, but prob of Asiatic origin—cf Arm *elegn-*, a reed, hence a flute. (Boisacq.)

element (whence elemental), elementary.

*Elementary* comes from L *elementārius*, the *-ārius* adj of L *elementum*, usu in pl *elementa*, the four simple substances or principles—air, earth, fire, water—of which the physical universe was anciently supposed to consist, hence elementary knowledge, hence, in E, the forces of Nature and, in sing, a living creature's natural medium: o.o.o.: ? for *elimentum* from *eligmentum*, from *ēligere*, to choose (the fundamental substances or the basic principles) from (a welter of physical phenomena). L *elementum* becomes OF-MF *element* (later *élé-*), adopted by E.

elephant; elephantiasis (Gr word—cf the element *-iasis*); elephantine (L *elephantīnus*, adj of *elephantus*, as below).—ivory, adj ivorine (OF *ivorin*, adj of *ivoire*, as in para 2).

1. *Elephant* derives from ME *elefaunt*: OF-MF *elefant*: L *elephantus* (cf learnèd and later *elephas*, gen *elephantis*), elephant, ivory: Gr ἐλέφαντος, *elephantos*, gen of ἐλέφᾱς, *elephās*, ivory, (later) elephant: ? orig 'the *ivory* beast'. The Gr *elephās* app consists of *el-*, o.o.o., perh an IE r *el-*, horn (perh cf ἔλαφος, *elaphos*, a stag: ? 'the *antlered* beast'), and *-έφᾱς*, *-ephās*, with s and r *eph-*, akin to L *ebur*, ivory, with s and r *eb-*, from an IE r *ebh-*, ivory: ? therefore 'the beast with the ivory horns' (tusks). Both the Gr *-ephas* and the L *ebur* come from Eg *abu* (whence Coptic *ebu*, *ebou*), elephant, a tusk of ivory, ivory—cf Eg *aab*, *ab*, ivory. (Note that the ME var *olifant* is adopted from OF-MF, where it predominates over *elefant*, and is akin to OE *olfenda*, *olfend*, OHG *olbanta*, *olbenta*, OS *olbhundeo*, Go *ulbandus*, ON *ūlfaldi*, which all mean 'camel'; this *ol-* (var *ul-*) form prob indicates a 'popular channel', perh a VL *oliphantus*.)

2. *Ivory*, present in ME, derives from AF *ivorie* and ONF *ivurie*, varr of OF-F *ivoire*, itself either from ML *ebor*, var of L *ebur*, ivory, or from *eboreum*, neu (employed as n) of *eboreus*, adj of *ebur*, o/s *ebor-*.

3. The *crux* obviously lies in the 1st element: *el-*, which cannot be the Ar article 'the', *el* (var *al*), which did not, by many centuries, exist so early as Gr *elephās*. Now, the *el-* of the Gr word is prob akin to Skt *ibha-*, elephant, rather than to Berber *elu*; nevertheless, *elu* and *ibha* (therefore Gr ἐλ-), as well as Akk *pīlu*, later H *pīl* and Ar *fīl*, are ult of prob the one origin, as Professor M. Cohen has suggested in *Essai comparatif sur le Chamito-Sémitique*, p. 170.

4. Subsidiarily, yet importantly, one must remember that the two kinds of elephant—the Indian and the African—were known to the ancients: the former being recorded in Skt as *ibha-* and in Gr as ἐλ- (*el-*), and presumably also in the Akk,

later H, Ar, as *pīlu*, *pīl*, *fīl*; the latter as Eg *abu* or *ebu*, the Berber *elu*; Berber *elu* is basically Hamitic, being perh independent but prob a blend of the Akk (and H and ? Ar) and the Eg words.

5. The Gr ἐλέφᾱς, *elephās*, is therefore both a phonetic and a semantic duplicate, consisting of the Indian elephant and the African elephant and their names: the one with an IE (app from Sem) origin, the other with a Ham origin (? influenced by Sem). These facts rather point to Gr ἐλέφᾱς being a very old word indeed, with the Sem and the Ham origins becoming lost at some point in what was, for the Greeks, pre-history.

elevate, elevation, elevator, elevatory. See LEVER, para 8.

eleven, eleventh; 'elevenses'. See ONE, final para.

elf (pl elves), elfin, elfish or elvish.

1. The 4th softens the 3rd; the 3rd=*elf*+adj *-ish*; the 2nd prob=*elfen* (*-en*, adj suffix); and *elf* derives from OE *aelf*, var *ylf*, akin to the syn ON *aelfr*, *ālfr*, and to MHG-G *alp*, a nightmare; perh cf ALB, but prob (Walshe) cf Skt *ṛbhúś*, a cunning artist (name of a genie).

2. The ON *ālfr* yields *oaf* (earlier, also *auf*), an elf's child, hence a changeling, hence an uncouth child, hence a dolt, a lout. Hence the adj *oafish*.

elicit. See DELICACY, para 6.

elide, elision. See LESION, para 3.

eligible, eligibility. See LEGEND, para 8, s.f.

eliminate, elimination, eliminatory; eliminant. See LIMIT, para 6.

elision. See LESION, para 3.

elite. See LEGEND, para 9.

elixir. See SERENE, para 3.

Eliza, Elizabeth (whence Elizabethan); Elise; Liza, Liz, Lizzie; Betty, betty.

*Eliza* (cf the F *Élise*) shortens *Elizabeth*: LL *Elisabeth*: LGr *Eleisabeth*, *Elisabet*: H *Elīsheba'*, lit 'God is (an) oath', hence consecrated to God. *Liza* is a pet-form of either *Eliza* or *Elizabeth*, and *Liz*—whence *Lizzie*—a further shortening; *Bet*, whence *Betty*, comes from the *-beth* of *Elizabeth* and has the humorous derivative (orig underworld) *betty*, a short bar used by thieves—cf the syn *jemmy* or *jimmy*.

elk; eland; lamb (n hence v).

1. An *elk* comes from ON *elgr*, akin to OE *eolh* and OHG *elaho*, MHG *elhe*, G *Elch*, elk, and ult to Skt *ṛśya*, antelope.

2. *Eland* is adopted from D *eland*, elk (MD *elant*, *elen*), akin to—perh from the MHG form of—G *Elend*, extn *Elentier*, elk, MHG *elen*, for *elhen*, from an oblique case of MHG *elhe* (Walshe), from OHG *elaho*; akin also to Lith *elnis*, elk, and to Gr *ellos*, deer.

3. *Lamb* descends direct from OE *lamb*, var *lomb*: intimately related to the syn OHG, OS, ON *lamb*, and to Go *lamb*, a sheep; perh related to Gr *elaphos*, *ellos*, deer, and to Lett *lôps*, cattle.

ell; elbow.

An *elbow*, lit an arm-bend, derives from OE *elboga*, var of *elnboga*, akin to OHG *ellinbogo*, MHG *ellenboge*, G *Ellenbogen*, *Ellbogen*, and ON *ölnbogi*. For the 2nd element, see BOW, to bend. The 1st element is OE *eln*, the forearm, hence an ell, ME *eln*, later *elne*, latest *ellen*, whence E *ell*: akin to OFris *elne*; to OHG *elina*, MHG *elene*, later—'the radical *-n* being taken as an inflexional ending' (Walshe), ? as in ME—*ele*, whence G *Elle*; to Go *aleina*; to ON *alin*; also to L *ulna* (s *uln-*), the forearm, hence the distance from elbow to wrist—an ell; to Gr *ōlenē* (s *ōlen-*); cf OIr *uile* (gen *uilenn*), Ga *uileann*, W and Cor *elin*, OC \**olēn-*, and, more remotely, Skt *aratnis*, elbow, ell, and several Sl words.

**ellipse, ellipsis, ellipsoid; elliptic,** with *-al* extn **elliptical.**

*Elliptic* derives, perh via EF-F *elliptique*, from Gr *elliptikos*, adj of *elleipsis*, a leaving, a falling short, from *elleipein*, to leave (*leipein*) in (*el-* for *en*): for *leipein*, cf LEND. Gr *elleipsis* becomes L *ellipsis* (adopted by E), pl *ellipses*, whence, by b/f, *ellipse*, whence, by suffix *-oid*, *ellipsoid*.

**elm,** direct from OE, is akin to OHG-MHG *elm* boum (G *Baum*, tree) and ON *almr*, themselves akin to L *ulmus* (s *ulm-*) and—? a metathesis—MIr *lem*, Ga *leamhan* (but Cor *elan*).

**elocution,** whence **elocutionary** and **elocutionist; eloquence, eloquent.** See LOQUACIOUS, para 4.

**elongate, elongation.** See LONG, para 11.

**elope, elopement.** See LEAP, para 4.

**eloquence, eloquent.** See LOQUACIOUS, para 4.

**else** (adj hence adv): OE *elles*, otherwise, prob orig the gen of a Gmc adj akin to L *alius*: cf OHG *elles*, otherwise, and Go *aljis*, other: cf also OIr *aile* and Gr *allos*, other, and cognates in Tokh A and B and in Arm; IE etymon, \**alios*. Cf ALIAS.

**elucidate, elucidation, elucidatory.** See the 3rd LIGHT, para 15.

**elude, elusive.** See LUDICROUS, para 6.

**elute, elution; eluriate.** See LAVA, para 9, s.f.

**Elysian, Elysium; Champs Elysées.**

*Elysian* substitutes *-an* for L *-us* in *Elysius*, Elysian, of *Elysium*, trln of Gr *Ēlusion*, elliptical for *Ēlusion pedion*, Elysian field, which, in L, became *elysii campi*, whence LL *elysei campi*, whence F *champs elysées* (C14, *c. elisies*), finally bestowed upon the finest avenue in Paris. The Gr *ēlusion* (ήλύσιον) perh derives from the Gr r *eluth-*, as in Homeric *ēluthon*, preterite of *eleathō*, I come or arrive: 'the field·of arrival' in the Gr heaven.

**elytroid, elytron.** See VOLUBLE, para 5.

**emaciate, emaciation.**

1. The latter derives, by anl, from the former; the former, from L *ēmaciātus*, pp of *ēmaciāre*, to render lean: int *ē*+*maciāre*, to render lean, from *maciēs*, leanness, itself from *macer*, lean (cf *aciēs*, sharp edge, and *ācer*, sharp), r *mac-*, akin to Gr *makros*, long, s *makr-*, r *mak-*, and to Hit *maklanza*, thin, lean, r *mak-*; IE r, \**mak-* or \**mek-*.

2. L *macer* becomes OF *maigre* (extant), *megre*; the latter is adopted by ME—hence E *meagre*, AE *meager*.

**emanate, emanation, emanative.**

'To *emanate*' derives from L *ēmānātus*, pp of

*ēmānāre*, to trickle out: *ē*, out ¦-*mānāre*, to trickle (s *mān-*), hence to distil; subsidiary LL *ēmānātiō*, o/s *ēmānātiōn-*, yields E *emanation*; *emanative* is an anl E formation. L *mānāre* app derives from a n akin to EIr *moin*, a marsh, peat-bog, fen, Ga *mōine*, a morass, peat, W *mawn*, peat.

**emancipate, emancipation,** etc. See CAPABILITY, para 8 (at *manceps*).

**emarginate, emargination.** See MARK, para 8.

**emasculate, emasculation.** See MALE, para 4.

**embalm.** See BALM, s.f.

**embank, embankment.** See BANK.

**embarcation.** See 3rd BARK, para 3.

**embargo,** legal restraint upon a ship. See BAR, para 8.

**embark, embarkation.** See 3rd BARK, para 3.

**embarrass, embarrassment.** See BAR, para 7.

**embassy; ambassador** (whence both **ambass-adress,** cf F *ambassadrice*, and **ambassadorial,** with aj suffix *-ial*).

*Ambassador* merely anglicizes MF-F *ambassadeur*, itself from It *ambasciatore*, from OProv *ambaissador*, answering to OProv *ambaissada*, whence It *ambasciata*, whence OF *ambassee*, whence E *embassy*. OProv *ambaissada* derives from O Prov \**ambaissa*, answering to ML *ambactia* (var *ambascia*), of Gmc origin: cf Go *andbahti*, OHG *ambahti* (G *Amt*, function), service, function, itself of C origin; cf Gaul \**ambactos* (Caesar's *ambactus*), servant, client, vassal, W *amaeth*, ploughman, husbandman (cf Cor *améthy*, to till), Cor *omager*, vassal. Cf also ML *abantonia*, maidservant, and L *ambāgēs*, a going about (see AMBIGUOUS). Note that Gaul \**ambactos* is for \**ambiactos*, from *ambi*, about, around, the L *ambi*, on both sides, all around; the C r is \**amb*, on both sides, around. Basic idea: one who goes about (husbandman) or is sent about (servant, vassal, ambassador).

**embellish, embellishment.** See BEAU, para 4.

**ember** (1), adj, as in *Ember days*: ME *ymber*: OE *ymber*, Ember days, app a confusion of L *quattuor tempora* or (*ieiūnia*) *quattuor temporum*, (fast of) the four seasons, the days of fast appointed by the Church for each of the four seasons of the year (cf the G *Quatember*, Ember days: L *quattuor tempora*), with OE *ymbryne*, a running about, a circuit, a cpd of *ymb*, about, around (L *ambi*: therefore cf AMBASSADOR)+*ryne*, a running, from *rinnan*, to RUN.

**ember** (2), a lighted coal, esp *embers*, smouldering remains of a fire: ME *eymbre*, earlier *emer*, *aymer*: OE *ǣmerge*: akin to OHG *eimuria* and ON *eimyrja*, ember, and ON *eimr*, steam; and prob to Gr *heuein* (s *heu-*), to singe.

**embezzle**—whence **embezzlement** (*-ment*) and **embezzler** (agential *-er*)—comes from MF *embesillier*: o.o.o.; perh from VL (? rather ML) \**imbecillāre*, to render feeble, from LL *imbēcillāri*, to be feeble, from L *imbēcillus* (or *-is*), feeble: f.a.e., IMBECILE. Basic idea: to enfeeble (someone) financially—by cheating him.

**emblem:** L *emblēma*, inlaid work, gen *emblē-matis*, o/s *emblēmat-*: Gr *emblēma*, gen *emble-*

*matos*, from *emballein*, to throw in, hence put on: *em-* for *en*, in+*ballein*, to throw: cf BALLISTIC. *Emblematic* derives from a probable LL *\*emblēmaticus*; *emblematize* is an anl E formation. For *blem-* (Gr *-blēma*), cf PROBLEM; for Gr *emballein*, cf EMBOLISM.

**embodiment, embody.** See BODY.

**embolism**: LL *embolismus*: Gr *embolismos*, from *emballein*, to throw in, to insert: cf EMBLEM.

**embonpoint.** See PUNGENT, para 23.

**emboss.** See the 1st BOSS.

**embrace,** v hence n; hence also **embracement** (*-ment*). 'To *embrace*' comes from OF-MF *embracer* (F *embrasser*): *em-* for *en*, in+*brace*, the two arms (cf BRACE)+inf *-er*.

**embrasure,** adopted from EF-F, derives from EF *embraser*, later *ébraser*, to enlarge (an opening): perh from OF-F *embraser*, earlier *braser*, to set alight, from OF *breze*, later *braise*, fire: cf BRAZIER. The sem development is obscure. (B & W.)

**embrocation,** adopted from MF-F, derives from *embrocātiōn-*, o/s of ML *embrocātiō*, from *embrocāt-*, s of *embrocātus*, pp of LL *embrocāre*, to treat with moist dressings, from LL *embroca* (var *embroce*), *embrocha*, a moist dressing, from Gr *embrokhē*, lit a sprinkling, hence a lotion, from *embrekhein*, to foment: *em-* for *en*, in+*brekhein*, to wet, to moisten; cognates in Lett and Cz.

**embroider, embroidery.** See BROIDER.

**embroil, embroilment.** See the 2nd BROIL.

**embryo;** for cpds, see the element *embryo-*. *Embryo*, adopted from ML, derives from ML *embryon*: Gr *embruon*, from *en*, in+*bruein* (s *bru-*), to swell, perh akin to ON *brum*, a bud, with IE r *\*bhreu-*, to swell. *Embryonic* has been influenced by MF-F *embryon*, embryo.

**emend, emendation.** See MENDICANT, para 3.

**emerald**: ME *emeraude*: MF *esmeraude* (F *émeraude*): OF *esmeralde*: VL *smaraldus*, an easement of L *smaragdus*: Gr *smaragdos*, int of Gr *maragdos*: app from India, for cf Prakrit *magarada*, Skt *marakata*: ? ult Sem, for cf H *bāreqeth*, ? 'the glistener', from *bāraq*, to glisten, and Akk *barraḳta*, emerald.

**emerge, emergent, emergence, emergency.** See MERGE, para 3.

**emeritus.** See MERIT, para 3.

**emersion.** See MERGE, para 3.

**emery, smear.** *Emery*=late MF-F *émeri*, earlier *esmeril*: It *smeriglio*: Gr *smiris, smeris*, (the basic form) *smuris*, akin to Gr *muron*, unguent: IE r,*\*smor-*, var *\*smer-*: cf ON *smyr*, fat, butter, OHG *smero*, grease, OHG-MHG *smirwen* (G *schmieren*), ON *smyrva*, to smear, Go *smaithr*, fatness (cf Lith *smarsas*, fat), OIr *smir*, marrow; perh also L *medulla*, marrow. The OE cognate *smeoru*, or *smeru*, grease, fat, becomes ME *smere*, whence E *smear*, n; 'to *smear*' derives from OE *smerian*, from the OE n.

**emesis, emetic.** See VOMIT, para 2.

**emeu.** See EMU.

**emigrant, emigrate, emigration, emigrator.** MIGRANT, para 3.

**eminence, eminent.** See MINATORY, para 3.

**emir.** See ADMIRAL.

**emissary** (adj, n). See MISSION, para 11.

**emission.** See MISSION, para 11.

**emit.** See MISSION, para 11.

**emollient.** See the 2nd MEAL, para 16, s.f.

**emolument.** See the 2nd MEAL, para 12.

**emotion,** whence **emotional; emotive.** Cf *motion*; see MOVE, para 12.

**empathic, empathy.** See PATHIC, para 2.

**emperor, empress; empire;—imperator, imperatrix; imperative** (adj hence n); **imperial** (adj hence n).

1. *Emperor* is adapted from OF *empereor* (acc, the nom being *empereḍre, emperere*): L *imperātor*, lit a commander, from *imperāre* (s *imper-*), to command: *parāre*, to make preparations+*in*, in, into, against, (directed) at: f.a.e., PARE. OF *emperere* has f *emperesse*, adopted by ME, whence *empress*: cf the LL *imperātrix*.

2. L *imperāre* (s *imper-*) has derivative *imperium*, power over a family, over a great household, over a state, hence supreme power, empire, an empire, with LL adj *imperiālis*, whence OF-MF *imperial* (var *em-*), adopted by ME; the various senses of the n arise naturally, either from emperors in general or from some particular emperor, e.g. the beard, from Napoleon III, Emperor of France, 1852–70. *Imperium* becomes OF *empirie* (var *emperie*, whence the obs E *empery*), later *empire*, adopted by E. On *imperāt-*, s of *imperātus*, pp of *imperāre*, there arises in LL the adj *imperātīuus* (gram and mandatory), ML *-īvus*, whence *imperative*.

**emphasis, emphasize, emphatic.** See FANCY, para 10.

**empire.** See EMPEROR, para 2.

**empiric,** n hence adj with extn **empirical,** and also **empiricism, empiricist.** An *empiric* represents the syn L *empiricus*: n from Gr *empeirikos*, experienced, mdfn of syn *empeiros*, itself from *en*, in+*peira*, a trial or experiment: f.a.e., PERIL. *Empeiros* accounts for Psy *empirism*.

**emplacement.** See *place* at PLANE.

**emplastration.** See PLASM, para 6.

**employ, employment.** See PLY, para 15.

**emporium** (whence the adj **emporial**): L *emporium*, merchandise: Gr *emporion*, a trading-station, a market, orig the neu of *emporios*, pertaining to commerce: *emporos*, a traveller, hence a trader: *em-* for *en*, in+*poros*, a path, a way (cf, sem, *voyager* and Can *voyageur*): f.a.e., FARE.

**empower.** See POWER.

**emprise.** See PREHEND, para 10.

**emption.** See EXEMPT, para 2.

**empty**—adj, whence n and v, also **emptiness**—comes from OE *āemetig*, idle, empty, from *āemetta*, rest, leisure, idleness, quiet, but lit an interval: *āe-*, not, hence no+the r of (*ge*)*mōt*, a meeting: f.a.e., MEET, v.

empyreal (adj and n), empyrean: LL *empyreus*, var *-ius*, on fire, fiery: Gr *empurios*, var *empuros*: *em-* for *en*, in+*pur*, fire: cf *pyre* and, f.a.e., FIRE.

emu, occ emeu, an ostrich-like Aus bird: Port *ema*, ostrich, but also crane: o.o.o.: perh cf Eg *āḥāu* and *genu*, a crane, and esp Eg *nau* or *nu*, an ostrich, for the latter could be vocalized to *enu* and eased to *emu*.

emulate, emulation; emulous.

The 3rd comes from L *aemulus*, whence *aemulāri*, to equal by imitating, to be a rival of, to try to rival, with pp *aemulātus*, whence 'to *emulate*'; on the pps *aemulāt-* is built *aemulātiō*, o/s *aemulātiōn-*, whence *emulation*. *Aemulus* itself is o.o.o., but prob it is akin to L *imitāri*, to imitate, and to L *imāgo*, image.

emulgent, emulsify, emulsion. See MILK, para 2.

emunctory. See MUCUS, para 1, s.f.

enable. See HABIT, para 5.

enact, whence enactment (-*ment*), is to put something into (*en*) the form of an *act*: f.a.e., AGENT.

enamel (v, hence n). See MELT, para 5.

enamor (AE), enamour. See AMATEUR, II, 3.

enate, enatic. See NATIVE, para 9.

encamp, encampment. See CAMP, para 3.

encaustic. See CAUSTIC.

enceinte. See CINCH, para 3.

encephalic, etc. See CEPHALIC.

enchain. See CHAIN, para 4.

enchant, -ed, -er, -ment. See CHANT.

enchase. See the 2nd CASE, para 5.

encircle, encirclement. See CIRCLE, para 3.

enclave, adopted from MF-F, derives from MF-F *enclaver*: VL *\*inclāuāre*, *-clāvāre*, to shut, enclose, with a key, from L *clāuis* (ML *clāvis*), a key.

enclitic. See CLIME, para 12.

enclose, enclosure. See CLOSE, para 7.

encomiastic, encomium.

The former derives from Gr *enkōmiastikos*, eulogistic, the adj of *enkōmion*, formed of *en*, in+ *kōmos*, a revel (f.a.e., COMEDY), and yielding L, whence E, *encomium*.

encompass, -ment. See PACE, para 5.

encore. See HOUR.

encounter. See COUNTER, adv.

encourage, encouragement. See CORDIAL, para 5.

encroach, encroachment. See CROOK, para 8.

encumber, encumbrance. See CUMBER, s.f.

encyclical. See CYCLE, para 2.

encyclopaedia (AE -pedia), whence encyclopaedic, -paedist (cf the F *encyclopédique*, *encyclopédiste*), is a Sci L word, trln of Gr *enkuklopaideia*, from *enkuklios paideia*, education (*paideia* from *paideuein*, to educate a child, from *pais*, a child: cf PEDAGOGUE) in the circle (*en*, in=*kuklos*, a circle: cf CYCLE)—sc, of the arts and sciences.

end, n and v (whence ending), endless.

'To *end*' derives from OE *endian* (cf OFris *enda*), from OE(-ME) *ende*, whence 'an *end*'; whence also OE *endelēas* (cf LESS). OE *ende* is akin to OFris *enda*, *ende*, OS *endi*, OHG *endi*, usu *enti*, MHG-G

ende, Go *andeis*, MD *int*, *ent*, *ende*, D *einde*, ON *endi*, *endir*, and also Skt *ántas*, itself prob akin to adv *anti*, opposite; IE etymon, *\*anti*, opposite: cf the prefix *anti-*.

endanger. See DANGER, para 3.

endear, endearment. See DEAR, para 2.

endeavor (AE), endeavour. See DEBT, para 7.

endemic. See DEMOCRACY, para 2.

endive, adopted from MF, comes from ML *endīvia*: L *endīuia*: varr *intubum*, *intubus*, *intiba*, *intibum*, *intibus*: LGr *intubon*, *intubos*, *entubon*, *entubos*, (dim) *entubion*: o.o.o.

endless. See END.

endocrine (glands: secreting internally): prefix *endo-*, within+*krinein* (s *krin-*), to sift or separate: f.a.e., CRISIS.

endogamy, endogenous, endoplasm: *endo-*, within +c/f ee -*gamy* (at -*gam*), -*genous* (at -*gen*), -*plasm* (cf PLASM).

endorse, endorsement. See DORSAL, para 3.

endow, endowment. See DOWAGER, para 2.

endue. See DUKE, para 9.

endurable, endurance, endure. See DURABLE, final para.

enema: LL from Gr *enema*, from *enienai*, to send in, hence to insert: *en*, in+*hienai*, to send.

enemy. See AMATEUR, III, 3.

energetic, energic, energize, energy; energumen; —erg.

1. The base lies in Gr *ergon*, work, s *erg-*, whence the *erg* of Phys: and *ergon* stands for *\*wergon*, IE etymon *\*uergom*: see WORK.

2. Gr *ergon* has derivative adj *energos* (lit, being at work: *en-*, in), whence prob the E *energic*, which perh, however, derives from *energy*, itself from LL *energia*, trln of Gr *energeia*, an -*eia* (cf -*ia*) derivative from *energos*; *energos* has derivative v *energein*, to be at work, be active, whence the adj *energētikos*, E *energetic*. *Energein* has pp passive *energoumenos*, (lit) activated, hence possessed of a devil, whence, via LL, the E *energumen*, one so possessed. 'To *energize*'=*energy*+*-ize*.

3. Gr *ergon*, work, occurs also in:

*allergy*, altered susceptibility, a Med term often misused: *all-*, for *allo-*, other+*-ergy*, Gr c/f *-ergeia*, -work; adj, *allergic*;

*parergon*, a by-work: adopted, via L, from Gr: *para*, beside+*ergon*; adj, *parergal*;

*synergy*, combined Physio action: Gr *sunergia*: *sun*, with, (hence) together+Gr c/f *-ergia*; derivative Gr adj *sunergētikos* yields E *synergetic*; *synergism*, *-ist*, are E anl formations from *synergy*.

enervate, enervation. See NERVE, para 6.

enfant terrible, a very difficult child. See TERRIBLE and INFANT.

enfeeble. See FEEBLE, para 2.

enfeoff. See FEE, para 2.

enfilade. See FILAMENT, para 7.

enforce, enforcement. See FORCE, para 3.

enfranchise, enfranchisement. Cf *franchise*; see FRANK, para 6.

engage, engagement. See the 2nd GAGE, para 2.

engender. See GENERAL, para 7.

engine, whence, by suffix -eer or -er, engineer, n whence v, whence engineering (adj and n). See GENERAL, para 23.

English, adj hence n and v; obvious derivatives Englishman, Englishry; England (New England), Englander; Angles, Anglia, Anglian, Anglican (adj hence n), Anglicism, Anglicize.

1. England (whence Englander—cf Hollander— and New England, whence New Englander) conflates OE Engla land, land of the Engles or Angles: the OE Angle, var Engle, the Angles, take their name from Angul, the 'angular', lit 'hook-shaped', district now called Schleswig, itself from OE angul, a hook: f.a.e., ANGLE. The Angles, with b/f Angle, derive imm from Angli, the L shape of the Gmc name; Angli yields Anglia and Anglian; Anglic, whence Anglicism, comes from ML Anglicus, English, from Angli in its later, more general, sense 'the English (people)'. Anglicus has the late ML mdfn Anglicānus, English, whence Anglican, whence Anglicanism.

2. OE Engle, the Angles, has adj Englisc, whence E English: adj suffix -ish, esp as applied to nationality, as in Irish.

engraft. See GRAFT.

engrain. See GRAIN, para 1.

engrave, engraver, engraving. See the 2nd GRAVE.

engross, engrossment. See GROSS, para 2.

engulf. See GULF.

enhance (whence enhancement: suffix -ment) derives from AF enhauncer, alteration of AF enhaucer, from MF enhaucier, var of OF-MF enhalcier, itself a var of OF ensalcier; ens, in, used int+alcier, to raise, to heighten, from VL *altiāre, from L altus, high: f.a.e., ALTITUDE.

enharmonic. See HARMONY, para 3.

enigma, enigmatic.

The adj derives, via LL aenigmaticus and perh via MF-F énigmatique, from Gr ainigmatikos, of or like or by an ainigma—whence, via L aenigma, the E enigma—itself from ainissesthai (s ainis(s)-, r ain-), to speak darkly, hence in riddles, from ainos (s ain-), a fable or an allegory: perh cf the Go inilo, a plea, or a reason, to be excused.

enjoin. See JOIN, para 17.

enjoy, enjoyment. See JOY, para 3.

enlace, enlacement. See DELICACY, para 2, s.f.

enlarge, enlargement. See LARGE, para 2.

enlighten, enlightenment. See the 3rd LIGHT, para 2.

enlist, enlistment. See 1st LIST.

enliven, etc. See LIFE.

enmity. See AMATEUR, III, 3.

ennead, enneatic. See NINE, para 7.

ennoble, ennoblement. See NOBILITY, para 1.

ennui. See ODIUM, para 6.

enorm, enormity, enormous. See NORM, para 4.

enough, enow. See ADDENDA TO DICTIONARY.

enounce. See NUNCIO, para 5.

enquire, enquiry. See QUERY, para 10.

enrage. See RAGE, para 3.

enrapt, enrapture; enravished, enravishment. See RAPT (heading).

enrich, enrichment. See RICH, para 2.

enrobe. See ROB, para 2.

enrol(l), enrol(l)ment. See ROLL, para 6.

ensample. See EXEMPT, para 2.

ensconce. See the 2nd SCONCE, para 2.

enscroll. See SHRED (heading).

ensemble. See SIMULTANEOUS.

enshroud. See SHRED (heading).

ensign. See SIGN, para 15.

ensilage, ensili. See SILO.

enslave, enslavement. See SLAVE (heading).

ensnare. See NARROW, para 2, s.f.

ensue. See SEQUENCE, para 7.

ensure. See CURE, para 8.

entablature. See TABLE.

entail. See the 2nd TAIL, para 2.

entangle, -ment. See TANGLE, para 2.

entelechy: LL entelechia: Gr entelekheia, from entelekhēs, complete, from en telei ekhein, lit to finally hold (hold good), hence to be complete: en, in+telos, end+ekhein, to have, to hold.

entente. See TEND, para 12.

enter, entrance, entrant, entry, entrée.

'To enter' comes, through ME enteren, entren, from OF-F entrer, from L intrāre: in, in, into+tra- for trans, across+-āre, inf suffix. Entrance, adopted from MF, derives from entrer, presp entrant, whence the E adj and n; OF-F entrer has OF-F derivative entrée, orig the f of the pp entré; whence entry. Cf:

enteric, enteritis. See DYSENTERY, s.f.

enterprise, enterprising. See PREHEND, para 10.

entertain, whence entertainment, represents OF-F entretenir, lit 'to hold together': entre (L inter)+tenir, to hold, L tenēre: f.a.e., TENABLE.

enthral(l). See THRAL.

enthusiasm, enthusiast, enthusiastic, with b/f the coll 'to enthuse'.

The n comes, via LL-ML enthūsiasmos, from Gr enthousiasmos, divine possession or inspiration, from enthousiazein, to be god-inspired, from entheos, god-inspired: en, in+theos, a god: f.a.e., THEISM. The Gr v has derivative agent enthousiastēs, whence E enthusiast; the subsidiary Gr adj enthousiastikos yields enthusiastic.

entice, enticement.

The latter is adopted from OF-MF, which derives it from OF-MF enticier, whence, via ME enticen, the E 'to entice': and enticier, o.o.o., prob derives from VL *intitiāre: in, in+L titiō, a firebrand, o.o.o., but perh (Malvezin[2]) for *tiptiō, from tepēre, to be warm, IE r *tep-, heat.

entire, entirety. See TACT, para 19.

entitle. See TITLE, para 5.

entity. See ESSE, para 12.

entomic, entomology. See TOME, para 7, and cf the element entomo-.

entrails: OF-F entrailles: ML intrālia, mdfn of L intrānea, contr of interānea, pl of interāneum, intestine, prop the neus of interāneus, internal, prob suggested by L extrāneus: inter, between, among+adj suffix -āneus. Cf enteric at DYSENTERY, s.f.

entrain. See TRACT, para 4, s.f.

entrance, a way in. See ENTER.

entrance, to enchant. See TRANSIENT (heading).

entrant. See ENTER.

entrap. See TRAP.

entreat, entreaty. See TRACT, para 17.

entrée. See ENTER.

entrench, entrenchment. See TRENCH, para 4.

entrepôt. See POSE, para 12, s.f.

entrepreneur. See ENTERPRISE, s.f.

entropy. See TROPE, para 5.

entrust. See TRUE, para 4, s.f.

entry. See ENTER.

entwine. See TWINE.

enucleate, enucleation. See NUCLEAR, para 4.

enumerable, enumerate, enumeration, enumerator. See NIMBLE, para 5.

enuresis, enuretic. See URINE, para 7.

envelop, envelope, envelopment. See DEVELOP, para 1.

envenom. See VENOM.

enviable, envious, envy (n, v). See VIDE, para 14.

environ, environment, environs. See VEER, para 2.

envisage. See VIDE, para 2.

envoi, envoy. See VIA, para 15.

envy, n and v. See VIDE, para 14.

envy, to strive (archaic). See VIE, para 2.

Eocene; eolith. See the element eo-.

eon. See AGE, para 3.

epaulet, epaulette. See SPOON, para 6.

epée. See SPOON, para 6.

ephemeral; ephemerid, ephemerides; ephemeris.

*Ephemeral*=Gr *ephēmer*os, of—lasting only—a day: *epi*, upon, over+Attic *hēmerā*, a day, Homeric *hēmar*, Doric and Aeolic *āmerā*: IE r, *āmōr-*, varr *āmar-*, *āmer-*, *āmur-*. Gr *ephēmeros* has derivatives *ephēmeron*, a day fly, pl *ephēmera*, whence Zoo *Ephemera*, and *ephēmeris*, diary, calendar, hence anything ephemeral, with o/s *ephēmerid-*, whence both E *ephemerid*, a May fly, and Gr pl *ephēmerides*, adopted by E for 'publications of transient worth or interest'.

epic, epos. See VOCABLE, para 2.

epicene: L *epicoenus*: Gr *epikoinos*, common (*koinos*, s *koin-*: akin to L *cum*, with, *comēs*, a companion) to (*epi*, upon), sc both sexes.

epicure; Epicurus; Epicurean, whence epicurean, both being adj (whence epicureanism) hence n.

The Gr philosopher *Epikouros*, lit 'the assister or ally', L *Epicūrus*, whence E *epicure*, has adj *Epikoureios*, whence L *Epicūreus*, whence E *Epicurean*. This man's far from voluptuous, far from self-indulgent philosophy has been misunderstood to imply a refined sensuousness.

epideictic. See DICT, para 23.

epidemic. See DEMOCRACY, para 2.

epidermis, the outer skin, is a Gr word: *epi*, upon, over+*-dermis*, c/f of *derma*, skin.

epidiascope. See SCOPE.

epiglottis. See GLOSS, interpretation.

epigram, epigrammatic, epigrammatist. See GRAMMAR, para 4.

epigraph—whence epigraphic, -graphist, -graphy. See GRAMMAR, para 8.

epilepsy, epileptic (adj hence n).

1. The latter derives, perh via EF-F *épileptique*, certainly via LL *epilēpticus*, from Gr *epilēptikos*, adj corresp to Gr *epilēpsia*, whence, via LL *epilēpsia* and perh via EF-F *épilepsie*, the E *epilepsy*: and Gr *epilēpsia* derives from *epilambanein*, to seize: *epi*, upon+*lambanein*, to take, pp *lēptos*, derivative n *lēpsis*.

2. The cpd *katalambanein* (*kata*, down), to seize upon, has derivative *katalēpsis*, whence *catalepsy* (cf EF-F *catalepsie*), with E adj, formed anl, *cataleptic*, used also as n.

epilogue. See LEGEND, para 28.

Epiphany. Cf the element -*phane* and see FANCY, para 7.

episcopacy, episcopal, episcopate. See BISHOP.

episode, episodic. See ODOGRAPH, para 3.

epistemology. See the element *epistemo-*.

epistle, epistolary.

The latter derives, via EF-F *épistolaire*, from L *epistolāris*, the adj of *epistola*, inferior to *epistula*, lit a sending, esp of a letter, hence the letter itself: trln of Gr *epistolē*, from *epistellein*, to send (*stellein*) to (*epi*): f.a.e., STALL. The L n becomes OF *epistle* (var *epistre*, F *épître*), adopted by ME.

epistrophe. See STRAP, para 3, s.f.

epitaph: (OF-MF *epitaphe*, from) L *epitaphium*, funeral oration: Gr *epitaphion*, prob the neu of *epitaphios*, delivered over (*epi*) a tomb (*taphos*, s *taph-*, akin to *taphros*, a grave, and *thaptein*, to bury, s *thapt-*).

epithesis, epithet, epithetic. See THESIS, para 9.

epitome, epitomize. See TOME, para 8.

epoch, whence epochal, derives—perh imm from EF *epoche*—from ML *epocha*: Gr *epokhē*, a check, hence a star's epoch (point of time), hence an historical period that is clearly defined: *epekhein*, to check: *epi*, upon+*ekhein* to hold, to have.

epode. See ODE, para 2.

eponym, eponymous. See NAME.

epos. See EPIC.

equability, equable. See para 5 (s.f.) of:

equal (adj, hence n and v), equality, equalize (whence equalization, equalizer); inequality; equable, equability; equate, equation, equator (whence equatorial); equity, equitable, inequitable, and iniquity, iniquitous;—egalitarian;—adequate, whence adequacy; inadequate, whence inadequacy;—equanimity, equanimous; equilibrate, equilibration, equilibrator, equilibratory; equilibrium, equilibrist; equinox, equinoctial;—such obvious cpds as equiangular—equidistance (perh from OF *équidistance*) and equidistant (EF-F *équidistant*, LL *aequidistans*, o/s-*distant-*: cf DISTANCE)—equilateral (EF-F *équilatéral*, ML *aequilaterālis*, from LL *aequilaterus*: cf LATERAL)—equipoise (cf POISE)—equipollent (MF-F *équipollent*, L *aequipollens*, o/s -*pollent-*: L *pollēre*, to be powerful: ? akin to *posse*, to be able)—equipotential (cf POTENT)—equivalent (MF-F *équivalent*, LL *aequiualens*, o/s -*ualent*, ML -*valent-*, from *aequiualēre*, to have equal power: cf

VALUE) and **equivalence** (via MF-F *équivalence* from ML *aequivalentia*—**equivocal** (LL *aequiuocus*, ML *-vocus*: cf VOICE) and **equivocate** (ML *aequivocātus*, pp of *aequivocāre*, to call by the same name, from LL *aequiuocus*) and, perh via MF-EF, **equivocation** (ML *aequivocātiō*, o/s *-vocatiōn-*: from the ML pp) and **equivoque** (MF-F adj, hence, EF-F n, *équivoque*, from LL *aequiuocus*, ML *-vocus*).

1. The key to all these words is the L *aequus*, (of ground, etc.) even, (of things, then of abstracts) equal: o.o.o.; but perh (Webster) cf Lith *aikstus*, level, wide, for *aequus* has s and r *aequ-*, and the IE r is perh *\*aikw-*; which, esp if *\*aikw-* is for *\*waikw-*, the etymon being *\*aikwos*, ? for *\*waikwos*, leads one to surmise a possible kinship to Gr *isos* (s and r *is-*), Arcadian and Cretan *\*wiswos*, s and r *\*wisw-*.

2. L *aequus* has the following derivatives relevant to E: *aequālis*; *aequāre* (pp *aequātus*, derivative adj, *aequābilis*); *aequitās*; and c/f *aequi-* (becoming E *equi-*).

3. L *aequālis* becomes E *equal*; its subsidiary *aequālitās* becomes MF-EF *equalité*, whence E *equality*; its opp, L *inaequālitās*, becomes MF *inequalité*, whence E *inequality*; E *equalize* derives from EF *equaliser*, which=EF *equal*+*-iser* (L *-izāre*).

4. *Aequālis* becomes OF-EF *equal*, whence F *égal*, whence *égalité*, equality, whence *égalitaire*, whence E *egalitarian*.

5. L *aequus* has derivative v *aequāre* (vt), to level, to render equal, hence to equal, to equalize. Its pp *aequātus* yields 'to *equate*'; subsidiary L *aequātiō*, o/s *aequātiōn-*, yields *equation*, and subsidiary agent LL *aequātor*, an equalizer, becomes E *equator* (cf the MF-F *équateur*). Also from *aequāre* derives *aequābilis*, equal in all its parts, capable of being equalled or equalized, hence equitable, (of temper) constant: whence E *equable*. Derivative *aequābilitās* becomes E *equability*.

6. L *aequus* has the further derivative *aequitās*, 'equalness', but usu in the sense of its E (via MF-F *équité*) derivative *equity*; MF *equité* (F *équité*) has the EF derivative *équitable*, whence E *equitable*. The neg *inequitable* is adopted from EF *inequitable*, itself from EF *inequité*, whence E *inequity*— contrast *iniquity*, ME *iniquitee*, OF-F *iniquité*, L *iniquitās* (o/s *iniquitāt-*), unevenness of ground, hence general inequality, from *iniquus*, uneven, hence of unequal, hence unfair, dealing: *in-*, not+ *-iquus*, c/f of *aequus*. The E *iniquitous*=*iniquity*+ adj suffix *-ous*; contrast MF-F *inique*, direct from L *iniquus*.

7. The L *aequāre* of para 5, with its pp *aequātus*, has a cpd *adaequāre*, to render truly level or equal, *ad-* (to) being int; its pp *adaequātus* yields E *adequate*, whence *adequacy*—cf *accuracy* from *accurate*. E forms the neg *inadequate*, whence *inadequacy*.

8. The (except to a 'Classic') non-obvious cpds of prime importance are these:

*equanimity*, EF *équanimité*, L *aequanimitās* (o/s *-animitāt-*), from L *aequanimis*, of an equal *animus* or mind or spirit; from the LL var *aequanimus* comes the E *equanimous*;

*equilibrate*, LL *aequilibrātus*, equally balanced, from LL *aequilibrāre*, to balance equally, from *libra*, a balance (cf LIVRE); derivative LL *aequalibrātiō*, o/s *-librātion-*, yields E *equilibration*; derivative ML *aequilibrātor* becomes E *equilibrator* which prompts the adj *equilibratory*;

*equilibrium*, L *aequilibrium*, from *aequilibris*, equally balanced, from *libra*; L *aequilibrium* becomes EF-F *équilibre*, whence F *équilibriste*, whence the E *equilibrist*, a tight-rope walker;

*equinox*, (perh via MF-F *équinoxe*, from) L *aequinoctium*, night (*nox*: cf NOCTURNAL) equal to day, with adj *aequinoctiālis*, whence E *equinoctial*.

**equanimity, equanimous.** See prec, para 8, and esp ANIMAL, para 6.

**equate, equation, equator.** See EQUAL, para 5.

**equerry**: by a confusion of F *écurie* (MF *escuerie*, ? from OHG *scūra*, barn), a stable, and OF-MF *escuier* (F *écuyer*), a squire (cf SCUTCHEON), and L *equus*, a horse (cf next): orig a large stable, hence the officer in charge.

**equestrian, equestrienne: equine; equitation.**

The 2nd is mock-F for the 1st in its n use; the 1st adds suffix *-ian* to *equestr-*, the o/s of L *equester*, adj of *equēs* (agential *-ēs*), horseman, from *equus*, a horse, as also is the adj *equīnus* (suffix *-īnus*), whence E *equine*; *equitation* comes from L *equitātiōn-*, o/s of *equitātiō*, horsemanship, from *equitāt-*, s of *equitātus*, pp of *equitāre*, to be an *equēs* or horseman. L *equus*, s *equ-*, is akin to Gaul *\*epos*, OE *eoh*, OS *ehu*, Go *aihwa-*, Skt *aśvas*.

**equidistance, equidistant.** See EQUAL, terms of ref, s.f.

**equilateral.** See EQUAL, terms of ref, s.f., and LATERAL, para 2.

**equilibrate, equilibration, equilibrator.** See EQUAL, para 8, and DELIBERATE, para 3.

**equilibrist, equilibrium.** See EQUAL, para 8.

**equiliteral.** See LETTER, para 7.

**equine.** See EQUESTRIAN.

**equinoctial, equinox.** See EQUAL, s.f.

**equip, equipage, equipment.** See SHIP, para 4.

**equipoise.** See PEND, para 9.

**equipollent; equipotential.** See EQUAL, terms of ref, cpds.

**equitable.** See EQUAL, para 6.

**equitation.** See EQUESTRIAN.

**equity.** See EQUAL, para 6.

**equivalence, equivalent.** See VALUE, para 16.

**equivocal, equivocate, equivocation, equivoque.** See EQUAL (heading, s.f.) and VOCABLE, para 9.

**era**, a chronological system, hence a fixed time-point for dating, hence an epoch, comes from LL *aera*, era, L items in an account, brass counters, the pl of *aes* (o/s *aer-*), brass: f.a.e., ORE.

**eradicable, eradicate, eradication, eradicator.** See RADICAL, para 8.

**erase, eraser, erasion.** See RASE, para 1.

**ere** (adv, early, soon, sooner; hence conj, before); **erst, erstwhile;** sep **early.**

The adv *ere* derives from OE *āēr*, prop a comp adv (sooner, earlier), hence also prep and conj: akin to OFris, OS, OHG *ēr*, Go *aīr*, ON *ār*, early, Gr *ēri*, in the early morning. The OE sup *āērest*, soonest, earliest, yields archaic E *erst*, formerly, with extn *erstwhile*, in former times, and is akin to OFris *ērst*, for *ērost* (and *-est* or *-ist*), OHG *ērist*.

erect, erectile, erection, erector. See REX, para 31.

eremic, eremite. See the first RARE, para 2.

erept, ereption. See RAPT, para 11.

erg. See ENERGETIC, para 1.

ergo. See REX, para 33.

Erin. See IRISH, para 1.

ermine; Armenia, Armenian.

1. *Ermine*, a weasel coated in pure white, hence its fur, is OF-MF *ermine* (F *hermine*), perh of Gmc origin, for cf OE *hearma*, OHG *harmo*, weasel, and the OHG dim *hermelēn*, weasel, in MHG esp the white winter fur (Walshe); but prob the f of the OF adj (*h*)*ermin*, Armenian, from L *Armenius*, and therefore elliptical for *Armenius mus*, Armenian rat—this weasel was 'so named because it abounded in Asia Minor' (B & W).

2. L *Armenius* is the adj of L *Armenia*, adopted from Gr; *Armina* in the inscriptions of the Achaemides, the royal house of Ancient Persia; ult, *Armina* or *Armenia* derives, app, from *Haykh* or *Haïk*, Noah's great-great-grandson, who settled there (*Genesis*, x, 3)—hence *Hayastan*, *Haiastan*, the Arm name of the country. (Enci It.)

erode, erodent. See RAT, para 3, s.f.

erogate, erogation. See ROGATION, para 7.

Eros; erotic (whence eroticism).

*Erotic* comes from Gr *erōtikos*, the adj of *erōs*, sexual love, personified as *Erōs*, whence E *Eros*, from *eramai*, Attic *eraō*, I love, s *era-*, perh akin to Skt *arıs*, amorous, desirous.

erosion, erosive. See RAT, para 3, s.f.

erotic. See EROS.

err, to wander, hence to fall into error, whence pa erring; erratic, erratum (pl errata); erroneous; error.

1. The base is L *errāre*, to wander, hence to be deceived, r *er-*, perh akin to Go *airz*jan, to stray. 'To err' has passed through OF-F *errer*. L *errāre* has the foll derivatives relevant to E:

*errāticus* (*errāt-*, s of pp *errātus*), whence *erratic*;

*errātum*, prop the neu of *errātus*;

*erronēus*, whence *erroneous*;

*error*, adopted by E, although perh via OF-MF *error* (F *erreur*).

2. The prefix-cpd *aberrāre*, to wander away (*ab*, away from), has presp *aberrans*, o/s *aberrant-*, whence the E adj *aberrant*, whence *aberrancy*; on *aberrāt-*, s of the pp *aberrātus*, arises *aberrātiō*, o/s *aberrātiōn-*, whence E *aberration*.

errand: ME *erande*, earlier *arende*, a message: OE *āērende*, akin to OFris *ērende*, OS *ārundi*, OHG *ārunti*, ON *erendi*.

errant: adj from OF-F *errant*, presp of *errer*, to travel; VL *iterāre*, to travel, from *iter*, a journey: cf *itinerant* and, f.a.e., ISSUE; partly confused with

OF *errer*, to wander (cf ERR). Derivative, *errantry* (suffix *-ry*), esp in *knight-errantry*.

erratic. See ERR.

erratum. See ERR.

erroneous; error. See ERR.

ersatz, adj, derives from G *Ersatz*, a substitute.

Erse. See IRISH, para 1.

erst, erstwhile. See ERE.

eruct: L *ēructāre*, to belch (*ructāre*) forth (*ē*), with pp *ēructātus*, s *ēructāt-*, whence *ēructātiō*, o/s *ēructātiōn-*, whence E *eructation*. *Ructāre* is an int of *rugāre* (attested in *ērugāre*), to belch: ult echoic.

erudite, erudition. See RUDE, para 3.

erupt, eruption, eruptive. See RUPTURE, para 6.

erysipelas. See RED, para 17.

erythrin(e), erythrism, erythrite. See RED, para 16.

escalade (n hence v), escalator. See ASCEND, para 4.

escal(l)op. See SCALLOP.

escape (v hence n), escapade, escapement, escapism, escapist; scape, scapegoat.

1. 'To *escape*': ME *escapen*: ONF *escaper* (OF-MF *eschaper*, whence F *échapper*): VL *excappāre*: L *ex*, out of (here, by extrication)+*cappa* (f.a.e., the garment CAPE). Cf the Sp *escapar* and It *scappare*.

2. It *scappare* has derivative *scappata*, whence EF-F *escapade*, adopted by E. *Escape*, v, adds *-ment* to form *escapement*, anl to OF-MF *eschappement*, F *échappement*. *Escapism* and *escapist* are hybrid E formations in abstract *-ism* and agential *-ist*.

3. 'To *escape*' has aphetic var '*scape*, whence the n *scape*.

escarp, escarpment. See SCARP.

eschalot. See SCALLION, para 2.

eschar. See the 2nd SCAR.

eschatology. See the element *eschato-*.

escheat. See CADENCE, para 7.

eschew (whence eschewal): ME *eschuen*, earlier *escheven*: OF-MF *eschiuver*, *eschiver*: like the OProv *esquivar*, from Frankish *skiuhan*: cf OHG *sciuhēn*, MHG *schiuwen*, G *scheuchen*, to scare away; f.a.e., SHY.

escort (n, hence—influenced by EF *escorter*—v): EF *escorte*: It *scorta*, a guide or a guard; from *scorto*, pp of *scorgere*, to discern, to lead: VL *excorrigere*, to thoroughly (int *ex-*) set right (*corrigere*: cf CORRECT and RIGHT.)

escritoire. See SCRIBE, para 8.

escrow. See SHRED, para 6.

escuage. See SCUTAGE, para 6.

escutcheon. See SCUTAGE, para 7.

Eskimo, whence the adj Eskimoan, usu written *Eskimauan*, was orig pl (F *Esquimaux*, It *Eschimesi*, Sp *Esquimales*) and has been adopted from the Danish reshaping of the Alg name for the tribes further north: cf the Abnaki *esquimantsic*, Ojibway *Askkimey*, raw-flesh eaters, Cree *askimowew*, he eats it raw.

2. By f/e from *Eskimo* (*dog*), in its E shortening

*Esky*, comes *Husky*, now *husky*, a tough Eskimo sledge-pulling dog, probably influenced by the coll sense 'strong' of HUSKY (adj).

**esophagus.** See the element *esophago-*.

**esoteric; exoteric.**

Whereas the latter comes, via LL *exōtericus*, from Gr *exōterikos*, external, from the ad *exō*, outside, from *ex*, out of, the former comes, via LL *esōtericus*, from Gr *esōterikos*, mdfn of *esōteros*, internal, from the adv *esō*, within, from *es*, var of *eis*, into.

**espalier.** See SPOON, para 7.

**esparto.** See the 2nd SPIRE, para 4.

**especial.** See SPECIAL, para 4.

**esperance, Esperanto.** See DESPAIR, para 2.

**espial; espionage.** See SPECTACLE, paras 19–20.

**esplanade.** See PLANE.

**espousal, espouse.** See DESPOND, para 4.

**esprit de corps.** See SPIRIT, para 4.

**espy.** See SPECTACLE, para 19.

**esquire.** See SCUTAGE, para 8.

**essay** (n and v), **essayist; assay** (n, v), whence **assayer, assaying.**

1. An *essay*=OF *essai*, a trial, an attempt, EF the literary composition, from OF-F *essayer*, to weigh, test, attempt, whence E 'to *essay*': and OF *essayer* derives, via VL *\*exagiāre*, from LL *exagium*, a weighing, hence a balance and also a fig testing, prob with ref to L *exigere* in its sense 'to weigh', but imm from Gr *exagion*, an assaying or testing. Cf EXACT and see ACT.—*Essayist* attaches agential -*ist* to E *essay*, n and v.

2. OF *essayer* (*essaier*) has ONF var *assaier*, whence 'to *assay*'; derivative ONF *asai* or *assai* yields the E n *assay*.

**esse, in; essence, essential** (adj hence n), **essentiality; quintessence, quintessential;—adsum;— interest** (n and v), whence pa **interested** and pa **interesting; disinterest** (n, v), pa **disinterested;— uninteresting;—absence, absent** (adj, v), **absentee, and presence, present** (adj, n, v), **presentable, presentation, presentative,** with **represent, representation, representative** (adj hence n); **prosit; entity;—is.**

1. The phrase *in esse*, in actual as opposed to potential being, exemplifies the L *esse*, to be, contr of *essere*: *es-*+euphonic -*s*-+inf suffix -*ere*. The r *es-* is very widely represented in the IE languages —Gr, L, Gmc, Sl, Skt, Hit, etc.—and is linked with ETYMOLOGY and SOOTH: that which is, exists; that which exists, is true.

2. *Esse* lacks both presp and pp; but presp *\*essens*, o/s *essent-*, is presupposed in certain words, and presp *ens* is a Phil creation (see para 12). On *essent-* is formed L *essentia*, being, whence OF-F, whence E, *essence*; its derivative LL adj *essentiālis* (of, by, for being) yields OF-F *essentiel* and E *essential*, whence the neg *inessential*; subsidiary LL *essentiālitās*, o/s *essentiālitāt-*, yields *essentiality*.

3. The fifth (and last, as well as the supreme) essence, i.e. power, of a natural body was, in medieval scholastic philosophy, known in ML as *quinta* (fifth) *essentia*: whence MF *quinte essence*, whence F *quintessence*, adopted by E, with adj *quintessential*—obviously after *essential*.

4. L *esse* has several prefix-cpds relevant to E: *abesse, adesse, interesse, praeesse, prodesse.*

5. *Abesse*, to be *ab* or away, has presp *absens*, where -*sens* is influenced by *sum*, I am; the o/s is *absent-*, whence, via MF-F, the E adj *absent*; derivative *absentia* passes through MF-F to become E *absence*. MF-F *absent* has derivative MF-F (*s'*)*absenter*, whence 'to *absent* oneself', whence *absentee*.

6. *Adesse*, to be *ad* or at, hence present, has *adsum*, I am here.

7. *Interesse*, to be *inter* or between, hence to be vitally concerned, hence to be important, esp in (e.g., *mihi*) *interest*, it is important—of interest— to (e.g., me): whence, via MF-EF *interest* (F *intérêt*), with intervention of ML *interesse*, usury (also, compensation), the EE *interess*, E *interest*. EE *interess* has derivative 'to *interess*', whence, via the pp *interess'd*, the E 'to *interest*'.

8. *Praeesse*, to be *prae* or before, hence in view, has presp *praesens* (with -*sens* as in *absens*), o/s *praesent-*, whence, via OF-MF (F *pré-*), the E adj *present*; from the n use of the OF-MF *present* comes the E n; the L derivative *praesentāre* becomes OF-MF *presenter* (F *pré-*) whence 'to *present*'. OF-MF *presenter* has derivative *presentable*, adopted by E. L *praesentāre*, pp *praesentātus*, has derivative *praesentātiō*, o/s *praesentātiōn-*, whence, via MF, the E *presentation. Presentative* is an E anl formation.

9. *Praesentāre* has subsidiary *repraesentāre*, whence OF-MF *representer* (F *repré-*), whence 'to *represent'*. Derivative L *repraesentātiō*, o/s *repraesentātiōn-*, passes through MF-F to become E *representation*, with derivatives *representational, representationism*, etc. The ML *repraesentātīvus* becomes, perh via EF-F, *representative*.

10. Like *adesse, prōdesse* (to be *prō* or forward, to be for, hence to be useful) affects E in a survival: *Prosit*, May he prosper, esp as a toast.

11. *Disinterest*, n, v=*dis*+E *interest*, n, v. The v yields *disinterested*, free of ulterior motives.

12. The Phil presp *ens*, as in para 2, has o/s *ent-* and is used as a Phil n (gen *entis*, pl *entia*), thing, material object; derivative ML *entitās*, o/s *entitāt-*, yields—perh via EF-F *entité*—the E *entity*. Cf Gr *ta onta*, existing—hence real—things, as in *ontology*: indeed, the L presp *ens* was created to translate the Gr presp *ōn*, gen *ontos*.

13. Akin to L *est*, he is, hence to syn Gr *esti* and Skt *asti*, is the E (from OE) *is*: cf OFris and OS *is*, and Go *ist*; also Lith *est* or *esti*, and Hit *ēszi*.

**essoin.** See SOOTH, para 3.

**establish, establishment.** See STABLE, adj.

**estacade.** See STAKE, para 4.

**estancia.** See STAND, para 9.

**estate.** See STAND, para 15.

**esteem** (v hence n); **estimable; estimate** (v hence n), **estimation, estimative.**

L *aestimāre*, to fix the price or the value of, or

to calculate it, has s *aestim-*; the L derivation from *aes*, brass, hence money, is prob the correct one. *Aestimāre* becomes MF-F *estimer*, whence 'to *esteem*'. L derivatives include *aestimābilis*, whence, prob via MF-F, the E *estimable*, and *aestimātiō*, o/s *aestimātiōn-*, whence, via MF-F, the E *estimation*; E *estimative* is an anl formation. *Aestimātiō* is built upon *aestimāt-*, s of the pp *aestimātus*, whence 'to *estimate*'.

**ester.** See ETHER.

**estival.** See the element *estivo.*

**estop, estoppage, estopped.** See STOP, para 3.

**estrade.** See STRATUM, para 4.

**estrange.** See STRANGE, para 1.

**estray.** See STRATUM, para 8.

**estreat.** Cf *treat*; see TRACT, para 16.

**estuary,** whence the adj *estuarine* (cf *riverine* from *river*), comes from L *aestuārium*, itself from *aestus* (gen -*ūs*), sea-swell, orig burning heat, hence the bubbling of boiling water; IE r, *\*es-*, as in Skt *édhas*, Av *aesmo*, OPer *hēzum*, firewood. Cf ETHER.

**esurience** derives from **esurient**, voracious: L *ēsurient-*, o/s of *ēsuriens*, presp of *ēsurīre*, to be hungry, desid of *edere*, f.a.e., EAT.

**etch** (whence the vn **etching** and the agent **etcher**): D *etsen*, to etch: MHG *etzen*, to corrode, OHG *ezzēn*: Gmc *\*atjan* caus of *\*etan*, to eat: f.a.e., EAT.

**eternal, eternity.** See AGE, para 3.

**etesian.** See WETHER, para 7.

**ethane**=*eth*er+Chem -*ane.*

**ether; ethereal,** whence **ethereality** and **etherealize; etherize; ester.**

1. *Ester* is a G blend of *äther*, ether+*saure*, acid: *äther*=L *aether*, whence E *ether*: *aether*=Gr *aithēr*, the upper air, clear sky, whence imaginatively by Sci for the liquid and the anaesthetic. Gr *aithēr* (s *aith*-) is akin to *aithein* (s *aith*-), to burn brightly, and to Skt *īdhryás*, of or like the brilliance of a clear sky; IE r, *\*aidh-*, to burn. Cf ESTUARY.

2. 'To *etherize*'=*ether*+-*ize*; but *ethereal* substitutes -*eal* for -*eous* and derives from L *aethereus*, var of *aitherius*, trln of Gr *aithērios*, the adj of *aithēr*.

**ethic,** obsol adj—now usu **ethical**—and current n, now usu **ethics** (cf *mathematics, politics*, etc.); **ethicize** (*ethic*, adj+-*ize*); **ethos.**

*Ethic*, n, derives, via MF-F *éthique* and L *ēthica*, from Gr *ēthika, ēthikē*, elliptical for *ēthikē tekhnē*, the moral art, from the adj *ēthikos* (whence, via L *ēthicus* and EF-F *éthique*, the E adj *ethic*)—itself from *ēthos*, character, whence L *ēthos*, adopted by E, esp in sense 'character and spirit of a people': intimately akin to Gr *ethos*, custom, Skt *svadhá* (IE r *\*suedh-*), prop one's own doing or action: *sva*, self (cf *suicide*)+*dhā*, to set.

**Ethiop,** an Abyssinian: L *Aethiops*: Gr *Aithiops*, prob from *aithe*in, to burn+*ōps*, face: 'a sunburnt, hence swarthy, man'. The derivative Gr adj *Aithiopikos* accounts for *Aithiopia* (*khōra*), whence L *Aethiopia* (*regiō*), the E *Ethiopia*; and syn Gr *Aithiopikos* becomes L *Aethiopicus*, whence E

*Ethiopic.* The E adj and n *Ethopian* app derives from *Ethiopia*. Gr *Aithiops*, however, is perh f/e for Eg *áthtiu-ábu*, robbers of hearts, ? conquerors, from *áthu*, robber, conqueror.

**ethnic** (with extn **ethnical**); c/f *ethno-*, q.v. for ethnology, etc.

*Ethnic*, racial, derives, via L *ethnicus*, from Gr *ethnikos*, the adj of *ethnos*, a nation, a race, prob akin to *ēthos*, character, and *ethos*, custom (qq.v. at ETHIC), their s and r being *ĕth*- and *ethnos* prob consisting of r *eth*-+infix -*n*-+formative -*o*-+nom -*s*; perh cf Hit *udnē*, *udni*, or *utne, utni.* (Hofmann; Sturtevant.)

**ethos.** See ETHIC.

**ethyl:** *eth*er (q.v.)+Chem -*yl.*

**etiolate** (whence *etiolation*), to blanch or bleach, hence to render sickly, as if from SciL *\*etiolatus* but, in fact, from F *étioler*, perh for s'*éteuler*, to become like straw, from MF-F *eteule*: OF-MF *esteule*, stubble or straw: L *stupula*, var of *stipula*, a cereal stalk, straw: f.a.e., STUBBLE.

**etiology.** See the element *etio-.*

**etiquette.** See STICK, para 16.

**Etruria, Etruscan.** See TOWER, para 3.

**étude.** See STUDENT, para 3.

**etymology, etymological, etymologist, etymologize; etymon.**

*Etymon,* the orig form of a word, is L *etymon*, trln of Gr *etumon*, the 'true' or lit sense of a word adjudged by its origin, prop the neu of *etumos*, real, hence true, an extn of syn *eteos*, intimately akin to *etazein* (s *etaz*-), to prove, to establish as true, with r *et*-, formed by psilosis from IE *\*set-*, etymon *\*setos*, being, existing, therefore true: cf ESSE and SOOTH.

*Etymon,* Gr *etumon*, c/f *etumo*-, figures in the notable cpd *etymology*: OF-F *étymologie*: L *etymologia*: Gr *etumologia*: *etumo*-+-*logia*, discourse, c/f from *logos*, word, speech (f.a.e., LOGIC). The derivative Gr adj *etumologikos* becomes L *etymologicus*, whence EF-F *étymologique* and E *etymological*; OF-F *étymologie* has derivatives EF-F *étymologiser* and EF-F *étymologiste*, whence E *etymologize, etymologist.*

**eucalypt** (approx, gum-tree) anglicizes Sci L *Eucalyptus*: Gr *eu-*, well+*kaluptos*, covered, the pp of *kaluptein* (s *kalupt*-), to cover or conceal: cf CALYPSO. The buds are well covered.

**Eucharist, eucharistic.** See YEARN, para 2.

**euchre,** orig AE (*euker*, 1841; *euchre*, 1845), with v senses deriving from the n, is variously said to be G (etymon carefully unnamed) and F (*écarté* corrupted!) and o.o.o. At a mere guess, I propose derivation from EUREKA: cf, sem, the origin of card-game *snap.*

**Euclidean** (or -**ian**) is the adj of *Euclid*: L *Euclīdes*: Gr *Eukleidēs*, ? 'The Glorious', app a mdfn of *\*eukleios*, glorious, attested by *Eukleios*, epithet of Zeus. The famous Gr geometer flourished c300 B.C.

**eugenic** (whence **eugenics, eugenist,** etc.): Gr *eugenēs*, well-born: *eu*, well+-*genēs*, c/f of *genos*, offspring, race, stock: cf GENERAL, para 2.

eulogist, eulogistic, eulogize, eulogy. See
LEGEND, para 30.

Eumenides. See MIND, para 2.

eunuch: L *eunuchus*: Gr *eunoukhos*, n from adj
'guarding the couch': *eunē*, couch+*ekhein*, to
have, hold, keep, keep safe.

eupepsia, eupeptic. See the element -*pepsia*.

euphemism, euphemistic, euphemize.

The 3rd comes from Gr *euphēmizein*, to use
terms of good omen, to speak favourably: *eu*,
well+a c/f of *phanai*, to speak (f.a.e., FAME).
Derivative *euphēmismos* becomes *euphemism*,
whence the anl E formation *euphemistic*.

euphonious, euphony. See PHONE, para 4.

euphuism (adj euphuistic). Literary affectation is
called *euphuism* after John Lyly's *Euphues* (Gr
*euphuēs*, well-born), eponymous hero of two works
published c1580. This n and this adj recall
*euphemism*, *euphemistic* (as above).

Eurasian. See ASIA.

eureka. See HEURISTIC.

Europe, European (adj hence n), europium.

The 3rd (an element)=*Europe*+Chem -*ium*; the
2nd=EF *européen*, F *europeén*, from L *Eurōpaeus*,
trln of Gr *Eurōpaios*, adj of *Eurōpē*, whence L
*Eurōpa*, whence F and E *Europe*. Prob 'the broad
country': Gr *eurus*, broad, wide: Europe being a
region narrow from N to S, wide from W to E.

eurhythmics. See RHYTHM.

euthanasia, adopted from Gr, represents *eu*, well
(hence painlessly)+a c/f of *thanatos*, death, akin
to Skt *ádhvanīt*, (a light) is extinguished.

evacuant, evacuate, evacuation, evacuee. See
VACANT, para 5.

evade. See VADE, para 3.

evagate, evagation. See VAGABOND, para 4.

evaluate, evaluation. See VALUE, para 17.

evanescence, evanescent. See VACANT, para 11,
s.f.

evangel, evangelic(al), evangelist. See ANGEL,
para 2.

evanish. See VACANT, para 11.

evaporate, evaporation. See VAPID, para 4.

evasion, evasive. See VADE, para 3.

Eve: OE *Ēfa*: LL *Eva*, *Heva*: H *Ḥawwāh*, later
pron *Ḥavvāh*, lit 'Life'.

eve, even, evening; evensong, eventide.

1. *Eve*, evening, is a ME var of *even*: OE *ēfen*,
*āēfen*: akin to OFris *ēvend*, OHG *āband* (MHG
*ābend*, G *Abend*), OS *āband*, ON *aptanr* (for
\**aftanr*), perh also Gr *opse*, at evening, late, and
*epi*, upon, after. The Gmc etymon is app \**āēbandaz*.
(Walshe.)

2. OE *āēfen* has cpds *āēfensang*, whence *evensong*,
and *āēfentīd* (cf TIDE), whence *eventide*.

3. OE *āēfen* has derivative *āēfnian*, (of time) to
approach evening, whence *āēfnung*, whence *evening*.

evection. See VIA, para 12.

even (1), adj (whence v) and adv. The adv *even*
derives from OE *efne*, itself from the OE adj *efen*,
*efn*: akin to OFris *even*, var *iven* (adv *evene*, *efne*)
—OS *eban*, OHG *eban*, MHG-G *eben*, Go *ibns*,
ON *iafn* (*jafn*). *Evenly*: OE *efenlīce*.

even (2), n. See EVE.

evening. See EVE, para 3.

evenly. See 1st EVEN, s.f.

evensong. See EVE, para 2.

event, eventual. See VENUE, para 13.

eventide. See EVE, para 2.

ever, whence the cpds everglade, evergreen,
everlasting, evermore; every, whence the cpds
everybody, everyone, everything, (in part) everywhere;—never.

1. *Never* derives from OE *nāēfre*, not (*ne*) ever
(*āēfre*).

2. OE *āēfre* becomes ME *aefre*, later *ever*, extant
in E: it is prob a mdfn or extn of *ā*, always, cf
OHG *io* or *eo*, G *je*, ever.

3. OE *āēfre*, ever+*āēlc*, each (cf EACH), combine
in ME to form *everilk*, *everich*, later *everi* and, as
in E, *every*.

4. OE *gehwāēr* (int *ge*-+*hwāēr*, where) becomes
ME *ihwer*, which occurs also in the ME phrase
*ever ihwer*, very soon apprehended as *every where*,
whence E *everywhere*.

eversion, evert. See VERSE, para 15.

every; everywhere. See EVER, paras 3 and 4.

evict, eviction. See VICTOR, para 5.

evidence (whence evidential), evident. See VIDE,
para 14.

evil (adj hence n): ME *evil*, *evel*, *ifel*, *ufel*: OE
*yfel*, *yfil*: cf OFris *evel* (adj and n), OS *ubil*, OHG
*ubil*, MHG-G *übel*, Go *ubils*, MD *evel*, D *euvel*:
o.o.o., but perh akin to OVER (OE *ofer*) and UP
(OE *up*, *upp*): 'basic idea: transgressing' (Webster).

evince. See VICTOR, para 5.

eviscerate, evisceration. See VISCERA, para 3.

evitable; inevitable, inevitability.

1. *Evitable*, avoidable, comes, perh via OF-F,
from ML *ēvitābilis*, L *ēuitābilis*, from *ēuitāre*, to
avoid: *ē*, out of, used int+*uitāre*, to avoid, s *uit*-,
perh (E & M) a freq of *uiēre* (s *ui*-), to weave or
plait.

2. L *ēuitābilis* has neg *inēuitābilis*, ML *inēv*-,
whence (perh via late MF-F) *inevitable*, whence anl
*inevitability*.

evocable, evocation, evocative, evocatory, evoke.
See VOCABLE, para 10.

evolute, evolution, evolutionary; evolve. See
VOLUBLE, para 4.

evulse, evulsion. See VELLICATE, para 6.

ewe: OE *ēwe*, usu *ēowu*: akin to syn OHG *ouw*
or *ou* MD *ooye*, *oye*, *ooy*, D *ooi*, and to Go
*awēthi* (? s *awe*-), a flock of sheep; to ON *aer*, ewe;
to OIr *oi*, ewe, *óisc*, sheep (Ga *òisg*); to L *ouis*,
Gr *oïs* (for \**owis*), Skt *ávis*, a sheep, esp a ewe—
cf OSl *ovĭnŭ*, ram, *ovĭca*, ewe, Lith *avìs*, ewe: IE
etymon, \**ouis*, s \**oui*, r \**ou*-; Gmc etymon, \**awi*.

ewer. See *aqua*, para 4.

exacerbate, exacerbation.

The latter comes from LL *exacerbātiōn*-, o/s
of *exacerbātiō*, formed on *exacerbāt*-, s of *exacer-
bātus*—whence 'to *exacerbate*'—pp of *exacerbāre*,
to irritate very much: int *ex*+*acerbāre*, to irritate,
from *acerbus*, extn of *ācer*, bitter: f.a.e., EAGER.

exact, adj, derives from L *exactus* (prop, a pp),

precisely weighed or determined, precise, from *exigere*, to weigh, to achieve, but also to drive out, hence to cause to come out, whence, via the pp *exactus*, the E 'to *exact*', the derivative L *exactiō*, o/s *exactiōn-*, yielding, via MF-F, the E *exaction*. L *exigere=ex*, out, here partly int+*igere*, a c/f of *agere*, to drive: f.a.e., ACT. *Exactitude*, adopted from EF-F, is an -*itude* derivative from F *exact*. *Exactive*=ML *exactīvus*, LL *exactīuus*, extn of adj *exactus*.—Cf EXAMINE.

2. L *exigere* has presp *exigens*, o/s *exigent-*, whence E *exigent*; derivative ML *exigentia* yields *exigency*; *exigence* is adopted from MF-F *exigence*. *Exigere* (s *exig-*) has derivative adj *exiguus*, strictly weighed, hence too strictly weighed, whence E *exiguous*; subsidiary L *exiguitās*, o/s *exiguitāt-*, yields *exiguity*.

**exaggerate, exaggeration, exaggerative, exaggerator.**

'To *exaggerate*' comes from L *exaggerātus*, pp of *exaggerāre*, to heap up: *ex*, out (of)+*aggerāre*, to heap, from *agger*, a heap, from *aggerere*, to bring(*gerere*, s *ger-*) to (*ag-* for *ad*): f.a.e., GERUND. On pps *exaggerāt-* arise *exaggerātiō*, o/s *exaggerātiōn-*, whence E *exaggeration* (cf the EF-F *exagération*); LL *exaggerātiuus* (ML -*īvus*), whence *exaggerative*; LL *exaggerātor*, an increaser or a spreader, whence E *exaggerator* (cf EF-F *exagérateur*).

**exalt, exaltation.**

'To *exalt*' comes, via OF-F *exalter*, from L *exaltāre*, to raise high: *ex*, out of, used int+*altus*, high+inf suffix -*āre*: f.a.e., ALTITUDE. The derivative LL *exaltātiō*, o/s *exaltātiōn-*, yields, via MF-F, the E *exaltation*.

**examine** (whence examinee, examiner, examining), **examination.**

'To *examine*'=MF-F *examiner*: L *examināre*, from *examen*, the needle or tongue of a balance, hence a weighing, a control, an examination: *\*exagsmen* (? rather *\*exagmen*), from *exigere*, to weigh: cf EXACT, para 2, and for the r, ACT. On *examināt-*, s of the pp *examinātus*, is formed *examinātiō*, o/s *examinātiōn-*, whence E *examination*.

**example.** See EXEMPT, para 5.

**exanimate.** See ANIMAL, para 5.

**exasperate, exasperation.** See ASPERITY.

**Exaudi.** See AUDIBLE, para 4.

**ex cathedra.** See CHOIR, para 1.

**excavate, excavation.** See CAVE, para 3.

**exceed.** See CEDE, para 7.

**excel, excellence, excellency, excellent; excelsior.**

L *excellere*, to rise above—whence, perh via EF-F *exceller*, 'to *excel*'—is simply to rise (-*cellere*) out of (*ex*), hence above, hence above others: f.a.e., HILL. The L presp *excellens*, o/s *excellent-*, becomes OF-F *excellent*, adopted by E; its derivative *excellentia* yields, directly, the E *excellency* and, via OF-F, the E *excellence*. The pp *excelsus*, used as adj, has comp *excelsior*, higher, loftier, hence the motto *Excelsior*, ever upward, ever higher.

**except** (prep, v), **exception, exceptional.** See CAPABILITY, para 7.

**excerpt** (v hence n)—whence excerptive, excerptor—comes from L *excerptus*, pp of *excerpere*, to extract: *ex*, out of+*carpere*, to pluck, to gather (fruit): f.a.e., HARROW. Derivative L *excerptiō*, o/s *excerptiōn-*, yields *excerption*.

**excess, excessive.** See CEDE, para 7.

**exchange, exchangeable.** See CHANGE, para 4.

**exchequer.** See CHECK, para 2.

**excise**, a duty levied upon goods (hence exciseman), is o.o.o.; but prob from MD *excijs*, var of *accijs*, *assijs*: OF *acceis*, var of *accens*: VL *\*accensus*, from *accensāre*, to tax: *ad*, to+*cens*us, a tax+inf suffix -*āre*; f.a.e., CENSUS. B & W prefer to derive MD *accijs*, *assijs*, from OF-F *assise*, a tax, itself from *asseoir*, to seat: cf ASSIZE.

**excitable, excite, excitement.** See CITE, para 3.

**exclaim; exclamation, exclamatory.** See CLAIM, para 7.

**exclude; exclusion, exclusive.**

'To *exclude*' derives from L *exclūdere*, to shut (-*clūdere*, c/f of *claudere*) out (*ex*): cf CLAUSE. The pp *exclūsus*, s *exclūs-*, has derivatives *exclūsiō*, o/s *exclūsiōn-*, whence (perh via MF-F) the E *exclusion*, and ML *exclūsīvus*, whence (perh via late MF-F *exclusif*) the E *exclusive*.

**excogitate, excogitation, etc.** See COGITATE, para 2.

**excommunicate, excommunication.** See COMMON, para 4.

**excoriate, excoriation.** See CUIRASS, para 2.

**excrement.** See EXCRETE, para 2.

**excrescence, excrescent.** See CRESCENT, para 7.

**excrete, excretion, excretive, excretory; excrement,** whence adjj excremental, excrementitious.

1. L *excernere*, to sift (*cernere*: cf CERTAIN) out (*ex*), has Med sense 'to evacuate'. The pp *excrētus* yields 'to *excrete*'; its neu pl *excrēta*, used as n, is adopted by Med; but *excretion* (cf EF-F *excrétion*), *excretive*, *excretory* (cf EF-F *excrétoire*) are anl E formations.

2. Med *excernere* has derivative *excrēmentum*, whence, prob via EF-F *excrément*, the E *excrement*.

**excruciate, excruciation.** See CROSS, para 4.

**exculpate, exculpation.** See CULPABLE, para 3.

**excurrent.** See COURSE, para 10.

**excursion, excursive, excursus.** See COURSE, para 10, at *excurrere*.

**excusable, excuse.** See CAUSE, para 6.

**execrable, execrate, execration.** See SACRAMENT, para 17.

**executant, execute, execution** (whence executioner), **executive** (adj hence n), **executor,** **executrix.** See SEQUENCE, para 9.

**exegesis, exegete, exegetic(al).** See SEEK, para 8.

**exemplar, exemplary, exemplify.** See para 5 of:

**exempt** (adj, v), **exemption** (in para 4); **emption, emptor; peremptory; pre-empt, -emption, -emptive; premium; prompt** (adj, n, v), **prompter, promptitude, promptness, promptuary**—cf **pronto** and **impromptu; redemption, redemptive, Redemptorist, redemptory**—cf **redeem,** whence redeemable (neg irredeemable) and **The Redeemer** (cf **ransom** (n, v)—cf also **irredentism, irredentist; sample** (n, hence v), **sampler** (para 5)—**ensample**—**example** (n, hence v, whence, in turn, **unexampled**), **exemplar, exemplary, exemplify, exemplification** (para 5); cf, sep, the **as-, con-, pre-, re-, sub-sume** vv and their corresp nn in *-sumption* and adjj in *-sumptive.*

1. At the base of all these words: L *emere,* (orig) to take, esp to take for—in exchange for—money, hence to buy: akin to OSl *imǫ,* Lith *imù,* I take, and Lith *iṁti,* OP *īmt,* to take; C affords several cognates; the European (rather than IE) r is app *\*em-,* to take.

2. L *emere,* to buy, has pp *emptus,* s *empt-,* whence both *emptiō,* a buying, a purchase, o/s *emptiōn-,* whence E *emption,* and agent *emptor,* as in *Caveat emptoi,* let the purchaser beware!

3. Several L prefix-cpds are relevant to E: *eximere, perimere, \*prae-emere, prōmere, redimere.*

4. *Eximere,* to take aside (*ex,* out of), hence to put aside, hence to remove, to chase away, to deliver, to free. Its pp *exemptus* yields the MF-F adj *exempt,* adopted by E; MF-F *exempt* has the MF-F derivative v *exempter,* whence 'to *exempt*'; derivative L *exemptiō,* o/s *exemptiōn-,* yields— perh via MF *exempcion,* EF-F *exemption,* the n *exemption.*

5. *Eximere,* pp *exemptus,* has a derivative *exemplum,* whence MF-EF *example* (F *exemple*), adopted by E. The earlier *essamplle* (OF) has var *ensample,* whence E *ensample,* whence 'to *en-sample*'; OF *essample* also becomes ME *asaumple,* later—by aphesis—*sample,* adopted by E, whence 'to *sample*'. L *exemplum* has derivative adj *exemplāris,* whence both the E *exemplary* and the L n *exemplar,* adopted by E; L *exemplar* becomes OF *essemplaire, essamplaire,* whence, by aphesis, the ME *samplere,* whence E *sampler,* orig a pattern. *Exemplum* has the ML cpd *exemplificāre* (*facere,* to make), whence 'to *exemplify*'; derivative *exemplificātiō,* o/s *-ficātiōn-,* yields *exemplification.*

6. *Perimere,* to take thoroughly (*per,* through, used int), to destroy, has pp *peremptus,* s *perempt-,* whence *peremptōrius,* destructive, (in Law) decisive, final, whence *peremptory.*

7. *\*Prae-emere,* to take before (*prae*), has derivative *\*prae-emium,* whence L *praemium,* the first-fruits (of booty) offered to the victory-granting divinity or to the victorious general before the distribution of spoil takes place, hence legitimate reward, profit; hence the E *premium.*

8. *\*Prae-emere* links with F *préemption* and the prob independent E *pre-emption,* whence, by b/f, 'to *pre-empt*' and, by anl, *pre-emptive* and *pre-emptory.*

9. *Prōmere,* to take—hence, put—forward (*prō*), hence to bring up to date, to publish, to express, has pp *promptus,* used also as adj, rendered available, readily available, hence agile, prompt; hence MF-F *prompt,* adopted by E, with derivative nn *prompt, promptness,* and derivative ME *prompten,* whence 'to *prompt*', whence *prompter.*

L *promptus,* adj, has derivatives LL *promptitūdō,* whence late MF-F, then E, *promptitude* (cf the suffix *-itude*), and LL *promptuārius,* available, with neu *promptuārium* used as LL n, 'storehouse', whence, as E *promptuary,* a book of ready reference.

10. The L adj *promptus* becomes Sp *pronto,* adj hence adv, the latter adopted by coll AE.

11. *Promptus,* adj, has the derivative n *promptus* (gen *promptūs*), occurring only in *in promptu,* ready to hand, usu with *esse,* to be, or *gerere,* to bear, carry, or *habēre,* to have or hold; hence EF-F *impromptu* (Molière, 1659), immediately, (esp) without preparation, hence an improvised theatrical act or short piece (B & W); hence E adj, adv, n.

12. To revert to the L prefix-cpds: *redimere,* to take back (*re-*), hence to buy back, hence, in LL, to buy back from the Devil; hence—cf MF-F *rédimer*—'to redeem'. *Redimere* has pp *redemptus,* s *redempt-,* with derivative *redemptiō,* a buying back, o/s *redemptiōn-,* whence OF-MF *redemption* (later *ré-*), ME *redempcioun,* E *redemption,* the Christian sense dating from early LL; *redemptive* is an E anl formation; the derivative adj *redemptōrius* (L *-ōrius,* E *-ory*) leads to *redemptory; Redemptorist* = F *rédemptoriste,* from the L agent *redemptor* (cf *emptor* in para 2).

13. L *redemptiō* also becomes OF *raençon,* contr to *rançon,* whence ME *raunson* (or *-soun*), whence the E n *ransom;* 'to *ransom*' prob derives from *rançonner,* itself from MF-F *rançon.*

14. L *in-,* not + *redemptus* combine to form It *irredento,* unredeemed, as in *Italia irredenta,* whence *irridentismo, irredentista:* E *irredentism, irredentist.*

**exequies, exequy.** See SEQUENCE, para 10.

**exercise, exercitation.** See ARK, para 3.

**exert, exertion.** See SERIES, para 13.

**exeunt** is the pl ('they go out') of **exit.**

**exhalant, exhale, exhalation.** See HALITOSIS, para 2.

**exhaust** (v hence n), **exhaustion, exhaustive; inexhaustible.**

'To *exhaust*' comes from L *exhaustus,* pp of *exhaurīre,* to draw or drain (*haurīre*) out (*ex*): *haurīre,* s *haur-,* r *\*hau-,* is akin to Gr *auein* (s and r, *au-*), to drain, and *exaustēr,* a hook for pulling flesh out of a pot, and ON *ausa,* to draw out, to drain. Derivative LL *exhaustiō,* o/s *exhaustiōn-,* yields E *exhaustion; exhaustible* and *exhaustive* are E anl formations, the former with neg *inexhaustible.*

**exhibit** (v hence n), **exhibition** (whence **exhibitioner, exhibitionism, exhibitionist**), **exhibitory.** See HABIT, para 11.

**exhilarate, exhilaration.** See HILARIOUS.

**exhort, exhortation, exhortative, exhortatory; hortation, hortative, hortatory.**

1. L *hortor* (s *hort-,* r *hor-*), I urge, encourage, is the freq-int of OL *horior* (s and r, *hor-*), I cause to wish, I urge, akin to Gr *khairō,* I rejoice, *kharmē* (s *kharm-,* r *khar-*), warlike ardour, Skt *háryati,* he takes pleasure in, is fond of; akin also to OHG *gerōn,* to desire, and OHG *gerno,* MHG

*gerne*, G *gern*, willingly; IE r, *\*gher-*, var *\*kher-*, to desire. (E & M; Hofmann; Walshe.) The pp *hortātus*, s *hortāt-*, has derivatives *hortātiō*, o/s *hortātiōn-*, whence E *hortation—hortātīuus*, ML *-īvus*, whence *hortative—hortātōrius*, whence *hortatory*.

2. The cpd *exhortāri* is an *ex* int of *hortāri*; whence, via OF-F *exhorter*, the E 'to *exhort*'. On *exhortāt-*, the s of pp *exhortātus*, are formed *exhortātiō*, o/s *exhortātiōn-*, whence, prob via OF-F, the E *exhortation—exhortātīuus*, ML *-īvus*, whence *exhortative—*and LL *exhortātōrius*, whence *exhortatory*.

3. Cf YEARN.

**exhumation, exhume.** See HOMO, para 5.

**exigency, exigent.** See EXACT, para 2.

**exiguity, exigous.** See EXACT, para 2.

**exile.** See SALLY, para 12.

**exist, existence, existent, existential** (whence **existentialism, -ist**). See SIST, para 5.

**exit**, L for 'he goes out' (pl *exeunt*), like L *exeat*, let him go out, is used as an E n, influenced by L *exitus* (gen *-ūs*), a going out, likewise from the inf *exīre*: f.a.e., ISSUE.

**exodus.** See ODOGRAPH, para 4.

**exogamy,** adj **exogamous.** See the element *gamo-*.

**exonerate, exoneration, exonerative.** See ONUS, para 3.

**exorable.** See ORATION, para 6.

**exorbitance (-ancy), exorbitant.** See ORB.

**exorcise (-ize), exorcism.** See SARTORIAL, para 2.

**exordium.** See ORDER, para 11.

**exoteric.** See ESOTERIC.

**expand, expanse, expansion, expansive.**
'To *expand*' comes from L *expandere*, (vt) to spread out: *ex*, used int+*-pandere*, to spread out, a nasal vt cognate of *patēre*, to lie open: f.a.e., PACE. Pp *expansus* has neu *expansum*, whence the E n *expanse*; derivative LL *expansiō*, o/s *expansiōn-*, affords us, perh via EF-F, *expansion*; *expansive* is an anl E formation.

**expatiate, expatiation.** See SPACE, para 3.

**expatriate (adj, n, v), expatriation.** See FATHER, para 9.

**expect, expectant, expectation.** See SPECTACLE, para 11.

**expectorant, expectorate, expectoration.** See PECTORAL, para 2.

**expedience (or -cy), expedient; expedite, expedition, expeditious.** See FOOT, para 10.

**expel.** See the 2nd PULSE, para 10.

**expend, expenditure; expense, expensive.** See PEND, para 20.

**experience** (n hence v); **experiment** (n hence v), whence **experimental; expert, expertise.**

1. The r of L *perītus*, experienced (f.a.e., PERIL), takes prefix *ex* to form *experīri*, to try out, to test, with presp *experiens*, o/s *experient-*, whence *experientia*, whence, via MF-F, the E *experience*. *Experīri* has derivative *experimentum*, whence, via OF-MF, the E n *experiment*; the LL vi *experimentāre* has perh suggested the E 'to *experiment*' (cf the MF-F *expérimenter*). Derivative ML

*\*experimentālis* (deduced from the ML adv *experimentāliter*) yields EF-F *expérimental* and (? thence) E *experimental*.

2. *Experīri* has pp *expertus*, whence the MF-F adj *expert*, adopted by E, with derivative n; EF-F derivative *expertise* has likewise penetrated E.

**expiable, expiate, expiation, expiatory.** See PITY, para 4.

**expiration, expiratory, expire, expiry.** See SPIRIT, para 9.

**explain, explanation, explanatory.** See PLANE, para 10.

**expletive.** See PLENARY, para 13.

**explicable, explicate, explication, explicative, explicatory.** See PLY, para 12.

**explicit.** See PLY, para 12.

**explode.** See PLAUDIT, para 3.

**exploit (n, v), exploitation.** See PLY, para 13.

**exploration, exploratory, explore** (whence **explorer**).
'To *explore*' derives, via EF-F *explorer*, from L *explōrāre*, to cry (*plōrāre*) out (*ex*) at, e.g., the sight of land or enemy, hence to spy out: cf DEPLORE and IMPLORE, and the OF-F *pleurer*. The pp *explōrātus*, s *explōrāt-*, has derivatives *explōrātiō*, o/s *explōrātiōn-*, whence late MF-F, then E, *exploration*, and *explōrātōrius*, whence E *exploratory*.

**explosion, explosive.** See PLAUDIT.

**exponent, exponible.** See POSE, para 10.

**export** (v hence n), whence **exporter; exportation.** Cf *import*; see the 3rd PORT, para 8.

**expose, exposé, exposition, expositor, expository.** See POSE, para 10.

**expostulate, expostulation.** See PRAY, para 7, s.f.

**exposure.** See POSE, para 10.

**expound.** See POSE, para 10, s.f.

**express (adj, n, v), expression, expressive.** See the 2nd PRESS, para 7.

**exprobate, exprobation.** See OPPROBRIOUS.

**expropriate, expropriation.** Cf *property*; see PROPER, para 4.

**expugnable.** See PUNGENT, para 15.

**expulse, expulsion, expulsive.** See the 2nd PULSE, para 11.

**expunge.** See PUNGENT, para 20.

**expurgate, expurgation, expurgator, expurgatory.** See PURGE, para 9.

**exquisite.** See QUERY, para 9.

**exsert, exsertion.** See SERIES, para 12.

**exsufflate, exsufflation.** See INFLATE.

**extant.** Cf *instant*; see STAND, para 25.

**extasy.** See STAND, para 7.

**extemporaneous, extemporary, extempore, extemporize.** See TEMPER, para 11.

**extend; extension, extensive; extent.** See TEND, para 11.

**extenuate, extenuation, extenuatory.** See TEND, para 25.

**exterior** (adj hence n); **extern** (adj hence n), **external; extima; extreme, extremity; extrinsic: interior** (adj hence n); **intern** (adj hence n), **internal, intima, intimate** (adj—whence **intimacy**—

and v, whence intimation)--cf the obs intimous; intrinsic.

1. This intimate set of complementaries originates in L (with several very close parallels in Gr and Skt): and they stem from L *ex*, out of (connoting 'outside'), and *in*, in, into (connoting 'inside'): cf, therefore, IN and the prefix *ex-*.

2. Whereas the L adj *exterior*, adopted by E (cf the late MF-F *extérieur*), is the comp of *exter* (var *exterus*), placed on the outside, L *interior*, adopted by E (perh via MF *interior*, F *intérieur*), is a comp of adj *\*interus*, placed on the *inside*, from the prep *inter*, in between. *Exter* has mdfn *externus*, whence E *extern*, with extn *external* (whence *externality*, *externalize*, etc.); *inter* has adj-mdfn *internus*, whence (like *extern*, prob via late MF-F) E *intern*, with extn *internal* (whence *-ity*, *-ize*, etc.)—perh imm from the ML subsidiary *internālis*.

3. *Exter* has sup *extimus*, outmost, with neupl *extima*, balanced by (the sup of *inter*, viz) *intimus*, inmost, with neupl *intima*; *extima* and *intima* are techh of An and Zoo. For *intimate*, see para 7.

4. But whereas L *exter* has another sup, *extremus* (? for *\*exterrimus*), whence MF, hence E, *extreme*, with L derivative *extremitās*, o/s *extremitāt-*, whence MF-F *extremité*, whence E *extremity*, L *inter*, *\*interus*, has no such subsidiary. But then *intestīnus* (see INTESTINE) has no counterpart *\*extestinus*.

5. The correspondence, however, continues in the L advv *extrinsecus*, *intrinsecus*, on the outside, on the inside, resp from *exter* and *inter* (*\*interus*), with *-secus* prob deriving from *sequi*, to follow: 'outside-following' and 'inside-following'. *Extrinsecus* yields the LL differentiated adj *extrinsicus*, external, whence the MF-F adj *extrinsèque*, whence, though perh direct from L, the E *extrinsic*; *intrinsecus* yields the LL adj *intrinsicus*, whence MF-F *intrinsèque*, whence E *intrinsic*.

6. The MF-F adj *interne* (cf para 2) has derivative F *interner*, whence 'to intern', whence—unless from F *internement* (from *interner*)—*internment*.

7. The L adj *intimus*, inmost, becomes MF-F and EE *intime*, which becomes the adj *intimate*—whence *intimacy* (for *\*intimatecy*: cf *accurate-accuracy*)—as if from L *intimātus*, pp of *intimāre*, to make inmost to, hence to make known to, itself from *intimus*: and this pp *intimātus* accounts for E 'to intimate', to notify. On the pp s *intimāt-* arises LL *intimātiō*, o/s *intimātiōn-*, whence, prob via MF-F, the E *intimation*.

**exterminable, exterminate, extermination, exterminator, exterminatory.** See TERM, para 7.

**extern, external** (-ity, -ize). See EXTERIOR, para 2.

**extima.** See EXTERIOR, para 3.

**extinct, extinction, extinctor; extinguish,** whence **extinguisher.** See TINGE.

**extirpate, extirpation, extirpator, extirpatory.**

'To *extirpate*' derives from L *extirpātus*, pp of *extirpāre*, for *exstirpāre*, to root out: *ex*, out+ *stirp-*, s of *stirps*, stem, root+inf suffix *-āre*. 'A

root *\*stirp-* would, in IE, be surprising' (E & M): nothing would surprise me in IE; moreover, what of Lith *stirpti*, to grow up, and *tirpti*, to become stiff (Webster)? Derivatives *ex(s)tirpātiō*, o/s *ex(s)tirpātiōn-*, and *extirpātor* yield E *extirpation*, *extirpator*; E *extirpatory* is an anl formation. Cf TORPID.

**extol.** See the 1st TOLL, para 3.

**extort, extortion, extortionate, extortive.** See TORT, para 4—and heading.

**extra,** adj (orig coll): b/f from *extraordinary*, q.v. at ORDER.—Cf the prefix *extra-*.

**extract** (obsol adj; n; v), **extraction, extractive, extractor.** See TRACT, para 15.

**extradite, extradition.** See TRADITION, para 2.

**extramundane.** See MUNDANE, para 2.

**extramural.** See MURAL.

**extraneous.** See STRANGE, para 2.

**extraordinary.** Cf *ordinary*; see ORDER, para 11.

**extrapolate, extrapolation,** which look so very Latin, blend *extra-*, outside of (hence beyond)+ inter*polate, interpolation*.

**extraterritorial.** See TERRA, para 3, s.f.

**extravagance, extravagant, extravaganza.** See VAGABOND, para 4.

**extravasate, extravasation.** See VASE, para 1.

**extravert.** See EXTROVERSION.

**extreme, extremity.** See EXTERIOR, para 4.

**extricate** (Zoo adj; ordinary v), **extrication, extricable** and its neg **inextricable;**—**intricate** (ordinary adj, rare v), **intricacy, intrigue** (n, v), **intriguer.**

1. Both the *ex-* and the *in-* words rest upon L *trīcae* (pl) trifles, (? hence ironically) embarrassments, sources of annoyance or causes of impediment; perh orig a farming term for weeds (E & M): o.o.o.; ? a dial var of *triuia*, trivial matters; more prob from Eg *tchāā*, a weed, straw (cf *tchā*, a stalk).

2. L *extrīcāre* (s *extrīc-*) would then mean, to free from weeds, hence to free from embarrassment or worry, with pp *extrīcātus*, whence both the adj and 'to *extricate*'; derivative LL *extrīcātiō*, a disentangling, o/s *extrīcātiōn-*, yields E *extrication*; derivative *extrīcābilis* yields *extricable*.

3. LL *inextrīcābilis* yields *inextricable*.

4. L *intrīcāre*, to entangle, has pp *intrīcātus*, whence the E adj *intricate*, whence (for *\*intricatecy*) *intricacy*. L *intrīcāre* becomes It *intrigare*, whence EF-F *intriguer*, whence 'to *intrigue*', whence an *intriguer*; F *intriguer* has derivative EF-F n *intrigue*, adopted by E.

**extrinsic.** See EXTERIOR, para 5.

**extroversion, extrovert** (adj hence n), with var **extravert.**

These are E formations in L *\*extrō-* (from *extrā*, beyond)+*-version*, -turning, -version, and *-vert*, -turned, -changed: ML *vertere*, pp *versus* (L *uertere*, *uersus*): f.a.e., VERSE. They connote 'outward-looking', as opp *intro-*, or inward, -looking.

**extrude, extrusible. extrusion, extrusive.** See THRUST, para 4.

**extund.** See PIERCE, para 2.

**exuberance, exuberant.** See UDDER, para 3.

**exude, exudation.** See SWEAT, para 3.

**exult, exultant, exultation.** See SALLY, para 14.

**eyas.** See NETHER, para 7.

**eye** (n hence v), whence **eyebrow, eyeful** (adj and coll n), **cyelash, eyeless, eyelet, eyesome, eyetooth, eyewash,** etc.

An *eye* derives, through ME *eye*, earlier *eie*, still earlier *eige, ege*, from OE *ēage*: akin to OFris *āge*, OS *ōga*, OHG *ouga*, MHG *ouge*, G *Auge*, Go *augō*, MD *oge, ouge*, D *oog*; ON *auga*; OSl *oko*, Lith *akis*; Arm *akn* (gen *akan*); L *oc*ulus (orig a dim); Gr *okkon*, eye (cf *osse*, the two eyes); Skt *ákši*; Hit tun-*ak*alas, eye of the sun. IE etymon, *\*okus* or *\*okes*; Gmc r, *\*aug-*; IE r *\*ok-*, to see.

**eyre** (or **itinere**), **justices in,** applied to judges on circuit: *eyre*, from OF-EF *eire*, var of OF-(archaic) F *erre*, a journey, itself either from OF-MF *errer*, to go, to walk (cf ERRANT), or from L *iter* or irreg from L *itinere*, abl of *iter*, a going, a journey, from *īre*, to go: f.a.e., ISSUE.

**eyrie, eyry,** var **aerie, aery,** a predatory bird's (esp an eagle's) nest: ME *eire*, var of *airie, air*, nest, origin: syn OF-F *aire*: prob from L *ārea*, threshing-floor, also an eagle's nest: o.o.o.—Cf DEBONAIR.

# F

**Fabian:** L *Fabiānus*, of or like Fabius Cunctator, Fabius the Delayer, foiler (by delaying tactics) of Hannibal, c210 B.C.

**fable (n, v), fabular, fabulist, fabulosity, fabulous; confabulate, confabulation; affable, ineffable.**

1. 'To *confabulate*' derives from *confābulātus*, pp of *confābulāri*, to talk (*fābulāri*) together (*con*); derivative LL *confābulātiō*, o/s *confābulātiōn-*, yields *confabulation*.

2. *Fābulāri*, whence OF-MF *fabler* and E 'to *fable*', derives from *fābula*, a fiction, a tale, from *fāri*, to speak, say, tell: f.a.e., FAME. *Fābula* becomes OF-F *fable*, adopted by E; derivative adjj *fābulāris, fābulōsus*, yield *fabular, fabulous* (cf MF-F *fabuleux*); derivative *fābulōsitās*, o/s *fābulōsitāt-*, yields *fabulosity*; erudite EF-F *fabuliste* (from *fābula*) becomes E *fabulist*.

3. *Fāri* has another cpd derivative v: *affāri*, to speak to (*af-* for *ad*), with derivative adj *affābilis*, speakable-to, easy to speak to, whence MF-F, then E, *affable*. Derivative L *affābilitās*, o/s *affābilitāt-*, becomes MF-F *affabilité*, whence *affability*.

4. LL *effābilis*, utterable, from *effāri*, to speak out (*ē*), yields the rare *effable*, and the neg *ineffābilis*, yields late MF-F, then E, *ineffable*; derivative LL *ineffābilitās* (o/s *-fābilitāt-*) yields *ineffability*.

**fabric, fabricate, fabrication, fabricative, fabricator.**

L *faber*, a workman in hard materials—f.a.e., FORGE—has gen *fabri*, o/s *fabr-*, whence the adj *fabricus*, f *fabrica*, used for a workshop, also for a fabric, whence MF-F *fabrique*, whence E *fabric*. *Fabrica* has derivative *fabricāre*, to make with one's hands, to build, to forge, with pp *fabricātus*, whence 'to *fabricate*'. On the pps *fabricāt-* are formed LL *fabricātiō*, o/s *fabricātiōn-*, whence (perh via late MF-F) *fabrication*, and *fabricātor*, adopted by E, which anl coins *fabricative*.

**fabulist, fabulous.** See FABLE, para 2.

**façade.** See para 3 of:

**face (n hence v), facer, facing; façade; facet; facetious; facies, facial;—deface, defacement; efface, effacement, (self-)effacing; surface (n, hence adj and v);—superficies, superficial (whence *superficiality*), superficiary.**

1. The imm base is L *faciēs*, form or shape, esp that of the front of the head—the face; *faciēs* (s *faci-*, r *fac-*) derives from *facere* (s *fac-*), to make: f.a.e., FACT. *Faciēs* is retained by Bio and Geol.

2. *Faciēs* has LL adj \**faciālis* (cf LL *faciāle* face-towel or handkerchief: Souter), ML *faciālis*, whence EF *facial*, adopted by E, whence as n.

3. *Faciēs* becomes LL and VL *facia*, whence both OF-F *face*, adopted by E, and It *faccia*, whence *facciata* (cf the E suffix *-ade*), whence EF-F *façade*, adopted by E. The derivative 'to *face*' yields the pa and vn *facing* and the agent *facer*.

4. Akin to L *faciēs* is L *facētus* (s *facēt-*, r *fac-*), finely made, elegant, witty, whence the obs E adj *facete*. Witty sayings, also humorous, esp if coarsely humorous, sayings are, in L, *facētiae* (pl of *facētia*, from *facētus*), partly adopted by E. *Facētia* becomes late MF-F *facétie*, with derivative adj *facétieux*, f *facétieuse*, whence E *facetious*.

5. E *face* has cpd vv *outface* and *reface*; L *faciēs* occurs in two vv:

*deface*, ME *defacen*, OF-EF *desfacier*: *des-* for L *dis-*+L *facies*+inf *-er*; hence *defacement*;

*efface*: OF-F *effacer*: *es-* for L *ex*, out+F *face*+*-er*; hence MF-F *effacement*, adopted by E. OF-F *effacer* has another derivative borrowed by E: EF-F *ineffaçable*, whence *ineffaceable*.

6. OF-F *face* has the OF-F dim *facette*, whence E *facet*, used derivatively in, e.g., 'many-*faceted*'.

7. L *faciēs* has cpd *superficiēs*, the fact of being placed above, hence surface, external aspect; adopted in tech E. LL derivative adjj *superficiālis, superficiārius*, yield E *superficial* (cf the MF-F *superficiel*) and *superficiary*.

8. L *superficiēs* becomes EF *superface*, duly contr to *surface*, adopted by E.

**facetious.** See para 4 (s.f.) of prec.

**facial; facies.** See FACE, paras 2, 1.

**facile, facilitate, facilitation, facility.** See FACT, para 6.

**facsimile.** See SIMILAR.

**fact** (cf artifact), **factice, factitious**—**fetish; facile, facilitate, facilitation, facilitative, facility**—cf the sep DIFFICULT, DIFFICULTY; **faction** (whence **factional**)—cf fashion—**factionary, factitious; factive—factitive; factor, factory** (whence **factorial**); **factual** (whence **factuality**); **facture**—cf **manufacture** (n and v, whence **manufacturer**), **manufactory; faculty, facultative;—feat, feature,** cp sep DEFEAT; **hacienda.**—All cpds are treated sep, whether they are full (except *artifact, manufacture*) or prefix-cpds; the latter include *affect* (*-ion, -ive, -ionate*), *confect, defect, effect, infect, perfect, prefect,* etc.; *deficient, proficient, sufficient,* etc.;

195

*deficit; counterfeit, forfeit, surfeit; comfit (com-*
*fiture), profit,* etc.; *artifice, artificial,* etc.; *benefac-*
*tion, -factor, benefice, beneficent, beneficial,* etc.;
*malefactor, malefic,* etc.; *refectory; suffice,* etc.; the
numerous vv in *-fy,* e.g. *liquefy.* Cf the sep AFFAIR,
FACE, FEASIBLE, FIAT, and perh OFFICE.

1. The base, clearly, is L *facere,* to make, *facio,*
I make, (secondarily) I place; preterite, *fēci,* s *fēc-;*
pp *factus,* s *fact-;* presp *faciens,* o/s *facient-.* The
predominant c/f is *-ficere,* with pp *-fectus* and
presp *-ficiens,* o/s *-ficient-.* L *fac-* (*fēc-*) is ult akin
to Gr ti*thēmi,* I place, L *dō* (inf *dare*), I give, (but
also) I place, and E *do;* the IE r is *\*dhe-,* var *\*dho-.*

2. Pp *factus* has neu *factum,* used also as n
'thing done', whence E *fact.* Cf *artifact,* a thing
made by man's skill: *arti-,* c/f of *ars* (o/s *art-*),
skill, art+*fact.*

3. On *fact-,* s of *factus,* are formed the foll
derivatives directly relevant to E:

*factīcius,* made by art, whence both the F adj—
hence the E n—*factice* and the E adj *factitious;* cf E
*fetich* or *fetish,* from Port *feitiço,* sorcery, a charm,
n use of adj 'artificial', from L *factīcius;*

*factiō,* action or manner of making or doing,
(but also) position, o/s *factiōn-,* whence, prob via
MF-F, the E *faction,* esp a group taking up a
political position; derivative LL n *factiōnārius* has
form-suggested both the F *factionnaire* and the E
*factionary;* the cognate adj *factiōsus* (*facti-+*
*-osus*) becomes, perh via late MF-F *factieux,* f
*factieuse,* the E *factious,* much influenced, in sense,
by the E n;

*factor,* adopted by E, perh influenced by MF-F
*facteur;*

LL *factōrium* (suffix *-ōrium*), an oil-mill or
-press (Souter), has suggested at least the form of
E *factory,* usu derived from late MF-EF *factorie*
(cf F *factorerie*), itself from L *factor;*

*factūra,* a making, whence MF-F, hence E,
*facture,* now rare outside of *manufacture,* derived,
via EF-F, from ML *manūfactūra,* a making by
hand (*manu,* abl of *manus:* f.a.e., MANUAL: cf LL
*manūfactilis,* hand-made); the F n *manufacture* has
the derivative EF-F v *manufacturer,* whence 'to
*manufacture*', whence *manufacturer; manufactory*
blends manu*facture+factory.*

4. L *factiō,* acc *factiōn*em, becomes OF *fazon,*
MF-F *façon,* whence ME *facioun, fasoun,* whence
E *fashion;* the F n has the derivative OF v *fazonner,*
later *façonner,* whence 'to *fashion*', whence *fashionable,* (lit) capable of being fashioned. The predominant social sense of *fashion* arose early in
C16, via the sense 'a special manner of making'
clothes.

5. E *fact* has its own derivatives: *factive* (adj
*-ive*)—contrast the similar *-ive* formation *factitive,*
causative, from L *factitare,* the freq of *facere;*
*factual,* being *fact*+adj *-ual,* after *actual.*

6. Reverting to *fac-,* the s of L *facere,* we find
several L derivatives directly relevant to E:

adj *facilis* (s *facil-*), 'doable', makable, hence
easily done or made; whence MF-F *facile,* adopted
by E derivative *facilitās,* o/s *facilitāt-* yields

MF-F *facilité,* therefore E *facility;* o/s *facilitāt-*
has an It derivative, *facilità,* whence *facilitare,* to
render easy, whence late MF-F *faciliter,* which
prompts E 'to *facilitate*', whence, anl, *facilitation*
and *facilitative;*

*facilis* has a further derivative—*facultās,* ability,
aptitude, o/s *facultāt-,* whence, via late OF-F
*faculté,* the E *faculty;* the derivative late EF-F adj
*facultatif,* f *-ive,* accounts for E *facultative.*

7. L *factum* (n) becomes OF-F *fait,* with OF-
MF var *fet,* both adopted by ME, the latter
emerging as E *feat.*

8. L *factūra* (as in para 3) becomes OF-MF
*faiture,* whence ME *feture,* whence E *feature,*
whence 'to *feature*'.

9. L *facere* has gerundial neupl *facienda,* things
to be done, form-adopted by OSp and thereby
sense-adapted to 'employment, hence a place of
employment, hence an estate', which duly becomes
Sp *hacienda* (cf *hacer,* to make or do), esp a large
estate, adopted by AE.

**faction, factious.** See prec, para 3.
**factitious.** See FACT, para 3.
**factitive.** See FACT, para 5.
**factor.** See FACT, para 3.
**factory.** See FACT, para 3.
**factotum.** See TOTAL, para 5.
**factual.** See FACT, para 5.
**facture.** See FACT, para 3.
**faculty.** See FACT, para 6, s.f.
**fad, faddist, faddy; faddle.** See ADDENDA.
**fade,** adj and v; whence **fadeless, unfading.**

The obsol adj *fade,* adopted by ME from OF-F,
comes from VL *\*fatidus,* a blend of L *fatuus,*
insipid+either L *sapidus,* tasty (B & W), sem more
prob, L *uapidus* (ML *vapidus*), stale (Webster),
unless perchance the L origin be simply *\*fatidus,*
mdfn of *fatuus.* OF *fade* has the derivative OF-MF
v *fader,* whence ME *faden,* whence 'to *fade*'.

**faecal, faeces**—AE **fecal, feces; defecate, defecation.**

1. L *faex,* occ *fex,* pl *faeces,* occ *feces,* wine-lees,
hence impure residue, hence, in Med E, *faeces,
feces,* excrement, is o.o.o.: ? of Eg origin. *Faecal,
fecal,* is an E formation, as if from L *\*f(a)ecālis.*

2. Derivative L *dēfaecāre,* to remove (*dē,* down
from) the lees or residue from, has pp *dēfaecātus,*
whence 'to *defecate*', as in L but with special vi
sense 'to void excrement'; derivative L *dēfaecātiō,*
o/s *dēfaecātiōn-,* yields *defecation.*

**faerie, faery.** See *fairy* at FATE.

**fag,** n (hence **fag-end**) and v (hence pa **fagged**).
The n app derives from 'to *fag*', to become,
hence to cause to become, weary: o.o.o.; but perh
from FLAG, to grow weary, to droop. The coll
*fag,* a cigarette, derives from the 'loose end' nuance
of the n; the school *fag* (n hence v) comes prob
from the v, perh as abbr of (esp the military)
*fatigue.*

**faggot** or **fagot** (n hence v, whence vn **fag(g)ot-
ing** in embroidery and ironwork): OF-F *fagot*
derivative MF-F v *fagoter*): OProv *fagot* (cf It
*fagotto*), perh from Gr *phákelos,* a bundle, a fagot,

s *phakel-*, r *phak-*, with *phak-* becoming *fag-* and another suffix substituted for *-elos*.

Fahrenheit: Gabriel *Fahrenheit*, a G physicist, the deviser, in 1710, of the mercury thermometer.

fail, whence the pa and vn failing; failure;—fallacious, fallacy—fallible, fallibility (negg infallible, infallibility);—false, falsification, falsify, falsity;—fault (n hence v), whence faultless and faulty;—faucet; faux pas.

1. The keyword is L *fallere*, to deceive, to escape from, hence the vr *se fallere*, to be deceived, to commit a fault; the s is *fall-*, the r *fal-*: prob cf OHG *fallan*, to fall (E FALL), and Gr *sphallein* (s *sphall-*), to cause to fall, and *phēlos*, deceitful.

2. L *fallere* has VL derivative *\*fallīre*, to deceive, esp to commit a fault, to fail, whence OF-F *faillir*, whence E 'to *fail*'; *faillir*, used as n, becomes, in ONF, *failer*, whence EF *failer*, whence E *failure*.

3. L *fall(ere)* has derivative adjj *fallāx*, deceptive, and ML *fallibilis*, deceivable, capable of mistakes. *Fallāx* has derivative n *fallācia* (pl *fallāciae*), whence E *fallacy*; derivative LL *fallāciōsus* yields *fallacious*.

4. ML *fallibilis* yields *fallible*, whence, anl, *fallibility*; the ML neg *infallibilis* yields *infallible*, whence *infallibility*.

5. *Fallere* has pp *falsus*, used also as adj, whence OF-MF *fals*, whence E *false*; derivative LL *falsitās*, o/s *falsitāt-*, becomes OF-MF *falsité*, *falseté*, whence ME *falste*, whence the refashioned E *falsity*. On the L c/f *falsi-* is built the LL-ML cpd *falsificāre*, to make (*-ficāre*, a c/f of *facere*, to make) false, whence, perh via MF-F *falsifier*, the E 'to *falsify*'; derivative ML *falsificātiō*, o/s *falsificātiōn-*, yields, perh via MF-F, the E *falsification*.

6. L *falsus* becomes OF-MF *fals*, with MF var *faus*, whence F *faux*, as in *faux pas*, false step (lit and fig); for *pas*, cf PACE.

7. L *fallere* has LL mdfn (? caus) *falsāre*, to falsify, whence OProv *falsar*, to falsify, create a fault in, bore through, with derivative MF n *falset*, whence EF-F *fausset*, whence E *faucet*, a water-tap.

8. *Fallere* has a VL *\*fallita* (n from *\*fallita*, f of *\*fallitus*, pp of VL *\*fallīre*, as in para 2): whence OF-MF *falte*, MF-F hence ME *faute*, with *-l-* restored in E *fault*. With the adj *faulty*, perh cf late MF-F *fautif*.

fain, adj hence adv; 'to fawn'.

1. *Fain:* ME *fayn*, earlier *fagen*: OE *faegen*: akin to OS *fagan*, ON *fegenn*, *feginn*, glad—to OE *gefēon*, OHG gi-*fehōn*, to rejoice, Go *fahēths*, joy —to OHG *fagēn*, to please: Gmc r, *\*feh-*.

2. OE *faegen* has derivative *faegnian*, to rejoice, with varr *fagnian* and esp *fahnian*, whence ME *fawnen*, to rejoice, (later) to welcome or flatter, whence 'to *fawn*': for cognates, cf para 1.

faint, faintness. Cf *feint*; see FEIGN, para 3.

fair (1), adj hence adv: ME *fair*, earlier *fayer*, earliest *faiger*: OE *faeger*, *faegr*: akin to OHG and OS *fagar*, Go *fagrs*, ON *fagr*, fit, hence pleasing to the eye, beautiful, and, further off, Skt *pajras* in

good condition, fit, strong: IE r *\*pak-*, firmly placed, firm. (Feist.)

fair (2), n: ME *faire*, earlier *feire*, adopted from OF-MF (cf the F *foire*): L *fēria*, a holiday (very rare before LL), pl *fēriae*, holidays, holy days (of festival): akin to L *festus*, of a holiday, joyous, whence the n *festum*, usu in pl *festa*: see *feast*.— Hence, *fairing*, a gift at, hence from, a fair.

fairy (n hence adj). See ADDENDA.

faith, whence faithful and faithless; fides, as in bona fides (good faith), fidelity; Fido; fiduciary; feal, fealty; fay and foy; auto-da-fé; cognates federal, federate, federation, treated sep —Prefix-cpds: affidavit—cf coll davy; affiance—cf fiancé, fiancée; confide, confidence, confidant, confident, confidential; defiance, defiant, defy; diffidence, diffident; infidel, infidelity; perfidious, perfidy.

1. *Faith*, ME *fayth*, *feith*, comes from OF *feit*, *feid*, from L *fidēs* (s *fid-*), intimately related to *fīdere* (LL *fīdēre*), with s *fid-*, to trust. Note that *fidēs* has derivative adj *fidēlis*; *fīdere*, derivative adj *fīdus*. The IE r is app *\*bheidh-*, var *\*bhidh-*, to believe; cf Gr *peith*esthai, to have trust or confidence, caus *peith*ein, to persuade, Homeric pt (aorist) *epith*on, and, for *fidēs*, the Gr n *pistis* (s *pist-*: perh for *\*pitsis*).

2. OF *feid*, *feit*, faith, becomes MF *fei*, whence archaic E *fay*; derivative EF-F *foi* yields archaic E *foy*.

3. L *fidēs* becomes Port *fé* (cf Sp *fe*), as in *auto-da-fé*, (lit) act of faith, hence the burning of a heretic; *auto*=L *actus* (gen *-ūs*).

4. L *fidēlis*, faithful, becomes, via OF-F, both the obs E *fidele* and the obs E *feal* (MF *feal*, var of OF-EF *fëel*, *fëeil*)—cf the obsol *fealty*, loyalty, from MF *fealté*, var of OF-EF *fëelté*, *fēalté*, from L *fidēlitās*, o/s *fidēlitāt-*, itself from *fidēlis*.

5. L *fidēlitās*, faithfulness, yields, prob via MF-F *fidélité*, the E *fidelity*.

6. The L negg *infidēlis*, *infidēlitās*, become MF-F *infidèle*, *infidélité*, whence E *infidel* (adj, whence n), *infidelity*, with diverging senses.

7. L *fīdus*, worthy of faith, faithful, reaches and survives in E only in the commonest of all dog-names *Fido*, prob via the It *fido*, trusty.

8. Perh from *fīdus* (? via *\*fīdūsia*: *fīdus*+abstract *-ia*), but perh direct from *fīdere*, to trust, derives L *fīdūcia*, trust, with derivative adj *fīdūciārius*, whence E *fiduciary*; *fiducial* is an E formation, in *-al*, from L *fīdūcia*.

9. The L prefix-cpds relevant to E are *affīdāre*, *confīdere*, *diffīdere*, *perfīdus*. ML *affīdāre*, to give, or swear, faith to (*af-* for *ad*, to), make an oath, has *affīdāvit*, he has made oath, adopted by Law as n 'a sworn statement', whence the coll *davy* (*affidavit*).

10. *Affīdāre* becomes OF-MF *afier*, MF *affier*, to trust, whence MF *afiance*, *affiance*, whence the ME-E n *affiance*, trust, faith; MF *afiance* has derivative MF-EF v *afiancier*, whence E 'to *affiance*', to pledge to marriage.

11. VL *\*fīdāre*, to entrust, becomes OF-F *fier*, whence the OF-EF n *fiance*, whence OF-F *fiancer*

(prop to take a pledge), with pp *fiancé*, f *fiancée*, both used as nn and then adopted by E.

12. *Confīdere* (int *con-*), to have trust or confidence, yields 'to *confide*'. Its presp *confīdens*, o/s *confīdent-*, becomes It *confidente*, whence EF *confidant*, f *confidante* (F *confident*, *-fidente*), adj used as n and duly adopted by E. The E adj *confident* app comes direct from the L o/s *confident-*. On *confident-* is formed L *confidentia*, whence E (and MF-F) *confidence*, whence *confidential*.

13. D *diffīdere* (*dif-* for *dis*, apart), to lack trust or confidence in, yields the obs 'to *diffide*'; its presp *diffīdens*, o/s *diffīdent-*, becomes E *diffident*; derivative *diffīdentia* becomes *diffidence*.

14. With L *diffīdere*, cf the VL *\*disfīdāre* (cf *\*fīdāre* in para 11), to renounce or abandon (implied by *dis-*) trust or faith in, orig a feudal term, which accounts for OF-EF *desfier* (EF-F *défier*), whence E 'to *defy*'; derivative OF-EF *desfiance* (EF-F *défiance*) becomes E *defiance*; the OF-EF presp *desfiant* (whence *desfiance*), EF-F *défiant*, becomes E *defiant*.

15. L *fidēs* has a derivative cpd adj *perfidus* (short *i*), perh explicable by *qui per fidem decipit*, (he) who deceives by means of faith or trust, as E & M point out; but (E & M) *per-* may connote deviation—unless *per*, through, with secondary sense 'across', connotes infringement. *Perfidus* has derivative *perfidia*, whence, prob via EF-F *perfidie*, the E *perfidy*; and *perfidia* has its own adj *perfidiōsus*, whence E *perfidious*.

**fake** (v hence n, whence adj), derivative agent **faker.**
This orig underworld term comes perh from MD-D *vegen*, to sweep, prob from G *fegen* (MHG *vegen*), to sweep, extensively used in sl (EW): cf, therefore, the obs E *feague*, to whip, of same Gmc origin. Cf the 2nd FIG.

**fakir**, a religious, vowed to poverty and often subsisting as a mendicant: perh via EF *fakir* (F *faquir*): Ar *faqīr*, poor.

**falcate; falchion;** cf the element *falci-*.
*Falcate*, scythe- or sickle-shaped, derives from L *falcātus*, itself from L *falx*, a scythe or a sickle, o/s *falc-*: prob akin to L *flectere*, to bend, pp *flexus* (f.a.e., FLEX), s *flex-*, with *falx* a metathesis for *\*flax-*, s of *\*flaxus*, var of *flexus*; and perh to Gr *phalkēs* (s *phalk-*), a ship's rib, which is, naturally, bent or curved. L *falx* has derivative VL *\*falciō*, o/s *\*falciōn-*, whence OF-MF *falchon* (var *fauchon*), whence E *falchion*, a slightly curved, broad-bladed sword. OF-MF *falchon, fauchon*, however, could be an aug of OF *fals*, MF-F *faux*, a scythe (DAF). Cf:

**falcon** is a reshaping of ME *faucon* (MF-F *faucon*, OF-MF var *faulcon*; earliest *falcun*), after the originating LL *falcōn-*, o/s of *falcō*, the hawk used in hunting other birds; OF-MF *faulcon*, MF-F *faucon*, has OF-MF derivative *falconier*, MF-F *fauconnier*, whence, via ME, the E *falconer*, and also MF-F *fauconnerie*, whence E *falconry*. LL *falcō* comes either from OHG *falcho*, cf ON

*falki*, or, more prob—because of its curved beak and wings—from L *falx*.

**faldistory; faldstool.** See STALL, para 8.
**fall**, pt fell, pp fallen; hence fall, n; vt fell.
1. 'To *fall*' derives from OE *feallan*, akin to OFris *falla*, OS and OHG *fallan* (G *fallen*), ON *falla*, and also to Lith *puólu*, I fall, *pulti*, to fall, and prob to Gr *sphallein*, to fell, and Skt *phálati*, it bursts; IE r, *\*pal-*, var *\*pel-*, with extnn *\*phal-*, *\*phel-*, and *s*-int *\*sphal-*, *\*sphel-*. (Walshe; Hofmann).—*Fall*, autumn, derives from 'the *fall* of the generic leaf'.
2. 'To *fell*' derives from OE *fellan* (cf OFris and ON *fella*), either the caus of OE *feallan* or, at the least, a caus from the r of *feallan*.

**fallacious, fallacy.** See FAIL, para 3. Cf:
**fallible** (and **fallibility**). See FAIL, para 4.
**fallow** (1), adj (pale-yellow): OE *fealu* or *fealo*: akin to OHG *falo* (G *falb*), MD *valuwe, vale, vael*, D *vaal*, ON *fölr*—to Lith *palvas*, L *pallidus* (s *pallid-*, r *pal-*), pale—to Gr *polios*, grey—Ve *palitás*, grey: f.a.e., PALE. Hence, **fallow deer.** Cf the 2nd FAVO(U)R.

**fallow** (2), n (hence adj and v): ME *falow*, ploughed land: akin to OE *faelging*, fallow land, OE *fea h*, OHG *felga*, a harrow: prob influenced, perh even at the early ME stage, by prec.

**false, falsify** (**falsification**), **falsity.** See FAIL, para 5.

**falter** (v hence n), whence pa and vn **faltering:** ME *falteren* or *faltren*: o.o.o. If of Gmc origin, it is perh akin to ON *faltrask*, to be burdened, encumbered, puzzled; EW, however, derives the ME word from ME *falden*, to fold—*falter* would then be a mdfn of *\*falder*, an *-er* extn of s *fald-*; if of Romance origin, it prob derives from VL *\*fallita* or, rather, from the derivative MF-F *fauter* (to commit a fault), which may well have orig existed as *\*faulter, \*falter*.

**falx**, as used in An and Zoo: see FALCATE.

**fame** (n hence v, usu as pa **famed**), **famous**—**infamy, infamous;** defame, defamation, defamatory; —sep FABLE, FABULOUS, with AFFABLE, AFFABILITY, and INEFFABLE, INEFFABILITY; sep INFANT, INFANCY (whence *enfant terrible*); sep INFANTRY;—**nefarious;** preface, prefatory; sep FATE (FATAL, etc.; where *fairy*).
1. *Fame*, adopted from OF-EF, comes from L *fāma* (s *fām-*), itself from L *fāri*, to speak: akin to Gr *phēmē* (s *phēm-*), a saying, report, rumour, (hence) public reputation, Doric *phāmā* (s *phām-*), *phanai* (s *phan-*), to speak, *phēmi* (s *phēm-*), I speak, and *phēmis* (s *phēm-*), conversation, renown; IE r, prob *\*bhā-*, to speak; etymon *\*bhāmi*, I speak.
2. *Fāma* has derivative adj *fāmōsus*, causing himself to be spoken of, (LL) renowned, whence (late MF-F *fameux* and) E *famous*.
3. The neg L *infāmis* (s *infām-*) has ML extn *infāmōsus*, whence E *infamous*; derivative *infāmia* (abstract *-ia*) becomes MF-F *infamie*, whence E *infamy*.
4. Other L prefix-cpds relevant to E are:

*dēfāmātus* (*dē-*, down, from), infamous, has derivative v *diffāmāre*, (prob) to publish, usu, by confusion, to decry, whence MF-F *diffamer*, whence ME *diffamen*, later *defamen*, whence 'to *defame*'; LL *diffāmātiō*, publication, a making known, later confused to mean 'a decrying', o/s *diffāmātiōn-*, yields, prob via MF-F *diffamation*, the ME *diffamacioun*, the E *defamation*—after *defame*; ML *diffāmātōrius* becomes, anl, *defamatory*;

*praefāri*, to say or speak beforehand (*prae-*, before), has derivative *praefātiō*, a preamble, o/s *praefātiōn-*, whence MF *preface* (F *préface*), adopted by E; hence 'to *preface*'. E *prefatory* is an anl formation.

5. Akin to L *fāri*, to speak, is L *fās*, divine law —that *which has been spoken* by the gods; its neg *nefās*, wrong, sin, crime, has derivative adj *nefārius* (clearly harking back to *fāri*), whence E *nefarious*.

6. The Gr-derived cognates, such as *anthem*, *blasphemy* (*blame*), *euphemism*, *phone*, are treated sep.

**familiar** (adj, hence n), **familiarity, familiarize, family; paterfamilias.**

1. *Family* comes from L *familia*, orig the servants and slaves of a great house, then the house itself with master, mistress, children—and the staff; it derives from *famulus*, f *famula*, a servant, from adj *famulus*: o.o.o.; ? Etruscan (E & M); ? rather (Webster) akin to Skt *dhāman*, house or household, s *dhām-*, .? also to Hit *dammaras*, a temple-servant. Perh, however, the formation of L *famulus* is *fa*+euphonic *m*+dim suffix -*ulus*, the r being *fa*- and of Medit origin: cf Eg *ha*, neighbourhood, whence *hau*, family, those in the master's immediate neighbourhood.

2. *Familia* has adj *familiāris*, of the (all-senses) family, hence intimate; hence also n, a friend of the family: whence OF-F *familier*, adopted by ME, whence the refashioned E *familiar*. Derivative L *familiāritās*, o/s *familāritāt-*, yields OF-F *familiarité*, whence E *familiarity*; *familiarize* is an E anl formation (cf the EF-F *familiariser*)—perh cf the LL *familiārescere*, to become intimate.

3. The master of the household is *paterfamilias*, (lit) father (cf PATER) of the family.

**famine; famish.**

1. 'To *famish*', usu as pa *famished*, derives, via ME *famen*, by aphesis from OF-MF *afamer* (*a-*= L *ad*, to, used int), F *affamer*, itself from L *famēs*, hunger, s *fam-*, r *fam-*: o.o.o.

2. *Famēs* has VL derivative *\*famina*, whence OF-F *famine*, adopted by E.

**famous.** See FAME, para 2.

**fan.** See WIND, para 8.

**fan**, sl become coll for 'enthusiast'. Short for *fanatic*.

**fanatic, fanatical, fanaticism.** See FANE.

**fancy** (n, hence adj and v), whence pa *fancied*, agent *fancier*, adj *fanciful*; **fantasy, fantastic; phantasy—phantasm, phantasmal, phantasmagoria —phantom.**—Cf the element *phanero-*.—**phaeton—**

**phenomenon** (pl **phenomena**), **phenomenal, phenomenology; diaphanous—Epiphany—theophany, tiffany; pant** (v, hence n); **phase, phasis—emphasis, emphasize,** emphatic; sep sycophancy, sycophant, sycophantic.

1. *Fancy* arises, in late ME, as a contr of *fantasy*, itself via OF-EF *fantasie* (EF-F *fantaisie*) from LL *fantasia*, var of L *phantasia*, idea, (but esp) apparition, adopted from Gr, where it means 'appearance, imagination', from *phantazein* (s *phantaz-*), to render visible, fig to the mind, an elaboration of *phainein*, to show, s *phain-*. *Phainō*, I show, is prob for *\*phaniō*, with IE etymon *\*bhanio* or *\*bhenio*, and IE r *\*bhan-* (var *\*bhen-*), itself a sem and phon extn of IE r *\*bha-*, to shine: cf Skt *bhāti*, it shines, is light, and, for *bhan-*, Skt *bhānus* light (of day, etc.).

2. The adj of *fantasy* is *fantastic* (cf the MF-F *fantastique*): ML *fantasticus*: LL *phantasticus*: Gr *phantastikos*, able to show or represent, from *phantazein*.

3. LL *phantasticus* accounts for obs *phantastic*; L *phantasia* for obsol *phantasy*.

4. Allied *phantasm* (whence *phantasmal*) is a reshaping of ME *fantasme*, adopted from OF-MF, itself from L *phantasma*, taken over from Gr, which derives it, by suffix -*asma*, from *phant-*, r of *phantazein* (as in para 1).—The SciL *phantasmagoria*, orig a magic-lantern show, combines either Gr *phantasma*+-*agoria*, arbitrarily from Gr *agora*, an assembly (the predominant theory), or Gr *phantasma*+the -*gory* of *allegory* (B & W); E *phantasmagoria* (whence adj *phantasmagoric*), 1802, prob reshapes F *fantasmagorie* (adj *fantasmagorique*), 1801. L *phantasma* becomes, in OF-MF, not only *fantasme* but also *fantesme* and notably *fantosme*, adopted by ME and soon written and pron *fantome* (cf EF-F *fantôme*), refashioned by E to *phantom*, used also as adj.

5. Closely akin to Gr *phainein* (s *phain-*) is Gr *phaein* (s *pha-*), to shine, with var *phaethein* (s *phaeth-*), presp *phaethōn*, personified as Phaethōn, the Sun God (Helios), or, more usu, his son, who, one day, somewhat disastrously drove the chariot of the sun, hence, via F *phaéton*, the E *phaeton*, an open, four-wheeled carriage.

6. *Phainein*, to show, has passive *phainesthai* (s likewise *phain-*), to be shown, i.e. to appear, with presp *phainomenos*, neu *phainomenon* (pl *phainomena*), which, as n, passes into LL as *phaenomenon* (pl -*na*), adopted by E. *Phenomenal* (cf the F *phénoménal*)=*phenomen*on+adj -*al*; *phenomenology*=*phenomen*on+-*logy*, q.v. at the element -*logia*.

7. The Gr *phan-*, a c/f of *phain-*, occurs in:

Gr *diaphanēs* (from *diaphainein*, to show *dia* or through), transparent, becomes ML *diaphanus*, whence E *diaphanous*;

Gr *epiphaneia* (from *epiphainein*, to show *epi* or to, i.e. to manifest), manifestation, becomes LL *epiphania*, esp in eccl sense, then OF-MF *epiphanie* (EF-Fé-), finally E *Epiphany*;

Gr *theophaneia*, physical manifestation of a

theos or god, becomes LL *theophania*, whence E *theophany*; the OF shape was *theophanie*, often *tiphanie*, also *tifenie* or *tiffenie*, whence, prob because of its transparency, the very thin silk, now muslin, named *tiffany*.

8. L *phantasia* (as in para 1) is assumed to have generated a derivative VL *pantasiāre*, for VL *phantasiāre*, to have a nightmare; whence OF-EF *pantaisier*, *pantoisier*, to be breathless (EF-F *pantois*), whence E 'to *pant*'.

9. Gr *phainein* has derivative *phasis*, adopted by SciL and SciE; whence late EF-F and E *phase* (of, e.g., the moon; hence, stage or aspect). Cf:

10. The Gr prefix-cpd *emphainein*, to show (*em-* for *en*) in, to indicate, has derivative *emphasis*, forcible expression, adopted by L and then by E (cf the EF-F *emphase*); derivative Gr adj *emphatikos* becomes LL *emphaticus*, whence E *emphatic* (cf EF-F *emphatique*); *emphasize* is an anl E formation.

**fane, fanatic, fanatical, fanaticism.**

1. *Fanaticism* is an anl E formation from the adj *fanatic*, whence, perh after the LL use of the L adj, the n *fanatic*, which duly takes its own adj *fanatical*: and *fanatic*, adj, represents L *fānāticus*, divinely inspired, lit of a *fānum* or temple, akin to L *fēriae*, religious festivals and therefore to E FEAST.

2. L *fānum* has derivative prefix-cpd adj *prōfānus*, lit before (*prō*) the temple, hence outside it, hence not holy, hence impious; whence, prob via MF-F, the E *profane*. Derivative *prōfānāre* becomes MF-F *profaner*, whence 'to *profane*'; on *prōfānāt-*, s of the pp *prōfānātus*, arises LL *prōfānātiō* o/s *prōfānātiōn-*, whence, perh via MF-F, *profanation*. *Prōfānus* has LL derivative *prōfānitās*, o/s *prōfānitāt-*, whence *profanity*.

**fandango** is a Sp word: o.o.o.: ? a redup of the L r *tang-* in *tangere*, esp as in *chordas tangere*, to pluck the strings (of the lyre). Cf TANGO.

**fanfare; fanfaronade.**

*Fanfare*, adopted from EF-F, derives from the EF-F v *fanfarer*, itself perh from EF-F *fanfaron*, a boaster or a swaggerer, adapted from Sp *fanfarrón*, mdfn of *fafarrón*, from Ar *farfar*, garrulous: echoic. *Fanfarrón* has derivative *fanfarronada*, whence EF-F *fanfarronade*, whence the E *fanfaronade*, a swaggering, an ostentatious display.

**fang**, a seizing, hence a predatory beast's long, sharp tooth, derives from the now dial *fang*, to seize: ME *fangen*, varr *fongen* and *fon*: OE *fōn*: akin to OE *feng*, OFris *feng*, *fang*, a seizing, a fang, OHG *fāhan* (pp *gifangen*), G *fangen*, Go *fāhan* (for *\*fanhan*), MD *vaen*, MD-D *vangen*, ON *fā*; also to L *pangere*, to fasten, and Skt *pasas*, a noose: cf PACT.

**fantail.** See WIND, para 8.

**fantasia** (It); **fantastic, fantasy.** See FANCY, para 2 (adj), para 1 (E n).

**far, farther, farthest** (*far*, adj + -*ness*).

1. *Far*, adv and adj, derive from OE *feor*, *feorr*, likewise both adv and adj: akin to OFris *fēr*, *fīr*, OS *fer*, *ferr* OHG *ferro*, adv, and OHG *ferrana*,

G *fern*, adj, Go *fairra*, ON *fjarri*, adv—to Gr *pera*, further (adv), and *peran*, beyond—to Skt *páras*, far (adv), and *pára*, forth—and to Hit *par(r)anda*, *parranta*, beyond, besides.

2. The advv *farther*, *farthest* app derive from the adjj *farther*, *farthest*; adj *farthest* is formed anl with adj *farther*, which—confused with *further*—stands for *farrer*, ME *ferrer*, comp of *far*; note, however, that *farther* equally well derives from ME *ferther*, a var of FURTHER.

**farce** (n and v), **farcical.**

The n *farce*, orig stuffing in cookery, is adopted from MF-F; it derives from MF-F *farcir*, to stuff, whence ME *farcen*, whence 'to *farce*', orig to stuff with forcemeat: and *farcir* comes from L *farcīre*, perh akin, by metathesis, to Gr *phrassein* (s *phrass-*), to fence, fortify, stop up; hardly to L *frequens* (see FREQUENT).

**fare**, to go, to journey; **fare**, a going, a journey, hence the charge made for it; **thoroughfare; -farer**, as in **wayfarer; farewell** (adj from n from v).

To *farewell* someone is to say *Fare* (thou, ye) *well*, 'Have a good journey!': cf VOLITION, para 15. A *thoroughfare* is a 'going, hence a way, through'. A *wayfarer* is one who *wayfares* (obs), from ME adj *weifarende*, journeying, from OE *wegfarende*, going one's *weg* or WAY. *Fare*, n, derives from OE *faru*, a journey, intimately akin to OE *faran*, to journey, whence 'to *fare*': akin to OFris *fara*, OHG, OS, Go *faran* (cf G *fahren*): Gmc r, *\*far-*; IE r, *\*per-*, var *\*por-*: cf Gr *poros*, a thoroughfare, and *poreuein*, to convey. Cf FERRY and FORD—POROUS and EMPORIUM.

**farinaceous; farrago.**

1. The former comes from LL *farīnāceus*, adj of L *farīna*, a fine meal—a term partly adopted by E. L *farīna* is an -*īna* extn of L *far* (gen *farris*), a sort of grain, esp the wheat called spelt, with cognates in OGmc (e.g., ON *barr*, cereals) and in C (e.g., OIr *bargen*, Cor *bara*, bread).

2. Derivative L *farrāgō* (*far* + connective or euphonic -*r*- + suffix -*āgō*), (a mash of) mixed fodder for cattle, hence a medley, esp a hodge-podge, has been adopted by E.

**farl** or **farle**: EE *fardel*: OE *fēortha dāel*, a fourth part (of an oatmeal cake): cf 'to DEAL' and FOUR.

**farm** (n, whence adj and v); **farmer; farming.** See FIRM, para 1.

**faro**, a card game, app derives from *Pharaoh*, generic title of the kings of ancient Egypt, perh because 'he' was formerly represented upon one of the cards: prompted by the earlier recorded F *pharaon* (cf It *faraone*), the game, from *Pharaon*, Pharaoh, itself from LL *Pharaon-*, o/s of *Pharao*: Gr *Pharaō* (gen *Pharaonos*): H *Par'ōh*: Eg *pr-'o*, a great house; Budge gives it as *per-āa*: *per*, house + *āa*, great.

**farrago.** See FARINACEOUS, para 2.

**farrier** (whence **farriery**): MF *ferrier*, OF *ferreor*: L *ferrārius*: *ferrum*, iron + agent -*ārius*: f.a.e., FERRIC.

**farrow** (n, hence v): OE *fearh*, a little, or young, pig: akin to syn OHG *farh* (cf G *Ferkel* from the

OHG dim *farhili*): Gmc r, *\*farh-*; IE r, *\*pork-* —cf L *porcus*; see PORK.

**fart**, v hence n: OE *feortan*: akin to G *farzen*: ult echoic. Cf PETARD, s.f.

**farther, farthest.** See FAR, para 2.

**farthing.** See FOUR, para 4.

**farthingale.** See ADDENDA.

**fasces; fascia; fasciate** (whence **fasciation**); **Fascicle; fascinate** (whence pa **fascinating**), **fascination, fascinative, fascinator; fascine** (n, hence v); **fascism, Fascist** (n, hence adj)—**Fascisti.**

1. L *fasces*, a bundle of authoritative rods, pl of *fascis*, a bundle, has s *fasc-*, prob akin to MIr *basc*, a neck-band, a collar, and therefore perh to BASKET.

2. L *fascis* has It derivative *fascio*, a bundle, hence a political group, whence both *fascismo*, hence *Fascism*, and *Fascisti*, hence *Fascists*.

3. Intimately related to L *fascis* is L *fascia* (*fasc-+-ia*), a band (of, eg., cloth), adopted by E in senses 'band' or 'sash', also for tech terms in An and Arch; derivative *fasciāre*, to wrap about with a band, pp *fasciātus*, whence the E Bot and Zoo adj *fasciate*.

4. *Fascis* has dim *fasciculus*, whence E *fascicle* and *fascicule*.

5. *Fascis* has further derivative *fascīna* (*fasc-+-ina*), a faggot, whence the EF-F, hence E, *fascine* of fortification.

6. Prob akin to *fascis* is L *fascinus*, var *fascinum*, a magical, usu pej, spell: *fascinus*, *-um*, 'may orig have designated a magical operation in which one tied up the victim' (E & M). Derivative *fascināre*, to cast a spell over, has pp *fascinātus*, whence 'to *fascinate*'; subsidiarily derivative *fascinātiō*, o/s *fascinātiōn-*, yields E *fascination*—LL *fascinātor* is adopted by E—but E *fascinative* is an anl formation (cf the syn LL *fascinātōrius*).

**fascinate, fascination.** See prec, final para.

**fash.** See FASTIDIOUS, para 2.

**fashion, fashionable.** See FACT, para 4.

**fast** (adj—whence adv, n, v); **fasten**, whence agent **fastener** and vn **fastening; fastness.**

1. 'The sense *swift* comes from the idea of keeping close to what is pursued' (Webster), the orig sense being 'firmly fixed, firm': ME *fast*, firm: OE *faest*: akin to OS *fast*, OFris *fest*, OHG *festi*, *fasti*, MHG *vest*, *veste*, G *fest*, firm, solid, MD *fast*, *vaste*, (also D) *vast*, ON *fastr*, and prob Arm *hast* (for *\*past-*), firm, and Skt *pastya*, home; IE r, *\*past-*, firm. The adv *fast* derives, through ME *faste*, firmly, (but also) swiftly, from OE *faeste*, firmly: cf syn OHG *fasto* and OFrsi *feste*. 'To *fast*' or abstain from food derives from OE *faestan* (cf OFris *festa*, to fasten, to abstain, OHG *fastēn*, ON *fasta*), itself from OE *faest*, firm; the n *fast*, abstinence, ME *fast*, *faste*, comes from the ON n *fasta*. *Fast*, a mooring rope, ME *fest*, comes from ON *festr*, a rope; 'to *fast*' or bind derives from OE *faestan*, to render *faest* or firm; but 'to *fasten*' derives from OE *faestnian*, likewise from the OE adj. *Fastness*, orig abstract OE *faestnes*

(*faest+-nes*, E *-ness*): cf G *Feste*, fortress, castle, from *fest*.

**fastidious** derives, prob via MF-F *fastidieuse*, f of *fastidieux*, from L *fastīdiōsus*, expressing aversion, disdainful, adj of *fastīdium*, strong aversion, loathing, disgust, app a blend of *fastus* (gen- *ūs*), disdain, haughtiness, and *taedium*, disgust; *fastus* itself is o.o.o. (E & M.)

2. Sc *fash*, to vex or trouble (someone), represents late MF-EF *fascher* (F *fâcher*), to vex, from LL *fastīdiāre*, from L *fastīdīre*, to repel with disdain, from *fastīdium*.

**fastness.** See FAST, s.f.

**fat, fatness, fatten** (whence **fattening**, pa and vn), **fatty.**—**pine** (tree); **pituitary, pituitous.**—**pome, pomade, pomatum, pomander; pomegranate; pommel** (n, whence v).

1. *Fat*, n (whence *fatty*), derives, like *fatness* and *fatten*, from adj *fat*: OE *faett*, from OE *faeted*, fattened: akin to OFris *fatt*, *fet*, OHG *feizit* (G *feist*), G *fett*, OS *\*fētid*, ON *feitr*; to L *opimus*, abundant, fat, *pinguis*, fat, stout, and *pīnus*, pine-tree; to Gr *píōn*, fat (adj), *píar* and *pimelē*, nn, fat; and to Skt *payate*, it swells or fattens, *pīvaras*, fat (adj), *pítu-darus*, pine-tree (cf the syn Gr *pítus*), the pine being resinous, gummy—therefore cf also the L *pītuīta*, gum, resin, (hence) mucus, phlegm. The IE r app veers from *\*pa-* to *\*pi-*, with extnn *\*pat-* and *\*pit-*, the latter with var *\*pin-*, *\*pim-*.

2. *Pine* (tree), ME *pine*, derives alike from OE *pīn* and from OF-F *pin*, both from L *pīnus*, as above.

3. L *pītuīta* (as above) yields the E adjj *pituitary* (gland), and, via the L derivative adj *pītuītōsus*, *pituitous*.

4. Perh akin to the L *pīnus* and *pītuīta* is L *pōmum* (pl *pōma*), a fruit, in LL esp an apple, whence, via VL *\*pōma*, the OF-MF *pome* (F *pomme*), whence E *pome*, an apple, now a Bot term.

5. L *pōmum* becomes It *pomo*, with derivative *pomata*, a cosmetic with an apple base, whence EF-F *pommade*, whence E *pomade*; *pomatum* is a Sci L formation (L *pōmum*+suffix *-atum*), prob suggested by the It word.

6. OF-MF *pome*, var *pom*, used also for the pommel of a sword, has dim *pomel*, adopted by ME, both as a surmounting 'ball' and as the knob on a sword hilt, whence E *pommel*, with predominant sense 'knob at front of a saddle-bow'; 'to *pommel*' was orig to beat with the pommel of a sword, and is, in C19-20, often spelt *pummel*.

7. *Pomander*, however, is a cpd: EE *pomamber*, for *pomeamber*: *pome*+AMBER: this is a mixed perfume, carried against infection.

8. Another cpd is *pomegranate*: ME *pomgarnet*: OF *pome grenate* or *pume grenate* (then *grenade*), lit a grained (i.e., large-pipped) apple: cf *grenade* at GRAIN.

**fate** (n, hence v, esp in pa **fated**)—whence **fateful; fatal, fatalism, fatalist, fatalistic, fatality.**

*Fate* is, by ME, adopted rom OF-MF: VL *fāta*: L *fātum* (pl *fāta*): orig the neus of *fātus*, spoken, pp of *fāri*, to speak (\**for*, I speak): 'that which has been spoken, hence decreed', hence 'a divine statement'. The derivative adj *fātālis*, whence MF-F and E *fatal*, bears the dual senses 'of fate, fateful' and 'deadly, resulting in death'; the further derivative, LL *fātālitās* (*fātālis*+ abstract-n suffix *-itās*), o/s *fātālitāt-*, becomes late MF-F *fatalité*, whence E *fatality*. Fatalism and fatalist (whence *fatalistic*) are hybrid formations from E *fatal*.

father (n hence v), whence fatherhood; fatherless; fatherly, whence fatherliness; godfather and grandfather; Vaterland.—II, Romance: padre; père and compère.—III, Latin: pater; paternal, paternity; patrician; patristic; patron, patronage, patronal, patronize—pattern (n hence v);—2nd-element cpds: (Jove, Jovial, and) Jupiter, q.v. sep at DIANA, paras 4, 3; perpetrate, perpetration, perpetrator—cf the literary impetrate, impetration, impetrative, impetrator; repatriate, repatriation—Romance repair, to go, resort—cf expatriate, expatriation;—1st-element cpds: paterfamilias, q.v. sep at FAMILY, para 3; paternoster—patter (v, hence n), chatter; patriarch (LL from Gr), patriarchal, patriarchate, patriarchic, patriarchy; patricide, parricide; (app cpd) patrimony, patrimonial; cf the element *patro-*, where see PATROLOGY and PATRONYMIC (LL from Gr).—IV, (Additional) Gr: patriot (compatriot), patriotic, patriotism, papa (cf pa; cf also poppa, pop); papacy, papal, papish, papism, papist, papistic, papistry; pope, popedom, popehood, popery—cf antipope.

1. *Fatherless* derives from OE *faederlēas* (cf the suffix *-less*); *fatherly* from OE *faederlīce* (cf *-like*); *father*, therefore, from OE *faeder*, through ME *fader*: and OE *faeder* is akin to OFris *feder*, OS *fadar*, OHG *fater* (MHG-G *vater*), Go *fadar* (once only—usu *atta*, cf para 20), ON *fathir*—and to L *pater*.

2. Whereas *godfather* derives from OE *godfaeder*, *grandfather* merely combines *grand*, great, and *father*—cf the OF-F *grandpère*.

3. L *pater*, father, gen *patris*, o/s *patr-*, becomes OF-F *père*, with MF-F cpd *compère*, from LL *compater*, godfather: cf LL *commater*, godmother (MF-F *commère*).

4. L *pater* becomes Sp, Port, It *padre*, a father in the Catholic Church, hence as a term for any Armed Services chaplain.

5. L *pater* is very closely akin to and perh derived from Gr *patēr*. The E coll *pater* is prob, at first, Public School sl.

6. The main simple L derivatives affecting E are these:

LL-ML *paternālis*, whence MF-F *paternel* and E *paternal*; itself from

*paternus* (cf *maternus*), of a or the father, with LL derivative *paternitās*, o/s *paternitāt-*, whence OF-F *paternité* and—prob from F—E *paternity*;

from pl *patres*, (lit) fathers, hence senators, comes the adj *patricius*, whence MF-F *patricien*, whence E *patrician*—cf *Patricia*, from L *patricia*, a well-born woman;

as if from LL or ML \**patrista*, a father of the Church, with adj \**patristicus*, come F *patristique* and E *patristic*, concerning the Church Fathers, whence the n *patristics*, a study of their lives, writings, doctrines;

*patrōnus* (cf *matrōna*), a (usu powerful or wealthy) guardian or protector, ML a guardian saint, whence OF-F *patron* (OF *patrun*), whence ME *patron*—extant—and *patroun*; derivative LL adj *patrōnālis* yields *patronal*; derivative ML *patrōnāticum* becomes MF-F, hence E, *patronage*; *patroness*=*patron*+*-ess*; *patronize* (cf F *patroner*) =*patron*+*-ize*.

7. OF-F *patron*, a patron, gained in C14 the secondary sense 'a model', which reached E in late ME and became, in E, *pattern* (esp in dressmaking), whence—after F *patroner*, (late C14 onwards) to reproduce from a model or pattern— 'to *pattern*'.

8. The E 2nd-element cpds deriving from L include:

*impetrāre*, to obtain,=*im-* for int *in-*+*patrāre*, to achieve, bring to pass, conclude, from *pater*: *patrāre*, to be effectually *pater* or master of—cf *ministrāre* from *minister*. The pp *impetrātus* yields the literary 'to *impetrate*', to obtain by request; derivatives *impetrātiō* (o/s *impetrātiōn-*), LL *impetrātīuus* (ML *-īvus*), *impetrātor*, become *impetration, impetrative, impetrator*.

*perpetrāre*, to effect=*per*, thoroughly+*patrāre*, to accomplish; pp *perpetrātus* yields 'to *perpetrate*'; LL derivatives *perpetrātiō* (o/s *perpetrātiōn-*) and *perpetrātor* become *perpetration, perpetrator*.

9. *Expatriate* and *repatriate* come from L *patria*, fatherland, elliptical for *terra*, land, *patria*, f of *patrius*, of the *pater* or father, thus:

L *expatriāre* (*ex*, out of) to banish, has pp *expatriātus*, whence both the adj (hence n) and v *expatriate*; hence, by anl, *expatriation*, cf:

LL *repatriāre*, to restore (connoted by *re-*) to the *patria* or fatherland, has pp *repatriātus*, whence the adj, n, v *repatriate*; derivative ML *repatriātiō*, o/s *repatriātiōn-*, yields E *repatriation*.

10. LL *repatriāre* has a Romance derivative: 'to repair', to go (back), to resort: OF-EF *repairier*: ME *repairen*. The E n *repair*, resort, concourse, etc., derives from OF-F *repaire*, itself from OF-EF *repairier*.

11. First-element L cpds of *pater* result in the foll E words: sep paterfamilias; *paternoster* and *patter*; *patriarch*; *patricide*; app cpd *patrimony*. *Paternoster*=L *pater noster*, our father: the Pater Noster, Our Father (, which art in Heaven). From the rapid or mumbling recitation of *pater*nosters, we get 'to *patter*', chatter or mumble, whence the n *patter*.

12. *Patriarch*, ME from OF-F *patriarche*, derives from LL *patriarcha*, itself from Gr *patriarkhēs*, from *patria*, lineage+*arkhos*, a chief or leader—cf the element *-arch*. Derivatives LL *patriarchālis*, ML *patriarchātus*, LL *patriarchicus* (Gr *patriarkhikos*), ML *patriarchia*, a cathedral (LGr

*patriarkhia*, a patriarch's office or diocese), yield E *patriarchal*, *patriarchate*, *patriarchic*, *patriarchy*.

13. *Patricide*, murder or murderer of one's father, derives from LL *patricīdium*, murder of father; but *parricide*, the crime, derives from L *parricīdium*, and *parricide*, the criminal, from L *parricīda*, in both of which the 2nd element is *-cide*, from L *-cīdere*, c/f of *caedere*, to strike down, (earlier) to cut down: cf CAESURA. The 1st element is prob, by assimilation, from L *pater*; improb from a lost L word akin to Doric Gr *pāos*, a parent. *Parricidal* = the L derivative adj *parricīdālis*.

14. *Patrimonial* comes from LL *patrimōniālis*, adj of L *patrimōnium*, whence, via OF-F *patrimoine* and ME *patrimoigne*, the E *patrimony*. L *patrimōnium* derives from L *pater*: c/f *patri-*+ suffix *-mōnium*: cf L *matrimōnium* and perh *alimōnia*, with modified suffix *-mōnia*. It is tempting to think that, for the *-mōnium* nn at least, the suffix might be *-mōnium* (s *mōni-*, r *mōn-*), akin to L *monēta*, money, s *monēt-*, r *\*mon-*: but this theory, phon sound, is sem unsound, the basic senses being discrepant.

15. Besides the fundamentally Gr words (*patriarch*, *patronymic*) above, we have two notable derivatives from Gr: *patriot* and *papa*. *Patriot* comes, via MF-F *patriote* and LL *patriōta*, from Gr *patriōtēs*, an *-ōtēs* ('native; inhabitant': cf Cypriot), derivative from *patrios*, established by one's ancestors, from *patēr*, father. Derivative adj *patriōtikos* becomes LL *patriōticus*, whence EF-F *patriotique* and E *patriotic*. E *patriotisme*, like F *patriotisme*, is an anl formation.—LL *patriōta* has (prob suggested by LGr *sumpatriōtēs*) prefix-cpd *compatriōta* (*com-*, c/f from *cum*, with), whence late MF-F *compatriote*, whence E *compatriot*.

16. Gr *patēr*, father, has the nursery var *papas* or *pappas*, whence—or at least thereby prompted —L *papa*, likewise of the nursery; prob adopted from the L is late MF-F *papa*, in turn adopted by E. Hence *pa*; hence the AE *pappy*, var of *poppa*, with shortening *pop*. Now, Gr *papas* acquires, in the LGr period, the sense 'bishop': hence *Papa*, the Patriarch of Alexandria. Likewise, L *papa* acquires in LL the sense 'bishop', esp 'archbishop', and finally, as *Papa*, 'the Pope': whence both ML *papātia*, whence E *papacy*, and ML *\*papālis*, of the Pope, deducible from ML *papālitās*, the Pope's office and dignity, whence, prob via MF-F, the E adj *papal*. App E anl formations, with some intervention by MF-F, are: *papish* (*-ish*, adj); *papism*, *papist*, *papistic*—cf the EF-F *papisme*, EF-F *papiste*, F *papistique*—and *papistry* (*-ry* for *-ery*).

17. LL *papa* (Gr *papas*), as above, is adopted by OE, whence ME *pape*, later *pope*—extant. The chief derivatives are *popedom* (OE *pāpdōm*); *popehood* (*pope*+*-hood*: cf OE *pāpanhād*); *popery* (*pope* +*-ery*);

18. *Antipope*, elected in defiance of the properly chosen *Pope*, was prob suggested by MF-F *antipape*, itself deriving from ML *antipapa*.

19. Gr *patēr* has acc *patera* and gen *patros* (whence the c/f *patro-*) and is akin to Skt *pitá*, father, pl *pitáras*, which, like L *patres*, means also 'ancestors'; cf also Skt acc sing *pitáram* (cf L *patrem*) and dat sing *pitré* (Gr and L *patri*). The IE etymon is app *\*pəter* (ə being 'neutral *e*'); IE r, *\*pət-*.

20. The extremely complex relationships of Gr *patēr*, L *pater*, E *father*, with Gr and L *tata*, nursery word for 'father'; with Gr and L—and Go—*atta* and Hit *attas*; with such syn C words as OIr *athir*, Ga *athair*, but W, Br, Cor *tād*, and Cor varr *tūs*, *tūt* (and *dās*); with Skt *attas*, and ult with *abbé*, *abbot* (of Sem origin, with Ham parallels): these relationships have not yet been fully interdistinguished either phon or sem. But, like *mother*, *sister*, *brother*, *father* seems, ult, to have both denoted an agent and perh also been of Medit origin (cf Eg *ab*, father).

**fathom** (n, v), whence **fathomless**.

'To *fathom*', orig to embrace, derives from OE *faethmian*, to embrace, itself from OE *faethm*, the embracing arms, hence the full, straight stretch of both arms, hence the measure fathom (6 feet): whence, through ME *fethme*, *fadme*, the E *fathom*: and OE *faethm* is akin to OFris *fethem*, OS *fathom*, fathom, and *fathmos*, the outstretched arms, OHG *fadam*, *fadum*, MHG *vadem*, G *Faden*, thread, fathom, ON *fathmr*, fathom; Gmc r, *\*fath-*; IE r, *pat-*, cf L *patēre*, to lie open, *pandere*, to lay open, Gr *petannunai* (s *petan-*, r *pet-*), to spread out, *petalos* (s *petal-*, r *pet-*), outspread, hence flat (cf PETAL), *patanē* (s *patan-*, r *pat-*), a flat bowl or dish. Cf PATENT.

**fatidical.** See DICT, para 11, and cf the element *fati-*.

**fatigue** (n, v); **indefatigable**, whence **indefatigability**.

*Indefatigable* derives from MF-F *indéfatigable*, itself from LL *indéfatigābilis*: *in-*, not+*\*défatigābilis*, from *défatigāre*, a *dē-* int of *fatigāre*, to exhaust, hence merely to weary: *fatigāre* has s *fatig-*, r *fati-*: prob from L *fatis*, a crevice, a crevasse, s *fati-*, r *fat-*. L *fatigāre* becomes MF-F *fatiguer*, whence 'to *fatigue*'; *fatiguer* has the MF-F derivative n *fatigue*, adopted by E.

**fatten, fatty.** See FAT.

**fatuity, fatuous.** See VAPID.

**faucal, fauces.** See SUFFOCATE, para 2.

**faucet.** See FAIL, para 7.

**fault, faultless, faulty.** See FAIL, para 8.

**faun; fauna.** See FAVOR, FAVOUR, para 2.

**fauteuil.** See STALL, para 9.

**faux pas.** See FAIL, para 6.

**favel.** See the 2nd FAVO(U)R.

(1) **favor** (AE), **favour**, n and v; **favo(u)rable**, **favo(u)rite** (whence **favo(u)ritism**).—**faun** (whence **faunal**), **fauna**, **Faunus**.

1. *Favo(u)r*, n, is adopted from OF-MF, from ML *favor*, L *fauor*, a kindly disposition towards, hence a mark thereof, an *-or* derivative of *fauēre* (s *fau-*), to treat warmly, be kindlily disposed to; IE r, prob *\*bhau-*. OF-MF *favor* (F *faveur*) has deriva-

tive OF-MF v *favorer*, whence 'to *favo(u)r*'. *Favo(u)rable* derives from OF-F *favorable*, itself from ML *favorābilis*, L *fauorābilis* (from *fauor*); *favo(u)rite* derives from EF *favorit*, f *favorite* (cf the F *favori*, f *favorite*), from It *favorito*, pp of *favorire*, to favour, from ML *favor* (L *fauor*).

2. On the L s *fau-* is formed *Faunus* (s *Faun-*, r *fau-*), the god of herds and crops: whence *faun*. The god *Faunus* acquires a prophetic sister, the LL *Fauna*, prob evoked by—and to complement—*Flora*; hence Sci L, Sci E, *fauna*, animals in general: cf *flora*, plant life in general.

(2) *favo(u)r*, as in, and only in, 'to *curry favour*', has been corrupted (from 'to *curry favel*') by the 1st *favo(u)r*: it stands for obs *favel*, a pale-yellow horse, adopted from OF, where it is elliptical for *cheval favel*, a pale-yellow horse: OF *favel*, adj, usu *falve*, comes from Gmc—see the 1st FALLOW.

**fawn** (1), n, a young deer, hence a reddish-yellow hue of brown (the colour of its coat), used derivatively as adj: OF(-F) *faon*, var of *feon*: VL *fētonem*, acc of *fētō*: from L *fētus*, a new-born animal: f.a.e., FETUS.

**fawn** (2), v, to cringe or toady. See FAIN, para 2.

**fay** (1), a fairy: OF-F *fée*: VL *fāta* (cf *Fāta*, the goddess of fate): neu pl (*fāta*)—apprehended as sing—of L *fātum*, q.v. at FATE.

**fay** (2), faith. See FAITH, para 2.

**feague.** See FAKE.

**feal, fealty.** See FAITH, para 4.

**fear** (n, v), whence **fearful, fearless, fearsome.** 'To *fear*', ME *feren*, earlier *faeren*, derives from OE *fǽran*, to terrify, itself from the source of fear, viz. danger, OE *fǽr* (also fear), whence, via ME *fere, feer*, the E n *fear*, fright, dread: and OE *fǽr* is akin to OFris *forfèra* (int *for-*), to terrify—to OHG *fāra*, MHG *vāre*, ambush, evil intent, MHG *gevāre*, treachery, G *Gefahr*, danger—to ON *fārr*, misfortune: Gmc r, *fǽr-*, *fer-*; IE r, *pēr-*, *per-*: cf L *perīculum*, danger, and perh Gr *peira*, an attempt, and E PERIL. (Walshe.)

**feasible** (whence **feasibility**) MF *faisible* (perh suggested by ML *facibilis*), var of MF-F *faisable*, from *fais-*, s of *faisant*, presp of *faire*, to make, to do: L *facere*: f.a.e., FACT, para 1.

**feast**, n and v; **festal, festival** (adj, whence n), **festive, festivity; -fest** (AE), **festa, fiesta, féte; festoon** (n hence v).—cf the 2nd FAIR and also FANE.

1. The AE *-fest* represents G *Fest* (MHG *vest*); *festa* is It, *fiesta* Sp, *fête* F; and all four derive from VL *festa*, holiday, sing n from *festa*, pl of *festum*, neus of adj *festus*, of or for a holiday: from *fēriae*, holidays: r *fes-*+thematic formative *-t-*+ declensional formative *u*+nominative *s*. The r *fes-* does not occur outside of the Italic languages: perh *fes-* comes from an IE r *dhes-*, extn of *dhē-* or *dhē-*, to place, to establish. (E & M.)

2. VL *festa* becomes OF-MF *feste* (whence *féte*), with derivative OF-MF adj *festal* (*-el*), adopted by E. But L *festum* has its own adj *festīuus*, ML *-īvus*, whence E *festive*; derivative *festiuitās*, ML *festīvitās*, o/s *festīvitāt-*, yields OF-MF *festivité*,

whence *festivity*. ML *festīvus* becomes the OF-EF adj *festival* (*-al*), adopted by E, which then converts it into n. VL *festa* becomes It, with aug *festone*, a holiday garland, whence F *feston*, whence E *festoon*.

**feat** (1), adj, ME *fete*, comes from OF *fait*, made, hence well made, pp of *faire*, from L *facere*: f.a.e., FACT.

**feat** (2), n. See FACT, para 7.

**feather** (n; hence v—cf OE *gefitherian*), whence the adj **feathery.**—**pen**, feather, whence, via the quill pen, a writing pen, whence 'to **pen**'; **pennate; pennon** and **pennant;** cf the elements *ptero-* and *strepsi-*.

1. *Feather*, ME from OE *fether*, is akin to OFris *fethere* (in cpds *-fether*), OHG *fedara*, MHG (and MD) *vedere* or *veder*, G *Feder*, ON *fiöthr*(*fjöthr*); to L *penna* and Gr *pteron* (also wing); to Skt *pattra*; and to Hit *pittar*, wing. Gmc etymon, *fether*; IE etymon, *peter* or *pter*. (Walshe.) Cf FERN.

2. L *penna* prob stands for *pet-s-na*, with r *pet-*, to fly: cf Gr *petomai*, Skt *pátāmi*, I fly. *Penna* becomes OF-F *penne*, whence ME *penne*, feather, hence a quill, whence E *pen*. Derivative *pennātus*, provided with feathers, hence winged, yields the *pennate* of Bio and Zoo.

3. OF-F *penne* has the OF-MF derivative *pennon, penon*, adopted by ME, whence E *pennon*, whence, in EE-E and app influenced by *pendant*, the alteration *pennant*.

4. For the matter of paras 2–3, see also the supplementary (and fuller) treatment at the 2nd PEN.

**feature.** See FACT, para 8.

**febrifuge** (cf the elements *febri-* and *-fugal*) and **feverfew; febrile; fever** (n, hence v), whence **feverish** (*-ish*, adj) and literary **feverous** (*-ous*).

1. *Feverfew*, a herb with juice thought to be efficacious against fever, derives from OE *fēferfūge*, a reshaping of LL *febrifuga*, var *-fugia*, the latter yielding late EF-F *fébrifuge*, whence E *febrifuge*; with anl derivative adj *febrifugal* (cf *centrifugal*); *febri-* is the c/f of L *febris*, a fever, and *-fuga* is an end-c/f from *fugāre*, to put to flight, itself from *fuga*, flight, from *fugere*, to flee (f.a.e., FUGITIVE).

2. L *febris* has the LL adj *febrīlis*, whence EF-F *fébrile* and E *febrile*.

3. *Febris* itself becomes OE *fēfer*, whence E *fever*.

**febrile.** See para 2 of prec.

**fecal, feces.** See FAECAL.

**feckless**, shiftless, inefficient, complements **feckful**, strong, efficient: these mainly Sc words have base *feck*, orig effect, now usu force, efficacy: and *feck* represents '*fect*, aphetic for *effect*.

**fecund, fecundate, fecundity.** See FEMALE, para 5.

**federal** (whence **federalism, federalist**); **federate** (adj, n, v), **federation, federative**—cf **confederacy, confederal, confederate** (adj, n, v), **confederation, confederative.**

1. Akin to L *fīdere* (s *fīd-*), to have faith or trust (in someone), and *fīdēs* (f.a.e., FAITH), is L *foedus*

(s *foed*-), a treaty, o/s *foeder*-, whence F *fédéral*, E *federal* (-*al*, adj); whence also *feoderatus*, bound by treaty, whence E *federate*, adj, with derivative n and v; and LL *foederātiō*, o/s *foederātiōn*-, whence MF-F *fédération*, whence E *federation*; and F *fédératif*, f *fédérative*, whence E *federative*.

2. LL has the derivative prefix-cpd *confoederāre*, to unite by treaty (LL *foederāre* is a re-shaping from *foederātus*), with pp *confoederātus*, whence the E adj *confederate* (with derivative n and v). Derivative LL *confoederātiō*, o/s *confoederātiōn*-, yields MF-F *confédération*, whence E *confederation*; *confederal* is an anl formation, after *federal*, as *confederative* is after *federative*. *Confederacy* perh derives from MF *confederacie*, from the LL n *confoederātus*, but prob represents *confederate*+ -*cy*, precisely as *accuracy*=*accura*te+-*cy*.

**fedora**: F *Fédora* (f PN), a Sardou drama published in 1882 and, in 1883, played in England and USA.; it became popular in America and there generated this name for, orig, a style of hat worn by the Russian princess, Fedora Romanoff. EW aptly compares TRILBY.

**fee** (n, whence v), a heritable estate (cf the legal *in fee simple*), hence a charge thereon, hence a fixed, monetary compensation: ME *fee*, fief, payment: (prob via AF *fee*, from) OF *fius, fieus*, acc *fiu, fieu*, MF-F *fief*: akin to OE *feoh*, cattle, hence property, whence the obs E *fee*, (personal) property; OHG *fihu, fehu*, MHG *vihe*, G *Vieh*, cattle, and Go *faihu*, ON *fē*, cattle, (hence) property, money, cattle being 'the oldest form of wealth' (Walshe): cf L *pecūnia*, money, from *pecū, pecus*, cattle (f.a.e., PECUNIARY).

2. MF-F *fief* is adopted by E, esp in sense 'feudal estate'; the derivative v *fieffer* becomes AF *feoffer*, whence legal 'to *feoff*' (with var *enfeoff*: AF *enfeoffer*: MF *enfieffer*); the AF v has pp *feoffé*, whence legal *feoffee*.

3. Of the same general Gmc origin is ML *feodum, feudum*—cf OHG *fehu*, cattle, and OHG *ōt*, possession, (hence) property, akin to OE *ēad*— whence hist *feud* or *feod*, a heritable right, distinct from the 2nd FEUD, enmity, quarrel. ML *feudum* has adj *feudālis*, whence E *feudal*, as in *the feudal system*, whence *feudalism*.

4. In the Scan group of the Gmc languages, we find an important cognate: the ON *fēlag*, a laying (-*lag*) together of property (*fē*-), hence a partnership, whence ON *fēlagi*, a partner, hence a comrade, whence late OE *fēolaga*, whence ME *felaghe*, later *felawe*, whence E *fellow* (with derivative v); derivative ME *felawscipe* (etc.) becomes E *fellowship* (suffix -*ship*).

**feeble**, whence **feebleness**; **enfeeble**, whence **enfeeblement**; **foible**.

1. The adj *feeble* derives from ME *feble*, adopted from OF-MF, which has the OF-MF var *foible*, which becomes an E n, 'weak point or part (esp moral)'; now, OF-MF *feble* is a metathesis of OF *flebe*, itself from L *flēbilis*, to be wept over, lamentable, an -*ibilis* derivative of *flēre* (s *flē*-), to weep (vi), to weep over: akin to OE *bellan* and

cognate *bylgan*, and ON *belia*, (of cattle) to bellow, and OHG *bellan*, to bark—cf, therefore, BELLOW.

2. OF-MF *feble* (var *feible, faible*) has derivative prefix-cpd v *enfeblir, enfeiblir* (*en*, in, used int), to deprive of strength: whence 'to *enfeeble*'.

**feed** (v, hence n)—pt, pp fed—whence **feeder** and **feeding**; **fodder** (n hence v); **food.—foster**, n (whence adj) and v, whence **fosterage** (*age*); **fosterchild, -mother.**

1. 'To *feed*'=OE *fēdan*, akin to OFris *fēda*, OS *fōdian*, Go *fōdjan*, OHG *fuottan*, which are all akin to OE *fōda*, ME *fode*, E *food*—and to OE *fōdor*, food for animals, whence E *fodder*, and therefore to OHG *fuotar*, MHG *fuoter*, G *Futter*, and ON *fōthr*, and again, though less nearly, the L *pābulum* (s *pāb*-, r *pā*-), food, fodder, *pānis* (s *pān*-, r *\*pā*-), bread, *pāscere* (s *pāsc*-, extn of *\*pās*-, r *\*pā*-), to pasture, therefore also to Gr *pateomai* (s *pate*-, r *pat*-, extn of *\*pa*). The Gmc r is app *\*fōd*-; the IE r, *\*pā*-, to eat, with extnn *\*pāb*-, *\*pān*-, *\*pās*-, *\*pat*-. Cf PASTOR (and *pasture* and *repast*).

2. Akin to OE *fōdor* and *fēdan* is OE *fōster* or *fōstor*, a nourishing, a rearing, whence the syn but obs E n *foster*; the OE cpds *fōstercild, fōstermōdor*, become *fosterchild, fostermother*. OE *fōster*, which has derivative v *fōstrian*, whence 'to *foster*', is akin to the syn ON *fōstr* and OS *fōster*, and to ON *fōstra*, a fostermother. The OE words suggest that, orig, they were freqq of *fēdan*, influenced by *fōdor*.

**feel**, v, whence n and **feeler** and pa, vn **feeling** (**unfeeling**, adj); pt, pa **felt** (**unfelt**, adj).—**palm** of hand (n hence v), whence, either from the leaf's resemblance to the hand's tracerled palm (Webster) or from 'the spreading fronds' (EW), the palm tree; **palmaceous; palmar, palmary; palmate; palmer; palmetto; palmist, palmistry; palmitic; palmus; palmy; palmyra.—palp, palpable (impalpable), palpate, palpation, palpatory; palpebral; palpitant, palpitate, palpitation; palpus,** whence adj **palpal.— psalm, psalmist, psalmody, psaltery.**

1. 'To *feel*' derives, through ME *felen*, from OE *fēlan*, akin to the syn OFris *fēla*, OS *gifōlian* (*gi*-, G *ge*-, int), OHG *fuolēn*, MHG *füelen*, G *fühlen*, MD *vuelen, volen*, (as in D) *voelen*; to ON *fālma*, to grope, fumble; also to L *palpāre*, to touch, to stroke; Gr *psallein*, to cause to vibrate, to shake, *psēlaphan*, to stroke, grope, the 2nd element being *haphaō*, I touch, stir, excite; Skt as*phāl*ayati, he shakes, flaps, strikes.

2. L *palma*, palm of the hand, could derive from *\*palpma*, 'the feeler', but is prob for *\*palama*, deriving from or intimately akin to the syn Gr *palamē*, s *palam*-, r *pal*-. (Some etymologists relate the Gr and L word to the PLACE group, basic idea 'flatness'.) Its derivatives include E *palm*, G *Palm* (the tree), OF-F *paume* (OF-MF *palme*)—cf OProv *palma*. Derivatives include *palmaceous* (-*aceous*, perh after *rosaceous*); *palmar*, from L *palmāris*, of the palm of the hand; *palmary*, from L *palmārius*, of palm trees, hence deserving the palm leaves, anciently a symbol of victory—cf *bear away the palm* and *the palm of martyrdom*; *palmate*, hand-

shaped, from L *palmātus*; the medieval *palmer* wore two palm leaves, crossed, to show that he had visited the Holy Land—from OF-F *palmier*, ML *palmārius*, n from the adj; *palmetto*, a fan palm, reshapes Sp *palmito*, dim of *palma*, a palm tree; *palmist*, hand-reading fortune-teller, is either a b/f from *palmistry* or short for EE *palmister*, and *palmistry*, ME *paumestry* (or *pau-*)=ME *paume*, palm of the hand+*maistrie* (E *mystery*), adopted from OF-MF; *palmitic*=F *palmitique*, a fatty acid occurring in palm oil; *palmy*=*palm* (tree)+adj *-y*, from association with palmy and pleasant shores and countries; *palmyra*, a tall African palm, derives from Port *palmeira*, a palm tree.

3. Note, however, that SciL *palmus* derives from Gr *palmos* (r *pal-*+formative *-m-*+declensional *-o-*+nominative *-s*), palpitation: cf para 8.

4. L *palpāre*, to touch, stroke, feel, becomes late MF-F *palper*, whence E 'to *palp*'. Derivative *palpābilis* yields, via late MF-F, the E *palpable*, whence *palpability*, with neg LL *impalpābilis*, whence *impalpable*, whence *impalpability*; derivative *palpātiō*, o/s *palpātiōn-*, yields *palpation*, whence, anl, *palpatory*; Med *palpate* comes from the pp *palpātus*. But L *palpus*, the soft palm of the hand, (? hence) a caress, whence Zoo *palpus*, a feeler, is prob the origin of *palpāre*.

5. *Palpebral* (of the eyelids)= LL *palpebrālis*, adj of L *palpebra*, an eyelid, characterized by its repeated movements in blinking, fluttering, etc., and therefore, like *palpus*, indicating the close kinship of the Gr words.

6. L *palpāre* has freq *palpitāre*, to be briskly agitated, to flutter. The presp *palpitans*, o/s *palpit-ant-*, becomes the E adj *palpitant*; pp *palpitātus* yields 'to *palpitate*'; derivative *palpitātiō*, o/s *pal-pitātiōn-*, accounts for *palpitation*.

7. Gr *palamē*, palm of the hand (cf para 2), becomes Zoo Sci L *palama*, the webbing of aquatic birds' feet, whence Zoo *palamate*, web-footed (cf PALMATE in para 2).

8. Gr *psallein*, to pull briskly and repeatedly, to twitch, to pluck at the strings of, eg., a lyre, to make vibrate (cf para 1), LGr to sing religious hymns, is either an echoic freq of *\*pallein*, to shake, IE r *\*pal-*, to move lightly, quickly, repeatedly, or a very early metathesis of syn *\*palassein*, extended from r *\*pal-* and formed like *malassein*, to render soft or supple. *Psallein* has these derivatives affecting E:

*psalmos*, orig a plucking of musical strings, later a song accompanied on the harp, whence LL *psalmus*, whence OE-E *psalm*, with adj *psalmic*;

LGr *psalmistēs*, LL *psalmista*, E *psalmist*;

LGr *psalmōidia*, a singing (*aeidein*, to sing) of psalms to the harp, later a collection of psalms: LL *psalmōdia*: OF-F *psalmodie*: E *psalmody*;

*psaltērion*, a stringed instrument: LL *psaltērium*, whence both MF *psalterion* (F *-érion*) and OF-MF *psalterie*, whence, via ME, the E *psaltery*, an ancient form of zither, and OE *psaltere*, E *psalter*, The Book of Psalms, with intervention, in the ME period, of OF *saltier* (from the LL word), the two

words affording an illuminating example of sense-differentiation arising so early as LL.

**feet.** See FOOT.

**feign,** whence pa *feigned*; **faint** (adj, hence v; from both, the n); **feint** (n, whence v); **fictile**, **fiction** (whence **fictional**), **fictitious**, **fictive**—cf **figment**; sep EFFIGY.

1. The base is the L *fingere*, to model in clay, hence to fashion in any plastic material, then to fashion or form, and finally to invent, imagine, even to pretend. *Fingere* becomes OF-F *feindre* (in OF-MF, a vr), with presp *feignant* (s *feign-*), whence ME *feinen* or *feignen*, the latter surviving as 'to *feign*'.

2. OF *feindre* has pp *feint*, whence the obs E *feint*, feigned; the OF *feint* has f *feinte*, used also, in MF-F, elliptically for *action* (or *chose*) *feinte*, a false appearance, a trick, whence the E n *feint*.

3. The OF-F pp *feint* has the OF-MF var *faint*, adopted by ME and extant in E, (orig) feigned, hence cowardly ('*Faint* heart never won fair lady'), lacking in spirit, hence lacking consciousness, our *faint*.

4. Nasal *fingere* has s *fing-*, but r *fig-*, as in the derivative *figmentum*, something fashioned, whence E *figment*, esp a thing fashioned by the imagination.

5. *Fingere* has pp *fictus*, a *fict-*, on which arise: *fictilis*, (capable of being) moulded, whence E *fictile*;

*fictiō*, a moulding or fashioning, o/s *fiction-* whence, via MF-F, the E *fiction*;

*ficticius*, whence E *fictitious*;

late MF-F *fictif* (f *-ive*), whence E *fictive*.

6. F.a.e.: FIGURE.

**feint.** See prec, para 2.

**feldspar,** earlier **feldspath**: both adopted from G: *Feldspat*, earlier *Feldspath*: *feld* (see FIELD)+*Spat*, earlier *Spath*, spar: and E *spar*, a non-metallic mineral occurring in a metalliferous vein, is adopted from MLG *spar*. The modern use of *spar* arises from a confusion of the MLG *spar* with G *Spath*, *Spat*. MLG *spar* is akin to OE *spaer*stān, chalkstone; this OE *spaer*, frugal, is the source of the E adj SPARE.

**felicitate, felicitation, felicitous, felicity**—cf **in-felicitous, infelicity; felix, felicia.**

1. The base is L *felix* (s and r *fēl-*), o/s *fēlic-*, fruitful, (specialized as) fortunate, prosperous, happy, whence the m PN *Felix*, with f *Felicia*. The L adj *fēlix* app derives from *\*fēla*, breast—cf FEMALE; orig, therefore, *fēlix* would have meant 'milk-giving or -supplying'. (E & M.) Cf *Arabia Felix*, the fertile region, opp *Arabia Deserta*.

2. On o/s *fēlic-* arises

*fēlicitās*, fertility, hence prosperity, happiness, with o/s *fēlicitāt-*, whence MF *felicité* (F *fé-*), whence E *felicity*, whence *felicitous* (*felicity*+adj *-ous*). On *fēlicit-* arises rare LL *fēlicitāre*, to render happy, with pp *fēlicitātus*, whence 'to *felicitate*,' esp to congratulate; *felicitation* derives from EF(-F) *félicitation*, erudite derivative of F *féliciter* (from *félicitāre*).

3. L *felix* has neg *infelix* (*in-*, not), whence *infelicitas*, o/s *infelicitat-*, whence EF-F *infélicité*, whence E *infelicity*, whence, anl, *infelicitous*.

feline, felinity. The latter derives, by suffix *-ity*, from the former; the former derives from VL *felinus*, from L *felineus*, of a (wild) cat, from *feles* (var *felis*), a cat, a wild cat: o.o.o.: perh cf Eg *pek*hat, the Cat-Goddess.

Felix. See FELICITATE.

fell (1), adj; felo de se, felon, felonious, felonry.

*Fell*, cruel, deadly, came into ME from OF *fel* (cfMD *fel*), fierce, cruel, the OF nom of OF-MF *felo* (F *fé-*), which, both adj and n, was adopted by ME for 'cruel' and 'a cruel man, esp a villain', whence E *felon*, whence the adj *felonious* (perh cf EF *felonnieux*, f *-ieuse*, treacherous, and EF *felonneux*, f *-euse*, cruel, wicked) and the n *felonry* (*-ry* for-*ery*); derivative OF-MF *felonie* (F *fé-*) becomes E *felony*. The legal *felo-de-se* is AL: *felo*, a villain+ *de*, concerning, of+*se*, oneself. Now AL *felo* derives either from VL *fello* (gen *fellonis*), perh from L *fel* (gen *fellis*), bile, with basic idea 'bitterness', hence 'venom', or, via Carolingian L *fello*, from a Frankish *fillo*, a reduction of *filljo*, a whipper, hence maltreater, esp of slaves, from a Frankish v that answers to OHG *fillen*, to whip (B & W).

fell (2), n, a skin or esp a hide: OE *fell*: cf OFris *fell*, OHG *fel*, MHG *vel*, G *Fell*, MD *velle*, MD-D *vel*, in cpds Go *-fill*, ON *fiall* and, in cpds, *-fell*: corresponding to L *pell*is, skin, hide, and Gr *pell*a, a milk-bowl or -pail, ? made of skin; Gmc r, *fil-*; IE r, *pel-*. (Walshe.) Cf FILM.

fell (3), n, orig a hill, now a (high) moor: ON *fjall*, mountain: akin to OHG *felis*, MHG *vels*, G *Fels*, a (great) rock; perh cf Gr *Pel*ion, a mountain in Thessaly.

fell (4), v, to cut down (a tree), beat or knock down (a person). See FALL, para 2.

felloe. See FELLY.

fellow, fellowship. See FEE, para 4.

felly, also felloe: ME *feli*, *felow*, *felwe*: OE *felg*: cf OHG *felaga*, *felga*, MHG *velge*, G *Felge*, MD *velge*, D *velg*: Walshe compares Skt *párśuš*, a rib.

felo-de-se; felon, felonious, felony. See the 1st FELL.

felt (n hence v), whence vn felting: OE *felt*: akin to OHG *filz*, MHG *vilz*, G *Filz*. These words are akin to Gr *pilos*, L *pilus*, a hat, and esp to ML *filtrum*, var *feltrum* (whence OF-F *feutre*, felt, fulled wool, esp used for straining a liquid), whence EF-F *filtre*, whence E *filter*; derivative EF-F *filtrer* becomes 'to *filter*'. ML *filtrum* has derivative v *filträre*, with pp *filträtus*, whence 'to *filtrate*'. Learnèd EF-F *filtration* (from *filtrer*) was adopted by E.

Cf PILE, hair.

2. Derivative EF-F s'*infiltrer* prob suggested 'to *infiltrate*' (*in-*, into); its EF-F derivative *infiltration* was adopted by E.

felucca. See LUG.

felwort. See FIELD, para 2, s.f.

female (n hence adj); feminine, femininity (femi-

neity), feminism, feminist, feminize; femme (fatale); cf effeminate, whence effeminacy.—fecund, fecundate (whence fecundative, fecundatory), fecundity.

1. *Effeminate* anglicizes L *effeminatus*, pp of *effeminare*, to make a *femina* or woman *ex*, out of.

2. *Femina*, woman (hence also wife), represents perh the reduction of a presp that answers to the rare *feminatus* (pp used as adj), form-resembles *alunna*, f of *alumnus*, from *alere*, to nourish, and lit means 'milk-giving', hence 'milk-giver' (breast-feeder).

3. L *femina* becomes OF-F *femme*.

4. *Femina* has these derivatives affecting E:
*femella*, little woman—OF-F *femelle*—ME *femelle*, whence, after *male*, the E *female*;
*femineus*, of a woman, whence E *femineity*;
*femininus*, of a woman, womanly—OF-MF *feminin* (F *fé-*), f *-ine*—E *feminine*, whence *femininity*. But *feminism*, *-ist*, *-ize*, come, perh with F encouragement, from *femin-*, s of *femina*.

5. L *femina*, s *femin-*, has r *fem-*, itself an extn of *fe-*, woman, essential physical femineity; this is the r of L *fecundus*, (of land, crops, females) fertile, E *fecund* (via MF-F *fécond*, f *féconde*). Derivative *fecundare*, pp *fecundatus*, yields 'to *fecundate*', to render fruitful, and derivative *fecunditas*, o/s *fecunditat-*, yields *fecundity*. The adjj *fecundative*, *fecundatory*, are E anl formations in *-ive*, *-ory*, from L *fecundat-*, s of the pp *fecundatus*. *Fecundus* is app an ancient participle: *fec-* (extn of *fe-*)+*-und-*, presp base (cf *facundus* from *fari*, to speak)+*-u-*, declensional formative+nom *-s*.

6. The r *fe-* occurs also in L *felix*, q.v. at FELICITATE, and in FETUS. It rests upon an IE r *dhe-*, to give suck to, with examples, not only in L but also in Gr; in C and Gmc; and in Skt.

7. Cf FILIAL.

femoral, femur. See the element *femoro-*.

fen: OE *fen* or *fenn*, marsh, primarily mud: akin to OFris *fene* or *fenne*, OS *fen*, OHG *fenna*, G *Fenn*, ON *fen*, marsh, and Go *fani*, mud, and, further off, Skt *pañka*, mud.

fence; fencible. See last para of:

fend, fender—cf fence, fencible, fencing; defend (whence defender), defence (AE *-nse*), defensive (adj hence n); offend (whence offender), offence (AE *-se*), offensive (adj hence n).—gonfalon, gonfanon.

1. L *fendere*, to strike or knock, appears in three prefix-cpds, of which only *defendere* and *offendere* concern E. It has s *fend-*, r *fen-*, and is akin to Gr *theinein*, to strike, Skt *gonim*, I wound severely, *hánti*, he strikes, *ghanás*, a club, Hit *kunanzi*, they strike; to OP *gun*nimai, we push, OSl *gün*ati, Lith *genù*, to chase, pursue; to ON *gun*nr, combat, OHG *gund*, war (cf OE *güth*, battle). The IE r is prob *gwhen-*, to strike.

2. OHG *gund* occurs in the OHG cpd *gundfano*, a war flag (for *fano*, cloth, cf E VANE): whence MF *gonfanon*, a kind of *gonfalon*, a princely ensign or standard; MF-F *gonfalon* is a dissimilation of OF *gonfanon*.

3. L *offendere* (*of-* for *ob-*, in front of, over against, on account of), to knock against, shock,

wound, becomes OF-MF *offendre*, whence E 'to *offend*'. The L pp *offensus* has derivative syn nn *offensum* and *offensa*, whence MF-F *offense*, adopted by ME with var *offence*; derivative EF-F *offensif*, f -*ive*, becomes E *offensive*. *Inoffensive* is likewise of F origin.

4. L *defendere*, to knock or strike away (connoted by *de*, down from), to repel, hence to protect, becomes OF-MF *defendre* (F *dé-*), whence 'to *defend*'. The L pp *dēfensus* has derivative syn nn *dēfensum* and *dēfensa*, whence OF-MF *defense*, adopted by ME with var *defence*; LL *dēfensibilis* (*dēfens*us+-*ibilis*), capable of defence, yields *defensible*; ML *dēfensivus* yields—perh via MF-F *défensif*, f -*ive*—*defensive*.

5. *Defence* acquired, by aphesis in late ME, the derivative n *fence*, orig an act, then a means, of defending oneself, esp in self-defence, usu with sword; the derivative v leads to the vn *fencing* and the agent *fencer*. Derivative *fencible*, able to defend or to be defended, now archaic, becomes n—'the *fencibles*', the Napoleonic Wars original of the Home Guards.

**fenestella; fenestra, fenestral, fenestrate.** See PENATES, para 3.

**fennel**: OE *fenol*: VL *\*fēnuc(u)lum*, for L *fēniculum* (or *faeni-*), dim of *fēnum* (*faenum*), hay, s *fēn*, *faen-*, perh an extn of the r *\*fē-* occurring in *fēcundus, fēlix, fēmina, fētus*, and therefore meaning 'product' (sc of the meadow), as E & M propose.

2. L *faenum Graecum*, (lit) Greek hay, an aromatic herb, becomes *faenugraecum*, whence MF *fenegrec*, soon *fenugrec*, whence E *fenugreek*.

**fenny**: *fen*+euphonic -*n*-+adj -*y*.

**fenugreek**. See FENNEL, para 2.

**feoff, feoffee**. See FEE, para 2.

**feral; ferine**. See FIERCE, para 2.

**Feringhee, Fering(h)i**. See FRANK, para 10.

**ferment (n, v), fermentation**.

The latter derives from LL *fermentātiō*, a leavening, o/s *fermentātiōn*-, from *fermentāt*us, pp of *fermentāre*, whence, via MF-F *fermenter*, the E 'to *ferment*': and *fermentāre* derives from *fermentum*, a leaven, esp yeast, whence, via MF-F, the E n *ferment*. *Fermentum=fer-* (as in *feruēre*, ML *fervēre*; cf FERVENT)+formative -*mentum*; IE r, *\*bher*-. The Gmc shape is seen in E BARM.

**fern** (whence *ferny*): OE *fearn*: akin to OHG *faram*, MHG *varm, varn*, G *Farn*, MD *varn* and (as in D) *varen*, and esp Skt *parṇa*, wing, feather, hence a feathery plant, esp a fern—cf Gr *pteron*, feather, wing, and *pteris*, bracken: cf, therefore, FEATHER.

**ferocious, ferocity**. See FIERCE, para 3.

**ferret** (n, whence v—cf the F *fureter*), with adj *ferrety*: MF-EF *fuiret*, whence MF-F *furet*, an *fet* dim of MF-EF *fuiron*, whence MF-F *furon* (s *fuir-, fur-*): VL *\*furiōnem*, acc of *furiō*, debasement or enlargement of LL *furō*, a cat, orig a thief, itself from L *fūr*, a thief: f.a.e., FURTIVE.

**ferric, ferrous, ferruginous**; cf the element *ferro-*, and sep FARRIER.

*Ferric*=L *ferrum*, iron+E adj suffix -*ic*; *ferrous*=*ferrum*+adj -*ous*; *ferruginous*=L *ferrūginus*, adj of *ferrūgō*, iron-rust, o/s *ferrūgin*-, from *ferrum* (r *fer*-): o.o.o.: perh of Hit origin—cf Ass *parzillu*, iron; more prob Eg—cf *parthal*.

**ferrule**. See WIRE, para 4.

**ferry** (v, whence n): ME *ferien*: OE *ferian*: akin to ON *ferja*, to ferry, and, further off, OE *faran*, to travel: f.a.e., FARE.

**fertile, fertility, fertilize** (whence **fertilization** and **fertilizer**).

*Fertile* comes, prob via MF-F, from L *fertilis*: *fer*-, r of *ferre*, to bear, carry+formative -*t*-+ the common adj suffix -*ilis*: f.a.e., BEAR, v. *Fertilis* has derivative *fertilitās*, o/s *fertilitāt*-, whence, prob via MF-F *fertilité*, the E *fertility*. MF-F *fertile* has EF-F derivative *fertiliser*, whence 'to *fertilize*'.

**ferule**, (obs) the giant fennel, hence a school master's stick; the fennel's stalks were anciently used as a cane for punishing schoolboys: L *ferula*, retained by Bot: perh from L *ferīre*, to strike; perh akin to L *festūca*, a straw, a light rod, itself perh from *\*ferstūca*.

**fervent, fervency; fervescent, fervescence; fervid; fervor** (AE), **fervour;—effervesce, effervescence, effervescent**.

1. 'To *effervesce*' derives from ML *effervescere*, L *efferuescere*, an *ex*- int of *feruescere*, to begin to boil, inch of *feruēre*, to boil, be boiling; presp (ML) *effervescens*, o/s *effervescent*-, yields *effervescent*, whence *effervescence*.

2. L *feruēre*, s *feru*-, r *fer*-, goes back to IE *\*bher*-, to bubble, to boil: cf Skt *bhuráti*, it is agitated, it bubbles; cognates in Gr, C, Arm, Alb. Cf FERMENT and BARM.

3. *Feruēre*, ML *fervēre*, has presp *fervens*, o/s *fervent*-, whence, via OF, the adj *fervent*; OF-F *fervent* has the MF-EF derivative *fervence*, whence obs E *fervence* and, by anl, *fervency*; the inch (ML) *fervescere* has presp *fervescens*, o/s *fervescent*-, whence *fervescent*, whence *fervescence*.

4. L *feruēre* has two derivatives affecting E: *feruidus*, ML *fervidus*, boiling, whence *fervid*; *feruor*, ML *fervor*, a boiling, heat, ardour, whence OF-MF *fervor* or *fervour* (cf F *ferveur*), E adopting the latter, AE the former (unless straight from the ML form).

**-fest, festa; festal; festival, festive, festivity**. See FEAST, para 1 for first two; para 2 for the others.

**festoon**. See FEAST, para 2.

**festuca**, adopted by Bot: see FERULE.

**fetal**. See FETUS.

**fetch** (v, whence n), to go and get (bring alor g, bring forward), derives, through ME *fecchen*, from OE *fecan*, var of *fetian*, akin to OE *faet*, a step, itself akin to FOOT. The presp is used derivatively as coll adj for 'attractive'.

**fête**. See FEAST, para 1.

**fetich**. See FACT, para 3 at *facticius*.

**fetid** (whence **fetidity**), evil-smelling: L *fetidus*, var of *foetidus*, from *fetēre*, var of *foetēre*, to smell bad, to stink, s *fet-, foet*-, perh akin to L *foedus*, repulsive, disgusting; both *foetēre* and *foedus* are o.o.o.—nevertheless, *foet-* and *foed-*, with prob r *\*foe-*, strikingly recall Eg *hua-t* (r *hua-*), stench, (adj) stinking.

2. *Foetēre*, *fetēre* has the further derivative *foetor*, *fetor*, stench, adopted by learnèd and Sci E.

**fetish.** See FACT, para 3 at *factitius*.

**fetlock.** See FOOT, para 3.

**fetor.** See FETID, para 2.

**fetter.** See FOOT, para 4.

**fettle** (v, whence n, as *in fine fettle*, in excellent condition) derives from ME *fettlen*, *fetlen*, to set in order, orig to gird up, from OE *fetel*, a girdle, akin to ON *fetill*, a strap, and OHG *fezzil*, a sword-belt, and *fazzōn*, to seize, equip, MHG *vazzen*, G *fassen*, to contain, grasp (cf OE *fatian*): f.a.e., VAT.

**fetus,** incorrectly **foetus**: L *fētus*, the bearing, the bringing forth, of a child, pregnancy, hence the newborn child, akin to—prob from—L *fētus* (adj), childbearing, fruitful, with s *fēt-*, r *fē-* (as in *fecund*, q.v. at FEMALE), essential physical femineity. Derivative adj *fetal*.

2. For derivative L *effētus*, lit 'having ceased to bear children', see EFFETE. Derivative L *superfētāre*, to conceive during pregnancy (*super*, over), has pp *superfētātus*, whence 'to *superfetate*', with derivative *superfetation*.

3. Cf the sep FAWN (1).

**feud** (1), a heritable right. See FEE, para 3.

**feud** (2), continued, usu active, hostility: ME *feide*: OF *feide*, *faide*: OHG ga-*fēhida* (int *ga-*), whence G *Fehde*: akin to OHG gi-*fēh*, OE *fāh*, OFris *fāch*, hostile, OE *fāēth*, OFris *fāithe*, *fēithe*, enmity, Go *-faihs*, deception: f.a.e., FOE. The spelling has been influenced by the 1st FEUD.

**feudal, feudalism.** See FEE, para 3.

**fever, feverish.** See FEBRIFUGE, para 3; at para 1, FEVERFEW.

**few** (whence **fewness**): ME *fewe*, earlier *feawe*: OE *fēawe*, the pl of *fēa*: akin to OE *fēa*, OFris *fē*, OS *fāh*, OHG fao, *fō*, ON *fār*, little, and to Go *fawai* (pl); to L *pauci*, few men, *pauca*, few things (and also to *pauper*, poor), and Gr *pauros*, little, in small number: cf, therefore, PAUCITY and POOR.

**fey,** doomed, hence—esp in Sc—appearing to be doomed to die, derives from OE *fāēge*, akin to OE *fāh*, inimical, and ON *feigr*, OHG *feigi*, doomed to die, G *feig*, cowardly: perh akin to the 2nd FEUD; f.a.e., FOE.

**fez:** F *fez* (EF *fes*): *Fez*, the capital of Morocco, where this felt cap was first made.

**fiancé, fiancée.** See FAITH, para 11.

**fiasco,** a flask or bottle (esp of wine), hence—? from 'dead marines' and smashed bottles—a crash, esp a resounding or ludicrous failure: via F, from It, *fiasco*, bottle, crash, of Gmc origin. The 'failure' sense may have an independent origin: it comes, in F, from *faire fiasco*, from It *far fiasco*, to make a failure, and this It *fiasco* is not certainly the 'bottle' *fiasco*. (See esp B & W.) Cf FLASK.

**fiat:** L *fiat*, let it be done, from *fiō*, I am made, I become, used as passive of *facere* but app of same r as *fuī*, I have been.

**fib** (n and v; whence **fibster**) prob derives from *fiddle faddle*, nonsense, a redup of *fable*.

**fiber** (AE) or **fibre**; **fibril, fibrillate** (whence **fibrillation**); **fibrin**; element **fibro-**; **fibrose, fibrous**; **fibrosis, fibrositis.**

*Fiber* comes straight from L *fibra* (o.o.o.), *fibre* from the MF-F form. The ML adj *fibrōsus* yields both *fibrose* and *fibrous*, the latter perh suggested by *fibreuse*, f of EF-F *fibreux*, from *fibre*. SciL coins the dim *fibrilla*, whence *fibril* and, by anl, *fibrillate*; Biochemistry coins *fibrin* (chem *-in*); Med introduces *fibrosis* (suffix *-osis*, denoting a diseased condition) and *fibrositis*, which=*fibroso-*, Sci c/f of *fibrōsus*+*-itis*, 'disease'. This L *fiber* is distinct from L *fiber*, a beaver.

**fibster.** See FIB.

**fickle** (whence **fickleness**), orig deceitful: ME *fikel*: OE *ficol*: cf OE *gefic*, deceit or fraud, *fācen*, deceit; L *piget*, it disgusts; and ult E FOE.

**fico.** See FIG.

**fictile.** See FEIGN, para 5.

**fiction, fictional, fictitious, fictive.** See FEIGN, para 5.

**fiddle** (n hence v, whence pa and vn **fiddling**); **fiddler** (**Fiddler's Green**); **fiddle-de-dee**; **fiddlesticks.** —**vielle, viol, viola, violin, violinist, violoncello** (abbr **'cello**), **violoncellist.**

1. 'To *fiddle*', in all senses, derives from the modern n; *fiddler*, OE *fithelere*, derives from the OE form of the n: *fithele* (ME *fithele*, later *fidele*). OE *fithele* prob comes from ML *fidula*; but ME *fidel*(e), prob from the ML var *fidella*; ML *fidusa* and *fidella* are dimm (cf L *fidicula*) of L *fidēs*, *fidīl*, lyre or guitar, b/f of pl *fidēs*, the strings of a lyre, itself o.o.o.; the derivation from VL-ML *vitula*, a fiddle, from L *Uitula*, ML *Vitula*, Goddess of Exultation or Victory (whence *uitulāri*, to sing or rejoice), is ingenious but far less prob. (The goddess's name is perh Sabine: E & M.)

2. *Fiddler's Green* is the sailor's paradise, with junketing to tunes on the fiddle; *fiddle-de-dee!* comes from the n *fiddle*, perh ref tuning-up thereon; *fiddlesticks!* comes from *fiddlestick*, the bow, so much less valuable than the fiddle itself.

3. *Vielle*, a large medieval viol, is adopted from F, of imm Gmc origin but ult from L *uitula*, ML *vitula* (as in para 1); *viol* derives from ME *vyell*, from OF-F *vielle*, perh influenced by OProv *viola*; E *viola* is adopted from It *viòla*, itself adopted from OProv *viola*, prob, like OF-F *vielle*, imm of Gmc origin.

4. It *viòla* has dim *violino*, whence (late MF-F *violon* and) E *violin*; derivative It *violinista* has suggested E *violinist*.

5. It *viòla* has also the aug *violone*, a double-bass viol, a term adopted by E; and It *violone* has dim *violoncello*, likewise adopted by E, which, in *violoncellist*, prob reshapes derivative It *violoncellista*. E *violoncello*, *violoncellist*, have aphetic derivatives *'cello*, *'cellist*.

**fidelity.** See FAITH, para 5.

**fidget,** v—hence n **fidget,** a restless person, and **fidgets,** restlessness, and **fidgety,** restless—is a freq

of *fidge* (now only dial), varr *fitch, fig, fike*: ME
*fiken*, to fidget: prob from, at the least akin to,
ON *fīkjask*, to desire eagerly, be eager.

**Fido.** See FAITH, para 7.

**fiducial, fiduciary.** See FAITH, para 8.

**fie!**, like *faugh!* and *foh!*, is merely echoic.

**fief.** See FEE, para 2.

**field** (n, whence adj and v)—fieldfare—field
marshal—felwort; sep **feldspar; veld, veldschoen.**

1. A *field* comes, through ME *fild*, earlier *feld*,
from OE *feld*: akin to OFris, OS, OHG *feld*, MHG
*velt*, G *Feld*, MD *veelt, velt*, (also D) *veld*; also,
with mutation, ON *fold*, OS *folda*, OE *folde*, earth,
land: Gmc r, *\*feld-*, var *\*fuld-*. If *field* is akin to E
*place* and *plane*, the IE r is *\*pelt-* or *\*palt-*, with
metathesis *\*plet-, \*plat-*, in Gr *platus*, flat, and
mdfn *\*plan-* in syn L *plānus*; cf Skt *práthati*, it
widens or broadens out. Cf FLAT and PLACE.

2. *Fieldfare* = ME *feldefare* = OE *feldeware*, ? for
*feldefare*: app—but perh only app—*felde*, field +
*fare*, a going (FARE);

*field marshal*, orig a kind of quartermaster-
general, merely anglicizes the slightly earlier G
*Feldmarschall*, which merely translates F *maréchal
de camp*;

*feldspar*, sep entry;

*felwort*: OE *feldwyrt* (cf WORT).

3. D *veld*, field, becomes, in Afr, grassland, however extensive, esp the *grass veld* of Natal and
Transvaal, and the *bush veld* in Cape Province;
*veldt* is an obs spelling. Afr *veldschoen*, prop a shoe
that is nailless and of untanned hide, is a f/e (after
*veld*) refashioning of Afr *velschoen*: *vel* (E *fell*),
skin, hide + *schoen*, a shoe.

**fiend** (whence **fiendish**: adj *-ish*): ME *fiend*,
earlier *feond*: OE *fēond*, orig the presp of *fēon*, to
hate (cf OHG *fīēn*, Go *fijan*, ON *fiā*): akin to
OFris *fīand, fīūnd*, OS *fīond*, OHG *fīant* (MHG
*vīant, vīent*), G *Feind*, Go *fijands*, ON *fiānde*, all
orig 'the enemy'; cf also Skt *píyati*, he scorns or
abuses.

**fierce** (whence 'to fiercen' and **fierceness); feral**
and **ferine; ferocious, ferocity.**—**theriac;** element
*therio*-; **treacle.**

1. *Fierce*: ME *fiers, fers*, both adopted from OF,
where they form the nom of *fier, fer*, fierce, savage
(cf the derivative *fier*, haughty, proud): L *ferus*,
wild (untamed), cruel, whence (elliptical for *fera
bēstia*) the n *fera*, a wild beast: akin to the syn
Aeolic Gr *phēr*, Thessalian *pheir*, varr of Gr *thēr*,
with elaboration—strictly a dim—*thērion*; IE
etymon, *\*ghēr, \*ghuer*—cf OLith *žverù*, of wild
beasts, Lith *žvéris*, wild beast, OP *swīrins* (acc),
wild beasts. (E & M; Hofmann.)

2. L *fera*, wild beast, has LL derivative adj
*ferālis*, bestial, cruel, whence E *feral*, and derivative L *ferīnus*, of or like a wild beast, whence the
learnèd E *ferine*.

3. L *ferus*, s *fer-*, has mdfn *ferōx*, savage and
untamable (cf *ātrōx* and *āter*), o/s *ferōc-*, gen
*ferōcis*, whence (cf the MF-F *féroce*) the E *ferocious*; derivative *ferōcitās*, o/s *ferōcitāt-*, whence
(cf the MF-F *férocité*) the E *ferocity*.

4. Gr *thērion*, a (wild) beast, has adj *thēriakos*,
whence the f *thēriakē* used as n, an antidote against
snake-venom, whence LL *thēriaca*, adopted by
(old) Med and often anglicized to *theriac*, the adj
to both being *theriacal*.

5. But this LL *thēriaca* must have had a dim
*\*thēriácula*, whence VL *\*triácula*, whence OF
*triacle*, adopted by ME, whence E *treacle*, with
'molasses' sense (first recorded late in C17) arising
from the fact that molasses formed an ingredient
in many a C16–17 *treacle* or 'sovereign remedy'.

**fiery.** See FIRE, para 2.

**fiesta.** See FEAST, para 1.

**fife.** See PIPE, para 4.

**fifteen, fifteenth; fifth; fiftieth, fifty.** See FIVE,
paras 4, 3, 5.

**fig** (1), the fruit: OF-F *figue*: OProv *figa*: VL
*\*fīca*: L *fīcus*, fig, fig-tree: app of Medit stock
(sem cf *uinum*, vine). The It derivative *fico*, common in Elizabethan times as a term of contempt—
as in Shakespeare's 'Steal! foh, a fico for the
phrase'—whence the C19–20 'I don't care a fig',
recalls the MF-F *faire la figue à quelqu'un*, to
mock, prop. snap one's fingers, in a rude gesture,
at someone; in L (cf Gr *sukon*) and It, F and E,
'fig' has obscene connotations, prob—despite the
usu accepted etymologies—present, etym, in F 'Je
m'en *fiche* de quelquechose', I mock at, don't care
a fig for, something.

**fig** (2), as in the coll phrase *in full fig*, in full
dress, derives from the obsol v *fig*, to dress
(smartly), put (a horse) into good form, a var of
*feague*, q.v. at FAKE.

**fight**, n, v (whence **fighting**, pa and vn); **fighter;**
pt and pp, **fought** (OE *feaht*).

*Fighter* derives from OE *feohtere* (cf OFris
*fiuchtere*), from the OE v *feohtan*, which becomes
ME *fehten, fihten*, whence E 'to fight'. Also from
*feohtan* comes OE *feoht* (cf OFris *fiucht*), which
becomes ME *feht*, later *fiht*, retained in
E 'a *fight*'. The OE *feohtan* is akin to OS and OHG
*fehtan*, MHG *vehten*, G *fechten*, OFris *fiuchta*:
Gmc r, *\*feht-*; IE r, *\*pekt-*: cf L *pectere* (s *pect-*),
to comb, and Lith *pèsti*, to pluck, and *pèstis*
(reflexive), to fight; basic idea, 'to pluck', then 'to
scuffle', finally 'to fight'. (Walshe.)

**figment.** See FEIGN, para 4.

**figura, figurable, figural, figurant, figurate,
figuration, figurative, figure** (n and v), **figurehead;
figurine; configuration; disfigure**, whence **disfigurement; prefigure, prefiguration; transfigure, transfiguration.**

1. L *figūra*, a thing shaped, the shape given to
something, a *figure* in most of the modern senses,
is *fig-*, the *n*-less r of *fingere*, to model in clay, to
mould, to form or shape (q.v. at FEIGN) + suffix
*-ūra*. The IE r is *\*dheig-* or *\*dheigh-*, to fashion
in or with earth, clay, etc.: cf Ve *déhmi*, I cement,
and Go *digands*, having moulded.

2. L *figūra* becomes OF-F *figure*, adopted by E.
'To *figure*' derives from OF-F *figurer*, from L
*figūrāre*, to fashion, give form to, from *figūra*;

*figurable*, from 'to *figure*'; *figural*, from LL *figūrālis*, from *figūra*.

3. Whereas *figurant*, m, and *figurante*, f, are adopted from the F presp, the adj *figurate* comes, like the obs v, from L *figūrātus*, pp of *figūrāre*. Derivative L *figūrātiō*, o/s *figūrātiōn*-, yields—prob via MF-F—*figuration*; derivative LL *figūrātīuus*, ML -*īvus*, yields—again prob via MF-F—*figurative*. L *figūra* becomes It *figura*, with dim *figurina*, whence F *figurine*, adopted by E.

4. *Figurehead* is lit the *figure* at a ship's *head* or bow.

5. L *configūrāre* (int *con*-) becomes 'to *configure*'; pp *configūrātus* yields 'to *configurate*'; derivative LL *configūrātiō*, o/s *configūrātiōn*-, yields *configuration*.

6. 'To *disfigure*' comes from MF *desfigurer* (*des*- for L *dis*-), from VL *\*disfigūrāre*, perh suggested by the sem very different LL *dēfigūrāre*.

7. 'To *prefigure*' derives, perh via EF-F *préfigurer*, from LL *praefigūrāre* (*prae*-, before); pp *praefigūrātus* becomes rare adj *prefigurate*; derivative LL *praefigūrātiō*, o/s *praefigūrātiōn*-, becomes *prefiguration*; derivative ML *praefigūrātīvus* becomes *prefigurative*.

8. LL *transfigūrāre*, to transform (*trans*, across), becomes OF-F *transfigurer*, whence late ME *transfiguren*, whence 'to *transfigure*', with pa *transfigured*; derivative *transfigūrātiō*, o/s *transfigūrātiōn*-, yields, via MF-F, the E *transfiguration*.

**Fiji**—whence **Fijian**, adj, whence n—derives from native *Viti*, as in Viti Levu, the largest of the Fiji Islands; *Viti* is the original pronunciation, *Fiji* a corruption due to Tongan influence; *Fiji* and *Viti*, therefore, are identical. The name applied, in pre-European days, only to *Na Viti*, a small island in the NW, and to *Na Viti Levu*. In these two names, as in *Na Vanua Levu*, The Big Land, *Na* is the article 'the' (and *Vanua* is 'land'), occurring after transitive verbs. *Viti*, which survives only as a place-name, prob means 'Clear (a way) with your hands', in an order given by Ndengei, leader of that migration, perh East African, which conquered the original Papuan stock. A second theory is that *Viti* is an EAfr place-name, transplanted by Ndengei. (With thanks to Mr Erle Wilson, author of those remarkable Nature-stories *Coorinna* and *Minado*.)

**filament** (see para 3) whence **filamentous** and Sci L **Filaria** (whence Sci E **filarial**); cf **filature**; **file**, orig a thread, hence a line, a row or a rank, a collection of papers set in chronological order (*in a row*), whence 'to **file**', walk in line, set in order, etc.; **fillet** (n hence v), F var **filet**, **filigrain** or -**grane**, **filigree**;—cpds: **defile**, to march off, file by file, and military and Topo n **defile**, **defilade**; **enfilade** (n hence v); **profile** (n, v)—cf **purfle** (v hence n), with pa **purfled**.—Prob akin: **hilum**; **nihil** (contr: **nil**), **nihilify**, **nihilism**, **nihilist**, **nihility** —cpd **annihilate**, **annihilation**, **annihilator**.—Perh akin: L **pilus**, E **pile**, hair; **pilose** or **pilous**; **pilosis**; **pilosity**; cf the element **pilo**-; cpd **depilate**, **depilator**, **depilatory** (adj hence n), **depilous**.

## General

1. The three L words concerned are *fīlum*, a thread or anything threadlike, hence a line; *hīlum*, a trifle, said by Festus to be so named because *grano fabae adhaeret*, it clings to the grain of a bean, the orig sense being either that ('a tiny mark') of Bot or, equally well, the tiny slender funicle stalk (L *fūniculus*, dim of *fūnis*, a cord or rope, itself formed r *\*fū*+formative -*n*-+declensional -*i*-+nom -*s*) attaching the ovule to its support; and *pilus*, a single hair or bristle.

2. All three L words are o.o.o. Several facts and several probabilities, however, are suggestive: *fīlum* is prob akin to Lith *gysla*, OP -*gyslo*, OSl *žila*, vein, artery, tendon, and to Arm *jil*, tendon (E & M; Webster), the r being, in L, *fī*-, and the IE r being *\*ghī*- or some var thereof; the L *fī*- is perh akin to the *fū*- of *fūnis*, cord; Latin *f* having multiple origins, an *f-h* alternation is valid—cf OL *Fercles* for *Hercles* (*Hercules*, Gr *Hēracleēs*), a fact relevant to the linking of *hīlum* to *fīlum*; *pilus* is prob akin to Gr *pilos*, felt—cf L *pilleus*, a felt cap, and the possibility of *pilos* orig meaning 'hair';— the sense common to *fīlum* and *pilus*, credibly also to *hīlum*, is 'thread' (cf the use of threads to represent hair); an IE *\*phīl*-, hair, (? hence) thread, could well become *\*fīl*, as in *fīlum*—to *\*hīl*-, as in *hīlum*—to *\*pil*-, as in *pilus*; this *\*phīl*- is an extn of *\*phi*-, becoming *\*fī*- or *\*hī*- or *\*pi*-: the differing quality of the thematic vowel (*ī*, *ĭ*) establishing no insuperable obstacle.

## L *Fīlum*

3. *Fīlum*, s *fīl*-, becomes both the OF-F *fil* and, through the derivative LL *fīlāre*, to thread (hence to spin), OF-F *filer*, the late MF-F n *file*; most E senses of *file* come from the latter. *Fīlum* has derivative ML *fīlamentum*, whence, prob via EF-F, the E *filament*; and *fīlāre*, pp *fīlātus*, has ML derivative *fīlātūra*, whence F *filature*, adopted by E. The learnèd adj *filose* derives from ML *\*fīlōsus*.

4. OF-F *fil* has the MF-F dim *filet*, a narrow band (for the hair), anglicized as *fillet*, the F *filet* being reserved for cookery.

5. From L *fīlum*+*grānum*, a grain (hence a bead), It forms *filigrana*, a kind of delicate ornamental work, whence EF-F *filigrane*, adopted by E and anglicized to *filigrain*, which, now archaic, has made way for the distorted *filigree*.

6. To note first prefix-cpd we note is *defile*, to file off: EF-F *défiler* (*dé*-, L *dē*-)+F *file*, row, rank; the F pp *défilé*, used as n, becomes the E n *defile*, a narrow passage, e.g. a gorge, in which troops can march only on a narrow front, esp in single file; derivative F *défilade* becomes E *defilade*, and v. Cf the suffix -*ade* and:

7. The MF-F *enfiler* (*en*, L *in*), lit to make a thread (*fil*) or line into, has derivative EF-F *enfilade*, adopted by E.

8. It *profilare*, which consists of *pro*-, L *prō*-, forward+*filo* (L *fīlum*)+inf -*are*, becomes 'to *profile*', to draw in vertical outline, esp laterally;

the ĭt derivative *profilo* yields the E n *profile*. Cf:

9. OF-EF *porfiler*, consisting of *por-* for L *prō-*, forward+*fil*, thread, line+inf *-er*, becomes (F *pourfiler* and) ME *purfilen*, whence the obs *purfile*, whence, by contr, 'to *purfle*', to trim (ornament) the hem or border of, whence the n *purfle*.

### L *Hīlum*

10. L *hīlum* (as in para 1) is form-adopted, sense-adapted, by Bot and, with Sci L var *hilus*, by An and Zoo.

11. The derivative yet predominant L sense 'however little, a mere trifle', combined with *ne-*, not, to form *nihilum*, nothing, usu shortened to *nihil* and further to *nīl*, accounts for E *nil*, nothing. *Nihil* occurs, as gen *nihili*, in the phrase *nihili facere*, to make, hence account, as nothing, to slight, whence E 'to *nihilify*'. ML *nihilitās* (*nihil-*+abstract *-itās*), nothingness, yields *nihility*. Other *nihil* derivatives in E—with aid from F—include *nihilism, nihilist, nihilistic*: cf the suffixes *-ism, -ist, -istic*.

12. LL has the prefix-cpd *adnihilāre*: *ad,* to +*nihil*, nothing+active inf suffix *-āre*; 'to bring to nothing', to destroy utterly. The assimilated ML form *annihilāre* (whence the E *annihilable*) has pp *annihilātus*, whence 'to *annihilate*'; derivative LL *adnihilātiō*, ML *annihilātiō*, o/s *annihilātiōn-*, yields, perh via MF-F, the E *annihilation*. E anl formations include *annihilator, annihilatory, annihilative*.

### L *Pilus*

13. L *pilus*, a hair, has derivative adj *pilōsus*, whence E *pilose* and *pilous*, hairy, the former with derivative *pilosity*; Med *pilosis*, the condition of having excessive hair=c/f *pil(o)-*+Med suffix *-osis*.

14. Derivative prefix-cpd *dēpilāre*, to take the *pilus*, hair, *dē*, or from off, to remove (a person's) hair, has pp *dēpilātus*, whence 'to *depilate*', whence, by anl, *depilation, depilator, depilatory* (hair-removing). *Depilous*, hairless, is anl formed from *de*+*pilous*.

**filbert** is aphetic for Norman F *noix de filbert*, nut of *Filbert*, i.e. St *Philibert*, whose commemorative day falls on August 22, early in the nutting season; his name derives from OHG *Filuberht*: lit, very (*filu*, G *viel*) bright (*berht, beraht*, E BRIGHT).

**filch**, to steal, whence *filchery*, comes from the C16–17 underworld: o.o.o. The underworld n *filch* means a thief's hooked stick, but app derives from the v; nor can 'to *filch*' come from the considerably later syn 'to *file*', from a *file* or pickpocket (akin to EF-F *filou*).

**file** (1), row, rank. See FILAMENT, para 3.

**file** (2), the abrasive tool: OE *fīl* (var *fēol*): akin to the syn OHG *fīhala*, MHG *vīle*, G *Feile* (also, polish), MD *vile* and, as in D, *vijl*, and perh OFris *fīāl*, wheel; cf, further off and uncertainly, L *pingō*, I paint, and Skt *pimśati*, he cuts (out) or forms. The derivative v has vn FILINGS.

**file** (3), to befoul. See FOUL, para 4.

**filial** (whence **filiality**, cf LL *fīliālitās*), **filiate**, **filiation**; **affiliate**, **affiliation**.

1. *Affiliate*, adj and v, comes from L *affīliātus*, pp of *affīliāre* (*af-* for *ad*, to), to adopt as a *fīlius* or son; *affiliation*, from the derivative ML *affīliātiō*, o/s *affīliātiōn-*; *affiliable*=*affiliate*+*-able*.

2. L *fīlius*, with f *fīlia*, daughter, is prob for *fēlius*: r *fē-*+extn *-l-*+formative *-i-*+declensional *-u-*+nom *-s*: and this *fē-* is that of *fēcundus* and *fēmina*—for both, see FEMALE. Orig, *fīlius* was common gender: 'he, she, whom the mother breast-feeds'. *Fīlius, fīlia*, have derivative LL adj *fīliālis*, whence E *filial*; derivative LL-ML v *fīliāre*, pp *fīliātus*, whence 'to *filiate*'; derivative LL *fīliātiō*, sonship, o/s *fīliātiōn-*, yields—perh via F—*filiation*.

3. L *fīlius* becomes OF *filz*, then *fiz* (F *fils*), whence, since C12, its use in E surnames (esp of F origin): connoting 'son (esp if illegitimate) of', as in *FitzHerbert*. Cf the Ga and Ir *Mac*, as in *MacDonald* (OIr *macc*, son), W *ap*, archaic for *ab*, as in *ap-Lloyd*, from OW *mab* or *map* (cf Br *ab, ap*, Cor *mab, map*), son, and the similar Ir *O'*, as in *O'Mara*, from *o*, descendant.

4. L *fīlius* becomes Sp *hijo*, as in *hijo de algo*, son of something (sc. important), whence, by contr, Sp *hidalgo*, son of a noble house (of the lower order), hence, a minor Sp nobleman.

**filibuster.** See BOOTY, para 3.

**filigrain** (or **-grane**); **filigree.** See FILAMENT, para 5.

**filings.** See the 2nd FILE, s.f.

**fill.** See FULL.

**fillet.** See FILAMENT, para 4.

**fillip.** See FLAP, para 4.

**filly.** See FOAL, para 2.

**film** (n hence v), whence the adjj **filmic** and **filmy**, derives from OE *filmen*, a thin skin or membrane, akin to OFris *filmene*, skin, hide, and Gr *pelma*, sole of foot, L *pellis*, skin—and to the 2nd FELL (skin); IE r, *\*pel-*.

**filose.** See FILAMENT, para 3, s.f.

**filter.** See FELT.

**filth**, whence **filthy.** See FOUL, para 4.

**filtrate, filtration.** See FELT.

**fimbriate, fimbriation.** See FRINGE, s.f.

**fin**, whence **finny**, derives from OE *finn*: cf MHG *pfinne*, var *vinne*, G *Finne*, and MD *venne, vinne*, (as in D) *vin*—and L *pinna*, fin, *penna*, feather, fin —and perh SPINE.

**final** (adj hence n), **finale, finalist, finality; fine,** adj (whence adv) and n (whence v)—**fineness**, from the adj—**finery**—**finesse** (n hence v); **finance** (n hence v), whence **financial**—cf **financier**; **finial; finical, finick, finicking, finicky; finis**—**finish** (v hence n), with paa **finishing, finished** (neg **unfinished**); **finite** (adj hence n), **finitesimal, finitive, finitude, finity,** with negg **infinite** (adj hence n), **infinitesimal, infinitive, infinitude, infinity.**—(Other) prefix-cpds: **affine** (adj, v), **affinition, affinitive, affinity; sep confine** (n and v), **confinement, con-**

finity; sep define (whence definable, neg indefinable), definement, definite (adj hence n), definition, definitive; refine (whence pa refined and pa, va refining), refinement, refiner, refinery.—Perh cf the sep DIKE and FIX.

1. All these words descend from L *fīnis*, limit or boundary of a field or a farm or an estate, hence, in pl *fīnes*, the boundaries of a large territory, the frontiers of a country or a state. L *fīnis* is o.o.o.—unless it orig meant either 'mark on a tree' (trees often serving as limits of a field) or a stake driven into the ground to mark a boundary, for then it could be a contr of *\*fingis*, a fixing, a being fixed, something fixed, nasal derivative of *figere*, to thrust in, to fix firmly (f.a.e., FIX). The transferred sense 'end' appears in 'He wrote *finis* to his book'.

2. L *fīnis* has the foll simple derivatives relevant to E:

LL *fīnālis* (orig Gram and Phil), limited, whence OF-F *final*, adopted by E, which acquires further senses; derivative LL *fīnalitās*, o/s *fīnālitāt-*, F *finalité*, E *finality*; *finale*, adopted ex It;

VL *\*fīnus*, brought to an end or a finish, esp if good: OF-F *fin*, f *fine*: ME *fin*, *fine*: E *fine*, adj; but the n *fine*, (obs) end, money paid as an end or a settlement, comes from L *fīnis*, via OF-F *fin*, end, settlement, and ME *fin*;

L *fīnīre*, to end or finish, becomes MF-F *finir* (OF *fenir*), with such forms as presp *finiss*ant and nous *finiss*ons, we finish, leading to E 'to finish';

L *fīnītus*, pp of *fīnīre*, is used also as adj, whence E *finite*; the neg *infīnītus* yields *infinite*;

L *fīnītīuus*, ML *-īvus*, becomes *finitive*; LL neg *infīnītīuus*, ML *-īvus*, E *infinitive*;

LL *infīnitās*, o/s *infīnitāt-*, becomes MF-F *infinité*, whence E *infinity*, whence, anl, the rare *finity*.

3. L *infīnītus* has a learnèd L derivative *infīnitesimus*, whence E *infinitesimal*, whence, anl, *finitesimal* (Math); cf *finitude*, neg *infinitude*, formed as if from L *\*(in)finitūdō*.

4. Whereas *finery* is an E *-ery* derivative from E adj *fine*, *finesse* is adopted from MF-F (*fin*, adj + *-esse*). *Financier* is adopted from late MF-F (*finance* + *-ier*), but *financial* = E *finance* + *-ial*. 'To finance' prob comes from MF-F *financer*, itself from the source of the E n—the MF-F *finance*, which, owing something to ML *financia*, prob comes primarily from OF-EF *finer*, to pay, a mdfn of OF *fenir*, MF-F *finir* (L *finīre*).

5. The Arch *finial*, a knot or bunch at the upper end of a pinnacle or canopy, represents L *finis*, end + n *-al*.

6. The adj *finical*, excessively neat or dainty, has b/f 'to finick', with pa *finicking*, and dim-b/f *finicky*, fussy over trifles; *finical* = E *fine*, adj + *-ical*, as in *tactical*.

7. There are, of L *finis*, several prefix-cpds affecting E: *adfinis*, *confinis*, *dēfinīre* and prob *\*refinīre*. *Adfinis*, later *affinis*, related (by marriage), bordering (on), becomes, via F, the obs adj and n and, from derivative ML *affīnāre*, the rare v

*affine*; derivative *affīnitās*, o/s *affīnitāt-*, becomes MF *afinite* (F *affinité*), ME *affinite*, E *affinity*; *affinition* and *affinitive* are anl E formations.

8. *Confine* and *define* and their close relations are treated sep at those head-words

9. 'To refine' (*re-*, again + *fine*, to make fine) owes something to EF-F *raffiner*, as *refinement* does to EF-F *raffinement* and *refinery* to late EF-F *raffinerie*; *refiner* comes straight from 'to refine'.

finance, financial, financier. See FINAL, para 4.

finch: OE *finc*: cf OHG *fincho*, MHG *vinke*, G *Fink*, MD *vinke*, D *vink*; remotely cognate but equally echoic is Gr *spingos* (σπίγγος); cf—but from Scan—the local E *spink*, chaffinch.

find (v hence n), pt and pp found, agent finder, va findings; foundling.

1. A *foundling* is a dim (*-ling*) found (OE *funden*) child.

2. 'To find' derives from OE *findan*: cf OFris *finda*, OS and OHG *findan*, OHG var *fintan*, MHG *vinden*, G *finden*, MD-D *vinden*, Go *finthan*, ON *finna*, and cf OHG *fendo*, a pedestrian; further off, L *pont-*, o/s of *pons*, bridge, Gr *pontos*, sea, Skt *panthas*, path. Cf therefore PATH and PONS.

fine, adj, adv, n, v. See FINAL, para 2.

finery; finesse. See FINAL, para 4.

finger (n hence v): OE *finger*: akin to OFris *finger*, OS and OHG *fingar*, MHG *vinger*, G *finger*, ON *fingr*, Go *figgrs*: perh akin to either FIVE (5 'fingers' on hand) or FANG (the fingers being 'the seizers').

finial. See FINAL, para 5.

finical, finicking, finicky. See FINAL, para 6.

finis. See FINAL, para 1.

finish. See FINAL, para 2.

finite. See FINAL, para 2.

finnan (haddock, Sc haddie) derives from Sc fishing-village of *Findon*, pron and occ written *Finnan*, formerly a noted centre of haddock-fishing.

Finnish is an *-ish* adj from Finn, whence also Finland; its c/f *Finno-* occurs in, e.g., *Finno-Ugric* (cf HUNGARIAN). A *Finn* perh comes, by b/f, from Tacitus's *Fenni*, Ptolemy's Φίννοι (*Phinnoi*).

finny. See FIN.

fiord. See 1st FRITH.

fir; quercus, quercine; sep CORK.

1. *Fir*, ME *firre*, prob comes from ON *fyri* (cf Dan *fyr*), var *fura*: akin to OE *furh*, OHG *forha*, MHG *vorhe*, G *Föhre*; all are akin either to L *quercus*, oak, and Skt *parkatī*, fig-tree (cf OHG *vereh*-eih, oak) or—as certain moderns (e.g., Walshe) hold—because of the fir's sharp needles, to L *perca*, the fish PERCH (Gr *pherkē*).

2. If L *quercus*, oak, is cognate, so are the adj *quercine* (LL *quercīnus*) and, from the cork-oak, CORK.

fire (n hence v), with numerous—and obvious—cpds; fiery; pyre; pyrite, pyrites, pyritic; cf the element *pyro-*; sep EMPYREAN.

1. *Fire* derives, through ME *fir*, var *fyr*, from OE *fyr*, akin to OFris *fiōr*, *fiūr*, OS *fiur*, OHG *fiur*,

*fuir*, MHG *viur*, *viuwer*, G *Feuer*, MD *vuy(e)r*, *fuer*, *vuer*, MD-D *vuur*, ON *fūrr*, *fȳrr*; also to Arm *hur*; Gr *pur*; Umbrian *pir*; Cz *pyr*, live coal; Hit *pahhur*, *pahhuwar*; Tokh A *puwar*, *por*; Skt *pu-*, flame. The IE r is prob *pu-*, to flame, with predominant extn *pur-*, a fire. Cf also the *fu-* of Go *funins*, gen of *fōn*, fire, syn ON *funi*. (Walshe; Hofmann.) The word is perh Medit: cf Eg *pa*, flame, fire, and perh *gara*, fire, furnace.

2. *Fiery*=ME *firie*, from ME *fir* (as above).

3. Gr *pur* (πῦρ), fire, has derivative *pura*, whence L *pyra*, whence E *pyre*, esp *funeral pyre* for the burning of a corpse.

4. E *pyrite* is a b/f from E *pyrites*, adopted from the L trln of the Gr adj *puritēs* in *puritēs lithos*, a stone for striking fire; hence the adj *pyritic*.

**firkin.** See FOUR, para 5.

**firm** (adj, n, v), whence **firmness; firmament** (whence **firmamental**); **affirm, affirmation, affirmative** (adj hence n); sep CONFIRM, etc.; **infirm, infirmary, infirmity.**—**farm** (n, hence adj and v), **farmer, farming.**—Cf sep THRONE.

1. A *farm* comes, via ME *ferme*, lease or rent, from MF-F *ferme*, a lease, hence a leased farm, from *fermer*, to make a firm agreement, i.e. contract, from L *firmāre*, to make firm, to confirm, from *firmus*, well fixed or established, solid, strong. MF-F *ferme*, leased farm, has MF-F agent *fermier*, ME *fermour*, E *farmer*.

2. L *firmus*, s *firm-*, is prob akin to Gr *thronos*, a (royal) seat, and Skt *dhármas*, a thing firmly set, a law, and *dhāráyati*, he holds fast or firm; *firmus* becomes OF-F *ferme*, whence E *firm* (adj); derivative *firmāre* (as above) becomes OF-F *fermer*, ME *fermen*, E 'to *firm*'; L *firmāre* becomes It *firmare*, with derivative n *firma*, signature, and Sp *firmar*, whence the n *firma*, and from both comes the E n *firm*, signature, hence, via the signatories, a business concern.

3. L *firmāre* has LL derivative *firmamentum*, firmness, hence authority and, in Eccl L, the prop of the sky, the sky itself, whence OF-F, hence E, *firmament*.

4. The prefix-cpd *affirmāre* (*af-*, for *ad*, used int) becomes OF-MF *affermer*, MF-F *affirmer*, ME *affermen*, E 'to *affirm*'; derivative L *affirmātiō*, o/s *affirmātiōn-*, becomes MF-F, hence E, *affirmation*; derivative *affirmātiuus* ML *-ivus*, becomes MF-F *affirmatif*, f *affirmative*, whence E *affirmative*.

5. L *firmus* has neg *infirmus*, whence MF-F *infirme* and E *infirm*; derivative *infirmitās*, o/s *infirmitāt-*, yields *infirmity*; derivative ML *infirmāria*, a hospital (cf LL *infirmans*, an invalid), yields *infirmary*.

**first** (whence **firstly**), adj hence adv and n, derives from OE *fyrst*, akin to OHG *furist*, first, the sup of *furi*, *fora*, cf E *fore*, and to *furisto* (G *Fürst*), prince: f.a.e., FORE.

**firth.** See 1st FRITH.

**fisc, fiscal;** sep **confiscate, confiscation.**

*Fiscal* (adj, whence n) is adopted from MF-F, from LL *fiscālis*, of the treasury, the adj of L *fiscus*, orig a basket, hence a lockable money-

basket, hence a royal or other State treasury, whence MF-F *fisc*, adopted by E: o.o.o., but perh of Medit stock.

**fish, fisher, fisherman, fishery, fishmonger, fishwife, fishy; piscary, piscator, piscatorial, piscatory, piscine, piscis;** cf the element *pisci-*.

1. 'To *fish*'—whence vn *fishing* and *fishery* (*-ery*) —derives, via ME *fischen*, *fissen*, etc., from OE *fiscian* (cf OHG *fiscōn* and OFris *fiscia* or *fiskenia*), itself from OE *fisc*, whence, via ME *fisch*, *fisc*, the E n *fish*: and OE *fisc* is akin to OFris and OS *fisk* or *fisc*, OHG *fisc*, MHG *visch*, G *Fisch*, MD *visc*, (as in D) *visch*, Go *fisks*, ON *fiskr*; to L *piscis* (s *pisc-*); to OIr *iasc* (for *\*piska*) or *aesc*, with gen *éisc*, Ga *iasg* (gen *éisg*), Cor *pisc*, *pisk*, *pysc*, *pysk*, Br *pisk*, *pesk*, W *pysc*, Mx *eeast*, *eease*, OC *\*eiskos* for *\*peiskos*.

2. The OE v has derivative *fiscere*, whence E *fisher*, with elaboration *fisherman*; *fishwife*=*fish*, n+*wife* in old sense 'woman'; *fishmonger*=*fish*, n+*monger*, vendor, merchant; *fishy*=*fish*, n+*y*, adj

3. L *piscis* is familiar as the horoscopical *Pisces* (pl). It has derivatives relevant to E:

*piscārius*, of fish(es) or fishing, whence the legal n *piscary*;

*piscātor*, fisherman, angler;

*piscātōrius*, whence *piscatory*, with elaboration *piscatorial*;

*\*piscīnus*, whence the adj *piscine*; the derivative n *piscīna*, fishpond or -tank, is adopted as an Eccl tech.

**fissate, fissile, fission, fissure** (n hence v); cf the element *fissi-*.

1. All these terms derive from L *fissus* (s *fiss-*), pp of *findere*, to split or cleave: and *findere* (s *find-*) derives from *\*fid-*, as in *bifidus*, *trifidus*, whence E *bifid*, *trifid*, cleft in two, in three; IE r, prob *\*bhid-*, to split—Skt *bhinádmi*, I split, and *bhindánti*, they split, representing the nasal infix of the present.

2. L derivatives formed on pp *fiss-* include ML *fissilis*, whence E *fissile*, splittable; LL *fissiō*, o/s *fissiōn-*, whence *fission*; LL *fissūra*, E *fissure*. *Fissate* is a Sci formation, as if from a VL *\*fissātus* (for L *fissus*).

**fist** (n hence v), whence **-fisted** and **fistic; fisticuff(s).**

1. *Fist* comes, through ME *fist*, var *fust*, from OE *fȳst*, akin to OFris *fest*, OHG-MHG *fūst*, G *Faust*, MD *fuest*, *vuest*, *vuust*, *vust*, MD-D *vuist*— and OSl *pęsti*; Gmc r *\*fust-*, IE r *\*pest-*, varr *\*pist-*, *\*pust-*; the Gmc being perh for *\*funst-*, the IE perh for *\*penst-*, varr *\*pinst-*, *\*punst-*. If *\*funst-*, *\*penst-* (etc.) are valid, *fist* could be akin to (E FIVE and) G *fünf*, but there could also be a connexion with L *pugnus*, fist (? a metathesis for *\*pungus*, itself from *\*punstus*).

2. *Fisticuff* is euphonic for *\*fistcuff*, a cuff or blow with the fist.

3. D *vuist*, fist, has a dial derivative *vuisten*, to take in the hand, hence to palm a coin or a gambling die, whence prob E 'to *foist*', to palm,

hence to insert or introduce illicitly or surreptitiously.

**fistula.** See element *fistuli-*. The adjj *fistulose*, *fistulous*, derive from the L adj *fistulōsus*.

**fit** (1), adj and v. The adj *fit*, ME *fyt*—although sense-influenced by ME *fete*, E FEAT (adj)—prob comes from ME *fitten*, to array, whence, with late senses influenced by the adj, 'to *fit*'; and ME *fitten* prob derives from ON *fitja*, to knit together, itself akin to OHG *fizza*, G *Fitze*, a skein. Adj *fit* has derivative *fitness*, v *fit* the derivatives *fitter* and *fitting* (pa and vn) and *fitment* (suffix -*ment*).

**fit** (2), n (false-archaic *fytte*), canto of a poem, a strain of music, derives from OE *fitt*, akin to G *Fitze*, skein, as in 1st FIT, and to Gr *peza*, an end, a border (therefore to E FOOT).

**fit** (3), n, (obs) a dangerous crisis, a paroxysm (e.g., epilepsy), comes from OE *fitt*, strife, conflict; but the OE word is o.o.o., although prob akin to FIGHT.—Hence *fitful*.

**fit** (4), v. See 1st FIT.

**fitch**, polecat, is short for *fitchew*: MF *fichau*, var of *fissel*: MD *fisse*, *visse*: o.o.o.

**fitful.** See 3rd FIT.

**fitment.** See 1st FIT, s.f.

**fitter**, n. See 1st FIT.

**fitting**, suitable. See 1st FIT.

**Fitz-** in surnames. See FILIAL, para 4.

**five**, game of fives; **fifteen, fifty; fifth, fifteenth, fiftieth.**—Gr *pente*: **pentacle, pentad, pentathlon, Pentecost** (whence **Pentecostal**); cf the element *pent(a-), pente-*, where see *pentagon, pentagram, pentameter, pentarchy, Pentateuch, penthemimer*.— L *quinque*: **'quin'; quinary, quinate, quincunx, quinquagenarian, quinquagenary, Quinquagesima**; cf element *quinque-*, where see *quinquennial*; L *quintus* (cf element *quint(i)-*, where see **quintessence**, whence **quintessential**), **quint, quintain, quintan, quintet, quintic, quintuple** (adj, whence v), **quintuplet, quintuplicate**, F *quinzaine* and *quinze*;— **keno.**

## I. Germanic

1. *Five*, ME *five* and earlier *fif*, derives from OE *fīf*, *fīfe*, akin to OFris and OS *fīf*, OHG *finf*, *funf*, MHG-G *fünf*, MD *vif*, *vive*, MD-D *vijf*, Go *fimf*, ON *fimm*; L *quīnque* (see section II); OIr *cóic*, Ga *còig* Mx *queig*—but OW *pimp*, Cor *pemp* or *pimp(pymp)*, Br *pemp*, *piemp*; Gr *pente* (see sec. III): f.a.e., see sec. IV.

2. *Fives*, a game similar to *hand*ball, is prob akin, as EW proposes, to the pugilistic *bunch of fives*, the fist, from the five 'fingers'.

3. *Fifth*=ME *fifthe*, earlier *fifte*: OE *fīfta*, from *fīf*.

4. *Fifteen* comes, through ME *fiftene*, from OE *fīftȳne*, five [and] ten; cf *thirteen, fourteen*, etc.; *fifteenth* represents ME *fiftenthe* (from *fiftene*), displacing ME *fiftethe, fyftethe*, from OE *fīftēotha*, fifteenth. Cf OFris *fiftēne*, 15, and *fiftēnda*, 15th.

5. *Fifty*=OE *fiftig*, five [times] ten, from OE *fīf(e)*; derivative OE *fiftigotha* finally becomes *fiftieth*. Cf OFris *fiftich*, 50, and *fiftichsta*, 50th.

## II. Latin

6. L *quīnque*, 5, has the foll derivatives relevant to E:

*quīnquāginta*, 50, whence the adj *quīnquāgēnārius*, whence E *quinquagenary*, with elaboration *quinquagenarian*, now used mostly as n;

*quīnquāgēsimus*, 50th (the ordinal of *quīnquāginta*), with f *quīnquāgēsima*, used in LL as n, elliptical for *q. diēs*, 'the 50th day', Whitsunday, but now the numerically loose Sunday before Lent;

*quīnquennis*, whence *quinquennial*—see element *quinque-*;

and, with *quīncu-* for *quīnque-*:

*quīncunx*, lit five-twelfths: *quīnque+uncia*: orig a coin ($\frac{5}{12}$ of the as), marked with 5 spots, hence a figure bearing, as a gambling 'five-spot' die bears, a spot in each corner and one in the middle, hence its special uses in Bot and Horticulture.

7. Intimately akin to L *quīnque* is L *quīni*, 5 each, with adj *quīnārius*, consisting of 5, arranged in sets of 5, whence E *quinary (system)*; *quīni* has suggested Bot *quinate*, growing in sets of 5.

8. The ordinal of L *quīnque* is *quīntus* (cf the syn Gr *pemptos*), 5th, whence the PN *Quintin*, F and now predominant E *Quentin*; whence also the OF *quint* (elliptically from L *quīnta pars*, 5th part), adopted and sense-adapted by E. The mdfn *quīntānus*, of the 5th rank, has f *quīntāna*, which, used as n, meant that street in a camp which separated the 5th from the 6th maniple (larger than a platoon but smaller than a company) and served as the camp's business-centre, and came, in ML, to designate an object at which, in that centre, the soldiers tilted: whence OF-F *quintaine*, whence E *quintain*.

9. L *quīntus* becomes It *quinto*, with dim *quintetto*, whence F *quintette* and E *quintet*. Cf the tech *quintic*: L *quint*us+adj -*ic*.

10. L *quīntus* has the LL cpd *quīntuplex*, fivefold: for the 2nd element, cf PLY. *Quīntuplex* becomes late MF-F *quintuple*, adopted by E, whence—anl with *triplet*—*quintuplet*, whence sl *quin*; *quīntuplex* has derivative ML *quīntuplicāre* (var of *quīnquiplicāre*), pp *quīntuplicātus*, whence—aided by *duplicate, triplicate, quadruplicate*—adj (whence n) and v *quintuplicate*, whence, again anl, *quintuplication*.

11. There remain two Romance words. L *quīndecim*, 15 (*quīnque*, 5+*decem*, 10), becomes OF-F *quinze*, adopted by E in card-game sense; its OF-F derivative *quinzaine*, lit 15 days, the E fortnight, partly adopted by E.

12. L *quīni*, 5 each (cf para 5), has acc f *quinas*, whence OF-F *quines*, which, by b/f, becomes F *quine*, a run of five winning numbers, which has app suggested the gambling game of *keno*, which prob, from its similarity to lotto, blends F *quine*, roughly pron *keen*, and lotto; this AE name (earlier *kino*, earliest *keeno*) perh came rather from a Louisianian or an ASp var of Sp (and Port) *quinas*, two 5's at dice, of same origin as OF *quines*.

## III. Greek

13. Gr *pente* (πέντε), Aeolic *pempe* (πέμπε), has Skt and other ancient cognates—see next section. It has the simple derivative *pentas*, o/s *pentad-*, whence LL *pentas*, *pentad-*, whence E *pentad*, a group of five: cf *duad* and *triad*. The ML derivative *pentaculum*—prob influenced by LL *pentagonus*, 5-cornered (*pentagon*, at *penta-* in Elements)— becomes MF-F, whence E, *pentacle*.

14. The Gr derivative *pentekonta*, 50, has ordinal *pentēkostos*, 50th, whence the LGr *pentēkostē* (*hēmera*), the 50th day, whence LL *pentecostē*, Pentecost, whence E *Pentecost*, orig a Jewish festival.

15. Apart from the cpds noted at *penta-*, *pente-*, in Elements, the only notable one is *pentathlon*, adopted from Gr; for Gr *athlon*, a contest, see ATHLETE.

## IV. Indo-European

16. The IE etymon is app *\*pénkwe*; cf Skt *páñca*, Av *pañca*, 5, Skt *pañcathás*, 5th, Per *panj*, 5, Tokh A *päñ*, 5, *pant*, 5th, Lith *penkì*, 5; cf the C *p-* forms in para 1; L *quīnque* stands for *\*pinque*; Gmc *\*finf* for *\*finhw* (cf para 1). Cf also the merely app more remote C forms in *c-* (or *q-*) and the Arm *hing*, 5. Improb related is Eg *pu-nu*, 5.

17. Cf the sep CINQUE and PUNCH (the drink); perh also related are FINGER and FIST.

'fiver', £5 (esp as banknote), hence $5 (esp as one bill): from FIVE; perh suggested by '*five-pounder*'.

fives (game). See FIVE, para 2.

fix (v hence n), whence fixer; fixate, fixation, fixative (adj, hence n); fixity; fixture.—Cpds: affix, infix, prefix, suffix, transfix, all orig vv, whence also nn, with derivatives as for the simple.

1. 'To *fix*' comes either from the obs adj *fix*, firmly placed or fastened, ME from MF-F *fixe*, from L *fixus*, pp of *figere*, to set firmly, drive (a stake) into the ground, hence senses as in E, or from MF-F *fixer*, or from ML *fixāre*, extn of *figere*, or again from *fixus*, pp of *figere*. *Figere*, s *fig-*, app has a European r *\*dheig-* (sense as *figere*) —cf Lith *dygti*, to sharpen to a point, and *degti*, syn with *figere*: cf, therefore, DIKE.

2. ML *fixāre* has pp *fixātus*, whence the Psy and Psychi 'to *fixate*'; derivative *fixātiō*, o/s *fixātiōn-*, yields late MF-F and E *fixation*; but *fixative* is an anl E formation. *Fixity* app derives from EF-F *fixité* (from adj *fixe*); *fixture* displaces obsol *fixure* LL *fixūra*, from *fix-*, s of pp *fixus*)—cf *mixture* and *mix*.

3. ML *adfixāre*, assimilated as *affixāre* (cf L *affigere*), to attach firmly (*ad*, to), yields 'to *affix*', whence anl *affixation*; L *infigere*, to fix *in*, in, has pp *infixus*, whence late MF-EF *infixer*, whence 'to *infix*', whence anl *infixion*; L *praefigere*, to fix in front of, has pp *praefixus*, whence late MF-EF *prefixer*, E 'to *prefix*', with anl derivatives *prefixation* and *prefixion*; L *suffigere*, to fasten under, hence behind, has pp *suffixus*, whence 'to *suffix*',

the n perh deriving from L *suffixum*, neu of *suffixus*, used as n, with anl derivative *suffixation*; and L *transfigere*, to pierce, has pp *transfixus*, whence 'to *transfix*', with anl *transfixation* and with *transfixion* from LL *transfixiō*, o/s *transfixiōn-*.

fizz (v, hence n): echoic; perh influenced by ON *fīsa*, to break wind, and OSw *fisa*, to fizzle. 'To *fizzle*'—whence the n—is a freq of *fizz*; *fizzy*, the adj of *fizz*, n.

flabbergast. See FLAP.

flabby (whence flabbiness). See FLAP, para 2.

flabellate (whence flabellation), flabellum; flageolet; flautist, flute; flout (v hence n).

1. The base is L *flāre*, to blow, *flō*, I blow, s and r *flā-*: but for the direct derivatives (and their cpds) of *flāre*, see FLATUS (also f.a.e.). *Flāre* has derivative *flābrum*, a breeze, with dim *flābellum*, a fan, retained by E as a tech; *flābellum* has LL derivative v *flābellāre*, to fan, pp *flābellātus*, whence the E adj *flabellate*, fan-shaped.

2. *Flābellum* becomes VL *\*flābeolum*, whence OF-MF *flajol*, var *flageol*, with MF-F dim *flageolet*, lit a small flute, adopted by E.

3. E *flautist*, flute-player, derives from It *flautista* (It-L agential *-ista*), from It *flauto*, flute, from Prov. But E *flute*, ME *floute*, *floite*, comes from EF-F *flûte*, OF-MF *flaüte*, *fleüte*, OF *flehutes*, from Prov *flaüt*, itself—though influenced by Prov *laut* (see musical LUTE)—from Prov *flaujol* (cf para 2); like OF-MF *flajol*, OProv *flaujol* perh derives from VL *\*flābeolum*, but is prob echoic, as indeed *flajol* may be.

4. OF-MF *flaüte*, *fleüte* have derivatives *flaüter*, *fleüter*, EF-F *flûter*, whence ME *flouten*, *floiten*, to play the flute, whence 'to *flute*'. Now ME *flouten* prob yields also 'to *flout*', to mock: cf D *fluiten* (from the OF v), orig to play the flute, but derivatively to jeer.

flaccid (whence flaccidity) comes from L *flaccidus*, LL derivative of *flaccus* (s *flac-*), drooping, flabby: '*Flaccus* has the doubled interior consonant characteristic of adjectives describing a physical deformity, cf *broccus*, *lippus*, etc.' (E & M); perh akin to Doric Gr *blāx* (gen *blākos*), soft, lazy, Ir *bláith*, soft, tender.

flacker. See FLICKER.

flag (1), plant: ME *flagge*; o.o.o., but prob Scan.

flag (2), in dial a turf or sod, in E a *flagstone* (prob a f/e elaboration): ON *flaga*, a flat stone, akin to Sw *flaga*, a flake, a crack, itself akin to ME *flawe*, later *flaw*, whence E *flaw*, a flake, breach, crack, hence a flaked or cracked part, hence a fault or defect, whence 'to *flaw*'; the n *flaw* is, at the least, prob Scan. ON *flaga*, flat stone, is akin to ON *flō*, a flat piece or surface, a layer, whence Nor *flo*, whence app E (ice)*floe*.

flag (3), a standard or banner: o.o.o., but perh from next: without a wind, it droops. Hence, 'to *flag*', to signal with, or as with, a flag.

flag (4), to hang loosely down, to droop, hence to become unsteady or weary: o.o.o., but prob akin to the 2nd FLAW.

flagellant (adj, n), flagellate (adj, n), flagellation,

flagellatory, flagellum; flog, whence agent flogger and pa, vn flogging; flail (n hence v).

1. L *flagellāre*, to flog, has presp *flagellans*, o/s *flagellant-*, whence E *flagellant*, a flogger, esp of himself, and pp *flagellātus*, whence adj and v *flagellate*; on the pp s *flagellāt-* is formed LL *flagellātiō*, o/s *flagellātiōn-*, whence E *flagellation*. L *flagellāre* derives from *flagellum* (prob a little whip), retained in Bio; *flagellum* is a dim of *flagrum*, a scourge, perh akin to ON *blaka*, esp the var *blakra*, to beat on this side and that, to beat to and fro, and to Lith *bluškyti*, to flog.

2. L *flagellāre*, s *flagel-*, therefore has r *flag-*, whence E 'to *flog*' could easily descend.

3. L *flagellum* becomes OF-MF *flaiel*, *flaël*, *flaële* (F *fléau*; cf OProv *flagel*), whence ME, whence E, *flail* (n).

flageolet. See FLABELLATE, para 2.

flagitious: prob via EF *flagitieux*, f *flagitieuse*: L *flāgitiōsus*, scandalous, disgraced: an *-ōsus* derivative of *flāgiti*um, a noisy moral protest, a scandal, hence the object of scandal, disgraceful conduct, disgrace: perh from, certainly allied very closely to, L *flāgitāre*, to demand bitterly or imperiously: both have the L r *flāg-*, make a din; IE r, the syn *bhlag-*: cf the *bhlag-* underlying *flag*ellum, *flagrum*, qq.v. at FLOG.

flagon, See ADDENDA.

flagrant, flagrancy; flagrante delicto; conflagrant, conflagrate, conflagration, conflagrative and conflagratory; deflagrable, deflagrate, deflagration.— fulgence, fulgent—effulgence, effulgent—refulgence, refulgent; fulgid; fulgor, fulgorous, fulgural, fulgurate, etc; fulminant, fulminate, fulmination, fulminatory, fulminic.

1. *Flagrancy* comes from L *flagrantia*, a flaming, from *flagrant-* (source of adj *flagrant*), o/s of *flagrans*, presp of *flagrāre*, to flame, burn (brightly), from etymon *flagra*, a flame; perh cf Nor *blakra*, to shine (brilliantly), (of lightning) to flash; L *flagrāre* is akin to L *fulgere*—see para 4.

2. Cpd *conflagrāre* (int *con-*), to catch fire, be on fire (esp with flames), has presp *conflagrans*, o/s *conflagrant-*, whence E *conflagrant*; pp *conflagrātus* yields *conflagrate*, vi and vt; derivative L *conflagrātiō*, o/s *conflagrātiōn-*, yields *conflagration*; adjj *conflagrative*, *conflagratory*, are anl E formations.

3. Cpd *dēflagrāre*, to be consumed in flame, to cease (connoted by *dē-*) to burn, s *dēflagr-*, accounts for *deflagrable*; pp *dēflagrātus* for 'to *deflagrate*'; derivative *dēflagrātiō*, o/s *deflagrātion-*, for *deflagration*.

4. Akin to L *flagrāre* is L *fulgere*, Classical *fulgēre*, (of stars) to shine, (of lightning) to flash. The IE r is app *bhlag-*, var *bhleg-*: cf Skt *bhrájate*, it shines. *Fulgēre* has presp p *fulgens*, o/s *fulgent-*, whence the E adj *fulgent*, whence *fulgence*, *fulgency*, rare as simples. Cf both *effulgence*, LL *effulgentia*, itself from L *effulgent-* (whence *effulgent*), o/s of *effulgens*, presp of *effulgere*, to shine out (*ē-*), hence forth, and *refulgence*, L *refulgentia*, from *refulgent-* (whence *refulgent*), o/s

of *refulgens*, presp of *refulgere*, to shine back (*re-*), to reflect brightly.

5. Simple *fulgēre* has other derivatives affecting E:

*fulgidus*, brilliant, whence *fulgid*;

*fulgor*, flash of lightning, thunderclap, adopted by E (var *fulgour*), with sense 'dazzling brightness' whence *fulgorous*;

*fulgur*, lightning, whence E *fulgurous* and L: *fulgurālis*, E *fulgural*;

*fulgurāre* (from *fulgur*), to flash (orig of lightning), with presp *fulgurans*, o/s *fulgurant-*, whence the adj *fulgurant*, and with pp *fulgurātus*, whence 'to *fulgurate*'; derivative *fulgurātiō*, o/s *fulgurātiōn-*, whence *fulguration*; cf Geol *fulgurite* (Min *-ite* attached to *fulgur*).

6. L *fulmen* (for *fulgmen*), thunderclap, thunderbolt, lightning, o/s *fulmin-*, has derivative v *fulmināre*, to be or emit, or strike with, lightning, with presp *fulminans*, o/s *fulminant-*, whence the adj *fulminant*, and with pp *fulminātus*, whence 'to *fulminate*', esp in derivative sense 'to inveigh'. Derivative *fulminātiō*, o/s *fulminātiōn-*, yields *fulmination*; derivative LL *fulminātor* has been adopted; but *fulminatory* is an E anl formation.

7. Chem *fulminic* (acid)=L o/s *fulmin-*+Sci *-ic*; it has a derivative n—*fulminate* being *fulmin*ic+ Chem suffix *-ate*.

flagstone. See the 2nd FLAG.

flail. See FLAGELLANT, para 3.

flair. See FRAGRANCE, para 2.

flak, anti-aircraft artillery, esp its fire: G *Fliegera*bwehr*k*anone, lit 'cannon protection against aircraft'.

flake (n hence v), a thin, flattish piece, scale, layer: ME *flake*: of Scan origin—cf Nor *flak*, a flat piece of ice, and L *plaga*, a flat extent or surface, perh orig something stretched out flat, itself o.o.o. The adj is *flaky*. Dial *flake*, a paling, is ult identical.

2. Akin, ult, is the flatfish named *fluke*, OE *flōc*, with several close Gmc cognates; *fluke*, the broad end of each arm of an anchor, is perh derivative—from its flatness. (Webster.) Prob from the derivative whaling *fluke* (lobe of a whale's tail) comes *fluke*, an accidental success or advantage, whence both 'to *fluke*' and the adj *fluky*.

flam (whence the redup flimflam) is perh short for Sc *flamflew*, a trinket or trifle: OF-MF *fanfelue* (whence by alteration, EF-F *fanfreluche*): ML *famfalūca* (It *fanfaluca*), var *famfolūca*, a bubble, perh via LL *pomfolyx* (zinc oxide) and almost certainly from Gr *pompholux*, bubble, (L Gr) zinc oxide.

flambeau. See FLAME, para 2.

flamboyant, whence flamboyance (or -ancy). See para 2 of:

flame, n and v (whence pa flaming); flambeau; flamboyant;—inflame, inflammable, inflammation, inflammatory.

1. 'To *flame*', ME *flamen*, comes from OF-MF *fiamer*, itself from OF-MF *flame* (F *flamme*), whence E 'a *flame*': and OF-MF *flame* derives

from L *flamma*: prob for *\*flagma*, from *flagrāre*, to burn, s *flagr-*, r *flag-*: see FLAGRANT.

2. L *flamma* has dim *flammula*, whence OF *flamble*, whence OF-EF *flambe*, whence MF-F *flambeau*, a flaming torch, adopted by E. OF-EF *flambe* has OF-F derivative *flamboyer*, with presp *flamboyant*, whence the E adj, lit 'having flamelike curves', hence 'ornate', whence *flamboyance*.

3. *Flamma* has also, perh via simple *flammāre*, a derivative prefix-cpd v *inflammāre*, to put a flame into (*in-*), whence OF *enflamer*, whence 'to *inflame*'; derivative *inflammātiō*, o/s *inflammātiōn-*, yields, perh via MF-F, *inflammation*; *inflammable*, adopted from EF-F, and *inflammatory*, adapted from F *inflammatoire*, represent erudite F formations from L *inflammāre*.

**flamenco; flamingo.** See FLANDERS, para 3.

**flan**, archaic and dial **flawn**: the former adopted from MF-F, the latter adapted from the OF-MF source, *flaon*: Gmc: cf Frankish *\*flado*, OHG *flado*, MHG *flade*, G *Fladen*, pancake, cake, flan: ult akin to Gr *platus*, flat: cf PLACE.

**Flanders;      Fleming,      Flemish;—flamenco; flamingo.—Wal(l)achian; Walloon; Wales, walnut, Welsh** (adj hence n), 'to **welsh**'.

1. *Flanders* owes something to F *Flandre* (cf G *Flandern*) and to the pl idea of D *Vlandeeren*, a count's domain formerly part of Belgium, Holland, France. F *Flandre* derives from ML *Flandri*, the inhabitan s of ancient Flanders, varr *Flandrenses* (prop a p$^t$ adj) and *Flamingi*: o.o.o.

2. Also lderivative are MD *Vlaming*, whence E *Fleming*, and MD *Vlaemisch*, *Vlamisch* (D *Vlaamsch*), whence E *Flemish*, adj hence n.

3. The Sp shape of 'Flemish' is *flamenco*, adj and n, adopted by E for 'Andalusian gypsy dancing (and singing)'; *flamenco* becomes syn Port *flamengo*, whence Po,rt *flamingo*, the bird, perh by a pun on Port *flamma* a flame, or by ref to medieval Flemish reputation for bright clothes and florid complexion (EW). But Sp *flamenco*, flamingo, could equally well have come from OProv *flamenc*, a flamingo (OProv *flama*, flame+suffix *-enc*, of Gmc origin), from its pinkish-and-scarlet plumage (B & W; Dauzat).

4. Inhabiting much of S. Belgium (the Flemings are mostly in the coastal areas) are the *Walloons*, from F *Wallon*, of Gmc origin: cf *Walachian*, occ *Wallachian*, adj and n, from G *Wallache*, *Walache*, a Wallachian, which, like ML *Walachia*, derives from OHG *Walah*, *Walh*, orig a Celt but here a Romance-speaker, *Walachia* being now a part of Rumania, whose language is based on Latin.

5. Thus we reach *Wales*, land of the *Wēalas*, Celts, Britons: OE *wealh*, a stranger or a foreigner (not of Saxon origin), hence a Celt, esp a *Welshman*. The adj of *wealh* is *wēlisc*, *wǣlisc*, whence adj (hence n) *Welsh*. Cf OHG *walh*, a Latin, with adj *walhisc*, MHG *welhisch*, Latin-, then Romance-speaking, G *welsch*, foreign. The ON *volskr*, Celtic, is illuminating, for it recalls Caesar's *Uolcae* (ML *Volcae*), a Celtic tribe, itself obviously of C origin (? *Uolk-*).

6. 'To *welsh*', to cheat (someone) by failing to pay his race-course winnings, perh comes, as EW first suggested, from the old E nursery-rhyme:

'Taffy was a Welshman, Taffy was a Thief,
Taffy came to my house and stole a leg of beef'

7. OE *wealhhnutu*, a walnut (ME *walnot*), is lit a Celtic or a foreign nut (OE *hnutu*): cf ON *valhnot*, as rendering of L *nux gallica*, Celtic, esp Gaulish, nut, and G *Walnuss*, MHG *walhesch nuss*.

8. Cf—esp with *Wales* (para 5)—Cornwall (see the sep CORNISH) and its F form, Cornouailles.

**flange** (n hence v); **flank** (n hence v); **flinch; flunk, flunky** (n hence v); **lank**, whence the prop dim **lanky; link** (of chain; hence v).

1. *Flange* comes from OF-MF *flangir*, to turn or bend, of Gmc origin. Cf para 3 and:

2. *Flank* represents OF-F *flanc*, from Frankish *\*hlanka*, hip—cf OHG *flancha*, hips, loins, and *hlanca*, side.

3. 'To *flinch*'—whence the n—comes from OF-MF *flenchir*, *flenchier*, prob of Gmc origin—cf MHG *lenken*, to turn or bend (G *lenken*, to guide), either from or akin to MHG *lanke*, side (of body), from OHG *hlanca*.

4. 'To *flunk*' (AE coll), to fail, e.g. an examination, is perh a blend of *flinch*+*funk*.

5. *Flunk(e)y*, pej for a liveried servant, is akin to—perh from—*flank*, and perh influenced by *flinch*. EW suggests that it is a dim (*-ey*, cf *-y*, *-ie*) from *flanker*, a side attendant.

6. *Lank*, tall and slim and lean derives from OE *hlanc*, lit flexible: akin to OHG *hlancha*, hips, loins, *hlanca*, side, OE *hlence*, link in coat of mail, G *Gelenk*, joint, MHG *gelenke*, waist ('where the body bends': Walshe). Cf:

7. *Link* (of chain) derives from ME *linke*, of Scan origin; akin to OE *hlence*.

**flank.** See prec, para 2.

**flannel.** See WOOL, para 3.

**flap**, n and v. The n derives from ME *flappe*, from *flappen*, whence also 'to *flap*': echoic: cf *flop* in para 5. Hence *flapper*.

2. From the adj *flappy* comes *flabby*, whence *flabbiness*; and *flabby*+*aghast*, i.e. *flabbaghast*, yields 'to *flabbergast*'—cf GHASTLY.

3. 'To *flap*' has the thinned derivative 'to *flip*', whence the n (including the drink); whence also the adj *flip*, nimble, lively, whence, in turn, *flippant*, whence *flippancy*; *flipper* is merely the instrumental (cf *flapper*) of 'to *flip*'.

4. 'To *flip*' has freq 'to *fillip*' (whence the n).

5. 'To *flop*'—whence both the n *flop* and the adj *floppy*—is a clearly echoic var (? influenced by *plop*) of *flap*.

**flare** (v hence n): o.o.o.; but, orig to flicker or flutter, it could derive from syn MD *vlederen*, D *fladderen*—cf MHG *flatern*, G *flattern*, to flutter; therefore cf *flitter* and *flutter*.

**flash** (v hence n and also the adj) is ME *flaschen*, prob imitative: cf ME *flaskien*, to splash; *flash*, orig to splash or to dash, partly owes its 'rapid brilliance of light' senses to *flame*. (EW notes the *fl-* of rapid movement and the *-sh* of sound.) *Flashy*, orig 'splashing', owes its later senses to the cant n *flash* (cf P²).

**flask.** See ADDENDA at flagon.

**flat**, adj, whence, in part, the n; whence entirely the v, with *-en* var **flatten; flatter, flattery.**

1. A *flat* or apartment=Sc *flet*: OE *flet*, ground, floor: akin to syn OFris and OS *flett*, OHG *flezz*, and to OHG *flaz*, level: all akin to ON *flatr*, level, whence ME, hence E, *flat*: cf, further off, L *plānus* and esp Gr *platus*, level (f.a.e., PLACE).

2. *Flattery* is ME *flaterie*, adopted from MF (F *flatterie*): from OF-MF *flater*, to caress, whence EF-F *flatter*, to flatter, whence through ME *flateren*, the E 'to flatter'. OF-MF *flater* varies OF-MF *flatir*, to flatten, esp by throwing to the ground, from Frankish *\*flat*, level, of Gmc origin (as in para 1).

**flatulent.** See para 2 of:

**flatus, flatulent.**—Cpds in *-flate, -flation*, etc.: **afflation, afflatus; conflate** (adj, v), **conflation; deflate, deflation** (whence **deflationist**), **deflator; inflate** (whence pa **inflated**), **inflatile, inflation** (whence **inflationary** and **inflationist**); **perflation; reflate, reflation; sufflate, sufflation**—(cf **exsufflate, exsufflation** and **insufflate, insufflation, insufflator.**— **souffle; surf.**—Perh cf sep FLAVOR.

1. All these words rest upon L *flāre*, to puff or blow, *flō*, I puff, blow, pp *flātus*, s *flāt-*, whence the n *flātus* (gen *-ūs*), a breathing, puffing, blowing: *flāre* is remotely akin to OE *blāwan*, 'to blow', to E 'to flow', and to L *follis*, a wind-filled bladder, bellows: all are ult echoic.

2. From the L n *flātus*, esp *flātus uentris*, wind in the stomach, learnèd EF-F derives *flatulent*, whence F *flatulence*: both of them get into E.

3. L *afflāre*, to blow at (L *ad*), hence upon, has derivative n *afflātus* (gen *-ūs*), applied esp to inspiration by a god; the anl E *afflation* is rare.

4. L *conflāre*, to blow *con-* or together, to (re)unite, pp *conflātus*, whence both adj and v *conflate*; derivative LL *conflātiō*, o/s *conflātiōn-*, yields *conflation*, esp a composite reading of texts.

5. Not the rare L *dēflāre*, to blow *dē*, down, upon, but *dē-*, down+*flātus*, pp of *flāre*, to blow, accounts for 'to *deflate*', to blow (the wind) *de*, out of; whence anl *deflation* and *deflator*.

6. L *inflāre*, to blow *in-*, into, or upon, hence to blow wind into, to cause to swell, has pp *inflātus*, whence 'to *inflate*'; derivative LL *inflātilis* becomes E *inflatile*, wind(-instrument); derivative L *inflātiō*, o/s *inflātiōn-*, becomes *inflation*.

7. L *perflāre*, to blow *per* or through, pp *perflātus*, has derivative *perflātiō*, o/s *perflātiōn-*, whence the Med *perflation*.

8. Not LL *reflāre* but *re-*, again+*-flate*, as in *inflate* (currency) explains commercial *reflate*, *reflation*.

9. L *sufflāre*, to blow *sub*, from below, hence to blow up, has pp *sufflātus*, whence 'to *sufflate*'; derivative L *sufflātiō*, o/s *sufflātiōn-*, yields *sufflation*. Both are commoner in *insufflate, insufflation* (and anl *insufflator*): LL *insufflāre*, to breathe or blow upon, pp *insufflātus*, derivative *insufflātiō*, o/s *insufflātiōn-*. Cf LL *exsufflāre*, to blow away, pp *exsufflatus*, derivatives *exsufflātiō* and *exsufflātor*: whence E *exsufflate, exsufflation, exsufflator*.

10. L *sufflāre* becomes OF-F *souffler*, pp *soufflé*, which is used as cookery n and adopted by E.

11. Here, perh, is the origin of *surf*, the swell of the sea as it approaches the shore, the breaking waves, esp their foam: late C16–17 *suffe, suff*, late C17–20 *surf*, with *r* perh (EW) from *surge*. *Suffe* could be a confused blend of OF-F *souffle* and It *soffio*, breath of wind, both ult from L *sufflāre*; far more prob, however, *suff* is a var of *sough*, a hollow moaning (as it were of the surf), with *r* intervening to form *surf*.

**flaunt** (v whence n and **flaunter, flaunting,** adj **flaunty);**—**planet, planetary.**

'To *flaunt*' (vi, ? hence vt) is akin to Nor *flanta*, OScan *flana*, to gad about—cf the EF-F *flâner*, to dawdle or idle; akin also to Gr *planasthai*, to wander about, itself perh imm from *planos*, vagrant, wandering.

2. Gr *planasthai* has derivative adj *planētēs*, wandering, hence n, wanderer, whence LL *planēta*, whence OF-MF, hence ME, *planete* E *planet*. OF-MF *planete*, EF-F *planète*, has the EF-F adj *planétaire* whence E *planetary*; the n *planetary* comes rather from LL *planētārius*, an astrologer. The IE r is perh *\*pela-*, to wander.

**flautist.** See FLABELLATE, para 3.

**flavor** AE, **flavour** (n hence v), whence vn **flavo(u)ring** and adj **flavorous.**

A *flavo(u)r* comes from OF-MF *flaor, flaur* (both dissyllabic), an odour good or bad: VL *\*flātorem*, acc of syn *\*flātor*, either from *flāt-*, s of *flātus*, pp of *flāre*, to puff or blow, or from syn LL *flātāre*, mdfn of *flāre*: cf therefore FLATUS.

**flaw** (1), a crack. See the 2nd FLAG.

**flaw** (2), a short, sudden gust of wind: of Scan origin—cf ON *flaga*, an onset or attack, and Nor *flaga*, sudden gust, squall; cf MHG (and MLG) *vlage*, onset, gust, and MD *vlage, vlaech*, D *vlaag*, gust, flaw.

**flawn.** See FLAN.

**flax**, whence **flaxen**: OE *fleax*; cf OFris *flax*, OHG *flahs*, G *Flachs*, and OHG *flehtan*, MHG *flehten*, G *flechten*, to plait: f.a.e., PLY.

**flay**, to skin: OE *fléan*: cf ON *flá* and MD-D *vlaen*, and several cognates in Sl.

**flea:** ME *fle* or *flee*: OE *fléa* or *fléah*: akin to OHG-MHG *flôh*, G *Floh*, MD *vo, vloe*, (as in D) *vloo*, ON *flô*: Gmc r, *\*flauh-*: 'Prob related to L *pūlex* [IE *\*plouk-* for *\*poul(e)k-* ?]. Not related to [G] *fliehen, Fliege*': Walshe.

**fleam.** See PHLEBITIS.

**fleck** (n, v), whence pa **flecked.**

'To *fleck*' comes from ON *flekka*, from ON *flekkr*, a spot (esp a freckle), whence, via ME *flek*, the E *fleck*: cf OHG *flecko*, MHG *flecke* G *Fleck*, and MD *vlecke, vlec*, D *vlek*; cf also OFris *flekka*, G *flecken*, to spot. Cf FLICK.

**flection, flector.** See FLEX.

**fledge.** 'To *fledge*', to feather, to rear until

plumage is mature, derives from the obs adj *fledge*, feathered, able to fly: ME *flegge*, var *flygge*: OE *flycge*, akin to OHG *flucchi*, G *Flügge*: f.a.e., FLY. *Unfledged* derives from OE *un-flycge*; *fledg(e)ling=fledge*, adj+dim *-ling*.

flee, pt and pp fled; flight.

1. *Flight* derives from OE *fliht*, *flyht*, a fleeing, a flying, from the OE forms of *flee* and *fly*: even in OE (esp as *flyht*), *flight* is a coalescence. (Walshe.)

2. 'To *flee*', ME *fleen*, *fleon*, OE *flēon* (for *fléohan*), is akin to OFris *fliā*, OS and OHG *fliohan*, MHG-G *fliehen*, ON *flȳia*, *flȳja*; cf also Go *thliuhan*, 'which shows that this word [G *fliehen*] is not primitively allied to *fliegen* [to FLY], though similarity of meaning has later caused them to be partly confused' (Walshe): o.o.o.

fleece: ME *flees*: OE *flēos*, akin to MHG *flies*, *flius*, *flūs*, G *Fliess*, MD *vlues*, *vluys*, (as in D) *vlies*; perh also MLG *flus*, G *Flaus*, woollen material; cf also L *plūma*, down: f.a.e., PLUME.

fleer. See JEER.

fleet (1), adj 'swift': prob from—at the least, akin to—ON *fliōtr*, *fljōtr*, swift: cf the 4th FLEET.

fleet (2), n, 'inlet, estuary; brook; drain': OE *flēot*, a place for vessels to *float* (see 4th FLEET), hence, an inlet, a river, akin to MD-D *vliet* and G *Fliess*, a small brook, therefore to *fliessen*, to flow.

fleet (3), n, 'a naval force': ME *flete*, earlier *fleote*: OE *flēot*, a ship, from *flēotan*, to float, to swim: f.a.e., next.

fleet (4), v, 'to float' (now dial), 'to flow, hence glide, swiftly', hence vt, as in Shakespeare's '*fleet* the time carelessly': ME *fleten*, earlier *fleoten*, to swim; OE *flēotan*, to swim, to float: cf OFris *fliāta*, OS *fliotan*, OHG *fliozzan*, MHG *fliesen*, G *fliessen*, to float, to flow, MD *vleten*, *vliten*, MD-D *vlieten*, to flow, ON *fliōta*, *fljōta*, to float, to flow; cf Lith *plusti*, to float, L *pluit*, it rains, Gr *pleō*, I sail, and esp Skt *plu* (var *pru*), to swim or flow; cf also

2. Akin is 'to *float*', ME *floten*, earlier *flotien*, OE *flotian*, to float, to swim (cf *flēotan*, to swim or float), akin to ON *flota*. The n *float* derives, through ME *flote*, from OE *flota*, a ship, a fleet, akin to ON *floti*, a float or raft, also a fleet, and OHG-MHG *flōz*, G *Floss*, a raft; OE *flota* prob derives from OE *flotian*.

3. ON *floti*, raft, fleet, accounts for OF-F *flotte*, a fleet, and the Gmc group exemplified in para 2 has, with Frankish intervention, led to OF-MF *floter* (F *flotter*), to float, whence MF *flotaison*, lit a floating, whence EF *flotsan*, *-en*, *-on*, finally E *flotsam*.

4. Reshaped F *flottation*, a floating, yields—as if for *floatation*—the E *flotation*. E *flotage*, a floating, etc., prob blends E *float*+F *flottage* (MF *flotage*).

5. But *flotilla* is adopted from the Sp dim of Sp *flota*, a fleet, from syn F *flotte* (para 3).

Fleming, Flemish. See FLANDERS, para 2.

flense: (perh via D *flenzen*) Da *flense*: cf Sw *flänsa*, Nor *flinsa*.

flesh (n, hence v); flesher; fleshly; fleshy, whence fleshiness.

Whereas *fleshy=flesh*, n+adj *-y*, *flesher=flesh*, v+agent *-er*; *fleshly* derives from OE *flǣsclīc*, fleshlike, adj of *flǣsc*, whence, through ME *flesc*, later *flesh*, the E *flesh*: and OE *flǣsc* is akin to OFris *flāsk*, *flēsk*, OS *flēsk*, OHG *fleisc*, MHG-G *fleisch* (flesh, meat), MD *vlees*, *vleis*, *vleysche*, *vleesche*, *vlesch*, D *vleesch*, ON *flesk*, pork, bacon: o.o.o.; perh cf FLITCH.

fleur-de-lis, fleuret, fleuron, fleury. See FLORA, para 8.

flex, flexibility, flexible (cf inflexible, etc.); flexile; flexion or flection; flexor, flector; flexuous, flexuosity; flexure, whence flexural.—circumflex; deflect, deflection (deflexion), deflective, deflector, deflex, deflexure; inflect, inflection (inflexion), inflectional (or -x-), inflective (or -x-), inflector, inflex; reflect, reflectance, reflection (whence reflectional), reflective (whence reflectivity), reflector, reflex (adj, n, v), reflexible, reflexive. Cf sep *falchion*, q.v. at FALCATE.

1. The root word is L *flectere*, to bend, curve (inward), pp *flexus*: perh akin to *plectere*, to plait, or interlace, pp *plexus*: IE r, perh *\*plek-*, var *\*phlek-*.

2. 'A *flex*' derives from 'to *flex*', itself from L *flex-*, s of pp *flexus*. On L *flex-* are formed these simple L derivatives affecting E:

*flexibilis*, whence, prob via MF-F, *flexible*; derivative LL *flexibilitās*, o/s *flexibilitāt-*, becomes MF-F *flexibilité*, whence E *flexibility*;

*flexilis*, whence *flexile*;

*flexiō*, o/s *flexiōn-*, whence both *flexion* and *flection*;

Sci L *flexor*, with anglicized var *flector*;

*flexuōsus*, whence *flexuous*; derivative LL *flexuōsitās*, o/s *flexuōsitāt-*, yields *flexuosity*;

*flexūra*, whence *flexure*.

3. L *flexibilis* has neg *inflexibilis*, whence *inflexible*, whence, anl, *inflexibility*.

4. The first L prefix-cpd, among vv, is *circumflectere*, to bend or curve about, pp *circumflexus*, whence n *circumflexus* (gen *-ūs*), whence 'a *circumflex* accent'; derivative LL *circumflexiō*, o/s *circumflexiōn-*, becomes E *circumflexion*.

5. L *dēflectere*, to turn, or be turned, away, yields 'to *deflect*'; pp *dēflexus* has derivative *dēflexiō*, o/s *dēflexiōn-*, whence *deflexion*, anglicized var *deflection*; *dēflexus* itself yields 'to *deflex*', whence, anl, *deflexure*; *deflective* (*deflexive*) and *deflector* are E anl formations.

6. L *inflectere*, to bend inwards, produces 'to *inflect*', whence, anl, *inflective* (*-flexive*) and *inflector*. Pp *inflexus* leads, anl, to E 'to *inflex*'; derivative *inflexiō*, o/s *inflexiōn-*, becomes—perh via late MF-F—*inflexion*, anglicized to *inflection*, whence *inflectional* (*-flex-*).

7. L *reflectere*, to bend back, to turn again (to refract light), becomes, prob via OF *reflecter*, 'to *reflect*', whence *reflectance* (*-ance*)—*reflective*, *reflexive* (cf the F *réflectif*, *réflexif*)—*reflector*; *reflexible* goes back to the L pp *reflexus*, whence

directly LL *reflexiō*, o/s *reflexiōn-*, E *reflexion* (also the ME and MF form), anglicized to *reflection*. L *reflexus*, pp, accounts for E *reflex*, adj; derivative n *reflexus* (gen *-ūs*), for the E n *reflex*; pp *reflexus*, for 'to *reflex*'. *Reflexology*=E *reflex*, n+connective *-o-+-logy*, discourse, science.

**flick**, n hence v, is imitative—and akin to FLECK.

**flicker** (v hence n, including the woodpecker so named): OE *flicorian*, akin to OE *flacor*, a fluttering, and OHG *flagarōn*, MHG-G *flackern*, to flicker, cf ON *flōkra* and, further off, L *plangere*, to beat, a nasalization of *plag-*: cf PLAIN, v. Dial *flacker*=ME *flakkeren*, from r of OE *flacor*.

**flier**. See FLY.

**flight**, a flying: see FLY; a fleeing, see FLEE, para 1. The former yields FLIGHTY.

**flimflam**. See FLAM.

**flimsy** (adj hence n) is app metathetic for filmsy, for *filmy*, adj of FILM.

**flinch**. See FLANGE, para 3.

**flinder**. See FLINT, para 1.

**fling** (v hence n), pt and pp flung (cf *far-flung*): ME *flingen* or *flengen*; (vi) to rush, (vt) to hurl: ON *flengja*, to flog, (but also) to hurl; cf Nor dial *flenja*, to hurl, to throw, and Sw *flanja*, to dash or rush: ? echoic. Cf the 2nd FLAW.

**flint** (whence flinty); flinder, usu pl flinders; plinth; splint—splinter (n hence v); split (v hence n), with pa and vn splitting;—splice (v hence n).

1. *Flinder*, ME *flender*, is akin to D *flender*, Nor *flindra* and ult to *flint*.

2. *Flint*, OE *flint*, is akin to OHG-MHG *flins*, and LG *flint*, flint, and LG *flinse*, *flise*, a stone slab, MD-D *vlint*, flint, MLG *vlintstēn*, flint stone; cf also Nor *flint* and, as 'splinter', ON *flīs*: clearly there are nasal and *n*-less forms: cf the Gr *plinthos*.

3. Gr *plinthos*, a brick or a tile, becomes L *plinthus*, whence E *plinth*, with Arch sense: and *plinthos*, s *plinth-*, is app of extremely ancient stock (perh not IE).

4. Akin to E *flint* and the other words in para 2 is *splint*, from MD *splint* (var *splinte*), of which MD *splinter* (var *splenter*)—whence the E n *splinter*—is app an extn. Cf:

5. Without *n* is E 'to *split*', from MD *splitten*: cf MHG *splitter*, a splinter.

6. Akin to all the words above is 'to *splice*', from MD *splissen* (D *splitsen*), akin to MHG *splīzen*, G *spleissen*.

**flip**. See FLAP, para 3.

**flippancy, flippant**. See FLAP, para 3.

**flirt** (v hence n), orig to throw rapidly or jerkily; whence, anl, **flirtation, flirtatious.**

'To *flirt*'—whence F *flirter*—comes from EF *fleureter*, to talk sweet nothings, F *conter des fleurettes*, *fleurette* being the dim of *fleur*, a flower: cf, sem, 'to say it with *flowers*': f.a.e., FLORA.

**flit** (v hence n), which has freq flitter (v hence n), derives through ME *flitten*, var *flutten*, to go (or to carry) away, from ON *flytja* (cf ON *fliōta*, *fljōta*, to float or swim): perh cf also MHG *flittern*, to flutter. Hence *flittermouse: flitter*, vi+*mouse*: cf G

*Fledermaus*, MHG *fledermus*, OHG *fledarmus*, a bat (for 1st element, cf MHG *fledern*, to flutter).

**flitch**: ME *flicche*: OE *flicce*, akin to the syn ON *flikki*, MLG *vlicke*, Lith *paltis*; prob ult to FLESH, for OE *flicce* seems to be both a 'thinning' of the form and a narrowing of the sense of OE *flǣsc*, flesh.

**flitter**. See FLIT.

**flivver**, whether a small, cheap car, or a failure or 'fizzle', is sl (AE): o.o.o.: perh from *failure* via *filure* and *filyer* and metathetic *fliyer*.

**float** (n, v). See the 4th FLEET, para 2. Hence **floater** and **floating**.

**flocculence, flocculent, flocculus, floccus**. See the 2nd FLOCK.

**flock** (1), orig a large company, hence esp of sheep or geese: OE *flocc*, company, flock: cf ON *flokkr*, a crowd, and MLG *vlocke*; perh cf MD *vloc*, which, however, is a var of MD *volc*, later *volk*, E FOLK—was OE *flocc* perh orig a metathesis for OE *folc*, folk, tribe, nation?—Hence 'to *flock*'.

**flock** (2) of wool, whence **flocky**: ME *flocce* (cf MHG *flocke*, OFris *flokk-*): OF-F (obsol) *floc*: L *floccus*, which, like its LL dim *flocculus*, is adopted by tech E. L *floccus* has derivative LL adj *floccōsus*, whence both *floccous* and *floccose*; *flocculent*—whence *flocculence*—is an anl E formation from *flocculus*. Floccus itself, s *floc-*, is a picturesque word and therefore it requires no other origin. Cf FLOSS.

**floe**. See the 2nd FLAG, s.f.

**flog**. See FLAGELLANT, para 2.

**flood** (n, whence v, whence **flooding**): ME *flod*, a flood, a stream, a flowing: OE *flōd*, a flowing, hence a stream, hence esp a stream in spate: akin to OFris and OS *flōd*, flood, OHG-MHG *fluot*, flood, river, sea, G *Flut*, flood, Go *flōdus*, ON *flōth*; cf also 'to FLOW' (cf ON *flōa*).

**floor** (n hence v, whence **flooring**, vn): OE *flōr*: cf MHG *fluor*, G *Flur*, m 'threshold, entrance-hall', f 'field', ON *flōr*, *flōrr*, floor, esp of a cow-stall; also OIr *lár* (for *plár*), Ga *lár*, W *llawr*, Cor *lear*, *lēr*, OC *lār-*, *plār-*, and L *plānus*, level (E PLAIN)—and FIELD.

**floosie** or -zie, **floosy** or -zy. See FLORA, para 15.

**flop**. See FLAP, para 5.

**Flora**, flora, floral; florate; floreal; Florence (Florentine), florence—florin; flores; florescence, florescent; floret (cf floscule); floriation; c/f flori-(esp floriculture, floriferous), q.v. in Elements; florid, whence floridity; Florida; florist, floristics, floristry; element *-florous*; floruit;—fleur-de-lis, fleuret, fleury, almost direct from F.—E words from F: flower (n hence v), whence pa and vn flowering, flowers and adj flowery; cf flour (n hence v), whence adj floury;—flourish (v hence n), whence pa and vn flourishing.—Cpds: deflorate (adj, v), defloration, deflorescence, deflower; effloresce, efflorescence (-ency), efflorescent; inflorescence, inflorescent.—Coll and sl: Florrie, Flossie—floosey, -sie (var floozie).—Sep FLIRT.— For Gmc cognates, cf BLOOM, BLOSSOM, (of flowers) 'to BLOW'.

1. Of all the L words and L derivatives, as of the R offshoots, the easily recognizable root is L *flōr-*, o/s of *flōs* (gen *flōris*), a flower, a word common to the whole of ancient Italy; no *f-* cognates exist outside L and R, but C and Gmc have r *\*bhlo-* (C var *\*bhla-*), which we see in *bloom, blossom*, BLOW (to blossom).

2. L *flōs* has pl *flōres*, used in Chem and Pharm, and the derivative *Flōra*, goddess of flowers and of all blossoming vegetation, with adj *Flōrālis*, of Flora, hence *Flōrālia* (neu pl), her festival, but F and E have vulgarized *Floral* to common *floral*, of flowers; the general L adj *flōreus* affects E only in the rare *floreal* (cf the F *Florēal*, April 20–May 10). Goddess *Flora* becomes generic *flora* or plant life, opp *fauna*, animal life; cf the Bot *florate* (as in *triflorate*, three-bloomed), perh form-influenced by ML *flōrātus*, adorned with embroidered flowers.

3. L *flōridus*, flowery, yields *florid*. The State of *Florida* was so named because the Sp explorer, Juan Ponce de León, 'reached its shores in 1513 during the Feast of the Flowers (*Pascua Florida*)': *Collier's Encyclopedia*.

4. *Flōs, flōr-*, has derivative v *flōrēre*, to grow like a flower, hence to flourish: cf *flōruit* (abbr *fl.*), he flourished—at a certain period. The presp *flōrens*, o/s *flōrent-*, has derivative *flōrentia*, a blooming, hence prosperity, whence the city of *Flōrentia*, anglicized as *Florence*: cf the It *Firenze*. Hence, *florence*, a gold coin first minted there. It *fiorino* (from *fiore*, a flower, from L *flōs, flōr-*), the same Florentine coin, was reshaped by MF-F to *florin*, adopted by E; the value decreased. L *Flōrentia* has adj *Flōrentīnus*, whence E *Florentine*, n and adj, with several derivative n senses.

5. *Flōrēre* has inch *flōrescere*, to begin to bloom, or, hence, to flourish, with presp *flōrescens*, o/s *flōrescent-*, whence E *florescent*, whence *florescence*.

6. L *flōs* has dim *flōsculus* (*-culus*), whence F, hence E, *floscule*; more usual in E is *floret*, from OF-MF *florete* (cf F *fleurette*), dim of OF-MF *flor*, from L *flōrem*, acc of *flōs*.

7. Of L form, although not of L origin, are *floriate* (or *floriated*), *floriation*; *florist*, influenced by late EF-F *fleuriste*—whence both *floristic*, whence, in turn, *floristics*, and *floristry*.

8. Almost pure F are:
*fleur-de-lis* (var *-lys*), lit flower of (the) lily, the royal emblem of France, with corrupted E form *flower-de-luce*;
*fleuret*, a light fencing-foil, adopted from EF-F; as a small flower, E *fleuret* adapts EF-F *fleurette* (OF-MF *florete*);
*fleury* (Her)= F *fleuri*, covered or ornamented with flowers, prop the pp of *fleurir* in its sense 'to cover with flowers, render flowery'.

9. Of the remaining simple E words coming, altered, from F are *flower, flour, flourish*.

10. *Flower* derives from ME, from MF, *flour*, var of *flor* (as in para 6). '*Flowers*' (menstrues) anglicizes MF-F *fleurs*, which comes from LL

*flōres*, which, influenced by L *flōres*, flowers, represents L (*menstrui*)*fluōres*, monthly flowings. Cf:

11. *Flour*, fine-ground wheat-meal, derives from ME *flour*, var *flure*, from MF *flour de farine*, the flower—i.e., the best—of (wheat-)meal, itself from L *flōs farīnae*. *Flour* is therefore a doublet of *flower*.

12. 'To *flourish*', ME *florisshen* or *flurisshen*, derives from such parts of OF-MF *florir*, var *flurir* (cf EF-F *fleurir*), as pp *florissant* (*flurissant*) and 'ils *florissent*' (*flur-*), they bloom, hence flourish; OF-MF *florir, flurir*, comes, via rare LL *flōrīre*, VL *\*flōrire*, from L *flōrēre* (as in para 4).

13. L prefix-cpds include *dēflōrēre*, with LL int *dēflōrāre*, to pluck, hence to devirginate (a woman), with pp *dēflōrātus*, whence adj and v *deflorate*; derivative *dēflōrātiō*, o/s *dēflōrātiōn-*, yields E *defloration* and late MF-F *défloraison*, learnèd F *défloration*. LL *dēflōrāre* becomes MF *desflorer*, later *deflorer*, whence ME *defloren*, whence, after *flower*, E 'to *deflower*'. The inch L *flōrescere* has cpd *dēflōrescere*, to begin to lose its flowers, to fade, with presp *dēflōrescens*, o/s *dēflōrescent-*, whence E *deflorescent*, whence, in turn, *deflorescence*.

14. The L inch *flōrescere* has also the cpds:
LL *efflōrescere*, to begin to break out (*ef-* for *ex*) into flower, whence 'to *effloresce*'; presp *efflōrescens*, o/s *efflōrescent-*, becomes *efflorescent*, whence *efflorescence*, var *efflorescency*;
LL *inflōrescere*, to begin to break into (*in*) blossom, has presp *inflōrescens*, o/s *inflōrescent-*, whence *inflorescent*, whence *inflorescence*.

15. The goddess *Flora* becomes any woman's first name, with pet-forms *Florrie* (and *Flo*) and *Flossie* (and *Floss*); the latter is so proletarian that it leads to the sl AE *floosie* (*-ey, -y, floozie*, etc.), a girl or woman of light character and usu of little breeding.

**florist.** See prec, para 7.

**floscule.** See FLORA, para 6.

**floss,** whence **flossy,** comes from F (*soie*) *floche*, soft or downy silk, floss silk, *floche* deriving from OF-(obsol)F *floc*: see the 2nd FLOCK.

**flotage, flotation.** See 4th FLEET, para 4.

**flotilla.** See 4th FLEET, para 5.

**flotsam.** See 4th FLEET, para 3.

**flounce** (1), vi, as in 'to *flounce* out of the room', is app of Scan origin (cf Sw *flunsa*, to plunge): ult, prob echoic; perh, however, a blend of *flop*+ *bounce* (EW).

**flounce** (2), vt, in dressmaking, whence the n, the pa **flounced**, the vn **flouncing**, 'eases' the earlier **frounce**, to gather into, hence to adorn with, pleats, itself coming, via ME *frouncen, froncen*, from OF-MF *froncier, froncir* (MF-F *froncer*), from OF-F *fronce*,-a wrinkle, of Gmc origin, prob Frankish *\*krunkja* (cf ON *hrukka*), a wrinkle.

**flounder** (1), n, a flatfish; AF *floundre*: OF-MF *flondre*, of Scan origin: cf Sw *flundra* and, ult, Gr *platus*, level, flat.

**flounder** (2), v, orig to stumble: perh a blend of *founder*, to sink+*blunder*.

**flour.** See FLORA, para 11.

flourish. See FLORA, para 12.

flout. See FLABELLATE, para 4.

flow (v hence n), whence pa flowing, derives from OE *flōwan*, akin to ON *flōa*, to flow, L *pluit*, it rains: cf the 4th FLEET, FLOOD, FLUENT.

flower. See FLORA, para 10.

flown (1), adj, as in '*flown* with wine': from 'to FLOW'.

flown (2), pp. See FLY.

fluctuant, fluctuate, fluctuation. See FLUENT, para 4.

'flu. See FLUENT, para 8.

flue (1), obs a chimney, now an enclosed passage-way for conveying air or gases: o.o.o.; prob connected with FLUENT and FLOW.

flue (2): cf FLUFF, see VELVET.

fluent, fluency; fluid, whence fluidity; flume; fluor, whence fluorescence, fluorescent, fluorite; fluvial; flux, fluxion;—fluctuant, fluctuate, fluctuation.—Prefix-cpds: affluence, affluent; confluence, confluent; effluence, effluent, effluvium, efflux; influence, influent, influenza ('flu), influx; refluent, reflux; superfluent, superfluity, superfluous.

1. Firmly at the base stands L *flu-*, s of *fluere*, to flow: cf Gr *phluein*, to flow abundantly, overflow; IE r, perh *bhleu-*, to flow (abundantly), prob orig to swell up (as water when boiled) and flow over. Perh, ult, this group is akin to that of the 4th FLEET, FLOOD, PLUVIAL (Jupiter Pluuius), where *pla-*, *ple-*, *plo-*, *plu-* app means 'to cause to flow'.

2. L *fluere* has presp *fluens*, o/s *fluent-*, whence the E adj *fluent*; derivative L *fluentia* accounts for *fluency*.

3. L *fluere* has derivative adj *fluidus*, whence the adj (hence the n) *fluid*, whence *fluidity*: cf the MF-F *fluide* and EF-F *fluidité*. The derivative n *flūmen*, a stream, a river, becomes OF-MF, whence ME, *flum*, whence, ult, the AE *flume*, a rivered gorge: derivative *fluor*, a flowing, has Min derivative *fluorite*; derivative L *fluxus*, a current, a wave, becomes MF-F, whence E, *flux*, and var *fluxiō*, likewise formed upon *flux-*, s of pp *fluxus*, has o/s *fluxiōn-*, whence MF-F, hence E, *fluxion*; derivative *fluuius* (orig an adj), a river, has adj *fluuiālis*, ML *fluviālis*, whence MF-F, hence E, *fluvial*.

4. L *fluxus* represents earlier *fluctus*, current, wave, which has derivative *fluctuāre*, (of the sea) to swell, be agitated, with presp *fluctuans*, o/s *fluctuant-*, whence the E adj *fluctuant*, and with pp *fluctuātus*, whence 'to *fluctuate*'; derivative *fluctuātiō*, o/s *fluctuātiōn-*, yields, perh via OF-F, *fluctuation*.

5. L *affluere*, to flow towards (*af-* for *ad*), has presp *affluens*, o/s *affluent-*, used also as adj, whence, prob via EF-F, the E *affluent*, flowing with goods and money; derivative L *affluentia* becomes EF-F *affluence*, adopted by E. On the pp *affluxus* arises ML *affluxus*, a flowing towards, whence EF-F and E *afflux*.

6. L *confluere*, to flow *con-* or together, has presp *confluens*, o/s *confluent-*, whence the E adj (hence

n) *confluent*; derivative LL *confluentia* yields *confluence*.

7. L *effluere*, to flow outwards, has presp *effluens*, o/s *effluent-*, whence the E adj, hence n, *effluent*; derivative LL *effluentia* yields *effluence*. *Effluere* has the further derivative *effluuium* (influenced by *fluuius*), ML *effluvium*, adopted by E, mostly with adapted senses and with adj *effluvial*. E *efflux*, anl with *afflux* and *influx*, was perh prompted by LL *effluxiō*, a flowing forth.

8. L *influere*, to flow in, has presp *influens*, o/s *influent-*, whence the E adj, hence n, *influent*; derivative LL *influentia* becomes both MF-F, whence E, *influence* and It *influenza*, a malady induced by the influence of the heavenly bodies, adopted by E, with coll shortening '*flu*; LL *influxus* (on the pp s) yields *influx*.

9. L *refluere*, to flow *re-* or back, has presp *refluens*, o/s *refluent-*, whence the E adj *refluent*, whence *refluence*; *reflux* is anl with *influx*.

10. L *superfluere*, to flow *super* or over, has presp *superfluens*, o/s *-fluent-*, whence E adj *superfluent*, flowing—or floating—above; *superfluere* has the derivative adj *superfluus*, overflowing, whence E *superfluous*, and the derivative LL *superfluitās*, o/s *-fluitāt-*, whence, perh via OF-F, the E *superfluity*.

fluff, fluffy. See ADDENDA.

fluid, fluidity. See FLUENT, para 3.

fluke, whence adj fluky. See FLAKE, para 2.

flume. See FLUENT, para 3.

flummery, orig soft food (pap): W *llymruwd* (var of *llymru*), a soft, sour oatmeal food.

flummox (coll), to bewilder: cf dial *flummock*: echoic.

flunk. See FLANGE, para 4.

flunk(e)y. See FLANGE, para 5.

fluor (whence fluoresce, etc.), fluorite. See FLUENT, para 3.

flurry (n hence v): prob imitative: cf HURRY and SCURRY. Perh a blend of *fluster* and *hurry*.

flush (1), adj, (orig) well-filled, hence well-supplied, prob derives from the liquid senses of:

flush (2), v hence n: ME *fluschen*, to rise rapidly, fly up: prob imitative; app influenced by *flash* and *blush*. The liquid senses, basically 'to rush', are intimately related.

fluster (v hence n) is of Scan origin: cf Ice *flaustra*, to be flustered: ? orig echoic.

flute. See FLABELLATE, para 3.

flutter (v hence n): OE *floterian*, to float here and there, to be wave-tossed, to flutter, perh a freq of *flēotan*: cf the 4th FLEET, para 2.

fluvial. See FLUENT, para 3, s.f.

flux, fluxion. See FLUENT, para 3.

fly (1), adj (sl): prob as quick as a *fly* to avoid capture or annihilation.

fly (2), n, orig any flying insect, comes, through ME *flie*, from OE *flȳge* (cf OHG *flioga*, MHG-G *fliege*), var of *flēoge*, prob from OE *flēogan*, to fly, whence:

fly (3), to move, above ground, on wings: ME *flien*, *fleyen* (etc): OE *flēogan*: cf OFris *fleāga*, OS *fliogan*, OHG *fliogan*, MHG-G *fliegen*, MD-D *vliegen*, to fly, Go us*flaugjan*, to cause to fly, ON *fliūga*, to fly: o.o.o.; but prob akin to FLOW; perh to L *plūma*, a feather.

2. Note the presp *flying*, pp *flown*, pt *flew*, agent *flyer* or *flier*. The *flying*-cpds are self-explanatory.

**foal** (n hence v): ME *fole*: OE *fola*: cf OFris *fola*, OS *folo*, OHG *folo*, MHG *vole*, G *Fohlen*, Go *fula*, ON *foli*: the *o-u* variation and the Gmc *f* and L-Gr *p* sound-change appear in cognate L *pullus*, young animal (chick), and Gr *pōlos*, young animal (colt): perh further cf L *puer*, boy, Skt *putra*, child, son, which suggest IE r *\*pu-*, young and growing (animal)—cf PUBERTY, PUERILE, PEDAGOGUE.

2. ON *foli*, foal, has derivative *fyl*, whence E *filly*.

3. L *pullus*, young animal, has ML mdfn *pullānus*, foal, whence OF-F *poulain*, colt, with dim *poulenet*, whence prob the Sc C17–18 *powny*, C18 *powney*, E C18–19 *poney*, C19–20 *pony*.

**foam** (n; hence v, unless from OE *fǣman*, from *fām*), derives, through ME *fome*, earlier *fame*, from OE *fām*: cf OHG-G *feim* and L *pūmex*, pumice, also, with initial *s-*, L *spūma*, foam, and Skt *spāma*, spit, foam—cf Skt *phénas*, scum, foam, and OSl *pena*, foam.—Hence, *foamy*.

**fob** (1), n, a small waistband pocket in men's trousers: app Gmc—cf E Prussian dial *fuppe*, a pocket.

**fob** (2), v, to cheat, hence to fob (something) **off** on (somebody), to trick him into accepting it: orig cant, prob of Gmc origin: cf G *foppen* and *fopper*, resp to lie, to befool, and liar, trickster, from C15–16 G cant *voppen* and *vopper*: ? ult echoic. Cf FOP.

**focal** (whence **focalize**) is the adj of E **focus**, adopted from L *focus*, hearth, hence the dwelling-place of the Lares and Penates—the household gods of the Romans, whence the E Math, Med, seismological senses; VL 'fire'. L *focus*, s *foc-*, perh comes from an IE r *\*bhok-* but is prob of non-IE origin (? remotely, by metathesis, Eg *tchesef*, fire, heat).

2. The VL sense 'fire' has derivative LL *focālia*, neu pl taken as f sing, whence MF *foail*, *foaille*, *fouaille*, *fuaille*, a faggot, kindling, whence E *fuel*, whence 'to *fuel*'.

3. The VL derivative *focārium*, fireplace (prob from an *-ārius* adj *\*focārius*, from VL *focu*s, fire), becomes OF *fuier*, MF-F *foyer*, a heated room, hence ult the *foyer* or lobby of a theatre, adopted by E.

4. The obs *fusil*, a flintlock musket, comes from MF-F *fusil*, from OF *fuisil*, var of *foisil*, from VL *\*focīle*, prop the neu of adj *\*focīlis*, from VL *focus*, fire.

5. The VL sense 'fire' of L *focus* becomes OF-F *feu*, with MF cpd *covrefeu*, *couevrefu* (lit, cover-fire), whence ME *curfu*, later *courfew*, whence E *curfew*: fires had, in the Middle Ages, to be either put out or, at the least, covered by a certain hour of the evening and people off the streets.

**fodder.** See FEED, para 1.

**foe** (foeman: OE *fāhman*, enemy man): ME *fo*, earlier *fa*: OE *fāh*: cf OFris *fāch*, OHG *gifēh*, hostile, Go *faih*, deception, bi*faih*, envy, covetousness: cf also the *p-* forms Skt *pišáčas*, a demon, and *pišuna*, malicious—Lith *pìktas*, wicked, L *piget*, it causes sorrow or shame. (Walshe.)

Cf the 2nd FEUD and also FICKLE.

**foetid, foetor:** obsol for fetid (fetor).

**fog**, heavy mist, is prob sense-adapted from Da *fog*, spray, driving snow: cf ON *fok*, spray, driving snow, and Nor dial *fuka*, sea fog.—Hence **foggy**.

Perh from *fog*, heavy mist, comes *fog*, after-grass, decaying grass.

**fogey** or **fogy**, usu *old fog(e)y*: o.o.o.: perh cf E *foggy*, covered with *fog* (ME *fogge*: o.o.o.) or after-grass; perh however from EF-F *fougueux*, quick- or hot-tempered (adj of EF-F *fougue*: It *foga*, impetuosity: L *fuga*, a fleeing, from *fugere*, to flee) —old men being characteristically quick-tempered.

**foible.** See FEEBLE, para 1.

**foil** (1), n, leaf, whence, from its thinness or lightness, a small practice sword: ME *foil* or *foile*: OF-MF *foil*, *foille* (also *fueil*, *fueille*)—cf EF-F *feuille*—VL *folia*, neu pl (apprehended as f sing) of L *folium*, a leaf: f.a.e., FOLIAGE.

**foil** (2), v, orig to trample underfoot, hence to defeat, hence to outwit: ME *foilen*: (irreg from) OF-F *fouler*, to trample, orig to *full* (cloth): f.a.e., FULL, v.

**foison.** See the 2nd FOUND, para 3, s.f.

**foist.** See FIST, para 3.

**fold** (1), n, as in 'sheep*fold*': ME *fold*, earlier *fald*: OE *fald*, var *falod*: of Gmc origin, esp LG: cf MD *vaelde*, *valde*, *vaelte*, *valt*, D *vaald*, a dung-pit, but also Da *fold*, sheepfold, pen.

**fold** (2), v hence n: ME *folden*, var *falden*: OE *fealdan*: akin to OHG *faltan*, MHG *valten*, G *falten*, Go *falthan*, ON *falda*, also, in cpds, OFris and OS *-fald*, OE *-feald*, E two*fold*, three*fold*, mani*fold*, etc: also akin, further off, to Gr di*plasios*, twofold, and Skt *puṭas* (for *\*pultas*), a fold. (Walshe.)

**folder, folding:** from prec.

**foliage, foliaceous; foliate** (adj, v), **foliation; folio; foliole; foliose, folious.**

1. L *folium*, a leaf, hence 'because the Sibyl inscribed her predictions upon palm leaves', a sheet for writing (E & M). *Folium* has s *foli-*, r *fol-*: prob akin to Gr *phullon* (r *phul-*), a leaf, with IE r *\*bhul-*, var *\*bhel-*; there are several cognates in C, as also, more remotely and less prob, in Gmc—cf ON *blath*, *blad*, OHG-MHG *blat*, G *Blatt*, OE *blaed* (E BLADE).

2. The abl *folio*, esp *in folio*, yields E *folio*.

3. L derivatives affecting E are:

*foliāceus*, leaf-shaped, whence *foliaceous*;

*foliātus*, leaved, whence *foliate*, adj (whence v), whence, anl, *foliation*;

LL *foliolum*, a small leaf, whence *foliole*;

*foliōsus*, leafy, whence both *foliose* and *folious*.

**folk**, whence, from pl *folks*, the coll AE **folksy;** **folk-moot** or **-mote; folklore** (*folk* + *lore*, q.v. at LEARN); **Herrenvolk.**

1. *Folkmoot*, a *moot* (q.v. at MEET, v) of the *folk* or people, derives from OE *folcmōt*, contr of *folcgemōt*. *Folk* itself derives from OE *folc*, akin to OFris and OS *folk*, OHG *folc*, MHG *volc*, G *Volk*, ON *fŏlk*, all perh allied to FULL; perh cf, further off, the L *plēbs*, the people, and the Gr *plēthos*, a multitude, from *pimplēmi*, I fill; the IE r is perh *\*pleodh-*.

2. G *Volk* has cpd *Herrenvolk*, race (people) of masters, the master race: cf HERR.

**follicle, folliculate, folliculose (and -ous), follis.**

L *follis*, orig a bellows, hence an inflated ball, hence a (leather) money-bag, a large purse, is akin to ON *böllr*, OHG *ballo*, a ball, also Gaul *bulga*, Ir *bolg*, a (leather) bag: perh ult akin to BULL. *Follis* has dim *folliculus*, a small bag, hence a husk or a pod, whence E *follicle*, with derivative anl adjj *follicular* and *folliculate*. *Folliculus* has derivative LL *folliculōsus*, whence the adjj *folliculose*, *folliculous*.—Cf FOOL.

**follow**, v (hence n), whence pa and vn **following**; **follower.**

A *follower*, ME *folwere*, derives from OE *folgere*, agent of *folgian*, var *fylgan*, whence, through ME *folgen*, later *folwen*, latest *foluwen*, the E 'to *follow*'. The OE *folgian*, *fylgan*, is akin to OFris *folgia*, *fulgia*, OS *folgon*, OHG *folgēn*, MHG-G *folgen*, ON *fylgia*. Of OHG *folgēn*, Walshe remarks that, app, it was orig a cpd: 'OHG *folá gan*, OE *ful-gangan*'—add MD *volligen*, contr to *volgen* (extant in D). He adds, 'The second element would then be *gehen* [E GO], while the first element seems to be *voll* [E adj FULL], but may represent some now obscure word'—perh *Volk*, FOLK.

**folly.** See FOOL.

**foment, fomentation.**

The latter comes from LL *fōmentātiō*, o/s *fōmentātiōn-*, a derivative of *fōmentāre* (pp *fōmentātus*), whence, via MF-F *fomenter*, the E 'to *foment*'. *Fōmentāre* derives from *fōmentum*, for *fouimentum* (ML *fovi-*), a hot lotion, from *fouēre* (ML *fovēre*), to warm or gently heat, to keep warm: caus, from the IE r furnishing Skt *dáhati*, Av *dažaiti*, he burns, OCz *dahneti*, to burn: perh cf DAY.

**fond**, adj, whence **fondness** and, as an *-le* freq, **fondle**; **fun**, v (hence n, whence adj **funny**, whence the AE coll n 'the **funnies**', comic papers or strips).

1. *Fond* derives from ME *fonned*, pp of *fonnen*, to be silly, to make a fool of: o.o.o.: prob of C origin—cf MIr *fonn*, pleasure, folly, and *fand*, *fann*, faint, weak, OIr and Ga *fann*, weak, faint, W and Cor *gwan*, Br *goann*, feeble, faint; OC *\*vannos* (MacLennan).

2. *Fun*, n, derives from 'to *fun*', itself from EE *fon*, to make a fool of, to fool with (cf EE *fon*, a fool or idiot), ME *fonnen* as in para 1.

**font** (1), as in printing. See 2nd FOUND, para 2.

**font** (2), a spring of water, **fontanel, Fontainebleau; fount, fountain.**

*Font*, OE *font*, represents L *font-*, o/s of *fons*, whence also, via OF-EF *font*, the E *fount*, which gathers special senses. *Fountain*, however, comes from OF-F *fontaine*, from LL *fontāna*, prop the f (sc *aqua*) of *fontānus*, of a *fons* or spring; and *fontāna* acquires, perh via ML *fontānella*, the EF-F dim *fontanelle*, adopted by E, which adapts it to *fontanel*, now only a tech of Med, An, Zoo. *Fontainebleau* is, as to the 2nd element, o.o.o.: perh *-bleau* is a contr of [de] *belle eau*.—L *fons* is f/e derived from *fund*ere, to pour out; prob akin to Skt *dhan*áyati, *dhán*vati, it runs or flows.

**food.** See FEED, para 1.

**fool**, n whence v and **foolery** and **foolish; folly.**

*Folly*, ME *folie*, is adopted from OF-F *folie*, itself from OF-MF *fol*, foolish, mad; as n, OF-MF *fol* (cf the F adj *fou*, *fol*, *folle*) is adopted by ME, whence E *fool*. OF *fol*, a fool, derives from LL *follis*, a fool, from L *follis*, bellows (hence a wind-bag): f.a.e., FOLLICLE.—That size of paper which is *foolscap* is so named because of the orig water-mark of a fool's cap (*fool's-cap*, *foolscap*) and bells.

**foot** (pl **feet**), hence v, hence vn **footing**; such obvious cpds as **football** (whence sl **footer**); **-fall, -hill, -hold, -loose, -man, -note, -pad, -step**, etc; **afoot**; sep FETCH; **fetlock; fetter**; sep FIT (of verse).—Latin: **pedal**, adj and n (whence v)—**sesquipedalian; pedary** and **pedate; pedestrian** (adj hence n); element **pedi-**, q.v., as in *pedicure*; **pedicel, pedicle, pedicule**; element *pedo-*, q.v., as in *pedometer*; **peduncle**, whence **peduncular; petiolate, petiole; pawn**—**peon.**—**biped, quadruped; expedience** (and **-ncy**), **expedient** (adj hence n), **expedite, expedition** (whence **expeditionary**), **expeditious; impede** (whence **impedance**), **impediment** (whence **impedimental**), **impedimenta; impeach, impeachment**—**appeach, appeachment**—**peach** (v) and sl 'peach';—**cap-a-pie; pedestal; pedigree; piedmont, piepowder;**—**repudiate, repudiation;**—cf the sep IMPAIR (v) and PEJORATIVE (with PESSIMIST).—Greek: elements **-pod, -poda, podo-**, qq.v.; **pilot** (n, v), **pilotage; podium** and **pew;**—**podagra; antipodes**, whence **antipodal**, adj, and **antipodean**, n; **octopod, octopus** (pl **octopodes**); **trapeze, trapezium, trapezius, trapezoid** (whence **trapezoidal**); **tripod.**

### Germanic

1. *Foot*: ME *foot*, pl *feet*, earlier *fot*, pl *fet*: OE *fōt*, pl *fēt*: cf OFris and OS *fōt*, OHG-MHG *fuoz*, MD *voot*, *vuet*, MD-D *voet*, Go *fōtus*, ON *fōtr*: Gmc r, *\*fōt-*. The sense 'measure of 12 inches' exists already in OE and OHG.

2. The adv—hence adj—*afoot* merely=*a-*, on+*foot*.

3. *Fetlock* derives from ME *fetlak* and its var *fitlok*: cf MHG *vizlach*, *vizzeloch* (G *Fissloch*): 1st element, akin to *foot*; 2nd, to LOCK of hair.

4. *Fetter*=OE *fetar*, *feter*, *fetor*: cf OFris *fitera*, to fetter (OHG *fezzarōn*, OE *feterian*, whence 'to *fetter*'), OHG *fezzara* (or *-era*), ON *fiōturr*; cf L *pedica* (cf *ped-*, o/s of *pēs*, foot), Gr *pedē*, fetter.

### Latin

5. L *pēs* (gen *pedis*), a foot, o/s *ped-*, is akin to Gr *pous*, o/s *pod-*: see next section. It has adj

*pedālis*, whence E *pedal*, of the foot (or feet); the neu *pedāle* becomes the It n *pedale*, whence EF-F *pédale*, whence E 'a *pedal*', orig a treadle. *Pedālis* has cpd *sesquipedālis*, 'of, containing, a foot and a half', *sesqui-* being a mdfn of *semi-*, half, and standing for *\*semisque*; hence Horace's *sesquipedālia* (*uerba*), words a foot and a half long, i.e. very long, whence the E adj *sesquipedalian*.

6. The rarer L adj *pedārius*, of the foot, becomes learnèd E *pedary*, esp 'of walking'. L *pedātus*, furnished with feet, yields Zoo and Bot *pedate*.

7. L *pedester* (occ *pedestris*, as *p. orātiō*, pedestrian speech), of the feet, hence lowly, humble, earth-bound, has o/s *pedestri-*, whence the E adj *pedestrian* (*-an*, adj). Cf the formation of *equestrian* from L *equus*.

8. L *pēs*, *ped-*, has dim *pediculus*, a little foot, hence a slender stalk, whence E *pedicule*, usu *pedicle* (mostly in An); Sci L has two dimm: *pedicellus*, whence E *pedicel*, used in Bot and An, and *pedunculus*, whence E Bot, An, Med *peduncle*. The L dim *petiolus*, esp a fruit stalk, becomes the *petiole* of Bot and Zoo, with adj *petiolar*; from *petiolus*, SciL derives *petiolatus*, anglicized as *petiolate* (Bot and Zoo).

9. L *pēs*, foot, has derivative LL *pedō*, a pedestrian, a foot-soldier, acc *pedōnem*, whence OF-MF *peon* (F *pion*), with var *paon*, with additional sense 'pawn' in chess, whence ME *poune*, later *pawne*, whence E *pawn*. LL *pedō*, o/s *pedōn-*, becomes (Port *peão* and) Sp *peón*, whence E *peon*, (India, Ceylon) foot-soldier, ordinary policeman, messenger, but now predominantly S Am, farm or wine, then any, manual worker.

10. Thus we reach the cpds, both full and merely prefixal. The L prefix-cpds include *expedīre*, to free (one's or another's) feet (*ped-*) from (*ex*) shackles or a trap, with presp *expediens*, o/s *expedient-*, whence, via MF-F, the E adj *expedient*; derivative LL *expedientia*, advantage, opportunity, yields E *expedience* (cf EF-F *expédience*) and *expediency* (perh ex *expedient*). The pp *expeditus* yields both 'to *expedite*', orig to set free, and the adj *expedite*; derivative *expedītiō*, o/s *expedītiōn-*, orig a freeing, yields, perh via MF-F, the E *expedition*, whence, anl, *expeditious*, prompt.

11. L *impedīre*, to put (someone's feet: *ped-*) in (*im-*) shackles, hence to prevent from walking, hence to hinder, yields 'to *impede*'; *impedimenta* is prop the pl of L *impedīmentum* (*imped*+connective *-i-+-mentum*), an obstruction, whence E *impediment*.

12. Cf LL *impedicāre*, to tangle someone's feet (*ped-*) in (*im-*) a *pedica* or trap, hence fetter, whence OF *empeechier*, MF *empechier*, *empeschier* (F *empêcher*), to hinder or prevent, whence ME *empechen*, whence E 'to *impeach*', esp in legal sense 'to charge with an official crime or misdemeanour'; OF-MF derivative *empeechement* (F *empêchement*) helps to form E *impeachment*.

13. OF *empeechier*, *empechier*, becomes AF *apecher*, whence ME *apechen*, whence 'to *appeach*' (whence *appeachment*), to impeach, whence the

equally obs 'to *peach*', to impeach, surviving as sl *peach* (*on*), to turn informer (against), to blab.

14. A less obvious L prefix-cpd is *repudium*, a 'back-footing', a (rejection indicated by) pushing back (*re-*) with the foot (*pede*, abl), esp a rejection of wife by husband, f/e related to *pudet*, it is a shame (*me pudet*, I am ashamed)—cf PUDENCY. *Repudium* has derivative *repudiāre*, to reject (esp a wife), with pp *repudiātus*, whence 'to *repudiate*'; derivative *repudiātiō*, o/s *repudiātiōn-*, accounts for late MF-F *répudiation* and E *repudiation*.

15. Full or true cpds include *cap-a-pie*, *pedestal*, *pedigree*, *piedmont*, *piepowder*. *Cap-a-pie*, (armed or dressed) from head to foot: adopted from MF (*de*) *cap a pié*, EF-F (*de*) *cap à pied*, now *de pied en cap*: L *pēs*, *pedem*, and *caput*, head.

16. *Pedestal*: EF-F *piédestal*: It *piedestallo* (or *-istallo*), foot of a stall, a place for sitting or standing:=*pie* (for *piede*: L *pēs*, *pedis*), foot+*di* (L *dē*), of+*stallo*, a support or a stall (see STALL).

17. *Pedigree* (n whence v, whence pa *pedigreed*): ME *pedegru*: MF *pié de grue*, lit 'foot of crane' (the bird: L *grus*): ref the resemblance of the three-line mark of descent to the three 'toes'.

18. Geog *piedmont*, adj and n, '(district) formed or situated at the base of mountain or mountains': from the *Piedmont* region of Italy (cf It *Piemonte*, F *Piémont*): L *Pedimontium*: L (*ad*) *pedes montium*, at the feet of the mountains, here the Alps. Cf MOUNTAIN.

19. *Piepowder* 'anglicizes' *piepowdre*, lit dusty-footed (traveller, esp an itinerant vendor): OF-MF *pié* (F *pied*), foot+*poudreux*, dusty, from *poudre*, dust (see POWDER): now only hist, in *court of piepoudre* (*-powder*), a fairground or market-place summary court.

20. Midway between prefixal and full cpds stand *biped* and *quadruped*. *Biped* comes, perh via EF-F *bipède*, from L *biped-*, o/s of *bipēs*, two-footed; *quadruped* (adj hence n)—perh via late MF-F *quadrupède*—from *quadruped-*, o/s of L *quadrupēs*, four-footed.

### Greek

21. Akin to L *pēs*, gen *pedis*, is Gr *pous*, gen *podos*, which has dim *podion*, a base or a pedestal, whence LL *podium*, under-part (of a structure), adopted by Arch for 'substructure'; the LL pl *podia*, apprehended as f sing, becomes OF *puie*, a raised place, MF *puye*, a parapet, later balcony, whence—perh via AF *pui*, a platform or stage— ME *puwe*, later *pewe*, then E *pew*, orig a preacher's stall.

22. Akin to Gr *pous*, o/s *pod-*, is Gr *pēdon* (s *pēd-*), an oar-blade, with pl *pēda*, a rudder, whence Byz Gr *\*pēdōtēs*, whence obs It *pedota* (var *-otta*), whence It *pilòta* (*-l-* perh from It *pileggiare*, to navigate). Prati less convincingly derives obs It *pedota* from obs It *pede*, foot. Either way, It *pilòta* yields MF-EF *pilot*, EF-F *pilote*, whence E *pilot*; F *pilot*, *pilote*, has derivative EF-F *piloter*, whence 'to *pilot*'; derivative late MF-F *pilotage* becomes E.

23. One Gr cpd has, via L, come unchanged into E: *podagra*, a seizure or catching (*agra*) of the foot (*podos*), gout.

24. In the other cpds, Gr *pod-* occurs in the 2nd place. Let us take them alphabetically, the 1st being (*the*) *antipodes*, orig the people, now the lands: L *antipodes*: Gr *hoi antipodes*, the people with feet (*podes*) opposite (*anti*): pl of adj *antipous* (gen *antipodos*).

25. *Octopus* (pl *octopodes*, anglicized as *octopods*; true E pl, *octopuses*): Sci L from Gr *oktōpous*, eight-footed (hence -tentacled): *oktō*, 8+*pous*, foot.

26. *Trapeze* comes from EF-F *trapèze*: LL *trapezium* (adopted by Geom): Gr *trapezion*, an irregular 4-sided figure, lit a little table, dim of *trapeza*, a 4-legged table, for *tetrapeza*, a 4-footed object: *tetra*, 4+*peza*, foot, mdfn of *pous*. *Trapezius* is an An Sci L derivative from *trapezium*. Gr *trapeza*, a 4-legged table, has derivative adj *trapezoeidēs*, table-shaped, trapezion-shaped, with -*eidēs*, -like, a c/f of *eidos*, form, shape, resemblance.

27. *Tripod*: LL *tripoda*: L *tripos*, gen *tripodis*, a tripod: Gr *tripous*, gen *tripodos*, a three-footed seat, n from adj; *tri-*, c/f of Gr *treis*, 3.

Indo-European

28. Whereas the Gmc r is *fōt-* (para 1), the L is *ped-*, the Gr *pod-*; and the IE r is *pod-* or *pōd*, with varr *ped-* or *pēd-*, and perh *pād-*. Notable cognates not already mentioned include: Skt *pāt*, acc *pádam*, gen *pādas*, foot, *padám*, footprints, *pattis* (cf OPer *pastiŝ*), foot-soldier; Tokh A *pe*, Tokh B *pai*, foot; Lith *péda*, foot, and *pešĉias*, on foot.

'**footling**' derives from FUTILE, q.v.

**foozle**, to bungle, perh owes something to FUTILE, but prob far more to G dial *fuseln*, to work very slowly, or clumsily, akin to G *fuschen*, better *pfuschen*, to bungle, with cognates in Da and Sw (Kluge).

**fop**, whence both **foppery** and **foppish**, derives from ME *fop*, *foppe*, a fool, akin to G underworld *foppen*, to jeer at, to cheat: cf the 2nd FOB.

**for** (prep; hence—elliptical for *for that*—conj): OE *for* or *fore*: akin to OFris *for*, *fore*, *fori*, *for*, OS *fora*, *furi*, *for*, OHG *fora* (whence MHG *vore*, MHG-G *vor*), *furi*, MHG-G *für*, Go *faur*, *faura*, ON *fyr-ir*; OIr *ro* (for *pro*); L and Gr *pro*; kindred L *prae*; OSl *pro*, Lith r *pra-*; Skt *pra-*, Av *fra-*: IE r of the prep, *prod-*. Cf also FORE and PRIOR.

**forage**, n and v (whence **forager**). 'To *forage*' comes from MF-F *fourrager*, itself from F *fourrage*, OF-MF *fourage*, var *forrage*, whence the E n: OF-MF *fourage*, *forrage* derives from OF *fuerre* (var *feurre*), which is of Gmc origin, prob the Frankish *fōdare*: cf OHG *fuotar* and E *fodder* (q.v. at FEED, para 1). Cf FORAY.

**foramen**, **foraminate** (adj and v), **foramination**, **Foraminifera**.

1. *Foramen*, orifice, adopted from L, derives from *forā*re, to pierce (cf BORE, to pierce), akin to

Epic Gr *pharoosi*, they plough. Derivative LL *forāmināre*, to perforate, has pp *forāminātus*, whence *foraminate*; *foramination* is an E anl formation; SciL coins the cpd *Foraminifera* (usu pl), a Zoo order: cf the element *-fer*, -bearing, -bearer.

2. *Forāre* has cpd *perforāre*, to bore, or pierce, *per* or through, with pp *perforātus*, whence the adj and v *perforate*; derivative ML *perforātiō*, o/s *perforātiōn-*, yields, perh via MF-F, the E *perforation*.

**foray** (v hence n): OF-MF *forer*, *forrer*, to pillage, from *forre*, var of *fuerre*, q.v. at FORAGE: orig to plunder for food.

**forbear** (whence **forbearance**): ME *forberen*: OE *forberan*: 1st element, adversative prefix *for-*; 2nd, see the v BEAR.

**forbid**, pt forbad(e), pt forbidden. See BID, para 2.

**force** (n, v); from n, **forceful**, **forcible**;—**enforce**, whence **enforcement.**—**fort**; **forte**; **fortissimo**; **fortify**, **fortification**—cf **fortress**; **fortitude.**—**comfort** (n, v), **comfortable** (neg **uncomfortable**), **comforter**, **comfortless**—**discomfort** (n, v); **effort**, whence **effortless.**

1. The n *force*, adopted from OF-F, derives from LL *fortia*, strength, from neu pl *fortia* (apprehended as f sing n) of L *fortis*, strong; and *fortia* has derivative VL *fortiāre*, whence OF-F *forcer*, whence 'to *force*'. L *fortis*, s *fort-*, perh stands for *forctis*, s *forct-*, with IE r *dherg-*, *dhergh-*. (E & M.)

2. Derivative MF-EF *forcible* is adopted by E.

3. 'To *enforce*' comes from OF-MF *enforcier* (*en*, L *in*): VL *infortiāre* (cf para 1).

4. *Fort*, adopted from MF-F (sc *lieu*, place), represents L *fortis*, strong; derivative OF-F *forteresse* (from adj *fort*) becomes E *fortress*; E *forte*, one's strong point, derives from F *le fort* (*à qq n*), one's strong point; Mus *forte* is adopted from It (L *fortis*), as also the sup *fortissimo*.

5. L *fortis* has LL derivative *fortificāre*, to strengthen (c/f *forti-*+*-ficāre*, c/f of *facere*, to make): hence F *fortifier*, whence 'to *fortify*'; derivative LL *fortificātiō*, o/s *fortificātiōn-*, becomes MF-F, then E, *fortification*.

6. L *fortis* has derivative *fortitūdō*, whence E *fortitude*.

7. The chief prefix-cpds are *comfort* and *effort*. *Comfort*, n, derives from OF-F *confort*, from OF-EF *conforter*—whence 'to *comfort*'; and *conforter* derives from LL *confortāre*, to strengthen considerably (int *con-*), from *fortis*. *Comfortable*= OF-EF *confortable*, from *conforter*. The MF-EF cpd *desconforter* (*des-*, L *dis-*) yields 'to *discomfort*'; the derivative MF-EF n *desconfort* yields the E n, and derivative MF *desconfortable* becomes obsol *discomfortable*.

8. *Effort* is adopted from F; MF-F *effort* derives from OF-MF *esfort*, for *esfors*, from *esforcier*, to force oneself (*es-*, L *ex*, out of, sc oneself): VL *exfortiāre*: cf *fortiāre* in para 1.

**forceps**. See CAPABILITY, para 8.

**forcible**. See FORCE, para 2.

**ford** (n hence v): OE *ford*: cf OFris *forda*, OS *ford*, OHG-G *furt*, MD *voort*, *vort*, D *voord*, a ford, ON *fiörthr*, a bay: cf FARE, FIORD, 1st FRITH, PORT (harbour).

**fore**, adv (hence adj and n): OE *fore*, adv and prep: akin to OFris *fora*, *fore*, *fori*, *for*, OHG *fora*, *furi*, G *faura* (cf FOR), and, further off, Skt *puras*, in front, and *purā*, formerly. Cf FOREMOST and FROM.

**forebear**, ancestor: *fore*, formerly+(to) *be*+ agential *-er*.

**forebode, foreboding**. See BODE, para 2.

**forecast** (v hence n): to CAST or calculate beforehand (FORE).

**foreclose** (whence **foreclosure**): OF-F *forclos*, excluded, pp of *forclore*: *for-* for *fors* (F *hors*), outside, L *foris*, out of doors+*clore*, to close (cf CLOSE).

**foregather.** See FORGATHER.

**forego**, to precede. See GO, para 2.

**forehead**: OE *forhēafod*: the front (FORE) of the HEAD.

**foreign**, adj, whence **foreigner, foreignness**, etc.: ME *foreine* or *forene*: OF-F *forain* (f *foraine*): LL *forānus*, situated on the outside, esp beyond one's own country: an *-ānus* adj from *forēs*, *foris*, out of doors, hence abroad, from *\*fora*, a door,—akin to L *foris* (occ *forēs*), pl *fores*, doors, esp outer doors: IE r, *\*dhwer-*, cf DOOR.

2. Akin to L *foris* is L *forum*, a market-place (out of doors), the centre of public business: adopted by E.

3. *Forum* has adj *forensis*, of the forum as the orig centre of law business; hence *forensic*, legal— esp in relation to speech.

4. The L adv *foris*, outside, has LL derivative *forestis*, usu in *silua* (ML *silva*) *forestis*, a wood outside, hence for the use of all, hence, by ellipsis, the ML n *forestis*, a wood, a forest, whence OF-MF *forest* (F *forêt*), adopted by ME; but app the ML *silva forestis* or *forestis silva* was orig applied, in so far as OF is concerned, to Charlemagne's royal forest, with *forestis* deriving—cf *forensis*— from *forum* in its special early ML sense 'court of the King's justice'. (B & W.) Hence OF-F *forestier*, whence E *forester*, orig a forest warden; and MF-EF *foresterie*, whence E *forestry*.

**foreknowledge**. A knowledge (see KNOW) beforehand (FORE).

**foremost**: OE *formest* (*fyrmest*), sup of *forma*, first, itself a sup from the r of FORE: akin to OFris and OS *formest*, *forma*, Go *frumists*, *fruma*: in E, drastically influenced by MOST.

**forensic**. See FOREIGN, para 3.

**forerunner**: a runner (see RUN) in front (FORE).

**foresee**. See SEE, para 2. Pt *foresaw*, pp *foreseen*.

**foreshow**: OE *forescēawian*.

**foresight**: late ME cpd of FORE and *sight* (q.v. at SEE). Cf the G *Vorsicht*.

**forest**. See FOREIGN, para 4.

**forestall**. See STALL, para 3.

**forester, forestry**. See FOREIGN, para 4.

**foretell**: to TELL before (FORE) the event.

**forethink**: OE *forethencean*. Extant in derivative *forethought*.

**forewarn**: to WARN beforehand (*fore*).

**forfeit** (adj, n, v); **forfeiture**.

OF-EF *forfaire*, to transgress, hence to forfeit, comes from ML *forisfacere*, lit to act (*facere*: see FACT) out of doors (*foris*: see FOREIGN), hence to act beyond (one's rights), to transgress; *forfaire* has pp *forfait* (cf ML *forisfactum*), which, used (OF-EF) as n, 'crime', becomes ME *forfet*, crime, hence the penalty for it, whence E *forfeit*, whence 'to *forfeit*'; the OF pp *forfait* becomes E adj *forfeit*; and OF *forfaire*, through its derivative *forfaiture* (MF-EF), yields *forfeiture*.

**forgather**, later often **foregather**: earliest (C16) as *forgad(d)er*, mostly Sc: *for-*, predominantly 'forward, to the fore'+*gad(d)er*, obs form of GATHER.

**forge** ahead: a corruption of FORCE (oneself) ahead. Influenced by:

**forge** (n and v), **forger, forgery**.

The 2nd and 3rd derive from 'to *forge*', from MF-F *forger*, OF *forgier*, L *fabricāri* or *-cāre*, from *fabrica*, a hard-material workshop (potentially a factory): f.a.e., FABRIC. L *fabrica* becomes OF-F *forge*, adopted by ME.

**forget**, pt *forgot*, pp *forgotten*; hence **forgetful**. **forget-me-not**, etc. See GET, para 3.

**forgive** (**forgave, forgiven**). See GIVE, para 3.

**forgo** (**forwent, forgone**). See GO, para 3.

**fork** (n hence v); **bifurcate, bifurcation**.

A *fork* comes, through ME *forke*, partly from OE *forca* (L *furca*) and partly from ONF *forque*, from L *furca*, s *furc-*, o.o.o. The derivative L adj *bifurcus*, LL *bifurcis*, in or of two branches, was blended with LL *furcātus*, fork-shaped (whence E *furcate*), to suggest EF-F *bifurquer*, E 'to *bifurcate*', (of roads) to fork; the anl EF-F *bifurcation* is adopted by E.

**forlorn**; **forlorn hope**.

1. ME *forlorn* is the pp of *forlesen*, to lose (*lesen*) utterly (connoted by *for-*): OE *forlēosan* (pp *forloren*): cf OHG *farliosan*, MHG *verliesen*, G *verlieren*, and Go *fraliusan*: see LOSE.

2. *Forlorn hope* derives, in C16, from D *verloren hoop*, lost band (of soldiers or sailors), e.g. a storming party: D *verloren*, pp of *verliezen*, to lose +*hoop*, akin to E HEAP.

**form**, n (whence **formless**, and v); **formal**, whence **formalism, formalist, formalize; formality; format**—**formation** (whence **formational**), **formative;**—**formula** (whence adj **formular**), **formulary, formulate** (whence **formulation**).—Cpds: **conform** (whence **conformable**), **conformation, conformator, conformity; deform** (whence pa **deformed**), **deformation, deformity; inform** (adj—and v, whence **informer**), **informal** (whence **informality**), **informant, information, informative; reform** (v hence n), **reformation, reformative, reformer, reformist; transform** (whence **transformer**), **transformation, transformative; uniform** (adj and n), **uniformity**.

1. The group rests firmly upon L *fōrma*, s *fōrm-*, shape, that which shapes, that which has been

shaped, but esp the shape imparted to an object: o.o.o., but perh by metathesis from syn Gr *morphē*, s *morph*-. L *fŏrma* becomes OF-F *forme* (OF-MF var *fourme*), whence E *form*; derivative OF-MF *fourmer*, later *former*, yields 'to *form*'.

2. L *fŏrma* has both the adj *fŏrmālis*, whence E *formal*, whence, aided by MF-F *formalité*, the E *formality*, and the derivative v *fŏrmāre*, with pp *fŏrmātus*, whence It *formato*, which, used as n, accounts for F *format*, adopted by E. On pp s *fŏrmāt*- arises *fŏrmātiō*, o/s *fŏrmātiōn*-, whence OF-F, whence E, *formation*; *formative* is an anl E formation, abetted by F *formatif*, f *formative*.

3. L *fŏrma* has dim *fŏrmula*, a pattern form, hence a regulation, adopted by E—L pl *fŏrmulae*, E pl *formulas*. Derivative L *fŏrmulārius* occurs esp in LL *fŏrmulāria* (sc *ars*, art), the science of legal formulae, whence E *formulary*. L *fŏrmula* becomes late MF-F *formule*, whence *formuler*, which prob suggested 'to *formulate*', as if from L \**fŏrmulātus*.

4. L *fŏrmāre* has prefix-cpds, the first being *cŏnfŏrmāre* (int *con*-), to fashion, arrange, whence, via OF-F *conformer*, E 'to *conform*'; on *cŏnfŏrmāt*-, s of the pp *cŏnfŏrmātus*, arise *cŏnfŏrmātiō*, o/s *cŏnfŏrmātiōn*-, whence EF-F and E *conformation*, and *cŏnfŏrmātor*, a fashioner, a framer, adopted by E in new sense; *conformity* derives, via MF-F *conformité*, from LL *cŏnfŏrmitās* (*cŏnfŏrm*-+-*itās*). *Conformist* (*conform*+-*ist*) occurs mostly in *nonconformist*: cf the complementary *nonconformity*.

5. *Dēfŏrmāre*, to disfigure (*dē*, down from, hence away from+*fŏrm*a, the shape+-*āre*), yields, perh via MF-F, 'to *deform*'; derivative *dēfŏrmātiō*, o/s *dēfŏrmātiōn*-, accounts for *deformation*; but *deformity* comes from MF-EF *deformité*, from L *dēfŏrmitās*, o/s *dēfŏrmitāt*-, from the adj *dēfŏrmis*, disfigured, hideous.

6. The adj *infŏrmis*, shapeless, hence of ill shape, becomes late MF-F *informe*, whence E *inform*; but 'to *inform*', ME *enformen*, derives from OF-MF *enformer* (MF-F *informer*), from L *infŏrmāre*, to put into (*in*-) shape (*fŏrma*), give shape to, hence, in F and E, to a person's thoughts, i.e. to instruct or tell him of.—*Informal*=*in*-, not+*formal*, but owes something to E adj *inform*.—*Infŏrmāre* has presp *infŏrmans*, o/s *infŏrmant*-, whence the E adj and n *informant*; the pp *infŏrmātus* has s *infŏrmāt*-, on which arises *infŏrmātiō*, o/s *infŏrmātiōn*-, whence MF *in*- or *enformacion* (F *information*), both adopted by ME, the *in*- form ending as E *information*; *informative* is an anl E formation.

7. L *refŏrmāre*, to re-form or to reform, becomes OF-F *reformer*, whence 'to *reform*', whence *reformer* and *reformist*; the n *reform*, deriving from the v, is influenced by EF-F *réforme* (from the v); derivative L *refŏrmātiō*, o/s *refŏrmātiōn*-, leads, prob through MF-F, to E *reformation*; *reformative* is anl E.

8. L *transfŏrmāre*, to change (connoted by *trans*, across) the *fŏrma* or shape of, becomes MF-F *transformer*, ME *transformen*, E 'to *transform*'; derivative LL *transfŏrmātiō*, o/s *transfŏrmātiōn*-,

becomes MF-F, then E, *transformation*; derivative ML *transfŏrmātīvus* becomes *transformative*.

9. L *ūnifŏrmis*, single (*ūni*-: cf ONE) in form, hence unvarying, becomes MF-F *uniforme*, whence the E adj *uniform*.—Used as n, F *uniform.e* becomes the E n *uniform*.—Derivative LL *ūnifŏrmitās*, o/s *ūnifŏrmitāt*-, becomes MF-F *uniformité*, whence E *uniformity*.

**formic, formaldehyde; pismire.**

*Formaldehyde*=*form*(o)-, c/f of *formic*+*aldehyde* (alcohol+*dehyd*rogenation+euphonic -*e*); and *formic*=L *formī*ca, an ant+Chem -*ic*. *Formīca* is a dissimilation of IE \**mormi*-, as in syn Gr *murmēx*—and as in the archaic pis*mire*, so named from its ejection (*pis*-=PISS) of the acid we call formic.

**formidable** (whence **formidability**); **marmoset.**

1. *Formidable*, arousing fear, hence impressively deterrent, is adopted from late MF-F, which takes it from L *formīdābilis*, from *formīdāre*, to dread, from the hunting-term *formīdŏ*, a scarecrow, hence dread: a picturesque redup (cf the Gr *mormŏ*, a scarecrow, bugbear, hence a monster): cf L *formīca* q.v. in prec.

2. Gr *mormŏ* app issues ult into the—orig a dim —MF-F *marmouset*, a grotesque carven image, hence an ape: whence E *marmoset*. Perh from MF-F *marmouset* comes, by contr, MF-F *marmot*, adopted by E; B & W, however, derive *marmot* from the echoic EF-F *marmonner*, to mutter (chatter mumblingly), and Webster less convincingly derives it from late OF-F *marmotte*, LL *musmontānus*, lit a mountain *mus* or mouse.

**formula, formulary, formulate, formulation.** See FORM, para 3.

**fornicate, adj and v; fornication** (Arch and sex); **fornicator; fornix.**

The base is L *fornix* (gen *fornicis*), o/s *fornic*-, s *forn*-, an arc, an arch, hence an arched vault, hence a vault, esp underground, hence an underground brothel, hence a low brothel: cf L *furnus*, an oven, and esp *fornāx* (o/s *fornāc*-, s *forn*-), a furnace, an oven, both an oven and a furnace being usu vault-shaped: cf, therefore, FURNACE. Some authorities, however, relate L *fornix* to L *firmus*, strongly placed or based. L *fornix*, an arch, a vault, adopted by E as an An and Bot tech, has L adj *fornicātus*, vaulted, whence the Arch adj *fornicate*; L *fornix*, a brothel, has the LL (esp Eccl) derivative v *fornicāri*, to frequent brothels, with pp *fornicātus*, whence 'to *fornicate*'; on *fornicāt*-, s of pp *fornicātus*, are built both LL *fornicātiō*, brothelling, hence unmarried sexual intercourse, o/s *fornicātiōn*-, whence—perh via OF-F—*fornication*, and the LL agent *fornicātor*, adopted by E.

**forsake**, pt **forsook**, pp **forsaken**. See SAKE, para 2.

**forswear** (**forswore, forsworn**), to swear *for*-against: OE *forswerian* (cf SWEAR).

**fort, forte.** See FORCE, para 4.

**forth**, OE *forth*, is akin to OFris and OS *forth*, MHG *vort*, G *fort*, and to the Go comp *faurthis*, formerly: cf FORE. It has many cpds, e.g. *forth-coming*, *forthright*, *forthwith*.

**fortieth.** See FOUR, para 3, s.f.

**fortification, fortify; fortitude; fortress.** See FORCE, paras 4–6.

**fortuitous; fortunate.** See:

**fortune,** n (whence **misfortune**) and v; **Fortuna; fortunate** (whence **unfortunate**), **Fortunate Isles; fortuitous** (whence **fortuitism**).—Cf sep BEAR, v.

1. The base is L *fors*, chance, o/s *fort-*, perh akin to L *ferre*, to bear, to bring, s *fer-*: *fors*, chance, is that which life *fert* or brings: cf BEAR, v.

2. *Fors* has a c/f *fortu-*, which we see in *fortuītus*, of or by chance, whence E *fortuitous*.

3. On *fort-*, o/s of *fors*, arises *fortūna*, chance, esp if lucky, *Fortūna*, the Goddess of Chance, esp if favourable, whence OF-F, hence ME, whence E, *fortune*. L *fortūna* has adj *fortūnātus*, whence *fortunate*; the neg L *infortūnātus* yields the obsol *infortunate*. By b/f from *fortūnātus* derives *fortūnāre*, to happen by chance, whence, perh via MF-EF *fortuner*, the now rare 'to *fortune*'.

4. *Fortūnātus* occurs notably in *Fortūnātae Insulae*, The Fortunate Isles, displacing *Fortūnātorum Insulae*, The Isles of the Blest, a rendering of Gr τῶν μακάρων νῆσοι, Isles of the Blest, whither, westward, passed the souls of the brave and the good.

**forty.** See FOUR, para 3.

**forum.** See FOREIGN, para 2.

**forward,** adj—whence n and v; **forwards,** adv, orig the gen of the OE adj *foreweard* or *forweard*, whence the E adj: *or(e)*, q.v. at FORE+-*ward*, implying direction, q.v. at WORTH, v.

**fosse; fossil,** adj hence n (whence **fossilize**).

The adj *fossil* comes, through EF-F *fossile*, from L *fossilis*, which can be dug out, from *foss-*, s of *fossus*, pp of *fodere*, to dig (up), excavate, whence also the n *fossa*, a ditch or a trench, whence, through OF-F *fosse*, the E *fosse*, occ *foss*. L *fodere* has IE r *bhod-*: cf OSl *bode*, I thrust or prick or pierce (pt *basŭ*), Lith *bedù*, I prick or excavate, Lett *badu*, I excavate, OP em-*bad*dusisi, (pp pl) plunged in misery; Lett *bedre*, a trench, W *bedd*, OW *bet*, Cor *bedh*, *beydh*, *beth*, Br *bez*, OC *bedh*, a grave, and Ga lea*baidh*, a bed: cf also, therefore, E *bed*, G *Bett* (OHG *betti*, MHG *bette*), Go *badi*, ON *bedr*, a bed: the first 'beds' having been hollows dug in the ground? (E & M; Walshe.)

**foster.** See FEED, para 2.

**foul** (adj hence v), **foulness; befoul; filth,** whence adj **filthy** (whence v); **file,** to befoul—to **defile,** whence **defilement; fulmar.**—**pus, purulent; putrid, putridity.**

1. The adj *foul*, filthy, disgusting, derives through ME *foul*, earlier *ful*, from OE *fūl*; cf OFris *fūl*, OHG-MHG *fūl*, G *faul*, Go *fūls*, ON *fūll*; cf also Lith *púti*, to decay or rot, L *pūtēre*, to rot, be decayed, and *pūs* (gen *pūris*), Gr *púon, púos*, pus, and Skt *pu-*, to stink (*pūyati*, it stinks or rots), *pútis*, rotten; IE r *pu-*, to stink or be rotten.

2. *Foulness* derives from OE *fūlness* (from *fūl*): cf OFris *fūlnisse*.

3. 'To be*foul*' is a *be-* int of 'to *foul*'.

4. OE *fūl* has both a *-th* derivative n *fȳlth*, whence ME *fulthe*, var *filthe*, whence E *filth*, and a derivative v *fȳlan*, whence ME *fulen*, later *filen*, whence EE 'to *file*', befoul, (hence) dishonour, now obsol dial and obs E, but fully extant in the only by f/e connected, rather literary 'to *defile*', to befoul, to ravish (a woman), strictly from ME *defoilen, defoulen*, from OF-MF *defouler, defuler, defoler*, to crush, lit to trample (*fouler*) down (*de*)—cf the v FULL (cloth).

5. OE *fūl* has ON cognate *fūll*, which, preceding ON *mār*, a sea mew (cf MEW, the bird), yields E *fulmar*, a gull named 'foul' because it ejects foul-smelling liquid in self-defence.

## Latin

6. As para 1 has shown, *pus*, a foul exudation, is adopted from L; on the L o/s *pūr-* arises the L adj *pūrulentus*, whence E *purulent*; derivative LL *pūrulentia* yields E *purulence*.

7. L *pūs* has r *pū-*, which recurs in the intimately cognate *pūtēre* (s *pūt-*), to decay, be decayed, to stink, whence the adj *pūtidus*, whence literary E *putid*. *Pūtēre* has another derivative adj: *pūter* (o/s *putr-*), rotten: whence *pūtrēre*, to rot, be rotten, s *pūtr-*, whence the adj *pūtridus*, whence E *putrid*, whence—cf *arid*, *aridity*—*putridity*. L *pūtrēre* has inch *pūtrescere*, presp *pūtrescens*, o/s *pūtrescent-*, whence E *putrescent*; whence *putrescence*. *Putrescible*, subject to decay, esp to rottenness, derives from LL *pūtrescibilis*, from *pūtrescere*. *Pūtrēre*, moreover, has cpd *pūtrefacere*, to cause (*facere*) to go rotten, whence late MF-F *putréfier*, whence 'to *putrefy*'; derivative LL *pūtrefactiō*, o/s *putrefactiōn-*, yields MF-F and E *putrefaction*; *putrefactive* is an anl E formation, perh suggested by F *putréfactif*.

**foumart.** See MARTEN, para 2.

**found** (1), to set or place solidly, to base or establish; **foundation; founder** (an establisher); 'to **founder**', to go to the bottom;—**fund** (n hence v, whence pa **funded**), whence **funds,** money—**fundament,** whence **fundamental; profound, profundity.**—**bottom** (n hence v), whence **bottomless**—**bottomry.**

1. To *found*, establish, derives from OF-F *fonder*, from L *fundāre*, to base firmly, from *fundus*, base, foundation, s *fund-*, IE r prob *bhund(h)-*: cf W *bon*, a base, OIr *bond*, sole of the foot, Ga *bonn, bun*ait, foundation. But there is an unnasalized IE r *bhud(h)-*: cf Skt *budhnaś*, ground, base, and OHG *bodam*, G *Boden*, bottom, ground; also a form *bhat-*, var *bhot-*, eased in ON *botn*, OE *botm*, foundation, base; again, a p- nasal var in Gr *pund*ax, ground, bottom, foundation, and *puthmēn*, base (e.g., foot of a mountain), bottom of the sea.

2. L *fundus* has derivatives affecting E:

*fundāre*, as above, whence *fundāmentum*, base, foundation, whence E *fundament*, with further senses 'groundwork' or 'underlying principle'; hence also the part on which one is most firmly based, one's seat, the buttocks (hence esp anus);

derivative LL adj *fundamentālis*, of the foundation, accounts for E *fundamental*;

LL *fundātiō*, from *fundāt-*, s of *fundātus*, pp of *fundāre*: whence MF *fundacion* (later *fondation*), whence E *foundation*;

LL *fundātor*, likewise from *fundat-*: whence OF-MF *fondeor*, *fondere*, whence—though partly direct from 'to *found*'—E *founder*, an establisher or originator.

3. 'To *founder*', basically 'to go to the *bottom*', hence to fall, stumble badly, (of a ship) to sink, derives from OF-MF *fondre*, to fall in (cave in), from *fond*, bottom, base, from L *fundus*.

4. 'To *fund*' derives from 'a *fund*', orig any basis or foundation, hence one's resources (energy, courage, but esp money): late MF-F *fond*, base, bottom, with E monetary sense from F pl *fonds*: OF *fonz*, MF *fonds*, base, bottom: VL *\*fundus* (gen *funderis*): L *fundus* (gen *fundi*).

5. L *fundus* has derivative prefix-cpd adj: *profundus*, whence EF-F *profond*, whence E *profound*; derivative LL *profunditās*, o/s *profunditāt-*, whence EF *profondité*, whence E *profundity*.

6. OE *botm* (cf, further, OFris *bodem*, OS *bodom*), cited in para 1, becomes ME *botme*, *botum*, whence *bottom*, with all the many E senses developing quite naturally. In MD the shape is *bodom*, *bodum*, (as in D) *bodem*; MD-D *bodem*, as in E, is applied also to (the lower hold of) a ship, with cpd *bodemerij*, which is anglicized to *bottomry*, the mortgaging of a ship.

**found** (2), to melt and mould, to cast, whence (metal-) **founder**; **foundry**; AE **font**, E **fount** (in printing); **fuse, fusible** (**fusibility**), **fusil, fusion** and **foison**; **futile, futility.**—L cpds: **confound, confuse, confusion; diffuse** (adj and v), **diffusible, diffusion, diffusive** (whence **diffusivity**); **effuse** (adj, v), **effusion, effusive; infundibulum, infuse, infusible, infusion** (whence **infusionism**), **infusive, Infusoria** (whence **infusorial**); **interfuse, interfusion; perfuse, perfusion, perfusive; profuse, profusion, profusive; refund**, to pour back again, hence to return (money)—**refuse** (adj, n; v), **refusal; suffuse, suffusion, suffusive; transfuse, transfusion.**—Gr: **chyle, chyme; sep alchemist, alchemy**, treated at CHEMICAL (CHEMIST, CHEMISTRY).—Gmc cognates: **geyser; gut** (n hence v); **ingot** (whence obs *lingot*: F *l'ingot*, the ingot).

1. 'To *found*', cast metal, comes, through OF-F *fondre*, from L *fundere*, basically to pour, hence to melt and mould (metal), with IE r *\*gheu(-d)-*, *\*ghud-*, var *\*dheu*, var *\*de-* or *\*do-*: cf OE *gēotan*, OS *giotan*, OFris *giāta*, Go *giutan* (pp *gutans*), OHG *giozan*, MHG *giezen*, G *giessen*, Gmc r *\*gut-*; Gr *kheein*, to pour; Skt *juhóti*, he pours (in libations). The L *fund*ere shows an *n*- infix, absent in pt *fūd*i and pp *fūs*us. For other Gr cognates, see para 16.

2. Whereas *foundry* comes from MF-F *fonderie* (from *fondre*), a *fount* or *font*, orig a process of casting or founding, now a set of printer's type of one style and size, represents MF-F *fonte* (from *fondre*).

3. The L pp *fūsus*, poured, melted (and moulded), yields 'to *fuse*'; on s *fūs-* arise late MF-F *fusible*, adopted by E—LL *fūsilis*, molten, whence the E *fusil*, made liquid by heat—L *fūsiō*, o/s *fūsiōn-*, whence *fusion*, of which *foison* (archaic 'abundance' and dial 'vitality'), adopted from OF-F (from the L acc *fūsiōn*em), is a doublet.

4. L *fund*ere, pt *fūd*i, has derivative adj *fūtilis*, flowing easily, esp frivolous, whence MF-F and E *futile*; derivative *fūtilitās*, o/s *fūtilitāt-*, yields late EF-F *futilité* and E *futility*.

### Latin Cpds of *fundere*, *fusus*

5. L *confundere*, to pour *con* or together, hence to mix utterly, to confuse, becomes OF-F *confondre*, whence 'to *confound*', with pa *confounded*. The pp *confūsus* yields, perh via the OF-F adj *confus*, the E 'to *confuse*', whence *confusable*; derivative *confūsiō*, o/s *confūsiōn-*, yields, prob via OF-F, the E *confusion*.

6. L *diffundere* (*dif-* for *dis-*, connoting dispersion), to pour out, has pp *diffūsus*, whence—perh via the MF-F adj *diffus*—both the adj and the v *diffuse* (whence *diffusible*); derivative LL *diffūsiō*, o/s *diffūsiōn-*, leads to EF-F and E *diffusion*; *diffusive* is an anl E formation.

7. L *effundere* (*ef-* for *ex*, out), to pour out, has pp *effūsus*, whence both adj and v *effuse*; derivative LL *effūsiō*, o/s *effūsiōn-*, accounts for *effusion*; with *effusive*, cf *diffusive*.

8. L *infundere*, to pour in(to), has an *-ibulum* (basically dim) derivative *infundibulum*, a funnel (esp for pouring grain), adopted by An, Zoo, Bot for a funnel-shaped part or organ. The pp *infūsus* yields 'to *infuse*', with various natural sense-developments; whereas *infusible=in*, into+*fusible*, *infusion*—whence, anl, *infusive*—derives from *infūsiōn-*, o/s of LL *infūsiō*, from the LL pps; the Zoo *Infusoria* (pl) owes something to LL *infūsōrium*.

9. L *interfundere*, to pour *inter*, between or among, has pp *interfūsus*, whence 'to *interfuse*'; derivative LL *interfūsiō*, o/s *interfūsiōn-*, explains *interfusion*.

10. L *perfundere*, to pour throughout (*per*), hence all over, has pp *perfūsus* and derivative LL n *perfūsiō*, o/s *perfūsiōn-*, whence resp 'to *perfuse*' and *perfusion* (whence, anl, *perfusive*).

11. L *prōfundere*, to pour *pro*, forth, esp freely, has pp *prōfūsus*, whence the E adj and v *profuse*, the former deriving from the derivative LL adj *prōfūsus*, lavish, unbounded; the derivative *prōfūsiō*, o/s *prōfūsiōn-*, becomes, perh via late MF-F, *profusion*, whence, anl, *profusive*.

12. L *refundere*, to pour *re-*, back, becomes MF-EF *refunder* (var *-fonder*), whence 'to *refund*', (obsol) to pour—hence, give—back, hence to return (money), reimburse, the latter sense (whence 'a *refund*') being influenced by *funds*, money (cf 1st FOUND, para 4).

13. *Refundere* has a VL freq *\*refūsāre*, to refuse, formed upon L *refūsus*, pp of *refundere*, which, in LL, has the additional sense 'to reject': whence

OF-F *refuser*, whence E 'to *refuse*', whence *refusable* and (-*al*, n) *refusal*. The n *refuse*, something rejected as worthless, hence leavings or rubbish, derives from ME *refuse*, either from OF 'chose *refuse*', f of pp *refus*, refused, rejected, or from OF-F *refus*, refusal, hence the subject of refusal, that which is rejected; the adj *refuse*, ME *refus*, prob derives from OF-F *refuse*, f of pp *refus*.

14. L *suffundere*, to pour below, hence from below, hence to overspread with or as with a liquid, has pp *suffūsus*, whence 'to *suffuse*'; derivative LL *suffūsiō*, o/s *suffūsiōn-*, yields *suffusion*, whence, anl, *suffusive*.

15. L *transfundere*, to pour *trans*, across, hence as from one vessel to another, has pp *transfūsus*, whence 'to *transfuse*'; derivative LL *transfūsiō*, o/s *transfūsiōn-*, leads to EF-F and E *transfusion*.

### Gr Cognates (other than *alchemist*, *chemistry*, etc.)

16. The *khu-* var in Gr—cf L *fūdi*, *fūsus*—occurs in *khulos*, juice, sap, from *kheein*, to pour; hence, via LL *chylos*, *chylus*, the late MF-F and E *chyle*; the var *khumos* becomes Sci L *chymus*, E *chyme*.

### Gmc Cognates

17. Akin to the Gmc words for 'to pour' mentioned in para 1 is ON *gjōta*, to pour, with freq *gjōsa*, to gush; cf Ice *geysa*, (e.g., of water) to rush, whence Ice *Geysir*, a particular hot spring, whence E *geyser*, any hot spring.

18. *Gut*, an intestine, is a b/f from *guts*, OE *guttas*, bowels, akin to OE *gēotan*, to pour (cf para 1), and MD *goto*, D *goot*, intestine.

19. *Ingot* was formed in ME: OE *in*, in+OE *goten*, pp of *gēotan*, to pour, a mould for metal-casting, hence the metal there cast.

**found** (3): pt, pp of **find**: esp in 'well *found*' (ship) and '*found* in clothes'.

**foundation.** See 1st FOUND, para 2.

**founder** (1), n, establisher. See 1st FOUND, para 2, s.f.

**founder** (2), metal-. From the 2nd FOUND.

**founder** (3), to fall or sink. See 1st FOUND, para 3.

**foundling.** See FIND, para 1.

**foundry.** See 2nd FOUND, para 2.

**fount** (1), fountain. See the 2nd FONT.

**fount** (2), printer's type. See 2nd FOUND, para 2.

**fountain.** See the 2nd FONT.

**four, fourth; fourteen, fourteenth; forty, fortieth.**

1. *Four*, ME *four*, earlier *fower*, earliest *feower*, derives from OE *fēower*, akin to OFris *fiōwer*, *fiōr*, *fiūwer*, OHG *fior*, MHG-G *vier*, OS *fiuwar*, *fior*, Go *fidwōr*, ON *fiōrir*; L *quat(t)uor*; Gr *tessares*, Attic *tettares*; Skt *catur-*; C and Sl cognates; IE r, app *\*kwetwor-*. OE *fēower*, contr *fēor*, has ordinal *fēortha*, ME *fourthe*, E *fourth*.

2. *Fourteen*, ME *fourten*, earlier *feowertene*, derives from OE *fēowertȳne* or *-tēne*, lit 4+10. Derivative OE *fēowertēotha* becomes ME *fourtethe* or *fourtend*, which blend into E *fourteenth*.

3. OE *fēower* has the further derivative *fēowertig* (lit $4 \times 10$), akin to OS *fiwartig*, contr to *fiartig*, Go *fidwōr tigjus*, ON *fiōrutīu*: whence ME *fowerti*, later *fourti*, latest *forti*, whence E *forty*. Derivative OE *fēowertigotha* ends as *fortieth*.

4. OE *fēortha*, 4th, has derivative *fēorthung*, lit a 'fourthing': ME *farthing*: E *farthing*.

5. In D, 4 is *vier*, with derivative *vierde*, 4th, whence, with dim *-kyn* (later *-kin*) attached, prob comes the EE *ferdekyn*, later *firkin*, the 4th part of a barrel.

6. L *quatuor* becomes OF-F *quatre*, whence EF-F *quatrain*, a set of 4, esp a stanza of four lines, adopted by E.

7. For the other Romance derivatives, see QUARTER and CARILLON (where also *quaternion*) and QUIRE (of paper).

8. Gr *tessares*, neu *tessara*, 4, has cpd *tessaragōnos*, 4-cornered, hence oblong or square; whence, by abbr, the L *tessera*, a square piece, e.g. of marble, with dim *tessella*, whence the adj *tessellātus*, whence E adj and v *tessellate*, with derivative *tessellation*.

**fowl** (n, v), **fowler.**

A *fowler* derives from OE *fugelere*, agent of *fugelian*, to seek, catch, kill wild fowl, whence 'to *fowl*': OE *fugelian* derives from OE *fugol*, whence ME *fugel*, *fowel* or *foule*, whence E 'a *fowl*': and OE *fugol* is akin to OFris *fugel*, OS *fugal*, OHG *fogal*, MHG-G *vogel*, Go *fugls*, ON *fugl*: Gmc r, app *\*fugl-*, dissimilation of *\*flugl-*, as in OHG *fliogan*, MHG-G *fliehen*, and E 'to FLY'. (Walshe.)

**fox** (n, hence v), whence **foxy; foxglove;—vixen,** whence **vixenish.**

1. The flower *foxglove* affords an example of folk-poetry: OE *foxesglōfa*, fox's glove. A *fox*, straight from OE, is akin to OHG *foha*, OHG-MHG *fuhs*, G *Fuchs*, Go *fauhō*, MD *vosse*, *voos*, MD-D *vos*, ON *fōa*, fox, cf ON *fox*, deceit (? orig an elliptical gen); perh also to Skt *púčcha*, a tail: ? 'the tailed (creature)', as Walshe proposes.

2. OE *fox* has f *fyxen*, whence dial *vixen*, whence E *vixen*.

**foy.** See FAITH, para 2.

**foyer.** See FOCAL, para 3.

**fracas,** adopted from late MF-F, comes from It *fracasso*, itself from *fracassare* (s *fracas-*), to break into pieces: o.o.o.; prob echoic—cf CRASH and SMASH.

**fraction,** whence both **fractional** and (perh after *caption-captious*) **fractious; fracture,** n hence v, hence also the adj **fractural; fragile, fragility**—cf **frail, frailty; fragment,** n, whence the v, also the adjj **fragmental, fragmentary,** and the tech n **fragmentation; frangible; frangipani** or **-pane.**—L cpds: **diffract, diffraction, diffractive; effraction; infract, infraction, infractor—infrangible—infringe** (whence **infringement** and **infringible**); **refragable,** and **irrefragable; ossifrage** and **saxifrage; refract, refraction, refractive, refractory; suffrage** (whence **suffragette**), **suffragan.**—Cf the sep (BREACH and) BREAK.

1. The origin of all these terms resides in L

*frangere*, to break, s *frang*-, a nasalization of *frag*-, whence, via *\*fragtus*, the pp *fractus* and, by lengthening, the pt *frēgi*; the IE r is *\*bhreg*-, the Gmc *\*bhrek*-: 'the MHG past pl *brâchen* (Go *brēkum*) corresponds exactly to L *frēgimus*' (Walshe): cf, therefore, BREAK. Skt offers several cognates.

2. The pres s *frang*- occurs in *frangible*, adopted from MF-EF, and in EF-F, hence E, *frangipane*, a 'rationalizing' of *frangipani*, from that It marquis *Frangipani* (lit, break-loaves or -bread) who invented the perfume, whence, by extn, the almond-flavoured pastry cream and also the shrub (only *-pani*).

3. The pp *fractus* leads to Arch *fractable* and Her *fracted*. On the s *fract*- arise:

L *fractiō*, a breaking, o/s *fractiōn*-, whence, via OF-F (L *fractiōnem*), the E *fraction*;

L *fractūra*, whence, prob via MF-F, *fracture*; cf the 2nd FRITTER.

4. On the *n*-less s *frag*- arise:

*fragilis*, easily broken, hence brittle or delicate, whence, prob via MF-F, the E *fragile*; derivative L *fragilitās*, o/s *fragilitāt*-, leads—very prob via OF-F *fragilité*—to *fragility*; both adj and n have doublets: *frail, frailty*, L *fragilis* becoming OF-MF *fraile* (varr *fresle, frele*), which, via ME, produces *frail*, and L *fragilitās* becoming OF-MF *fraileté*, which, again via ME, produces *frailty*;

*fragmen*, a piece broken off, whence LL *fragmentum*, whence late MF-F, hence E, *fragment*, whence, by anl, *fragmentation*.

## Compounds

5. L *diffringere* (*dif-* for *dis-*, connoting dispersal +-*fringere*, c/f of *frangere*), to break into pieces, has pp *diffractus*, whence 'to *diffract*'; derivative *diffractiō*, o/s *diffractiōn*-, yields *diffraction*, whence, anl, *diffractive*. *Diffrangible* is an E formation: *dif-*, as in *diffringere*+*frangible* (para 2).

6. *Effringere* (*ef-* for *ex*, out), pp *effractus*, has derivative LL *effractūra*, which perh suggests MF-F, hence E, *effraction*, a forcible breaking open (of house, chest, etc.).

7. *Infrangible*, unbreakable, derives from LL *infrangibilis* (*in-*, not+*\*frangibilis*); *infringe* comes from L *infringere*, to break into, pp *infractus*, whence *infractiō*, o/s *infractiōn*-, whence E *infraction*; *infractor* is adopted from LL-ML *infractor*.

8. L *refringere*, to break back, has presp *refringens*, o/s *refringent*-, whence *refringent*, whence *refringency*, and pp *refractus*, whence 'to *refract*'; derivative LL *refractiō*, o/s *refractiōn*-, becomes E *refraction*, whence anl, rather than from LL *refractīuus*, ML -*īvus*, the E *refractive*. L *refractārius* may have prompted E *refractory* (*-ory*, adj), stubborn.

9. The L *n*-less s *frag*- occurs in several E words (*refractory* is perh one of them) not, by most, imm associated with *frangere*; they end in -*frage* or, derivatively, -*fragable* and -*fragan*. In *ossifrage* and *saxifrage* the sense of 'breakage' can be detected: whereas *ossifrage*, familiarly, for the osprey,

'break-bones', is L *ossifraga* or -*fragus* (*os*, bone, c/f *ossi*-), *saxifrage*, lit 'rock-breaker', is L *saxifraga*, from adj *saxifragus* (*saxum*, a rock, c/f *saxi*-: cf SAXON), perh because it grows in crevices.

10. L *refragāri*, to break back, esp to oppose, is a -*frag*- var of *refringere* (para 8); it has ML derivative *refragābilis*, opposable, hence controvertible, much less used than the neg *irrefragable*, incontrovertible, LL *irrefragābilis* (*ir-* for *in-*, not).

11. ML has *suffrangere* (*suf-* for *sub*, below), which is paralleled by the earlier *suffrāgāri*, to support, esp with one's vote, whence prob *suffrāgium*, (political) support, whence OF and E *suffrage*; some etymologists, however, relate L -*frāgāri* to the E v *bray*. Aided by *suffrāgant*-, o/s of *suffrāgans*, presp of *suffrāgāri*, but deriving imm from ML *suffrāgāneus*, an -*āneus* adj-become-n from *suffrāgium*, is OF-F *suffragant*, adj and n, whence E *suffragan*, any bishop in an assistant subordinate role.

**fragile.** See prec, para 4.

**fragment, fragmentary.** See FRACTION, para 4, s.f.

**fragrance, fragrant; flair.**

1. *Fragrance*, adopted from MF-EF, derives from LL *fragrantia*, an -*ia* derivative of *fragrant*-, o/s of *fragrans*, presp of L *fragrāre*, to smell sweet, s *fragr*-, perh akin to Skt *ghrāti*, it smells (good or bad). From L *fragrantem*, acc of *fragrans*, derives MF-EF *fragrant*, adopted by E.

2. L *fragrāre*—prob via VL *\*flagrāre*—becomes OF *flairer*, whence the n *flair*, whence, via ME *flaire*, odour, the E *flair*, with modern F sense.

**frail, frailty.** See FRACTION, para 4.

**frame,** v hence n; derivatively the Am sl **frame-up,** and **framework.**

'To *frame*', ME *framen*, earlier *framien*, to be useful or profitable, hence to shape or fashion (in building), derives from OE *framian*, to profit, from OE *fram*, var of *from* (cf FROM), forth, (as prep) from, the idea being that of furthering: akin to OE *fremman*, *fremian*, OFris *fromia*, OHG *frummen*, ON *fremja*, *frama*, to further.

**franc.** See FRANK, para 4.

**France.** See FRANK, para 5.

**franchise.** See FRANK, para 6.

**Francis.** See FRANK, para 7.

**Franciscan.** See FRANK, para 7.

**francolin.** See FRANK, para 8.

**frangible.** See FRACTURE, para 2.

**frangipane, -pani.** See FRACTURE, para 2.

**frank,** adj (hence v), whence **frankness; Frank,** whence **Frankish; frankfurter; frankincense; franklin; frankpledge,** cf **frankalmoign.—franc; France** and **French** (whence **Frenchify); franchise,** n, whence **disfranchise** (whence **disfranchisement),** cf **enfranchise** (whence **enfranchisement); Francis** (cf **Francois, Frances)** and **Franciscan;** c/f **Franco-,** as in **Francophil(e)** and **Francophobe,** cf the elements -*phil(e)* and -*phobe*; **francolin; lingua franca; Feringhee.**

## The *frank* Forms

1. The adj *frank* comes from OF-F *franc*, free, hence frank, from OF-F *Franc*, a Frank: ML *Francus*, a Frank, hence *francus*, free: (*Francus*, from) OHG *Franko*, a Frank—member of a Gmc people on the Rhine. 'The Frankish conquerors in early France (*Frank*reich) were the only "free" men or nobles, hence OF *franc* generally means "of noble birth". The name OHG *Franko* of the Franks is derived from OS *franko* "spear" (ON *frakke*); cf the name of the Saxons from *sahs* "sword" ' (Walshe). Cf also OE *franca*, a javelin, and ON *frakka, frakkr*, brave, bold.

2. A *frankfurter* is a *Frankfurter* sausage, orig made at *Frankfurt*, Frankfort, in Germany, at 'the Ford of the Franks': *frankincense*=OF-F *franc*, free, hence pure+*encens* (cf INCENSE); *frankpledge* =a *frank*, free, *pledge*, perh by misapprehension of OE *frithborh*, peace surety or pledge; *frankalmoign*, a free *almoign*, from AF *almoign* or *almoigne*, app from OF-MF *almosne* (cf ALMS), this term belonging, like the prec, to English history.

3. Equally historical—but extant in the surname *Franklin*—is *franklin*, a freeman, later a free-holder: ME *frankelein*, prob ult from ML *franchi-lānus*, the AF *fraunclein* forming app the intermediate stage.

## The *franc* Forms

4. A *franc* derives from '*Franc*orum rex', the device borne by the coin first struck in 1360 by 'the king of the French'. (B & W.)

5. *French* derives from OE *frencisc*, adj of *Franca*, a Frank; *France*, however, is the F name, from ML *Francia*, from *Francus*, a Frank (para 1).

6. OF-F *franc*, free, has derivative OF-F *fran-chir*, to free, whence OF-F *franchise*, a freeing, hence freedom, but also magnanimity; the political sense, adopted by E, comes much later. *Franchir* has a MF cpd *enfranchir* (*en-*, L *in*, used int), to set free, with a var pp *enfranchisé*, whence 'to *enfranchise*'.

7. *François* is the F, *Francis* the E, derivative from OF *Franceis*, a Frank, from LL *Franciscus*, of Gmc origin: cf *Frank* in para 1. *Franceis* has f *Franceise*, whence *Frances*. In ML, *Franciscus* has become a font-name; St *Francis* established mon-asteries and nunneries; hence *Franciscānus*, of St Francis, whence the *Franciscāni*, E *Franciscans*.

8. Obscurely connected is *francolin*, a genus of partridge: MF-F *francolin*: It *francolino*, perh elliptical for *uccello francolino*, with *francolino* a dim of *franco*, free, from OF *franc*. The 'freedom' has been explained thus: the birds becoming rare, it was forbidden to kill them, and so they were free to fly and live unmolested; but there is no record of this prohibition. (Prati.)

9. It *franco* occurs also, but in the orig sense 'Frankish', in *la lingua franca*, the language of the Franks: consisting basically of It, but containing also Sp, F, and also Gr and Ar, it served as the common language of the Mediterranean sea and ports. Cf:

10. OF *Franc*, a Frank, became Ar *Faranji*, var *Ifranji*, whence Per *Farangi, Firingi*, whence, in India, the Hind *Feringi* or *Feringhee*, a European. The virility and energy of the Franks has caused the widening sense implied in *Feringi* and in *lingua franca*.

**frankalmoign.** See prec, para 2.
**frankfurter.** See FRANK, para 2.
**frankincense.** See FRANK, para 2.
**franklin.** See FRANK, para 3.
**frankpledge.** See FRANK, para 2.
**frantic.** See FRENZY, para 2.

**frater, fraternal, fraternity, fraternize**; cf element *fratri-* (as in **fractricide**); **fratry;—friar, friary;—pal** (n hence v), whence adj **pally;—phratry.—brother** (n hence v)—archaic pl **brethren** (ME *bretheren*)—whence **brotherhood** (cf suffix -*hood*) and **brotherly** (adj suffix -*ly*);

### Indo-European

1. L *frāter*, brother, is akin to Gr *phratēr*, var *phratōr*, member of a brotherhood, a clansman, and to Skt *bhrātṛ*, Av *brātar*. Apart from L and Gr, the predominant form is *b(h)r-*: cf OSl *bratrŭ* (OP *brāti*; Lith *brolis*, note the *bro-*; Cz *bratr*); W *brawd*, pl *brodyr*—Cor *brodar* (or -*er*), *bruder*, *breder*—Br *brér*, pl *bredér*—Mx *braar*—Ga *bràthair*, pl *bràithrean*—OIr *brāthir*—OC *\*brāter*; ON *brōthir* (Da, Sw *broder*); Go *brōthar*, OHG-MHG *bruoder*, G *Bruder*, OS *brothar*, OFris *brōther*, OE *brōthor*: Gmc etymon, *\*brōther*; IE etymon, *\*bhrāter*, and IE r *\*bhrāt-*. Note the remoter cognates Tokh A *pracar* and Tokh B *procer*.

### Sanskrit

2. Skt *bhrātṛ* becomes Gypsy *pral* (European continent) and *pal* (England), the latter getting into cant and finally into sl.

### Greek

3. Gr *phratēr* has an -*ia* derivative *phratria*, a clan, later a political brotherhood: whence E *phratry*.

### Latin

4. L *frāter*, retained in the Catholic Church, has derivatives *frāternus*, which in ML becomes *frāternālis*, whence E *fraternal* (cf OF-F *fraternel*), and which has derivative *frāternitās*, o/s *frāter-nitāt-*, whence, prob via OF-F *fraternité*, the E *fraternity*; *fraternize, fraternization*, owe much to F *fraterniser, -nisation*, erudite EF formations from *fraternel*. The hist *fratry*, religious brotherhood, derives from ML *frātria*, from *frātr-*, o/s of L *frāter*.

5. L *frāter* becomes OF *fradre, fredre*, MF *frere*, whence F *frère* and ME *frere*, whence, with sense-change, the E *friar*. The *friar bird* is bald. A *friary* is a collection of friars: cf *priory* from *prior*, but cf also OF *frarie*, MF-F *frairie* (ML *fratria*).

English

6. As para 1 shows, OE *brōthor* has many Gmc cognates. It becomes ME, whence E, *brother*.

American English

7. In the southern (not SW) United States, *brother* was, by the Negroes, contr to *br'er*, usu written *brer*, as *Brer* Rabbit in Joel Chandler Harris's Uncle Remus stories.

**fraud, whence fraudful, fraudless; fraudulence (or -cy), fraudulent; defraud, defraudation, defraudment;** perh akin to sep FRUSTRATE.

1. *Fraud* comes, through MF-F *fraude*, from L *fraus*, o/s *fraud-*: o.o.o., the relationship to L *frustra* (see FRUSTRATE) being prob f/e. *Fraus* has derivative v *fraudāre*, whence the adj *fraudulentus*, EF hence E *fraudulent*; derivative *fraudulentia* becomes EF, hence E, *fraudulence*.

2. *Fraudāre* has cpd *dēfraudāre*, to cheat, esp of money: whence MF-EF *defrauder*: E 'to *defraud*'. Derivative LL *dēfraudātiō*, o/s *dēfraudātiōn-*, passes through MF-EF to become *defraudation*; *defraudment* prob derives from 'to *defraud*'—cf, however, MF *defraudement* (from *defrauder*).

**fraught.** See FREIGHT.

**fray,** n. See AFFRAY.

**fray,** v. See FRICTION, para 3.

**frazzle.** See FRICTION, para 4.

**freak** (whence adjj **freakish** and **freaky**), orig a caprice, is o.o.o.: but perh cf ME *frek*, quick, bold, from OE *frec*, bold, whence EE *freck*, insolent, eager, whence dial *freck*, lusty, hale. Akin to OE *frec* is Go *-friks*, -greedy, whence MD *frisc*, fresh, whence MF *frisque*, lively, whence 'to *frisk*', whence both 'a *frisk*' and *frisky*.— Cf the distinct G *frech* (OHG *freh*).

**freckle** (n hence v) is an E dim of ME *freken*, from ON pl *freknur*, spots, freckles, cf ON *freknottr*, freckly: o.o.o.

**free,** adj—hence adv and n; to **free; freedom, freeman, freemason, freestone,** akin to sep **Friday** and **friend** and **defray.**

*Free*, ME *fre*, var *freo*, derives from OE *frēo* or *frēoh*, var *frī*: cf OFris, OS, OHG-MHG *frī* (G *frei*), Go *freis*, cf ON *frithr*, love, peace, OE *frithu*, OHG *fridu*, peace, Go *frijōn*, to love: cf remotely yet significantly Skt *priyás*, beloved, and *prīyate*, he loves. 'To *free*', ME *freen*, earlier *freoien*, derives from OE *frēogan* (contr *frēon*), from *frēo*: cf OFris *frīa*, contr (?) of *frīaia*, from *frīa*. *Freedom*=OE *frēodōm* (cf the suffix *-dom*), akin to OFris *frīdōm*; *freeman*=OE *frēoman*, akin to OFris *frīmann*; *freemason*, from the freemasons' former independence of local guilds; *freestone* is easily cut —cf the F *pierre franche*.—Cf FRIEND.

**freebooter.** See BOOTY, para 2.

**freedom; freemason.** See FREE.

**freeze,** v hence n, pt **froze,** pp **frozen; frost** (n hence v), whence **frosty** (cf OE *fyrstig*).—**prurient** (whence prurience), prurigo.

1. 'To *freeze*', ME *fresen*, earlier *freosen*, derives from OE *frēosan*: cf OHG *friosan*, MHG

*friesen*, G *frieren*, and ON *friōsa*, to freeze, and Go *frius*, frost, cold.

2. OE *frēosan* is akin to OE *frost* (var *forst*), frost: cf OFris (var *forst*), OS, OHG, ON *frost*.

3. Go back to L, we find the expected *p-* forms: *pruīna*, hoar frost, and, the basic idea being 'a tingling sensation', *prūrīre*, to feel hot, hence to itch, and *prūna*, a live coal: cf Skt *pruşvá*, hoar frost, and *pruşţa*, burnt. *Prūrīre*, to itch, has presp *prūriens*, o/s *prūrient-*, whence E *prurient*, and a derivative *prūrīgō*, an itching, the itch, adopted by Med.

**freight,** n hence v (whence **freighter); fraught.**

The adj *fraught*, laden, like the archaic 'to *fraught*', derives from *fraught*, a cargo, (earlier) freight: ME *frauht, fraucht*: MD *vracht*, a var of *frecht*, whence ME *freyte*, whence *freight* (cost of transportation): cf OHG *frēht*, earnings, compensation, reward, fee, as if for Go *\*fra-âihts*: cf the E prefix *for-* and OWN—Go *âih*, I have; G *eigen*, OHG *eigan*, one's own. (Walshe.)

**frejol.** See FRIJOL.

**French** (whence Frenchify). See FRANK, para 5.

**frenzy,** n hence v (whence pa **frenzied); frantic— phrenetic; phrenic;** cf the element *-phrenia, phreno-* as in *phrenology*.

1. *Phrenic*, like F *phrénique*, derives from Gr *phrēn* (o/s *phren-*), the heart, usu the mind. The Gr adj is *phrenitikos*, from *phrenēsis* (var *phrenitis*), a disease of the mind, from *phrēn*; *phrenitikos* becomes L *phreneticus*, whence E *phrenetic*, own used only in Med and Psy.

2. L *phreneticus* becomes late OF-MF *frenetique* (F *fréné-*), whence ME *frentik*, whence E *frantic*. Gr *phrenēsis* becomes LL *phrenesis*, whence ML *phrenesia*, whence MF *frenesie* (F *fréné-*), adopted by ME, whence F *frenzy*.

**frequency, frequent** (adj and n), **frequentation, frequentative; infrequent.**

*Infrequent* derives from *infrequent-*, o/s of L *infrequens*, neg (*in-*, not) of *frequens*; derivative L *infrequentia* yields *infrequency*. Now L *frequens*, o/s *frequent-*, dense, abundant, hence crowded, numerous, much-visited, is o.o.o.; its kinship with L *farcīre*, to stuff (see FARCE), is extremely doubtful. The o/s *frequent-* yields (MF-F *fréquent* and) E *frequent*, orig crowded; derivative *frequentia* becomes E *frequency*. The derivative L *frequentāre* becomes (OF-F *fréquenter* and) E 'to *frequent*'; on *frequentāt-*, s of pp *frequentātus*, arise both *frequentātiō*, o/s *frequentātiōn-*, whence E *frequentation*, and LL *frequentātīuus*, ML *-īvus*, whence (F *fréquentatif*, f *-ive*, and) E *frequentative*, gram adj and also as n.

**fresco.** See para 4 of:

**fresh** (adj hence adv and n), whence **freshen, freshet** (*-et*, n), **freshman, freshness, freshwater; afresh; refresh** (whence **refresher), refreshment; fresco**—cf al fresco.

1. The adj *fresh* derives, via ME *fresch*, from OF-MF *fresche*, f of *fres, freis* (cf F *frais, fraîche*): O Gmc *\*frisk*, fresh of temperature, hence unfaded, unwithered, also recent: cf OHG *frisc*. The var ME

*fersch* derives from OE *fersc*, akin to ON *ferskr*, and OHG *frisc*, MHG-G *frisch*, prob to Lith *prieskas*, perh to L *priscus*. Note that AE *fresh*, impudent, comes from the quite distinct G *frech*, insolent (OHG *freh*, greedy).

2. The adv *afresh*, again=*a*-, on+*fresh*, adj; cf *anew* from NEW.

3. *Refreshment* comes from MF *refreschement*, itself from OF-MF *refreschir* (var *refreschier*), whence ME *refrechen*, *refreshen*, whence 'to *refresh*'; and OF-MF *refreschir*=*re*-, again+ *fresch*-, c/f of *fresche* (para 1)+inf suffix -*ir*.

4. From Gmc comes It *fresco*, fresh; *al fresco* is 'in the fresh (air)'—in the open air; the *fresco* of painting is, like F *fresque*, from It *fresco*, from *dipingere a fresco*, to paint upon a fresh, still moist plaster. (B & W.)

**fret** (1), n, whence **fretwork**, was, in ME, applied esp to ornamental network, esp that used as a hairnet: ME *fret*, earlier *frette*: OF-F *frette*, latticework: OF-F *fretté* (pp), *freté*, *fresté*, adorned with interlaced work: *fret*, an ornament or an adornment: OE *fraetwe*, ornaments.

**fret** (2), n, the ridge set across the fingerboard of a stringed instrument: app from OF-MF *frete*, MF-F *frette*, a ring, a band, from OF-MF *freter* (MF-F *fretter*), perh a metathesis of *ferter*, to fasten, from VL *firmitāre*, to secure, from L *firmitās*, firmness, from *firmus*, solidly fixed: f.a.e., FIRM. (Dauzat.)

**fret** (3), v, orig to eat or consume, hence to eat, or gnaw, away, hence vi to be worn by either irritation or anxiety, hence a state of irritated agitation, whence **fretful**: ME *freten*, to eat: OE *fretan*: cf Go *fra-itan*, to devour, OHG *frezzan*, MHG *frezzen*, G *fressen*, to eat greedily: OHG *fr*-, Go *fra*-, is the int G prefix *ver*- (cf the syn MHG *verezzen*); and -*ezzen*, -*itan*, is G *essen*, E EAT. (Walshe.)

**friable** (whence **friability**): prob via EF-F, certainly from L *friābilis*, from *friāre*, to reduce, rub, grind, to little pieces: f.a.e., FRICTION.

**friar, friary**. See FRATER, para 5.

**fribble**, a trifler, to trifle. See FRIVOLOUS.

**frication, fricative**. See para 1 of:

**friction** (n hence v), whence **frictional**; **frication**, **fricative** (adj hence n); **fray**, to wear or rub into shreds, to ravel, whence pa and vn **fraying**; **frazzle**, v hence n; **fry**, young fish (fishes).

1. L *friāre*, to rub small (see FRIABLE), has what is app an enlarged form: *fricāre* (s *fric*-), to rub, with pp *fricātus* and, commoner, *frictus*: on s *fricāt*- arise LL *fricātiō*, o/s *fricātiōn*-, whence E *frication*, whence, anl, *fricative* (adj -*ive*). But, *friāre* and *fricāre* being o.o.o., the latter is prob the original and very prob echoic.

2. On *frict*-, the commoner pp s, arises *frictiō*, o/s *frictiōn*-, whence EF-F and E *friction*.

3. L *fricāre* becomes OF-MF *freier* (EF-F *frayer*), to rub, whence both F *frayer* and E 'to *fray*'.

4. 'To *frazzle*' is app a freq (-*le*) of 'to *fray*', influenced perh by *fraze*, unevenness of edge, itself

prob from 'to *fray*'; the n *frazzle* occurs mostly in coll *worn to a frazzle*, utterly exhausted.

5. OF-MF *freier* (para 3) has varr *friier* and *froiier*, with further sense 'to spawn', whence MF *fri* (varr *frai*, *froi*, *froie*; F *frai*), whence ME *fri*, later *fry*, extant in E for 'young fishes'. A less prob origin has been proposed: ON *frae* (cf Go *fraiw*), seed.

**Friday**: OE *frīgedaeg*, the day (cf DAY) of the goddess *Frīg*: cf the ON goddess *Frigg* (cf OHG *Frīa*), Odin's wife, akin to OE *frēo*, free (cf FREE). With OE *frīgedaeg*, cf OFris *frīgendei*, *frīadei*, OHG *frīatag*, MHG *frītac*, G *Freitag*, ON *frīādagr*.

**friend** (n hence v), **friendly** (whence **unfriendly**), **friendship**; **befriend**, an int (*be*-) of *friend*, v.

*Friend*, ME *frend*, earlier *freond*, derives from OE *frēond*, n from the presp of *frēon*, contr of *frēogan*, to love: cf the other nn from prespp, OFris *friōnd*, *friūnd*, OS *friund*, OHG-MHG *friunt*, G *Freund*, Go *frijonds*, ON *fraendi*. Derivative OE *frēondlīc* (cf OFris *friōndlīk*) becomes E *friendly*; OE *frēondscipe*, E *friendship* (cf OFris *friōndskip*). Akin to FREE.

**Friesian**. See FRISIAN, para 1.

**frieze** (n hence v). See FRIZ.

**frigate** (whence **frigate bird**, long-flighted and rapacious): EF-F *frégate*: It *fregata*: prob aphetic for L *aphracta*, pl—apprehended as sing—of *aphractum* (var -*actus*), trln of Gr *aphrakton*, orig *aphraktos*, elliptical for *aphraktos naus*, an undecked (lit, unguarded, uncovered) ship: *a*-, not+ *phraktos*, pp of *phrassein*, to fence, to guard.

**fright**, n and v (whence **frighten**); from n: **frightful**, whence **frightfulness**; **affright**, v hence n.

'To *affright*' comes from ME *afright*, orig a pp from OE *afyrhtan*, to terrify, int of OE *fyrhtan*, to frighten, whence ME *frigten*, whence 'to *fright*', whence 'to *frighten*': cf OE *forhtian*, to fear, itself akin to OS *forhtian*, OHG *furhten*, Go *faúrhtjan*. The n *fright*, ME *frigt*, aberrant *freyht*, derives from OE *fryhto*, var of *fyrhto*, akin to OS and OHG *forhta*, G *Furcht*, Go *faúrhtei*, fear.

**frigid, frigidity**—**frigidaire**; **refrigerate, refrigeration, refrigerative, refrigerator, refrigeratory** (adj hence n).

1. *Frigidity* comes, prob via F, from LL *frīgiditās*, o/s *frīgiditāt*-, from L *frīgidus*, (very) cold, an -*idus* adj from *frīgēre* (s *frīg*-), to be cold, from *frīgus*, cold, coldness, o/s *frīgor*-, c/f *frīgori*-, as in L *frīgorificus*: cf the element *frigo*-, *frigori*-. L *frīgus* answers exactly to Gr *rhigos* (ῥίγος), for *srīgos*; with L *frīgeō*, cf Gr *rhīgeō*. The Gr word is o.o.o.

2. As 'any electric refrigerator', *frigidaire* is loose and coll, deriving from the trade-name *Frigidaire*, prob suggested by L *frigidārium*, a cooling-off room, orig the neu of *frigidārius*.

3. L *frīgēre*, to be cold, has caus *frīgerāre*, to render cold, superseded by its prefix-cpd *refrigerāre*, where *re*- has a vaguely int force. Presp *refrigerans*, o/s *refrigerant*-, yields the E adj, whence n, *refrigerant*. Pp *refrigerātus* accounts for

'to *refrigerate*'; derivative *refrīgerātiō*, o/s re-*frīgerātiōn-*, for *refrigeration*; derivative LL *refrīgerātīuus* (ML *-īvus*), for refrigerative; *refrigerator* is an E anl coinage; but *refrigeratory* comes from the L adj *refrīgerātōrius* (suffix *-ōrius*) and LL n *refrīgerātōrium*.

**frijol** or **frijole** (occ **frejol**)=Sp *frijol* (var *frejol*), earlier *frisol*: L *faseolus* (var *phasēlus*): Gr *phasiolos*, mdfn of *phasēlos*, a haricot bean, prob akin to—perh from—Gr *phakos*, a lentil; ? cf Alb *bathë*, a kind of bean, and OP *babo*, a bean, and, if so, then L *faba*, F *fève*.

**frill** (n, whence v), whence adj **frilly** (whence coll n **frillies**), is o.o.o. To relate it to F *frileux* (OF *friuleus*, MF *friuleux*), shivery, is far-sought: why not, both the sem and the phon resemblances being so much closer, relate the n *frill* to F *vrille*, tendril (of vine)? *Vrille*, influenced by *virer*, derives from EF *ville* from MF *veïlle* from ML *vīticula*, L *uīticula*, tendril of vine, dim of *uītis*, vine, as in *viticulture*.

**fringe** (n hence v): ME from OF-MF *frenge* (F *frange*): VL *frimbia*, by metathesis from LL *fimbria*, b/f sing from L *fimbriae*, fringes of garment, o.o.o.; derivative L *fimbriātus*, fringed, accounts for Bot and Zoo *fimbriate*, whence *fimbriation*.

**frippery** (cheap finery; orig, cast-off clothes) derives from EF-F *friperie*, from MF *freperie*, from OF-MF *freper*, to crumple (clothes), from OF *frepe*, metathesis of *ferpe*, var of *felpe*, a fringe, (collectively) old clothes, from ML *faluppa*, fibre, straw, hence anything worthless, recorded (C10) only in pl *faluppae*, o.o.o.

**Frisian** is adj and n, esp for the LG language of *Fries*land (OFris *Fresland*); **Friesian** is adj and n for the cattle; and both go back to the ancient Gmc tribe of *Frisii*, whence *Frisia*, their country. ML uses the forms *Frisones*, var *Fresones*; the name perh means 'The Brave'.
2. The name recurs in EF-F *cheval de frise*, usu in pl *chevaux* . . .; 'horse (horses) of *Frise* or *Friesland*': mistranslation of D *friese ruiter*, 'horseman or cavalryman of Friesland', this defensive device (esp against cavalry) being reputed to have originated there. Cf the syn G *spanischer Reiter*, 'Spanish cavalryman'. (B & W.)

**frisk, frisky.** See FREAK, s.f.

**frith** (1), a narrow inlet of the sea, is a metathesis of ME *firth*, whence **firth**: ON *fiörthr*, whence, via Nor *fiord*, the E FIORD. Cf FORD and, f.a.e., PORT (harbour).

**frith** (2), wooded country, occurs in ME and derives from OE *fyrhthu*, woodland—cf OE *frith-geard*, enclosed land. OE *frith*, peace, is akin to FREE.

**fritter** (1), n, portion of fried batter: OF-F *friture*: LL *frīctūra*, from *frīgere*, to fry: f.a.e., 2nd FRY.

**fritter** (2), v, to waste piecemeal, derives from the obsol n *fritter*, a fragment: OF-MF *freture*, var of *fraiture*: L *fractūra*—cf *fracture* at para 3 (s.f.) of FRACTION.

**frivolity, frivolous; fribble,** n and v.
*Fribble* derives, humorously, from 'to be *frivolous*', perh influenced by the 2nd FRITTER; *frivolity* from F *frivolité*, from the OF-F adj *frivole*, which, like E *frivolous*, derives from ML *frivolus*, L *friuolus*, perh akin to *friāre*, to rub away, q.v. at FRIABLE.

**friz,** usu **frizz,** v hence n (whence **frizzy**); hence the freq (*-le*): **frizzle,** v hence n, whence **frizzly**; **frieze,** a coarse, shaggy woollen cloth; prob also the Arch **frieze.**
'To *friz(z)*', to curl (hair), derives from EF F *friser*, to curl, crimp, dress the hair, from MF *frise*, frieze, this being also the source of *frieze*, the woollen cloth. The Arch *frieze* derives from EF-F *frise*, app from ML *frisium*, var of *phrygium*, broidery, fringe, prob prompted by L *phrygiae* (*uestes*), lit 'Phrygian garments', garments, or garment-fabrics, embroidered with gold, the Arch ornament being likened to such embroidery.—As for *friz(z)*, however, it is possible to derive *friser*, as B & W derive it, from *fris-*, the late MF-EF r of certain forms of *frire*, to fry, ref meats (esp if fine-cut) tending, while they fry, to curl up like frizzy locks of hair.

**fro.** See FROM.

**frock,** n—orig a coarse monastic gown—whence v, esp in neg pp **unfrocked**: OF-F *froc*: Frankish *hrok*: cf OHG-MHG *roc*, G *Rock*, OFris *rokk*, and also OE *rocc*, coat: ? of C origin—cf OIr *ruckt*, jacket.

**frog** (n hence v), whence **frogman** and **leap-frog** or **leapfrog**, derives from OE *frogga*: cf the syn OE *forsc, frosc*, OHG *frosc*, MHG-G *frosch*, ON *froskr*; perh cf ON *frauth, frotha* (see FROTH), if the basic idea is 'slimy'; perh rather cf Skt *právatē*, he hops (Walshe), with basic idea 'the hopper'. Prob the *frog* in a horse's hoof and perh the *frog* on a military coat derive from the jumping amphibian. Cf:

**frolic,** adj, whence n (whence **frolicsome**) and v, comes from D *vroolijk*, a *-lijk* elaboration of MD *vrō*, akin to syn MHG *frō* (OHG *frao, frō*, G *froh*), joyous, whence G *fröhlich*; cf also ON *frār*, nimble, and esp Skt *právatē*, he hops; therefore cf prec.

**from; fro,** whence **froward** (cf the dial **fromward(s)**, away, away, from: OE *framweard*).
1. *Fro*, ME *fro*, earlier *fra*, both prep 'from' and adv 'away', derives from ON *frā*, intimately related to ON *fram*, forwards (cf *framr*, very brave), and to OFris *fram*, from, OS *fram*, out, OHG *fram*, ON *fram*, forwards, and to Go *fram*, from, and esp to OE *fram*, var *from*, the latter surviving into E. The basic idea of the prep *from* is 'forwards out of'; of the group, 'forward' (adj)—cf Gr *promos*, lit one who is forward, in the van, a leader; therefore cf FORE.

**frond, frondage, frondescent, frondose;** cf element *frondi-*.
*Frondose* comes from L *frondōsus*, leafy, from *frons* (gen *frondis*), o/s *frond-*, leaves collectively, a leafy branch, foliage, whence E *frond*, whence

collective *frondage* (*-age*). The adj *frondescent* derives from *frondescent-*, o/s of *frondescens*, pp of *frondescere*, to put on leaves, inch of *frondēre*, to be in leaf, from *frond-*. L *frons, frondis*, is o.o.o., kinship with L *gramen*, E GRASS, being very dubious; a more likely cognate is C *brond-*, to swell, increase (cf Cor *bron*, breast, udder, Br *bronn*, breast), 'the coming of leaves being a true swelling of the trees' (Malvezin).

front, n whence adj and v and also **frontage; frontal**, adj, n; **frontier** (n hence adj), whence **frontiersman; frontlet;** cpd **frontispiece;** cf element *fronto-*.—Prefix-cpds: **affront,** v hence n and the adj **affrontive; confront** (whence **confrontment), confrontation; effrontery.**

1. L *frons* (gen *frontis*, o/s *front-*), forehead, is o.o.o.; perh it is akin to MIr *broine*, prow of ship; possibly *frons, frondis,* and *frons, frontis*, were orig identical, with basic sense 'swelling' or 'projection', esp a 'swelling or swollen projection'. From L *frontem*, acc of *frons*, derives OF-F *front*, forehead, adopted by E, with derivative senses rapidly developing, parallel to those of F.

2. *Frontal*, a forehead ornament, comes, prob via EF-F, from L *frontāle*, prop the neu of the adj *frontālis*, whence E *frontal*. Cf *frontlet*, from MF *frontelet*, dim of OF-F *frontel*, var of *frontal*, from L *frontāle*.

3. *Frontier* derives from MF *frontiere* (F *-ière*), from *front*, forehead, from L *frontem*, acc of *frons*.

4. *Frontispece* anglicizes (after PIECE) the EF-F *frontispice*: LL *frontispicium*, a small wavy moulding at edge of a table, the façade of a building (Souter), esp of a church, in short the part first meeting the eye: *fronti-*, c/f of *frons*, brow+ *-spicium*, from *-spicere* (c/f of *specere*), to look at —cf SPECULATE.

5. LL has the cpd *affrontāre*, to knock one's forehead *ad* or against, to strike against, whence— prob aided by OF-MF *afronter* (EF-F *aff-*)—E 'to *affront*', whence, perh aided by EF-F *affront*, 'an *affront*'. ML *confrontāre*, to come front to front (*con-*, together), yields, prob via MF-F, 'to *confront*'; derivative ML *confrontātiō*, o/s *confrontātiōn-*, becomes MF-F and E *confrontation*. LL *effrons*, without (*ef-* for *ex*, out of) forehead (to blush with), shameless, becomes MF *effronté*, whence EF-F *effronterie*, whence E *effrontery*.

**frontier.** See prec, para 3.

**frontispiece.** See FRONT, para 4.

**frost, frosty.** See FREEZE, para 2.

**froth** (n hence v), whence **frothy** (*-y*, adj): ME *froth*, earlier *frothe*: ON *frotha, frauth*: cf OE *āfrēothan*, to froth, and prob Skt *prothati*, he snorts; perh, therefore, cf FROG. Ult, it is prob echoic.

**frounce,** n, v. See the 2nd FLOUNCE.

**froust, frouzy.** See FROWST.

**froward.** See FROM.

**frown,** v hence n: ME *frounen*: MF *froignier* (F *se ren frogner*): prob from MF *froigne*, a scowling face or expression: Gaul *\*frogna*, nostrils: cf W

*ffroen*, Ga *sròn*, OIr *srón*, nose, Ga *sròin*, a huff, OC *\*srokna*, nose.

**frowst,** occ **froust,** stale air, musty odour, is a b/f from **frowsty** (**frousty**), musty or fusty, var of earlier **frowzy** (**frouzy**), musty, slovenly and unkempt, perh from EE *frowy*, rank-smelling, itself app from OE *thrōh*, rancid. (EW.)

**frozen.** See FREEZE.

**fructify, fructification.** See FRUIT, para 4.

**frugal, frugality.** See para 6 of:

**fruit** (n hence v), whence **fruitful, fruitless, fruity; fruition;**—**fracture, fructification, fructify; frugal, frugality;** cf the element *frugi-*; **usufruct.**

1. L *frui* (s *fru-*, short for *\*frug-*), to have the full use, hence the enjoyment, of, akin to OE *brūcan*, OFris *brūka*, OS *brūcan*, OHG *brūkhan* (G *brauchen*), Go *brukjan*, to utilize, and OE *bryce*, Go *brūks*, usable: cf *frūg-*, the o/s of L *frūx*, fruit. The IE r would be *\*brugh-*, with a formative *-we-*.

2. *Frui* has pp *frūctus*, s *frūct-*, whence the n *frūctus* (gen *frūctūs*), a full use, hence enjoyment, with further senses 'fruits, i.e. products, of the earth, esp of trees and shrubs, hence fruit in the modern sense'. L *frūctus* becomes OF-F *fruit*, adopted by ME and preserved by E. The doubly agential E *fruiterer* (cf MF-F *fruitier*) prob originates in the now rare *fruitery*, from EF-F *fruiterie*, a fruit storehouse, from MF *fruiterie*, fruit collectively.

3. *Frui* has a secondary pp *fruitus*, s *fruit-*, whence LL *fruitiō*, o/s *fruitiōn-*, whence, prob via late MF-EF, the E *fruition*, full use and enjoyment, hence a successful realization.

4. L *frūctus*, n, has adj *frūctuōsus*, whence literary *fructuose*, which perh suggested the Chem *fructose*, strictly L *frūctus*+Chem *-ose*; it also has the cpd *frūctificāre*, to render fruitful, bear fruit, whence OF-F *fructifier*, whence 'to *fructify*', the derivative LL *frūctificātiō*, o/s *frūctificātiōn-*, becoming *fructification*.

5. L *ūsus et frūctus*, use and enjoyment, shortens to *ūsus frūctus*, thence *ūsusfrūctus*, thence, via the abl *ūsūfrūctū*, LL *ūsūfrūctus*: whence E *usufruct*, the beneficiary being a *usufructuary* (LL *ūsūfrūctuārius*).

6. The L *frūctus*, fruits of the earth, fruit, has syn *frūx*, usu pl *frūges*, s *frūg-* (cf para 1), r *fru-*; on its dat *frūgi*, for fruit, hence fit for fruit, hence fit to be used and enjoyed, esp temperately, arises LL *frūgālis*, whence, prob via EF-F, the E *frugal*; derivative L *frūgālitās*, o/s *frūgālitāt-*, yields, prob via late MF-F, the E *frugality*.

**frump** (n, v), **frumpish.** See RUMPLE.

**frustrate; frustration,** whence, anl, **frustrative, frustratory.**

Both the adj and the v *frustrate* derive from L *frustrātus*, pp of *frustrāri*, var *frustrāre*, to drag things out, (vt) to render (an action) vain, to circumvent, deceive, a person, from the L adv *frustra*, in vain, uselessly, itself o.o.o.—though, just possibly, akin to L *fraus*, q.v. at FRAUD. Derivative L *frustrātiō*, o/s *frustrātiōn-*, and LL adj *frustrātōrius*, account for E *frustration* and *frustratory*.

**fruticose**, shrub-like, derives from L *fruticōsus*, adj of *frutex*, s *frut-*, a shrub, o/s *frutic-*: o.o.o.; but *frut-* could, like *frug-*, be an extn of *fru-*, r of *frui*, to use and enjoy; *fruticose*, therefore, is perh akin to FRUIT.

**fry** (1), young fish(es). See FRICTION, para 5.

**fry** (2), v, pt and pp **fried**; sep **fritter**.

'To *fry*' comes, through ME *frien*, from OF-F *frire*, from L *frīgere*, to roast, grill, fry, s *frīg-*, perh echoic: cf Gr *phrug*ein, to grill, and Skt *bhrjjati*, he grills or roasts, which, full parallels, are imperfect cognates.

**fuchsia** (whence **fuchsine**: Chem *-ine*) is a flowering shrub named after the G botanist Leonhard *Fuchs* (1501–66); cf FOX.

**fucic**. See FUCOID.

**fuck**, v hence n, is a SE word classed, because of its associations, as a vulgarism. The derivative expletive **Fuck (it)**!—derivative agent **fucker**—and vn and pa **fucking**, except when lit (then, they are likewise vulgarisms), belong to low sl. *Fuck* shares with *cunt* two distinctions: they are the only two SE words excluded from all general and etym dictionaries since C18 and the only two SE words that, outside of medical and other official or semi-official reports and learned papers, still could not be printed in full anywhere within the British Commonwealth of Nations until late 1961.

That *fuck* cannot descend straight from L *futuere* (whence OF-F *foutre*) is obvious; that the two words are related is equally obvious. That it cannot derive unaided from G *ficken*, to strike, (in popular speech) to copulate with, is clear; it is no less clear that the E and G words are cognates. 'To *fuck*' app combines the vocalism of *futuere*+the consonantism of *ficken*, which might derive from *\*fücken* (only dubiously attested).

Now, L *futuere* is formed similarly to L *battuere*, to strike, hence to copulate with a woman. With both, cf Ir *bot*, Mx *bwoid*, penis; *battuere*, says Malvezin, is borrowed from C and stands for *\*bactuere*; and *futuere* recalls the C r *\*buc-*, a point, hence to pierce (Malvezin); cf also Ga *batair*, a cudgeller, and Ga *buail*, EIr *bualaim*, I strike. Both L *battuere* and L *futuere* (cf L *fustis*, a staff, a cudgel: ? for *\*futsis*) could have got into L from C, which, it is perh worth adding, had orig no *f*: basic idea, 'to strike', hence (of a man) 'to copulate with'. Nevertheless, the source prob long antedates both L and C: a strikingly ancient etymon is app afforded by Eg *petcha*, (of the male) to copulate with, the hieroglyph being an ideogram of unmistakably assertive virility. The Eg word has a close Ar parallel.—A Medit word?

**fucoid** (*fuc*us+adj suffix *-oid*), like the acid **fucic** (*fuc*us+Chem *-ic*), derives from L *fūcus* (s *fūc-*), rock lichen, used as a dark-red, or purple, dye, and adopted by E, esp in Bot for a genus of Algae (seaweed): akin to Gr *phūkos* (s *phūk-*), seaweed, itself app of Sem origin—cf H *pūk*, paint.

**fuddle**, to confuse, render tipsy, esp in pa *fuddled*, tipsy, is o.o.o.; like the obs syn *fuzzle*, it is prob echoic.

**fudge!**, Nonsense!, is prob of Gmc origin; **fudge**, to contrive, to counterfeit—whence the sweet or candy *fudge*—may be for 'to *forge*' but is prob a var of obs *fadge*, to get on well, itself app of LG origin.

**fuel**. See FOCAL, para 2.

**fug** is orig Sc for E *fog*.

**fugacious, fugacity**. See para 3 of:

**fugitive**, adj and n; **fugacious, fugacity; fugue**, whence adj **fugal; centrifugal; refuge, refugee; subterfuge**;—for **feverfew**, see FEBRIFUGE, para 1.

1. L *fugere* (s *fug-*), to flee, vi and vt, has derivative *fuga*, a fleeing, whence *fugāre*, to put to flight: cf Gr *pheugein* (s *pheug-*), to flee; IE r, *\*bheug-*, to flee.

2. *Fugere*, pp *fugitus*, has derivative LL adj *fugitīuus* (ML *-īvus*), whence MF-F *fugitif*, adopted by ME, whence the reshaped E *fugitive*; the derivative n *fugitīuus*, ML *-īvus*, becomes, again via F, the E n *fugitive*.

3. The further derivative L adj *fugāx*, o/s *fugāc-*, yields E *fugacious*, tending to flee, hence evanescent; the LL derivative *fugācitās*, o/s *fugācitāt-*, yields *fugacity*.

4. L *fuga* (as para 1) becomes It *fuga*, whence EF-F *fugue*, with a special Mus sense, adopted by E.

5. The cpd *centrifugal*, fleeing the centre= *centri-*, c/f of *centrum* (see CENTER)+*-fugal*, as if from L *\*fugālis*, adj of *fuga*.

6. The obs v 'to *refuge*', whence *refugee* (unless from F *réfugié*), derives from L *refugere*, to flee (*fugere*) back (*re-*), hence to safety, whence L *refugium*, a place to which to flee back, a place of safety, whence OF-F *refuge*, adopted by E.

7. A *subterfuge*, adopted from MF-F, derives from LL *subterfugium*, a secret flight, from L *subterfugere*, to flee *subter* or under, hence secretly, adv from prep *sub*, under.

**fugue**. See prec, para 4.

**fulcrum**, whence the adj **fulcral**, is adopted from L *fulcrum* (s *fulcr-*, r *fulc-*), a support, from *fulcīre* (s *fulc-*), to uphold, support, prop (up): o.o.o.; but the IE r *\*bhelg-*, to prop, has exact cognates in OE *bealca*, ON *bjalki*, E BALK.

**fulfil**. See FULL.

**fulgence, fulgent**. See FLAGRANT, para 4.

**fulgid**. See FLAGRANT, para 5.

**fulgural, fulgurant, fulgurate, fulguration, fulgurite**. See FLAGRANT, para 5.

**full** (1), adj, whence **fulness** and **fulsome; fulfil**, whence **fulfilment; fill**, v and n.

1. The adj *full*, straight from OE, is akin to OFris and OS *full* (OFris var *foll*), OHG *fol*, MHG *vol*, G *voll*, MD *vul*, *volle*, MD-D *vol*, Go *fulls*, ON *fullr*, with Gmc r *\*full-*; the IE r veers between *\*pler-* and *\*plen-*, as in Gr *plērēs* and L *plēnus*, with E derivatives, e.g. PLENARY, treated sep.

2. OE *full*, var *ful*, has cpd *fulfyllan*, ME *fulfullen*, var *fulfillen*, whence 'to *fulfil*'.

3. OE *fyllan* becomes ME *fullen*, var *fillen*,

whence 'to *fill*'; and OE *fyllan* has derivative n *fyllo*, whence 'a *fill*'.

**full** (2), v, 'to *full* cloth', ME *fullen*, comes from OF-MF *fuler*, MF-F var *fouler*, from VL \**fullāre*, from L *fullō*, a cloth-fuller, o.o.o., but perh akin to Skt *bhāla*, lustre, and, if so, akin to BALD. L *fullō* has an OE agent in *-ere* (E *-er*): *fullere*, whence E *fuller*, a cloth-fuller, whence *fuller's earth*, an earthy clay-like substance used in fulling cloth.

**fulmar.** See FOUL, para 5.

**fulminant, fulminate, fulmination, fulminic.** See FLAGRANT, para 6.

**fumaric; fumarole; fumatory.** See FUME, para 3.

**fumble,** to feel, or move, or otherwise act, clumsily, whence pa and vn **fumbling** and agent **fumbler,** is a derivative of the now only dial *famble*, to stutter, from ME *famelen*, influenced by LG *fummeln* and D *fommelen*.

**fume,** n (whence fumy) and v; **fumaric, fumarole, fumatorium, fumatory; fumet; fumigant, fumigate, fumigation, fumigator, fumigatory; fumitory; fumose** (and **fumous**), whence **fumosity;—perfume** (n and v), **perfumer, perfumery.**—The Gr cognates —thyme, thurible, typhoid, typhoon, stew, etc.—are treated sep at THYME.

1. L *fūmus*, smoke, s *fūm-*, is akin to Skt *dhūmás* and OSl *dymŭ*, and app to Gr *thumos*, spirit: f.a.e., THYME. *Fūmus* becomes OF-MF *fum* (OF-F *fumée*), whence E *fume*. The derivative L *fūmāre* becomes OF-F *fumer*, whence 'to *fume*', orig to smoke (vi).

2. The foll L derivatives concern E:

*fūmōsus*, smoky, whence *fumose* and *fumous*;

LL *fūmāriolum*, chimney-pot, smoke-vent, whence F *fumerolle*, whence E *fumarole*, such a hole in lava as permits gases to escape;

*fūmigāre*, to expose to smoke, with presp *fūmigans*, o/s *fūmigant-*, whence E adj, hence n, *fumigant*, and with pp *fūmigātus*, whence 'to *fumigate*'; derivative *fūmigātiō*, o/s *fūmigātiōn-*, yields *fumigation; fumigator, fumigatory*, are E anl formations.

3. *Fumaric*, a crystalline acid, represents L *fūmār*ia, the plant fumitory + Chem *-ic*: and *fumitory* itself = ME *fumetere*, MF-F *fumeterre*, i.e. L *fūmus*, smoke, (of) *terra*, the ground (cf TERRACE). Cf *fumet*, adopted from EF-F, an *-et* derivative of OF *fum*, smoke: 'fume, hence odour, of meat, esp game, and occ of wine'. *Fumatory* is the adj (whence n) of SciL *fumatorium*, an airtight compartment for the generation of smoke.

4. The n *perfume* derives from EF-F *parfum*, itself from EF-F *parfumer*—whence 'to *perfume*'—from It *perfumare*: L *per*, through, hence thoroughly + *fumare*. E *perfumer, perfumery*, though coming straight from 'to *perfume*', owe something to EF-F *parfumeur*, F *parfumerie*.

**fumigate, fumigation, fumigator.** See prec, para 2.

**fumitory.** See FUME, para 3.

**fumosity, fumous.** See FUME, para 2.

**fun.** See FOND, para 2.

**funambulist.** See the element *funi-*.

**function,** n hence v (? suggested by F *fonctionner*)

and **functional; functionary; fungible;—defunct; perfunctory,** whence **perfunctoriness.**

1. *Function* derives from *functiōn-*, o/s of L *functiō*, the performing of a task, from *funct-*, s of *functus*, pp of *fungī*, to acquit oneself of, to perform, s *fung-*, akin to Ve *bhuṅkté*, he has the enjoyable use of, he enjoys, and, without *-n-*, *bhújam* (acc), enjoyment; perh cf Go us*baugj*an, to sweep out; IE r, \**bhreug-*, to have full use of.

2. *Functiō* yields also—via the acc *functiōn*em— the EF-F *fonction*, whence the agent *fonctionnaire*, which prompts E *functionary*; the legal adj *fungible*, however, comes from ML res *fungībiles*, fungible things.

3. *Fungī* has two prefix-cpds affecting E:

*dēfungī*, to complete (*dē-* used int) the performance of, with pp *dēfunctus*, applied esp to one who has wholly done with life, is dead, whence E *defunct*;

*perfungī*, to discharge in detail, the int force of *per-* becoming lost, so that the sense becomes 'to perform merely as a duty'; whence the LL adj *perfunctōrius*, whence E *perfunctory*.

**fund.** See 1st FOUND, para 4.

**fundament; fundamental.** See 1st FOUND, para 2.

**funeral,** adj and n; **funerary; funereal; funest.**

L *fūnus* (s *fūn-*), a funeral, o/s *fūner-*, is o.o.o.; just possibly, *fūnus* is ult akin to DEAD. LL adjj *fūnerālis, fūnerārius*, lead to *funeral* (adj), *funerary*; L adj *fūnereus* leads to E *funereal*, with *-eal* substituted for *-eous*. The n *funeral* comes from MF-F *funérailles* (pl): ML *fūnerālia*, the funeral rites (hence a funeral), prop the neu pl of the adj *fūnerālis*. *Fūnus* has a further derivative adj: *fūnestus*, tending to a funeral, hence mortal, deadly, whence, prob via MF-F *funeste*, the literary *funest*, portending death.

**fungi.** See FUNGUS.

**fungible.** See FUNCTION, para 2.

**fungus,** pl **fungi; fungoid;** cf the element *fungi-* (as in *fungicide*); **sponge,** n (hence v, whence **sponger),** whence **spongy** (cf L *spongius*); **spunk,** whence **spunky.**

1. *Fungus* (s *fung-*), adopted from L, was orig applied to mushrooms, toadstools, puffballs, etc.: either deriving from or akin to Gr *sphongos* (σφόγγος), var of *spongos* (σπόγγος), sponge, s *spong-*, itself akin to syn Arm *sung*, var *sunk*. The adj *fungoid* = *fung*us + *-oid*, -like.

2. Gr *spongos* has the further var *spongia* (σπογγία), whence L *spongia*, whence MF *esponge* (F *éponge*), whence the E n *sponge*.

3. L *spongia* becomes EIr *spongc*, tinder, whence Ir *sponcc* (cf Ga *spong*), sponge, hence—by superficial resemblance—touchwood, a tinder made from fungus, hence a spark, hence the coll mettle, pluck, (obsol) anger: sem, cf G *Feuerschwamm*, lit fire-fungus, hence touchwood, tinder, spunk. (MacLennan.) *Spunk* comes from the Ir-Ga words.

**funicle, funicular, funiculus.**

The 1st anglicizes the 3rd, which, adopted by An, Zoo, Bot, is the dim ('little cord') of L *fūnis* (s *fŭn-*), a cord, a rope: o.o.o.; if for *\*fulnis*, it could be akin to L *fīlum*, a thread. *Funicular*, adj hence n, represents *fūniculus*+adj *-ar*.

**funk** (coll), n—with adj **funky**—hence v, app comes from Flemish *fonck*, perturbation, perh akin to obs E *funk*, smoke, steam, stench. (EW.)

**funnel** (n hence v): ME *fonel*: Prov *founil*: L *fundibulum*, var of *infundibulum*, q.v. at 2nd FOUND, para 8.

**funny.** See FOND, para 2.

**funny bone.** See HUMERAL.

**fur**, n (whence **furry**) and v (whence **furred**).

The n *fur* derives from ME *furre*, itself from *furren*, whence 'to *fur*': and ME *furren* comes from OF-MF *fuerrer*, *fuerer* (varr *forrer*, *forer*), from OF-MF *fuere*, fur, of Gmc origin; cf OHG *fōtar*, *fuotar*, MHG *fuoter*, G *Futter*, the lining of a coat, and Go *fōdr*, sheath of sword; perh ult cf Skt *pâtra*, a container.—*Furrier*=*fur*+euphonic *r*+agential *-ier*: cf the MF-F *fourreur*.

**furbish**, to scour, or rub, bright, to burnish, hence, esp as **refurbish**, to renovate: through late ME (*fur-*, *for-*), from OF-MF *furbir*, *forbir*, esp in such forms as presp *furbissant* and 'Nous *furbissons*', we furbish: Old W Gmc *\*furbjan*, MHG *furben*, to clean. (B & W.)

**furcate.** See FORK.

**furibund; furious.** See FURY.

**furl** (v hence n): F *ferler*: EF *frêler*, orig *fresler*: o.o.o.—perh (Webster) from OF-MF *fermlier*, to tie (*lier*) fast, firmly (*ferme*, adj, firm): cf FIRM+LIGAMENT.

**furlong; furrow.**

ME *furlong* derives from OE *furlong* (var *-lung*): a furrow long, this being the average length (220 yards, roughly the side of a 10-acre square) of a furrow in old English farming. E *furrow*—whence 'to *furrow*'—derives from ME *forow*, earlier *forgh*, earliest *furgh*, from OE *furh*, akin to OFris *furch*, OHG *furh*, MHG *furch*, G *Furche*, furrow, ON *for*, trench, W *rhych*, furrow, L *porca*, the raised part between furrows; prob IE r, *\*pork-*.

**furlough.** See the 1st LEAVE, para 2.

**furnace:** ME *fornais* (var *forneis*): OF *fornais*, *fornaise*: L *fornāx*, furnace, acc *fornācem*: L *furnus*, oven, akin to L *formus*, warm, Gr *thermē*, heat: f.a.e., WARM.

**furnish**, whence agent **furnisher** and vn **furnishing; furniture.**

'To *furnish*' derives from OF-MF *furnir* (F *fournir*), var *fornir*, to furnish, to do (completely), esp in such forms as presp *furnissant* and (nous) *furnissons*, we furnish: OHG *frumjan*, to further, to do completely, akin to OE *framian*, to further, to profit. OF *fornir* has derivative MF *forneture*, later *forniture*, F *fourniture*, E *furniture*.

**furor, furore.** See FURY.

**furrier.** See FUR, s.f.

**furrow.** See FURLONG.

**furry.** Adj of FUR.

**further**, adj, adv, v; **furthest; furtherance**, from *further*, v, and **furthermore**, from the adv.

1. The adj *further*, ME *further*, *forther*, derives

from OE *furthra*, a comp from the s of FORTH; the adv derives from OE *furthor*, *furthur*, likewise from the s of FORTH. Cf OFris *farther*, *further*, OS *furthor*, adv, and OHG *furdir*, adv (G *furder*), comp of *fort*, forwards, and OHG *fordar*, MHG-G *vorder*, adj. OE *furthra* has derivative v *fyrthran* (var *-rian*), whence ME *furthren* (var *forthren*), whence 'to *further*'.

2. Late in ME, there arises, to balance the comp *further*, the adj and adv *furthest* (early varr *fyrthest*, *forthest*).

**furtive** derives, prob via MF-F *furtif*, f *furtive*, from ML *furtīvus*, L *furtīuus*, theft-, hence thief-, like: L *furtum* (s *furt-*), a theft: L *fūr*, a thief, akin to Gr *phōr* (φώρ): prob *fūr* derives from *ferre*, to carry (implication 'away'), precisely as *phōr* derives from *pherein*, to carry. IE r *\*bher-*: cf 'to BEAR'.

2. *Fūr* has dim *fūrunculus*, a little thief, whence that thief of health, a *furuncle* or boil.

**fury; furibund, furious; furor, furore; infuriate, infuriation.**

1. *Fury* comes, through MF-F *furie*, from L *furia*, itself, like *furor* (whence It *furore*) and *furibundus* (whence obsol *furibund*—cf the suffix *-bund*), and *furiōsus*, whence, via MF *furieus* (F *furieux*), the E *furious*, from *furere*, s *fur-*, to be mad, to be agitatedly and profoundly angry, akin to Gr *thorein* (s *thor-*), to rush or dart forth, and *thorubos* (s *thorub-*, r *thor-*), a great noise, tumult, and Skt *dvaraiti*, he rushes forth. (E & M.)

2. *Furia* has derivative *furiāre*, to render furious, with ML int *infuriāre*, with pp *infuriātus*, whence 'to *infuriate*', whence, anl, *infuriation*.

**furze:** ME *firse*: OE *fyrs*: cf Gr *puros*, wheat, OSl *pyro*, spelt, Cz *pýr*, furze, OP *pure*, broom (the shrub), and also, because made from wheat, Skt *pūras*, bread: prob IE etymon, *\*purs*.

**fuse** (1), n, impregnated cord (etc.) for detonating: It *fuso*, from L *fūsus*, a spindle: from the shape. L *fūsus*, said to be o.o.o., prob derives from syn Eg *khes*. Occ spelling: **fuze**. Cf FUSEE.

**fuse** (2), v, to melt, hence to merge. See 2nd FOUND, para 3.

**fusee**, occ **fuzee**: MF-F *fusée*, a fusee, orig a spindleful: ML *fūsāta*: ? elliptical for *fūnis* (cord) *fūsāta*: from L *fūsus*, a spindle—cf the 1st FUSE. Cf:

**fuselage**, adopted from F, derives from MF-F *fuselé*, spindle-shaped, from OF-F *fuseau*, a spindle, from OF *\*fus*, from L *fūsus*. Cf prec.

**fusible.** See the 2nd FOUND, para 3.

**fusil** (1), adj. See the 2nd FOUND, para 3.

**fusil** (2), a light flintlock. See FOCAL, para 4. OF-F *fusil* has derivatives *fusiller*, whence *fusillade*, adopted by E, and EF-F *fusilier*, likewise adopted.

**fusilier.** See prec.

**fusillade.** See 2nd FUSIL.

**fusion.** See 2nd FOUND, para 3.

**fuss**, n, whence both 'to *fuss*' and **fussy**, is o.o.o.—but prob echoic; perh, however, cf G *fusseln*, to walk unsteadily, to 'play feet ("footy")'; EW, more prob, proposes Nor-Da *fjas*, foolery, nonsense—? rather the obs Da *fas*.

fust. See FUSTY.

fustian (n hence adj): ME *fustyan*, var *fustane*: MF *fustaigne*: ML *fustăneum*, a blend,? rather a confusion, of ML *xylinum* (Gr *xulinon*, neu of *xulinos*, of or from *xulon* or wood)+L *fustis*, a wooden club, a cudgel, itself o.o.o. B & W treat ML *fustăneum* as a translation of Septuagint Gr *xulina lina*, cotton, lit tissue of wood: cf the ML definition of *fustăneum* as *lana de legno*, lit wool coming from wood, and cf sem the G *Baumwolle*, cotton, lit wood-wool. This etym is more prob than that which derives MF *fustaigne* from *Fustat*, a suburb of Cairo.

fustic. See PISTACHIO.

fusty, musty, derives from the now dial *fust*, a strongly musty smell, from the obs *fust*, a wine-cask (made of wood), adopted from OF (cf F *fût*), from L *fustis*, a staff or stave—cf FUSTIAN.

futile, futility. See the 2nd FOUND, para 4.
Futilitarian blends *futility*+utili*tarian*.

futtock, a crooked timber in lower part of a ship's compound rib, prob eases *foothook*.

future, adj hence n (cf F *le futur*), derives from MF-F *futur*, itself from L *futūrus*, future participle of *esse*, to be: cf *fu*it, he has been, Gr e*phu*, he has grown, Skt *ábhũt*, he has been. *Futurity* is an E formation, as if from L \**futūritās*; *futurism*, *futurist* (whence *futuristic*) derive from F *futurisme*, *futuriste*, trlnn of It *futurismo*, *futurista*, themselves from *futuro* (L *futurus*).

fuze. See 1st FUSE.

fuzee. See FUSEE.

fuzz, fuzzy.
The former is a b/f from the latter: and the latter app comes from LG *fussig*, loose, fibrous, spongy (perh cf D *vez*el, fibre, filament). Kipling's *Fuzzy-Wuzzy* is a rhyming redup of *fuzzy*, the *wuzzy* being prob suggested by *woolly*, these Sudanese tribesmen having thick, abundant, woolly hair.

fytte. See 2nd FIT.

# G

gab, v hence n, coll for '(to) prattle or chatter', is perh echoic, but cf *gab*, Sc var of the dial and sl gob, mouth (Ga and Ir *gob*); the freqq are 'to gabble', whence the n, and the echoic 'to gobble', whence gobbler (a turkey cock). *Gobble*, to eat hastily, is a different word.

gabardine. See GABERDINE.

gabble. See GAB.

gaberdine, gabardine.
The fabric, usu *gabardine*, derives from the medieval coarse woollen frock or coat, now usu *gaberdine*: Sp *gabardina*: MF *gaverdine*, var of MF *galvardine*: ? from MHG *wallevart* (G *Wallfahrt*), lit 'wandering journey', i.e. a pilgrimage: ? because such garments were affected by pilgrims.

gabion. See CAVE, para 1.

gable (n hence v): MF-EF *gable*: ON *gafl*, akin to OHG *gibil*, MHG *gibel*, G *Giebel*, gable, and Go *gibla*, battlement, pinnacle: cf also OHG *gebal*, Gr *kephalē*, head: Gmc r, *gebhal-*; IE r, *ghebhal-*. (Walshe.)

Gad! See GOD, para 5.

gad (1), n, a spike, a goad, whence gadfly. See the 1st YARD.

gad (2), v, to roam, wander about: perh by b/f from the now dial *gadling*, a wanderer, a vagabond: OE *gaedeling*, a companion, ? a *-ling* derivative from, or from the r of, OE *gaed*, companionship; f.a.e., GATHER.

gadfly, a goading fly. Cf 1st *gad*, q.v. at 1st YARD.

gadget is o.o.o.; perh a dim of *gage* (var of *gauge*), an instrument for measuring, *gaget* (dim *-et*) becoming *gadget*; perh, however, cf GASKET.

Gael, whence Gaelic (adj hence n); Goidelic.
Both the 1st and *Goidel-*, s of the 3rd, derive from Ga *Gàidheal*, which, like Ir *Gaedheal*, *Gaoidheal*, derives from MIr *Gōedel*, OIr *gōidel*, OC *goidelos*, a Celt, esp if Irish—cf *Gaul* (L *Gallus*), a Celt, esp of ancient Gaul, L *Gallia*, esp *Gallia Transalpina* (approx France). L *Galli*, the Gauls, whence sing *Gallus* (whence *Gallia*), is prob of C origin: ? 'The Strangers' (? OC *gallos*), perh because they came to W Europe from much further east.

gaff (n; hence v—cf the EF-F *gaffer*), an iron spear for striking, hence an iron hook for securing and lifting, heavy fish, turtles, etc.: MF-F *gaffe*: OProv *gaf*: prob of C origin (OC *gab-*, to catch,

seize), perh (B & W) from Go *gaffan*, to catch or seize.

gaffer and gammer are mainly dial contrr of *grandfather* (via *granfer*) and *grandmother*.

gag, to retch, to cause to retch, hence to silence, whence a *gag*, orig something thrust into the mouth, hence a joke, etc.: echoic.

gage (1), n. See GAUGE.

gage (2), n, something deposited as security, hence (obs) to pledge, (archaic) to wager; engage (whence pa engaging), engagement; wage (n and v), wager; wed (whence pa wedded), wedding, wedlock.
1. 'To *gage*' comes from OF-MF *gagier* (MF-F *gager*), from OF-F *gage*, a pledge: Frankish *wadi*, cf Go *wadi*, a pledge, and OHG *wetti*, a pledge, MHG *wette*, pledge, contract, stake, G *Wette*, pledge, bet: cf WED in para 4.
2. OF-MF *gagier* has the cpd OF *engagier*, MF-F *engager* (*en*, in, into, used int), whence 'to *engage*', whence —unless from OF-F—*engagement*.
3. The OF-F n *gage* has the ONF var *wage*, adopted by ME and retained by E, orig as a pledge (obs), later a recompence (obs), finally money paid for work or other service, now usu in pl *wages*. Derivative ONF *wagier* (cf OF *gagier*) becomes ME *wagen* becomes 'to *wage*', orig to pledge, later to stake, to hazard, hence to engage in (a struggle, esp a war). ONF *wagier* has derivative *wageure* (cf the MF-F *gageure*), whence ME *wager*, orig a pledge, hence a stake, a wager, a bet.
4. The OHG *wetti*, a pledge (as para 1), has an exact cognate in OE *wedd*, whence the now dial *wed*, a pledge, a wager. This OE *wedd* derives from OE *weddian*, to pledge, covenant, promise to marry (vt), to marry, whence ME *wedden*, to pledge, to marry, whence 'to *wed*'. OE *weddian* has derivative *weddung*, a pledging, hence a marriage ceremony, whence E *wedding*. *Wedlock*, however, ME *wedlok*, earlier *wedlac*, derives from OE *wedlāc*, betrothal: OE *wedd*+abstract-n suffix *-lāc*, akin to OE *lāc*, a game, sport.
5. OE *weddian* is akin to OFris *weddia*, to pledge, to promise, Go *gawadjōn*, to betroth, ON *vethja*, G *wetten*, to pledge, promise, vow, cf the OE and OFris nn *wedd*, OHG *wetti*, Go *wadi*, ON *veth*, ML *vadium*, L *uas* (o/s *uad-*, as in gen *uadis*), all meaning 'a pledge', cf L *uadimōnium* (s *uadi-*, r *uad-*), a security; cf also L *uadāri* (s *uad-*), to receive a pledge, accept a security, and Lith

243

*vaduōti*, to redeem a pledge. The L words perh come from OGmc.

**gaggle**, to cackle, with derivative n, a cackling, hence a flock of geese on the water, is echoic—and obviously akin to, ? a thickened form of, CACKLE.

**gaiety.** See GAY.

**gain, n and v, gainful; regain.**

1. *Gain*, n (whence *gainful*), is adopted from EF(-F) *gain*, contr of OF *gaain*, itself from OF *gaaignier*, whence OF-F *gagner*, whence 'to gain' (whence *gainer*): and OF *gaaignier* derives either from Frankish *waidanjan, to procure food, take booty, or from OHG *weidanōn* (G *weiden*), to pasture, to hunt for food, from OHG *weida* (G *Weide*), pasture, itself akin to ON *veithr*, OE *wāth*, a hunting; cf OIr *fiadach*, the chase, and Skt *veti*, he pursues; ? cf L *uēnāri*, to hunt.

2. 'To *regain*', whence the nn *regain* and *regainer*, prob=*re-*, again+'to *gain*', but perh derives from OF-F *regagner* (*re-*+*gagner*).

**gainly**, graceful, is taut, the adj suffix -*ly* being added to the now dial adj *gain*, direct (of roads), convenient, useful, (of persons) deft, ME *gayn*, earlier *geyn*, from ON *gegn*, straight, direct (cf AGAIN); the commoner *ungainly*, clumsy, derives from the ME adj *ungeinliche*, from ME *ungein*, inconvenient, the *un-* neg of ME *geyn*.

**gainsay**, to contradict: ME *geinseien*, aphetic for *ageinseien*: to '*say* against'.

**gait.** See the 2nd GATE.

**gaiter** (n hence v): F *guêtre*: EF *guietre*: prob Frankish *wrist, ankle—therefore cf WRIST.

**gala** (n hence adj): F, from It, *gala*: MF *gale*, merrymaking: MD *wale*, wealth: f.a.e., WEAL. OF *gale* perh derives rather (B & W) from MF-EF *galer*, to make merry: Gallo-Roman *walāre*, to live pleasantly: Frankish *wāla*, akin to the E adv WELL, therefore to WEAL.

2. Now, MF-EF *galer* has presp *galant*, making merry, which, as adj, becomes in C17 'well-mannered, esp towards women', whence E *gallant*, in this sense often pron as F *galant*, the sense 'brave' going back to MF-EF. Derivative EF-F *galanterie* yields E *gallantry*.

**galaxy**; adj *galactic*; cf element *galact(o)-*. See LACTAM, para 2.

**gale**, 1 (of air), is ult akin to YELL; cf OE *galan*, ON *gala*, to sing, and Da *gal*, furious.

**gale**, 2 (tribute, licence). See GIVE, para 4.

**gale**. 3 (obs v, and n -*gale* in, e.g., *nightingale*). See YELL, para 2.

**galilee.** See GALLERY.

**gall** (1), bile, hence ult the Am sl *gall*, effrontery, impudence. See GOLD, para 3.

**gall** (2), excrescence or swelling of plant-tissue: ME, from OF-F, *galle*: L *galla*: o.o.o.; perh cf Skt *glau*, ball. Hence *gallic* (acid). Cf GANGLION and:

**gall** (3), a chafed spot, derives from ME *galle*, from OE *gealle*, a blister, ult from L *galla*, a gall-nut. ME *galle* has derivative v *gallen*, to chafe, whence 'to *gall*'.

**gallant, gallantry.** See GALA, para 2.

**galleass.** See GALLEY, para 3.

**galleon.** See GALLEY, para 2.

**gallery; galilee.**

*Gallery* descends, via MF-F *galerie* (cf the It *galeria*, later *galleria*), from ML *galeria*, app an -*eria* alteration of ML *galilea*, var of *galilaea*, vestibule or inner porch of a church, app from the PlN *Galilaea*, Galilee, ref the Scriptural 'Galilee of the Gentiles' (Matthew, iv, 15), the sem development being tricky, not impossible. At least we know that ML *galilea*, vestibule, became MF *galilee*, adopted by E.—LL *Galilaea* is a trln of Gr *Galilaia*, an -*ia* ('country') derivative from H *Gālīl*, 'the region or district', from *gālīl*, region, district.

**galley; galleon; galleass.**

1. A *galley*, a large, low, one-decked vessel (whence its kitchen), derives, in ME, from OF-MF *galie*, var *galee* (whence F *galée*, a printer's galley —from its shape), from ML *galea*, from Byz Gr *galea* (var *galaia*), perh, by phon and sem change, from Gr *galeē*, a weasel.

2. OF-MF *galie* has MF aug *galion*, answering to Sp *galeón*, aug from ML *galea*: and the MF-F *galion*, aided by Sp *galeón*, or vice versa, yields E *galleon*.

3. ML *galea*, adopted by It, has It aug *galeazza*, whence MF *galéasse* (var -*éace*, -*iace*), whence obsol E *galleass*.

4. *Galley* combines with WASP to form *galliwasp*, ? orig 'a wasp that infested ships in WI ports' (Webster), but now applied to a lizard and a lizard fish of CA and the WI. Cf *gallipot*: app *galley*+POT.

**Gallic**=L *Gallicus*, Gaulish, of Transalpine Gaul (approx France); adj of *Gallia*, Gaul, and *Galli*, the Gauls: cf GAEL. From *Gallicus*, EF-F derives *gallicisme*, whence E *Gallicism* (or *g-*). L *Gallicus*, moreover, has the extn *Gallicānus*, Gaulish, (ML) pertaining to the Church of France, whence E *Gallican*, whence—or from F *gallicanisme*—*Gallicanisme*. L *Gallia*, Gaul, participates in the Chem element *gallium*, which has adj *gallic*. Cf the element *Gallo-*.

**gallic**, adj, both of the 2nd GALL and of *gallium* (see GALLIC).

**galligaskins.** See GRECIAN.

**gallimaufry, a** culinary hash; hence any (absurd) medley: MF-F *galimafrée*: MF-EF *galer*, to rejoice, make merry (f.a.e., GALA)+Picard *mafrer*, to eat much, from MD *maffelen*. (B & W.)

**gallinaceous, gallinule.**

The latter derives from L *gallīnula*, chicken, dim of *gallīna*, hen, with adj *gallīnāceus*, whence *gallinaceous*: and *gallīna* is the f of *gallus*, a cock, s *gall-*, r *gal-*, either from *Gallus*, a Gaul, or from the IE r present in YELL.

**gallipot.** See GALLEY, para 4, s.f.

**gallium.** See GALLIC, near end.

**gallivant**, whence agent *gallivanter* and vn *gallivanting*, is app a dial deviation of 'to *gallant*', to play the gallant: cf *gallant* at GALA, para 2.

**galliwasp.** See GALLEY, para 4.

**gallon:** ME, from ONF, *galon*, with var OF *jalon*, *jallon*, prob an aug from *gal-*, r of LL *galleta*, a liquid measure: o.o.o.: ? C.

**galloon.** See GARLAND.

**gallop,** n, derives from OF-F *galop*, itself from the source of 'to *gallop*': the derivative MF-F *galoper*, whence 'to *gallop*', is partly a var of ONF *waloper*: Frankish *wāla hlaupan*, to run (cf LOPE) well (cf the adv WELL). MF-F *galoper* has derivative EF-F *galopade*, whence E *gallopade*. ONF *waloper* leads to dial 'to *wallop*', to move quickly but heavily, hence, esp coll, to flog or thrash: whence *wallop*, (dial) a gallop, (coll) heavy blow (usu *walloping*, a thrashing, a heavy beating or defeat), hence, in E sl, beer, which used to 'pack a *wallop*'.

**gallows** (pl *gallowses*), n hence adj: ME *galwes* (pl): OE *galga*, *gealga* (sing), a gallows, a cross: akin to OFris *galga*, OS and OHG *galgo*, MHG *galge*, gallows, cross (of Christ), G *Galgen*, gallows, Go *galga*, ON *galge, -gi*, cross (of Christ): Gmc r, *galg-*, IE r *ghalgh-*: cf Lith *žalga*, Arm *jalk*, a pole. Cf GIBBET and nautical JIB.

**galoche.** See GALOSH.

**galoot.** See GILLIE, para 2.

**galore,** in plenty: Ir *go leōr*, enough.

**galosh,** occ **galoshe,** often occurs in its OF-F form *galoche*, either (B & W) from Gaul *gallos*, with r akin to *gal-*, as in OF-F *galet*, a pebble, or from LL *gallicula*, dim of Cicero's *gallica*, elliptical for L *solea gallica*, Gaulish sandal.

**galvanic, galvanism, galvanization, galvanize:** F *galvanique*, F *galvanisme*, F *galvanisation*, F *galvaniser*, all coined during 1797–1802 (B & W): after an It physicist, Luigi *Galvani*, who in 1780 discovered animal electricity. Cf the element *galvano-*.

**gamb.** See GAMBOL, para 4.

**gambade.** See GAMBOL.

**gambit.** See CHANGE, final para.

**gamble** (v hence n, hence also **gambler** and **gambling**) is app a freq from ME *gamenen*, to play, disport oneself, from OE *gamenian*, from *gamen*, a game, sport, whence ME *gamen*, later *game*, adopted by E; 'to *game*', orig to play, disport oneself, derives from ME *gamenen*; **gamester,** *gambler=game*, n+agential *-ster*. One object of sport is the quadruped or, later esp, the bird; whence *gamekeeper*. The adj *game*, plucky, comes from gamecocks used in cockfighting. The adj *gamey*, *gamy*, has developed a special sense.

2. ME *gamen*, a game, sport, becomes one particular indoor game, *gammon*, now *backgammon*, prob 'because the men are often set *back*' (Webster).

3. OE *gamen*, var *gomen*, a playing, a game, a sport, is akin to OFris *game*, *gome*, ON, OS, OHG *gaman*, MHG *gamen*, mirth, fun, and Sw *gamman*, Da *gammen*, a playing, a game.

**gambol** (n hence v): EE *gambolde*, var of *gambalde*: (? influenced by GAMBLE, from) late MF-F *gambade*, a leaping or a skipping, adopted

by E in sense 'a horse's spring': Prov *gambado*, an *-ado* derivative of Prov *gambo*, leg: LL *gamba*, var *camba*, fetlock, pastern, thin leg: Gr *kampē*, a joint.

2. LL *gamba* becomes ONF *gambe* (OF-F *jambe*), with ONF dial dim *gamberel*, whence E *gambrel*, orig a horse's hock, hence a large hook for the suspension of carcases.

3. ONF *gambe*, leg, has an ONF derivative in *-on*: *gambon* (MF-F *jambon*, adopted by culinary E), whence E *gammon*, now in specialized sense, 'flitch or ham of smoked bacon'.

4. ONF *gambe* becomes Her *gamb*. Cf the cant, then low s, *gams*, legs—esp a girl's.

**gambrel.** See prec, para 2.

**game,** adj, n, v. See GAMBLE, para 1.

**gamester.** See GAMBLE, para 1.

**gamete;** cf the element *gamo-*. See the element *-gam* and esp *monogamy*.

**gamey.** See GAMBLE, para 1, s.f.

**gamma.** See GAMUT.

**gammer.** See GAFFER.

**gammon** (1), backgammon. See GAMBLE, para 2. Whence prob the sl *gammon*, deceptive nonsense, and its derivative v: cf, sem, the coll '*legpull*'.

**gammon** (2), of bacon. See GAMBOL, para 3.

**gamp** (coll), an umbrella: from Mrs *Gamp*, in Dickens's *Martin Chuzzlewit*, 1843–4.

**gams** (sl). See GAMBOL, para 4.

**gamut; gamma.**

*Gamut*, entire range, (earlier) the entire series of notes in music, (earlier still) Guido d'Arezzo's 'great scale', (orig) the 1st or lowest note of that model scale, devised c1040: Gr γ or *gamma*, prop the 3rd letter of the Gr alphabet; of Sem origin, *gamma* occurs in E esp in *gamma rays*.—In 'the great scale', the notes are named by letters+the syllable of the successive hexachords, *ut* (now usu *do*) being the 1st syllable; Mus *ut* is ML, from the L introductory conj *ut*, as in LL *dico ut*, I say that. *Gamma ut* becomes *gamut*. OF-F has *gamme*.

**gamy.** See GAMBLE, para 1, s.f.

**gander; gannet; goose--gooseberry, gooseflesh, gooseneck, goose step—goosey, goosy** (whence sl **goo-goo); goshawk; gosling; gossamer—gosmore.**

1. *Gander*, male goose, derives from OE *gandra* (var *ganra*), akin to G dial *gander*, var *ganter*, and OF-MF *gante*, var *jante*, wild goose, L *ganta*, small-tailed white goose, ? of Gmc origin.

2. Akin to *gander* is *gannet*, from OE *ganot*, a sea or fen duck, a goose-like seagull, akin to MD-D *gent*, OHG *ganazzo*, MHG *ganzer*, G *Ganserich*, gander.

3. Cf, therefore, OHG-G and D *gans*, goose, ON *gās*, OE *gōs* (pl *gēs*), ME *gos*, E *goose* (pl *geese*): cf also OIr *gēis*, wild duck, swan, Lith *žąsìs*, OP *sansy*, L *anser* (for *hanser*), Gr *khēn* (Doric *khan*), Skt *hamsī*, *hamsas*, goose. The Gmc r is *gans-*; the IE *ghans-*; *-s* is app a suffix. (Walshe; E & M.)

4. OE *gōs* adds, in ME, the dim suffix *-ling* to form *gosling*, a young goose, retained by E. The

adj of *goose* is *goosey*, *goosy*, like a goose, hence foolish, whence 'make *goo-goo* eyes'.

5. Of the *goose*-cpds, perh the most important are:

*gooseberry*, cf BERRY; perh *gooseberry* is f/e for a lost cpd of different form: cf OF-MF (and current dial) *grosele*, F *groseille*, from MD *croesel*, dim of *kroes* (var *kruus*), curly, cf MHG *krūs*, G *kraus*, curly, and G *Krausbeere* (dial *Krauselbeere*), curly berry (from its beard);

*gooseflesh*, from a goose's rough skin; hence fig;

*goshawk*, OE *gōshafoc*, (lit) goose hawk;

*gooseneck*, anything resembling a goose's curved neck;

*goose step*, a goose-like marching step.

6. A disguised cpd is *gossamer*, ME *gossomer*, *gossemer*, revealingly *gosesomer*, app for *gos somer*, i.e. goose summer, ref both to a period of summer-like weather in November when, formerly, geese were habitually eaten, and to the filmy substance (cobwebs) floating, or settling on bushes and grass, in calm, esp in calm autumnal, weather; hence any filmy or gauzy fabric.

7. In certain E diall, *gossamer* means 'the down on plants', a sense contributing to *gosmore*, a weedy herb with hairy or feathery bristles.

**gang**, n and v (whence **ganger**); **gangster**; **gangway**.

Whereas the 4th derives from OE *gangweg* (cf WAY), a 'going' way, a passage, the 3rd merely adds agential *-ster* to the n *gang*: and the n *gang*, a going, hence those going together, comes straight from OE and is akin to syn OFris, OHG-G, MD-D, Da *gang*; to ON *gangr* and Go *gaggs* (pron *gangs*), a lane, a street. All these nn prob derive from the answering vv, e.g. OHG and OS *gangan*, Go *gaggan* (pron *gangan*), ON *ganga*: cf Skt *jánghā*, leg, foot, Lith *žengti*, to walk or step, and *pražanga*, trespass: perh ult akin to GO (OE *gān*: cf G *gehen*).

**ganglion** is adopted from LL *ganglion*, a subcutaneous tumour, a swelling, an excrescence, from Gr *ganglion* (γαγγλίον), ? a gutturo-nasal (*-ng-*) derivative from IE r *gal-*, var *gel-*, to swell, to form a ball: cf the 2nd GALL.

**gangrene** (n hence v): prob via late MF-F *gangrène*: L *gangraena*: Gr *gangraina*: ? for *gangrasnia*, from *gangrōn*, greedy eater, corroder, canker, or *gangrān*, to corrode or canker, from *graō*, I eat greedily, corrode. (Hofmann.) Adj: *gangrenous*, perh from EF-F *gangréneux*, f *-euse*.

**gangster**; **gangway**. See GANG.

**ganister**. See GNEISS.

**gannet**. See GANDER, para 2.

**gantlet**, as in *run the gantlet* (not *gauntlet*), derives from earlier *gantlope*, from Sw *gatlopp*, lit a running (*lopp*) down a lane (*gata*), hence the military *run the gantlet*, through a lane of fellow-soldiers striking at the offender as he runs.

**gantry** (occ **gauntry**); **chantier**; **shanty**.

1. The 1st and 2nd come from ONF *gantier*, MF-F *chantier* L *cantērius*, *canthērius*, a gelding,

(later) any horse, hence a vine-prop, hence in house-building, Gr *kanthēlios*, a pack ass, dim of *kanthos*, a nag: sem cf EASEL and 'clothes-*horse*'.

2. In Can F, the F *chantier* takes the sense 'hut, or small, rough, temporary dwelling': whence E *shanty*.

**gaol**, **gaoler**. See CAVE, para 2.

**gap** (n hence v); **gape** (v hence n), whence **gaper**. ME *gap* comes direct from ON: and ON *gap* derives from ON *gapa*, whence ME *gapen*, whence 'to *gape*'; derivative adj, *gapy*. The ON v is akin to MHG-G *gaffen* (? for *gapfen*), to gape: ult an expressive, almost echoic, word.

**gar**, elliptical for *garfish*, occ called *gar pike*; **garlic**; **goad**; **gore** of land and 'to *gore*', to pierce, now only of quadrupeds wounding with horn or tusk; cf sep **auger**; **gerfalcon** or **gyrfalcon**.

1. *Gar* derives from OE *gār*, a spear, which occurs in OE *gārlēac* (cf LEEK), whence ME *garlek*, E *garlic*.

2. OE *gār* has derivative *gāra*, a small piece of land, shaped like a spearhead, i.e. triangular, whence ME *gare*, later *gore*, retained by E, as in *Kensington Gore*, with derivative Her, dressmaking, naut senses. Prob from ME *gare*, *gore*, comes 'to *gore*', to pierce as with a *gār* or spear. Cf OFris, OS, OHG *gēr*, ON *geirr*, a spear, and OHG *gēro* (G *Gehre*), ON *geiri*, gore of land; cf, ult, Gr *khaios* (for *khaisos*), a shepherd's crook, and Skt *hēšas*, a missile: IE r, perh *ghairs-*, often eased to *ghais-*, a spear, a javelin, itself an extn of *ghei-*, to pierce.

3. *Gerfalcon* (or *gyr-*) derives from ME, from MF, *gerfaucon*, an *-on* extn of *gerfauc* (F *gerfaut*), earlier *gerfalc*, *girfalc*, of Gmc origin: cf MHG *girfalc*, *gerfalc*, and ON *geirfalki*, spear, falcon (cf FALCON).

4. Prob akin to OE *gār*, spear, is OE *gād*, spear, arrow, point, ME *gode*, E *goad*, esp a sharp-pointed staff to urge cattle: cf Langobard (Lombard) *gaida*, a spear, and Gaul *gaiso-*, spear, from IE *ghais-* (as in para 2, s.f.).

**garage** (n hence v) is adopted from F, which derives it from MF (? OF) *garer*, to protect, to pay heed to: Frankish *warōn*, cf OHG bi*warōn*, MHG *warn*, to observe, G *wahren*, to protect, OHG *wara*, attention; f.a.e., the adj WARE.

**garb**. See GEAR, para 2.

**garbage**, offal, hence animal, then also vegetable, refuse, is usu said to be o.o.o.; but does it not derive from EF *garbuge* (from its EF var *gaburge* comes, by metathesis, F *grabuge*), itself (Dauzat) from Genoese dial *garbüdjo*, from It *garbuglio*, a confused intrigue, hence confusion, a mess, *garbuglio* being (app as a *gar-* int) from It *bugliare*, to be agitated or confused, as Prati shows.

**garble**, whence pa **garbled** and n **garble**, derives from It *garbellare* (s *garbel-*), itself from Ar *gharbala*, to sift, from Ar *ghirbāl*, a sieve, itself from LL *crībellum*, dim of L *crībrum*, a sieve, akin to L *cernere*, to sift (s *cern-*), q.v. at DISCERN.

**garden** ( n hence v, whence **gardener**: cf the OF-F *jardinier*); whence PN **Garden**, whence **gardenia**, after the Am botanist Alexander Garden (1730–1791).

A *garden* derives from ME, from ONF, *gardin* (OF-F *jardin*), mdfn of ONF *gart* (OF *jart*), from Frankish *\*gardo*, cf OFris *garda*, OS *gardo*, OHG *garto*, MHG *garte* (gen *garten*), G *Garten*, garden, OHG *gart*, OE *geard*, ON *garthr* (E *garth*), an enclosure, a yard. ML (C10) *gardinium*, prob Gallo-Roman, perh represents *\*hortus gardīnus*, an enclosed garden, cf Go *garda*, an enclosure.

F.a.e., YARD.

**garfish.** See GAR.

**gargantuan,** earlier *Gargantuan*, is the adj of *Gargantua*, the gigantic king and eponymous 'hero' of Rabelais's satirical romance (1535). Possessing a huge appetite, he naturally owes his name to his gullet: cf the Sp and Port *garganta*, gullet, throat: f.a.e., GARGLE.

**garget.** See para 1 of:

**gargle** and **gurgle; gargoyle;** cf **garget** and see GARGANTUAN.

1. *Garget*, ME var *gargat*, throat, derives from OF-MF *gargate*, throat, gullet, an *-ate* derivative from the echoic r *garg-*, with an ancient var *gurg-*, as in L *gurges*, whirlpool. *Garget* now means an inflammation of the throat in pigs and cattle.

2. This echoic *garg-* occurs also in MF-F *gargouiller* (*-ouiller*, pej suffix), closely akin to MF *gargoule*, EF-F *gargouille*, throat: from *gargouiller* comes 'to *gargle*', whence 'a *gargle*'; cf It *gorgogliare*, to gargle, from L *gurguliō*, gullet, which perh suggested 'to *gurgle*', prob an echoic var of *gargle*.

3. L *gurguliō*, gullet, windpipe, has s *gurgul-*, r *gurg-*; it becomes EF *gargouille*, a waterspout, esp a grotesquely carved waterspout, projecting from a gutter of the roof, whence E *gargoyle*.

4. Cf GORGE, para 1; cf also *jargon* at GORGE, para 6.

**gargoyle.** See prec, para 3.

**garish,** unrecorded before C16, is o.o.o.: perh (OED, Webster, EW) from obs *gaure*, to stare: cf *garing* (*gauring, gouring*)-*stock*, a gazing-stock.

**garland,** n hence v (with prefix-cpd **engarland**); **galloon.**

1. ME *garland* derives from MF-EF *garlande* (cf OProv *garlanda*), perh from Frankish *\*weron*, akin to MHG *wieren*, to encircle, to adorn.

2. Akin, perh, is *galloon*, a tape-like trimming, from EF-F *galon*, from OF-F *galonner*, to adorn (the head) with ribbons—cf either, with Webster, MF *garlander*, var *galander*, to adorn with wreaths, or, with B & W, MF *galant* (E GALLANT).

**garlic.** See GAR, para 1.

**garment.** See WARN, para 5.

**garner.** See GRAIN, para 5.

**garnet.** See GRAIN, para 5, at end of *granatus* subdivision.

**garnish, garnishment, garniture.** See WARN, para 5.

**garotte.** See GARROTE.

**garret.** See WARN, para 6.

**garrison.** See WARN, para 5.

**garrote, garrotte,** occ **garotte.**

'To *garrote* (*-otte*)' derives from EF-F *garrotter*, to pinion, (C19–20) to strangle, itself from MF-F *garrot*, a staff or stick, var of MF *guaroc*, bolt of a crossbow, itself from OF *garokier*, var of *warokier* (*-quier*), prob from Frankish *\*wrokkan*, to turn violently, to twist (e.g., the neck of). F *garrot* becomes Sp *garrote*, with sense 'a throttling instrument', duly taken back by F and taken over by E, and thus accounting for the *-ote* (as opp the F *-otte*) form.

**garrulity, garrulous.** See CARE, para 5.

**garter:** ONF *gartier* (OF *jartier*, MF *jarretier*, MF-F *jarretière*), from ONF *garet* (OF-MF *jaret*, MF-F *jarret*), the bend of the human knee, dim (*-et*) of dial ONF *garre* (dial OF *jarre*), cf OProv *garra*: of C origin—cf Cor and Br *gar*, leg, and W *gar*, shin, lower part of thigh.

**garth.** See the 1st YARD and cf GARDEN.

**gas, gaseous, gasify.** See CHAOS, para 1.

**gash,** n, derives from 'to *gash*', itself from EE *garsh*, from late ME(-EE) *garse*, from ONF *garser* (OF-EF *jarser*), to scarify, prob (B & W) from VL *\*charissāre*, for *\*charassāre*, mdfn of LL *charaxāre*, to carve, from Gr *kharassein*, to cut a notch in, hence, as in cpd *enkharassein*, to scarify; IE r, perh *\*gher-*, to scratch.

**gasket,** a line for securing a furled sail, is o.o.o.: perh from syn It *gaschetta*, cf EF-F *garcette*, rope's end, little cord, orig a little girl (fig from *garce*, girl, from OF-F *gars*, acc *garçon*, boy). Perh cf GADGET.

**gasoline** (or *-ene*)=*gas*+*ol-*, oil+Chem *-ine*.

**gasp,** v hence n and **'gasper'** (cigarette): ME *gaspen*, earlier *gaispen*, to gasp, to yawn: ON *geispa* (for *\*geipsa*), to yawn—prob either a freq of ON *gapa*, to gape, or simply echoic.

**gastric, gastronomy.** See the element *-gaster*.

**gate** (1), an opening, for passage, in a barrier (wall, fence, etc.): ME *gate, gat:* OE *gaet, gat, geat*, akin to OFris *gat, jet*, OS and ON *gat*, and perh to:

**gate** (2), now mostly dial for way, path, going (esp walking), with var spelling **gait**, now the SE word for manner of walking on foot. ME *gate* derives from ON *gata*, akin to Go *gatwō*, OHG *gazza*, MHG *gazze*, G *Gasse*, a lane. 'Perh brought from Scandinavia by the Goths; prob an extn with suffix *-wō* of OS, ON *gat* "hole" (OE *geat*, E *gate* in usual sense)', says Walshe: therefore cf prec.

**gather,** whence agent **gatherer** and vn **gathering;** cf sep *gad*, to roam.

1. 'To *gather*' comes, through ME *gaderen*, from OE *gaderian* (contr *gadrian*): cf OFris *gaderia* (contr *gadria*), MD *gaderen* (also D), *gederen*, MHG *gate, gegate*, companion, (occ) husband, G *Gatte*, husband (marriage companion), OE *gegada*, companion, and *gaed*, companionship: ult akin to GOOD (f.a.e.).

2. Intimately akin to the OE and other OGmc terms just mentioned are OE *gador, geador*, OFris *gader*, MHG *gater*, together. Note that OE *gador* takes prefix *to-*, i.e. the OE prep *tō*, and thus forms

OE *tōgador* (*-ore*), *tōgaedre*, *tōgaedere*, whence ME *togedere*, whence *together*: cf OFris *to gadera*.

**gauche** is adopted, together with its derivative **gaucherie**, from F, where orig (late C14) it meant 'left-handed'. F *gauche* derives from MF *gauchir*, to make detours, from syn OF *guenchir*, either from Frankish *\*wankjan* or from syn OHG *wanchan* (MHG-G *wanken*), to waver, vacillate, in both origins influenced by OF *gauchier*, *gaucher*, to trample. (Dauzat.)

**gaucho**, a Sp-Amerindian cowboy of the pampas, is a S Am Sp word, app from Araucan *cauchu*, a wanderer.

**gaud, gaudy.** See JOY, para 4.

**gauffer, gaufre, gaufrette.** Cf *gopher* but see WEAVE, para 5.

**gauge** (loosely **gage**), a measure, an instrument for measuring, derives from ONF *gauge* (MF-F *jauge*), itself from ONF *gauger* (MF-F *jauger*), to measure exactly; perh, however, the ONF and OF vv derive from the nn, with origin perh either in Frankish *\*galgo*—cf OHG *galgo* (pl *\*galga*), a perch, a crutch, gallows, windlass, as B & W hold, or in *gallicum* (sc *metrum*), a Gaulish measure, as others maintain, or in Basque *galga*, a gauge, as I propose, the Basques being notably deft and ingenious.

**Gaul** (whence **Gaulish**, adj hence n). See GAEL.

**gaunt** (whence **gauntness**): C15 *gawnt*, C16–17 *gant*: prob of Scan origin. Cf dial (E and Shetlands) *gant*, a tall, thin person.

**gauntlet**: MF-F *gantelet*, double dim (*-el*, *-et*) of OF-F *gant*, a glove: Frankish *\*wanth*, cf MD *want* and ON *\*vantr*, *vöttr*.—Also loose for GANTLET, q.v.

**gauze** (whence **gauzy**) derives from EF-F *gaze*, either from the Palestinian city of *Gaza* (Ar *Ghazzah*) or from Ar *gazz*, floss silk.

**gavel** (1), a sheaf-quantity of mown grain: ONF *gavelle* (OF-F *avelle*), orig a heap: of C origin— cf OIr *gabāl*, a grasping, from *gabim*, I grasp or take, OC r *\*gab-*, to take, to contain.

**gavel** (2); **kevel.**

*Gavel*, a presiding officer's mallet for ensuring silence, is o.o.o., but perh akin to *kevel*, a hammer for stone-shaping or -breaking, itself o.o.o., but prob akin to naut *kevel*, a strong cleat or timber for fastening a vassel's heavy lines. This naut *kevel* derives from ONF *keville* (OF-F *cheville*), from ML *clāvicula*, L *clāuicula*, dim of ML *clāvis*, L *clāuis*, a key: cf CLAVICLE.

**gavel** (3), a tribute. See GIVE, para 4, where also *gavelkind*.

**gavotte**, adopted from EF-F, derives from Prov *gavoto*, dance of the *Gavots*, as Provençals call the inhabitants of the Alps; *gavot* derives from Pyrenean F *gave*, pre-L *\*gaba*, throat, gullet, goitre, perh of C origin; cf ML *gabarus*.

**gawk**, n whence coll v and the adj **gawky**: cf dial *gawk*, left-handed, and dial *cack-* (var of *keck-*) *handed*.

**gay, gaiety.**

The latter comes from OF-F *gaieté*, from OF-F

*gai*, whence E *gay*: and OF *gai* derives from Frankish *\*gāhi* – cf OHG *gāhi*, impetuous, sudden, sharp (MHG *gāch*, *gaehe*, G *jäh*), perh akin to OHG *wāhi*, good, beautiful; Walshe, however, suggests that OHG *gāhi*=g-*ahi*, akin to L *ōcior*, swifter.

**gaze** (v hence n), **gazebo.**

The latter prob=*gaz*(e)+*-ebo*, mock-L for 'I shall gaze', after L *uidebo*, ML *videbo*, I shall see. 'To *gaze*', ME *gasen*, is prob of Scan origin: cf Nor dial and Sw dial *gasa*, to stare; perh cf GAPE.

**gazelle**, adopted from MF-F, comes from Ar *ghazāl*, *ghazāla*.

**gazette** (n hence v), **gazetteer.**

The latter anglicizes EF-F *gazettier*, *gazetier*, from EF-F—whence E—*gazette*: It *gazzetta*: Venetian *gazeta*, orig a small coin, hence—from the price of the first news-sheet sold in Venice— a news-sheet (in full, *gazeta delle novità*), as B & W propose.

**gear** (n hence v); **garb** (n hence v).

1. *Gear*, ME *gere*, either derives from approx syn ON *gervi* or is worn down from OE *gearwe*, equipment, clothing, armour: cf OFris *gare*, OHG *garwī*, contr of *garawī*, dress; cf also OE *gearu*, *gearo*, ready, whence the obs and dial E *yare*, ready, lively, active.

2. With OHG *garawī*, *garwī*, cf It *garbo*, grace, graceful or beautiful form, whence EF *garbe* (now *galbe*), graceful contour or outline, whence E *garb*.

**gebir.** See KAFFIR, para 2.

**gecko**: Mal *geko'*, from its cry.

**gee** (1), interjection: for **Gee**: from *Jesus*.

**gee** (2), n, coll for a horse:, ? from *Gee up!*, prob for *Get up!*, Get moving as addressed to a horse.

**gee** (3), v (mostly Am coll and E dial), to agree, to fit: o.o.o.: ? orig nursery aphesis and easement of *agree*.

**geese.** See *goose* in para 3 of GANDER.

**geezer** (sl), old person: prob from obs *guiser*, an actor (see GUISE), but perh introduced by sailors and soldiers from Malta (? *gisem*, the human body, hence a man).

**Gehenna**, adopted from LL, comes from Gr *Géenna*, from post-Biblical H *Gē Hinnōm*, Valley of Hinnom (near Jerusalem), where the Jews had sacrificed to Moloch and thus caused the place to become accursed and later to become syn with 'hell'. (B & W.)

**geisha**, a Japanese professional singing-and-dancing girl, is adopted from Jap, where, deriving from Ch, it means 'artist'; it combines *gei*, art, esp of singing or dancing+*sha*, person.

**gel.** See JELLY (heading).

**gelatin(e), gelatinous.** See JELLY, para 2.

**geld** (1), a Crown tax. See YIELD, para 2.

**geld** (2), to castrate; **gelding.**

The latter derives from ON *geldtngr*, from ON *geldr*, barren, akin to OSw *galder*, OE *geld*, OHG *galt*, barren. ON *geldr* has derivative v *gelda*, whence ME *gelden*, whence 'to *geld*'.

gelid: L *gelidus*: f.a.e., COLD.—Cf *glacial* at GLACÉ.

gelignite. See JELLY, para 3.

gelseminine, Gelsemium. See JASMINE, s.f.

gelt, money. See YIELD, para 4.

gem (n, hence v): ME, from OF-F, *gemme*: L *gemma*, bud, the 'eye' of a vine, hence, from resemblance of form and colour, a precious stone, thence a jewel, indeed anything brilliant and valuable: either from IE *\*gembhma*, cf Lith *žémba*, it buds or sprouts, or from IE r *\*gem-*, to press, to press out, to bud or sprout. (E & M.)

2. *Gemma*, a bud, a bud-like formation, is retained by Bot. Derivative *gemmātus*, provided with buds, yields *gemmate* and 'to *gemmate*'; LL *gemmifer*, bud-bearing, gem-producing, yields *gemmiferous*; the dim *gemmula* yields *gemmule*.

3. Perh cf:

gemini; geminate, gemination.

*Gemini*, The Twins of Astr, is the pl of L *geminus*, twin, double, adj and n: prob, with 'popular' or f/e substitution of *g* for *y*, *geminus* (s *gemin-*, ? r *\*gem-*) is akin to Skt *yamás*, yoked, linked, twin, Av *yemō*, twin, Lett *junis*, double fruit, cf Ir *emuin*, twins; but perh akin to Gr *gemō*, I am full, OSl *žímǫ*, I press (cf GEM, para 1, s.f.), Ir *gemel*, a bond. (E & M.)—Cf GIMBAL.

gemmate, gemmation, gemmule. See GEM, para 2.

'gen', information, news, derives from that consecrated phrase of the fighting Services, 'for the *gen*eral information of all ranks'.

gendarme, gendarmery. See GENERAL, para 28.

gender. See GENERAL, para 4.

gene. See GENERAL, para 3.

genealogical, genealogist, genealogy. See para 25 of:

general, adj, n, v (mostly in out-general), generality, generalize, whence generalization; genus, pl genera; gene; generable, generate, generation, generative, generator—degenerate, degeneration, degenerative—regenerate, regeneration, regenerative, regenerator; generic; generosity, generous; genesis, genetic (whence genetics, geneticist); genital (whence genitals); genitive, adj hence n (whence genitival); genitor, geniture—progenitor, progeniture; gender—engender; genre; genius, genial; gens—Gentile, gentility—gentle (whence gentleness, gentleman, gentlewoman)—genteel—gentry—jaunty; genuine (whence genuineness); germ, germen—german, germane—germinal—germinant, germinate, germination, germinative—germule.—Other prefix-cpds: congener, congeneracy, congeneric—congenial (whence congeniality), whence neg uncongenial—congenital (adj hence n); indigenous; ingenious, ingenuity—ingenuous (whence ingenuousness), neg disingenuous—engine (n, v), engineer (n, v), engineering, enginous—cf gin, a contrivance; progeny.—Other cpds: eugenic, whence eugenics, eugenism; gendarme, gendarmerie; genealogical, genealogist, genealogy; homogeneity, homogeneous; primogenitary, primogenitor, primogeniture—primogenous.—Cf sep the 'born' group: COGNATE, NATAL, NATION (NATIONAL, etc.),

NATURE, and, as the keyword, NATIVE.—Cf also the Gmc group, likewise sep: KIN (keyword), KIND, KINDRED, KING: a group running parallel to the *genus* group above.—Cf sep the less obvious BENIGN, MALIGN.

### Indo-European

1. The base of the *general* group is L *genere*, to engender, s and r *gen-*; *genere* was displaced by the redup syn *gignere* (s *gign-*), with extended sense 'to produce, to cause'. The principal derivative of *gen*ere is the n *gen*us, birth, stock, race, hence any group of beings having a common origin, esp if also possessing natural resemblances, hence class or kind: cf Gr *genos*. The IE r is *\*gen-*, to engender, with implied derivative sense (as esp in the sep NATIVE group), to be born. With *genos*, *genus*, cf Skt *jánas*-; with Gr *egenonto*, they were born, cf Skt *ajananta*; with L *gens* (para 14 below), cf Skt *ganus*: indeed the relationships between Gr-L and Skt are strikingly numerous and intimate.

### Greek

2. Cf *genealogy* (para 25) and *homogeny* (para 26) below. For hydro*gen*, oxy*gen*, see the elements *hydro-* and *oxy-*. But Gr *gignomai* (for *\*gigenomai*), I am born, which has r *gen-*, possesses the important derivative *genesis*, a coming into being or a natural development, duly adopted by L and incorporated by E (cf the EF-F *genèse*); cf *Genesis*, the first book of The Bible. Gr *genesis* has adj *genētikos*, whence, perh via F *génétique*, the E *genetic*.—Direct Gr descent occurs also in *eugenic*, which, perh influenced by *genetic*, derives from *eugenēs*, well-born.

### Latin—mostly Simples

3. L *genus* (gen *generis*, o/s *gener-*), pl *genera*, has been adopted by Logic and by Sci, esp Bio. The Bio *gene* derives from *genus*.

4. In F, the L o/s *gener-* becomes both late OF-F *genre*, orig esp *le genre humain* (prompted by the L *genus humānum*), adopted by E, and, in OF-EF, *gendre*, with excrescent *d* (excised by F); *gendre* becomes ME *gender*, sex of all animals, now mostly a gram tech.

5. L *genus*, o/s *gener-*, has adj *generālis*, (orig) generic, (then) general, whence OF-MF *general* (F *général*), adopted by E; MF *capitaine general* (C14) becomes, in C15, the elliptical n *general* (F *général*), likewise adopted by E. L *generālis* has LL derivative *generālitās*, whence MF-F *généralité* and E *generality*; F *général* has derivative EF-F *généraliser*, whence 'to *generalize*', whence *generalization*.

6. L *genus*, o/s *gener-*, has the derivative v *generāre*, to engender, to generate, with presp *generans*, o/s *generant-*, whence the Geom n *generant*. The pp *generātus* (s *generāt-*) yields 'to *generate*'. On *generāt-* arise *generātiō*, o/s *generātiōn-*, whence, via OF, *generation*; LL *generātīuus*, ML *-īvus*, whence *generative*; and agent *generātor*, adopted by E, with derivative

'instrument' senses. *Generable* derives from L *generābilis* (*generāre+-ābilis*).

7. *generāre* also becomes OF-MF *gendrer* (var *genrer*), whence the obs 'to *gender*'; extant, however, is the cpd 'to *engender*', to beget: OF-F *engendrer*: L *ingenerāre*: int *in-+generāre*.

8. L *generāre* has two notable prefix-cpds: *dēgenerāre* and *regenerāre*. *Dēgenerāre*, to fall *dē*, off from, the *genus* or stock, has pp *dēgenerātus*, whence both the adj and the v *degenerate*, whence *degeneracy*, for *\*degeneratecy*; derivative LL *dēgenerātiō*, o/s *dēgenerātiōn-*, accounts for late MF-F *dégénération* and E *degeneration*; *degenerative* is an anl E formation. *Regenerāre* (*re-*, again) has presp *regenerans*, o/s *regenerant-*, whence *regenerant*; pp *regenerātus* (s *regenerāt-*) explains both adj and v *regenerate*, whence *regeneracy*; derivative LL *regenerātiō*, o/s *regenerātiōn-*, leads, through OF-F, to *regeneration*; whereas *regenerative* is an E formation, *regenerator* is adopted from LL.

9. L *genus*, stock, has the specialized sense 'good (noble) stock', with adj *generōsus*, whence, via MF *genereux* (F *généreux*), f *genereuse*, the E *generous*; derivative L *generōsitās*, o/s *generōsitāt-*, whence, via late MF-F, the E *generosity*.

10. L *genus*, in its tertiary sense 'sort or kind, class', acquires in erudite EF-F the adj *générique*, whence E *generic*.

11. L *genere*, pp *genitus* (s *genit-*), has derivative adj *genitālis*, pertaining to procreation, whence E *genital*; the n *genitals*, sexual parts, was prompted by L *genitālia*, prop the neupl of the adj.

12. On L *genit*us arise both *genitor*, adopted by E, and *genitūra*, adapted by E as *geniture*: both more common in the cpds *progenitor*, *progenitūra*, the former adopted, the latter (as *progeniture*) adapted, by E. Also on *genit-*, s of pp *genitus*, arises the adj *genetīuus*, pertaining to sexual reproduction, original, generic, hence, in LL, applied to the 'of' or classifying case in L (and Gr) declensions, whence the E *genitive*, adj then— with its own adj *genitival*—n.

13. L *genere*, to beget, has derivative *Genius*, a god presiding over birth, esp of a potential great or talented or otherwise remarkable person, hence, as in *Genius loci*, the tutelary god of a place; finally, a person thus aided, as in the E adoption. L *genius* has adj *geniālis*, possessed of unusual powers, hence dedicated to those powers, hence joyous; L *geniālis* also harks back to its v, for an early sense is 'concerned with procreation, hence with marriage'. All these senses are known in E, but the 'procreative' and 'nuptial' senses are obs, 'of genius' is obsol, 'cheerful, happy-natured, jovial' predominates, with the allied sense 'favourable' (e.g., climate) still active.—L *geniālis* has LL derivative *geniālitās*, o/s *geniālitāt-*, whence *geniality*. Cf *congenial* in para 20.

14. Another important derivative of *genere* is the n *gens*, orig 'the group of all those who, in the male line, descend from a common (free) male ancestor' (E & M), hence a clan. The adj is *gentīlis*, belonging to the clan, hence, in LL, a non-Roman, a foreigner, and, in LL-ML, a non-Jew, a non-Christian, esp in *gentīles*, Gentiles, the latter coming into E straight from L, the former through OF-F *gentil* (f *gentille*), itself from L *gentīlis*. The derivative L *gentīlitās* becomes E *gentility*, with its current sense influenced by OF *gentilité* (L *gentīlitāt*em, acc.).

15. It is OF-F *gentil* which accounts for E *genteel*, (orig) of good birth, (later) invincibly respectable; it also accounts for E *gentle* (ME *gentil*, direct from OF). *Gentlewoman* complements *gentleman* (whence *gentlemanly*, whence *gentlemanliness*), which derives from ME *gentilman*, a well-born man, prompted by syn OF *gentils hom* (whence F *gentilhomme*),

16. Partly from OF *gentil* (para 14) and partly from OF-(obsol)F *gent*, well-born, hence gracious, comes OF-MF *genterise* (var *gentelise*), whence ME *gentrise*, whence ME *genterie*, contr to *gentrie*, whence E *gentry*. Certainly from OF-F *gentil*, perh also partly from OF-F *gent*, f *gente*, come EE (now only dial) *genty* and the var EE *janty*, whence E *jaunty*, (obs) gentlemanly, hence stylish, hence sprightly.

17. L *gen*ere perh has, through the n *genus*, the further adj *genuīnus* (suffix *-īnus*, E *-ine*), of the true *genus* or stock, native (not foreign), authentic, whence E *genuine*, with additional senses 'frank' and 'sincere'. E & M, however, convincingly derive *genuīnus*, from *genu*, knee.

18. Obscurely from L *genus* rather than from L *genere*, derives L *germen* (s *germ-*), o/s *germin-*: clearly *gener-*, o/s of *genus*, and prob Skt *janman*, *janiman*, birth, hence origin (cf *jánas-*, race, a creature), have operated: prob *germen* is a contr of *\*genermen*. L *germen*, a seed, a bud, a shoot, hence descent, becomes, through its s *germ-*, the OF-F *germe*, whence E *germ*. Derivative *germināre*, to bud, has pp *germinātus*, whence 'to *germinate*'; the derivative *germinātiō*, o/s *germinātiōn-*, yields EF-F and E *germination*; presp *germinans*, o/s *germinant-*, accounts for the adj *germinant*, but adj *germinal* is adopted from F, which, taking it from LL *germinālis*, uses it mostly as n—*Germinal*, one of the Revolutionary months. *Germinative* is an E formation, and *germule* is a *-ule* dim of E *germ*.

19. This *germ-* s occurs also in *germānus* (adj suffix *-ānus*, E *-an*), of the same race, esp of the same parents, authentic, whence OF-F *germain*, adopted by ME with var *german*, as in *brother-german*, full brother, and *cousin-german*, first cousin. The var *germane* (cf F *germaine*, f of *germain*) predominantly signifies 'relevant'.

Latin: the other prefix-cpds

20. L *genus*, o/s *gener-*, has the cpd adj *congener*, of the same (implied by *con-*, together) race, adopted by E and used as n, with adjj *congeneric*, *congenerous*, and with subsidiary n *congeneracy*. But *congenial* is of E formation: *con-+genial* (as in para 13). *Congenital*, influenced by *genital* (para

11), derives from L *congenitus*: *con*+pp *genitus*: present at birth, hence inborn.

21. L *indigena*, a native, lit one born (*-gena* from Gr *-genēs*) within (*indu*, var of *endo*: cf syn Gr *endon*) the clan, has LL adj *indigenus*, whence E *indigenous*.

22. L *genus*, rather than *genere*, has a cpd adj *ingenuus*, born within (*in-*) the clan, hence freeborn, hence frank: whence E *ingenuous*. Its derivative *ingenuitās* (o/s *ingenuitāt-*) means frankness, candour, ingenuousness, but its E sense has, in C19–20, been predominantly that of a n answering to E *ingenious*, which derives, prob via MF-F *ingénieux*, f *ingénieuse*, from *ingeniōsus*, adj of *ingenium*, inborn quality, esp of talent or even of genius (cf *genius* in para 13). L *ingenuus*, ingenuous, survives in MF-F *ingénue*, f of *ingénu*, ingenuous; the F, hence the E, theatre employs *ingénue* as n.

23. L *ingenium*, natural ability, LL ingenious invention, becomes OF-F *engin*, with derivative senses 'skill' and 'machine'—esp 'engine': whence E *engine*, whence prob, by agential suffix *-eer*, an *engineer*, although the earlier *enginer* owes something to OF-MF *engignier* (or *-neor*), a contriver, adviser, from OF-EF *engignier*, to contrive, to invent, from VL *ingeniāre*, from L *ingenium*. The adj *enginous*, of or like an engine, sense-adapts the obs *engenous*, ingenious, crafty, from OF-MF *engignos*, itself from L *ingeniōsus*, esp in its LL sense 'ingenious'. From OF-F *engin* comes, by aphesis, ME *gin*, a contrivance, a device, whence E *gin*, a trap or a snare.

24. A cpd of *gignere* (para 1) is *prōgignere*, to engender *prō* or forward, hence to have offspring, whence *prōgeniēs* (s *prōgeni-*), bodily issue (a child), descent: whence OF-MF *progenie*, adopted by ME: whence *progeny*.

Full Compounds, Greek and Latin

25. Gr accounts for *genealogy* and *homogeny*. From Gr *genea* (var *gennea*), descent, akin to *genos*, derives *genealogos* (*logos*, discourse, disquisition: cf LOGIC), a genealogist, whence *genealogia*, genealogy, whence LL *genealogia*, OF-MF *genealogie* (F *généalogie*), ME *genealogi* or *genelogie*, whence E *genealogy*. Derivative EF-F *généalogiste* leads to *genealogist*; late MF-F *généalogique* to *genealogic*, extended to *genealogical*.

26. Gr *genos*, stock, race, has an adj c/f *-genēs*, as in *homogenēs* (*homos*, same), whence ML *homogeneus*, whence E *homogeneous*; derivative ML *homogeneitās* yields *homogeneity*; derivative Gr *homogeneia* yields Bio *homogeny*.

27. LL *prīmogenitor*, first (*prīmo-*, c/f of *prīmus*) genitor (cf para 1), is adopted by E; ML *prīmogenitūra* (cf *geniture* in para 11) becomes *primogeniture*, the right of the first-born, with anl adj *primogenitary*; ML *prīmogenius* and L *prīmigenus* combine to suggest E *primogeneous*.

28. The cpd *gendarme*, adopted from EF-F, is a b/f from the MF-F pl *gensdarmes*: *gent*, people +*de*, of+*armes*, weapons—as if a translation of L *\*gentes armorum*. F *gensdarmes* has derivative

late MF-F *gendarmerie*, a body or force of gendarmes: adopted by E, which often anglicizes to *gendarmery*.

generate, generation, generative, generator. See prec, para 6.

generic. See GENERAL, para 10.

generosity, generous. See GENERAL, para 9.

genesis. See GENERAL, para 2.

genet, a long-tailed, civet-like carnivore: MF-F *genette*: Ar *djarnait* (*jarnayt*). The Sp *gineta* is first recorded three centuries later than the F word.

genetic, genetics. See GENERAL, para 2.

geneva. See GIN (the drink).

genial, geniality. See GENERAL, para 13.

geniculate, geniculation. See GENUFLECT.

genital. See GENERAL, para 11.

genitive. See GENERAL, para 12.

genitor, geniture. See GENERAL, para 12.

genius. See GENERAL, para 13.

genre. See GENERAL, para 4.

gens. See GENERAL, para 14.

genteel. See GENERAL, para 15.

gentian: ME *gencyane*: MF-F *gentiane*: L *gentiāna*, prop the f of the adj of *Gentius*, the Illyrian king reputed to have discovered it.

gentile, Gentiles. See GENERAL, para 14.

gentility. See GENERAL, para 14.

gentle; gentleman, gentlewoman. See GENERAL, para 15.

gentry. See GENERAL, para 16.

genuflect, genuflection; geniculate, geniculation. The base is L *genū* (s and r *gen-*), knee, akin to Hit *genu*, knee, and the syn Gr *gonu* (s and r *gon-*) and Skt *jánu*. The LL cpd *genuflectere*, to bend the knee, to kneel, becomes 'to *genuflect*', to kneel in worship; LL derivative *genuflexiō*, o/s *genu-flexiōn-*, becomes *genuflexion* or *-flection*. L *genū*, moreover, has dim *geniculum*, adopted by An; derivative *geniculātus*, bent like a knee, yields *geniculate*, and the LL derivative *geniculātiō*, o/s *geniculātiōn-*, yields *geniculation*.

genuine. See GENERAL, para 17.

genus. See GENERAL, para 1.

geocentric. See the element *geo-*.

geode, geodesic, geodesy. See the element *geo-*.

geography; geographer, geographic(al).

*Geographic*, with extn in *-al*, derives from LL *geographicus*, trln of Gr *geōgraphikos*, which, like *geōgraphos* (whence ML *geographus*, whence, with E *-er* for L *-us*, *geographer*), follows from Gr *geōgraphia*, a writing (*-graphia*) about the earth (*gaia*, *gē*), adopted by L, whence late MF-F *géographie*, whence E *geography*. For *-graphy*, cf the element *-graph* and see GRAPH. Gr *gē* is the Attic form answering to Homeric *gaia* (cf Doric *ga*, Ionic *geē*), for *\*gawia*, the earth, o.o.o.

geology; geologic(al), geologist.

Without Gr or L (even ML) antecedents, *geology* and its agent and adj imitate the prec. Contrast:

geometry; geometric(al), geometer (occ geometrician).

*Geometric* comes, via L *geometricus* and perh via MF-F *géométrique*, from Gr *geōmetrikos*;

*geometer* is adopted from LL, the L form being *geometra*, var of *geometres*, from Gr *geōmetrēs*; and both are intimately related to Gr *geōmetria* (from *geōmetrein*, to measure (*metrein*) land—cf *meter* at MEASURE), L *geometria*, whence—perh via OF-MF *geometrie* (later *géo-*), the E *geometrý*.

**georgette** is elliptical for *crêpe Georgette*, from a celebrated F modiste, Madame *Georgette* de la Plante.

**Georgian** is the E adj both of *George* and of the Russian and the American *Georgia*, the latter from King George II of England, the former being, in Ru, *Grusia*; the L adj *georgicus* (Gr *geōrgikos*) occurs in Virgil's *Georgics* or (*carmina*) *georgica*, songs of husbandry. The PN *George* comes, via OF *George* (F *Georges*), from LL *Georgius*, trln of Gr *Geōrgios*, from *geōrgos*, husbandman; *gē*, land (cf GEOGRAPHY, s.f.)+*ergon*, labour (cf ERG).

**geranium.** See CRANE, s.f.

**gerent.** See GERUND, para 2.

**gerfalcon.** See GAR, para 3.

**germ.** See GENERAL, para 18.

**German, Germanic, Germany; germanium.**

The Chem element (*-ium*) *germanium* derives from L *Germānia* (whence *Germany*), which, like L *Germānicus* (whence *Germanic*), derives from L *Germānus*, a German, b/f from *Germāni*, orig the great invading tribes in C3 B.C., hence all Teutons. Perh the name is of C origin: ? 'The Noisy Men', from C *\*gar*, to shout. But Holder derives L *Germāni* from *\*Geramani*, *\*Geramanniz*, 'The Greedy Men': OHG *gër*, greedy (IE r, *\*gher-*) +OHG *man*. The 'Spear Men' theory (OHG *gēr*, cf OE *gār*, a spear) is obs.

**german.** See GENERAL, para 19.

**germander.** See HOMO, para 4, s.f.

**germane.** See GENERAL, para 19.

**germanium.** See GERMAN.

**germen.** See GENERAL, para 18.

**germinal, germinate, germination.** See GENERAL, para 18.

**gerrymander** recalls Elbridge *Gerry*, governor of Massachusetts, who so redistributed the electoral districts that a certain district accidentally acquired a dragonish outline; a famous painter compared this outline to a sala*mander* and thus, in 1812, elicited from the editor of *The Centinel* the punning alteration *Gerrymander*, whence the Am n and v for the manipulation of electoral districts. (Thus John Fiske, cited by Webster; so too DAE and Mathews.)

**gerund** (whence adj **gerundial**), **gerundive; gerent,** esp **vice-gerent; gest, geste—jest** (n, hence v— whence **jester**); **gestate, gestation, gestatory; gesticulate, gesticulation, gesticulator, gesticulatory; gesture,** n, whence v (whence **gesturer**) and the adj **gestural;**—**congeries**—cf **congest, congestion, congestive; digest** (n and v), **digester, digestible, digestion, digestive—** cf **indigestible, indigestion, indigestive; egest, egestion, egestive; ingest, ingestible, ingestion, ingestive; register** (n and v), **registrant, registrar, registration, registry; suggest, suggestible,**

**suggestion, suggestive.**—Cf the sep EXAGGERATE and perh CAST.

1. The base of all these words is L *gerere* (s *ger-*), to bear or carry, to take on oneself, take charge of, to perform or accomplish: o.o.o.: perh akin to CAST.

2. The LL derivative *gerundium* becomes E *gerund*; LL *gerundīuus*, ML *-īvus*, becomes *gerundive*. The presp *gerens*, o/s *gerent-*, yields the obs adj, whence the n, *gerent*, esp in *vice-gerent*, from ML *vicegerens*, o/s *-gerent*; derivative ML *vicegerentia* yields *vicegerency*.

3. *Gerere* has pp *gestus* (s *gest-*), neupl *gesta* (things performed, deeds, exploits), which, apprehended as f sing, yields OF-(archaic)F *geste*, exploit, hence a tale of exploits, adopted by ME, with E var *gest* (obsol).

4. ME *geste*, deed, exploit, tale, has var *jeste*, which becomes E *jest*, duly specialized to 'humorous or witty tale, a joke', whence 'to *jest*', whence *jester*, perh slightly reminiscent of L *gestor*.

5. *Gerere*, pp *gestus*, has freq *gestāre* (s *gest-*), soon becoming virtually syn with its source. The pp *gestātus* (s *gestāt-*) yields 'to *gestate*'; derivative L *gestātiō*, o/s *gestātiōn-*, yields *gestation*, a bearing, esp of child in womb; the similarly derivative L *gestātōrius* yields *gestatory*.

6. On the pps *gest-* arises another v: *gestīre*, to make *gestus* or gestures; *gestīre* is supplanted by *gesticulāri*, with presp *gesticulans*, o/s *gesticulant-*, whence the E adj *gesticulant*, and with pp *gesticulātus*, whence 'to *gesticulate*'; derivative *gesticulātiō*, o/s *gesticulātiōn-*, becomes MF-F and E *gesticulation*; likewise derivative *gesticulātor* is adopted by E; *gesticulatory* is an anl E formation.

7. Pps *gest-* occurs yet again in ML *gestūra*, way of carrying, mode of action; whence E *gesture*.

### Prefix-Compounds

8. The s and r *ger-* appears in the n *congeriēs*, a carrying *con-* or together, a collection, adopted by E esp for an indiscriminate collection or aggregation.

9. L *congeriēs* derives imm from *congerere*, to carry, hence to bring, together. The pp *congestus* yields 'to *congest*'; derivative *congestiō*, o/s *congestiōn-*, leads to E—perh via MF-F—*congestion*; *congestive* is an anl E formation.

10. L *dīgerere*, to bring apart (*di-* for *dis*), to separate, arrange, hence to digest, has pp *dīgestus*, whence directly 'to *digest*' and, from the neu *dīgestum* (pl *dīgesta*), used as n, the n *digest*; as derivative LL *dīgestībilis* yields *digestible*, so derivative LL *dīgestīuus*, ML *-īvus*, yields *digestive* (cf the MF-F *digestif*); *digestion* represents *dīgestiōn-*, o/s of *dīgestiō-*, from pp *dīgestus*.

11. Cf *indigestible*, from LL *indigestībilis* (*in-*, not); *indigestion*, via MF-F, from LL *indigestiō*, o/s *indigestiōn-*; and the anl E formation *indigestive*.

12. Complementaries are L *ēgerere*, to carry *ē*, out, to discharge, and *ingerere*, to bring in, esp for digestion: pp *ēgestus* becomes 'to *egest*', pp

*ingestus* becomes 'to *ingest*'; as L *ēgestiō*, o/s *ēgestiōn*-, becomes *egestion*, so LL *ingestiō*, o/s *ingestiōn*-, becomes *ingestion*; *egistible*, *ingestible*, and *egestive*, *ingestive* are anl E formations.

13. *Regerere*, to carry back (*re*-), esp to a list or a book, hence to record or register, has pp *regestus*, whence the neupl *regesta*, used in LL for a list, a register, whence ML *regestum*, a list or register, altered to *regestrum*, var *registrum*, whence MF-F, hence ME, *registre*, whence E *register*; 'to *register*' comes from MF-EF *registrer*, from ML *registrāre*, var *regestrāre*, from the ML n. The ML v has presp *registrans*, o/s *registrant*-, whence MF *registrant*, whence the E n *registrant*; the pp *registrātus* accounts for the rare 'to *registrate*'; derivative ML *registrātiō*, o/s *registrātiōn*-, leads to *registration*; derivative ML *registrārius*, an official recorder, becomes *registrary*, now only in the University of Cambridge, the predominant term being *registrar*, influenced by the ML agent but deriving from EE *registrer*, itself from MF-EF *registreur*, from MF-EF *registrer*. Either by contr from late ME-EE *registery* or from 'to *register*'+ -*ry*, comes *registry*.

14. L *suggerere*, to carry, hence bring, hence put, underneath (*sug*- for *sub*-, under), hence to furnish and finally, to suggest, has pp *suggestus*, whence 'to *suggest*', whence, anl, both *suggestible* and *suggestive*; derivative *suggestiō*, o/s *suggestiōn*-, becomes, prob via OF-F, the E *suggestion*, whence Psychi *suggestionism* and *suggestionize*.

**gesso.** See GYPSUM.

**gest, geste.** See GERUND, para 3.

**gestate, gestation, gestatory.** See GERUND, para 5.

**gesticulant, gesticulate, gesticulation, gesticulator.** See GERUND, para 6.

**gesture, n and v.** See GERUND, para 7.

**get,** pt **got,** pp **gotten** (obs, except in AE and in al¹ cpds); **beget** and **misbeget,** pp **misbegotten; forget,** pp **forgotten;** cognate GUESS, v hence n.— Cf the sep *-prehend* of APPREHEND, COMPREHEND, REPREHEND, and, f.a.e., PREHENSILE.

1. 'To *get*' derives from ME *geten* from ON *geta*, akin to OE *-gietan*, *-gitan*, OS bi*getan*, OHG bi*gezzan*, Go bi*gitan*, to find, OB *gad*ati, to guess, OIr *gataim*, I take or steal, L prae*hend*ere, to grasp or seize, *praed*a, booty, Gr *khand*anein, to hold: IE r, prob *\*ghed*- or, with *-n-* infix, *\*ghend-*, to hold or grasp. (Hofmann; Walshe.)

2. 'To *beget*' derives, via ME bi*geten*, bi*giten*, to beget, (orig) to get, from OE be*gitan*, to get (*be*-+ -*gitan*): 'to *beget*' is to get additionally or on the side, there being a collaborator. 'To *misbeget*' is modern: *mis*-, wrongly+'to *get*'.

3. 'To *forget*' derives, via ME for*geten*, for*yeten*, from OE for*gitan*, for*gietan* (*for*-, connoting omission or failure+*-gitan*): cf OHG fir*gezzan*, MHG ver*gezzen*, G ver*gessen*, and OS far*getan*.— The flower *forget-me-not* was prompted, not by G *Vergissmeinnicht* but by its original, the MF *ne m'oublie mie* and *ne m'oubliez mie* (F *ne m'oubliez pas*).

**geyser.** See the 2nd FOUND, para 17.

**ghastly.** See GHOST.

**ghebir.** See KAFFIR, para 2.

**gherkin** is aphetic for D *agurkje* (as if *\*agurkkin* or *-kjin*), dim of *agurk*, var of *augurk*, cucumber, from Polish *ogórek* (gen *ogórka*), *ogúrek*, from MGr *angourion* (ἀγγούριον), *angouron* (ἀγγουρον) watermelon, from Iranian *angôrah*. (Walshe.)

**ghetto,** adopted from It, derives from Venetian *ghèto* or *gèto* (It *gètto*), in C14 a foundry: in 1516, the Jews of the city of Venice were expelled to a Venetian islet named *Ghèto* or *Gèto*, from a foundry situated there, and all other ghettos took their name from this Venetian ghetto: prob from ML *\*jectus*, for ML *\*jactus* (L *iactus*), a casting or founding, from *iacere*, to throw or cast. (Prati.)

**ghost** (n hence v), **ghostly**—**ghastly.**

1. The third derives from ME *gastli*, earlier *gastlich*, from ME *gasten*, to terrify, from OE *gāestan*, from *gāst*; *gastlich* has var *gostlich*, whence *ghostly*. ME *gastlich* derives from OE *gāstlīc*, ghost-like, where 'ghost'=spirit, soul, breath, the breath of God, OE *gāst*. OE *gāst*, which becomes ME *gast*, var *gost*, whence *ghost* ('spelling with *gh*- due to Caxton's Flemish compositors—cf OFlem *gheest*': Walshe), is akin to OFris *gāst*, OS *gēst*, OHG-G *geist*, spirit, ghost; with OE *gāestan*, to alarm, cf the syn Go us-*gais*jan. The Gmc r is prob *\*gais*-, the IE prob *\*ghais*-, with var *\*ghois*-: cf Skt *hêḍas* (for *\*hêzdas*), anger, as Walshe does.

2. *Aghast* derives from ME *agast*, *agasted*, pp of *agasten*, to alarm, to terrify, where *a*-, OE *ā*-, is an int.

**ghoul** (whence **ghoulish**) is Ar *ghūl*, a grave-robbing, corpse-eating spirit: from *ghāla*, to seize.

**giant,** whence **giantess** and **giantism; gigantic.**

*Giant*, ME *geant*, represents ONF *gaiant* (OF *jaiant*): VL *\*gagantem*, acc of *\*gagas*, alteration of LL *gigas*, L *Gigas*, a Myth character (gen *Gigantis*): Gr *gigas* (rare), *Gigas* (gen *Gigantos*): o.o.o.; perh a redup (*gi-ga*-) of a simple *\*ga*-, large (creature). Whereas *gigantesque* is adopted from EF-F, from It *gigantesco* (from *gigante*, from the L o/s *gigant*-), *gigantic*=that o/s+*-ic*; hence *gigantism*.

**giaour.** See KAFFIR, para 2.

**gib** (1). See GIBBET.

**gib** (2), **Gib,** a male cat, derives from *Gilbert* (OF *Guillebert*, of Gmc origin—cf OHG *Willibert*, Bright Will); cf OHG *Giselberht*, OF *Gilebert*, whence the F *G*-. App from *Gib*, pet-form of *Gilbert*, is the surname *Gibbon*, whence possibly (Skeat) the ape *gibbon;* the ape's name, however, is adopted from F, where it is prob a distortion of Hind *bojīnā*, from Per *bōzīna*, monkey, as Webster suggests.

**gibber,** to speak with rapid unintelligibility, has derivative **gibberish** (*-ish*, n, connoting speech or language) and an origin that, like **jabber,** is echoic.

**gibbet,** a gallows, whence the v, derives from ME, from OF-F, *gibet*, dim of *gibe*, a staff, perh from

Frankish *gib- or *gibb-, forked stick: cf E dial gib, a notched or hooked stick, whence perh the tech gib, a notched or tapered removable plate in a machine. Prob from E gibbet comes E jib, a crane's projecting arm.

**gibbon.** See the 2nd GIB.

**gibbosity, gibbous.**

The former comes from MF-F gibbosité, an erudite -ité (E -ity) derivative from LL gibbōsus, hunch-backed, whence MF-F gibbeux, f gibbeuse, whence E gibbous; gibbōsus derives from L gibbus, var gibber, a hump, both forms being also adjj. L gibber, gibbus, are expressive words, with s gibb- and r gib-: cf Lett gibbis, hunch-backed, gibt, to be curved; perh cf Gr kuphos (κῦφος), hump, and kuphos (κῡφός), bent forward; IE r, perh *kub-, var *kup-, to curve or bend. (E & M; Hofmann.)

**gibe** (1) or **jibe**, v hence n, sneer, scoff, is o.o.o.: but cf D gijbelen, to giggle, to sneer, app the freq of a v *gijben.

**gibe** (2), to agree. See JIBE.

**giblets**, a fowl's edible viscera, is the pl of giblet: ME gibelet: OF-MF gibelet, a dish of birds' flesh, an eased form of *giberet, dim of OF-F gibier, the chase (esp for birds), var of gibiez, from Frankish *gabaiti, cf MHG geneize, a hunting with falcons. (B & W.)

**gid**, a sheep's disease; **giddy.** See GOD, para 7.

**gift.** See GIVE, para 2.

**gig**, a whirling top, prob therefore—from its lightness and manoeuvrability—the light, two-wheeled, one-horsed carriage: echoic: cf Da gig, a whirligig (top). Whirligig=a whirly, or whirling, gig or top.

**gigantic, gigantism.** See GIANT, s.f.

**giggle**, v hence n, is prob a thinning of gaggle and therefore prob akin to CACKLE.

**gigolo.** See JIG, para 3.

**gilbert**, in El, derives from Wm Gilbert (cf the 2nd GIB), that E physician and physicist (1540–1603) who, in 1600, published De Magnete, a great work.

**gild** (1), n. See guild at YIELD, para 3.

**gild** (2), to gilt. See GOLD, para 6.

**gild** (3), to pay taxes. See YIELD.

**gill** (1), fish's: ME gile: cf ON gjölnar, gills, and Sw gel or gäl, jaw; more remotely cf Gr kheilos, lip, and khelanē, lip, jaw: IE etymon, perh *ghelnos, r *ghel-. (Hofmann.)

**gill** (2), liquid measure: OF-MF gille, var gelle, a wine-measure: LL gillō, gellō, a water-pot, a large earthen vessel esp for wine, ML var gellus: perh cf Macedonian Gr gullas, a cup, and H gulla, a round (earthen) vessel.

**gill** (3), Gill, Gillian. See JILL.

**gillie** or **gilly**; **galoot.**

1. Gillie derives from Ga gille (var gillu), itself from EIr gilla (Ir giolla), all meaning boy or lad, and manservant esp if young.

2. Perh akin to these C words is galoot, varr galloot and early geloot, orig sl for a soldier (–1812), then in the Navy for an inexperienced marine (–1835). The form geloot, however, perh

indicates a D origin: ? gelubt, eunuch, or (EW) a corruption of genoot, companion.

**gillyflower**: ME gilofre, clove: by metathesis from syn OF-F girofle: L caryophyllon: Gr karuophullon, clove-tree: karuo-, c/f of karuon, nut (cf CAREEN)+phullon, leaf. Sem cf EF-F giraflée, gillyflower, because it smells like cloves.

**gilt**, adj and n. See GOLD, heading.

**gimbal** is a mdfn (? after cymbal) of **gimmal**, n, which is a doublet of the adj gemel, twin, coupled, adopted from OF-MF (cf the OF jumel, MF-F jumeau), from L gemellus (s gemel-), twin, a dim of geminus (f.a.e., GEMINI). E gemel is used also as n, as in gemel hinge, but esp in pl, as in Her bars gemels, and as (obs) gemels, twins or pairs.

2. From gimbal, a pair—hence a series—of interlocking rings, and from gimbals, 'a contrivance for permitting a body to incline freely . . . or for suspending anything, as a barometer, ship's compass, etc., so that it will remain plumb' (Webster),—from these, either or both, prob comes AE (orig sl) gimmick, a secret, or a clever, device, app either influenced by gimcrack (Webster) or blended with trick.

**gimcrack** (n hence adj), a fanciful scheme (obs), a contrivance (obsol), a showy ornament, app cpds the now dial gim, spruce, neat+Sc and dial crack, showy or boastful lad (cf CRACK, n); gim prob eases the Sc (and dial) jimp, spruce, slender, itself o.o.o. EW, however, starts from earlier form jimcrack and ingeniously proposes an alteration '(after name Jim) from ME gibecrake, inlaid woodwork'.

**gimlet**: EF gimbelet: MF guimbelet, with F dim -et for D dim -kin: MF wimbelquin (F vilebrequin) or wimbelkin: MD wimmelkijn, dim of wimmel, an auger; from the MD var wimpel comes, through ONF, the ME-E wimble, gimlet, auger.

**gimmal.** See GIMBAL, para 1.

**gimmick.** See GIMBAL, para 2.

**gimp.** See WIMPLE, para 2.

**gin** (1), drink. See ADDENDA TO DICTIONARY.

**gin** (2), trap. See ENGINE, para 1; cf GENERAL, para 23, s.f.

**gin** (3), native woman, is an Aus aboriginal word.

**ginger; gingerbread.**

The latter is f/e for gingebras, mdfn of gingembras, from ML gingiber, from LL zingiberi, from Gr zingiberis (ζιγγίβερις), akin to—perh (Hofmann) ult from—the Pali shape (siṅgivera-) of Skt śṛṅgavera, itself perh from a Dravidian source. L gingiber is adopted by OE, to become E ginger, with intervention, in ME, from OF gimgibre, gengibre, MF-F gingembre. (See esp Alan S. C. Ross's masterly monograph, Ginger, 1952.)

**gingerly** probably comes from OF genchor or gençor, the comp of gent, well-born, gracious, handsome, from L genitus, born, esp well-born: f.a.e., GENERAL.

**gingham**: F guingan: Mal giṅgaṅ, striped, hence a striped fabric.

**gingival; gingivitis.**
*Gingival* tacks adj *-al* to ML *gingīva*, L *gingīua*, usu in pl *gingīuae*, the gums: o.o.o. *Gingivitis* tacks *-itis*, connoting disease, to ML *gingīva*.

**gip,** to cheat. See EGYPT, para 4.

**Gipsy.** See EGYPT, para 3.

**giraffe:** EF *giraffa* (F *girafe*), adopted from It *giraffa* (cf Sp *azorafa*, *a-*=Ar *al*, the): Ar *zirāfah*, var *zarāfah*.

**girandole; girasol(e).** See GYRATE, para 3.

**gird** (1), pt and pp **girded:** to strike, to sneer at (also vi): ME *girden*: identical with the next entry: app 'first used of striking with a belt or whip, the lash circling round the one struck' (Webster).

**gird** (2), to encircle, esp with a belt, pt *girded* (or *girt*), pp *girt*: ME *girden* (*gerden*, etc.): OE *gyrdan*: akin to OFris *gerda*, OS *gurdian*, OHG *gurtēn*, G *gürten*, Go bi*gairdan*, ON *gyrtha*: perh ult cf YARD. Hence the structural *girder*.

2. Intimately akin to—indeed, prob from—OE *gyrdan*, s *gyrd-*, is OE *gyrdel*: cf OFris *gerdel*, OHG *gurtil*, MHG-G *gürtel*, and ON *gyrthill*. The Hit *gir*, a girdle, suggests that OGmc *gerd-*, *gird-*, *gurd-*, perh represents a Gmc int *-d* extn of IE *\*ger-, gir-, gīr-, gur-* (cf Gr *guros*), a circle, a ring.

3. *Girth*, orig a broad belt or strap, derives from ON *girthi, gerthi*, var *gjörth* (cf *gyrtha*, to encircle, gird): cf Go *gairda*, a girdle. *Girth* has an easement *girt*, esp in structural tech senses.

**girder** (structural). See prec, para 1, s.f.

**girdle.** See the 2nd GIRD, para 2.

**girl,** whence **girlish,** derives from ME *girle*, varr *gerle, gurle*: o.o.o.: perh of C origin: cf Ga and Ir *caile*, EIr *cale*, a girl; with Anglo-Ir *girleen* (dim *-een*), a (young) girl, cf Ga-Ir *cailin* (dim *-in*), a girl. But far more prob, *girl* is of Gmc origin: Whitehall postulates the OE etymon *\*gyrela* or *\*gyrele* and adduces Southern E dial *girls*, primrose blossoms, and *grlopp*, a lout, and tentatively LG *goere*, a young pierson (either sex). Ult, perh, related to L *puer*, *puella*, with basic idea '(young) growing thing'.

**gist.** See JOIST.

**gitano.** See EGYPT, para 5.

**gittern.** See ZITHER.

**give,** pt **gave,** pp **given; gift,** n hence v, whence pa **gifted; forgive, forgiveness; gavel** (tribute), **gaveler, gavelkind.**

1. 'To *give*', ME *given*, is a N form of OE *gifan, giefan*; there has, in the ME period, been influence by ON *gefa*, to give. Akin are OFris *jeva*, OS *gebhan*, OHG *geban*, OHG-G *geben*, Go *giban*, MD-D *geven*: cf also OIr *gabim*, I take ('the same action regarded from the opposite point of view': Walshe). The C r *\*gab-*, to take, to receive, is akin to L *hab-*, as in *habēre*, to hold, to possess.

2. The n *gift*, ME *gift*, derives from ON *gift*, akin to OE *gift* (cf *give* above), OHG *gift* (preserved in *Mitgift*), OS *gift*, OFris *jeft, jefte*, Go *gifts* (in cpds).

3. OE *giefan, gifan*, has cpd *forgiefan, -gifan*, ME *foryiven*, later *forgiven*, whence 'to *forgive*';

and OE *forgifan* has derivative n *forgifnes*, whence *forgiveness*.

4. Akin to OE *giefan, gifan*, is OE *gafol*, whence ME *gavel*, tribute, periodical fee (esp as rent), whence *gavel(l)er*, usurer (obs), a miner's licence (or *gale*, from ME *gavel*). ME *gavel* has cpd *gavelkynde*, E *gavelkind*, formerly a kind of landtenure.

**gizzard** derives, with *-ard* substituted for *-er*, from ME *giser*: OF *giser* (later *gisier*, F *gésier*): VL *gigērium*: by b/f from L *gigēria*, poultrycntrails offered as sacrifice, (later) gizzard: perh of Iranian origin; perh also akin to L *iecur*, liver. (B & W; E & M.)

**glabrous,** See GLAD, para 2.

**glace, glacial, glaciate (glaciation), glacier, glacis.**

1. L *glaciēs* (s *glaci-*, r *glac-*), ice, the base of this group, is akin to L *gelū*, a freezing, hence cold (n): f.a.e., COLD.

2. *Glaciēs* has relevant derivatives:

L *glaciālis*, icy, whence MF-F, whence E, *glacial*;

LL *glaciāre*, to freeze, with pp *glaciātus*, whence 'to *glaciate*', whence, anl, *glaciation*; *glaciāre* becomes OF-F *glacer*, to freeze, pp *glacé*, frozen, hence smooth as ice; also from *glacier, glacer*, comes MF-F *glacis*, sloping ground;

VL *\*glacia*, ice, whence VL *\*glaciārium*, whence F, thence E, *glacier*.

**glad, gladly; gladden; gladness.—glade; Everglades.—glabrous.**

1. The adj *glad*, whence 'to *gladden*' (*-en*, v suffix), derives from OE *glaed*, shining, bright, (hence) joyous, glad, whence both OE *glaedlīce*, E *gladly*, and OE *glaedness*, E *gladness*: and OE *glaed* is akin to OS *glad*, OFris *gled*, OHG-MHG *glat*, shining, bright, smooth, G *glatt*, smooth, MD-D *glad, glat*, smooth, ON *glathr*, bright, glad; cf also OB *gladūkū*, Lith *glodùs*, smooth, and L *glaber*, (of face) hairless, hence smooth: perh ult akin to GLASS; cf GLIDE.

2. L *glaber* (whence EF-F *glabre*) has LL mdfns *glabrus* and *glabrōsus*, the latter prob originating the E *glabrous*, smooth, (of surface) hairless.

3. *Glad*, shining, bright, seems to have originated *glade*, an open—hence, sunny—space in a wood. Hence the A *everglade*, lit 'always, i.e. interminably, (a) glade', a low-lying, swampy region, esp in the Floridan *Everglades*.

**gladiator** (whence **gladiatorial:** cf LL *gladiātoricius*), adopted from L, derives from L *gladius*, a sword, with dim *gladiolus* (pl *gladioli*), little sword, hence the flower *gladiolus* or *sword lily* (cf the G *Schwertlilie*), so named from its swordshaped leaves. L *gladius*, s *gladi-*, r *glad-*, is prob of C origin.

**gladiolus.** See prec.

**gladly, gladness.** See GLAD, para 1.

**Gladstone bag.** This sort of travelling bag was named in honour of W. E. Gladstone (1809–98), who, with Benjamin Disraeli (1804–81), dominated British political life for a generation. Cf the adj, hence n, *Gladstonian*.

**glair,** white of egg, hence a bookbinding paste, with adjj *glaireous* (cf the MF-F *glaireux*) and *glairy,* derives, perh via OF-F *glaire,* from VL *\*clāria,* from L *clārus,* bright, clear: cf CLEAR.

**glamor** (AE), **glamour;** whence adj **glamorous** and v **glamorize.**

*Glamo(u)r* was vogue'd by Scott for 'magic, a magical charm': on the basis of *grammar* in the sense usu attached to obsol *gram(m)arye*: 'magic, occult science', powers often, in medieval times, attributed to the learned.

**glance,** n, derives from 'to *glance*', orig to glide harmlessly from the object struck: app from OF-MF *glacier,* to slip or slide (prop, to freeze), from L *glaciāre,* to freeze: f.a.e., GLACÉ. There has app been a double intervention: prob by E GLINT (v, hence n) and perh by MHG *glanst,* brilliance, or MHG *glanz,* splendour, cf OHG *glanz,* brilliant, shining.

**gland; glanders; glandular; glandule.**

*Glandular* is the adj, both of *gland* (*-ular*) and of *glandule*(*-ar*), the latter from L *glandula,* dim of *glans* (o/s *gland-*), an acorn, hence any object shaped like an acorn. *Glanders* derives from MF *glandres,* from L *glandulae,* pl of *glandula*. *Gland,* an acorn (obs), whence the Bot and Aer senses, is adopted from OF-F, from L *glandem,* acc of *glans;* but the Med *gland* comes from EF-F *glande,* refashioned from MF *glandre,* from L *glandulae*. L *glans* (f) has r *glan-:* cf the *balan-* (contr to *\*blan-*) of Gr *balanos:* IE r, perh *\*glen-,* var *\*guelen-* or *\*gelen-,* as the Arm, Lith, OSl cognates suggest.

**glare** (v, hence n, whence adj **glary;** pa **glaring**), to shine dazzlingly, hence to look brightly and angrily (*at* someone): ME *glaren:* akin to, perh from, MD (and MLG) *glaren,* to glow, OE *glaeren,* glassy, ON *gler,* glass. Cf *glaze,* q.v. at:

**glass** (n, hence v; hence also the adj **glassy**); **glaze** (v hence n, whence adj **glazy**), **glazier;** cf the sep GLARE and, more remotely, GLOW and LURID.

ME *glasier,* whence *glazier,* derives, as also does ME *glasen,* whence 'to *glaze*', from ME *glas,* glass, whence obviously *glass:* and ME *glas,* var *gles,* derives from OE *glaes,* akin to OHG-MHG *glas,* amber, glass, G *Glas,* glass, OFris *gles,* glass, but also to OE *glaer,* amber, OE *glāēre,* resin, ON *gler,* glass—cf GLARE; cf also L *glaesum, glēsum,* amber, of Gmc origin; doubtfully cf L *lūridus,* q.v. at LURID; less doubtfully GLAD and GLIDE.

**glaucous,** now usu yellowish-green, orig greenish-blue: L *glaucus:* Gr *glaukos* (? for *\*gelaukos*), adj, bluish-green: ult from IE r *\*gel-,* to shine brightly.

**glaze, glazier.** See GLASS.

**gleam** (n, hence v); **glim; glimmer** (v hence n); **glimpse** (v hence n);—**glisten; glister; glitter** (v hence n);—**glee.**

1. *Gleam,* whence the adj **gleamy,** comes, through ME *gleam, glem,* from OE *glǣm,* akin to OS *glīmo,* brightness, and OHG *glīmo, gleimo,* the gleamer, i.e. a glowworm.

2. Dial and sl *glim,* n, is app short for *glimmer,* n, from 'to *glimmer*', from MHG *glimmern*—cf MHG-G *glimmen,* to gleam, to glow, and therefore OFris and ON *glīa,* to glow, to shine.

3. MHG *glimsen,* app a freq of MHG *glimmen,* becomes EE *glimse,* whence—? influenced by 'peep' and 'appear'—'to *glimpse*'.

4. Akin to those E vv is 'to *glisten*', ME *glistnen* (? with *t* from ME *gliteren*), var of *glisnen,* from OE *glisnian,* to shine, esp to glisten, akin to—perh a mdfn of—the syn OE *glisian,* therefore to OFris *glisia* and OHG *glīzzan,* MHG *glīzen,* G *gleissen,* to gleam.

5. Akin to ME *glistnen* is ME *glistren,* whence 'to *glister*' ('All that *glisters* is not gold'): app *glistren* is a blend of *glistnen* and *gliteren*.

6. ME *gliteren,* whence 'to *glitter*', derives from ON *glitra,* akin to OE *glitenian,* OS *glītan,* Go *glit*manjan, to shine, to gleam; also to OHG *glīzzan* (cf para 4). With both *glisten* and *glitter,* cf MHG-G *glitzern,* to glitter, freq of *glitzen,* to sparkle, itself an int of MHG *glīzen,* G *gleissen,* to gleam.

7. Akin to ON and OFris *glīa,* to shine, to glow (cf para 2), is ON *glȳ,* glee, itself intimately akin to OE *glēo,* ME *gleo,* later *gle,* E *glee:* cf also OIr *glē,* shining, bright, clear, and *glēse,* a gleam, and perh OB *ględati,* to look.

8. The IE r is prob *\*ghlei-,* to shine, with extn *\*ghleid-,* itself with varr *\*ghleim-, \*ghleis-, \*ghleit-,* with such elaborations as *\*ghleimps-* and *\*ghleist-*. For a notable cognate, cf Gr *klidē,* flashily luxurious living, hence arrogance. Ult, the word is expressive, esp pictorial.

**glean,** whence **gleaner,** derives from ME *glenen:* MF *glener* (EF-F *glaner*—cf OProv *glenar*): LL *glenāre* or *glennāre,* to gather the grain left by a reaper, hence fig: of Gaul origin—cf OIr do*glinn,* he gathers, dí*ghlaim,* I gather, Ga dío*ghlum,* gleanings. The C r is *\*glen(n)-,* to gather.

**glebe,** with adjj **glebal** (LL *glēbālis*), **glebous** (L *glēbōsus*), **gleby** (*glebe*+*-y*): L *glēba* (or *glaeba*), a small or smallish round mass, esp a clod of earth, hence soil, land: akin to CLIP, to embrace —cf Lith *glebiu,* I embrace. The important element is *gl-:* cf that of L *glomus* (cf GLOMERATE), app with var *\*glemus,* any small, close-packed object (e.g., ball, skein)—that of L *globus,* ball, sphere—and that of L *glūten* (cf GLUE), as E & M have shown.

**glee.** See GLEAM, para 7.

**gleet,** Med for a morbid discharge, comes, through ME *glet, glette,* from OF-MF *glete, glette,* clay, earthy slime, pus, mucus, from ML *glitem,* acc of *glis* (o/s *glit-;* r *gli-*), clay, perh from Gr *glia* (r *gli-*), glue: akin to GLUE.

**glen,** a narrow (and secluded) valley: C: cf EIr *glenn, glend,* Ir and Ga *gleann,* Cor *glen, glyn;* OC *\*glennos*.

**glib** (whence **glibness**), smooth or slippery, hence very, esp too, ready and fluent of speech: Gmc: cf D *glibberig* (r *glib-*), slippery, hence glib, and *glibberen* (r *glib-*), to slide. The r *glib-* is app a mutation from MD *glid-,* as in MD *gliden,* D *glijden,* to glide: cf next.

**glide** (v, hence n and the agent **glider**) descends from OE *glīdan*, akin to OFris *glīda*, MHG *glīten*, G *gleiten*, MD *gliden*, D *glijden*: cf OHG-MHG *glat*, G *glatt*, smooth, shining, and OE *glaed*, shining, joyous: therefore cf GLAD and perh GLASS.

**glim; glimmer.** See GLEAM, para 2.

**glimpse.** See GLEAM, para 3.

**glint** (v, hence n): ME *glenten*, to glance (turn aside), to gleam: of Gmc origin: cf Sw dial *glinta*, to slide, ON *glan*, brilliance, MHG *glanst*, brilliance, OHG *glanz* (adj), shining, MHG-G *glanz* (n), splendour.

**glisten.** See GLEAM, para 4.

**glister.** See GLEAM, para 5.

**glitter.** See GLEAM, para 6.

**gloaming** (with b/f n and v **gloam**): OE *glōmung*, from OE *glōm*, dusk: cf GLOSS and GLOW.

**gloat** (v, hence n) derives from ON *glotta*, to smile derisively or scornfully: cf MHG-G *glotzen*, to stare, to gloat; perh cf OB *ględeti*, to look. (Walshe.)

**globe**, whence **global**; **globate**; **globose**; **globule**, whence **globular** and **globulin** (Chem *-in*).

*Globule*, adopted from EF-F, comes from L *globulus*, dim of *globus*, ball, sphere, globe: f.a.e., GLEBE, s.f. *Globus* has adj *globōsus*, whence E *globose*, and derivative *globāre*, to make a ball of, pp *globātus*, whence E *globate*.

**glomerate, glomeration.** See CLAM.

**gloom**, v, hence n, whence **gloomy**; **glower**, v, hence n; **glum.**

1. 'To *gloom*' derives from ME *gloumen*, akin to MD *gloemen*, *glomen*, (vi, vt) to obscure, and MD *gloem*, *gloom*, cloudy, hazy, MLG *glomen*, to render turbid; cf para 3.

2. Akin to MD *gloemen*, *glomen*, are D *gluren*, MLG *glüren*, to leer, and EFris *gluren*, to look sharply at: from this implied Gmc source app comes 'to *glower*'.

3. ME *gloumen* has var *glomen*, to look sullen: whence the E adj *glum*.

**Gloria.** See GLORY, para 1.

**glorify; glorious.** See paras 2, 3 of:

**glory, glorious, glorify, glorification; Gloria,** whence elaboration **Gloriana.**

1. *Gloria*, PN, merely personifies L *glōria* (s *glōri-*, r *glōr-*), renown, fame, esp if good: o.o.o.: ? for *\*gnōria* (s *\*gnōri-*, r *\*gnōr-*), a being known —cf *ignore*, not to know.

2. L *glōria* becomes OF-MF, whence ME, *glorie*, whence E *glory*. (Cf the F *gloire*.) Its adj is *glōriōsus*, whence OF-MF *glorious* (var *glorios*), adopted by E; cf the F *glorieux*.

3. L *glōria* has LL cpd *glōrificus*, glory-making, glorious, whence LL *glōrificāre*, to render glorious, whence OF-F *glorifier*, whence 'to *glorify*'; cf the element *-fic*, L *-ficus*, c/f of *facere*, to make, to render.

**gloss** (1), lustre (n, hence v), whence the adj **glossy**: Gmc: cf MHG *glosen*, to glow, and Ice *glossi*, a blaze: perh an int of the OGmc r of GLOW.

**gloss** (2), interpretation, hence v: ME, from OF-F, *glose*: L *glóssa*, a hard word needing to be made clear: syn Gr *glóssa*, prop the tongue, hence language, Attic *glótta*: akin to Gr *glókhis* (s *glókh-*, r *glók-*), a (projecting) point, as is the tongue: orig an expressive, a pictorial word. The adjj are *glossal* and *glottal*.

2. L *glóssa* has derivative *glóssārium*, a store (connoted by *-ārium*) of words, hence E *glossary*. 'To *gloze*' derives from ME *glosen*, to explain, from OF-F *gloser*, from OF-F *glose*.

3. Attic Gr *glótta* has derivative adj *glóttikos*, whence *glottic*, and derivative n *glóttis*, whence SciL-ScE *glottis*, with cpd *epiglottis* (adj *epiglottal*) —Gr *epiglóttis*.

**glossy.** See the 1st GLOSS.

**glottal, glottic, glottis.** See the 2nd GLOSS, esp para 3.

**glove** (whence **glover**): ME *glove*, earlier *glofe*: OE *glóf*, akin to ON *glófi*, glove—cf ON *lófi*, palm of the hand: f.a.e., LUFF.

**glow** (v, hence n)—whence **glow-worm**—derives from OE *glówan*, akin to OHG *gluoēn*, MHG *glüejen*, G *glühen*, MD *gloeyen*, *gloyen*, D *gloeien*, ON *glóa*, and to OFris and ON *glía*. Cf GLOAMING.

**glower**, to look scowlingly. See GLOOM, para 2.

**gloze**, n and v. See the 2nd GLOSS, para 2.

**glucose**, whence **glucoside** (Chem *-ide*); **glycerin** (or *-ine*).

*Glucose*, adopted from F, comes irreg from Gr *gleukos* (s *gleuk-*), must, sweet wine, akin to Gr *glukos* (s *gluk-*), sweet, which has mdfn *glukeros* (s *gluker-*, r *gluk-*), whence F *glycérine*, whence E *glycerine* (Chem *-ine*), with var *glycerin*. Gr *glukus* is prob for *\*dlukus*—cf L *dulcis*, q.v. at DULCET.

**glue**, n, v; hence adj **gluey**; **gluten, glutinous, glutinate, glutinative; agglutinate, agglutination, agglutinative**—cf **deglutinate, deglutination.**

1. 'To *glue*' comes from OF-MF *gluer*, itself from OF-F *glu*, whence the E n *glue*: and OF *glu* derives from LL *glūs* (s *glū-*), o/s *glūt-*; *glūs* derives from L *glūtis*, var of *glūten*, glue, adopted by E, with derivative sense 'the adhesive element in dough'. Now, the effective element of *glūten* is *\*gl-*, with varr *\*gle-*, *\*glo-*, *\*glu-*: cf GLEBE, s.f. Also cf CLAY.

2. *Glūten*, o/s *glūtin-*, has two derivatives relevant to E:

*glūtinōsus*, whence *glutinous*;

*glūtināre*, to glue, pp *glūtinātus*, whence 'to *glutinate*', whence *glutination*; on pp s *glūtināt-* is formed LL *glūtinātīuus*, ML *-īvus*, sticky, whence *glutinative*.

3. Two cpds of *glūtināre* concern E:

*agglūtināre*, to glue *ad*, to or against, with pp *agglūtinātus*, whence the adj and v *agglutinate*, whence *agglutination* and *agglutinative*;

*dēglūtināre*, to remove the glue *de* or from, to unstick, with pp *dēglūtinātus*, whence 'to *deglutinate*', whence *deglutination*.

**glum.** See GLOOM, para 3.

**glut** (v, hence n), to satiate: ME *glotten*, to satiate: MF-EF *glotir*, *gloutir*, to swallow, cf the

derivative MF *glotoier*, to eat greedily: L *glutīre*,
*gluttīre*, to swallow, s *glut-*. The ME *glotten* was
influenced by ME *glut*, a glutton, itself from OF
*glout, glot, glos*, gluttonous, a glutton, the noun
of OF *gloton, glutien, glouton* (extant), whence ME
*gloton, glutun*, whence E *glutton* (whence adj
*gluttonous*); derivative MF *gloutonnie, glotonie*,
lead, through ME *glotonie*, etc., to E *gluttony*.
OF-F *glouton*, OF *gloton, gluton*, represents L
*glutōn*em, *gluttōn*em, acc of *glut(t)ō*, a glutton,
with o/s *glut(t)ōn-*. L *glut(t)ō*, akin to L *gluttīre*,
to swallow, derives from L *gluttus*, throat, gullet,
itself akin to *gluttīre*.

**gluten; glutinate, glutinative, glutinous.** See
GLUE, para 2.

**glutton, gluttony.** See GLUT.

**glycerin(e).** See GLUCOSE. Cf the element *glyco-*.

**glyph, glyphic; glyptic.**

The Gr *gluphein* (s *gluph-*), to carve, has pp
*gluptos*, whence the adj *gluptikos*, concerned with
carving, whence F *glyptique*, whence E *glyptic*.
*Gluphein* has derivative n *gluphē*, a carving, whence
E *glyph*, a carved figure, a sculptural pictograph.
F.a.e., CLEAVE, to split.

**gnarled**, knotty, twisted, is a var of **knurled**, prop
the pp of 'to *knurl*', from *knurl*, a small excrescent
knot, dim of *knur*, (a tree's) hard, knotty excrescence, from ME *knorre*, of Gmc origin, with
cognates in D and G: cf MHG *knoche*, knot in a
tree. Of the various Gmc nn beginning with *kno-*,
Walshe has remarked that they all mean 'something hard, prominent & lumpy'.

**gnash**: ME *gnasten, gnaisten*, with *-h* for *-t-*,
prob anl with late ME-E CLASH: cf ON *gnīsta* (?
for *\*gnaista*), Fris *gnastern*, to gnash, and ON
*gnastan*, a gnashing: ult echoic.

**gnat; to nag** and to **gnatter or natter**.

1. *Gnat* (whence the *gnat-catcher* birds) comes
straight from OE *gnaet*, akin to OE *gnīdan*, to rub,
ON *gnit*, and LG *gnatte*, a gnat.

2. Akin to *gnat* is *gnaw* (pt *gnawed*, pp *gnawn*),
ME *gnawen*, OE *gnagan*: cf OHG *gnagan*, MHG
*gnagen*, MHG-G *nagen*, and ON *gnaga*, to gnaw:
ult echoic.

3. Akin to *gnaw*, esp in its *gnag-, nag-* forms,
is 'to *nag*', to gnaw (now dial), hence to irritate by
petty scolding and fault-finding: prob imm of
Scan origin.

4. Akin is dial *gnatter*, to talk much and idly,
to grumble persistently, now usu spelt *natter* (also
sl): clearly influenced by CHAT and its derivative
*chatter*.

**gnathal, gnathic, -gnathous**: adjj from Gr
*gnathos*, jaw, as is **gnathism**: f.a.e., the element
*-gnatha*.

**gnatter.** See GNAT, para 4.

**gnaw.** See GNAT, para 2.

**gneiss; ganister.**

The latter comes from G dial *ganster*, which,
like G *Gneiss* (whence E *gneiss*), varr *Gneis* and esp
*Gneist*, derives, because of its lustre, from MHG
*ganeiste*, a spark, itself from OHG *gneisto*, akin to
QN *gneisti* and OE *gnāst*.

**gnome** (1), a fabled tiny being, is adopted from
EF-F, which takes it from Paracelsus's C16 L
*gnomus*, perh from Gr *gnomē*, intelligence: gnomes
are reputedly intelligent (B & W). Therefore cf:

**gnome** (2), a maxim; **gnomic; gnomon, gnomonic;
gnosis, gnostic, Gnostic, Gnosticism; agnostic** (adj
hence n), **agnosticism; diagnose, diagnosis, diagnostic, diagnostician; prognosis, prognostic** (adj
and), **prognosticate, prognostication, prognosticator.**

1. Dissyllabic *gnome*, a maxim, is Gr *gnōmē*,
intelligence, hence an expressed example thereof.
*Gnōmē* has adj *gnōmikos*, whence, perh via LL
*gnōmicus*, the E *gnomic*.

2. The s *gnōm-* occurs also in Gr *gnōmōn*, a
knower, hence a sundial's index (knower of time)
and a carpenter's square; hence the erudite, Sci,
tech E *gnomon*. The Gr adj *gnōmonikos* becomes L
*gnōmonicus*, whence E *gnomonic*.

3. The s *gnōm-* has r *gnō-*, as in Gr *gnōsis*, knowledge, a seeking to know, a means of knowing:
hence erudite E *gnosis* and Med and Psy *-gnosis*.

4. Gr *gnōsis* has adj *gnōstikos*, excellent at knowing, whence LL *gnosticus*, whence E *gnostic*, esp
in *Gnostic*, whence *Gnosticism*, a philosophico-
religious cult.

5. *Agnostic*, however, is formed differently: Gr
*agnōsto*s, unknown, hence unknowing: *a-* not+
*gnōstos*, known, var of *gnōtos* (cf L *nōtus*)+E *-ic*.
Hence *agnosticism*.

6. 'To *diagnose*' is a b/f of *diagnosis*, from Gr
*diagnōsis*, from *diagignōskein*, to distinguish, lit
to know *dia*, through. Derivative Gr *diagnōstikos*,
able to distinguish, yields *diagnostic*, adj (hence n),
whence *diagnostician*: cf *technician* from *technic*.

7. *Prognosis*, adopted from LL, derives from Gr
*prognōsis*, a knowing *pro-* or beforehand, a forecast, esp in Med. Derivative Gr adj *prognōstikos*
becomes ML *prognosticus*, whence the E adj
*prognostic*; the n *prognostic* derives, through F and
ML, from Gr *prognōstikon*, prop the neu of the
adj. The ML *prognosticum* (prop the neu of
the adj) has derivative *prognosticāre*, to foretell (a
medical condition) from the symptoms, hence to
predict in general; the pp *prognosticātus* yields 'to
*prognosticate*'; derivative ML *prognosticātiō*, o/s
*prognosticātiōn-*, yields, perh via F, *prognostication*;
*prognosticator* is an anl E formation.

8. The Gr ss *gnōm-, gnōs-, gnōt-*, all come from
Gr *gignōskein*, (obviously a redup of the *gnōskein*
attested by Epirote Gr), to know: cf the syn OL
*gnōscere*, L *nōscere*, OIr *gnāth* (cf Gr *gnōtos*),
known, OHG *knāu*, I know; cf Skt *jānámi*, I
know; cf also E CAN (where, at para 5, cf *know*).

**gnomon.** See prec, para 2.

**gnosis; gnostic.** See the 2nd GNOME, paras 3-4.

**gnu** comes from *nqu* in the language of the Cape
Bushmen of SAfr.

**go**, pt went (see wend), pp gone (OE *gān*); **forego,**
whence **foregoing, foregone; forgo,** pt **forwent,** pp
**forgone; outgo** (out, prep+go), whence **outgoing,**
adj hence n.—Cf the distantly related, sep treated
**heir (hereditary, inherit,** etc.).

1. 'To *go*' (whence the coll n *go*) comes, through ME *gon*, earlier *gan*, from OE *gān*: cf OFris and OS *gān*, OHG-MHG *gān*, *gēn*, G *gehen* (an extn), Crimean Go *geen*: IE r, perh *\*ghē-*, as in Gr kik*hēmi*, I reach, cf Skt *jihīte*, he goes forth. (Walshe.)

2. 'To *forego*' (to go *fore* or before, to precede) derives from OE *foregān*; cf the G *vorgehen*.

3. 'To *forgo*' (to go *for-* or without) derives from OE *forgān*; cf the G *vergehen*, to go past, pass away, transgress.

**goad.** See GAR, para 4.

**goal** (whence **goalkeeper**, coll **goalie**) derives from ME *gol*, o.o.o.; but cf OE *gǣlan*, to hinder. EW cfs, sem, L *mēta*, limit, boundary, hence goal.

**goanna**, occ **goana**, is an at first coll form of (a confused Bio confusion with) IGUANA.

**goat, goatee, goatish.**

*Goatish* merely tacks adj *-ish* to *goat*, as *goatee* tacks *-ee* thereto, this particular style of beard (tufted on the chin) resembling a he-goat's beard. *Goat*, ME *goot*, var *gat*, derives from OE *gāt*. akin to OHG-MHG *geiz*, G *Geiss*, she-goat, Go *gaits* (cf *gaitein*, kid), ON *geit*, the Gmc r being app *\*gait-*: cf L *haedu*s, he-goat, young goat (kid), the IE r being app *\*ghaid-* (Walshe).

**gob** (1), mouth. See GAB. Cf:

**gob** (2), a lump: OF-MF *gobe*: app from a Gallo-Roman *\*gob* (cf Ir *gob*, mouth), whence MF-EF *gobet*, a mouthful, whence E *gobbet*.

**gobbet.** See prec.

**gobble** (1), echoic, as of a turkey cock. See GAB.

**gobble** (2), to eat hastily, is a freq, formed from *\*gob*, to swallow, from MF-F *gober*, from OF-MF *gobe*, as at the 2nd GOB. Cf:

**goblet**: ME, from MF-F, *gobelet*, dim (*-et*) of OF *gobel*, itself a dim (*-el*) of Gallo-Roman *\*gob*, as at the 2nd GOB, this C origin (B & W) being more prob than derivation from LL *cuppa* (CUP).

**goblin**; ME, from MF-F, *gobelin*: ML *gobelinus*, app either a dim of VL-ML *cobalus*, from Gr *kobalos*, an outright knave, hence in pl mischievous sprites ('invoked by rogues': L & S), or, less prob, from MHG *kobolt* (G *Kobold*: cf COBALT), a familiar sprite, itself ult from *kobalos*.

**goby; gudgeon.**

The latter, ME *gojon*, comes from MF-F *goujon*, from L *gōbiōn*em, acc of *gōbiō*; the L var *gōbius* indicates origin in Gr *kōbios*, app of Medit stock (Hofmann). The L o/s *gōbi-* leads to E *goby*. Easily caught, the *gudgeon* acquires the secondary sense, a simpleton. The tech, esp naut, *gudgeon* app results from a confusion of MF-F *gond*, hinge, with MF-F *goujon*.

**God, god** (whence **goddess**); **godhead**; **godlike**; **godly** (whence **godliness**); **godfather** and **godmother** —**goddaughter** and **godson**; **godsend**; **good-by** (or -bye), **good day** and **night**; **Godspeed**; **Golly, Gosh!**; **gospel**; **gossip** (n, hence v) and **sib**; **gid**—**giddy**;— **bigot** (whence **bigoted**), **bigotry**;—such PNN as **Goddard, Godfrey, Godwin**, not treated here.

1. The Supreme Being *God* is '*the* god': and *god*, OE *god*, is akin to OFris, OS, MD (var *got*) -D

*god*, OHG-MHG *got*, G *Gott*, Go *guth*, ON *goth*, *guth*: perh orig 'the (one, the being, hence the deity) invoked': Walshe cfs the 'Skt *-hūta* (for *\*ghūta*) "invoked" (deity)', *huta* being the pp of *havate*, he calls upon (a god); perh cf also Ga and OIr *guth*, voice, OC *\*gutus* (r *\*gut-*).

2. *Godlike*, which=*god*+adj *-like*, is a doublet of *godly*, which=*god*+*-ly* (OE *-līc*), like. So *godless*=*god*+*-less*, without. *Godhead* derives from ME *godhed*, which=*god*+abstract *-hed*, *-head*.

3. The *god-* relationships imply 'in God', not by blood:

*goddaughter:* OE *goddohtor*—cf DAUGHTER;
*godson:* OE *godsunu*—cf SON;
*godfather:* OE *godfaeder*—cf FATHER;
*godmother:* OE *godmōdor*—cf MOTHER.

4. A *godsend* is for earlier *God's send*, God's sending or message (ME *sande*, OE *sand*, cf *sendan*, to send); cf SEND, para 2. As *Godspeed* or *God-speed* is a contr cf *God speed you*, God prosper you!, so *good-bye* (later *-by*)=*God bwye*, for *God bw'ye*, for *God be wi' ye*, i.e. *God be with ye!* Cf *good day*, for God give you a good day; *good morning* (*morrow*), God give you a good morning (to-morrow's day); *good night*, God give you a good night; and so forth.

5. Exclamatory *gosh*, orig *Gosh*, is euphem for *God*; cf the old-fashioned *Gad* and its cpd *begad* (by God), the latter worn down to *egad*; cf the childish *golly*.

6. With *begad* perh cf *bigot*, adopted from OF-F. In C12, *bigot* was an insult addressed by Frenchmen to Normans; the word then went underground for three centuries. OF *bigot* prob, but no more than prob, represents OE-ME *bi god* (or *God*). The sense 'superstitious hypocrite' (hence that of 'religious fanatic') perh comes from the violent contrast between rough, uncivilized men's religious invocations and their crude behaviour; cf the C14 F *godon*, Englishman, from his addiction to *God damn* (it). Derivative late MF-F *bigoterie* accounts for E *bigotry*.

7. The *god-* terms are straightforward; the *good-*, easily discernible. But *gid* and *giddy*, like *gospel* and *gossip*, are much less obvious. *Gid*, a disease affecting sheep, is a b/f from *giddy*, a notable symptom being the animal's tendency to run about in circles until it falls: and *giddy*, ME *gidi*, silly, mad, derives from OE *gydig*, mad: lit, possessed (connoted by adj suffix *-ig*) by a god (*\*gyd*, as attested in OE *gyden*, a goddess): cf, sem, *enthusiastic*.

8. Whereas *gospel*, ME *gospel*, earlier *godspel*, derives from OE *godspell*, perh *god-spell*, God's tidings, but prob *god spell*, good tidings (cf GOOD and SPELL, n), *gossip* (ME *gossib*, earlier *godsib*) derives from OE *godsibb*, a person spiritually related to God. Obsol *sib*, related, derives from OE *sibb*; *sib*, a relation, derives from OE *sibb*, var *gesib*. OE *sibb*, *-sib*, is akin to OHG *sippa*, MHG *sippe*, consanguinity, G *Sippe*, one's kin, and esp to OFris *sibbe*, cf OS *sibbea* (or *-ia*) and Go *sibja*; perh cf also Skt *sabhấ*, a village community— notoriously inter-related. (Walshe.)

goffer. Cf *gauffer* and *gopher*, but see WEAVE, para 7.

goggle, goggles. See JIG, para 6.

Goidelic. See GAEL.

goiter, goitre; adj goitrous.

1. The adj derives from F *goitreux*, f *goitreuse*, from *goitre*, adopted by E and Americanized as *goiter*. The EF(-F) *goitre*, borrowed from a dial of the Rhone valley, is a b/f from OF-EF *goitron*, throat, gullet, which, in the MF of SE France, took the sense 'goitre', a thyroid-gland protuberance on the neck. OF *goitron* derives from VL *\*gutturiōnem*, acc of *\*gutturiō*, from L *guttur*, throat. (Dauzat.)

2. From L *guttur*, EF learnedly derives the adj *guttural*, adopted by E and derivatively used also as n. *Guttur* is o.o.o.—but (B & W) it strikingly resembles Hit *kuttar* (dat *kuttani*), neck, itself perh akin to Hit *kuttas* (dat *kutti*), side or wall.

gold (n, hence adj)—goldsmith; golden—Golden Age, the;—gild, v, pp gilded or gilt, the latter used derivatively, now usu as n; gall; guilder, gulden.—yellow (adj, hence n and v); yolk.

1. *Gold*, OE *gold*, is akin to OFris, OS, OHG and G *gold*, Go *gulth*, ON *gull*; Gmc r, *\*gulth*; IE r, *\*gholt-*, var *\*ghelt-*, extn of *\*ghel-*, var *\*ghol-*. The IE r *\*ghel-* (var *\*ghol-*) is seen in OS and OHG *gelo*, MHG *gel*, G *gelb*, yellow, akin to OE *geolo*, *geolu*, ME *yelwe*, later *yelow*, E *yellow*, and to ON *gull*, gold, *gulr*, yellow. Cf, further, L *heluus* (adj), pale-yellow, and Gr *khloos* (s *khlo-*, ? for *\*khelo-*), a greenish-yellow colour (cf the sep CHLORAL-CHLORINE group), and Skt *hari*, yellow, and *hiranya*, gold.

2. OE *geolu* (s *geol-*) yellow, has derivative *geoleca*, contr to *geolca*, whence ME *yelke*, later *yolke*, whence E *yolk*, the yellow part of an egg.

3. Intimately akin to OE *geolu* is OE *gealla*, ME *galla*, *gal*, E *gall*, bile; cf OHG and OS *galla*, G *Galle*, ON *gal*; cf also L *fel* and Gr *kholē* (cf the sep CHOLER and, at the element *mela-*, *melano-*, the cpd *melancholy*).

4. To return to *gold*: the cpds are self-evident; *goldsmith*, however, descends straight from OE and has an id OFris cognate.

5. ME *gold* has adj *golden*; the var ME *gulden* derives from OE *gylden*. E *golden* appears in many fig terms, as, e.g., *the golden age*, imitative of L *aureus*, golden, used with *aetās*, age, or *saecula*, centuries, or *tempus*, time.

6. OE *gold* has derivative v *gyldan*, to overlay thinly with gold, hence as if with gold; hence 'to *gild*'. (For *gilt*, cf heading.)

7. D and G *gulden*, golden, hence a gold coin, has—but only in E—the monetary var *guilder*. The MHG *guldēn* is elliptical for *guldēn phenninc*, lit 'golden penny'.

goldfinch. See FINCH.

golf first occurs in late ME and app comes from MD *colf* (var *colve*: cf D *kolf*), a club: cf MD *colven*, to play a game with clubs or sticks, and OHG *kolbo*, MHG *kolbe*, G *Kolben*, ON *kolfr*, a club: ult, therefore, *golf* is prob akin to CLUB.—*Golf* has derivative 'to *golf*', whence *golfer*.

Golgotha. See CALVARY.

golland. See GOWAN.

golliwog, better golliwogg, derives from *Golliwogg*, a fanciful name—? after *polliwog*, (now mostly AE for) a tadpole, ME *polwigle* (it *wiggles* its *poll* or head)—for the shaggy-haired, rather grotesque black doll of the Golliwogg books illustrated, the first in 1895, by Florence K. Upton and written by her mother, Bertha Upton; the last of them appeared in 1909. Florence Upton was born, of British parents, in the U.S.A., where the Golliwogg books were first published.

Golly, golly. See GOD, para 5.

gombeen man. See CHANGE, para 1.

gondola, general It from Venetian, either (B & W) a dim from Gr *kondu*, a vase (cf, sem, OF-F *vaisseau*, E *vessel*, q.v. at VASE), or, more prob (Prati), imitative of the craft's motion, from Venetian *\*gondolare*, to undulate, perh an alteration of *dondolare*, to rock or swing, vi *dondolarsi*. (The ML *gondula* occurs, at Venice, before the year 1094.) Derivative It *gondoliere* becomes EF-F *gondolier*, adopted by E.

2. It *dondolare* has an obs var *dandolare*, s *dandol-*, whence 'to *dandle*'.

gone. See GO, heading.

gonfalon or gonfanon. See FEND, para 2.

gong is either Javanese *gon* or the likewise echoic Mal *gun*; perh it derives from both.

gonidium; gonophore, gonorrhoea. See, in Elements, the 2nd *-gon*.

good (adj, hence adv and n), goodly, goodness.

The 3rd derives from OE *gōdnes* (cf *-ness*); the 2nd from OE *gōdlic* (cf adj *-ly*); both OE words from OE *gōd*, whence the adj *good*. OE *gōd* is akin to OFris and OS *gōd*, Go *iōths*, OHG-MHG *guot* (G *gut*), ON *gōthr*: basic gdea, 'suitable'—cf OSl *godu*, a suitable time, and *goditi*, to be suitable (hence, pleasing).

good-by(e); good day (night, etc.). See GOD, para 4.

goody, coll adj hence n, is a pet-form (*-y*, *-ie*) of the adj GOOD, perh influenced by *goodly*.

googly. See JIG, para 7.

goon, a thug: a word coined by comic-strip artist E. C. Segar (†1939), his *Goons* being subhuman creatures: prob a blend of *gorilla*+*baboon*, or perh of *goof*+*baboon*.

goose. See GANDER, para 3; GOOSEBERRY, id., para 5.

gopher. See WEAVE, para 8.

gore (1), of land. See GAR, para 2.

gore (2), slime, filth (obs), hence clotted blood: OE *gor*, dirt, filth, akin to OHG and ON *gor*, also Ga *gur*, a festering, and OIr *gur*, W *gōr*, pus, OC *\*goru-*. (MacLennan).—Hence the adj *gory* (*-y*).

gore (3), to pierce or stab (obs), hence (of a horned beast) to wound, perh derives from ME *gore*, var of *gare*, OE *gār*, a spear.

gorge, n and v—cf disgorge; ? gorgeous; gorget; ingurgitate, ingurgitation—regurgitate, regurgitation; gurgle, q.v. at sep GARGLE, para 2; for garget, see GARGLE, para 1; for gargoyle, see id., para 3; jargon, n and v; sep DEVOUR and sep VORACIOUS.

1. 'To *gorge*' is to fill one's *gorge* or throat, gullet: MF-F *gorger*, from OF-F *gorge*, throat, from VL *\*gorga*, from LL *gurga*, gullet, from L *gurgēs*, whirlpool, abyss, and, in popular L, gullet (to judge by, e.g., *ingurgitāre*), with s *gurg-*; IE s, *\*gurg-*, var *garg-* (cf GARGLE), app an extn of *\*gur-*, *\*gar-*: ult echoic. Cf VORACIOUS.—*Gorge*, a rocky ravine, derives, via F, from L *gurgēs*, abyss.

2. 'To *disgorge*' comes from MF *desgorger* (F *dégorger*): *des-* (L *dis-*)+*gorger*.

3. 'To *ingurgitate*' comes from L *ingurgitātus*, pp of *ingurgitāre*, to pour into the *gurges* or gullet; derivative LL *ingurgitātiō*, o/s *ingurgitātiōn-*, yields *ingurgitation*: cf *regurgitation*, from ML *regurgitātiō*, itself from ML *regurgitātus* (whence 'to *regurgitate*'), pp of *regurgitāre*: *re-*, back+LL *gurgitāre*, to swallow, from L *gurgēs*.

4. OF-F *gorge*, throat, has the MF dim *gorgete* (cf F *gorget*), a piece of throat-armour; whence E *gorget*.

5. OF-F *gorge*, throat, has derivative *gorgias*, a neckerchief, a ruff, with which late MF-EF *gorgias*, vain, ultra-fashionable, might ult be id; DAF, however, derives the adj *gorgias*—whence E *gorgeous*—from the Ancient Gr rhetorician *Gorgias*, notorious for luxurious living and ornate oratory.

6. The IE s *garg-* (para 1), has, in F, the var *arg-*, as in OF-F *jargon*, OF var *gargon*, any noise made in the throat, as the warbling of birds, the modern sense arising in late MF: the former sense was adopted by ME (e.g., Chaucer), the latter by E. OF-F *jargon* has OF-F derivative *jargonner*, whence 'to *jargon*', now obsol.

gorgeous. See prec, para 5.

gorget. See GORGE, para 4.

gorgon, any terrifying or very ugly person, esp woman, derives from *Gorgon*, one (esp Medusa) of three horrifying, snaky-haired sisters in Gr mythology: Gr *Gorgō*, gen *Gorgon*os: an *-ō* suffix (connoting 'person' or 'being') derivative of Gr *gorgos*, terrible, horrifying, s *gorg-*: akin to OIr *garg*, wild and fierce, and Arm *karcr*, hard, bold, strong. (Hofmann.) MIr and OSl cognates suggest an IE r *\*greg-* (Boisacq). The adj is *gorgonesque*.

gorilla is a SciL b/f from Gr *gorillai*, 'hairy humans', mentioned, in C5 B.C., by Hanno the Carthaginian voyager as an African word—i.e., West African.

gormandize (n, hence v); gourmand (adj, hence n), gourmandise; gourmet; groom (n, whence v)—cf *bridegroom*, q.v. at BRIDE.

*Gormandize*, gluttony, is obs; *gormandize*, art and delight of eating, is rare for its original, the MF-F *gourmandise* (abstract *-ise*), from the MF-F *gourmand*, greedy, perh an alteration of late MF *gormet*, by metathesis from MF *gromet*, a servant, esp a wine-merchant's, whence *gourmet*, with derivative sense (first in C16) 'wine-taster, connoisseur of wine, hence epicure'. OF *gromet*, which is o.o.o., becomes late ME *grome*, then *grom*, whence *groom*, orig a servant, esp if young (cf, sem, KNIGHT)—but for the *groom* of *bridegroom*, see HOMO.

gorse. See HEARSE, para 9.

gory. See the 2nd GORE, s.f.

Gosh, further euphemized to gosh. See GOD, para 5.

goshawk. See GANDER, para 5. Cf:

gosling. See GANDER, para 4. Cf:

gosmore. See GANDER, para 7; cf SUMMER, para 2.

gospel. See GOD, para 8.

gossamer. See GANDER, para 6; cf SUMMER, para 2.

gossip. See GOD, para 8.

gossoon eases *garsoon*, 'English' for F *garçon*, boy, (young) manservant.

got. See GET.

Goth, Gothic (adj, hence n; hence also **Gothicism** and Gothicize); Ostrogoth and Visigoth.

1. *Gothic* derives—prob not via F *gothique*—from LL *Gothicus* (for *Gotthicus*), adj of LL *Gothi*, better *Gotthi*, the Goths, from Gr *Gothoi*, better *Gotthoi* (Γότθοι), app from the Go s *Gut-* in *Gutthiuda*, the Gothic people: cf OSw *Gutan-* and ML *Gutani*: perh 'the *good* people'.

2. *Ostrogoth*, an East Goth, comes from LL *Ostrogothae* or *-gothi*, earlier *Austrogoti*, of Gmc origin—prob 'the splendid Goths, taken later as, the eastern Goths' (Webster). Cf *Visigoth*, from ML *Visigothi*, LL *Uisigothi*, of Gmc origin—lit 'the noble (or good) Goths' (LL *Uisi*—being akin to Skt *vasu*, good), apprehended later, by f/e, as the western Goths. (See esp Feist.)

gouge (n, hence v) is adopted from OF-F, which takes it from LL *gubia*, a hollowed chisel (Souter): prob of C origin—cf OIr *gulban* (s *gulb-*), var *gulpan*, OW *gilbin*, Ga *guilb* (gen *gulbann*), a beak; OC *\*gulbanos*. (MacLennan.)

gourd; cucurbit.

*Gourd* comes from MF-F *gourde*, a contr derivative of L *cucurbita*, whence obviously *cucurbit*, a flask shaped like a gourd, also a common field pumpkin. L *cucurbita* is akin to—perh ult from—Skt *carbhaṭas*, this being no 'doubtless accidental coincidence' (E & M)! It is app a Medit word: Eg shows *garagantesi*, gourd, pumpkin.

gourmand, gourmet. See GORMANDIZE.

gout (whence gouty), orig as '*gout* of blood', later in Med sense, OF-MF *goute*, var of OF-F *goutte*, from L *gutta*, a drop of water, blood, etc.: r *gut-*, ? akin to the syn Arm *kat*'n (E & M): prob imitative.

2. OF *goute*, a drop, has derivative OF-MF *gutiere*, *goutiere* (F *gouttière*), lit a receptacle (connoted by *-iere*, F *-ière*) for drops of water, a course—an open pipe—for rainwater on a roof or in a road: hence ME *gotere*, later *gutere*: hence E *gutter* (whence 'to *gutter*'). Hence the at first sl *guttersnipe*, a 'snipe' of the roadway gutters.

**govern, -ance, -ess, -ment, -or; Gouverneur; gubernatorial; cybernetics.**

1. 'To *govern*' comes from OF-MF *governer* (F *gou-*): L *gubernāre* (s *gubern-*), to steer or pilot, hence to govern: syn Gr *kubernan*, perh of Medit stock, if neither Thracian nor Macedonian; perh cf Skt *kubhanyús* (s *kubhan-*), adj 'dancing, pirouetting' (steering one's steps). The derivatives MF *governance*, MF *governesse*, OF-MF *governement*, OF-MF *governeor*, account for the next four words; *Gouveneur* (Morris) is the F *gouverneur*.

2. L derivative *gubernāculum* (suffix *-aculum*) is adopted by An; agent *gubernātor* leads to E *gubernatorial* (adj *-ial*).

3. Gr *kubernan*, to steer, control, has derivative adj *kubernētikos*, skilled in steering, etc., whence, as if from *ta kubernētika, the modern *cybernetics*, the science of vast computators and 'mechanical brains'.

**gowan** derives from North Country dial *gowlan*, *gollan* (whence E *golland*), varr of *golding*, a gold-coloured or -centred, usu field-, flower: f.a.e., GOLD.

**gown** (n, hence v): ME *goune*: OF-MF *gone*, var of OF-EF *gonne*: LL *gunna*, a leather garment, app of Gaul origin.

**graal.** See GRAIL.

**grab** (v, whence n); **grabble.**
The latter derives from MD *grabbelen*, freq of *grabben*—whence 'to *grab*'. Cf OSl *grab*iti, to seize, and Skt *gṛbhṇāti*, he seizes.

**grace** (n and v), whence directly **graceful** and **graceless**—cf **disgrace** (n, v), whence **disgraceful; gracious, graciosity;** obs adj **grate, grateful, gratitude**—cf **ingrate** (adj, hence n), **ingratitude**—cf also **ingratiate**, whence, anl, **ingratiation, ingratiatory; gratify, gratification; gratis, gratuitous, gratuity;** obsol **gratulate, gratulation, gratulatory**—cf **congratulate, congratulation, congratulatory.**

1. *Grace*, adopted from OF-MF (F *grâce*), derives from L *grātia*, gratitude, something that merits gratitude, a service rendered, hence influence, credit, favour, from *grātus*, received with favour, agreeable, (also) conscious of favour, prob akin to Skt *gūrtás*, celebrated (in religious sense), pleasing, dear, *gír* (gen *girás*), a song of praise, *gṛṇáti*, he sings of, praises, and Lith *gìrti*, to praise, and *girtas*, celebrated, dear. (E & M, after Walde.)

2. OF *grace* has derivative MF *gracier*, whence 'to *grace*'.

3. L *grātia* becomes It *grazia*, whence *disgrazia* (L *dis-*), whence EF-F *disgrâce*, whence E *disgrace*; and It *disgrazia* has derivative *disgraziare*, whence EF-F *disgrâcier*, whence 'to *disgrace*'.

4. L *grātia* (s *grāti-*) has derivative adj *grātiōsus*, in favour, amiable, whence OF-MF *gracious* (whence F *gracieux*), adopted by E. Derivative late MF-F *gracieuseté* leads to E *graciosity*, much rarer than *graciousness* (*gracious+-ness*).

5. L *grātus* becomes the long-obs E *grate*, agreeable, grateful, whence *grateful* itself; *gratitude*, however, perh via MF-F, comes from LL *grātitūdō* (from *grātus*).

6. L *grātus* has neg *ingrātus* (*in-*, not), whence MF-F *ingrat*, f *ingrate*, whence E *ingrate*; derivative LL *ingrātitūdō* yields, perh ∮ a MF-F, the E *ingratitude*. But 'to *ingratiate*' is an E formation—a cpd of *in*, into+*gratia*, favour: to bring into favour, usu reflexively (*ingratiate oneself*).

7. L *grātus* has the cpd *grātificus*, favour-making, gratitude-causing (cf the element *-fic*), with derivative *grātificāri*, to render a service to, to please by doing so, whence MF-F *gratifier*, whence 'to *gratify*'; derivative L *grātificātiō*, o/s *grātificātiōn-*, yields—perh via MF-F—*gratification*.

8. L *grātia* has abl pl *grātiīs*, with favours, graciously, freely; its contr *grātis*, used as adv, has been adopted in various IE languages.

9. App from a lost s *grātu-* comes L *grātuïtus*, freely rendered (cf *fortuïtus* from *fort-*, o/s of *fors*, chance): whence E *gratuitous* (cf the late MF-F *gratuit*). Derivative ML *grātuïtās*, o/s *grātuïtāt-* (cf the late MF-F *gratuité*), accounts for E *gratuity*, orig graciousness, a gracious act, debased to a tip or even a bribe.

10. L *grātia* has derivative *grātulāri*, to render thanks (to the gods), to felicitate, with presp *grātulans*, o/s *grātulant-*, whence the literary adj *gratulant*, and with pp *grātulātus*, whence 'to *gratulate*'; derivative *grātulātiō*, o/s *grātulātiōn-*, becomes *gratulation*, and LL *grātulātōrius* becomes *gratulatory*.

11. *Grātulāri* has cpd *congrātulāri*, to felicitate warmly (*con-* implies 'thoroughly'), with presp *congrātulans*, whence the adj *congratulant*, and pp *congrātulātus*, whence 'to *congratulate*'; derivative *congrātulātiō*, o/s *congrātulātiōn-*, yields, perh via EF-F, *congratulation*; *congratulatory* is an anl E formation.

**gracile, gracility.**
The latter derives, perh via late MF-F *gracilité*, from L *gracilitās*, o/s *gracilitāt-*, from *gracilis*, slender, esp gracefully slender, whence, perh via F, the E *gracile*. *Gracilis*, s *gracil-*, app has r *grac-*; cf *gracentes*, presp pl of a v *gracere*: o.o.o.

**gracious.** See GRACE, para 4.

**grackle.** Cf CROAK.

**gradation.** See para 3 of:

**grade** (n, hence v)—cf **gradus; gradate, gradation** (whence **gradational**); **gradient; gradual** (whence **gradualism, gradualness**); **graduate** (n and v), **graduation, graduator; gressorial.**—Cpds: **aggradation—aggress, aggression, aggressive, aggressor; congress** (and Congress), **congression** (whence **congressional**), **congressive; degrade, degradation—degree, degression, degressive; digress, digression, digressive** or **digressory; egress, egression; ingredience, ingredient—ingress, ingression, ingressive; introgression; progress** (n, hence v), **progression** (whence **progressional, progressionism** and **progressionist,** cf **progressism**), **progressive** (whence **progressivism, -ist**); **regress** (n and v), **regression, regressive; regressor; retrograde** (adj and v), **retrogradation—retrogress** (v), **retrogression, retrogressive;** transgress, **transgression, transgressive, transgressor.**

1. *Grade*, a step, a stage, adopted from EF-F, comes from L *gradus* (gen *gradūs*; s *grad-*), intimately akin to L *gradī* (s *grad-*), to step, walk, go, seen in the *-gredient*, *-gree*, *-gress* cpds: both n and v are akin to Av aiwi-*gered*mahi, we begin, OSl *gręḍǫ*, I come, Lith *grìdyti*, to go, to walk; app there are cognates in C (*gred-*) and in Go. (E & M.)

2. *Gradus* survives in E mostly as an ellipsis of *Gradus ad Parnassum*, A Step to, or a Stage towards, Parnassus, the title of a once-famous book on Latin versification.

3. L *gradus* has derivative *gradātiō*, o/s *gradātiōn-*, whence (perh via MF-F) *gradation*, whence, by b/f, 'to *gradate*'.

4. Also from L *gradus* come the ML adj *graduālis*, whence E *gradual* (adj, whence n), and the ML v *graduāre*, to admit to a ML *gradus* or degree, with gerundive *graduandus*, whence Sc *graduand*, one about to receive a degree, and with pp *graduātus*, whence both 'a *graduate*' and 'to *graduate*', the derivative *graduātiō*, o/s *graduātiōn-*, yielding *graduation*; *graduator* is an anl E formation.

5. L *gradī*, to step, walk, go, has presp *gradiens*, o/s *gradient-*, whence the adj—hence, in turn, the n—*gradient*. The pp *gressus*, s *gress-*, prompts the Zoo *Gressoria* and *gressorial*, adapted for walking.

## Compounds

6. *Aggradation* (adj in *-al*)=*ag-* for *ad-*, to+ *gradation*. The L cpd *aggredi*, to approach, hence to assail, has pp *aggressus*, whence 'to *aggress*'; derivative *aggressiō*, o/s *aggressiōn-*, becomes EF *aggression* (F *agression*), adopted by E—hence, anl, *aggressive* (cf F *agressif*); derivative LL *aggressor* is adopted by E (cf F *agresseur*, MF *aggresseur*).

7. L *congredī*, to walk, go (hence, come), *con* or together, has pp *congressus*, with s *congress-*, whence the n *congressus* (gen *-ūs*), whence E *congress*, often particularized to *Congress*. Whereas *congression*, from *congressiōn-*, o/s of derivative L *congressiō*, is obs, its E derivative adj *congressional* thrives; *congressive* is an anl E formation.

8. Whereas *degression* (whence anl *degressive*) comes from L *dēgressiō*, from *dēgress-*, s of *dēgressus*, pp of *dēgredī*, to go down, *degradation* comes from LL *dēgradātiō* (o/s *dēgradātiōn-*), a reduction in rank, from *dēgradātūs*, pp of LL *dēgradāre*, to reduce in rank, whence, via EF *degrader* (F *dé-*), the E 'to *degrade*'.

9. LL *dēgradāre* has derivative VL *dēgradus*, whence OF *degret*, soon *degré*, whence, via ME *degre*, the E *degree*. More prob, however, the OF *degret*, *degré*=*de*+*gret*, *gré*, step, without recourse to LL or VL.

10. L *digredī* (*di-* for *dis-*, apart), to walk, go, apart, has pp *digressus*, whence 'to *digress*'; derivative *digressiō*, o/s *digressiōn-*, passes through OF-F and ME to become E *digression*, whence the adj *digressional*; *digressive* comes from LL *digressīuus*, ML *īvus*, but *digressory* is an anl E formation.

11. L *ēgredī*, to walk, go (hence come), *ē* or out, has pp *ēgressus*, s *egress-*, whence the n *ēgressus* (gen *-ūs*), whence E *egress*; derivative *ēgressiō*, o/s *ēgressiōn-*, produces *egression*.

12. L *ingredī*, to walk, go (hence come), in, has presp *ingrediens*, o/s *ingredient-*, whence the obsol adj *ingredient*, whence *ingredience*; the E n *ingredient* comes from F *ingrédient*, used as early as EF as a pharmaceutical n.

13. L *ingredī* has pp *ingressus*, s *ingress-*, whence n *ingressus* (gen *-ūs*), whence E *ingress*; derivative L *ingressiō*, o/s *ingressiōn-*, yields *ingression*, whence, anl, the adj *ingressive*.

14. L *introgredī*, to go *intro* or within, has pp *introgressus*, s *introgress-*, whence, anl, the erudite E *introgression* (cf the LL n *introgressus*).

15. L *prōgredī*, to step, walk, go (or come) *prō* or forward, has pp *prōgressus*, s *prōgress-*, whence n *prōgressus* (gen *-ūs*), whence, perh via MF, the E *progress*, whence 'to *progress*'; derivative L *prōgressiō*, o/s *prōgressiōn-*, yields—perh via MF-F—*progression*, whence, anl, *progressive*, perh prompted by MF-F *progressif*, f *-ive*.

16. L *regredī*, to step, go, back, has pp *regressus*, whence 'to *regress*'; the E n *regress* comes from the L n *regressus* (gen *-ūs*), from the pp; derivative *regressiō*, o/s *regressiōn-*, becomes *regression*, whence, anl, *regressive* and *regressor*.

17. L *retrogradī*, to step, go, backwards (*retro*), yields 'to *retrograde*'; its derivative adj *retrogradus* yields the adj *retrograde*; derivative LL *retrogradātiō*, o/s *-gradātiōn-*, accounts for *retrogradation*. *Retrogradī*, to go backwards, has pp *retrogressus*, whence 'to *retrogress*'; derivative LL n *retrogressus* (gen *-ūs*) becomes the rare E n *retrogress*, whence, anl, *retrogression* (perh from F *rétrogression*) and *retrogressive*.

18. L *transgredī*, to step, go, *trans* or across, has pp *transgressus*, whence, perh via MF-F *transgresser*, the E 'to *transgress*'; derivative *transgressiō*, o/s *-gressiōn-*, becomes OF-F and E *transgression*, and LL *transgressīuus*, ML *-īvus*, becomes *transgressive*; LL *transgressor* is adopted by E.

graft (1) of tree; n hence v, whence **graftage**.

A *graft* derives (? influenced by *craft*) from ME *graff*: OF-F *greffe*, graft or scion (cion): OF *grefe*, var of *grafe*, stylus: LL *graphium*, a grafting knife: L *graphium*, stylus: Gr *graphion*, var of *grapheion*, stylus: Gr *graphein*, to write: cf *graph*, q.v.—f.a.e. —at GRAMMAR.

graft (2), sl for 'work' (hence the sl v): SE *graft*, a spade-depth, a spadeful: cf ON *gröftr*, a digging, and, f.a.e., the 2nd GRAVE.

grafter is the agent of 'to *graft*', as at GRAFT (1) and (2). Sl *grafter* has thinning *grifter*.

grail, var graal: OF *graal*: VL *cratalem*, accof *cratalis*, a chalice: L *crātēra*, that var of L *crāter* which is formed from Gr *kratēra*, acc of *kratēr*, a cup: f.a.e., CRATER.

grain (n, hence v); engrain, with anglicized var ingrain; gram, kinds of pea and bean; cf the elements *gramini-* (*gramino-*) and *grani-* (*grano-*);

granadilla; granary; pomegranate; grange; granite, granitic; granose; granule, granular, granulate, granulation; gravy; grenade, grenadier;—garner; garnet;—sep CORN; kernel; churn; perh cf the sep CHURL.

1. 'To *engrain*' derives from ME *engreynen*, to dye scarlet: OF *en graine*, in(to) grain (seed), esp in sense 'dye', latterly influenced by sense 'texture'. OF-F *graine* derives from L *grāna*, pl (apprehended as f sing) of *grānum* (para 4).

2. *Gram*, a plant grown for its seed, derives from Port *grão*, from L *grānum*.

3. *Granose* derives from L *grānōsus*, adj of *grānum*.

4. L *grānum*, a grain, a seed, hence a particle, has s *grān-*, attested also in C, OSl, Lith, Go: cf OIr *grán*, Ga *gràn*, Br *gran* or *gren*, Mx *grain*, W *grawn*; OSl *grüno*; by metathesis, Go *kaurn*.

5. L *grānum* has certain derivatives relevant to E:

*grānārium* (*gran-*+'receptacle' *-arium*), whence *granary*; in MF, *granārium* becomes *grenier* (as still in F) with MF metathesis *gernier*, whence ME *gerner*, with var *garner*, adopted by E, whence 'to *garner*';

*grānātus*, adj 'like or of grain or seeds', whence the n *grānātum* (sc L *malum*, a fruit; ML, sc *pomum*, an apple), with LL var *grānāta*, f sing from L pl (*mala*) *grānāta*, both *grānātum* and *grānāta* meaning lit 'a fruit, esp an apple, rich in seeds'. ML (*pomum*) *grānātum* becomes OF *pume* (later *pome*, etc.) *grenate*, whence MF *pume grenade*, whence EF(-F) *grenade*, a pomegranate, a sense long obs in E, which, however, retains the EF-F derivative sense 'projectile', the F derivative *grenadier* being likewise adopted; note that the long-obs *granate*, a pomegranate, from both LL *grānāta* and L *grānātum*, survives in *pomegranate*, reshaped in EE from ME *pomgarnet*, from MF *pome grenate*; note also that in OF *pome grenate*, *grenate* is f of the adj *grenat*, which occurs in OF *jagonce grenat*, lit 'grained hyacinth', whence MF-F *grenat*, that semi-precious stone the garnet, which, adopted by ME, acquires the metathesis *garnet*, retained by E;

VL *\*grānica*, whence OF *grange*, adopted by E; LL *grānulum*, a little grain or seed (dim of *grānum*), whence *granule*, whence, anl, *granular*; *granulate* is a b/f of *granulation*, adopted from late EF-F, which derives it from the v *granuler* (from L *grānulum*).

6. L *grānum* becomes It *grano*, with derivative *granire*, to render grain- or seed-like, pp *granito*, used as n for the 'grainy' rock, whence late EF-F *granit* and E *granite* (whence the adj *granitic*).

7. ML *grānāta*, pomegranate, remains *granata* in Sp, which forms the dim *granadilla*, passion-flower fruit—like the pomegranate, full of seeds; derivative is Sp *granadillo*, the tree bearing grana-dillas.

8. OF-MF *grané* deriving from *graine* but influenced by LL *grānāta*, means 'grained'—containing grains; used as n, it was misread, by English

cooks, to become ME *grave*, whence E *gravy*: many gravies do contain grains of some sort. (OED; EW.)

9. From the sep treated CORN (cf Go *kaurn*—as in para 4 above), or rather from OE *corn*, derives the dim OE *cyrnel*, ME *curnol*, *kirnel*—and *kernel*, retained by E.

10. Perh akin to OE *cyrnel* is OE *cyrin*, ME *chirne*, *cherne*, E *churn*, whence 'to *churn*'. As Webster very neatly puts it, the basic idea is 'cream (cf G. dial. *kern*, cream), the kernel of the milk, becoming granular in churning'.

gram (1). See GRAIN, para 2.

gram (2), gramme. See GRAMMAR, para 1.

gramary or gramarye. See para 1*a* of:

grammar, grammarian, grammatical, grammatist; gramarye; cf the element *gram-*, *gramo-* (as in *gramophone*, cf *-phone*); anagram, whence anagrammatic(al); epigram, epigrammatic(al), epigrammatist; program(me), whence, anl, programmatic(al); telegram; sep GLAMO(U)R.—graph (cf the element *-graph*), graphic, graphite; epigraph, whence, anl, epigraphic, epigraphist, epigraphy; telegraph (n, hence v), telegraphic, telegraphist, telegraphy.—sep GRAFT (1); sep CARVE.

1. *Grammar*, the Latin language (C14–16), the general subject (C14 onwards), hence a book of grammar (C16 onwards), derives from late ME *gramer*, *gramere*, from OF-MF *gramaire* (MF-F *grammaire*) a semi-learnèd, irreg derivative from L *grammatica*, trln of Gr *grammatikē* (elliptical for *g. tekhnē*, the art of alphabetical characters, the art of reading and writing), prop the f of *grammatikos*, skilled in grammar, adj from *gramma*, a letter of the alphabet, lit something written or for writing, hence also—from the marking—a small weight (whence F *gramme*, E *gram*), perh for *\*graphma*, from *graphein* (s *graph-*), to scratch or carve, hence to scratch or carve marks or characters, hence to write: akin to OE *ceorfan* to notch, nick, cut (whence CARVE, q.v. sep), MHG-G *kerben*, to notch or nick, MHG *kerve*, a notch, Lett *grebiu*, I carve; IE r, *\*gerbh-*.

1*a*. Late ME *gramer(e)* has varr *gramery*, *gramory*, whence *gramary* or *gramarye*, (obs) grammar or learning, (whence) magic: all learning is mysterious to the illiterate.

2. L *grammatica* has LL adj *grammaticālis*, whence MF-F and E *grammatical*; OF-MF *gramaire* has the MF adj, hence n, *gramarien* (cf the F *grammairien*), whence E *grammarian*; Gr *gramma* (o/s *grammat-*) has derivative v *grammatizein*, to teach the alphabet, to be a scribe, whence the agent *grammatistēs*, becoming ML *grammatista*, F *grammastiste*, E *grammatist*.

3. The chief *gram-* cpds in E are *anagram*, *epigram*, *program*, *telegram*. *Anagram* (whence *anagrammatic*, *anagrammatist*, etc.) derives from EF-F *anagramme*, from LG *anagramma*, reversal (connoted by *ana-*) of letters.

4. *Epigram*: MF-F *épigramme*: L *epigramma*, epigram, from Gr *epigramma*, a writing *epi* or upon, an inscription, an epigram, from *epigraphein*,

to write upon (cf *epigraph* below); derivative LL *epigrammaticus* becomes *epigrammatic*; LL *epigrammatista*, from Gr *epigrammatistēs*, yields *epigrammatist*.

5. *Program* (E, often *programme*, adopted from late EF-F): LL *prōgramma*, a writing before (*pro-*) the public, a proclamaton, adopted from Gr, from *prographein*, to write before, i.e. in public.

6. *Telegram* is modern: *tele-*, from afar+-*gram*, as in *epigram* and *program*.

7. From the Gr c/f -*graphos*, comes E -*graph*, as in the two prefix-cpds below: from -*graph* comes E *graph*.The adj *graphic*=L *graphicus*, trln of Gr *graphikos*, of, by, for writing, from *graphein*, to write. *Graphite*=G *Graphit*, which, like F *graphite*, is a learnèd derivative from Gr *graphein*.

8. The two chief -*graph* prefix-cpds are *epigraph* and *telegraph*. *Epigraph* comes, perh via late EF-F *épigraphe*, from Gr *epigraphē*; cf *epigram* in para 4 above.

9. *Telegraph* derives from F *télégraphe*; *telegraphic* and *telegraphist* prob derive from F *télégraphique* and *télégraphiste*; *telegraphy* is an anl E formation.

**grampus**: EE *graundepose*, the 1st element deriving by f/e from F *grand*, big: OF *graspeis, -pois*, earlier *craspois, -peis*: L *crassus*, fat+*piscis*, fish: cf CRASS and FISH.

**granadilla.** See GRAIN, para 7.

**granary.** See GRAIN, para 5.

**grand** (adj, hence n); **grandee; grandeur; grandiose; grandfather** (whence **granfer**, whence **gaffer**) and **-mother** (whence **grannam** and **granny**), **-daughter** and **-son**, all from **grand**, adj,—but for *grandfather*, cf FATHER, para 2;—**aggrandize, aggrandizement.**

1. *Aggrandizement* derives from EF-F *agrandissement*, itself from MF-F *agrandir*, from whose presp *agrandissant* and other *agrandiss-* parts comes 'to *aggrandize*'; *agrandir*=*a-* (F *à*), L *ad*, to +*grandir*, from L *grandīre*, from the adj *grandis* (s *grand-*), whence, via OF-F *grand*, the E *grand*. The L *grandis* is perh a nasalized derivative of IE r *\*grad-*, var *\*grod-*: cf Lett *graods*, strong, and ? E GROW.

2. L *grandis* becomes Sp *grande*, which, used as n, fathers E *grandee*; OF-F *grand* has the OF-F derivative *grandeur*, adopted by E; L *grandis* becomes It *grande*, with extn *grandioso*, whence F and E *grandiose*.

**grange.** See GRAIN, para 5 at *granica*.

**granite, granitic.** See GRAIN, para 6.

**grannam, granny.** See GRAND, heading.

**granose.** See GRAIN, para 3.

**grant**, n and v (whence *grantee* and *grantor*).

A *grant*, ME *grant* or *graunt*, derives from OF *graant*, itself from OF *graanter*, var of *craanter*, for *creanter*, to promise, from VL *\*crēdentāre*, to make believe, from L *crēdent-*, o/s of *crēdens*, presp of *crēdere*, to believe: cf CREED.—OF *graanter* becomes ME *graunten, granten*, whence 'to *grant*'.

**granular, granulate, granulation, granule.** See GRAIN, para 5.

**grape**: by semantic b/f from OF *grape* (F *grappe*), a bunch of grapes: OF *graper* (varr *craper* and *grafer*), to gather grapes, orig to gather (? prop, to pull) with hooks: ? Frankish *\*krappa*, a hook—cf OHG *krāpfo*, contr of *krampfo*, a hook: cf CRAMP. B & W suggest that a bunch of grapes was, in OF, named *grape* because of the shape-resemblance of a bunch to a hook (OF *grafe, grape*).—Such cpds as *grapefruit* and *grapevine* are self-explanatory.

**graph, graphic, graphite.** See GRAMMAR, para 7.

**grapnel; grapple.** See CRAMP.

**grasp**, n and v. See GRIP, para 5.

**grass** (n, hence v), whence **grassy** (adj -*y*); whence also, e.g., **grasshopper** and **grass widow**; **graze** (to feed on grass), whence **grazier**—cf *glasier* from *glass*.

1. *Grass*, ME *gres*, var *gers*, OE *graes*, var *gaers*: cf OFris *gres, gers*, OHG-G *gras*, OS *gras*, grass, and Go *gras*, herb; cf also L *grāmen* (? for *\*grasmen*), grass, and E GREEN and GROW: Gmc r, *\*grā-*, var *\*grō-*; IE r, *\*ghra-* or *\*ghrā-*. (Walshe.)

2. OE *graes* has derivative v *grasian*, whence ME *grasen*, whence 'to *graze*': orig, to feed (vt, then vi) on grass.

**grate** (1), n, for fire: ML *grāta*: L *crātis*, hurdle: cf HURDLE.

**grate** (2), v, to scrape, with pa **grating**. See SCRATCH, para 2.

**grateful.** See GRACE, para 5.

**gratification, gratify.** See GRACE, para 7.

**gratis.** See GRACE, para 8.

**gratitude.** See GRACE, para 5.

**gratuitous, gratuity.** See GRACE, para 9.

**gratulate, gratulation.** See GRACE, para 10.

**gravamen.** See para 3 of:

**grave** (1), adj; **gravamen; gravity; gravitate, gravitation;—aggravate, aggravation;—gravid;— grief, grieve, grievance, grievous; aggrieve.**

1. The adj *grave* is adopted from MF-F, from ML *gravis*, neu *grave*, L *grauis*, neu *graue*, heavy, s *grau-*: cf the syn Skt *gurús*, Av *gourús*, Gr *barus*, Go *kaurus*, perh Ir *bair*, Lett *grūts*, L *brūtus*; also cf Skt *garimā*, Gr *baros*, heaviness; IE r,*\*gur-*, var *\*gar-*, there being either contr (? from *\*garauis*) or metathesis (? *grau-* for *\*garu-*) in L *grauis*.

2. L *grauis* has derivative *grauitās*, ML *gravitās*, whence late OF-F *gravité* and E *gravity*: and *grauitās* has the SciL derivative *gravitāre*, pp *gravitātus*, whence 'to *gravitate*'; the subsidiary SciL *gravitātiō*, o/s *gravitātiōn-*, yields *gravitation*.

3. L *grauis* has also the derivatives:

LL *grauāmen*, ML *gravāmen*, adopted by E, esp in legal sense;

*grauidus*, ML *gravidus*, heavy with child, whence E *gravid*;

*grauāre*, ML *gravāre*, to weigh upon, with cpd *aggrauāre*, ML -*vāre*, to make heavy or, esp, heavier, with pp *aggrauātus*, ML -*vātus*, whence 'to *aggravate*'; derivative *aggrauātiō*, o/s *aggrauātiōn-*, ML *aggravātiōn-*, accounts for *aggravation*.

4. ML *aggravāre*, prob via a popular *\*aggrevāre*, becomes OF-MF *agrever*, with *il agrieve*, he renders heavy: whence ME *agreven*: whence (cf 'il *agrieve*') 'to *aggrieve*', now mostly in pa *aggrieved*.

5. L *grauāre* (cf para 3, s.f.) becomes VL *\*greuāre*, *\*grevāre*, whence OF-EF *grever*, ME *greven*, E 'to *grieve*' (cf OF 'il *grieve*'); OF *grever* has derivative *grevance*, whence, anl, E *grievance*; the likewise derivative OF-MF n *gref* and its MF-F var *grief* are adopted by ME, whence E *grief*; MF *gref* has the derivative adj OF-MF *grevos*, MF *grevous*, whence, anl, E *grievous*.

**grave** (2), n, a burial place in the earth, derives from OE *graef*, intimately akin to OE *grafan*, to dig, hence to engrave (to dig in wood or stone), whence 'to *grave*', now mostly in cpd *engrave* (influenced by EF *engraver*); the artistic n *gravure*, adopted from OF-F, comes from OF-F *graver*, of Gmc origin. With *grave*, n and v, cf OS *graf*, OFris *gref*, G *Grab* (cf *Graben*, ditch, moat, MHG *grabe*, OHG *grabo*), ON *gröf*, OSl *grobŭ*, and the vv OFris *grēva*, OHG *graban*, MHG-G *graben*, Go *graban*, ON *grafa*, to dig, OSl *pogrebǫ*, to bury: Gmc r, *\*grab-*, var *\*greb-*; IE r, *\*ghrebh-*, *\*ghrobh-*. (Walshe.) Cf GROOVE and GRUB.

**grave** (3), v, to dig. See prec.

**grave** (4), v, to clean. See next, s.f.

**gravel** (n, hence v): OF *gravele* or OF-F *gravelle*, dim of *grave*, *greve* (F *grève*), a sandy shore: either of C origin (cf Br *grouan*, gravel, W *gro*, coarse gravel, Cor *grou*, *grouan*, *grean*, Ga *grin*neal, MIr *grin*nel, EIr *grìan*, gravel, the Ga and MIr words meaning also the sea-bottom) or (B & W) from a pre-L *\*grava*, sand, sand-pit, hence a sandy shore. From EF *grave*, F *grève*, comes the naut *grave* (whence '*graving* dock'), to clean a vessel of, e.g., barnacles and then pay it over with pitch (Webster).

**gravid.** See 1st GRAVE, para 3.

**graving dock.** See GRAVEL, s.f.

**gravitate, gravitation.** See 1st GRAVE, para 2.

**gravity.** See 1st GRAVE, para 2.

**gravure.** See 2nd GRAVE.

**gravy.** See GRAIN, para 8.

**gray** (E and AE) and **grey** (mostly E), adj, hence n; hence also **grayness, greyness** (*-ness*); **graylag, grayling, greyhound; grilse, grisette, grizzle;—roan.**

1. Both *gray* and *grey* go back, through ME *gray*, *grey*, to OE; *grāēg* and *grēg*. Cf OFris *grē*, which will account for both of the OE forms, OHG *grāo*, MHG *grā*, G *grau*, MD *gra*, *grau*, D *grauw*, ON *grār*; perh cf L *rāuus* (ML *rāvus*), ? for *\*hrāuus*. (Walshe.) IE r, *\*ghra-*, var *\*ghre-*.

2. The *graylag* or grey wild goose, app=*gray* +*lag* (goose), the last of a flock of geese; *greyhound*=ME *grehound* (or *-hund*)=OE *grīghund*, cf ON *greyhundr*; *grayling*=*gray*+*-ling*, one of certain qualities.

3. *Grilse*, a young salmon after its first return from the sea, app derives, by metathesis, from OF-MF *grisel*, *grisle*, somewhat grey, from OF-F

*gris*, grey; OF-MF *grisel* also explains the adj *grizzle*, now usu *grizzled*, (rather) grey-haired, whence 'to *grizzle*' or become grey, whence prob *grizzle*, to whimper or fret—prob from *grizzling* skies betokening rain. The adj *grizzle* has derivative adj *grizzly*.

4. OF-F *gris*, grey (of Gmc origin), has the OF-F dim *grisette*, orig dim (adj), then a grey woollen fabric, finally a young working-class woman, because affecting dresses made therefrom.

5. L *rāuus*, grey, tawny, has derivative *\*rāuānus*, whence Sp *roano*, whence MF *roan* (F *rouan*), adopted by E.

**graze** (1), to feed on grass. See GRASS, para 2.

**graze** (2), to scrape, or to rub in passing, whence n: o.o.o.: Webster proposes source in *graze*, to 'cut the grass', but why not 'crop, eat, the grass'?

**grazier.** See GRASS, heading.

**grease** (n, hence v), whence **greaser** and **greasy.** See CRASS, para 2.

**great** (adj, hence adv and n), whence **greatness; groat.**

1. The silver coin named *groat*, ME *grote*, earlier *groot*, is adopted from MD-D *groot*, great, thick, MD var *grot*: and MD *groot* is akin to OE *grēat*, whence E *great*: cf OFris *grāt*, OS *grōt*, OHG-MHG *grōz*, G *gross*; Gmc r, *\*grout-* (Walshe).

2. Note that E *gross*, massive, burly, (unpleasantly) fat, is independent.

**grebe:** EF-F *grèbe*, MF *grebe*: o.o.o.: perh because its nest, built of reeds, resembles a crib or manger; like *crèche*, it could derive from Frankish *\*kripja* (G *Krippe*).

**Grecian** (adj, hence n), **Grecism, Grecize;** cf the element *Greco-*; **Greece; Greek** (adj, n); cf *fenugreek* at FENNEL.

1. *Grecian* derives from L *Graecia*, whence also *Greece*; *Graecia* is an *-ia* or 'region, country' derivative from L *Graecus*, both adj and n, whence *Greek*, adj and n; *Graecus* is a trln of Gr *Graikos*. Orig the *Graikoi* were a tribe in W Greece; the Italians applied the name to the inhabitants of Greece as a whole—Aristotle was the first Greek to do so. The name is thought to be of Pelasgian origin: prob, therefore, it is a Medit word.

2. Gr *Graikos* has derivative *Graikizein*, to speak Greek, whence, in part, E *Grecize*; *Grecism* derives from ML *Graecismus*, anl with other *-ismus* (Gr *-ismos*) formations.

**greed; greedy.**

The former comes, by b/f, from the latter, which comes, through ME *gredi*, from OE *grāēdig*, akin to the syn OS *grādag*, OHG *grātag*, Go *grēdags* (cf *grēdus*, hunger), ON *grāthugr*: cf Skt *gardha*, greediness, and Lith *gardus*, palatable (worthy of greed).

**Greek.** See GRECIAN, para 1.

**green** (adj, hence n and v), **greenery; greenback, greengage, greening.**

1. *Green*, ME *grene*, derives from OE *grēne*: cf OFris *grēne*, OS *grōni*, OHG *gruoni*, MHG *grüene*, G *grün*, ON *groenn*: cf OHG *gruoěn* MHG

*grüejen*, to grow (green): akin to sep GRASS and GROW.

2. *Green* has an *-ery* derivative *greenery* and many cpds, mostly self-explanatory. A *greenback* is an A legal-tender note, with green-hued devices on the back. A *greengage* is a greenish-yellow plum, named after Sir William Gage, who, c1725, imported it from France: cf *greening*, a green-skinned apple, from MD *groeninc* (MD-D *groen*, green).

**greet, greeting; regret** (n, v), **regretful, regrettable.**

*Regretful*=*regret*, n+*-ful*; *regrettable*, adopted from EF-F, derives from OF-MF *regreter*, EF-F *regretter* (*re-*, back), whence also the OF-F n *regret*, adopted by E; 'to *regret*' comes from OF-MF *regreter*, var of OF *regrater*, of Gmc origin: cf ON *grāta*, to weep, akin to syn OE *grāetan, grētan*, ME *greten*, E 'to *greet*', now archaic and dial, and Go *grētan* and prob Skt *hrādāte*, he roars. With OE *grētan*, ME *greten*, E *greet*, to address, cf OFris *grēta*, OS *grōtian*, Go *grōtjan*, OHG *gruozēn*, to accost, MHG *grüezen*, accost, greet, G *grüssen*, greet, ON *groeta*. The basic sense of 'to *greet*' is either 'to call' (Webster) or 'to cause to shout (in reply)' (Walshe). Note that the n *greeting*, salutation, goes back to OE *grēting*, vn from *grētan*.

**gregal, gregarian, gregarious, gregaritic;— aggregate** (adj—whence n—and v), **aggregation** (whence anl **aggregative** and **aggregator**); **congregant, congregate** (adj and v), **congregation** (whence **congregational,** whence **Congregationalism** and **Congregationalist**), **congregative, congregator; egregious; segregant, segregate** (adj—whence n—and v), **segregation** (whence, anl **segregative, segregator**); cf sep AGORA and ALLEGORY.

1. The base is L *greg-*, o/s of *grex*, herd, flock, hence company of persons: cf OIr *graig*, herd (of horses), W and Ga *greigh*, Br *gré*, OC *\*gragis*, with *greigh* meaning esp 'stud of horses'; cf also Gr *ageirō*, I gather or assemble, and *agora*, an assembly—Lith *gurgulys*, a swarm—and perh Skt *gaṇás*, herd, flock, company, crowd, and *grāma*, company, community.

2. L *grex*, o/s *greg-*, has adj *gregālis*, whence E *gregal*, and *gregārius*, whence both *gregarious* and, with *-ian* for *-ious*, *gregarian*; Geol *gregaritic*= *gregar*ious+adj *-itic*.

3. L *grex* has prefix-cpds *aggregāre* (*ag-* for *ad-*, to), *congregāre* (*con-* together), *ēgregius* (*ē-*, out of, away from), *sēgregāre* (*sē-*, apart from, aside).

4. *Aggregāre*, to bring together (at or to a given point), has pp *aggregātus*, whence adj and v *aggregate*; derivative LL *aggregātiō*, o/s *aggregātiōn-*, yields *aggregation*.

5. *Congregāre*, to gather together, has pp *congregātus*, whence adj and v *congregate*; derivative *congregātiō*, o/s *congregātiōn-*, produces—prob via OF-MF *congregacion—congregation*; derivative LL *congregatiuus* (ML *-ivus*) and LL *congregātor* lead to *congregative* and *congregator*. *Congregant*, n, derives from L *congregant-*, o/s of the presp *congregans*.

6. L *ēgregius*, (apart from the herd, hence) distinguished, outstanding, excellent, becomes E *egregious*.

7. L *sēgregāre*, to separate (orig, from the herd), has presp *sēgregans*, o/s *sēgregant-*, whence the E n *segregant*; the pp *sēgregātus* yields adj and v *segregate*; derivative LL *sēgregātiō*, o/s *sēgregā-tiōn-*, accounts for *segregation*.

**grenade, grenadier.** See GRAIN, para 5.

**gressorial.** See GRADE, para 5.

**grew.** See GROW.

**grewsome:** occ var of GRUESOME.

**grey, greyhound.** See GRAY—the hound at para 2.

**grid and gridiron; griddle; grill, n and v; grille and grillage.**

1. *Grid* is a b/f from *gridiron*: and *gridiron* derives from ME *gredirne*, a f/e mdfn (by confusion with ME *iren*, iron) of ME *gredire*, either slovenly or illiterate for ME *gredil*—var *gridel*, whence E *griddle*, a gridiron: and ME *gredil* prob comes from OF-MF *\*gredil*, a var of OF *graïl*: cf MF-EF *grediller*, to scorch.

2. 'To *grill*' comes from OF-F *griller*, itself from OF(-F) *gril*, a gridiron, a var of OF-F *grille*, OF varr *graïl, graïle*, from VL *\*grāticula*, for L *crāticula*, although *gril* comes perhaps rather from VL *\*grāticulum*, for L *crāticulum*; both *crāticula* and *crāticulum* are dim derivatives from L *crātis, crātēs* (strictly, pl), a hurdle, with LL var *grātis, grātēs*: cf CRATE. As a hurdle is openwork, though of wood, so a grille, or grating, is openwork, though usu of metal.

**grief, grievance, grieve, grievous.** See 1st GRAVE, para 5.

**griffin, griffon, gryphon:** resp the E, OF-F, imitation-L form: E *griffin*, ME *griffon*, OF *grifoun*, MF-F *griffon*, OHG *grīf, grīfo*, L *gryphus*, var *gryps*, Gr *grups*, either deriving from or at the least akin to Gr *grupos*, curved, hooked, hook-nosed: cf Ass *kurub*, a fabulous winged monster. (Walshe.)

**grifter.** See GRAFTER.

**grig,** earliest as 'boon companion' (*merry grig* or *Grig*), is *Grig*, pet-form of *Gregory*; modern sense 'cricket' or 'grasshopper' derives, by f/e, from *merry as a cricket*; with *merry Grig*, cf *merry Andrew*. (EW.)

**grill; grille.** See GRID, para 2.

**grilse.** See GRAY, para 3.

**grim** (whence **grimness**); **grimace** (n, hence v); **grime** (n, hence v), whence **grimy; grum; grumble; grumpy;—chagrin,** n and v.

1. *Grim*, OE *grim*, is akin to OFris and OS *grinm*, OHG-MHG *grim*, G *grimm*, ON *grimmr*: app a thinning of such forms as ON *gramr*, an enemy, the devil, OE *gram*, OHG-G *gram*, hostile (*Gram*, grief): Gmc r *\*grim-*, *\*gram-*; IE r, *\*ghrem-*, *\*ghrom-*.

2. Perh of Gmc origin is *grimace*, adopted from MF-F, from OSp *grimazo*, a grimacing counten-ance, prob from Go *\*grima*, spectre, terror: cf OE *grīma*, a spectre, from OE *grim*. (Dauzat.)

3. OE *grīma*, spectre, also a mask or a visor

(as ON *grūma*), is at least akin to MD be*grimen*, to sully, to dirty, and Fl *grijm*, both of which are intimately akin to E *grime*.

4. Akin to *grim* is *grumble*, from EF syn *grumeler*, var of MF-F *grommeler*, app a freq of OF-MF *grommer*, itself prob from MD *grommen* (cf Fl *grommelen*): cf the MD varr *grimmen*, *grimmelen*. OF-MF *grommer*, var *gromer*, is, however, perh a var of OF-MF *gronir*: see GRIN, para 5.

5. Clearly connected with *grim* is the mostly dial *grum*, morose or surly, either deriving from or at the least akin to Da *grum*, fierce, angry; cf the dial and coll *grumpy*, with dial var *grumphy*, app from the echoic *grumph*, a grunt.

6. Akin to the *gram* terms noted in para 1 is OF-MF *graim*, sorrowful, with var *graing* or *grain*, whence OF-MF *graignier*, to be sorrowful, perh with MF int *chagraigner*, *chagrigner*, whence EF-F *chagriner*, whence 'to *chagrin*'; the E n *chagrin* is adopted from EF-F *chagrin*, which comes either from *chagriner* or from the MF adj *chagrin*, sad, discomfited, much disappointed. (The foregoing is a merely provisional statement, the etymology of *chagrin* being obscured with doubts and interventions; with *cha-*, if indeed an int, cf Gmc *ge-* and AE *ker-*.)

**grimace.** See para 2 of prec.

**grime, grimy.** See GRIM, para 3.

**grin** (v, hence n): ME *grinnen*, earlier *grennen*: OE *grennian*: akin to ON *grenja*, to grin, to howl, G *grinsen*, to grin, and OHG *grīnan*, MHG *grīnen*, G *greinen*, to grin, to whine, and therefore prob to *groan*. A dog grins when it snarls, a boy when he laughs.

2. 'To *groan*' — whence 'a *groan*' — comes, through ME *gronen*, earlier *granen*, earliest *granien*, from OE *grānian*, akin to OHG *grīnan* (as above) and to OHG *granōn*, to grunt.

3. 'To *grunt*'—whence 'a *grunt*'—comes, through ME *grunten*, from OE *grunnettan*, extn of *grunian*, to grunt, akin to MHG-G *grunzen*, to grunt: orig, echoic—cf L *grunnīre* (s *grunn-*, r *grun-*), with early var *grundīre* (s *grund-*, r *grun-*), to grunt, and its derivative *grunnitus* (early var *grunditus*), a grunt.

4. 'Mrs *Grundy*', proponent of the proprieties, occurs in Morton's *Speed the Plough*, a comedy produced in 1798: the name is perh a blend of *grunty*, addicted to grunting (in disapproval), and the EF-F *grondeuse*, a female growling scolder, from MF-F *gronder*, vi to growl, vt to scold, from L *grundīre*.

5. L *grunnīre* becomes OF-MF *grunir*, *gronir*, EF-F *grogner*, to grunt or grumble; from OF *gronir* (s *gron-*) comes, by metathesis, OF *gornart*, *gornard* (pej suffix *-art*, *-ard*), whence the E fish *gurnard*, *gurnet*: 'it makes a grunting sound when caught' (EW).

**grind** (v, hence n), pt, pp (and pa) **ground**; hence **grinder, grindery; grist.**

*Grist*, OE *grīst*, comes from OE *grindan*, whence 'to *grind*': and *grindan* is akin to Lith *grendu*, I scrape, or rub violently, L *frendere*, to grind (esp

corn), to gnash, Gr *khrainein*, to touch lightly, to smear (cf CHRISM), and *khondros* (for *\*khrondros*), a grain; IE r *\*ghren-*, with extn *\*ghrend-*; *\*ghren-* itself prob a mdfn of *\*gher-*, to rub.

**grip** (n, v); **gripe** (v, hence n); **grippe; grope;**— **grasp** (v, hence n).

1. 'To *gripe*' descends from OE *grīpan*, akin to OFris *grīpa*, OS *grīpan*, MD *gripen*, D *gripjen*, Go *greipan*, ON *grīpa*, also OHG *grīfan*, MHG *grīfen*, G *greifen*, and Lith *gribti*; Gmc r, *\*ghreib-*, to grasp firmly, to seize.

2. OE *grīpan* has derivative OE *gripe* (cf OFris *grip*), whence 'a *grip*'; 'to *grip*' derives from OE *grippan*, app from the OE n *gripe*, perh however a thinning of the OE v *grīpan*.

3. Akin to the Gmc words of para 1 are Frankish *\*grīpan*, to seize, and *\*grip*, a seizing or grasping, whence the syn MF-F v *gripper* and MF-F n *grippe*. The malady (*la*) *grippe*, approx influenza, arises in C18 and 'would be so named because it seizes (its victim) suddenly' (B & W); to postulate origin in Ru *khrip*, hoarseness—an echoic word— is supererogatory.

4. Akin to OE *grīpan* is OE *grāpian*, to touch, to handle, ME *grapien*, later *gropen*, whence 'to *grope*'.

5. Akin to OE *grāpian* is ME *graspen*, to grope, grasp at, whence 'to *grasp*': cf LG *grapsen*, to grasp, and MD *grapen*, to seize, grip, grasp.

**grippe.** See prec, para 3.

**grisette.** See GRAY, para 4.

**grisly; grizzly (bear).**

The *grizzly*, a large, powerful creature, *Ursus horribilis*, is a var of *grisly*, not from *grizzly*, rather grey. *Grisly*, inspiring horror, comes, through ME *grisly*, earlier *grislich*, from OE *grislīc*, causing one to *-grīsan* or shudder: cf the syn OFris *grislik*, OHG *grisenlīch* and MD *griselijc* and G *gruselig*.

**grist.** See GRIND.

**gristle** (whence **gristly**) comes straight from OE: cf OFris *gristel*, *grestel*, *gerstel*, MLG *gristel*.

**grit** (1), sand, esp if hard and rough, hence 'to *grit*' (e.g., one's teeth), hence also the adj **gritty**— this *grit* derives, via ME *greet*, var *greot*, from OE *grēot*, sand, grit: cf OFris *grēt*, OS *griot*, OHG *grioz*, MHG *griez*, sand, G *Griess*, gravel, groats, ON *griōt*, pebbles, stones. Cf:

**grit** (2), coarse meal, now **grits**: OE (pl) *grytta*, *gryttan*: cf OHG *gruzzi*, MHG-G *grütze*, groats. Cf, therefore, E *groats*, ME *grotens* (pl), OE *gratan* (pl), perh for *\*grotan*—cf OE *grot*, a grain or a particle; cf also ON *grautr*, groats, and Lith *grúdas*, grain, corn, kernel, OSl *gruda*, a clod.

**grizzle, grizzled.** See GRAY, para 3.

**grizzly,** adj. See GRAY, para 3, s.f.

**grizzly,** n, elliptical for *grizzly bear*. See GRISLY.

**groan.** See GRIN, para 2.

**groat.** See GREAT.

**groats.** See the 2nd GRIT.

**grocer** (whence **grocery**). See GROSS, para 3.

**grog, groggy; grogram.**

*Groggy*, unsteady on one's feet, suggests that the victim has had too much *grog*, orig rum and water, hence any intoxicant, so named because, in 1740, Admiral Vernon ordered the sailors' rum to be diluted: he was known as 'Old *Grog*', from the *grogram* cloak he wore in dirty weather. *Grogram* anglicizes F *gros grain*, large grain—hence, coarse texture—hence a coarse-textured fabric. Cf GROSS and GRAIN.

**groin**, varr **groyn**, **groyne**. See GROUND, para 3.

**groom** (1), an ostler. See GORMANDIZE, s.f.

**groom** (2), as in *bridegroom*. See HOMO, para 14.

**groove** (n, hence v): ME *groof* (var *grofe*), MD *groeve* (var *grove*; D *groef*), akin to ON *gröf*, OHG *gruoba*, MHG *gruobe*, G *Grube*, and Go *gröba*; akin also to GRAVE, n.

**grope**. See GRIP, para 4.

**groper** (fish). See GROUPER.

**grosbeak**. See heading, s.f., of:

**gross** (adj, whence v; n, from F *gros* used as n); **engross** (with pa **engrossing** and pa **engrossed**), whence **engrossment**; **grocer**, whence **grocery**; sep **program**, where **grosgrain** is implied; **grosbeak** (EF-F *grosbec*, big-beak).

1. The adj *gross*, relatively very large, hence coarsely big and fat, hence coarse, derives from OF-F *gros*, f *grosse*, from LL *grossus*, f *grossa*, big and fat, coarse (esp food or mind), prob of C origin, *grossus* being app for *\*grossos*, itself eased from *\*grodsos*, from the C r *\*grod-* (var of *\*grad-*), to increase (vt, vi) in size: cf MIr, W, Br, Cor *bras*, Ir and Ga *breas*, large, bulky, corpulent, coarse.

2. OF-F *gros* has MF-F derivative *engrosser* (MF varr *engrossier*, *engroissier*) to make or render thick or large, whence 'to *engross*', esp to write large and fair.

3. OF-F *gros* has MF-F agent *grossier*, enlarger, late MF-EF vendor (merchant) in bulk, whence E *grocer*, orig a wholesaler; OF *grossier* was perh suggested by ML *grossārius*, an *-arius* derivative of LL *grossus*.

**grot**, **grotto**; **grotesque** (adj and n); cf the sep CRYPT.

1. *Grot*=EF-F *grotte*=It *grotta*, which, by anl with the multitudinous It nn in *-o*, becomes E *grotto*: and It *grotta* derives from VL *\*grupta*, alteration of VL *\*crupta*, itself from LL *crypta*, a cave, hence a hidden underground passage, hence a vault: f.a.e., CRYPT.

2. It *grotta* has adj *grottesco*, whence n *grottesca*, elliptical for *pittura grottesca*, ref the decorated grottos once fashionable in Italy; the It n becomes EF-F *grotesque*, n, which acquires the sense 'ridiculous face or figure', whence the F adj; the F n and adj are adopted by E. (B & W.)

**grouch**. See GRUDGE, para 2.

**ground** (n, whence adj and v), **groundling**, **groundsel**; **groin** (**groyn**, **groyne**).

1. In Arch, *groundsel*=*ground*+SILL; the medicinal herb *groundsel* comes, through ME *grundswilie*, from late OE *grundeswylige*, var of *grundeswelge*, mdfn of OE *gundeswelge*, app *gund(e)*, pus +*-swelge*, swallower, from *swelgan*, to swallow: 'pus-absorber'—from its being used in poultices. *Groundling*=*ground*+*-ling*, one belonging to or

having the quality of: a *groundling* is a fish that, like the loach, keeps close to the bottom, hence a spectator that, frequenting the pit of a theatre, is presumed to lack judgement and taste.

2. *Ground* itself, ME *ground*, earlier *grund*, derives from OE *grund*, foundation, earth: cf OFris and OS *grund*, OHG-MHG *grunt*, G *Grund*, MD *grunt*, *gront*, D *grond*, Go *grundu-*, Scan *grund*, ON *grunnr*; Gmc r, *\*grun-*.

3. Akin to OE *grund* is OE *grynde*, abyss, whence, app, ME *grynde*, whence the eased EE *grine*, whence—influenced by LOIN—the E *groin*, the depression between lower belly and upper thigh, hence its use in Arch and in Eng—where occ *groyn*, *groyne*, obs elsewhere.

**groundling**. See prec, para 1, s.f.

**groundsel**, both senses. See GROUND, para 1; for the herb, cf the 2nd SWALLOW, para 3.

**group**. See CROP, para 4.

**grouper**, with a f/e var **groper**, is a kind of sea bass that frequents warm waters: and it anglicizes Port *garoupa*, o.o.o.—Webster cfs Galibi (F-D Guiana) *groupy*, a distinct species of fish. In the Sp of CA this fish is called *garopa* (Santamaria).

**grouse** (1), a game bird, is o.o.o.: perh (Webster) cf OF *greuce*, some unspecified food, from ML *gruta*, a vaguely domestic bird; perh rather (EW) the EE form *grewys*, pl used collectively, indicates a wrong-sensing of ME *grewe*, a crane, from OF-F *grue* (cf Port *grou*), crane, itself, through VL *\*grūa*, from L *grūs* (gen *grūis*), s *grū-*, well represented, with varr, in IE. (Whitehall approves EW's suggestion.)

**grouse** (2), to grumble. See GRUDGE, para 3.

**grove**, a tree-group smaller than a wood, derives from OE *gräf* and app lacks kindred, at least in IE.

**grovel** is a b/f from the ME adv *grovelinge*, *grufelinge*, on one's face, prone, misapprehended as presp of syn ME *groffe*, *gruf*, from ON *grūfa* in *ā grūfa*, grovelling, from *grūfa*, to grovel: ? from Gmc *\*gruben*, to cower (down), as Holthausen suggests.

**grow**, pt **grew**, pp **grown**; **growth**.

*Growth* derives from 'to *grow*', much as ON *gröthr* (*gröthi*) derives from ON *gröa*, to grow. 'To *grow*' derives from OE *grōwan*, akin to syn OFris *gröia*, OHG *gruoēn*, MHG *grüejen* (both also 'to grow, become, green'), MD *groyen*, *groeyen*, D *groeien*, ON *gröa*: akin, therefore, to GREEN and GRASS.

**growl** (v, hence n), whence **growler**, SE agent and sl container, may be natively echoic but prob comes from MF *grouler* (MF-F *grouiller*), itself from MD *grollen*: cf *grumble*, q.v. at GRIM, para 4.

**grown**; **growth**. See GROW.

**groyn(e)**. See GROUND, para 3.

**grub** (v, whence app the n, whence both the adj **grubby** and the cpds **grub-stake** and **Grub Street**) derives from ME *grubben*, var of *gruben*, akin to OHG *grubilōn*, MHG *grübilen*, to dig, grub, poke about, investigate, whence G *grübeln*, to rack one's brains; hence akin also to OHG *graban*, MHG-G *graben*, to dig: f.a.e., the 2nd GRAVE.

grudge (v, hence n), with derivative int (*be-*) begrudge; grouch (v, hence n; hence also the adj grouchy); grouse (v, hence n and the agent grouser). Sem: to give grumblingly.

1. 'To *grudge*' comes, through EE *grutch*, ME *grutchen*, var of *gruchen*, to grumble, from MF *groucher*, var *groucier*, itself a var of MF *grocier*, a worn-down var of OF-MF *groucier*, to growl; prob akin to *grunt*, q.v. at GRIN, para 3; ult echoic ?

2. 'To *grouch*' prob comes from ME *gruchen*.

3. 'To *grouse*' perh comes from OF-MF *groucier* (as in para 1).

grue. See GRUESOME.

gruel was adopted from OF *gruel* (F *gruau*), app a dim of the syn OF-EF *gru*: Frankish *\*grūt*: cf OHG *gruzzi*, therefore cf GRIT, coarse meal.

gruesome, occ var grewsome, tacks adj suffix *-some* to dial 'to *grue*', to shiver with fear: cf MD (and MLG) *gruwen*, with MD var *grouwen* (and freq *gruwelen, gruelen*); cf also OHG *gruēn*. Ult echoic.

gruff (whence gruffness): MD *grof, groef, grouf* (for *gerouf*): cf OHG *gerob*, thick, MHG *grof*, strong, G *grob*, coarse; perh ult akin to GREAT.

grum. See GRIM, para 5.

grumble. See GRIM, para 4.

grumpy. See GRIM, para 5.

Grundy, Mrs. See GRIN, para 4.

grunt. See GRIN, para 2.

gryphon. See GRIFFIN.

guana. See IGUANA.

guano. See the element *guani-*.

guarantee, guarantor, guaranty. See WARN, para 7.

guard (n, v), guardian, guard-room. See WARD, paras 9 and 1.

guava: via the obsol var *guaba*, from Sp *guayaba*, the fruit (cf *guayabo*, the tree): Arawakan, from Cariban, prob ult from Tupi: cf Taino *guayavá* and Tupi *guajava*. (Webster; Santamaria.)

gubernatorial. See GOVERN, para 2.

gudgeon. See GOBY.

Guelph. See WHELP, para 2.

guerdon. See LUCRE, para 3.

guernsey comes from *Guernsey*, as jersey from *Jersey*, these being two of the Channel Islands, noted for their fishermen, themselves notable for their knitted woollen, buttonless jackets, so suitable for their work. *Guernsey* comes, via F, from L *Sarnia*, of C origin; *Jersey*, from L *Caesarea* (insula), Caesar's Island.

guerre, C'est la. See WAR, para 2.

guerrilla, guerrillero. See WAR, para 3.

guess (v, hence n): ME *gessen*: perh of Scan origin, but prob imm from MD *gessen*, var *gissen*: akin, ult, to ON *geta*, to get, to guess: cf GET.

guest. See HOSPICE, para 10.

guffaw (*guf-faw'*) is echoic.

guidance, guide. See VIDE, para 10.

guild or gild (n), a common-pursuited association. See YIELD, para 3.

guilder. See GOLD, para 7.

guile. See VICTIM, para 3.

guillemot. See VOLITION, para 11.

guillotine, n and v. 'To *guillotine*' represents F *guillotiner*, itself from (la) *guillotine*, which, adopted by E, derives, in 1790, from Dr J. G. *Guillotin* (1738-1814), who, in 1789, recommended its use. This surname derives from F *Guill*aume, William.

guilt, guilty.

The latter derives from OE *gyltig*, adj of *gylt*, (a) crime, whence ME *gult* or *gilt*, which app blend into E *guilt*. OE *gylt* is o.o.o.: ? akin to OE *scyld*, ON *skuld*, sin, guilt, and the approx syn OHG *sculd*, MHG *schult, schulde*, G *Schuld*, and therefore ult to E *shall* and *should*.

guimp(e). See WIMPLE, para 2.

guinea, a gold coin worth 21 shillings, is a *Guinea* (*coin*), reputed to be minted of gold from Guinea in West Africa; likewise the *guinea cock—fowl— hen* comes from Guinea; and *Guinea* is a Port form of *Gineua*, the name brought to medieval Europe by Arabs, who thus adapted a Negro word.—Note that *guinea pig* is prob f/e for *Guiana pig*, for this little quadruped comes from SAm; unless, perhaps, the *guinea* derives from *Guineamen*, those traders who, after taking slaves to the WI, picked up goods and oddities from the WI and from Northern SAm and conveyed them to Britain and the Continent of Europe.

guipure. See VIBRATE, para 5.

guise. See ADDENDA TO DICTIONARY.

guitar: MF-F *guitare*: Sp *guitarra*: Ar *qītāra*: Gr *kithara*. Zither, adopted from G (cf OHG *zitera*), derives from L *cithara*, likewise from Gr *kithara*, itself app imported: prob cf Hit *katras*, ? a tambourine-player; perh from PlN *Kithairon* (L & S).

gulden. See GOLD, para 7.

gules. See GULLET, s.f.

gulf (n, hence v); engulf.

'To *engulf*' = *en-*, in(to) + *gulf*, but was prob suggested by EF-F *engouffrer* (OF *engolfer, engoulfer*): and *gulf* anglicizes MF-F *golfe* (cf MD-D *golf*), from It *golfo*, from LL *colfus*, from LGr *kolphos*, a gulf, from Gr *kolpos*, gulf, bay, orig bosom; akin to OE *hwealf*, (the sky's) vault, and G *wolben*, MHG *welben*, ON *hvelfa*, to vault or arch, Go *hwilftrjōs*, a coffin. (Walshe.)

gull (1), the sea bird: app 'the (well-) *beaked* bird': OC *\*gulbanos*, OIr *gulban*, OW *gilbin*, Ga *guilb* (gen *gulbann*), a beak, and W *gwylan*, Br *gwelan*, Cor *guilan, gullan*, a gull; OC r, prob *\*gulb-*, a point (Malvezin).

gull (2), to deceive, trick, defraud, whence *gull*, one easily deceived, perh derives from the now dial *gull*, a young bird, esp a gosling ('The silly goose!')—prob from ON *gulr*, yellow: cf *yellow* at GOLD, para 1.—Hence *gullible*.

gullet and gully; gules.

*Gully*, a narrow valley, a ravine, derives from EE

*gullet*, itself from ME *golet*, the throat, from OF *goulet*, dim of *gole*, *goule*, throat (MF-F *gueule*), from L *gula*, itself akin to E *gurgle*, q.v. at GARGLE. The MF pl *gueules*, lit 'gullets', becomes, in C13, an Her term for 'red', whence ME *goules*, E *gules*: from the redness of the gullet. (The Per *gul*-rose etymology is obs.)

**gullible** (whence **gullibility**). See the 2nd GULL, s.f.

**gully.** See GULLET.

**gulp** (v, hence n): D *gulpen*: clearly echoic.

**gum** (1), of the mouth: ME *gome*: OE *gōma*, palate (in pl: jaws): cf OHG *goumo*, MHG *goume*, G *Gaumen*, ON *gōmr*, Lith *gomurys*, palate; cf also Gr *khaunos* (adj), gaping, and therefore *khaos*, abyss, space: the IE r is prob *\*gha-*, with var *\*ghau-* and with nasal extn *\*ghaun-*, *\*ghaum-*. Cf CHAOS.

**gum** (2), a sticky substance, whence 'to **gum**' and adj **gummy**, derives from ME *gumme*, earlier *gomme*—adopted from OF-F, which thus adapts LL *gumma*, mdfn of L *gummi*, var *cummi*, trln of Gr *kommi*, itself from Eg *qemài* (*ķmj-t*), the exudation of the acanthus.

**gumbo** (AE), prop a soup thickened with okra-pods, hence loosely any thick soup, hence, among tramps, a stew: either from the element *-ngombo* of such Negro words as *kingombo* and *ocingombo* (Webster) or, more precisely, from a Bu word of Angola (Mathews).

**gun** (n, hence v), whence **gunner**; many self-explanatory cpds, but note **gunwale** (often pron **gunnel**), which=*gun*+*wale*, ship's or boat's side, q.v. at WALL, 'because the upper guns were pointed from it' (Webster).

A *gun* derives from ME *gunne*, var *gonne* (1339), either from OF *engon*, var of *engin*, a device, f.a.e. ENGINE, as Webster proposes, or, more prob (as EW), from the f name *Gun*hild, applied, in ML of 1330-31 as *Gun*ilda, to a mangonel (a military stone-throwing engine), for cf, sem, the famous C15 *Mons Meg* of Edinburgh and the no less famous 1917-18 *Big Bertha* that shelled Paris.

**gurgle.** See GARGLE, para 2, s.f.

**gurnard, gurnet.** See GRIN, para 5.

**gush** (v hence n), with pa **gushing.** 'To *gush*' is ME *guschen*, clearly echoic.

**gusset**: MF-F *gousset*, gusset, (orig) armpit: dim (*-et*) of *gousse*, a husk or a pod: o.o.o.

**gust** (1), of wind: ON *gustr*, akin to ON *gjōsa*, to gush: cf GEYSER. Ult echoic.

**gust** (2), taste, whence 'to **gust**' or relish; **gusto**; **gustation, gustative** or **gustatory**;—**degust, degustation; disgust** (n, v), whence pa **disgusting** and adj **disgustful; ragoût,** usu written **ragout.**

1. *Gusto*, adopted from It, derives from L *gustus* (gen *-ūs*), akin to Skt *juṣáte*, he enjoys (the use of), and ult akin to CHOOSE. *Gustus* becomes E *gust*. Derivative L *gustāre*, to taste, to enjoy the taste of, has derivative *gustātiō*, o/s *gustātiōn-*, whence E *gustation*; the E adjj *gustative* and *gustatory* are formed anl.

2. *Gustāre* has cpd *dēgustāre* (int *dē-*), whence 'to *degust*'; derivative LL *dēgustātiō*, o/s *dēgustā-tiōn-*, yields *degustation*.

3. L *gustus* becomes OF *goust*, with MF derivative cpd v *desgouster* (*des-*, L *dis-*, apart), whence E 'to *disgust*'; *desgouster* has derivative n *desgoust* (F *dégoût*), whence the E n *disgust*.

4. F *goût* (L *gustus*), taste, has the MF-F derivative cpd v *ragoûter*, to restore (connoted by *re-*) one's taste, whence the EF-F n *ragoût*, a spiced stew, adopted by E; *ragoûter* was perh suggested by L *regustāre*.

**gut(s).** See the 2nd FOUND, para 18.

**gutta(-)percha**: Mal *gëtah*, gum+*përca*, the tree exuding it. By a sort of erudite f/e—the kind of thing one gets in the ghostly 'ab*h*ominable'—Mal *gëtah* has been assimilated (as EW points out) to L *gutta*, a drop of water or other liquid.

**gutter; guttersnipe.** See GOUT, para 2.

**guttural.** See GOITER, para 2.

**guy** (1), a guide rope: OF *gui* or *guie*, a guide, from OF-MF *guier*, to guide, from Frankish *\*uitan*, *\*witan*, to indicate a direction: cf E *guide*, q.v. at VIDE, para 10.

**guy** (2), a ragged, ludicrous—even grotesque—effigy of *Guy* Fawkes of the Gunpowder Plot: F *Guy*, var *Gui*: LL *Uitus* (ML *Vitus*), as in 'St *Vitus*'s dance', rendering F 'danse de Saint-*Guy*' (cf the E var 'St *Guy*'s dance'): the child martyr Vitus was invoked by epileptics, said to have danced before his image.

**guzzle** (v, hence n) prob comes from MF *gosillier*, to vomit—by passing through the *gosier* or gullet, from Gaul *geusiae*, attested in C5; the E *-u-* was perh suggested by L *guttur*, gullet, throat (cf GOITER).

**gymnasium, gymnast, gymnastic(s)** See NAKED, para 4.

**gynecocracy, gyneocracy.** See the element *-gyn*.

**gyp**, a swindler, to swindle. See EGYPT, para 4.

**gypsum; gesso.**
The latter, adopted from It, derives from L *gypsum*, adapted from Gr *gupsos* (γύψος), chalk; the derivative LL adj *gypseus* yields E *gypseous*; Gr *gupsos* is of Sem origin—cf Ar *jibs*, mortar.

**Gypsy.** See EGYPT, para 3.

**gyrate, gyration, gyratory; gyre;** cf the element *gyro-*, but for **gyroscope**, see the element *-scope*; **girasol; cower.**

1. 'To *gyre*' or turn round derives from LL *gyrāre*, to turn (vi, vt), itself from *gyrus*, whence E *gyre*, a revolution or the path tracked by one: from Gr *guros*, s and r *gur-*, as in IE, where it extends *\*geu-*, to bend (vt): cf Arm *kor* (*cuṙ*), bent, crooked, *kuṙn*, the back, and Ga *guairs*geach, curled, curly, Ir *gúaire*, hair of the head, and Ga *guairdean*, vertigo, Ir *gúairdean*, a whirlwind.

2. LL *gyrāre* has pp *gyrātus*, whence 'to *gyrate*', whence LL *gyrātiō*, o/s *gyrātiōn-*, whence E *gyration*, whence, anl, the adj *gyratory*.

3. LL *gyrāre* becomes It *girare*, with two cpds affecting E: *girandola*, a cluster of radiating

rockets, a radiating fountain, EF-F *girandole*, adopted by E; *girasole*, adopted, perh via EF-F, by E, with var *girasol*, the heliotrope, a sunflower, 2nd element from L *sol*, sun (cf SOLAR).

4. Akin to Gr *guros* is 'to *cower*' (to make oneself *round* and small, through fear): ME *couren*, prob of Scan origin—cf Nor *kūra*, Sw *kura*, to cower,

themselves akin to syn G *kauern*, MLG *kūren*; ? cf D (and MD) *hurken*, MD *huerken, hoorken, horken*, to squat.

**gyrfalcon.** See GAR, para 3.

**gyroscope.** See the element *-scope* and cf GYRATE.

**gyve.** See WIRE, para 2, s.f.

# H

h comes, through L *h*, from the Gr 'rough breathing' (', as in ἅγιος, *hagios*, holy), itself from a Phoen letter corresponding to H *cheth*, indicative of a very guttural 'breathing' or aspirate.

**habeas corpus** is L for '(See that) you have the *corpus* or body', a legal term: a medieval writ, implying that the person accused must be produced in court. For *corpus* see CORPS; *habeas* is the subj of *habēre*, to hold, to have, as in HABIT.

**habena, habenula.** See HABIT, para 2.

**habendum.** See HABIT, para 3.

**haberdasher** (whence **haberdashery**) app derives from AF *happertas*, a stuff or fabric: o.o.o.: ? OF *happetas* or *happatas*, for OF *happe a tas*, hook (orig, scythe)+*a* (F *à*), for+*tas*, heap (sc *de draps*, of clothes). OF *happe* derives either from Gmc *happa*, scythe, hook, or from OF-F *happer*, of Gmc origin (cf D *happen*, to seize): ? an ult echoic *hap(p)-*, to seize, take hold of, hold. EW proposes: *haberdasher* as agent, hence dealer, connoted by *-er*, in *haberdash*, small wares, with the *haber-* of EE *haber*dupois, avoirdupois, but he, like so many others, slides away from *-dash-*.

**habile.** See HABIT, para 4.

**habiliment.** See HABIT, para 6.

**habilitate, habilitation.** See HABIT, para 7.

**habit** (n, v), **habitable, habitant** (whence **habitancy**), **habitat, habitation**—cf **cohabit, cohabitant, cohabitation,** and **inhabit, inhabitable, inhabitant** (whence **inhabitancy**), **inhabitation; habile, hability**—**able, ability; habiliment,** whence **habilimentation; habilitate, habilitation**—**rehabilitate, rehabilitation; habitual, habituate** (whence, anl, **habituation), habitude, habitué; habena** (**habenula); habendum.**—The *-hibit* cpds: **adhibit, adhibition; cohibit, cohibition; exhibit** (v, hence n), **exhibition** (whence **exhibitional, exhibitioner, exhibitionism, exhibitionist), exhibitor, exhibitory; inhibit** (whence **inhibitable, inhibitive), inhibition, inhibitor, inhibitory; prohibit, prohibition** (whence **prohibitionary, prohibitionism, prohibitionist), prohibitive, prohibitor, prohibitory; redhibition.**—Less obvious derivatives of L *habēre*: **aver,** n; **binnacle;** sep **debit** (debt, etc.); sep **gavel,** sheaf of mown grain, bundle of hay, etc.; **malady; prebend** (whence **prebendal), prebendary**—cf **provender.**

1. The centre of this constellation of words lies in the L *habēre* (s *habē-*; r *hab-*), to hold (vt, vi), hence to occupy or possess, hence to have. 'L

*habē-* is to [OIr *gabim*], Ir *gaibim* [ss *gab-*, *gaib-*], "I take", what OHG *habē-* (*habēn*, "to have") is to L *capio* [s *cap-*], Go *hafja*': E & M. Akin to L *hab-*, therefore, is the *gab-* (*gaib-*) of OIr-Ir and of Lith *gabenti* (to bring); the IE r might be *\*ghab-* or *\*khabh-*.

2. L *habē-*, s of *habēre*, appears in *habēna*, a thong or other strap that controls, preserved in An, with adjj *habenal, habenar*; its dim *habēnula* is commoner, even in An.

3. The legal *habendum* is form-adopted (and sense-adapted) from L: (which is) to be had: neus of gerundive *habendus*.

4. L *habēre* has adj *habilis* (*-ilis*, cf E *-ile*), able, hence well able, to hold, hence to control, whence MF-F, hence E, *habile*, adroit; derivative L *habilitās* (o/s *habilitāt-*) yields *hability*.

5. F *habile* has the MF var *hable*, often *able*, adopted by ME; hence 'to *disable*' and 'to *enable*'. The MF *habilité*, var *abilité*, becomes *ability*, whence *disability* and *inability* (perh influenced by ML *inhabilitās*).

6. MF-F *habile*, in nuance 'suitable', has, f/e, the derivative MF-F *habiller*, to make fit, hence ready, hence to clothe, whence MF-F *habillement*, equipment, clothing, whence E *habiliment*. But *habiller*, earliest as *abillier*, is prop 'to *dress* a log of wood', from MF-F *bille*, a (dressed or hewn) log: cf E *billet*.

7. L *habilitās* has ML derivative *habilitāre*, to render fit, with pp *habilitātus*, whence 'to *habilitate*'; derivative ML *habilitātiō*, o/s *habilitātiōn-*, becomes *habilitation*. ML *rehabilitāre*, to render fit again (*-re*), pp *rehabilitātus*, and the derivative *rehabilitātiō*, yield *rehabilitate* and *rehabilitation*.

8. L *habēre* has pp *habitus*, s *habit-*, whence the n *habitus* (gen *-ūs*), state or condition, appearance, dress, whence OF-F *habit*, OF-MF var *abit*, both adopted by ME and the former surviving. The n *habitus* has ML adj *habituālis*, whence *habitual* (cf MF-F *habituel*), and LL v *habituāre*, to condition, with pp *habituātus*, whence 'to *habituate*'; the pps *habit-* has the further derivative n *habitūdō*, manner of being, hence of doing, whence MF-F, hence E, *habitude*. LL *habituāre* becomes MF-F *habituer*, with pp *habitué*, later also n, adopted by E.

9. L *habēre* has freq *habitāre* (s *habit-*), to have often, used also int, to dwell; hence OF-F *habiter*, whence 'to *habit*', to dwell (obs), to dress. Derivative LL *habitāblis*, in which to dwell, hence fit to

273

dwell in, becomes OF(-F) *habitable*, adopted by E. OF-F *habiter*, to dwell, has presp *habitant*, whence also n, adopted by E, where largely displaced by *inhabitant*: L *habitat*, he (she, it) dwells, becomes F and E *habitat*, natural abode. The pp *habitātus*, s *habitāt-*, has derivative *habitātiō*, o/s *habitātiōn-*, whence OF-F, hence E, *habitation*.

10. L *habitāre* has two L prefix-cpds: (a) LL *cohabitāre*, to dwell with another, esp in marriage or concubinage, whence 'to *cohabit*', the presp *cohabitans*, o/s *cohabitant-*, yielding the n *cohabitant*, and the pp-derivative LL *cohabitātiō*, o/s *cohabitātiōn-*, yielding *cohabitation*; and (b) L *inhabitāre*, to dwell in, whence OF *enhabiter*, whence ME *enhabiten*, whence, by reversion to the L form, E 'to *inhabit*'; derivative LL *inhabitābilis* becomes *inhabitable*; presp *inhabitans*, o/s *inhabitant-*, becomes the MF, hence E, n *inhabitant*; the LL pp-derivative *inhabitātiō*, o/s *inhabitātiōn-*, becomes *inhabitation*, an inhabiting.

11. The predominant prefix-v c/f of *habēre* is *-hibēre*, as in:

*adhibēre*, to hold *ad* or to, i.e. to apply, with pp *adhibitus*, whence 'to *adhibit*'; derivative *adhibitiō*, o/s *adhibitiōn-*, gives us *adhibition*;

*cohibēre*, to hold *co-* (for *con-*, from *cum*, with) or together, to contain, to restrict, has pp *cohibitus*, whence 'to *cohibit*'; derivative LL *cohibitiō*, o/s *cohibitiōn-*, accounts for *cohibition*;

*exhibēre*, to hold out (*ex*) or forth, to offer, to exhibit, has pp *exhibitus*, whence 'to *exhibit*'; derivative LL *exhibitiō* (o/s *exhibitiōn-*), LL *exhibitor*, LL *exhibitōrius*, yield resp *exhibition* (prob via F), *exhibitor*, *exhibitory*;

*inhibēre*, to maintain in, hence to arrest, and to exercise authority over, has pp *inhibitus*, whence 'to *inhibit*'; derivative *inhibitiō* (o/s *inhibitiōn-*) explains *inhibition*; derivative LL *inhibitor* gets itself adopted; derivative ML *inhibitōrius* explains *inhibitory*, with an anl var *inhibitive*;

*prōhibēre*, to hold *prō* or forward, hence out of the way, hence to prevent (hence order the prevention of), has pp *prōhibitus*, whence 'to *prohibit*'; derivative LL *prōhibitiō* (o/s *prōhibitiōn-*) becomes MF-F, hence E, *prohibition*; derivative *prohibitor* is adopted; derivative *prōhibitōrius* becomes *prohibitory*, with now predominant var *prohibitive*, app from EF-F *prohibitif*, learnedly formed in *-if*, f *-ive*, from the L pp *prōhibitus*;

*redhibēre*, to (cause to) hold again, hence to (cause to) take back (*red-* for *re-*), has pp *redhibitus*, with derivatives legal LL *redhibitiō*, o/s *redhibitiōn-*, whence legal E *redhibition*—LL *redhibitor*, adopted—and LL *redhibitōrius*, whence *redhibitory*.

12. The less obvious E derivatives from L *habēre*, as listed at the end of the heading, are perh best treated alphabetically. *Aver*, property (obs), hence a cart-horse or a working ox, an old horse (now only E dial), derives from OF *aver*, var of *aveir* (F *avoir*), property, esp horses or cattle, from L *habēre*.

13. *Habitāre*, to dwell, has derivative *habitā-*

*culum* (pl *habitācula*), a dwelling-place (whence, via OF-F, the rare E *habitacle*), which, by aphesis, becomes Port *bitacola*, a binnacle, whence, prob influenced by E *bin*, the E *binnacle*, which 'houses' a ship's compass.

14. *Habēre* in its nuance 'to be in this state or that condition' (vi 'hold') occurs in the phrase *male habitus*, ill-kept, hence (of persons), unwell, whence OF-F *malade*, ill, whence OF-F *maladie*, whence E *malady*.

15. L has a prefix-cpd unmentioned in para 11: the Plautinian *praehibēre*, to hold *prae* or before, forth, to offer, to furnish. Far commoner is the contr *praebēre*, to present, to furnish, with gerundive *praebendus*, with LL neu pl *praebenda*, things to be furnished or supplied, a subsistence, whence MF-F *prébende*, whence E *prebend*, orig a daily allowance (at meals), hence a stipend granted by, e.g., a cathedral estate; derivative ML *praebendārius*, whence MF-F *prébendier*, accounts for *prebendary*, the holder of a stipend.

16. LL *praebenda*, a subsistence, becomes—by confusion of L *prae* with L *pro*—the OF-F *provende*, OF-MF *provendre*, both adopted by ME, with the latter yielding E *provender*.

**habitable, habitant, habitat, habitation.** See prec, para 9.

**habitual, habituate, habituation, habitude, habitué.** See HABIT, para 8.

**hachure.** See the 3rd HATCH, s.f.

**hacienda.** See FACT, para 9.

**hack** (1), a riding horse. See HACKNEY.

**hack** (2), to cut roughly or irregularly, whence **hacksaw; hackle**—**heckle; haggle; haggis; hatchel; —higgle**, cf **higgledy-piggledy;—hay**, cf **haywire; —hew**, pp **hewn;—hoe** (n, hence v).—**incus; incuse;** cf the sep CAUSE and CODE.

1. 'To *hack*' (whence the n *hack*) derives from ME *hakken*, from OE *haccian* and, in cpds, *haccian*, akin to OFris *hakkia*, MD and MLG-MHG *hacken*; ult, prob echoïc.

2. Perh a freq of *hack* is *hackle*, to comb (flax), with derivative n. With *hackle*, n and v, cf the syn n and v *hatchel*, resp from ME *heckele* (akin to MD *hekel*, MHG *hechel*, *hachel*), and from ME *hechelen* (akin to MD-D *hekelen*).

3. ME *hechelen* has syn var *hekelen*, whence 'to *heckle*', with derivative sense 'to badger'.

4. Akin to OE *haeccan* is the syn ON *höggva*, whence Sc *hag*, with freq *haggle*, to hack, hatchel, etc., hence to argue with a vendor, hence to wrangle, whence the agent *haggler*. Sc *hag* has derivative n *haggis*, a *minced*-meat dish.

5. *Haggle* has the 'thinned' derivative var 'to *higgle*', whence the rhyming redup *higgledy-piggledy*.

6. With 'to *hack*', cf 'to *hew*' (whence *hewer*), from OE *hēawan*, akin to the syn OFris *hāwa*, var *houwa*, OS *hauwan*, OHG *houwan*, MHG *houwen*, G *hauen*, MD *hauen*, D *houen*, ON *höggva*; cf also OSl *kovati*, to strike, hammer, forge, Lith *kova*, a battle, and *káuju*, I forge, MIr *cuad*, to strike, (hence) to fight, Gaul *\*cot-*, to strike, to forge, L

*cūdō*, I strike, stamp, forge, and *incūs* (? for *\*incuds*), an anvil. The Gmc r is app *\*hau-* or *\*hauw-*; the IE, *\*kau-*, to strike, forge, hew. (Walshe.)

7. OHG *houwan* has derivative n *houwa*, with Frankish var *\*hauwa*, whence OF *houe*, ME *howe*, E *hoe*.

8. L *incūs*, anvil, lit that into (*in*) or upon which one strikes (*cūdit*), is adopted by SciE, esp in An and Zoo; akin to L *incūs* is L incūdere, to forge (by striking with a hammer), pp *incūsus*, whence the E adj and v *incuse*.

9. Reverting to the Gmc r *\*khau-*, to strike, to hew, we find that akin are OHG *houwi, hewi*, MHG *höu*, G *Heu*, hay, Go *hawi*, (cut) grass, ON *hey*, hay—and OE *hieg, hīg, hēg*, whence, through ME *hei*, the E *hay*; the basic idea is 'grass that is mown or *cut*', 'the *cut* (grass)'.

**hackle.** See prec, para 2.

**hackney** (n, hence v); **hack** (n, hence v).

A *hack* or workaday riding horse is a b/f from the syn *hackney*, whence *hackney* (carriage) and *hackney*, a drudge, now *hack*, a literary drudge: and *hackney*, ME *hakeney* or *hakenai* (earliest as AL *hakeneius*), is elliptical for *Hakeney* (etc.) *horse*, a horse of *Hackney*, in Middlesex and now a borough of London; *Hackney* is OE *Hacan īeg*, Haca's isle. The derivative 'to *hackney*' orig meant to use a horse for common purposes.

**hacksaw.** See the 2nd HACK, in heading.

**had**, pt and pp of HAVE: resp OE *haefde* and OE (*ge*)*haefed*.

**haddock**: ME *haddok* or *hadok*: prob from MF *hadot* and EF *hadou*: o.o.o. The r is clearly *had-*: but whence?

**Hades**: Gr *Haidēs* ("Aιδης), the god of the underworld, hence the realm of the dead, hence, in LGr-MGr, hell: prob for *\*Haiwidēs* (\*Aιϝίδης) and from *aiānēs* (αἰἄνής), grim, terrible, itself from *aiei* (αἰεί), always: 'lasting for ever'. (Hofmann.)

**haemophilia, haemorrhage, haemorrhoids** (archaic *emerods*, from OF *emmeroides*—cf RHEUM, para 3)—see the element *haema-*, var *haemo-*; **anaemia**, whence **anaemic**, and AE **anemia**, whence **anemic**—Gr *anaimia*, a lacking (*an-*, without) of blood. The adj is *haemal*, of, for, with blood; AE *hemal*.

**haft.** See HEAVE, para 3.

**hafnium** is a Chem-element -*ium* derivative of L *Hafnia*, Copenhagen: it occurs in a Nor zircon.

**hag; hagberry; haggard.** See HAW, paras 2-3.

**haggis.** See the 2nd HACK, para 4, s.f.

**haggle.** See 2nd HACK, para 4.

**hagiarchy, hagiography, hagiolatry, hagiology.** See the element *hagio-*.

**hail** (1), n, from the skies: OE *haegel, hagol*: akin to OHG *hagal*, MHG-G *hagel*, and ON *hagl* —prob also to Gr *kakhlēx*, a pebble, ? for *\*kakhlos* (Hofmann).

**hail** (2), v, to salute or greet. See WHOLE, para 3.

**hair**, whence **hairy**: ME *her*, earlier *haer*: OE *hāer*: cf OFris *hēr*, OS *hār*, OHG-MHG *hār*, G *Haar*, ON *hār* and several syn modern Scan words;

cf also ON *haddr*, a woman's head of hair (Gmc *\*khazd-*, extn of *\*khaz-*; IE *\*kĕs-*). Walshe.

**hake.** See HOOK, para 4.

**halation.** See HALO.

**halberd.** See the 2nd BARB.

**halcyon** (n, hence adj); **auk**.

1. *Halcyon*, adopted from L, represents Gr *halkuōn*, a kingfisher, with *h-* caused by that of Gr *hals*, sea, the correct Gr form being *alkuōn*, which has the further derivative, the syn L *alcēdō*. Gr *alkuōn* is o.o.o.: ? a loan-word. This bird was fabled by the Greeks to nest at sea, about the time of the winter solstice, and, during incubation, to calm the waves; hence, a calm period, hence calm and peaceful.

2. Prob akin to Gr *alkuōn* is *auk*, of Scan origin: cf ON *ālka*, Sw *alka*, Da *alke*, with several C cognates.

**hale** (1), adj, (robustly) healthy. See WHOLE, para 3.

**hale** (2), v. See HAUL.

**half**, adj (whence adv) and n: OE *healf*, var *half*, adj and n: cf OFris and OS *half*, OHG *halb*, MHG *halp*, G *halb*, Go *halbs*, ON *hālfr*, all adjj, and Go *halba*, ON *hālfa*, n, cf OFris *halfte* and the Central G *halfte*, n: cf also Skt *klptás*, cut, and L *scalpere*, to cut, s *scalp-*. The adj therefore is basically 'cut (off)'; the n, 'a part cut off'. (Walshe.)

2. *Half* has derivative 'to *halve*'—aided by *halves*, the pl of *half*, n.

**halibut.** See HOLY, para 2.

**halidom!**, by my. See HOLY, para 2.

**halitosis; exhale, exhalant, exhalation; inhale, inhalant, inhalation.**

1. *Halitosis*=*hālit*us, a breath+suffix -*osis*, connoting disease: and *hālitus* derives from *hālāre*, to breathe, also to emit an odour, itself akin to L *anhēlāre*, to be out of breath, to puff, orig echoic.

2. Derivative *exhālāre*, to breathe *ex* or out, becomes OF *exhaler*, whence 'to *exhale*'; its derivative LL *exhālātiō*, o/s *exhālātiōn*-, becomes, via MF-F, the E *exhalation*; presp *exhālans*, o/s *exhālant*-, becomes adj, hence n, *exhalant*.

3. Derivative LL *inhālāre*, to breathe upon, becomes E 'to *inhale*', to breathe *in*; presp *inhālans*, o/s *inhālant*-, becomes adj, hence n, *inhalant*; derivative *inhālātiō*, o/s *inhālātiōn*-, becomes *inhalation*; *inhalator* is an anl E formation.

**hall**, whence, via Goldsmiths' Hall (where gold and silver articles were formerly stamped), **hall-mark; hell**, whence **hellish** and such cpds as **hellcat, hellfire, hellhound** (OE *helle hund*); **hold** of a ship; **hole**, n (whence adj **holey**) and v; **hollow**, adj, whence n and v, and **hollowness; howe; hulk**, n, hence v; **hull**, n, hence v (whence **huller**).—**cell, cellular, cellule, Celluloid, cellulose; cellar** (n, hence v), **cellarage, cellarer; occult**, adj (hence n) and v, **occultation, occultism, occultist; clandestine.** —Cf the sep: CALYPSO and CILIARY (and SUPER-CILIOUS) and COLOR (AE), COLOUR (n and v), COLO(U)RABLE, COLORADO, COLORATION, COLORATURA, and CONCEAL and HELMET.

1. The IE r of the entire group is *\*kel-*, to hide,

varr *kal-, *kil-, *kol-, *kul-, as in Gr kaluptein
and L celāre, to hide, Gr kalia, a hut, Gr koleos,
a sheath, L cella, small room, cellar, (LL) cell,
L cilium, eyelid, L occultāre, to conceal. IE app has
the varr *khal-, *khel-, *khol-, *khul-, whence the
Gmc hall, hell, hole, hull, etc. Note, too, the var
represented by Skt śālā, a house.

2. Hall, a large house, but esp a large, high
apartment or room, comes, through ME halle or
hal, from OE heal or heall, akin to OS and OHG
halla, MHG-G halle, a hall, and ON höll, a large
house.

3. Hell, orig the place of the dead, comes unchanged from OE and is akin to OFris helle, OS
hellia, OHG hellia, hella, MHG helle, G Hölle,
MD helle, hille, (as in D) hel, Go halja, hell, and
ON Hel, the goddess of the dead; cf also OIr cel,
death, and celim, I conceal (OE helan).

4. Although the -d is caused by hold, to contain,
a ship's hold derives, through ME hol or holl, from
MD hool, hole, (as D) hol, hole in the ground,
hence hold of a ship (hole, or hollow part).

5. Intimately related to this hold, therefore, is
hole, ME hol or hole, OE hol, a hole or a cavern,
from the OE adj hol, hollow: cf MHG hol, a cave,
prop the OHG-MHG adj hol, hollow, used as n,
the G adj being hohl and the G n being the very
closely related Höhle; cf also the ON adj holr and
Go ushulōn, to hollow out, and esp OFris hol,
hollow, also a hollow. The OE n hol has derivative
v holian, whence 'to hole'.

6. Akin to the OE adj hol is the OE holh, a
hollow, whence the ME adj holgh, later holow,
E hollow.

7. Howe, a depression or hollow in land, e.g. a
shallow valley, is a Sc derivative (adj before n)
from OE hol, a hole.

8. Certainly akin to the prec Gmc words, esp
to hell, is hull; prob akin, esp to hole, is hulk, orig
a ship, esp if heavily built, now the carcase of a
wrecked or dismantled or abandoned ship, hence
any clumsily bulky person or thing, from ME
hulke, a heavy ship, sense-shifted (cf RUM, adj)
from OE hulc, a light and speedy ship, akin to
MD hulc, hulke, holc, and OHG holcho.

9. Hull, orig a husk or a pod, hence the frame
of a ship, derives, via ME hul, from OE hulu, akin
to OHG hulla, MHG-G hulle, a covering, a sheath,
a husk, G hullen, Go huljan, OS hullian, OFris
hella, to cover, also OE and OS helan, OFris hela,
to cover, conceal, hide; therefore cf E hell.

### Latin

10. Akin to OE helan is the syn L celāre,
affecting E mostly in the cpd concelāre: see the
sep CONCEAL.

11. Either deriving from or intimately cognate
with L celāre is L cella, whence, via OF-EF then
ME celle, the E cell. The dim cellula becomes
EF-F and E cellule and has, in F, the derivative
adj cellulaire, whence E cellular; likewise F is
cullulose (Chem -ose); Celluloid, with suffix -oid,
is a trade-name.

12. L cella, in its sense 'a (small) store-room',
has derivative adj cellārius, with neu cellārium
used as n 'pantry', whence OF-MF celier (EF-F
cellier), whence ME celer, celler, whence E cellar,
now esp a wine-cellar, whence cellarage (collective
-age). Cellarer derives from OF-MF celerier, from
celier; perh prompted by LL cellārius, keeper of a
(wine-)cellar, prop the adj used as n.

13. L celāre, to hide, has derivative adv clam
(for *celam: complementary to palam, publicly,
openly), secretly, very much in private. Hence the
adj clandestīnus (form-influenced by intestīnus,
internal): whence, perh via MF-F clandestin, the E
clandestine.

14. The L s cel- has var cul- in occulere (oc- for
ob-, as in obstruct), to cover up, obscure, hide, with
pp occultus, whence the E adj occult. 'To occult'
derives, however, from L occultāre, to conceal,
hide, an int of occulere; on occultāt-, s of pp
occultātus, arises occultātiō, o/s occultātiōn-,
whence E occultation; occultism and occultist
derive from adj occult.

hallelujah. See ALLELUIA.

halliard. See HAUL.

hallmark. See HALL heading.

halloo (v, hence n): EE hallow: MF-EF halloer,
to pursue (game) with shouts, an echoic var of
MF-EF haler, to excite dogs by shouting hale!,
var of hare!, itself with var haro!, clearly echoic.
Cf HARASS.—Hence hallo!, with thinning hello!,
and with var hullo!, itself with redup derivative
hullabaloo, and var hollo.

hallow, hallowed, Halloween. See HOLY, para 3.

hallucinate (vt from vi), hallucination (whence,
by suffix -osis, connoting a disease, hallucinosis),
hallucinator (whence perh the adj hallucinatory,
unless it=hallucination+adj -ory).

1. Hallucinator, a person erring because of
hallucinations, is adopted from LL; like L
hallucinātiō (o/s hallucinātiōn-, whence E hallucination), it is formed upon hallucināt-, s of hallu-
cinātus, pp of hallucināri, to wander in one's mind,
LL var of L alucināri, itself from the syn Gr aluein
(s alu-, r al-), akin to Gr alē (s and r, al-), a homeless wandering, a restless roaming: o.o.o.; but cf
the -ul- of L ambulāre (Boisacq).

halo (n, hence v); photographic halation; cf the
element halo-.

Halation=halo+suffix -ation; and halo=L halo,
acc of halos, trln of Gr halōs, a threshing-floor,
usually round, hence the sun's or the moon's
disk, hence a circle about it: cf OSw lo, a threshing-
floor, and perh Skt lūnati (lū-na-ti), he cuts off
or away. (Hofmann.) Cf also Hit halis (acc halen,
dat hali), an enclosure, a halo about the moon.

halt (1), adj, lame, derives from OE healt, akin
to syn OFris and OS halt, Go halts, OHG halz,
ON haltr; more remotely to L clādēs, an injury,
and Gr kolobos, kolos, mutilated; also to Ru
koldyka, limping. Derivative OE healtian becomes
ME halten, whence 'to halt' or limp.

halt (2), n and v, in or of marching. See HOLD,
para 2.

**halter.** See HELVE, para 2.

**halve.** See HALF, para 2.

**halyard.** See HAUL.

**Ham.** See the element *Hamito-*.

**ham,** a thigh and its buttock, hence a ham of bacon; cpds, e.g. **hamstring,** a tendon above and behind the knee, hence 'to hamstring', and **hamfatter,** from a Negro song 'The *Hamfat* Man', whence the syn A sl **ham,** an inferior actor, whence 'to ham'. A *ham* comes straight from OE; cf OHG *hamma,* MD *hamme* (as in G dial) and *ham* (as in D); also Gr *knēmē,* lower part of leg, and OIr *cnāim,* a bone.

**hamadryad.** Cf *dryad,* q.v. at TREE, para 2, s.f.

**hamartiology.** See the element *hamartio-*.

**hamburger** (AE) was prompted by its syn, *Hamburg steak,* finely chopped beef, esp (*hamburger*) a sandwich containing a grilled cake thereof; reputedly from the great G port of *Hamburg,* lit 'the home city'—it being orig a centre of missionary work.

**hame** (in harness) comes from OE *hama,* a cover, a skin: cf MD *hāme,* a hame, OHG *hamo,* ON *hamr,* skin, covering; cf also OFris *hamethe, hemethe,* OHG *hemithi,* G *Hemd,* a shirt; therefore cf CHEMISE. Gmc r, *\*ham-;* IE r, *\*kam-.*

**Hamitic.** See the element *Hamito-*.

**hamlet.** See HOME, para 2.—The fish so named is o.o.o.: prob of Amerind origin.

**hammer** (n, hence v): ME *hamer:* OE *hamer,* var *hamor:* cf OFris *hamer,* OHG *hamar,* MHG *hamer,* G *Hammer,* MD-D *hamer,* ON *hamarr* (orig rock, the primitive ON hammer being made of stone, this being app the general IE origin): cf, further, OSl *kamy,* Lith *akmuo,* stone, Gr *akmōn,* anvil, Skt *áśmā,* stone, anvil, hammer. (Walshe.)

**hammock** (1). Cf *hummock,* q.v. at HUMP.

**hammock** (2), a swinging, suspended bed: Sp *hamaca,* of Caribbean origin: cf Yukuna *hamaca* and Taino *amaca,* a sleeping-net (Webster, who aptly cfs *macaw*): prob via Sp contacts with Haiti. 'Haïtian word': Santamaria.

**hamper** (1), n, is an easing of obs *hanaper:* OF *hanapier,* a sense-adapted *-ier* derivative from OF-F *hanap,* a drinking-vessel: Frankish *\*hnap:* cf OE *hnaep,* OHG *hnapf* (ML *hanappus*).

**hamper** (2), v: ME *hampren:* cf LG *hampern, happern,* and D *haperen:* ? a nasal var of a r *\*hap-,* to seize, capture, take (akin to L *capere*), as in ON *haptr,* a serf.

**hamster,** a marmot-like rodent: G *Hamster,* OHG *hamēstro,* field-mouse: o.o.o.; but cf OSl *chomēstorŭ,* Lith *staras.* (Walshe.)

**hamstring.** See HAM.

**hanaper.** See the 1st HAMPER.

**hand** (n, hence adj and v), whence the adj **handy** (cf D *handig*); very many cpds, mostly self-explanatory—but note **handbook, -cuff, -fast, -ful, handicap** (n, hence v), **handicraft, handiwork, handsel** (n, hence v), and var **hansel, handsome, handspike; underhand,** adj and adv; **handle,** n and v.

1. A *hand* comes straight from OE, which has var *hond:* cf OFris *hand* (var *hond*), OS *hand,*

OHG-MHG *hant,* G *Hand,* Go *handus,* MD *hant,* D *hand,* ON *hönd,* Sw *hand,* Da *haand:* prob akin to OE *hentan,* ON *henda,* to catch, and E HUNT, the *hand* being then 'the grasper'. (IE r, ? *\*kent-,* varr *\*kant-, \*kont-.* Walshe.)

2. *Hand* cpds worth noting etym include:

*handbook: hand+book:* prompted by G *Handbuch* (cf OE *handbōc*);

*handcuff: hand+cuff* (of sleeve): app not by f/e from OE *handcops,* hand-rope or -fetter, manacle;

*handfast,* a clasping of hands in agreement, esp of marriage (whence the archaic *handfasted,* betrothed): *hand+fast,* adj, n, v;

*handful:* OE *handfull;*

*handicap,* with modern sporting sense (whence that of 'disadvantage') deriving from an old sport, characterized by forfeit money hand-held in a *cap:* easement of *hand-in-cap;*

*handicraft,* form-influenced by next: EE *handcraft:* OE *handcraeft;*

*handiwork:* ME *handiwerc:* OE *handgeweorc* (OE *geweorc,* work, a *ge-* int of syn *weorc*);

*handkerchief.* See CHIEF, para 8;

*handsel:* ON *handsal,* handsale, a bargain ratified by a handshaking, ON *sal* being a var of ON *sala* (E *sale*);

*handsome* (whence *handsomeness*), orig dextrous: *hand+*suffix *-some,* -like;

*handspike:* influenced by E *spike* but deriving from D *handspeak,* lit 'hand-pole'.

3. *overhand* and *underhand* are advv, whence adjj, the latter implying concealment or, at the least, slyness.

4. OE *hand* has OE derivative *handle,* lit a little (connoted by dim *-le*) hand; preserved throughout E. 'To *handle*' comes, through ME *handlen,* from OE *handlian,* imm from OE *handle* and ult from OE *hand:* orig to touch, or to feel, with the hand or hands, OE *handlian* is akin to OFris *handelia* (var *hond-*) and OHG *hantalōn,* to touch thus, MHG-G *handeln,* to bargain, to act.

**handicap, handicraft** or **-work.** See prec, para 2.

**handkerchief.** See CHIEF, para 8.

**handle,** n, v. See HAND, para 4.

**handsel; handsome.** See HAND, para 2, cf SALE, para 2.

**hang,** pt and pp **hanged** and (vi) **hung; hanger; hangdog, hangfire, hangman, hangover; hank, hanker, hanky-panky;** sep HINGE.

1. 'To *hang*' comes, through ME *hangen,* var *hongien,* from OE *hangian* (vi), *hōn* (pp *hongen:* vt): cf OFris *hangia, hongia,* vi, and OS *hangōn,* vi, and OHG *hangēn,* MHG *hangen,* G *hängen, hangen,* vi, and OHG *hangēn,* MHG *hengen,* G *hängen,* vt, and OHG *hāhan,* MHG *hāhen,* cf Go *hāhan,* OE *hōn,* all vt, and ON *hanga,* vi: Gmc r, *\*khang-,* IE r *\*kenk-,* varr *\*kank-, \*konk-:* cf Skt *śaṅkatē,* he hesitates (*hangs* in the balance), and perh L *cunctāri,* to delay (vi).

2. Of the cpds, the foll are worth noting:

*hangdog* (adj, n): (a person) fit only to be 'strung up' like a dog—or perh to hang a dog;

*hangfire,* orig of a gun that is long in going off;

*hangman*=a man to hang another;

*hang-over* (n, hence adj): something hanging (=left) over from the past.

3. The presp and vn *hanging* occur in var cpds; instrumental or agential *hanger* (the short, curved sword, perh influenced by obs D *hangher*) occurs, agentially, in *hanger-on*.

4. Prob akin to *hang* is the now mostly dial 'to hank', ME *hanken*, ON *hanka*, to coil; 'a *hank*' or coil, loop, naut ring, (dial) handle, is also of Scan origin—cf ON *hanki*, a hasp, *hönk* (var *hangr*), a coil, Da *hank*, a handle, but cf also MD *hanc*, var *hang*, a handle.

5. *Hank*, in its dial senses 'control, influence' and 'bad habit', has a redup derivative, the coll *hanky-panky*, syn with and prob prompted by HOCUS-POCUS.

6. Perh a freq, either of 'to hank' or of 'to hang', or, more prob, a derivative from Fl *hankeren*, to long (for), is 'to hanker': cf D *hunkeren*, to hanker, freq of *hangen*, to hang: to *hanker* for something is to *hang* about, eyeing or waiting longingly for it.

**hangar** is adopted from F, where earliest (1502) as *hanghart* in N France; o.o.o.: prob either from MD *ham-gaerd*, an enclosed space (cf E *-ham*, a pasture, in PlN terms) or, more likely, from ML *angārium*, a shed where horses are shod, perh from the r of *hang*, horses being hung up for easier shoeing (B & W).

**hanger.** See HANG, para 3.

**hank**, n, v.; **hanker**; **hanky-panky.** See HANG, resp paras 4, 6, 5.

**Hansard**, the periodic official report of British Parliamentary proceedings, long compiled (1774 onwards) by Messrs *Hansard*: lit 'member of the G *Hanse*' (or *Hanseatic* League), a vast league of merchants in the later Middle Ages: MLG *hanse*, merchants' guild: OHG *hansa* (id in Go), a troop.

**hansel.** A var of *handsel*, q.v. at HAND, para 2, and SALE, para 2.

**hansom** is elliptical for the *Hansom cab*, invented by Englishman John A Hansom, who patented it in 1834.

**hap** (n and v), **hapless, haply**—**haphazard, mayhap** and **perhaps**; **happen** (whence vn **happening**), AE **happenchance**; **happy**, whence **happily** (adv *-ly*) and **happiness** (*-ness*), also **happy-go-lucky** and (one's) **happy hunting grounds.**

1. *Hap*, chance, an event exemplifying chance, comes, through ME *hap*, earlier *happe*, from ON *happ*, good luck, akin to OE ge*haep*, convenient or suitable; from the ME *hap(pe)* comes ME *happen*, to have the good luck to, hence to have any sort of luck, hence, impersonally, to befall or chance: ME *happen* yields the now archaic 'to hap'; it also, perh through its var *hapnen*, yields 'to happen'. The humorous *happenstance*=a circum*stance* that simply *happens*.

2. *Hapless*, unlucky, merely tacks *-less* to *hap*, good luck; *haply* merely adds the adv *-ly*. The now archaic and dial *mayhap* (var *mayhaps*—after *perhaps*)=*it may hap* (happen): sem cf *maybe*,

perhaps. *Perhaps* itself=*per*, through, by+*haps*, happenings: sem cf *perchance*.

3. *Hap* in its orig sense 'good luck' has derivative *happy*: *hap*+euphonic *p*+adj *-y*. *Happy-go-lucky* is applied to one who is quite happy to trust to luck. *Happy hunting grounds*=the region occupied, after death, by hunters and warriors of the N Amerind peoples; hence, very loosely among whites, Heaven, or worse still, any place favourable to one's activities.

**haploid; haplology.** See the element *haplo-*.

**happen, happening; happily, happiness, happy.** See HAP, resp paras 1, 3.

**hara-kiri** is adopted from Jap: lit, a belly-cutting.

**harangue**, n and v.

A *harangue*, adopted from MF-F, comes from MF *arenge*: ML *harenga*: OHG *hari*, army+*hringa*, ring, hence an assembly. Derivative EF-F *haranguer* yields 'to harangue'. But EF-F *haranguer* was perh influenced by It *aringare*; and MF *arenge* perh derives from It *aringa*, and both of the It words from It *aringo*, a public place for horse-racing and popular assemblies; if that be so, as B & W suggest, then It *aringo* derives from Go *\*hriggs* (pron *\*hrĭngs*)—cf Frankish *hring*, whence F *rang*, rank. Cf HARBINGER.

**harass** (whence **harassment**) comes from EF-F *harasser*, an aug of MF *harer*, to excite hunting dogs, from the OF-F cry *hare!*: cf HALLOO.

**harbinger; harbor** (AE) or **harbour** (n and v), whence **harbo(u)rage** (suffix *-age*).

1. *Harbinger*, orig one who goes ahead and finds accommodation, hence one who lodges or acts as host, derives irreg from ME *herbergeour*, one who supplies lodging, from syn OF-MF *herbergeor* (agential *-eor*, cf L *-or*), from OF-MF *herbergier* (OF-MF *hébergier*), to provide lodging, from *herberge*, lodging, an inn (F *auberge*), from OHG *heriberga*, shelter for soldiers: *heri*, army (cf HARRY)+OHG *bergan* (MHG-G *bergen*), to preserve, bring to safety (cf Go *bairgan*, OE *beorgan*).

2. Akin to OHG *heriberga* (MHG-G *herberge*) is ON *herbergi*, whence prob ME *herberge*, then *herberwe*, finally *herbore*, whence the E n *harbo(u)r*. 'To *harbour*' derives from ME *herboren, herberen*, earlier *herberwen*, earliest *herbergen* (from *herberge*). (Walshe.)

**hard**, adj, adv, n; **harden; hardihood; hardly; hardness; hardy** (whence **hardiness**);—**Reynard**;—? **harsh**, whence **harshen, harshness**.

1. The adj *hard*, ME *hard*, earlier *herd*, derives from OE *heard*: cf OFris *herd*, OS *hard*, OHG *harti*, MHG *harte, herte*, G *hart*, Go *hardus*, MD *harde* (cf D *hard*), *haerde, herde, hart*, ON *hardr*, Da *haard*, with Gmc r *\*hard-*; IE r, *\*kart-*, as in Gr *kartos*, strength, with metathesis *kratos*—cf the adj *kratus*, strong. (Walshe.)

2. OE *heard* has derivative adv *hearde*, whence the E adv *hard*, and the further adv *heardlīce*, whence *hardly*; derivative *heardness* becomes *hardness*; but *harden* goes back only to ME *hardenen*,

*hardnen*, from the ME adj *hard*—cf OFris *herda*, OS *herdian*, to harden.

3. Of the above-exemplified Gmc origin is OF *hardir* (cf OHG *hartjan*, Go *hardjan*), to render bold, with pp *hardi*, which, used as adj, becomes E *hardy*, whence *hardihood* (-*hood*).

4. Gmc *hard* (etc.) has the OHG cpd—a man's name—*Reginhart*, Strong in Counsel (cf Go *ragin*, counsel), which becomes MD *Reynard*, adopted by E and, through the C13 beast-epic, *Roman de Renard*, coming to mean a fox; OF-MF *Renard* (whence F *renard*, a fox) was orig *Renart*, from the OHG name, prob via Frankish.

5. Prob akin to E *hard* is E *harsh*: ME *harsk*, app of Scan origin—cf also MLG-G *harsch* and esp MD *hars*, *harse*, *harst*.

6. For the Gmc and IE rr, cf the r of CANCER.

**hare** (n, hence v), whence **harrier** (runner); **haze** (n, hence v), whence **hazy**; **xanthic**, **xanthous**—cf the element *xantho*-.

1. The *hare*, usu grey- or brown-furred, goes back to OE *hara*, akin to ON *here*, *heri* (cf Da *hare*, Sw *hara*) and to OFris *hasa*, OHG *haso*, MHG-G *hase*: cf also OE *hasu*, ON *höss*, grey, grey-brown, OHG *hasan*, grey, and L *cānus* (for *\*casnus*), light-grey. The Gmc r is app *\*has*- or *\*haz*-, with extn *\*has(a)n*-; IE r, app *\*kas*-, extn *\*kas(a)n*-. Cf Skt *śáśas*, OP *sasnis*, a hare. App orig 'the grey (quadruped)'. (Walshe.)

2. With OE *hasu*, *heasu*, grey, cf the otherwise unexplainable E *haze*, a light vapour or greyness or smoke that slightly lessens vision; cf dial *haze*, to be foggy. Decidedly derivative is AE *haze*, to bully: bullying produces haziness of mind.

3. App akin to the Gmc and other old words noted in para 1 is the Gr *xanthos* (ξανθός), fair, yellow, yellowish-brown, app from IE r *\*kasn*- in var *\*khasn*, for *xanthos*, s *xanth*-, prob has r *xan*-. Gr *xanthos* becomes E *xanthous*, yellow(ish); the var *xanthic* represents F *xanthique*, which=Gr *xanthos*+F adj suffix -*ique*.

**harem**: Ar *ḥarīm*, anything forbidden, hence the women's quarters in a (great) household, these being prohibited to strangers: *ḥarama*, to forbid.

**haricot** (bean): EF-F *haricot*: Sp *ayecote*, *ayo-cote*: Nahuatl *ayecotli*. In transition to F, the Sp *ayccote* got itself involved with MF-F *haricot*, stew (? via a stew made with beans), itself from MF *harigoter*, to cut (esp meat) into small pieces.

**hark; harken.** See HEAR, para 2.

**Harlequin**, whence **harlequin**, **harlequinade**, **harlequinesque**.

1. Basic *Harlequin* is adopted from EF-(obs)F, the EF-F *arlequin* deriving from It *arlecchino*, itself from EF *Herlekin* or *Hierlekin*, var *Hellequin*, a demon or a goblin, the *maesnie Hierlekin* (*Hellequin*) denoting a retinue of evil spirits seen in the night air: *Hierlekin* is perh of Gmc origin and perh corresponds to a ME *\*Herle king* (King Harilo), possibly one of the names of Wodan. (B & W.) I prefer DAF's derivation of *Hierlekin* from G-Fl *hellekin*, a devil, a dim -*kin* offshoot

from the Gmc r of E *hell* and G *Hölle*. The modern conception owes much to the adaptation in the It Commedia dell' Arte.

2. EF-F *arlequin* has derivative *arlequinade*, whence E *harlequinade*; *harlequinesque* comes from It *arlecchinesco*, adj of *arlecchino*.

**harlot** (whence **harlotry**), a rogue, a male menial, hence a loose woman, esp a prostitute: ME *harlot*, *herlot*, both adopted from MF, which has var *arlot*, all with predominant sense 'young man, esp if debauchee or idler or rogue': o.o.o.: ? of C origin—perh cf Ga *àl-òg*, a young man (*àl*, offspring+*òg*, young, OIr *óc*).

**harm**, n (whence **harmful** and **harmless**) and v. 'To *harm*', ME *harmen*, comes from OE *hearmian*, itself from the OE n *hearm*, whence E *harm*: and OE *hearm* is akin to OS and OHG-G *harm*, OFris *herm*, ON *harmr*, distress, grief; cf also OSl *sramŭ*, shame.

**harmonic** (adj, hence n), **harmonica**, **harmonious**, **harmonist**, **harmonium**, **harmonize**, **harmony**; **disharmonic**, **disharmonious**, **disharmony**—**enharmonic**.

1. *Harmony* descends, via ME and OF, from L *harmonia*, adopted from Gr: from Gr *harmos*, a joining or fitting, akin to Gr *arthron*, a (bodily) joint: IE *\*ar*-, to fit, join (hence, add), as in L *a ma*, martial arms. Cf, therefore, the 2nd ARM and ARTHRITIS.

2. Gr *harmonia* has adj *harmonikos*, whence LL *harmonicus*, whence MF-F *harmonique* and E *harmonic*; the L adj has f *harmonica*, whence the E musical instrument; OF-F *harmonie* has, perh prompted by LGr *harmonios*, the MF-F adj *harmonieux*, f *harmonieuse*, whence E *harmonious*; *harmonist* is an E anl formation; *harmonize* derives from late MF-F *harmoniser* (from *harmonie*); *harmonium* is adopted from F (*harmonie*+-*ium*).

3. *Disharmonic* and *disharmonious* derive, anl, from *disharmony*, an E anl formation, perh suggested as opp to *enharmonic*, which, influenced by *harmonic*, derives from LL *enarmonius*, from Gr *enarmonios* (*en*-, in).

**harness**, v, derives from ME *harneisen*, from ME *harneis*, whence the E n *harness*; ME *harneis*, adopted from OF-F *harneis*, var of OF-MF *herneis*: ON *\*hernest*, provisions (*nest*) for an army (*herr*), on anl of ON *vegnest*, provisions for the road—for a journey (*veg*). Cf HARANGUE and see HARRY.

**harp** (n, v), **harper**, **harpist**; **harpsichord**;— **harpoon** (n, hence v).

1. 'To *harp*' derives from OE *hearpian* (whence OE *hearpere*, E *harper*, dislodged by the mod E *harpist*, which=*harp*+agent -*ist*), itself from OE *hearpe*, whence ME *harpe*, E *harp*. OE *hearpe* is akin to OHG *harpfa*, MHG *harphe*, *harfe*, G *Harfe*, and ON *harpa*: o.o.o.: prob, either from crooked shape or from fingers crocked, from a Scan r akin to ON *herpask* (r *herp*-), to contract (e.g., one's fingers): perh cf Gr *harpagē*, a hook (LL *harpāgō*, grappling iron).

2. LL *harpa*, of Gmc origin, appears in the It cpd *arpicordo* (It *corda*, a string, L *chorda*, cf

CORD), whence MF *harpechorde*, whence E *harpsichord*.

3. Prob akin to *harp* is *harpoon*: OF-F *harpon*: an *-on* aug of OF-F *harpe*, a claw: OF-MF *harper*, to grapple: app of Gmc origin—cf ON *herpask* (para 1, s.f.).

**Harpy** (whence **harpy**, a rapacious person, usu woman). See RAPT, para 10.

**harridan** is an *-an* alteration of F *haridelle*, a jade (worn-out horse): EF *aridelle*: from the r *har-* of the many F dial words for a horse (cf OF-F *haras*, a stud of horses).

**harrier** (1), runner=*hare*+euphonic *r*+easement *i*+agent *-er*.

**harrier** (2), one who harries=*harry*, with *i* for *y* +agent *-er*.

**harrow** (1), farming implement, hence v; **harvest**, n hence v; whence **harvester**; sep CARPEL.

A *harrow* derives from ME *harwe*, akin to and perh deriving from ON *harfr*, var *herfi*, and akin to *harvest*: ME *harvest* or *hervest*: OE *haerfest*, itself akin to OFris *herfst*, OS *herbhst*, OHG *herbist*, MHG *herbest*, G *Herbst*, ON *haust*—and to L *carpere*, to pluck, and Gr *karpos*, fruit.

**harrow** (2), to distress or oppress: OE *hergian*, q.v. at:

**harry**, to raid or plunder: ME *haryen*, earlier *herien*: OE *hergian*, akin to ON *heria*, OHG *-heriōn*, *-herjōn* (cf G *verheeren*, to devastate); therefore also to OE *here*, OFris *here*, *hire*, OHG *heri*, MHG *her*, G *Heer*, Go *harjis*, ON *herr*, an army, and, further off, MIr *cuire*, a troop, *cath*, battle, battalion, Ga *cath*, battle, Cor and W *cad*, battle, with OC r *\*cat-*, to fight, do battle; OP *karjis*, army, Lith *kâras*, war; OPer *kāra*, army; Gr *koíranos* (for *\*korjanos*), a general: IE r, ? *kăr-*, army: ? ult id with *\*kar-*, strong.

**harsh.** See HARD, para 5.

**hart**, a stag; **hartebeest**. See HORN, para 6.

**Harvard** University: *Harvard* College (1639), founded by the Rev. John *Harvard* (1607–38), an Englishman; softening of *Harward*: OE *Hereweard* (E *Hereward*), 'army-guardian', military general.

**harvest.** See the 1st HARROW.

**hash**, n, derives from 'to *hash*', to cut (meat) small: MF-F *hacher*: OF-F *hache*: f.a.e., the 3rd HATCH.

**hashish.** See ASSASSIN.

**hasp**, v, derives, by metathesis, from OE *haepsian*, from OE *haepse*, var *haesp*, whence ME *hesp* or *hasp*, the latter adopted by E: and OE *haepse* is akin to G *Haspe*, a hasp, MHG *haspe*, OHG *haspa*, a reel of yarn, and ON *hespa*, a skein: Gmc etym, ? *\*hapsa* (Walshe): basic idea, ? 'to catch hold of, catch, grasp'. Perh cf APSE.

**hassock**, a tussock, as in OE *hassuc* (s *hass-*), hence a small cushion resembling one; cf the suffix *-ock*. Perh orig applied to coarse, very dry grass, grey in colour and therefore akin to OE *hasu* (s *has-*), grey: cf HARE

**haste**, n and v; **hasten**; **hasty**, whence **hasty pudding** (quickly and easily made) and **hastiness**; **hastings**.

*Haste*, ME *hast* or *haste*, comes, as do OFris *hāst* and G *Hast*, from OF *haste* (F *hâte*), which, however, derives from Gmc *\*haisti*: cf OHG *heisti*, impetuous, violent, OE *hǣste*, violent, and *hǣst*, violence; also cf Go *haifsts*. OF *haste* has derivative OF-MF v *haster* (F *hâter*), whence ME *hasten*, whence 'to *haste*'—whence, in turn, E 'to *hasten*'; OF-MF *haste* also has OF-MF derivative adj *hastis* (acc *hastif*, whence F *hâtif*), with var *hasti*, whence E *hasty*, presp *hasting*, has pl n *hastings* (now dial), early vegetables, esp peas.

**hat**, n—hence v (esp in pa *hatted*), whence *hatter*, whence, through folklore, *mad as a hatter* (cf Lewis Carroll's 'the *mad hatter*').

*Hat* descends from OE *haet* or *haett*, akin to ON *hattr*, hat, and *höttr*, hood, OHG-MHG *huot*, G *Hut*, hat, therefore to OE *hōd*, E *hood*; prob ult to L *cassis*, a helmet (? for *\*catsis*): if that be so, the IE r is perh *\*khat-*. The E phrase *a* (or *the*) *hat trick*, orig and still applied in cricket to a bowler taking a wicket with each of three successive balls (from *him*), app arises in an old custom whereby, in recognition of his feat, the bowler received a hat.

**hatch** (1), n, door, gate, **hatchway** (*hatch*+*way*); **hack**, a frame or a grating; **heck**, a door.

*Hatch*, ME *hacche*, derives from OE *haec*, akin to MLG *heck*, MD *hecke* or *hec* (D *hek*): o.o.o. *Hack* is akin: it prob derives from OE *haca*. *Heck* is app a Sc, and N dial, var of *hack*.

**hatch** (2), to produce young from eggs: ME *hacchen*, akin to G *hecken*, MHG *hęcken*, which Kluge derives from a Gmc r *\*kak-*, the penis— cf MHG *hagen*, a bull. Hence then *hatch*, a hatching, the young that are hatched.

**hatch** (3), to mark with shadow lines (hence n), whence the vn **hatching**; **hachure**; cf sep HASH.

'To *hatch*' derives from MF-F *hacher*, to chop, from OF-F *hache*, an axe, from Frankish *\*hăppja* —cf OHG *happa*, a sickle-shaped knife, and syn OProv *apcha*. (B & W.) OF-F *hache* has MF-F dim *hachette*, whence E *hatchet*. MF-F *hachure* (from *hacher*) has been adopted by E.

**hatchel.** See the 2nd HACK, para 2.

**hatchet.** See the 3rd HATCH.

**hatching** (in engraving). See heading of 3rd HATCH.

**hatchment** corrupts *achievement*: see ACHIEVE.

**hatchway.** See the 1st HATCH.

**hate**, n (whence **hateful**) and v; **hatred**;—**heinous**.

1. 'To *hate*', ME *haten*, earlier *hatien*, derives from OE *hatian*, intimately akin to the OE n *hete*, whence, through ME *hete* and later—strongly influenced by the ME v *hatien*—*hate*, the E *hate*: the OE n and the OE v are resp akin to OFris *hat*, Go *hatis*, OHG-MHG *haz*, G *Hass*, ON *hatr*, MIr *caiss*, all meaning 'hate', and Gr *kēdos* (cf ACCIDIA), care, sorrow, affliction; and, for the v, OFris *hatia*, OHG *hatan*, *hatjan*, OHG *hazzōn*, MHG *hazzēn*, G *hassen*, ON *hata*, to hate, and OS *hatōn*, *hatan*, to be hostile towards, also to OHG *hezzēn* (for *\*hatjan*), MHG-G *hetzen*, to pursue, to hunt.

2. The ME v *hatien* has derivative *hatreden* (*-reden* from OE *rāeden*, condition, stipulation: cf *kindred*), later *hatred*.

3. Frankish \**hatjan*, to hate, becomes OF(-F) *haïr*, whence OF-MF *haïne* (F *haine*), with derivative OF-MF adj *haïnos* (F *haineux*), whence ME *heynous*, whence E *heinous*, hatefully bad.

**hatter.** See HAT.

**haughty**: OF-F *haute*, f of *haut*, high, from L *altus* (cf ALTITUDE): influenced by OS and OHG *hoh* (cf Go *hauhs* and see HIGH).

**haul** (v, hence n), whence **haulage** (*-age*) and **haulier** (agential *-ier*); **hale**, v.

'To *hale*' or haul derives from ME *halen*, whence also EE 'to *hall*', E 'to *haul*', cf *halyard* (*halliard*, occ *haulyard*), EE *hallier*, from 'to *hall*': and ME *halen* comes from OF-F *haler*, itself from ON *hala*, akin to OFris *halia*, OS *halōn*, OHG *halōn*, *holōn*, MHG *holn*, G *holen*, to fetch, pull, haul, and OE *geholian*, to get or acquire; perh cf Gr *kalōs*, a rope, a hawser. The Gmc r is prob \**hal-*; the IE т, \**kal-*; and the basic idea, 'to fetch'.

**haulm.** See CULM.

**haunch**; ? **hunch** (v, hence n), **hunchback**; ? **hunker**, v, and **hunkers**, n.

1. *Haunch* (prop the hip; loosely *haunches*, the region of hips and adjoining upper thighs and buttocks), derives from ME, from OF-F, *hanche*, from Gmc \**hanka*, cf MD *hanke*, ED *hancke*.

2. AE *hunkers*, haunches, prob derives from ED *hancke*, as also prob does the AE *hunker*, to squat: so the o.o.o. *hunch*, to bow the back, (earlier) to push, as with shoulders or elbows or hips, is perh a dial var of 'to *haunch*' (from the n). *Hunchback*, a bowed, hence a humped, back, prob eases *hunched back*; cf *humpback*, q.v. at HUMP. The orig AE coll *hunch*, a strong, intuitive guess, derives, according to Webster, 'from the gambler's superstition that it brings luck to touch the hump of a hunchback'.

**haunt** (n, v). See HOME, para 3.

**hautboy**: late MF-F *hautbois*, lit 'wood (*bois*) high (*haut*), esp in tone': cf *haughty* and, f.a.e., ALTITUDE.

**Havana.** See para 3 of:

**have**, pt and pp **had**; **haven** (n, hence v), whence **havenage** (*-age*)—cf **havana**; **behave**, **behavio(u)r**.

1. 'To *have*' derives, through ME *haven*, earlier *habben*, from OE *habban*, akin to OFris *habba* or *hebba*, OS *habbian* or *hebbian*, Go *haban*, OHG *habēn*, MHG-G *haben*, MD-D *hebben*, ON *hafa*; prob also to G *haben*, MHG *heben* or *heven*, OHG *heffēn*, OS *hebbian*, Go *haffjan*, ON *hefia*, OE *hebban*, E HEAVE, q.v. sep; and perh to L *capere*, to contain, hold, take, as in E *captive*. (Of G *haben*—therefore inferentially of E *have*—Walshe, voicing the opinion of every reputable scholar, says that 'the resemblance to Lat. *habēre*, which extends to the terminations, can only be fortuitous': but to postulate fortuitousness merely because L *h* normally becomes Gmc and C *g* (as in Ir *gaib*im, I take) is to go perh too far: there

may have been either conservatism or persistence or recalcitrance.) The IE r is app \**kap-*, to take.

2. Akin to OE *habban*, to have, is OE *haefn* or *haefene*, whence E *haven*: cf G *Hafen*, from MLG *havene* (MHG *habene*, ? extn of MHG *habe*), and ON *höfn* (cf Da *havn*).

3. A *Havana* is elliptical for a *Havana cigar*, made in or near *Havana*, Sp la *Habana*, the capital of Cuba: lit, 'the Haven'.

4. *Have* has the notable prefix-cpd *behave*, where *be-* is an int. Derivative *behavior* (AE) or *behaviour* has been influenced by the distinct archaic and dial *havio(u)r*, ME *havour* (with *h-* from ME *haven*, to have), OF *aveir* or *avoir*, n use of inf 'to have', L *habēre*. *Behaviour* has subsidiaries *behavio(u)rism* and *behavio(u)rist*, whence, in turn, *behavio(u)ristic*.

**haven**, whence **havenage**. See prec, para 2.

**haversack**: EF *havresac*, earlier EF *habresac* (as still in F diall): G *Habersack*, sack, or bag, for oats: LG *Hafer*, G *Haber* (OHG *habaro*): cf syn OSw *hafre* and prob the Gr *kakhrus*, parched barley. (Walshe.)

**havoc.** See HEAVE, para 4.

**haw**, with such cpds as **hawfinch** (cf FINCH) and **hawthorn** (OE *hagathorn*, var *haegthorn*: cf THORN); **hag**, **haggard**—cf **hagberry**; **hay**, a hedge; **hedge** (n, hence v), whence **hedgehog**;—**quay**.

1. *Haw*, a hawthorn berry, derives from OE *haga*, whence ME *hawe*, whence the now obs E *haw*, a fence, a hedge (? orig of hawthorn), hence the yard or grounds of a house. The obs *hay*, a hedge or the space enclosed thereby, comes from OE *hege*, very closely akin to OE *haga*: and akin to both of these OE words is OE *hegg* or *hecg*, whence ME *hegge*, later *hedge*, retained by E: cf OHG *hegga* or *hecka*, MHG *hegge* or *hecke*, G *Hecke*, hedge, themselves akin to G *Hag*, an enclosure, orig a hedge, MHG *hac*, OHG *hag*, OS *haga*—cf ON *hagi*, *hage*, enclosure, pasture.

2. Akin to ON *hege*, OE *hegg*, etc., is ON *heggr*, cognately surviving in Da *haeggebaer*, so closely resembling the E *hagberry*, with its var *hackberry*.

3. Akin to OE *haga*, hedge, OHG *hag*, hedge, also a grove, is OE *haegtesse*, whence, by lopping off the 2nd element, the ME *hegge*, var *hagge*, whence E *hag*, a female demon, with basic meaning, hedge (or wood) woman, hence wild woman (cf, sem, 'the *wild man* of the *woods*'); cf OHG *hagazussa*, MHG *hekse*, G *Hexe*, of which 'the first element seems to be *hag* [hedge], the second perh. as in Norw. (dial.) *tysja* "fairy"; Gaelic *dusii* "demons" ' (Walshe). The 1st element app occurs in MF *hagard*, prob of Gmc origin and possibly meaning orig 'of the hedges (and woods)', hence 'wild', applied esp to an untamed hawk, hence 'wild-looking'; perh influenced in EE by *hag*, a witch. With MF-F *hagard*, cf ME *hagger*, wild, untamed, an untamed hawk, clearly operative in E *haggard*; cf also MHG-G *hager*, lean, haggard. The MHG, ME word is o.o.o.

4. Of the same IE r as *haw*, hedge, but through C, is **quay**, ME *key*, OF *kai* or *cay* (F *quai*): cf

OBr *cai* (Br *kaé*), Cor *kea, ke,* W *cae,* hedge, OIr *cae, cai,* house (enclosed by a hedge): the OF word prob deriving imm from a Gaul \**caio* (cf OBr *caiou,* ramparts, and L *cau*lae, fence, hedge). The OF *cai,* hedge, developed the senses 'wall'—'embankment'—'quay'.—Derivative F *quayage*—cf the C12 ML *caiāgium*—has been adopted by E. (B & W; Holthausen.)

**hawk** (1), the bird. See HEAVE, para 5.

**hawk** (2), to clear one's throat, is echoic.

**hawk** (3), to sell itinerantly; **hawker,** itinerant merchant, a peddler. See HOOK, para 2.

**hawse:** EE *halse:* ON *hals,* neck, hence part of a ship's bows: f.a.e., COLLAR.

**hawser:** OF-MF *haucier* (F *hausser*), to hoist: VL \**altiāre,* to put high, to raise: from L *altus,* high: cf ALTITUDE.

**hawthorn.** See the heading of HAW.

**hay** (1), mown grass. See the 2nd HACK, para 9.

**hay** (2), hedge. See HAW, para 1.

**hazard,** n and v; **hazardous.**

*Hazard,* orig a game of chance played with dice, is adopted from OF *hasart,* MF-F *hasard,* from Ar *al-zahr,* the die, through Sp *azar,* unforeseen disaster, itself of the same origin. The derivative EF-F adj *hasardeux* prob suggested E *hasardous;* the derivative MF-F v *hasarder* certainly yielded 'to *hazard*'.

**haze.** See HARE, para 2.

**hazel** (whence hazelnut): ME *hasel:* OE *haesel,* akin to OHG *hasala,* MHG-G *hasel,* and ON *hasl:* Gmc r, \**xasala;* IE r \**kosolo-;* cf Ir *coll* (for \**cosl*) and L *corulus* (for \**cosulus*). (Walshe.)

**hazy.** See HARE, para 2.

**he, him, his; hence, here, hither; it, its; she— her, hers.**

1. The personal pronoun, 3rd person sing, is, in OE, *hē,* m; *hēo,* f; *hit,* neu: whence, resp, *he;* not *she,* q.v. in para 7; and, through ME *hit,* later *it,* the E *it,* whence EE *it's,* whence E *its.*

2. OE *hē* is akin to OFris and OS *hē, hī,* OHG *hē,* cf MD *he, hi,* D *hij;* also to words in L and Gr— cf, e.g., the pronominal element *e-* in Gr *ekei,* there—and, more remotely, in other IE languages.

3. OE *hē* has dat *him,* whence the E *him* (orig the indirect object).

4. OE *hē* has gen *his,* of him, whence both the possessive pronoun and the possessive adj, E *his.*

5. OE *hē* has derivative advv (1) *heonan, heonon, heona, hina,* whence, with gen *-s* added, ME *hennes, hens,* whence E *hence,* with several Gmc cognates; (2) *hēr,* MF *her,* E *here,* with Gmc cognates; (3) *hider,* ME *hider,* later *hither,* E *hither,* with very close Gmc cognates.

6. OE *hēo,* she, has gen and dat sing *hire,* whence ME *hire, here, hir,* whence E *her,* pronoun, whence *her,* adj, whence *hers* (gen suffix *-s*).

7. But the E *she* comes from a different r: through ME *she* (earlier *scae*), varr *sche, scheo, scho*:? from OE *sēo,* var *sīo,* f of the article 'the', orig a demonstrative pronoun: cf OHG *siu,* MHG *siu, sie, sī,* G *sie,* OS *siu;* cf also Skt *syā,* this one.

**head,** n hence adj and v (whence **header, head-**

ing); many cpds, all obvious; **behead,** whence **beheadal; ahead.**

1. *Head:* ME *hed,* earlier *heved,* earliest *heaved:* OE *hēafod,* akin to OE *hafud,* OFris *hāved, hāft, hāud,* ON *höfuth,* Go *haubith,* OHG *houbit,* MHG *houbet, houbt,* G *Haupt*—to L *caput*—Skt *kapālam* (skull): f.a.e., CHIEF, para 1.

2. *Behead:* ME *biheden,* earlier *bihefden:* OE *behēafdian:* prefix *be-+hēafod+*inf suffix.

3. *Ahead=a-,* on+*head:* in the front, forwards.

**heal, health, healthy.** See WHOLE, paras 4-5.

**heald.** See HEAVE, para 6.

**heap,** n, comes, via ME *heep, heap,* from OE *hēap,* whence OE *hēapian,* whence 'to *heap*': and OE *hēap* is akin to OFris *hāp,* OS *hōp,* OHG *hūfo, houf,* MHG *hūfe, houfe,* G *Haufen,* MD *hoep, houp,* (as D) *hoop,* also to OSl *kupŭ,* Lith *kaúpas,* all 'heap': cf Skt *kaofa,* mountain ('a great heap').—Cf HIVE.

**hear,** pt and pp **heard;** vn **hearing,** agent **hearer; hearsay** (from 'I *hear say*', I hear it said); **hearken** or **harken; hark.**

1. 'To *hear*', ME *heren,* derives from OE *hēran, hȳran, hīeran:* cf OFris *hēra,* OS *hōrian,* OHG *hōrēn,* MHG *hoeren,* G *hören,* MD *horen, hoeren,* MD-D *hooren,* Go *hausjan,* ON *heyra:* Gmc r, ? \**hauz-;* IE r, ? \**kauz-:* cf Gr *akouein* (? for \**akousein*), perh lit (Walshe) 'to have a *sharp ear*': IE r \**ak-,* sharp+\**ous-,* var \**aus-,* ear (cf EAR).

2. Akin to *hear* is the syn *hark,* ME *herken,* from that 'lost' OE v (cf OFris *herkia,* OHG *hōrechēn,* MHG *hōrchēn,* G *horchen,* MD *horken,* all prob intt of the simple 'to *hear*' forms) which accounts for OE *heorcnian,* often in contr *hercnian,* whence ME *hercnien, hercnen,* whence E 'to *hearken*', with var *harken,* influenced by *hark.*

**hearse, herse; rehearse,** whence **rehearsal** (suffix *-al,* connoting 'activity');—**hirsute;—horrendous; horrent; horrible; horrid; horrify, horrific; horripilate, horripilation; horrisonant; horror;—abhor, abhorrent** (whence **abhorrence**);—**gorse;—ordure, ordurous;—urchin—herisson;** sep CAPRICE.

1. *Herse,* now rare, is a var of *hearse:* ME *herse:* OF-MF *herce,* a harrow, an ornamental framework over a coffin (whence, ult, the predominant modern sense), a portcullis (F, cf E, *herse*): L *hirpic*em, acc of *hirpex* (o/s *hirpic-*), a harrow, prob akin to L *hirsūtus,* prickly (see para 3): L *hirpex,* var *irpex,* derives from Samnite *hirpus, irpus,* a wolf: cf L *hircus* (cf Sabine *fircus*), he-goat.

2. OF-MF *herce,* a harrow, has derivative OF-MF v *hercier* (cf ML *hirpicāre*), to harrow, with OF-MF prefix-cpd *rehercier,* to harrow *re-* or again, hence to repeat: whence ME *rehercen, rehersen,* whence 'to *rehearse*'.

3. L *hirsūtus,* shaggy, bristly, is akin also to L *hirtus,* hairy, (esp) stiff-haired, whence Bot *Hirtella,* f of SciL dim *hirtellus; hirsūtus* becomes E *hirsute.* All these L words are akin to L *horrēre* (see para 5).

4. With L *hirsūtus,* cf Skt *hṛṣyati,* he bristles, itself akin to Gr *khēr,* hedgehog, whence perh L \**her,* L *er,* with derivative syn extn *erīcius,* second-

arily a hedgehog-like, obstructive machine of war, whence, via a form *ericiō, acc *ericiōnem, the OF-MF *her çon*, whence F *hérisson*, whence E *herisson*, hedgehog (obs), the obstruction (hist). The MF var *herichon*, esp in the mdfn *irechon*, becomes ME *irchoun*, with var *urchon*, whence E *urchin*, orig a hedgehog, hence a mischievous boy, esp if raggedly dressed.

5. L *hirpex, hirtus, hirsūtus, ericius* are all, very prob, akin to L *horrēre*, (of human hair) to stand on end, esp with fright, hence to shudder with fear, itself perh (E & M) akin to Skt *hárṣate*, his hair bristles with joy, *ghárṣus*, excited—cf Arm *garšim*, I have a horror of.

6. *Horrēre* (s *horr-*) has presp *horrens*, o/s *horrent-*, whence the literary adj *horrent*, bristling, bristly; it also has the foll L derivatives affecting E:

   *horrendus*, causing a shudder of fear or extreme disgust: E *horrendous*;
   *horribilis*: OF-F, whence ME-E, *horrible*;
   *horridus*, bristly, hence savage-looking, hence horrible: E *horrid*;
   *horror*, a bristling with fear, a shudder, extreme fear or disgust: OF-MF *horror* (F *horreur*): ME *horrour*: E *horror*.

7. *Horrēre* has several prefix-cpds; by far the most important is *abhorrēre*, to remove oneself with *horror* from (*ab*), hence to feel horror at or towards: whence 'to *abhor*'. Presp *abhorrens* became in LL an adj, meaning 'repulsive': from its o/s *abhorrent-* comes the E *abhorrent*.

8. The chief full-cpds of *horrēre* are perh:

   *horrificāre*, to cause (*-ficare*, c/f of *facere*, to make) to *horrēre* or bristle, esp with fear, whence 'to *horrify*'; the derivative adj *horrificus* becomes EF *horrifique* and E *horrific*;
   LL *horripilāre*, (of the *pilus*, hair) to bristle, esp with fear, hence to shudder, the pp *horripilātus* yielding both 'to *horripilate*' and, via the derivative LL *horripilātiō*, o/s *horripilātiōn-*, E *horripilation*;
   *horrisonus*, dreadful-sounding, whence, as if via a derivative ML pa *horrisonans*, the E *horrisonant*.

9. There remain two notable E words: *gorse* and *ordure*. *Gorse*, from OE *gorst*, is akin to L *hordeum* (s *hord-*, r *hor-*), barley, app for *horzdeum* or *horsdeum*, much as *horrēre* is perh for *horsēre*; with OE *gorst*, cf OHG *gersta*, MHG-G *gerste*, barley (Walshe.)

10. *Ordure*, adopted from OF-F, is a *-ure* derivative of OF *ord*, repulsively dirty, disgustingly filthy: from L *horridus* (s *horrid-*), prob through *hord-*, contr of *horrid-*. E *ordure* has adj *ordurous* (cf the F *ordurier*).

**heart**, n (whence **hearty**, whence **heartily** and **heartiness**) and v (whence **hearten**, whence **dis-hearten**, with paa **heartening**, **disheartening**); numerous cpds, all self-explanatory, but notably: **heartbreak** (**-broken**), **-burn**, **-felt**, **-less**, **-rending**, **heart's ease** (lit and, of a flower, fig); **heartsick** (cf OE *heortsēoc*), Sc **heartsome**, **-string**, **-whole**.

*Heart*, ME *harte*, earlier *herte*, with var *heorte*, derives from OE *heorte*: cf OFris *herte* (*hirte*), OS *herta*, OHG *herza*, MHG *herze*, G *Herz*, Go

*hairtō*, MD *herte, hert, harte*, MD-D *hart*, ON *hiarta*; cf also Gr *kardia* (and *kēr*), L *cor* (gen *cordis*)—and Lith *širdis*. See the sep *cordial* (*-cardiac*) group.

**hearth**: ME *harthe, herth*: OE *heorth*, akin to OFris and OS *herth*, OHG *herd*, MHG *hert*, G *Herd*, MD *hert, herte, heert, hart*. Cf also Lith *karstas*, hot; L *carbō* (? for *khardho-*), a coal—see sep CARBON; perh L *cremāre*, q.v. at CREMATE; perh Gr *keramos*, earthenware (fired in a kiln), with adj *keramikos*, whence E *ceramic*, whence the n *ceramics*.

**hearty**. See heading of HEART.

**heat**, n and v (whence **heater** and AE dial and coll **het-up**, excited); **hot**, adj (hence n and v), whence **hotness** (*-ness*).

'To *heat*', ME *heten*, derives from OE *hǣtan*, akin both to OE *hǣtu* (var *hǣto*), whence, through ME *haete*, later *hete*, the E n *heat*, and to OE *hāt*, whence, through ME *hat*, later *hot*, the E adj *hot*. The OE adj is akin to OFris and OS *hēt*, OHG-MHG *heiz*, G *heiss*, MD *heit*, MD-D *heet*, ON *heitr*, and, further off, the Lith *kaitrus*: the Gmc r is app *hait-*; the IE, *koid-*. (Walshe.) The OE n *hǣtu, hǣto*, is akin to OFris *hēte*, OHG *hizzea, hizza, heizi*, MHG-G *hitze*, Go *heito* (fever), MD *heet, heit*, MD-D *hitte*, ON *hite, hiti*; cf also Lith *kaitrà*, incandescence. In general, the nn derive from the adjj.

**heath** (whence the adj **heathy**), **heathen**, **heathen-dom, heathenish**; **heather**, whence adj **heathery**; ? **hoyden**, whence **hoydenish**.

1. *Heath*, ME *heth*, waste land (or heath), the plant heath or heather, from OE *hǣth*, waste land, heathland (heath), the plant; the plant app comes from the land, because it grows there. Akin to OE *hǣth* are MHG-G *heide*, MD *hede* and (as D) *heide*, ON *heithr*, waste land, a heath, cf Go *haithi*, a field, and, further off, OIr *ciad*, OW *coid*, both for a forest; cf also L *būcētum*, a pasture for cattle (cf *bucolic*): Gmc r, *haith-*; IE r, *koit-*. (Walshe.)

2. App from ON *heithr*, waste land, a heath, comes ME *hathir*, var *hadder*: E *heather*.

3. *Heathen*, ME *hethen*, derives from OE *hǣthen*, prob 'he of the *hǣth* or heath', hence 'he of the (remote) country districts': cf OFris *hēthen*, OS *hēthin*, adjj, OFris *hēthenmann* and *hēthena*, nn, OHG *heidano* (perh cf Arm *hethanos*, from Gr *ethnos*, a people, a nation), MHG *heiden*, G *Heide*, MD *heiden*, n, and *heiden, heidin*, adj, Go *haithno* (heathen woman), ON *heidinn, heithinn*, adj. The sem parallel to PAGAN cannot be pushed very far.

4. The Go *haithnō*, female heathen, suggests the not impossible derivation of *hoyden*, a lout (obs), a rough, bold girl, from D *heiden*, a heathen, (but also) a boor.

**heathen**. See prec, para 3.

**heather**. See HEATH, para 2.

**heave**, pt and pp **heaved** and **hove** (OE pt *hōf*); **haft; havoc; hawk** (the bird); **heald—heddle; heavy, heaviness; heft** (n and v), **hefty**.—For the numerous L *capere* cognates, see CAPABILITY.

1. 'To *heave*' (whence the n) comes, through

ME *heven*, earlier *hebben*, from OE *hebban*, (vt) to move up or along, to lift (now usu effortfully): cf OFris *hebba*, OS *hebbian*, OHG *heffēn* (pt *huob*), MHG *heven* and, as in G, *heben*, MD-D *heffen*, Eastern MD *heven*, Go *hafjan*, ON *hefia*, *hefja*: all corresp exactly to L *capere* (r *cap-*), to take, grasp, seize; cf also Gr *kōpē*, a handle; prob cf HAVE.

2. From, or at the least akin to, ME *heven*, is E dial and coll *heft*, to heave, and a heaving, the latter yielding the dial and coll adj *hefty*, weighty, somewhat roughly vigorous.

3. Akin to, perh from, OE *hebban* is OE *haeft*, a handle (now esp of a knife): E *haft*, that by which one raises an object. Cf OFris *heft*, *hefte*, OS *hafta*, OHG *hefti*, MHG *hefte*, D and G *Heft*, a handle, MHG *haft*, a holding, a hold, ON *hepti*—and Gr *kōpē* (as in para 1).

4. Prob of the same Gmc origin as *heave* is *havoc*, adapted from OE-MF *crier havot*, to cry havoc, *havot* being pillage or plunder, akin to—prob from—OF-MF *haver*, to take, prob from OF-MF *hef*, a hook, itself prob from OHG *heffēn* (as in para 1). (DAF.)

5. Akin to *havoc* is the predatory *hawk*: ME *hauk*, earlier *havek*, OE *hafoc*, dial var *heafoc*: cf OFris *havek* and *hauk*, OHG *habuh*, MHG *habech*, G *Habicht*, ON *haukr*: each Gmc n deriving very prob from the 'heave' v.

6. From the r of *heave* comes OE *hefeld*, whence E *heald*, a harness in weaving, also known as a *heddle*, from OE *\*hefedl*, earlier form of *hefeld*. (OED.)

7. Akin to OE *hebban* is OE *hefig*, whence ME *hevi*, whence E *heavy*; derivative OE *hefignes* yields *heaviness*. The OE *hefig* is akin to OS *hebhig* (*hefig*), OHG *hebīg*, *hevīg*, MD *hevich*, ON *höfigr*, *höfugr*; cf also OE *hefe*, a weight.

**heaven, heavenly.**

The latter derives from OE *heofonlīce* (cf *-like*), the adj of OE *heofon*, whence through ME *heofene*, later *hefen*, latest *heven*, the E *heaven*: and OE *heofon* is akin to OS *hevan* (*hebhan*), LG *heven*, *heben*, and also, at a simple remove, akin to OFris *himel*, *himul*, OS *himil*, OHG *himil*, MHG *himel*, G *Himmel*, Go *himins*, ON *himenn*, *himinn*. The Gmc r is app *\*heman-*, var *\*himin-*, and that r could even be akin to that of CAMERA.

**heaviness, heavy.** See HEAVE, para 7.

**hebdomad, hebdomadal, hebdomadary.** See SEVEN, para 3.

**Hebe:** Gr *Hēbē*, goddess, personification of *hēbē*, youthfulness, youthful strength: IE etymon, *\*iega*, *\*iegua*—cf Lith *jegiù*, I have the strength (to . . .).

**Hebraic, Hebraism, Hebraist, Hebraize, Hebrew** (n, hence adj).

The base is H '*Ibhrī*, 'one who is, or comes, from across' the river Euphrates (Webster), esp a Jew, from H *ēbher*, from beyond: whence Aram *Ebrai*, Gr *Hebraïos*, L *Hebraeus*, ML *Ebreus*, OF-MF *Ebreu* (F *Hébreu*), ME *Ebreu*, E *Hebrew*. But since '*Ibhrī* is orig an adj form (*-ī*), '*Ibhrī* might well, as Enci It proposes, derive from a remote ancestor

'*Ebher*. Gr *Hebraïos* has adj derivative *Hebraïkos*, LL *Hebraicus*, E *Hebraic*, and derivative v *hebraïzein*, to speak Hebrew, whence 'to *Hebraize*'—cf the F *hébraïser*—to render or become Jewish. *Hebraism* and *Hebraist* add *-ism* and *-ist* to *Hebraic*, but owe something to F *hébraïsme* and *hébraïste*.

**hecatomb.** See HUNDRED, para 2.

**heckle.** See the 2nd HACK, para 3.

**hectic:** late MF-F *hectique*: LL *hecticus*: Gr *hektikos*, consumptive, (orig and mainly) habitual, from *hexis*, a habit of body or mind, from *ekhein*, to have (f.a.e.: SCHEME): cf, sem, HABIT from L *habēre*, to have. Cf:

**hector,** to bully, derives from *hector*, a bully, itself from L *Hector*, trln of Gr *Hektōr*, lit one who holds firm, from *ekhein*, to hold, to have: cf prec and, f.a.e., see SCHEME.

**heddle.** See HEAVE, para 6.

**hedge.** See HAW, para 1. The *hedgehog*, which is a hedge-haunter, resembles a pig only in its snout.

**hedonic, hedonism, hedonist.** See SUAVE, para 3.

**heed,** v—hence n, whence both *heedful* (*-ful*) and *heedless* (*-less*)—comes, through ME *heden*, from OE *hēdan*, akin to OHG *huotēn*, MHG *huëten*, to protect, OHG *huota*, protection, MHG *huote*, (esp) supervision of women to prevent illicit love-affairs, G *Hut*, a guarding, heed, OFris *hēda*, *hoda*, *huda*, watch over, guard, take care of. (The OE v prob derives from the Gmc r occurring in OHG *huota*.)

**heel** (n, hence v); **hock** (of, e.g., a horse), n, hence v; **coxa.**

1. *Heel*, ME *heele* or *hele*, derives from OE *hēla*, for *\*hōhila*, dim of OE *hōh*, heel: cf OFris *-hēl*, *hēla*, MD *hiele* or, as D, *hiel*, ON *haell*.

2. OE *hōh*, heel, becomes E *hock*: cf ON *hā*-sin, the sinew in the hock, and prob L *coxa* (? for *\*cocsa*), hip, hip-bone, itself retained by An and Zoo, and akin to Skt *kakṣā*, *kákṣas*, armpit, and EIr *coss*, Ga *càs*, foot, and perh OHG *ahsa*, the part behind the knee-joint.

**heft, hefty.** See HEAVE, para 2.

**hegemony.** See SEEK, para 7.

**Hegira,** Mohammed's flight from Mecca: either via Sp *hegira* or via ML *hegīra*: Ar *hijrah*, flight, departure, from Ar *hagara*, to depart.

**heifer:** ME *hayfare*: OE *hēahfore*: o.o.o.: ? 'high-farer' (EW).

**height, heighten.** See HIGH, para 3.

**heinous.** See HATE, para 3.

**heir, heiress, heirloom; hereditable, hereditament, hereditary, heredity—heritable, heritage, heritance, heritor—inherit, inheritable, inheritance, inheritor—disinherit.**

1. *Heiress*=*heir*+f suffix *-ess*; *heirloom*=*heir*+*loom* in its earlier sense of 'tool' (almost 'chattel'); and *heir* itself derives from ME *heir*, *eir*, both adopted from OF (cf the F *hoir*): from VL *\*hērem* for L *hērēdem*, acc of *hērēs*, prob akin to Gr *khēros*, bereaved, and Skt *jahāti*, he leaves (e.g., an heir) or abandons.

2. L *hērēs*, an heir, o/s *hērēd-*, has derivative LL

*hērēditāre*, to inherit, whence both ML *hērēditābilis*, whence, via MF, *hereditable*, heritable, and ML *hērēditamentum*, whence E *hereditament*, heritable property. *Hērēs* has the further derivative *hērēditās*, o/s *hērēditāt-*, whence, via OF-F *hérédité*, the E *heredity*; *hērēditās*, s *hērēdit-*, has derivative *hērēditārius*, whence late MF-F *héréditaire* and E *hereditary*.

3. *Hērēditāre* becomes OF-MF *heriter* (F *hériter*) with OF derivatives *heritable*, *heritage*, *heritance*, all adopted by E; derivative OF-MF *heritier* becomes E *heritor* (L *-or* substituted for F *-ier*).

4. *Hērēditāre* has LL prefix-cpd *inhērēditāre*, to appoint (someone) as heir, whence MF *enheriter*, whence ME *enheriten*, to leave a heritage to, (also) to inherit, whence 'to inherit', whence *inheritable* and *inheritor*; derivative MF *enheritance* becomes E *inheritance*. *Inherit* has the dissociative off-shoot, *disinherit*.

**heliacal.** See SOLAR, para 4; cf SUN, para 3.

**helianthus.** See the element *heli(o)-*.

**helical, helicine, helicoid** (extn **helicoidal**); **helicopter**—see the element *heli-*; **helix**; cf the element *helico-* at *heli-*.

The first two adjj are E formations from *helic-*, o/s of L *helix*, adopted from Gr *helix*, adj and n, (anything) twisted or rolled, (a) spiral, o/s *helik-*, c/f *heliko-*, whence the Gr adj *helikoeidēs*, whence the F *hélicoïde* and E *helicoid*. Gr *helix* and var *helikē* derive from *elissō*, Attic *helittō*, I turn about or around, twist, roll (vt), akin to OE *wilwan* (*wilwian*) and Go *walwjan*, to roll (vt); *elissō* is prob for *\*ewelissō*, r *\*ewel-*, perh a vocalization of IE r *\*wel-*, varr *\*wal-* and *\*wil-*.

**heliocentric, heliograph, heliotrope.** See the element *heli(o)-*.

**Helios, helium.** See SOLAR, para 4.

**helix.** See HELICAL.

**hell.** See HALL, para 3.

**Helladic, Hellas.** See HELLENE.

**hellebore**, a poisonous herb, derives from L *helleborus* (var *elleborus*), trln of Gr *helleboros* (var *elleboros*): o.o.o.: ? ult akin to L *uērātrum*, Bot *Veratrum*, occ known as 'false hellebore' and itself o.o.o.

**Hellene, Hellenic, Hellenism, Hellenist, Hellenistic, Hellenize; Helladic, Hellas; Hellespont.**

The *Hellespont* or Dardanelles is the *pontos* (s *pont-*: f.a.e., PONS) of *Hellas* or Greece; and *Hellas*, adj *Helladikos*, whence *Helladic*, is an *-as* derivative of *Hellēn* (Ἕλλην), the o.o.o. eponymous originator of the Gr race: hence, Ἕλληνες, *Hellēnes*, the *Hellenes* or Greeks, with derivatives *Hellēnikos*, E *Hellenic*—*Hellēnismos*, E *Hellenism*—*Hellēnistēs* (*-istēs*), E *Hellenist*, whence *Hellenistic*, perh after Gr *hellēnistiki*, in Gr fashion—*Hellēnizein*, E *Hellenize*.

**hello!** See HALLOO, s.f.

**helm** (1), rudder: ME *helme*: OE *helma*, akin to OFris, OS, OHG *helm*, ON *hjalmr*: PGmc *\*helmo-* (Kluge): cf HELVE.

**helm** (2); **helmet**. *Helm*, helmet, comes straight from OE; *helmet*, however, is adopted from

OF-MF, where it is the dim of OF-MF *helme* (C8 *helmus*), from Frankish *\*helm*, therefore id with E *helm*, akin to prec.

**helot**, a serf, derives from *Helot*, a serf of Sparta: L *Helotes*, *Hilotai*, trlnn of Gr *Heilōtes*, *Heilotai*, all pl: either from the enslaved inhabitants of the Laconian town of *Helos* or, more prob, from Gr *haliskesthai*, to be made captive, itself akin to L *uellere* (r *uel-*), to tear, or pull violently, away, Go *wilwan*, to take forcibly; *haliskesthai* has s *halis-*, r *hal-*. Hence *helotism*.

**help**, n (whence **helpful** and **helpless**) and v; **helpmate, helpmeet.**

*Helpmeet* rationalizes *helpmate*, which corrupts the Biblical '*help meet*'—suitable—'for him' (Eve, for Adam). *Help*, n, is OE *help*, akin to OFris *helpe*, OS *helpa*, OHG *hёlfa*, *hilfa*, MHG *hёlfe*, *hilfe*, G *Hülfe*, *Hilfe*, ON *hjalp*. 'To help', ME *helpen*, is OE *helpan*, akin to OFris *helpa*, OS *helpan*, OHG *helfan*, MHG-G *helfen*, Go *hilpan*, ON *hialpa* (*hjalpa*); cf Lith *šelpiù*, I help.

**helter-skelter**, in confused haste, is an echoic redup: cf, sem, *hurry-scurry* and, phon, G *holter-polter* and D *holderdebolder*.

**helve**: ME *helve*, earlier *helfe*: OE *helf*, *hielf*, *hylf*: akin to the 1st HELM and prob to Lith *kilpa*, a stirrup.

2. Akin to OE *helf* is OE *haelftr*, ME *helfter*, later *helter*, latest *halter*, extant in E: cf MD *halfter* (as D), *haelter*, *halter*, and OHG *halftra*. MHG-G *halfter*.

**hem** (1), a border or edge, hence the v: OE *hem* or *hemm*, akin to MD and MHG-G *hemmen*, to confine, hem in, hinder, whence E *hem*, usu *hem in*, to surround (e.g., a foe): perh cf OE and E dial *ham*, a pasture, and Gr *kēmos* (s and r *kēm-*), a muzzle.

**hem** (2), to hinder or confine. See prec.

**hem** (3), to clear one's throat ('to hem and haw'), derives from the echoic interjection *hem!* of warning, with its reinforced var *ahem!*

**hemal.** See HAEMOPHILIA, s.f.

**hemicycle; hemisphere.** See the element *hemi-*; for the latter, cf SPHERE, para 2.

**hemlock**: ME *hemlok*, *hemeluc*: OE *hymlīc*, *hymlīce*, *hemlīc*: o.o.o. The suffix *-līc* ('-like') suggests that the OE n was orig an adj: perh *hymlīc(e)* is a contr of *hymelelīc*, '(a herb) like the hop-vine or the bryony or the convolvulus', the OE *hymele* being applied indifferently to all three vine-like or climbing herbs; there may even be some obscure pun on the deadliness of the hemlock—and of the products of the hop.

**hemp**, whence the adjj **hempen** and the mostly dial **hempy**; cf the sep CANVAS, where also *cannabis*.

*Hemp*, ME *hemp*, is an easing of OE *henep* or *haenep*: cf ON *hampr*, OS *hanap*, OHG *hanaf*, MHG *hanef*, G *Hanf*, MD *hanep*, *hannep*, *hennip*, and, as in D, *hennep*; cf also Gr *kannabis* (L *cannabis*), OB *konoplja*, Pol *konop*, Lith *kanãpės*. The Gmc, Gr, OSl words app go back to 'some old E European language': Walshe cites a Cheremiss and a Zyrjän word, these two languages being

Finno-Ugric: 'a wandering culture-word of wide diffusion'.

**hen** (whence **henbane**—cf BANE)—whence 'to **henpeck**' or nag at; cf the sep CANT, where *chant, enchant, chanticleer, charm,* are treated.

*Hen* comes straight from OE *hen,* which has varr *henn, haen*: the f of OE *hana,* cock: cf OHG *henna, heninna,* MHG-G *henne,* hen, and, for 'cock', OHG *hano,* MHG *hane, han,* G *Hahn,* OFris and Go *hana,* ON *hani.* The OGmc 'cock' words prob mean 'the chanter or singer', for they are akin to L *canere* (r *can-*), to sing, and its int *cantāre*—to Gr *ēïkanos,* cock, lit 'singing in the dawn' (*ēōs*)—and several C words: IE r, either *\*kan-* or, more prob, *\*khan-,* to sing.

**hence** (whence **henceforth**). See HE, para 6.

**henchman**: ME *hencheman* or *henxman,* a groom: app OE *hengest, hengist,* a horse+*man.* With OE *hengest,* cf OFris *hengst* and *hanxt,* OHG *hengist,* a stallion, a gelding, MHG *hengest,* G *Hengst,* stallion, and ON *hestr* (for *\*henhistr*); prob akin to Skt *šankus,* (of horses) nimble. (Walshe.)

**hendecagon; hendecasyllable.** See the element *hendeca-.*

**hendiadys.** See the element *hen(o)-.*

**henna,** dye from the leaves of the tropical shrub *henna*: Ar *hinnā',* whence with *al,* the, prefixed, the ML *alchanna,* whence—cf Sp *alcana*—*alkanna,* a herb of the borage family; Sp *alcana* has dim *alcaneta,* whence *alcanet,* a herb and its derivative dye.

**henpeck.** See the heading of HEN.

**henry,** the unit of El inductance, is named from an American physicist, Joseph *Henry* (1797–1878): and *Henry,* surname from given name, is OF-F *Henri,* from G *Heinrich,* from OHG *Haganrih,* lit the 'ruler' (*-rih*: cf L *rex*) 'of an enclosure' (OHG *hag, haga*: cf HAW, para 1, s.f.). Given-name *Henry* has pet-form *Harry,* whence *Hal.*

**hepar; hepatic.** See the element *hepato-.*

**heptad; heptagon.** See SEVEN, para 2.

**her.** See HE, para 6.

**Hera.** See HERO, s.f.

**herald,** n, whence—after OF *herauder*—v and **heraldic** (cf the late MF-F *héraldique*) and **heraldry** (*-ry* for *-ery,* connoting 'profession' or 'subject').

*Herald,* already in ME (var *heraud*), derives from MF *heralt* (var *heraut,* whence F *héraut*), earliest as *hirauz,* from Frankish *\*hariwald,* the chief (cf OHG *waltan,* to have power over, to govern) of an army (cf OHG *hari, heri*: see HARRY): cf Tacitus's Batavian chief *Charioualda* and OE *Harald* or *Harold.*

**herb; herbaceous; herbage; herbal** (adj, hence n) —whence **herbalist; herbarium, herbary; herborize; herbose, herbous;**—sep ARBO(U)R in a garden; **yerba;**—cf the element *herbi-,* where, e.g., *herbivorous.*

1. *Herb,* ME from OF-F *herbe,* derives from L *herba*; o.o.o.: 'doubtless a survival of some pre-Latin rustic word' (E & M).

2. In Sp, L *herba* becomes *hierba,* whence SAm Sp *yerba,* known in E as an ellipsis of *yerbu de maté* or commonly *yerba maté,* from which maté

(Sp *mate,* from Quechuan *mate,* calabash) or Paraguayan tea is made.

3. The following L derivatives of *herba* affect E: *herbāceus,* grassy, whence *herbaceous*;

LL *herbārium,* a grassy place, a herbal, adopted by E, with derivative *herbary*; *herbōsus,* grassy, LL green like, or as, grass, whence both *herbose* and *herbous.*

4. Through F come:

*herbage,* an adoption from OF-F: *herbe*+*-age*;

*herborist,* from EF-F *herboriste,* which suggests *herboriser,* whence

*herborize,* with subsidiary *herborization* (F *herborisation*).

5. But *herbal*=E *herb*+adj *-al.*

**herculean** derives from *Herculean,* of *Hercules,* L adaptation of Gr *Hēraklees* (whence the L and E var *Heracles*), lit 'glory (*kleos*) of *Hera*', the Gr goddess.

**herd,** v, derives from **herd** (of animals), ME *herd,* var *heorde,* from OE *heord,* whence OE *heorde,* var *hierde,* ME *heorde, herde,* E *herd,* a herdsman (*herd's man*): and OE *heord* is akin to OHG *herta,* MHG *herte* and, as in G, *herde*—Go *hairda*—ON *hiörth* (*hjörth*)—and, further off, Skt *sárdhas*; cf Lith *keřdžius,* a shepherd. The Gmc r is *\*herd-*; the IE r, *\*kerdh-.* (Walshe.)

2. *Shepherd* derives, via ME *schepherde* or *-hirde,* from OE *scēaphyrde,* the first element being the source of SHEEP.

**here.** See HE, para 5.

**hereditament, hereditary, heredity.** See HEIR, para 2.

**heresy, heretic.** See SERUM, para 3.

**herisson.** See HEARSE, para 4.

**heritable, heritage, heritor.** See HEIR, para 3.

**herma; hermaphrodite; hermeneutic,** whence **hermeneutics; Hermes, hermetic,** with extn **hermetical.**

1. A *herma* or pillar-shaped image with a head of the Gr god Hermes, Gr *Hermēs* (L *Herma*), the Olympian messenger and therefore a bearer of secrets. Gr *Hermēs,* o.o.o., has the ML derivative adj *hermeticus,* with esp ref to Hermes Trismegistos (thrice-greatest): whence *hermetic.*

2. Hermes and Aphrodite (cf APHRODISIAC) had a son *Hermaphroditos,* who, bathing, found himself unicorporally merged with a nymph, whence *hermaphroditos,* L *hermaphroditus,* E *hermaphrodite,* a person double-sexed.

3. Gr *Hermēs* has acc *Hermēn,* which perh suggested Gr *hermēneus,* an interpreter (? orig of Olympian messages), otherwise o.o.o.; Boisacq and Hofmann propose a PGr *\*herma* or *\*hermos,* a speech or a reply, with r *\*wer-,* to say or speak. The derivative v *hermēneuein* has dependent adj *hermēneutikos,* whence E *hermeneutic.*

**hermit, hermitage; eremite.** See the 1st RARE, para 2.

**hern.** See HERON.

**hernia.** See YARN; cf the element *hernio-.*

**hero, heroic, heroine, heroism.**

The last derives from EF-F *héroïsme* from MF

*héro*s, trln of Gr *hērŏs*, whence, via L *heroe*s, pl of
L *heros* (from Gr), the E *hero*. Gr *hērŏs* has adj
*hērŏĭkos*, L *heroïcus*, MF-F *héroïque*, E *heroic*
(whence n *heroics*); the derivative Gr f *hērŏĭnē*
becomes L *heroĭna*, EF-F *héroĭne*, E *heroine*. Gr
*hērŏs*, s *hērŏ-* r *hēr-*, is akin to L *seruāre* (ML
*servāre*), to safeguard, s *seru-*, r *ser-*: cf SERVANT.
Akin is the Gr goddess *Hēra* (Attic *Hērē*), app for
\**Hērwa*, precisely as *hērŏs* is for \**hērowos*: cf
Av *haurvaiti*, he keeps guard over. The basic
sense of both *Hera* and *hero* would therefore be
'protector'.

**heron** (whence **heronry**), occ **hern**; **egret** and
**aigrette**.

*Egret*, a white-plumed heron, derives from F
*aigrette*, EF-F *egret*, tuft of feathers (sense and
form adopted by E), from MF *egreste*, heron, from
OProv *aigreta*, mdfn (*-eta* for *-on*) of OProv
*aigron*, prob from Frankish \**haigiro* (cf OHG
*heigir*), whence also OF-MF *hairon* (F *héron*),
whence ME *heiroun*, *heroun*, *heron*, occ contr to
*hern*; whence both E *heron* and E *hern*. Akin to
OHG *heigir*, var *heigri*, are ON *hegri* and OE
*hrāga*, heron; earlier history, obscure.

**herpes, herpetic.** See REPTILE, para 8.
**Herr.** See HOAR, para 2.
**herring.** See HOAR, para 4.
**hers.** See HE, para 6.
**herse.** See HEARSE, para 1.
**Herzog.** See DUKE, para 1, s.f.
**hesitate; hesitancy, hesitant, hesitation.**

*Hesitancy* derives from L *haesitantia*, a stammering, LL delay, from *haesitant-* (whence E *hesitant*),
the o/s of *haesitans*, presp of *haesitāre*, int formed
from *haes-*, p of *haesus*, pp of *haerēre*, to stick fast,
hence to hesitate. *Haesitāre* has pp *haesitātus*,
whence 'to *hesitate*'; derivative *haesitātiō*, o/s
*haesitātiōn-*, accounts for *hesitation*. L *haerēre* has s
*haer-*, perh akin to Lith *gaisti*, to hesitate, to
temporize. The cpds *adhaerēre*, *cohaerēre*, *in-*
*cohaerēre*, *inhaerēre*, occur in the sep ADHERE
(*adherent, adhesion, adhesive*)—COHERE (*coherent,*
*cohesion*)—INCOHERENT—INHERE (*inherent*).

**Hesper, Hesperian, Hesperides, hesperidium,**
**hesperis, Hesperus.** See WEST, para 4.

**hessian**, coarse sacking, derives from *Hessian* (as
in *Hessian boots*, often *hessians*), adj and n from
*Hesse*, from G *Hessen*, a region of SW Germany:
and *Hessen* derives from LL *Hessi*, var of *Hessii*,
from C2 (A.D.) *Assii*, app id with Tacitus's *Chatti*,
a Gmc tribe. (Enci It.)

**hest.** See BEHEST.
**hesternal.** See YESTER.
**heterodox; heterogeneous; heterosexual.** See the
element *heter(o)-*. For the 1st, see esp DOGMA,
para 3.
**het-up.** See the heading of HEAT.
**heuristic**, serving to reveal (esp to persuade):
from Gr *heuriskein*, to discover, whence also
*eureka* (Gr *heurēka*, I have found): s *heurisk-*, r
*heur-*: IE r, perh \**uer-*: cf OIr *fúar*, I have found.
**hew** (pt *hewed*, pp *hewn*), whence *hewer*. See the
2nd HACK, para 6.

**hexagon, hexameter, hexapod.** See the element
*hex(a)-*.
**heyday.** See HIGH, para 1.
**hiatus.** See YAWN, para 2.
**hibernacle, hibernaculum; hibernal; hibernate,**
**hibernation;—Himalaya** (whence the adj **Hima-**
**layan**);—**chimera, chimerical.**

1. *Hibernacle*, winter quarters, derives from L
*hibernāculum*, a winter residence, pl *hībernācula*,
winter quarters, from *hībernus*, wintry, akin to L
*hiems* (o/s *hiem-*), Gr *kheima, kheimōn* (s *kheim-*),
OSl *zima* (cf Lith *žĕma*), all 'winter', Skt *hima*, m
'winter', neu 'snow', and, in C, the OW *gaem*, Ir
*gaim*, OC \**gaimo-* or \**gaiamo*; cf also Hit *gim-*
*manza*. The IE r is app \**ghai-*, var \**khai-* (*khei-*).

2. In L, the r is *hī-*: cf *hībernus*, wintry, whence
the neu pl as n, *hīberna*, winter quarters, whence
*hībernāre*, to go into winter quarters, with pp
*hībernātus*, whence 'to *hibernate*'; late derivative
*hībernātiō*, o/s *hībernātiōn-*, yields *hibernation*.
*Hibernus* has LL mdfn *hībernālis*, whence the
erudite *hibernal*.

3. Corresp to L *hī-* is Gr *khi-*, as in *khimaros*,
f *khimaira*, the latter a goat that has passed one
*winter* (year) and has its first kids, whence Gr
myth *Khimaira*, a *goat*-bodied monster, whence L
*Chimaera*, whence E *chimaera*, usu written *chimera*,
whence—perh from EF-F *chimérique* (from MF-F
*chimère*, from L *chimaera*)—the adj *chimeric* (*-ic*),
mostly in extn *chimerical*.

4. Skt *hima*, snow (cf para 1), joins with Skt
*ālaya*, residence, to form *Himālaya*, the abode of
the snows.

**Hibernian, Hibernicism.** See the element *Hiberno-*
and, f.a.e., IRISH, para 2.
**hiccup**—often f/e written *hiccough*—is EE
*hickup* or *hickock* or even *hicket*: as clearly echoic
as, say, the MF-F *hoquet*.
**hick.** See RICH (heading).
**hickory** (earliest as *hickery*) is short for C17 AE
*pokhickery* (or *-ory*) or *pokickery* (*-ory*): Virginian
Amerind *powcohickora* or *pawcohiccora*, prop the
'milk' pressed from the pounded kernels.
(Mathews.)
**hid.** See the 3rd HIDE.
**hidalgo.** See FILIAL, para 4.
**hidden.** See 3rd HIDE.
**hide** (1) of land. See CITY, para 2, s.f.
**hide** (2) of a beast, comes, through MF *hide*,
earlier *hude*, from OE *hÿd*, akin to OHG-MHG
*hūt*, G *Haut*, ON *hūth*: Gmc r, prob \**hud-* or
\**huth-*, IE r app \**kut-* (? extn of \**ku-*, to cover or
hide): cf OP *keuto*, hide, L *cutis* (s *cut-*), skin, Gr
*kutos* (s *kut-*), hollow vessel—also L *scūtum* (s
*scūt-*), a shield, and Skt *skáuti, skunāti*, he covers:
therefore cf CUTICLE. Prob cf:
**hide** (3), to conceal, pt *hid*, pp *hidden*: ME *hiden*,
earlier *huden*: OE *hÿdan*, akin to OFris *hūda*, Gr
*keuthein*, to conceal, Skt *kuhara*, prob Serbian
*kuća*, a house, perh E HOUSE.
**hideous:** ME *hidous* (F *hideux*, f *hideuse*),
adopted from OF, var of *hisdos*, the adj of *hide*,
var of *hisde*, a great fright, horror, perh of Gmc

origin (B & W) but perh rather (DAF) from *hispidum*, neu of L *hispidus*, bristling, bristly, shaggy, akin to *hirsūtus*, E *hirsute* (cf HEARSE, para 3).

**hidrosis, hidrotic.** See HYDRA.

**hie,** to strive (obs), to hasten: ME *hien*, earlier *hihen*, earliest *highen*: OE *hīgian*, to strive, to hasten: cf MD *higen*, D *hygen*, to pant, be eager or desirous: perh ult echoic.

**hierarchy.** See the element *hier(o)-*.

**hieratic.** See the element *hieratico-*.

**hieroglyphic; hierophant.** See the element *hiero-*; for the 2nd, see also *-phane*.

**higgle; higgledy-piggledy.** See the 2nd HACK, para 5.

**high** (adj, hence adv and n); many cpds (mostly obvious), e.g.: highboy (AE for E *tallboy*)—high-brow (adj, hence n)—high-flying and -flown—high-handed (hand held authoritatively high)—high hat, a topper, hence adj high-hat, aristocratic, snobbish, supercilious—high-jack (whence hijack), whence high-jacker (hijacker), prob f/e from *hi, Jack!*, a halting call—highlands—high light (high, therefore large and powerful), whence 'to high-light'—high-minded—the high sea, usu pl—highway, whence highwayman; highness; height, whence heighten; heyday.

1. E *high* derives, via ME *high*, earlier *hegh* or *hey* (surviving in *heyday*)—cf '*high* days and holy days', later ' . . . holidays')—earliest *heh*, from OE *hēah*, often contr to *hēh*: cf OFris *hāch* or *hāg* (adv *hāge*), OS *hōh*, OHG-MHG *hōh*, (contr of) *hōch*, G *hoch*, Go *háuhs*, MD *hooch, hoge*, D *hoog*, ON *hār*; cf also ON *haugr*, a mound or a highland, MHG *houc*, a hill, Lith *kaukarà*, hill, and *kaūkas*, a swelling or a boil; cf also Go *háuhei*, OHG *hōhī*, MHG *hoehe*, G *Höhe*, height. (Walshe.)

2. OE *hēah* has derivative *hēahnes*, whence *highness*.

3. Either deriving from or, at the least, akin to OE *hēah, hēh*, is OE *hēahthu, hēhthu*, with var *hīehthu*, whence ME *heighthe*, later *heighte*, whence E *height*: cf Go *haúhitha*, OHG *hōhida*, MD *hoocheit* (D *hoogte*), ON *haeth*.

**hijack, hijacker.** See prec, in heading.

**hike** (v, hence n) is app a dial var of HITCH, the dial use preceding the coll: and dial *hike* means 'to move swingingly', hence, vi, 'to move oneself thus, to swing along'.

**hilarious** (cf hilary), hilarity, exhilarant, exhilarate, exhilaration, exhilaratory.

1. *Hilarious* adds *-ious* to *hilar-*, s of L *hilaris* (or *-rus*), merry, whence *hilaritās*, acc *hilaritātem*, whence MF-F *hilarité*, whence E *hilarity*; the L adj, which has derivative *Hilarius*, whence *Hilary*, is a trln of Gr *hilaros*, via *\*helaros*, from *\*hilēmi* (I am gracious), well attested; the PGr r is prob *hil-*. (Hofmann.)

**hill** (whence the AE rhyming redup hill-billy), whence hilly; holm, islet; sep COLUMN; sep CULMINATE (CULMINATION, etc.); sep COLOPHON; sep CELT, CELTIC; sep EXCEL, EXCELLENCE, EXCELLENT.

*Hill*, ME *hil*, var *hul*, derives from OE *hyll*: cf MD *hille, hil, hul*, Go *hallus*, a rock, OS *holm*, a hill, ON *holmr*, islet (cf the intimately related OE *holm*, hill, hence—'hill (arising from the sea)'— an island, whence E *holm*, islet); also, further off, L *collis* (? for *\*colnis*), a hill, *columen*, height, *culmen*, a summit, *excellere*, to excel, *celsus*, (very) high, Gr *kolōnos*, hill, *kolophōn*, summit, Lith *kélti*, to raise, *kalnas*, a mountain, perh OB *čelo*, forehead. The IE r is prob *\*kel-*, to rise, to reach up. (Feist.)

**hilt:** OE *hilt* (*hilte*): akin to OS *hilta, helta*, OHG *helza*, ON *hjalt*: perh ult akin to the v HOLD.

**hilum, hilus.** See FILAMENT, para 10.

**him.** See HE, para 3.

**Himalaya, Himalayan.** See HIBERNACLE, para 4.

**hind** (1), adj. See HINDER, adj.

**hind** (2), a farm servant: ME *hine*: OE *hīne, hīna*, prop the gen pl of *hīwan*, domestic servants: f.a.e., CITY.

**hind** (3), the female of the red deer (m *stag*): cf OHG *hinta*, MHG-G *hinde*, ON *hind*. 'The *-d* is perh a suffix, the root being *\*him-* (cf Gr *kemas* "young deer", Skt *śámas* "hornless")': Walshe.

**hinder** (1), adj; hind, adj, whence hindmost and hindquarters; hinterland; behind (adv, hence prep and n), whence behindhand.

1. *Behind*, adv, derives from OE *behindan*, an int cpd of *be-*+*hindan*, behind: and *hindan*, whence ult, though indirectly, the E adj *hind*, of the end or rear, as in derivative *hindquarters*, is itself intimately akin to the OE adv *hinder*, behind (OFris *hindera*): cf the OHG *hintar*, MHG *hinter*, *hinder*, G *hinter*, Go *haintr*, *hindar*, all prepp and prob orig a neu comp adj, with the OE *hinder* akin to OE *hine*, hence (? further hence'—further behind): Walshe adduces the IE neu comp element *-terom* and neatly cfs, sem, the Gr *proteros*, former, with neu *proteron* used as adv 'in front'. Cf HINDER (2).

2. The G prep *hinter*, behind, not the G adv *hinten*, behind, occurs in the cpd n *Hinterland*, the land behind (the coast): adopted by E.

**hinder** (2), v, whence hindrance: ME *hinderen*, *hindren*: OE *hindrian*, prob from the OE adv *hinder*, behind, much as G *hindern*, MHG *hindern*, OHG *hintarōn*, to hinder, derives from the OHG prep *hintar* (MHG-G *hinter*). With OE *hindrian*, cf also the syn OFris *hinderia*, MD *hindren*, (as in D) *hinderen*, ON *hindra*.

**Hindi.** See INDIA, para 4.

**hindmost.** See the heading of 1st HINDER.

**hindrance.** See the 2nd HINDER.

**Hindu, Hindustan, Hindustani.** See INDIA, para 4.

**hinge** (n, hence v): ME *heng, heeng*: perh from MD *henge* (D *heng, hengsel*)—vv *hengen, hingen*— cf LG *henge*: akin to E HANG.

**hinny.** See WHINE, para 2.

**hint** (n, hence v) is a thinned derivative of ME *henten*, to catch (cf the obs EE *hent*, a grasping), from OE *hentan*, to catch, to pursue: f.a.e., HUNT.

**hinterland.** See the 1st HINDER, para 2.

**hip** (1) of body (whence 'to *hip*'), whence prob the **hipe** of wrestling. See HIVE, para 3.

**hip** (2), berry: ME *hepe*: OE *hēope*, prob imm from OE *hēopa*, a bramble, a briar: cf OS *hiopo*, OHG *hiufo*, a bramble, and perh OP *kaāubri*, thorns.

**hipe.** See the 1st HIP.

**hipparch; hippodrome.** See the element *hipp(o)-*.

**hippopotamus,** adopted from L, comes from Gr *hippopotamos*, for *hippos potamios*, horse (*hippos*) of the river (*potamos*), the latter Gr word occurring also in *Mesopotamia* (cf the element *meso-*). Gr *hippos* has IE etymon *\*ekwos*: cf L *equus*, with adj *equīnus*, whence E *equine*; cf also OIr *ech*, OE *eoh*, Tok B *yakwe*.

**hire,** n and v; **hireling.**

The latter, although prompted by OE *hȳrling,*= *hire*, n+n-suffix -*ling*. *Hire*, n, ME *hire*, var *hure*, comes from OE *hȳr*, o.o.o.: akin to OFris *hūre*, a lease, MD-MLG *hūre*, G *Heuer*. 'To *hire*', ME *hiren*, earlier *huren*, comes from OE *hȳrian*, app from the n: cf G *heuern*, LG *hüren*, MD *huyren, hueren*, MD-D *huren*.

**hirsute.** See HEARSE, para 3, and cf the element *hirsuto-*.

**Hirtella.** See HEARSE, para 3.

**his.** See HE, para 4.

**Hispania, Hispanic.** See SPAIN, paras 1, 4.

**hiss** (v, hence n): ME *hissen*: echoic—cf the echoic var in G *zischen*, MHG *zispen*, OHG *zispan*.

**hist.** See HUSH, para 2.

**histology.** See the element *histo-*.

**historian, historiated, historic,** etc. See para 2 of:

**history; historian, historiated, historic** (extn **historical**), whence **historicity; historiographer** (see at element *historico-*); **prehistoric, prehistory;**— **story** (n, hence v), with differentiation **storey.**

1. *History* anglicizes L *historia*, adopted from Gr, where it derives (abstract suffix -*ia*) from the adj *histōr*, knowing, hence erudite, itself an agent (-*ōr*) from *eidenai* (for *\*weidenai*), to know, r *eid*-: IE r, *\*weid*-, connoting vision, which subserves knowledge: cf Gr *eidos*, form (IE etymon *\*weides*), akin to Skt *védas*-, knowledge aspect, and E WIT: Gr *histōr*, therefore, is for *\*wistōr*.

2. L-from-Gr *historia* becomes OF-MF *estoire*, whence MF-F *histoire*, whence MF-F *historien*, whence E *historian*; the derivative late MF adj *historique* (LL *historicus*, Gr *historikos*, from *historia*) contributes to E *historic*; L *historia* has derivative LL *historiāre*, to record in *history*, with pp *historiātus*, whence the adj *historiate*, now usu in pp form *historiated*; the rare E *historial*, historical, derives from LL *historiālis* (*historia+-ālis*, E -*al*).

3. E *prehistory* and *prehistorical* owe something to F *préhistoire* and *préhistorique*: F *pré-*, L *prae-*, before.

4. *Story*, (orig) history, a history, hence any narrative, whether true or fictional, derives from ME *storie*, prob aphetic and metathetic for OF-MF *estoire* (as in para 2), but perh direct

from LL-ML *storia*, existing from C5 A.D. onwards and deriving aphetically from L *historia*.

5. *Story* (AE) or *storey* (E), the inhabited or inhabitable floor—or rather the set of rooms and passages thereon—of a building, takes its sense from C12–15 AL *historia* used thus and prob denoting, orig, 'a tier of painted windows or of sculptures on the front of a building' (OED)—a view anticipated by EW and shared by Webster.— Hence, e.g., E 'three-*storeyed*' and AE 'four-*storied*'.

**histrionic.** See the element *histrio-*.

**hit** (v, hence n): ME *hitten* (var *hytten*): OE *hittan*: ON *hitta,* to meet with, to find: perh akin to OE *hentan*, to seize, q.v. at HINT; prob akin to L *caedō*, I strike, cut down.

**hitch,** to move jerkily (hence n), prob derives from syn *hotch*, which likewise occurs, along with *hatch*, in late ME: and *hotch* perh derives from syn OF-F *hocher* (cf F *hocher la tête*, to nod one's head), itself prob through Frankish from the G r of MHG *hotzen*, to shake.

**hither.** See HE, para 5.

**Hittite** is a b/f from H *Ḥittīm* (s *Ḥitt*-), the Hittites, with E suffix -*ite(s)* substituted for the H pl. -*īm*. The H name adapts *Khatti*, as the Hittites called themselves; *Khatti* was used also by their Mesopotamian neighbours. (Enci It.)

**hive** (n, hence v); sep **heap**; **hip** of body —**coop** (n, hence v), **cooper.**—**couvade, covey; cube** (n, hence v), **cubic, cubism**—**cubicle, cubicular**—**cubit; concubine** (whence, unless adopted from MF-F, **concubinage**); **accumbency, accumbent; decumbency, decumbent; incumbency, incumbent** (adj, hence n); **recumbency, recumbent;**—**incubate, incubation, incubator; incubus;**—**succumb, succumbence, succumbent; succubus.**

1. *Hive* comes, through ME *hive*, earlier *hyve* and *huive*, from OE *hȳf*, akin to ON *hūfr*, a ship's hull, Lith *kúopa*, a heap, L *cūpa*, a tub or a cask, Gr *kúpē*, cavity, *kupellon*, a beaker, Skt *kū́pas*, cavity, pit, hollow, and *kūpikā*, a small jug: IE r, prob *\*keu*-, extn *\*keup*-, with basic sense 'a curving or an arching'.

2. L *cūpa* prob becomes ME *cupe* or *coupe*, a basket, whence E *coop*; ME *cupe*, however, could derive from OE *cype*, a cask, itself akin to the L word. *Cooper*, ME *couper* or *cowper* (cf the surnames *Cooper, Couper, Cowper*), app derives from MD *cuper* (var *cuyper*) or MLG *kuper*.

3. Akin to *hive* is the *hip* of the body, ME *hip*, earlier *hippe*, earliest *hupe*, from OE *hype*: cf OHG-MHG *huf*, G *Hüfte*, hip, Go *hups*, hip or loin, ON aptr*huppr*, a horse's flank, Gr *kubos*, the hollow near the hips, L *cubitus*, elbow, and *cubāre*, to be lying down. Here, the basic idea has been modified to something like 'to bend at a joint, to form a hollow or a curve there'.

4. Both L *cubāre*, to be lying down, and its n-infix var -*cumbere* (easement of *\*cunbere*), occurring only in cpds and connoting the accomplishment of the act, have considerably impinged upon E.

5. *Cubāre* has cpds *concubina*, a woman lying
down *con* or with a man, whence, via MF-F, the E
*concubine*, and *incubāre*, to lie upon (*in-*), with pp
*incubātus*, whence 'to *incubate*', to sit upon (eggs)
and hatch (them); derivatives *incubātiō* (o/s *in-
cubātiōn-*) and *incubātor* become E *incubation*,
*incubator*. *Incubāre*, s *incub-*, has LL derivative
*incubus*, a nightmare, 'popularly supposed to be a
demon *lying on* a sleeper' (Souter), hence any person or thing that burdens. Cf *succubus*, which ('a
female demon sleeping with men') is adopted from
ML and which, after *incubus*, derives from L
*succuba*, a whore, itself from *succubāre* (for *sub-
cubāre*), to lie under. Cf *succumb* in para 8, s.f.

6. *Cubāre* becomes OF-MF *cover* (F *couver*),
applied to birds sitting upon eggs, whence the
OF-MF n *covée*, whence ME *cove, covy*, whence E
*covey*. F *couver* has the EF-F derivative *couvade*,
lit a brooding and hatching, esp, among primitive
peoples, a father's going to bed while his wife is
in childbed, adopted by E.

7. *Cubāre* has derivative *cubiculum*, a place to
sleep (bedroom), whence E *cubicle*, with senses
diverging from that of L; derivative adj *cubiculāris*
becomes E *cubicular*.

8. L *-cumbere* (as in para 4) occurs in these cpds
relevant to E:

*accumbere*, to lie beside, to sit down at (*ad*)
table, has presp *accumbens*, o/s *accumbent-*,
whence the E adj *accumbent*, reclining, leaning,
whence *accumbency*;

*dēcumbere*, to set oneself down (*dē*) at table or
in bed, has presp *dēcumbens*, o/s *dēcumbent-*,
whence the E adj *decumbent*, lying down, whence
*decumbency*;

*incumbere*, to lie, or rest, upon (*in-*), hence, in
LL, to be incumbent upon, has presp *incumbens*,
o/s *incumbent-*, whence E *incumbent*, whence *incumbency*;

*recumbere*, to lie back (*re-*), to recline, has presp
*recumbens*, o/s *recumbent-*, whence E *recumbent*,
whence *recumbency*;

*succumbere*, to lie under (*sub*), hence to submit to
discipline, to give way, yield, fall, whence 'to
*succumb*'; presp *succumbens*, o/s *succumbent-*,
becomes E *succumbent*, whence *succumbency*.

9. Associated, f/e, with L *cubāre* is L *cubitus*
(gen *cubiti*), the elbow, with var *cubitum* mostly
reserved for the derivative sense 'a cubit', whence E
*cubit*: cf, sem, the relation of *ell* and *elbow*, qq.v.
at ELL. The L word prob derives from Gr *kubiton*,
elbow, say E & M; but Hofmann and others hold
that Gr *kubiton* derives from L *cubitum*. Certainly,
the elbow being that upon which one leans in
reclining, the association of *cubitus* (gen *-i*) with
*cubāre* might be rather more than merely f/e; the
rare L *cubitus* (gen *cubitūs*), the fact of being recumbent, clearly derivative from *cubāre*, may be
a learnèd differentiation from *cubitus*, (mostly)
elbow, *cubitum*, (mostly) cubit.

10. Akin to L *cubāre* (s *cub-*) is L *cubus*, whence
MF-F, hence E, *cube*; *cubus* is a trln of Gr *kubos*,
a hip-hollow, vertebra, hence a cube, with deriva-

tive adj *kubikos*, whence L *cubicus*, MF-F *cubique*,
E *cubic*. F *cube* has Art derivatives *cubisme* and
*cubiste*, whence E *cubism* and *cubist*.

**hoar** (adj, hence n), whence **hoarfrost** (cf *frost* at
freeze) and extn **hoary** (adj *-y*); **horehound**; **Herr**;
**herring**; perh **hue** (n, hence v, esp in pp **-hued**),
whence **hueless** (*-less*).

1. The adj **hoar**, ME *hor*, earlier *har*, derives from
OE *hār*, grey, old (and grey-haired): akin to OFris
*hēr*, grey, OHG-MHG *hēr*, old, distinguished, G
*hehr*, distinguished, exalted, and ON *hārr*, grey
with age; cf also EIr (and Ga) *cīar*, dark (OC
**kīro-*), and perh OB *sěrŭ*, grey.

2. The OHG *hēr*, old, distinguished, has comp
*hēriro*, contr to *hērro*, older, whence MHG *hērre,
herre, hēr*, whence *Herr* (pl *Herren*), master, lord;
already in OHG used as n: a loan-trans of ML
*senior* (lit 'older') as title of respect—cf F *seigneur*,
sieur, It *signor*, Sp *señor*. (Walshe.) Note the cpd
*Herrenvolk*, master race (lit FOLK).

3. OE *hār*, grey, has cpd *hārhūne, hārehūne*, lit
'grey *hūne* or plant' (the Marrubium Vulgare):
ME *horehune*: E *horehound*, with intrusive *-d*, by
f/e, from *hound*.

4. Perh akin to OE *hār* is the s of OE *hǣring,
hēring* (? the 'greying', sc 'fish'), whence, via ME
*hering*, the E *herring*: cf the OFris *hereng* (or *hering*), OHG *hering* and esp *hāring* (MHG *herinc*, G
*Hering*). Less prob is a relationship with OE *here*,
OHG *heri* (G *Heer*), army, 'owing to the fish's
habit of travelling in shoals' (Walshe).

5. Prob akin to OE *hār*, grey, is OE *hēow, hīew,
hēw*, shape, appearance, colour, ME *heow*, later
*hew*, whence EE *hew*, form, colour, and E *hew*,
colour: akin to Go *hiwi*, form, appearance, ON
*hȳ*, bird's down (predominantly grey), OE *hǣwen*,
bluish-grey, blue, and, more remotely, to OSl *sivŭ*,
grey, and Skt *śyāva*, brown; anterior etym,
dubious.

**hoard**, n and v.

'To *hoard*', OE *hordian*, derives from OE *hord*,
whence the E n *hoard*: and OE *hord* is akin to OS
*hord*, OHG-MHG-G *hort*, Go *huzd*, ON *hodd*:
Gmc r, **huzda-*, IE r **kuzdhó-* (? for **kudhtó-*)—
perh cf Gr *kusthos*, a hollow, and certainly cf
HIDE, to conceal. (Walshe.)

**hoax** (n, hence v). See JOKE, para 5.

**hob** (1), a rustic, hence a sprite (usu *hobgoblin*).
See ROBERT, para 5.

**hob** (2) of fireplace. See HUB.

**hobble** (v, hence n) has the prob derivative
**hobbledehoy**, a clumsy youth, perh from his awkward movements, with *hoy* rhyming on *boy* and
with euphonic *de*: for the formation of the cpd, cf
D *hobbeldebobbel*, joltingly, bumpingly, redup of
D *hobbel*, knob, hump, bump. 'To *hobble*', ME
*hobelen, hoblen*, is akin to—? derived from—MD
*hobelen* or, as in D, *hobbelen*, to hobble, app a
freq of MD **hoben*, D *hobben*, to be tossed, or
swung back and forth, to rock, ult echoic. Either
from MD **hoben* (D *hobben*) or from MD *hobelen,
hobbelen*, comes ME *hoby* (var *hobyn*), orig an
ambling horse, hence, fig, a subject one is con-

stantly riding; the elaboration *hobbyhorse* was at first a morris-dance figure of a horse. Prob akin to this *hobby* is the small medieval falcon called *hobby*: ME *hoby*: MF *hobet* (or *hobé*), dim of MF *hobe*, a falcon, prob from MF *hober*, to stir, from OF-MF *hobeler*, to skirmish, itself from MD *hob(b)elen*, to hobble.

**hobbledehoy.** See prec.

**hobby**, both 'horse' and 'small falcon'; **hobby-horse.** See HOBBLE, latter half.

**hobnob**, to be on familiarly intimate terms, perh derives from the obs drinking toast or catch-phrase, *Hobnob!*, earlier *Hob or nob* (*Hob and nob*), roughly meaning 'Give and take', itself app from the obsol adv *hobnob*, at random, EE *habnab*, prob from ME *habbe*, have+*nabbe*, have not, themselves from OE *haebbe*+*naebbe* (*ne*, not+ *haebbe*).

**hobo** (AE) is, according to Webster and Mathews (and EW and OED), o.o.o.; DAE, Godfrey Irwin and myself support the suggestion that *hobo* represents *ho! bo*, i.e. *ho! beau* (for *hello! beau*), known to have been a tramps' formula of address in the 1880's and 1890's.

**Hobson's choice** (no choice) derives from Cambridge livery-stables owner Thomas Hobson (d. 1631), who insisted that every customer should take the horse standing nearest the door. (Webster —after EW.)

**hock** (1), of a horse. See HEEL, para 2.

**hock** (2) is short for obs *hockamore*, from *Hoch-heimer*, adj become n: 'wine of *Hochheim*' in Germany.

**hockey**, o.o o., perh comes from MF *hoquet*, a bent or curved stick, hence a shepherd's crook, from MF *hoc*, a hook, from syn MD *hoek*: f.a.e., HOOK: cf, sem, the origin of the game of CRICKET.

**hocus; hocus-pocus.** See JOKE, para 5.

**hod** (whence **hodman**), a bricklayer's handle-tray, comes from MD *hodde*, *hode*, akin to ME *hotte*, from MF *hote* (F *hotte*), a dosser, or basket carried on the *dos* or back, from Frankish *\*hotta* (cf G dial *Hotte*, *Hotze*).

**Hodge.** See ROBERT, para 6.

**hodge-podge.** Cf *hotch-potch*, but see POT, para 7.

**hodiernal.** See DIANA, para 12.

**hodman.** See HOD.

**hoe** (n, hence v). See the 2nd HACK, para 7.

**hog** (n, hence v), with obvious cpds, e.g., **-back, -fish, -gum, -wash, -weed,** and **hogshead** (a *hog's head*, prob from shape); **hogget.**

*Hogget*, orig a 2nd-year boar, then also a year-ling sheep, is orig a dim of *hog*, a pig: OE *hogg*: ? of C origin—cf OIr *torc*, wild boar, Ga *torc*, W *turch*, boar, OC *\*torkos*, (wild) boar.

**Hogmanay**, the Sc New Year's Eve, in C17 *hog-mane*, *hogmynae*, is o.o.o.: prob not of British C origin, but perh cf OF *aguilanneuf*, New Year's Day or a new year's gift (OED): ? 'for this new year': OF *a*, F *à*, for | *gui*, L *huic*, dat of *hic*, this+ *an*, year+*neuf*, new.

**hoist**, v hence n: EE *hoise* (extant in dial), earlier *hysse*: MD *hischen*: cf LG *hissen*, whence both G

*hissen* and F *hisser*. Ult origin obscure: ? echoic from accompanying cries or shouts.

**hoity-toity**: ? for dial *\*highty-tighty*, a rhyming redup (on *high*), app suggested by '*high* and *mighty*'.

**hokey-pokey; hokum.** See JOKE, para 5, s.f.

**hold** (1) of ship. See HALL, para 4.

**hold** (2), to guard (obs), grasp firmly and long, retain, pt **held**, pp **holden** (archaic except in int **beholden**); hence **hold**, n, and agent **holder** and vn **holding**; dial var **holt**; **behold**; **halt** (n, hence v).

1. 'To *hold*', ME *holden*, earlier *halden* and *healden*, derives from OE *haldan*, with var *healdan*, to grasp, keep, retain, restrain, hence to hold, occupy, possess: akin to syn OFris *halda*, OS *haldan*, ON *halla* (for *\*halda*), to hold, and Go *haldan*, OHG *haltan*, to keep or pasture cattle, G *halten*, to hold. The basic idea is perh 'to guide (as in tending cattle), to rule', with derivative 'to hold up, to check', as Walshe has suggested.

2. MHG-G *halten*, to hold, has derivative n *Halt*, a stop, whence late EF-F *halte*, whence E *halt*.

3. OE *healdan* has int *behealdan*, to hold firmly, esp in one's sight: ME *bihalden*, later *biholden*: E 'to *behold*', esp to gaze at; the primary meaning survives in the pa *beholden*.

4. Perh akin to the Gmc vv are Gr *kellein* (s *kell-*, r *kel-*), to drive (esp cattle), and its cognate *boukolos*, cow-herd, herdsman: therefore cf CELE-BRATE (and *celerity*).

**hole.** See HALL, para 5.

**holiday; holiness.** See HOLY, para 2.

**holism** (whence the adj **holistic**). See the element *hol(o)-*, s.f.

**Holland; holland, hollands.**

*Holland*, adopted from D, derives from MD *Holtlant*: *holt*, a wood+*lant*, land: applied orig to the Dordrecht region, 'the nucleus of Holland' (SOED).—The fabric *holland* is elliptical for EE *Holland cloth*; *hollands*, Dutch gin, derives from the D adj *hollandsch* (cf adj *Scots* and liquor *Scotch*).

**hollo!** See HALLOO, s.f.

**hollow** (whence **hollowness**). See HALL, para 6.

**holly; holm** (oak).

1. *Holly* comes, through ME *holi*, earlier *holin*, from OE *holen*, or *holegn*, r *hol-*: cf OS-OHG *huls* or *hulis* (r *hul-*), MHG *huls*, MD *huls* or *hulse*, D and G *hulst*, ON *hulfr* (r *hul-*); cf also Ir *cuileann* (Ga *cuillean*), W *celyn*, Cor *celin*, Br *kelen*, and the 'midway' Mx forms *hullin*, *hollyn*. The IE r is app *kel-*, to prick.

2. OE *holen*, holly, has ME deviation *holm*, holly (now dial), holm oak.

**hollyhock.** See HOLY, para 2, s.f.

**holm** (1), islet. See HILL.

**holm** (2), holm oak. See HOLLY, para 2.

**holocaust.** See CAUSTIC, para 2, and cf the element *holo-*.

**holograph.** See element *holo-*.

**holster; housings** (trappings).

1. *Holster*, adopted from D, comes from MD

*holfter*: cf G *Holfter*, holster, from MHG *hulfter*, agential from OHG *huluft*, shell, case, sheath: IE r, *\*kel-*, to cover.

2. With MHG *hulfter*, cf MLG *hulfte*, case, sheath, and its cognate—? rather derivative—the ML *hultia*, whence OF-MF *houce* (F *housse*), late ME-EE *house*, whence E *housing*, (an ornamented) saddlecloth (obsol), whence *housings*, trappings.

**holt** (1), a wood, comes unchanged from OE: cf OHG-MHG *holz*, a wood, a forest, timber, G *Holz*, wood, timber, MD *holt*, D *hout*, OFris-OS *holt*, wood, timber, ON *holt*, a wood, with cognates in C, Sl, Gr: Gmc r, *\*hult-*; IE r, *\*keld-*, var *\*kold-*. (Walshe.) Cf HOLLAND.

**holt** (2). See the 2nd HOLD (heading).

**holy, holiness; holiday; hollyhock; halibut;** by my **halidom!; hallow, Halloween.**

1. *Holy*, ME *holi*, earlier *hali*, derives from OE *hālig*, akin to OFris *hēlich*, OS *hēlag*, OHG *heilag*, MHG *heilec*, G *heilig*, MD *heilich, helich*, D *heilig*, Go *hailags*, ON *heilagr*—cf ON *heill*, a good omen, and OIr *cél*, omen, and prob OE *hāl*, whole, healthy (E *hale*, q.v. at WHOLE).

2. OE *hālig*, holy, has derivative *hālignes*, whence *holiness*; E *holy+day=holy day*, whence *holiday*; OE *hālig* has further derivative *hāligdōm*, whence *halidom*, holiness, esp in the 'Wardour Street English' *by my halidom!* The ME *hali*, holy, occurs in *halibut*, i.e. *hali+but*, var *butte*, a flounder—cf D *heilbot*; the ME var *holi* occurs in ME *holihoc* (whence *hollyhock*), i.e. *holi+hoc* (OE-ME), a mallow.

3. OE *hālig*, holy, possesses yet another derivative: *hālgian*, to make holy, to sanctify, ME *halgien*, later *halwen*, latest *halowen*, whence 'to *hallow*', with pa *hallowed*. The n *hallow*, a saint or a shrine, survives only in *Allhallows*, All the Saints (in heaven), hence All Saints' Day, and in *Halloween*, the *e'en* or evening preceding All Saints' Day.

**homage.** See HOMO, para 6.

**hombre.** See HOMO, para 13.

**home** (n, hence adj, adv, v), whence **homeless, homely** (whence **homeliness**), **homer** (agential *-er*), and such obvious cpds as **home-made, -sick, -spun, -stead** (cf OE *hāmstede*), **-ward** (cf OE *hānweard*), **-work;—ham,** in PlNn; **hamlet;—haunt** (v, hence n).

1. *Home*, ME *hom*, earlier *ham*, derives from OE *hām*, home, house with land, estate, akin to OFris *hām, hēm*, OS *hēm*, MD *heem, heim*, OHG-G *heim*, home, Go *haims*, village, ON *heimr*, world, village, *heima*, home; also to OP *seimins*, a farm, Lith *šeimà*, a family, ? orig a homestead, and Gr *kōmē*, a village, and perh Gr *keitai*, he is recumbent, Skt *kayati*, he is lying down; IE r, *\*kei-*.

2. OE *hām* acquires in PlNn the sense 'group of dwellings', as in *Nottingham, West Ham*, etc. But *hamlet* derives from ME *hamelet*, adopted from MF *hamelet*, dim of MF *hameau*, hamlet, itself from OF *ham*, of Gmc origin (as above).

3. OE *hām*, an abode or dwelling, has derivative *hāmetan*, to house, which has cognate ON *heimta*,

to bring (cattle) home (from pasture), whence OF *hanter*, to dwell in, hence to frequent: whence ME *hauten*, E 'to *haunt*'.

**homeopathy** (cf the F *homéopathie*). See the element *home(o)-*.

**homer.** See HOME (heading).

**Homer, Homeric.**

*Homer*, L *Homērus*, Gr *Homēros*, prob neither Cumaean for 'blind' nor a var of the Cretan PN *Homaros*, as two 'schools' have proposed, but simply a particularization of Ionic and Attic Gr *homēros* (ὅμηρος), a hostage, as the Enci It maintains. The derivative adj is *Homērikos*, L *Homēricus*, F *homérique*, E *Homeric*, esp in 'Homeric laughter', irrepressible laughter, suggested by and, prop, ref to the Olympian gods' *asbestos gelōs*, inextinguishable laughter, in *The Iliad*, I, 599: cf F *rire homérique* and G *homerisches Gelachter*.

**homicidal, homicide.** See HOMO, para 7.

**homiletic, homily.**

The adj derives, perh via LL *homilēticus*, from Gr *homilētikos*, from *homilein*, to be in the company of, akin to or derived from *homilos*, an assembly (itself from *homos*, identical: f.a.e., SAME), whence Gr *homilia*, assembly, LGr a sermon, adopted by LL, whence OF *omelie* (F *homélie*), adopted by ME, whence, after LL, the E *homily*.

**hominoid.** See HOMO, para 8.

**hominy,** made from dry maize by removing the husk and then breaking the kernels into particles coarser than in corn meal, is aphetic for the obs but syn *rockahominy*, of Alg origin: cf Virginian *rokahamĕn*, meal derived from parched corn: a cpd of *rok*, meal (grain coarsely ground)+*aham*, pounded +*mĕn*, grain. (Webster; DAE.)

**homme de lettres.** See para 13 of:

**homo** (h. sapiens); **hombre** and the card-game **ombre**, AE **omber; homme** (d'esprit); **hominoid; homuncle, homunculus;—homage; homicide,** whence **homicidal; human, humane, humanism, humanist** (whence **humanistic**), **humanity** (whence 'the **humanities**' and **humanitarian**—cf the F *humanitaire* and the suffix *-arian*), **humanize** (whence **humanization**); **inhuman, inhumane, inhumanity—superhuman.—humus, humate, humation**—cf **exhumate, exhumation, exhume,** and **inhumate, inhumation, inhume; humiliate, humiliation, humility; humble,** adj hence v.—**camomile, chameleon; chthonian—autochthon, autochthonous; germander.—bridegroom.**

1. *Homo sapiens*, man the sapient (cf SAPID), glorifies mere *homo*, generic 'man': L *homō*, s and r *hom-*, pl *homines*, o/s *homin-*, c/f *homini-* (see Elements), OL *hemō* (whence *nemō*, nobody: contr of *ne*, not+*hemō*): 'the *earthy* one, the *earth*-born', from L *humus*, earth (soil, ground), loc *humi*, on the ground.

*Indo-European*

2. L *humus* has r *hum-*: cf Gr *khthōn* (χθών), with loc *khamai* (χαμαί), on the ground; Ve *kṣás* (loc *kṣámi*), Hit *tekan* (cf *takan*, to the ground),

Tokh A *tkaṃ*, Tokh B *kan*; cf also Lith *žeṁe* and OSl *zemlja*; perh OIr *dū* (gen *don*), earth. C affords for 'man' such cognates as Br *dēn*, Cor *dēn* and *dhēn*, W *dȳn*, Ga and OIr *duine*, OC *dunjós*.— A perh merely accidental 'likeness' to the Gr, L, Tokh words occurs in Eg *khui*, earth, ground; cf Eg *Kami*, Egypt (? '*The* Land'); the word is prob of Medit stock, for Semitic also affords a suspiciously close parallel. The IE r is app *khem-* with varr *kham-*, *khom-*, *khum*, with *n* occ for *m*: and this IE r for 'earth' is perh a nasal extn of Medit *khe-*, varr *kha-*, *kho-*, *khu-*.

3. Gr *khthōn*, earth, affects E, both by its derivative adj *khthonios*, of or in or under the earth, the s *khthoni-* yielding E *chthonian*, and by its cpd *autokhthōn*, of or from the earth, or the land, itself (*autos*, self: cf the element *auto-*), whence L *autochthon*, an aborigine, a native, adopted by E, with derivative adj *autochthonous*, indigenous.

4. Gr *khamai*, on the ground, occurs notably in three E words: *camomile, chameleon, germander*, resp from Gr *khamaimelōn*, 'earth apple' (from the scent of the bloom), whence L *chamomilla* (imm from the Gr pl *-mela*), LL *camomilla*, MF-F *camomille*, E *camomile*; Gr *khamaileōn*, 'lion on the ground—dwarf lion', L *chamaeleon*, E *chameleon*, with derivative adj *chameleonic*; Gr *khamaidrus* (*drus*: f.a.e., TREE), LGr *khamandrua*, ML *gamandra*, further corrupted to *germandra*, OF *gemandree*, MF *germandree*, E *germander*, a wall plant.

### Latin

5. L *homō* has dim *homunculus*, adopted by E and then anglicized to *homuncle*.

6. *Homō* has ML senses 'servant, vassal', with derivative *homināticum* (o/s *homin-*+suffix *-āticum*: cf *viaticum*), whence OF-MF *homage* (F *hommage*), adopted by E: ML 'acknowledgement of oneself as another's vassal' develops the sense now current.

7. *Homō* has cpds *homicīda*, man-slayer, and its derivative *homicīdium*, a man-slaying: both become OF-F, hence E, *homicide*.

8. *Homō* itself has no direct adj, not even the expected *hominālis* (cf *nōminālis* from *nōmen*), for *hominoid* is an E formation (L o/s *homin-*+adj *-oid*); but in its stead, with the senses of *homō*, out of *humus* whence it arises, the adj *hūmānus* (s *hūm-*+adj suffix *-ānus*). *Hūmānus* becomes OF-F *humain*, whence E *human*; the secondary *humane* descends straight from *hūmānus*. *Hūmānus* (s *hūmān-*) has the *-itās* (F *-ité*, E *-ity*) derivative *hūmānitās*, o/s *hūmānitāt-*, whence, via OF-F *humanité*, the E *humanity*. *Humanité* leads to EF-F *humaniste*, which leads to *humanisme* (cf G *Humanismus*): these two become E *humanist, humanism*. *Humanize* owes something to EF-F *humaniser*. The sense-evolutions of E *human-humane* have, in the main, followed the sense-evolution of L-LL-ML *hūmānus*.

9. *Hūmānus* has neg *inhūmānus*, MF-F *inhumain*, E *inhuman*, whence (after *humane*) the complementary *inhumane*; derivative *inhūmānitās*, o/s *in-*

*hūmānitāt-*, becomes MF-F *inhumanité*, E *inhumanity*. But *superhuman* (cf EF-F *surhumain*) and *suprahuman* are E anl cpds: cf the prefixes *super-* and *supra-*.

10. L *humus*, earth, soil, is adopted by F and by E, both of which use it in a special sense.

11. L *humus* has several L derivatives relevant to E: e.g., *humāre* (s *hum-*), to bury (the dead), with pp *humātus*, whence the now archaic E adj *humate*; derivative *humātiō*, o/s *humātiōn-*, yields the rare *humation*. *Humāre* has the cpds (1) ML *exhumāre*, whence, via EF-F *exhumer*, the E *exhume*, with obsol var *exhumate* from the L pp *exhumātus*, the derivative *exhumātiō*, o/s *exhumātiōn-*, yielding EF-F and E *exhumation*, and (2) *inhumāre*, to bury (*in-* being int), whence—cf the MF-F *inhumer*—'to *inhume*', the obsol var *inhumate* deriving from the L *inhumātus*, s *inhumat-*, whence the n *inhumātiō*, o/s *inhumātiōn-*, whence late MF-F and E *inhumation*.

12. A more important derivative of L *humus* is the adj *humilis* (*hum-*+*-ilis*), on the ground or of the earth, hence physically, thence morally, lowly; whence OF-F *humble*, OF-MF *umble*, both adopted by ME, the former prevailing into E. Derivative *humilitās*, o/s *humilitāt-*, becomes OF-MF *humelité*, OF-F *humilité*, the latter becoming ME *humilite*, whence E *humility*. *Humilis* has the LL derivative v *humiliāre*, with pp *humiliātus*, whence 'to *humiliate*'; derivative LL *humiliātiō*, o/s *humiliātiōn-*, becomes MF *humiliation*, adopted by E.

### Romance

13. F intervention has been noted in paras 6-9, 11-12. The L *homō* becomes OF *huem*, whence F *homme*, as in *homme de lettres*, anglicized as 'man of letters'. *Homō* also becomes Sp *hombre*, current also in SW U.S.A. as a coll; Sp *hombre*, adopted by F, takes, in its card-game sense, the more Gallic form *ombre*, itself adopted by E.

### Germanic

14. L *homō* is akin to OHG and OS *gomo*, Go *guma*, ON *gumi*, OFris and OE *guma*; the last occurs in OE *brydguma* (cf OHG *brutigomo*, G *Bräutigam*, OFris *bredgoma*, OS *brudigomo*), ME *brudgume*, later *bridegome*, whence, under the influence of GROOM, the EE-E *bridegroom*.

**homogeneity, homogeneous; homologous; homonym.** See, for the 1st, GENERAL, para 26, and cf the element *homo-*, where also the 2nd and the 3rd.

**homophone, homophonous.** The latter derives from Gr *homophonos*, same-sounding, whence also F *homophone*, whence E *homophone*, with its own tech adj *homophonic*.

**homuncle, homunculus.** See HOMO, para 5.

**hone** (n, hence v): OE *hān*, a stone: cf ON *hein*, whetstone, Gr *kōnos*, a cone, Skt *śāṇa*, whetstone (cf Av *saēni-*, top, summit). Cf CONE.

**honest, honesty.**
The latter derives, via ME *honeste, oneste*, honour, from OF *honesté, onesté*, from L *honestāt-*,

o/s of *honestās*, respectability, honour, itself from *honestus*, respectable, honourable, honoured, a derivative of *honōs* (later *honor*): see HONOR. *Honestus* becomes OF *honeste*, *oneste* (cf F *honnête*), whence ME *honeste* (*onest*), later *honest*, extant in E. Derivative MF *deshoneste* and *deshonesté* yield *dishonest*, *dishonesty*.

**honest John.** See JOHN, s.f.

**honey**: ME *honi*, earlier *huni*: OE *hunig*, *huneg*, akin to OFris *hunig*, OS *hunig*, *honeg*, OHG *honang*, *honag*, G *Honig*, ON *hunang*, and, further off, Gr *knēkos*, saffron, saffron-hued (Doric *knākos*), yellow, and Gaul *canecon*, Skt *káñakam*, gold, and perh OP *cucan*, brown. The Gmc 'honey', therefore, is prob elliptical for 'the *yellow* substance'. (Boisacq.)

OE has cpd *hunigcamb*, whence *honeycomb*, and cpd *hunigsūce* (*-sūge*), privet, from which the bee can suck honey, whence—cf SUCK, para 2—*honeysuckle*. *Honeymoon* jocularly refers to the fact that no sooner is the moon at the full than it begins to wane.

**honk**, n hence v, is echoic.

**honor** (AE), **honour**, n and v; **hono(u)rable**, **honorarium**, **honorary**, **honorific** (adj, hence n); **dishono(u)r**, n and v, and **dishono(u)rable**; sep **honest**, **honesty**.

1. The nn *honor* and *honour*, both already in ME, represent varr of the OF derivative from L *honor*, a b/f from *honor-*, o/s of *honōs*, an honour awarded to someone, an office of honour, hence a quality worthy of honour: s and r *hon-*, o.o.o.: perh from the IE r *hen-*, to swell.

2. L *honor* has the foll derivatives relevant to E:

*honorāre*, to show honour to, becomes OF-F *honorer*, whence ME *honoren*, *honouren*, whence 'to honour';

*honorābilis* (from *honorāre*), whence OF-F *honorable*, adopted by E, with var *honourable* prompted by *honour*;

*honorārius*, done as an, or bestowing, honour, (later) honorific, whence—perh via late MF-F *honoraire*—the E *honorary*; the neu *honorārium*, with *donum* (gift) understood, is adopted by E;

*honorificus*, honour-making (*-ficus*, from *facere*, to make), becomes—perh via late MF-F *honorifique*—the E *honorific*.

3. L *honorāre* has LL cpd *dēhonorāre* (*dē-*, away from), to dishonour, which prompted ML *dishonorāre*—whence OF-MF *deshonorer* (F *dés-*), whence ME *deshonouren*, whence 'to *dishonour*'; the n *dishonour* comes from OF-MF *deshonor*, from OF-MF *honor* (*honour*); *dishono(u)rable* represents MF-EF *deshonorable*.

**hooch** is short for obsol *hoochinoo*, from *Hoochinoo*, the Tlingit tribe better written *Hutsnuwu*, lit 'Grizzly Bear Fort': orig applied to illicit strong drinks made by these Indians, hence by all Indians, hence to any liquor, esp spirits, made clandestinely. (Mathews.)

**hood** (n, hence v), whence the game of obs **hoodman-blind** (blindman's buff) and also **hood-**

**wink**, lit to blind by covering someone's eyes (cf WINK).

A *hood*, ME *hood*, earlier *hod*, derives from OE *hōd*: cf OFris *hōde*, OHG-MHG *huot*, helmet, hat, G *Hut*, hat, MD *huet*, *hoet*, *hoot*, D *hoed*; cf the slightly remoter OE *haett* (E *hat*), L *cassis*, helmet, Skt *chattra*, parasol.

**hoodlum**, orig and still mainly AE: Bavarian dial *hodalum*, var of *huddellump*, lit a ragged beggar or rogue, ragamuffin, hence a scoundrel; both elements of the G cpd mean 'rag(s)'.

**hoodoo.** See VOODOO.

**hooey.** See BALLY, s.f.

**hoof**, pl **hooves** (now usu **hoofs**), whence 'to **hoof** it', whence dial and sl **hoofer**.

*Hoof*, OE *hōf*, is akin to OFris and OS *hōf*, OHG-MHG *huof*, G *Huf*, MD *hoof*, MD-D *hoef*, ON *hōfr*, Skt *śaphás*, Av *safa-*: Gmc r, *hōf-*; IE r, *\*kōph-*, var *\*kāph-*, both also with short vowel.

**hook** (n, hence v), whence pa **hooked** and agential-instrumental **hooker** and adj **hooky** and such cpds as **hook-up** and **hookworm**; sep **hockey**; **hawker**, peddler (whence, by b/f, 'to **hawk**' or sell itinerantly), and **huckster**; **hake**.

1. *Hook*, ME *hok*, comes from ME *hōc*, akin to OHG *hāgo*, *hāko*, G *Haken*, MD *hake*, *hoec*, D *haak*, ON *hake*, *haki*; Gmc r, app *\*hek-* or *\*hōk-*, that which serves to hook on to, to catch.

2. *Hawker* comes from LG *Höker*, itself from MLG *hōke* (MHG *hucke*), a dealer or trader: cf the syn D *heuker*. The form *hawker* owes much to *hawker*, a falconer, (later) a peddler of hawks.

3. D *heuker* derives from MD *hoeker*, which has f *hoekster*, with var *hokester*, whence ME *hokester*, later *hukster*, whence E *huckster*, petty retailer, peddler, hence a pettily mercenary fellow.

4. In E dial, *hook* has a var *hake*, whence, from its peculiar fin-development, the fish *hake*: cf Nor *hake*fish, the 'hook fish' or hake, and, both sem and phon, the OHG *hahbit*, *hechit*, G *Hecht* and OE *hacod*.

**hooligan** arose, in the 1890's, from association with a rumbustious family named *Houlihan* in Southwark, London. (P.)

**hoop**, n hence v; geog **hope**.

1. *Hoop*, ME *hoope*, earlier *hope* or *hop*, derives from OE *hōp*, akin to OFris *hōp*, a hoop, MD *hoop*, *houp*, *hoep*, archaic D *hoep*, D *hoepel*; to Lith *kabē*, a hook; to Gr *kuphos* (s *kuph-*, r prob *kup-*).

2. Also akin to all those words are ON *hōp*, a small bay, and *hōpr*, a bay, and, in cpds, the OE *hop*, whence the archaic when not dial E *hope*, a small bay, an inlet, a sloping plain, a fen or a marsh.

**hoopla.** See WHOOP, s.f.

**hoopoe.** See DUPE, para 2.

**hooray.** See HUZZA.

**hoosegow.** See JUS.

**hoot**, v hence n, is echoic: cf ME *hoten*, *huten*, the Sc *hoot!* or *hoots!*, Sw and Nor *huta*, G *Hupe*, hooter (mechanical), and the Da var *tude*, a hoot.

**hop** (1), plant: ME *hoppe*: MD *hoppe* (D *hop*):

cf OHG-MHG *hopfe*, G *Hopfen*, and perh G *hlufo*, a briar.

**hop** (2), to move by short, usu successive, leaps, hence such a leap, comes, through ME *hoppen*, to hop, to dance (cf the coll *hop*, a public dance or ball), from OE *hoppian*: cf MHG *hupfen*, G *hüpfen*, and its int *hopsen*, likewise 'to hop'; cf also MD *huffen*, with var (? orig freq) *hubbelen*, D *huppelen*, and ON *hoppa*; perh also Gr *kubistan*, to dance, to tumble, and Skt *kubhanyús* (adj), dancing, both with ult r *kub-*; IE r, *\*kub-*, var *\*kup-*.

2. Hence *hop-o'-my-thumb*, a midget: perh imm from 'Hop on my thumb!'; hence also the agent *hopper*, as, e.g., in *grasshopper*. But *hopper*, a hop-picker, obviously derives from the 1st HOP.

**hope** (1), geog feature. See HOOP, para 2.

**hope** (2), in *forlorn hope*. See FORLORN HOPE.

**hope** (3), n and v, of expectant desire; whence **hopeful** and **hopeless**.

'To *hope*' derives from OE *hopian*, itself intimately akin to the late OE n *hopa*, aphetic for earlier *tōhopa*: cf the vv MLG *hopen*, rare MHG *hoffen*, G *hoffen*, MD *hopen*, and the nn OLG *tōhopa*, MLG *hope*, MD *hope* and, as in D, *hoop*, and, prob from OLG, the late ON *hop*, and G *Hoffe*. Jespersen connects G *hoffen*—hence E 'to hope' and the E n—with G *hüpfen*, hence with E 'to hop'; if rightly, the basic idea would be 'a leaping, or to leap, with expectation'. (Walshe.)

**hopper.** See the 2nd HOP, para 2.

**hopscotch** derives from 'to HOP a SCOTCH or line'.

**hora, horal, horary** (adj, hence n); **horoscope**—cf the 1st element *horo-*, q.v. for *horologe*; **hour**, whence **hourglass** and **hourly**;—**yore**; **year** (whence **yearling**—cf the n suffix *-ling*), **yearly**.

1. Eccl *hora*, a book of hours, is L *hōra*, an hour, with adjj *hōrālis*, whence *horal*, and *hōrārius*, whence *horary*.

2. L *hōra* derives from Gr *hōra* (ὥρα), a season, hence a period of the day, an hour, whence *Hōrai*, the three goddesses presiding over the seasons of the year, whence also the cpd *hōroskopos*, lit 'hour-surveyor' (cf SCOPE and the element *-scope*), that part of a zodiacal sign which comes above the horizon at a given moment, hence a diagram that, showing the twelve signs in position, enables astrologers to predict a person's life, a sense occurring already in Gr, whence the L *hōroscopus* (cf the LL *hōroscopīum*, an instrument for casting nativities), whence EF-F, hence E, *horoscope*, the adj *horoscopic* going back, through LL *hōroscopicus*, to Gr *hōroskopikos*.

3. L *hōra* becomes OF *hore*, varr *ore*, *ure*, whence ME *hore* (varr *ure*, *our*), later *hour*, E *hour*.

4. With Gr *hōra*, a season of the year, cf OE *gēar*, whence, through ME *yeer*, *yer*, the E *year*; the derivative OE adj *gēarlīc*, 'year-like', becomes E *yearly*, and the derivative OE adv *gēara*, formerly, becomes ME *yare*, whence EE *yore*, extant only in *of yore*, lit 'from formerly', hence ' long ago'.

5. OE *gēar*, a year, is akin to OFris *jēr* (*iēr*), OS *jār*, OHG-MHG *jār*, G *Jahr*, Go *jēr*, MD *jaer*, jair, D *jaar*, and ON *ār* (for *\*jār*): cf also OSl *jara*, Pol *jar*, Cz *jaro*, Spring, and Av *yāre*, Skt *-yār-* in cpds, Gr *hōros*, a year, pl *hōroi*, annals, which brings us back to Gr *hōra*, a season of the year (esp Spring), part of a day, esp an hour, L *hōra*, F *heure* (OF *hore*, *ure*, *eure*, etc.), E *hour*, as in paras 1–3, esp 2. The Gmc r is app *\*jāer-*; the IE, app *\*jēr-*, with varr *\*jār-* and (as in Gr) *\*jōr-*. The semantic 'contradiction' between 'year' and 'hour' arises by oscillation between the orig 'season of the year' and the derivative 'season of the day'; 'season of the year' increases to 'full year', and 'season of the day' decreases to 'hour'. Walshe aptly cfs Serbian *god* or *godina*, a year, with Cz *hodina*, Pol *godzina*, an hour. The derivation of IE *\*jēr*, a season of the year, a year, from IE *\*je-* or *\*ie-*, perh rather or also *\*ei-*, to go, as in L *eō*, I go, *īre*, to go, Gr *eimi*, I go, is conjectural, as Boisacq remarks; this derivation presupposes, perh correctly, that a season, a year, an hour, represent divisions of time—of that which goes by or passes.

**horde; ordu**—Urdu.

*Horde*, adopted from EF-F from G, comes from Pol *horda*, itself from Tu *ordu*, camp, army, used in E for a Tu military district or army corps. Besides moving west into *horde*, the Tu *ordu* moves east into Per *urdu*, thence into Hind *urdū*, prop the language of camps, hence the Per Moslemized form of Hind, hence any Hind, esp that spoken by Europeans: *Urdu*.

**horehound.** See HOAR, para 3.

**horizon, horizontal**; cf the element *horismo-*; **aorist**.

1. Whereas ME *orisonte*, MF *orizonte*, derives from *horizont-*, o/s of L *horizon*, E *horizon* is reshaped by adoption of L *horizon* (gen *horizontis*), trln of Gr *horizōn* (gen *horizontos*), elliptical for 'ho *horizōn* kuklos', the *bounding*, i.e. limiting, circle, from *horizein*, to bound or limit, from *horos*, a boundary, perh for *\*worwos*, with IE r *ueru-*, to draw. (Hofmann.) Learnedly from EF-F *horizon* comes the EF-F adj *horizontal*, adopted by E.

2. Gr *horizein* has pp *horistos*, used as adj 'definable', with neg *aoristos*, not (*a-*, privative) definable, hence indefinite, esp in relation to other past tenses: whence the E *aorist*, adj, hence n; *aoristic*, adj, recalls Gr *aoristikos*.

**horme, hormic, hormone.** See SERUM, para 2.

**horn**, animal's; hence anything horn-shaped, esp the musical instrument; hence 'to **horn**' and such obvious cpds as *hornbeam* (cf BEAM), *-bill*, (BILL, beak), *-blende* (adopted from G; cf BLENDE), *-book* (BOOK), *-pipe* (PIPE), *-tail* (TAIL), *-work* (WORK), and the adj *horny* (*-y*).—**corn** on foot; **cornea, corneous; corner** (n, hence v), whence **cornerstone** (cf STONE); **cornet; cornicle; cornu cornute; cornucopia** and **unicorn**, and sep CAPRICORN, q.v. at CAPER.—**hart; hartebeest.**—Cf the sep CEREBRAL (and its group).

1. An animal's *horn*, straight from OE, is akin to OFris, OS, OHG-G *horn*, Go *haúrn*, ON *horn* and, in a rune, *horna*, the Gmc r being *\*hurn-*

and the IE r being *ker-*, with varr *kar-* and *kor-*: cf EIr and Ga *còrn*, a drinking-horn (OC *korno*), and W *corn* (pl *cyrn*), Cor *corn* or *korn* (pl *kern*) Br *korn*, Mx *cayrn*, the animal's horn, W *karn*, a hoof, and Galatian (a C language) *karnon*, a trumpet, s *karn-*; cf also Gr *krangōn*, a crab, s *krang-*, a nasalized form of *kran-*, itself app a metathesis of *\*karn-*, and Skt *śṛṅga*, a horn, r *śṛṅ-*; cf the var in Gr *keras*, a horn, r *ker-*, as in sep CEREBRAL. (Walshe.)

2. L *cornū*, animal's horn, hence the substance of which horns are composed, hence a corn on the foot, becomes OF and hence, in the last sense, E *corn*. L *cornū*, adopted by An, has adj *corneus*, whence E *corneous*, horny, and the An and Zoo *cornea*, adopted from Med ML *cornea*, either as if from L *cornea* (pars), horny part, sc 'of the eye', or (B & W) more prob elliptical for *cornea tunica* —cf L *tunica oculorum*, lit 'the eyes' tunic'.

3. L *cornū* has ML derivative *corneria*, a place (or a point) where two converging lines or sides meet: whence OF *corniere*, whence ME-E *corner*.

4. L *cornū* has dim *corniculum*, whence E *cornicle*; and OF *corn*, horn, has the MF-F dim *cornet*, the musical horn, adopted by E, and the further dim MF-EF *cornette*, a cavalry standard, hence a cavalry officer bearing the standard, whence E *cornet* (obs); the C18 head-dress E *cornet* also derives from F *cornette*.

5. L *cornū* has derivative adj (pp-style) *cornūtus*, horned, whence E *cornute*, and the cpds *capricornus*, whence *Capricorn*, q.v. at CAPER; *cornū copiae*, LL *cornūcopia*, horn of plenty (cf COPY), adopted by E and other modern languages; *ūnicornis*, a trans of Gr *monokerōs*, one-horned (sc 'animal'), whence MF-EF, hence ME, *unicorne*, E *unicorn*—for the 1st element, cf the element *uni-* and see ONE.

6. Akin to Gr *keras* (s *ker-*), a horn, and *keraos*, horned, are L *ceruus* (s *ceru-*, r *cer-*), a stag, and Lith *karve* (s *karv-*, r *kar-*), a cow, and esp the Gmc group represented by OFris *hert*, OHG *hiruz*, MHG *hirz*, G *Hirsch*, Old D *hirot*, MD *heert*, *herte*, *hart*, *hert*, D *hert*, ON *hiörtr*, OE *heorot*, *heort*, ME *heort*, later *hert*, latest *hart*, E *hart*, a stag, esp the male of the red deer. ED *hart* combines with D *beest* (cf BEAST) to become Afr *hartebeest*, a large SAfr antelope.

7. Prob cf:

**hornet** shows the influence of HORN upon the orig OE *hyrnet*, akin to OHG *hornaz*, OHG-MHG *hornūz*, G *Horniss*, MD *huersel*, *hursel*, *horsel*, D *horzel*; cf also Lett *sirsis*, Lith *širšone* and, for 'wasp', *širšuo*, and L *crābrō* (for *\*crāsrō*), hornet, and prob Gr *keras*, a horn. Walshe thinks it a cpd, with 1st element deriving from Gmc r *\*hurz-*.

**horny.** See HORN (heading).

**horologe.** See the 1st element *horo-*.

**horoscope.** See HORA, para 2.

**horrendous, horrent.** See HEARSE, para 6.

**horrible.** See HEARSE, para 6.

**horrid.** See HEARSE, para 6.

**horrify.** See HEARSE, para 8.

**horripilant, horripilation.** See HEARSE, para 8.

**horrisonant.** See HEARSE, para 8.

**horror.** See HEARSE, para 6, s.f.

**hors d'oeuvre.** See OPERA, para 6.

**horse** (n and v), whence the adj **horsey** or **horsy** and such obvious cpds as **horseback, -block, -bush**, chestnut (? formerly held either nutritious or medicinal for horses), **-fish, -flesh, -fly, Guards, -hair, latitudes** (naut humour), **-leech, -man, marine** (Service humour), **-power, -radish** (tall and coarse), **-shoe, -tail, -weed, -woman; walrus;** sep COURSE (where also CURRENT).

1. *Walrus*, adopted from D, which has var *walros*, is of Scan origin—cf ON *hrossvalr* (whence OE *horshwael*)—and is prop a kind of WHALE, known as a 'horse whale'; ON *hrossvalr* has been confused with ON *rosmhvalr*, a walrus.

2. E *horse* is OE *hors*, akin to OFris *hors*, *hers*, *hars*, OS *hers*, *hross*, OHG-MHG *ros*, G *Ross*, ON *hross*, themselves prob akin to L *currō*, for *\*cursō*, I run. The v 'to *horse*' goes back to OE *horsian*, from the n *hors*.

**hortation, hortative, hortatory.** See EXHORT, para 1.

**horticulture**, whence **horticultural** and **horticulturist**. See the element *horti-*; cf COHORT and COURT and, for the 2nd element, *cult-*.

**hosanna**, adopted from Eccl LL, is itself a trln of Gr *hosanna*, an attempt—? via Aram—at H *hōshī'āh nnā*, save [us] now, we pray.

**hose**, a long stocking or a legging hence a modern stocking, hence, from tubular shape, a flexible, usu rubber, waterpipe, hence 'to **hose**'; hence **hosier**, whence **hosiery**.

*Hose* descends from OE *hosu* and is akin to ON *hosa*, a legging, a stocking, OHG *hosa*, MHG *hose*, a gaiter, G *Hose*, trousers, MD *hoosse*, *hose*, D *hoos*, legging, gaiter: perh orig 'a covering'—cf Skt *kōśas*, a container.

**hospice; hospitable; hospital, hospital(l)er, hospitality; hospitate; hostel, hostler (and ostler), hostelry; hotel, hotelier; spital; host (3), hostess; hostage**—**hostile, hostility.**—**guest** (n, hence v).

1. *Hospice*, a house of shelter and sustenance for travellers, is adopted from MF-F: L *hospitium*, hospitality, an *-ium* derivative from *hospes*, acc *hospitem*, a receiver of strangers, a host, hence, by reciprocity, a guest. L *hospes*, *hospit-*, has further derivatives affecting E, as e.g.:

*hospitāre*, to receive a stranger, to receive as a guest, pp *hospitātus*, whence the now rare 'to *hospitate*'; whence also, as if from ML *\*hospitābilis*, the MF *hospitable*, adopted by E;

*hospitālis*, of or befitting the reception of strangers or guests, LL most hospitable, whence the now rare E adj *hospital*; L *hospitālis* has neu *hospitāle*, used in ML as n, a var of L *hospitālis domus* (house), a hospice, hence, in MF and late ME-EE, a place of refuge and maintenance for the needy and the aged: OF-MF *hospital* (F *hôpital*), adopted, as 'hospice', by ME, the modern sense arising in C16;

*hospitālitās* (from *hospitālis*), o/s *hospitālitāt-*, whence OF-F *hospitalité*, whence E *hospitality*.

2. OF-MF *hospital* has OF-F derivative *hospitalier*, prob suggested by ML *hospitālārius*, a monk in a house affording hospitality to pilgrims and other travellers, hence E *hospital(l)er*; also the erudite derivative (1801), *hospitaliser*, whence the horrible E 'to *hospitalize*'. In late ME, *hospital* was, by aphesis, shortened to *spital*; after EE, obs; and never applied to a religious house.

3. ML *hospitāle* becomes OF-MF *hostel*, adopted by ME; derivative OF-MF *hostelier* (*ostelier*) yields ME *hosteler*, *osteler*, a guest in a hospice or hostel; ME *hosteler*, adopted by E, survives only in sense 'a student living in a hostel', but ME *osteler* becomes E *ostler* and—under the influence of *horse* pron *hoss*—'degraded' in sense to 'stableman'. OF-MF *hostel* has another derivative: OF-MF *hostelerie*, whence ME *hostelrie*, E *hostelry*.

4. OF-MF *hostel* becomes F *hôtel*, whence E *hotel*, and OF-MF *hostelier* becomes F *hôtelier*, hotel-keeper, whence E *hotelier*.

5. L *hospes*, guest, host, acc *hospitem*, became, by contr, OF-MF *hoste* (*oste*), adopted by ME, whence EE *host*, host, guest, E 'host, landlord', with a spec sense in Bot. Derivative MF *hostesse* (*ostesse*) yields E *hostess*.

6. L *hospes* has, prob as a contr of ML *\*hospitāticum*, a ML derivative n *hostāticus* (var *ostāticum*), whence OF-MF *hostage* (*ostage*; F *otage*), lodging, shelter, hence a guest, esp if lodged as a hostage, hence a hostage, adopted by E.

7. L *hospes*, guest, host, has s *hosp-*; L *hostis*, a stranger, hence a guest, but hence also an enemy, this last sense predominating in L from c30 B.C. onwards, mainly because *hospes* successfully competes in sense 'guest',—*hostis* has s *host-*. The r common to both *hospes* and *hostis* is *hos-*, prob with basic sense either 'shelter, refuge' or 'food' or perh 'shelter, with food'. Perh, even more fundamentally, the orig basic sense is 'food (with shelter) as a means of preservation': if that were so, L *hospes* (? also *hostis*) might be akin to L *sospes*, safe and sound, (as n) protector, preserver —cf the Roman goddess *Iunō* (ML *Junō*) *Sospita*, Juno the Preserver: perh, despite the generally accepted etym of the Gr words, cf Gr *sōtēr*, preserver, saviour, applied esp to Zeus (cf Eg *Suter*, the Saviour-God), agent (*-tēr*) from *sōein*, var of *sōizein*, to save (cf *sōs*, safe and sound), esp if the r be *sōs-*. Tentatively I suggest an IE r *\*ksōs-*, var *\*ksos-*, issuing into Gr *sōs-* (L *sos-* in *sospes*) and L *hos-*. (But cf the Gmc cognates in para 10.) The word may be Medit.

8. L *hostis*, in its later sense 'enemy', acquires, in ML, the sense 'army' (from the pl *hostes*, enemies): whence OF-MF *host* (*ost*), adopted by ME and, in EE, acquiring sense 'multitude'. The derivative adj *hostīlis* accounts, perh via late MF-F, for E *hostile*; subsidiary *hostīlitās*, o/s *hostīlitāt-*, accounts—prob via MF-F *hostilité*—for *hostility*.

9. App akin to L *hostis*, a stranger, an enemy, is

L *hostia*, an expiatory victim offered to the gods, a sacrifice, whence OF *oiste*, whence ME *oyste*, later *oste*, latest *host*, extant in E, now only for the Eucharistic wafer; L *hostia* becomes also MF-F *hostie*, which has perh intervened.

10. Akin to L *hostis*, a stranger, a guest, is the Gmc set of terms: OHG-MHG *gast*, stranger, guest, G *Gast*, guest—OS *gast*—OFris *jest*—MD-D *gast*—Go *gasts*—ON *gestr*, proto-Norse *-gestir* (Runic)—and, perh imm from QN, the OE *gaest*, *giest*, whence *guest*. (Cf also OB *gostĭ*.) The Gmc etymon is *\*gastiz*; the IE, *\*ghostis*. (Walshe.)

**hospitable.** See prec, para 1.

**hospital, hospital(l)er.** See HOSPICE, para 1 at *hospitalis*, and para 2.

**hospitality.** See HOSPICE, para 1, s.f.

**host,** receiver of guests—an army—Eccl term. See HOSPICE, paras resp 5, 8, 9.

**hostage.** See HOSPICE, para 6.

**hostel, hosteler, hostelry.** See HOSPICE, para 3.

**hostess.** See HOSPICE, para 5.

**hostile, hostility.** See HOSPICE, para 8.

**hostler.** See HOSPICE, para 3.

**hot.** See HEAT.

**hotch-potch.** See POT, para 7.

**hotel, hotelier.** See HOSPICE, para 4.

**Hottentot** is adopted from Afr, where lit it denotes a stutterer or a stammerer, from the predominant clicks of Hottentot speech: a pun on the sounds '*hot* and (D *en*) *tot*', recalling D *hateren*, to stammer, and *tateren*, to stutter.

**hough** is a Sc and N dial var of horse's *hock*, q.v. at HEEL, para 2.

**hound.** See CANINE, para 2.

**hour, hourly.** See HORA, para 3.

**house** (1), n (dwelling) and v; hence such obvious cpds as **houseboat, -breaker (-breaking), -fly, -hold** (whence **-holder**; cf MD *huysholt, huushoud*: OED), **housekeeper (-keeping), -leek, -maid, -wife** (ME *husewif*); **husband,** whence 'to husband', **husbandly, husbandman, husbandry,** and, prob via *\*husby*, the pet-form **hubby; husk** (n, hence v), whence the adj **husky; hussy; husting, hustings.**—Perh cf HOSE.

1. 'To *house*' derives from OE *hūsian*, itself from the OE n *hūs*, whence ME *hus*, later *hous*, whence E *house*: and OE *hūs* is akin to OFris and OS *hūs*, OHG-MHG *hūs*, G *Haus*, MD *hues, huus, huys*, D *huis*, Go gud*hūs*, house of God, a temple, ON *hūs*: perh also cf G *Haut*, E HIDE and 'to HIDE'. Basic idea: a covering, a shelter.

2. The head of the house is normally the *husband*, OE *hūsbonda*, from ON *hūsbōndi*, householder, husband; *bōndi* stands for *\*būandi*, from *būa*, to dwell. The householder in the country used formerly to be mostly a farmer, whence obsol *husbandman*, a farmer, and *husbandry*, farming.

3. ME *husewif* has var *huswif*, with dial var *hussif*, adopted by E as the pron of *housewife*, a little bag or case for needle, thread, pins, scissors, etc. Dial *hussif* has influenced the contr of *housewife* into *hussy*, orig, but long obs for, 'housewife'.

4. ON *hūs*, house, had a cpd *hūsthing*, lit 'house assembly', hence a council, ON *thing* being 'assembly' (though also 'thing'—see THING): hence OE *hūsting*, a council, an assembly, ME *husting*, retained by E, orig for a council, hence a legal court, hence the Guildhall platform where the presiding officials sat, whence *husting*, usu pl *hustings*, in its political sense.

5. MD *huus*, a house (as in para 1), has a MD cpd *huuskijn*, a little (D dim -*kijn*, E -*kin*) house, whence ME *huske*, a fruit's or seed's 'little house', whence E *husk*, whence *husky*, of or like husks, full of husks, whence, husks being dry and therefore tending to rustle, a *husky* voice, whence, such voices often belonging to spirit-drinking toughs, a *husky* fellow, strong and hardy.

**house** (2), **housings** (trappings). See HOLSTER, para 2.

**Houyhnhnm.** See WHINE, heading and para 1.

**hovel**: ME *hovel*, var *hovyl*: o.o.o.: perh cf MF *huvelet*, a penthouse, app a dim of MF *huve*, a bonnet, from Gmc \**huba*—perh ult cf HAT.

**hover** (v, hence n): ME *hoveren*, to hover, to linger, (? an int, ? a freq, ? freq-int) from ME *hoven*, to hover, to linger: prob from MD-MLG *hoven*, to dwell, to linger: ? akin to L *habitāre* (cf HABIT, para 9).

**how**, adv: ME *how*, earlier *hou*, earliest *hu*: OE *hū*, app an old instr from—or from the stem of—OE *hwā*, who, *hwaet*, what: cf OFris *hū*, *ho*, OS *hwō*, OHG *hweo*, with var *wio*, whence MHG-G *wie*, MD *hu*, D *hoe*, Go *hwaiwa*, *aiwa*: from IE etymon \**kwoivos*, what—cf Gr *poîos*, what like? Cf WHAT, WHO, WHICH.

**howbeit**, be that as it may (archaic), although (obs): *how*, with force of 'however' (adv)+*be* (subj)+*it*.

**howe.** See HALL, para 7.

**however**, adv=*how* (in what manner, in whatever manner)+-*ever*, used as a time-int suffix; hence the conj.

**howitzer**: G *Haubitze*: early G *haufnitz*: Cz *houfnice*, a siege-warfare catapult. EG *haufnitz* arose during the Hussite wars of C15. (Walshe.)

**howl**, whence 'howler'. See ULULANT, para 3.

**howlet.** See ULULANT, para 4.

**hoy**, a small coasting freighter, now a heavy barge: MD *hoey*, *hoei* (cf D *hui*, *heu*), varr of MD *hoede*, *hode*, *huede*, app from MD *hoeden*, *hoden*, *huende*, whence MD *hueden*, to guard, protect, akin to OHG *huotēn*, MHG *hüeten*, to protect, OHG *huota*, protection: cf HEED.

**hoyden.** See HEATH, para 4.

**hub**, the cylindrical centre of a wheel; **hob** of fireplace; **hobnail**.

*Hub* is a var, prob orig dial, of *hob* in its senses 'that part of a fireplace which affords a flat surface on either side of the grate and is level with its top' and 'round peg or pin used as a target' (whence *hobnail*); *hub* assumes the specific sense 'the central part of a wheel'. The basic idea common to *hob* and *hub* seems to be 'protuberance' (OED); and *hob* perh derives from *Hob* (see the 1st HOB) as a

familiar name for a familiar object or device (EW) —cf the multiple senses of *jack* from *Jack*.

**hubbub** is app of C, esp Ir, origin: cf EIr *abu*, a war cry, Ga *ubub!*, redup of syn *ub!*, signifying aversion, *ubh ubh!*, signifying incredulity, and *ubarraid*, confusion, bustle, W *ub!*, alas, and the n and v *ubain*, howl, moan: ult echoic. Cf HULLA-BALOO.

**hubby.** See HOUSE (heading).

**hubris.** See HYBRID.

**huckleberry** is a dial var (whence *Huckleberry Finn*) of *hurtleberry*, which, arising in C16, has a C17-20 var, orig dial but now predominant, *whortleberry*, perh influenced by WHORL; -*berry* has been f/e added to ME \**hortel* or \**hortle*, substituting suffix -*el* or -*le* to the -*e* of OE *horte*, a whortleberry: o.o.o.: ? akin to OE *wyrt*, ME *wurt*, E *wort*, plant, herb, q.v. at WORT.

**huckster.** See HOOK, para 3.

**huddle** (v, hence n) is app a dial, orig freq, derivative of ME *hoderen* (contr *hodren*: cf LG *huderen*, to cover up), to huddle, wrap up, akin to ME *huden*, to HIDE: basic idea, prob to crowd together for protection, esp in a hidden—or at least a safe—place: ? cf, ult, HEED. The -*le* was perh suggested by the -*els* of ME *hüdels*, from OE *hȳdels*, a hiding-place. App the sl *oodles* is of the same origin.

**hue.** See HOAR, para 5.

**huff** (v, hence n), is, like PUFF, echoic: '*huffed* up with air' is syn with '*puffed* up . . .'. Hence *huffy*, overblown, insolent, apt to take offence.

**hug** (v, hence n) app comes from ON *hugga* (s *hug*-), to comfort or soothe, as a mother hugging her child: prob orig echoic from the accompanying words of comfort or sounds of lullaby.

**huge**, ME *huge*, *hoge*, is prob apheatic for OF *ahuge*, *ahoge*, enormous, itself app a prefix-cpd of *a* (F *à*, in, on, at, L *ad*)+*hoge*, a height, a hill, of Gmc origin: cf OHG *hōhē* (G *Hohe*), Go *hāuhei*; cf also OHG *hōh*, *hōch* (G *hoch*), MD *hooch*, *hoge*, D *hoog*, high. Perh, however, OF *hoge*, *hogue*, ? *huge*, hill, eminence, derives from OC \**uc*-, an eminence, whence \**uxellos*, as in the PIN *Uxello-dunum*; \**uc*- occurs in OBr *uhel*, Br *huel*, Cor *ūghel*, W *uchel*, high—in the obs Cor prefix *ugh*-, high-, above-, cf Br *ahué*, above (prep); seductive is Cor *uthek*, *uthic*, *uthyc*, huge, esp if it be akin to *ūghel*, high.

**huggermugger** (n, mostly in *h*-, hence adj and esp adv, clandestinely) prob completes the anglicization manifest in AIr *cuggermugger*, a whispering, a low-voiced gossiping, from Ir *cogair!*, whisper!: Cf EIr *cocraim*, I whisper or conspire, Ga *cogar*, a whisper, and *cogair* (var *cagair*), to whisper: ? ult echoic.

**Huguenot.** See OATH, para 2.

**hulk.** See HALL, para 8.

**hull.** See HALL, para 9.

**hullabaloo; hullo!** See HALLOO, s.f.

**hum** (v, hence n), whence, as in **humming bird**, pa and vn **humming** and the adj **humdrum** (redup, suggested by DRUM, of *hum*) and the sl AE **hum-**

**dinger,** which prob glances at the now dial *ding*, to strike, or, more prob, at the echoic *dingdong*—*hum* is no less echoic than the MHG-G *hummen* and the orig freq MD *hummelen* and, as still in D, *hommelen*. Cf HUMBLEBEE.

**human, humane, humanist, humanism, humanitarian, humanity, humanize.** See HOMO, para 8.

**humate, humation.** See HOMO, para 11.

**humble.** See HOMO, para 12.

**humblebee:** ME *humbel-bee, humbylbee, hombulbe*, which f/e adds *bee* to ME *\*humbel* (\**humbyl*, etc.), itself from MHG *humbel* (later *hummel*, as in G), from OHG *humbal*, humblebee: cf the syn MD *hummel, homel*, (as in D) *hommel*, and several Scan and Lith cognates: clearly 'the insect that *hums*'—see HUM.

2. The var *bumblebee* (C16 onwards) was prob, at first, a nursery word, with assimilation of *h* to *b* perh suggested by *buzz* and ME *bommen*, to hum, and E *boom*. (Walshe.)

**humble pie.** See LOIN, both heading and para 4.

**humbug,** imposture, sham, hypocrisy, hence the person guilty thereof, hence to deceive, was orig (c1750) sl: o.o.o.: prob suggested by '*hum* and haw', ref to temporizing, and perh also by *bug*bear.

**humdrum.** See HUM.

**humdudgeon**=C18 sl *hum*, a deception+DUDGEON.

**humeral** is the E-formed adj of L *humerus*, shoulder, adopted by An and Zoo, but, in L, better written *umerus*: cf the Go *ams*, Gr *ōmos*, Skt *áṃsas*: IE r, \**am*-, varr *ōm*- and *um*-.

**humid, humidify, humidity, humidor.** See HUMOR, para 4.

**humiliate, humiliation, humility.** See HOMO, para 12.

**humming bird.** See HUM (heading).

**hummock.** See HUMP.

**humor** (AE), **humour**, n hence v; **humoral**, whence **humoralism; humoresque; humo(u)rist**, whence **humoristic; humorous.**—**humid, humidify, humidity, humidor.**

1. *Humour* and *humor*, both in ME (with varr *umor, umour*), are adopted rom OF: L *hūmor*, better *ūmor*, from *hūmēre*, better *ūmēre*, to be moist, akin to L *ūuidus* (ML *ūvidus*), contr *ūdus*, Gr *hugros*, ON *vökr*, moist, prob to Skt *ukṣati*, he sprinkles (cf ox), and perh OIr *fūal*, urine: IE r, prob \**ug*-, with var \**udh*-, moist.

2. In old Physio, animals had four fluids, which determined human temperament and health: hence 'in a good or a bad *humour*'.

3. From L *hūmor*, F derives *humoral*, of or by the humours, adopted by erudite E. The general E adj is *humorous*, from LL *hūmorōsus*, var of LL *ūmorōsus*, very moist, hence juicy, succulent (Souter), from (*h*)*ūmor*. *Humo*(*u*)*rist* is an E formation; *humoresque* comes from G *humoreske*—influenced by *picturesque*.

4. L (*h*)*ūmēre* has a derivative adj (*h*)*ūmidus*, whence, prob via MF-F *humide*, the E *humid*; derivative *hūmiditās*, o/s *hūmiditāt*-, yields—prob via MF-F *humidité*—the E *humidity*. *Humidify*=

*humid*+element *-fy* (to make); *humidor*, a receptacle for preventing cigars from becoming dry, merely adds agential *-or* to *humid*.

**hump** (n hence v), **humpback; humpty-dumpty; hummock,** Topo **hammock; hunk.**

1. *Hump* is of Gmc origin, prob either D or LG: cf D *homp* and MD *humpelen*, D *hompelen*, to hobble (walk with back humped), and LG *hump*, hump, hunk, *humpel*, hump, hill: prob cf Gr *kumbē*, a hollow vessel, therefore cf E *hip* (q.v. at HIVE).—Hence *humpback*—cf *hunchback*.

2. *Hump* has an altered redup: *humpty-dumpty* (from *dump*), glorified in a nursery rhyme.

3. Perh akin to *hump* is *hummock*, a rounded knoll: ? for \**humpock*, after *hillock*. It has an AE var *hammock*, used esp in Florida.

4. App akin to *hump* but perh influenced by *hunch* is *hunk*, a large lump: cf Fl *hunke*.

**humpy** (Aus), an aboriginal's, hence any primitive, hut: Aboriginal *oompi*.

**humus.** See HOMO, paras 2 and 10.

**Hun,** whence **Hunnian, Hunnic, Hunnish.**

*Hun* is a b/f from OE *Hūne* or *Hūnas*, the Huns, itself prob from LL *Hūni* (ML, usu *Hunni*), with less correct var *Chūni* or *Chunni*, prob from Ch *Han* (var *Hiong-nu*): cf Skt *Huṇa*, Gr *Ounnoi* or *Khounoi*, and also ON *Hūnar* and OHG *Hūni* (G *Hunnen*). These invaders from Asia overran and terrorized Europe c372-453 A.D., Attila dying in the latter year. Cf the G derivative *Hune*, MHG *hiune*, a giant. (Walshe.)

**hunch, hunchback.** See HAUNCH, para 2.

**hundred,** whence **hundredth; hecatomb.**

1. *Hundred*, already in OE, is an elaboration of OE *hund*, 100, the 2nd element, *-red*, being akin to Go *rathjō*, a reckoning, as in *ga-rathjan*, to count: cf OFris *hundred*, var *hunderd*, OHG *hunderit*, MHG-G *hundert*, Go *hund*: Gmc etym \**hunda* or \**hundam*; IE etym, ? \**kentom*: cf L *centum* and E CENT.

2. Akin to L *centum* is Gr *hekaton*: with both, cf Skt *śatám*, Av *satem*. Gr *hekaton* has cpd *hekatombē*, the 2nd element deriving from r of Gr *bous*, an ox (cf *bovine* at BEEF): this sacrifice of 100 oxen became L *hecatombe*, whence E *hecatomb*.

**hung.** See HANG.

**Hungarian, Hungary.** See OGRE, para 2.

**hunger** (n, v), **hungry.**

The latter derives from OE *hungrig* (cf OFris *hungerich*), the adj of *hungor*, hunger, to which is intimately related the OE *hyngrian*, to be hungry, ME *hungren* (influenced by the n), E 'to *hunger*'. The OE *hungor* is akin to OFris *hunger*, OHG *hungar* (also in OS), MHG-G *hunger*, MD *hunger*, (as D) *honger*, Go *hūhrus* (for \**hunhrus*), cf Go *huggrjan* (*hugg*-, pron *hung*-), to hunger; ON *hungr*; Lith *kankà*, distress, suffering, torment; Gr *henkei*, he suffers from hunger. The Gmc r is either \**hung*- or ? \**hunk*-; the IE, \**kenk*-, with varr \**kank*-, \**konk*-.

**hunk.** See HUMP, para 4.

**hunker, v; hunkers.** See HAUNCH, para 2.

**hunkydory,** AE sl *hunky*, in good condition, from

AE *hunk*, a goal in children's games+ *-dory*, a very approx rhyming redup.

hunt, v (hence n), whence hunter, huntress, and vn hunting (cf hunting ground—huntsman being a *hunt's man*.—Cf the sep HINT and HIT.

'To *hunt*' comes, by way of C12-13 *hunten*, *huntien*, from OE *huntian*, akin to Go *-hinthan*, to seize, and OE *hentan*, to try to capture, to capture; IE r, *\*kent-* (Feist).

hurdle, n (hence v, whence hurdler), orig a movable frame, made of wattle twigs: ME *hurdel*, *hirdel*, OE *hyrdel*, prob a dim from the r of such Gmc words as ME *hyrde*, OHG-MHG *hurt*, G *Hürde*, MD *hurde*, D *horde*, a hurdle, Go *haúrds*, ON *hyrd*, a door: basic sense, 'wickerwork': Gmc r, *\*hurdi-*; IE r, perh *\*ker-*, with varr *\*kar-*, *\*kor-*, *\*kur-*, with exx in L (*crātes*, wickerwork: see CRATE), Gr (*kartalos*, a basket), Skt, C, OP.

hurdy-gurdy is ult echoic; imm, perh a blend of E dial *hirdy-girdy*, an uproar+*hurly-burly* (see next).

hurl (v, hence n), whence the game hurling and its player or hurler; hurly-burly.

1. 'To *hurl*' derives from ME *hurlen*, var *hourlen*, app echoic: cf Fris *hurreln*, (of wind) to blow in gusts, E *hurry*, OF *houler*, to hurl: prob from the r of *hurtle*, q.v. at HURT; if that be so, the *-l* is a freq suffix.

2. Perh from *hurl* is *hurly-burly*; cf, however, the app echoic (obsol) *hurly*, uproar, confusion: cf the orig exclamatory EF-F *hurluberlu*, likewise a rhyming redup (G *hurliburli*): ult echoic.

hurrah. See HUZZA.

hurricane: Sp *huracán*: Taino *huracan*, *hurricán*, an evil spirit of the sea, hence a hurricane. (Webster; Sp authorities prefer Carib *huracán*.)

hurry (v, hence n), with pa hurried and pa, vn hurrying, perh comes either from the echoic dial *hurr*, to snarl, or from ME *horien*, to befoul, but prob is akin to HURL, the r of both being app *hur-*. The redup *hurry-scurry* was prompted by SCURRY.

hurt (v, hence n), whence hurtful; whence also the freq hurtle (ME *hurtlen*).

The basic sense of *hurt* is 'to strike': ME *hurten*: OF *hurter* (MF-F *heurter*), to strike, knock, thrust, etc.: prob (B & W) via Frankish, from OGmc *hurt-*, to butt (someone, something) as a ram does —cf ON *hrutr*, a ram (cf ON *hjörtr*, a stag); cf also MHG *hurt*, an impact, a shock, and *hurtec* (G *hurtig*), rapid, and prob ON *hrjōta*, to break or burst (something). Ult echoic.

husband, husbandman, husbandry. See HOUSE, para 2.

hush (v, hence n), hushaby; hist! and whist!

1. The ME *hussht* is thought to be 'silenced', pp of a lost v of echoic origin ('having been said *hush!* to'). *Hushaby!*, hush!, blends *hush*+ *lullaby*.

2. *Hist!* is a weakened var of *whist!*, be silent!, whence both the AIr 'Hold your *whist!*', lit 'maintain your silence' but now mostly 'be silent', and the archaic when not dial adj *whist*, silent, (of,

e.g., woods) still: clearly echoic: cf the G *pst!* (*bst!* and weakened *st!*), existing also in E, usu as *psst!* —mostly, as by spivs, to attract attention.

husk. See HOUSE, para 5.

husky (1), adj. See HOUSE, para 5, s.f.

husky (2), n. See ESKIMO, para 2.

huso. See ISINGLASS.

hussar. See COURSE, para 9.

hussif. See HOUSE, para 3.

hussy. See HOUSE, para 3.

husteron proteron. See HYSTERIA, para 2.

husting(s). See HOUSE, para 4.

hustle (v, hence n), whence hustler, derives, by metathesis (? prompted by BUSTLE), from D *hutselen*, to shake continually or continuously, the freq of *hutsen*, to shake; both vv exist already in MD; *hutsen* is prob the int of an echoic v (? cf HIT).

hut (n, hence v—whence hutment): MF *hutte*: either MHG *hütte* or OHG *hutta* (for *\*huttia*): prob cf OHG *huota* (G *Hut*), protection, and therefore E 'to HIDE'.

hutch: ME, from OF, *huche*: ML *hutica* (C8): o.o.o.: ? cf prec.

huzza (cf G *hussa*) is as clearly echoic as, say, *hurrah* (cf G *hurra*), with its frequent var *hurray* or *hooray*.

hyacinth, hyacinthine; jacinth.

The 3rd, ME *iacynth*, *iacynt*, derives from OF-MF *iacinte*, itself from L *hyacinthus* (whence E *hyacinth*), trln of Gr *huakinthos*, the flower, hence a gem, app for *\*wakinthos*—cf the Cretan monthname *Bakinthos*; of Aegean but pre-Gr origin (Hofmann). Derivative Gr adj *huakinthinos*, L *hyacinthinus*, becomes E *hyacinthine*.

hyaline, sea-clear, hence, n, a clear sea: LL *hyalinus*: Gr *hualinos*, adj of *hualos*, glass: cf the element *hyalo-*.

hybrid, whence hybridity, is n, hence adj, and, like EF-F *hybride*, it represents L *hybrida*, the piglet resulting from the union of wild boar and tame sow: from Gr *hubris*, violation, excessive pride, adopted in latter sense by E as university sl. *Hubris* app cpds Cyprian Gr *hu*, upon+a cognate of Gr *briaros*, strong. (Boisacq.)

Hydra; hydrate.

The latter=*hydr-* (as in *Hydra*)+Chem n-suffix *-ate*. *Hydra* adopts the L form of Gr *Hudra*, a nine-headed serpentine monster, PN from *hudra*, *hudros*, a water-snake, akin to Skt *udrás*, a water-beast: cf *otter* and, f.a.e., WATER.

hydrant=*hydr-*, as in prec+suffix *-ant*.

hydrate. See HYDRA.

hydraulic (adj, hence n, whence hydraulics): late MF-F *hydraulique*; L *hydraulicus*, trln of Gr *hudraulikos*, adj of *hudraulis* (or *-aulos*), a water organ: element *hydr(o)-*, water+*aulos*, a flute.

hydro is short for '*hydropathic* establishment', where *hydropathic* is the adj of *hydropathy*, a water cure: cf the element *-pathic*.

hydrochloric=the element *hydro-*+*chloric*, q.v. at CHLORAL.

hydrogen: F *hydrogène*, water (Gr *hudōr*) resulting—cf the element -*gen* and, f.a.e., GENERAL— from the combustion of this gas.

**hydrography**, whence the adj **hydrographic**, derives from EF-F *hydrographie*, a description (cf the element -*graph* and, f.a.e., GRAMMAR) of water, esp of the ocean.

**hydrometer** is a *meter* (q.v. at MEASURE) of the specific gravity of liquids (Gr *hudōr*, water).

**hydropathic, hydropathy.** See HYDRO.

**hydrophobia.** See the element -*phobe*.

**hydroplane** is a motoboat that 'planes (see *plane* at PLAIN) over the water (Gr *hudōr*, c/f *hudro*-).

**hydrostat,** whence **hydrostatic** (whence **hydrostatics**). See the element -*stat*.

**hyena** (EE **hyaena**). See the 1st SOW, para 3.

**hygiene**—whence both **hygienic** (unless from F *hygiénique*), whence **hygienics** and **hygienist**—represents EF-F *hygiène*, from Gr *hugieinon*, n use of the neu of *hugieinos*, of or for (good) health, the adj of *hugieia* (var *hugeia*), whence the Goddess of Health *Hugieia*: from *hugiēs*, healthy, with IE etymon \**sug(u)ijēs*, lit 'well (IE *su*-)- living' (Gr *zēn*, to live).

**hygrometer** is a meter of atmospheric moisture (Gr *hudōr*, water); perh suggested by EF-F *hygromètre*; cf the element *hygro*-.

**Hymen**, the Gr god of marriage; **hymen**, the virginal membrane broken during the consummation of marriage; **hymeneal**, of or by or for or at (a) wedding, a marriage; cf the element *hymeno*-;— **hymn**, orig a bridal song, hence a song of praise, esp of Deity, **hymnal** (adj, hence n), **hymnary**, **hymnody** (whence **hymnodist**), **hymnology** (whence **hymnologist**).

1. The general source is Gr *humēn*, a membrane, esp the virginal, akin to Skt *syūman*, a band, a suture, hence prob to E SEAM: and app this Gr physio *humēn* is id with Gr *humēn*, a bridal song, perh orig the cry greeting the announcement of virginity removed, whence *Hymen* as above; the Gr terms become L *Hymen* and L *hymen*. Wedding *humēn* has adj *humenaios*, L *hymenaeus*, hence— with -*eal* substituted for -*eous*—the E *hymeneal*.

2. Akin to, perh deriving from, Gr *humēn*, marriage cry, hence marriage song, is Gr *humnos*, whence L *hymnus*, whence OF-F *hymne*, whence E *hymn*, with derivative adjj *hymnal* and *hymnic*. (OE *ymen*, *hymen* took a slightly different course.) Whereas L *hymnus* has the ML derivative *hymnārium*, -*ārium* connoting 'a receptacle of', whence *hymnary*, Gr *humnos* has the cpd *humnōidos* (a professional singer in a religious cult), which prompts *humnōidia*, hymn-singing (*ōidē*: cf ODE), whence *hymnody*. *Hymnology* prob derives from F *hymnologie*: cf the element -*logy*, discourse.

**hyoid**, shaped like a *Y*: F *hyoïde*: Gr *huoeidēs*, of the form (-*eidēs*: cf the E suffix -*oid*) of the Gr letter '*upsilon*' (bare or mere *u*).

**hyperbola, hyperbole, hyperbolic.**

The geom *hyperbola* is a SciL derivative of Gr *huperbolē*, a throwing (*bolē*) beyond (*huper*): cf the element *hyper*- and BALLISTICS, *bolē* deriving from *ballein*, to cast or throw. *Hyperbole*, in rhetoric, is adopted from the L trln of *huperbolē*, which has

adj *huperbolikos*, excessive, exaggerated, LL *hyperbolicus*, EF-F *hyperbolique* and E *hyperbolic*.

**hyperborean.** See BOREAL.

**hypercritical.** See CRISIS, final sentence.

**hyphen** (n, hence v), whence **hyphenate**, whence **hyphenation**, is adopted from LL, which takes it from Gr *huphen*, prop *huph'hen* (ὑφ' ἕν), under one, hence into one, i.e. together: Gr *hupo*, under (cf the element *hypo*-)+*hen*, neu of *heis*, one (cf the *en*- of ENTITY).

**hypnosis, hypnotic, hypnotism, hypnotist, hypnotize.** See SOMNOLENCE, para 6.

**hypochondria, hypochondriac** (ML *hypochondriacus*). See the element *chondri*- and cf the element *hypo*-.

**hypocorisma**, a pet-name, and its adj **hypocoristic**.

The former, adopted from LL, represents Gr *hupokorisma*; the latter derives from Gr *hupokoristikos*. The Gr words=*hupo*-, c/f of *hupo*, under (E *hypo*-)+derivatives from *korizesthai*, to caress, s *koriz*-, r *kor*-: cf Gr *korē*, a girl.

**hypocrisy, hypocrite, hypocritic,** now in extn **hypocritical.**

The adj *hypocritic(al)* derives from Gr *hupokritikos*, the adj of *hupokritēs*, a stage actor, hence one pretending to be what he is not, esp a hypocrite, whence LL *hypocrita*, var *ypocrita* becoming OF *ypocrite*, *ipocrite*, both adopted by ME, whence, by reversion to LL *hypocrita* or to Gr *hupokritēs*, the E *hypocrite*. Hypocrisy, ME *ypocrisie*, *ipocrisie*, adopted from OF, goes back to LL *ypocrisis*, better *hypocrisis*, trln of Gr *hupokrisis*, a play-acting, hence simulation, hence hypocrisy, itself from *hupokrinein*, to play a stage-part, to answer one's fellow-actor: *hupo*-, from *hupo*, under (E *hypo*-)+*krinein*, to sift, hence to decide (*krinesthai*, to dispute): cf CRISIS and esp CERTAIN.

**hypodermic** is the -*ic* adj—cf **hypodermal**, the -*al* adj—of SciL *hypoderma*: prefix *hypo*-+Gr *derma*, the skin (cf the element -*derm*): 'under the skin'.

**hypogastric**, from F *hypogastrique*, is the adj of SciL *hypogastrium*: Gr *hupogastrion*, the lower belly or paunch: *hupo*, under, beneath+*gastēr*, belly (cf GASTRIC).

**hypostasis** (whence **hypostasize**), **hypostatic.**

The 3rd derives from Gr *hupostatikos*, the adj of *hupostasis*, subsistence, substance, LL *hypostasis*, adopted by E; Gr *hupostasis* comes from *huphistasthai*, to stand (*histasthai*, middle voice of *histanai*, to cause to stand) under (*hupo*); cf *stasis* and f.a.e., STAND.

**hypotenusal, hypotenuse** (incorrectly **hypothenuse**). See TEND, para 27.

**hypothec, hypothecary, hypothecate, hypothecation.** See THESIS, para 10.

**hypothesis** (whence **hypothesize**); **hypothetic(al).** See THESIS, para 11.

**hyssop**: ME *hysope*, a re-shaping of ME *ysope*, adopted from OF-MF (F *hysope*): L *hysopus*, *hyssopus*, trln of Gr *hussōpos*, an aromatic herb: either from H *ēzōb* or from a Sem cognate.

hysteria; hysteric (whence hysterics), now in -al extn hysterical.

1. *Hysteria* is a SciL formation, in -*ia*, from E *hysteric* or from its L orig *hystericus*, a trln of Gr *husterikos*, the adj of *hustera*, womb, perh elliptical for *hustera mētra*, a later, or the latter, womb, where *mētra* is akin to *mētēr*, mother: cf L *mātrix*, womb, akin to L *māter*, mother. Gr *hustera* is the f of *husteros*, the latter (adj): IE etym *\*udteros*—cf Skt *uttáras*, the higher, the later, and L *uterus*

(perh for *\*uderos*), womb, itself, like L *mātrix*, adopted by E. *Uterus* has LL derivative adj *uterinus*, whence—perh via late MF-F *utérin*—the E *uterine*.

2. Gr *husteros* has neu *husteron*, preserved in E in the phrase *hysteron proteron* (cf the LL shortening *hysteroproteron*), the later before the earlier, a rhetorical figure depending upon a reversal of sense, as in Webster's ex 'He is well and lives'.

# I

I, pronoun. See EGO, para 1.

iamb, iambic (adj. hence n), iambus.

*Iambic* comes, like EF-F *iambique*, from L *iambicus*, trln of Gr *iambikos*, adj of *iambos*, whence L *iambus*, adopted by E but there less common than iamb (EF-F *iambe*, L *iambus*): but Gr *iambos* is o.o.o.: perh (Hofmann) for *\*wiambos* —cf Gr *dithurambos*, whence E *dithyramb*. Sturtevant has proposed a derivation from Gr *iainein* (s *iain-*), to warm, to cheer; iambics are an enlivening metre.

iatric, medical: Gr *iatrikos*, adj of *iatros*, a physician, from *iasthai*, to heal. Cf the element *iatro-*.

Iberia, whence Iberian (adj, hence n); Iberic; Iberis, a pepperwort.

*Iberis* represents Gr *ibēris*, prob from growing in *Ibēria*, the L name (var *Hibēria*) of the Sp peninsula, though also of Asiatic Georgia, an ancient and medieval kingdom lying between the Black Sea and the Caspian. The L adj is *Ibēricus*, whence E *Iberic*. The ancient Spaniards were the L *Ibēres* (*Hibēres*), trln of Gr *Ibēres*, itself, according to ancient Gr tradition, from Gr *ibēr*, the name of some undetermined animal.

ibex, adopted from L, is o.o.o.; prob of (Swiss) Alpine origin—like L *camox* (surviving in CHAMOIS).

ibis, adopted from L, comes from Gr: alteration, with Gr suffix *-is*, of Eg *hab* or *heb*.

ice (n, hence adj and v), iceberg, icicle, icy; Iceland, Icelandic (adj, hence n).

*Ice* derives, via ME *is, iis*, from OE *īs*, akin to OFris, OS, OHG-MHG *īs*, G *Eis*, MD *iss, isse*, D *ijs*, ON *īss*, prob also to Av *isav-*, frosty. The cpd *iceberg*, lit 'mountain of ice', ult of Scan origin, perh comes imm from MD *ijsberch* (D *ijsberg*); cf BERG. Similarly *Iceland* is 'Land of Ice', the native name being *Ísland*; hence *Icelandic*. *Icicle* derives from ME *isikel*, a f/e extn of OE *gicel*, icicle, with ME *is* (OE *īs*) added superfluously; cf ON *jökull*, icicle. *Icy* represents OE *īsig*.

ichneumon, a mongoose or a mongoose-like mammal, is adopted from L: from Gr *ikhneumōn*, lit 'the tracker', sc 'of crocodiles' eggs': from *ikhneuein* (s *ikhneu-*), to track, hunt after or out, itself from *ikhnos*, a footprint, a track, s *ikhn-*, r *ikh-*, from IE *\*eigh-*, to go, an extn of *\*ei-*, to go (as in the Gr and L vv). The ichneumon being so very highly regarded in Ancient Egypt, I suspect a

Gr f/e rationalization of Eg *khatra*, an ichneumon —cf Eg *Khatri*, the Ichneumon-God.

ichnology. See the element *ichno-*.

ichor: LL *īchōr*, bloody matter: Gr *ikhōr* (ἰχώρ), the juice that, instead of blood, flows in the veins of the gods, hence various Med and Sci senses: o.o.o., app non-Gr: perh a pre-vocalization (*i-*) of *\*khōr*, from Hit *kar-*, the r of Hit *karimm-* or *karimn-*, a god (gen *karimnas*, dat *karimmi*), which has adj *karinmas, karimnas*, of a god, divine (8turtevant).

ichthyology, whence ichthyological, ichthyologist; ichthyosaurus. See the element *ichthyo-*.

icicle. See ICE.

icon (for cpds, e.g., iconoclast, see the element *icono-*), adopted from L, represents Gr *eikōn*, app for *\*weikōn* (or *-on*): perh cf Lith pa*veiklas*, an example, a pattern, and i-*vykti*, to hit upon, prove right, arrive at. (Hofmann.)—The adj *iconic* derives from L *īconicus*, Gr *eikonikos*.

icy. See ICE, s.f.

id ('the ego and the *id*'): G *Id*, from G *Idioplasma* (E *idioplasm*: elements *idio-* and *-plasm*). The Bio preceded the Psychi sense.

idea, ideal (adj, hence n), idealism, idealist (whence idealistic), idealize (whence idealization), ideate (whence ideation, whence ideational), idée fixe; ideology (whence ideological and ideologist); idol (whence idolize) and eidolon, idolater; idolatrize and idolatrous from idolatry; eidetic; idyl or idyll, whence idyllic; cf the elements *ideo-idolo-, eido-*; cf also the sep WIT, esp f.a.e.

1. *Idea*, adopted from L, itself borrowed from Gr *idea* (ἰδέα), a concept, derives from Gr *idein* (s *id-*), to see, for *\*widein*. L *idea* has derivative LL adj *ideālis*, archetypal, ideal, whence EF-F *idéal* and E *ideal*, whence resp F *idéalisme* and E *idealism*, also resp *idéaliste* and *idealist*, and, further, *idéaliser* and *idealize*. L *idea* becomes MF-F *idée*, with cpd *idée fixe*, a fixed idea, adopted by E Francophiles; it also has ML derivative *\*ideāre*, pp *\*ideātus*, whence the Phil n *ideātum*, a thing that, in the fact, answers to the idea of it, whence 'to *ideate*', to form in, or as an, idea.

2. From Gr *idea*, F erudites formed the c/f *idéo-*, esp in *idéologie* (1796), whence E *ideology*. (For other *ideo-* cpds, see that element.)

3. Akin to Gr *idein*, to see, hence to *idea*, is Gr *eidos* (s *eid-*), that which is seen, hence the form or shape, hence a figure; whereas its dim, *eidōlon* an

image in the mind, hence a physical image, hence an idol, is retained in erudite E, its derivative adj *eidētikos* becomes E *eidetic*, esp in Psy.

4.° Gr *eidōlon* becomes LL *īdōlon*, further latinized as *īdōlum*, MF-F hence ME *idole*, E *idol*. *Eidōlon* has c/f *eidōl(o)-*, seen best in *eidōlolatreia*, worship of physical objects, esp of images or idols, whence, by contr, LL *īdōlolatria*, OF-MF *idolatrie*, E *idolatry*; the cognate *eidōlolatrēs* becomes LL *īdōlatrēs*, MF *idolatre*, F *idolâtre*, E *idolater*.

5. Gr *eidōlon* has a var, perh rather Gr *eidos* has the secondary dim, the LGr *eidullion*, a short lyrical poem (a sense arising somewhat obscurely), whence L *idyllium*, whence E *idyll* (idyl)—cf the EF-F *idylle*.

**idem.** See para 1 of:

**identic, identical, identify** (whence **identification**), **identity; idem.**

1. The base is L *īdem* (pron and adj), precisely that, hence the same: m *īdem*, f *eadem*, neu *idem*: app from the L pron *is*, *ea*, *id*, that+particle *-dem* (of IE origin).

2. L *īdem* has LL derivative *īdentitās* (for *\*īdemitās*), o/s *īdentitāt-*, whence, prob via MF-F *identité*, the E *identity*; *īdentitās* gains, in ML, the adj *īdenticus*, whence EF-F *identique* and E *identic*, usu in extn *identical*; the ML s *ident-* recurs in ML *īdentificāre*, to make or render identical, whence EF-F *identifier* and E *identify*.

**ideology.** See IDEA, para 2.

**Ides** (of March), seven days beginning, e.g., on March 15: L *īdūs* (gen *īduum*), pl: prob of Etruscan origin, as Varro says, and app meaning 'division' of a month.

**idiocy, idiot, idiotic; idiom, idiomatic; idio-syncrasy,** whence, after *idiomatic*, the adj **idio-syncratic;** the element *idio-*.

These words derive from Gr *idios*, proper or peculiar to oneself, private: dial *widios*, for older *\*whedios* (Argive): IE r, *\*sued-*, separated, separate, apart, akin to L *sed* and privative prefix *sē-*. Gr *idios* has the foll derivatives relevant to E:

*idiōtēs*, a private person (not holding public office), hence an ignorant person, L *idiōtēs*, *idiōtā*, with additional sense 'a simple-minded person', MF *idiote. ydiot*, EF-F *idiot*, E *idiot*, with modern sense; whence *idiocy* (cf *accuracy* from *accurate*)—cf F *idiotie*;

hence *idiōtikos*, L *idiōticus*, ignorant, E *idiotic*; *idioun*, to make proper, render peculiar, whence *idiōma*, LL *idiōma*, EF-F *idiome* and E *idiom*;

hence *idiōmatikos*, whence F *idiomatique* and E *idiomatic*;

*idiosunkrasia* (ἰδιοσυγκρασία)—whence *idiosyn-crasy*—var of *-sunkrasis*, a blending, itself=*sun*, with+*krasis*, from *kerannunai*, to mix: cf the element *-crase*.

**idle** (adj, hence n and v, whence **idler**); **idleness,** whence archaic contr **idlesse.**

*Idleness* derives from OE *īdelnes* (*-nes*, E *-ness*, abstract suffix)—cf the OFris *īdelnisse*—from OE *īdel*, vain, useless, empty, whence ME *idel*, E *idle*:

and OE *īdel* is akin to OFris *īdel* (cf the adv *īdle*), OS *īdal*, OHG *ital*, MHG *itel*, G *eitel*, MD *idel*, *ydel*, D *ijdel*: o.o.o.: perh cf Gr *aithein* (s *aith-*), to burn, *aithōn*, burning, smoky, with basic idea of a brightness that has little substance: cf EDIFY.

**idol, idolater, idolatry, idolize.** See IDEA, para 4.

**idyl** (**idyll**), **idyllic.** See IDEA, para 5.

**if,** whence the coll adj **iffy,** extremely hypo-thetical, hence risky: ME *if*, earlier *gif*: OE *gif*, akin to OFris *jef* (occ *jeft*), *ef*, *jof*, *of*, OS *ef*, *of*, if, OHG *ibu*, *uba*, *oba*, MHG *obe* or *ob*, G *ob*, whether, if, MD *of* (as in D), *off*, *ofte*, *ocht*, *ochte*, Go *jabai*, if, whether, and *ibai*, lest, ON *ef*, if: orig, perh an instrumental of a Gmc n for 'doubt'—cf OHG *iba*, doubt—in sense 'on (the) doubt that', hence 'on condition that', as Webster and Walshe suggest; perh rather from the OG r of 'to *give*'—cf OFris *jeft*, if, alongside *jeft*, a gift—in sense '*granted* that', hence 'suppose . . .', hence 'if'.

**igneous; ignescent; ignite, ignition;** cf L *ignis fatuus*, 'foolish [cf FATUITY] fire', the gleam (E *will-o'-the-wisp*) that, arising from marshy ground, tends to mislead travellers; cf the element *igne(o)-* or *igni-*.

L *ignis*, fire, a fire, IE etymon *\*egnis*: cf Skt *agnís*, fire; Hit *Agnis* (? Fire-God); OSl *ogni*, Lith *ugnis*, Lett *uguns*, fire. Derivative adj *igneus* becomes E *igneous*; derivative *ignītus*, on fire, leads to LL *ignīre*, to set on fire, pp *ignītus*, whence 'to *ignite*'; (from *ignis*) inch LL *ignescere*, to become hot, catch fire, has presp *ignescens*, o/s *ignescent-*, whence the E adj *ignescent*. *Ignition*, E and F, app derives from L *ignītus*, but as if from L *\*ignītiō*, o/s *\*ignītiōn-*.

**ignoble.** See NOBLE.

**ignominious, ignominy.** See NAME, para 10.

**ignoramus; ignorance, ignorant; ignoration, ignore.**

L *ignōrāre*, not to know, derives from *ignārus*, not knowing, ignorant: *ig-*, for *in-*, not+*gnārus*, knowing, well-informed, akin to OL *gnōscere* (L *nōscere*), to begin to know: cf *gnostic* and, f.a.e., KNOW.

*Ignoramus* is prop the L for 'we do not know'; *ignorant*=L *ignorant-*, o/s of *ignorans*, presp of *ignorāre*, and *ignorance*=derivative L *ignorantia*; *ignoration* comes from L *ignorātiō*, from the pp *ignorātus*; *ignore*—prob via MF-F *ignorer*, from *ignorāre*.

**iguana;** Aus coll form **guana**—carried still further in **goanna; Iguanodon.**

The last is a SciL cpd: *iguana*+*-odon*, connoting 'teeth'. *Iguana*, adopted from Sp, is of Caribbean origin, prob from Carib *ihuana* or *iuana*; cf the extinct Taino *iguana*.

**ileum.** See ILIUM.

**ileus.** See the 1st JADE, s.f.

**ilex:** L *īlex*, holm-oak: ? akin to Gr *aigilops*, an oak bearing edible acorns; if so, prob of Medit origin.

**iliac.** See JADE.

**Iliad** (Homer's): L *Iliad-*, o/s of *Ilias* (gen *Iliadis*): Gr *Ilias* (gen *Iliados*), elliptical for *Ilias*

*poiēsis*, poem about *Ilios* or *Ilion*, Ilium, city of
*Ilos*, son of Tros, the founder of Troy, poetically
*Ilium.*

**ilium** and **ileum**, An terms, are adopted from L,
where they represent varr of *īle*, refashioned from
*īlia*, flanks, the groin: o.o.o.

**ilk**, n, arises from 'of that *ilk*', of the same (sc
'estate, property'): Sc *ilk*: ME *ilke*, the same:
OE *ilca*, itself a cpd of the r in Go *is*, he (cf L *is*,
that one)+OE *gelīc*, like (adj).

**ill** (adj, hence adv), whence **illness**, derives,
through ME *ill*, from ON *illr*; the E n *ill* is adopted
from the ON n *ill*, evil, bad health, intimately akin
to *illr*, evil, in bad health, itself o.o.o., but perh
either akin to OIr *elc*, worthless, evil, or deriving
from ON *īthila*, akin to OFris, OE *īdel*, worthless,
vain (see IDLE).

**illation, illative.** See the 1st TOLL, para 6.

**illegal, illegality.** See LEGAL, para 2, s.f.

**illegible.** See LEGEND.

**illegitimacy, illegitimate.** See LEGAL, para 4, s.f.

**illiberal.** See LIBERAL, para 2.

**illicit.** See LICENCE, para 1.

**illimitable.** See LIMIT, para 3, s.f.

**illiterate,** whence **illiteracy.** See LETTER, para 3,
s.f.

**illness.** See ILL.

**illogic, illogical.** See LEGEND, para 21, s.f.

**illude.** See LUDICROUS, para 7.

**illume, illuminate, illumination,** etc. See the 3rd
LIGHT, para 16.

**illusion, illusive.** Cf ILLUDE, but see LUDICROUS,
para 7.

**illustrate, illustration, illustrative, illustrator;
illustrious.** See the 3rd LIGHT, para 18.

**image** (n, hence v—cf the F *imager*—and
**imagist**), **imagery; imaginable, imaginary, imagination, imaginative, imagine; imago, imaginal;—
imitable** (and **inimitable**), **imitate, imitation,
imitative, imitator.**—Cf the sep EMULATE (EMULA-
TION).

1. *Image* is adopted from OF-F *image*, a shortening of OF *imagene*, from L *imāginem*, acc of
*imāgō*, o/s *imāgin*-: from the r of *imitāri* (para 3).
Derivative MF *imagerie*, adopted by ME, becomes
*imagery*. The L *imāgō* is retained, but given new
senses, by E Zoo and Psy, with adj *imaginal*, perh
suggested by the LL adj *imāginālis*, figurative.

2. *Imāgō* has derivative LL v *imāgināri* (*im*- for
*in*, into), occ *imāgināre*, to form an image of,
whether in one's own or another's mind, whence
MF-F *imaginer*, whence 'to *imagine*'; derivative
LL *imāginābilis* yields, perh via MF-F, *imaginable*;
LL *imāginārius, imaginary*, perh via late MF-F
*imaginaire*; LL *imāginātiō*, o/s *imāginātiōn*-,
OF-F *imagination*, adopted by E; MF-F *imaginatif*,
f *imaginative* (app *imagina*tion+-*if*, -*ive*), adopted
by E.

3. L *imāgō*=*im*-, to picture+-*āgō* (cf *uorāgō*
from *uorāre*). This r *im*- (o.o.o.) occurs—perh
rather, it recurs—in L *imitāri* (OL -*are*), to seek to
reproduce the image of, to imitate. (E & M.)
*Imitāri* has pp *imitātus*, whence 'to *imitate*'.

Derivative LL *imitābilis* and its LL neg *inimitābilis*
become, via F, the E *imitable, inimitable*; derivative L *imitātiō*, o/s *imitātiōn*-, becomes MF-F and
E *imitation*; LL *imitātīuus*, ML -*īvus*, becomes
*imitative*; L agent *imitātor* is adopted by E—cf
the MF-F *imitateur*.

**imbecile** (adj, hence n), **imbecil(l)ity.**

The latter comes, via MF-F *imbécillité*, from L
*imbēcillitās*, feebleness, o/s *imbēcillitāt*-, from L
*imbēcillus*, feeble, whence late MF-F *imbécile*, E
*imbecile*: an *im*- for *in*-, not, derivative from *baculum*, a staff: lit, therefore, 'without staff' or 'unable
to grasp a staff'. Cf BACILLUS.

**imbibe:** L *imbibere*, to drink (*bibere*) in (*im*- for
*in*-, in, into): f.a.e., BIBULOUS.

**imbricate, imbrication.** See NEBULA, para 5.

**imbroglio.** See the 2nd BROIL, para 2.

**imbrue:** ME *embrewen, embrowen*, to stain: MF
*embreuver*, to soak: VL *\*imbiberāre*, from *bibere*,
to drink. Cf IMBIBE and BEVER.

**imbue.** See NEBULA, para 6.

**imitate, imitation, imitative, imitator.** See
IMAGE, para 3.

**immaculate.** See the 1st MAIL, para 1, s.f.

**immanence, immanent.** See MANOR, para 6.

**immaterial.** See MATTER, para 1, s.f.

**immature, immaturity.** See MATURE, para 4.

**immeasurable.** See MEASURE, para 5.

**immediacy, immediate.** See MEDIAL, para 8.

**immemorable, immemorial.** See MEMORY, paras 4
and 5.

**immense, immensity.** See MEASURE, para 8.

**immeasurable.** See MEASURE, para 5.

**immerge, immerse, immersion.** See MERGE,
para 4.

**immigrant, immigration.** See MIGRANT, para 4.

**imminence, imminent.** See MINATORY, para 3.

**immission, immit.** See MISSION, para 12.

**immitigable.** See MITIGATE, para 2, s.f.

**immix, immixture.** See MIX, para 9.

**immobile, immobility, immobilize.** See MOVE,
para 5.

**immoderate.** See MODAL, para 5, s.f.

**immodest.** See MODAL, para 7, s.f.

**immolate, immolation.** See the 2nd MEAL,
para 12.

**immoral, immorality.** See MORAL, para 4.

**immortal, immortality, immortalize.** See MORTAL,
para 1.

**immovable.** See MOVE (heading).

**immune, immunity, immunize.** See the 1st MEAN,
para 5.

**immure.** See MURAL.

**immutable.** See MUTABLE, para 6.

**imp,** n (whence adj **impish**) and v.

*Imp*, a shoot, a graft or scion, hence a child,
hence a mischievous child, derives from OE *impa*,
from OE *impian*, to engraft, hence to fasten
(wings) on, whence 'to *imp*' and *impian*, s *imp*-,
comes from LL *impotus*, a graft, from Gr *emphutos*,
engrafted, from *emphuein*, to implant: *en*, in(to)+
*phuein* (s *phu*-), to produce: f.a.e., PHYSIC.

**impact.** See PACT, para 4.

impair, adj and n. See PAIR, para 3.
impair (v), impairment. See PESSIMISM, para 3.
impale. See PACT, para 9.
impalpable. See FEEL, para 4.
impanate, impanation. See PANTRY, para 11.
imparity. See PAIR, para 3.
impart, impartial. See PART, para 21 and heading.
impartible. See PART, para 4.
impassable. See PACE, para 4.
impasse. See PACE, para 4.
impassible; impassion, impassionate, impassioned; impassive, impassivity. See PATIENCE, resp. paras 2—4, s.f.—5.
impasto. See PASTE, para 3.
impatience, impatient. See PATIENCE, para 2.
impeach, impeachment. See FOOT, para 12.
impeccable. See PECCABLE.
impecunious. See PECULIAR, para 5, s.f.
impedance, impede, impediment, impedimenta. See FOOT, para 11.
impel. See the 2nd PULSE, para 12.
impend. See PEND, para 21.
impenetrable. See PENATES, para 1.
impenitence, impenitent. See PAIN, para 5.
imperative; imperator, imperatrix. See EMPEROR, para 2, s.f., and para 1; cf PARE, para 4.
imperceptible. See CAPABILITY, para 7.
imperfect, imperfection. See PERFECT, para 2.
imperforate. See PERFORATE.
imperial, imperialism, etc.; imperious. See EMPEROR, para 2.
imperil. See PERIL (heading).
imperishable. See PERISH.
impermanence, -manent. See MANOR.
impersonal, impersonate. See PERSON, para 3 and heading.
impertinence, impertinent. See PERTAIN, para 2.
imperturbable. See TURBID.
impervious. See VIA, para 15 (at pervius).
impetigo. See PETITION, para 5.
impetrate, impetration. See FATHER, para 8.
impetuosity, impetuous, impetus. See PETITION, para 5.
impiety. See PITY, para 3.
impinge, impingement. See PACT, para 4.
impious. See PITY, para 3.
implacable. See PLEASE, para 2.
implant, implantation. See the 2nd PLANT, para 3.
implement. See PLENARY, para 14.
implicate, implication; implicit. See PLY, para 14.
imploration, implore. See DEPLORE, para 2.
implosion. Anl with EXPLOSION, q.v. at PLAUDIT.
imply. See PLY, para 15.
impolite. See POLISH, para 3.
imponderable. See PEND, para 12.
imponent. See POSE, para 11.
import; importance, important; importation, importer. See the 3rd PORT, para 9.
importunate, importune, importunity. See the 2nd PORT, para 7.

impose, whence pa imposing; imposition. See POSE, para 11.
impossibility, impossible. See POSSE, para 2.
impost, impostor, imposture. See POSE, para 11.
impôt. See POSE, para 11.
impotence, impotent. See POSSE, para 4.
impound. See POUND, enclosure.
impoverish, impoverishment. See POOR, para 1, s.f.
impracticable, impractical. See PRACTIC, heading and para 4.
imprecant, imprecate, imprecation. See PRAY, para 5.
impregnable. See PREHEND, para 11A.
impregnate, impregnation. See NATIVE, para 9, s.f.
impress (1), to levy. See the 1st PRESS, para 2.
impress (2), to stamp; impression, impressive. See the 2nd PRESS, para 8.
imprest, a levy, a loan. See the 1st PRESS, para 2.
imprimatur; imprint, See the 2nd PRESS, paras 8 and 9.
imprison, imprisonment. See PREHEND, para 4, s.f.
improbable. See PROVE, para 3.
improbation. See PROVE, para 9.
improbity. See PROVE, para 2.
impromptu. See EXEMPT, para 11.
improper, impropriety; impropriate. See PROPER, paras 2 and 5.
improve, whence improvement, improver; approve, to profit by; prow, adj, and prowess; prude, prudery, prudish.

1. The archaic prow, brave, derives, as ME, from OF prou (var preu, F preux), acc of proz, from VL *prōdis, useful, profitable, from LL prōde, used for prō, forward, in prōde est, instead of L prōdest, to be useful. (B & W.) OF proz has derivative OF-MF proece, proesce (F prouesse): whence E prowess.

2. EF prude derives from MF preude femme, a strong woman, a modest one, preude being the f of preu, var of prou (as above); EF-F prude is adopted by E, whence prudish; prudery comes from EF-F pruderie, from EF prude.

3. Legal approve, to profit by, derives from MF-E aprover, to cause to profit: a-, L ad, to+ *prover, from OF proz or L prōd- (in prōdest)—as in para 1. Derivative MF-EF approuvement yields legal approvement.

4. 'To improve' alters C16-17 emprove, from C15-16 emprowe or emprow: F en+prou (as in para 1).
improvidence, improvident. See VIDE (heading).
improvisation, improvise: F improvisation, anl from F improviser, from It improvvisare, from improvviso, from ML imprōvisus, L imprōuīsus: im- for in-, not+prouīsus, pp of prouīdēre: cf VIDE, para 14.
imprudence, imprudent. See PRUDENCE.
impudence, impudent. See PUDENCY, s.f.
impudicity. See PUDENCY.
impugn. See PUNGENT, para 16.

**impuissance, impuissant.** See POSSE, para 5.

**impulse, impulsion, impulsive.** See the 2nd PULSE, para 12.

**impunity.** See PAIN, para 4.

**impure, impurity.** See PURE, para 2.

**imputable, imputation, impute.** See the 2nd COUNT, para 3.

**imsonic.** See SONABLE, para 5.

**in,** adv (whence adj) and prep, whence the cpd **into; inner, inmost,** whence—after *inner*—*innermost;*—**inn; inning,** usu **innings.**

1. An *inn* comes from OE *inn*, a place within, i.e. a room, a house, akin to ON *inni*, a house, and also to—indeed, prob deriving from—the OE adv *inn* (*inne*), within, esp indoors. This OE adv has derivative *innung*, a taking in, a gathering (cf OFris *inning*), an enclosing, hence the modern games sense.

2. OE *inn, inne,* within, internally, has comp *innerra* (cf OFris *inra* and OHG *innaro*), whence E *inner*; it also has the double sup *innemest*, id in ME, whence, by confusion with *most*, the E *inmost*.

3. That OE adv *inn(e)*, whence the E adv *in*, is intimately akin to—prob it derives from—the OE prep *in*, whence the E prep *in*: and this OE prep *in* is akin to OFris, OS, OHG-G, MD-D, Go *in*, ON *ī* (by lost *-n* and lengthened *i*-); OIr *in*-; OP *en*; OL *en*, L *in*; Cretan and Cyprian Gr *in*, Gr *en*. The IE etymon is *\*en*.

**inability.** See HABIT, para 5.

**inaccessible** (LL *inaccessibilis*, neg of LL *accessibilis*): f.a.e., CEDE.

**inaccuracy, inaccurate:** cf *accuracy, accurate*, qq.v. at CURE.

**inactive, inactivity.** Cf *active*-: see ACT.

**inadequacy, inadequate.** See EQUAL, para 7.

**inadvertence, inadvertent.** See VERSE, para 15.

**inalienable.** See ALIAS.

**inamorata, -ato.** See AMATEUR, 11, 3.

**inane.** See VACANT, para 13.

**inanimate.** See ANIMAL, para 5.

**inanition, inanity.** See VACANT, para 13.

**inappropriate.** See PROPER.

**inarticulate.** See ARTICULATE.

**inattention, inattentive.** See TEND, para 7.

**inaudible.** See AUDIBLE, para 2.

**inaugural, inaugurate, inauguration.** See AUGMENT, para 5, s.f.

**incalculable.** See CALCAREOUS.

**incandescence, incandescent.** See CANDID, para 2.

**incantation, incantatory.**

The latter is an anl E formation, perh prompted by L *incantātor*, an enchanter; the former, adopted from MF-F, comes from LL *incantātiō* (o/s *incantātiōn*-), enchantment, from *incantātus*, pp of *incantāre*, to chant (*cantāre*) a spell over (connoted by *in*-) someone: cf *enchant* (enchantment) and CANT (2).

**incapability, incapable; incapacitate, incapacity.** See CAPABILITY, esp para 2.

**incarcerate, incarceration.** See CANCEL, para 2.

**incarnadine.** See CARNAGE, para 2.

**incarnate, incarnation.** See CARNAGE, para 2.

**incautious.** See CAUTION, para 3.

**incendiary.** See CANDID, para 3.

**incense.** See CANDID, para 3.

**incentive:** L *incentīuus*, setting the tune.

**inception, inceptive.** See CAPABILITY, para 7.

**incertitude.** See CERTAIN, para 4.

**incessant.** See CEASE, s.f.

**incest, incestuous.** See CASTE, para 5.

**inch.** See ONE, para 5.

**inchoacy** = *inchoate* + -*cy*: **inchoate** derives from L *inchoātus*, irreg for *incohātus*, pp of *incohāre*, to begin: o.o.o.: perh *in*, into, onto + *cohum*, that part of the yoke to which the shaft is attached. Derivative **inchoātiō** (o/s *inchoātiōn*-), irreg for *incohātiō*, yields **inchoation.**

**incidence, incident, incidental.** See CADENCE, para 7.

**incinerate, incineration, incinerator.** See CINDER, para 5.

**incipient.** See CAPABILITY, para 7.

**incise, incision, incisive, incisor.**

L *caedere*, to cut (cf *ceasura*), has cpd *incīdere*, to cut into, with pp *incīsus*, whence the E Bot and Zoo adj, and the v, **incise;** derivative L *incīsiō* (o/s *incīsiōn*-) and ML *incīsīvus* and LL *incīsor* (surgeon) yield E **incision** (prob imm from MF-F), **incisive** (perh via MF-F *incisif*), **incisor**—with special Zoo sense.

**incite, incitement.** See CITE, para 4.

**incivility:** MF-F *incivilité*: LL *incīuīlitātem,* acc of *incīuīlitās* (ML -*cīvīlitās*): cf *civil*, q.v. at CITY.

**inclemency, inclement.** See CLEMENCY, para 2.

**inclinable, inclination, incline** (n, v). See CLIME, para 9.

**inclose, inclosure.** Anglicized varr of **enclose, enclosure.**

**include, inclusion, inclusive.** See CLAUSE.

**incognito,** adopted from It, derives from L *incognitus*, not (*in*-) known (*cognitus*): f.a.e., CAN, v.

**incoherence** = *incoherent* + -*ce*; **incoherent** = *in*-, not + *coherent*, q.v. at COHERE: f.a.e., HESITATE.

**income.** See COME, para 3.

**incommensurable, incommensurate.** See MEASURE, para 6, s.f.

**incommode, incommodious.** See MODAL, para 13.

**incommunicable.** See COMMON, para 4.

**incomparable.** See PAIR, para 9.

**incompatibility, incompatible.** See PATIENCE, para 7, s.f.

**incompetence, incompetent.** See COMPETE, para 1.

**incomplete.** See COMPLEMENT, para 1.

**incomprehensible, incomprehension.** See PREHEND, para 8.

**inconceivable.** See CAPABILITY, para 7.

**incongruence, incongruent; incongruity, incongruous.** See CONGRUENCE, para 1.

**inconscient.** See SCIENCE (heading).

**inconsequence, inconsequent.** See SEQUENCE, para 8, s.f.

**inconsiderable, inconsiderate.** See CONSIDER.

**inconsistency, inconsistent.** See SIST, para 3.

**inconsolable.** See SOLACE.

inconstancy, inconstant. See STAND.
incontaminable. See TACT, para 14.
incontestable. See TESTAMENT, para 8.
incontinence, incontinent. See CONTAIN, para 2, s.f.
inconvenience, inconvenient. See CONVENE, para 1, and cf VENUE, para 14.
incorporate, adj and v; incorporation. See CORPORAL, para 4.
incorporeal. See CORPORAL, para 4.
incorrect. See REX, para 27.
incorrigible. See REX, para 27.
incorrupt, -ible, -ion. See RUPTURE, para 4.
increase. See CRESCENT, para 8.
incredible; incredulous. See CREED, para 3.
increment; increscent. See CRESCENT, para 8.
incriminate, incrimination. See CRIME, para 4.
incrust; incrustation: EF-F incruster, L incrustāre, to cover with a crust, f.a.e., CRUST; perh via EF-F incrustation, from derivative LL incrustātiō, o/s incrustātiōn-.
incubate, incubation, incubator; incubus. See HIVE, para 6.
inculcate, inculcation. See KICK, s.f.
inculpate, inculpation. See CULPABLE, para 2.
incumbency, incumbent. See HIVE, para 8.
incunabula, whence the adj incunabular, is adopted from the L pl incūnābula, a cradle, a birthplace: in-, in+cūnābula, from *cūnāre, to cradle, from cūnae, a cradle: o.o.o.
incur. See COURSE, para 10 (at incurrere).
incurable (LL incurabilis): f.a.e., CURE. Cf:
incurious. See CURE, para 2, s.f.
incursion. See COURSE, para 10 (at incurrere).
incus. See the 2nd HACK, para 8.
ind. See INDIA.
indebted. See DEBT, para 4.
indecency, indecent. See DECENCY, para 1.
indecision, indecisive. See DECIDE, para 3.
indeclinable. Cf decline; see -cline at CLIME.
indecorous, indecorum. See DECENCY, para 3.
indeed. See DO.
indefatigable. See FATIGUE.
indefinite: L indēfinītus: in-, not+dēfinītus, defined: cf DEFINE.
indelible. See DELETE.
indelicate. See DELICACY.
indemnification, indemnify, indemnity. See DAMN, para 5.
indent, indentation, indention, indenture. See TOOTH, para 8.
independence, independent. See PEND, para 16, s.f.
indeterminable, indeterminate, indeterminism. See TERM, para 5.·
index. See DICT, para 13.
India (cf poetic Ind); India ink, Indiaman, India rubber (now usu indiarubber); Indian, adj (from India), hence n; Indian corn—I. file—I. hemp—I. red—I. summer; Indiana, orig Indiana Territory (ref Red Indians); Indic; indic, indican, indigo, indium, indole, indolin(e), indulin.—Indus.—Hindi; Hindu (obsol Hindoo), Hinduism, Hindustan,
Hindustani;—Scinde, Sind or Sindh; Sindhi; sendal, sindon.—tamarind.

1. India is L from Gr India, a Geog -ia ('region') derivative of Indos, whence L, hence E, Indus, the river; Gr Indos itself derives from OPer and Av Hindu, India, akin to Skt sindhu, a river, hence Sindhu, the river Indus, hence the region traversed by that river.

2. Skt Sindhu becomes both E Sindh, often written Sind, archaic Scinde, and Ar Sind, with adj Sindī, used as n, and usu represented by E as Sindhi.

3. Skt Sindhu, the region of the Indus, has Gr derivative sindōn, linen—later, cotton—of Sind, whence L sindon, a fine fabric, adopted by E, although now only hist; L sindon becomes, with different suffix (-al), the MF-EF cendal, whence E cendal or sendal.

4. OPer and Av Hindu, India, becomes Per Hind, with derivative Hindū, a native of India, adopted by AE, the E usage preferring the sense 'a follower of Hinduism' (Hindu+-ism), a non-Moslem native. Per Hindu has derivative Hindūstān, the country (-stan: cf Pakistan) of the Hindu: whence the Hindustani word Hindūstānī, an Indian, used in E as adj, hence as Hindustani, the most important dial (with sub-dialect Urdu) of W Hindi. Hindi represents Hind hindī (adj used as n), from Hind Hind, India, adopted from Per.

5. Hind, India, is also the Ar form, with adj hindī, which occurs in tamār hindī, the Indian date (tamar or tamr, prop a dried date): whence—cf the late MF-F tamarin (earlier tamarinde)—the Port, Sp, It tamarindo, whence E tamarind, the tree Tamarindus indica.

6. That indica is the f of L Indicus, belonging to India, from Gr Indikos, the adj of Gr India: whence E Indic.

7. But indic is the E adj of Chem E indium, itself a SciL formation: L indicum (neu of Indicus)+Chem -ium.

8. Gr Indikos, Indian, has neu Indikon, which, used as n indikon, means either the indigo plant or its product: indikon becomes L indicum, whence Sp índico, with var índigo: whence E and F indigo. L indicum, indigo, has the Sci derivative indican: indicum+Chem suffix -an (-ane). E indigo has derivative indol or indole: indigo+Chem -ol (-ole); and indol(e) has subsidiary indolin or indoline, the suffix being Chem -in or -ine; cf indulin or induline, which suggests a loose blend—influenced by indolin(e)—of indigo+anilin or aniline.

9. India (para 1) has many cpds, the etym most notable being perh:
India ink, or Indian ink, orig came from China (whence China, or Chinese, ink)—prob via India;
Indiaman, orig an East India Company sailing vessel—for the -man, cf 'man-of-war';
India rubber, caoutchouc or rubber, the rubber tree being traditionally associated with India, but mostly growing further E.

10. Indian, however, has far more cpds, some of them associated with the West Indies, so named

by Columbus, who thought he had sailed so far W as to have reached the E Indies. Among them are these:

Indian corn, orig maize grown by the Red Indians;

Indian file, in, in single file—the customary Red Indian method of passing through a wood;

Indian hemp, the common hemp of India, whence a variety cultivated in NA;

Indian red, prop but less usu Persian red, is a pigment deriving from a reddish, iron-bearing earth coming orig from the Persian Gulf;

Indian summer, an, mild, sunny weather in late autumn (or even in early winter), comes from NA and perh orig referred to the longer period of activity afforded to the Indians.

indican. See INDIA, para 8.

indicate, indication, indicative, indicator. See DICT, para 14.

indict, indictment. See DICT, para 7 (at indicere).

indifference, indifferent. See DIFFER.

indigence, indigent.

Indigence, adopted from MF-F, derives from L indigentia, neediness, from indigent-, o/s of indigens, presp of indigēre, to be in need of: indu, within+egēre, to be needy, to lack or need: several dubious cognates in OGmc. Indigent, adopted from MF-F, comes from L indigentem, acc of presp indigens.

indigenous. See GENERAL, para 21.

indigestible, indigestion. See GERUND, para 11.

indignant, indignation; indignity. See DECENCY, para 5.

indigo. See INDIA, para 8.

indirect, indirection. See REX, para 30.

indiscreet, indiscretion; indiscrete. See DISCREET, s.f.

indiscriminate, indiscrimination. See DISCRIMIN-ANT, s.f.

indispensable. See PENSION, para 19.

indisposed, indisposition. See POSE.

indisputable. See PUTATIVE.

indissoluble. See LOSE, para 4.

indistinct, indistinguishable. See STICK.

indite. See DICT, para 7 (at indicere).

indium. See INDIA, para 7.

individual (adj, n), -ism, -ist, -ity, -ize; individ-uate, individuation. See DIVIDE, para 1.

indivisible. See DIVIDE, para 3.

indoctrinate, indoctrination. See DOCILE, para 2 (at doctrina).

Indo-European: Gr Indo- (c/f of Indos, see INDIA)+European, q.v. at EUROPE.

indol(e). See INDIA, para 8.

indolence, indolent.

The former comes, perh via MF-F indolence, from LL indolentia, freedom from pain, from indolent- (whence EF-F and E indolent), o/s of indolens, adj formed of in-, not+dolens, presp of dolēre, to be in pain: cf DOLOR.

indolin(e). See INDIA, para 8.

indomitable. See TAME.

indoor, adj, and indoors, adv: in, within+DOOR.

indorse, indorsement. Var of endorse; see DORSAL.

indubitable. See DOUBT, para 2, s.f.

induce, inducement; induction, inductive. See DUKE, para 6 (at inducere).

indue. See DUKE, para 9 (at endue).

indulge, indulgent. See LONG, para 12

indulin(e). See INDIA, para 8.

indurate, induration. See DURABLE, para 3.

Indus. See INDIA, para 1.

industrial (whence industrialism, industrialist, industrialize); industrious, industry. See STRUC-TURE, para 7.

inebriate, inebriation. See EBRIETY, para 3.

ineffable. See FABLE, para 4.

ineffaceable. See FACE, para 5, s.f.

ineffective; ineffectual; inefficacious, inefficient, and their nn. Merely the negg of effective, effectual, efficacious, efficient: cf EFFECT.

inelegance, inelegant. The negg of elegance, elegant: see LEGEND, para 10, s.f.

ineligibility, ineligible. See LEGEND, para 8, s.f.

ineluctable, inevitable. See RELUCTANCE, para 2.

inenarrable. See NARRATE, s.f.

inept, ineptitude. See APT, para 3.

inequality. See EQUAL, para 3.

inequitable, inequity. See EQUAL, para 6.

ineradicable. See RADICAL, para 8.

inert, inertia.

The latter, adopted from L, derives from L iners, o/s inert-, unskilled, whence E inert: in-, not+-ers, o/s -ert-, c/f of ars, o/s art-, q.v. at ART.

inessential=in-, not+essential, q.v. at ESSE.

inestimable: OF: L inaestimabilis, not reckon-able: f.a.e., ESTEEM.

inevitability, inevitable. See EVITABLE, para 2.

inexact, -itude. The neg of exact, q.v. at ACT.

inexcusable. See CAUSE, para 7.

inexhaustible. See EXHAUST, s.f.

inexistence, inexistent. See SIST, para 5.

inexorable. See ORATION, para 6.

inexpiable. See PITY, para 4.

inexplicable. See PLY, para 12.

inexpressible. See PRESS.

inexpugnable. See PUNGENT, para 15.

inexterminable. See TERM, para 7, s.f.

inextricable. See EXTRICATE, para 3.

infallibility, infallible. Cf fallible; see FAIL.

infamous, infamy. See FAME, para 3.

infancy, infant, Infanta; infanticide; infantile; infantry.

1. L infans, o/s infant-, c/f infanti- (as in infanticide: LL infanticīdium, child-murder), is lit a non-speaker: in-, not+fans, presp of fāri, to speak (cf FABLE). E infant is a Renaissance re-shaping of ME enfaunt, from OF-F enfant, from L infantem, acc of infans; derivative L infantia yields infancy—cf F enfance. Infanta, daughter of a Sp or a Port king, is the f of Infante, son thereof: from L infant-. The L adj infantilis yields infantile.

In LL, *infans* came to mean youth, young man, son, whence It *infante*, with further sense 'foot soldier', itself having derivative *infanteria*, foot-soldiery, whence EF-F *infanterie*, whence E *infantry*.

**infatuate, infatuation.** See VAPID.

**infect, infectant, infection, infectious, infective; disinfect, disinfectant, disinfection.**

1. 'To *infect*' derives from L *infectus*, pp of *inficere*, to put in, hence to steep, hence to stain or colour, hence to corrupt, to infect: *in-*, in+-*ficere*, c/f of *facere*, to put, to make: f.a.e., FACT. The L pp *infectus* becomes the MF adj *infect*, whence late MF-F *infecter*, with presp *infectant*, whence the E adj, later n, *infectant*. Derivative LL *infectiō*, o/s *infection-*, leads, via MF-F, to E *infection*, whence —three centuries earlier than F *infectieux*— *infectious*; *infective* comes, perh via MF-F *infectif*, from L *infectīuus*, ML *-īvus*, of, by, for dyeing.

2. Late MF-F *infecter* has EF-F subsidiary *désinfecter*, whence 'to *disinfect*'; its presp *désin-fectant* becomes the E adj, hence n, *disinfectant*.

**infelicitous, infelicity.** See FELICITATE, para 3.

**infer; inference,** whence **inferential** (cf *conse-quence—consequential*).

*Inference* derives from scholastic ML *inferentia*, an *-ia* derivative from *inferent-*, o/s of *inferens*, presp of *inferō*, I carry in(to), ML I logically deduce: *in*, in(to)+*ferō*, I carry: f.a.e., FERTILE.

**inferior, inferiority; infernal; inferno.**

*Inferior* is adopted from L, where it forms the comp of the adj *inferus*, situated below, akin to the syn Skt *ádharas*. L *inferior* becomes late MF-F *inférieur*, whence (reshaped by L *inferior*) EF-F *infériorité*, whence E *inferiority.—*L *inferus* has the doublet *infernus*, which in LL becomes *Infernus*, Hell, whence It *Inferno* (as in Dante), whence the generalized *inferno*, adopted by E. LL *Infernus* has derivative adj *infernālis*, whence, prob via OF-F, the E *infernal*, orig as in 'the *infernal* regions', euphem for hell.

**infertile** and **infertility** come, via Renaissance F, from LL *infertilis* and its derivative *infertilitās*: f.a.e., FERTILE.

**infest:** MF-F *infester*: LL *infestāre*, to infest, L to attack, from L *infestus*, directed at (*in-*), esp against, hence hostile: cf L mani*festus* (E *manifest*), app 'taken i n, or brought to, the hand (*manus*)', hence 'evide nt', *-festus* being prob akin either to Skt *dharṣati* he attacks, or to L *ferre*, to bring. (Webster; E & M; mdfn, E.P.) The derivative LL *infestātiō*, o/s *infestātiōn-*, becomes E *infestation*.

**infidel, infidelity.** See FAITH, para 6.

**infiltrate, infiltration.** See FELT.

**infinite, infinitesimal, infinitive, infinitude, infinity.** See FINAL, para 2, s.f., and 3.

**infirm, infirmary, infirmity.** See FIRM, para 5.

**infix.** See FIX, para 3.

**inflame, inflammable, inflammation, inflamma-tory.** See FLAME, para 3.

**inflate, inflation.** See FLATUS, para 6.

**inflect, inflection; inflex, inflexion.** See FLEX, para 6.

**inflexible.** See FLEX, para 3.

**inflict, infliction.**

The latter derives from LL *inflictiōn-*, o/s of *inflictiō-*, itself deriving from the imm source of 'to *inflict*': L *inflictus*, pp of *infligere*, to strike (*fligere*) something onto(*in-*) somebody, to inflict upon or with: cf CONFLICT.

**inflorescence.** See FLORA, para 14, s.f.

**influence, influential, influenza; influx.** See FLUENT, para 8.

**inform, informal(ity), information, informative, informer.** See FORM, para 6.

**infraction, infractor.** See FRACTION, para 7.

**infrangible.** Cf FRANGIBLE: f.a.e., FRACTION.

**infrequency, infrequent.** See FREQUENCY.

**infringe,** whence **infringement.** See FRACTION, para 7.

**infundibulum.** See 2nd FOUND, para 8.

**infuriate, infuriation.** See FURY, para 2.

**infuse, infusion.** See the 2nd FOUND, para 8.

**ingenious, ingenuity; ingénue, ingenuous.** See GENERAL, para 22, and, from another angle, ENGINE, paras 2–3.

**ingest, ingestible, ingestion.** See GERUND, para 12.

**inglorious**=*in-*, not+*glorious*, q.v.

**ingot.** See the 2nd FOUND, para 19.

**ingrain** is a var of *engrain*, q.v. at GRAIN.

**ingrate, ingratiate, ingratitude.** See GRACE, para 6.

**ingredient.** See GRADE, para 12.

**ingress.** See GRADE, para 13.

**inguinal.** See the element *inguino-*.

**ingurgitate, ingurgitation.** See GORGE, para 3.

**inhabit, inhabitant, inhabitation.** See HABIT, para 10.

**inhalant, inhalation, inhale.** See HALITOSIS, para 3.

**inhere, inherence, inherent.**

*Inherence* comes, perh through EF-F *inhérence*, from scholastic ML *inhaerentia*, itself from *inhaerent-*, o/s of ML *inhaerens*, adj from L *inhaerens*, presp of *inhaerēre*, to cling or stick or be attached (*haerēre*) to (*in-*), whence 'to *inhere*': f.a.e., HESITATE. ML *inhaerent-*, perh aided by EF-F *inhérent*, accounts for E *inherent*.

**inherit, -ance, -or.** See HEIR, para 4.

**inhibit, inhibition.** See HABIT, para 11.

**inhospitable,** adopted from MF-EF, comes from ML *inhospitābilis*: *in-*, not+L *hospitābilis*, hos-pitable: f.a.e., HOSPICE.

**inhuman, inhumane, inhumanity.** See HOMO, para 9.

**inhumation, inhume.** See HOMO, para 10.

**inimical.** See AMATEUR, III, 3.

**inimitable.** See IMAGE, para 3.

**iniquitous, iniquity.** See EQUAL, para 6, s.f.

**initial; initiate, initiation, initiative, initiator, initiatory.**

The L *initiāre*, to set going, is an inch of *inīre*, to enter, hence to begin: f.a.e., ISSUE. Its pp *Initiātus* accounts for 'to *initiate*'; derivative *initiātiō*, o/s *initiātiōn-*, for late MF-F and E *initiation*; the LL agent *initiātor* is adopted by E

—hence prob the adj *initiatory*. *Initiative* is adopted from a learned EF-F derivative from L *initiāre*. *Initial* (adj, hence n) comes from LL *initiālis*, the adj of *initium*, a beginning, itself from *inīre*.

**inject, injection, injector.**

'To *inject*' derives from ML *injectus*, L *injectus*, pp of *iniicere, inicere*, to throw in(to): *in*, in, into+ *-iicere, -icere,* c/f of *iacere,* to throw, very intimately akin to *iacēre*, to be lying on the ground (cf *adjacent*). Derivative *iniectiō*, ML *injectiō*, has o/s *injectiōn-*, whence E *injection*; derivative *iniector* is, in its ML form, adopted by E.

**injudicious.** See DICT, para 17.

**injunction.** See JOIN, para 14

**injure, injurious, injury.** See JURY, para 3, s.f.

**injustice.** See JURY, para 5.

**ink, n,** whence 'to ink' and inky, comes, through ME *inke*, earlier *enke*, from OF-MF *enque* (cf F *encre*), from LL *encaustum*, from Gr *enkauston*, prop the neu s of *enkaustos*, burnt (*kaustos*) in (*en*): f.a.e., CAUSTIC and IN.

**inland, n,** hence adj: *in*, within+LAND.

**inlay, n,** derives from the v: and the v=to LAY in.

**inlet, n,** derives from the partly obs v, which= to LET in. Cf LET, para 2.

**inmate.** See the 1st MATE, s.f.

**inmost.** See IN, para 2.

**inn.** See IN, para 1.

**innascible, innate.** See NATIVE, para 9.

**innavigable.** See NAUTIC, para 7.

**inner.** See IN, para 2.

**innervation, innerve.** See NERVE, para 6.

**inning(s).** See IN, para 1.

**innocence, innocent.** See NOXIOUS, para 2.

**innocuous.** See NOXIOUS, para 3.

**innominable, innominate.** See NAME, para 9, s.f.

**innovate, innovation, innovator.** See NOVA, para 5.

**innuendo.** See NUTANT, para 1, s.f.

**innumerable.** See NIMBLE, para 5.

**inobedience, inobedient.** See AUDIBLE, para 5, s.f.

**inobservance, inobservant.** See OBSERVABLE, s.f.

**inoculate, inoculation.** See OCULAR, para 4.

**inoffensive.** See FEND, para 3, s.f.

**inoperable, inoperative.** See OPERA, para 5.

**inopportune.** Cf *opportune*; see PORT, n, para 7.

**inordinate.** See ORDER, para 12.

**inorganic.** See ORGAN, para 6.

**inquest.** See QUERY, para 10, s.f.

**inquietude.** See QUIET, para 7.

**inquire, inquiry.** See QUERY, para 10.

**inquisition, inquisitive, inquisitor.** See QUERY, para 10.

**insane, insanitary, insanity.** See SANE, para 2.

**insatiable, insatiate.** See SAD, para 3.

**inscience, inscient.** See SCIENCE, para 6.

**inscribe; inscription.** See SCRIBE, para 13.

**inscroll.** See SHRED (heading).

**inscrutable.** See SHRED, para 8.

**insect,** See the 2nd SAW, para 11.

**insecure, insecurity.** See CURE, para 6.

**insemination:** cf sow (2); lit 'an into-sowing'—cf *seminary* (b).

**insensate.** See SENSE, para 3.

**insensibility, insensible; insensitive.** See SENSE, para 4.

**inseparable.** See PARE, para 8.

**insert, insertion.** See SERIES, para 4.

**inside** (adj, adv, n). See SIDE (heading).

**insidiate, insidious.** See SIT, para 14.

**insight:** O.E. *insiht*, a seeing within: *in*+*sight*, q.v. at SEE.

**insignia.** See SIGN, para 15.

**insignificance, insignificant.** See SIGN (heading).

**insincere, insincerity.** See SINCERE.

**insinuate, insinuation.** See SINE, para 4.

**insipid, insipidity.** See the 1st SAGE, para 2.

**insist, insistence, insistent.** See SIST, para 6.

**insolate, insolation.** See SOLAR, para 5.

**insolence, insolent.** See SALLY, para 16.

**insolubility, insoluble; insolvable.** See LOSE, para 7.

**insolvency, insolvent:** negg of *solvency, solvent*: see LOSE.

**insomnia, insomniac.** See SOMNOLENT, para 3.

**insouciance, insouciant.** Ult cf SOLICIT.

**inspect, inspection, inspector.** See SPECTACLE, para 12.

**inspiration, inspire.** See SPIRIT, para 10.

**inspissate,** to thicken (e.g., a liquid): L *inspissātus*, pp of *inspissāre*: *in-*, used int+*spissāre*, from *spissus*, thick: basic idea, 'pressed'.

**instability.** See STABLE.

**install, installation, instalment.** See STALL, para 3.

**instance, instant.** See STAND, para 26.

**instantaneous.** See STAND, para 26.

**instate.** See STAND, para 16.

**instaur, instauration, instaurator.** See STORE, para 1.

**instead.** See STAND (heading).

**instep.** See STEP.

**instigate, instigation, instigator.** See STICK, para 4.

**instil(l), instillation.** See the 3rd STILL, para 2.

**instinct, instinctive.** See STICK, para 7.

**institute, institution.** See STAND, para 27.

**instruct, instruction, instructive, instructor.** See STRUCTURE, para 5.

**instrument, instrumental.** See STRUCTURE, para 6.

**insubordinate, -ation.** See ORDER, para 14, s.f.

**insubstantial,** neg of *substantial*. Cf *substance*— see STAND.

**insufferable.** See SUFFER.

**insufficiency, insufficient.** See SUFFICE.

**insufflate, -flation, -flator.** See FLATUS, para 9.

**insula, insular, insularity.** See the 1st SOLE, para 6.

**insulate, insulation, insulator.** See the 1st SOLE, para 6.

**insulin.** See the 1st SOLE, para 6.

**insult, n and v.** See SALLY, para 15.

**insuperable.** See SUPER, para 3.

**insupportable.** See the 3rd PORT, para 13.

**insurable, insurance, insure.** See CURE, para 9.

insurge, insurgence, insurgent; insurrection. See SURGE, para 3.

insurmountable. See MINATORY, para 10, s.f.

insusceptibility, insusceptible. See CAPABILITY, para 8, s.f.

intact, intactile. See TACT, para 18.

intake. See TAKE, para 2.

intangible. See TACT, para 3.

integer, integral; integrant, integrate, integration; integrity. See TACT, para 16.

integument. See TEGUMENT.

intellect, intellection, intellectual. See LEGEND, para 11.

intelligence, intelligent, intelligentsia; intelligible. See LEGEND, para 11.

intemperance, intemperate. See TEMPER, para 4.

intempestive. See TEMPER, para 9.

intend, intendant. See TEND, paras 12 and 21.

intense, intensify, intension, intensity, intensive. Cf *tense*—see TEND, para 13.

intent (adj and n), intention, intentional, intentive. See TEND, para 14.

inter (v), interment. See TERRA, para 5.

interact, -action. To ACT, an ACTION, between (L *inter*).

intercalary, intercalate, intercalation. See CALENDAR, para 2.

intercede. See CEDE, para 8.

intercept, -ion, -ive, -or. See CAPABILITY, para 7.

intercession, intercessor. See CEDE, para 8.

interchange. See CHANGE, para 5.

intercolumniation. See COLUMN.

intercostal. See COAST, para 2.

intercourse: OF-MF *entrecors*. later *-cours*, exchange, from *entre*, L *inter*, between+*cors*, later *cours*, course: cf *current* and, f.a.e., COURSE.

interdict, interdiction. See DICT, para 7 (at *interdicere*).

interest. See ESSE, para 7.

interfere, interference.

The latter is an *-ence* derivative of the former, which comes from MF-EF *entreferir*, to knock together, orig of a trotting horse: *entre*, L *inter*, between+*ferir*, L *ferīre*, to strike.

interfuse, interfusion. See the 2nd FOUND, para 9.

interim, a meantime: L *interim*, meanwhile: *inter*, between+the temporal-adv suffix *-im* (as in *olim*, formerly). For E n from L adv, cf *alias*.

interior. See EXTERIOR, para 2.

interject, interjection, interjective, interjector.

These words flow from L *interiicere* (*intericere*), to throw between, pp *interiectus*, ML *-jectus*, precisely as *inject, injection,* etc., from L *iniicere*: see INJECT.

interlace. Cf LACE—see DELICACY.

interlard. See LARD.

interline, interlinear. See LINE.

interlocution, interlocutor. See LOQUACIOUS, para 5.

interloper. See LEAP, para 5.

interlude. See LUDICROUS, para 8.

intermeddle. See MIX, para 4, s.f.

intermediary, intermediate. See MEDIAL, para 7.

interment. See TERRA.

intermezzo. See MEDIAL, para 7.

interminable, interminate. See TERM, para 2.

intermission; intermit, intermittent. See MISSION, para 13.

intermix, intermixture. See MIX, para 9.

intermural. See MURAL.

intern, internal. See EXTERIOR, para 2.

international (-ism, -ist, -ize). See NATIVE, para 10.

internecine. See NOXIOUS, para 5.

internment. See EXTERIOR, para 6.

internuncio. See NUNCIO, para 6.

interpel, interpellate, interpellation. See the 2nd PULSE, para 13.

interpolate; interpolation; interpolator: L *interpolātus*, pp cf *interpolāre*, to form anew, hence to falsify by insertion; *interpolātiō*, o/s *-ātiōn-*; LL *interpolātor*: *inter*, between, perh+a derivative of *polīre*, to polish. Cf EXTRAPOLATE.

interpose, interposition. See POSE, para 12.

interpret, -ation, -er. See PRICE, para 7.

interregnum. See REX, para 15.

interrogate, -rogation, -rogative, -rogatory. See ROGATION, para 8.

interrupt, -ion. See RUPTURE, para 7.

interscribe, interscription. See SCRIBE, para 14.

intersect, intersection. See the 2nd SAW, para 12.

intersert, intersertion. See SERIES, para 15.

interspace, interspatial. See SPACE, para 4.

intersperse, interspersion. Cf *disperse*—see SPARSE, para 5.

interstice, interstitial. See STAND, para 28.

interval: MF-F *intervalle*: ML *intervallum*, L *interuallum*, a space *inter*, between, *ualla*, ML *valla*, ramparts or walls: cf WALL.

intervene, intervention. See VENUE, para 15.

interview. Cf *view*—see VIDE, para 14.

intestable, intestacy, intestate. See TESTAMENT, para 6.

intestinal, intestine.

The former=the n *intestine*+adj *-al*, unless it was adopted from EF-F; *intestine*, adj, derives from L *intestīnus* (from *intus*, within, from *in*, in); *intestine*, n, derives from L *intestīna*, orig the neu pl of *intestīnus*.

intima; intimacy, intimate (adj, v), intimation. See EXTERIOR, para 7.

intimidate, intimidation. See TIMID.

intitule. See TITLE, para 5.

into. See IN (heading).

intolerable, intolerance, intolerant. Cf TOLERABLE—see the 1st TOLL, para 5.

intonation, intone. See TEMPER, para 30.

intort, intortion. See TORT, para 10.

intoxicant, intoxicate, intoxication. See TOXIC, para 3.

intractable. See TRACT, para 6.

intransigent, whence *intransigence* (cf the F *intransigeance*), derives from F *intransigeant*, itself from Sp *intransigente*; L *-n-*, not+*transigent-*, o/s of *transigens*, presp of *transigere*, to transact:

*trans*, across+*agere*, to play, do business: f.a.e., ACT.

intransitive. Cf TRANSIT, q.v. at TRANSIENT.

intreat, intreaty. See TRACT, para 17.

intrepid, intrepidity. See TREPID, para 3.

intricacy, intricate. See EXTRICATE, para 4.

intrigue. See EXTRICATE, para 4.

intrinsic. See EXTERIOR, para 5.

introduce, introduction, introductory. See DUKE, para 6 (at *introducere*).

introit: MF-F *introït*: L *intrŏitus* (gen *-ūs*), a going in, from *introïre*: *intrŏ*, within, inwards (cf the prefix *intro-*)+*īre*, supine *itum*, to go: f.a.e., ISSUE.

intromission, whence, anl, the adj intromissive; intromit, intromittent. See MISSION, para 14.

introspect, whence, anl, introspection, introspective.

L *intrŏspicere*, to look inside, has pp *intrŏspectus*, whence 'to *introspect*': prefix *intrŏ-*+-*spicere*, c/f of *specere*, to look: f.a.e., SPECTACLE.

introversion, introvert. See VERSE, para 15.

intrude, whence intruder; intrusion, intrusive. See THRUST, para 5.

intuition, intuitive. See TUITION.

intussusception, the taking up of one part (esp in Med) into another: L *intus*, within+*susception* (*sub*+*capere*, to take)—cf SUSCEPTIBLE.

inumbrate, inumbration. See UMBRA, para 7.

inundant, inundate, inundation. See UNDA, para 4.

inure. See URE.

inutile, inutility. See USE, para 2.

invade, whence invader. See VADE, para 4.

invalid, adj and n; invalidate, invalidation. See VALUE, para 18.

invariable. See VARY.

invasion. See VADE, para 4.

invection, invective; inveigh. See VIA, para 12.

inveigle. See OCULAR, para 5.

invent, invention, inventive, inventor, inventory. See VENUE, para 16.

inverse, inversion, invert. See VERSE, para 15.

invertebrate. See VERSE, para 7, s.f.

invest. See VEST, para 3.

investigable, investigate, investigation, investigator. See VESTIGE, para 2.

investiture, investment, investor. See VEST, heading and para 3.

inveteracy, inveterate. See WETHER, para 6.

invictus. See VICTOR, para 2.

invidious. See VIDE, para 13.

invigilate, etc. See VIGOR, para 6.

invigorate, invigoration. See VIGOR, para 4.

invincible. See VICTOR, para 2.

inviolable, inviolate. See VIS, para 2.

invisibility, invisible. See VIDE, para 2.

invitation, invitator, invite. See VIE, para 2.

invocation. See VOCABLE, para 10.

invoice. See VIA, para 15.

invoke. See VOCABLE, para 10.

involucre. See VOLUBLE, para 4.

involuntary. See VOLITION, para 3.

involute, involution. See VOLUBLE, para 4.

involve. See VOLUBLE, para 4.

invulnerable. See VULN.

inward (adj and adv), whence inwardness; inwardly; inwards, adv. *Inwardly*, adv, derives from OE *inweardlīce*, from the OE adv *inweard*, which consists of OE *in* (E IN)+the element-suffix *-weard* (E *-ward*).

iodic. See:

iodine, whence the nn iodate and iodide (Chem suffixes *-ate* and *-ide*) and the adj iodic (suffix *-ic*); cf the element *iodo-*.—Viola, violaceous, violet.

1. *Iodine* is an E chem (*-ine*) elaboration of F *iode*, iodine: Gr adj *iodēs*, of the form (*eidos*) of, i.e. like, a violet; *ion*, for *\*wion*, app of Medit stock.

2. Akin to Gr *ion*, *\*wion*, is L *uiola*, ML *viola*, a violet (plant and flower), whence the girl's name *Viola*. Its adj *uiolāceus*, ML *vi-*, yields E *violaceous*. ML *viola* becomes OF-F *viole*, with OF-MF dim *violete* (F *violette*), whence E *violet*.

ion (in Phys Chem), whence ionium (Chem *-ium*) and ionize, whence ionization, represents Gr *ion*, neu of *iōn*, presp of *ienai*, to go: cf ITINERARY and ISSUE.

Ionian, adj hence n; Ionic, adj hence n. The former derives from L *Iōnius*, var of *Iōnicus*, whence *Ionic*; and *Iōnicus* is a trln of Gr *Iōnikos*, adj of *Iōnia*, either the land of the legendary founder *Iōn* or, more prob, a Grecization of Eg *Ḥa-nebu*, a very old name for those who lived in the Mediterranean islands, hence, later, esp the Ionians: perh a Medit word.

ionium, ionize. See ION.

iota; jot.

An *iota*, L *iōta*, Gr *iōta*, is Gr ι, the E *i*; the sense 'a particle' comes either from '*iota* subscript', a tiny ι written under a long vowel, or from the fact that ι is the smallest Gr letter; hence E *jot*, n hence v. Gr *iōta* is akin to H *yōdh*.

I.O.U.=*I owe you.*

ipecac is a frequent shortening—cf the F *ipéca*—of ipecacuanha, adopted from Port: Tupi *ipe-caagoéne* or *ipekaaguéne*, lit either 'small roadside emetic plant' (Webster) or 'knotty plant' (Dict of the Sp Academy).

iracund. See IRASCIBLE, para 1.

Irak or Iraq, whence the adj Iraqi, is Ar al-'*Irāq*, from Middle Per *ērāk*, Persian. Cf:

Iran, whence the adj Iranian, is Per *Irān*, Persia, akin to ARYAN.

Iraq, Iraqi. See IRAK.

irascible, whence irascibility; irate; iracund, ire. —oestrus, whence the adjj oestrous, oestrual.

1. L *īra* (s and r *īr-*), anger, becomes OF *ire*, adopted by E; hence Shakespeare's *ireful*. L *īra* has adj *īrācundus*, with *-cundus* a var of the suffix *-bundus*, 'full of'; hence the rare E *iracund*. But it also has the derivative *īrāsci*, to be angry, whence LL *īrāscibilis*, prone to anger, whence, prob via OF-F, the E *irascible*; the pp *īrātus* becomes the E adj *irate*.

2. L *īra* (? for *\*eisa*) is prob akin to Homeric *hieros*, quick, lively (cf 'quick-tempered' and 'of a

lively temper')—Skt *işirás*, lively—ON *eira*, to rush forward; to Av *aẹšmo*, anger, and Lith *aistra*, a violent passion; and to Gr *oistros*, a gadfly, hence its sting, hence the sting of desire, hence (strong) sexual desire, latinized as *oestrus*, adopted by E Physio and Zoo, with var *oestrum*. (E & M; Hofmann.)

iridescence, from iridescent; iridium; iris, whence irisation; cf the elements *iridio-* and *irido-*.

1. The *iris* of the eye, like that of the garden, derives from L *iris*, a rainbow, the plant, from Gr *iris*, a rainbow, the ocular iris: L *Iris* (gen *Iridis*): Gr *Iris* (gen *Iridos*), Homer's Goddess of the Rainbow, var *Eiris*: app for *\*Wiris*, *\*Weiris*, with IE r *\*wei*, *\*uei-*, to bend, bow, curve: ? therefore akin to E WIRE.

2. From L *iris*, o/s *irid-*, rainbow, SciL derives *iridium* (Chem *-ium*), with adjj *iridious* and *iridic* (*acid*). App prompted by LL *uiridescere*, ML *viridescere*, to grow green, with pp *uiridescens*, o/s *uiridescent-*, whence E *viridescent*, is E *iridescent*, with b/f *iridesce*, to be iridescent, to display a rainbow-like range and interaction of colours.

Irish (adj hence n), whence Irishism, Irishry; Erse, adj hence n; Ireland; Eire—Erin; Hibernia, whence Hibernian (adj, hence n).

1. *Irish*, ME *Irisc*, an *-isc* adj from the s of OE *Iras* (cf ON *Īrar*), the Irish, from OIr *Ériu*, itself from OIr *Ēire*, Ireland, whence E *Eire*; the var *Erin* derives from the OIr dat *Ērinn*—cf Ga *Éirim*; *Ireland*, however, comes from OE *Īrland*, var of *Īraland*, land of the Irish. *Erse* was orig a C14–15 Sc var (*Erish, Ersh*, etc.) of ME *Irisc*.

2. The OIr dat *Ērinn* leads—app by confusion with L *Hibēria* (var of *Ibēria*), the Sp peninsula—to L *Hibernia*, Ireland, with adj *Hibernicus*, whence E *Hibernic*, whence *Hibernicism*, an Irishism. Yet the influence of L *Hibēria* in the formation of L *Hibernia* arises not entirely from a confusion: ult the two words are prob cognates.

irk, whence irksome (ME *irksum*), derives from ME *irken*, to weary (vt) or to become weary: o.o.o.: perh (Webster) cf Sw *yrka*, to urge, but prob (EW) from ME *irk*, distasteful, weary, from or akin to OE *earg*, timid, wretched (? cf Chaucer's *erke*, lazy), itself akin to OFris *erg*, OHG *arg*, MHG *arc*, and perh (Walshe) to Av *eregant*, disgusting.

iron. See ORE, para 2 for the n, para 3 for the adj.

ironic, ironical, ironist, irony.

*Ironical* is an *-al* elaboration of *ironic*, which, like MF-F *ironique*, derives from LL *īrōnicus*, ironical, Gr *eirōnikos*, deceitful, adj of *eirōneia*, dissimulation, from *eirōn*, one who, in speaking, dissembles, orig the presp of *eirō* (s *eir-*), I say or speak, perh by metathesis for *\*weriō*; akin to Gr *rhētōr*—see RHETORIC. Gr *eirōneia* becomes L *īrōnia*, whence—cf the MF-F *ironie*—the E *irony*; E *ironist* prob derives from F *ironiste* (*ironie+iste*).

irradiance; irradiate, irradiation. See RAY, para 4.

irrational. See REASON, para 4.

irreal, irreality. See the 1st REAL, para 1.

irreclaimable, irreconcilable, irrecoverable, irredeemable, are simply *ir-* for *in-*, not, negg of *reclaimable*, etc., themselves merely *re-*, back-, cpds from *claim*, etc. So, too, for all *ir-* negg not specifically entered in this dict.

irredentism, irredentist. See EXEMPT, para 14.

irrefragable. See FRACTION, para 10.

irrelevance, irrelevant. See RELEVANCE.

irregular, -ity. See REX, para 18.

irreligion, irreligious. See LIGAMENT, para 11.

irreparable. See PARE, para 7, s.f.

irresoluble; irresolute, irresolution. See LOSE, para 8.

irrevocable. See VOCABLE, para 10, s.f.

irrigable, irrigate, irrigation. See RAIN, para 2; cf RUN, para 3.

irritable, irritant, irritate, irritation. Ult akin, perh, to RUN, *irritate* derives from L *irrītātus*, pp of *irrītāre*, to arouse, hence to vex, perh akin to Gr *orinō*, I arouse: cf LL *prōrītātor*, a quarrelsome fellow. L *irrītāre* has presp *irrītans*, o/s *irrītant-*, whence the adj, hence n, *irritant*; the pp has derivative *irrītātiō*, acc *irrītātiōnem*, MF-F *irritation*, adopted by E; the inf has the LL derivative *irrītābilis*, whence EF-F and E *irritable*.

irrupt, irruption. See RUPTURE, para 8.

is. See ESSE, para 13.

ischiadic, ischial, ischiatic, ischium. See SCIATIC, para 2.

Isis. See OSIRIS.

isinglass: by f/e from ED *huysenblas*, bladder (*blas*) of the *huso* (OHG *huso*, G *Hausen*) or large sturgeon: a gelatin made from the air bladders of sturgeons.

Islam, whence Islamic, Islamism; Moslem, Muslim, Mussulman; salaam.

*Islam*=Ar *Islām*, submission (to God), from *aslama*, to submit (vi); *Moslem* is the E form of Ar *Muslim*, a believer (in Mohammed's faith), also from *aslama*; the syn *Mussulman* is Per and Tu *Musulmān*, from Ar *Muslim*. *Aslama*, to submit, to seek place, yields *salam*, peace, whence E *salaam*, n hence v.

island is taut, being OE *īland*, *īgland*: *īg*, *īeg*, island+*land*. The *-s-* has been influenced by:

isle, islet. See the 1st SOLE, para 7.

isobar. Cf the elements *-iso-*, equal-, and *-bar*, -weight (*baro-*, as in *barometer*).

isolate, isolation. See the 1st SOLE, para 8.

isomeric, isomerous. Cf the elements *iso-*+ *-mer, mero-*.

isomorph, -ic, -ous. See the element *iso-*; cf MORPHEUS.

isosceles. See the element *iso-*; cf *-sceles*.

isotherm. See the element *iso-*; cf THERM.

isotope. See the element *iso*; cf TOPIC.

isotype. See the element *-type*; cf the element *iso-*.

Israel, Israelite, Israelitic or Israelitish.

*Israel*, LL (usu *Isruhol*) from Gr *Israēl*, derives from H *Yisrā'ēl*, contender (*yisra*, from *sārāh*, to fight, contend) with God (*Ēl*, God, orig a Syrian god, the word being common throughout the Sem languages). Gr *Israēl* has derivative *Israēlitēs* (*-itēs*, a descendant), whence LL *Israēlīta*, whence E *Israelite*; and *Israēlitēs* has LGr derivative adj *Israēlitikos* (cf LL *Israhēlīticus*), whence *Israelitic*, usu anglicized to *Israelitish*.

issue, n hence v (whence issuable and, influenced by F, issuant, whence—again influenced by F—issuance); cf the sep ambition, circuit, coit, commence, county, errant (and aberrant), exit, eyre, initial, introit, itinerant, janitor, obituary, perish, preterit, sedition, sudden, transient, all from L *īre*, and also, these from Gr, the sep enema and isthmus.

The n *issue* is adopted from OF, which has var *eissue*, from *issir* (cf the OProv *eissir*), to go out, from L *exīre*: *ex*, out + *īre*, to go, with supine *itum*: cf *it*, he goes, and *itur*, there is a going, and *iter*, a going, a journey. L *īre*, to go (*eō*, I go), has such cognates as Gr *ienai*, to go (*eimi*, εἶμι, I am about to go), Skt *émi*, I go, *éti*, he goes, Lith *eiti*, he goes; C affords several cognates. The IE r is *ei-, var *i-*, to go. Cf:

isthmian; Isthmian, isthmian, isthmic, isthmoid.

*Isthmus*, adopted from L, comes from Gr *isthmos*, a narrow passage, a neck of land, an isthmus, akin to Gr *eisithmē*, an entrance, (lit) a going-in: *eis*, into + *i-*, the r of *iendi*, to go (f.a.e., ISSUE) + *-thmē*: cf *ithma* (*i-* + *thma*), a going. Cf also ON *eith*, isthmus.

Gr *isthmos* has adjj *isthmikos*, whence *isthmic*, and *isthmios*, whence *isthmian* (*-ian* for *-ious*): Gr *isthmios* occurs mostly as *Isthmios*, as in the orig forms of the Isthmian League and the Isthmian Games, ref the isthmus joining the Gr mainland with the Peloponnese.

it. See HE, para 1.

Italian (adj hence n), whence Italianism (unless from It *italianismo*), Italianize; Italianate; Italic (adj, hence n), whence italic, whence italicize; Italiote; Italy, whence italite (*Italy* + Geol *-ite*).

1. *Italian* derives from It *italiano*, adj (hence n) of It, from L, *Italia*, app for *Uitalia* (cf Oscan *Uiteliù*), from *uitulus*, a calf, ancient Italy being rich in cattle. (Gr *Italia* and *italos*, a bull, app derive from the L words.)

2. *Italianate* (or *Italianized*, cf F *italiniser*) derives from It *italianato*, pp of *italianare*, to render Italian, from *italiano*.

3. *Italic*, adj, derives from L *Italicus* (cf Gr *Italikos*), adj of L *Italia*: the printing type so named was first used by an Italian, Aldus Manutius, in a 'Virgil' he printed in 1501, and it comes into E via EF-F *italique*.

4. *Italiote*, a Gr inhabitant of Italy, derives from Gr *Italiōtēs*, from Gr *Italia*.

itch, n, derives from ME *icchen*, to itch, whence, obviously, also 'to itch': but *icchen* is a var of earlier *yicchen*, from OE *giccan*, with derivative n *gicce*, whence, partly, the n *itch*. OE *giccan* is akin to OHG *jucchēn*, MHG-G *jucken*, and MD *juecken, jucken, jocken, joken*, D *jeuken*: o.o.o.: ? echoic.—Hence itchy (*-y*, adj).

item, whence itemize.

L *item*, proleptic 'thus', is akin to L *ita*, both retrospective and prospective 'thus' and, like it, from *id*, it, the neu of *is, ea, id*, he, she, it; *item* has perh been influenced by *idem*, the neu of *īdem, eadem, idem*, the same (person m and f, thing neu). Cf Skt *īti* (Av *uiti*) and Umbrian *itek*, thus. The IE r is prob *id-*, alternating with *it-*. Cf:

iterate, iteration, iterative.

1. Both the obs adj and the current v *iterate* derive from L *iterātus*, pp of *iterāre*, to repeat, hence to go on repeating, from the adv *iterum*, for the 2nd time, app orig the neu of an adj *iterus*, another: cf the Skt adj *ītaras*, other, another. *Iterum* is akin to L *item* (see prec) and therefore to L *is, ea, id*, he, she, it. Derivatives LL *iterābilis*, L *iterātiō* (o/s *iterātiōn-*), LL *iterātīuus* (a gram term), ML *iterātīvus*, yield resp *iterable, iteration, iterative* (perh imm from MF-F *itératif*, f *itérative*).

2. The cpd LL *reiterāre*, to repeat (*iterāre*) again (*re-*), hence to say over and over again, has pp *reiterātus*, whence 'to reiterate'; derivative LL *reiterātiō*, o/s *reiterātiōn-*, becomes E *reiteration*; but *reiterative* is anl on *iterative*.

itineracy, itinerancy; itinerant; itinerary, adj and n.

*Itineracy* is an easement of *itinerancy*, itself for *itinerantcy* (abstract suffix *-cy*), from *itinerant*, E adj from LL *itinerant-*, o/s of *itinerans*, presp of *itinerāri* (s *itiner-*), to go on a journey, from L *iter*, a going, a walk (esp if long), a journey, with o/s *itiner-*, whence the LL adj *itinerārius* (*-ārius*), of or for a journey, hence of or for a road, whence the E adj *itinerary*; *itinerārius* has neu *itinerārium*, which, used as LL n, the planned course of a journey, accounts for E 'an *itinerary*'. L *iter*, s and r *it-*, is intimately akin to L *itum*, the supine of *īre*, to go: cf L *it*, he goes: f.a.e., ISSUE.

its: orig, in EE, *it's*: *it*, neu pron + possessive *'s* (orig *-es*).

ivied. See IVY, s.f.

ivory. See ELEPHANT, para 2.

ivy: OE *īfig*: cf OHG *ebihewe, ebahewi*, by f/e for *ebewe, ebawi*, there having been interference by OHG *hewi* (G *Heu*), hay: MHG *ephöu*: G *Efeu*. (Walshe.)—Hence the pa ivied.

2. The MHG *ephöu* suggests kinship with Gr *iphuon* (s *iphu-*), spike-lavender: o.o.o.

# J

**j, J.** Capital *J* follows, anl, from small *j*: and in
E words, it usu indicates either a direct L or a
Romance (mostly F) origin. L *j* was orig an
elongated *i* and was 'first used in cursive writing to
indicate an initial *I* [*i*]'; 'in the semi-vocalic sense'
it did not occur until c800 A.D. and, even then,
'only in S Italy and Spain' (Souter). In E, 'the
regular and practically uniform sound of *j*, as in
*jet* (=*dzh*), the same as *g* in *gem*, dates from the
11th century' (Webster).

**jab** (v, hence n); **job** (to stab, to jab), v hence n.
App the former is a var of the latter: and the latter
derives from ME *jobben*, to peck, itself o.o.o. but
prob echoic.

**jabber** (v, hence n) is prob echoic: ? an altered
freq of 'to *gab*': cf GABBLE.

**jacaranda**: Port, from Tupi, *jacarandá*.

**jacinth.** See HYACINTH.

**jack** (1), an EI fruit: Port *jaca*: Mal *cakka*, this
fruit: Skt *cakra*, a round object: ? ult akin to L
*circus* and *curuus* (ML *curvus*)—CIRCLE and
CURVE.

**jack** (2), a popular name for various quadrupeds
(*jackass*), birds (cf *jackdaw, laughing jackass*) and
fishes, and esp for various objects (cf *jackboot*),
devices and contrivances, esp if mechanical (*jackknife*): *Jack*, the very common pet-form of *John*,
the world's commonest font-name. *Jack*, although
used for *John*, derives from OF *Jaques* (F *Jacques*),
James, ML *Jacōbus*, LL *Iacōbus*, LGr *Iı̆kóbos*, H
*Ya'aqōbh*, lit 'supplanter'. LL *Iacōbus* has adj
*Iacōbaeus*, whence E *Jacobean*; ML *Jacōbus* has F
derivative *Jacobin*, adopted by E, and ML derivative *Jacōbita*, whence *Jacobite*. The C17 coin
*jacobus* is named after James I of England.

2. The Jack cpds are self-explanatory: e.g., *jack-
in-the-box, Jack-of-all-trades, jackpot, jack rabbit*.
—'To *jack*' derives from the n.

3. In C14 F, *Jacques* or *Jaques* designated the F
peasant, whence *la Jacquerie*, the great Peasant
Rising of 1357. *Jaques* has derivative *jaque*, a
peasant's short, close-fitting jacket, whence, 1375,
the dim *jaquette*, whence E *jacket*, whence 'to
*jacket*'.

4. OF-MF *Jaques* is partly adopted by EE:
hence \**Jaques' house*, Jack's house (a privy),
whence, via *Jakes* (later *Jake*), an E pet-form of
*Jacob*, \**Jakes'* (or *Jake's*) *house*, whence, by ellipsis,
\**Jakes'* (*Jake's*), whence the C16 *jakes*, a privy:

cf Sir John Harington's punning title, *The Meta-
morphosed Ajax*, 1596.

**jackal**: Tu *chaqāl* (*tchaqāl*): Per *shagāl* (*shaghāl*):
Skt *sr̥gāla* (*śr̥gāla*): ? 'the scavenger' (perh, however, cf Hit *šaggal*, fodder, forage).

**jackaroo**, occ **jackeroo**: *Jack* (see 2nd JACK)+
euphonic -*a*- or -*e*-+kanga*roo*, perh assisted by
walla*roo*.

**jackass; jackdaw** (cf DAW). See the 2nd JACK.

**jacket.** See the 2nd JACK, para 3.

**jackknife.** See the 2nd JACK.

**Jacob, Jacobean, Jacobin, Jacobite, jacobus.** See
the 2nd JACK.

**jaculate, jaculation, jaculator, jaculatory; ejacu-
late, ejaculation, ejaculator, ejaculatory.**

1. 'To *ejaculate*' derives from ML *ējaculātus*, L
*ēiaculātus*, pp of *ēiaculāri*, to hurl forth: *ē*, out+
*iaculāri*, to hurl, from *iaculum*, a dart, orig the neu
of the adj *iaculus*, of or for throwing, casting hurling, from *iacere*, to throw, akin to *iacēre*, to be
lying on the ground, orig because thrown there;
the s and r are *iac*-. The IE r is app \**je*-: cf L
*iectus*, thrown; prob cf also Gr *hiēmi* (for \**yi-yē-
mi*), I throw, pt *hēka*. The c/f of *iacere*, to throw,
is -*iicere*, often contr to -*icere*, and in E it occurs
esp in the pp form -*iectus*, as in *abject, deject,
inject, object, project, reject, subject*; cf the -*jacent*
(whence -*jacency*) words from *iacēre*—e.g.,
*adjacent*.

2. L *iaculāri* has derivatives *iaculātiō*, o/s
*iaculātiōn*-, whence E *jaculation*; *iaculātor*, tepidly
adopted (as *j*-) by E; LL *iaculātōrius*, whence
*jaculatory*; *jaculative* is an anl E formation.

3. E formations anl with those derivatives are
these: *ejaculation, ejaculative, ejaculator, ejaculatory*.

**jade** (1), in Min; **ileac, ileum, iliac, ilium.**

*Jade*, adopted from F, is elliptical and aphetic
for Sp 'piedra de ijada', stone of (the) side: *ijada*,
flank or side of the human body, hence a pain in
the side: the Middle Ages supposed this stone to
be able to cure that pain. *Ijada* comes from L *īlia*,
the flanks, a flank, the groin, whence, by b/f, the
s *īle, ileum, īlium*, the 2nd and 3rd being adopted
by Med; the adj of E *ileum* is *ileac*. The adj *iliac*,
obs for *ileac*, is now, by An, used for 'of the *ilium*,
but it owes something to EF-F *iliaque*, of or fo'r
colic, from L *īliācus*, from L *īleus*, colic, trln of
Gr *eileos*, an intestinal obstruction. L *īleus*, earlier
*īleos*, is used by Med for a grave, painful com-

316

plaint; the Gr *eileos* prob derives from *eilein* (s *eil-*), to roll up.

jade (2), a horse usu inferior or worn out, hence, usu pej, a wench; hence also 'to *jade*', to exhaust (a horse) or, usu by surfeit, a man or his appetite, mostly as pa *jaded*. E-ME *jade* is app a var of Sc *yade*, var *yaud* (also in E dial), from ON *jalda*, a mare, of Fin origin.

jag (n prob from v), orig a pendant notched into a garment's hem, thence both a sharp projection and the v to project sharply, the adj *jagged* app deriving from the n: o.o.o.: prob echoic; perh cf JOG. Note that *jag*, a small load, is a different word, whence A sl *jag*, a 'load' of liquor: likewise o.o.o.

Jagannath. See JUGGERNAUT.

jaggery. See SUGAR, para 4.

jaguar: a Port and Sp word: Tupi *jaguára*, any large feline, but often a dog: cf Tupi *aguara*, the crab-eating raccoon.

jail (n and v), jailer (or *-or*). Cf *gaol*, *gaoler*—but see CAVE, para 2.

Jahveh, Jahweh. See YAHWEH.

jakes. See the 2nd JACK, para 4.

jalap, adopted from F (earliest as *xalapa*), derives from Sp *jalapa*, first obtained at the Mexican town of *Jalapa*, by the Aztecs named *Xalapan*: *xalli*, sand+*apan*, in the water.

jalouse; jalousie. See ZEAL, para 4.

jam, the fruit product, like *jam*, a congestion or the resulting stoppage, derives from 'to jam', to crowd, squeeze, block, and is app a var of the now only dial *cham*, to chew, itself from CHAMP, to bite and chew noisily.—The adj is *jammy*.

jamb (esp of a door) has var *jambe*, which indicates its origin: OF-F *jambe*, leg, esp in *jambe de force*, a main rafter: f.a.e., GAMBOL. Cf:

jambon. See GAMBOL, para 3.

jambone. See:

jamboree, orig AE (1864) and orig meaning the holding of the five highest cards at euchre, is, like the AE *jambone* (1864), the playing, at euchre, of a lone hand with cards exposed, o.o.o. (DAE): ? resp luck and hazard when *jammed* into one hand. The element *-bone* could be a humorous var of *-boree*; and *-boree* could, as EW proposes, derive from *boree*, EF-F *bourrée*, a rustic, therefore lively, dance: note that *bourrée* derives from MF-F *bourrer*, to stuff tightly, to jam, itself from OF-F *bourre*, a coarse dress-material, from LL *burra*, perh the f of the L adj *burrus*, reddish.

James, adopted from F, is prop the Béarnais (SW France) form of OF-MF *Jaques*, EF-F *Jacques*: f.a.e., JACOB. Its pet-forms *jemmy* and *jimmy* are sl (orig cant) names for a burglar's short crowbar. (P[1].)

jammy. See JAM.

Jane (F *Jeanne*, ML *Joanna*: cf JOHN) becomes A sl *jane*, girl, woman, and has pet-form *Jenny*, as in *spinning jenny*: sem cf *betty* from *Elizabeth*. (The old Genoese coin *jane*='coin of *Genoa*': cf ML *Janua* and F *Gènes*.)

jangle (n, v); jangler; jangling, pa and vn from 'to *jangle*'.—jingle, n from v.

'To *jingle*', ME *ginglen*, *gingelen*, is prob a thinning of ME *janglen*, E *jangle*, to clatter, (ME) to quarrel noisily: OF-MF *jangler*, itself o.o.o. but prob from MD *jangelen*, to clatter, to jingle (D *jengelen*, to jingle), app echoic. OF-MF *jangler* has the OF-MF derivative agent *jangleor*, whence E *iangler*.

janitor, adopted from ML, is L *iănitor*: *iănua*, a door, from *Iānus*, ML hence E *Janus*, God of Doors, looking both forwards and backwards: for the formation of *iănitor*, cf that of *portitor* from *portus* (orig syn with *porta*, door, gate), this *-itor* perh deriving from *itum*, supine of *īre*, to go (cf ISSUE), but prob being syn with agential *-ator* (basically *-or*). *Iānua* is app for *\*ienua*, s *ienu-*, r *ien-*, o.o.o.

2. The god *Iānus* has a month consecrated to him: *Iānuārius* (suffix *-ārius*, connoting 'owner of'), OL *Ienuārius*, sc *mensis*, a month; *Iānuārius*, ML *Jānuārius*, whence E *January*, came to be regarded as the month when the year, still facing winter, also faces spring.

January. See prec, para 2.

Janus. See janitor, para 1.

Japan; Japanese (adj, n), whence sl, now coll, Jap; to japan, whence japanner; japonica.

1. *Japanese* is the *-ese* n and adj of *Japan*, whence *japan*, for *Japan varnish*; hence 'to *japan*'. *Japan* derives, via EF-F *Japon*, from Ch *Jihpén*, a shortening of *Jih-pên-kuo*, land of the origin of the sun. *Jihpén* becomes also It *Giappone*.

2. The Jap pron of *Jihpên* is *Nihon* or *Nippon*: *hon*, origin+*nichi* (or *nitsu*), the sun. *Nippon* is the official Jap name, adopted by the U.S.A.; hence, after *Japanese*: *Nipponese*, whence the A sl, now coll, *Nip*.

3. F *Japan* is latinized as *Japonia*, with SciL adj *Japonicus*, whence *japonica*, camellia.

jape (v, hence n), to jest: o.o.o.: ? MF *japer* (F *japper*), to yelp, itself echoic (cf YAP)+E 'to GAB'.

Japhet is an eased form of Japheth: LL, from Gr *Japheth*, from H *Yehpheth*, enlarged, a son being doubly an increase. The E adj is *Japhetic*, whence the n *Japhetic*, either a group of non-IE languages in Europe and W Asia or the Caucasian languages.

japonica. See JAPAN, para 3.

jar (1), a broad-mouthed, usu earthenware vessel: late MF-F *jarre*: Prov *jarra*: Ar *jarrah* (*djarra*), a large earthenware vessel for water.

jar (2), to sound gratingly, hence to be discordant, hence vt to clash with: echoic: perh from ME *charken*, to creak, itself from OE *cearcian*, to creak, to gnash, ? for *cracian* and therefore akin to CREAK.—Hence, the bird aptly known as *nightjar*, var *nightchur*.

jargon (1), speech. See GORGE, para 6.

jargon (2), gem; occ jargoon. See ZIRCON.

jasmine, occ jasmin; jessamine (dial jessamy); gelsemium.

*.asmin(e)* derives from F *jasn in* (first as *jassemin*, in 1500), coll Ar *yasmīn*, Ar *yāsamīn*, Per *yāsaman*. The EF *jassemin* has var *jessemin*, whence E *jessamine*. The Ar words yield also early It *gesmino*, which, influenced by It *gèlso*, mulberry (fruit or tree), becomes It *gelsomino* and late ML *gelseminum*; the latter accounts for E *gelseminine* (Chem *-ine*), the former and the latter jointly produce SciL *Gelsemium*.

**jasper**: ME *jaspre*, var *jaspe*: adopted from late MF *jaspre* (cf EF *jaspere*), var of OF-F *jaspe*: L, from Gr, *iaspis*, s *iasp-*: of Sem origin—esp H *yāshpheh* (cf Ar *yashb*)—prob via Phoen.

**jaundice** (n, hence v—whence **jaundiced**) derives from ME *jaunis*, with intrusive *d* perh after 'glanders': OF-F *jaunisse*, an *-isse* derivative from OF-F *jaune*, yellow, earlier *jalne*: L *galbinus*, yellowish, an *-inus* dim of *galbus*, yellow: o.o.o.: ? C, the Cor forms being suggestive.

**jaunt; jaunting car; jaunce, jounce.**

'To *jaunt*'—whence the n—orig to prance, then to go hither and yon, finally to ramble, esp on pleasure, is prob id both with E dial *jaunt*, to jolt, whence 'a *jaunting* car', and with obs *jaunce*, to prance, and—? influenced by *bounce—jounce*, to jolt; *jaunce* app derives from MF *jancer*, to sweep, EF to rub, the idea perh being 'to sweep along'. *Jaunt* and *jaunting* (car) may owe something to:

**jaunty.** See GENERAL, para 16, s.f.

**javelin**: F *javeline*, a C15 dim of OF-F *javelot*, of C origin: cf W *gaflach*, a feathered lance, a barbed spear, Cor *geu, gew, gu* (cf *gȳa*, to spear), Mx *ga*, EIr *gae, gai*, Ga *gath*, dart or javelin: OC *\*gaison* (Malvezin; MacLennan), from *\*gais*, to throw or cast (Malvezin).

**jaw** (n, hence v): perh a blend of E 'to chaw' (see CHEW)+OF-F joue, the cheek, as Webster proposes; EW suggests that C14-15 *jowe, jow—jawe*, *jaw* not occurring before late C15—comes from OF(-F) *joue*, itself perh from VL *gabata*, a bowl, (sl) the cheek, but has been influenced by 'to chaw' or by *jowl* or by both; OED entirely rejects F *joue* and proposes *\*chow(e)*, a var of *chaw*.

**jay**, adopted from OF (cf OF and OProv *gai*): LL *gāius*, f *gāia*, prob from the PN *Gāius*—a common process in the naming of the more familiar creatures. LL *gāius, gāia* could, however, be echoic, with the PN deriving as nickname from it, as many etymologists admit.—The sl sense derives from the SE sense.

**jazz**, v hence n, like JUKE (box), is orig an A Negro word: and both are traceable to W Africa. Both, moreover, refer ult to sexual activity and excitement; hence to excitant music. Among the Gullahs of SE U.S.A., a *juke house* is a brothel (Mathews).

**jealous, jealousy.** See ZEAL, para 3.

**jeans,** (working) trousers or overalls, were orig made of the twilled cotton cloth known as *jean*, perh from F *Gênes*, Genoa.

**jeer** (v, hence n): ? a blend of EE *fleer* (ME

*flerien*, of Scan origin), to mock+an ironic CHEER.

**Jehovah.** See YAHWEH.

**jehu**, a coachman, alludes to the Biblical *Jehu* (2 *Kings*, ix), who led a furious attack made with chariots. *Jehu*=H *yēhū*', o.o.o.—perh 'Jeh is he'.

**jejune.** See DINE, para 1.

**jelly** (n, hence v), **jelloid; gel** (n, hence v)—from **gelatin** (**-ine**), whence also **gelatinize** and **gelatinous** (cf F *gélatineux*, f *-ineuse*); **gelignite; gelose,** whence **gelosin.**

1. *Jelly*, ME *gely*, derives from OF-F *gelée*, jelly, frost, itself from L *gelāta*, elliptical for *res gelāta*, something frozen, from *gelāre*: f.a.e., COLD. *Jelloid*=jelly+*-oid*, like. A *jellyfish* has a jelloid body.

2. L *gelāta* has It dim *gelatina*, whence EF-F *gélatine*, E *gelatine*, with var *gelatin*. Gelatin(e)+ Chem *-ose* explains *gelose*.

3. *Gelatin(e)* occurs also in *gelignite*: gelatin+L *ignis*, fire+the explosives suffix *-ite*, as in *cordite*, *dynamite*, *lyddite*.

**jemmy.** See JAMES.

**jennet**, a small Sp horse, whence a female ass: MF-F *genet*: Sp *jinete*, prop a lightly armed cavalryman, hence his horse: Ar *Zenāta* (*Zanātah*), a Berber tribe famed for its daring cavalry. (B & W.)

**jenneting** is a variety of apple, ripe soon after St *John's* Day (June 24): F dial *pomme de Jeannet* (dim of *Jean*), cf F *pomme de Saint-Jean*: the *-ing* is prob that of, e.g., *wilding*, a wild plant or its fruit, esp a wild apple.

**jenny.** See JANE.

**jeopardy**, whence the adj **jeopardous** and the vv **jeopard** (by b/f) and **jeopardize.**

*Jeopardy*, ME *jupartie*, earlier *juperti*, earliest *jeuparti*, represents OF-MF *jeu parti*, a divided, hence equally shared, hence even game, a dilemma: ML *jocus partītus*: OF-F *jeu*, from ML *jocus* (L *iocus*), f.a.e. JOKE+OF-F *parti*, pp of *partir*, to divide, to share, f.a.e., PART.

**jerboa** is a SciL word (var *gerboa*), formed from Ar *yarbū*'.

**jeremiad**, a bitter lamentation or denunciation, hence loosely a doleful tirade, comes from the Lamentations of *Jeremiah*: F *jérémiade*, an *-ade* (E *-ad*) derivative of *Jérémie* (whence *Jeremy*), the prophet *Jeremiah*: LL *Jeremias*: H *Yirmĕyāh*, Exalted of *Yah* the Lord.

**jerk** (v of movement, hence n, whence the adj **jerky**), like the partly syn **yerk** (v, hence n), is o.o.o.: ? echoic.

**jerk** (2). See:

**jerkee, charqui;** to jerk (beef), whence **jerked beef** and simple **jerk.**

*Jerkee* is an A dial var (Western) of *charqui*, meat—esp beef—cut into strips and dried in the sun (cf the SAfr BILTONG and the origin of BUCCANEER): Sp *charqué*: Quechuan (Peruvian Amerind) *charqui*, dried meat. *Jerkee* leads, by f/e ref to 1st. JERK, to the v *jerk*, to sun-dry strips of meat.

**jerky**, adj. See the 1st JERK.—As n, var of JERKEE.

**Jerry**, a German soldier (hence ship or 'plane), was orig *Gerry*, a pet-form derivative of German: cf *Ger*, *Gerry*, pet-forms of PN *Gerald*.

**jerry**, E sl for a chamber pot, derives, not from *Jeremiah* but from *jeroboam*, a bottle either ten or twelve times as large as an ordinary one, hence a large bowl, itself from *Jeroboam*, 'a mighty man of valour' (1 *Kings*, xii).

**jersey**. See GUERNSEY.

**Jerusalem artichoke** is, as to *Jerusalem*, a f/e corruption of It *girasole* (E *girasol*: cf GYRATE), a sunflower with a tuber that serves as a vegetable; *artichoke* is, by f/e, added ref the true ARTICHOKE. —*Jerusalem*=LL *Hierūsalēm*, Gr *Hierousalēm*, trln of an Aram word (H *Yĕrūshālaim*), orig without *h*-: Ass *Ur-sa-li-immu*: the Eg Tell El-Amarna tablets (c1450 B.C.) *Uru-sa-lim*: prob meaning, 'City, or Possession, of Peace'.

**jess**. See the 2nd JET, para 5.

**jessamine, jessamy**. See JASMINE.

**jest, jester**. See GERUND, para 4.

**Jesuit, Jesuitic, Jesuitism, Jesuitry; Jesus and Jesu.**

Orig, *Jesuit* was a nickname for a member of the Society, or Company, of Jesus: *Jesus*+*-ita*, descendant. The F form *Jésuite* has adj *jésuitique*, whence E *Jesuitic*, with *-al* elaboration *Jesuitical*; E *Jesuit* has derivatives *Jesuitism* (cf the F *jésuitisme*) and *Jesuitry*, with suffix *-ry*. (See esp P².) *Jesus* itself derives, through ML *Jēsus*, LL *Iēsus*, trln of LGr *Iēsous*, from H *Yēshūa'*, prob 'Jehovah (or Yahveh) is salvation': cf YAHWEH. The mostly poetical *Jesu* was orig a voc

**jet** (1), a glossy-black mineral: MF *jet*, contr of OF *jayet* (cf F *jais*): L *gagātem*, acc of *gagātes*: Gr *gagātēs*, elliptical for *lithos gagatēs*, stone of *Gagas*, a river and town of Lycia in S Asia Minor.

**jet** (2) of water, also v; **jetsam** and **jettison** (n hence v); **jetton; jetty; parget**.—**jess**.—**jitney**—**jut** (v, hence n).—For the *-ject*, *-jection*, *-jective* cpds, see sep **abject, conject(ure), deject, eject, inject, interject, object, project, reject, subject, traject**, etc.

1. A *jet* comes from OF-MF *get* (F *jet*), from OF-MF *geter*, a merely scriptural var of *jeter*, to cast or throw, whence 'to *jet*': and OF-F *jeter* comes from VL *\*jectāre*, for L *iactāre* (ML *jactāre*), freq of *iacere*, to throw: f.a.e., JACULATE, para 1.

2. OF-MF *geter* has MF derivative *getaison*, a throwing, whence E *jettison*, now esp a casting of goods overboard; *getaison* also becomes the E doublet *jetsam*, that which is thrown overboard— sem cf *flotsam*. OF-MF *geter* has another derivative relevant to E: the MF *geton*, F *jeton*, E *jetton*, a counter used in book-keeping, later in card-playing. Perh from F *jeton* comes also AE *jitney*, sl for a nickel (5 cents).

3. *Jetty*, however, comes from EF-F *jetée*, an *-ée* formation from *jeter*: something thrown out, from the land into the sea.

4. OF-MF *geter* has the OF cpd *pargeter*, to throw (something) all over (*par*=L *per*, throughout) a surface: hence ME *pargeten*, whence 'to *parget*', to coat or cover with plaster, with vn *parget(t)ing*.

5. OF-MF *get*—as in para 1—has the OF-EF var *giet*, with pl *gies* or *giez*, used as that Falconry n which becomes E *jess*.

6. 'To *jet*' has the var (unrecorded before late C18), prob orig Sc, or perh N dial, 'to *jut*', and mostly as vi.

**jetsam**. See prec, para 2.

**jettison**. See the 2nd JET, para 2.

**jetton**. See 2nd JET, para 2.

**jetty**. See 2nd JET, para 3.

**Jew** (whence **Jewish**), **Jewry; Judaic, Judaism** (whence, anl, **Judaist**), **Judaize; Judas, Jude; Yiddish** (n, hence adj), whence the sl **Yid**.

1. A *Jew* derives from OF *juieu*, var *juiu*, both recorded in C12 and deriving from ML *Jūdaeum*, acc of *Jūdaeus*, LL *Iūdaeus*, trln of LGr *Ioudaîos*, itself from H *Yĕhūdhi*, a person of H *Yĕhūdhāh*, Gr *Ioudaia*, LL *Iūda*, ML *Jūda*, E *Judah*. Lit '(The) Praised', *Yehūdhāh* from being the name of the founder becomes the name of his tribe; from tribe to kingdom, and, after the return (early C6 B.C.) of the Jews from Babylon, the new Hebrew state.

2. OF *juiu* has derivative *juiuerie*, whence ME *Jewerie*, E *Jewry*.

3. LGr *Ioudaîos* has derivative adj *Ioudaïkos*, LL *Iūdaïcus*, ML *Jūdaïcus*, E *Judaic*—derivative n *Ioudaïsmos*, LL *Iūdaïsmus*, ML *Jūdaïsmus*, E *Judaism*—and derivative v *Ioudaïzein*, LL *iūdaïzare*, E *Judaize*.

4. H *Yĕhūdāh*, Judah, has derivative LGr *Ioudas*, LL *Iūdas*, ML *Jūdas*, retained as the name of the traitor Apostle, Judas Iscariot, hence for any traitor and also, as *judas* (F and E), for a peephole in wall or door; *Judas* becomes fully anglicized as *Jude*. The adj *Judas*, applied esp to human hair, derives from the medieval tradition that the Apostle Judas was red-haired; a *Judas tree*, because he reputedly hanged himself on one; *Judas priest!* is an A euphem for *Jesus Christ!*

5. ML *Jūdaeus* becomes G *Jude*, a Jew (OHG *judeo*, *judo*; MHG *jüde*), with adj *jüdisch*, whence *jüdisch-deutsch* (*Sprache*), Jewish-German (speech), whence the n *Jüdisch*, whence E *Yiddish*: cf the learnèd syn *Judaeo-German*. (Walshe.)

**jewel** (n, hence v), **jeweller, jewellery** or **jewelry**. See JOKE, para 4.

**jib** (1), a crane's projecting arm. See GIBBET, s.f.

**jib** (2), a triangular sail, derives from 'to **jib**' or shift, itself a thinning of naut *jibe*, (of a sail and its boom) to shift suddenly and violently from one side to the other, with var *gybe*: D *gibjen* (var *gipjen*), with Scan cognates. 'To *jib*' is derivatively used of a horse.

**jibe** (1), to shift. See prec.

**jibe** (2), to sneer. See 1st GIBE.

**jibe** (3), AE (coll) for 'to agree, to harmonize': o.o.o.: but perh from the *jibe* recorded at 2nd JIB, the basic idea being 'to shift in unison'.

**jig** (v, hence n), whence **jigger** in its mechanical

and tech senses; cpd **jigsaw**; **jiggle**.—**jog** (v, hence n); **joggle**; **goggle** (v, hence n, esp **goggles**); **googly**. —**gigolo**.—? **jink** (v, hence n, esp **jinks**, esp if high), whence **jinker**.

1. 'To *jig*', to dance springily, to hop about, comes from MF *giguer*, to hop (about), to dance, var *ginguer*: prob from MF *gigue*, a fiddle, perh imm from MHG *gīge* (G *Geige*), prob ult from ON *gīgia* (*gīgja*), a fiddle: cf ON *geiga*, to move crosswise, as a manipulated fiddle-bow normally does. (Walshe.) Hence a *jig saw* (sawing machine), whence a *jigsaw*, a puzzle with pieces of wood made with such a saw.

2. 'To *jig*' has freq *jiggle*: *jig*+euphonic *-g-*+ freq suffix *-le*; hence n *jiggle* and adj *jiggly*.

3. MF *gigue*, a fiddle, has derivative sense 'leg', whence F *gigolette*, a prostitute, whence, by b/f, *gigolo*, a man living on a prostitute's earnings, whence E *gigolo*, a paid male dancing partner or escort.

4. MF *ginguer* (var of *giguer*: as in para 1) perh, leads to *jink*, to move with sudden turns (as in dancing), to dodge about, unless *jink* be purely echoic.

5. Partly echoic or, at the least, imitative, with some ref to *jig*, is 'to *jog*', which partly derives from the now dial *shog*, q.v. at SHOCK. 'To *jog*' has freq *oggle*: cf *iggle*.

6. With *joggle*, cf 'to *goggle*', ME *gogelen*, which, sem, is to joggle one's eyes; hence a *goggle* and a *goggler*, the latter esp for a fish with large, bulging eyes.

7. 'To *goggle*' has var—obs, except in dial—*google*, whence prob the cricketing *googly*.

**jigger** (1), a mechanical device. See prec (heading).

**jigger** (2), a parasitic flea. See CHIGGER.

**jiggle**. See JIG, para 2.

**jigsaw**. See JIG, para 1, s.f.

**Jill**. See:

**jilt** (n, hence v) is a contr of Sc *jillet*, a giddy, esp if flirtatious, girl: dim of *jill*, (feminine) sweetheart: var of *gill*: Gill, Jill, pet-forms of *Gillian*; cf 'Jack and Jill'. *Gillian* derives from F *Juliane*, ML *Jūliana* (LL *Iūliana*), derivative of ML *Jūlia*, L *Iūlia*: cf JULY.

**jimmy**. See JAMES.

**jimp**. See GIMCRACK.

**Jimson weed** derives from the obsol *Jamestown* (in Virginia) *weed*: cf *Jimson*, a Sc pron of *Jameson* (James's son).

**jingle**. See JANGLE.

**Jingo**, a bellicose patriot (cf the F *chauvin*), derived in 1878 from the chorus of an immensely popular E music-hall song: 'We don't want to fight, but by jingo if we do, We've got the ships, we've got the men, we've got the money too'. The oath *by jingo!* is either—suggested by *by Jove!*—euphem for *by Jesus!* or derived from Basque *Jinko* (var *Jinkoa*), God.—Hence *jingoism*, prob after *chauvinism*.

**jink**, v (whence **jinker**); **jinks**, n. See JIG, para 4 and heading.

**jinn** is prop the pl of *jinni* (occ anglicized as **jinnee**), adopted from Ar; orig a hostile demon, later a supernatural being subject to magical control.

**jinriksha**, anglicized to **jinrickshaw** and then shortened to **rickshaw**, comes almost straight from Jap: *jin*, a man+*riki*, power+*sha*, a carriage. With *riki*, one is tempted to cf E REX—and prob rightly.

**jinx** or **jynx**, hoodoo, bad luck, a 'Jonah': SciL-ML *jynx*, pl *jynges*, L *iynx*, Gr *iunx* (ἴυγξ), the wryneck, used in the casting of spells: o.o.o.

**jitney**. See the 2nd JET, para 2, s.f.

**jitters, the**, extreme nervousness, whence the adj **jittery**, app derives from **jitter**, to be very nervous, act very nervously: A sl (c1920) become coll; adopted by E c1943. Perh echoic.

**Joan, Joanna**. See JOHN, para 2.

**job** (1), of work, whence 'to **job**', whence **jobber** and **jobbing** (vn), which jointly produce **jobbery**. *Job*, orig a lump, a piece, prob derives from ME *jobbe*, a lump; hence a piece of work. Perh cf:

**job** (2). See JAB.

**Jock; jockey** (n, hence v).

*Jock* is the Sc form of *Jack*, q.v. at the 2nd JACK, para 1: and *Jock* has dim *Jockie, Jockey*, whence, because he's small, *jockey*, whence 'to *jockey* for position', hence, vt, to cheat or trick.

**jocose, jocosity, jocular**. See JOKE, para 2.

**jocund, jocundity**.

The latter derives from ML *jocunditās* (o/s *jocunditāt-*), LL *iocunditās*, for L *iūcunditās*, from L *iūcundus*, helpful, (hence) pleasant: the r *iu-* of *iuuō* (ML *juvō*), I help, (hence) afford pleasure to+ the suffix *-cundus* of, e.g., *fēcundus*; L *iuuāre*, ML *juvāre*, is o.o.o. The adj *iūcundus* has, by the f/e influence of *iocus* (see JOKE), the inferior LL var *iocundus*, whence MF *jocund* (*jocond*), whence ME *jocunde*, E *jocund*.

**joe; joey**. See JOSEPH, s.f.

**jog; joggle**. See JIG, para 5.

**John**, whence the dim **Johnny** or **Johnnie**; cpds, e.g. **John Bull**—**Doe**—**dory**—**Hancock**; **Johnson** (*John's son*—cf *Jackson*, Jack's son), whence, via Dr Samuel *Johnson*, **Johnsonese**; **Johannes**, whence **Johannine**; **johannite**; **Joan, Joanna**—cf *Jean* (m, f) and sep JANE and JENNETING; Don **Juan**; **shoneen; zany**.

1. The most important IE varr of *John* are G *Johann* (whence *johannite*) or *Johannes* (whence *Hans*); D *Jan*; F *Jean*, f *Jeanne* (E *Jean*); Sp *Juan*, esp in *Don Juan*, a refined profligate, popularized in and for E by Byron's long narrative poem so titled; It *Giovanni*, with Venetian pet-form *Zanni*, whence It *zanni*, a merry-Andrew, whence EF-F *zani*, whence E *zany*; Ru *Ivan*; Ga *Iain*, anglicized as *Ian*; Anglo-Ir *Sean*, Ir *Seon* (imm from E *John*) —with dim *Seoninen*, whence Anglo-Ir *shoneen*, a 'little'—i.e., would-be—gentleman, prob after Anglo-Ir *squireen*: all of which, like E *John*, derive from ML *Jōhannes*, earlier *Jōannes*: LL *Iōhannes*: LGr *Iōannēs*: H *Yōḥānān*, 'God (*Yōh-*: cf YAHWEH) is gracious'.

2. ML *Jōannes* has f *Jōanna*, adopted by E and

then shortened to *Joan*; E *Joan of Arc*= F *Jeanne d'Arc*.

3. The chief cpds are *John Bull*, the typical-Englishman's name, the type being instituted by Dr John Arbuthnot in *The History of John Bull*, 1712: *John*, the commonest E male given-name+ *bull*, the animal he has so successfully reared; *John Doe* (and Richard Roe), a convenient legal fiction, chosen for much the same reason; *John Dory* (or *Doree*), a fish good for eating, *John* because common, *Dory* for DORY—cf the old song *John Dory*, a F privateersman; *John Hancock*, AE for a signature, from the first (and very clear) signature of the A Declaration of Independence.—Cf the A *honest John*, an honest citizen. There are many other *John* or *Johnny* terms, but all self-explanatory, being based upon the fact that, throughout the IE world, *John* is easily the commonest given-name.

4. Cf, sem, the 2nd JACK.

**johnny-cake.** See JOURNEY.

**join** (v, hence n), pt and pp **joined; joinder; joiner; joint** (adj, n, v), **jointer, jointure;** cpds: **adjoin** (whence **adjoining**)—**conjoin, conjoint**—**disjoin, disjoint** (whence **disjointed**), **disjointure**—**enjoin, enjoinder**—**rejoin, rejoinder**—**subjoin, subjoinder.**—**junction, junctive, juncture;** cpds: **adjunct** (adj, hence n), **adjunction, adjunctive**—**conjunct, conjunction, conjunctive, conjunctivitis, conjuncture** —**disjunct, disjunction, disjunctive**—**injunction, injunctive**—**subjunct, subjunction, subjunctive** (adj, hence n).—**junta, junto.**—**jugal, jugate, jugum; jugular, jugulum; conjugal, conjugant, conjugate** (whence **conjugacy**), **conjugation, conjugative; subjugate, subjugation, subjugator.**—**jumentous.**—**joust,** occ **just,** n and v (whence **jouster, jousting**); **jostle** (v, hence n).—**yogi** (whence **yogism**)—cf *Yuga.*— **yoke,** perh **yokel.**—**zeugma** (whence **zeugmatic**); **zygoma, zygon, zygosis, zygote, zygous**—cf **syzygy.**—Perh cf the sep JONQUIL and the sep JUS (as in JUST).

1. This constellation of terms is so clear that it would be a pity to disunite them: and they exemplify many of the interactions operating within the IE family of languages. Nor is the constellation so vast that it cannot be lucidly and conveniently treated under the one heading.

## I. Indo-European

2. For most of the terms, the effective origin lies in L *iungere*, to join, s *iung-*, ML *jung-*; for many others, in the cognate L *iugum*, a yoke, s *iug-*, ML *jug-*; of both sub-groups, certain members come through R; Gr and Skt supply the remainder.

3. L *iung-*, with nasal-infix (*-n-*), or rather the more basic *iug-*, is akin to Gr *zug-* in the n *zugon*, a yoke, and to its var form *zeug-*, as *zeugma* (see para 7) and *zeugos*, a yoke. With L *iugum*, Gr *zugon*, cf Skt *yugám* and Hit *jugan, jukan*, perh better *yugan, yukan* (dat *yuki*); other cognates are, e.g., OSl *igo*; Go *iuk, juk*, OHG *joh*, MHG-G *och*, OE *geoc*, E *yoke*; C affords several examples.

With the nasal L *iungo* (pp *iunctus*, ML *junctus*), Gr *zeugnumi*, I yoke, cf Skt *yunákti*, Lith *jungti*, he yokes, Skt *yuñjánti*, they yoke, Lith *jùngas*, a yoke. With L *iunctus*, contrast the syn Skt *yuktás*, and with L *iunctiō*, a yoking, a joining, contrast the syn Skt *yuktis*. In short, the distribution of the nasal and the other forms is, as one would expect, irreg; the *-n-* forms predominate.

4. The IE r is app *\*ieug-*, to bind together, to yoke, to join, itself an extn of *\*ieu-*, var *\*ieo-*, to bind, with ult r perh *\*ie-* (*\*ye-*), varr *\*io-* (*\*yo-*) and *\*iu-*, to bind.

## II. Sanskrit

5. The Skt *yoga*, union (cf para 3), becomes Hi *yoga*, a mental, hence also a spiritual, discipline of Hinduism, adopted, as a word, throughout the IE countries. Derivative Skt *yogīn* becomes Hi *yogī*, a follower—a practiser—of yoga; hence E *yogi*.

6. Very intimately akin to Skt *yoga*, union, is Skt *yugá-* (Hi *yug*), a yoke, hence an age ('a yoke of years'); hence *Yuga*, one of Hinduism's Four Ages of the World.

## III. Greek

7. Gr *zeugma* (o/s *zeugmat-*), a joining, from *zeugnumi*, I yoke or join, is adopted by L Rhetoric, hence by E.

8. Gr *zugon*, a yoke, is adopted, in its SciL form *zygon*, by E An, with derivative adj *zygous*; derivative Gr *zugōsis*, balancing, becomes E Bot and Zoo *zygosis*; derivative *zugoun*, to yoke, has n *zugōma*, whence An and Zoo *zygoma*, a yoking, o/s *zugōmat-*, whence the E anl adj *zygomatic*; *zugoun*, moreover, has pp *zugōtos*, yoked, whence the Bio n *zygote*, with derivative adj *zygotic*.

9. Gr *zeugnumi*, inf *zeugnunai*, combines with *sun-*, with, to form the derivative *suzugia*, a joining together, whence LL *syzygia*, whence the E *syzygy* of Astr, Math, Zoo.

## IV. Latin—Simple Derivatives

10. L *iugum*, ML *jugum*, is adopted by Bot and Zoo; its derivative adj *iugālis*, ML *j-*, becomes the SciE *jugal*; the derivative v *iugāre* has pp *iugātus*, ML *jugātus*, which becomes the SciE adj *jugate*. L *iugum* has dim *iugulum*, ML *jugulum*, the part which joins neck to shoulders and chest, adopted by Zoo; its SciL adj *jugularis* becomes E *jugular*.

11. L *iugum* has a derivative *\*iugmentum*, eased to *iumentum*, a team of draught animals, hence a draught animal, esp the horse, whence the Med E adj *jumentous*.

12. The nasal form is *iungere* (s *iung-*), to yoke, join, with pp *iunctus*, whence E *-junct*: see para 14. Derivative *iunctiō*, o/s *iunctiōn-*, ML *junctiōn-*, becomes E *junction*; LL *iunctīuus*, ML *junctīvus*, becomes *junctive*; LL *iunctūra*, ML *j-*, becomes *juncture*.

## V. Latin Compounds

13. The relevant cpds of L *iugum*, *iugālis*, pp *iugātus*, derivative n *iugātiō* (o/s *iugātiōn-*), LL agent *iugātor*, are these:

*coniugāre*, to join together, to marry, pp *coniugātus*, ML *conjugātus*, whence E *conjugate*, adj (hence n) and v; derivative *coniugātiō*, o/s *coniugātiōn-*, yields *conjugation*, whence, anl, the adj *conjugative*; the n *conjugant*, however, derives from *coniugant-*, o/s of *coniugans*, presp of *coniugāre*;—

*coniux*, ML *conjux*, husband, wife, each being joined to the other, app=*con-*, with+*iug*um+ nom -*s*: *coniugs* becomes *coniux*, gen *coniugis*, o/s *coniug-*, whence the adj *coniugālis*, ML *conjugālis*, F and E *conjugal*;—

*subiugāre*, to put under (*sub*) the yoke (*iugum*), hence under one's power, pp *subiugātus*, ML *subjugātus*, whence 'to *subjugate*'; derivative LL *subiugātiō*, o/s *subiugātiōn-*, becomes *subjugation*; derivative ML *subjugātor* is adopted by E.

14. The relevant L cpds of *iungere* are these:

*adiungere*, to join *ad* or to, pp *adiunctus*, ML -*junctus*, whence the E adj *adjunct*; derivative *adiunctiō*, o/s *adiunctiōn-*, whence E *adjunction*; LL *adiunctīuus*, ML *adjunctīvus*, E *adjunctive*;—

*coniungere*, to join *con-* or together, pp *coniunctus*, whence E *conjunct*; derivative *coniunctiō*, o/s *coniunctiōn-*, OF hence E *conjunction*; LL *coniunctīuus*, ML *conjunctīvus*, whence both E *conjunctive* and (suffix -*itis*) E *conjunctivitis*; ML *conjunctūra*, E *conjuncture*;—

*disiungere*, to unyoke (*dis-*, apart), to disunite, pp *disiunctus*, E *disjunct*; derivative *disiunctiō*, o/s *disiunctiōn-*, E *disjunction*; *disiunctīuus*, ML *disjunctīvus*, E *disjunctive*;—

*iniungere*, to join *in-*, into, hence onto, hence to impose, pp *iniunctus*, whence E *injunct*, rare adj; derivative *iniunctiō*, in LL an enjoining, an order, o/s *iniunctiōn-*, E *injunction*, whence anl *injunctive*;—

*sēiungere*, to separate (privative *sē-*), pp *sēiunctus*, whence the rare *sejunct* and, from *sēiunctiō*, the rare *sejunction* and its anl derivative *sejunctive*;—

*subiungere*, to join under (*sub*) the yoke, to subject to the yoke, LL to subjoin, pp *subiunctus*, whence *subjunct*; derivative LL *subiunctiō*, o/s *subiunctiōn-*, E *subjunction*; LL *subiunctīuus*, ML *subjunctīvus*, E *subjunctive*.

## VI. Romance—Spanish

15. L *iunctus*, f *iuncta*, ML *juncta*, becomes, as n, the Sp *junta*, a council or tribunal, partly adopted by E; hence, the corruption *junto*, a faction— prompted by the very numerous Sp nn in -*o*.

## VII. Romance—French

16. L *iungere*, ML *jungere*, becomes OF-F *joindre*, which, used as n, accounts for the E n *joinder*; OF *joindre*, perhaps rather *joignant*, presp, or 'ils *joignent*', they join, produces ME *joignen*, later *joinen*, whence 'to *join*'. Derivative OF-MF *joigneor* becomes ME *joynour*, whence E *joiner*. The pp *joint* becomes the E adj *joint*; the derivative OF-F n *joint* or *jointe* becomes the E n *joint*, whence 'to *joint*', whence *jointer*. But E *jointure*,

adopted from OF-F, derives from ML *junctūra*, LL *iunctura* (as in para 12).

17. The relevant F cpds, deriving from L but following the pattern of *joindre*, are:

MF-EF *ajoindre* (ML *adjungere*: para 14), EF reshaping it to *adjoindre*—ME *ajoinen*—reshaped E 'to *adjoin*';

OF-F (archaic) *conjoindre* (ML *conjungere*)—'to *conjoin*'; the OF-F pp *conjoint* is adopted by E;

MF-F *disjoindre* (OF *desjoindre*, ML *disjungere*): E 'to *disjoin*'; the MF pp *disjoint* is adopted by E, with anl derivative *disjointure*;

Late OF-F *enjoindre* (ML *injungere*) becomes both the E n *enjoinder* and, anl with other -*join* vv, 'to *enjoin*'; cf:

MF-F *rejoindre* (*re-*, again+*joindre*) yields both a '*rejoinder*' and 'to *rejoin*';

MF-EF *subjoindre* (ML *subjungere*), whence— after *rejoinder*—*subjoinder* and, after other -*join* vv, 'to *subjoin*'.

18. A less obvious debt to F is 'to *joust*', var 'to *just*': ME *jousten*, *justen*: OF *jouster*, *juster*, earliest *joster* (cf F *jouter*): ML *juxtāre*: LL *iuxta*, very close to (prep), L *iuxta*, so close as to touch (adv): from L *iugsta*: *iug-*, r of *iugum*+formative *s*+adv suffix -*ta*. The OF v *joster*, *juster*, *jouster* has derivative OF-MF n *joste*, *juste*, *jouste*, whence ME *just*, *joust*, extant in E.

19. ME *jousten*, *justen*, have late ME-EE freq *joustle*, *justle*, soon *jostle*—orig, jousting terms— the 1st obs by 1700, the 2nd obsol by 1900 and obs by 1950, the 3rd extant.

## VIII. Germanic

20. 'To *yoke*' derives from OE *geocian*, itself from the source of the E n *yoke* (ME *yok*): OE *geoc*, akin to OHG *joh*, Go *yuk*, ON *ok* (? worn-down from Gmc r *juk-*): cf para 3. Unless a dim (-*el*) from *yoke* of oxen—perh he was orig a plough-man—*yokel* (at first, c1800, cant; then sl; by c1850, SE) is difficult to explain, the dial sense 'woodpecker', even if *green*, being unsatisfactory.

**joint, jointure.** See prec, para 16.

**joist; gist.**

The former app arises from a dial pron of the latter: whereas the former, ME *giste*, is adopted from OF-MF *giste* (F *gîte*), from ML-VL *jacitum*, from ML-VL *jacēre*, L *iacēre*, to be lying on the ground (f.a.e., JACULATE, para 1), the latter is adopted from OF *gist*, (he) lies on the ground (F *gît*), from OF-MF *gesir* (later *gésir*), from ML *jacēre*, L *iacēre*: the latter is that foundation of a legal case without which it would not *lie* (be admissible), and the former is a beam *lying* from wall to wall.

**joke** (n, hence v, whence **joker**); **jocose, jocosity; jocular, jocularity; juggle, juggler, jugglery; jewel** (n, hence v), **jeweller, jewellery** or **jewelry;** sep JEOPARDY;—**hoax** (n, v)—**hocus-pocus—hokey pokey—hokum.**

1. *Joke* derives from ML *jocus* (s *joc-*), L *iocus* (s *ioc-*), a joke or a jest, orig a verbal game, app

akin to Lith *juokas*, a joke, mirth; the Gmc cognates occ proposed are extremely doubtful.

2. L *iocus* has L adj *iocōsus*, ML *jocōsus*, whence *jocose*, whence *jocosity*, prob after *jocularity*, from LL *ioculāritās*, wittiness, from LL *ioculāris*, (as n) a wit, (also adj) witty, whence *jocular*.

3. L *iocus* has a dim *ioculus*, whence *ioculāri*, to jest, whence OF-EF *jogler*, with var *jugler*, to jest, hence to be a jester or entertainer, e.g. a tumbler or esp a juggler, whence ME *juglen*, E 'to juggle', whence 'a juggle'. L *ioculāri* has agent *joculātor*, ML *joculātor*, whence, via the acc *joculātorem*, the OF-EF *jogleor*, varr *joglere* and *jugleor*, whence ME *jogelour* and *juglur*, whence E *juggler*; OF-EF *jogler*, *jugler*, has the OF-MF derivative *joglerie*, *juglerie*, whence E *jugglery*.

4. L *iocus* has the VL adj *iocālis*, ML *jocālis*, whence OF *joel*, var *juel*, a plaything, hence a trinket, hence a jewel, unless OF *joel* derives imm from OF-F *jeu* (ML *jocus*, L *iocus*): *joel* and *juel* become, in ME, resp *jowel* and *juel*, the latter becoming E *jewel*. OF *juel* has both agent MF *juelier*, whence E *jeweller*, and collective MF *juelerie*, whence E *jewellery* and AE and E *jewelry*.

5. The ML *jocus* has app produced the prob orig jugglers' mock-L catch-phrase *hocus-pocus* (? sc 'what a *jokus*!'), whence *hocus*, n and v, and prob, by contr, *hoax*, n hence v; the sl *hokum* prob arose as a mock-L neu (*hocum*) of the *hocus* of *hocus-pocus*. Moreover, *hokey-pokey* is merely *hocus-pocus* anglicized, this being its orig sense, whence arises that of 'cheap ice-cream sold by itinerant vendors'. (The It *O, che poco* is f/e nonsense, for the phrase means, not 'Oh, how cheap!' but 'Oh, how little!'—hardly a good slogan.)

**jollification; jollity.** See:

**jolly** (1), adj, whence **jolliness; jollify,** whence **jollification; jollity.**

The naut sl *jolly*, a marine, and 'to jolly', to render (someone) jolly, hence to banter, derive, the former prob, the latter certainly, from the adj *jolly*, itself from ME *joly*, from OF *joli* (orig *jolif*), merry (whence F *joli*, pretty), prob from ON *jōl* (q.v. at YULE). E *jolly* has the coll derivative *jollify*, to render (-*fy*) jolly, hence to make merry; and OF *joli* has the MF derivative *joliete* (E -*ety*), whence ME *jolite* (three-syllabled), whence *jollity* (-*ity*).

**jolly** (2), n, is short for **jolly boat**, a partly f/e derivative from Da *jolle*, a yawl; *yawl* itself prob comes rather from MLG *jolle* (cf D *jol*), a ship's small boat; E *yawl* acquires the sense 'a light sailing vessel'. Hence *yawler*, one of its crew.

**Jolly Roger, the.** See ROBERT, para 6.

**jolt** (v, hence n); **jowl.**

The former, o.o.o., perh derives from *jole*, an EE var of *jowl*, and, if so, orig means 'to knock on the head' or 'to butt with the head'. *Jowl*, jaw, jawbone, cheek, blends OF-F *joue*, cheek, with ME *chauel*, itself for *chavel*, from OE *ceafl*, jaw, akin to the syn MHG *kiver* (G *Kiefer*) and ON *kiaptr* (*kjaptr*) and perh OIr *gap*, mouth; *jowl*, a

dewlap, and *jowl*, a fish's head, are prob id with *jowl*, jaw, cheek.

**Jonah,** bringer of bad luck, derives from the Biblical *Jonah* (H *Yōnāh*, lit a dove), cast overboard by superstitious sailors.

**jonquil:** EF-F *jonquille*: Sp *junquilla*, jonquil, orig a reed: dim of *junco*, a rush: ML *juncus* (cf the OF-F *jonc*), L *iuncus*, s *iunc*-: perh from *iungere*, to join, s *iung*-: if so, cf JOIN. The jonquil has reed- or rush-like leaves.

**jordan.** See:

**Jordan almonds:** by f/e from ME *jardyne almaunde*: OF-F *jardin*, a garden + *almaunde*, q.v. at ALMOND. *Jordan,* (obs) a narrow-necked vessel for liquids, (dial and sl) a chamberpot, prob derives from *\*Jordan bottle*, a bottle containing water brought by pilgrims from the river Jordan, famous in Biblical history.

**joseph,** a riding-cloak, any C18 cloak, derives from Biblical Joseph's 'coat of many colours': ML *Jōsēphus*, LL *Iōsēphus*: LGr *Iōsēph*: H *Yōsēph*, 'He shall add' (? to the family). Pet-form: *Joe*, with dim *Joey*: both occurring in sl and coll E, ref some famous tenant's given-name.

**joss.** See DIANA, para 5.

**jostle.** See JOIN, para 19.

**jot,** n hence v. See IOTA.

**joule** derives from an E physicist, James P. *Joule* (1818–89). Hence the Phys adj *joulean*.

**journal, journalese, journalism, journalist.** See DIANA, para 9.

**journey,** etc. See DIANA, para 10.

**joust,** n, v. See JOIN, para 18.

**Jove; jovial** (whence **joviality**). See DIANA, para 4.

**jowl,** whence -*jowled* and **jowly.** See JOLT.

**joy** (n, v), **joyance, joyful, joyless, joyous; enjoy, enjoyable, enjoyment; rejoice,** whence pa and vn **rejoicing; gaud** (n, v), **gaudery, gaudy,** adj and n.

1. The n *joy*, ME *joye*, OF-F *joie*, derives from L *gaudia*, pl of *gaudium* (s *gaudi*-, r *gaud*-), itself from *gaudēre* (s and r *gaud*-), to be joyous, whence, via LL *\*gaudīre* and OF-MF *joīr* (F *jouir*), the E 'to *joy*': and the r *gaud*- is a -*d* extn of *\*gau*-, itself an extn of the IE *\*ga*- present in Gr *gaiein* and *ganumi*, I rejoice, and *gauros*, proud.

2. *Joyful* and *joyless* merely add the suffixes -*ful* and -*less* to the n *joy*; *joyance*, however, derives from OF-MF *joiance* (from *joīr*), and *joyous* from OF-MF *joyous*, var of *joious* (EF-F *joyeux*), itself a var of *joios* (from *joie*).

3. OF-MF *joīr* has cpds MF *enjoīr*, whence 'to enjoy', whence *enjoyable* and *enjoyment*, and OF-EF *esjoīr*, an *es*- (L *ex*-) int of *joīr*, this *esjoīr* combining with *re*-, again, to form OF-EF *resjoīr*, to rejoice (esp 'ils *resjoīssent*', they rejoice), whence 'to *rejoice*'.

4. L *gaudēre* becomes VL *\*gaudīre*, whence OF-EF *gaudir*, whence app the ME n *gaude*, whence E *gaud*, (obs) a jest, (then) a trinket, whence 'to *gaud*' and *gaudery* and the adj *gaudy*; the n *gaudy* however, prob derives from L *gaudium*, joy, with

the E university sense perh influenced by the imperative *gaudē*, rejoice!

**jubilance**, from **jubilant**; **jubilarian**; **jubilate**, v, and **Jubilate**, n; **jubilation**, **jubilatory**, **jubilee.**—**yodel** (v, hence n); perh **yowl** (v, hence n).

1. *Jubilant*, adj, derives from *jūbilant-*, o/s of ML *jūbilans*, presp of *jūbilāre*, LL *iūbilāre*, to utter cries of joy, L *iūbilāre*, to shout, to shout after (domestic animals): IE r, *\*yū-*: cf Gr *iuzō*, I shout or shriek, *iugē*, a cry or shout of either joy or woe, and, for the r, the echoic *iū*, a cry of wonder. L *iūbilāre* has pp *iūbilātus*, whence 'to *jubilate*'; *Jubilate* is that psalm (100th—Vulgate 99th) which begins 'Jubilate', Shout ye with joy. Derivative L *iūbilātiō*, o/s *iūbilātiōn-*, yields OF-F, whence E, *jubilation*, whence, anl, the adj *jubilatory*. A *jubilarian* (*-arian*), ML *jūbilārius* (*-ārius*), is one who is celebrating a *jubilee*: MF-F *jubilé*: ML *jūbilaeus*, LL *iūbilaeus*, better *iōbelēus*: LGr *iōbēlaios* (suffix *-aios*): H *yōbēl*, a ram's horn, hence a trumpet: the LL *iōbelēus* having been influenced by L *iūbilum*, a shout, from *iūbil*āre. (Souter; E & M.)

2. ML *jūbil*āre acquires, ult, a G cognate: *jodeln*, whence 'to *yodel*'. The G word derives imm from the exclamatory *jō*, itself clearly, though remotely, akin to the Gr *iū* of para 1.

3. ML *jūbil*āre perh acquires the further cognate 'to *yowl*', imm from ME *youlen*.

**Judaic**, **Judaism**, **Judaize**. See JEW, para 3.

**Judas** and **judas**; **Judas tree**. See JEW, para 4.

**judge** (n, v), **judgement**. See DICT, para 15.

**judicable**, **judicate**, **judication**, **judicature**. See DICT, para 16.

**judicial**, **judiciary**, **judicious**. See DICT, para 17.

**jug** (pitcher, ewer), n hence v, app derives from *Jug*, a pet-form of *Joan* or *Joanna* (cf *Meg*, for *Margaret*); hence *jug*, any woman, but esp a servant; *Joan* was formerly a common name among servants. Perh, sem, cf MOP.

**jugal**, **jugate**. See JOIN, para 10.

**juggernaut** derives from *Juggernaut*, an anglicized form of *Jagannath*, an idol of Krishna at Puri in Orissa, India: Hi *Jagannāth*, Lord of the World: Skt *jagannātha*. The E senses arise from the former, completely erroneous belief that devotees allowed themselves to be crushed beneath the wheels of the idol perambulating at an annual festival.

**juggle**, **juggler**, **jugglery**. See JOKE, para 3.

**jugular**, **jugulum**. See JOIN, para 10, s.f.

**jugum**. See JOIN, para 10.

**juice**, whence **juicy**; **verjuice.**

*Juice*, ME *juis*, earlier *juse*, derives from MF-F *jus*, juice, gravy, broth, from syn ML *jūs*, L *iūs*: cf Skt *yús*, broth. MF-F *jus* has the MF-F cpd *verjus*, for *vert jus*, green juice—the juice of green fruit. (Cf VERD.) MF *verjus* becomes ME *vergeous*, etc., whence E *verjuice*.

**jujitsu** is a var of and now commoner than *jujutsu*: Jap *jūjutsu*: *jū*, pliant+*jutsu*, art: the yielding art.

**jujube**, adopted from F (EF *jajube*), comes from LL *zizufum*, from L *ziziphum*, trln of Gr *zizuphon*, itself from OPer *zīzafūn*.

**juke**. See JAZZ.

**julep**, adopted from F, comes into MF from OProv *julep* or OSp *julepe*, from Ar *julāb*, itself from Per *gulāb*, rose water: *gul*, a rose+*āb*, water.

**julienne**. See:

**July**; **Julia**, **Julian**, **julienne**, **Juliet**, **Julius.**

*July*, AF *Julie*, derives from ML *Jūlius*, L *iūlius* (*mensis*), the Julian month, a month named for Caius *Iūlius* Caesar, born in it: *Iūlius* was a clan name. L derivatives include *Iūlia*, whence *Julia*; *Iūliānus*, whence E *Julian* and F *Julien*, whence, presumably, after a famous chef, *julienne*; L *Iūlia* has LL dim *Iūlitta*, ML *Jūlitta*, whence F *Juliette*, E *Juliet*.

**jumble** (v, hence n) is perh an easing of the syn ME *jompren*: ? cf JUMP.

**jumbo**, any very large person or thing, cf *Jumbo*, a generic name for elephants, from *Jumbo*, a particularly large African elephant in the London Zoo of the early 1880's: prob from either MUMBO-JUMBO or Kongoese *nzombo*, a python. (Webster.)

**jumentous**. See JOIN, para 11.

**jump** (1), a loose jacket, an under-bodice, whence **jumper**; **jupe**, **jupon.**

A *jump* is prob f/e (? after 'to *jump*') for earlier *jup*, from *juppe*, adopted from EF *juppe*, a var of OF(-F) *jupe*, a skirt, etc., itself perh via Sp *aljuba*, a long woollen Moorish garment, from Ar *jubbah* (*al-* being merely the Ar 'the'), such an outer garment; OF-F *jupe* has the MF-F derivative *jupon*, and both words have been partly adopted by E.

**jump** (2), to leap high, whence the n, derives from ML *jumpāre*: o.o.o.: perh ult echoic. Hence a *jumper* and the pa, vn *jumping*; the n *jump* has adj *jumpy*.

**jumper** (1). See the 1st JUMP.—**jumper** (2). See the 2nd JUMP.

**jumpy**. See 2nd JUMP, s.f.

**junction**, **junctive**, **juncture**. See JOIN, para 12.

**June**: OF-F *juin*: ML *Jūnius*, L *Iūnius*, the name of a Roman clan: cf, sem and perh phon, JULY.

**jungle**, whence the adj **jungly**, derives from Hind *jaṅgal*, desert or forest, two senses merging, sem, in that of jungle: Skt *jaṅgala*, waste ground, wilderness, desert: cf the sem development of *wilderness*, q.v. at WILD.

**junior**. See JUVENILE, para 1.

**juniper**: ML *jūniperus*, L *iūniperus* (varr *iūnipirus* and LL *iniperus*, ML *giniperus*): OL *\*ieniperus*: ? akin to L *iuncus*, a rush or a reed; perh of Medit stock. Cf:

**junk** (1), orig a piece of old rope, hence old cordage, hence any old materials, prob comes from Port *junco*, junk, earlier cordage, earliest a reed or rush: ML *juncus*, L *iuncus*, a reed, a (bul)rush: prob Medit—cf Eg *ganu*, reed.

**junk** (2), an Oriental, esp a Ch, sailing ship: Port *junco*: Jav *joṅ*.

**junket** (n, hence v), orig a cream cheese, comes from It *giuncata*, a cream cheese served in a reed- or rush- or wicker-basket: an *-ata* derivative of *giunco*, a rush, ML *juncus*, L *iuncus*: cf the 1st JUNK.

Juno, whence (after statue*sque*) **Junoesque, is** L *lūnō*, the consort of Jupiter: o.o.o.

**junta; junto.** See JOIN, para 15.

**jupe.** See the 1st JUMP.

**Jupiter.** See DIANA, para 3.

**jupon.** See the 1st JUMP.

**Jurassic:** F *jurassique*, of the *Jura* mountains, with false suffix *-assique* (*-asique*), *-assic*, from F *triasique*, E *Triassic*, adj of the Geol system known as *Trias* (L from Gr *trias*, a set of three).

**jurat:** MF-F *jurat*: ML *jūrātus* (n from pp): L *iūrātus*, sworn, pp of *iūrāre* (s *iūr-*), to swear. Cf the LL adj *iūrātōrius*, formed in *-ōrius* upon *iūrāt-*, s of pp *iūrātus*: hence, via ML *jūrātōrius*, the E *juratory*. See, f.a.e., JUS, and cf:

**juridic(al).** See DICT, para 11.

**jurisconsult; jurisdiction; jurisprudence.** For *juris-* (L *iūris*, gen of *iūs*, law), see the element *juris-*; for the 2nd elements, cf CONSUL—DICT, para 11—PRUDENCE. The 1st and the 3rd prob come imm from late MF-F *jurisconsulte* and EF-F *jurisdiction*, both from L cpds.

**jurist** (whence **juristic**). See para 3 of the 2nd JURY.

**juror.** See para 2 of 2nd JURY.

**jury** (1), adj, as in **jury mast** and **jury-rigged**, occurs earliest in *jury mast*, a temporary mast, which app tacks MAST to an aphetic derivative of OF-MF *ajurie*, contr of OF-MF *adjutorie*, assistance, relief, from ML *adjutōrium*, assistance, support, L *adiutōrium*, from *adiutāre*, to aid, to support (cf *adjutant*).

**jury** (2), n, **juror;** sep JURAT and JURIDICAL; **jurist**—**abjure, abjuration, abjuratory; adjure, adjuration, adjuratory; conjure, conjuration, conjurator, conjurer** (and **conjuror**), **conjury; injure, injurious. injury; perjure** (whence pa **perjured** and **perjurer**), **perjurious, perjury;**—**just** (adj, hence adv and n; v **justice** (and **injustice**), **justiciar, justiciary; justify, justifiable, justification, justificative, justificatory; adjust** (whence **adjuster**), **adjustment,** with *re-* cpds; sep JUDGE, etc., q.v. at DICT, para 15, JUDICATE (ib, para 16), JUDICIAL and JUDICIOUS (ib, para 17) and PREJUDICE (18*a*).

1. The effective basis of all these words is L *iūs*, ML *jūs*, gen *iūris*, ML *jūris* (o/s *iūr-*, *jūr-*), orig a religious formula having the force of law, but, in L-LL-ML, *iūs* (*jūs*) is law, hence justice: cf the Ve formula *yós* '(Your) welfare!'; perh cf also Alb *jē*, permission, and OIr *uisse*, just, right; ? ult akin to L *iugum*, a yoke, and *iungere*, to join. ML *jus* is retained in many European, incl E, legal phrases.

2. L *iūs* has o/s *iūr-*, whence *iūrāre* (s *iūr-*), ML *jūrāre*, orig to pronounce a ritual formula, but predominantly to swear on oath. From the pp *iūrātus*, s *iūrat-*, comes the agent *iūrātor*, ML *jūrātor*, whence OF-MF *jureor*, whence E *juror*. ML *jūrāre* becomes OF-F *jurer*, whence OF-MF *jurée*, an oath, hence a juridical inquiry, which becomes E *jury*, with the new sense 'a body of persons sworn to give a true verdict in a court of law'—adopted, late in C17, by F.

3. ML forms upon the o/s *jūr-* the n *jūrista* (*-ista*, Gr *-istēs*, E *-ist*), whence, app via MF-F *juriste*, the E *jurist*. More important is L *iniūrius*, unjust, whence—perh via MF-F *injurieux*—the E *injurious*; derivative L *iniūria*, OF-F *injure*, E *injury*; thence the derivative v *iniūriāri*, MF-F *injurier*, E 'to *injure*'.

Compounds of L *iūrāre*, ML *jūrāre*

4. The cpds relevant to E are these:

*abiūrāre*, to swear *ab* or away, to deny upon oath, whence 'to *abjure*'; derivative LL *abiūrātiō*, o/s *abiūrātiōn-*, whence *abjuration*, whence, anl, *abjuratory*.

*adiūrāre*, to swear *ad* or to, hence to adjure, whence, perh via EF-F *adjurer*, 'to *adjure*'; derivative *adiūrātiō*, o/s *adiūrātiōn-*, whence *adjuration*, and LL *adiūrātōrius*, whence *adjuratory*.

*coniūrāre*, to swear *con* or together, to conspire, hence, in LL, to beg urgently, hence, in ML, to exorcise, to avert by prayer, hence also by magic: whence MF-F *conjurer*, E 'to *conjure*', long obs in its orig sense; derivative *coniūrātiō*, o/s *coniūrātiōn-*, whence, via MF-F, the E *conjuration*; the ML agent *conjūrātor* is adopted by legal E; MF-F *conjurer* has derivative *conjureur*, which perh suggested the E *conjurer* (modern sense) and *conjuror*, a co-swearer upon oath; *conjury* app='to *conjure*' +n-suffix *-y*.

*periūrāre*, to swear *per-*, thoroughly, esp against the facts, whence OF-F (*se*) *parjurer*, whence the reshaped 'to *perjure*'; derivative OF *parjurie* leads to reshaped E *perjury*, whence—unless from L *periūriōsus*—*perjurious*.

*Just* and *Justice*

5. L *iūstus*, ML *jūstus*, conformable to law, derives from *iūs*, law; hence, via OF-F *juste*, the E *just*. Derivative *iūstitia* leads, via OF-F, to E *justice*. The negg *iniūstus*, *iniūstitia*, pass through MF-F and OF-F to become E *injust* (obs—now *unjust*) and *injustice*. The OF-MF derivative v *justicier* becomes 'to *justice*' (obs); its OF-F derivative *justiciable* is adopted by E; ML *jūstitiārius* (*-ārius*), later *jūsticiārius*, becomes the E n *justiciar*, whence the Sc extn *justiciary* (cf the OF-F n *justicier*).

6. The derivative LL cpd *iūstificāre*, ML *j-*, to render just, to justify, becomes OF-F *justifier*, whence 'to *justify*'; derivative LL *iūstificātiō*, o/s *iūstificātiōn-*, yields—perh via OF-F—*justification*, whence, anl, *justificatory*; MF-F *justifiable* (*-able*) is adopted by E; EF-F *justificatif*, f *-ive*, yields *justificative*.

7. OF-F *juste* has derivative MF-F cpd *ajuster* (*a-*=*à*, L *ad*, to+*juste*+inf ending *-er*), whence 'to *adjust*'; derivative MF-F *ajustement* produces *adjustment*. The related OF-F *rajuster* (*re-*, again+ *ajuster*) prompts, although it does not generate, the E *readjust*, whence, anl, *readjustment*.

**just,** adj. See prec, para 5.

**just,** n (a tourney). See JOIN, para 18.

justice, justiciable, justiciar, justiciary. See JURY, para 5.

justifiable, justification, justificative, justify, See JURY, para 6.

justle. See JOIN, para 19.

jut. See the 2nd JET, para 6.

Jute is a b/f from *Jutes*, an Englishing of Bede's ML *Jutae*, Juti, which=OE *Eōtas*, a var of *Iōtas*, app from ON *Iōtar*, the people of (the etym-derivative) *Jut*land.

jute: Bengali *jhuṭo* (var *jhōṭo*), jute: Skt *jūṭa*, var *jaṭā*, a braid of hair, hence matted hair, hence a fibrous root.

juvenal, juvenescent. See paras 2 and 3 of:

juvenile (adj, hence n), juvenility, juvenal (and Juvenal), juvenescent; rejuvenate; junior (adj, hence n), whence juniority (after *seniority*).—young (adj, hence n), whence—after *younker*—youngster (suffix -*ster*); younker; youth, whence youthful.

1. *Junior*, adopted from ML *junior*, is L *iunior* (s *iuni-*, r *iun-*), younger, the comp of *iuuenis*, ML *juvenis*, young, hence a young man or woman, s *iuuen-*, r *iuu-*: cf Skt *yúvā*, young, acc *yúvānam* (cf L *iuuenem*, ML *juvenem*)—with *a* for *u* in Av *yava*, young, and Skt *yávīyas-*, younger, and *yáviṣṭhas*, youngest; cf also OSl *junŭ* and Lith *jáunas*—W *ieuanc*, OW *iouenc*, OIr *óac*, *óc*, Ga *òg*, Cor *iouenc*, *iunc*, *yowynk*, *yonk*, OC *\*yovnko-*, cf L *iuuencus*, ML *juvencus*, a young bull, *iuuenca*, a heifer (*iuuencus* being orig an adj)—Go *juggs* (pron *yoongs*)—OFris, OS, OHG *jung*, MHG *junc*, G *jung*—ON *ungr*—OE *geong*, *gung*. Gmc etymon is *\*jungaz*, for *\*juwungaz*; the IE etymon is *\*juwenkos*.

2. L *iuuenis*, young person, has these relevant derivatives:

*iuuenālis* (after *uirginālis*), youthful, whence E *juvenal*, as in '*juvenal* plumage'; hence an EE n, a young man (cf Shakespeare's 'my tender juvenal'); L *iuvenālis* becomes n in the satirical poet *Iuuenālis*, ML *Juvenālis*, E *Juvenal*, whence the adj *Juvenalian*;

*iuuenīlis* (after *puerīlis*), ML *juvenīlis*, young, whence (F and) E *juvenile*; derivative L *iuuenīlitās*, ML *juvenīlitās*, yields E *juvenility*.

3. L *iuuenis*, young, has relevant derivatives:

LL *iuuenescere*, to become young, grow young again, presp *iuuenescens*, o/s *iuuenescent-*, ML *juvenescent-*, whence E *juvenescent*;

and—perh rather from *iuuenis*, young man—Horace's *iuuenāri*, to talk or act like a young man, with pp *iuuenātus* (ML *juvenātus*), whence, aided by *iuuenis*, young man, the E *rejuvenate*, to make young again, to restore (a measure of) youth to, whence *rejuvenation*; cf 'to *rejuvenesce*', to make or become young again, from ML *rejuvenescere*, with presp *rejuvenescens*, o/s *rejuvenescent-*, whence E *rejuvenescent*, whence *rejuvenescence*.

4. OE *geong*, *gung*, becomes ME *yong*, *yung*, whence E *young*. OE *geong* has derivative *geoguth* or *geogoth*—a collective n—prob an easing of *\*geonth*: ME *yeogethe*, *yuwethe*, *yuhethe*, *youhthe*, *youthe*: E *youth*. The particular 'young person' (still in EE), following naturally from the collective 'young persons', becomes fully established as 'young man' only c1750. With OE *geogoth*, *geoguth*, cf OS *juguth*, OFris *jogethe*, OHG *jugund*, MHG *jugent*, G *Jugend*, Go *junda*: Gmc r, *\*jugunth-*; IE r, *\*juwent-* (cf L *iuuentus*, ML *juventus*, youth, whether an abstract or a collective concrete).

5. Akin to OE *geong* is the syn MD *jonc* (D *jong*), whence MD *jonchere*, *jongheer*, *jongher*, *joncker*, *jonker*, D *jonkheer*, *jonker*, lit a young lord (cf the G *Herr*), whence EE *younker*, a young nobleman or a young gallant, hence, in E, a youth, hence the coll sense 'child'.

juxtapose. See POSE, para 13, and sem, cf *joust*, q.v. at JOIN, para 18.

jynx. See JINX.

# K

Kaffir, rarely Kafir; Gheber or Gebir—cf Giaour.

1. *Kafir*, member of a SAfr Bu race, hence its language, derives from the obsol *Kafir*, a non-Mohammedan, an infidel: Ar *Kafīr*, from *kafara*, to be, in religion, a sceptic: one of many instances of the influence exercised by medieval Ar traders and explorers and soldiers upon the IE languages.

2. Ar *kafīr*, an infidel, becomes Per *gabr*, whence F *guèbre*, whence E *Gheber* or, as in W.S. Landor's poem (1798), *Gebir*; cf *giaour*, as in Byron's poem (*The Giaour*, 1813), from Tu *giaur*, from Per *gaur*, a var of *gabr*.

kail. See COLE, para 2. (Cf KALE.)

Kaiser. See CAESAR, para 3.

kaka, a Maori echoic name for a large NZ parrot, has derivative kakapo, the NZ owl parrot.

kale. See COLE, para 2.

kaleidoscope. See the element -*scope* and cf *telescope*.

kalmuck or kalmuk, a shaggy cloth, derives from *Kalmuck, Kalmuk*, member of a Buddhist Mongol tribe (whence the language): Turki *kalmuk*, that body of a nomadic Tatar tribe which remains at home: lit, 'the *has-remained*', for *kalmuk* is orig the pp of *kalmak*, to remain (at home).

Kanaka, a South Sea Islander, esp a Melanesian imported into the Queensland sugar plantations, derives from Polynesian *kanaka*, a man: *Kanakas* are, to themselves, '*The* Men'. (Cf 'We Are *the* People' in P⁴.)

kangaroo; wallaroo; wallaby.

These words represent two Aus Aboriginal vv: *kanga* and *walla*, to leap or jump, with two n-suffixes: -*roo* and -*by* (possibly orig complete words meaning 'quadruped'): either 'the jumpers' or 'the jumping (quadrupeds or animals)'. There is no good reason to doubt that all three names are, or orig were, of native origin.

kaolin (whence the adj kaolinic), adopted from F, derives from Ch *Kaoling*, where this pure white clay was first extracted: Pekinese *kao-ling*, a high hill.

kapok: Mal *kapok* (cf Jav *kapuk*).

karakul, occ caracul, the glossy black coat—used as fur—of newborn lambs of the *Karakul* breed of sheep in Bokhara: *Karakul*, a lake of the Pamir region in Central Asia: *kara*, black+*kul*, lake. Turki *kara* (Tu *qarah*), black, occurs in many a Central and Western Asiatic Pl N, e.g. the famous *Karakoram* (or -*um*) mountain range.

karma (whence the adj karmic), the Buddhist and Hindu principle of moral and spiritual causation, is adopted from Hi, itself from Skt, *karma*.

karoo or karroo, an arid plateau of SAfr, whence *the Great Karroo*, app derives from Cape Province Hottentot word for 'red soil'.

kasher. See KOSHER.

Kashmir. See CASHMERE.

katydid, a noisy NA insect, is named from its shrill note *katydid-katydid* or, f/e, *Katy did—Katy did*.

kauri, a fine NZ tree, is Maori: ? lit, from its hardness, 'iron', as the Tahitian, Paumotan, Samoan cognates imply (Tregear).

kay. See the 2nd KEY.

kayak, an Eskimo canoe, is naturally of Eskimo origin—prob the Hudson Bay *keiyak*.

kea, a large NZ parrot, is a Maori word, prob echoic: cf KAKA.

kedge, a small anchor, may derive from 'to *kedge*', to use one: o.o.o.: perh cf E dial *cadge,* to tie or bind, ME *caggen*, a var of CATCH.

kedgeree: Hi *khicṛī*, from *khichreé*, a dish basically of rice, flavoured with sesamum.

keel (1) of a ship; keelhaul.

To *keelhaul* is to haul or hale (a man) along the ship's keel: D *kielhalen*. *Keel* derives either from ON *kjölr* or from OHG *kiol* (MHG-G *kiel*); the latter leads to the D *kiel*. There has prob been confusion between the Gmc (? esp Scan) origins of *keel* (1) and (2); perh the two words are ult id.

keel (2), a fat-bottomed lighter or barge: MD *kiel*, a sea-going vessel, akin to OE *cēol* and ON *kjöll* (*kiöll*).

keelson (var kelson) is app, like G *Kielschwein*, of Scan origin: cf the D *kolzwijn*, MD *colzwijn*, -*swijn*. The 1st element is prob that of KEEL (1); the 2nd may be a corruption of Nor *svill* (E SILL).

keen (1), adj, whence keenness. See CAN, para 2.

keen (2), n and v: a wailing of lamentation, to wail in lamentation: Ir *caoine*, n, and *caoinim*, I wail: with the latter, cf OIr *cáinim* (var *cóinim*), Ga *caoin*, W *cwyno*, Br *keinal*.

keep (v, hence n), whence agent keeper and pa, vn keeping and keepsake (something one keeps for the sake of the giver).

1. 'To *keep*', ME *kepen*, derives from OE *cēpan*, to observe or notice, to desire to seek, to keep

(the semantic chain or, at the least, interconnexions are worth noting): cf ON *kōpa*, MD *capen*, MLG *kapen*, MHG *kapfen*, to gaze or stare. The origins of this v need to be clarified still further.

2. Such cpds as *housekeeper* and *upkeeper*, however, present no difficulty.

keg is a—? orig Cockney—deviation from *cag*, C16 *cagge*, late ME *kag*, akin to and prob deriving from ON *kaggi*, a cask: o.o.o.

kelp: EE *kilp* or *kilpe*: ME *culp* or *culpe*: o.o.o.

kelpie, kelpy, a horse-like water-spirit, is of C origin: cf esp Ga *cailpeach*, *calpach*, *colpach*, heifer, colt, from EIr *colpthach*, a heifer.

kelson. See KEELSON.

kelter. See KILTER.

ken. See CAN, para 1.

kennel. See CANINE, para 3.

keno. See FIVE, para 12.

Kent. See CANTER.

Kentucky bluegrass, a meadow grass growing best in *Kentucky*, itself perh Amerind for 'prairie'.

kepi: F *képi*: Swiss G *Kaeppi*, dim of *Kappe*, bonnet (E CAP).

kerchief. See CHIEF, para 8.

kermes. See CARMINE.

kermess or kermiss. See CHURCH, para 4.

kernel. See GRAIN, para 9.

kerosene: Gr *kēros*, wax (cf L *cēra*)+the Chem *-ene* of, e.g., *benzene* and *gasolene*.

kestrel: ME *castrel*: MF *cresserelle*: ? VL *cristarellus*, from L *crista*, crest: f.a.e., CREASE.

ketch, a sailing vessel rather like a yawl, app derives—? by Cockney deviation (cf KEG)—from late ME *catch*, perh from 'to CATCH'.

kettle, whence, from its shape, kettledrum: ME *ketel*: ON *ketill*, which, like OE *cetel*, derives from L *catillus*, dim of *catīnus*, a (large) deep vessel, prob akin to Gr *kotulē*, a bowl, a cup, and Skt *cātvāla*, a hole: basic idea, 'hollow(ness)'.

kevel. See the 2nd GAVEL.

kewpie, a wingèd, chubby-faced infant fairy, drawn by Rose O'Neill (†1944), hence an imitative doll: orig (c1911) AE: *Cupid*; prob from the chubby and wingèd representations of Cupid by It artists.

key (1) of door, whence keyboard, -hole, -stone, etc., is ME *key*, earlier *keye*, earliest *kay*, from OE *cǣg* (var *cǣge*): cf OFris *kai* or *kei*, prob OHG-MHG *kidel*, MHG *kil*, G *Keil*, a wedge, itself prob akin to OE *cīna*, a crevice, E *chine*, with Gmc r *ki-*, to split, to open up, to open; very prob akin to ON *kīll*, a long, narrow inlet (cf the AE *kill*, channel, stream).

key (2), a low island, esp a Floridan islet, also written kay or cay: Sp *cayo*: Taino *cayo*, var *caya*, an islet. (The spelling *key* shows the influence of 1st KEY, formerly pron *kay*: Webster.)

khaki (adj, hence n): Hind *khākī*, dust-coloured: Per *khāk*, dust, earth.

khan (1), a prince as in 'Genghiz *Khan*', is Turki *khān*.

khan (2), a resthouse on a traders', or a pilgrims', route, is Ar-Per *khan*, whence, through Hi and

Hind, channelled by the Gypsies, the E underworld *ken*, inn, etc. Cf the approx syn Eg *khen*.

kibitz, to be inquisitive, is a Yiddish, hence AE coll, b/f from Yiddish, hence AE coll, *kibitzer*, a meddlesome onlooker, from coll G *kiebitzen*, to look on—esp over a player's shoulder—at cards, from underworld G *Kietitz* or *Kibitz*, an inquisitive onlooker, from G *Ki(e)bitz*, a peewit, a plover, MHG *gabiz*, ult echoic; for the G bird-name, cf Bavarian *Geibitz* and, for E *peewit*, cf the LG *kīwit*.

kibosh (n, hence v), sl, occurs first in 'put the *kibosh* on', to dispose of, to settle, hence, influenced by *bosh*, nonsense, it becomes 'nonsense': o.o.o.: ? Yiddish.

kick, n, derives from the v: ME *kiken*: o.o.o.: ? echoic, but perh akin to L re*calcit*rare, to kick (*calcitrāre*) back (*re-*), presp *recalcitrans*, o/s re*calcitrant-*, whence E recalcitrant, whence *recalcitrance*—unless imm from F *récalcitrance* (from EF-F *récalcitrant*). L *calcitrāre* is a freq of *calcāre*, to kick, to tread on, from *calx*, heel, o/s *calc-*: and *calcāre* has derivative cpd *inculcāre*, to tread down or in or into, to force in, hence to force knowledge into or on, with pp *inculcātus*, whence 'to inculcate'; derivative LL *inculcātiō*, o/s *inculcātiōn-*, becomes inculcation, whence, anl, inculcatory, perh after the LL agent *inculcātor*, adopted by E.

kickshaw. See CAUSE, para 9.

kid (n, hence v): ME *kid* or *kide*: ON *kith*, akin to OHG-MHG *kiz*, *kizze*, G *Kitze*. Hence the dim *kiddie* (*-y*) and the adj *kiddish*. For 'to kidnap', see NAB, para 2.

kidney. See the 1st EGG, para 2.

kill (1), a channel, a stream. See the 1st KEY, s.f.

kill (2), to slay, whence killer and killing (pa and vn), derives from ME *killen*, var of *kellen*, to strike, to kill: o.o.o., but prob akin to *quell*.

2. 'To quell' comes, sense-weakened, from ME *quellen*, OE *cwellan*, to kill, causative of OE *cwelan*, to die: cf OE *cwalu*, death, esp by slaughter, and OS *quellian*, OHG *quellēn*, MHG *queln*, G *quälen*, to grievously torment (causative of OHG *quēlan*, to suffer torment, OHG *quāla*, a torment or tormenting), ON *kvelja* (*kvelia*), to torment, to kill: cf also Lith *gēlia*, he hurts. (Walshe.)

killick, a small anchor: o.o.o.: EW well conjectures an orig *keel-lock*, perh influenced by D *kiel*.

kiln (n, hence v): ME *kilne*, var *kulne*: OE *cyln*, var of *cylen*: L *culīna*, a kitchen, itself akin to the syn L *coquīna*, from *coquere*, to COOK.

kilo is short for *kilometer* and *kilogram*: cf the element *kilo-*.

kilt, Sc garment, derives from *kilt*, to tuck up, of Scan origin: cf Da *kilte op*, to tuck up, akin to Sw *kilta*, lap, and Go *kilthei*, womb, itself akin to OE *cild*, child.

kilter (var kelter), usu out of, out of order, in bad condition: o.o.o.: perh from MD *kelter*, a wine-press: *out of kelter* would then be applied to a wine-press not properly locked, hence to the contents of such a press.

**kimono** is adopted from Jap.

**kin** (n, hence adj), whence **kinsfolk, kinship, kinsman; kind** (adj—whence **kindness**—and n); **kindly** (whence **kindliness**); **kindle**, to bring forth young; **kindred** (n, hence adj); **kindergarten;**— **king** (n, hence adj and v)—whence the dim **kinglet**, the adj **kingly**, the abstract n **kingship**, and such obvious cpds as **kingbird, kingfisher, king-of-arms, king's counsel; kingdom;**—prob **knight** (n, hence v), whence **knightly** (cf OE *cnihtlīc*, boyish); **knighthood;**—cf the sep GENERAL and NATIVE groups.

### Kin and Kind

1. *Kin* derives, through ME *kin*, var *cun*, from OE *cynn*, kindred, (one's own) kind, people or race: cf OE *cennan*, to beget, OFris *kenn* (*kinn*), OS *kunni* (*cunni*), OHG *kunni* (*chunni*), MHG *kunne*, Go *kuni*, ON *kyn*, kin, race: cf also L *gign*ere, to beget, *gen*us, race (see GENERAL), Gr *gen*ea, birth, race, Skt *ján*as, race.

2. The adj *kind*,' innate, native, hence—e.g., of feelings—natural, hence esp benevolently natural (cf the obs sense 'of good birth' and the E dial senses 'favourable and 'thriving'): OE *cynde*, for *gecynde*, prob a pp used as adj and certainly very intimately related to the OE n *gecynd*, *cynd*, whence ME *cunde*, var *kinde*, whence the E n *kind*, nature, orig human; cf the adj *kindly*, from OE *cyndelīc*, for *gecyndelīc*, adj of OE *gecynd*.

3. *Kindred* is, after the n *kind*, a re-shaping of ME *kinrede*, *kynrede*, var *kunreden*, a cpd consisting of derivatives from OE *cynn* (as in para 1)+ -*rǣden*, -condition (cf READY): cf *hatred*.

4. Akin to OE(*ge*)*cynd* is OFris, OS, OHG *kind*, a child, G *Kind*, themselves akin to the Go adj -*kunds*, descended from, and ON *kundr*, son. The G *Kind* occurs in *Kindergarten*, children's garden, hence classes—a school—mainly conducted, when possible, in a garden or, at worst, a playing field; adopted by E and occ anglicized as *kindergarden*.

5. ME *cunde*, *kinde* (the n *kind*) have derivatives *cundlen*, *kindlen*, whence the now rare 'to *kindle*' or give birth to young.

### King

6. OE *cynn* has derivative *cyning*, with patronymic suffix -*ing* ('a man of noble birth'); the contr OE form *cyng* becomes E *king*; with OE *cyning*, cf the OFris *kening*, *kining*, OS *kuning* (*cuning*), OHG *kuning*, *kunig*, MHG *kunec*, G *König*, MD *coninc*, *cueninc*, *conich*, D *koning*, ON *konungr* (cf ON *konr*, a nobleman). OE *cyning* has derivative *cyningdōm*, whence *kingdom* (suffix -*dom*; cf 'to *deem*').

### Knight

7. Prob akin to OE *cynn* (E *kin*) is OE *cniht*, var *cneoht*, a boy, hence a youth, hence an attendant (at Court or in a noble house), hence a military follower (of the King): cf OHG *kneht*, a boy, a squire, MHG *kneht*, a man, warrior, but also, late,

a subordinate, whence G *knecht*, a servant (parallel is the sem development of KNAVE); cf also MD *cnecht*, occ *cnacht*, orig a youth, D *knecht*. OE *cniht* had derivative *cnihthād*, youth (the state of), whence ult E *knighthood*, the state or condition (cf the suffix -*hood*) of a knight, the order of knights.

**kind**, adj and n. See prec, para 2.

**kindergarten.** See KIN, para 4.

**kindle** (1), to bring forth young. See KIN, para 5.

**kindle** (2), to set afire: a freq derivative (in -*le*) from ON *kynda* (s and r, *kynd*-), to set afire, aided by ON *kyndil-l*, a torch: cf the barely possible origin, the OS *quindla*, to set afire.

**kindly**, adj. See KIN, para 2, s.f.

**kindred.** See KIN, para 3.

**kine.** See COW.

**kinema, kinematic.** See CINEMA.

**kinesis, kinetic.** See CINEMA, para 1.

**king, kingdom, kingly, kingship.** See KIN, para 6.

**kink**, n (hence v), whence the adj **kinky; akimbo.**

*Kink* is adopted from MD *kinc*- (in *kinchorn*), D *kink*, a twist (or a coil) in a rope: cf MLG *kinke*, a twist, and ON *kengr*, a bend. Also prob ult Scan in origin is *akimbo*, with one or, usu, both hands on hip with elbow turned outward: ME *in kenebowe*: cf Ice *kengboginn*, crooked. (EW.)

**kinnikinnic** or -*kinic* or -*kinnick*: of Alg origin: perh (Webster) Massachusett *kinikkinuk*, a mixture (esp for smoking)—cf Ojibway *kiniginige*, he mixes—but prob from either the Creek or the Chippewa dial of Alg: lit, what is mixed (Mathews).

**kino**, a tree-product used in Med and in dyeing: Mandingo (a Negro language of western Sudan) *keno*.

**kinsfolk, kinship, kinsman.** See KIN (heading).

**kiosk**: F *kiosque*, orig (EF) a garden pavilion: Tu *kieushk* (*kiūshk*), a pavilion: Per *koushk* (*kūshk*), portico.

**kip** (n, hence v), orig a brothel, then a lodging house, then a bed, finally a sleep: orig underworld, now sl: prob ult from OE *cip*, brothel, but in its C18-20 uses much influenced by D and Da words approx syn.

**kipper** (n, hence v) comes from OE *cypera*: o.o.o.

**kirk.** See CHURCH, para 3.

**kirsch** is short for G *Kirschwasser*, (lit) cherry water: cf CHERRY and WATER.

**kirtle.** ME *kirtel*, earlier *curtel*: OE *cyrtel*: akin to ON *kyrtill*: either derived from or, at the least, influenced by L *curtus*, short: cf *curtal*, see CURT.

**kiss**, v (whence, at the ME stage, the n), whence **kissing crust**: ME *kissen*, var *cussen*: OE *cyssan*: cf OFris *kessa*, OS *cussian*, OHG *chussēn*, G *küssen*, ON *kyssa*, to kiss, and, for the n, OFris, OS, OE *koss*, OHG-MHG *kus*, G *Kuss*, ON *koss*, OE *coss*: ult echoic—cf Hit *kuwass*-, to kiss.

**kist**, n. See CIST.

**kit** (1), a wooden tub, a basket for fish; hence, from assorted contents, personal equipment: ME *kitt*, var *kyt*: MD *kitte*, var *kit*, D *kit*, a jug.

**kit** (2). See CAT.

**kitchen**, whence **kitchener**: ME *kichen(e)*, var

*kuchene*: OE *cycene*: L *coquīna*, from *coquere*, to cook: f.a.e., COOK.

**kite**, a smallish hawk famous for graceful flight, hence the flying contrivance, hence also as v: ME *kyte*: OE *cȳta*, perh akin to MHG *kuze*, G *Kauz*, a screech-owl.

**kith.** See CAN, para 3.

**kitten, kittenish.** See CAT, last par.

**kittiwake**, a kind of gull, is echoic of its cry.

**kittle**, ticklish, hence 'touchy', derives from the now dial *kittle*, to tickle, hence to puzzle: ME *kytellen*: MD *kitelen*, akin to G-MHG *kitzeln*, OHG *chizilōn*, ON *kitla*, to tickle: prob echoic. 'To *tickle*' is itself a 'transposition of consonants for *kittle*' (Walshe).

**kitty** (1). See CAT, last para.

**kitty** (2), a receptacle, a pool of money, is o.o.o.: perh a dim of the 1st KIT. The Hon. Peter Rodd brilliantly suggests this catena: *kitty*, *Kitty*, dim of *Kate* (pet-form of *Catharine*, *-erine*), erudite pun on F *quête*, as in *faire la quête*, to take up the collection in church: OF-MF *queste*, seeking, cf E *quest*. Cf, sem, the approx syn F sl 'la *cathérine*' (or *C——*).

**kiwi**, the N.Z. 'national' bird, is echoic of its cry: cf KAKA and KEA.

**klaxon.** See LAUGH, para 3.

**kleptomaniac** derives, anl, from **kleptomania**, a mania (see MIND, para 4) for theft; cf the element *klepto-*.

**klipspringer.** See SPRING, para 2.

**knack**, whence the adj **knacky**, derives from 'to *knack*' (ME *cnak*), to strike together so as to make a sharp sound, akin to the equally echoic MHG-G *knacken*, to break by cracking, and Sw *knaeka*, to knock, and therefore akin also to 'to *knock*' (whence the nn *knock*, *knocker*, *knocking*), ME *knokken*, *knoken*, OE *cnocian*, var *cnucian*, itself related to ON *knoka*, all ult echoic.—*Knick-knack* is a redup of the n *knack*: knick-knacks tend to get knocked together. Cf the 2nd KNAP.

**knap** (1), a hill-top, a knoll: OE *cnaep*, a knob, the top, akin to OFris *knapp* and ON *knappr*. Hence *knapweed*, a plant with a knob-like cluster of flowers. Cf KNOB.

**knap** (2), to rap or snap, hence nn **knap** and **knapper**: echoic: cf (G from) D *knappen*, MD *cnappen*, to crack, to bite, to eat. D has the cpd (C16+) *knapzak*, whence G *Knappsack* and E *knapsack*, lit an eating-bag.

**knapper.** See prec.

**knapsack.** See the 2nd KNAP, s.f.

**knapweed.** See the 1st KNAP.

**knave**, whence **knavery** and **knavish**, derives from ME *knave*, knave, earlier servant, earliest boy or youth, from OE *cnafa*, boy, youth: akin to OHG *chnapo*, MHG-G *knabe*, boy, and, less clearly, to OE *cnapa*, boy, youth, OFris *knapa*, boy, youth, OHG *knappo*, MHG *knappe*, young squire, G *Knappe*, an attendant or squire, MD *cnape*, *cnappe*, *cnaep* (cf the D *knaap*), a youth, a servant, ON *knapi*, an esquire or squire; anterior etym, unknown.

**knead**, whence **kneader** and **kneading**, derives, via ME *kneden*, from OE *cnedan* (s *cned-*), akin to OS *cnedan*, OHG *knetan* (s *knet-*), MHG-G *kneten*, MD *cnedan*, ON *knotha*, to knead, and OSl *gnesti*, to press, *gnedo*, I press: basic idea, to press repeatedly with the hands.

**knee** (n, hence v); **kneel** (pt, pp **knelt**), whence **kneeler** and **kneeling.**

1. *Knee*, ME *kne*, var *cneo*, OE *cnēo*, is akin to OFris *knē*, usu *knī*, OS *cneo* (*kneo*, var *knio*), OHG (and Go) *kniu*, MHG-G *knie*, MD *cnie*, *cne*, *cnee*, D *knie*, ON *knē*; also to L *genū* and Gr *gonu*, and to Skt *jǎnu*—cf Tokh B *kenī* and Hit *gēnu*, *ginu*, var *genus*. Linking with para 2 is Hit *kaniniya*, to kneel, or bow down, with vn *kaniniyawwar*. IE r, perh *\*gnu-*: cf the Gr *gnu*petein, to sink to one's knees.

2. 'To *kneel*', ME *knelen*, earlier *cneolien*, derives from OE *cnēowlian*, to go to, be on, one's knees, from *cnēo*, a knee: cf MD *cnielen*, D *knielen*.

**knell**, n, comes, through ME *knel*, var *cnul*, from OE *cnyll*, *cnell*, a sound of bells, itself from *cnyllan*, ME *knullen*, later *knillen* and *knellen*, E 'to *knell*', akin to MGH *erknellen*, to resound, G *knallen*, to clap (cf *Knall*, a loud report); ult echoic.

**knickerbockers**, shortened to **knickers** (shortened, in sl, to **knicks**), derives from *Knickerbockers*, short breeches, gathered at the knee, from Diedrich *Knickerbocker*, the fictitious author of Washington Irving's *A History of New York* (' . . . to the end of the Dutch Dynasty'), 1809, and a typical Dutchman.

**knick-knack.** See KNACK, s.f.

**knife** (n, hence v), pl **knives**: ME *knif*: OE *cnīf*, perh from ON *knīfr*: cf MD *cnijf* (D *knijf*), *cnief*, MLG *knīf*, MHG *knīf*, *knip*, G *Kneif*, *Kneipf*, cf LG *knīpen*, G *kneifen*, to nip: therefore cf 'to NIP'.

**knight, knighthood, knightly.** See KIN, para 7. A *knight-errant*, an adventure-seeking, *wandering* knight, whence *knight-errantry*.

**knit** (pt and pp **knit** or **knitted**), whence **knitter** and **knitting**; **knot** (n, hence v) and **knout.**

1. 'To *knit*', ME *knitten*, var *knutten*, derives from OE *cnyttan*; cf ON *knyta*, intimately akin to ON *knytja*, cf also MLG *knutten*, LG *knutten*, G *knutzen*: perh, in PGmc, a thinned form of the closely related words in:

2. 'To *knot*' derives from 'a *knot*', ME *knot*, earlier *knotte*, OE *cnotta*, akin to OFris *knot*, OHG *knoto*, *knodo*, MHG *knode*, *knote*, G *Knoten*, 'another puzzling word of the *kno-* series' of words 'all meaning something hard, prominent and lumpy' (G *Knollen*, *Knopf*, *Knoten*), as Walshe points out; akin also to ON *knūta*, *knūtr*.

3. From ON *knūta*, *knūtr*, a knot, comes—prob through the Varangians—the Ru *knut*, a knotted whip, whence both J. J. Rousseau's *knout* (1772), adopted by E, and G *Knute*, a knout.

**knob** (whence **knobbed** and **knobby**), weakened in certain senses, esp in sl, to **nob** (adj **nobby**), derives from ME *knobbe*, prob from LG *knobbe*,

itself akin to MD *cnop*, *cnoppe*, D *knop*, *knoop*, a
bud, OHG-G *knopf*, bud (OHG only), button,
knob, OFris *knopp*, a knob, Sw *knopp*, bud: cf the
remarks on *knot*, q.v. at KNIT, para 2. Prob from
MD *cnop*, *cnoppe*, derive ME *knop*, *knoppe*, E *knop*,
a knob.

**knock, knocker.** See KNACK.--Hence *knock-about*, *knockdown*, *knockout*, etc.

**knoll** (whence **knolly**, adj): OE *cnoll*: cf ON
*knollr*, MHG-MLG *knolle*, MD *cnol*, a knoll, ED
*knolle*, a ball, a bunch, D *knol*, a turnip: cf the
remarks in para 2 of KNIT.

**knop.** See KNOB, s.f.

**knot** (whence **knotty**). See KNIT, para 2.

**knout.** See KNIT, para 3.

**know; knowledge.** See CAN, paras 5 and 6.

**knuckle** (n, hence v), whence **knucklebone**,
**-duster**, etc., and adj **knuckly**.

ME *knokel* or *-il*, OE *cnucel*: cf OFris *knokel*,
MLG *knokel*, MHG *knochel*, *knuchel* (OHG
\**knuchilo*), G *Knöchel*, MD *cnockel*, D *knokkel* or
*kneukel*: a dim group from the etymon *knok*, seen
in MD *cnoke*, D *knok* (var *knook*) and rare MHG
*knoche*, G *Knochen*, a bone: Gmc r, \**kno-* (cf
remarks on *knot*, q.v. at KNIT, para 2), with var
\**knu-*: cf ON *knúi*, a knuckle.

**knur, knurl, knurled.** See GNARLED.

**koala**, the Aus 'native bear', is a native word,
prob echoic of its cry.

**kobold.** See COBALT.

**kodak** is prop *Kodak*, a trade-name of arbitrary
formation: ? '*accurate code*' reversed; ? rather
echoic of the sound made by the release.

**kohl.** See ALCOHOL.

**koine** is Gr *koinē* (*dialektos*), common language:
f.a.e., COMMON.

**kopje.** See the 1st COP.

**Koran**, the: Ar (*al*) *Qur'ān*, the reading, from
*qara'a*, to read.

**kosher** (anglicized as **cosher**) is occ—and better—
**kasher**, ritually clean: H *kāshēr*, fitting, proper.

**kraal.** See CORRAL.

**kris**, occ **kreese**, often **creese**: Mal *kris* (pron as
*crease*).

**krone** (coin) is the G form of CROWN.

**krypton**: Gr *krupton*. neu of *kruptos*, hidden: cf
*cryptic* at CRYPT.

**kudos**: coll from university sl: adopted from Gr
*kudos*, glory: perh (Hofmann) aphetic from
a*kou*ein, to hear.

**Kuklux** (or **Ku-Klux**) **Klan**: the circle (Gr *kuklos*)
*clan*.

**Kultur**: G form of E *culture*: f.a.e., CULT.

**kümmel** is adopted from G, where the 'liqueur'
sense derives from that of 'caraway seeds', with
which it is flavoured: MHG *kümel*: OHG *chumil*:
L *cumīnum* (whence, rather via MF-F *cumin*, OF
*coumin*, than via OE *cymen*, the ME, hence E,
*cumin*): Gr *kúmīnon*, of Sem origin—cf Ass
*kamūnu*, H *kammōn*, Ar *kammūn*—or perh even of
Medit origin (cf Eg *tepena*).

**kumquat** (occ anglicized to *cumquat*), a Ch citrus
fruit, comes into E from the Cantonese pron of
Pekinese Ch *chin-chu*, (lit) golden orange.

**Kurd** (whence **Kurdish**, adj hence n), with
'region' cpd **Kurdistan** (cf *Afghanistan*), prob
derives from the r of Sumerian *Qard*a, Gr *Kard*ukoi,
although perh from the LGr *Kurt*ioi, a Median
tribe. (Enci It.)

**Kyrie eleison.** See CHURCH, para 5.

**kyrin(e).** See CHURCH, final para.

# L

laager. See the 2nd LIE, para 3.

labdanum. See LAUDANUM.

label, n hence v, is adopted from MF *label*, perh an 'eased' var of MF *lambel*, Her term, dim of MF-F *lambeau*, a kind of fringe, itself a nasalized derivative of Frankish *\*labba*, presumed from OHG *lappa*, a hanging piece of cloth, a flap: f.a.e., the 1st LAP.

labelloid, labellum; labial, labiate. See the 2nd LAP, para 3.

labile. See LABOR at para 1; cf *lapse*.

labium. See the 2nd LAP, para 3.

labor (n, v), labour; laboratory; laborious; labourer, AE laborer; labo(u)rite;—belabour; collaborate, collaboration, collaborative, collaborator; elaborate (adj, v), elaboration;—labile; lapse (n, v); collapse, elapse, prolapse, relapse.

1. The effective base is L *lābi*, to glide, to slip, (hence) to fail: perh a denasalized cognate of Skt *lamb*ate, he leans. *Lābi* has derivative *lābilis*, tending to slip, whence E *labile*. The pp *lapsus* has two derivatives relevant to E:

*lapsus* (gen *lapsūs*), a slipping, whence *lapse*, n;

LL *lapsāri* (freq of *lābi*), to slip repeatedly, whether physically or morally, whence 'to *lapse*', with several new senses.

2. *Lābi* has many cpds; four notably concern E:

*collābi*, to slip together (*col-* for *con-*, with), to collapse, with pp *collapsus*, whence 'to *collapse*';

*ēlābi*, to slip or glide away (connoted by *ē-*, out of), pp *ēlapsus*, whence 'to *elapse*';

*prōlābi*, to slip forward (*prō-*), pp *prōlapsus*, whence 'to *prolapse*';

*relābi*, to slip *re-* or back, pp *relapsus*, whence 'to *relapse*', whence 'a *relapse*'.

3. Closely akin to *lābi* and prob deriving from it is the n *labor*, a (heavy) weight, under which one totters or staggers, hence fatigue, hence work which causes fatigue: whence OF-MF *labor*, OF-F var *labour* (cf the differentiated OF-F *labeur*), whence AE *labor*, E *labour*, whence *labo(u)rite*. L *labor* has derivative *laborāre*, to bend under a (heavy) weight, to be engaged in heavy, hence difficult work, hence to be in difficulty or in pain, whence OF-MF *laborer*, OF-F *labourer*, ME *laboren*, *labouren*, AE 'to *labor*', E 'to *labour*', whence *labo(u)rer*. 'To *labo(u)r*' has int 'to *belabo(u)r*': cf the int prefix *be-*.

4. The L n *labor* has adj *labōriōsus*, whence OF-MF *laborios*, E *laborious*.

5. L *laborāre* has pp *laborātus*, s *laborāt-*, upon which arises ML *laborātōrium*, a place in which to work, whence EF *laboratoire* and the slightly earlier E *laboratory*, now always scientific.

6. *Laborāre* has two cpds important for E:

*collaborāre*, to work *col-* or together, pp *collaborātus*, whence 'to *collaborate*'; derivative ML *collaborātor*, adopted by E, leads, anl, to *collaboration*, whence, anl, *collaborative*;

*ēlaborāre*, to obtain, or achieve, by hard work or with difficulty, pp *ēlaborātus*, used also as adj 'achieved with difficulty', whence the E adj *elaborate* and also 'to *elaborate*'; derivative LL *ēlaborātiō*, o/s *ēlaborātiōn-*, explains *elaboration*, whence anl *elaborative* and *elaborator* and the obs *elaboratory*, a laboratory.

laboratory. See prec, para 5.

laborious. See LABOR, para 4.

labour. See LABOR.

Labrador, whence labradorite (Min -*ite*), a feldspar found there, prob derives from the fact that Gaspar Corte-Real, partial rediscoverer in 1500, took back to Portugal a cargo of Eskimo slaves (*labrador*es, mod Port *lavradores*)—cf the early It name, *Terra del Laboratore* (L *laborātor*, a toiler).

labrose; labrum. See the 2nd LAP, para 3.

laburnum: L: o.o.o.: perh Etruscan.

labyrinth, whence labyrinthine, derives from L *labyrinthus*: Gr *laburinthos*, orig applied to Eg and Cretan palaces of many halls interconnected by tortuous passages, hence a maze: app a Lydian, possibly a Carian, word, deriving from Lydian *labrus*, a two-edged battle-axe: ? 'palace of the two-edged axe'. (Boisacq.)

lac (1) or lakh, 100,000, esp rupees: Hi *lākh*: Skt *lakṣa*, a lac, orig a mark or sign.

lac (2)—lacquer (n, hence v)—the colour lake; shellac.

1. *Lac*, an insect-derived resinous substance, is either Hi *lākh* or, more prob, Per *lak*, from Skt *lākṣā*.

2. Per *lak* becomes Ar *lakk*, whence OProv *lacca*, whence MF-F *laque*, whence the pigment *lake*. (B & W.)

3. Per *lak* becomes, prob via ML *lacca*, the Port *lacoa*, *laca*, whence Port *lacre*, a kind of sealing wax, whence EF *lacre*, whence E *lacquer* (obsol *lacker*).

4. F *laque* has the tech cpd *laque en écailles*, lac

LACE 333 LAIN

in 'scales' (thin plates), trans by E as '(thin-)*shell*ed *lac*': *shellac*.

**lace** (n, v). See DELICACY, para 2.

**lacerate, laceration** (whence anl **lacerative**).

*Laceration* derives, perh via MF-F *lacération*, from L *lacerātiōn-*, o/s of *lacerātiō*, formed on *lacerāt-*, s of *lacerātus*—whence 'to *lacerate*'—pp of *lacerāre*, to tear into pieces, mangle, lacerate, closely akin to, perh from, the adj *lacer*, torn, lacerated, akin to Gr *lakis*, *lakos*, a tear, a rent, perh akin to Pol *lach*, Ru *loxma*, a rag, a tatter: IE r, ? *lakh-*, to tear small. Cf *lizard*, q.v. at LEG.

**lacert-** cpds. Cf *lizard*, q.v. at LEG.

**lacery**; from *lace*, q.v. at DELICACY, para 2.

**laches.** See LANGUID, para 3.

**lachrymal, lachrymation, lachrymatory, lachrymose.** See the 1st TEAR, paras 1, s.f., and 2.

**lack; lackadaisical.** See LANGUID, paras 14 and 15, resp.

**lacker.** See the 2nd LAC, para 3, s.f.

**lackey:** MF-F *laquais*, by aphesis from MF *alacays*: Catalonian *alacay*, a military man-servant (cf Sp *alacayo*), var of Cat *alcay*: Ar *al-kaid*, (military) chief. The semantic degradation arose when, the Christians reconquering Spain from the Arabs, the Moorish chiefs were reduced to subordinate positions. (B & W.)

**laconic, laconism, laconize.**

The adj *laconic* derives, perh via EF-F *laconique*, from *Laconic*, LL *Lacōnicus*, Gr *Lakōnikos*, of a *Lakōn*—a Laconian or Spartan, hence pithily or tersely brief, in the Laconian manner. Gr *Lakōn* (whence *Lakōnia*, L *Lacōnia*) has derivative *Lakōnizein*, whence 'to *laconize*', to imitate the Laconians, esp in speech, whence *Lakonismos*, EF-F *laconisme*, E *laconism*.

**lacquer.** See the 2nd LAC, para 3.

**lacrosse.** See CROOK, para 6.

**lactam and lactim; lactarene** (or -ine); **lactary, lactase; lactate** (n), **lactation; lacteal** (adj hence n), **lacteous, lactescent** (whence **lactescence**), **lactic, lactiferous, lactify** (whence **lactification**); **lactol, lactone, lactose, lactyl;**—**lettuce;**—**galaxy, galactic,**

1. The prob base is Gr *gala*, milk, gen *galaktos*; the s and r *gal-* is perh metathetic for *gla-*, extn *glak-*, whence L *lac*; cf the Homeric *glagos*. Kinship with MILK, not proven, is at least possible.

2. Gr *gala*, gen *galaktos*, has adj *galaktikos*, whence E *galactic*, milky; the secondary adj *galaxias* occurs in *galaxias kuklos*, milky circle, whence the n *galaxias*, adopted by L, whence both F *galaxie* and E *galaxy*, the Milky Way, hence a vast assemblage of stars, hence an assembly of brilliant persons.

3. L *lac*, gen *lactis*, o/s *lact-* (cf the var *lacte*, potent in R), has the foll derivatives relevant to E: *lacteus*, milky, whence E *lacteous* and anl *lacteal* and (? prompted by *galactic*) *lactic*, whence *lactyl* (Chem *-yl*); *lactārius*, supplying milk, whence *lactary*; *lactescere*, to be changed into milk, presp *lactescens*, o/s *lactescent-*, whence *lactescent*; LL *lactātiō*, o/s *lactātiōn-*, whence *lactation*;

formed upon *lactāt-*, s of *lactātus*—whence *lactate* v and n—pp of *lactāre*, to give suck.

4. E words anl formed include *lactific, lactify, lactiferous*: see the element *lacti-*.

5. App E yet L is *lettuce*: ME *letuse*: OF-F *laitues* (pl of *laitue*), apprehended as a sing; L *lactūca* (*herba*), the 'milky herb', from an unrecorded adj *lactūcus*: its juice is milky.

6. Sci formations include:
*lactarene, -ine*: *lactarius*+Chem *-ene, -ine*;
*lactone*: *lact-* (o/s of *lac*)+Chem *-one*: whence *lactam* (*lactone*+*amino*) and *lactim* (*lactone*+*imido*) and *lactol* (*lactone*+*-ol*);
*lactose*: *lact-*+Chem *-ose*: whence *lactase* (*lactose*+Chem *-ase*).

**lacuna, lacunar.** See the 1st LAKE, paras 3 and 4.

**lacustrine.** See the 1st LAKE, para 2.

**lad**: ME *ladde*: OE *Ladda*, personal name: o.o.o. The equally obscure *lass*, ME *lasse*, is perh —via a glottal stop—a contr of *laddesse* (*ladess*).

**ladder.** See the the 2nd LEAN, para 2.

**lade,** pt **laded,** pp **laden; ladle** (n, hence v); **larboard; last,** a load (obs), a weight; **lathe.** (But not **load.**)

1. 'To *lade*', whence the vn 'bill of *lading*', derives from OE *hladan*, to pile up or heap, to load: cf OFris *hlada*, OS *hladan*, OHG *ladan*, MHG-G *laden*, MD-D *laden*, Go *-hlathan*, ON *hlatha*, to load, also OSl *klasti*, to spread, *klado* I put: Gmc r, *hlath-*; IE r, ? *klad-* (Walshe).

2. OE *hladan* has further sense 'to draw (water), to drain', whence OE *hlaedl*, a large, cup-headed spoon: E *ladle*.

3. Derivative ME *ladeborde*, the loading 'board' or side of a ship, is influenced by 'starboard' to become *larboard*.

4. Akin to OE *hladan* is OE *hlaest*, whence *last*, a weight of approx 4,000 pounds: cf OFris *hlest*, OHG *hlast*, MHG-G *last*, MD-D *last*, ON *hlass*. Cf BALLAST.

5. Prob akin to *lade* is *lathe*, a rotating machine-tool, app of Scan origin: cf Da drei*elad*, a turning-lathe. Perh, however, *lathe* is, as EW suggests, a differentiated form of LATH, the primitive lathe being worked by a spring-lath.

**Ladin.** See LATIN, para 3.

**ladle.** See para 2 of LADE.

**lady.** See LOAF, para 4.

**lag,** adj, v. See LANGUID, para 14.

**lager** (1). Var of *laager*, q.v. at the 2nd LIE, para 3. Cf:

**lager** (2), beer. See the 2nd LIE, para 3.

**laggard.** See LANGUID, para 14, s.f.

**lagniappe** is a Creole word: F *la*, the+a F shape of Sp *napa* (syn with *lagniappe*), a Sp shape of var *yapa*, adopted from Quechuan *yapa*, a present to a customer (A. W. Read); others postulate an African origin for the Sp word.

**lagoon.** See the 1st LAKE, para 5.

**lai.** See LAY, n.

**laic, laicize.** See LAY, adj.

**laid.** See the 2nd LIE (heading).

**lain.** See the 2nd LIE (heading).

**lair.** See the 2nd LIE, para 5.

**laird.** Cf *lord* but see LOAF, para 6.

**laissez faire.** See LANGUID, para 11.

**laity.** See LAY, adj.

**lake** (1) of water; **lacuna, lacunar, lacunose—lagoon** (whence **lagoonal**); **lacustrine;—loch, lough.**

1. *Lake*, ME *lake*, earlier *lac*, is adopted from OF-F *lac*: L *lacus*, s *lacu-*, r *lac-*, to which are akin the syn OE *lagu*, OHG *lahha*, MHG-G *lache*, a pool; ON *lögr*; EIr (whence Ga) *loch*, cf Mx *logh*, Br and Cor *lagen*, W *llagad*, OC *\*laku-*; Gr *lakkos*, a reservoir, a hole in the ground; OSl *loky*, lake, marsh (cf W *llagad*).—*Lake* has derivatives *laker, lakish, lakist, laky.*

2. L *lacus* (gen *lacūs*) has adj *lacustris*, whence EF-F *lacustre*, whence, with suffix *-ine* otiosely added, the E *lacustrine.*

3. L *lacus*, r *lac-*, has derivative *lacūna*, a lake-like body of water as at Venice, a pool, a pond, prob orig the f of an adj *\*lacūnus*; *lacūna* comes to mean a cistern, (in VL) a cavity, hence a gap, this last being adopted by E; the L adj *lacūnōsus* becomes E *lacunose.*

4. L *lacūna* has the Arch LL derivative *lacūnar*, sunk panels, adopted by E.

5. L *lacūna* becomes It (orig Venetian) *laguna*, whence F *lagune* and E *lagoon.*

6. EIr—whence Ga—*loch* is adopted by E for Sc lakes and closely land-locked arms of the sea. *Loch* is also mod Ir, often, by E authors, re-written *lough.*

**lake** (2), pigment. See the 2nd LAC, para 2.

**lake** (3), to play or sport; coll **lark**, to play about, hence n (whence the adj **larky**).

'To *lark*', o.o.o., makes the best sense if derived, perh by a coll deviation, from 'to *lake*', itself now only E dial, from ME *laken, laiken*, from ON *leika* (cf OE *lācan*), akin to Go *laikan* and, further off, Lith *laigyti*, to run wild, and Skt re*jate*, he shakes (e.g., with laughter) or trembles (e.g., with pleasure).

**lam**, to thrash (now sl); whence, anl with '*beat it*', to depart hurriedly, **take it on the lam** (A cant, then sl). To *lam* is ult akin to ON *lemja*, to beat, hence to the adj **lame.**—*Lambaste* merely adds BASTE.

**lama:** Tibetan *blama*. Hence **lamaism.**

**lamb** (n, hence v). See ELK, para 3.

**lambency, lambent.** See the 2nd LAP, para 2.

**lame** (1), adj, hence v, hence also **lameness:** OE *lama*: cf the syn OFris *lam* (var *lom*), OHG-MHG *lam*, G *lahm*, MD *lam, laem*, D *lam*, ON *lami*; cf also OIr *laime*, an axe, and OB *lomiti*, to break.—Cf LAM.

**lame** (2), a thin, usu metal, plate or sheet; **lamé; lamina, laminate** (adj, v)—hence, anl, **lamination; lamella—omelet; lamellule; laminose.**

1. That rich fabric, *lamé*, adopted from France's 'la haute couture', is 'the *laminated* (fabric)', from MF-F *lame*, likewise adopted by E: L *lamna*, contr of *lāmina*, o.o.o.—prob a loan-word, perh Chaldean.

2. L *lāmina*, adopted by tech E, has SciL derivative *laminatus*, whence both adj and v *laminate* (cf the F *laminer*). The derivative LL adj *lāminōsus* yields *laminose*, var *laminous*; the derivative dim *lāmella* (contr of *\*lāminella*), adopted by SciE, becomes OF *lemelle* (F *lamelle*), whence MF *alumelle*, whence, with new suffix, MF *alumette*, whence MF *\*alemette*, whence, by metathesis, late MF *amelette*, whence, influenced by ML *ōvum*, an egg, the EF *omelette*, adopted by E, which anglicizes it as *omelet*. (B & W.)—L *lāmella* itself acquires a dim, the LL *lāmellula*, whence E *lamellule*; the resp adjj are *lamellar, lamellular.*

**lament** (n, v), **lamentable** (L *lāmentābilis*), **lamentation.**

*Lamentation* derives, via MF-F, from L *lāmentātiōn-*, o/s of *lāmentātiō*, from *lāmentāt-*, s of *lāmentātus*, pp of *lāmentāri* (s *lāment-*), to lament, whence, via MF-F *lamenter*, the E 'to *lament*'; *lāmentāri* derives from L *lāmentum*, whence the E n *lament*: and *lāmentum* is a nasal cognate of L *lātrāre*, to bark, the ult r of both being *lā-*: cf Arm *lam*, I weep; prob echoic.

**lamina, laminate, lamination.** See the 2nd LAME, para 2.

**Lammas(tide).** See LOAF, para 3.

**lammergeier (-geyer):** G *Lämmergeier*: *Lammer*, pl of *Lamm*, a lamb (cf ELK, para 3)+*Geier*, a vulture (MHG *gire*, OHG *gir*, app from OHG *giri*, greedy: cf YEARN).

**lamp** (n, hence v), **lampadary;** ? **lampas** (a textile); **lantern** (n, hence v).

1. *Lamp*, ME *lamp*, earlier *lampe*: LL *lampada*, orig an acc of L *lampas* (gen *lampadis*): Gr *lampas* (gen *lampados*), from *lampein* (s *lamp-*), to shine: a nasal form of an IE r *\*lap-*, to shine (brightly), with varr *\*laip-*, *\*leip-*, perh *\*lep-* and *\*lop-*: cf ON *leiptr*, lightning, Lith *liepsnà*, OP *lopis*, a flame, Lith *lópe*, light, OIr *lassaim*, I shine or flame, s *lassa-*,* r *lass-*, for *laps-*. (Hofmann.) L *lampas* has ML derivative *lampadārius* (*lampad-*+*-ārius*), a lamp-tender, whence the ML n *lampadārium*, an ornamental lamp-standard (or *-post*); hence E *lampadary* in its two resp senses.

2. The rich ornamental textile fabric *lampas*, adopted from F, is usu said to be o.o.o.: ? from LL *lampas*, brilliance, esp lustre; from L *lampas*, a lamp.

3. Gr *lampein* (s *lamp-*), to shine, has another relevant Gr derivative: *lamptēr*, a torch, whence, influenced by L *lucerna*, oil-lamp (from *lūx*, light), the L *lanterna*, whence OF-F *lanterne*, whence E *lantern.*

**lampas** (1), fabric. See prec, para 2.

**lampas** (2), horses' disability, also *lampers*. See the 2nd LAP, para 4.

**lampoon.** See the 2nd LAP, para 5.

**lamprey; limpet.**

*Lamprey*, ME from OF *lampreie*, derives from ML *lampr(a)eda*, by f/e influence from L *lambere*, to lick, from LL *naupreda*: perh of Gaul origin—? a nasal form of OC *\*lap-* (var *\*lab-*), to tear, the lamprey feeding by tearing flesh from the fish to which they attach themselves.

2. ML *lampreda*, lamprey, limpet, becomes OE *lempedu* (s *lemped-*), whence, by a further 'thinning' of the 1st vowel and by a natural transition from *d* to *t*, the E *limpet*.

Lancaster (whence Lancastrian, adj hence n), Lancashire.

The latter, late ME *Lancastreshire*, merely adds SHIRE to the ancient town of *Lancaster*, Domesday Book *Loncastre*, a Roman *castra* (cf CASTLE) or fort on the River *Lune* (Ekwall).

lance (n, v), lancer, lancet; lancelet (-*let* dim of *lance*, n); lanceolate, whence anl lanceolation;—launch (v, hence n);—élan.

1. 'To *lance*' (Med from military) comes from OF *lancier*, itself from LL *lanciāre* (var *lanceāre*), from L *lancia*, *lancea*, whence OF-F *lance*, ME *launce*, E 'a *lance*': and *lancia* comes from Gaul *lancia*, *lankia*, from OC *\*lanc-*, to throw or cast: cf Ga *lann*, *lainne*, Ir *laigen*, OIr *lann*, prob the MX *slean*. The C r *\*lanc-*, *\*lank-*, perh nasalizes an IE r *\*lagh-*; cf the Gr *lakkaino*, I dig, and, with *n* and with vocalic change, the Gr *lonkhē*, a lance.

2. *Lancer* derives from EF-F *lancier*, from *lance*; *lancet*, from OF-F *lancette*, an -*et(te)* dim of *lance*.

3. *Lanceolate* derives from LL *lanceolātus*, adj from LL *lanceola*, dim of *lancea*, var of *lancia*.

4. 'To *launch*' derives from ME *launchen*, to throw (a lance): ONF *lanchier* (OF *lancier*): LL *lanceāre*, var of *lanciāre*, to handle, or to pierce with, a spear, from *lancea*, *lancia*.

5. *Elan*, a dashing eagerness, adopted from F, derives, in C15, from OF-MF-F *élancer*, to cast forth (*é-*, L *e-*, out of) as if a lance, from *lancer* (L *lanceāre*).

land (n, hence v), whence pa landed and pa, vn landing; such obvious cpds as landfall, landgrabber, landlady after landlord, landlubber, landmark (OE *landmearc*), landscape (D *landschap*, akin to OE *landscipe*), landsman (land's man: OE *landes mann*), landward (suffix -*ward*); landau, whence the dim landaulet(te); lande;—lawn (sward), whence, eg., lawn tennis (opp *tennis*, played on an enclosed, usu roofed, court) and the adj lawny.

1. *Land*, OE *land* (var *lond*), is akin to OFris *land*, *lond*, OHG-MHG *lant*, G *Land*, Go *land*, MD *lant*, MD-D *land*, ON *land*, land, region—EIr *land*, region, an open space, Ga *lann* (pron *lawn*), enclosure, land, W *lann*, Cor *lan*, enclosure, Br *lann*, a lande, OC *\*landa*—OP *linda*, a valley, OSl *ledina*, *ledo*, waste land, a heath—F *lande* (Gaul *\*landa*), heath, moorland (esp if infertile), partly adopted by E.

2. G *Land*, land, occurs in the G Rhenish city *Landau* (*Au*, water-meadow, OHG *ouwa*, akin to L *aqua*, water), where the four-wheeled, covered horse-carriage known as a *landau* was first made.

3. F *lande* had OF var *launde*, whence ME *launde*, later *laund*, whence E *lawn* (cf Br *lann*, Ga *lann*, as above), orig a glade.

landau. See prec, para 2.

lande. See LAND, para 1, s.f.

landscape. See the 2nd SCAPE and cf LAND (heading).

lane: ME-OE *lane*, varr *lone*, *lanu*: cf OFris *lane*, *lone*, MD *lane*, *laen*, D *laan*, a lane, and ON *lön*, a row of houses.

language (whence -languaged), langue d'oc (and langue d'oïl), languette (usu anglicized as languet); lingua franca (see FRANK, para 9), lingual (whence bilingual, etc.), linguist, linguistic (adj, whence linguistics)—lingula, whence lingulate, linguloid; lingo.—tongue (n, hence v), whence -tongued, tongueless, tonguer, tonguing, tonguester; prob tang (a snake's or a knife's or a flavour's), whence the now dial 'to *tang*'; perh tongs.

1. The best starting-point is at L *lingua*, the tongue, whence OF-F *langue*, whence OF-F *langage*, ME *langage*, whence, influenced by F *langue*, the E *language*, for L *lingua* is either f/c—after L *lingere*, to lick—for OL *dingua*, or (E & M) a Sabine dial var thereof, with IE r *\*dinghw-*: cf OPer *hizbāna-* (Per *zubān*); Skt *jihvá*, Av *hizu-*; OSl *językŭ*, Lith *lēžuwis*, OP *inzuwis*; OIr *tenga* (Ir *tenge*, gen *tengad*), Ga *teanga*, Mx *chengey*, with Br and Cor cognates lacking the *n*; ON *tunga* (Sw *tunga*, Da *tunge*); Go *tuggō* (pron *tungō*), OHG *zunga*, MHG *zunge*, tongue, language, G *Zunge*, tongue, MD *tong(e)*, *tung(e)*, D *tong*, OS *tunga*, OFris *tunge*, OE *tunge*, ME *tunge* and *tonge*, jointly producing E *tongue*. The 'tongue-language' dualism is as widespread as it is natural.

2. OF-F *langue* has in MF-F the virtual cpds *langue d'oc*, *lange d'oïl*: language of *oc*, Prov for 'yes'; language of *oïl*, OF of the Loire basin and northwards for 'yes' (hence F *oui*). The MF-F dim *languette*, little tongue, has been adopted by E in its F sense 'anything shape-resembling a tongue'.

3. L *lingua* has ML adj *linguālis*, whence F and E *lingual*. On the learnèd F s *lingu-* arise F *linguiste*, whence E *linguist*, and the F adj *linguistique*, whence E *linguistic*; with E *linguistics*, cf F 'la *linguistique*'.

4. L *lingua* has dim *lingula*, adopted by An and Zoo.

5. L *lingua* becomes Prov *lingo*, form-adopted and sense-adapted by E.

6. With E *tongue* (para 1), prob cf E *tang*, a serpent's tongue (now only dial), a fang, a prong, the tang of a knife, hence, from stinging or pricking sensations, a sharp, lingering taste: ME *tange*: ON *tangi*, a pointed projection.

7. With E *tongue*, hence with E *tang*, perh cf E *tongs*: ME *tonge*, earlier *tange*: OE *tange* or *tang*, a 'biting' or gripping device: cf OFris *tange*, *tonge*, OHG *zanga*, MHG-G *zange* (cf OHG *zangar*, biting, sharp), ON *töng*: prob cf also Gr *daknō* (s *dakn-*), I bite, Skt *daśáti* (? for *\*dankhéti*), he bites, and Alb *danĕ*, tongue. (Walshe; Hofmann.)

languet. See prec, para 2.

languid, languish (whence languishing, languishment), languor (whence languorous); laches; lack (n, v), lackaday, lackadaisical slack (adj, n, v), slacken, slackness, slacks—slake; lag (adj, n, v), laggard; laissez-faire; lax, laxation, laxative, laxity—relax, relaxant, relaxation, relaxatory and relaxative; lease (n, v), lessee, lessor—release (n, v); **relish** (n, v); **relay** (n, v)—cf **delay** (n, v); **lea** (a measure); **leash** (n, hence v); **lush** (adj).

1. *Languid* comes, perh via EF-F *languide*, from L *languidus* (s *languid*-, r *langu*-, an extn of *lang*-), adj formed from *languēre*, to be or feel faint or over-relaxed, s *langu*-, r *lang*-, whence also *languor*, a feeling of faintness, whence OF, hence ME whence E, *languor*. *Languēre* has a VL var *languīre*, whence OF-F *languir*, whence, esp from such forms as presp *languiss*ant and 'nous *languiss*ons', we languish, the ME *languissen*, *languishen*, E 'to *languish*'.

2. Akin to L *languēre* is L *laxus*, relaxed, slack, lazy, whence E *lax*. *Laxus* has derivatives *laxāre*, to loosen or slacken, pp *laxātus* (whence E 'to *laxate*'), whence both LL *laxātiō*, a slackening, o/s *laxātiōn*-, whence E *laxation*, and the LL *laxātīuus*, causing slackness, ML *laxātīvus*, esp in Med sense, whence MF-F *laxatif*, f *laxative*, whence E *laxative*, adj hence n; and L *laxitās*, whence F *laxité* and E *laxity*.

3. L *laxāre*, s *lax*-, has LL *laxicāre*, to become shaky, whence OF *laschier*, whence the adj *lasche* (F *lâche*), with derivative MF abstract n *laschesse*, whence E *laches*, laxness, negligence, hence, esp in Law, culpable negligence.

4. L *laxāre* has cpd *relaxāre* (*re*-, again), to let loose, to slacken, whence 'to *relax*', whence the paa *relaxing* and *relaxed*; the presp *relaxans*, o/s *relaxant*-, yields *relaxant*. On *relaxāt*-, the s of the pp *relaxātus*, arise *relaxātiō*, a slackening, o/s *relaxātiōn*-, whence, as in F, *relaxation*, and the adj *relaxātōrius*, loosening, whence *relaxatory*, with E anl var *relaxative*.

5. L *relaxāre* becomes OF *relaissier*, whence ME *relessen*, E 'to *release*'. *Relaissier* has derivative n *relais*, var *reles*, with legal sense (MF) influenced by LL 'freeing of a prisoner'; hence ME *reles*, E 'a *release*'. *Releasement* comes from 'to *release*'.

6. L *laxāre*, to loosen or slacken, acquires the LL sense 'to let or allow', whence OF *laissier*, to allow (also, to leave), var *lessier* (F *laisser*), whence E 'to *lease*', mostly in legal sense. OF *laissier* has derivative n *lais*, with var *les*, whence late ME *lese*, *leas*, whence E 'a *lease*', a legal permission to occupy or use.

7. OF *lessier* has var *lesser*, pp *lessé*, allowed, hence 'a person *allowed*' (the use or occupation of property); whence the E *lessee*, whence, anl, the agent *lessor*.

8. OF *laissier*, in its secondary sense 'to let go', has (cf para 5) the cpd *relaissier*, to let (someone) go back, to leave (someone, hence also something) behind, with derivative n *relais*, *reles* (as in para 5), what is left behind, hence the lingering taste of what one eats, ME *reles*, E *relish*, whence 'to *relish*'.

9. OF *laissier* has derivative OF-F n *laisse*, a leash, var *lesse*, whence, prob, ME *leece*, *lees*, *lese*, whence E *leash*; OF *laisse* perh, however, derives from ML *laxa*, a leash, from L *laxus*, loose, ? by ellipsis from *corda laxa*, a loose rope or cord; but, in either event, the n *leash* arises because it is a cord held loosely.

10. OF *laissier* has the OF derivative var *laier*. to let or allow, in itself of no consequence to E, Its two chief cpds are important:

OF *deslaier* (OF *des*-, L *dis*-, E prefix *dis*-), *delaier*, to postpone, becomes ME *delaien*, E 'to *delay*'; the derivative OF-MF n *delai*, F *délai*, becomes 'a *delay*';

MF *relaier* (OF *re*-, L *re*-, back), applied to keeping fresh dogs in reserve, on a hunt, hence, in C16, to horses, becomes late ME-E 'to *relay*'; the derivative MF n *relai*, later *relais*, becomes 'a *relay*'.

11. The F *laisser*, to allow, has imperative *laissez*, which occurs in *laissez faire*, let (people) do (as they wish); hence the n *laissez-faire*, non-interference, adopted by E.

12. OF *laissier*, varr *lessier*, *lesser*, has, as we've seen, derivative n *lais*, var *les*, whence E *leas*, which, apprehended as pl, yields a b/f *lea*, a (varying) measure of yarn—usu 300 yards for linen, 120 for cotton: cf *leash*.

13. OF *lasche*, loose (as in para 3), becomes the ME, now only dial, *lash*, loose, hence (of persons) flabby and (of fruit or grass) soft and watery or wet, whence, prob, the adj *lush*, juicy, luxuriant.

14. Akin to L *laxus*, loose, is the E n *lack*, ME *lac*, prob from MD *lac*, a deficiency, a fault, but perh from the cognate ON *lakr*, deficient, inferior; the intimately related 'to *lack*', ME *lacken*, prob derives from MD *laken*, to be deficient in; certainly the MD n and the MD v are akin to the L adj, with which cf the OIr-MIr *lacc*, Ir and Ga *lag*, feeble, W *llag*, loose (obs), sluggish. Prob of that implied C origin is the E adj *lag*, sluggish (obs), last, as in *lag end*, latter end. Hence, 'to *lag*', to linger, and the obsol *lag*, one who, or that which, is late or last; hence also *laggard*, adj hence n: *lag*, adj+euphonic *g*+pej suffix *-ard*.

15. *Lack*, in its earlier senses 'loss' and 'shame', has f/e influenced *alas*! to become *alack*!, esp in *alack the* (or *a*) *day*!, alas the day; *alackaday*! has, by aphesis, become *lackaday*!, with f/e var *lackadaisy*!, whence the adj *lackadaisical*.

16. *Lack* and *lag* together bring us to the adj *slack*, whence the n and the v *slack*, with extn *slacken*, and the abstract n *slackness* and the loose, informal trousers known as *slacks*. *Slack*, loose (physically, mentally, morally), ME *slak*, is OE *slaec*, akin to OS *slak*, OHG *schlack*, *slah*, ON *slakr*, a group akin to ON *lakr*, deficient, MD *lac*, deficiency, MIr *lacc*, feeble (as in para 14)—cf also Gr *lagaros*, slack, (of animal's flanks) hollow, s *lagar*-, r *lag*-.

17. OE *slaec*, slack, has derivative *slaecian*, *slacian*, to become slack, ME *slaken*, to become, but also to render, slack, hence to 'slacken' thirst, to *slake* it.

18. To the OE words in paras 16–17, add L *laxus*, slack, a non-nasal cognate of *languēre* (r *lang*-), to be faint, as in para 1: add also Gr *lēgein*, s and r *lēg*-, to cease, and the variously nasalized *lagnos* (s *lagn*-, r *lag*-), weakened by debauchery, *langōn* (λάγγων) a sluggard, *langazō*

($\lambda\alpha\gamma\gamma\dot\alpha\zeta\omega$), I lag or slacken. The IE r emerges as
*lag-, varr *lēg- and *lĕg (and app *log-), with a
prob int form *slag-, varr *slēg- and *slĕg- (also
*slog-), to be loose or soft, hence flabby; both the
lag- (etc.) and the slag- (etc.) forms have -n- varr.

**laniard.** See lanyard at the 2nd NET, para 5.

**lank, lanky.** See FLANGE, para 6.

**lanolin(e),** purified wool-fat: L lāna, wool+L
oleum, oil+Chem suffix -in, -ine: cf the elements
lani-(lano-) and -ol.

**lantern.** See LAMP, para 3.

**lanthanum:** a SciL Chem-element name from Gr
lanthanein, to forget: f.a.e., LETHAL.

**lanugo.** See VELLICATE, para 1, s.f.

**lanyard,** occ laniard. See the 2nd NET, para 5.

**lap** (1), a garment's loose part, a fold, hence a
particular part of the human body in sitting
position, hence ME lappen, 'to lap' or fold;
dewlap; lapel—cf the sep LABEL; lappet.

1. A lap derives from OE laeppa, akin to OFris
lappa, OHG lappa, MHG lappe, G Lappen, a rag,
MD lappe or, as in D, lap, a patch, a piece (of,
e.g., cloth), ON leppr, piece (of cloth), a fold, and
lapa, to hang loose, therefore to L labāre, to totter,
intimately akin to L lābī, to slide or glide, to slip:
cf LABOR, para 1.—Note that many tech senses of
lap, n, derive imm from the v.

2. ME lappe occurs in the cpd dewlappe, E
dewlap (cf the Da doglaep), the 1st element being
DEW, ref the moistness of this pendulous fold of
skin under the neck of oxen.

3. Lap, n, has two dim derivatives: lapel (-el)
and lappet (lap+euphonic p+-et).

**lap** (2), v, to take up with the tongue and into
the mouth, as a cat does, comes, through ME
lappen or lapen, from OE lapian: cf OHG laffan,
LG lappen, Ice lepja, Sw läppja, Da labe, also Gr
laptein, to lap up, and, with nasal infix, L lambere,
to lick, prob also, therefore, L labium, the lip; cf,
further, Arm lap'el, to lick, and Alb l'ap, to lap
(water). The IE r is prob *lab-, with var *lap-, to
lick, to lap. (Hofmann.) Ult: echoic.

2. L lambere (s lamb-, ult r *lab-), to lick (orig
of dogs, then of men), becomes applied to flames
'licking at', e.g., a building; hence, via the presp
lambens, o/s lambent-, the E adj lambent, whence
lambency.

3. L labium, a lip, is rare—and a b/f from labia,
lips, intimately akin to L labra, lips (the sing
labrum is rare and prob b/f), later applied mostly
to vessels, as occ also labia. Both labium and
labrum have been adopted by tech and sci E,
with derivative adjj labial (ML labiālis), labiose,
and labral, labrose (L labrōsus). The L dim
labellum has E derivative labelloid.

4. Akin, ult, to OE lapian, to lap, is OF laper,
which, in EF, becomes nasalized to lamper, to
guzzle, whence, app, the horses' disease lampas,
adopted by E, which then adapts it as lampers.

5. EF-F lamper, to guzzle, has lampons, let us
drink, whence lampon (C17), a drinking song,
hence, such songs being often ribald and occ
scurrilous, and usu abusive, a song satirically

aimed at a person, whence the E lampoon, whence
'to lampoon'.

6. L labium has Gmc cognates, e.g. OE lippa,
ME lippe, E lip (whence 'to lip'), OHG lefs (var
leffur), LG lefze, MHG-G lippe, OFris lippa, MD
leppe, then lippe, finally lip (as in D), Sw läpp, Da
laebe.

**lapel.** See the 1st LAP, para 3.

**lapidary,** whence lapidarian; lapideon, lapideous;
lapis lazuli; lapidate, lapidation—dilapidate, dilapidation.

1. E lapis lazuli, a precious stone of azure hue,
is adopted from MF-F: lazuli represents Ar
lâzaward, from Per lâdjeward, lapis lazuli, the
lapis being added tautologically.

2. L lapis, a stone, is o.o.o., although possibly
akin to Gr lepas, a bare rock. From the o/s lapid-
derives the LL adj lapidārius, full of stones (L
lapidōsus), working with stones, hence ML
lapidārius (L lapicīda), a worker in stone: hence
resp the E adj and the E n. The derivative lapidāre,
to throw stones at, has pp lapidātus, whence 'to
lapidate'; derivative lapidātiō, o/s lapidātiōn-,
yields lapidation.

3. Lapidāre has cpd dilapidāre (di- for dis-, apart),
to scatter, as one scatters stones, hence to squander.
The pp dilapidātus yields 'to dilapidate'; derivative
LL dilapidātiō, o/s dilapidātiōn-, accounts for
dilapidation; the LL agent dilapidātor is adopted
by E.

**lappet.** See the 1st LAP, para 3.

**lapse.** See LABOR, para 1.

**lapwing.** See LEAP, para 3; cf WENCH, para 4.

**larboard.** See LADE, para 3.

**larceny** (whence larcenous): a -y derivative from
F larcin: contr of OF larrecin: L latrōcinium,
robbery, theft; a -cinium derivative of latrō, a
robber, but orig a (Greek) mercenary soldier,
hence a brigand: akin to Gr latron, pay, e.g. a
soldier's: s latr, r lat-, IE r *la- or *le-.

**larch:** G Lärche (MHG lerche): L laricem, acc
of larix (o/s laric-), o.o.o.—prob either C or
Alpine.

**lard,** v, derives from (OF-)F larder, itself from
F lard, a pig's back-fat, OF-MF lard, bacon, whence
the E n; L lārdum, contr of lāridum: akin to Gr
lārīnos, fattened, fat: IE r, ? *lar-. Perh akin
to LARGE.

**Lares.** See LARVA.

**large** (adj, hence adv, n, v), whence largeness—
cf largesse; Mus largo;—enlarge, whence enlargement.

1. It largo and OF-F large both derive from L
largus, abundant, hence generous, hence, in LL-
ML, large: perh akin to Skt dirghas, long. OF-F
large, adopted by E, with sense '(by comparison)
big' gradually predominating, has the OF-F
derivative largesse, largeness (obs), generosity,
adopted by E; AE usu spells it largess.

2. OF-F large has the MF cpd enlargier (en-,
L in, in, into, used int), whence—unless from MF-F
enlargir—'to enlarge'.

**lariat:** Sp la (the) reata (rope or cord): reata,

from *reatar*, to tie together: *re-*, again, back+*atar*, to tie (L *aptāre*): cf APT.

**lark** (1), the bird, whence, folklorishly, the plant *larkspur*, shaped like a lark's spur: ME *larke*, partly a contr of ME *laverock*: OE *lāwerce*, var *lāferce*: cf OHG *lērahha*, MHG *lēwreche*, *lēreche*, G *Lerche*, LG *lewerke*, MD *lawerke*, *leewerke*, *leewerike*, *leeuweric*, D *leeuwerik*, ON *lāērvirki* (cf Da *lerke*, Sw *lärka*): 'a cpd of obscure origin' (Walshe)—?, rather, echoic.

**lark** (2), to play about (hence n). See the 3rd LAKE.

**larkspur.** See the 1st LARK.

**larky.** See *lark* at the 3rd LAKE.

**larrikin**, a lawless and noisy, usu young or youngish, street loafer: Midlands dial *larrikin*, a mischievous youth, akin to rare dial *larrick*, lively, and Yorkshire dial *larack*, to be actively mischievous, to 'lark' about. (EDD.) App all these words are dial varr of 'to *lark*', q.v. at the 3rd LAKE.

**larrup** (coll) either derives from D *larpen*, to thresh (Webster), or blends *lather* and *wallop* (EW).

**larva, larval, larvate; Lares.**

*Larval* comes from ML *larvālis*, L *laruālis*, ghostly, the adj of ML *larva*, L *larua*, a ghost (of the dead, pursuing the living), hence a mask: s *laru*, r *lar-*, as in L *Lares*, tutelary gods of the fields and then of the house, esp of the hearth, as in *Lares et Penatēs*, household gods, partly adopted by E, with additional sense 'household goods': *Lares* (sing *Lar*) and *larua* seem to be either of Etruscan origin or of Sabine origin with an Etruscan suffix.—L *larua* has derivative *laruātus*, ML *larvātus*, masked, whence E *larvate*; and ML *larva* prompts the SciE dim *larvule*. The Ent and Zoo senses of *larva* derive, picturesquely yet naturally, from the L.

**laryngeal, larynx.**

The former derives from the o/s *larung-* of Gr *larunx* (λάρυγξ), the larynx; cf LL *laryngotomia* (Gr *larungotomia*), laryngotomy. Gr *larunx* perh represents a nasal 'answer' to L *lurcāre*, to eat greedily. (Hofmann.)

**lascar:** Hind *lashkar*, prop an army, apprehended as *lashkarī*, of the army, hence a soldier, whence loosely a sailor: Per *lashkar*: Ar *al-'askar*, the (*al*) army. Ar *'askar*, army, has adj, hence n, *'askarī*, a soldier, whence *Askaris*, native soldiers that, in E Africa, serve a European power.

**lascivious; list**, (archaically) to be inclined or pleased (to do), hence (of a ship) to incline to one side; **lust** (n, hence v), whence **lustful** (cf OE *lustfull*, eager, desirous) and **lustless** and also **lusty**.

1. *Lascivious*, wanton, lustful, derives from ML *lasciviōsus*, LL *lasciuiōsus*, from L *lasciuia*, wantonness, lust, from *lascīuus*, wanton, orig merely 'playful' and applied esp to children and animals: akin to Skt *lasati*, he plays, and *lālasas*, desirous—to Gr *lastē*, a wanton woman, and *lasthē*, mockery; also to Ru *lasyj*, desirous, and

OSl *laska*, flattery, *laskrŭdĭ*, desire; Go *lustus* and OFris, OS, OHG-MHG-G, OE *lust*, MD *list*, *lost*(*e*), *lust*(*e*), D *lust*, ON *loste*, *losti*, pleasure, desire. The IE r is *lăs-* or *lăs-*, to be eager or desirous.

2. The r of OE *lust*, pleasure, has derivative *lystan*, to be pleasing, whence ME *lusten*, whence, for form, 'to *lust*', which, however, takes its modern sense from *lust*, n, in its modern sense. OE *lystan* also becomes ME *listen*, whence the now, except naut, archaic 'to *list*'.

**lash** (1), adj. See LANGUID, para 13.

**lash** (2), stroke of a whip, the flexible part of a whip, whence perh eye*lash*, derives from ME *lasche*, from ME *laschen*, to move violently, to rush, to strike, prob imitative but perh from the next; *laschen* becomes 'to *lash*'.

**lash** (3), to bind. See DELICACY, para 3.

**lass.** See LAD.

**lassitude.** See LATE, para 4.

**lasso.** See DELICACY, para 5.

**last** (1), adj (whence adv). See LATE, para 3.

**last** (2), n, a load. See LADE, para 4.

**last** (3), of boot or shoe: OE *lāst*, var of *lāest*, a footstep, a trace or a track, (late) a last: cf ON *leistr*, the foot below the ankle, esp the underfoot, Go *laists*, a track, OHG-MHG *leist*, G *Leisten*, a last, MD *leist*, (also D) *leest*. Cf:

**last** (4), to remain existent, to endure: ME *lasten*: OE *lāestan*, to perform or achieve, to continue (one's, its) existence, orig to follow in the tracks or footsteps of: OE *lāest*, footstep, track, course (see prec): cf OFris *lasta*, *lesta*, OS *lēstian*, OHG *leistēn*, MHG-G *leisten*, to perform. Hence the pa *lasting*.

**latch**, fastener; **latch**, to fasten; **latchet.** See DELICACY, para 4.

**late; later, latter; latest, last.—lassitude; alas!**

1. *Late*, adv and adj, derives from OE *laet*, slow, sluggish, hence tardy, hence late, ME *lat*, E *late*: cf OFris *let*, OS *lat*, MD *late*, *laet*, D *laat*, late; OHG-MHG *laz*, tardy, G *lass*, idle, weary, Go *lats*, slow, weary, ON *latr*, slow, tardy; cf the cognates of LET, to hinder, to allow; cf also L *lassus* (for *lădtus*)—see para 4.

2. The comp of *late*, adj and adv, is *later*, which, in its modern pron, dates only from C16; *latter*, sense-differentiated in E, answers to ME *laetter*, from OE *laetra*, the comp of *laet*. Cf the OFris *letera*, *letora*, and MD *later*.

3. The sup of *late* is *latest* (late ME onwards), with modern pron hardly antedating C16; *last*, sense-differentiated in E, is ME *last*, a metathesis of ME *latst*, deriving from OE, where it is a contr of *latest*, var of *latost*, the sup of *laet*, adj, and *late*, adv. Cf the OFris *lest*, OS *lezto*, MD *latest*, *laest*, *lest*.

4. L *lassus*, falling forward, bowed, esp with weariness or illness, hence weary or faint, has derivative *lassitūdō*, whence MF *lassitude*, adopted by E. *Lassus* becomes OF-F *las*, whence the OF *a las* (*alas*), ah, weary or, esp, unfortunate (and

unhappy), sc that I am!: ME *allas, alas*: E *alas*—cf the F derivative *hélas* (via *hé las*).

**lateen.** See LATIN, para 2.

**latent,** whence **latency** (for *\*latentcy*); **lethargic, lethargy; Lethe.**

1. *Latent* derives from L *latent-*, o/s of *latens*, presp of *latēre*, to lie hidden, s and r *lat-*: akin to Gr *lathros*, hidden, and *lēthē*, forgetfulness, and the nasalized *lanthanesthai*, to forget, and *lanthanein*, to escape notice, both with s *lanthan-*, r *lanth*; akin also to OSl *lajati*, to lie in wait for.

2. Gr *lēthē*, forgetfulness, whence L *Lēthē*, the River of Forgetfulness, whence E *Lethe*, forgetfulness (personified), is intimately akin to Gr *lanthanesthai*, to forget, itself the middle voice of *lanthanein*, to lie hidden, to escape notice (aorist *elath*on, perfect *lelēth*a): IE r, perh *\*ladh-*, alternating with *\*lēdh-*, to be hidden.

3. The Gr adj *lēthargos*, forgetful, is very closely akin to the adj *laithargos*, secretly biting, the two words deriving from an IE r *\*laidh-*, var *\*leidh-*, mdfns of *\*lādh-*, *\*lēdh-*. *Lēthargos* has derivative *lēthargia*, ML *lēthargia*, E *lethargy*, with rather doubtful MF-ME intervention; derivative Gr *lēthargikos* becomes LL *lēthargicus*, MF *lethargique* (F *léthargique*), E *lethargic*.

**later.** See LATE, para 2.

**lateral;** cf the element *lateri-* (*latero-*); **latitude,** whence **latitudinal** and **latitudinarian** (adj, hence n).—Cpds: **collateral** (adj, hence n), **equilateral; dilate—dilatant, dilatate, dilatation, dilatative.**—Perh cf LATIN.

1. *Lateral* derives from L *laterālis*, the adj of *latus* (o/s *later-*), flank (of body), side: prob akin to *lātus*, wide, broad; indeed, prob—like *later* (o/s *later-*), a brick—deriving from it.

2. *Laterālis* occurs in such cpds as ML *collaterālis* (*col-* for *con-*, with, hence accompanying), whence E *collateral*, and LL *aequilaterālis* (*aequi-*, c/f of *aequus*, equal), equal-sided, E *equilateral*.

3. L *lātus*, broad, wide, is o.o.o.; despite authoritative opinion, *lātus* could be ult akin to Gr *platus* (cf PLACE). Its derivative *lātitūdō* becomes (MF-F and) E *latitude*, which has, on the L o/s *lātitūdin-* and anl, perh, with *marginal*, formed the adj *latitudinal* and also, with suffix *-arian*, *latitudinarian*.

4. *Lātus*, wide, has cpd *dīlātare*, to widen by separation (connoted by *di-* for *dis-*, apart), whence, app via MF, 'to dilate'. The presp *dīlātans*, o/s *dīlātant-*, yields the E adj, hence n, *dilatant*; pp *dīlātātus* yields the adj *dilatate*; derivative LL *dīlātātiō*, o/s *dīlātātiōn-*, yields, prob via MF-F, *dilatation*, whence, anl, *dilatative*.

**latest.** See LATE, para 2.

**latex:** L *latex*, a fluid: perh, via Sicilian Gr, from Gr *latax*, wine-lees: if so, cf EIr *lathach*, fluid mud (OC *\*lātāka*), and OHG *letto*, G *Letten*, moist loam.

**lath:** ME *laththe, latthe*: OE *laett*: cf OHG *latta*, MHG-G *latte*, and D *lat*; cf also W *llath*, OIr *slath*, Ga *slat*, a rod or staff, OC *\*slattâ*.

2. OHG *latta* becomes OF *latte*, whence the late MF derivative in *-is* (cf OF-F *treille—treillis*)—*lattis*, lath-work, ME *latis*, E *lattice*.

**lathe,** a machine tool. See LADE, para 5.

**lather,** whence 'to **lather'** (cf, however, OE *lēthrian*, to lather): OE *lēathor*, washing-soda: cf ON *lauthr* and LAVE.

**lathy:** lath+adj *-y*.

**Latin** (adj, hence n: cf *Greek*, adj hence n), **Latinism** (or *l-*), **Latinist, Latinize** (or *l-*); **Ladin; lateen;—Latium,** whence the adj **Latian.**

1. *Latium*, the It region in which Rome lies and of which the Campagna di Roma forms the greater part (? therefore from *lātus*, wide, broad, s and r *lāt-*), has s *Lati-* and r *Lat-*; its adj, formed with *-īnus*, is *latīnus*, s *latīn-*, whence OF-F *latin* and E *Latin*. Derivative *latīnitās* becomes MF-F *latinité*, E *Latinity*; derivative LL *latīnizāre* becomes EF-F *latiniser*, E *latinize*; *Latinism* and *Latinist* are anl formations, perh aided by EF-F *latinisme*, late MF-F *latiniste*, and It *latinismo*, *-ista*.

2. The F 'voile *latine*', a 'Latin' sail, characteristic of the Mediterranean, yields E *lateen*: cf the It *vela latina*.

3. L *latīnus* (adj) becomes It *latino*, Alpine It *ladino*, whence E *Ladin*, any Rhaeto-Romanic dialect.

**latitude, latitudinal, latitudinarian.** See LATERAL, para 3.

**latrine.** See LAVE, para 7.

**latten:** ME *latoun, laton*: MF *leiton, laton* (F *laiton*): OProv *leton, laton*: aphetically from OSp *alatón*: Ar *al*, the+Ar *latun*, copper: OTu *altan*, gold (B & W).

**latter.** See LATE, para 2.

**lattice.** See LATH, para 2.

**Latvia, Latvian.** See LETT.

**laud** (n, v), **laudable, laudation, laudative** and **laudatory; lied,** n; **lyra** (whence **lyrate**), **lyre** (whence, from the spread of the male's tail-feathers, **lyre bird**), **lyric** (adj, hence n), whence the extn **lyrical** and the nn **lyrician, lyrist.**—Cf ALLOW, which L *allaudāre* has influenced.

1. The n *laud* derives from OF *laude*, from L *laudem*, acc of *laus*, praise, esp if spoken, o/s *laud-*: o.o.o.: but prob akin to Ir *lauaidim*, I mention, esp in praise, OIr *lúad*, news, speech, Ga *luadh*, a mentioning; perh cf also OE *lēoth*, ON *lióth*, OS *lioth*, Go *liuth*, OHG *leod, liod*, G *Lied*, a song, and Go *liuthan*, to sing praises.

2. L *laus*, o/s *laud-*, has derivative v *laudāre* (s *laud-*), to praise, whence 'to laud'. Derivative L *laudābilis* yields *laudable*; on *laudāt-*, s of the pp *laudātus*, arise *laudātiō*, o/s *laudātiōn-*, whence *laudation—laudātiuus*, ML *-īvus*, whence *laudative* —LL *laudātōrius*, whence *laudatory*.

3. Behind *laus*, there is r *lau-*; behind the Gmc words, the r *lēu-, liu-* (*leo, lio-*): perh cf *lu-*, the ult r behind Gr *lura* (s and r *lur-*), a lyre: L *lyra*, retained by Mus and An: OF, hence ME, *lire*: reshaped E (and F) *lyre*. Gr *lura* has derivatives *lurikos*, L *lyricus*, whence F *lyrique* and E *lyric*;

*lurismos*, F *lyrisme*, E *lyrism*; *luristēs*, F *lyriste* and E *lyrist*.

**laudanum**, whence **laudanin(e)** (*laudan*um+ Chem *-in*, *-ine*), is a SciL word, prob from ML *laudanum*, var of L *lādanum*, *lēdanum*, a resinous juice from the Cyprian shrub *lada*, *leda*, *ledon*: Gr *lēdanon*, from the shrub *lēdon*, itself o.o.o.: perh Medit. Paracelsus was app the first (early in C16) to apply *laudanum* to an opiate preparation; Thomas Sydenham (C17) to use it in liquid form.

**laugh** (v, hence n), whence **laughable** and the pa and vn **laughing**; **laughter**; **clang** (v, hence n), **clangor** or **clangour**, **clangorous**; **klaxon**.

1. 'To *laugh*', ME *laughen*, earlier *laghen*, *lauhen*, derives from OE *hlaehhan*, varr *hlehhan*, *hliehhan* and *hlyhhan*: cf OFris *hlakkia*, OHG *hlahhan*, *lahhan*, MHG-G *lachen*, Go *hlahjan*, MD-D *lachen* (MD var *lachgen*), ON *hlaeja*; also, much further off, L *clang*ere. *Laughter* derives from OE *hleahtor*, itself from the OE v: cf OHG *hlahtar*, *lahtar*, MHG *gelehter* (*ge-*, orig an int), G *Gelachter*, MD-D *gelach*, ON *hlatr*. The Gmc r is *\*hlah-*; the IE r, *\*klak-*: cf OIr *cluiche*, a joke, and, nasalized, L *clangere*, *clangor*.

2. L *clangor* (s *clang-*), adopted by E, derives from *clang*ere, (of large birds) to cry, (of the human voice, of musical instruments) to sound or resound, and has derivative ML adj *clangorōsus*, whence E *clangorous*. L *clangere* has s and r *clang-*, nasalization of *\*clag-*, var of IE *\*klak-*: ult echoic. *Clangere* yields 'to *clang*', prob akin to Gr *klangē* (κλαγγή), a clang or a loud twang.

3. Akin to those Gr and L words is Gr *klazō* (for *\*klangiō*), I make a loud or piercing sound, presp *klazōn* and future *klanxō* (κλάγξω): hence, rather confusedly, *Klaxon*, a trade-name, hence *klaxon*, any similar noise-making device.

**laughter** (1). See prec.

**laughter** (2). See the 2nd LIE, para 5, s.f.

**launch** (1), a warship's boat: either (OED and Webster) Sp and Port *lancha*, a pinnace, app from Mal *lanca*, a three-masted boat; or (EW) Sp *lancha*, pinnace, from Port *lanchara*, from Mal *lancharan*, a swift warship, from Mal *lanchar*, swift; or (several reputable Sp philologists) Sp *lancha*, launch, pinnace, by alteration of LL *planca*, a slab, a plank, from *planca*, the f of the LL adj *plancus*, flat-footed, app a nasal cognate of Gr *plax* (gen *plakos*), anything flat: ? ult akin to *plain*, *plane*.

**launch** (2), v. See LANCE, para 4.

**launder** (n, hence v), **laundress**, **laundry**. See LAVA, para 4.

**laureate**. See para 2 of:

**laurel** (n, hence v, whence the pa **laurelled**); **Laura** (whence Min **laurite**: suffix *-ite*), **laurus** whence the adj **lauric** and Chem n **laurin**—cf LL *laurīnum*, bay-tree oil); **laureate** (ad, hence n), whence, anl, **laureation**; **laurustine**; **Laurence**, with anglicizing var **Lawrence** and the adj **Laurentian**.

1. *Laurel* derives from ME *lorel*, a var, with change of suffix, of *lorer*, var *laurer*, from OF-MF *lorier*, OF-F *laurier*, from OF *lor*, itself from L *laurus* (s and r, *laur-*), a laurel tree or shrub, hence, laurel leaves being sacred to Apollo and used for crowning triumphant generals, a triumphal crown: o.o.o.: but prob, like Gr *daphnē*, of Medit stock. Hence the It given-name *Lauro*, f *Laura*.

2. L *laurus* has adj *laureus*, whence *laurea* (sc *corona*), a crown of laurels, whence *laureātus*, crowned with laurels, whence the E adj **laureate**. *Laurus*, laurel tree+*tinus*, the laurustine, suggests to the scientists *Laurustinus*, whence *laurustine*, a laurel-like shrub with evergreen leaves.

**lava**, whence **lavatic** and **lavic**; **lave**, **lavabo**, **lavage**, **lavation**, **lavatory**, **lavement**, **laver** (seaweed; washing bowl); **lavish** (n, hence adj and v); **latrine**; **launder** (n, hence v), **launderer** (from the v), **laundress** (*launder*, n+f suffix *-ess*), **laundry**; sep **lather**; **loment**, whence **lomentaceous**; **lotion**, **lotic**; **lye**.—Cpds: **abluent**, **ablution**; **alluvial**, **alluvion**, **alluvium**; **colluvial**, **colluvies**; **diluent** (adj, hence n), **dilute** (adj and v), **dilution**—cf **diluvial**, **diluvian** (whence **diluvianism**), **diluvium**—cf, therefore, **deluge** (n, hence v); **elute**, **elution**, **elutriate**—cf **eluvium**.—Cf the sep LAVENDER.

1. *Lava* is an It word, orig Neapolitan for such torrential rain as overflows the streets, from It *lavare*, from L *lauāre* (ML *lavāre*), to wash oneself, to wash, s *lau-*, ML *lav-*, as in OF-F *laver*, whence—assisted by OE *lafian* (perh from ML *lavāre*)—the ME *laven*, whence 'to *lave*'. L *lauāre* is akin to the syn L *luere*, s and r *lu-*, itself akin to Gr *louein*, to wash, s *lou-*, r *lou-*, app a mdfn or extn of *lo-*; cf also Arm *loganam*, I wash myself— OIr *lōathar*, pelvis, Br *louein*, to urinate—OHG *louga*, MHG *louge*, G *Lauge*, OE *lēah*, lye, ON *laug*, a warm bath. The IE r is prob *lo-*, with var *lu-* and with extn *lou-* or *lau-*.

2. L *lauāre* (s *lau-*), to wash, has the foll simple derivatives relevant to E:

*lauābō*, ML *lavābō*, I shall wash, occurs in the Psalm, Vulgate xxv, AV xxvi; verses 6–12, beginning 'Lavabo inter innocentes', are recited, at the Mass, by the priest while he washes his hands, hence *lavabo*, the liturgical act, hence the towel, hence the basin, hence a wash-basin and its fittings (Webster);

*lauātiō* (from pp *lauāt*us), a washing, ML *lavātiō*, o/s *lavātiōn-*, whence *lavation*;

LL *lauātōrium*, ML *lavātōrium*, a wash-basin, whence, in E, a wash-place, whence the combination of that with urinal and water-closet(s); hence also OF-MF *lavoir* (EF-F *lavoir*), ME *lavour*, E *laver*, a water-bowl or a wash-basin, (Jewish) a large vessel for water, baptismal water; cf

*lauer*, ML *laver*, a water plant, hence, in Bot, several kinds of seaweed, hence a dish made of their pickled fronds.

3. Simple derivatives passing through F include: *lavage*, adopted from MF-F, from OF-F *laver*, from ML *lavāre*;

*lavement*, adopted from OF-F, deriving from OF-F *laver* but perh suggested by LL *lauamentum*, ML *lavamentum*;

*lavish*, adj, from the obs n *lavish*, from EF-F *lavasse*, late MF-EF *lavache*, a very heavy fall of rain, from Prov *lavaci*, from ML *lavātiō* (as in para 2).

4. Also through F comes *launder*, a washer-woman (obs), later a conduit, a trough, with derivative v 'to *launder*': ME *lander*, short for *lavender*: OF *lavandiere*, a laundress, from ML *lavandāria*, LL *lauandāria*, itself from *lauandus*, due or fit to be washed, from *lauāre*. Cf *laundry*, ME *lavendrie* (influenced by ME *lavender*), MF *lavanderie*, prob formed anl from OF *lavandiere*.

5. L *lauāre*, vi and vt, has a parallel, rather than a var, *lauere*, vt, with pp *lautus*, with var *lōtus*; on the pp *lōt*us is formed LL *lōtus* (gen *lōtūs*), a washing, with s *lōt-*, whence—prompted by E *lotion*—the E adj *lotic*. On the same L s *lōt-* arises LL *lōtiō*, a washing, o/s *lōtiōn-*, whence, perh via MF-F *lotion*, the E *lotion*.

6. The L pp s *lōt-* app rests upon the IE r *lo-*: cf the L *lōmentum*, something that serves for washing, a soap, a cosmetic wash, ? hence a bean meal (used as such a wash): hence the Bot *loment*, whence—anl with *saponaceous*—the adj *lomentaceous*.

7. L *lauāre* has, through pp *lauāt*us, the further relevant derivative *lauātrīna*, usu shortened to *lātrīna*, orig a wash-basin, hence a water-closet, whence, *lātrīna* being apprehended as pl, the MF *latrines*, whence the rare F sing *latrine*; hence the E *latrines* (the earlier form) and *latrine*.

8. As we saw, late in para 1, L *lauāre* is akin to OHG *louga*, G *Lauge*, lye, itself akin to the syn OE *lēah*, whence E *lye*: cf also D *loog*, lye.

9. L *lauere* has c/f *-luere*, whence—so numerous are the prefix-cpds—*luere*, to wash. The chief cpds relevant to E are these:

*abluere*, to remove (connoted by *ab*) by washing, hence to cleanse, to purify, with presp *abluens*, o/s *abluent-*, whence *abluent*, adj hence n, and with pp *ablūt*us, whence LL *ablūtiō*, o/s *ablūtiōn-*, whence, perh via MF-F, the E *ablution*;

*alluere*, to wash against (*ad*, towards), to bathe, whence both *alluuiō*, ML *alluviō*, o/s *alluviōn-*, whence, prob via EF-F, the E *alluvion*, and the adj *alluuius*, with neu *alluuium*, which, used as n (ML *alluvium*), is adopted by E, whence the adj *alluvial*;

*colluere* (*col-* for *con-*, with, connoting extension), to sprinkle all over, to wash, whence *colluuiēs*, ML *colluviēs*, a 'gathering' of washing-water, off-scourings, dregs, adopted by E, whence the anl adj *colluvial*;

*dīluere*, to wash away (*di-* for *dis-*, apart), hence to dilute, with presp *dīluens*, o/s *dīluent-*, whence the E adj, hence n, *diluent*, and with pp *dīlūtus*, whence the E adj and v *dilute*, the derivative *dīlūtiō*, o/s *dīlūtiōn-*, yielding *dilution*;

*dīluere* has the further derivative *dīluuium*, ML *dīluvium*, inundation, a deluge, adopted by E; the derivative LL adj *dīluuiālis*, ML *dīluviālis*, yields *diluvial*, with var *diluvian*, whence *diluvianism*;

ML *dīluvium* becomes OF-MF *deluge* (F *dé-*), whence E *deluge*, whence 'to *deluge*';

*ēluere*, to remove (*ē-*, out of, from) by washing, hence to wash, to purify, with pp *ēlūtus*, whence 'to *elute*'; derivative LL *ēlūtiō*, o/s *ēlūtiōn-*, yields *elution*; the inf s *ēlu-* has derivative *ēluuiēs*, ML *ēluviēs*, an out- or over-flowing, whence, anl with *alluvium*, the SciE *eluvium*;

*ēluere* has cognate *ēlutriāre*, to rinse out, to decant, pp *ēlutriātus*, whence 'to *elutriate*'.

**lavabo; lavation; lavatory.** See prec, para 2.

**lave.** See LAVA, para 1.

**lavender** is explained either (OED, EW, Webster) as from AF *lavendre*, from ML *lavendula*, var of *livendula*, a dim of ML *lividus*, L *liuuidus* (cf LIVID), or as from AF *lavendre*, alteration of MF-F *lavande*, adopted from It, from (after B & W and Dauzat) ML *lavanda*, f of *lavandus*, serving to wash, hence cleanse, from *lavāre*, L *lauāre*, to wash (cf LAVA, para 1): because it perfumes a cosmetic wash. AF *lavendre* was prob influenced by ML *lavandārio*, var *lavanderia*, in the shortened form *lavandria*, the ML word meaning lit 'things applied to washing', neu pl of *lavandārius*, suitable for washing (hence, cleansing)'.

**laver,** washing-bowl, seaweed. See LAVA, para 2, s.f.

**lavish.** See LAVA, para 3.

**law, lawful, lawless.** See the 2nd LIE (to be prostrate), para 6.

**lawn (1),** sward. See LAND, para 3.

**lawn (2),** a fine linen (later, cotton) fabric: C15–16 *laun*, *laune*: (linen from) the F town of *Laon*, medievally famous for its manufacture.

**lawyer.** See the 2nd LIE (to be prostrate), heading; cf para 6.

**lax, laxation, laxative, laxity.** See LANGUID, para 2.

**lay (1),** adj, whence **layman** and **laity** (*lai-* for *lay*+suffix *-ity*): ME, from OF-archaic F *lai*: LL *laïcus*: Gr *laïkos*, of the *laos* or people. 'To *laicize*' —cf the F *laïciser*—derives from the adj *laic* (LL *laïcus*)—cf the MF-F *laïc*, *laïque*. Cf LEWD and LITURGIC.

**lay (2),** n, song, ballad: ME *laye*, earlier *lai*: OF-F *lai*: of C origin—cf OIr *lāed*, *lōid*, Ir *laid*, Ga *laoidh*, song, poem. Cf LUDICROUS.

**lay (3),** v.; **layer,** a stratum. See the 2nd LIE (to be prostrate), para 2.

**lazuli,** in *lapis lazuli*. See LAPIDARY, para 1.

**lazy,** whence 'to *laze*' and **laziness:** EE *laysy*: perh MLG *lasich*, var *losich*, feeble—perh cf G *lasch*, flabby, itself perh akin to G *los*, loose, free, MHG-OHG *los*, free, frivolous (therefore E LOOSE); cf also OFris *lās*, loose.

**lea (1),** meadow. See the 3rd LIGHT, para 4.

**lea (2),** a measure. See LANGUID, para 12.

**leach.** See LEAK, para 2.

**lead (1),** the metal; **leaden.**

The adj *leaden*, OE *lēaden*, derives from OE *lēad*, whence, through ME *leed* and *led*, the E n *lead*: and OE *lēad* is akin to MD *loot*, *lood*, D *lood*, MHG *lōt*, lead (G *Lot*, a plummet): prob of

C origin, for cf OIr *lúaide* (Ga *luaidhe*, Mx *leoaie*); prob OC etymon, *loudiā* (MacLennan).

**lead** (2), to guide (whence—cf OFris *lēde*—'a *lead*'), pt and pp **led**, hence **leader; leitmotiv.**

'To *lead*', derives from ME *leden*, from OE *lǣdan*, itself akin to OFris *lēda*, OS *lēdian*, OHG *leitēn*, MHG-G *leiten* (whence G *Leitmotiv*, lit 'leading motive', in Mus a strongly marked melodic phrase, adopted by E), Go *laidjan*, ON *leitha*: prop a causative—'to make go'—from the etymon (? *līthan*) of that Gmc word for 'to go' which we see in OE *līthan*, ON *lītha*, Go *-leithan*, to go, OHG *galīdan*, to travel: cf (the IE *r-l* alternation in) Av *raēth-*, to depart, hence to die. (Walshe.) Cf the sep LOAD.

**leaden.** See the 1st LEAD.

**leader,** whence **leadership.** See the 2nd LEAD.

**leaf,** n (hence v and -leaved), pl leaves; whence **leafage** (prob after **foliage**), **leaflet** (dim *-let*) and **leafy** (adj *-y*);—**libel** (n, hence v), whence **libellant, libelee,** and **libellous; librarian, library.**

1. *Leaf*, ME *leef* or *lef*, derives from OE *lēaf*, akin to OFris *lāf*, OS *lōf*, Go *laufs*, OHG *loub*, MHG *loup*, G *Laub*, MD-D *loof*, ON *lauf*, and Lith *lapas*, all 'leaf', some also 'foliage': cf also L *liber*, bast, Lith *lupti*, to peel, OSl *lubŭ*, bark, and nasalized Skt *lumpati*, he breaks: basic idea, 'to peel, to strip' (Webster). The IE r is app *lubh-*, with varr *lābh-*, *lēbh-*, *libh-*, *lobh-*.

2. L *liber* (s and r *lib-*), OL *leber*, representing a notable vocalic change, means primarily 'bast' (fibre between the wood and the outer bark of esp a tree), hence, because—before papyrus was introduced—'that on which one writes, paper', hence finally 'book'. On the o/s *libr-* arises the adj *librārius*, of or for or in a book, hence *librāria*, a bookshop, and *librārium*, a library. The derivative L *librārius*, used with L *scrība*, a scribe, means a copyist or a secretary, whence MF *libraire* (OF *livraire*), copyist, author, whence MF *librairie*, a library, whence late ME *librairie*, E *library*, whence *librarian*, perh suggested by the L and F words. (The modern F senses 'bookseller' and 'bookshop' arose in C16.)

3. L *liber* has dim *libellus*, little book, pamphlet, journal, memorandum, letter, etc., whence OF *libel*, *libelle*, a legal document, whence MF *libelle diffamatoire* (cf ML *libellus diffāmatōrius*), whence, ult, the E *libel*, whence—perh aided by late MF-F *libeller*—'to libel'.

**league** (1), a covenant. See LIGAMENT, para 4.

**league** (2), a distance usu of 3 miles: OF *legue* (whence F *lieue*): LL *leuga* or *leuca*: Gaulish, says St Jerome c400 A.D.: perh (Malvezin[1]) for OC *leuva*, from OC *leu-*, to divide: 'division (of a road or a journey)'.

**leaguer,** a camp. See the 2nd LIE, para 4.

**leak,** n (whence—cf ON *lekr*—**leaky**) and v (whence **leakage**); **leach,** v hence n (whence **leachy**).

1. 'A *leak*' derives either from 'to *leak*' or from ON *leki*; 'to *leak*', from ON *leka*, akin to MD *leken*: cf also OE *leccan*, to moisten, OIr *legaim* (r

*leg-*), to moisten, W *llaith*, moist, OC *lego*, I flow, ? from OC *li-*, liquid, wet, moist (Malvezin), and therefore akin to L *līmus*, mud, slime, perh ult to LICK.

2. OE *leccan* (s *lecc-*, r *lec-*), to moisten, aided by ON *leka*, to leak, yields 'to *leach*', now mostly in tech senses.

**leal, lealty.** See LEGAL, para 3.

**leam.** See the 3rd LIGHT, para 3.

**lean** (1), adj, whence **leanness** and the whaling v 'to *lean*': ME *lene*: OE *hlǣne*, perh akin to Lett *kleins*, feeble, but perh to G *klein* (cf CLEAN).

**lean** (2), v, to incline, whence pa and vn **leaning; ladder,** n hence v.—Cf the sep CLIME.

1. 'To *lean*', ME *lenen*, derives from OE *hlinian*, var *hleonian*, akin to OHG *hlinēn*, MHG *linen*, *lenen*, G *lehnen*, OS *hlinōn*, MD *lenen*, D *leunen*, and, further off, L *clīnāre*, Gr *klinein*.

2. That which *leans* against a wall and is used for climbing is a *ladder*, ME *laddre*, OE *hlaedder* or *hlaeder*, from the Gmc r of 'to *lean*': cf OFris *hladder*, *hledder*, *hlēdere*, OHG *hleitara*, *leitara*, MHG-G *leiter*.

**leap,** n, derives from—cf OFris *hlēp*—'to *leap*': ME *lepen* or *leapen*: OE *hlēapan*, to jump, to run, akin to OFris *hlāpa*, to go, to run (cf *hlāpia*, to jump), OS *āhlōpan*, OHG *hlauffan*, *loufan*, MHG *loufen*, G *laufen*, MD *lopen*, D *loopen*, to run, Go *hlaupan*, to run, to jump, perh cf Lith *klubti*, to stumble.

2. ON *hlaupa* leads through ME *loupen*, *lopen*, to E 'to *lope*', to leap (obs), to canter, to run as if cantering; and ON *hlaup*, a leap, to the E n *lope*; with the derivative agent *loper*, cf MD *loper*.

3. *Lope* occurs in such E prefix-cpds as *elope*, *gallop* (treated sep), *interlope*, *orlop*, and, cognately, in *lapwing*, ME *lap wynke* or *leepwynke*, OE *hlēapwince*, lit 'a wavering leap' (OE *wincian*, to wink, and *hlēapān*, to leap).

4. 'To *elope*' comes, through AF *eloper* (*a*, F *à*, L *ad*, to), prob from ME *lopen*, *loupen*, to run, to leap, or perh from some other Gmc syn (cf paras 1 and 2). Hence *elopement*.

5. 'To *interlope*' is a b/f from *interloper*, itself prob from D *enterlooper*: *enter*, from F *entre* (L *inter*), between+*looper*, runner.

6. *Orlop*, a ship's lowest deck, comes from D *overloop*, (lit) a running over, hence a covering, from *overloopen*, to *loopen* or run *over*, over.

**learn,** pret and pp **learned** (whence the pa) and **learnt, learner** (OE *leornere*), **learning** (OE *leornung*); **lore;** sep **last** (of boot; v, to endure); **deliration, delirious, delirium** (e.g. tremens).

1. 'To *learn*' derives, through ME *lernen*, var *leornen*, from OE *leornian*, akin to OFris *lernia*, OHG *lernēn*, *lirnēn*, MHG-G *lernen*, OS *līnōn*, MD *leernen*, *lerenen*: perh inch from the r of the caus Gmc v represented by OE *lǣran*, to teach, and the syn OFris *lēra*, OS *lērian*, OHG *lērēn*, *lērran*, MHG *lēren*, G *lehren*, MD *leeren*, D *leren*, Go *laisjan*: to teach is to cause to understand, (lit) to lead someone on his way. Cf also OE *lǣst*, a track,

hence a last (cf the 3rd and 4th LAST), OHG wagan-*leisa*, a track (rut) caused by a waggon, OHG-MHG *leist* (G *Leisten*), a shoemaker's last, Go *laists* and MHG *leis*, a track, and prob Go *lais*, I know; cf, further off, the L *līra*, a furrow; OP and OSl afford cognates. Clearly, therefore, the IE r is *\*lī-* (varr *\*lai-*, *\*lei-*), with extnn *līr-*, *līs-* (Go *lais-*, OHG *leis-*), varr *lēr-* (*lāēr-*), *lor-*.

2. Very closely akin to OE *lāēran*, to teach, is OE *lār*, a teaching, instruction, hence the knowledge taught: ME *lare*—var *lore*, adopted by E. Cf OFris *lāre*, OS and OHG *lēra* (G *Lehre*), MD *lere*, *leere*, (as D) *leer*.

3. L *līra*, a furrow, is retained by Zoo for a hair-like ridge. The derivative *līrāre*, to furrow, has the cpd *dēlīrāre* (s *dēlir-*), to leave—connoted by *de-*, down from—the furrow, hence to get off the right track, to lose one's way, hence to go out of one's mind. Derivative *dēlīrātiō* (from *dēlīrāt-*, s of the pp *dēlīrātus*), o/s *dēlīrātiōn-*, becomes E *deliration*; derivative *dēlīrium* (suffix *-ium*) is adopted by E, as is the Med *delirium tremens*, trembling delirium; *delirious*=delirium+adj *-ous*.

**leary.** See LEERY.

**lease.** See LANGUID, para 6.

**leash.** See LANGUID, para 9.

**least** (adj, hence adv and n); **less**, adj (hence n) and adv—**lessen** and **lesser**, both from the adj; **lest**.

1. The key-word is *less*. The adv *less*, OE *lǣs*—cf OFris and OS *līs*—prob derives from the adj *less*, ME *lesse*, OE *lǣssa*, akin to OFris *lessa*, var *lessera* (perh influencing E *lesser*): the comp of a lost Gmc positive, with an IE base implied by Lith *liesas*, thin (? earlier 'slight', ? earliest 'little'). Cf *loose* at LOSE.

2. The answering sup is *least*, ME *lest*, *last*, OE *lǣst*, contr of *laesast* or *laesest*, akin to OFris *lēst*, contr of *lērest*.

3. The conj *lest* comes, through ME *leste* (for *les te*), from OE 'thȳ *lǣs the*', the less that: *thȳ*, instr of *sē*, the; *lǣs*, (adj) less; *the*, which, that—a relative particle.

**leather** (n, hence adj and v), whence **leathery**—cf **leathern** (OE *letheren*, from *lether*).

*Leather* is ME, from OE, *lether*, akin to OFris and OS *lether*, OHG *ledar*, MHG-G *leder*, MD *ledder*, *ladder*, D *leder* (*leer*), ON *lethr*; cf also EIr (and Ga) *lethar*, *leathar*, W *lledr*, OC *\*lētro-* (MacLennan).

**leave** (1), permission ('by your leave!'), now esp permission to be absent; **furlough**; **lief** (var **lieve**; comp **liefer**, **liever**, sup **liefest**, **lievest**), adj hence adv—cf **belief**, **believe** (whence **believer**); **leman**; **livelong**; **love**, **lovable**, **lovely**, **lover**; **libido**.

1. *Leave*, ME *leve*, OE *lēaf*, is akin to MHG *loube*, ON *leyfi*, permission, OHG-MHG ur*loup*, ur*lop*, ON or*lof*, permission (esp to depart), G Ur*laub*, leave of absence, OHG ir-*loubēn*, MHG er*louben*, G er*lauben*, Go us-*laubjan*, to permit or allow.

2. MHG *erlouben* has the var *verlouben* (whence prob the G *Verlaub*, permission), which has perh

prompted the MLG *vorlof* and which is certainly akin to MD-D *verlof*, leave of absence, whence EE *furloff*, E *furlough*.

3. OE *lēaf*, permission (as in para 1), is akin to OE *geleafa*, a believing, which, under the influence of OE *belīfan*, *belēfan* (whence ME *bileven*, E 'to believe'), results in ME *bileafe* (var *belive*), whence E *belief*. With OE *geleafa*, cf OHG *giloubo*, MHG *geloube*, G *Glaube*; with OE *belīfan*, *belēfan*, cf OE *gelīfan*, Go *galaubjan*, OS *gilōbian*, MHG *gelouben*, G *glauben*.

4. OE *lēaf*, permission, is also akin to OE *lēof*, dear, pleasing, which, joined to OE *mann*, man, produces ME *leofmon*, later *lefman*, latest *lemman*, whence EE-archaic E *leman*, orig a lover, then a paramour.

5. OE *lēof*, dear, pleasing, becomes ME *leof*, later *lef* and *lefe* or *leef*, whence E *lief*, archaic as adj and obsol as adv ('He would as lief die as live').

6. ME *lefe* (etc), dear, occurs in *lefe long*, lit 'dear long', i.e. 'very long', *lefe* being a mere int: hence E 'the *livelong* day, or night'—cf G *die liebe lange Nacht* (EW)—where *livelong* has gained the nuance 'tediously long', often debased to 'entire'. *Livelong* has perh suggested *lifelong*, as *long* as *life*, itself increasingly debased.

7. To revert to OE *lēof*, dear, pleasing, we find a cognate group of words rather more important than *lief* and *live*long. 'To *love*' goes back to OE *lufian*; the n *love*, ME *luve*, to OE *lufu*. *Lufu* has adj *luflīc*, loving, hence fit for or worthy of love, hence beautiful, *lovely*, etc. *Lover* comes straight from 'to *love*', as also does *lovable*.

8. Akin to OE *lēof*, dear, and OE *lufu*, love, are OFris *liāf*, OS *liof*, OHG *liob*, *liub*, MHG *liep*, G *lieb*, Go *liufs*, ON *liūfr*, OSl *ljubŭ*, with IE etymon *\*leubhos*, Gmc *\*liubhaz* (Walshe); and, for 'love', OHG *liubī*, MHG *liebe*, joy, G *Liebe*, love—OSl *ljuby* (n) and *ljubiti* (v)—L *lubet* (s and r *lub-*), it pleases, with var *libet* (cf *libīdō*, desire, esp if sexual)—Skt *lúbhyati* (r *lubh-*), he desires. The IE r is app *\*leabh-*, with varr *\*leubh-*, *\*loubh-*.

9. The r *lib-* of L *libet*, a thinned form of *lubet*, it pleases, recurs in L *libīdō* (o/s *libīdin-*), lust, adopted by Psy; derivative L *libīdinōsus* becomes, perh via MF-F *libidineux*, f *libidineuse*, the E *libidinous*.

**leave** (2), to permit, or to cause, to remain. See LIFE, para 7.

**leaven.** See LEVER, para 4.

**lebensraum.** See LIFE, para 6.

**lecher, lecherous, lechery.** See LICK, para 2.

**lectern; lection, lectionary, lector; lecture: lecturer.** See LEGEND, paras 2–4.

**lectual.** See the 2nd LIE, para 13.

**lecture, lecturer.** See LEGEND, para 4.

**led.** See the 2nd LEAD.

**ledge.** See the 2nd LIE (be prostrate), para 8.

**ledger.** See the 2nd LIE, para 8.

**lee** (1), now always LEES, dregs. See the 2nd LIE, para 11.

**lee** (2), shelter ('in the lee of'—hence adj), ME

*lee*, shelter, derives from OE *hlēo* (for *hlēow*), shelter or protection, akin to OFris *hlē*, OS *hleo*, D *lij*, ON *hlē*: ult akin to CALDRON.—Hence, *leeway* (cf WAY).

**leech** (1), edge of a sail. See LIGAMENT, para 4.

**leech** (2), a physician, ? hence, because so widely employed by early physicians, a blood-sucking worm: ME *leche*: OE *lǣce*, akin to OFris *lētza*, OS *lāki*, Go *lēkeis*, ON *laeknari*: ? akin to OIr *līaig*, enchanter, magician, conjurer, hence a physician, and consequently to Skt *lapati*, he talks.

**leek.** See LOCK (1), para 2.

**leer** (v, hence n), orig to look askance, ? particularly down one's cheek: perh from EE *leer*, OE *hlēor*, cheek: cf OS *hlēor*, *hlēar*, *hlīor*, *hlīer*, Frankish *chleura*, ON *hlȳr*: cf also such C words as OIr and Ga *clūas*, W *clust* (cf OC *\*kloustā*), ear, and Cor *grüth*, cheek or jaw: ? ult akin to Gr *ous* (prob for *\*ousos*), ear.

**leery** or **leary**, knowing, sly, suspicious: orig cant, then low sl: perh from prec, but prob from dial *lear* (cf E *lore*), learning, hence cleverness, smartness: cf, sem, the older cant *peery*, sly, suspicious (P and P¹): EW proposes dial *lear* influenced by E *leer*.

**lees**, dregs. See the 2nd LIE, para 11.

**leeway.** See the 2nd LEE, s.f.

**left** (1), adj, hence n, whence coll **leftist,** a Socialist; **leper, lepra, leproid, leprosy, leprous; lepid.**

1. *Left*, on the left hand, hence the left-hand quarter, comes through the syn ME *left*, varr *lift*, *luft*, from rare OE *left*, *lyft*, weak, cf OE *lyftādl*, palsy: perh an extn of OE *lēf*, weak (as also in OFris and OS), cf OE *lēfung*, palsy, paralysis.

2. Prob cognate to OE *left*, weak, is *leper*, from ME, from OF, *lepre* (F *lèpre*), leprosy, from L *lepra*—adopted by Med—from Gr *leprā*, itself perh from *lepra*, neu pl of *lepros* (s *lepr-*, r *lep-*), scaly, for in leprosy the skin flakes away in small scales: cf *lepos* (s, r *lep-*), a scale or a husk, and *lep*ein, to scale or husk: IE r *\*lep-*, to scale.

3. L *lepra* has LL adj *leprōsus*, whence OF-MF *leprous* (var *lepros*), adopted by E; whence, by b/f, *leprosy*—cf the EF *léproserie* from *lepros*.

4. Akin perh to Gr *lepos*, a scale, *lepros*, scaly, and esp to *leptos* (prop the pp of *lepein*), scaled, husked, hence thin or small, is L *lepidus* (s *lepid-*, r *lep-*), dainty, whence the obsol literary E *lepid*, charming, pleasant.

**left** (2), pt and pp of 'to *leave*', q.v. at LIFE.

**leg**, n, hence v, hence also the adj **leggy; lizard** and **alligator; lobster** and **locust.**

1. *Leg*, ME *leg*, earlier *legge*, comes from ON *leggr*, the leg or merely its calf (cf ON arm*leggr*, the arm), akin to Lombard *lagi*, thigh, OSl *lakŭtĭ*, lower arm. Gmc r, perh *\*leg-*, var of *\*lag-*; IE r, prob *\*lak-*.

2. Prob akin to *leg* is L *lacertus* (s *lacert-*, ult r ? *lac-*), a muscle, mostly in pl *lacerti*, muscles of the upper arm, hence muscles in general: and app id is L *lacerta* (fem), *lacertus* (m), a lizard: cf,

sem, the relation of *muscle* to *mouse*. Zoo has adopted L *lacerta* for the Sci name of a lizard; but *lacertus* has been more potent, for, via OF-MF *laisard* (F *lézard*) and derivative ME *lesard*, it yields E *lizard*.

3. L *lacertus*, moreover, becomes Sp *lagarto*, lizard, whence Sp *el lagarto de Indias*, 'the lizard of the [West] Indies' or the cayman (American alligator), which, prob in its debased shortening *aligarto* (1591), accounts for E *alligator*; *aligarto* owes much to a 'learnèd' f/e ref to L *alligāre*, to tie or attach, as B & W suggest.

4. Perh akin to L *lacerta*, *-us*, lizard, is L *locusta*, var *lacusta*, a grasshopper or a locust, but also a lobster, both senses app ref, both phon and sem, to the cognates Gr *lēkan*, to jump, Lett *lékt*, *lezu*, to jump, *lékat*, to hop, *lékas*, 'jumpings' of the heart, and Lith *lekiù*, fly. The r *\*lac-* (or *\*lak-*), as in L *lacerta*, has varr *\*lek-* (or *\*lik-*) and *\*loc-* (or *\*luc-*): basic idea, ? 'to bend', hence esp to bend the muscles, etc., in jumping or darting and in flying, derivatively 'to jump, leap, dart about'— cf even the 'jumping' of muscles that ripple. These reptiles, crustaceans, insects, limbs have much in common.

5. L *locusta*, grasshopper, locust, becomes OF-F *locuste* and—perh therefrom—E *locust*.

6. L *locusta*, lobster, perh blends, phon, with OE *loppe*, spider, to produce OE *loppestre* (var *lopystre*), lobster, whence ME *lopster* and later *lobster*, the latter extant in E.

**legacy.** See para 5 of:

**legal, legalism, legalist, legality, legalize— illegal, illegality; legist**—cf lex; **legacy, legate** (cf LEGATEE), **legation**—cf delegacy, **delegate, delegation,** and **relegate, relegation; legitim, legitimate** (adj, hence v and **legitimacy), legitimation, legitimize** —**illegitimacy, illegitimate; legislate, legislation, legislative, legislator; colleague**—cf **college, collegial, collegiate, collegium**—cf again privi*lege*, q.v. at PRIVATE; **leal, lealty**—cf **loyal, loyalist, loyalty,** and **disloyal, disloyalty.**

1. The entire group rests upon L *lēx* (prob for *\*lēgs*), o/s *lēg-*, law, orig religious and then governmental. *Lēx* is o.o.o.—unless, as is prob, it derives from L *legere*, to collect; for the latter group, see LEGEND.

2. L *lēx* occurs in several Law cpds; its ML derivative *lēgista* becomes F *légiste*, whence E *legist*, a jurist. The derivative adj *lēgālis* (*lēg-*+ adj suffix *-alis*)—later than *lēgitimus* (see para 4)— becomes, prob via MF-F, the E *legal*; derivative ML *lēgālitās* beomes MF-F *légalité*, whence E *legality*; *legalize*, *legalization* represent EF-F *légaliser*, *légalisation*, themselves from *légal*. ML *illēgālis* becomes MF-F *illégal*, whence MF-F *illégalité*: whence the E *illegal, illegality*.

3. L *lēgālis* becomes OProv and OF *leial*, (orig) legal, (then) loyal, whence the mostly Sc *leal*, whence *lealty*. But OF *leial* becomes MF *loial* and F *loyal*, adopted by E, whence *loyalism* and *loyalist*; derivative MF *loialté* (F *loyauté*) becomes E *loyalty*. Both *disloyal* and *disloyalty* are adopted

from OF-MF *desloial, desloialté* (etc), where *des-* is L *dis-*, apart.

4. The L adj *lēgitimus* becomes MF-F *légitime*, which, used as a Law n, yields the E Law term *legitim*. The derivative ML *lēgitimāre*, to render legitimate, has pp *lēgitimātus*, whence E *legitimate*, both adj and hence n; derivative ML *lēgitimātiō*, o/s *lēgitimātiōn-*, leads to MF-F *légitimation* and E *legitimation*. The MF-F *légitime* has derivatives *légitimiste*, whence E *legitimist* (*legitimize* is an anl E formation), and MF-F *illégitime*, which perh suggested the E *illegitimate*, whence *illegitimacy*.

5. L *lēx*, law, o/s *lēg-*, has derivative *lēgāre*, by law, hence officially, to entrust to someone the duty, or the right, to do something, hence the right to inherit. The pp *lēgātus* is used as n, 'one who is so entrusted'—whence OF-F *légat*, whence E *legate*, an envoy. This *lēgātus* (gen *lēgāti*) and *lēgātus* (gen *lēgātūs*), an official mission, prob combines with *lēgātiō*, a diplomatic mission, o/s *lēgātiōn-*, whence OF-F *légation*, E *legation*, to form ML *lēgatia*, the office or dignity of a legate, whence MF *legacie*, whence E *legacy*, now only in legal sense.

6. *Lēgāre* has two cpds affecting E; with prefixes *de-, re-*, used int:

*dēlēgāre*, to send on, entrust with, a formal mission, to delegate, with pp *dēlēgātus*, whence both the n and the v *delegate*, whence *delegacy*; the derivative *dēlēgātiō*, o/s *dēlēgātiōn-*, accounts for *delegation*;

and *relēgāre*, to send on a mission, a commission, a duty, with pp *relēgātus*, whence 'to *relegate*'; derivative *relēgātiō*, o/s *relēgātiōn-*, explains *relegation*.

7. Either from the r of *lēgāre* or directly from *lēg-*, o/s of *lēx*, come the interlinked *collēga*, a person elected along with (*col-* for *con-* for *cum*, with) another, or merely associated professionally with him, and *collēgium*, a body of such persons, prob orig in a religious college. Whereas *collēgium*, partly adopted by E, becomes MF *college* (F *collège*), fully adopted by E, *collēga* becomes late MF-F *collègue*, adapted by E to *colleague*. *Collēgium* has adj *collēgiālis*, whence, perh via MF-F, *collegial*, and the ML *collēgiātus*, member of a college, whence E *collegiate*, now mostly an adj.

8. The gen *lēgis*, of (the) law, occurs in the L virtual cpds *lēgis latiō*, the carrying—hence passing—of a law or of laws, and *lēgis lator*, the 'carrier' of a law: whence resp the E *legislation* and the E *legislator*: whence, by b/f, 'to *legislate*'; *legislative* and *legislature* are anl E formations.

**legate, legatee, legation.** For the 1st and 3rd, see prec, para 5; the 2nd was prompted by both *legate* and *legacy*.

**legend** (n, hence v), **legendary; lectern, lection** and **lesson** (n, hence v); **lectionary, lector; lecture** (n, whence **lecturette**; hence v—whence **lecturer**); **legible, legion, legionary; legume**, whence, as if from L, **leguminose** and **leguminous; ligneous, lignite, lignose** (adj, hence n), **lignum**.—L cpds of *legere*: **collect** (n, v), **collection, collective** (whence

**collectivism, collectivist, collectivity**), **collector**—cf **coil** (v, hence n) and **cull** (v, hence n and also **cullage**); **diligence, diligent; elect** (adj—whence n—and v), **election** (whence **electioneer**), **elective** (whence **electivity**), **elector**, whence **electoral** and **electorate**—**elegance, elegant**—**eligible**, whence **eligibility**—**elite; intellect, intellection, intellective, intellectual** (whence **intellectualism, ist-**), **intellectuality**—**intelligence, intelligent, intelligential, intelligentsia**—**intelligible**, whence, anl, **intelligibility; neglect**, n (whence **neglectful, neglective**) and v (whence **neglector**—cf LL *neglector*)—**negligee**, anglicized form of **négligé**—**negligence, negligent, negligible; predilection; prelect, prelection, prelector** (**praelector**); (sep) **privilege** and **sacrilege** (**sacrilegious**); **select** (adj, v), **selection** (whence **selectionism**), **selective** (whence **selectivity**), **selectman, selector**.—From Gr *legein*: **lexical** (cf **lexigraphy**) and **lexicon** (cf **lexicographer, -graphic, -graphy, -logy**); **logia**—**logic, logical, logician**, and **illogic, illogical**—**logistic**—**logos** (cf LOGARITHM, LOGOGRAM, LOGOGRAPHIC, LOGOGRAPHY, LOGOMACHY, LOGORRHOEA, LOGOTYPE).—Gr prefix-(pds: **analectic, analects; analogical, analogous, analogue, analogy; apologetic, apologia, apologist, apologize, apologue, apology; dialect, dialectal, dialectic** (adj and n), whence **dialectical, dialectician**—cf **dialogue; duologue, eclogite, eclogue; epilogue; eulogist, eulogistic, eulogy**—cf **dyslogistic, dyslogy; monologue; paralogism, paralogy; prolegomenon**, pl **prolegomena; prologue; syllogism, syllogistic; tetralogy** and **trilogy**.—Cf the not certainly cognate group at LEGAL.

I. Latin: *A*, simple *legere*

1. L *legere* (s and r *leg-*), to gather (esp fruit), hence to collect, to assemble, hence to choose, hence—cf E *gather*, to form an impression (that), loosely to deduce—to read, perh (E & M) via such phrases as *legere oculis*, to assemble (the alphabetical letters) with the eyes, and *scriptum legere*, to gather or collect as being written, to find written: cf Gr *legein* (s, r *leg-*), to enumerate or reckon, to say (by choosing one's words),—*legere* has gerundive *legendus* (cf gerund *legendum*), fit, or needing, to be read, whence, via the neu pl *legenda* apprehended as n 'things to be read' and finally—perh aided by *historia legenda*—as a sing, the ML *legenda*, a life-story, the narrative of an important event, whence OF-MF *legende* (EF-F *lé-*), with additional EF sense 'explanatory inscription'; the orig senses pass into C14 ME, the additional into EE. ML *legenda* acquires the alternative *legendārius* (*liber*), a book of legends, which passes into C16 E for a collection of saints' lives, whence, later in the century, comes the corresp adj, which gradually develops the wider sense 'fabulous'. *Legere* has LL adj *legibilis*, whence E *legible*.

2. *Legere* has pp *lēctus*, s *lēct-* whence *lēctiō* (as in the *varia lectio* of scholarship), a reading, with o/s *lēctiōn-*, whence both E *lection* and, from acc *lēctiōnem*, the OF-F *leçon*, with derivative

sense 'a teaching', whence ME *lessoun*, whence E
*lesson*. *Lēctiō* has the ML derivative *lēctiōnārius*,
*-ārium*, a book of Church 'readings', whence E
*lectionary*. On the pps *lēct-* arises the agent *lēctor*,
adopted by E, extant only as University lecturer,
esp in G *Lektor*.

3. Pps *lēct-* has the early ML derivative *\*lec-
tōrium*, a place for reading, attested by the contr
*lectrum*, a reading desk in a church, whence OF
*leitrun, letoren, lettrun*, ME *lettron, lettorne*, (with
*c* from LL-ML) *lectorn*: E *lectern*.

4. *Lēct-* has yet another derivative relevant to
E: ML *lēctūra*, a reading, esp of Scripture or of a
University lecture: MF-F *lecture*, adopted by E.

5. But the inf s *leg-*, to gather or assemble, recurs
in that important Roman word *legiō*, orig a
choosing, hence, because only the best men were
chosen, the Roman army's *legiō* or regiment, o/s
*legiōn-*, acc *legiōnem*, whence OF-MF *legion* (F
*légion*), ME *legioun*, E *legion*. Derivative *legiōn-
ārius*, adj hence, as in Caesar, n, becomes MF-F
*légionnaire* and E *legionary*.

**I, B:** Prefix-cpds of *legere*

6. The principal cpds affecting E are *colligere,
dīligere, ēligere, intellegere, neglegere, sēligere.
Colligere* (*col-* for *con-*, with), to gather together,
to collect, has pp *collectus*, whence 'to collect';
whence also, through the f *collecta* used, in LL and
esp ML, as Eccl n, the Eccl E *collect*; both v and
n owing something to MF. The foll L derivatives
have influenced E: LL *collectiō*, o/s *collectiōn-*,
whence, prob via MF-F, *collection*; LL *collectīuus*
(ML *-īvus*), whence, perh via MF-F *collectif*, the
E *collective*; ML *collector*, adopted by E. L
*colligere* becomes OF *coillir*, whence 'to coil', to
gather together esp a rope. OF *coillir* has var
*cuillir* (F *cueillir*), whence ME *cullen*, E 'to cull'
fruit, hence flowers, etc., and fig, as indeed in OF
and in LL-ML.

7. *Dīligere*, to gather apart (*di-* for *dis-*), to
prefer, to like very well, has presp *dīligens*, o/s
*dīligent-*, whence OF-F *diligent*, adopted by E;
derivative *dīligentia* becomes OF-F, whence E,
*diligence*, the obs 'stage-coach' sense being adopted
from F, where it is elliptical for *carrosse de
diligence*, where *diligence* bears the C17 F sense
'haste' (B & W).

8. *Eligere*, to gather out (*ē-*), to set apart, to
choose, has pp *ēlectus*, whence both adj and v
*elect*; derivative *ēlectiō*, o/s *ēlectiōn-*, yields OF-F,
whence E, *election*; derivative LL *electīuus*, ML
*-īvus*, yields, perh via MF-F, *elective*; LL *ēlector*
is adopted by E (cf the MF-F *électeur*); LL
*ēligibilis* (*elig-+ibilis*) becomes, perh via MF-F,
*eligible*.

9. L *ēligere* becomes VL *\*exlegere*, whence
OF-MF *eslire*, with pp *eslit*, f *eslite*, which, used
as n (? elliptical for *partie eslite*), becomes OF-MF
*eslite*, EF-F *élite*, adopted by E.

10. *Legere* must have had an int *\*legāre*—
attested by *\*elegāre*, surviving in the presp *ēlegāns*,
o/s *ēlegant-*, whence OF *elegant* (F *élégant*),

whence the E word; derivative L *ēlegantia* becomes
MF *elegance*, adopted by E. The derivative L
*inēlegāns*, LL *inēlegantia*, become, perh with F
aid, E *inelegant, inelegance*.

11. L. *intellegere*, to choose from among (*intel-
=inter*, between, among), hence to understand, to
know, to perceive, has presp-used-as-adj *intellegens*,
o/s *intellegent-*, whence, or rather from the var
*intelligent-*, the E *intelligent*; derivative *intelle-
gentia, -igentia*, yields—prob via OF—*intelligence*.
Derivative LL *intellegentiālis*, var *-ig-*, becomes
*intelligential. Intelligentsia*, adopted from Ru,
comes from It *intelligenzia* (L *intelligentia*). The pp
*intellēctus*, s *intellect-*, has derivative nn *intellēctus*
(gen *-ūs*), whence, prob via MF-F, *intellect*, and ML
*intellectiō*, o/s *intellectiōn-*, whence *intellection*;
the derivative adjj ML *intellectīvus*, whence
*intellective*, and LL *intellēctuālis*, whence, perh via
MF-F *intellectuel*, the E *intellectual*, the derivative
LL *intellēctuālitās* becoming *intellectuality*. LL
*intellegibilis* (*intelleg-+ibilis*), var *-ig-*, becomes
MF-F, whence E, *intelligible*. The L negg *inintelle-
gentia, inintellegibilis* perh suggested *unintelligence*
(and *-ent*), *unintelligible*: cf the corresp EF-F
words.

12. L *neglegere*, var *-ig-*, combines *neg-* for *nec*
(from *ne*), not, to mean 'not to gather or assemble',
hence to disdain, to neglect. Presp *neglegens*, o/s
*neglegent-*, var *-ig-*, becomes MF *negligent* (F *nég-*),
adopted by E; derivative *neglegentia*, var *-ig-*,
becomes OF-MF *negligence* (F *né-*), adopted by E.
The pp *neglēctus*, s *neglect-*, whence 'to neglect',
has derivative ML n *neglēctus* (gen *-ūs*), whence
E *neglect*. *Negligible* derives from a non-existent
L *negligibilis*; a woman's *negligee*, from EF-F
*négligé*, pp used as n.

13. ML *praediligere* (*prae-*, before+*dīligere*, as
in para 7), to prefer, has pp *praedilēctus*, whence
both the rare E adj *predilect* and the F *prédilection*,
E *predilection*.

14. L *praelegere*, to announce or, esp, to comment upon what one is about to read, pp *praelēctus*,
whence 'to prelect', has derivatives *praelēctiō,
praelēctor*, whence E *praelection, praelector*, AE
*pre-*.

15. L *sēligere* (*sē-*, connoting separation or
privation), to choose from a number, to select,
has pp *sēlēctus*, whence both the adj and the v
*select*, whence AE *selectman* (chosen annually).
On *sēlēct-*, s of *sēlēctus*, arise both LL *sēlēctiō*, o/s
*sēlēctiōn-*, E *selection*, whence, anl, *selective*, and
LL *sēlēctor*, adopted by E.

**I, C:** L Cognates of *legere*, to gather

16. Prob deriving from *legere*, s *leg-*, is *legūmen*
(suffix *-umen*), 'what one gathers or picks'—a
vegetable, orig esp peas and beans: whence EF-F
*légume*, E *legume*. On the o/s *legūmin-*, EF formed
the adj *legumineux*, f *-euse*, whence E *leguminous*
(and *-ose*).

17. One also gathers wood for the fire; prob L
*lignum*, wood, derives from *lig-*, the predominant
c/f of *legere*. Adopted by E (esp in SciL *lignum*

*vitae*, (lit) tree of life), *lignum*, s *lign-*, has F, hence E, derivative *lignite* (Min suffix *-ite*) and L adj *ligneus*, whence E *ligneous* (cf F *ligneux, -euse*).

II.   Greek: *A*, Simple *leg*ein and simple *log*os

18. Akin to L *leg*ere, to gather, to read, is Gr *leg*ein, to gather, hence to count, hence to recount, hence to say or speak, with its complementary *logos*, which, exhibiting the characteristic Gr alternation between *-e-* vv and *-o-* nn, means a counting, a reckoning—proportion—explanation, statement—rule or principle—a reason, reasoning, reason—continuous statement, a narrative, a story —a speech—verbal expression (often a sentence, a saying, a phrase, rarely a word)—a discourse or a disquisition. (L & S.)

19. Gr *legein* has simple derivative *lexis* (? for *\*legsis*), phrase, word, with adj *lexikos*, whence E *lexic*, mostly in extn *lexical*; Gr *lexikos* has neu *lexikon*, which, elliptical for *lexikon biblion*, a word- or phrase-book, means a glossary, a dictionary, E *lexicon*: cf *-lexia* and *lexico-* in Elements.

20. *Logos* appears in E in most of its Gr meanings. At Element *-loger* are noted the chief *logo*-cpds, except *logarithm*, q.v. at ARITHMETIC, para 2.

21. Gr *logos* (s *log-*) has derivative *logia*, sayings (of, e.g., Christ), prop the neu pl of adj *logios*, and the more important adj *logikos*, whence, via LL *logicus* and EF-F *logique*, the E adj *logic*, in extn *logical*. Gr *logikos* combines with *tekhnē*, art, to form *logikē* (*tekhnē*), whence LL *logicē*, soon and predominantly *logica*, whence OF-F *logique*, ME *logike*, E *logic* (n). From LL *logicus*, learnèd MF-F *logicien*, whence E *logician*. *Logic* (n), *logical*, have negg *illogic* (n), *illogical*, both owing something to the F adj *illogique*.

22. Gr *logos* in its sense '(a) counting or reckoning', has derivative *logizesthai*, to calculate, with adj *logistikos*, concerned with (esp the accountancy of) financial administration, whence E *logistic*, of, for, in, with logic or, esp, financial calculation, and, as n, symbolic logic, prob influential in the formation of that modern horror *logistics*, the 'quartermastery' of military operations, imm from F *logistique*, elliptical for *l'art logistique* and deriving from F *logis*, a lodging, from *loger*, to lodge, q.v. at LODGE.

II, *B*:   Prefix-Compounds of *leg*ein and *log*os

23. *Legein* and *logos* have numerous prefix-cpd derivatives. Perh the most important of those affecting E are the foll:—

24. *Analegein* (*ana-*, on, up), to gather up, to collect, has pp *analektos*, neu pl *analekta*, which, as n ('literary gleanings'), becomes L *analekta*, E *analects*, with adj *analectic*. Akin to, perh deriving from, *analegein* is *analogos*, proportionate, whence L *analogus*, E *analogous*; derivative Gr *analogia*, adopted by L, becomes MF-F *analogie* and E *analogy*. The secondary Gr adj *analogikos* becomes L *analogicus*, whence EF-F *analogique* and E *analogic*, now usu *analogical*. Whereas *analogue*, adopted from EF-F, comes from the L-Gr adj

*analogus, analogos, analogist* is an anl E formation and *analogize* goes back to Gr *analogizein*, whence *analogismos*, whence *analogism*.

25. Gr *apologos*, a story, becomes L *apologus*, late MF-F *apologue*, adopted by E: and *apologos* has derivative *apologia*, a spoken or written defence, adopted by LL, whence MF-F *apologie* and E *apology*. *Apologist* derives from EF-F *apologiste*; *apologize*=*apology*+*-ize*; *apologetic* derives, perh via late MF-F *apologétique*, from LL *apologēticus*, from Gr *apologētikos*, from *apologizesthai*, to speak in defence, from *apologia*.

26. *dialegesthai*, to converse, has pp *dialektos*, which, used as n, becomes L *dialectus* (gen *-ūs*), EF-F *dialecte*, E *dialect*, whence adj *dialectal*. The Gr n *dialektos* has adj *dialektikos*, whence OF-F *dialectique* and E *dialectic*, adj. The n *dialectic* reshapes ME *dialatik*, from OF-MF *dialetique*, from L *dialectica*, elliptical for *dialectica ars*, trln of Gr *dialektikē*, elliptical for *dialektikē tekhnē*, from *dialektikos*. *Dialectician*=F *dialecticien*, learnedly formed by MF from L *dialecticus*.

27. Gr *dialegesthai*, to converse, has corresp n *dialogos*, whence L *dialogus*, OF-F *dialogue*, adopted by E. Derivative LL *dialogista* yields E *dialogist*. Gr *dialogos* has derivatives *dialogismos*, adopted by LL, whence E *dialogism* (in Logic), and *dialogikos*, whence LL *dialogicos*, E *dialogic*, now usu *dialogical*.

28. *Duologue* is an afterthought (*duo-*, two) from *monologue*, itself adopted from MF-F, from Gr *monologos*, speaking (*-logos*) alone (*mono-* from *monos*). Cf *epilogue* and *prologue*: the former being OF-F *épilogue*, LL *epilogus* (influenced by LL *epilogium*), Gr *epilogos*, a concluding speech, etc., corresp to *epilegein*, to say something in addition (*epi*, besides; lit, upon); the latter, from OF-F *prologue*, L *prologus*, Gr *prologos*, a speech (*logos*) before (*pro*): both have derivatives in *-ist* and *-ize*, modelled upon Gr.

29. Gr *eklegein*, to pick *ek-* or out, to select, with corresp adj *eklogos*, whence prob *eklogē*, a choice, a literary selection, esp a type of pastoral poem, whence L *ecloga*, EF-F *églogue* (var *églogue*), E *eclogue*; Gr *eklogē* leads also to Min *eclogite* (*-ite*).

30. Gr *eulogia*, lit a well (*eu*)-speaking, adopted by LL, is also adopted by learnèd E; the ordinary E shape is *eulogy*, with subsequent anl formations *eulogist, eulogistic, eulogize*. European erudition has coined the complementary *dyslogy*, an ill (*dys-*, Gr *dus-*)-speaking, with adj *dyslogistic*. Cf *syllogistic*, L *syllogisticus*, Gr *sullogistikos*, adj of *sullogismos* (from *sullogizesthai*, to reckon all together: *sul-* for *sun-*, with, hence together), whence L *syllogismus*, OF *sil(l)ogisme* ME *silogisme*, E *syllogism*, Logic's scheme or apparatus of reasoning. Cf Logic's *paralogism*, a false method of reasoning: perh via F *paralogisme*, certainly from LL *paralogismus*, Gr *paralogismos*, from *paralogizesthai*, to reason *para-* or to the side, hence falsely; the Gr var *paralogia* has been adopted by E.

31. Gr *prolegein*, to say *pro* or beforehand, hence to state preliminarily, has passive presp *prolegomenos*, stated preliminarily, neu *prolegomenon*, used as n, and, in pl *-omena*, adopted by the learnèd.

32. Ancient Gr drama employs—apart from *prologue*, etc.—two terms that have become literary techh: *tetralogia*, a group of four plays, whence E *tetralogy*, four interrelated or sequential works; and *trilogia*, a group of three plays, hence E *trilogy*, any three sequential works.

### III. Indo-European

33. The very close relationship of L *legere* to Gr *legein* is already clear. The IE r is *\*leg-*, to gather: cf Alb mb-*l'eth*, I gather, mb-*l'oda*, I gathered. (Hofmann.)

**legerdemain** consolidates, substantivizes, anglicizes F *léger de main*, light of hand: as if from ML *levis* (L *leuis*) *dē manū*: cf LEVER and MANUAL.

**leghorn,** whether plaited straw or domestic fowl (*Leghorn*), comes from *Leghorn*, a f/e anglicism for It *Livorno*, a port in Tuscany.

**legible.** See LEGEND, para 1, last sentence.

**legion, legionary.** See LEGEND, para 5.

**legislate, legislation, legislative, legislator, legislature.** See LEGAL, para 8.

**legist.** See LEGAL, para 2.

**legitim, legitimacy, legitimate, legitimize.** See LEGAL, para 4.

**legume, leguminous.** See LEGEND, para 16.

**leisure.** See ADDENDA TO DICTIONARY.

**leitmotiv.** See the 2nd LEAD.

**leman.** See the 1st LEAVE, para 4.

**lemma.** See DILEMMA.

**lemming,** a sub-Arctic rodent, is adopted from Nor and Da *lemming:* cf ON *lemendr*, pl of *lōmundr*, and Lapp *luomek*: perh akin to OSl *lajati*, L *latrāre*, to bark: ? orig the barker.

**lemon; lime** (fruit)—**Limey.**

1. *Lemon*, from MF-F *limon*, from OProv *limun* from Ar *laymūn*, better *līmūn*; *lime*, adopted from EF-F, from Prov *limo*, from Ar *līma*, of which *līmūn* is app an Ar-Per deviation—coined to name another variety of citrus.

2. MF-F *limon* has the EF-F derivative *limonade*, whence, after *lemon*, the E *lemonade*: and E *lime* has AE *lime-juicer*, a British ship, hence sailor, from the *lime juice* served, against scurvy, on British ships, whence sl *Limey*, a British sailor, hence soldier, hence, from c1942, also civilian.

**lemur,** an arboreal quadruped, is so named because it is active at night: b/f from L *lemures*, ghosts active at night: s *lemur-*; r, app *lem-*: cf Gr *lam*uros, greedy, *lam*os, maw, crop, *lamiai*, ghosts that devour children, and perh Lett *lam*ata, a mousetrap: 'basic idea: open jaws' (Webster).

**lend** (whence **lender**), pt and pp **lent; loan.**— L-derived cognates: **delinquent** (adj, hence n), **delinquency; relinquish** (whence **relinquishment**)— cf **relic, relict,** therefore also **derelict** (adj, hence n), **dereliction.**—Gr-derived cognates: sep ECLIPSE

(ECLIPTIC) and ELLIPSE (ELLIPTIC)—Gmc cognates: sep ELEVEN and TWELVE.

1. 'To *lend*', ME *lenen*, OE *lǣnan*, derives from OE *lǣn*, a loan, itself intimately related to ON *lān*, whence ME *lane*, var *lone*, whence E *loan*: with the OE and ON nn, cf OE *lēon*, to lend, OFris *lēn*, a loan, *lēna*, to lend or to borrow, OHG *līhan*, to borrow, MHG *līhen*, to borrow or to lend, G *leihen*, to lend, Go *leihwan*, to lend, also OFris *līa*, ON *ljā*, to lend: basic idea, ? to leave money with (someone, for his use): itself a specialization of the IE idea, to leave (hence, to abandon)—as in the cognate Lith *likti*, Gr *leipein*, to leave, Lith *lieku*, I leave, and, with nasal infix, OP po-*linka*, he remains (*leaves* himself behind), L *linquere*, to leave, and—exhibiting that further IE characteristic, the alternation of *l* and *r*—Skt *riṇākti*, he leaves or abandons (cf Skt *rékṇas*, heritage). The Gmc r is prob *\*lihw-*; the IE r, app *\*leikw-*, var *\*likw-*, with nasal var *\*linkw-*.

2. L *linquere* has the cpd *relinquere*, to leave *re-* or behind, whence MF *relinquir*, with such forms as presp *relinquissant* and 'Nous *relinquissons*', we relinquish, whence E 'to *relinquish*'.

3. *Relinquere* has pp *relictus*, whence the E adj *relict*; *relict*, a widow, represents L (coniux) *relicta*.

4. *Relinquere* has adj *relicuus, reliquus*, left behind or over, whence the n *reliquiae*, remains, whence OF-F *relique*, whence E *relic*.

5. *Relinquere* has the strengthened form *dērelinquere* (*de-* used int), to abandon utterly, pp *dērelictus*, whence the E adj *derelict*; on the pp s *dērelict-* arises *dērelictiō*, o/s *dērelictiōn-*, whence *dereliction*.

6. L *linquere* has another prefix-cpd: *dēlinquere*, to fail (connoted by *de-*, down from) in one's duty, presp *dēlinquens*, o/s *dēlinquent-*, whence the E adj *delinquent*; derivative LL *dēlinquentia* accounts for *delinquency*.

**length, lengthen, lengthy.** See LONG, para 3.

**lenience, lenient; lenitive** (adj, hence n), **lenitude, lenity.**

At the base, stands L *lēnis*, soft to the touch, hence gentle: akin to OSl *lēnŭ*, Lett *lēns*, mild, lazy. *Lēnis* has derivative *lēnīre*, to soften, presp *lēniens*, o/s *lēnient-*, whence E *lenient*, whence *leniency*. Derivative *lēnitās*, o/s *lēnitāt-*, becomes OF-EF *lenité*, whence E *lenity*. The var *lēnitūdō* yields *lenitude*; ML *lēnitīvus*, MF-F *lénitif*, E *lenitive.*—Perh cf LET, to permit.

**lens.** See LENTIL.

**Lent.** See LONG, para 4.

**lent.** See LEND.

**Lenten.** See LONG, para 4.

**lenticel; lenticular.** See para 2 of:

**lentil—lenticel—lenticular; lens,** whence **-lensed** and **lensless.**

1. *Lens* is form-adopted, sense-adapted from L, where it means 'lentil': a double convex lens shape-resembles a lentil seed. L *lēns* is a nasal cognate of Gr *lathuros*, a vegetable pulse; cf OSl

*lęšta*, lentil, and, for L *lēns*, the OHG *linsī*, G *Linse*, Lith *leñšis*, lentil.

2. L *lēns* has var *lentis*, with dim *lenticula*, E *lenticule*, L adj *lenticulāris*, E *lenticular*. Learnèd F has formed the dim *lenticelle*, whence E *lenticel*; *lentil*, however, derives from OF *lentille*, itself app from VL *\*lentīcula*, var of L *lenticula*.

**leo** (whence **Leo**, cf the closely related **Leonard**), **leonine**; **lion, lioness, lionize**; **leopard** (and **pard** itself); sep CHAMELEON and DANDELION.

1. L *leo*, a lion, has o/s *leōn-*, whence the adj *lēonīnus*, whence—perh via OF-MF *leonin*, f *leonine*, F *léonine*)—the E *leonine*: Gr *leōn*, gen *leontos*: perh Sem, for with the Homeric var *līs* (acc *līn*) cf the H *lajiš*: prob Medit, for several Eg words for a lion, e.g. *ri* and *rema*, suggest one of those famous *r-l*, *l-r* alternations.

2. L *leō*, acc *leōnem*, becomes OF *leon*, with OF-F var *lion*, adopted by E; OF-EF has f *lionnesse*, whence E *lioness*; *lionize*, to treat as a 'lion' or celebrity, is an anl E formation.

3. *Leopard*, adapted from EF-F *léopard* (OF *leupart*, MF *liepart*), comes imm from L *leopardus*, trln of Gr *leopardos*, cpd of *leōn+pardos*, a pard or panther, L *pardus*, OF hence E *pard*. *Pardos* is a var of the Gr syn *pardalis*, akin to Skt *prdāku*, panther, tiger: prob Medit, there being an almost certain Eg cognate.

**Leonnoys**. See LYONNESSE.

**leopard**. See LEO, para 3.

**leper**. See the 1st LEFT, para 2.

**lepid**. See the 1st LEFT, para 4.

**Lepidoptera**=the scaly fliers: cf the elements *lepido-* (and LEFT, para 4) and *ptero-*.

**lepra, leprosy, leprous**. See LEFT, para 3.

**Lesbian**: perh via F *lesbien*: L *Lesbius*: Gr *Lesbios*, adj of *Lesbos*, that Aegean island where 'burning Sappho loved and sang': the sexual deviation known as *Lesbianism* is attributed to her eccentric loving.

**lèse-majesté**. See para 2 of:

**lesion**: OF-MF *lesion*, EF-F *lésion*: L *laesiōn-*, o/s of *laesus*, from *laesus*, pp of *laedere*, to strike or wound, hence to damage or injure; s *laed-*; perh cf ON *lesta* (? for *\*ledsta*), to maltreat.

2. Cf *lèse-majesté*—occ, in AE, *lese* (or *leze*) *majesty*—adopted from MF-F, which forms it from legal ML *crimen laesae majestatis*, an accusation, hence crime, of injured majesty (sovereign power): cf *majesty* at MASTER. The form *leze* occurs in MF.

3. *Laedere* has c/f *-lidere*, notably in *collidere*, to clash together, E 'to *collide*', LL pp *collisus*, whence LL *collisiō*, o/s *collisiōn-*, late MF-F and E *collision*, and in *ēlidere*, to strike out, hence off, E 'to *elide*', pp *ēlisus*, whence *ēlisiō*, o/s *ēlisiōn-*, E *elision*.

**less**, adj and adv. See LEAST, para 1.

**lessee**. See LANGUID, para 7.

**lessen; lesser**. See LEAST (heading).

**lesson**. See LEGEND, para 2.

**lessor**. See LANGUID, para 7.

**lest**. See LEAST, para 3.

**let**, to hinder (whence the n, as in 'without *let* or hindrance'), and *let*, to leave or relinquish (archaic, except in 'to *let* alone, to *let* be'), to allow or permit, are closely inter-related. *Let*, to hinder, comes, through ME *letten*, from OE *lettan*, to delay (cf LATE), to hinder: cf OFris *letta*, OS *lettian*, OHG *lezzēn*, to hinder, to hurt, G *verletzen*, to injure, Go *-latjan*, MD-D *letten*, ON *letia* (*letja*), to hinder. *Let*, to leave, to allow, comes, through ME *leten*, earlier *laeten*, pt *let*, *lat*, from OE *lāetan*, pt *lēt*: cf OFris *lēta*, OS *lātan*, OHG *lāzzan*, MHG *lāzen*, G *lassen*, Go *lētan*, MD-D *laten*, ON *lāta*, to allow, perh Go *lats*, weary—and, further off, Lith *léidmi* (s *léid-*), I let, L *lassus* (? for *\*ladsus*), weary (cf LATE, para 4), Gr *lēdein* (s and r *lēd-*), to be weary: Gmc r *lāet-*, IE r *lēd-*, var *lēid-* (Feist): perh with basic idea 'to let go' (Webster); *let*, to hinder, perh has basic idea 'to not let go'. The ult IE r might well be *\*lē-*, thus admitting to the sem group the IE words in *lēn-*, as L *lēnis*, gentle.

2. *Let*, to allow, has derivatives *inlet*, a letting in, something let in, and *outlet*, a letting out, something let out.

**lethal**: L *lēthālis*, better *lētālis*, adj of *lētum*, death, with inferior var *lēthum* caused by Gr *lēthē*: o.o.o.: perh cf Gr *lemos*, famine, *loimos*, pestilence; IE r, ? *\*lei-*, var *\*lī-*, to remove. (Hofmann.)

**lethargic, lethargy**. See LATENT, para 3.

**Lethe**. See LATENT, para 2. *Lethean*=L *Lēthaeus* (Gr *lēthaios*)+adj suffix *-an*.

**Lett**, whence the adjj **Lettic, Lettish**, derives from G *Lette*, itself from Lett *Latvi*, whence *Latvija*, whence E *Latvia*, whence *Latvian*. Akin to *Lithuanian*, n from the adj of *Lithuania*, app a semi-L reshaping in *-ania* of Lith *Lietuva*.

**letter** (n hence v), **belles-lettres; literal; literate** (whence **literacy**) and its neg **illiterate** (whence **illiteracy**); **literary; literature, littérateur**.—Cpds: **alliterate, alliteration, alliterative; equilateral; obliterate, obliteration; transliterate, transliteration**.

1. *Letter*, an alphabetic character, derives, via ME from OF *lettre*, from L *littera*, superior to the var *litera*, an alphabetic character, with pl *litterae*, a letter, then also any written work, hence literature: from this collective *litterae*, therefore, derive both *letter*, an epistle, and *letters*, literature, as in F, whence E, *belles-lettres*, fine literature, aesthetic literature, esp poetry, drama, essays, whence *bellelettrist*, whence the var *belletrist*, with adj *belletristic*.

2. The once popular relationship to L *linere*, to smear, pp *litus*, is largely discredited. As E & M remark, the L alphabet having been, prob via Etruscan, borrowed from Gr, *littera* itself would not improb come from Gr: perh from *diphthera*, a tablet (Hesychius, glossed by Bréal): for the *d-l* mutation, cf Gr *dakruma*—OL *lacruma*, L *lacrima*.

3. L *littera* has three adjj affecting E: *litterālis*, var *literālis*, MF *literal* (F *littéral*), E *literal*, whence *literalism*;

*litterārius*, var *literārius*, E *literary* (cf EF-F *littéraire*);

*litterātus*, var *literātus*, E *literate*; neg *illiterātus*, E *illiterate*.

4. L *litterātūra*, whence F *littérature*, and its var *literātūra*, whence E *literature*, meant the art of writing and reading (in LL, literature), and imitated Gr *grammatikē* (*tekhnē*).

5. Two R words have been partly adopted by cultured E: It *literati*, pl of *literato*, from L *literātus*; F *littérateur*, from L *litterātor*, var *literātor*, one versed in grammar.

### Compounds

6. A rare ML *alliterātiō*, o/s *alliterātiōn-*, yields *alliteration*, whence the anl *alliterative* and the b/f 'to *alliterate*'; perh there did exist a v *allitterāre* (*al-* for *ad*, to), prefix-cpd of LL *litterāre*, to indicate by letters (Souter).

7. *Equiliteral* is an E formation: the element *equi-*, equal(ly)+*literal*.

8. L *oblitterāre*, var *obliterāre*, to efface (connoted by *ob-*) the letters, hence to destroy, also to cause to forget, has pp *oblit(t)erātus*, whence 'to *obliterate*'; derivative *obliterātiō*, o/s *obliterātiōn-*, accounts for *obliteration*; LL agent *oblit(t)erātor* is adopted by E.

9. *Transliterate* (*trans*, across) is an E formation anl with *obliterate*; with *transliteration* as an anl derivative.

**Lettic, Lettish.** See LETT.

**lettuce.** See LACTAM, para 5.

**leucite, leucocoma, leukemia.** See the 3rd LIGHT, para 20, and cf the element *leuco-*.

**Levant, levant.** See LEVER, para 3.

**levator.** See LEVER, para 4.

**levée and levee.** See LEVER, para 6.

**level** (n, whence adj and v); **libra, librate, libration, libratory; lira; litre,** AE **liter; livre;** cpds **deliberate** (adj, v), **deliberation, deliberative, deliberator,** and sep **equilibrate, equilibration, equilibrator, equilibratory, equilibrist, equilibrium.** —Perh akin: **libate, libation, libatory**—and therefore **littoral.**

1. *Level*, ME *level*, a var of ME *livel*, adopted from OF, derives from VL *libellum*, an alteration of L *libella*, a level, esp a water or a plumb level, dim of *libra*, any object used for weighing, hence a balance, a pair of scales, and also a weight of about 12 oz avoirdupois, thence the Roman monetary unit (E & M). L *libra* is perh akin to L *lībāre*, to pour, but prob, to judge by Sicilian Gr *lītrā*, a pound weight, adj *lītraios*, deriving from an IE r *līthrā-*, app either of pre-IE or of Medit origin—? cf, at least sem, the Eg *beqsu* and *sekhekh*.

2. The constellation *Libra* personifies L *lībra*, a pair of scales. *Lībra*, moreover, has derivative *lībrāre*, to balance, to weigh, pp *lībrātus*, whence 'to *librate*', to vibrate like a balance, to be poised; derivative *lībrātiō*, o/s *lībrātiōn-*, yields *libration*, whence the anl adj *libratory*.

3. L *lībra* becomes It *lira*, the monetary unit of

Italy. In F it becomes *livre*, a 'pound' weight (approx) and value; F *litre*, however, derives from EF *litron*, an obsolete measure, itself from ML *lītra*, a liquid measure, from Gr *lītrā*.

4. L *lībrāre* has cpd *aequilībrāre*, whence 'to *equilibrate*', *equilibrium*, etc., qq.v. at EQUAL. App also from *lībrāre* comes L *dēlīberāre* (for *\*dēlībrāre*, to weigh thoroughly, *de-* being int), to consider very carefully, pp *dēlīberātus*, whence both adj and v *deliberate*; derivative *dēlīberātiō*, o/s *dēlīberātiōn-*, becomes, prob via MF-F *déliberation*, the E *deliberation*; derivative *dēlīberātīuus*, ML *-īvus*, becomes *deliberative*; the L agent *dēlīberātor* is adopted.

5. If L *libra* has s *lībr-*, r *līb-*, and Gr *lītrā* has s *lītr-*, r *līt-*, then there may well be an IE r *\*li-*, a liquid, occurring also in e.g. *liquid* and *libation*. L *lībāre*, to pour, esp to a god, pp *lībātus*, whence 'to *libate*'; derivative *lībātiō*, o/s *lībātiōn-*, yields *libation*; the adj *\*lībātōrius* (deduced from LL *lībātōrium*, a vessel used in religious libations) yields *libatory*. Cf the Gr *leibein* (s and r, *leib-*), to pour, to offer a libation.

6. Cf L *lītus* (s and r, *līt-*), seashore, which has var *littus*, o/s *lit(t)or-*, with adj *lit(t)orālis*, whence the E adj, hence n, *littoral*: cf the Lith *lieti*, to pour—to be compared also with L *lībāre*, Gr *leibein*.

**leven.** See the 3rd LIGHT, para 3.

**lever,** n hence v (whence **leverage**); **levant** (n, v); **Levant, Levantine; levator; levee and levée and levy** (n, hence v); **levity**—**levitate, levitation; leaven** (n, hence v); cpds: **alleviate, alleviation, alleviative, alleviator**—**elevate, elevation, elevator.** —**relief** (and **bas-relief**), **relieve** (whence **reliever**). —**light** in weight, **lighten,** to become or make less in weight, **lighter,** a barge, **lights, lungs;** prob **lung** itself.

1. The *-lev-* (*-lief*, *-lieve*) words all come from L *leuis*, ML *levis*, light in weight; syn E *light* and prob *lung* are Gmc cognates; the L and E words are akin to Alb *l'eh*, Lith *leñgvas*, *lengvùs*, OSl *l'igŭ-kŭ*, light, OIr *laigiu*, smaller (therefore lighter), Gr *elakhus*, slight, small, Skt *laghús*, rapid, light; the Gmc r is app *\*līht-*, ? for *\*linht-*; the IE r, prob *\*lengw-* (var *\*legh-*), with L *leuis* perh for *\*lenguis* (Walshe).

### Latin and Romance Simples

2. *Lever*, ME *levour*, OF *leveor*, derives from *lever*, to raise, from ML *levāre*, L *leuāre*, from *leuis*, ML *levis*, light; L *leuāre* means both to lighten a load and, in LL, to raise.

3. *Leuāre* has presp *leuans*, o/s *leuant-*, ML *levant-*, whence the OF adj *levant*, as in *le soleil levant*, the rising sun, hence, in MF, n 'the rising sun', whence 'the *Orient* or East', adopted in E *Levant*, now only of the E Medit countries; the lit sense is preserved in legal *levant and couchant*, straying animals' period of trespass. F *le Levant* has derivative adj *levantin*, f *-ine*, adopted by E and used also as n *Levantine*. 'To *levant*' or abscond

=Sp *levantar*, lit to raise, hence to (raise oneself and) go from place to place.

4. *Levator*, in An and Surgery, is a SciL (? suggested by the ML) agent from ML *levāre*. ML *levāmen*, yeast, L *leuāmen*, a lightening, becomes OF *levain*, adopted by ME with var *levein*, becomes *leaven*.

5. L *leuis* has derivative *leuitās*, ML *lev-*, lightness, o/s *leuitāt-*, whence *levity*, whence, anl, *levitate* (opp *gravitate*), with anl derivative *levitation*.

6. E *levée*, whence *levee*, a reception held by the sovereign, distorts F *levé*. AE *levee*, an embankment against flooding, derives from late OF-F *levée*, which also originates the much older *levy* of taxes or of troops. Both *levé* and *levée* derive from *levé*, pp of OF-F *lever*.

### L and R Compounds

7. LL *alleuiāre* (*al-* for *ad-*, to), ML *alleviāre*, to lighten, has pp *alleuiātus*, ML *allevi-*, whence 'to *alleviate*'; derivative ML *alleviātiō*, o/s *alleviātiōn-*, yields *elleviation*, whence, anl, *alleviative* and *alleviator*.

8. L *ēleuāre*, ML *-vāre*, to raise *e* or out of, hence up, has pp *ēleuātus*, ML *-vātus*, whence 'to *elevate*'; derivatives *ēleuātiō* and LL *ēleuātor*, ML *ēlevātiō* (o/s *ēlevātiōn-*) and *ēlevātor*, become *elevation* and *elevator*.

9. L *releuāre*, ML *-vāre*, to raise again, becomes OF-F *relever*—note esp *il relieve*, he raises again— whence ME *releven*, 'to *relieve*'. OF-F *relever* has the OF-F derivative *relief*, a raising-up, raised work (whence *bas-relief*, prompted by It *bassorilievo*, low relief-work, and adopted by E), adopted by ME as *relef*, whence E *relief*.

### Gmc Cognates

10. *Light* in weight, ME *light*, earlier *liht*, derives from OE *līht*, var *lēoht*: cf OFris *līchte*, var *liuchte*, OHG *līhti*, MHG *līhte*, G *leicht*, Go *leihts*, MD *lichte*, D *licht*, ON *lēttr*. ME *light* has derivative *lightenen*, whence 'to *lighten*', to become or make less heavy; D *licht* has v *lichten*, to make lighter, hence to unload, with agent *lichter*, whence E *lighter*, a barge for unloading; *light*, not heavy, has derivative *lights*, lungs of beasts, prob from *light meats*, because lungs are relatively light.

11. OE *līht*, not heavy, has derivative *līhtan*, prop to take one's weight from a horse, i.e. to dismount, hence, in general, to descend from any conveyance or, of a bird, to land: 'to *light*'. OE *līhtan* has two prefix-cpds, *ālīhtan* (*ā-*, on) and *gelīhtan* (int *ge-*), from either or both of which comes ME *alihten*, E 'to *alighten*'.

12. The lungs (cf para 10, s.f.) are 'the lightest internal organs': *lung*, ME *lunge*, OE *lungen*, is akin to OFris *lungen*, *lungene*, OHG and OS *lunga*, MHG-G *lunge*, MD *lungen(e)*, *longen(e)*, *longer*, *longe*, D *long*, ON *lungr*. (Walshe.) Perh, with Holthausen, cf also Arm *lanjk*, chest.

**Leviathan**: ML *Leviathan*, LL *Leuiathan*: H

*liwyāthān*, variously a huge crocodile, a whale, or even—away from water—a dragon, hence, in C19–20 E, any huge and formidable creature. The H word is either (Enci It) an extn of the r *lwh*, therefore 'the coiled or tortuous creature', or a cpd of two rr, meaning 'great fish' and 'fastened', therefore 'a huge fish covered with scales', i.e. a crocodile (Ency. Americana).

**levigate, levigation.**
The latter derives from ML *lēvigātiōn-*, o/s of *lēvigātiō*, L *lēuigātiō*, a smoothing, from *lēuigātus* —source of 'to *levigate*'—pp of *lēuigāre*, to smooth: *lēuis*, smooth (contrast *lēuis*, light in weight, q.v. at LEVER), s *lēui-*, perh after *mītigāre*, from *mītis*, soft; prob *-igāre* derives from *agere*, to drive, hence to render (over a long time).

**levin.** See the 3rd LIGHT, para 3.
**levitate, levitation.** See LEVER, para 5.
**levity.** See LEVER, para 5.
**lew.** See LUKEwarm.
**lewd**, whence **lewdness**: ME *lewede*, vile, (earlier) ignorant, (earliest) lay: OE *lǣwede*, of the laity (not of the clergy): o.o.o.—but prob cf LAY, adj.
**lewis; lewisite; lewisson.** See LOUIS, para 2.
**lex.** See LEGAL, paras 1 and 2.
**lexical; lexicographer; lexicon.** See LEGEND, para 19.
**liability, liable.** See LIGAMENT, para 4.
**liaison.** See LIGAMENT, para 1.
**liana**: EF-F, from Antilles F, *liane*, itself prob borrowed from a dial of W France, the orig dial word being prob *liarne*, var *lierne*, themselves varr of *liorne*, which, in the passage from *viorne* (ML *vīburnum*, L *uīburnum*), clematis, shows the influence of F *lier*, to bind (cf LIGAMENT, para 1, s.f.).
**liar.** See the 1st LIE.
**libate, libation.** See LEVEL, para 5.
**libel** (n, v), **libellous.** See LEAF, para 3.
**liberal** (adj, hence n Liberal; hence also Liberalism and liberalize), **liberality**—cf **illiberal, illiberality**; **liberate, liberation, liberator**; **Liberia**, whence **Liberian**, adj hence n; **libertinage, libertine** (whence **libertinism**); **liberty**, whence **libertarian** (after *humanitarian* from *humanity*); **livery**, n—cf **deliver, deliverance, deliverer, delivery.**

1. L *liber*, free—whence prob *Līber*, the Roman god of growth—is akin to the syn Gr *eleutheros*, perh also to the OGmc words for 'people', as, e.g., OE *lēod*, OFris *liōd*, OS *liud*, OHG *liuti*, MHG *liute*, G *Leute*, esp if these words orig meant 'free people' as opp slaves (Walshe).

2. L *līber* has the foll simple derivatives relevant to E:

*līberālis*, OF-MF whence E *liberal*, the derivative *līberālitās*, o/s *līberālitāt-*, passing through MF-F *līberalité* to become *liberality*; the negg *illīberālis*, *illīberālitās* yielding, prob via F, the E *illiberal*, *illiberality*;

*līberāre*, to set free, has pp *līberātus*, whence 'to *liberate*'; derivative *līberātiō*, o/s *līberātiōn-*, yields MF-F *libération* and E *liberation*; derivative *līberātor* is adopted by E;

*Liberia*, 'the free country': regional *-ia* tacked to *liber* by SciL;

*lībertās*, o/s *lībertāt-*, MF-F *liberté*, ME *liberte*, E *liberty*;

▓ *lībertus*, a freedman, with adj *lībertīnus*, whence, via EF-F, *libertine*, adj hence n, *libertinage* being adopted from EF-F (*libertin*+suffix *-age*).

3. *Līberāre* has ML sense 'to give, deliver up': OF-F *livrer*, whence MF *livree* (F *livrée*), clothes provided by lords to retainers, then, c1500, the modern sense: ME *livere* (trisyllabic): E *livery*.

4. L *līberāre* has LL cpd *dēlīberŏ* (int *de-*), I set free, 'perh corrupt for *ēlīberŏ*' (Souter): OF-MF *delivrer* (F *dé-*), to set free, to hand something over to someone: 'to *deliver*'. Derivative OF-MF *delivrance* becomes E *deliverance*; OF-MF *delivreor*, E *deliverer*; EF-F *délivre*, afterbirth, has perh helped E *deliver* to become, prob after *livery*, E *delivery*.

**libidinous, libido.** See the 1st LEAVE, para 9.

**Libra.** See LEVEL, para 2.

**librarian, library.** See LEAF, para 2.

**librate, libration.** See LEVEL, para 2.

**lice.** See LOUSE.

**licence,** n, and **license,** v (whence pa **licensed** and **licensee**), **licentiate** (adj, hence n), **licentious; leisure,** whence **leisured; licit** and **illicit.**

1. L *licēre*, to be permissible, used impersonally, as *licet, licitum est*, has pp *licitus* used as adj, whence E *licit*; neg *illicitus* becomes *illicit*. *Licēre* is app o.o.o.

2. The presp *licens*, o/s *licent-*, has derivative *licentia*, liberty or permission to do something, hence excessive liberty, whence OF-F, hence ME, *licence*, whence 'to *licence*', still common in AE, although E has, for the v, decided to use the var *license*. L *licentia* has derivative adj *licentiōsus*, whence EF-F *licencieux* (f *-ieuse*) and E *licentious*. Derivative ML *licentiāre*, to allow to do anything, has pp *licentiātus*, whence the adj and n *licentiate*.

**lich,** as in lich gate. See LIKE, para 5.

**lichen,** whence **lichenoid** (*-oid*) and **lichenous** (*-ous*), is adopted from the L trln of Gr *leikhēn*, akin to Gr *leikhein*, to lick. Cf LICK.

**licit.** See LICENCE, para 1.

**lick** (v, hence n), whence sl **at full lick** and **lickety-split; lickerish** (**liquorish,** influenced by *liquor*)—**lecher, lecherous, lechery;** sep LICHEN; **ligula, ligule, ligulate—lingula, lingulate; electuary.**

1. 'To *lick*' derives from OE *liccian*, akin to OHG *lecchōn*, MHG-G *lecken*, OS *likkōn*, Go bi*laigan*, to lick, OIr *ligim*, Arm *lizem*, L *lingo* (nasal infix), Gr *leikhō*, I lick, OSl *lizati*, Skt *lḗḍhi* (for *\*leighti*), later *lihati*, he licks: IE r *\*leigh-*, with var *\*sleigh-*, attested by ON *sleikia*, MHG *slecken*, G *schlecken*, to lick. (Hofmann.)

2. *Lickerish* is for earlier *lickerous*, from the ONF shape of OF-MF *lecheros*, whence E *lecherous*; OF *lecheros* derives from OF-MF *lecheor* (var *-eur*), a glutton, a libertine, whence ME *lechour, lechur*, E *lecher*; OF *lecheor* derives from OF-MF *lechier* (F *lécher*), to lick, of Gmc origin.

3. L *lingere*, to lick, s and r *ling-* (nasal form of PL *\*lig-*), has derivative *lingula*, usu eased to *ligula*, a spoon, hence, influenced by *lingua*, the tongue, a little tongue of, e.g., leather, a little strap; *ligula*, its E derivative *ligule, lingula*, all occur in Bot, An, Zoo, with Sci derivative adjj *ligulate, lingulate*.

4. Gr *leikhein*, to lick, appears both in sep LICHEN and in *electuary*, ML-LL *ēlectuārium*, var of LL *ēlectārium*, a medicinal lozenge, an *-ārium* derivative from Gr *ekleikton*, from *ekleikhein*, to lick *ek-*, out of (e.g., a plate).

**licorice** or—? influenced by *liquor*—**liquorice**: ME *licoris*: OF-MF *licorece, licorice*: LL *liquiritia*: L *glycrrhiza*: Gr *glukurrhiza*: Gr *glukus*, sweet+ *rrhiza*, root. Cf e.g. *glu*cose and *radic*al.

**lictor.** See LIGAMENT, para 3.

**lid** (n, hence v, whence *-lidded*): OE *hlid* (lit a cover), lid, door: cf OE and OS *hlīdan*, to cover or shut, and OFris *hlid*, OHG *hlit* or *lit*, MHG *lit*, lid, G (Augen)*lid*, (eye)lid, ON *hlith*, gate(way): perh cf 'to LEAN'.—Hence *lidless*.

**lie** (1), n and v (pt, pp lied, presp lying), a falsehood, to speak a falsehood; **liar.**

*Liar*, ME *liere*, derives from ME *lien*—whence 'to *lie*'—from OE *lēogan*, intimately related to OE *lyge*, whence 'a *lie*': and OE *lyge, lēogan*, are akin to OHG *lugin* (n), OFris *liâga* and OHG, OS *liogan* (v), G *Lüge, lügen*, Go *liugn* (n), *liugan* (v), ON *lygi* (n), *lȳga* (v), also to OSl *lŭgati*, to lie: IE r, *\*leugh-*, varr *\*lough-* and esp *\*lugh-*. (Walshe.)

**lie** (2), to be prostrate, pt lay, pp lain; **lay** (v, hence n), pt **laid**, pp **laid**, whence **layer; laager, lager—leaguer** (a camp), **beleaguer; lair** (n, hence v—whence **lairage**); **laughter,** a clutch of eggs; **law,** whence **lawful, lawless, lawyer** (*-yer*=*-ier*, var of agential *-er*)—cf **outlaw,** n and v (whence **outlawry**); **ledge** and **ledger; lees,** dregs; **ligger; litter** (n, hence v)—cf **lectual** and **coverlet; lochia; log** (n, hence v—whence **logger**), **loggerhead,** 'be at loggerheads'; **low** (adj, hence adv, n), comp **lower** (whence 'to lower'), sup **lowest**—with many obvious cpds, e.g. **lowland,** and with derivative **lowly** (adj suffix *-ly*).

1. *Lie*, to be prostrate, to be situated, ME *lien*, earlier *liggen* (whence the dial *ligger*, coverlet, footbridge, flat stone laid over tomb, a baited line left for night fishing), derives from OE *licgan*, akin to OHG *liggan*, MHG *ligen*, G *liegen*, Go *ligan*, MD *licgen, ligen*, (as in D) *liggen*, ON *liggja*; akin also to the syn OSl *ležati*, Gr *lexasthai*, and to OIr *lige*, L *lectus*, Gr *lekhos*, a bed; IE r, *\*legh-*, to be lying flat.

2. The corresp caus v is 'to *lay*' (to cause to be lying flat), ME *leien*, earlier *leggen*, OE *lecgan*: cf OHG *legēn*, MHG-G *legen*, Go *lagjan*, MD *lecgen, legen, leigen*, (as in D) *leggen*, ON *leggja, legia*; cf also MIr *leigid*, he lays himself down, OSl *ložiti*, to lay down.

3. Afr *laager*, var *lager*, is a camp, often (orig) defensively ringed with waggons; cf G *Lager*, a bed, a storeroom or -house, whence, with *Bier*, beer, understood, *lager*, because stored before use.

**4.** With Afr *laager*, cf *leaguer*, a camp, from the D source of *laager*: *leger*, a camp. The derivative 'to *leaguer*', to besiege, is commoner in the cpd *beleaguer*, from D *belegeren*: *be-*, as in E+*leger*+ inf suffix *-en*.

**5.** Akin to MD-D *leger*, which means also 'bed, couch, lair', is OE *leger*, whence E *lair*: cf OFris *leger*, OHG *legar*, G *Lager*, Go *ligrs*, couch, bed. With all these words, cf ON *látr*, *láttr*, a place where animals put their young, whence prob the dial *laughter*, a clutch of eggs.

**6.** A law being that which is *laid* down, *law* not too surprisingly comes, through ME *lawe*, earlier *laghe*, from OE *lagu*, law, akin to and prob from ON *lög*, law, orig the pl of *lag*, a layer or stratum, a due place, syn OS *lag*, OFris *laga*.

**7.** The ON cpd *ūtlagi*, an outlaw, and *ūtlagr*, outlawed, become OE *ūtlaga*, later *ūtlah*, whence 'an *outlaw*'; 'to *outlaw*' derives from OE *ūtlagian* (from *ūtlaga*).

**8.** ME *leggen*, to lay (cf para 2 above), is the prob source of ME *legge*, a bar, whence E *ledge*, a bar—hence a strip—laid along a surface, as a shelf, esp on a wall of rock. The same ME *leggen*, to lay, produces ME *legger*, which has var *lidger*, influenced by and perh even deriving from ME *liggen*, to be lying down, to be situated: *lidger* and *legger* app combine to give us *ledger*, prop a book always lying in one place and open to inspection.

**9.** OE *licgan*, to lie flat, is akin to the syn ON *liggja*, whence ON *lāg*, the trunk of a felled tree (cf OS-OHG *lāga*, OFris *lēga*), whence ME *logge*, whence both the E *log* and the syn E dial *logger*; the latter, in its sense 'block of wood', joins with *head* to form *loggerhead*, a stupid fellow (in short, a *blockhead*), but, 'in nautical language orig a bar-shot with a cannon-ball at each end. Hence to *be at logger-heads* (cf *at daggers drawn*)': EW.

**10.** That which is lying down or lying flat is as low as it can get: and this is the source of *low* itself, ME *low*, earlier *louh*, earliest *lah*, from ON *lāgr*, itself akin to OFris *lēg*, *lēch*, MD *leech*, *lege*, *laech*, *lage*, D *laag*.

**11.** That which lies down and then naturally settles, as at the bottom of a cask, is *lee*, now always *lees*: OF-F *lie*, ML *lia*, prob of C origin: cf, as in para 1, OIr *lige*, a lying (down), a bed. Malvezin postulates an OC *\*leg-*, to be lying down, and cfs Br *lec'hid*, lees.

**12.** L *lectus* (s and r *lect-*), a bed, a couch, has a VL derivative *\*lectāria*, whence OF-MF *litiere* (F *litière*), whence ME *liter*, a bed, a litter, whence E *litter*, a portable, usu curtained and always shafted couch, hence, or from the sense 'bed', the collective, recently borne young of esp a sow; the straw, etc., used for bedding tends to become scattered, hence scattered rubbish.

**13.** L *lectus* has LL adj *lectuālis*, whence Med *lectual*, as in 'a *lectual* disease', confining the sufferer to bed (Webster). L *lectus* becomes OF(-F) *lit*, a bed, as in ME *coverlyte* (*cover-* from OF *covrir*, to cover), whence *coverlet*.

**14.** Akin to Gr *lekhos*, bed (as in para 1) is Gr *lokhos*, a lying-in, hence childbirth, with derivative adj *lokhios*, with neupl *lokhia* used as n, whence SciL *lochia*, postnatal discharges.

**lied**, n. See LAUD, para 1, s.f.

**lief.** See the 1st LEAVE, para 5.

**liege** (adj, hence n—and also **liegeman**): ME *lege*, *lige*: OF-MF *liege*, OF-F *lige*: LL *\*liticus*, *\*leticus*, varr of LL *laeticus*, (of land) 'cultivated by serfs', from LL *laetus*, 'a (foreign) serf (who tills Roman soil)'—in Souter's definition: LL *laetus* is of Gmc origin: cf OE *frēolǣta*, Go *fralēts*, a freed serf, a freedman, OFris *lethar*, freedmen: prob akin to E LET, to allow.

**lien.** See LIGAMENT, para 3.

**lieu.** See LOCAL, para 5.

**lieutenant**, whence **lieutenancy**. See LOCAL, para 5.

**lieve.** See the 1st LEAVE, in heading; cf *lief* in para 5.

**life** (pl **lives**), with numerous—and rather obvious—cpds; **lifelike**, **lifeless**; **live**, adj (cf **alive**) and v (whence pa, vn **living**), whence **relive** —**livelihood**—**lively**—**liven**, **enliven**; **liver**, organ of body, whence **liverish**, **livery**—cf **liverwort**, **liverwurst**; **Lebensraum**; **leave**, to permit, or to cause, to remain.

**1.** *Life*, OE *līf*, is akin to OFris (and OS) *līf*, OHG *līb*, MHG *līp*, life, body, G *Leib*, MD-D *lijf*, body, ON *līf*, life, body. Derivative OE *liflīc*, living, yields *lively* and the reshaped *lifelike*; derivative *liflēas* (cf OFris *liflās*), yields *lifeless*; derivative ME *livelode*, earlier *liflode*, whence, by f/e, the E *livelihood*, combines OE *līf*+OE *lād*, way, maintenance.

**2.** The adj *live* is aphetic for *alive*, ME *on live*, OE *on līfe*, (being) in life; *līfe* is dat of *līf*.

**3.** 'To *live*' (whence *livable*), ME *liven*, var *livien*, OE *libban*, var *lifian*, is akin to OFris *-līva*, OS *-līban*, to remain, OFris *libba*, OS *libbian*, OHG *lebēn*, MHG-G *leben*, Go *liban*, MD-D *leven*, to live, ON *lifa*, to remain, to live, and, further off, Gr *liparein* (s *lipar-*, ult r *lip-*), be sticky, hence to persist, *liparēs*, persistent, and, still further, Skt *limpati* (with nasal infix), he smears, *lipta*, smeared, hence adherent, cf Lith *lipti*, to adhere; cf Go bi-*leiban*, OHG bi-*līban*, to remain. The Gmc r is app *\*lībh-* (or *\*libh-*), var *\*laibh-*, and the IE r, app *\*lip-*, var *\*leip-*: the basic idea, 'to be sticky'— hence 'to adhere'—hence 'to remain or stay'—esp 'to stay alive'—hence simply 'to live'. (Walshe; Webster.)

**4.** 'To *liven*' prob derives from the adj *live*; 'to *enliven*' either intensifies *liven* or derives from *en-*, in(to)+*life*, eased to *liv-*+v suffix *-en*.

**5.** *Liver*, the bile-secreting organ, derives from OE *lifer*, prob from OE *lifian* (as in para 3): cf OFris *livere*, OHG *lebara*, MHG-G *leber*, ON *lifr*; cf also Arm *leard* and perh Gr *liparos*, sticky. (Walshe.) Cf the cpds *liverwort* (WORT) and *liverwurst*, prompted by G *Leberwurst*, a sausage containing much liver.

**6.** G *leben*, to live, hence, as n, living, has cpd *Lebensraum*, room—i.e., space—to live.

7. Akin to 'to *live*' is 'to *leave*', permit or cause to remain: ME *leven*: OE *lǣfan*: cf OE *lāf*, that which is left, a remnant, and the OGmc vv recorded in para 3.

**lift** (1), sky. See:

**lift** (2), to raise, hence as n (a raising, a being raised; sky); **loft, aloft.**

1. *Lift*, the sky, the atmosphere, now dial and archaically poetic, derives from OE *lyft*, air, and is akin to *loft*, orig the sky, now as in *hay-loft*: ME *loft*, a loft, a height, air: OE *loft*, air. *Lofty* clearly derives from ME *loft*, a height; and *aloft*=*a*-, on, hence in+*loft*, air.

2. OE *loft* derives from ON *lopt* (for \**loft*), air, heaven, hence a loft: and both ON *lopt* and OE *lyft* are akin to OHG-MHG-G *luft*, Go *luftus*.

3. To put in the air, to raise in the air—cf G *lüffen*, to air, to raise—is to *lift*: ME *liften*, var *lyften*: ON *lypta*, akin to, prob deriving from, ON *lopt*, air, the sky.

**lift** (3), to steal; whence **shoplifter** (cf SHOP).

This 'to *lift*' prob derives from prec, but perh derives ult from the Gmc r in Go *hlifan*, to steal (*hlifus*, a thief), itself akin to the syn L *clep*ere and Gr *klept*ein.

**ligament** and **ligature; liable**, whence, anl, **liability; liaison;** sep **liana; lictor; lien; league,** a covenant, whence v; naut **leech.**—Cpds: **ally** (v, hence n), **alliance,** cf **rally,** to reunite, hence as n, and contrast **rely,** whence **reliable, reliance, reliant;**—**obbligato** and **obligate** (adj and v), **obligation, obligatory, oblige** (whence pa **obliging**), cf **disobligation, disoblige** (whence **disobliging**); **religate, religation**—**religion, religiosity, religious** (adj, hence n)—cf **irreligion, irreligiosity, irreligious.**

1. *Ligament* derives, perh via EF-F, from L *ligāmentum*, anything that ties one part (etc.) to another: *lig-*, s and r of *ligāre*, to bind+*-a-*, sign of the 1st L *conjugation*+suffix *-mentum* (cf E *filament*, ML *fīlāmentum*, from L *fīlāre*, to spin). On *ligāt-*, s of pp *ligātus* (whence to *ligate*), arise LL *ligātūra*, whence MF-F, hence E, *ligature*, and L *ligātiō*, o/s *ligātiōn-*, whence E *ligation*, and LL *ligātor*, adopted by surgery; the L o/s *ligātiōn-* influences the derivation of MF-F *liaison* —adopted by E—from OF-F *lier*, to bind (from *ligāre*).

2. L *ligāre* is akin to ON *līk*, a cord, esp a bolt-rope, MHG ge*leich*, a joint, MLG *līk*, a binding, a bandage, Alb *l'ith*, I bind, *l'ithe*, a band or a bond.

3. Prob akin to L *ligāre* is L *lictor* (? for \**ligtor*, contr of *ligātor*), the Roman officer affected to the carrying of the fasces. Certainly akin to—perh the suggester of—L *ligāmentum* is the syn L *ligāmen*, whence OF *lieien*, whence, influenced by *lier*, the F *lien*, adopted by E Law in sense 'a charge—due because of debt—upon property'.

4. Whereas *leech*, the edge of a square sail, comes from LG (cf MLG *līk*, as in para 2), *liable* comes from OF-F *lier*, and *league*, a covenant, from MF-F *ligue*: It *liga*, var of *lega*: from It *legare*, from L *ligāre*. to bind.

**Prefix-Compounds of *ligāre***

5. 'An *ally*' (cf F *allié*) derives from 'to *ally*', ME *alien*, OF *alier* (F *allier*), L *alligāre*, to bind (*al-* for ad) to, pp *alligā*tus, whence the n *alligātiō*, o/s *alligātiōn-*, whence *alligation*. OF *alier* has derivative OF-MF *aliance* (F *alliance*) ME *aliaunce*, E *alliance*. OF *alier* itself combines with *re*-, again, to form OF-F *rallier*, to reunite e.g. dispersed troops, whence 'to *rally*'.

6. But 'to *rely*' has derived from ME *relien*, to rally, from late OF-F *relier*, to bind again, from the syn L *religāre*. *Rely* has derivatives *reliable* (influenced by *liable*)—*reliance*, as if from F—*reliant*, as if from F *reliant*, presp of *relier*.

7. L *obligāre*, to tie about, to bandage, hence to face with the duty to, to put under an obligation (to), becomes MF *obligier*, MF-F *obliger*, whence 'to *oblige*'; LL *obligātiō*, o/s *obligātiōn-*, and LL *obligātōrius* become, via MF-F, the E *obligation*, *obligatory*. Both of these LL words are formed upon L *obligā*tus, pp of *obligāre*: and *obligātus* accounts for 'to *obligate*' and the Bio adj *obligate* and for the It Mus term *obbligato*.

8. MF-F *obliger* has MF derivative *desobliger* (F *dés-*; L *dis-*), whence 'to *disoblige*', whence anl *disobligation*.

9. L *religāre*, to bind *re-* or again, has pp *religā*tus, whence 'to *religate*', whence, anl, *religation*.

10. Prob deriving from, certainly very closely akin to, L *religāre* (s *relig-*), to bind again, hence, int, to bind strongly, is *religiō* (s *relig-*), a binding back, or very strongly, sc to one's faith or ethic, o/s *religiōn-*, as in the acc *religiōnem*, whence OF-F *religion*, adopted by E; in ML, *religiōsus*—whence OF-F *religieux*, whence E *religious*—was also a n, 'one in a religious order, a monk or a friar, hence (*religiōsa*) a nun'. The ML derivative *religiōsitās*, o/s *religiōsitāt-*, yields EF-F *religiosité* and E *religiosity*.

11. *Religiō* has LL neg *irreligiō*, o/s *irreligiōn-*, whence—perh via EF-F—*irreligion*; LL *irreligiōsus* and its derivative *irreligiōsitās* naturally—and again via F—become *irreligious* and *irreligiosity*.

**ligger.** See the 2nd LIE, para 1.

**light** (1), adj: bright. See the 3rd LIGHT.

**light** (2), adj: of little weight. See LEVER, para 10.

**light** (3), n, brightness—adj, bright—v, to illuminate (whence the vn **lighting**), to shine; **lighten**—**enlighten, enlightenment; lightning; leven** or **levin;** **lea** (meadow); **Loki.**—L: **lux; lucent; Lucia, Lucius, Lucy; Lucifer; lucid, lucidity; lucubrate, lucubration; luminary, luminous; luna, lunacy, lunar, lunatic ('loony'), lunation, lunette**—cf **demilune** and **sublunary; luster** (AE), **lustre, lustrous** perh **luxuriant, luxuriate, luxurious, luxury, de luxe.** —L cpds: **elucidate, elucidation, elucidatory**— **illume, illuminant, illuminate, illuminati, illumination, illuminative, illuminator, illumine**—**limn**— **illustrate, illustration, illustrative, illustrator,** and **illustrious.**—**pellucid.**—Gr: **leucite, leucoma, leukemia,** cf the element *leuco-*; **lynx,** whence the adj **lyncean.**

## Germanic and Indo-European

1. Both 'to *light*', illumine, OE *lȳhtan*, *līhtan*, and *light*, bright, derive from OE *lēoht*, illumination, ME *liht*, later *light*, retained by E: and OE *lēoht* is akin to OFris *liächt* (n, light, a candle, and adj, bright), OS *lioht*, OHG *lioht*, MHG *lieht*, G *Licht*, light, a candle, Go *liuhath*, MD *lucht*, *locht(e)*, *lecht*, *liecht*, (as in D) *licht*, with adj *lucht*, *liechte*, *lichte*, and differently suffixed ON *līos* (*ljōs*), a light; to OIr *lóche*, brightness, *lócharn*, a light, a lamp (cf the F *lucarne*); to OSl *luči*, light (n), *luča*, a ray of light; to Arm *lois*, *loys*, a light, with gen *lusoy*; L *lūx* (gen *lūcis*), a light, brightness, *lūcēre*, to shine; Gr *leukos*, shining, white; Skt *rōčĭs* (for *raučĭs* for *leukĭs*), a light, *rōcatē*, it shines, *rōcaṇas*, brilliant, Hit *lukke-*, to be light, to become day, *lukkes-*, to become light, *lukitta*, next day; Tokh A *luk-*, to shine. The Gmc r is *liuh-*; the IE r, *leuk-*. (Walshe.) The word is perh Medit: ? cf the Eg metathetic complements *ukheb*, *ubekh*, to shine, to be bright, and *ubekht*, brilliance.

2. OE *lȳhtan* (*līhtan*) acquires the ME mdfn *lightenen*, whence 'to *lighten*', to shine, grow lighter; *lighten* has the int *enlighten*, perh ult from OE *inlīhtan*, whence *enlightenment* (suffix *-ment*). 'To *lighten*', to shine, to flash, has vn *lightening*, which, as an electrical discharge and flash in the sky, is contr to *lightning*.

3. Akin to OE *lēoht*, illumination, is OE *lēoma*, brightness, ME *leome*, var *leme*, then *leem*, E *leam*, a flash, a blaze, now only Sc (and N dial); and akin to ME *leome*—? orig a scribal error for it —is ME *levene*, the now archaic E *leven* or *levin*, lightning.

4. Also akin to OE *lēoht*, (a) light, is OE *lēah*, *lēa*, ME *lay*, *ley*, E *lea*, pastureland, a meadow, which is open to the sun and therefore, at times, drenched with light.

5. Akin to ON *līos*, (a) light—as in para 1—is ON *leygr*, flame, with var *logi*, to which is perh related the ON *Loki*, the mischievous god of Scan mythology, esp if he were orig a god of fire. (Webster.)

## Latin

6. The L r is *lūc-*, seen basically in *lūcēre*, to shine, and *lūx* (for *lūcs*; gen *lūcis*), light, esp that of day. Prob from *lūx* are the PNN *Lūcius*, f *Lūcia* (whence F *Lucie*, E *Lucy*); certainly a cpd is the adj *lūcifer*, light-bringing (c/f *lūci-+-fer*, -bringing), whence *Lūcifer*, the Morning Star; *Lūcifer*, Satan, is a creation of EcclL.

7. *Lūcēre*, to shine, has presp *lūcens*, o/s *lūcent-*, whence the E adj *lucent*, whence *lucence*, usu *lucency*.

8. *Lūcēre* has derivative adj *lūcidus*, shining, brilliant, dazzling-clear, whence late MF-F *lucide* and E *lucid*; derivative LL *lūciditas*, o/s *lūciditāt-*, becomes late MF-F *lucidité* and E *lucidity*.

9. The L r *lūc-* prob appears in *lūmen* (? for *lūcmen*), light, usu a light, o/s *lūmin-*, adj *lūmin-ōsus*, whence MF-F *lumineux*, f *lumineuse*, whence E *luminous*; subsidiary ML *lūminōsitās*, o/s *lūminōsitāt-*, becomes *luminosity*. *Lūmen* has the further adj *lūmināris*, neu *lūmināre*, as in the n *lūmināre*, a torch, usu in pl *lūmināria*, whence OF-MF *luminarie* (cf F *luminaire*), whence E *luminary*. *Lūmen* has also the deriv v *lūmināre*, to illumine, presp *lūminans*, o/s *lūminant-*, whence the E adj, hence n, *luminant*; pp *lūminātus*, whence 'to *luminate*'; derivative LL *lūminātiō*, o/s *lūminā-tiōn-*, becomes *lumination*, and LL *lūminātor*, giver of light, adopted by, though now obs at, the University of St Andrews. *Luminescence* derives from *luminescent*, as if from *lūminescent-*, o/s of *lūminescens*, presp of *lūminescere*, to begin to grow light, inch of *lūmināre*. Cf the *illum-* cpds in para 16.

10. *Lūx*, o/s *lūc-*, has derivative *lūcubrum*, a small fire, ? hence a lamp, lamp-light, whence *lūcubrāre*, to work by lamp-light, pp *lūcubrātus*, used by LL as adj '(of a literary work) carefully composed', whence the E literary adj and n *lucubrate*; derivatives *lūcubrātiō*, o/s *lūcubrātiōn-*, and *lūcubratōrius* (adj suffix *-ōrius*) yield *lucubration* and *lucubratory*.

11. L *lūna*, the moon, prop 'the luminous', represents either a contr of *lūcĕna* or orig the f of an adj *lūnus*, with *-na* the f of the IE adj formative *-no-*. The OF-F form *lune* is adopted by Geom and, in the cpd *demilune* ('half-moon'), by fortification; the late OF-F dim *lunette* has been much more widely accepted.

12. L *lūna* has three adjj relevant to E:

L *lūnāris*, whence OF-F *lunaire*, whence E *lunar*; SciL *sublūnāris* becomes E *sublunary*, '(of things) beneath the moon'—'earthly, not heavenly';

LL *lūnāticus*, living in the moon, subject to the moon's changes, hence epileptic, hence (ML) mad, cf sem the L *fānāticus*, E *fanatic*; thence MF-F *lunatique*, E *lunatic* (adj hence n); whence *lunacy*— cf *loony*, for *luny*, from *lunatic*;

*lūnātus* (from the pp), moon-shaped, whence E *lunate*, crescent-shaped; derivative ML *lūnātiō*, o/s *lūnātiōn-*, accounts for Astr *lunation*.

13. Akin to—and formed in the same way as— *lūmen*, is L *lustrum*, (a) light, whence *lustrāre*, to light up, illumine, It *lustrare*, whence the It n *lustro*, late MF-F *lustre*, E *lustre* and AE *luster*, whence 'to *lustre* or *luster*'. E *lustrous* perh derives from F *lustreuse*, f of *lustreux*, adj of *lustre*. Cf the cpds *illustr-* in para 18.

14. Perh akin to L *lūcēre*, to shine, is L *luxus* (gen *luxūs*), excessive indulgence in creature comforts and sensual pleasures, flashy living, whence EF-F *luxe*, as in *de luxe*, of luxury, adopted by E in '*de luxe* cars, models, etc.'; E & M, however, derive the n *luxus* from the adj *luxus*, dislocated, sprained, whence, by the way, *luxāre*, to dislocate, pp *luxātus*, whence 'to *luxate*', with derivative LL *luxātiō*, o/s *luxātiōn-*, E *luxation*. The L n *luxus* has extn *luxuria* (var *luxuriēs*), sybaritic and sensual living, OF-MF *luxurie* (cf F *luxure*), E *luxury*; derivative adj *luxuriōsus* becomes OF-MF *luxurius*, E *luxurious*; the derivative v *luxuriāri*, to be excessive, to grow over-abundantly, has presp *luxurians*,

o/s *luxuriant-*, whence EF-F and E *luxuriant*, whence, anl, *luxuriance*, and has pp *luxuriātus*, whence 'to *luxuriate*'.

### Latin compounds

15. L *lūcidus* has LL derivative *ēlūcidāre*, to bring the inner *lux* or light *ē* or out of, to explain thoroughly esp a difficult matter, pp *ēlūcidātus*, whence 'to *elucidate*', whence, anl, *elucidation* (perh after EF-F *élucidation*) and *elucidatory*.

16. L *lūmināre* gives way to the orig int (*il-* for *in-*) *illūmināre*, whence OF-F *illuminer*, whence 'to *illumine*'; the pp *illūminātus* yields both the adj (hence n) and v *illuminate* and also, partly via It, *illuminati*, lit 'persons lit up'. Derivatives LL *illūminātio* (o/s *illūminātiōn-*) and LL *illūminātor*, shedder of light, ML illuminator of books, lead, the former prob via OF-F, to *illumination* and *illuminator*; and *illuminative* perh owes something to F *illuminatif*, f *-ive*.

17. ML *illūmināre*, to illuminate books (sem from the bright initial capital letters affected by medieval scribes), becomes MF *enluminer* (in OF, to render brilliant, to light up, from the L senses of *inlūmināre*, a mostly learnèd var of *illūmināre*), whence ME *enluminen*, whence, by aphesis, *luminen*, duly contr and thinned to late ME *limnen*, whence 'to *limn*'; *luminen* has agent *luminer*, whence, anl, *limner*.

18. L *lustrum* (see para 13) has two int derivatives in *il-* (for *in-*, into):

*illustris* (s *illustr-*), very luminous, brilliant, hence famous, whence both MF-F *illustre* and E *illustrious*;

*illustrāre*, to render very luminous, hence brilliant, hence illustrious, hence, in late ML, a synonym of scribal *illūmināre*; the pp *illustrātus* becomes 'to *illustrate*'; derivative LL *illustrātiō*, o/s *illustrātiōn-*, becomes, prob via MF-F, *illustration*; *illustrative* is an anl E formation; the LL agent *illustrātor* is adopted by E.

19. L *lūcidus* (para 8) has int (*pel-* for *per-*, thoroughly *pellūcidus*, notably clear: whence *pellucid*.

### Greek

20. Gr *leukos*, bright, hence white (para 1), has c/f e *leuko-* (see Elements at *leuco-*) and s *leuk-*, which becomes Sci European *leuc-*, as in *leucite*, from G *Leucit*; *leucoma*, SciL from Gr *leukōma*—cf the suffix *-oma*—from *leukos*; AE *leukemia*, E *leukaemia*, SciL cpd of Gr *leukos+-emia*, Gr *-aimia*, connoting 'blood'.

21. Akin to Gr *leukos* is Gr *lunx* (λύγξ)—a nasal form of \**lux* (λύξ)—gen *lunkos* (λύγκος), which, in L trln, yields *lynx* (gen *lyncis*), adopted by E: the quadruped was prob so named from the *bright* colour of its keen and flashing eyes. Cf, phon, OHG-MHG *luhs*, G *Luchs*, OE *lox*, Lith *lúšis*.

light (4), to dismount. See LEVER, para 11.

light (5), to illuminate. See the 3rd LIGHT, para 1.

lighten (1), to brighten. See the 3rd LIGHT, para 2.

lighten (2), to render less heavy. See LEVER, para 10.

lighter, a barge. See LEVER, para 10.

lighting. See the 3rd LIGHT (heading).

lightness=the *-ness* of *light*, bright (OE *lihtnes*), and of *light*, not heavy.

lightning. See the 3rd LIGHT, para 2, s.f.

lights, lungs. See LEVER, para 10, s.f.

ligneous, lignite, lignum. See LEGEND, para 17.

ligula, ligulate. See LICK, para 3.

Liguria, ligurite. See LOVAGE.

like, adj (whence conj, n, prep) and adv (OE *gelīce*, from adj *gelīc*) and v; likely (adj, hence adv); liken; likeness, likewise, liking (n); dislike (v, hence n)—unlike, unlikely, unlikeness.—lich- or lych-gate.

1. The adj *like*, ME *lik*, earlier *ilik*, earliest *gelic*, derives from OE *gelīc* (int *ge-+līc*, body), having the same, or a common, body—hence form or shape, hence appearance—as, therefore similar: cf OS *gilīk*, OHG *gilīh*, MHG *gelīch*, G *gleich*, Go *galeiks*, MD *gelike*, D *gelijc*, ON *līkr*, prob aphetic for the var *glīkr*. Akin to OE *līc*, body, are OFris and OS *līk*, OHG *līh*, MHG *līch*, *līche*, body, G *Leiche*, corpse, Go *leik*, body, corpse, MD *like*, D *lijc*, ON *līk*, body. Note also OFris *līk*, similar, and *līke*, similarly.

2. *Likely*, akin to OE *gelīclīc* but from ON *līkligr*; hence *likelihood*;

*liken*, ME *liknen* (cf OFris *līkna*), from the ME adj *lik*;

*likeness*, ult from OE *gelīcnes*;

*likewise*, in like *wise* or manner—cf the n WISE.

3. *Liking*, OE *līcung*, is the vn of 'to *like*', ME *liken*, to please, OE *līcian*, prob aphetic for the var *gelīcian*, to please: cf OHG *līchēn*, to be like, hence to be suitable, hence to please: OE (*ge*)*līcian* is therefore akin to OE *gelīc*, like, similar. The now only dial *like*, to compare, make a likeness of, derives from the adj and has been superseded by *liken*.

4. *Alike* derives from OE *onlīc*, in (the) like, similar, or, with prefix *a-* for prefix *ge-*, from OE *gelīc*; *belike*, archaic except in dial, prob represents *be-* for *by+like*, adj; 'to *dislike*'=*dis-*, apart, hence n+*like*, v; *unlikely* (adj, hence adv)—whence *unlikelihood*—extends *unlike*, adj, itself merely *un-*, not+*like*.

5. *Lich-* or *lych-gate* is a usu roofed gateway in which the bier is placed to await the clergyman: *lich*, the better spelling, derives from OE *līc*, body.

lilac. See ANILINE.

liliaceous. See LILY.

Lilliputian is the adj (hence n) of *Lilliput*, Swift's land (*Gulliver's Travels*, 1726) of tiny people: *lil* for *li'l*, a nursery (and dial) slovening of *little+* connective *-i-+*C17–18 *put*, a (rustic) fellow, app of C, prob W, origin.

lilt, v (hence n), whence the pa lilting, comes from ME *lülten*, to sing, or strike up, loudly: o.o.o.: Webster cfs the Nor *lilla* or *lirla*, to sing high: ult, prob echoic.

lily, liliaceous.
The latter derives from LL *līliāceus*, of a lily, L

*līlium*, OE *lilie*, E *lily*: prob (medial *l* for *r*) from Gr *leirion*, which, if its r be *leir-*, would come (initial *l* for aspirated *r*) from Eg *hrr-t* (*-t* merely indicating the f gender), as Coptic *hrēri*, var *hlēli*, more clearly shows. (Hofmann.)

**limaceous**, snail-like, is anl formed (cf *testaceous*) from L *limāc-*, o/s of *limāx*, a snail, the Zoo *Limax*: f.a.e., the 1st LIME.

**limb** (1), a member of the human body, whence **-limbed**: ME, from OE, *lim*, with intrusive *b* from the 2nd LIMB: cf ON *limr*, limb, and *lim*, a tree's 'limb' or branch, and, with different suffix, OE *lid*, *lith*, OFris and OS *lith*, OHG *lith*, *lid*, cpd *gelid*, MHG *gelit*, G *Glied*, D *gelid*, *lid*, Go *lithus*: perh ult akin to LIMIT, q.v. in para 1.

**limb** (2), edge, border; **limbate, limbic, limbous, limbus** and **limbo**.

*Limb*, as used tech, is influenced by F *limbe*: both from L *limbus*, border: o.o.o.; but the r being prob *lim-*, I suspect kinship with L *līmes*, a bordering path or road, hence a boundary, q.v. at LIMIT. Derivative LL *limbātus*, bordered, yields the Bot and Zoo *limbate*; the ordinary, though literary, E adj is *limbic*; *limbous* is the characteristically E adj of *limbo*, which sem derives from L *in limbo*, on the edge, EcclL on the boundary between heaven and hell, cf ML *limbi*, MF-F 'les *limbes*', the region inhabited by these intermediate souls. Prob cf the adj LIMP.

**limber** (1), pliant, supple, is app akin to—perh a dial mdfn of—the adj LIMP and, if that be so, akin to the 2nd LIMB.

**limber** (2), the shaft of a carriage, hence the detachable fore-part of a gun-carriage: prob—? influenced by the 1st LIMB—from F *limonière*, a waggon with its shafts, from (by f suffix *-ière*) OF-F *limon*, a shaft, o.o.o., but, like several other 'carriage' words, prob from C (B & W), although perh from OE-ON *lim*, branch of tree.

**limbers**, gutters on each side of a ship's keelson, comes—phon cf *limn* from ME *luminen*—from OF-F *lumières*, lights, ult from L *lūmen*, light, q.v. at 3rd LIGHT, para 4: sem cf *lights* as in *skylights*.

**limbic.** See the 2nd LIMB.

**limbo, limbous.** See the 2nd LIMB, s.f.

**limbus** (Bot and Zoo). See the 2nd LIMB.

**lime** (1), glue, as in **birdlime** (to catch birds), hence a caustic; hence such cpds as **limehouse** (whence London's **Limehouse**)—**limelight**—**limestone**; **slime**, whence **slimy**; **slick**, adj and v (whence the AE **slicker**, oilskin, trickster), and **sleek**; **loam**, whence **loamy**; sep **limaceous**; **liniment**; sep **delete, deletion; oblivion, oblivious, obliviscence** (or **-escence**); sep **polish, polite**; sep **slip, glide** or **slide away**; **slowworm**.

1. *Lime*, orig glue, birdlime, much later a caustic, derives from OE *līm*: cf OHG-MHG, OS, ON *līm*, G *Leim*, glue, birdlime, MD *lime* and, as in D, *lijm*; L *līmus*, mud, slime, *lino*, I smear; Gr *leimax*, a snail (whence, via L, the E *limaceous*), *leimōn*, a moist meadow (whence Min *limonite*), *leimax*, id, also a snail, *limnē*, a marsh, *alinein*, to smear;

also, with the IE prefix *s-*, OSl *slina*, spittle, OIr *sligim*, I smear, ON *slīm*, OHG *slīm*, MD-D *slijm*, mire: basic idea: slime or slimy. The Gmc r is *\*līm-*, var *\*laim-*; the IE r, *\*leim-*, var *\*loim-* (Walshe). With 'to *lime*', from OE *līman*, cf OS *līmian*, OHG *līmēn*, to glue, to cause to stick, OE *gelīman*, to glue together, L *oblīmāre*, to cover with mud or slime.

2. *Slime* derives from OE *slīm*, with cognates as above; akin to the adj *slick* (whence *slickness*), from ME *slike*, whence also *sleek* (whence 'to *sleek*' and *sleekness*); ME *slike*, prob deriving from ON *slīkr*, smooth, is akin to OE *slīcian*, to smoothe, which, accounting for 'to *slick*' (make sleek), is itself akin to OHG *slīchan*, MHG *slīchen*, to walk smoothly or with dignity, G *schleichen*, to slink, MD *sliec* and, as in D, *slijk*, mud.

3. Akin to OE *līm*, glue, is OE *lām*, ME *lam*, E *loam*, a clayey, hence moist, earth: cf G *Lehm*, loam, clay, LG *lēm*, MHG *leime*, OHG *leimo*, MD *liem, leim, leme*, (as in D) *leem*.

4. Akin to OE *līm*, birdlime, glue, are OE *slīw*, *slēo*, a fish (notably slimy), Nor *slo*, a blindworm, and to the *slā-* of OE *slāwyrm*, the blindworm or *slowworm* (cf WORM).

5. Akin to L *līmus*, mud, mire, slime, is L *linere*, var *linīre* (s and r *lin-*), to smear, whence LL *linīmentum*, something smeared on, whence EF-F and E *liniment*.

6. L *linere* has cpd *oblinere* (prefix *ob-*), to rub out, to efface: and akin is L *oblīuisci*, ML *oblīvisci*, to have something in one's mind effaced, i.e. to forget, whence *oblīuiō*, ML *oblīviō*, o/s *oblīviōn-*, whence, via the acc *oblīviōnem*, the MF-EF *oblivion*, adopted by E; derivative adj *oblīuiōsus*, ML *oblīviōsus*, whence *oblivious*. *Oblīuisci* has presp *oblīuiscens*, o/s *oblīuiscent-*, ML *oblīviscent-*, whence the adj *obliviscent*, forgetful, whence the n *obliviscence*.

**lime** (2), fruit-tree. See LEMON.

**lime** (3), linden tree. See LINDEN, para 1.

**limen.** See LIMIT, para 5.

**Limerick**, nonsense verse, app blends the ideas conveyed by Father Matthew Russell's *learic* (Edward *Lear*+lyric) and the refrain 'Will You Come up to *Limerick*?' (EW.) Perh also contributory is the *Limerick hook*, an angler's fish-hook first made at Limerick.

**Limey.** See LEMON, s.f.

**liminal, liminary.** See para 5 of:

**limit** (n, v, whence the pa **limited, limiting**), **limitarian, limitary, limitate, limitation, limitless** (*limit*, n+*-less*, without); **lintel**; cpds **delimit, delimitation** —**illimitable.**—Cognates: **limen, liminal, liminary**; cpds: **eliminant, eliminate, elimination, eliminative, eliminator, eliminatory**—**oblique** (adj, hence n; v), **obliquity** (whence **obliquitous**)—**preliminary** (adj, hence n)—**sublimant, sublimate** (adj, n, v), **sublimation, sublimatory**—**sublime, sublimity**—**subliminal.**

1. 'To *limit*' comes, via MF-F *limiter*, from L *līmitāre*, to set a *limes* or boundary to: L *līmes*, a road bordering a domain, hence a boundary, hence

a limit, has o/s *līmit-*, acc *līmitem*, whence MF-F *limite*, whence E *limit*: and *līmes* (r *līm-*) is prob akin to L *līmen*, threshold, *līmus* (s, r *līm-*), LL var *līmis*, oblique, and, without a nasal, *līquis*, oblique; prob akin also to the 1st LIMB (of the body).

2. L *līmes*, o/s *līmit-*, has these additional derivatives affecting E:

*līmitāris*, of or for a boundary, whence E *limitary*, whence the n *limitarian*;

derivative *līmitāre*, to delimit, to limit, pp *līmitātus*, whence 'to *limitate*'; subsidiary *līmitātiō*, o/s *līmitātiōn-*, yields MF-F *limitation*, adopted by E.

3. L *līmitāre* has cpd *dēlīmitāre*, F *délimiter*, E 'to *delimit*'; pp *dēlīmitātus* yields 'to *delimitate*'; subsidiary LL *dēlīmitātiō*, o/s *dēlīmitātiōn-*, yields F and E *delimitation*. *Illimitable*, however, merely = *limitable* (from 'to *limit*') preceded by *il-* for *in-*, not.

4. *Līmes* has dim *līmitellus*, whence, via VL *\*lintellus*, the OF *lintel*, adopted by E.

5. Prob akin to L *līmes* is L *līmen* (o/s *līminis*; r *līm-*), which means both the lintel and the step or threshold of a door affording entry to a house: *līmen superum*, upper 'limit', and *līmen inferum*, lower 'limit'. The L adj is *līmināris*, EF-F *liminaire*, E *liminary*; *liminal* is an E formation.

6. *Līmen* has cpd *ēlīmināre*, to chase from (*ē-*) the *līmen* or threshold, to expel, (LL) to exclude (a thing), with presp *ēlīminans*, o/s *ēlīminant-*, whence the E adj hence n *eliminant*; pp *ēlīminātus* leads to 'to *eliminate*'. The anl formations *elimination, eliminator, eliminatory* owe much to the corresp F derivatives of late MF-F *éliminer* (from *ēlīmināre*).

7. Derivative *postlīminium*, the right to return to one's country after (*post*) having left one's threshold, is retained by modern Law.

8. Diplomatic *preliminaries* derives from syn EF-F *préliminaires*, from adj *préliminaire*—whence E *preliminary*, adj—which = *pré-*, L *prae-*, before + *liminaire* (as in para 5).

9. Whereas *subliminal* is a Psy formation from L *sub*, below + *līmin-*, o/s of *līmen*, threshold, sc 'of consciousness' + adj suffix *-al* (cf *liminal*), *sublime* derives, perh via MF-F, from L *sublīmis*, neu *sublīme*, coming up from below the threshold, rising in the air, hence lofty, hence morally very lofty: either 'that below which is the *līmen* or threshold' or, more prob from *līmus*, oblique, 'that which rises obliquely, that which climbs a steep slope, hence lofty' (E & M): for *līmus*, cf para 1. Derivative *sublīmitās*, o/s *sublīmitāt-*, becomes MF-F *sublimité*, whence E *sublimity*; and derivative *sublīmāre*, to elevate, has pp *sublīmātus*, whence the adj and v *sublimate*. In ML, *sublīmātus* is, in the neu, *sublīmātum*, used as a Chem n, whence the E Chem n *sublimate*; cf the Chem adj hence n *sublimant*, from L *sublīmant-*, o/s of *sublīmans*, presp of *sublīmāre*. Derivative LL *sublīmātiō*, elevation, exaltation, o/s *sublīmātiōn-*, accounts for *sublimation*, whence, anl, *sublimatory*.

10. Akin to L *līquis*, oblique (as in para 1), is

L *oblīquus*, oblique, hence indirect, whence—prob via MF-F—*oblique*; the v 'to *oblique*' comes from F *obliquer*, from F *oblique*. Derivative LL *oblīquitās*, o/s *oblīquitāt-*, yields—via MF-F *obliquité*— *obliquity*.

**limn, limner.** See the 3rd LIGHT, para 17.

**limonite.** See the 1st LIME, para 1.

**limousine**, a closed motorcar, is adopted from F: sense-change from F *limousine*, a hood orig affected by the *Limousins* or inhabitants of the old Central French province of *Limousin*, from Augustoritum *Lemouicensium*, the L name of Limoges, chief town of the region, from L *Lemouices*, ML *Lemovices*, a Gallic tribe (perh 'the warriors of Lemos').

**limp**, adj, unrecorded before 1706, is akin to 'to *limp*', occurring in ME: both have app MHG cognates and both are related to SLAP.

**limpet.** See LAMPREY, para 2.

**limpid, limpidity.** See LYMPH, para 2.

**limy:** adj of the 1st LIME.

**linage.** See LINE.

**linden** was orig the adj of *lind*, a linden tree, OE *lind*, var *linde*: cf OHG *linta*, MHG-G *linde*, ON *lind*, also Ru *lipa*. *Lime*, linden tree, dissimilates *\*line* for *\*lind-tree* (Walshe).

2. *Lithe*, flexible, pliant, (obs) gentle, mild, OE *līthe* (app for *\*linthe*), is akin to OHG *lindi*, MHG *linde*, G *gelinde*, gentle, ON *linr*, L *lentus*, flexible, supple, hence soft, lazy, slow, perh an extn of L *lēnis*, smooth, gentle (cf LENIENCE). The Gmc r is *\*linth* (issuing into *lind, lint*) and the IE r, *\*lēnt-*, extn of *\*lēn-* (Walshe); the basic idea is perh 'flexible', as is the bast—cf Ru dial *lut*, linden bast —of a tree (Webster). *Lithe* has mdfn *lithesome*, whence, by thinning, *lissom*.

3. L *lentus* has derivative *lentāre*, to render flexible, to bend, with cpd *allentāre*, to cause to become slower, to retard, whence OF-EF *alenter*, var (more usual) *alentir*, whence EF-F *ralentir*, to slacken; the app much earlier E 'to *relent*' must owe something to L *relent*escere, to begin to grow slack, the inch of *\*relentāre*, to bend, or become supple, again. The obs derivative n *relent*, a relenting, has derivatives *relentless* and *relentment*.

**line**, a thread, string, cord or rope (cf 'fishing *line*'), hence any of these used in measuring, hence a drawn line, descends from OE *līne*, cord, line, intimately related to and prob derived from OE *līn*, flax, whence the now rare E *line*, flax, its fibre, spun flax, linen, linen thread: and is therefore akin to OFris *līne*, OHG *līna*, MHG *līne*, G *Leine*, cord, leash, MD-MLG *line*, D *lijn*, L *līnea*, a linen thread, hence string, hence line, itself from L *līnum*, flax, hence any object made from it, esp linen, a thread, a rope, itself akin to Gr *linon*; whereas prob the ON *līna* and perh the Go *lein* come from L, the Sl words (e.g., Ru *lĭn*, Lith *linaĭ*), prob come from Gr; the C words (e.g., OIr *lín*, OW *llin*, Ga *lion*, Cor *lín*, Br *lin*, OC *\*līnu*) are perh loans from, but more prob cognates of, L *līnum*. Gr *linon* has derivative *linaiā*, cord, line— cf L *līnea*, whence OF-F *ligne*, line, which has much influenced the ME-E senses of the native E *line*; as *linaiā* was orig the f of adj \**linaios*, so *linea* was orig (*līnea restis*) the f of adj *līneus*. Similarly the known Gr adj *lininos* has influenced OFris *linnen*, OHG *linīn*, MHG *līnen*, OE *līnen*, all orig adjj, becoming the modern nn G *Leinen* and E *linen*, the E adj *linen* pursuing a parallel course from OE. The European etymon is prob \**linom*, r *lin-*, itself perh an extn of an ult r \**li-*, ? flax. I suspect the word to be Medit, even though Eg *ḥemā*, flax, and *meni*, linen cloth, be hardly encouraging.

2. Whereas *linage*, number of amount of lines, derives from E *line*, *lineage*, descent through a line of progenitors, derives from ME *linage*, OF-F *lignage*, from OF *ligne* (L *līnea*).

3. Several simple L derivatives of *līnea* concern E:

*līneālis*, MF-F *linéal*, E *lineal*;

*līneāre*, to trace a line, whence *līneāmentum*, EF-F *linéament*, E *lineament*;

*līneāris*, E *linear*, with the anl E formations *collinear*, *rectilinear*.

4. *Līneāre*, to trace a line, has pp *līneātus*, whence the E adj and v *lineate*; derivative *līneātiō*, o/s *līneātiōn-*, becomes *lineation*. But these two words are much less common than *delineate* and *delineation* (whence the anl *delineator*), from LL *dēlīneātiō* and its source *dēlīneātus*, pp of *dēlīneāre*, to delineate, an int (*de-*) of *līneāre*.

5. *Līneāre* has the further cpd *collīneāre*, to direct in a straight (connoted by *col-* for *con-*, together) line, pp *collīneātus*, whence 'to *collineate*'; derivative *collīneātiō*, o/s *collīneātiōn-*, leads to *collineation*. *Collīneāre*, by a false reading of its var *collīniāre* (LL), becomes ML *collīmāre*, with pp *collīmātus* and subsidiary *collīmātiō*, o/s *collīmātiōn-*, whence resp the Astr and Phys 'to *collimate*' and *collimation*, whence, anl, the *collimator* of Optics; both *collimation* and *collimator* owe much to F.

6. Not from L but from F comes 'to *align*', OF-F *aligner*, to put in (*a-* for *à*, to, in) a line (*ligne*); derivative MF-F *alignement* results in E *alignment*.

7. Reverting to L *līnum*, flax, linen, we find another derivative relevant to E: *linteus*, made of linen, with neu *linteum* used as n, 'linen cloth', LL *linta*, ME *lynete*, *lynnet*, later, by contr, *lynt*, whence E *lint*. But MF-F *linotte*, whence, because this bird delights in flax seeds, E *linnet*, is a dim of OF-F *lin* (L *līnum*), flax.

8. *Līnum*, flax, combines with L *oleum*, oil, to form *linoleum* (now often shortened to *lino*), orig a soldified linseed oil, now a floor-covering partly made with this oil: and *linseed* itself derives from OE *līnsǣd*, seed of flax: cf OE *līn* (in para 1 above) +SEED.

9. The E n *line* has, from one sense or another, the foll derivatives:

'to *line*', to cover the inner surface of (e.g., a cloak), to form a line; *liner*, from a line of ships;

*linesman* (railway or telephone lines); *lining* of garment; c/f *lino-*, as in *linotype*.

**lineage**, descent. See prec, para 2.
**lineal**. See LINE, para 3.
**lineament**. See LINE, para 3.
**linear**. See LINE, para 3.
**lineate, lineation**. See LINE, para 4.
**linen**. See LINE, para 1.
**liner**. See LINE, para 9.
**linesman**. See LINE, para 9.
**ling** (1), a fish. See LONG, para 5.
**ling** (2), a kind of heather, comes from ON *lyng*, perh akin to OE *lōh*, a strap, a thong, with basic idea 'to bend' (in the wind?).
**linger**. See LONG, para 6.
**lingerie**, adopted from late MF-F, is a late MF derivative (*-erie*, E *-ery*) from OF-F *linge*, a linen garment, from L *linea* (*uestis*), f of *lineus*, made of linen: f.a.e., LINE, para 1.
**lingo**. See LANGUAGE, para 5.
**lingua franca**. See FRANK, para 9.
**lingual, linguist, linguistic(s)**. See LANGUAGE, para 3.
**lingula, lingulate**. See LICK, para 3.
**liniment**. See the 1st LIME, para 5.
**lining** of garment. See LINE, para 9.
**link** (1), of chain. See FLANGE, para 7.—Hence *linkage*.
**link** (2), a ridge, a bank: OE *hlinc*: akin to the 2nd LEAN, q.v. Hence *links*, a seaside golf-course, from the dunes, hence any golf-course.
**link** (3), a torch: prob from ML *inch*inus, var of *lichinus*, itself from Gr *lukhnos*, a (portable) lamp, akin to *leukos*, bright, white: f.a.e., the 3rd LIGHT. —Hence *linkboy*, *linkman*.
**linkage**. See the 1st LINK.
**linn**, a pool below a waterfall: partly from Ga *linne* and partly from the syn OE *hlynn*: cf OIr *lind*, liquid: ult from the C r \**li-*, liquid.
**Linnaean**, AE **Linnean**, refers to the Bot classification set forth, in his *Systema Naturae*, 1735, by the Sw naturalist Karl von *Linné*, 1707–1778, latinized as *Linnaeus*.
**linnet**. See LINE, para 7.
**linoleum**. See LINE, para 8.
**linotype**=line o(f) type.
**linseed**. See LINE, para 8.
**linsey-woolsey**: a rhyming redup (prompted by WOOL) of the earlier *linsey*, a coarse linen-and-wool cloth made at *Lindsey* in Suffolk.
**lint**. See LINE, para 7.
**lintel**. See LIMIT, para 4.
**lion, lioness, lionize**. See LEO, para 2.
**lip**, n, hence adj and v. See the 2nd LAP, para 6.
**lipo-words**. See Elements.
**liquate, liquation**. See LIQUEFY, para 2.
**liquefacient, liquefaction**. See para 5 of:
**liquefy; liquescent**—cf **deliquesce, deliquescent** (whence **deliquescence**); **liquid** (adj, hence n); **liquidate, liquidation, liquidator; liquidity, liquor** (n, hence v) and **liqueur; liquate, liquation**.—obs **delay**, to allay; **prolix, prolixity**.

1. L has three interrelated vv: *liqui*, to flow, *liquēre*, to be clear, to be liquid, to be filtered, *liquāre*, to filter, to clarify, (LL) to melt. As in the fruitful derivatives *liquidus* and *liquor*, the r is *liqu-*, IE r *leikw-*, var *likw-*, which seems to be akin to—and perh the passive complement of—the active nasal *linkw-*, to leave, abandon, as in L *linquere*, q.v. at LEND, para 2.

2. *Liquāre* has pp *liquātus*, whence the 'to liquate' of metallury; derivative LL *liquātiō*, o/s *liquātiōn-*, yields *liquation*, a melting, a fusion. The LL prefix-cpd *dēliquāre*, to melt or strain *dē-* or away, passes through VL to become MF-F *délayer*, whence the now obs 'to *delay*', to dilute.

3. *Liquēre*, to be fluid, has simple derivatives: *liquidus*, clear, fluid, liquid, MF-F *liquide*, E *liquid*;

*liquor*, fluidity, hence also a fluid, a liquid, adopted by E as a reshaping of ME *licour*, *licur*, adopted from OF-MF; adopted from F is *liqueur* '(L *liquor*), with specialized sense.

4. *Liquidus* has LL derivative *liquidāre*, to melt, pp *liquidātus*, whence 'to *liquidate*'—whence, anl, *liquidation*, perh imm from F—and *liquidator*; derivative L *liquiditās*, o/s *liquiditāt-*, yields late MF-F *liquidité*, whence E *liquidity*.

5. *Liquēre* combines with *facere*, to make, to form the cpd *liquefacere*, MF-F *liquéfier*, E *liquefy*, whence *liquefiable*; the presp *liquefaciens*, o/s *liquefacient-*, whence the E adj, hence n, *liquefacient*; the pp *liquefactus* appears in E *liquefactive* and in LL *liquefactiō*, o/s *liquefactiōn-*, whence EF-F *liquéfaction* and E *liquefaction*.

6. *Liquēre* has inch *liquescere*, presp *liquescens*, o/s *liquescent-*, whence *liquescent*. The cpd *dēliquescere*, to melt away, to dissolve, explains 'to *deliquesce*'; its presp *dēliquescens*, o/s *dēliquescent-*, explains *deliquescent*.

7. The same IE r prob occurs in L *lixa*, elliptical for *lixa aqua*, running water, from the adj *lixus*, f *lixa*, attested in L *prōlixus*, app applied orig to water flowing *prō*, forward, hence overflowing, but mostly, in LL-ML, to speech that overflows: whence, prob via late OF-F *prolixe*, the E *prolix*, verbose. The derivative L *prōlixitās*, prob via MF-F *prolixité*, becomes *prolixity*.

**liquorice.** See LICORICE.

**liquorish**, lecherous. See LICK (heading).

**lira.** See LEVEL, para 3.

**lisp** (v, hence n): ME *lispen*: aphetically from OE *wlispian*, itself from the adj *wlisp*, lisping, stammering, speaking inarticulately: cf OHG *lispan*, to stammer, and the MHG-G derivative freq *lispeln*, to lisp: echoic.

**lissom.** See LINDEN, para 2, s.f.

**list** (1), an edge or border, a selvage, OE *liste* (cf ON *lista*)—whence, by fusion with OF-MF *lice*, the lists or enclosing barriers of a medieval tourney, Frankish *listia*, OHG *lista*, a border, the E *lists*; the modern sense is adopted from F *liste*, itself borrowed, in C16, from It *lista*, which, like OF *liste*, a border, comes from OHG *līsta*, a strip, a border. The OGmc r *līst-* perh contains the occ IE infix -*s*-: if so, it is prob akin, as Walshe suggests, to L *lītus*, seashore, the 'border' of the ocean.

Hence 'to *list*', to put a list or border on, to make a list of; hence also the adj *list*, made of strips of cloth, as in '*list* slippers'.

**list** (2), to hearken. Cf *listen*, but see LOUD, para 2.

**list** (3), to wish. See LASCIVIOUS, para 2. Hence, (of a ship) to incline, to lean, whence 'a *list*'.

**listen.** See LOUD, para 2.

**lit**, pp, hence adj. See the 3rd LIGHT.

**litany** is a reshaping of ME, from OF-EF, *letanie*: LL *litania*: Gr *litaneia* (s and r *litan-*), a prayer, akin to *litaneuein* (s *litaneu-*, r *litan-*), to pray, with ult r *lit-*, as in *lit*esthai, to pray, and *litē*, a prayer.

**liter.** See LEVEL, para 3.

**literal.** See LETTER, para 3.

**literary.** See LETTER, para 3.

**literate.** See LETTER, para 3.

**literature.** See LETTER, para 4.

**litharge**, found in silver-bearing ore, is reshaped from ME, from MF, *litarge* (later *litharge*): L *lithargyrus*: Gr *litharguros*: *lith*os, a stone + *arguros*, silver.

**lithe.** See LINDEN, para 2.

**lithia**, SciL from Gr *lithos*, a stone; **lithic**, Gr *lithikos*, adj of *lithos*; **lithite** and **lithium**, Sci derivatives from *lithos*; c/f *litho-*, see Elements; such cpds as **eolith** (Gr *ēōs*, dawn)—**megalith** (Gr *megas*, great)—**monolith** (Gr *monos*, alone): Gr λίθος, s and r λιθ-, *lith-*: o.o.o.

**Lithuania (-ian).** See LETT.

**litigant** (adj, hence n), **litigate**, **litigation**, **litigious**.

1. The group rests upon L *lit-*, o/s of *līs*, a dispute, a lawsuit, OL *stlis*, perh akin to OE *slīthe*, cruel, hurtful, and, if that be so, certainly to LOATH. The L *līs*, gen *lītis*, has derivative *lītigāre*—perh for *lītem agere*, to play a (collective) lawsuit—to dispute at law, with presp *lītigans*, o/s *lītigant-*, whence *litigant*, and pp *lītigātus*, whence 'to *litigate*'; derivative LL *lītigātiō*, o/s *lītigātiōn-*, yields *litigation*. On *lītig-*, the s of *lītigāre*, arises *lītigium*, a quarrel, a dispute, with adj *lītigiōsus*, whence, prob via MF-F *litigieux*, f *litigieuse*, the E *litigious*. Cf LOATH.

2. From VL *exlītigāre*, OF derives *esligier*, to free from the law, to buy, whence ME *aleggen*, to advance as evidence, E 'to *allege*'.

**litmus**: SciL reshaping of ON *litmose*, a lichen used for dyeing: *litr* (silent *r*), a colour, hence a dye + *mosi*, E MOSS.

**litre.** See LEVEL, para 3.

**litter.** See the 2nd LIE, para 12.

**littérateur.** See LETTER, para 5.

**little**—belittle; loiter; lout.

1. *Little*, ME *litel*, var *lutel*, derives from OE *lȳtel*, perh orig a dim of OE *lȳt*, little, few: cf OS *luttil*, OHG *luzzil*, MHG *lützel*, LG *lütt*, Go *leitils*, MD *lettel*, *littel*, (as in D) *luttel*, the var OFris *littik*, and prob the OSl *ludŭ*, foolish, MIr *luta*, the little finger, but only very improb the Cor *lȳth*, feeble: Gmc r, *lut-*, IE r *lud-*. (Walshe.)

2. *Little*, preceded by the int *be-*, gives us 'to belittle', whence *belittlement* and *belittler*.

3. OE *lȳt* and *lȳtel* are akin to OE *lytig*, Go *liuts*, deceitful, OE *lot*, deceit, *lūtian*, to lurk, themselves perh akin to MD *loteren*, to be loose, MD-D *leuteren*, to loiter, late ME *loitren*, E 'to *loiter*', whence *loiterer* and pa, vn *loitering*.

4. Perh akin to the OGmc words mentioned in para 1 is the now archaic *lout*, to stoop or bow, OE *lūtan*, ME *luten*, later *louten*: and OE *lūtan* is akin to the syn ON *lūta*, whence (or very closely akin) the ON *lūtr*, stooping, hence *lout*, a bumpkin, hence any uncouth fellow, whence *loutish* (*-ish*, adj).

**littoral.** See LEVEL, para 6.

**liturgic** (with extn **liturgical**), **liturgy** (whence **liturgist**: agential *-ist*).

*Liturgic* derives from L Gr *leitourgikos*, the adj of LGr *leitourgia*, a public service to God, from Gr *leitourgia*, any public service, LL *liturgia*, the service of the Mass, EF-F *liturgie*, E *liturgy*: *lit-* is akin to Gr *laos*, *leos*, the people, and *ourgia* to E WORK.

**live,** adj. See LIFE, para 2.

**live,** v. See LIFE, para 3.

**livelihood; lively.** See LIFE, para 1.

**livelong.** See the 1st LEAVE, para 6.

**liven.** See LIFE, para 4.

**liver.** See LIFE, para 5.

**liverwort, liverwurst.** See LIFE, para 5; for the latter, cf WURST, para 2.

**livery,** adj. See LIFE (heading).

**livery,** n. See LIBERAL, para 3.

**livid, livor; sloe;** doubtfully the sep LAVENDER.

L *liuēre*, ML *livēre*, to be lead-coloured, to be livid, has derivatives *liuidus*, ML *lividus*, whence, perh via MF-F *livide*, the E *livid*, and *liuor*, ML *livor*, adopted by Med. The L *liuēre*, s *liu-*, perh has r *li-*: cf OIr *lí*, Ga *lì*, Cor *liu*, *lyw*, W *lliw*, OC *līvos*, colour, lustre, and OSl *sliva*, a plum, OHG *slēha*, MHG *slēhe*, G *Schlehe*, a wild plum, a sloe, itself akin to OE *slā*, ME *slo*, E *sloe*.

**living,** pa and vn of 'to live', q.v. at LIFE, para 3.

**livor.** See LIVID.

**livre.** See LEVEL, para 3.

**lizard.** See LEG, para 2.

**llama;** Sp *llama*: Quechuan (SAm) *llama*.

**llanero, llano, llanura.** See PLANE, para 8.

**llyn:** W var of *linn*.

**lo!,** OE *lā*, a purely echoic interj, has, in ME (hence in E), been influenced by ME *lōke*, look!, from the imperative of ME *lōken*, to look—unless, as is less prob, the reverse be true, viz. that E *lo*, behold!, represents ME *lōke* look, because of ME *lo*, OE *lā*, 'there!' (cf F *la*, in *oh, la, la!* with *là*, there).

**loach:** MF-F *loche*: o.o.o.: app id with F dial (Western) *loche*, a slug, and prob deriving, through a C-L *laukka*, for Gaul *leuka*, from Gr *leukos*, white (B & W).

**load** (n, hence v), whence pa **loaded** and pa, vn **loading; lode, lodestar.**

1. Much influenced sem by LADE, load, ME *lode*,

load, way, is phon id with *lode*, which, ME *lode*, derives from OE *lād*, a way, hence a journey, via the EE sense 'carriage, conveyance', carrying persons on their way and also carrying loads: OE *lād* is akin to OE *līthan*, to go, travel, and to ELEAD (v), as appears in *lodestar*, a guiding star, cf dial *lode*, a path, a road; the Min senses of *lode*, 'a deposit filling a rock-fissure', hence 'a tabular deposit' and the AE sense, all following naturally. *Lodestone* is more usu spelt *loadstone*.

**loaf,** pl **loaves; lord** (n, hence v), whence **lordly**—cf **lordship; laird**, whence **lairdly; lady** (n, hence adj), whence **ladylike; ladybird; Lammas**, whence **Lammastide** (cf TIDE, orig season, time).

1. *Loaf*, orig bread in general, comes, through ME *lof*, var *laf*, from OE *hlāf*: cf EHG *hleib*, *leib*, MHG *leip*, G *Laib*, Go *hlaifs*, ON *hleifr*, OSl *chlēbǔ* (perh from OGmc), bread, and perh L *lībum*, a sacrificial cake, itself o.o.o. *Loaf*, OE *hlāf*, is prob Medit: cf Eg *hebnen-t* and *khanf* (var *khenfu*), a sacrificial cake.

2. The o.o.o. *loaf*, to idle, whence *loafer*, might come from the generic notion of 'bread the staff of life' and the particular notion of 'a loaf of bread, a flask of wine, and thou beside me in the wilderness—and wilderness were paradise enow'. More prob, however, EW is right in deriving this orig Am word from G dial *lofen*, G *laufen*, to run, as in *Landlaüfer*, landloper, vagabond.

3. OE *hlāf* occurs in three cpds important to E, the first being *hlāfmaesse*, loaf Mass—the feast of the First Fruits—August 1: whence *Lammas*.

4. The second is *hlāfdīge*, loaf-kneader, cf (for the 2nd element) DAIRY: ME *lafdi*, later *lavede*, latest *ladi*: E *lady*. A *ladybird* is a *Lady bird*, a 'bird' of Our Lady—an example of religious folklore.

5. The third is *hlāfweard*, loaf-ward or -guardian (cf WARD), soon contr to *hlāford*; ME *laverd*, var *loverd*, latest *lord*: E *lord*. OE has the derivative *hlāfordscipe*, whence E *lordship*, orig the state or rank of a lord.

6. In Sc, *hlāford* becomes *laird*; perh cf (Sc) *larde* or *lard*.

**loaf,** to idle. See prec, para 2.

**loam.** See the 1st LIME, para 3.

**loan.** See LEND, para 1.

**loath** or **loth**, adj; **loathe**, v, whence vn **loathing** and adj **loathsome**.

'To *loathe*', to feel disgust or extreme aversion for, derives from OE *lāthian*, to be hateful, itself from OE *lāth*, odious, whence ME *loth*, *looth*, E *loath* or *loth*: and OE *lāth* is akin to the syn OFris and OS *lēth*, OHG *leid*, ON *leithr*, also OHG *leid*, pain, G *Leid*, harm, sorrow; prob cf Gr a*litein*, to sin, and *loig*os, disaster. Cf LITIGANT.

**lob,** pollack, lugworm, (now dial) a heavy (and dull) person, something short and thick and heavy, hence 'to *lob*', to let fall heavily, throw lazily, whence, as in cricket or lawn tennis, a lobbed ball; hence app **loblolly** (cf LOLL) and **looby**, a (heavily) awkward, clumsy person, usu male, and **lubber** (cf LOOBY and the Sw dial *lubber*), a clumsy fellow, esp seaman, with adj **lubberly** and cpd **landlubber.**

A *lob*, ult echoic, is akin to and perh imm from MLG *lobbe*, a plump person or, usu, quadruped, cf Fris *lob* or *lobbe*, a short hanging lump, e.g. of fat, and Da *lub* or *lubbe*, a pollack.

lobate. See LOBE.

lobby. See LODGE, para 4.

lobe; lobate; cf the element *lobato-*.

*Lobate*, having lobes, is a Sci formation from SciL *lobus* (dim *lobulus*, E *lobule*), whence EF-F, hence E, *lobe*—from Gr *lobos*, a (small) rounded projection, akin to Gr *lep*ein, to scale. Cf SLEEP.

lobelia: the Sci, esp Bot, suffix *-ia* tacked onto the Flemish botanist Matthias de *Lobel* or L'Obel (1538–1616).

loblolly. See LOB.

lobo. See WOLF, para 4.

lobster. See LEG, para 6.

lobule. See LOBE.

local, locale, locality, localize, locate, location, locative, locator; allocate, allocation; collocate, collocation, collocative; dislocate, dislocation, dislocatory.—lieu; lieutenant.

1. L *locus* (s and r *loc*-), a place, as in *locus classicus*, an important, esp the most important, passage ('place' in a book) on a given subject, is o.o.o.—but prob akin to STALL.

2. The derivative adj is LL *locālis*, whence MF-F, hence E, *local*, used also as n; also from F *local* comes E *locale*. F *local* has derivatives *localiser*, whence 'to localize'; *localisation*, whence *localization*; *locality*, although imm from EF-F *localité*, goes back to LL *locālitās* (o/s *locālitāt*-), situation.

3. L *locus* has derivative *locāre*, to place, with pp *locātus*, whence 'to locate'; derivative *locātiō*, o/s *locātiōn-*, becomes, perh via EF-F, *location*, and derivative *locātor*, a contractor, is sense-adapted by E; *locative*, perh imm from MF-F *locatif* (orig, legal), is anl with all the other L-named grammatical cases (*nominative*, *vocative*, etc.).

4. ML *allocāre*, lit to place at or to, has pp *allocātus*, whence 'to allocate'; derivative ML *allocātiō*, o/s *allocātiōn-*, leads to *allocation*; L *collocāre*, lit to place with, pp *collocātus*, yields 'to collocate', and derivative *collocātiō*, o/s *collocātiōn-*, yields *collocation*, whence, anl, *collocative*; ML *dislocāre*, lit to place apart, pp *dislocātus*, yields 'to dislocate'; derivative ML *dislocātiō*, o/s *dislocātiōn-*, yields *dislocation*, whence, anl, *dislocatory*.

5. L *locus* becomes OF-F *lieu*, adopted by E in the phrase 'in *lieu* of'. Derivative MF-F *lieutenant*, adopted by E, is lit *lieu-tenant*, one who is 'placeholding'.

6. Cf the sep COUCH.

loch. See LAKE, para 6.

lochia. See the 2nd LIE, para 14.

lock (1), of hair, OE *locc*, is akin to OFris and OS *lokk*, OHG-MHG *loc*, G *Locke*, MD *loke*, D *lok*, ON *lokkr*, and, further off, L *luxus* (*luk*sus), dislocated, Gr *lug*os, a pliant twig, a withe, *lug*izein, to bend.

2. Akin to OE *locc* is OE *lēac*, often contr to

*lēc*, whence E *leek:* cf OHG *louh*, MHG *louch*, G *Lauch*, MD *loke*, *looc*, D *look*, ON *laukr* (cf ON *lok*, weed).—Cf *garlic* at GAR, para 1.

lock (2), fastening, as for a door, whence locksmith (cf SMITH), lock-up, etc., as well as 'to lock', whence locker; locket.

1. *Lock*, including that on a canal, derives from OE *loc*, an enclosure, or that which ensures one, i.e. a fastening: cf OFris *lok*, a lock, a castle, OHG *loh*, MHG *loch*, a lock, an enclosure, a hole, G *Loch*, a hole, ON *lok*, a fastening, a lock: cf also the vv OE *lūcan*, OFris *lūka*, OS and Go *-lūkan*, OHG *lûhhan*, MHG *lūchen*, ON *lūka*, to fasten, to lock: perh ult akin to the 1st LOCK, the two words sharing the basic idea 'to bend, hence to close', as Webster proposes.

2. OE *loc*, a lock, a latch, is retained or, rather, borrowed by AF, which, passing to late OF, acquires the OF-F dim *loquet*, a little latch or lock, whence E *locket*.

loco, A sl for 'crazy', is the ASp sl *loco*, mad, from ASp *loco*, that poisonous herb of the Western US and of SAm which AE usu calls *locoweed*; Sp *loco* is Port *louco*, of Araucan (central SAm) origin.

locomotive, adj hence n, is anl formed from *locomotion*, movement 'from a place', L *loco*, abl of *locus*, q.v. at LOCAL.

locoweed. See LOCO.

locum tenens, L for '(one) holding the place' for another: cf *lieutenant* at LOCAL, para 5.

locus classicus. See LOCAL, para 1.

locus standi. See STAND, para 10.

locust. See LEG, para 5.

locution. See LOQUACIOUS, para 1.

lode, lodestar, lodestone. See LOAD.

lodge, n and v, the latter having agent lodger and pa, vn lodging; lodgement; loge and loggia; dislodge, whence, anl, dislodgement;—lobby, n hence v (whence lobbying and lobbyist); cf *logistics* at LEGEND, para 22.

1. 'To *lodge*,' ME *loggen* (pron *lodgen*), derives from OF-MF *logier* (whence F *loger*), itself from OF *loge*, a leafy bower, an arbour, prob from ML *laubia*, var *lobia*, porch or gallery, from the syn OHG *louba* (MHG *loube*, id, G *Laube*, bower, with sense influenced by OHG *loub*, MHG *loup*, G *Laub*, foliage—cf LEAF), prob akin to ON *lopt* (E *loft*, q.v. at the 2nd LIFT, paras 1, 2); B & W, however, derive OF *loge* imm from Frankish *\*laubja*, which, they imply, comes from OHG *loub*, foliage. The IE r is app *\*laubh-* (Walshe).

2. OF-MF *logier* has the MF-F derivative *logement*, whence E *lodgement*, orig a place at which to lodge. OF *logier* has the OF-MF cpd *deslogier*, *desloger* (*des-*, L *dis-*, apart), whence 'to *dislodge*'.

3. Whereas F *loge* has been partly adopted by E in sense 'stall', esp in a theatre, the It *loggia* (from OF-F *loge*) is partly adopted in sense 'a roofed open "porch" forming an almost integral part of a house'.

4. ML *lobia* (var of *laubia*, as in para 1) has var

*lobium*; from either *lobia* or *lobium* could *lobby* orig an eccl term (OED), have come.

**loess.** See LOSE, para 3.

**loft** (n, hence v), **lofty.** See the 2nd LIFT, paras 1 and 2.

**log.** See the 2nd LIE, para 9.

**loganberry**: found, 1881, by the jurist and skilful gardener J. H. Logan (1841–1928). DAE.

**logarithm, logarithmic.** See ARITHMETIC, para 2.

**loge.** See LODGE, para 3.

**loggerhead; be at loggerheads.** See the 2nd LIE, para 9.

**loggia.** See LODGE, para 3.

**logia.** See LEGEND, para 21.

**logic, logical, logician.** See LEGEND, para 21.

**logistic,** with extn **logistical.** See LEGEND, para 22.

**logistics.** See LEGEND, para 22.

**logodaedaly, logogriph, logorrhoea.** See the element *-loger*; for the 3rd, cf RHEUM, s.f.

**logos.** See LEGEND, passim in paras 20–22.

**log-rolling; logwood.** These AE terms have arisen, the former from a friendly co-operative rolling of logs to a stream, the latter because it is wood imported as logs from WI and CA into the U.S.

**loin** and **sirloin; lumbar** and **lumbago; numbles** and **umbles,** whence **umble** (or f/e **humble) pie,** whence f/e 'to **eat humble pie'.**

1. *Loin,* usu in pl, derives from ME *loyne,* from the MF dial *loigne,* var of OF-F *longe,* itself, via VL *\*lumbea,* from L *lumbus,* usu in pl *lumbi*: cf the differently vowelled OE *lenden,* OFris *lenden,* OS *lendin,* OHG *lentī,* MHG-G *lende,* ON *lend*: Gmc r, *\*landw-*; L *lumbus* being perh for *\*lundwus.* (Walshe.)

2. *Sirloin,* EE *surloyn,* derives from MF *sur-loigne,* lit 'over-loin'.

3. The adj *lumbar* derives from LL *\*lumbāris,* attested by LL *lumbāre* (prop the neu of the adj), a loincloth; and *lumbago,* adopted from L *lumbāgō,* represents *lumb-+-āgō,* var of the suffix otherwise formed in *-īgō* and *-ūgō.*

4. *Umbles* (whence the rare *humbles* and the f/e *humble pie*) is an aphetic var of *numbles* (var *nombles*), adopted from MF, where the predominant *nomble* is a var of OF *lomble,* var *lumble,* from LL *lumbellus,* a small haunch (mostly in cookery), dim of L *lumbus.*

**loiter.** See LITTLE, para 3.

**Loki.** See the 3rd LIGHT, para 5.

**loll; Lollard.** See LULL, para 2.

**lollipop, lolly.** The former = *lolly + pop* (it into your mouth); and the ? orig dial *lolly* is prob short for *loblolly,* a thick broth or gruel, app a rhyming redup on LOB.

**Lombard, Lombardesque, Lombardy; lumber,** (obs) a pawnbroker's shop, hence articles stored in pawn (obs), whence both old, not valuable things stored away, and (smallish) sawn timber, whence *lumberjack* (*Jack,* a man), hence, in part, 'to *lumber',* to heap untidily, to clutter (a room) with.

1. *Lombard,* n hence adj, is adopted from F,

taking it from It *Lombardo,* a contracted derivative from LL *Longobardus* (var *Langobardus,* influenced by OGmc), which EW, in a private letter of mid-January, 1950, suggests is '(The Men of) the Long Axes' (OHG *barta,* MHG-G *Barte*), rather than '(of) the Long Beards' (OHG-G *bart*), which supposes a *b-d* alternation. Walshe, relating *Barte,* a broad axe, to *Bart,* a beard, remarks that 'the axe-blade hangs like a beard (the name of the *Langobardi* possibly derived from this)'; the *Longobardi,* mentioned by Tacitus, were orig a N German tribe, noted for their ferocity. The var *Longobardi* had the ML derivative *Longobardia,* It *Lombardia,* F *Lombardie,* E *Lombardy.* It *Lombardo* had adj *Lombardesco,* whence *Lombardesque.*

2. E *Lombard,* in its derivative sense 'banker' or 'moneylender' (famous in medieval and early modern Lombardy), hence a bank or even a pawn-shop, soon lost its capital *L*: and *lombard,* banker, moneylender, became, by C17, *lumber.* The history of the sense-related v is obscure, for 'to *lumber'* is app—though prob only app—considerably earlier than the n.

**loment, lomentaceous.** See LAVA, para 6.

**London** (whence **Londoner** and the obsol **Londonese,** Cockney speech): Tacitus (A.D. 115–117), *Londinium*; LL *Londinum* (predominant), varr *Lundinium, Lundinum*: app of C origin, OC *\*lond-,* wild, bold, as in OIr *lond,* wild, Ga *lonn,* powerful, irascible, perh Br *lon,* a (wild) beast. *Londinum,* r *Lond-,* has s *Londin-,* perh imm from a PlN *\*Londinos.* (Ekwall.)

**lone; lonely.** See ONE, para 10.

**long,** adj (hence n) and adv and v (whence the pa, vn **longing**); obvious cpds, e.g. **longboat, long-bow, longhorn, long-lived, longshoreman** (for **alongshore-man**), **longspur** (a bird with a very long hind-claw), **longtail, longways** or **-wise; along;—longanimity; longitude; elongate, elongation; oblong; prolong, prolongation;—length, lengthen, lengthy;—Lent, Lenten;—ling** (fish); **linger; lounge** (v, hence n), whence **lounger** and **lounging; lunge** (n, hence v);—**indulge, indulgence, indulgent; purloin,** whence **purloiner.**

1. *Long,* adv, derives from OE *lange,* itself from the OE adj *lang,* which in its var *long* becomes E: MD (and MHG) *lanc,* D *lang,* ON *langr* (pron thus), and the differently vocalized MIr *long,* L *longus,* long, (prob) Gr *lonkhē* (λόγχη), a lance (the *long* weapon), (perh) Skt *dīrgha,* long.—'To *long'* derives from OE *langian,* to grow long (potentially tedious; cf OE *langsum,* tedious), in its presumably derivative impersonal use 'to cause longing or desire in' (*Langath thē āwuht,* Does it discontent thee at all?—Do you desire anything?); the former certainly derives from OE *lang,* long.

2. OE *lang,* long, has cpd *andlang,* by the side of, against or closely parallel to the length of, where *and-* is akin to Gr *anti,* over against; *andlang* becomes ME *anlong,* later *along,* E *along.* Hence *alongside,* prep and adv.

3. OE *long, lang,* vowel-mutates in the cognate

OE *lengthu*, ME *lengthe*, E *length*: cf ON *lengd*, OFris *langhēd*, *lengethe*, and, in general, E *strength* and *strong*. Hence *lengthen* (v suffix *-en*) and *lengthy* (adj *-y*).

4. Akin to OE *lang* is OE *leng*ten, *lenc*ten, the 2nd element, *-ten*, being akin to the r in DIANA (cf Go *sinteins*, daily, Lith *dienà*, day): cf OHG *lengizin*, contr to *lenzin*, with var *lenzo*, MHG *lenze*, G *Lenz*, Spring: 'the lengthening of days'. OE *lencten* becomes ME *lenten*, later *lente*, E *Lent*; the adj *Lenten* arose in ME.

5. The *ling* is a long fish: ME *lenge*: perh from ON *langa*.

6. 'To *linger*' is to be long in moving or departing: a freq of ME *lengen*, to tarry, from OE *lengan*, to lengthen, prolong, put off, from the Gmc r of OE *lang*, long.

### Transitional

7. 'To *lounge*', to move lazily, to stand or sit lazily, is perh a b/f from EF *lungis*, a tall, slow fellow, from MF *longis*, a slow fellow, mainly if not wholly from L *longus*, partly also perh from the Apocryphal-Gospel *Longinus* or, more prob, the Mystery-Plays *Longius*, that centurion who pierced the side of Christ, a name prob deriving from, or at the least cognate with, L *longus*.

8. A *lunge*, a long-armed thrust or stroke, has EE var *longe*, aphetic for the obs Fencing term *allonge*, adopted from MF, from OF-F *allonger*, to lengthen, from OF-F *long*, from L *longus*.

9. 'To *purloin*' derives, via AF, from OF-EF *purloigner*, OF-MF *purloignier*, to retard: *pur-* (F *pour*), L *prō*+*loin*, far off, L *longe* (from *longus*)+ inf *-er*. Orig 'to put far off or away', *purloin* develops—quite naturally—the sense 'to put oneself at a distance with, to make off with', hence simply 'to steal'.

### Latin

10. *Long*us has derivative *longitūdō* (abstract-n suffix *-itūdō*), whence, perh via EF-F, the E *longitude*, whence, anl, *longitudinal*, and the LL cpd (with *animus*, mind, heart) *longanimis*, whence LL *longanimitās*, o/s *longanimitāt-*, whence OF-F *longanimité*, whence E *longanimity*.

11. LL *ēlongāre*, to lengthen *ē-* or out, has pp *ēlongātus*, whence the E adj and v *elongate*; derivative *ēlongātiō* (o/s *ēlongātiōn-*), LL removal, ML a prolonging, lengthening-out, becomes, via OF, *elongation*; L *oblongus*, rather long, hence oblong, yields *oblong*; LL *prōlongāre*, to lengthen *pro-* or forward, to prolong, becomes MF *prolonguer* (F *prolonger*), whence 'to *prolong*', and derivative LL *prōlongātiō*, o/s *prōlongātiōn-*, yields, via MF-F, *prolongation*.

12. Prob akin to L *longus* is L in*dulg*ere, to be long-suffering towards, hence to be kind to, hence to be over-kind to (*in-*)—cf Skt *dīrgha*, Gr *dolikhos*, OSl *dlūgŭ*, long—whence 'to *indulge*'. The presp *indulgens* has o/s *indulgent-*, whence the E adj

*indulgent*; derivative L *indulgentia* yields MF-F and (perh from F) E *indulgence*.

**longanimity.** See ANIMAL, para 6, and cf LONG, para 10.

**longitude.** See LONG, para 10.

**loo** (1), the card-game, is short for *lanterloo*: F *lanturlu*, contr of *lanturelu*, from *lanturelu*, an arbitrary refrain-word in a fashionable song of Richelieu's period (1630's).

**loo** (2), a water-closet, derives either from F *l'eau*, the water, cf Sc *Gardyloo!*, Beware the water! (F *gare à l'eau*); or, less prob, from OF-F *lieu*, place, as in *lieux* d'aisance, a 'lavatory'.

**looby.** See LOB.

**look** (v, hence n), whence **look-out, good-looker, good-looking, onlooker, overlook**, etc., comes through ME *lōken* from OE *lōcian*, akin to OS *lōcōn*, to look, and OHG *luogēn*, MHG *luogen*, G *lugen*, to look out.

**loom** (1), n, orig a tool, but long predominantly a frame for weaving: ME *lome*: OE *gelōma*, utensil, tool: cf OE *andlōman*, for *andgelōman*, utensils, and obs D *allaam*, for *\*andlame* (var *\*antlame*), the *and-* being akin to Gr *anti*, over against.

**loom** (2), to rise and fall, as the sea does, the obs origin of the sense, to come indistinctly into sight, as over the horizon, hence appear impressively or exaggeratedly: o.o.o.: perh (EW) from ON *ljōma*, to gleam, akin to OE *lēoma*, a gleam, a ray of light, themselves akin to L *lūmen*, light, a light: f.a.e., the 3rd LIGHT.—Hence the n *loom* ('loom of the land above the horizon') and vn *looming*.

**loon** (1), a bird, is a var of the syn *loom*, of Scan origin: cf ON *lōmr*, itself from echoic *lō-*, cf the *lā-* of L *lātrāre*, to bark. (Holthausen.)

**loon** (2), Sc for a (worthless) fellow, a lad: Sc varr *loun, lown*: prob cf MD *loen*, a stupid fellow.

**loony.** See the 3rd LIGHT, para 11, at *lunaticus*.

**loop** (n, hence v): ME *loupe*: ? of C origin—cf EIr *lúpaim*, Ga *lùb*, Mx *loob*, bend, fold, loop. The adj is *loopy*, whence prob the sl *loopy*, crazy —cf sl 'round the *bend*'.

**loophole**=the obs *loop*, a small (narrow) opening, ME *loupe*, app from MD *lupen, luepen, luipen*, to look slyly+HOLE.

**loose, loosen, looseness.** See LOSE, para 2.

**loot** (n, hence v, whence **looter**): Hind *lūt*: denasalized from Skt *lun̠ati*, he plunders.

**lop** (1), to cut branches or leaves from a tree (whence **loppings**), hence (**lop off**) to cut the head or the limbs off: rare OE *loppian*, perh akin to:

**lop** (2), to hang loosely, whence **lop-eared** and **lopsided**, is prob akin to the 1st LAP (a fold)—but perh cf LOB.

**lope.** See LEAP, para 2.

**loppings.** See the 1st LOP.

**loquacious, loquacity; locution; collocution** (whence anl **collocutor**), **colloquial** (whence **colloquialism**), **colloquy**—**elocution** (whence **elocutionary, elocutionist**), **eloquence, eloquent**—**inter-**

**locution**, whence, anl, **interlocutor, interlocutory—obloquy—prolocutor.**

1. The base of all these words is L *loqui*, to speak, presp *loquens*, o/s *loquent-*, pp *locūtus*, s *locūt-*, with derivative *locūtiō*, the act or a manner of speaking, o/s *locūtiōn-*, whence, prob via MF-F, the E *locution.—Loqui* has IE r *\*lokw-*, o.o.o., but perh akin to Gr *laskein* (? for *\*lakskein* for *\*lokskein* for *\*lokwein*), to prattle, to speak loudly, to shout; perh (E & M, approving H. Pedersen) akin to C *-tluch*ur in OIr *atluchur*, I thank, *duttluchur*, I pray.

2. *Loquī* has derivative adj *loquāx*, talkative, o/s *loquāc-*, whence (F *loquace* and) E *loquacious*; derivative *loquācitās*, o/s *loquācitāt-*, whence (late MF-F *loquacité* and) E *loquacity*.

### Compounds

3. L *colloqui*, to speak *col-* (for *con-*, from *cum*) with someone, to converse, has pp *collocūtus*, whence *collocūtiō*, o/s *collocūtiōn-*, whence, perh via F, *collocution; colloqui* has derivative n *colloquium*, whence *colloquy*, whence *colloquial*.

4. *Eloqui*, to speak *ē-* or out, to declaim, has presp *ēloquens*, o/s *ēloquent-*, whence, prob via MF-F, *eloquent*; derivative L *ēloquentia* yields, prob via OF-F, *eloquence*. On the pp *ēlocūt*us arises *ēlocūtiō*, o/s *ēlocūtiōn-*, whence EF-F *élocution* and E *elocution*.

5. *Interloqui*, to interrupt (someone, some persons) in order to speak, has pp *interlocūt*us, whence both LL *interlocūtiō*, an interruptive speech, o/s *interlocūtiōn-*, whence *interlocution*, and EF-F *interlocuteur*, prompting the E *interlocutor*.

6. *Obloqui*, to speak *ob-* or against, has LL derivative *obloquium*, whence *obloquy*, a censorious speech, hence a bad reputation, disgrace.

7. *Prōloqui*, to speak *prō-* or forward, hence openly, has pp *prōlocūt*us, whence the agent *prōlocūtor*, adopted by E.

**loquat** represents the Cantonese pron of Pekin Chinese *lu*² *chü*², lit a rush orange.

**lord, lordly, lordship.** See LOAF, para 5.

**lore.** See LEARN, para 2.

**lorikeet**=*lory*+parra*keet*.

**loriot.** See AUREATE.

**lorn.** See LOSE.

**lorry** was orig the Sc and North Country var of Yorkshire and Lancashire *lurry*, a flat, sideless dray, from dial *lurry*, to lug, to pull, therefore ult echoic, unless (EW) it be metathetic for earlier *rolley, rulley*, a coal-mining truck, which *rolls* along.

**lory**: Mal *lūrī* (var of *nūrī*).

**lose** (pt, pp lost), whence agent **loser** and pa, vn **losing;** loss and **loess;** loose, adj hence v, hence also **loose-strife** (trans of Bot *Lysimachia*: via L from Gr *lusis*, a loosing+Gr *makhē*, a battle, strife) and **loosen**, whence pa, vn **loosening**, and **looseness; lorn**, as in **love-lorn** and **forlorn.**—**lyse, lysis,** and **lytic**: cf the cpds **analyse** (or **-lyze**), **analysis, analyst, analytic—catalyse (-lyze), catalysis, cat-**alyst, catalytic—paralyse (-lyze), paralysis, paralytic**, cf **palsy**, n, hence v (whence **palsied**).—**solve, solvable, solvate, solvency, solvent** (adj, hence n) and **soluble, solute** (adj, hence n), **solution**: cf the cpds **absolve, absolvent**, and **absolute** (whence **absolutism, absolutist**), **absolution—dissoluble, dissolute, dissolution, dissolve, dissolvable, dissolvent—insoluble, insolubility, insolvent** (whence **insolvency**) —**irresoluble, irresolute, irresolution—resolute, resolution, resolve** (v, with pa **resolved**; hence also n), **resolvent.**—Cf the suffix *-less*.

### Indo-European

1. 'To *lose*', ME *losien*, to lose, earlier to be lost, OE *losian*, to become lost, to be destroyed (cf OE *los*, destruction, E *loss*), is akin to ME *leosen*, to lose—pp *loren*, often contr to *lorn* (retained by E) —from OE *lēosan*, to lose, with pp *-loren*, as in E-ME *forlorn*, pp of ME *forlesen*, to wholly lose, from OE *forlēosan* (pp *forloren*); akin to OE *lēas*, OFris *lās*, OS and OHG *lōs*, G *los*, Go *laus* (cf *usluneins*, a setting free, a release), ON *lauss*, free; to L *luere*, to loose, and *luēs*, the plague; to Gr *luein*, to loose, and *lusis*, a loosing; to Skt *lunáti*, he cuts off, *lavís, lavítram*, a sickle; and to Hit *lāiska-*, to unloose, app an aug of *lāi-*, to loose. The IE r, clearly, is *\*lū-* or *\*leu-* (both with vowels now long, now short), to detach, set free.

### Germanic

2. Akin to *lose* is the adj *loose*, ME *loos*, earlier *lous*, earliest *laus*, from ON *lauss*, free, loose: and akin to both is *loss* (see para 1), sem influenced by 'to *lose*', phon influenced by *lost*.

3. OHG *lōs*, free, bare, has derivative *lōsēn*, MHG *loesen*, G *lösen*, to free, to loosen, whence dial *löss*, an unstratified deposit of loam, whence E *loess*.

### Latin

4. L *luere*, to loose, perh imm from the syn Gr *luein*, appears, even in L, mostly in the cpd *soluere*, to detach, set loose or free, where *so-* is a var of the privative or separative *sē-*; the ML form *solvere* yields 'to *solve*', whence *solvable*. The presp *soluens*, o/s *soluent-*, ML *solvent-*, accounts for *solvent*, whence *solvency*; the pp *solūtus* accounts for *solute*, and the derivative *solūtiō*, o/s *solūtiōn-*, for *solution* (prob via OF-F); LL *solūbilis* (*solu*ere+ *-(i)bilis*), for *soluble*, whence, anl, *solubility*.

5. Soon apprehended by L as a simple v, *soluere* promptly acquires its own prefix-cpds, notably *absoluere, dissoluere, resoluere. Absoluere—*int (connoted by *ab-*) of *soluere—*ML *absolvere* becomes 'to *absolve*'; the pp *absolūt*us yields the adj, hence n, *absolute*; the derivative LL *absolūtiō*, the act of freeing, esp from sin or blame, o/s *absolūtiōn-* yields, via OF-F, *absolution*.

6. *Dissoluere*, ML *dissolvere*, explains 'to *dissolve*', whence *dissolvable*; presp *dissoluens*, o/s *dissoluent-*, ML *dissolvent-*, E *dissolvent*, adj hence n; pp *dissolūt*us, E *dissolute*, and derivative *dissolūtiō*, o/s *dissolūtiōn-*, E (perh from OF-F) *dissolution*; L *dissolūbilis*, E *dissoluble*.

7. L *solūbilis* has neg *insolūbilis*, whence E *insoluble*; derivative LL *insolūbilitās* gives us *insolubility*; formed anl from L *in-*, not+E *solve* are *insolvable* and *insolvent*.

8. L *resoluere*, ML *resolvere*, yields 'to *resolve*'; ML presp o/s *resolvent-* yields *resolvent*; pp *resolūt*us, E *resolute*, and derivative *resolūtiō*, o/s *resolūtiōn-*, MF-F *résolution*, E *resolution*; LL *resolūbilis*, E *resoluble*. The negg LL *irresolūbilis*, irreversible, and LL *irresolūtus*, incapable of being loosened or untied, prompt the forms of *irresoluble* and *irresolute* (whence, perh after EF-F, *irresolution*), which take their meanings from the E *re*-words.

## Greek

9. Gr *lu*ein, to loose, set free, has derivative *lusis*, a freeing, whence SciL *lysis*, whence *lysin* (Chem *-in*) and, via F *-lyser*, the c/f e *-lyse*, *-lyze*, whence the Chem v *lyse*. Gr *lu*ein has derivative agent *lutēs*, whence SciL *-lytes*; derivative adj *-lutikos* becomes SciL *-lyticus*, whence F *-lytique* and E *-lytic*, whence the Chem *lytic*. More important to E are the cpds.

10. Gr *analuein*, to unloose (cf the prefix *ana-*, on, up), hence to resolve into elements, has derivative n *analusis*, ML *analysis*, E *analysis*; its adj *analutikos* becomes LL *analyticus*, EF-F *analytique* and E *analytic*. ML *analysis* becomes EF-F *analyse*, whence the EF-F v *analyser*, whence 'to *analyse*, *-lyze*'; whence also the late EF-F *analyste*, E *analyst*.

11. Gr *kataluein*, to dissolve (*kata-*, down, connoting wholly) has derivative *katalusis*, whence SciL *catalysis*, whence the anl *catalyse*, *-lyze*, *catalyst*, *catalytic*.

12. Gr *paraluein*, to loosen—hence disable—*para*, at or in the side, has derivative *paralusis*, whence Med L *paralysis*, whence E *paralysis* and OF-F *paralysie*, whence EF-F *paralyser*, whence 'to *paralyse*, *-lyze*'; derivative Gr *paralutikos* becomes Med L *paralyticus*, MF-F *paralytique*, E *paralytic*.

13. OF-F *paralysie* becomes ME *parlesie*, softened (*r* to *l*) to *palesie*, whence E *palsy*.

**loss.** See prec, para 1.

**lost.** See LOSE (heading).

**lot** (n, hence v), **lottery, lotto; allot, allotment.**

1. A counter used in assigning a duty, a reward, etc., hence that which befalls, esp in an auction (e.g. of land); hence a large lot, coll 'a lot': OE *hlot*, akin to OE *hlēotan*, to cast lots: cf OFris *hlot*, OS *hlōt*, OHG *hlōz* or *lōz*, MHG *lōz*, G *Los*, Go *hlauts*, MD *lod*, *lott*, (as in D) *lot*, ON *hluti*, *hlutr*, also Lett *hļūtas*, fate, and perh Hit *luzzi* (? for *\*lutzi*), 'goods and labor due the state from all . . . not explicitly exempted' (Sturtevant); cf also OHG *hliozan*, to gain by lot.

2. Akin to those OGmc words is Frankish *hlōt* or *lōt*, whence EF-F *lot*, whence It *lotto*, a lot, whence the E card-game *lotto*. It *lotto* has derivative *lotteria*, whence E *lottery*.

3. AF has, in C14, the cpd *aloter* (cf the EF-F

*allotir*), whence EE 'to *alot*, *allot*', the latter retained by E; derivative AF *alotement* yields, in EE, *allotment*.

**loth.** See LOATH.

**Lothario**, a gay seducer (male), was orig a heartless rake in Nicholas Rowe's *The Fair Penitent*, 1703: a blending of F *Loth*aire and It *Lotario*: f.a.e., LUTHERAN.

**lotic, lotion.** See LAVA, para 5.

**lottery; lotto.** See LOT, para 2.

**lotus,** adopted from L, comes from Gr *lōtos* a reshaping of H *loṭ*.

**loud** (adj, adv), whence **loudness; listen** (whence **listener, listening**) and syn **list.**—**ablaut** and **umlaut; client, clientèle** (AE *-ele*), cf **clio;** perh cf the sep GLORY (GLORIFY, GLORIOUS, etc.).

1. The adv *loud* derives from OE *hlūde*, from the OE adj *hlūd*, whence ME *lud* and later *loud*, the latter retained by E: and OE *hlūd* is akin to OFris and OS *hlūd*, OHG *hlūt* or *lūt*, MHG *lūt*, G *laut*, MD *luut*, *lude*, D *luid*; L *in*clutus (int *in-*), Gr *klutos*, Skt *śrūtás*, famous; OIr ro-*cluinethar*, he hears; Arm *luay*, I have heard. Every one of the adjj was orig the pp of a v 'to hear'—e.g., L *-clutus* answers to *clu*ere, to be called, and Gr *klutos* to *klu*ein, to hear, *klei*ein, to celebrate. (OB *slovo*, a word, represents prefix *s-*+r *lov-*+ending *-o*.) The IE r is app *\*kleu-*.

2. The archaic *list*, to hearken, derives from ME *listen*, var of *lusten*, from OE *hlystan*; 'to *listen*' derives from ME *listnen*, var *lustnen*, themselves mdfnn of ME *listen*, *lusten*, OE *hlystan*, itself from OE *hlyst*, (sense or act of) hearing: cf OS *hlust*, hearing, OHG *hlosēn* (very closely akin to OHG *\*hlūskēn*, MHG *lüschen*, G *lauschen*), ON *hlust*, ear, *hlusta*, to listen; cf also Lith *klausýti*, to hear, and the L and Gr vv noted above.

3. Akin to G *laut*, loud, is G *Laut*, a sound, MHG *lūt*, the latter with var *liute* (OHG *lūti*), resonance, voice. G *Laut* occurs in the rather ambiguously named *Ablaut*, lit an off (*ab-*) sound, and *Umlaut*, lit an about (*um-*) sound. (Walshe.)

4. L *clu*ere, to be named, hear oneself named, has a differently vowelled cognate: *cli*ens, a dependant as opp a patron, o/s *client-*, whence, perh via MF(-F) *client*, the E *client*; derivative EF(-F) *clientèle*, adopted by E, derives from L *clientēla*, with suffix *-ēla* as in *sequēla* (E *sequel*). The fact that a dependant is called by the name of his patron overrides, perh, E & M's phon objection.

5. Gr *klei*ein, to celebrate or tell of and thus render famous, has derivative *Kleiō*, lit the Proclaimer, hence the Muse of History: L *Clio*.

**lough.** See LAKE, para 6.

**Louis, louis, Louisa** (Louise), **Louisiana, louisine; Lewes; Lewis, lewis, lewisite; Lulu, lulu.**

1. OHG *Hluthawig*, lit 'famous warrior', becomes OF of *Louis*, 'rendered fashionable by the Carolingians' (Dauzat) in 751–987. The f *Louise* becomes—perh cf It and Sp *Luisa*—E *Louisa*. The coin *louis* is short for *louis d'or*, a golden louis,

first struck by Louis XIII in 1640. The silken fabric *louisine* commemorates some manufacturer or dress-designer *Louis* or some modiste *Louise*. *Louisiana* anglicizes F *Louisiane*, from Louis XIV.

2. Now, the British PN *Lewis* merely anglicizes F *Louis*; *lewis* (var *lewisson*) the building term prob recalls that early builder who introduced it, whereas the Chem *lewisite* refers to the A chemist W. Lee Lewis (b. 1878) and Min *lewisite* refers to the E mineralogist W. J. Lewis (1847–1926).

3. *Lulu* is a pet-form of *Louis* and, usu, of *Louise* (*Louisa*): hence, prob, the A sl *lulu*, as in 'It's a *lulu*' (superlative): perh cf, sem, the sl use of *daisy*.

**lounge.** See LONG, para 7.

**lour.** See the 3rd LOWER.

**louse:** ME *lous*: OE *lūs* (pl *lȳs*, whence E *lice*): cf OHG-MHG *lūs*, G *Laus*, MD *luse, luus*, MD-D *luis*; ON *lús*; MBr *louen*, Cor *lowen*, W *lleuen*. The word is perh C: cf the C r *\*lou-*, to stink.

**lout,** n, v. See LITTLE, para 4.

**louver** (AE) and **louvre** (cf the *Louvre* in Paris), in Arch, derive from ME *lover*, adopted from OF, which has var *lovier*: OHG *lauba* (G *Laube*), q.v. at LODGE, para 4.

**lovable.** See the 1st LEAVE, para 7.

**lovage; Liguria** (whence **Ligurian**), **ligurite.**

*Ligurite=Ligur*ia, where it was first found + the *-ite* of Min and Geol; L *Liguria*, a region of N Italy, is named after the L *Ligures*, an ancient people, pl of *Ligus* (o/s *Ligur-*), whence the L adj *Ligusticus*, neu *Ligusticum*, whence *ligusticum*, this specific plant of Liguria, whence the LL corruption *leuisticum*, ML *levisticum*, with debased var *levistica*: OF *leuesche, luvesche*: E *lovage*.

**love** (v, n), **lovely, lover.** See the 1st LEAVE, para 7.

**low** (1), adj. See the 2nd LIE, para 10.

**low** (2), to moo, whence the vn **lowing**: ME *louwen*: OE *hlōwan*: cf OHG *hluojēn* and MD *loeyen, loyen*, D *loeien*: clearly echoic.

**lower** (1), adj. See the 2nd LIE, heading, s.f.

**lower** (2), v, to cause to descend. See the 2nd LIE, heading, s.f.

**lower** (3), v, to frown or look sullen, with var *lour*; **lurk,** whence **lurker.**

1. 'To *lower*': EE, and still occ, *lour*: ME *louren, lowren, lūren*, to frown, to lurk: MD *lueren* and (as D) *loeren*: cf MHG and MLG *lūren*, G *lauern*, to lie in wait, to lurk; cf also ON *lūra*, to slumber.

2. 'To *lurk*', ME *lurken*, var *lorken*, is akin to ME *lūren*: cf Fris *lurken*, to shuffle, or sneak, along. Dial var: *lurch*. Torp cfs L *luscus*, one-eyed, half-blind, and proposes a Scan *\*lu-*, to watch in the dark, lie in wait, etc.

**lowly.** See the 2nd LIE, heading, s.f.

**lox** (AE), smoked salmon: New York City Yiddish spelling of G *Lachs*, salmon, MHG-OHG *lahs*: cf OE *leax*, ON *lax*, Lith *lāšiša* (cf Pol *losoś*): Gmc r, *\*lahs-*; IE r, *\*lak-*, var *\*lok-*, with an *-s*

suffix: 'a word common to the N Sea and Baltic languages' (Walshe).

**loxia,** Med for wryneck, Zoo (*Loxia*) for a crossbill. Cf the (orig, Gr) element *loxo-*.

**loyal, loyalist, loyalty.** See LEGAL, para 3.

**lozenge:** MF *losenge* (1294 in Her, C14 in Geom): from the shape implied by Gaul *\*lausa*, a stone slab (B & W), and C-L *lausiae*, stone slabs: for the C origin, cf OIr *lia*, a stone, and the Gr (? of C origin) *lāas*, Attic var *lās*, a stone.

**lubber.** See LOB.

**lubric, lubricant, lubricate, lubrication, lubricious, lubricity, lubricous.**

L *lūbricus*, slippery, hence LL lascivious, yields E *lubricous*, with varr *lubricious* and (via MF-F *lubrique*) the now rare *lubric*; derivative LL *lūbricitās*, o/s *lūbricitāt-*, MF-F *lubricité*, E *lubricity*; and *lūbricāre*, to render slippery, esp greasy, with presp *lūbricans*, o/s *lūbricant-*, E adj hence n *lubricant*, and pp *lūbricātus*, E adj and v *lubricate*, whence, anl, *lubricator* and, for sense, *lubrication* (cf LL *lūbricātiō*, a slipping, o/s *lūbricātiōn-*). Ult akin to SLEEVE.

**lucency, lucent.** See the 3rd LIGHT, para 7.

**lucerne,** occ **lucern,** a forage herb, derives from EF-F *luzerne*: Prov *luzerno*, with sense transferred from *luzerno*, a glow-worm, lucerne having shiny grains: OProv *luzerna*, a lamp: VL *\*lūcerna*: L *lūcerna*, (oil-)lamp, from *lūcēre*, to shine: f.a.e., the 3rd LIGHT. (B & W.)

**lucid, lucidity.** See the 3rd LIGHT, para 8.

**Lucifer,** so bright before his fall. See the 3rd LIGHT, para 6, and cf the element *luci-*.

**luck,** whence **luckless** and **lucky** (neg **unlucky**), derives by aphesis from MD *gluc*, contr of *geluc*, var *gelucke*, cf D *geluk* and *luk*: akin to MLG *gelucke*, MHG *gelücke*, G *Glück*: perh of Scan origin—? cf G *locken*, MHG *lucken*, OHG *locchōn*, to entice, itself perh from the syn ON *lokka*. (Walshe.)

**lucrative, lucre; guerdon.**

*Lucre* comes, perh via late MF-F, from L *lucrum*, gain, profit, akin to OIr *lōg, luag*, ON *laun*, OHG *lōn* (G *Lohn*), Go *laun*, OE *lēan*, reward, and prob to Gr apo*lauein*, to benefit from: Gmc r, *\*lau-*, with extn *\*laun*; IE r, *\*low-* (Walshe).

2. L *lucrum* has derivative *lucrāri*, to gain, whence *lucrātīuus*, profitable, ML *lucrātīvus*, whence—via MF-F *lucratif*—E *lucrative*.

3. OHG *lōn* has cpd *widarlōn* (*widar*, against, cf *widdershins*), ML *widerdonum* (L *donum*, a gift, substituted for *lōn*): OF-EF *guerredon*, contr to MF-EF *guerdon*, adopted by Chaucer in C14.

**lucubrate, lucubration, lucubratory.** See the 3rd LIGHT, para 10.

**Lucy.** See the 3rd LIGHT, para 6.

**ludicrous,** whence, anl, **ludicrosity; ludo; victor ludorum;**—**allude, allusion** (whence **allusive**); **collusion,** whence **collusive; delude, delusion** (whence **delusive**); **elude, elusion** (whence **elusive**); rare **illude, illusion,** whence **illusionism, illusionist,** anl **illusive; interlude,** whence **interludial; prelude** (n, whence **preludial,** v), **prelusion** (whence **prelusive**), prelusory; prolusion, prolusory.—Cf the sep LAY, a song.

1. L *lūdus*, a game, s and r *lūd-*, is perh of C origin: cf OIr *lōid*, a song, MIr *lāidim* (r *lāid-*), I exhort, admonish, with OC r *\*leut-* or *\*lut-*, to be joyous; *lūdus* perh derives from *\*loidos*. Perh cf also Gr *loidoros*, insulting, s *loidor-*, ult r *\*loid-*.

2. ML *victor* (L *uictor*) *lūdōrum*, victor of the games; *ludo*, played with counters on a board, is L *lūdō*, I play, intimately akin to *lūdus*. The primary L adj of *lūdus* is *lūdicer*, neu *lūdicrum*, which, used as n, suggests the subsidiary adj *lūdicrus*, whence E *ludicrous*.

3. *Lūdere*, to play, has many prefix-cpds, the alphabetical first being *allūdere*, to touch—connoted by *al-*, *ad*, to—playfully, play with, jest at, hence to touch jokingly upon, whence 'to allude'; upon the pp *allūsus* is formed the LL *allūsiō*, o/s *allūsiōn-*, whence, perh via EF-F, *allusion*.

4. L *collūdere*, to play *con-* or together, hence to connive, has pp *collūsus*, whence *collūsiō*, o/s *collūsiōn-*, whence, prob via MF-F, *collusion*.

5. L *dēlūdere*, to play deceptively (connoted by *dē-*) with, to deceive, whence 'to *delude*', has pp *dēlūsus*, whence *dēlūsiō*, o/s *dēlūsiōn-*, whence *delusion*.

6. L *ēlūdere*, to play from, parry the blow of, whence 'to *elude*', has pp *ēlūsus*, whence LL *ēlūsiō*, o/s *ēlūsiōn-*, E *elusion*.

7. L *illūdere*, to play against, to mock, whence 'to *illude*', has pp *illūsus*, whence *illūsiō*, o/s *illūsiōn-*, whence, prob via OF-F, *illusion*.

8. LL *interlūdere*, to play *inter* or between times, or at intervals, has ML derivative *interlūdium*, a game between two periods of business, hence something light introduced to relieve heaviness, as in a medieval morality or mystery, ME *enterlude*, reshaped as E *interlude*.

9. L *praelūdere*, to play *prae* or beforehand, as an introduction, whence 'to *prelude*', has the ML derivative *praelūdium*, a preliminary entertainment, esp play, whence, perh via EF-F, *prelude*; on the pp *praelūsus* arise both *praelūsiō*, o/s *praelūsiōn-*, E *prelusion*, and LL *praelūsōrius*, E *prelusory*.

10. L *prōlūdere*, to play *pro-* or in advance, to attempt, to prelude, has pp *prōlūsus*, whence both *prōlūsiō*, o/s *prōlūsiōn-*, E *prolusion*, and LL *prōlūsōrius*, E *prolusory*.

11. To offset *prelude*, Mus has coined *postlude*—L *post*, after.

ludo. See prec, para 2.

luff (n, hence v): ME *luf*, *lufe*, *loofe*, windward side: OF *lof*, some contrivance for altering a ship's course: MD *lōf*: perh of Scan origin (? *\*lof*, cf Sw *lof*).

2. MD *lōf* (D *loef*) prob gives rise to *aloof*: *a-*, on+*loof*, the windward side (cf D *te loef*, to windward).

lug, n and v; luggage, lugsail (whence prob lugger).

*Lug*, to pull (as by ear or hair), to drag, ME *luggen*, is of Scan origin, prob Nor and Sw *lugga*, to pull by the hair, from *lugg*, forelock, o.o.o., but perh akin to OE *lūcan*, to pull up weeds, with many OGmc cognates; *lug*, a flap, an ear, is very closely related to, perhaps even derived from, the v—as *luggage* and *lugsail* certainly are. *Lugger*, a vessel carrying lugsails, perh owes something to fe*lucca*, which comes from It *feluca*, from Sp *faluca*, perh from Ar *fulk*, a ship.

lugubrious: L *lūgubris*, of or for mourning: L *lūgēre*, to be in mourning: akin to, ? rather from, Gr *lugros* (s *lugr-*, r *lug-*), sad, and—the *r-l* alternation—Skt *rujati*, he breaks, Lith *lužti*, to break; sem base, 'the violent ritual manifestations of mourning' (E & M).

lukewarm; lew.

*Lukewarm* is a senseless elaboration of the now dial *luke*, lukewarm, and prob distorts the now dial *lew*, itself from OE *hlēow*, akin to OE *hlēo*, a shelter: in a shelter, one is warm; warmth connotes shelter. *Luke*, ME *lewk*, has perh (EW) been influenced by D *leuk*, cool, dry, snug.

lull (v, hence n), lullaby; loll (whence pa, vn lolling), Lollard.

1. 'To *lull*', ME *lullen*, is clearly echoic: cf G *lullen*, D *lullen*, *lollen*, to hum a tune to, to lull, MD *lollen*, to mumble or mutter, to doze, L *lallāre*, to sing to sleep (perh for *la-la*, comforting sounds+*-are*), and Skt *lolati*, he moves to and fro, *lulita*, swinging. *Lullaby* perh=to *lull* a child to sleep+*a*+*b*'*y* for *baby*, but perh=*lull*+a comforting dissyllable.

2. ME *lullen* has var *lollen*, esp in sense 'to hang loosely, to droop', whence 'to *loll*'. MD *lollen*, to mumble, has agent *lollaerd*, a mumbler, esp as pej *Lollaerd*, a mumbler of prayers and psalms.

lulu. See LOUIS, para 3.

lumbago, lumbar. See LOIN, para 3.

lumber (1), n, (a jumble of) miscellaneous articles. See LOMBARD, para 2.

lumber (2), to clutter. See LOMBARD, both heading and para 2.

lumber (3), to walk heavily and clumsily: o.o.o.: prob akin to Fris *lomen*, to walk slowly and stiffly, to limp, from OFris *lom* (var *lam*; cf E LAME), lame; perh influenced by such E words as dial *clump*, *clumper* (var *clumber*), to walk heavily, and prob, in part at least, echoic. Hence the pa *lumbering*.

luminant, luminary, luminescence, luminous. See the 3rd LIGHT, para 9.

lump (n, hence v—including 'If you don't like it, you must *lump* it', to swallow as a lump, however disagreeable), whence agent lumper and adj lumpy: cf the prob equally echoic obs D *lompe*, a heavy piece: cf also CLUMP.

lunacy, lunar, lunate, lunatic, lunation, lune, lunette. See the 3rd LIGHT, para 12.

lung. See LEVER, para 12.

lunge. See LONG, para 8.

lupin or lupine, n, and lupine, adj; lupus, whence adj lupous; lobo. See WOLF, para 3.

lurch (1), n, v, a sudden roll, to roll suddenly, to

one side, is o.o.o.; a conflation of C18 *lee-larch*,
late C17 *lee-latch*, it perh derives—orig as a redup?
—from OF-F *lâcher*, to let go; form prob influenced by:

**lurch** (2), to prowl, now only dial, is a var of
*lurk*, q.v. at the 3rd LOWER, para 2.

**lure**, n and v; **allure** (v, hence n), whence **allure-
mènt**.

1. 'To *lure*' derives from EF-F *leurrer* (MF
*loirer, loirier*), from F *leurre*, a falconer's bird-like
contrivance for recalling hawks, whence the E 'a
*lure*': and EF-F *leurre*, late OF-MF *loirre* (cf
OProv *loire*), derives from Frankish *\*lopr*, bait,
lure—cf MHG *luoder*, G *Luder*, perh akin to OHG
*ladōn*, MHG-G *laden*, to summon.

2. EF-F *leurrer* has cpd *aleurrer, alurer*—to
recall (a hawk), lit 'to bring *a* (F *à*, L *ad*), to, the
*leurre*, lure'—whence late ME *aluren*, E 'to *allure*',
with derivative n *allurement*, partly displaced by
*allure*, which, although from 'to *allure*', was app
prompted by F *allure*, gait, the sem key being 'a
seductive gait'. F *allure* is OF *aleure*, from *aler* (F
*aller*), to go, to walk: cf the E *alley*.

**lurid**, whence the rare **luridity** and the normal
**luridness**, derives from L *lūridus*, yellowish, an
-*idus* derivative of *lūror* (r *lūr*-), a yellowish hue,
prob akin to Gr *khlōros* (r *khlōr*-), greenish-yellow:
cf YELLOW.

**lurk, lurker.** See the 3rd LOWER, para 2.

**luscious**, o.o.o., is prob aphetic for *delicious*, with
*licious*—not unknown among children—altered to
*luscious*, perh under the influence of:

**lush**, whence prob the sl **lush**, a drunkard, and
certainly **lushness.** See LANGUID, para 13.

**lust.** See LASCIVIOUS.

**luster**, gloss. See the 3rd LIGHT, para 13.—For
the rare sense 'lustrum', see LUSTRAL, s.f.

**lustful.** See LASCIVIOUS.

**lustral** is the L *lūstrālis*, adj of *lūstrum*, a five-
yearly purification, whence *lūstrāre*, to purify, pp
*lūstrātus*, whence 'to *lustrate*'; derivative *lūstrātiō*,
o/s *lūstrātiōn*-, becomes *lustration*. The L *lūstrum*,
which is employed by literary E for 'a period of
five years' and is occ anglicized as *lustre*, AE *luster*,
is prob akin to L *lauāre*, to wash, q.v. at LAVA.

**lustre, lustrous.** See the 3rd LIGHT, para 13.

**lustrum.** See LUSTRAL.

**lusty.** See LASCIVIOUS.

**lutanist, lute.**
The former derives from ML *lutanista*, from ML
*lutana*, a lute, itself prob from OProv *laut*, whence,
via MF *leüt* (F *luth*), the ME-E *lute*, a stringed
instrument: and OProv *laut*, like Sp *laud*, derives
from Ar *al-'ūd*, the (Ar *el*) piece of wood.—Cf
FLUTE.

**lute** (2), a clay element. See POLLUTE, s.f.

**Lutheran** is the adj of Martin *Luther* (1483–
1546), the leader of the G Reformation: OHG
*Chlodochar, Chlothacar*, whence *Chlothar*, whence
*Hlotar* and *Hludher*, which combine to form late
OHG *Luther*: lit, Illustrious Warrior. Cf *Lothario*.

**lux**, L for 'light, brightness'. See the 3rd LIGHT,
para 1.

**luxate, luxation.** See the 3rd LIGHT, para 14.

**luxe, luxuriant, luxuriate, luxurious, luxury.** See
the 3rd LIGHT, para 14.

**lycanthropy.** See the element *lyco-*.

**lyceum** is the Common Noun form of L *Lyceum*,
trln of Gr *Lukeion*, that gymnasium at Athens
where Aristotle lectured: named from the neighbouring *Lukeion* or temple of Apollo *Lukeios*, an
epithet representing either '(the god) of Lycia' in
Asia Minor or 'the wolf(-killer)', from Gr *lukos*,
a wolf—f.a.e., WOLF.

**lych-gate.** See LIKE, para 5.

**lye.** See LAVA, para 8.

**lying**: pa and vn of LIE, paras 1 and 2.

**lymph, lymphatic; limpid, limpidity; nubile**,
whence **nubility; nuptial** (adj, hence n, esp in pl);
**connubial;—nymph.**

1. The n *lymphatic* derives from the adj, itself
from L *lymphaticus*, distracted, frantic, (love-)mad,
a sense obs in E, the E adj going back to the sense
of the source: L *lympha*, water, whence EF-F
*lymphe* and E *lymph*, (poetic and obsol for) water,
with that special sense in An and Physio which
affects the adj in '*lymphatic* ducts and *l.* system'.
L *lympha* is perh a LGr reshaping of OL *limpa*, var
of *lumpa*, a dissimilation of Gr *numphē*, a goddess
of moisture, of springs, etc.

2. OL *limpa* app acquires the L adj *limpidus*,
water-like, hence as clear as water, whence, prob
via late MF-F *limpide*, the E *limpid*; derivative
LL *limpiditās*, o/s *limpiditāt*-, becomes late EF-F
*limpidité* and E *limpidity*.

3. Gr *numphē*, goddess of waters, hence a
nymph, also a young girl, becomes L *nympha*,
nymph, young woman, bride, whence OF, hence
ME, *nimphe*, E *nymph* (cf F *nymphe*), with adj
*nymphal* (cf LL *nymphālis*, of a spring); the adj
*nymphean* goes back to Gr *numphaios*.

4. Gr *numphē* is akin to Gr *nuos*, Arm *nu* (gen
*nuoy*), L *nurus*, daughter-in-law, Alb *nuse*, bride.
The IE r is app *\*neu*-, with *s*- var *\*sneu*-: cf ON
*snor*, OHG *snur*, G *Schnur*, Skt *snušá*, daughter-in-
law. (Hofmann.)

5. The IE *\*neu*- occurs in L *nūbere* (s *nūb*-, r
*nū*-), to marry, whence *nūbilis*, (of a girl) able to
marry, whence EF-F and E *nubile*. The cpd
*cōnūbium* (*co*- for *con*-, from *cum*, with), marriage,
has adj *cōnubiālis*, later *connubiālis*, whence E
*connubial*.

6. L *nūbere*, to marry, has pp *nuptus*, whence
*nuptiae* (f pl), a wedding, with adj *nuptiālis*, whence
MF-F and E *nuptial*.

**lynch**, in 1835 as v (whence the agent **lyncher**
and the pa, vn **lynching**), derives from **lynch law**,
earlier **Lynch law** (1811), earliest **Lynch's law**
(1782), 'named after Captain William *Lynch*
(1742–1820), of Pittsylvania County, Virginia, and
later of Pendleton District, South Carolina': a
compact drawn up in 1760 by Lynch and his
neighbours, to enable them to deal summarily,
orig not necessarily by hanging, with such lawless
characters as were—or seemed to be—beyond the
reach of the law. (Mathews.) Another Lynch

(Charles, 1736–96), a Virginian planter and Justice of the Peace, had perhaps something to do with the rapid spread of the term *Lynch('s) law*. (Webster.)

lynx. See the 3rd LIGHT, para 21.

Lyonnesse, occ Leonnoys, derives from MF *Leonois*, OF *Loenois* or *Loonois*, ML *Loonia*, app ult from the r of *Lothian* in Scotland but, in Arthurian legend, applied to a fabled country, lying between Cornwall and the Scilly Isles.

lyre, lyric(al), lyricism, lyrist. See LAUD, para 3. The Aus *lyre bird* has a lyre-shaped tail.

lyse, lysin, lytic. See LOSE, para 9.

# M

ma. See MAMA (heading—cf para 1).

ma'am. Cf *madam, madame*, at DAME.

Mac in surnames. See FILIAL, para 3.

macabre, adopted from F (1842 as adj), comes from F *danse macabre, macabre* being a scribal error for EF (danse) *Macabré*; cf OF *Macabré*, Macchbaeus, and ML (C15) *chorea Macchabeorum*, a *danse macabre*—lit, of the Maccabees, leaders of a Jewish revolt in C2 B.C. The sem association is obscure. (B & W.)

macadam, whence macadamize; tarmac.

The word *tarmac* stands for the trade-name *Tarmac*, for *tar macadam*, a bituminous road-binder, hence a road or surface thus treated; *macadam* derives from the Sc engineer, John L. *McAdam* (1756–1836), who, c1820, invented the process.

macaroni, whence the C18 fops the Macaronis; macaroon; macaronic.

Tubular *macaroni* re-spells the It pl *maccaroni*, dial var of *maccheroni*, prob (Prati) from the obs It *maccare*, to break, to break up. *Maccheroni* has jocular adj *maccherònico*, applied to verse that intermingles L with other IE languages, either in words only or in entire verse-lines, whence EF-F *macaronique*: whence E *macaronic*. *Maccheroni* has sing *maccherone*, with dial var *maccarone*, whence C17–18 E *macaron*, whence *macaroon*.

Macassar, as in *Macassar oil*, whence (to counteract its effects upon chair-backs) *antimacassar*, is a var of *Makassar*, a district and its seaport in the Celebes.

macaw (cf the EF *mecou*): Port *macó*: (prob) Tupi *macaúba*, the macaw palm, for the bird feeds on its fruit: a blend of Arawak *macoya* (from *amaca*, a hammock)+Tupi *úba*, tree. (Webster.) But Dauzat and B & W may be right in saying that the word is African (Bu, to be more precise) and was imported into Brazil by the Portuguese.

mace (1), club. See MATTOCK, s.f.

mace (2), a spice: ME *maces*, apprehended as pl: MF-F *macis*: ML *macis*: scribal error for L *macir*, the rind of an Indian root: LGr *maker* (var *makeir*): 'vox Indica' (Du Cange).

Macedon, Macedonia, Macedonian (adj, hence n), macédoine.

The last, a—usu, culinary—medley, is adopted from F, where it jests upon the diversity of races in *Macedonia*. Gr *Makedōn*, a Macedonian, has adj *Makedonios*, L *Macedonius*, E *Macedonian*; hence *Makedonia*, L *Macedonia*.

macerate, maceration. See MASON, para 2.

Machiavellian derives from Niccolo *Machiavelli* (1469–1527), Italian diplomat, ref the political principles enunciated in *Il Principe*, The Prince, 1513.

machicolate, machicolation. See MASSACRE, para 2.

machination. See para 2 of:

machine (n, hence adj and v), whence machinery and machinist (imm from EF-F *machiniste*); machinate, machination, machinator; mechanic, adj (now always in extn mechanical), hence 'a mechanic'—mechanics—mechanism, whence anl mechanistic, mechanize; cf the element *mechano-*.—Cf ult MAY (v).

1. *Machine*, adopted from MF-F, comes, through L *māchina*, invention, an invention, a machine, a device, a trick, from Gr *mēkhanē*, or rather from Doric *mākhanā*, from Gr *mēkhos*, Dor *makhos*, means, esp an expedient: akin to the Gmc 'may' words: f.a.e., MAY (v).

2. L *māchina* has derivative *māchināri*, to devise, esp to plot, with pp *māchinātus*, whence 'to machinate'; derivative LL *māchinātiō*, o/s *māchinātiōn-*, yields MF-F, whence E, *machination*; derivative L *māchinātor* is adopted by E.

3. Gr *mēkhanē* has adj *mēkhanikos*, LL *mēchanicus*, E *mechanic*; Aristotle's(?) (*ta*) *mēkhanika*, (the) mechanical things, becomes E *mechanics*. *Mēkhanē* has derivative n *mēkhanēma*, an engine, whence app the LL *mēchanisma*, whence E *mechanism*, and derivative v *mēkhanesthai*, to invent, to devise, which perh prompted 'to *mechanize*'.

macintosh. See MACKINTOSH.

mackerel: MF *maquerel* (later *maquereau*): ML *macarellus*: o.o.o.: but cf ML *megarus*, EIr *magar*, a small fish, and Ga *maghar*, a young fish, a shellfish. Being a spotted fish, it could derive from OC *\*mac*, to strike, to bruise (Malvezin).

mackinaw, a short, heavy coat, is short for *Mackinaw coat*: CanF *mackinac*: prob from *Mackinac* (Michigan), 'where stores were formerly distributed to the Indians': itself short for CanF *Michilimackinac*: Ojibway (Alg tribe) *mitchimakinâk*, great turtle. (Webster; DAF. Mathews notes that this etym has been contested).

mackintosh, prop but now rarely macintosh, a

371

waterproof cape, invented by an Sc chemist, Charles *Macintosh* (1766–1843).

**macrocosm**, great world, opp *microcosm*, small world: cf the element *macro-* and the r of COSMETIC (Gr *kosmos*, world).

**macula, maculate.** See the 1st MAIL, para 1.

**mad**, whence 'to **madden**', whence the pa **maddening**—**madly**—**madness; maim** and **mayhem; to mangle.**

1. *Mad* comes from OE *gemāed*, pp of a lost v from the adj *gemād*, mad: cf OS *gemēd*, OHG *gimeit*, foolish, also Go *gamaidans* (acc pl), crippled, ON *meitha*, to hurt, Lith ap*maitinti*, to wound, Gr *mistullein* (s *mistul-*, r \**mist-*), to cut into (small) pieces. IE r, perh \**mait-*, to hew.

2. Go *gamaidans* is akin to MHG *meidenen*, to castrate, MHG *meidem*, a gelding, Go *maidjan*, to alter, to adulterate, hence also to ME *maymen*, whence 'to maim', whence 'a maim'; ME *maymen* is a contr of ME *mahaymen*, from OF *mahaignier* (varr *mes-* and *me-*), to mutilate, to wound, of Gmc origin—perh the Go words cited here.

3. In Law, the n *maim* is spelt *mayhem*; ME *maheym*; OF *mahaing* (or *me-*), from *mahaignier*.

4. OF *mahaignier* acquires in AF the freq *mahangler*, soon contr to *mangler*, whence 'to *mangle*', to wound, hence to hack or bruise, repeatedly, whence the pa *mangled* and the vn *mangling*.

**madam, madame.** See DAME.

**madder**, a herb: ME *mader*: OE *maedere*: cf the syn OHG *matara*, MHG *matere, metere*, and ON *mathra*.

**made**: pt, pp of MAKE.

**Madeira.** See MATTER, para 3.

**Madeleine, Madelon.** See MAUDLIN.

**mademoiselle.** See DAMSEL.

**madness.** See MAD.

**madrepore**: F *madrépore*: It *madrepora*: It *madre*, mother (cf MATER heading)+either It *poro*, a pore, or Gr *pōros*, a soft stone—for both, see PORE.

**madrigal** comes, perh via F, from It *madrigale*: o.o.o.—perh, for obscure reasons, from LL *matricālis* (herba), an everlasting, n.

**maelstrom.** See the 2nd MEAL, para 2.

**maenad.** See MIND, para 5.

**maestro.** See MASTER (heading).

**maffick** is to rejoice publicly and hilariously, as England did upon the relief (1st May 1900) of *Mafeking* during the Boer War.

**magazine**, a warehouse or storehouse (e.g., of arms or cartridges), hence, in C18, a 'storehouse' of information or entertainment, esp in a periodical: F *magasin*: MF *magazin*: It *magazzino*: Ar *makhāzin*, pl of *makhzan*, storehouse.

**Magdalen(e).** See MAUDLIN.

**mage.** See MAGIC.

**magenta**, the dye (whence the colour), was discovered soon after the battle (1859) of *Magenta* in Italy.

**maggot**: ME *madok*, prob with *Maggot*, obs pet-form of *Margaret*, intervening: dim of OE *matha*, worm, maggot: cf ON *mathkr*, Go *matha*,

OS *matho*, OHG *mado*, MHG-G *made* (also MD-D), maggot, and Skt *mātkuṇa*, a bug.

2. Prob from ON *mathkr* comes ME *mathek*, maggot, with var *mawke*, whence the now only Sc and dial *mawk*, whence *mawkish*, maggoty, (hence) squeamish, (hence) tending to render squeamish, (esp) nauseatingly sentimental.

**magic** (adj, n), **magician, mage;** cf the element *magico-*.

*Mage*, a magician, is a gallicism, from L *magus*, which has adj *magicus* (after Gr *magikos*), whence MF-F *magicien*, whence E *magician*. The n *magic* comes from OF *magique* (prob via LL *magica*) from L *magicē*, trln of Gr *magikē*, elliptical for *magikē tekhnē*, magical art, *magikē* being the f of *magikos*, adj of *magos*, a magician, a sorcerer, from *Magos* (pl *Magoi*), a Magus (L form, with pl *Magi*) or member of the priestly caste of Media and Persia, from OPer *Magu*. L *magicus*, magical, becomes MF-F *magique*, E *magic*, now mostly in the extn *magical*.

**magister, magisterial, magistral, magistrand; magistrate**, whence **magistracy.** See MASTER, para 13.

**magma.** See MAKE, para 3.

**Magna Carta** or *Charta*: ML for The Great Charter, signed by King John in 1215: cf (*magnitude* at) MASTER and CHART.

**magnanimity, magnanimous.** See ANIMAL, para 6.

**magnate.** See MASTER, para 5.

**magnesia** (whence the SciL **magnesium**) is adopted from ML, which thus reshapes Gr *hē Magnēsia lithos*, the Magnesian stone: Magnesia, a district in Thessaly.

2. An inhabitant of Magnesia is Gr *Magnēs*, used as adj in *ho Magnēs* (*lithos*) and the var *hē Magnētis* or *Magnētēs* (*lithos*), the magnet, whence L *magnes* (gen *magnetis*), OF-hence-ME *magnete*, E *magnet*. The true Gr adj of *Magnēs*, a Magnesian, is *Magnētikos*, LL *magnēticus*, EF-F *magnétique* and E *magnetic*, whence, anl, *magnetism* and *magnetize*.

3. ML *magnesia* becomes, by metathesis, It *manganese*, whence F *manganèse*, E *manganese*, whence, via the s *mangan-*, both *manganite* (Min *-ite*) and *manganic* (adj *-ic*), *manganous* (adj *-ous*).

**magnet, magnetic, magnetism.** See prec, para 2.

**magnific, Magnificat, magnification, magnificence, magnificent, magnify; magniloquent; magnitude; magnum, magnum opus.** See MASTER, paras 4–6; for *magnum opus*, cf also OPERA, para 1.

**magofer.** See WEAVE, para 8.

**magpie.** See MARGARET, para 1.

**maguey.** See MESCAL.

**Magyar** is adopted from Hung: earlier *Mogyeri*: app a cpd of a derivative from *Manśi*, a Vogul, an Ostyak+Tu *eri*, a man.

**maharaja, maharani, mahatma.** See MASTER, para 2; cf REX, para 35.

**mah-jongg** (or, loosely, *-jong*) comes from the Cantonese pron of a Pekinese word meaning 'house sparrow': ? from the noise made by the players.

mahogany: obs WI Sp *mahogani*: ? Arawakan.

Mahomet, Mahometan. See MOHAMMED.

Mahori. See MAORI.

maid, maiden (whence maidenly), maidenhair, maidenhead, maidenhood.

*Maid* shortens *maiden*, ME *maiden*, earlier *meiden*, OE *maegden*: cf OE *maegth*, OFris *maged*, *megith*, OS *magath*, OHG *magad*, MHG *maget*, G *Magd* (maidservant), Go *magaths*, answering to OE *magu*, Go *magus*, ON *mögr*, OIr *macc*, OW *map*, Cor *māb*, *māp*, Br *mab*, Ogam *maqva*, son (MacLennan). *Maidenhair* (fern) is named from its delicate fronds; *maidenhead* is a var of *maidenhood*, OE *maegdenhād*.

maigre. See MEAGER.

mail (1), armour; macula, maculate—immaculate; maquis, maquisard; mascle, whence the adj mascled.

1. *Mail*, ME *maile*, earlier *maille*, OF-F *maille*, comes from L *macula*, a spot or blemish, hence, from the spotted coats of certain quadrupeds, the mesh of a net: o.o.o. Derivative *maculāre*, to spot or blemish, has pp *maculātus*, whence the E adj and v *maculate*; subsidiary LL *maculātiō*, o/s *maculātiōn-*, yields *maculation*; E *macular*=L *macula*, adopted by An and Med+adj suffix -*ar*. The LL neg adj *immaculātus*, unspotted, unblemished, (hence, fig) unstained, yields *immaculate*.

2. L *macula* becomes It *macchia*, whence, via Corsica, the F *makis*, now *maquis*, both being orig pl: these groups of shrubs or bushes form, as it were, spots or blemishes upon the Corsican mountain-slopes (B & W). Hence, in World War II, the F *maquisard* (suffix -*ard*), a member of the Resistance: cf, esp, George Millar, *Maquis*, 1945.

3. Prob from L *macula*, via ML *mascla*, var of *macla*, var of *macula*, derives AF *mascle* (F *macle*), adopted by ME for 'spot' and 'mesh', thence, in late ME-E, (Her) 'lozenge'; the ML, hence OF, -*s*- app comes from the intervention of OHG *masca*, mesh.

mail (2), a bag, e.g. a mail-bag, hence letters, hence 'to mail' or send through the post: ME, from OF-MF, *male* (F *malle*), a bag or a wallet: Frankish *malha*: OHG *malha*, *malaha*, wallet, akin to D *maal*.

mail (3), payment, tribute, tax, obs except in Sc, ME *male*, OE *māl*, tribute, price, derives from ON *māl*, an agreement, (orig) speech: cf OE *māēl*, speech, OS-OHG *mahal*, meeting-place, speech, Go *mathl*, meeting-place, esp a market: cf *moot* at MEET.

2. Hence *blackmail*, tribute exacted by freebooters in the Border Country: *black*, because crippling and disheartening. Hence 'to *blackmail*'.

maim. See MAD, paras 3, 4.

main (adj, n). The OE *maegen*, strength, akin to OHG *magan* and ON *megin*, yields both the E n *main*, with derivative sense 'considerable expanse', whether of land or of sea (as in *the Spanish Main*), and derivatively the adj *main*, influenced by ON

*megn*, strong; cf also MAY, v. The n *main* in card-games prob derives from the adj.

mainmortable. See MANUAL, para 21.

mainor (-our). See MANUAL, para 15.

mainprise (-prize). See MANUAL, para 21.

maintain, maintenance. See MANUAL, para 21, s.f.

maître d'hotel. See MASTER (heading).

maize: Sp *maíz*: either Haïtian Arawak or the very closely related Taino (an extinct Caribbean tribe) *mahis* or *mahiz*—as written first (1553) in F—or *mayz*.

majestic, majesty (cf *lèse-majesté*, q.v. at LESION). See MASTER, para 11.

majolica, adopted from It, derives from *Majolica*, early name of Majorca, where the ware was made. *Majorca* answers to ML *major*, L *maior* (see MASTER), the larger, as *Minorca* to L *minor* (see MINOR), the smaller.

major, majority; majordomo; majuscule. See MASTER, para 7.

make, to form (whence the n), whence maker and making(s), pt and pp made; such obvious prefix-cpds as remake and unmake; magma; match (n, hence v).

1. 'To *make*', ME *maken*, earlier *makien*, OE *macian*, is akin to OFris *makia*, OS *makōn*, OHG *mahhōn*, MHG-G *machen*, MD *maicken*, *maecken*, (as in D) *maken*: the nuances 'make' and 'build' derive from 'to fit together', itself prob from 'to knead' (hence, imm, 'to mould'—hence 'to fashion'): Gmc r ('to fit together'), *mak-*; IE r ('to knead'), *mag-*, as in Gr *magis*, dough, *mageus*, kneader, and *massein* (for *magsein*), to knead.

2. The sense 'to fit together' is strong in *match*, a spouse, hence an exact counterpart: ME *macche*: OE ge*maecca*: cf OE ge*maca*, whence the obs *make*, a spouse, an accepted lover, OS *gimako*, spouse, OHG *gimah*, fitting, convenient, ON *makr*, suitable, and *maki*, spouse.

3. Akin to Gr *massein*, to knead, is Gr *magma*, a thick unguent, form-adopted—via L—and sense-adapted by E Pharmacy and Geol.

malacca. See MALAYAN.

malachite. See MALLOW.

maladdress. See REX, para 9.

maladroit. See REX, para 7.

malady. See HABIT, para 14.

malaise. See EASE, para 2.

malapert. See PERT.

malaprop, whence the adj malapropian and the n malapropism, derives from Mrs *Malaprop*, maker of felicitous verbal confusions, in Sheridan's *The Rivals*, 1775. Her own name puns the F *mal à propos*, badly to the purpose, adopted by E as *malapropos*, adj, adv, n: *mal*, L *male*, badly+*à*, L *ad*, to+*propos*, cf the E *proposition*.

malaria (whence malarial): adopted from It, for *mala aria*, bad air. *Malarin*=*malaria*+Chem -*in*.

Malayan is the adj (hence n) of 'a **Malay**' and of **Malaya**, the earliest term, recorded first (644 A.D.) as *Malayu*; *Malay* owes something to F *Malais*.

Very closely akin is *Malacca*, a port and district in Malaya: cf *malacca*, a *Malacca* cane.

**malcontent** (adj, hence _n_): F: *mal*, badly+ *content*, pleased.

**male** (adj, hence n)—**mallard**—**masculine, masculinity; masculate** and **emasculate**, whence, anl, **emasculation** and **emasculative.**

1. *Male*, OF *male* (F *mâle*) for *masle* for *mascle*, derives from L *masculus*, of a or the male, hence the male, a dim adj and n, from *mās*, a male, o/s *mar-*: perh akin to MARRY.

2. OF *male* has the OF-(dial)F derivative *malart* (suffix -*art*, cf E -*ard*), a wild drake: E *mallard*, the common wild drake or duck.

3. L *masculus*, n, acquires the LL adj *masculīnus*, late OF-F *masculin*, E *masculine*; derivative MF-F *masculinité* prompts E *masculinity*.

4. L *masculus*, n, has LL *masculātus*, whence the rare 'to *masculate*', to render masculine. The derivative LL cpd *ēmasculāre*, to deprive of masculinity, has pp *ēmasculātus*, whence 'to *emasculate*'; *emasculation* is perh after F *émasculation*, formed anl from *émasculer*.

5. The orig vulgar L *masturbāri* has pp *masturbātus*, whence 'to *masturbate*', whence anl *masturbation*; derivative L *masturbātor* is adopted by E. E & M propose a phon and sem distortion of Gr *mastropeuein* (s *mastropeu-*, r *mastrop-*); but is not *masturbāri* rather a corruption of *mās*, *'male seed'* (semen)+*turbāre*, to disturb or agitate?

**malediction.** See DICT, para 7 at *maledicere*.

**malefactor** is adopted from L: from *male*, badly +*facere*, to make, to do.

**malefic, maleficence.** See MALICE, para 3.

**malevolence, malevolent.** See VOLITION, para 2.

**malice, malicious; malign** (adj, v)—**malignant**— whence **malignance** or **-ancy**—**malignity.**

1. L *malus*, bad, wicked, with adv *male*, OF-F *mal*, E *mal-*, as in *malcontent* and *malevolent*, app has IE r *\*mel-* alternating with *\*mal-*: cf Av *mairya-* (r for *l*), bad, Gr *meléos*, vain, Lett *maldīt*, to go astray, Lith *mēlas*, deception, lie, Ir *mellaim*, I deceive, MIr *mell*, (a) sin, OIr *maldacht*, malediction.

2. L *malus* has derivative *malitia*, mischievous evil, OF-F *malice*, adopted by E; derivative L *malitiōsus* becomes OF-MF *malicius* (EF-F *malicieux*), whence E *malicious*.

3. L *malus* has c/f *mali-*, as in *malignus* (opp *benignus*, E *benign*), for *\*malignos*, *-gnos* being prob the *gno-* of OL *gnōscere* (L *nōscere*), to know +nom ending -*s*. *Malignus* becomes OF-MF *maligne* (EF-F *malin*, f *maligne*), whence E *malign*; derivative LL *malignāre*, to render evil, ML to harm, to malign, becomes OF-MF *malignier*, whence 'to *malign*', the LL presp *malignans*, used as adj 'evil-hearted', o/s *malignant-*, yielding E *malignant*, whence, anl, *malignancy*; derivative L *malignitās* becomes OF-F *malignité*, whence *malignity*.

4. The L adv *male* occurs in many words sense-deducible from their 2nd element: as, e.g., *malefic* (cf late MF-F *maléfique*), *maleficence*, (an) evil-

working, and *malevolent, malevolence*, (an) evil-wishing (cf VOLITION; contrast *benevolent*).

**malinger,** whence agent **malingerer** and pa, vn **malingering,** derives from EF-F *malingre*, sick or sickly, weak, o.o.o.: perh (Webster) OF *mal*, badly +OF *heingre*, lean, emaciated, or OF-F *malade*, ill+*heingre*; or (B & W) *malade*+OF m*ingre*, ailing, the latter perh blending OF-F *maigre*, thin, emaciated, and *heingre*, var *haingre*, itself o.o.o., although prob of Gmc origin; *heingre*, however, is far more prob (DAF) akin to OE *hungrig*, OFris *hungerich*, hungry, and OE *hungor*, OFris *hunger*, OHG *hungar* (MHG-G *hunger*), ON *hungr*, hunger. Improb is the derivation (EP) of *malinger* from VL or ML *\*malingerere*, to introduce, or apply, or force oneself evilly (upon someone), hence to malinger.

**malison.** Cf *malediction* but see DICT, para 7 (at *maledicere*).

**malkin** and **grimalkin; merkin;** Matilda and Maud.

*Grimalkin* is an alteration of *graymalkin*, a grey (she-)cat; *malkin*, occ *mawkin*, is a dim (cf the suffix -*kin*) of *Maud*, from OF *Mahaut*, of the same Gmc origin as *Matilda*, from F *Mathilde*, from OHG *Machthilt*, 'Mighty Battle Maid': OHG *maht* (G *Macht*), power+OHG *hiltia*, battle+ 'girl' or 'woman' understood. App from *malkin* comes *merkin*, false pubic hair (of the female): cf, sem, the obsol sl *pussy*.

**mall** or **maul,** a heavy club or hammer, hence 'to **maul**', to treat roughly and injuriously; **malleable**— **malleate, malleation; mallet; malleus** (whence **malleal);—pall-mall,** whence, from being sited upon an old pall-mall alley, *Pall Mall* in London.— Perh ult cf the 2nd MARCH and the 2nd MEAL.

1. The obs game of *pall-mall* (wooden ball and mallet) derives from EF *palemail*, from It *palla-maglio*: *palla*, ball (cf the spherical BALL)+*maglio*, a mallet, from L *malleus*, mallet, hammer, s *malle-*, r *mal(l)-*, perh akin to OSl *mlatŭ*, hammer, and perh, ult, of C origin, Malvezin proposing OL *\*macleus*, from OC *\*mac-*, to strike.

2. L *malleus*, retained by An and Zoo, becomes OF-F *mail*, whence ME *malle*, E *mall*, mostly n, and its var *maul*, now mostly as v. OF-F *mail* has early MF-F dim *maillet*, whence E *mallet*.

3. L *malleus* has derivative *\*malleāre*, to hammer, with real pp-used-as-adj *malleātus*, whence 'to *malleate*'; subsidiary ML *malleātiō*, o/s *malleātiōn-*, yields *malleation*. From L *malleus*, erudite EF coined *malléable*, whence E *malleable*; derivative F *malléabilité* prompted E *malleability*.

**mallard.** See MALE, para 2.

**malleable; malleation.** See MALL, para 3.

**mallee,** a eucalypt shrub, esp a thicket or brush-wood of these shrubs: an Aus aboriginal word.

**mallet.** See MALL, para 2.

**malleus.** See MALL, para 1.

**mallow:** ME *malwe*: OE *mealwe*: ML *malva* (whence E *malvaceous*): L *malua*, akin perh to Gr *malakos*, soft, and prob to Gr *malakhē*, a mallow, whence, from the colour of the leaves, *malakhitēs*, var *molokhitēs*, app malachite, whence, via L, the OF *melochite*, E *malachite*. Gr *malakhē* is very prob a Medit word.

**malm.** See the 2nd MEAL, para 3.

**malodorous:** *mal-*, badly+*odorous* (f.a.e., ODIUM).

**malpractice:** *mal-*, from L *malus*, bad, evil+ PRACTICE.

**malt, maltose.** See MELT, para 3.

**Malta**, whence **Maltese** (adj, hence n), derives, by contr, from L *Melĭta*, earlier *Melĭte*, from Gr *Melĭtē* (adj *Melĭtaios*), which, the Phoenicians having colonized the island c1000 B.C., is prob Phoen: cf the Ar name *Mālĭṭah*. The tri-consonantal r *M-L-T* app either means 'place of refuge' or stands for Malta's ethnic deity.

**maltreat**, whence **maltreatment**. See TRACT, para 9.

**malvaceous.** See MALLOW.

**malus.** See MELON, para 4.

**mama** or **mamma** (mother), whence the nursery **mammy** and, via the nursery var **mummy**, the nursery and coll **mum; ma**, prob from *mama*; AE **momma** (orig an illit var of *mamma*), whence AE **mom**.—L **mamma**, the female breast, adopted by An and Zoo; **mammal**, adj hence n—cf Zoo **Mammalia; mammary; mammilla, mammillary.**

1. The safest starting-point is afforded by L *mamma*, primarily a woman's breast, hence a young child's name for its mother: hence the E *mamma*, mother (esp as voc), often in var *mama*, influenced perh by F *maman* and prob by Sp *mamá* and certainly, as a linguistic var, by the long-vowelled, one-*m*'d Sl cognates. L *mamma* is very closely akin to and perh derived from Gr *mamma* (μάμμα), var, ? orig the voc, of *mammē* (μάμμη). Cf also Alb *mēmĕ* and—in C—Ir, Cor, Br *mam*, mother, MIr *mamm*, breast, EIr *mumme*, Ga *muime*, wet-nurse. Gr *mammē*, *mamma*, is prob a redup: cf the Gr *maia* (μαῖα), voc *ma* (μᾶ). That all the ancient dissyllabic 'breast-mother' words are redupp seems prob in the light of Skt *mă*, mother, and in that of languages other than IE; the basic *mă*, which has var *mē* or *mĕ*, represents that most fundamental of all sounds, the cry or murmur of a babe for the breast. It seems not unlikely that this *ma* or *me* occurs in Eg *mentĭṭi*, the two female breasts, and in the syn Eg *mest*-t, breast, which vividly points to syn Gr *mazos* (cf Amazon): cf the Bu *ĕme* (approx) and the Aus aboriginal—? orig a dissimilation—*namma*, breast. Perh cf the *ma-* of MATER, q.v.

2. L *mamma*, breast, has derivative adj LL *mammālis*, whence *mammal*; *mammary*=*mamma* +adj suffix -*ary*. L *mamma* has dim *mammilla* (better *mamilla*), a nipple, adopted by An; the derivative adj *mamillāris*, inferior *mammillāris*, yields E *mammillary*. The Sci adj *mammate*, having breasts, was suggested by LL *mammātus*, pp of *mammāre*, to give suck, to suck.

**mamba**, a deadly Afr snake, derives from Zulu *im-amba* (for *in-amba*): cf the Swahili *mamba*, a crocodile.

**mamma**, mother. See MAMA.

**mammal, mammary, mammate, mammilla, mammillary.** See MAMA, para 2.

**mammon:** LL *mammōna*, orig *mammōnas*, both occ with one medial *m*: Gr *mamōnas* (μαμωνᾶς): from Aram, prob orig Punic, *māmōna*, riches: the sense (*M-*) 'demon of riches' occurs in LL. (Souter.)

**mammoth** (n, hence adj): Ru *mammot*, varr *mamont*, *mamant*: Ostyak *mamut*.

**mammy.** See MAMA (heading).

**man,** n, comes straight from OE (cf 'to *man*'— OE *mannian*—from the OE n), which has varr *mann*, *manna*, and *mon*, *monn*: cf OFris *mann*, *monn* (cf the Sc *mon*), OS-OHG (and MHG) *man*, G *Mann*, Go *manna* (cf the tribal deity *Mannus* in Tacitus's *Germania*, 98 A.D.), ON *mathr*, for **manthr*, itself for **manr*: cf also Skt *mánuš*, a person, and the Indian god *Manu*—and, for a vowel-changing form, OHG *mannisco*, var *mennisco*, MHG *mensche*, G *Mensch*, a human being, a person. IE r, perh **ghmon-*: cf L *homō*. The very attractive theory that *man* derives from the IE r of Skt *man-*, to think, Gr *menos*, mind, spirit, L *mens*, mind, E *mind*, is now discredited; it may yet be proved correct. (Walshe.)

2. *Manhood* certainly=*man*+abstract -*hood*; *mankind* prob=*man*+*kind* (*kin*), but it owes something to OE *mancynn*; as *manlike*=*man*+*like*, so *manly* (whence *manliness*)=*man*+-*ly*; *manikin*, var *mannikin*, derives from obs D *manneken* (MD *mannekijn*, whence EF-F *mannequin*, orig a figurine —cf D *mannetje*); *mannish* prob=*man*+euphonic -*n-*+-*ish* (adj), but owes something to OE *men(n)isc* (cf Go *mannisks*, ON *mennskr*), human.

3. To *unman*=*un-*, not (as used in vv)+*man*; *unmanly*=*un-*+*manly*. **Superman** (G. B. Shaw, 1903), which formally = L *super-*, beyond, superior to+*man*, translates Nietzsche's (earlier Goethe's, and even C16) *Ubermensch*, an 'over', hence vastly superior, person (usu apprehended as a male), an 'overman': cf the F translations *superhomme*, 1893, and *surhomme*, 1898: Nietzsche's relevant work, *Zarathustra*, appeared in 1883–85.

4. 'To *manhandle*', to treat roughly, orig 'to move by one's own, or by other, *human* force', is lit 'to *handle* as a *man* (not a machine) does'.

**mana**, the Polynesians' non-physical immanent controlling power of the universe, is a Poly word, which I suspect to be akin to Skt *man-*, to think, *mánas-*, sense, meaning (cf MIND), and to have been introduced by ancient traders from India.

**manacle.** See MANUAL, para 3.

**manage, management, manager.** See MANUAL, para 5.

**manatee:** Sp *manati*: Cariban, with cognates in other Caribbean languages.

**Manchester:** ME *Manchestre*: Domesday Book *Mamecestre*, which=L *Mamucium* (from Old British *Mamucion*)+OE *ceaster* (cf CASTLE). From the ML form *Mancunium*, comes the adj hence n *Mancunian*.

**Manchu** (adj, n), whence **Manchuria** (whence adj,

hence n, **Manchurian**), is a modern name, app derived from the Tatar name *Niu-chi* (or *Jurchin*), the Tatar people that overran N China in C12.

**mancipate, mancipation, mancipatory, mancipium.** See MANUAL, para 8. For the 1st, see also CAPABILITY, para 8.

**Mancunian.** See MANCHESTER.

**mandamus.** See MANUAL, para 9.

**mandarin,** a higher Ch bureaucrat, hence **Mandarin,** the Ch spoken by court and officials, derives, via Sp *mandarin*, from Port *Mandarim*: Mal *mantri*, a minister of state, borrowed from Hind: Skt *mantrin*, an adviser or counsellor: Skt *mantra*, advice, counsel: Skt *man-*, to think, as in *mányate*, he thinks: f.a.e., MIND. Hence *mandarin*, elliptical for *m. orange*.

**mandatary, mandate, mandative, mandatory.** See MANUAL, para 9.

**mandible,** whence **mandibular.** See MANGE, para 5.

**mandioc.** See MANIOC.

**mandolin; bandore.**

*Mandolin* derives, via F *mandoline*, from It *mandolino*, dim of *mandola*, a violent metathesis of LL *pandōrium*, var of *pandūrium*, itself an *-ium* derivative of LL *pandūra*, whence, via Port *bandurra* (? rather Sp *bandurria*), the E *bandore*; the var *pandore*, adopted from F, reflects *pandora*, the It shape of LL *pandūra*; the It var *pandura* also occurs in Mus. In all these terms, there are an ancient stringed instrument and a modern one (mandolin or 'mandolin-type'); cf the orig AE *banjo* (1774), either the Negro slaves' attempt at E and F *bandore*, or, as Mathews holds, a Negro slaves' importation of a genuinely Afr word, adopted by Europe, mostly from the WI, c1840. LL *pandūra* represents LGr *pandoura*, a three-stringed guitar: o.o.o.: perh Medit.

**mandragora, mandrake.**

The latter comes, through ME *mandrage*, earlier *mandragore* (? influenced by MF), from OE *mandragora* (surviving in E): L, from Gr, *mandragoras*: perh from a physician *Mandragoras* (Hofmann). The late ME *mandrake* is f/e (*man*+*drake*), because of the large forked root's supposed resemblance to the forked human.

**mandrill,** a large WAfr baboon, f/e cpds E *man* +E *drill*, a (smaller) WAfr baboon: EF-F sl *drille*, a vagabond soldier, often 'in rags': MF *drille*, a rag: OF *\*druille*, from OF *\*druillier*, to tear into rags: perh via syn OBr *druilla*: OHG *durchilōn*, to tear (into pieces, into rags): from OHG *durah* (MHG *durh*, G *durch*), through, prob via OHG *durhil*, *durkil*, MHG *durkel*, honey-combed; prob cf, ult, Gr *trōglē*, a hole, with IE r *\*trog-*, var *\*trug-*. (B & W; Walshe.)

**manducate, manducation, manducatory.** See MANGE, para 4.

**mane** (whence, e.g., long-maned): OE *manu*: cf OFris *mana, mona*, OHG *mana*, MHG *mane* (pl *mene*), G *Mahne*, MD *mane, maen*, D *maan*, ON *mön*—OIr *mong*, hair, *muin*, nape of neck, Cor *mong*, Ga *mong, muing*, mane—L *monīle*, necklace

(cf OIr *muinél*, nape)—Doric Gr *mannos*, necklace —Skt *mányā*, nape. Prob of C origin (Gaul, say both E & M and Hofmann); with IE etymon *\*monī*—for the *\*mon-* var, cf the Gr *monnos*, OSl *monisto*, necklace.

**manes,** spirits of the dead. See MATURE, para 2.

**maneuver** (AE). See MANUAL, para 14.

**manganese, manganic, manganite, manganous.** See MAGNESIA, para 3.

**mange,** a skin disease, whence the adj **mangy**; **manger** (for horses' fodder);—**manducate, manducation, manudactory; mandible,** whence, anl, the adj **mandibular**;—**munch** (v, hence n).

1. *Munch*, ME *monchen, manchen*, perh partly from MF *manger* (OF *mangier*, to eat), is basically echoic; in its mod form, it prob blends the obs E *mange* or the F *manger*, to eat, with c*runch*.

2. E *mange*, ME *manjewe*, derives from OF *manjue* or *mangeue*, an eating, hence an itching, from OF *manjuer*, OF-MF *mangier* (MF-F *manger*), to eat, from L *mandūcāre*, to eat (orig, popular L), to chew, from the n *mandūcus*, a glutton, from *mandere*, (of animals) to chew, hence (of persons) to eat greedily: perh (E & M) akin to several Gr words (ss *math-, mus-, mast-*) for 'jaw', 'mouth', 'to chew', and to MW-W *mant*, jaw.

3. L *mandūcāre* has derivative VL *\*mandūcátoria* (cf the LL *mandūcātor*, eater), whence OF-MF *maingeure* (F *mangeoire*), whence E *manger*.

4. L *mandūcāre* has pp *mandūcātus*, whence 'to *manducate*'; derivative LL *mandūcātiō*, o/s *mandūcātiōn-*, yields *manducation*, whence, anl, *manducatory*.

5. And L *mandere* has derivative *mandibulum* (suffix *-ibulum*, cf the *-abulum* of *stabulum* from *stare*), whence LL *mandibula*, EF-F *mandibule*, but MF hence E *mandible*.

**manger.** See prec, para 3.

**mangle** (1), a domestic machine; **mangonel,** a complicated medieval stone-throwing machine.

The latter, adopted from OF-MF, comes from ML *mangonum* (military sense), from LL *manganum*, a mechanism, trln of Gr *manganon*; the former, from D *mangel*, from *mangelen*, to mangle, from MD *mange*, a mangle, but also a mangonel, ult from Gr *manganon*. Gr *manganon*, the military machine, a pulley-axis, orig a means of bewitchment or deception, is an extn of the Gr r *mang-*, a deception, to deceive, by means of beauty: cf Skt *mañjus*, extn *mañjulás*, beautiful, very attractive, *mangalam*, good luck, Tokh A *mank*, a sinner, guilt, OP *manga*, a whore, MIr *meng*, deceit: IE r, *\*mang-* or *\*meng-*, to charm, to deceive. (Hofmann.)

**mangle** (2), the mangrove; **mangrove.**

The former, adopted from Sp, comes from Taino (extinct Caribbean language) *mangle*, the tropical, maritime shrub or tree we call a *mangrove*, which=this *mangle*+E *grove*: f/e, prompted by the fact that mangroves grow in groves or groups.

**mangle** (3), to hack severely. See MAD, para 4.

**mango; mangosteen.**
The latter, an EI tropical fruit, comes from Mal *mangustan*, app an extn or a cpd of Mal *manga* (from Tamil *mān-kāy*), whence, via Port *manga*, the E *mango*, likewise a tropical fruit.

**mangonel.** See the 1st MANGLE.

**mangosteen.** See MANGO.

**mangrove.** See the 2nd MANGLE.

**mangy.** See MANGE (heading).

**manhandle.** See MAN, para 4.

**manhood.** Scc MAN, para 2.

**mania; maniac; manic.** See MIND, para 3.

**manicate.** See MANUAL, para 4.

**manicure, manicurist.** See MANUAL, para 10.

**manifest** (adj, n, v), **manifestation, manifesto.** See MANUAL, para 11.

**manifold:** OE *manigfeald*: see MANY and FOLD.

**manihot.** See MANIOC.

**manikin.** See MAN, para 2.

**Manila,** occ **Manilla,** capital and principal city of the Philippine Islands, whence its application to cigars, envelopes, grass, hemp, etc.: Tagalog (orig a Mal race) *manilad*, place of *nilads*—white blossoming shrubs growing profusely around Manila bay. (Ency Brit.)

**manioc,** cassava: EF-F: Tupi *manioca*. Cf Oyampi (NW Brazil) *manihoc*, the plant, whence, via EF, *manihot*, and Tupi *mandioca* or *mandihoca*, the root, whence, via Port and Sp, *mandioc*.

**maniple, manipular.** See MANUAL, para 12.

**manipulate, manipulation, manipulative, manipulator.** See MANUAL, para 13.

**mankind; manly.** See MAN, para 2.

**manna:** LL *manna*: LGr τὸ μάννα (*manna*): Aram *mannā*: H *mān*, What is this?

**mannequin,** adopted from F. See MAN, para 2.

**manner, mannered, mannerism, mannerly.** See MANUAL, para 6.

**mannish.** See MAN, para 2.

**manoeuvre.** See MANUAL, para 14.

**manor** (whence **manorial**), **manse** and **mansion; menage, menagerie, menial.**—Cpds: **immanent** (whence **immanence, -cy**); **permanence** (var **-cy**), **permanent** (whence 'perm')—cf **pearmain; remain** (n, v), **remainder**—**remanent** (whence **remanence**), **remnant** (adj, n).

1. The structure rests upon L *manēre* (s *manē-*, r *man-*), to rest, to remain, hence to dwell: cf Arm *mnam*, I remain, Gr *menein* (s and r, *men-*), Av *man-*, Per *māndan*, to remain, and perh Tokh A *mäsk-* (? for *\*mansk-*), to be, and also OIr *mendat*, a residence, Ga *mainne*, a delay: IE r, *\*men-*, to remain.

2. L *manēre* becomes OF-MF *manoir*, to stay, to dwell, whence OF-F *manoir*, a village, a habitation (esp the most important one in a village: the *manor house*): ME *maner*: E *manor*.

3. L *manēre* has pp *mans*us, whence ML syn nn *mansa*, *-sus*, *-sum*, a farm, whence E, *manse*, a farmhouse, hence any homestead, hence, in Scotland, a minister's house; whence also *mansiō* (o/s *mansiōn-*), a staying, a residing, a residence,

whence OF-MF, hence E, *mansion*, now a rather grand house.

4. L *mansiō*, o/s *mansiōn-*, has derivative ML adj *mansiōnāticus*, of or for a house(hold), whence, via a VL n *\*mansiōnāticum*, the OF-MF *maisnage*, EF-F *ménage*, a household, partly adopted by E; its EF-F derivative *ménagerie*, administration of a household, hence a place where domestic animals are cared for, hence, in the 1670's, the modern F sense, whence E *menagerie*.

5. The E adj (hence n) *menial*, ME *meyneal*, derives from ME *meinie*, which, with its modern var *meiny*, is preserved as an hist term meaning 'body of feudal retainers or household': OF *meisniée, maisniée,* varr of *maisnie* (ME *mayne*): VL *\*mansiōnāta*, from L *mansiōn-*.

## Compounds

6. LL *immanēre*, to remain in (*im-* for *in-*) its own place, to remain in, has presp *immanens*, o/s *immanent-*, whence the E adj *immanent*, applied esp to the indwelling spirit.

7. L *permanēre*, to remain *per* or throughout, hence to the end, hence to last, has presp *permanens* o/s *permanent-*, whence the OF-F, thence E, adj *permanent* (hence as n); derivative ML *permanentia* yields OF-F, whence E, *permanence*.

8. L *permanēre* has the VL var *\*permanere*, whence OF-MF *parmaindre*, to last, whence OF-MF *parmain, permain,* a long-keeping apple, whence late ME *permayn(e), parmain, parmayn(e),* etc.: E *pearmain*. Thus EW, who, in 1921, exploded the derivation from VL *parmanus*, of *Parma* in Italy.

9. L *remanēre*, to stay *re-* or back, to remain, becomes OF-MF *remaindre* (esp il *remaint*, he remains), whence 'to remain'; the derivative MF n *remain* is adopted by E, but now always in pl *remains*. OF-MF *remaindre*, used as n, becomes E *remainder*, whence 'to remainder'. L *remanēre* has presp *remanens*, o/s *remanent-*, whence the E adj *remanent*, whence *remanence (-cy)*; and OF-MF *remaindre*, var *remanoir*, has presp *remanant, remenant,* used also as OF-MF n, whence, resp, the E adj and n *remnant*.

**manse; mansion.** See prec, para 3.

**manslaughter,** which=MAN+*slaughter* (q.v. at SLAY), anglicizes *homicide*.

**mansuetude.** See MANUAL, para 16.

**manta; mantel** (whence **mantelpiece**) and **mantle** (n, hence v—whence **mantling**); **mantelet** and **mantilla; mantua.**

1. Sp *manta*, a horse-cloth, a cape, hence in Zoo, derives from VL *\*manta*, from LL *mantum* (C7) or LL *mantus* (early C4), a mantle; one or other of these two forms must have existed in L, for L has the obvious dim *mantellum*, used by Plautus, c200 B.C., for a veil or a covering, and soon thereafter current for a cloak, a mantle: o.o.o.: Isidore of Seville (early in C7) postulated a Sp origin: it is, in fact, prob Basque—cf Basque *mantar* (*manthar*), a chemise, a plaster (which *covers*).

2. *Mantel* and *mantle* are sem divisions of one

word (cf *manteau*, a cloak, and *manteau de chemineé*, a mantelpiece): ME *mantel* (var *mentel* from OE *mentel*, from L): OF-MF *mantel* (F *manteau*), a cloak: L *mantellum*.

3. Whereas OF *mantel* has the OF-F dim *mantelet*, adopted by E, Sp *manta* has dim *mantilla*, adopted by E.

4. The old *mantua*, a loose-bodied robe, confuses F *manteau* and E *mantua*, a C17 fabric made at Mantua (Italy).

**mantis**, esp in 'the *praying mantis*', is SciL from Gr μάντις, a prophet, s *mant-*, r *man-*: cf Skt *múnis*, a seer, and perh ult Skt *mátis*, L *mens*, mind. The cognate Gr *manteia*, prophecy, occurs in many E *-mancy* cpds, e.g. *necromancy*.

**mantle, mantling.** See MANTA, para 2.

**mantua.** See MANTA, para 4.

**manual, manus.**—Simple derivatives: **manacle** (n, hence v); **manage**, whence **manageable, management, manager** (whence **managerial**); **manicate; manner**, whence **mannered, mannerism, mannerist, mannerly.**—*Man-* (*main-*), *mani-*, *manu-* cpds: **mancipate, manicipation, mancipatory; emancipate, emancipation, emancipator, emancipatory.**—Sep: LEGERDEMAIN.—**mandamus, mandatory, mandate, mandative, mandatory**—cf Maundy Thursday; **manicure** (n, hence v), whence **manicurist; manifest** (adj, n, v), **manifestation** (whence, anl, **manifestative,** often contr to **manifestive**), **manifesto; maniple, manipular, manipulation** (whence, by b/f, **manipulate**), whence, anl, **manipulative** and **manipulator; manoeuvre** (n, v) and AE **maneuver**—cf **mainor** or **mainour; mansuetude**—cf **mastiff; manubrium; manufactory, manufacture, manufacturer**—sep at FACT, para 3, s.f.; **manumission** (whence **manumissive**), **manumit; manure** (n, v); **manuscript** (adj, n), whence **manuscriptal; mainmortable—mainprise**—**maintain, maintenance.**—*Mand-* cpds: **command** (v, hence n), **commandant, commander, commandery, commandment, commando**—cf **commandeer; demand** (n, v), whence **demander, demanding; —commend** (v, hence n), **commendatary, commendation, commendatory—recommend, recommendation, recommendatory.**

1. The adj *manual* comes from L *manuālis*, an *-ālis* derivative from *manus*, gen *manūs* (s and r, *man-*), the hand, of Italic origin (Umbrian and Oscan), with Gmc cognates—cf OE *mund*, OHG-MHG *munt*, ON *mund*, all primarily 'hand', all secondarily 'guardianship, protection'—cf OFris *mund*, protection (not hand), and G *Vormund*, a guardian, and MHG *vormunde*, OHG *foramundo*, protector (*fore*, G *vor*, before); perh cf also OC *\*mana*, hand, implied in Cor *maneg*, a glove.—Is there ult a connexion with HAND?

2. The L adj *manuālis*, neu *manuāle*, has the LL-ML derivative *manuāle*, a handbook, whence both the syn EF-F *manuel* and the syn E *manual*. And L *manus* itself is retained in Roman Law and in international An and Zoo.

### Simple Derivatives of L *manus*

3 *Manus* has dim *manicula* (cf E *-ule*), little

hand, whence OF-EF *manicle*, adopted by ME, whence—? after *tentacle—manacle*.

4. *Manus* has derivative *manica*, a sort of glove, then a sleeve, whence *manicātus*, gloved, sleeved, whence E *manicate*.

5. *Manus* becomes It *mano*, whence *maneggiare*, to control by hand, whence 'to *manage*' and, via the It derivative n *maneggio*, the E n *manage*. It *maneggio* becomes, in its riding-school sense, the EF-F *manège*, adopted by E.

6. Besides *manuālis*, *manus* has the syn adj *manuārius*, whence the VL n *\*manāria*, way of handling, whence OF-MF *maniere* (cf the OF adj *manier*, f *maniere*, manual, adroit, supple, (finally) well-mannered): ME *manere*: E *manner*, fundamental in '*manner* of doing something' and cultural in 'perfect *manners*'. E *mannered, mannerism, mannerist* owe something to EF-F *maniéré*, F *maniérisme*, F *maniériste*.

7. *Manus* has one obscurely formed derivative: *manubrium*, a handle, adopted by An and Zoo, which coin the adj *manubrial*.

### *Man-* (F *main-*), *mani-*, *manu-* Compounds

8. *Manus* has the *cap*ere (to take) cpd *manceps*, he who takes in or into his hand(s), he who acquires, whence *mancipium*, a taking, hence a thing taken, in hand, a property, hence a slave, hence *mancipāre*, to sell, with pp *mancipātus*, whence 'to *mancipate*'; derivative *mancipātiō*, o/s *mancipātiōn-*, yields *mancipation*, in Roman Law the transfer of a slave, whence, anl, the adj *mancipatory*. *Mancipāre* has cpd *ēmancipāre*, to take *ē*, out of, slavery, pp *ēmancipātus*, whence 'to *emancipate*', to free; derivative *ēmancipātiō*, o/s *ēmancipātiōn-*, yields *emancipation*; LL *ēmancipātor* is adopted by E, which then forms, anl, the adjj *emancipatory* and *emancipative*.

9. *Manus* has the *dare* (to give) cpd *mandāre*, to entrust (something) to, hence to charge (someone) with, to command, to recommend to, whence, via OF *mander*, the obs 'to *mand*'; *mandamus*, we charge or command, has become a Law n; derivative LL *mandātārius* yields *mandatary*, and LL *mandātōrius* yields *mandatory*. The pp *mandātus* has neu *mandātum*, used as n, whence *mandate* (cf the F *mandat*), an official order, a prescript; the Sc *mandation* comes from LL *mandātiōn-*, o/s of *mandātiō*; *mandator* is adopted from L; *mandative* comes from LL *mandātīuus* (ML *-īvus*). Cf *Maundy* Thursday, from the injunction to wash the feet of the poor (*John*, xiii, 5 and 34), esp, later, on the *Thursday* of Holy Week: ME *maunde*, a command, OF-MF *mande*, L *mandātum*.

10. Only at the F stage does *manicure*, the care (F *cure*, L *cūra*) of the hands, arise; the adopted E word acquires the derivative *manicurist* (*-ist*).

11. L *manufestus*, lit either 'given' or 'taken' by the hand, hence palpable or obvious, has var *manifestus*, whence, perh via OF-F *manifeste*, the E adj *manifest*. Derivative L *manifestāre*, to render evident, accounts—perh via OF-F *manifester*—for 'to *manifest*'. The E n *manifest* derives from the

EF-F *manifeste*, from It *manifesto*, itself adopted by E, from It, from L, *manifestāre*. Derivative L *manifestātiō*, o/s *manifestātiōn-* leads, perh via OF-F, to E *manifestation*.

12. L *manus* has cpd *manipulus* (early var *manupulus*), a handful of men, esp a military section, whence the MF-EF *manipule*, contr to *maniple*, the latter adopted by E, where extant only as an Eccl term for an ornamental handkerchief carried in the hand; the derivative L adj *manipulāris* becomes E *manipular*. Prob the 2nd L element derives from *plēre*, to fill (cf *plēnus*, full).

13. MF-EF *manipule* has erudite F derivative *manipulation*, duly adopted by E, which therefrom coins, anl, 'to *manipulate*' (cf F *manipuler*), whence, in turn, *manipulator* (cf F *manipulateur*).

14. VL *manuopera*, work by hand, from VL *manu operāre*, to work by hand, becomes OF *manuevre*, whence F *manoeuvre*, adopted by E; the VL v becomes OF *manuevrer*, F *manoeuvrer*, whence 'to *manoeuvre*': for both n and v, the A spelling is *maneuver*. Hence *manoeuvrable*, *maneuvrable*.

15. The OF n *manuevre*, manual labour, hence the necessary materials, has derivative AF *meinoure*, whence the Law term *mainour* or *mainor* or rare *manner*.

16. L *manus* has, with *suēscere*, to accustom (from *sui*, of one's own, from the adj *suus*, one's own), the cpd *mansuēscere*, to accustom oneself to, whence *mansuētus*, accusto med, hence domesticated, tame, gentle, whence the obsol E *mansuete*; derivative L *mansuētudō* becomes, perh via MF-F, *mansuetude*. L *mansuētus* has derivative VL *\*mansuētinus*, tamed, hence a watch-dog, whence OF *mastin*, whence ME *mastif* (with *-if* from OF *mestif*, a mongrel dog), E *mastiff*.

17. For *manufacture*, *manufactory*, etc., see FACT, para 3, s.f.

18. L *manus* forms with *ēmittere*, to send (*mittere*) forth (*ē-*), the cpd *manumittere*, (lit) to send forth by, or from, the hand, hence to release, free, a slave, whence 'to *manumit*'; derivative *manumissiō*, o/s *manumissiōn-*, becomes MF-F, hence E, *manumission*.

19. The OF *manuevrer* of para 14 has var *manouvrer*, with derivative sense 'to till the soil', whence E 'to *manure*', now mostly 'to fertilize' the soil, whence the n.

20. L *manu scriptus*, written (cf SCRIBE, a writer) by hand, whence the E adj *manuscript*, acquires the LL *manuscriptiō*, a written paper, which suggested ML *manuscriptum*, something hand-written, whence the E n *manuscript*.

21. F *main-* cpds, besides *mainour* (para 15), include:

*mainmortable*, adopted by E: an *-able* derivative of F *mainmorte*, (lit), dead hand; the E *mortmain*, from OF *mortemain*, from ML *mortua manus*, (lit) dead hand, i.e. lands possessed by Eccl institutions: ecclesiastics were, medievally, held to be, in Civil Law, dead;

AF *mainprise*, (lit) hand taken, whence the now

only hist E *mainprise* or *-prize*: from MF *mainprendre*, to undertake suretyship, to go bail, the 2nd element deriving from L *prehendere*, to seize (OF-F *prendre*, to take);

OF-F *maintenir*, whence 'to *maintain*': VL *\*manutenire*, from VL *manutenere*, from L *manu tenēre*, to hold (*tenēre*, cf TENABLE), hence to keep, in the hand; derivative OF-EF *maintenance* is adopted by E.

## *Mand-* Compounds

22. L *mandāre* (para 9) has VL cpd *\*commandāre*, whence OF-MF *comander*, whence ME *comaunden*, var *commanden*, whence 'to *command*', whence 'a *command*', perh influenced by OF *comande* (F *commande*). OF-MF *comander* has derivative OF-MF *comandement* (later *commandement*), whence E *commandment*; also *comandant*, presp used as n, whence E *commandant*; also OF-MF *comandeor*, whence E *commander* (cf F *commandeur*); and also MF-F *commanderie*, whence E *commandery*. 'To *commandeer*' (whence vn *commandeering*) comes—via Afr *kommandeeren*, as in E, itself from D *kommandeeren*, to command —from F *commander* (OF *comander*). Afr *commando*, from D, is adopted from Port *commando*, itself from It or L.

23. L *mandāre* has L cpd *dēmandāre*, to entrust (*mandāre*) from (*de*) oneself, whence LL 'to demand': OF-F *demander*: E 'to *demand*'; the derivative OF-F n *demande* yields 'a *demand*'.

24. The 'prompter' of VL *\*commandāre* was L *commendāre*, an int (connoted by *con-*, with, together) of *mandāre*: 'to entrust utterly to, to recommend a person, (euphem) to command': whence 'to *commend*', whence Eccl and Legal 'a *commend*'. Derivative L *commendābilis* becomes EF, hence E, *commendable*; L *commendātiō* (from the pp *commendā*tus), o/s *commendātiōn-*, becomes OF-F, hence E, *commendation*; the ML n *commendatārius* yields the E n *commendatary*, and the LL adj *commendātōrius* yields the E adj *commendatory*; the ML agent *commendātor* is adopted as an E Law and Eccl term.

25. L *commendāre* develops its own cpd: the virtually syn ML *recommendāre*, whence 'to *recommend*', whence *recommendable*; derivative ML *recommendātiō*, o/s *recommendātiōn-*, accounts for *recommendation* (cf the OF-F *recommandation*), whence, anl, *recommendatory*.

**manubrial, manubrium.** See prec, para 7.

**manufacture, manufacturer, manufactory.** See FACT, para 3, s.f.

**manumission, manumit.** See MANUAL, para 18.

**manure.** See MANUAL, para 19.

**manus.** See MANUAL, para 1.

**manuscript.** See MANUAL, para 20.

**Manx** (adj, hence n): *Mansk*, contr of *Manisk*: prob from a Scan adj: from C *Man*, the Isle of Man: W *mān*, small (sc island)—cf the Cor prefix *man-*, small.

**many** (adj, hence n); c/f *mani-*, as in the adj

**manifold** (cf OFris *manichfald*), of, or with, many a fold.

*Many:* ME *mani* (var *moni*): OE *manig* (var *monig*): cf OFris *manich, monig,* OS and OHG *manag,* MHG *manec,* G *manch,* MD *manich, menich,* D *menig,* Go *manags,* OSl *mŭnogŭ,* many, and OIr *menicc,* frequent (cf the prec), also modern Scan.

**Maori; Mahori,** the Polynesian languages regarded as one. With *Maori,* app orig an adj, perh cf the *Moriori* or natives of the Chatham Islands in the S. Pacific; ? 'the *Big* Men' or 'the *Indigenous* Men'.

**map** (n, hence v); **nappe, napery, napkin; nape** of neck; **apron.**

1. *Map*: MF *mappe*monde: OF *mapa*monde: ML *mappa* mundi, lit 'napkin, or small sheet, of the world' (cf LL *mappa,* a linen book): L *mappa,* a napkin, a cloth thrown into the ring as a signal to start the games or other public show: a Carthaginian word (i.e., of a Phoen dial), says Quintilian (C1 A.D.).

2. L *mappa* is dissimilated in F *nappe,* sense-adapted by E Geol and Geom. OF *nape* has derivative *naperie,* whence E *napery,* and E takes OF-MF *nape* and derives the dim *napkin* (*-kin*); moreover, the obscure ME-E *nape* of the neck is perh a sense-adaptation of OF-MF *nape,* for it is the flat part.

3. OF *nape* has the further derivative *naperon* (F *napperon*), whence ME *napron,* whence, *a napron* being apprehended as *an apron,* the E *apron.*

**maple:** OE *mapul*trēow, maple tree, varr *mapolder, -ulder:* cf ON *möpurr* (for *\*mapulr*) and OHG *mazzaltra, -oltra:* Gmc r, app *\*mapl-.* (Walshe.)

**maquis, maquisard.** See the 1st MAIL, para 2.

**mar.** See SMART, para 2.

**marathon:** *Marathon race:* Gr *Marathōn:* the victory gained by the Greeks in 490 B.C. was announced to the waiting Athenians by a messenger running from *Marathon* to Athens.

**maraud** (whence pa and vn **marauding**), **marauder.**

The latter derives from F *maraudeur,* which derives from F *marauder,* to raid and plunder, whence 'to *maraud*': and F *marauder* derives from EF *maraud,* a vagabond, itself perh humorous from the central and western F dial *maraud,* a tom-cat, itself echoic. (B & W.)

**marble** (n, hence adj and v—whence **marbled**); **marmoreal.**

*Marble* derives from ME *marbel,* var (*l* for *r*) of ME-from-OF *marbre,* dissimilation of L *marmor:* Gr *marmaros,* orig a boulder, a large stone, hence—influenced by *marmairein,* to gleam or shimmer—marble: cf Skt *márīcis,* var *marīcī,* a ray or beam of light; and perh L *merus,* pure. (Hofmann.)

2. L *marmor* has adj *marmoreus,* whence F *marmoréen* and E *marmoreal.*

**marc.** See the 2nd MARCH, para 2.

**March:** OF *march,* var of *marz* (F *mars*): L

(*mensis*) *Martius,* month of *Mars* (gen *Martis*), God of war: OL *Mauors* (gen *Mauortis*): perh cf Gr *mar*nasthai, to fight, and therefore ult akin to E MAR.

2. L *Mars* has adj *martiālis,* whence E *martial.*

**march** (1), a border, usu in pl **marches**; with cognate v. See MARK, para 3.

**march** (2), to walk like a soldier, with cognate n; **démarche; marc; mush,** to journey afoot, usu with dogs, through the snow.

1. 'A *march*' derives from F *marche,* from late MF-F *marcher,* to march, whence 'to *march*'; this F sense derives from OF-MF *marcher,* to trample (stamp on with one's feet): either from the approx syn Frankish *\*markōn* or from VL *\*marcāre* (id), itself from LL *marcus,* a hammer, from syn L *marculus* (later apprehended as a dim): prob akin to L *malleus,* a hammer (cf MALL, para 2).

2. OF-MF *marcher,* to trample, has the OF-MF cpd *demarcher,* to trample *de-* or down, whence EF-F *démarche,* which, in its modern diplomatic sense 'step', is adopted by E; its other derivative, the EF-F *marc,* the residue after grapes have been trampled for wine, is also adopted.

3. The Can *mush* (also a call to the dogs) app shortens *Mush on!,* Press on, a 'Hobson-Jobson' of the F Can hunters', trappers', fur-sledders' *Marchons!* ('March on!'), addressed to their huskies. (Webster.)

**marchioness.** See MARK, para 4, s.f.

**marchpane** and (imm from G) its var **marzipan** both derive from It *marzapane,* C14–15 *marciapane:* Venetian *matapan:* ML *matapanus,* a Venetian coin (imitated from the Ar) with an enthroned Christ, a small box: Ar *mauthabān,* a king seated, esp as figured on a coin. C14 It developed the sense 'a (fancy) box for sweetmeats, esp for this sweetmeat'; MF (C14 *marcepain,* C15 *massepain*—as still) borrowed this sense; C16 EF inaugurated the modern sense, which E adopted. (B & W, Dauzat; Prati.)

**mare** (1), female horse: ME, from OE, *mere,* OE varr *mīere, mȳre:* f of OE *mearh,* horse: cf OFris *merie,* OS *meria,* OHG *meriha, merha,* MHG *merha,* G *Mähre,* MD *marie, merie,* D *merrie,* ON *merr;* with OE *mearh,* horse, cf OFris *mar,* OHG *marh, marah,* ON *marr.* Perh of C origin: cf EIr and Ga *marc,* OW *march,* Cor *margh* (and *march*), Br *marh,* a horse; OC *\*markā,* mare, and *\*markos,* horse.

2. OHG *marah* cpds with *scalc,* a servant (cf OE *scealc*), to form *marahscalc,* horse-servant, MHG *marschale,* overseer of armed retainers: either the latter becomes OF-MF, hence ME, *mareschal,* whence (F *maréchal* and) E *marshal,* or the former becomes LL *mariscalcus,* whence OF *mareschal.* The OF word developed into *maréchal-ferrant,* blacksmith, and into *maréchal,* a marshal of the army; in E, the latter sense (influenced by G *Marschall*) is obs, except in *Field Marshal.* 'To *marshal*' follows naturally from the military *marshal.*

**mare** (2), incubus, is obs except in *nightmare*

(which oppresses one at night); it derives from OE *mara*, akin to the syn OHG and ON *mara*, MHG *mare*, G *Mahr*, Cz *mŭra*, Pol *mora*, OIr *mor*-rigain, queen of the elves, and perh to Skt *mṛṇāti*, he crushes (cf SMART).

Margaret (pet-forms **Margie**, **Mag(gie)**, **Meg**), with var **Margery** (OF *Margerie*, of id origin as *Margaret*), itself with var **Marjorie** or **-ry**; **margaric**, **margarin** and **-ine**; **margarita**—cf **margarite** and **marguerite**.—magpie.

1. **Magpie**=**Mag**, short for *Maggot*, from F *Margot*, dim of *Marguerite*, from L *margarīta* (next para)+E-ME *pie*, OF *pie*, L *pica*, a magpie, akin to L *picus*, woodpecker, and Skt *pika*, the Indian cuckoo: hence ult to E *peck* and *pick*, vv, and *pike*, n.

2. The L *margarīta*, a pearl, forms the true base, even though it derives from Gr *margaritēs*, elliptical for *margaritēs lithos* (stone), from *margaron*, a pearl, from *margaros*, a pearl-oyster, itself app of Eastern origin: cf the cognate Skt *mañjarī*, a pearl, but also a flower-bud, which prob forms the orig sense, for it is clearly the more basic one. *Margarita* survives as an Eccl term, and its predominant late OF-F derivative *margarite*, orig a pearl, as a Min term. The F form occurs in the adopted-by-E flower-name *marguerite*, from the MF *margerite* (var of *margarite*, a pearl).

3. Gr *margaron*, pearl, has a direct erudite-F derivative: *margarique*, whence E *margaric*; from *margarique* comes the F *margarine*, whence Chem E *margarin* and ordinary F *margarine*.

**marge**, **margent**. See MARK, para 7.

**margin**, **marginal**. See MARK, para 7.

**margrave**, **margravine**. See MARK, para 4.

**marguerite**. See MARGARET, para 2, s.f.

**Maria**, **Marian**, **Mariana**; **Marianne**; **marigold**. See MARY.

**marijuana** or **marihuana**: ASp *mariguana*, var *marihuana*: o.o.o. For *mariguana*, a 'vulgar Mexican name for the common hemp'—whence its A use—Santamaria tentatively suggests origin in *Mariguana*, one of the islands forming the Bahamas.

**marinade**, **marinate**. See the 2nd MERE, para 3.

**marine**, **mariner**. See 2nd MERE, para 3.

**Mariolatry**; **Marion**, **marionette**; **Marist**. See MARY.

**marish**. See the 2nd MERE, para 7.

**marital**. See MARRY, para 2.

**maritime**. See the 2nd MERE, para 4.

**marjoram**: ME *marjoran*: MF *marjorane*, *-aine*, app an alteration of MF *mariolaine* (o.o.o.), ? by f/e from ML *marjorana*, var of *marjoraca*: prob aphetic from L *amāracus* and *-cum*: Gr *amarakos* or *-on*: o.o.o.: ? orig Dravidian (Hofmann).

**Marjorie**, **-y**. See MARGARET (heading).

**mark**, the coin. See para 1 of the next, where also *mark*, boundary, sign.

**mark**, v, derives from ME *marken*, earlier *merken*, from OE *mearcian*, itself from OE *mearc*, var *merc*, a limit or boundary, hence a boundary-sign, whence, via ME *marke*, *merke*, the n *mark*,

(obs) a limit, (hence) goal, target, hence the indication thereof, hence any sign. OE *mearc*, *merc*, E *mark*, is perh related to E *mark*, the coin, OE *marc*, app from Gaul L *\*marcum*, var of LL *marca*, a boundary, a territory, of Gmc origin: the predominant form *mark*—*marc* being now obsol—owes something to G *Mark*, the coin, from MHG *mark* or *marke*, a ½ lb of silver (or of gold), from syn ML *marca*, prob from LL *marca*, boundary, with orig meaning 'divided in two' (Walshe). Note that, whereas ON *mörk* is the weight, ON *mark* is the sign.

2. Akin to OE *mearc*, *merc*, boundary, frontier, are the syn OFris *merke*, OS *marca*, Go *marka*, OHG *marcha*, MHG *march*, *marc*, *marke*, G *Mark*; cf OHG *marcha*, var *morcha*, MHG *marke*, an inscription, sign, mark, G *Marke*, a token, a mark; also ON *mörk*, a forest, 'since forests often formed frontiers' (Walshe)—L *margō*, edge, border—Av *marezu*, frontier—Per *marz*, frontier country—and OIr *brú*, contr of *bruig*, var of *mruig*, frontier; perh Hit *mark-*, to cut up, hence to divide. IE r, *\*mar-*, with var *\*mer-*, and with extnn *\*marg-* and *\*mark-*.

3. Prob from OHG *marka*, or a Frankish cognate, comes OF-F *marche*, adopted by ME, whence E *march*, a border country, usu in pl *marches*.

4. Corresp to OHG *marka*, OE *mearca*, is MD *merke*, *maerc*, *maerke*, *marke* (D *merk*), whence MD *marcgrave* (cf G *Markgraf*), a borderland-country lord or governor, whence E *margrave*; the D f *markgravin* becomes E *margravine*. Cf E *marquis* (the var *marquess* owes much to the Sp *marqués*), adopted from MF-F, from OF *markis* or *marchis*, from ML *markensis*, from LL *marca*, boundary, hence march, hence any territory (as in para 1); derivative MF-F *marquisat*, whence E *marquisate*, derives from It *marchesato*, from *marchese*, marquis; corresp to MF-F *marquise* (OF *marchise*), f of F *marquis*, is E *marchioness*, from ML *marchionissa*, from ML *marchiō*, a marquis, from *marca*, a border country.

5. Perh from Gmc *\*marc*, a pledge, closely akin to ON *mark*, a sign, and its cognates, is *marque*, as in *letter of marque*: late MF *marc*, soon also *marque*: OF *merc*: OProv *marca*, a seizing, reprisal: syn ML *marca*: cf OProv *marcar*, from ML *marcāre*, to seize, esp as a pledge. Moreover, MF *marque*, a sign (MF *marc*, OF *merc*), has derivative MF *marqueter*, to chequer, surviving esp in the pp *marqueté*: whence late MF-F *marqueterie*, inlaid work, whence E *marquetry*.

6. MF *marque*, a sign, a mark, owes much to the originating MF-F v *marquer* (OF *mercher*), to mark, to indicate: and *marquer* has the EF-F cpd *remarquer* (MF *remercher*, *remerquier*), whence 'to *remark*'; 'a *remark*'=EF-F *remarque*, from *remarquer*; *remarkable*=EF-F *remarquable*, from *remarquer*.

7. The cognate L *margō*, edge, margin, becomes MF *marce*, late MF-F *marge*, adopted by E, now only poetical. *Margō* has gen *marginis*, o/s *margin-*, whence ME *margine*, E *margin*. Late MF-F *marge*

has derivative v *marger* (? prompted by late Classical L *margināre*), which, blending with *margin*, produces the n and adj *margent*. Erudite EF coins the adj *marginal*, adopted by E; *marginalia*, however, derives, as neu pl used as n, from the SciL adj *marginalis* (o/s *margin-*+*-alis*). L *margināre* has pp *marginātus*, whence the erudite E adj *marginate*, whence, anl, *margination*.

8. *Margināre* has, moreover, the cpd *ēmargināre*, to margin *ē-* or out, hence to remove the margin of, with pp *ēmarginātus*, whence 'to *emarginate*'; the E adj *emarginate*, however, bears the imposed sense 'having a notched margin', whence, anl, *emargination*.

9. Akin to MF-F *marquer* and likewise of Gmc origin (cf OHG *merken*, to mark) is Sp *marcar*, which has the cpd *demarcar* (*de*, down from, out of, hence int), to mark the boundaries, whence the n *demarcación*, whence, in C18, the F *démarcation*, whence E *demarcation*, whence, by b/f, 'to *demarcate*'.

**marker**: agent of 'to *mark*': prec, para 1.

**market** (n, hence v—whence **marketable**): ME, from ONF, *market*: OF *merchiet* (MF-F *marché*): L *mercātus* (gen -*ūs*): from *mercāt-*, s of *mercātus*, pp of *mercāri*, to trade in: from *merc-*, o/s of *merx* (for *\*mercs*), merchandise, (VL) business, affairs: closely akin to L *m rcēs* (gen *mercēdis*), price paid for goods, hire, wages, and perh akin to *merēre* (-*ēri*), to earn, hence to deserve, therefore cf MERIT.—Cf the sep MERCER and MERCY.

### L *merx*

2. *Mercāri* has presp *mercans*, o/s *mercant-*, whence It *mercantile*, adopted by EF-F, whence by E; hence *mercantilism*.

3. *Mercāri* has VL mdfn *\*mercatāre*, presp *mercatans*, o/s *mercatant-*, whence the OF n *marcheant* or -*chant*, whence (F *marchand* and) ME *marchant*, whence the re-shaped E *merchant*, whence the occ 'to *merchant*', whence *merchantable*. OF *marcheant* has derivative OF *marcheandise*, whence (F *marchandise* and) ME *marchandise*, whence E re-shaped *merchandise*, whence 'to *merchandise*'.

4. *Mercāri* has cpd *commercāri*, to trade together, whence MF-F *commercer*, whence obsol 'to *commerce*'; *commercāri* has derivative n *commercium*, merchandise, commercial relations, whence MF *commerque*, late MF-F *commerce*, adopted by E, with derivative adj—as in F—*commercial*, whence *commercialism*, *commercialize*.

5. The Roman god of commerce was *Mercurius* (*merc-*+*-urius* for -*ārius*), whence E *Mercury*, who, a lively and speedy messenger, gave his name to the element *mercury*, popularly known as *quick*silver. The derivative L adj *mercuriālis* becomes EF and E *mercurial* (F *mercuriel*).

### L *mercēs*

6. *Mercēs* has derivative adj *mercēnārius*, whence, prob via MF-F *mercénaire*, the E *mercenary*, whence also n.

**marksman** is for earlier *markman*: *mark*, target+ *man*. Hence *marksmanship*.

**marl** (1), n: MF-EF *marle*: Gaul L (ML) *margila*: L *marga*, which Pliny says is of Gaul origin.

**marl** (2), nautical v, derives from D *marlen*, a freq from MD *māren* (varr *meeren*, *meren*), to fasten, to moor; *marline*, as in *marline-* or *marlin-* or *marling-spike*, is for *marling*, from D *marling* (from *marlen*), influenced by D *marlijn* (D *maren*+ *lijn*, line).

2. MD *māren*, prob imm, generates late ME *moren*, E 'to *moor*', to secure (esp a ship), whence *moorage* and *moorings*: cf OE *māērels*, a mooring rope, and MD *mēre* (var *meer*), a stake.

**marlin(e)-spike**. See prec, para 1.

**marmalade**. See MELON, para 5.

**marmoreal**. See MARBLE, para 2.

**marmoset; marmot**. See FORMIDABLE, para 2.

**maroon** (1), orig chestnut colour, now usu reddish blue, whence as adj: F *marron*, chestnut-coloured: EF-F *marron*, a large chestnut: It *marrone*, orig Milanese dial: o.o.o.—? Ligurian.

**maroon** (2), whence, in the WI a fugitive Negro slave, or his Negro descendant: EF-F *marron*: EF *cimaroni*: ASp *cimarrón*: OSp *cimarra*, brushwood, says Webster, but the Dict of the Sp Academy derives it from *cima*, a mountain-top: such slaves fled to the mountains. Hence 'to *maroon*', to abandon (someone) on a desolate shore.

**marque**. See MARK, para 5.

**marquee**: F *marquise*, from MF-F *marquise*, marchioness, perh because orig an 'aristocratic' (large and handsome) tent: cf MARK, para 4.

**marquess**. See MARK, para 4.

**marquetry**. See MARK, para 5, s.f.

**marquis, marquisate**. See MARK, para 4.

**marriage**. See MARRY, para 2.

**marrow**, the soft tissue filling the cavities of bones, hence pith, hence (*vegetable*) marrow: ME *marowe*, *marouh*, *mary*, etc.: OE *mearg*, *mearh*: cf OFris *merch*, *merg*, OS *marg*, OHG *marag*, *marg*, MHG *marc*, G *Mark* (neu), MD *maerch*, *merch*, *morch*, *murch*, D *merg*, ON *mergr*, marrow, also syn Skt *majjan* and Av *mazga* (also, brains), and OSl *mozgŭ*, OP *musgeno*, Ru *mozg*, brains: Gmc r, *\*mazg-*, marrow.

**marry**, pt and pp (whence pa) **married; marriage**, whence **marriageable**.

1. 'To *marry*', ME *marien*, comes from OF-F *marier*, from L *marītāre*, to marry, from *marītus*, husband (cf the later *marīta*, wife), orig an adj 'coupled, married', perh from *mar-*, the o/s of *mās*, a male: cf Skt *máryas*, young man, lover, Gr *meirax*, a youth, a girl, Lith *merga*, girl, *martì*, bride; also cf, in C: Brito*martis* (name of Artemis) and Cor *mergh*, Br *merh*, W *merch*, girl.

2. The derivative L adj *marītālis* yields, perh via late MF-F, the E *marital*; *marriage*, however, derives from ME, from OF-F, *mariage*, from *marier*, from L *marītāre*.

**Mars**. See MARCH, para 1.

**marsh** (whence **marshy**). See the 2nd MERE, para 5.

marshal. See 1st MARE, para 2.

marshmallow: OE *merscmealwe*: cf MARSH and MALLOW.

marsupial: SciL *marsupialis*, pouched, as in Zoo *Marsupialia*: from L *marsupium*, pouch, trln of Gr *marsupion*, dim of *marsupon*, var of *marsipos*, a bag: perh cf Av *marshū*, belly.

mart is adopted from MD *mart*, var of *marct* (D *markt*): f.a.e., MARKET.

marten: ME *martern*, metathesis of ME *martrin*: OF-MF *murtrine*, orig the f of *martrin*, contr of OF-MF *marterin*, adj of OF-F *martre*, a marten: OGmc *marthor*—cf OHG *mardar*, MHG-G *marder*, ON *mörthr*, OE *mearth*: perh ult cf the MARRY words.

2. OE *mearth* combines with OE *fūl*, foul, to form ME *fulmard*, var *folmard*, whence E *foumart*, polecat.

martial. See MARCH, para 2.

Martian (adj, hence n): L *Martius*, adj of *Mars*, o/s *Mart-*: f.a.e., MARCH.

martin; martinet; martlet.
The 1st, adopted from EF-F, derives from *Martin*, from L *Martinus*, an *-inus* adj of *Mars*, o/s *Mart-*: cf prec; see (f.a.e.) MARCH. Orig a F dim of *martin* is EF-F *martinet* (syn of the bird *martin*), whence the surname *Martinet*, whence a drill-system devised by an officer so named, whence a severe disciplinarian—adopted by E; with *-elet* for *-inet*, EF-F *martelet* (syn of the bird *martin*) derives from *martinet*, with Her sense adopted by E; F *martelet* yields E *martlet*.

martingale, adopted from EF-F, derives either from Prov *martengalo*, app from Prov *martengau*, an inhabitant of *Martigues* in Provence, or, more prob, from Sp *almártaga*, a rein, itself from Ar *al*, the+*mirta'ah*. (B & W.)

martlet. See MARTIN, s.f.

martyr, martyrdom. See MEMORY, para 2.

marvel, marvellous. See MIRACLE, para 5.

Mary: LL, from LGr, *Maria*, var of LGr *Mariam*: H *Miryām*, whence also E *Miriam*. LL *Maria* becomes OF-F *Marie*, partly adopted by E; F *Marie* has dim *Marion*, adopted by E; the F cpd *Marianne* (ANN) becomes E *Marian*, but the adj *Marian* derives from LL *Maria* or, in E Hist, from *Mary*; *Marist*=F *Mariste*, from F *Marie*. Whereas *Mariolatry*=LGr *Maria*+'combiner' *-o-*+*-latry*, Gr *-latreia*, -worship, *marionette* anglicizes EF-F *marionnette*, from F *Marionnette*, dim of F *Marion*. —*Mary* has pet-forms *May*; *Molly* (whence *Moggy*), shortened to *Moll*, whence *moll*, cf *doll* from *Doll*, from *Dolly*, from *Dorothy*; *Polly*, *Poll*. —And *Maryland* merely anglicizes *Terra Mariae*, Lord Baltimore's naming of the territory in honour of Henrietta *Maria*, queen of Charles I of England.

marzipan. See MARCHPANE.

mascara, Tuscan red, hence a Tuscan-red cosmetic for the eyelashes: ? from Prov *mascara*, to blacken (the face)—or from Sp *máscara* (see MASK), ult from Ar *mácjara*, a buffoon, a clown, because of the heavily made-up faces of clowns—or from *Mascara*, an important Algerian trading-centre.

mascle, mascled. See the 1st MAIL, para 3.

mascot anglicizes F *mascotte*: Prov *mascoto*, a lucky charm: Prov *masco*, sorceress: syn Longobardic *masca*: o.o.o. (B & W.)

masculine. See MALE, para 3.

mash (n, hence v, whence the sl masher): OE *masc-* or *mãx-* (OE *mãxwyrt*, mash-wort) in cpds: cf MLG *mēsch*, MHG *meisch*, G *Maisch*: cognates in Scan and Sl: IE r, *meigh-*, to crush, to mash.

2. *Mash*, n, has dial var *mush*, with the derivative coll sense 'mawkish sentimentality'.

mashie, an iron golf-club: Sc re-shaping of F *massue*, a club (weapon), perh influenced by *mattock*.

mask (n, hence—prompted by EF-F *masquer*—v)—hence pa masked and agent masker; maskoid (*mask*, n+*-oid*, -like); masque, the F spelling, retained esp for the C16-17 plays so named; masquerade (EF-F *mascarade*, It *mascherata* from *maschera*, a mask), n hence v (whence masquerader). A *mask*=EF-F *masque*=It *maschera*, earlier *mascara*: Ar *maskharah*, a buffoon: Ar *sakhira*, to burlesque, to ridicule.

maslin. See MIX, para 3.

masochism (whence, anl, masochist, whence masochistic) derives from that Austrian novelist, Leopold von Sacher-*Masoch* (1835-95), who described it. Delight in being hurt, *masochism* is opp *sadism*, delight of hurting, from (F *sadisme*, from) the Comte de *Sade* (1740-1814), who described it—whence *sadist*, whence *sadistic*.

mason (whence Freemason), whence masonic (whence M-); masonry (whence M- and Freemasonry), from MF-F *maçonnerie*, from OF-F *maçon*, a mason. F *maçon* derives from *machiōn*em, the acc of late LL *machiō*, prob from Frankish *makjo*, builder, mason, from *makōn*, to make: cf MAKE.

2. OF *masson*, *maçon*, however, perh derives from *mac-*, the r of L *macerāre* (s *macer-*), to soften, esp by soaking or immersion; the pp *macerātus* explains 'to macerate', as its derivative *macerātiō*, o/s *macerātiōn-*, does *maceration* (cf EF-F *macération*).

masque, masquerade. See MASK.

Mass, cf Christmas, Lammas, Michaelmas, but see MISSION, para 4.

mass, the form, or a large quantity, of matter, whence the adj and—? indebted to MF-F *masser*—the v; massif, massive; massy (*mass*, n+adj *-y*);—amass, whence amassment.—Cf the sep MINGLE.

1. 'To amass' derives from OF-F *amasser*: *a-*, F *à*, L *ad*, to+*masser*, from *masse*, from L *massa*, whence, via OF *masse*, the ME *masse*, E *mass*.

2. L *massa*, a mass, orig a lump or heap of paste, derives from Gr *maza*, a paste of barley flour, hence a barley cake, hence, in LGr, a lump, hence a mass: prob, esp if for *magia* or *maggia*, akin to Gr *massein* (? for *magsein*), to knead—cf Gr *magus*, a kneaded lump: IE r, *mag-*, to knead.

Less prob of Sem or Ham origin (? cf Eg *am* or *amm*, grain, esp wheat or barley).

3. OF-F *masse* has late MF-F adj *massif*, f *massive*: hence E *massive*. The Geol n *massif*, adopted from F, is the F adj used as n.

**Massachusetts**, the A State, derives from the pl of *Massachuset*, member of an Alg tribe (long extinct): Massachuset *Massa-adchu-es-et*, (those living) at or about the big hill: *massa*, big+*wadchu*, hill+*-es*, dim suffix+*-et*, locative suffix 'at, about'. (Webster; Mathews.)

**massacre**, n and v; **machicolate** (adj, v), **machicolation**.

1. 'To *massacre*' derives from MF-F *massacrer*, itself from MF-F *massacre*, whence the E n: and MF-F *massacre* derives from OF *maçacre*, varr *macecre, macecle*; o.o.o., but perh from OF *\*mache-col*, butcher, (lit) one who strikes or crushes the neck (*col*) of the beasts he kills.

2. *Machicolation* (in Arch: an opening between corbels) derives, anl, from *machicolate* (adj, v), itself from ML *machicolātus*, pp of *machicolāre*, to provide with openings for shooting or dropping missiles, etc.: MF *machicoler*: from MF *machecolis* (F *mâchicoulis*): perh (B & W) an alteration of *\*machiscoulis*: *\*machis*, from *macher*, to crush+ *coulis*, a flowing, from *couler*, to flow.

**massage** (n, hence v); **masseur, masseuse.**

*Massage*, adopted from F, derives from F *masser*, to massage, whence *masseur*, f *masseuse*, both adopted by E: and F *masser*, in this sense, comes, not (as often stated) from Port *amassar*, to knead, from *massa*, dough, L *massa* (cf MASS, para 2), but (B & W) from Ar *mass*, to touch, esp to palpate: the practice, after all, was introduced into Europe from the East.

**massif; massive.** See MASS, para 3.

**mast** (of ship): OE *maest*: cf OHG-G *mast*, MD *maste* and, as in D, *mast*, ON *mastr* (? from OHG or MLG): cf the syn L *mālus* (for *\*mādus* for *\*masdus*), perh influenced by L *pālus*, a stake, and also MIr ad-*mat*, timber: Gmc r, *\*mast-*; IE r, *\*mazd-*. (Walshe.)

**mast** (2), nuts. See MEAT, para 2.

**master**, n, whence **masterful** and **masterly;** hence also adj, whence **masterpiece**, and v (cf the MF-F *maîtriser*); **mastery** (cf pal*mistry* at PALM); **mister**, a thinned form, influenced by **mistress**, whence the coll **missus** and, by contr, **miss**, whence **missy**; F *maître* (OF *maistre*), as in *maître d'hotel*, a major-domo, a hotel-manager, and It *maestro*, both partly adopted by E.—L **magister**, E **magistral** (cf **mistral**) and **magisterial**—**magistrand** and **magistrate** (whence **magistracy**); **Magna Carta**—**magnanimous, magnanimity**, sep at ANIMAL, para 6— **magnate**—**magnific, Magnificat, magnification** (whence, anl, **magnificative**), **magnificence, magnificent, magnifico, magnify, magnitude**—**magnum; majesty.** whence **majestic**: **major** (cf **majuscule**), **majority**—cf **mayor, mayoralty**—Majorca, see MAJOLICA; **marino**; **May** (month) and **may**; **maxim** —cf **maximum** (whence **maximal**).—**maha, maharaja, maharani, mahatma.**—Cf the element

*magni-*, where, e.g., *magniloquence.*—For the derivatives from Gr *megas*, great, see *mega-* in Elements.—Gmc: **mickle**, var **muckle; much**, whence **muchness.**

### I. Indo-European

1. All these words derive from one or other of the Skt, Gr, L, L-via-R, Gmc derivatives from the IE r *\*mag-*, var *\*meg-*, with extnn *\*magh-* and *\*megh-* (L *magn-* exhibiting a different radical suffix); even *\*mag-*, *\*meg-*, are *-g-* extnn of the still more fundamental *\*ma-* or *\*me-*, with varr *\*mi-*, *\*mo-*, *\*mu-*, big: cf OE *micel, mycel*, great, from mc Gr *\*mik-*; L *magn*us, great—*maior*, greater—*maximus* (? for *\*magsimus*), greatest; Gr *mega*, much, *megas* (f *megale*), great; Skt *mah-, mahat-, máhi*, great, *máhas, majmán-*, greatness, cf *mahēyān*, greater, and *mahisthas*, greatest; Hit *mah*, strong, *makkess-*, to become great, *mekkis*, great, numerous, pl *meggaes*, and *mekki*, very, much: cf Tokh A *mak*, Tokh B *makī-*, great, much, Alb *math* and Arm *mec*, great (instr *mecaw*): cf also MIr *mag*, great, and *māl* (from extn *\*magl-*), nobleman, prince, *mass* (from *\*magsos*), important, OC r *\*mag-*, var *\*mac-*, great, perh akin to *\*mac-, mag-*, to nourish,—with the C var *\*magal-*, cf the *megal-* of Gr *megalē*.

### II. Sanskrit

2. Skt *mah-*, great, occurs in the Singhalese *maha*, a species of monkey, a species of deer. *Maharaja* is Skt *maharaja*, great king (*raja*, cf L *rex*); *maharani*, Hi *maharānī*, great queen (cf L *regīna*); *mahatma*, a (Hindu) sage, Skt *mahātman*, (lit) great soul (*ātman*).

### III. Greek

3. See Elements at *mega-* (where also *megalo-*): e.g., *megaphone* and *megalomania*.

### IV. Latin *magnus*

4. L *magnus*, great, retained in the names of ancient and medieval kings and medieval alchemists and others, has f *magna*, as in *Magna Carta* (or *Charta*), The Great Charter, cf *chart* at the 1st CARD; the neu *magnum* is, in E, used as n for a 2-quart bottle.

5. *Magnus* has two simple derivatives affecting E:

LL *magnātes*, leading people, and LL *magnātus*, a leading man, a nobleman, (Oriental ML) a prince; hence, by b/f, the F *magnat* (Rousseau, 1772), a (Polish) grandee; whence E *magnate* (Burke, 1790);

L *magnitūdō*, greatness, whence E *magnitude*.

6. For cpds, see *magnanimus* at ANIMAL, para 6; cf *magni-* in Elements; but note esp:

*magnificus* (adj), great-making or -rendering, whence, perh via MF-F *magnifique*, the obsol E *magnific*; whence also the It title *Magnifico*, whence E *magnifico*, a grandee;

derivative *magnificāre*, to enlarge, whence, perh via OF-F *magnifier*, the E *magnify*; *magnificat*, it enlarges, hence glorifies, occurs in Christian European literature as *Magnificat*, My soul doth magnify the Lord (*Luke*, i, 46–55); on the pp *magnificāt*us arises the LL *magnificātiō*, praise, o/s *magnificātiōn-*, whence, as to form only, the E *magnification*;

likewise derivative from *magnificus* is the syn LL *magnificens*, o/s *magnificent-*, whence both MF-EF and E *magnificent*; subsidiary LL *magnificentia* becomes MF-F and E *magnificence*.

### V. Latin *māior* (neu *māius*), greater

7. L *māior* is for OL *maiior*, itself from *\*magyōs* (r *mag-*+suffix element *yō-*+nom ending *-s*); it becomes ML *major*, whence OF-F *majeur* and EF-F and E *major*, with derivative F *majorité* (ML *majoritās*) yielding E *majority*, the attainment of 21 years, *majority* in the other senses coming straight from E *major*. ML *major domūs*, the head of the household, becomes It *maggiordomo*, which joins with the syn Sp *mayordomo* to produce F *majordome* and E *majordomo*. Based on the neu *māius* is the L dim derivative *māiusculus*, a little greater, whence, via (*litera*) *māiuscula*, the EF-F *majuscule*, adopted by E.

8. In OF, L *māior*—already in LL used as n— becomes *maire*, adopted by ME, whence *mayor*, whence *mayoress* (cf LL *māiōrissa*, the chief slave-woman); derivative MF *mairalté* yields *mayoralty*.

9. From ML *mājōrīnus*, of a larger kind, hence, as n, an overseer, via the ML contr *mērīnus*, over-seer of pastures, comes the syn Sp *merino*, whence (OED, EW, Webster) a special breed of sheep reared in Estremadura; perh, however (B & W), Sp *merino* derives from *merīnī*, the adj of Bani-*Merīn*, the great Ar dynasty of late medieval Morocco and members of an important Berber tribe that specialized in sheep-raising.

10. From the ancient Italic goddess *Māia* (for *Maiia*; ancient var *Māiesta*)—? for (*dea*) *māia*, the greater goddess, f of *\*māius*, prob akin to *magnus* and perh an ancient var of *māior*—comes *Māius mensis*, Maia's month, whence, by ellipsis, *Māius*, OF-F *mai*, E *May*, whence the Spring-blooming, spiny shrub *may*, applied esp to the hawthorn and its bloom.

11. *Māiesta*, that ancient var of *Māia*, suggests that rather from some ancient var of *māior*, greater, than direct from *māior* itself, derives L *māiestas*, greatness, esp grandeur, ML *mājestas*, whence, via OF-F *majesté*, the ME *majestee*, whence E *majesty*, whence, anl, *majestic*.

### VI. L *māximus*, greatest

12. L *māximus* (var *māxumus*), for *\*magsomos* (r *mag-*+formative element *-som-*+declensional *-o-*, later *-u-*+case-ending *-s*), has neu *māximum*, which, used as n, is adopted by E for 'the greatest value, size, quantity, speed, etc.' The elliptical L *māxima* (? for *m. sententia*), the greatest sentence, hence thought or axiom, becomes MF-F *maxime*, whence E *maxim*.

### VII. L *magis*, more, rather

13. Closely akin to—and perh, as a contr of *magnis*, with great (things), hence greatly, deriving from—*magnus* is the adv *magis*, whence L *magister*, lit a greater (person), hence a superior, chief, master, much as L *minister* derives from *minus*, less (*minor*, lesser): partly adopted by E. The derivative L adj *magistrālis*, masterly, becomes F and E *magistral*; its LL mdfn *magisterius* has neu *magisterium*, which, used as LL n for 'body of teachers', etc., yields *magistery*; either imm from *magisterium* or as an extn of *magisterius* is the LL adj *magisteriālis*, of teaching, ML of command, whence *magisterial*.

14. L *magistrālis*, masterly, dominant, becomes OProv *maistral*, whence Prov *mistral*, esp as n, 'dominant wind', adopted by E; B & W, however, derive *maistral* from OProv (and OF) *maistre*, master (cf para 16).

15. L *magister* has LL derivative *magistrāre*, to master, hence to rule, to teach, whence ML *magistrandus*, lit one to be trained, hence a university student in his final year, hence Sc *magistrand*. *Magister* has the further derivative *magistrātus*, lit control of the people, hence a magistrate's function and the magistrate himself: *magistrātus* (gen *-ūs*) produces EF-F *magistrat* and E *magistrate*; derivative EF-F *magistrature*, adopted by E, is rare for *magistracy* (*magistra*te+*cy*; cf *accuracy* from *accurate*).

### VIII. OF *maistre*

16. L *magister* becomes OF-MF *maistre* (F *maître*), adopted by ME, whence E *master*; sem, OE-from-L *magister* has contributed. Derivative OF-MF *maistrie* leads to *mastery*.

17. OF *maistre* has MF f *maistresse* (F *maîtresse*), adopted by ME, which partly anglicizes it as *maistress*, whence, by thinning (cf *mister* from *master*), the E *mistress*.

### IX. Germanic

18. *Much* (adj, hence adv and n), great, esp in size or degree, derives from ME *muche*, var *moche*, from earlier *muchel*, var *mochel*, from OE *mycel*, var *micel*; ME *muchel* has var *mikel* (? ON *mikill*), whence *mickle*, now Sc (*meikle*) and dial. OE *mycel* (*micel*) is akin to OS *mikil*, OFris *mikili*, OHG *michil*, *mihhil*, *mihil*, MHG *michel*, Go *mikels*, *mikils*, ON *mikell*, *mikill*, *mykill*: Gmc r, *\*mikil-*. The parallel E *muckle* is a var—influenced by *much*—of *mickle*.

**mastic; masticate, mastication.** *Mastic*, OF *mastic*, LL *masticum*, *mastichum*, Gr *mastikhē*, gum mastic, is akin to 'to *masticate*', from *masticātus*, pp of LL *masticāre*, to chew, from Gr *mastikhan*, to gnash the teeth, and *mastax*, mouth, mouthful, morsel: akin, ult, to MOUTH.

**mastiff.** See MANUAL, para 16, s.f.

**mastodon.** See the element *-odon*. Cf:

**mastoid,** (lit) breast-shaped: Gr *mastoeidēs*: *mastos*, breast+*-eidēs*, cf the E suffix *-oid*.

masturbate, masturbation. See MALE, para 5, and TURBID, para 4.

mat (1), adj. See MATT.

mat (2), n (hence v, whence matted): OE *matt*, varr *meatt*, *meatte*: L *matta*, a rush-mat: o.o.o., but presumably a borrowing; perh Punic (a dial of Phoen), as Webster proposes—for the form, cf L *mappa* (E MAP)—yet perh rather Medit: tentatively I propose a cognate, ? even the origin, in Eg *smait*, a mat, a couch, wherein *s-* could be that ancient quasi-prefix *s-* which we see in, e.g., Gr (*stegos*, *tegos*); certainly an IE, perh even a Medit, quasi-prefix.

matador. See the 2nd MATE.

match (1), for ignition: ME *macche*, a candle- or a lamp-wick, a small torch: OF *meshe* (F *mèche*): VL *micca*: L *myxa*: Gr *muxa*, lamp-wick, (orig) nasal *mucus*: f.a.e., MUCUS.

match (2), a spouse (obs), some person or thing equal to another, a harmonious pair, etc., hence 'to *match*'. See MAKE, para 2.

mate (1), n: ME *mate*: prob MLG *mate*, *māt*, a companion, prop a messmate: cf OHG gi*mazzo*, messmate, and OHG-MHG *maz*, OS *mat*, ON *matr*, food: cf also, therefore, MEAT.—Hence INMATE (*in*, adv).

mate (2), v, to baffle or utterly fatigue (obsol), to checkmate: OF-F *mater*, to fatigue, overcome, checkmate, itself from OF-F *mat*, defeated, not from Ar *māt* (cf *checkmate* at CHECK) but from L *mattus*, suffering from a hangover, perh for *maditus*, VL var of L *madidus*, wet, hence tipsy, from *madère*, to be wet. (B & W.) Cf MATT.

maté, a tea-like stimulant of SAm: prob via F *maté* (EF *mati*); from Sp *mate*: Quechuan *mate*, anciently *mati*, a calabash.

mater, as in alma mater (L: kindly or gracious mother) and in schoolboy sl; maternal, maternity; matrical, matrix, pl matrices, whence, anl, the adj matricular; for matri- cpds (e.g., *matriarch*), see *matri-* in Elements; matriculate (adj, n, v), matriculation; matrimonial, matrimony; matron (whence matronage and matronly), matronal.—European R forms: It, Sp, Port madre, F mère.—Gr: Demeter; metropolis, metropolitan (adj, hence n).—Gmc: mother (n, hence adj and v), whence motherhood, mother-in-law (and stepmother), motherly.—Perh akin is the 2nd MOTHER (slimy membrane) and prob akin is MATTER, both treated sep.

### Indo-European

1. Corresp to *pater*, L *māter*, mother, affords a good starting-point, for Doric Gr has *mátēr* (Attic *mētēr*) and Skt has *mātā* (*mātṛ*)—cf the OSl and Ru *mate*, *mati* (gen *matere*, *materi*), Lett *māte*; OP po*matre*, mother-in-law; cf, with sense 'wife', the revealing Lith *móte*; in C: OIr *máthir* (Ga *màthair*), Mx *moir*, OC *māter*; Arm *mair* (gen *maur*); peripherally: Tokh A *mācar*, Tokh B *mācer*; centrally the Gmc: OE *mōdor*, OFris *mōder*, OS and Go *mōdar*, OHG *muotar*, MHG *muoter*, G *Mutter*, MD *moder*, D *moeder*, ON *mōthir* (cf Da and Sw *moder*). The IE base is *mat-*, mother,

itself a precision-extn of *ma-*, breast (cf MAMA): the f 'breast-feeder' answers to the m 'producer': *mā-*+agent *-tēr*, and *pa-*+*-tēr*. For the suffix *-ter*, cf *brother* (L *frater*, Gr *phratēr*, etc.) and *sister* and *daughter*.

### Greek

2. Gr *mētēr* (μήτηρ), acc *mētera*, gen *mētros*, affects E in two cpds:

Gr *Dēmētēr*, E *Demeter*, the goddess of the fruitful soil, perh lit 'mother of the gods' (cf DIANA)—my theory, at least as prob as the others (Gr *dē* for *gē*, earth; and Gr *zeia*, barley);

*mētropolis*, the mother (c/f *mētro-*) city (Gr *polis*, see POLICE), ref esp Athens and her colonies: LL *mētropolis*, mother-city: MF, hence EE, *metropole* (F *métropole*), and E *metropolis*; the derivative LL adj *mētropolītanus*—perh suggested by LL *mētropolīta*, from Gr *mētropolītēs*, a native, an inhabitant, of a metropolis—becomes late MF *metropolitain*, whence E *metropolitan*. (Cf POLICE, para 5.)

### Latin

3. L *māter* has the foll derivatives relevant to E: adj *māternus*, whence—either via the derivative learnèd MF-F *maternel* or from the popular ML *maternālis* attested by the popular ML adv *maternāliter*—E *maternal*; learnedly from MF *maternel*, late MF—perh after ML *maternitas*, syn of *Mater Ecclesia*, Mother Church—coins *maternité*, whence E *maternity*;

*mātrimōnium*, legal maternity, marriage for a woman, is formed after *patrimōnium* (E *patrimony*) —hence OF, whence ME, *matrimoine*, whence *matrimony*; derivative adj *mātrimōniālis* becomes MF-F *matrimonial*, adopted by E.

*mātrix*, womb (cf the Gr *mētra*), acc *mātrīcem* (MF-F *matrice*), adopted by SciE and, after F, endowed with new senses; derivative LL adj *mātricālis* yields E *matrical*; *mātrix* in LL means also a public register, with the syn dim *mātricula*, whence in ML, a register of university students, whence ML *immātriculāre*, to enroll students, pp *immātriculātus*, whence, by aphesis, the EE-E *matriculate*—cf the late MF-F *immatriculer* (there being no *matriculer*); hence, anl, *matriculation*—cf EF-F *immatriculation*—and, as if from *matriculant-*, o/s of ML *mātriculans*, presp of *mātriculāre*, the E *matriculant*, a matriculating student.

*mātrōna* (corresp to L *patrōnus*), a married woman, or a widow, esp with children: like *māter*, a dignified word, whence, prob via OF-F *matrone*, the E *matron*; derivative adj *mātrōnālis* yields, perh via F, *matronal*.

### Romance

4. It madre, mother, occurs in *madrepore*, q.v.; OF-F *mère* in *commère*, corresp to *compère*, these being radio-ex-music-hall terms.

### Germanic

5. OE *mōdor*, mother, as in para 1, becomes ME

*moder*, whence, perh under the influence of ON *mōthir* but prob under that of OIr and MIr *māthir*, the E *mother*, whence 'to *mother*'; OE *mōdor* has adj *mōdorlīc*, whence E *motherly*.

**material** (adj, n), **materialism, materialist, materialize**. See MATTER, para 1.

**maternal, maternity**. See MATER, para 3.

**mathematic** (obsol adj, whence **mathematical**), **mathematician, mathematics; mathesis**, whence, anl, the adj **mathetic** (cf Gr *mathēteos*);—**polymath** (whence, anl, **polymathic**) and **polymathy**.—Ult cf the sep MIND.

1. *Polymath*, a person extremely and diversely erudite, derives from the Gr adj *polumathēs*, learnèd in many subjects; *polymathy*, from Gr *polumathia*, much and numerous learning: Gr *polu*, much (E *poly-*)+derivatives from *manthanein*, to learn, with aorist s *math-*: cf Skt *medhā*, intelligence, and E MIND.

2. Gr *manthanein* has the var *mathein*, whence *mathēsis*, learning (esp in mathematics), whence, via LL, the E *mathesis*. Another derivative, *mathēma*, that which is learnt, has pl *mathēmata*, learning, esp mathematics, with adj *mathēmatikos*, whence ML *mathematicus*, MF-F *mathématique* and E *mathematic*. From MF-F *mathématique* comes the EF-F n *mathématique*, mathematics, whence EE *mathematic*, n, later—after *physics*, *ethics*, etc. —*mathematics*. The MF-F *mathématicien* becomes E *mathematician*.

**Matilda**. See MALKIN.

**matin, matins** (early-morning Eccl services); **matinal, matinée; matutinal**.

*Matin*, a morning song, orig the morning, is adopted from OF-F: L *mātūtīnum*, n from *mātūtīnum tempus*, morning-time, from *mātūtīnus*, of the morning, from *Mātūta*, the ancient Italic goddess of the morning (Roman Aurora): akin to *mātūrus*, seasonable, early: f.a.e., MATURE. *Mātūtīnus* has LL extn *mātūtīnālis*, whence *matutinal*, early. OF *matin*, morning, has OF-F adj *matinal*, adopted by E; it also has OF-F derivatives *matinée*, orig the entire morning (cf *soirée* and *soir*), with sense-changes in F, hence in E, and the Eccl pl OF-F *matines*, whence E *matins*.

**matriarch**, whence **matriarchal, matriarchate, matriarchy; matricide**. See *matri-* in Elements and, f.a.e., MATER, para 1.

**matriculant, matriculate, matriculation**. See MATER, para 3.

**matrimonial, matrimony**. See MATER, para 3.

**matrix** (pl **matrices**). See MATER, para 3.

**matron, matronal, matronly**. See MATER, para 3, s.f.

**matt**, adj and n, var **mat**: F *mat*, n, a dull colour: EF-F *mat*, adj, dull-coloured, lustreless: OF *mat*, downcast, afflicted, hence (of foliage) withered, whence MF (of weather) sombre, dull: either (B & W) from L *matus, mattus*, suffering from a 'hangover', wine-sad or -heavy, perh dial from *\*maditus*, soaked (cf the modern sl *soaked*, drunk), pp of *madēre*, to be soaked with water; or (Webster, Dauzat), from Ar *māt* (see the 2nd MATE), an

etymology now somewhat discredited. Hence 'to *mat* or *matt*' glass or a metal.

**matter** (n, hence v), whence 'a **matter of fact**', whence the adj **matter-of-fact**; **material**, adj, hence —prob influenced by the militarily adopted F n *matériel* (from the MF-F adj *matériel*)—n; *material*-adj derivatives: **materialism, materialist, materiality, materialize** (whence **materialization**), all perh influenced by the resp F *matérialisme*, EF-F *matérialiste*, late MF-F *matérialité*, F *matérialiser*, all from LL adj *māteriālis*;—**Madeira**. —Prob ult akin to L *māter*—as at MATER, esp para 1.

1. The adj *material* derives from LL *māteriālis*, of bodily substance, of the perishable substance of the human body and of earthly things, secular (Souter), from L *māteria*, var *māteriēs*, bodily or solid matter, earlier timber, earlier the hard part of a tree, orig the substance of which the *māter* consists, *māter* being the trunk, which produces the shoots; *māter*, therefore, is here a transferred use of *māter*, mother (see MATER, para 1). *Immaterial* derives from the LL neg *immāteriālis*.

2. Whereas OF-F *matière* derives rather from L *māteriēs*, E *matter* perh derives, via ME *matere*, rather from L *māteria*, stuff, matter.

3. L *māteria* becomes Port *madeira*, wood, whence the well-wooded island *Madeira*, hence the wine made there.

**mattock; mace** (a club, a staff).

*Mattock*, OE *mattuc*, substitutes *-ock*, OE *-uc*, for the dim *-eola* of L *mateola*, a mallet: cf Skt *matyá*, club, harrow. L *mateola* has a base *\*matea* (*\*mattea*), whence, perh via a VL *\*matia* or *\*mattia*, the OF *mace* (F *masse*), adopted by E.

**mattress**: MF *materas* (late MF-F, with *l* for *r*, *matelas*): It *materasso*: Ar *matras* (*maṭraḥ*), something thrown, hence laid down, esp a mattress, from *taras* (*taraḥ*), to throw.

**maturate, maturation, maturative**. See para 3 of:

**mature** (adj, hence v), **maturity**—cf **maturescent** (whence **maturescence**); **immature, immaturity**—cf **premature, prematurity; manes**, ancestral spirits.— Cf the sep MATIN.

1. *Maturity* derives, perh via late MF-F *maturité*, from L *mātūritās*, o/s *mātūritāt-*, from *mātūrus*, produced at the right or favourable moment, hence fully developed, itself, like the goddess *Mātūta*, built, with abstract formative *-tu-*, from the IE r *mā-*, good: cf Hit *mai-*, to ripen, the OL adj *mūnis*, var *mānis*, good, and the L *māne*, in the morning: cf the syn OIr and Ga *maith*, Ga var *math*, OIr var *maid*, W and Br *mad* (OBr *mat*), OC *\*matis*, var *\*matos*, good.

2. OL *mānis*, good, has L pl *mānēs*, used as n, the good (gods), euphem for *dī inferi*, later a family's ancestral spirits worshipped as gods.

3. L *mātūrus* has derivative v *mātūrāre*, to ripen or to cause to ripen, with pp *mātūrātus*, whence 'to *maturate*'; derivative *mātūrātiō*, o/s *mātūrātiōn-*, yields, perh via MF-F, *maturation*; derivative F *maturatif*, f *-ive*, explains E *maturative*. *Mātūrāre* has inch *mātūrescere*, to begin to ripen, presp

*maturescens*, o/s *maturescent-*, whence the E adj *maturescent*.

4. *Mātūrus* has neg *immātūrus*, whence *immature*; derivative *immātūritās*, o/s *immātūritāt-*, becomes *immaturity*; it also has the *prae-* (before) cpd *praemātūrus*, whence *premature*, whence, anl, *prematurity*.

5. Late ME-E *demure* is o.o.o.: either it adds an unclear *de-* (?, at least orig, int) to late ME *mure*, modest, mature, from OF *meür* (F *mûr*), L *mātūrus* (OED); or it elliptically represents MF *de meüre* (F *mûre*) *façon* or *pensée*, of mature or modest behaviour or thought (as Webster hints); or it derives from OF *de murs*, of manners (F *moeurs*, L *mores*), presumably with *bonnes* understood—most improb; or it comes from AF *demurer*, var of OF *demorer*, *demourer*, to retard, *se demorer* (*-mourer*), to dwell, to abstain, from ML *dēmorāre*, from LL *dēmorāri*, to dwell, remain, continue, a vaguely int *dē-* cpd of *morāri*, from *mora*, a delay (cf MORATORIUM)—perh imm from the AF pp *demuré*, and certainly comparable, sem, with *staid*, from 'to *stay*', the implied orig sense being 'hanging back' (EW), a very attractive theory; or (EP)—deducible both from Palsgrave's 'sadly, gravely, seriously, wysly, *demeurement*' (1530), aomittedly recorded, so far, nowhere else, and also from LL *dēmātūrāre*, to hasten (Souter), ? also to render very (int *dē-*) mature, over-mature, staid—it very properly derives from MF *\*demeür* (f *\*demeüre*), mature, grave, modest, from syn ML *\*dēmātūrus*.

**matutinal.** See MATIN.

**Maud.** See MALKIN.

**maudlin; Magdalen, Madeleine, Madelon.**

The 4th is a var of the 3rd, which, like E *Magdalen* or *-ene*, comes from LL *Magdalena*, from LGr *Magdalēnē*, (a woman) of *Magdala* in Palestine: from Mary Magdalene derive both the fig sense of *Magdalen* and *maudlin*, from EE *Maudlin*, ME *Maudeleyne*, OF *Maudelene*, var of *Madeleine*, LL *Magdalene*, she being, by the painters, usu represented with eyes red and swollen from weeping.

**maul.** See MALL.

**Maundy** Thursday. See MANUAL, para 9, s.f.

**Mauresque; Mauretania.** See MOOR, para 1 and para 4.

**mauve:** MF-F *mauve*, mallow, ML *malva*, L *malua* (f.a.e., MALLOW): from the colour of the common mallow's petals.

**maverick** (AE): an unbranded calf, hence fig, also as v: from the Texan cattle-owner Samuel Maverick (1803–70), who often neglected to brand his calves. (Mathews.)

**maw:** ME *mawe*: OE *maga*: akin to OFris *maga*, OHG *mago*, MHG *mage*, G *Magen*, ON *magi*: perh also to Let *mąks*, bag, and Lith *makas*, pouch.

**mawkish.** See MAGGOT, para 2.

**maxilla, maxillary** (adj, hence n).

*Maxillary* derives from L *maxillāris*, adj of *maxilla*, jaw or jawbone, adopted by An and Zoo: and *maxilla* is—cf *axilla* and *ala*—a dim of *mala*, (upper) jaw, itself o.o.o. (E & M.)

**maxim, maximal, maximum.** See MASTER, para 12.

**May,** month. See MASTER, para 10.

**may** (1), a shrub, its bloom. See MASTER, para 10.

**may** (2), v; **might,** v and n; **dismay** (v, hence n).—Cf the sep MACHINE and MAIN.

1. *May* derives from OE *maeg*, I am able, pt *meahte*, later *mihte*, whence *might*, v: cf OHG *magan*, MHG *mugen*, *mügen* (cf G *mögen*), OFris *muga*, Go *magan*, ON *mega*, to be able: cf also OSl *mogǫ*, I can, and prob Gr *mēkhos*, means (as ult in MACHINE).

2. With OE *meahte*, I was able, cf the intimately cognate OE *meaht*, var *miht*, power, whence E *might*: cf OFris *mecht*, var *macht*, OHG-MHG *maht*, G *Macht*, OS *maht*, Go *mahts*, ON *māttr* (for *\*mahtr*): prob cf also Skt *māyā*, magical power, and perh Eg *nāsht*, strength, from *nāsh*, to be strong. Derivative OE *meahtig*, *mihtig*, becomes *mighty*.

3. The Gmc r *\*mag-*, to be able, occurs in VL *\*exmagāre*, to deprive—connoted by *ex-*, out of—of strength or power, whence OF-EF *esmaier* (cf the syn OProv *esmagar*, *esmaiar*), to frighten badly, to perturb, whence, with *des-* (L *dis-*) for *es-* (L *ex-*), the AF *desmaier*: ME *desmaien*, later *dismaien*: E 'to *dismay*'.

**Maya** (whence the adj, hence n, **Mayan**; whence also their language, **Mayathan**), member of a highly civilized tribe of CA: presumably of CAmerind origin, and prob akin to—perh derived by metathesis from—*Zamnā*, the early Mayas' culture-god.

**maya,** magical power. See MIME, para 1; cf the 2nd MAY, para 2.

**mayhap.** See HAP, para 2.

**mayhem.** See MAD, para 3.

**mayonnaise,** elliptical for *sauce mayonnaise*, var of *mahonnaise*, f of *mahonnais*, the adj of Port Mahon in Minorca: but why?

**mayor, mayoralty, mayoress.** See MASTER, para 8.

**mazard.** See MEASLES.

**maze,** n (whence **mazy**) and v; **amaze,** v, whence the nn **amaze** and **amazement.**

'To *amaze*' derives from OE *āmasian*, app an int *a-+-masian*, prob akin to the Scan orig of Nor dial *masast*, to lose one's senses. From OE *-masian* comes ME *masen*, *mazen*, whence 'to *maze*' or bewilder; and from ME *mazen* comes the ME, hence E, n *maze*.

**mazer; mazzard.** See MEASLES, para 2.

**me; mine, my.** *Me*, OE *mē* (acc, dat), is prob a var, prompted by L *mē* and Gr *me*, of OE *mec* (acc only)—cf ON *mek*, *mik*, OS and Go *mik*, OHG *mih*, G *mich*, D *mij*; further off, L *mē* (also the OIr form), OL *mēd*, Gr *me*, *eme*, Skt *mā*; still further off, Hit am*muk*, am*mug*-. The Gmc r is *\*me-*; the IE r, *\*eme-*.

2. *My*, early ME *mī*, derives from ME, from OE, *mīn*, my, mine: cf OFris, OS, OHG *mīn*, MHG

*mīn*, G *mein*, Go *meins*, ON *minn*, OGmc *\*mino-*, all from OGmc *\*me-*.

**mead** (1), a potent drink. See AMETHYST.

**mead** (2), a grassy field; **meadow**.

The latter comes from OE *māedwe*, the gen of *māed*, E *mead*: and OE *māed* is akin to OFris *mēde*, OS *mada*, OHG *matoscrech*, (lit) meadow hopper, a grass-hopper, MHG *mate* and, as in G, *matte*; prob akin to L *metere*, to mow (see the 1st MOW).

**meager** (AE) or **meagre**. See EMACIATE, para 2.

**meal** (1), a repast. See MEASURE, para 13.

**meal** (2), grain—usu cereal—coarsely ground, whence the adj **mealy**, whence **mealy-mouthed**; **mealie, mealies; maelstrom; malm**, with dial var **maum; mellow**, adj, whence the v and **mellowness; mild; mill**, cf **miliary** and **millet; moil; molar** (teeth); **mold** (AE) or **mould**, friable earth, humus, whence 'to mo(u)lder' and mo(u)ldy; **mole**, blood clot, **molinary, moline; mollescent, mollification, mollify**—cf **mollusc** (AE **mollusk**), **molluscoid, molluscous; mulch** (n, hence v) and dial **melch; mullein; muller**, cf dial **mull** (dry mould, dust); **multure;**—**immolate, immolation; emolument;** perh the sep MALL (or MAUL) and its dim MALLET and also the sep MELT (with MALT, MILT, spleen, and SMELT)—and perh *mildew*, q.v. at MEL, para 4.

1. *Meal*, grain coarsely ground, derives from ME *mele*, OE *melu*, var *melo*: cf OFris *mele*, OS *mẹlu*, OHG *melo*, MHG *mel*, G *Mehl*, MD *mele*, *meele*, D *meel*, ON *miöl* (*mjöl*)—cf also OS, OHG, Go *malan* (G *mahlen*), ON *mala*, and Lith *malti*, L *molere*, Gr *mullein*, to grind, also Hit *malla-* (*mallānzi*, they grind or crush). IE r, *\*m\*l* (esp *\*mel-*), with * running through the vocalic gamut from *a* to *u*.

2. D *malen*, to grind, hence to whirl round, combines with *stroom*, stream, to form *maelstroom* (now *maal-*), a whirlpool, orig the famous one off the W coast of Norway. Hence, E *maelstrom*.

3. Akin to OE *melu*, meal, is OE *mealm*, E *malm*, a soft, grey, friable limestone: cf ON *malmr*, ore, OS-OHG *melm*, G *Mulm*, dust, Go *malma*, sand; hence *malmstone* (or *malm rock*).

4. Akin to OE *melu* or *mealm* is OE *myl*, ME *mul*, E (now dial) *mull*, dry mould, dust, dirt: cf MD and MLG *mul*, dust, G *Müll*, garbage. ME *mul* has derivative *mullen* to pulverize, whence E 'to *mull*', to pulverize or powder, and E instr *muller*, a stone (etc.) used as a pestle: cf ON *mylja*, OHG *mullen*, to grind or crush.

5. Akin to OE *melu*, *mealm*, *myl*, is OE-ME *molde*, AE *mold*, E *mould*, soft, friable earth, esp humus: cf the syn OFris *molde*, OHG *molt*, *molta*, Go *mulda*, ON *mold*.

6. Akin to, perh from, OE *melu*, *melo*, meal, is ME *melwe*, E *mellow*; meal is soft and easily worked.

### Latin *molīna* and *mola*

7. A *mill*, whether contrivance or machine or building, whence 'to *mill*', derives from ME *mille*, earlier *melle*, *mulle*, earliest *milne*, from OE *myln*, contr of *mylen*: LL *molīna*, mill: L *mola*, millstone,

mill; L *molere*, to grind, akin to Gr *mullein* (corresp to n *mulē*, LGr *mulos*). The other OGmc words likewise come from *molīna*. Derivatives: *miller* (cf G *Müller*)—*millstone*—*windmill*.

8. Perh akin to L *mola* and *molīna* or, rather, to the IE r, *\*mel-* (para 1, s.f.), is L *milium*, millet, whence OF-F *mil*, with syn dim MF-F *millet*, adopted by E; certainly akin to L *milium* are Gr *melinē* and Lith *malnos*. *Milium* has adj *miliārius*, whence E *miliary*.

9. L *milium* becomes Port *milho*, with additional sense 'maize': hence Afr *milje*: SAfrE *mealie*, a maize-spike, and pl *mealies*, maize.

10. LL *molīna* answers to the adj *molīnus*, of a *mola* or mill(stone), whence the Her adj *moline*; the adj of *molīna* is LL *molinārius*, whence E *molinary*. *Mola*, however, has adj *molāris*, whence E *molar*, whence n (a 'grinder' tooth).

11. Gr *mulē*, a mill, has the secondary sense 'a hard uterine formation', retained in L *mola* and becoming Med *mole* (distinct from *mole*, blemish).

12. L *mola* has two derivative cpds notably affecting E:

*ēmolumentum*, orig a sum paid to a miller for grinding (*molere*, to grind) out one's corn, hence a profit, whence, prob via MF-F *émolument*, the E *emolument*;

*immolāre*, to strew sacrificial meal upon (a victim), hence to sacrifice, has pp *immolātus*, whence 'to *immolate*'; derivative *immolātiō*, o/s *immolātiōn-*, becomes MF-F, whence E, *immolation*.

13. L *molere*, to grind, has n *molitiō*, a grinding, which prompts the syn ML *molitūra*, whence MF *moulture* (F *mouture*), whence the hist E *multure*, a fee for corn-grinding (cf *emolument*).

### Latin *mollis*, soft

14. Less than very prob, yet rather more than merely perh, akin to L *molere* (s and r *mol-*), to grind, is L *mollis* (s *moll-*, r *mol-*), soft, tender, whether physically or morally: cf Skt *mṛdús*, weak, mild, Gr *amalos*, tender, and perh Gr *mōlos*, enfeebled, and *malakos*, soft.

15. L *mollis*, neu *molle*, yields—via F—the Mus *molle*. The derivative *mollitiēs*, softness, is adopted by Med; the mdfn *molluscus*, soft-shelled, neu *molluscum*, used also as n, becomes F *mollusque*, whence E *mollusc* (AE *mollusk*), whence *molluscoid* (*-oid*) and (perh from L *molluscus*) *molluscous*. *Mollis* has v *mollīre*, with VL var *\*molliāre*, to soften, whence OF-MF *moillier*, *muiller* (F *mouiller*), to soften, esp by steeping, whence ME *moillen*, to soak, to wet, hence to soil, whence, as *moil*, to soil one's hands, to work very hard.

16. L *mollīre* has the inch derivative *mollescere*, to grow soft, presp *mollescens*, o/s *mollescent-*, whence the E adj *mollescent*. From *mollis* comes— perh prompted by the LL adj *mollificus*, softening —ML *mollificāre*, to render soft, whence MF-F *mollifier*, whence 'to *mollify*'; derivative ML *mollificātiō*, o/s *mollificātiōn-*, becomes—via EF-F *mollification*— E *mollification*. *Mollīre* has the int cpd *ēmollīre*, to soften *ē-* or out, with presp

*ēmolliens*, o/s *ēmollient-*, whence E *emollient*, adj hence n.

17. Akin to L *mollis*, soft, is OE *melsc*, mellow, soft, whence the now dial E *melch*, soft, (of weather) mild: hence, app, the ME *molsh*, soft, sodden (cf the G dial *molsch*, soft, beginning to rot): hence the E *mulch*, a cover—orig, of wet straw—of straw or leaves to protect plant-roots or, derivatively, to keep fruit clean; hence 'to *mulch*' (dress with mulch).

18. L *mollis* becomes OF *mol*, whence, prob—because its leaves are woolly and its down very soft —MF *molaine*, *moleine* (F *molène*), whence ME *moleyne*, E *mullein* (occ *mullen*).

### E *mild*

19. L *mollis* is app for *\*molduis* (cf *mold*, *mould* in para 5): and this OL *\*mold-* is very prob akin to the Gmc *\*mild-* occurring in E *mild*, OE *milde*: cf OFris *milde*, OS *mildi*, mild, OHG *mildi*, *milti*, MHG *milte*, kind, generous, G *mild*, Go *mildeis*, MD *melde*, *milt*, *milde*, D *mild*, ON *mildr*, mild; cf the OC r *\*mel-* (app a var of *\*mal-*, soft) in OIr *meld*, mild, *meldach*, complaisant, and the var r *\*mal-* in Gr *malthakos*, gentle, feeble, perh an extn or a mdfn of Gr *malakos*, soft, and in OP *maldai* (pl), young, OSl *mladŭ*, tender, young.—Hence *mildness*.

**mealies.** See prec, para 9.

**mealy, mealy-mouth(ed).** See the 2nd MEAL (heading).

**mean** (1), adj: ordinary, hence inferior, stingy, (AE coll) petty-minded: ME *mene*: aphetic for OE *gemāene*, general, common: cf OHG *gimeini*, MHG *gemeine*, OFris *mēn-* (in cpds) and *mēne*, Go *gamains*, MD *gemene*, *gemeene*, D *gemeen*, all '(held) in com mon'—cf G *gemein*, vulgar (pej); cf also L com*mūnis* (s com*mūn-*), OL com*oinis* (s com*oin-*). The*ga-*, *ge-* prefix is int; of the base, the Gmc etymon is *\*mainiz*, the IE etymon is *\*moinis* (Walshe).

2. The basic idea is app 'to exchange' (Webster): cf L *munus*, a civic obligation, hence a gift, and *munia*, obligations, official duties, (civic) services, and, without the *-n-* infix, Skt *mayate*, he exchanges. *Munia* has cpd *municipium*, as in *municipal*, q.v. at CAPABILITY, para 8. *Munus* has the cpd adj *munificus*, gift-making, generous, lavish, whence E *munific* (obs), whence, anl, *munificent*; *munificence* derives from L *munificentia*, anl from *munificus*.

3. L *munus* has o/s *muner-*, as in the derivative *munerāre*, to make a present of, with cpd *remunerāre*, to reward (*re-*, back, again), pp *remunerātus*, whence 'to *remunerate*'; derivative *remunerātiō*, o/s *remunerātiōn-*, accounts, prob via MF-F, for *remuneration*, whence, anl, *remunerative*.

4. For *commune*, *communion*, *community*, etc., see sep COMMON.

5. L *munus* has derivative neg adj *immunis*, free from public obligation or service: whence, ? via MF, the E *immune*. Derivative L *immunitās*, o/s *immunitāt-*, becomes MF-F *immunité*, whence E

*immunity*, whence, anl, 'to *immunize*', whence *immunization*.

6. Cf the sep MUTATION, etc.

**mean** (2), adj: intermediate, hence average. See MEDIAL, para 10.

**mean** (3), n: the average. See MEDIAL, para 10.

**mean** (4), v (to have in mind; to signify), whence ill- and well-meaning and -meant; meaning, n, and moan, n, hence v, whence moaner and moaning—cf bemoan.

1. 'To *mean*', pt and pp *meant*, comes, through ME *menen*, from OE *māenan*, to recite or tell, hence to state an intention, to intend: cf OFris *mēna*, OS *mēnian*, OHG *meinēn* (cf G *meinen*, to think, to mean), MD *meinen*, *menen*, (as in D) *meenen*, to say, to mean; cf also OB *mēniti* and perh Hit *mema-*, to say: Gmc r, *\*main-*; IE r, *\*moin-*. (Walshe.)

2. Akin to *mean* is *moan*, n: ME *mone*, earlier *mane*: OE *\*mān*, from OE *māenan*, to complain, very prob id with OE *māenan*, to recite. OE *māenan*, to complain, has int *bemāenan*, ME *bimēnen*, whence, under the influence of *moan* itself, 'to *bemoan*'.

**meander** (n, hence v—whence the pa and vn **meandering**): a winding or turn of a stream, hence a winding course or path: L *maeander*; Gr *maiandros*: Gr *Maiandros*, that Phrygian river—now the *Menderes*—which was anciently proverbial for its extremely winding course.

**meaning**, n, whence **meaningful**. See the 4th MEAN (heading).

**means**, as in 'ways and *means*'. See *mean*, n, at MEDIAL, para 10.

**meant.** See the 4th MEAN, para 1.

**measles**, whence, as if from the old sing, the pa **measled**: ME *masel*, pl *maseles*: cf the syn D *mazelen* (MD *maselen*) and G *Masern*, pl of G *Maser*, a vein, a streak, OHG *masar*, a knotty excrescence; cf OE *maser*, a knot in wood, and even OHG *māsa*, a scar. (Walshe.)—Hence, *measly*, lit 'measled', hence sl 'contemptible'.

2. Akin to OHG *masar* (as above) and MD *maser*, excrescence on a maple (cf ON *mösurr*, a maple), is ME *maser*, E *mazer*, a large drinking bowl, ? orig of maple wood.

**measurable.** See para 5 of:

**measure** (n and v), **measurable** (hence the neg **immeasurable**), **measureless**, **measurement**, **measurer**, pa and vn **measuring**; **mensal** (monthly), **menses**, **menstrual**, **menstruant**, **menstruate**, **menstruation**, **menstruous**; **mensurable** (and **incommensurable**, **immensurable**), **mensural**, **mensuration** (whence, anl, **mensurative**); **mens(e)-** in: **commensurable**, **commensurate**, **commensuration**—**dimensible**, **dimension** (whence **dimensional**)—**immense**, **immensity.**—**moon** (n, hence v), whence **moony** and such visual cpds as **moonbeam**, **-calf**, **-fish**, **-flower**, **-light** (**-lit**), **-shine**, **-stone**, **-struck**: cf **Monday**, also **month, monthly.**—**meter** and **metre**, **metric** (with extn **metrical**); cpds: **diameter**, **diametral**, **diametric** (extn **diametrical**)—**parameter**, whence, anl, **parametric(al)**—**perimeter**, whence,

anl, **perimetric** and (after *symmetry*) **perimetry**—
**symmetry**, whence, anl, **symmetric(al)**, cf **sym-**
**metrize**, with negg **asymmetry** and **asymmetric(al)**;
**catamenia.**—**meal**, a repast; **piecemeal.**—Cf the sep
MODE (where *moderate, modest*, etc.) and the sep
MEDICAL (where *meditate*).

## Indo-European

1. The idea of 'to measure' and 'a measure' lies
at the back of all these words: Gr, L, Gmc. L
*mētīrī*, to measure, has s and r *mēt*-, an extn of IE
*\*mē*-, to measure: and this *\*mē*- is seen also in the
pp *mēnsus*, measured, with s *mēns*- occurring in LL
*mēnsūra*, a measuring, and L *mēnsis*, a month;
this s *mēns*- has r *mēn*-, as also in Gr *mēnē*, moon,
and *mēn*, month (measured by the moon), with
Gmc var *mān*- or *mon*- (E *moon*). The IE *\*mē*-
appears, although in the var *me*-, in Gr *metron*,
a measure. On an IE scale, cf Skt *māti* (and
*mimāti*), he measures, *mắtrā*, a measure, *mita*-, to
measure, *mātis*, a measure, esp in sense 'exact
knowledge' (cf Gr *mētis*, prudence, cunning); OE
*maēth*, a measure, and OE *maēl*, Go *mēl*, (a
measured length of) time; OSl *mĕnŭ*, a measure,
and Lith *mĕnuo*, moon, month, Tokh A *mañ*,
moon, month, and Tokh B *meñe*, month; Go
*mēnōths*, month, OHG *māno*, moon; Skt *mās*-,
*mắsas*, month, moon; perh cf Hit *mehur* (gen
*mēhunas*), time, esp a point of time, and hieroglyphic Hit *meinu*las, crescent of moon. The
changes of the moon afforded the earliest measure
of time longer than a day (measured by the sun).

For the var *med*-, see MEDICAL; for the subsidiary var *mod*-, see MODE.

## Greek

2. Gr *mēnē*, moon, has the cpd adj *katamēnios*,
monthly, whence *ta katamēnia* (neu pl), 'the
monthlies' or *menses*: Med *catamenia*.

3. IE *mē*- has var *me*-, as we see in Gr *metron*
(perh for *\*medstron*), a means of measuring, a
measure, a rule, a verse or Mus metre; s *metr*-, r
*met*- (extn of *me*-). *Metron* becomes L *metrum*,
MF *metre* (F *mètre*), E *metre*, AE *meter*. Derivative Gr adj *metrikos* becomes L *metricus*, late
MF-F *métrique*, E *metric*. The n *metric*, prosody,
derives from F *la métrique*, elliptical for *l'art
métrique*.

4. The chief Gr prefix-cpds affecting E are:
*diametros* (adj, hence n)—*dia* being 'through'—
L *diametrus*, MF *diametre*, adopted by ME,
whence *diameter*; LL *diametrālis*, MF-F *diamétral*,
E *diametral*; Gr *diametrikos*, E *diametric*; whence,
anl, the SciE *parameter*, whence *parametric*;

*perimetros* (*peri*, round about), adj hence n, L
*perimetros*, later *-us*, whence, anl, E *perimeter*,
whence *perimetric*;

*summetria* (*sun*-, with, together), a just proportion, L *symmetria*, EF *symmétrie* (F *symétrie*), E
*symmetry*, whence, anl, *symmetrical*; the Gr neg
*asummetria* yields *asymmetry* (cf F *asymétrie*),
whence—prompted by Gr *asummetros*—*asymmetrical*.

## Latin

5. L *mētīrī*, to measure, has pp *mēnsus*, whence
L *mēnsūra*, whence VL *mēsūra*, whence OF-F,
hence ME, *mesure*, E *measure*; LL *mēnsūrālis*
becomes learnèd E *mensural*. Derivative LL
*mēnsūrāre*, VL *mēsūrāre*, becomes OF-F *mesurer*,
E 'to *measure*'; derivative LL *mēnsūrābilis*, VL
*mēsūrābilis*, becomes OF-F *mesurable*, whence E
*measurable*. LL *mēnsūrābilis* also becomes erudite
E *mensurable*. The LL neg *immēnsūrābilis* becomes
*immensurable*.

6. *Mēnsūrāre* has further derivatives: the pp
*mēnsūrātus* yields the rare 'to *mensurate*'; the subsidiary *mēnsūrātiō*, o/s *mēnsūrātiōn*-, yields *mensuration*, orig a measuring. CF LL *commēnsūrāre*,
to measure by comparison, whence *commēnsūr-
ābilis*, MF-F, hence E, *commensurable*; the pp
*commēnsūrātus* becomes the E adj *commensurate*,
and the subsidiary *commēnsūrātiō*, o/s *-ātiōn*-,
explains *commensuration*; the neg LL *incommēn-
sūrabilis* gives us MF-F, hence E, *incommensurable*,
which anl suggests E *incommensurate*.

7. The *mēns*- of the L pp *mēnsus* has two other
important prefix-cpd derivatives: *dīmētīrī*, to
measure exactly, and *immēnsus*, unmeasured.
*Dīmētīrī*, to measure thoroughly (*di*- for Gr *dia*,
throughout), has pp *dīmēnsus*, whence *dīmēnsiō*,
o/s *dīmēnsiōn*- whence, via MF-F, the E *dimension*,
whence, anl, *dimensible*.

8. L *immēnsus*, not (*in*-) measured, hence, as adj,
not—at least, not easily—measurable, hence huge,
vast, becomes MF-F *immense*, adopted by E;
derivative M *immēnsitās*, o/s *immēnsitāt*-, becomes
MF-F *immensité*, whence E *immensity*.

9. L *mēnsis* (s *mēns*-, r *mēn*-), a month, has pl
*mēnses*, retained by Med in a specialized sense. The
derivative LL adj *mēnsuālis* (suffix *-uālis*: cf
*annuālis* from *annus*, a year) yields erudite E
*mensual* and F *mensuel*. The L *mēnstruus*, monthly,
has neupl *mēnstrua*, used as n in Med sense,
whence LL *mēnstruāre*, with pp *mēnstruans*, o/s
*mēnstruant*-, whence the E adj *menstruant*, and
with pp *mēnstruātus*, whence 'to *menstruate*',
whence, anl, *menstruation*. Also from L *mēnstrua*
come both LL *mēnstruālis*, whence—perh via
MF-F *menstruel*—E *menstrual*, and LL *mēn-
struōsus*, whence E *menstruous*.

## Germanic

10. E *moon*, ME *mone*, OE *mōna*, is akin to
OFris *mōna*, OS and OHG *māno*, MHG *māne*,
Go *mēna*, MD *mane, maen*, D *maan*, ON *māni*:
cf para 1.

11. E *month*, ME *moneth*, OE *mōnath* (? *mōna*,
moon+abstract suffix *-th*), is akin to OFris
*mōnath*, OHG *mānōd*, MHG *mānōt*, G *Monat*,
Go *mēnōths*, ON *mānathr* (*-uthr*). Derivative OE
*mōnathlīc* becomes E *monthly*.

12. E *Monday* (whence *Mondayish*), ME *mone-
day*, earlier *monenday*, OE *mōnandaeg*, lit 'day of'
—hence, 'sacred to'—'the moon' (cf, sem, the L
*lunae dies*), is akin to OFris *mōnandei*, OHG
*mānetag*, MHG *māntac*, G *Montag*, ON *mānadagr*.

13. Akin to the OGmc words for 'moon' and 'month' are those for 'measure', esp a measure of, a point in, time, an occasion: e.g., OE *māel*, a measure, an appointed time, hence—via ME *māel*, *mele*, a repast—the E *meal*: perh imm from ON *māl*, measure, time, meal-time, meal: cf MHG *māl*, G *Māhl*, meal, Go *mēl*, time: cf para 1.

14. *Meal* has the cpd *piecemeal*, ME *pecemele*: ME *pece*+*mele* from OE *māelum*, dat pl of *māel*, a measure.

**meat** (whence **meaty**); sep MATE, companion; **mast**, collective nuts; for MASTODON, see the element -*odon*; **must**, n.

1. *Meat*, orig food in general (as still in EE), hence animals', esp quadrupeds', flesh used as food: ME, from OE, *mete*: cf OFris *mete*, OS *meti*; with the intimately cognate shorter OE *maet*, cf OS *mat*, OHG *maz*, ON *matr*. OGmc r, *\*mat-*, *\*mati-*; IE r, *\*mad-* (cf OIr *maisse*, food—for *\*mad-tja*). Walshe.

2. Akin to OE *maet* is OE *mast*, E *mast*, nuts, esp as food for pigs: cf MHG-G *mast* and esp Skt *mēdas*, fat (n).

3. Akin to OE *maest* is OE-E *must*, grapes' expressed juice before fermentation, hence juice in state of fermentation: L *mustum*, elliptical for *mustum uinum*, new wine: *mustus*, new, young, fresh: perh cf L *muscus*, moss: ? IE r *\*mus-*, mould, mustiness.

**Mecca**, a desirable goal (esp if a place), derives from *Mecca*, that Arabian city which, Mohammed's birthplace, is the Moslems' holiest city: Ar *Makkah*, with triliteral r *M-K-H*: Ptolemy the Geographer called it, c130 A.D., *Macoraba*: o.o.o.

**mechanic** (adj, hence n), **mechanical**, **mechanism**, **mechanize**, etc. See MACHINE, para 3.

**medal**, **medallion**. See METAL, para 3.

**meddle**, **meddler**, **meddlesome**. See MIX, para 4.

**media**, in Phon, is elliptical for L *media uox* (ML *vox*), lit 'middle sound', *media* being the f of *medius*, intermediate, in the middle; but *media* is also the neupl of L *medius* and, in E, used as the Sci pl of *medium*, q.v. in:

**medial**; **median**—cf **mitten** (with shortened **mitt**) —**mizzen**—**mezzanine**—cf also **intermezzo**; **mediant**; **mediate**, adj (whence **mediacy**) and v, and **mediation** (whence, anl, **mediative**), **mediatize**, **mediator** (whence the f **mediatress**)—cf **immedial**, **immediate** (whence **immediacy**)—cf also **intermediary** and **intermediate**; **mediocre**, **mediocrity**; **medium**, Sci pl **media**; **mediety** and **moiety**; **mean**, intermediate, **middling**, hence **mediocre**—whence both the n (as in 'the golden *mean*') and **meanness**, also **meantime** and **meanwhile**;—L-derived cpds in *medi*- or *medio*- (see Elements), mostly self-explanatory, but note **mediaeval** (**medieval**), q.v. at AGE, para 2, and **mediterranean** (whence M—).— Gmc: **mid** (adj), **midst**—cf **amid**, **amidst**, **midshipman** (a sailor—junior officer—in *mid* or middle *ship*) and other easy cpds, e.g. **midday** (OE *middaeg*), **midland**(s), **midnight** (OE *midniht*), **midway** (OE *midweg*), **midwife** (ME *midwif*), whence **midwifery**; **middle**, adj and n (whence v), with such

obvious cpds as **middle-class** (adj), **middleman**, **middle west** (**mid-west**), and the less obvious **Middlesex**, (district of) the Middle Saxons, OE *Middelseaxan*, Domesday *Midlesexe*; **middling**, adj, hence n.—Gr: **mesial**, adj of **mesion**; **meson**: qqv at elements *mesio*-, *meso*- (where note *Mesopotamia*) and, f.a.e., para 1—as follows.

### Indo-European

1. *Medial* comes from LL *mediālis*, situated in the middle, a mdfn of the L *medius*, middle. With s *medi*- and r *med*-, *medius* is akin to Homeric and Aeolian Gr *messos*, Attic *mesos*, varr of an etymon *\*medhios* or, say others, *\*methjos*—cf Cretan *mettos*; to Skt *mádhyas*; OC etymon, perh *\*medios*, with r *\*med*-, as in these 'answers' to L *medium*: OIr *medón*, Ga *meadhon*, MW *mwyn*, Mx *mean*; to Arm *mēj*, n; to OB *mežda* (for *\*medja*), a border; to Go *midjis*, OHG *mitti*, OS *middi*, OE *midd*, middle (adj). The IE etymon is app *\*medhyos*; the IE r, *\*medh*-, the middle, extn *\*medhy*-, n, *\*medhyo*-, adj.

### Greek

2. See the elements *mesio*- and esp *meso*-.

### Latin

3. The L adj *medius* has neu *medium*, used also as n; adopted by E. In addition to LL *mediālis*, *medius* has extn *mediānus*, whence E *median*. *Medius* has derivative LL *mediāre*, to cut in half, to be at the middle (of), with presp *medians*, o/s *mediant*-, whence the It n *mediante*, whence E *mediant*, and with pp *mediātus*, whence both the adj *mediate* and 'to *mediate*'; subsidiary LL *mediātiō*, o/s *mediātiōn*-, passes through late MF-F *médiation* to become E *mediation*, and subsidiary LL *mediātor* is adopted by E; 'to *mediatize*', however, derives from the F *médiatiser*, formed eruditely from MF-F *médiation* and *médiateur*.

4. L *medius* has LL derivative *medietās*, the middle, centre, a half, whence E *mediety*; whence, via the acc *medietātem*, the OF *meitiet*, whence F *moitié* and E *moiety*.

5. LL *medietās* has derivative VL *\*medietāna*, a mitten (which is 'halved' between thumb and fingers), whence OF-F *mitaine*, adopted by ME, whence E *mitten*; B & W, however, derive *mitaine* from the syn OF *mite*, itself o.o.o.

6. L *mediānus* (as in para 3) becomes It *mezzano*, whence, elliptical for *vela* (sail) *mezzana*, the It n *mezzana*, whence EF-F *misaine*, whence E *mizzen*. It *mezzano*, middle, has dim *mezzanino*, which, used as n, becomes the late EF-F Arch term *mezzanine*, adopted by E.

7. Also It is *intermezzo*, adopted by E as a Mus term: n, from L *intermedius*, situated in the *medius*, or middle, between (*inter*). *Intermedius* becomes the now rare E *intermedial*; the neu *intermedium*, used by LL as n for 'an intervening space' (and partly adopted by SciE), becomes the EF-F *intermède*, (obs) E *intermede*; the derivative EF-F adj *intermédiaire* becomes E *intermediary*, adj

hence n. Prob from the LL n *intermedium* derives the ML adj *intermediātus*, whence E *intermediate*, adj hence n.

8. Whereas the rare *immedial* (*im-* for *in-*, not) is an anl E formation from *medial*, *immediate* derives, perh via MF-F *immédiat*, from LL *immediātus*, not (*im-*) mediated, hence next.

9. L *medius* has the further extn *mediocris*, a cpd with obscure 2nd element, perh the app dial *ocris*, a height, a hill (cf Umbrian *ocar*): 'situated at mid-height', hence 'well poised', hence 'moderate' or 'average', often pej: hence late MF-F *médiocre*, E *mediocre*; derivative L *mediocritās*, o/s *mediocritāt-*, becomes MF-F *médiocrité*, whence E *mediocrity*.

10. L *mediānus*, situated in the middle (as in para 3), becomes OF *meien*, adj hence n: ME *mene*: E *mean*.

11. L *medius*, s and c/f *medi-*, has the notable LL cpd *mediterraneus*, situated between two lands (*terra*, a land: f.a.e., TERRA), applied esp to the land-locked sea and soon used as n therefor: E *mediterranean*.

### Germanic

12. The E adj *mid*, which lacks a comp but has sup *midmost* (OE *midmest*), derives from OE *midd*, with cognates as in para 1; the OE adv *middes* occurs in the phrase *in middes*, which, influenced by *middest* (a sup of *mid*), becomes *in the middest*, whence E *midst*.

13. With *mid*, *midst*, cf *amid*, *amidst*. *Amid* comes from ME *amidde*, itself from earlier ME *amiddes*, whence *amidst*: and ME *amiddes* (gen *-s*, used as adv suffix) comes from OE *on middan*, in the middle, the n *midde* deriving from the adj *midd*.

14. The n *middle* derives from OE *middel*, from the OE adj *middel*, whence, via ME *middel*, the E adj *middle*. The OE adj *middel* is akin to OFris *middel*, OHG *mittil* (whence the MHG-G n *mittel*, means), MD-D *middel*: all the OGmc forms represent extnn of the simple adj (OE *midd*, etc., as in para 1). The adj *middling*, orig 'intermediate', recorded first in 1495 (OED), app derives from *mid*, adj+*-ling* as used in adjj.

**mediate, mediation, mediatize, mediator.** See prec, para 3.

**medicable.** See para 2 of:

**medical, medicament, medicate, medication** (whence, anl, **medicative**), **medicatory; medicine**, n (whence **medicinal**) and v, **medico;—remedy**, n (whence **remediless**) and v, **remediable** (and **irremediable**), **remedial.—meditant, meditate, meditation, meditative.—mete**, to measure, whence **meter**, an instrument that measures, whence, in turn, **meterage.—**Cf the rather closely related MEASURE and MODE, treated sep.

### Medicine

1. *Medical* derives, via EF-F *médical*, from L *medicālis*, adj of *medicus*, a physician, itself orig an adj, deriving from *mederi*, to attend medically

(to), s and r *med-*, itself an extn of the IE r *me-*, to measure: f.a.e., MEASURE, para 1.

2. L *medicus*, physician—whence It *medico* (cf Sp *médico*), adopted as E coll—has derivative *medicāre*, attend medically, which has these derivatives affecting E:

LL *medicābilis*, capable of healing—a sense obs in E *medicable*;

*medicāmentum*, MF-F *médicament*, E *medicament*, whence *medicamental*, *medicamentous*;

*medicātiō*, o/s *medication-*, whence, perh via EF-F *médication*, the E *medication*;

LL *medicātōrius*, with healing power, whence E *medicatory*;

*medicīnus*, of or by or for a physician, whence, via *medicīna ars*, the physician's art, the n *medicīna*, whence, via OF-MF and ME, *medicine*, whence, partly, 'to *medicine*', partly from OF-MF *medeciner*;

LL *medicīnālis* (from *medicīna*), of or for or by healing, whence, via OF, the E *medicinal*.

3. L *mederi* has the derivative *remedium*, a medical tending that brings back (*re-*) health; whence, via OF-MF *remede* (F *remède*), the E *remedy*; 'to *remedy*' derives, via OF-MF *remedier*, from L *remediāre* (from *remedium*). Derivative LL *remediālis* produces E *remedial*; derivative L *remediābilis* produces *remediable*, with the neg *irremediābilis* explaining *irremediable*.

### Meditation

4. L *mederi*, orig to attend to (any person or thing), has the freq *meditāri*, to apply oneself to, to study, to reflect upon, with presp *meditans*, o/s *meditant-*, whence the E adj and n *meditant*; the pp *meditātus* yields 'to *meditate*'; derivative *meditātiō*, o/s *meditation-*, passes through OF-MF to E *meditation*; derivative LL *meditātīuus*, ML *-īvus*, becomes OF-MF *meditatif* (f *-ive*), whence E *meditative*.

### Measurement

5. Whereas L *medicus* is a measurer of man's ills and injuries and *meditation* is the thought-measuring of an idea, a fact, a thing, the IE r *me-*, to measure, is displayed openly in OE *metan*, whence 'to *mete*', akin to OFris *meta*, OS *metan*, OHG *mezzan*, MHG *mezzen*, G *messen*, Go *mitan*, MD-D *meten*, ON *meta*; cf also Gr *medesthai* (s and r *med-*), to attend to, to estimate, and OIr *midiur* (r *mid-*), I judge. Cf the 1st MEET.

**mediety.** See MEDIAL, para 4.

**medieval, medievalism**, etc. See AGE, para 2.

**mediocre, mediocrity.** See MEDIAL, para 9.

**meditant, meditate, meditation, meditative.** See MEDICAL, para 4.

**mediterrane, Mediterranean.** See MEDIAL, para 11, and TERRA, para 6.

**medium** (n, hence adj). See MEDIAL, para 3.

**medlar**, tree, its fruit: ME *medler*, the tree, adopted from OF-MF; var of OF-MF *meslier*, the tree, from OF-EF *medle*, var of *mesle*, the fruit, var *mesple* (with MF var *nesple*, whence F *nèfle*): L *mespila*, varr *-lus*, *-lum*, with dissimilated var *nespila*: Gr *mespilē*, var *mespilon*: perh orig Ch— cf LOQUAT.

**medley.** See MIX, para 6.

**medulla** (whence the adj **medullar**), **medullary.** The latter derives from L *medullāris*, adj of *medulla*, marrow (filling the cavities of bones), adopted by Sci: perh for *\*merulla* (deducible from several Italic dialects), with *-d-* suggested by L *medius*, middle: if that be so, cf the syn OIr *smiur*, EIr *smir*, Ga *smior*, and the *s*-less W *mēr*, Cor *maru*; moreover, if that be so, L *medulla* is akin to E SMEAR.

**Medusa** (whence the jellyfish *medusa*), adopted from L *Medūsa*, is a mere trln of Gr *Medousa*, one of the Gorgons: f of *Medōn*, Lord, prop the presp of *medein*, to take care of, to protect, to rule over: r *med-*, extn of IE *\*me-*, to measure: cf MEDICAL, para 1, and MEASURE, para 1.

**meed**, a due reward or recompense: ME *mede*: OE *mēd*: cf the syn OFris *mēde*, OS *mēda*, OHG *mēta*, *mieta*, MHG *miete* (cf G *Miete*, rent, hire), Go *mizdō*, OSl *mīzda*; Gr *misthos* (for *\*mizdhós*), Av *mīžda*, Skt *mīḍha* (for *\*mizdhá*), booty.

**meek** (whence **meekness**): ME *mēk*, a contr of *mēoc*: ON *mjūkr*, mild, gentle, soft: cf Go *mūka-mōdei*, gentleness, MLG *mūke*, MD *muke*, D *muik*: ult akin to MUCUS (f.a.e.).

**meerschaum.** See MERE, n, and cf SKIM, para 2.

**meet** (1), adj (suitable, fitting): ME *mete*: OE *gemǣte*, akin to OE *metan*, to measure, q.v. at MEDICAL, para 5.

**meet** (2), v (whence the vn **meeting**), hence n; pt and pp **met.**

'To *meet*', ME *meten*, OE *mētan*, is akin to OFris *mēta*, OS *mōtian*, Go gamōtjan, ON *moeta*, to meet, therefore also to ON *mōt* and OE ge*mōt*, in cpds *-mōt*, a meeting, whence E *moot*, now only hist; OE *-mōt* has derivative *mōtian*, to meet for talk or discussion, ME *motien*, later *moten*, E 'to *moot*', now archaic, even for 'to discuss', yet extant in 'a *moot* case or point', one requiring or worthy of discussion.

**Meg.** See MARGARET (heading).

**megalomania** is SciL for 'delusion of (one's own) grandeur': 'great madness': cf the elements *megalo-* and *-mania*. Cf:

**megaphone**, 'great voice': cf the element *mega-*. For this, as for prec, see, f.a.e., MASTER, para 1.

**megrim.** See MIGRAINE.

**meinie, meiny.** See MANOR, para 4.

**meiosis, meiotic.**

The latter derives from Gr *meiōtikos*, the adj of *meiōsis*, diminution, from *meioun*, to diminish (vt), from *meiōn*, smaller, akin to *minuein* (L *minuere*), to diminish: IE r, *\*mei-*, to diminish.

**mel**, honey (Pharm); **melilite, melilot, mellifluous**, all three at element *meli-*; **mellite** (L *melli*, c/f +Min *-ite*), whence **mellitic**;—**molasses; mulse**;—**mildew.**

1. L *mel*, honey, gen *mellis*, c/f *melli-*, is akin to Gr *meli*: cf Hit *melit* (var *milit*: cf OIr *mil*),

honey, and *meliddus* (var *mil-*), sweet; cf also *mead*, q.v. at AMETHYST.

2. L *mel* has LL adj *mellāceus*, honey-like, hence sweet, whence, via the n *mellācium*, Port *melaço* (cf Sp *melaza*, whence EF-F *mélasse*), whence EE *melasses*, whence—violently, yet Britannically— E *molasses*. The Chem adj *melassic* derives from the F *mélasse*.

3. Akin to L *mel* is L *mulsus*, mixed with honey, whence *mulsum* (sc *uīnum*), wine strongly flavoured with honey: E *mulse*.

4. A Gmc cognate of L *mel*, Gr *meli*, perh occurs in OE *meledēaw*, *mildēaw*, whence E *mildew*; but the sense agrees ill with the presumed orig meaning 'honey-dew', and well with the sense 'meal (or flour)-dew', as prob in the cognate OHG *militou*, MHG *miltou*, G *Mehltau*: cf OE *melu*, E *meal*, grain coarsely ground. (Walshe.)

**melancholia, melancholic, melancholy; melanian, melanic, melanin, melanism, melanite, melanoid, melanosis** (whence **melanose**), **melanous; melasma; Melanesia**—see Elements at *mela-*;—**mullet, surmullet; mule,** slipper.

1. *Melancholy*, ME from OF *melancolie* (F *mé-*), derives from LL *melancholia*, now a Med and Psy term in E: Gr *melankholia*: Gr c/f *melan-*+an *-ia* abstract derivative from *kholē*, gall, bile (f.a.e., CHOLER): 'black bile', hence an extremely depressed, long-lasting mood. Gr *melas*, o/s *melan-*, f *melaina* (cf Skt *malinī*), is akin to Skt *malinás*, filthy, black, *mlānas*, black, *mala-*, filth, dirt; cf also OHG *māl*, a mark, a spot, and Lith *mēlynas*, blue: IE r, *\*mel-*, varr *\*māl-* and *\*mōl-*, dirty, dark. (Hofmann.)

2. Gr *melankholia* has adj *melankholikos*, LL *melancholicus*, F *mélancolique* (F *mé-*), E *melancholic*.

3. The Gr *melas*, through its c/f *melan-*, directly affects E in the foll words:

*melanian* (*-ian*) and *melanic* (*-ic*), adjj, as are *melanoid* (*-oid*) and *melanous* (*-ous*);

*melanin* (Chem suffix *-in*) and *melanite* (Min suffix *-ite*); cf the Zoo *melanism* (*-ism*), whence, anl, *melanistic*;

*melanosis*, Gr *melanōsis*, a becoming black, from *melanousthai*, to become black, from c/f *melan-*.

4. The Med *melasma* (with derivative adj *melasmic*) is adopted from Gr ('a black spot'): *melas*+suffix *-asma*.

5. Akin to Gr *melas*, black, is Gr *mullos*, a red mullet, L *mullus*, whence, prob, the OF-F, orig dim, *mulet*, adopted by ME, whence, by Classical re-shaping, E *mullet*. With the red mullet, cf, both phon and sem, the L *mulleus*, and the Lith *mulvas*, reddish.

6. E *surmullet*, a red mullet, is adopted from F: OF *sormulet*: OF *sor* (F *saure*: cf SORREL)+OF *mulet*.

7. L *mulleus*, reddish, is, as n, used elliptically for *mulleus calceus*, a reddish shoe, i.e. of red leather: hence, prob via MD *mule* (later *muyle*: D *muil*), the EF-F *mule*, adopted by E for a backless slipper.

Melbourne, Aus city, was, c1836, named for the E statesman Lord *Melbourne* (1779–1848): PlN *Melbourne*, either 'middle stream' or 'mill stream'. The adj, hence 'inhabitant', is *Melburnian*.

melch. See the 2nd MEAL, para 17.

mêlée. Cf *medley*; see MIX, para 6.

melic. See MELODY.

melilite; melilot. See the element *meli-*.

meliorable, meliorant, meliorate, melioration (whence, anl, meliorative; meliorism, meliority; ameliorable, ameliorant, ameliorate, amelioration (whence, anl, ameliorative and ameliorator).—Cf the sep MULTITUDE.

1. *Ameliōrāre* (*ad*, to, used int) does not exist in L; ML, however, possesses the rare *ameliōrāri*, to be in better health: and to it, something is perh owed by the OF *ameillorer*, to render better, from OF *meillor*, better (L *melior*); Voltaire re-shapes the OF *ameillorer* to *améliorer*, which E, after *meliorate*, turns into *ameliorate*; the derivative MF *amelioration*, F *amélioration*, becomes E *amelioration*, whence, prompted by the simple *meliorable*, etc., the subsidiaries *ameliorable*, etc.

2. L *meliōrāre*, to render better, has presp *meliōrans*, o/s *meliōrant-*, whence the E n *meliorant*, and pp *meliōrātus*, whence 'to *meliorate*'; the inf s *meltōr-* suggests *meliorable*; the pps has derivative LL *meliōrātiō*, o/s *meliōrātiōn-*, whence *melioration*.

3. Whereas *meliority* derives from ML *meliōritās*, o/s *meliōritāt-*, *meliorism* and *meliorist*=L *melior*, better+*-ism*, *-ist*. L *melior*, s *meli-*, r *mel-*, is akin to Gr *mallon* (r *mal-*), rather, and *mala*, very, and prob to the L adj *multus* (s *mult-*, OL r *\*nul-*), much, many a (cf MULTITUDE).

mell, to mix or meddle. See MIX, para 5.

mellay. Cf *medley*; see MIX, para 6.

mellifluous. See the element *meli-*.

mellow. See the 2nd MEAL, para 6.

melodic, melodious, melody. See ODE, para 5.

melon; malus and pepo; marmalade; camomile, q.v. at HOMO; pompion, pumpkin.

1. *Melon*, OF *melon*, derives from *mēlōn*em, acc of early LL *mēlō*, 'fruit of the gourd *or* water melon *or* quince' (Souter), but esp of the 2nd: short for LGr *mēlopépōn*, a watermelon, (lit) an apple-shaped melon: *mēlon*, an apple+*pepōn*, a (large) melon.

2. Gr *pepōn* becomes—Pliny onwards—L *pepō* (gen *peponis*), adopted by E as a Bot term. Gr *pepōn* is lit '(a fruit) cooked (by the sun)': cf the element *-pepsia*.

3. Gr *mēlon*, an apple (cf Gr *mēléā*, *mēlis*, apple-tree), is o.o.o.: perh from the Aegean island *Mēlos* (Hofmann); perh, however, the plant being indigenous to tropical Africa and southern Asia, *mēlon* is a Medit word.

4. Gr *mēlon* becomes or, at the least, prompts the L *mālum*, an apple, *mālus*, an apple-tree; the latter is adopted as a Bot term.

5. *Marmalade* (occ *marmelade*) comes from F *marmelade*, EF *mermelade*: prob via Sp *mermelada*: Port *marmelada*: an *-ada* derivative from

Port *marmelo*, quince: dissimilated from L *melimēlum*, a honey- or sweet-apple: Gr *melimēlon*, a sweet apple, esp a quince-grafted apple: *meli*, honey (f.a.e., MEL)+*mēlon*, apple (as in paras 1, 3).

6. The now only dial *pompion*, *pumpion*, whence, with dim suffix *-kin*, the E *pumpkin*, is a var of EE *pompon*, adopted from late MF-EF, which nasalizes *popon*, itself a var of late MF-EF *pepon*, from L *peponem*, acc of *pepō* (as in para 2).

melos, song, melody. See ODE, para 5.

melt (v, hence n) pt, pp (hence pa) melted—presp, hence pa and vn, melting; obs pp, now only adj, molten (OE *gemolten*); cf malt, n, hence v (whence pa malted), maltose (*malt*, n+Chem *-ose*); —smelt, v, whence smelter, smeltery, pa and vn smelting; cf smalt, whence smaltine, smaltite (Min suffixes *-ine*, *-ite*); prob milt, spleen; enamel.

1. 'To *melt*' derives from OE *meltan*, vi, sense-assisted by OE *mieltan*, *myltan*, vt: cf ON *melta*, to digest, Gr *meldein* (vt), to melt, and perh L *mollis*, soft: IE r, prob *\*meld-*.

2. Akin to *melt* is *smelt*, to fuse (ore): MD or MLG *smelten*: cf OHG *smelzan*, MHG *smelzen*, G *schmelzen*, to melt, vi, and the vt OHG-MHG *smelzen*, G *schmelzen*.

3. Akin to OE *meltan*, *mieltan*, to melt (vi, vt), is OE *mealt*, E *malt*, grain (usu barley) softened by steeping and thereupon allowed to germinate: cf ON *malt*, OHG-G *malz* (cf the OHG adj *malz*, melting away, and ON *maltr*, rotten), MD *malt*, *molt*, *moud*, D *mout*.

4. Akin to the v *smelt* is the n smalt, adopted from EF-F: It *smalto*, coloured glass, of Gmc origin: cf OHG *smelzan* (as in para 2), but esp OHG *smelzi*, G *Schmelz*, enamel, and cf MLG *smalt*, OHG-MHG *smalz*, G *Schmalz*, fat or lard, which melt easily and, in one form, result from cooking.

5. *Enamel* itself (v, hence n) derives from AF *enameler*, earlier *enamayller*: *en-*, in(to)+*amayl*, OF *esmail* (F *émail*), earlier *esmal*, from a lost *\*esmalt*: Frankish *\*smalt*, deduced from OHG *smelzi*, enamel.

6. Akin prob to OE *mealt*, malt, and *melt*an, to melt, is OE *milte*, the spleen: cf OFris *milte*, OHG *milzi*, MHG *milze*, G *Milz*, MD *melte*, *milte*, D *milt*, ON *milte*, *milti*.

member, part—esp limb—of the human body, hence a person in a group or a community; hence membral; dismember, dismemberment;—membrane, whence, prompted by L *membranus*, the adj membranous; membranelle, membranule;—meninges, whence, anl, meningeal and meningism, cf meningitis;—mensa, mensal.

1. *Member*, ME from OF *membre*, derives from L *membrum* (senses as in heading): s *membr-*, r *memb-*, extn of IE *\*mem-* or *\*men-*, base of *\*mēmsro-*, var of *\*mēmso-*, part of a (living) body: cf Gr *mēn*inx, membrane, Skt *māṃsám*, Tokh B *misa*, Arm *mis*, Alb *miš*, OSl *męso*, Go *mimz*, flesh; perh also cf Gr *mēros*, thigh, and OIr *mēr*, a piece of flesh, and very prob cf Skt *mās* (? for *\*mēs* for *\*mēms*), flesh.

2. L *membrum* becomes OF-F *membre*, whence OF-MF *desmembrer*, to tear limb from limb, whence 'to *dismember*'; derivative MF *desmembrement* yields *dismemberment*.

3. L *membrum* has adj *\*membrānus*, of the body's limbs, whence, elliptical for *carō membrāna*, flesh covering the limbs, the n *membrāna*, skin covering the limbs, hence membrane: whence, perh from EF-F, the E *membrane*. The L dim *membranulum*, *-ula*, yields E *membranule* and prompts the SciL *membranella*, whence Zoo *membranelle*.

4. Gr *mēninx* (μῆνιγξ), skin, membrane, has gen *mēningos* (μῆγιγγος), whence the SciL *meninges* (cf LL *mēninga*, the dura mater membrane), the three membranes encasing both the brain and the spinal cord: and *meninges*+the 'disease' suffix *-itis* accounts for *meningitis*.

5. Perh akin to Gr *mēninx* and L *membrum* is L *mēnsa*, a table; this is a good guess only if the orig sense was 'a *meat* board' or even '*meat* itself'. But the somewhat discredited old etymology '*mēnsa* for *mēnsus*, pp of *metīrī*, to measure' is preferable, for it might well have originated in *tabula mēnsa*, 'a *measured* plank (hence collectively, set of planks)'. L *mēnsa* has LL adj *mēnsālis*, whence the erudite E *mensal*.

memento. See MIND, para 14.

memoir. See para 4 of MEMORY.

memorabilia, memorable, memorandum. See para 4 of MEMORY.

memorial (adj, hence n). See para 5 of MEMORY.

memorize. See the heading of:

memory (whence 'to *memorize*'); memoir (often in pl), whence memoirist; memorabilia; memorable; memorandum, pl memoranda, often shortened, coll, to memo, memos; memoria, memorial (adj, hence n), whence memorialist, memorialize; memoriae; immemorial; commemorable, commemorate, commemoration, commemorative, commemorator;— remember, remembrance, remembrancer; cf perh moratorium, moratory; cf prob mourn, mourner, mournful, mourning (pa and vn).—Gr: martyr (n, hence v), martyrdom, martyrize, martyry —and martyrology, whence, anl, martyrological and martyrologist.

## Indo-European

1. The L starting-point is *memor*, mindful; the Gr, *martus* (gen *marturos*), a witness; and the Gmc, OE *murnan*, to grieve. The resp rr are *mem-*, *memor* being a redup; *mart-*, prob an extn of *\*mar-* (cf the Skt suffix *-t*); *murn-*, prob an extn of *\*mur-*. Cf the Gr *merimna*, solicitude, anxiety, and *mermeros*, solicitous, anxious, the former an ancient extn, the latter a redup, of *\*mer-*, itself a var of *\*mar-*; cf Skt *smárati*, he remembers, with that *s-* prefix which we find in, e.g., Gr; OLith *merëti*, to be anxious, and Serbo-Croatian *máriti*, to grieve over; Go *maúrnan*, OHG *mornēn*, to mourn; if L *mora*, a delay, be indeed cognate, then cf OIr *maraim*, I remain, and Ga *mair*, to last, *mairneal*, dilatoriness; cf also W *marth*, sorrow, anxiety, Cor *mar*

(obs), a doubt, *moreth*, grief, regret, Br *mār*, (a) doubt, with OC r *\*mar-*, to be anxious, itself with an *s-* var, as in Ga *smùr*, sadness; Arm *mormok*, regret, sorrow. The IE r, therefore, is prob *\*mer-* or *\*smer-* (Hofmann), with varr *\*mar-* and *\*smar-*, *\*mor-*, *\*mur-* and *\*smur-*, to be anxious, to grieve.

## Greek

2. Gr *martus* (o/s *martur-*), a witness, has Aeolic and Doric var *martur* (o/s *martur-*), which, in LGr, takes the sense 'witness of God, witness to one's faith': hence LL *martyr*, adopted by OF, OE, etc.; E *martyr* has derivative *martyrdom* (*-dom*). LL *martyr* has these derivatives affecting E:

LL *martyrizāre*, to suffer martyrdom, whence, in ML, to inflict it upon, whence, prob via OF-F *martyriser*, 'to *martyrize*'; derivative ML *martyrizātiō*, o/s *martyrizātiōn-*, produces *martyrization*;

LL *martyrium*, martyrdom, hence a martyr's memorial (shrine, chapel, etc.), adopted by E and also anglicized as *martyry*;

ML *martyrologium*—cf the element *-logy* (at *-loger*)—whence, prob via MF-F *martyrologie*, the E *martyrology*.

## Latin

3. L *mora*, a stopping, a pause, (orig *mora temporis*) a delay, is retained by E as a legal and prosodic term. The derivative *morāri*, to delay (vi and vt), acquires its own derivative, the LL adj *moratōrius*, causing delay, dilatory, whence (F *moratoire* and) E *moratory*, mostly—as in LL, ML —in Law. *Moratōrius* has neu *moratōrium*, which, in modern times, becomes a general European banking term—c1875 in Britain, c1890 in France —with its own adj *moratorial*.

4. L *memor*, mindful, has the foll derivatives affecting E:

*memoria*, memory, hence a remembrance, hence the pl *memoriae*, memoirs: OF-MF *memoire* (F *mé-*), with var *memorie*, adopted by ME, whence *memory*; OF-MF *memoire* gains, in MF, the sense 'memorandum', whence, aided by L *memoriae*, the pl *mémoires*, one's personal history, history from the personal angle: whence E *memoir* and *memoirs*, etc.;

*memorāre*, to recall to mind, to celebrate the memory of, hence simply to relate, to narrate; derivative *memorābilis*, worthy of remembrance, yields *memorable* (cf late MF-F *mémorable*), and its neupl *memorābilia* has been partly adopted by E; the neg *immemorābilis* becomes *immemorable*; derivative *memorandus*, worthy or needing to be remembered, has neu *memorandum*, neupl *memoranda*, form-adopted, sense-adapted, by E (cf the F *mémorandum*); pp *memorātus*, derivatives *\*memorātiō* and LL *memorātīuus* (ML *-īvus*), produce the obs or rare 'to *memorate*', *memoration*, *memorative*—cf *commemorate*, etc., in para 6.

5. L *memoria* develops its own adj *memoriālis*, whence MF, hence E, *memorial* (F *mé-*); the derivative LL *memoriāle* (orig the neu of the adj), a 'sign of remembrance, memorial, monument'

(Souter), becomes the MF n *memorial* (F *mé-*), adopted by E; the ML neg *immemoriālis* yields *immemorial*.

6. *Memorāre* (as in para 4) has cpd *commemorāre*, a mere int (implied by *com-*, from *cum*, with) of the simple v; derivative *commemorābilis* gives us *commemorable*; pp *commemorātus* brings 'to *commemorate*'; derivative LL *commemorātiō*, o/s *commemorātiōn-*, passes through OF-MF to become E *commemoration*, and the EF-F derivative *commémoratif*, f *-ive*, leads to E *commemorative*; derivative LL *commemorātor* is extant in E.

7. *Memorāre* has the derivative var *memorāri*, to remember, with LL (merely int) cpd *rememorāri*, to call back to one's own mind, to remember, whence, by a partial dissimilation of OF *\*rememrer* (contr of *\*rememorer*—as in EF), the OF *remembrer*, whence 'to *remember*'; derivative OF-MF *remembrance* is adopted by E, orig in the F senses 'memory' and 'memorandum'; the now rare derivative 'to *remembrance*' has derivative agent *remembrancer*, extant mostly in the E Supreme Court *Remembrancer*.

### Germanic

8. 'To *mourn*', ME *mournen*, derives from OE *murnan*: see para 1.

**men.** Pl of MAN.

**menace.** See MINATORY, para 1.

**ménage, menagerie.** See MANOR, para 4.

**mend** (v, hence n; hence also vn **mending**) is aphetic for *amend*, q.v. at MENDICANT.

**mendacious, mendacity.** See MENDICANT, para 2.

**Mendelian** is the adj, **Mendelism** the abstract n, corresp to **Mendel's Law**, a Bio law governing inheritance: discovered by the Augustinian abbot, Gregor J. Mendel (1822–84).

**mendicant** (whence **mendicancy**), **mendicity**; **mendacious, mendacity**; **amend** (whence **mend**), **amende, amendatory, amendment, amends**; **emend, emendate, emendation, emendatory**.

1. The base is L *menda* (var of *mendum*), a physical defect, hence a fault, esp in a text: o.o.o.: perh cf W *mann*, a physical blemish or defect, Cor *mans*, maimed, crippled, and Skt *mindā*, a physical defect: IE r, *\*men-* or *\*min-*, with var *\*man-*, a physical defect.

2. L *mendum, -da*, has two simple derivatives relevant to E:

*mendāx*, gen *mendācis*, whence E *mendacious*; with derivative LL *mendācitās*, o/s *mendācitāt-*, whence E *mendacity*;

*mendīcus*, *\*having physical defects, \*infirm*, (hence) poor, hence, as n, a beggar; derivative *mendīcāre*, to beg for alms, has presp *mendīcans*, o/s *mendīcant-*, whence the E adj, hence n, *mendicant*; another derivative, *mendīcitās*, o/s *mendīcitāt-*, yields, via OF-F *mendicité*, the E *mendicity*.

3. L *mendum, -da*, has a cpd-v derivative: *ēmendāre*, to remove (connoted by *e*, out of) the faults of, to correct, whence 'to *emend*', to correct (a literary work, esp a text); the pp *ēmendātus*

explains the unwanted 'to *emendate*'; derivative *ēmendātiō*, o/s *ēmendātiōn-*, gives us *emendation*; derivative agent *ēmendātor* has been adopted; derivative LL *ēmendātōrius* yields *emendatory*. *Emendable*=L *ēmendābilis*.

4. *Ēmendāre* becomes OF-F *amender*, whence ME *amenden*, E 'to *amend*'; derivative OF-F *amende*, partly adopted in the phrase *amende honorable*, has pl *amendes*, adopted by ME, whence E *amends* (to make). Derivative OF-F *amendement*, adopted by ME, soon becomes *amendment*. *Amendatory*='to *amend*'+emend*atory*.

**menhaden**, a herring-like fish abounding off the N Atlantic coast and much used, even by the Amerindians, as a fertilizer: of Alg origin: cf Narragansett *munnawhat*, fertilizer, and Massachuset *munnóquohteau*, he manures the soil. (Webster.)

**menhir.** See DOLMEN. Perh cf Eg *men*, a stone, and *meni*, a stony hill, a mountain.

**menial.** See MANOR, para 5.

**meninges, meningitis.** See MEMBER, para 4.

**meniscus:** SciL from Gr *meniskos*, little moon, dim of *mēnē*, moon: f.a.e., MEASURE.

**menopause.** See PAUSE and cf the element *meno-* (1).

**mensa, mensal.** See MEMBER, para 5.

**menses.** See MEASURE, para 9.

**menstrual, menstruate, menstruation, menstruous.** See MEASURE, para 9.

**mensual.** See MEASURE, para 9.

**mensurable, mensural, mensurate, mensuration.** See MEASURE, paras 5, 6.

**mental, mentality.** See MIND, para 10.

**Mentha** (whence **menthyl**: suffix *-yl*), **menthane** (occ **menthan**), **menthol**, whence **menthene** (=*menth*ol+Chem *-ene*) and **mentholated**; **mint**, whence the pungent **peppermint** and the **spearmint** with its *spire*-shaped inflorescence.

1. The Bot *Mentha* is L *mentha*, var *menta*, the aromatic plant mint: perh suggested by Gr *mintha, minthē*: ? from Asia Minor.

2. *Menthol*=E *Mentha*+Chem *-ol*; from *menthol*, G forms *Menthan* (*-an* is E *-ane*, a Chem suffix), adopted by E, now usu *menthane*.

3. OE *minte*, whence E *mint*, app blends L *menta* and Gr *mintha*; cf MF *mente*, EF-F *menthe*.

**mention.** See MIND, para 13.

**mentor.** See MIND, para 2.

**menu.** See MINOR, para 6.

**Mephistophelean** (**-ian**) is the adj of the devil *Mephistopheles* in Goethe's *Faust* (1808, 1831): G: o.o.o.: ? from L *mephitis* (see next).

**mephitic** (LL *mephiticus*, var *mefiticus*) is the adj of L *mephitis, mefitis*, a noxious exhalation from the earth, but also, prob the earlier, *M-*, the name of a goddess averting such exhalations: o.o.o.

**mercantile.** See MARKET, para 2.

**mercenary.** See MARKET, para 6.

**mercer**, OF-F *mercier*, orig a merchant, like **mercery**, OF-F *mercerie*, orig merchandise, derives from L *merx* (gen *mercis*), wares: f.a.e., MARKET, para 1.

mercerize=the v suffix -ize attached to John Mercer (1791–1886), the E calico-printer inventor of the process.
mercery. See MERCER.
merchandise; merchant. See MARKET, para 3.
merciful, merciless. See MERCY.
mercurial, mercury, Mercury. See MARKET, para 5.

mercy, whence merciful (whence unmerciful) and merciless: ME from OF-F merci derives from LL mercēs (gen mercēdis), pity, mercy, from L mercēs, hire, reward: cf MARKET, para 1.

mere (1), adj, clear, hence pure, (hence) this and nothing else; cf sep MORGANATIC and MORN(ING), MORROW.

Mere derives, perh via OF mier, from L merus: cf OE āmerian (int a-), to purify; perh cf Skt máricis, a ray of light.

mere (2), n, the sea (obs), a (small) lake, a pond: ME from OE mere, sea, lake: cf OFris mere, OS meri, Go marei and mari-, OHG mari, meri, MHG mer, G Meer, MD maer, D meer, ON marr; OIr muir (gen mora), Ga muir (gen mara), Cor and EW mor, OC *mori (prob cf Armorica); Lith mãrés and OSl morje (cf Ru móre); F dial mare, pond; L mare, sea; perh Skt maryā́dā, seashore, and prob Gr amárā, a conduit. IE r: *mar-; basic idea, 'liquid'.

2. ME mere, lake, has cpd meremaide, mermayde, whence E mermaid, whence, anl, merman.

3. L mare, sea, has adj marīnus, OF-F marin, E marine; the derivative F n marine becomes also E. The F adj marin (whence the n marin, a sailor, E marine) has EF-F derivative mariner, to put into salt water, whence late EF-F marinade, a brine (in cooking), adopted by E; 'to marinate' app fuses— or perh rather, confuses—the F pp mariné and F and E marinade. E mariner, imm from OF-F marinier, seaman, sailor, derives ult from the ML marinārius, n, from L marīnus. The E adj marine has cpd submarine, prob suggested by F sousmarin, which, by becoming, late in C19, a n, has prompted also the E naval n submarine, whence the C20 submariner, one who serves in a submarine.

4. From mare itself comes L maritimus, MF-F maritime, adopted by E.

5. Akin to L mare is OE merisc (prob orig an adj), with contr var mersc, whence ME mersch, E marsh, whence marshy (-y, adj): cf MLG-G marsch, marsh, moor.

6. Akin to OE mersc is OE mōr, a moor, a morass, a swamp, ME mor, E moor (no longer a swamp): cf MLG mor, MHG muor, G Moor, a swamp, OHG muor, sea, D moer, moor. The derivative OE mōrland, fenland, now means predominantly (heathy) moors, which may have bogs and do connote wasteland.

7. With marsh, cf marish, marshy, earlier (and still in dial) a marsh: OF mareis, soon marais: like OProv maresc, from Frankish *marisk—perh via ML mariscus.

8. OF marais also became D moeras (cf D moer, a moor), whence E morass, boggy ground, a swamp.

mère. See MATER (heading).
meretricious. See MERIT, para 4.
merganser: SciL cpd of L mergus, a diving bird (from mergere, to dip: see next entry)+L anser, a goose.

merge, whence the commercial merger and the pa-vn merging; cf sep MERGANSER; obsol merse and mersion; demerse (whence the adj demersal, sinking to the bottom), demersion; emerge, emergence, emergency, emergent, and immerse (whence pa immersed and immersible), immersion; submerge (whence pa submerged), submergent (whence submergence and submergible), and submerse (whence submersed, submersible), submersion.

1. Merge derives from L mergere, to dive, to dip, with pp mersus, whence the rare 'to merse' or dip in a liquid, with derivative LL mersiō, o/s mersiōn-, whence E mersion, now very rare outside of the cpds. L mergere is akin to Lith mazgoti, to wash (by repeatedly dipping), and Skt májjati, he dives, he bathes; IE r, *mezg-, with var *mazg-, to plunge in(to) water.

2. L mergere has cpds dē-, ē-, im-, submergere. Dēmergere, to plunge down, to sink, has pp dēmersus, whence the obs v demerse, with extant Bot pa demersed; derivative LL dēmersiō, o/s dēmersiōn-, yields demersion.

3. Ēmergere, to come to the surface (of an enveloping liquid), gives us emerge; presp ēmergens, o/s ēmergent-, E emergent; the ML derivative ēmergentia, E emergency; pp ēmersus yields 'to emerse' (as counterpart to immerse), whence the Bot adj emersed; its LL derivative ēmersiō, o/s ēmersiōn-, E emersion.

4. Immergere, to plunge in(to), is, in practice, an int of mergere, and yields E immerge; presp immergens, o/s -ent, yields immergent, whence immergence. The pp immersus, whence 'to immerse', has LL derivative immersiō, o/s immersiōn-, whence MF-F, hence E, immersion.

5. Submergere, to plunge under, becomes 'to submerge'; presp submergens, o/s -ent-, becomes submergent; pp submersus accounts for the adj and v submerse; its derivative LL submersiō, o/s submersiōn-, for OF-F, whence E, submersion.

meridian, See DIANA, para 13. The L source meridiānus has ML extn meridiōnālis, whence, via MF-F, meridional, southern, southerly.

meringue, adopted from F, is o.o.o.
merino. See MASTER, para 9.
meristem; merism. See para 5 of:
merit (n, v), meritorious; meretricious; demerit, whence, anl, demeritorious; (professor) emeritus; Bio merism, Bot meristem, Bio meristic.

1. 'To merit' derives from MF-F mériter, itself from the source of the E n merit: OF-MF merite (F mé-): L meritum, orig the neu of meritus, pp of merēre, to receive as one's share or as the price, hence, via merēre (or -ēri) stipendia, (of a soldier) to earn one's pay, to deserve. Meritum has the adj meritōrius, whence meritorious.

2. OF merite has the MF derivative demerite, where de- (F dé-) is L dis-, apart from, (hence)

not: hence the E n *demerit*. The now archaic 'to *demerit*' comes from the derivative MF *demeriter*. Both the OF *merite* and the MF *demeriter* perh owe something, in form, to L *dēmeritus*, pp of *dēmerēre*, to deserve well (int *dē-*).

3. L *ēmerēre*, to gain by service (connoted by *e-*, out of), has pp *ēmeritus*, whence its retention in academic circles for a professor with long and honourable service; perh influenced by the derivative L n *ēmeritus*, a soldier time-expired.

4. L *merēre* has derivative *meretrīx*, she who has earned her pay, hence a prostitute, with adj *meretrīcius*, whence E *meretricious*, now used only fig, as in 'meretricious charms'.

5. L *merēre*, s and r *mer-*, is akin to Gr *meros*, a share, a division or part of something, and *mei*resthai, to obtain as one's share: cf Hit *mark-*, to divide: IE r, *\*mer-*, prob with var *\*smer-* (Hofmann). *Meros+-ism* explains Bio *merism*; but the *merism* of Rhet derives from Gr *merismos*, a partition or division, from *meros*, whence *merizein*, to divide, with pp *meristos*, whence both the Bot *meristem*, tissue having cells actively divisible, and the Bio *meristic*, divisible.

**merkin**. See MALKIN, s.f.

**merl, merle**. See OUZEL, s.f.

**merlin**: ME *merlion*, aphetic for OF *esmerillon* (F *émerillon*): from OF *esmeril*: prob from Frankish *smiril*: cf OHG *smirl* (G *Schmerl*).

**mermaid, merman**. See the 2nd MERE, para 2.

**merry**, whence **merriment** (*-ment*); **mirth**, whence **mirthful, mirthless**.

*Mirth*, ME *mirthe*, earlier *merthe, murthe*, derives from OE *mirhth, myrgth, myrth*, from OE *myrige, myrge*, pleasant, whence, via ME *murie, mirie, merie*, pleasant, merry, the E *merry*: and the OE adj is akin to Go ga*maurgjan*, to shorten, and OHG *murg-, murgi*, short: so many brevities are agreeable. The IE r is perh *\*mergh-*, short, brief.

**mesa**, a hill's flat top, a natural terrace, with steep sides, is, along with its dim *meseta*, adopted from Sp: L *mēnsa*, a table: f.a.e., MEMBER, para 5.

**mescal**: Sp *mezcal*: ASp *mexcal*: Aztec *mexcalli*, a drink from juice of the fleshy-leaved maguey (itself a Sp word, prob from Taino, certainly Caribbean).

**mesentery**, whence the adj **mesenteric**. See the element *meso-*.

**mesh** (n, hence v), whence **meshy** and also **enmesh** (whence **enmeshment**), prob derives from obs D *maesche*, var of obs D *masche* (D *mass*): cf OE *māsc, māēscra*, OS *māsca*, OHG *māsca*, MHG-G *masche*, mesh, knot, ON *möskvi*, also Lith *māzgas*, knot, *megsti*, to knot, to weave nets.

**mesial**. Cf the element *mesio-*.

**mesmeric, mesmerism, mesmerist, mesmerize**, all derive from the G doctor F. A. *Mesmer* (1733–1815), who, at Vienna, first (c1775) publicized hypnotism.

**Mesopotamia**. See the element *meso-*.

**mesquite**: Sp *mezquite*: Aztec *misquitl*.

**mess** (n, hence v), a quantity of food put out at a meal, a course, a group habitually taking a meal, and, likewise derivatively, a hodge-podge, esp if disagreeable: ME from OF-MF *mes* (F *mets*): VL *missum*, a course, prop the neu of *missus*, pp of *mittere*, to let go, to send: f.a.c., MISSION.

**message, messenger**. See MISSION, para 5.

**Messiah, Messias**.

The latter is LL from L Gr *Messias*, from Aram *mĕshīḥā*, whence E *Messiah*: H *māhsīaḥ* (*māhsīos*), anointed: cf, sem, CHRIST. The adj *Messianic* derives from F *messianique* from late MF-F *Messie* from LL *Messias*.

**messuage**: AF *mesuage*, app a scribal error for OF-MF *mesnage*: cf *ménage* at MANOR, para 4.

**mestizo**. See MIX, para 8.

**met** (1): pt, pp of 'to meet'; (2), *mete*orologist.

**metabola, metabolic, metabolism**.

The 3rd adds *-ism* to E *metabola*, from LL from Gr *metabolē*, a fundamental change, a metamorphosis: *metaballein*, to change: *meta*, between, after+*ballein*, to throw: cf BALLISTIC. The derivative Gr adj *metabolikos* becomes *metabolic*, often in extn *-al*.

**metal** (n, hence adj and v), **metallic; metalliferous** and **metallurgy**, whence **metallurgic(al)** and **metallurgist;—medal** (n, hence v, esp in int cpd **bemedalled**; hence also **medallist**) and **medallion; mettle**, whence **mettlesome**.

1. *Metal*, adopted into ME from OF-MF *metal* (F *métal*), comes from L *metallum*, which, like its imm source, the Gr *metallon*, means orig a mine, derivatively a metal: akin to, perh deriving from, Gr *metallan*, to search after, seek out, itself o.o.o.: perh Medit, several Eg words sem relevant being phon suggestive. Derivative Gr *metallikos* becomes L *metallicus*, whence late MF-F *métallique* and E *metallic*.

2. Two cpds merit a notice:

*metalliferous*: L *metallifer*, metal-bearing (cf the element *-fer*);

*metallurgy*: SciL *metallurgia*: from Gr *metallourgos*, a metal-worker (cf Gr *ergon*, work), or *metallourgein*, to work a mine.

3. L *metallum* has derivative VL *\*metallia* (*monēta*), a metal coin, whence It *medaglia*, late MF-F *médaille*, E *medal*; It *medaglia* has aug *medaglione*, whence EF-F *médaillon*, E *medallion*.

4. E *metal*, used fig for the temper of a sword, came to designate also a person's temperament, esp in fortitude, with a natural tendency, fixed c1700, to the differentiated spelling *mettle*.

**metamorphic, metamorphism, metamorphose, metamorphosis**.

Gr *metamorphoun*, to transform, has derivative *metamorphōsis*, whence, via L, the E word; on the base *metamorph-* arise the 1st and 2nd; the 3rd derives from EF-F *métamorphoser*, from *métamorphose*, from L *metamorphosis*. The prefix *meta-* connotes 'change'; for *-morph-*, the body of the cpd, see MORPHEUS.

**metaphor, metaphoric** (with extn *-al*).

The latter derives, via MF-F *métaphorique*, from Gr *metaphorikos*, the adj of *metaphora*, whence, via L, the MF-F *métaphore*, whence *metaphor*: and Gr *metaphora* derives from *metapherein*, to transfer: *pherein*, to carry, *meta-*, beyond.

**metaphysic** and **metaphysics; metaphysical** and **metaphysician.** See PHYSIC, para 6.

**metatarsus.** Cf TARSAL and EF-F *métatarse* and the prefix *meta-*.

**metathesis, metathetic.** See THESIS, para 12.

**mete,** to measure. See MEDICAL, para 5.

**metempsychosis.** See PSYCHE, para 4.

**meteor, meteoric, meteorism, meteorite, meteorize; meteorology, meteorological,** (anl formed) **meteorologist.**

1. *Meteorological* is an *-al* extn of obsol *meteorologic*, Gr *meteōrologikos*, the adj of *meteōrologia*, a discourse (*-logia*: cf LOGIC) about the atmosphere; the 1st element forms the source of E *meteor*, which, perh via MF *meteore* (F *mé-*), comes from scholastic ML *meteōra* from ML *meteōrum* from Gr *meteōron*, something high in the air; orig the neu of *meteōros*, high in the air: *meta*, beyond+*eōra*, contr of *aiōra*, a hovering, from—or, at the least, akin to—*aeirein*, to raise.

2. ML *meteōra* has adj *meteōricus*, whence, perh via EF-F *météorique*, the E *meteoric*; F *météore* has derivative *météorite*, whence E *meteorite*. Gr *meteōros*, high in air, has v *meteōrizein*, to raise high, whence 'to *meteorize*'; derivative Gr *meteōrismos*, a raising, becomes Med E *meteorism*, flatulence—cf Hippocrates' *meteōrizesthai*, to suffer from flatulence.

**meter** (1), AE for Mus and verse *metre*. See MEASURE, para 3.

**meter** (2), as for gas and electricity. See MEDICAL (heading).

**methane, methanol.** See METHYLENE.

**metheglin,** mead: W *meddyglyn* (cf Cor *medheklyn*): W *meddyg* (L *medicus*), a physician+W *llyn*, liquor (cf *linn*, a pool).

**methinks.** See THINK, para 1.

**method, methodic** (whence extn **methodical**), **Methodism, Methodist** (whence **Methodistic**), **methodology.** See ODOGRAPH, para 5.

**methylene,** whence **methyl,** whence **methane** (whence **methanol**) and **methylate** (*methyl*+ *alcohol*ate), n hence v (whence **methylated**), and its adj **methylic:** F *méthylène*: Gr *methu*, wine+ *hulē*, wood+Chem suffix *-ène* (E *-ene*): Science's 'answer' to the truly E *wood spirit*.

**meticulous:** EF-F *méticuleuse*, f of *méticuleux*: L *metīculōsus*, formed—anl with *perīculōsus* from *periculum*—from *metus*, fear: o.o.o.; but the r *met-* recalls that of L *metīrī*, to measure, extn of IE *me-* (cf MEASURE, para 1): excessive measuring of, hence excessive thought about, a situation or a potentiality causes fear.

**métis.** See MIX, para 8.

**metonymy** (whence **metonymic**): prob via EF-F *métonymie*: LL *metonymia*: Gr *metonumia*: *meta-*, prefix of change+*onuma* (var of *onoma*), a name.

**metre, metric.** See MEASURE, para 3.

**metropolis, metropolitan.** See MATER, para 2, and cf the element *-pole*.

**mettle.** See METAL, para 4.

**mew** (1), a gull: OE *māēw*: echoic, as are OS *mēh*, MLG *mēhe* (whence G *Möwe*), D *meeuw*, ON *mār* (pl *māvar*).

**mew** (2), a cage for *moulting* hawks, hence confinement (obsol), hence *mews*, orig the royal stables (built where the kings' hawks had been housed), hence a range of stables, now esp if converted to houses and apartments: ME *mewe*, earlier *mue*: OF-MF *mue*, a moulting, from *muer*, to moult, from OF-F *muer*, to change: L *mutāre*: f.a.e., MUTABLE. OF *muer*, to moult, becomes ME *muen*, E 'to *mew*' or moult, also (obs) to shed horns.

**mew** (3), to moult. See prec, s.f.

**mew** (4), to miaow (hence n): echoic: cf G *miauen* and the E cognate *miaow*, which has var *miaul*, perh imm from OF-F *miauler*. Almost a blend of *mew* and *miaul* is 'to *mewl*'.

**mewl.** See prec, s.f.

**Mexican** (adj, hence n) prob derives imm, by suffix *-an*, from **Mexico,** but perh derives either from F *Méxicain* or from obs Sp *Mexicano* (Sp *Mejicano*), the adj of obs Sp *Mexico* (Sp *Méjico*). The *Mexicanos* were orig those Aztec (most important of the Nahuatl) tribes who, before the Sp Conquest, settled in the country: and the name prob comes either from Aztec *mizquitl*, desolate land, or from *Mixitli*, the Aztec god of war. (Santamaria.)

**mezzanine.** See MEDIAL, para 6.

**mezzo-soprano.** See SUPER, para 4.

**mezzotint.** See the element *mezzo-*.

**miasma,** a noxious exhalation, hence a contaminating influence: SciL, from Gr, *miasma*, pollution, from *miainein*, to pollute, with s *miain-* an extn of s *miai-*, extn of r *mia-*: IE r, *\*mei-* or *\*mai-*, to dirty, as in OHG *meil, meila*, MHG *meil*, a (dirty) spot, a stain, MHG *meil*, defect, sin, and perh in Lith *máiva*, a morass. The Gr gen *miasmatos* leads to the adjj *miasmatic* and *miasmatous*, app being superseded by *miasmal* and *miasmic* (from E *miasma*).

**miaul, miaow.** See the 4th MEW.

**mica,** whence the adj **micaceous**—cf *rosaceous* from *rosa*; **micelle,** whence **micellar; microbe,** whence **microbic** and **microbism.**

1. *Micelle* anglicizes *micella*, the SciL dim of L *mīca*, a particle or morsel, a crumb, a grain, adopted by Min for a group of crystals: the r *mīc-* is prob akin to that of Gr *mikros*, small, var *smikros*: cf OHG *smāhi*, small.

2. From Gr *mikros*, F coins *microbe*, a tiny organism (Gr *bios*, life): the F surgeon Sédillot's pun (1878) on the Gr adj *mikrobios*, short-lived. (B & W.)

**Michaelmas,** with its **daisy,** is the festival—celebrated with a *mass*, on September 29—of the archangel *Michael*, LL *Michaël*, LGr *Mikhaēl*, H *Mīkhā'ēl*, Who is like God? Pet-forms, *Mick* (esp for an Irishman) and *Mike*.

**mickle.** See MASTER, para 18.

**microbe.** See MICA, para 2.

microcosm, micrometer; microphone, whence sl-become-coll mike; microscope. See the element *micro-*.

mid. See MEDIAL, para 12.

midday. See MEDIAL (heading).

midden: ME *midding*: cf Da *mödding*, an easing of *mögdynge*, a heap (*dynge*) of dung (*mög*): cf the now dial E *ding*, to throw (akin to DINT), and MUCK.

middle; middling. See MEDIAL, para 14.

midge, whence midget (dim *-et*), ME *mydge*, var *migge*, comes from OE *mycg* or *mycge*: cf OS *muggia*, OHG *mucca*, MHG *mücke*, gnat, fly, G *Mücke*, gnat, midge, MD *mugge*, D *mug*, Da *myg*, Sw *mygga*, ON *mȳ*, gnat, midge; L *musca*, Gr *muia*, ÖSl *mucha*, Ru *muxa*, a fly; Alb *mīze*, gnat. The IE r is app *mu-*, prob echoic; with extnn *mug-* and esp *mus-*.

2. L *musca*, a fly, is retained by Zoo, with derivative *Muscidae* (*-idae*, descendants). The derivative adj *muscārius* yields, via SciL, the Chem n *muscarine*.

3. L *musca* becomes Sp *mosca*, with dim *mosquito*, orig a little fly: adopted by E in its derivative and soon its exclusive sense.

4. L *musca* becomes It *mosca*, with dim *moschetto*, a sparrowhawk, whence—via OF *moschet*, later *mousket* (F *mouchet*)—the E *musket*, a male sparrowhawk; C14 It *moschetto*, a crossbow (cf the C14 *moschetta*, a crossbow dart), becomes, in CC16-17, the larger sort (fired from a rest) of arquebuse, finally a musket (superseded by the rifle): whence EF *mosquet* (1581), soon (c1590) *mousquet*, whence E *musket*. EF *mousquet* has derivatives EF-F *mousquetaire*, whence E *musketeer*, and EF-F *mousqueterie*, whence *musketry*. The large-bored CC16-17 moschettone (aug of *moschetto*) becomes EF-F *mousqueton*, whence E *musketoon*.

midmost; midnight. See MEDIAL (heading).

midshipman. See MEDIAL (heading).

midst. See MEDIAL, para 12.

midway; midwife. See MEDIAL (heading).

mien, although perh influenced by 'demean oneself', to behave, prob derives from late MF-F *mine*, facial appearance, itself app from Br *min*, (bird's) beak, (quadruped's) muzzle, hence a person's face: extn of OC *mi*, little. (Malvezin.)

might (n and v), mighty. See the 2nd MAY, paras 1 and 2.

mignon; mignonette. See MITIGATE, para 3.

migraine is adopted from (OF *migraigne*, MF-)F *migraine*: by aphesis from LL *hēmicrānia*: trln of Gr *hēmikrania*, lit '(pain in) the half (*hēmi-*) of the head (*kranion*)'—cf CRANIUM. MF *migraine* becomes ME *mygrene*, later *migrym*, whence E *megrim*, obsol for 'migraine', obs (as *megrims*) for 'low spirits'.

migrant (adj, hence n), migrate, migration, migrator, whence—or from *migrate*—anl migratory;—emigrant (adj, hence n), emigrate, emigration (whence, anl, emigratory), émigré; immigrant, immigration (whence, anl, immigratory); remigrant, remigrate, whence, anl, remigration;

transmigrant, transmigrate, transmigration (whence, anl, transmigratory and transmigrative).

1. L *mīgrāre*, to change one's residence, hence to depart, even for another country, has s *mīgr-*, r *mīg-*, prob an extn of *mei-*, to change: cf Gr *ameibein*, to exchange, and Skt *mayate*, he exchanges: cf, therefore, the 1st MEAN, para 2.

2. *Mīgrāre* has presp *mīgrans*, o/s *mīgrant-*, whence the E adj *migrant*; pp *mīgrātus*, whence 'to *migrate*'; derivative *mīgrātiō*, o/s *mīgrātiōn-*, becomes late MF-F, whence E, *migration*; derivative LL *mīgrator* is adopted by E.

3. L *ēmīgrāre*, (vi) to move from a place, (LL) to transfer from one place to another, has presp *ēmīgrans*, o/s *ēmīgrant-*, whence the adj *emigrant*; pp *ēmīgrātus*, whence 'to *emigrate*'; derivative LL *ēmīgrātiō*, o/s *ēmīgrātiōn-*, E *emigration*. F *émigré* is prop the pp of *émigrer* (L *ēmīgrāre*).

4. L *immīgrāre*, to come to settle in (*im-* for *in*, in, into), has presp *immīgrans*, o/s *immīgrant-*, E adj and n *immigrant*; pp *immīgrātus* yields 'to *immigrate*'; *immigration* is adopted from F, which forms it as if from *immīgrātiōn*em, acc of LL or ML *immīgrātiō*, from *immīgrāre*.

5. L *remīgrāre*, to return to one's former residence or native place or homeland, has presp *remīgrans*, o/s *remīgrant-*, E n and adj *remigrant*, and pp *remigrātus*, 'to *remigrate*'; the E words, however, perhaps rather=*re-*, back+*migrant*, *migrate*.

6. L *transmīgrāre*, (vi) to move across (*trans*) in changing residence, hence (LL) to transport, has presp *transmīgrans*, o/s *transmīgrant-*, whence the E adj and n *transmigrant*; pp *transmīgrātus*, whence 'to *transmigrate*'; derivative LL *transmīgrātiō*, emigration, (in EcclL) metempsychosis, o/s *transmīgrātiōn-*, MF-F, whence E *transmigration*, esp of souls.

Mikado: Jap: either 'honourable door': *mi*, august, honourable+*kado*, a door (prob of IE origin); or 'noble place': archaic Jap *mi*, great, noble+Jap *to*, a place.

mike (1), n. See at MICROCOSM.

mike (2), v. See MOOCH.

mil. See MILE (heading).

Milan. See MILLINER.

milch. See MILK.

mild. See the 2nd MEAL, para 19.

mildew. See MEL, para 4.

mile, whence mileage (collective *-age*) and the orig sl, then coll, now familiar SE miler; mil and mill ($\frac{1}{1000}$ of an A dollar), both from L *mille*, a thousand; millenary; millennium; millepede—cf, at the element mille- (*milli-*), milligram and millimeter—millepore; million (whence the adj millionary), millionaire (whence millionairess).

1. E *mile*, OE *mīl*, derives from L *mīlia*, a thousand as quantity, esp elliptical for *mīlia passuum*, a thousand of paces: var of OL *mīllia*, prop the pl of *mīlle*, a thousand: prob akin to the syn Gr *khīlioi* (Hofmann); perh (Webster), however, to Gr *homilos*, a throng—cf MILITANT, para 1.

2. L *mīlle* has derivative *mīllēnī* (*-nae*, *-na*), a thousand each, whence LL *mīllēnārius*, containing a thousand, whence *mīllēnārium*, period of 1,000 years, whence resp the E adj and n *millenary*; as n, *millenary* has given way to the SciL, hence E, *millennium* (*annus*, a year).

3. The L cpd *mīllepeda*, (creature having) 1,000 feet (L *pedes*), yields EF-F *mille-pieds* and E *millepede*; the cpd *millepore*, however, derives from F *millépore*, (organism having) 1,000 pores (f.a.e., PORE), i.e. a species of coral.

4. L *mīlle* remains *mille* in It, which forms, in *-one*, the aug *millione* (now *milione*), whence MF-F *million*, adopted by E; C18 F coins *millionnaire*, whence E *millionaire*.

**miliary.** See the 2nd MEAL, para 8.

**milieu**, adopted from F,=OF *mi*, middle (L *medius*)+*lieu*, place (cf LOCAL).

**militant** (whence **militancy**), **militarism** (whence anl, **militaristic** and perh **militarize**, whence **demilitarize**), **military** (adj, hence—assisted by the F n *militaire*—n), **militate** (whence, anl, **militation**), **militia** (whence **militiaman**).

1. All these terms derive from L *mīlit-*, o/s of *mīles*, a soldier, esp an infantryman: o.o.o.: for the suffix *-es*, cf *eques*, horseman, and *pedes*, a foot-soldier (L *pēs*, a foot, gen *pedis*); for the s and r *mīl-*, perh cf Skt *mēla*, an assembly, and Gr *homilos*. a throng: ? 'one of a(n armed) throng'. Perh cf MILE, esp if L *mīlia* derives from OL *\*mīlia*, a multitude, hence a large number.

2. L *mīles*, soldier, has adj (OL *mīlitārius*) *mīlitāris*, whence MF-F *militaire*, whence E *military*; it also has derivative n *mīlitia*, military service, adopted by E, with new senses 'a body of soldiers' and, subsidiarily but soon predominantly, 'a body of citizens trained as soldiers, but serving as such only in emergency'; moreover, it has derivative v *mīlitāre*, to be a soldier, esp to serve on a campaign, with presp *mīlitans*, o/s *mīlitant-*, whence E *militant*, and with pp *mīlitātus*, whence 'to *militate*'.

3. The foll E words prob owe much to the corresp F terms: *militarism* to F *militarisme*; *militarist* to F *militariste*; *militarize* to F *militariser*, and *militarization* to F *militarisation*;—*anti*(-) *militarism*, *-militarist*, to F *anti-militarisme*, *-iste*; *demilitarize*, *-ization*, to F *démilitariser*, *-isation*.

**milk** (n, v)—whence **milksop** and **milky**—and **milch**, adj; **emulgent**, **emulsify**, **emulsion**.

1. The adj *milch*, as in *milch cows*, derives from ME *mielch*, *milche*, adj of ME *milc*, whence E *milk*, n: ME *milc* derives from OE *milc*, varr *meolc*, *meoloc*, *meoluc*, *mioluc*, whence OE *meolcian*, *milcian*, whence 'to *milk*': and OE *milc* is akin to OFris *melok*, OHG *miluh*, MHG-G *milch*, Go *miluks*; ON *miōlk*, Da (and D) *melk*; OIr *melg*. With OE *milcian* and esp with the very closely linked *melcan*, to milk, cf OFris *melca*, OHG *melchan*, MHG-G *melken*, ON *miolka*; L *mulg*ere, G a*melg*ein, to milk, bou*molg*os, cow-milker, cow-hand; perh Skt *mrjati*, he wipes, or

rubs, off, *mārsti*, he removes by rubbing. The IE r is perh *\*melg-*, to milk.

2. L *mulgēre* has cpd *ēmulgēre*, to milk *ē-* or out, to milk dry, hence to drain, with presp *ēmulgens*, o/s *ēmulgent-*, whence E adj, hence n, *emulgent*, and with pp *ēmulsus*, whence SciL *ēmulsiō* (o/s *ēmulsiōn-*), E *emulsion*, orig the 'milk' rubbed out of almonds, hence, in Pharm, a smooth, 'milky' medicine; hence *emulsify* (*emulsion*+*-fy*) and Chem *emulsin* (*emulsion*+Chem *-in*).

**mill** (1), for grinding. See the 2nd MEAL, para 7.

**mill** (2), a thousandth part. See MILE (heading).

**millenary.** See MILE, para 2.

**millennium**; **millepede**, **millepore.** See MILE, resp paras 2 and 3; for the 1st, cf ANNUAL, para 3.

**millet.** See the 2nd MEAL, para 8.

**milligram**, **millimeter.** See the element *mille-*, *milli-*.

**milliner**, whence **millinery**; **Milan.**

*Milliner* 'corrupts' *Milaner*, an inhabitant of Milan, hence such a Milanese as, in England, imported feminine finery—cf *Milan point*, a lace formerly made at *Milan*, It *Milano*, prob Livy's *Mediolanum*; L *medius*, middle+C *lan*, land, *lano*, a plain (Enci It).

**million**; **millionaire.** See MILE, para 4.

**milreis.** See REX, para 10.

**milt** (1), spleen. See MELT, para 6.

**milt** (2), a fish's reproductive glands, or their secretion: either from the syn Da *milt* or, by confusion with **milt** (1), for earlier *milk* used in this sense.

**mime** (n, hence v); **mimesis**, **mimetic**, **mimetite**; **mimic** (adj, hence n and v), whence **mimicry** (*-ry* for *-ery*, exercise, art); **mimosa**; **mimeograph**, v, from *Mimeograph*, a copying device, from Gr *mimeisthai*, to imitate (cf GRAPH);—**maya**, magical power.

1. *Maya*, Skt *māyā*, is perh akin to Bulgarian *iz*mama, deception (? orig by imitation), and to Gr *mim*eisthai, to imitate, prob from *mimos*, a play of real life imitated grotesquely: IE r, *\*mei-*, varr *\*mai-*, *\*mi-*, to deceive—cf OHG *mein*, false, deceptive.

2. Gr *mimos* (μῖμος) becomes L *mīmus*, whence EF-F and E *mime*; derivative adj *mimikos* becomes L *mīmicus*, EF-F *mimique* and E *mimic*; derivative n *mimēsis*, imitation, is, via its LL trln *mīmēsis*, adopted by E, and its adj *mimētikos*, LL *mīmēticus*, becomes *mimetic*; derivative agent *mimētēs*, imitator, joins with the Min suffix *-ite* to form *mimetite*, which 'mimics' pyromorphite.

3. Gr *mimos* and L *mimus* also mean 'actor'; SciL takes L *mimus* and coins *mimosa*, whose leaves shrink at a touch of the hand.

**mina.** Var of MYNA.

**minaret**, adopted from EF-F, comes from Tu *menārei* (*manārai*), itself from Ar *manāra*, light-house, hence, from the shape, the slender tower of a mosque.

**minatory**—**commination**, **comminatory**; **menace**, n and v (whence the pa **menacing**).

1. 'To *menace*' derives from OF *menacier* (F

*menacer*), from the OF-F n *menace*, adopted by E: L *minācia*, from the adj *mināx* (o/s *mināc-*), threatening, (lit) projecting, hence projecting forbiddingly, from *mināri*, to project, overhang, but soon and esp to threaten, from *minae* (pl), a projection, the overhang of, e.g., a rock: prob from an IE r *\*men-* (varr *\*min-*, *\*mon-*, perh *\*man-*), to jut out, project: cf, therefore, L *mōns*, a high, steep hill, a mountain; cf also W *mynydd*, OBr *-monid*, Br *menez*, Cor *menedh*, *monedh*, Ir *monadh*, mountain (Ga *monadh*, moor and mountains).

2. L *mināri* has derivative adj *minātōrius*, whence F *minatoire*, whence E *minatory*; the cpd *commināri* (int *com-* for *con-*, from *cum*, with), to threaten, has pp *comminātus*, whence 'to *comminate*'; derivative *comminātiō*, o/s *comminātiōn-*, yields *commination*; derivative LL *comminātīuus* (ML *-īvus*) yields *comminative*, and LL *comminātor*, threatener, adopted by E, and ML *comminātōrius*—perh via EF-F *comminatoire*—*comminatory*.

3. L *minae*, a projection, s and r *min-*, has, via an ill-attested *minere*, to jut, these cpds:

*ēminēre*, to detach itself by projecting, to raise itself out of, has presp *ēminens*, o/s *ēminent-*, whence, perh via MF-F, the adj *eminent*, the derivative *ēminentia* becoming, perh via MF-F, *eminence*, with var *eminency*;

*imminēre*, to project above or over, to dominate, presp *imminens*, o/s *imminent-*, MF-F and E *imminent*, the derivative *imminentia* yielding *imminence*;

*prōminēre*, to jut forward, presp *prōminens*, o/s *prōminent-*, E *prominent*, the derivative *prōminentia* yielding *prominence*;

*ēminēre* has cpd *praeēminēre*, to jut upwards and *prae-*, in front of, presp *praeēminens*, LL adj, o/s *praeēminent-*, E *pre-eminent*, the derivative LL *praeēminentia* yielding *pre-eminence*.

All four E adjj and all four E nn prob owe something to the OF-MF forms.

4. Prob akin to L *prōminēre* is L *prōmunturium*, LL *prōmuntōrium*, ML *prōmontorium*, whence E *promontory*, land jutting high from and well forward into the sea.

5. L *mināri*, to threaten, has the rustic and popular LL derivative *mināre*, to threaten, hence to shout at, animals as one drives them, hence to drive them with shouts, hence simply to drive or guide them, with LL cpd *prōmināre*, to drive forward (*prō*), whence late MF-EF *promener*, to take for a walk (whence F *se promener*, to go for a walk), whence EF-F *promenade*, adopted by E, with derivative sense '(artificial) place for a walk'.

6. LL *mināre*, to drive or lead animals, becomes OF-F *mener*, to lead, with OF-F cpds *amener* (*a-*, L *ad*, to, towards), to lead up, whence AF *amenable*, adopted by E: 'leadable, bringable', hence 'answerable'; hence 'easily bringable'; hence 'tractable'. OF *mener*, lead, has the further prefix-cpd OF-EF *demener*, to conduct (*de-* being vaguely int), whence *se demener*, to conduct oneself, to behave, whence the syn E 'to *demean* oneself';

whence *demeanure* (*-ure*), whence *demeanour*, (AE) *demeanor*. The E neg is 'to *misdemean* oneself' (*mis-*, wrong, wrongly), to behave badly, whence the agent *misdemeanant* and the abstract *misdemeano(u)r*.

### L *mōns*, a mountain

7. L *mōns*, gen *mōntis*, o/s *mōnt-*, becomes OF-F *mont* and OE *munt*, whence ME *munt* and then—influenced by F—*mont* and finally *mount*, extant in E; moreover, L *mōns* has derivative VL *\*montāre*, to climb a hill or mountain, hence to climb, hence to mount, OF-F *monter*, ME *monten*, then *mounten*, E 'to *mount*'. The Canadian NW *Mounted* Police are, coll, 'the *Mounties*'.

8. L *mōns* has adj *montānus*, whence the erudite *montane*: cf the 'high' State of *Montana*, as if for *regiō montāna*, mountainous region. The ML *ultramontānus*, beyond (*ultra*) the mountains, becomes E adj, hence n, *ultramontane*. L *transmontānus* becomes It *tramontano*, whence E *tramontane*.

9. L *montānus* has LL var *montāneus*, whence the VL n *\*montanea*, var *\*montania*, whence OF-MF *montaigne* (F *montagne*), whence ME *montaine*, later—influenced by *mount*—*mountaine*, whence E *mountain*. Perh, however, ME *montaine*, like the MF var *montene*, comes from LL *montāna*, a mountain, from *montānus*. *Mountain* has derivatives *mountaineer* (cf the MF adj *montanier*, from ML *montānārius*) and *mountainous* (perh, however, via F from LL *montāniōsus*).

10. *Mount* occurs in the foll prefix-cpds:

*amount*, n, from *amount*, v: into ME from OF-MF *amonter* (*a-*, L *ad*, towards), to ascend, hence to advance, to increase: *amont*, upwards: L *ad montem*, to(ward) the mountain;

*dismount*, v: *dis-+mount*: anl with OF-MF *desmonter* (*des-*, L *dis-*), to descend: *des-+monter*;

*paramount*: OF *par amont*, above, on top: *par* (L *per*), through, by+*amont*, above;

*remount*, n, from *remount*, v: OF-F *remonter*: *re-*, again+*monter*;

*surmount* (whence *surmountal*: *-al*): ME *surmounten*: OF-F *surmonter* (OF var *sor-*): *sur-* (*sor-*), L *super*, over+*monter*. The EF-F derivative neg *insurmontable* becomes *insurmountable*.

11. Pl Nn from L *mōns*, mountain, are very numerous. Here are a few of the best known:

*Montana*, see para 8, and *Vermont*, lit 'green mountain';

*Montenegro*, lit 'black mountain'; the region about a famous Montenegrin landmark;

*Monterey*, lit 'king's mountain': ASp; cf:

*Montevideo*: ML *vidēo*, I see+Sp *monte*, mountain;

*Montreal*: F *Montréal*, royal mountain.

**mince, mincemeat, mincer.** See MINOR, para 8.

**mind** (n, hence v—whence, in cpds, **-minded**; **minder**), whence **mindful** and **mindless**; **remind**, to bring *re-*, or back, to *mind*—whence **reminder**.—Latin: **mental**, whence **mentality**; **demented**, **dementia**;—**Minerva**;—**mention**, n and v (whence

mentionable); comment (n, v), commentary, commentate, commentation, commentator;—memento;
(reminisce, from) reminiscence, reminiscent;—
monish (whence monishment)—monition, monitor
(whence monitorial)—cf admonish (whence admonishment), admonition, admonitory; premonition;
monument, monumental; — monetary; money
(whence moneyed), moneyer—demonetize, whence
demonetization—mint (n, hence v—whence minter),
whence mintage.—Greek: Eumenides;—mania,
maniac (adj, hence n), manic, cf dipsomania, dipsomaniac, and nymphomania, nymphomaniac; sep
MATHEMATIC; maenad; -mancy, see the element;—
mnemonic, mnesic; amnesia (whence amnesiac);
amnesty;—automat, automatic, automaton (Gr pl
automata), automatous;—sep MONSTER (etc.);—sep
MANDARIN.

### Indo-European

1. Mind, ME minde, munde, derives from OE
gemynd: cf OFris minne, OS minnia, OHG minna,
love, Go gamunds, ON minni, remembrance; Lith
menas, understanding, minti, to think, minéti, to
mention; L mēns (o/s ment-), mind, mentiō, a
mention, meminisse, to remember, monēre, to
warn; Gr menos, mind, intention, force, mnasthai,
to remember, mainesthai, to rave; Skt mánas,
mind, spirit, manyate, he thinks: IE r, *men-, to
use one's mind, to think.

### Greek

2. Gr Eumenides, the well-minded, or well-
disposed, hence the gracious ones, is euphem for
the Erinyes or avenging spirits of Gr myth: eu,
well (adv)+menos, spirit. Menos in its sense 'purpose' is clearly present in Gr Mentōr, the counsellor friend of Odysseus in Homer's epic, hence E
mentor, a wise counsellor: men-+agential -tor, var
of -ter.

3. Closely akin to Gr menos is Gr mania, madness, whence, via L, the E word. Whereas the
derivative Gr adj maniakos becomes LL maniacus,
whence MF-F maniaque, whence E maniac, the
derivative adj manikos imm becomes manic.

4. Of the numerous -mania cpds, note esp:
   dipsomania: SciL: Gr dipsa, thirst, c/f dipso-+
mania;
   kleptomania: SciL: Gr kleptēs, a thief;
   nymphomania: SciL: Gr numphē, young woman.
The adjj end, anl, in -maniac.

5. Gr mania is closely akin to mainesthai, to act
as a madman, whence mainas (gen mainados, o/s
mainad-), a nymph attendant upon, and participating in the orgiastic rites of, Dionysus: hence,
via L maenas, o/s maenad-, the E maenad.

6. Akin to Gr mainesthai and mania are Gr
mantis, seer, and manteia, oracle, divination, in
cpds -mantia, LL -mantia, OF -mancie, E -mancy,
preserved in numerous cpds, all deriving from—
or modelled upon—the Gr. Note esp necromancy,
q.v. at the element -mancy.

7. Akin to the Gr words already mentioned is
mnáomai, I remember, whence mnēsis, remem-

brance, and mnēstis, memory, the former with adj
mnēsios, whence E mnesic, the latter with anl E
adj mnestic. Mnasthai, to remember, has presp
mnēmōn, whence the adj mnēmonikos, whence E
mnemonic (hence n); mnemonics, the art, or means,
of improving memory, was prompted by the syn
Gr (ta) mnēmonika (prop, neu pl)—cf the LL
mnēmonicum, an aid to memory.

8. Gr mnēsis has the approx neg amnēsia, forgetfulness, adopted by Psy and esp by Psychi;
hence—perh after maniac—the E amnesiac, one
suffering from amnesia; the adj is amnesic.
Amnēsia has derivative amnēstéō, I forget, whence
amnēstia, forgetfulness, hence a pardon; the adj
amnēstos, forgotten, forgetful, yields E amnestic.
Amnēstia becomes L amnestia, EF amnestie (F
amnistie), E amnesty.

9. Akin to Gr man-, main-, men-, is Gr -matos
as in automatos, (thinking, hence) acting for itself:
with Gr mat-, cf Gr math- as in mathesis, activity
of learning, and in the sep MATHEMATIC; cf also
Skt mata, thought. The Gr neu automaton is used
as n, pl automata, both adopted by E; derivative
Gr automatismos, adopted by LL, becomes F
automatisme and E automatism. Gr automatos
becomes EF-F automate, n, whence G Automat,
n, whence E automat; F automate acquires adj
automatique, whence E automatic; Gr automatos
becomes E automatons. Modern automation=
automatic action+station.

### Latin

10. L mēns, mind, s mēn-—cf Gr menos, spirit,
courage, purpose, s men-—has derivative LL adj
mentālis, whence, prob via MF-F mental, the E
mental; derivative F mentalité leads us to mentality.

11. Mēns, o/s ment-, has prefix-cpds āmentia,
lack (connoted by a-) of mind, and dēmentia,
madness (dē- connoting 'departure from' sanity):
both adopted by Med and Psi. They derive from
āmēns, mindless, o/s āment-, and dēmēns, mad,
o/s dēment-, whence, via F dément, the rare adj
dement; dēmēns has derivative dēmentāre, to
deprive of reason, send mad, whence 'to dement',
whence the much commoner pa demented.

12. Perh akin to L mēns and Gr menos is L
Minerua, ML Minerva, adopted by E; if so, Min-
is app a thinned form of the mon- of monēre, to
warn (see para 17).

13. L mentiō, a bringing to mēns or the mind, has
acc mentiōnem, whence OF-F, hence E, mention;
derivative EF-F mentionner produces 'to mention'.

14. L meminisse, to remember, memini, I
remember—both, perfect form, present sense—
recall Gr memona, I remember. The imperative
memento, as in Memento mori, Remember to die,
becomes n, F mémento, E memento.

15. Meminisse, to remember, s memin-, has two
prefix-cpd derivatives affecting E: comminisci, to
imagine, com-, with, being used int; reminisci,
to call re-, back, to mind. Comminisci has int commentāri, to have in, to recall to, the mind, to
reflect upon, hence to study, to treat, in detail, of

a subject, hence to edit a text: MF-F *commenter*: E 'to *comment*'. The derivative MF-EF n *comment* was adopted by E. The adj *commentārius*, used elliptically for *commentārius liber* (book), becomes n, with var *commentārium*: perh via late MF-F *commentaire*, the E *commentary*. *Commentāri* has pp *commentāt*us, whence 'to *commentate*'; derivative *commentātiō*, o/s *commentātiōn-*, yields *commentation*; derivative *commentātor* is adopted (cf MF-F *commentateur*).

16. *Reminiscī*, to call back to mind, has presp *reminiscens*, o/s *reminiscent-*, whence E *reminiscent*; derivative LL *reminiscentia* became late MF-F *réminiscence*, whence E *reminiscence*, whence, by b/f, 'to *reminisce*'.

17. The L r *men-*, to think, acquires the caus derivative *monēre* (r *mon-*), to cause someone to think (hence, to remember), hence to call someone's attention to, esp as injunction: whence VL *\*monestāre*, OF *monester*, ME *monesten*, (? after *admonish*) 'to *monish*', now archaic. On *monit-*, s of the pp *monitus*, arise *monitiō*, o/s *monitiōn-*, whence (prob via MF) the E *monition—monitor*, adopted—*monitōrius*, whence *monitory*.

18. *Monēre* has cpd *admonēre*, to remind, or warn, strongly (int *ad-*): VL *\*admonestāre*: OF *admonester* (often *am-*): ME *amonesten*: anl with other E *-ish* from F vv, 'to *admonish*', whence *admonishment* (cf the OF-EF *amonestement*). Derivative *admonitiō*, o/s *admonitiōn-*, passes through OF-MF to become E *admonition*; *admonitor* is adopted; LL *admonitōrius* explains *admonitory*.

19. *Monēre* has other cpds, esp *praemonēre*, to warn in advance, whence, anl, 'to *premonish*'; on *praemonit-*, s of pp *praemonitus*, arise LL *praemonitiō*, o/s *praemonitiōn-*, E *premonition—praemonitor*, E *premonitor—*LL *praemonitōrius*, E *premonitory*.

20. *Monēre* has derivative *monimentum* (*mon-*+ connective *-i-*+*mentum*), with the var, more usual, *monumentum*, anything that recalls the mind, esp the memory, to people, esp a tomb or a statue: OF-F *monument*, adopted by E. The late derivative adj *monumentālis* yields *monumental*.

21. The Gr Goddess of Memory, *Mnēmosunē* (cf para 7), adopted by Romans, became *Monēta*, epithet of Juno='The Warner': hence, Juno's temple at Rome: thence, coinage being struck there, *monēta*, a mint, hence the minting process: hence, *monēta*, coins, money in its cash form. The derivative LL adj *monētarius* accounts for *monetary*; *moneta+-iser* (E *-ize*)=F *monétiser*, whence 'to *monetize*', whence *monetization* (F *monétisation*).

22. Derivative F *démonétiser*, *démonétisation* produce 'to *demonetize*', *demonetization*.

23. L *monēta*, cash, becomes OF-F *monnaie*: ME *moneie*: E *money*. Derivative EF-F *monnayeur* yields E *moneyer*, minter; MF-F *monnayage* yields the now only hist *moneyage*.

24. L *monēta*, a mint, coins, becomes OE

*mynet*, coins, money: CC15-17, *mynt*: E *mint*, with sense 'place of coining' long predominant.

**mine** (1), adj and pron. See ME, para 2.

**mine** (2), n and v (whence pa, vn **mining**); **miner**; **mineral** (adj and n), whence **mineralize** (whence **mineralization**) and **mineralogy** (whence, anl, **mineralogical** and **mineralogist**).

1. A *miner* derives from MF *mineor* (F *mineur*), agent of OF-F *miner*, whence 'to *mine*'. A *mine* is adopted from OF-F, prob—like OProv *mina*—of C origin: cf EIr *mianach*, ore, Ga *mèin*, *mèinn*, ore, a mine, Cor *moina*, a mine, *mūn* (*muyn*), ore, W *mw̄n*, ore, a mine, Br *min*, Mx *meain*, a mine: OC *\*meini*, var *\*meinni* (MacLennan).

2. *Mineral*, n, comes from late MF-F *minéral*, from ML *minerāle*, prop the neu of ML adj *minerālis*, whence late MF-F *minéral*, whence E *mineral*: and ML *minerālis* derives from ML *minera*, ore, a mine, prob of C origin (as above). From *minéral*, F derives *minéralogie* (for *\*minéralologie*: cf *-logy*, science, at the element *-loger*): whence E *mineralogy*.

**Minerva.** See MIND, para 12.

**minery**: MF *miniere* (F *-ière*): ML *mineria*, a place where mining is being done, var of *minera*, *mināria* (MINE, para 2).

**mingle**, whence **mingler** and **mingling**, is a late ME freq of ME *mengen* from OE *mengan*, akin to MHG-G and D *mengen*, OS *mengian*, ON *menga*, to mix, to blend, perh orig to knead together— cf Lith *mìnkyti*, to knead—and, f.a.e., MASS, para 2.

**miniate**, adj (rare) and v, **miniature** (whence— perh via F—**miniaturist**), **minium**; cf the sep CARMINE.

*Minium*, red lead, the colour vermilion, is adopted from L: Iberian, 'the Romans getting all their cinnabar from Spain' (Webster)—cf Basque *armineá*. L *minium* has derivative *miniāre*, to paint or ornament with minium; the pp *miniātus* yields adj and v *miniate*; on the pp s *miniāt-* arises ML *miniātūra*, a miniating, a rubrication, whence, via It, the EF-F and E *miniature*, the sense 'illumination (of a page) with vermilion letters' passing naturally into sense 'a (very) small painting', esp a portrait.

**minim**; **minimize**, **minimum**. See MINOR, para 1 and esp para 4.

**minion.** See MITIGATE, para 3.

**minish.** See DIMINISH, para 1, s.f.

**minister**, **ministerial**, **ministrant**, **ministration**, **ministry.** See MINOR, para 9.

**minium.** See MINIATE.

**miniver.** See VACILLANT, para 5.

**mink**, a slender, semi-aquatic quadruped, resembling a weasel, was orig native to N Europe, therefore of Scan origin: cf Nor and Da *mink*, Sw *menk*.

**minnesinger** is G *Minnesinger*, a singer of *Minne* or love: cf MIND, para 1.

**minnow.** See MINOR, para 14.

**Minoan** (adj, hence n) substitutes suffix *-an* for suffix *-ius* of L *Mīnōīus*, trln of Gr *Mīnōīos*, adj of

*Mīnōs*, a generic for 'king' (cf *Pharaoh* and *Caesar*), from *Mīnōs*, son of Zeus and Europa.

minor (adj, hence n), Minorca, minority; minus, minuscule; minimus, minim, minimize, minimum (whence minimal); minute, adj and n (whence v), minuteman, minutia (usu in pl minutiae); minuet; menu; sep minish (q.v. at DIMINISH, where also DIMINUTION, etc.); mince, mincing; minister (n, v), ministerial, ministrant, ministrate (obs), ministration, ministrative, ministrator, ministry—cf administer (whence, anl, administerial and administrable), administrant, administration, administrative, administrator; minstrel;—minnow.

### Indo-European

1. L *minor*, lesser, neu *minus*, has sup *minimus*—all three, retained by E—but no positive, meaning 'little', to complement the series *magnus*, large, great, *maior* (ML *major*), *maximus*: clearly, however, there was very prob a L r *\*min-* corresp to an IE r *\*men-*, var *\*min-*, little, itself an extn of *\*mī-*, var *\*mei-*: cf Gr *minuein*, to lessen, reduce, Skt *minóti*, he lessens (hence, damages), and *mīyate*, he or it becomes less, fades away; Cor *minow*, *menow*, little, Br *mén* (pl *méneu*), young of an animal, Ga *mean* (pron *min*), *mion*, little, *meanbh* (EIr *menbach*), very little, OC *\*menoos*, *\*menuos*, little; OFris *minu*, OHG *min*, (adv) less, OFris *minnera*, *minra*, OS and OHG *minniro*, MHG *minner*, *minra*, Go *mins*, less (adv), *minniza*, lesser, ON *minni*, lesser, *minnr*, less (adv).

2. L *minor* has ML derivative *minoritās*, acc *minoritātem*, whence OF-F *minorité*, whence E *minority*. In Sp, L *minor* becomes *menor*, whence *Menorca*, whence *Minorca*.

3. L *minus* prompts the dim *minusculus*, rather small, whence EF-F *minuscule*, adopted by E as counterpart of *majuscule*.

4. L *minimus*, smallest, accounts, prob via It *minima*, for the Mus *minim*; its neu *minimum* becomes an E (and F) n; the anl E *minimize* prob owes something to F *minimiser*.

5. L *minor* is very closely akin to L *min*uere, to lessen, with pp *minūtus*, used also as adj, whence the E adj *minute*. The n *minute*, a second of time (whence the other senses), derives, prob via MF-F *minute*, from ML *minūta*, prop the f of the adj *minūtus*, (? for *minūta pars temporis*): cf the A, now only hist, *minuteman*, a militiaman holding himself ready at a minute's notice. L *minūt*us has *-ia* derivative *minūtia*, mostly in pl *minūtiae*, small points, trifling details, adopted by erudite E.

6. L *minūtus* becomes OF-F *menu*, whence, in its sense 'detailed', the EF-F n *menu*, adopted by E. OF *menu* has dim *menuet* (*-et*), orig adj, whence, in EF-F, the n *menuet*, a dainty dance, whence E *minuet*.

7. L *minuere* has, relevant to E, these cpds: *comminuere* (int *com-* for *con-*, together, altogether), to break into (little) pieces, with pp *comminūt*us, whence 'to *comminute*'; derivative *comminūtiō*, o/s *comminūtiōn-*, becomes E *comminution*;

*dēminuere*, corrupted to *dīminuere*, to lessen by removal of a part, pp *dēminūtus*, *dīminūtus*: see DIMINISH:

8. From *minūtus*, adj, VL coins *\*minūtiāre*, whence OF *mincier* (F *mincer*), whence 'to *mince*' —lit, to make small; hence *mincemeat* and *mincer* and the pa *mincing* (manners, steps, speech), overdainty.

9. Complementary to and prompted by L *magister*, from *magis*, more, is L *minister*, from *minor*, one who serves or assists another, hence at a religious cult, hence of a public office, finally one at the head of a political department—cf 'minister of religion' or 'of the Crown': hence E *minister*, a re-shaping of ME, from OF-F, *ministre*, from L *minister*. The derivative LL adj *ministeriālis*, ministering, becomes EF-F *ministériel*, whence *ministerial*; derivative *ministerium*, a ministering, becomes EF-F *ministère*, whence *ministry*. L *minister* has, moreover, the derivative v *ministrāre*, to serve, with presp *ministrans*, o/s *ministrant-*, whence the E adj, hence n, *ministrant*, and with pp *ministrāt*us, whence the obs 'to *ministrate*'; derivative *ministrātiō*, o/s *ministrātiōn-*, yields *ministration*, whence, anl, *ministrative*, and the derivative LL adj *ministratōrius*, serving, yields *ministratory*.

10. LL *ministeriālis* is used also as n—'a public orderly or official'—whence OF *ministral*, *menestrel* (whence F *ménétrier*), servant, (later) minstrel, whence ME *minstrale* (var *menestral*), whence E *minstrel*. OF *menestrel* has derivative *menestrelsie* (*-alsie*), whence E *minstrelsy*.

11. L *ministrāre* has cpd *administrāre* (where *ad-* is vaguely int), to serve, hence, later, to govern: whence, partly via MF-F, 'to *administer*'. Presp *administrans*, o/s *administrant-*, explains the E adj, hence n, *administrant*. Pp *administrāt*us yields 'to *administrate*'; derivative *administrātiō* becomes, perh via MF-F, the E *administration*; derivative *administrātīuus* (ML *-īvus*) becomes *administrative*, and derivative LL *administrātōrius* becomes *administratory*; derivative *administrātor* is adopted —cf the OF-F *administrateur*.

12. Perh influenced by Cor *minow*, small, is E *minnow*, which descends from OE *myne*: cf the syn OHG *muniwa*.

Minorca. See prec, para 2.

minority. See MINOR, para 2.

Minos. See MINOAN.

Minotaur, L *Mīnōtaurus*, Gr *Mīnōtauros*, is that *tauros* or bull of *Minos* to which, in Myth, human sacrifices were made in Crete. Cf MINOAN.

minster, a monastery (obs), hence a church, esp *York Minster* (cathedral): OE *mynster*: LL *monasterium*: cf MONK and, f.a.e., MONAD.

minstrel, minstrelsy. See MINOR, para 10.

mint (1), plant. See MENTHA, para 3.

mint (2) for coin. See MIND, para 24.

minuet. See MINOR, para 6.

minus, adj, hence n and prep. See MINOR, para 1.

minuscule. See MINOR, para 3.

minute, adj, n, v; minuteman; minutiae. See
MINOR, para 5.

minx, C16 *mincks*, C17–18 *minks*, prob comes
from LG *minsk*, wench, hussy, akin to G *Mensch*,
(C17) maidservant, (C19–20) prostitute: orig an
adj 'of mankind': f.a.e., MAN.

miracle, miraculous; mirage; mirific; mirror (n,
hence v);—admire (whence admirer), admirable,
admiration, admirative;—marvel (n, v), marvellous.
—smile, v (whence agent smiler and pa, vn
smiling) hence n;—prob cf smirk, v (whence
smirker and smirking) hence n.

1. *Miraculous* derives from MF-F *miraculeux*,
f *miraculeuse*, from OF-F *miracle*, adopted by E:
LL *mīrāculum*, a miracle, L *m.*, a prodigy: L
*mīrārī*, to wonder, to wonder at: L *mīrus*, astonishing, strange, wonderful: OL r *mīr-*, to look (at),
esp with astonishment: IE r, perh *mei-*: cf the Gr
*meidáō*, I smile. App the IE *mei-* has an s-prefix
var *smei-*: cf OSl *smijati se*, to laugh, Skt *smáyate*,
he smiles, *smerás* (adj), smiling, MHG *smielen*,
var *smieren*, ME *smilen*, OE *smearcian*, to smile.

2. L *mīrāri*, to wonder (at), has the VL derivative
*mīrāre*, to look, esp with attention: OF-F *mirer*,
whence F *mirage*, adopted by E. OF *mirer* has the
derivative *mireor*, var *mirour*, the latter adopted
by ME, whence E *mirror*.

3. L *mīrus* has cpd *mīrificus* (-*ficus*, from -*ficere*,
c/f of L *facere*, to make), whence MF-F *mirifique*,
whence E *mirific*.

4. L *mīrāri*, to wonder, has cpd *admīrārī* (*ad-*
vaguely int), to wonder at, usu favourably, whence
E 'to *admire*'. Derivative L *admīrābilis* becomes,
perh via MF-F, the E *admirable*. On *admīrāt-*, s
of pp *admīrātus*, arises *admīrātiō*, o/s *admīrātiōn-*,
whence prob via MF-F, the E *admiration*; MF-F
*admiratif*, f -*ive*, leads us to E *admirative*.

5. L *mīrāri*, to wonder at, has derivative
*mīrābilis*, wonderful, whence LL *mīrābilia*, things
worth wondering at, whence OF(-F) *merveille*,
whence ME *mervaile*, whence E *marvel*; 'to
*marvel*' is ME *merveilen*, OF *merveillier*, from OF
*merveille*, whence also OF *merveillos* (F *merveil-
leux*), whence ME *merveillous*, whence *marvellous*.

6. ME *smilen* (as in para 1) becomes 'to *smile*';
OE *smearcian*, var *smercian*, becomes ME *smirken*,
E 'to *smirk*', now always affectedly or too com-
placently.

mirage. See para 2 of prec.

mire (n, hence v), whence miry; quagmire.
A *mire* came into ME from ON *mȳrr*, a swamp:
cf MOSS, q.v. *Quagmire* merely attaches *quag*, to
shake, a dial var of QUAKE, to *mire*.

mirific. See MIRACLE, para 3.

mirk, mirky. See MURK.

mirror. See MIRACLE, para 2.

mirth, mirthful, mirthless. See MERRY.

miry. See MIRE.

misadventure: OF *mesaventure*. Cf *adventure* at
VENUE, para 4.

misanthrope, misanthropic, misanthropy.
The 1st derives, prob via EF-F *misanthrope* and
perh via LL *mīsanthrōpus*, from Gr *misanthrōpos*,

hater of mankind (*anthrōpos*, generic man), the 1st
element being *misos*, hatred, s and r *mis-* (cf
*mis*ein, to hate): o.o.o. Derivative *misanthrōpia*
produces EF-F *misanthropie* and E *misanthropy*;
*misanthropic* derives, anl, from E *misanthrope*.

misbeget, misbegotten. See GET, para 2.

miscalculate=*mis-*, amiss+*calculate* (q.v. at
CALCAREOUS); miscall=*mis-*+CALL; miscarry
(whence miscarriage)=*mis-*+CARRY.

miscegenation. See the element *misce-*.

miscellanea, miscellaneous, miscellany. See MIX,
para 2.

mischance. See CADENCE, para 5.

mischief, mischievous. See CHIEF, final para.

misconduct, n and v. See CONDUCT, para 4.

miscreant. See CREDENCE, para 6, s.f.

misdeed: OE *misdǣd*: *mis-*, wrong, wrongly+
*deed* (cf DO).

misdemeanant, misdemeanor (AE) or -our. See
MINATORY, para 6, s.f.

misdirect, misdirection. See DIRECT, para 2.

misdoubt, merely =*mis-*, wrongly+DOUBT; perh
cf the MF *mesdoubter*.

mise, as in *mise en scène*. See MISSION, para 2.

miser, n—whence miserly (-*ly*, adj)—comes from
the archaic adj *miser* ('wretched'), itself adopted
from L *miser*, wretched, miserable, whence L
*miserāri*, to take pity on, whence *miserābilis*,
pitiable, whence MF(-F) *misérable*, whence E
*miserable*. L *miser* has also derivative *miseria*,
whence OF-MF *miserie* (MF-F *misère*), adopted
by ME, whence E *misery*.

2. L *miserāri* has cpd *commiserāri* (*com-* for *con-*,
together—vaguely int), to pity, with pp *com-
miserātus*, whence 'to *commiserate*'; on the pps
*commiserāt-* arises *commiserātiō*, o/s *commiserā-
tiōn-*, whence OF-F *commisération*, whence E
*commiseration*, whence, anl, *commiserative*.

misericord. See CORDIAL, para 2, and cf the
element *miseri-* and MISER, para 1.

miserly; misery. See MISER, resp the heading and
para 1.

misfire; misfit. Prefix *mis-*, wrongly+FIRE, FIT.

misfortune. See FORTUNE (heading).

misgive (whence misgiving); misgovern; mis-
guide; mishap; misinterpret, misjudge, mislay, mislead (perh directly from OE *mislǣdan*), obsol
mislike (prob imm from OE *mislīcian*, to displease),
mismanage, misname. All combine prefix *mis-*,
wrongly, badly, with the keyword.

misnomer. See NAME, para 7, s.f.

misogamy, hatred of marriage; misogyny (whence
misogynist), hatred of women; misology, hatred
of argument. The 1st element is *miso-*, c/f of
Gr *misos*, hatred (cf MISANTHROPE); the 2nd
elements, from resp Gr *gamos*, *gunē*, *logos* (lit,
discourse).

misplace (whence misplacement); misprint. Prefix
*mis-*, wrong, wrongly+PLACE, PRINT (see PRESS).

misprise. See PRICE.

misprision. See PREHEND, para 11.

misprize, occ misprise. As 'to misvalue' (usu
-*prize*), it=*mis-*, amiss+'to *prize*', q.v. at PRICE;

as 'to misunderstand', it=*mis*-+a F derivative of
PREHEND, to seize, to grasp.

mispronounce (whence, anl, mispronunciation);
misrepresent (whence, anl, misrepresentation);
misrule (v, hence n); all=*mis*-, wrongly+the
keyword it precedes.

miss (1), unmarried woman, esp in address. See
MASTER (heading).

miss (2), to fail to hit, meet, find, see, etc.;
hence n, hence also the pa missing. 'To *miss*',
*missan*, is akin to OFris *missa*, OHG *missēn*, G
*missen*, to miss, and to Go *maidjan*, to change:
therefore cf MUTABLE.

missal. See MISSION, para 4.

missel (thrush). See MISTLETOE.

misshape, misshapen. See SHAPE (heading).

missile. See MISSION, para 3.

missing (persons). See MISS (2).

mission (n, hence v), whence adjj missional and
missionary (hence as n); mise; missal; missible;
missile (adj, n); missive; sep mess; message,
messenger; Mass, as in CHRISTMAS, LAMMAS,
MICHAELMAS, qq.v. sep; mittimus.—Cpds: admissible, admission, admit (whence admittance); commissar, commissariat, commissary, commission (n,
whence v), commissioner, commissure, commit
(whence the nn commitment, committal (whence the
neg n non-committal, whence the adj), committee;
demise (n, hence v), demiss, demission (whence
demissionary), demit; dismiss (whence dismissal),
dismission (whence, anl, dismissive); emissary (n,
hence adj), cf the purely abstract n emission
(whence, anl, emissive, whence, in turn, emissivity),
emit, emittent; immit; intermission (whence, anl,
intermissive), intermit, intermittent (whence, anl,
intermittence, var -ency); intromission, intromit;
sep manumission, manumit, qq.v. at MANUAL, para
18; omission (whence, anl, omissible, omissive),
omit; permissible, permission (whence, anl, permissive), permissory, permit (v, hence n), whence
permittance and permittivity; premise (n, hence v),
whence the adj premisory and the (in Logic) var
premiss; pretermission, pretermit; promise (n, hence
v), promissive, promissory—cf compromise; remise
(n, v), remiss, remissible, remission, remissive,
remit, remittance, remittent; submiss (obsol), submission (whence, anl, submissible, submissive),
submit (whence submittal); transmissible, transmission (whence, anl, transmissive), transmit
(whence transmittance, transmitter, pa trans-
mitting).

1. The base is L *mittere*, to let go, cause to go,
send, with r *mit*-, perh akin to Av *maīth*-, to send;
the pp is *missus*, s *miss*-, equally potent in R
etymologies.

2. L *mittimus*, we send, has become the name of
a legal writ; OF-F *mettre* (L *mittere*) has pp *mis*, f
*mise*, the latter being used also as MF-F n for 'a
putting, a setting', esp in the theatrical *mise en
scène*.

3. The L pp *missus* (? for *\*mitsus*) has s *miss*-,
whence:

LL *missibilis*, capable of being thrown, whence
E *missible*;

L *missilis*, capable of being sent, esp of being
thrown, whence the E adj *missile*; used as n, the
L neu *missile*, a thing (esp a weapon) for throwing,
is adopted by E;

L *missiō*, a sending or dispatching, a release, a
discharge, o/s *missiōn*-, whence (EF-F and) E
*mission*, persons sent, esp on religious duty; the
derivative *missionary* perh owes something to
EF-F *missionnaire*;

ML *\*missivus*, prompted by Eccl senses of
*missiō*, is deduced from late MF 'lettre *missive*',
whence the EF-F n *missive*, adopted by E.

4. The L pp *missus*, f *missa*, neu *missum*, becomes
a n, not only in F *mise* (as in para 2 above) and
MESS (q.v. sep), but also in LL *missa*, the Liturgy,
the Mass, the Eucharist, perh from LL *Congregatio*
(or, more prob, *Contio*) *missa est*—The gathering
is now dismissed—pronounced by the officiating
priest 'at close of the Vigil and other offices'
(Souter); whence both OF-F *messe* and OE
*maesse*, ME *messe* (prob from MF) and esp *masse*,
whence E *mass*, usu *Mass*; LL *missa*, Mass,
gained, in ML, the adj *missālis*, whence (as in
*missālis liber*, book of the *Mass*) the ML n *missāle*,
the book of the Mass for any Eccl year, whence
E *missal* (MF *messel*, EF-F *missel*).

5. The L pp *missus* has VL derivative *\*missāticum*, ML *missāticum*, whence OF-F *message*,
adopted by E; B & W, however, derive OF *message* from OF *mes*, sent, corresp to the L pp
*missus*: *mes*, pp+euphonic *s*+suffix *-age*. OF
*message* has derivative OF *messagier*, MF(-F)
*messager*, adopted by ME, whence, with intrusive
*n* (cf *passenger* from *passage*), the E *messenger*.

Compounds of and from L *mittere*, pp *missus*

6. The pattern of derivation from the L cpds
into the R languages and into E is remarkably
uniform. In the latter, *-mittere* becomes *-mit*;
presp *-mittens*, o/s *-mittent*-, E *-mittent*, whence
the *-ence*, *-ency* nn; *-missus*, pp and adj, E *-miss*,
but if via F, *-mise* (whence *-misory*); *-missiblis*, E
*-missible*; *-missiō*, o/s *-missiōn*-, E *-mission*; ML
*-missivus* (LL *-missiuus*), E *-missive*; L *-missor*,
scantily adopted; ML *-missōrius*, E *-missory*, and
L *-missārius*, E *-missary*. The *-able* and *-ance* (cf E
*-ence*) subsidiaries are E formations, on the pattern
of multitudinous other adjj in *-able* and nn in
*-ance*.

7. L *admittere*, to allow to approach (*ad*-,
towards), E 'to *admit*'; pp *admissus*, whence LL
*admissibilis*, MF-F and E *admissible*, and L
*admissiō*, EF-F and E *admission*, whence, anl, the
adjj *admissive*, *admissory*.

8. L *committere*, to send, hence put, together,
hence to entrust to, hence also to undertake, to
risk, E 'to *commit*'. On pp *commissus* arises LL
*commissārius*, contributory, ML *commissārius*, an
office-holder, whence E *commissary* and MF-F *com-
missaire*, the latter yielding E *commissar*, and the F
*commissariat*, adopted by E. L *commissus* has the

derivative *commissiō*, whence, prob via MF-F, the E *commission*; MF-F *commission* has EF-F agent *commissionnaire*, whence both E *commissionaire* and E *commissioner*. L *commiss*us has also the derivative *commissūra*, a sending, hence putting, hence joining together, whence MF-F *commissure*, adopted by E; the derivative LL adj *commissūrālis* becomes E *commissural*. L *committere* becomes OF-F *commettre*, pp *commis*, whence, in MF-F, a n, whence AF *committé*, whence *committee*, in EE a person to whom a duty is entrusted, hence, in E, a body of such persons.

9. L *dēmittere*, to send down, hence away, yields 'to *demit*', to dismiss (obsol), to relinquish; pp *dēmiss*us yields the adj *demiss*, humble, and, via L *dēmissiō*, o/s *dēmissiōn-*, the MF-F *démission* and E *demission*, and, via F *demis*, f *demise*, the legal n *demise*, whence 'to *demise*'.

10. L *dīmittere*, to send in opposite directions (*dī-* for *dis-*, apart), prob, via its pp *dīmiss*us, suggested 'to *dismiss*', as if from L *\*dismissus*; hence, anl, *dismission* (cf L *dīmissiō*, o/s *dīmissiōn-*).

11. L *ēmittere*, to let escape, to expel (e.g., breath), accounts for 'to *emit*'; presp *ēmittens*, o/s *ēmittent-*, becomes *emittent*; pp *ēmiss*us has derivative *ēmissiō*, o/s *ēmissiōn-*, MF-F *émission* and E *emission*, whence, anl, *emissile*; its further derivative *ēmissārius*, an agent sent forth to gather information or to further certain interests, becomes *emissary* (cf EF-F *émissaire*).

12. L. *immittere*, to send, or let, in (*im-* for *in-*), gives us 'to *immit*'; pp *immiss*us has derivative *immissiō*, o/s *immissiōn-*, E *immission*.

13. L. *intermittere*, to allow an interval *inter* or between, hence to interrupt, produces 'to *intermit*'; its pp *intermittens*, o/s *intermittent-*, the EF-F and E adj *intermittent*; pp *intermiss*us has derivative *intermissiō*, o/s *-missiōn-*, MF-F and E *intermission*.

14. L *intromittere*, to send *intro* or within, to let into, hence to introduce, yields 'to *intromit*'; its pp *intromiss*us has, anl, suggested *intromission*, *intromissible*, *intromissive*.

15. L *omittere* (for *\*obmittere*), to let escape, to omit, produces 'to *omit*'; pp *omiss*us has derivative LL *omissiō*, o/s *omissiōn-*, E *omission* (perh via MF-F).

16. L *permittere*, to send or let through, hence to grant entry to, to allow, whence 'to *permit*'; pp *permiss*us has derivative *permissiō*, o/s *permissiōn-*, whence, prob via OF-F, the E *permission*; derivative F *permissif*, f *-ive*, perh suggested E *permissive*; F *permissible* is an anl formation.

17. L *praemittere*, to send before, has pp *praemiss*us, f *praemissa*, whence the ML n *praemissa* (sc *sententia*), the MF *premisse*, F *prémisse*, the E *premiss*, with var *premise*, the latter now mostly in non-Logical senses.

18. L *praetermittere*, to send, let go, beyond, hence to let pass, becomes 'to *pretermit*'; pp *praetermiss*us has derivative *praetermissiō*, o/s *-missiōn-*, E *pretermission*.

19. L *prōmittere*, to send, hence put, in front, hence to engage to (do something), pp *prōmissus*, whence LL *prōmissa* (? for *res*, thing, that is promised), a promise, whence, via OF-F, the E *promise*; LL *prōmissīuus* (ML *-īvus*) and *prōmissor* become E *promissive* and *promissor* (prompting both legal *promisor* and ordinary *promiser*), the latter L word having ML derivative *prōmissōrius*, whence E *promissory*. The obs 'to *promit*' has the SciL agent *promittor*.

20. L *prōmittere* has itself the legal cpd *comprōmittere*, (of both parties) to delegate or refer a decision to an arbiter, whence 'to *compromit*'; pp *comprōmiss*us has neu *-missum*, used, in LL-ML, as the corresp n, whence MF-F *compromis*, whence E *compromise*, n hence v; derivative LL *comprōmissārius* becomes *compromissary*, and derivative ML *comprōmissiō* becomes *compromission*.

21. L *remittere*, to send back, hence to relax (vt), gives us 'to *remit*' (whence *remittal*); presp *remittens*, o/s *remittent-*, the adj *remittent*, whence *remittence*, var *remittance*; pp *remissus* becomes E *remiss*, and its derivative *remissiō*, o/s *remissiōn-*, becomes, prob via OF-MF (F *ré-*), *remission*; derivative LL *remissibilis* and *remissīuus* (ML *-īvus*) yield MF-F, hence E, *remissible* and *remissive*. The pp *remissus* has the LL derivative *remissa* (? sc *res*, thing), forgiveness, whence EF-F *remise*, adopted by E; hence—perh aided by the derivative F *remiser*—'to *remise*'.

22. L *submittere*, to send, hence put, under, to subjugate, E 'to *submit*', has pp *submissus*—whence the obsol adj *submiss*, syn of *submissive*—with derivative *submissiō*, o/s *submissiōn-*, whence, prob via OF-MF, the E *submission*.

23. L *transmittere*, to send across (*trans-*), to cause to pass, E 'to *transmit*', has pp *transmiss*us, with derivatives LL *transmissibilis*, EF-F and E *transmissible*, and L *transmissiō*, o/s *-missiōn-*, MF-F and E *transmission*, and LL *transmissōrius*, of transport, E *transmissory*.

**Mississippi; Missouri.**

In both of these Amerind river-names, the 1st element is Ojibway (an Alg tribe) *misi*, big; in the former, the 2nd element is Ojibway *sipi*, river, the full Ojibway name being *Misisipi*; in the latter, *-souri* is app Illinois for 'muddy', the AE word deriving, by aphesis, from Illinois *Emissourita*, var *Oumessourits*, the name for the tribe dwelling by the river. (Webster.) *Missouri*, however, is stated by Mathews to bear the prob meaning 'People of the Big Canoes'.

**missive.** See MISSION, para 3.

**Missouri.** See MISSISSIPPI.

**misspend: misstate** (whence **misstatement**): *mis-*, wrongly+SPEND, STATE.

**missus; missy.** See MASTER (heading—at *mistress*).

**mist** (n, hence v), whence **misty**: **mizzle**, to drizzle (hence n), whence **mizzly**.

1. The n *mist* comes straight down from OE *mist*: cf OS (and D) *mist*, mist, ON *-mistr*, fine or misty rain, with Gmc r *\*mihst-*; cf also OB *mĭgla*, Lith *miglà*, mist, OB *mĭgla*, fog; Arm *mēg*,

Gr *omíkhlē*, Skt *mih*, mist, and Skt *mégha-*, a cloud; prob (Walshe) cf also OHG-G *mist*, Go *maíhstus*, dung, and perh, with nasal infix, L *mingere*, to make water, partly for the sem reason that, from fresh dung and urine, steam arises: IE r, ? *\*migh-*, var *\*megh-*, to form mist, be misty.

2. The now mainly dial *mizzle* derives from late ME *miselen* (? as freq *\*mistelen* from ME *mist*): cf the syn LG *miseln* and D dial *miezlen*.

3. Cf MISTLETOE.

**mistake**, v (hence n), pt **mistook**, pp **mistaken**: ON *mistaka*: f.a.e., TAKE.

**mister.** See MASTER (heading).

**mistime:** *mis-*, wrongly+ to TIME.

**mistletoe; missel** (thrush).

*Mistletoe*, OE *misteltān*, is—like the corresp ON *mistelteinn*—tautological, for it merely tacks OE *tān*, a twig, to OE *mistel*, mistletoe—whence, via the obs EE *mistele*, *missel*, mistletoe, the bird *missel*, which feeds on the berries; OE *mistel* is akin to OHG *mistil*, MHG-G *mistel*. The OE *mistel* perh derives from OHG *mistil*, which app derives from OHG *mist*, dung, for 'mistletoe is propagated by the excrement of birds which eat the berries' (Walshe).

**mistral.** See MASTER, para 14.

**mistress.** See MASTER, para 17.

**mistrial; mistrust:** *mis-*, wrong, wrongly+TRIAL, TRUST.

**misty.** See MIST.

**misunderstand(ing), misuse** (v, hence n), **miswrite** (cf OE *miswrītan*): *mis-*, wrongly+understand (q.v. at STAND)—USE—WRITE.

**misusage, misuse.** See USE, para 9, s.f.

**mite:** OE *mīte*, a minute arachnid, akin to OHG *mīza*, MD (and LG) *mite*, D *mijt*: Gmc r, *\*mit-*, tiny insect. The sense 'small coin or sum', as in 'the widow's *mite*', comes into ME from MD (from the 'arachnid' sense).

**miter.** See MITRE.

**Mithra** is *Mithras*: L from Gr *Mithras*: OPer *Mithra*, a Per god of light, akin to the Ve *Mitra*, an Ancient Indian god of the sun. The adj is either *Mithraic*, from E *Mithra*, or *Mithriac*, from LL *Mithriacus*, of Mithras.—Perh cf MITRE.

**mitigate, mitigation, mitigative, mitigatory, mitigable, mitigant; immitigable; mignon, mignonette, minion.**

1. L *mītis*, soft, smooth, gentle, mild, whence spring all these words, is akin to OIr *mōith*, soft, tender, (perh) EIr *mīn*, fine, delicate, Ga *mīn*, OW *mwyn*, smooth, W *mwydion*, soft parts: OC *\*mitta*, soft, mild, *\*mit-*, to be soft or mild (Malvezin) and OC *\*mēnos*, smooth. The IE r, therefore, is perh *\*mī*, var *\*mē-*.

2. L *mītis*, soft, mild, has derivative *mītīgāre*, to soften, render mild, with presp *mītigans*, o/s *mītigant-*, whence the E adj, hence n, *mitigant*; with pp *mītigātus*, whence 'to *mitigate*'. On the pps *mītigat-* arise *mītigātiō*, o/s *mītigātiōn-*, whence, perh via MF, the E *mitigation*, and LL *mītigātīuus* (ML *-īvus*), soothing, whence E *mitigative*, and

*mītigātōrius*, E *mitigatory*. LL *\*mītigābilis* yields E *mitigable*; LL *immītigābilis*, E *immitigable*.

3. The F adj *mignon*, dainty, is partly adopted by E, which, in *mignonette*, adapts the late MF-F dim *mignonnette*; F *mignon* is thoroughly anglicized in *minion*. But B & W contest the C origin (EIr *mīn*, as above) of late MF-F *mignon* and make it akin to EF-F *minet*, familiar name for 'cat'.

**mitosis; mitosome.** See the element *mito-*.

**mitral, mitrate.** See:

**mitre:** AE **miter:** late OF-F *mitre* (whence the adj *mitral*, adopted by E): L *mitra*, headband, turban (whence the adj *mitrātus*, turban-wearing, E *mitrate*): Gr *mitra*: perh from Ve *Mitra* or, more prob, its OPer cognate, *Mithra* (as above).

**mitt; mitten.** See MEDIAL, para 5.

**mittimus.** See MISSION, para 2.

**mix** (v; hence n, also in cpd **mix-up**), whence pa **mixed** and agent **mixer** and pa, vn **mixing; mixtion, mixture;—maslin; meddle,** whence **meddler** and **meddlesome; intermeddle; mell,** to mix, meddle; **medley;** F *mêlée*, E **mellay**—cf **pell-mell; mestizo** and **métis; misce-** cpds, see the element *misce-*; **miscellanea, miscellaneous, miscellany.**—Prefix-cpds: **admix, admixtion, admixture; commix, commixtion, commixture; immix, immixture; intermix,** whence, anl, **intermixture;** cf **permix, permixtion, permixture,** all from *permixtus*, pp of L *permiscēre*, to mix *per* or thoroughly.

1. 'To *mix*' derives from earlier *mixt*, mixed (pp), from F *mixte*, L *mixtus*, pp of *miscēre*, to mix, to mingle: cf OE *miscian* (prob from L *miscēre*), OHG *miskan*, MHG-G *mischen* (perh from *miscēre*); cf Gr *meignumi*, I mix, *emigēn*, I mixed, also the var *misgō*, I mix; cf also Skt *misrás*, mixed (adj); there are, moreover, C and Sl cognates. The IE r is *\*meik-*, var *\*meig-*, to mix. (E & M.)

2. On *mixt-*, s of pp *mixtus*, arise LL *mixtiō*, o/s *mixtiōn-*, MF-F, hence E, *mixtion*, mixture (obs), hence a kind of cement, and L *mixtūra*, whence, via EF-F, *mixture*, and the dim adj *miscellus*, mixed, with subsidiary *miscellānus*, var *miscellāneus*, whence E *miscellaneous*; the neu pl *miscellānea*, used as n (lit, things mingled), a potpourri, becomes EF-F *miscellanées*, with sing *\*miscellanée*, whence E *miscellany*.

3. L *mixtūra* becomes OF-MF *mesture*, whence MF *mestueil*, *mestoil*, whence MF *mesteillon*, a dish made of various grains, whence ME *mestylyon*, contr to *mestlyon*, whence E *maslin*, now dial.

4. L *miscēre* has, in VL, the derivative freq *\*misculāre*, whence OF-MF *mesler* (F *mêler*), with a (perh popular) var *medler*, whence ME *medlen*, to mix, whence E *meddle*, to mix (obs), both vt and, derivatively, vi, hence to interfere. The cpd *intermeddle* (*inter-*, among, between) comes from ME *entremedlen*, to mix together, from MF *entremedler*, var of OF-MF *entremesler*: *entre* (L *inter*)+*mesler*.

5. OF *mesler* has another var: MF *meller*, whence ME *mellen*, E 'to *mell*', to mix, to meddle, now mostly dial.

6. OF *mesler* has derivative OF-MF *meslee*, whence F *mêlée*, partly adopted by E, which prefers *mellay*, from OF-MF *mellee*, var of *meslee*; *meslee* has the further var *medlee*, adopted by ME, whence E *medley*.

7. OF *mesle* has the int redup *mesle mesle*, with var—soon ousting its parent—OF-MF *pesle mesle* (*p-* for *m-* to avoid repetition), whence F *pêle-mêle*, whence E *pell-mell*, in a rapidly moving disorder, hence furiously.

8. Both the F *métis* (f *métisse*), a mixed-blood, whence Can half-breed and AE octoroon, and Sp *mestizo*, a mixed-blood, loosely any half-breed (AE), come, the former via OF-MF *mestis*, from LL *mistīcius*, *mixtīcius*, from L *mixtus*, mixed, used as adj.

### Prefix-Compounds

9. The prefix-cpds all (except for *unmixed*) derive from L and follow a regular pattern, thus:

L *admiscēre* (*ad-*, towards), to add something to a mixture, has pp *admixtus*, also used as adj, whence EE *admixt*, which, apprehended as a pp, yields, by b/f, 'to *admix*', whence, anl, *admixture*; *admixtion*, however, derives from L *admixtiōn-*, o/s of *admixtiō*, from the pp *admixt*us;

L *commiscēre*, to mix *com-* or together, pp *commixtus*, whence EE *commixt*, apprehended as a true E pp, whence, by b/f, 'to *commix*'; derivative L *commixtūra* yields *commixture*; derivative LL *commixtiō*, o/s *-mixtiōn-*, yields *commixtion*;

L *immiscēre*, to mix in (with something), pp *immixtus*, whence EE *immixt*, which, taken as an E pp, produces, by b/f, 'to *immix*', whence, anl, *immixture*;

L *intermiscēre*, to mix in among (other things), pp *intermixtus*, EE *intermixt*, which, taken as an E pp, produces, by b/f, 'to *intermix*', hence, anl, *intermixture*, displacing *intermixtion* (LL *intermixtiō*).

**mizzen.** See MEDIAL, para 6.

**mizzle**, to drizzle. See MIST, para 2.

**mnemonic, mnesic, mnestic.** See MIND, para 7.

**moa**, extinct large N.Z. bird: Maori word.

**moan.** See the 4th MEAN, para 2.

**moat**: OF *mote*, small hill, mound, dike, bank: cf OProv *mota*, mound, hence a château built upon a height: ? of C origin: C *\*mot*, a mound, ? ex *\*moc*, a swelling. Id with OF-F *motte*, a mound, which B & W think to be of pre-L origin.

**mob** (n, hence adj and v): L *mobile uulgus* (ML *vulgus*), the fickle populace: cf:

**mobile, mobility, mobilize** (whence **mobilization**) —cf *immobile*, etc.; hence **demobilize** (sl 'to **demob**'), **demobilization.** See MOVE, para 5.

**mocassin**, perh better—certainly, in AE, usu— **moccasin**: of Alg origin: cf Narragansett *mocussin* and Massachusett *mokhisson* (Webster), Alg *mawcahsun* (Funk & Wagnall).

**mock** (v, hence n, whence adj), whence agent **mocker** and pa, vn **mocking**; **mockery.**—Perh **Momus.**

1. *Mōmus*, L trln of Gr *Mōmos*, god of mockery

and censure, personifies Gr *mōmos*, ridicule, s *mōm-*, r perh *\*mō-*. Perh akin to

2. Gr *mōkos*, a mocker, s *mōk-*, r perh *\*mō-*, to ridicule or mock: whence, unless the F v be purely echoic (as, indeed, the Gr words may have been), the OF-MF *mocquer*—F *moquer* (cf the syn OProv *mocar*): whence certainly the ME *mokken*, whence E 'to *mock*'; derivative OF-MF *mocquerie*, EF-F *moquerie*, produces E *mockery*. The *mocking bird* is gracelessly imitative.

**modal, modality; mode**—cf **outmoded** and F **démodé**—whence **modeless; model** (n, whence v— cf the F *modeler*), whence the pa, vn **modelling** (AE **modeling**) and the agent **model(l)ist; moderant, moderantism, moderate** (adj, whence **moderatism**; hence the v), **moderation, moderator**—cf **immoderate, immoderation; modern** (adj, hence n), whence **modernism, modernist,** and **modernity, modernize** (whence **modernization**); **modest, modesty**—negg **immodest, immodesty; modicity (immodicity), modicum; modify** (whence **modifiable** and **modifier**), **modification** (whence, anl, **modificative** and **modificatory**); **modiolus;** F *la mode*, **modish, modiste; modulate, modulation, modulator** (? hence **modulatory**), **module** (whence, anl, the adj **modular**), **modulus;** L *modus operandi*, method of working, and **m. vivendi**, way of life; **mould**, AE **mold**, matrix, hence form, shape, hence the v, whence agent **mo(u)lder** and vn **mo(u)lding**.—Cpds: **commode, commodious, commodity**—cf **ditty bag**—cf also **accommodate, accommodation** (whence, anl, **accommodative**); **incommode, incommodious, incommodity.**—Cf the sep MEASURE and MEDICAL (where, at para 5, to *mete* or measure).

### I. The base: L *modus*

1. L *modus*, a measure, hence a measure one should not exceed, a limit, hence manner, way of doing something or of behaving: whence, perh via late MF-F, the E *mode*. *Modus*, s and r *mod-*, is very closely akin to L *medērī*, to measure, with s and r *med-*: cf MEASURE, para 1.

### II. Simple Derivatives of *modus*

2. *Modus* has ML adj *modālis*, whence E *modal*; derivative ML *modālitās*, o/s *modālitāt-*, becomes EF-F *modalité*, whence E *modality*. From F *la mode*, fashion (in dress, etc.), comes E *mode*, fashion, with derivatives *modish* and *outmoded*; the F *démodé*, no longer in fashion, is partly adopted by E, which fully adopts *modiste*.

3. *Modus* has dim *modulus*, a small measure, hence a poetic metre, a melody, whence, perh via EF-F, the E *module*. Derivative *modulāri*, to regulate, has pp *modulātus*, whence the E adj (obsol) and v *modulate*; subsidiary *modulātiō*, o/s *modulātiōn-*, becomes late MF-F and E *modulation*, and agent *modulātor* is adopted.

4. L *modulus* has the VL var *\*modellus*, whence It *modello*, whence EF-F *modèle*, whence E *model*. *Modulus* also becomes OF *modle*, with var *molle* (whence F *moule*), which combine to form ME *molde*, whence E *mould*, AE *mold*, whence—prob

influenced by OF *modler*, MF *moler* (F *mouler*)—
'to *mo(u)ld*'.

5. L *modus* has derivative v *moderāri* (influenced
by *medērī*), var *moderāre*, to keep within measure,
to regulate. The presp *moderans*, o/s *moderant-*,
produces the E n *moderant*; *moderantism* prob
comes from F *modérantisme* (from *modérant*). The
pp *moderātus* yields both the adj and the v
*moderate*; derivative *moderātiō*, o/s *moderātiōn-*,
becomes MF-F *modération*, whence E *moderation*,
and derivative agent *moderātor* is adopted. The neg
*immoderātus* and *immoderātiō*, o/s *immoderātiōn-*,
explain *immoderate*, *immoderation*.

6. L *modus* has abl *modo*, with measure, esp of
time, hence as adv, just now, very recently, with
the LL derivative *modernus* (cf *hodiernus*, from
*hodie*, today), whence MF-F *moderne*, whence E
*modern*.

7. From *modus*—like *moderāri*, influenced by
*medēri*, and esp by the *\*modes-* var of *modus*—
comes the adj *modestus*, keeping oneself within
measure, well regulated, whence MF-F *modeste*,
whence E *modest*; derivative *modestia* becomes
MF-F *modestie*, E *modesty*; the neg *immodestus*
and *immodestia* become, perh via EF-F, the E
*immodest*, *immodesty*.

8. *Modus* itself has an *-icus* adj: *modicus*,
measured, moderate, with derivative LL *modicitās*,
o/s *modicitāt-*, EF-F *modicité*, the rare E *modicity*,
with neg *immodicity* prompted by *immodesty*.
*Módicus* has neu *modicum*, which, used as n, gives
us *modicum*, a little.

9. *Modus*, influenced by *modērī*, has mdfn
*modius*, a measure of capacity (esp for corn), with
dim *modiolus*, adopted by An.

### III. Compounds

10. *Modus* has derivative *modificāre*, to make
(*-ficare*, a c/f of *facere*) limited, to limit or regulate,
whence MF-F *modifier*, whence 'to *modify*';
derivative *modificātiō*, o/s *modificātiōn-*, supplies,
perh via MF-F, *modification*.

11. The remaining cpds are prefix-cpds:
*commodus*, conforming to measure, hence convenient, advantageous, with neu *commodum* used
as n, whence late MF-F *commode*, borrowed by
E; the n *commodum* acquires, in ML, the adj
*commodiōsus*, whence, perh via F *commodieux*, f
*-ieuse*, the E *commodious*; *commodity* derives, via
MF-F *commodité*, from L *commoditās* (o/s *com-
moditāt-*), from *commodus*.

12. *Commodity* perh explains the sailor's '*ditty*
bag', ? for '*commodity* bag'.

13. *Commodus* has neg *incommodus* (whence F
*incommode*, inconvenient), with subsidiary v *in-
commodāre*, to cause inconvenience to, whence
late MF-F *incommoder*, whence 'to *incommode*'.
Derivative *incommoditās*, o/s *incommoditāt-*,
passes through MF-F *incommodité* into E *incommodity*; *incommodious*=*in-*, not+*commodious*.

14. *Commodus* has derivative v *commodāre*, to
adjust, hence to render a service to, with pp
*commodātus* (neu *commodātum*) and derivative

*commodātiō*, o/s *commodātiōn-*, whence *commodate* (n), *commodation* (obs), *commodatum*. The
cpd *accommodāre*, to adapt, hence to afford help,
e.g. shelter, to, pp *accommodātus*, whence *accom-
modātiō*, o/s *-ātiōn-*, gives us the obsol adj, and the
v, *accommodate* and *accommodation*.

**model.** See prec, para 4.

**moderate, moderation, moderator.** See MODAL,
para 5.

**modern, modernist, modernize.** See MODAL,
para 6.

**modest, modesty.** See MODAL, para 7.

**modicity.** See MODAL, para 8.

**modification, modify.** See MODAL, para 10.

**modiolus.** See MODAL, para 9.

**modish.** See MODAL, para 2.

**modiste.** See MODAL, para 2.

**modulate, modulation, modulator.** See MODAL,
para 3.

**module, modulus.** See MODAL, para 3.

**modus operandi, m. vivendi.** See MODAL (heading).

**Mogul.** See MONGOL.

**mohair; moire, moiré.**

**Mohair**, a fine fabric made from the hair of
Angora goats, comes from It *moccaiaro* (*-jaro*),
itself from Ar *mukhayyar*, a (coarser) fabric. From
E *mohair*, late EF-F derives *moire*, a watered
mohair, hence a watered silk; whence F *moirer*, to
'water' (a fabric, esp silk), with pp *moiré*, itself
used as a F n and an E adj, n, v.

**Mohammed**, whence **Mohammedan** (adj hence
also n), whence **Mohammedanism; Mahomet.**—Cf
**Muslim**, q.v. at ISLAM.

*Mohammed* derives from Ar *Muḥammad*, which
personifies *muḥammad*, worthy of praise; *Mahomet*
is the F form—cf the F adj *mahométan*.

**moiety.** See MEDIAL, para 4.

**moil.** See the 2nd MEAL, para 15, s.f.

**moire, moiré.** See MOHAIR.

**moist, moisten, moisture.** See MUCUS, para 4.

**moke**, a donkey, (Aus) a horse: sl and o.o.o.:
cf Skelton (C16), '*Mocke* hath lost her shoe',
which points to a dial var of *Moggy*, itself a var
of *Maggy*, pet-form of *Margaret*. (EW.)

**molar** (1), of a mass. See the 3rd MOLE (heading).

**molar** (2), for grinding. See the 2nd MEAL, para
10.

**molasses.** See MEL, para 2.

**mold** (1), friable earth. See the 2nd MEAL, para
5.

**mold** (2), shape. See MODAL, para 4.

**mole** (1), animal: ME *molle*: OFris *moll*—cf
MLG *mol* (var *mul*) and esp MD *molle*, var *mol*
(as in D): prob 'the *earth*-creature'—cf OHG *mult-
wurf*, MHG *moltwerfe*, G *Maulwurf*, lit 'soil-
thrower': f.a.e., the 2nd MEAL, para 5, *mo(u)ld*.

**mole** (2), a small congenital protuberance: OE
*māl*: cf OHG-MHG *meil*, a stain, Go *mail*, a
wrinkle: ? cf Gr *miainein*, to pollute.

**mole** (3), a mass, massive structure, breakwater,
whence the adj **molar; molecule**, whence the adj
**molecular** (cf the F *moléculaire*); **molest, molesta-**

tion;—demolish (whence demolishment—cf the F *démolissement*), demolition.

1. This *mole* derives from EF-F *môle*, from It *molo*, from MGr *môlos*, from L *môlēs*, a mass, esp of stone, a dike, a breakwater: perh akin to Gr *môlos*, strain, great physical effort or exertion, and OHG *muodi* (G *müde*), ON *môthr*, weary: IE r, \**mo-*, to make an effort, bestir oneself, with extn \**mol-*, n.

2. L *môlēs* acquires, in C17 F, the erudite dim *molécule*, whence E *molecule*; in L, it has adj *môlestus*, (too) heavy, hence painful, hence troublesome: hence the v *môlestāre*, to be a burden—hence a trouble—to, OF-F *molester*, whence 'to molest', and MF-F *molestation*, adopted by E.

3. *Môlēs* has derivative *môlīri*, to make an effort at, to set moving, with cpd *dēmôlīri*, to pull effortfully *dē-* or down, whence MF *demolir* (F *dé-*), whence, via such parts as presp *demolissant* and 'nous *demolissons*', we pull down, the E 'to *demolish*'; derivative L *dēmôlitiō*, o/s *dēmôlitiōn-*, becomes MF-F *démolition*, E demolition.

**mole** (4), a uterine growth. See the 2nd MEAL, para 11.

**molecule, molecular.** See the 3rd MOLE, heading and para 2.

**molest, molestation.** See the 3rd MOLE, para 2.

**molinary, moline.** See the 2nd MEAL, para 10.

**mollescent; mollify, mollification.** See the 2nd MEAL, para 16.

**mollusc, AE mollusk.** See the 2nd MEAL, para 15.

**Molly.** See Mary.

**mollycoddle**=*Molly*, obs sl for a milksop+ CODDLE.

**Moloch**, a Semitic deity ('the abomination of the Ammonites'): LL *Moloch*: LGr *Molokh*: H *Môlekh*, akin to H *melekh*, king (cf Phoen *milk*) and prob deriving from it, with *-o-* perh from H *bôsheth*, shame. (EnciIt.) Hence *moloch*, an evil doctrine to or for which humanity is sacrificed; hence also a formidable-looking (though harmless) Aus lizard.

**molt.** See MOULT.

**molten**, adj from pp of MELT.

**molybdenite, molybdenum.** See PLUMB.

**mom.** See MAMA (heading).

**moment, momentaneous, momentary, momentous, momentum.** See MOVE, para 7.

**momma.** See MAMA (heading).

**Momus.** See MOCK.

**monachal, monachate.** See MONK, para 1.

**monad**, a unit: like EF-F *monade*, from LL *monad-*, o/s of *monas*, adopted from Gr *monas* (o/s *monad-*), from *monos*, sole, single, alone, with s and r *mon-*: cf Gr *mānos* (s and r *mān-*), thin, sparse, and Skt *manǎk* (s *man-*), a little, Tokh B *meṅki*, less, lesser, Lith *meṅkas*, little, trivial, OIr *menb*, little. The Gr adj *monadikos* produces *monadic*.

**monarch** (whence **monarchism, monarchist**), **monarchic, monarchy.**

Gr *monarkhēs*, *monarkhos*, one who governs alone—whence LL *monarcha*, whence E *monarch* (and MF-F *monarque*)—derives from *monos*, alone (see prec)+*arkh*ein, to be first, hence to rule; derivative *monarkhikos*, *monarkhia*, yield resp—via LL and app via MF-F—the adj *monarchic* and the n *monarchy*.

**monastery, monastic.** See MONK, para 2.

**Monday.** See MEASURE, para 12.

**monetary, monetize.** See MIND, para 21.

**money, moneyage, moneyer.** See MIND, para 23.

**mong** (dial). See MONGREL.

**monger:** OE *mangere*, agent of *mangian*, to be a trader: L *mangō*, a vendor that decks out and furbishes his wares (in order to deceive), also esp a slave-trader: Gr *manganon*, a means of deception: f.a.e., the 1st MANGLE.

**Mongol** (whence **Mongolia, Mongolian, Mongolism, Mongoloid**); **Mogul.**

The latter, lit a Mongol, esp one of the Mongol conquerors of India, particularly The Great Mogul or ruler of Mongolian India (CC16–early 18), hence derivatively a magnate (*mogul*),—*Mogul* comes from Per *Mughul*, a Mongol; in fact, from the source of *Mongol* itself: Mongolian *Moṅgol*.

**mongoose:** Marathi *mungus*: almost a blend of Skt *musa*, rat or mouse (habitual victims of the mongoose)+Skt a*ngusa,* mongoose.

**mongrel; mong; among.**

*Mongrel*=the now dial *mong*, to mix+*-rel* for *-erel*, as in *cockerel*; 'to *mong*' app derives from *mong*, a mixture, a mingling, which derives from late ME-EE y*mong*, among, from OE *gemang*, which, moreover, drops its prefix *ge-* and takes instead OE *on*, in, to produce ME-E *among*. This OE *gemang* is basically 'a mingling', hence 'a crowd', from *gemengan*, to mingle: f.a.e., MINGLE.

**monial.** See MULLION.

**monish.** See MIND, para 17.

**monism:** Gr *mon*os, alone, single+*-ism*, a philosophy: cf *dualism* and *pluralism*.

**monition, monitor, monitory.** See MIND, para 17.

**monk**, whence **monkery, monkish; monachal, monachate; monastery, monastic.**

1. Gr *monos* (f.a.e., MONAD) has derivative *monakhos*, a solitary, hence, in LGr, a monk, whence LL *monachus*, VL \**monicus*, OE *munuc*, E *monk*. LL *monachus* has LL adj *monachālis*, whence *monachal*, and a derivative n *monachātus* (gen *-ūs*), the monastic state, whence *monachate*.

2. Gr *monos* has derivative v *monazein*, to live alone, be a solitary, whence *monastēs*, a solitary, with adj *monastikos*, LL *monasticus*, E *monastic* (late MF-F *monastique*), and with subsidiary *monastērion*, LL *monastērium*, E *monastery* (MF-F *monastère*).—Cf the sep MINSTER.

**monkey:** perh MLG *Moneke*, an ape's name: a dim (*-ke*: cf *-kin*) from *mon-*, of R origin—cf Sp *mono*, f *mona*, It *mona*, *monna*, from Tu *maimón*, from Ar *maimún*. The MLG shape is prob due to MD *monec*, *munic* (D *monnik*), a monkey, ref 'the brown-capped head' (EW): cf, sem, the SAm monkey called the *capuchin*.

**monochord:** via MF-F: LL *monochordon*: Gr *monokhordon*, prop the neu of *monokhordos*, with a single string: *monos* (f.a.e., MONAD)+*khordē* (CHORD).

**monochrome**: Gr *monokhrōmos*, of a single *khrōma* or colour: f.a.e., MONAD and CHROMATIC.

**monocular**, one-eyed: L *monoculus*, a hybrid of Gr *mon*os, single+L *oculus*, eye.

**monodrama**. See the element *mono-*.

**monody**. See ODE, para 6, and cf the element *mono-*.

**monogamist** derives from **monogamy**, EF-F *monogamie*, LL *monogamia*, adopted from Gr, from Gr *monogamos*, single-wived, which leads, via LL *monogamus*, to E *monogamous*. For *mono-*, c/f of *monos*, alone, single, cf MONAD; for Gr *gamos*, marriage, cf GAMETE.

2. Largely anl to *monogamy, monogamous, monogamist*, are:

*bigamy*, MF-F *bigamie*, from MF *bigame*, which, like E *bigamous*, derives from LL-ML *bigamus*, twice-married; *bigamist* is anl;

*polygamy*, EF-F *polygamie*, LL *polygamia*, Gr *polugamia*, multiple marriage, from *polugamos*, much-married, whence E *polygamous*; *polygamist* is anl;

*cryptogam*, F *cryptogame*, from *cryptogamie*, SciL *cryptogamia*: *crypto-*, Gr *krupto-*, c/f of *kruptos*, hidden (cf CRYPT)+Gr *gamos*, marriage; hence the anl adj *cryptogamous*.

**monogram**; **monograph**: LL *monogramma*, adopted from Gr: *monos*, single+*grammē*, a line (cf GRAMMAR); E formation in *mono-* (c/f)+*graph*, q.v. at GRAMMAR.

**monolith** (whence **monolithic**): EF-F *monolithe*, n: LL *monolithus*, Gr *monolithos*, consisting of a single (*monos*: cf MONAD) stone (*lithos*).

**monologist** derives from *monologue*, q.v. at LEGEND, para 28.

**monomania**: F *monomanie*, reshaped after *mania* (q.v. at MIND, para 3). Hence, anl, *monomaniacal*.

**monopolist** and **monopolize** derive from **monopoly**: L *monopōlium*: Gr *monopōlion*, the right to sell (*pōlein*) alone (*monos*), certain goods.

**monosyllable**, **monosyllabic**. See SYLLABLE, para 3.

**monotheism, monotheist**. See THEISM, para 2.

**monotone, monotonous, monotony**.

The 1st=n from F adj *monotone*, which, like E *monotonous*, derives from LL *monotonus*, from Gr *monotonos*, of one (*monos*) tone (*tonos*: cf TONE), whence Gr *monotonia*, adopted by LL, whence late EF-F *monotonie* and E *monotony*.

**monotype**: *mono-*, c/f of Gr *monos*, single (cf MONAD)+*type* in its printing and Bio senses: similar—in form—to *linotype*.

**monseigneur, monsignor; monsieur**. See SENILE, para 4, s.f.

**monsoon**: ED *monssoen* (D *moesson*): Port *monçao* or perh Sp *monzón*: Ar *mausim, maucim*, a time, hence a season, esp that of these winds.

**monster, monstrous, monstrosity; monstrate, monstration, monstrable, monstrance; muster**, n and v; **demonstrable, demonstrate, demonstration, demonstrative, demonstrator**—cf **remonstrance, re-**

**monstrant, remonstrate, remonstration** (whence, anl, **remonstrative, remonstrator**).

1. *Monster* derives, via ME from OF-F *monstre*, from L *mōnstrum*, an omen portending the will of the gods, hence a supernatural being or object, hence a monster: from *monēre*, to warn: cf MIND, para 17. Derivative LL *mōnstrōsus* becomes MF *monstreux* (F *monstrueux*), f *monstreuse*, E *monstrous*; subsidiary *mōnstrōsitās*, o/s *mōnstrōsitāt-*, yields *monstrosity*.

2. Derivative *mōnstrāre*, to be an omen of, loses its religious character when it passes into common speech and comes to mean 'to point out, to show'. The presp *mōnstrans*, o/s *mōnstrant-*, has derivative ML *mōnstrantia*, whence, via OF-EF, the Eccl E *monstrance*; the pp *mōnstrātus* becomes the obs 'to monstrate', and its subsidiaries *mōnstrātiō*, o/s *mōnstrātiōn-*, *mōnstrābilis*, the obs *monstration, monstrable*.

3. L *mōnstrāre* has the VL var *\*mōstrāre*, whence OF-MF *mostrer*, with var *mustrer*, whence ME *mustren*, to show, hence to bring together in order to show, hence E 'to *muster*'; the E n *muster*, ME *moustre*, derives from OF-MF *mostre*, from *mostrer*.

4. *Mōnstrāre* has two prefix-cpds affecting E:

*dēmōnstrāre*, to point out forcibly, to prove, with derivatives *dēmōnstrābilis*, E *demonstrable*—presp *dēmōnstrans*, o/s *dēmōnstrant-*, E *demonstrant*—pp *dēmōnstrātus*, E 'to *demonstrate*'—subsidiaries *dēmōnstrātiō*, o/s *dēmōnstrātiōn-*, MF-F *démonstration*, E *demonstration*, and LL *dēmōnstrātīuus* (ML *-īvus*), MF-F *démonstratif*, f *-ive*, E *demonstrative*, and *dēmōnstrātor*, adopted by E;

ML *remōnstrāre*, to show again, point back to, as a fault, with presp *remōnstrans*, o/s *remōnstrant-*, whence both E *remonstrant* and MF *remonstrance* (F *remontrance*), adopted by E; and with pp *remōnstrātus*, whence 'to *remonstrate*', the derivative ML *remōnstrātiō*, o/s *remōnstrātiōn-*, yielding E *remonstration*.

**Montana**. See MINATORY, para 11.

**month, monthly**. See MEASURE, para 11.

**Montreal**. See MINATORY, para 11, s.f.

**monument, monumental**. See MIND, para 20.

**mooch** (whence **moocher**, a skulker, hence a loiterer) is akin to the now dial *miche* (whence 'to *mike*'), to skulk, to loiter illicitly, as in '*miching* mallecho': ME *mychen*, to pilfer, OF-EF *muchier, mucier*, to conceal, (vr) to lurk: cf MHG *miuchelingen*, G *meuchlings*, treacherously, OHG *mūhhōn*, to attack from ambush, *mūhhilāri*, an assassin, OIr for-*múigthe*, hidden, MIr *múchaim*, I conceal, L *muger*, a cardsharper: European r: ? *\*mugh-*, var *\*mug-*, to lurk. (Walshe.)

**mood**, in grammar, sem derives from *mode*, manner (cf MODAL), but takes the form of *mood*, temper of mind, whether permanent or, as now usu, at a particular time: ME *mood*, earlier *mod*: OE *mōd*, mind, heart, courage, feeling: cf the syn OFris (and OS) *mōd*, OHG-MHG *muot* (G *Mut*, courage), MD *moede*, D *moed*, and Go *mōths* (gen *mōdis*), ON *mōthr*, anger; cf also Doric Gr

*mānis*, Attic *mēnis*, anger: Gmc r, \**mod-*, \**modh-*;
IE, \**ma-*. (Walshe.) *Moody*—whence *moodiness*—
derives from OE *mōdig*, courageous.

**moon.** See MEASURE, para 10.

**moor** (1), n. See the 2nd MERE, para 6.

**moor** (2), v. See the 2nd MARL, para 2.

**Moor**, whence **Moorish; morisca, morisco; Moro;
Mauresque; Mauretania;—morris** (dance).

1. *Moor*, a NAfr Arab, (hence) or Berber,
(hence) or Arab-Berber: OF-F *More*, var of
*Maure*: L *Maurus*, a Moor, whence *Mauretania*:
Gr *Mauros*, personification of *mauros*, (very) dark,
aphetic for the syn *amauros*, s *amaur-*, o.o.o.

2. L *Maurus* becomes Sp *Moro*, applied in E to
a Moslem of the Philippines.

3. L *Maurus* has ML adj *mauriscus*, whence Sp
*Morisco*, used in E for a Moor of Spain and, as
*morisco*, a Moorish dance; the Sp var *morisca*
(*danza*) becomes MF-F *morisque*, whence EE
*morys* and *morish*, whence E *morris*.

4. The F adj *morisque* becomes—anl with the
numerous adjj in (Sp *-isco* and) F *-esque*—the
MF-F *moresque*, E *Moresque*, with var *Mauresque*.

**moorings.** See the 2nd MARL, para 2.

**Moorish.** See MOOR (heading).

**moose:** Massachusett (Amerind) *moos*, varr *mos,
mus*: of Alg stock: 'he strips or eats off' the young
bark and twigs of trees. (Mathews.) Sem, cf
CARIBOU.

**moot**, adj and n and v. See the 2nd MEET, s.f.

**mop** (n, hence v), whence the dim *moppet* (*mop*+
euphonic *p*+dim *-et*), derives from ME *mappe*,
var of earlier *mapple*: ? from *Mabel* as a given-
name common among housemaids: dim of *Mab*,
of C origin—cf MIr *Mebd*.

**mope** (whence **mopish**, now usu **moping**), to act
in a daze (dial), hence dejectedly: cf LG *mopen*, to
gape, and Sw dial *mopa*, to sulk.

**mopoke** (mostly NZ); by f/e, **morepork** (mostly
Aus). Echoic.

**moppet.** See MOP.

**moraine**, adopted from F, derives from Savoyard
*morēna*, from dial *mor*, *morre*, a snout. (B & W.)

**moral** (adj, whence n, whence **morals**), whence,
anl, **moralism** and **moralist; morality; moralize**
(whence **moralization**); **morale; mores; morose,
morosity**.—Cpds: **amoral**, whence **amorality:** **demoralize, demoralization; immoral, immoralist,
immorality**.

1. *Mōres*, used learnèdly for ethical folkways,
is the pl of L *mōs* (o/s *mōr-*), a way of carrying
oneself, hence esp of behaving; a custom as
determined by usage, not by law: o.o.o.

2. The L adj is *mōrālis*, whence, via OF-F,
*moral*; from F *moral* used as n comes E *morale*.
L *mōrālis* has LL derivative *mōrālitās*, o/s *mōrā-
litāt-*, OF-F *moralité*, E *morality*; MF-F *moraliser*
yields 'to *moralize*'.

3. L *mos*, in its nuance 'character', has the
derivative pej 'bad mood', whence the adj *mōrōsus*,
in a bad mood, sullen, E *morose*; derivative L
*mōrōsitās*, o/s *mōrōsitāt-*, accounts for E *morosity*
(cf late MF-F *morosité*).

## Compounds

4. The prefix-cpds are all of F origin, *amoral*
being adopted, *amorality* being adapted (F *amor-
lalité*), from F; *demoralize*=F *démoraliser*, *demoralization*=F *démoralisation*; *immoral* is adopted,
*immorality* adapted (F *immoralité*), *immoralist*
adapted (Andre Gide's *L'Immoraliste*, 1911), from
F.

**morass.** See the 2nd MERE, para 8.

**moratorium, moratory.** See MEMORY, para 3.

**Moravia**, whence **Moravian** (adj, hence n), is
prob of C origin.

**moray:** prob Port *moreia*: L *muraena*: Gr
*muraina*: o.o.o.

**morbid, morbidity, morbific.** See MORTAL, para
11.

**mordacious, mordacity; mordant, mordent; mor-
dicate, mordication.** See MORSEL, paras 3, 2, and 5.

**more** (adj 'greater', hence adv and n), whence
**moreover; most**.

1. *More*, ME *more*, var *mare* (cf the adv *mo*,
earlier *ma*), derives from OE *māra* (adv *mā*): cf
OFris *māra*, adj, *mā* and *mār*, *mēr* and *mē*, adv;
OS *mēra*, adj, and *mēr*, adv; OHG *mēro*, adj, *mēr*,
adv, G *mehr* (adv); MD *mere, merre*, adj and adv,
*mee*, adv, D *meer*, adv; Go *màis*, adv, and *màiza*,
adj: ON *meiri, meirr*, adj; OIr *más*, greater, *mór*
(var *már*), great, *māu*, *mō*, more (adv), Ga *mór*,
W *mawr*, Br and Cor (also *mēr*, *mūr*) *maur*,
OC \**maros*, great; Homeric Gr enkhesi*mōros*
(ἐγχεσίμωρος), great with—famed for—the *enkhos* or spear: perh from prehistoric C of Asia
Minor; prob (Hofmann) from an IE etymon
\**mēros*, var \**mōros*, great, very large.

2. Akin to the OE adj *māra*, greater, is the OE
adj *māēst*, greatest, ME *mest, mast*, later *most*, E
*most*, adj; derivative OE *māēst*, adv, leads to E
*most*, adv; the n derives from the adj. OE *māēsst*
is akin to OFris *māst*, OS *mēst*, Go *maists*,
OHG-MHG *meist*, greatest, G *meist* (adv), most,
ON *mestr*, greatest; the *o* in late ME-E *most* was
app prompted by that of ME-E *more*.

**morepork.** See MOPOKE.

**mores.** See MORAL, para 1.

**Moresque.** See MOOR, para 4.

**morganatic:** EF-F *morganatique*: ML 'matri-
monium ad *morganaticam*': ML *morganatica*, a
morning gift: OHG *morgangeba*, gift (*-geba*: E
GIVE) of the *morgan* (G *Morgen*) or morning.

**morgue.** See MORTAL, para 4.

**moribund.** See MORTAL, para 9.

**morisca, morisco.** See MOOR, para 3.

**Mormon** derives, not from Gr *mormōn*, a monster, but from The Book of *Mormon* (1830),
'discovered' and written by Joseph Smith, founder
of the sect: E *more* (adv)+(the non-existent) Eg
*mon*, great: 'the *better*' religion of the Latter-Day
Saints.

**morn**—ME *morn*, earlier *morwen*, whence ME
*morwening*, later *morning*, E *morning*, with *-ing* as
in *evening*: earliest ME, from OE, *morgen*: cf OFris
*orgen, mergen*, OS and OHG *morgan*, MHG-G

*morgen*, Go *maúrgins*, ON *morgunn, morginn*: cf, further off, Lith *mirgēti*, to wink, blink, twinkle, Gr *marmairein*, to flash, Skt *marīci*, ray of light: cf, therefore, the 1st MERE and MURK.

2. ME *morwen* has var *morwe*, whence E *morrow*, morning, hence as in *on the morrow*, the next day. Hence *to-morrow* (TO).

**Moro.** See MOOR, para 2.

**Morocco** (whence **Moroccan-** cf the F adj *marocain*, whence EF-F n *maroquin*), whence the fine leather, *morocco*, first made there, derives from It *Marocco*: Sp *Marruecos*: Ar *Marrakish*.

**moron**, whence **moronic; oxymoron; sophomore**, whence **sophomoric**.

*Moron* is Gr *mōron*, neu of *mōros*, stupid, akin to Skt *mūra*; *oxymoron* is Gr *oxumōron*, neu of *oxumōros*, pointedly (or shrewdly) foolish—cf the element *oxy-*; AE *sophomore* derives from Gr *sophos*, wise (cf SOPHISM), and *mōros*: the wisely foolish second-year student at a university.

**morose, morosity.** See MORAL, para 3.

**morpheme.** See para 2 of:

**Morpheus; morphia, morphine, morphic; morphology; morphosis;**—cf the element *morph-*;— **amorphous; dimorphism.**

1. The base is furnished by Gr *morphē*, shape or form: IE r, ? *\*morgh-* or perh a dissyllabic *\*meregh-*; L *forma* is perh a metathesis of Gr *morphē*.

2. *Morphē* has derivative *Morpheus*, the shaper of dreams; prop the god of dreams, he is popularly apprehended as the god of sleep. The E adj *morphic*=Gr *morph*ē+E suffix *-ic*; *morphosis*= Gr *morphōsis*, from *morphoun*, to shape, from *morphē*; *morphology*=*morph*ē+connective *-o-*+*-logy*, science (cf LOGIC).

3. From Gr *Morpheus*, G derives *Morphin*, whence F, hence E, *morphine* (Chem suffix *-in*, *-ine*); and from *morph*ine comes *morphia*, with the SciL (from L) suffix *-ia*. But *morpheme*=F *morphème* (*-ème*), from Gr *morphē*.

4. Gr *amorphos* (*a-*, without), formless, becomes E *amorphous*; Gr *dimorphos* (*di*=*dis*, twice), two-formed, becomes E *dimorphous*, with Sci var *dimorphic*, adj corresp to *dimorphism*.

**morris** (dance). See MOOR, para 3.

**morrow.** See MORN, para 2.

**morsel** and **morsal; mordacity, mordacious; mordant** (whence **mordancy**) and **mordent; mordicate, mordication;**—**remorse**, whence both **remorseful** and **remorseless.**—Cf the sep SMART and SMIRCH.

1. All these words go back to L *mordēre*, to bite, s *mord-*, r *mor-*: o.o.o.: perh cf OHG *smerzo* (G *Schmerz*)—Gr *smerdnos*, horrible—and esp Skt *mardati*, he crushes: the *s* of SMIRCH and SMART, as of those G and Gr words, could be the IE prefix *s-*.

2. The presp *mordens*, o/s *mordent-*, becomes It *mordente*, whence G *Mordent*, adopted by E as a Mus term; *mordant*, however, is adopted from F, where it is the presp of OF-F *mordre* (from *mordēre*).

3. The L s *mord-* occurs in the adj *mordāx*, biting,

o/s *mordāc-*, whence E *mordacious*; derivative L *mordācitās*, o/s *mordācitāt-*, yields *mordacity*.

4. The L pp *morsus*, s *mors-*, issues into the E adj *morsal*, sharp-biting, cutting; it also has the derivative n *morsus* (gen *morsūs*), a biting, a bite, whence OF-F *mors*, with OF dim *morsel* (F *morceau*), a little bite, hence the quantity bitten off by a person, a small piece, and duly adopted by E.

5. The LL extn *mordicāre*, to bite painfully, has pp *mordicātus*, whence 'to *mordicate*.; derivative LL *mordicātiō* (o/s *mordicātiōn-*), colic, becomes E *mordication*, a gnawing pain.

6. The L cpd *remordēre*, to bite back or again, connotes 'to bite afterwards', as one's conscience does; hence the obs *remord* (n, v). The pp is *remors*us and has the ML derivative n *remorsus* (gen *-ūs*), whence MF *remors* (F *remords*), adopted by ME, whence E *remorse*.

**mort.** See para 5 of:

**mortal, mortality**—**immortal, immortality,** anl **immortalize** (cf the EF-F *immortaliser*); **mort; mortgage** (n, hence v); **mortification, mortify; mortician, mortuary** (adj, n); **mortmain**—see MANUAL, para 21;—**morbid, morbidity, morbific; moribund; morgue; murrain;**—**amortize; post-mortem;**—**murder,** n whence **murderous,** and v, whence **murderer.**

1. The basic word is L *mors*, death, o/s *mort-*, whence the adj *mortālis*, OF-MF *mortal* (F *mortel*), adopted by E; derivative L *mortālitās* (o/s *mortālitāt-*) becomes OF-F *mortalité*, E *mortality*. The neg LL *immortālis* and its derivative *immortālitās* pass through OF-MF to become E *immortal, immortality*.

2. L *mors* (s and r *mor-*) is intimately related to *morī*, to die, s and r *mor-*. The IE r is app *\*mer-*, to die, attested by the cognates in Skt, Arm, OSl, Lith.

3. L *morī* has pp *mortu*us, whence the L *mortuārius* (*-ārius*), of, by, for the burial of the dead, whence, via MF-F *mortuaire*, the E adj *mortuary*; the n *mortuary* derives from MF-F *mortuaire*, from ML *mortuārium*, prop the neu of the adj. AE *mortician* app=*mort-* (o/s of L *mors*)+*physician*.

4. But a *morgue*, where the lost or murdered dead are exposed, is prob unconnected with L *mors*, death, for E *morgue* is adopted from EF-F; as late as 1611, the F term was defined as 'a place where prisoners were examined on entry into prison'; in C15 it meant 'a haughty air'—o.o.o.

5. The L pp—hence also adj—*mortuus* became VL *mortus*, whence F *mort* (f *morte*), which occurs in MF-F *mortgage*, lit 'dead gage' (pledge)— adopted by E. The OF-F n *mort* (L *mort*em, acc of *mors*), death, adopted by E, is there obs except as a hunting term for 'the death' of a deer and the horn-call sounded thereat. The now dial n *mort*, a large quantity or number, derives either sem from the obs E *mort*, death, or from the E adj *mortal* used int.

6. The L cpd *mortificus*, death-making (*-ficus* from *-ficere*, c/f of *facere*, to make), hence death-dealing, yields the rare E *mortific*; derivative LL *mortificāre*, to put to death, becomes OF-F

*mortifier* (with senses gradually widening and weakening), whence 'to *mortify*'; subsidiary LL *mortificātiō*, o/s -*ficātiōn*-, becomes OF-F *mortification*, adopted by E.

7. The ML cpd *admortisāre*, var *amortisāre*, to extinguish (lit, to put to death: L *ad*+*mortem*+ML v suffix -*isāre*, var of LL-ML -*izāre*, from Gr -*izein*)—e.g., a debt—becomes ME *amortisen*, E 'to *amortize*'; derivative ML *amortisātiō* (var of *admortizātiō*), o/s *amortisātiōn*-, yields E *amortization*.

8. L *post mortem*, after death, explains the E adj, hence n, *post-mortem*.

9. L *morī*, to die, has derivative adj *moribundus*, being—or appearing to be—about to die, whence *moribund*.

10. *Morī* has the VL varr *morīre*, *morīri*: whence OF-MF *morir* (F *mourir*), whence OF-MF *morine*, a plague, ME *moreine*, E *murrain*.

11. Perh akin to L *mors*, death, and *morī*, to die, is L *morbus* (s *morb*-, r *mor*-), a disease; despite E & M's 'The resemblance to *morior* must be fortuitous', L *morb*- could well be an extn of the r *\*mor*-: cf OIr *marb* (cf OW *marw*), OC *\*marvos*, dead. The foll derivatives concern E:

*morbidus*, diseased, becomes (EF-F *morbide* and) E *morbid*, whence *morbidity*;

LL *morbificus*, disease-causing (cf LL *morbificāre*, to cause illness), yields F *morbifique* and E *morbific*.

12. Akin to L *morī* and *mors* is E *murder*, n, and *murder*, v: ME *morder*, *morther*, and v *mortheren*, *murtheren*: OE *morthor* and v *myrthrian*: cf OE, OFris, OS, ON *morth*, MD *mord*, D *moord*, Go *maurthr*, (a) murder, and OFris *morthia*, Go *maurthrjan*, to murder; cf also OSl *mrēti*, to die, and Skt *marate*, he dies.

**mortar.** See SMART, para 3.

**mortgage.** See MORTAL, para 5.

**mortician.** See MORTAL, para 3, s.f.

**mortific, mortification, mortify.** See MORTAL, para 6.

**mortise** (n, hence v): F *mortaise*: MF *mortoise*: Ar *murtazz*, fastened—or fixed—in, pp of *razza*, to fit something into something else.

**mortmain.** See MANUAL, para 21.

**mortuary,** adj and n. See MORTAL, para 3.

**Mosaic:** ML *\*Mosaïcus*, adj of LL *Mōsēs*—unless direct from LGr *Mosaïkos*—from LGr *Mōsēs* (Μωσῆς): H *Mōsheh*: perh Eg *mesu*, child, boy, son, the babe being discovered, in the bulrushes, by the Pharaoh's daughter.

**mosaic.** See MUSE, para 2.

**Moscow.** See MUSCOVITE.

**mosey.** See VADE, para 6.

**Moslem.** See ISLAM.

**mosque:** EF-F *mosquée*: It *moschea*: Ar *masjid* (N Afr Ar *masgid*), place where one worships: Ar *sajada*, to bow down in worship.

**mosquito.** See MIDGE, para 3.

**moss** (n, hence v), whence **mossy; mother,** lees, a slimy membrane forming upon fermenting liquids, whence the adj **mothery; mundificant, mundify;** cf the sep LITMUS.

1. *Moss*, a bog, hence the plant thriving there, comes, through ME *mos*, a bog, from OE *mos*, a marshy place (? from ON *mosi*, id), and, through ME *mos*, moss, from ON *mosi*, moss: cf OE *mēos*, OHG-MHG *mos*, G *Moos*, MD *moss* and, as in D, *mos*, moss; OSw *mos*; OSl *mŭchŭ*, *mŭxŭ*, Ru *mokh*, moss, and Lith *mūsaī*, mildew; L *muscus*, moss: IE r, *\*mu*-, to be damp; with extnn *\*mus*-, var *\*mos*, and perh *\*mun*-, as in L *mundus*, clean, ? prop 'washed clean', from '*\*washed*'.

2. L *mundus*, clean, well cared for, has the LL cpd *mundificāre*, to make (LL -*ficāre*, L -*ficere*, c/f of L *facere*, to make) clean, whence 'to *mundify*' or cleanse; presp *mundificans*, o/s *mundificant*-, yields the E adj hence n *munificent*.

3. Prob akin to L *muscus*, moss, and *mundus*, cleansed, is E *mother*, lees, etc., which, form-influenced by MOTHER, female parent, derives from MD *modder*, mud; therefore cf the sep MUD.

**most.** See MORE, para 2.

**mot,** word. See MUTE, para 4.

**motatorious, motatory.** See MOVE, para 4.

**motet.** See MUTE, para 4.

**moth:** ME *mothe*: OE *moththe*: cf late MHG *mot*, *matte*, G *Motte*, MD *mutte*, *motte*, D *mot*, and ON *motti*; perh cf OHG *mado*, MHG-G *made*, maggot.

**mother** (1), female parent. See MATER, para 5.

**mother** (2), lees, slimy membrane. See MOSS, para 3.

**motherless; motherly:** OE *mōdorlēas*; OE *mōdorlīc*. Cf MATER, para 5.

**motif.** Cf *motive*; see MOVE, para 2.

**motile.** See MOVE (heading).

**motion, motionless.** See MOVE, para 2.

**motivate, motivation.** See MOVE, para 2.

**motive.** See MOVE, para 2.

**motley**—whence, via *motley'd*, **mottled**, whence, by b/f, 'to **mottle**', whence the vn **mottling**—derives from ME *motteley*, itself either from OF and perh ult from LL-ML *\*mustēlātus*, weasel-hued, from L *mustēla*, weasel (o.o.o.), as Webster proposes, or, as EW, from AF *\*moitelé*, from F *moitié*, half, anl with *écartelé*, quartered, or (EP) from *motelé*, pp of MF-EF *moteler*, to heap into MF-EF *motels* or little *motes* (F *mottes*) or mounds, with an effect like that of brown or black wormcasts upon the earth's green surface.

**motor,** whence **motorist, motorize,** etc. See MOVE, para 2, s.f.

**mottle, mottled.** See MOTLEY.

**motto.** See MUTE, para 4.

**mould** (1), friable earth. See the 2nd MEAL, para 5.

**mould** (2), shape, form. See MODAL, para 4.

**mound** (n, hence v): ED *mond*, MD *mond*, var of MD *mont*, *munt*, protection, very closely akin to the syn OFris *mund* and OHG-MHG *munt*: cf the -*mund* of G *Vormund*, guardian, MHG *vormunde*, OHG *foramundo*, protector, and esp ON *mund*, protection, (orig) hand (cf L *manus*, q.v. at MANUAL).

**mount**, n and v. See MINATORY, para 7.

**mountain, mountaineer, mountainous.** See MINATORY, para 9.

**mountebank** derives, by f/e, from It *montimbanco*, (he who) mounts (It *montare*, to mount) upon (*im-* for *in-*, from *in*) a bench (It *banco*), perh via late MF *montenbancque* (Godefroy): cf the syn It *saltimbanco* (It *saltar*, to leap), whence the EF-F *saltimbanque*. From a bench he cries his wares.

'**Mounties, the'.** See MINATORY, para 7, s.f.

**mourn**, whence **mournful**, etc. See MEMORY, paras 1 and 8.

**mouse** (n, hence v), whence **mousey** or **mousy**; pl **mice**; **muscle, muscular; mussel; musk**; cf the sep MONGOOSE; **myosotis**.

1. *Mouse*, ME *mous*, earlier *mus*, derives from OE *mūs*, pl *mȳs*: cf OS *mūs*, OHG-MHG *mūs*, G *Maus*, MD *mues, muus, muys*, D *muis*, ON *mūs*; Arm *mukn*, Alb *mī*; OSl *myšī*; L *mūs* (gen *mūris*), Gr *mus*; Skt *mūs*, OPer *mūš*; Hit or, rather, Luwian *mashuil*: IE r *\*mus-*.

2. Gr *mus* also means 'a muscle': cf L *musculus*, a little mouse, hence any object resembling one, esp a muscle (as seen rippling in arm or leg): whence MF-F *muscle*, adopted by E. From F *muscle*, erudite F coins both *musculaire*, whence E *muscular*, and *musculature*, adopted by E.

3. L *musculus* has the further transferred sense 'mussel': whence OE *musle*, ME *musselle*, E *mussel*.

4. Skt *mūs*, mouse, has derivative *muṣka*, scrotum, vulva, whence OPer *mushk*, a substance obtained from sac under the abdominal skin of a male musk deer and, when dried, used as a perfume: LGr *moskhos*, var *moskos*: LL (Tertullian, A.D. c220) *muscus* (prob after L *muscus*, moss): MF-F *musc*: ME *musc, musk*: E *musk*.

5. Gr *mus* (gen *muos*, c/f *muo-*, E *myo-*) has cpd *muosōtis*, lit 'mouse-ear', the flower reshaped by SciL as *myosotis*.

**moustache.** See MUSTACHE.

**mouth** (n, hence v), whence **mouthful, mouth-piece**, etc., derives from OE *mūth*: cf the syn OFris and OS *mūth*, Go *munths*, OHG (and G) *mund*, ON *munnr*, and, further off, Gr *mastax*, mouth, mouthful, morsel, and L *mandere*, to chew, and perh L *mentum*, chin. Cf the sep MUSTACHE and MASTIC.

**move** (v, hence n), whence—unless from OF-MF *movable*—**moveable** (**movable**)—with neg **immovable**—**mover**, '**the movies', moving; motile**, anl with *audile, tactile*, etc.; **movement; motorious, motatory; motion** (n, hence v), whence **motion picture** and **motionless; motive** (adj, hence n, hence v)—cf the corresp MF-F *motif*—whence **motivate**, whence **motivation; motor** (n, hence adj and v), whence **motor car** (**motorcar**), **motorist, motorize** (whence **motorization**); **motorium;—mobile, mobility, mobilization, mobilize**, cf **immobile, immobility, immobilization, im-**

**mobilize**, and, anl, **demobilization, demobilize; moment, momentaneous, momentary, momentous, momentum.**—Prefix-cpds: **amotion, amove; commotion, commove; demote, demotion; emotion** (whence **emotional**, whence **emotionalism**) and **emotive; promote** (whence **promoter**), **promotion** (whence **promotional** and, anl, **promotive**), **promovent; remove** (v, hence n), whence **removable** and **removal**—cf **remote** (whence **remoteness**) and **remotion**, whence, anl, **remotive; submotive=***sub-*, connoting 'secondary'+*motive*, n.

1. 'To *move*', ME *moven*, derives from OF-MF *mover*, from OF *movoir* (F *mouvoir*): ML *movēre*, L *mouēre*, to set, or to set oneself, going: s and r *mou-*, akin to Gr a*meu*sasthai, to become displaced, to pass beyond; Lith *màuju, màutí*, to pass in rubbing; Skt *mívati*, he displaces, and kāmamūtas, impelled by desire: IE r, *\*meu-*, to move.

2. L *mouēre* has pp *mōtus*, which explains *-mote* in, e.g., *promote*. On pp *mōt*us arise:

L *mōtiō* (o/s *mōtiōn-*), movement, MF-F *motion*, adopted by E;

LL *mōtiuus*, ML *-īvus*, capable of moving: OF-F *motif*, f *motive*, E *motive*; the E n *motive* is adopted from MF-F *motive*, from the adj. The derivative F *motiver* (C18+)prob suggested 'to *motivate*';

rare L agent *mōtor*, he who, that which, sets moving, adopted by E (cf the late MF-F *moteur*);

LL *mōtōrius*, capable of moving, (hence) moving, with neu *mōtōrium*, used as a n, 'the power of moving', adopted by SciE.

3. OF *movoir* has derivative OF-MF *movement* (F *mou-*), adopted by E.

4. L *mouēre* has the LL aug-freq *mōtāre* (vt), to keep moving, with pp *mōtātus*, whence agent *mōtātor*, whence E *motatorious*.

5. L *mouēre*, s and r *mou-*, perh has the OL base *\*mō-*, as in L *mōbilis*, capable of moving, whence, via OF-F, the E adj *mobile*; derivative *mōbilitās*, o/s *mōbilitāt-*, passes through OF-F *mobilité* to become *mobility*. The LL negg *immōbilis*, *immōbilitās*, yield—via MF-F—*immobile* and *immobility*. Derivative F *immobiliser*, whence *immobilisation*, explains 'to *immobilize*' and *immobilization*.

6. Anl is F *démobiliser*, whence, anl, *démobilisation*: hence 'to *demobilize*' and *demobilization*.

7. The ult OL base *\*mō-* occurs also (cf para 5) in L *mōmen*, superseded by *mōmentum* (contr of *\*mouimentum*), impulsion, hence a weight determining physical impulsion or inclination, adopted by E. The weight on a pair of scales being usu light, there arises the sense 'small division', hence 'a small division of time': OF-F *moment*, adopted by E. L *mōmentum*, a moment of time, has these derivatives relevant to E:

LL *mōmentāneus*, ephemeral, temporary, E *momentaneous*;

L *mōmentārius*, ephemeral, E *momentary*, also in sense 'at every moment'; but

L *mōmentōsus* means 'prompt, rapid'. E *momentous*, and is strongly tinged with the 'weight' sense, hence 'important (at that or this moment)'.

8. *The psychological moment* derives, in sense 'most suitable or advantageous moment', from F *moment psychologique*, orig (but very briefly and restrictedly) in the sense of the G (Bismarck's) *Psychologisches Moment*, that 'weight upon the hearts and minds' of a people—that spiritual shock —which would be felt by the French because of the G bombardment of Paris in the latter part of the Franco-Prussian War of 1870–71. (B & W.)

Prefix-Compounds of L *mouēre*

9. *Amouēre* (ML *amovēre*), to put aside, set at distance (*a-*, away from), becomes legal AF *amoever*, whence 'to *amove*', to dismiss from office. The L pp *amōt*us has derivative *amōtiō*, o/s *amōtiōn-*, legal E *amotion*.

10. L *commouēre* (ML *-movēre*), to set in motion, to move strongly, to perturb, becomes OF-MF *commoveir*, ME *commoeven*, E 'to *commove*'—much rarer than *commotion*, adopted from OF-F, from *commōtiōn-*, o/s of L *commōtiō*, from *commōtus*, pp of *commouēre*.

11. L *dēmouēre* (ML *-movēre*), to move (vt) away from, turn aside, hence to chase away, has pp *dēmōtus*, whence the AE 'to *demote*', opp *promote*, in the Armed Forces.

12. L *ēmouēre* (ML *-mov-*), to move out from, to move out of (someone), to strongly affect the feelings, with pp *ēmōtus*, which influences the formation of EF-F *émotion*—from *émouvoir* (ML *ēmovēre*)—whence E *emotion*; anl F *émotif*, f *émotive*, yields E *emotive*.

13. L *prōmouēre* (ML *-movēre*), to move—hence, to push—forward, has presp *prōmouens*, o/s *prōmouent-*, whence, via ML, the legal n *promovent*, and pp *prōmōtūs*, whence 'to *promote*'; derivative LL *prōmōtiō*, o/s *promōtiōn-*, whence MF-F *promotion*, adopted by E.

14. L *remouēre*, to move (hence to lead, to force) back; ML *removēre*, gives us—perh not via OF—'to *remove*'; the pp *remōtus* furnishes *remote*—its derivative *remōtiō*, o/s *remōtiōn-*, the E *remotion*—and its LL derivative adj *remōtiuus*, ML *-īvus*, the E *remotive*.

**movement.** See prec, para 3.

**mow,** to cut grass, whence agential **mower** and pa, vn **mowing**; pp **mown** (cf *sow, sown*); cf sep the 2nd MEAD (meadow); aftermath.

1. 'To *mow*', ME *mowen*, var *mawen*, derives from OE *māwan*: cf OHG *māen*, MHG *maejen*, G *mähen*, MD *mayen, maeyen*, D *maijen*; OBr *metetic*, harvested, Br *médein*, to cut the crops, *medereh*, harvest season, Cor *medé, medi*, to mow, to reap, MIr *meithel*, a reaping-party; L *metere*, Gr a*man*, to reap: European r, *\*med-*, to cut or mow grass.

2. Akin to OHG *māen*, to mow, is OHG *mād*, MHG *māt*, G *Mahd*, OE *māeth*, mowing-time, whence the *-math* of *aftermath*, a second mowing, a second crop of grass in one season, hence consequences, cf the now dial *math*, a mowing or its produce; also akin is Gr a*mētos*, a harvest.

**Mozarab.** See ARAB, para 5.

**mucedin, mucedinous.** See MUCUS, para 2.

**much** (adj, hence adv and n). See MASTER, para 18.

**mucid.** See MUCUS, para 3.

**mucilage, mucilaginous.** See MUCUS, para 2.

**muck** (n, hence v), whence **mucky**, as well as **muckrake** and **muckworm**, is ME *muk*, of Scan origin: cf ON *myki*, dung, OE *moc, muc*, ? L *mūcus* and *ēmung*ere, to wipe one's nose: ? ult echoic.

**muckle.** See MASTER, para 18.

**muckrake, muckworm.** See MUCK.

**mucoid, mucous.** See resp the heading and para 2 (s.f.) of:

**mucus,** whence Chem **mucin** (*muc-*+Chem *-in*) and **mucoid** (*muc-*+*oid*); **mucous; mucedin, mucedinous; mucilage, mucilaginous;—emunctory;—mycelium;—muggy;—moist** (whence **moisten, moistness**), **moisture**.

1. L *mūcus*, nasal secretion, burnt end of a wick, adopted by E (and, e.g., F) in the former sense, is closely akin to L *mūcor*, mildew, mould: indeed, both (s and r *mūc-*) derive from or are very intimately cognate with L *mūcēre* (s, r *mūc-*), to go mildewy or mouldy, VL var *muccāre*: cf Gr *muxa*, slime, nasal mucus, L *mung*ere, to blow or wipe one's nose, usu in the int *ēmung*ere, pp *ēmunctus*, whence LL *ēmunctōrium*, a pair of candle-snuffers, whence Med E *emunctory*, any excretory organ: IE r, perh *\*meug-*, var *\*mug-*, slippery, slimy. Perh cf MUCK.

2. L *mūcus* has the foll derivatives relevant to E:
*mūcēdō*, mucus, whence *mucedin* (Chem suffix *-in*); on the L o/s *mucedin-* arises the E adj *mucedinous*;
LL *mūcilāgō*, a musty juice, whence MF-F *mucilage*, adopted by E; the E adj *mucilaginous*= L *mūcilāgin-* (o/s of *mucilago*)+*-ous*;
*mūcōsus*, whence *mucous* (and EF-F *muqueux*),—whence also EF-F *mucosité*, E *mucosity*.

3. L *mūcēre* has derivative adj *mūcidus*, whence E *mucid*.

4. L *mūcidus* becomes VL *\*muccidus*, var *\*muscidus*, mildewy, whence OF *moiste* (F *moite*), adopted by ME, whence *moist*; derivative MF *moistour* (F *moiteur*), whence E *moisture*.

5. Gr *muxa* has corresp adj *mukēs*, slimy, hence a mushroom, whence SciL *mycelium*.

6. Akin to Gr *mukēs* and L *mūcus* are ON *mygla*, to become mouldy, and *mugga*, fine rain, and, of Scan origin, ME *mugen*, to drizzle, and E dial *mug*, fine rain, a mist: whence the adj *muggy*, (of weather) damp, hence close, oppressive.

**mud** (n, hence v), whence **muddy** (adj, hence v, with pa **muddied**); **muddle** (v, hence n), whence **muddler** and pa, vn **muddling**.

1. 'To *muddle*' is lit 'to render muddy, hence turbid', hence to obscure the minds of, to confuse: in short, it prob=*muddy*, adj+freq suffix *-le*;

2. *Mud*, ME *mudde*, var *modde*, derives either from MLG *mudde* or from MD *modde*, mud, cf MD *modder, mudder*, mud, slime, dregs (cf E *mother*, lees: q.v. at MOSS, para 3), and late

MHG-G *moder*, mould; cf also OB *myti*, to wash, and Skt *mūtram*, urine: IE r, *\*meu-*, esp the var *\*mu-*, damp, with extn *\*mud-*, *\*mut-*.

**muff** (n, hence v, 'to handle as if with muffs, hence clumsily'); **muffin**; **muffle** (n, v), whence **muffler**.

1. A *muff* comes from D *mof*: Walloon *mouffe*: MF-F *moufle*, a mitten: ML *muffula*, a fur-lined glove: o.o.o.; perh akin to the wild sheep called the *mouflon*, F *mouflon*, It dial *muflone* (Corsican *muffolo*), L dial *mufro*, o/s *mufron-*.

2. Prob akin to *muff* is—? as a dim—*muffin*, perh from the softness and also from the shape: cf the MF *moufflet*, soft bread.

3. Certainly akin to *muff* is *muffle* (from MF-F *moufle*, mitten), anything that wraps up, envelops, hence obscures the view or deadens sound; 'to *muffle*' app comes rather from F en*moufler*, and from 'to *muffle*' obviously derives *muffler*.

**mufti**, civilian dress worn by anyone entitled to wear a uniform, prob derives from *in mufti*: F *en mufti*, applied to an Army officer (F or E) acting as a magistrate and, in this role, dressed 'like a *mufti*' or Mohammedan expounder of the law (loosely, a judge)—an interpretation I owe to the late Field Marshal Lord Wavell. A *mufti* derives from Ar *mufti*, active participle of *aftā* (a conjugation of *fatā*), to decide a point of law (OED).

**mug** is prob of Scan origin: cf Sw *mugg*, Nor *mugge* (or *-ga*); cf also Fris *mukke*. The sl sense 'face' comes from faces painted on mugs; unless it be from a PN, *muggins*—cf *juggins*—could have the same origin, many such faces being so foolish.

**muggins.** See prec.

**muggy.** See MUCUS, para 6.

**mugwump** is of Alg origin, prob the Massachuset *mugquomp*, a chief.

**mulatto.** See MULE.

**mulberry**: ME *mulberie*, *murberie* (cf OHG *mūrberi*, *mōrberi*): *mul*, for *mur*+*beri*, E BERRY: *mur*, from OF-MF *mure*, var of *moure*: VL *mora*: L *mōrum*, mulberry, trln of Gr *moron* (var *mōron*), r *mor-*: IE r, *\*mer-*, black.

2. L *mōrum* has ML derivative *morata*, OF *moree*, E *murrey*, mulberry-colour.

3. Gr *moron* has, along with Gr *sukon*, a fig, helped, by f/e, to shape Gr *sukomoros*, of Sem origin (cf H *shiqmāh*): Gr *sukomoros* becomes L *sycomorus*, OF *sicamor* (F *sycomore*), ME *sicamour*, E *sycamore*.

**mulch.** See the 2nd MEAL, para 17.

**mulct** derives, prob via F *mulcter*, from L *mulctāre*, inferior form of *multāre*, to inflict a fine upon, hence to punish by depriving (of something): prob either Samnite or Oscan. Hence the adj *mulctary*, *-uary*.

**mule** (1), whence **mulish**; **muleteer**; **mulatto**.

*Mulatto* derives from the Sp (and Port) adj *mulato*, f *-ata*, of mixed breed, from *mulo*, a mule, from L *mulus*, f *mula*, whence OE *mūl* (cf ON *mūll*) and OF *mul*, f *mule*, whence E *mule*: and L *mulus* is akin to Gr *mukhlos*, ass, and Alb *mušk*, mule. OF *mul* has MF-F dim *mulet*, whence EF-F *muletier*, a mule-driver, whence E *muleteer*.

**mule** (2), slipper. See MELANCHOLIA, para 7.

**mulga** is an Aus aboriginal word.

**mull**, dry mould, dirt. See the 2nd MEAL, para 4.

**mullein**, **mullen**. See the 2nd MEAL, para 18.

**muller**, a stone used as pestle. See the 2nd MEAL, para 4.

**mullet.** See MELANCHOLIA, para 5.

**mullion** is a characteristically E refashioning of OF *\*moienel*, var of *\*meienel*, medial—cf the OF *moinel*, a sally port—from L *mediānus*: f.a.e., MEDIAL, para 1. The OF *\*moienel* and *\*meienel* do exist, but in a totally different sense (hunting horn). EW suggests that *mullion* corrupts *monial* (a mullion) and, noting that E *monial*, like OF *moinel*, derives from ML *moniālis*, lit a monk, cfs G *Mönch*, a monk, also a mullion.

**mulse.** See MEL, para 3.

**multifarious.** See the element *multi-*.

**multiple** and **multiplex**; **multiplication**, **multiplicity**, **multiply** (whence **multiplier**). See PLY, para 26.

**multitude**, whence, anl, **multitudinous**, is adopted from OF-F: L *multitūdō*, itself from *multus* (adj), much, *multi*, many: cf the element *multi-*. The s is *mult-*; the r, *mul-*: cf the Gr adv *mala*, much.

**multure.** See the 2nd MEAL, para 13.

**mum** (1), mother. See MAMA (heading).

**mum** (2), theatrical v. See MUMMER.

**mum!** Be quiet—whence *mum*, silent, and *mum*, silence—is echoic.

**mumble** (v, hence n), whence **mumbler**, **mumbling**, comes from ME *momelen*, ult echoic (cf MUM!): akin to MD *mummelen*, var—as in D—*mommelen*, and to G *mummeln*. Cf MUMP.

**mumbo-jumbo**, a meaningless incantation, meaningless talk, earlier a bugaboo, earliest *Mumbo-Jumbo*, a tutelary genius or god of the Mandingos in the W Sudan: (in a Mandingo dial) *mama dyambo*: *mama*, ancestor+*dyambo*, pompon, hence esp its wearer. (Webster.)

**mummer**, **mummery**; **to mum**.

*Mum*, to act in a dumb show or in disguise, is akin to and perh from MUM!: cf the OF-EF *momer*, to disguise oneself, whence late MF-EF *momerie*, a masquerade, whence E *mummery*, a masking or masquerade, (hence) a pretentious or hypocritical or ludicrous ceremony or performance; also from OF *momer* derives *momeur*, with var *mommeur*, whence E *mummer*, one who mums, hence (pej) any actor or actress. OF *momer* perh meant, orig, to grimace with astonishment or fear: cf Sp and Port *momo*, a grimace, and F (childish) *momo!*, indicative of fear or astonishment (B & W).

**mummify.** See the 2nd MUMMY, para 2.

**mummy** (1), childish for 'mother'. See MAMA (heading).

**mummy** (2), a body treated with preservatives and then entombed, derives from MF-F *momie*, from ML *mumia*, from Ar *mūmīa* (or *mūmiya*), a mummy, earlier the bitumen with which the ancient Egyptians plastered the enbalmed corpses; Ar *mūmīa* derives from Per *mūm*, wax.

2. F *momie* has derivative *momifier*, whence 'to

*mummify'*, whence—or from F *momification*—*mummification*.

**mump**, to mumble, hence to beg numblingly, hence to be sulky, prob derives from MD-D *mompelen*, MD varr *mommelen, mummelen*, to mumble: cf MUMBLE. Hence the n *mump*, now mostly in pl *mumps*, which, as *the mumps*, denotes the sulks, whence prob, from the sufferer's appearance, *mumps* the disease; from the n *mump* comes also the obsol *mumpish*, sulky, sullenly dull.

**munch.** See MANGE, para 1.

**mundane** (whence **mundanity**) comes, like late OF-F *mondain*, f *mondaine* (as in *demi-mondaine*), from L *mundānus*, of this world, hence, in LL, worldly, pagan: and *mundānus* is the adj of *mundus*, the universe (as trans of Gr *kosmos*), hence our world therein: o.o.o.; perh—the earth clearly being a body in motion—akin to L *mouēre*, to move; f.a.e., MOVE.

2. L *mundānus* has the LL cpd derivative *extramundānus*, beyond this world: E **extramundane**, which prob suggested **supramundane**, above this world.

**mundificant, mundify.** See MOSS, para 2.

**muncipal, municipality.** See CAPABILITY, para 8.

**munificence, munificent.** See the 1st MEAN, para 2.

**muniment; munition, ammunition.**

The 3rd derives from F *amunition*, formed by apprehending *la munition* as *l'amunition*; MF-F *munition*, collective for all the means of defence, including notably food and weapons: *munītiōn*em, acc of L *mūnītiō*, from *mūnītus*, pp of *mūnīre*, to fortify, OL *moenīre*, from *moenia*, walls, esp if defensive: o.o.o.: perh not even akin to L *mūrus*, wall.—*Mūnīre* has derivative *mūnimentum*, a defence, hence a protection, hence legal **muniments**, title-deeds.

**mural** (adj, hence n), whence **extra-mural**, outside the walls, i.e. external; **immure.**

'To *immure*', to wall in, derives from ML *immurāre*; *im-* for *in-, in*, in, into+*mūrus*, a wall+inf suffix *-āre*. *Mūrus*, s *mūr-*, perh has r *mū-*; if so, then cf L *moenia*, q.v. at MUNIMENT. *Mūr*us has adj *mūrālis*, whence MF-F *mural*, adopted by E.

**murder** (n, v), **murderer, murderous.** See MORTAL, para 12.

**murex, muricate.**

The latter derives from L *mūricātus*, having sharp points, from *mūrex*, a shell-fish yielding a purple dye, hence the dye itself: o.o.o.: prob Medit.

**murk** (occ **mirk**), adj, darkened, dark, obscure, hence as n, whence, in turn, the adj **murky** (*mirky*): ME *mirke, merce*: OE *mirce*: cf the ON *myrkr* and modern Scan cognates, also Lith *mirgēti*, to glimmer: perh ult akin to MORN.

**murmur** (n, v), **murmurous.**

'To *murmur*' comes from OF-F *murmurer*, L *murmurāre*, from the n *murmur*, whence, via OF-F *murmure*, the E n *murmur*; the derivative adj L *murmuriōsus* acquires the LL var *murmurōsus*, whence, prob via MF *murmuros*, the E **murmurous**. Echoic (cf the L *susurrus*), *murmur* is akin to Arm

*mṙmṙam* (for *\*murmuram*), I growl, Gr *mormurein* (s *mormur-*), to 'grumble' as it boils, and to Skt *murmuras*, a crackling fire, *marmaras*, rustling, roaring, noisy. All these words are perh redupp of *\*mur-* or *\*mor-* or *\*mar-*, themselves echoic: cf Lith *murmēti*, to murmur.

**murrain.** See MORTAL, para 10.

**murrey.** See MULBERRY, para 2.

**musca, muscarine.** See MIDGE, para 2.

**muscat, muscatel.**

The latter, a sweet, rich wine, is adopted from MF, where it forms, orig, a dim (*-el*) of MF-F *muscat*, the same wine, its grape, adopted from OProv, where, orig, it meant 'smelling like *musk*', from LL *muscus*: f.a.e., MOUSE.

**muscle.** See MOUSE, para 2.

**muscology.** See the 2nd element *musci-*.

**Muscovite** (n, hence adj) derives, by suffix *-ite* (inhabitant), from *Muscovy* or Ancient Russia—cf the F *Muscovite* from *Moscovie*. *Muscovy* comes from F *Muscovie*, earlier *Moscovie*, itself from Ru *Moskva*, Moscow, capital of that kingdom and so named because it stands on the river *Moskva*, app a cpd with a Ru r for 'water': cf Fin *va*, water. Note that *Muscovy duck* is f/e for *musk duck*, 'so called from its odor during the breeding season' (Webster): f.a.e., MOUSE, para 4.

**muscular, muscularity.** See MOUSE, para 2.

**Muse; museum; music, musical, musician;—mosaic.**

1. In Gr Myth there were nine goddesses presiding over song, poetry, the arts, hence E *Muse*, one of them, derivatively one's inspiring genius, esp in poetry: OF-F *Muse*: L *Mūsa*: Gr *Mousa*, perh for *\*Monthia*, from *manthanein* (s *manthan-*, r *manth-*), to learn: IE base, perh *\*mendh-*, to direct one's MIND towards something. (Hofmann.)

2. Gr *Mousa*, pl *Mousai*, s *Mous-*, has derivative *mouseion*, a temple of the Muses, hence, in LGr, an establishment recording and propagating the cultivation, by the people, of the arts and sciences: L *mūseum*, adopted by E. The Gr *mouseion* is prop the neu of the adj *mouseios*, of the Muses, whence ML *musaīcus* (adj), whence *musaīcum* (n, prop the neu of the adj), var *mosaīcum*, It *mosaico* (n), EF-F *mosaïque*, E *mosaic*; the sem chain is rather vague.

3. The Gr adj *mouseios* has var *mousikos*, which occurs in *mousikē tekhnē*, art of the Muses, hence esp, as *mousikē*, music (lyric poetry being set to music), whence LL *mūsica*, whence EF-F *musique*, whence EE *musick*, E *music*. LL *mūsica* has ML derivative adj *mūsicālis*, MF-F *musical*, adopted by E; MF-F *musicien* becomes E *musician*.

**muse** (v, hence n)—cf **amuse, amusement; musette; muzzle.**

1. 'To *muse*' comes from OF *muser*, to loiter, to reflect, prob orig to stay with muzzle in air, from OF *\*mus*, attested by OF-F *museau*, OProv *mus*, It *muso*, ML *musum*, var *musus*, muzzle, animal's mouth: o.o.o.

2. OF-F *muser* has OF-F cpd *amuser*, to cause to stand with muzzle in air, (hence) to bemuse,

whence 'to *amuse*'; derivative late MF-F *amusement* was adopted by E.

3. OF *muser* has derivative n *muse*, whence the MF-F dim *musette*, ref *muser* in its special MF sense 'to play the bagpipes'; *musette*, adopted by E, acquires one or two additional Mus senses.

4. ML *musum*, *musus* has dim *musellum*, whence MF *musel*, whence ME *mosel*, E *muzzle*; 'to *muzzle*' comes from MF-F *museler*, from *musel*, which, by the way, B & W derive from OF *\*mus* (as in para 1).

**museum.** See MUSE, para 2.

**mush** (1), n. See MASH, para 2.

**mush** (2), Canadian v. See the 2nd MARCH, para 3.

**mushroom**: ME *muscheron*: MF *mouscheron* (F *mousseron*): perh from OF-F *mousse*, moss (cf MOSS, para 1), but, the OF form being *meisseron*, the F word more prob derives, via the acc *mussiriōnem*, from LL *mussiriō*, a word that, proper to the N of France, is perh of pre-L origin. (B & W; E & M.)

**mushy.** Adj of MUSH (1).

**music, musical, musician.** See MUSE, para 3.

**musk.** See MOUSE, para 4.

**muskeg**, a (usu tussocky) sphagnum bog: of Alg origin—cf Cree *muskeg*, Ojibway *mashkig*, a swamp, and Shawnee *muskiegui*, a pool, a lake. (Mathews.) Cf:

**muskellunge**, a large NAm pike: of Alg origin— cf esp Ojibway *mashkinoje*, a large pike: akin to prec.

**musket, musketeer, musketry.** See MIDGE, para 4.

**muslin**: EF-F *mousseline*: It *mussolina*: coll Ar *mūṣili*, (adj) of Mosul (Ar al-*Mawṣil* or approx *Musul*), the Mesopotamian city where it was orig made.

**muss** is a coll form (mostly AE) of MESS.

**mussel.** See MOUSE, para 3.

**Mussulman.** See ISLAM.

**must** (1), n. See MEAT, para 3.

**must** (2), v: ME *moste* (pt), could, was obliged to (cf pres *moot*, *mot*): OE *mōste* (pt—cf pres *mōt*): akin to OFris *mōta*, OS and Go *-mōtan*, OHG *muozan*, MHG *muëzen*, G *müssen*, MD *mueten*, *moten*, (as in D) *moeten*, all pres inf, with slightly intervarying senses: perh akin to E *mete*, to measure; if that be so, the basic idea would be 'to be allotted (a portion, a duty, etc.)'.

**mustache** (var **mous-**): late MF-F *moustache*: It *mostaccio*, var of *mostacchio*: prob via ML *mustacia*: LGr *mustaki*: Gr *mustax*, gen *mustakhos*, upper lip, hence mustache: akin to Gr *mastax* (gen *mastakhos*), mouth: therefore cf MOUTH.

**mustang**, a half-wild horse of the SW states of U.S.A.: Am Sp *mestengo* (whence the—at least, orig—superior var *mestang*, now obsol): Sp *mesteño*, belonging to the *mesta* or graziers taken collectively: ML *mixta*, a mixture: L *mixta*, f of *mixtus*, pp of *miscēre*, to mix.

**mustard**: MF *moustarde* (F *moutarde*): OF *moust* (F *moût*): L *mustum*, must (cf MEAT, para 3):

in being prepared for use, mustard was mixed with must.

**muster.** See MONSTER, para 3.

**musty** is both the adj of *must*—q.v. at MEAT, para 3—and a sep adj meaning 'damp' (obs), 'affected with mouldiness, rank', perh for *moisty*, an obs var of *moist*, q.v. at MUCUS, para 4.

**mutable, mutability, mutant, mutate, mutation** (whence, anl, **mutative**), **mutatory**; **mutual** (whence **mutualism, mutuality, mutualize**), **mutuary, mutuum.** —Prefix-cpds: **commutable, commutant, commutate, commutation, commutative,** anl **commutator, commute** (whence **commuter**); **immutability, immutable; permutable, permutate, permutation** (whence, anl, **permutator** and **permutatory**), **permute** (whence **permuter**); **transmutation** (whence, anl, **transmutative**), **transmute** (whence **transmutable** and **transmuter**).

### Indo-European

1. All these words rest upon the firm base of L *mūtāre* (vt, vi), to change, exchange: s and r, *mūt-*, which, having IE cognates *met-*, *mit-*, *maid-* or *meid-*, is app a *-t-* or *-th-* extn (cf the *-b-* extn in Gr *ameibō*, I exchange) of an ult IE r *\*mei-*, to change, to exchange: cf Skt *methati*, he alternates, *mithás*, alternately; OSl *mitĕ*, *mitusŭ*, alternately, and Lett *mitét*, to change; Go *maidjan*, to change. Cf, further, Skt *mayate*, he exchanges, and the 1st MEAN.

### Simple *mūtāre*, to change

2. The presp *mūtans*, o/s *mūtant-*, yields the E adj, hence n, *mutant*; the pp *mūtātus* yields the n and v *mutate*. On the pps *mūtat-* arise:

*mūtatiō*, o/s *mūtātiōn-*, whence OF-F *mutation*, adopted by E;

LL *mūtātōrius*, whence *mutatory*.

3. On the pres s *mūt-* is formed *mūtābilis*, whence *mutable*; derivative *mūtābilitās*, o/s *mūtābilitāt-*, becomes OF-F *mutabilité*, whence *mutability*.

4. Also on the pres s *mūt-* is formed the adj *mūtuus*, exchanged, hence reciprocal, mutual: MF-F *mutuel*, E *mutual*; E *mutuality* perh owes something to EF-F *mutualité*. L *mūtuus* has neu *mūtuum*, which, via *mūtuum argentum*, becomes n 'a loan of movables, returnable in kind but without interest', adopted as a legal term; the derivative L adj *mūtuārius* becomes E *mutuary*.

### Prefix-Compounds

5. L *commūtāre*, to change *com-*, with, to exchange, gives us 'to *commute*'. Derivative *commūtābilis* explains *commutable*; presp *commūtans*, o/s *commūtant-*, E *commutant*; pp *commūtātus*, 'to *commutate*'; its derivative *commūtātiō*, o/s *commūtātiōn-*, OF-F *commutation*, adopted by E, and derivative ML *commūtatīvus*, E *commutative*.

6. L *mūtābilis* and *mūtābilitās* have negg (*im-* for *in-*, not) *immūtābilis*, *immūtābilitās*, whence E *immutable* and, perh via MF-F *immutabilité*, E *immutability*.

7. L *permūtāre*, to change, or exchange, *per-* or

thoroughly, becomes MF-F *permuter*, whence 'to permute', whence *permutable*. The pp *permūtātus* yields 'to *permutate*'; derivative *permūtātiō*, o/s *permūtātiōn*-, becomes OF-F *permutation*, adopted by E.

8. L *transmūtāre*, to change *trans* or across, to change utterly (from one nature to another), yields 'to *transmute*'; derivative *transmūtātiō*, o/s *transmūtātiōn*-, becomes MF-F *transmutation*, adopted by E. *Transmutability* is perh indebted to F *transmutabilité*.

**mute** (adj, hence n and v), whence **muteness** (*-ness*) and **mutism**; **mutescent**, whence **mutescence**. —**motto**; **mot, motet**.

1. The adj *mute* derives from L *mūt*us, dumb, with s *mūt*- and ult r *\*mū*-: 'Doubtless at first said of animals that can utter only *mū* [cf E *moo*]; then applied to human beings [incapable of distinct speech]; finally to inanimate objects' (E & M). This r *mu*- occurs also in, e.g., L *muttīre* (*mutīre*), to mutter; Gr *mu*, a groan, and *mundos, mudos, mukos*, dumb; Skt *mūkas*, dumb; Arm *munj*, dumb.

2. L *mūtus* has LL derivative *mūtēscere*, to become mute, with presp *mūtēscens*, o/s *mūtēscent*-, whence E *mutescent*.

3. Akin to L *muttīre*, *mutīre*, to mutter, to mumble, is ME *muteren*, whence 'to *mutter*', whence the n *mutter* and the pa, vn *muttering*.

4. L *muttīre* has derivative LL-VL n *muttum*, a mutter, a mumbling, a grunt, whence OF-F *mot*, orig applied to a word as uttered, whence It *motto*, an uttered word, a saying, whence, in latter sense, the E *motto*. The F *mot* exists for E in the partially adopted *bon mot*, a witticism; the MF-F derivative *motet* (dim *-et*)—cf the It *mottetto*—is adopted as a Mus term.

**mutic, muticous.** See para 2 of:

**mutilate** (adj, v), **mutilation** (whence, anl, **mutilatory**).

1. 'To *mutilate*' derives from L *mutilātus*, pp of *mutilāre*, *to de-horn, to maim, from *mutilus*, de-horned (lacking horns), hence maimed; the derivative LL *mutilātiō*, o/s *mutilātiōn*-, yields— perh via MF-F—*mutilation*.

2. Akin to the L adj *mutilus* is the L adj *muticus*, docked, whence Zoo *mutic* and Bot *muticous*: cf OIr *mut*, short, Ga *mutach* (s *mut*-), short and thick, *mùtan*, stump of a finger, OC *\*mut*, thick (and short), whence *\*muttos*, f *\*mutta*, whence the Comtois (E France) *mout*, *moute*, and—? via *\*mustos* or *\*mussos*—the F *mousse*, de-horned, hornless.

3. The origin of the group, therefore, is European, esp C, *\*mut*, short, esp by shortening.

**mutineer, mutinous, mutiny** (n, hence v).

The 2nd derives from the 3rd; the 1st from F *mutinier*, itself from MF-F 'se *mutiner*', to rebel, whence EE 'to *mutine*' (to mutiny), whence E 'a *mutiny*'. MF-F 'se *mutiner*' derives from MF-F *mutin*, rebellious, stubborn, from OF-MF *muete*, a riot (F *meute*), from (? VL—)ML *movita*, a movement, esp if quarrelsome or hostile, from ML *movēre, L *mouēre*, to MOVE.

**mutism.** See MUTE (heading).

**mutt** (sl), a fool, (? hence) a dog, esp if mongrel, derives from the coll *mutton-head*, a dullard, itself by b/f from coll *mutton-headed*, dull. Cf MUTTON.

**mutter.** See MUTE, para 3.

**mutton** (whence **mutton-bird, -chop** (hence of whiskers), **-fish, -grass**, etc., for one sem reason or another): ME *motoun*: MF *moton*, easement of OF *molton, multun*, a sheep of either sex, but esp a ram, occ a wether: ML *multō*, acc *multōn*em: of C origin—cf OIr *molt*, Ga *molt, mult*, Cor *mols, molz*, Br *maout, mout*, W *mollt*, a wether, OC *\*moltos, \*multos*: per from C *\*mol*-, to be gentle. (Malvezin, who quotes the F proverbial phrase, *doux comme un mouton*, as gentle as a sheep.)

**mutual, mutuality**, etc. See MUTABLE, para 4.

**mutuary, mutuum.** See MUTABLE, para 4.

**muzzle** (n, v). See MUSE, para 4.

**my.** See ME, para 2.

**myall** (1), a hard- and fragrant-wooded acacia of SE Aus: Aboriginal (State of Victoria). Perh cf:

**myall** (2), an Aus native still uncivilized, hence adj 'wild': Aboriginal: ? cf prec.

**mycelium.** See MUCUS, para 5.

**mycology**, the science of fungi. See the element *-myces*.

**myelic** (adj), of the spinal cord. Cf the element *myel(o)*-.

**myna** or **mynah**, with varr **mina, minah**: Hi *maina*.

**myopia, myopic.** See the element *-ope*.

**myosotis.** See MOUSE, para 5.

**myriad** (n, hence adj): LL *myriad*-, o/s of *mȳrias* (gen *mȳriadis*), trln of Gr *murias* (gen *muriados*), the number of ten thousand, from *murioi*, 10,000 (adj), prop the pl of *murios*, numberless, innumerable: cf EIr *mūr*, abundance, Ga *mùr*, a countless number, Cor *mūr*, large, great, many; perh cf Gr *plēmūra, plemūris*, a flux, and therefore also Epic Gr *mūro*mai, I flow (Boisacq).

**myrmidon**, a hireling follower, earlier a loyal retainer, derives from *Myrmidon*, b/f from L *Myrmidon*es, pl, from the Gr pl *Murmidones*, a Thessalian troop accompanying Achilles to the Trojan War: f/e associated with *Murmidōn*, son of Zeus, who, in the guise of an ant (*murmēx*), deceived yet another maiden.

**myrrh**: ME *myrre, mirre* (influenced by OF *mirre*): L *myrrha*: Gr *murrha*: of Sem origin: cf H *mōr*, myrrh, and *mōr*, bitter, and also Ar *murr*, Aram *mūrā*, bitter. Perh cf Eg *kher*, myrrh.

2. From the same Sem r *mūr* comes Gr *murtos* (*mur*-+formative *-t*-+declensional *-o*-+nom suffix *-s*): L *murtus*, var *myrtus*: ML derivative dim *myrtillus*: MF-F *myrtille, mirtille*, myrtleberry (cf F *myrtille*, bilberry): E *myrtle*.

**myrtle.** See para 2 of prec.

**myself**: *my* (see ME, para 2)+*self* (q.v.).

**mystagogic, mystagogue.** See para 4 of:

**mysterious**—cf **mysterial**—**mystery; mystic** (adj, hence n)—whence **mystical** and **mysticism** (cf the F *mysticisme*) and **mysticity** (cf F *mysticité*)—

mystification, mystify; mystagogic, mystagogue, mystagogy.—Akin to sep MUTE.

1. Whereas the rare *mysterial* derives from LL *mystērialis*, secret, mystical, *mysterious* derives from MF-F *mystérieux*, f *mystérieuse*, the former word from L *mystērium* (in LL, the Divine secret), the latter from OF *mystere* (F *mystère*), itself likewise from *mystērium*, whence also the E *mystery*: and L *mystērium* is merely a trln of Gr *mustērion*, itself akin to Gr *mustēs*, (lit) close-mouthed, hence, as n, an initiate into a religious mystery: *mu*, a groan (cf MUTE, para 1)+the agential suffix -*istēs*. Contributory to *mustēs* is *mūo*, I shut my mouth (and close my eyes).

2. The Gr n *mustēs* has derivative adj *mustikos*, L *mysticus*, MF *mistique* (earliest, *misticque*; EF-F *mystique*), E *mystic*.

3. F *mystère* acquires, somewhat arbitrarily in C18, the derivative *mystifier*, whence 'to *mystify*'; the F derivatives *mystification* and *mystificateur* become, resp by adoption and by adaptation, the E *mystification* and *mystificator*.

4. Gr *mustēs* has the derivative cpd *mustagōgos*: a leader or trainer—*agōgos*, (adj) leading, from *agein*, to lead (cf AGENT)—of *mustai* or initiates: L *mystagogus*: whence, ? via Rabelais's *mystagogue*, the E *mystagogue*; *mystagogy* and *mystagogic* come, via ML *mystagogia* and *mystagogicus*, from Gr *mustagōgia*, *mustagōgikos*, themselves from *mustagōgos*.

mystic, mystical, mysticism, mysticity. See heading and para 2 of prec.

mystification, mystery. See MYSTERIOUS, para 3.

myth, mythical (whence, anl, mythicism, mythicist, mythicize and mythify); mythologic, with extn mythological—mythologize—mythology.

1. Like the F *mythe*, the E *myth* derives, via L *mȳthus*, from Gr *muthos*, speech, a narrative, a fable or myth: o.o.o.: perh cf Lith *maudžù*, *maũsti*, to yearn for, OSl *mysle*, thought, and perh, with the IE prefix *s*-, OIr *smūainim*, I think: IE r, perh *\*mud-* or *\*mudh-*, to think, to imagine.

2. Gr *muthos* has adj *muthikos*, LL *mȳthicus*, whence, perh via MF-F *mythique*, the E *mythic*, with extn *mythical*. It also has the cpd *muthologia*, a discourse (-*logia*, from *logos*, q.v. at LOGIC) upon fables, whence LL *mȳthologia*, whence MF-F *mythologie*, whence *mythology*; derivative Gr *muthologikos* yields LL *mȳthologicus*, MF-F *mythologique*, E *mythologic*; hence, anl, E *mythologist* (perh from F *mythologiste*) and *mythologize*. The further cpd *muthopoios*, (adj) myth-making, becomes E *mythopoeic*: cf *poetic* and POEM. Gr *muthopoios* has derivative *muthopoiïa*, LL *mȳthopoeia*, the making (invention) of myths, adopted by erudite E.

myxo- cpds. Cf the elements -*myxa* and *myxo*-. Note *myxoid*, mucus-like: *myx*- (Gr *muxa*), mucus + -*oid*, resemblin.

# N

nab, to seize; nap and kidnap, whence kidnapper; nobble.

1. *Nab* is a mainly sl var of the mainly dial *nap*, to catch or seize, app of Scan origin: cf Sw *nappa*, to catch, to snatch, and Da *nappe*, to twitch, to pull: Gmc r *\*knapp-*, IE r *\*knabh-*, *\*khneb-*: cf Lett *knābt*, Lith *knibti*, to pluck, to pull, pinch, Gr *knaptō*, I scratch, tear, full (cloth). (Torp.)

2. *Kidnap* is to *nap* or seize a child or *kid* (hence, much later, anybody): orig an underworld term. (P¹.)

3. App *nab* once had a var *\*nob*, of which *nobble* is a freq (*nob*, for *nab*+euphonic *b*+freq -*le*), as in 'to *nobble* or drug a horse': orig race-course cant, then sl. (P and P¹.)

nabob; nawab. *Nabob*, like EF-F *nabab*, derives from Hind *nabāb* (Hi *navvāb*, *navāb*): Ar *nuwwāb*, pl of *nā'ib*, governor of a province, hence, fig, a splendid personage; *nawab* from Hi *navāb*.

nacre, a shellfish producing mother-of-pearl, the pearl itself: EF-F *nacre*: EIt *naccaro* (It *nacchera*): Ar *naqqārah*, a drum, whence also MIt *nacchera*, MF *nacaire*, ME *nakere*, E *naker*, a kettledrum. (The intervention of ML *nacara*, kettledrum, the shellfish, *nacchara*, the shellfish, seems unnecessary: cf B & W.) The sem link between the drum and the pearl-producing shellfish, hence the pearl, is prob Ar *naqīr*, hollowed.

nadir: MF *nador* (? a mere scribal error), EF-F *nadir*: Ar *naḍīr*, opposite (the ZENITH).

nag (1), a small, hence (pej) any, horse: ME *nagge*: cf D *negge* and G *Nickel* (dim of *Nikolaus*), an undersized horse. (EW.)

nag (2), to irritate. See GNAT, para 3.

Nahua, Nahuatl, Nahuatlan.

The 3rd is the adj (IE -*an*) of the 2nd, which is app the adj (Uto-Aztec -*tl*)—hence n (the language) —of the 1st, a native of CAm and part of Mexico, one of a closely related group of Amerind peoples, the most important being the Aztecs. *Nahua* is a native word, perh short for *Nahuatlachi*, the clear-speakers, the clear-speaking (people).

naiad. See NOURISH, para 2.

naïf. See NATIVE, para 7.

nail (n, v), agnail; unguis, ungula, ungulate; onyx, sardonyx.

1. 'To *nail*' derives from OE *naeglian*, from OE *naegel*, whence 'a *nail*': and OE *naegel*, var *naegl*, orig a finger-nail, hence, from shape, a wood or metal nail, is akin to OFris *neil*, *nīl*, OS and OHG

*nagal*, MHG-G *nagel*, MD *negel*, MD-D *nagel* nail, Go ga*nagljan*, to nail; ON *nagl* (finger), *nagl* (metal), with modern Scan cognates; OIr *ingen*, OW *eguin*; Lith *nāgas*, Ru *nogot'*; L *unguis*; Gr *onux* (o/s *onukh-*); Skt *nakhás*, *nakhám*—cf Per *nāxun* (? for *\*nākhsun*): IE r, *\*nagh-*, var *\*nogh-*, as in Gr, with some kind of prefix *o-*, cf the *u-* of L *unguis*. (E & M; Hofmann; Walshe.)

2. *Agnail* comes, as an easement, from OE *angnaegl*, where *ang-*, 'painful', is id with that of *anguish* and ANGRY.

3. L *unguis*, fingernail, toenail, claw, hoof, is adopted by Sci, which likewise adopts the dim *ungula*, claw, whence LL *ungulātus*, hoofed, E *ungulate*.

4. Gr *onux* (ὄνυξ), fingernail, claw, hoof, hence —from the transparency—that veined gem the onyx, becomes L *onyx*, when e, prob via OF-F, the E *onyx*. Gr *onux* has the cpd *sardonux*, L *sardonyx*, adopted by E: 'the *Sardian* onyx', that of *Sardeis* (L *Sardis*), the capital of Lydia in the W of Asia Minor. The chalcedony named *sard* is, in Gr, *sardios* (*lithos*), the Sardian stone, whence *sardion*, whence L *sarda*, E *sard*.

naïve, naïveté. See NATIVE, para 7.

naked, whence nakedness; nude (adj, hence n), nudity—denudant, denudate, denudation (whence, anl, denudative), denude;—gymnasium, gymnast, gymnastic.

1. *Naked* comes from OE *nacod*, nude: cf OFris *nakad*, naked, OHG *nachut*, *nackut*, MHG *nacket*, G *nackt*, Go *naqaths*, MD *naect*, *naket*, D *naakt*, ON *nakinn* (and *nökk*vithr); OIr *nocht*, Ga *nochta* (cf lom*nochd*, *nochd*aidh), EW *noeth*, OC *\*noqtos*; OSl *nagŭ*, Lith *nuógas*; L *nūdus*; Skt *nagnás*; Hit *nekumanza*, *nikumanza*; cf also Gr *gumnos*, which, like Hesoid's *lumnos*, is difficultly aberrant (? metathetic)—cf the lesser aberrancy in Arm *merk*. The -*d* and -*t* forms app derive from the pp of a lost IE v *\*nog-*, to bare. (Boisacq; Walshe.)

2. L *nūdus*, naked, becomes E *nude*; derivative LL *nūditās*, o/s *nūditāt-*, yields MF-F *nudité*, whence E *nudity*.

3. L *nūdus* has derivative *nūdāre*, to bare, with pp *nūdātus*, whence the obsol *nudate*; derivative ML *nūdātiō*, o/s *nūdātiōn-*, becomes obsol *nudation*. The L v, however, has cpd *dēnūdāre*, whence —perh via late MF-F *dénuder*—'to *denude*'; the presp *dēnūdāns*, o/s *dēnūdant-*, yields the E adj, hence n, *denudant*; pp *dēnūdātus* yields 'to

*denudate*', and its LL *derivative dēnūdātiō* yields —prob via late MF-F *dénudation—denudation*.

4. Gr *gumnos*, naked, has s *gumn-* and r *gum-* (? for *mug-* for *\*nug-* for *\*nog*, as at end of para 1). *Gumnos* has the derivative *gumnas*, one who exercises naked, as men did in Ancient Greece; this form (with gen *gumnados*) app suggests *gumnazein*, to exercise naked, whence the agent *gumnastēs*, a trainer, whence, via EF-F *gymnaste*, the E *gymnast*; the derivative adj *gumnastikos* becomes L *gymnasticus*, MF-F *gymnastique*, E *gymnastic*, whence the n *gymnastics*. *Gymnasium*, adopted from LL, derives from Gr *gumnasion* (from *gumnazein*).

**naker.** See NACRE.

**namby-pamby** derives, by rhyming redup, from *Nam*, a pet-form of *Ambrose*, ref the E poetaster Ambrose Phillips (1675?–1749), master of flaccid and simple-minded, yet often agreeable, pastoral verse.

**name**, n (whence ME *nameles*—perh after MD *nameloos*—E **nameless** and **namely**, ME *nameliche*, perh after OFris *namelik*, and **namesake**, from *name's sake*, one named in memory or honour of the name of another) and v (whence pa, vn **naming**); **nomen, agnomen, cognomen, praenomen** —**nomenclator, nomenclature**—**nominal** (whence **nominalism**)—**nominable**—**nominate** (adj and v), **nomination, nominative, nominator, nominee**— **denominate** (ad and v), **denomination** (whence **denominational**, whence **denominationalism**), **de- nominative, denominator** — **innominate**; — **noun, Proper Noun** (peculiar to one subject), **pronoun, pronominal**—**ignominious, ignominy**—**misnomer**— **nuncupate, nuncupation, nuncupative**—**renown**, n and v (whence pa **renowned**); **nom de guerre** and **nom de plume**; **surname**:—**onomastic, onomasticon, onomatopoeia** (q.v. at the element *onomato-*), **onomatous**—**anonym, anonymity, anonymous**, cf **pseudonym** (whence, anl, **pseudonymity**), **pseudo- nymous**; **synonym, synonymous** (whence **synony- mity**), **synonymy** (whence, anl, **synonymize**)—cf **antonym**, whence, anl, **antonymous**.

## I. Indo-European

1. 'To *name*' derives from OE *namian* (cf OFris *namia*, OS *namōn*), from OE *nama*, whence 'a *name*': and OE *nama* is akin to OFris *nama* (var *noma*), OS and OHG *namo*, MHG-G *name*, Go *namō*, MD *name, naem*, D *naam*; ON *nafn* (for *\*namn*), Da *navn*; OIr *ainm, ainmm*, Ga *ainm*, OW *anu*, W *enw*, Mx *ennym*, obs Cor *honua, honwa*; Arm *anun*, Alb *emen*; L *nōmen*; Gr *onoma*; Skt *nắman-*; Tokh A *ñom*, B *nem*; Hit *lāman*; perh cf Lapp *namma*, Fin *nime-* (? cf OSl *imę* and OP *emmen*), Hung *név*, of the Finno-Ugric family of languages. The Gmc r is *\*nam-*; the IE, prob *\*nem-*, with varr *\*nom-* and *\*nōm-* and with the sure consonantal base *n-m*. With the Gr *o-*, cf the *o-* of *onyx* (q.v. at NAIL); cf the other pro- thetic vowels, e.g. the C *a-* and *e-*. (Hofmann; E & M; Walshe.)

## Greek

2. Gr *onoma* (dial *onuma*), name, has gen *onomatos*, o/s *onomat-*, occurring in various full cpds and in the E adj *onomatous*. *Onoma* has derivative *onomazein*, to name, whence the adj *onomastikos*, of or for or by naming, whence E *onomastic*; via the neu *onomastikon*, used as n elliptical for *onomastikon biblion* (a book), comes the ML *onomasticon*, a glossary or a list of names, esp of personal names, adopted by erudite E.

3. Gr *onoma* has the foll prefix-cpds relevant to E:

*anōnumos*, nameless (*an*, not), whence, via LL *anōnymus*, both the E *anonymous* and the EF-F *anonyme*; the latter, used derivatively as n, becomes the E *anonym*, an unnamed author; *anonymity* is formed anl from *anonymous*;

*pseudōnumos* (*pseudēs*, false), whence both E *pseudonymous*, whence anl *pseudonymity*, and late EF-F *pseudonyme*, the latter, used derivatively as n, yielding E *pseudonym*;

*sunōnumos* (*sun*, with, implying likeness), whence, via ML *synōnymus*, both the E *synonymous* and the OF-F *synonyme*, which, used also as n, yields E *synonym*; *synonymy* comes, sense-changed and prob via EF-F *synonymie*, from LL *synōnymia*, a synonym, itself from Gr *sunōnumia*; cf the opp:

*antōnumia*, a word used instead of another, whence E *antonym*, serving as the complement of *synonym*, as 'bad' is the antonym of 'good'.

## Latin

4. L *nōmen*, name, occurs in three prefix-cpds used occ by erudite E:

*agnōmen* (pl *agnōmina*), an additional—usu honorary—*cognomen* in Roman names, as in 'Publius Aemilius Scipio *Africanus*': *ag-* for *ad*, to(wards);

*cognōmen* (*cog-* for *con-*, with), pl *cognōmina*, the family name, the third of the usual three Roman names, as in 'Marcus Tullius *Cicero*'; hence an E surname, loosely a nickname;

*praenōmen* (*prae*, before, in front), pl *praenōmina*, the first of the usual three Roman names, as in 'Marcus Tullius Cicero', corresp to the modern first name; the L *nōmen* is, in personal designa- tions, the name of the *gens* or clan.

5. *Nōmen* has the full cpd *nōmenclātor*, a slave whose office it is, in a court of law, to call the names of the clients, *-clātor* representing *calātor*, caller, summoner; hence, anl, *nōmenclātūra*, a call- ing of names, hence a system of naming, whence, perh via EF-F, the E *nomenclature*.

6. *Nōmen*, gen *nōminis*, has c/f *nōmin-*, as in *nōminālis*, of or for or by a name, whence, perh via EF-F, the E *nominal*. It also has derivative *nōmināre*, to name, whence *nōminābilis*, worthy of mention, E *nominable*; the pp *nōminātus* yields both adj and v *nominate*; derivative *nōminātiō*, o/s *nōminātiōn-*, yields, perh via MF-F, *nomination*; and likewise derivative *nōminātīuus*, ML *-īvus*, MF-F *nominatif*, E *nominative*; the LL agent

*nōminātor*, adopted by E, has suggested its E complement, *nominee*.

7. *Nōmen*, s and r *nom-*, becomes OF-F *nom*, as in *nom de guerre*, lit war-name (as of an adventurer), hence a pseudonym, and *nom de plume*, pen-name—not a true F term. Moreover, the OF *sournom*, ME *sournoun*, has suggested the E *surname* (*sur*, E *sur*, L *super*, upon+*name*); hence 'to *surname*'. Besides, OF *nom* (etc.) has the derivative v *nommer*: respectively these two words have OF-F prefix-cpds *renon* (Cí2; F *renom*) and *renommer* (C11), whence ME *renoun*, EE *renoun*, E *renown* (n, v). OF *nommer* has the MF cpd *mesnommer* (*mes-*, L *minus*, less), to misname, which, apprehended as n, produces the E *misnomer*, a misnaming, a wrong name.

8. *Nōmen* has also given us *noun*, from OF *non* and *nun*, varr of *nom*. Cf *pronoun*, which reflects the influence of *noun* upon the MF-F *pronom*, LL *prōnōmen*(*prō*, on behalf of); the derivative LL adj *prōnōminālis* leads, perh via F, to E *pronominal*.

9. But *nōmināre* (as in para 6) has several prefix-cpds relevant to E:

*dēnōmināre* (int *dē-*), to designate by a name, pp *dēnōminātus*, whence both adj and v *denominate*, with subsidiary *dēnōminātiō*, o/s *dēnōminātiōn-*, MF-F *dénomination*, E *denomination*; anl formed LL *dēnōmināṭīuus*, ML *-īvus*, E *denominative*; LL *dēnōminātor*, adopted by E, esp in Math.

LL *innōminābilis* (*in-*, not+*nōminābilis*: para 6), E *innominable*; cf LL *innōminātus* (*in-*, not+*nōminātus*: para 6), lacking a name, E *innominate*, esp in *innominate bone* (in the pelvis).

10. With L *innōminātus*, cf L *ignōminia* (*ig-* for *in-*, not), deprivation of one's good name, whence late MF-F *ignominie*, whence E *ignominy*; derivative *ignominiōsus* becomes late MF-F *ignominieux*, f *ignominieuse*, whence E *ignominious*.

11. *Nōmen* has also the less obvious cpd *nuncupāre*, to take (*capere*: cf CAPABILITY, para 1) the name (*nōmen*), hence to invoke or proclaim: *nōmen*, become *nun-*+*capere*, become *cup-*+the different inf-ending *-āre*. The pp *nuncupātus* yields 'to *nuncupate*'; derivative *nuncupātiō*, o/s *nuncupātiōn-*, gives us *nuncupation*, and derivative LL *nuncupātīuus*, ML *-īvus*, *nuncupative*.

nameless; namely. See prec (heading).

Nancy: perh ME mine *Annis*, Agnes, confused with or, at the least, influenced by *Ann(e)*. Hence *Miss Nancy*, an effeminate man, hence *Nancy* (whence occ *nancy*), a passive male homosexual, often, in sl, *nancy* boy. Cf NANNY.

nankeen is a cloth made orig at *Nankin* or *Nanking*, which, in Pekinese, means 'Southern Capital'.

nanny, a children's (usu in-living) nurse. See ANN. So *nanny goat*, female goat, is a *Nanny* goat.

nap (1), a short sleep, derives from 'to *nap*': ME *nappen*: OE *hnaeppian*, akin to OHG *hnaffezēn* and perh to Da and Nor *nap*, snap, 'with idea of quick closing of the eyes; cf coll Nor *nippe*, to take a nap, i.e. to nip the eyes to' (EW): ult echoic.

nap (2), in cards. See NAPOLEON.

nap (3), of cloth. See MAP, para 2.

nape of neck. See MAP, para 2.

napery. See MAP, para 2.

naphtha—whence naphthalene (whence naphthol) and naphthene—is adopted from L, itself from Gr, *naphtha*: akin to Akkadian *napṭa* (cf Per *nafṭ*), naphtha, and prob Av *napta*, moist.

napkin. See MAP, para 2.

Napoleon (whence Napoleonic), napoleon; nap at cards (n, hence v).

The 20-francs gold coin the *napoleon* is named after the first Emperor *Napoleon*: F *Napoléon*: It *Napoleone*, from a Corsican name perh derived from the OGmc r attested by *Nibelungen*, Children of the Mist (cf L *nebula*, fog, cloud, OHG *nebul*, MHG-G *nebel*: see NEBULA), and f/e reshaped after *Napoli* and *leone*, as if the It word meant 'Lion of Naples'. (Dauzat, *Dict. éty. des noms de famille.*) Also named after him is the card game *napoleon*, usu shortened to *nap*, whence the horse-racing sense.

nappe, sheet. See MAP, para 2.

narcissism (whence, anl, narcissistic), Narcissus, narcissus.

The flower is named after that self-adoring youth of Gr Myth who, falling in love with his own reflection, ended as this flower, whence, via G *Narcissismus* and F *narcissisme*, the E *narcissism* of Psychi. *Narcissus*, adopted from L, is a trln of Gr *Narkissos*, perh—because of the plant's sedative properties—akin to Gr *narkē*, torpor (Hofmann). Therefore cf:

narcose, Med adj, is a b/f from narcosis, which has ordinary adj narcotic (whence, anl, narcotism, narcotize: cf the F *narcotisme*, *narcotiser*). *Narcotic* derives from MF-F *narcotique*, ML *narcōticus*, Gr *narkōtikos*, itself from *narkoō*, I benumb, from *narkē*, numbness, torpor, orig a muscular cramp: prob cf Arm *nergev*, slender, orig shrunken, and perh cf OHG *narwa*, a scar, and, with the IE prefix *s-*, ON *snara*, a noose. (Hofmann.) Also from Gr *narkoun*, to benumb, derives *narkōsis*, whence SciL-Med E *narcosis*; *narcotine* is adopted from F (from *narcotique*).

nard. See SPIKE, para 2.

nares; narine. See NOSE, para 8.

naringin. See ORANGE, para 2.

nark (1), a police spy, hence to spy: Romany *nāk*, nose. (Orig cant; still sl.)

nark (2), to irritate, tease, in E dial, hence in Aus sl, whence, in Aus sl, a tease, esp a spoil-sport; derivative adj narky: perh from 1st NARK; perh from F, either EF-F *narquois*, sly, bantering, or, more prob, from EF-F *nargue!*, expressive of scorn or defiance, EF-F *narguer*, to set at defiance, cock a snook at, app (B & W) from *nargue!*, but possibly vice versa, with *narguer* of Gmc origin (cf G *nörgeln*, *nergeln*, to nag, to tease), as Dauzat suggests.

narrate, narration, narrative, narrator.

L *narrāre*, to tell the particulars of an event or an act, is akin to L *ignōrāre*, to be ignorant of, hence to E CAN (f.a.e.). The pp *narrātus* yields 'to *narrate*'; derivative *narrātiō*, o/s *narrātiōn-*, LL *narrātīuus*, ML *-īvus*, and *narrātor* become resp *narration* (perh via OF-F), *narrative* (perh via EF-F *narratif*, f *-ive*), *narrator* (perh via· EF-F *narrateur*). The L adj *narrābilis* has negg *innarābilis* and, from *ēnarrāre*, to tell forth, *inēnarrābilis*, the latter giving us, perh via EF-F, the E *inenarrable*.

narrow (adj, hence n and v), whence narrowness, comes, through ME *narwe*, earlier *naru*, from OE *nearu*: cf OFris *nare*, OS *naru*, *naro*, OHG *narwa*, MHG *narwe*, G *Narbe*, a scar, lit the drawing-together of a wound, and perh cf also Lith *narys*, a loop, *nérti*, to thread a needle.

2. Those OGmc and Lith words have cognates exhibiting the IE prefix (? orig int) *s-*: e.g., OHG-MHG *snuor*, G *Schnur*, a cord, *schnurren*, to shrink, Go *snōrjō*, a wicker basket, Da *snor*, a cord, Av *snāvarĕ*, a cord—and OE *snearh*, a cord, and esp OE *snearu* (from syn ON *snara*), a noose, a snare, whence E *snare*, whence 'to *snare*', with int *ensnare*, whence *ensnarement*.

narwhal. See WHALE, para 2.

nasal, nasality, nasalize. See NOSE, para 6.

nascency, nascent. See NATIVE, para 2.

nasturtium. See NOSE, para 7.

nasty, whence nastiness, is ME *nasty* and, ? earlier, *nasky*, prob of Scan, certainly of N European, origin: cf the syn Sw dial *naskug*, *nasket*, and perh cf D *nestig*, dirty, ugly (cf E dial *nast*—? for *\*nask*—dirt).

nasute. See NOSE, para 6.

Natal, natal, natality. See NATIVE, para 4.

natant, natatory. See NOURISH, para 8.

nation, national, nationality. See para 5 of:

native (adj, hence n), nativity; neif—cf naïf, naïve, naïveté; nation, national, whence nationalism, nationalist, nationality (cf the F *nationalité*), nationalize—cf the F *nationaliser*—whence nationalization—cf anti-national, denationalize (-ization) and international (*inter*, between, among+*national*), whence internationalism, etc.; Natal, natal, natality —cf prenatal and noel; nascency, nascent—cf renascence (renaissance), renascent (renaissant); natural, whence naturalism and naturalist (prob imm from EF-F *naturaliste*) and naturalize (prob imm from EF-F *naturaliser*), whence naturalization —cf naturality—nature; connatural; denaturalize (-ization)—denaturant, denature; supernatural, whence supernaturalism; unnatural (*un-*, not+ *natural*); obs nate—cf adnate (whence, anl, adnation) and agnate, agnation and cognate, cognation and connate, whence anl connation, and enate, whence, anl, enation, and innascible, innate; pregnancy, from pregnant—cf impregnate; eigne; puisne—puny, whence puniness. Cf the sep GENERAL and KIN groups: f.a.e.

Simples

1. The base of the entire group is L *nāscī*, to be born, with presp *nāscens*, o/s *nāscent-* and pp *nātus*, s *nāt-*: OL *\*gnāscī*, attested by OL *gnātus*

(L *nātus*): s *gnāsc-* is akin to the *gen-* of *genus*, q.v. —f.a.e.—at GENERAL; cf KIN.

2. L *nāscens*, o/s *nāscent-*, becomes E *nascent*; derivative LL *nāscentia*, E *nascency*. Cf LL *nāscibilis*, capable of being born: rare E *nascible*.

3. L *nātus*, born, yields *nate*, surviving only in cpds. But the s *nat-* occurs in those fruitful L derivatives *nātālis*, *nātiō*, *nātīuus* (ML *-īvus*), *nātūra*.

4. The L adj *nātālis*, of birth, hence (from *nātālis diēs*) of one's birthday, whence late MF-F, hence E *natal*,—*nātālis* derives imm from the L n *nātus* (gen *nātūs*), birth. Hence, prob after *mortality*: *natality* (cf F *natalité*). In LL, *nātālis* becomes also n, whence F *noël*, E *Noël*, Christ's birthday, hence Christmas. The province of *Natal* in SAfrica was first—by a European—discovered by Vasco da Gama on Christmas Day, 1497.

5. L *nātiō*, orig (a) birth, hence a creature's entire offspring at one time, hence a clan's off-spring, hence a people's, hence that people itself: acc *nātiōnem*, whence OF *nacion*: ME *nacioun*: E (reshaped after L) *nation*. EF-F *nation* has EF-F adj *national*, adopted by E.

6. L *nātīuus*, ML *nātīvus*, becomes MF-F *natif*, f *native* ,whence E *native*; derivative LL *nātīuitās*, o/s *nātīuitāt-*, ML *nātīvāt-*, becomes OF-F *nativité*, whence E *nativity*.

7. ML *nātīvus* becomes OF *neïf*, whence the now only hist E *neif* (occ f *neife*), one born a serf. OF *neïf* has extant var *naïf*, f *naïve*, adopted by E; the MF-F derivative *naïveté*—prompted by the ML *nātīvitās*—is likewise adopted by E, with anglicized var *naivety*.

8. L *nātūra*, (orig) birth, hence an inborn char-acteristic, character, disposition, etc., yields OF-F, hence E, *nature*. The derivative adj *nātūrālis* yields OF-EF *natural*, whence (EF-F *naturel* and) E *natural*; subsidiary LL *nātūrālitās* explains E *naturality*.

Compounds

9. L *nāscī*, to be born, has the foll prefix-cpds relevant to E:

*adnāscī*, to grow *ad*, to or upon (something), presp *adnāscens*, o/s *adnāscent-*, whence the E adj *adnascent*, whence *adnascence*, and pp *adnātus*, whence the Zoo and Bot adj *adnate*;

*agnāscī*, to be born additionally (*ag-* for *ad*, to, towards) to, pp *agnātus*, EF-F *agnat*, E *agnate*, adj hence also n; derivative L *agnātiō*, o/s *agnātiōn-*, yields *agnation*;

*\*cognāscī*, to be born together, hence blood-related, has pp *cognātus* used as adj, whence E *cognate*; derivative *cognātiō*, o/s *cognātiōn-*, E *cognation*; subsidiary LL *cognātīuus*, ML *-īvus*, E *cognative*;

LL *connāscī*, to be born at the same time as, has pp *connātus*, whence the E adj *connate*; the related LL *connātūrālis*, of the same nature as, explains E *connatural*;

the rare *dēnāscī*, to perish (? 'be born down from life'), pp *dēnātus*, has no E derivatives but perh suggested the OF-F *dénaturer*, to remove the nature of, hence to change—for the worse—the nature of, whence 'to *denature*';

*ēnāscī*, to be born from, hence (of growths) to spring up, pp *ēnātus*, whence the adj *enate*, with extn *enatic*, related on the mother's side;

*innāscī*, to be *in*born, with pp *innātus*, whence *innate*, inborn (cf EF-F *inné*); contrast LL *innāscibilis* (*in*-, not+*nāscibilis*, as in para 2), incapable of being born;

*praegnāns*, var of *praegnās*, (adj) being with child: *prae*, before+*-gnās*, *-gnāns*, from *gnāscī*, to be born: o/s *praegnant*-: E *pregnant*; whence, anl, *pregnancy*. *Praegnās* has derivative *praegnāre*, to be with child, LL to render pregnant, with its pp *praegnāta* used as adj; and *praegnāre* has the LL derivative int *impraegnāre*, to render pregnant, attested by the pp-adj *impraegnātā*; hence 'to *impregnate*'. Derivative ML *impraegnātiō*, o/s *impraegnātiōn*-, gives us *impregnation*, whence, anl, *impregnator*;

*renāscī*, to be born again, presp *renāscens*: OF *renestre*, MF-F *renaître*, presp *renaissant*, whence MF-F *renaissance*, both adopted by E, which anglicizes them as *renascent*, *renascence*.

10. Such cpds as *anti-national* (*anti*-, against), *denationalize* (*de*-, down or away from, connoting removal), *denaturalize*, *international* (*inter*, between, among), *supernatural* (ML *supernātūrālis*), *unnatural* (*un*-, not) hardly need particular treatment; most of them owe something, either phon or sem (or both), to the corresp F words.

11. There remain, however, two or three words not imm explicable: *eigne* and *puisne* and *puny*. *Eigne*, in Law the first-born, derives from MF-F *aîné*, OF *aisné*: *ainz*, before (adv) (VL *\*antius*, from L *antea*)+*né*, born (f *née*), L *nātus*.

12. *Puisne*, lesser, junior (esp judge), derives from OF *puisné*, later-born: OF-F *puis*, then, VL *\*postius*, L *postea*, afterwards+*né*. The later F form *puîné*, younger, becomes E *puny*, with its entirely natural sense-development.

**natron.** See NITRE, para 4.

**natter.** See GNAT, para 4.

**natty.** See NEAT, adj, para 2, s.f.

**natural, naturalist, naturality, naturalize, nature.** See NATIVE, para 8—and heading.

**naufragous.** See the element *nau*-.

**naught** is a var of **nought**: ME *nought*, *naught*, earlier *naht*, *nawiht*: OE *nāht*, *nōht*, contrr of *nāwiht*, *nōwiht*: *ne*, not+*ā*, ever+*wiht*, thing: lit, therefore, not ever a thing, nothing. Hence the adj **naughty**, worthless (obs), hence wicked (obsol), hence merely misbehaving, mischievous, cf the obs (except in Sc) *noughty*, worthless, bad; whence *naughtiness*.

2. **Ought**, now illit, and its var *aught*, anything, clearly derive, therefore, from OE *āwiht*, through ME *awiht*, contracting to *aught* and *ought*.

**nausea; nauseate** (whence pa **nauseating**), whence, anl, **nauseation; nauseous.** See para 2 of:

**nautic** (whence **nautics**), superseded by extn **nautical; nautilus; Argonaut; nausea, nauseant,**

**nauseate, nauseous; noise** (n, hence v), whence **noiseless** and **noisy; naval** (whence **navalism**), **nave** (of church) and **nef, navicella** (cf **nacelle**), **navicula, navicular, navy; navicert** (see the element *navi*-); **navigable, navigate, navigation, navigator,** cf **navvy.**

### Indo-European

1. The primary etymon is Gr *naus* (ναῦς, dissyllabic); the secondary, L *nāuis* (ML *nāvis*); cf Skt *nắvas* with *nāuis*, and Skt *nāús* with ναῦς: IE, *\*nāus*, with s *\*nāu*-, r prob *\*nā*-. Of the numerous IE cognates, the foll are at least notable: OIr *nau* (gen *nōe*), *naust*, place for a boat, W *nausum*; ON *nōr*; Arm *naw* (gen *nawi*); OPer *nau*-; OE *nōwend*, a mariner.

### Greek

2. Gr *naus* has two derivatives important for E: *nausia*, Ionic *nausiē*, and *nautēs*. *Nausia* (var *nautiā*), seasickness, becomes L *nausea*, adopted by E; derivative L *nauseāre*, to make seasick, has presp *nauseans*, o/s *nauseant*-, whence E *nauseant*, adj hence n, and pp *nauseātus*, whence 'to *nauseate*', whence *nauseation*; derivative L *nauseōsus* gives us *nauseous*.

3. *Nautēs*, a sailor—with adj *nautikos*, L *nauticus*, late MF-F *nautique*, E *nautic*—has the mdfn *nautilos*, with additional sense 'a kind of shellfish, supposed to possess a membrane serving as a sail', whence L *nautilus*, adopted by E.—E *Argonaut*= L *Argonauta*=Gr *Argonautēs*, a sailor in the good ship *Argo*, under the leadership of Jason: a pre-Homeric story.

4. *Noise*, adopted by ME from OF *noise*, noisy strife, a din, derives from L *nausea*, the sem link being afforded by the noise made by an ancient shipful of passengers groaning and vomiting in bad weather.

### Latin

5. L *nāuis*, ML *nāvis*, a ship, becomes the E *nave* of a church, churches being often compared with ships—perh prompted by OF-F *nef*, OF-MF ship, OF-F *nave*; *nef* is extant in E in a couple of specialized yet obvious senses.

6. *Nāuis* (*nāvis*) has the foll derivatives concerning E:

L *nāuālis*, ML *nāvālis*, whence MF-F, hence E, *naval*;

LL dim *nāuicella* (ML *nāvi*-), adopted by Art; hence OF-F *nacelle*, which, as part of an aircraft, is adopted by E;

L dim *nāuicula*, adopted by Eccl and Bot E; its derivative adj *nāuiculāris* becomes *navicular*;

VL *nāuia*, ML *nāvia*, OF-MF *navie*, a fleet, adopted by ME, whence E *navy*; OF *navie*, however, perh comes rather (DAF) from L *nāuigia*, neupl (of *nāuigium*, a ship: from *nāuigāre*: see next para) taken as a sing n.

7. *Nāuis* has cpd *nāuigāre*, to sail a ship (*nauem*+*-igere*, c/f of *agere*, to drive, to direct), whence *nāuigābilis* and neg *innāuigābilis*, whence, perh

via late MF-F, the E *navigable*, *innavigable*. The presp *nāuigans*, o/s *nāuigant-*, ML *nāvigant-*, yields the rare adj, obs n *navigant*; the pp *nāuigātus*, ML *nāvi-*, gives us 'to *navigate*'; derivative *nāuigātiō*, o/s *nāuigātiōn-*, ML *nāvi-*, passes through MF-F to become *navigation*; derivative *nāuigātor*, ML *nāvigātor*, is adopted—cf the EF-F *navigateur*. E *navigator* explains *navvy*, much of whose work is done in wet conditions.

nautilus. See prec, para 3.

Navaho, Americanized form of Navajo: Sp 'Apaches de *Navajo*': Tewa (a tribe of New Mexico) *Navahú*, that Tewa village owning 'great fields' which lay close to the Spaniards' first encounter with the Navajos. (Webster.)

naval. See NAUTIC, para 6.

nave (1) of church. See NAUTIC, para 5.

nave (2) of wheel. See OMPHALIC.

navel. See OMPHALIC.

navicella; navicula, navicular. See NAUTIC, para 6.

navigable, navigate, navigation, navigator. See NAUTIC, para 7.

navvy. See NAUTIC, para 7, s.f.

navy. See NAUTIC, para 6, s.f.

nawab. See NABOB.

nay, ME *nei*, ON *nei* (*ne*, not+*ei*, ever). Cf AY.

Nazi: G N*ati*onalso*zi*alistische (sc *Partei*, party).

neap, adj, usu in '*neap* tides', the least in a lunar month, OE *nēp flōd*, where *nēp* is o.o.o.: perh cf *naep*en, scarcely, and the *nipp-* of Nor *nippílo*, neap tide; certainly cf OE *forthganges nēp*, (scant of advance, hence) unable to advance.

near, adv (hence adj, prep, v), comp nearer (cf OE *nēarra*, adj) and sup nearest: OE *nēar*, comp of *nēah*, nigh: for the change from comp to positive, cf ON *naer*, prop a comp but meaning both 'nearer' and 'near'. OE *nēah*, which becomes ME *neih*, later *neigh*, latest *nigh*, whence E *nigh*, is akin to OFris *nēi*, *nī*, adj and adv, OS *nāh*, id, OHG *nāh*, MHG *nāch*, G *nahe*, adj, and OHG *nāhe*, adv, Go *nēhw*, *nēhwa*, id, MD-D *na*, id, ON *nā-*, id; perh ult cf Skt *na*śati, he attains.

2. OE *nēah*, nigh, has sup *nīehst, nyhst, nēhst*, the 3rd becoming E *next*, adj, hence adv.

3. OE *nēah* has a cpd *nēahgebūr*, often contr to *nēhgebūr*, lit a near fellow-dweller, whence ME *neighebour*, E *neighbour*, AE *neighbor*: cf OHG *nāhgibūr*, MHG *nāchgebur*, G *Nachbar*, and—without the *ge*-'together' prefix—MD *nabuer*, *nabur*, MD-D *nabuur*, ON *nābūi*: for the 2nd element, cf BOOR.

4. Cf sep ENOUGH in ADDENDA TO DICTIONARY.

neat (1), adj, whence neatness; net, adj—cf natty; nitid, nitidous.

1. *Nitidous*, like its rare var *nitid*, comes from L *nitidus*, brilliant, hence elegant, LL clean, an *-idus* adj (cf *splendidus* from *splend*ēre) from *nit*ēre, to be shining, brilliant, dazzling; the presp *nitēns*, o/s *nitent-*, leads to F *nitence* and E *nitency*, brilliance, lustre. The L *nit*ēre has s *nit-*, perh an extn of an IE r *\*ni-*, *\*nei-*, to shine: cf Ir *ni*am, a flash of lightning, and OIr *necht*, brilliant.

2. L *nitidus* becomes OF-F *net*, bright, hence clean, adopted by E in sense 'clean of extraneous matter'—the commercial *net*, free of charges, often (for clarity) spelt *nett*; F *net* becomes anglicized as *neat*, with coll mdfn *natty*, perh influenced by OF-F *nettoyé*, pp of *nettoyer*, to cleanse, from OF *net*.

neat (2), n, oxen collectively, whence *neatherd*, cowman: OE *nēat*: cf OFris *nāt*, OHG *nōz*, ON *naut*: basic sense, useful property—cf OE *nēotan*, OS *niotan*, Go *niutan*, ON *niōta*, to enjoy the use of, and OE *nytt*, OHG-MHG *nuz*, G *Nutzen*, Lith *nauda*, use (n).

neb. See NIB.

Nebraska, whence adj, hence n, Nebraskan, takes its name from the State's principal river, which in Otoe Amerind is *Ne-brath-ka*, Shallow Water; *-aska* perh after Alaska.

nebula (occ anglicized nebule), whence the adj nebular—cf *tabular* from L *tabula*; nebulated nebulé; nebulite, nebulium; nebulosity, nebulous; nephelite, nephelium, nepheloid—and cf the element *nephelo-*.—nimbose, nimbus.—imbricate (adj, v), whence imbrication.—imbue.

1. *Nebula* (pl *nebulae*), in E a gaseous celestial structure, is adopted from L *nebula*, vapour, mist, cloud, whence *nebulōsus*, misty, cloudy, whence E *nebulous* (cf the late MF-F *nébuleux*, f *nébuleuse*); the derivative LL *nebulōsitās*, cloudness, o/s *nebulōsitāt-*, yields *nebulosity*—perh after late MF-F *nébulosité*. L *nebula* has derivative LL *nebulāre*, to becloud, hence to obscure, with pp *nebulātus*, whence both the E *nebulate* (adj), usu *nebulated*, and the F *nébulé*, adopted by E heralds as *nebulé*, consisting of cloudlike curves. From L *nebula*, SciL derives *nebulium* (Chem element *-ium*), and E derives *nebulite* (Min *-ite*).

2. L *nebula* has s and r *nebul-*, akin to Gr *nephelē*, a cloud; that the IE r is *\*neb-* or rather *\*nebh-* appears from OSl *nebo*, sky, Gr *nephos*, a cloud, Skt *nábhas*, mist, cloud, sky, and Hit *nebiš*, *nepis*, sky; there are Gmc and C cognates—cf OHG *nebul*, MHG-G *nebel*, OS *nebhal*, fog, and OE *nifol*, dark, ON *niōl*, darkness, night—also OIr *nél*, Ga *neul*, *nial*, a cloud, W *niwl*, Cor *niul*, mist, fog, OC etymon *\*neblos*; cf the nasal var presented by L *nimbus* in para 4.

3. With L *nebula*, cf esp the Gr *nephelē*, a cloud, whence E *nephelite* (cf the F *néphéline*). *Nephelē* has dim *nephelion*, adopted by LL, the plant burdock, which SciL converts to Bot *Nephelium*. *Nepheloid*, cloudy=*nephelē*+*-oid*, -like.

4. The IE var *nib-* is nasalized in L *nimbus*, a cloud rain-charged, hence a golden cloud enveloping the gods, E *nimbus* (F *nimbe*): cf, more imm, the Pahlavi (C3-9 Per) *namb*, moisture. Derivative *nimbōsus* yields *nimbose*.

5. L *nimbus* has perh been influenced by L *imber*, which, indeed, is prob, ult, akin. *Imber*, rain(-shower), has derivative *imbrex* (gen *imbricis*), a gutter tile, whence *imbricāre*, to form like a gutter tile, to cover with such tiles, pp *imbricātus*, whence the E adj and v *imbricate*.

6. With *imbricāre* and esp its source *imber*, cf the L *imbuere*, to drench or saturate, whence 'to *imbue*', to impregnate, hence to instil profoundly; perh cf Gr *aphuein*, to dip, and Skt *ambus*, water.

**necessary, necessitate, necessitous, necessitude, necessity.**

1. The L base is app '*necesse* est', it is an unavoidable duty or task: and prob *necesse* is the neu of an adj *necessis*, deriving from L *ne*, not+ *cessis*, a yielding, from *cessus*, pp of *cēdere*, to retire, hence to yield, orig to go, to arrive: f.a.e., NOT and CEDE.

2. *Necesse* has these derivatives affecting E:
*necessārius* (adj suffix -*ārius*), whence, perh via OF-MF *necessaire* (F *né-*), the E *necessary*, adj, hence—as in F—n;
*necessitās*, o/s *necessitāt-*, OF-MF *necessité* (F *né-*), ME *necessite*, E *necessity*; hence:
ML *necessitāre*, to render necessary (cf LL *necessāre*), pp *necessitātus*, whence 'to *necessitate*'; L *necessitūdō*, E *necessitude*.

3. OF-MF *necessité* has derivative MF *necessiteux* (F *né-*), f *necessiteuse*, whence E *necessitous*.

**neck** (n, hence adj and v), whence **neck and crop, neck and neck, neck-cloth, neckerchief** (for *neck kerchief*), **necklace, necktie; nook,** whence **nookery.**

1. *Neck*, ME *necke*, OE *hnecca*, nape of neck, the neck, is akin to OFris *hnekka*, OHG *hnac*, MHG *nac*, G *Nacken*, nape of neck, and ON *hnakki*, nape, neck; prob also to OIr *cnocc*, a hill, a hump. (Walshe.)

2. Akin to that group is E *nook*, a tapering or narrowing place, esp a corner, ME *nok*, nook, corner, angle—cf the Nor dial *nok*, a bent figure.

**necromancer, necromancy.** See the elements *-mancy* and *necro-*.

**necropolis.** See the element *necro-*.

**nectar; nectarine; nectary.** See NOXIOUS, para 6.

**Ned; neddy.** See EDWARD.

**need** (n and v), whence **needful, needless, needy; needs,** adv.

*Needs*, necessarily, derives from OE *nēdes*, gen of *nēd*, var—along with *nȳd*—of *nēod, nīed, nēad*, whence, via ME *neod, nede*, later *need*, the E n *need*: and OE *nēad* (*nēod, nīed*, etc.) is akin to OFris *nēd*, OS *nōd*, OHG-MHG *nōt*, G *Not*, Go *nauths*, ON *nauthr*, distress, compulsion, and, in Sl, the OP *nauti-*, distress, and OB *naviti*, Cz u-*navit*, to tire.

'To *need*' derives from OE *nēodian, nīedian*, etc., from the OE n: cf OFris *nēda*, OS *nōdian*.

**needle** (n, hence v). See NERVE, para 7.

**needs,** necessarily; **needy.** See NEED.

**neese, neeze.** See SNEEZE.

**nef.** See NAUTIC, para 5.

**nefarious.** See FAME, para 5.

**negate, negation, negative** (adj, hence n and **negativism, negativity), negator, negatory.**—cpds: **abnegate, abnegation** (whence, anl, **abnegative), abnegator; denegate** (obs), **denegation** (obsol)—cf **deny,** whence **deniable** (neg **undeniable) and denial; renege,** whence, anl, **renegation**—cf **renegade** (n, hence adj).

1. All these words come from L *negāre*, to say No, hence to refuse (something or oneself), to deny the existence of, with pp *negātus*: *neg-* for *nec*, not+inf ending -*āre*: 'to *no!*' *Negātus* yields 'to *negate*'; derivatives *negātiō* (o/s *negātiōn-*); L *negātiuus* (ML -*īvus*), adj, LL n (? for *sententia negātīua*); LL *negātor*; LL *negātōrius*; these lead resp to *negation*, perh via OF-F *négation*; *negative*, perh via MF-F *négatif*, f *négative*; *negator*; *negatory* (cf the C16–18 F *négatoire*).

2. L *abnegāre* (*ab-*, from, here int), to refuse, deny, LL to renounce, has pp *abnegātus*, whence 'to *abnegate*'. The LL derivatives *abnegātiō* (o/s *abnegātiōn-*), *abnegātīuus* (ML -*īvus*), *abnegātor*, resp become E *abnegation* (perh via late MF-F *abnégation*), *abnegative, abnegator*.

3. L *dēnegāre*, to deny, to refuse, to repudiate, has pp *dēnegātus*, whence 'to *denegate*'; the LL derivative *dēnegātiō*, o/s *dēnegātiōn-*, becomes *denegation*. But *dēnegāre* also becomes OF *deneier*, later *denier* (F *dénier*), whence ME *denaien*, later *denien*, whence 'to *deny*'. The derivative F *indéniable* perh prompted E *undeniable*.

4. ML *renegāre*, to deny again, go back upon, to repudiate or renounce, yields 'to *renege*', obsol except at cards. The pp *renegātus* is used also as 'one who denies his faith': whence Sp *renegado*, whence E *renegade*.

**neglect, negligee, negligence, negligent.** See LEGEND, para 12.

**negotiable, negotiate, negotiation, negotiator.** See OTIOSE, para 2.

**Negress.** See NEGRO, para 2.

**Negrillo; Negritic, Negrito.** See para 3 of:

**Negro, Negroid** (adj, hence n); **Negress; Nigger; Negrillo—Negrito,** whence **Negritic; Niger,** whence **Nigeria,** whence **Nigerian** (adj, hence n); **nigrescent,** whence **nigrescence; nigricant; nigrify; Nigritian; nigrities, nigritude; nigrosine; nigrous; denigrate; niello; darnel.**

1. The effective origin of this group is afforded by the L adj *niger*, black, s and r *nig-*: o.o.o.: perh cf the Gr a*nigros* (*a-*, merely prothetic), impure, unclean, akin to Gr *knephas*, darkness, and *knephaios*, dark, sombre: IE r, *neigh-*, filthily— hence, very—black.

2. L *niger* becomes Sp (and Port) *negro*, soon used also as n for '*black* man', esp in Africa; adopted by E, better *Negro*. L *niger* becomes EF-F *nègre*, whence the f *négresse*, whence E *negress*, better *Negress*. EF-F *nègre* becomes EE *neger*, whence the now derog and always coll *nigger*, a Negro, hence most improp of a non-African 'black' man; hence the adj and v *nigger*.

3. *Negrillo*, lit a little Negro, is adopted from Sp and applied to the Bushmen of Africa; Sp *negro* has another dim—*negrito*, whence E *Negrito*, applied to all 'little Negroes', including Negrillos.

4. L *niger*, black, occurs in such river-names as the three or four rivers named *Rio Negro* in SAm and the *Niger* of central WAfrica, perhaps the same as Pliny's *Nigris* and Ptolemy's *Nigeir*.

5. L *niger*, o/s *nigr-*, c/f *nigri-*, has the foll derivatives affecting E:

*nigrescere*, to become black, presp *nigrescens*, o/s *nigrescent-*, E *nigrescent*;

*nigricāre*, to be rather black, presp *nigricans*, o/s *nigricant-*, E *nigricant*;

LL *nigrificāre*, to blacken, whence 'to *nigrify*'; *nigritia*, blackness, whence ML *Nigritia*, Sudan, whence *Nigritian*;

*nigritiēs*, blackness, adopted by Med; *nigritūdō*, blackness, whence literary E *nigritude*; LL *nigrus*, black, E *nigrous*.

6. L *niger* leads also to *nigrine*, which=*nigr-*+adj *-ine*); *nigrosine*, which app=*nigrous*+Chem *-ine*.

7. L *niger*, black, has the dim *nigellus*, rather black, i.e. dark, whence both the SciL herb *Nigella* and, via the derivative ML n *nigellum*, the It *niello*, a dark metallic alloy of sulphur, hence inlay metal work in which this alloy is used—adopted by E.

8. The L adj *nigellus* has the derivative LL n *nigella*, the plant black cummin, whence OF *neiele* (C12), *neelle*, whence MF-F *nielle*, whence, with an o.o.o. 1st element *dar-*, the dial F *darnelle*, ME-E *darnel*. *Dar-* is perh akin to E *tare*, a vetch, but, in The Bible, a grainfields weed, usu said to be darnel: ? appositive 'weed *nielle*'.

9. L *niger*, o/s *nigr-*, has derivative *nigrāre*, to blacken, with cpd *dēnigrāre* (*dē-* used int), to blacken thoroughly, with pp *dēnigrātus*, whence 'to *denigrate*' esp a person's character; derivative LL *dēnigrātiō*, o/s *dēnigrātiōn-*, becomes E *denigration*, whence, anl, the agent *denigrator*.

**neif.** See NATIVE, para 7.

**neigh** (v, hence n): ME *neien*: OE *hnǣgan*: akin to ON *gneggja*, Ice *hneggja*, OS *hnēgian*, OHG *hneigen*, MHG *nēgen*: echoic.

**neighbor, -bour,** etc. See NEAR, para 3.

**neither,** adj, hence adv, conj, pronoun. See EITHER.

**nema.** See nerve, para 3; cf the element *nemato-*.

**nemesis.** See NIMBLE, para 7.

**neo-** words collectively. See the element *neo-*; perh note esp *neologism*, from F *néologisme*, a learnèd formation (cf LOGIC); and *neophyte*—perh via late MF-F *néophyte*—from LL *neophytus*, newly planted (cf the Eccl LL *neophyta*, a woman newly converted): trln of Gr *neophutos*.

**nephelite, nephelium, nepheloid.** See NEBULA, para 3.

**nephew, niece; nepotism; neve.**

1. *Nephew*, ME *neveu* or *nevou*, from OF, derives from L *nepōs*, o/s *nepōt-*, with r *nep-*, akin to Skt *nápāt* (acc *nápātam*, cf L *nepōtem*), OPers *napā*, Skt f *naptís*, OLith *nepotis*, *neputis*, f *nepte*; OE *nefa*, OHG *nevo*, f *nift*, MHG *neve*, G *Neffe*; ON *nefi*; Ir *necht*, W *nith*; with merely prothetic *a-*, the Gr *anepsios* (cf OSl *netĭjĭ*), first cousin.

2. *Niece*, ME *nece*, *nice*, OF *niece* (F *nièce*), derives from VL *\*neptia*, var of LL *nepta*, itself a var of LL *neptis* (? for *\*nepotis*: *-is*, f suffix), from L *nepōs*, orig of common gender.

3. The L o/s *nepōt-* accounts for It *nepote*, nephew, whence *nepotismo*, applied orig to the favour enjoyed by Popes' nephews at the Papal Court in Rome, whence EF-F *népotisme*, whence E *nepotism*.

4. OE *nefa* became ME *neve*, EE *nevve*, whence the dial *nevvy*.

**nephria, nephridium, nephrism, nephrite, nephritic, nephritis, nephrology** (see the element *nephro-*).

1. The Gr *nephros*, a kidney, is akin to Praenestian L *nephrōnes* and OHG *nioro*, MHG-G *niere*, ON *nȳra*; OGmc *\*niura-* for *\*nigura-*, and IE *neghurōn-* (Walshe) or *\*neguhron-* (Hofmann).

2. From Gr *nephros*, s *nephr-*, SciL derives *nephria*, Bright's disease; Med E *nephric*, of the kidneys, is *nephr-*+adj *-ic*; cf Med *nephrism* (*-ism*), a morbid kidney-condition, and G *Nephrit*, whence E *nephrite*, with Min suffix *-ite*.

3. Gr *nephros* has adj *nephritikos*, LL *nephriticus*, E *nephritic*; *nephritis* is a SciL formation (*nephr-*+the 'disease' suffix *-itis*)—cf Med *nephrosis* (*nephr-*+the similar Gr Med suffix *-ōsis*).

**nepotism.** See NEPHEW, para 3.

**Neptune,** adj **Neptunian,** derive from L *Neptūnus*, orig a god of springs and streams, later God of the Sea, adj *Neptūnius*: cf Ve *apā́ṃ nápat*, Av *apąm napá*, descendant (cf para 1 of NEPHEW) of the waters. (E & M.)

**Nereid, nereid, nereis.** See NOURISH, para 3.

**Nero, Neronian** (whence, anl, **Neronize,** to treat, or to act, tyrannically and cruelly).

*Neronian* derives from L *Nerōniānus*, adj of *Nerō*, o/s *Nerōn-*, of Sabine origin: IE r, *\*ner-*, a warrior, akin to *\*uir* (*\*wir-*), as in L *uir* (ML *vir*), a man—cf VIRILE.

**nerve** (n, hence adj and v), **nerval** (adj, n), **nervate** (whence, anl, **nervation**), **nervine** (adj, hence n), **nervose, nervosity, nervous** (whence **nervousness**), **nervule** (whence, anl, **nervular** and **nervulose**), Med **nervus, nervy** (from *nerve* and esp from pl *nerves*); L cpds: **enervate, enervation; innervate** (whence, anl, **innervation**), **innerve.**—Gr: **neural** (whence **subneural**), **neuration, neuric, neurine, neuritic, neuritis, neuroid, neuroma, neuron** (whence **neuronism**), **neurosis, neurotic** (whence **neuroticism**); Gr cpds: **neuralgia** (whence **neuralgic**), see the element *-neura*; **neurasthenia** (whence **neurasthenic**), see the element *-asthenia*; **neuropath** (whence **neuropathic**), see the element *-path*; cognate **nema** (whence *nematite*: Min *-ite*)—cf the element *nemato-*.—Gmc cognates: **needle** (n, hence adj and v), whence **needle-fish, -point, -woman, -work,** etc.; **snood** (n, hence v).

Indo-European

1. *Nerve* derives, like OF-F *nerf*, from ML *nervus*, L *neruus*, a sinew, hence a nerve, s *neru-*, akin to—perh a metathesis of—Gr *neuron*, a cord, fibre, nerve, s and r *neur-*: cf Arm *neard*, sinew, and with IE prefix *s-*, Skt *snáva*, Av *snāvarĕ*, a strong cord, a tendon, Tokh B *sñaura*, nerves, OHG *senawa* (G *Sehne*), a tendon, Lett *snaujís*, a lace, a snare: IE base, perh *\*snēwro-*, whence, by popular

inversion, *nerwo-, whence the L neruus; with ult IE r *sne-, var *sneu-. (Hofmann; E & M.)

## Greek

2. Gr neuron, sinew, tendon, hence both a cord made of sinew and, in pl neura, nerves in the modern sense, is retained in SciE. On the s neur- arise the adj neural, perh after nerval (see para 4), and the var neuric, cf Gr neurikos, perh cf neurotic, and neuroid (-oid, resembling); the nn neurine (Chem -ine), neurite, neuritis (whence, anl, neuritic), neuroma (-oma), neurosis (-osis)—whence, anl, neurotic. Neuration is anl with nervation.

3. The cognate Gr nēma, a thread, is—via LL— adopted by Zoo; imm from Gr néō, I spin, L nēre, to spin.

## Latin

4. L neruus, ML nervus, whence E nerve, has adj neruālis, ML nervālis, E nerval. The simplex *neruāre, ML *nervāre, is attested by a cpd; hence E nervate, as if from the ML pp *nervātus, tied up, bound.

5. L neruus has these other derivatives affecting E:

LL neruīnus, ML nervīnus, E nervine;

L neruōsus, whence E nervose and predominantly nervous, the latter perh via MF nervouse, f of MF nervous (EF-F nerveux, f nerveuse);

hence L neruōsitās, strength (from 'sinew' neruus), ML o/s nervōsitāt-, whence EF-F nervo-sité, whence E nervosity, in C19-20 '(extreme) nervousness';

L dim neruulus, ML -vulus, whence E nervule.

Nervure, adopted from F, is however a MF coinage in -ure (cf musculature) from MF-F nerver, to furnish with nerves.

6. L neruus has two prefix-cpds affecting E:

ēneruis (var ēneruus), ML ēnervis, lacking sinews, hence weak, nerveless, whence ēneruāre, to deprive of sinews, pp ēneruātus, ML ēnervātus, whence 'to enervate'; the derivative LL ēneruātiō, o/s ēneruātiōn-, yields enervation;

LL inneruis (in-, not), without sinew, may have, in form, suggested the E 'to innerve' and, anl, 'to innervate', both of which, however, mean 'to supply with nervous strength', in-, into, being here int.

## Germanic cognates

7. A needle, ME nedle, derives from OE nāedl, akin to OFris nēdle, OS nādla, nāthla, Go nēthla, OHG nādala, MHG nādel, G Nadel, ON nāl (a contr?); cf also OIr snathat, Ga snathad, needle, and OIr snāthe, sinew, thread.

8. Akin to OIr snāthe, a thread, is OE snōd (? orig a pp), whence E snood, a fillet worn, by a woman, around the hair: cf Lett snāte, a linen cover.

nescience, nescient. See SCIENCE, para 7.

nesh, moist, tender, hence weak, sickly, now dial: OE hnesc, hnesce: cf Go hnasqus, soft, tender, West Frisian nesk, tender, and perh (Walshe) OHG

hnascōn, nascōn, MHG-G naschen, to nibble (esp sweet things); ? also Skt khắdati, he chews (Feist).

ness. See NOSE, para 5.

nest, nestle, nestling. See NETHER (and cf SIT), paras 3-4.

net (1), adj, clear. See NEAT, adj, para 1.

net (2), n, a catching-device made of twine (etc.), hence v, whence the vn netting; nettle (nautical); node (whence nodal), nodose, nodosity, nodule (whence nodular and anl nodulate, whence nodula-tion); noose, n hence v; dénouement; lanyard; ouch.—nexus; annex (n and v), annexation, annexion; connect (whence connector, -er), connec-tion (connexion), connective (whence connectivity); connex, connexity.

1. Net, OE net, is akin to OFris -net, OS netti, OHG nezzi, MHG netze, G Netz, Go nati, MD nette, D net, ON net; cf L nassa (? for *natta), a fish-basket, nōdus, a knot, and Skt nahyati, he binds. Cf also L nectere, to bind; indeed the basic idea is 'to bind, to knot'; the IE r is perh *nedh-.

2. Prob akin to net is the nautical nettle, a line of rope yarn, earlier knittle, from 'to knit', q.v. sep.

3. L nōdus, a knot, yields E node. The derivative L adj nōdōsus becomes nodose, and the subsidiary LL nōdōsitās, o/s nōdōsitāt-, becomes nodosity. The L dim nōdulus yields nodule. The derivative L nōdāre, to knot, becomes OF noer (F nouer), with cpd denoer (F dénouer), to unknot (de, down from), whence EF-F dénouement, an untying, esp of a theatrical plot, adopted by E.

4. L nōdus becomes Prov nous, whence E noose.

5. Akin to OHG nezzi, G Netz, a net, is OHG nestila, a knot of ribbons, a bandage, a strap; akin to nestila, and from the Gmc r it contains, is OF lasne, a strap, a thong, whence OF lasniere, F lanière, whence ME layner (EE lainer), whence, with new suffix (? suggested by the nautical yard), lanyard or laniard.

6. Of OGmc origin—cf the OHG nusca, nuscha (akin to nezzi, etc.)—is OF nusche, nousche, a neck-lace or a collar, whence ME nouche, whence (a nouche being apprehended as an ouche) the later ME ouche, whence the obsol E ouch, a brooch, a clasp.

## L nectere

7. Nectere, to intertwine, bind, fasten, tie, has pp nexus, whence the n nexus (gen -ūs), an inter-twining, binding, tying, adopted by E, esp for an interconnection, with adj nexal.

8. L nectere has, relevant to E, two prefix-cpds, one being adnectere, to attach to, usu assimilated annectere, with pp annexus, whence the n annexus (gen -ūs), whence prob the MF-F annexe, whence the E n annexe, usu annex; 'to annex' app comes from MF-F annexer, from the L pp annexus. Possibly, however, the MF-F n annexe comes, in some senses at least, from L annexum, neu of pp annexus. The derivative LL annexiō, o/s annexiōn-, accounts for E annexion. The nn annexiō and

*annexus* prompted the ML *annexātiō*, o/s *annexā-tiōn-*, whence *annexation*.

9. The other L prefix-cpd is *conectere*, to bind (or attach) *co-* or together; faultily—but in ML predominantly—*connectere*, whence 'to *connect*', whence *interconnect*. On *con(n)ex*us, the pp, arise: *con(n)exiō*, o/s *con(n)exiōn-*, whence MF-F *connexion*, adopted by E, which anglicizes it *connection*, after *connect*; *con(n)exīuus*, ML *-īvus*, E *connexive*; *connexus* (gen *-ūs*), E *connex*. *Connexity* derives from late MF-F *connexité*, from the MF-F adj *connexe*, from the L pp *connexus*.

**nether**, lower, whence **Netherlands** (whence **Netherlander**) and **nethermost; beneath** and **underneath; nest** (n, hence v), **nestle, nestling; nidal, nidamental, nidation, nidatory, nidificant, nidificate** (whence **nidification**), **nidifugous, nidify, nidulant, nidulus, nidus; niche; eyas.**

### Indo-European

1. *Nether*, ME *nethere*, earlier *nithere*, OE *nithera*, comes from the OE adv *nither*, *nithor*, downward, akin to OE *neothan*, below, beneath: cf OFris *nether*, *nither*, OS *nithar*, OHG *nidar*, MHG *nider*, G *nieder*, MD-D *neder*, ON *nithr*, down (adv); further off, Skt *nitharám*, downwards, from *ni*, down (adv): IE r, *\*ni-*, down.

### Germanic

2. *Beneath*, ME *benethe*, earlier *bineothan*, derives from OE *beneothan*, *benythan*: prefix *be-*+*neothan*, downward, beneath; and *underneath*, ME *undernethe*, from OE *underneothan*, *undernythan*—cf UNDER.

3. *Nest*, OE *nest*, is akin to OHG-MHG-G *nest*, Skt *nīḍas* (for *\*nizdas*), seat, rest, OB *gnězdo*, Lith *līzdas* (for *\*nizdas*), L *nīdus* (for *\*nisdus*); several C cognates; Gmc r, *\*nest-*, and IE r, *\*nizd-*: a very ancient IE cpd of *\*ni-*, down (adv)+*\*sed-*, to sit. a place in which to sit down.

4. OE *nest* has derivative *nestlian*, to nest: E 'to *nestle*'. The ME-E *nestling* (cf MD *nestelinc*) prob=*nest*+*ling*, a creature belonging to, but perh=*nestling*, presp—used as n—of *nestle*.

### Latin

5. L *nīdus*, a nest, adopted by Sci, acquires the E adj *nidal*—and derivative n *nidation* and adj *nidatory*, both formed as if from *\*nīdātus*, pp of *\*nīdāre*, to nest. Derivative *nīdāmentum*, materials for a nest, acquires the Zoo E adj *nidamental*. The dim *nīdulus*, adopted by E, has v *nīdulāri*, presp *nīdulans*, o/s *nīdulant-*, E *nidulant* (adj), nestling, and pp *nīdulātus*, E 'to *nidulate*', whence, anl, *nidulation*. The cpd *nīdificāre*, to build a nest, yields 'to *nidify*'; its presp *nīdificans*, o/s *nīdificant-*, E *nidificant*, adj; its pp *nīdificātus*, 'to *nidificate*'. *Nidifugous*, nest-fleeing=*nīdi-*, c/f of L *nīdus*+*-fugous*, from L *fugāre*, to flee (vt).

6. A *niche* is adopted from MF-F *niche*, recess in a wall, from OF *nichier* (F *nicher*), from VL *\*nīdicāre*, to nest, from L *nīdus*; and OF *nichier* (F *nicher*) gives us 'to *niche*'. B & W, however, derive

the MF-F n *niche* from It *nicchia*, mdfn of *nicchio*, a shell, perh from L *mitulus*, Gr *mutilos*, a mould.

7. *Eyas* (C15 *eyes*) derives, by way of *a nias* (*niais*) taken as *an iais*, from OF-F *niais*, foolish, lit fresh from the nest: *\*nīdācem*, acc of VL *\*nīdāx*, from L *nīdus*.

**netting.** See the 2nd NET (heading).

**nettle** (1), the plant: OE *netle*, *netele*: cf OHG *nezzila*, MHG *nezzel*, G *Nessel*, and MD *netele*, *nettel*, D *netel*: perh akin to NET, n.

**nettle** (2), nautical term. See the 2nd NET, para 2.

**neume.** See PNEUMA.

**neural, neuric, neuritis, neuroma, neuron, neurosis, neurotic.** See NERVE, para 2.

**neurasthenia, neurasthenic.** See STHENIA.

**neuter** (adj, hence n); **neutral** (adj, hence n) and **neutrality** and **neutralize; neutron;** cf the element *neutro-*.

1. *Neuter* is either adopted from L, or adapted from MF-F *neutre* (from L *neuter*); the L adj *neuter*, neither, simply combines *ne-*, not (f.a.e., NOT)+*uter*, either.

2. Derivative *neutrālis* becomes E *neutral*, perh via the obs F *neutral*; *neutrality* derives, perh via MF-F *neutralité*, from ML *neutrālitās*, o/s *neutrālitāt-*; *neutralize* from EF-F *neutraliser*.

3. From L *neuter*, SciE derives *neutron*—cf *proton*, *photon*, etc.

**Nevada, névé, nival, niveous, nivosity; snow** (n, hence adj and v), whence **snowy** and such obvious cpds as **snowball, -drop, -fall, -flake,** etc.

1. *Snow*, ME *snawe*, *snowe*,=OE *snāw*: cf OFris *snē*, OS and OHG *snēo*, MHG *snē* (gen *snēwes*), G *Schnee*, Go *snaiws*, MD *snee*, D *sneeaw*, ON *snāer* (with modern Scan cognates); OIr *snechta*, Ir and Ga *sneachd*, Mx *sniaghtey*; OSl *snēgŭ*, Lith *sniégas*; Skt *snēhaš*, stickiness. (Walshe.)

2. In Gr and L, initial *s-* has disappeared: the Gr acc *nipha*, nom *\*nix*, gen *\*niphos* (s and r *niph-* stands for *\*sniph-*) and L *nix* for *\*snix* (for *\*snigws*): cf L *nīuit* and Gr *neiphei*, *niphei*, it snows, and, in C, the W *nyf*, snow.

3. L *nix* has gen *niuis*, o/s *niu-*. The foll derivatives affect E:

*niuālis*, ML *nivālis*, E *nival*;
*niueus*, ML *niveus*, E *niveous*;
*niuōsus*, ML *nivōsus*, the very rare E *nivose*—cf the F Revolutionary month *Nivose*; hence, anl, *nivosity*.

4. The derivative L adj *niuātus*, ML *nivātus*, becomes Sp *nevado*, f *nevada*, as in the Sierra *Nevada* mountain ranges, whence the State of *Nevada*.

5. *Névé*, mountaineers' word for partly compacted snow, came into F, via an Eastern dial of F (cf Savoyard *névi*), from ML *nivem*, acc of *nix*.

**never.** See EVER, para 1.

**nevvy.** See NEPHEW, para 4.

**new.** See NOVA, para 6.

**newel.** See NUCLEUS, para 6.

**newfangle; newfangled.** See NOVA, para 7.

**newly.** See NOVA, para 6.

**newmarket,** certainly the long, loose coat and prob the card game, derives from *Newmarket* (England), famous for its racing stables and its horsey types.

**news.** See NOVA, para 6. Hence NEWSBOY, NEWSPAPER, etc.

**newt.** ME *newte*, by apprehending earlier *an ewte* as *a newte*: earlier ME *evete*: OE *efete*, a lizard, whence E *eft*: o.o.o.

**New Zealand.** See SEA, para 1.

**nexal.** See the 2nd NET, para 7.

**next.** See NEAR, para 2.

**nexus.** See the 2nd NET, para 7.

**Nez Percé.** See NOSE, para 6.

**Niagara,** whence the fire-fighters' large, revolving nozzle, platform-mounted, is an Iroquoian word.

**nib** of pen derives from *nib*, var *neb*, a bird's beak: akin to MLG *nibbe*, it descends from OE *nebb* (whence *neb*)—cf MLG *nebbe* and ON *nef* (? for *nebh*). There are also some *s*-prefix cognates: cf OHG *snabul*, MHG *snabel*, G *Schnabel*, D *sneb*, MD-D *snavel*, OFris *snavel*, Lith *snápas*.

2. *Neb, nib,* app have dim *neble, nible,* whence—? influenced by *nip,* to compress sharply—*nipple.* Cf:

**nibble** is of Gmc origin (cf LG *nibbelen* and D *knibbelen*); it is also the freq of 'to NIP'.

**nice** (whence **niceness**), **nicety.** See SCIENCE, para 7.

**niche.** See NETHER, para 6.

**nick,** a small notch (hence v), hence a point in time; **nock** (of an archer's bow: a tip of horn, with notches for holding the string, hence such—whence any—notch).

*Nick* is app a thinning of *nock*: and *nock*, ME *nocke,* is akin to MD *nocke* (D *nok*) but prob from OSw *nock, nocka*: ? orig echoic.

**nickel** (the coin, from the metal): G *Nickel*: Early Modern High German Kupfer*nickel*, lit 'copper devil' (cf 'Old Nick', The Devil): 'because in spite of its colour it yields no copper' (Walshe): for the 1st element, see COPPER.

**nickname:** ME 'an *ekename*', surname, nickname. For the formation, cf NEWT.

**nicotine** (whence **nicotinian, nicotinic**) is adopted from F, which, in 1836, thus reshaped earlier *nicotiane,* adapted in 1570 from SciL *herba nicotiana,* 'grass of *Nicot*': Jean Nicot, that F ambassador at Lisbon who, in 1560, sent some tobacco to Catherine de Médicis. (B & W.)

**nidal, nidamental, nidation, nidificate, nidifugous, nidulant, nidulus, nidus.** See NETHER, para 5.

**niece.** See NEPHEW, para 2.

**niello.** See NEGRO, para 6.

**nifty,** attractively smart (A sl), from *magnificat,* says Bret Harte in 1869: ? rather from L 'Magnifi*cate*', Magnify ye! (cf the obs *magnificate,* to magnify) or, as EW proposes and as Whitehall agrees, from *magnificent,* or possibly, as Mathews suggests, from *\*snifty,* having a pleasant smell.

**Nigella.** See NEGRO, para 6.

**Niger, Nigeria, Nigerian.** See NEGRO, para 3 and heading.

**niggard,** a very stingy person, a miser—whence the adj **niggardly**—prob derives from ME *nig,* such a person+the pej suffix -*ard*; *nig-* is app of Scan origin—cf Nor dial *gnigga, gnikka,* to be stingy. Cf NIGGLE.

**nigger.** See NEGRO, para 2.

**niggle,** now esp to potter, to be finicky, orig to cheat pettily: app Scan (cf Nor dial *nigla*): prob cf NIGGARD. Hence the pa, vn *niggling.*

**nigh.** See NEAR, para 1.

**night** (n, hence adj and v; cf **benighted,** pp of *benight,* with int *be-*), **nightly** (adj, OE *nihtlic,* hence adv); cpds, all self-explanatory, as, e.g., **nightcap, nighthawk, nightingale** (para 2), **nightjar, nightmare, nightshade, nightwalker.**—**noctule, nocturn** and **nocturnal; nocturne;** cf the element *nocti-;* sep EQUINOX, EQUINOCTIAL; **nycteris;** cf the element *nycti-.*

1. *Night,* ME *niht,* OE *niht,* var of *neaht,* is akin to OFris *nacht,* OS and OHG-MHG *naht,* G *Nacht,* Go *nahts,* MD *nach* and, as in D, *nacht;* ON *nātt, nōtt;* OIr in*nocht,* tonight, Ga *nochd,* W *nos,* Br *noz,* Cor *nōz, nōs,* OC *\*nokti;* Alb *natĕ;* OSl *noštĭ,* Lith *naktìs;* Gr *nux* (gen *nuktos*)—L *nox* (gen *noctis*); Skt *nakta, náktiš.* The Gmc etymon is *\*nahts;* the IE, *\*nokts,* with Hit *nekuz* (? for *\*nekuts,* for *\*nokuts*) a mere vocalic var.

2. Of the *night* cpds, one merits special attention: *nightingale,* ME from OE *nihtegale,* lit a nightsinger: cf OS and OHG *nahtigale,* MHG *nahtegale,* G *Nachtigall;* for the 2nd element, cf YELL.

3. L *nox,* o/s *noct-,* has adj *nocturnus,* whence the ML n *nocturna,* whence Eccl E *nocturn; nocturnus* becomes F *nocturne,* which, used as n (in Mus, a night-piece), is adopted by E. *Nocturnus* acquires the LL mdfn *nocturnālis,* whence *nocturnal.* The derivative *noctua,* an owl, acquires the SciF *noctule,* a large brown bat, adopted by E.

4. Cf *Nycteris,* a genus of Am bats: Gr *nukteris,* a bat, from *nukt-,* o/s of *nux,* night.

**nightingale.** See prec, para 2.

**nightjar.** See the 2nd JAR, s.f.

**nightmare.** See the 2nd MARE.

**nigrescent; nigricant; nigrify; nigrities; nigritude; nigrous.** See NEGRO, para 4. Cf *nigrine, nigrosine,* in para 5.

**nihilify; nihilism, nihilist; nihility; nil.** See FILAMENT, para 11.

**Nihon.** See JAPAN, para 2.

**Nile; Nilot** (or **Nilote**), **Nilotic.**

*Nilotic* comes, via L *Nilōticus,* from Gr *Neilōtikos,* from *Neilōtēs,* a native of the Nile country: Gr *Neilos,* the River Nile, L *Nīlus,* F and E *Nile. Neilos* is o.o.o.; one Eg name is *Aur-Aa,* Great River.

**nimble** (whence **nimbleness**); **nim, nimmer;**—**numb** (adj, hence v—with int **benumb**), whence **numbness;** — **numismatic, numismatist;** — **nomad, nomadic;** — **nemesis.** — **number** (n, v), whence **numberless; numeral, numerate, numeration, numerous,** with cpds *e-, i-.*

1. *Nimble*, ME *nimel* (var *nemel*), ? orig 'quick to grasp or take', derives from ME *nimen*, OE *niman*, to take, akin to OFris *nima*, *nema*, OS and OHG *neman*, MHG *nemen*, G *nehmen*, Go *niman*, MD-D *nemen*, ON *nema*, to take, and, further off, the Gr *nemein*, to distribute, and, with *e-o* alternation, *nomos*, anything distributed or allotted, and L *numerus*, number.

2. OE *niman*, ME *nimen*, become 'to *nim*', to take, esp to steal, now (and long) only dial; hence the obsol *nimmer*, a thief.

3. OE *niman*, pp *numen*, ME *nimen*, pp *nume*, taken, seized, hence adj (with deadened feeling), whence *numb*.

## Latin

4. L *numerus*, a number, s *numer-*, prob has r *num-*. The foll simple derivatives affect E:

LL adj *numerālis*, whence, perh via late MF-F *numéral*, the E *numeral*, adj, hence n; cf *numerical*, prob suggested by EF-F *numérique*, learnedly formed from *numerus*;

L *numerāre*, to count, number, whence *numerābilis*, E *numerable*; presp *numerans*, o/s *numerant-*, E adj *numerant*, used in counting; pp *numerātus*, whence the E adj and v *numerate*; derivative *numerātiō*, o/s *numerātiōn-*, whence, perh via MF-F *numération*, the E *numeration*, whence, anl, *numerative*; LL *numerātor*, adopted by E;

LL *numerārius*, arithmetician, ML adj, whence EF-F *numéraire*, whence E *numerary*;

L *numero*, prop the abl of *numerus*, becomes It *numero*, number, whence the EF-F *numéro*, whence F *Nº*, adopted by E;

L *numerōsus*, E *numerous*; derivative LL *numerōsitās*, o/s *numerōsitāt-*, E *numerosity*.

5. L *numerus* has the foll prefix-cpds affecting E:

*ēnumerāre*, to count *ē-* or out, whence, anl, *enumerable*; the pp *ēnumerātus* yields 'to *enumerate*'; derivative *ēnumerātiō*, o/s *ēnumerātiōn-*, whence, via EF-F *énumération*, the E *enumeration*, whence, anl, *enumerative*; LL *ēnumerātor*, adopted by E;

*innumerābilis*, E *innumerable*;

LL *supernumerārius*, finding oneself (itself) in excess, whence *supernumerary*, adj hence also n.

6. L *numerus* becomes OF-F *nombre*, whence ME *nombre*, var *noumbre*, whence E *number*; L *numerāre* becomes OF-F *nombrer*, ME *nombren*, var *noumbren*, whence 'to *number*'.

## Greek

7. Gr *nemein* (s and r *nem-*), to distribute, has derivative *nemesis* (suffix *-esis*), distribution, whence *Nemesis*, goddess distributor of retribution, adopted by E.

8. Gr *nomos*, anything allotted, hence usage, custom, whence E *nomism* and all the cpds in *nomo-*, q.v. in Elements. The Gr adj *nomikos*, customary, becomes erudite E *nomic*. *Nomos* has two very fruitful c/ff: *-nomos*, one who deals with —a subject; *-nomia*, connoting a field of laws or

principles governing a subject, and occurring in E as *-nomy*. Among the most important *-nomy* cpds are these:

*astronomy*, OF-F *astronomie*, L from Gr *astronomia*, from *astronomos*, an astronomer: cf the element *astro-*, the adj *astral*, the n STAR; the Gr adj *astronomikos* passes through L and EF-F ·to become E *astronomic*, with its extn *astronomical*; *astronomer* (agent *-er*) was perh suggested by LL *astronomus*;

*autonomy* (whence *autonomic*), self-government, Gr *autonomia*, from the adj *autonomos*, whence E *autonomous*: cf the element *auto-*;

*binomial*, (in Math) two-termed: *bi-*, two, twice +*-nomial*, var of *nomic*;

*economy*, q.v. sep.

9. Also from Gr *nemein* comes the Gr adj *nomas*, pasturing, hence roaming the country in search of pasture, which, used as n (one who does this), with gen *nomados*, becomes L *nomas*, gen *nomadis*, o/s *nomad-*, whence, perh via EF-F *nomade*, the E *nomad*. The derivative Gr adj *nomadikos* becomes E *nomadic*.

10. *Nomos*, custom, has derivative *nomisma*, anything sanctioned by custom, esp the current State coin, whence L *nomisma*, with var *numisma*, whence erudite EF-F *numismatique*, whence E *numismatic*; the n *numismatics* derives from F la *numismatique*, and *numismatist* from F *numismatiste*.

**nimbose, nimbus.** See NEBULA, para 4.

**nincompoop,** a simpleton: o.o.o.: perh—after *ninny*—a slovening of '*non compos* mentis', not of sound mind.

**nine,** whence **ninth** (cf OE *nigotha*) **nineteen,** whence **nineteenth** (cf OE *nigontēotha*); **ninety** (whence **ninetieth**).—Latin: **November, novena, novenary, novendial, novennial; none** (canonical hour), **nones**—cf **nonagenarian, nonane, noon** (whence **nooning), noontide.**—Greek: **ennead, enneatic.**

## Indo-European

1. E-ME *nine* derives from OE *nigon*, var *nigan*: cf OFris *nigun*, *niugun*, OS *nigun*, OHG *niun*, MHG *niun*, *niune*, G *neun*, Go *niun*, MD *negene* and, as in D and LG, *negen*; ON *nīu*, with modern Scan cognates; OIr *noi*, Ga *naoi*, *naoidh*, *naodh*, EW-W *naw*, Cor *nau*, *naw*, *nawe*, Br *nau*; L *nouem* (ML *novem*), Gr *ennea*, Skt *náva*; and perh E *new* (q.v. at NOON), for 'the IE word for eight (cf *acht*) is dual in form ($=2 \times 4$), so that an old system of counting by fours appears to have existed; 9 would then mark the first of the third series of tetrads' (Walshe): Gmc r, *\*niwan-*, IE r *\*newon-*, *\*newn-*.

## Germanic

2. *Nine* has the cpd *nineteen*, OE *nigontȳne* or *-tēne*, lit 'nine' *plus* 'ten'; cf *ninety*, OE *nigontig*, lit 'nine' *by* 'ten (times)'.

## Latin

3. L *nouem* (perh for *\*nouen*), 9, occurs in

*Nouember* (*mensis*), ML *November*, the ninth month of the Roman year; E *November*, F *novembre*. Derivative ML *novēna*, a nine days' devotion, is extant in Eccl E: cf Eccl *novendial*, a nine days' feast, L *nouendiāle*, prop the neu of adj *nouendiālis*, of the ninth *dies* or day. *Nouem* has derivative *nouēnārius*, of the number 9, whence E *novenary*, and the LL cpd adj *nouennis*, nine *anni* (or years) old, whence E *novennial*, recurring every ninth year.

4. L *nouem* has ordinal *nōnus*, ninth, whence, via *nōna* (sc *hōra*, hour), the ninth hour in Ancient Roman reckoning, hence, in LL, the canonical hour or an office recited then, whence OF-F *none*, adopted by E. *Nones*, however, is the ninth day before the Ides: via MF-F *nones*: from L *nōnae*.

5. L *nōnāgēnārius* (*nōnāgēni*, 90 each+*ārius*) yields *nonagenarian*, adj hence n; L *nōnāgēsimus*, 90th, yields *nonagesimal*. E formations from L *nōnus* include *nonane* (*nonus*+Chem *-ane*) and Math *nonary* (form-prompted by L *nōnārius*, of the ninth hour).

6. L *nōna* (hōra), 'the ninth hour' (3 p.m.), becomes OE *nōn*, orig as in L, but, the hour of the Eccl service being moved from 3 p.m. to 12 a.m., also—and soon predominantly—midday: E *noon*. Cf *noontide*, midday, from OE *nōntīd*, orig the ninth hour.

### Greek

7. Gr *ennea*, app for *\*ennewa*, has gen *enneados*, o/s *ennead-*, whence E *ennead*, a group or set (cf the suffix *-ad*) of nine. The derivative Gr adj *enneadikos* becomes LL *enneadicus*, whence E *enneadic*; the LL var *enneaticus* explains the E var *enneatic*.

**ninny.** See NOXIOUS, para 2, s.f.

**nip** (v, hence n), whence agent **nipper**, pa and vn **nipping**, adj **nippy**: ME *nippen*: cf MD *nīpen* (D *nipjen*, *knipjen*), to pinch, and Lith *knibti*, to pluck: prob cf *nap* (4), q.v. at NAB, para 1.

2. The sl *nipper*, a young boy, derives from cant *nipper*, a pickpocket; young—or, at any rate, small—boys making the best pickpockets.

**nipple.** see NIB, para 2.

**Nippon.** See JAPAN, para 2. Hence the AE *Nipponese*, whence A sl *Nip*, a Japanese.

**nippy.** See NIP (heading).

**nirvana:** Skt *nirvāṇa*, (of, or like, a candle) extinguished: cf Pali *nibbāna*, extinction.

**nit**, egg of louse: OE *hnitu*: cf MD *nette*, *nete*, D *neet*, OHG *hniz*, *niz*, G *Niss*, and prob Arm *anic*, Gr *konis* (perh for *\*knis*), a louse: IE r, *\*knid-*, to sting (cf Gr *knīdē*, a nettle).

**nitency, nitid, nitidous.** See NEAT, para 1.

**niter** (AE) or **nitre**; **nitrate**, whence **nitrator**; **nitric**; **nitrify**, **nitrification**; cf the element *nitro-*; **nitrogen** (whence **nitride**), whence **nitrogenize**, **nitrogenous**; **nitrous.**—**natron**; **trona.**

1. E *nitre*, AE *niter*, derives from MF-archaic F *nitre*: L *nitrum*, native soda: Gr *nitron*: H *nether*: Eg *ntṛj* (*netrà*), natron; ult idea, perh 'to cleanse' (cf Eg *netrà*).

2. F *nitre* has derivatives: *nitrate*, adopted by E, whence 'to *nitrate*'; *nitrique*, whence E *nitric*; *nitrifier*, whence 'to *nitrify*'; subsidiary *nitrification*, adopted by E; *nitrogène*, whence E *nitrogen*—cf the element *-gen*.

3. L *nitrum* has adj *nitrōsus*, whence E *nitrous*.

4. Gr *nitron* becomes Ar *naṭrūn*, whence Sp *natrón*, whence F, hence E, *natron*.

5. Ar *naṭrun*, with SciL suffix *-a* tacked on, yields Sw *trona*, adopted by E Min.

**nitwit**, orig A sl, now AE and E coll, is a 'nix' (G *nichts*, nothing) wit, a know-nothing: cf WIT.

**nival, niveous, nivosity.** See NEVADA, para 4, and cf the element *nivi-*.

**nix.** See NITWIT.

**Nº**, number. See NIMBLE, para 4.

**no**, adj and adv; sep NAY; **none**; **not**; sep NON.

*No*, not so, ME *no*, var *na*, derives from OE *nā*: OE *ne*, not+*ā*, ever (cf *aye*). But the adj *no*, ME *non*, earlier *nan*, derives from OE *nān* (*ne*, not+*ān*, one: cf ONE), whence, via ME *nan*, *non*, *noon*, *none*, the E *none*, pronoun—whence archaic adj. *Not*, ME *noht*, *naht*, earliest *nawiht*, derives from OE *nāwiht* (*ne*, not+*ā*, ever+*wiht*, a thing however small).

**Noachian; Noah; Noah's ark.**

*Noah*, H *Nōaḥ* (lit, rest or comfort), was commander of the ark during the Biblical Deluge, whence the child's toy called a *Noah's ark* (cf ARK); adj *Noachic* or, more usu, *Noachian*.

**nob**, head (sl), hence a swell. See KNOB.

**nobble.** See NAB, para 3.

**nobby**, very smart (sl). Adj of *nob*, a swell.

**nobility; noble** (adj, hence n)—whence **nobleman** (**-woman**), **nobleness; noblesse oblige;**—**ennoble**, whence **ennoblement.**—Akin to KNOW, q.v. at CAN.

1. 'To *ennoble*' derives from MF-F *ennoblir*: *en*, into+*noble*, well-born (person)+ *ir*, inf suffix: to turn into a noble.

2. E *nobility* derives from OF-EF *nobilité* (superseded by MF-F *noblesse*, as in *noblesse oblige*, noble birth imposes obligations): L *nōbilitātem*, acc of *nōbilitās*, itself from *nōbilis*, whence, via OF-MF *nobile*, and MF-F *noble*, the E adj *noble*.

3. L *nōbilis* is intimately related to and, indeed, prob derived from *nō-*, the ult r of L *nōscere*, to know: 'knowable, known', hence 'well-known', hence 'well-born', hence 'high-born', hence 'noble'. For *nōscere*, see CAN.

**noblesse oblige.** See prec, para 2.

**nocent.** See NOXIOUS, para 2.

**nock.** See NICK.

**noctambulant; noctiluca; noctivagous.** See the element *noct(i)-*.

**noctule, nocturn, nocturnal, nocturne.** See NIGHT, para 3.

**nocuous.** See NOXIOUS, para 3.

**nod** (v, hence n); **noddle**, n and v; **noddy** and syn **noodle.**

1. 'To *nod*', ME *nodden*, is perh akin to OHG *hnōtōn*, *genutōn*, to shake, and prob akin to L

*nut*āre, to nod the head repeatedly, freq of *\*nu*ere, to nod the head; if that be so, cf also Gr *neu*ein, to nod, and Skt *nauti, návate*, he budges, he turns (the head). The IE r is perh *\*nu-*, var *\*nau-* with extnn *\*naut-*, *\*not-*, *\*nōd-*.

2. Whereas 'to *noddle*' is a freq of 'to *nod*', a *noddle*, jocose for a head, earlier the nape of the neck, derives from ME *nodle, nodel*, which, o.o.o., perh derives from the lost origin of dial *nod*, nape of neck.

3. Perh from 'to *nod*' comes *noddy*, a simpleton; cf, sem, the adj *noddy*, inclined to drowse, therefore only half-awake.

4. App from *noddy*, simpleton—perh allied with *noddle*, head—comes *noodle*, simpleton, which has, of course, nothing to do with the alimentary paste *noodle* (usu in pl *noodles*): G *Nudel*, vermicelli: cf Silesian *knudel*: perh cf G *Knödel*, a dumpling. (Walshe.)

nodal. See the 2nd NET, para 3.
noddle. See NOD, para 2.
noddy. See NOD, para 3.
node, nodose, nodular, nodule. See the 2nd NET, para 3.
Noël, Christmas. See NATIVE, para 4.
noetic. See NOUS, para 1.
nog; noggin.

*Noggin*, a small cup, hence a small cupful, is o.o.o., but perh akin to *nog*, a brick-sized peg, hence a (large) projecting pin, itself o.o.o., but more prob akin to Norfolk *nog*, strong ale, ? hence any strong drink with an egg beaten in; even this *nog* is o.o.o.—? for *knock*, from the 'punch' it carries.

noise, whence noisy. See NAUTIC, para 3.
noisome. See ODIUM, para 7.
nolition. See VOLITION, para 6.
nolle prosequi—familiarly, nol. pros. See VOLITION, para 6.
nomad, nomadic. See NIMBLE, para 9.
nombles. See LOIN, para 4.
nom de guerre. See NAME, para 7.
nomen. See NAME, paras 1, 4 (s.f.), 7.
nomenclator, nomenclature. See NAME, para 5.
nomic. See NIMBLE, para 8.
nominal, nominate, nomination, nominator, nominee. See NAME, para 6.
nomism. See NIMBLE, para 8.
non, L for 'not'. See Prefixes.
nonage, the being a legal minor, is adopted from MF: *non*, not+*age* (F *âge*), not (the full) age.
nonagenarian; nonagesimal; nonary. See NINE, para 5.
nonce. See ONE, para 13.
nonchalance, nonchalant. See CALORIC, para 2.
nonconformist, nonconformity. See FORM, para 4, s.f.
nondescript, not (hitherto) described, hence not easily described: L *non*, not+L *dēscriptus*, described—cf SCRIBE.
none. See ONE, para 12.
nonentity, a person of no account, derives from *non-entity*, a not-existing: cf ENTITY.

nones. See NINE, para 4.
nonesuch, some thing or person unequalled: *none*, pronoun+*such*. Cf NONPAREIL.
non-existence, -existent. See SIST, para 5.
nonpareil. See PAIR, para 4.
nonplus, v, derives from *nonplus*, n, a state—a point—in or at which 'not (L *non*) more (L *plus*)' can be done.
nonsense, nonsensical. See SENSE, para 2.
non sequitur. See SEQUENCE, para 3.
noodle, (1) and (2). See NOD, para 4.
nook. See NECK, para 2.
noon; noontide. See NINE, para 6.
noose. See the 2nd NET, para 4.
nor, ME *nor*, is a contr of ME *nother*, from OE *nāwther, nōwther*, contr of *nāhwaether, nōhwaether*: *ne*, not+*hwaether*, whether. Cf *neither* at EITHER.
Nordic. See NORTH, para 3.
Norfolk dumplings were orig made (and later applied to the natives), Norfolk jackets orig worn, in *Norfolk* county, England: 'The Northern Folk' —opp *Suffolk*, 'The Southern Folk'—of East Anglia. Cf NORTH.
norm; normal (adj hence n)—whence normalcy (AE), normality, normalize; normative (after *formative*).—Cpds: abnormal (whence abnormality), abnormous; anormal; enorm, enormity, enormous.

1. The L *norma*, a carpenter's square, hence a rule of conduct, is o.o.o.: perh an adaptation— after L *forma*, a concrete form, a mould, hence shape—of Gr *gnōrimos*, a carpenter's square; if that be so, cf NOTABLE and KNOW and CAN.

2. L *norma* becomes OF-F *norme*, whence— unless direct from L—the E *norm*. The derivative L adj *normālis*, patterned or made with a carpenter's square, hence, in LL-ML, conforming to rule, becomes MF-F *normal*, whence—unless direct from L—the E *normal*.

3. The L prefix-cpd *abnormis*, away from (*ab*) the rule, yields the now rare *abnormous* (cf *enormous*); derivative L *abnormitās* gives *abnormity*; *abnormal*=L *abnormis*, influenced by *anormal*, adopted from MF-F *anormal*, itself from ML *anormālis*, a fusion—? orig a confusion—of L *anomalus* (see ANOMALOUS) and L *normālis*.

4. L *ēnormis*, out of (*ē-*) the square or the rule, becomes MF-F *énorme*, whence the obsol E *enorm*, displaced by *enormous* (from L *ēnormis*); derivative L *ēnormitās* becomes MF-F *énormité*, whence E *enormity*.

Norman. See NORTH, para 4.
normative. See NORM (heading).
Norn, an ancient Norse goddess of fate, is ON *Norn* (pl *Nornir*): perh cf ME *nurnen*, to say (? orig in prophecy or warning), and Sw dial *norna, nyrna*, to warn secretly.
Norse, Norseman. See para 4 of:
north, n, hence adj (whence norther, a north wind) and v (whence northing); obs norther, further north, with extn northerly; northern; Northman— cf Norman; northward; northwest—cf northeast; northward; Nordic; Norse, adj, hence n and also Norseman; sep NORFOLK; Northampton;

**Northumbria,** whence **Northumbrian** (adj, hence n); **Norway, Norwegian** (adj, hence n).

1. *North,* OE *north,* is akin to OFris and OS *north,* OHG *nord,* MHG *nort,* G *Nord* (but OF *north,* whence F *nord,* comes from OE) and *Norden,* MD *nort,* later *noort,* D *noord,* and ON *northr;* further off, Oscan *nertrak,* on the left, Umbrian *nertru,* from the left, and Gr *nerteros,* nether: basic idea of *north* is 'left (with eastern orientation)', as Webster remarks—cf the ult origin of SOUTH; but the IE r is perh *\*ner-,* under (Hofmann).

2. *Northerly* tacks *-ly* to obs *norther,* further north, from OE *northerra,* adj, and *northor,* adv; *northern* derives from OE *northerne; northward* (whence *northwardly*), from OE *northweard; northwest,* direct from OE; *northeast,* however, is *north+east.*

3. *Nordic* anglicizes the SciL *nordicus,* of the north: cf F *nordique,* derived rather from F *nord.*

4. *Northman,* an ancient Scandinavian, derives, at least partly, from OE *northman; Norseman* is a *Norse* man, *Norse* deriving from D *Noorsch,* a Norwegian, from *noordsch,* northern, MD *nordsch, nortsch;* cf OFris *norsk,* contr of *northesk. Norman,* however, comes from OF *normant*—nom *normans, normanz*—whence F *Normand:* and OF *normant* comes, through Frankish *\*nortman* and perh through C9 ML *nortmannus,* from OGmc (cf OE *northman,* OFris *northmann*).

5. *Norway* derives from late ML *Norwegia,* earlier *Norvegia,* from ON *Norvegr:* ON *northr,* north+*vegr,* way (cf WAY); also from ML *Norwegia* derives *Norwegian*—cf the F *Norvégien* from *Norvège.*

6. *Northumbria* is a latinized form of *Northumberland,* ON *Northymbralond,* land of the *Northymbre,* Dwellers *North* of the River *Humber.* (Ekwall.)

**Norway; Norwegian.** See prec, para 5.

**nose** (n, hence v), with many obvious cpds— **nosebag, nosepiece,** etc., but note **nosegay**—and adj **nosey** or **nosy; nostril,** cf **nozzle** (n, hence v) and **nuzzle; naze** and **ness;**—L: **nasal,** whence **nasality** and **nasalize**—cf the F *nasalité* and *nasaliser;* **nasute; nasturtium;** Nez Percé;—**nares, narine.**

1. *Nose,* OE *nosu,* is akin to OFris *nose,* OHG *nasa,* MHG-G *nase;* ON *nös* (with modern Scan cognates); Lith *nósis,* OSl *nos,* OP *nozy;* L *nāsus,* nose, and *nārēs,* nostrils; Skt *nāsā.*

### Germanic

2. *Nosegay,* a posy, cpds *nose+*the n (from adj) *gay,* something showy: something bright that one holds to the nose.

3. *Nostril,* ME *nostrill,* earlier *nosethril,* earliest *nosethirl,* derives from OE *'nosthyrl: nos-,* c/f of *nosu,* nose+*-thyrl,* c/f of *thyrel,* a hole, an opening, n from adj *thyrel,* for *thyrhel,* pierced, from *thurh,* through (cf THROUGH).

4. *Nose* has dim *nozzle* (for *\*nossle*); cf 'to *nuzzle',* to thrust (etc.) with the nose—a vowel-changed freq of 'to *nose'.*

5. OE *nosu,* nose, has cognate *naes, nes* (cf ON *nes*), a *nose-like* projection of land into sea, a promontory, whence, like the E *naze* (? influenced by F *nez*), the E *ness.*

6. L *nāsus,* nose, has adj *nāsūtus,* long-nosed, keen-nosed, whence E *nasute;* ML *nāsāle,* a nose-piece, becomes, via MF *nasal, nasel,* the E n *nasal;* the E adj *nasal* is rather adopted from EF-F, formed learnedly from MF-F *nez* (OF *nes*), nose, which occurs in *Nez Percé* (pl *Nez Percés*), lit Pierced-Nose, the F name of several W Amerind tribes.

7. L *nāsus* has the cpd *nasturtium,* a cress, lit a nose-twist: *nas-,* s of *nāsus+turt-,* corruption of *tort-,* s of *tortus,* pp of *torquere,* to twist (f.a.e., TORT): which, however, is perh f/c.

8. Akin to L *nāsus* is L *nārēs,* the nostrils, adopted by Med, with adjj *narial* and *narine* (-*ine*), the latter perh suggested by OF-F *narine,* a nostril.

**nosism.** See US, para 3.

**nostalgic** derives from *nostalgia,* homesickness: SciL term: *nost-,* s of Gr *nostos,* a return to one's home+Gr *algia,* pain (as in *neuralgia*).

**nostril.** See NOSE, para 3.

**nostrum.** See US, para 3.

**not.** See NO.

**notabilia.** See para 2 of:

**notable, notabilia, notability; notary,** whence **notarial, notariate, notarize; notate, notation** (whence **notational**)—whence, anl, **notative** and **notator; note** (n and v), whence **notebook, noteless, noteworthy; notice,** n, hence v—whence **noticeable; notify, notification; notion,** whence **notional, notionary; notoriety, notorious,** cf the Sc **notour.** —Cpds: **annotate, annotation** (whence, anl, **annotative), annotator; connotation** (whence, anl, **connotative), connote; denotation** (whence **denotative), denote; prenotation.**

1. The imm source of all these words is L *nota,* a manner of designating, a means of recognition, a brand, a mark: deriving from or intimately related to *nōtus,* pp of *nōscō,* I begin to know, *nōuī,* I know. L *nōscere,* to (begin to) know, OL *gnōscere,* pp *gnōtus,* is akin to Gr *gignōskein,* to know (*gi-,* redup of the r+IE r *\*gnō-,* to know+ *-sk-,* IE formative element+*-ein,* inf suffix), with pp *gnōtos;* to OIr *gnáth,* and Skt *jñātás,* known, both so clearly and so very closely related to the syn Gr *gnōtos* and L (*g)nōtus;* Lith *žinóti,* OSl *znati,* to know; OE *cunnan,* to know, *cann* or *can,* I know, therefore E CAN; many OGmc cognates; Skt *jānāti,* he knows, OHG *-knaan,* E KEN; OE *cnāwan,* E KNOW.

2. L *nota,* a mark, becomes OF-F *note,* adopted by E. The derivative L *notāre,* to designate with brand or mark, becomes OF-F *noter,* whence 'to *note'. Notāre* has derivative *notābilis,* worthy of note, whence MF-F *notable,* adopted by E; *notābilis* has neupl *notabilia,* used as n 'things worth noting' and adopted by Continental and E erudites.

3. L *nota,* in its sense 'mark in or of writing', has derivative *notārius,* secretary, whence, via OF-MF

notarie (MF-F *notaire*), the E *notary*, with legal sense taken from late MF. *Notariate* perh derives from EF-F *notariat*.

4. L *notāre* has pp *notātus*, whence the E adj and rare v *notate*; on the s *notāt-* arises *notātiō*, o/s *notātiōn-*, whence, perh via MF-F, the E *notation*.

5. L *nōtus*, known, has derivative *nōtitia*, a being recognized or known, whence MF-F *notice*, adopted by E; its derivative *nōtificāre*, to make known, becomes MF-F *notifier*, whence 'to notify', the subsidiary ML *nōtificātiō*, o/s *nōtificātiōn-*, passing through MF-F to become E *notification*; and its LL derivative *nōtiō* (o/s *nōtiōn-*), notoriety, (but also) definition, a species of knowledge, becomes—perh via EF-F—the E *notion*.

6. L *nōtus*, known, has the LL *-ōrius* extn *nōtōrius*, causing to be known, whence—cf the MF-F *notoire*—the E *notorious*; derivative ML *nōtōrietās*, o/s *notōrietāt-*, becomes—perh via the late MF-F *notoriété*—the E *notoriety*. The Sc *notour*, notorious, app blends the F *notoire* and the L *nōtōrius*.

7. L *notāre* has several prefix-cpds relevant to E, the alphabetical first being *annotāre*, to put marks or notes *ad* or against, at, to, pp *annotātus*, whence 'to annotate'; derivative *annotātiō*, o/s *annotātiōn-*, yields, perh via MF-F, the E *annotation*; agent *annotātor* is form-adopted by E.

8. ML *connotāre* (int *con-*), to mark or note, hence to suggest, becomes 'to connote'; derivative *connotātiō*, o/s *connotātiōn-*, becomes *connotation*.

9. L *dēnotāre*, to mark or note down, to signify, yields MF-F *dénoter*, whence 'to denote'; derivative *dēnotātiō*, o/s *dēnotātiōn-*, yields late MF-F *dénotation*, whence E *denotation*.

10. L *praenotāre*, to mark, hence to note, beforehand (*prae-*), becomes 'to prenote'; derivative LL *praenotātiō*, o/s *praenotātiōn-*, becomes *prenotation*. But *prenotion*, a presentiment, derives from L *praenōtiō* (*prae-+nōtiō*, as in para 5, s.f.), o/s *praenōtiōn-*.

notary. See prec, para 3.

notation. See NOTABLE, para 4.

notch (n, hence v): perh via *a notch*, mistakenly for *an otch*: MF *oche*: OF *osche* (F *hoche*), from OF *oscher* (F *hocher*), *oschier*, to notch: o.o.o.; but cf NICK.

note, whence note-book, -case, -worthy. See NOTABLE, para 2.

nothing (whence nothingness)=*no*+*thing*. Cf *anything*.

notice, n—hence v, whence noticeable. See NOTABLE, para 5.

notification, notify (whence notifiable). See NOTABLE, para 5.

notion. See NOTABLE, para 5, s.f.

notochord. See the element *noto-*.

notoriety, notorious. See NOTABLE, para 6.

nototribe. See the element *noto-*.

notour. See NOTABLE, para 6.

Notre Dame, the cathedral of Our Lady: MF-F *notre* (OF-MF *nostre*), from L *noster* our+OF-F

*dame*, lady, from L *domina*, mistress of the house (*domus*).

notwithstanding=*not*+*withstanding*, presp of *withstand*, to resist (successfully), q.v. at STAND.

nougat, adopted from F, comes from Prov *nougat*, OProv *nogat*, from *noga*, nut: via VL, from L *nux* (gen *nucis*), a nut: lit, 'made with nuts': f.a.e., NUCLEUS.

nought. See NAUGHT.

noumenal, noumenism, noumenon. See NOUS, para 1, s.f.

noun. See NAME, para 8.

nourish (whence the pa nourishing), nourishment; nurse (n, hence v), whence nursemaid and pa, vn nursing, cf nursery and nursling; nurture, n hence v; nutricial, nutricism; nutrient, nutriment, nutrimental, nutrition, nutritious (whence, anl, nutritive). —natant, natation;—naiad, naid; nereid, Nereis, Nereus.

Indo-European

1. *Nourishment* derives from OF *norrissement*, from *norrir*, varr *norir*, *nurir*, *nurrir* (F *nourrir*), whence, via such forms as presp *norissant* and 'nous *norissons*', we nourish, the ME *norisen*, *norischen*, whence 'to nourish': and OF *norir*, *nurir*, etc., derives from L *nūtrīre*, to give milk to, hence to feed, to nourish: akin to L *nūtrīx*, a nursing mother, a foster-mother; akin also to L *natāre*, to swim, a freq of *nāre*, to float, and to Gr *naein*, to flow: all are var derivatives from an IE r *\*sneu-*, varr *\*snau-*, *\*snu-*, to give milk to, as in Skt *snauti*, she gives milk, *snāti*, he bathes, MIr *snāim*, I swim: a good example of the ubiquitous IE prefix *s-*. Ult IE r, prob *\*(s)na-*.

Greek

2. Gr *naō*, I flow, has derivative *naias* (gen *naiados*), a water nymph, whence L *naias* (gen *naiadis*), whence E *naiad*—perh via MF-F *naiade*; with contr *naid*.

3. Akin to Gr *naias* is Gr *Nēreus*, a sea god, whence, via L, E *Nereus*; any of his daughters is *Nērēis* (f suffix *-is*), gen *Nērēidos*, L *Nērēis*, gen *Nērēidis*, E *Nereïd*.

Latin

4. L *nūtrīre* (as in para 1) has presp *nūtriens*, o/s *nūtrient-*, whence the E adj nutrient. *Nūtrīre* has derivative *nūtrīmentum*, whence E *nutriment*; derivative LL *nūtrīmentālis* yields *nutrimental*. On the pp *nūtrītus* arises LL *nūtrītiō*, o/s *nūtrītiōn-*, whence MF-F *nutrition*, adopted by E; *nutritious*, however, derives from L *nūtrīcius*, *nūtrītius*, from *nūtrīx*, nursing mother; *nutritory*, nutritive, derives from LL *nūtrītōrius*, from *nūtrītus*.

5. L *nūtrix*, gen *nūtrīcis*, yields the obsol *nutrice*, a nurse; from the L o/s *nūtrīc-* come both the E adj *nutricial* and the n *nutricism* (*-ism*) in Biol.

6. The L adj *nūtrīcius* (from *nūtrix*) has f *nūtrīcia*, used also as LL n for foster-mother, nurse: OF *nurrice*, *norrice* (F *nourrice*): ME *nurice*,

*norice*, later *nors*, *nurse*, E *nurse*, whence *nursling* and, from the v, *nursery* (cf the F *nourricerie*).

7. The L pp *nūtrītus* has yet another relevant derivative: LL *nūtrītūra*, OF *norriture*, *norreture* (F *nourriture*), ME *noriture*, contr to *norture*, whence, reshaped after the L original, E *nurture*.

8. L *natāre*, to swim, has presp *natans*, o/s *natant*-, whence E *natant*; and pp *natātus*, whence *natātiō*, o/s *natātiōn*-, whence EF-F and E *natation*.

**nous; noetic; noumenal, noumenism, noumenon** (pl **noumena**);—**paranoia**, whence (after *maniac*) **paranoiac**, adj hence n, whence, in turn, **paranoid**.

1. *Nous*, (Phil) mind, whence (orig, University sl) ready wit, shrewdness, is adopted from Gr *nous* (Attic νοῦς), a contr of *noos* (νόος), mind—cf *noéō*, I take thought, I perceive, whence *noēsis*, intellectual grasp, whence *noētikos*, intellectually apprehensible, E *noetic*. Gr *noein*, to perceive, has pp *noumenos*, with neu *noumenon* used as n 'a thing perceived, or thought', whence the Phil terms *noumenal* (perh after *phenomenal*) and *noumenism*. With the metaphysical, esp Kantian *noumenon*, cf the derivative F *noumène*.

2. Gr *nóos*, mind, has derivative -*noia*, as in *paranoia* (*para*, beside), madness (cf, sem, '*beside* oneself'), adopted by alienists; with derivative *paranoiac*, cf the F *paranoïaque* (from F *paranoïa*).

**nouveauté.** See para 3 of:

**nova, novum, novus; novalia, novate, novation** (whence **novative, novatory**), **novator, novity; novel** (adj, n)—whence **first, novelette** (cf It *noveletta*), hence **novelettish**, and second, **novelist**, whence **novelistic**, and, third, **novelize; novelty** (cf the EF-F *nouveauté*); **novella, nouvelle; Novial; novice, noviciate** (-**itiate**); L cpds: **innovant, innovate, innovation** (whence, anl, **innovative**), **innovator** (whence, anl, **innovatory**); **renovate, renovation** (whence, anl, **renovative**), **renovator** (whence, anl, **renovatory**).—Gr: **neon**, cf the element *neo*- and note esp **neolithic, neologism, neophyte**.—Gmc: **new** (adj, adv, n), **newfangle** (whence **newfangled**), **newly, newness, news** (whence **newsboy, newsman, newspaper**, the coll adj **newsy**)—**anew**—**renew**, whence **renewal**; prob akin, ult, to sep NOW.

### Indo-European

1. *Nova*, a temporarily 'new' star, *novum*, as in Francis Bacon's *Novum Organum*, and *novus*, as in *novus homo* (new man), are resp the f, neu, m of ML *novus*, L *nouus*, new, most recent, s and r *nou*-: cf Gr *neos* (for \**newos*) and Skt *návas*; cf also Hit *newas*, Tokh A *ñu*; OIr *nūe*, W *newydd*, Br *névez* (early *nouuid*), OC \**novios*; OSl *novŭ*, Lith *naujas* (cf Skt *návyas*); Go *niujis*, OHG *niuwi*, MHG *niuwe*, G *neu*, OS *niuwi*, OFris *nīe*, *nī*, OE *nīwe*, *nēowe*; ON *nȳr*. The Gmc r is \**niwj*, with -*j*- an extn id with that of Lith *nawjas* and the longer Skt var *návyas*; the IE r being \**new*- (or \**neu*-), with var \**nu*-. (Hofmann; Walshe.)

### Greek

2. Gr *neos*, new, has neu *neon*, whence the Chem

gaseous element *neon*. Of the many *neo*- cpds, at least three deserve sep mention:

*neolithic*, of the new stone age: cf LITHIC;

*neologism*, a new word, imm from F *néologisme*, and *neology*, the use or science of new words, imm from F *néologie*; cf LOGIC;

*neophyte*: perh via late MF-F *néophyte*: LL *neophytus*: LGr *neophutos*, a new convert: Gr *neophutos*, newly engendered or planted: Gr *phutos*, grown (cf *phuton*, a plant): *phuein*, to grow: f.a.e., PHYSIC.

### Latin

3. L *nouus* (s and r *nou*-) has the foll simple derivatives affecting E:

*nouāle*, a field new-ploughed, pl *nouālia*, ML *novālia*, retained in Sc Law;

*nouāre*, to make new, pp *nouātus*, ML *novātus*, legal E 'to *novate*'; derivative *nouātiō*, o/s *nouātiōn*-, ML *novātiōn*-, obsol E *novation*; agent *nouātor*, ML *novātor*, adopted by E, but obsol;

*nouellus* (dim of *nouus*), ML *novellus*, whence OF-MF *novel*, whence E *novel*, adj; the LL *nouellae* (*constitūtiōnes*) perh suggested the VL *nouella*, prop neupl, whence ML *novella*, f sing n, whence—via derivative It *novella*—the late MF-F *nouvelle*, a short or middle-length story, whence E *novel*, with sense gradually enlarging to that of full-length story (the F *roman*); It *novella* and its derivative the Sp *novela* are occ used by scholars; the It dim *novelletta* perh suggested the E *novelette* (more prob E *novel*+dim suffix -*ette*); E *novelist*, prob *novel*+-*ist*, was perh suggested by EF-F *nouvelliste* or even the It *novellista* or Sp *novelista*.

LL *nouellitās* (from *nouellus*), o/s *nouellitāt*-, MF-EF *novelté*, E *novelty*; MF-EF *novelté* became EF-F *nouveauté*, partly, in pl -*tés*, adopted by commercial E for 'novelties';

LL *nouitās*, o/s *nouitāt*-, ML *novitāt*- MF-EF *novité*, E *novity*;

*nouītius*, better *nouīcius*—extn of *nouus* used as n —a newly acquired slave, hence, in LL, an Eccl probationer, whence OF-F *novice*, adopted by E; *noviciate* and *novitiate* come, the former prob via EF-F *noviciat* (? imm from *novice*) and the latter app imm from ML *novītiātus* (gen -*ūs*), from ML *novītius*.

4. Otto Jespersen's new 'universal language' *Novial*=*novus*+*i*nternational *a*uxiliary *l*anguage.

5. The relevant L prefix-cpds are:

LL *innouāre* (int *in*-), to make new, to renew, presp *innouans*, o/s *innouant*-, ML -*vant*, Bot adj *innovant*, pp *innouātus*, E 'to *innovate*'; derivative *innouātiō*, o/s *innouātiōn*-, whence, perh via MF-F, the E *innovation*; ML *innovātor*, adopted by E;

L *renouāre*, to make new again, to renew, pp *renouātus*, E 'to *renovate*'; derivative LL *renouātiō*, o/s *renouātiōn*-, ML -*vation*, whence, perh via MF-F *rénovation*, the E *renovation*; ML *renovātor*, adopted by E.

### Germanic

6. The OE adj *nīwe*, *nēowe*, becomes ME *newe*,

E *new*; the E adv *new* derives from OE *nīwe* (from the adj). Much as the syn F *les nouvelles* comes from the adj *nouveau*, f *nouvelle*, so does E *news* come from *new*. The adv *newly* goes back to OE *nīwlīce*; *newness* to OE *nīwnes*.

7. *Newfangle*—whence the adj *newfangled*—derives from ME *newefangel*, a novelty: *newe*, new +*fangel*, a silly device or contrivance, app a dim from ME *fangen*, to seize or grasp: a *grasping* or taking-up of something *new*.

8. The adv *anew* is lit 'of (*a-* for *of*) new': cf the F *de nouveau* and ML *de novo* (lit, from new), afresh.

9. 'To *renew*'=*re-*, again+the obs 'to *new*', from OE *nīwan*: cf the OF *renoveler*, MF-F *renouveler*, from OF-MF *novel*, MF-F *nouveau*.

**novel**, adj. See prec, para 3.

**novel**, n; **novelette**; **novelist**. See NOVA, para 3 (at *nouellus*).

**novella**. See NOVA, para 3 (at *nouellus*).

**novelty**. See NOVA, para 3 (at *nouellitās*).

**November**. See NINE, para 3.

**novena, novenary, novendial, novennial**. See NINE, para 3.

**Novial**. See NOVA, para 4.

**novice, noviciate** (or **novitiate**). See NOVA, para 3, s.f.

**novity**. See NOVA, para 3 (at *nouitās*).

**now**, ME *nou*, earlier *nu*, OE *nū*, is akin to OFris, Go, OS, OHG *nu*, MHG *nu, nuon*, G *nu* (well), *nun* (now), ON *nū*; OSl *nyné*, Lith *nù, nūnai*; L *nunc*; Gr *nu, nun, nūni*; Skt *nu, nū, nūnám*; Hit and Tokh A *nu*, then: ult akin to NEW.

**nowadays**=*now*+*a*, on+*days*: in these days.

**nowel**. See NUCLEUS, para 6.

**nowhere**. OE *nāhwǣr*: cf NO and WHERE.

**nowise**: (in) *no wise* (manner): cf WISE, n.

**noxal**. See para 1 of:

**noxious**—**obnoxious**; **noxa, noxal**; **nocent**—**innocent** (adj, hence n), **innocence** and **innocency**—**ninny**; **nocuous**—**innocuous**; **nuisance**; **internecine** and **pernicious**; **nectar, nectareous, nectarine, nectary**; cf the element *necro-*.

1. *Obnoxious* derives from L *obnoxiōsus*: perh the prefix *ob-*+*noxius*, harmful. *Noxious* derives from L *noxius*, from *noxa*, harm, injury, retained by E as a Med term, with adj *noxal* (L *noxālis*): and *noxa*, prob for *\*nocsa*, derives from *nocēre* (s and r *noc-*), to cause—to prepare—the death of, hence, by a weakening of the sense, to be (very) harmful to; *nocēre*, in short, was orig a caus (marked by verb *-o-* from noun *-e-*) from *nex* (gen *necis*), death, esp if violent. L *nex* is prob akin to Gr *nekros* (adj), dead, hence a dead body. The IE r is app *\*nek-*, to cause to die: cf Skt *nāçayáti*, he causes to die.

2. *Nocēre*, has presp *nocens*, o/s *nocent-*, whence E *nocent*, harmful; derivative LL *nocentia* becomes E *nocency*. These two words are overshadowed by the negg *innocent*, from OF-F *innocent*, from *innocent-*, o/s of the L adj *innocens*, incapable of doing harm, hence guiltless, and *innocence*, var *innocency*, from OF-F *innocence*, from L

*innocentia*, from *innocens*. From a*n innoc*ent comes —via *a n*innoc*ent*—*ninny*.

3. *Nocēre* has derivative adj *nocuus*, whence E *nocuous*; the neg *innocuus* yields *innocuous*.

4. *Nocēre* becomes VL *\*nocere*, whence OF-F *nuire*, presp *nuisant*, whence the OF-(archaic)F n *nuisance*, harmfulness, harm, adopted by E, with gradually weakening senses.

5. L *nex*, (violent) death, o/s *nec-*, has two prefix-cpds affecting E:

*internecāre* (*inter-* used int), to slay to the last person, with derivative adj *internecīnus*, mutually murderous, E *internecine*;

*perniciēs* (int *per-*; *-nic-* from *nec-*), massacre, hence merely ruin, (heavy) loss, with derivative *perniciōsus*, destructive, MF-F *pernicieux*, f *pernicieuse*, E *pernicious*.

6. Akin to *nex* is the very odd Gr cpd *nektar*, a death-overcoming (drink), the drink of the Olympian gods, whence—via L *nectar*—the MF-F and E *nectar*, any delicious potion: r *nek-*, as in Gr *nekus*, a corpse, *nekros*, dead+*-tar*, from Skt *tarás*, victorious (cf *tarati*, he overcomes). Gr *nektar* has adj *nektareos*, L *nectareus*, E *nectareous*, with varr *nectareal, nectarean, -ial, -ian*, and esp *nectarine*, whence—via *nectarine peach*—the n *nectarine*, a delicious smooth-skinned variety of peach. The E *nectar* has derivative *nectary*, Bot SciL *nectarium*, a nectar-secreting gland.

**nozzle**. See NOSE, para 4.

**nuance**, adopted from MF-F: from OF *nuer*, to cloud, to shade: from OF-F *nue*, a cloud: VL *\*nūba*: L *nūbēs*: cf obs W *nudd*, fog, and Cor *nuibren*, cloud.

**nub** is a var of *knub*, itself a var of KNOB; hence AE *nubbin*, a small (or an imperfect) ear of corn; hence also the dim *nubble*, with adj *nubbly*.

**nubile**. See LYMPH, para 5.

**nuclear** (occ var **nucleal**); **nucleate** (adj, v), whence **nucleation** and **nucleator**; **nucellus**—cf **nucleus**, whence **nuclein** (Chem *-in*) and **nucleoid**—**nucleolar**, from **nucleolus**—**nux, nucal, nucament, nucule; enucleate**, whence **enucleation**.—**Nut**, whence **nutcracker, nuthatch** (ME *notehach, nuthake*)—and **nutty; nutmeg**; sl **nuts**;—**newel, nowel**.

1. All these words derive from or are akin to L *nux*, a nut, o/s *nuc-*: cf OIr *cnú*, Ga *cnù*, var *cnò* (pl *cnothan*), W *cneuen*, Cor *cnyfan*, OC *\*knovā*; ON *hnot*; OHG-MHG *nuz*, G *Nuss*, MD *nuete, note, notte, not*, D *noot*: Gmc r, *\*hnut-*; IE (W European only), *\*knud-*.

2. E *nut*, ME *nute*, derives from OE *hnutu*—cf ON *hnot* above. The cpd *nutmeg*, ME *notemuge*, consists of ME *note*, var of *nute*, nut+*muguette*, itself an alteration of (noix) *muscade*: OProv *muscada*, f of *muscat*, smelling like MUSK.

3. L *nux*, retained in the orig ML *nux vomica*, lit a nut to make one vomit, has LL adj *nucālis*, whence E *nucal*; derivative *nucāmenta*, fir-cones, gives us the Bot *nucament*; dim *nucella* suggests SciL *nucellus*; dim *nucula* becomes *nucule*.

4. Dim *nuculeus* has contr *nucleus*, kernel, adopted by several IE languages. From its s *nucle-*

spring both F *nucléaire* (for the form, cf the ML *nucleárius*, a nut-bearing tree), whence E *nuclear*, and E *nucleal*; also the L v *nucleăre*, to form a kernel, pp *nucleătus*, whence the E adj and v *nucleate*. The prefix-cpd *ēnucleăre*, to remove the kernel from, has pp *ēnucleătus*, whence 'to *enucleate*'.

5. L *nucleus* duly acquires a LL dim of its own: *nucleolus*, a little kernel, adopted by Sci.

6. *Nowel* and *newel* both derive from ME *nowell*: OF *nouel*, *noiel*, fruit-stone, newel: ML *nucăle*, prop the neu of LL-ML *nucălis*, of or like a nut, nut-shaped.

**nucule.** See NUCLEAR, para 3.

**nude.** See NAKED, para 2.

**nudge** (v, hence n) is of Scan origin: cf Nor dial *nuggja* (var of *nugga*), to push gently: ? ult echoic.

**nudity.** See NAKED, para 2.

**nugacious, nugacity, nugatory; nugae.**

L *nūgae*, trifles, is o.o.o.: ? for \**nucae*, nut-shells, from *nuc-*, o/s of L *nux*, a nut. Derivative adj *nūgāx*, o/s *nūgāc-*, becomes E *nugacious*; subsidiary LL *nūgācitās*, o/s *nūgācitāt-*, becomes *nugacity*. L *nūgae* has also the derivative v *nūgāri*, to trifle, whence the adj *nūgātōrius*, E *nugatory*.

**nugget** is app a dim of E dial *nug*, a lump, a block; whence *nuggety*.

**nuisance.** See NOXIOUS, para 4.

**null,** adj, hence (after *annul*) v; **nullify; nullification; nullity;—annul,** whence *annulment*.

1. 'To *annul*', ME *anullen, adnullen*, MF *anuller* (F *annuler*), *adnuller*, derives from LL *annūllāre, adnūllāre*, to bring to nothing: *ad*, to+*null*us, not any+inf suffix *-āre*: and *nūllus* itself=*ne*, not+*ūllus*, any, akin to *ūnus*, one, q.v. at ONE. L *nūllus* becomes OF-F *nul*, whence E *null*.

2. L *nūllus* has the ML derivative *nūllitās*, whence, perh via MF-F *nullité*, the E *nullity*, and the LL cpd *nūllificāre*, whence 'to *nullify*', with derivative *nūllificātiō*, o/s *nūllificātiōn-*, whence *nullification*.

**numb, numbness.** See NIMBLE, para 3.

**number.** See NIMBLE, para 6.

**numbles.** See LOIN, para 4.

**numen.** See NUTANT, para 3.

**numeral; numerate, numeration, numerator; numerical, numerous.** See NIMBLE, para 4.

**numinism, numinous.** See NUTANT, para 3.

**numismatic(s), numismatist.** See NIMBLE, para 10.

**numskull** is a *numb-skull*: cf, sem, the G *Dummkopf*.

**nun; nunnery.**

The latter derives from late ME *nunnerie*, earlier *nonnerie*: a blending of ME *nunne* (whence *nun*) and OF-F *nonne*+suffix *-erie, -ery*. Nun, OE *nunne*, derives from Eccl LL *nonna*, a nun, also later a child's nurse: very prob a nursery word, akin to Gr *nanna*, aunt, and Skt *nanā*, mother, Alb *nanë*, mother, (wet-) nurse.

**nuncio,** a Papal permanent representative abroad: It *nuncio*, obs var of *nunzio*: L *nūntius*, messenger: perh \**nouentius*, for \**nouiuentius*, one

new- (L *noui*, c/f of *nouus*) coming (L *uent*um, supine of *uen*ire) with a message.

2. L *nūntius* has derivative *nūntiāre*, with pp *nūntiātus*, whence *nūntiātiō*, o/s *nūntiātiōn-*, obs E *nunciation*, whence, anl, *nunciative* and *nunciatory*; LL agent *nūntiātor*. This v and its derivatives figure most in the cpds *annūntiāre, dēnūntiāre, ēnūntiāre, internūntiāre, praenūntiāre, prōnūntiāre, renūntiāre*.

3. L *annūntiāre, adnūntiāre*, to bear, hence to deliver, a message *ad*, to, becomes OF *anoncier* (F *annoncer*), ME *anounce*, E 'to *announce*', whence *announcement* and *announcer*. The pp *annūntiāt*us, whence the obsol 'to *annunciate*', has derivative *annūntiātiō*, o/s *annūntiātiōn-*, E *annunciation* (perh via OF-F *annonciation*), whence, anl, *annunciative*; derivative LL *annūntiātor* becomes *annunciator*, which perh suggests *annunciatory*.

4. D *dēnūntiāre* (int *dē-*), to declare solemnly, to cite as a witness, becomes OF *denoncer* (F *dé-*), whence, after *announce*, the E 'to *denounce*', whence *denouncement* and *denouncer*. The presp *dēnūntians* accounts for the adj *denunciant*; pp *dēnūntiātus*, for 'to *denunciate*'. The L derivatives *dēnūntiātiō* (o/s *-iōn-*)—LL *dēnuntiātīuus* (ML *-īvus*)—*dēnūntiātor* become resp *denunciation* (perh via MF-F *dénonciation*)—*denunciative*—*denunciator* (cf the MF-F *dénonciateur*).

5. L *ēnūntiāre*, to make known *ē-* or abroad, becomes EF-F *énoncer*, whence, after *announce*, 'to *enounce*'. The pp *ēnūntiātus* yields 'to *enunciate*'. The L derivatives *ēnūntiātiō* (o/s *-iōn-*)—*enūntiātiuus* (ML *-ivus*)—LL *ēnūntiātor* give us resp *enunciation* (cf late MF-F *énonciation*)—*enunciative* (cf MF-F *énonciatif*)—*enunciator*, whence, anl, *enunciatory*.

6. L *internūntiāre* becomes the obs 'to *internounce*'; *internūntius*, an intermediary, becomes It *internunzio*, whence, after *nuncio*, the E *internuncio*.

7. L *praenūntiāre*, to announce beforehand, becomes obs 'to *prenunciate*'; its derivative *praenūntius* leads to the Sci adj *prenuncial*.

8. L *prōnūntiāre*, to announce *prō-* or publicly, becomes OF-F *prononcer*, ME *pronouncen*, E 'to *pronounce*', whence *pronouncement, pronouncer*, pa *pronouncing*. On the pp *prōnūntiāt*us arise *prōnūntiātiō* (o/s *-iōn-*), in LL 'pronunciation', OF *pronunciation* (MF-F *pronon-*), adopted by E—LL *prōnūntiātīuus* (ML *-īvus*), E *pronunciative*—*prōnūntiātor*, E *pronunciator. Unpronounceable* was perh suggested by EF-F *inprononçable*; *pronunciamento* eases Sp *pronunciamiento*.

9. L *renūntiāre*, to announce in reply, (but also) to announce the retirement of, hence, esp in Eccl L, to reject: whence MF-F *renoncer*, ME *renouncen*, E 'to *renounce*', whence *renouncement* and *renouncer*. On the pp *renūntiāt*us arises *renūntiātiō* (o/s *-iōn-*), MF-F *renonciation*, E *renunciation*, whence, anl, *renunciative* and *renunciator*.

**nuncle.** See UNCLE.

**nuncupate, nuncupation, etc.** See NAME, para 11.

**nunks, nunky.** See UNCLE.

**nunnery.** See NUN.

**nuptial.** See LYMPH, para 6.

nurse, nursery, nursling. See NOURISH, para 6.

nurture. See NOURISH, para 7.

nut. See NUCLEAR, para 2.

nutant, nutate, nutation; innuendo; numen, numinism, numinous.

1. L *nūtāre*, to nod one's head frequently, with presp *nūtans*, o/s *nūtant-*, E adj *nutant*, and pp *nūtātus*, whence 'to *nutate*', and derivative *nūtātiō*, o/s *nūtātiōn-*, E *nutation*, is a freq of *nuere*, to nod the head, which has prefix-cpd *innuere*, to nod the head *in-* or to, esp as a sign, with gerund *innuendum*, abl *innuendo*, by nodding, hence by hinting, adopted by E, first as legal 'namely', hence the explanation itself, hence, in general use, an insinuation.

2. L *nuere*, to nod, has s and r *nu-*: cf the syn Gr *neuein* (s and r *neu-*) and also Sk *nāuti* (s, r *nau-*), *návate* (s *nav-*), he budges or stirs; perh cf also Ru *nukati*, to awaken, and prob cf the thinned form in OHG *nicchēn*, MHG-G *nicken*, to nod; IE r, \**neu-*, to nod. (Hofmann.)

3. L *nuere*, r *nu-*, has derivative *nūmen* (cf the Gr *neuma*), a divine nod (of, e.g., approval), hence divine power, hence (LL) a divinity, hence, in E, a divine presiding spirit; on the o/s *nūmin-* arise both *numinism* and *numinous*.

nuthatch. See NUCLEAR (heading).

nutmeg. See NUCLEAR, para 2.

nutricial, nutrient, nutriment, nutrition, nutritious. See NOURISH, paras 4–5.

nutty. See NUCLEAR (heading, s.f.).

nux vomica. See NUCLEAR, para 3.

nuzzle. See NOSE, para 3.

nyctalopia. See the element *nycti-*.

Nycteris. See NIGHT, para 4.

nylon is, as the manufacturers have told me, an arbitrary formation: neither *N.Y.* (New York)+ *Lon*don, as EW suggests, nor *ni*trogen+arbitrary *-lon*, as Webster proposes.

nymph, whence nymphal. See LYMPH, paras 3–4.

nympholepsy, nympholept. See the element *-lepsia*.

nymphomania, whence nymphomaniac. See MIND, para 4.

# O

**-o.** See Suffixes.

**-o-.** See Suffixes—an interpolation.

**o,** vocative; **oh!** and **ho!**
The 3rd is both an aspiration of the 2nd and a var of *ha!*; the 1st itself is orig exclamatory, as is the *hi* of *hi* (you), *there!* All such utterances—they cannot properly be called words—are common not only to all the IE languages but also to many others.

**O',** as in *O'Donnell*, means 'descendant': see FILIAL, para 3.

**o'** is short for *of*, as in 'The top o' the morning to you!'; also for *on*—cf the *a-* of *aboard*.

**oaf, oafish.** See ELF, para 2.

**oak,** whence **oaken** (cf ME *oken*, from *ok* or *oke*), comes—through ME *oke*, *ok*, var *ak*—from OE *āc*: cf OFris and OS *ēk*, OHG *eih*, MHG *eich*, G *Eiche*, MD *eike*, D *eik*, an oak; ON *eik*, a tree; cf, further off, the L *aesculus* (for *\*aeg-sculus*), mountain oak, and Gr *aigilōps*, a kind of oak: IE r, *\*aig-*.

**oakum:** OE *ācumba*: *ā-*, out (cf Go *ur-*, *us-*)+*cemban*, to comb, from *camb*, a comb (cf COMB).

**oar** (n, hence v): OE *ār*; akin to ON *ār* and its modern Scan cognates; to Fin *airo*; and perh, without *r*, to Gr *oiāx*, a tiller, Serb and Cz *oje*. (Holthausen.)

**oasis,** whence the adjj **oasal, oasitic,** is adopted from L from Gr *oasis*, of Eg origin: cf Eg *Uakh-t*; the Great Oasis, lit 'fertile region'—*Uah*tiu, dwellers there—and esp *uakh*, to be green, to bloom, to flourish; cf also Copt *ouahe*, oasis. The Eg base, therefore, is *uah-*.

**oast:** ME *ost*: OE *āst*: cf MD *ast, est, este,* D *eest* and prob L *aest*us, a burning heat.

**oat:** ME *ote*, var *ate*: OE *āte*, pl *ātan*: o.o.o.: one is, however, tempted to compare Lettish *auza* and OSl *ovĭsŭ*, which would bring us to L *auēna* (F *avoine*).

**oath:** ME *othe, oth,* var *ath*: OE *āth*: cf OFris and OS *ēth*, Go *aiths*, OHG *eid*, MHG *eit*, G *Eid*, MD *eyd, eit, eet*, D *eed*, ON *eithr*, OIr *oeth*, which, lit 'a going', suggests kinship with L *itus* (gen *itūs*), a going, prob from *it*um, the supine of *īre*, to go: ? basically 'a going together—in agreement'.

2. G *eid* has cpd *eidgenoss*, a confederate (*genoss* being a comrade): Swiss F *eydguenot*, softened to C16 F *eiguenot*, whence, by blending with the name of the Genevan syndic *Hugues* Bezanson, the EF-F *Huguenot*, a C16–17 F Protestant: adopted by E.

**oatmeal,** late ME *ote-meel, -mele,* cpds OAT+MEAL, ground grain.

**obbligato.** See LIGAMENT, para 7, s.f.

**obduracy, obdurate.** See DURABLE, para 4.

**obedience, obedient; obeisance; obey.** See AUDIBLE, para 5.

**obelisk, obelize, obelus.**
The 1st, a tapering pillar, derives from LL *obeliscus*, a little spit, Gr *obeliskos*, dim of *obelos* (o.o.o.), a spit (as over a fire), hence a pointed pillar, whence LL *obelus*, adopted by E; derivative Gr *obelizein*, to mark with an obelus or obelisk, yields 'to *obelize*'. For a spit-like sign in a manuscript, or in print, *obelisk* is now obsol, *obelus* customary.

**obese, obesity.** See EDIBLE, para 3.

**obey.** See AUDIBLE, para 5.

**obfuscate, obfuscation; subfusc.**
LL *obfuscāre*, to blacken, to obscure, has pp *obfuscātus*, whence 'to *obfuscate*'; derivative *obfuscātiō*, o/s *obfuscātiōn-*, becomes *obfuscation*. *Obfuscāre*=*ob-*+*fuscāre*, to darken, from *fuscus*, dark, dun, akin to DUSK. The cpd *subfuscus*, rather dark (*sub*, under), yields *subfuscous*, now often *subfusc*.

**obit, obiter dictum, obituary** (n, hence adj).
*Obit*, a funeral service, derives, via OF, from L *obitus*, from *obīre*, to encounter, go to meet (*ob*, against+*īre*, to go), in the derivative sense 'to die' (from *obīre mortem*, to meet with death). Intimately akin to L *obīre* is L *obiter*, on the way (*iter*, a journey), in passing, as in *obiter dicta*, incidental sayings (hence writings). *Obitus* has the ML derivative *obituārius*, a death-notice, whence the E n *obituary*, whence *obituarian*.

**object** (n, v), whence **objectify**, whence **objectification;** **objection,** whence **objectionable; objective** (adj, hence n), whence **objectivity; objector.**
The n *object* derives, like MF-EF *object*, EF-F *objet*, from ML *objectum*, L *obiectum*, a thing thrown, hence put, before, hence a thing presented to one's attention, prop the neu of *obiectus*, pp of *obicere* (contr of *obiicere*), to throw before, hence to oppose: *ob*, against, before | *-iicere, -icere,* the c/f of *iacere*, to throw. From the pp *obiectus*, ML *objectus*, comes, perh via MF-F *objecter*, 'to *object*'. Derivative LL *obiectiō*, o/s *obiectiōn-*, ML *objectiōn-*, yields OF-F, whence E, *objection*; the

derivative ML adj *objectīvus* yields MF-F *objectif* and, perh independently, E *objective*; the derivative LL agent *obiector*, ML *objector*, is adopted by E.

**objurgate, objurgation, objurgatory.**

L *obiurgāre*, to chide, consists of *ob*, against+ *iurgāre*, to dispute, to quarrel, itself perh from *ius*, law, a right. The pp *obiurgātus*, ML *objurgātus*, gives us 'to *objurgate*'; derivative *obiurgātiō*, o/s *obiurgātiōn-*, becomes *objurgation*, and derivative *obiurgātōrius*, *objurgatory*.

**oblate** (adj, hence n) derives from L *oblātus*, pp of *offerre*, to offer (see OFFER); derivative LL *oblātiō*, o/s *oblātiōn-*, becomes, prob via OF-F, *oblation*.

**obligate, obligation, obligatory, oblige.** See LIGAMENT, para 7.

**oblique, obliquity.** See LIMIT, para 10.

**obliterate, obliteration, obliterator.** See LETTER, para 8.

**oblivion, oblivious, obliviscence.** See the 1st LIME, para 6.

**oblong.** See LONG, para 11.

**obloquy.** See LOQUACIOUS, para 6.

**obnoxious.** See NOXIOUS, para 1.

**oboe:** It *oboe*: EF-F *hautbois*, whence E *hautboy*: *haut*, high-toned, from L *altus* (cf ALTITUDE)+ *bois*, wood.

**obreption, obreptitious.** See REPTILE, para 2.

**obrogate, obrogation.** See ROGATION, para 9.

**obscene, obscenity.**

The latter derives from EF-F *obscénité*, from L *obscēnitāt*em, acc of *obscēnitās*, from *obscēnus*, varr *obscaenus*, *obscoenus*, whence, via EF-F *obscène*, the E *obscene*. L *obscēnus*, obscene, orig and prop of bad augury (hence ugly): o.o. ?.: perh *ob-*, against+*scaena*, a stage (SCENE); perh—though even less likely—*obs*, c/f of *ob*+*caenum*, mud, filth.

**obscurant,** whence **obscurantism; obscuration,** whence **obscurative; obscure** (adj, v), **obscurity.**

The L adj *obscūrus* (opp *clārus*) app=*ob*, against +*-scūrus*, akin to Skt *skutás*, covered (adj), and perh to OHG *scūr*, *scūra* (G *Scheuer*), a barn, where the light tends to be dim. *Obscūrus* becomes OF-F *obscur*, whence E *obscure*; derivative *obscūritās*, o/s *obscūritāt-*, becomes OF-F *obscurité*, whence E *obscurity*. *Obscūrus* has the further derivative *obscūrāre*, to darken, OF-F *obscurer*, E 'to *obscure*'; the presp *obscūrans*, o/s *obscūrant-*, yields the n *obscurant*; pp *obscūrāt*us has derivative *obscūrātiō*, o/s *obscūrātiōn-*, E *obscuration*.

**obsecrate, obsecration, obsecrator.** See SACRAMENT, para 18.

**obsequent; obsequies; obsequious; obsequy,** whence **obsequial.** See SEQUENCE, para 11.

**observable, observance, observant, observation, observatory, observe, observer.**

The base is afforded by L *obseruāre* (ML *observāre*), to watch over (physically, morally), to respect, to heed appropriately: *ob-*, over, against, etc.+*seruāre* (ML *servāre*), to keep safe, preserve,

conserve. ML *observāre* becomes OF-F *observer*, whence 'to *observe*', whence *observer*. Derivative *obseruābilis* accounts for MF-F and E *observable*. The presp *obseruans*, o/s *obseruant-*, becomes MF-F *observant*, adopted by E; derivative L *obseruantia* yields MF-F *observance*, adopted by E. The pp *obseruātus* has derivative *obseruātiō*, o/s *obseruātiōn-*, whence, via ML, the late MF-F *observation*, adopted by E, whence, anl, *observatory*—cf the EF-F *observatoire*. The neg *inobseruans* and its derivative *inobseruantia* have, perh via EF-F, yielded *inobservant*, *inobservance*.

**obsess, obsession** (whence **obsessional, obsessive**), **obsessor.** See SIT, para 15.

**obsidian** (whence **obsidianite**): LL *obsidiānus*, an opaque stone: L (Pliny's) *Obsidiānus lapis*, stone of *Obsidius*, an error for *Obsius*, who discovered it in Ethiopia.

**obsidional.** See SIT, para 15.

**obsignate, obsignation.** See SIGN, para 16.

**obsolescent,** whence **obsolescence; obsolete,** whence **obsoleteness, obsoletism.**

The L *obsolescere*, to wear out gradually, hence to fall gradually into disuse, cpds *ob-*+an inch derivative of *solēre*, to be in use, to be customary. Its presp is *obsolescens*, o/s *obsolescent-*, whence the E adj *obsolescent*; its pp *obsolētus* is used also as adj, whence *obsolete*.

**obstacle.** See STAND, para 29.

**obstetric,** etc. See STAND, para 29.

**obstinacy, obstinate.** See STAND, para 29.

**obstreperous.** See STREPENT.

**obstriction.** See the 2nd STRAIN, para 10.

**obstruct, obstruction** (whence **obstructive**). See STRUCTURE, para 8.

**obtain, obtention.** See TENABLE, para 6.

**obtest, obtestation.** See TESTAMENT, para 10.

**obtrude, obtrusion, obtrusive.** See THRUST, para 6.

**obtund, obtundent; obtuse.** See PIERCE, para 2.

**obumbrant, obumbrate, obumbration.** See UMBRA, para 8.

**obvention.** See VENUE, para 17.

**obverse, obvert.** See VERSE, para 15.

**obviate, obviation, obvious.** See VIA, para 15.

**obvolute, obvolvent.** See VOLUBLE.

**occasion, occasional.** See CADENCE, para 7.

**occidence, occident, occidental.** See CADENCE, para 7.

**occipital, occiput.** See CHIEF, para 2; cf the element *occipito-*.

**occlude; occlusion,** whence, anl, **occlusive.**

'To *occlude*', to shut up or confine, also to shut out, derives from L *occludere* (*ob-*+*claudere*, to shut), which has pp *occlus*us, whence ML *occlusiō*, a shutting, o/s *occlusiōn-*, whence, perh via F, the E *occlusion*.

**occult, occultation, occultism.** See HALL, para 14.

**occupant** (whence **occupancy**), **occupation, occupy** (whence **occupier**). See CAPABILITY, para 4.

**occur, occurrence.** See COURSE, para 10 (at *occurrere*).

**ocean, oceanic,** cf the element *oceano-*; **Oceania, Oceanus.**

An *ocean*, adopted from OF (F *océan*), derives from L *ōceanus*, trln of Gr *ōkeanos*, strictly Homer's *Ōkeanos* (L *Oceanus*) or great river encompassing the earth: perh cf Skt *āsáyānas*, lying over against. The learnèd EF-F derivative *océanique* becomes E *oceanic*. *Oceania*, the lands and waters of the central Pacific Ocean, is a Modern L formation.

**ocellar, ocellate(d), ocellus.** See OCULAR, para 2.

**ocelot**, a large spotted cat ranging from Texas to Patagonia, is adopted from F: perh via Sp *ocelote*: from Aztec (Nahuatl) tha*locelotl*, lit a 'field (*thalli*) jaguar (*ocelotl*)'.

**ocher** (AE) or **ochre**, whence **ocherous, ochreous, ochrous**; cf the element *ochro-*. *Ocher, ochre* derives from MF-F *ocre*: L *ōchra*: Gr *ōkhra*, from *ōkhros*, pale, esp pale yellow: perh (Hofmann) cf Skt *-āghras* in *vyāghrás*, a tiger

**ochlocracy.** See the element *ochlo-*.

**octachord, octagon, octahedron, octameter, octangular.** See the element *octa-*.

**octant; octave; October; octonary; octoroon**

L *octō*, 8, is akin to Gr *oktō*: f.a.e., EIGHT. Its ordinal is *octāuus*, ML *octāvus*, whence the E adj *octave*, the n being adopted from F, which takes it from ML *octāva* (*pars*), eighth part. Derivatives of *octō* include the Modern L *octans*, o/s *octant-*, whence the Geom *octant*, and *octoni*, 8 each, with derivative *octōnārius*, whence *octonary*. *Octōber* the eighth month of the Roman year, is elliptical for *octōber mensis*; the adj suffix *-ber* connotes 'of (a) month'. *Octoroon*, offspring of a quadroon and a white, cpds *octo-+-roon* as in *quadroon*.

**octopus.** See FOOT, para 25.

**octoroon.** See OCTANT, s.f.

**octuple**, 8-fold=*octu-*, c/f of L *octo*, 8+*-plex*, a fold (cf PLY).

**ocular, oculate, oculist, oculus**; cf the element *oculo-*; **ocellar, ocellate, ocellated, ocellus; œil-de-bœuf, œillade; ogle; inoculate, inoculation** (whence, anl, **inoculative**), **inoculator; inveigle**, whence **inveigler; antler**; cf the sep EYE and OPTIC.

1. L *oculus*, an eye (whence *oculist*), retained in E Arch, is akin to Hit tun-*akalas*, eye of the sun: 'Here, the suffix *-lo-* indicates an active being, of the animated sort, and has no diminutive value' (E & M). The L word prob has Gr cognates: cf OPTIC.

2. L derivatives relevant to E include: the adj *oculāris*, of the eye, whence *ocular*; *oculātus*, furnished with eyes, whence *oculate*; the dim *ocellus*, little eye (retained by Zoo), with E derivative *ocellar* (*-ar*, adj suffix); derivative *ocellātus*, furnished with little eyes, yields *ocellate*, often anglicized as *ocellated*.

3. L *oculus*, VL *oclus*, becomes OF-F *oeil*, as in *œil-de-bœuf*, lit 'ox's eye', retained by Arch; derivative MF-F *œillade* (*œil*+euphonic *-l-*+suffix *-ade*) is partly adopted by E for an amorous glance, the E 'an *ogle*, usu *ogling*', which derives from 'to *ogle*', from LG *oegeln*, the freq of *oegen*, to look at, to eye, cf D *oogen*, to eye, from *oog*,

an eye, MD *oge*, an eye, *ogen*, to eye: cf OE *ēage*, OFris *āge*, OHG *ouga*, all akin to L *oculus*.

4. L *oculus* has LL derivative v *oculāre*, to eye, with cpd *inoculāre*, lit to put an eye into, to put a bud or graft—a derivative sense of *oculus*—into, to engraft, with pp *inoculātus*, whence 'to *inoculate*', orig to graft (a tree) by budding, hence the Med sense; the derivative *inoculātiō*, o/s *inoculātiōn-*, becomes E *inoculation*, and derivative agent *inoculātor* is adopted by E.

5. ML has *aboculīs* (app *ab*, from, hence without +*oculis*, abl p of *oculus*, var *aboculus*, blind; hence OF-F *aveugle*, with derivative OF-F *aveugler*, to blind, whence AF *enveogler*, whence late ME *envegle*, whence 'to *inveigle*', orig to throw deceptive dust into the eyes of, hence to blind and lead astray, hence to entice away, to ensnare guilefully.

6. L *ante oculos*, before (in front of) the eyes, becomes the VL *\*antoculāris*, set before the eyes, hence that which is set there (sc *ramus*, a branch), OF *antoillier*, ME *auntelere*, E *antler*. (EW.)

**odd** (adj, hence n), whence **oddity** (*-ity*) and **oddment** (*-ment*); **odds**.

*Odd*, ME *odde*, comes from ON *oddi*, a point or a tip, hence the odd or third point or angle of a triangle, hence an odd number, a triangle, a tongue of land: cf ON *oddr*, point, e.g. of a weapon, OE *ord*, OHG-MHG *ort*, a point, G *Ort*, a place; cf also Lith *usnis*, a thistle (notably pointed), and Alb *usht*, an ear of corn. *Odd*, adj, used as n, has pl *odds*, uneven or unequal things.

**ode; epode, palinode; comedy, comedian, comedic, comic** (whence **comical**), **Comus; melody, melodic, melodious**, and (from *melo*dy) **melodism, melodist, melodize**, cf the element *melo-*; **monody, monodic; parody, parodic, parodist; prosody**, whence **prosodic; rhapsody, rhapsodic** (whence **rhapsodical**) and, from *rhapsody*, **rhapsodist** and **rhapsodize; threnode** or **threnody**, whence **threnodic** (cf **threne, threnetic, threnos**); **tragedy** (whence **tragedize**), **tragedian, tragedienne, tragic** (adj, hence n), extended as **tragical**; cf the element *tragi-* and **tragopan**.

1. *Ode*, adopted from late MF-F, derives from L *oda*, var of *odē*, from Gr *ōidē*, a song, esp if lyric: contr of *aoidē*, from *āeidein*, to sing: IE r, app *\*a-ud-*: cf Skt *vádati*, he sings, he plays music, and *vadinti*, to call.

2. Gr *ōidē* and *āeidein* have numerous cpds, of which the two most obvious are perh *epaidein*, to sing to, whence the adj *epōidos*, singing to, sung after, used also as n ('aftersong'), whence LL *epōdos, epōdus*, F *épode*, E *epode*; and *palinōidia* (*palin*, again+a var of *ōidē*), a song of recantation, LL *palinōdia*, whence, via MF-F, the E *palinode*.

3. But far more important is Gr *kōmōidia*: *kōmos*, a musical and dancing festivity, which, as *Kōmos*, a god of festive mirth, yields L, hence E, *Comus*+*ōidia*, a singing: L *comoedia*: MF *comedie* (F *comédie*): E *comedy*. The derivative Gr adj *kōmōidikos*, L *comoedicus*, becomes *comedic*. EF-F *comédien* and its f, *comédienne*, lead to E *comedian, comedienne*.

4. Gr *kōmos* has adj *kōmikos*, L *comicus*, MF-F *comique*, E *comic*, adj hence n.

5. The Gr cpd *melōidia*, a choral song (from *melōidos*, musical, lit melodious, from *melos*, a tune, lit a limb or member+*aoidos*, musical, a singer), becomes LL *melōdia*, OF *melodie* (F *mélodie*), E *melody*. The derivative Gr adj *melōidikos* becomes LL *melōdicus*, (EF-F *mélodique* and) E *melodic*; *melodious* derives from MF *melodieus* (F *mélodieux*), from *melodie*.

6. Gr *monōidia* (from the adj *monōidos*, singing *monos* or alone) becomes LL *monōdia*, E *monody*; derivative Gr *monōidikos* yields *monodic*.

7. Gr *parōidia* (*para*, beside), L *parōdia*, (EF-F *parodie* and) E *parody*, whence 'to *parody*' (cf the F *parodier*), has adj *parōidikos*, whence, anl, *parodic*; EF-F *parodie* has EF-F agent *parodiste*, whence E *parodist*.

8. Gr *prosōidia*, a song (from *ōidē*) with accompaniment (connoted by *pros*, to), becomes L *prosōdia*, (EF-F *prosodie* and) E *prosody*; derivative Gr *prosōidiakos* becomes LL *prosōdiacus*, whence E *prosodiac*.

9. Gr *rhapsōidia* (from *rhapsōidos,* a rhapsodist; *rhaptein*, to sew, hence to unite) becomes L *rhapsōdia*, EF *rhapsodie* (F *rapsodie*), E *rhapsody*; derivative *rhapsōidikos* yields *rhapsodic*.

10. Gr *thrēnōidia*, a song of *thrēnos* or lamentation, yields *threnody*. Gr *thrēnos*, a dirge, LL *thrēnus*, E *threne* (cf F *thrène*), has adj *thrēnikos*, LL *thrēnicus*, E *threnic*; the modified Gr adj *thrēnetikos* becomes *threnetic*. Gr *thrēnos* derives from *thréomai*, I cry aloud: IE r, *dhre-* (var *dher-*), a loud or a confused noise: cf OE *drēam*, a joyous din (itself akin to E *dream*), OHG *treno*, a resounding, a droning, and Skt *dhrónati*, he sings. (Hofmann.)

11. Gr *tragōidia*, app lit 'goat song', from *tragos*, a he-goat (IE r, *trag-*, *treg-*)—cf the Asiatic pheasant named *tragopan*, in L a fabulous bird of Ethiopia, from Gr *Tragopan*, Goat Pan—this Gr *tragōidia* passes through L *tragoedia* and MF *tragedie* (F *tragédie*) to become ME *tragedie*, E *tragedy*. OF *tragedie* has derivative MF *tragedien*, F *tragédien*, f *tragédienne*: E *tragedian* and *tragedienne*. Influenced by *tragōidia*, Gr adj *tragikos*, goatish, acquires the sense 'of or for (a) tragedy', whence L *tragicus*, (EF-F *tragique* and) E *tragic*. The L cpd *tragicocomoedia* becomes, by contr, LL *tragicomoedia*, EF-F *tragicomédie*, E *tragicomedy*; the anl EF-F adj *tragicomique* leads to *tragicomic*.

Odin, odinite. See WEDNESDAY, para 2.

odious, odium; odiometer; odor (AE), odour, odo(u)r of sanctity, odorous and malodorous; odoriferous; olfactory; redolent; ozone; annoy, annoyance; ennui; noisome;—Ulysses; Odysseus, Odyssey.

1. *Odious* comes from MF *odieus* (EF-F *odieux*), from L *odiōsus*, adj of *odium*, itself adopted by E. L *odium* prob derives imm from *ōdi*, I hate: cf Gr *odussomai*.

2. L *ōdi* and *odium*—? orig to dislike, a dislike

of, the smell of—are perh akin to L *odor*, a smell: cf *olēre* (for *odēre*), Gr *ozein* (? for *odzein*), Lith *uosti*, to emit a smell, and Arm *hot*, a smell, *hotim*, I smell an odour.

3. L *odor* becomes OF *odor*, MF *odour* (F *odeur*), both adopted by ME, the latter explaining E *odour*, the former (along with L *odor*) explaining AE *odor*. The derivative adj *odōrus* becomes—perh via MF *odoreux*—the E *odorous*, anl, *malodorous*. L *odorifer*, odour-bearing, leads to E *odoriferous*; the ill-formed E *odiometer* should be *odorimeter*, smell-measurer.

4. *Odo(u)r of sanctity* translates the F *odeur de sainteté*, a pleasant odour—cf LL *odor*, incense—supposed to have been emitted by the corpses of saints.

5. L *olēre*, to exhale an odour, has two cpds relevant to E:

*olefacere* (for *odefacere*), to cause to smell, has shortened form *olfacere*, with pp *olfactus*, whence the adj *olfactōrius* (attested by *olfactōrium*, a scent-box), whence E *olfactory*;

*redolēre*, to diffuse a smell (good or bad), has presp *redolens*, o/s *redolent-*, whence MF-EF, whence E, *redolent*; derivative MF-EF *redolence* becomes E.

6. L 'esse alicui *in odio*', to be in hatred to someone or something, to feel intense dislike of or discomfort at, leads both to the OF n *enui*, F *ennui*, a weary dissatisfaction or even disgust, adopted by E, and hence to AF *anui*, with var *anoi*, both adopted by ME and the latter surviving as the n *annoy*, now archaic. The L 'esse alicui *in odio*' becomes VL *inodiāre* (cf LL *inodiāre*, to render loathsome), OF-MF *enuier* (F *ennuyer*), AF *anuier*, with var *anoier*, whence MF *anoien*, E 'to *annoy*'; AF *anoier* has derivative *anoiance*, adopted by ME, whence E *annoyance*.

7. Both the n and the v *annoy* had, by aphesis, the derivative *noy*, long since obs; the n *noy* acquired the adj *noysome*, soon spelt *noisome*.

8. Gr *ozein*, to emit a smell (good or bad), has presp *ozōn*, whence the n *ozone*. The Gr *odussomai* (I hate), postulated in para 1 and, in certain parts, attested in old Gr poetry, has s *oduss-* and prob the ultimate r *od-* (cf the L r in *ōdi*, I hate, and *odor*). Derivative is the name *Odusseus*, perh via the adj *odussos*, irritated, irritable; hence *Odysseus*, with derivative *Odusseia*, the story of Odysseus, whence L *Odyssea*, whence F *odyssée* and E *Odyssey*. *Odysseus* is less prob 'the wayfarer', for *hodos* (way) is unlikely to become *odos*.

9. But *Odussos* has, in Attic, the var *Olusseus*, whence the L *Ulysses*, adopted by E.

odograph (occ hodograph) and odometer; cathode, whence cathodic—whence, anl, anode, anodic; episode, episodic (whence episodical); exodus, Exodus; method (whence methodology), methodic (whence methodical), Methodism, Methodist; period, periodic (whence periodical, adj hence n); synod, synodal, synodic (whence synodical).

1. All these words derive from Gr *hodos* (ὁδός), a way, a road, hence a journey, hence also a way,

manner, means of doing something: cf OSl *chod*iti, to go, L *cēd*ere, to go, and Skt *sad-* in *asad-*, to come to, to reach: IE r, *\*sed-*, to go, ult id with *\*sed-*, to sit, ? orig to go to sit.

2. The *cathode* of El (cf the complementary *anode*) derives from Gr *kathodos*, a descent: *katá*, down+*hodos*, way.

3. Gr *epeisodios* (adj), coming in besides (*epi*, upon, besides+*eis*, in(to)+*hodios*, adj c/f of *hodos*), has neu *epeisodion*, used as n 'a coming in besides, an episode', whence EF-F *épisode*, adj *épisodique*: whence E *episode*, adj *episodic*.

4. Gr *exodos*, a going *ex* or out, becomes LL *exodus*, adopted by E, as also LL *Exodus*, from LGr *Exodos*, the Israelites' going out of Egypt.

5. Gr *methodos* (*meta*, after) becomes L *methodus*, EF-F *méthode*, E *method*; derivative Gr *methodikos* becomes LL *methodicus*, late MF-F *méthodique*, E *methodic*. *Method*, applied to religion, has derivatives *Methodism, -ist*.

6. Gr *peri*, around, combines with *hodos* to form *periodos*, a going round, hence a period of time, hence also of a complete, well-rounded sentence: L *periodus*: MF-F *période*: E *period*; derivative Gr *periodikos* becomes L *periodicus*, MF-F *périodique*, E *periodic*.

7. Gr *sun*, with+*hodos*=Gr *sunodos*, a meeting, LL *synodus*, a conjunction, an assembly of bishops, a Church council (Souter), EF-F *synode*, E *synod*; derivative LL *synodālis* becomes MF-F *synodal*, adopted by E; derivative Gr *sunodikos* becomes LL *synodicus*, whence (F *synodique* and) E *synodic*.

8. E *odograph* and *odometer* are, lit, (journey, hence) distance-describer (cf *graph* at GRAMMAR) and distance-measurer, the former being of E formation, the latter deriving from Gr *hodometron* (cf *metre* at MEASURE).

**odontic, odontoid.** See TOOTH, para 12.

**odor, odorous, odour.** See ODIUM, para 3.

**Odysseus, Odyssey.** See ODIUM, para 8.

**oecumenical.** See the element *-oeca*.

**Oedipus** is Gr *Oidipous*, Club-Foot; the *O. complex* derives from the myth that Theban Oedipus unwittingly married his mother.

**œil-de-bœuf; œillade.** See OCULAR, para 3.

**œnology, œnomancy.** See the element *œno-*; for *œnology* cf VINE, para 2.

**œsophagus.** See the element *esophago-*.

**œstrous, œstrual, œstrus.** See IRASCIBLE, para 2.

**of** and **off** (adv, hence adj—whence n—and prep).

The latter derives from ME *of*, orig id with the prep *of*, OE *of*, adv and prep: and OE *of*, var *aef*, of, from, hence off, is akin to OFris *of*, *af*, OS and Go *af*, MD *of*, *off*, *aff*, *af*, *ave*, D *af*, OHG *aba*, MHG *abe*, G *ab*, ON *af* (as also in Da and Sw), from; cf L *ab* (app for *\*ap*), away from, from, by, and the syn Gr *apo* (before a vowel, *aph-*) and Skt *ápa*, away, back; cf also Umbrian *ap*-ehtre, from outside, and Hit *appa*, again, back (adv), off, away. The Gmc etymon is *\*abha*, *\*abh*, *\*af*; the IE etymon *\*apó* or *ápo*. (Walshe.) Cf:

**offal** eases *off-fall*, that which falls off or is allowed to fall off; adv *off*+n *fall*.

**offence, offend, offender, offense, offensive.** See FEND, para 3.

**offer** (n, v), **offering, offertory.**

An *offer* derives from OF-F *offre*, itself from OF-F *offrir*, from L *offerre*, to bring (*ferre*) before (*ob*), to present, to offer, to sacrifice, whence also OE *offrian*, to offer, esp to sacrifice, ME *offrien*, later *offren*, whence 'to *offer*'. OE *offrian* has derivative vn *offrung*, a gift, a sacrifice, whence *offering*; *offertory*, however, comes—prob via MF-F *offertoire*—from ML *offertōrium*, an offering of money in church, from LL *offertōrium*, a place of sacrifice, from *offerre*, to sacrifice.

**office** (n, hence v)—cf **officer** (n, hence v); **official** (adj, hence n), whence **officialdom** and **officialism**—cf **officious; officiary; officiant, officiate; officinal.**

1. At the base of this group is the L *officium*, performance of work, work, a task, hence a public duty: app lit a work-doing: *opus*+*-ficere*, c/f of *facere*, to do, to make. L *officium* becomes OF-F *office*, adopted by ME.

2. L *officium* has ML derivative agent *officiārius*, whence the E n and adj *officiary*; *officiārius* becomes MF-F *officier*, whence E *officer*. Derivative LL *officiālis*, of a public duty or office, becomes E *official*; its derivative *officiālitās*, o/s *officiālitāt-*, yields *officiality*.

3. The L adj *officiōsus*, conformable to duty, becomes (EF-F *officieux* and) E *officious*; the derivative sense 'complaisant', present already in LL and in EF, explains the modern E sense.

4. L *officium* also has the derivative ML *officiāre*, to perform one's public duty, with presp *officians*, o/s *officiant-*, whence the E n *officiant*; the pp *officiātus* gives us 'to *officiate*'; with these two words, cf the MF-F *officier* (v) and the EF-F *officiant* (n).

5. With L *officium*, cf L *officīna*, workshop, contr of *opificina*, from *opifex*, a workman (*opus*+*-ficere*, c/f of *facere*: cf para 1): whence ML *officīnālis*, belonging to or characteristic of a workshop, esp an apothecary's: whence E *officinal*, (of drugs) stocked by apothecaries, now by A drugstores and E chemists.

**offish**: off, adj, connoting 'at a distance'+the dim or moderative *-ish*.

**often** is a reinforcement of late ME *ofte*, itself a lengthening of ME *oft*, from OE *oft*, frequently, whence directly—i.e., unchanged—the now archaic *oft*: cf OFris *ofta*, OS *oft*, *ofto*, OHG *ofto*, MHG *ofte*, G *oft*, Go *ufta*, OSw *ofta*, ON *opt*: perh all from ON *of*, a (large) quantity (Walshe); perh akin to L *opus*, work, *opēs*, abundance, riches (Feist).

**ogam, ogham, ogum**, an early Ir script, represents Ir *ogham*, MIr *ogom*, *ogum*, an invention attributed to *Ogma* mac Eladan, Son of Science (Learning), himself akin to Gaul *Ogmios*, god of eloquence. Cf the Ga *oghum*, ogam writing, (derivatively) occult science.

**ogive**, adopted from F, goes back to MF *ogive*,

varr *orgive*, *augive*, esp the latter, which predominated over the two others until C18: o.o.o.: but perh from OF-F *auge*, a trough, a flume, from its shape; or perh from Sp *algibe*, a vaulted cistern, from Ar *al*, the+*g'ubb*, a well. (B & W; Dauzat.)

**ogle.** See OCULAR, para 3.

**ogre, ogress; ogreish** or **ogrish; Ugrian—Hungarian, Hungary.**

1. *Ogreish*, often contr to *ogrish*, merely tacks *-ish*, of, like, to E *ogre*, which is adopted from late EF-F; F *ogre*, which has f *ogresse*, whence E *ogress*, comes either from L *Orcus*, god of death, hell (cf OSp *huerco*, a devil, hell), as B & W propose and uphold, or from OF *Ogre*, a Hungarian, from ByzGr *Ogōr*, as Dauzat prefers.

2. ByzGr *Ogōr* became Hung *Ogur*, a Hungarian, early Ru *Ugri* (pl), whence *Ugrian* and, anl, *Ugric*, with c/f *Ugro-*. The Hung *Ogur* and early Ru *Ugri* are nasalized in ML (of Germany) *Ungarus*, whence *Ungaria*, whence E *Hungaria*, later *Hungary*, whence *Hungarian*, adj, hence n.

**ogum.** See OGAM.

**Ohio** state is named from the river: Iroquoian *Ohionhilo*, lit 'the beautiful river' or perh 'the beautiful *oheyo*, *ohio*, or great river'.

**ohm:** G physicist (El), Georg Simon *Ohm* (1787–1854), author of *Ohm's law*. Hence *megohm*, a million ohms: *meg-*, *mega-*, great.

**oil**—whence **oiler** and **oily** and such obvious cpds as **oilfish** and **oilskin**—derives from ME *oile*, adopted from OF-MF *oile*, *oille* (cf F *huile*), from L *oleum*, itself an adaptation (? after L *olēre*, to emit a smell) of Gr *elaion*, olive-oil. Note that L *oleum* answers to L *olea*, an olive-tree, with var *olīua* (cf Gr *elaia*), ML *olīva*, whence OF-F *olive*, olive-tree, an olive, adopted by E. The basic Gr *elaia* is for *\*elaiwa*, hence *elaion* for *\*elaiwon*: like Arm *eul*, prob from an Aegean speech—Hofmann suggests Cretan.

2. L *olīua* has the foll derivatives relevant to E: *olīuārius*, of or like olives, whence *olivary*—cf the E formation *olivaceous*;

*olīuētum*, an olive-grove, whence *olivet*. *Olivine*, whence *olivinite*, is an E formation: *olive*+the Min suffix *-ine*: cf the F *olivine*.

3. L *oleum*, olive-oil, and *olea*, olive-tree, an olive, have the foll relevant L derivatives:

SciL *Olea*, the genus of true olives;

L *oleāginus* (var *oleāgineus*), adj of *olea*: whence, perh via MF-F *oléagineux*, the E *oleaginous*;

L *oleāster*, wild olive-tree, adopted by E;

LL *oleātus*, made with olive-oil, has prob suggested the Chem n *oleate*;

L *olei-*, c/f of *olea*, and *oleo-*, c/f of *oleum*; adopted by E, as in *oleiferous*, *oleograph*, *oleomargarine*: see *olei-*, *oleo-* in Elements;

L *oleōsus*, whence *oleose*.

4. E words not directly from L *olea*, *oleum*, include:

*olefiant*: F *oléfiant*, oil-forming: L *ole*(um)+ *-fiant* from *-ficiens*, presp of *-ficere*, c/f of *facere*, to make; hence the Chem *olefin* or *-fine*: *olef*iant+ Chem suffix *-in*, *-ine*;

*oleic*, Chem adj: L *ole*um, olive-oil, hence oil+ adj *-ic*: cf the F *oléique*;

*olein*: L *ole*um, oil+Chem *-in*: cf the F *oléine*.

5. ML formed the cpd *petroleum*: *petra*, a rock +*oleum*, oil: adopted by E. ML *petroleum* became MF-F *pétrole*, whence E *petrol*; the adj is *petrolic*. The Pharm SciL *petrolatum*=*petrol*+suffix *-atum*.

6. Gr *elaion*, olive-oil, and *elaia*, olive-tree, an olive, occur only in Sci terms, such as the Chem adj *elaidic*, whence *elaidin*.

**oinology.** See the element *oeno-* and cf VINE, para 2.

**oinomancy.** See the element *oeno-*.

**ointment.** See UNCTION, para 3.

**O.K.** is prob not, as formerly believed, from Choctaw *oke*, var *hoke*, meaning 'Yes, it is', but perh rather (as proposed by Allan Walker Read) from the banners of the *O.K.* Club, the Democratic party's political club of 1840: app for *Old Kinderhook*, the nickname of Martin van Buren (president of the U.S.A. in 1837–41), whose birthplace was *Kinderhook* in the State of New York.

**okapi** is adopted from Mbuba, the language of the Bambuba, an important Negro tribe of Central Africa.

**Oklahoma**, whence the sl *Okies*, natives thereof: '(land of the) Red Indians': Choctaw *okla*, people +*hummu*, red.

**old** (adj, hence n), whence the comp **older** and the sup **oldest**; Sc var **auld**;—**eld**;—**elder** (adj, hence n), **eldest; elderly**, from **elder; alderman**, whence **aldermanate** and **aldermanic;—adult** (adj, hence n); **adolescence, adolescent** (adj, hence n); cf the sep ABOLISH (ABOLITION) and COALESCE (COALITION)—ALIMENT—ALTITUDE—ALUMNUS —EXALT—PROLETARIAN—WORLD.

1. *Old*, ME *old*, var *ald*, derives from OE *ald*, var *eald*: cf OFris *ald*, var *old*, OS *ald*, OHG-MHG-G *alt*, Go *altheis*, MD *alt*, *olt*, *out*, D *oud*; G *alt* is a pp formation from a v answering to Go *alan*, to grow up: cf ON *ala*, to bear or produce, OIr *alim*, I nourish or rear, L *alere*, to nourish, and its inch *alescere*, to be nourished, to begin to grow, to grow, and Gr *aldēskein*, to grow up, and its caus *ald*ainein, to nourish, cause to grow up, strengthen (L & S): IE r, *\*al-*, to nourish.

2. OE *eald*, old, has derivative n *eldo*, *yldo*, *yldu*, whence *eld*, old age (now dial), antiquity (archaic).

3. OE *eald* has comp *ieldra*, *eldra*, *yldra*, E *elder*, and sup *ieldest*, *yldest*, E *eldest*.

4. OE *eald* has derivative *ealdor*, the head of a family, with cpd *ealdorman*, which in its variant *aldormon* (*-man*) becomes *alderman*, gradually sense-changing from 'governor of a territory' to 'member of a council': cf OFris *aldermann* (or *-monn*), a senior, a forebear.

5. L *alere*, to nourish, has inch *alescere*, to begin to grow, which has cpd *adolescere*, to grow *ad*, (connoting) up, with presp *adolescens*, o/s *adolescent-*, whence the E adj *adolescent*; the n *adolescent* perh owes something to the MF-F n. On *adolescent-* is formed L *adolescentia*, whence

MF-F *adolescence*, adopted by E. The pp *adultus* yields *adult*.

**Olea; oleaginous; oleaster; oleate; olefiant, olefin; oleic, olein; oleose.** See OIL, paras 3-4.

**oleander.** Ult akin to *rhododendron*.

**oleo-** terms. See the elements at *olei-, oleo-*.

**olfactory.** See ODIUM, para 5.

**olibanum,** frankincense, is adopted from ML: Ar *al-lubān* (*al*, the): cf Gr *libanos*, incense, from H.

**oligarch, oligarchic** (whence the extn **oligarchical**), **oligarchy:** Gr *oligarkhēs, oligarkhikos, oligarkhia*: *olig-* for *oligo-*, c/f of the adj *oligos*, little, *oligoi*, few+derivatives of *arkhein*, to rule or govern. *Oligos* is akin to Gr *loigos*, misfortune, illness, disease, death—hence to Lith *ligà*, disease, and Alb *l'ik*, emaciated, evil. (Boisacq.)

**olio.** See OVEN, para 2.

**olivaceous, olivary, olive, olivet, olivine.** See OIL, paras 1 (at end: *olive*) and 2.

**olla podrida.** See OVEN, para 2.

**-ollop** is an echoic element; recorded here, both because it is not in the usual sense an element at all and because it occurs in such picturesque words as *dollop, gollop, jollop, wallop* (occ represented, in dial, as *wollup*).

**ology,** jocular for a branch (esp if Sci) of knowledge. The *-o-* is a connective; *-logy* derives from Gr *-logia*, q.v. in Elements: Cf *ism*, as in 'ologies and isms'.

**Olympiad; Olympian** (adj, hence n); **Olympic** (adj, hence n—esp in pl); **Olympium; Olympus.**

All come from Gr *Olumpos*, that mountain which the Ancient Greeks believed to be the dwelling-place of the gods: Gr *Olumpias*, L *Olympias* (gen *Olympiadis*), F *olympiade*; LL *Olympiānus*, from L *Olympius*; Gr *Olumpikos*, L *Olympicus*—whence, prompted by Gr *ho Olumpikos agōn*, the Olympic competition, *the Olympic Games*, instituted in 776 B.C. and formerly called *the Olympian Games*; Gr *Olumpeion*, L *Olympium*; Gr *Olumpos*, L *Olympus. Olumpos*, var *Elumpos*, is a PIN o.o.o.: the religious significance of this mountain, situated on the Macedonian-Thessalian border, prob arises from the fact that it is the highest in the Gr peninsula.

**omber, ombre** (card game). See HOMO, para 13.

**omega,** whence **omegoid** (*-oid*) is $\omega$, capital $\Omega$, the last letter of the Gr alphabet: lit 'great *O*', it complements *omicron*, 'little *o*'. Hence, *alpha and omega*, the beginning and the end, *alpha* being the 1st letter of that alphabet.

**omelet, omelette.** See the 2nd LAME, para 2.

**omen, ominous; abominable, abominate, abomination.**

1. *Ominous* derives from L *ōminōsus*, the adj of *ōmen* (o/s *ōmin-*), an augury—adopted by E—OL *osmen*, prob for *\*augsmen*, from *augēre*, to increase, whence *augur*.

2. L *ōmen* has derivative *ōmināri*, to presage, pp *ōminātus*, whence the obs 'to ominate'. The cpd 'to abominate' derives from *abōminātus*, pp of *abōmināri*, to reject or repel as a bad omen, which,

as if from *ab ōmine*, is a cpd of *ōmināri*; the derivative LL *abōminātiō*, accursèd conduct, o/s *abōminātiōn-*, becomes OF-F *abomination*, adopted by E; derivative LL *abōminābilis* (*abōmināri*+ *-abilis*), accursèd, becomes OF-F *abominable*, adopted by E.

**omental, omentum.** Perh cf ABDOMEN.

**omission, omit.** See MISSION, para 15.

**omneity.** See OMNIUM.

**omnibus.** See BUS.

**omnifarious, omnipotent, omniscient, omnivorous.** See the element *omni-*; for the 3rd, cf SCIENCE, para 8.

**omnium** (in finance and commerce)=L *omnium*, of all (things; here, shares); gen pl of the adj *omnis*, all; cf the jocular *omnium gatherum*, a gathering (E *gather*+L neu ending *-um*), a miscellaneous collection. L *omnis*, whence the erudite *omneity* (as if from L *\*omneitās*: *omne*, all (neu sing)+abstract *-itās*), is o.o.o.

**omoplate.** See the element *omo-* (1).

**omphalic, omphalos;** cf the element *omphalo-*.

The adj *omphalic* derives from Gr *omphalikos*, the adj of *omphalos*, navel, hence the central part, esp the boss or knob of a shield: akin to the syn L *umbilicus*, itself related to L *umbō*, boss of a shield. L *umbilicus*, adopted by Med, has LL adj *umbilīcālis* (var of *umbilīcāris*), whence E *umbilical*. The Gr and L words are akin to Skt *nabbhis*, navel—cf OP *nabis* and OE *nafala*, E *navel*.

**on** (prep, hence adj, adv, n) and obvious cpds (e.g., *oncoming*); **onto; don, v.**

1. The prep *on* derives from ME-OE *on* (ME-OE var *an*): cf OFris *on*, OS *an, ana*, OHG *ana*, MHG *ane*, G *an*, Go *ana*, ON *ā* (cf the ME reduced forms *a, o*); cf also the *an-* of L *anhelāre*, to pant, Gr *ana*, Av *ana*, and OB, Ru *na*: Gmc etymon, *\*anam*; IE etymon, *\*aná, ano* (Walshe).

2. Prep *on*+prep *to* combine to produce *onto*; *do*, to put+*on*, adv produce *don*—cf *doff, do+off*.

**onager:** L *onager*, var of *onagrus*: Gr *onagros*, contr of *onos* (ass) *agrios* (of the fields—wild).

**once.** See ONE, para 13.

**oncome, oncoming.** See COME, para 3.

**ondine.** See UNDA, para 2.

**one** (adj, hence n), whence **oneself, oneness,** and such obvious cpds as **one-sided; a, an; alone, lonely** (whence **loneliness**); **none; once, nonce; anon; any; atone,** whence **atonement; eleven.**—Latin: **Una, union** (and **onion**), **unique, unit, unite, unitive, unity; unanimity, unanimous, unicorn, uniform** (**uniformity**), **unison, universe** (etc.), **univocal; uncia, uncial—onza—ounce—inch; disunion, disunite—reunion, reunite.** Cf the sep NULL.

### Indo-European

1. *One*, with pron *w-* a survival from an obs spelling in *w-*, derives from ME *one*, ? earlier *on*, ? earliest *an*, from OE *ān*: cf OFris *an*, usu *en*, OS *ēn*, OHG-MHG-G *ein*, Go *ains*, MD *en, een*, D *een*; ON *einn* (cf Sw *en*, Da *een*); OIr *óen, oin, óenán*, Ir *aon*, Ga *aon, aonan*, Cor *onan, onen, onon*, (on playing cards) *un*, W *un*, obs Br *unan*, Br *eunn*

(for *eun), Mx un, unnane; OP ains, and OSl inokŭ, unique; L ūnus, OL oinos, one, and Gr oinos (οἰνός) and oinē (οἰνή), the '1' or ace on dice—cf the Homeric oios (for *oiwos), sole; and prob the Skt ēkas, one, sole. The Gmc etymon is *ainaz; the IE, *oinos (Walshe).

## Latin

2. L ūnus (s and r ūn-) has f ūna, neu ūnum, and c/f ūni-, q.v.—for cpds—in Elements. F ūna becomes Spenser's Una, a fair lady whose name has become a frequent 'Christian'.

3. L ūnus has the foll simple derivatives affecting E:

ūnicus (cf, in formation, Go ainaha and OS ēnug): late MF-F unique, adopted by E; the learnèd F derivative (from unique), unicité, becomes E unicity;

LL ūniō, oneness, union, unity, o/s ūniōn-, becomes OF-F union, adopted by E;

ūnīre, to make one of, to unite, has pp ūnītus, whence 'to unite'; the cpd disunite (dis-, apart) was prob suggested by MF-F désunir, and disunion by MF-F désunion,—note that F désunir was itself perh suggested by LL disūnīre, to sever; reunite, deriving from ML reūnītus, pp of reūnīre, to make one again, to bring together again, perh owes something to MF-F réunir, as reunion prob owes something to MF-F réunion;

ūnitās, oneness, o/s ūnitāt-, becomes MF-F unité, whence E unity, whence, by b/f, unit;

LL ūnītiuus, ML ūnītivus, becomes E unitive.

4. L ūniō app has, in LL, the derivative form ūniō, o/s ūniōn-, with senses 'large pearl' and esp 'onion': whence MF-F oignon, whence E onion.

5. Akin to, perh deriving from L ūnus is L uncia, a unit that is a twelfth part, esp of a foot length or of a pound weight, the latter becoming both the OF unce, ME unce, whence, influenced by F once, the E ounce, and the Sp onza and It oncia. L uncia, one-twelfth of a foot, becomes OE ynce, ME unche, inche, E inch; its derivative adj unciālis, an inch high, becomes the E uncial, hence, as n, a large-written letter, or a script in such letters.

6. The most important full L cpds of ūnus are, in respect of E, perhaps these:

ūnanimus (or -mis), of one animus or mind, in complete agreement, becomes E unanimous, cf the F unanime; derivative L ūnanimitās, o/s ūnanimitāt-, becomes MF-F unanimité, whence unanimity; cf ANIMAL, para 6;

ūnicornis (after Gr monokerōs, one-horned), of one cornu or horn, is used, esp as n, for a fabulous quadruped: MF unicorne: E unicorn;

ūniformis, of one forma or form: MF-F uniforme, E uniform; the E n derives from the F n uniforme (C18+), from the adj; derivative LL ūniformitās, o/s ūniformitāt-, becomes MF-F uniformité, whence uniformity;

ūniversus—see next para;

LL ūniuocus, ML ūnivocus, whence univocal.

7. L ūniuersus, ML -versus, turned with a single impetus—hence, turned wholly—towards a single unity, turned into one, combined into an entity (a whole): is used in the sing with collective nouns and in the pl for 'all together', ūniuersi being opp singuli, taken piecemeal. Cicero and later Phil writers employed the neu ūniuersum (ML -versum) as a n: hence EF-F univers, whence E universe. Universus has the foll L derivatives relevant to E:

ūniuersālis, ML ūniversālis: OF-MF universal (F universel): adopted by E. The derivative LL ūniuersālitās (opp L singularitās), ML ūniversālitās, o/s ūniversālitāt-, becomes MF universalité, whence universality; cf the E derivative formations universalism, -ist (whence -istic), -ize, all perh prompted by F;

ūniuersitās, rare in L ('totality')—as LL, a legal term for a corporation—in ML, ūniversitās, a college, a university: MF-F université: E university.

## Germanic

8. OE ān, one (adj), becomes the indefinite article an, a, whence the reduced form a, used before consonants.

9. OE ān combines with OE on, in, to form, in ME, anan, later anon, retained by E: lit 'in one' (sc 'moment').

10. OE ān, one (adj), connotes 'alone', a sense extant in ME, where we find al on, al one, all (i.e., utterly) alone: whence E alone. By aphesis, alone becomes lone. Compare only, ME only, anly, earlier onlich, anlich, OE ānlīc: 'like one', like one only, lonely (a sense now only dial), hence the only one of its class, sole; hence the adv.

11. ME at on, later at one, also, later, written solid (attone, atoon, etc.), at one, hence in concord or agreement, has suggested EE-E 'to atone'.

12. OE ān, one, combines with ne, not, to form nān, ME nan, later non, later noon, latest none, adopted by E.

13. ME an, on, one, has adv anes, ones (-es, the gen case-suffix: OE ānes), whence E once; cf E nonce, for 'the nonce', the one (sc 'use' or 'occasion'), occurring orig, and now only, in 'for the nonce': ME 'for the nones', from ME 'for then ones', where the -n of 'then' recalls the -m of OE thǣm, dat of the article sē.

14. Pronoun any derives from the adj any: ME aenig and aeni, eni and ani: OE āēnig, a sense- and form-mdfn of ān, one: cf OFris ānich, usu ēnig, OHG einag, einīg, MHG einec, G einig, MD enich (dial var eenic), D eenig.

15. Not imm recognizable as a cpd of 'one' is eleven, ME enleven, OE endleofan, endlufon: cf OFris andlova, alvene, elvene, elleva, OS ellevan, OHG einlif, MHG einlif, eilef, early G eilf, G elf, Go ainlif, ON ellefo: all meaning, lit, 'one leave'— in full, '(ten and) one leave over', hence 'ten+one left over': 10+1=11. For the formation, cf TWELVE.

Oneida. See the 2nd SENECA, s.f.

oneiromancy. See the element oneiro-.

onerary, onerous. See ONUS, para 2.

onion. See ONE, para 4.

only. See ONE, para 10.

onomastic, onomasticon. See NAME, para 2.

onomatopoeia, onomatopoeic. See the element *onomato-*.

onset is a *set*(ting) *on*, an attack.

onslaught. See SLAY, para 2.

onto. See ON, para 2.

ontological, adj of ontology. See the element *onto-*.

onus is adopted from L *onus* (o/s *oner-*; s and r, *on-*): cf Skt *ánas*, a dray or a waggon; perh cf also Gr *ania*, Lesbian Gr *onia*, chagrin (a weight upon one's mind and temper), and *anios*, importunate. (E & M.)

2. Derivative adj *onerārius* yields *onerary*; derivat ve adj *onerōsus*, E *onerous*; derivative v *onerāre* has cpd *exonerāre*, to free (connoted by *ex-*) from an *onus* or burden, pp *exonerātus*, whence 'to *exonerate*'; derivative LL *exonerātiō*, o/s *exonerātiōn-*, whence *exoneration* (cf the EF-F *exonération*).

onward (adv, hence adj), onwards (adv): towards —connoted by *-ward*, *-wards*—a point further *on*. Cf the suffix *-ward(s)*, connoting direction.

onyx. See NAIL, para 4.

onza. See ONE, para 5.

oodles. See HUDDLE.

ooze (n, both senses; v), oozy. See VIRULENT, para 2.

opacity. See OPAQUE.

opal, whence opalescent and opaline (perh after F *opalin*) and opaloid: L *opalus*: Gr *opallios*: Skt *upala*, a stone, esp a precious stone.

opaque, opacity.

The latter derives from late MF-F *opacité*, from L *opācitās*, o/s *opācitāt-*, abstract n from *opācus*, shaded, shady, dark, whence, via late MF-F, the E *opaque*: o.o.o.: ? akin to Gr *opsis*, sight, *opōpa*, I have seen, *ōps*, an eye.

open, adj and v (whence *ope*, dial 'an opening' and poetic 'to open'); hence the agent opener and the pa, vn opening; hence also reopen, reopening.

'To *open*' derives from OE *openian*, itself from the OE—whence E—adj *open*, akin to OFris *open*, var of *epen*, *epern*, OS *opan*, OHG *offan*, MHG-G *offen*, MD *oppen*, MD dial *apen*, MD-D *open*, ON *opinn*, OSw *ypin*; prob related to E *up* and G *auf*: 'for development of meaning cf *aufmachen*' (to open), as Walshe has noted.

opera (whence operatic), operetta; operand, operant, operate, operation (whence operational), operative (adj, hence n), operator, operose, opus, opuscule; co-operate, co-opcration, co-operative, co-operator—inoperable, inoperative; hors d'œuvre; —avera and average, forms of feudal service; cf the sep OFFICE.

1. The entire group derives from L *opus*, work, itself adopted by E, esp in Mus and in medieval names of embroidery, and also in *magnum opus*, a great work, esp in size or in time needed for writing it; its pl is *opera*, therefore its o/s *oper-*. L *opus* is akin to L *opis*, gen of *\*ops* (attested by *Ops*, an ancient goddess of the harvest, her

festival being the *Op*alia), meaning both 'abundance, hence riches, strength', and 'aid'; akin also to Skt *āpas* (gen *āpasas*), work; in Gmc, cf ON *efni*, material to be used, *efna*, to accomplish, OE *aefnan*, *efnan*, to perform. (E & M; Holthausen.)

2. The neupl *opera* becomes a sep f sing *opera*, work, whether as activity or as result, whence It *opera*, work, hence a composition, esp musical, adopted by E; the It dim *operetta* is likewise adopted. L *opera* has adj *operōsus*, whence *operose*; the L dim of L *opus* is *opusculum*, whence late MF-F *opuscule*, adopted by E.

3. Both from L *opus* and from L *opera* derives L *operāri*, LL *operāre*, with gerundive *operandus*, whence the Math E n *operand*; presp *operans*, o/s *operant-*, whence the E n *operant*; pp *operātus*, whence 'to *operate*', with derivatives *operātiō*, o/s *operātiōn-*, MF-F *opération*, E *operation*, and LL *operātīuus*, efficacious, ML *operātīvus*, whence, perh via F, the E *operative*, and LL *operātor*, adopted by E.

4. The LL prefix-cpd *coöperāri* has pp *coöperātus*, whence 'to *co-operate*'; derivative LL *coöperātiō*, o/s *coöperātiōn-*, MF-F *co-opération*, E *co-operation*; derivative LL *coöperatīuus*, ML *-īvus*, (F *co-opératif* and) E *co-operative*; derivative LL *coöperātor*, adopted by E.

5. LL *operābilis* produces *operable* (cf the F *opérable*), with neg *inoperable* (cf F *inopérable*), perh aided by LL *inoperātus*, inactive; cf the anl *inoperative*.

6. L *opera*, work, becomes OF *oevre*, *uevre* whence F *œuvre*, with the EF-F cpd *hors-d'œuvre*, adopted by E.

7. L *opera* also becomes OF *oevre*, var *ovre*, whence app ML *avera*, adopted by E for a feudal service; ML *avera* (prob influenced by ML: OF-MF *aver* property) has derivative *averagium*, whence, perh via MF *average*, the ME *average*, a feudal tenant's service.

opercle, operculate, operculum.

The 3rd (whence the 1st), adopted from L, derives from L *operīre*, to cover (as with a lid); *operculum* has derivative *operculāre*, to furnish with an *operculum*, lid, the pp *operculātus* yielding the E adj *operculate*. L *operīre* could=*ob*, before, hence against, hence connoting an opp or a neg +*aperīre*, to open; the usual theory, however, is that *aperīre* and *operīre* prefix *ap-* (for *ab-*) and *op-* (for *ob-*) to a simple *\*uerīre*, which has correspondences in the Balto-Slavic languages (E & M).

ophthalmia, ophthalmic. See the element *ophthalmo-*.

opiate. See OPIUM.

opine, opinable, opinion, opinionated (whence, anl, opinionative); opt, optative, option; co-opt, co-optation (whence, anl, co-optative).

1. *Opinable* derives from L *opīnābilis*, from L *opīnāri*, to hold an opinion, to be of the opinion, whence MF-F *opiner*, whence 'to *opine*'. Derivative L *opīniō*, o/s *opīniōn-*, becomes OF-F *opinion*, adopted by E; hence the obs v *opinionate*, with pp *opinionated*, extant as adj.

2. *Opīnāri* is akin to L *optāre*, to choose, to wish, whence EF (? also MF)-F *opter*, whence 'to *opt*'; derivative LL *optatiuus*, ML *-īvus*, becomes *optative*; intimately related to *optāre* is L *optiō*, the faculty of choosing, hence a free choice, o/s *optiōn-*, whence OF-F *option*, adopted by E.

3. The LL cpd *coöptāre*, to choose together, to choose by election, yields 'to *co-opt*'; derivative *coöptatiō*, o/s *-iōn-*, yields, perh via F, *co-optation*.

**opium; opiate; opopanax.**

*Opium*, adopted from L, derives from Gr *opion*, poppy-juice, dim of *opos*, vegetable juice: perh cf OSl *soku*, juice of plants or fruits, and OP *sackis*, Lith *sakai* (pl), resin, gum, Let *svakas*, resin. L *opium* has the ML derivative adj *opiātus*, soporific, whence the n *opiātum*, a soporific, whence E *opiate*. Gr *opos* has cpd *opopanax*, with 2nd element *panax*, a sort of plant, from the adj *panakēs*, all-healing: cf, at element *opo-*, the cpd *opobalsam*.

**opossum**, an A marsupial (when caught, it pretends to be dead—hence 'to *play possum*', to feign illness or ignorance or absence), hence an Aus phalanger: of Alg origin: cf Virginian *apäsûm*, Ojibway *wâbassim*, a white animal. (Webster.)

**opponent.** See POSE, para 14.

**opportune, opportunist, opportunity.** See the 2nd PORT, para 6.

**oppose, opposite, opposition.** See POSE, para 14.

**oppress, oppression, oppressive, oppressor.** See the 2nd PRESS, para 10.

**opprobrious, opprobrium; exprobrate, exprobration.**

*Opprobrious* derives, perh via MF-F *opprobrieux*, f *opprobrieuse*, from L *opprobriōsus*, the adj of *opprobrium*, infamy, adopted by E. *Exprobration* derives from L *exprobrātiōn-*, o/s of *exprobrātiō*, severe censure, from *exprobrāt-*, s of *exprobrātus* —whence 'to *exprobrate*'—pp of *exprobrāre*, to censure severely. These are *op-* (for *ob-*) and *ex-* (used int) prefix-cpds deriving from *probrum*, a reproach, a deed worthy of reproach, prop the neu of the adj *prober*, worthy of reproach, reproached: app *prober* represents IE *pro-bher-os*: *pro-*, forward+*bher-*, to carry (cf 'to BEAR')+formative *-o-*+nom case-ending *-s*. (E & M.)

**oppugn, oppugnant.** See PUNGENT, para 17.

**opt, optative.** See OPINE, para 2.

**optic** (adj, hence n), also in *-al* extn **optical; optician; optics;** cf the element *opto-*.

1. *Optics*, imm from the adj *optic*, was suggested by Gr *ta optika*, the things (matters) of the sight, *optika* being the neupl of the adj *optikos*, of the sight, whence, via ML *opticus* and MF-F *optique*, the E *optic*; the passage of *optics* from *ta optika* was eased by the EF-F n *optique* and ML *opticē*, from Gr *optikē*, elliptical for *optikē tekhnē*, art of vision. The MF-F adj *optique* has the EF-F derivative *opticien*, whence E *optician*.

2. The Gr adj *optikos* is closely akin to Gr *opsis*, vision, sight, *opsomai*, I shall see, *osse*, the two eyes, and less closely to Gr *ōps*, eye, face: also to L *oculus*, an eye (q.v. at OCULAR), and to EYE.

3. Gr *opsis* and *optikos* appear in two prefix-cpds:

Gr *autopsia*—whence E *autopsy* (perh via EF-F *autopsie*)—from *autoptos*, seen (*optos*) by oneself (*autos*), and the corresp true adj *autoptikos*, whence E *autoptic*; *-opsia* may be regarded as a c/f of *opsis*;

Gr *sunopsis*, a seeing-together (*sun*, with), a collective view, whence LL *synopsis*, adopted by E, and the corresp adj *sunoptikos*, whence EF-F *synoptique*, whence E *synoptic*.

**optimal, optimate; optimism, optimist** (whence **optimistic**), **optimum.**

*Optimal* is the adj of E *optimum*, adopted from the neu (*optimum*) of L *optimus*, the best, var *optumus*, app derived from *ops*, gen *opis*, q.v. at OPERA, para 1. L *optimus* has L derivative *optimātes*, members of the Roman nobility, whence, by b/f, the E *optimate*, and learnèd F derivative *optimisme* and, anl, *optimiste*, whence E *optimism* and *optimist*.

**option.** See OPINE, para 2.

**optometer.** See the element *opto-*.

**opulence, opulent.** See COPY, para 2.

**opus, opuscule.** See OPERA, resp para 1 and para 2.

**or** (1), conj of alternatives: ME *or*, earlier *other*, *outher*, *auther*: OE *āwther*, contr of *āhwaether*: *ā*, aye+*hwaether*, whether; perh, however, ME (*or*) *other* comes from OE *oththe*, with the *-r* due to the influence of the preceding *other*, *outher*, either (OED): OE *oththe* (var *eththa*) is akin to OHG *odar* (rare), *odo*, *eddo*, MHG *ode*, G *oder*, and Go *aiththau*.

**or** (2), conj of time, 'before': ON *ār*, formerly influenced by OE *āēr*, before (cf ERE).

**or** (3), n, 'gold': F *or*, L *aurum*. Cf AUREATE.

**oracle, oracular.** See ORATION, para 3.

**oral, orle; orifice,** whence **orificial; orotund,** whence **orotundity; oscular, osculate, osculation, osculatory—oscillate, oscillation,** whence, anl, **oscillator** and **oscillatory; ostiary, ostiole** (whence, anl, **ostiolar**), **ostium—usher** (n, hence v).

1. *Oral* prob derives from LL *ōrālis*, of or for or by the mouth, from L *ōs*, mouth, gen *ōris*, o/s *ōr-*: cf L *ōra*, coast, border, OE *ōr*, a front, *ōra*, border, ON *ōss*, mouth of river, MIr *ā*, mouth, Skt *ās*, mouth, L *ōsculum* (dim of *ōs*), little mouth, hence a kiss, and L *ōstium*, Lith *uesta*, *uestas*, river-mouth, Let *uõsta*, *uosts*, a port, OSl *usta* and OP *austis*, mouth.

2. On the L o/s *ōr-* is formed *ōrificium*, a mouth-like opening, whence MF-F *orifice*, adopted by E; *orotund*, however, derives, by contr, from Horace's *ore rotundo*, with round mouth; *orle*, adopted from F, derives from OF *ourle*, border, edge (of garment), from VL *orulus* or *orulum*, dim of L *ōra*, border.

3. L *ōsculum*, (little mouth, hence) a kiss, has derivative *ōsculāri*, to kiss, with pp *ōsculātus*, whence 'to *osculate*'; derivative *ōsculātiō*, o/s *osculātiōn-*, yields *osculation*, whence, anl, *osculatory*.

4. L ōs, mouth, bears also the sense 'face', with dim ōscillum, a (little) mask, esp of Bacchus; masks of Bacchus were, esp in vineyards, suspended from trees and bushes, so that they were agitated by the wind, hence ōscillāre, to swing (like masks in the wind: E & M), with pp ōscillātus, whence 'to oscillate'; derivative ōscillātiō, o/s ōscillātiōn-, becomes oscillation.

5. L ōstium, river-mouth, has also the sense 'gate, door', whence ōstiārius, a doorkeeper, Eccl E ostiary; ōstium has the VL or C6 dial var ūstium, whence VL ūstiārius, doorkeeper, OF uissier (F huissier), ME uschere, ussher, E usher. L ōstium, moreover, has the dim ōstiolum, a little door, whence E ostiole.

**orange, orangeade, orangery; aurantium; naringin.**

1. The descent of orange is long, yet clear: ME orange, earlier orenge: MF orenge (F orange): OProv auranja (influenced by aur, gold—from the colour), earlier aranja, earliest naranja: Sp naranja: Ar nāranj, Per nārang, Skt nāranga, orange-tree, akin to—? from—Tamil naru, fragrant. The OF ō- is perh caused by the F city of Orange, through which the fruit must have passed in its passage to the north (B & W); the change from naranja to aranja was caused by confusion of the -n of the indefinite article un, un naranja becoming un aranja (Dauzat). The EF-F derivative orangeade was adopted by E; the EF-F orangerie became orangery.

2. Skt nāranga has var nāraṅgī, whence Marathi nāriṅgī, an orange, whence the Chem E naringin (Chem suffix -in).

**orang-utan:** Mal oraṅ utan, lit wild (utan) man (oraṅ).

**orant; orate.** See:

**oration,** whence, by b/f, 'to orate'—orator, whence oratorical—oratorio—oratory; orant; orison; oracle, oracular; orison.—Cpds: adorable, adoration, adore (whence adorer); exorable and inexorable; peroration (whence, by b/f, 'to perorate'), whence perorational and, anl, perorative, peroratory (adj).

1. L ōrāre (s and r, ōr-), to pronounce a ritual formula, hence to pray, to plead, has presp ōrans, o/s ōrant-, whence the Eccl n orant. On ōrāt-, s of the pp ōrātus, have arisen ōrātiō (preserved in oratio obliqua and recta), o/s ōrātiōn-, whence E oration—ōrātor, whence OF oratour (F orateur), whence E orator—ōrātōrius, whence, via ars ōrātōria and late MF art oratoire, the art of oratory, and whence, via LL ōrātōrium, a place to pray, the ME oratorie, E oratory (cf the F oratoire); LL ōrātōrium becomes It oratorio, whence, from the musical services held in the oratory of St Philip Neri in Rome, the name of a religico-musical composition (B & W).

2. L ōrātiō (o/s ōrātiōn-), a speech, acquires in LL-ML the sense 'prayer': whence MF oreison, orison, a prayer, the form orison being adopted by E; since c1800, literary.

3. Also from L ōrāre derives L ōrāculum, OF-F oracle, adopted by E; derivative ōrāculārius yields oracular.

4. L ōrāre is o.o.o.; but the so-called folk-etymology ōrāre from ōs, mouth, is prob correct, for ōs means also mouth-as-organ-of-speech.

5. L ōrāre has three prefix-cpds: adōrāre, exōrāre, perōrāre. Adōrāre, to address a prayer ad or to, becomes OF-F adorer, whence 'to adore'; derivative L adōrābilis becomes EF-F and E adorable; derivative L adōrātiō, o/s adōrātiōn-, becomes MF-F and E adoration.

6. L exōrāre (ex- used int), to pray urgently, has derivative exōrābilis, whence exorable; the neg inexōrābilis, incapable of being moved by prayer, becomes late MF-F inexorable and, prob independently, E inexorable.

7. L perōrāre, to plead per or throughout, hence to the end, hence to finish one's plea in a summing-up, has pp perōrātus, whence perōrātiō, o/s perōrātiōn-, whence peroration (cf the EF péroration and late EF-F péroraison).

**orb—orbicular, orbiculate—orbit, whence orbital; exorbitant, whence, anl, exorbitance, exorbitancy.**

Exorbitant derives from exorbitant-, o/s of exorbitans, presp of exorbitāre, to get out of (ex), hence off, the course or orbita, course, track, orig a rut, the trace of a wheel, whence, perh via MF-F orbite, the E orbit. L orbita derives from orbitus, shaped like an orbis, a round, a circle, e.g. a wheel, a ball, a globe, whence, perh via MF-F orbe, the E orb. The L dim orbiculus, a little orb, becomes orbicle; the derivative LL adj orbiculāris becomes MF-F orbiculaire, whence E orbicular; the from-orbiculus-derivative orbiculātus, shaped like a (little) orb, yields orbiculate.—L orbis, s orb-, r ? orb-, ? *or-, is o.o.o.: perh cf Hit *ūrkis (acc ūrkin), a trace, a track, and ūrkiya, to trace or track.

**orb** (2), in Arch: see ORPHAN, para 2.

**orchard.** (Cf the 1st YARD.) Orchard, ME orchard, orchiard, comes from OE orceard, var of OE ortgeard, with ort- akin to L hortus, a garden: cf Go aurtigards, a garden.

**orchestra,** whence orchestral and orchestrate (whence orchestration), is form-adopted from L, which takes it from Gr orkhēstra, the place (a circular space in front of the proscenium) for the chorus of dancers, the modern E sense being aided by its earlier occurrence in EF-F orchestre; Gr orkhēstra derives from orkheisthai, to dance, itself akin to Skt ṛghāyati, he trembles or raves: IE r, *ergh-, to tremble, to dance, itself perh an extn of *er-, to move, go, come: cf Gr erkhomai, I come or arrive. (Hofmann.)

**orchid,** whence, anl, orchidaceous (adj suffix -aceous: cf rosaceous and violaceous); orchis, whence orchitis (-itis, denoting a disease); cf the element orchi-.

The Gr orkhis, a testicle, hence—from the shape of its tubers—an orchid (Bot Orchis), becomes L orchis, the plant, with faulty gen orchidis, o/s orchid-, whence the E orchid. Gr orkhis is akin to Av erezi, the two testicles, the scrotum, Alb herde, testicle, Arm *orji-kh*, testicles, and *orji*, not castrated, Lith *eřžilas*, a stallion, MIr *uirgga*, Ir *uirge*, testicle: IE etymon, \**orghi-*, testicle: perh a Medit word, ? cf Eg *asti*, testicles.

**ordain.** See ORDER, para 5.

**ordeal.** See the 1st DEAL, para 3.

**order** (n and v), whence the adj **orderly** (whence the n)—whence also **disorder**, whence **disorderly**; **ordain, ordainer, ordainment; ordinal** (adj, hence n); **ordinary** (adj and n); **ordinance and ordnance and ordonnance; ordinand; ordinate, ordination;— ornament** (whence **ornamental** and **ornamentation**), **ornate, ornature.**—L cpds: **adorn, adornment; exordium; extraordinary; primordial, primordium; inordinate; subordinate** (adj, hence v), **subordination.**

1. The base of the group is supplied by L *ōrdō*, a tech term for the order of the threads in the woof, hence, in non-tech language, a row, a rank, hence order in general (things in due succession or place): o/s *ōrdin-*, whence the v *ōrdināre*, to put or set in order. L *ōrdō* derives from—or is, at the least, intimately related to—L *ōrdīri*, to weave (a woof), setting the threads in order: both the s and the r of both *ōrdō* and *ōrdīri* are *ord-*: IE r, \**or-*, perh with var \**ar-* (as in L *artus*, Gr *arthron*, a joint).

### Simples

2. L *ōrdō*, retained by E in several tech and Sci senses, has the LL Gram adj *ōrdinālis*, whence, perh via EF-F, the E *ordinal*; the normal L adj is *ōrdinārius*, whence OF-AF *ordinarie*, whence E *ordinary*, adj and earlier noun, several of the later senses of the adj prob deriving imm (like MF-F *ordinaire*) from L *ōrdinārius*.

3. L *ōrdō*, acc *ōrdin*em, becomes OF *ordene*, whence OF-F *ordre*, adopted by ME, whence E *order*; ME *ordre* has derivative v *ordren*, whence 'to *order*'. 'To *disorder*'=*dis-*+*order*, v; *disorder*, n=*dis-*+*order*, n, influenced by late MF-F *désordre*.

4. The derivative *ōrdināre*, to set in order, has gerundive *ōrdinandus*, whence E *ordinand*, one about to be ordained into the Church; pp *ōrdinātus* yields the Zoo adj *ordinate* and the now rare v 'to *ordinate*'. In LL, *ōrdināre* acquires the sense 'to ordain into the Church'; derivative *ōrdinātiō*, o/s *ōrdinātiōn-*, has both the Classical and the Eccl sense, whence OF-F *ordination*, adopted by E; the agent *ōrdinātor* is partly adopted. The ML *co-ōrdināre* and LL *co-ōrdinātiō*, and the LL *prae-ōrdināre*, *prae-ōrdinātiō*, yield *co-ordinate*, *pre-ordinate*, and their corresp nn.

5. L *ōrdināre* becomes OF *ordener* (cf the n *ordene* in para 3), ME *ordeinen*, E 'to *ordain*'; derivative OF-MF *ordenement* becomes E *ordainment*, and the OF-MF agent *ordeneor* ends in E *ordainer*. 'To *pre-ordain*' owes something to F *préordonner* (LL *prae-ōrdināre*).

6. OF *ordener* becomes, in late MF, *ordonner* (prob showing the influence of *donner*), whence

MF-F *ordonnance*, arrangement (of parts in a whole), adopted by E.

7. But, seen differently, MF *ordonnance* derives from OF *ordenance*, from *ordener*; and OF-MF *ordenance* is adopted by ME, with late var (after the L original) *ordinance*, retained by E. The ME word, lit 'an ordering, an arrangement', derivatively means 'supplies', which, with the latter sense fully established during C16, sees the contr *ordnance* established not before C17.

8. L *ōrdināre* is very closely akin to *ōrnāre*, which is app—but perh only app—a contr of *ōrdināre*. L *ōrnāre*, to equip, to arrange, hence to embellish (the predominant sense), has derivative *ōrnāmentum*, whence OF-F *ornement*, adopted by ME, whence, reshaped after L, the E *ornament*. The L pp *ōrnātus* accounts for *ornate*; derivative LL *ōrnātura*, for *ornature*.

### L Compounds affecting E

9. *Adōrnāre*, where *ad* is merely int, soon specializes as 'to embellish': OF *aorner* (ME *aournen*), reshaped by MF to *adorner*: ME *adornen* (*adournen*): 'to *adorn*'; derivative MF *adornement*, E *adornment*.

10. *Exōrdīri* (*ex-*+*ōrdīri*), to mount a woof, lay a warp, begin a web, has derivative *exōrdium*, which soon acquires the non-tech sense 'a beginning, an introduction', esp of a discourse: adopted by E.

11. *Extraōrdinārius*, a sense-cpd of *ōrdinārius*, derives from *extrā ōrdinem*, outside (*extra*) the order (that is customary); hence *extraordinary* (cf the MF-F *extraordinaire*).

12. L *inōrdinātus*, not (*in-*) set in order, hence lacking in order, hence lacking in proportion, yields *inordinate*.

13. *Prīmōrdium*, the first (*prīm-*, pre-vocalic c/f of *prīmus*, first) beginning, is adopted by learnèd E; derivative LL adj *prīmōrdiālis* leads—perh via late MF-F—to *primordial*.

14. ML *subōrdināre*, to set in a lower (*sub-*) order, has pp *subōrdinātus*, used also as adj: whence *subordinate*; derivative *subōrdinā tiō*, o/s *subōrdinātiōn-*, yields EF-F, and E, *suboraination*. *Insubordinate* and *insubordination* are E negg in *in-*, but they perh owe something to F *insubordonné* and *insubordination*.

**ordinary.** See prec, para 2.

**ordnance.** See ORDER, para 7.

**ordo; ordonnance.** See ORDER, resp para 2 and para 6.

**Ordu.** See HORDE.

**ordure**, whence **ordurous**, is adopted from OF-F *ordure*, a *-ure* derivative from the OF adj *ord*, filthy, repulsively dirty: by contr from L *horridus*, *-orrid-* becoming *ord*. Cf, therefore, *horrid*.

**ore; iron** (n, adj, v), **ironmonger, ironmongery;** akin are the sep ERA and the sep ESTEEM (ESTIMABLE, ESTIMATE, ESTIMATION).

1. *Ore*, as a Min term, derives, through ME *ōr*, from OE *ār*, copper, brass: cf OHG *ēr*, ore, brass, iron, and OHG-MHG *ērīn*, G *ehern*, brazen,

OFris *ēren*, OE *āēren*, brazen, Go *aiz*, ore, brass, ON *eir*, brass, copper; cf also L *aer-*, o/s of *aes* (OL *ais*), copper, bronze, hence money, and Skt *áyas*, ore, iron: IE r, *\*ais-*, (a lump of) bronze or copper, later used to designate iron.

2. *Iron*, n, ME *iren*, OE *īren*, *īsern*, *īsen*, is akin to OFris *īrsen*, *īrser*, *īsern*, *īser*, OS *īsarn*, OHG *īsarn*, *īsan*, MHG *īsern*, *īser*, G *Eisen*, Go *eisarn*, MD *iser*, *isere*, *iseren*, D *ijzer*, ON *iārn*, *īsarn*, a loan from C ('The early Celts were leading iron-workers': Walshe): cf OIr *iarnn*, *iārn*, *iarand*, *iarund*, Ga *iarunn*, Gaul *īsarna*, W *haiarn*, *heiyrn*, *heyrn*, Br *houarn*, Cor *hoarn*, *hoern*, *horn* (pl *hern*), Mx *yiarn*, OC *\*eisarno-*, *eiserno-*.

3. The adj *iron* derives from OE *īren*, var *īsen*: cf OHG *īsarnīn*, MHG *īserīn* (for *īsern-īn*), G *eisern*.

**oread.** See ORIENT, para 7.

**orectic.** See REX, para 34.

**Oregon**, occurring in so many NA plant and bird names, derives from the territory drained by the river *Oregon* (now the Columbia): o.o.o., but prob Amerind.

**organ**, **organic** (whence **organicism**), **organism** (whence **organismal**), **organist**; **organization**, **organize** (whence **organizer**); **organon** and **organum**; **orgue**;—**disorganization**, **disorganize**; **reorganization**, **reorganize**;—cf the element *organo-*; ult akin to WORK.

1. *Organ* derives, via MF-F *organe*, the musical instrument, a part of the human body, from L *organum*, trln of Gr *organon*, s *organ-*, r *org-*, akin to s and r *erg-* of Gr *ergon*, work: f.a.e., WORK. Both Gr *organon* and L *organum* are used in erudite E.

2. The derivative Gr adj *organikos* becomes L *organicus*, MF-F *organique*, E *organic*; L *organum* has ML derivative *organista*, whence MF-F *organiste*, whence E *organist*; F *organe*, part of body, has derivative *organisme*, whence E *organism*. LL *organum*, a church organ, becomes MF-F *orgue*, by some rather obscure contr process; the derivative F military senses are adopted by E.

3. LL *organum*, church organ (a sense possessed by LGr *organon*), has LL derivative *organizare*, to play the organ (sense possessed by LGr *organizein*), which form-suggested the ML *organizāre*, to furnish with organs or parts, to invest with organic structure, whence, via MF-F *organiser*, 'to *organize*'; derivative ML *organizātiō*, o/s *organizātiōn-*, whence, prob via late MF-F *organisation*, the E *organization*.

4. 'To *disorganize*' and *disorganization* derive from EF-F *désorganiser* and F *désorganisation*, native F formations; *inorganic* derives from EF-F *inorganique*, the neg of *organique*; *reorganize* and *reorganization* owe something to F *réorganiser*, *réorganisation*.

**orgasm**, whence **orgasmic**: EF-F *orgasme*: Gr *orgasma*, *orgasmos*: *organ*, to 'boil' with ardour, swell with lust: cf Gr *orgē*, impulse, and Skt *ūrjā*, sap, vigour (? esp if sexual): IE r, *\*uerg-*, to swell.

**orgiac**, **orgiastic**. See ORGY.

**orgue**. See ORGAN, para 2, s.f.

**orgy**, **orgiac**, **orgiast**, **orgiastic**.

1. *Orgy* derives from F *orgie*, a b/f from the late MF-EF pl *orgies*: L *orgia*, pl: Gr *ta orgia*, secret rites, esp in the cult of Dionysus (Bacchus): *\*orgion*, akin to Gr *ergon*, work: cf ORGAN and, f.a.e., WORK.

2. The derivative Gr adj *orgiakos* becomes F *orgiaque* and E *orgiac*; derivative *orgiazein*, to practise these rites, has agent *orgiastēs*, whence E *orgiast*, and adj *orgiastikos*, whence E *orgiastic*.

**oriel**, a recessed window projecting from a wall: ME *oriel*: OF *oriol*, a sill, a gallery or a corridor: ML *oriolum*, portico, hall: o.o.o.: ? *or-*+connective *-i-*+dim *-olum*; *or-* represents ML *\*orum*, orig a VL var or derivative of L *ōra*, border, edge.

**orient** (adj, n, v) and **oriental** (whence **orientalism**, **orientalist**), adj hence n, all also *O-*; **orientate** and, anl, **orientation**, from *orient*, n; cpds: **disorientate**, **disorientation**; **reorient**, **reorientate**, **reorientation**.—**origin**, **original** (adj, hence n), **originality**, **originate** (whence **originator**), **origination** (whence, anl, **originative**); **aborigine**, **aboriginal**.—**abort**, **abortient**, **abortion**, **abortive**.—**oread**.

1. At the root of the entire group, lies L *orīrī*, to rise, esp of the sun and the moon, hence to arise, have a beginning, spring up, even to be born, with pp *ortus*: the s and the r are *or-*, to rise; cf Gr n*eortos*, newborn, *ormenos* (pp), stirred up, *ormenos*, a sprout or shoot of a plant: and this *or-* is a var of the IE r *\*er-* (var *\*ar-*), to stir up—cf Skt *árnas*, (of waves) rolling, and Zend *ar-*, to be stirred up or excited.

2. L *orīrī* has presp *oriens*, o/s *orient-*, whence the adj *orient*. L *oriens* is also elliptical for *sol oriens*, the rising sun, hence, as *Oriens*, the Orient or East, OF-F *Orient*, adopted by E. The L *Oriens*, the East, esp E Asia, has adj *orientālis*, whence OF-F *oriental*, adopted by E, whence the n *Oriental*.

3. F *orient*, the east, has late MF-F derivative *orienter*, whence 'to *orient*', whence, in part, 'to *orientate*' and, prob after F, *orientation*; F *orienter* has the EF-F cpd *désorienter*, whence 'to *disorient*', largely superseded by 'to *disorientate*', whence *disorientation*; hence, anl, 'to *reorient*', now usu *reorientate*, whence, anl, *reorientation*.

4. L *orīrī* has cpd *aborīrī*, to disappear, to die, *ab-* connoting 'away from' (life), with pp *abortus*; hence *abortāre*, whence 'to *abort*'; also from pp *abortus* come *abortiō*, o/s *abortiōn-*, whence *abortion*, and *abortīuus*, ML *abortīvus*, whence, perh via MF-F *abortif* (f *abortive*), the E *abortive*; *abortiens* (presp of LL *aborīre*), o/s *abortient-*, leads to the E adj *abortient*, syn of *abortifacient* (L *abortus*, n+*facient-*, o/s of *faciens*, presp of *facere*, to make).

5. Deriving from L *orīrī* is *orīgō*, source (of a spring), an origin, acc *orīginem*, whence MF-F *origine*, whence E *origin*. Derivative L adj *orīginālis* becomes MF-F *original* (and MF-F *originel*), adopted by E; the F use of *original* as n perh

prompted the E n, but note that, as 'original form' of an artistic or literary work, the E *original* prob arose in ML *orīgināle*, prop the neu of the adj. The LL mdfn *orīginārius* (adj) became MF-F *originaire*, whence the now obsol E *originary*; LL *orīginātiō*, an etymology, o/s *orīginātiōn-*, became, prob via MF-F, the E *origination*; *originality*, however, derives imm from late EF-F *originalité*, imm from F *original* but perh prompted by the LL adv *orīgināliter*.

6. L *orīgō*, pl *orīgines*, has the cpd pl *Aborīgines*, prob suggested by *ab origine*, from—hence of— the origin, sc 'the original country': applied first to the inhabitants of Latium: hence, by b/f, an *aborigine* or native inhabitant of a country (cf the f/e F *aborigène*, altered after *indigène*): hence, anl, the adj *aboriginal*, whence the Aus *Aboriginalities*, news or history, etc., of the Aus aborigines, called, in sl, *abos* (sing *abo*).

7. Ult akin to L *orīrī* is Gr *oros*, a mountain— rising high above the surrounding country; hence *Oreias*, a mountain nymph, L *Oreas*, o/s *Oread-*, whence E *oread*, any mountain nymph.

**orifice.** See ORAL, para 2.

**oriflamme,** adopted from F, comes from OF *orie flambe*, golden banner: *orie*, from L *aureus*, golden (adj of *aurum*, gold)+*flambe* (later *flamme*) in its sense 'banner': influenced by ML *aurea flamma*, the red banner of the F kings, orig of the Abbots of St Denis. (B & W.)

**origan.** See the 2nd element *ori-*.

**origin, original, originality, originate, origination.** See ORIENT, para 5.

**oriole.** See AUREATE.

**orison.** See ORATION, para 2.

**orle.** See ORAL, para 2.

**orlop.** See LEAP, para 6.

**ormolu,** orig ground gold, now brass imitative of gold: F *or moulu*: *or*, gold+*moulu*, pp of *moudre*, L *molere*, to grind (cf MILL). OF-F *or*: L *aurum*; OL *ausom*: cf OP *ausis*, Tokh A *uās, väs*.

**ornament, ornamental; ornate, ornature.** See ORDER, para 8.

**ornery** (dial AE) distorts *ordinary*: cf the deterioration of *common, mean, vulgar*.

**ornithologist, ornithology.** See the element *-ornis*.

**oro-** terms, all erudite and most tech: see the elements *oro-*; e.g., *orotund* comes at the 3rd *oro-* (but see also ROLL, para 18).

**orphan** (n, hence v), whence **orphanage; orb** (in Arch); **robot.**

1. *Orphan* derives from LL *orphanus*, trln of Gr *orphanos*, orphaned, an orphan: s *orphan-*, r *orph-*: IE r, *orb-*, extnn *orbh-*, *orph-*: cf Arm *orb*, an orphan, and L *orbus*, deprived, esp of one's parents. IE *orb-* has the basic var *arb-*, with extn *arbh-*: cf Skt *árbhas*, little,weak, a child. A different sense-development has taken place in OHG *arbi*, *erbi*, G *Erbe*, Go *arbi*, OIr *orbe*, inheritance, and OHG *arbeo*, G *Erbe*, Go *arbja*, OIr *orbe*, heir.

2. L *orbus*, bereft, becomes OF *orb*, MF-EF *orbe*, blind, F *orbe*, lightless, blank, whence the old Arch *orb*, a recessed panel.

3. Akin to Go *arbi, arbja* (as in para 1), is Go *arbaiths*, labour, toil, trouble, distress, syn OHG *arabeit* and MHG *arebeit* (G *Arbeit*, work), OSl *rabota*, Cz (and Pol) *robota*, servitude, forced labour. Cz *robota* occurs in Karel Capek's *R.U.R.*, Rossum's Universal Robots, published—and played—in Britain and U.S.A. in 1923: there a *robot* was an artificially manufactured person, mechanically efficient but soulless.

**Orpheus, Orphic.**

The adj derives, via L *Orphicus*, from Gr *Orphikos*, adj of *Orpheus*, whence, via L, the E *Orpheus*, in myth a Thracian poet and musician, player of a most persuasive lyre: o.o.o.

**orpiment.** See PAINT, para 5, s.f.

**orrery:** named in honour of Charles Boyle (1676–1731), 4th Earl of *Orrery*.

**ort,** morsel, scrap: OFris *ort*: app the *or-* of *ordeal* (see 1st DEAL, para 2)+part of OE *etan*, ME *eten*, E ea*t* (cf OFris *eta*).

**ortho-** terms: see Elements at *orth(o)-*. But for *orthodox* (*orthodoxy*), see DOGMA, para 3.

**ortolan,** a bird frequenting garden-hedges, has a name adopted from EF-F (earliest as *hortolan*), from Port, *ortolan*, the bird, orig a gardener: L *hortolānus*, gardener, from *hortulus*, dim of *hortus*, a garden: cf *horti*culture and, f.a.e., the 2nd YARD.

**oryx:** sense-changed from L *oryx*, some kind of antelope or gazelle: Gr *orux*, id, from *orux*, any sharp digging-tool, from *oruss*ein, to dig: because of its sharp horns.

**oscillate, oscillation, oscillator.** See ORAL, para 4. Cf:

**osculate, osculation, osculatory.** See ORAL, para 3.

**osier.** See AQUA, para 5.

**Osiris,** husband of the goddess Isis, is, in Eg myth, the king of the netherworld and the judge of the dead: L, from Gr, *Osīris*: Eg *Ás-àr* or *Us-àr*: cf Eg *Ást* (*-t* merely indicating f gender), whence Gr, hence L, *Isis*, whose name, in Eg, is also represented as *'îse* (Coptic *êse*); a name meaning, lit, 'seat' (cf, ult, SIT)—perh that forming the throne of mighty Osiris.

**Osmanli.** See OTTOMAN.

**osmium**—whence **osmate** (Chem suffix *-ate*) and **osmic**—is a SciL derivative of Gr *osmē*, a smell: cf Gr *ozein*, to smell, and L *odor* (q.v. at ODIOUS).

**osmosis,** whence, anl, the adj **osmotic,** derives from Gr *ōsmos*, an impulse, from *ōthein*, to impel

**osprey.** See para 2 of:

**ossature, osselet, osseous, ossicle, ossification, ossify, ossuary; ossifrage, osprey; osteal, osteitis;** cf the elements *ossi-* and *oste(o)-*;—**oyster; ostracism, ostracize.**

1. L *os* (gen *ossis*), a bone, is akin to Gr *osteon*: cf Skt *ásthi*, Av *astam* (gen pl), Alb *asht*, Arm *oskr*, W *asgwrn*, Br *ascorn*, Cor *ascorn, asgorn, asgarn*: IE r, perh *ass-*, var *oss-*.

2. Derivative L adj *osseus* produces *osseous*; s *osse-*, as in Chem *ossein*; dim *ossiculum*, E *ossicle*; L *ossuārius* (*oss-*+formative *-u-*+adj *-ārius*) has LL derivative *ossuārium*, whence *ossuary*; L

*ossifragus* (adj), bone-breaking, whence (sc *auis*, bird) *ossifraga*, whence the E *ossifrage* and, via OF *osfraie* (F *orfraie*), the E *osprey*.

3. OF(-F) *os* has the OF-F dim *osselet*, adopted by E, and the F *-ature* (L *-ātūra*) derivative n, *ossature*, likewise adopted by E. Erudite late C17 F coined *ossifier* (L *ossi-*, c/f of *os*+*-fier*, LL *-ficare*, L *-ficere*, c/f of *facere*, to make), whence 'to *ossify*'; derivative F *ossification* is adopted by E.

4. Gr *osteon* has c/f *osteo-* or, before a vowel, *oste-*, whence the E *osteal* and *osteitis*: suffixes, adj *-al* and 'disease' *-itis*.

5. Akin to Gr *osteon* is Gr *ostreon*, whence L *ostreum*, var *ostrea*, LL var *ostria*, whence both MF *oistre*, whence E *oyster*, and MF *uistre*, whence F *huître*.

6. Akin to Gr *ostreon*, hence to Gr *osteon*, is Gr *ostrakon*, a hard shell (bone-like), hence a piece of earthenware, a tile, a tablet used for voting, whence *ostrakizein*, to banish by vote, whence 'to *ostracize*', the modern sense arising in C18 F *ostracisme* (Gr sense, C16-17), whence E *ostracism*; EF *ostracisme* derives from LL *ostracismus*, trln of Gr *ostrakismos* (from *ostrakizein*).

**ostensible, ostensive; ostent, ostentation, ostentatious.** See TEND, paras 15-16.

**osteology.** See the element *-otic*.

**osteology.** See the element *ost-*. Cf *osteopathy*, with 2nd element *-pathy*, q.v. at element *-path*.

**ostiary, ostiole, ostium.** See ORAL, para 5.

**ostler.** See HOSPICE, para 3.

**ostracism, ostracize.** See OSSATURE, para 6.

**ostrich:** ME *ostriche* (var *ostrice*): OF *ostrusce* (EF *ostruce*, F *autruche*): popular ML-LL *avis(auis) strūthiō*, 'the ostrich bird': *auis*, bird (cf AVIARY)+LL. *strūthiō*, from Gr *strouthiōn*, ostrich, mdfn of *strouthos*, a bird, esp an ostrich: o.o.o.: perh from a PGr etymon *strousthos*, from IE *trozdos* (var *trousthos*)—if so, cf THRUSH.

2. LL *strūthiō* accounts for the E adj *struthious*, of or for or like an ostrich or ostriches.

**Ostrogoth.** See GOTH, para 2.

**other** (whence **otherness** and **otherwise**), adj hence pron: OE *ōther* (adj and pron), one of two, either, the second of two: cf OFris *ōther*, OS *ōther*, *ōthar*, *āthar*, OHG *andar*, MHG-G *ander*, MD-D *ander*, Go *anthar*, ON *annarr*: Gmc etymon, *antheraz*; IE etymon, *ánteros*: cf Skt *antarás*, *anyas*, Lith *añtras*, other, next, second. (Walshe.)

**Othin.** See WEDNESDAY, para 3.

**otiant.** See OTIOSE.

**otic:** LL *ōticus*: Gr *ōtikos*, of the *ous* (gen *ōtos*) or ear, akin to L *auris* (? for *ausis*), ear.

**otiose, otiosity, otiant; negotiable, negotiant, negotiate, negotiation, negotiator.**

1. L *ōtium* (s *ōti-*, r *ōt-*), leisure, is o.o.o. The derivative *ōtiāri*, to be at leisure, has presp *ōtians*, o/s *ōtiant-*, whence the E adj *otiant*, at rest, unemployed; derivative adj *ōtiōsus*, idle, at leisure, becomes *otiose*, and its own derivative the LL *ōtiōsitās* becomes, perh via MF-EF *otiosité*, the E *otiosity*.

2. The opp of L *ōtium* is *negōtium* (*neg-* for *nec-* for *ne-*, not) busyness, hence business. Derivative

*negōtiāri*, to do business, has presp *negōtians*, o/s *negōtiant-*, whence—cf the EF-F *négociant*—the E n *negotiant*. The pp *negōtiātus* yields 'to *negotiate*'; derivatives *negōtiātiō* (o/s *negōtiātiōn-*) and *negōtiātor* become *negotiation* (cf late MF-F *négociation*) and *negotiator* (cf MF-F *négociateur*).

**otology.** See the element *-otic*.

**otter,** ME *oter*, OE *otor*, is akin to OHG *ottar*, MHG-G *otter*, MD-D *otter*, ON *otr*; cf also OSl *vydra*, Lith *údra*, Skt *udras*, Gr *hudōr*, water: therefore cf, ult, WATER.

**Ottoman**—whence, perh via F, the *ottoman* of furniture—is adopted from F: It *Ottomano*: ML *Ottomānus*: Ar *'Uthmāni*, belonging to *'Uthmān*, Othman, which has the Tu var *'Osmān*, with adj *'Osmānli*, whence OF and E *Osmanli*, a Western Turk.

**oubliette,** adopted from MF-F, derives from OF-F *oublier*, to forget, VL *oblitare*, from L *oblītus*, pp of *oblīuisci*: cf *oblivious*, q.v. at LIME (1).

**ouch,** a clasp. See the 2nd NET, para 6.

**ought** (1), anything, is now illit for *aught*, q.v. at NAUGHT, para 2.

**ought** (2), v. See OWE (heading).

**ounce** (1) in weight. See ONE, para 5.

**ounce** (2), a leopard-resembling cat: F *once*, influenced by OUNCE (1): by *lonce* taken as *l'once*, from MF *lonce*: VL *luncea*: L *lyncea*, f of *lynx* (cf LYNX).

**our, ours, ourselves.** See US.

**ousel.** See OUZEL.

**oust.** See STAND, para 30.

**out** (adv, hence adj and n), ME *out*, *oute*, *ut*, OE *ūt*, is akin to OFris, OS, Go *ūt*, to OHG-MHG *uz*, G *aus*, MD *ut*, *ute*, *uet*, *ud*, *uud*, D *uit*, ON *ūt*, out; and to Skt *ūd-*, outwards, upwards.

2. The cpds are numerous and obvious; two are old—*outlaw*, OE *ūtlah*, earlier *ūtlaga*, from ON *ūtlagi* (n; *ūtlagr*, adj); *outward* (adj, hence adv), OE *ūteweard*, *ūtweard*. The adv *outwards* derives from OE *ūtweardes*, orig the gen of the adj. With *outlandish*, cf OE *ūtlendisc*, foreign.

3. The comp *outer* and sup *outmost*, irreg *outermost*, are modern; the old forms are *utter*, OE *ūttra*, *ūtera*, etc., akin to OFris *ūtra*, *ūtera*, and *utmost*, OE *ūtmest*, *ūtemest*. Like *outermost*, *uttermost* is irreg.

**outlaw,** n. See prec, para 2, and cf the 2nd LIE, para 7. 'To *outlaw*': OE *ūtlagian*.

**outlet.** See LET, para 2.

**outmoded.** See MODAL, para 2.

**outrage, outrageous.** See ULTERIOR, para 7.

**outright.** See REX, para 3.

**outward, outwards.** See OUT, para 2.

**ouzel, ousel:** ME *osel*: OE *ōsle* (prob for *amsle*): cf OHG *amsala*, MHG-G *amsel*: perh cf the syn L *merula* (? for *mesula*), whence OF-F *merle*, hence E *merle*, *merl*. (Walshe.)

**oval, ovary, ovate, ovoid, ovule, ovum;** cf the elements *oo-* and *ovario-*, *ovi-*.

The L *ōuum*, ML *ōvum*, PL *ouom*, an egg, is akin to Gr *ōion*, *ōon*, PGr *ōuion*, IE *ōuiom*, var *ōuom*: cf EGG and prob L *auis*, a bird. ML *ōvum* is adopted by Sci; *ovule* comes from F (dim from ML *ōvum*); *ovoid*=*ov*-+adj *-oid*; *ovate*=ML *ōvātus*, L *ouātus* (*ōu*-+-*ātus*); *oval*, adopted from EF-F, =*ov*-+adj *-al*. Ovary=SciL *ōvārium* (*ov*-+ -*ārium*, connoting a receptacle).

**ovation** comes, perh via EF-F, from ML *ovātiōn*-, L *ouātiōn*-, c/f of *ouātiō*, a Roman victory-celebration inferior to a triumph: from *ouātus*, pp of *ouāre*, to utter shouts of joy, hence to celebrate an ovation: perh cf the Gr *euoi*, a cry of joy uttered at the festival of Bacchus.

**oven; olio—olla podrida.**

1. *Oven*, OE *ofen* (*ofn*), is akin to OFris *oven*, OHG *ovan*, MHG *oven*, G *Ofen*, Go *aúhns*, MD *aven*, MD-D *oven*, ON *ofn*: Gmc etymon, *\*uhwnaz*; IE etymon, *\*ukwnos*—cf Gr *ipnos*, stove, and L *aula*, *aulla*, Skt *ukhás*, a pot: early ovens were pot-shaped. (Walshe.)

2. L *aul*(*l*)*a* has var *olla*, retained by Sp: and Sp *olla*, a pot, hence a dish of stewed meat, not only becomes E *olla* but, in the phrasal cpd *olla podrida*, lit a rotted, hence rotten, pot, hence a medley, is adopted by EF-F and by E.

**over** (adv and prep, hence adj and n) derives from OE *ofer*: cf OFris *over*, MD-D *over*, OS *obhar*, OHG *ubar* (adv *ubiri*), MHG-G *über*, Go *ufar*, ON *yfir*: cf also L *super* (? IE prefix *s*-+ *\*uper*), Gr *huper* (ὑπέρ), Skt *upari*—and OE *ufan*, (from) above. The IE etymon is prob *\*uper*, var *\*uperi*. (Hofmann.)

2. The cpds are very numerous and entirely obvious; among the old ones are 'to *overcome*', OE *ofercuman*; to *overdo*, OE *oferdōn*; to *overdrive*, OE *oferdrīfan*; to *overflow*, OE *oferflōwan*; to *overgo*, OE *ofergān*; to *override*, OE *oferrīdan*; to *oversee*, OE *ofersēon*; to *overwork*, OE *oferwyrcan*.

3. Akin to OE *ufan* and *ofer* is OE *efes*, brink or brim, hence eaves, ME *evese* (pl *eveses*), E *eaves*, whence, by b/f (implicit in ME), a sing *eave*. OE *efes* has var *yfes*, as in the cpd *yfesdrype*, water dripping from the eaves, hence the ground onto which the water drips, hence E *eavesdrop*, hence 'to *eavesdrop*' or stand there, esp in order to learn (chiefly by listening) what goes on inside.

**overture:** OF *overture* (F *ouverture*): VL *\*opertūra*, alteration of: L *apertūra*: f.a.e., APERIENT.

**overweening.** See VENERABLE, heading; cf para 10.

**overwhelm.** See WHELM (heading).

**oviduct; oviparous.** See the element *ovario*-.

**Ovis,** in Zoo a sheep: ML *ovis*: L *ouis*, with s and r, *ou*-: cf Gr *oïs* and Skt *avis*, a sheep, and OHG *ouwi*, E *ewe*.

**ovoid, ovule, ovum.** See OVAL.

**owe,** pt **owed** but formerly **ought**, which, becoming specialized in sense, duly became a separate v, and pp *owed* but formerly *owen*, which became specialized as an adj *owen*, itself coalescing with the adj *own*; **own**, adj and v, the latter yielding **owner** (whence **ownership**)—cf **disown.**

1. 'To *owe*', ME *owen*, earlier *awen*, earliest *aghen*, (latest sense) to owe, earlier to own, possess,

have, OE *āgan*, to have, is akin to OFris *āga*, OS *ēgan*, *aigan*, ON *eiga*. 'To *disown*' is modern: *dis*-, apart+*own*, v.

2. 'To *own*', ME *ohnien*, earlier *ahnien*, OE *āgnian*, derives from the OE adj *āgen*, own, whence, via ME *aughen*, *awen*, later *owen*, the E adj *own*: and the OE adj *āgen*, own, is prop the pp of OE *āgan*, to have, to possess: cf these OGmc adjj: OFris *ēgen*, *ein*, OS *ēgan*, OHG *eigan*, G *eigen*, MD *egen*, *eigin*, MD-D *eigen*, ON *eiginn*.

**owl,** ME *oule*, earlier *ule*, OE *ūle*, is akin to OHG *ūwila*, MHG *iule*, G *Eule*, OS *ūwila*, MD *hule*, *uul*, *ule*, D *uil*, ON *ugla*: echoic from its cry.—Dim *owlet*; adj *owlish*.

**own,** adj and v. See OWE, para 2.

**ox,** pl **oxen; Oxford; aurochs.**

1. An *ox* comes from OE *oxa*, akin to the syn OFris *oxa*, OHG *ohso*, MHG *ohse*, G *Ochse*, *Ochs*, Go *aúhsa*, ON *uxi*, *oxi*; Gmc *\*uhsan*-, IE *\*uksan*: cf W *ych*, Br *egen*, ox, Skt *ukšan*, ox, bull: orig sense, bull; basic sense, the besprinkler—cf Skt *ukṣati*, he emits semen.

2. *Oxford* is OE *Oxnaford* (Domesday: *Oxeneford*), ford of the oxen, whence also the ML *Oxonia*, whence the E adj, hence n, *Oxonian*.

3. OHG *ohso* tautologically combines with OHG *ūr* (cf OE *ūr*, ON *ūrr*, aurochs) to form OHG *ūrohso*, MHG *ūrohse*, G *Auerochs*, whence E *aurochs*.

**oxalic, oxalis.** The adj *oxalic* derives from F *oxalique*, an -*ique* derivative from L *oxalis*, a kind of sorrel, taken over from Gr, which derives it from *oxus*, pungent (cf OXYGEN). *Oxalis* is adopted by Bot.

**Oxford.** See OX, para 2.

**oxidate, oxidation, oxide** (whence **oxidize**).

1. 'To *oxidate*' derives from F *oxider* (now *oxyder*), whence F *oxidation* (now *oxy*-), adopted by E: and F *oxider* derives from F *oxide* (now *oxyde*): a blend of *oxygène*+*acide*.

2. *Peroxide*=prefix *per*-, used int+*oxide*.

**Oxonian.** See OX, para 2.

**oxter:** OE *ōhsta*: cf AXIS, q.v.

**oxygen:** F *oxygène* (Lavoisier, 1786): *oxy*-, from Gr *oxus*, sharp, pungent, acid+the element -*gène* (E -*gene*); the F derivative *oxygéner* has prompted E 'to *oxygenate*' and prob *oxygenize*. Gr *oxus*, s and r *ox*-, perh stands for *\*ok-s-us*: cf L *occa*, a harrow, and, ult, EDGE.

2. For *oxymoron*, see the 1st element *oxy*- and cf MORON.

3. *Paroxysm* (with adjj in -*al*, -*ic*) derives from MF-F *paroxysme*, itself—perh via ML—from Med Gr *paroxusmos*, from *paroxunein*, to irritate, lit to sharpen excessively: *para*, beyond+*oxunein*, to sharpen, from *oxus*, sharp.

**oyer, oyez.**

The former derives from the n use of AF *oyer* (as in legal *oyer and terminer*): OF *oïr* (F *ouïr*), to hear: L *audīre*: f.a.e., AUDIBLE. AF *oyer* has imperative *oyez*, hear ye.

**oyster.** See OSSATURE, para 5.

**ozone.** See ODIUM, para 8.

# P

pa, father. See FATHER, para 16.

pabulum, adopted from L *pābulum* (s *pābul-*, r *pāb-*), is akin to *pāscere*, to nourish, esp to cause flocks and herds to eat, pp *pāstus*; cf PASTOR. The adj is pabular, from L *pābulāris*.

pace (n, hence v); pass (n and v), passable (and impassable), passage, passenger, passe-partout, passus; Passover, passport, password, pastime; compass (n, v), encompass; surpass, whence the pa surpassing; trespass (n, v), trespasser;—paten, patina, qq.v. at PAN; sep PETAL, PETALIFEROUS; sep SPANDREL, sep SPAWN, sep EXPAND (expansion); and sep FATHOM.

1. A *pace*, or step taken in walking, derives from ME *pace*, earlier *pas*, adopted from OF(-F) *pas*: L *passus* (gen *passūs*), a pace or step, orig a spreading or stretching of the legs in walking, from *passus*, pp of *pandere*, to spread or stretch: perh a nasal derivative of *patēre* (? orig *padēre*), to be or lie open, to extend (vi), and, if so, akin also to Av *pathanō*, stretched out; L *patēre* is prob akin to L *spatium* (q.v. at SPACE). If the IE r were *pa-*, a pace, to pace, then one would compare Hit *pāi*, to go, *panzi*, they go.

2. OF *pas* also becomes E *pass*, a pace (obs), a way through, e.g., mountains; *pass*, an act of passing, a permit, etc., derives from MF-F *passe*, from OF-F *passer*, to pass, from VL *passāre*, from the L n *passus*; also from *passer* comes 'to pass', to move, proceed, go through, to exchange or be exchanged.

3. Cpds of *pass*, or of F *passer*, are *passover*, esp *Passover* (in afflicting the Egyptians, God *passed over* the Israelites)—*passe-partout*, adopted from EF-F—*passport*, imm from EF-F *passeport* (*passe*, he passes+*port*, harbour)—*password* (a *word* allowing one to *pass*)—*pastime*, something that enables one to *pass* the *time* agreeably (cf the late MF-F *passe-temps*).

4. Simple derivatives of *pass*, or of its F original, include:
*passable*, adopted from MF-F, from *passer*, with E neg *impassable*—cf *impasse*, adopted from F;
*passage*, adopted from OF-F, from *passer*;
*passenger*, with intrusive *n* (cf *messenger*—*message*): ME, from MF(-F), *passager*, from *passage*;

5. Prefix-cpds include:
to *compass*—whence 'to *encompass*'—from OF-F *compasser*, VL *compassāre*, to pace off with equal steps, from the L n *passus*; OF *com-*

*passer* has derivative OF-F *compas*, orig a measure, a rule, whence E *compass*;
to *surpass*, from EF-F *surpasser* (*sur*, L *super*, over+*passer*);
to *trespass*, from OF *trespasser*, to pass across, to transgress (F *trépasser*, to die), VL *transpassāre* (L *trans*, across+the n *passus*); OF *trespasser* has derivative OF n *trespas* (F *trépas*), whence E *trespass*, n; derivative OF *trespasseor* becomes ME *trespassour*, E *trespasser*.

pachyderm. See the element *pachy-*.

pacific (Pacific), pacifism, pacification, pacify. See PACT, para 12.

pack (n, hence v, whence packer—cf MD *packer*, D *pakker*—and packing), package, packet (whence packet boat, whence the F *paquebot*); obvious cpds: packsack, packsaddle, packthread.

1. The n *pack*, ME *pakke*, is app of LG origin: cf MD *pac*, D *pak*, and MLG *packe, pak*, G *Packe*; cf also W *beich, baich*, Cor *bedh*, Br *bech*, a burden. With 'to *pack*', cf MD *packen*, D *pakken*.

2. *Package* either=*pack*+suffix *-age* or derives from D *pakkage*; *packet* derives from AF *pacquet*, dim from ME *pakke*.

pact, paction; compact (adj, whence n and v), compaction; impact (adj, n, v), impaction, and impinge, whence impingement; dispatch (v, hence n); page (of book), paginate, pagination; pageant, whence pageantry; propaganda (whence propagandist), propagate, propagation (whence, anl, propagative and propagatory), propagator; pole, a stake (whence v), poleaxe, and pale, a stake, also v —cf impale, impalement; sep FANG; peace, whence peaceable and peaceful—cf pax, pacific, pacify.

1. *Paction*, an agreement, derives, perh via MF, from L *pactiōn-*, o/s of *pactiō*, itself from *pactus*, pp of *pacisere* (orig an inch v), to covenant: akin to L *pāc-*, o/s of *pāx* (for *pācs*), the fact, or the act, of making, or coming to, an agreement between two belligerents, hence *Pāx*, the Goddess of Peace, hence also a peaceful agreement, a peace, peace. From the pp *pactus* comes also the n *pactus, pactum*, an agreement, whence MF *pact* (later, as in F, *pacte*), whence E pact.

2. L *pāciscere*, pp *pāctus*, is akin to L *pangere* (? a nasal form of *pagere*), to knock into the ground or fix firmly, to fasten, to conclude, with pp *pāctus*; to the syn Gr *pēgnunai*; perh—but only perh—to Skt *pásas*, a noose, a bond, and Av *pas-*,

461

to bind; certainly, however, to the OGmc words noted at FANG.

3. L *pāciscere* has the int (*com-*) prefix-cpd *compācisci*, with pp *compāctus*, whence the n *compāctus*, var *compāctum*, an agreement, whence the E syn *compact*. But *compact*, a compacted body, and 'to *compact*', to press closely together, join firmly, derive from the E adj *compact*, itself from L *compactus*, pp of *compingere*, to bring together tightly, to form a close-knit whole: *com-* for *con-*, from *cum*, with+*-pingere*, c/f of *pangere*, to fasten.

4. The cpd *impingere* is an int (*im-*) of *pangere*; in LL its dominant sense is perh 'to be driven against, to fall upon': hence 'to *impinge*'. The pp *impāctus* yields the obs adj, the v, hence also the n *impact*; derivative L *impāctiō*, o/s *impāctiōn-*, yields *impaction*.

5. But a *dispatch* derives—cf Sp *despacho*, from *despachar*—from 'to *dispatch*': and 'to *dispatch*' derives either from Sp *despachar* or from It *dispacciare*: *dis-*, L *dis-*, apart+a v 'to fasten' deriving, prob via VL, from *pāct*us, pp of *pangere*. The forms in *des-* show F influence. B & W think that the It and Sp vv derive from MF *despeechier* (F *dépêcher*) and make *despeechier* a *des-* derivative from *empeschier* (F *empêcher*), which is of completely different origin.

6. That L *pang*ere is a nasalized form of a PL *pag*ere rather follows from the existence of L *pāgina*, orig a trellis, then a column of writing, finally a page, whence, via OF *pagene*, the MF-F *page*, adopted by E. Derivative LL adj *pāginālis* becomes E *paginal*; derivative LL *pāgināre*, to construct, to compose, to write, has pp *pāginātus*, whence 'to *paginate*', whence, anl, *pagination*.

7. In AL, *pāgina* came to mean a stage's movable scaffold, and what was exhibited thereon (cf the Gr-LL *pēgma*, a scaffolding, and the 'to construct' sense of LL *pāgināre*); hence ME *pagen*, later *pagent* (? after *extend*, *extent*): E *pageant*.

8. Akin to L *pangere* is, also, L *propāgēs* (var *propāgo̧*), a layered branch or stock of a vine, a slip: *pro-*+r *pāg-*. *Propāgēs* has derivative *propāgāre*, to reproduce by slips, to propagate, with pp *propāgātus*, whence 'to *propagate*'; derivative *propāgātiō*, o/s *propāgātiōn-*, becomes, via MF-F, the E *propagation*; derivative agent L *propāgātor* is adopted by E. *Propaganda*—like F *propagande* —derives from *Congregatio de propaganda fide*, 'the council dealing with propagating the Faith', the Catholic Church's Congregation of Propaganda, founded in 1622: compare the College of Propaganda, instituted a few years later for the education of priests destined for missions.

9. A *pale* or stake, hence 'slab' of a fence, derives from MF(-F) *pal*, from L *pālus*, a stake, a pole: cf *pāla*, anything one drives, or fixes, into the ground: IE etymons, *puk-sl-o-s* and *pak-sl-a*, a stake. MF-F *pal* has derivative, to enclose as with stakes or pales, whence 'to *pale*'; cf 'to *impale*', from EF-F *empaler*, to drive a stake into, also enclose with a palisade: *em-*, for *en-*, in(to)+

*paler*. Derivative EF-F *empalement* has prompted *impalement*.

10. L *pālus*, a stake, has VL derivative *\*palicea*, whence OProv *palissa*, with derivative *palissada*, whence MF-F *palissade*, whence E *palisade*. The F word, however, could be *palis* (from *pal*)+ orthographic *-s-*+*-ade*. Cf PALACE.

11. L *pālus*, stake, becomes OE *pāl*, whence ME *pol*, *pole*, E *pole*; the ME cpd *pollax*, *polax*, becomes *poleaxe*, AE *poleax*: cf AX(E).

12. Reverting to L *pāx* (see para 1), we find that, apart from its Eccl senses, it has the derivative cpd adj *pācificus* (*pāci-*, c/f of *pāx*+*-ficus*, derivative of *-ficāre*, c/f of *facere*, to make), peace-causing, whence MF-F *pacifique*, whence E *pacific*, whence 'the *Pacific* (Ocean)', so named by Magellan because, during his voyage (1520–21) to the Philippines, it behaved very calmly. L *pācificus* has derivative *pācificāre*, whence MF-F *pacifier*, whence 'to *pacify*'; the derivative *pācificātiō*, o/s *pācificātiōn-*, leads, via late MF-F, to *pacification*.

13. L *pāx*, acc *pācem*, becomes OF *paiz*, MF *pais*, the latter adopted by ME; ME *pais* becomes late ME *pees*, whence E *peace*. Derivative OF-F *paisible* becomes ME *peisible*, whence, after *peace*, the E *peaceable*.

**pad** (1), a path or a road, whence the v; from n and v, **footpad**. This *pad* is of LG origin: cf MD *paden*, to walk along a path, MD *pader*, a path-walker, and D-LG *pad*, a path: f.a.e., PATH.

**pad** (2), a cushion (furniture, hence foot)—hence v (whence the vn **padding**)—is o.o.o.—but '*pad* of foot' does suggest an ult kinship to PAD (1).

**pad** (3), an open pannier, is a dial var of *ped*, ME *pedde*, o.o.o.; the dial derivative *pedder* became—? after *meddler*—ME *pedlere*, whence *pedlar*, *peddler*, whence, by b/f, 'to *peddle*'.

**padding.** See the 2nd PAD.

**paddle** (1), used in rowing-boats, is o.o.o.: ? from the 3rd PAD. Hence *paddle wheel* and *paddle steamer*.

**paddle** (2), to wade in shallow water, is prob a freq of *pad*, to walk: cf the G dial *padde n*, to walk short-paced, to paddle. Perh cf prec.

**paddock,** an enclosed field. See PARK, para 2.

**Paddy.** See PATRICK.

**paddy,** unmilled rice: Mal *padi*.

**padlock** is perh a *lock* shaped like a shallow basket (cf the 3rd PAD).

**padre.** See FATHER, para 4.

**paean; paeon, paeonic** (adj, hence n); **peony.**

1. A *paean*, adopted from L, derives from Gr *paian*, itself from *Paian*, the Healer, app from *paiein*, to strike, to touch forcibly, to touch so as to heal, *Paian* 'The Healer' being an epithet applied to Apollo and *paian* orig a song of praise to Apollo; it began *iè paiéon* (Ionic form of Attic *iō paiōn*), 'lo! the healer' (*ίὴ παιήων*). Perh cf, ult, 'to PAVE'.

2. Gr *paian*, song of praise, has Attic form *paiōn*, whence the metrical foot (‒◡◡◡) known in L and E as *paeon*; the derivative Gr adj *paiōnikos* becomes L *paeonicus*, whence E *paeonic*.

3. Attic *Paiōn*, the Healer, has derivative *paiōnia* (his flower), L *paeonia*, OE *peonie*, whence—although partly via OF *peone*, MF *pyone* (F *pivoine*)—E *peony*.

**pagan** (n, hence adj), **paganic, paganism, paganize; paynim; peasant** (n, hence adj), whence **peasantry**.

1. *Pagan* (ME-E) derives from LL *pāgānus*, a heathen, from L *pāgānus*, a civilian, earlier a peasant, orig a villager, from L *pāgus*, a village, a rural district, orig a boundary post stuck into the ground: prob from *pangere*, to stick (something) into (esp the ground), to fix firmly, and therefore akin to *pāx* (something firmly established): *pang*- is a nasal var of r *pag*-.

2. LL *pāgānus*, a heathen, has derivative adj *pāgānicus*, whence E *paganic*, and derivative n *pāgānismus*, whence, perh via EF-F *paganisme*, E *paganism*; learnèd F *paganiser* becomes 'to *paganize*'.

3. LL *pāgānismus* becomes OF *païenisme*, whence ME *painime, painim*, heathendom, later a heathen, whence E *paynim*, now archaic.

4. L *pāgus*, a rural district, has LL derivative *pāgēnsis*, an inhabitant thereof, whence OF *païsenc* (*-enc*, from Gmc *-ing*, 'a native'),. whence MF *païsent, païsant*, whence ME *paissaunt*, whence E *peasant*.

**page** (1): of book. See PACT, para 6.

**page** (2): at court: MF *page*: It *paggio*: prob from Gr *paidion*, dim of *pais* (o/s *paid*-), a boy: f.a.e. PEDAGOGUE.

**pageant, pageantry.** See PACT, para 7.

**paginal, paginate, pagination.** See PACT, para 6.

**pagoda,** a temple: Port *pagode*: Tamil *pagavadi*: Skt *bhagavatī*, belonging to a deity, from *bhagavat*, a deity.

**pagro.** See PORGY.

**Pahlavi.** See PARTHIA.

**paid.** See PAY.

**paideutics.** See PEDAGOGIC, para 2.

**pail.** See PEG.

**paillasse, palliasse; paillette, pallet** (bed).

The 2nd anglicizes the 1st; the 1st, adopted from F, derives from It *pagliaccio*, VL *paleaceum*, prop the neu of *paleaceus*, adj (*-aceus*) of L *palea*, chaff, straw: cf syn Skt *palāva*, OSl *plēva*, and perh L *pellis*, a skin. *Pallet* anglicizes F *paillette*, dim of *paille*, straw, L *palea*.

**pain** (n, v), whence **painful, painless, painstaking; penal** (whence **penalize**), **penalty**—**penance**—**penitence, penitent** (adj, hence n)—**impenitence, impenitent**—**penitential, penitentiary; subpoena; repent, repentance, repentant**—**repine**—**pine** (v);—**punish, punishment**—**punitive,** anl **punitory**—**impunity;**—cf the sep PATIENCE.

1. *Subpoena* is a modern Law Latin coinage from L *sub poena*, under penalty: L *poena*, penalty, punishment, hence torment, pain, becomes OF(-F) *peine*, penalty, pain, adopted by ME, whence E *pain*; 'to *pain*', ME *peinen*, derives from OF *peiner*, from *peine*.

2. L *poena* is a trln of Doric Gr *poinā*, var of

Attic *poinē*, legal compensation, a fine, hence expiation, punishment: cf Av *kaēnā*, punishment, revenge, OSl *cēna*, Lith *kaina*, reward, Skt *kayate*, he revenges, exacts punishment; IE r, *kei*-, varr *kai*-, *koi*-, to reckon (count), hence to make a reckoning.

3. L *poena* has adj *poenālis*, whence, via OF-MF *penal*, F *pénal*, the E *penal*; derivative ML *poenālitās, penālitās*, becomes late MF-F *pénalité*, whence E *penality* (obs), whence, by contr, *penalty*.

4. *Poena* has the v *poenīre* (rare), with predominant var *pūnīre*, to take vengeance upon, exact a penalty from, punish: OF *punir*, whence, via such parts as presp *punissant* and 'nous *punissons*' (we punish), the ME *punischen, punisshen*, E 'to *punish*', whence *punishable* (cf the MF-F *punissable*); OF *punir* has derivative *punissement*, whence *punishment*. The L pp *pūnītus* has neg *impūnitus*, with derivative *impūnitās*, whence MF-F *impunité*, whence *impunity*. On the pps *pūnīt*- are formed *pūnītiō*, o/s *pūnītiōn*-, whence, via MF-F, the now rare *punition*, and ML *pūnītivus*, whence *punitive*.

5. L *poenīre* has caus *poenitēre*, var *paenitēre*, to cause to repent, hence also to repent; presp *pacnitens*, o/s *paenitent*-, becomes MF *penitent* (F *pé*-), E *penitent*; derivative LL *paenitentia*, regret for sin, becomes OF *penitence* (F *pé*-), E *penitence*. The more Gallic OF *peneance, penance*, becomes ME *penaunce*, E *penance*. The L neg *impaenitens*, o/s *impaenitent*-, and its derivative *impaenitentia*, become—perh via EF-F *impénitent* and late MF-F *impénitence*—the E *impenitent, impenitence*. L *paenitentia* has, moreover, the LL derivative *paenitentiālis*, concerned with penitence, whence, perh via MF-F *pénitential* (cf the more general *pénitentiel*), the E *penitential*. Also on the s *paenitent*- arises the ML *paenitentiāria* (prob the f of an adj *paenitentiārius*), a tribunal examining cases of conscience, confession, absolution, etc., whence, ult, the modern sense of 'a house of correction' (prison).

6. L *poena* becomes OE *pīn*, penalty, pain, whence OE *pīnian*, to torment, ME *pinen*, to torment, hence also to suffer torment, whence 'to *pine*', now only vi. 'To *repine*' simply tacks prefix *re*- to *pine*.

7. 'To *repent*', however, derives from the OF-F v '(se) *repentir*', a *re*- cpd of OF '(se) *pentir*', from VL *penitīre*, from L *paenitēre* in its impersonal use, as in *me paenitet*, it causes me regret or repentance; derivative OF-F *repentance* is adopted by E, as is the OF-F presp *repentant*.

**paint** (v, hence n), whence **painting**—**painter; pict, Pict** (whence **Pictish**)—cf **depict, depiction; pictorial, picture** (n, hence v), **picturesque** (adj, hence n); **pigment** (n, hence v), **pigmentary**—**pimento, orpiment; pinto;**—**picric, picrite;**—**file,** the instrument, whence 'to *file*', and, from its rough, granulated skin, the **filefish,** and the vn **filings.**

1. 'To *paint*', ME *peinten*, derives from *peint*, f *peinte*, pp of OF-F *peindre*, from L *pingere*, to paint; *painter*, from OF-MF *peintor*, from

*pinctor*em, acc of VL *pinctor*, var of L *pictor*. L *pingere*, s and r *ping-*, pp *pictus*, s *pict-*, r ? *pic-*, is akin to Skt *piṅkte*, he paints, *piṅgas*, reddish brown, *piñjáras*, reddish yellow; the IE r is app *peig-*, to paint, closely linked to *peik-*, to adorn —whether by incision, hence by writing, or by laying-on colour: cf Skt *pinsáti*, he adorns, OSl *pisati*, to write (cf *pěgǔ*, many-hued), OP *peisāt*, he writes, Lith *piesti*, to write, to draw, Tokh B *pinkaṃ*, he writes.

2. The L pp *pictus* yields the rare *pict*, to paint, whence *Picti*, a f/e re-shaping of OE *Peohtas*, the Picts.

3. L *pingere* has cpd *dēpingere*, to describe by painting or drawing, with pp *dēpictus*, whence 'to depict'; derivative LL *dēpictiō*, o/s *dēpictiōn-*, becomes E *depiction*.

4. On the L pp s *pict-* arise both *pictor*, a painter, with derivative adj *pictōrius*, s *pictōri-*, whence E *pictorial* (cf LL *pictōria*, painting, for *pictōria ars*), and *pictūra*, a painting, whether process or product, whence *picture*. L *pictor* becomes It *pittore*, with derivative *-esco* (F, E *-esque*) adj *pittoresco*, whence F *pittoresque*, whence—after *picture*—the E *picturesque*.

5. That L *ping*ere is a nasal development of a PL r *pig-*, appears from L *pigmentum* (suffix *-mentum*), whence OF-F *pigment* and, perh independently, E *pigment*; the derivative L adj *pigmentārius* yields *pigmentary*. L *pigmentum* becomes Sp *pimienta*, Port *pimenta*, whence, prob by confusion with Sp *pimiento* (same origin), the E *pimento*. Cf E *orpiment*: OF-F *orpiment*: L *auripigmentum*, pigment of gold (*aurum*).

6. Two other R derivatives affecting E are (1) *pintado*, chintz (obs), Cape pigeon, guinea fowl: Port *pintado*, pp of *pintar*, to paint; and (2) *pinto*, a piebald horse or a Pakawa Indian (tattooed): Sp *pinto*, painted.

7. *picrite* derives from Gr *pikros*, bitter, with Min suffix *-ite*, much as *picric* (acid) derives from *pikros*, with general adj suffix *-ic*: picric acid is used in dye-making, and *picrite* contains a large percentage of magnesia (slightly bitter): *pikros*, s *pikr-*, r *pik-*, app derives from PGr *peik-* (cf para 1).

**painter** (1). See prec, para 1.

**painter** (2)—of boat. See PEND, para 5.

**pair** (n, hence v), **impair** (adj, hence n); **par, parity, disparity, imparity, nonpareil; peer, peeress, peerless, compeer; compare** (v, hence n), **comparable (incomparable), comparator, comparison, comparative; disparage, disparagement; umpire** (n, hence v);—perh **pornocracy, pornographer, pornographic, pornography;**—cf the sep PART, q.v. at PARSE.

1. The effective base of most of these words is the L adj *pār*, equal, hence an equal: o.o.o.: perh cf Hit *pariyas*, app 'of a pair': perh also cf Gr *pornē* (s *porn-*, r *por-*), a prostitute (cf *pornos*, debauchery), from or akin to Gr *pernēmi*, I sell (and export), Gr prostitutes having orig been *bought* slaves (L & S): prob the VL *pāria* (see

para 6) was orig 'a term of barter, akin to L *parāre* to value equally, . . . Av *pairyeinte* they are compared, OIr *renim* [? for *prenim*] I sell' (Webster): cf LL *pāriāre* (from *pāria*), to make, or be, equal, to traffic.

2. Gr *pornē*, a prostitute, occurs in the learnèd E cpd *pornocracy*, government (*-cracy*: Elements) by prostitutes. The Gr cpd *pornographos*, a writer on prostitution, whence F *pornographe*, has suggested E *pornographer, pornographic, pornography* (F *pornographie*).

3. L *pār*, n, esp as 'equal', is adopted by E. The derivative LL *paritās*, o/s *paritāt-*, becomes MF-F *parité*, whence E *parity*; neg LL *imparitās* becomes MF-F *imparité*, E *imparity*, the L n deriving imm from the neg adj *impār*, whence F-E *impair*. Anl with *imparitās* is LL *disparitās*, o/s *disparitāt-*, whence EF-F *disparité*, whence E *disparity*.

4. L *pār*, equal, has extn *parilis*, which perh suggested LL *pariculus* (prop a dim), whence OF-F *pareil*, with neg MF-F *nonpareil*, adopted by E as adj, whence n.

5. L *pār*, n, becomes OF-MF *per* (late MF-F *pair*), E *peer*, a person of equal rank, hence, as for MF *per*, a nobleman; hence *peerage* and *peeress* and the adj *peerless*, having no peer or equal. Cf the n *compeer*: ME *comper*: MF *comper*: L *compār*, adj and n.

6. L *pār*, adj, has neupl *pāria*, whence the VL n *pāria*, a pair, OF-F *paire*, ME *pair*, E *pair*, two of a kind.

7. With *disparity* (para 3, s.f.), cf 'to *disparage*': OF-MF *desparagier* (F *déparager*), to marry unequally: *des-*, L *dis-*, apart+*parage*, extraction, lineage, from *per*, of equal high birth; derivative OF-MF *desparagement*, a misalliance, becomes E *disparagement*, misalliance (obs), disgrace (obsol), detraction.

8. With *nonpareil* (para 4), cf *umpire*: EE 'an *umpire*' for 'a *numpire*': ME *nompere* (*nounpere*): OF *nomper*, earlier *nonper*: *non*, not+*per*, equal.

9. L *pār*, equal, has the derivative int *compār* (cf para 5, s.f.), reciprocally alike, hence n, a like person or thing, and *compār* itself has derivative *comparāre*, to render alike, to treat as alike, whence OF-F *comparer*, whence 'to *compare*'. Derivative L *comparābilis* becomes OF-F *comparable*, adopted by E, and the L neg *incomparābilis* becomes OF-F *incomparable*, likewise adopted. On *comparāt-*, s of the pp *comparātus*, arise the agent *comparātor*, adopted by E; *comparātiō*, o/s *comparātiōn-*, OF-F *comparaison*, E *comparison*; *comparātīuus* (ML *-īvus*), MF-F *comparatif*, f *comparative*, adopted by E.

**pajama** (mostly AE), **pyjama** (mostly E), now—except as adj—only in pl: Hind *pājāmā, paijāmā*, a Mohammedan's loose trousers, lit a 'leg-garment': Per *pā, pāi*, a leg+*jamāh*, garment.

**pakeha**: Maori for a white man, orig and esp a Briton: either 'foreign' (sc person) or 'turnip-coloured', i.e. pale, i.e. fair.

**pal** (n, hence v). See FRATER, para 2.

palace, palatial, palais de danse; palatine, palatinate; paladin; palsgrave.

1. *Palace*, ME from OF-F *palais* (cf *palais de danse*, dance-'palace'), derives from LL *palātium*, a royal abode, itself—because Caesar Augustus had his there—from L *Palātium*, the Palatine Hill of Rome; *Palatium* is perh akin to L *pālus*, a stake, the hill having prob, and very early, been a *palisaded* place (Webster).

2. *Palatial*, the adj of *palace*, represents L *palāti-*, s of *palātium*+adj suffix *-al*; the L adj is LL *palātīnus*, from L *Palātīnus*: MF-F *palatin*, E *palatine*. Derivative MF-F *palatinat* becomes E *palatinate*. The E adj and the E n connote '(having) royal privileges'.

3. In LL, the *palātīni* (pl of *palātīnus* used as n) were high-ranking officials; in ML, *palātīnus* was an official of the royal palace, whence It *paladino*, whence EF-F *paladin*, one of the twelve peers of France, whence E *paladin*, orig the champion of a medieval king or prince, now a legendary, esp if medieval, hero.

4. LL-ML *palātium*, a palace, becomes D *palts*, which has ED cpd *paltsgrave* (D *paltsgraaf*), whence E *palsgrave*, a count palatine: cf G *Pfalzgraf*. His wife is a *palsgravine*: D *paltsgravin*: cf G *Pfalzgräfin*.

paladin. See prec, para 3.

palaeobotany, palaeography, etc. See Elements at *palaio-*.

palais de danse. See PALACE, para 1.

palama, palamate. See FEEL, para 7.

palankeen, but usu palanquin: (like F *palanquin*, from) Port *palanquim*: Javanese *pëlaṅki*: Prakrit *pallaṅka*: Skt *palyaṅka*, var (*l* for *r*) of *paryaṅka*, palanquin, earlier a bed, earlier a sitting posture, orig a loin-cloth: cpd of *pari*, around (cf Gr *peri*)+ prob *ancati*, it curves or goes, but pcrh *anka*, a curving, a curve. Prakrit *pallaṅka* becomes Marathi *pālkhī*, *pālkī*, Hind *pālkī*, Anglo-Indian *palkee* or *palki*.

palate, whence palatable and—unless adopted from F—palatal, whence palatalize, whence palatalization; palatine; from *palate*: palation, palatitis; cf the element *palato-*; perh peel, a shovel.

1. *Palate*, roof of mouth, derives from L *palātum* (var *palātus*): o.o.o.: perh akin to L *pāla*, a shovel (itself perh related to L *pandus*, curved), whence, via OF *pele* (F *pelle*), the ME *pele*, E *peel*, a shovel.

2. From L *palātum*, learnèd F derives the adjj *palatal* and *palatin*, the latter yielding E *palatine*.

palatial; palatinate, palatine. See PALACE, para 2.

palatine (2), palatal. See PALATE, para 2.

palation, palatitis. See PALATE (heading).

palaver. See PARABLE, para 3.

pale (1), adj (and v), whence paleness; pallid, pallor; appal or appall (whence appalling), hence, by aphesis, 'to pall'; cf the sep FALLOW, adj.

1. 'To *pale*' derives from OF-F *pâlir*, itself from OF-F *pâle*, whence E *pale*: and OF *pâle* derives from L *pallidus* (whence E *pallid*), itself from *pallēre*, to be, to go, pale, whence *pallor*, adopted

by E (cf the F *pâleur*): and *pallēre*, s *pall-*, r *pal-*, is akin to Ve *palitás*, grey, Gr *pelitnos* (Ionic *pelidnos*), livid, sombre, Lith *pìlkas*, grey, *palvas*, pale, OHG *falo*, livid, pale.

2. OF *palir* has cpd *apalir*, *apallir*, to become, to render, pale, with *a-* for L *ad*, used int: ME *apallen*, later *appallen*, E 'to *appal*', to become pale (obs), to cause to become pale.

pale (2), a stake; hence as v. See PACT, para 9.

paleobotany, -graphy, -lithic, -logy, paleontology. See the element *palaio-*.

Palestine, whence Palestinian.

The adj derives from L *Palestīnus* (var of *Palaestīnus*), adj of *Palestīna*, var of *Palaestina*, trln of Gr *Palaistinē*, itself from H *Pelesheth*. The inhabitants were, in H, *Pelistīm* or *Pelishtīm* (cf Ar *Filastīn*), whence Gr *Philistinoi*, LL *Philistini*, both pl, whence, by b/f, the F sing *Philistin*, whence E *Philistine* (n, hence adj). Strictly, the Philistines inhabited S.W. Palestine; 'after harassing the Israelites for centuries they were finally assimilated by the native Semites' (Webster) and were regarded as barbarians, hence *Philistine*, an unenlightened person, hostile to art, literature, thought, the transition being aided, both in E and in F, by G *Philister*, a G universities' (orig, theological students') slang name—at Jena as early as C17—for a townsman, hence outsider, hence any ignorant person. First used in France by Théophile Gautier in 1847 (B & W), *Philistine* was 'introduced into England by Matthew Arnold (cf *Judges*, xvi, 9)' (Walshe). Hence *Philistinism*.

palette; pallet, implement with flat blade and a handle. The painter's *palette*, adopted from F, derives, as a dim (*-ette*), from L *pāla*, a shovel (cf *peel* at PALATE, para 1, s.f.): and from F *palette* comes the E implement *pallet*.

palfrey: ME *palefrai*: OF *palefrei* (F *palefroi*): ML *palefredus*, *palafredus*, for (*r* becomes *l*) ML *parafredus*, a contr var of ML *paraveredus*, from LL *paraueredus*, 'post horse *for the lesser highways and out-of-the-way places*' (Souter), the ML form accounting also for the OHG-MHG forms that end up as G *Pferd*, horse: a hybrid of Gr *para*, near, beside+LL *ueraedus*, *ueredus*, a courier's horse, a post horse (Souter), the latter being of C origin: cf W *gorwydd*, a trained horse (app a cpd: *go-rhwydd*); the rare Cor *verh*, a horse; Gaul *woredos*, app a cpd: *wo*+*redos*, the latter intimately related to Gaul-L *raeda*, *reda*, a cart, a waggon, from the C r *red-*, *ret-*, to run. (Walshe; Malvezin.)

Pali: Skt *pāli*, line, hence a series: from the series of Buddhist religious writings.

palimpsest, palindrome, palinode. See the element *pali-*; for *palinode*, see also ODE, para 2.

palisade. See PACT, para 10.

palkee, palki. See PALANQUIN, s.f.

pall (1), a rich stuff for garments (obs), hence a fine covering cloth, esp over a coffin (whence *pallbearer*), a cloak: ME *pal*: OE *pael*: L *pallium* (s *palli-*, r *pall-*), a covering cloth, a man's cloak, a toga, closely akin to L *palla*, a woman's cloak:

o.o.o.: perh (*r* becoming *l*) cf Gr *pharos*, a kind of garment (E & M), or, less prob, the L *pellis*, skin (Webster). As used in An and Zoo, *pallium* has adj *pallial*. Cf PALLIATE.

pall (2), v. See the 1st PALE (heading).

palladium; Pallas.

The Chem element *palladium* (suffix *-ium*) is derived by SciL, from the asteroid *Pallas*, itself named after the Gr tutelary goddess *Pallas* Athena, whence *Palladion*, L *Palladium*, a famous protective statue of her, whence E *palladium*, any potent safeguard.

Gr *Pallas*, gen *Pallad*os, personifies *pallas*, maiden.

pall-bearer. See the 1st PALL.

pallet (1), a bed. See PAILLASSE, s.f.

pallet (2), implement. See PALETTE.

pallial. See the 1st PALL, s.f.

palliasse. See PAILLASSE.

palliate, palliation, palliative (adj, hence n).

'To *palliate*', to cloak or disguise (obs), hence to mitigate, derives from LL *palliātus*, cloaked, from *palliāre*, to conceal, orig to cover with a *pallium*, q.v. at the 1st PALL. Derivative ML *palliātiō*, o/s *palliātiōn*-, and ML adj *palliātivus* yield—perh via F—*palliation* and *palliative*.

pallid. See the 1st PALE, para 1.

pallium. See the 1st PALL, s.f.

pall-mall. See MALL, para 1.

pallor. See the 1st PALE, para 1.

palm; palmar, palmate; palmer; palmetto; palmistry. See FEEL, para 2.

palmus. See FEEL, para 3.

palmy. See FEEL, para 2, s.f.

palp, palpable, palpate, palpation. See FEEL, para 4.

palpebral. See FEEL, para 5.

palpitant, palpitate, palpitation. See FEEL, para 6.

palsgrave. See PALACE, para 4.

palsy. See LOSE, para 13.

palter is prob a b/f from paltry, trashy, petty, contemptible, which, like dial *paltry, peltry, palt, pelt*, rags, rubbish, prob derives from LG: cf LG *paltrig*, ragged, from *palte*, a rag, a tatter.

paludal; paludine; paludous, marshy: resp L *palūd*-, o/s of *palūs*, a marsh+adj suffix *-al*; L *palūd*-+adj *-ine*; L *palūdōsus*, marshy: and L *palūs* (r *pal*-) is akin to Skt *pal*valam, a marsh, a large pond, and Lith *pēlkē*, a marsh: the IE r is app *pal*-, varr *pel*-, *pil*-, to pour (water), as in Lith *pilù, pìlti*, and, ? metathetic, L *pluit*, it rains (cf PLUVIAL).

pam. See PAMPHLET, para 2.

Pampa, the great grassy plain of SArgentina; pampas, vast treeless plains S of the Amazon; joint adj, pampean (*pampa, pampas*+suffix *-ean*). *Pampa* and *pampas*, both adopted from Sp, derive from Quechua (and Aymara) *pampa*, a plain.

pamper, whence pa pampered and vn pampering, app comes from the syn LG *pamperen*, caus of *pampen*, to live softly and luxuriously, itself prob from *pampe*, thick pap, perh a nasal var of the r of PAP.

pamphlet, whence pamphleteer (n, hence v): ME *pamflet*, contr of *pamfilet*: OF *pamfilet*, for *Pamphilet*, a small book: a popular dim (*-et*) of *Pamphilus*, short form of the C12 poem *Pamphilus seu de Amore*, 'Pamphilus, or Concerning Love', which prob owed much of its tremendous popularity to its remarkable characterization of an old bawd.

2. L *Pamphilus*, Loved by All (Gr *Pamphilos*), becomes F *Pamphile*, whence the card-game *pamphile*, whence E *pam*.

Pan, whence Panpipe(s); panic, adj, whence n (whence panicky), whence v.

The n *panic* prob owes something to Gr *to panikon deima*, fear caused by Pan, often elliptically *to panikon*: *panikon* is the neu of adj *panikos*, of Pan, whence EF-F *panique* (whence the n *panique*), whence the E adj *panic*. Gr *panikos* is the adj of *Pan* (itself duly adopted by L, hence by E); and Gr *Pan*, var *Paiōn*, Arkadian *Paōn*, perh derives from Skt *Pūṣán*-, a Vedic god, the protector and increaser of herds (Hofmann).

pan (1), a part. See PANE.

pan (2), a utensil, whence pancake and panhandle, whence panhandler (handler of a pan or bowl or cup for alms), whence, by b/f, 'to panhandle'; pannikin; paten or patin; penny, pfennig.

1. *Pan*, broad and shallow and (except in *saucepan*) usu open, derives from ME, from OE, *panne*, which, perh via ON *panna*, derives prob from ML *panna*, contr of L *patina*, a cooking bowl, itself from Gr *patanē*: akin to Gr *patakhnon* and L *patera*, a large flat vase, and therefore to Hit *pittar*, a plate.

2. Very closely akin to, prob a mere var of, L *patina* is L *patena*, a plate, whence MF-F *patène*, whence ME *pateyne*, E *patten*; the E var *patin* is prob influenced by L *patina*.

3. Akin to OE-ME *panne* are MD *panne*, D *pan*, and OHG *pfanna*, MHG-G *pfanne*, a pan; the D dim *pannekijn* becomes E *pannikin*.

4. Perh from OHG *pfanna* is OHG *pfenning*, MHG *pfenninc* later eased to *pfennic*, whence G *Pfennig*, a G penny, akin, obviously, to E *penny*, ME *peni*, OE *penig*, easement of *pening, penning* (var *pending*): cf ON *penningr* and MD *pennic, penninc*, and, as in D, *penning*, and OFris *pennig, penning, pannig, panning* (cf OFris *panne*, a pan); the OGmc suffix *-ing* is that occurring also in *shilling*. The sem link is: 'made in a *pan*' (Walshe)—or perh '*pan*-shaped' (Webster). And, by the way, the A sl *pan*, a face, as in 'dead *pan*', an expressionless face or, hence, its owner, derives from seeing one's face mirrored in the bottom of a well burnished frying-pan belonging to a goldminer or, maybe, a housewife: cf, sem, *dial* and *clock*(-face).

pan-, 'all-', in cpds. See the element *pan*-.

panacea. See the element *pan*-.

panache. See the 2nd PEN, para 4.

Panam. See PANTRY, para 2.

panama is elliptical for *Panama hat*, formerly distributed mainly from Panama City, CA.

pancake. See the 2nd PAN (heading).

pancreas. See the element *pan-*.

panda is o.o.o.: ? Tibetan.

pandanus is a SciL re-shaping of Mal *pandan*.

pandar. See PANDER.

pandect, a complete digest: F *pandecte*: LL *pandectes* (pl), Justinian's collection of laws: Gr *pandektēs*, n from adj 'all-receiving': *pan*, neu of *pas*, all+*-dektēs*, receiving, from *dekhesthai*, to receive.

pandemic. See DEMOCRACY, para 2.

pandemonium, whence adj pandemoniac. See the element *pan-*.

pander, n (var *pandar*, obsol), whence v; Pandarus.

A *pander*, or sexual intermediary, derives from Chaucer's *Pandare* or, adopted from L, *Pandarus*: Gr *Pandaros*, in *The Iliad*: the intermediary between Troilus and Cressida: the E popularity of the word owes a little to Boccaccio's Pandaro and much to Shakespeare's *Troilus and Cressida*.

Pandora. See the element *pan-*.

pandore, pandura. See MANDOLIN.

pane (1), a piece, and pan, a part; panel (n, hence v).

1. *Pane*, a piece, usu square, of cloth (obs), hence a piece or a facet, a division or compartment as, e.g., of a window, derives, like *pan*, a part or a division, from ME *pan*: OF *pan*: L *pannus*, a piece of cloth, a rag, influenced, in several senses, by the cognate L *panis*, a panel. L *pannus* prob belongs to the IE group typified by *\*pen-*, (vi) to hang: f.a.e., PEND.

2. *Panel*, ME from MF *panel*, derives from VL *\*pannellus*, dim of L *pannus*, and prob also from VL *\*panellus*, dim of L *panis*, a panel.

pane (2); peen.

1. A *pane* or *peen*, that end of a hammer's head which is opp the face, derives, the former from OF-MF *pane* (F *panne*), the latter perh from the MF var *penne*: prob from VL *\*patina*, app from Gr *pathnē*, var of *phatnē*, a crèche, but perh from that Gmc r which is represented by MD *penne*, D *pen*, a pin, and by G *Pinne*, pane of a hammer (f.a.e., PIN).

panegyric. See the element *pan-*.

paneity. See PANTRY, para 5.

panel. See the 1st PANE, para 2.

pang, n, hence v—esp in pp panged; prong whence the quadruped pronghorn.

*Pang*, a sharp pain, is o.o.o.; but app it blends— or, if you prefer, confuses—E *pain* and ME *prange*, var of *pronge*, a sharp pain, prob intimately related to ME *pronge*, *prange*, a fork, hence the tine of a fork: cf MLG *prange*, a (sharp) stick, *prangen*, to pinch, and MHG-G *pranger*, a pillory, and Go ana*praggan* (pron *-prangan*), to afflict, oppress: ? ult echoic.

panhandle, panhandler. See the 2nd PAN (heading).

panic, panicky. See PAN.

panification. See PANTRY, para 7.

Panjab (Punjab), Panjabi; punch, the drink.

1. *Panjabi* is prop the adj (indicated by *-i*) of *Panjab*, the land of the 'five rivers' (Indus and tributaries). With *pan-*, cf Skt *pañca*, 5; the E pron *pun-* occurs also in *pundit*, prop *pandit*; f.a.e., FIVE, para 16.

2. *Pan-* app recurs in *punch*, a drink consisting of five ingredients.

panjandrum. See CONUNDRUM.

pannage. See PASTOR, para 7.

pannam. See PANTRY, para 2.

pannier. See PANTRY, para 3.

pannikin. See the 2nd PAN, para 3.

panoply. See the element *pan-*.

panorama, whence panoramic. See the element *-orama*.

Panpipe. See PAN (heading).

pansy. See PEND, para 11, s.f.

pant, to breathe hard. See FANCY, para 8.

pantaloon, with pl yielding, by abbr, pants and, by dim, pantalets or pantalettes.

*Pantaloon* anglicizes EF-F *pantalon*, recorded for 1651 in modern sense and for 1550 thus, 'L'un vêtu en Pantalon, l'autre en Zani' (cf ZANY): It *Pantalone*, contr of *Pantaleone*, a long-trousered character, always a Venetian, of It comedy: from St *Pantaleon*, held in high regard by the Venetians (B & W): lit 'entirely lion', hence 'exceptionally courageous'.

pantechnicon. See the element *pan-*.

pantheism, Pantheon. See THEISM, para 2, and cf the element *pan-*, s.f.

panther is a Classical re-shaping of ME, from OF, *pantere*: L *panthera*: Gr *panthēr*: akin to Skt *puṇḍārīkas*, a tiger: perh to E PARD. Derivative L *pantherīnus* yields *pantherine*.

pantile combines *pan*, a dish, and a roof *tile*: from the shape.

pantomime, pantomimic.

The adj derives from L *pantomimicus*, from the n *pantomimus*, whence, via EF-F, the E *pantomime*, orig 'he who mimes everything', as in L and in the orig Gr *pantomimos*: *pantos*, of everything, *mimos*, q.v. at MIME.

pantry, whence pantryman; pannier; 'pannam', ? 'Panam'; paneity; pastille; panification;—prefix-cpds: accompany, accompaniment, whence, anl, accompanist; appanage; companion (n, hence v), whence companionable, companionage (? suggested by F *compagnonnage*), companionate—company, n and v; impanate, impanation.

1. Behind all these terms, the L *pānis* (s and r *pān-*), bread, stands unmistakable: app from PL *\*pasnis*, *pānis* is prob akin, ult, to L *pāscere* (s *pāsc-*, r *pās-*), to nourish, q.v. sep at PASTOR. If that be so, the IE r would be *\*pa-*, to nourish: cf Gr *pateomai* (s *pate-*, r *pat-*), I eat—lit, I nourish myself.

Simples

2. L *pānis* has acc *pānem*, which suggested the obs cant *pannam*, *-um*, bread, and perh blended with *Paris* to form the F sl *Panam*, Paris.

3. The derivative L adj *pānārius* has neu *pānārium*, used as n for 'bread-basket': whence OF, hence ME, *panier*, E *pannier*.

4. L *pānis* becomes OF-F *pain*, whence—perh influenced by ML *panetārius*, a baker—the OF-F *paneterie*, bread-store, whence ME *panetrie*, contr to *pantrie*, whence *pantry*.

5. In LL, *pānis* acquires the special sense 'the Eucharist'; whence the learnèd E *paneity*, the quality of being bread.

6. *Pānis* has dim *pāstillum*, a small loaf, hence, because shaped like such a loaf, a pastille; the L, in the 2nd sense, becomes EF-F *pastille*, adopted by E.

## Compounds

7. LL forms the cpd *pānificāre*, to make bread, whence EF-F *panifier*, with derivative *panification*, adopted by E.

8. More numerous are the prefix-cpds, of which the most important group is that of *companion*, *company*, the latter from ML *compānia*, lit the sharing of bread with another, the former from ML *compāniō*, o/s *compāniōn-*, via OF-F *compagnie* and via OF-F *compagnon*; 'to company' was prob suggested by OF *compagnier*.

9. OF *compagnier* has OF cpd *acompagnier* (or *acc-*), MF-F *accompagner*, whence 'to accompany'; the derivative, orig Mus, MF-F *accompagnement* becomes E *accompaniment*.

10. OF *pain* has a further cpd: MF-F *apanage*, whence E *apanage*, orig the provision made for young members of the royal family, now usu *appanage*: from OF-MF *apaner*, to support, (lit) to nourish: ML *appānāre*, to supply with bread: *ap-*, for *ad*, to+*pān-*, s of *pānis*+inf *-āre*.

11. L *pānis* has the Theo ML cpd *impānāre*, to embody in bread, with pp *impānātus*, whence the E Theo adj *impanate*; derivative ML *impānātiō*, o/s *impānātiōn-*, yields *impanation*.

**pants**, trousers. See PANTALOON (heading).

**pap**, a nipple, hence anything nipple-shaped, ME *pappe*, cf Lith *papās*, nipple, may ult be akin to *pap*, soft food, cf MD *pappe* (MD-D *pap*); the latter is prob, the former perh, akin to L *pappa*, a child's word for food. Therefore cf PAPILLA.

**papa.** See FATHER, para 16.

**papacy, papal.** See FATHER, para 16.

**Papaver, papaverine.** See POPPY.

**papaw (pawpaw); papaya.**
The former derives from Sp *papayo*, the papaw tree; the latter is adopted from Sp *papaya*, its fruit: of Caribbean origin, esp Antillean Carib *papaya* (the fruit).

**paper** (n, hence v), whence **papery; papier mâché; papyrus**, cf the element *papyro-*; **taper** (n, hence v), whence **taperwise**, like a taper, whence the adj **taper.**

1. E *paper*, like F *papier* (as in *papier mâché*, lit 'chewed paper'—cf MASTICATE), derives from OF-F *papier*: L *papȳrus*, the tall sedge from which the Ancient Egyptians made a sort of paper (E *papyrus*) and which grew also in Near and Middle Eastern countries: Gr *papuros*; o.o.o., but prob Eg.

2. In LL-ML, *papyrus* meant also a wick and, in ML, also a small wax candle (the orig sense of the E *taper*): whence, by dissimilation, OE *tapur*, later *tapor*, then *taper*, whence E *taper*, now usu a long thin candle or waxed wick, hence, via the v, the adj *tapering*.

**papilla**, whence—cf *mammillary* from *mammilla* —**papillary; pappus; papule**, whence **papular; pimple**, whence **pimply**; cf the sep PEPPER.

1. *Papilla*, a nipple, LL a pustule, a pimple, is adopted from L, where, meaning orig (in L) a small bud, it is a dim, very closely related to L *papula*, a pimple, LL a nipple, adapted by Med E as *papule*. The r of both words is *pap-*.

2. Perh akin to *papilla* and *papula* is L *pappus* (s *papp-*, r *pap-*), the beard or down forming the cotton-like crest of certain plants, but orig a grandfather, an old man: trln of Gr *pappos*, intimately related to Gr *pappas*, *pappa*, whence L *pappas*, *pappa*, (familiarly) father, perh id with L *pappa*, nourishment, food: see PAP.

3. L *papilla* and *papula* are akin to Lith *papās* and Skt *pippalaka*, a nipple, themselves closely akin to the Lith *pampti*, to swell up, a nasal form of *\*papti*. Cf *pimple*, which perh represents a thinned nasal cognate of the syn L *papula*; for the thinning, perh cf the non-nasal OE *piplian*, to have herpes. With the basic *pap-*, perh cf the Hit *pappars-*, to sprinkle or pour, *pap*arashun, I sprinkled or poured.

**papillon.** See PAVILION, para 1.

**papism; papist**, whence **papistic, papistry.** See FATHER, para 16.

**pappus.** See PAPILLA, para 2.

**pappy** (1), adj=PAP+euphonic *-p-*+adj *-y*.

**pappy** (2), n, papa. See FATHER, para 16.

**paprika.** See PEPPER, para 2.

**Papua**, whence the adj, hence n, **Papuan**, derives from Mal *papuwa*, frizzled, the New Guinea natives having frizzy hair.

**papule.** See PAPILLA, para 1, s.f.

**papyraceous** (L *papȳrāceus*) and **papyral** (E suffix *-al*) are adjj of **papyrus**, q.v. at PAPER, para 1.

**par**, adj, n. See PAIR, para 3.

**parable** (n, hence v)—**parabola** (whence Geom **parabolic** and **paraboloid**)—**parabolical; palaver** (n, hence v) and **parlary; parle, parley** (n, hence v), **pourparler**—**parlance**—**parlatory**—**parlor** (AE) or **parlour**—**parliament**, whence **parliamentary**, whence **parliamentarian; parol, parole** (n, hence v).

1. Geom *parabola* belongs to SciL, from L *parabolē*, a placing beside; the form is that of LL *parabola*, a similitude, a proverb, esp a parable, from the syn LGr *parabolē*: from *paraballein*, to throw (*ballein*: cf BALLISTICS) beside (*para*), hence to compare. Derivative Gr *parabolikos*, in its LGr sense, becomes LL *parabolicus*, whence late MF-F *parabolique*, whence E *parabolic*, now usu (except in Geom) in extn *parabolical*.

2. LL *parabola*, proverb, parable, becomes

MF-F *parabole*, adopted by ME, which promptly contracts it to *parable*.

3. In ML, *parabola* acquires the further senses 'word' and 'tale, story': whence Port *palavra* (cf the Sp *palabra*), whence E *palaver*, with several new, very naturally derivative senses.

4. ML *parabola*, word, becomes OF-F *parole*, word in general, speech, whence E *parole* or, in Law, *parol*, esp *by parol*, by word of mouth. Military and legal *parole* derives from F *parole* in its special sense 'word of promise', itself prob from Eccl L *parabola Christi*, the word(s) of Christ.

5. LL *parabola* has ML derivative *parabolāre*, whence OF-F *parler*, to speak, whence ME *parlen*, E 'to *parle*' (obsol); app from the OF-F pp *parlé*, f *parlée*, comes E *parley*. *Parabolāre* becomes It *parlare*, whence E *parlary*, that jargon of C19-20 itinerant actors, circusmen, showmen, which is based upon It words.

6. The OF-EF cpd v *pourparler* becomes, in C16, n, adopted by E as a diplomatic term; the OF-MF *parlance* (*parler*+suffix -*ance*) has likewise been adopted by E.

7. OF *parleoir* (from *parler*), whence F *parloir*, has, by confusion with *parleor*, a speaker, the var *parleor*, whence ME *parlur*, *parlour*, E *parlour*, AE *parlor*; this OF *parleor* owes something to ML *parlatōrium* (for *\*parabolatōrium*), a room—orig in a monastery or a nunnery—for conversation with visitors, whence Eccl.E *parlatory*.

8. OF-F *parler* has the OF-F derivative *parlement* (suffix -*ment*), perh suggested by ML *parlamentum*, for both orig meant 'conversation, hence a conference'; hence ME *parlement*, whence—influenced by the ML var *parliamentum*—the E *parliament*, a conference; as in MF, so in late ME, the term came to designate a judicial, hence a political, assembly, whence *Parlement*, *Parliament*, whence, influenced by EF-F *parlementaire*, the E *parliamentary*.

**parachute** is a device *para*-, against (see Prefixes), a *chute* or fall (see CADENCE).

**parade.** See PARE, para 2, s.f.

**paradigm.** See DICT, para 23.

**paradise,** whence the adjj **paradisiac(al)** and **paradisal,** derives from ME *paradis*, adopted from OF(-F) *paradis*: LL *paradīsus*, the Garden of Eden: Gr *paradeisos*, a park, a pleasure garden: MPer *\*paridaiza*, a nobleman's park: cf Av *pairidaēza*, an enclosure—*pairi*, about, around (cf Gr *peri*)+*daēza*, a wall (cf Gr *teikhos*, *toikhos*): cf also Syriac *pardēza*, a garden, from H *pardeš*, enclosed garden, from Per. (Hofmann.) The sense 'abode of the blest, heaven', occurs as early as Tertullian; hence the LL adj *paradisiacus*, whence E *paradisiac* (cf F *paradisiaque*), often in extn *paradisiacal*.

2. LL *paradīsus* becomes VL *\*parauisus*, ML *\*paravisus*, MF *parevis*, later *parvis*, paradise, later (*parvis*) a forecourt, because, early in the Middle Ages, the forecourt of St Peter's, Rome, was, in Eccl L, named *Paradīsus*.

**parados.** See DORSAL, para 4.

**paradox, paradoxical.** See DOGMA, para 3.

**paraffin,** (obsol) **paraffine:** G *Paraffin*: L *parum*, too little+*affin*is, related: from its Chem inactivity.

**paragon** (n, hence v) is adopted from EF-F *paragon* (F *parangon*): It *paragone*, a model: prob from MGr *parakonē*, a polishing stone, from Gr *parakonan*, to rub against: *para*, beside+*akonē*, a whetstone.

**paragraph** (n, hence v—whence **paragrapher**): MF-F *paragraphe*: ML *paragraphus* (cf LL *paragraphē*, 'brief summary of a subject *before passing to another*': Souter): from Gr *paragraphos* (sc *grammē*), a marginal stroke or line, from *paragraphein*, to write (*graphein*: cf *graph*, q.v. at GRAMMAR, para 7) in the margin (*para*, beside).

**parakeet.** Cf *parrot* and see PETER, para 10.

**parallactic** derives from Gr *parallaktikos*, adj of *parallaxis*, whence, via EF-F *parallaxe*, the E **parallax;** Gr *parallaxis* derives from *parallassein*, to change slightly, to deviate: *para*, beside+*allassein*, to change.

**parallel** (adj, hence n and v): EF-F *parallèle*: L *parallelus*: Gr *parallēlos*, lit of two or more lines (lying) beside each other: *para*, beside+*allēlōn*, of each, or one, another, from *allos*, other (cf *alias* and *else*).

**parallelogram.** See the element *paralleli*-.

**paralogism, paralogy.** See LEGEND, para 30, s.f.

**paralysis, paralytic, paralyze.** See LOSE, para 12.

**parameter, parametric.** See MEASURE, para 4.

**paramount.** See MINATORY, para 10.

**paramour.** See AMATEUR, II, 3.

**paranoia, paranoiac.** See NOUS, para 2.

**parapet.** See DORSAL, para 4.

**paraphernalia** derives elliptically from ML '*paraphernalia* bona' (*bona*, goods): from LL from Gr *parapherna* (pl), property other than the marriage portion: *para*, beside, besides+*phernē*, a bride's dowry, itself akin to *pherein*, to bring.

**paraphrase, paraphrastic.** See PHRASE, para 2.

**paraphysis**=Gr *para*, beside+*phusis*, nature, SciL *physis*, q.v. at PHYSIC.

**parapodium,** a SciL formation: Gr *para*, beside +*pod*-, o/s of *pous*, a foot (f.a.e., FOOT), suffix -*ium*.

**parasite** (whence **parasitism**), **parasitic(al);** cf the element *parasito*-.

*Parasitic*, whence the extn *parasitical*, derives, via L *parasiticus*, from Gr *parasitikos*, adj of *parasitos*, itself prop an adj for '(eating) *sitos*, food, beside (*para*)' another, esp at table.

**parasol.** See SOLAR, para 5, s.f.

**parataxis.** Cf TAXIS.

**parathyroid.** Cf THYROID.

**paravane.** See VANE.

**parboil.** See BOIL, para 2.

**parcel.** See PART, para 7.

**parcener.** See PART, para 9.

**parch.** See PIERCE, para 5.

**parchment; Pergamene, pergameneous, Pergamon** or **Pergamum.**

1. *Parchment* derives from ME, from OF(-F), *parchemin*, which represents a VL *\*particaminum*, a confused blend of *parthica* (pellis), lit 'Parthian skin' (some Parthian texts are, in the fact, written

on parchment)+LL *pergamēnum*, (a sheet of) parchment, ML *pergamēna* (prop a neupl become f sing), var *pergamīna*, parchment: the former from L *pergamēnus*, of Pergamum, the latter from Gr *pergamēnē*, '(skin) of Pergamon', an ancient city of Mysia in NW Asia Minor; at Pergamon the art of preparing sheepskins for writing on was invented. The *-t-* of the E *parchment* derives from ML *pergamentum*, var of LL *pergamēnum*, with *-t-* for 'part*hica*' (as above).

2. Gr *Pergamon* has adj *Pergamēnos*, whence L *Pergamēnus*, whence E *Pergamene*, with varr *Pergamenous, Pergameneous*.

**pard.** See LEO, para 3.

**pardon, pardonable, pardoner.** See DONATION, para 3.

**pare,** whence vn **parings; parade** (n, hence v); **parry** (v, hence n)—cf 'to spar', as in boxing.— Prefix-cpds: sep APPAREL (APPARATUS); **imperative, imperator**—cf the sep EMPEROR (EMPIRE); **prepare—preparation, preparative, preparatory; rampart; repair,** to mend—**reparable** and neg **irreparable—reparation, reparatory; separable** (and **inseparable), separate, separation, separative, separator**—cf **sever** (whence **severable), several, severalty, severance**—**dissever, disseverance;** cf the prefix *para-* (cf *parry*) in sep PARACHUTE, PARAPET, PARASOL; cf the cognate PARENT, the perh cognate PAUPER, the prob cognate PART, and the element *-parous*.

### Indo-European

1. In the L words, the r is basically *par-*, as in *par*āre, to prepare, *par*ere, *to procure, to produce (a child), *par*s, a part, with var *per-*, as in re*per*ire, to find, and pau*per*, poor; the r *per-* occurs also in Lith *per*iù, *per*éti, to hatch; in Gr, the r is *por*-, as in e*por*on (aorist), I procured; in Skt, the r is *pur*-, as in *pūr*tám, a wage—that which one procures by producing. The IE r, therefore, is perh *\*per-*, to procure, hence to produce, to prepare.

### Latin Simples

2. To 'prepare' an apple is to *pare* it: OF *pare*, to prepare, hence to arrange, hence to trim, to adorn: L *parāre*. But *parāre* acquires, in It *parare*, the further senses 'to prevent, to ward off', whence the EF-F *parer*, to ward off a thrust or blow in fencing, whence 'to *parry*'. L *parāre* becomes Sp *parar*, to prepare, with the further sense 'to stop' (esp to stop a horse short), whence *parada*, orig of stopping a horse, hence a stopping or halting of a group of cavalrymen, hence of soldiers in general, hence an assembling for exercise, hence the assembly itself: whence EF-F *parade*, adopted by E.

3. With 'to *parry*', cf 'to *spar*', as a boxer does: from the EF vr *s'esparer* (F *s'éparer*), to kick (vi): from It *sparare*, to kick: from It *parare*, as above.

### Latin Prefix-Compounds

4. L *imperāre*, for *\*imparāre*, to prepare (*parāre*) against or for (*in*), hence to give orders against or

for, hence to order, has agent *imperātor* and LL adj *imperātiuus*, ML *imperātīvus*, whence, perh via MF-F *impératif*, f *impérative*, the E *imperative*.

5. L *praeparāre*, to produce, or make ready, *prae* or beforehand, to prepare, becomes MF-F *préparer*, whence 'to *prepare*'; derivative *praeparātiō*, o/s *praeparātiōn-*, becomes MF-F *préparation*, E *preparation*, and LL *praeparatōrius*, E *preparatory*; and MF-F *préparatif*, f *préparative*, yields E *preparative*.

6. The VL *\*anteparāre*, to prepare (esp to defend oneself), becomes OProv *antparar*, eased to *amparar*, whence MF *emparer*, to fortify (whence EF-F *s'emparer* de quelquechose, to take possession of something), with late MF-F cpd *remparer* (*re-*, again, used int), whence late MF-F *rempart*, whence E *rampart*.

7. L *reparāre*, to procure again, to procure in exchange, hence to restore or mend, becomes OF *reparer* (F *réparer*), whence 'to *repair*'; derivative L *reparābilis* becomes late MF-F *réparable*, whence E *reparable*; derivative LL *reparātiō*, o/s *reparātiōn-*, becomes MF-F *réparation*, whence E *reparation*, whence, anl, *reparative, reparatory*. The L neg *irreparābilis* becomes MF-F *irréparable*, whence E *irreparable*.

8. L *sēparāre*, to prepare *sē-* or apart, to separate, has derivative *sēparābilis*, whence late MF-F *séparable* and E *separable*; the L neg *insēparābilis* yields MF-F *inséparable* and E *inseparable*. The L pp *sēparātus* accounts for E *separate*, adj and v alike; derivative *sēparātiō*, o/s *sēparātiōn-*, becomes MF-F *séparation*, whence E *separation*; LL *sēparātiuus*, ML *-īvus*, yields E *separative*; the LL agent *sēparātor* is adopted by E; the anl F *séparatiste* becomes E *separatist*.

9. L *sēparāre* becomes VL *\*sēperāre*, whence OF *sevrer*, to separate (MF-F to wean), whence 'to *sever*'; derivative OF *sevrance* becomes AF *severance*, adopted by E. The LL cpd *dissēparāre* becomes OF *dessevrer*, whence 'to *dissever*'; derivative OF *dessevrance* leads to E *disseverance*.

10. L *sēparāre* app has derivative adj *sēpar*, separate, with ML extn *sēparālis*, whence AF *several*, adopted by E; derivative AF *severalté* (*severauté*), whence E *severalty*.

**paregoric** (adj, hence n—a soothing medicine), often in extn **paregorical**: LL *parēgoricus*: Gr *parēgorikos*, extn of the adj *parēgoros*, addressing (an assembly), hence encouraging or, esp, soothing: *para*, beside, in the company of+*agora*, an assembly.

**parent** (n, hence adj), **parentage, parental; parturient, parturition; repertory.** Cf the element *-para, -parous*, 'producing young'.

1. L *parere* (s and r, *par-*), *\*to procure, hence to produce young, is akin to L *parāre* (s and r, *par-*), to procure, to prepare: cf, therefore, PARE, para 1, and OE *fearr*, a bull, Gr *poris* (s and r, *por-*), calf, and Skt *pṛthuka*, the young of any animal: IE r, prob *\*per-*.

2. *Parere* has presp *parens* (o/s *parent-*), which, used as n, becomes OF-F *parent*, adopted by E;

derivative L *parentālis* becomes E *parental*; and derivative OF *parentage* is adopted by E.

3. *Parere* has desid *parturīre*, to desire to give birth, with pp *parturiens*, o/s *parturient-*, whence the E adj *parturient*; derivative LL *parturitiō*, o/s *parturitiōn-*, yields *parturition*, childbirth.

4. The basic sense of *parere*—'to procure'— occurs in the cpd *reperīre*, to procure for oneself, hence to find, with pp *repertus*, whence LL *repertōrium*, a list or a catalogue, whence (late MF-F *répertoire* and) E *repertory*, with theatrical sense influenced by the F word, which directly yields E *repertoire*: a list, specialized as a list of plays, becomes a stock of plays; hence (*repertoire* only) a fund of, e.g., good stories.

**parenthesis, parenthetical.** See THESIS, para 13.

**parergal, parergon.** See ENERGETIC, para 3.

**par excellence,** adopted from F, is lit 'by excellence': *par*, L *per+excellence*, as in E (cf EXCEL).

**parget, pargetting.** See the 2nd JET, para 4.

**parhelion.** See SOLAR, para 6.

**pariah**: Port *paria*: Tamil *paṛaiyan*, member of a low (but not the lowest) caste, lit a drummer, from *paṛai*, a drum. The sense 'outcast', as in F *paria* and E *pariah*, is a sense-degradation peculiar to Europe.

**parietal.** See the element *parieto-*.

**parings.** See PARE (heading).

**Paris** (1), the city, with adj (hence n) **Parisian**. The former is adopted from F, the latter derives from F *parisien*, f *parisienne*, adj of *Paris*, which, like It *Parigi*, derives from L *Parisii*, the Gallic tribe whose capital was *Lutetia*, whence the literary F *Lutèce*; both L names are prob of C origin.

**Paris** (2), the herb, is elliptical for ML *herba paris*, from L *pār*, equal, a pair: from its even or symmetrical parts, and by a f/e connexion with *Paris* (o.o.o.), that Trojan prince who abducted the beautiful Helen.

**parish, parishioner.** See ECONOMIC, para 4.

**parity.** See PAIR, para 3.

**park** (n, hence v); **parquet, parquetry; paddock.**

1. *Park*, ME *parke*, earlier *parc*, is adopted from OF-F *parc*: Barbaric (early) ML *parcus*, contr of *parricus*: prob of PGmc origin (*\*parrak*, *\*parrik*) —cf OHG *pfarrih, pfarrich, pferrich*, whence G *Pferch*, a small enclosure of land, a fold or pen: itself perh from Go *\*parra*, an enclosure—preserved in OProv *parran*, enclosure, esp an enclosed garden, and Sp *parra*, a trellis. (B & W.) Perh rather of C, esp Gaul, origin.

2. PGmc *\*parrak* would explain OE *pearroc*, a fence, an enclosure, E *parrock*, now only E dial and Sc, whence, ? by easement, E *paddock*, an enclosed field.

3. OF-F *parc* has MF-F dim *parquet* (with MF var *parchet*), small enclosure, and then, in C16, that part of a law-court where the judges sat, from the bar that separates this part from the rest, hence, in carpentry, a small enclosure with board floor, hence a type of flooring first used there; derivative F *parqueterie* becomes E *parquetry*. (B & W.)

**parlance.** See PARABLE, para 6.

**parlary.** See PARABLE, para 5.

**parlatory.** See PARABLE, para 7.

**parle; parley.** See PARABLE, para 5.

**parliament, parliamentary.** See PARABLE, para 8.

**parlor, parlour.** See PARABLE, para 7.

**parlous.** See PERIL, para 1.

**Parnassian, Parnassus.**

The former derives from F *parnassien*, adj. of *Parnasse*: L *Parnassus*: Gr *Parnassos*, var *Parnasos* (cf It *Parnaso*), a Gr mountain sacred to Apollo (as God of Poetry) and the Muses: o.o.o.

**parochial.** See ECONOMIC, para 5.

**parodist, parody.** See ODE, para 7.

**parol, parole.** See PARABLE, para 5.

**paroli**—whence the AE **parlay** (v, hence n)—is adopted from F, itself from It, *paroli*, the using of orig stake+winnings as new stake: mdfn of It *paro*, equal, from L *pār*.

**paronomasia; paronymous.**

The former, adopted from the L grammarians, is ult a Gr word, derived from *paronomazein*, to form a word by making a small change: *para*, beside+*onomazein*, to name, from *onoma*, name: f.a.e., NAME. The latter derives from LL *parōnymon*, from Gr *parōnumon*: *para+onuma*, var of *onoma*.

**parotid** is lit 'near the ear': via L from Gr *parōtid-*, o/s of *parōtis*: *para*, beside+*ous*, o/s *ōtid-*, ear.

**paroxysm.** See OXYGEN, para 3.

**parquet, parquetry.** See PARK, para 3.

**parrakeet.** See PETER, para 10.

**parricide.** See FATHER, para 13.

**parrock.** See PARK, para 2.

**parrot.** See PETER, para 10.

**parry.** See PARE, para 2.

**parse.** See PART, para 12.

**Parsee (-si).** See PERSE, para 1.

**parsimonious, parsimony.**

The former derives from the latter, much as F *parcimonieux* (f *-ieuse*) does from late MF-F *parcimonie*: the E and F nn derive, resp, from L *parsimōnia* and from its var, *parcimōnia*: *parsi-*, c/f of *parsus*, pp of *parcere*, to spare+the suffix *-mōnia*: *parcere* is o.o.o. Sem, 'what one—grudgingly—spares'.

**parsley**: ME *persely*, metathesis of *peresil*, adopted from OF *peresil* (whence, by contr, the F *persil*): like OE *petersilie*, from ML *petrosīlium*, parsley: LL *petroselīnum, petroselīnon*, rock parsley: Gr *petroselīnon*: *petro-*, c/f of *petra*, a rock, and of *petros*, a stone (cf PETER)+*selīnon*, parsley, itself perh from the Gr river-name *Selinous*. (Hofmann.)

**parsnip**: ME *parsnepe*: a blend of ME *nepe*, a turnip+OF *pasnaie* (F *panais*), parsnip, the latter from L *pastināca*, parsnip, carrot, perh akin to L *pastinum*, a hoe, itself perh akin to *pangere*, to thrust into the ground (f.a.e., PACT).

**parson, parsonage, parsonical.** See PERSON, para 6.

**part,** n and v (whence **parter** and vn **parting**); **partial, partiality**—with derivative negg **impartial, impartiality; partible, impartible; particle, parti-**

cular (adj, hence n), **particularism, particularity, particularize, particulate**—perh cf **pernickery**—**parcel** (n, hence v); **partisan, -izan; partite** (as in tripartite), **partition, partitive; partner** (n, hence v), whence **partnership** (suffix -*ship*); **parse**, whence the vn **parsing; parti, party.**—Cognate **portion** (n, hence v). whence **portionable**, **portional** (unless imm from LL *portiōnālis*), **portioner, portionist** (cf ML *portionista*), **portionless.**—Full cpds of *part*: sep JEOPARDY; **participable, participant** (whence **participance**), adj hence n, **participate**, adj and n, **participation** (whence **participative**), **participator** (whence **participatory**)—**participial, participle; parti-colo(u)r, -colo(u)red; partake**, whence **partaker**, vn **partaking.**—Prefix-cpds of *part*, n and v: **apart, apartment; compart, compartition, compartment** (whence **compartmental**); sep COUNTERPART—**depart** (whence **departer, departing**), **department** (whence **departmental**), **departure; dispart**, whence, anl, **dispartment; impart**, whence, anl, **impartment; repartee, repartition.**—Prefix-cpds of **portion**, n and v: **apportion, apportionment; proportion** (n and v), **proportionable, proportional, proportionate**—**disproportion** (n, hence v), whence, anl, **disproportionable, disproportional, disproportionate.**

### Indo-European

1. In all these words, the base is L *pars* (s *par-*), o/s *part-*, with one section deriving imm from the cognate *portiō* (s *porti-*, r *port-*, PL r *\*por-*), o/s *portiōn-*: cf, in L, *parere*, *\*to procure, (hence) to produce children, *parare*, to procure, to prepare, L pau*per*, poor, qq.v. at, resp, PARENT, PARE, POOR; cf, in Hit, *pars-, parsiya*, to break, to divide; cf, in Gr, *pernēmi*, I sell, s and r *pern-*, PGr *\*per-*, and epo*ron*, I procured; in C, *\*perna*, a part, a leg, a thigh, a ham—cf Gr *perna*, a ham, and L *perna*, a leg, thigh, ham—the s being *pern-*, the r *\*per-*, as implied by Malvezin[1]; in Skt, *pūrta*, a reward, *pūrtám*, wages: IE r, *\*per-*, with varr *\*par-*, *\*por-*, *\*pur-*: basic idea, to procure; hence to cause to be procured (to make ready; to sell), to produce (e.g., children), to prepare; hence, also, to allot, whence a part.

### Simples of L *pars*, gen *part*is

2. A *part*, ME *part*, derives both from OE *part* (L c/f *part-*) and from OF *part* (L acc *partem*), both from L *pars*; 'to *part*', from OF *partir*, to divide, from VL *\*partīre*, from L *partīri*, from *part-*, c/f of *pars*: the sense 'to part from' (somebody) arises in MF 'soi *partir* de quelqu'un', lit 'to divide oneself from him', whence, almost imm, both '*partir* de qqn', part from someone, and *partir* (d'un endroit), to depart from a place. (See esp B & W.)

3. L *pars, part-*, has derivative adj LL *partiālis*, whence, via MF-F *partial* (cf F *partiel*), the E *partial*; derivative MF-F *partialité* yields E *partiality*.

4. L *partīri*, to divide, has adj LL *partībilis*, divisible, with neg LL *impartībilis*, whence E *partible, impartible* The pp *partītus* yields E

*partite*, mostly in *bipartite, tripartite*: L *bipartītus, tripartītus*. On the pp s *partit-* arises *partītiō*, a sharing, a division, o/s *partītiōn-*, whence, via OF-F, the E *partition*, whence to *partition*'; and EF-F *partitif*, f *partitive*, accounts for E *partitive*.

5. L *pars* has dim *particula*, a little part, whence, perh via late MF-F *particule*, the E *particle*. The derivative LL adj *particulāris* becomes MF *particuler* (F *particulier*), adopted by ME, reshaped by E to *particular*; derivative LL *particulāritās* becomes MF-F *particularité*, whence E *particularity*. MF-F *particulariser* and F *particularisme* have led to *particularize* and *particularism*. Derivative *particulāre* has pp *particulātus*, used by LL as adj, whence learnèd E *particulate*.

6. Perh either *particulate* or *particular* has blended with *pernicious* to produce the coll *pernickety*, finical, finicky, fussy.

7. The L dim *particula* app has the VL var *\*particella*, whence MF-F *parcelle*, whence E *parcel*.

8. L *pars, part-*, becomes It *parte*, whence *partigiano*, one who takes the part of—supports—another, with dial varr *partisano, partezan*, whence late MF-F *partisan*, adopted by E, with var *partizan*.

9. The L acc *partītiōn*em (cf para 4) became, by contr, the OF *parçon*, a sharing, a share, booty, whence OF *parçonier*, var *parcenier*, an associate, whence EF-F *parçener*, a joint heir in an estate, itself adopted as an E Law term; now, *parcener* blends with ME *part*, a share, to form ME *partener*, whence E *partner*—which, by re-exportation, becomes F *partenaire*.

10. OF *partir*, to divide, has pp *parti*, which, as adj, yields E *party*, as in *party wall*; the c/f is *parti-*, as in *parti-colo(u)red*.

11. The OF-F pp *parti*, divided, becomes, in MF, also n, 'that which is divided or shared', whence 'a person', partly adopted by E, esp in 'a very eligible *parti*'. This F n has had a share in the genesis of E *party*, which, however, derives mainly from OF-F *partie*, part of a whole, with a number of derivative senses.

12. L *pars*, a part, is used by the grammarians for 'a part of speech', elliptically for *pars oratiōnis*: hence, perh via OF *pars* (*parz*), the E 'to *parse*'—another indication of the influence of L on E grammar.

### Simple of L *portiō*, gen *portiōn*is

13. L *portiō*, acc *portiōnem*, becomes OF-F *portion*, adopted by E; the derivative MF-F *portionner* yields 'to *portion*', now rare.

### Full Compounds of *part*

14. L *pars*, c/f *parti-*, combines with *capere* (c/f -*cipere*), to take, to form the adj *particeps*, part-taking, share-taking, sharing, whence *participium*, a sharing, ML a participle, whence MF-F *participe*, with MF var *participle*, adopted by E; the MF -*iple* form was prob influenced by the L adj *participiālis*, whence E *participial*.

15. L *particeps* has also the important derivative *participāre*, to have a share (in), with derivative LL adj *participābilis*, whence E *participable*; with presp *participans*, o/s *participant-*, whence the E adj, hence also n, *participant*; and with pp *participātus*, whence the now rare adj, and the v, *participate*. On the pp s *participāt-* arise both the LL *participātiō*, o/s *participātiōn-*, whence MF-F *participation*, adopted by E, and the LL agent *participator*, adopted by E.

16. L *particeps* and *participāre* prob suggested the E *part-taking*, *part-taker*, soon eased to *partaking*, *partaker*, whence, by b/f, 'to *partake*', to share (usu vi).

### Prefix-Compounds of *part* (n and v)

17. The L phrase *a parte*, from a part, i.e. separately, becomes OF *a part* (F *à part*), whence the E adv, hence occ adj, *apart*. L, hence It, *a parte* has derivative *appartare*, to separate, whence *appartamento*, a separate suite of rooms, whence F *appartement*, whence E *apartment*.

18. L *partīri*, to divide, has the LL cpd *compartīri*, to divide and share with (*com-*), whence E 'to *compart*' (obs); derivative ML *compartitiō*, o/s *compartitiōn-*, yields E *compartition*. *Compartīri* becomes, prob via VL *compartīre*, the It *compartire*, with derivative *compartimento*, whence EF-F *compartiment*, whence E *compartment*.

19. OF *partir*, to divide, has cpd 'soi *departir*', to divide, hence separate, oneself, hence to go away, whence ME *departen*, to divide, to depart, whence 'to *depart*'. OF *departir*, to divide, has not only the OF-MF derivative *departement*, orig the action of dividing, F *département*, whence E *department*, but also derivative *departeüre*, division, separation, hence a parting, a going away, whence E *departure*.

20. The L cpd *dispartīri*, to divide and separate (connoted by *dis-*, apart), has var *dispartīre*, whence OF *despartir*, whence 'to *dispart*', used derivatively also as n.

21. L *partīri* has the LL cpd *impartīri*, var *impartīre*, to give a share of, to accord or grant, and becomes MF-F *impartir*, whence 'to *impart*'.

22. OF *partir*, to divide, (later) to depart, has cpd *repartir*, to depart again, (later) to reply, whence MF-F *repartie*, a reply, esp a witty one, whence E *repartee*; the other derivative *répartir* (OF-F), to divide again, (but usu) to distribute, perh suggested the E *repartition*, formed as if from L *repartitiō*.

### Prefix-Compounds of *portion*

23. OF *portion* has derivative *portionner*, with the MF cpd *apportionner*, to divide and—connoted by *ap-*, L *ad*, to—assign, whence 'to *apportion*'. Derivative F *apportionnement* prob suggested E *apportionment*.

24. L *portiō* occurs in the phrase *prō portiōne*, as a (due) share, conformably to the shares of each person, whence the n *prōportiō*, o/s *prōportiōn-*, MF *proporcion*, adopted by ME, whence, as in the

EF-F reshaping, the E *proportion*; derivative OF *proporcionner*, F *proportionner*, yields 'to *proportion*'. Derivative LL *proportiōnālis* becomes MF-F *proportionnel* and, prob independently, E *proportional*; subsidiary LL *prōportiōnalitās*, o/s *prōportiōnalitāt-*, becomes MF-F *proportionnalité* and E *proportionality*. As if from the L v *prōportiōnāre* come both LL *prōportiōnābilis*, whence E *proportionable*, and LL pp-as-adj *prōportiōnātus*, whence E *proportionate*.

25. EF-F *proportion* has derivative EF-F cpd *disproportion*, adopted by E; subsidiary EF-F *disproportionner* has suggested 'to *disproportion*'. *Disproportionable*, *disproportional*, *disproportionate* have all been formed anl with *proportionable*, etc.

**partake.** See prec, para 16, and cf TAKE, para 2.

**parterre.** See TERRA, para 4, s.f.

**parthenian, parthenic, Parthenium, Parthenon.**

The 1st is an anglicized var (*-ian* for *-ic*) of the 2nd, which derives from Gr *parthenikos*, adj of *parthenos* (for a wild guess, see VIRGIN, para 1) (o.o.o.), a maid, a virgin; *parthenikos* is a var of *parthenios* (*parthenos*+adj *-ios*), whence—prop the neu of that adj—the n *parthenion*, whence, via L, the Bot *Parthenium*, a woody herb, so named for its white flowers, white connoting virginity. Gr *parthenos* has derivative *Parthenōn*, temple of the goddess Athena, L *Parthenon*, adopted by E.

**Parthia**, whence the adj, hence n, **Parthian; Parthian shot—parting shot;—Pahlavi, var Pehlevi.**

1. *Pehlevi* is a var of *Pahlavi* (whence the coin *pahlavi*), adopted from Per *Pahlavi*, the chief Per language of c200-800 A.D.: from OPer *Parthava*, Parthia, a country to the SE of the Caspian Sea, with inhabitants of an app Turkoman stock. OPer *Parthava* becomes Gr, hence also L, *Parthia*, the natives being Gr *Parthoi*, L *Parthi*, adj *Parthus*, whence—unless imm from *Parthia*—the E adj *Parthian*.

2. Notable mounted archers, the Parthians used, after each discharge of their bows, to turn their horses as if in flight: whence *Parthian shot*: whence, f/e, *parting shot*.

**partial, partiality.** See PART, para 3.

**partible.** See PART, para 4.

**participable, participant, participate, participation, participator.** See PART, para 15, and cf CAPABILITY, paras 4, 8.

**participial, participle.** See PART, para 14.

**particle.** See PART, para 5.

**parti-colo(u)red.** See PART, para 10.

**particular, particularity, particularize.** See PART, para 5.

**particulate.** See PART, para 5, s.f.

**parting.** See PART (heading).

**parting shot.** See PARTHIA, para 2.

**partisan (1), party-man.** See PART, para 8.

**partisan (2) or -zan, a halberd.** See PIERCE‘ para 6.

**partition, partitive.** See PART, para 4.

**partizan.** See PART, para 8, and PIERCE, para 6.

**partner, partnership.** See PART, para 9.

**partridge:** ME *partriche* (cf the Sc *partrich*), var

of *pertriche*: OF *pertris* (var *perdriz*, cf F *perdrix*): a partial metathesis of OF *perdis*: L *perdic*em, acc of *perdix*, adopted from Gr: ? echoic of the whirring wings of the rising bird (Hofmann).

**parturient, parturition.** See PARENT, para 3, and cf the element *parturi-*.

**party**, adj. See PART, para 10.

**party**, n. See PART, para 11.

**party wall.** See PART, para 10.

**parvenu.** See VENUE, para 18.

**parvis.** See PARADISE, para 2.

**Pasch, paschal; pasqueflower.**

*Paschal* reshapes OF-F *pascal*, adj of OF *pasche*, whence, via ME *pasche*, the E *Pasch*, the Passover: LL *pascha*: LGr *paskha*: H *pesaḥ*, from *pāsah*, to pass over. OF *pasche* has var *pasque*, whence *pasqueflower*.

**pash** (v, hence n), to hurl, to smash, is echoic: cf *bash, crash, dash, mash, smash*.

**pasha.** See CHECK, para 4.

**Pashto.** See PATHAN.

**pasqueflower.** See PASCH.

**pass**, n and v. See PACE, para 2.

**passable, passage.** See PACE, para 4.

**passenger.** See PACE, para 4.

**passe-partout.** See PACE, para 3.

**passible.** See PATIENCE, para 3.

**passion, passional, passionate.** See PATIENCE, para 4.

**passive, passivity.** See PATIENCE, para 5.

**Passover.** See PACE, para 3.

**passport.** See PACE, para 3.

**passus.** See PACE, para 1.

**password.** See PACE, para 3.

**past**, adj hence n: orig the pp of 'to *pass*', q.v. at PACE.

**paste** (n, hence v), whence the adj **pasty; pasty**, n, and **pastry** and **patty; pastose** and **impasto; pastel** and **pastiche.**

1. *Paste*, adopted from OF *paste* (whence F *pâte*), derives from LL *pasta* (whence It and Sp *pasta*), a pastry cake: trln of Gr *pastē*, sauce mixed with flour (cf Gr *pasta*, barley porridge), akin to *pastos*, sprinkled, esp with salt, pp of *passō*, I sprinkle.

2. LL *pasta* has derivative ML *pastīcius*, pastry, var *\*pastīcium*, whence *\*pastīciare*, to cook pastry, whence OF *pastissier*, which, soon used as n, has MF derivative *pastisserie*, which app combines with E *paste* to form E *pastry*.

3. OF *paste* has OF derivative *pasté*, whence E *pasty*, n; F *pâté*, whence E *patty*.

4. LL *pasta* becomes It *pasta*, paste, dough, with adj *pastoso*, whence E *pastose*; It *pasta* has the further derivative *impastare*, to make *im-* or into a paste (whence E 'to *impaste*'), whence the n *impasto*, a 'doughy'—i.e., thick—application of pigment to canvas, adopted by E painters.

5. LL *pasta*, paste, has dim *pastellus*, a seal, or its impression, in wax, whence It *pastello*, whence EF-F *pastel*, adopted by E; and VL *\*pastīcium* (as in para 2) becomes It *pasticcio*, a paste, hence a hodge-podge, literary or musical, whence EF-F *pastiche*, adopted by E, now—as in F—only of a direct imitation.

**pastel.** See prec para.

**pastern.** See PASTOR, para 5.

**pasteurize.** See PASTOR, para 3.

**pastiche.** See PASTE, para 5.

**pastille.** See PANTRY, para 6.

**pastime.** See PACE, para 3.

**pastor** (whence **pastorate**), **pastoral** (whence **pastoralist**), **pastorale, pastorium; pasteurize**, whence **pasteurization; pasture** (n, hence v), **pasturage, pastural; pastern; repast**; sep PABULUM; **pannage.** Akin to sep FEED (FOOD).

1. *Pastor*, orig a shepherd, ME *pastour*, derives from OF *pastor, pastur*: L *pāstor*, agent from *pāst-*, s of *pāstus*, pp of *pāscere*, to nourish, pasture, feed: s *pāsc-, pāst-*, r *pās-*, extn of *pā-*, as in *pābulum*, food: app akin to the *\*pāt-, \*pet-*, attested by Gr *pateomai*, I eat, and Go *fōdjan*, to nourish. Cf PANTRY, para 1, s.f.

2. L *pāstor* has adj *pāstorālis*, whence, perh via MF-F, E *pastoral* (adj, hence n) and It *pastorale*, which, used as n, is adopted by E for a Mus composition of pastoral life. The adj *pāstōrius*, of or for a shepherd, has the Southern U.S. derivative *pastorium*, a Protestant parsonage.

3. OF *pastor, pastur* becomes F *pasteur*, whence the PN *Pasteur*, esp that famous F chemist, Louis Pasteur (1822–95), who invented this way of sterilizing milk, whence F *pasteuriser* and its subsidiary, *pasteurisation*, whence E 'to *pasteurize*' and *pasteurization*.

4. L *pāscere*, pp *pāstus*, has the LL derivative *pāstūra*, OF *pasture* (F *pâture*), adopted by E; the derivative OF-MF v *pasturer* (F *pâturer*) app contributes to E 'to *pasture*', and the subsidiary OF-MF *pasturage* (F *pâturage*) is adopted by E. The E adj *pastural*, although perh aided by the ML n *pasturalis*, app=E *pasture+-al*.

5. The L adj *pāstōrius* has the VL derivative *\*pāstōria*, a shackle put on beasts as they graze, attested by It *pastoia*; hence the MF *pasture*, a horse's pastern, whence late MF-EF *pasturon* (F *paturon*), whence, by contr, the late ME *pastron*, whence the E *pastern*.

6. L *pāscere* becomes OF *paistre*, with cpd *repaistre* (*re-*, again, is vaguely int), to feed; and *pāscere*, pp *pāstus*, has derivative n *pāstus* (gen *-ūs*), food, whence OF *past*, food, hence a meal; both contribute to OF-MF *repast* (F *repas*), a meal, adopted by E.

7. On the L pp s *pāst-* arose also *pāstiō*, a pasturing, o/s *pāstiōn-*, whence the LL *pāstiōnāticum* (suffix *-āticum*), whence OF *pasnage* (F *panage*), whence the E legal term *pannage*, (the right of) feeding swine in a wood, hence the fee therefor.

**pastose.** See PASTE, para 3.

**pastry.** See PASTE, para 2.

**pastural, pasture.** See PASTOR, para 4.

**pasty**, adj and n. See PASTE, heading and para 3.

**pat**, n and v, (to deliver) a light, flat-handed stroke or blow, is prob echoic: cf such words as *bat* and *spat*. Prob from the v derives the adv *pat*, neatly, timely, hence easily, fluently.

**patch, patchwork, patchy.** See PIECE, para 10.

**pate,** recorded first in ME, is o.o.o.

**patella,** L dim of *patina*, a bowl: f.a.e., the 2nd PAN. Cf:

**paten.** See the 2nd PAN, para 2.

**patent** (adj, hence n, hence v, whence **patency**) derives from L *patent-*, o/s of *patens*, presp of *patēre*, to be or lie open: akin to Av *pathanō*, stretched out. The corresp L adj is *patulus*, open, distended, whence E *patulous*: cf the sep PETAL. Also from *patēre* comes Sp *patio*, an open court- (yard).

**pater.** See FATHER, paras 1 (s.f.) and 5.

**paterfamilias.** See FAMILY, para 3.

**paternal; paternity.** See FATHER, para 6.

**paternoster.** See FATHER, para 11.

**path,** whence · **pathfinder, pathway, footpath,** derives from OE *path, paeth*: cf OFris and OS *path*, MD *paden*, to walk along, D *pad* (cf the 1st PAD), OHG *pfad*, MHG *pfat*, G *Pfad*: ? Scythian —cf Av *pathā*, akin to Skt *pathā*, a way, a road. Akin to FIND.

**Pathan; Pashto.** A *Pathan* or member of the principal race of Afghanistan, derives from Hind *Paṭhān*, by b/f from Afghan *Pēṣṭāna*, Afghans, pl of *Pēṣṭūn*. Their language is *Pashto*—often anglicized as *Pushtu*—from *Pēṣṭūn*.

**pathic,** L *pathicus*, Gr *pathikos*, derives from Gr *pathos*, suffering, adopted—perh via LL—by E with accruing senses: from *path*ein, to suffer, akin to the syn Gr *paskh*ein, and to the nasal, app basic *penthos*, sorrow, mourning, hence akin to Lith *kenčiù, kentēti*, to suffer. Gr *pathos* has adj *pathētos*, susceptible to pain or suffering, with extn *pathētikos*, LL *pathēticus*, E *pathetic* (F *pathétique*). Cf the element *patho-*, as in *pathology*.

2. The chief cpds are

*antipathy*, L *antipathia*, Gr *antipatheia*, a passion (*-patheia*) against (*anti*) someone, with adj—after *pathetic—antipathetic* (contrast F *antipathique*);

*empathy*, Gr *empatheia*, sympathetic (connoted by *em-*, for *en*, in) understanding or suffering, with adj *empathic*;

*sympathy*, L *sympathia*, Gr *sumpatheia*, a feeling (*sum-*, for *sun*) with another; adj *sympathetic*, Gr *sumpathētikos*; and v *sympathize* (whence *sympathizer*), EF-F *sympathiser*, from MF-F *sympathie*.

**patible.** See para 6 of:

**patience, patient; passible, passion** (whence **passionless**), **passional, passionate, passive, passivity** —cf **impassionate, impassioned, impassive—impatience, impatient; compassion, compassionate**—**dispassionate; patible**—cf **compatible, compatibility—incompatible, incompatibility;—penury, penurious.**

1. Of the *pat-* and *-pat-* words, the base is L *patī*, to suffer, to endure, to be patient; app the s and r *pat-* is an extn of IE *pa-*, which has varr *pē-*, as in Gr *pēma*, suffering (n), and *pō-*, as in Gr talai*pōros*, unhappy, unfortunate, and *pe-*, as in Gr *penēs*, poor, *penomai*, I work painfully, and *po-*, as in Gr *ponos*, pain, punishment: perh cf

also L *paenitet*, it causes regret or remorse, and Skt *pāpman*, harm.

2. L *patī* has presp *patiens*, o/s *patient-*, whence OF *pacient*, adopted by ME; like F, E reshapes *pacient* to *patient*. Derivative L *patientia* becomes OF *pacience, patience*, the latter adopted by ME. The L negg *impatiens* and *impatientia* yield—via OF—the ME *impacient, impacience*, E *impatient, impatience*.

3. L *patī* has pp *passus*, s *pass-*, whence LL *passibilis*, capable of suffering, whence OF-F *passible*, adopted by E; the LL neg *impassibilis* becomes MF-F *impassible*, adopted by E. The subsidiary LL *passibilitās*, o/s *passibilitāt-*, and *impassibilitās*, pass through OF-F to become E *passibility, impassibility*.

4. On the pp s *pass-* arises LL *passiō* (o/s *passiōn-*), endurance of ill or illness, suffering, whence OF-F *passion*, adopted by E, which takes most of its modern senses from MF-F; the derivative LL adj *passiōnālis* becomes E *passional*, and the subsidiary ML n *passionāle*, prop the neu of the adj, becomes E *passional*, a book of martyrs. In ML, *passiō*, o/s *passiōn-*, acquires the adj *passiōnātus*, whence (MF-F *passionné* and) E *passionate*; and in MF, *passion* acquires the v *passionner*, whence the now rare 'to *passion*', to affect with— to be moved with—passion. The int *impassion*, pp as adj *impassioned*, and *impassionate*, adj and v, owe much to It *impassionare* and *impassionato*.

5. Also on the pp s *pass-* arises L *passīuus*, ML *passīvus*, susceptible to suffering, hence, in LL, passive (as in grammar): whence, perh via MF-F *passif*, f *passive*, the E *passive*. Derivative LL *passīuitās*, ML *passīvitās*, o/s *passīvitāt-*, becomes— perh via F *passivité*—the E *passivity*. The negg *impassive, impassivity* are anl E formations.

6. L *patī*, s *pat-*, has derivative *patibilis*, sensitive, (but also) supportable, bearable, whence the now rare E *patible*.

7. Prefix-compounds of *patī*, etc., not already treated include *compassion*, adopted from OF-F, from LL *compassiōn-*, o/s of *compassiō*, from *compass*us, pp of LL *compatī*, to suffer with (*com-*) another, to feel pity, hence the anl *compassionate*, adj and v; derivative LL *compassibilis* and *compassīuus*, ML *-īvus*, become the rare *compassible, compassive*; the ML-from-*compatī* derivative *compatibilis* passes through MF-F to become E *compatible*, and the F subsidiary *compatibilité* yields *compatibility*; the ML *incompatibilis* and its attester *incompatibilitas* have passed through MF-F into E *incompatible, incompatibility*.

8. Gr *penēs*, poor, s and r *pen-*, has a cognate in L *pēnūria*, extreme poverty, whence, via EF-F *pénurie*, the E *penury*; derivative ML *pēnūriōsus*, MF *penurieux*, f *penurieuse*, leads to *penurious*.

**patin.** See the 2nd PAN, para 2.

**patina,** a film or a glaze, is adopted from It and usu said to be o.o.o.: perh, however, it derives from verdigris forming upon a disused *patina* (E *paten*), a shallow dish, q.v. at the 2nd PAN, para 2. —Hence *patinous*, coated with a patina.

**patio.** See PATENT.

**patois; patrol,** n and v; **patten.**

1. Behind all three words we find the late OF-F *patte*, a paw, a foot, akin to OProv *pauta* and Cat *pota* and the Gallo-Roman PN *Pauto*: either C, Malvezin postulating OC *\*patta*, the flat part of the foot, from the C r *pat-*, var of *bad-*, to be broad, perh cf Cor *paw*, *baw*, a paw; or (B & W) from some such pre-C stratum as Illyrian.

2. *Patois*, adopted from MF-F, has the suffix *-ois* of *françois* (F *français*), French, and its r expresses the uncouthness of the people speaking a rural dialect: (perh via OF *patoier*, to paddle, and certainly) from *patte*. (B & W.)

3. A *patrol* derives from EF-F *patrouille*, from late MF-F *patrouiller*, to 'paddle' in the mud, to go through puddles, a var of OF-F *patouiller* (for *\*pattouiller*) to paddle, to paw, from *patte*; the suffix *-ouiller* is that of *barbouiller*, to daub. (B & W.)

4. *Patten*, a clog, a sabot, derives from MF-F *patin*, orig a shoe, then a skate, app a dim of *patte*.

**patriarch, patriarchal.** See FATHER, para 10.

**patrician.** See FATHER, para 6.

**patricide.** See FATHER, para 13.

**Patrick** derives from OIr *Patricc*, itself from L *patricius*, nobly born. Its pet-forms are **Pat** and **Paddy** and **Patsy**, the 2nd being often used as sl for an Irishman; hence, app, *be in a paddy*, to be angry—cf sl *scotty*, angry. The f *Patricia*=L *patricia*, f of *patricius*; f.a.e., FATHER.

**patrimony.** See FATHER, para 14.

**patriot, patriotic, patriotism.** See FATHER, para 15.

**patristic, patristics.** See FATHER, para 6.

**patrol.** See PATOIS, para 3.

**patrology.** See the element *patri-*.

**patron, patronage, patronize.** See FATHER, para 6, s.f.

**patronymic.** See the element *-onym*.

**patten.** See PATOIS, para 4.

**patter** (1), n from v: glib talk. Cf *paternoster*; see FATHER, para 11, s.f.

**patter** (2), n from v: to run short-steppingly: freq of PAT.

**pattern.** See FATHER, para 7.

**patty.** See PASTE, para 3.

**patulous.** See PATENT.

**paucity.** See the element *pauci-*.

**pauldron.** See PAWL.

**paunch,** whence **paunchy:** OF *panche*, var of *pance* (F *panse*): L *panticem*, acc of *pantex*, belly (*pantices*, intestines): o.o.o.

**pauper.** See POOR, para 2.

**pause,** whence **pausal;** menopause, whence **menopausic; pose,** to place.

1. *Menopause* combines *meno-*, c/f of Gr *mēn*, a month+*pause*, n: cf the L-become-Med-E *menses*. 'To *pause*' (cf EF-F *pauser* and L *pausāre*, to cease) derives from 'a *pause*': and *pause*, n, is adopted from MF-F *pause*, from L *pausa*, from Gr *pausis*, from *pauein*, to cause to stop, also vi, to cease: r *pau-*: o.o.o.

2. L *pausa* has derivative *pausāre*, (vi) to stop, to cease, hence, in Eccl LL, to rest (in death); in spoken LL, *pausāre* takes over, from L *ponere*, the sense 'to place, to put', whence OF-F *poser*, to rest (surviving in 'se *reposer*', to rest), but also and finally only, to place or put, whence 'to *pose*'; the derivative EF-F n *pose* is adopted by E, as is the derivative *poseur*.

3. The cpds of 'to *pose*' can very easily cause a quite spectacular confusion: the simplest, most logical treatment is to deal with all of them, along with the *-pone*, *-posit* (*-position*) cpds, at the 2nd PONE.

**pavan** (anglicizes **pavane,** adopted from EF-F, itself from Sp *pavana*, mdfn of *pavo*, a peacock, from ML *pavo*, *pavus* (L *pāuō*, *pāuus*), a peacock, o.o.o.—but, like Gr *taos*, of presumably Asiatic origin. A slow, stately dance, resembling a parade of strutting peacocks.

2. L *pāuō*, *pāuus* becomes OE *pāwa*, with var *pēa*, whence the f/e ME *pecok*, E *peacock*, where *-cock* is the male of the hen.

**pave** (whence **paver**—cf MF-F *paveur*—and **pavior, paviour), pavé, pavement; putation, putative; pit,** n (cavity), hence v, whence the pa **pitted.**

1. 'To *pave*' derives from OF-F *paver*: VL *\*pavāre*, ML *pavīre* (L *pauīre*), to beat, or tread, earth down to level it: perh akin to L *putāre*, Lith *piauti*, to cut. F *paver* has pp *pavé*, used also as n and adopted by E. The L derivative *pauimentum*, ML *pavimentum*, becomes OF-MF *pavement*, adopted by E.

2. Prob akin is *pit*, a cavity, ME *pit*, var *put*, OE *pytt*, app from L *puteus*, a well, s *pute-*, r *put-*.

3. Prob akin to L *puteus*, a hole cut in the ground, esp a well, is L *putāre*, to prune (loosely, to cut), hence to 'prune' an account, to count or calculate, app akin to Skt *pūtás*, purified; the pp *putātus* has derivatives *putātiō*, a pruning, LL an estimating, and LL *putātīuus*, ML *putātīvus*, believed, supposed, whence, perh via MF-F *putatif*, the E *putative*.—For the cpds of *putāre*, see the 2nd COUNT.

**pavilion; papillon,** a tiny European dog.

1. The latter, adopted from F, is so named from the shape of its ears and it derives from F *papillon*, a butterfly, from L *pāpiliōnem*, acc of *pāpiliō*, a butterfly, akin to OS *fīfoldara*, *fifalde*, OHG *fīfaltra*, MHG *vīvalter*, G *Falter*, ON *fífrildi*: cf also G *pallō*, I shake, the other forms, esp L *pāpiliō*, representing an int redup (Walshe).

2. In LL, *pāpiliō* means also—? orig in soldiers' sl—a large tent, from the resemblance of the curtains that closed it to a butterfly's wings: whence OF *paveillon*, MF-F *pavillon*, ME *pavilon*, later *pavilioun*, *pavilion*, E *pavilion*.

**pavior, paviour.** See PAVE (heading).

**paw,** n, hence v: ME *pawe*, var of *powe*: OF *poue*, var of *poe*: cf OProv *pauta*, therefore cf para 1 of *patois*; cf also MLG *pōte*, MD *pote* and, as in D, *poot*, and G *Pfote*.

**pawl,** occ **paul** or even **pall,** in machinery a sliding bolt or a pivoted tongue: app from F *épaule*, a shoulder, OF *espaule* (cf *epaulet* and, f.a.e., SPOON), whence *espauleron*, whence, by aphesis and prob by contamination of *cauldron*, the E *pauldron*, var *pouldron*.

**pawn** (1), in chess. See FOOT, para 9.

**pawn** (2), a deposit at a moneylender's, whence 'to pawn' and **pawnbroker**: OF *pan*, var of *pand*, a pledge, a surety: cf the syn MLG *pand* and OHG-MHG *pant*, G *Pfand*: perh cf L *pondus*, a weight (f.a.e., the weight POUND).

**pax.** See PACT, paras 1 and 13.

**pay** (1) a vessel's bottom: MF *peier*: L *picāre*, to cover with tar, from L *pix*, tar, pitch: cf Gr *pissa*, pitch: f.a.e., FAT.

**pay** (2), to compensate monetarily (whence **payable** and **payee**), and such compensation (whence **paymaster**); **payment.** The last derives from MF-F *paiement*, itself from OF *paier* (F *payer*), from L *pācāre*, to pacify, in VL to appease, hence to pay: from L *pāc-*, o/s of *pāx*, peace: f.a.e., PACT. Also from OF *paier* comes the MF-F *paie* (F *paye*), whence the E n *pay*.

**paynim.** See PAGAN, para 3.

**pea** comes, by b/f, from EE *pease*, sing—but extant, mostly in dial, as a collective pl: ME *pese* (pl *pesen*): OE *pise* (pl *pisan*): LL *pisa*, f sing from L *pisa*, pl of *pisum*: Gr *pison*, var *pisos*: o.o.o. (? Thracian-Phrygian: Hofmann). Hence, by shape-resemblance, *peanut*, the nut-like seed of the Brazilian herb *Arachis hypogaea*.

**peace, peaceable, peaceful.** See PACT, para 13.

**peach** (1), n. See PERSE, para 1.

**peach** (2), v. See FOOT, para 13.

**peacock.** See PAVAN, para 2.

**peak** (n and v), **peaked, peaky.** See PICK, para 3.

**peal.** See APPEAL.

**peanut.** See PEA, s.f.

**pear; perry; pyrus, pyriform.**

1. *Pear*, ME-OE *pere*, derives from LL *pera*, var of *pira*, f sing from L *pira*, pl of *pirum*, a pear, the 'parallel' of L *pirus* (gen *pirī*), a pear-tree: o.o.o.; perh an aphetic derivative of an IE r *api-* represented by Gr *apios*, pear-tree, and *apion*, pear. The ML form *pyrus* has been adopted by Bot, with c/f *pyri-*, as in *pyriform*, pear-shaped.

2. The fermented liquor made from pears is *perry*: MF *peré*: from OF *pere*.

**pearl** (n, hence v), whence the adj **pearly**, whence **'Pearlies'**, Cockneys jacket-adorned with pearl buttons; from *pearl*: **pearled, pearlite** (Min *-ite*)— cf **perlite**, from F *perle*; **purl** (liquor).

1. A *pearl*, ME *perle*, derives from MF-F *perle*, itself from ML *perna*, a pearl, from L *perna*, a mussel, a ham, either via ML *perla*, a pearl, or via It *pèrla*—cf the Neapolitan and Sicilian *perna*, pearl. The *n-l* change was perh caused by L *sphaerula*, a globule. Perh cf the Gr *pterna*, ham, heel, and Skt *parṣṇi, pắršniš*, heel, and therefore Go *fairzna*, OHG *fersana*, MHG *versene, verse*, G *Ferse*, a heel.

2. The spiced or bittered malt liquor known as *purl* derives, perh, from F *perlé*, (of liquor) beaded,

lit pearled, from MF-F *perler*, to take the shape of a pearl.

**pearmain** has nothing to do with *Parma* in Italy: see MANOR, para 8.

**peart.** See PERT.

**peasant, peasantry.** See PAGAN, para 4.

**pease.** See PEA (heading).

**peat.** See PIECE, para 11.

**peavey**, occ **peavy**, a lumberman's hook, prob derives from its inventor, Joseph *Peavey*, a New England blacksmith, c1872. (Mathews.)

**pebble** (n, hence v), whence **pebbly**, derives, by b/f, from OE *papolstān* (var *popelstān*), a small roundish stone: perh, as EW suggests, 'imitative of rattling sound'.

**pecan**, earlier *paccan*, the nut, or the tree, of a hard-wooded hickory, is of Alg origin: cf Ojibway *pagân*, any hard-shelled nut.

**peccable** and **impeccable; peccadillo; peccancy; peccant.**

L *peccāre*, to sin, has derivative ML *peccābilis*, prone to sin, whence E *peccable*; the ML neg *impeccābilis* yields *impeccable*. The presp *peccans*, o/s *peccant-*, is, in LL, used as adj, whence E *peccant*; derivative LL *peccantia* yields *peccancy*. From the pp *peccātus* is formed the n *peccātum*, whence Sp *pecado*, with dim *pecadillo*, anglicized as *peccadillo*.

L *peccāre* has s *pecc-*, r *pec-*: ? IE *pik-*, to be angry—cf L *piget*, it irks (me).

**peccary**: ASp *pecari*, varr *pécari, paquiro, paquira*: Cariban, as in Chayma *pekera* and Aparai *pakira* (*paquira*).

**peck** (1), a measure of weight, ME from OF *pek*, is akin to PITCHER, ME *picher*, OF *pichier*, app (*p* for *b*) via OGmc from LL *becarium* (cf E *beaker*): cf MF-F *picotin*, a peck, MF *picote*, a wine measure, ML *picotinus*, a grain measure, ML *picotus*, a liquid measure: cf also OHG *bikeri*, a pitcher, and OF *bichet*, a grain measure, *pichet*, a salt measure, OF-EF *pichier*, a liquid measure, mdfn (*p* for *b*) of syn OF-MF *bichier*: LL *becarium* prob derives from Gr *bikos*, a wine-vase, o.o.o.

**peck** (2), v, hence n; **pecker; peckish.** See PICK, para 2.

**pecten; pectinate**, whence **pectination.**

*Pectinate*, adj and v, derives from L *pectinātus*, comb-shaped, from the pp of *pectināre*, to comb, from *pectin-*, o/s of *pecten*, a comb, itself akin to *pectere*, to comb, Gr *pekein*, pp *pektos*. L *pecten*, derivatively any comb-like object, is adopted by E.

**pectoral**, adj and n, derives, prob via OF-F, from L *pectorālis*, adj, with neu *pectorāle* used as n: from *pector-*, o/s of *pectus*, the breast in sense of chest: perh cf L *pexus*, woolly, hairy, and Skt *pakṣmala*, hairy, shaggy; perh also cf PECTEN.

2. L *pectus, pector-*, has derivative *expectorāre*, to eject (phlegm) *ex* or from the *pectus* or chest, with presp *expectorans*, o/s *expectorant-*, whence the E adj, hence n, *expectorant*, and with pp *expectorātus*, whence 'to *expectorate*', whence anl *expectoration*.

**peculate, peculation.** See para 3 of:

**peculiar** (adj, hence n), **pecularity; peculate, peculation; pecuniary, pecunious, impecunious,** whence anl **impecuniosity.**

1. The phon and sem base is L *pecū*, livestock, one's flocks and herds, hence also money, since in the IE civilizations and, indeed, in the Sem and the Ham, cattle formed the earliest assessable wealth; 'property in livestock', hence 'wealth in livestock', hence 'money', are the senses attaching to the derivative L *pecūnia*.

2. L *pecū* (pl *pecua*) and its syn *pecus* (gen *pecoris*) are akin to OLith *pekus*, OP *pecku*, livestock (cattle); to syn Skt *páçu* (*pāśu*); and to Go *faihu*, OE *feoh*, ON *fē*, cattle, money, and OHG *fihu*, MHG *vihe*, G *Vieh*, cattle. Cf, therefore, the sep FEE.

3. L *pecū* has dim *pecūlium*, that small part of a herd or a flock which is given, as his own property, to the slave acting as herd, hence private property, hence, from dishonest appropriation of a beast, theft of property entrusted to one's care: whence *peculāri*, to commit such a theft, pp *peculātus*, whence 'to *peculate*', esp at expense of the State; derivative LL *peculātiō*, o/s *peculātiōn-*, becomes *peculation*.

4. More directly from L *pecūlium*, private property, comes *peculiāris*, whence—perh via C16 F *peculier*—the E *peculiar*; derivative LL *peculiāritās*, o/s *peculiāritāt-*, yields *peculiarity*, whence—cf *particularize*—the anl 'to *peculiarize*'.

5. L *pecūnia*, property in cattle, hence money, has adj *pecūniārius* (LL var *pecūniāris*), relating to money, whence—prob via MF-F *pécuniaire*—the E *pecuniary*; *pecūniōsus*, rich, becomes MF-F *pécunieux*, f *pécunieuse*, and E *pecunious*, now much rarer than its neg *impecunious*, from F *impécunieux*, f *-ieuse*; *im-*, for *in-*, not+*pécunieux*.

**ped,** a basket. See the 3rd PAD.

**pedagogic** (whence **pedagogics**), **pedagogue, pedagogy; pederasty; paideutics; pedant** (whence **pedantic), pedantism, pedantry;** cf the element **pedo-** (*paedo-*); prob cf the sep PUERILE.

1. This group rests upon Gr *pais*, o/s *paid-*, c/f *paido-*, a boy, hence a child: PGr *\*pawis*, gen *\*pawidos*, cf Old Attic *paus*, gen *pawos*: cf Skt *putrás*, son, boy, child, L *puer*, boy, child: IE r, prob *\*pu-*, with varr *\*pou-* and *\*peu-*, little, a young child (Hofmann).

2. On the Gr o/s *paid-* is formed Gr *paideuein*, to teach, whence the adj *paideutikos*, whence 'hē *paideutikē* (tekhnē)', the art of teaching, education, whence the E *paideutics*—cf *ethics* from *ethic*.

3. But the principal impact of Gr *pais, paid-*, upon E comes from two cpds, the lesser being *paiderastēs*, boy-lover (*paido-+-erastēs*, agent from *erān*, to love, cf EROS), whence the abstract n *paiderastia*; whence, resp, the EF-F *pédéraste*, E *pederast*, and EF-F *pédérastie*, E *pederasty*.

4. More important is the Gr cpd *paidagōgos*, lit child-leading, -leader, orig a slave leading children to school, whence L *paedagōgus*, n, whence MF *pedagogue* (F *pédagogue*), adopted by E; the Gr derivatives *paidagōgia, paidagōgikos*, pass through late MF-F *pédagogie*, EF-F *pédagogique*, to become E *pedagogy, pedagogic*.

5. L *paedagogus* has the ML derivative *paedagōgāre*, to teach, be a teacher, with presp *paedagogans*, o/s *paedagogant-*, whence, app, the It n *pedante*, a schoolmaster, hence he who never stops being one, whence C16 F *pedant* (later *pédant*), adopted by E; the C16 F derivatives *pedanterie* (F *pé-*) and *pedantisme* (F *pé-*) yield E *pedantry* and *pedantism*; *pedantic*, whence *pedanticism*, is an E var of C16 *pedantesque* (F *pé-*).

**pedal.** See FOOT, para 6.

**pedant, pedantic, pedantry.** See PEDAGOGIC, para 5.

**pedate.** See FOOT, para 6.

**peddle, peddler.** See the 3rd PAD.

**pederast, pederasty.** See PEDAGOGIC, para 3.

**pedestal.** See FOOT, para 16.

**pedestrian.** See FOOT, para 7.

**pediatric.** See the 1st *pedo-* in Elements.

**pedicel, pedicle, pedicule.** See FOOT, para 8.

**pedigree.** See FOOT, para 17.

**pediment** is prob a learnèd f/e corruption— after *pedi-*, c/f of L *pes*, a foot—of earlier *periment*, itself app a less learnèd corruption of *pyramid*.

**pedlar.** See the 3rd PAD.

**pedograph, pedology.** See the 2nd *pedo-* in Elements.

**pedometer, pedomotive.** See the 3rd *pedo-* in Elements.

**pedro.** See PETER, para 9.

**peduncle** anglicizes SciL *pedunculus*, lit a little foot (L *pes*, c/f *ped-*): f.a.e., FOOT.

**pee.** See PISS, para 3.

**peek** (v, hence n); its syn **peep** (v, hence n); its virtual syn **peer.** The second is prob, after *peep*, to chirp feebly, an alteration of the first, which derives from ME *piken*, o.o.o.—but perh akin to *peer*, itself o.o.o.—possibly aphetic from ME *apperen*, q.v. at APPEAR.

**peel** (1), a stake, a palisade, a palisaded enclosure (all obs), hence a small castle, derives from syn ME *pel*, from OF *pel*, a stake, from L *pālus*: cf the 2nd PALE.

**peel** (2), a shovel. See PALATE, para 1, s.f.

**peel** (3), to deprive of hair, hence of rind, etc., whence the corresp n **peel** and the vn **peeling,** usu in pl; **pelage; pill,** to plunder, **pillage** (n, hence v); sep **pile,** hair, **pilose, depilate, depilatory, depilous; piligan; Poilu; pellet** and medical **pill,** whence **pillbox; plush** and **pluck,** v; **platoon;** sep CATERPILLAR.

1. 'To *peel*', ME *pelen, pilen*, app derives in part from OE *pilian*, vi, to peel, and in part from OF *peler*, vt, to remove the hair from, to peel, itself partly from OF *pel*, var of OF-F *peau*, skin, from L *pellis*, and partly from L *pilāre*, to deprive of hair, from *pilus*, a hair—cf *pelage*, a quadruped's coat of wool or fur or hair, adopted from late MF-F, from OF *pel*, hair, and *Poilu*, F sl for a F soldier, from late MF-F *poilu*, hairy, earlier *pelu*, from *pel*.

2. L *pilus*, a hair, whence E *pile*, as of a carpet, is akin to Gr *pilos*, felt (n), and perh to L *fīlum*, a

thread. Cf FILAMENT, q.v. for *pilose, depilatory,* etc.

3. With 'to *peel*', cf 'to *pill*' or plunder, ME *pillen, pilen,* partly from OE *pilian,* to strip, *to peel, and partly from MF(-F) *piller,* to plunder, o.o.o.—but prob, ult, either from L *pilleum,* a rag (B & W), or from L *pīlum,* a pestle, a javelin (Webster). Derivative MF-F *pillage* has been adopted by E.

4. L *pilus,* hair, perh has derivative *pila,* a ball, whence OF *pile,* whence E *pill,* the 'little ball' of Med; the L dim *pilula* becomes MF-F *pilule,* adopted by E; cf *pellet,* from OF(-F) *pelote,* from ML *pelota,* mdfn of *pilota,* from L *pila;* cf also *platoon,* from late MF-F *peloton,* dim of *pelote* and, in C16, acquiring the sense 'group of soldiers'.

5 That odd-looking word *piligan,* a kind of moss, derives from SciL *Piligena,* a blend of *pili-,* an inferior c/f of Gr *pilos,* felt (n)+the element *-gen*.

6. E *plush* derives from F *pluche,* a contr (? orig phon only) of EF-F *peluche,* itself either from It *peluzzo,* (lit) little hair, dim of *pelo,* hair (L *pilus*) or, less prob, from OF-MF *peluchier* (F *pelucher*), to pick out, to pluck, from VL *piluccare,* ? a freq from L *pilāre,* to deprive of *pilus* or hair.

7. Prob from *piluccāre* derives, by contr, the late OE *pluccian* (var *ploccian*), E 'to *pluck*', to pick out, to cull, to strip of (e.g., feathers): cf It *piluccare,* to gather grapes; ON *plokka, plukka,* MHG-G *pflücken,* MD *plocken, plucken,* D *plukken.* 'To *pluck*' generates a *pluck,* act of plucking, hence that which is plucked, hence the heart, lungs, windpipe of an animal killed for food, hence —cf *heart* in sense 'courage'—the (orig sl) sense 'courage' (cf, sem, *guts*).

**peeler,** a policeman. See ROBERT, para 3.

**peen.** See the 2nd PANE.

**peep** (1), to cheep, to chirp feebly, ME *pepen,* is echoic: cf ME *pipen,* to pipe (cf PIPE), and L *pipīre, pipiāre.* Hence n. Cf PIPE.

**peep** (2), to peer. See PEEK.

**peer** (1), n. See PAIR, para 5.

**peer** (2), to glance sharply. See PEEK.

**peerage; peeress; peerless.** See PAIR, para 5.

**peeve,** a coll v, hence n, is a b/f from **peevish,** ME *pevische,* var *peivesshe:* o.o.o.

**peewee** derives from **peewit,** better **pewit:** echoic: cf KIBITZ, s.f.

**peg,** n, hence v; **pail.**

*Peg,* ME *pegge,* app derives from MD *pegge:* cf MD-MLG *pegel,* a gauge-rod or water-mark, and OE *paegel,* a wine-measure; OE *paegel* app becomes—influenced by OF *paiele,* a pan (L *patella*)—ME *payle,* E *pail.*

**Pegasus,** L *Pegasus,* Gr *Pēgasos* (from *pēgē,* a spring of water), is that myth wingèd horse which, with a blow of his hoof, caused Hippocrene, the Muses' inspiring fountain (fig, source of inspiration), to gush from Mt Helicon.

**pegmatite.** See the element *pegmato-*.

**Pehlevi.** See PARTHIA, para 1.

**pejorative.** See PESSIMISM, para 2.

**pekin; Pekinese, Pekingese; Peiping.**

The silk fabric *pekin* anglicizes F *pékin,* from F *Pékin,* corresp to E *Peking,* now called *Peiping;* derivative adj, hence n, *Pekingese* is applied esp to a small dog originating in China. *Peking*=Ch *Pe-king,* Capital (*king*) of the North (*pe*).

**pelage.** See the 3rd PEEL, para 1.

**pelagian** and **pelagic.** See ARCHIPELAGO.

**pelecan.** See PELICAN.

**pelerine.** See PEREGRINE, para 2.

**pelf; pilfer.**

*Pelf,* orig booty, stolen goods, derives from OF *pelfre,* o.o.o.: *pelfre* has derivative *pelfrer,* to rob, despoil, whence, by 'thinning', to *pilfer* (cf the long obs syn 'to *pelf*').

**pelican,** occ *pelecan,* derives from LL *pelicānus,* var of LL *pelecān* (acc *pelecāna*), trln of Gr *pelekán* (acc *pelekana*): cf Gr *pelekas* (acc *pelekanta*), a woodpecker: therefore cf Gr *pelekeus,* an axe, in Lesbian Gr a hammer, and Skt *paraśus* (*pársús*), an axe: prob Mesopotamian—cf Ass-Babylonian *pilakku* and, *b* for *p,* Sumerian *balak,* an axe. (Hofmann; Webster.)

**pelisse,** adopted from OF-F, derives from LL *pellīcia,* a cloak, app elliptical for *uestis pellīcia,* garment 'made of fur' (*pellīcius*), prop 'made of skin', from L *pellis,* skin: cf the n PELT.

**pell; pellagra, pellagrous.** See PELT, n, paras 2, 3.

**pellet.** See the 3rd PEEL, para 4.

**pellicle.** See PELT, n, para 2.

**pellitory** derives—*l* for *r*—from ME *paritorie:* OF *paritoire,* var of *paritaire* (F *pariétaire*): L *parietāria,* from the adj *parietārius,* from *pariet-,* o/s of *pariēs,* a wall: o.o.o. Cf the element *parieto-*.

**pell-mell.** See MIX, para 7.

**pellucid,** whence **pellucidity.** See the 3rd LIGHT, para 19.

**pelmet** anglicizes F *palmette,* dim of *palme,* q.v. at FEEL, para 2.

**pelorus,** a navigating instrument, derives from Hannibal's pilot *Pelorus;* cf *Pelorus Jack,* a porpoise that, following ships plying the Wellington Straits, was famous in N.Z. of late C19–early 20. *Pelorus* app derives from Gr *pelōros,* monstrous.

**pelota,** adopted from Sp and parallel to OF-F *pelote,* a ball, comes, via VL *pilotta* (a dim), from L *pila,* a ball: cf the 3rd PEEL, para 4.

**pelt** (1), a skin or fell, as of a sheep or, now esp, of a fur-bearing animal, **peltry; pell** and **pellicle** (whence **pellicular**); **pellagra, pellagrous.**

1. A *pelt* app derives, by b/f, from *peltry:* OF-MF *peleterie* (F *pelleterie*), a collective, in *-erie,* from OF *peletier* (F *pelletier*), itself from OF *pel,* from L *pellis,* a skin, s *pell-,* r *pel-:* prob cf Homeric *pella, pellis,* a milk-bowl, ? orig of leather: cf also the n FELL.

2. OF *pel* becomes E *pell,* a skin or a hide (both obs), whence a roll of parchment, whence a record in parchment, whence the obs *Master of the Pells,* and L *pellis* has dim *pellicula,* whence—perh via EF-F *pellicule*—E *pellicle.*

3. *Pellagra*, adopted from It (whence the F *pellagre*), blends Gr *pell*a, *skin, *hide+Gr Med suffix *-agra*, from *agra*, a catching or seizing, as in Gr *podagra*, hence Med E, gout, lit a seizure of the *pode*s or feet. It *pellagra* has adj *pellagroso*, whence E *pellagrose*, *pellagrous*; cf E *podagrous*, from L *podagrōsus*, and *podagric*, from L *podagricus*, from Gr *podagrikos*.

**pelt** (2), vt and vi, to strike (with) a series of usu vigorous blows, derives from ME *pelten*, var *pilten* (whence the obs 'to *pilt*'), to push or thrust, both being app varr of syn ME *pulten*, itself perh from—at least, very prob akin to—L *pultāre*, to strike, to beat, repeatedly, a freq of *pellere*, to push, hence to strike: f.a.e., PULSE, to throb.

**peltate**. See the element *pelti-*.

**peltry**. See the 1st PELT.

**pelvic** (cf the element *pelvi-*) is the learnèd E adj —cf *pelvien*, the learnèd F adj—of ML *pelvis*, L *peluis*, a basin: cf Gr *pelux*, a bowl, and Skt *pālavī*, a sort of vase.

**pemican** now usu (as in F) **pemmican**, derives from Cree *pəmikkân*, var of *pimikkân*, from *pimiz*, fat, grease. The Crees are a Canadian, esp Manitoban, branch of the Algonquins.

**pen** (1) an enclosure, and **pen**, to enclose. See PIN, para 4.

**pen** (2), a feather, hence a quill for writing, whence **penknife** and **penmanship**, hence also 'to pen'; **pennant**, **pennon**; **pencel** and **pennoncel**; **pennate** and **pinnate**; **pinion**, n, a wing, a feather, hence v; **panache**.—Cf the elements *penni-*, *-ptene*, *-ptera*, and also E FEATHER.

1. A *pen* derives from ME *penne*, feather, quill, adopted from late OF-MF, from L *penna*, a wing, a large feather, ML a writing pen: OL *pesna*, perh for **pesna*, that which serves for flying, IE **pet-*, to fly, cf Gr *petomai*, I fly, and Skt *pátram*, a feather.

2. OF-MF *penne* has the OF-MF derivative *pennon*, with var *penon*, adopted by ME, whence E *pennon*, whence—? after *pendant*—the syn *pennant*, a flag that flies out lengthways like a long, waving plume. OF-MF *penon* has both the dim *penoncel*, whence the obsol E *pennoncel*, often contr to the obsol *pencel*, and the var *pignon*, whence ME-E *pinion*, a (part of a) bird's wing.

3. L *penna*, a feather, has derivative *pennātus*, furnished with wings or with feathers, whence E *pennate*, winged, feathered; and the perh orig mere var L *pinna*, a feather, a wing, has derivative *pinnātus*, feathered, whence E *pinnate*, feather-like; dim *pinnula*, a small feather, yields E *pinnule*, whence, anl, *pinnulate*.

4. *Panache*, adopted from F *panache*, late MF-EF *pennache*: It *pennaccio*, var of *pennacchio*, from *penna*, a feather, from L.

**pen** (3), a headland. See PENGUIN.

**penal, penalty**. See PAIN, para 3.

**penance**. See PAIN, para 5.

**penates; pencil** (n, hence v); **penetrable** (whence, anl, **penetrability**), **penetralia, penetrant** (adj, hence n), **penetrate, penetration, penetrative, penetrator**—cf neg **impenetrable**, whence **impenetrability**; **penicillate; penicillin, penicillium; penis.**—**fenestra, fenestral, fenestrate, fenestration, fenestella; defenestration**.

1. *Penātes*, gods of the Roman household, gods of the interior, derives from L *penes* (r *pen-*), inside, in the interior of, which has derivative adv *penitus* and derivative adj *penitus*, interior, hence both *penetrālis*, internal, with neupl *penetrālia*, the innermost, hence most secret parts, adopted by learnèd E, and *penetrāre*, vt, to go right inside, whence *penetrābilis*, whence, perh via MF-F *pénétrable*, the E **penetrable**; the LL neg *impenetrābilis*, obscure, incomprehensible, yields MF-F *impénétrable*, whence E **impenetrable**. L *penetrāre* has presp *penetrans*, o/s *penetrant-*, whence, perh via F, **penetrant**. The pp *penetrātus* gives us 'to **penetrate**', whence the pa *penetrating*; derivative *penetrātiō*, o/s *penetrātiōn-*, becomes MF-F *pénétration* and, perh independently, E **penetration**; derivative ML *penetrātivus* yields **penetrative**, and LL *penetrātor* is adopted by E.

2. Prob, with *-n-* infix, from an IE r **pe-*, as in G *peos* and Skt *pásas*, penis, is L *pēnis*, the male member, adopted by many European nations as the Med or tech word; perh, however, despite the vowel change (? imposed as differentiation), L *pēnis* derives from or is, at least, akin to L *penes*, inside: 'the withinner, the penetrator'. From *pēnis* in its sense 'tail'—superseded by *cauda*—comes the dim *pēnicillus*, a painter's brush, cf that other dim, *pēniculus*, a brush, a broom; the VL var **pēnicellus* becomes MF *pincel* (F *pinceau*), whence ME *pencel*, E **pencil**. L *pēnicillus* has suggested both the E **penicillate**, pencil-shaped, and the Sci *Penicillium*, a fungus bearing conidiophores with tufts at their ends; whence the Biochem **penicillin** (*Penicill*ium +Chem suffix *-in*).

3. Prob distinct from, yet perh—by a *p-f* alternation—cognate with, L *penes*, within, is L *fen*estra, orig a mere hole made in a wall in order to admit light, hence a window; the L word is adopted by An with the new sense 'a small opening', as is the dim *fenestella* by Arch; but whereas the adj *fenestrate*, having many openings, derives from L *fenestrātus*, provided with windows, the adj *fenestral*=L *fenestra*+E adj suffix *-al*, as if from L **fenestrālis*.

4. The adj *fenestrate* has prompted the learnèd *defenestration*, the act of throwing somebody *de*, from, a *fenestra* or window.

**pence**. See PENNY.

**pencel**. See the 2nd PEN, para 2.

**penchant**. See PEND, para 6.

**pencil**. See PENATES, para 2.

**pend**, whence the pa, whence the prep, **pending** (cf F *pendant* from *pendre*), **pendant**—**pendent, pendentive; pendicle; pendulous, pendulum, pendule; —painter** (a rope); **penchant;—pensile; pension** (n, hence v), **pensionary, pensioner, pensionnaire, pensive, pensum, pensy**—cf **pensée** and **pansy**—c also **poise** (n and v), **peso, peseta**.—Cognate: **pondus, ponder** (whence **pondering**), **ponderable**, ponderant (whence **ponderance**), **ponderate** (adj, v), **ponderation, ponderosity, ponderous.**—Cpds: **append, appendage, appendant** (adj, hence n), **appendicitis, appendix, appendicle** (whence anl **appendicular** and **appendiculate**); **appentice** and **penthouse; compendent** (whence **compendency**), **compendious, compendium**—**compensable, compensate, compensation, compensative,** anl **compensator** (whence **compensatory**); **depend** (whence **dependable**), **dependant, dependent, dependence** (whence **dependency**)—and the neg **independent,** whence **independence,** with var **independency; dispend, dispendious**—**dispensable** (cf **indispensable**), **dispensary, dispensation** (whence, anl, **dispensative**), **dispensator, dispensatory, dispense, dispenser**—**spence, spencer, spend** (whence **spender** and pa, vn **spending**), **spendthrift, spent; equipoise** and **counterpoise; expend** (whence **expenditure**), **expense; impend, impendent; imponderable; perpend**—**perpendicular; prepense; preponderant** (whence **preponderance,** with var **-ancy**), **preponderate, preponderation; propend, propendent**—**propense, propension, propensity; stipend, stipendiary; suspend** (whence **suspender**), **suspense** (adj, n), **suspension, suspensive** (whence anl **suspensoid**), **suspensor,** whence anl **suspensorium** and **suspensory.**

### Indo-European

1. In this constellation, there are two vv with the one s *pend*-: *pendēre*, vi, to be hanging or suspended, and *pendere*, vt, to hold in suspension, to suspend, hence to weigh, esp to weigh money, hence to pay, to evaluate; both vv have pp *pēnsus,* with its neu *pēnsum* used as n, whence *pēnsāre,* which is syn with *pendere*; and the s and r *pend*- has var *pond*- in L *pondus,* weight. Prob the r *pend*- is an extn of IE *\*pen-,* to weigh. For the vi *pendēre*-vt *pendere* alternation of form and sense, cf *iacēre*, to be lying on the ground, and *iacere*, to cause to lie on the ground, i.e. to throw or cast.

### Simples

2. 'To *pend*' derives, via OF-F *pendre,* from L *pendēre*, to be hanging; and the F presp *pendant,* used (already in OF) as n, is adopted by E; the adj *pendent,* deriving from the F presp, shows the influence of L *pendent-,* o/s of *pendens,* presp of *pendēre*; the L o/s *pendent-* occurs in the EF-F n *pendentif,* whence E *pendentive.*

3. *Pendulous* derives from L *pendulus,* hanging, suspended, from the common r *pend-*; hence, anl, *pendulosity. Pendulus* has neu *pendulum,* used by SciL as a n, adopted by E; F *pendule* likewise comes from *pendulus.*

4. *Pendulus* has the dim *pendiculus,* a cord, whence, in part, the E *pendicle. Pendiculus* has the cpd *perpendiculum,* a plumb line (obs E *perpendicle*), with derivative LL adj *perpendiculāris,* whence MF *perpendiculier, perpendiculer* (F *perpendiculaire*), whence E *perpendicular.*

5. L *pendere* app had a pp *\*penditus,* whence VL *\*penditōrium,* whence OF *pentoir,* a suspensory cord, whence the naut E *painter.*

6. With L *pendiculus,* cf the L adj *\*pendicus,* whence VL *\*pendicāre,* to lean, whence MF-F *pencher,* with presp *penchant,* used as n in EF-F and thereupon adopted by E.

7. L *pēnsus,* pp of *pendere,* to suspend, to weigh, to pay, has adj *pēnsilis,* pendent, whence E *pensile,* and derivative n *pēnsiō* (acc *pēnsiōnem*), a paying, (a) payment, salary, rent or hire, whence MF-F *pension,* adopted by E; F *pension,* a boarding-house, is modern. Derivative MF-F *pensionner* becomes 'to *pension*', and its own derivative MF-F *pensionnier* becomes E *pensioner.* L *pēnsiō, pēnsiōn-,* has ML agent *pēnsiōnārius,* a pensioner, whence both E *pensionary* and F *pensionnaire,* partly adopted by E in the modern sense 'boarder'.

8. The L pp *pēnsus,* weighed, has neu *pēnsum,* used in LL-ML as n, a weight of wool distributed to the maids for spinning, hence a task; in the latter sense, it has been adopted in some secondary schools. More importantly, the L n *pēnsum,* a weight, becomes VL *pēsum,* whence OF *peis,* soon —under influence of L *pondus*—*pois* (F *poids*), adopted by ME, whence E *poise;* note, however, that OF has var *peise* (perh imm from LL *pēnsa,* a weight), whence *poise,* a weight, balance. 'To *poise*' derives from ME *poisen,* from MF 'il *poise*', from OF-F *peser,* to weigh, from VL *\*pēsāre,* from L *pēnsāre,* orig an int of *pendere.*

9. OF *pois* has cpd OF *contrepois* (F *contrepoids*), whence, ult, the E *counterpoise;* cf the anl formed *equipoise,* equality in weight, and *avoirdupois,* ME *avoir de pois,* adopted from MF, lit 'goods (property, *avoir*) of weight'.

10. LL *pēnsum,* VL *\*pēsum,* a weight, becomes the syn Sp *peso,* which acquires the sense 'a Spanish, or a Mexican, dollar', which, silver, weighs heavy; its dim is *peseta.*

11. L *pēnsāre,* to weigh, to judge, becomes OF-F *penser,* to think, whence OF-F *pensif,* f *pensive,* whence E *pensive;* the OF nom sing *pensis* yields Sc and dial *pensy,* thoughtful. OF-F *penser* has derivative OF-F *pensée,* a thought, as in *arrière-pensée,* an after thought; *pensée,* moreover, became, in EF-F, a flower-name, whence E *pansy.*

12. L *pondus,* weight, is notable for its derivatives:

*ponderāre,* to weigh, MF-F *pondérer,* E 'to *ponder*'; hence LL *ponderābilis,* late MF-F *pondérable,* E *ponderable,* with neg *imponderable;* presp *ponderans,* o/s *ponderant-,* E *ponderant;* pp *ponderātus,* whence the E adj and v *ponderate;* its derivative *ponderātiō,* o/s *ponderātiōn-,* whence, perh via EF-F *pondération,* the E *ponderation;*

*ponderōsus,* heavy, E *ponderous;* hence ML *ponderōsitās,* o/s *ponderōsitāt-,* E *ponderosity.*

### Compounds

13. L *appendere* (*ad,* to+*pendere,* suspend), to hang (something) on to or from, becomes OF-F *appendre,* E 'to *append*', whence—perh after LL *appendicia,* appendages—*appendage;* the F presp *appendant* is adopted by E as adj, hence n. Deriva-

tive L *appendix* is adopted by Sc, and on its o/s *appendic-* is formed *appendicitis* (Med suffix *-itis*); its dim *appendicula* yields *appendicle*. F *appendre* has late MF-F derivative *appentis*, whence both the obs E *appentice*, a penthouse, and, by aphesis, the obs *pentis* and *pentice*, whence, by f/e (HOUSE), *penthouse*.

14. L *compendere*, to weigh together, hence to weigh, has presp *compendens*, o/s *compendent-*, E Math adj *compendent*; derivative *compendium*, LL a short cut, an epitome, is adopted by E; LL adj *compendiōsus* becomes MF-F *compendieux*, f *-ieuse*, E *compendious*.

15. With L *compendere*, cf L *compēnsāre*, to weigh (several things) together, to balance together, whence MF-F *compenser*, with derivative *compensable*, adopted by E; the L pp *compēnsātus* yields 'to *compensate*'. On the pp s *compēnsāt-* arise *compēnsātiō*, o/s *compēnsātiōn-*, whence, prob via MF-F, the E *compensation*, and LL *compēnsātiuus*, ML *-ivus*, E *compensative*.

16. L *dēpendēre*, to be suspended or hanging down (from), hence to derive from or rely upon, becomes OF *dependre* (F *dé-*), E 'to *depend*'; whereas the L presp gives us *dependent*, the F presp gives us *dependant*. Derivative MF-F *dépendance* yields E *dependence*. The EF-F neg *indépendant* and its subsidiary *indépendance* leads to *independent, -ence*.

17. L *dispendere*, to weigh out, distribute, spend, becomes OF-MF *despendre*, whence 'to *dispend*'; derivative L *dispendium* has LL adj *dispendiōsus*, whence E *dispendious*, costly, extravagant.

18. 'To *dispend*' has been superseded by 'to *spend*', ME *spenden*, by aphesis from OF *despendre*, to spend also to weigh out or distribute, with derivative n *despense*, whence, aphetically, both the E, now only dial, *spense*, expenditure, expense, and the Sc *spence*, a pantry; derivative OF *despensier* becomes, by aphesis, the now only Hist E *spencer*. 'To *spend*' has cpd *spendthrift*, lit a spender of savings, and pp *spent*.

19. Orig the int of L *dispendere* is *dispēnsāre*, OF *dispenser*, E 'to *dispense*', with agent *dispenser* (owing something to OF *despensier, despenseor*) and adj *dispensable*, the neg *indispensable* prob coming direct from the EF-F word. *Dispēnsāre* has pp *dispēnsāt*us, whence *dispēnsātiō*, o/s *dispēnsātiōn-*, OF-F *dispensation*, adopted by E, and LL *dispēnsātiuus*, ML *-ivus*, E *dispensative*, and *dispēnsātor*, OF-F *dispensateur*, AF *dispensatour*, E *dispensator*, and LL *dispēnsatōrius*, E *dispensatory*. Note that *dispensary*, whence F *dispensaire*, comes from 'to *dispense*'.

20. L *expendere*, to pay in full, yields 'to *expend*', whence *expendable*; the derivative ML agent *expenditor*, a disburser, occurs in E Hist, and on it is anl formed *expenditure*. The pp *expēnsus* becomes, in its f *expēnsa*, LL for an expense, money for expenses, with the ML var *expensum*, whence OF *espense* and AF *expense*, whence E *expense*, whence *expensive*.

21. L *impendēre*, to hang into, to hang over,

yields 'to *impend*'; its presp *impendens*, o/s *impendent-*, explains the E adj *impendent*.

22. L *perpendere*, to weigh *per-* or exactly, hence to examine carefully, becomes 'to *perpend*'.

23. L *praeponderāre*, to weigh more, to exceed in weight, has presp *praeponderans*, o/s *praeponderant-*, whence E *preponderant*, and pp *praeponderātus*, whence 'to *preponderate*', with derivative LL *praeponderātiō*, o/s *praeponderātiōn-*, E *preponderation*.

24. L *prōpendēre*, to be hung in front, yields 'to *propend*'; its presp *prōpendens*, o/s *prōpendent-*, yields the adj *propendent*; its pp *prōpēnsus* is used also as adj 'hanging, hence inclining, forward', E *propense*, and the L derivative *prōpēnsiō*, o/s *prōpēnsiōn-*, becomes *propension*, almost superseded by *propensity* (*propense+-ity*).

25. With *propense*, cf *prepense*: L *prōpēnsus* has perh influenced OF *purpenser*, to plan beforehand, lit to think (*penser*) forward (*pur-*, var *pour-*, for *pro-*); the OF pp *purpensé* led to ME *purpensed*, whence EE *prepensed*, pp, whence the E adj *prepense*.

26. L *pendere*, to weigh, to pay, has the cpd OL \**stipipendium*, whence, by contr, L *stipendium*, the 1st element being *stips* (gen *stipis*, c/f *stipi-*), a small piece of money: 'payment of a small sum', e.g. as alms, hence, in LL, *stipendia* (pl), the revenues of the Church, hence, in ML, *stipendium*, a priest's salary, whence, prob via MF, the E *stipend*; the derivative L adj *stipendiārius* becomes, perh via EF-F *stipendiaire*, the E *stipendiary*, salary-receiving.

27. L *suspendere*, lit to hang *sub* or under, i.e. to hang up, becomes OF *souspendre, suspendre* (as in F), whence 'to *suspend*', lit and fig. The LL pp *suspēnsus* becomes the late MF-F adj *suspens*, whence E *suspense*; the E n *suspense* derives, by b/f, from 'in *suspense*', trans of the late MF-F adv phrase, *en suspens* (from the adj). L *suspēns*us has these derivatives affecting E: LL *suspensibilis*, E *suspensible*; *suspēnsiō*, o/s *suspēnsiōn-*, OF-F, whence E, *suspension*; ML *suspēnsīvus*, MF-F *suspensif*, f *-ive*, E *suspensive*; *suspēnsōrius*, neu *-ōrium*, as LL n, whence the E adj and n; ML agent *suspēnsor*, adopted by E.

**pendant; pendent; pendentive.** See prec, para 2.

**pendicle.** See PEND, para 4.

**pending.** See PEND (heading).

**pendule, pendulous; pendulum.** See PEND, para 3.

**peneplain** (or -plane); **peninsula**, whence—after *insular*—**peninsular**; **penult, penultimate; penumbra**, whence **penumbral**.

1. *Pene-* or, before a vowel, *pen-* represents the L adv *paene*, almost, occ written *pēne*: o.o.o. *Peneplain* is an anl E formation, after *peninsula*, which derives from L *paeninsula*, an 'almost *insula* or island' (f.a.e., SOLE, adj).

2. *Penult* shortens *penultima*, the last syllable but one: L *paenultima* (*syllaba*): f of *paenultimus*, last but one: *paene+ultimus*, last. From *penultima* comes, after ULTIMATE, the adj *penultimate*.

3. *Penumbra* is a SciL formation, as if from L

*paenumbra, an 'almost (paen-) shadow (umbra)':
f.a.e., UMBRA. Cf the F pénombre.

penetrable, pentralia, penetrant, penetrate, penetration, penetrative. See PENATES, para 1.

penguin; pen, a headland.

Penguin, app orig the great auk, seems to represent W pen, head + W gwyn, white; both W pen and W gwyn have numerous cognates in other C languages. Pen, in its derivative sense 'headland', occurs, e.g., in Cor surnames beginning with Pen-.

penicillate; penicillin, Penicillium. See PENATES, para 2.

peninsula, peninsular. See PENEPLAIN.

penis. See PENATES, para 2.

penitence, pentitent, penitential, penitentiary. See PAIN, para 5.

penknife, orig used for cutting quills to write with. See the 2nd PEN (heading).

pennant. See the 2nd PEN, para 2.

pennate. See 2nd PEN, para 3.

pennon, pennoncel. See 2nd PEN, para 2.

Pennsylvania, whence adj (hence n) Pennsylvanian, is lit 'the Sylvania, or Sylvan Country, of William Penn', that E Quaker (1644–1718) who, in 1681, founded the settlement that was to grow into a State. For the formation, cf Transylvania, Rum -silvania, formerly a province in East Hungary; for -sylvania, see, f.a.e., SILVAN.

penny. See the 2nd PAN, para 4. The pl pennies, numerical, becomes, by contr, pence, collective.

pennyroyal is f/e for ME puliall royal, itself via an AF royal elaboration of MF peuliol (C14), earlier poulioel (C13), from VL *puleium, mdfn of L pūleium (cf LL pulēiatum, pennyroyal wine), itself a contr of pūlegum, so named because anciently this kind of mint, with pungently aromatic leaves, was used against the pūlex (o/s pūlic-) or flea: cf F herbe aux puces, herb for (i.e., against) fleas. (Enci It.)

pennywort is a wort or herb with leaves round like pennies.

penology. See the element peno-.

pensée. See PEND, para 11.

pensile. See PEND, para 7.

pension, pensionary, pensioner. See PEND, para 7.

pensive. See PEND, para 11

pensum. See PEND, para 8.

pensy. See PEND, para 11.

pent, adj, is the pp of pend, var of pen, to enclose, q.v. at PIN.

pentacle, pentad. See FIVE, para 13.

pentagon, pentagram, pentameter, Pentateuch. See the element penta-.

pentathlon. See FIVE, para 5.

Pentecost. See FIVE, para 14. Cf PINKSTER.

penthouse. See PEND, para 13, s.f.

penult, penultimate. See PENEPLAIN, para 2; cf ULTERIOR, para 6.

penumbra. See PENEPLAIN, para 3; cf UMBRA, para 9.

penurious, penury. See PATIENCE, para 8.

peon, whence peonage. See FOOT, para 9.

peony. See PAEON, para 3.

people, n and v; populace, popular, popularity (whence, anl, popularize, whence popularization), populate, population, populous—cf depopulate, depopulation;—public (adj, hence n), publican, publication, publicist, publicity, publish (whence publisher)—cf republic, whence republican; pueblo; —perh akin are plebe, plebeian (adj, hence n), plebiscite, plebs.

1. People, ME people, poeple, OF poeple, pueple (F peuple), derives from L populus, a State's citizens collectively, s popul-, IE r perh *popl-, ? var *pupl-, with -b- varr *pobl-, *publ-, as in the L corresp adj pūblicus; L plēbs (var plēps), c/f plebi-, the generality of non-noble Roman citizens, (later) the populace, is perh a contr of *polebs (var *poleps).

2. OF pueple has v puepler, poepler (F peupler), whence 'to people'.

3. L populus has derivative adjj populōsus, whence E populous, and populāris, of the people, democratic, whence, perh via OF populeir, MF-F populaire, the E popular; derivative LL populāritās, populousness, fellow-citizenship, comradeship, but also general opinion (Souter), o/s populāritāt-, becomes late M F-F popularité, hence E popularity; late EF-F populariser (from L populāris) fathers E 'to popularize'. Populace is adopted from EF-F, which thus adapts It popolaccio, a pej extn of popolo (L populus). L populus has, moreover, the LL-ML v populāri, populāre, to people, with pp populātus, whence 'to populate'; derivative LL populātiō, o/s populātiōn-, the people, yields—perh via late MF-F—the E population.

4. LL populātiō and LL-ML populāri, -āre, are not to be confused with Classical L populāre, -āri, to devastate (populātiō, devastation) which perh represent a b/f from L dēpopulāre, to deprive—or reduce the number—of people; dē-, down from, connoting descent, reduction, deprivation + populus + inf suffix -āre, -āri. Dēpopulāre has pp dēpopulātus, whence 'to depopulate'; derivative dēpopulātiō, o/s dēpopulātiōn-, yields depopulation.

5. The corresp adj pūblicus, only perh akin to populus, passes through MF-F public, f publique, to become E public; derivative L pūblicānus, adj and n, passes through OF-F publicain into E publican; derivative pūblicāre, to render public, has pp pūblicātus, whence the LL n pūblicātiō, o/s pūblicātiōn-, whence MF-F, hence E, publication. F public has derivatives publiciste and publicité, whence E publicist and publicity, whence, anl, 'to publicize'. 'To publish', ME publisshen, derives from OF-F publier, with incorrect -ish anl with that of astonish, from L pūblicāre.—With public-house (orig, as often still, public house), cf the F maison publique (lit, public house), a brothel, and LL pūblicus locus (lit, public place), a latrine, and perh LL pūblica, a public street, elliptical for pūblica uia.

6. L pūblicus occurs in the important cpd respūblica, lit 'the public res or affair', whence MF-F république, whence E republic, whence—

aided by EF-F *républicain*—the adj, hence n, *republican*.

7. L *populus*, a people, becomes Sp *pueblo*, a village—cf OF *poblo* and later OF *pueble*.

8. L *plēbs*, as in para 1, becomes MF-F *plèbe*, whence E *plebe* (obs), the Roman plebs, the common people, whence, at least in part, the AE *plebe*, a freshman at West Point or at Annapolis. The derivative L adj *plēbeius* becomes MF-F *plébéien*, whence E *plebeian*; and the derivative cpd *plēbiscītum* (c/f *plebi-+scītum-*, from *scītus*, adj from the pp of *scīre*, to know, hence, in LL, also to decide, to decree): a decree or decision made by the Roman *plebs*; whence MF-F *plébiscite*, with modern sense arising in 1792; hence as EE-E *plebiscite*.

**pep**, n hence v, is a sl abbr of PEPPER.

**pepo.** See MELON, para 2.

**pepper** (n, hence v), whence the adj **peppery** and such obvious cpds as **pepperbox, -corn** (OE *piporcorn*), **-grass, -mill, -mint, -pot, -tree, -wort**; the sl **pep**, whence sl **peppy**; **paprika**; **pipal**; **Piper, piperin(e), piperonal; pimpernel**.

1. *Pepper*, ME *peper*, OE *pipor*, derives from LL *piper* (gen *piperis*), itself from—or at the least akin to—Gr *péperi*, prob (Hofmann) via Persia from India—cf (*l* for *r*) Skt *pippalī*, peppercorn, a grain of pepper, and *pippala*, a berry.

2. App from Gr *péperi* comes Hung *paprika*, Turkish pepper, whence—perh via G—the E *paprika*.

3. Skt *pippala*, a berry, also denotes the sacred fig tree of India (*Ficus religiosa*), whence Hind *pīpal*, E *pipal*.

4. L *piper* becomes Bot *Piper*, the true pepper, usu a climbing shrub: whence Chem *piperin, -ine* (perh suggested by the LL-ML adj *piperīnus*), whence, in turn, *piperitone* (Chem suffix *-one*) and, adopted from G, *piperonal*; cf *piperate*, n, and *piperic*, adj: *piper*, pepper+Chem *-ate*, Chem *-ic*.

5. The LL-ML adj *piperīnus* app has derivative LL *pimpinella*, a plant with medicinal qualities (Souter)—cf It *pimpinella*, OProv *pempinella*—whence ML *pimpernella*, whence MF-F *pimprenelle*, whence E *pimpernel*. (OF *piprenelle* came perh from a VL *piperinella*, from LL *piperīnus*.)

**pepsin, peptic.** See the element *-pepsia*. (*Peptone*= Gr *pepton*, neu of *peptos*, cooked+Chem suffix *-one*.)

**per**, adopted from L *per*, through (whence F *par*), is akin to Gr *peri*, Aeolic *per*, round about (cf, sem, E *about*), beyond, and the syn OPer *paryi* and Skt *pári*.

**peradventure**, which has prompted **perchance**, derives from ME *per aventure*, from OF *par aventure*. Cf prec.

**perambulate, perambulation.** See AMBLE, para 4.

**perceive.** See CAPABILITY, para 7.

**percentage; percentile.**

*Percentage* is an *-age* n formed from *per cent*, (so much) per hundred, from L *per centum*; the adj is *percental*. *Percentile*=*percent*age +adj *-ile*.

**perception, perceptive.** See CAPABILITY, p. 7.

(The Psy n *percept*=L *perceptum*, prop the neu of *perceptus*, pp of *percipere*.)

**perch** (1), the fish; **perciform**; ? **pulchritude**, whence **pulchritudinous** (cf *multitudinous* from *multitude*).

1. *Perch*, ME *perche*, derives from MF-F *perche*: L *perca*: Gr *perkē*, itself akin to Gr *perkos*, speckled, dark (cf *perknos*, dark), and Skt *pŕśni*, speckled; IE r, prob *\*perk-*, speckled, spotted.

2. L *perca* has c/f *perci-*, as in E *perciform*, perch-like.

3. Perh akin to L *perca*, Gr *perkē*, etc., is L *pulcher* (f *pulchra*), beautiful, whence *pulchritūdō*, beauty, whence E *pulchritude*.

**perch** (2), a measure of length, ME from MF(-F) *perche*, comes from L *pertica*: ? of C origin.

**perch** (3), to alight and settle, as a bird does: MF-F *percher*: from MF *perche*, as in prec.

**perchance.** See PERADVENTURE.

**Percheron**, a heavy draught horse, is, in F, lit a 'native of Le *Perche*', a famous horse-breeding district of NW France.

**perciform.** See the 2nd PERCH.

**percipient.** See CAPABILITY, para 7.

**percolate**, n and v; **percolation**, whence, anl, **percolative** and **percolator**.

The Pharm n *percolate* derives from L *percōlātum*, prop the neu of *percōlātus*, pp of *percōlāre*, to cause (a liquid) to be strained through interstices: *per*, through+*cōlāre*, to be filtered, to flow, to strain (a liquid); *percōlātus* yields both E 'to *percolate*' and L *percōlātiō*, o/s *percōlātiōn-*. *Cōlāre* derives from L *cōlum*, a filter, a sieve: o.o.o.

**percurrent.** See COURSE, (at *percurrere* in) para 10.

**percuss, percussion** (whence, anl, **percussive**), **percussor, percutient**: all derive from L *percutere*, to strike *per-* or violently, *-cutere* being the c/f of *quatere*, to shake (f.a.e., QUASH), hence to strike; the presp *percutiens*, o/s *percutient-*, yields the E adj hence n *percutient*; the pp *percussus* yields E 'to *percuss*' and L *percussiō*, o/s *percussiōn-*, whence, perh via MF-F, the E *percussion*.

**perdition; perdu.**

The former derives, via ME *perdicioun* and OF *perdicion* (MF-F *perdition*), from L *perditiōn-*, o/s of *perditiō*, from *perditus*, pp of *perdere*, to lose, ruin, destroy: *per*, through+*-dere*, c/f of *dare*, to put (hence, via 'put into the hands of', to give). L *perdere* becomes OF-F *perdre*, pp *perdu*, lost, hence, in E, lost to view.

**perdurable, perdure.** See DURABLE, para 7.

**peregrine** (adj, hence n), whence **peregrinoid** (suffix *-oid*, *-resembling*); **pelerine**—cf **pilgrim, pilgrimage; peregrinate, peregrination, peregrinator, peregrinity.**

1. The L adj *peregrīnus*, travelling abroad, coming from abroad, (hence) concerning foreign parts (cf LL *peregrīna*, foreign parts)—whence E *peregrine*, foreign, exotic—derives from the L advv *peregrē*, from abroad, and *peregrī*, in or to

foreign parts, themselves very closely akin to L *peragrāre*, to travel from or to or in foreign parts: *per*, through+*agrōs*, acc of *agri*, the fields+inf suffix -*āre*—sc *īre*, to go, or *ambulāre*, to walk. (For *agri*, pl of *ager*, c/f *agri*-, cf '*agri*culture'.)

2. L *peregrīnus* has the LL var *pereger*, with LL var *peleger*, which—after *peregrīnus*—prompts the ML *pelegrīnus*, of a pilgrim, hence as n, a pilgrim: whence OF *pelerin* (F *pèlerin*), adj and n, f *pelerine*, used, centuries later (*pèlerine*), for a woman's fur cape, esp with long ends hanging down in front, whence E *pelerine*.

3. OF *pelerin* app had a var *\*pelegrin*, to judge by ME *pelegrim*, later *pilegrim*, latest *pilgrim*, extant in E. OF *pelerin* had derivative v *peleriner*, to go on a pilgrimage, with derivative n *pelerinage* (F *pè*-), later *pelrimage*, adopted by ME and duly re-shaped to *pilgrimage*, extant in E.

4. L *peregrīnus* has derivative *peregrīnāri*, LL *peregrīnāre*, to travel abroad, with pp *peregrīnatus*, whence 'to *peregrinate*'; derivatives *peregrīnātiō* (o/s *peregrīnātiōn*-) and *peregrīnātōr* become E *peregrination* (prob via OF *peregrination*, F *péré*-) and *peregrinator*. *Peregrīnus* has abstract n *peregrīnitās*, the being a foreigner, o/s *peregrīnitāt*-, whence—perh via EF-F *pérégrinité*—the E *peregrinity*.

**père.** See FATHER, para 3.

**peremptory.** See EXEMPT, para 6.

**perennial.** See ANNUAL, para 4.

**perfect** (adj—hence v, whence **perfecter**), **perfectible** (whence, anl, **perfectibility**), **perfection** (whence **perfectionism**, **perfectionist**), **perfective**; negg **imperfect** (adj, hence n), **imperfection** (whence, anl, **imperfective**); **pluperfect**, adj, hence n; cf, f.a.e., the sep FACT.

1. A *perfect* thing is one 'made, or done, thoroughly': L *perfectus*, pp of *perficere*, to make or do thoroughly: *per*-, through(out)+-*ficere*, c/f of *facere*. The archaic *parfit* is ME (e.g., Chaucer), adopted from OF *parfit* (cf thè F *parfait*), from L. From *perfectus*, learnèd F coins *perfectible*, whence *perfectibilité*: cf the E *perfectible*, *perfectibility*. On L *perfectus* arise *perfectiō*, whence, via the acc *perfectiōn*em, the F *perfection*, adopted by E, and LL *perfectiuus*, ML *perfectivus*, whence E *perfective*.

2. L *perfectus* has derivative neg adj *imperfectus*, whence E *imperfect*; derivative LL *imperfectiō*, acc *imperfectiōnem*, becomes OF-F *imperfection*, adopted by E.

3. The LL *plusquamperfectus* (*plus*, more+ *quam*, than+*perfectus*, completed) of the grammarians became EF-F *plus-que-parfait*; E has drastically coined the contr *pluperfect*.

**perfervid** is *per*- or thoroughly *fervid*, q.v. at FERVENT.

**perfidious, perfidy.** See FAITH, para 15.

**perflation.** See FLATUS, para 7.

**perforate, perforation.** See FORAMEN, para 2.

**perforce** anglicizes F *par force*, by force. Cf PERADVENTURE.

**perform**, whence **performance** and **performer**, derives from ME *performen*, earlier *parfourmen* (these two forms being influenced by *form* and perh by L *performāre*, to form thoroughly), earliest *parfournen*, from OF-EF *parfornir*, *parfournir*: *par*-, L *per*-, thoroughly+*fournir*, *fornir*, to complete, to furnish (f.a.e., FURNISH).

**perfume, perfumery.** See FUME, para 4.

**perfunctory.** See FUNCTION, para 3.

**perfuse, perfusion.** See the 2nd FOUND, para 10.

**pergameneous.** See PARCHMENT, para 2.

**pergola**, adopted from It, comes from L *pergula*, a shed, a vine arbour, perh from *pergere*, to proceed with, from *regere*, to guide.

**perhaps.** See HAP, para 3.

**pericarditis** is an inflammation (connoted by Med suffix -*itis*) of the **pericardium**, a SciL trln of Gr *perikardion*, orig the neu of *perikardios*, near the heart: *peri*, round about (cf PER) the *kardia* or heart.

**pericarp**, like F *péricarpe*, derives from Gr *perikarpion*: *peri*, round about+*karpos*, fruit.

**pericycle**: Gr *perikuklos*, spherical. Cf prec two entries.

**peridium**: Gr *peridion*, dim of *pera*, a leather pouch.

**perigee**: EF-F *périgée*: from Gr *perigeios*, (passing) around the *gē* or earth.

**peril**, n, hence v—usu **imperil**, with *im*- for *in*, into; **perilous**—cf **parlous**;—**piracy**, **pirate** (n, hence v), **piratic**, **piratical**.

1. *Parlous* stands for *perlous*, a contr of *perilous*, from OF *perillous*, var of *perilleus* (F *périlleux*), from L *perīculōsus*, adj of *perīclum*, contr of *perīculum*, an attempt, hence a risk, danger, akin to *perītus*, experienced, and to Gr *peira*, a trial or attempt, and *peiran*, to attempt.

2. Gr *peiran* has agent *peiratēs*, a robber at sea, L *pīrāta*, MF-F *pirate*, adopted by E. Derivative Gr *peirateia* becomes ML *pīrātia*, whence E *piracy*; and derivative Gr *peiratikos* becomes L *pīrāticus*, whence E *piratic*, now usu in extn *piratical*.

**perimeter.** See MEASURE, para 4.

**perineal** is the adj of **perineum**, SciL trln of Gr *perinaion*, *perineos*: *peri*, round about+*inaō*, I urinate or defecate (cf Skt *iṣṇāti*, he discharges).

**period, periodic, periodical, periodicity.** See ODOGRAPH, para 6.

**periosteum** is a SciL coinage from Gr *periosteos*, round (*peri*) the bones (*osteon*, a bone). Hence *periosteal*.

**peripatetic**, adj hence n, derives from late MF-F *péripatétique*: L *peripatēticus*: Gr *peripatētikos*, walking about, from *peripatein*, to walk (*patein*) about (*peri*): cf Gr *patos*, a path, a step: perh cf the 1st PAD.

**peripheral** (cf the F *périphérique*) derives irreg from **periphery**: EF-F *périphérie*: LL *peripheria*: Gr *periphereia*, lit a carrying (-*phereia*, from *pherein*, to carry) around (*peri*).

**periphrasis, periphrastic.** See PHRASE, para 2, s.f.

**periscope, periscopic.** See SCOPE.

perish, whence perishable (? prompted by MF-F *périssable*) and the paa perished, perishing; imperishable, partly prompted by EF-F *impérissable*, but imm from *perishable*.

'To *perish*', ME *perisshen*, *perissen*, derives from *periss*ant, presp, and the pres pl *periss*ons, *periss*ez, *periss*ent, of OF *perir* (F *périr*), from L *perīre*, to go through, hence to come to nothing or be lost: *per*, through+*īre*, to go: f.a.e., ISSUE.

peristaltic (Physio): Gr *peristaltikos*, compressing as it clasps, from *peristellein*, to envelop: *peri*, round about+*stellein*, to place.

peristyle. See the element *-stylar*.

peritoneal is the adj of *peritoneum*: LL *peritonaeum*: Gr *peritonaion*, from *peritonos*, stretched around (*peri*): f.a.e., TONE.

periwig. See PETER, para 12.

periwinkle (1), a trailing herb or its flower; vetch; vinculum.

1. *Periwinkle*—prob influenced by the mollusc *periwinkle*—derives from ME *pervenke*, *pervinke*, themselves—the former via ONF *pervenke* (MF-F *pervenche*), the latter via OE *perwince*—from ML *pervinca*, L *peruinca*, from L *peruincīre*, int (*per-*) of *uincīre*, to bind or twine, itself o.o.o.

2. L *uincīre* has derivative *uinculum*, something that ties, binds, joins together, adopted, in its ML form vinculum, by An and Math.

3. Akin to L *uincīre* is the denasalized L *uicia*, ML *vicia*, whence OF *vece*, with var *veche*, adopted by ME, whence E vetch. With L *uicia*, ML *vicia*, cf Lett *vīkne*, a tendril

periwinkle (2), a mollusc; winkle.

This *periwinkle*—perh influenced by the 1st—app derives from OE *pinewincle*, a shellfish, with *pine-* perh deriving from L (from Gr) *pinna*, var *pina*, a mussel, and *-winkle* is OE *-wincle*, which, recorded only in cpds, seems to be a dim of *wince*, a reel, a winch (f.a.e., WINCH)—from the convoluted shell (EW).

perjure, perjury. See JURY, para 4, s.f.

perk, to rise, esp jauntily, in order to see, ME *perken*, is app a var of 'to *perch*'—see the 3rd PERCH. Hence, perky, lively and self-confident.

perks is a sl derivative of *perquisites*, q.v. at QUERY.

perlite. See PEARL (heading).

permanence, permanent. See MANOR, para 7.

permanganate, permanganic. The former= *permangan*ic+Chem suffix *-ate*; the latter=prefix *per-*+*manganic*, which=*mangan*ese+*-ic*: f.a.e., MAGNESIA.

permeable, whence, anl, permeability; permeate, permeation, whence, anl, permeative; negg impermeable, whence impermeability.

1. *Impermeable* derives from LL *impermeābilis*, perh via EF-F *imperméable*; *permeable* from LL *permeābilis* (cf EF-F *perméable*), from L *permeāre*, to pass (*meare*) through (*per*): and *meāre* has s and r *me-*, prob akin to *migrāre* and *mūtāre*: cf OSl *mimo*, across, athwart. On the pp *permeātus*—whence 'to *permeate*'—is, anl, formed the E *permeation*.

2. Cf, ult, ZENITH.

permissible, permission, permit. See MISSION, para 16.

permutation, permute. See MUTABLE, para 7.

pernicious. See NOXIOUS, para 5.

pernickety. See PART, para 6.

peroneal, peroneus, peronium, all An terms, come from Gr *peronē*, the fibula, the 3rd imm from its dim *peronion*.

perorate, peroration. See ORATION, para 7.

peroxide is an *oxide* (see OXYGEN) with a high proportion—connoted by the int *per-* (L *per*, through)—of oxygen. Hence as v.

perpend. See PEND, para 22.

perpendicular. See PEND, para 4.

perpetrate, perpetration, perpetrator. See FATHER, para 8.

perpetual, perpetuate, perpetuation (whence, anl, perpetuator), perpetuity.

*Perpetual* is a reshaping of OF-F *perpétuel*, from L *perpetuālis*, mdfn of *perpetuus*, continuing throughout, lasting for ever, from *perpet-*, o/s of *perpes*, lasting throughout, uninterrupted: *per*, through, *per-*, throughout+*pet*ere, to seek: f.a.e., PETITION. On *perpetuus* arise both *perpetuitās*, o/s *perpetuitāt-*, MF-F *perpétuité*, E perpetuity, and *perpetuāre*, to render lasting throughout or for ever, pp *perpetuātus*, whence 'to *perpetuate*'; derivative ML *perpetuātiō*, o/s *perpetuātiōn-*, becomes *perpetuation*.

perplex, perplexity. See PLY, para 27

perquisite, perquisition. See QUERY, para 11.

perrier. See PETER, para 7.

perron. See PETER, para 7.

perry. See PEAR, para 2.

perscribe, perscription. See SCRIBE, para 15.

perscrutate, perscrutation. See SHRED, para 9.

perse, Persia (whence Persian, adj, hence n); Persicaria, whence persicary; persienne and persiennes; peach.

1. The colour *perse*, dark blue, is adopted from F *perse*, prop the f of the OF-F adj *pers*, from ML *persus*, a form-and-sense mdfn of L *persicus*, peach-coloured, from *Persicus*, Persian (obs E *Persic*), adj of *Persia* (Gr ἡ Περσίς, *Persis*); OPer *Pārsa*, whence *Pārsi*, a Persian, whence E *Parsee* or *Parsi*); L *Persicus*=Gr *Persikos*, adj of *Persēs*, a Persian, itself—by the Greeks—derived from the Myth *Perseus*, slayer of the Medusa. Gr *Persikos* or *Persikon*, the latter elliptical for *Persikon mēlon*, Persian fruit, i.e. the peach, became L *persicum*, LL *persica* (neupl as f sing) and VL *\*pessica*, whence OF *pesche*, later *peche* (F *pêche*), ME *peche*, E peach.

2. The Bot *Persicaria* is derived by SciL from L *persicum*; whence *persicary*. And *persienne*, painted (or printed) cotton (or cloth), orig made in Persia, is adopted from F, where it is elliptical for *toile persienne*, Persian cloth, *persienne* being the f of MF-F *persien*, adj derived from the older adj *perse*, of Persia; and *persiennes* (f pl used as n), Venetian blinds, are supposed to have come from Persia.

persecute, persecution, persecutor. See SEQUENCE, para 12.

perseverance, persevere. See SEVERE, para 3.

Persia, Persian; Persicaria, persicary; persienne(s). See PERSE.

persiflage, adopted from F, derives from *persifler*, to quiz: *per-*, vaguely int+*siffler*, to hiss, to whistle, from VL *sifilāre* (attested by LL *sifilātiō*, a hissing in the theatre, L *sībilātiō*), from L *sībilāre*, ult echoic (cf SIBILANT).

persimmon is of Alg origin—cf Cree *pasiminan*, Lenape *pasīmĕnan*, dried fruit. (Webster.)

persist, persistence, persistent. See SIST, para 7.

person, persona, personable (from *person*), personage, personal (whence personalize, whence personalization), personality, personalty, personate (adj and v, whence personation), personative, personator (cf the derivative impersonate, impersonation, impersonator), personify, personification, personnel; impersonal, impersonality; parson (whence, from its colouring, the parson bird), parsonage, parsonic(al), parsonify; squarson.

1. *Person*, ME *person* and earlier *persone*, derives from OF *persone* (late MF-F *personne*): L *persōna*, orig a mask (Gr *prosōpon*), as worn in the Ancient Classical theatre, hence the role attributed to this mask, hence a character, a personage, hence—already in Cicero—a person, hence in Gram: and L *persōna*, a mask, is prob of Etruscan origin, for cf Etruscan *phersu*, app a mask or a masked person; both *persōna* and *phersu* may well be akin to Gr πρόσωπον, *prosōpon*, var *prosōpeion* (E & M). The Gr *prosōpeion*, a mask, is a derivative of *prosōpon*, a mask, orig and prop the face: *pros* (πρός), towards, at+*ōpa* (ὦπα), eye, the face.

2. L *persōna* is retained by E (*persona*) in several erudite or tech senses.

3. L *persōna* has the following derivatives affecting E:

ML *personāgium*, an Eccl duty or office, MF *personage*, id, (late MF) a personage (F *personnage*), E *personage* (cf *parsonage* in para 6);

LL *personālis* (often opp *materiālis*), relating to a person, OF *personal* (F *personnel*), E *personal*; derivative LL *personālitās*, o/s *personālitāt-*, MF *personalité*, EF-F *personnalité*, E *personality*; MF *personalité* becomes AF *personaltie*, whence the E Law term *personalty*, a sense going right back to L *persōna* in its LL sense 'a person *in the eyes of the law*', hence 'legal status' (Souter)—*persōna* as opp *rēs*, property;

the LL neg *impersōnālis* becomes E impersonal and OF *impersonal* (F *impersonnel*), with derivatives *impersonality* and *impersonnalité*;

L *persōnātus*, masked, hence disguised, hence feigned, whence E *personate*, both adj and v; hence anl:

LL *persōnātiuus*, ML *persōnātivus*, E *personative*, and ML *persōnātor*, adopted by E.

4. OF *persone*, MF and F *personne* has derivative late EF-F *personnifier*, whence 'to personify'; F *personnification* becomes E *personification*.

5. OF *personal*, MF and F *personnel*, personal,

becomes a n ('total number of persons attached to a Service'), opp *matériel*; adopted by E.

6. ME *persone*, *persoun*, etc., acquires the sense '*parson*' (already by 1250); the spelling *parson* is adopted from AF *parson*, earlier *parsone*, itself perh suggested by MF, esp Picard, *parsoune*. (OED.) AF has likewise influenced the change from ME *personage*, in its Eccl sense (from ML *personāgium*, q.v. in para 3), into *parsonage*. *Parson* has direct E derivatives *parsonic* (adj -*ic*), with extn *parsonical*, and *parsonify* (*parson*+ connective -*i-*+-*fy*, to make, render).

7. *Parson* blends, irreg, with *squire* to form *squarson*, a landowner+clergyman, hence a fox-hunting parson.

personnel. See prec, para 5.

perspective; perspicacious, perspicacity; perspicuous, perspicuity. See SPECTACLE, para 13.

perspiration, perspire. See the 2nd SPIRIT, para 11.

persuade, persuasion, persuasive. See SUAVE, para 3.

pert is aphetic for ME-from-OF *apert*, open, free, hence impudent, from L *apertus*, pp of *aperīre*, to open; cf the archaic *malapert*, from OF *mal apert*, badly opened, ill-taught or -bred. *Peart* is a dial form of *pert*.

pertain; pertinence (var pertinency), pertinent; impertinence, impertinent.

1. 'To *pertain*', ME *partenen*, derives from OF *partenir*, from L *pertinēre*, in its sense 'to concern': *per*, through+*c/f* of *tenēre*, to hold (f.a.e., TENABLE). *Pertinēre* has presp *pertinens*, o/s *pertinent-*, MF-F *pertinent*, adopted by E; derivative late MF-F *pertinence* is likewise adopted.

2. L *pertinens*, as adj, has LL neg *impertinens* (o/s *impertinent-*), lit not belonging, irrelevant, whence MF-F *impertinent*, adopted by E, with sense 'impudent' coming from F; derivative late MF-F *impertinence* is likewise adopted.

3. With 'to *pertain*', cf 'to *appertain*', ME *apperteinen*, earlier *aperteinen*, from OF *apartenir* (F *appartenir*), L *appertinēre*, to belong to, an *ad*-cpd of *pertinēre*. OF *apartenir* has derivative *apartenance*, whence AF *apurtenance*, whence E *appurtenance*.

perthite (Min) was discovered at *Perth* in Ontario, Canada.

pertinacious, pertinacity.

The former derives from L *pertināx* (*per-*, thoroughly+*tenāx*, tenacious); derivative ML *pertinācitās*, o/s *pertinācitāt-*, becomes MF-F *pertinacité*, E *pertinacity*. Cf *tenacious* at TENABLE; and, for formation, cf PERTAIN.

pertinence, pertinent. See PERTAIN.

perturb, perturbation. See TURBID, para 5, s.f.

pertuse, pertusion. See PIERCE, para 2.

Peru; Peruvian bark, cinchona, a native product of Peru. Like F *péruvien*, *Peruvian* is the adj, hence n, of *Peruvia*, SciL name of *Peru*, a name given by the Spaniards, taking it, app, from the small river *Pirù*, var of *Birù*.

peruke. See PETER, para 11.

**perusal, peruse.** See USE.
**Peruvian bark.** See PERU.
**pervade.** See VADE, para 6.
**pervagate, pervagation.** See VAGABOND, para 4, s.f.
**pervasion, pervasive.** See VADE, para 6.
**perverse, perversion, perversity; pervert.** See VERSE, para 15.
**pervigilate, pervigilium.** See VIGOR, para 6.
**pervious.** See VIA, para 15.
**pes,** L *pēs* (gen *ped*is), the foot. See FOOT, para 1.
**peseta.** See PEND, para 10.
**pesky.** See PEST, para 2.
**peso.** See PEND, para 10.
**pessary:** LL *pessārium* (-*ārium*), pessary, from L *pessum*, var of *pessus*, pessary: Gr *pessos* (Attic *pettos*), an oval stone used in games, LGr (in Med) a pessary: prob of Sem origin—cf Aram *pīsā*, *pīssā*, a stone, a tablet. (Boisacq.)
**pessimism, pessimist, pessimistic; pejorative; impair,** v.

1. *Pessimism* merely tacks -*ism* to L *pessim*us, the worst, and *pessimist* is an anl derivative: opp *optimism, optimist.* L *pessimus* is prob for \**pedsimus*, resting upon \**pedyōs*-, as in that \**pedyōr* which becomes L *peiior*, contr to *peior*, worse, neu *peius*: and \**pedyōs*- is app akin to Skt *pádyate*, he falls, 'worse' and 'worst' representing a progressive 'fall' from 'bad'. (E & M.)

2. L *peior*, worse, has LL derivative *peiōrāre*, to make worse, to become worse, with pp *peiōrātus*, ML *pejōrātus*, whence 'to *pejorate*', whence, anl, *pejorative.* Cf *pejorism*=ML *pejor*+ -*ism* and answers *meliorism* (L *melior*, better).

3. LL *peiōrāre* has the VL int \**impeiōrāre*, ML *impejōrāre*, whence OF *empeirier* (F *empirer*), ME *empeiren*, E 'to *impair*'; OF *empeirier* has derivative *empeirement*, whence, via ME forms in *em*-, *en*-, the E *impairment.*

**pest, pestiferous, pestilence, pestilent, pestilential.**
A *pest*, or plague, derives, via EF-F *peste*, from L *pestis*, s and r *pest*-; o.o.o.: ? cf Hit *pasihāti*, to crush, trample. L *pestis* has the foll derivatives affecting F:
*pestifer*, with var *pestiferus*, E *pestiferous*;
*pestilens*, o/s *pestilent*-, E *pestilent*; derivative *pestilentia*, OF-F *pestilence*, adopted by E; OF-F *pestilence* has EF-F adj *pestilentiel*, whence E *pestilential.*

2. As if from a very prob adj \**pesty*, comes the coll AE *pesky.*

**pestle,** n and v; **pistil, pistillate; piston; pile,** arrowhead; **ptisan, tisane.**

1. 'To *pestle*' derives from OF *pesteler*, from OF *pestel*, which, adopted by ME, yields *pestle*, n: and OF *pestel* comes from L *pistillum*, *pistillus*, a pestle, a dim of *pīlum*, a pestle, but also (? orig a club: Webster) a javelin, whence OE *pīl*, a stake, a dart, E *pile*, obs as dart and spike but extant as arrowhead and, in Arch, a long, slender piece of timber or steel.

2. *Pistillum*, *pistillus*, although a dim of *pīlum*, is therefore akin to *pinsere*, to pound (e.g., grain),

to crush, pp *pistus*; indeed, *pīlum*, a pounding-device, and *pīla*, a mortar, are—whatever the origin of *pīlum*, a javelin—usu derived from *pinsere.* The ult IE r is perh \**pī*-, to pound or crush, with extn \**pīs*- (nasalized as *pins*-) and perh extn \**pīl*-.

3. L *pistillum*, var *pistillus*, becomes, by shape-resemblance, the late EF-F, whence E, *pistil* of a flower, whence, anl, the adjj *pistillar* and *pistillate.*

4. On L *pist*-, s of *pistus*, pp of *pinsere*, LL builds *pistāre*, to pound, whence It *pistare*, var *pestare*, whence It *pistone*, a piston (cf *pestone*, a large pestle), whence EF-F *piston*, orig a pounder, later a piston: whence E *piston.*

5. Akin to L *pinsere*, LL *pistāre*, VL \**pisāre*, to crush or pound, is Gr *ptiss*ein, to crush, to husk or peel, whence *ptisanē*, peeled barley, barley water, whence LL *ptisana*, barley-gruel, often written *tisana*: whence MF *tisane*, occ, in EF-F, *ptisane*: whence E *ptisan, tisane.*

**pet,** n and v; both senses. See PIECE, para 8.

**petal** (whence -**petalled**, pa), whence **petaloid** and **petalous; petalite; petalody;**—c/ff **petali**-, as in **petaliferous**, petal-bearing (cf the element -*fer*), and **petalo**-.

1. *Petal*, like F *pétale*, comes from C17 Bot SciL *petalum*, trln of Gr *petalon*, a leaf, a plate of metal, from *petalos*, broad, flat, outspread, akin to Gr *petannumi* (Attic future *petō*, r *pet*-), I broaden, I lay open: cf PATENT. SciL *petalum* prob owes something to LL *petalum*, plate of metal.

2. The Min *petalite* (Min suffix -*ite*) is so named from its occurrence in *foiated* masses; and, *petalody* is a Bot n, derived from Gr *petalōdēs* leaf-like, with -*ōdēs* a post-c/f of *eidos*, a form.

**petard, petardeer** or -**ier; fart.**
*Petardeer* (obs) anglicizes EF-F *pétardier*, agent of *pétarder*, to petard, from EF-F *pétard*, detonator, lit 'farter', from MF *peter* (EF-F *péter*), to explode, orig to break wind, from MF-F *pet*, a wind-breaking, from L *pēditum*, itself from *pēdere* (pp *pēditus*), to break wind. The L r *pēd*- app derives from an IE r \**perd*-, as in Gr *perdomai*, I break wind, with var \**pard*-, as in Gr *epardo*n, I broke wind, and Skt *pardate*, he breaks wind; with Gmc *f* for Gr and L (etc.) *p*, we get the E 'to *fart*', whence the n.

**Peter** (whence the underworld **peter**, a safe, etc.), with dim **Peterkin**, whence the contr **Perkin**, whence **Perkins;** modern pet-form **Pete;** cf It *Pietro* and Sp (and Port) *Pedro*, and F *Pierre*, LL *Petrus.* Latin derivatives: **petrean** and **petrine**, **Petrine; petrify,** whence **petrification; petrol**, **petrolatum**, **petroleum** (whence **petroleous**), **petrolic; petrosal**, **petrous; saltpetre.**—Romance derivatives: **petrel; petronel** and **perrier; perron** and **pier; pierrot; pierrette; parrot**—**parrakeet; peruke** and **periwig** and **wig;** sep PARSLEY.

### Indo-European

1. *Peter* derives from LL *Petrus*, trln of LGr *Petros*, a personification of Homeric Gr *petros*, a stone, mdfn of *petra*, a rock: o.o.o.: perh a Medit

word—cf Hit *perunas*, a stone, a rock, and *pirwa*, a rock, and, more doubtfully, Eg *batgā* and *beḥus* (? *b-* for *p-*)—*haqar-t*—*pertchan* (?)—*tekhanu*, *tekhnu* (? *t-* for *p-*).—With LL *Petrus*, cf the Eccl LL use of *petra* for 'the Rock (of Faith)' and *fundati super petram*, (they who are) founded upon that Rock, i.e. Christians. (Souter.)

### Latin derivatives: direct

2. L and LL *petra*: *Petrus*:: Gr *petra*: LGr *Petros*, Gr *petros*,—these forms have the foll derivative adjj relevant to E:
Gr *petraios* (from *petra*), L *petraeus*, LL *petreus*, E *petrean*;
LL *petrālis*, E *petral*;
Gr *petrinos* (πέτρινος), LL *petrinus*, rare E *petrine*, the LL and E words prompting *Petrine*, of, by, for, like, the apostle Peter;
L *petrōsus*, whence both *petrosal* and *petrous*.
3. L *petra*, a rock, a stone, has in ML the cpd *sal petrae*, *salpetrae*, rock salt, whence MF *salpietre* (F *salpêtre*), whence, after *salt*, the E *saltpetre* or AE *saltpeter*.
4. The ML *petroleum*, a contr of *petrae oleum*, rock-oil, oil from the rocks, hence from the earth, is adopted by E; ML *petroleum* becomes MF-F *pétrole*, whence E *petrol*, whence *petrolic*; the Pharm *petrolatum* app=*petrol*+that -*atum* which becomes Chem -*ate*.

### Romance derivatives

5. *Petrel*, C18 *petril*, C17 *pitteral*, derives either from *\*peterel*, for *\*Peterel*, '(a bird of St) Peter', with suffix -*el* as in *cockerel*, or from the LL-ML *Petrellus* or *Petrillus*, dimm of *Petrus*: St Peter walked upon the sea (*Matthew*, xiv, 29) and, feeders upon surface-swimming organisms and ships' refuse, these birds appear to walk upon it—a sem reason far from being necessarily f/e.
6. L *petra* becomes It *pietra*, a stone, hence the flint for a gun, with derivative *pietronello*, contr to *petronello*, whence the now only Hist E *petronel*, a large carbine of the late C16–17, unless, as is possible, the E *petronel* be a reshaping of EF-F *petrinal*, which derives from OF *peitrine* (F *poitrine*), ult from L *pector-*, o/s of *pectus*, the chest: this firearm was supported against the chest (Dauzat).
7. L *petra* became OF-F *pierre*, whence MF *perriere*, var *perrier*, a stone-throwing engine, adopted by E, which adds a sense. Also from OF *pierre* comes OF-F *perron* (aug -*on*), a large stone, esp one used as a base, adopted by E, which adds a sense.
8. OF *pierre* occurs also in the form *piere*, to which is perh akin the ML (esp AL) *pera*, whence AF *pere*, ME *pere* (var *per*), E *pier*, orig an intermediate support, usu of stone, for a bridge: cf Picard and Walloon OF *piere*, *pire*, a breakwater. (EW.)
9. LL *Petrus* becomes Sp *Pedro*, whence the card-game *pedro*; it also becomes F *Pierre*, with pet-form *Pierrot*, m, and *Pierrette*, f, the former

being applied to a jesting character in pantomime, whence E *pierrot*.
10. OF-F *Pierrot* has ME var *Perrot*, itself with var *Parrot*, adopted by ME, whence the birdname *parrot*. Perh from MF *parrot* (var of *perrot*, a parrot) comes the MF *paroquet* (F *perroquet*), whence E *parakeet*, occ *parrakeet*. B & W, however, derive MF *paroquet* from It *parrochetto*, a playful dim of *parroco*, a curé, from LL *parochus* (cf *parish* at ECONOMIC, para 4).
11. *Peruke* anglicizes late MF-F *perruque*, trln of It *perrucca*, var *parrucca*, dressed hair, o.o.o.—but possibly akin to MF *paroquet*, EF-F *perroquet*, for the It *perrucca*, like the OProv *peruca*, perh meant, orig, 'with hair resembling a parrot's ruffled feathers' (Webster).
12. MF-F *perruque* became, not only E *peruke* but now obs E *perwyke*, eased to *perewyke*, whence E *periwig*, whence, by a thoroughgoing aphesis, the E *wig*.
13. F has coined a cpd: EF-F *pétrifier* (L *petri-*, c/f of *petra*+F -*fier*, LL -*ficāre*, var of L -*ficere*, c/f of *facere*, to make), whence E 'to *petrify*'; whence, anl, *petrification* (cf EF-F *pétrification*).

**petiolar, petiolate, petiole.** See FOOT, para 8, s.f.
**petit, petite.** See PIECE, paras 1 and 2.
**petition** (n, hence v, whence **petitioner**; hence also **petitionary**); **petitory**; **petulance, petulant.**—Cpds: **appetence, appetency, appetent, appetible, appetite, appetition, appetitive, appetize** (from *appeti*te), whence **appetizer**; **compete, competence** (var -*ency*), **competent, competition** (whence, anl, **competitive**), **competitor**, whence **competitory**; **impetigo, impetuosity, impetuous, impetus**; sep PERPETUAL; **repeat** (v, hence n; hence also **repeater**), **repetend, repetition,** whence, anl, **repetitious** and **repetitory.**
1. *Petition* derives from OF *peticion*, EF-F *pétition*, from L *petītiōnem*, acc of *petītiō*, from *petīt*us, pp of *petere*, to try to obtain, to seek, to beg: the IE r *\*pet-* occurs in, e.g., Gr, but with senses 'to fall' and 'to fly': cf FEATHER.—Derivative LL *petitōrius*, emulous, yields E *petitory*.
2. From a freq derivative *\*petulāre* comes L *petulans*, presp used as adj, with o/s *petulant-*, whence MF-F *pétulant*, whence E *petulant*; derivative L *petulantia* becomes EF-F *pétulance*, whence E *petulance*.
3. L *appetere* (*ap-* for *ad*, to, towards), to try to seize, to attack, hence to desire violently, with presp *appetens*, o/s *appetent-*, E *appetent*; derivative L *appetentia* becomes E *appetency*, the var *appetence* deriving from EF-F *appétence* (from *appetentia*). From the L pp *appetī*tus derive *appetītiō*, o/s *appetītiōn-*, E *appetition*, and the n *appetītus*, whence OF *apetit* (EF-F *appétit*), ME-E *appetite*. EF-F *appétit* has derivative *appétitif*, f -*ive*, whence E *appetitive*. The pa *appetizing* owes something to the MF-F *appétissant*; *appetible*, however, is L *appetībilis*, desirable.
4. L *competere*, to meet the requirements, to seek *com-* or along with another, whence, perh via MF-F *compéter*, the E 'to *compete*'. The L

presp *competens, o/s competent-*, becomes MF-F *compétent* and E *competent*; derivative L *competentia*, agreement, adequacy, becomes MF-F *compétence* and E *competence*. On the pp *competitus* arise both LL *competītiō*, rivalry, o/s *competītiōn-*, whence E *competition*, and LL *competītor*, whence MF-F *compétiteur*, whence E *competitor*.

5. L *impetere*, to seek *im-*, at, after, to attack, has derivative *impetīgō*, whence Med *impetigo*, with adj *impetiginous* prompted by LL *impetīginōsus*. Derivative *impetus* (gen *-ūs*), assault, shock, is adopted by E; its LL adj *impetuōsus* becomes MF-F *impétueux*, f *-euse*, whence E *impetuous*, and the subsidiary ML *impetuōsitās*, o/s *impetuōsitāt-*, becomes MF-F *impétuosité*, whence E *impetuosity*.

6. L *repetere*, to attack again, seek again, yields OF *repeter*, MF-F *répéter*, whence 'to *repeat*'; the gerundive *repetendus* becomes the E Math n *repetend*. On the pp *repetītus* arises L *repetītiō*, o/s *repetītiōn-*, MF-F *répétition*, E *repetition*. E *repetitory* perh owes something to the L agent *repetītor*.

**petral, petrean.** See PETER, para 2.

**petrel.** See PETER, para 5.

**petrifaction, petrify.** See PETER, para 13.

**petrine** and **Petrine.** See PETER, para 2.

**petrography.** See the element *petri-*.

**petrol, petrolatum, petroleum, petrolic.** See PETER, para 4.

**petrology.** See the element *petri-*.

**petronel.** See PETER, para 6.

**petrosal, petrous.** See PETER, para 2.

**petticoat.** See PIECE (heading).

**pettifogger.** See PIECE, para 6.

**pettiness.** See PIECE (heading).

**pettish.** See PIECE (heading, s.f.).

**pettitoes.** See PIECE, para 7.

**petty.** See PIECE, paras 1 and 6.

**petulance, petulant.** See PETITION, para 2.

**petunia** is a SciL derivative from EF-dial F *petun*, tobacco, from Port *petum, petume*, either from Guarani *petume* (B & W) or from Tupi *petúm, putúma* (Webster).

**pew.** See FOOT, para 21.

**pewee, pewit,** varr **peewee, peewit:** echoic: cf MHG *gībiz*, G *Kiebitz*, and LG *kīwit*. (Walshe.) Cf KIBITZ.

**pewter** (n, hence adj), **pewterer.** The latter comes from OF *peautrier, peutrier*, agent of *peautre, peutre*, varr of OF-MF *peltre*, tin: o.o.o.: ? Ligurian (Webster).

**pezograph.** See the element *pezo-*.

**pfennig.** See the 2nd PAN, para 4.

**phacoid; phacolith.** See the element *phaco-*.

**phaeton.** See FANCY, para 5.

**phagocyte; sarcophagus.**

The Bio and Med *phagocyte* (cf the element *-cyte*) exemplifies the element *phago-*, from Gr *phagein*, to eat. The terminal *-phage, -phagous, -phagus, -phagy*, occur in such words as *anthropophagous, -phagy*, man-eating (adj, n), and *sarcophagous*, Zoo adj for 'feeding on flesh'; and esp *sarcophagus*, a tomb, a coffin, orig a limestone that,

used by the Greeks, 'ate' the corpses deposited in it: L *sarcophagus*, trln of Gr *sarkophagos* (adj), flesh-eating: *sarko-*, c/f of *sarx*, flesh+*-phagos*, E *-phagous*.

**phalange, phalanger; phalanstery, phalanx.**

The 2nd derives, in SciL, from the Zoo *phalange*, which is adopted from F *phalange*, orig (C13) a phalanx, from LL *phalanga*, from Gr *phalang-*, o/s of φάλαγξ, *phalanx*, line of battle (adopted, via L, by E), orig a big, heavy stick, a log: IE r, prob *bhelag-* or ? *bhelaks-*, a piece of wood (Boisacq). From F *phalange*, a phalanx, Fourier (1772–1837) coined—after 'mona*stère*', monastery—*phalanstère* (a community), anglicized as *phalanstery*.

**phalarope**, a small shore-bird, is adopted from F: SciL *Phalaropus*: Gr *phalaro-*, c/f of *phalaris*, a coot+*pous*, a foot.

**phallic** (whence **phallicism), phallus.**

*Phallic* derives from Gr *phallikos*, adj of *phallos*, a penis, whence L *phallus*, adopted from E; and Gr *phallos* derives from IE r *bhel-*, to swell—cf the E BALL, a sphere.

**phantasm, phantasmagoria, phantasy, phantom.** See FANCY, paras 3–4.

**Pharaoh.** See FARO.

**Pharisaic**, of the Pharisees; **pharisaical**, hypocritically formal; **Pharisee.**

The 2nd is an *-al* extn of the 1st, which derives, prob via Calvin's *pharisaïque*, from Eccl LL *Pharisaïcus*, trln of LGr *Pharisaikos*, adj of LGr *Pharisaios*, a Pharisee, from Aram *perīshaiyā*, pl of *perīsh*, corresp to H *pārūsh*, separated, hence exclusive: cf *Matthew*, iii, 7. LL *Pharisaïcus* becomes MF *Pharisé* (F *Pharisien*), whence E *Pharisee*.

**pharmaceutic**, with extn **pharmaceutical** and derivative **pharmaceutics** and, anl, **pharmaceutist; pharmacopoeia;—pharmacy**, whence, anl, **pharmacist.** See the element *pharmaco-*.

**pharyngeal** is the adj of **pharynx**, SciL trln of Gr *pharunx* (akin to Gr *pharanx*, a ravine), gen *pharungos*, E c/f *pharnyg(o)-*, as in **pharyngitis.**

**phase, phasis.** See FANCY, para 9.

**pheasant:** ME *fesant*: MF *faisant*, early MF (and F) *faisan*: L *phasianus*: trln of Gr *phasianos*: elliptical for *phasianos ornis*, lit 'the *Phasian* bird': *Phasis*, a river in Colchis—a region in what has become Georgia, in Transcaucasia.

**phene.** See the element *phen-*, which combines with the Chem element *-ol* to produce *phenol* and with the Chem *-yl* to produce *phenyl*.

**phenomena, phenomenal, phenomenology, phenomenon.** See FANCY, para 6.

**phenyl.** See PHENE, s.f.

**phial** and **vial.**

1. The former derives from ME *fiole*: OF *fiole*, MF *phiole*: either from OProv *fiola* (from ML) or direct from ML *fiola, phiola*: L *phiala*, a flat, shallow cup (or bowl): Gr *phialē*: o.o.o.

2. ME *fiole* has var *viole*, whence, anl, E *vial*.

**Philadelphia** is adopted from the Gr for 'brotherly love': *adelphos*, a brother+*phil-*, connoting affection. See the element -*phil* and cf next entries.

**philander**, to flirt, whence **philanderer** and the pa, vn **philandering**, prob derives from E *Philander* (the Gr PN *Philandros*, from adj *philandros*, manloving: the element *phil-*+*andros*, gen of *anēr*, a man) used as the stock name for a lover in early romances, as EW has noted. (Could the n *Philander* have been influenced by the F *filandre*, fibre, esp as pl *filandres*, gossamer? *Filandre* is for *filande*, from *filer*, to thread.)

**philanthropic, philanthropy** (whence, anl, **philanthropist**).

The adj *philanthropic*—cf the F *philanthropique*—derives from Gr *philanthrōpikos*, corresp to *philanthrōpia*—whence LL *philanthrōpia*, whence E *philanthropy* (cf late EF-F *philanthropie*)—from *philanthrōpos* (adj), mankind-loving: element *phil-*+*anthrōpos*, man in general.

**philatelic** and **philatelist** (cf F *philatéliste*) derive, anl, from **philately**: F *philatélie*, created in 1864 by the collector Herpin: element *phil-*+*\*atelie*, from Gr *ateleia*, incompleteness (privative *a-*+*-teleia*, from *telos*, an end or purpose), immunity, esp from taxation, ref Gr *ex ateleias*, freely, with a Gallic pun on F '*franco* de port', carriage-free. (B & W.)

**philippic**, an oratorical invective, derives from L *Philippicus*, trln of Gr *Philippikos*, pertaining to *Philippos*, Philip—Philip of Macedon, against whom the Gr orator Demosthenes fulminated. *Philippos*=Horse-Loving; *hippos*, a horse. Cf:

**Philippine** is the adj (hence n) of 'the *Philippines*', Sp *Filipinas*, elliptical for *Islas Filipinas*: *Filipino*, adj of Sp *Felipe* (cf It *Filippo*), Philip II (of Spain), from L *Philippus*. Cf prec.

**Philistine.** See PALESTINE.

**philologian** and **philologer** are *-ian*, *-er* varr of **philologist**, an *-ist* derivative of **philology**, whence —unless direct from EF-F *philologique* (from *philologie*)—**philologic**, now usu **philological**: and **philology** derives from MF-F *philologie*, from L *philologia*, a love of learning, (later) philology: Gr *philologia*, love of learning, from *philologos*, fond of learning, orig *phil-*, fond of, *-logia*, talking, a discourse, from *logos*, a word, speech, a discourse (f.a.e., LOGIC).

**philosopher, philosophic** (with extn **philosophical** and with anl derivative **philosophize**), **philosophy**.

The Gr *philosophos*, a lover of *sophia* or wisdom, *sophia* deriving from *sophos*, wise (f.a.e., SOPHISM), becomes L *philosophus*, OF-F *philosophe*, adopted by ME, which deviates with *philosophre* (? influenced by MF-F *philosopher*, to philosophize), whence E *philosopher*. *Philosophic* comes, like MF-EF *philosophique*, from L *philosophicus*, trln of Gr *philosophikos*, from *philosophia*, itself from *philosophos*; Gr-become-L *philosophia* yields OF-F *philosophie*, whence E *philosophy*.

**philter** (AE) or **philtre**: MF-F *philtre*: L *philtrum*: Gr *philtron*: instr, connoted by *-tron*, from *philein*, to be fond of, from *philos*, fond: f.a.e., the element -*phil*.

**phlebitis, phlebotomy**. See the element *phlebo-*. The LL *phlebotomus* (Gr *phlebotomos*, instrument for cutting the veins) passed through a contr VL form to become OF-MF *flieme* (F *flamme*), whence E *fleam*.

**phlegm, phlegmatic.**

1. The latter derives, via MF, from L *phlegmaticus*, trln of Gr *phlegmatikos*, adj of *phlegma*, a flame, hence an inflammation, hence mucus, from *phlegein*, to burn, ult akin to BLACK. Grhence-LL *phlegma* becomes MF *fleugme, fleume*, the latter adopted by ME, whence, reshaped from the Gr word, the E *phlegm*.

2. Corresp to the Gr v s *phleg-* is the Gr n s *phlog-*, as in *phlox* (for *\*phlogs*), a flame, a blaze, gen *phlogos*, o/s *phlog-*, whence *phlogizein*, to set ablaze or on fire, whence *phlogistos*, burnt, hence inflammable, whence medieval SciL *phlogiston*, the hypothetical principle of fire; moreover, Gr *phlox* has the derivative sense, 'plant with a flamecoloured bloom', L *phlox*, such a flower, hence the Bot *Phlox*. Gr *phlegein* has IE r *\*bhleg-*, with metathetic var *\*bhelg-*, as in Skt *bhárgas*, a shining, splendour. (Hofmann.)

**phloem**, in Bot, is adopted from G, which adapts the form and sense of Gr *phloos* (s and r *phlo-*), bark, akin to *phleō*, I teem, am overfull.

**phlogiston; phlox.** See PHLEGM, para 2.

**phobia**—whence **phobic**, whence, anl, **phobism, phobist**—is a SciL reshaping, in abstract *-ia*, of Gr *phobos* (s *phob-*), dread, a strong fear, a feardetermined aversion. Rare as simples, both *phobia* and *phobic* and also *phobe*, '(one) having a phobia', occur very often in cpds: see the element -*phobe*.

**phoebe**, an American flycatcher, is prob so named, after Gr Myth *Phoebe* (*Phoibē*), from its cry: cf *pewee*. Gr *Phoibē* is the f of *Phoibos*, God of the Sun, personification of *phoibos*, shining, bright.

**Phoenician** (adj, hence n); **Phoenix, phoenix.**

*Phoenician* derives, via F *phénicien* and L *Phoenicius*, from L *Phoenicē*, trln of Gr *Phoinikē*, Phoenicia, from *Phoinix*, a Phoenician, whence *phoinix*, a date palm (Bot *Phoenix*), lit 'the Phoenician (tree)', and the bird, lit 'the Phoenician (bird)', whence, via L *phoenix*, both OF *phenix* (F *phénix*) and E *phoenix*. Gr *Phoinix*, a Phoenician, is perh akin to Gr *phoinos, phoinios*, blood-red. The sem succession and interaction are obscure. The date-palm, the bird, and the colour 'purple' or 'scarlet' senses of Gr *phoinix* all follow naturally from *Phoinix*, a Phoenician; and *Phoinix* could be an *-ix* derivative of *phoinos*, blood-red, purple, if the Phoenicians were so named because they wore purple or scarlet robes. Prob, however, Gr *Phoinikes*, Phoenicians (cf L *Poeni*, the Carthaginians), represents, as Boisacq suggests, the influence of Gr *phoinos*, blood-red, purple, upon Eg *Poun-t*, a collective name for the Semites of the E Medit hinterland.

**phone** (whence **phonic**), **phoneme** (whence **phonemic**), **phonetic** (whence **phonetics, phonetician**, phoneticize); c/ff *phono-*, as in **phonogram** (*-gram*), **phonograph** (*-graph*), **phonology** (*-logy*: cf LOGIC), and *-phone*, as in **telephone**, whence **telephonic**, **telephonist**, **telephony**; cpds: **euphony**, whence **euphonic** and **euphonious**; ? **diphthong**, whence **diphthongal**.

1. Gr *phōnē*, a sound, whence E *phone*, a speech-sound, is the n corresp to *phēmi*, I speak, and is perh akin to *phthongē* (φθογγή), voice, and *phthongos* (φθόγγος), a speech-sound, a word, and *phthengomai* (φθέγγομαι), I speak: IE r, at least of *phēmi*, *phōnē*, is prob \**bhā-*, to speak.

2. Gr *phōnē* has derivative *phōnēma* (suffix *-ēma*), a sound regarded objectively as an element of speech: F *phonème*: E *phoneme*. Also from *phōnē* comes *phōnein*, to produce a sound, whence *phōnētos*, spoken, with extn *phōnētikos*, whence SciL *phonēticus*, whence F *phonétique* and E *phonetic*.

3. *Phonograph* derives from F *phonographe*, and *telephone* derives from F *téléphone*, modelled on *télégraphe*.

4. From *phōnē*, Gr derives *euphōnos*, well (*eu*), hence sweetly, voiced, whence *euphōnia*, whence, via LL, the EF-F *euphonie*, whence E *euphony*.

5. Gr *phthongos* has cpd *diphthongos* (*di-* for *dis*, twice), whence, via LL *diphthongus*, the F *diphthongue*, whence E *diphthong*.

**phoney.** See ADDENDA.

**phonograph.** See PHONE, para 3.

**phosphorescence, phosphorescent; phosphoric** and **phosphorous**, from **phosphorus**.

The last derives from L *Phosphorus*, the Morning Star, Gr *Phōsphoros*, from *phōsphoros*, light-bringer: cf the elements *phos-* and *phor-*. The F form *phosphore* has derivatives *phosphorescence* and *phosphorescent*, prob influencing the E. words, and *phosphate* (Chem *-ate*), adopted by E Cf:

**photic** derives from Gr *phōt-*, o/s of *phōs*, light. The element *photo-* occurs notably in **photograph** (cf the element *-graph*), whence **photographic** and **photography** and, via the v **photograph**, the agent **photographer**.

**phragma**, in Zoo, derives from Gr *phragma*, a fence.

**phrase** (n, hence v), whence **phrasal** and, via the Gr c/f *phraseo-*, **phraseology** (element *-logy*: cf LOGIC); cpds: **antiphrasis**, whence, anl, **antiphrastic**; **paraphrase** (n, hence v), **paraphrastic**; **periphrasis**, **periphrastic**.

1. *Phrase*, adopted from EF-F, derives from L-from-Gr *phrasis*, from *phrazein*, to indicate, to explain: ? PGr r \**phrad-*.

2. Gr *phrazein* has three cpds affecting E:

*antiphrazein*, to express antithetically, whence *antiphrasis*, adopted, via L, by E;

*paraphrazein*, to say the same thing, but in other words, whence *paraphrasis*, whence, via L, the EF-F *paraphrase*, adopted by E; derivative adj *paraphrastikos*, whence, via ML *paraphrasticus*, the E *paraphrastic*;

*periphrasis* (*peri*, round about), adopted, via L,

by E; derivative adj *periphrastikos*, whence, via LL *periphrasticus*, the E *periphrastic*.

**phratry.** See FRATER, para 3.

**phrenetic, phrenic.** See FRENZY, para 1.

**phrenology**, whence **phrenological** and **phrenologist.** See the element *-phrenia*.

**phthisic**, via OF and L, from Gr *phthisikos*, is the adj of *phthisis*, adopted by E; from *phthíein*, to waste away. Cf the element *phthisio-*.

**phycology.** See the element *phyco-*.

**phylactery**, whence the adj, hence n, **phylacteric**, comes, via LL *phylactērium*, from Gr *phulaktērion*, a safeguard, from *phulaktēr*, a watcher or guard, from *phulassein*, to watch over, to guard: o.o.o.

2. Gr *phulassein* has cpd *prophulassein*, to guard *pro-*, forward, hence against, with derivative adj *prophulaktikos*, whence EF-F *prophylactique* and E *prophylactic*.

**phylon**, from Gr *phulon*, a tribe, a race, and **phylum**, the SciL trln thereof. See the element *phylo-*, were also *phylogeny*. Cf:

**physic**, adj (whence, influenced by the n, **physics**) and n, **physical**, **physician**, **physicist** (from *physic*, adj, and *physics*), **physique**; cf the element *physico-*, *physio-*, but note, here, **physiognomy** (whence **physiognomic** and **-gnomist**) and **physiological**, **physiology** (whence, anl, **physiologist**); **metaphysic** (adj, with extn in *-al*, and n), **metaphysics**, whence, anl, **metaphysician** (perh imm from late MF-F *métaphysicien*).

1. The adj *physic* derives, via OF and L, from Gr *phusikos*, natural, adj of *phusis*, nature, s *phus-*, r *phu-*, as in *phulon*, *phulē*, a tribe, a race (see prec entry), *phuton*, a plant, whence E *phyte* in cpds, and esp in *phuein*, to cause to grow, to engender, and *phunai*, to be produced, i.e. to be born: IE r, \**bheu-*, to grow, exemplified in all the principal IE languages.

2. The Gr adj *phusikos* has derivative (*hē*) *phusikē* (*tekhnē*), the science of nature, L *physicē*, *physica*, OF *phisique*, *fisique* (cf F *physique*) physics, ME *fisike*, *phisike*, whence reshaped E *physic*.

3. L *physicus* has the ML extn *physicālis*, whence E *physical*; in LL, *physicus* is used also as n, 'a doctor of medicine', whence OF *physicien*, *phisicien*, *fisicien*, ME *fisicien*, later *fisician*, whence reshaped E *physician*; the OF-F adj *physique* becomes, in C18, n (? elliptical for *constitution physique*), duly adopted by E.

### Compounds

4. Gr *phusis* has cpd *phusiognōmia* (2nd element from *gnōmōn*, one who knows, hence an examiner, a judge), whence LL *physiognōmonia*, soon contr to *physiognōmia*, 'science of determining character from the features' (Souter), whence, via MF-F *physionomie* and comparable ME forms, the reshaped E *physiognomy*. The E adj *physiognomic* perh owes a little to the LL *physiognōmicus*.

5. Gr *phusis* has also the more important cpd *phusiologia*, L *physiologia*, EF-F *physiologie*, E

*physiology.* The derivative Gr adj *phusiologikos* becomes LL *physiologicus,* whence E *physiological.*

6. Aristotle's *meta ta phusika,* lit 'after, hence beyond, the physical things (or Nature)', becomes the ML n *metaphysica,* neu pl, whence, anl, E *metaphysics;* the derivative ML adj *metaphysicus* becomes E *metaphysic,* now usu *metaphysical;* the E n *metaphysic* derives, perh via MF-F *métashysique,* from ML *metaphysica,* ? elliptical for *cientia metaphysica,* from adj *metaphysicus.*

**physical; physician.** See prec, para 3.

**physiognomy.** See PHYSIC, para 4.

**physiological, physiology.** See PHYSIC, para 5.

**physique.** See PHYSIC, para 3.

**phyte,** whence **phytic.** Cf PHYSIC, para 1, s.f., and, for *phyto-* cpds, see the elements *-phyte, phyto-.*

**pianissimo, pianist, piano, pianoforte.** See PLANE, para 7.

**piaster** (AE) or **piastre.** See PLASM, para 7.

**piazza.** See PLANE, para 13.

**pibroch.** See PIPE, para 3.

**pica.** See PICK, para 5, s.f.

**picador.** See PICK, para 10.

**picaninny,** occ **piccaninny,** often **pickaninny,** in A and WI usage a Negro or other coloured child, hence in Aus an Aboriginal and in N.Z. a Maori child, derives from Sp *pequeñito,* dim of *pequeño,* little, from *pico,* a point, hence a small part—or perh rather from Port *pequenini,* dim of syn *pequeno.*

**Picard,** a native or the dialect of **Picardy,** F *Picardie* (recorded in C13), from *Picard*: o.o.o.; perh from OF *pic,* a pike (f.a.e., PICK).

**picaresque,** adopted from F, derives from Sp *picaresco,* adj of *pícaro,* a rogue (*picaro* in Port), itself from *picar,* to wound lightly, lit to prick. Sp *pícaro* has aug *picarón,* whence E *picaroon.*

**picayune**—whence A sl **piker**—orig a small A Sp coin, then a five-cent piece, finally something very small, esp if of slight value, derives from F *picaillon,* a C18 copper coin of Savoy and Piedmont: Prov *picaioun,* dim of *picaio,* collective coins, money in cash; perh 'money that rings', from Prov *pica,* to sound, to ring. (B & W.)

**piccaninny.** See PICANINNY.

**piccolo** is, in It, 'a *small* flute'.

**picine.** See PICK, para 6.

**pick,** a tool. See para 9 of:

**pick,** to pierce or prick, to clear of unwanted matter, to pluck or gather (esp fruit), hence to choose, to separate as desirable, whence 'to **pick up',** whence the n **pick-up;** hence n; hence also pa **picked,** agent **picker,** vn **picking** (often in pl); hence also such cpds as **toothpick, picklock** and **pickpocket;—pick,** the tool, with cpd **pickaxe,** AE **pickax—pica—picador—pike,** the weapon and the fish, cf **pickerel—peak, peaked—picket** (n hence v), **piquet, pique, piquant** (whence **piquancy);—picnic—pickle,** n hence v;—perh **picric—peck,** v, to strike with the beak, hence n, hence also the agent **pecker,** as in **woodpecker,** and the adj **pecky** and the coll adj **peckish;—pink,** to pierce; **pinch** (n hence v), **pincers;—**prob **pitch,** to thrust into

the ground, hence to erect (a tent) and to throw, whence the n **pitch,** 'act of throwing, place for throwing' (in cricket, baseball, etc.), and agent **pitcher,** va and vn **pitching;** perh cf the sep POKE, to prod or thrust; **pie,** the bird (also **magpie**), the dish, perh the type, prob the Eccl term;—prob cf the sep SPIKE.

### Indo-European

1. The IE r is *\*pik-,* with—at least in Gmc—an occ var *\*pek-;* basic sense, either 'a sharp point' or, better, 'to pierce or prick', or, more prob, 'the birds mag*pie* and wood*pecker*', whence, because of their sharp bills and 'pecking' habits, the ideas 'sharp point' and 'to pierce, to prick': cf L *pīca,* a magpie, and *pīcus,* a woodpecker; Umbrian *peico* (cf the L acc *pīcum*) and *peica* (cf the L acc *pīcam*); perh Gr *pikros,* bitter (*sharp* to the taste; *biting* the tongue); Skt *pikás,* the Indian cuckoo; perh, with the IE prefix *s-,* the OHG *speh, speht,* MLG-G *specht,* ON *spāetr,* the woodpecker—cf the sep SPIKE.

### The -e- Variants

2. The *\*pek-* (*\*pec-*) var of the IE r may, as C suggests (Malvezin and Malvezin[1]), have var *\*bek-,* as in BEAK, treated sep. But to avoid that alluring side-issue and to keep on the course:

'to peck' is a var of 'to *pick*' (para 9 below), to pierce—cf MLG *pecken,* to pierce; from the derivative n, in sense 'a stroke, a light blow', comes *pecky,* the Forestry adj; and from *peck* in its now dial senses 'to throw' (vt) and 'to pitch forward' (vi) comes *pecky,* tending to stumble; '*peck* at' (something) leads to *peckish,* hungry;

the agent *pecker,* esp as 'a bird that pecks at wood', occurs usu as *woodpecker,* a modern formation.

3. *Peak,* a sharp tip or pointed end, is a var of *pike* (see para 8); *peak,* a hilltop, a mountain crest, was earlier *pike,* from the syn Sp and Port *pico,* collateral with *pica,* of L origin (cf para 1 above). E *peak* has derivative 'to *peak',* now mostly in the pa *peaked,* and the derivative *peaky, sharp*-featured through ill-health.

### The -i- Words: Greek

4. Gr *pikros,* bitter, yields F *picrique* and E *picric* (acid), whence *picrate* (Chem *-ate*) and *picrite* (Min *-ite*) and *picrol* (Element *-ol*). Perh, however, Gr *pikros* is of another origin: see PAINT, para 7.

### The -i- Words: Latin

5. L *pīca,* a magpie, becomes OF, whence ME-E, *pie;* for *magpie,* see MARGARET, para 1. Perh because orig made with magpies, ME *pie,* a dish with pastry crust over meat, fish, etc., could be the same word, as also could Eccl *pie, pye* (also ME), a collection of rules for determining the service for the day, as in '*pie* (or *pye*) book', perh 'from

some resemblance to the colors of the bird' (Webster); moreover, the culinary *pie* could, from its miscellaneous contents, have originated the printers' *pie*, type in confusion, hence a medley. With Eccl *pie*, cf the type named *pica*, perh 'once used in printing the service book' (Webster), from ML *pica*, a collection of these rules.

6. L *pīcus*, a woodpecker, has pl *pīci*, whence the Zoo *Pici*; *pīc*us accounts for the Zoo adj *picine* (*-ine*).

7. L *pīcus* has VL var *\*piccus*, whence *\*piccāre* (cf It *piccare* and Sp *picar*), whence OF-F *piquer*, whence E 'to *pique*'; the derivative F n *pique* is adopted by E, as also is the F presp *piquant*. Derivative EF-F *piquet*, a game of cards, is likewise adopted, and derivative MF *piquet*, a stake (cf the E '*picket* fence'), whence the C18-20 military *piquet*, becomes E *picket*. Prob from F *piquer* comes *piquenique* (a redup), whence E *picnic*, whence 'to *picnic*'; certainly from OF-F *piquer* comes late MF-F *piqûre*, adopted by Med E.

8. Akin to F *piquer*, which some say it originates, is OF-F *pic*, whence (unless from *piquer*) the MF-F *pique*, a foot-soldier's weapon, whence E *pike*, whence, mainly from its head, shaped like the tip of that weapon, and partly from its elongate form, the fish *pike*. The weapon *pike* (although cf the Nor dial *pēk*, a sharp mountain-top) app led to the mostly N. Eng dial *pike*, a peaked hill-top. The fish *pike* has dim *pickerel* (for *\*pikerel*), occ corrupted to *pickering*.

9. The n *pick*, a long-handled garden tool pointed at one or both ends, partly derives from 'to *pick*' or pierce, partly varies *pike*, a pick, a pickaxe (senses obs except in dial), a prick, a prickle (now only dial), from OF *pic*, and, in its form, partly blends OF *pic*, a pick, pickaxe, and *pike*, the weapon, but in its sense comes straight from that OF *pic*.—The v 'to *pick*', ME *piken*, deriving from OF-MF(-F) *piquer*, was influenced by the v of OE *pīcung*, a pricking, and perh by ON *pikka*, to pierce, as with a sharp-pointed tool—cf the syn MLG *pikken* and G *picken*, MHG *bicken*, to peck (Walshe),

10. The *picador* or lance-bearing teaser of the bull is adopted from Sp, where it forms the agent of *picar*, to prick (cf para 7).

11. OF-F *pic*, a pick, has the nasalized derivatives *pince* or *pinque*, a supporting stake, a pointed tool; the latter has perh suggested E 'to *pink*' or perforate, pierce, stab; 'to *pink*', however, could nasalize 'to *pick*' or pierce.

12. EF-F *pince*, however, perh (like OProv *pinsar*) comes rather from OF *pincier* (F *pincer*) from VL *\*pinctiāre*, a blend of VL *\*piccāre* (see para 7) and VL *\*punctiāre* (from L *punctum*, a pricking, a point); *\*pinctiāre*, *pincier*, *pinsar*, orig, like It *pinzar* and Sp *pinchar*, signified 'to prick or pierce'. OF *pincier* led, ? via ONF, then AF, to ME *pynsours*, whence E *pincers*.

13. OF *pincier*, to pierce or prick, later to pinch, became ONF *\*pinchier*, whence ME *pinchen*, whence 'to *pinch*'.

? Germanic

14. 'To *pitch*' or fix in the ground, later (cf the heading) to throw, derives from ME *picchen*, which strikingly resembles ME *piken*, MLG *pikken*, ON *pikka*, to pierce, esp with a sharp tool (cf para 9, s.f.). Hence *pitchfork*.

15. *Pickle*, a preservative brine, hence 'to *pickle*' and that which is pickled, a *pickle*, esp in pl *pickles*, derives from ME *pykyl*, *pekille*, app from MD *peeckel*, *pekel*, perh lit 'that which is sharp on the tongue'—cf MD *peken*, *pecken*, *picken*, D *pikken*, to pierce, to use a pick on, etc.

**pickaback**, whence, by f/e, **piggyback**, derives from *a pick back*, by f/e from *a pick pack*, where *pick* is a thinned redup of *pack*, a bundle, and where *a* is 'on' (cf *aback*, on or at one's back)—cf F *à pic*, vertically.

**pickaninny.** See PICANINNY.

**pickerel, pickering.** See PICK, para 8, s.f.

**picket.** See PICK, para 7.

**pickings.** See PICK (heading).

**pickle**, preservative brine. See PICK, para 15.

**picklock, pickpocket.** See PICK (heading).

**pick-up.** See PICK (heading).

**picnic.** See PICK para 7.

**picrate, picric, picrite.** See PICK, para 4, and PAINT, para 7.

**Pict.** See PAINT, para 2.

**pictograph.** See the element *picto-*.

**pictorial.** See PAINT, para 4.

**picture.** See PAINT, para 4.

**picturesque.** See PAINT, para 4, s.f.

**piddle.** Cf *pizzle*, q.v. at PISS, para 2.

**pidgin**, occ **pidgeon**, by f/e **pigeon**. See BUSY, para 2.

**pie** in all senses. See PICK, para 5.

**piece**, n, hence adj and v; **apiece, pièce de résistance, piecemeal, piecework** (simply *piece*+ *work*);—**patch**, n hence adj and v; **patchwork** (*patch*+*work*), **patchy** (*patch*+adj *-y*)—**petit, petite, petty** (whence **pettiness**)—**petticoat** (*petty*, little+ *coat*), **pettifogger** (whence **pettifoggery** and, by b/f from *pettifogger*, **pettifog**, whence the pa **pettifogging**), **pettitoes; pet**, n hence adj and v (whence **pettable** and va, vn **petting**)—and **pet**, a fit of ill-humour, whence **pettish; peat**, whence **peaty.**

Indo-European

1. According to Daužat and B & W, the OF-F *petit* (f *petite*)—therefore E *petty*—is of different origin from F *pièce*, therefore from that of E *piece*. Those etymologists derive *petit* from 'a root *pitt-*, belonging to the language of the nursery and expressing "smallness" and occurring in LL *pitinnus*, "little", "little boy" ' (prob after E & M), but they add 'Solely Gaulish-Roman, cf OProv and Catalan *petit*'; and of OF-MF *piece*, EF-F *pièce*, they say: 'Same word as *petia* in ML, cf *et alia petia*, "and another piece (of land)", c730 A.D.', comparing It *pezza* and Sp *pieza* (cf also Port *peça*), and add: 'From a Gaul *\*pettia* for

*pettis, which may be presumed from the W peth and the Br pez'—cf also Cor peth, pith. I derive OF piece, not from ML petia but from its var pecia; other varr are petium (pecium) and petius (whence Sp pecio, a fragment)—the recorded dimm are peciola and petiolum.

2. The LL pitinnus is app a var of the syn pisinnus or pissinus, little, cf LL pisinna, a little girl. (Souter.) These -s-, -ss- forms help us to relate OF-F petit to OF-MF piece, EF-F pièce.

3. The evidence of C may be severely condensed thus:—In C, b and p are interchangeable—and frequently interchanged. Of the C r pic Malvezin says, 'Form of bic, little'; of bic, var beic, he says, 'Hence: (the etymons) beicos and biccos, in the OIr becc, the Ga beic; and a derivative bicanos, in the Br bihan, with same sense "little", and the cpd Morbihan, little sea'. Malvezin also notes the C r pet, app of basic idea 'little, a part' (esp in the space-time continuum), and continues, 'In our [i.e., F] word petit; in the dial petion and petiot C14]', a (very) small child; 'in pièce, from petia, and dial pète, connoting a form *peta'.

4. Both the C r bic, var *bec, little, and the syn extn *bican- are well represented in the ancient and modern C tongues, thus:

OIr becc, Ir and Ga beag (pron beg); Ir beccán, Ga beagan;

Mx beg;

W bechan, bychan;

Cor bechan, bichan, bȳghan (often contr to bȳan);

Br bihan.

5. Sem, the link is: a piece is a small or very small part (a bit, a fragment) of something. Phon, the C peth (or pith), pez, a piece, represent the p varr of C bec (bic), little. In short, we are here confronted with prob two cognate groups; if, however, one group is primary, that group is very prob the 'little' one.

### The F petit, E petty Group

6. The from-F-adopted petit is now only a Law term for 'small' or 'insignificant'; the F petite is applied to small, neatly built girls and women. OF-MF petit, adopted by ME, with later var pety, duly becomes petty, which figures in pettifogger, app a tautological cpd of petty+obs fogger, a monetary trickster, o.o.o.—but cf LG fokker, a usurer.

7. By early etymologists treated, f/e, as being for petty (little) toes, the odd word pettitoes, pig's feet used as food, but prob, at first, a beast's heart, lungs, liver, etc., app derives either from the sing pettytoe, as in a pygges pettytoe, a pig's pettitoe, from MF petite oye, giblets, lit 'little goose', i.e. little parts of a goose, or from MF petitose, goose offal (? from petites oies, little geese): MF-F oie, goose, derives from OF oue, from LL auca, a goose, from VL *auica, goose, from L auis, a bird. With LL auca, cf the It and Sp oca.

8. From F petit used as n, 'little one' or 'child'— cf the endearment mon petit, ma petite—comes the

E pet, a tame animal treated as a dear companion, hence a (usu young) human being treated similarly: prob thence comes pet, a fit of ill-humour, for spoiled children and young people tend to sulk and to have little control of their tempers.

### The piece Group

9. E piece derives from late MF piece, ME pece: OF pece, var of piece: f.a.e., para 1. Apiece, for each, was orig a piece. The F pièce de résistance is lit 'piece of resistance', the main dish of a meal, hence the chief article or feature. Piecemeal, piece by piece, derives from ME pecemele: ME pece, a piece+a derivative from OE maelum, for or by measures, from mael, a measure, hence a portion: see also MEASURE, final para.

10. E patch derives from ME pacche: o.o.o.; but prob akin to—? a dial var or mdfn of—ME pece.

11. E peat, orig a piece of turf cut for and used as fuel, hence, particularly or generally, semi-carbonized vegetable matter (esp mosses) used as fuel: ME pete: ML peta, prob akin to ML petia (as in para 1).

pied, of two colours (esp black and white), hence occ of more, derives from pie, a magpie: f.a.e., PICK, para 5.

piedmont. See FOOT, para 18.

piepoudre, piepowder. See FOOT, para 19.

pier. See PETER, para 8.

pierce (whence piercer and piercing)—piercel (gimlet), a dim from pierce, influenced by EF-F perce, gimlet; parch (whence parching); partisan or -zan, a sort of pike or halberd; obs tund, to pound or beat—contund, contuse, contusion, contusive—extund—obtund, obtundent, obtuse (adj and v), obtusion, obtusity—pertuse, pertusion—retuse; —stut, stutter (v, hence n), whence stutterer and pa, vn stuttering.

1. 'To pierce' derives, via ME percen, from OF percer, var of percier; VL *pertusiāre, from L pertūsus, pp of pertundere, to pound or beat (tundere) through (per), hence to pierce: and tundere, to strike, beat, pound, s and r tund-, is akin to Ve tundānás, knocking (against), tundate, he knocks against: a nasal var of IE r *tud-, as in Skt tudáti, he knocks (against). L tundere yields the obs 'to tund'.

2. Tundere occurs in the foll cpds relevant to E: contundere, to beat or pound strongly (int con-), to crush, whence 'to contund', rare for 'to contuse', from the pp contūsus, s contūs-, whence contūsiō, o/s contūsiōn-, whence, via MF-F, the E contusion; contusive perh derives from F contusif, f -ive (from contusion);

extundere, to beat out (ex), whence the rare 'to extund';

obtundere, to beat towards (ob) or against, hence to blunt (the edge of an instrument), to dull, whence 'to obtund'; presp obtundens, o/s obtundent-, explains the Med adj hence n obtundent; the pp obtūsus, blunted, dulled, is used also as adj, 'blunt' or 'dull', whence the E obtuse, perh via EF-F obtus; derivative LL obtūsiō, o/s *obtusiōn-*, becomes the obsol *obtusion*, and LL *obtūsitās*, o/s *obtūsitāt-*, becomes *obtusity*;

*pertundere* (as in para 1) has pp *pertūsus*, whence 'to *pertuse*'; derivative *pertūsiō*, o/s *pertūsiōn-*, yields *pertusion*;

*retundere*, to strike, beat, pound back, gives us the obsol 'to *retund*'; the pp *retūsus* gives us the Bot adj *retuse*.

3. The IE r *\*tud-*, *\*teud-*, has the var *\*stud-*, *\*steud-* (IE prefix *s-*), with Gmc var *\*stut-*, as in Go *stautan*, knock against, push, and OHG *stōzan*, MHG *stōzen*, G *stossen*, ON *stauta*, *steyta*, to push. Prob cf the L *stupēre*, to be knocked stupid (hence, to remain stupid, hence to be stupid), with s *stup-* and r *\*stup-*, an *s-* mdfn of that IE r *\*tup-*, *\*teup-*, which we see in Gr *tuptein* (*tupt-*, extn of *tup-*), to strike, and in Skt *tupáti*, he strikes—cf *tudáti* in para 1.

4. The IE *\*stud-*, *\*steud-*, has the *t-*for-*d* var *\*stut-*, *\*steut-*, as in ME *stuten*, late ME *stutte*, *stute*, whence EE and dial *stut*, to *push* one's tongue too hard, to stutter, whence the EE-E freq *stutter*: cf MLG *stoteren*, G *stottern* (from LG *stoteren*, int of *stossen*), MD *stoteren*, D *stotteren*.

5. 'To *parch*' derives from ME *parchen*, var of *perchen*: perh, ref *piercing* heat, from ONF *parchier*, var of *perchier*, cf OF *percier*, var of *percer* (cf para 1).

6. A *partisan*, *-zan* comes from EF *partisane* (now *pertuisane*; late MF *pourtisaine*)—itself from It *partesana*, var *partigiana* (influenced by *partigiano*, party-man), from *pertugiaire*, from VL *\*pertūsiāre* (as in para 1).

**Pierre, pierrette, pierrot.** See PETER, para 9.

**pietism, piety.** See PITY, para 2.

**piffle,** whence the adj **piffling,** is perh (EW) a blend of *piddling* and *trifling*.

**pig,** whence **piggery** (*-ery*) and **piggish** (*-ish*) and such obvious cpds as **pigfish** (a grunting fish), **pig-headed, pig-iron** (cast into *pigs*, crude castings so called from their large size), **pignut** (beloved of pigs), **pigskin, pigsty** (see STY), **pigtail, pigweed**— and the not entirely obvious **pigsney** (*pig's nye*; *nye* being *eye* preceded by the *n* rather of *an* than of *mine* and *thine*), now only dial for a sweetheart; dim, **piggy** or **piggie,** with redup **piggy-wiggy.**

'A *pig*'—whence 'to *pig* it' or live like a pig— derives from ME *pigge*: *b* for *p*, cf the LG *bigge* and the D *big*, *bigge*, which, note well, has the MD form *pigge*: o.o.o.

**pigeon** (1), the bird: ME *pigeon*, var of *pejon*: MF *pijon*: LL *pīpiōnem*, acc of *pīpiō*, from LL *pīpīre*, to whimper, to make the sound *peep*: echoic (IE *\*pi-*). Cf PIPE.

**pigeon** (2), speech. See BUSY, para 2.

**pigment, pigmentary.** See PAINT, para 5.

**pigsney, pigsty.** See PIG (heading, s.f.).

**pika,** an A and Asiatic rodent, derives from Tungusic (E. Siberia) *peeka*.

**pike** (all senses). See PICK, para 8.

**piker** (A sl). See PICAYUNE.

**pilaster—pile** (pillar)—**pillar,** n hence v, all derive from L *pīla*, a pillar, esp a breakwater:

o.o.o.: ? cf (*r* for *l*) the Hit *pirwa*, a rock, ? also *pir*, a house. L *pīla* has It derivative *pilastro*, whence EF-F *pilastre*, whence E *pilaster*, a pier, a column; *pīla* becomes MF-F *pile*, adopted by E, with sense 'large heap' deriving from the obs 'breakwater' (a mass of rocks and stones); *pīla* has the VL derivative n *\*pīlāre* (? suggested by L *pīlārium*, pedestal for a funerary urn), whence MF *piler* (F *pilier*), adopted by ME, whence E *pillar*.

**pilch,** a light saddle, an infant's garment covering the napkin or diaper, derives—prob via F rather than from OE *pylce*—from LL *pellicia*, a cloak, elliptical for *pellicia uestis*, garment of fur or skin, *pellicius* being an adj of *pellis*, skin: f.a.e., the E FELL, a skin, a hide.

**pilchard,** var **pilcherd,** derives from the syn EE *pilcher*: ? *\*pilch*+suffix *-er*, with pej *-ard* substituted later for *-er*.

**pile** (1), a column (obs), a great heap (whence 'to *pile*'). See PILASTER.

**pile** (2), hair, hence the 'hair' of a carpet; **pilose** (**pilosity**), **pilous.** See FILAMENT, para 13, and cf the 3rd PEEL, para 2.

**pile** (3), a blade of grass, an arrow head. See PESTLE, para 1.

**pilfer.** See PELF.

**pilgrim, pilgrimage.** See PEREGRINE, para 3.

**piligan.** See the 3rd PEEL, para 5.

**pill** (1), the Med n. See the 3rd PEEL, para 4.

**pill** (2), to plunder, to peel; **pillage.** See the 3rd PEEL, para 3.

**pillar.** See PILASTER.

**pilled,** peeled: pp as adj: cf the 2nd PILL.

**pillion:** Ga *pillean* (cf Ir *pillīn*): from Ga (and Ir) *peall*, a covering, a hide: EIr *peall*, earlier *pell*, a horse: cf L *pellis*, a hide: f.a.e., FELL, skin, hide.

**pillory,** n hence v, derives, in ME, from OF *pilori*: ML *pilorium*, prob an *-orium* derivative of L *pīla*, pier, column. (B & W.)

**pillow,** n, hence v and cpd **pillowcase** and adj **pillowy:** ME *pilwe*: OE *pyle* or *pylu*: ML *pulvīnus*, L *puluīnus*, cushion, pillow: o.o.o.: ? an *-īnus* derivative of a lost *\*pulu*, itself from an IE *\*pul-*, a short log, a billet, the earliest 'pillow'—? cf Hit *pulpule*, either the trunk of a tree or some kind of tree, with *pulpul-* a redup of *\*pul-*, (a block of) wood, piece of a tree: sem cf Eg *urs*, a cedar or other wood pillow.

**pilose.** See the 3rd PEEL, para 2.

**pilot, pilotage.** See FOOT, para 22.

**pilous.** See the 3rd PEEL, para 2; cf FILAMENT, para 13.

**pilule.** See the 3rd PEEL, para 4.

**pilum,** a heavy javelin. See PESTLE, para 1.

**pimento, pimiento.** See PAINT, para 5.

**pimp,** n hence v: EF-F *pimpant*, smart, seductive, adj from the presp of late MF-EF *pimper*, to be seductively dressed: nasal mdfn of MF *piper*, to deceive by seduction, to wheedle: L *pipāre*, var of *pipīre*, (of a bird) to peep or cheep, hence to murmur seductively.

**pimpernel.** See PEPPER, para 5.

**pimple.** See PAPILLA, para 3.

pin (n, hence v), whence pinafore (*afore*, in front), pinfish ('from their sharp dorsal spines': Webster), pin money (a wife's pocket-money), pintail, with long central tail feathers; pint; pintle;—pen, an enclosure, 'to pen', with old pp pent.

1. *Pin*, ME *pinne*, derives from OE *pinn*, a pin, orig a peg: cf MD *pinne*, *penne*, D *pin*, MLG *pinne*, ON *pinni*; perh cf Ga *prine*, a pin, and MIr *benn*, a point.

2. The liquid measure *pint* derives from ME *pinte*, adopted from OF: cf OProv and Sp *pinta* and MD *pinte*: o.o.o.: perh orig of Gmc origin and at first meaning 'a pin' or rather 'a peg'.

3. The *pintle* of Ordnance and Mechanics derives from *pintle*, OE *pintel*, penis: phon, cf MLG *pint*, penis, and sem, cf *prick*.

4. *Pen*, a small enclosure (for, e.g., sheep), derives, through ME *penne*, from OE *penn*: a vocalic var of OE *pinn*, a peg or a pin. OE *penn* has the derivative v *pennian*, as in OE on-*pennian*, to unfasten; hence ME *pennen*, E 'to *pen*', to bolt (a gate: obs), to shut in.

piña. See the n PINE.

pinafore. See PIN (heading).

pince-nez: F, lit 'pinch-nose': f.a.e., PICK.

pincers. See PICK, para 12.

pinch. See PICK, para 13.

pinchbeck, an alloy (copper-zinc), hence spurious, derives from a Fleet Street London watchmaker, Christopher *Pinchbeck* (d. 1732).

Pindar, Pindaric (adj, hence n). *Pindaric* comes from L *Pindaricus*, trln of Gr *Pindarikos*, adj of *Pindaros*, L *Pindarus*, F *Pindare* and E *Pindar*.

pine (1), the tree. See FAT, para 2.

pine (2), to languish. See PAIN, para 6.

pineal: EF-F *pinéal*: L *pinea*, pine-cone: cf the 1st *pine*, q.v. at FAT.

pineapple, orig a pine-cone: cf the 1st *pine*, q.v. at FAT.

ping is echoic; hence the redup ping-pong, now called 'table tennis'.

pinguefy: LL *pinguefiō*, I become fat, L *pinguefacere*, to render (*facere*) fat (*pinguis*).—*pinguid*: from L *pinguis*, ? after *languid*.—*pinguin*, an A tropical plant: SciL, perh from *pinguis*.

pinion (1), a bird's wing. See the 2nd PEN, para 2, s.f.

pinion (2), in machinery. Cf *pinnacle*, but see SPINE, para 5.

pink (1), adj, derives from:

pink (2), a carnation, hence both the colour (whence the adj) and the sense 'perfection, a paragon' (Shakespeare's 'the very *pink* of courtesy' and the Cockney's coll 'in the *pink*' of health): EE *pinke*, *pynke*, *pincke*, *pinck*: o.o.o.: perh from the v *pink*, 'as if the edges were picked out' (Webster).

pink (3), a small, narrow-sterned coastal vessel, is adopted from D *pink*, MD *pinke*: o.o.o.

pink (4), a minnow, now a young salmon: earlier *penk*: of Gmc origin—cf G dial *pinke*.

pink (5), to pierce or perforate. See PICK, para 11.

pinkeye: An eye that is pink (acute conjunctivitis).

Pinkster, Whitsunday or Whitsuntide (esp in New York)—whence *pinkster* (for *Pinkster flower*, blooming at that season)—is adopted from D ('in regions of early Dutch influence': Mathews): ult from Gr *pentēkostē*—cf E *Pentecost*, q.v. at FIVE, para 14.

pinna. See the 2nd PEN, para 3.

pinnace: F *pinace*, *pinasse*: prob from Sp *pinaza*, itself from *pino*, from L *pīnus*, a pine tree, hence a boat built from one. (B & W.)

pinnacle. See SPINE, para 6.

pinnate. See the 2nd PEN, para 3.

pinnulate; pinnule. See the 2nd PEN, para 3.

pinochle, occ pinocle, an A card game, is app a blend of earlier *penuchle* and *binochle:* 'the form of the word and the relation of the game to bezique suggest Fr. origin' (Webster): perh MF-F *pinacle* (cf E *pinnacle*), ref the facts that two packs (cf, sem, CANASTA) and only the cards higher than '8' are used and that one can meld, e.g., four kings, a meld being permitted only after one wins the preceding trick.

pinole, edible seeds used for making flour, flour sweetened with such seeds, is a Sp adaptation of Nahuatl (Aztec) *pinolli*. (Webster; Whitehall.)

piñon, a pine nut or seed, is Sp *piñón*, from *pino*, a pine tree: f.a.e., FAT, para 2.

pint. See PIN, para 2.

pintado. See PAINT, para 6.

pintail. See PIN (heading).

pintle. See PIN, para 3.

pinto. See PAINT, para 6.

Pinus. See FAT, para 2.

pioneer (n, hence v): OF *peonier*, a foot soldier, later (*pionnier*) an Army 'labourer', finally a forerunner in a new, uncivilized land: tautological agent (-*ier*) from OF *peon*, foot soldier (F *pion*, in chess): L *pedōnem*, acc of *pedō*, one who goes on foot: cf E *pawn*, q.v. at FOOT, para 9.

pious. See PITY, para 2.

pip (1), a poultry disease: ME, from MD, *pippe*: VL *\*pipita*: L *pituita*, phlegm: cf *pituitary*, q.v. at FAT, para 3.

pip (2), on cards: earlier *peep*: o.o.o.

pip (3), of fruit. See PIPPIN.

pip (4), v, is a var of *peep*, to cheep.

pipal. See PEPPER, para 3.

pipe (n and v); many cpds, all obvious (pipe of peace, from an old N Amerindian custom); piper; pipette; thinned form of v: pip; sep PEEP, to cheep; sep PIGEON; pibroch; fife.

1. Ult, both the n and the v *pipe* come from L-ML *pipāre*, *pipiāre*, *pipīre*, varr of echoic *pip-*, extn of IE *\*pi-*, a bird's cry, to cry thus. 'To *pipe*', orig as a bird does, derives from OE *pīpian* from L *pipiāre*; a pipe, orig a wind instrument, from OE *pīpe*, from ML *pīpa*, from *pipāre*. A *piper* derives from OE *pīpere*, from *pīpe*.

2. L *pipāre* becomes OF-F *piper*, whence the OF-F n *pipe*, a reed used as a musical instrument,

a tube, whence the late MF-F dim *pipette*, adopted
by E.

3. The E n *pipe* becomes Ga *piob* (pron *peeb*), a
pipe (tube), esp a Sc Highland bagpipe, whence
*piobaire*, a piper, whence *piobaireachd*, pipe music,
whence E *pibroch*, elaborate musical variations for
the bagpipe.

4. ML *pīpa* becomes OHG *pfifa*, MHG *pfife* (G
*Pfeife*), whence E *fife*.

**Piper** (pepper plant), **piperin**. See PEPPER,
para 4.

**piper** (player on the pipe). See PIPE, para 1.

**pipette.** See PIPE, para 2.

**pipit**, a small A bird, is as echoic as, say,
PEWEE (PEWIT), q.v.

**pippin**, a seed, whence, by abbr, **pip**: ME *pipin*,
var of *pepin*, a seed: OF-MF *pepin* (F *pépin*; F dial
*pipin*): as in the Sp *pepita* and It *pippolo*, 'the
repetition of *p* expresses the tininess of the object'
(B & W).

**piquancy, piquant; pique.** See PICK, para 7.

**piquet.** See PICK, para 7.

**piqûre.** See PICK, para 7, s.f.

**piracy, pirate, piratical.** See PERIL, para 2.

**pirl.** See the 3rd PURL.

**pirouette**, v, derives from EF-F *pirouetter*, itself
from EF-F *pirouette*, adopted by E: late MF
*pirouet*: ? (Webster) a blend of *pivot*+*girouette*, a
weathercock.

**piscary, piscatorial, Piscis.** See FISH, para 3.

**pismire**, an ant. See FORMIC, s.f.

**piss** (v, hence n), hence dial 'a **pissing while**', a
moment; **pizzle; piddle**, whence the pa **piddling**,
trifling; **pee**, v hence n.

1. 'To *piss*', ME *pissen*, derives from MF-F
*pisser*, OF *pissier* (cf OFris *pissia*), VL *pissiāre*
(cf It *pisciare*); ? cf Hit *pisan*, a vessel for water:
ult echoic.

2. Perh akin is *pizzle*, an animal's—e.g., a bull's
—penis: app a dim—cf LG *pesel* with D *pees*, MD
*pese*, a sinew.

3. 'To *piss*' app has softened dim *piddle*, syn, also
to trifle, and the childish—? orig euphem—*pee*.

**pistachio; fistic, fustic.**

1. *Pistachio* anglicizes It *pistacchio*: L *pistacium*,
the nut, LL *pistacia*, the tree: Gr *pistakion*, the
nut, from *pistakē*, the tree: OPer *pistah*, the
nut.

2. Gr *pistakē* becomes Ar *fustuq*, whence Sp,
whence F, *fustoc*, whence E *fustic*; and Ar *fustuq*
has the coll form *fistuq*, whence ML *fisticum*,
whence the now obs E *fistic*.

**pistil, pistillate.** See PESTLE, para 3.

**pistol**: EF-F *pistole*: G *Pistole*: late MHG
*pischol*, var *pisschula*: Cz (c1421) *pišt'al*, *pišt'ala*,
lit 'hand fire-arm'. (Walshe.)

**piston.** See PESTLE, para 4.

**pit** (1), a cavity. See PAVE, para 2.

**pit** (2), a fruit-stone. See PITH.

**pita** (plant fibre): Sp: prob Quechuan *pita*, fine
thread.

**pitapat**: easement of *pitpat*, redup of PAT.

**pitch** (1), black, sticky substance: ME *pich*: OE

*pic*: L *pix*, o/s *pic-*: cf Gr *pissa*, Attic *pitta*: IE r,
*pi-*, fat (adj, n): cf *pine* at FAT, para 2. Adj: *pitchy*.

**pitch** (2), a throw, a place for throwing balls, to
throw. See PICK, para 14.

**pitcher** (vessel). See the 1st PECK.—**pitcher**, as in
baseball: see PICK, para 4.

**pitchfork.** See PICK, para 14.

**piteous.** See PITY, para 6.

**pith**, whence pithy (whence **pithiness**); **pit** (fruit-
stone). *Pith* derives from OE *pitha*; *pit* is adopted
from D *pit*, MD *pitte*, kernel, cf Fris and LG *pit*,
pith, kernel: o.o.o.

**pithecan**, loosely 'ape-like': Gr *pithēkos*, an ape,
? lit '*hateful* creature': IE r, *bhidh-*: cf L *foedus*,
frightful, outrageous. (Hofmann.) Cf the element
*pithec(o)-*.

**pithy.** See PITH (heading).

**pitiable, pitiful, pitless.** See PITY, the 1st at para
6, the others in the heading.

**pittance.** See PITY, para 7.

**pituitary.** See FAT, para 3.

**pity**, n, hence v (cf MF *piteer*, MF-F *pitoyer*);
**piteous; pitiable; pitiful, pitiless** (*piti-* for *pity-*+
*-ful, -less*); **pittance;—piety, pietas, pietism** (whence
**pietist**, whence pietistic), **pious; impious, impiety;**—
**expiable (inexpiable), expiate, expiation, expiator,
expiatory.**

1. The base of all these words is the L *pius*,
dutiful to one's gods and one's parents: with s
and r *pi-*, the word is of Italic orgin, well attested
in Oscan, Umbrian, Volscian.

2. L *pius* becomes OF *pieus*, F *pieux*, f *pieuse*
and, perh independently, E *pious*. Derivative L
*pietās*, o/s *pietāt-*, becomes OF-MF *pieté* (F
*piété*), whence E *piety*; on the s *piet-*, G has coined
*Pietismus*, whence E *pietism*.

3. L *pius, pietās* have negg *impius, impietās*
whence E *impious* and *impiety*, the latter perh via
OF-MF *impieté* (F *impiété*).

4. *Pius* has derivative *piāre*, to purify, to perform the due rite for, to expiate, with cpd *expiāre*
(*ex-* used int), to expiate, with derivative LL
*expiābilis*, whence F and E *expiable*; the neg
*inexpiābilis* becomes late MF-F and E *inexpiable*.
The pp *expiātus* yields 'to expiate'; derivative
*expiātiō*, o/s *expiātiōn-*, yields OF-F and, perh
independently, E *expiation*; derivative LL *expiātor*
is adopted by E; derivative LL *expiātōrius* becomes
EF-F *expiatoire* and, perh independently, E *expiatory*.

5. L *pietās* has acc *pietātem*, whence OF *pitet*,
varr *pité, pitée* (MF-F *pitié*), piety, also pity,
whence ME *pite* (dissyllabic), whence E *pity*,
which, like F *pitié*, means only 'compassion'.

6. L *pietās* has the VL derivative adj *pietōsus*,
whence OF *pitos*, later *pitous* (MF-F *piteux*, f
*piteuse*), whence ME *pitous*, whence, influenced by
the MF f *piteuse*, the E *piteous*. The MF *piteer*, var
*pitier*, has the MF derivative *piteable*, with var
*pitiable*, retained by F and adopted by E.

7. OF *pité*, in sense 'pity', has OF derivative
*pitance*, pity, hence a monk's portion of food: the
subsistence of monks and nuns was generally

assured either by pious foundations or by the charity of the faithful (DAF): hence ME *pitance*: whence E *pittance*.

**pivot** (n, hence—unless from EF-F *pivoter*—v) is adopted from OF-F *pivot*: o.o.o., but perh (B & W) from an IE r *pu-, *pi-, attested by Angevin (F dial) *pue*, tooth of a weaver's comb, prong of a harrow, OProv *pua* (now *pivo*), tooth of a comb, Sp *pua*, var *puga*, a point.

**pixy**, occ **pixie**, a mischievous fairy, is o.o.o.; cf E dial *pisky* (? a metathesis of a Scan word) and Sw dial *pyske* (*pysk*), a goblin.

**pizzle.** See PISS, para 2.

**placable.** See PLEASE, para 2.

**placard**, n, hence v; **placket**; **plaque, plaquette.**

1. A *placard* is adopted from F: a poster, C16, from an official document or notice that is not folded, C16: app for *plaquard, from MF-F *plaquer*, from MD *placken*, to piece together, to paste or stick on or together, whence MD *placke*, a piece or a patch, also a coin: the MD v is prob echoic (EW). EF-F *plaque* (dim *plaquette*, adopted by E) —whence E *plaque*—comes partly from MD *placke* and partly from MF *plaquer*.

2. The MD n *placke* (D *plak*) becomes, as coin, the obs E *plack*, with form perh influencing E *placket*, a petticoat, now a slit in skirt or petticoat; *placket*, which app has the dim suffix *-et*, might be a distortion of *placard*, as Webster suggests and Whitehall states.

**placate, placation, placatory.** See PLEASE, para 3.

**place.** See PLANE, para 12.

**placebo.** See PLEASE, para 4.

**placement.** See PLANE, heading—cf para 12.

**placenta, placentary, placentation.** See PLANK, para 2; cf the element *placo-*.

**placer.** See PLANE, para 13.

**placet.** See PLEASE, para 4.

**placid, placidity.** See PLEASE, para 5.

**placitum.** See PLEASE, para 4.

**placket.** See PLACARD, para 2.

**placoid**, scaly: *plac-+-oid*: *plac-* for *placo-*, from Gr *plax*, o/s *plak-*, a tablet, a flat plate, a scale.

**plagal; plagiarism, plagiarist, plagiarize, plagiary.**

1. Behind these words lies Gr *plagios* (s *plagi-*, r *plag-*), crooked, oblique, hence, fig, treacherous; cf Gr ta *plagia*, the sides, *plagos*, a side, related by Hofmann to *pelag*os, the open sea (cf ARCHI-PELAGO).

2. Gr *plagios* becomes L *plaga*, a Mus mode, whence ML *plagalis*, of that mode, whence E *plagal*.

3. From Gr *plagios*, LL derives *plagium*, a kid-napping, whence LL *plagiārius*, a plunderer, a kidnapper (of another's slaves), whence the E *plagiary*, n hence adj, whence *plagiar-ism, -ist, -ize*.

**plague**, n, whence v and the adj **plaguey** or **plaguy**: L *plāga*, a (severe) blow, hence a plague: prob from Gr *plēgē*, from *plēssō*, I strike or wound; less likely, an *n*-less derivative of L *plangere*, orig to strike, later to mourn (vt)—cf the 2nd PLAIN, para 1.

**plaice.** See PLANE, para 15.

**plaid**: Ga *plaide*, a blanket, app a contr deriva-tive of *peallaid*, a sheepskin, from *peall*, a skin or hide: cf PILLION.

**plain** (1), adj and n. See PLANE, para 6.

**plain** (2), to mourn (vi); **plaint, plaintiff, plaintive; plangent** (whence **plangency**), **plangor**, whence **plangorous; complain, complainant, complaint.**

1. The group rests upon L *plangere* (s and r *plang-*), to strike, esp *se plangere*, to strike one's breast in grief, hence *plangere*, to lament: echoic. (Cf PLAGUE.)

2. L *plangere* becomes OF-F *plaindre*, ME *playne*, E 'to *plain*', obs except in the cpd. Presp *plangens*, o/s *plangent-*, yields E *plangent*; deriva-tive L *plangor* is adopted by E. On the pp *planct*us arises the n *planctus* (gen *-ūs*), whence OF-F *plainte*, whence ME *plaint*, retained by E; the derivative OF-F adj, hence n, *plaintif* becomes the E n *plaintiff* and, via the f *plaintive*, the E adj *plaintive*.

3. The ML cpd *complangere* (*com-* used int) becomes OF *complaindre*, whence 'to *complain*'; the derivative OF-F n *complainte* becomes E *complaint*; E *complainant*, orig an adj, derives from OF-F *complaignant*, presp of the v.

**plain(-)song.** See PLANE, para 6.

**plait.** See PLY, para 5.

**plan.** See PLANE, para 4.

**planar, planarian, planate, planation.** See PLANE, para 5.

**planch, planche, planchette.** See PLANK.

**plane**, adj, n, v (whence **planer**), **planish; acro-plane**, whence '**plane** (aircraft)—cf **volplane;**— **plan**, n hence v (whence **planner** and the pa, vn **planning**), and **planless;—planarian, planate, plana-tion; planula;—plain**, adj (whence **plainness**) and n;—**plano; piano, pianoforte, pianissimo, pianist; llano, llanura.** Cpds of *plane* and *plain* (adj, n): **complanate, complanation; explain, explanate, explanation, explanatory;** for *plani-*, *plano-* cpds, see the Elements.—Perh cf the sep treated PLANT group.—**place** (n, hence v—perh prompted by EF-F *placer*), **placement** (perh adopted from F, perh from the E v), **placer** in mining; cpds of *place*, v: **displace**, whence **displacement; emplace-ment;** and **replace**, whence **replacement;—plaice: plaza** and **piazza; plat; plate** (n, hence v—whence **plater**) and **plateau; platitude**, whence, anl, **plati-tudinous** and **platitudinarian; platband, platform, Plattdeutsch; platen, platina, platinize, platinum, platten;** ? **Plato, Platonic** (whence, anl, **Platonism** and **Platonist); platypus**—cf the element *platy-*; **Plautus, Plautine; splat**, n, hence v.—**plot** of ground, the 'scheme' sense being influenced by **complot** (n, v)—whence 'to **plot**', whence **plotter** and **plotting.** —Cf the sep FLAT (FLATTEN, etc.).

### Indo-European

1. Sem, the basic idea is that of 'flat' (hence of 'flatness'), whence that of 'easy to see or determine'

PLANE

(hence 'easy to build upon', etc.): this fact illuminates the identity of *plane* or *plain* with *plat* or, in the Gmc mode, *flat*; on the other hand, it shows up the fundamental difficulty of relating *plant* (herb, shrub, etc.) to them, although the *plant* or sole of a foot may be related rather to *plane*, *plat*, etc., than to the growing *plant*. Phon, the IE r is app *pla-* (meaning 'flat', hence 'to widen'), with extn *plat-*, as in Gr *platus*, and with extn *plan-*, as in L *plānus*, and prob with extn *plag-*, as in L *plaga*, a flat surface, a district, a zone; cf—with r for l—the Skt *práthati*, he flattens out. In Hit we find what is app a metathesis of *pla-*: *pal-*, as in *palhis*, broad.

### The *plane, plain, -plain* Group

2. The L adj *plānus*, flat, level, hence straightforward, clear, becomes E *plane*; derivative L *plānum*, prop the neu of the adj, becomes the E n *plane*, a level surface, and the tool *plane* derives from the syn LL *plāna*; derivative L *plānāre*, to level, LL to make smooth, becomes EF-F *planer*, whence 'to *plane*', and also MF *planir*, whence, via such parts as presp 'planissant' and 'nous planissons', the E 'to planish'.

3. L *plānum* becomes EF-F *plan*, a plane, whence F *aéroplan, biplan, monoplan*, whence E *aeroplane, biplane, monoplane*; F *vol plané*, lit 'planed, hence glided, flight', yields 'to volplane', to glide in an aircraft.

4. EF-F *plan* acquires, in C16, the sense 'a design': influenced by It *pianta*, L *planta*, sole of foot.

5. L *plānum*, a flat surface, a plane, has the derivative LL adjj *plānāris*, whence E *planar*, and *plānārius*, on level ground, whence E *planarian*, adj hence n. L *plānāre*, to flatten, LL to make smooth, has pp *plānātus*, whence the E adj *planate*, whence, anl. *planation*. From the L n *plānum*, SciL coins the Zoo dim *planula*.

6. L *plānus* became OF-MF *plain*, flat, level, surviving in *plain-chant*, whence E *plain song*, an Eccl chant or chanting. This adj *plain* was adopted by ME (var *plein*, whence the confusion with F *plein*, full). The L n *plānum*, in sense 'a plain', becomes OF *plain* (the F *plaine* derives rather from the f of the adj), whence ME *plein, plain*, the latter retained by E.

7. Several other R derivatives of L *plānus* and n *plānum* have got into E. For instance, the It *piano*, flat, hence, in Mus, softly, is adopted by E, along with its sup *pianissimo*. It *piano* combines with It *forte* (L *forte*), strongly, loudly, to form the Mus instrument *pianoforte*, whence, prob via F *piano-forte* (Voltaire, 1774), the E *pianoforte*; the It, hence F (1798), hence E *piano* is an abbr. (B & W.) The derivative It *pianista* becomes F *pianiste*, whence E *pianist*.

8. L *plānus*, level, becomes Sp *llano*, level, whence the n use, esp in ASp, whence *llanero*, a plainsman, a cowboy; derivative Sp *llanura*, flatness, occurs in ASp as 'plains country', the plains.

Compounds in *-plane* (*-planation*) and *-plain*.

9. L *plānāre*, to flatten or level, has cpd *complānāre*, with pp *complānātus* (*com-* used int), whence both the v (obs) and the adj *complanate*, whence, anl, *complanation*, a levelling, perh suggested, in form, by the LL *complānātiō*, o/s *complānātiōn-*.

10. L *explānāre*, to flatten, hence spread, out, both lit and before the mind, yields 'to *explain*'; the pp *explānātus* gives us the Bot adj *explanate*; derivative *explānātiō*, o/s *explānātiōn-*, yields *explanation*; and derivative LL *explānātōrius* leads to *explanatory*.

### The *place* Group

11. Akin to L *plānus*, flat, level, is the syn Gr *platus* (s and r *plat-*), which occurs purely in the *platy-* cpds, notably *platypus*, a SciL coinage, from LGr *platupous*, '(a) flat- or broad-footed (creature)', used occ as nickname.

12. Gr *platus* has f *plateia*, used by LGr for 'a public place, a public square', whence L *platēa*, a wide street, whence, via VL *plattea*, the OF-F *place*, predominantly a city square, adopted by ME, orig a city square, hence an open space, a space, and finally a locality, E *place*. Gr *platus* has extn *platikos*, broad, hence general, whence LL *platicus*, whence E *platic*.

13. VL *plattea* becomes It *piazza*, Sp *plaza*, G *Platz*, all in the 'city square' acceptation. From the s of *plaza*, Sp derives *placel*, a sandbank, with var (r for l) *placer*, which acquires a mining sense, adopted by E.

### Compounds of *place*, v.

14. F *placer* has cpdd *desplacer* (F *dé-*), whence to *displace*', whence—perh after F—*displacement*; EF-F *emplacement*, adopted by E; EF-F *replacer*, whence 'to *replace*', whence *replacement*.

### Other *plat-* Derivatives

15. *Plaice*, ME *plais*, derives from MF *plaïs* (F *plie*): L *platessa*, a flatfish, a plaice; ult from Gr *platus*, f *plateia*, flat, broad.

16. The now only dial *plat*, flat, and the derivative n *plat*, a flat surface, a small piece of ground (orig flat), derive, in ME, from OF-F *plat*, f *platte*, flat, level, from LL *platēa* (cf para 12).

17. A *plate*, whether metallic or culinary, reaches ME from OF-MF *plate*, a sheet or plate of metal, prob elliptical for *lame plate* (later *platte*), a flat sheet (of metal). The OF adj *plat* has the OF-F derivative *plateau*, basically 'something flat': adopted by E.

18. *Platitude*, adopted from late EF-F, derives, by suffix *-itude*, from the F adj *plat*: anl with *altitude, latitude*, etc. Also from F come the Arch *platband*, EF-F *plate-bande*, and *platform*, late MF-F *plate-forme*. But *Plattdeutsch*, the LG of N Germany, is adopted from G: *platt*, flat + *Deutsch*, German: cf D *platteland*, countryside (Walshe). G *platt* comes from F.

19. *Platen*, a flat plate of metal, derives from F *platine*: C18 Sp *platina* (now *platino*), from Sp *plata*, silver, either from OProv *plata*, a plate of metal, or from syn OF *plate* (as in para 17). The Sp *platina* is, in Chem, used for crude native platinum: and *platinum* itself is its SciL derivative, with the anl E derivative *platinize*. *Platten*, however, is a sort of blend of the adj *plat* and 'to *flatten*'.

### Miscellaneous

20. Gr *plat*us, flat, level, hence broad or wide, perh (EnciIt) accounts for Gr *Platōn*, ? a nickname 'The Broad-Minded' or 'The Versatile': hence L, whence E, *Plato*. The Gr adj *Platōnikos* becomes L *Platonicus*, whence F *platonique* and E *Platonic*, whence *Platonic* (or spiritual) *love*.

21. *Plautus* is L *plautus*, lit 'flat', hence '(the) flat-footed (one)'; the derivative adj *Plautīnus* affords us *Plautine*.

22. With *plat*, flat, cf a chair's *splat* or flat upright middle piece of wood in the back. The word is puzzling: have we here the IE prefix *s*- (usually int)?

23. With a *plat* of ground, cf a *plot* of ground; indeed, this *plot* is prob a var of that *plat*. *Plot*, a secret scheme, has app been influenced by *complot*, from OF-F *complot*, OF var *complote*, orig a closely packed crowd, prob from *\*comploter*, contr of *\*compeloter*, to form into a ball (*pelote*), as Webster proposes. Derivative MF-F *comploter* yields 'to *complot*'. Clearly, however, the literary *plot* and 'to *plot*' could equally well be aphetic for '(to) *complot*'.

'**plane**, n hence v, now usu **plane**. See prec (heading).

**planet, planetary.** See FLAUNT, para 2.

**plangency, plangent, plangor, plangorous.** See the 2nd PLAIN, para 2.

**planish.** See PLANE, para 2, s.f.

**plank** (n, hence v—whence vn **planking**); **planch, planchette; placenta, placental, placentary, placentation.**

1. A *plank*, ME *planke*, derives from ONF *planke*, corresp to OF-F *planche*: LL *planca*, perh the f (taken as n) of the adj *plancus*, flat, usu flat-footed. OF-F *planche* becomes E *planch*, a plank (now dial); the MF-F dim *planchette* is adopted by E.

2. With LL *planca*, cf the *n*-less Gr *plax* (gen *plakos*, o/s and r *plak*-), a flat surface, anything flat and broad; cf Lett *plakt*, to become flat. Gr *plax* has derivative *plakous*, a flat cake, whence, from the acc *plakounta*, the L *placenta*, perh influenced by *placent*-, o/s of *placens*, presp of *placēre*, to please: hence the SciL *placenta* of Zoo and An. The derivative L adj *placentārius* yields E *placentary*, with var *placental*. *Placentation* is an anl formation, based upon *placentate*, possessing a placenta, itself formed anl.

**plankton**, adopted from G, derives from Gr *plankton*, prop the neu of the adj *planktos*, wandering, from *planesthai*, to wander: akin to *planet*.

**plant** (1), sole of foot: OF-F *plante*: L *planta*: prob a nasal derivative of IE *\*plat*-, q.v. at PLANE, para 1. The adj is *plantāris*, E *plantar*. *Planta* has derivative *plantāgō*, named from its flat leaves: from the acc *plantāginem* comes MF-F *plantain*, adopted by E.

2. *Planta* has derivative *plantāre*, to stamp the ground with one's foot, with cpd *supplantāre*, to put one's foot under (*sup*- for *sub*) another, to trip him up, to upset him: OF-F *supplanter*, orig to upset: E 'to *supplant*', whence *supplanter*. Derivative LL *supplantātiō*, o/s *supplantātiōn*-, becomes, prob via MF-F, the E *supplantation*.

**plant** (2), a herb, shrub, (young) tree, a sprig, a slip; to **plant**, whence **planter; plantation;—implant**, whence, anl, **implantation; transplant**, whence, anl, **transplantation.—clan**, whence **clannish.**

1. L *planta*, a shoot, sprout, or a slip, cutting, lacks the modern sense (represented by L *herba*), which arose in the R languages and has been adopted by the Gmc: o.o.o. Some senses of the n derive from the derivative v *plantāre*, to put something into the ground to start it growing.

2. *Planta* becomes OF-F *plante* and OE *plante*, whence E *plant*; *plantāre* becomes OF-F *planter* and OE *plantian*, whence 'to *plant*'. Derivative *plantātiō*, o/s *plantātiōn*-, becomes MF-F and, prob independently, E *plantation*.

3. LL *implantāre*, to ingraft, becomes It *impiantare*, to place (in), whence EF-F *implanter*, whence 'to *implant*'; derivative EF-F *implantation* is adopted by E.

4. LL *replantāre*, to plant again, becomes MF-F *replanter*, whence 'to *replant*', whence, anl, *replantation*.

5. LL *transplantāre* becomes MF-F *transplanter* and, prob independently, E *transplant*: derivative EF-F *transplantation* perh suggested the E word (otherwise formed anl).

6. L *planta* becomes OIr *cland*, offspring, hence a tribe, with eased var *clann*, whence Ga *clann*, descendants, tribe, whence E *clan*, all the larger family bearing the one name. With OIr *cland*, cf W *plant*, children, *planta*, to beget children, and Cor *plans*, *planz*, a plant, *plansa*, to plant.

**Plantagenet** comes, through F, from L *planta*, a sprout+*genesta*, a broom plant: orig, prob a MF nickname.

**plantago:** Bot term, from L *plantāgō*, q.v. at the 1st PLANT, para 1, s.f.

**plantain** (1), a weed. See 1st PLANT, para 1, s.f.

**plantain** (2). See BANANA.

**plantation.** See the 2nd PLANT, para 2; the heading, for **planter.**

**plantigrade.** See the 2nd element *planti-*.

**planula.** See PLANE, para 5, s.f.

**plaque, plaquette.** See PLACARD.

**plash** (1), to cut lightly, then bend and intertwine, e.g. branches, derives from OF-MF *plassier* (varr *plaissier, pleissier, plessier*), from VL *\*plaxāre*, *\*plexāre*, either via an intermediate *\*plectiāre* or direct from L *plexum*, the supine of *plectere*, to intertwine (reeds, branches, etc.).

2. From VL *plexāre*, via ONF *plechier* (F *plécher*)—a var of OF *plessier*—comes ME *plechen*, whence E 'to *pleach*' or unite by interweaving or interlacing.

**plash** (2), to splash, whence **plashy**. See SPLASH.

**plasm** (whence **plasmic**), **plasma**; **ectoplasm**, **protoplasm**, with adjj in *-ic*; cf the elements *plasmato-*, *plasmo-*; **plaster** (n, whence v, whence **plasterer**, **plastering**) and **emplaster**—cf the elements *-plast*, *plasto-*; **plastic** (adj and n, whence **plastics**), whence **plasticism**, **plasticity**, **plasticize**; **plastid**; **plastron**; cf the element *-plasty*; **piaster** (AE), **piastre**.

1. *Plasm* derives from *plasma*, the fluid part of blood, a sense-adaptation of LL *plasma*, anything moulded, hence anything formed, adopted from Gr *plasma*, gen *plasmatos*, itself from *plassein*, to mould, hence to form: IE r, *\*pela-*, to spread, often contr to *\*pla-*.

2. Of the cpds in *-plasm*, perh the two best known are *ectoplasm*, where *ecto-* means 'outside', and *protoplasm*, from G *Protoplasma*, where *proto-* means 'first, virginal'.

3. Gr *plassein*, to mould, has derivative adj *plastikos*, whence L *plasticus*, whence EF-F *plastique* and E *plastic*; *hē plastikē tekhnē*, the plastic art, elliptically *hē plastikē*, becomes LL *plastica*, a thing created by the hands, whence E *plastic*, a sculptor (obs), something that is plastic, whence *plastics*, plastic surgery.

4. The agent of *plassein* is *plastēs*, f *plastis*, with pl *plastides*, whence G *Plastiden* (pl), whence Biol E *plastid*.

5. *Plassein* has prefix-cpd *emplassein*, to daub into or upon, with derivative *emplastron*, whence L *emplastron*, a plaster, adopted by Pharm; derivative LL *emplastrāre*, to apply a plaster to a wound, etc., has ML derivative *emplastrātiō*, o/s *-ātiōn-*, whence Med *emplastration*.

6. L *emplastrum* has the ML aphesis *plastrum*, with farming and building senses: hence, with sense from the L cpd and form from the simple, the OE-E *plaster*, whence the v—perh suggested by OF-EF *plastrir* (EF-F *plâtrer*), itself from OF-MF *plastre* (F *plâtre*), prob from ML.

7. L *emplastrum* becomes It *impiastro*, whence It *piastra*, orig a sheet of metal, whence—perh via Sp—the EF-F *piastre*, a coin (Turkey, Egypt), adopted by E.

8. It *piastra*, sheet of metal, has the derivative *piastrone*, whence late MF-F *plastron*, a metal breastplate, whence, C17 onwards, the Zoo and other senses, adopted by E.

**plaster.** See prec, para 6.
**plastic, plastics.** See PLASM, para 3.
**plastid.** See PLASM, para 4.
**plastron.** See PLASM, para 8.
**plat** (1), adj and n. See PLANE, para 16.
**plat** (2), v. See PLY, 5.
**platband.** See PLANE, para 18.
**plate.** See PLANE, para 17.
**plateau.** See PLANE, para 17.
**platen.** See PLANE, para 19.

**platform.** See PLANE, para 18.
**platic.** See PLANE, para 12, s.f.
**platina, platinize, platinum.** See PLANE, para 19.
**platitude.** See PLANE, para 18.
**Plato, Platonic.** See PLANE, para 20.
**platoon.** See the 3rd PEEL, para 5, s.f.
**Plattdeutsch.** See PLANE, para 18.
**platten.** See PLANE, para 19, s.f.
**platypus.** See PLANE, para 11.
**Platz.** See PLANE, para 13.

**plaudit** (whence **plaudtory**), **plausible**, whence **plausibility**; **applaud**, **applause**; **explode** and **explosion**, **explosive**, whence, resp, the Phon **plosion**, **plosive**.

1. L *plaudere*, to beat or strike, esp to strike hand against hand, has s and r *plaud-*, var *plod-*: echoic. The imperative pl *plaudite*, Clap your hands!, yields the E n *plaudit*. On *plaus-*, s of pp *plausus*, arises L *plausibilis*, worthy of applause, whence EF-F and, prob independently, E *plausible*, both with a new meaning, soon to predominate. The neg *implausible* is an E formation.

2. The cpd *applaudere* (*ap-* for *ad-* used int), becomes MF-F *applaudir* and, perh independently, E *applaud*; E *applause* is formed, anl, after the syn L simple n *plausus* (gen *-ūs*).

3. L *explōdere*, to chase away (connoted by *ex-*) by clapping one's hands, becomes 'to *explode*', orig as in L; derivative L *explōsiō*, o/s *explōsiōn-*, yields (F and) E *explosion*, whence, anl, the adj *explosive* (cf F *explosif*, f *-ive*).

**Plautine, Plautus.** See PLANE, para 21.

**play**, n and v; with such obvious derivatives and cpds as **player** (OE *plegere*), **playful**, **playing**, **playboy**, **playground**, **playwright**.

The n *play* derives from OE *plega*, app from *plegian*, *plegan*, whence, through ME *pleien*, comes 'to *play*': akin prob to MD *playen*, *pleyen*, to frolic, and perh to OHG *pflegan*, MHG *pflegen*, to pay attention to, G *pflegen*, be answerable for: o.o.o.

**plaza.** See PLANE, para 13.
**plea.** See PLEASE, para 11.
**pleach.** See the 1st PLASH, para 2, and PLY, para 6.
**plead, pleader, pleading.** See PLEASE, para 11.
**pleasance.** See PLEASE, para 7.
**pleasant, pleasantry.** See para 7 of:
**please**, whence the pa, vn **pleasing**; **pleasance**, **pleasant**, **pleasantry**; **pleasure** (n, hence v), whence **pleasurable**; **displease** (whence pa **displeasing**), **displeasure**;—**placability**, **placable** (**implacable**, **implacability**), **placate**, **placation**, **placatory**; **placebo**, **placet**, **placitum**; **placid**, **placidity**;—**complacence** (var **complacency**), **complacent**, cf **complaisance**, **complaisant**; **displacency**;—**plea**, **plead** (whence pa, vn **pleading**), **pleadable**, **pleader**.

1. L *plācāre*, to appease, to pacify, and *placēre*, to please, form complementary aspects of PL s *\*plac-*, app from an IE r *\*plac-*, *\*plak-*, as in Tokh B *plaki*, agreement, mutual understanding.

2. *plācāre* (s and r *plac-*) has derivative *plācābilis*, whence MF-F, hence ME-E, *placable*; derivative L *lācābilitās*, o/s *-itāt-*, becomes *placability*. The L

neg *implācābilis* becomes late MF-F *implacable*, adopted by E; derivative *implācābilitās* becomes *implacability*.

3. *Plācāre* has pp *plācātus*, whence 'to *placate*'; on s *plācāt-* arise *plācātiō*, o/s *plācātiōn-*, and LL adj *plācātōrius*, whence resp *placation* and *placatory*, with anl var *placative*.

4. L *placēre* (s and r *plac-*), to afford satisfaction or happiness to, has *placet*, it pleases, and pp *placitus*, neu *placitum*, used as ML n, adopted by E Law for a court decree; the future *placēbō*, I shall please, has passed into F as an Eccl and Med term.

5. *Placēre*, s *plac-*, has adj *placidus*, orig pleasing, soon peaceable, easy-going, with derivative *placiditās*, o/s *placiditāt-*; hence, resp, *placid* (cf late MF-F *placide*) and *placidity* (cf F *placidité*).

6. *Placēre* becomes OF *plaisir* (MF-F *plaire*), almost imm used also as n (retained by MF-F); whereas the v passes through ME *plaisen, plesen*, to become 'to *please*', the n passes through ME *plesir*, later *plesure*, to become *pleasure*.

7. MF-F *plaire* has presp *plaisant*, whence E *pleasant*; derivative MF-F *plaisance* yields E *pleasance*, orig a pleasing, now usu a pleasure ground; *plaisant* has the further MF-F derivative *plaisanterie*, whence E *pleasantry*.

8. OF *plaisir*, v, has the cpd *desplaisir* (MF-F *déplaire*), whence 'to *displease*'; used as n, the OF *desplaisir* (MF-F *déplaisir*) yields E *displeasure* (cf para 6).

9. L *placēre* has cpd *complacēre* (int *com-*), to be very pleased, presp *complacens*, o/s *complacent-*, used as adj, whence E *complacent*; derivative ML *complacentia* yields *complacence*. *Complacēre* becomes OF-F *complaire*, presp *complaisant*, used in MF-F as adj, whence the E word; derivative MF-F *complaisance* is likewise adopted.

10. The L cpd *displicēre* has presp *displicens*, o/s *displicent-*, whence the n *displicentia*, reshaped by ML to *displacentia*, whence E *displacency*.

11. The *placitum* of para 4, as a Law term, becomes OF-EF *plaid* (varr *plait, pled*), adopted by ME with later varr *plai, plee*, whence E *plea*; and OF *plaid* has the derivative v *plaidier*, later *plaider*, whence ME *plaiden, pleden*, whence 'to *plead*'; derivative OF-F *plaidable* and OF *plaideor* (F *plaideur*) become E *pleadable* and *pleader*.

**pleasure.** See prec, para 6.

**pleat.** See PLY, para 5.

**plebe, plebeian, plebiscite, plebs.** See PEOPLE, para 8.

**pledge** (n, hence v—cf the OF *plegier*, F *pleiger*); **plevin** and **replevin.**

1. *Pledge* comes from OF-EF *plege*, var *pleige*, a guarantee, from ML *plebium*, var *plevium*, app of Gmc origin: cf OS *plegan*, to be answerable for. DAF derives the OF n from the OF v, which it makes a var of *plevir*, to guarantee, to pledge oneself, (with *l* for *r*) from L *praebēre*, to offer.

2. The OF *plege, pleige* is a var of, or has the MF var, *plevie*, itself with var *plevine*, whence the Law term *plevin*. OF *plevir* has the MF cpd *replevir*, to give security for, whence the AF n *replevine*, whence E *replevin*; MF *replevir* becomes the corresp v *replevy*.

**plein-air.** See PLENARY (heading).

**Pleistocene**, ref the Geol period imm preceding the present: Gr *pleistos*, most (sup of *polus*, much) + *kainos*, fresh, new.

**plenary; plenarty; plenipotentiary; plenish**, whence **plenishment**—cf **replenish**, whence **replenishment; plenitude; plenty** (whence **plentiful**), **plenteous; plenum; plein-air**, lit 'full'—hence 'open' —'air', short for *en plein air* and adopted from F; —**plethora, plethoric.**—Nn in *-plement* and *-pletion*, vv in *-plement* and *-plete*, with related adjj, etc.: **accomplish, accomplishment; complement** (whence **complemental, complementary**), **complete, completion**—cf the neg **incomplete** (whence, anl, **incompletion**) and the doublet **compliment** (n, v), whence, anl, **complimentary; compline; deplete, depletion**, whence, anl, **depletive; explement, expletive** (adj, hence n); **implement** (n, hence v), **implementiferous; replete, repletion; supplement** (n, hence v), whence, anl, **supplemental, supplementary** —**supply**, v hence n.

1. The L r is *plē-*, as in the simple *plēre*, to fill, genuine only in the cpds *complēre, deplēre, implēre*, etc., and in the adj *plēnus*, full. The IE r *\*plē-* occurs also in, e.g., Gr pim*plēmi*, I fill, *plē*tho, I am full, and, with *r* for *l*, in Ve *áprāt*, he has filled, Skt *prātás*, full; this IE r has the var *\*pēl-*, to fill—cf, with *f* for *p*, the Go *fulls*, full, therefore cf the sep FULL (where *fill*).

### Latin *plēnus*

2. L *plēnus*, full, has neu *plēnum*, used as n 'a space full of water'; whence E *plenum*. The c/f *plēni-* occurs esp in LL *plēnipotens*, fully potent, o/s *plēnipotent-*, whence E *plenipotent*; derivative ML *plēnipotentiārius* becomes EF-F *plénipotentiaire* and, perh independently, E *plenipotentiary*. Derivative *plēnitūdō*, fullness, becomes OF-MF *plenitude* (EF-F *plénitude*), adopted by E.

3. L *plēnus* has the LL extn *plēnārius*, whence *plenary*; whence also OF-MF *plenier* (F *plénier*), whence MF *pleniereté*, with contr *plenerté*, whence E *plenarty*, (the state of) a benefice fully occupied.

4. The OF-F adj *plein* (L *plēnus*) has derivative MF *plenir*, to fill, presp *plenissant*, whence 'to *plenish*'. The MF cpd *replenir*, to fill again, hence to re-stock, has presp *replenissant*, whence ME *replenissen*, E 'to *replenish*'.

5. L *plēnus* has the ML derivative *plēnitās*, the state of being full, with acc *plēnitātem*, whence OF-EF *plenté*, abundance, ME *plentee*, E *plenty*. Derivative OF-EF *plentious* becomes E *plenteous*.

### Greek *plēthein*

6. Gr *plēthein*, to be, to become, full, has derivative *plēthōrē*, whence LL *plēthōra*, fullness of habit (Souter), adopted by E; the derivative Gr adj *plēthōrikos* becomes LL *plēthōricus*, whence EF-F *pléthorique* and, independently, E *plethoric*.

Latin *plēre, to fill

7. L complēre, to fill up (com- is int), becomes
OF-MF complir, presp complissant, whence 'to
complish' or fulfil, superseded by accomplish, itself
from OF-MF acomplir, F accomplir (ac- for ad-,
used int), with presp acomplissant (cf ils acomplis-
sent, they fulfil), whence ME acomplissen, var
-isen, E 'to accomplish'; derivative MF acomplisse-
ment (F accom-) finally yields E accomplishment.

8. L complēre has pp complētus, whence—perh
via MF-F complet, f complète—the E adj complete
and the v 'to complete'; the LL neg adj incomplētus
yields incomplete. Derivative LL complētiō, o/s
complētiōn-, yields completion; and LL complētīuus,
ML -īvus, tending or helping to complete, gives us
completive.

9. Complēre has derivative complēmentum, an act
of filling up or filling out, LL a fulfilling, whence—
cf the MF-F complément, orig in the LL sense—
E complement. E complementary perh owes something to late EF-F complémentaire.

10. Complēre app has the VL var *complīre,
whence Sp complir (cumplir), to complete, to perform what is due, hence complir (cumplir) con
alguien, to be polite to someone, with derivative
complimiento (cum-), whence It complimento,
whence, in turn, EF-F compliment, adopted by E,
orig as 'a civility'; derivative EF-F complimenter
affords us 'to compliment'.

11. In LL, the pp complētus is used in complēta hōra, occ in pl complētae hōrae, a church
service completing the religious day, soon (LL)
elliptically complēta, whence OF-MF complie
(MF-F complies): ME complie: E complin, now
usu compline; with -in perh (EW) from the Eccl
matins.

12. L dēplēre, to empty, has pp dēplētus, whence
'to deplete'; derivative dēplētiō, o/s dēplētiōn-,
yields depletion.

13. L explēre, to empty (determined by ex, out
of), but also to fill completely (determined by the
int use of ex-), has derivative explēmentum, that
which fills up or completes, whence E explement.
On the pp explētus arises LL explētīuus, ML
explētīvus, supplementary, redundant, whence the
E adj expletive, whence the n, an expletive being
an unnecessary word.

14. L implēre, to fill up (im- vaguely int), to fulfil,
has derivative implēmentum, a filling up, whence E
implement, with additional senses; hence the
archaeological implementiferous, tool-bearing (cf
the element -fer).

15. L replēre, to fill again, to fill up, has pp
replētus, whence the MF-F replet, hence the E adj
replete; derivative LL replētiō, o/s replētiōn-, completion, fulfilment, becomes MF-F replétion,
whence E repletion, with additional sense 'over-
fullness'.

16. L supplēre, lit to fill from below (sup- for
sub), hence to fill up, hence to supply, has derivative supplēmentum, whence MF-F supplément and,
prob independently, E supplement, and LL deriva-

tives supplētīuus, ML -īvus, and supplētōrius,
whence suppletive (rare) and suppletory. Supplēre
becomes the badly formed MF souploier, later
souplier and supplier (badly formed), the last being
taken into ME and finally becoming E 'to supply'.

plenipotentiary. See prec, para 2.
plenish. See PLENARY, para 4.
plenitude. See PLENARY, para 2.
plenteous, plenty. See PLENARY, para 5.
plenum. See PLENARY, para 2.
pleonasm, pleonastic.

The adj derives from Gr pleonastikos, adj of
pleonasmos, whence, via LL pleonasmus, the EF-F
pléonasme and the E pleonasm; Gr pleonasmos=
pleon, neu of pleōn, greater, more+suffix -asmos
(E -asm). Cf PLURAL.

plethora, plethoric. See PLENARY, para 6.
pleura, pleurisy, pleuritic; cf the element pleuro-,
esp for cpds.

Gr pleuron, the side, mostly in pl pleura, the side,
esp the ribs, is o.o.o., but perh ult akin to Gr
platus, flat (cf PLANE). Adopted by Med, pleura
has the E adj pleural. Gr pleura has derivative
pleuritis, adopted by LL, whence MF pleurisie (F
pleurésie), whence E pleurisy; pleuritic comes, via
MF and LL, from the Gr adj pleuritikos.

plevin. See PLEDGE, para 2.
plex, plexure, plexus. See PLY, para 4.
pliable. See PLY (heading).
pliant. See PLY, para 4.
plicate, plicatile, plication, plicator. See PLY,
para 3.
pliers. See PLY (heading).
plight (1), condition or state, derives from AF
plit, a fold, a plait, hence a manner, a state or
condition (cf ME plet)—a var of OF pleit: f.a.e.,
PLY. The -gh- perh comes from:—
plight (2), a pledge, derives from ME pliht, an
engagement, earlier (a) danger, from OE pliht,
danger; 'to plight', from OE plihtan, to expose to
danger, from the n. Cf OFris plicht, OHG-MHG
pliht, care, obligation, G Pflicht, duty, OS plegan,
to pledge.
Plimsoll is elliptical for Plimsoll's mark (occ
line), the load-line safety mark on ships: from its
procurer (1876), Samuel Plimsoll, M.P.
plinth. See FLINT, para 3.
plod—whence agent plodder and pa, vn plod-
ding—is echoic: cf the syn D ploeteren.
plonk. See PLUNK.
plot, n (both senses) and v. See PLANE, para 23.
plough. See PLOW.
plover. See PLUVIAL, para 2.
plow (E and AE) or plough (E only), n hence v,
with such obvious derivatives and cpds as plower,
plowing, plowman, plowshare (cf G Pflugschar), E
forms usu plough-: ME plouh or plow: (late) OE
plōh, prob from ON plōgr (cf Sw plog): cf OHG
pfluog, MHG pfluoc, G Pflug, and MD ploech,
plouch, D ploeg: ? of Rhaetian origin. (Walshe.)
ploy. See PLY (heading).
pluck, n (whence PLUCKY) and v. See the 3rd
PEEL, para 7.

**plug,** n hence v, comes from MD *plugge* (D *plug*): cf MLG *pluck* (OHG *phloc*, G *Pflock*) and Sw *plugg*: ? ult echoic, from the noise of insertion.

**plum,** whence the adj **plummy,** comes from OE *plūme*: (with *l* for *r*) from LL *prūna,* f from L neu pl *prūna,* sing *prūnum*: Gr *prounon,* easement of earlier *proumnon* (tree *proumnos*), o.o.o.: ? from Asia Minor, perh Phrygian. (Hofmann.)

2. LL *prūna* becomes OF-F *prune,* adopted by E; the dim OF-F *prunelle* prob suggested the Bot *Prunella,* and certainly the transferred sense of *prunelle* led to E *prunella,* a woollen stuff app orig sloe-coloured.

**plumage.** See PLUME.

**plumate.** See PLUME, para 2.

**plumb** (n hence adj), a lead weight, derives from OF-F *plomb* (C12 varr *plon, plom, plun*): L *plumbūm*: prob of Iberian origin, lead having orig come from Spain. The derivative *plumbāgō* has been adopted by E; the L adj *plumbeus* becomes *plumbeous.* The n *plumb* has derivative 'to *plumb*', whence *plumber* and vn *plumbing.*

2. OF *plom* has dim OF *plommée,* MF var *plommet,* adopted by ME, whence the reshaped *plummet,* whence 'to *plummet*'.

3. L *plumbūm* has VL derivative \**plumbiāre,* with extn \**plumbicāre,* to plumb, whence OF-MF *plongier* (F *plonger*), whence ME *plongen,* later *plungen,* whence 'to *plunge*', whence 'a *plunge*' and *plunger* (cf MF-F *plongeur*).

4. Perh akin to L *plumbūm* is the syn Gr *molubdos,* whence *molubdaina,* a vein of silver mingled with lead, whence L *molybdaena,* whence SciL *molybdenum,* whence, in turn, *molybdenite* (Min suffix *-ite*). From Gr *molubdos,* Sci has coined the adjj *molybdic* and its syn *molybdous,* both meaning 'of or like molybdenum'.

Hofmann aptly cfs Basque *berun,* lead.

**plumbago.** See prec, para 1.

**plumbeous,** of or like lead (esp in colour). See **plumb,** para 1, s.f.

**plume,** n hence v (prob suggested by OF-F *plumer,* L *plūmāre*), orig to strip of feathers, derives from OF-F *plume,* L *plūma*: o.o.o.; perh cf Lith *plūnksna,* a feather (E & M). E *plumage* is adopted from MF-F *plumage,* itself from *plume* but perh suggested by LL *plūmācium,* a feather bed.

2. The L derivatives *plūmātus, plūmōsus, plūmula* have duly become E *plumate, plumose, plumule.*

3. Cf the sep FLEECE.

**plummet.** See PLUMB, para 2.

**plumose.** See PLUME, para 2.

**plump,** blunt (obs), well rounded, hence rather, but not very, fat: MD *plump,* var of *plomp* (*plomb*), blunt—cf MLG *plump,* 'orig, falling, heavy, clumsy, and of imitative origin' (Webster). The MD-MLG adjj prob derive from the corresp vv MLG-MD *plumpen,* MD *plompen,* clearly echoic: and from MD *plumpen* (*plompen*) E derives 'to *plump*', to fall, heavily or suddenly or clumsily, with several intimately derivative senses and the adv *plump.* Prob from the ideas conveyed by adj

and v alike, E derives the n *plump,* a cluster or group, e.g. of ducks.

**plumule.** See PLUME, para 2.

**plunder** (v, hence n): G *plündern,* to plunder, from late MHG *plundern,* to plunder, but orig to remove household goods, from MHG *plunder,* household goods (whence G *Plunder,* lumber, ? orig household goods relegated to an attic or a storehouse, hence rubbish): app introduced into England 'by men who had served in the 30 Years' War' (1618–1648). (Walshe).

**plunge, plunger.** See PLUMB, para 3.

**plunk,** occ **plonk:** echoic: the v, prob from the interjection.

**pluperfect.** See PERFECT, para 3.

**plural,** adj, hence n; **plurality,** whence, anl, **pluralism, pluralist, pluralize; plus.**

*Plural* derives, either direct or via OF *plurel* (EF-F *pluriel*), from L *plūrālis,* itself from *plūr-,* o/s of *plūs,* more, akin to Gr *pleon,* neu of *pleōn,* var of *pleiōn*: IE r, \**plē-.* (Cf PLEONASM.) Derivative LL *plūrālitās,* o/s *plūrālitāt-,* yields- MF-F *pluralité,* whence E *plurality.*

**plurivocal.** See VOCABLE, para 9.

**plush.** See the 3rd PEEL, para 6.

**Pluto,** God of the Underworld (Gr Myth), is adopted from L *Plūto*: from Gr *Ploutōn* (var *Plouteus*), with adj *Ploutōnios,* whence, via L *Plūtōnius,* the E *Plutonian* (var *Plutonic,* prob from F *plutonique*): perh, as Plato says, akin to Gr *Ploutos* (L *Plutus*), God of Wealth, from *ploutos,* wealth, itself akin to *polus,* much.

**plutocracy, plutocrat.** See the element *-cracy,* 2nd para.

**pluvial, Jupiter Pluvius; plover.**

1. *Pluvial* derives from ML *pluviālis,* L *pluuiālis,* adj of *pluuia,* rain, from *pluuius,* rainy—*Jupiter Pluvius* being Jupiter in his role of Rain God: and *pluuius* derives from *pluere,* to rain, s and r *plu-*: cf Skt *plavayati,* it overflows, and Gr *plunō,* I wash.

2. L *pluuia,* rain, has VL derivative \**pluuiārius,* \**pluviārius,* lit the rain bird (because flocks arrive with the rainy season), whence OF *plouvier, plovier* (EF-F *pluvier*), whence E *plover.*

**ply,** to fold, to bend, whence **pliable** and **pliers; plica, plicate, plicatile, plication, plicator, plicature; plex, plexal, plexure, plexus.**—Simple derivatives: **pliant** (whence **pliancy**); **plait, plat, pleat; pleach.**— Cpds of L *plicāre*: **applicable, applicant, application,** whence, anl, **applicative, applicator, applicatory, appliqué**—**apply,** whence **appliance; complicate** (whence **complicacy**), **complication,** whence **complicative; deploy,** whence **deployment**—**display,** v hence n, and **splay,** adj and v (whence n); **explicable** (**inexplicable**), **explicate, explication, explicative** (whence, anl, **explicatory**), **explicator**—**explicit**— **exploit,** n and v (whence **exploiter**), **exploitation; implicate** (adj and v), **implication** (whence, anl, **implicative**)—**implicit**—**imply**—cf **employ** (v, n), whence, by aphesis, the n **ploy** and, directly, **employee, employer, employment; replica**—**replicate** (adj and v), **replication,** whence, anl, **replicative**—

**reply**, v hence n; **suppliant** (adj, n), whence **suppliance**—**supplicant, supplicate, supplication, supplicator,** anl **supplicatory.**—Cpds of L *plexus*, pp and n, and of *-plex*: **simplex, simplicist, simplicity, simplify** (**simplification**), **simple** (adj, n); **complex** (adj, n), **complexion, complexity**—**complice, complicity**—**accomplice; duplex**—**duplicand, duplicate** (adj, hence n and v), **duplication** (whence, anl, **duplicative**), **duplicator**—**duplicity**—**double,** adj (hence n) and v, **doublet, doubloon; triplex, triplicate** (adj, hence n and v), **triplication**—**triplicity**—**triple** (adj, hence n and v), whence, after *doublet*, **triplet; quadruplex, quadruplicate, quadruplication, quadruple**—**quintuple** (whence **quintuplet**), hence, anl, **quintuplicate**—and so on; **multiple, multiplication, multiply; perplex** (adj, v), **perplexed, perplexity; supple** (adj, hence v) and **souple**—**supplejack.**—Cf the sep entries at FLAX and FLEX.

1. *Ply*, to fold or bend, ME *plien*, comes from OF-F *plier* (cf the doublet OF *ploier*, F *ployer*), from L *plicāre*, to fold; cf the intimately related L *plectere*, to intertwine, to weave, pp *plexus*, and Gr *plekein*, to plait, to weave: IE r, *\*plek-*, to intertwine, to plait.

2. *Ply* in the sense 'to use, wield, practise frequently or diligently', derives, by aphesis, from the cpd *apply* (oneself)—see para 8.

3. L *plicāre* has the ML derivative *plica*, a fold, adopted by Med and Bot. The pp *plicātus* yields both the pa and the v *plicate*, whence such anl forms as *plication* (prob after F), *plicative, plicator*: four words that partly set the pattern for the cpds. The cpds have, app, omitted to utilize the simple *plicatile*, from L *plicātilis*, and few have utilized the simple *plicature*, from L *plicātūra*.

4. L *plectere*, to intertwine, has, via the pp *plexus*, the derivative n *plexus*, a network, adopted by E, with adj *plexal*; hence 'to *plex*', to form one. Also from E *plexus* comes, anl, *plexure*.

### Simple Derivatives

5. L *plicāre* becomes OF *plier*, with presp *pliant*, whence the E adj; the irreg L pp *plicitus, plicitum*, used as n, becomes OF *pleit*, whence ME *pleyt, playt*, E *plait*, hence 'to *plait*', with var *plat*, of which *pleat* is a var, with sense promptly differentiated.

6. L *plectere* becomes VL *\*plectiāre*, whence OF *plessier*, with ONF var *plechier* (F *plécher*), whence ME *plechen*, E 'to *pleach*'.

### Compounds of L *plicāre*, to fold or bend

7. L *applicāre*, to bend oneself *ad* or towards, hence to address oneself to, has presp *applicans*, o/s *applicant-*, whence the E adj, hence n, *applicant*, and pp *applicātus*, whence the E adj *applicate*; derivative L *applicātiō*, o/s *applicātiōn-*, becomes MF-F, hence E, *application*. MF-F *appliquer* (from L *applicāre*) has derivative MF *appliquable*, EF-F *applicable*, adopted by E; pp *appliqué* is adopted by E as an adj.

8. L *applicāre* also becomes OF *aplier* (cf para 1), whence ME *aplien*, E 'to *apply*'.

9. L *complicāre*, to fold together, has presp *complicans*, o/s *complicant-*, whence the E adj *complicant*, and pp *complicātus*, whence the E adj and v *complicate*; derivative LL *complicātiō*, o/s *complication;* whence MF-F and E *complication*.

10. L *displicāre*, to unfold (*dis-*, apart), becomes OF *despleier*, whence ME *displaien*, E 'to *display*', whence, by aphesis, 'to *splay*', to display (obs), to open out, whence both the adj and the n *splay*.

11. OF *despleier* becomes F *déployer*, whence *déploiement*: hence the E 'to *deploy*' and *deployment*. (Cf para 1.)

12. L *explicāre*, to unfold, hence to explain, has derivative *explicābilis*, whence EF-F and E *explicable*; the L neg *inexplicābilis* becomes F and, perh independently, E *inexplicable*. The pp *explicātus* becomes the obsol adj and the v *explicate*; derivative *explicātiō*, o/s *explicātiōn-*, becomes MF-F and, prob independently, E *explication*—L *explicātīuus*, ML *-īvus*, E *explicative* (perh via EF-F *explicatif*)—L *explicātor*, adopted by E. The LL-ML *explicit* is short for *explicit(um est volumen)* and for *explicit(us est liber)*, 'the book has been completely unrolled'; then, at end of MS, as if vi, 'here endeth' (Souter). Cf the E adj *explicit*, which comes, through late MF-F *explicite*, from that same pp *explicitus*.

13. L *explicitum*, neu of *explicitus*, becomes OF *espleit*, var *esploit*, revenue, force, an achievement, adopted by ME, whence—as in F—the E *exploit*; OF *esploit* has OF-MF derivative *esploitier* (F *exploiter*), whence 'to *exploit*'. *Exploitable* and *exploitation* perh owe something to the id MF-F and F forms.

14. L *implicāre*, lit to fold in, hence to entangle, hence to involve, hence to engage (labour), has presp *implicans*, o/s *implicant-*, hence, in Logic, the E *implicant*, and pp *implicātus*, whence the E adj and v *implicate*; derivative *implicātiō*, o/s *implicātiōn-*, whence MF-F and, perh independently, E *implication*. The irreg or var pp *implicitus* becomes late MF-F *implicite* and, perh independently, E *implicit*.

15. L *implicāre* also becomes OF *emplier*, whence 'to *imply*' (cf the formation of *apply* and *reply*, cf also para 1), whence EF *emploier*, F *employer*, with that sense 'to engage (labour)' which occurs in ML; derivative EF-F *emploi* becomes the E n *employ*.

16. L *replicāre*, to fold back or again, hence to repeat, becomes It *replicare*, whence It *replica*, a reproduction, adopted by E; the L pp *replicātus* yields the E adj and v *replicate*; derivative *replicātiō*, o/s *replicātiōn-*, yields OF-MF *replication*, adopted by E. *Replicāre* becomes OF *repliier* (F *replier*), to bend back, whence, with L secondary sense restored, ME *replien*, E 'to *reply*'.

17. Rather from L *supplex*, bowed to one's knees (see para 28), than from *\*subplicāre*,—but conveniently treated here,—is L *supplicāre*, to kneel before (someone: in entreaty), with presp *supplicans*, o/s *supplicant-*; whence the E adj-hence-n

*supplicant*, whence *supplicancy*. The pp *supplicātus* yields 'to *supplicate*'; derivative *supplicātiō*, o/s *supplicātiōn-*, becomes OF-F, hence E, *supplication*, and agent *supplicātor* is adopted by E. *Supplicāre* becomes OF *souploier*, MF *souplier*, late MF-F *supplier*, presp *suppliant*, adopted by E as adj, hence n.

Compounds of L *plexus*, folded, and, as n, a folding, and of *-plex* (in adjj)

18. L *simplex* is for \**semplex*: *sem-*, as in L *semel*, once+*-plex*, -fold (as in *manifold*): 'of one fold', hence 'single', hence—via 'single-minded'—'simple'. *Simplex*, which is adopted by E for 'uncompounded', hence as n, becomes OF-F *simple*, adopted by E; C13–16 F *simple médecine* (opp *médecine composée*)—cf ML *simplex medicīna* —becomes, in C16, the n *simple*, a medicinal plant (B & W), adopted by E.

19. L *simplex* has o/s *simplic-*, as in derivative *simplicitās*, whence OF-F *simplicité*, adopted by E; hence the anl *simplicist*. Subsidiary LL *simplicitūdō* becomes E *simplicitude*. ML *simplificāre* (*-ficāre*, L *-ficere*, c/f of *facere*, to make) becomes late MF-F *simplifier*, whence 'to *simplify*'; derivative late MF-F *simplification* is adopted by E.

20. L *complecti*, to entwine around, to embrace, to comprise, has pp *complexus*, whence the late EF-F adj *complexe* and, independently, the E adj *complex*; the n *complex* derives from L n *complexus* (gen *-ūs*), an embrace, a connexion, a network. Derivative from the L pp is *complexiō*, o/s *complexiōn-*, combination or collection, ML temperament, which becomes OF *complexion*, adopted by E, esp in the ML sense; *complexity*, however, comes from the E adj—cf E *complexité* from *complexe*.

21. In LL, the L pp-become-adj *complexus* acquires the n *complex*, a partner or a colleague, hence, esp as pej, a confederate: hence MF-F *complice*, adopted by E, but now archaic; derivative late MF-F *complicité* becomes E *complicity*. *Accomplice* prob=*a complice*.

22. L *duplex*=*duo*, two+*-plex* ('two-fold') and is adopted by E, as adj, hence n; the mdfn *duplus* becomes E *duple*; derivative LL *duplātiō* yields *duplation*. Derivative *duplicāre*, to double, has gerund *duplicandum*, whence, from *duplicando* (by doubling), the E *duplicand*. The pp *duplicātus* gives us the adj, hence n and v, *duplicate*; derivative *duplicātiō*, o/s *duplicātiōn-*, yields F and E *duplication*, and the LL agent *duplicātor* is adopted by E. L *duplex* has LL derivative *duplicitās*, whence, via MF-F *duplicité*, the E *duplicity*. The LL *reduplicāre* leads to *reduplicate*, etc.

23. L *duplus* becomes OF *duble*, MF-F *double*, adopted by E as adj, whence the n; 'to *double*', ME *doublen*, derives from MF-F *doubler*, OF *dobler*, from LL *duplāre*, from *duplus*. F *double* has dim OF *doblet*, MF-F *doublet*, adopted by E; the orig OF sense was 'a stuff made of two materials'. L *duplus* becomes Sp *doble*, whence the Sp *doblón*, when EF-F *doublon*, whence E *doubloon*.

24. L *triplex*, three-fold (*tri-*, c/f of *tres*, neu *tria*, 3+*-plex*), is adopted by E (adj, hence n); derivative *triplicāre* has pp *triplicātus*, whence the E adj (hence n) and v *triplicate*, and subsidiary LL *triplicātiō* becomes *triplication*. The L mdfn *triplus* becomes MF-F, hence E, *triple*, whence, anl, *triplet*. LL *triplicitās* (from *triplex*) yields *triplicity*.

25. L *quadruplex*, four-fold, *quintuplex*, five-fold, and their derivatives—anl with those of *duplex* and *triplex*—yield *quadruple* (*-plex*), *quintuple*, and *quadruplicate*, *quintuplicate*, etc.

26. L *multiplex*, manifold, is adopted by E; the derivative MF-F *multiple* is also adopted. Derivative L *multiplicāre* becomes OF-F *multiplier*, whence 'to *multiply*', whence *multiplier*; derivative L *multiplicātiō* (o/s *-ātiōn-*), LL *multiplicātiuus* (ML *-īvus*), LL *multiplicātor*, LL *multiplicitās* (o/s *-itāt-*), yield MF-F, hence E, *multiplication*—E *multiplicative*—E *multiplicator*—OF-F *multiplicité*, whence E *multiplicity*.

27. L *perplexus*, lit thoroughly (*per*) intertwined (*plexus*), hence involved, confused, becomes MF *perplex* (EF-F *perplexe*), adopted by E, whence, anl, the pa *perplexed*, whence the E 'to *perplex*'; derivative LL *perplexitās* (o/s *-itāt-*) becomes MF-F *perplexité*, whence E *perplexity*.

28. The L adj *supplex*, bending *sub* or low, hence kneeling, becomes OF *supple*, *sople*, MF-F *souple*, adopted by ME, but now mostly Sc; hence 'to *souple*'. The E adj *supple* comes from ME *souple*; hence 'to *supple*'. The *supplejack* is a pliant-stemmed vine, whence canes, etc., are made; *jack* is the instrumental form of *Jack* used for devices, machines, etc.

**pneuma, pneumatic, pneumonia; neume.**

*Pneumatic*, like EF-F *pneumatique*, derives from L *pneumaticus*, trln of Gr *pneumatikos*, adj of *pneuma*, air, wind, breath, from *pnein*, to blow: echoic (cf ANIMAL). Adopted by erudite E, *pneuma* has the ML derivative *neuma*, a group of notes sung while one breath lasts, whence late MF-F *neume*, adopted by E. Cognate Gr *pneumōn*, pl *pneumones*, the lungs, has derivative *pneumonia*, adopted by SciL, hence by E; the adj *pneumonic* derives from Gr *pneumonikos*.

**poach** (eggs). See POCK, para 5.

**poach** (2), to thrust, to trespass, whence **poacher** and **poaching**; **pochard**; **poke** (v), whence **poker** (utensil and prob the game).

1. 'To *poach*', earlier *poche*, derives from MF *pocher*, to thrust, hence to encroach upon, from MLG *poken*, to poke; prob akin to MD *pochen*, *puchen*, to boast, talk big, bluff. Derivative F *pochard*—perh from the F source of 1st POACH— is adopted by E for a species of European duck.

2. MLG *poken* (cf G *pochen*, to knock or beat, to boast) becomes ME *poken*, whence 'to *poke*' or thrust, prod. With the game *poker*, essentially an exercise in bluffing (whence *poker-faced*), cf G *Pochspiel*, lit 'boast game', D *pochspel*.

**pochard.** See para 1 of prec.

**pochette.** See para 2 of:

**pock** (n, hence v) and **pox** (n, hence v), **smallpox**;

pocket (n, hence v) and pochette; poke, a sack or bag; poach (eggs); pouch, n hence v; puck and pug, elf, and pooka; pucker, v hence n.

1. *Pock*, a pustule—pl *pocks*, soon *pox*, syphilis —comes, through ME *pokke*, from OE *pocc*, var *poc*: cf MD and MLG *pocke* (G *Pocke*), 'prob connected with LG *pogge* "frog" and OE *pohha* "pocket". Orig. meaning "to swell" ' (Walshe). E *smallpox*=a disease characterized by *small pocks* or pustules.

2. *Pocket*, ME *poket*, derives from AF *pokete*, dim of ONF *poke*, *poque*, bag, pouch; *pochette*, adopted from F, is OF *pochette*, dim of OF-F *poche*, pocket, from Frankish *\*pokka*.

3. OF *poche* has N var *poque*, *poke*, whence ME-E *poke*: cf MD *poke* and OE *pocca*, mdfn of OE *pocc* (as in para 1).

4. OF *poche* has the further var *pouche*, adopted by ME, whence E *pouch*.

5. Early in MF, OF-F *poche* has derivative *pocher*, esp in *pocher les yeux*, prob 'to make them swell like pouches', whence, app, late MF-F *pocher les oeufs*, to cook eggs so that the white envelops the yolk, as in a bag (B & W): whence E 'to *poach* eggs'.

6. Akin to OE *pocca* (var *pohha*), a bag, is OE *puca*, ME *pouke*, E *pook* and *puck*, a hobgoblin, often as *Puck*—cf Kipling's book-title *Puck of Pook's Hill* (1906). With *pook*, cf *pooka*, an Ir goblin, from Ir *puca*: cf EIr *boccánach*, Ga *bòcan*, a goblin, and Cor *bucca*, a ghost.

7. E *puck*, hobgoblin, has var—? orig dial—*pug*, an elf, a loved one (both senses obs), hence a small, alert quadruped (mostly dial), esp a small, compact dog.

8. E *poke*, a bag, has EE-E derivative freq *pucker*, to crinkle as a bag does: cf F *faire des poches*, to pucker (OED).

pocket. See prec, para 2.

pocky. Adj of POCK (para 1).

pococurante, indifferent, hence an indifferentist: It *poco curante*, little-caring: *poco* from L *paucus*, little, *pauci*, few+*curante*, from It-from-L *curare*, to care about: f.a.e., CURE.

pod (n, hence v) of plant. EE *pood*: o.o.o.

podagra. See FOOT, para 23, and the 1st PELT, para 3, s.f.

podgy. See PUDDING, para 3.

podium. See FOOT, para 21.

podo-words. See the element.

poem, poesy (and posy), poet (and poet laureate), poetaster, poetic (often in extn poetical), poetics, poetize, poetry; poiesis, poietic.

1. Behind this group stands the Gr *poiein*, to make or construct: r *poi*-: IE r, *\*quei*- (Hofmann), var *\*quoi*- (Boisacq), to construct, to make—cf Skt *cáyati*, he constructs or arranges, var *cinóti*, cf OB *činiti*, to arrange, and Skt *cītís*, arrangement, collection.

2. Gr *poiein* has agent *poiētēs*, var *poētēs*, whence L *poëta*, OF-F *poète*, ME *poete*, E *poet*—cf sem, the mainly Sc *maker*, a poet. What he makes is particularly a *poem*, MF-F *poème*, L *poēma*, Gr

*poēma*, var of *poiēma*; generally, either *poesy*, EF-F *poésie*, L *poēsis*, Gr *poēsis*, var of *poiēsis*, or *poetry*, ME *poetrie*, ML *poëtria*—app a blend (? a confusion) of LL *poētīa*, poetry+L *poetria* (Gr *poiētria*), a poetess. The adj *poetic* derives from late MF-F *poétique*, L *poēticus*, Gr *poiētikos*; *poetics* app derives from Aristotle's treatise; EE-E *poetaster* prob comes from Erasmus (1521: OED): cf, sem, *criticaster*. *Poetize* derives from late MF-F *poétiser*, an erudite formation.

3. Gr *poiēsis* is occ used (*poiesis*) in erudite E for creative power or the creative act, with the corresp adj *poietic* (Gr *poiētikos*).

pogrom comes from the Ru for 'devastation', itself from *gromit'*, to batter.

poiesis, poietic. See POEM, para 3.

poignancy, poignant. See PUNGENT, para 10.

Poilu. See the 3rd PEEL, para 1, s.f.

poind. See POUND, v.

point (n, v), pointel, pointer, pointillism, pointless; point-blank and point-device. See PUNGENT, para 8.

poise. See PEND, para 8.

poison (n, v), poisoner, poisonous. See POTABLE, para 3.

poke (1), pocket, pouch, sack. See POCK, para 3.

poke (2), to thrust or prod; hence n. See the 2nd POACH, para 2.

poker: utensil from prec; game, perh from prec (2nd POACH, para 2).

Polack, a Pole, occurs in Shakespeare's *Hamlet* (I. i. 63)—hence, in part, the coll AE use; mostly from G *Polack*, pej of *Pole*, a Pole; the correct word for a native of *Poland* is Pole, and the adj for both is *Polish*. *Poland*, app influenced by E *land* (contrast, e.g., the G *Polen* and the F *Pologne*), prob derives from MHG *Polān*, a Pole, pl *Polāne*, from Pol *Poljane*, lit field-dwellers, from Pol *pole*, a field (OED): ? cf Ru *polesee*, forest land.

2. The F adj *polonais*, Polish, is, in the f *polonaise*, used elliptically for *danse polonaise*, a Polish dance; Sw, hence E, *polska*, a Swedish dance, is lit 'a Polish dance', from Sw *polsk*, Polish; and ML *Polonia*, Poland, has Chem derivative *polonium* (Chem suffix -*ium*).

3. But *polka*, often stated to come ult from Pol *Polka*, a Polish woman, in fact comes, via F and perh G, from Cz *pŭlka*, a half-step, from Cz *pŭl*, a half. (Walshe.)

polar, polarity, polarize. See the 2nd POLE.

Pole. See POLACK, para 1.

pole (1), a stake. See PACT, para 11.

pole (2), either extremity of an axis or of a sphere, whence the North and South Pole; polar, whence polarity; polarize (whence polarization); cf such cpds as polarimeter and polariscope—see the element *polari*-;—pulley.—Ult akin to sep WHEEL.

1. E, from ME, *pole* derives from MF-F *pôle*: L *polus*: Gr *polos*, a pivot, hence an axis, hence a Geog pole, s and r *pol*-: cf Gr *pelō*, I turn (vi), am in motion, IE etymon *\*quelō*, I am in motion, I stir or move (Hofmann): f.a.e., WHEEL.

2. MF-F *pôle* has EF-F adj *polaire*, whence—
unless from ML *polāris*—the E *polar*. EF-F *polaire*
has derivative *polariser*, whence *polarisation*;
whence 'to *polarize*' and perh *polarization*.

3. Gr *polos* app has LGr derivative *\*polidion*,
whence OF-MF *polie* (F *poulie*), ME *poley*, later
*puly*, E *pulley*.

**poleax** (AE), **poleaxe**. See PACT, para 11.

**polecat**: ME *polcat*, lit 'poultry cat' (from its
fondness for poultry): by f/e from MF *pole* (var of
MF-F *poule*), a hen, a fowl: L *pulla*, f of *pullus*, a
chicken, orig the young of any animal: s *pul-*, perh
extn of that IE *\*pu-* which occurs in L *puer*, a boy,
orig a child: 'a grow-er'; basic sense prob 'to
grow'.

2. MF-F *poule* has MF-F dim *poulet*, var *polete*,
adopted by ME: whence E *pullet*. MF *poulet*,
adopted by ME, becomes *pulte*, whence E *poult*,
a young turkey; ME *pulte* has—from MF *pouletier*
—the agent *pulter*, E *poulter*, now only in the
*Poulters'* Company, the ordinary word being now
its derivative *poulterer*; OF-F *poulet*, moreover, has
derivative *pouleterie* (perh suggested by *pouletier*),
whence ME *pultrie*, E *poultry*.

3. Cf PULLULANT.

**polemic** (adj, hence n), esp in pl **polemics**; with E
extn **polemical**; hence **polemicist** (*-ist*).
*Polemic*, of, in, for, by a verbal attack, derives—
like F *polémique*—from Gr *polemikos*, of, by, for
war, the adj of *polemos*, war, s *polem-*: cf Gr
*pelemizō*, I sct in motion, s *pelem-*, prob an extn of
IE r *\*pel-*, to shake: cf the 2nd PULSE, para 1.

**polenta**. See POLLEN, para 1.

**police** (n, hence v), whence **policeman**; **policy**
(science, or the tactics, of government); **polity**,
**politic** (with extn **political**, now sense-differentiated), whence **politician** (cf *technician* from *technic*),
**politics**.—**polis**, esp in **Acropolis**—**cosmopolis**,
**cosmopolitan** (adj, hence n), **cosmopolite** (whence
**cosmopolitism**)—**metropolis**, **metropolitan** (adj,
hence n), **metropolite**; cf the element *-pole*.

1. Clearly the base rests firmly in Gr *polis*, a
city, hence a state: s and r, *pol-*: cf Lith *pilìs*, a
citadel, a castle, and—*r* for *l*—Skt *pùr*, *pùram*,
*puris*, a castle, a fortress, a town, a city.

2. Gr *polis*, city, has agent *politēs*, a citizen, with
adj *politikos*, of a citizen, of the citizens, of the
state: L *politicus*: MF-F *politique*: E *politic*, whence
the n *politics*, perh suggested by Gr *hē politikē*
(sc *epistēmē*), the political knowledge, hence the art
and science of government.

3. Gr *politēs* (s *polit-*), a citizen, has derivative
abstract n *politeia*, whence LL *politia*, citizenship,
government, administration, which has, in MF,
two offshoots: *policie*, political organization—
whence E *policy*—soon with var *police*, still in
same sense, the modern one arising in Fénelon's
*L'Education des Filles*, 1687, and borrowed, c1730
(OED), by E: perh prompted by LGr *politeia*,
police regulations; the 2nd being late MF (and
J. J. Rousseau) *politie*, E *polity*, form of government, constitution of a state.

## Compounds

4. The *Acropolis* of Athens particularizes,
already in Gr, the common n *akropolis*, a citadel:
*akros*, at the crest or highest point+*polis*, city.

5. A *metropolis* is lit '(the) mother-city' whence
spring the colonies: via LL from Gr *mētropolis*,
*mētro-* being a c/f of *mētēr*, mother (see MOTHER).
The F form *métropole* becomes E *metropole*, now
rare. LL *mētropolis* has LL adj *mētropolitānus*, of a
metropolis, whence, as n, a metropolitan bishop:
whence, resp, the E adj and the E n, the former
perh imm from late MF-F *métropolitain*. The LL
derivative *mētropolita*, citizen of a metropolis,
becomes E *metropolite*.

6. A *cosmopolis* is lit a world (*cosmos*, Gr
*kosmos*) city, but the sense does not exist in Gr;
the E sense is a b/f from Gr *kosmopolitēs*, a citizen
of the world, whence EF-F *cosmopolite*, adopted
by E, which coins—after *metropolitan*—the adj
*cosmopolitan*.

**policy** (1), science of government. See prec,
para 3.

**policy** (2), an insurance certificate. See TEACH,
para 3.

**polio** is a shortening, orig coll, of **poliomyelitis**.
See the element *polio-*.

**polis**. See POLICE, para 1.

**Polish**. See POLACK, para 1.

**polish** (v, hence n), whence **polisher**; **polite**
(whence **politeness**), **politesse**; **impolite**, whence
**impoliteness**.

1. 'To *polish*', ME *polischen*, *polishen*, derives
from the present-tense-pl and presp s *poliss-* of
OF-F *polir*, from L *polīre*, perh from an IE *\*peld-*,
extn of *\*pel-*, to strike, hence to polish by striking.
(E & M.)

2. L *polīre* has pp *poīltus*, whence E *polite*.
*Politesse*, borrowed from EF-F *politesse*, a reshaping, after the L pp, of OF-F *poli*, adj from pp.

3. L *polītus*, used as adj, has neg *impolītus*,
whence E *impolite* (contrast F *impoli*).

**polite**. See prec, para 2.

**politic** (**political**). See POLICE, para 2.

**politician**. See POLICE (heading).

**politics**. See POLICE, para 2, s.f.

**polity**. See POLICE, para 3, s.f.

**polka**. See POLACK, para 3.

**poll** (1), the head, esp the top and back; hence
'to **poll**'; **pollard** (adj, hence n, hence v); **tadpole**.

1. *Poll*, head, comes, through ME *pol* or *polle*,
from MD *polle*, poll, app a mdfn of MD *pol*, top,
crest: cf (*b* for *p*) the L *bul*la, a bubble: f.a.e.,
BULB.

2. 'To *poll*,' remove the hair, horns, top branches,
etc., has pp *polled*, whence, with substitution of
suffix *-ard*, the EE-E adj *pollard*, anl with other
adjj (and nn) in *-ard*.

3. *Poll* has the cpd *tadpole*: ME *tade* or *tadde*,
a toad (see TOAD)+*pol*, head: the young toad and
the young frog have very large heads.

**poll** (2), as in the University of Cambridge's *poll*

*degree,* a degree without honours: from Gr 'hoi *polloi*', the many, the multitude, the rabble.

**pollack,** occ **pollock,** prob comes from the syn Ga *pollag*; perh akin to POOL, a pond.

**pollard.** See the 1st POLL, para 2.

**pollen, pollinate** (whence **pollination**), **pollinium**— and **polenta**; **powder** (n, v), whence the adj **powdery**; **pulse** (edible seeds) and **poultice** (n, hence v), **pulvereous** and syn **pulverulent,** whence **pulverulence** —**pulverize,** whence **pulverization, pulverizer, pulverizing**—**pulvis et umbra.**

1. *Pollen* is L *pollen,* a fine meal obtained from cereal grains, hence a very fine powder. From its o/s *pollin-* is formed the ML *pollināta,* whence, unless merely anl, 'to *pollinate*' and SciL *pollinium.* An app irreg derivative of *pollen* is L *polenta,* a fine barley meal, adopted by It with new sense 'a thick porridge' and, in that guise, known in Britain.

2. Akin to L *pollen* is L *puls* (o/s *pult-*), a meal porridge: whence OF-MF *pols, pouls,* a collective pl: whence ME *pols, puls*: E *pulse.* L *puls* has pl *pultes,* with ML sense 'pap': whence E *pultes,* E *poultice.*

3. Also akin to L *pollen* is L *puluis,* ML *pulvis* (o/s *pulver-*), dust (esp of arena or battlefield), as in the Classical tag, *pulvis et umbra,* dust and shadow. Derivative adjj *puluereus, puluerulentus* yield *pulvereous, pulverulent,* dusty, tending to crumble to dust; derivative LL *puluerizāre,* ML *pulverizāre,* becomes MF-F *pulvériser,* whence 'to *pulverize*'.

4. L *puluis* has acc *puluerem,* ML *pulverem,* whence OF *puldre, pouldre, poldre,* whence MF-F *poudre,* adopted by ME, whence E *powder*; 'to *powder*' comes from MF-F *poudrer,* earlier *pouldrer.*

5. With L *puls,* occ *pultis,* cf the syn Gr *poltós,* s *polt-.* The L r, therefore, wavers between *pol-* and *pul-*; the Gr r wavers between *pol-* (*polt-* is an extn) and the app more basic *pal-*, as in *palē,* fine meal, dust; cf Skt *pálalam,* ground seeds (of the sesame plant). The IE r is prob *pel-*, dust.

**pollock.** See POLLACK.

**pollute, pollution.**

The n comes—prob via OF-F *pollution*—from *pollūtiōn-,* o/s of LL *pollūtiō,* from *pollūt-,* s of *pollūtus,* pp of *polluere,* to render thoroughly filthy, to defile: app for *por-* (sometimes for *per-*, throughout, as here, sometimes for *pro-*, forward) +*luere,* to make dirty, perh a var of L *lutāre,* to plaster with mud, from L *lutum,* mud, akin to Gr *lumē,* a soiling, Homeric Gr *luthron,* blood mingled with dust, and Cor *lued,* Ir *loth,* EIr (and Ga) *làthach,* mud.—From L *lutum,* mud, clay, derives E *lute,* a clay cement.

**polo:** Balti (Indus Valley dial) *polo,* the ball used in the game, hence the game: cf Tibetan *pulu,* polo, and—? a loanword—*bolo,* a ball.

**polonaise.** See POLACK, para 2.

**polonium.** See POLACK, para 2, s.f.

**polony.** Cf BOLONEY.

**polska.** See POLACK, para 2.

**poltergeist,** a G word, is lit a 'noisy ghost':

*Polter,* noise, from *poltern,* to make a great noise, ult echoic+*Geist,* spirit (f.a.e., GHOST).

**poltroon, poltroonery:** EF-F *poltron* and its EF-F derivative *poltronnerie*: It *poltrone,* a colt, hence a coward (colts being easily alarmed), from *poltro,* a colt, ult from L *pullus,* a young animal (B & W): cf E *pullet,* q.v. at POLECAT.

**poly,** a herb: L *polium*: G *polion,* app the neu of *polios,* grey: cf FALLOW.

**polyandry** (adj *-androus*). See the element *andro-.*

**polyanthus.** Cf the element *anth-,* but see ANTHOLOGY, para 3.

**polychrome,** many-hued: via F, from Gr *polukhrōmos.* Cf CHROMATIC.

**polygamist, polygamous, polygamy.** See MONOGAMIST, para 2, and cf the element *poly-.*

**polyglot.** See the element *poly-,* and see GLOSS (comment).

**polygon:** LL *polygonum,* n, from Gr *polugonos,* many-angled: cf the element *-gon.*

**polymath.** See MATHEMATIC, para 1.

**Polynesia,** whence **Polynesian** (adj, hence n). See the element *poly-.*

**polyp, polypus.** See the element *poly-*; cf FOOT.

**polyphonic, polyphony:** Gr *poluphōnos,* many-sounded, and *poluphōnia.* Cf the element *poly-* and PHONE.

**polysemia, polysemant.** See elements *poly-* and *sema-* (para 2).

**polysyllabic, polysyllable.** See SYLLABLE, para 3.

**polytechnic.** See the element *poly-* and TECHNIC.

**pomade, pomander.** See FAT, paras 4, 5.

**pomato** blends potato and to*mato.*

**pomatum.** See FAT, para 7.

**pome, pomegranate.** See FAT, para 8; cf GRAIN, para 5.

**pomeranian**=*Pomeranian dog. Pomerania,* a Baltic province of Prussia, app comes, like G *Pommern,* from Pol *Pomorze,* '(Land) by the Sea'. (Enci It.)

**Pomfret cake.** See PONS, para 5.

**pommel.** See FAT, para 6.

**Pommy,** Aus sl for a newcomer from Great Britain, esp England: *pome*granate, ref his or her rosy cheeks.

**pomp, pomposity, pompous; pompon** and **pompadour.**

1. *Pomp,* ME *pompe,* derives, via MF-F, from L *pompa,* trln of Gr *pompē,* lit a sending, hence a procession, esp if sumptuous and solemn, hence organized magnificence, from *pempein,* to send: Gr r, *pemp-*: o.o.o.

2. L *pompa* has LL adj *pompōsus,* whence, via MF-F *pompeux,* f *pompeuse,* the E *pompous*; derivative LL-ML *pompōsitās,* o/s *pompōsitāt-,* yields *pomposity.*

3. Influenced by, yet prob not from, late MF-EF *pomper,* to dress oneself magnificently, is F *pompom,* an ornamental ball for women's robes: rather is it an arbitrarily picturesque redup.

4. But *Pompadour,* a style of dress, a style of headdress, derives from the Marquise de *Pompadour* (1721–64) Louis XV's mistress, whose name

derives from a locality in Corrèze, a department of
S Central France, perh from L *pompa*, though prob
of C origin.

**pompion.** See MELON, para 6.

**pompon.** See POMP, para 2.

**pomposity, pompous.** See POMP, para 2.

**poncho,** adopted from Sp, is Araucan (S Am)
*poncho*, perh better written *pontho*.

**pond** is a doublet of **pound** (an enclosure), for it
was orig an enclosed body of water.

**ponder, ponderable, ponderous.** See PEND, para 2.

**pone** (1), n, is, in AE, short for **corn pone**, corn
bread; *pone* is of Alg origin—cf Virginian *äpán*,
something baked, esp bread, from *äpen*, she bakes
(Mathews).

**pone** (2), v; **ponent.** See POSE, para 2.

**poney.** See FOAL, para 3.

**pongee:** Pekinese *pen-chi*, home-woven, home
loom.

**poniard.** See PUNGENT, para 14.

**pons** (pons asinorum); **pont, pontage, pontifex,
pontiff, pontifical, pontifical pontificate, pont-levis,
ponton, pontoon; Pontefract, Pomfret** (**Pomfret
cake**); **punt** (n, hence v) (whence **punter**), **punty** and
**pontil; Transpontine.**

1. L *pons*, a bridge, retained by An and Zoo, and
aspic'd in the outmoded Geom *pons asinorum* or
'asses' bridge', has o/s *pont-*, so clearly present in
all the E words coming straight from L: o.o.o.:
perh cf Gr *pontos*, sea—regarded as a means of
crossing from land to land (E & M; Hofmann);
Skt *pánthas*, like OSl *poti* and OPr *pintis*, means a
path. If the word *pons* be basically Italic, it could
represent the nom *-s* attached to *pon-*, the s—and
extn r—of *ponere*, to place.

2. *Pont*, a ferry (S Afr), comes imm from D
*pont* (MD *pont, ponte*), a ferryboat, from the
L o/s *pont-*.

3. L *pons* has the foll derivatives relevant to E:
*pontō*, a ferry, a pontoon, o/s *pontōn-*, whence
OF-F *ponton*, whence E *pontoon* and the occ AE
syn *ponton*; L *pontō*, s *pont-*, in Caesar's *Gallic
Wars* a punt, also becomes OE-E *punt*;

LL *pontīlis*, of or like a bridge, yields the rare
adj *pontile*; the derivative LL n *pontīle*, a bridge-
like structure, becomes F *pontil*, occ used in E
but much less common than its derivative *punty*
(in glass-making);

cf the bridge-toll *pontage*, adopted from late
MF-EF *pontage* (F *pont+-age*).

4. L *pons* has the important cpd *pontifex* (gen
*pontificis*), *bridge-builder, a priest important in
Roman religion and so named because, anciently,
Rome was essentially 'the City of the Bridge'
(E & M), hence, in LL, a bishop (later, the Pope).
L *pontifex*, acc *pontificem*, becomes late MF-F
*pontife*, whence E *pontiff*. The L adj *pontificius*
yields E *pontificial* (*-al* for *-ous*), of a pontifex or
a Pope; the L adj *pontificālis* yields late MF-F
*pontifical*, adopted by E, now usu in the sense
'oracular' or 'dogmatically authoritative'. The
derivative L n *pontificātus* (gen *-ūs*) passes through
late MF-F *pontificat* into E *pontificate*. The E v

'to *pontificate*' takes its form from the n *pontificate*
and its sense from *pontifical* (oracular, etc.)—cf the
F *pontifier* (from *pontife*).

5. L *pons* occurs in the E PlN *Pontefract*, from
ML *Pontefractus*, 'Broken Bridge'—whence AF
*Pontfreit*, whence the pron *pumfrit* and the spelling
*Pomfret*, whence the *Pomfret cake* orig made in
this Yorkshire town.

6. OF-F *pont*, a bridge, has the cpd OF *pons
leveïs*, MF-F *pont-levis*, a drawbridge, adopted by
E, now usu a term in formal horsemanship.

7. From *pont*, F learnedly coins *transpontin*,
whence E *transpontine*, situated on or belonging
across (L *trans*) the bridge, applied esp to melodrama formerly popular in S London.

**pont.** See prec, para 2.

**pontage.** See PONS, para 3, s.f.

**pontifex; pontiff.** See PONS, para 4.

**pontifical, pontificate** (n and v), **pontificial.** See
PONS, para 4.

**pontil.** See PONS, para 3.

**pont-levis.** See PONS, para 6.

**ponton.** See PONS, para 3.

**pontoon.** See PONS, para 3.

**pony,** occ **poney.** See FOAL, para 3.

**poodle:** G *Pudel*, 'said to be for *Pudelhund*'
(Walshe), i.e. 'puddle-hound', from LG *pudeln*, to
splash about in water.

**pook, pooka.** See POCK, para 6.

**pool** (1), a pond, a small lake: OE *pōl*: cf OFris
*pōl*, MD *puel, poil*, a pool, a morass, D *poel*, a pool,
LG *pool*, OHG-MHG *pfuol*, G *Pfuhl*; cf Ga *poll*,
Cor *pol, pul*; perh (Walshe) cf Lith *balà*, OB *blato*,
a swamp.

**pool** (2), a stake—now usu an aggregated stake
—deposited by each player in certain games, hence
a type of billiards: EF *poule*, a player's stake in
card games, later in others too, from OF-F *poule*,
a hen (layer of an egg a day). Hence 'to *pool*'.

**poop** (1), n, hence v: MF *pope* (late MF-F
*poupe*): OProv, rather than It and Sp, *poppa*: L
*puppis*: o.o.o.: perh an Italic confusion of Eg *pehui*,
the stern of a boat, and Eg *tepi*, the hindmost part
of a boat's stern.

**poop** (2), v (hence n), to toot, gulp, break wind:
ME *poupen, popen*: all echoic—cf MD *puppen*, to
bubble.

**poor,** whence adv, whence adj, **poorly; poverish**
(whence **poverishment**), **poverty—impoverish**
(whence **impoverishment**); **pauper** (n, hence adj),
whence **pauperize,** whence **pauperization.**

1. *Poor*, ME *pore*, earlier *poure*, is adopted from
MF *poure*, a var of OF-MF *povre* (EF-F *pauvre*),
from L *pauper*; derivative L *paupertās* becomes OF
*poverté* (EF-F *pauvreté*), whence ME *poverte*
(trisyllabic), whence *poverty*; OF *pouverir* (cf VL
*pauperāre*) has var *poverir*, presp *poverissant*,
whence E 'to *poverish*', now mostly dial. 'To *impoverish*' derives, anl, from MF *empovrir* (*em-* for
*en-*, from L *in-* used int).

2. *Pauper*, n, derives from L *pauper*, poor (orig
of soil): s *paup-*, extn of the r *pau-* that occurs in
*paucus*, pl *pauci*, few, and *paullus*, little.

pop (1), n. See FATHER, para 16.

pop (2), v hence n: echoic: cf the 2nd POOP. Freq: *popple*.

pope, popery. See FATHER, para 17.

popinjay: ME *popingay*, earlier *papejay*; influenced by E JAY in its transit from OF *papegai*: OProv *papagai*: Sp *papagayo*: Ar *babaghā*.

poplar: ME *popler*: OF *poplier* (MF-F *peuplier*): agential extn of OF *pople* (var *peuple*): L *populus*, a poplar: ? cf Gr *ptelea*, an elm.

poplin: EF *papeline*: perh from It *papalina*, n from f of *papalino*, of the *Papa* or Pope, because made at papal Avignon.

poppa. See FATHER, para 16.

poppet. A var of *puppet*, q.v. at PUP, para 4.

popple. See the 2nd POP.

poppy, whence pa poppied; Papaver, whence the adjj papaverine, papaverous (cf ML *papāvereus*, L *papāuereus*).

*Poppy* is OE *popig*, *popaeg*, ult from L *papāuer*, ML *-āver*: o.o.o.: perh Medit—? cf Eg *peqer*, poppy-seed.

populace, popular, popularity, popularize; populate, population; populous. See PEOPLE, para 3.

porbeagle. See PORK, para 3.

porcelain. See PORK, para 4.

porch. See the 2nd PORT, para 2.

porcine. See PORK, para 1.

porcupine. See PORK, para 6.

pore (1), n; porosity, porous.

1. *Pore*, minute orifice, is adopted from MF-F *pore*: L *porus*: Gr *poros*, orig a passage: f.a.e., FARE.

2. MF-F *pore* has derivative MF-F adj *poreux*, f *poreuse*, whence E *porous*; subsidiary MF-F *porosité* becomes E *porosity*.

pore (2), v, to gaze intently: ME *pouren*, *puren*: o.o.o.: ? from MF *purer*, from *pūrāre*, to cleanse, to pass through a sieve, hence to examine, from *pūrus*, clean, pure.

porgy, a food fish, app derives from the fish *pargo*, adopted from Sp and Port: L *pagrus*, mdfn of *phagrus*, trln of Gr *phagros* (o.o.o.). *Porgy* is mainly AE, *pargo* mainly E.

pork, whence porker, porky, and, because of its grunt, porkfish; porcine;—porbeagle; porcelain and purslane; porcupine and porpentine; porpoise.—Cf the sep FARROW.

1. L *porcus*, a pig male or female, is akin to OE *fearh* (see FARROW) and to several Sl words, e.g. Lith *paršas*. The L adj *porcīnus* becomes MF-F *porcin*, whence E *porcine*.

2. L *porcus* becomes OF-F *porc*, whence ME *porc*, E *pork*, with sense 'pig's flesh' deriving from F.

3. E *porbeagle*, a viviparous shark, perh comes, f/e, from F *porc*, a hog+E *beagle*.

4. *Porcelain* derives from EF-F *porcelaine*, MF *pourcelaine*: It *porcellana*, orig 'the porcelain'—or 'the Venus'—'shell': It *porcello*, L *porcellus*, dim of *porcus*: 'the shell has the shape of a pig's back, and a surface like porcelain' (Webster); B & W, however, derive It *porcellana* from L *porcella*, a

young sow, f of *porcellus*, and explain the semantics thus: 'so called from the resemblance of the shell's opening to a sow's vulva'.

5. L *porcus* has influenced L *portulāca* (o.o.o.), the plant purslane, into the form *porcilāca*, whence the irreg MF *pourcelaine*, *porcelaine*, whence E *purslane*.

6. *Porcupine*, ME *porkepyn*, derives from MF, from OProv, *porc-espin*, from It *porcospino*, lit 'spiny pig' (cf SPINE); *porpentine* is an EE, esp a Shakespearean, var.

7. *Porpoise* comes, via ME *porpoys*, var *porpeys*, from MF *porpois*, var of *porpeis*; a contr of L *porcus pisces*, lit a pig fish, a hog fish.

pornocracy. See PAIR, para 2.

pornographer, pornographic, pornography. See PAIR, para 2.

porosity, porous. See PORE, para 2.

porphyrogenite, porphyrite, porphyry. See PURPLE, para 3, and cf the element *porphyro-*.

porpoise. See PORK, para 7.

porridge; porringer. See POT, para 8.

port (1), wine: shipped from *Oporto* (now *Porto*): Port *o* (the) *porto* (harbour): 'the harbour' *par excellence*. Therefore see:

port (2), harbour, and the cognate port, a gate; portal; porte-cochère; portcullis, porthole, portreeve; porch; porter; portico; ? Portingale, Portugal, Portuguese (and Portuguese man-of-war), Portugee; —opportune, opportunism, opportunist, opportunity —importunate, importune (adj, v), importunity.

1. *Port*, a harbour, derives partly from OE, partly from OF-F, *port*, both from L *portus* (gen *-ūs*), orig a mountain pass and a gate, a door, basically, therefore, a passage; hence a harbour; and *port*, a gate, derives from OF-F *porte*, a door, from syn L *porta*. In L, the senses become differentiated, *portus* coming to denote a harbour: s and r *port-* is an extn of IE r *por-*, a var of *per-*, to cross, to go through (cf L *per*, through): cf the sep E FORD (*f* for *p*); Av *peretuš*, a passage, a ford; Skt *pāráyati*, he causes to traverse, Gr *peirō*, I traverse, go through; L *portāre*, to cause to pass, to transport, to bring to port; hence, to carry—with E derivatives treated in the next entry. (E & M.)

### Derivatives of L *porta*, gate, door

2. L *porta* has LL *portārius*, a doorkeeper, whence OF-F *portier*, whence E *porter*, doorkeeper; derivative L *porticus* (gen *-ūs*), a covered passage supported by a colonnade, becomes It *portico*, adopted by E. L *porticus* also becomes OF-F *porche*, adopted by ME, whence E *porch*; the VL adj *portālis* has neu *portāle*, whence ML *portāle*, a large gate or door, MF *portal* (late MF-F *portail*), adopted by E; F *porte-cochère*, a large gate admitting coaches (EF-F *coche*), is adopted by E, AE omitting the accent.

3. The chief cpds are *portcullis*, MF *porte coleïce*, lit a sliding door, *coleïce* being the f of OF-EF *coleïz*, ult from L *colāre*, to filter (whence F *couler*, to glide); and *porthole* (cf HOLE).

Derivatives of L *portus*, (passage), harbour

4. Prob from *portus*, harbour, comes *port*, the left side of a ship as you look from stern to bow; certainly, *portreeve*, OE *portgerēfa*, from *port*, a market town, from *port*, a harbour, and OE *gerēfa*, (by aphesis) ME *reve*, E *reeve*—cf *sheriff*, ME *shereve*, OE *scīrgerēfa*, where E *scīr*=E SHIRE.

5. Another full cpd is *Portugal*, known in the Middle Ages as *Portucale*, the region behind the L *Portus Cale*, port of Cale, on the left bank of the Douro; cf It *Portogallo*. The adj, hence n, *Portuguese* (whence the b/f *Portugee*) derives from Port *portuguez* or its Sp shape *portugués*; cf F *portuguais*. *Portuguese man-of-war* is a sailors' name for the Siphonophora of Sci: it has a sail-like crest that enables it to float on the surface.—*Portingale* is a late ME-EE name for Portugal, hence also for a Portuguese.

6. L *portus* has a notable prefix-cpd: *opportūnus* (for *obportūnus*), lit of a wind blowing *ob*, towards, port, hence favourable at a given moment; whence MF-F *opportun*, f *opportune*, adopted by E. Derivative L *opportūnitās*, acc *opportūnitātem*, yields MF-F *opportunité*, whence E *opportunity*. The F derivatives *opportunisme*, *opportuniste*, account for *opportunism*, *opportunist*.

7. L *has*, for *opportūnus*, created the opp *importūnus*, not blowing towards port, hence not, at a given moment, favourable: whence late MF-F *importune*, whence E *importune*, adj, displaced by *inopportune*, from LL *inopportūnus*. The v *importune* derives from EF-F *importuner* (from *importun*); *importunity*, from late MF-F *importunité*, from *importūnitātem*, acc of LL *importūnitās* (from *importūnus*); *importunate*, as if from ML *importūnāre*, pp *importūnātus*.

**port** (3), to carry, now only military; **portable** (whence **portability**); **portage**; **portamento**; **portative**; **portly**; **porter** (carrier), whence **porterage** and **porterhouse**; **portas** (**-ass, -hors, -house**), **portfire**, **portfolio**; **portmanteau**.—Cpds from L *port*āre, to carry, and its L derivatives: **apport**, n and v; **asport**, **asportation**; **comport**, **comportment**; **deport**, **deportation**, **deportment**; **disport**, n and v—cf **sport** (n, v), whence **sportful**, **sporting**, **sportive**, **sportsman**, **sporty**; **export** (v, hence n and **exporter**), **exportation**; **import** (v, hence n and, anl, **importation**, also **importer**), **importance**, **important**; **purport**, n, v; **rapport**; **report** (n, v), whence **reportable**, **reporter**, **reporting**, **reportorial**; **support** (v, hence n), **supportable** (and **insupportable**), **supportance**, **supporter**; **transport** (n, v; whence **transportable** and **transporter**), **transportation**.

1. L *port*āre, to carry, is akin to L *portus* and *porta*: see the 2nd PORT, para 1, esp s.f.; also cf FARE. Hence OF-F *porter*, E 'to *port*'. Derivative LL *portābilis* yields MF-F *portable*, adopted by E; LL *portātor* yields OF *porteor* (MF-F *porteur*)—acc of *portere*—whence E *porter*, carrier of burdens, whence *porter*, orig a drink fit for *porters*, whence *porterhouse*, where porter and, later, other malt

liquors were sold, whence *porterhouse steak*, orig the sort of steak you'd expect to find there. From OF-MF *porter*, MF forms both the adj *portatif*, f *portative*, adopted by E, and the n *portage*, likewise adopted by E. The Mus term *portamento*, however, is adopted from It (from It, from L, *portāre*). The E n *port*, a manner of carrying, carriage, demeanour, is adopted from MF-F *port*, from the v; hence the adj *portly*, with narrowing sense.

2. N-cpds, mostly deriving from or imitative, either of F cpds of OF-F *porter*, or of It cpds of It *portare*, to carry, include:

*portas* (*-ass*), varr *porthors*, *porthouse*, a medieval breviary, ME *portous*, *porthos*, MF *porte-hors*, lit a 'carry-outdoors'—an easily portable prayer-book;

*portfire*, suggested by F *porte-feu*, lit a 'carry-fire';

*portfolio*, adapted from It *portafoglio*, var *portafogli*, lit a 'carry-leaf, -leaves' (i.e., sheets of paper): *porta*, it carries+*foglio*, pl *fogli* (cf E *folio*): cf F *porte-feuille*;

*portmanteau* (obs *-mantua*, *-mantle*): EF-F *porte-manteau*, lit a 'carry-cloak' (cf MANTLE).

Compounds of L and R *portāre*, to carry

3. Whereas *apport* is adopted from OF-F *apport*, from *apporter*, from L *apportāre*, to bring (*ap-* for *ad*, towards), the rare *asport*, to carry off, comes from L *asportāre*, to carry away (*as-* for *abs-*, from *ab*, away from), pp *asportāt*us, whence *asportātiō*, o/s *asportātiōn-*, E *asportation*, a (felonious) removal.

4. L *comportāre* (*com-*, with) becomes MF-F *comporter*, esp in 'se *comporter*', whence E 'to *comport* oneself'; derivative late MF-F *comportement* yields E *comportment*.

5. L *dēportāre*, to carry *dē* or away, yields the EF 'se *déporter*', to behave oneself (irrelevant senses in OF-MF), whence *déportement*, whence E *deportment*; the lit sense occurs in F *déporter*, to banish (a criminal). whence 'to *deport*'; E *deportation* comes imm from F *déportation*, itself from L *dēportātiōn*em, acc of *dēportātiō*, from *dēportātus*, pp of *dēportāre*.

6. The archaic E *disport*, ME var *desport*, merriment, games, derives from OF-MF *desport*, from 'se *desporter*', to amuse oneself, from ML *disportāre* (attested by *disportat*), where *dis-* denotes 'apart' and connotes 'apart, or away, from business or gravity'; 'se *desporter*' yields 'to *disport*' oneself, to make merry, play games.

7. From that v comes, by aphesis, E 'to *sport*' or play; the E n *sport* comes from the ME n *disport*.

8. L *exportāre*, to carry abroad (*ex*, out of), yields 'to *export*'; derivative L *exportātiō*, o/s *exportātiōn-*, yields *exportation*.

9. L *importāre*, to carry in (*im-* for *in*), esp to bring into a country, becomes E 'to *import*', whence the trade n. But *import*, something important, importance, significance, derives from 'to *import*', to be important or significant, from the

syn EF-F *importer*, 'formed to serve as verb for *importance* and *important*' (B & W), which, arising, the former in C14, the latter in C15, derive from ML *importāre*, to be of importance, from L *importāre*, and have been adopted by E.

10. The E n *purport* is adopted from MF *purport*, from OF-MF *purporter*, varr *pourporter, porporter*, from VL *prōportāre*, lit to carry *prō-* or forward, bear forth; *purporter* becomes E 'to *purport*'.

11. The F-become-E *rapport* ('to be en rapport' or, AE, 'in rapport') derives from MF-F *rapporter*; *re-*, again, afresh+*apporter* (cf para 3).

12. 'To *report*' derives from OF-F *reporter*, from L *reportāre*, to carry *re-*, back or again (in LL, occ weakened to 'to carry or bear'); OF *reporter* has OF-F derivative n *report* (or *raport*), whence the E n. The E senses have been influenced by MF-F *rapporter*, as above, esp from its EF-F senses 'to bear news of, to relate'; E *reporter* owes something to F *rapporteur*; E *reportage* is borrowed from F.

13. L *supportāre* (*sup-* for *sub*, under, from below), to convey, LL to bear or endure, becomes OF *sorporter* and MF-F *supporter*, whence 'to *support*', whence the n—unless adopted from late MF-F *support*. Derivative late MF-F *supportable* and its neg *insupportable* go straight into E; *supporter* derives from 'to *support*', whence also *supportance*.

14. L *transportāre* becomes OF-MF *tresporter*, late MF-F *transporter*, E 'to *transport*'; the derivative MF-F n *transport* is adopted by E; derivative L *transportātiō*, o/s *transportātiōn-*, yields—perh via F—the E *transportation*.

**portable; portage.** See prec, para 1.

**portal.** See the 2nd PORT, para 2.

**portamento.** See the 3rd PORT, para 1, s.f.

**portas, portass.** See 3rd PORT, para 2.

**portative.** See 3rd PORT, para 1.

**portcullis.** See 2nd PORT, para 3.

**porte-cochère, (AE) -cochere.** See 2nd PORT, para 2.

**portend, portent, portentous.** See TEND, para 17.

**porter** (1), carrier. See the 3rd PORT, para 2.

**porter** (2), doorkeeper. See 2nd PORT, para 2.

**porterage.** See 3rd PORT (heading).

**porterhouse steak.** See 3rd PORT, para 1.

**portfire.** See 2nd PORT, para 2.

**portfolio.** See 3rd PORT, para 2.

**porthole.** See 2nd PORT, para 3, s.f.

**portico.** See 2nd PORT, para 2.

**portion.** See PART, para 13; for derivatives, the heading.

**portly.** See the 3rd PORT, para 1, s.f.

**portmantle** (archaic), **portmanteau.** See 3rd PORT, para 2.

**portrait, portraiture, portray, portrayal.** See tract, para 18, and cf the heading.

**portreeve.** See the 2nd PORT, para 4.

**Portugal; Portuguese** (man-of-war), whence the coll *Portugee*. See the 2nd PORT, para 5.

**Portulaca.** Cf PORK, para 5.

**pose,** v (hence n), whence posed, pa, and agent poser; posit, *posite, position (whence positional), positive (whence positivism, positivist), positor, positure, post (to place; position), postage, postal, posture (whence postural); the corresp pone (a writ) and 'to *pone', *ponend, ponent (adj, hence n), and derivative ponency, *ponible.—Compounds of *pone, to place, and of *pose (n, v), *position*, etc.: antepone (obsol), anteposition; appose, apposite, apposition, appositive; circumpose, circumposition; compone, component (adj, hence n), compose (whence pa composed and agent composer), composite (adj, hence n), composition, compositive, compositor, compost (n, hence v), composture, composure—cf compound, v and n; contraponend, contrapose, contraposition (whence, anl, contrapositive); depone, deponent (adj, hence n), depose (whence deposal), deposit (n, v), depositary (and depository), deposition (whence, anl, depositive), depositor—cf dépôt (AE depot); dispone, disponent, dispose (whence disposable and disposal), disposition, dispositive; exponent (whence exponential), exponible, exposé, exposition (whence, anl, expositive), expositor, expository, exposure—cf expound; imponent, impose (whence imposer, imposing), imposition—cf superimpose, superimposition—impot, impostor, imposture; interpone, interpose, interposition—cf entrepôt; juxtapose, juxtaposition; opponent (adj, hence n; hence also opponency), oppose (whence opposal), opposite (adj, hence n), opposition (whence, anl, oppositive)—cf the irreg appose, and esp pose, to nonplus, and puzzle, n hence v; postpone (whence postponement), postpose, postposition (whence, anl, postpositive); praepositor, praepostor, praepositure (AE pre-), prepose, preposition (whence prepositional), prepositive—cf provost; propone, proponent, propose (whence proposal), proposition (whence propositional)—cf propound; purpose, n (whence purposeful, purposive) and v; repone, repose, n (whence reposeful) and v (L and F senses), reposit, reposition, repositor, repository; sepone, sepose; superpose, superposition; suppose (whence supposal), supposition (whence, anl, suppositive), supposititious, suppository, suppost—cf presuppose, presupposition; transponible, transpose (whence transposal and transposer), transposition (whence, anl, transpositive and, directly, transpositional).

1. With one remarkable exception, the entire structure rests clearly and firmly upon L *ponere*, orig to put aside, hence simply to put or place or set. The s *pon-* is app an extn of an IE r *po-*, var *pa-*, perh aphetic for the r in Gr *apo*, away from (with -*b*- var in L *ab*), and *epi*, upon, and Skt *ápa*, away. (E & M; Hofmann.)

Simples

2. The pres s *pon-* occurs in the E v *pone, to place, seen in many prefix-cpds; in the legal and card-game n *pone*, from L *pone*, place thou; in *ponent*, from L *ponent-*, o/s of the presp *ponens*; in *ponend and *ponible*, attested by several prefix-cpds.

**2A.** The L pp *positus*, s *posit-*, occurs in:

*Posit*, to place firmly, prob from pp *positus*, perh from the supine *positum*;

*position*, from OF-F *position*, from L *positiōnem*, acc of *positiō* (o/s *positiōn-*), from *posit*us;

*positive*, from ME *positif*, adopted from MF, from ML *positīvus*, L *positīuus*; derivative F *positivisme* becomes E *positivism*;

*positor*, lit a placer, adopted from L (*posit-*+ agential *-or*);

*positure*, from L *positūra*, position, whence, by contr, EF-F *posture*, adopted by E;

*post*, the place where a soldier stands on guard, hence an assigned position, whence both a trading station and one's earning position: late MF-F *poste* (m): It *posto*: LL *postum*, contr of *positum*, orig the neu of pp *positus*;—hence 'to *post*' or station (someone) in a given place;

*post*, orig a man stationed in a series along a road, e.g. a courier, hence the vehicle used, hence the state packets or, later, mail carried, whence *in post-haste*, speedily, whence *posthaste*, hastily: from F *poste* (f), orig (C15) a relay of horses: It *posta*, either the f of *posto*, pp of *porre*, to place or set, from L *ponere*, or from LL *posta*, contr of *posita*, orig the f of pp *positus*;—hence 'to *post*', to travel with relays of horses, from late MF-EF *poster*, from *poste*;—*postage*, *postal*=E *post*, mail (letters, etc.)+*-age*, adj *-al*:

**3.** The exception is *pose*. The n *pose*, a sustained posture, adopted from late EF-F *pose*, derives from OF-F *poser*, to place (definitely or firmly), whence the syn E to *pose*'. Now, OF *poser* comes from LL *pausāre*, to place, from L *pausāre*, to pause, from L *pausa*, a pause: f.a.e., PAUSE, para 1. That is true; but the *pos-* of OF *poser* was, as early as LL, influenced by *pos-*, the r of *posit-*, s of *positus*, pp of *ponere*, and therefore it would hardly be wrong to say that, analogically, OF-F *poser*, hence E 'to *pose* or place', comes, ult, from L *ponere*. The same view is, by extn, valid for the cpds in *-pose*: one cannot abruptly sever them from the cpds in *-pone*; or, if you prefer, the E-from-F *-pose* cpds derive from F *poser*, but the F cpds themselves were, except *juxtapose*, prompted by the L cpds.—For 'to *pose*' or puzzle, see para 14.

### Compounds both Manifest and Aphetic

**4.** L *anteponere*, to place *ante* or before, in front, becomes 'to *antepone*'; the pp *anteposit*us has, anl, suggested E *anteposition*. L *apponere* (*ap-* for *ad-*, towards) is better represented: the pp *appositus* yields E *apposite*, and the derivative *appositiō*, o/s *appositiōn-*, the F, whence the E, *apposition*; cf 'to *appose*', to place (something) before or opposite (someone), from F *apposer*, from *poser*.

**5.** L *circumponere*, to place *circum* or around, has pp *circumposit*us, whence LL *circumpositiō*, o/s *circumpositiōn-*, whence E *circumposition*, whence, anl and by b/f, 'to *circumpose*'.

**6.** L *componere*, to put *con-* or together, yields the obs *compone*; the presp *componens*, o/s *component-*,

yields the E adj *component*, whence *componency*; the pp *compositus* is used also as adj 'formed of parts', whence E *composite*; derivative L *compositiō*, o/s *compositiōn-*, becomes MF-F, whence E, *composition*, and LL agent *compositor*, an arranger, an inventor, is adopted by E, prob after MF-F *compositeur*. But 'to *compose*' derives from OF-F *composer*, which, in one opinion, = *com-*+ OF *poser* and, in the other, L *compos-* (as in pp *compositus*)+F inf ending *-er*. The L derivative *compositūra* and its contr *compostūra* yield the obs E *compositure* and, via F, *composture*; the L pp *compositus* has the VL derivative n *\*composita*, *\*composta*, whence OF-F *compost*, adopted by E. E *composure*='to *compose*'+the *-ure* of *compositure*, *posture*, etc.—L *componere* also becomes OF-MF *componre*, var *compondre*, whence ME *compounen*, whence E 'to *compound*': cf *expound* in para 10 and *propound* in para 17. The ME pp *compound* becomes the E adj *compound*; the v has derivatives *compound*, n, *compounder*, *compounding*.

**7.** L *contraponere*, to set over against, has gerundive *contraponendus*, neu *-ponendum*, whence the *contraponend* of Logic; the pp *contrapositus* has the LL derivative *contrapositiō*, o/s *contrapositiōn-*, whence *contraposition* and, anl, *contrapositive*; 'to *contrapose*' derives from EF-F *contreposer*: *contre-* (L *contra*)+OF-F *poser*.

**8.** L *dēponere*, to put *dē-* or down, ML to state under oath, yields 'to *depone*'; presp *dēponens*, o/s *dēponent-*, yields *deponent*; pp *dēposit*us yields 'to *deposit*'—the n *deposit* comes from L *dēpositum*, orig the neu of the pp, and *dēpositum* also becomes MF-F *dépôt*, adopted by E; derivative LL *dēpositārius*, a trustee, yields *depositary* (cf MF-F *dépositaire*); LL *dēpositor* is adopted by E, and LL *dēpositōrium* becomes *depository*. 'To *depose*' blends two F vv, one old (*deposer*), the other (*déposer*) modern.

**9.** L *disponere*, to set *dis* or apart, in different places, gives us 'to *dispone*', which, like most of the *-pone* cpds, is a Law term; presp *disponens*, o/s *disponent-*, accounts for *disponent*; pp *dispositus* has derivative *dispositiō*, o/s *dispositiōn-*, whence OF-F *disposition*, adopted by E, the sense 'temperament' going back to LL; the anl MF-F *dispositif*, f *-ive*, becomes E *dispositive*. 'To *dispose*' derives from OF-F *disposer*. The derivative *predispose*, *predisposition* perh owe something to F.

**10.** L *exponere*, to put out, LL to interpret or explain, yields the obsol 'to *expone*', whence, anl, *exponible*; presp *exponens*, o/s *exponent-*, becomes *exponent*; pp *expositus* becomes the rare 'to *exposit*'; derivative L *expositiō*, o/s *expositiōn-*, LL an interpretation, becomes OF-F, whence E, *exposition*; LL *expositor*, a textual critic, passes into E; ML *expositōrius* yields *expository*. 'To *expose*'—whence *exposure* (cf *composure*)—derives from OF-F *exposer*; the F pp *exposé* becomes a late EF-F n, adopted by E.—Moreover, L *exponere* becomes OF-MF *espondre*, whence ME *expounen*, *expounden*, whence 'to *expound*': cf *compound* (para 6) and *propound* (para 17). Hence *expounder*.

11. L *imponere*, to place, hence lay, into or upon, explains the obsol *impone*; presp *imponens*, o/s *imponent-*, E *imponent*; pp *impositus*, neu *impositum*, becomes MF *impost*, F *impôt*, both adopted by E. Th L derivative agent *impositor* is, in LL, contr to *impostor*, a deceiver, whence, via EF-F *imposteur*, the E *impostor*, and subsidiary LL *impostūra* yields, via EF-F, the E *imposture*; derivative L *impositiō* (o/s *impositiōn-*) passes through MF-F into E *imposition*, whence the school s *impot*, occ *impo*. 'To *impose*' derives from MF-F *imposer* (*im-*+OF-F *poser*), prompted by L *impos*itus. 'To *superimpose*', whence, anl, *superimposition*, was perh prompted by F *surimposer*, but it derives, anl, from *superimpos*itus, pp of ML *superimponere*.

12. L *interponere*, to set between, to insert, affords us the rare 'to *interpone*'; pp *interpositus* has derivative L *interpositiō* (o/s *interpositiōn-*), LL *intervention*, whence—perh via OF-F—the E *interposition*. 'To *interpose*' derives from MF-F *interposer*. Cf *entrepôt* (AE *entrepot*), adopted from EF-F, which forms it upon *dépôt*.

13. As if suggested by L *\*iuxtaponere*, ML *\*juxtaponere* (cf ML *juxtāre*), with derivative *\*juxtapositiō* (o/s *-positiōn-*), learnèd F coins (1690) *juxtaposition*, whence, by b/f, F *juxtaposer*: hence E *juxtaposition* and 'to *juxtapose*'.

14. L *opponere*, to set *ob* or against, has presp *opponens*, o/s *opponent-*, whence E *opponent*, and pp *oppositus*, whence MF-F, whence E, *opposite*; derivative L *oppositiō*, o/s *oppositiōn-*, becomes OF-F *opposition*, adopted by E. 'To *oppose*' derives from OF-F *opposer*. 'To *oppose*' is corrupted to ME-EE *appose*, to put questions to, whence *apposer* (obs), a questioner or examiner: hence, by aphesis, the EE 'to *pose*' or question, hence (E) to baffle or nonplus, whence *poser*, an examiner (obs), a baffling question or problem. ME-EE *appose*, to question, has the late ME-EE derivative *apposal*, whence, prob via *\*posal*, the E *puzzle*.

15. LL *postponere*, to place after, L to defer, yields 'to *postpone*', whence *postponable*; the pp *postpos*itus has LL derivative *postpositiō* (o/s *-positiōn-*), a placing after, a postponement, whence E *postposition*. 'To *postpose*' derives from EF-F *postposer* (*post-*+OF-F *poser*).

16. L *praeponere*, to place *prae* or before, hence to set (someone) over (others), has ML agent *praepositor*, contr *praepostor*, adopted by E: cf the LL *praeposita*, an abbess, from the f of the pp *praepos*itus. Derivative *praepositiō* (o/s *-positiōn-*) becomes late MF-F *préposition*, whence E *preposition*; LL *praepositiuus*, ML *-ivus*, becomes E *prepositive* (cf F *prépositif*); LL *praepositūra* becomes E *praepositure*, AE *prepositure*. 'To *prepose*' derives from late MF-F *préposer*. The pp *praepos*itus is, in LL, used as n, 'one set in authority', whence, by influence of *prōponere*, to set forward (pp *prōpositus*)—see next para—the LL

var *prōpositus*, whence OF *provost* (cf the F *prévôt*) and OE *profost*: whence the E *provost*; *provostry* derives—perh after MF *prevosterie* (cf the F *prévôté*, OF *prevosté*)—from *provost*.

17. L *prōponere* yields 'to *propone*'; presp *prōponens* (o/s *-ponent-*), *proponent*—opp *opponent*; pp *prōpos*itus has derivative *prōpositiō*, o/s *prōpositiōn-*, whence OF-F, hence E, *proposition*. Gallicized, after OF-F *poser*, from *prōponere* is OF-F *proposer*, whence 'to *propose*'. 'To *propone*' itself has—via the var *propoune*—become 'to *propound*'.

18. Influenced by L *prōponere*, OF-F *poser* has the OF-MF cpd *pourposer*, *purposer* (*pour*, *pur*, *por* derive from L *prō*, forward), whence ME *purposen*, E 'to *purpose*'; the derivative OF-MF n *porpos*, *pourpos*, becomes ME *purpos*, E *purpose*.

19. L *reponere*, to put back, becomes legal 'to *repone*'. The pp *repos*itus yields 'to *reposit*' (cf *deposit*); derivative LL *repositiō*, o/s *repositiōn-*, E *reposition*; LL *repositōrium*, E *repository*, whence prob, anl, E *repositor*. App from pp *repos*itus comes E 'to *repose*' in its senses 'to restore' (obs), 'to set' (e.g., trust in someone). But 'to *repose*', to lay at, or to, rest, vi to rest, derives from OF-F *reposer*, from LL *repausāre*, to rest (vt and vi): cf the OF *poser* in para 3. OF *reposer* has derivative OF-F n *repos* (cf LL *repausātiō*), whence—influenced by 'to *repose*'—the E n *repose*.

20. L *sēponere*, to place or set *sē-* or in hiding or aside, hence to reserve, yields the rare 'to *sepone*'; cf the rare syn 'to *sepose*', app from the L pp *sēpos*itus.

21. L *superponere*, to place *super* or above, has pp *superpos*itus, whence LL *superpositiō* (o/s *-positiōn-*), whence F and E *superposition*; learnèd F *superposer* (*super*+*poser*, as in para 3) yields 'to *superpose*'.

22. L *supponere*, to place *sub* or under, hence to substitute, becomes 'to *suppone*' (obs). The pp *suppos*itus has neu *suppositum*, used by scholastic ML as a n, whence the E adj *supposital*. Derivative L *suppositiō*, ML a hypothesis, yields MF-F *supposition*, adopted by E. The subsidiary L *supposītīcius*, var *supposititius*, yields E *supposititious*; and subsidiary *suppositōrius*, placed underneath, has derivative Med n *suppositōrium*, whence MF-F *suppositoire* and E *suppository*. LL *suppositiuus*, ML *-ivus*, becomes *suppositive*. The L pp *suppos*itus and supine *suppos*itum app prompted MF-F *supposer* (cf OF-F *poser*), whence MF *supposen*, E 'to *suppose*'.—MF-F *supposer* itself acquires a cpd: the late MF-F *présupposer* (*pré-*, L *prae-*, before), whence 'to *presuppose*'; derivative late MF-F *présupposition* becomes *presupposition*.

23. L *transponere*, to place across or beyond, yields, anl, *transponible*; pp *transpositus* has derivative LL *transpositiō* (o/s *transpositiōn-*), a change of position, whence—prob via the late MF-F word—E *transposition*. 'To *transpose*', however, derives from OF-F *transposer*, from L *transpos*itus (and supine *transpos*itum)—gallicized after OF-F *poser* (as in para 3).

**poser**, a puzzling question. See prec. para 14, where also *pose*, to nonplus.

**poseur.** See PAUSE, para 2.

**posit.** See POSE, para 2^A.

**position.** See POSE, para 2^A.

**positive, positivism.** See POSE, para 2^A.

**positor, positure.** See POSE, para 2^A.

**posology.** See the element *poso-*.

**posse** and **posse comitatus; possible, possibility—impossible, impossibility; potence, potency, potent, potentate, potential—impotence, impotent—omnipotence, omnipotent,** qq.v. at the element *omni-*,—cf *plenipotentiary* at PLENARY, para 2,—**prepotence, prepotent; puissance, puissant—impuissance, impuissant; power** (n, hence v), whence **powerful, powerless;** cf the scp DESPOT (DESPOTIC, DESPOTISM) and the sep POSSESS.

1. The n *posse*, a small force that has legal authority, as of a sheriff and his deputies, or of police, derives from the Law term *posse*, short for *posse comitatus*, which, in ML, means 'power of the county' (cf COUNT, a person of high rank). ML *posse*, power, derives from L *posse*, to have power, lit to be able: for *\*potse*, from PL *\*potesse*, to be able: from a PL r *\*pot-*, able, hence strong, powerful: cf L *potis*, s and r *pot-*, orig 'a master, a possessor, of', hence 'having, esp exercising, one's ability or mastery or power', displaced by *potens*, which, the presp of *posse*, is soon used also and mostly as adj. With L *potis*, master or possessor (of), cf Skt *pátis*, master, husband, and Gr *pósis*, Tokh A *pats*, Lith *patìs*, *pàts*, husband, and, with *f* for *p*, Go *-faths*, master (in *brūthfaths*, bridegroom); cf also the *-pot-* of Gr *despotēs*, (prop) master of the house. (E & M; Hofmann.)

2. Either from L *posse*, to be able, or from L *possum* (*\*potsum*), I am able, comes L *possibilis*, (that which is) able (to be done), MF-F *possible*, adopted by E; derivative L *possibilitās* (o/s *-itāt-*) becomes MF-F *possibilité*, whence E *possibility*. The neg L *impossibilis* and LL *impossibilitās* become MF-F *impossible*, adopted by E, and MF-F *impossibilité*, whence *impossibility*.

3. The L presp and adj *potens* has o/s *potent-*, whence E *potent*; derivative *potentia* yields E *potency* and OF-EF *potence*, adopted by E. L *potentia* has LL adj *potentiālis*, whence E *potential* (adj, hence n)—cf EF-F *potentiel*; hence *potentiality*. Derivative L *potentatus* (gen *-ūs*), power, esp if political, LL a powerful person, yields MF-F *potentat*, whence E *potentate*.

4. The L neg *impotens*, o/s *impotent-*, and its derivative *impotentia*, become MF-F *impotent* and *impotence*, both adopted by E; L *praepotens*, o/s *praepotent-*, and its derivative *praepotentia* yield *prepotent* and *prepotency*, the var *prepotence* deriving from EF-F *prépotence* (from the L word).

5. L *posse* has the VL var *\*potere*, whence OF *povoir*, *pouvoir*, with pres forms *pois-*, *puis-* (cf Je *puis*, I can), whence the OF-F adj *puissant*, adopted by E; derivative OF *poissance*, MF-F *puissance*, is likewise adopted, as are the neg MF-F *impuissance* and *impuissant*.

6. The OF v *povoir* had earlier forms *pooir*, *poeir*, *\*podeir* (cf *podir*, recorded for 842); it becomes, as early as C12 and first in the form *poeir*, a noun, with early var *pooir*: whence ME *poer*, var *pouer*: hence E *power*. (Dauzat.)

**possess** (whence pa **possessed**), **possession, possessive, possessor, possessory; dispossess,** whence, anl, **dispossession.**

1. L *potis*, a master of (esp, property)—see POSSE, para 1—has derivative *\*potsidēre*, L *possidēre*, lit to sit (*-sidēre*, c/f of *sedēre*), as master of, i.e. to be master of (property), with mdfn *possīdere*, to make oneself master of, to occupy, with pp *possessus*, whence—perh via MF-EF *possesser*—'to possess'; derivative L *possessiō*, o/s *possessiōn-*, yields—prob via the OF-F word—the E *possession*; derivative *possessīuus*, ML *-īvus*, yields—perh via late MF-F *possessif*, f *-ive*—the E *possessive*; derivative *possessor* is adopted by E (cf MF-F *possesseur*); and *possessōrius* becomes *possessory*.

2. MF-EF *possesser* has cpd *despossesser*, whence 'to dispossess'. But *prepossess* is an entirely E formation with *pre-*, in advance; hence, anl, *prepossession* and *prepossessive*.

**posset,** a hot drink of milk curdled with ale or wine: ME *possot*, *poshote*: o.o.o.: cf the dubious MF *possette*.

**possibility, possible.** See POSSE, para 2.

**possum,** esp **play p.** See OPOSSUM.

**post** (1), an upright piece of timber, etc., serving as stay (e.g., of a fence), hence as v: ME *post*: OE and OF *post*: L *postis*, a door-post: perh cf Gr *pastas*, a stake, a post, ? for *\*parastas*, that which stands beside (*para*)—here, beside the open space of the doorway. (Hofmann.)

**post** (2), a station, to station; a relay, a coach, the mail—and the corresp v. See POSE, para 2.

**post-.** See POSTERIOR, para 1.

**postage, postal.** See POSE, para 2, s.f.

**postchaise**=*post*, as in POST (2)+F *chaise*, a chair.

**poster,** a large bill or placard displayed publicly, was orig a notice affixed to a POST (1).

**poste restante,** adopted from F, is lit '*post* (letters, etc.) resting'—i.e., remaining until called for by the addressee; *restante* is the f of *restant*, presp of *rester*, to remain.

**posterior,** adj, hence n (usu *posteriors*, buttocks)—**posteriority; posterity; postern; posthumous; preposterous;** cf the element *postero-*; **postil.**

1. The L prep *post*, after, derives from OL *poste* from PL *\*posti* (*\*pos-ti*); PL r *\*pos-* is perh akin to Gr *epi*, upon, after, and therefore app an extn of the IE r *\*po-* occurring in L *ponō*, I place.

2. The L derivatives affecting E are:
*posterus*, coming after, with derivative *posteritās*, o/s *posteritāt-*, whence MF-F *postérité*, whence E *posterity*, and with comp *posterior*, coming still later, adopted by E (cf late MF-F *postérieur*), the LL derivative *posterioritās*, o/s *posterioritāt-*, yielding *posteriority* (cf late MF-F *postériorité*), complementing *priority*;

*postumus*, last of all, becomes—by f/e association with *humus*, soil, ground—the LL *posthumus*, whence E *posthumous*, esp born after the father's death or published after the author's;

LL *posterula*, a back gate or door, at first a dim of LL *postera*, a back gate or door, ? orig elliptical for *postera ianua*, from *posterus*: whence OF-early MF *posterle*, whence OF-MF *posterne* (F *poterne*): whence E *postern*;

*praeposterus*, having the sense before-behind or, as we'd say, back to front or the cart before the horse: whence E *preposterous*.

3. Perh from L *post*, after, comes E *postil*, an annotation: MF-EF *postille*: ML *postilla*: perh elliptical for *post illa verba*, after those words, or, more prob, simply a contr of *post illa*, after those things. MF *postille* has derivative late MF-F *apostiller*, to make a marginal note, whence the EF-F n *apostille*, adopted by E and anglicized as *apostil*. (B & W.)

**posthaste.** See POSE, para 2A.

**posthumous.** See POSTERIOR, para 2.

**postil.** See POSTERIOR, para 3.

**postilion** or **postillion**: EF-F *postillon*: It *postiglione*, from *posta*: cf E *post* at para 2A (s.f.) of POSE.

**postliminium.** See LIMIT, para 7.

**postlude.** See LUDICROUS, para 11.

**postman; postmark; postmaster, postmistress; post office.** Obvious cpds of the 2nd *post* (q.v. at POSE, para 2A)+MAN, etc.

**postmeridian**: L *postmeridiānus* (adj), after noon: cf *post* at POSTERIOR, para 1, and *meridian*, q.v. at DIANA, para 13.

**post-mortem.** See MORTAL, para 8.

**postnatal, postnate**: ML *postnātus*, born later: cf NATIVE.

**postpone, postponement.** See POSE, para 15.

**postpose, postposition.** See POSE, para 15.

**postscribe, postscript.** See SCRIBE, para 15.

**postulant, postulate, postulation, postulatory.** See PRAY, para 7.

**posture.** See POSE, para 2A.

**posy**, orig a rhymed sentiment, hence—prob from 'the language of flowers'—a bouquet, is a contr of *poesy*, q.v. at POEM, para 2.

**pot** (n, hence v), **potter, pottery, poteen; pottage; pottle; pot-boiler, -hook, -house, -hunter, -luck, -sherd, -shot, -walloper; potpourri; potash, potass, potassium; putty; hotchpotch and hodgepodge;— porridge; porringer.**

1. *Pot*, an earthen vessel, derives from late OE *pott*, which, like OF-F *pot* (whence EF-F *pot de chambre*, E *chamber pot*, whence both *chamber* in this sense and E *pot* pron *pō*), prob comes from some VL derivative (cf ML *pottus*) of *pōtāre*, to drink: cf the L *pōtōrium*, a drinking vessel (cf Gr *potērion*, drinking-cup): f.a.e., POTABLE.

2. OF *pot* has OF-F agent *potier*, a maker of pots, whence, in part, the E *potter*; derivative MF-F *poterie* leads to *pottery*. OF-F *pot*, moreover, has the MF-F derivative *potage*, adopted by E cookery but, elsewhere, anglicized as *pottage*,

and the EF-F cpd *pot-pourri*, lit 'rotten pot'—a trans of the Sp *olla podrida*. The MF dim *potel* (cf MF *potet*) is adopted by ME, whence E *pottle*.

3. OF-F *pot* has a further notable derivative: the OF-F *potée*, a potful, (later) a cement made orig in a pot—in short, the E *putty*, for *\*potty*.

4. E *pot* becomes Ir *pota*, later *poite*, with dim *poitín*, a small pot, hence whiskey made in a private still: whence AIr *poteen*.

5. Akin to OE *pott*- E *pot* is MD-D *pot*, with cpd *potasch*, lit 'pot-ash', whence both E *potash* and late EF-F *potasse*, whence E *potass*, whence, in 1808, Sir Humphry Davy's Sci L *potassium*.

6. E *pot*, a vessel, esp for cookery or for drinking, has the foll cpds:

*pot-belly*, *potbelly*, shaped like one;

*pot-boiler*, something written, painted, composed hastily to keep the domestic pot boiling;

*pot-hook*, in handwriting, derives from a pot's *S*-shaped hook;

*pot-house*, *pothouse*, a tavern, pots of ale being served there, hence *potboy* and *potman*;

*pot-hunter*, orig a parasite, now a contestant that, in sports, plays only for the trophies;

*pot-luck*, *potluck*, usu *to take potluck*, to be prepared for an informal meal;

*potsherd*, a shard or fragment of an earthenware pot;

*potshot*, orig a shot fired to kill something for the pot, hence a chancy or unskilled shot;

*pot-valiant, -valo(u)r*: (with) the courage that comes from liquor;

*pot-walloper*, lit one who boils (*wallops*) his own pot, later a scullion, a sea cook.

7. *Pot* occurs in *hotchpotch*, for earlier *hotchpot*, itself from MF-F *hochepot*, lit a shake-pot; *hoche-* comes from MF-F *hocher*, OF *hocier*, to shake, of Gmc origin. *Hotchpotch* has the 'blunted' var *hodgepodge*.

8. E contains two 'disguised' derivatives from F derivatives of F *pot*: *porridge* from *pottage* from MF-F *potage*, the *-rr-* coming perh from ME *porree*, an orig leek pottage, from OF-EF *porrée*, from L *porrum, porrus*, a leek, prob of Medit stock —cf Gr *prason* (E & M); and *porringer*, earlier *pottinger*, var of *pottanger*, which, with intrusive *n*, stands for *\*pottager*, from MF-F *potager* (from *potage*).

**pot**, a hole. See POTHOLE.

**potable; potation, potatory; potion**—cf poison (n, v), whence poisoner, poisoning, poisonous.

1. *Potable*, adopted from late MF-F, derives from LL *pōtābilis*, drinkable, from *pōtāre*, to drink, s and r *pōt*-: cf Gr *potos*, a drinking, and *posis* (? for *\*potsis*), a drink, *pinein*, to drink, OSl *piti*, to drink, Skt *pībati*, he drinks: IE r *\*pi-*, to drink, with extnn *\*pib-*, *\*pin-*, *\*pit-*.

2. *Pōtāre* has pp *pōtātus*, whence *pōtātiō*, o/s *pōtātiōn-*, MF-EF, whence E, *potation*, and *pōtātor*, adopted but rare, and *pōtātōrius*, whence *potatory*.

3. Intimately akin to *pōtāre* is the adj *pōtus*, having drunk and having been drunk: whence *pōtiō*, a drink, esp a love-potion or a poison:

indeed, from *pōtiō*, o/s *pōtiōn-*, comes both MF-EF *potion*, adopted by E, and the gallicized MF-F *poison*, likewise adopted. 'To *poison*' derives from MF-F *poisonner*, suggested by LL *pōtiōnāre*, to give to drink, from the n *pōtiō*.

**potage.** See POT, para 2.

**potash, potass, potassium.** See POT, para 5.

**potation.** See POTABLE, para 2.

**potato:** Sp *patata*, orig the sweet potato: a *p* for *v* var of Sp *batata*, the sweet potato: adopted from Taino (an extinct Caribbean language).

**potator, potatory.** See POTABLE, para 2.

**potbelly** (whence **potbellied**), **potboiler.** See POT, para 6.

**poteen.** See POT, para 4.

**potence, potency, potent, potential.** See POSSE, para 3.

**pother.** See PUT, para 2.

**pothole,** a large hole, tacks *hole* to the now mainly Sc and N dial *pot*, of Scan origin: prob akin to the Sw dial *pott*, varr *putt*, *pit*, and therefore to PIT, a hole. Nevertheless, *pothole* could equally well be a cpd of POT and HOLE.

**pothook, pothouse, pothunter.** See POT, para 6.

**potion.** See POTABLE, para 3.

**potlatch** comes, with f/e form and via Chinook jargon, from Chinook *patshatl*, a giving, a gift.

**potluck, potman.** See POT, para 6.

**potpourri.** See POT, para 2.

**potsherd, potshot.** See POT, para 6.

**pottage.** See POT, para 2.

**potter** (1), n. See POT, para 2.

**potter** (2), v, is a freq of the now dial *pote*, a var of the v *poke*, q.v. at POACH, para 2.

**pottery.** See POT, para 2.

**pottle.** See POT, para 2, s.f.

**pot-valiant, pot-walloper.** See POT, para 6.

**pouch.** See POCK, para 4.

**pouf.** See PUFF, para 2.

**pouldron.** See PAWL, s.f.

**poulter, poulterer.** See POLECAT, para 2.

**poultice.** See POLLEN, para 2.

**poultry.** See POLECAT, para 2, s.f.

**pounce** (1), n (a powder). See the element *pumici-*.

**pounce** (2), v (to swoop down), derives from *pounce*, a bird's claw. See PUNGENT, para 11.

**pound** (1), an enclosure: OE *pund*, only in cpds: o.o.o. Hence, 'to *pound*', now usu in the orig int form, 'to *impound*'. From pp of *pen*, enclose?

**pound** (2), a unit of weight, the gold unit of value: OE *pund*: L *pondo*, meaning 'in weight': akin to PEND, where cf esp *ponderous*. Hence *poundage* and, from 'weight', *poundal* and *pounder*.

**pound** (3), to beat as with a pestle, to pulverize: ME *pounen*: OE *punian*, to bray, to bruise, whence also the now dial var 'to *pun*'.

**poundage; poundal; pounder** (weight). See the 2nd POUND.

**pour:** ME *pouren*: o.o.o.: ? orig 'to filter or strain' and therefore from the syn MF *purer*, ult from L *purus* (cf PURE).

**pourparler.** See PARABLE, para 6.

**pout** (1), a fish: OE *-pūte*, as in *ǣlepūte*, an eelpout: cf the D *puit*, a frog: basic idea, prob 'inflated', as in Sw *puta*, to be inflated. Therefore akin to:

**pout** (2), to puff out, thrust out, the lips: ME *pouten*: cf Sw *puta*, to be inflated—hence also Skt *budbuda*, redup of r *\*bud-*, swollen, to be swollen. Cf prec—and perh PUDDING.

**poverish; poverty.** See POOR, para 1.

**powder.** See POLLEN, para 4.

**power, powerful, powerless.** See POSSE, para 6.

**powwow** (n, hence v), a (noisy) conference, a sense orig AE and still coll, derives from 'Indian conference', itself from Alg 'medicine man': cf Narragansett *powáw*, Massachusett *pouwaw*, medicine man (DAE), from a r 'to dream': 'he derives his art from his dreams' (Mathews).

**pox.** See POCK, para 1.

**praam,** occ **pram,** a flat-bottomed Nor boat: D *praam*; MD *praem*, *prame*: cf LG *prahm*, from Sl *pram*, akin to FARE (Walshe).

**practic** (adj, n), **practicable, practical, practice** (n; AE n and v) and **practise** (v), **practician, practitioner; chiropractic; impracticable, impractical; pratique; praxis; pragmatic** (adj, hence n), whence, anl, **pragmatism** and **pragmatist.**

1. *Practical* (whence the neg *impractical*) is an extn of the late ME-E (obsol) adj *practic*, from MF *practique* (soon *pratique*): ML-LL *practicus*: Gr *praktikos*, able in, fit for, doing, active: from *prassein*, Attic *prattein*, to do, to do habitually; akin to *perā*, *perān*, over, beyond, via *\*prā-ko*, leading over, or through, and beyond (Hofmann).

2. Gr *praktikos* has the derivative n *praktikē*, ? elliptical for *hē praktikē tekhnē*, the practical art, i.e. technology: whence LL-ML *practicē*, MF *practique* (F *pratique*, borrowed by E and used in naut sense), ME *practike*, E *practic* (now only Sc), whence *practics*; cf *chiropractic*, often *chiropractics*, manual manipulation of the spine—from Gr *kheir*, the hand (our element *chiro-*).

3. 'To *practise* or, AE, *practice*' derives, via ME *practisen*, from MF *practiser*, for MF *practiquer* (late MF-F *pratiquer*), from ML *practicāre*, from LL *practicē*; hence the n *practise*, later—influenced by the LL n—*practice*.

4. Late MF-F *pratiquer* has the EF-F derivative *praticable*, which at least prompted the E *practicable*, precisely as the EF-F neg *impraticable* prompted *impracticable*. The MF *practicien* (later *praticien*) suggested *practician*, which in turn generated the irreg and unnecessary *practitioner*.

5. Gr *prassein*, to do (habitually), has the derivative n *praxis*, habitual action, practice, adopted by scholastic E. More generally interesting is the derivative *pragma*, a thing done, o/s *pragmat-*, whence the adj *pragmatikos*, whence L *pragmaticus*, esp in sense 'skilled in business', whence E *pragmatic*, whence William James's *pragmatism*.

**praelection, praelector.** See LEGEND, para 14.

**praenomen.** See NAME, para 4, s.f.

**praepositor, praepostor.** See POSE, para 16.

**praetor,** for an ancient Roman magistrate, is

adopted from L: for *praettor*, lit a goer (-*itor*) before (*prae*); the L adj *praetōrianus* yields *praetorian*.

**pragmatic, pragmatism.** See PRACTIC, para 4.

**prairie; pratincole**, whence **pratincolous.**

*Prairie*, adopted from F ('a large meadow'), is for OF *praerie*, formed, with suffix -*erie*, from OF-F *pré*, a meadow, from L *prātum*, itself o.o.o. Sci combines L *prātum*+L *incola*, an inhabitant, to give us *pratincole*, lit a meadow-inhabiter.

**praise.** See PRICE, para 3.

**Prakrit**, whence **Prakritic; Sanskrit**, whence **Sanskritic.**

*Prakrit* derives from Skt *prakṛta*, original or natural, hence usual, common, hence vulgar; *pra-* is akin to E FOR. *Sanskrit* derives from Skt *saṁskṛta*, (lit) made together, hence prepared or artificial, hence elaborate or polished, highly cultivated; *saṁs-*, from *sam*, together (cf E SAME). The common element -*krit* derives from the Skt r *kṛ*, to make, to do.

**pram** (1), boat. See PRAAM.

**pram** (2) is a contr abbr of *perambulator*, q.v. at AMBLE, para 4.

**prance**, whence **prancer** and pa, vn **prancing**, derives from ME *praunen*: perh (Webster) from MF *paravancier*, int (*par-* for L *per-* used thus) of OF *avancier* (MF-F *avancer*): cf ADVANCE.

**prank**, n and v; **prink.**

*Prank*, a piece of mischief, is o.o.o.—unless, as prob it does, it derives from 'to *prank*' or adorn gaily, now usu in the thinning, 'to *prink*': and 'to *prank*' derives from or is, at the least, akin to MLG *prank*, pomp, display, adornment: cf G *Prunk*, ostentation, and MLG-MHG-G *prangen*, and MD-D *pronken*, to adorn oneself.

**prase, prasine.**

The latter, as n, derives from *prasine*, adj, which derives from L *prasinus*, trln of Gr *prasinos*, adj of *prason*, a leek; *prasinos* is a mdfn of the adj *prasios*, whence L *prasius*, whence the F n *prase*, adopted by E; *prase*, however, perh comes direct from Gr *prasos*, var of *prason*. The nn *prasine* and *prase* denote minerals of a leek-green colour; the former as already in the LL n *prasinus* (Gr *prasinos*).

**prate**, whence **prater**, has freq **prattle** (perh, however, direct from MLG *prätelen*), whence **prattler** and pa, vn **prattling**, and itself comes from MD-MLG *präten*: ? ult echoic.

**pratincole.** See PRAIRIE.

**pratique.** See PRACTIC, para 2.

**prattle, prattler.** See PRATE.

**prawn:** ME *prane* or *prayne*: o.o.o.

**praxis.** See PRACTIC, para 4.

**pray, prayer, praying mantis; prie-Dieu; prithee; precarious, precation** (obs)**, precative, precatory; deprecable, deprecate, deprecation, deprecative, deprecatory; imprecant, imprecate, imprecation,** whence, anl, **imprecator** and **imprecatory;—postulant, postulate, postulation, postulator, postulatory** —cf **expostulate, expostulation** (whence, anl, **expostulatory**).

1. 'To *pray*', ME *preien*, derives from OF-MF *preier* (MF-F *prier*): VL-LL *precāre*: L *precāri*: L *prec-*, o/s of *prex* (attested by oblique cases and pl), a request, hence esp a prayer: prob akin to L *procus*, a wooer, and *poscere*, to ask or demand, and to Skt *prechati*, he asks, *praśnás*, a question, OE *fricgan*, to inquire, OHG *prāgēn*, *frāhēn*, G *frāgen*, OS *frāgōn*, Go *fraihnan*, to ask (questions): IE r, *prĕk-* or *prēk-*, var *prok-*; Gmc r, *freh-*, *frāeh-*, var *frāeg-*. (Walshe.)

2. L *precāri* has derivative adj *precārius*, obtainable only by prayer, not assured, with f *precāria*, used by VL as n, whence OF-MF *preiere* (MF-F *prière*), adopted by ME, whence—after 'to *pray*'— the E *prayer*.

3. Straight from L *precārius* comes E *precarious* (cf the MF-F *précaire*); the L pp *precātus* has derivative *precātiō*, o/s *precātiōn-*, whence E *precation*, extant only in cpds—LL *precātīuus*, ML -*īvus*, E *precative*—and LL *precātōrius*, E *precatory*.

4. The L cpd *dēprecāri*, to avert (connoted by *de-*), by prayer, has derivative LL *dēprecābilis*, E *deprecable*, and pp *dēprecātus*, whence 'to *deprecate*', with derivatives *dēprecātiō*, o/s *dēprecātiōn-*, OF *deprecation* (F *dépré-*), E *deprecation*—LL *dēprecātīuus*, ML -*īvus*, E *deprecative*—and LL *dēprecātōrius*, late MF-F *déprécatoire* and, perh independently, E *deprecatory*.

5. L *imprecāri*, to pray, rarely for, usu against (*in-*), someone, has pp *imprecans*, o/s *imprecant-*, E *imprecant*, and pp *imprecātus*, E 'to *imprecate*', with derivative *imprecātiō*, o/s *imprecātiōn-*, MF-F *imprécation* and, perh independently, E *imprecation*, whence, anl, *imprecator* and *imprecatory*.

6. Remaining are: *praying mantis* (*Mantis religiosa*), from its reverent posture; *prie-Dieu*, adopted from F, is '(a stool on which one kneels to) pray to God'; *prithee* derives from ME-EE *preythe*, (I) pray thee.

7. Akin to L *precāri* is L *poscere*, to ask (see para 1), which app has the freq *postulāre*, to demand, presp *postulans*, o/s *postulant-*, whence the E n *postulant*, whence *postulance* or *postulancy*, and pp *postulātus*, whence the obs adj *postulate* and 'to *postulate*', with the n *postulate* deriving from L *postulātum*, a request, prop the neu of the pp. That pp *postulātus* has derivative *postulātiō*, o/s *postulātiōn-*, whence E *postulation*. The cpd *expostulāre*, to demand vehemently (int *ex-*), has pp *expostulātus*, whence 'to *expostulate*'; derivative *expostulātiō*, o/s *expostulātiōn-*, yields *expostulation*.

**preach, preacher, preachment.** See DICT, para 9.

**preamble.** See AMBLE, para 3.

**prebend, prebendary.** See HABIT, para 15.

**precarious.** See PRAY, para 3.

**precative, precatory.** See PRAY, para 3.

**precaution, precautionary.** See CAUTION, para 4.

**precede, precedence, precedent.** See CEDE, para 9.

**precentor:** LL *praecentor*, from *praecinere*, to sing before: f.a.e., cf CHANT.

**precept, preceptor.** See CAPABILITY, para 7.

**precession.** See CEDE, para 9.

**précieuse.** See PRICE, para 4.

**precinct.** See CINCH, para 4.

**preciosity, precious.** See PRICE, para 4.

**precipice; precipitance, precipitant, precipitate, precipitation, precipitous.** See CHIEF, para 4.

**précis; precise, precisian and precision.**

*Précis* is adopted from EF-F: n use of the MF-F adj *précis*, whence, with the senses new in F, the E *precise*. The adj *précis* derives from L *praecīsus*, succinct, adj use of the pp of *praecīdere*, lit to cut off *prae-* or in front, hence simply to cut off, to shorten, *-cīdere* being the c/f of *caedere*, to cut: cf CAESURA. The L pp-adj *praecīsus* has derivative *praecīsiō*, o/s *praecīsiōn-*, whence, perh via EF-F *précision*, the E *precision*. But the E adj *precise* acquires its own derivative: *precisian*, where the suffix *-ian* is agential.

**preclude; preclusion,** whence, anl, **preclusive.**

*Preclusion* derives from L *praeclūsiōn-*, o/s of *praeclūsiō*, from *praeclūsus*, pp of *praeclūdere*, to shut *prae-* or in front, hence to place a barrier before (someone), to shut out, whence 'to *preclude*'. Cf CLOSE.

**precocious, precocity.**

The latter derives from late EF-F *précocité*, itself from the adj *précoce*, which, like E *precocious*, derives from L *praecoc-*, o/s of *praecox* (gen *praecocis*), cooked—hence ripened—beforehand, hence early, hence too early, from *praecoquere*, to cook in advance: f.a.e., COOK.

**preconceive, preconception.** See CAPABILITY, para 4.

**precurrent; precursor.** See COURSE, para 10 (at *praecurrere*).

**predator, predatory.** See PREY, para 1.

**predecessor.** See CEDE, para 9, s.f.

**predestinate, predestination; predestine.** See DESTINATION.

**predeterminant, predetermination, predeterminate, predetermine.** See TERM, para 6.

**predicament.** See DICT, para 8, s.f.

**predicate** (adj, v, v), **predication.** See DICT, para 8.

**predict, prediction, predictive.** See DICT, para 7, s.f.

**predilection.** See LEGEND, para 13.

**predispose, predisposition.** See POSE, para 10, s.f.

**predominant, predominate, predomination.** See DOMESTIC, para 6 (at *dominatus*, s.f.).

**pre-eminence, -eminent.** See MINATORY, para 3.

**pre-empt, -emption, -emptise, -emptor.** See EXEMPT, para 3.

**preen,** orig vt 'to trim (feathers) with beak', app takes the sense of earlier *prune*, to preen, and the form of *preen*, to fix with a pin, from the now dial *preen*, a pin, a brooch, OE *prēon*, a bodkin, a clasp, akin to ON *priōnn*, a nail. The now obsol *prune*, to trim or dress, ME *prunen, pruinen*, derives from MF *poroindre*, to anoint (*oindre*), the *por-* (L *pro-*) being here int: cf *ointment* at UNCTION.

**preface, prefatory.** See FAME, para 4.

**prefect, prefecture.**

The latter derives, perh via MF-F *préfecture*,

from L *praefectūra*, itself formed from *praefect*us, pp of *praeficere*, to place *prae* or before, to set over, *-ficere* being a c/f of *facere*, orig to put: f.a.e., FACT. L *praefectus*, used as n, becomes OF-MF *prefect* (MF *prefet*, late MF-F *préfet*), adopted by E.

**prefer, preferable, preference, preferent, preferential, preferment.**

'To *prefer*', whence *preferable* (cf the F *préférable*) and *preferment* (*-ment*), derives from MF-F *préférer*, itself from L *praeferre*, lit to carry (*ferre*) in front (*prae-*): cf the *-fer* of *confer, defer, infer*, etc. The pp *praeferens*, o/s *praeferent-*, becomes E *preferent*; on L *praeferent-*, F forms the late MF-F *préférence*, whence E *preference*; *preferential* is the anl adj of *preference*.

**prefiguration, prefigure.** See FIGURE, para 7.

**prefix.** See FIX, para 3.

**preform, preformation:** L *praeformāre*, LL *praeformātiō*: *prae*, before+*formāre*, to shape: f.a.e., FORM.

**pregnancy, pregnant.** See NATIVE, para 9.

**prehend, prehensible, prehensile, prehension**—whence, anl, **prehensive, prehensor; prise,** usu **prize,** a lever, to lever—cf the syn **pry; prison** (n, v), **prisoner, prisoner's** base—cf **imprison, imprisonment.**—Cpds of L *prehendere* or of derivative F *prendre* (n *prise*): **apprehend, apprehensible, apprehension, apprehensive**—whence, anl, **misapprehend, misapprehension**—cf **apprise** and **apprentice, n** (whence the v), whence **apprenticeship** (suffix *-ship*), whence also the aphetic **prentice** (n, hence adj); **comprehend, comprehensible, comprehension, comprehensive,**—negg **incomprehensible, incomprehensibility,** anl **incomprehension:**—cf **comprise; obs deprehend** (L *dēprehendere*); **enterprise,** n hence the obsol v, whence pa **enterprising**—cf **emprise** and **entrepreneur; impregnable; misprision; reprehend, reprehensible, reprehension**—cf **reprisal, reprise; surprise,** n and v (whence **surprisal,** pa **surprising**). —cf the sep PREY.

1. The base of this group is supplied by L *praehendere* (Plautus has *prehendere*); *prae*, before (sense lost in our word)+*\*hendere*, to grasp, app attested, without *n*, in *praeda*, q.v. at PREY, but not in ON *henda*, OE *gehendan*, to seize, these being from the old forms of HAND.

### Simples

2. L *praehendere, prehendere*, yields E *prehend*, to seize; and L *prehensiō* (from pp *prehensus*), o/s *prehensiōn-*, yields *prehension*; *prehensible* is formed anl with, e.g., *comprehensible*; *prehensile* derives from F *préhensile*, itself formed anl from *préhension*.

3. L *prehendere* has the contr *prendere*, whence OF-F *prendre*, pp *pris*, f *prise*, whence the OF-F n *prise*, a taking, seizing, capturing, whence ME *prise*, E *prize*, a lever, whence 'to *prize*', to move or force with a lever, esp 'to *prize* open'. *Prize*, a lever, apprehended as a pl, gives us *pry* a lever, whence 'to *pry*', to move, raise, with a lever.

4. L *prehensiō* has the contr *prensiō*, whence the VL *\*presiō*, o/s *presiōn-*, acc *presiōnem*, whence the OF-F *prison*, adopted by E, whence the now rare 'to *prison*'; derivative OF-MF *prisonier* (MF-F *prisonnier*) explains E *prisoner*. The ancient game *prisoner's base* was orig *prisoners' bars*; the station, or *base*, at first represented prison bars. The cpds OF-MF *emprisoner*, MF-F *emprisonner*, and MF-F *emprisonnement* duly became E 'to *imprison*' and *imprisonment*.

## Compounds

5. L *apprehendere* (with *ap-* for *ad-*, used int), to seize, hence to grasp with the mind, yields 'to *apprehend*'—prob via MF-F *appréhender*; much as E *apprehension* prob comes from L *apprehensiō*, o/s *apprehensiōn-*, via MF-F *appréhension*. Derivative LL *apprehensibilis* becomes *apprehensible*; and derivative ML *apprehensīvus*, *apprehensive*.

6. L *apprehendere* becomes OF-F *apprendre*, pp *appris*, f *apprise*, whence 'to *apprise*', give (someone) notice of. In OF-MF, *apprendre* has var *aprendre*, with MF derivative *aprentiz*, itself with MF-EF var *apprentis* (F *apprenti*), whence ME *aprentis*, E *apprentice*. The form *prentice* occurs already in late ME.

7. L *comprehendere*, to grasp thoroughly (int *con-*), both lit and fig, gives us 'to *comprehend*'. On the pp *comprehensus* arise *comprehensibilis*, whence *comprehensible* (cf late MF-F *compréhensible*), with derivative LL *comprehensibilitās*, whence *comprehensibility*; *comprehensiō*, o/s *comprehensiōn-*, whence late MF-F *compréhension* and, perh independently, E *comprehension*; LL *comprehensīuus*, ML *-īvus*, whence *comprehensive*.

8. The L neg *incomprehensibilis*, whence LL *incomprehensibilitās*, yields *incomprehensible* and *incomprehensibility*.

9. L *comprehendere* becomes MF-F *comprendre*, pp *compris*, f *comprise*, whence 'to *comprise*'.

10. *Enterprise*, adopted from OF-F, derives from *entrepris*, f *entreprise*, pp of OF-F *entreprendre* (*entre*, L *inter*+*prendre*), whence MF-F *entrepreneur*, adopted by E. The archaic *emprise* derives from MF *empris*, f *emprise*, pp of *emprendre*, to undertake, from VL *\*imprendere* (for *\*imprehendere*).

11A. *Impregnable*—whence *impregnability*—derives, with an intrusive *g* (prob after *impregnate* or *pregnant*), from MF-F *imprenable*, untakable, uncapturable, the neg of OF-F *prenable*, from OF-F *prendre*, to take, from LL *prendere*, a contr of L *prehendere*.

11. *Misprision*, (in Law) misdemeanour, (ordinarily) misapprehension (archaic), derives from MF *mesprision*, from OF (*se*) *mesprendre*, MF-F (*se*) *méprendre*, lit to take oneself (se) amiss (*mes-*, L *minus*; E *mis-*).

12. L *reprehendere*, lit to take (and lead) back, to hold back, to check, hence to blame, accounts for 'to *reprehend*'. On the pp *reprehensus* are formed.

LL *reprehensibilis*, whence MF-F *répréhensible*, E *reprehensible*, whence, anl, *reprehensibility*; L *reprehensiō*, o/s *reprehensiōn-*, OF-MF *reprehension*, MF-F *répréhension*, E *reprehension*.

13. L *reprehendre* becomes OF-F *reprendre*, pp *repris*, f *reprise*, the latter used, in MF-F, as n, adopted by E (with derivative v); it also becomes It *riprendere*, whence OIt *ripresaglia* (f sing), whence ML *represalia*, which, apprehended as neu pl, becomes MF *reprisailles*, whence EF-F *représailles*, whence, by b/f, the E *reprisal*.

14. In E, both the n and the v *surprise* come from MF-F *surprendre* (OF *sorprendre*), the v from the pp *surpris*, f *surprise*, the n from the derivative MF-F n *surprise*, in modern sense only since C16: OF *sor*, L *super*, over, above+*prendre*: perh suggested by VL *\*superprendre*, for *\*superprehendere*. (B & W.)

**prehistoric, prehistory.** See HISTORY, para 3.

**prejudge; prejudice, prejudicial.** See DICT, para 18A.

**prelacy, prelate** (whence **prelatic** or **prelactical**), **prelation, prelature.**

*Prelacy* derives from ML *praelatia*, an *-ia* formation from ML *praelātus*, a prelate, cf LL *praelātus*, a noble, n use of the adj *praelātus*, preferred, from L *praelātus*, used as pp of *praeferre*, lit to carry forward, hence to prefer: see PREFER. ML *praelātus*, a prelate, becomes OF *prelat* (MF-F *prélat*), ME *prelat*, E *prelate*. Derivative LL *praelātiō* (o/s *praelātiōn-*) passes through MF to become E *prelation*, much as ML *praelatūra* passes through late MF-F *prélature* to become E *prelature*.

**prelection, prelector.** See LEGEND, para 14.

**preliminary.** See LIMIT, para 3.

**prelude, prelusory.** See LUDICROUS, para 9.

**premature.** See MATURE, para 4.

**premeditate, premeditation:** L *praemeditātus*, pp of *praemeditāri* (*prae*, beforehand), and its derivative *praemeditātiō*, o/s *-meditātiōn-*. Cf *meditate*, q.v. at MEASURE.

**premier; première.** See PRIME, para 4.

**premise** and **premiss.** See MISSION, para 17.

**premium.** See EXEMPT, para 7.

**premonish; premonition, premonitory.** See MIND, para 19.

**prenotation, prenote, prenotion.** See NOTABLE, para 10.

**prentice.** See PREHEND, para 6, s.f.

**prenuncio.** See NUNCIO, para 7.

**preoccupation, preoccupy:** L *praeoccupātiō* (o/s *-ātiōn-*), from *praeoccupātus*, pp of *praeoccupāre*, to possess beforehand, whence, via late MF-F *préoccuper*, the E 'to *preoccupy*'.

**preordain, preordination.** See ORDER, para 5 and, for the n, para 4, s.f.

**preparation, preparatory, prepare.** See PARE, para 5.

**prepense.** See PEND, para 25.

**preponderance, preponderant, preponderate, preponderation.** See PEND, para 23.

**prepose.** See POSE, para 16.

preposition. See POSE, para 16.

prepositor, prepositure; prepostor. See POSE, para 16.

prepossess, whence, anl, prepossessing. See POSSESS, para 2.

preposterous. See POSTERIOR, s.f.

prepotence, prepotent. See POSSE, para 4.

prepuce, whence the adj preputial; pustule (whence pustular), pustulate, pustulation, pustulous.

1. *Prepuce*, the foreskin, derives from OF *prepuce*, MF-F *prépuce*: L *praeputium*: app *prae-*, in front+*putium*, perh akin to White Ru *potka*, penis, and Lith *pusti*, to blow, to swell, and *pusli*, a vesicle, a bladder, hence also to Gr *phusa*, a bubble, a bellows, and the echoic Skt-E *phut*, therefore to L *pustula*, varr *pussula*, *pūsula*, a bubble, a pimple.

2. L *pustula* becomes MF-F *pustule*, adopted by E; the derivative EF-F adj *pustuleux*, f *pustuleuse*, yields E *pustulous*. In LL, *pustula* has derivative *pustulāre*, vi and vt, to (cause to) break out in pimples, with presp *pustulans*, o/s *pustulant-*, whence E *pustulant*, and with pp *pustulātus*, whence 'to *pustulate*'; derivative LL *pustulātiō* (o/s -*ātiōn-*) yields *pustulation*.

prerogate, prerogation, prerogative. See ROGATION, para 10.

prerupt, preruption. See RUPTURE, para 9.

presage. See SEEK, para 6.

presbyopia, presbyopic. See the element *presby-*.

presbyter; Presbyterian, whence Presbyterianism; presbytery; priest, priesthood.

*Presbyterian*, designating a sect, derives from the adj *presbyterian*, of or by or in or for a *presbyter*, an elder, adopted from LL *presbyter*, an elder in the early Christian church, the term being pagan and deriving from LL *presbyter*, a senior, from LGr *presbuteros*, an Eccl elder, Gr *presbuteros*, a senior, from the adj 'older', the comp of Gr *presbus*, an old man, old, important, orig 'going in front, taking precedence' (L & S): two elements, *pres-* akin to L *prae-*, in front+*bu-*, IE var *gu-*, an ox, *presbus* being orig '(an ox) leading the way' (Boisacq).

2. LGr *presbuteros*, a church elder, has derivative *presbuterion*, whence LL *presbyterium*, whence OF *presbiterie* (MF-F *presbytère*), whence E *presbytery*.

3. Akin to and perh ult deriving from LL *presbyter* is OE *prēost* (cf the OF-MF *prestre*, MF-F *prêtre*), ME *preost*, var *prest*, E priest, whence *priestess* and *priestly*; derivative OE *prēosthād* becomes *priesthood*. But Walshe thinks that OE *prēost* comes rather from L *praepositus*: one who is set over a congregation.

prescience, prescient. See SCIENCE, para 9.

prescribe; prescript, prescriptible, prescription, prescriptive. See SCRIBE, para 17.

presence, present (adj, n, v), presentation. See ESSE, para 8.

presentient, presentiment. See SENSE, para 17.

presentment: OF *presentement* (MF-F *pré-*), from *presenter*: cf ESSE, para 8.

preservation (whence, anl, preservative, adj hence n); preserve (v, hence n), whence preserver.

*Preservation* derives from MF-F *préservation*, formed anl from LL *praeseruāre*, to observe (a custom), whence MF-F *préserver*, whence 'to *preserve*'. Cf CONSERVE.

preside, presidency, president, presidential, presidium. See SIT, para 16.

presignification, presignify. See SIGN, para 17.

press (1), as in press gang; press, to commandeer; prest;—impress, imprest.

1. *Press*, a compulsory enlistment, is for *prest*, a loan, enlistment for advance pay (both obs): OF-MF *prest* (MF-F *prêt*), a loan, from OF-MF *prester* (MF-F *prêter*, to lend): LL *praestāre*, to lend (money), L *praestāre*, to supply: f.a.c., STAND. OF-MF *prester* becomes 'to *prest*' (obs), whence 'to *press*'.

2. E *prest*, n and v, has the prefix cpd *imprest*, n and v; and *press*, v, has prefix cpd *impress*, to levy (money) for the state, to force into enlistment.

press (2), to squeeze, crowd, a being squeezed or crowded,—whence agent presser and pa pressing and pressible; pression (obsol); pressive (from E *press*); pressor; pressure;—print (n and v), whence printable, printer, printing, printless.—Compounds of *press*, *print*, also of the L c/f -*prim-*: appressed, appressor, appressorium; compress (n, v), compression (whence, anl, compressive), compressor; depress (whence depressant), depression (whence, anl, depressive), depressor; express, adj (whence n) and v, whence expressible (and inexpressible), expression, expressive (and inexpressive), expressor; impress (v, hence n, hence also impressible), impression, impressionable, impressionism; impressionist, impressive (neg unimpressive)—imprimatur—imprint, n and v; oppress, oppression, oppressive, oppressor; repress (whence repressible, whence irrepressible), repression, repressive, repressor—reprimand, n and v; sprain, v, hence n; suppress (whence suppressible), suppression (whence, anl, suppressive), suppressor.

1. L *premere*, to press (lit and fig), to squeeze, pp *pressus*, has r *pre-*, which could well be the IE r, perh with metathetic var *\*per-*: cf L *prelum* (s *prel-*, r *pre-*), a wine-press, and perh Ru *peret'*, to press, OSl *pirati*, to trample, Lith *perti*, to thrash, flog; perh also Skt *sphuráti*, he knocks with the foot. (E & M.)

2. On the L pp *pressus* is formed the freq *pressāre*, whence OF-F *presser*, whence 'to *press*'; the n *press* derives from OF-F *presse* (from *presser*). Also from pp *pressus* comes *pressiō*, o/s *pressiōn-*, MF-F *pression*, adopted by E—LL *pressor*, adopted by E—*pressūra*, OF-EF *pressure*, adopted by E.

3. L *premere* becomes OF-MF *preindre*, pp *preint*, f *preinte*, used as MF n, adopted by ME with var *printe*, whence E *print*; 'to *print*' derives from ME *printen*, from ME *printe*.

Compounds

4. L *apprimere* (*ap-* for *ad*, to, towards), to press

to, hence to fit closely to, has pp *appressus*, whence 'to *appress*', used only in the Bot and Zoo pa *appressed*; cf the SciL (Bot) *appressorium*, consisting of *appress*us+*-orium*.

5. L *comprimere*, to press *con*- or together, has pp *compressus*, whence the LL int *compressāre*, to press hard, whence the OF-EF *compresser*, whence 'to *compress*'; the derivative MF-F n *compresse* yields É *compress*. Derivative L *compressiō*, o/s *compressiōn-*, passes through MF to become E *compression*; derivative ML *compressīvus* becomes —perh via MF-F *compressif*, f *compressive*—the E *compressive*; derivative L *compressor* is adopted by E.

6. L *dēprimere*, to press *dē*- or down, has pp *dēpressus*, whence the LL int *dēpressāre*, to press down hard; E 'to *depress*' could derive from either the L pp or the LL inf. The pp *dēpressus* has derivatives *dēpressiō*, o/s *dēpressiōn-*, whence, perh via MF-F *dépression*, the E *depression*, and *dēpressor* (crusher of weakness), whence perh the form of the tech E *depressor*.

7. L *exprimere*, to press out, has pp *expressus*, whence the OF-F adj *expres*, f *expresse*, E *express*; 'to *express*' derives from MF *expresser*, *espresser*, from OF-F *presser* after the L. Derivative L *expressiō*, o/s *expressiōn-*, becomes MF-F *expression*, adopted by E; the F *expression* has anl derivative *expressif*, f *-ive*, whence E *expressive*. Derivative LL *expressor* provides at least the form of E *expressor*.

8. L *imprimere*, to press onto or upon, has the modern offshoot, *imprimatur*, let it be printed, hence as n. The pp *impressus* yields 'to *impress*'; its derivative *impressiō*, o/s *impressiōn-*, passes through MF-F to become E *impression*, whence, anl, *impressive*. F *impression* has derivatives *impressionable*, *impressionisme*, *impressioniste*: whence E *impressionable*, *impressionism*, *impressionist*.

9. L *imprimere* becomes MF-F *empreindre*, pp *empreint*, f *empreinte*, which, used as MF-F n, yields 'an *imprint*'; 'to *imprint*' derives from ME *imprenten*, earlier *empreynten*, from MF *empreinter*, from *empreinte*.

10. L *opprimere* (*op*- for *ob*), to squeeze, to crush, has pp *oppressus*, with ML int *oppressāre*, whence MF-F *oppresser*, E 'to *oppress*'; derivative L *oppressiō*, o/s *oppressiōn-*, passes through OF-F to become E *oppression*; late MF-F *oppressif* (from *oppresser*) yields E *oppressive*, which, however, may—like the F word—derive from ML *oppressīvus*; L *oppressor* (from pp *oppressus*) is adopted by E—perh via MF-F *oppresseur*.

11. L *reprimere*, to press *re*- or back, to check, has gerundive *reprimendus*, with f *reprimenda* used elliptically for *culpa reprimenda*, a fault to be checked, hence a scolding, EF *réprimende*, later *réprimande*, whence E *reprimand*; derivative EF *réprimender*, later *réprimander*, gives 'to *reprimand*'.

12. L *reprimere* has pp *repressus*, whence 'to *repress*'; derivative LL *repressiō*, o/s *repressiōn-*, whence, perh via late MF-F *répression*, the E

*repression*; derivative OF-F *répressif*, f *-ive*, yields E *repressive*. The L agent *repressor* is adopted by E.

13. To interpolate! 'To *sprain*' derives, by aphesis, from MF *espreindre*, from VL *\*expremere*, for L *exprimere*: 'to press (a muscle, etc.) *out of* place'.

14. L *supprimere*, to press *sub* or under (hence to put down), to press under foot, hence to cause to disappear, to subjugate, has pp *suppressus*, whence 'to *suppress*'; derivative L *suppressiō* (o/s *suppressiōn-*), LL concealment, becomes E (and EF-F) *suppression*, and LL *suppressor*, hider (of another's slaves) supplies the form of E *suppressor*.

**prest.** See 1st PRESS, para 1.

**prestidigitation, prestidigitator.** See DICT, para 3, s.f.

**prestige, prestigious.** See the 2nd STRAIN, para 11.

**presto:** adopted from It (adj, hence adv): LL *praestus*, quick: L *praesto*, quickly: ? from L *praesto*, I am at the head of.

**presume, presumable, presumption, presumptive, presumptuous.** See SUMPTION, para 4.

'To *presume*' derives from OF-MF *presumer* (MF-F *présumer*), from L *praesumere*, to take *prae*- or in advance, hence to take for granted: for *sumere*, see SUMPTUARY. Derivative L *praesumptiō*, o/s *praesumptiōn-*, yields—perh via OF-MF *presomption* (MF-F *pré*-)—E *presumption*; anl LL *praesumptiuus*, bold, contentious, ML *praesumptivus*, conjectural, yields MF-F *présomptif*, f *-ive*, whence the reshaped E *presumptive*; the LL mdfn *praesumptuōsus*, conceited, audacious, (pej) self-confident, becomes OF-MF *presomptueux*, f *-ueuse* (MF-F *pré*-), whence E *presumptuous*.

**presuppose, presupposition.** See POSE, para 22, s.f.

**pretend, pretender; pretence, pretension, pretentious.** See TEND, para 18.

**preterit,** now usu **preterite** (adj, hence n): MF *preterit* (later *prétérit*): L *praeteritum* (*tempus*): *praeteritus*, pp of *praeterīre*, to go (*īre*) beyond (*praeter*), pass by: cf prefix *preter*- and ITINERARY. —Derivative LL *praeteritiō* (o/s *-itiōn-*) becomes, perh via EF-F *prétérition*, the E *preterition*, a being passed over, a passing over (in silence).

**pretermission, pretermit.** See MISSION, para 18.

**preternatural:** ML *praeternātūrālis*; *praeter*, beyond+*nātūra*, nature.

**pretext.** See TECHNIC, para 13, s.f.

**pretty** (adj, hence adv), whence **prettify, prettily, prettiness:** ME *prati*: OE *praettig*, sly, cunning, the adj (*-ig*) of *praet*, *praett*, deceit, cunning: cf ON *prettugr*, tricky, deceitful, adj of *prettr*, a trick.

**pretzel** comes, as Walshe notes, from the Upper German pron of G *Bretzel*: MHG *brezel*: OHG *brezitella*: ? from VL *\*braciola* (cf LL *brac(c)hi-olum*), dim of VL *bracia*, f sing from L *brac(c)hia*, pl of *brac(c)hium*, an arm.

**preux chevalier.** See PROUD, para 1, s.f.

prevail (whence pa **prevailing**), **prevalence**, **prevalent**. See VALUE, para 19.

**prevaricate, prevarication, prevaricator**. See VACILLANT, para 8.

**prevent, prevention, preventive**. See VENUE, para 19.

**previous**. See VIA, para 15.

**previse, prevision**. See VIDE, para 14.

**prey**, n and v; **predator, predatory;—depredate, depredation, depredator, depredatory**.

1. 'To *prey*' derives from OF-MF *preier, preër*: L *praedāri*, from *praeda*, booty, OL *praida*: perh from the r of L *praehendere, prehendere*, to seize. The n *prey*, ME *preie*, OF *preie*, comes from *praeda*. *Praedāri* has agent *praedātor*, whence E *predator*; derivative *praedātōrius* becomes E *predatory*.

2. *Praedāri* has LL cpd *dēpraedāri, -praedāre*, to plunder or thieve, pp *dēpraedātus*, whence 'to *depredate*'; derivatives *dēpraedātiō* (o/s *-ātiōn-*) and *dēpraedātor* yield *depredation* and *depredator*, the latter acquiring, anl, the adj *depredatory*.

**Priapean, priapism, Priapus**.

*Priapean* (verse) derives from, L *Priapeius*, of *Priapus*, trln of Gr *Priapos*, the God of Virility: o.o.o.: ? from Asia Minor: but perh rather cf Skt *sápas*, penis. The Med *priapism*=LL *priapismus*, earlier *-ismos*=Gr *priapismos*=Priapos+ suffix *-ismos*.

**price**, n (whence **priceless**) and v; **prize**, n and v, 'value', and **apprize** and **misprize**, to undervalue; **precious, précieuse, preciosity; praise** (v, hence n)— **appraise**, whence **appraisal, appraisement, appraiser** —**dispraise**, v, hence n; **appreciable, appreciate, appreciation** (whence, anl, **appreciative** and **appreciator**)—**depreciable, depreciate, depreciation** (whence **depreciative, depreciator, depreciatory**).— **interpret, interpretable, interpretation** (whence, anl, **interpretative**), **interpreter**, (from *interpret*) **interpretive**.

1. L *pretium*, a price paid for goods or service, hence also a reward, has s *preti-*, r *pret-*: o.o.o., unless, as seems not improbable, akin to L *interpres*, o/s *interpret-*, an intermediary, a commercial agent, a negotiator, hence an interpreter: *inter*, between, among+*pres* (? for *prets*), *a trafficker, gen *pretis*, r *pret-*.

## Simples and their Prefix-Compounds

2. L *pretium* becomes OF-MF *pris* (MF-F *prix*), adopted by ME, whence E *price*; 'to *price*' derives from the n rather than from ME *prisen*, to value, which, the source of the syn 'to *prize*', comes itself from MF *prisier*, OF *preisier*, LL *pretiāre*, to value, to prize, from L *pretium*. *Prize*, v, occurs in the prefix-cpds *apprize*, to put a value on (*ap-*, L *ad*), from MF *aprisier* (cf *appraise* in para 3), and *misprize*, to misvalue, to scorn, from MF *mesprisier*, OF *mespreisier* (cf the F *mépriser*): *mes-*, L *minus*, E *mis-*+*preisier, prisier*.

3. OF *preisier* becomes ME *preisen*, whence 'to *praise*', whence the n *praise*. There are two cpds:

*appraise*, which, prob after the corresp L cpd, is formed of *ap-* (for *ad-*)+*praise*;

*dispraise*, ME *dispreisen*, MF *despreisier* (*des-*, L *dis-*+*preisier*).

4. L *pretium* has adj *pretiōsus*, whence OF-MF *precios*, MF-F *précieux*, f *précieuse*, partly adopted by E for '(an) affectedly literary (woman)': hence E *precious*. Derivative L *pretiōsitās*, o/s *pretiōsitāt-*, becomes MF-F *préciosité*, whence E *preciosity*.

## Latin Compounds and English Derivatives

5. LL *appretiāre*, to value *ap-* for *ad*, i.e. at a price, has pp *appretiātus*, whence 'to *appreciate*'; *appretiāre* becomes MF-F *apprécier*, with derivatives late MF-F *appréciable*, late MF-F *appréciation* (perh suggested by LL *appretiātiō*, acc *appretiā-tiōnem*), EF-F *appréciatif* (f *-ive*), EF-F *apprécia-teur*, whence, resp, *appreciable, appreciation, appreciative, appreciator*.

6. L *dēpretiāre*, to price *dē-* or down, has pp *dēpretiātus*, whence to *depreciate*; it becomes F *déprécier*, with derivatives *dépréciable* and *dépré-ciation*, which have perh influenced E *depreciable* and *depreciation*; *depreciator* (cf F *dépréciateur*) comes from LL *dēpretiātor*, a cheapener.

## Interpretation

7. L *interpres* (o/s *interpret-*), negotiator, agent, hence interpreter, has derivative *interpretāri*, to explain, to interpret, whence MF *interpreter* (F *inter-préter*), whence 'to *interpret*'; L derivative *interpre-tātiō* (o/s *-ātiōn-*) becomes OF-MF *interpretation* (later *interprétation*), adopted by E, and LL deriva-tive *interpretātor* prob influenced MF *interpreteur* (imm from the MF v), whence the E *interpreter*. LL *interpretābilis* yields *interpretable*; whereas *inter-pretive* comes from 'to *interpret*', the now less usual *interpretative* comes from the obs 'to *interpretate*' (L *interpretātus*, pp of *interpretāri*).

**prick** (n, v), whence the dim **pricket; prick-eared, prick song; pricker**, from 'to *prick*'; **prickle** (n, hence v), whence **prickly**—whence **prickly heat** and **prickly pear**; ? **prig**, whence **priggish**.

1. A *prick*, orig the mark made by anything sharply pointed, hence a tapering point (e.g., a thorn, a goad), a sting, derives from OE *prica*, a point or a dot: cf MD *pric, pricke*, D *prik*, LG *prick* or *pricke*, and several Scan cognates. Akin to, prob deriving from, OE *prica* is OE *prician*, to pierce slightly, whence E 'to *prick*', with many naturally effluent senses, e.g. 'to ride with spurs'; cf ON *prīca*, to beat, and, syn with E, LG *pricken*, MD *priken*, D *prikken*, Sw *pricka*. *Prick-eared* refers to sharp, pointed ears; *prick song*, to the 'points' or notes.

2. OE *prica* has dim *pricel*, whence a *prickle*: cf MD *prikel*, D *prikkel*, LG *prickel*: with the v, cf G *prickeln*, MHG *prekeln*, MD *prikeln*, D *prikkeln*.

3. Sl *prig*, to steal, perh derives from *prick*, to stick a sharp point into something in order to remove it. A *prig*, orig a fellow, then a tiresomely self-sufficient or virtuous fellow, perh derives from

sl *prig*, a thief, from the v; the thieving *prig*, n and v, was orig an underworld term (P¹). The too obviously virtuous fellow might, however, draw his name from 'to *prick*' in its now dial sense 'to adorn'.

**pride.** See PROUD, para 2.

**prie-Dieu.** See PRAY, para 6.

**priest, priesthood, priestly.** See PRESBYTER, para 3.

**prig,** n and v. See PRICK, para 3.

**prim.** See PRIME, para 3.

**primacy.** See PRIME, para 5, s.f.

**primage.** See PRIME (heading).

**primary.** See PRIME, para 4.

**primate.** See para 5 of:—

**prime,** adj and n and—mostly from that adj or that n—v; **prim**; **primacy**, **primate**; naut **primage**, from adj *prime*; **primary** (adj, hence n)—cf **premier** and **première**; **primeval**; **primer**; **primero**; **primitive** (adj, hence n); **primogeniture**; **primordial**, **primordium**; **primrose**; **primula**; **primus.**—**prior** (adj, n), **priority**, **priory**; **prince** (whence **princely**) and **princess**; **principal** (adj, hence n), **principality**, **principate**; **principium**; **principle** (n, hence v), whence pa **principled**, with neg **unprincipled**; **Priscian**; **pristine.**

1. In L *primus*, first, earliest, the sup corresp to the L comp *prior*, earlier, and prob occurring in L *pristinus*, existing in, or as if in, its first state, and L *priscus*, syn except that the thing no longer exists, we have a set of derivatives from—or, at the least, cognates with—the OL adv *pri*, forwards, from in front: akin to the virtually syn OL adv *pro*; cf also the Homeric adv and Attic prep and conj *prin*, before: the IE r is *pri-*, before. (Boisacq.) In L, *prim-*, *prin-*, *pris-*, are therefore extnn of *pri-*.

2. L *primus*, (the) first, is retained by E in certain special usages; the portable stove so named is prop *Primus*, a trade-name. L *primus* becomes the OF-MF adj *prin*, f *prime* (surviving only in phrases); hence the E adj. The Eccl E *prime*, the first hour of the Eccl day, derives from OE *prim*, from L *prima* (*hora*), f of *primus*; derivative is *prime*, one's maturity, the best part, etc. 'To *prime*' derives mainly from the adj; in sense 'to trim' (a shrub, a tree), it perh owes something to the 3rd PRUNE (to trim); 'to *prime* or put into working order' is to establish, or to restore, what should be its *first* condition.

3. OF-MF *prin* has—influenced by the f *prime* —the var *prim*, which, in the derivative MF-EF sense 'fine or delicate', yields the E *prim*, formally precise or neat, (later) stiffly or fussily decorous.

4. L *primus*, first, has mdfn *primarius*, orig a military term for 'of the first rank'—cf the LL sense 'a leader'; hence E *primary*. L *primarius* becomes OF-F *premier*, f *première*, first in rank, later first in appearance, whence the n *première*, first showing of a play, elliptical for *première représentation*. Largely displacing *prime minister*, the n *premier* is elliptical for *premier minister* (c1680–1740: OED). ML *primarius*, used as n

(? for *p. liber*, primary book) for 'prayer book', var *primarium*, becomes, in C14, E *primer*, first used in its modern sense late in C15. L *primarius* becomes Sp *primero*, whence *primera*, a card game, re-shaped by E to *primero*.

5. L *primus* has the derivative *primas*, one who belongs to a leading family, hence a leading person, in LL the chairman of a Church council, a metropolitan bishop (Souter), in ML the head of the Church: from the acc *primatem* comes OF-F *primat*, adopted by ME, whence E *primate*. Derivative ML *primatia*—cf LL *primatus*, gen -*us*—becomes MF *primacie* (EF-F *primatie*), whence E *primacy*.

6. L *primus* has derivative adv *primitus*, in the first place, whence the adj *primitiuus*, ML *primitivus*, first-born: MF-F *primitif*, f *primitive*, adopted by E.

7. In ML, *primus* has the derivative n *primula*: whence, prob by illiterate corruption, OF-MF *primerole*, altered, after *rose*, to OF-F *primerose*: ME *prymerose*: E *primrose*.

8. The foll cpds will be found:

*primeval*, at AGE, para 2;

*primogeniture*, at GENERAL, para 27—cf *primogenous*, ib, para 27, s.f.;

*primordial*, at ORDER, para 13.

9. For *prince* and *princess*, see CAPABILITY, para 8 at *princeps*—where also are treated *principal*, *principate*, as well as (para 8, s.f.) *principle*.

10. Akin to L *primus* are both *priscus* and *pristinus*, as in para 1. *Priscus* has derivative *Priscianus*, a famous Roman grammarian: E *Priscian*, often used generically, as in 'breaking Priscian's head' or flouting grammar. *Pristinus* yields E *pristine*, fresh and unspoilt.

11. L *prior*, coming before, earlier, is adopted by E; the ML derivative *prioritas*, o/s *prioritat-*, becomes MF-F *priorité*, whence *priority*. In ML, *prior* is used as n, adopted by both OF and OE, whence, perh rather from OF-MF than from OE, the ME *priour*, *prior*, E *prior*; MF *prioresse* becomes E *prioress*, and OF-MF *prioré* (F *prieuré*) becomes E *priory*.

**primer.** See prec, para 4, s.f.

**primeval.** See AGE, para 2; cf PRIME, para 1.

**primitive.** See PRIME, para 6.

**primero.** See PRIME, para 4, s.f.

**primogeniture.** See GENERAL, para 27; cf PRIME, para 1.

**primogenous.** See GENERAL, para 27, s.f., and cf PRIME, para 8.

**primordial.** See ORDER, para 13; cf PRIME, para 8.

**primrose.** See PRIME, para 7.

**primula.** See PRIME, para 7.

**primus.** See PRIME, para 2.

**prince, princess.** See CAPABILITY, para 8, at *princeps.*

**principal; principate.** See CAPABILITY, para 8, at *princeps.*

**principle.** See CAPABILITY, para 8, at *princeps.*

**prink.** See PRANK.

**print**, whence **printer, printing.** See the 2nd PRESS, para 3.

**prior, priority, priory.** See PRIME, para 11.

**Priscian.** See PRIME, para 10.

**prism**: LL, from Gr, *prisma*: from Gr *prizein*, extn of *priein*, to saw; perh cf Alb *priš*, to break up; IE r, ? *\*perĕi-*, to break into small pieces. (Boisacq.) On the Gr o/s *prismat-* are formed F *prismatique* and E *prismatic.*

**prison, prisoner.** See PREHEND, para 2.

**pristine.** See PRIME, para 10.

**prithee.** See PRAY, para 6.

**private** (adj, hence n), whence **privacy** (for *\*privatecy*) and **privateer** (agential *-eer*); **privation, privative; privity, privy** (adj, hence n; hence also **privily**); cpd **privilege** (n, v); prefix-cpd **deprivation** (whence, anl, **deprivative**), **deprive.**

1. At the base, lies OL *prīuus*, taken in isolation, singular, owned by one person. '*Prīuus* could have issued from *\*prei-u-os* [*pri-u-os*]: that which is in front, hence that which is isolated from the rest' (E & M): if that be so, cf PRIME, para 1.

2. OL *prīuus* has derivative *prīuāre*, ML *prīvāre*, to put aside, to exempt, hence to deprive of, with pp *prīuātus*, ML *prīvātus*, used as adj, hence also as n 'a private person'; hence the E adj *private.* Derivative *prīuātiō*, ML *prīvātiō*, o/s *prīvātiōn-*, leads through MF-F to E *privation*; derivative L *prīuātīuus*, ML *prīvātīvus*, to E *privative.*

3. L *prīuātus*, ML *prīvātus*, becomes OF-F *privé*, whence E *privy*; derivative MF *priveté*, adopted by ME, whence *privity.*

4. OL *prīuus* acquires the cpd *prīuilēgium*, ML *prīvilēgium*, a law affecting a private person (L *lex*, o/s *leg-*, a law), whence OF-MF *privilege* (MF-F *privilège*), adopted by ME; and OF *privilege* has MF derivative v *privelegier* (F *privilégier*), whence 'to *privilege*'.

5. L *prīuāre* has the ML cpd *dēprīvāre*, whence (MF *depriver* and E) 'to *deprive*'; the ML derivative *dēprīvātiō*, o/s *dēprīvātiōn-*, yields E *deprivation.*

**privet**, a Eurasian shrub widely used for hedges, is, in Sc, *privie*: perh, therefore, from the privacy it ensures—cf *privy* at PRIVATE, para 3. Perh, however, it is a f/e alteration of *\*primet*, from *prime*, to prune.

**privilege.** See PRIVATE, para 4.

**privity, privy.** See PRIVATE, para 3.

**prize** (1), a lever; to lever. See PREHEND, para 3.

**prize** (2), a reward; to value. See PRICE, para 2.

**probabilism, probability, probable.** See PROVE, para 3.

**probant.** See PROVE, para 4.

**probate, probation, probationary, probative.** See PROVE, para 4.

**probe**, n and v. See PROVE, para 5.

**probity.** See PROVE, para 2.

**problem, problematic** (with extn in *-al*).

The latter derives from late MF-F *problématique*, LL *problēmaticus*, Gr *problēmatikos*, the adj of Gr *problēma*, L *problēma*, MF-F *problème*, ME *probleme*, E *problem.* Gr *problēma* is lit 'a thing thrown forward', esp for the mind to solve: Gr

*pro*, forward+*blēma*, a throwing, something thrown, from *ballō*, I throw: f.a.e., BALLISTIC.

**proboscis.** See the element *proboscidi-.*

**procedure, proceed, proceedings; process, procession, processional.** See CEDE, para 10.

**proclaim; proclamation.** See CLAIM, para 8.

**proclivity, proclivous.** See CLIVUS, para 4.

**proconsul**, one acting *pro* or for a consul, hence, in E, a governor of a province, is adopted from L; adj, *proconsular* (L *proconsulāris*).

**procrastinate, procrastination.**

The latter derives, perh via F, from L *procrastinātiōn-*, o/s of *procrastinātiō*, from *procrastinātus*, pp of *procrasināre*, to bring *pro* or forward until *cras*, tomorrow, to make it a matter for tomorrow; *procrastinātus* yields 'to *procrastinate*'.

**procreate, procreation, procreative, procreator.** See CREATE, para 3.

**Procrustean** derives from *Procrustes*, that legendary highwayman of Attica who stretched or abbreviated his victims to fit them to the length of an iron bed: L: from Gr *prokroustēs*, agent of *prokrouein*, to beat out and so to stretch: *pro*, forward+*krouein*, to beat or strike, a v with Sl cognates.

**proctor.** See CURE, para 4.

**procuration, procurator; procure, procurer.** See CURE, para 3.

**procurrent, procursive.** See COURSE, para 10 (at *procurrere*).

**prod** (n, hence v), a pricking with a pointed instrument or remark, is app akin to the now only dial *brod*, a thorn, a goad, ME *brod*, ON *broddr*: cf BRAD.

**prodigal** (adj hence n), **prodigality.**

*Prodigal*, adj, is adopted from late MF-EF *prodigal*, app a b/f from MF-F *prodigalité*, whence E *prodigality*; and MF *prodigalité* derives from LL *prodigalitātem*, acc of *prodigalitās*, itself—influenced by *liberalitās*—from L *prodigus*, wastefully extravagant, from *prodigere*, to dissipate (one's substance), orig to drive (*agere*) before (*pro*) oneself: f.a.e., ACT.

**prodigious; prodigy.**

The former derives—perh via late MF-F *prodigieux*, f *prodigieuse*—from L *prōdigiōsus*, adj of *prōdigium*, a prophetic sign, hence a marvel, hence something or someone extraordinary, whence E *prodigy*: *prō*, before+*adagium* (see ADAGE), with *-ag-* thinned to *-ig-.*

**produce** (v, n); **product, production, productive.** See DUKE, para 6 (at *producere*).

**proem**, whence **proemial**: ME, from MF, *proheme* (F *proème*): L *prooemium*: Gr *prooimion*: *pro*, before+*oimē*, a song.

**profanation, profane** (adj, v), **profanity.** See FANE, para 2.

**profess, profession** (whence **professional**, adj, hence n), **professive, professor, professorial.**

'To *profess*' is a b/f from ME *professed*, bound by a religious vow: syn OF-MF *profes* (F *profès*), f *professe*: syn LL *professus*, f *professa*, from L *profess*us (f *-fessa*), declaring (adj), from the pp of *profitēri*, to declare: *pro*, before+*-fitēri*, c/f of *fatēri*, to admit, confess: cf CONFESS. Derivative L *professiō* leads, via the acc *professiōnem*, to OF-F *profession*, adopted by E; LL *professīuus*, ML *-īvus*, yields *professive*; L *professor*, a (public) teacher, becomes MF-F *professeur* and, perh independently, E *professor*; L *professōrius* becomes, with different suffix, *professorial*.

**proffer**, ME *profren, proferen*, comes from MF *proffrir*, contr of *poroffrir*: *por* (F *pour*), for+ *offrir*, to offer, VL *\*offerire*, L *offerre* (cf OFFER).

**proficiency, proficient.** The former derives from the latter, itself from L *prōficient-*, o/s of *prōficiens*, presp of *prōficere*, which, in LL, means 'to advance, to develop': *prō-*, forward+*-ficere*, for *facere*, to make: f.a.e., FACT. Cf PROFIT.

**profile.** See FILAMENT, para 8.

**profit**, n and v; **profitable**; from the n, both **profiteer** and **profitless**.

*Profitable*, adopted from OF-F, derives from OF-F *profiter*, whence E 'to *profit*'; OF *profiter* derives from OF-F *profit*, whence the E n; and OF *profit* derives from the L n *prōfectus*, advance, improvement, profit, from *prōfectus*, pp of *prōficere*, to progress, hence to yield a profit: *prō*, forward+*-ficere*, c/f of *facere*, to make: f.a.e., FACT.

**profligate** (adj, hence n), whence **profligacy**: L *prōflīgātus*, pp of *prōflīgāre*, to strike or fling *prō*, forward, hence to the ground; *-flīgāre*, for *flīgere*, to strike down: cf Gr *phlib*ein, to press hard —cf also AFFLICT, CONFLICT, INFLICT.

**profound, profundity.** See the 1st FOUND, para 5.

**profuse, profusion.** See the 2nd FOUND, para 11.

**prog** (now only dial), to forage, hence food, derives from—or from the same source as— ME *prokken*, to forage, which has MD, MLG, also Scan cognates.

**progenitor, progeniture.** See GENERAL, para 12.

**progeny.** See GENERAL, para 24.

**prognosis; prognosticate, prognostication.** See the 2nd GNOME, para 7.

**program, -gramme.** See GRAMMAR, para 5.

**progress, progression, progressive.** See GRADE, para 15.

**prohibit, prohibition, prohibitive.** See HABIT, para 11.

**project** (n, v), **projectile** (adj, hence n), **projection, projector** (from 'to *project*').

L *prōiicere*, contr *prōicere*, to cast forward, is a prefix-cpd: *prō*, forward+*-iicere*, c/f of *iacere* (ML *jacere*), to cast or throw: cf JET. Its pp *prōiectus*, ML *prōjectus*, yields 'to *project*'; the neu *prōiectum*, ML *prōjectum*, yields the n *project*. LL *prōiectīuus*, ML *-īvus*, becomes E *projective*; *projectile* is a learnèd F derivative, in *-ile*, from ML *prōject*us.

**prolapse.** See LABOR, para 2.

**prolation, prolative.** See the 1st TOLL, para 6.

**prolegomena, prolegomenon.** See LEGEND, para 31.

**prolepsis, proleptic.**

The latter comes from Gr *prolēptikos* adj of *prolēpsis*, whence, via LL, the E *prolepsis*, lit a taking in advance: Gr *pro*, forward+*lēpsis*, from *lambanein*, to take: cf CATALEPSY.

**proletarian** (adj, hence n), **proletary, proletariat.**

The 1st is a mdfn of the 2nd, which derives from L *prōlētārius*, adj of *prōlēs*, offspring; L *prō*, forward+*alere*, to nourish: cf ALIMENT. *Proletariat* adapts F *prolétariat*, itself from F *prolétaire* (L *prōlētārius*).

**proliferate, proliferation.** See the element *proli-*.

**prolific**, whence **prolifiacy**: EF-F *prolifique*: ML *prōlificus*: *prōli-*, c/f of *prōlēs*, offspring (q.v. at PROLETARIAN)+*-ficus*, -making, from *facere*, to make (f.a.e., FACT).

**prolix, prolixity.** See LIQUEFY, para 7.

**prolocutor.** See LOQUACIOUS, para 7.

**prologue.** See LEGEND, para 28, s.f.

**prolong, prolongation.** See LONG, para 11.

**prolusion.** See LUDICROUS, para 10.

**promenade.** See MINATORY, para 5.

**Promethean** is the adj of **Prometheus**, which, adopted from L, is the Gr *Promētheus*, the Forethinker, n from *promēthēs*, forethoughtful: *pro*, forward+perh a derivative from *menos*, mind.

**prominence, prominent.** See MINATORY, para 3.

**promiscuity, promiscuous.**

The former derives from F *promiscuité*, learnedly formed from L *prōmiscu*us, confused, whence E *promiscuous*: *prō*, for, instead of+*miscē*re, to mix: f.a.e., MIX.

**promise, promissive, promissory.** See MISSION, para 19.

**promittor.** See MISSION, para 19, s.f.

**promontory.** See MINATORY, para 4.

**promote, promotion.** See MOVE, para 13.

**prompt, promptitude, promptuary.** See EXEMPT, para 9.

**promulgate, promulgation, promulgator, promulge.** See VULGAR, para 2.

**prone**, whence **proneness; pronation.**

The 3rd derives from *prōnātiōn-*, o/s of ML *prōnātiō*, itself from the source of E *prone*: L *prōnus*, leaning forward, hence inclined to (do something): from *prō*, forwards (for *-nus*, cf *infernus*: E & M): cf Skt *pravaṇa*, inclined (lit and fig).

**prong.** See PANG.

**pronominal, pronoun.** See NAME, para 8.

**pronounce, pronouncement.** See NUNCIO, para 8.

**pronto.** See EXEMPT, para 10.

**pronunciamento; pronunciation.** See NUNCIO, para 8.

**proof.** See PROVE, para 6.

**prop**, n, hence v (cf the syn MD *proppen*): ME, from MD, *proppe*, a stake or pole that supports, later a stopper or stopple: cf MLG *prop, proppe*, a plug, G (C18+) *Pfropfen*, a stopper, a cork, from LG: Walshe, however, thinks that the LG-MD words are unrelated to E *prop* and that they are akin to L *propāgō*, a shoot for grafting (OHG *phrofa*), and therefore to:

propaganda, propagate, propagation. See PACT, para 8.

propel, propeller. See PULSE, para 14.

propend. See PEND, para 24.

propensity. See PEND, para 24.

proper, propriety and property; proprietary (adj, n) and proprietor; improper, impropriety; appropriate (adj, v, whence appropriator), appropriation; expropriate, whence expropriator and expropriation; impropriate, whence impropriation and impropriator.

1. *Proper* derives, as ME *propre*, from OF-F *propre*, from L *proprius*, private or peculiar to oneself, prob (E & M) from *prō prīuō* (*prīuus*, ML *prīvus*, private), by private and particular right. Derivative *proprietās*, o/s *proprietāt-*, particular character (peculiarity), hence a private possession, becomes OF-F *propriété*, whence E *propriety*, orig private property; OF-MF *propriété* also becomes ME *proprete*, later, by metathesis, *properte*, whence E *property*. L *proprius* acquires, in LL, the extn *proprietārius*, a proprietor, and, as adj, belonging to a proprietor, whence the E n and adj *proprietary*, which, as n, generates, with suffix *-or* for *-ary*, *proprietor*.

2. L *proprius* has neg *improprius*, with derivative *improprietās*, whence, via MF-F *impropre*, *impropriété*, the E *improper*, *impropriety*.

3. The L cpd *appropriāre*, to make private *ad*, or to, oneself, has pp *appropriātus*, whence both the E adj and the E v *appropriate*; derivative *appropriātiō*, o/s *appropriātiōn-*, yields *appropriation*.

4. ML *expropriāre*, to deprive of (connoted by *ex-*) private property, hence to take the property, has pp *expropriātus*, whence 'to *expropriate*'.

5. ML *impropriāre*, to take into (*im-* for *in*) one's own property, to appropriate (a benefice), has pp *impropriātus*, whence the E adj and v *impropriate*.

prophecy (n), prophesy (v); prophet, prophetic.

Gr *prophētēs*, lit 'a speaker out' (*pro*, forth+ *phanai*, to speak: f.a.e., FAME), becomes LL *prophēta*, OF *prophete* (MF-F *prophète*), adopted by ME, whence *prophet*. Derivative Gr *prophēteia* becomes LL *prophētīa*, OF *prophetie* (MF-F *prophétie*), ME *prophecie*, E *prophecy*. 'To *prophesy*', ME *prophesien*, derives from MF *prophecier*, short for OF *prophetiser* (MF-F *prophétiser*), from LL *prophētizāre* (var *prof-*), from Gr *prophētizein*, from *prophētēs*: cf the syn LL var *prophētāre*, var *prof-*, suggested by the Gr var *prophēteuein*. *Prophetic* comes, perh via late MF-F *prophétique*, from LL *prophēticus*, trln of Gr *prophētikos*, adj of *prophétēs*; *prophetess*, prob via EF-F *prophétesse*, perh suggested by LL *prophētissa* (Gr *prophētis*).

prophylactic. See PHYLACTERY, para 2.

propinquity, propinquous.

1. The former derives from L *propinquitāt-*, o/s of *propinquitās*, itself from the source of *propinquous*, that is near: L *propinquus*, from the adv *prope*, near (? an extn, in sense as in form, of *pro*, forwards).

2. *Prope* has comp *propior*, nearer, with sup *proximus*, nearest (adj; adv, *proxime*), as in the abl *proximo*, used in commerce for 'in the next month (L *mense*)'; from *proximus* comes, with *-al* for *-ous*, the E adj *proximal*. *Proximus* has derivatives *proximitās*, whence late MF-F *proximité*, whence E *proximity*, and *proximāre*, to approach. pp *proximātus*, whence the E adj and v *proximate*.

3. *Proximāre* has the LL cpd *approximāre*, to come near to (*ad*), approach to, with pp *approximātus*, whence the E adj and v *approximate;* derivative LL *approximātiō*, o/s *approximātiōn-*, yields MF-F *approximation*, adopted by E.

propitiate, propitiation, propitiator, propitiatory, propitious.

L *propitius*, favourable, is akin to Gr *propetēs*, (lit) falling forward, hence well-disposed, therefore to L *petere*, to hasten towards, to seek; it becomes MF *propicius* (cf OF-F *propice*), whence E *propitious*. Derivative L *propitiāre* has pp *propitiātus*, whence 'to *propitiate*'; whence LL *propitiātiō*, o/s *propitiātiōn-*, and LL *propitiātor* and LL *propitiātōrius*, whence, resp, *propitiation*, *propitiatory*, *propitiatory*.

propone, proponent. See POSE, para 17.

proportion, proportional, proportionate. See PART, para 24.

proposal, propose, proposition. See POSE para 17.

propound. See POSE, para 17, s.f.

proprietary, proprietor, propriety. See PROPER, para 1.

propulsion, propulsive. See PULSE, para 14.

prorogate, prorogation, prorogue. See ROGATION, para 11.

proruption. See RUPTURE, para 10.

prosaic. See VERSE, para 15.

proscenium. See SCENE, para 3.

proscribe, proscription, proscriptive. See SCRIBE, para 18.

prose. See VERSE, para 15.

prosecute, prosecution, prosecutor. See SEQUENCE, para 13.

proselyte, whence proselytism and proselytize, derives from ME *proselite*, from MF *proselite* (F *prosélyte*), LL *prosēlitus*, var of *prosēlytus*, LGr *prosēlutos*, a proselyte, orig—in Gr—a newcomer: *pros*, toward+*-ēlutos*, from *ēluthon*, I came, with r *\*luth-*, akin to OIr *lod*, I went (Webster).

prosit. See ESSE, para 10.

prosodiac, prosodic, prosody. See ODE, para 8.

prosopopoeia. See the element *prosopo-*.

prospect, prospective, prospector, prospectus. See SPECTACLE, para 14.

prosper, prosperity, prosperous. See DESPAIR, para 4.

prostate. See STAND, para 7.

prosthesis, prosthetic. See THESIS, para 14.

prostitute, prostitution. See STAND, para 31.

prostrate, prostration. See STRATUM, para 6.

protagonist. See the element *-agonist*.

protean. See PROTEUS.

protect, protection, protective, protector, protectorate; protégé. See TECHNIC, para 10.

**protein:** G *Protein*: Gr *prōteion*, neu of *prōteios*, primary: mdfn of Gr *prōtos*, first: f.a.e., PROTON.

**protend, protension, protensity.** See TEND, para 19.

**protest, protestant, protestation.** See TESTAMENT, para 11.

**Proteus, protean.**

The latter (orig *Protean*) is formed with adj suffix *-an* from *Proteus*, adopted from L: from Gr *Prōteus*, a sea god notable for ability to change his shape: perh a *-eus* derivative from *prōtos*, first.

**prothallium.** See THALLIC.

**prothesis, prothetic.** See THESIS, para 15.

**prothonotary.** See PROTON.

**protocol.** See the element *proto-*.

**proton** is a SciL derivative of Gr *prōton*, neu of *prōtos*, first, itself from *pro-*, forwards, before; cf the prefix *pro-*. For the E derivatives (e.g., *protoype*) of *prōtos*, see the element *proto-*; see sep PROTEIN above; *prothonotary* is irreg for *protonotary*, from LL *prōtonotārius*, a chief clerk (Gr *prōto*, c/f+*notārius*, cf E *notary*); for *protoplasm*, see PLASM, para 2; for *protozoic*, cf the element *zo-*.

**protract, protraction, protractor.** See TRACT, para 18.

**protrude, protrusion, protrusive.** See THRUST, para 7.

**protuberance, protuberant.** See THIGH, para 6.

**proud; pride.**

1. *Proud* derives from ME *proud*, var *prout*, earlier *prud*, var *prut*, from OE *prūd*, var *prūt*: OF *prud-*, var of *prod-*, in the OF cpd *produme*, MF-F *prud'homme*, loyal man (the orig OF adj is *proz*, acc *preu*, from VL *\*prodis*, from): LL *prode*, as in *prode est*=L *prodest*, it is useful or advantageous, where the *-d-* is euphonic, *prod-* or *prode* standing for *pro-*, forward (connoting 'advantage'). Ult from OF *preu* comes MF-F *preux*, as in *preux chevalier*, 'a verray parfit gentil knight', adopted by literary E. OF-MF *preu* has var *prou*, used also as n: whence the ME-now archaic E *prow*, valiant, valour (prowess).

2. OE *prūt* has derivative *prȳte*: ME *prute*, later *prude*, latest *pride* (dissyllabic): E *pride*. Cf IMPROVE, para 1.

**prove, provable; probe (n, v), probability, probable**—cf **improbable, improbability**—**probate** (obs adj, hence n), **probation** (whence **probationary** and **probationer**), **probative, probator** (hist), **probatory, probity; proof** (n, adj).—Cpds: **approbate, approbation** (whence, anl, **approbative** and **approbatory**, the latter perh after the L agent *approbator*)—**disapprobation**—cf **approve** (whence **approval, approver**) and **disapprove; disprove, disproof; improbation**—**improbity; reprobate** (adj, v), **reprobation** (whence, anl, **reprobative, reprobatory**)—cf **reprove, reprovable,** and **reproof.**

1. The effective basis is afforded by L *probus*, upright, honest, good: *pro-*, forwards+*-bus*, occurring also in *superbus* (*super*, over+*-bus*) and deriving from an IE *\*bhos*, going (cf Gr *bainō*, I go: *bai*+*-n+o*), or *\*bus* (*bu-s*), with *bu-* a *b*-for-*f*

var of the *fu-* of L *fui*, I have been, and therefore denoting 'being'. The 'going forward—hence, in the open—hence, uprightly' theory is proposed by E & M; the 'being forward—hence, in the open—hence, upright' theory, by Webster. (Both, extended by the author.)

Simples

2. L *probus* has derivative *probitās* (o/s *probitāt-*), uprightness, strict honesty, whence, prob via late MF-F *probité*, the E *probity*; the L neg *improbitās* yields *improbity*.

3. From *probus* comes also *probāre*, to find or think good, also to cause to be found good, to test. Derivative *probābilis* and its subsidiary *probabilitās* pass through late OF-F *probable* and late MF-F *probabilité* to become E *probable, probability*; the L neg *improbābilis* becomes late MF-F *improbable*, adopted by E and having its anl EF-F subsidiary *improbabilité*, whence E *improbability*.

4. *Probāre* has presp *probans*, o/s *probant-*, whence the E adj *probant*, and pp *probātus*, whence the E adj, hence n (whence v), *probate*; derivatives *probātiō*, o/s *probātiōn-*, *probātiuus* (ML *-ivus*), *probātor* become E *probation, probative, probator*; *probatory* owes something to the LL *probatōria* (sc *epistula*).

5. *Probāre* also has derivative LL *proba*, a test, hence a successful test—a proof; hence the surgical *probe*. 'To *probe*' derives mainly from the n, partly from L *probāre*.

6. LL *proba* becomes OF-MF *prueve*, var *preve* (cf F *preuve*), whence ME *preve*, var *prefe*, later—influenced by the E v—*prove*, var *profe*, whence E *proof*. 'To *prove*' comes from OF *prover* (MF-F *prouver*)—from L *probāre*. The MF derivative *provable*, EF-F *prouvable*, has suggested E *provable*.

Compounds

7. L *approbāre*, an int (*ap-* for *ad* used int) of *probāre*, means both 'to approve' and 'to cause to be approved'. The pp *approbātus* yields 'to approbate'; derivative *approbātiō*, o/s *approbātiōn-*, becomes MF-F, whence E, *approbation*, and the anl EF-F *approbatif*, f *-ive*, becomes E *approbative* (unless imm from the E n). L *approbāre* passes into MF as *approver* (EF-F *approuver*), whence ME *aproven*, E 'to approve'. *Approbation, approve* have E negg *disapprobation, disapprove* (whence *disapproval*), the latter perh indebted to EF-F *désapprouver*.

8. OF *aprover* has the further derivative *desprover*, whence, with reversion to L *dis-*, the E 'to disprove', whence, anl (after *proof*), the E *disproof*.

9. L *improbus*, dishonest, not upright—as in para 2—has derivative *improbāre*, not (*im-*) to approve, i.e. to disapprove, to blame, pp *improbātus*, with derivative *improbātiō*, o/s *improbātiōn-*, whence E *improbation*, whence, anl, *improbative* and *improbatory*.

10. L *probāre* has the further cpd, the LL *reprobāre*, to test again, to reprove, pp *reprobātus*,

whence both the adj (whence the n) and the v *reprobate*; derivative LL *reprobātiō*, o/s *reprobātiōn-*, becomes—perh via late MF-F *réprobation*—the E *reprobation*; LL *reprobator* is adopted by E. 'To *reprove*' derives from ME *reproven*, OF-MF *reprover* (EF-F *réprouver*), LL *reprobāre*; *reproof*, from ME *reproef*, earlier *reprove*, MF *reprove*, *reprueve*, formed—after OF-MF *prueve*—from the v.

provection. See VIA, para 12.

provedor. See VIDE, para 14.

provenance, provenient. See VENUE, para 20.

Provençal, Provence. See PROVINCE.

provender. See HABIT, para 16.

proverb, proverbial. See VERB, para 7.

provide, providence, provident, providential. See VIDE, para 14.

province, provincial (whence provincialism); Provence, Provençal.

*Provençal* (adj, hence n) is the F adj of *Provence*, from ML *prōvincia*, a province: '*the* province'. ML *prōvincia* becomes early MF-F *province*, adopted by E, as also is the MF-F adj *provincial*. ML *prōvincia* is L *prōuincia*, orig a magistrate's charge or duty, hence esp the administration of a conquered territory, hence that territory itself: o.o.o.; perh a loan. (Any talk of *prō*, in place of, and of *uincere*, ML *vincere*, to conquer, is prob, as E & M imply, merest f/e. Yet, f/e or not, I suggest that *prōuincia*=\**prōuintia*, contr of *prōuidentia*.)

provision, provisional, proviso, provisor, provisory. See VIDE, para 14.

provocation, provocative, provoke. See VOCABLE, para 10.

provost, provostry. See POSE, para 16, s.f.

prow (1), adj. See IMPROVE, para 1; cf PROUD, para 2.

prow (2), of a ship: MF-F *proue*: C13 *proe*: OProv *proa* (cf Genoese *prua*): (by dissimilation from) L *prōra*: Gr *prōira*: app from *pro*, in front—cf Skt *pūrva*, (situated) in front, first; perh cf *pravanás*, steep. (B & W; Hofmann.)

prowess. See IMPROVE, para 1.

prowl (v, hence n), whence prowler and prowling, comes from ME *prollen*, to rove in search (e.g., of food): o.o.o.

proximal, proximate, proximity, proximo. See PROPINQUITY, para 2.

proxy. See CURE, para 5.

prude. See IMPROVE, para 3.

prudence, prudent, prudential, are doublets of *providence*, etc.: f.a.e., see VIDE: *prudence* and *prudent* come, via MF-F and OF-F from L *prūdentia* and its source *prūdens*, o/s *prūdent-*, an adj from L *prōuidens*, foreseeing, presp of *prōuidēre*, to foresee. Cf also PROVISION.

prudery, prudish. See IMPROVE, para 3.

prune (1), n. See PLUM, para 2.

prune (2), v. See PREEN.

prune (3), v, to cut off the superfluous twigs, branches, shoots of: C17–18 *pruin, pruine*, C16–17 *proine* (OED): MF *proignier*, contr of *prooignier*, itself perh for MF \**porroignier*, int (*por*, L *per*) of *rooignier*, to clip: VL \**rotundiāre*, prop to round off: L *rotundus*, round: f.a.e., ROTUND.

prunella. See BROWN, para 5.

prurient, prurience, pruriency; prurigo, pruriginous; pruritus, pruritic. See FREEZE, para 3.

Prussia, whence Prussian (adj, hence n); prussiate; prussic;—spruce, n hence adj hence v.

1. E *Prussia*, from ML *Prussia*, derives, as does G *Preussen*, from ML *Prussi*, a *p*-for-*b* contr of *Borussi*, the orig Baltic, then the Gmc, inhabitants of the present East Prussia; ML had the alternative form *Borussia* (from *Borussi*). From F (*la*) *Prusse* comes *bleu de Prusse*, blue of Prussia, Prussian blue: whence both F *acide prussique* and *prussiate*: whence, resp, E *prussic acid* and E *prussiate*.

2. ML *Prussia* became ME *Pruce*, with var *Spruce*, whence, the tree being earliest known as a native of that country, the evergreen, handsome *spruce*, whence *spruce*, smartly and neatly dressed, whence the coll 'to *spruce*' or dress neatly and smartly.

pry (1), to force with, or as with, a lever. See PREHEND, para 3, s.f.

pry (2), to look closely or inquisitively: ME *prien*: o.o.o.: ? a confusion of 1st PRY and SPY.—Hence the pa, vn *prying*.

psalm, psalmist, psalmody, psalter, psaltery. See FEEL, para 8.

pseudigraphous; pseudonym, pseudonymous. See the element *pseudo-* and, for *pseudonym*, also NAME, para 3.

psilo-, psittaco-, psoro- cpds. See these elements.

psst! See HUSH, para 2.

Psyche, psyche; psychic (whence psychical), whence, anl, psychism and psychist; psychosis, whence—after *neurotic*—psychotic.—Cpds: metempsychosis; psychiatry, whence, anl, psychiatric and psychiatrist; pyschoanalysis (whence—after the *analysis* derivatives—psychoanalytic, psychoanalyst, psychoanalyze); psychology, whence, after *logic* and its derivatives, psychologic (now usu psychological—for p. moment, see MOVE, para 8) and psychologist; psychopathy, whence psychopathic and, by b/f, psychopath—qqv at the element *-path*.

1. The Gr goddess *Psukhē* ($\Psi \bar{v} \chi \dot{\eta}$), Goddess of the Soul or Spirit, personifies *psūkhḗ*, a breath, the breath of life, the spirit or soul or mind-and-spirit; cf L *spiritus* (E SPIRIT). As *spiritus* is akin to *spirāre*, to breathe, so is *psūkhē* to *psūkhein*, to breathe: both words are notably echoic; two of the four prob most remarkable echoic words in the IE group, the third and most remarkable being L *anima*, breath, soul, the fourth being the Gr *atmos*, vapour, air (cf Skt *ātman*, breath, soul). Gr *psūkhō*, I breathe, represents the out-, followed by the in-, breathing.

2. Gr *psūkhḗ*, the soul, becomes, via L *psȳchē*, the E *psyche* of Psy and esp of Psychi; cf *Psyche*, via L *Psȳchē*. The derivative Gr adj *psukhikos* yields E *psychic* and F *psychique*; LL *psȳchicus*,

bearing—at first sight, very oddly—the contrary sense of materialistic, carnal (Souter), did not intervene.

3. Gr *psúkhē*, in its sense 'mind', had the derivative *psúkhoun*, to breathe life into, to animate, whence *psūkhōsis*, animation, which, misapprehended as 'state of the psyche, state of mind', became the *psychosis* of the psychiatrists.

4. Gr *psúkhoun* had the prefix-cpd *empsúkhoun* (*em-* for *en-*, in, into, used int), to animate, which itself, after *psūkhōsis*, acquired the prefix-cpd *metempsūkhōsis*, the passing—connoted by *meta*, beyond—of one person's soul, after death, into another body: whence LL *metempsȳchōsis*, E *metempsychosis*.

*Psychi-, Psycho-*Compounds

5. From Gr *psūkhḗ*, mind, and Gr *iātreia*, (the art of) healing (cf *iātros*, healer, physician, from *iainō*, I heal), SciL has formed *psychiatria*—cf F *psychiâtrie*, from *psychiâtre*—whence E *psychiatry*.

6. The *psycho-* cpds, formidable in appearance, are, in formation, easy and simple, the generally known ones being:

*psychoanalysis*: a SciL joining of *analysis* to *psycho-*;

*psychology*=*psycho-*+*-logy*, discourse, from Gr *-logia*, from *logos* (f.a.e.: LOGIC); prob aided by EF *psychologie* (or *psi-*), modern sense only in 1754 (Bonnet)—from the G *Psychologie* of the philosopher Christian, Baron Wolff (1679–1754); EF *psychologie* (*psi-*) derives from the modern L *psychologia*, coined by Melanchthon (1497–1560), who himself app took it from the modern Gr title Ψυχολογία, *Psūkhologia*, used, in 1590, by the G philosopher Rudolf Göckel (B & W; Enci It);

*psychopathy*=*psycho-*+*-pathy*, suffering, feeling, emotion (cf PATHIC).

**psychiatry.** See prec, para 5.

**psycho-** words in general. See that element.

**psychoanalysis.** See PSYCHE, para 6.

**psychology.** See PSYCHE, para 6.

**psychopathy.** See PSYCHE, both heading and para 6, s.f.

**psychosis.** See PSYCHE, para 4.

**ptarmigan:** Ga *tàrmachan*: o.o.o.: ? 'the settler' —cf Ga *tàrmaich*, to settle.

**pteridology; pterodactyl.** See the element *-ptera*.

**ptisan.** See PESTLE, para 5.

**Ptolemaic, Ptolemy.**

The former derives from Gr *Ptolemaikos*, adj of *Ptolemaios*, whence L *Ptolamaeus*, F *Ptolémée*, E *Ptolemy*: and *Ptolemaios* derives from *ptolemos*, var of *polemos*, war (cf POLEMIC).

**ptomaine:** It *ptomaina*: an *-ina* derivative of Gr *ptōma*, a corpse, itself from *piptein*, to fall. Cf **ptosis,** a SciL derivative of Gr *ptōsis*, a falling (from *piptein*).

**puberal, puberty** (whence **pubertal**), **pubes, pubescence, pubescent, pubic, pubis** (from the L var of *pūbēs*).

1. *Puberal* derives from L *pūber*, an adult, a var of *pūbēs*, gen *pūberis*. Orig an adj, *pūbēs*, an adult,

is prob id with L *pūbēs*, that hair which, covering much of the pelvis, indicates the ability to generate, or to bear, children. Perh cf Skt *pumắn* (gen *puṃsás*), a man: if *pum-* and *pūb-* be extnn of an IE r *pu-*, L *pūbēs* is akin to L *puer*, a boy: cf PUERILE.

2. L *pūber-*, o/s of *pūbēs*, an adult, has derivative *pūbertās*, whence—perh via late MF-F *puberté*—the E *puberty*.

3. L *pūbēs*, pelvic hair, has s and o/s *pūb-*, whence the E adj *pubic*. Also from *pūb-* derives *pūbescere*, to become covered with hair or down, to become sexually adult, with presp *pūbescens*, o/s *pūbescent-*, whence, perh via EF-F *pubescent*, the E *pubescent*; derivative F *pubescence* is adopted by E.

**public** (adj, n); **publican.** See PEOPLE, para 5.

**publication, publicist, publicity, publicize; publish, publisher.** See PEOPLE, para 5.

**puce** is *flea*-coloured: F *puce*, from *puce*, a flea: L *pūlicem*, acc of *pūlex*: cf Gr *phulla*.

**Puck, puck.** See POCK, para 6.

**pucker.** See POCK, para 8.

**puckish,** from **Puck** (see POCK, para 6).

**pudding; puddening; puddle; pudgy;** sep POODLE; sep POUT.

1. *Pudding* has ME var *poding*: cf OE *puduc*, a wen, E dial *puddy*, pudgy, and LG *puddig*, stumpy, thick, (? basically) swollen: ? a Gmc r *pud-*, to be swollen. From the dial var *pudden* comes the naut *puddening*, a thick fender of rope yarn—from the softness.

2. Prob akin to OE *puduc*, a wen, is OE *pudd*, a ditch, whence the ME dim *puddel* (*podel*), E *puddle*: cf the G dial *pfudel* (*pudel*), a puddle.

3. Akin to dial *puddy* (as in para 1) is the orig and still mainly dial *pudgy*, the adj of the Sc, and N dial, *pudge*, a short, thick person, itself with a var—or, at the least, a, cognate—*podge*, anything sticky, a mire, whence app, the adj *podgy*, syn with *pudgy*.

**pudency, pudent**—**pudend,** whence **pudendal**— **pudic, pudicity; impudence, impudent**—cf **impudicity.** (Not *repudiate*.)

L *pudēre* (s and r *pud-*), to be ashamed, is o.o.o. The presp *pudens* has o/s *pudent-*, whence E *pudent*, bashful, modest; derivative LL *pudentia* yields *pudency*. Gerundive *pudendus* has neu pl *pudenda*, used as n—'genitals'; the neu s *pudendum* is used in mod L for 'vulva'. From r *pud-* comes *pudicus*, whence MF-F *pudique*, whence *pudic*; the neg *impudicus* has derivative *impudicitās*, whence *impudicity*, shamelessness. *Pudens*, as adj, has neg *impudens*, o/s *impudent-*, whence EF-F, whence E, *impudent*; derivative *impudentia* yields EF-F *impudence*, adopted by E.

**pudgy.** See PUDDING, para 3.

**pueblo.** See PEOPLE, para 7.

**puerile, puerility; puerperal, puerperium.**

*Puerile* derives, perh via late MF-F *puérile*, from L *puerīlis*, adj of *puer*, a child (between infancy and adolescence), hence esp a boy; the derivative *puerīlitās* yields, perh via late MF-F *puérilité*, the E *puerility*. *Puer*, moreover, has cpd *puerpera*, a woman in childbirth (*-pera* from *parere*, to bring forth a child: cf PARENT), whence E *puerperal* (esp with *fever*); derivative L *puerperium*, child-birth, is sense-adopted by Med E. — Cf the sep PUPIL (at PUP).

**puff** (n, v), whence **puffer, puffin** (puffy-eyed), pa and vn **puffing**, adj **puffy**, and also such obviously derived cpds as **puff adder** and **puffball; pouf.**

1. The n *puff*, ME *puf*, derives from ME *puffen*, whence 'to *puff*': and *puffen* is prob from OE *pyffan*, to breathe out: cf also G and MLG *puffen*, to buffet, MD-D *puffen*, to blow: ult, echoic.

2. From the syn and cognate EF-F *pouffer* comes *pouf*, jokingly employed for a woman's bonnet (C18–mid 19) and then (C19+) a large, flat cushion used as a seat—adopted by E.

**pug**, an elf, a small quadruped (esp dog). See POCK, para 7.

**pugilism, pugilist, pugilistic.** See PUNGENT, para 12.

**pugnacious, pugnacity.** See PUNGENT, para 13.

**puisne.** Cf *puny*; see NATIVE, para 12.

**puissance, puissant.** See POSSE, para 5.

**puke** (v, hence n), whence **pukish** and **puky**, is perh a de-sibilated derivative of **spew**, after MHG-G *spucken*, to spit, to spew, but perh independent and merely echoic.

**pulchritude.** See the 1st PERCH and cf the element *pulchri-*.

**Pulex.** See PUCE.

**pull** (v, hence n) whence, **puller, pullery, pullover:** OE *pullian*, to pull, to pluck: cf syn LG *pulen*: o.o.o.: ? ult akin to L *uellere*, to pull violently, to pluck.

**pullet.** See POLECAT, para 2.

**pulley.** See the 2nd POLE, para 3.

**pullulant, pullulate, pullulation.**

L *pullulāre*, to bear young, hence to teem, derives from *pullulus*, dim of *pullus*, the young of an animal, esp a chicken (cf *pullet* at POLECAT, para 2), also a bud. The presp *pullulans*, o/s *pullulant*, leads to the E adj *pullulant*; the pp *pullulātus*, to 'to *pullulate*', and the derivative LL *pullulātiō* (o/s *pullulātiōn-*), propagation, to *pullulation*.

**pulmonary**, of or like the lungs, whence the Zoo syn *pulmonar*; whence also, anl, **pulmonate** and **pulmonic** (? imm from F *pulmonique*) and cpd *pulmoniferous* (cf *-ferous* at the element *-fer*). *Pulmonary*, like EF-F *pulmonaire*, derives from L *pulmōnārius*, adj of *pulmō*, a lung, o/s *pulmōn-*: perh metathetically from an IE r *pleum-*, to breathe, as in Gr *pleumōn*, a lung.

**pulp** (n, whence v), whence the adj **pulpy**: EF-F *pulpe*: late MF *poulpe*: L *pulpa*, flesh (esp the lean of meat), pith: o.o.o.: ? cf Hit *pulpulī*, ? trunk of tree.—Derivative L *pulpōsus* yields E *pulpous* (cf F *pulpeuse*, f of *pulpeux*).

**pulpit:** L *pulpitum*, a trestle, a scaffold, in LL 'the platform from which the reader read scripture in church . . .; a pulpit' (Souter): o.o.o.

**pulpous, pulpy.** See PULP.

**pulque**, a fermented drink, is adopted from Sp, which gets it app from a Mexican Amerindian source.

**pulsant.** See the 2nd PULSE, para 3.

**pulsate, pulsation, pulsator, pulsatory.** See 2nd PULSE, para 3.

**pulse** (1), edible seeds. See POLLEN, para 2.

**pulse** (2) of the heart, hence v; **pulsate, pulsatile, pulsation, pulsator** (whence, anl, **pulsatory**); **pulsion**, whence, anl, **pulsive**; **push** (v, hence n), whence **pusher, pushful, pushing**.—Compounds, whether in *-pulse, -pulsion, -pulsive, -pulsory*, or in *-pel* (var *-peal*), *-pellant, -pellate, -pellation*; or in *-pellent*: **appeal** (n, v), **appellant, appellate, appellation, appellative**—**appulse, appulsion**, whence, anl, **appulsive; compel, compellation, compellent**—**compulsion, compulsive, compulsory; dispel; expel, expulse, expulsion, expulsory; impel, impellent**—**impulse, impulsion, impulsive; interpel, interpellant, interpellate, interpellation, interpellator; propel, propellant, propellent, propeller**—**propulsation, propulsion** (whence, anl, **propulsive**), **propulsor; repel, repellent** (whence **repellence**)—**repeal** (n, v)—**repulse** (n, v), **repulsion, repulsive, repulsory.**

1. At the base, stands L *pellere*, to push, hence to chase, hence to chase away (to rout): s *pell-*, r *pel-*: IE r *pel-*, varr *pal-*, as in Gr *pallō*, I shake, and *pol-*, as perh in Gr *polemizō*, I agitate violently, *polemos*, war (cf POLEMIC); with the Gr r *pal-*, perh cf—with *b* for *p*—Sumerian *bal-*, to cause to revolt, and—with *r* for *l*—Hit *parh-*, to drive (horses) at a gallop (Sturtevant).

2. L *pellere* has presp *pellens*, o/s *pellent-*, whence E *-pellent*, and pp *pulsus*, whence the n *pulsus* (gen *-ūs*), a push, a shaking, hence, in Med, prob elliptical for *pulsus uēnarum*, the beating or throbbing of the heart, as indicated in the wrist: ME *puls*: E *pulse* (cf EF-F *pouls*). 'To *pulse*' or throb comes straight from the n, but *pulse*, to drive (obs), comes from L *pulsāre*, to push or drive, to beat or strike, from the n *pulsus*.

3. L *pulsāre* acts, in usage, as an int (and freq) of *pellere*. The presp *pulsans*, o/s *pulsant-*, becomes the E adj *pulsant*; the pp *pulsātus* yields 'to *pulsate*', and its derivative *pulsātiō*, a beating, a striking, o/s *pulsātiōn-*, becomes—perh via MF-F *pulsation* —E *pulsation*; its agential derivative *pulsator* is adopted by E; its ML derivative *pulsātilis*, pulsating, becomes E *pulsatile*. L *pulsiō*, o/s *pulsiōn-*, E *pulsion*, derives, however, from *pulsus*, pp of *pellere*.

4. L *pulsāre*, to push, to strike, becomes OProv *polsar*, later *poussar*, whence MF *poulser*, later *pousser*, to push, the sense 'to grow' arising only in C16; late MF-F *pousser* yields 'to *push*', whence 'a *push*'—perh influenced by the syn late MF-F *pousse*.

5. L *pellere*, moreover, has—although only in cpds—the mdfn *pellāre*, to push oneself, esp to address oneself to, as in *appellāre, compellāre, interpellāre*, the first two existing alongside *appellere, compellere*. In E: *-pellant, -pellate, -pellation*, etc.

(Paras 1–5: with thanks to E & M.)

## Compounds

**6.** L *appellāre*, to address oneself *ad* or to, to invoke, to summon, has presp *appellans*, o/s *appellant-*, whence—perh via F—E *appellant*, adj hence n, and pp *appellātus*, whence the E adj *appellate*; derivative *appellātiō*, acc *appellātiōnem*, yields EF-F *appellation*, adopted by E, and derivative LL *appellātīuus*, ML *-īvus*, becomes the E adj *appellative*, the E n deriving from LL *appellatiuum* (sc *nomen*). L *appellāre* passes into OF as *apeler* (EF-F *appeler*), whence ME *apelen*, later *appelen*, whence 'to *appeal*'; the n *appeal* derives from ME *appel*, *apel*, from OF-MF *apel* (late MF-F *appel*), from OF *apeler*.

**7.** L *appellere*, to push *ad* or towards, (of a ship) to touch land, with pp *appulsus*, whence the n *appulsus* (gen *-ūs*), whence E *appulse*, now mostly in Astr; whence, anl, *appulsion*.

**8.** L *compellere*, to drive *con-* or together, hence (*con-* used int) to urge, LL to force (to do something), becomes—prob via MF-EF *compeller* (or *-ir*)—'to *compel*'; presp *compellens*, o/s *compellent-*, yields the adj *compellent*. The pp *compulsus* has derivative LL *compulsiō*, o/s *compulsiōn-*, whence, perh via F, *compulsion*, whence—perh suggested by F *compulsif* (f *-ive*)—*compulsive*; the ML derivative *compulsōrius* gives us *compulsory*. But *compellation* (whence, anl, *compellative*) derives, of course, from L *compellātiō*, o/s *compellātiōn-*, from *compellātus*, pp of *compellāre*, to accost, (later) to accuse.

**9.** L *dispellere*, to scatter (connoted by *dis-*) and drive away, yields 'to *dispel*'.

**10.** L *expellere*, to push, to drive, out, becomes 'to *expel*'; the presp *expellens*, o/s *expellent-*, accounts for the Med adj (hence n) *expellent*, irreg *expellant*.

**11.** L *expellere* has int *expulsāre*, to drive out (violently), whence, via late MF-F *expulser*, 'to *expulse*'; *expulsion*, however, derives—via the MF-F word—from L *expulsiō*, acc *expulsiōnem*, from *expulsus*, pp of *expellere*; as derivative ML *expulsīuus* becomes *expulsive*, so derivative LL *expulsōrius* becomes *expulsory*.

**12.** L *impellere*, to push, or drive, into or onto (*im-* for *in-*) or towards, becomes 'to *impel*'; its presp *impellens*, o/s *impellent-*, the adj, hence n, *impellent*. From the pp *impulsus* come: the n *impulsus* (gen *-ūs*), whence E *impulse*; *impulsiō*, acc *impulsiōnem*, MF-F *impulsion*, adopted by E; LL *impulsīuus*, ML *-īvus*, whence, perh via late MF-F *impulsif* (f *-ive*), E *impulsive*.

**13.** L *interpellāre*, to interrupt (connoted by *inter*, between) by speaking, becomes late MF-F *interpeller*, whence Sc legal *interpel*; the pp *interpellātus* yields 'to *interpellate*'; derivative LL *interpellātiō*, acc *interpellātiōnem*, becomes late MF-F *interpellation*, adopted by E, and derivative LL *interpellātor* is adopted by E (cf the EF-F *interpellateur*).

**14.** L *prōpellere*, to push, or drive, *prō* or forward, furnishes us with 'to *propel*', whence *propeller*; the presp *prōpellens*, o/s *prōpellent-*, with *propellent*, adj hence n. The pp *propulsus* leads, anl (after *compulsion*), to *propulsion* and to *propulsor*. The obs 'to *propulse*' derives from L *propulsāre*, int of *propellere*.

**15.** L *repellere*, to push, or drive, *re-* or back, explains 'to *repel*'; presp *repellens*, o/s *repellent-*, explains the E adj (whence *repellence* or *repellency*)—hence n—*repellent*; pp *repulsus*, E 'to *repulse*'—the E n *repulse*, however, from the L derivative *repulsa*; derivative LL *repulsiō*, o/s *rep:ulsiōn-*, E *repulsion* (perh cf the MF-F *répulsion*), whence, anl, *repulsive* (cf late MF-F *répulsif*); derivative LL *repulsōrius*, the rare E *repulsory*.

**16.** OF *apeler* (as in para 6) forms the OF cpd *rapeler* (MF-F *rappeler*), to summon *re-* or back, whence 'to *repeal*'; the E n *repeal* derives from OF *rapel* (from *rapeler*).

**pulsometer** is merely a 'pulse-measurer': cf prec and METER.

**pulverize; pulverulent.** See POLLEN, para 3.

**puma**, a cougar, is adopted by Sp, which adopts it from Quechuan.

**pumice.** See the element *pumici-*.

**pummel:** var of **pommel**, q.v. at FAT; para 6.

**pump**, n, hence v: ME *pumpe*, earlier *pompe*: app imm from MD *pompe* (D *pomp*): prob (B & W) from It *pompa*: ? VL *\*pompa*, of echoic origin, opp the more tech L *tromba*. Walshe, like Webster, prefers origin in Sp *bomba* (also echoic).

**pumpkin.** See MELON, para 6.

**pun** (1), a play on words, hence v: o.o.o.: perh (Webster) from It *puntiglio*, a quibble (cf the E *punctilio*, q.v. at PUNGENT); but prob (EW) a C17 clipped form of the syn EE *punnet*, var *pundigrion*, itself perh from the It word; EW appositely cfs the F *pointe*, a verbal conceit. At one time, I entertained the idea that *pun* might afford an early example of blend: *puzzle+conundrum*, with *con*-pron *cun-*. Agent: *punster*.

**pun** (2), to beat, to pound. See the 3rd POUND.

**Punch.** See PUNCHINELLO.

**punch** (1), the drink. See PANJAB, para 2.

**punch** (2), a short, thick draught horse, prob comes, by abbr, from PUNCHINELLO.

**punch** (3), to hit with the fist, hence as n. See PUNGENT, para 11, s.f.

**puncheon.** See PUNGENT, para 11.

**Punchinello**—whence **Punch**—or **punchinello:** Neapolitan dial *Pulcinella* (adopted by It), a figure in regional farce, perh from It *pulcina*, a chicken (from L *pullus*, as in *pullet*, q.v. at POLECAT, para 2); the Neapolitan var *Polecenella* becomes F *Polichinelle*. (Prati.)

**punctate, punctation.** See PUNGENT, para 3.

**punctilio, punctilious.** See PUNGENT, para 4.

**punctual, punctuality.** See PUNGENT, para 5.

**punctuate, punctuation.** See PUNGENT, para 6.

**punctum.** See PUNGENT, para 2.

**puncture.** See PUNGENT, para 7.

**pundit:** Hindi *paṇḍit*, from Skt *paṇḍita*, a learnèd man—esp in Hindu lore.

**pungent** (cf the obs **punge**), whence **pungence**,

pungency; punct, punctum—punt, v; punctate, punctation, punctator; punctule; punctilio, punctilious; punctual, punctuality; punctuate, punctuation (whence, anl, punctuative, punctuator); puncture, n hence v; pounce, a talon, hence to leap on, as with talons; punch, to hit with the fist, hence n; puncheon; point (n, v), point-blank, point-device (or -devise), pointer (from *point*, v), pointless (*point*, n+*-less*), pointsman (*points*, pl n+*man*)—pointel—pointillism; poignant, whence poignancy. —L *pugil*: pugilant, pugilism, pugilist; cf pygmy.—cpds of L *pungere*: compunct (obs), compunction (whence, anl, compunctious)—expunction, expunge (whence, anl, expungible). L *pugnāre*: poniard; pugnacious, pugnacity; expugn (obs), expugnable—neg inexpugnable; impugn, impugnation; oppugn, oppugnant, oppugnation; propugn (obs), propugnaculum, propugnation, propugnator; repugn, repugnance, repugnant, repugnatorial.—Cpds from F: appoint, appointment; counterpoint; disappoint, disappointment; embonpoint.

### Indo-European

1. L *pungere*, to prick, has s *pung-*, with pp *punctus*, s *punct-*; L *pugil*, a boxer, has s *pug-*, r *pug-*; *pugnus*, fist, has s *pugn-*, r *pug-*. The L *pung-*, *punct-*, represents a nasal var of the r *pug-* of *pugil* and *pugnus*; basic idea, to strike; IE r *\*peug-* or *\*pug-*: cf the Gr *pugmē* (s *pugm-*, r *pug-*), fist. One strikes with the fist.

L *pungere*, to prick: Direct Derivatives (Simple)

2. *Pungere* yields the obs 'to *punge*' or goad. The presp *pungens*, o/s *pungent-*, yields pungent. The pp *punctus* has neu *punctum*, retained by Sci, with derivative *punct*; the dim *punctulum* yields punctule. L *punctum* also becomes Sp *punto*, a point, esp in a game, whence, perh via F *ponte*, the E punt, esp in a game against the bank; the corresp 'to *punt*' derives rather frcm the E n than from F *ponter*.

3. L *punctum* gains, in ML, the derivative *punctāre*, to point, esp to mark with points or dots, pp *punctātus*, whence the E adj punctate and the E n punctation and agent punctator.

4. The LL dim *punctillum*, a little point, becomes It *puntiglio* (cf Sp *puntillo*), whence E punctilio; the derivative It adj *puntiglioso* has at least suggested the E punctilious.

5. L *punctum*, as n, has var *punctus* (gen *-ūs*), with ML adj *punctuālis*, whence E punctual (cf the late MF-F *ponctuel*); derivative ML *punctuālitās*, o/s *punctuālitāt-*, becomes punctuality.

6. L *punctus*, a point, has, in ML, the v *punctuāre*, to point out, to define, pp *punctuātus*, whence the adj and v punctuate, developing the sense 'to separate sentences, etc., with *points*'—perh influenced by LL *punctum* in sense 'a punctuation mark'; derivative ML *punctuātiō*, o/s *punctuātiōn-*, leads to punctuation (cf EF-F *ponctuation*).

7. L *punctus*, pp of *pungere*, has derivative *punctūra*, whence E puncture.

L *pungere*: Indirect Derivatives (Simple)

8. L *punctum*, a point, a dot, becomes OF-F *point*, adopted by ME; in several senses, E point (n) prob derives rather from F *pointe*, from L *puncta*, prop the f of the pp *punctus*. 'To *point*', ME *pointen*, comes from MF-F *pointer*, from the OF n *point*. The adj point-blank derives from the adv, itself perh from F *de pointe en blanc*, from a point into the white (of the target); point-device or -devise, from ME *at point devis*, at point exact, OF-MF *devis*, exact, fixed, from L *diuīsus*, (sharply) divided.

9. OF *point* has MF derivative *pointel*, tip of a lance, where ME *pointel*, a stylus, now a tech of Bot and Zoo. OF-F *point* has the further derivative EF *pointiller*, to strew with dots, pp *pointillé*, used as n in painting, with late C19 derivatives *pointillisme*, *pointilliste*, both adopted by E and both, by AE, deprived of the *-e*.

10. L *pungere* becomes OF *poindre*, to prick, presp *poignant*, ME *poynant* (*-aunt*), E poignant, with sense 'keenly affecting the senses, hence very moving', arising in C18 F.

11. Pounce, a bird's talon, app derives from ME *ponson* or *ponchon* or *punchon*; the last certainly yields E puncheon, a dagger (obs). Puncheon, a large cask, although perh of different origin, prob derives from *puncheon*, a die, a punch, a figured stamp, from a mark or sign 'punched' into the wood: and the latter *puncheon* (id with the 'dagger' one) derives, in ME, from MF *poinchon*, var of *poinçon* (as still in F), from *punctiōnem*, acc of L *punctiō*, a point, from the pp *punctus*. MF *poinçon* has MF-F derivative *poinçonner*, whence—with form prob affected by ME *punchon*—'to punch'.

L *pugil*

12. L *pugil*, a boxer, s and r *pug-*, is intimately related to *pugnus* (s, r *pug-*), a fist: whence E pugilism and pugilist and anl pugilistic; derivative L *pugilāre*, to box, pp *pugilans*, o/s *pugilant-*, accounts for the E adj pugilant. Corresp to L *pugnus* is the syn Gr *pugmē*, with adj *pugmaios*, of the size, esp the length, of a fist, hence the n *Pugmaios* one of a myth race of dwarves: L *Pygmaeus*, E Pygmy, whence the common n *pygmy*.

Simple Derivatives of L *pugnus*

13. L *pugnus*, a fist, has derivative *pugnāre*, to strike, hence to fight, with one's fists, hence to fight generically, whence *pugnāx*, combative, gen *pugnācis*, whence E pugnacious; derivative *pugnācitās*, o/s *pugnācitāt-*, gives us pugnacity.

14. L *pugnus* becomes OF-F *poign*, whence, though perh not imm, the EF-F *poignard*, whence E poniard.

Compounds of *pugnāre*

15. L *expugnāre*, to fight (a garrison) out of a place, hence to take by assault, yields MF *expugner*, whence 'to *expugn*'; derivative L *expugnābilis* becomes MF, hence E, expugnable. The L neg

*inexpugnābilis* becomes late MF-F *inexpugnable*, adopted by E.

16. L *impugnāre*, to fight *in*, against, passes through MF *impugner* into ME *impugnen*, E 'to *impugn*', now to assail verbally, to question pugnaciously; derivative L *impugnātiō*, o/s *impugnātiōn-*, becomes *impugnation*.

17. L *oppugnāre*, to deliver battle *ob*, around, yields 'to *oppugn*', to assail; presp *oppugnans*, o/s *oppugnant-*, E *oppugnant*; *oppugnātiō* (from pp *oppugnātus*), o/s *oppugnātiōn-*, E *oppugnation*.

18. L *repugnāre*, to fight back, i.e. backwards, to repel by fighting, yields—perh via MF-F *répugner*—'to *repugn*' or oppose; presp *repugnans*, o/s *repugnant-*, becomes MF *repugnant* (EF-F *ré-*), adopted by E, as is MF *repugnance* (F *ré-*). Derivative L *repugnatōrius* explains Zoo E *repugnatorial*, serving to repel—fitted for repelling —the enemy.

### Compounds (direct) of L *pungere*

19. L *compungere* (*com-* for *con-*, used int), to prick severely, LL to prick one's conscience, has pp *compunctus*, whence *compunct* (obs), conscience-stricken; derivative LL *compunctiuus*, ML *-ivus*, yields *compunctive*, and derivative LL *compunctiō* (o/s *compunctiōn-*), remorse, repentance, becomes OF-MF *compunction* (EF-F *componction*), adopted by E.

20. L *expungere*, to prick out, to mark (with dots) for deletion, becomes 'to *expunge*', whence, anl, *expungible*, erasable; derivative LL *expunctiō* (from pp *expunctus*), o/s *expunctiōn-*, yields *expunction*.

### Compounds, via French, of L *punctus* (pp) and *punctum* (n)

21. From L *punctum*, a point, derives—after *punctāre* (cf para 3)—VL *appunctāre*, to bring to (*ap-* for *ad*) the point, to fix the points of a contract or an agreement (perh cf LL *appungere*, to 'attach a critical point (*to a passage in a book*': Souter), whence MF *apointer* (EF-F *appointer*), orig a legal term that perh derives rather (B & W) from OF *point*, a point: whence ME *apointen*, later *appointen*, whence 'to *appoint*'. Derivative MF-F *appointement* leads to E *appointment*.

22. MF *apointer* has its own cpd: MF *desapointer* (EF-F *désappointer*), to dismiss from an *apointement* or office; whence 'to *disappoint*', in that sense, the modern E sense arising only in C16, whence the modern F sense.

23. Late MF-F *contre-point* is anglicized as *counterpoint*; EF-F *embonpoint*, plumpness, esp a 'corporation', from *en bon point*, in good point or form or condition, is adopted by E.

**punish, punishment; punition, punitive.** See PAIN, para 4.

**Punjab, Punjabi.** See PANJAB.

**punk**, a prostitute (late C16–early 18, then archaic), whence, prob, the A sl senses 'young tramp'—'worthless young fellow', etc., is o.o.o.; the Asl *punk* is prob influenced by AE *punk*, wood so dry as to be crumbly, hence fit only for burning (of Alg orig—cf Lenape *punk*, ashes, powder: Webster); the E sense perh conceals a learnèd pun on L (*femina*, or *puella*, *saepe*) *punc*ta, a woman, or a girl, frequently punctured. Adj: *punky*.

**punster.** See the 1st PUN, s.f.

**punt** (1), boat. See PONS, para 3.

**punt** (2), to gamble. See PUNGENT, para 2.— Hence the gambling *punter*.

**punty.** See PONS, para 2.

**puny.** See NATIVE, para 12.

**pup** (n, hence v), from **puppy; puppet** (whence **puppetry**), and **poppet; pupa** (c/f **pupi-**), whence **pupal** and **pupate; pupil** (of eye; scholar, whence **pupilage**), **pupillary.**—Cf the sep PUERILE.

1. *Puppy*, orig a toy dog, derives from MF-F *poupée*, itself from VL *puppa*, a doll, from L *pūpa*, a girl child, hence a puppet, a doll, orig a nursery word, prob from L *puer*, orig any child (f.a.e., PUERILE).

2. L *pūpa* is sense-adapted by SciL to mean 'an insect in the intermediate stage'.

3. *Pūpa* has dim *pūpillus* (m), *pūpilla* (f), which in L Law, came to designate a child, esp an orphan child, in the charge of a guardian or of a tutor, whence the sense 'young scholar': whence MF-F *pupille*, orig in the L legal sense: whence E *pupil*. The L derivative adj *pūpillāris* yields *pupillary*. L *pūpilla* also denoted the pupil of the eye, 'so named because of the tiny image reflected there' (E & M): MF-F *pupille*, E *pupil*.

4. VL *puppa* becomes dial MF-EF *poupe*, with late MF-F dim *poupette*, little doll, whence ME *popet*, whence both *poppet* and, re-shaped after L, *puppet*.

**pupil.** See prec, para 3.

**puppet.** See PUP, para 4.

**puppy.** See PUP (heading).

**purblind.** See PURE, para 7.

**purchase** (v and n), whence **purchasable, purchaser.** See CATCH, para 3.

**purdah:** Urdu, from Per, *pardah*, a veil.

**pure, purity**—negg **impure, impurity; purée; purify, purification, purificatory; purin** or **purine; purism, purist;** Puritan (whence **puritan**), whence Puritanical (whence p-) and Puritanism (whence p-); **purblind;**—**depurant, depurate, depurative** (whence, anl, **depuration** and **depurator**).—**purge** (v, hence n), **purgation, purgative** (adj, hence n), **purgatory,** adj and n (whence **purgatorial**); **expurgate** (adj, n), **expurgation** (whence, anl, **expurgative, expurgator, expurgatory**), **expurge.**

1. Standing behind all these terms is L *pūrus*, spotless, unsoiled, hence (lit and fig) pure, s *pūr-*, r perh *pū-*: cf Skt *pūtás*, purified, pure, *pūnáti*, he purifies, cf *pavate*, he cleanses or purifies, but prob not L *putus*, unmixed, pure.

2. L *pūrus* becomes OF-F *pur*, f *pure*: ME *pur*, *pure*: E *pure*. The LL derivative *pūritās*, o/s *pūritāt*, becomes OF *purté*, MF-F *pureté*, whence ME *purte*, *purete*, whence—after the L—*purity*. The L neg *impūrus* and its LL derivative *impūritās* (o/s *impūritāt-*) become MF-F *impur* (f *impure*)

and *impureté* and, perh independently, EE-E *impure*, *impurity*.

3. L *pūrus* has derivative *pūrāre*, to purify, whence MF-F *purer* (pp *puré*), whence the MF-F n *purée*, a sieved soup, adopted by E; but the F-looking *purin* or *purine*=L purus+SciL *uricum, uric acid+the Chem suffix *-in*.

4. The late C16-mid 17 *Puritan* adds the n-from-adj *-an* to LL *pūritās*.

5. OF-F *pur* has the EF-F derivatives *purisme*, *puriste*, whence E *purism*, *purist*.

6. L *pūrus* has the cpd v *pūrificāre* (c/f *pūri-*+ *-ficāre*, a c/f of *facere*, to make), with pp *pūrificātus*, whence *pūrificātiō*, acc *pūrificātiōnem*, whence OF-F *purification*, adopted by E; 'to *purify*' derives from OF-F *purifier* (from *pūrificāre*). Derivative LL *pūrificātōrius* yields *purificatory*.

7. Whereas *purblind* derives from ME *pur blind*, wholly blind, *depurant*, 'to *depurate*', *depurative* derive from ML *dēpūrant-*, o/s of the presp *dēpūrans—dēpūrātus*, pp—*dēpūratīvus* (adj from the pp s).

### L *pūrgāre*

8. L *pūrāre* has the OL derivative *\*pūrigāre* (cf L *iūrāre—iūrgāre*: E & M), whence, by contr, L *pūrgāre*, to purify, to cleanse (lit and fig): whence OF *purgier*, MF-F *purger*: whence 'to *purge*', whence 'a *purge*'—prob suggested by F *purge*, juridical in late MF-EF, medical since C17. On the L pp *pūrgātus* are formed L *pūrgātiō*, acc *pūrgātiōnem*, OF-F *purgation*, adopted by E, and *pūrgātīuus*, ML *-īvus*, MF-F *purgatif*, f *-ive*, *purgative*, and LL *pūrgātōrius*, E *purgatory* (adj); the n *purgatory* comes, prob via OF-F *purgatoire*, from ML *pūrgātōrium* (prop the neu of the LL adj: cf LL *pūrgātōrium*, a purgative, a means of cleansing: Souter) in the Eccl sense.

9. L *pūrgāre* has the cpd *expūrgāre* (*ex-* used int), to purify, cleanse, purge, with pp *expūrgātus*, whence the adj (obsol) and v *expurgate*; derivative *expurgātiō*, o/s *expurgātiōn-*, yields *expurgation*; the very probable ML *\*expūrgatorius* perh accounts for *expurgatory*.

**purée.** See prec, para 3.

**purfle.** See FILAMENT, para 9.

**purgation, purgative, purgatory.** See PURE, para 8.

**purge.** See PURE, para 8.

**purification, purificatory, purify.** See PURE, para 6.

**purin** or **purine.** See PURE, para 3.

**purism, purist.** See PURE, para 5.

**Puritan, puritanical, Puritanism.** See PURE, para 4 and heading.

**purity.** See PURE, para 2.

**purl** (1), n: a liquor. See PEARL, para 2.

**purl** (2), v: to ripple, swirl, eddy, hence as n. To *pirl* or *purl*, to ripple, is of Scan origin—cf Nor *purla* (Sw *porla*), to ripple, to murmur: prob echoic.

**purl** (3), v, as in embroidery, derives from 'a *purl*' or border, edging, made with gold (or silver)

thread or with twisted wire: earlier *pirl*, n, from *pirl*, v: It *pirlare*, to twirl about: app from It *pirolo*, a spinning top; prob akin to PIROUETTE. (EW.)

**purlieu** is a f/e corruption—after F *lieu*, a place —of AF *puralee* (var *poralee*), from OF-MF *puraler* (*poraler*), to go through, hence to survey: *pur-*, L *per*, through+*aler* (F *aller*), to go—cf E *alley* at AMBULANCE.

**purloin.** See LONG, para 9.

**purple** (n, hence adj and v); **purpura, purpurate** (adj)—**purpure**—**purpureal** and **purpureous**—**purpurescent**—**purpuric** (**acid**)—**purpurin**—**purpurite**; **porphyry**, (whence **porphyritic**), **porphyrogenite**.

1. *Purple* derives from ME *purpel*, an *l*-for-*r* metathesis of ME *purpre*, adopted from OF-MF *purpre* (C11, *porpre*; EF-F *pourpre*), rather than adapted from OE *purpure*: L *purpura*, a purple dye, a purple fish: Gr *porphura*, the fish, hence the dye obtained therefrom: o.o.o., perh (Hofmann) from Asia Minor.

2. L *purpura* is sense-adapted by Med; its derivatives *purpurātus, purpureus*, become E *purpurate, purpureous* (var *purpureal*); Her *purpure* survives from ME, which derives it from L *purpura*. *Purpurescent*=L purpura+the inch suffix *-escent*; *purpuric*=L purpura+adj *-ic*; *purpurin*=L purpura +Chem *-in* (cf the F adj *purpurin*); *purpurite*=L purpura+Min *-ite*.

3. Gr *porphura* has derivative adj *porphuros, porphureos*, whence ML *porphyreus*, It *porfiro*, OF *porfire*, EF-F *porphyre*, E *porphyry*. Gr exhibits also the adj *porphuritēs*, which, used as n (elliptical for *porphuritēs lithos*), becomes L *porphyrites*, a purple-hued precious stone, whence E *porphyrite*. LGr *porphurogennetos*, lit 'born of porphyry', passes through ML *porphyro genitus* into E *porphyrogenite*, a son born into the purple.

**purport.** See the 3rd PORT, para 10.

**purpose.** See POSE, para 18.

**purpura, purpurate, purpure, purpureal (-eous), purpuric, purpurin, purpurite.** See PURPLE, para 2.

**purr,** v, hence n, is eminently echoic: cf MURMUR (*mur-mur*).

**purse** (n, hence v), whence **purser; bursar, bursary**—cf BOURSE; **disburse, disbursement; reimburse, reimbursement;—sporran.**

1. *Purse*, ME *purse*, earlier *purs*, OE *purs*, derives—*p* for *b*—from LL *bursa*, a leather bag, itself adopted from Gr: o.o.o.:?

2. LL *bursa* becomes OF *borse*, later MF-F *bourse*, purse, hence the exchange of money, hence *la Bourse*, the Stock Exchange of Paris; in E, *bursa* is used by An and Zoo for a sac, with adj *bursal*. *Bursar*, whether in the E or in the Sc sense, derives either from ML *bursārius* (bursa+*-ārius*) or from the late MF-F *boursier*; *bursary*, from ML *bursāria*, prop the f of adj *bursārius*.

3. MF *bourse* has MF-F derivative *desbourser* (later *débourser*), to pay out (connoted by *des-*, L *dis*) from one's purse, whence 'to *disburse*'; *disbursement*, imm from the v, perh owes something to EF-F *déboursement*, precisely as 'to *reimburse*'

and *reimbursement* owe something to late MF-F *rembourser* and *remboursement*.

4. LL *bursa* is akin to, it may even (*b* becoming *p*, with an int *s-* prefixed) have generated, E *sporran*, Ga *sporan*: cf the syn MIr *sboran*.

**purslane.** See PORK, para 5.

**pursuance, pursuant, pursue, pursuer, pursuit, pursuivant.** See SEQUENCE, para 7.

**pursy,** short-winded: AF *pursif*: MF-F *poussif* (*pouss*er+adj *-if*), 'from *pousser* in the sense "to breathe hard" ' (B & W): from L *pulsāre*: f.a.e., the 2nd PULSE.

**purulence, purulent.** See FOUL, para 6.

**purvey, purveyance, purveyor.** See VIDE, para 14.

**purview.** See VIDE, para 14.

**pus.** See FOUL, para 6.

**push.** See the 2nd PULSE, para 4.

**Pushta.** See PATHAN.

**pusillanimity, pusillanimous.** Cf the element *pusilli-*, but see ANIMAL, para 6.

**puss** (1), a cat, whence **pussy,** whence 'to **pussyfoot**' or walk stealthily like a predatory cat: o.o.o., but prob echoic of a cat spitting: cf D *poes*, cat, and Ga *puis*, cat, *piseag*, kitten, ? also W *pws*, an expelled breath, an utterance: prob also Sumerian *pū* (gen *pī*), the mouth.

**puss** (2), the face: A sl and dial: Ir *pus*, a lip, the lips, (usu pej) the mouth.

**pustule.** See PREPUCE, para 2, and cf the element *pustuli-*.

**put,** to thrust or throw, hence to place firmly, hence the mainly dial n **put,** with golfing var **putt;** hence also the agent **putter** (two pronn) and the vn **putting;** hence, further, **input** and **output;**—perh **pother** and **bother.**

1. 'To *put*', ME *putten*, earlier *puten*, OE *putian*, var *potian*, to thrust or push: cf Ice *pota*, D *peuteren*, MD *peuderen, poderen*, to stir, to fumble: ? ult echoic.

2. *Pother*, n hence v, and *bother*, v hence n, are o.o.o., but perh both akin to 'to *put*': cf esp the MD *peuderen, poderen*. There is, however, some reason to suppose that *pother*, earlier *pudder*, owes its modern form to *bother*, and that *bother* is independent and of C origin (EW)—cf Ir *bodhraim*, EIr *bodraim*, I deafen (someone) with noise, Ga *bodhair*, to deafen, and Ga *bodhar*, OIr *bodar*, deaf.

**putative.** See the 2nd COUNT, para 2.

**putid.** See FOUL, para 7.

**putrefaction, putrefy; putrescence, putrescent; putrescible; putrid, putridity.** See FOUL, para 7.

**putt.** See PUT (heading).

**puttee:** Hi *paṭṭi*, a bandage, prop a strip (of cloth): Skt *paṭṭikā*: Skt *paṭṭa*, perh akin to Skt *pattra*, a feather, a wing, hence a leaf: for Skt *pattra*, cf FEATHER.

**putty.** See POT, para 3.

**puzzle.** See POSE, para 14, s.f.

**pycni- (pycno-), pyelo-, -pygal (-pygous),** words in. See the elements *pycno-, pyelo-, -pygal*.

**pygmy.** See PUNGENT, para 12, s.f.

**pygo-.** See the element *-pygal*.

**pyjama.** See PAJAMA.

**pylon,** orig a gateway (building): Gr *pulōn*, a gateway: Gr *pulē*, a gate: o.o.o.: ? cf, with *l* for *r*, the Skt gōpuram, a city-gate.

**pyloric** is the adj of An *pylorus*: cf the element *pyloro-*.

**pyo-,** words in. See that element.

**pyramid** (n, hence v), whence—unless from ML *pÿramidālis*—the adj *pyramidal*, derives from OF-F *pyramide*: LL *pÿramida*: L *pyramis*, o/s *pyramid-*: Gr *pūramis*, o/s *puramid-*: prob either from Eg *pi-mar*, the pyramid (Webster), or ironically from Gr *pūramis*, a sort of cake.

**pyre.** See FIRE, para 3.

**Pyrenean** derives from L *\*Pyrēnaeus*, attested by *Pyrēnaei* (*montes*), suggested by Gr *ta Purēnaia orē*, the mountains of *Purēnē*; the range, also called simply *Purēnē* (L *Pyrene*), derives either, first, from a Danubian city *Purēnē*, visited by traders from Massilia (Marseilles), or (Webster), myth, from *Purēnē*, a girl beloved of Hercules and buried there, *Purēnē* being prob, at least orig, a nickname 'Roundhead', from *purēn*, a knob, a fruit-stone (cf the element *pyreno-*).

**pyreno-, pyrgo-,** words in. See those elements.

**pyriform.** See PEAR, para 1, s.f.

**pyrites.** See FIRE, para 4.

**pyrogenic, pyromania; pyrotechnic.** See the element *pyro-*.

**pyroxene.** See the element *-xene*.

**Pyrrhic,** esp in *Pyrrhic victory*, one too dearly gained. The Gr King *Pyrrhus*, L from Gr *Purrhos*, in defeating the Romans, 279 B.C., lost a very high proportion of his soldiers and exclaimed, 'One more such victory over the Romans, and we are utterly undone'. *Purrhos* is prob of same origin as *Purrhō*, the Gr philosopher known to us as *Pyrrho*: 'The Red-Haired', from Gr *pur*, q.v. at FIRE.

**pyrrho-,** words in. See that element.

**Pyrus.** See PEAR, para 1, s.f.

**Pythagorean** or **-ian,** whence **Pythagoreanism,** derives from L *Pythagoreus*, trln of Gr *Puthagoreios*, adj of *Puthagoras*, E *Pythagoras*, a famous early Gr philosopher.

**pytho-,** words in. See that element.

**python** derives from L *Python*, Gr *Puthōn*, the great primeval serpent slain by Apollo at *Puthō*, the very ancient name of Delphi and its surrounding district; hence the huge, non-venomous snakes we call *pythons*.

**pyx, pyxis** (pl **pyxides**). *Pyx* derives from a ML sense acquired by the L *pyxis*, a box, trln of Gr *puxis*, a box, orig one made of boxwood: an *-is* or 'derivative, or descended, from' alteration of Gr *puxos*, the box tree or its wood: cf BOX. *Pyx* is Eccl; *pyxis*, Hist, An, Bot.

**pyxie,** when not a bad spelling of pixy, an A evergreen creeper, is perh a confusion between Gr *puxos*, box tree, L *pyxis*, and *pixy*.

**pyxis.** See PYX.

# Q

**quab.** See QUAVER, para 2.

**quack** (whence **quackery**) is an echoic v, hence n: cf MD *quacken, quaken* (D *kwakken*), MHG-G *quaken*, to quack, ON *kvaka*, to twitter. MD has the cpd *quacksalver* (D *kwakzalver*), one who quacks or boasts about his salves: whence E *quacksalver*, whence E *quack*, a Med charlatan.

**quad** is coll short for *quadrangle* and has, as var, the sl*quod*, a prison, from a prison's courtyard; for *quadrant, quadrat, quadruped, quadruple, quadruplet, quadruplex*, see f.a.e., next.

**quadra**, whence **quadric; quadragenarian; Quadragesima, Quadragesimal**—cf **quarantine; quadral; quadrant** (adj, n), whence **quadrantal; quadrat, quadrate** (adj, n), whence **quadratic**—**quadrature; quadrual; quadrille.**—Cpds in *quadr-*: **quadrangle, quadrangular; quadrennial** (see ANNUAL, para 3); **quadriform; quadrilateral** (adj, hence n: cf the element *quadri-*); **quadrillion; quadripartite** (see the element *quadri-*); **quadrivium; quadrumana**, whence **quadrumanous; quadruped** (see FOOT, para 20); **quadruple, quadruplet, quadruplicate** (see PLY, para 25).—**quart, quartan, quartation; quarter** (n, hence v, whence **quartering), quarterage, quartermaster; quartern; quartet, quartette; quartile** (adj, hence n); **quarto.**—**quatern, quaternary; quaternion** —cf **carillon; quaternity.**—**quatorzain; quatrain; quatral; quatrefoil; quadrille; quadroon.**—**quarry.**— Sep QUIRE (of paper) and SQUAD, SQUADRON and SQUARE.

## Indo-European

1. Primary to the entire group is L *quattuor*, 4, of which *quadr-* (*quadra-, quadri-, quadru-*) is the c/f; the ordinal is *quārtus*; the adv, *quāter*. Akin to *quattuor* are Skt *catvāras*, neu *catvāri*, Gr *tettares* (Attic) or *tessares* or *tetores* (Doric), c/f *tetra-*, OIr *cethir*, OSl *četyre*; the IE etymon is app *\*kuetuor-* or *\*kwetwor-*.—The Gmc cognates are treated sep at FOUR; the Gr at TETRA-.

2. L *quattuor* has the VL var *\*quattor*, whence OF-F *quatre*, as in *quatrefoil*, a four-leaved flower (*quatre*+OF *foil, foille*—cf F *feuille*); derivative EF-F *quatrain* is adopted by E—cf *quatorzain*, a 14-lined poem, a sonnet, from MF-F *quatorzaine*, from *quatorze*, 14, from VL *\*quattordecim*, L *quattuordecim*, lit '4+10'. App from F *quatre*, comes Gram *quatral*, with var *quadrual* from the L *quadr-*.

3. The cognate L adj *quadrus*, square, occurs

mostly as n *quadra*, a square, esp in Arch, whence its use in European Arch, e.g. a plinth; E *quadra* has adj *quadral*. In L, *quadra* has derivative *quadrāre*, to square (vt and vi), with pp *quadrans*, o/s *quadrant-*, whence the E adj, hence n, *quadrant*, with many tech senses, and with pp *quadrātus*, whence E *quadrate*, adj hence n (var *quadrat*); An exhibits *quadrātus* used as n. Derivative L *quadrātūra* becomes *quadrature.*—L *quadrus* acquires, in Sp, the n *quudro*, a battle square, with dim *cuadrilla*, whence EF-F *quadrille*, with new senses: adopted by E.

4. L *quattuor*, 4, has cognate *quadrāgintā*, 40, with adj *quadrāgēsimus*, 40th, whence LL *Quadrāgēsima*, Lent, also Quadragesima Sunday, both senses adopted by Eccl E; derivative LL *quadrāgēsimalis*, yields E *quadragesimal*. Akin to L *quadrāgintā* is L *quadrāgēni*, whence *quadrāgēnārius*, forty years old, whence in LL a man of that age, whence E *quadragenarian*.

5. L *quadrāgintā*, 40, becomes *\*quadranta*, whence VL (LL) *quarranta*, whence It *quaranta*, with derivative *quarantina*, a set of 40, esp of 40 days, whence—cf the OF-F *quarantaine*—the E *quarantine*; the legal *quarantine* owes much to ML *buarentena* (from LL-VL *quarranta*).

## Compounds in *quadr-*

6. *Quadrangle:* LL *quadrangulum*, a quadrangle: L *quadrangulus*, 4-cornered (cf ANGLE); derivative LL *quadranguláris* yields *quadrangular*;

*quadrennial:* see ANNUAL, para 3;

*quadriform:* LL *quadriformis*, 4-shaped (cf FORM);

*quadrilateral:* EF-F *quadrilatéral*, from EF *quadrilatère*: L *quadrilaterus*: c/f *quadri-*+*-laterus*, from *later-*, o/s of *latus*, a side;

*quadrillion:* EF-F *quadrillion* (F var *quatrillion*): *quadr-*+*million* (cf MILE);

*quadripartite:* L *quadripartītus*, pp of *quadripartīri*, to divide into 4 parts—cf PART;

*quadrivium:* ML form of LL *quadriuium*, a group of 4 Math sciences, from L *quadriuium*, a four-ways (*uia*, ML *via*, a way or road), a crossways;

*Quadrumana*, in Zoo a group of 4-handed mammals: a SciL formation: *quadru-*, var of *quadri-*+L *manus*, hands (cf MANUAL);

*quadruped:* see FOOT, para 20;

*quadruple:* EF-F *quadruple:* L *quadruplus*, var of

*quadruplex*, 4-fold, o/s *quadruplici-*: see PLY, para 25.

## L *quārtus*

7. L *quārtus*, 4th, becomes OF-EF *quart*, whence —cf the L derivative nn *quārta*, *quārtum*—the MF-F n *quart*, var *quarte*: whence E *quart*. L *quārtus* has extn-mdfn *quārtānus*, whence *quārtāna*, elliptical for *quārtāna febris*, quartan fever, occurring every four days (reckoned inclusively): MF-F *quartaine* and, prob independently, E *quartan*. *Quartation* is an anl E formation, as if from L *\*quārtātiō*.

8. L *quārtus* has the further extn *quārtārius*, the fourth part of a measure: OF-F *quartier*: E *quarter*. Derivative MF-EF *quarterage* is adopted by E. *Quartermaster* imitates F *quartier-maître*. *Quartern*, ME *quarteroun*, derives from MF-F *quarteron*, from OF-MF *quartier*; *quartet*, var of *quartette*, from F *quartette* (It *quartetto*); *quartile*, from ML *quārtilis* (from *quārtus*); *quarto*, from L n *quārtō*, in fourth.

9. L *quāter*, four times, acquires *quāterni*, four each, whence the E adj (obs), hence n (obsol), *quatern*; derivative *quāternārius* yields *quaternary*, adj hence n—cf late MF-F *quaternaire*; derivative LL *quāterniō*, o/s *quāterniōn-*, becomes E *quaternion*, orig a set of 4—cf *carillon*, which, adopted from F, derives from MF *quarelon*, from VL *\*quādriniō*, o/s *\*quādriniōn-*, reshaped, after the *quadr-* words, from L *quāterniō*; and derivative LL *quāternitās*, o/s *quāternitāt-*, yields *quaternity*.—Cf the sep QUIRE (2).

10. L *quārtus*, 4th, becomes Sp *cuarto*, with derivative aug n *cuarterón*, a quarter-Negro: whence E *quadroon*, reshaped after the L and E *quadr-* words.

## English *quarry*

11. Reserved to the end because it looks so different from the *quadra* simples is *quarry*: ME *quarey*, perh influenced by ML *quareia*: earlier ME *quarrere*: OF *quarriere* (MF *quarrière*: F *carrière*): an *-iere* (F *-ière*) derivative of L *quādrus* or *quādrum*, a square, or squared, stone, from the adj *quādrus*, square.

quadragenarian. See prec, para 4, s.f.
Quadragesima. See QUADRA, para 4.
quadrangle, quadrangular. See QUADRA, para 6.
quadrant. See QUADRA, para 3.
quadrat, quadrate (whence quadratic), quadrature, quadratus. See QUADRA, para 3.
quadrennial. See ANNUAL, para 3.
quadric. See QUADRA (heading).
quadrilateral. See QUADRA, para 6.
quadrille. See QUADRA, para 3, s.f.
quadrillion. See QUADRA, para 6.
quadripartite. See QUADRA, para 6.
quadrivium. See QUADRA, para 6.
quadroon. See QUADRA, para 10.
quadrual. See QUADRA, para 2, s.f.
Quadrumana. See QUADRA, para 6.
quadruped. See FOOT, para 20.

quadruple, quadruplet, quadruplicate, quadruplication. See PLY, para 25.
quaestor. See QUERY, para 3.
quaff is app a var—? from long *s* taken as *f*—of the obs syn 'to *quass*', itself from MLG *quassen*: perh echoic.
quagga is of SAfr native origin: cf Zulu *qwara*, 'in which *r*=G. *ch* in *ach*' (Webster).
quaggy, quagmire. See MIRE.
quahog (AE) is of Alg origin: an aphetic (esp Narragansett) var of an Amerind word represented by Massachusett *poquahoc*, a hard-shelled clam (cf the syn Pequot *p'quaghhaug*). The four best A dictt complement one another in a most illuminating way.
quail (1), the bird: OF-MF *quaille* (F *caille*): ML *quaccula*: echoic.
quail (2), orig to perish, is perh id with the now only dial *quail*, to curdle: OF-MF *coaillier* (F *cailler*), cf It *quagliare*: L *coagulāre*, to coagulate: cf *coagulate* at COGENT. The modern sense 'to shrink or cower' prob owes something to the somewhat timorous bird.
quaint, orig skilful, knowledgeable, prudent, hence crafty, is ME *queint*, earlier *cointe*, adopted from OF-MF, which derives it from L *cognitus*, pp of *cognōscere*, to know (*cog-* for *con-*, used int+ *nōscere*, to know): f.a.e., CAN.
quake, v (hence n), whence quaker, whence Quaker; whence also pa, vn quaking and adj quaky; earthquake.—quetch.—Cf QUAG, as in *quagmire*, q.v. at MIRE.

1. *Earthquake* is simply a *quake* or trembling of the *earth*. 'To *quake*' comes from OE *cwacian*, akin to OE *cweccan*, to vibrate: cf Ice *kwija*, to move or stir: ? orig echoic.

2. The now dial *quetch*, to move (obs), to twitch, is, like *quag*, a var of *quake*; hence *quetch grass*, quaking grass.

quale; qualification (and, anl, qualificatory), qualify, whence disqualify, disqualification; quality, qualitative.

*Quale*, in Psy, is adopted from L, where it forms the neu of *quālis*, of what kind; akin to *qui, quis*, who (relative, interrogative): f.a.e., WHO. *Quālis* has derivative *quālitās*, o/s *quālitāt-*, whence, via OF-F *qualité*, the E *quality*; derivative LL *quālitātiuus*, ML *-īvus*, whence—perh via late MF-F *qualitatif*—the E *qualitative*. Derivative ML *quālificāre*, to give definition to, to limit, and its n *quālificātiō*, o/s *quālificātiōn-*, pass through late MF-F and EF-F to become 'to *qualify*' and *qualification*.—Complementary and akin is *quantity*, q.v. at QUANTIC.

qualm, whence qualmish and qualmy, orig denoted a sudden nausea or faintness or fear, and is akin to G *Qualm*, black smoke (LG and D: *kwalm*, Sw *kvalm*), MHG *twalm*, stupor: o.o.o.: sem cf *vapours* (EW). Connexion with OE *cwealm*, (violent) death, pestilence, has not been conclusively disproved; the predominant ME form of OE *cwealm* is *cwalm*, death, slaughter, torture.
quamash. Var of camas(s).

quandary, a dilemma, perplexity, is o.o.o.: ? an easing of L *quam dare*, how (in what manner) to give?, How much, or in what way, shall I (or you or he) give?, or a contr, or perh blend, of L *quando dare*, when to give?, When (exactly) shall I (etc.) give?, or of *quantum dare*, how much to give?, How much shall I give?

quandong (occ quantong or quandang), the Aus 'native peach', is of Aboriginal origin.

quantic and quantum and quantulum; quantify (whence, anl, quantification and, directly, quantifier); quantity (whence quantize), quantitative.

1. *Quantulum* is prop the neu of L *quantulus*, dim of *quantus* (f *quanta*), how big or large, neu *quantum*, how much, which, used as n, occurs in 'the *quantum* theory'; whereas *quantic*, adj, is *quant*um +*-ic*, *quantic* the n represents *quant*us+*-ic*. L *quantus*, *-a*, *-um* derives from L *quam*, how, how much.

2. *Quantus* has LL derivative *quantitās*, a specified amount or sum, whence, via the acc *quantitātem*, the OF-F *quantité*, whence E *quantity*; whereas derivative ML *quantitātivus* yields *quantitative*, ML *quantificāre* yields 'to *quantify*'.

3. Cf the complementary and cognate *quality*, q.v. at QUALE: f.a.e., WHO.

quantulum; quantum. See prec, para 1.

quarantine. See QUADRA, para 5.

quarrel (1), a square-headed bolt or arrow, hence, in Arch, a square of glass, a small square pavingstone: ME *quarel*, *quarrel*: OF-MF *quarrel*: VL *\*quadrellus* or *\*quadrellum*, dim of L *quadrus*, adj, *quadrum*, n, (a) square: f.a.e., QUADRA.

quarrel (2), discord. See QUERY, para 6.

quarry (1), orig (a part of) the entrails given to hounds that have brought a beast to bay or to a hawk that has killed, hence a prey: ME *querre* or *quirre*: MF *cuiriée* (F *curée*): either (B & W) imm from OF-F *cuir*, from L *corium*, a beast's skin regarded as potential leather (cf CORTEX), or (Webster) from *cuirié*, pp of OF *cuirier*, var of OF-F *curer*, to clean (cf CURE), esp to eviscerate, influenced by ML *corāta*, entrails, from L *cor*, heart (cf CORDIAL).

quarry (2), an open excavation, hence v. See QUADRA, para 11.

quart. See QUADRA, para 7.

quartan. See QUADRA, para 7.

quartation. See QUADRA, para 7.

quarter, whence quartering and quarterly. See QUADRA, para 8.

quartermaster. See QUADRA, para 8.

quartern. See QUADRA, para 8.

quartet, quartette. See QUADRA, para 8.

quartile. See QUADRA, para 8.

quarto. See QUADRA, para 8, s.f.

quartz, adopted from G, is o.o.o.: but the MGH *quarz* prob derives from MHG *quarc*, a dwarf, 'like *Kobalt* from *Kobold*' (Walshe).

quash, to dash to pieces, to crush, is id with quash, to annul, for both derive from OF-MF *quasser* (later *casser*), from L *quassāre*, to shatter, int of *quatere* (pp *quassus*), to shake, itself prob echoic. Whereas *quash*, to annul, to render void, has been sense-influenced by LL *cassāre*, to annul, from *cassus*, empty (akin to *carēre*, to lack), *quash*, to crush, has been sense-influenced by 'to SQUASH'.

quasi is L *quasi*, as if: prob for *quam* (as) *si* (if).

Quassia, the tree, hence quassia, the drug extracted therefrom, is a SciL derivative from Graman *Quassi*, that Surinam Negro who, c1730, discovered the drug's virtues.

quatern, quaternary. See QUADRA, para 9.

quaternion. See QUADRA, para 9.

quaternity. See QUADRA, para 9, s.f.

quatorzain. See QUADRA, para 2.

quatrain. See QUADRA, para 2; cf FOUR, para 6.

quatrefoil. See QUADRA, para 2.

quaver, v hence n, whence semiquaver, etc.; quiver, v hence n.—quab; squab.

1. 'To *quiver*' or tremble is a thinning of 'to *quaver*', which is a freq of the now dial *quave*, from ME *cwavien*: cf Sw dial *kvabba* and G *quabbeln*, to quiver, MLG *quabbe*, a bog: all are prob echoic.

2. The small fish named *quab* derives from MD *quabbe* (D *kwabbe*); and *squab*, a young bird (esp a young pigeon), is of Scan origin—cf Sw dial *skvabb* (*kv-*=*kw*), a var of *kvabb*, anything quivery and soft and thick, and *skvabba*, a var of *kvabba*, a fat woman, and also *kvabba*, to quiver.

quay. See HAW, para 4.

quean. See QUEEN, para 2.

queasy, orig unsettled or uncertain, now unsettled of stomach or of conscience or taste, is o.o.o.: prob cf Nor *kveis* (pron *kw-*), a 'hangover', and ON *kveisa*, a boil, a whitlow, and perh (Holthausen) Gr *deisa*, slime, filth.

Quebec perh derives from an Alg word for 'contraction'—of the St Lawrence river—as the EnciIt proposes.

queen (n, hence v), queenly; quean.

1. *Queen*, ME *quen* or *quene*, a queen, comes from OE *cwēn*, a woman (esp a wife), hence '*the* woman' of a country, its queen: cf OS *quān*, woman, wife, Go *qēns*, ON *kvān*, wife, queen—Gr *gunē* (OSl *žena*), woman—Skt *jani*, woman, hence wife, cf Skt *ganá*, a goddess: IE etymon, prob *\*gwunā*, woman. (Hofmann.) OE *cwēn* has adj *cwēnlīc*, womanly, whence, in part, E queenly.

2. OE *cwēn*, a woman, is modified as *cwene*, akin to the syn OS and OHG *cwena*, Go *qinō*, ON *kona*, a harlot: whence E *quean*, a slut, a harlot, whence the Sc and Northern E dial sense 'a girl' and also the sl sense 'a pathic'.

queer, adj, hence n and v; thwart, adj, hence both the naut n and the v 'to baffle'.

1. *Queer*, as used in C16 Scots, app=queried, questionable, and is perh independent of C16–18 cant, where it=worthless, inferior, hence dishonest, criminal, hence, in sl, dubious, unwell. The cant-hence-sl term prob derives from MHG *twer* (OHG *dwerah*, *twerh*), G *quer*, (adv) athwart: perh cf L *torquere*, to twist (IE r, *\*twerkw-*), as Walshe suggests.

2. MHG *twer*, *twerch*, OHG *dwerah*, are akin to ON *thverr*, transverse, neu *thvert*, whence ME

*thwert*, E *thwart*: cf OE *thweorh*, transverse, perverse, MD *dwers*, *dwersch*, *dwaers*, *dwars* (D
*dwars*), transverse, (lit and fig) cross-grained, and
Go *thwairhs*, angry.

**quell.** See the 2nd KILL, para 2.

**quench,** whence the pa, vn **quenching,** derives
from ME *quenchen*: OE -*cwencan* in *ācwencan*,
caus of *cwincan*, *ācwincan*, to grow less, to disappear: cf OFris *quinka*, to dwindle, to fade away,
and *utquinka*, to be extinguished, to die out.

**quercine, quercus.** See FIR, para 2.

**querimonious, querimony.** See QUERY, para 5.

**quern,** a primitive grain-mill, a small hand-mill:
OE *cwyrn*, *cweorn*: cf ON *kvern* (*kv=kw*), OHG
*quirn*, Go -*quairnus*: ? ult akin to cereal CORN.

**querulent, querulous.** See para 5 of:

**query,** v (whence **querist**) and n:—**quest** (v, n);
**quaestor;** **question** (v, n), whence **questionable** and
**questioner;** **questionary,** **questionnaire;**—querimonious, anl from **querimony; querulent, querulous;
quarrel,** v hence n.—Cpds: **acquest**—**acquire**
(whence **acquirement**), **acquisition, acquisitive;** conquer, conqueror—conquest, conquistador; disquisition; exquisite; inquest—cf inquire, whence **inquiry**
—cf **enquire,** whence **enquiry**—**inquisition, inquisitive, inquisitor; perquisite, perquisition, perquisitor;
request,** n, v—cf **require** (whence **requirement),
requisite** (adj, hence n), **requisition.**—Cf **wheeze.**

1. L *quaerere* (s and r *quaer*-), to seek, make an
inquiry about, inform oneself of, hence to seek to
obtain, to ask for, is o.o.o.: perh it is akin to L
*querī*, to utter plaintive cries, hence to complain,
and, if that be so, it is prob akin to 'to *wheeze*'
(whence the n), ME *whesen*, which derives from or
is, at the least, akin to ON *hvaesa*, to hiss, itself
related to Skt *śvasiti*, he breathes audibly, sighs,
snorts.

### Simples from L *quaerere*

2. The n *query* app derives from L *quaere*, ask
thou!, imp of *quaerere*; the v, either from the E n
or, less prob, from *quaerere*, to ask, or *quaerō*, I
ask—cf the OF-EF *querre*, late MF-F *quérir*.

3. L *quaerere* has pp *quaesītus*, occ contr to
*quaesta*, whence the VL n *\*quaesta*, whence
OF-MF *queste* (late MF-F *quête*), whence E *quest*;
derivative OF-MF *quester* (late MF-F *quêter*)
yields 'to *quest*'. On the pp s *quaest*- arises the agent
*quaestor*, a magistrate in the criminal courts,
adopted by E, with anl adj *qu(a)estorial*.

4. Also on *quaest*- is formed *quaestiō*, a querying,
acc *quaestiōnem*, whence OF-F *question*, adopted
by ME; 'to *question*' derives partly from the E n
and partly from MF-F *questionner* (from *question*).
Whereas the adj *questionary* derives from the E n
*questionary*, the n itself derives from LL *quaes-
tiōnārius*, a judicial torturer extracting answers;
*questionary*, n, serves also as an anglicized form of
EF-F *questionnaire*.

### Simples from L *querī*

5. *Querī*, to complain, has the LL derivatives
*querimōnia* (for the suffix, cf *alimōnia*, E *alimony*),

whence E *querimony*, with adj *querimonious*—prob
after *ceremonious*—LL *querulōsus* (var of LL
*querellōsus*), complaining, quarrelsome, whence E
*querulous*—and ML *querulāri*, to complain, presp
*querulans*, o/s *querulant*-, whence (though partly
after *querulous*) E *querulent*.

6. *Querī* has the L derivative, mostly legal n
*querella* (*querēla*), whence OF-MF *querele* (and,
as in F, *querelle*), ME *querele*, E *quarrel*; whence,
in part, 'to *quarrel*', which owes something to OF-F
*quereller* (from *querelle*).

### Compounds from L *quaerere*

7. *Quaerere* has a number of cpds important to
E. The L c/f is -*quīrere*, s -*quīr*-, with pp -*quīsītus*.
*Acquīrere*, to seek, to procure, additionally, yields
'to *acquire*'; from the pp *acquīsītus* are formed
*acquīsītiō*, o/s *acquīsītiōn*-, whence—perh via
MF-F—the E *acquisition*, and LL *acquīsītīuus*, ML
-*īvus*, whence E *acquisitive*. Pp *acquīsītus* has neu
*acquīsītum*, which, used as n, has the VL contr
*\*acquestum*, whence OF-MF *acquest* (late MF-F
*acquêt*), adopted by E.

8. L *conquīrere* (int *con*-), to seek for, to recruit
or requisition, LL to conquer, has the VL var
*\*conquerere*, to acquire, to conquer, whence OF-EF
*conquerre* (soon also *conquerir*, F *conquérir*),
whence 'to *conquer*'; derivative OF-MF *conquereor*
becomes E *conqueror*. OF *conquerre* has pp *conquest*, f *conqueste*, which, used as MF n (EF-F
*conquête*), becomes the E *conquest*. *Conquistador*,
with pl *conquistadores*, as in 'the C., or Sp conquerors of CA and Peru', is taken from Sp, which
derives it from *conquistar*, to conquer, from ML
*conquistāre*, from *conquīsītum*, supine of *conquīrere*.

9. L *exquīrere*, to seek *ex* or out, to seek carefully for, yields the obs 'to *exquire*'; pp *exquīsītus*,
used as adj 'refined, elegant', yields *exquisite*, adj
hence n. The almost syn *disquīrere*, pp *disquīsītus*,
has derivative *disquīsītiō*, o/s *disquīsītiōn*-, whence
*disquisition*.

10. L *inquīrere*, to search *in* or into, yields 'to
*inquire*'; 'to *enquire*', reshaped from the L, derives
from ME *enqueren*, from OF-early MF *enquerre*
(MF *enquerir*, F *enquérir*), from VL *\*inquaerere*,
from L *inquīrere*. On the pp *inquīsītus* are formed L
*inquīsītiō*, whence, via the acc *inquīsītiōnem*, the
OF-F *inquisition*, adopted by E—LL *inquīsītīuus*,
ML -*īvus*, whence E *inquisitive*—L *inquīsītor*,
whence, prob via late MF-F *inquisiteur*, the E
*inquisitor*—and ML *inquīsītōrius*, whence EF-F
*inquisitorial*, adopted by E. *Inquest* is reshaped,
after L, from ME *enqueste*, adopted from OF-MF
*enqueste* (late MF-F *enquête*), either orig the f of
pp *\*enquest*, from OF *enquerre*, from VL *\*inquaerere*, from L *inquīrere* (B & W), or from VL
*\*inquaesīta*, n from *\*inquaesītus*, pp of *\*inquaerere*
(Webster).

11. L *perquīrere*, to seek on all sides, to diligently
ask for, has pp *perquīsītus*, neu *perquīsītum*, which,
used as n, accounts for E *perquisite*; derivatives LL
*perquīsītiō*, o/s *perquīsītiōn*-, and L *perquīsītor*

**become** E *perquisition* (perh imm from late MF-F) and *perquisitor*.

12. L *requīrere*, to ask *re-* or again for, yields 'to require', ME *requiren*, earlier *requeren*, from OF-MF *requerre* (MF-F *requérir*), from VL *\*requaerere* (from *requīrere*). The L pp *requīsītus* gives us *requisite*; derivative *requīsītiō*, o/s *requīsītiōn-*, becomes OF *requisition* (MF-F *ré-*), adopted by E. 'To *request*' derives from OF-MF *requester* (F *requêter*), from the OF-MF n *requeste* (F *requête*), adopted by ME, whence E *request*: and OF *requeste* derives either from OF *request*, pp of *requerre*, or from VL *\*requaesīta*, prop the f of the pp of *\*requaerere*.

**quest.** See prec, para 3.

**question, questionary, questionnaire.** See QUERY, para 4.

**quetch.** See QUAKE, para 2.

**quetzal,** loosely **quezal,** a brilliant CA bird, derives from Sp *quetzal*, short form of *quetzale*: Nahuatl *quetzalli*, a tail feather—esp of the *quetzaltototl*, as the Aztecs call the bird, itself= *quetzalli* (from *quetza*, it stands up)+*tototl*, a bird. Cf the Aztec god *Quetzacoatl*, lit '(the) plumed serpent': *quetzalli*+*coatl* (or *cohuatl*), a serpent, lit 'hurting thing'. (Webster.)

**queue.** See CUE.

**quib** (obs), whence the dim **quibble** (n, hence v— whence **quibbler**), derives from L *quibus*, to whom, as in 'to whom it may concern': dat pl of *qui*, who: f.a.e., WHO.

**quick, quicken, quickness, quicksand, quicksilver.** See VIVA, para 7 and heading.

**quid** (1), for chewing. See CUD.

**quid** (2), sl for £1 (coin or sum), is o.o.o.; but prob suggested by L *quid pro quo*, something for something, hence a fair exchange. L *quid* is the neu of *quis*, who?: whence the scholastic ML *quidditās* o/s *quidditāt-*, whence E *quiddity*: cf the archaic *quillet*, a quibble, perh a slovening of *quidlibet*, anything you please, from *quid tibi libet*, What pleases thee?

**quiesce, quiescence, quiescent.** See para 2 of:

**quiet** (adj—whence **quieten**; n; v)—**quietism, quietist**—**quietude**—**quietus**—**quiesce, quiescence, quiescent; coy,** whence **coyness; quit** (adj and v), **quittance; quite.**—Prefix cpds: **acquiesce, acquiescence, acquiescent**—cf **acquit** (whence **acquittal), acquittance; disquiet** (adj n, v), **disquietude**—cf **inquiet** (adj, v), **inquietude; requiem, requiescat in pace, requiescence**—cf **requite,** whence **requital; tranquil** (whence **tranquillize), tranquillity.**— Cf the sep WHILE (AWHILE, WHILOM).

1. *Quiet*, n, derives from L *quiēt-*, o/s of *quiēs*, repose, calm, hence peace; *quiet*, adj, from L *quiētus*—prob orig the pp of *quiēscere*, to rest, itself from the n *quiēs*—via MF-EF *quiet*; 'to *quiet*', from LL *quiētāre*, to put to rest, from *quiētus*. The E n *quietus* derives from ML *quiētus est*, he is quiet, implying the 'at last' of death. *Quiētus* has derivative LL *quiētūdō*, whence *quietude*, literary for ordinary *quietness* (*quiet*, adj+*-ness*). L *quiētus*

**becomes** It *quieto* (now *cheto*), whence *quietismo*, *quietista*, whence E *quietism, quietist*.

2. *Quiētus* displaced the adj *quiēs* (gen *quiētis*), whence *quiēscere*, to be or keep quiet, to rest, whence 'to *quiesce*'; presp *quiēscens*, o/s *quiēscent-*, yields *quiescent*, and the derivative LL *quiēscentia* yields *quiescence* and *quiescency*.

3. L *quiētus* becomes VL *\*quētus*, whence OF *quei*, MF-F *coi*, E *coy* (whence *coyness*).

4. L *quiētus* becomes VL *\*quītus*, whence the OF-F adj *quitte*, whence the E adj *quit*, whence the n *quits*; ML *quītus* has derivative vi *quītāre*, whence OF-F *quitter*, whence ME *quitten, quiten*, E 'to *quit*'. OF *quitter* acquires, via the presp *quittant*, the n *quittance*, adopted by ME, where often *quituance*. In C13-17, the adj *quit* had the var *quite* (also a var in MF), whence the ME-E adv *quite*. The legal *quitclaim* (v, hence n) derives from MF *quite clamer*, to declare quit or free or clear.

### Prefix-Compounds

5. L *acquiēscere*, to give oneself *ad*, to, rest, hence to find one's rest, or peace (in something), becomes late MF-F *acquiescer*, whence 'to *acquiesce*'; the L presp *acquiēscens*, o/s *acquiēscent-*, yields *acquiescent*, whence—unless from EF— *acquiescence*.

6. The OF v *quitter* has cpd *acquiter* (MF-F *acquitter*), whence ME *acquiten*, E 'to *acquit*'; derivative *acquitance* (MF-F *acquittance*) yields E *acquittance*.

7. *Disquiet, disquietude* simply prefix *dis-*, implying 'want of', to *quiet*; cf *inquiet*, adj and n, from L *inquiēs*, o/s *inquiēt-*, adj and n; derivative LL *in-quiētūdō* yields *inquietude*, and derivative *inquiētāre*, 'to *inquiet*' (obsol).

8. L *quiēs*, n, has cpd *requiēs*, a rest again, a respite, hence simply rest: whence, via '*Requiem* aeternam dona eis, Domine' (Grant them eternal rest, O Lord: the Introit of the Mass begins thus), the E *requiem*. The corresp v *requiēscere*, presp *requiēscens*, o/s *requiēscent-*, yields both the rare adj *requiescent*, whence, anl, *requiescence*, and the LL tag *Requiescat in pace*, May he rest in peace!

9. Prob akin to L *quiēs* is L *tranquillus*, calm (esp of the sea): app *trans*, across, beyond, (hence) all the way across or through+*-quillus*, perh for *\*quītlus* (for *\*quiētlus*): ? 'calm throughout'. L *tranquillus* yields late MF-F *tranquille* and, perh independently, E *tranquil*; the derivative L *tranquillitās*, o/s *tranquillitāt-*, yields OF-F *tranquillité*, whence *tranquillity*; and EF-F *tranquilliser* (from *tranquille*) perh suggested 'to *tranquillize*'.

**quiff** is a sl var of **coif**.

**quill,** ME *quil*, is akin to MHG *kil*, G *Kiel* (cf LG *quiele*): o.o.o.

**quillet,** a quibble. See the 2nd QUID.

**quilt** (n, hence v); **quoit,** orig a discus, whence the game **quoits.**

1. *Quilt*, ME *quilte*, derives from OF-MF *cuilte, coilte* (late MF-F *coite*, with var *couette*), itself from L *culcita*, a bed, a cushion; akin to Skt *kūrca*, a bundle.

2. *Quoit*, ME *coite*, ? orig a flat stone, app comes
—with changed sense—from MF-F *coite*.

**quin.** See FIVE, para 10.

**quina.** See QUININE.

**quinary, quinate.** See FIVE, para 7.

**quince**: a b/f from MF *quynes*, pl of *quyne*, var of
*coyn*: MF *coin* (F *coing*): OF *cooin*: L *cotôneum*,
var of *cydônium*: Gr *kudônion*, a quince, prop the
neu of *kudônios* (indeed, *kudônion malon*, the
Cretan fruit, occurs), either an extn of the adj
*Kudôn*, Cretan (cf *Kudônea* or *-nia*, Cydon, a
Cretan town), or a mdfn of *Kutônion*, a city of
Asia Minor and therefore from a language of that
country. But the earliest Gr form is *kodumalon*,
with *kodu-* prob the true Near East name of the
fruit; both of the PIN origins would then, as
Boisacq suggests, be mere f/e explanations.

**quincuncial** (L *quincunciālis*) is the adj of *quincunx*, q.v. at FIVE, para 6, s.f.

**quinine, quinic, quina, quinol: cinchona.**

1. *Quina* is the Sp name of both the cinchona
bark and hence of the alkaloid extracted therefrom: and whereas *quinine* (occ *quinin*)=*quina*+
Chem *-ine*, *-in*, *quinic*=*quina*+adj *-ic*; the Sp *quina*
is aphetic for Quechuan *quinquina*.

2. *Cinchona* is a SciL derivative from the Conde
de *Chinchón*, name of a C17 Sp viceroy of Peru:
his wife recommended its use (discovered by the
Jesuits) after having been cured by this *Peruvian* (or
*Jesuits'*) *bark*. The name *Cinchona* is applied to the
tree; *cinchona* to its bark, hence to the drug.
*Chinchón* itself is an aug of Sp *chinche*, a bed-bug,
L *cīmex*.

**quinquagenary, Quinquagesima.** See FIVE, para 6.

**quinquennial.** See ANNUAL, para 3.

**quinsy** derives, by either contr or slovening,
from ML *quinancia*, from Gr *kunankhē*, a dog-
collar (*kuōn*, a dog, gen *kunos*+*-ankhē*, a constriction, from *ankhein*, to squeeze, constrict),
hence a very sore throat.

**quint; quintain.** See FIVE, para 8.

**quintal**, adopted from MF-F, derives from ML
*quintāle*, an *l*-for-*r* reshaping of Ar *qinṭar*, itself, via
Byz Gr *kentēnarion*, from LL *centēnārium*, 100
pieces (of gold): orig the neu of the adj *centēnārius*,
from L *centum*, 100.

**quintessence.** See ESSE, para 3.

**quintet, quintette.** See FIVE, para 9.

**quintuple, quintuplet, quintuplicate.** See FIVE,
para 9; cf PLY, para 25.

**quinzaine, quinze.** See FIVE, para 10.

**quip** (n, hence v, whence **quipster**): C16 *quippy*:
o.o.o., but prob from L *quippe*, indeed, Is that so?,
used sarcastically: *\*quidpe*, What then?

**quire** (1). See CHOIR, para 2.

**quire** (2), orig 4, later 24 (occ 25), sheets of
paper: ME *quair*, *quaer*: OF-MF *quaer*, MF *caer*,
*caier* (F *cahier*): VL *\*quaternum*, a set of 4 sheets
of paper, or a sheet folded in 4: L *quāterni*, 4 each,
from *quāter*, 4 times: cf para 9 of QUADRA.

**quirk**, whence **quirky**, is o.o.o.: prob Scan (? cf
Nor *kvark*—pron *kwark*—throat).

**quirt** derives, by thinning and shortening, from
Mexican Sp *curta*, a short riding whip: obscurely
from Sp *cuarta*, a fourth part, L *quārta*, elliptical
for *quārta pars*: f.a.e., QUADRA.

**quit,** adj and v. See QUIET, para 4.

**quitch** (grass). See the 1st COUCH; cf VIVA,
para 8.

**quitclaim.** See QUIET, para 4.

**quite.** See QUIET, para 4.

**quits** (n). See QUIET, para 4.

**quittance.** See QUIET, para 4.

**quiver** (1), n, for arrows, recorded first in C14,
derives from AF *quiveir*: OF-MF *cuivre*, var of
*cuevre*: OHG *kochar*, *kochāri* (MHG *kocker*, G
*Köcher*), cf OE *cocur*: o.o.o. (Walshe.)

**quiver** (2), to vibrate or tremble. See QUAVER,
para 1.

**qui-vive.** See VIVA, para 1, s.f.

**quixotic**, whence, anl, **quixotism, quixotry,** refers
to the eccentric, generous idealism of Don *Quixote*,
eponymous hero of Cervantes's satiric romance
published in 1605, 1615. The name *Quixote*
personifies Sp *quixote* (now *quijote*), a cuisse or
thigh-piece, ref the fact that this knight rode forth
in armour; *quixote* derives, with suffix *-ote*, from
L *coxa*, hips, thigh.

**quiz**, orig an odd or eccentric person; later one
who banters, also a piece of bantering, a jest;
hence 'to *quiz*' or banter: hence 'to *quiz*' or
examine orally, whence 'a *quiz*', such an examination—senses that go back to the prob origin of the
old n and v: either a person exciting in*quis*ition*s*,
or, if the basic sense was *\**'a person asking odd
questions', a person ludicrously in*quis*itive.

**quod.** See QUAD.

**quoin.** See COIN.

**quoit, quoits.** See QUILT, para 2.

**quorum** is the L *quorum*, of whom (pl), from a L
phrase used formerly in the commissioning of
justices of the peace: 'a select body of these
justices' becomes 'any sufficiency of members
entitled to transact business': f.a.e., WHO.

**quota, quotient, quotiety, quotity; quote** (whence
**quotable** and **quoter**) and **quotation,** whence, anl,
**quotative.**

1. The imm and effectual base of this tight little
group is afforded by L *quot*, How many?, as in
*Quot homines, tot sententiae*, So many persons, so
many opinions: akin to L *quis*, Who?, *quī*, who
(relative): f.a.e., WHO.

2. L *quot* has derivative adj *quotus*, In what
number?: whence, elliptical for *quota pars* (How
numerous a part or proportion?), the ML *quota*,
a part-share, a proportion (of countable objects),
adopted by E. From ML *quota*, learnèd late
MF(-F) formed—after *quantitié*, quantity—*quotité*,
whence E *quotity*.

3. L *quot* has the further derivative *quoties* or
*quotiens*, How many times?: whence the learnèd
late MF-F *quotient*, adopted by E.

4. From L *quoties*, but prob influenced by
*quotity*, E has coined *quotiety*.

*Quote*

5. Either from L *quotus* or perh from ML *quota*, ML forms *quotāre*, to distinguish by numbers, hence to divide a literary work into not only chapters but also verses: whence—perh aided by late MF *quoter* (EF-F *coter*), to number (the parts of)—the E 'to *quote*'. Derivative ML *quotātiō*, o/s *quotātiōn-*, yields E *quotation* (as also in late MF).

quoth, quotha; bequeath (whence bequeathal) and bequest.

1. *Quotha=quoth'a*, said he (dial *'a* for *he*): a sarcastic interj, sem id with 'Sez you!' The archaic *Quoth* I, or he (she), said, derives from the OE pt *cwaeth*, from *cwethan*, to say, to speak: cf OFris *qùetha*, OS and OHG *quethan*, OHG var *quedan*, Go *qithan* (pt *qath*), ON *kvetha*: o.o.o., but perh (Feist) cf L *uetō*, I forbid.

2. OE *cwethan* has cpd *becwethan* (int *be-*), to affirm, esp in a will: ME *biquethen*: E 'to *bequeath*'.

3. OE *cwethan* has the derivative or, at the least, the cognate *cwide*, a saying: whence ME *bicwide*, with var *biquide*, later corrupted—? after *quesi*—to ME *biqueste*: whence E *bequest*.

quotidian. See DIANA, final para. (Cf the element *quot-*.)

quotient. See QUOTA, para 3.

quotiety; quotity. See QUOTA, para 4; para 2, s.f.

# R

Ra, the Zeus of Ancient Egypt, personifies Eg *ra* or *rē'*, the sun, for, lit, he is 'the shining, or resplendent, one'.

Rab. See ROBERT, para 2.

rabban. See RABBI.

rabbet. See the 2nd BAT, para 3.

rabbi, rabbinical, rabbinism, rabbinist; rabban and rabboni.

1. *Rabbi*, adopted from LL, derives from LGr *rhabbi*: H *rabbī*, lit 'my great one', from H *rabh*, the great one—whence E *rab*, master or teacher. *Rabbī* has pl *rabbīn*, whence, by b/f, the EF-F *rabbin*, a rabbi, whence the EF-F adj *rabbinique*, whence E *rabbinic*, var *rabbinical*. F *rabbin* has the further derivatives *rabbinisme*, *rabbiniste*, whence E *rabbinism*, *rabbinist*.

2. Aram exhibits the cognate *ribbōni*, lit 'my great master': whence H *rabbōni*, E *rabboni*. Aram *ribbōn* has var *rabbān*, adopted by H, whence E *rabban*.

rabbit: ME *rabet*: MF-F *rabot*, carpenter's plane, prob orig a rabbit: perh from MD *robbe*, dim *robbeken*, a rabbit, prob orig the nickname 'Robert' (EW).

rabble (1), a bar used in puddling iron: MF *roable*, later *rable* (F *râble*): L *rutābulum*, a fire shovel, app from *ruere* (s and r *ru*-), to overturn, to fall suddenly upon.

rabble (2), a swarm of animals (obs), hence a mob: ME *rabel*, a pack of hounds: o.o.o.: ? akin to—and, from the noise it makes, deriving from —MD-D *rabbelen* (LG *rabbeln*), to chatter, E (now dial) *rabble*: prob ult echoic— cf *babble*.

rabboni. See RABBI, para 2.

Rabelaisian: EF-F *rabelaisien*, adj of François *Rabelais* (1490–1553), satirist and humorist. The name *Rabelais* was perh orig an adj of *Rabel*, itself occ a dim from Prov *raba* (F *rave*), the plant rape. (Dauzat.) Rabelais was often grossly robust.

rabic, rabid. See RAGE, para 2.

raccoon. See COON.

race (1), n hence v, (to) rush, run fast (whence racer, racing): ME *ras*: ON *rās*, a leap, a running, akin to OE *rǣs*, a running: prob echoic.

race (2), a family, a tribe, a people, whence racial, racy: EF-F *race*: It *razza*: prob L *ratio*, a species, in medieval scholastic Phil (Walshe).

race (3), a root. See RADICAL, para 3.

race (4), to scratch. See RASE, para 4.

raceme, racemic. See RAISIN.

rachis, rachitic, rachitis. See the element *rachi*-, 2nd para.

rack (1), neck and spine, now the foresaddle, of a carcass: OE *hreacca* (*hreca*), neck.

rack (2), a rush or a shock (obs), a mass of wind-driven clouds: akin to ON *rek*, something that has drifted ashore, and *reka*, to drive or thrust, with numerous Scan cognates; akin also to *wrack*, q.v. at WRECK.

rack (3), a set of bars, or a single bar, hence in torture, hence v (cf the OGmc words): ME *racke*, var of *rekke*: (prob) MD, MLG *rec*, a framework, *recken*, to put on one and stretch (OHG *recchēn*, Go *-rakjan*): caus of OGmc *\*rikan*; IE r *\*rig*-, as in OIr *rikim* and L por*rig*o, I stretch: cf, therefore, REACH. Whence *rackrent*, an excessively high rent.

rack (4). A var of *wrack*, q.v. at WRECK.

rack (5), a path. See the 2nd RAKE.

rack (6), a horse's gait: o.o.o.: ? id with (1) or, more prob, with the v in (3).

rack (7), as in *rack-punch*, is short for *arrack*, from Ar *'araq*, spirituous liquor.

rack (8), to draw (wine) off from the lees: aphetically from Prov *arraca*, to treat (wine) thus: from Prov *raca*, the skins and stems of pressed grapes. Cf RAISIN.

rack and ruin. See WREAK, para 3; cf the 2nd RACK.

racket (1), a din (whence rackety and the v, whence, in turn, racketeer), is o.o.o. but prob echoic: perh, in part, suggested by the rattle of dice in the long-obsolete game so named, although, obviously, the game could, theoretically, have come from the noise. The AE sense derives from the E underworld.

racket (2), in ball-games: EF-F *raquette* (modern sense): MF *raquette*, palm of the hand (used before the implement was): vulgar Ar *rāḥet*: Ar *rāḥat*. palm of hand. The indefensible form *racquet* arises from a confusion of E racket and F raque*tt*e.

racoon. See COON.

racy. See the 2nd RACE.

raddle. See RED, para 2.

radial, radian, radiant, radiate, radiation, radiator. See the 2nd RAY, para 3.

radical (adj, hence n), whence radicalism, radicalize; radical and radicle and radicule (whence, anl, radicular, radiculous), radicose; radix and radish and race, a root; radicand, radicant, radicate.—Cpds: déraciné; eradicable (whence ineradi-

546

cable), eradicate, eradication (whence, anl, eradicative) eradicator.—Cognate: root (n, hence v), whence rootless and rooty; wort.—Also: ramus (rame), ramulus (whence, anl, ramular), ramose, ramulose (irreg ramelose).—Cf the sep LIQUORICE (AE LICORICE) and ORCHARD—and perh the sep RAY group.

1. There is app an IE r *rā-, to derive, as a growing plant, from (the soil, a tree), to grow out of or off from. In L, *rā- has the extnn *rād- (Gr rhād-) and *rām-; in Gmc, rād- has the var rōt-, with further changes or manifestations in wort. Sem, the root-branch alternation presents no difficulties, and it has phon support: E & M compare, sem, the Skt šaka, a branch, šaknis, a root, and, phon, W gwraidd, roots, gwrysgen, branch (with initial w), and Gr rhiza, a root, rhadamnos, young shoot, branch. With Gr rhiza, cf the element rhizo- and the E derivatives rhizoid and rhizome (Gr rhizōma).

2. L rāmus, a branch, and its dim rāmulus survive in SciE; their resp adjj rāmōsus and rāmulōsus yield E ramose (var ramous) and ramulose (var ramulous), whence the irreg Bot ramelose. Ramage, boughs, is adopted from EF-F (from OF-MF rame, from L rāmus). In ML, rāmus acquires the cpd rāmificāre, to form branches, hence to branch out, with derivative rāmificātiō, acc rāmificātiōnem: whence MF-F ramifier and EF-F ramification: whence 'to ramify' and ramification.

## L rādix

3. L rādix, a root, acc rādicem, o/s rādic-, becomes OF-early MF raïs, raïz, whence E race, a root, esp of ginger.

4. On the o/s rādic- arises the LL adj rādīcalis, having roots, (deeply) rooted, whence the MF-F and, prob independently, the E radical. L rādix has dim rādicula, whence E radicule, rare for the more anglicized radicle; var radicel perh imitates F radicelle. The L adj of rādix is rādicōsus, whence radicose.

5. Rādix, retained by Sci, becomes It radice, whence EF radice, F radis, whence E radish, with sense narrowed from 'root' to 'radish' as early as in It.

6. L rādix has LL derivative rādicāre, to root, with presp rādicans, o/s rādicant-, whence the E adj radicant, and gerundive rādicandus, whence the Math n radicand, and pp rādicātus, whence the now rare adj and v radicate.

## Compounds from rādix

7. L rādix has the LL extn rādicina, whence OF-F racine (whence the PN Racine—cf E Root), with the MF-F cpd déraciner, to uproot, pp déraciné, used occ in literary E, with anl E derivative deracinator, whence deracination.

8. LL rādicāre has the cpd ērādicāre, to root out, whence LL ērādicabilis, E eradicable; pp ērādicatus yields 'to eradicate', and its LL derivatives ērādicatiō (o/s ērādicātiōn-) and ērādicātor become E eradication and eradicator.

## Gmc root and wort

9. Gmc *rot- (as in para 1) occurs in ON rōt, a root, whence OE rōt, ME rote, later roote, E root.

10. Akin to ON rōt and to L rādix, Gr rhadix, is —with initial w—E wort, ME wort, earlier wurt, OE wyrt, a root, a herb: cf OS wurt, Go waúrts, root, OHG-MHG wurz, root, herb, G Wurz, herb, and—without the w—ON urt, cf Da urt and Sw ört.

radicel, radicle, radicule. See prec, para 4.
radio. See RAY, para 2.
radish. See RADICAL, para 5.
radium. See RAY, para 2.
radius. See RAY, para 2.
radix. See RADICAL, para 5.
radula. See RASE, para 4.

raff (whence raffish) and riffraff; raffle (n, hence v);—ravel (whence ravelling), whence unravel, with pa, vn unravelling.

1. Raff, a jumble, esp if worthless, hence dregs or scum, whence the redup riffraff, app derives from the now dial raff, to rake, hence to jumble, together: and 'to raff' prob derives from EF raffer (cf the C16 n raffe), a var of EF-F rafler, orig a dicing term, itself from MF-F rafle (dicing term), app from MD raffel (dicing term): of Gmc origin— ? cf MHG-G raffen, to snatch away, and ON hrapa, to hasten. (Dauzat; Walshe.) MF-F rafle becomes ME rafle, E raffle, a dicing game, hence a kind of lottery, whence 'to raffle'.

2. Akin is 'to ravel': MD ravelen (D rafelen)— cf LG reffeln, reb(b)eln.

raffia derives from a word (and product) of Madagascar: rafia (whence SciL Raphia), var raofia.

raft, orig a rafter, later a log float: ME raft: either by shortening from OE raefter, whence, direct, E rafter, or from ON raptr, a rafter: with OE raefter, cf also MLG rafter and OS rehter.

rafter. See prec.

rag, n hence v, ME ragge, OE ragg (attested by the adj raggig, whence E raggy), comes from ON rögg, a tuft, also anything shaggy, whence shagginess, whence both Nor rugga, a coarse rug (cf ruggig, shaggy), and, perh not direct, the E rug (n, hence v), whence rugged, orig 'shaggy'·

2. Akin to ON rögg and E rug is E rough, ME rough, earlier rugh, earliest ruh, OE rūh, akin to OHG rūh, MHG rūch, G rauh, rough, coarse: cf Lith raúkas, L rūga, a wrinkle, and Skt rūkšás, rough. (Walshe.) The E adj rough has derivative n and v rough (with extn roughen) and roughness, and many cpds, e.g. rough-and-ready, rough-and-tumble, rough-cast, rough-hew, rough-rider, roughshod.

3. L rūga, a wrinkle, has adj rūgōsus, whence E rugose and, perh via late MF-F rugueux, f rugueuse, the var rugous; derivative LL rūgōsitās, o/s rūgōsitāt-, yields E rugosity and EF-F rugosité. The cpd corrūgāre (cor- for int con-), to wrinkle considerably, has pp corrūgātus, whence the E adj and v corrugate, whence, anl, corrugation.

4. E rag occurs in sl the red rag or tongue and in

the archaic 'to *bullyrag*', to bully by scolding, hence to badger: whence the sl 'to *rag*' or scold, hence to make fun of, whence the corresp n.

**rage,** n and v (whence pa **raging**), and **enrage; rabic, rabid** and **rabies**—cf **rave** (v, hence n), hence **raving** (pa, vn)—**reve, rêve, reverie.**

1. This small group stands upon the base formed by L *rabere* (s and r *rab-*), to be furiously angry: cf Skt *rábhas*, impetuosity, violence, *rabhasás*, impetuous: IE r, prob *rebh-*, to be impetuous.

2. L *rabere* has derivative adj *rabidus*, whence E *rabid*, and n *rabiēs*, the 'madness' of a 'mad' dog, adopted by Med E; from *rabies*, learnèd F derives *rabique*, whence E *rabic*.

3. L *rabiēs* soon added the sense 'violent anger, violent passion', whence VL and rare LL and occ ML *rabia*, whence OF-F *rage*, adopted by E; derivative OF-F *rager* becomes 'to *rage*'. The OF-MF cpd *enrager* (*en*, L *in*, into), to cause to rage, becomes 'to *enrage*'.

4. L *rabere* becomes, influenced by LL-VL *rabia*, *rabiāre*, whence perh MF *raver*, later *resver* (whence EF-F *rêver*), to wander, to be delirious, with modern sense 'to dream while awake' hardly before C18; MF *raver* yields ME *raven*, E 'to *rave*'.

5. MF *resver* has derivative *resverie*, delirium, EF-F *rêverie*, with modern sense hardly before C18: whence E *reverie*. The rare 'to *reve*'=F *rêver*, which has n *rêve*, occurring in Gallic E.

**raglan,** a loose, unbelted, but orig a caped, overcoat, derives from General Lord *Raglan* (1788–1855).

**ragman rolls; rigmarole.**

The latter derives, by slovening, from *ragman roll*, b/f of *ragman rolls*, those rolls (deeds on parchment) in which, 1291 and 1293, the Scottish lords and gentlemen swore allegiance to Edward I of England, there being an obscure ref to *ragman*, ME *rageman*, a state, or a papal, document, esp that of an act (1276) of Edward I for the hearing of ancient wrongs; this ME *rageman*, usu said to be o.o.o., is in fact o.o.o.—but perh it comes, by metathesis, from OF-F *parchemin*, parchment.

**ragoût,** AE ragout. See GUST, para 4.

**raid, raider.** See RIDE, para 3.

**rail** (1), a bar from one post to another, whence **railroad** (whence v) and **-way**: ME *raile*: MF-EF *reille*: VL *regla*, contr of L *regula*, a wooden ruler: cf *regular*: f.a.e., REX.

**rail** (2), a wading bird: MF *raale* (EF-F *râle*): prob echoic.

**rail** (3), to scold: late MF-F *railler*: OProv *ralhar*, to jest at (someone): ult echoic. Derivative EF-F *raillerie* becomes E *raillery*. Also from MF-F *railler* comes 'to *rally*' or banter.

**raiment.** See ARRAY, para 2.

**rain,** n (whence **rainy**) and v; **rainbird**, supposed to presage wet weather; **rainbow** (OE *regnboga*), whence **rainbow trout**.—**irrigable, irrigant, irrigate, irrigation** (whence **irrigational** and, anl, **irrigative**), **irrigator.**

1. *Rain*, ME *rein*, OE *regn*, is akin to OFris *rein*,

OS and OHG *regan* MHG-G *regen*, Go *rign*, ON *regn*; 'to *rain*', OE *regnian*, is akin to OFris *reinia*, Go *rignjan*, G *regnen*: and both are akin to L *rigāre* (s and r *rig-*), to water, to irrigate (a field), itself o.o.o.

2. L *rigāre* has cpd *irrigāre* (*in-*, int rather than 'into'), s *irrig-*, whence E *irrigable*. Presp *irrigans*, o/s *irrigant-*, yields the E adj, hence n, *irrigant*; pp *irrigātus* yields 'to *irrigate*', and derivatives L *irrigātiō*, o/s *irrigātiōn-*, and LL *irrigātor* become *irrigation* and *irrigator*.

**raise** (v, hence n) and **rise** (v, hence n), whence **riser, rising,** and pt **rose,** pp **risen; arise,** pa and vn **arising;—rouse** (pa **rousing**), whence **arouse.—rear,** with vn **rearing.**

1. To *raise*, ME *reisen*, comes from ON *reisa*, caus of ON *rīsa*, to rise. Intimately akin to ON *rīsa* is OE *rīsan*, whence 'to *rise*': with both, cf OFris *rīsa*, OS and OHG *rīsan* (also OHG *reisa*, MHG *reise*, a journey: Walshe), Go *-reisan*.

2. OE *rīsan* has cpd *ārīsan* (*ā-*, approx 'out'), a form occurring also in OS, cf Go *urreisan*, to arise: whence 'to *arise*', which has perh prompted 'to *arouse*', cpd of 'to *rouse*', to cause to arise from covert or bed, which, o.o.o., is conceivably a secondary (? orig dial) caus of 'to *rise*'.

3. OE *rīsan* has a caus cognate *rāēsan*, with the phon and sem var *rāēran*, to raise or elevate, whence ME *raeren* or *reren*, 'to *rear*', to elevate, hence to bring up a child; with OE *rāēsan*, cf ON *reisa*, to raise (as in para 1).

**raisin; raceme,** whence **racemic.**

*Raisin* derives from OF-MF *raizin, reisin* (F *raisin*): VL *racēmus*: L *racēmus*, a bunch of grapes or berries: prob akin to Gr *rhāx* (gen *rhāgos*) in that both words prob diverge from a Medit r. L *racēmus* yields the Bot E *raceme*

**raja,** E rajah. See REX, para 35.

**rake** (1), implement: OE *raca, racu*: cf OHG *rehho*, MHG *reche*, G *Rechen*, MLG and MD *rake*, a rake, ON *reka*, a shovel, also Go *rikan*, to heap up (with, or as with, a rake), to collect, prob Gr *oregein*, to stretch out, perh L *rogus*, a funeral pyre. (Walshe.) Prob cf the sep RECKON.

**rake** (2), a path or track, var **rack**: ME *rakke, rake*: partly ON *rāk, raku*, a stripe or a streak, a track, and partly OE *racu, race*, a hollow path, e.g. the dry bed of a stream: cf OS *raca*. Gmc r, *rac-*.

**rake** (3), v, to use a rake on: partly, prob mainly, from (1); partly of Scan origin—cf Ice *rake*, to rake away, and ON *raka*, to rake. Hence *raker*.— A *rakehell* (archaic) is lit a 'hell-raker': whence *rake*, a dissolute fellow, whence *rakish*.

**rake** (4), v, to incline: o.o.o.: perh cf Sw *raka*, to reach, and therefore REACH itself. Hence as n.— Hence *rakish*, as in 'at a *rakish* angle'.

**rake** (5), v, to move fast (as in 'a *raking* stride'): OE *racian*: cf the 2nd RACK and see WREAK.

**rakehell.** See the 3rd RAKE, s.f.

**raking,** adj. See the 5th RAKE.

**rakish,** debauched: see the 3rd RAKE, s.f.—Inclined: see the 4th RAKE.

rally (1), to banter, lightly mock. See the 3rd RAIL.

rally (2), to reunite, hence to rouse to action. See LIGAMENT, para 5.—Hence the n, finally in tennis sense.

ram (n, hence v), the male sheep, noted for its butting, hence an engine of war, comes straight from OE (var *ramm*): cf OHG-MHG and MD-D *ram* and prob ON *ramr*, (very) strong, and OB *raměnz*, violent. (Walshe.)

ramage, boughs. See RADICAL, para 2.

ramble, v hence n. See AMBLE, para 6.

rambunctious. See ROBUST (heading).

ramentum. See RASE, para 4.

ramification, ramify. See RADICAL, para 2, s.f.

ramose. See RADICAL, para 2.

ramp (v, hence n), whence rampage, whence rampageous—cf rampant, whence rampancy; romp (n and v, whence rompers and pa, vn romping); rumple, n, v; rimple (v, hence n).

1. 'To *ramp*', orig to creep or crawl, hence to stand menacingly, to climb, ME *rampen*, derives from the sem id OF-F *ramper*, from Frankish *\*rampōn*, earlier *\*hrampōn*, to creep or crawl, with *hr-* echoic of effort. OF-F *ramper* has presp *rampant*, whence the E adj, orig in Her.

2. ME *rampen* bears the secondary sense 'to be boisterous', whence *ramp* (obs), a bold, esp a sexually bold, woman, whence *romp*, a romping girl; hence 'to *romp*', whence, in turn, *romp*, a boisterous frolic; *rompers*, orig *romper*, denotes a dress suitable for young children to play in.

3. Akin to Frankish (*h*)*rampōn* are OHG *rimpfan*, to wrinkle, MHG *rimpfen*, later, as still in G, *rümpfen*, OE *gehrumpen* (int prefix *ge-*), wrinkled, and MD *rompelen*, *rumpelen*, whence, imm, the E 'to *rumple*'; MD *rompel*, *rumpel*, yields the E n. Perh, however, 'to *rumple*' derives rather from MHG-G *rumpeln*, to rumple, int of late MHG *rummelen* (G *rummeln*), cf D *rommelen*, to rattle.

4. Akin to OE *gehrumpen*, wrinkled, and MHG *rimpfen*, to wrinkle, are MLG-MD (and D) *rimpel*, a wrinkle, *rimpelen*, to wrinkle: whence, prob, the E n and v *rimple*, unless *rimple* be simply a thinning of *rumple*.

rampage. See prec (heading).

rampancy, rampant. See RAMP, heading and para 1, s.f.

rampart. See PARE, para 6.

ramrod is a rod you ram home.

ramshackle. See SEEK, para 3.

ramulose, ramulus, ramus. See RADICAL, para 2.

ranch, rancher, ranchero, rancho.

*Rancher* (*ranch*+agent -*er*) owes something to ASp *ranchero*, agent of ASp *rancho*, whence AE, hence E, *ranche*, now usu *ranch*: and ASp *rancho* derives from Sp *rancho*, a soldiers' mess, hence a mess hut (esp of soldiers), hence any hut: OHG *hring*, MHG *rinc* (G *Ring*), a ring, a circle, hence an assembly: cf RANGE, para 1.

rancid; rancor (AE), rancour (E), adj rancorous.

L *rancēre* (s and r *ranc-*), to be rancid, has adj *rancidus*, whence E *rancid*, and LL n *rancor*, acc

rancorem, whence OF-MF *rancor* (F *rancoeur*), var *rancur*, whence ME-E *rancour*, AE *rancor*; derivative OF-MF *rancoros*, *rancuros*, becomes E *rancorous*. L *rancēre* is o.o.o.

rand; the Rand. See RIM, para 2.

random. See RIM, para 3.

randy. See RIM, para 4.

range (n and v), whence ranger, ranging (pa, vn), rangey or, usu, rangy; arrange, arrangement (whence disarrange, disarrangement)—derange (whence pa deranged), derangement;—rank, n (whence ranker) and v (whence ranking, pa, vn); rink;—ring, a circlet, hence v (pt rang or rung, pp rung), whence ringer and ringing, pa, vn.—Cf the scp RANCH and HARANGUE.

1. At the base of the entire group stands, on the F side, Frankish *\*hring*, a circle, a ring, and, on the Gmc, OHG *hring*, a ring: cf OFris, OS, OE *hring*, MD and MHG *rinc*, MD *ryng*, D and G *ring*, Go *\*hriggs* (pron *hrings*), Crimean Go *rinck*, ON *hringr* (and modern Scan cognates): Gmc etymon, *\*hrengaz*; IE r, *\*krengh-*, var *\*krongh-*: cf OB *krogŭ*, a circle. (Walshe.)

2. OE *hring* becomes E *ring*; with this *i* form, cf E *rink*, orig Sc (a course, a race), earlier Sc *renk*, from OF-MF *renc*.

3. OF *renc*, from Frankish *\*hring*, a circle, a ring, becomes OF-MF *ranc*, whence the late MF-F *rang*; whence also E *rank*, a line or row, whence 'to *rank*'.

4. OF-MF *ranc* has the derivative OF-F v *ranger*, to set in a line, OF-MF var *rangier*, whence 'to *range*'; the OF-MF derivative n *range* (late MF-F *rangée*) becomes E *range*.

5. OF-F *ranger* has the OF-F cpds *arranger*, derivative MF-F *arrangement*, and OF-MF *déranger*, late MF-F *déranger*, derivative EF-F *dérangement*: whence ME *arayngen*, E 'to *arrange*', and E *arrangement*—and E *derange*, *derangement*.

rani. See REX, para 35.

rank, adj: OE *ranc*, proud, strong: cf MD *ranc*, *ranke*, D *rank*, erect, slender, and ON *rakkr*, slender, bold: perh ult akin to E *right*, q.v. at REX.

rank, n and v. See RANGE, para 3.

rankle. See DRAGON, para 3.

ransack. See SEEK, para 3.

ransom. See EXEMPT, para 13.

rant, whence ranter and ranting and perh the archaic rantipole (? *rant*+connective -*i*-+*pole*, var of *poll*, head): MD *ranten*, *randen*, to dote, to be in an extravagant rage: o.o.o.—? echoic.

rap (1), a smart, quick, not very severe blow: app echoic, with Scan cognates: cf SLAP.

rap (2), to snatch. Cf *rape*, to seize, q.v. at RAPT, para 2.

rapacious, rapacity. Cf *rape*, to seize, q.v. at RAPT, para 4.

rape (1), a turnip (obs), hence a forage plant (whence rape oil): L *rāpa* (var *rāpum*): cf Gr *rhapus* (var *rhaphus*), turnip, akin to Gr *rhaphanos* (var -*anē*), radish, in Attic a cabbage: Gmc and Sl cognates: ? a Medit word.

**rape** (2), the pomace of grapes, hence a filter;
**rappee.**

1. *Rape* derives from late MF-F *râpe*: ML *raspa*,
seeded grapes: ? from OGmc *raspōn*, to rasp, to
grate. (Dauzat.)

2. F *râpe* derives imm from MF *raspe*, whence
the MF *rasper*, EF-F *râper*, to grate, with pp
*râpé*, f *râpée*, whence E *rappee*, a coarse snuff.

**rape** (3), a Sussex topographical division: o.o.o.:
? OE *rāp*, a rope, used in measuring. (EW.)

**rape** (4), to snatch forcibly, hence to plunder or
ravish. See RAPT, para 2.

**rapid, rapidity.** See RAPT, para 4.

**rapier**: EF-F *rapière*: late MF *espée rapière* (F
*épée*, sword): o.o.o.: perh a pej sl expression 'rasping, or grating, sword' from *râper*.

**rapine.** See RAPT, para 5.

**rappee.** See the 2nd RAPE, para 2.

**rapport.** See the 3rd PORT, para 11.

**rapt,** adj, whence **enrapt** and **rapture** (whence
**enrapture**), whence **rapturous; rapt,** n; **rape,** v and
n, whence **rap,** v and n, '(to) snatch'; **rapacious,
rapacity; rapid, rapidity; rapine** and **ravine; raven,
ravin,** v—**ravin, raven,** n—**ravenous; ravish** (whence
**ravishing**), **ravishment** (whence **enravishment**),
**ravissant** (and **-ante**); **ravage,** n, v; **raptatorial.**—A
prob Greek cognate: **Harpy,** whence **harpy,** whence
**harpy bat** and **harpy eagle.**—Cpds from L *rapere*:
**correption; direption; erept, ereption; surreption,
surreptitious.**

1. L *rapere*, to seize and forcibly remove, to take
by force, has s and r *rap-*, pp s *rapt-*; the cpds are in
*-ripere*, pp *-reptus*. The IE r is prob *rap-*, with var
*rep-* (senses as for *rapere*): cf Lith ap-*rėpiu*, I
take forcibly, Alb *rjep*, I take, carry off, perh the
Gr pcp *ereptomenos*, eating greedily, and prob, by
metathesis of the IE r, Gr h*arpazo*, I seize or
snatch.

2. L *rapere* becomes OF-MF, hence AF *raper*,
ME *rapen*, to seize, E 'to *rape*', with sexual sense
added; *rap*, to snatch, is a thinned var.

3. L *rapere* has pp *raptus* (f *rapta*), s *rapt-*:
whence E **rapt,** adj. The n *rapt* derives from L
*raptus* (gen *-ūs*), from the pps *rapt-*.

4. On the L press *rap-* is formed L *rapāx*, o/s
*rapāc-*, whence MF-F *rapace* and E *rapacious*;
derivative L *rapācitās*, o/s *rapācitāt-*, yields late
MF-F *rapacité* and E *rapacity*. Also on *rap-* is
built *rapidus*, tending to carry away, hence impetuous, hence (very) fast, with derivative *rapiditās*,
o/s *rapiditāt-*, whence EF-F *rapide* (adj, hence n)
and *rapidité*, whence E *rapid*, adj and n, and
*rapidity*. With the n F *rapide*, E *rapid*, cf the ML
pl n *rapida*, the rapids of a river.

5. Likewise from *rap-* comes L *rapīnae*, plunder-
ings, hence plunder, whence, by b/f, the sing LL
*rapīna*, a plundering, plunder: whence OF-F
*rapine*, adopted by E. Also from LL *rapīna*
descends the OF-F *ravine*, orig impetus, rapine, the
topographical sense being recorded first in 1388
(B & W): whence E *ravine* (orig, impetus).

6. From OF-MF *ravine*, impetuosity, rapine,
derives the now archaic *ravin*, rapine, rapacity,

predacity, with var *raven*—prob indebted to the
OF-MF var *raveine*; OF-MF *ravine*, rapine, has
derivative OF-EF v *raviner*, whence 'to *ravin*', now
usu 'to *raven*', and derivative OF-MF adj *ravinos*,
rapacious, predacious, whence E *ravenous*, rapacious (archaic), eager for food.

7. L *rapere* becomes VL *rapīre*, whence OF-F
*ravir*, with presp *ravissant* (f *ravissante*), used also
as adj in F and in Gallic E; from such forms as
*ravissant* and 'nous *ravissons*' comes ME *ravissen*,
later *ravischen* or *ravishen*, whence 'to *ravish*', with
fig sense deriving from late MF-F. Derivative
MF-F *ravissement* produces *ravishment*.

8. OF-F *ravir* has late MF-F derivative *ravage*,
adopted by E; derivative EF-F *ravager* supplies
us with 'to *ravage*'.

9. On the L pps *rapt-* is formed the L agent
*raptor*, adopted by SciE, with pl *raptores*; *raptātor*,
pl *raptātores*, however, is the agent of *raptāre*, int
of *rapere*. LL *raptōrius* (*rapt-+ōrius*) explains
E *raptorious*, usu *raptorial*, whence, anl, the E
*raptatorial*, var *raptatory*.

## A Greek Cognate (?)

10. Gr *harpazein* (s *harpaz-*, r *harp-*), to seize, has
the app derivative *Harpuia*, whence L *Harpyia*,
later *Harpya*, whence (late MF *arpe* and) EF-F
*harpie*, whence E *Harpy*, a fabulous, rapacious
Gr monster, whence the Common Noun, C17 in
F, but C16 in E.

## Compounds from L *rapere*, c/f *-ripere*, pp *-reptus*

11. L *corripere* (int *cor-* for *con-*), to seize
violently or suddenly, hence, in LL, to shorten, pp
*correptus*, has derivative *correptiō*, o/s *correptiōn-*,
whence E *correption*, a shortened pronunciation;
L *diripere*, to tear (*di-* for *dis-*, i.e.) asunder, has LL
derivative *direptiō*, o/s *direptiōn-*, whence the now
Hist *direption*, a plundering, pillage; L *ēripere*, to
snatch away, pp *ēreptus*, whence LL *ēreptiō*, o/s
*ēreptiōn-*, whence resp 'to *erept*' and *ereption*.

12. Finally, L *surripere*, to snatch (*sur-* for *sub*,
under, hence) from under, hence secretly, has pp
*surreptus*, with derivatives

*surreptiō*, o/s *surreptiōn-*, whence E *surreption*;
*surreptīcius*, clandestine, secret, whence E *surreptitious*—cf MF *surreptice*, later *subreptice*, reshaped on the L var *subreptīcius*.

**raptatorial, raptatory; raptor, raptorial, rap-
torious.** See RAPT, para 9.

**rapture, rapturous.** See RAPT (heading).

**rare** (1), **rarity; rarefaction** (whence, anl, **rarefac-
tive**) and **rarefy,** whence the pa **rarefied.**—**hermit,
hermitage; eremic, eremite, eremitic.**

1. *Rarity* derives, like EF-F *rareté*, from *rāritāt-*,
o/s of L *rāritās*, from *rārus*, whence, perh via
EF-F, the E *rare*. The cpd *rārefacere* and its ML
derivative *rārefactiō*, o/s *rārefactiōn-*, yield MF-F
*rāréfier*, *raréfaction*, whence E *rarefy*, *rarefaction*.
L *rārus*, having many intervals or gaps, hence
sparse, hence rare, has s and r *rār-*, app an extn
of an IE r *rā-*, var *rē-*, as, with other extnn, in Gr

erēmos, solitary, Lith retas, rare, and, with l for r, Skt virala, rare (Webster).

2. Gr erēmos, solitary, has derivative erēmia, solitude, hence a desert, whence erēmitēs, lit a desert-dweller, whence LL erēmīta, var herēmīta, whence OF-MF ermite and hermite, both adopted by ME, whence E hermit and, reshaped after LL erēmita, the archaic eremite. The OF-MF (h)ermite has derivative MF (h)ermitage, both adopted by ME, the h- form surviving in E. Gr erēmia, a desert, has adj erēmikos, whence E eremic; and LL (h)erēmīta acquires LL adj (h)erēmīticus, whence E eremitic.

rare (2), not thoroughly cooked, dial var rear, derives from ME rere, OE hrēr: ? cf OE hrēren, OHG hruorēn, MHG rüeren, G rühren, ON hroera, to stir.

rarefaction, rarefy, rarity. See the 1st RARE, para 1.

rascal, rascality. See para 6 of:

rase and erase, whence erasion and erasure—cf abrade, abrasion, abrasive; race, to scrape; raze— cf razee—razor; perh rasp (n, v), raspberry; radula, ramentum; rash on skin; rascal, whence rascality.—Cf the sep RAPPEE and perh the sep RAT.

1. 'To erase' derives from L ērāsus, pp of ērādere, to scrape, hence to rub, out: ē-+rādere, to scrape or scratch, to scrape or scratch away; 'to abrade' derives from L abrādere, to scrape ab-, off, with pp abrāsus, whence abrāsiō, o/s abrāsiōn-, whence abrasion, whence, anl, abrasive.

2. 'To rase' derives from OF-F raser, from VL *rāsāre, from rāsus, pp of L rādere: and rādere, s and r rād-, is prob akin to Skt rádati, he scrapes or scratches.

3. 'To raze', with sense-deviation in E, likewise comes from OF-F raser; razee is a var. Razor, ME rasor, derives from OF-MF rasor (OF var rasur; F rasoir), from LL rāsorium, a scraper, a burin, from rāsus, pp of rādere. Prob suggested by rāsorium is the E adj rasorial.

4. 'To race' or scratch, slash, is a var of rase. The Zoo radula is sense-adapted from L rādula, a scraper, from rādere; likewise adopted is rāmentum (prob for *rādimentum), something scraped off.

5. A rasp derives from ME, from MF, raspe (cf F râpe), itself from OF-MF ràsper (F râper), whence 'to rasp'; OF-MF rasper, of Gmc origin (cf OHG raspōn), is perh akin to VL *rāsāre. Raspberry stands for EE raspis berry, taut for raspis, a raspberry, app id with raspis (wine), prob from OF-MF vin raspé, with raspé perh orig the pp of rasper, to scrape. (Webster; B & W.—All very confused and hypothetical.)

6. A rash on the skin derives from OF-EF rasche, rache, skin eruption, scurf, from VL *rāsica, from *rāsicāre, to scratch often, freq of L rādere. From OF rasche, rache, app derives, prob via a dial, the OF-MF rascaille, the rabble, adopted by ME, whence the E rascal, a scurvy fellow, whence the adj rascally.

rash (1), adj (orig 'lively'), whence rashness: ME

rasch, prob adopted from MLG rasch (cf MD rasc), or from MHG rasch, from OHG rasc, dashing, lively: cf ON röskr: o.o.o. (Walshe.)

rash (2), n. See RASE, para 6.

rasher of bacon: o.o.o.: ? from the obs rash, to slash, to cut—a var of RASE.

rashness. See RASH, adj.

rasorial. See RASE, para 3, s.f.

rasp, n v (whence rasper, rasping). See RASE, para 5.

raspberry. See RASE, para 5, s.f.

rasper, rasping. See RASP.

rat (n, hence v), ratten, ratton, 'ratty'; rodent.— Cpds from L rōdere: corrode, corrosion, corrosive; erode, erodent, erosion (whence, anl, erosive).

1. Rat, ME rat or ratte, OE raet, is akin to MD rat (also D), ratte, rotte, OHG ratta, MHG-G ratte, OS ratta, and prob akin to L rōdere, to gnaw. E dial exhibits the var ratten, whence prob the E 'to ratten', to rob of tools or machinery; the now dial ratton, however, comes rather from the MF-F dim raton. The sl ratty, angry, easily angered, derives from ratty, of or like a rat, rats being fierce creatures.

2. L rōdere has presp rōdens, o/s rodent-, whence the E adj hence n.

3. The cpd corrōdere (int cor- for con-) yields MF-F corroder, whence 'to corrode'; the pp corrōsus has derivatives corrōsiō, acc corrōsiōnem, and corrōsiuus, ML corrōsivus, whence MF-F corrosion, adopted by E, and MF-F corrosif, f -ive, E corrosive. Likewise through EF come 'to erode' and erosion, from L ērōdere, to gnaw away, and its derivative ērōsiō, the pp ērōdens leading to erodent.

ratchet; rock, a distaff, and rocket (n, hence v).

1. Ratchet derives, ? irreg, from EF rochet, a bobbin, a distaff, in MF the extremity of a jousting lance, from Frankish *rokka, a distaff, id with OHG roccho, MHG rocke, G Rocken, a distaff; cf OIr rogait, a spindle. MHG rocke is id in MD, whence prob ME rokke, roc, the now Hist E rock, a distaff.

2. The firework rocket comes either from EF rocquet (var of rochet) or, more prob, from It rocchetta, earlier rocchetto, dim of rocca, a distaff, of the same OGmc origin; a rocket, with its stick, resembles a distaff.

rate, n and v. See REASON, para 2.

rate (2), to chide, ME raten, ? aphetic for ME araten, to chide or rebuke, app from OF areter, to accuse (L reputāre, to compute, repute, impute).

rathe; rather.

The latter derives from OE hrathor, the comp of hrathe or hraethe, quickly, the adv of OE adj hraeth, quick, whence the archaic rathe, early (obs: 'quick'), as in Milton's 'the rathe primrose': and akin to OE hraeth, var hraed, are, e.g., OHG hrad and ON hrathr.

ratification, ratify. See REASON, para 6.

rating, n. See REASON, heading and para 2.

ratio. See REASON, para 3.

ratiocinate, ratiocination, ratiocinative. See REASON, para 5.

ration, rational, rationale, rationalism, rationalist, rationality, rationalize, etc. See REASON, para 3.

ratiuncle. See REASON, para 3, s.f.

ratline or ratlin, a small transverse rope (naut): a f/e alteration (to *rat* and *line*) of earlier *radelyng*: perh, as EW pertinently proposes, from naut and dial *raddle*, to intertwine, from *raddle*, var of *raddling*, dim of the obs *rathe*, a rail.

ratoon, a sprout or shoot of cottonplant or sugarcane: Sp *retoño*, from *retoñar*, to sprout again, either *re-*, again+*toñar*, to sprout, or from the syn EF-F *rejeton* (from *rejeter*, ML *rejectāre*, to throw forth again).

rattan: Mal *rotan*.

ratten. See RAT, para 1.

rattle, ME *ratelen*, is akin to MD-D *ratelen* and MHG *razzeln* (G *rasseln*), freq of *razzen*, to rattle, to roar: echoic.—Hence *rattler*, *rattling*, *rattlesnake*, etc.

ratton. See RAT, para 1.

ratty. See RAT, para 1, s.f.

raucity, raucous.

1. The former derives, like late MF-F *raucité*, from *raucitāt-* (acc *raucitātem*), o/s of L *raucitās*, from L *raucus*, whence, like late MF-F *rauque*, the E *raucous*: and L *raucus* derives from L *rauis*, hoarseness or huskiness: prob echoic and therefore akin to Skt *rauti*, he roars, and L *rūmor*, (loud) noise—cf RUMOR.

2. With the IE r *rū-*, var *rau-*, cf OE *rūn*, a secret or mystery, hence a rune, akin to syn ON *rūn*, Go, OS, OHG *rūna*, a secret, hence a secret conversation, and to OIr *rūn*, Cor *ryn*, W *rhēn*, OC *rūnā*.

ravage. See RAPT, para 8.

rave. See RAGE, para 4.

ravel. See RAFF, para 2.

raven (1), the bird, OE *hraefn*, is akin to OHG *hraban* (MHG *raben*), extn of OHG *rabo* (MHG-G *rabe*), and to ON *hrafn*—and more remotely to L *coruus* and Gr *korax*: ult echoic.

raven (2), v and n; ravenous. See RAPT, para 6.

ravin, n and v. See RAPT, para 6.

ravine. See RAPT, para 5, s.f.

ravish, ravishing, ravishment; ravissant, ravissante. See RAPT, para 7.

raw (adj, hence n and v), whence rawness, derives from OE *hræw*, with var *hrēaw*: cf OHG *rāo*, contr *rō*, MHG *rō* (gen *rāwes*), G *roh*, ON *hrār*: Gmc r *hrāew-*; IE r, *krew-*, var *krow-*: cf L *cruor*, gore, Gr *kréas*, flesh, Skt *kraviš*, raw meat. (Walshe.) Cf, therefore, the sep CRUDE.

ray, n (a light-spoke, prob also the fish), hence v; hence also rayless and, in part, rayon;—radius, radial, radiant (whence radiance), radiate, radiation, radiator (from *radiate*); irradiate, irradiation; radio, whence many obvious cpds; radium.

1. The fish *ray* derives from MF-F *raie*, from L *raia*, prob akin to, or even (from the ossature, resembling the spokes of a wheel) deriving—by contr—from L *radius*, whence, via OF-F *rai*, the E *ray* of light. Orig a pointed rod or stick or wand, hence a ray of light or the spoke of a wheel,

L *radius* is o.o.o. but perh akin to L *rādix*, a root, with IE r *rā-*: cf RADICAL, para 1.

2. *Radius*, adopted by E, has E derivatives *radial* (unless adopted from late MF-F *radial*, which= L *radius*+adj *-al*); *radio*, usu short for *radiotelegraphy*, where *radio-* is the c/f of L *radius*; SciL *radium*, with Chem *-ium* substituted for L *-ius*.

3. L *radius* has derivative *radiāre*, to emit rays (hence spokes, etc.), with presp *radians*, o/s *radiant-*, whence the E adj *radiant*, and with pp *radiātus*, whence 'to *radiate*'; derivative L *radiātiō*, o/s *radiātiōn-*, becomes late MF-F and, prob independently, E *radiation*.

4. *Radiāre* has the cpd *irradiāre* (*ir-* for *in-*, here used int), with presp *irradians*, o/s *irradiant-*, whence E *irradiant*, whence *irradiance*, and with pp *irradiātus*, whence the adj and v *irradiate*; derivative LL *irradiātiō*, o/s *irradiātiōn-*, yields *irradiation*.

rayon. See prec (heading).

raze. See RASE, para 3.

razee. See RASE, para 3.

razor, razorial. See RASE, para 3.

re, as in the L tag *in re*. See the 1st REAL, para 5.

reach (1), to stretch, hence n, whence reachless, overreach (*over*+*reach*).

'To *reach*', ME *rechen*, derives from OE *rǣcan*: cf OE *reihhēn*, MHG-G *reichen*, MD *reken*, MD-D *reiken*, and perh (Walshe) L *regere*, to direct in a straight line (f.a.e., REX).

reach (2) is a dial var of RETCH.

react, reaction, reactive, reactor, reagent, etc, merely prefix *re-*, again, to *act* (etc.) and *agent*, qq.v. at ACT.

read—whence readable and reader (OE *rǣdere*) and reading (OE *rǣding*)—derives, via ME *reden*, earlier *raeden*, from OE *rǣdan*, to counsel, to interpret, to read: cf OFris *rēda*, OS *rādan*, OHG *rātan*, MHG *rāten*, G *raten* (to advise, to guess), MD *raiden* or, as in D, *raden*, Go *-rēdan*, ON *rātha*: cf also OSl *raditi*, to take thought for, and perh the *rat-* of *ratus*, pp of L *rēri*, to compute, to think: cf therefore REASON.

2. OE *rǣdan*, to counsel, has both the derivative n *rǣd*, whence the archaic *rede*, advice, interpretation, a story, and the cognate *rǣdels* (*rǣdelse*)—cf the G *rätsel*—whence ME *redels*, whence, the *s* being apprehended as that of the pl, the later ME *redel*, *rydel*, whence E *riddle*, a conundrum.

readjust, readjustment. See JURY, para 7, s.f.

ready (adj, hence n and v), whence readiness and already (*all*+*ready*): ME *readi*, earlier *redi*: OE *rǣde*, aphetic for *gerǣde*, akin to OFris *rēde*, OHG *biretti*, equipped, ready, MHG *bereite* (also *gereite*), G *bereit*, Go *garaiths* (established), MD *gereit*, *gereet*, D *gereed*, and MD *bereit*, *bereet*, D *bereid*, ON *g-reidr*, *greithr*: prob akin to RIDE.

2. Akin to OE *rǣde* is OE *rǣdan*, to arrange, whence ME *reden*, whence, app, the Sc—and the North Country and Midlands E dial—*redd*, to put in order, to clean or clear, to tidy.

reagent, suggested by *react*, is a Chem term: f.a.e., ACT.

real (1), adj (hence n), whence realism and realist (whence realistic), influenced by F *réalisme, réaliste*; reality, realize (whence realization); realizable, irrealizable, realty, Realtor; res—in re—rebus—reify.—Cpds: irreality, cf unreality, unreal; surrealism, surrealist;—for republic, republican, see PEOPLE, para 6.

1. The rare *irreality* derives from the rare *irreal*, from F *irréel*, neg of MF-F *réel*, f *réelle*; *unreal* (whence *unreality*)=*un-*+*real*. *Surrealism* and *surrealist* derive from F *surréalisme, surréaliste*, where *sur-* is L *super*, above, hence beyond.

2. The E adj *real* derives from MF *real* (MF-F *réel*), itself from LL *realis*, adj of *rēs* (s and r *ré-*), property, a property, a thing, hence an orig business affair: cf Vc *rām, rās*, acc sing and pl, riches, Skt *reván*, rich, and MW *rāi*, goods, riches: IE r, *\*rē-*, property.

3. The LL adj *realis* later (ML) develops the scholastic n *realitās*, whence the late MF-F *réalité* and, prob independently, the E *reality*. 'To *realize*' derives from EF-F *réaliser* (from MF *real*); E *realizable* and *realization*, and also E *irrealizable*, owe something to F *réalisable*, EF-F *réalisation*, F *irréalisable*, all from *réaliser*.

4. *Realty*, real estate, which=*real*, adj+*-ty* (for *-ity*), no longer clashes with *realty*, royalty, realm, now obs; with *realty-reality*, cf *specialty-speciality*. *Realty*, real estate, acquires the AE agent *Realtor*, Member of National Real Estate Boards.

5. Latinisms include *in re*, in the matter, hence concerning; *rebus*, a particular kind of riddle, is L *rebus*, with things, via EF-F *rébus*; *reify*, to invest with reality, whence *reification*, is lit 'to make property of'.

real, a coin. See *regal* at REX, para 10.

realm. See REX, para 5.

realtor, realty. See the 1st REAL, para 4.

ream (1), n: ME *reme*: MF *rayme* (EF-F *rame*): Sp *resma*: Ar *rizmah*, a bundle, esp of paper.

ream (2), v, to widen an opening in (whence reamer): ME *remen, rimen*: OE *rȳman*, to extend or enlarge, from *rūm*, space, room, whence, via ME *roum*, the E *room* (with an additional, a narrow sense), whence 'to *room*', whence *roomer*. With OE *rūm*, space, cf OHG-MHG *rūm*, G *Raum*, OS *rūm*, ON *rūm*, and OFris *rūm*, Go *rūms*, OE *rūm*, spacious, roomy. The IE r is app *\*ru-*, spacious: cf L *rūs*, the country (the open spaces), and prob Av *ravō*, free or open space. (*Roomy*=*room*, n+adj *-y*: cf G *geräumig*.)

reanimate. See ANIMAL, para 5.

reap, reaper. See RIPE, para 2.

rear, adj, derives from rear, n, aphetic for *arrear*, n (now usu *arrears*), itself from the obs adv *arrear*, ME *arere*, from OF-MF *ariere* (MF-F *arrière*), from VL *\*ad retrō*, taut for L *retrō*, backwards.

2. The F cpd *arrière-garde*, soldiers guarding the rear, becomes, by aphesis, the AF *reregard*, whence E *rearguard*; *rearward* is relatively modern (cf *-ward*). *Reredos*, coined by AF, is AF *rere*, for

rear-, situated behind+AF (from OF-F) *dos*, back, L *dorsum*.

rear, to raise. See RAISE, para 3.

reason, n (whence reasonless) and v (whence reasoning), reasonable; rate, n hence v (whence rateable or ratable, rating); ratify, ratification; ratio, ration (n, hence v), rational, rationale, rationalism, rationalist (whence rationalistic), rationality, rationalize (whence rationalization)—cf irrational (whence, anl, irrationality); ratiuncle; ratiocinant, ratiocinate, ratiocination, ratiocinative; arraign, arraignment, and deraign.—Perh cf the sep HUNDRED.

1. The entire group rests upon L *ratus*, pp (s *rat-*) of *rērī*, to count, calculate, reckon, hence to think: o.o.o.: ? from an IE r *\*ra-* or *\*re-* (var *\*rē-*), to count. (The Go *rathjō*, reason, is prob a borrowing; I suspect a Medit origin—perh cf Ar *raqm*, a number, and even the Eg metatheses *ḥebs, ḥesb*, to count.)

2. The L pp *ratus* acquires, by ellipsis for *rata pars*, a calculated share, the ML n *rata*, whence AF, whence E, *rate*.

3. In L, *ratus* acquires the n *ratiō*, a counting, an account, hence a manner, or the faculty, of counting, hence judgement, reason, method, form and senses adopted or adapted from R by E. L *ratiō* has acc *ratiōnem*, whence MF-F *ration*, adopted by E; the F derivative *rationner* prob suggested 'to *ration*', whence *rationing*. L *ratiō* has adj *ratiōnālis*, whence E *rational*—perh via OF-F *rationnel*; the n *rationale* is adopted from LL *ratiōnāle*, prop the neu of *ratiōnālis*. Derivative LL *ratiōnālitās*, o/s *ratiōnālitāt-*, yields *rationality*. Learnèd F *rationaliser, rationalisme, rationaliste* perh suggested *rationalize, rationalism, rationalist*. The L *ratiuncula*, dim of *ratiō*, gives us the Math *ratiuncle*.

4. L *ratiōnālis* has neg *irratiōnālis*, whence *irrational*.

5. L *ratiōcināri*, to calculate, hence to reason, has presp *ratiōcinans*, o/s *ratiōcinant-*, whence E *ratiocinant*, adj, and pp *ratiōcinātus*, whence the adj and v *ratiocinate*; derivative *ratiōcinātiō*, acc *ratiōcinātiōnem*, yields late MF-F *ratiocination*, adopted by E, and anl LL *ratiōcinātiuus*, ML *-ivus*, yields *ratiocinative*.

6. L exhibits a notable cpd: ML *ratificāre*. *Ratificāre*, to fix by calculation, to validate, becomes MF-F *ratifier*, whence 'to *ratify*'; derivative ML *ratificātiō*, acc *ratificātiōnem*, yields late MF-F *ratification*, adopted by E.

7. L *ratiōnem*, acc of *ratiō*, becomes OF-F *raison*, ME *resoun*, E *reason*; derivative OF-F *raisonner* becomes 'to *reason*', and subsidiary MF *raisonable* (F *raisonnable*) becomes ME *resonable*, E *reasonable*.

8. In LL, *ratiō* has the further sense 'legal cause', whence VL *\*arratiōnāre*, to summon before a court, whence MF *araisnier*, ME *arainen*, E 'to *arraign*'; derivative MF *araisnement* becomes E *arraignment*.

9. The implied VL *\*ratiōnāre* occurs in legal

MF *deraisnier*, to plead, to vindicate, whence 'to *deraign*'.

**reave**, pp **reft**. See ROB, para 3; **reaver**, ibid, para 4.

**rebate**. See the 2nd BAT, para 3.

**rebel** (adj, n, v), **rebellion**, **rebellious**.

The adj and n *rebel* derive from the OF-F adj, hence n, *rebelle*, from L *rebellis*, akin to L *rebellāre*, to fight back, to rebel, cpd of *bellāre*, to make war, from *bellum*, war: cf BELLICOSE. *Rebellāre* becomes OF-F *rebeller*, whence 'to *rebel*'; derivative L *rebelliō*, acc *rebelliōnem*, yields MF-F *rébellion*, whence E *rebellion*, whence, anl, *rebellious*.

2. See REVEL.

**rebound**, v hence n, derives from OF-F *rebondir*, to bound back: cf the v BOUND.

**rebuff**, v, comes from EF *rebuffer*, itself from EF *rebuffe*, whence the E n; EF *rebuffe* derives from It *rebuffo*, var of *rabuffo*, from *rabbuffare*, to jostle or hustle: *re-*, again, used int+*buffare*, to puff out one's cheeks: cf BUFFOON. (B & W.)

**rebuke**, v, hence n: AF *rebuker*: MF *rebuchier*, to repel: *re-*, back+MF *buschier*, to strike, from OF-MF *busche* (F *bûche*), a piece of wood: ? Frankish *būsk*, a stick.

**rebus**. See the 1st REAL, para 5.

**rebut**, whence **rebuttal**, prob derives from late MF-F *rebuter* (cf OF-F *rebouter*), to knock back, to repulse: *re-*+*buter*, from MF-F *but*, from Frankish *būt*, a log. Cf BUTT.

**recalcitrance**, **recalcitrant**. See KICK.

**recall**, v hence n: *re-*, back+CALL.

**recant**, whence, anl, **recantation**: L *recantāre*, to sing 'back', to recall one's words: *re-*+*cantāre*, to chant, int of *canere*, to sing. Cf CHANT.

**recapitulate**, **recapitulation**. See CAPITAL, s.f.

**recapture**, **recast**=*re-*, back, again+the simples.

**recede**. See CEDE, para 11.

**receipt**. See CAPABILITY, para 7.

**receive**. See CAPABILITY, para 7.

**recension**. See CENSOR, para 2.

**recent**, whence **recency**, derives, via late MF-F *récent*, from L *recent-*, o/s of *recēns*, newly arrived, fresh: ? *re-*, again, afresh, used int+*-cēns*, akin to Gr *kainos*, new, and Skt *kanīna*, young, and OSl *koni*, a beginning. Cf RINSE.

**receptacle**: L *receptāculum*, from *receptāre*, int of *recipere*, to receive, pp *receptus*: cf CAPABILITY, para 7.

**reception**, **receptive**. See CAPABILITY, para 7.

**recess**, **recession**, **recessive**. See CEDE, para 11.

**recherché**. See CIRCLE, final sentence.

**recidivism**, **recidivist**, **recidivous**. See CADENCE, s.f.

**recipe**: L *recipe*, Take (it back)!: orig a Med formula.

**recipient**: L *recipient-*, o/s of *recipiens*, presp of *recipere*, to receive: cf CAPABILITY, para 7.

**reciprocal**, **reciprocant**, **reciprocate**, **reciproca-tion** (whence, anl, **reciprocative**, **reciprocatory**), **reciprocity**.

*Reciprocal*, like F *réciproque*, derives from L *reciprocus*, going backwards and forwards (like the

sea), hence alternating, working both ways: **recoprocos*: **recos*, from *re-*, backwards+**procos*, from *pro-*, forwards. Derivative *reciprocāre* has presp *reciprocans*, o/s *reciprocant-*, whence E *reciprocant*, and pp *reciprocātus*, whence 'to *reciprocate*'; derivative LL *reciprocātiō*, o/s *reciprocātiōn-*, yields *reciprocation*. *Reciprocus* has LL n *reciprocitās*, o/s *reciprocitāt-*, whence F *réciprocité*, E *reciprocity*.

**recital**, **recitation**, **recitative**, **recite**. See CITE, para 5.

**reck** (v, hence n), **reckless**; **reckon**, whence **reckoner**, **reckoning**.

1. 'To *reck*' comes, through ME *recken*, earlier *recchen*, from OE *reccan*, var of *recan*, to take heed: cf MHG *ruochen* (*geruochen*), OS *rōkjan*, ON *roekja*: o.o.o. The adj *reckless*=OE *reccelēas*, *rēcelēas*: **recce* or **rēce*, from the v+*-lēas*, E *-less*.

2. Akin to OE *reccan*, *rēcan*, is OE *gerecenian*, to explain, whence ME *rekenen*, E 'to *reckon*': cf OFris *rekenia*, *reknia*, MD-D *rekenen*, OHG *rechann*, MHG-G *rechnen*, to count, Go *rahnjan*, to calculate, and, further off, the Skt *račáyati*, he regulates. (Walshe.)

**reclaim**, **reclamation**. See CLAIM, para 9.

**reclinate**, **reclination**, **recline**. See CLIME, para 11.

**recluse** (adj, n), **reclusion** (whence, anl, **reclusive**).

Both the E adj and the E n *recluse* derive from OF-F *reclus*, f *recluse*, orig the pp of OF-MF *reclure*, from *reclūdere*, LL to shut back, hence up, L to open: *re-*, back+*-clūdere*, c/f of *claudere*, to shut or close: cf CLAUSE. Derivative ML *reclūsiō* (from the pp *reclūsus*), o/s *reclūsiōn-*, leads to *reclusion*.

**recognition**, **recognitive**, **recognize**. See COGNI-TION, paras 3 and 4.

**recoil**, v hence n: ME *recoilen*: OF-F *reculer*: *re-*, backwards+OF-F *cul*, backside+inf *-er*: L *cūlus*: cf Skt *kūla-*, as a rearguard, and OIr *cúl* (Ga *cùl*), W and Cor *cil*, the back.

**recollect**, **recollection**. See COLLECT, para 2.

**recommence**, **recommencement**. See COMMENCE.

**recommend**, **recommendation**, **recommendatory**. See MANUAL, para 25.

**recompense**, n and v: MF-F *récompense*, n, from *récompenser*: LL *recompensāre*: *re-*, again, back+*compensāre*, (lit) to weigh together: f.a.e., PEND.

**reconcile**, **reconciliation**. See CONCILIATE, para 1.

**recondite**; **abscond**; **sconce**, a candlestick.

L *condere*, to put together, to store=*con-*, to-gether+*-dere*, c/f of *dare*, to put, (later) to give: f.a.e., DATA. The cpd *abscondere* is to put away (*abs-*), to hide away: whence 'to *abscond*', to hide oneself away. From the L pp *absconsus* comes ML *absconsa*, by aphesis *sconsa*, a screened lantern or candlestick, whence—via MF—the ME *skonse*, E *sconce*. The cpd *recondere*, to store back, i.e. out of the way, hence to hide, has pp *reconditus*, whence the E adj *recondite*.

**reconnaissance**. See COGNITION, para 3, s.f.

**reconnoitre**, AE **reconnoiter**: F *reconnoître* (now

*reconnaître*): OF *reconoistre*, to recognize: cf COGNITION, para 3.

**reconsider, reconstitute:** simply *re-*, again + the simples.

**reconstruct, reconstruction.** See STRUCTURE, para 3.

**record** (n, v), **recorder.**

The n *record* is adopted from OF-MF *record*, memory, a memory, which derives it from OF-EF *recorder*, to remember for oneself, to recall to another, whence ME *recorden*, E 'to *record*': and OF-EF *recorder* derives from L *recordāri*, to remember: *re-*, back + *cord-*, o/s of *cor*, heart, mind + inf *-āri*, i.e. to bring back to mind: f.a.e., CORDIAL. OF-EF *recorder* has agent *recordeor*, a rememberer, a relater, a minstrel (whence the Mus instrument), in AF a magistrate, a sense extant in E.

**recount, recountal.** See the 2nd COUNT, para 6.

**recoup** derives from OF-F *recouper*, orig to cut back: *re-* + *couper*, to cut: cf *coppice*. Derivative OF-F *recoupement* gives us *recoupment*.

**recourse.** See COURSE, para 4.

**re-cover.** See COVER, para 3.

**recover** (regain), **recovery.** See CAPABILITY, para 5.

**recreant.** See CREDENCE, para 6, s.f.

**recreate, recreation, recreative.** See CREATE, para 4.

**recrescence, recrescent.** See CRESCENT, para 9.

**recriminate, recrimination.** See CRIME, para 5.

**recrudescence, recrudescent.** See CRUDE, para 2.

**recruit** (n, v), **recruitment.** See CRESCENT, para 9.

**rect.** See REX, para 23.

**rectangle,** whence, anl, **rectangular.** See the element *rect-*: f.a.e., REX.

**rectification, rectify.** See REX, para 23.

**rectilinear:** Element *recti-* + *linear*, q.v. at LINE.

**rectitude.** See REX, para 23.

**rector, rectory.** See REX, para 23.

**rectum.** See REX, para 24.

**recumbency, recumbent.** See HIVE, para 8.

**recuperate, recuperation.** See CAPABILITY, para 4.

**recur, recurrence, recurrent.** See COURSE, para 10 (at *recurrere*).

**recusancy, recusant.** See CAUSE, para 8.

**red** (adj, hence n); **red tape; redd; redden, reddish, redness,** all from *red*, adj: **raddle** and **ruddle; rud** and **rudd, ruddock** and **ruddy; russet; rust; rubella, rubellite; rubeola; rubescent,** whence **rubescence; rubric** (n, hence adj), **rubricate** (adj, v, whence **rubrication** and **rubricator**); **ruby**—cf **rubine; rubefacient; rubor; rutilant, rutile; rufous; rouge,** n, hence adj and v; **rowan; roil**—cf **rubiginous; rubicund, rubicundity; rubidic, rubidine, rubidium; ? ribbon** (n, hence v, whence the int **beribboned**), with f/e var **ribband** or **riband;**—**erythrin, erythrism, erythrite,** cf the element *erythro-*; **erysipelas.**

1. *Redd*, fish spawn, comes from E dial *red*, spawn (from colour); *red tape*, excessive routine, refers to the tape used for tying documents. The

adj *red*, ME *red*, earlier *reed*, *read*, derives from OE *rēad*: cf OFris *rād*, OS *rōd*, OHG-MHG *rōt*, G *rot*, Go *rauths*, MD *rode*, D *rood*, ON *rauthr*; Lith *raúdas*, Cz *rudý*; L *rūfus* (for *\*roudhos*); EIr *rúad*, OW *rudd*, Cor *rūd*, OC *\*roudos*: IE etymon, *\*roudhos*, Gmc *\*rauthaz*. 'In some languages the base is *\*rudhir-*: Skt *rudhirás*, Gr ἐρυθρός [*eruthros*], L *ruber*' (Walshe).

2. Akin to OE *rēad*, red, is OE *rudu*, a ruddy colour, whence E *rud*, with dim *ruddle*, with var *raddle*; OE *rudu* has adj *rudig*, whence *ruddy*. E *rud* has, esp for the fish, the var *rudd*; and OE *rudu* has derivative *rudduc*, a robin, whence E *ruddock*.

3. Akin to OE *rudu* is OE *rūst* (prob also *rust*), E *rust*, that reddish coating which iron forms if long exposed to damp air: cf OHG-MHG-G *rost*, MD *rost* and, as in D, *roest*, Let *rūsa*, rust, *rusta*, brown colour, and other Sl cognates. (Walshe.) Derivative OE *rustig* becomes E *rusty*.

4. *Russet*, however, derives from OF-MF *rousset*, f *roussette*, dim of OF-MF *ros*, *rus*, *rous* (F *roux*), red, reddish, from L *russus*, akin to L *ruber*, red.

5. L *ruber*, red, o/s *rubr-*, has a lost extn *\*rubrīcus*, surviving in *rubrīca* (sc *terra*, earth), red earth, red chalk (used for colouring): MF *rubriche*, later *rubrique*: ME *rubriche*, later *rubrike*: E *rubric*, red ochre (obs), hence a portion (of MS, etc.) coloured red. Derivative LL *rubrīcāre* has pp *rubrīcātus*, whence the E adj and v *rubricate*.

6. Intimately related to L *ruber* is L *rubēre* (s and r *rub-*), to be red, with inch *rubescere*, presp *rubescens*, o/s *rubescent-*, whence the E adj *rubescent*.

7. L *ruber* has dim *rubellus*, reddish, whence Med *rubella*, a skin disease, and Min *rubellite*, a gem, and tech *rubelle*, a kind of red. The cpd *rubefacere*, to make red, has presp *rubefaciens*, o/s *-facient*, whence *rubefacient*.

8. The Med *rubeola* is a SciL derivative from L *rubeus* (from *rubēre*), red, whence OF-MF *rubi* (MF-F *rubis*), the gem ruby, whence E *ruby*. The dye *rubine*, orig a ruby, derives from ML *rubinus*, an extn of *rubeus*.

9. L *rubēre* has derivative adj *rubidus*, whence both the rare E *rubid*, *rubidic*, and the Chem *rubidine* and *rubidium*; its derivative n *rubor*, redness, is adopted by Med for inflammation of the skin.

10. Also from *rubēre* derives *rubicundus*, whence (late MF-F *rubicond* and) E *rubicund*; derivative ML *rubicunditās*, o/s *rubicunditāt-*, leads to *rubicundity*.

11. L *ruber* has the perh orig dial var *rūfus*, whence E *rufous* and the PN *Rufus*; the dim *rufulus*, reddish, yields *rufulous*.

12. Akin to L *ruber*, but with s and r *rut-* for *rub-*, is L *rutilus*, of a golden red, whence G *Rutil*, F *rutile*, E *rutile*, a brilliant reddish-brown mineral. *Rutilus* has derivative *rutilāre* (vt), to turn red, presp *rutilans*, o/s *rutilant-*, whence E *rutilant*.

13. Akin to *ruber* is the syn *rōbus*, var *rubus*, whence *rōbīgō*, *rūbīgō*, mildew, rust, with LL adj

*rūbiginōsus*, whence E *rubiginose, rubiginous*. From L *rōbīgō*, via VL *\*rōbīcula*, derives OF-MF *rouil* (MF-F *rouille*), mud, rust, with derivative OF-F *rouiller*, whence E 'to *roil*' or render turbid, hence to vex.

14. L *rubeus* becomes OF-F *rouge*, adopted by E.

15. Ult akin to *rubeus* and *red* is the red-berried *rowan* (tree), imm of Scan origin—cf Nor *raun, rogn*, ON *reynir*. Cf the likewise not easily recognizable *ribbon*, ME *riban*, from MF *riban* (late MF-F *ruban*), app of Gmc origin—perh from the MD *ringhband*, a neckband or necklace (B & W), but perh from some syn of Go *rauths*, red, for, as Webster acutely remarks, the sem original is perh 'a red band'.

## Greek

16. Gr *eruthros*, red (cf para 1, s.f.), has these E derivatives: *erythrin, erythrine* (Chem *-in, -ine*); *erythrism* (Med *-ism*), with anl adj *erythritic*; *erythrite* (Min *-ite*).

17. App a cognate cpd of *eruthros* is Gr *erusipelas*, whence Med L, hence E, *erysipelas*, adopted by E; the 2nd element, *-pelas*, derives from Gr *pella*, skin, *erusi-* being a var of c/f *eruthro-*.

**red tape.** See RED, para 1.

**redan.** See TOOTH, para 9.

**redd** (1), n. See RED, para 1.

**redd** (2), v. See READY, para 2.

**reddition.** See RENDER, para 3.

**rede.** See READ, para 2.

**redeem, redeemer, redemption, redemptory.** See EXEMPT, para 12.

**redhibition.** See HABIT, para 11.

**redintegrate, redintegration.** See TACT, para 17.

**redirect, redirection.** See DIRECT, para 2.

**redivivus.** See VIVA, para 6.

**redolence, redolent.** See ODIUM, para 5.

**redouble:** F *redoubler*: f.a.e., DOUBLE.

**redoubt,** a small strongplace. See DUKE, para 9.

**redoubtable.** See DOUBT, para 4.

**redound.** See UNDA, para 4.

**redress.** See REX, para 9.

**redshank** and **redstart** are birds with pale-red legs and chestnut-red *start* (OE *steort*) or tail.

**reduce, reduction.** See DUKE, para 6 (at *reducere*).

**redundance, redundancy, redundant.** See UNDA, para 4.

**reduplicate, reduplication.** See PLY, para 22, s.f.

**reed,** whence *reedy* and *reedbuck* (trans of D *rietbok*, partly anglicized as *rietbuck*: D *riet*, a reed, a (bamboo) cane): ME *rede*, earlier *reod*: OE *hrēod*: cf OFris *hriād*, MD *ried, reet*, G *Riet*, MHG *riet*, OHG *riot*, earlier *hriot*, OS *hriod*: OGmc etymon *\*hreutha* (Kluge).

**reef,** a chain of rocks: ME *riff*: ON *rif*, prob id with ON *rif*, a rib, app the origin of the *reef* of a sail (ME *riff*)—f.a.e., RIB—whence 'to *reef*', whence the agent, whence the garment, *reefer*.

**reck** (n and v), whence *reeky*, smoky, whence *Auld Reekie*, Old Smoky, Edinburgh—cf *The Big Smoke*, London, and *Reykjavik* (ON *reykr*, smoke +*-vik*, bay, ML *vīcus*, L *uīcus*), Smoky Bay.

1. *Reek*, n, derives from OE *rēc*; the v from OE *rēocan*, to steam or smoke: cf OFris *rēk*, n, and *rēka*, v, OS *rōk*, OHG *rouh*, MHG *rouch*, G *Rauch*, and OHG *riohhan*, to steam or smoke, MHG-G *riechen*, to smell, ON *riūka*, to smoke. The OGmc r is perh *\*reuk-* or *\*rauk-* (Kluge).

2. The mostly diai *roke*, fog, mist, smoke, prob derives from D—cf MD *roke, rooc*, D *rook*, smoke.

**reel,** a lively Sc dance, app comes from **reel**, 'a revolvable device on which yarn or thread is wound' (Webster)—itself from OE *hrēol*, akin to OFris *hreil* and ON *hrāell* of cognate meanings. Hence 'to *reel*', to whirl, to sway dizzily.

**reeve** (1), n. See the 2nd PORT, para 4.

**reeve** (2), naut v., to pass, e.g. a rope, through an opening: prob (EW) from It *refare*, to thread, from *refe*, a strong thread, a twisted thread, itself either (Prati) from It *ripe* (rare and o.o.o.), a thread, or (EW) from OHG-MHG *reif*, a rope, a loop, and therefore akin to ROPE.

**refection, refectory.**

The former comes, via OF-MF *refection* (F *réfection*), from L *refectiō*, acc *refectiōnem*, lit a re-making, LL *food*, from *refectus*, pp of *reficere*, from *facere*, to make: f.a.e., FACT. Also on the pps *refect-* is formed LL-ML *refectōrium*, a dining-room, whence OF *refectoir*, MF *refectoire* (F *ré-*), whence E *refectory*.

**refer,** whence **referable** and **referee; referendary, referendum** (whence **referendal); referent,** whence, anl, **reference,** whence **referential.**

'To *refer*' derives, perh via MF *referer* (F *référer*), from L *referre*, to carry (*ferre*: f.a.e., BEAR, v) back (*re-*). The presp *referens*, o/s *referent-*, yields the adj, hence n, *referent*. *Referendary*, an arbitrator, derives from LL *referendārius*, an official charged with reports and petitions; *referendum* is prop the neu of the gerundive *referendus*.

**refine, refinement, refinery.** See FINAL, para 8.

**reflate, reflation.** See FLATUS, para 8.

**reflect, reflection** (or **reflexion), reflective, reflector; reflex,** etc. See FLEX, para 7.

**refluent; reflux.** See FLUENT, para 9.

**reform, reformation** (whence, anl, **reformatory), reformer, reformist.** See FORM, para 7.

**refract, refraction, refractory.** See FRACTION, para 8.

**refragable.** See FRACTION, para 10.

**refrain** (1), burden of a song: MF-F *refrain*, from OF-F *refraindre*, to break back or off, hence to modulate: VL *\*refrangere*: L *refringere*: *re-*, back+*-fringere*, c/f of *frangere*, to break: f.a.e., FRACTION.

**refrain** (2), to check: ME *refreinen*: OF-MF *refrener* (F *réfréner*): L *refrēnāre*, to hold back with the *frēnum* or reins.

**refresh, refreshment.** See FRESH, para 3.

**refrigerant, refrigerate, refrigeration, refrigerator.** See FRIGID, para 3.

**refuge, refugee.** See FUGITIVE, para 6.

refulgence, refulgent. See FLAGRANT, para 4.

refund. See the 2nd FOUND, para 12.

refurbish. See FURBISH.

refusal; refuse, adj, n, v. See the 2nd FOUND, para 13.

refutation, refutatory, refute.

'To *refute*' derives from L *refūtāre*, to repulse, esp in argument, a cpd of the same simple *\*fūtāre*, as occurs in *confūtāre*, whence the sep CONFUTE: perh an int of *fundere*, to pour. On the pp *refūtātus* are formed *refūtātiō*, o/s *refūtātiōn-*, whence *refutation*, and LL *refūtātōrius*, whence *refutatory*.

regain=*re-*, back+*gain*: cf OF-F *regagner*.

regal. See REX, para 12.

regale, to entertain agreeably or richly, derives from EF-F *régaler*, from late MF-EF *régale* (F *régal*), from OF-F *gale*, pleasure: cf GALLANT.

regalia, regality. See REX, para 12.

regard (n, v), regardant, regardful, regardless. See WARD, para 11.

regatta: It *regat(t)a*: Venetian *regata*, a gondola race, orig a challenge: Venetian *regatar*, to compete, to be rivals, prob from It *gato*, a cat, 'cats having the reputation of being very quarrelsome' (B & W).

regency. See REX, para 19.

regenerate (adj, v), regeneration. See GENERAL, para 8.

regent. See REX, para 19.

regicide. See REX, para 13.

regime, regimen, regiment, regimental. See REX, paras 20 and 21.

regina. See REX, para 14.

region, regional. See REX, para 22.

register, registrand, registrant, registrar, registrary, registration, registry. See GERUND, para 13.

regius. See REX, para 12, s.f.

regnal, regnant. See REX, para 15.

regrate (masonry and commerce); regrater. See SCRATCH, para 3.

regress, regression, regressive. See GRADE, para 16.

regret, regretful, regrettable. See GREET.

regular, regularity, regularize; regulate, regulation, regulative, regulator, regulatory; reguline, regulus. See REX, paras 17 and 18.

regurgitate, regurgitation. See GORGE, para 3.

rehabilitate, rehabilitation. See HABIT, para 7.

rehearsal, rehearse. See HEARSE, para 2.

Reich. See REX, para 1.

reification, reify. See the 1st REAL, para 5.

reign, n, v. See REX, para 15.

reimburse, reimbursement. See PURSE, para 2.

rein (n, hence v): ME *reyn, rene*: OF-MF *resne* (F *rêne*): VL *\*retina*, from L *retinēre*, to hold back: f.a.e., TENABLE.

reincarnate, reincarnation. See CARNAGE, para 2.

reindeer. See DEER.

reinforce=*re-*, again+*force*, v: cf F *renforcer*. Hence, reinforcement.

reins. See RENAL.

reinstate, reinstatement. See STAND, para 16.

reintegrate; reintegration: LL *reintegrātus*, pp of *reintegrāre*; derivative LL *reintegrātiō*, o/s *reintegrātiōn-*; cf *integrate* at ENTIRE.

reitbok, reitbuck. See REED.

reiterate, reiteration. See ITERATE, para 2.

reject, adj (hence n) and v (whence rejector); rejection, whence, anl, rejective. *Rejection* derives from ML *rejectiōn-*, o/s of *rejectiō*, L *reiectiō*, from *reiectus*, pp of *reicere, reiicere*: *re-*, back+*-iicere*, c/f of *iacere*, to throw.

rejoice. See JOY, para 3.

rejoin, rejoinder. See JOIN, para 17.

rejuvenate, rejuvenation; rejuvenesce, rejuvenescence. See JUVENILE, para 3, s.f.

relapse. See LABOR, para 2, s.f.

relate, relation (whence relationship), relative (whence relativity), relator; correlate, correlation, correlative.

1. 'To *relate*' derives from *relātus*, pp of *referre*, to carry back; derivatives *relātiō*, o/s *relātiōn-*, LL *relātiuus*, ML *-ivus*, LL *relātor*, become E *relation, relative, relator*.

2. Anl with *relate* is *correlate*, perh suggested by LL *correferre*, to report at the same time, pp *correlātus*, whence ML *correlātiō*, o/s *correlātiōn-*, whence *correlation*, and ML *correlātivus*, whence *correlative*: cf EF-F *corrélation* and MF-F *corrélatif*, f *-ive*, perh intervening.

relax, relaxation. See LANGUID, para 4.

relay. See LANGUID, para 10.

release. See LANGUID, para 5.

relegate, relegation. See LEGAL, para 6.

relent, relentless. See LINDEN, para 3.

relevance derives from relevant, itself from scholastic ML *relevant-*, o/s of *relevans*: *re-*, back +*levāre*, L *leuāre*, to raise: f.a.e., LEVER. Hence, anl, *irrelevant*, whence *irrelevance*.

reliable, reliance, reliant. See LIGAMENT, para 6.

relic. See LEND, para 4, s.f.

relict. See LEND, para 4.

relief, relieve. See LEVER, para 9.

religate, religation. See LIGAMENT, para 9.

religion, religious. See LIGAMENT, para 10.

relinquish, whence relinquishment. See LEND, para 2. Cf:

reliquary: MF-F *reliquaire*: ML *reliquārium*: L *reliquiae* (pl), akin to *relinquere*, to leave behind.

relish. See LANGUID, para 8.

reluctance derives from reluctant: L *reluctant-*, o/s of *reluctans*, presp of *reluctāri*, to struggle back or again, LL to force oneself to do something: *re-*, back, again+*luctāri*, to struggle, akin perh to Gr *lugizein*, to bend, to twist about, and therefore to E LOCK.

2. *Luctāri* has also a cpd *ēluctāri*, to struggle to get free (connoted by *e-*, out of), whence *ēluctābilis*, with neg *inēluctābilis*, irresistible, whence E *ineluctable*.

rely. See LIGAMENT, para 6.

remain, remainder. See MANOR, para 9.

remand, v hence n: OF-EF *remander*, to send word again, to send a new order: LL *remandāre*, to reply: *re-*, back, again+*mandare*, to give (*dare*) into the hands (*manus*) of: cf MANDATE.

remanent. See MANOR, para 9.

remark. remarkable. See MARK, para 6.

remediable, remedial, remedy. See MEDICAL, para 3.

remember, remembrance, remembrancer. See MEMORY, para 7.

remigrant, remigrate, remigration. See MIGRANT, para 5.

remind, reminder. See MIND (heading).

reminiscence, reminiscent. See MIND, para 16.

remiss, remissible, remission, remit, remittance. See MISSION, para 21.

remnant. See MANOR, para 9.

remonstrance, remonstrant (adj, hence n), remonstrate (whence remonstrator), remonstration (whence, anl, remonstrative). See MONSTER, para 4.

remora, adopted from LL ('a sucking sea-fish': Souter), is a sense-adaptation of L *remora*, a delay or a hindrance: f.a.e., MORATORIUM.

remorse, whence remorseful and remorseless. See MORSEL, para 6.

remote. See MOVE, para 14.

remount, n, v. See MINATORY, para 10.

removal, remove. See MOVE, para 14.

remunerate, remuneration, remunerative. See the 1st MEAN, para 3.

renaissance. See NATIVE, para 9, s.f.

renal; reins, kidneys, loins.

*Renal*, of the kidneys, derives—cf EF-F *rénal*—from LL *rēnālis*, adj of L *rēn*, a kidney, pl *rēnēs*, whence OF-F *reins*, adopted by E; L *rēn* is o.o.o.

renascence, renascent. See NATIVE, para 9, s.f.

rencounter, n: MF-F *rencontre*. Cf *encounter*, q.v. at COUNTER, adv.

rend (pt, pp rent), with dial var rent, whence the n rent; rind.

'To *rend*' or remove, or tear, violently, derives from ME *renden*, OE *rendan*, akin to the syn OFris *renda* (cf the OFris n *rend*), var *randa*, and perh to Skt *randhra*, a slit or a split; prob also to OE-E *rind*, orig the bark of a tree or a crust of bread; cf OHG *rinta*, MHG-G *rinde*, bark, rind, itself perh (Walshe) akin to G *Rand*, edge.

render (v hence n), whence renderer and rendering; rendezvous; rendition—cf reddition; rent, a monetary return, hence 'to rent'—cf rental; surrender, n and v.

1. 'To *render*' or give (e.g., pay) back, hence to melt, to recite, etc., comes from OF-F *rendre*, from VL *\*rendere*, influenced by *prendere* but deriving from L *reddere*: *re-*, back, again+*-dere*, c/f of *dare*, to give: f.a.e., DATA.

2. OF-F *rendre* has the EF-F derivative n *rendezvous*, from *Rendez-vous*, Give yourselves up!, and the MF-EF derivative *rendition*, adopted by E.

3. With *rendition*, cf *reddition*, adopted from MF-F, which took it from *redditiōn-*, o/s of LL *redditiō*, from *redditus*, pp of *reddere*.

4. OF-F *rendre* has a further derivative, the OF-F *rente*, which owes something to VL *\*rendita*, from *\*renditus*, pp of *\*rendere*. The derivative MF *renter* yields 'to *rent*' or pay money for use of.

5. *Rental*, however, is adopted from AF, which takes it from AL *rentale* (? for ML *\*renditāle*).

6. *Surrender* is adopted from AF, which uses as n the AF v *surrender*, from MF *surrendre*, to deliver: OF-MF *sur-*, over, L *super*+*rendre*.

rendezvous. See prec, para 2.

rendition. See RENDER, para 2.

renegade. See NEGATE, para 4.

renege. See NEGATE, para 4.

renew, whence renewal. See NOVA, para 9.

rennet. See RUN, para 2.

renounce. See NUNCIO, para 9.

renovate, renovation, renovator. See NOVA, para 5.

renown. See NAME, para 7.

rent (1), adj ('torn'). See REND (heading).

rent (2), a tear, a split. See REND.

rent (3), a monetary return; also v. See RENDER, para 4.

rental. See RENDER, para 5.

renunciation. See NUNCIO, para 9.

re-organization, re-organize. See ORGAN, para 4.

re-orient, re-orientation. See ORIENT, para 3, s.f.

rep or repp, occ reps, a fabric: F *reps*: E *ribs*, pl of RIB, q.v.: from its ribbed surface.

repair (1), to go, to resort. See FATHER, para 10.

repair (2), to mend. See PARE, para 7.

reparable, reparation, reparatory. See PARE, para 7.

repartee. See PART, para 22.

repartition. See PART, para 22.

repast. See PASTOR, para 6.

repatriate, repatriation. See FATHER, para 9.

repay (whence repayment): MF-EF *repaier*: *re-*, back+*paier*, to pay: f.a.e., PAY.

repeal. See the 2nd PULSE, para 16.

repeat, v (whence repeater), hence n. See PETITION, para 6.

repel, repellent. See the 2nd PULSE, para 15.

repent, repentance. See PAIN, para 7.

repercussion: MF-F *répercussion*: L *repercussiōn*em, acc of *repercussiō*, from *repercussus*, pp of *repercutere*: *re-*, back, again+*percutere*, to strike (*quatere*) hard (*per-*, throughout, from *per*, through): cf PERCUSS.

repertoire, repertory. See PARENT, para 4.

repetend; repetition, repetitious. See PETITION, para 6.

repine. See PAIN, para 6.

replace, replacement. See PLANE, para 14.

replant. See the 2nd PLANT, para 4.

replenish, replenishment. See PLENARY, para 4.

replete, repletion. See PLENARY, para 15.

replevin, replevy. See PLEDGE, para 2.

replica, replicate, replication. See PLY, para 16. Cf:

reply. See PLY, para 16.

repone. See POSE, para 19.

report, reportage, reporter. See the 3rd PORT, para 12.

repose, repository. See POSE, para 19.

repp. See REP.

reprehend, reprehensible, reprehension. See PRE-
HEND, para 12.

represent, representation, representative. See
ESSE, para 9.

repress, repression, repressive, repressor. See the
2nd PRESS, para 12.

reprieve, v hence n: ME-EE *repry* (F *repris*, pp of
*reprendre*—cf *reprise*, q.v. at PREHEND, para 13),
influenced by ME *repreven* (cf *reprove* at PROVE,
para 10).

reprimand. See the 2nd PRESS, para 11.

reprint, v hence n=*re-*, again+*print*.

reprisal. See PREHEND, para 13.

reprise. See PREHEND, para 13.

reproach, n, derives from OF-F *reproche*, itself
from OF-F *reprocher*, whence 'to *reproach*': and
OF-F *reprocher* comes from VL *repropiāre*, to
again (*re-*) come close to (*propiāre*, from L
*prope*, adv and prep 'close (to)'—cf *propinquus*, adj
'close'): cf APPROACH.

reprobate, reprobation. See PROVE, para 10.

reproduce=*re-*, again+*produce* (q.v. at DUKE,
para 6); reproduction, prob anl from *reproduce*, but
perh imm from EF-F *réproduction*; *reproductive*,
perh imm from F *réproductif*, f *réproductive*.

reproof. See PROVE, para 10. Cf:

reprove. See PROVE, para 10.

reps. See REP.

reptant, reptation. See para 1 of:

reptile, Reptilia, both with derivative adj reptilian; reptant, reptation; obreption, obreptitious;
surreption.—serpent, serpentine (adj, n); serpiginous;
serpigo; serpolet; Serpula, whence, anl, serpuline;—
herpes, Herpestes, herpetic, herpetism—and cf the
element *herpeti-, herpeto-*.

1. *Reptile*, adj, derives from LL *reptilis*; the n,
from LL *reptile* (? for *animal reptile*, a creeping
animal), pl *reptilia*; both from L *reptum*, supine of
*rēpere*, to creep, which has freq *reptāre*, presp
*reptans*, o/s *reptant-*, whence the E adj *reptant*,
and derivative n *reptātiō*, o/s *reptātiōn-*, whence E
*reptation*.

2. L *rēpere*, supine *reptum*, is akin to Lett
*raptiês*, to creep, and Lith *replioti*, to go on all
fours, to crawl. *Rēpere* has cpd *obrēpere*, to creep
up to (*ob*), supine *obreptum*; the derivatives L
*obrēptiō*, o/s *obrēptiōn-*, and LL *obrēpticius*, yield
E *obreption* and *obreptitious*. The cpd *surrēpere*, to
creep upon (*sur-* for *super*), has derivative LL
*surrēptiō*, o/s *surrēptiōn-*, whence E *surreption*, a
moral lapse.

3. Perh akin to L *rēpere*, to creep, is L *serpere*,
to glide, to creep, esp as a snake does. *Serpere* is
akin to the syn Gr *herpein* (cf *herpeton*, a snake)
and to Skt *sarpás*, a snake, lit a creeping animal,
and *sárpati*, he creeps. E & M regard L *serpere*,
s and r *serp-*, as an extn of IE *ser-*, to go, to flow;
is *serpere* perh rather a contr (with vocalic change)
of *serēpere*, to creep, or glide, away: *se-*(*sē* or *sĕ*),
connoting apartness or removal+*rēpere*?

4. L *serpere* has presp *serpens*, o/s *serpent-*,
which, used as n (elliptical for *serpens bestia*, a
creeping or gliding beast), becomes OF-F *serpent*,

adopted by E; *the Serpent*, or Devil, represents LL
*Serpens*. The derivative LL adj *serpentīnus* becomes
OF-F *serpentin* (f *-ine*), whence E *serpentine*; the
E n *serpentine* owes its senses to OF-MF *serpentin*,
EF-F *serpentine*.

5. L *serpere* has the ML derivative *serpīgo*, a
creeping skin-disease, e.g. ringworm, adopted by
Med. On the o/s *serpīgin-* are formed the EF adj
*serpigineux*, f *serpigineuse*, and—prob independently—the E adj *serpiginous*.

6. *Serpolet*, the wild thyme, is adopted from
EF-F: Prov *serpolet*, dim of *serpol*: L *serpullum*:
from *serpere*, but after the syn Gr *herpullos*.

7. Zoo SciL *Serpula* sense-adapts L *serpula*, a
little snake, irreg dim of *serpens*, a snake.

### Greek

8. Akin to L *serpere*, to creep, to glide, is the syn
Gr *herpein*, s and r *herp-*, whence *herpēs*, a creeping
skin-disease, adopted—via L and perh via EF-F
*herpès*—by Med; the derivative Gr adj *herpētikos*
becomes E *herpetic* (cf F *herpétique*); with E
*herpetism*, cf F *herpétisme*.

9. Also from Gr *herp*ein comes Gr *herpēstēs*, a
creature that creeps: whence the SciL *Herpestes*
(including the mongoose).

republic, republican. See PEOPLE, para 6.

repudiate, repudiation. See FOOT, para 14.

repugn, repugnance, repugnant. See PUNGENT,
para 18.

repulse, repulsion, repulsive. See the 2nd PULSE,
para 15.

reputable, reputation, repute. See the 2nd COUNT,
para 3, s.f.

request. See QUERY, final sentence.

requiem. See QUIET, para 8.

require, requirement. See QUERY, para 12.

requisite, requisition. See QUERY, para 12.

requital derives, by the n-suffix *-al*, from requite,
which stands for the earlier *requit*: *re-*, back+*quit*,
q.v. at QUIET, para 4.

reredos. See REAR, adj, para 2.

rescind, rescission, rescissory. See the 2nd SHED,
para 4.

rescribe; rescript, rescription, rescriptive. See
SCRIBE, para 19.

rescue (v, hence n), whence rescuer, comes from
ME *rescouen*: OF *rescourre* (var *rescorre*, confused
with OF *rescorre*, to run back): *re-*, back+*escorre*,
to shake, to move, from L *excutere*, to shake,
hence to drive, out (*ex*, out of+*-cutere*, c/f of
*quatere*, to shake: cf QUASH).

research. See CIRCLE, para 6.

resect, resection. See the 2nd SAW, para 13.

resemblance, resemble. See SIMILAR, para 13.

resent, resentful, resentment. See SENSE, para 18.

reservation, reserve (n, v), reservist, reservoir.

*Reservation* derives from MF-F *réservation*,
itself from OF *reserver* (EF-F *réserver*), whence
via ME *reserven*, the E 'to *reserve*'; whence also the
MF-F n *réserve* (whence F *réserviste*, whence E
*reservist*), whence the E n *reserve*. *Reservoir* derives
from EF-F *réservoir*. The OF *reserver* itself derives

from ML *reservāre*, LL-L *reseruāre*: *re-*, back+
*seruāre* (ML *servāre*), to keep. Cf CONSERVE,
OBSERVE, PRESERVE. The pa *reserved* owes something to F *réservé*.

reside, residence (and -cy), resident, residential;
residual, residuary, residue, residuum. See SIT,
paras 17 and 18.

resign, resignation. See SIGN, para 18.

resile, resilience, resilient. See SALLY, para 13.

resin (whence resinoid), resinous; rosin; retinol.

1. *Resin* derives from MF-F *résine*, L *rēsīna*, Gr
*rhēsinē*, var of *rhētinē*, perh akin to *rhéō*, I flow.
Derivative L *rēsīnōsus* yields EF-F *résineux*, f *-euse*,
and, prob independently, E *resinous*.

2. *Retinol*=Gr *rhētīnē*+*-ol*, oil (L *oleum*).

3. *Rosin*, a var of *resin*, derives from MF
*roisine*, var of *raisine*, a f/e var (after *raisin*, a
grape) of *résine*.

resist, resistance, resistant, resistible. See SIST,
para 8.

resolute, resolution. See LOSE, para 8.

resolve. See LOSE, para 8.

resonance, resonant, resonator. See SONABLE,
para 5.

resort, v and n: both from OF-F, where the n
derives from the v: *re-*+*sortir*, to go out: cf *sort*,
q.v. at SERIES. The E senses accord with the F.

resound. See SONABLE, para 2.

resource, resourceful. See SURGE, para 5.

respect, respectable, respectful, respective. See
SPECTACLE, para 15.

respiration, respirator, respiratory, respire. See
SPIRIT, para 12.

respite. See SPECTACLE, para 15.

resplendence, resplendent. See SPLENDID, para 3.

respond, response, responsible, responsion. See
DESPOND, para 3.

rest (1), stopping-place, repose, refreshment, to
pause, refresh oneself, whence resting, pa and vn,
and restful, restless (perh imm from OE *restlēas*).

'To *rest*' comes from OE *restan*, var *raestan*, akin
to OFris *resta*, OS *restian*, OHG *restan*, var *rastōn*,
G *rasten*; the n *rest*, pause, repose, comes from
OE *rest*, var *raest*, akin to OHG *rasta*, MHG
*raste*, a day's march, a rest, G *Rast*, rest, and syn
OHG *resti*, rest—cf Go *rasta*, ON *röst*, a stage on
a journey, and Go *razn*, a house. 'The term appears
to derive from the nomadic period: "resting-place
for the night" ' (Walshe).

rest (2), a remainder, to remain. See STAND,
para 32.

restaur; restaurant; restaurateur, restauration.
See STORE, para 2.

restitute, restitution, restitutory. See STAND,
para 33.

restive. See STAND, para 32, s.f.

restless. See the 1st REST (heading).

restoration, restorative, restore. See STORE,
para 2.

restrain, restraint. See the 2nd STRAIN, para 12.

restrict, restriction, restrictive. See the 2nd
STRAIN, para 12.

result, resultant. See SALLY, para 17.

resume, résumé, resumption, resumptive. See
SUMPTION, para 5.

resurgence, resurgent; resurrect, resurrection.
See SURGE, para 5.

resuscitate, resuscitation. See CITE, para 6.

retable. See TABLE, para 4, s.f.

retail, retailer. See the 2nd TAIL, para 6.

retain, retainer. See TENABLE, para 7.

retake. See TAKE, para 2.

retaliate (whence retaliator), retaliation (whence,
anl, retaliatory); talion, lex talionis.

1. *Talion*, adopted from late MF-F, derives
from *tāliōn*em, acc of L *tāliō*, the law—*lex
tāliōnis*—of 'an eye for an eye, a tooth for a tooth':
prob akin to OIr *tale*, MIr *taile*, pay, W *talu*, to
pay, *tāl*, compensation, Cor *taly*, *tylly*, *dāl*, to pay
to recompense.

2. L *tāliō* has a *tāli-*, which app recurs in ML
*retāliāre*, to return like (injury) for like, pp
*retāliātus*, whence 'to *retaliate*', whence, anl,
*retaliation*.

retard, retardation, retardative. See TARDY,
para 1.

retch (whence the vn retching): OE *hrǣcan*, to
clear one's throat, akin to—perh deriving from—
OE *hrāca*, spittle, (an) expectoration: cf ON
*hrāki*, spittle, *hraekja*, to spit, to hawk, and OHG
*hrāhhisōn*, to hawk (? also MHG *riuspern*, G (*sich*)
*räuspern*, to hawk, and MLG *ruspen*, to belch).

retention, retentive, retentor. See TENABLE, para
7.

retiary. See RETICULAR.

reticence, reticent. See TACIT, para 2.

reticular, reticulate (whence, anl, *reticulation*),
reticule; retiarius, retiary, reticella.

L *rēte*, a net, is o.o.o.: ? Medit (cf Eg *skhet*, a
net). Its dim is *rēticulum* (adopted by An and Zoo),
whence F *réticule*, whence E *reticule*; the It dim
*reticella* is adopted by E for 'a needle-point lace'.
From *rēticulum*, L derives *rēticulātus*, whence E
*reticulate*; *reticular* derives from SciL *rēticulāris*.
L *rēte*, c/f *rēti-*, has derivative *rētiārius*, a gladiator
armed with net and trident, whence E *retiary*, used
also as adj.

2. L *rēte* has the ML extn *rētina*, that net-like,
sensitive membrane of the eye which receives the
image: adopted by Sci (cf the MF-F *rétine*); its
adj is *retinal* (-al).

retina. See prec, para 2.

retinol. See RESIN, para 2.

retinue. See TENABLE, para 7.

retire, retirement. See TIRADE, para 1.

retort, retortion. See TORT, para 11.

retouch. See TOUCH, para 3.

retrace. See TRACT, para 2, s.f.

retract, retractation, retraction, retractor. See
TRACT, para 20.

retreat. See TRACT, para 21.

retrench, retrenchment. See TRENCH, para 4.

retribute, retribution, retributive. See TRIBUTE,
para 8.

retrieval, retrieve, retriever. See TROUBADOUR,
para 3, s.f.

**retro-** words. See, in general, the prefix *retro-* (L *retrō*, backwards). Note, in particular, these terms:

*retro(-)active*: cf F *rétroactif*;

*retrocede, retrocession*: L *retrōcēdere*, to go backwards, LL *retrōcessiō*, o/s *retrōcessiōn-*, F *rétrocession*;

*retroflex*, bent backwards: cf FLEX;

*retrograde*: see GRADE, para 17;

*retrogression*: see GRADE, para 17;

*retropulsion*, a driving, hence, forcing, backwards: cf the 2nd PULSE;

*retrospect, retrospection, retrospective*: see SPECTACLE, para 17;

*retroversion, retrovert*: see VERSE, para 15.

**retrude, retrusible, retrusion.** See THRUST, para 8.

**return.** See TURN, para 3.

**retuse.** See PIERCE, para 2, s.f.

**Reuben.** See RUBE.

**reunion; reunite.** See ONE, para 3.

**revalescence, revalescent; revalidate.** See VALUE, para 20.

**reve, rêve.** See RAGE, para 5.

**reveal.** See VEIL, para 3.

**revehent.** See VIA, para 12.

**reveille.** See VIGOR, para 6.

**revel,** n, is adopted from OF-MF *revel*, a revolt, hence din or disorder, hence merrymaking, from OF-MF *reveler*, to revolt, make a din, make merry, whence 'to *revel*': and OF-MF *reveler* derives from L *rebellāre*, to revolt: cf REBEL.

**revelation, revelatory.** See VEIL, para 3.

**revenant.** See VENUE, para 21.

**revenge, revengeful.** See DICT, para 21, s.f.

**revenue.** See VENUE, para 21.

**reverberant, reverberate, reverberation, reverberatory.** See VERVAIN, para 3.

**revere, reverence, reverend, reverent, reverential.** 'To *revere*' comes, prob via EF-F *révérer*, from ML *reverēri*, L *reuerēri*, a *re-* int of *uerēri*, to fear: akin to E WARY. The L presp *reuerens* and its derivative *reuerentia*, the gerundive *reuerendus*, yield resp—perh via F—the E *reverent, reverence* (adj *reverential*), *reverend*.

**reverie.** See RAGE, para 5.

**revers, reversal, reverse, reversible, reversion, reversionary; revert.** See VERSE, para 15.

**revest, revestment.** See VEST, para 3.

**revet, revetment.** See VEST, para 3.

**review, reviewer.** See VIDE, para 14.

**revile.** See VILE.

**revise, reviser, revision.** See VIDE, para 13.

**revisit.** See VIDE, para 12.

**revival** (whence **revivalism, revivalist**), **revive, revivification, revivify.** See VIVA, para 6.

**revocable, revocation, revocatory.** See VOCABLE, para 10, s.f.

**revoke.** See VOCABLE, para 10, s.f.

**revolt, revolting.** See VOLUBLE, para 4, at *reuoluere*, s.f.

**revolution, revolutionary, revolutionize.** See VOLUBLE, para 4, s.f.

**revolve, revolver, revolving.** See VOLUBLE, para 4, s.f.

**revue.** See VIDE, para 14.

**revulse, revulsion, revulsive.** See VELLICATE, para 7.

**reward.** See WARD, para 17.

**rex; regal, regale, regalia, regality; regina; raja** (**maharaja**) **and rani** (**maharani**)—cf raj; **regency, regent; regicide; régime, regimen, regiment** (whence **regimental**); **region, regional; regius;**—**real,** n, **and realm; Roy** (cf *vive le Roi!*), **royal, royalism, royalist; Reich; reis, milreis; rix-dollar; rect, rectitude, rector** (whence **rectoral, rectorial**), **rectum** (whence the adj **rectal**); **rectification, rectify** (whence **rectifier**); **rial, ryal; rye,** gentleman;—**regula and Regulus; regular** (adj, hence n), **regularity—irregular, irregularity; regularize, regularization; regulate,** whence, anl, **regulation, regulative, regulator;—rule,** n also v, whence **ruler** and pa, vn **ruling; misrule,** v, hence n;—**right** (adj, adv, n, v), **right whale, righteous, righteousness, rightful, rightly, rightness; aright**—**downright**—**outright**—**upright;**—**regnal, regnant** (whence **regnancy**)—**regnum and reign** (n, v)—**interregnum.**— Cpds in *-rect*: **arrect, arrector; correct** (adj, v), **correction, corrective, correctness, corrector**—negg **incorrect, incorrection, incorrectness; direct** (adj, v), **direction, directive, directness, director, directory**—**indirect, indirection**—**dirge**—**droit** and **adroit; erect, erection, erector.**—Cpds in *-rigible*: **corrigible, corrigibility**—negg **incorrigible, incorrigibility; dirigible.**—**dress** (n, v), **dressage, dressing; address**—**maladdress**—**redress.**—**ergo.**—Cf sep RICH and perh REACH; cf also SURGE.

I. Germanic

1. *Reich*, the German Empire, in 1919–45 the German Republic, derives from MHG *rîche*, OHG *rîhhi*, realm, itself from OC *\*rīg-*, a king (cf OIr *rí*), akin to OFris *rīke* and *rēx*. Hence *Reichsmark*, the G monetary unit, and *Reichswehr*, the G militia.

2. *Right*, adj, ME *right*, earlier *riht*, derives from OE *riht*, akin to OS and OHG-MHG *reht*, G (and D) *recht*, MD *richt*, Go *raihts*, ON *rēttr*, also to L *rectus*, straight, and perh Gr *orektos*, stretched (out), upright. OE *riht*, adj, is used also as n, whence the E n *right*, and it has derivatives *rihte*, adv, whence the E adv *right*, the v *rihtan*, whence 'to *right*', the adv *rihtlīce*, whence *rightly*, the abstract n *rihtness*, whence *rightness*, the cpd *rihtwīs* (*wīs*, wise), ME *rightwise, rightwys*, E *righteous*, with derivative adv *rihtwīslīce*, E *righteously*, and derivative n *rihtwīsness*, E *righteousness*.—A *right whale* is prob so named because it is the typical whale, the norm in whales.

3. *Right* has the foll prefix-cpds:

*aright*, correctly: *a-*, on (+*the*)+*right*, straight, right;

*downright*, adv 'straight down', hence adj: *down*, prep (+*the*)+*right*, straight;

*outright*, adv, hence adj: lit 'straight *out*';

*upright*, adj, hence adv and n: OE *upriht* (*uppriht*), lit 'being *up* the *straight*', hence 'erect'.

## II. Romance: A, French

4. The name *Roy* comes from an OF-MF var of MF-F *roi*, itself a var of OF *rei*, from L *rēgem*, acc of *rēx*, king; *Vive le roi* is '(Long) live the king!' The adj is OF *reial*, OF-MF *roial*, EF-F *royal*: ME *rial, riall, ryal*, then *roial*, EE-E *royal*. The ME forms *rial(l)* and *ryal* survive in the now only Sc *rial*, royal, magnificent, and the late ME-EE coin *rial* or *ryal*. The OF-MF *roial* has derivative *roialté*, with var *royaulté* (F *royauté*), whence E *royalty*.

5. The OF adj *reial*, var *real*, has OF-MF derivative *realme*, a kingdom, adopted by E; hence E *realm*.

6. The OF-F adj *droit*, straight, hence upright and also 'on or to the right' (the right hand being normally the more exact), cf E '*right* (hand)', was, in its derivative n use, adopted by E Law, esp in *droits*, dues. The F adj *droit* derives from L *dīrēctus*—cf *direct* in para 28 below.

7. The F adj *droit* has the OF-F cpd *adroit*, situated, or placed, *à droit* or on the right, hence skilful, adopted by E, whence *adroitness*; in C16, F *adroit* acquires *maladroit* (*mal à droit*)—cf, sem, *gauche*—likewise adopted by E; cf *maladdress*.

8. Also from L *dīrēctus* (para 28 below) comes VL *directiāre*, whence OF *drecier* (? for *directer*), MF-F *dresser*, to direct, hence to arrange, to dress, hence also, in EF-F, to train a horse, whence F *dressage*, adopted by E; MF-F *dresser* yields 'to *dress*', whence 'a *dress*' and the vn *dressing*.

9. *Drecier, dresser* has the prefix-cpds OF *adrecier*, MF-F *adresser*, to direct, or to direct oneself in a given direction, whence ME *adressen*, to adorn, etc., whence 'to *address*', the derivative MF-F n *adresse*, direction, EF-F skill, combining with the E v to yield the E n *address*; and OF *redrecier*, to make straight again, MF-F *redresser*, to straighten, whence 'to *redress*', whence the E n *redress. Maladdress* derives from F *maladresse*, which blends, as it were, *maladroit*, clumsy, and *adresse*, skill.

9A. See also paras 13, 15, 16, 18, 19, 20, 21, 22, 23.

## III, B. Spanish and Portuguese

10. That old Sp coin, the *real*, derives from the Sp adj *real*, royal, from L *regālis*: cf, sem, the E *sovereign*. Cf the Port *reis* (pl of Port *real*), discontinued in 1911; hence the Port *milreis* (lit, *mil*, 1,000+*reis*), likewise discontinued in 1911; the Brazilian *milreis* survives.

## III. Latin: A, *rēx*

11. L *rēx*, a king, was orig, it seems, a commander, a president, as in *rēx sacrōrum*; it prob stands, with vocalic change from short to long *e*, for *\*regs*, from *regere* (s and r *reg*-), to guide or direct, in a straight line, hence to have the direction, the command, of (persons). The lit sense occurs in

*rēctus*, straight, whence the moral sense; cf *rectangle* at the element *recti-*.

12. L *rēx* becomes the E PN *Rex*. The o/s is *rēg*-, whence the adj *rēgālis*, worthy of a king; whence, perh via OF-MF *regal* (MF-archaic F *régal*), the E *regal*; the neu *rēgāle* becomes E *regale*, a royal prerogative, usu in pl *regalia*, now applied to the emblems and symbols thereof, hence to any ceremonial, esp if official, dress. L *rēgālis* has the ML derivative *rēgālitās*, o/s *rēgālitāt-*, whence, perh via MF, the E *regality*. —The secondary adj *rēgius* occurs in *Regius Professor*.

13. L *rēx*, o/s *rēg*-, acquires in ML the cpd *rēgicīda*, king-slayer, and *rēgicīdium*, a kingslaying, whence EF-F *régicide*, whence E *regicide*.

14. L *rēx* has f *rēgīna* (*rēg*-, o/s of *rēx*+the f suffix *-īna*), seen on British coins; hence the adj in *-al*: *reginal*.

15. L *rēx*, s *rēg*-, has derivative *rēgnum*—prob a contr of *\*rēgīnum*, neu of adj *\*rēgīnus* (cf PN *Rēgīnus*, PIN *Rēgīnum*, perh *rēgīna*)—the control exercised and the power possessed by a king, hence his kingdom, has ML adj *regnālis*, whence E *regnal. Rēgnum* becomes OF-MF *regne* (EF-F *règne*), var *reigne*, orig kingdom, whence ME *regne, reyn*, whence E *reign*. 'To *reign*,' ME *reinen*, earlier *regnen*, derives from OF-MF *regner* (EF-F *régner*): LL *rēgnāre*, from *rēgnum*. The cpd *interrēgnum*, from *inter*, between+*rēgna*, the reigns, is retained by E; *regnant*=L *rēgnant-*, o/s of *rēgnans*, presp of *rēgnāre*.

16. The dim of *rēx* is *rēgulus* (*rēg-*+dim suffix *-ulus*), a kinglet, whence the PN *Regulus*. The f *rēgula*, a straight piece of wood, esp a measuring-bar, a ruler, hence, fig, a pattern of conduct, a discipline, becomes OF-MF *reule* (*riule, rieule*)— cf the Walloon *rule*—whence ME *reule*, E *rule*; 'to *rule*' comes from OF-MF *reuler* (*rieuler*, etc.), from LL *rēgulāre*, itself from *rēgula*.

17. LL *rēgulāre*, to keep straight, has pp *rēgulātus*, whence 'to *regulate*'.

18. L *rēgula* has adj *rēgulāris*, whence OF *reguler* (MF *regulier*, F *régulier*), adopted by ME, whence, re-formed upon the L word, the E *regular*; the MF-F derivative *régularité* becomes E *regularity*. The Eccl LL *irrēgulāris* and its derivative *irrēgulāritās*, o/s *irrēgulāritāt-*, yield—prob via MF—the E *irregular, irregularity*.

## III. Latin: B, *regere*

19. L *regere*, to guide straight, has presp *regens*, o/s *regent-*, whence, perh via MF-F *régent*, the E *regent*, adj and n; derivative LL *regentia*, office of ruler, yields—perh via late MF-F *régence*—the E *regency*.

20. L *regere*, s *reg*-, has derivative *regimen*, a guiding, a governing, adopted by MF and, prob independently, by E—esp in Med sense. The late MF-F shape, *régime*, has also been adopted by E, esp as 'form of government'.

21. L *regimen* has the LL doublet *regimentum*, a direction for government, hence governance;

hence, via MF-F *régiment* (military sense borrowed from G), the E *regiment*, whence 'to *regiment*'.

22. Also from the s *reg-*, derives L *regiō*, o/s *regiōn-*, a straight line (esp if a boundary), hence a frontier, hence a quarter or a district: whence OF *region*, MF-F *région*, whence E *region*; derivative LL *regiōnālis*, whence—cf EF-F *régional*—the E *regional*, whence *regionalism* (cf the F *régionalisme*).

23. The pp of *regere* is *rēctus*, whence, in E, the obs adj and the Phil n *rect* and the element *rect(i)-*, as in *rectangle* and *rectilinear*, or *-rect*, as in *correct*, *erect*, etc. Cf *rectify* and *rectification*, resp adapted and adopted from MF-F *rectifier* and *rectification*, from LL *rectificāre* and *rectificātiō*, o/s *rectificātiōn-*; *rectifiable* is adopted from F.

24. L *rēctus*, s *rēct-*, has the LL derivative *rēctitūdō*, straightness (lit and fig), whence—perh via MF-F—the E *rectitude*. Also from *rēctus* comes L *rēctor*, a guide, controller, director, adopted by E, with ML derivatives *rectoratus* (gen *-ūs*) and *rectoria* (*domus*), whence E *rectorate* and *rectory*; E *rectoral* is perh adopted from EF-F.

25. *Rectum* is the SciL *rēctum* (*intestinum*), the straight (part of the great) intestine.

### III. Latin: C, Compounds of *regere*, esp of pp *rēctus*

26. L *regere* has several prefix-cpds relevant to E, e.g. *arrigere*, to straighten *ad* or towards or upwards, with pp *arrēctus*, with ears erect, hence eagerly attentive, whence E *arrect* and the SciL *arrector*.

27. More important is *corrigere*, to straighten (*cor-* for *con-*, used int), lit and fig. The neu gerundive *corrigendum*, (something) to be straightened or set right, has, with its pl *corrigenda*, been adopted by learnèd IE; *corrigibilis*, correctable, becomes MF-F *corrigible*, adopted by E, and the LL neg *incorrigibilis* becomes MF-F and E *incorrigible*. The pp *corrēctus*, used also as adj, yields the E adj, whence v, *correct*. Derivatives *corrēctiō*, o/s *corrēctiōn-*, and *corrēctor* and LL *corrēctiuus* (ML *-ivus*) become MF-F *correction*, *correcteur*, *correctif* (f *-ive*), whence E *correction*, *corrector*, *corrective* (adj, hence n). The neg *incorrēctus* becomes (MF-F and) E *incorrect*; LL *incorrēctiō*, o/s *incorrēctiōn-*, becomes (EF-F and) E *incorrection*. *Correctitude* blends the adj *correct*+*rectitude*.

28. L *dīrigere*, to lead, or guide, in various directions, hence merely to guide, has presp *dīrigens*, o/s *dīrigent-*, whence E *dirigent*; *dirigible* —cf F *dirigeable*—represents *dīrig-*+adj *-ible*. The pp *dīrēctus* yields both the adj—cf the F *direct*— and the v *direct*; derivatives LL *dīrēctiō*, o/s *dīrēctiōn-*, LL *dīrēctor*, LL *dīrēctōrius*, its derivative n *dīrēctōrium*, yield resp (MF-F and) E *direction*—AF *directour*, E *director—directory*, adj —*directory*, n, and F *directoire*, as in the period of the *Directoire*. The ML adj *dīrēctivus* and its 'derivative' *dīrēctiva litera* (or *epistola*) account for the E adj and n *directive*.

29. L *dīrigere* has imperative *dīrige*, Direct *thou!*: whence, via the Catholic *Dirige, Domine*, ... *viam meam* (in the Office for the Dead), the E *dirge*.

30. The pp *dīrēctus*, used as adj, has neg *indīrēctus*, whence—perh via late MF-F—the E *indirect*.

31. L *ērigere*, to straighten out, hence to raise straight, has pp *ērēctus* (used also as adj), whence the E adj and v *erect*; derivative LL *ērēctiō*, o/s *ērēctiōn-*, becomes, perh via late MF-F *érection*, the E *erection*; the LL agent *ērēctor* becomes E *erector*. From *ērēctūs*, pp, learnèd F has derived *érectile*, whence E *erectile*.

32. L *surgere* (? for *\*subrigere*), to rise: see SURGE.

33. The L *ergō*, therefore, 'is doubtless formed from the preposition *e* [*ex*, out of]+the abl of a vn of *regō* [I guide straight]': E & M.

### IV. Greek

34. Perh akin to L *regere*, pp *rēctus*, is Gr *oreg*ein, to stretch for, to reach towards, pp *orekt*os, whence the adj *orektikos*, whence the Phil *orectic*, appetitive. Cf the 1st REACH (2).

### V. Sanskrit

35. Hindi *rāj*, n, rule or reign, and Hindi *rājā* (from Skt *rājan*) have become E *raj* and *raja* or *rajah*; the Hindi f *rānī* (Skt *rājñī*) becomes E *rani* or *ranee*. The cpds *maharajah*, *-raja*, and *maharanee*, *-rani*, derive from Skt *mahārāja* (*mahat*, great) and Hindi *mahārāni*: lit, 'great king' and 'great queen': with *rājā*, cf L *rēx*; with *rānī*, cf L *rēgīna*.

### VI. Indo-European

36. Clearly the IE r of all those words is *\*reg-*, to set straight, to lead or guide straight, hence, as n, a true guide, hence a powerful one, hence a chief, a king; perhaps the basic sense of *\*reg-* is 'a straight line' or, better, 'a movement straight from one point to another, hence a movement along a straight line'. (E & M.)

**Reynard.** See HARD, para 4.

**rhabdite.** See VERVAIN, para 4.

**rhamnus.** See VERVAIN, para 4.

**rhapontic.** See RHUBARB, para 2.

**rhapsodic(al), rhapsody.** See ODE, para 9, and cf WRAP, para 2.

**rhea**, the SAm ostrich, comes fancifully from L *Rhea*, Gr *Rhéā* ('*Ρέā*), 'the mother of the gods': derived by Chrysippus from Gr *rheo*, I flow, 'because rivers flow from the earth'.

**rhematic, rheme.** See RHETOR.

**rhematology.** See the element *rhemato-*. Cf prec.

**Rhenish, rhenium, Rhine.**

The 1st blends and alters L *Rhen*us, the Rhinc+ G rhein*isch*, of the Rhine; *Rhine* blends, phon, L *Rhenus* and G *Rhein*; *rhenium*, a rare Chem element=*Rhen*us+Chem *-ium*. L *Rhēnus* derives from Gaul *Renos*, perh akin to RISE.

**rheostat.** See the element *rheo-*.

**rhetor, rhetoric, rhetorical, rhetorician; rhematic, rheme.**

*Rhematic*=Gr *rhēmatikos*, adj of *rhēma* (gen *rhēmatos*), a word, whence adj *rhēmatikos*, whence E *rheme* and *rhematic*: and Gr *rhēma* is akin to Gr *rhētōr*, a teacher of oratory, whence, via LL, the learnèd E *rhetor*: both *rhēma* and *rhētōr*, for *whrēma* and *whrētōr*, derive from *eirō* (for *weriō*), I say: f.a.e., VERB. Gr *rhētōr* has adj *rhētorikos*, whence L *rhetoricus*, whence the obs E adj *rhetoric*, now in extn *rhetorical*. The Gr adj *rhētorikos* has f *rhētorikē*, used as n, elliptical for *r. tekhnē*, the art of the rhetor or orator: whence MF *rhetorique* (F *rhétorique*), ME *retorike*, whence the reshaped E *rhetoric*. F *rhétorique* has derivative *rhétoricien*, whence E *rhetorician*.

**rheum, rheumatic, rheumatism; catarrh,** whence **catarrhal—diarrhoea,** AE **diarrhea,** whence **diarrh(o)eal, diarrh(o)eic—haemorrhoid,** AE **hemorrhoid,** whence **h(a)emorrhoidal—logorrhoea,** AE **-rhea;** ult cf STREAM.

1. *Rheum*, old-fashioned word for the common cold, is reshaped from ME *reume*, adopted from OF-MF (later *rheume*, F *rhume*): LL *reuma*, var of *rheuma*, adopted from Gr: from *rhéō*, I flow, inf *rhein*: cf STREAM.

2. Gr *rheuma* has adj *rheumatikos*, whence, via LL *rheumaticus*, the late MF-F *rhumatique*, E *rheumatic*; EF *rheumatisme* (F *rhumatisme*) becomes E *rheumatism*.

3. Gr *rhein*, to flow, has several cpds affecting E: *katarrhein*, to flow *kata* or down, whence *katarrhoos*, *-rrhous*, whence LL *catarrhus*, late MF-F *catarrhe*, E *catarrh*;

*diarrhein*, to flow *dia* or through, whence *diarrhoia*, LL *diarrhoea*, adopted by E (cf the MF-F *diarrhée*);

*haimorrhoos*, flowing with *haima* or blood, whence *haimorrhoïs*, o/s *haimorrhoïd-*, pl *haimor-rhoïdes*, whence L *haemorrhoidae*, MF *emeroydes* (archaic E *emerods*), EF-F *hémorroïdes*, reshaped E *haemorrhoids*; the sing refers to one 'varicosal' swelling;

SciL *logorrhoea*, a flow of *logoi* or words: erudite E.

**Rhine.** See RHENISH.

**rhinoceros,** adopted from L, is the Gr *rhinokerōs*, '(the) horny-nosed (beast)': cf the element *rhino-*. The adj *rhinocerotic*=LL *rhinocerōticus*, Gr *rhino-kerōtikos*.

**rhizoid, rhizome.** See RADICAL, para 1, s.f.

**rhododendron.** See element *-rhodin* on p. 943.

**rhomb, rhombus.** See VERVAIN, para 4.

**rhubarb; rhapontic.**

1. *Rhubarb* derives from EF-F *rhubarbe*, var of MF *reubarbe*: ML *reubarbarum, rheubarbarum,* either 'the barbarian root' (L *barbarus*), from *rheu*, according to Isidore of Seville (C7) a 'barbarian' word meaning 'root', or, if the ML var *rhabarbarum* be taken as primary, from LL *rha* (var *ra*), rhubarb, from Gr *rha* (var *rhéon*), from *Rha*, the Volga, as Rabelais declares (B & W);

*Rha*, the Volga, perh derives from Gr *rhein*, to flow—'*the* flow-er'?

2. The LL var *ra* (ML *rha*) *ponticum*, both written also as one word, lit 'rhubarb of the *Pontus*' in Asia Minor, becomes EF-F (now archaic) *rhapontic*, adopted by E for the domestic rhubarb.

**rhumb** perh blends *rhomb*+either EF-F *rumb* or (the certainly-from-L-*rhombus*) Port and Sp *rumbo*: o.o.o.

**rhyme,** n and v (whence **rhymer** and **rhymester,** and pa, vn **rhyming**), with archaizing var **rime; rhythm, rhythmic** or **rhythmical;** ult cf STREAM.

1. *Rhyme* or *rime* derives from ME *rime* or *ryme*, var *rym*: OF-F *rime*, either from L *rhythmus*, rhythm, ML verse, from Gr *rhuthmos*, a measured movement, a poetic measure, app akin to *rhein*, to flow, or from some OGmc source—cf OE, OFris, MHG *rīm*, a number or a sequence; note, however, that the MHG and OFris words perh derive from the OF *rime*.

2. L *rhythmus* becomes EF *rithme*, later EF–C19 F *rhythme* (later *rythme*), whence E *rhythm*; the adj *rhythmic*, often in extn *rhythmical*, derives either from EF–C19 F *rhythmique* (later *rythmique*), itself from LL-ML *rhythmicus*, Gr *rhuthmikos* (*rhuthmos*+*-ikos*), or direct from LL-ML *rhythmicus*.

**rhynco-** words. See the element *rhynch(o)-*.

**rhyo-** words. Cf the element *rhyo-*.

**rhyparo-, rhypo-** words. See the element *rhyparo-*.

**rhythm, rhythmic.** See RHYME, para 2.

**ria.** See RIVER, para 7.

**rial.** See REX, para 4.

**rib,** n, hence v, whence **ribber** and **ribbing; naut ribband;** cf sep REEF.

The naut *ribband*, a long and narrow piece of timber, merely joins *band* to *rib*: and *rib* of ship (etc.) derives from *rib* of the animal body: OE *rib, ribb*: cf OFris *ribb* (var *rebb*), OHG *rippa*, MHG-G *rippe*, ON *rif*, OSI *rebro*, and perh OHG *reba*, MHG-G *rebe*, a vine, and Gr *orophos*, a reed, *orophē*, a roof of reeds, akin to *erephein*, to cover with a roof: IE r, perh *rebh-*, to arch over (Hofmann).

**ribald, ribaldry.**

The latter derives from ME *ribaldrie*, var of *ribaudrie*, from MF *ribauderie*, itself from OF-MF *ribault*, var of *ribaut*, var of *ribaud* (still in Walloon), from OF-MF *riber*, to be wanton, from OHG *rīban* (MHG *riben*), to be amorous, orig to rub—cf OHG *hrība*, a prostitute.

**riband.** Cf *ribbon*, q.v. at RED, para 15.

**ribband** (1). See RIB.

**ribband** (2). See:

**ribbon,** occ var **ribband, riband.** See RED, para 15.

**rice,** whence **ricey,** derives from ME *ris, rys*: MF *ris* (F *riz*): It *riso*: by aphesis from LL *oriza*: L *oryza*: Gr *oruza*, var *oruzon*: either deriving, via East Iranian, from or akin to Skt *vrīhis*, rice (cf Afghan *vrižĕ*), prob from some indigenous South Asiatic language. (Hofmann.)

**rich, riches; enrich,** whence **enrichment;** cf, ult, REX.

1. *Riches* derives from ME *richesse*, MF(-F) *richesse*, wealth, OF *richesse*, power: OF *riche*, powerful, MF-F wealthy+suffix *-esse*: OF *riche* derives from Frankish *\*rīki*, powerful: f.a.e., REX. But E *rich* derives from ME *riche*, a blend of OE *rīce*, powerful, rich+OF-MF *riche*; OE *rīce* is akin to OFris *rīke*, OS *rīhhi* (G *reich*), Go *reiks*, powerful, and ON *rīkr*, powerful, rich: f.a.e., REX.

2. OF *riche* has OF(-F) cpd *enrichir*, to make rich: *en*, L *in*, used int+*riche*+inf *-ir*. Hence the E 'to *enrich*'; derivative *enrichment* perh prompted by MF-F *enrichissement*.

**Richard.** See DICKENS . . ., s.f.

**riches.** See RICH.

**rick** (1), of hay; **ridge**; **ruck**, undistinguished members of crowd.

1. *Rick*, ME *reke*, derives from OE *hrēac*, akin to ON *hraukr*, rick, *hroki*, a heaped-up mass, MD *roke*, *roic*, *rooc*, D *rook*, rick; perh, ult, to CROSS.

2. *Ridge*, ME *rigge*, OE *hrycg*, is akin to MD *rigge*, *ric*, *regge*, *rugge*, D *rug*, OHG *hrukki*, *rucki*, G *Racken*, ON *hryggr*, and to the *rick* words.

3. *Ruck*, orig a heap or stack, is of Scan origin: cf ON *hraukr* (as in para 1 above), var *hrūga*, and Nor dial *ruka*.

**rick** (2), a sudden or painful twist of neck, back, ankle, (as v) so to twist, is a var of syn *wrick*, n hence v: ME *wricken*, to twist or jerk, akin to D *wrikken*. Cf MD *wrigen*, to twist, whence the MD-D freq *wriggelen*, akin to MLG *wriggeln*, whence the E 'to *wriggle*' (whence the n). Cf, further, WRY.

**rickets**, whence **rickety**. See the element *rachi-*, 2nd para.

**rickshaw.** See JINRIKSHA.

**ricochet**, adopted from MF-F, orig designated '(an) endless repetition' (modern sense, C17): o.o.o.

**rictus**, adopted from L, derives from *rictus*, pp of *ringere*, to show one's teeth: cognates in Sl: IE r, *\*reng-*, to grin.

**rid**, whence **riddance**: ME *ryddan* (var *ruden*): ON *rythja*, to clear (land): cf OE *āryddan*, to strip, and *hryding*, a clearing, a patch of cleared land, syn ON *ruthning*, and perh OHG ar-*riutan*, to extirpate (lit).

**ridden.** See RIDE.

**riddle** (1), a sieve, OE *hriddel*, an *l*-for-*r* var of *hridder*, is akin to OHG *rītara*, MHG *rīter*, G *Reiter*—to OIr *crīathar*—to L *crībrum*: f.a.e., CERTAIN. (Walshe.)

**riddle** (2), a conundrum. See READ, para 2.

**ride**, pt **rode**, pp **ridden**; **rider**;—**raid** (n, v), whence **raider**, **raiding**;—**road**, whence **roadstead**, **roadway**, **roadster**;—cf the sep RILL.

1. 'A *ride*' derives from 'to *ride*': ME *riden*, *ryden*: OE *rīdan*: cf OFris *rīda*, OHG *rītan*, MHG *rīten*, G *reiten*, LG *riden*, ON *rītha*—OIr *riadaim*, I ride or travel, *riad*, a riding, a driving, Gallo-L *rēda*, a cart; also OE *rād*, a journey—see para 3. Prob cf READY.

2. OE *rīdan* has agent *rīdere*, whence *rider*.

3. *Rīdan* has the further derivative *rād*, the act

of riding, hence a journey: ME *rade*, var *rode*: E *road*, which has the Sc var *raid*, a riding, esp if hostile, hence 'to *raid*'.

**ridge.** See the 1st RICK, para 2.

**ridicule**, **ridiculous.** See RISIBLE, para 2.

**riding** (1), an administrative district of Yorkshire: OE *\*thriding*, attested in L documents, the *th-* disappearing because of its clash with prec *-th* of *North Riding*: ON *thrithjungr*, the 3rd part (there being three Ridings), from *thrithi*, 3rd: f.a.e., TRI-.

**riding** (2), pa and vn. See RIDE.

**ridotto.** See DUKE, para 8.

**rietbuck.** See REED (heading).

**rife**: OE *rife*: cf the syn ON *rīfr* and MLG *rīve*, MD *rijf*, *rive*, also ON *reifa*, to bring forward, to manifest.

**riffle**, n, v; **ripple**, n, v; **rip** (of water); **ruffle**, v.

All these words are o.o.o.; prob *riffle* is a thinning of *ruffle*, and perh *ripple* is a blend of *riffle*+*rip* of water; *rip* may owe something to RIP (1). Not impossibly the *p* words represent *n*-less varr of *rimple* and *rumple*, qq.v. at RAMP, paras 4 and 3.

**riffraff.** See RAFF, para 1.

**rifle** (1), to despoil or plunder, whence **rifler** and **rifling** (plundering): OF-MF *rifler*, to plunder (F, to plane): OHG *riffilōn*, to tear by rubbing; cf ED *rijffelen*, to rub or scrape, to plunder; ? freqq of, e.g., OFris *rīva*, MLG *rīven*, ON *rīfa*, to tear.

2. From ON *rīfa*, comes ME *riven*, E 'to *rive*' or tear apart, to rend asunder, with pp *riven*, used also as adj. Cf RIFT.

**rifle** (2), v hence n, whence the **rifle bird**, from its cry; **rifling** (grooving).

The firearm derives, by b/f, from *rifled* (i.e., grooved) *gun*, from 'to *rifle*' or groove internally: from OF-F *rifler*, to scrape or file: cf prec, para 1.

**rifling**, grooving. See prec.

**rift**, n hence v, is of Scan origin—cf the syn Da *rift* and ON *ripa* and ON *rīfa*, q.v. at the 1st RIFLE.

**rig**, to fit (esp naut), to furnish, hence n, is of Scan origin: cf Nor and Sw *rigga*, Da *rigge*, to rig, and Nor, Sw *rigg*, Da *rig*, the n: o.o.o. Agent: *rigger*; vn: *rigging*, esp of ship.

**right** (adj, n, v), **righteous**, **rightly**, **rightness**. See REX, para 2.

**right whale.** See REX, para 2, s.f.

**rigid**, **rigidity**; **rigor** (*r. mortis*), **rigour**, **rigorous**, **de rigueur**.

L *rigēre*, to be stiff or inflexible, s and r *rig-*, is o.o.o.: prob akin to L *frīgus*, o/s *frīgor*, coldness, and *frīgidus*, cold; cf also Gr *rhīgos* (from *\*srīgos*), frost, the cold. *Rigēre* has two derivatives notably affecting E:

*rigidus*, whence late MF-F *rigide* and, prob independently, E *rigid*, the LL derivative *rigiditās*, o/s *rigiditāt-*, yielding *rigidity* (cf F *rigidité*);

*rigor*, adopted by Med E, esp in *rigor mortis*, the stiffness of death, and by AE, E preferring *rigour*, already in ME, which adopts it from MF (F *rigueur*),—the derivative LL *rigorōsus*, severely cold, ML also fig, becoming MF-F *rigoureux*, f *rigoureuse*, whence E *rigorous*. The phrase *de rigueur*, compulsory, indispensable, comes from F *être de rigueur*, to be compulsory or indispensable.

**rigmarole.** See RAGMAN ROLLS.

**rigor, rigorous, rigour.** See RIGID.

**rile** is a var, mostly AE, of *roil*, q.v. at RED, para 13.

**rill** prob derives from LG *rille*—unless from D *ril*; prob akin to MLG *ride*, a brook, OE *rīthe*, a stream, OIr *riathor*, a torrent, ? Ga *srùlag*, a stream, and Skt *rītī*, a stream; prob, therefore, cf RIDE.

**rim** (n, hence v), **rand, the Rand, random, randy.**

1. *Rim* comes from OE *rima*, akin to the syn OFris *rim* and to ON *rimi*, a raised strip of land, at, e.g., the edge of a field.

2. Prob akin to OE *rima*, etc., is OE, hence E, *rand*: cf OHG *rant*, boss of shield, MHG *rant*, rim of shield, hence rim in general, G *Rand*, edge; *the Rand*, in SAfr, shortens and anglicizes *Witwatersrand* (MD *rant*, MD-D *rand*)—in Afr, 'White Waters Ridge'. With OE *rand*, cf ON *rönd*, and perh (Walshe) OHG *rama*, a support, MHG *rame*, G *Rahmen*, a frame.

3. Perh akin to OHG *rant* is the OGmc origin of the OF-MF phrases *à randon* and *de randon*, rapidly, suddenly, violently, where *randon* means 'rapidity' or 'impetuosity'; hence ME *randon*, whence the eased EE *random*, impetuosity, force, whence E *at random*, haphazardly. (But *randon* could well derive from a Frankish *\*rant*, a running, a course, from OHG *rennēn* (MHG-G *rennen*), to run, as B & W hold.)

4. *Randy*, lecherous, derives from obs *randy*, loud- or coarse-spoken, ult akin to *random*.

**rime** (1), a white frost: OE *hrīm*: cf ON *hrīm*, MD-D *rijm*, and also OHG *hrīfo*, MHG *rīfe*, G *Reif*, OS *hrīpo*, MD *ripe*, D *rijp*, hoar-frost.

**rime** (2), in verse. See RHYME.

**rimple.** See RAMP, para 4.

**rind.** See REND.

**ring** (1), a circlet (whence **ringworm**), hence 'to **ring**' or surround. See RANGE, para 2.

**ring** (2), vi and vt, to (cause to) sound clearly or resonantly, pt **rang** (occ **rung**), pp **rung**: OE *hringan*: echoic—cf ON *hringja*, MD *ringhen*, D *rinkelen*. Hence the agent **ringer** and the pa, vn **ringing**.

**rink.** See RANGE, para 2.

**rinse** (v, hence n): ME *rinsen*, earlier *rincen*: MF(-F) *rincer*: OF *reincier*: app from VL *\*recentiāre*, to make fresh, from LL *recentāre*, to refresh, from L *recēns*, fresh: cf RECENT.

**rio.** See RIVER, para 7.

**riot** (n, v—whence **rioter, rioting**). 'To *riot*' derives from OF-MF *rioter*, *rihoter*, to quarrel, whence OF-MF *riote* (F *riotte*, archaic), E *riot*: o.o.o.: ? echoic. OF *riote* has MF derivative *riotous*, adopted by E.—Cf the 2nd RUT.

**rip** (1), n, of water. See RIFFLE.

**rip** (2), to tear asunder, hence n, is, ult prob **echoic**: cf Flem *rippen*, MLG *reppen*, MD *riten*,

D *rijten*—also Sw *reppa* and Da *reppe, rippe*. Hence agent *ripper* and pa, vn *ripping*.

**ripa, riparian.** See RIVER, paras 1 and 2.

**ripe**, whence **ripen; ripeness;—reap**, whence **reaper** and pa, vn **reaping**.

1. *Ripeness* comes from OE *rīpeness*, a *-ness* derivative of OE *rīpe*, whence E *ripe*: cf OS *rīpi*, MD *ripe*, D *rijp*, OHG *rīfi*, MHG *rīfe*, G *reif*: o.o.o.

2. Akin to OE *rīpe* is OE *rīpan*, to cut with sickle or scythe, perh orig to cut (grass, cereals) when ripe, var *reopan, repan*: ME *ripen, reopen, repen*: E 'to reap'.

**ripple.** See RIFFLE.

**Rip van Winkle**, one far behind the times, comes from the eponymous hero of a story in Washington Irving's *The Sketch Book*, 1819-20: cf, sem, *The Story of Sleepy Hollow* in the same collection.

**rise**, pt **rose**, pp **risen**; pa, vn **rising**. See RAISE, para 1.

**risible, risibility** (cf EF-F *risibilité*); **ridicule** (n, hence v), **ridiculous** (whence, anl, **ridiculosity**); **deride, derision** (whence, anl, **derisive**), **derisory.**

1. *Risibility* derives from LL-ML *rīsibilitās*, o/s *rīsibilitāt-*, from LL *rīsibilis*, laughable, whence, via late MF-F, the E *risible*: and LL *rīsibilis* derives from *rīsus*, pp of *rīdēre*, to laugh, also to laugh at, s and r *rīd-*, prob akin to Skt *vrīdate*, he is ashamed (perh from being laughed at), with IE r *\*krīd-*.

2. *Rīdēre* has derivative adj *rīdiculus* (for *\*rīditlos*), laughable, used also as n 'a buffoon', the neu *rīdiculum* being also used as n 'something to be laughed at, also a joke, a witticism', whence the late MF-F adj *ridicule*, hence, in C17-18, n, adopted by E, whence 'to *ridicule*'. The L adj *rīdiculus* and the LL *rīdiculōsus* (from the L n *rīdiculum*) combine to yield E *ridiculous*.

3. L *rīdēre* has the prefix-cpd *dērīdēre*, to laugh *dē-* or down, whence 'to *deride*'; the pp *dērīsus* has derivatives L *dērīsiō*, o/s *dērīsiōn-*, whence MF-F *dérision*, whence E *derision*, and LL *dērīsōrius*, worthy of derision, whence both late MF-F *dérisoire* and E *derisory*, and LL *dērīsibilis*, whence the rare E *derisible*.

**risk** (n, v), whence **risky**—cf the F **risqué**, partly adopted by E.

'To *risk*' derives from EF-F *risquer* (with pp *risqué* used as adj), itself from the EF-F n *risque*, whence E 'a *risk*'; F *risque* comes from It *risco* (now *rischio*): o.o.o.

**Risorgimento.** See SURGE.

**rissole**: MF-F *rissole*: earlier MF *roissole* (cf OF *rousole*, from *roux*, red, f *rousse*): VL *\*russeola*, prop the f of the LL adj *russeolus*, red (cf LL *russulus*, reddish): L *russus*, red—cf the E *rust* at RED, para 3.

**rite; ritual** (adj, hence n), whence **ritualism** and **ritualist** (prompting **ritualistic**).

*Ritual* derives from L *rītuālis*, adj of *rītus* (gen *-ūs*), a religious rite, whence E *rite*: s *rītu-*, r *rīt-*; IE r, *\*rīt-*, prob an extn of *\*rī-*, number, hence order. Cf Gr *nēritos*, numberless, and *arithmos*, number, OE, OHG, ON, OIr *rūn*, number, calculation.

**rivage.** See RIVER, para 4.

**rival, rivalry.** See RIVER, para 8.

**rive** (1), n. See RIVER, para 4.

**rive** (2), pp **riven.** See the 1st RIFLE, para 2.

**river, riverain, riverine** (cf Aus Riverina); **rivage;** Rive Gauche; rival, rivality, rivalry; ripa, riparian (whence, anl, the var **riparial**); ? **rivose, rivulose, rivulet; ria** and **rio;** dubiously **rivet,** n hence v.— Cpds: **arrive, arrival, arriviste; corrival,** whence **corrivalry; derive** (whence **derivable), derivant, derivate, derivation, derivative.**

1. We are concerned with two L words: *rīpa*, bank of river, occ shore of sea, whence the adj *rīpārius*, and *rīuus*, ML *rīvus*, a brook, adj *rīuālis*, ML *rīvālis*: although they are not certainly cognate, they prob share an Italic r *rī-, akin to the *rhei-* of Gr *rhein*, to flow, and perh to the IE r *sreu-*, to flow: IE int prefix *s-+*reu-* (cf L *rīu-*).

### L *rīpa*

2. *Rīpa*, a river-bank, is retained by learnèd E, esp in An; its adj *rīpārius* yields both *riparious* and, with *-ian* substituted for *-ious*, *riparian*.

3. Most authorities attribute *arrive* to a VL *arrīpāre* (for *adrīpāre*), to come to the bank; they should, I think, add that OF-F *arriver* has prob been influenced by *dērīuāre* and perh by *corrīuāre*. OF-F *arriver*, OF var *ariver*, becomes ME *ariven*, E 'to arrive'; MF *arriver* leads to AF *arrivaille*, adopted by ME, whence E *arrival*; F *arriviste* (agential *-iste*) has been adopted by E.

4. *Rīpa* becomes OF-F *rive*, as in *la Rive Gauche*, the Left Bank of the Parisian Seine; whence OF-F *rivage*, partly adopted by E.

5. L *rīpārius*, of the river-bank, has the ML derivative *rīpāria* (prob elliptical for *terra rīpāria*), land rimm behind river-bank or sea-shore, whence both It *riviera*, as in 'the *Riviera*', and OF-MF *riviere* (later *rivière*), MF var *rivere*, adopted by ME, whence E *river*; the modern sense appears as early as C12. Derivative C16 F *riveran*, then *riverain*, is adopted by E, with var *riverine*.

### L *rīuus*, ML *rīvus*, a brook

6. *Rīuus* has dim *rīuulus*, ML *rīvulus*, whence It *rivolo*, with further dim *rivoletto*, whence the reshaped E *rivulet*. Whereas *rivulose* is formed from ML *rīvulus*, *rivose* is formed from ML *rīvus*.

7. *Rīuus* becomes Sp *río*, a river, occurring in many PlNn; Sp *río* has derivative *ría*, estuary, creek, or a long, narrow inlet.

8. *Rīuus* has adj *rīuālis*, ML *rīvālis*, of the river bank, whence *rīuāles* (ML *rīvāles*), the inhabitants of the river-bank, whence, from the idea of those on opposite banks, rivals in love, whence, by b/f, *riuālis*, a rival, and the derivative *rīuālitās*, ML *-vāl-*, whence late EF-F *rivalité* and, prob independently, E *rivality*, virtually superseded by *rivalry* (rival+-ry).

9. Doubtfully cognate is E *rivet*, a headed pin or bolt used for joining two pieces, adopted from a MF-F derivative of OF-F *river*, thus to join perh (Webster) from VL *rīpāre*, to make (a ship) fast to the *rīpa* or shore, but prob (B & W) from MD *wrīven* (D *wrijven*), to cause to turn. Note that MD possesses *rivet*, a rivet, and also the v *riveren*, to rivet.

10. L *rīuus* has the LL derivative *rīuāre*, to carry water, with the foll cpds:

LL *corrīuāre*, to cause to flow together (*cor-* for *con-*), and, after *rīuālis*, the ML *corrīvālis*, a competitor (cf the LL *corrīuium*, a confluence of rivers), whence EF-archaic F *corrival*, adopted by E—but now rare;

LL *dērīuāre*, to flow, hence come, *dē-* or from, whence MF *deriver* (F *dé-*), whence 'to derive'; derivative LL *dērīuābilis* (ML *-rīv-*) has perh influenced *derivable*; *dērīuātiō*, o/s *dērīuātiōn-* (ML *-rīv-*) yields late EF-F *dérivation* and, perh independently, E *derivation*; LL *dērīuatiuus*, ML *-ivus*, yields late MF-F *dérivatif* and, perh independently, E *derivative*; the LL pp *dērīuātus* (ML *-riv-*) accounts for the adj, hence n, *derivate*, and the presp *dērīuans*, o/s *dērīuant-*, ML *dērīvant-*, for the adj, hence n, *derivant*.

**rivet.** See prec, para 9.

**Riviera.** See RIVER, para 5.

**rivose.** See RIVER, para 6.

**rivulet, rivulose.** See RIVER, para 6.

**roach** (1), the fish: ME, from ONF, *roche*, var of *roce*: ML *rocea*: o.o.o.

**roach** (2), rock: see ROCK (heading).

**roach** (3), naut: o.o.o.

**road, roadster, roadway.** See RIDE, para 3.

**roam,** whence **roamer** and **roaming,** derives from ME *romen*, o.o.o.: improbably by aphesis from OE *arǣman*, to arise, and therefore akin to *rise*, q.v. at RAISE; or, despite the very general scorn poured on the notion, not impossibly from 'pilgrimages to *Rome*'.

**roan.** See GRAY, para 5.

**roar,** v, hence n (cf OE *gerār*), hence also **roarer** and pa, vn **roaring:** ME *roren*, earlier *raren*, from OE *rārian:* cf OHG-MHG *rēren*, G *röhren*, MLG *rāren*, MD *rēren:* perh cf Skt *rāyati*, he bellows: ult, echoic. (Kluge.)

**roast,** n, v, whence **roaster** and **roasting; roster.**

1. 'A *roast*' derives, partly from OF-MF *rost* (from *rostir*), partly from 'to *roast*', itself from OF-MF *rostir* (F *rôtir*): Frankish *hraustjan:* cf OHG *rōstēn*, to roast, from OHG *rōst* (G *Rost*), a gridiron or a grate, perh akin to OHG-MHG *rōr* (G *Rohr*), a reed, and—note the form—the syn Go *raus*. (Walshe.)

2. Intimately akin to OHG-G *rōst* and OHG *rōstēn* are MD *rosten* (MD-D *roosten*), to roast, and MD *roster* (MD-D *rooster*), a gridiron, hence —from the parallel bars corresp to parallel lines— a list: hence E *roster*.

**Rob.** See ROBERT, para 2.

**rob, robber, robbery; reave** (pt **reaved,** pp **reft), reaver**—cf **bereave,** whence **bereavement; robe,** n hence v—**disrobe**—**enrobe**—**wardrobe.**

1. *Robbery* derives from MF *roberie, robber* from MF *robeor,* both F words coming from OF-MF *rober,* to rob, whence ME *robben,* E 'to rob': OF *rober* comes from OF *robe,* booty, whence, in MF-F—from booty in form of robes— a gown, a robe, adopted by ME: and OF-F *robe* comes from W Gmc *\*rauba,* booty: cf OHG *roub,* MHG *roup,* G *Raub,* spoil, robbery, and OHG *roubōn,* MHG *rouben,* G *rauben,* Go bi-*raubōn,* to which are prob akin the Go *raupjan,* to pluck, and OHG *roufēn,* MHG *roufen,* G *raufen,* to pluck, to fight, and, perh akin, the ON *riūfa,* L *rumpere* (nasalized *\*rup-*), to break.

2. OF-F *robe,* gown, robe, has the foll cpds relevant to E:

OF *desrober,* to despoil, to strip, hence, in MF, also to disrobe (vt), prob the prompter of 'to *disrobe*';

MF *enrober,* to furnish with robes, whence 'to *enrobe*';

MF-F *garde-robe,* with ONF var *warderobe,* adopted by ME, whence *wardrobe*—cf the v WARD.

3. With Go bi-*raubōn* (int *bi-*), to despoil, cf the syn OFris *birēva* and OE *berēafian,* ME *bireven,* E 'to *bereave*'. OE *berēafian* is the int of OE *rēafian,* ME *reven,* E 'to *reave*', akin to OFris *rēva,* to rob, itself akin to the OGmc words noted in para 1—to which add, e.g., ON *reyfa,* to rob, and OE *rēofan,* to break. Cf RUPTURE.

4. OE *rēafian* has agent *rēafere,* whence E *reaver.* **robe.** See prec, para 1.

**Robert,** whence **Roberts** (*Robert's* son) and **Robertson; Rob, Rob Roy, Robbie—Bob, bob, Bobbie, bobby—Rab, Rabbie; Robin** (whence **Robins and Robinson), Robin Goodfellow, Robin Hood**—and **robin; Dobbin; Hob, hob, hobgoblin; Hodge; Rupert; Roger, roger; Roderick; Roland and Orlando.**

1. *Robert,* adopted from F, itself adopted from OHG (varr *Hrodperht, Ruopert,* etc.), means 'fame-bright' (bright in fame): OHG *hruod-, ruodh-,* is akin to OE *hrōth,* a vocalic var of *hrēth,* glory, cf the syn ON *hrōthr;* and *-perht, -berht, -bert,* akin to OHG *beraht,* OE *beorht* (E *bright*). OHG *Ruopert* becomes G *Ruprecht* and E *Rupert.*

2. *Robert* has pet-form abbr *Rob,* dim *Robbie,* with Sc varr *Rab, Rabbie; Bob* 'assimilates' *Rob* and has dim *Bobbie* or *Bobby.* A *bobby* or policeman—whence humorously the syn *Robert*— derives from Mr, later Sir, *Robert* Peel (whence also *peeler*), who was Home Secretary when (1828) the Metropolitan Police Force was organized. A *bob,* or shilling, perh commemorates some topically famous Bob of the late C18.

3. F *Robert* has pet-form *Robin,* soon independent and duly adopted by E; the *robin* is merely one of several PN origins of bird-names; F *Robin* itself acquires the dim *Robinet,* whence E *robinet,* a chaffinch. The PN *Robin* occurs in the names of at least two folk-lore 'heroes':

*Robin Goodfellow,* a syn of *Puck*;

*Robin Hood,* legendary redresser of social wrongs.

4. *Dobbin,* a (prob dial) var of *Robin,* is a traditional E name for a farm horse; hence *dobbin,* any farm horse, esp if gentle.

5. *Hob,* a dial var of *Rob* (for *Robert* and *Robin*), becomes *hob,* a rustic, hence a rustic sprite, hence any sprite, with elaboration *hobgoblin* (cf GOBLIN).

6. *Hodge,* a rustic, is prop a var of *\*Rodge,* pron of *Rog,* pet-form of *Roger,* adopted from F, from OF *Rogier:* cf OHG *Hrothger, Rothger, Hrotger, Hrodger,* lit '(the) Spear-Famous', famed for, or with, his spear: 1st element as in *Robert,* 2nd the OHG *gēr* (OE *gār*), a spear. Often applied, as PN, to a bull, *Roger* leads to the sl v *roger* (loosely *rodger*), to copulate with (a woman). Cf *the (Jolly) Roger,* nickname of pirates' black flag with cross-bones. *Hodgkin,* whence *Hodgkins* and *Hodgkinson,* is a dim (*-kin*) of *Hodge.*

7. *Roderick* blends ML *Rodericus* and OHG *Hroderich, Ruodrich* (G *Roderich*): 1st element as in *Robert,* with 2nd akin to RICH: lit, '(the) Rich in Fame'; pet-form *Rod,* dim *Roddy.*

8. *Roland,* adopted from the name famous in F chivalry, is of Gmc origin: cf *Hruodland, Hrodland, Ruodland* (or *-lant*), lit '(the) Land-Famous'—cf LAND. Pet-form: *Roly.* Var: *Rowland,* pet-form *Rowley.* The It var *\*Rolando* becomes, by metathesis, *Orlando.*

9. *Rob,* as in para 2, occurs in *Rob Roy* (lit, Red Rob), a famous late C17-early C18 Sc outlaw, Robert MacGregor, hence, a light canoe, esp built for river work, from *Rob Roy,* pseudonym of that John McGregor who, in 1865, devised it.

**Robin** and **robin.** See ROBERT, para 3.

**robinet.** See ROBERT, para 3.

**roble.** See ROBUST, para 3.

**robot.** See ORPHAN, para 3.

**Rob Roy** (canoe). See ROBERT, final para.

**roborant, roborate; roboreous.** See ROBUST, para 4; para 2, s.f.

**robur, roburite.** See para 2 of:

**robust,** whence **robustious** (whence, prob, the AE (sl) **rumbustious,** var **rambunctious**) and **robustness; roble; roborean** or **-eous; robur, roburite; roborant** (adj, hence n), **roborate** (whence, anl, **roboration** and **roborative**)—cf **corroborant** (adj, hence n), **corroborate, corroboration, corroborative** and **corroboratory.**

1. *Robust* derives—prob via MF-F *robuste*— from L *robustus,* oaken, hence hard and tough (lit and fig), the adj of OL *rōbus,* L *rōbur,* the red oak (o/s *rōbor-*), s and r *rōb-;* IE r, prob *\*rudh-,* red: cf RED.

2. *Robur* is used by E for the British oak; the fig sense of L *rōbur* is 'vigour' or 'strength', recurring in, e.g., E *roburite* (Min *-ite*), a mining explosive. Derivative L *rōboreus* yields E *roboreous,* with var *roborean.*

3. L *rōbur,* an oak, becomes Sp *roble,* adopted by AE for several species of Californian and Mexican oak.

4. L *rōbur,* o/s *rōbor-,* has derivative v *rōborāre*

to strengthen, presp *rōborans*, o/s *rōborant-*, whence E *roborant*; the pp *rōborātus* yields the now rare 'to *roborate*'.

5. L *rōborāre* has the cpd *corrōborāre*, to strengthen (*cor-* for *con-*, here vaguely int), with presp *corrōborans*, o/s *corrōborant-*, whence E *corroborant*, and with pp *corrōborātus*, whence the E adj (archaic) and v *corroborate*; derivative LL *corrōborātiō*, a strengthening, o/s *corrōborātiōn-*, whence MF-F, hence E, *corroboration*; the anl EF-F *corroboratif*, f *-ive*, becomes E *corroborative*, whence, anl, *corroboratory*.

**roc.** See the 2nd ROOK (chess).

**rocaille.** See the 1st ROCK, para 2.

**rochet**, Eccl vestment: OF-F *rochet*: dim (*-et*), from Frankish *\*rok*: cf ML *roccus*, OHG-MHG *roc* (G *Rock*), OE *rocc*, ON *rokkr*, a coat, and, prob, OIr *rucht*, a jacket. (Walshe.)

**rock** (1), a cliff, or a peak, of stone, hence a large, esp if fixed, stone, whence **rockery** (*-ery*) and **rocky**; dial **roach**; **rocaille**; **rococo**.

1. The now only dial *roach*, a rock or a stony hill, hence gravelly soil, derives from ME, from OF-F, *roche*; *rock*, however, derives from ME *rokke*, from ONF *roque*. Both OF *roche* and ONF *roque* come from *\*VL rocca* (whence also It *rocca* and Sp *roca*): o.o.o.; presumably pre-L.

2. From EF-F *roc* we have both EF-F *rocaille*, artificial rockwork, and, orig a workshop tech, the F *rococo*, ornamentation employing rocaille, hence any florid ornamentation, hence adj 'florid'.

**rock** (2), a distaff. See RATCHET, para 1, s.f.

**rock** (3), to move (vt, hence vi) as in a cradle, comes from OE *roccian*: cf OHG *rucchēn*, MHG *rucken*, G *rücken*, ON *rykkia*, to jerk, push, pull, and OHG-MHG *ruc*, G *Ruck*, ON *rykkr*, a jerk: ? echoic.—Hence *rocker* and *rocking* chair—*horse*—etc.

**rocket** (1), a plant: EF-F *roquette*: It *rochetta*, var of *rucchetta*: (? a dim of) It *ruca*: apethically from L *ērūca*, colewort: o.o.o. (B & W.)

**rocket** (2), a firework. See RATCHET, para 2.

**rococo.** See the 1st ROCK, para 2.

**rod**: ME, from OE, *rodd*: app akin to ON *rudda*, a club, with cognates in the modern Scan diall.

**rode.** See RIDE (heading).

**rodent.** See RAT, para 2.

**rodeo.** See ROTA, para 12.

**Roderick.** See ROBERT, para 7.

**Rodomont, rodomontade.** See ROTA, para 13.

**roe** (1), deer: ME *ro*: OE *rā* (var *rāha*): cf ON *rā*; OS and OHG-MHG *rēh*, G *Reh*, with OS-OHG var *rēho*; MD *re*, MD-D *ree*; 'prob connected with OIr *ríach*, "grey, spotted" ' (Walshe).

**roe** (2), fish-eggs: app for C17(–19) *rone*, dial var *roan*: late ME *rowne*, EE-E (now dial) *rown*: ON *hrogn*, akin to OHG *rogan*, MHG *roge*, G *Rogen*, roe.

**rogation** (whence, anl, **rogatory**) and **Rogation Sunday**; **rogue**, whence **roguery** and **roguish**. From cpds of L *rogāre*: **abrogate, abrogation** (whence, anl, **abrogative**), **abrogator**; **arrogance, arrogant,** arrogate, arrogation (whence arrogative), arrogator; corvée; derogate, derogation (whence derogative), derogator, derogatory; erogate, erogation; interrogant, interrogate, interrogation, interrogative, interrogator, interrogatory; obrogate, obrogation; prerogate, prerogation, prerogative (adj, n); prorogate, prorogation, prorogator, prorogue; subrogate, subrogation; supererogate, supererogation (whence, anl, supererogatory); surrogate (adj, n, v), surrogation.

1. *Rogation Sunday* comes next before the *Rogation days*, three days of supplication preceding Ascension Day: from *rogation*, a petition, hence—from LL—a litany, from L *rogātiō*, o/s *rogātiōn-*, from *rogātus* (whence obs E *rogate*), pp of *rogāre*, to address oneself to (hence prob akin to L *regere*, q.v. at REX), to question, to ask or petition: s and r *rog-*.

2. Perh from L *rogāre* comes the o.o.o. *rogue*, a rough beggar (or begger): C16–17 *roag*, *roog*, C16 *rooge*, earliest *roge*: perh cf LL *roga*, largesse, and certainly cf Martial's use of *rogātor*, petitioner, for a beggar. More prob, however, E *rogue* form-adopts and sense-adapts MF-F *rogue*, arrogant, offensive, itself app from ON *hrōkr*, arrogant—just possibly aided by MF-F *arrogant* (Dauzat).

Compounds of *rogāre*

3. *Rogāre* bears also a 'parliamentary' sense: 'to propose' a law or a regulation, with cpd *abrogāre*, to demand the repeal, the cessation of: *ab-*, away from. The pp *abrogātus* yields the E adj and v *abrogate*; derivative *abrogātiō*, o/s *abrogātiōn-*, yields—perh via the MF-F word—*abrogation*; LL *abrogātor*, an abolisher, is adopted by E.

4. L *adrogāre* (*ad-*, towards), to ask for, appears mostly as *arrogāre*, to appropriate for oneself, to adopt (an heir); presp *arrogans*, o/s *arrogant-*, becomes OF *\*arrogant*, MF-F *arrogant*, adopted by E, the L derivative *arrogantia* producing OF-F *arrogance*, likewise adopted; pp *arrogātus* yields 'to arrogate', with '*arrogate* to oneself' prompted by L *sibi arrogāre*. Derivative *arrogātiō*, o/s *arrogātiōn-*, yields *arrogation*; and derivative LL *arrogātor* becomes E.

5. L *corrogāre*, to beg or demand together (*cor-* for *con-*), to procure by asking, to invite effectually, has pp *corrogātus*, f *corrogāta*, whence—? for *opera corrogāta*—the LL n *corrogāta*, a contribution, ML labour exacted by the authorities: whence OF *corovée*, almost imm contr to *corvée*; adopted by E.

6. L *dērogāre*, to annul (negation connoted by *de-*, down from), LL to disparage, with pp *dērogātus*, whence the E adj and v *derogate*. The LL derivatives *dērogātiō* (o/s *dērogātiōn-*), *dērogātiuus* (ML *-ivus*), *dērogātor*, *dērogātōrius* become E *derogation*, perh via late MF-F *dérogation* —*derogative—derogator—derogatory*.

7. L *ērogāre*, to spend, pp *ērogātus*, yields the obsol *erogate*; derivative LL *ērogātiō*, o/s *ērogātiōn-*, yields the obsol *erogation*.

8. L *interrogāre*, to ask the advice of, to question, has presp *interrogans*, o/s *interrogant-*, whence E

*interrogant*, n, and pp *interrogātus*, whence 'to *interrogate*'; derivatives *interrogātiō* (o/s *interrogātiōn-*), LL *interrogātiuus* (ML *-ivus*), LL *interrogātor*, LL *interrogātorius* yield E *interrogation*, prob via the MF-F word—*interrogative* (cf EF-F *interrogatif*)—*interrogator* (cf EF-F *interrogateur*)—*interrogatory* (cf late MF-F *interrogatoire*).

9. L *obrogāre*, to repeal, or to modify, a law, has pp *obrogātus*, whence 'to *obrogate*'; derivative *obrogātiō*, o/s *obrogātiōn-*, yields *obrogation*.

10. LL *praerogāre*, to question in advance, has pp *praerogātus*, whence the rare 'to *prerogate*'; derivatives LL *praerogātiō* (o/s *-rogātiōn-*), *praerogātiuus* (ML *-ivus*), asked before others for his opinion, voting before the rest, its derivative n *praerogatiuua* (ML *-iva*), give us resp E *prerogation* (rare)—*prerogative*, adj—the n *prerogative*, via MF-F *prérogative*.

11. L *prōrogāre* (*prō-*, forwards), to postpone, hence to prolong, has pp *prōrogātus*, whence 'to *prorogate*'; derivative *prōrogātiō*, o/s *prōrogātiōn-*, becomes MF-F, whence E, *prorogation*; LL *prōrogātor*, a cashier, suggests the rare E *prorogator*, a postponer. But *prōrogāre* yields also 'to *prorogue*' (parliament)—by way of late MF-EF *proroguer* (EF-F *proroger*).

12. L *subrogāre*, to propose (someone) as an alternative, has pp *subrogātus*, whence 'to *subrogate*'; derivative LL *subrogātiō*, o/s *-rogātiōn-*, yields *subrogation*, perh via late MF-F.

13. *Subrogāre* has the assimilated var *surrogāre*, pp *surrogātus*, whence the E adj (hence n) and v *surrogate*; derivative LL *surrogātiō*, o/s *-rogātiōn-*, yields *surrogation*.

14. L *ērogāre*, in sense 'to pay', has the LL cpd *superērogāre* (often contr to *supērogāre*), to pay or spend in, or as an, excess, pp *superērogātus*, whence 'to *supererogate*'; derivative LL *superērogātiō* (o/s *rogātiōn-*) yields *supererogation*.

Roger; roger. See ROBERT, para 6.

rogue, roguery, roguish. See ROGATION, para 2.

roi. See REX, para 4.

roil. See RED, para 13.

roister. See RURAL, para 5.

roke, fog. See REEK, para 2.

Roland. See ROBERT, para 8.

rôle, role. See para 1 of:

roll, n and v; hence roller and rolling; rôle, anglicized as role; roly-poly; ? rollick, whence rollicking; roulade, rouleau, roulette; rowel; control (n, v), controllable (from the v), controller, comptroller; enroll (or enrol), enrol(l)ment.—rota, rotal, rotary (whence rotarian), rotate, rotation (whence, anl, rotative and rotatory), rotator; rote; rotifer; rotula, rotulet, rotulus;—rodeo; Rodomont, rodomontade; roué; barouche; Rotten Row.—rotund, rotunda, rotundity—cf orotund, whence, anl, orotundity; round, adj (whence adv, prep, v and, in part, the n),/ whence roundabout, rounder, rounders, roundhouse, rounding, roundness, roundsman, the Roundheads, the Round Table; roundel, roundelay—cf rondeau, rondel or rondelle; rondo; rondure;—around.

## I. The *roll* Sub-Group

1. 'A *roll*' derives, in its 'movement' senses, from the v, but for the rest from ME *rolle*, from MF *rolle*, OF *role*; the C15-16 F var *roole* produces the F *rôle*, adopted by E, in theatrical, hence general, sense—from 'the roll on which an actor's part was written' (Webster). OF *role* derives from VL *rotulus*, a roll of 'paper', from L *rotulus*, a little wheel, dim of L *rota*, a wheel: cf Skt *ráthas*, a car or a chariot, OHG *rad*, MHG *rat*, G *Rad*, OFris *rath*, Lith *rátas*, OIr and Ga *roth*, W *rhod*, a wheel, and Lith *ritu*, I roll: Gmc r, *\*rath-*; IE r, *\*roth-* (Walshe).

2. 'To *roll*,' ME *rollen*, derives from MF *roller*, OF *roler*, *rouoller* (cf F *rouler*): VL *\*rotulāre*: L *rotulus*, *rotula*, dimm of *rota*. 'To *roll*' acquires the redup *roly-poly*, in dial a ball-game, in E a pudding.

3. 'To *rollick*' or walk swaggeringly, hence also to frolic, app blends *roll*+frolic (in EE, often fro*lick*).

4. OF-F *rouler*, to roll, has these derivatives adopted by E:

EF-F *roulade*, a 'run' in Mus;

late MF-F *rouleau*, lit a little roll, more prob from *role*, var *roole*, as in para 1;

OF-F *roulette*, with OF-MF varr, lit a little roll, perh rather from *role*, *roole*.

5. Rather from LL *rotella*, a small wheel, than from the syn L *rotulus*, comes OF-MF *rouele*, *rouelle*, MF-F *rouelle*, whence E *rowel*, a little wheel (obs), esp that on horses' spurs.

6. OF-MF *role*, *rolle*, has two prefix-cpds affecting E: MF *enroler* (F *enrôler*) and MF *contrerole*, EF-F *contrôle*. MF *enroler*, to inscribe *en*, in, hence on, a roll, hence, ca 1700, in military sense, becomes 'to *enroll*'; derivative MF-F *enrôlement* becomes E *enrol(l)ment*.

7. MF *contrerole*, a roll, hence a register, kept in duplicate, becomes E *counter-roll* (archaic); the EF-F *contrôle* becomes E *control*. MF *contrerole* has late MF derivative *contreroller*, whence EF-F *contrôler*, whence 'to *control*'. Derivative MF *contreroleur* (EF-F *contrôleur*) yields ME *conterroller*, whence, influenced by the EF-F n, the E *controller*; the Official E *comptroller* is a f/e alteration, after F 'les *comptes*', commercial accounts.

## II. L *rota*, continued

8. L *rota*, a wheel, acquired in C16 Pontifical L the sense 'an eccl tribunal whose members dealt, in due turn, with matters submitted to it', whence, ult, the E sense, 'duty-list, orig of soldiers'. The derivative LL adj *rotālis* becomes E *rotal*; the more usual var, LL *rotārius*, yields *rotary*. The derivative v *rotāre*, to cause to turn like a wheel, i.e. in a circle, has pp *rotātus*, whence *rotate*, and 'to *rotate*'; derivative L *rotātiō*, o/s *rotātiōn-*, yields MF-F and, prob independently, E *rotation*, and derivative LL *rotātor*, although in a special, quite different sense, prob suggested the E *rotator*.

9. Prob from L *rota* in its ML sense 'a public road or way, hence a regular course', derives *by rote*, hence, by b/f, *rote*, a regular course of study, hence repetition.

10. From L *rota*, a wheel, SciL forms the cpd *rotifer*, lit a circle (hence a disc)-bearer, applied, by Zoo, to a class of minute, multi-celled aquatic organisms.

11. The L dimm *rotulus, rotula*, and LL dim *rotella*, all adopted by E, are techh; *rotulus*, a written roll, has the anglicized var *rotulet*.

12. L *rota* and *rotāre* have, in the R languages, several not imm recognizable derivatives: *rodeo, rodomontade, roué, barouche. Rodeo* has been adopted by AE from AmSp *rodeo*, a mustering (and a counting) of cattle, hence the place into which they are mustered, from AmSp *rodear*, to muster, from Sp *rodear*, to surround, from L *rotāre*.

13. *Rodomont*, a brave yet boastful warrior king, and a Moorish hero, in It epics of late C15–early C16, derives, via EF, from It *Rodomonte* (or *Roda-*), lit a roller-away of mountains: It dial *rodare*, to roll away+It *monte*, a mountain; hence the It *rodomontata*, boastfulness, EF *rodomontade*, adopted by E.

14. *Roué*, a debauchee, is adopted from F, where it arose in C18: n from *roué*, lit 'broken on the wheel', pp of *rouer*, to break on the wheel, from OF *roer*, to shape like a wheel, from L *rotāre*. (Dauzat.)

15. *Barouche* comes from G *Barutsche*: It *baroccio*, alteration of *biroccio*: ML *\*birotium* (var *birodium*), var of ML *birotum*: LL *birotus*, a two-wheeled carriage, n use of LL *birotus*, two-wheeled: *bi-*, from *bis*, twice+*rota*.

16. English, however, affords a still more heavily disguised derivative: 'Rotten Row': prob for '*Rotan* Row': C18–mid-19 cant *rotan*, a wheeled vehicle: L *rotam*, acc of *rota*.

### III. Both *rotund* and *round*

17. L *rota*, a wheel, has a further adj: *rotundus*, shaped like a wheel, hence circular, round: whence E *rotund*. Derivative *rotunditās*, o/s *rotunditāt-*, yields *rotundity* (cf MF-F *rotondité*). L *rotundus* has f *rotunda*, used in LL as n 'a circle', whence— reshaped from late MF-F *rotonde*, a rotunda—the E *rotunda*.

18. With L *rotundus*, employed fig for (a) well-rounded style of speaking, hence of writing, cf Horace's *ore rotundo*, with round mouth, i.e. enunciating fully and clearly: whence E *orotund*.

19. L *rotundus* passes through VL *\*retundus* into OF-MF *reont* (OF var: *roont*), with f *reonde, roonde*, whence late MF-F *rond*, f *ronde*: whence ME *roonde*, late ME-EE *rownd*, E *round*. The E n derives, in part, from the F n—MF *reond*, later *rond. The Roundheads*, or Parliamentary party in the reign of Charles I, were so named by the Cavaliers apropos their close-clipped heads; *the Round Table* seated King Arthur and his knights.

20. The foll F derivatives of *rond* concern E, the first four being verse-forms:

MF-F *rondel* (prop a dim of *rond*, n), a roundelay, adopted by E, with anglicized var *roundel*;

MF-F var *rondelle*, adopted by E;

MF-F *rondelet*, whence E *roundelay*;

late MF-F *rondeau*, adopted by E;

late MF-F *rondeur*, roundness, whence E *rondure*.

21. Late MF-F *rondeau* became It *rondò*, mostly as a Mus term and, as such, adopted by E.

22. After the simples comes the prefix-cpd *around*, which (adv, hence prep) consists of *a-*, on +*round*, n: cf the MF *à la reonde*, EF-F *à la ronde*, lit 'in the round'.

23. 'To *surround*' has been influenced by *round* but does not derive from it: see UNDA.

**rollick, rollicking.** See prec, para 3.

**roly-poly.** See ROLL, para 2.

**Romaic.** See ROME, para 2.

**romaine.** See ROME, para 3, s.f.

**Roman.** See ROME, para 3.

**Romance.** See ROME, para 5.

**romance (n, v), romancer.** See ROME, para 5.

**Romanesque.** See ROME, para 7.

**Romanic.** See ROME, para 2, s.f.

**Romanism, Romanist.** See ROME (heading).

**Romanity, romanium, Romanize.** See ROME (heading).

**Romans(c)h.** See ROME, para 5.

**romantic (adj, hence n), romanticism, romanticist, romanticize.** See ROME, para 8.

**romaunt.** See para 6 of:

**Rome**, whence **Romish; Romaic** and **Romic; romaine; Roman** (adj, hence n), whence **roman, Roman candle, Roman holiday,** etc., and **Romish, Romanism, Romanist, Romanity** (? rather from LL *Romanitās*), **romanium** (perh from *Romanus*); **romance (n, v), romancer; Romanesque; Romanize; romantic** (adj, hence n,) whence **romanticism** and **romanticist; romaunt; Rumania** (var **Roumania**), whence **Rumanian** (adj, hence n)—cf **Rumelia,** whence **Rumelian; perh rum,** adj—whence **rummy,** adj, whence, app, the chancy card-game; ? ROAM, q.v. sep.

1. E *Rome*, adopted from OF-F, derives from L *Rōma* (whence It *Roma*): o.o.o., but prob either Italic or Etruscan; cf Italic *Rumon*, an ancient name of the River Tiber, Rome being 'the settlement, then town, finally city on the Tiber'; more likely from Etruscan *Ruma*, the name of an Etruscan clan. (EnciIt.)

2. The derivative Gr name is *Rhōmē*, with adj *Rhōmaïkos*, whence ML *Rōmaïcus*, whence E *Romaic*. Contrast the phon n *Romic*, which= *Rom*(an letters)+adj, hence n, suffix *-ic*. Cf *Romanic*, from L *rōmānicus*, extn of *rōmānus*.

3. The true L adj is *rōmānus*, whence, prob via OF-F *romain*, f *romaine*, the E *Roman*; the *roman*, orig *Roman* (cf *italic*, orig *Italic*), of printing owes something to F *romain*, recorded in C17, the characters having been invented, 1466, by the F printer Jenson; *romaine*, the Cos lettuce, is adopted

from F, where (C17 onwards) it is elliptical for *laitue romaine*, lit 'Roman lettuce'.

4. The firework *Roman candle* originated in Italy; *Roman holiday*, originating in Byron's '[gladiators] butchered to make a Roman holiday', refers to the games in the Circus of imperial Rome.

5. *Romance*, v, derives from F *romancer*, app from F *roman*, a novel, not from the F *romance*, which, however, does originate the Mus *romance*. The literary *romance* comes from ME *romance*, earlier *romans*, adopted from early MF *romans* (C13-17, *romant*; C16+, *roman*), from OF *romanz*: VL \**rōmănicē*, in the Roman way, (esp) in Latin: L *rōmănicus*, Roman: L *Rōmānus*, a Roman (orig an adj). The adj *Romance*, as in 'a *Romance* language', comes from F 'une langue *romance*' (now 'une langue *romane*'), from MF *romans*, OF *romanz*, something translated from Latin, hence written in French. Cf, in general, para 8; cf, in particular, *Romansch*, from F dial (of the Swiss Grisons) *rumansch*, lit 'Roman'. The late MF-F derivative *romancier*, writer of romances, has suggested E *romancer*.

6. MF-EF *romant* becomes E *romaunt* (archaic): cf *romaunce*, a ME var of *romance*.

7. *Romanesque* has, esp among the semi-erudite, caused some confusion, there being prop two distinct words: *Romanesque* and *romanesque*. Whereas the former derives from It *romanesco*, Roman, in the Roman style, with form influenced by F *romanesque*, the latter comes straight from EF-F *romanesque*, in the style of a romance, romantic.

8. *Romantic* derives from late EF-F *romantique*, from the already archaic *romant* (as in para 5 above). MF-EF *romant* acquired, in C14, the sense 'a verse romance of adventure', hence, in C15, 'prose romance of chivalry', whence the modern sense 'a novel'.

9. The L adj *rōmānus* has the LL derivative *Rōmānia* (territorial -*ia*), the Roman world, the Roman Empire existing early in our era: this LL word has influenced the formation of modern L *Rumania* from Rum *Ruman*, Rumanian, a var of Rum *Roman*, Rumanian, ult from L *Rōmānus*. Cf *Rumelia*, the C15-19 name of the Tu possessions on the Balkan peninsula.

10. The coll-from-sl-from-cant *rum*, inferior, odd, shady, orig denoted 'superior, excellent, (very) fine'; the C16-18 var *rome* (cf the C17 *room* or *roome*) suggests that, as John Camden Hotten proposed, *rum*, excellent, fine, derives either from *Rome* or from L-ML *rom*anus. For the form *rum*, cf Tu *rūmî*, belonging to the ancient Romans, and Ar *Rūmî*, belonging to Rome; for the sense, note Poe's 'the grandeur that was Rome' and the many favourable connotations of *Roman* and of such phrases as *rōmāno more*, in the Roman way, i.e. candidly, frankly.

**Romic.** See prec, para 2.
**Romish.** See ROME (heading), esp in ref to the Catholic Church.
**romp, rompers.** See RAMP, para 2.

**ronde.** See ROLL, para 19.
**rondeau.** See ROLL, para 20.
**rondel, rondelle.** See ROLL, para 20.
**rondo.** See ROLL, para 21.
**rondure.** See ROLL, para 20.

**rood**, a crucifix, a square measure of land, comes, through ME *rode*, from OE *rōd*, a crucifix, a land-measure: cf OFris *rōd*, *rōde*, a crucifix, OS *rōda* and OHG *ruota*, MHG *ruote*, G *Rute*, MD *rode*, *rouede*, D *roede*, a staff—and perh L *ratis*, a raft.

**roof** (n, hence v)—whence **roof-tree**—ME *roofe*, earlier *rof*, comes from OE *hrōf*, a roof, a top or covering: cf ON *hrōf*, *hrāf*, a boat-shed, MD *roof*, *rouf*, D *roef*, a cabin, MLG *rōf*, a penthouse, a covering: app with C and Sl cognates.

**rook** (1), the bird, whence **rookery**: ME *rook*, earlier *rok;* OE *hrōc*: echoic, as are the Gmc, L, Gr cognates—cf esp the Gr *hrōzein* (s *hrōz*-), to caw or croak.

**rook** (2), in chess: ME *rok*: OF-EF *roc*: Sp *roque*: Ar *rokh*, var of *rukkh*: Per *rukh*, orig the fabulous bird *roc*.

**rooky** (sl), a recruit. See CRESCENT, para 10.
**room, roomy.** See the 2nd REAM.

**roost** (n, hence v), whence **rooster**: ME *rooste*: OE *hrōst*, a perch, a roof's framework: cf MD *roest*, OS *hrōst*, a hen-roost, ON *hrōt* and Go *hrot*, a roof.

**root** (1). See RADICAL, para 9. Its freq is *rootle*.
**root** (2), vi, to applaud noisily: 'prob from *rout*, to shout, roar' (Webster); perh from the grunting of pigs as they *root* about for food.

**rope** (n, hence v, whence **ropeable**), whence **ropey** or **ropy**, of or like rope; **stirrup** and **stirrup cup**.

1. *Rope*, ME *roop*, *rop*, earlier *rap*, comes from OE *rāp*: cf OFris *rāp*, OS *rēp*, a rope, Go *skauda-raip*, a latchet, OHG-MHG *reif*, a rope, a loop, a hoop, G *Reif*, a hoop, MD *roop*, *roip*, (also D) *roep*, ON *reip*, a rope: o.o.o.

2. OE *rāp*, a rope, has cpd *stigrāp* (for the 1st element, cf STY), whence ME *stirop*, E *stirrup*: cf OHG *stegareif*, MHG *stegereif*, ON *stigreip*. A *stirrup cup* was orig a cup of usu wine, taken by a departing rider, hence any farewell, or parting 'glass of something'.

**roric**, dewy; **rosemary**, whence **Rosemary**.
*Roric*=L *rōr*-, o/s of *rōs*, dew+adj -*ic*; *rōs* is akin to Skt *rásas*, humidity, Ve *rasâ*, dew, and to OSl *rosa*, Lith *rasa*, dew. From *rōs*, dew, and *marīnus*, of the sea, LL forms *rōsmarīnus*, the shrub rosemary: whence ME *rosmarine*, later *rosemaryn* (f/e influence of ROSE), whence E *rosemary* (f/e influence of the Virgin *Mary*); cf the MF-F *romarin*.

**Rosa; rosaceous; Rosalind; rosary; rose**, whence **rosy**—cf **vin rosé; roseal** and **roseate** and **roseous; rosellate** and **rosulate; rosette**. Cf the element -*rhodin*.

1. *Rose* (n, hence adj), OE *rose*, comes from L *rosa*, akin to or perh arising (? via \**Rhodia*, with suffix -*ia*, 'originating in') from Gr *rhodon*, app for \**wrodon*: prob Medit—cf the Av *vareda*

(whence Arm *vard*) and, with *g* for *w*, the Per *gul*; cf also the Eg *uartá*.

2. L *rosa* has adjj *rosāceus*, whence E *rosaceous*; *rosārius* (see next para); *roseus*, whence E *roseous*, varr *roseal* and *roseate*; SciL *rosellātus* and *rosulātus*, whence E *rosellate* and *rosulate*.

3. L *rosārius* has neu *rosārium*, used also as n 'rose garden', hence, in ML, a rose garland for crowning the Virgin, whence, perh from the colour, a string of beads fingered in counting one's prayers, hence a series of prayers: E *rosary* (cf late MF-F *rosaire*).

4. OF-F *rose* has the MF-F dim *rosette*, adopted by E.

5. F *rose* has MF-F adj *rosé*, rosy, whence *vin rosé*, ordinary red wine: E sl 'the *rosy*'.

6. L *rosa* becomes the R feminine PN *Rosa*, adopted by E; and E adapts Sp *rosa linda*, pretty rose, as *Rosalind*: cf *Rosabella*, anglicized as *Rosabel*, from L *rosa bella*, a lovely rose.

**rosemary.** See RORIC.

**rosette.** See ROSE, para 4.

**rosin.** See RESIN, para 3.

**roster.** See ROAST, para 2.

**rostrum**: L *rōstrum*, a ship's beak, orig any beak: from *rōsus*, pp of *rōdere*, to gnaw; the L adj *rōstrālis* yields *rostral*; cf *rodent*, q.v. at RAT, para 2.

**rosy.** See ROSE, heading (the adj) and para 5 (the n).

**rot** (v, hence n), **rotten.**

'To *rot*' comes from ME *rotien*, OE *rotian*, akin to ON *rotinn*, rotten, whence, in fact, ME *rotin*, later *roten*, E *rotten*: cf also ON *rotna*, OFris *rotia*, OS *rotōn*, MD *roten*, D *rotten*, to rot. The sl sense 'nonsense' follows naturally from the standard sense; sl *rotter*= 'to *rot*'+orthographic *-t-*+agent *-er*.

**rota, rotal, rotary, rotate, rotation, rotator, rotatory.** See ROLL, para 8.

**rote,** custom, repetition. See ROLL, para 9.

**rotella.** See ROLL, para 11.

**rother.** See RUNT.

**rotifer.** See ROLL, para 10.

**rotor**: contr of *rotator*, q.v. at ROLL, para 8.

**rotten.** See ROT.

**Rotten Row.** See ROLL, para 16.

**rotter.** See ROT, s.f.

**rotula, rotulet, rotulus.** See ROLL, para 11.

**rotund—rotunda—rotundity.** See ROLL, para 17.

**rouble.** See RUPEE, para 2.

**roué.** See ROLL, para 14.

**rouge.** See RED, para 14.

**rough, roughen, roughness.** See RAG, para 2.

**roulade, rouleau, roulette.** See ROLL, para 4.

**round** (adv, adj, n, v). See ROLL, para 19.

**roundel, roundelay.** See ROLL, para 20.

**Roundhead; Round Table.** See ROLL, para 19, s.f.

**roup,** the poultry disease, comes from *roup*, hoarseness, from *roup*, clamour (obs), from 'to *roup*', to shout, to call, hence to speak, hoarsely, from MD *rouepen*, *ruepen*, *ropen*, *roepen*: cf OE

*hrōpan*, Go *hrōpjan*, OHG *hruofan*, *ruofǎn*, G *rufen*, to call: echoic.

**rouse** (1), a carousal, is aphetic for CAROUSE.

**rouse** (2), to awake, whence **rousing.** See RAISE, para 2.

**roust** is a dial var of the prec; hence **roustabout**—cf the dial **rouse-about,** a bustler.

**rout** (1), a roaring or shouting, derives from the now only dial 'to *rout*', to roar or shout: ON *rauta*: echoic.

**rout** (2), a throng (obs), whence a fashionable assembly, a confused flight. See RUPTURE, para 2.

**route.** See RUPTURE, para 2.

**routine.** See RUPTURE, para 2.

**rove** (1), whence tech **roving,** is prob a var of the 2nd REEVE.

**rove** (2), in archery, hence to ramble or wander, hence **rover,** a rambler or wanderer, and **roving,** wandering; **rover,** a pirate.

'To *rove*' prob derives, by scribal confusion, from MF *rouer*, to ramble or roam, from L *rotāre*, to turn as a wheel does, but is certainly influenced by *rover*, a pirate (as in *sea rover*, a sea robber), ME *rovere*, MD *rover*, a robber, from MD *rōven*, to rob—cf E *reave* (q.v. at ROB, para 3) and its agent *reaver*.

**row** (1), a continuous line or series of persons or things: ME *rowe*, earlier *rawe* and *rewe*: OE *rāw* and *raew*, akin to OHG *rīga*, a line, MHG *rīhe*, G *Reihe*, a series, and to Skt *rēkhā*, a line.

**row** (2), a brawl, a din, prob comes either from the 1st ROUSE apprehended as a pl or from the 1st ROUT. Hence 'to *row*' or quarrel, and the adj *rowdy*. But the *d* of the adj suggests that *row* is perh ult akin to the *rau-* of L *raucus* and *rauus*, hoarse, harsh, and to L *raudus* (var *rōdus*, *rūdus*), a rude mass, from the IE r *\*ru-*, to bellow—cf L *rugīre*, to roar, and Skt *aru-*, to bellow.

**row** (3), to oar a boat along, whence **rower,** oarsman, comes from OE *rōwan*: cf ON *rōa*, MD *roeyen*, *royen*, D *roeien*, also to OE *rōther*, ME *rother*, E *rudder*, OFris *rōther*, OHG *ruodar*, MHG *ruoder*, G *Ruder*, an oar, a rudder, perh also, further off, OIr *rāme*, L *rēmus*, Gr *eretmos*, Skt *arītras*, an oar, and therefore to an IE *\*rā-*, varr *\*rē-* and *\*rō-*, to row (a boat).

**rowan.** See RED, para 15.

**rowdy.** See the 2nd ROW.

**rowel.** See ROLL, para 5.

**Rowland,** whence **Rowlands, Rowlandson,** is a var of *Roland*, q.v. at ROBERT, para 8.

**rowlock** 'corrupts' the earlier *oarlock* (OAR+LOCK).

**Roy** (roy). See REX, para 4.

**royal, royalty.** See REX, para 4.

**rub,** v hence n, hence **rubber,** the agent, and, from the use of caoutchouc for erasers, **rubber,** the vegetable substance; hence also the pa, vn **rubbing.**

'To *rub*', ME *rubben*, is of Gmc origin: cf Fris *rubben*, Nor *rubba*, Da *rubbe*, Sw *rifva* (*f* for *b*): ? ult echoic. Perh cf:

**rubbish,** whence **rubbishy; rubble.**

1. *Rubbish* comes from ME *rubus, robys, robous*; perh, orig, that which is rubbed off, e.g., bricks or stones.

2. *Rubbel*, from ME *robyl* or *robel*, is clearly akin, both phon and sem, to *rubbish*. Hence the adj *rubbly*.

**rube**, AE sl for a rustic, derives from *Rube*, pet-form of *Reuben*, from H *Rê'ūbēn*, (lit) Behold a son. Cf, sem, the syn *hick*, from *Hick*, a rural var of *Dick*, pet-form of *Richard*.

**rubefacient.** See RED, para 7.

**rubella, rubellite.** See RED, para 7.

**rubeola.** See RED, para 8.

**rubescence, rubescent.** See RED, para 6.

**Rubicon,** to cross, or pass, the, to commit oneself irrevocably, comes from Julius Caesar's precipitation of civil war by crossing the river *Rubicon*, which separates Cisalpine Gaul from Italy. Hence the use of *Rubicon* in card-games. *Rubicon* derives from L *Rubicon-*, o/s of *Rubico*, that river, perh so named from a *red* soil in its region.

**rubicund.** See RED, para 10.

**rubidic, rubidine, rubidium.** See RED, para 9.

**rubiginous.** See RED, para 13.

**rubine.** See RED, para 8.

**ruble.** See RUPEE, para 2.

**rubor.** See RED, para 9.

**rubric, rubricate, rubrication.** See RED, para 5.

**ruby.** See RED, para 8.

**ruche** (n, hence v—whence **ruching**): F *ruche*, as a dressmaking term: MF *rouche*, earlier *rousche* or *rusche*, bark of tree, hence a beehive (made with bark): ML *rūsca*, bark: of C origin, presumably Gaulish—cf OIr *rúsc*, Ga *rùsg*, Cor *rusc*, OC *rūsk-*.

**ruck** (1), a heap, the mediocre part of a crowd. See the 1st RICK, para 3.

**ruck** (2), a crease, whence the v: ON *hrukka*: f.a.e., WRINKLE.

**ruckus; ruction.**

The former, dial and sl, app blends *ruction*+*rumpus*; the latter, orig AIr, derives from the Irish insur*rection* of 1798 (The Ruction), the vowel *e* becoming *u* by assimilation to the preceding *u*.

**rud,** red (n), whence the fish **rudd.** See RED, para 2.

**rudder.** See the 3rd ROW.

**ruddle.** See RED, para 2.

**ruddock.** See RED, para 2, s.f.

**ruddy.** See RED, para 2.

**rude,** whence **rudeness; rudiment,** whence **rudimentary** (cf the F *rudimentaire*); **erudite, erudition.**

1. ME-E *rude* is adopted from MF, from L *rudis*, in the crude state, hence unpolished, gross: akin to L *rūdus*, crushed stones, debris: both, o.o.o.

2. *Rudis* has the LL derivative *rudīmentum*, incompetence, ignorance, hence an element or first principle of learning: prob influenced by *elementum* (cf ELEMENT). Hence later MF-F and, perh independently, E *rudiment*.

3. Also from *rudis* comes LL *ērudīre*, to form by training, with pp *ērudītus*, used also as adj: cf, sem, the LL *ēruderāre*, to clear of rubbish, (fig) to purify. Hence late MF-F *érudit*, f *érudite*, and, prob independently, E *erudite*. Derivative LL *ērudītiō*, o/s *ērudītiōn-*, yields late MF-F *érudition* and E *erudition*.

**rue** (1), the herb, is adopted from MF-F: L *rūta*: Gr *rhutē*: o.o.o.

**rue** (2), to feel regret or be repentant, also n 'regret' or 'compassion', whence **rueful; ruth,** pity, whence **ruthless.**

1. *Rue*, n, comes from OE *hrēow*, sorrow, itself from OE *hrēowan*, to cause sorrow to, whence, through ME *reouwen, rewen*, the E 'to *rue*': cf OFris *hriōwa*, OS *hreuwan, hrewan*, OHG *riuwan*, MHG *riuwen*, G *reuen.*

2. Akin to OE *hrēow* (cf OHG *hriuwa*, pain, MHG *riuwe*, sorry, G *Reue*, repentance), is OE *hrēowe*, var *hrēow*, sad, whence ME *reowthe, reuthe*, E *ruth*: cf ON *hrygth*, sorrow.

**ruff** (1), at cards. See TRIUMPH, para 3.

**ruff** (2), a wheel-shaped collar (C16–17), whence, from its 'collar' of feathers, a common sandpiper; hence 'to **ruff**', to arrange in, or as if in, a ruff, whence to disorder; **ruffle,** to make a ruff of, to cause wrinkles in, to discompose, to irritate, whence the n 'that which is ruffed or plaited or gathered'.

'A *ruff*' is app a shortening of 'a *ruffle*', from ME-E 'to *ruffle*': cf EFris *ruffeln*, LG *ruffelen*, to crumple: perh ult echoic. The group is sem confused and phon obscure.

**ruff** (3), a fish, ME *ruffe, rowe*, prob derives from ME *rough, rugh*: f.a.e., RAG, para 2.

**ruffian** (n, hence adj), orig a pimp: EF-F *rufian*, MF *rufien*: It *ruffiano*: o.o.o., but prob Gmc—cf MLG *ruffer*, a pimp. Prob akin is 'to *ruffle*', to become rough or turbulent, hence (*ruffle it*) to swagger, ME *ruffelen*, to brawl, to swagger, app of Gmc origin—cf LG *ruffeln*, freq of MLG *ruffen*, to fornicate. Hence agent *ruffler* and pa, vn *ruffling.*

**ruffle** (1), to wrinkle, and the originating n. See the 2nd RUFF and cf RIFFLE.

**ruffle** (2), to swagger. See RUFFIAN.

**rufous.** See RED, para 11.

**rug.** See RAG, para 1.

**Rugby** football, whence sl **rugger** (the Oxford *-er*), arose at *Rugby* School, situated at *Rugby* in Warwickshire: from *Rokebi*, from *Rocheberi*: prob '*Hroca's* burg' or fort. (Ekwall.)

**rugged.** See RAG, para 1.

**rugger.** See RUGBY.

**rugose, rugosity.** See RAG, para 4.

**ruin** (n and v); **ruinate** (adj and v), whence **ruination; ruinous.**

*Ruinous* derives from OF-MF *ruineux*, f *ruineuse* (cf LL *ruīnōsus*), which, like MF-F *ruiner*, whence 'to *ruin*', comes from L *ruīna*, a falling or a crumbling, pl *ruīnae*, fallen or crumbled buildings, monuments, etc., in LL a Christian's downfall: from *ruere*, to fall in pieces, to crumble away, also vt, to cause to do this: L s and r, *ru-*: IE r, prob *ru-, to shatter.—*Ruīna* has the LL derivative *ruīnāre*, to crumble away, pp *ruīnātus*, whence the E adj and v ruinate, whence, anl, ruination.

rule, whence ruler (both agent and instrument) and ruling, pa and vn. See REX, para 16.

rum (1), adj. See ROME, para 10.

rum (2), n, the sugar-cane spirit, is short for the syn *rumbullion* (obs), app a var of the cant *rum booze*, excellent liquor: cf BOOZE.

Rumania, Rumanian. See ROME, para 9.

rumble, to make a low yet heavy, rolling sound, as thunder does, hence n, hence also the pa, vn rumbling: ME *romblen*: cf late MHG *rummelen* and MD-D *rommelen*: app freqq of a Gmc *rom-, *rum-, to make a noise, akin to L *rūmor* (cf RUMOR).—Hence rumble-tumble, a heavy cart, and prob rumble seat.

rumbustious. See ROBUST (heading).

Rumelia. See ROME, para 9.

rumen, ruminant, ruminate (adj, v), rumination (whence, anl, ruminative), ruminator.

*Rumen* is adopted from L *rūmen*, the first stomach of cud-chewers, also the belly, a gullet: o.o.o.: perh cf Akk *rimmu*, (?) womb. Now, *rūmen* has o/s *rūmin-*, whence *rūmināri* (occ *-āre*), to chew the cud, with presp *rūminans*, o/s *rūminant-*, whence E, and EF-F, *ruminant*, adj hence n, and with pp *rūminātus*, whence both the adj and the v ruminate; derivatives L *rūminātiō*, o/s *rūminā-tiōn-*, and LL *rūminātor* become MF-F and E rumination and E ruminator.

rummage, n hence v, is aphetic for MF *arrumage* (F *arrimage*), from *arrumer*, to stow goods, esp in a ship's hold, varr *arumer*, *aruner*, *arruner*: from MF *run*, a ship's hold, from Gmc *rūm*, as in OHG(-MHG) *rūm* (G *Raum*), and OE, ON *rūm*, a space: cf *room* at the 2nd REAM.

rummy, strange also the card-game. See ROME, heading, s.f.

rumor, rumour; rumorous.

The adj *rumorous* derives from MF *rumoreux*, f *-euse*, itself from MF *rumor*, var *rumour* (cf the F *rumeur*), whence the AE rumor and the E rumour: L *rūmor*. Akin to L *rūmor* are Skt *ráuti*, he roars or shouts, OSl *rjuti*, to cry, Gr *ōruomai*, I roar or yell; IE r, *reu- or *rū-, to cry or shout. —Cf rune at RAUCITY, para 2.

rump: ME *rumpe*, of Gmc origin: cf MHG-G *rumpf*, trunk, rump, MD *rump* (D *romp*).

rumple. See RAMP, para 3.

rumpus is o.o.o.: perh orig University sl, from Gr *rhombos*, a bull-roarer, kettle-drum, spinning-top. (EW.)

run, v, hence n (cf OE *ryne*); hence also runner and pa, vn running and such obvious cpds as runaround, runaway, run-on, runway, etc., and as outrun.—Cf RUNNEL below.

1. 'To *run*' comes prob from ME *runnen* (var *ronnen*), pp of *rinnen*, var *rennen*, pt *ran*, from OE *rinnan*; but perh, in part, from OFris: cf OS, OHG, Go *rinnan*, ON *rinna*, OFris *renna*, *rinna*, *runna*, to run, to flow; cf more remotely OSl *roniti*, to pour out, and Skt *arṇas*, a wave a stream. The exact

sem and phon originations and interactions are at once complicated and obscure.

2. ME *rennen* has derivative *rennet*, extant in E: cf OE *gerinnan* (int *ge-*), to curdle.

3. Prob akin to OE *rinnan*, to run, to flow, is L *rigāre*, to besprinkle, to water (e.g., a field), with cpd *irrigāre* (*ir-* for *in-* used int), pp *irrigātus*, whence 'to irrigate'; derivative *irrigātiō*, o/s *irrigātiōn-*, yields irrigation.

runagate, from ME *renegat*, from ML *renegātus*, a renegade (cf *renegade* at NEGATE, para 4), has, by f/e, been confused with 'to *run*' and the Sc and dial E adv *agate* (*a-*, on+*gate*, way), lit 'on the way', hence 'happening (amiss)'.

rune, whence the adj runic (cf the F *runique*). See RAUCITY, para 2.

rung, orig a staff, a cudgel, ME *ronge*, comes from OE *hrung*, a staff, a pole: cf Go *hrugga* (pron *hrunga*), a staff, MD *ronghe*, *ronge*, *runge*, *rung*, a prop, a rung, MHG-G *runge*, a rung; perh a nasalized cognate of L *crux*, a cross, o/s *cruc-*.

runic. See RUNE.

runnel, a rivulet: ME *rinnel*, *rinel*, form-influenced by 'to *run*'.

runner, running. See RUN.

runt, an undersized cow or ox, hence other domestic animal, comes from Sc *runt*, an old cow, hence an old withered woman, and is akin to MD *runt* (varr *rent*, *rint*), D *rund*, a cow, a bullock: nasalized cognates of OE *hrīther* (*hrȳther*), a horned beast, whence ME, whence dial E, *rother*, with which cf OHG *hrind*, MHG *rint*, G *Rind*, an ox. All these words prob derive from IE r *ker-*, horn (Walshe).

runway. See RUN (heading).

rupee; ruble or rouble.

1. The *rupee* or principal silver coin of India, derives from Hi *rūpiyah*, var *rupayā*: Skt *rūpya*, coined silver, from *rūpa*, form, shape.

2. Perh from Hi *rūpiyah*—? via Persia—comes the Ru *rubl'*, whence E *r(o)uble*.

Rupert. See ROBERT, para 1, s.f.

ruption, ruptive. See para 2 of:

rupture (n, hence v), ruption (whence, anl, ruptive); rout, a throng (obs), hence a fashionable assembly and a disordered flight; route (n, hence v), routine (n, hence adj).—Cpds in *-rupt*, *-ruption*, etc.: abrupt (whence abruptness), abruption: corrupt (adj, v), corruptible, corruption, corruptive; disrupt (adj, v), disruption (whence, anl, disruptive); erumpent, erupt, eruption (whence eruptive); interrupt, interruption (whence interruptive); irrupt, irruption (whence irruptive); prerupt; proruption.

1. All these terms rest upon L *rumpere* (s *rump-*), to break, pp *ruptus* (s *rupt-*): the r is *rup-*; *rump-* being a nasalization. The L word has cognates in Gmc, in Sl, in Skt.

2. On *rupt-*, s of the pp, L forms LL *ruptiō* (o/s *ruptiōn-*), a rupture, and ML *ruptūra*; whence E ruption and, perh via MF-F, rupture; also VL *rupta* (? for *turba rupta*), whence OF-MF route, a troop, a throng, whence the syn EE rout, whence

the E senses; also VL *rupta* (for *uia*—ML *via*— *rupta*), a broken, hence well-beaten, way, a customary road, whence MF-F *route*, adopted by E, with var *rut* soon acquiring a special sense. MF-F *route* has derivative EF-F *routine*, the following of a beaten track, likewise adopted by E.

## Compounds

3. L *abrumpere*, to break *ab* or off, pp *abruptus*, used also as n, yields the adj, whence the v, *abrupt*; derivative *abruptiō*, o/s *abruptiōn-*, yields *abruption*.

4. L *corrumpere*, to break entirely (*cor-* for *con-*, used int), hence to break up morally, has pp *corruptus*, whence the adj and v *corrupt*; from the derivative *corruptiō*, o/s *corruptiōn-*, comes OF-F *corruption*, adopted by E, and from the LL derivative *corruptibilis*, neg *incorruptibilis*, come *corruptible* and *incorruptible*; from LL *corruptiuus*, ML *-ivus*, E *corruptive*.

5. L *disrumpere*, to break *dis-* or asunder, has pp *disruptus*, whence the adj and v *disrupt*; from derivative L *disruptiō*, o/s *disruptiōn-*, E *disruption*.

6. L *ērumpere*, to bring out by breaking, esp in *sē ērumpere*, to precipitate oneself out from, hence to make a sortie, has presp *ērumpens*, o/s *ērumpent-*, whence the adj *erumpent*, and pp *ēruptus*, whence 'to *erupt*'; derivative *ēruptiō*, o/s *ēruptiōn-*, E *eruption* (cf MF-F *éruption*), whence anl—although cf the F *éruptif*—*eruptive*.

7. L *interrumpere*, to break between, to cut by breaking, hence fig, has pp *interruptus*, whence 'to *interrupt*'; derivative *interruptiō*, o/s *interruptiōn-*, becomes (MF-F and) E *interruption*.

8. L *inrumpere*, usu *irrumpere*, to break upon, to force an entry upon, to force the entrance of, has pp *irruptus*, whence 'to *irrupt*'; derivative *irruptiō*, o/s *irruptiōn-*, whence (late MF-F and) E *irruption*.

9. L *praerumpere*, to break (from) in front, has pp *praeruptus*, used as syn of *abruptus*: whence E *prerupt*, suddenly broken off, hence precipitous (cf the LL n *praeruptus*, gen *-ūs*, a steep precipice); derivative *praeruptiō*, o/s *praeruptiōn-*, rare E *preruption*.

10. L *prōrumpere*, to break violently *prō-* or to the front, has pp *prōruptus*, with LL derivative *prōruptiō*, o/s *prōruptiōn-*, rare E *proruption*.

**rural** (whence **ruralism** and **ruralize**), **rurality**, **Ruritania** (whence **Ruritanian**); **rus in urbe**; **rustic** (adj, hence n), **rusticate**, **rustication**, **rusticity**;— **roister**, n, hence v.

1. L *rūs* (gen *rūris*), country as opposed to town —cf *rus in urbe*, country in a city, i.e. a garden suburb—has r *rū-* and therefore is ult akin to Av *ravō*, an open space, and to the syn OHG *rūm* (cf *room* at the 2nd REAM).

2. *Rūs* has two adjj, the LL *rūrālis*, from the o/s *rūr-*, and the L *rūsticus*, from *rūs* itself. *Rūrālis*, becomes MF-F *rural*, adopted by E; the derivative ML *rūrālitās* yields *rurality*.

3. *Rūsticus* becomes MF-F *rustique* and E *rustic*; derivative LL *rūsticitās*, o/s *rūsticitāt-*, becomes late MF-F *rusticité* and E *rusticity*

4. *Rūsticus*, has, moreover, the derivative v *rūsticāri*, (of a townsman) to live in the country, with pp *rūsticātus*, whence 'to *rusticate*', whence the University sense; derivative L *rūsticātiō*, o/s *rūsticātiōn-*, becomes *rustication*.

5. Irreg from *rūsticus* comes OF-MF *ruste*, var *ruiste*, boorish, rough, violent, whence the MF n- extnn *rustre* and *ruistre*, the latter yielding EE-E *roister* (archaic), a noisy reveller, a brawler, whence EE-E 'to *roister*', whence a *roisterer*.

**ruse**, a trick, trickery: MF-F *ruse*, orig a hunting term: from OF *reüser*, MF-F *ruser*, orig to recoil or cause to recoil or give way or turn aside, hence in MF to make detours in order to throw dogs off the scent: (prob via a VL sense, from) L *recusāre*, to refuse. (B & W.) Cf the 2nd RUSH.

**rush** (1), the plant; **bulrush**.

*Bulrush* comes from ME *bulrysche*, *bolroysche*, a 'bole-rush' (a large rush): cf BOLE, stem. *Rush* itself comes from ME *rusch*, earlier *risch*, from OE *rysc* or *risc*: cf MHG *rusch*, *rusche*, and MLG *rusch*, *risch*, MD *rusch*, *ruysch*, *resch*, *risch*, D *rus*.

**rush** (2), to move violently or very hastily, whence n: ME *russhen*: AF *russher*, earlier *russer*: MF *ruser*: OF *reüser*: see RUSE.—Hence the pa, vn *rushing* and the agent *rusher*. Cf the 1st RUSTLE.

**rusk**: Sp *rosca*, a twist, or a roll, of bread, earlier something circular, earliest a turning-and-twisting machine; although existing also in Port and Cat, it is o.o.o.

**Russ; Russia**, whence **Russian**, adj hence n; **Ruthenia, Ruthenian, ruthenium**.

1. *Russ*, obs for a Russian, derives from F *Russe*, a Russian (adj *russe*): Ru *Rus'*, Russians, prob orig the Scandinavians wandering eastwards into Russia—cf Fin *Ruotsi*, Scandinavians. Also from Ru *Rus'* come F la *Russie*, It and E *Russia*, whence *Russian*.

2. In ML, the Russians were *Rutheni*, whence *Ruthenia* (territorial *-ia*), orig Russia, whence both E *Ruthenian* and Chem *ruthenium*, an element present in a metal discovered in the Ural Mountains.

**russet**. See RED, para 4.

**Russia, Russian**. See RUSS, para 1.

**rust**. See RED, para 3.

**rustic, rusticate, rustication, rusticity**. See RURAL, paras 3 and 4.

**rustle** (1), to sound as dry leaves moving, hence the n *rustle* and the pa, vn *rustling*: ME *rustle* or *rustel*, prob earliest *rouschel*: echoic: cf D *ritselen*, to rustle, MD *rutselen*, to glide, and MHG *riuschen*, *ruschen*, G *rauschen*, to rustle, to roar, to rush, and, ult, Skt *rṓṣati*, is angry: *rustle*, therefore, is prob a freq of 'to RUSH'.

**rustle** (2), AE sl for 'to act energetically', hence 'to obtain thus', whence **rustler**: a blend of *rush* and *hustle*.

**rusty**. See RED, para 3.

**rut** (1), a well-worn track, hence a regular, monotonous course. See RUPTURE, para 3.

**rut** (2), sexual impulse, esp the season thereof, in quadrupeds, hence v: EF-F *rut*, modern sense:

MF *ruit*, sexual roaring, bellowing, lowing: OF *ruit*, roaring, bellowing: L *rugītus*, a roaring, etc.: from *rugīre*, to roar: echoic.—Cf RIOT.

**ruth**, pity. See the 2nd RUE, para 2.

**Ruthenia, Ruthenian, ruthenium.** See RUSS, para 2.

**ruthless.** See the 2nd RUE, para 2.

**rutilant, rutile.** See RED, para 12.

**ryal.** See REX, para 4.

**rye** (1), the cereal: ME *ry*, *rie*, *reye*: OE *ryge*, akin to OFris *rogga*, OS *roggo*, OHG *roggo*, *rocco*, MHG *rocke*, G *Roggen*; to ON *rugr*; to Lith *rugys*, pl *rugiai*, with Ru and OB cognates.

**rye** (2), Gypsy for 'gentleman': Romany *rei*, *rai*, lord: cf *raja* at REX, para 35.

# S

*s*, 'the whispering and hissing letter', occurs initially in many echoic words; as a final, *-s* denotes the nom sing of a vast number of IE adjj and nn. This letter comes, via L, from Gr from Phoen (cf H *shīn*): see esp Walshe.

**Saba, Sabaean.** See SHEBA.

**Sabbath, Sabbatarian** (n, hence adj); **Sabbatic**—now usu in extn **Sabbatical**, whence **sabbatical**—**Sabbatism; sabbat.**

1. From H *shābath*, to rest, comes *shabbāth*, rest, esp the Jewish weekly day of rest: LGr *sabbaton*: LL *sabbatum*: both OF and OE *sabat*: MF-F *sabbat* and ME *sabat, sabath*: E *Sabbath*, the Christian day of rest; the LL n *sabbatārius* yields the E n *Sabbatarian*.

2. LGr *sabbaton* has adj *sabbatikos*: LL *sabbaticus*: EF-F *sabbatique* and E *Sabbatic*. The *Sabbath* falling on every seventh day, *Sabbatical* becomes *sabbatical*, as in *sabbatical year, s. leave of absence*.

3. LGr *sabbaton* has v *sabbatizein*, to observe the day of rest: LL *sabbatizāre*: E 'to *Sabbatize*'; LGr *sabbatizein* has derivative *sabbatismos*, whence LL *sabbatismus*, E *Sabbatism*.

4. In MF, *sabbat* acquires the sense 'witches' nocturnal gathering', adopted by E, which, however, prefers *witches' Sabbath*.

**saber.** See SABRE.

**Sabir.** See the 1st SAGE, para 7.

**sable; zibeline.** *Sable* is adopted from OF-F *sable* (cf MHG-G *zobel*), the animal, hence the fur: ML *sabellum*: of Sl origin—cf Pol *sabol*, Ru *sobol'*. The syn *zibeline* is likewise adopted from EF-F *zibeline*, MF *sibeline* (cf the OF *sebelin*), from It *zibellino*, also of Sl origin. (B & W.)

**sabot** and **savate; sabotage** (n, hence v). *Sabot*, a wooden shoe, is adopted from MF-F *sabot*, OF *çabot*, and blends OF-F *savate*+OF-MF *bot* (MF-F *botte*),two forms of shoe. *Sabot* has derivative MF-F *saboter*, to knock with the foot, hence to shake or torment, hence to work carelessly, whence F *sabotage*, adopted by E.

**sabre,** AE **saber,** whence the **sabre-** (or **saber-**) **toothed tiger; shabble.**

1. *Sabre*, whence *saber*, is adopted from EF-F *sabre* (occ EF var, *sable*): G *Sabel* (now *Säbel*): late MHG *sabel*, var *sebel*: prob from Hu *száblya* (from *szabni*, to cut), perh via Pol *szabla*: cf Ru *sablya*.

2. The now only Sc *shabble*, a cutlass, esp if old

and rusty, hence—? influenced by *shabby*—an inferior thing or contemptible person, prob comes from the Pol rather than from the Hu form.

**sac** and **sack** (n, hence v); **sackcloth and ashes; sachet** and **satchel;** cf the element *sacci- (sacco-)*.

1. The source is Sem, prob H *saq*, a hair-shirt, also a bag (cf Ass *chaqqu*, shirt, and Sumerian *shagadu*, an under-garment): Gr *sakkos* (s *sakk-*, r *sak-*): L *saccus* (s *sacc-*, r *sac-*): whence both OF-F *sac*, adopted by E, esp in its Sci senses, and OE *sacc*, ME *sacke*, E *sack*, a large, oblong bag. 'To *get the sack*,' to be dismissed from one's job, prob arises from the dismissed person's stuffing his clothes into a sack. Hence 'to *sack*'.

2. *Sackcloth and ashes* is (the, orig Biblical, wearing of) *sackcloth*—a coarse cloth—next to the skin and ashes on one's brow, as a penance: app a trans of LL *saccus et cinis*.

3. OF *sac* has OF(-F) dim *sachet*, finally adopted by E; L *saccus* has dim *saccellus*, whence OF-MF *sachel*, adopted by ME and then, in E, adapted as *satchel*.

**saccharate, saccharic, saccharin** or **saccharine, saccharinic.** See SUGAR, paras 2 and 3.

**sacellum.** See SACRAMENT, para 4.

**sacerdotal,** whence **sacerdotalism.** See SACRAMENT, para 8.

**sachem** and **Grand Sachem; sagamore.** Orig a supreme chief among the Algonquins, hence, in AE, a political chief, *sachem* is an Alg word: cf esp Narragansett *sâchimau*. Hence *the Grand Sachem* or the head of Tammany.—Akin is *sagamore*, prop, in Abnaki (Alg), the chief of a tribe. (Mathews.)

**sachet.** See SAC, para 3.

**sack** (1), a large, oblong bag. See SAC, para 1.

**sack** (2), a strong, white wine: earlier *seck*, for *wyne seck*, dry wine: EF-F *vin sec*: L *siccus*, dry.

**sack** (3), pillage, of, e.g. a city, after capture, hence the v: late MF-F *sac*: It *sacco*: prob from ML *saccāre*, VL *\*saccāre*, to pillage, from putting the plunder into a *saccus* or sack.

**sackcloth.** See SAC, para 2.

**sacral.** See para 4 of:

**sacrament, sacramental** (whence **sacramentalism**); **sacramentarian, sacramentary; sacrarium; sacred,** whence **sacredness; sacerdotal; sacrifice** (n, hence v), whence **sacrificial; sacrilege,** whence **sacrilegious; sacring** and **sacring bell; sacrist, sacristan, sacristy**—cf **sexton;** (os) **sacrum, sacral; sacellum;**

—sanct, sancta, sanctum, Sanctus; sanctimony, whence sanctimonious; sanction (n, hence v); sanctitude and sanctity; sanctuary; sanctify, sanctification; saint (n, hence v), whence saintly; San—Santo, Santa—Sao; sainfoin.—sacrosanct, whence, anl, sacrosanctity.—Prefix-cpds from L *sacrāre*, to consecrate: consecrate (adj, v), consecration (whence, anl, consecrative and consecratory), consecrator; desecrate, whence, anl, desecration and desecrator and desecratory; execrable, execrate, execration (whence, anl, execrative and execratory), execrator; obsecrate, obsecration (whence, anl, obsecratory), obsecrator.

### L *sacer*

1. L *sacer* is primarily 'sacred'; hence—for that which violates the sacred is accursed—'accursed'; whence the double sense of F *sacré*. The L word has cognates in the ancient Italic languages and also in Etruscan (the prob origin).

2. L *sacer*, o/s *sacr-*, has many derivatives and cpds, e.g. *sacramentum*, a deposit made to the Gods, hence, from the accompanying oath, an oath, whence, in LL, the Christian sense: whence OF-MF *sacrament*, MF-F *sacrement*: both adopted by ME, the former surviving. Derivative LL *sacramentālis* yields *sacramental* (also in EF); ML *sacramentārius*, agent, becomes E *sacramentary*, as also does LL-ML *sacramentārium*, a service book, these two L words deriving from adj *\*sacramentārius*.

3. Also from L *sacr-* comes *sacrārium*, a shrine, with Christian senses in LL-ML, adopted by Eccl E.

4. *Sacer* has neu *sacrum*, as in Med L *os sacrum*, the lowest spinal vertebra, whence Med E *sacrum*, whence, via Med L *sacrālis*, the adj *sacral*. L *sacrum*, a sacred place, has dim *sacellum*, adopted by Eccl E, with sense 'a small chapel'.

5. *Sacer* has derivative v *sacrāre*, to treat as, to render, sacred, whence OF-F *sacrer*, ME *sacren*, pp *sacred*, whence the adj *sacred*. For the cpds of *sacrāre*, see paras 8–10 below; ME *sacren* becomes 'to *sacre*', whence the pa, vn *sacring*, as in *sacring bell*.

6. *Sacer* has ML agent *sacrista*, whence the now rare *sacrist*, a sacristan: and *sacristan* itself derives from ME *sacristane* (cf the EF-F *sacristain*)—from ML *sacris ānus*, prop the adj of *sacrista*, which, moreover, has the *-ia* derivative *sacristia*, whence —perh via MF-F *sacristie*—the E *sacristy*.

7. ML *sacristānus* becomes MF *secrestein*, whence, irreg, the ME *sekesteyn*, contr to *sexteyn*, whence E *sexton*.

8. *Sacer* has three important full cpds: *sacerdōs*, a priest; *sacrificium*, an offering to a god; *sacrilegus*, a stealer of sacred things. L *sacerdōs*—*sacer* +-*dōs*, from *dare*, to give, *dō*, I give, basically I place. Its adj *sacerdōtālis* becomes MF-F *sacerdotal*, adopted by E.

9. L *sacrificium* derives from *sacrificus*, sacrificial, from *sacrum facere*, to perform a sacred

ceremony; *sacrificium* becomes OF-F *sacrifice*, adopted by E.

10. L *sacrilegus*, a gatherer—hence a stealer—of sacred things=*sacri-*, c/f of *sacer*+-*legus*, from *legere*, to gather. *Sacrilegus* has derivative *sacrilegium*, whence OF-MF *sacrilege*, MF-F *sacrilège*, whence E *sacrilege*.

### L *sanctus*

11. L *sancīre*, to render sacred, hence inviolable, whence—cf the double sense of *sacer*—to proclaim execrable, hence to solemnly forbid, hence to punish. Basically, *sanc-* is a nasalized *sac-*. The derivative adj, from pp *sanctus*, rendered sacred or inviolable, is potent in E.

12. L *sanctus* becomes the now rare E adj *sanct* and the OF-F adj *saint*, adopted by E; both F and E soon became also n. L *sanctus* becomes It *santo*, f *santa*; Sp *San*; Port *São*: all known to E from their occurrence in Pl Nn. L *sanctus*, from '*Sanctus, sanctus, sanctus*, Holy, holy, holy', in a Church service, is an Eccl E n; as is its f *sancta*; the neu *sanctum*, used for 'a holy place', becomes general E, after being Eccl LL-ML (as, e.g., in *sanctum Domini*, the Eucharist).

13. L *sanctus*, holy, has the foll derivatives relevant to E:

*sanctimōnia* (suffix *-mōnia*), MF-F *sanctimonie*, E *sanctimony*;

*sanctiō*, o/s *sanctiōn-*, MF-F and E *sanction*, with its double meaning;

*sanctitās*, o/s *sanctitāt-*, E *sanctity*—ME *saunctite*, *saintete*, from MF forms; syn *sanctitūdō* E *sanctitude*;

*sanctuārium*, a sacred place or depository: MF-F *sanctuaire* (OF *saintuaire*), E *sanctuary*;

the LL cpd *sanctificāre*, to render holy, MF *sanctifier* (OF-MF *saintifier*), E *sanctify*; pp *sanctificātus*, whence LL *sanctificatiō*, o/s *-ficātiōn-*, OF-F, whence E, *sanctification*;

*sacrosanctus*, both sacred and holy, whence E *sacrosanct* and EF-F *sacro-saint*.

14. The OF-F adj *saint* has—by confusion with *sain* (L *sānus*), healthy—the cpd EF-F *sainfoin* (*foin*, L *fēnum*, hay), adopted by E; but perh *sain*, healthy, is the correct 1st element, the spelling *sainct-foin* (1549) coming from confusion with MF *sainct*. (B & W.)

### Prefix-Compounds of L *sacrāre*

15. L *sacrāre*, to render sacred, has several cpds affecting E. The first is *consacrāre*, usu *consecrāre* (*con-* vaguely int), to consecrate, with pp *consecrātus*, whence adj and v *consecrate*; derivative *consecrātiō*, o/s.*consecrātiōn-*, OF-MF *consecration* (MF-F *consé-*), adopted by E; LL *consecrātor*, adopted by E.

16. L *dēsacrāre*, usu *dēsecrāre*, to desecrate, has pp *dēsecrātus*, whence the adj and v *desecrate*.

17. L *exsecrāre*, often in the eased form *execrāre*, to execrate, has derivative *exsecrābilis*, *execrābilis*, whence *execrable* (cf late MF-F *exécrable*); the pp *exsecrātus*, *execrātus*, yields the adj and v

*execrate*; derivative *ex(s)ecrātiō*, o/s *ex(s)ecrātiōn-*, yields *execration*, perh via MF-F *exécration*; LL *ex(s)ecrātor* is adopted by E.

18. L *obsecrāre*, to ask for religious reasons or in the name of the gods, has pp *obsecrātus*, whence 'to *obsecrate*'; derivatives L *obsecrātiō* and LL *obsecrātor* become E *obsecration*, *obsecrator*.

**sacrarium.** See prec, para 3.

**sacre.** See SACRAMENT, para 5.

**sacred.** See SACRAMENT, para 5.

**sacrifice, sacrificial.** See SACRAMENT, para 9.

**sacrilege, sacrilegious.** See SACRAMENT, para 10.

**sacrist, sacristan, sacristy.** See SACRAMENT, para 6.

**sacrosanct.** See SACRAMENT, para 13.

**sacrum.** See SACRAMENT, para 4.

**sad,** whence **sadden, sadly, sadness,** derives from ME *sad*, sated, tired, satisfied, from OE *saed*, sated, satisfied: cf OS *sad*, OHG-MHG *sat*, G *satt*, Go *saths*, ON *saddr*, *sathr*, OIr and Ga *sathach* (cf EIr and Ga *sàith*, Ga *sath*, plenty, enough), L *sat*, *satis*, enough, *satur*, sated; various Sl, Gr, Skt cognates; IE r, *sā-*, *sa-*.

2. 'To *sate*' is app a contr of *satiate*, which derives from L *satiātus*, pp of *satiāre*, to provide with enough, hence with more than enough (gluttony exceeding capacity), from *sati-*, c/f of *satis*, enough. Also from *sati-* comes L *satietās*, acc *satietātem*, whence OF-F *satiété*, whence E *satiety*.

3. The pp *satiātus*, used as adj, has neg *insatiātus*, whence *insatiate*. The cognate LL *satiābilis* yields *satiable*; the neg *insatiābilis*, MF-F *insatiable*, adopted by E; derivative LL *insatiabilitās* (o/s *-itāt-*) becomes *insatiability*.

4. The L c/f *sati-* has var *satu-*, attested by *satur*, replete or sated with food; the f *satura*, used elliptically for *satura lanx* (a composite dish), becomes *satira*, a macédoine of fruits or vegetables or a composite dish of meats, hence a mixed literary composition, esp the satires of Horace and Juvenal: whence MF-F *satire*, adopted by E; the derivative L adj *satiricus* yields late MF-F *satirique*, whence E *satiric*, often in the extn *satirical*; anl *satirist* and *satirize* perh owe something to F *satiriste* and EF-F *satiriser*.

5. L *satur*, replete, has derivative *saturāre*, to fill with food, to render replete or sated, to satisfy utterly, later to dye richly, to smear, pp *saturātus*, whence the adj and v *saturate*; derivative LL *saturātiō*, o/s *saturātiōn-*, gives *saturation*. The presp *saturans*, o/s *saturant-*, explains the Sci adj, hence n, *saturant*.

6. L *satis* has the cpd *satisfacere*, to do, or give, enough for or to someone, which leads to MF *satisfier* (displaced by *satisfaire*), whence 'to *satisfy*'; derivative L *satisfactiō*, acc *satisfactiōnem*, produces OF-F *satisfaction*, adopted by E; LL *satisfactōrius*, yielding satisfaction, penitential, becomes the Theo MF-F *satisfactoire*, whence E *satisfactory*, with secular senses added (cf the F *satisfaisant*). *Dissatisfy*, whence, anl, *dissatisfac-*

*tion*, and *unsatisfied* (cf F *insatisfait*), are E formations.

7. VL coins the phrase *ad satis*, enough, much, whence OF-F *assez*, enough, (until C16) much: OF-MF var *asez*, whence AF *asetz*, esp in the Law term *aver assets*, to have, hence own, enough (to pay one's debts and meet one's other obligations): whence *assets*, one's realizable property.

**saddle,** n and v (whence **saddler, saddlery, saddling**), whence **unsaddle.** 'To *saddle*' comes from OE *sadelian*, from OE *sadol*, whence ME *sadel*, E *saddle*: and OE *sadol* is akin to OFris *sadel*, MD *sadel*, D *zadel* (cf MD *sadelen*, to saddle), OHG *satul*, MHG *satel*, G *Sattel*, ON *söthull*; prob to OB *sedlo* and therefore to L *sella*, hence to E *settle* and *sit*.

2. Most of the cpds are modern; note, however, *saddlebow*, ME *sadelbowe*, OE *sadulboga*—cf G *Sattelbogen*, OHG *satilpogo*.

**sadism, sadist, sadistic.** See MASOCHISM.

**sadly, sadness.** See SAD (heading).

**safari,** basically an expedition, hence esp for hunting, derives ult from an Ar adj (connoted by *-i*) for 'of, for, on, by a journey or travel', but imm from Swahili *safari*, journey, expedition, esp when used for *msafara*, a hunting exped tion—cf Swahili *safiri*, to go on an expedition.

**safe** (adj, hence n), **safe-conduct, safeguard, safety; sage** plant; **save** (v and prep), **savings, saviour; salvable, salvage** (n, hence v), **salvation, salvatory, salve** (to save), **salver, salvo;—salutary, salutation, salutatory** (adj, n), **salute** (n, v);—**salubrious, salubrity.**—Akin to the sep SOLID, SOLEMN, SOLICIT—and to *holism* (cf *catholic*).

1. *Safe* derives from ME *sauf*, adopted from OF-F *sauf* (f *sauve*): ML *salvus*, L *saluus*, entire, intact, with moral senses added by LL-ML: akin to L *salūs*, good health, safety, *salūbris*, wholesome, salutary, *sollus*, entire, *solidus*, solid, resistant; Gr *holos*, entire; Skt *sárvas*, entire, intact.

2. L *saluus*, ML *salvus*, has the ML derivative n *salvitās*, acc *salvitātem*, whence OF-EF *salveté*, var *sauveté*, whence E *safety*, and the LL derivative v *saluāre*, ML *salvāre*, to save, to heal, whence both 'to *salve*', to provide an explanation of, hence to justify, hence also to maintain one's honour, promise, credit, etc., and OF *salver*, MF-F *sauver*, E 'to *save*', whence the pa, vn *saving*, whence *savings*.

3. Of the *safe* cpds, two are worth noting: *safe-conduct*, from OF-F *sauf-conduit*; *safeguard* (n, hence v), from MF-F *sauvegarde*, whence the F v *sauvegarder*: cf WARD, para 10.

4. L *saluus* has derivative *saluia*, ML *salvia*, from its—at least reputed—medicinal properties: whence MF-F *sauge*, E *sage*.

5. Other derivatives of *saluus*, ML *salvus*, affecting E include:

*ML *salvābilis*, salvable, OF-EF, whence E, *salvable*, prob owing something to 'to *salve*' (para 2 above);

ML *salvagium*, late MF-F *salvage*, adopted by E; LL *saluātiō*, o/s *saluātiōn-*, ML *salvātiōn-*, whence OF-F *salvation*, adopted by E, with its own subsidiaries *salvationism*, *salvationist*;

LL *saluātor*, a saver or rescuer, *Saluātor*, ML *Salvātor*, the Redeemer, whence OF *salveor*, MF *sauveor* (*-eour*), var *saveor* (*-eour*), ME *saveour*, *saviour*, whence E *saviour*, AE *savior*, esp *the Savio(u)r*;

LL *saluatōrium*, deliverance, ML *salvatōrium*, a receptacle (esp for ointment), E *salvatory*; from the assumed L adj *saluatōrius* comes the E adj *salvatory*.

6. LL *saluāre*, ML *salvāre*, becomes Sp *salvar*, with special sense 'to taste' the food and drink of royalty and nobility before they do: whence Sp *salva*, such tasting, whence a salver: whence late EF-F *salve*: E *salver*. And from ML *salvo jure*, law (hence, a right) being safe, comes the now rare E *salvo*, a proviso, safeguard; but a military *salvo* comes from It *salva*, a salute, hence a volley, prob from ML *Salve* (L *Salue*), Hail!, the voc of *salvus* (L *saluus*), safe, unharmed, well, apprehended as the imp of *saluēre*, to be well.

### L *salūs*, (good) health, safety

7. As L *saluus* has s *salu-*, so has L *salūs*, o/s *salūt-*. The adj of *salūs* is *salūtāris*, whence MF-F *salutaire* and E *salutary*. Also from *salūs* comes *salūtāre*, to wish good health to, hence to greet, with pp *salūtātus*, whence both *salūtātiō*, o/s *salūtātiōn-*, whence late MF-F *salutation*, adopted by E, and LL *salūtātōrius*, whence E *salutatory*. L *salūtāre* yields 'to salute'; a *salute* derives from MF-F *salut*, from L *salūtem*, acc of *salūs*.

### L *salūber*, healthy

8. Also from *salūs* comes *salūber*, var *salūbris*, whence late MF-F *salubre* and E *salubrious*; derivative *salūbritās*, acc *salūbritātem*, yields late MF-F *salubrité* and E *salubrity*.

**saffron, safranine, safrole; zaffer** or **zaffre.** *Saffron*, ME *saffran*, derives from OF-F *safran*: ML *safranum*: Ar-Per *za'faran*—cf Ar *aṣfar*, yellow. The ML form suggested the Chem *saffranin* or *saffranine*; the F, *safrol* or *safrole*: cf the Chem suffixes *-in*, *-ine*, and *-ol*.

2. Influenced by the 'saffron' words is *zaffer* or *zaffre*, an impure cobalt oxide: either F *zafre* or It *zaffera*: Ar *ṣufr*, yellow copper.

**sag** (v, hence n), whence pa, vn **sagging**: late ME *saggen*: cf MLG-LG *sacken*, D *zakken*, with Scan cognates: ? ult echoic.

**saga.** See SAY, para 2.

**sagamore.** See SACHEM, s.f.

**sage** (1), adj, hence n, is adopted from OF-F, which takes it from VL *\*sapius* (presupposed by Petronius's *nesapius*, imbecile), from L *sapidus*, pleasant to the taste, LL prudent, wise, itself from *sapere*, (of things) to have a pleasant taste, hence (of persons) to have good taste or judgement: IE r, *\*sap-* or *\*sep-*.

2. L *sapidus* yields E *sapid*, whence, anl, *sapidity*: cf the F *sapide* and *sapidité*. *Sapidus* has neg *insipidus*, tasteless, whence, perh via EF-F *insipide*,

the E *insipid*; derivative EF-F *insipidité* prob suggested *insipidity*.

3. L *sapere* has presp *sapiens* (also adj, as in *homo sapiens*), acc *sapientem*, whence OF-EF *sapient*, adopted by E; derivative L *sapientia* becomes OF-F *sapience* (archaic), adopted by E; *sapientia* acquires the LL adj *sapientiālis*, whence late EF-F and E *sapiential*.

4. L *sapere* has derivative n *sapor*, taste, savour, hence also sense of taste, whence LL *sapōrus*, extn *sapōrōsus*, pleasant to the taste, which app combine to yield E *saporous*; SciL coins *sapōrificus*, whence E *saporific*.

5. L *sapor*, acc *sapōrem*, becomes OF *savor*, MF *savor*, *savour* (F *saveur*), whence ME *savur*, *savour*, *savor*: E *savour*, AE *savor*. 'To savour' comes from MF-F *savourer*, MF-OF *savorer*, from *savor*. Whereas *savoury*, adj hence n, derives—perh influenced by LL *sapōrātus*—from MF-F *savouré* (OF *savoré*), pp of *savourer*, *savorous* derives from OF-MF *savoros*, var *-eros*, either from *savor* or direct from LL *sapōrōsus*.

6. L *sapere*, in its LL senses, became OF-F *savoir*, to know, as in late EF-F *savoir-faire*, a knowing how to act, and in late EF-F *savoir-vivre*, a knowing how to live, both—at least, partially—adopted by E. The OF-MF presp *savant* (superseded by *sachant*) soon became the n 'man of learning'; as such, adopted by E.

7. L *sapere*, in its LL senses, became Sp *saber*, to know, which, esp in the phrase *Sabe usted?*, Do you know, yields the sl n and v savvy. The Sp *saber* passes into Lingua Franca as *sabir*, which, esp in Molière's jargonic *Si ti sabir*, If you know, and, still more, in the Lingua Franca perfunctory phrase *Mi non sabir*, Me not know, has produced the Philological *Sabir*, the late Lingua Franca spoken in the ports of N Africa. (B & W.)

**sage** (2), the plant. See SAFE, para 4.

**sagitta**, whence **sagittal** and, via SciL, **sagittate**; **Sagittaria, Sagittarius.** *Sagittaria*, an aquatic herb, is a SciL derivative from the L adj *sagittārius*, of a *sagitta* or arrow, whence the Astr *Sagittarius*, the Archer: L *sagitta* is o.o.o.—? Scythian or Parthian.

**sago**, extracted from the sago palm of Malaya, derives from Mal *sāgū*.

**Sahara**: lit 'the desert', hence '*the* desert' (the world's largest): Ar *sahrā*, desert.

**sahib**: Hind *sāhib*: Ar *ṣāḥib*, *ṣaheb*, lord, master, companion.

**said.** See SAY (heading).

**sail** (n, v), whence pa, vn **sailing** and instr **sailer**, agent **sailor**.

'To *sail*' derives from OE *seglian*, *segelian*, from *segl*, or its var *segel*: cf OFris *seil*, as also in Da and MD (D *zeil*); OHG *segal*, MHG-G *segel*; ON *segl*: perh orig 'a cut piece of material', akin to L *secāre*, to cut. (Walshe.)—The cpds are self-explanatory.

**sain**, v. See SIGN, para 2.

**sainfoin.** See SACRAMENT, para 14.

**saint**, whence **saintly.** See SACRAMENT, para 12.

Saint Elmo's fire is named after the patron saint of sailors.

**Saint Vitus's dance.** See the 2nd GUY.

**sake,** a dispute, fault, obs, hence a purpose, a motive, a reason, hence an advantage or benefit ('for your *sake*'), derives from ME *sake*, lawsuit, fault: OE *sacu,* strife, lawsuit: cf OFris *sake, seke,* thing, matter, dispute, strife, OHG *sahha,* MHG *sache,* dispute, lawsuit, G *Sache,* thing, matter, Go *sakjō,* strife, MD *sake (zake), saec,* matter, lawsuit (D *zaak*), ON *sök,* lawsuit, guilt: f.a.e., SEEK. Cf also SEIZE.

2. OE *sacu* has v *sacan,* to contend (cf OFris *seka,* Go *sakan,* to quarrel, ON *saka,* to contend, to accuse), with cpd *forsacan,* to oppose (*for-*, against), whence 'to *forsake*', pt *forsook,* pp *forsaken.*

**sal,** as in *sal volatile.* See SALT, paras 1 and 3.

**salaam.** See ISLAM.

**salacious, salacity.** See SALLY, para 2.

**salad.** See SALT, para 9.

**salamander:** OF-F *salamandre:* L from Gr *salamandra:* o.o.o. The Myth sense arose with Paracelsus in C16: its fire-defying properties originated the 'stove' sense.

**salary.** See SALT, para 4.

**sale,** whence **salesman** (*sale's man*); **sell,** pt and pp **sold; handsel.**

1. *Sale,* late OE *sala,* is adopted from ON *sala.* Akin is 'to *sell*', ME *selle,* varr *sillen, sellen,* OE *sellan, syllan,* to deliver, to sell: cf OHG *sala,* n, and *sellen,* v, and the vv OFris *sella,* OS *sellian,* to deliver, sell. Go *saljan,* to offer a sacrifice, ON *selja,* to sell; perh cf LGr *helō,* I shall take, Gr *heilon,* I took; perh also EIr *selb,* Ga *seilbh,* W *helw,* property. IE r, perh *\*kel-,* to take.

2. ON *sala* has var *sal,* sale, bargain, with cpd *handsal,* lit a 'hand-sale', hands being clasped to seal the bargain: whence E *handsel,* often eased to *hansel.*

**saleratus.** See SALT, para 3, s.f.

**salicin(e).** See SALLOW, para 1, s.f.

**salience, salient.** See SALLY, para 3.

**salina.** See SALT, para 3.

**saline, salinity.** See SALT, para 3.

**saliva, salivary.** See para 2 of:

**sallow,** adj and n; **salicin(e), Salix; saliva, salivary, salivate, salivation, salivous.**

1. The adj *sallow,* pale reddish-yellow, OE *salu,* is akin to OHG *salo,* MD *salu, saluw,* D *zaluw,* Ice *sölr,* dirty-yellow. Both phon and sem akin to OE *salu* is OE *sealh,* ME *salwe,* later *sallow,* a broad-leaved willow: cf OHG *salaha* (G *Salweide,* from the OHG var *salewīda*), MHG *salhe,* ON *selja,* OIr *sail,* L *salix.* The L word, adopted by Bot, has o/s *salic-,* whence Chem *salicin(e)* and *salicyl.*

2. Perh akin to L *salix,* willow (and OE *salu,* sallow) is L *salīua,* ML *salīva,* the fluid secreted in the mouth; hence E *saliva.* L *salīua* has adjj *salīuārius* and *salīuōsus*—ML *salīvārius* and *salī-vōsus*: E *salivary* (cf EF-F *salivaire*) and *salivous.* *Salīua* has derivative v *salīuare,* pp *salīuātus,* ML

*salivātus,* whence 'to *salivate*'; derivative *salīuātiō,* o/s *salīuātiōn-,* ML *salīvātiōn-,* yields EF-F and E *salivation.*

**sally,** n hence v; **salience, salient** (adj, hence n); **salacious, salacity; salmon; saltant, saltate, salta-tion, saltator, saltatory; saltier, saltire; saltigrade, saltimbanco.**—Prefix-cpds: **assail, assailant, assail-ment**—assault, n and v; **desultor, desultory; exile, n, v**—**exult, exultance or -cy, exultant, exultation; insult** (n, v—whence **insulting), insultation**—**in-solence, insolent; resile, resilience, resilient, resilium** (whence the adj **resilial**)—**result** (v, hence n), **resultant** (whence **resultance**), whence, anl, **resulta-tive; somersault** (n, hence v).

1. All these words descend from *sal-,* the s and r of L *salīre,* to leap; its c/f is *-silīre,* as in *exile* and *resile*; its freq is *saltāre,* which has c/f *-sultāre,* as in *exult* and *insult*; *-sail,* for L *salīre,* arises in F, i.e. at an intermediary stage. Akin to *salīre* are Gr *hallesthai,* to leap, and Skt uc*ha*lati, he leaps up: IE r, *\*sal-* or *\*sel-,* to leap.

*L salīre*

2. *Salīre,* s *sal-,* to leap, hence to gush forth and, vt, (of quadrupeds) to cover the female, has adj *salāx,* lustful, o/s *salāc-,* whence EF-F *salace* and E *salacious*; derivative L *salācitās,* o/s *salācitāt-,* yields EF-F *salacité* and, prob independently, E *salacity.*

3. L *salīre* has presp *saliens,* o/s *salient-,* whence E *salient,* whence *salience.*

4. *Salīre* becomes OF-F *saillir,* whence the MF-F n *saillie,* whence E *sally.*

5. Prob akin to L *salīre,* r *sal-,* is L *salmō* (*salm-,* an *-m* extn of *sal-*), a salmon, acc *salmōnem,* whence MF-F *saumon,* ME *saumoun,* later, by a reshaping, *salmon.* The salmon is a 'leaper'.

*L saltāre*

6. L *saltāre,* to leap repeatedly, hence to dance, has presp *saltans,* o/s *saltānt-,* whence Her *saltant,* and pp *saltātus,* whence 'to *saltate*'; L derivatives *saltātiō,* o/s *saltātiōn-, saltātor, saltātōrius,* yield E *saltation, saltator* (esp in Zoo), *saltatory* (whence *saltatorial*). L *saltātōrius* has the ML derivative *saltātōrium,* a stirrup, whence MF-F *sautoir,* an Her term that becomes E *saltire* or *saltier.*

7. Both L *saltāre* and L *saltus,* a leap (from *salīre*), have, although not occurring in L itself, the c/f *salti-: saltigrade,* having legs suitable for leaping—cf GRADE; *saltimbank* or *-banque* or *-banco,* the 1st anglicizing the 2nd, adopted from EF-F, the 2nd gallicizing the 3rd, which is It, lit (he who) leaps on a *banco* or bench.

8. L *saltus,* a leap, combines with L *supra,* above, to form Sp *sobresalto,* whence—rather than from Prov *sobresaut* or MF-F *soubresaut*—the E *somer-sault,* dial var *summerset.*

Prefix-Compounds from *-silīre*

9. L *salīre* has the foll cpds affecting E: *assilīre, dēsilīre, \*exsilīre, resilīre.* Assilīre, to leap *ad* or at, upon, becomes VL *\*assalīre,* whence

OF *asalir*, MF *asaillir* (F *assaillir*), whence ME *asailen*, E 'to *assail*'; the presp OF *asalant*, MF *asaillant*, later *assaillant*, is adopted by E. The MF *assaillement* becomes E *assailment* (obs).

10. Akin to L *assilīre* is L *assultus* (*ad*+*saltus*, gen -*ūs*, a leap, a leaping), whence VL *\*assaltus*, whence OF-MF *assalt*, MF *assault* (MF-F *assaut*), whence, via ME, the E *assault*; 'to *assault*' derives from MF *assalter*, *assaulter* (from the n).

11. L *dēsilīre*, to leap *de-* or down, supine *dēsultum*, has agent *dēsultor*, adopted by erudite E for 'a circus rider leaping from horse to horse'. Also from the supine s *dēsult-* comes the adj *dēsultōrius*, leaping about, unsteady, whence E *desultory*.

12. L *\*exsilīre* has prompted LL *exsiliāre*, often eased to *exiliāre*, to drive out, to banish, whence MF *essillier* (var *eissillier*), whence the reshaped EF-F *exiler*, whence 'to *exile*'; the ME-E n *exile* comes from MF *exil*, a reshaping of OF *essil*, var *eissil*, from L *exilium*, an easing of *exsilium*, from *\*exsilīre*.

13. L *resilīre*, to leap back, to recoil, becomes EF *resilir* (later -*ir*), whence 'to *resile*', to recoil, to retract. The presp *resiliens*, o/s *resilient-*, yields *resilient*, whence *resilience*, var *resiliency*. From *resilīre*, SciL has coined the Zoo *resilium*.

### Prefix-Compounds from -*sultāre*

14. L *exsultāre*, usu eased to *exultāre*, to leap vigorously (*ex-* used int), hence to exult, becomes late MF-F *exulter*, whence 'to *exult*'; the L presp *exultans*, o/s *exultant-*, yields *exultant*.

15. L *insultāre*, to leap *in* or upon, to attack, becomes late MF-F *insulter*, whence 'to *insult*'; the derivative EF-F n *insulte*, deriving from the F v, displaces the late MF-EF *insult*, itself from LL *insultus*, deriving from *insult-*, the s of *insultum*, supine of *insilīre*, to leap upon, but influenced by Cicero's *insultāre*, to insult. The E n *insult* comes either from MF-EF *insult* or from LL *insultus*.

16. Perh akin to L *insultāre* is L *insolescere*, to be insolent, with presp *insolescens*, whence—? by contr—L *insolens*, o/s *insolent-*, whence E *insolent*; derivative L *insolentia* yields *insolence*. Cf the id F words. L *insolescere*, however, perh derives rather from *solēre*, to be accustomed (to do something).

17. L *resultāre*, to leap back, LL to rise again (cf LL *resultātiō*, a reverberation, an echo), ML to be or form a consequence, yields late MF-F *résulter* and E 'to *result*'; presp *resultans*, o/s *resultant-*, yields *resultant*, adj; the n *resultant* prob derives from Sci EF-F *résultante*.

**salmagundi**, a mixture of pickled herring and chopped meat: EF-F *salmigondis*: o.o.o.: Webster cfs It *salame*, salt meat (L *sal*, salt), and It, from L, *condire*, to pickle (cf CONDIMENT): I suggest that Rabelais's *salmigondin* is one of his verbal fantasias and that, in it, he playfully, arbitrarily mutilates the LL *salimuria* (Gr *halmuris*), sea-salt, hence brine, hence a pickle.

**salmon.** See SALLY, para 5.

**salon, saloon.** The latter, like the former, derives from late EF-F *salon*: It *salone*: aug of *sala*, a hall: It *sala*, like F *salle*, OF *sale*, is of Gmc origin: cf OHG-MHG *sal* (G *Saal*), ON *salr* (OE *sele*), hall, and Go *saljan*, to dwell: perh ult akin to L *sedēre*, to sit—cf SADDLE and SIT.

**Salopian** is the adj (hence n) of *Salop*, Shropshire: a shortening of late C11-12 *Salopescira*, a Normanized shape of Domesday Book *Sciropescire*, itself an alteration of C11 (and prob earlier) *Scrobbesbyrigscire*, 'the shire with Shrewsbury as its head' (Ekwall).

**salse.** See SALT, para 5.

**salsify:** EF-F *salsifis* (earliest—1600—as *sercifi*): C16 It *sassifrica* (It *sassefrica*), var of *salsefica*: C14 It (*erba*) *salsifica* (B & W): ? 'salt-making herb'—cf *salse* at SALT, para 5.

**salsilla.** See para 6 of:

**salt**, n (whence salty, whence saltiness) and adj, both leading to the v, whence salting, saltings; many cpds, e.g. saltbush (*salt*+*bush*), saltcellar (ME *salt seler*: taut from *salte*, salt+*seler*, var of *saler*, from MF-F *salière*, saltcellar, from L *sal*, salt), saltpan, saltpetre, AE saltpeter (see PETER, para 3), saltweed (cf WEED), saltwort (cf WORT); saltern;—sal volatile, saleratus; saline, whence salinity; salad; salary, whence salariat and salaried;—salse; salsilla; sauce (n, hence v), saucer; sausage; souse, a vinegar'd dish, whence the v;—silt (n, hence v), whence silty.—Cf the element *halo-*.

### E salt

1. *Salt*, adj, OE *salt*, var of *sealt*, app derives from the n *salt*, OE *sealt*: cf OFris *salt*, adj, OS, Go, ON *salt*, n, OHG-MHG-G *salz*, MD *sout*, D *zout*; EIr and Ga *sál*, salt-water, OIr *salann*, salt, Cor *sál*, *zál*, adj, and *salla*, *zalla*, n, W *hal*, salt, n, adj, with Chem n *halan*; Lett *sāls*, OB *solĭ*; Tokh B *sālyi*; L *sāl*; Gr *hals* (? for *\*sals*): cognates in Finno-Ugric (Walshe). IE r, *\*sal-*.

2. OE *sealt* has cpd *sealtaern*, *sealtern*, lit a salt-house (OE *aern*, *ern*): whence E *saltern*.

### L sāl

3. L *sāl*, salt, gen *salis*, occurs in such combinations as *sal ammoniac* (cf AMMONIA) and *sal volatile* (cf VOL). Its adj is *salīnus*, whence—perh via EF-F *salin*, f *saline*—the E *saline*. Salina, a salt-marsh, a depository of crystallized salt, a saltworks, is adopted from Sp, which draws it, by b/f, from the L pl *salīnae*, saltworks, from *salīnus*. From SciL *sāl aerātus*, aerated salt, comes *saleratus*.

4. L *sāl* has a second adj: *salārius*, relating to salt, with neu *salārium* used as n for 'sum of money paid to soldiers to enable them to purchase their salt', hence 'pay, wages': whence AF *salarie*, whence E *salary*.

5. L *sāl* has v *salere*, *salire*, to salt, with pp *salsus* used as adj 'salted, salty': whence It *salsa*, a mud volcano or volcanic spring, 'because often impregnated with salts' (Webster), whence F *salse*, adopted by E.

6. L *salsus* has f *salsa*, used by VL as n 'a salty

seasoning', hence 'a sauce'; adopted by Sp, *salsa* acquires the sense 'a kind of garlic', with dim *salsilla*, a WI and SAm plant.

7. The VL n *salsa* becomes OF *salse*, MF *sausse*, later *sauce*, adopted by E; late MF-F *saucer* perh suggested 'to sauce'. Derivative OF-MF *saussiere*, later *saucière*, yields E *saucer*.

8. L *salsus*, salted, has the VL derivative *salsīcius*, seasoned with salt, whence *salsīcia*, seasoned meal (cf LL *salsīcia farta*, sausages), whence OF-F *saucisse*, ONF *saussiche*, ME *sausige*, E *sausage*.

9. L *sāl* becomes Prov *sal*, whence *salar*, to salt, whence *salada*, a dish of salted vegetables, esp lettuce or cress, whence MF-F *salade*, whence E *salad*.

### OHG *salz*

10. Akin to OHG *salz*, salt (n), as in para 1, is OHG *sulz*, *sulza*, MHG *sülze*, salt water, G *Sülze*, brine, a pickle: whence OF *solz*, later *souz*, later *sous*, something pickled, whence the syn E *souse*, varr *souce*, *sowse*, whence the sense 'a steeping, a drenching'; hence 'to *souse*' or pickle, hence to drench or immerse.

11. Akin to OHG *sulza*, salt water, and *salz*, salt, is the Nor (dial) and Da *sylt*, a salt-water swamp, of the same origin—app Scan—as ME *sylt*, whence E *silt*.

**saltant, saltate, saltation, saltatory.** See SALLY, para 6.

**saltcellar.** See SALT (heading).

**saltern.** See SALT, para 2.

**saltier.** See SALLY, para 6, s.f.

**saltigrade.** See SALLY, para 7.

**saltimbanco, -bank, -banque.** See SALLY, para 7.

**saltire.** See SALLY, para 6, s.f.

**salpeter, -petre.** See PETER, para 3.

**salubrious, salubrity.** See SAFE, para 8.

**saluki:** Ar *salūqi*, of *Salūq*, an ancient S Arabian city.

**salutary.** See SAFE, para 7.

**salutation, salutatory, salute.** See SAFE, para 7.

**salvable.** See SAFE, para 5.

**salvage.** See SAFE, para 5.

**salvation.** See SAFE, para 5.

**salvatory.** See SAFE, para 5, s.f.

**salve** (1), a healing ointment: OE *sealf*: cf OHG *salba*, MHG-G *salbe*, LG *salwe*, D *zalf* (MD *salf*), and also Go *salbōn*, to anoint; Gr *olpē* (for *\*solpē*), an oil-bottle, *elpos*, oil, fat; Tokh A *ṣälyp*, Tokh B *ṣalype*, fat, butter, oil,; Skt *sárpiš*, grease, clarified butter. IE r, *\*selp-*, fat, oil. (Hofmann.)

**salve** (2), to explain, justify, save. See SAFE, para 2.

**salver**, tray. See SAFE, para 6.

**salvo.** See SAFE, para 6.

**Sam**, short for **Samuel** (LL *Samuel*, LGr *Samouël*, H *Shemūël*, His name is El or God, occurs in *Sam Browne* (*belt*), from General Sir Samuel Browne (1824–1901), and in *Uncle Sam*, perh from that meat-inspector (*Samuel* Wilson, locally 'Uncle Sam') who, c1812, stamped barrels of meat with '*U.S.*—E.A.'. for 'United States—

Elbert Anderson', the contractual supplier of meat (Webster). From *Uncle Sam* comes the World War I sl *Sammy*, an American (private) soldier.

**Samaria, Samaritan.** The latter (LL *Samaritānus*) —as in 'a good *Samaritan*' (*Luke*, x, 30–7)—is a native of the former, a kingdom (and its capital) in Palestine: H *Shōmerōn*.

**same** (adj, hence adv and pron), whence **sameness**; dial 'to *sam*';—**some** (adj, hence pron)—cf the suffix *-some*—with such obvious cpds as **somebody** (cf BODY), **somehow** (cf HOW), **someone** (cf ONE), **something** (cf THING), **sometime, sometimes** (cf TIME), **somewhat** (cf WHAT), **somewhere** (cf WHERE);—Sanskrit, q.v. at PRAKRIT;—semper (L), sempiternal (q.v. at AGE, para 4);—simile; similar, similarity, and dissimilar, dissimilarity—cf assimilate, assimilation, assimilative, and dissimilate whence, anl, dissimilation, dissimilative; similitude and dissimiltude; simulacrum; simulate (adj and v), simulation (whence, anl, simulative), simulatory, simulator—and dissimulate, dissimulation (whence, anl, dissimulative), dissimulator;—semblable, semblance (whence, anl, semblative), semble—cf assemblage, assemble, assembly—dissemblance, dissemble (whence dissembler)—resemblance, resemble;—simultaneous, whence simultaneity;—simple, simplicity, simplify, qq.v. at PLY, paras 18–19;—single (adj, hence n and v), whence singleness and such cpds as single-handed, -hearted, -minded—cf singlet, singleton; singular (adj, hence n), singularity;—seem (whence pa, vn seeming), seemly (adj, hence adv);—cf the sep HYPHEN and HOMILY and ANOMALOUS).

### Indo-European

1. *Same*, ME *same*, derives from the ON *samr* (cf Da *samme*): cf OE *same*, adv, and OS *sama*, *samo*, OHG *sama*, adj and adv, and Go *sama*, adj; C r *sam-*, var *sem-*, similar, as in OIr *semail*, an image, a likeness, Ga *samhail*, like (adj), OBr *hemel* for *\*semel*, similar; OB *samŭ*; Skt *samás*, same; Gr *homos*, same, *homoios*, similar, *homalos*, even (whence *anomalous*); L *similis*, similar, *singulus*, single, *semper*, always, *semel*, once. C also Gr *hama*, together with, OHG *samant*, MHG *sament*, together, and G *samt*, together with; OE *samnian* (whence the now dial 'to *sam*'), OFris *samnia*, OHG *samanōn*, MHG *samenen*, G *sammeln*, OS *samnōn*, ON *samna*, to collect (to bring *together*). Akin to ON *samr*, adj, and OE *same*, adv, is OE *sum*, ME *som*, E *some*: cf OFris, OS, OHG *sum*, Go *sums*, MD *som*, ON *sumr*. In all, the basic idea is 'single' or 'united'.

2. The IE r is app *\*sem-*, single: L *similis* prob derives from PL *\*semelis*—cf OL *semol*, L *simul*; with L *sim-*, var *sin-* (as in *singulus*), cf Go *simle*, OHG *simble*, once. In Gr *homos*, we glimpse an IE var *\*som-*, occurring also in Tokh A *ṣoma-*, Tokh B *somo-*, the same, similar. (Hofmann.)

### Sanskrit

3. The Skt word most notable for E is *Sanskrit*, q.v. at PRAKRIT.

## Greek

4. Gr *homos*, one and the same, derives from IE *\*somos*, corresp to Skt *samás*, even or level, similar, identical; *homalos*, even, similar, like *homoios*, similar, like, is a mdfn of *homos*. See the elements *homalo-*, *homeo-* (or *homoeo-* or *homoio-*), *homo-*; notable E words are *anomalous*, *homeopathy* (*homoeo-*), *homily*—all treated elsewhere. (Cf, more distantly, *hyphen*.)

## Latin: i, *similis*

5. L has no *sem-* word meaning '(one and the) same'; only a word for 'of the same kind or general features'—'approximately the same'—'similar': *similis*, with s *simil-* an extn of *sim-* (for *sem-*). Its neu, *simile*, used as n in Rhetoric, has been adopted by E: cf the *similis*-derivative *similitūdō*, MF-F *similitude*, adopted by E. From *similis*, EF formed *similaire*, whence E *similar*, whence *similarity*—cf the rare C17–18 F *similarité*. Hence the anl E formations *dissimilar*, *dissimilarity*, prompted by L *dissimilis*; cf *dissimilitude*, prob adopted from the MF-EF word, from L *dissimilitūdō*, from *dissimilis* after *similitūdō*.

6. *Dissimilis* also lies behind *dissimilate*, *dissimilation* (cf LL *dissimilāre*, to be different), formed as complementaries to *assimilate*, *assimilation* (cf late MF-F), from LL *assimilātus*, pp of *assimilāre*, to make similar, and its derivative *assimilātiō*, o/s *assimilātiōn-*: from the adj *assimilis*, eased form of *adsimilis* (*ad*, towards); *assimilative* comes from LL *assimilatiuus*, ML *-ivus*.

## Latin: ii, *simul*

7. L *simul*, at the one—the same—time, was orig the OL neu of *similis*; it occurs in E in *simultaneous* (cf F *simultané*), which, suggested by *momentaneous*, recalls, in form, the ML *simultaneus*, simulated. With derivative *simultaneity*, cf the F *simultanéité*.

## Latin: iii, *simulāre*

8. *Simulāre*, deriving, via the old neu *simul*, from *similis*, means 'to represent exactly, to copy, to imitate', hence 'to feign'. The pp *simulātus* yields the adj and v *simulate*; derivatives *simulātiō* (o/s *simulātiōn-*), *simulātor*, LL *simulatōrius* yield *simulation* (adopted from MF-F), *simulator*, *simulatory*. Also from *simul*āre comes *simulācrum* (suffix *-ācrum*), a painted or sculptured representation, an image, hence a spectre or phantom: adopted by E (cf OF-F *simulacre*).

9. *Simulāre* has cpd *dissimulāre*, pp *dissimulātus*, whence 'to *dissimulate*'; derivatives *dissimulātiō* (o/s *dissimulātiōn-*) and *dissimulātor* become, via OF-F *dissimulation* and late MF-F *dissimulateur*, the E *dissimulation* and *dissimulator*.

10. Influenced by L *simulāre* but deriving rather from LL *similāre*, to resemble, is OF-F *sembler*, to resemble, but also—app imm—to seem, whence OF-F *semblable*, resembling, seeming, apparent—OF-EF *semblance*—OF-F *semblant*, all adopted by E, but now archaic.

11. From L *simul* comes VL *\*assimulāre*, to bring together (*as-* for *ad*, towards), which app combines with LL *assimilāre*, to make similar, to produce OF-F *assembler*, whence 'to *assemble*'; derivatives late MF-F *assemblage* and OF-F *assemblée* yield *assemblage* and *assembly*.

12. Cf the origin of 'to *dissemble*' (whence *dissembler*), to feign, mask, disguise: a blending of earlier *dissimule* (from MF-F *dissimuler*—cf para 9 above) and *dissemble*, to be different, unlike (from OF-MF *dessembler*). *Dissemblance*, a dissembling, comes from 'to *dissemble*', influenced by the earlier (now obs) *dissemblance*, unlikeness (from OF-MF *dessemblance*).

13. Cf also 'to *resemble*', from OF-MF *resembler* (EF-F *ressembler*), lit to be similar, or like, again, to resemble (someone): OF-F *re-*+*sembler*. The MF derivative *resemblance* (F *ress-*) is adopted by E.

## Latin: iv, *singulus*

14. L *singulus*, single, is an extn in form, a mdfn in sense, of the L r *sim-*. Via the acc *singulum*, it becomes OF-EF *single* (var *sengle*, as also in ME), adopted by ME. *Singulus* has the extn *singulāris*, whence OF-MF *singuler* (late MF-F *singulier*), adopted by ME, whence the reshaped E *singular*; derivative L *singulāritās* becomes OF-F *singularité*, whence E *singularity*.

15. E *single* has derivative *singlet*, orig an *un*lined waistcoat, imitating and complementing *doublet*; and *singleton*: *single*+euphonic *t*+*one*, influenced by the PN *Singleton*.

## Latin: v, *simplex*

16. L *simplex*, lit 'of one fold', has the 1st element *sim-*, var of the *sin-* of *singulus*: for the E derivatives, see PLY, paras 18–19.—For L *semper*, cf *sempiternal* at AGE, para 4.

## Germanic

17. For *same*, see para 1 above; for *some* (IE *\*somos*), see ib, s.f., and cf para 4.

18. Akin to OE *same* (adv) and ON *samr* (adj), same, and to OE *sēman*, to reconcile (make one again), is ME *sēmen*, *sēme*, to befit, and, vi, to become, to appear to be, whence 'to *seem*': cf ON *soemr*, fit, becoming (adj), and *sōma*, to beseem, ON *soemr* has extn *soemiligr*, comely, whence E *seemly*. The cpd 'to *beseem*' derives from late ME *bi-sēme* (*bi-* used int).

**samite.** See SIX, para 7.

**samovar,** adopted from Ru, is lit a 'self-boiler'.

**sampan:** earlier *champan* or *champana*: Port *champana*, *champão*: Sp *champán*: prob from Panama and Colombia—cf Chocoan *jampua*, var *jamba*, a canoe. From Port, the word travelled to Malaya and China; the *s-* form derives imm from Ch *san-pan*.

**samphire** contracts and mutilates F 'l'herbe de *Saint Pierre*', St Peter's herb.

**sample** (n, v), **sampler.** See EXEMPT, para 5.

**Samson,** whence the naut, whence the logging, Samson (or *s-*) post, whence the syn **samson; samsonite,** from the *Samson* mine in the Harz mountains of Germany.—*Samson,* become generic for an immensely strong man, figures in *Judges* (xiii): LL *Samsōn,* earlier *Sampsōn:* LGr *Sampsōn:* H *shimshōn,* 'Sun's Man'.

**Samuel.** See SAM.

**San,** in PlNn. See SACRAMENT, para 12.

**sanable, sanative, sanatorium, sanatory.** See SANE, para 3.

**sanct.** See SACRAMENT, para 12.

**sancta.** See SACRAMENT, para 12.

**sanctification, sanctify.** See SACRAMENT, para 13.

**sanctimonious, sanctimony.** See SACRAMENT, para 13.

**sanction.** See SACRAMENT, para 13.

**sanctitude, sanctity.** See SACRAMENT, para 13.

**sanctuary.** See SACRAMENT, para 13.

**sanctum.** See SACRAMENT, para 12.

**Sanctus.** See SACRAMENT, para 12.

**sand** (n, hence v), **sandy; sabuline, sabulite, sabulose** and **sabulous.**

*Sabuline* is an *-ine* adj, *sabulite* a Chem *-ite* n, from L *sabul*um, sand, adj *sabulōsus,* whence *sabulose* and *sabulous:* L *sabulum* is ult akin both to Gr *psammos* and the aphetic *ammos, psamathos* and *amathos,* and to OE-ME-E *sand:* and OE *sand* is imm akin to OFris *sand* (var *sond*), OHG-MHG *sant,* G *Sand,* ON *sandr:* prob cf also Skt *bhas-,* to grind (Walshe).—The adj *sandy* derives from OE *sandig* (adj suffix *-ig*).

2. The cpds are all either absolutely or relatively obvious: e.g., *sandpiper,* from its haunting sandy shores; *sandman,* ref sleep causing eyes to feel as if sand were in them.

**sandal:** OF-F *sandale:* L *sandalium:* Gr *sandalion,* dim of *sandalon* (whence Per *sandal*): o.o.o.: ? Parthian.

**sandalwood.** See CANDID, para 4.

**sandman; sandpiper.** See SAND, para 2.

**sandwich** comes from the 4th Earl of *Sandwich* (1718–92), that passionate gambler who once spent some twenty-four hours at table without refreshment other than slices of cold beef placed between pieces of toast.

**sandy.** See SAND, para 1, s.f.

**sane, sanity**—**insane, insanity; sanative, sanatorium, sanatory; sanitary,** whence **sanitarium; sanitate, sanitation**—and the neg **insanitary.**

1. *Sane,* like F *sain,* derives from L *sānus* (cf *sani-*): o.o.o.: perh aphetic for *\*isānus,* from the IE r present in Gr *iainō,* I heal (prob for *\*isaniō*), corresp to IE *\*isniō:* cf Skt *isanyáti,* he progresses. (Hofmann.)

2. L *sānus* has derivative *sānitās,* good health, o/s *sānitāt-,* whence E *sanity.* The L neg *insānus,* in bad health, and its derivative *insānitās,* o/s *insānitāt-,* yield *insane, insanity.* The transition from physical to mental health is normal.

3. L *sānus* has v *sānāre,* to render healthy, to heal or cure, whence *sānābilis,* E *sanable;* on the pp *sānāt*us arise LL *sānātiuus,* ML *-ivus,* healing, E

*sanative,* and the syn LL *sānatōrius,* whence the adj *sanatory* and the SciL *sanatorium.*

4. From L *sānitās,* learnèd F derives the adj *sanitaire,* whence E *sanitary* (anl neg *insanitary*): cf the LL *sānitans,* a healing, implying *\*sānitāre,* to keep-on healing (a freq of *sanāre*), with pp *\*sānitātus* and derivative *\*sānitātiō,* o/s *\*sanitātiōn-,* whence 'to *sanitate*' and *sanitation,* which, like SciL *sanitarium,* prop issue, anl, from *sanitary.*

5. L *sānus* has the ML derivative *sānicula,* a plant with reputed healing properties, whence E *sanicle.*

6. Perh cf SAD.

**sangfroid.** See para 2 of:

**sanguinary, sanguine, sanguineous, sanguinous; consanguineous, consanguinity; sangfroid.**

1. L *sanguis,* blood, s *sangu-,* r *sang-,* is o.o.o.: ? by a guttural metathesis of the IE r present in Skt *asnás,* blood.

2. *Sanguis* has the var *sanguen,* whence—perh rather than from *sanguis*—the OF *sanc,* later *sang,* as in the EF-F *sangfroid,* (lit) cold blood.

3. *Sanguis,* o/s *sanguin-,* has the adj *sanguineus,* whence both *sanguineous* and—via OF-F *sanguin*—*sanguine. Sanguineus* acquires the varr L *sanguinārius,* whence *sanguinary* (cf EF-F *sanguinaire*), and LL *sanguinōsus,* whence *sanguinous* (cf MF-EF *sanguineux*).

4. *Sanguineus* has cpd *consanguineus,* of the same parental blood (*con-,* with), whence derivative *consanguinitās:* hence the E *consanguineous, consanguinity.*

**Sanhedrin.** See SIT, para 2.

**sanicle.** See SANE, para 5.

**sanies, sanious.** The latter derives from L *saniōsus,* adj of *saniēs,* the watery-blood discharge from a wound: o.o.o.—but prob akin to *sanguis,* q.v. at SANGUINARY.

**sanitarium, sanitary, sanitation.** See SANE, para 4.

**sanity.** See SANE, para 2.

**sannup,** a married A Indian, complementing *squaw:* of Alg, esp Abnaki, origin: basic sense, 'full-grown, hence a complete, man'.

**Sanskrit.** See PRAKRIT; cf SAME, para 1.

**Santa Claus:** D *Sant Nikolaas:* St Nicholas of Asia Minor, who died A.D. c345, was that patron saint (seamen, merchants, children), who, on Christmas Eve, bore gifts to children.

**Santo; Sāo.** See SACRAMENT, para 12.

**sap** (1), of plants, whence the v 'to drain', comes from OE *saep:* cf OHG-MHG *saf,* G *Saft,* ON *safi,* prob L *sapa,* must (of wine), perh L *sapor,* flavour.—Hence *sapless* and *sapling. Sappy:* OE *saepig.*

**sap** (2), an undermining, to undermine, hence a trench and the v, to build a trench in (the ground). The n *sap* comes from EF-F *sape,* itself from the source of 'to *sap*': late MF-F *saper,* from MF-F *sape,* a mattock: (early) ML *sappa:* o.o.o.

2. The military *sapper* owes something to EF-F *sapeur* (from *saper*).

**sapid, sapidity.** See the 1st SAGE, para 2.

sapience, sapient, sapiential. See the 1st SAGE, para 3.

sapless, sapling. See the 1st SAP.

sapodilla and dilly; Sapota, sapote. *Dilly*, a WI tree, derives from *sapodilla*: Sp *sapotillo* (var *zapo-*): dim of *sapote* (var *za-*), adopted by E, whence the Sci *Sapota*: Aztec *tzapotl* or *zapotl*, short for *cuauhzapotl*, the 1st element representing Aztec *cuauhitl*, a tree. (Santamaria.)

saponaceous, saponification, saponify, saponin, saponite. See SOAP, para 2.

sapor, saporific, saporous. See the 1st SAGE, para 2.

Sapota, sapote. See SAPODILLA.

sapper. See the 2nd SAP, para 2.

Sapphic. See SAPPHO.

sapphire, sapphirine. See SATURN, para 5.

Sappho, Sapphic, Sapphics. The 3rd=verse in *Sapphic* forms; *Sapphic* (cf the F *saphique*)=L *Sapphicus*, Gr *Sapphikos*, adj of *Sapphō* (Σαπφώ), poetess of c600 B.C.

sappy. See the 1st SAP.

saraband: EF (occ *sarabante*)-F *sarabande*: Sp *zarabanda*: Ar-Per *serbend*, a kind of dance.

Saracen, whence Saracenics; sarrazin;—sarcenet or sarsenet; sarsen. *Saracen* derives, by b/f, from LL *Saracēni*, trln of LGr *Sarakēnoi*: o.o.o., but presumably Sem: perh cf modern Ar *Sawāriqah*, pl of *\*Sariqī*, an Oriental, from Ar *sharqī*, Oriental (Enci It); B & W adduce a Medieval Ar *sharqīyīn*, the Orientals, from *sharqī*.

2. The F word corresp to E *Saracen*, adj, is *sarrasin*, var *-zin*, whence, elliptical for *blé sarrasin* (*-zin*), Saracen wheat, the E *sarrazin*, buckwheat.

3. The MF-F adj *sarrasin* (*-zin*) derives from the n *Sarrasin* (*-zin*), whence, by contr, the ME *Sarzin*, adj *sarzin*, whence the AF dim *sarzinett*, whence E *sarsenet* or *sarcenet*, a soft silken fabric.

4. *Saracen stone*, a heathen (large) stone or monument, becomes, by contr and ellipsis, *sarsen*, a sandstone block.

sarcasm, sarcastic; sarcode, sarcoid, sarcoma, sarcophagus; sarcosis; cf the element *sarco-*.

1. The origin lies in Gr *sarx*, flesh (gen *sarkos*, c/f *sarko-*), pl *sarkes*, slices of meat: prob from an IE r for 'to cut'. *Sarx* has derivative *sarkazein*, to tear flesh, to bite one's lips in rage, hence to sneer: whence *sarkasmos*, a flesh-tearing, a sneering, LL *sarcasmos*, esp in Rhetoric, var *sarcasmus*, EF-F *sarcasme*, E *sarcasm*. F *sarcasme* has adj *sarcastique*, whence E *sarcastic*, whence the sl and dial *sarky*.

2. Gr *sarx*, o/s *sark-*, has the cpd adj *sarkōdēs*, fleshy (2nd element: *eidos*, form), whence both the Biol n *sarcode* and the Med adj *sarcoid*; and the nn *sarkōma* (suffix *-ōma*, q.v.), a tumour, whence E *sarcoma*, any malignant growth; and *sarkōsis*, E *sarcosis*.

3. From *sarx*, Gr forms also the cpd adj *sarkophagos*, flesh-eating, whence E *sarcophagous* (cf the element *-phaga*); *sarkophagos*, used elliptically for *s. lithos*, lit a flesh-eating stone, is applied to a limestone that, serving as a coffin, quickly disintegrates the corpse: whence L *sarcophagus*, adopted by E.

sard, sardonyx. See NAIL, para 4.

sardine; Sardinia, Sardinian;—sardonic, whence sardonicism.

1. *Sardine*, adopted from F, derives from L *sardīna*: Gr *sardēnē*, from Gr *Sardō*, Sardinia, with var *Sardōnē*, whence the thinned L *Sardinia*, adj *Sardiniānus*, E *Sardinian*.

2. Gr *Sardō* has adj *Sardónios*, whence, perh, *sardánios gelōs*, later *sardónios gelōs*, whence, imitatively, the L *sardonicus risus* (*sardonicus* from Gr *Sardōnikos*, extn of *Sardónios*), EF *ris sardonic*, F *rire sardonique*, whence the adj *sardonique*, whence E *sardonic*. The sem link is app this: the *Sardonia herba* (later, elliptically, *sardonia*), lit the Sardinian herb (L *Sardonius* from Gr *Sardonios*), 'renders men insane, so that the sick person seems to laugh' (Paré, C16: B & W). Learnèd f/e has perh intervened.

sardonyx. See NAIL, para 4.

sargasso, a floating seaweed—whence both the Sargasso Sea and the Bot Sargassum—derives from Port *sargasso* (var *sargaço*: cf the Sp *sargazo*): app from Port *sarga*, var *sargo*, a kind of grape: o.o.o.: ? cf Sp *sarga*, a kind of willow, from L *salix*.

sari; sarong. The Mal *sarong* answers to the Hindu woman's *sari*: Mal *saroñ*, *sārung*, to Hi *sarī* (or *sarhī*): the former perh, the latter certainly, from Skt *śāṭī*. Mal *sārung*, however, may derive— as OED proposes—from Skt *sāranga*, variegated.

sark (garment). See CUTTY SARK.

sarrazin. See SARACEN, para 2.

sarsaparilla, a CAm shrub, hence a derivative: ASp *zarzaparrilla* (Sp *z. de Indias*): from its resemblance to the two plants, *zarga*, a shrub+*parrilla*, dim of *parra*, a vine: *zarza*, from Ar *xaraç*, a prickly plant; *parra*, as also in Port, o.o.o.

sarsen, sarsenet. See SARACEN, paras 4 and 3.

sartorial, sartorius (muscle). Both come, the latter via SciL, from L *sartor*, a tailor, lit a patcher, from *sartus*, pp of *sarcīre*, to patch or mend, orig to re-sew: o.o.o. SciL *sartorius* was prob suggested by LL *sarsōrius*, relative to patching, from LL *sarsor*, var of *sartor*. The *sartorius* muscle—man's longest—'noticeably assists in rotating the leg to the position assumed in sitting like a tailor' (Webster).

2. Perh akin to L *sarcīre* is Gr *herkos*, a fence, with its cognate *horkos*, an oath (fencing one about), whence *horkizein*, to bind with an oath, with cpd *exorkizein* (*ek-*, *ex-*, out), to swear (evil spirits) out from a man: LL *exorcizāre*: MF-F *exorciser*: E 'to *exorcize*'. Derivative Gr *exorkismos*, LL *exhorcismus*, usu *exorcismus*, yields late MF-F *exorcisme*, whence E *exorcism*, whence *exorcismal*; derivative Gr *exorkistēs* becomes LL *ex(h)orcista*, EF-F *exorciste*, E *exorcist*.

sash of window, and as worn. See the 2nd CASE, final para.

Saskatchewan, Saskatoon, saskatoon. The shrub *saskatoon*, like the city *Saskatoon*, represents a contr of *Saskatchewan*, itself aphetic for the Cree—an Alg dial—*misâskwatomin*, lit 'berry of the tree with much wood' (Webster); *misâskwat*, the tree of much wood.

**sassafras**, from Sp *sasefrás*, is perh a blend (? rather a confusion) of Sp *saxafrax*, saxifrage, with an Amerind word.

**sassy**, impudent, is certainly a dial var; *sassy*, a W Afr tree, is reputedly a corruption; of E *saucy*.

**Satan** (whence **Satanism** and **Satanist**), **Satanic**. The adj derives from late MF-F *satanique*, imm from F *Satan* but prob influenced by LGr *satanikos*, the adj of LGr *satan, satanas*, whence LL *satan, satanâs*, whence F and E *Satan*: and LGr *satan(as)* represents H *ṣāṭān*, adversary (whence 'The Adversary').

**satchel.** See SAC, para 3.

**sate.** See SAD, para 2.

**sateen.** See SATIN, para 2.

**satellite** (n, hence adj), whence the Astr adjj **satellitic, satellitory, satelloid**: MF-F *satellite*: L *satellitem*, acc of *satelles*, a bodyguard: o.o.o.: 'perh Etruscan, the first Roman king to whom legend attributes bodyguards being Tarquin the Proud' (E & M), himself of Etruscan origin.

**satiate, satiety.** See SAD, para 2.

**satin**, whence **satinwood**; **sateen**, whence **sateenwood**; **satiné**; **satinette**, with AE var **satinet**. *Satin*, adopted from MF-F (MF var *zatany*), prob derives—perh via Sp *aceituni*—from Ar *zaytūnī*, orig the adj 'of *Zaytūn*', the Ar name of the great medieval Ch seaport *Tzu-t'ing* (now *Chuanchow*, F *Tsia-Toung*), where the fabric was first manufactured.

2. Whereas *sateen*, a cottony satin, 'anglicizes' the F *satin*, *satiné*, a Brazilian hardwood with a satin-like sheen, derives from the pp of EF-F *satiner*, to render like satin, and *satinette* is adopted from F (*satin*+dim *-ette*).

**satire, satiric(al), satirist, satirize.** See SAD, para 4.

**satis**, enough. See SAD, para 1.

**satisfaction, satisfactory, satisfy.** See SAD, para 6.

**satrap.** See CHECK, final para.

**saturate, saturation.** See SAD, para 5.

**Saturday.** See para 4 of:

**Saturn, Saturnalia** (whence **Saturnalian**), **Saturnian, saturnine; Saturday;—sapphire, sapphirine.**

1. *Saturn*, like F *Saturne*, derives from L *Sāturnus*, itself o.o.o., the association with *serere*, to sow, pp *satus*, being f/e: perh Etruscan (E & M)—cf the Etr god *Satre*; perh rather Oriental—cf para 5; ? Medit—cf Eg *Sba âmenti* (*tcha pet*), Saturn.

2. L *Sāturnus* has the adj *sāturnius*, as in *sāturniī uersūs*, whence E *Saturnian verse*; hence E *Saturnian* (cf EF-F *saturnien*). From L *Sāturnīnus*, of Saturn, F derives *saturnin*, orig a Med adj, whence E *saturnine* (opp *jovial*).

3. L *Sāturnus* has yet another adj: *Sāturnālis*, whence, via the neu pl, the n *Sāturnālia*, the festival—unofficially, a carnival—of Saturn, whence E *saturnalia*, a period of licence.

4. L *Sāturnus* combines with OE *daeg*, day, to form OE *Saeternesdaeg*, Saturn's day, contr to *Saeterndaeg* and still further to *Saeterdaeg*, whence ME *Saterdai*, whence E *Saturday*.

5. Skt exhibits *śanipriya*, lit 'dear to Saturn' (*śanis*, the planet Saturn), hence, by f/e, a sapphire, whence—via Sem (cf H *sappīr*)—the Gr *sappheiros* (σάπφειρος), L *sapphirus* (LL *saphīrus*), OF *safir*, MF-F *saphir*, E *sapphire*. The L adj *sapphirīnus* yields *sapphirine*. (Hofmann.)

**satyr, satyriasis.** As 'lecher', *satyr* derives from MF-F *satyre*, from L *Satyrus*, trln of Gr *Saturos*, a sylvan demigod addicted to riotous and lascivious ways: perh from IE *sator* (*setor*), 'a sower', cf L *sator*. (Hofmann.) Derivative Gr *saturiasis*, insatiable sexual desire in the male, becomes LL *satyriāsis*, adopted by Med—cf the element *-iasis*.

**sauce**, whence **saucy**. See SALT, para 7.

**saucepan.** See the 2nd PAN, para 1; cf SALT, para 7.

**saucer.** See SALT, para 7.

**saucy.** See SAUCE.

**sault.** See SALLY, para 6.

**saunter**, v (hence n), whence pa, vn **sauntering** and agent **saunterer**, is o.o.o.: ? for MF *s'aunter*, not 'to adventure oneself' but 'to advance oneself, move forward', for *s'auanter*, for *s'avanter*, from OF-F *avant*, forward, before: for the *u*, cf MF *s'aunter*, var of *s'avanter* (F *se vanter*), to boast; the reflexive connotes effort.

**Sauria**, whence both **saurian** (adj, hence n) and **saury**, is a SciL neu pl, based upon Gr *saura* or *sauros*, a lizard: o.o.o.: ? (with Boisacq) for *psauros*, akin to Gr *paukros*, agile, restless.— Cf the c/f *sauro-*.

2. The best known E cpd is *dinosaur*, one of the *Dinosauria* (*dino-* from Gr *deinos*, terrible).

**sausage.** See SALT, para 8.

**savage** (adj, hence n and v), **savagery**; **silva, sylva—silvan, sylvan—Silvanus, Sylvanus**, cf **Pennsylvania** and **Transylvania**, with adjj (hence nn) in *-ian*; **silvics** and **silviculture; Silvia, Sylvia; Silvester, Sylvester**.

1. *Savage*, orig of the forest, hence untamed, hence cruel, derives from OF-F *sauvage*—whence *sauvagerie*, whence E *savagery*. OF *sauvage* comes from ML *salvāticus*, from VL *saluāticus*, a var of L *siluāticus*, living in the woods, an adj of L *silua*, ML *silva*, a wood or forest, inferior spelling *sylua, sylva*: o.o.o.

2. ML *silva, sylva*, is retained by tech E. The E adj *silvan*, var *sylvan*, derives from late MF-F *silvain, sylvain*, from ML *Silvānus*, var *Sylvānus*, L *Siluānus, Syluānus*, a god of the woods and fields, from *silua, sylua*.

3. From *siluānus*, adj, comes *siluāna, syluānia*, ML *-vania*, wooded country, whence both *Pennsylvania*, founded by William *Penn*, and *Transylvania*, now a province of central Rumania, from *trans*, across; discovered in Trans*ylvania* was *sylvanite* (Min *-ite*).

4. ML *silva* leads to *silvics* and the approx syn

*silviculture*, forestry; cf *silvicolous*, forest-inhabiting, from L *siluicola*, an inhabitant of the woods.

5. L *silua* has a further adj: *siluester* (or *siluestris*), var *syluester* or *-tris*, ML *-vester*, *-vestris*, whence MF-F *silvestre*, *sylvestre*, and E *Sylvester*.

6. L *silua* has derivative PN *Siluius*, ML *Silvius*, var *Sylvius*, f *Silvia*, *Sylvia*, adopted by E.

**savanna, savannah**, a treeless plain: Sp *zavana* (now *sabana*): Taino (WI) *zabana*.

**savant.** See the 1st SAGE, para 6.

**savate.** See SABOT.

**save.** See SAFE, para 2, s.f.

**savior (AE), saviour.** See SAFE, para 5.

**savoir-faire** and **-vivre.** See the 1st SAGE, para 6.

**savor, savorous, savory** (adj, hence n). See the 1st SAGE, para 5.

**savory**, an aromatic mint, derives from ME *saverey*—with *-v-* perh from OF-EF *savoré*, tasty —from OE *saetherie*, itself from L *satureia*: o.o.o.

**savour, savoury** (adj, hence n 'a relish'). See the 1st SAGE, para 5.

**savoy (cabbage)** derives from *Savoy cabbage*, trans of F *chou de Savoie*. *Savoy*=F *Savoie*, in SE France, formerly It *Savoia* in NW Italy: app (Enci It) 'The Country of Fir-Trees', (with *p* becoming *v*) from an Italic, ? orig C, r *sap-*, a fir-tree (cf the F *sapin*). Hence F *Savoyard*, an inhabitant of Savoy; E *Savoyard*, an admirer of the Gilbert & Sullivan operas, derives from the *Savoy* Theatre (London), where, from *Iolanthe* (1882) onwards, they were produced.

**savvy.** See the 1st SAGE, para 7.

**saw** (1), a maxim. See SAY, para 2.

**saw** (2), a tool (hence the v), whence **sawyer** (agential *-yer*, for *-ier*); **seesaw; scythe** (n, hence v); **sedge**, whence **sedgy; sickle; sect**, a section (distinct from religious **sect**)—**sectile**—**section** (n, hence v), whence **sectional**, whence **sectionalism**, **-ist**, **-ize**—**sector**, whence **sectorial; secant; secateur(s); segment** (n, hence v), whence **segmental** and **segmentary**—**segmentate**, whence, anl, **segmentation; dissect, dissection** (whence, anl, **dissective** and **dissector**); **insect** (adj, n), **insectarium** (anglicized as **insectary**), **insectile; insection; intersect, intersection** (whence **intersectional**); **resect, resection** (whence **resectional**); **subsection; transect**, whence, anl, **transection;**—perh the sep SAIL.

1. *Saw*, ME *sawe*, comes from OE *sagu* or *sage*: cf OHG *saga*, var *sega*, G *Säge*, MD *sege*, *sage*, *zage*, D *zaag*, ON *sög*: further off, L *secāre*, to cut, *sécula*, a sickle, *secūris*, an axe (cf OSl *sekyra*): IE r *sek-*, to cut, with cognates in C and Sl.

2. From the motion of a *saw* in use, comes, by redup, the juvenile pastime of two persons sitting at either end of a plank and keeping it moving: a *seesaw*.

3. Akin to the Gmc words noted in para 1 is *scythe*, influenced by OF-F *scier*, to saw, in the passage from ME *sithe*, itself from OE *sithe*, var *sigthe*: cf OHG *seganse*, sickle, scythe, MHG *segense*, *sengse*, G *Sense*, scythe, OS *segasna*, scythe, ON *sigthr*, sickle.

4. Akin to the Gmc words of paras 1 and 3 is

*sedge*, ME *segge*, OE *secg* (cf OE *secg*, a sword), cf LG *segge*: ? because often cut by the ancient English.

5. Akin to all the Gmc words so far mentioned, and also esp to L *sēcula*, is *sickle*, ME *sikel*, OE *sicel* or *sicol*: cf OHG *sihhila*, MHG-G *sichel*.

## L *secāre*, to cut

6. L *secāre* has presp *secans*, o/s *secant-*, whence E *secant*, adj (hence n); E *secateur* represents F *sécateur*, formed anl (*-ateur*) from L *secāre*.

7. L *secāre* has the irreg (supine *sectum* and) pp *sectus*, whence the rare E *sect*, a section, a cion.

8. On the L pp *sectus*, have been formed the foll L words relevant to E:

*sectilis*, cuttable, whence—perh via EF-F (obs) —*sectile*;

*sectiō*, o/s *sectiōn-*, a cutting, a piece cut off, late MF-F *section*, adopted by E;

L *sector*, a cutter, EF-F *secteur* and E *sector*.

9. L *secāre* has derivative *segmen*, a piece or portion cut off, usu in extn *segmentum*, s *segment-*, EF-F *segment*, adopted by E; derivative *segmentātus* yields *segmentate*.

## Compounds of *secāre*

10. L *dissecāre*, to cut apart, has pp *dissectus*, whence 'to *dissect*'; derivative LL *dissectiō*, o/s *dissectiōn-*, yields EF-F and E *dissection*.

11. L *insecāre*, to cut in or into, has pp *insectus*, whence both the E adj *insect* and the E n *insect* (L *insectum*, neu of the pp), its body being so sharply cut-into that it almost seems divided; derivative LL *insectiō*, o/s *insectiōn-*, accounts for E *insection*, but E *insectile* is an anl formation; derivative ML *insectārium* (*-ārium* connoting 'receptacle'), a place for the breeding of insects, is adopted by E.

12. L *intersecāre*, to cut between, has pp *intersectus*, whence 'to *intersect*'; derivative *intersectiō*, o/s *intersectiōn-*, produces MF-F and E *intersection*.

13. L *resecāre*, to cut back, to cut off, has pp *resectus*, whence 'to *resect*'; derivative *rese tiō*, o/s *resectiōn-*, produces EF-F and E *resection*.

14. *Subsection* has nothing to do with L *subsecāre*, to cut under; it simply=*sub-*, subordinate+ E *section*. *Transect* and *transection*=*trans*, across +*-sect*, *section*.

**saw** (3), pt of SEE.

**sawyer.** See the 2nd SAW (heading).

**sax**, a sword. See SAXON, para 2.—2. Short for **saxophone**, where also **saxhorn** and **saxtuba**.

**saxifrage.** See FRACTION, para 9, and cf the elements *saxi-* and *-frage*.

**Saxon** (n, hence adj), cf **Anglo-Saxon; Saxony; sax**, a sword.

1. *Saxon*, adopted from F, derives from LL *Saxō*, o/s *Saxōn-*, of Gmc origin: cf OE *Seaxe*, *Seaxan*, Saxons, app orig 'men of the (long) knife': OE *seax*, a knife or a dagger, syn OHG *sahs*, OFris *sax*, knife, sword, and *Saxa*, a Saxon, *Sax-land* (*-lond*), Saxony: perh—'knives being orig

made of stone' (Webster)—akin to L *saxum*, a rock, a stone: ? cf also L *secāre*, to cut.

2. OE *seax* becomes E *sax*, a short sword, hence a builder's chopper; and LL *Saxō*, o/s *Saxōn-*, has LL derivative *Saxōnia* (territorial *-ia*), whence *Saxony*.

3. *Anglo-Saxon*, n hence adj, derives from ML *Anglo-Saxōnes*, from earlier *Angli Saxōnes*, the English, taut combining LL *Angli*, the English, L the Angles, with *Saxōnes*, the Saxons of Saxony, later the English. Cf ENGLISH.

**saxophone**: invented, app c1860, by the Belgian Adolphe *Sax* (1814-94), *saxo-* being the c/f and *-phone* the Gr *phōnē*, voice, tone. Earlier came his *saxhorn* (cf HORN); anl are *saxtromba* (cf *trombone* at TRUMPET) and *saxtuba* (cf TUBA).

**say**, pt and pp **said** (OE *saegde*), presp and vn **saying** and agent **sayer** (as in *soothsayer*); **saga**; **saw**, a saying, a maxim;—cf the sep SEE, v.

1. 'A *say*' derives from 'to *say*', and 'to *say*' from ME *sayen*, *seyen*, earliest *seggen*, from OE *secgan*: cf OS *seggian*, LG *seggen*, MD *secgen*, *seggen*, D *zeggen*, ON *segia*, to say, and the OFris nn *sega*, a speaker, *sege*, a speech, all from a Gmc r *\*sagja-*, whereas OHG *sagēn* (G *sagen*) comes from the var *\*sagai-*: IE r, *\*sek-* (varr *\*sak-*, *\*sok-*), to say, as in the OL imp *insece*, Tell, Relate (cf Gr *ennepe*, from en*sepe*); Lith *sakýti*, to say; OB *sočiti*, to notify; cf also, with *h* for *s*, the OW *hepp*, he says. (Walshe; Hofmann.)

2. Akin to ON *segia* is ON *saga*, a story, adopted by E: cf the intimately related OHG *saga* (G *Sage*, a tale), OFris *sege*, OE *sagu*, a speech, a recital, the last yielding, via ME *sawe*, the E *saw*.

**scab** (n, hence v), whence **scabby**; **scabies**, **scabious** (adj and n), **scabish**; **scabrid**, **scabrous**; **shab**, **shabby**; **shave** (n, v), whence **shaver** and pa, vn **shaving**—cf **shaveling**.

1. *Scab*, ME *scab*, *scabbe*, derives from ON *skabb*, a scab, mange: cf Da and Sw *skab*, Nor *skabb*.

2. Very closely akin to ON *skabb* is the syn OE *sceabb*, varr *sceb*, *scebb*, *scaeb*, with *sc-* pron *sh-*, whence ME *shabbe*, a scab (now dial), hence a paltry fellow (obs sl), whence the adj *shabby*, whence *shabbiness*: cf the senses of *scabby*.

3. OE *scaeb*, *sceabb*, *sceb(b)* and ON *skabb* are akin to L *scabiēs*, roughness of the skin, the mange, from *scabere*, to scratch (oneself), to shave: L r, *scab-*; IE r, *\*skebh-*, varr *\*skabh-*, *\*skobh-*, to scratch, as in Go *skaban*, Lith *skabiù*, *skōbti*, to scratch, Gr *skaptein*, to dig.—L *scabiēs* has adj *scabiōsus*, scabby, whence E *scabious*; the plant *scabious* derives from ML *scabiōsa* (*herba*), reputed to cure scabies; the plant *scabious* becomes, by (? dial) corruption, *scabish*, the field scabious.

4. The L r *scab-* occurs also in L *scaber*, wrinkled, rough, mangy, o/s *scabr-*, as in L *scabrātus*, whence E *scabrate* (*-ate*, adj). *Scaber* has the LL extn *scabrōsus*, rough, wrinkled, whence EF-F *scabreux*, f *scabreuse*, whence E *scabrous*, and another LL extn *scabridus*, slightly ·scabrous, whence E *scabrid*.

5. Akin to L *scabere*, to scratch, to shave, is 'to shave', ME *shaven*, earlier *schaven*, OE *scafan* or *sceafan* (*sc-* pron *sh-*): cf OHG *scaban*, MHG-G *schaben*, to scrape, to shave, Go *skaban*, to scratch, to shear, MD-D *schaven*, ON *skafa*, to shave—cf also Lith *skabus*, sharp.—OE *sceafan* has derivative n *sceafa*, a carpenter's plane, whence syn E *shave*; the other senses of the E n *shave* derive from 'to *shave*'. From his tonsure, comes *shaveling* (dim suffix *-ling*), a priest; from the infrequency of his need to shave, a youth.

6. Prob cf SCAFFOLD.

**scabbard.** See SHARE, para 10.

**scabies**, **scabious** (adj and n). See SCAB, para 3.

**scabrid**, **scabrous**. See SCAB, para 4.

**scaffold**, n hence v, whence **scaffolding**: ME *scaffold*: ONF *escafaut*: MF *escafote*, a shell, dim of MF *escafe*, var *scaphe*, a shell: L *scapha*, a light boat, a skiff: Gr *skaphē*, a trough: prob IE r, *\*skebh-*, var *\*skabh-*, as for SCAB.

**scalar**, ladder-shaped, L *scalāris*, adj of *scāla*, whence E *scale*, q.v. at ASCEND, para 1.

**scalawag**, var **scallawag**, **scallywag**, and **scallaway**: o.o.o.: ? from *Scalloway*, a former capital of the Shetlands, ref the Shetland ponies or perh the small Shetland cattle. (Webster.)

**scald** (1) or **skald**. See SCOLD.

**scald** (2), to burn with water, hence n; hence also the pa, vn **scalding**. 'To *scald*' comes from ME *scalden*: by aphesis from ONF *escalder*: OF *eschalder* (later *eschauder*, finally *échauder*): LL *excaldāre*, also—by aphesis—*scaldāre*, to bathe, or to cook, in hot water: L int *ex-*+L *caldāre*, to warm, to heat, from *caldus*, warm: f.a.e., CALDRON.

**scale** (1), a ladder, hence the v. See ASCEND, para 4.

**scale** (2), a balance: ME *scale*, var *scole*, ON *skāl*, a bowl, hence, from things being weighed in one, a balance: cf OHG *scala*, MHG *schāle*, G *Schāle*, a drinking-vessel, OS *skala*, a cup, ON *skāl*, a drinking-vessel, whence the Scan toast *Skol!* Akin to:

**scale** (3), a fish's or a reptile's, hence the v: ME *scale*, *skale*: OF-MF *escale* (late MF-F *écale*, husk), a husk, a cup: via ONF from Frankish *skala*, a husk, a fish's scale, an egg-shell: cf the OGmc words cited in prec and the Go *skalja*, a tile: prob akin to ON *skilia*, to split. Cf SCALLOP and SHALE.

**scalene**: L *scalēnus*, unequal-sided: Gr *skalēnos*; akin to Gr *skelos*, the thigh; IE r, *\*skel-* (*\*squel-*), to bend.

**scaling**: pa and vn of *scale* (1) and (3).

**scallaway.** See SCALAWAG.

**scallion; shallot, eschalot.**

1. *Scallion*, a shallot, a leek, comes from ME *scalyon*: by aphesis from ONF *escalogne*, var of OF *eschalogne* or *eschaloigne*: VL *\*scalōnia*: L *ascalōnia*; elliptical for *a. caepa*, onion of *Ascalon*, a Palestinian seaport: adj of *Ascalō*, o/s *Ascalōn-*: Gr *Askalōn*: app of Sem origin, prob Canaanite; during the Crusades, it was known as *Escalone*.

2. OF *eschalo(i)gne*, by change of suffix, becomes MF *eschalette*, var *eschalotte* (F *échalotte*), whence both E *eschalot* and, by aphesis, E *shallot*.

**scallop**, n hence v, whence **scalloping**; **scalp**, n hence v.

1. *Scallop*, a bivalvular mollusc, whence the dressmaking sense, derives, by aphesis, from MF *escalope*, a shell, an animal-matter scale: of Gmc origin—cf SCALE (3) and MD *schelp(e)*, *schilpe*, *scholpe*, *schulpe*, D *schelp*, *schulp*.

2. *Scalp* (ME id) comes from ON *skalpr*, a sheath, akin to the MD words in para 1.

**scalpel**. See SHELL, para 2.

**scaly**: adj of the 3rd SCALE.

**scamble** (v, hence n); **shamble**, adj, n, v (whence **shambling**); **scrabble** (v, hence n) and **scramble**, v, hence n—hence also A sl **scram**; **scrap**, n hence v (whence **scrapper** and **scrapping**); **scrape** (v hence n), whence **scraper** and **scraping**.

1. *Scamble* (now mostly dial), to scramble, stumble along, sprawl, and, vt, to scatter, to collect, or to remove, bit by bit, to trample clumsily, is echoic.

2. Echoically (at least) akin is 'to *shamble*', to walk with unsteady or shuffling awkwardness; it derives from the adj *shamble*, walking thus, awkwardly unsteady, as in 'He has *shamble* legs', itself from the n *shamble*, a stool (obs), a bench, esp in a butcher's shop, hence a slaughterhouse, whence *shambles*, a scene of slaughter: ME *schamel*, from OE *sceamol* or *scamel* (*sc-* pron *sh-*), stool, bench: L *scamellum*, dim of *scamnum*, stool, bench, form: nasal derivative from IE *skabh-*, to support—cf Skt *skabhnáti*, he supports, props up, and *skambhás*, a support, a pillar.

3. 'To *scramble*' is a nasal var of 'to *scrabble*', to scrape or scratch with hands or feet, hence to scramble or clamber, and to scrawl or scribble. 'To *scrabble*' comes from MD-ED *schrabbelen*, freq of MD-ED *schrabben*, to scratch or scrape: echoic.

4. *Scrap*, a (left-over) fragment of food, a detached piece, coll 'a fight with fists' (cf *scrape*, a predicament), ME *scrappe*, comes from ON *skrap*, prob orig 'something scraped off' and certainly very closely akin to, if not derived from, ON *skrapa*, to scrape, whence, app, OE *scrapian*, ME *scrapien*, later *scrapen*, E 'to *scrape*': cf the syn MD *schrappen* (D *schrapen*), var of *schrabben* (cf above), MLG-G *schrapen* (MHG *schraffen*), with int G *schrappen*; cf also Lett *skrabt* (Walshe).

**scamp** (1), a rogue. See CAMP, para 4.

**scamp** (2), to perform hastily and imperfectly. See SCANT, para 2.

**scamper**, to run fast or in haste. See CAMP, para 4.

**scan**. See ASCEND, para 1.

**scandal**, **scandalize**, **scandalous**. See ASCEND, para 2.

**Scandinavia**, whence **Scandinavian**. See AQUA, para 8. The Chem *scandium* = ML *Scand*ia, Scandinavia + Chem *-ium*.

**scansion**. See ASCEND, para 1.

**scant**, adj hence v; hence also the extn **scanty** (whence—after *panties*—the sl **scanties**); to **scamp**, whence the pa, vn **scamping**; **skimp**, adj, hence n (whence **skimpy**) and v; **scrimp**, whence **scrimpy**; **shrimp**, n and v; **shrink**, whence **shrinkage**, **shrinker**, **shrinking**—pt **shrank** or **shrunk**, pp **shrunk** or **shrunken** (also pa).

1. *Scant*, ME *skant*, derives from ON *skamt* or *skammt*, the neu of *skam(m)r*, short: cf OE and OHG *scamm*, short.

2. Akin to ON *skam(m)r* is ON *skemma*, OHG *skemmēn*, to shorten, which, along with ON *skamt* and E *scant*, have app suggested E 'to *scamp*' or shorten one's work on (something) by doing it hastily or carelessly.

3. 'To *scamp*' has the thinned derivative 'to *skimp*', perh imm from the adj *skimp* (? prompted by *scant* and pa *scamped*).

4. With both 'to *scamp*' and 'to *skimp*', cf 'to *scrimp*', to provide (someone) with insufficient money, to provide insufficient money for (something): perh influenced by 'to *shrink*'.

5. 'To *shrink*', ME *shrinken*, earlier *schrinken*, comes from OE *scrincan*: cf MD *schrinken*: prob related intimately to a *shrimp*, ME *shrimpe*, so named because it looks shrivelled, and perh deriving from MHG *schrimpfen* (G *schrumpfen*), to shrink—cf, without the IE prefix *s-*, the syn MD *crimpen*, *crempen*, D *krimpen*. Note that in Gmc words, *scr-* (*skr-*) is usu representational or picturesque, and often echoic.

**scantle**: ONF *escanteler* (OF-MF *eschanteler*), to break into cantles: *es-* (L *ex-*, out of) + *cantel* (OF *chantel*). Cf CANTLE.

**scantling** is for earlier *scantillon*, aphetically from ONF *escantillon*, MF *eschantillon* (F *échantillon*), a standard measure or weight, mdfn of MF *eschandillon*, dim of *escandille* (cf OProv *escandil*), from VL *scandīlia*, from L *scandere*, to mount: cf ASCEND. (B & W.)

**scanty**. See SCANT (heading).

**scape** (1), to—or an—escape. See ESCAPE, para 3.

**scape** (2), a scenic view or painting, derives from *landscape*, earlier *landskip*, from ED *landschip* (D *landschap*), MD *lantschip*, *-schep*, *-schap*: cf OE *landscipe*, a region, and the E suffix *-ship*.

**scape** (3), in Bot and Zoo. See SHAFT, para 2.

**scapegoat**, orig a goat bearing the sins of the people and allowed to 'escape' into the wilderness: cf SCAPE (1).

**scapegrace** is one who has 'escaped' from religious grace.

**scaph-** and **scapo-** words. See those elements.

**scapula**, whence the adj **scapular**; **scapular**, n, **scapulary**. *Scapula*, the shoulder-blade, is adopted from LL *scapula*, a b/f from L *scapulae*, the shoulders: o.o.o.: perh cf Gr *skaptein* (s *skapt-*, r *skap-*), to hollow out. The LL derivative *scapulāre*, a monk's working garment, becomes EF-F *scapulaire* (cf the C13 *capulaire*, C14 *chapulaire*), whence E *scapular*; the ML extn *scapulārium* accounts for the E var *scapulary*.

**scar** (1), an isolated, esp if protruding, rock, hence a clinker; **skerry.** *Scar,* ME *skar,* earlier *skerre,* derives from ON *sker,* a rocky isle, whence —? orig a dim—the E *skerry*: f.a.e., the v SHEAR.

**scar** (2), a wound- or a burning-mark left in the skin, whence the v, whence the pa **scarred** and the vn **scarring; eschar,** (Med) a dry scab.

1. *Eschar* derives from MF-EF *eschare* (var *-arre*: F *escarre*): L *eschara*: Gr *eskhara*: o.o.o.— perh (Hofmann) cf OSl *iskra,* a spark. The derivative Gr adj *eskharōtikos,* LL *escharōticus,* yields E *escharotic.*

2. *Scar* derives either, by aphesis, from ONF *escare* (MF *eschare*), or from LL *scara,* aphetic for L *eschara.* Sem, *scar* owes something to the obs E *scar,* a crack, from the now only dial *scarth,* a cleft, from ON *skerth* (f.a.e. SHARD).

**scar** (3), a chink. See prec, final sentence.

**scarab, scarabaeus.** See CARBINE.

**scarce** (whence 'to scarcen'), **scarcity.** The n derives from ME *scarsete,* from ONF *escarseté,* itself from ONF *escars,* whence ME *scars,* E *scarce*: and ONF *escars,* OF-MF *eschars,* avaricious, derives from VL *\*excarpsus,* from L *excerptus,* pp of *excerpere,* to pluck out, to gather (cf E *excerpt*): *ex,* out (of)+*carpere,* to pluck fruit, hence to gather: f.a.e., HARROW.

**scare** (v, hence n), whence the pa **scared** and the dial and coll **scary; scarecrow,** orig something to scare a generic *crow.*

'To *scare,*' ME *skerren,* derives from ON *skirra,* itself from ON *skjarr,* shy, timorous: o.o.o.

**scarf** (1), pl *scarves,* comes—with *f* for *p*—from ONF *escarpe,* a pilgrim's wallet, usu worn round the neck, OF-MF *escharpe* (F *écharpe*), *escherpe,* such a wallet (OF), hence, in MF, a broad band worn around the body: Frankish *\*skerpa*: L *scirpus,* a reed (cf *scirpea,* a reed basket): o.o.o.

2. By metathesis, L *scirpus* becomes LL (*\*scrippus* and) *scrippum,* whence ME *scrippe,* E *scrip* (archaic), a pilgrim's wallet.

**scarf** (2), to join (pieces of timber or metal), comes from the n *scarf,* a joint (in building): ON *skarfr*: cf OE *scearfian,* to scrape, and *sceorfan,* to gnaw, to bite, and perh (Walshe) Gr *skorpios,* a scorpion.

2. Akin to those OE vv is OE *sceorf,* with var *scurf* prevailing into E: cf also OHG *scorf,* MHG-F *schorf,* a scab, scurf, and ON *skurfur* (pl). *Scurf* has adj *scurfy,* eased to *scurvy,* whence the disease.

**scarification, scarify.** See SCRIBE, para 5.

**scarlatina.** See para 2 of:

**scarlet** (n, hence adj), **scarlatina** (whence **scarlatinous**).

1. *Scarlet,* ME *scarlet,* earlier *scarlat,* orig a fabric, hence its usu colour, is aphetic for OF-MF *escarlate* (F *écarlate*): ML *scarlātum*: Per *säqirlāt*: Ar *siqillāt,* a fabric decorated with seals (as for letters): via LGr from L *sigillātus,* decorated with *sigilla* (LGr *sigillia*) or seals: f.a.e., SIGN.

2. From ML *scarlātum,* Med has coined *scarlatina* (cf the F *scarlatine*).

**scarp,** the parapet side of a trench, a steep descent, whence 'to *scarp*', is aphetic for *escarp,* from EF *escarpe,* from It *scarpa,* from Go *\*skrapa,* deduced from MHG *schrof,* a cliff. The EF *escarpe* originates both EF *escarper,* whence F *escarpement,* whence E *escarpment,* and EF-F *contrescarpe,* whence E *counterscarp.*

**scat.** See SCATTER.

**scathe,** n, 'whence **scatheless,** and v, whence **scathing** (orig a presp) and **unscathed.**

*Scathe,* injury, ME *scathe,* comes from ON *skathi*: cf OFris *skatha,* OS *skatho,* OHG *scado,* MHG *schade,* G *Schaden*; cf also Gr *askēthēs,* not (*a-*) harmed (*-skēthēs,* from *\*skēthos,* injury); there are several C cognates. 'To *scathe,*' ME *scathen,* comes from ON *skatha*: cf OFris *skathia,* OE *sceathan, sceththan,* OHG *scadōn,* MHG-G *schaden,* Go *skathjan,* MD-D *schaden.* The IE r is prob *\*skedh-,* var *\*skadh-,* to injure. Perh cf SCATTER.

**scatology,** whence **scatological.** See the element *scato-.*

**scatter** (v, hence n), whence the pa **scattered,** the vn **scattering;** hence also the A sl **Scat!** (Run away!) and the orig humorous **scatteration** and the adj **scattery** (whence—prob assisted by **scatterbrained**—the sl **scatty,** crazy); **shatter** (v, hence n), whence the pa, vn **shattering** and the adj **shattery; skedaddle** (v, hence n); perh cf the sep SKID.

1. *Scatter* and *shatter* are doublets: the origin of the former is ME *scateren*; of the latter, its var *schateren*: either deriving from or, at the least, akin to MLG *schateren*: ult echoic, as in the cognate Gr *skedannunai,* to split up or strew about: cf also Skt *skadhatē,* he splits; IE r, prob *\*skhed-,* to split up. (Hofmann.)

2. App from Gr *skedannunai,* to split up, comes the coll E *skedaddle,* to run hurriedly away, esp in fear: ? some scholarly wit's blend of Gr *skedan-nunai*+either '*paddle* away' or '*saddle* up (and depart)'.

**scavenge, scavenger; scavage.** 'To *scavenge*' is a b/f from *scavenger,* itself deriving—with intrusive *n,* as in E *passenger* from F *passager*—from ME *scavager,* an official concerned with *scavage,* a toll medievally exacted from foreign merchants for the display, or the offer, of goods for sale: AF *scawage,* by aphesis from ONF *escauwage,* from *escauwer,* to examine (goods): of Gmc origin: f.a.e., SHOW.

**scena.** See para 2 of SCENE.

**scenario.** See para 2 of:

**scene, scenery—scenario, scena—scenic; proscenium.—squirrel.—shine** (v, hence n), presp hence pa **shining,** pt and pp **shone; shimmer** (v, hence n), with pa, vn **shimmering.—scintilla, scintillant, scintillate, scintillation.—stencil** and **tinsel.—sheer,** bright, hence unclouded, hence pure.

Indo-European

1. *Scene* derives from MF-F *scène*: L *scēna,* var

*scaena*: (perh via Etruscan from) Gr *skēnē* (Doric *skānā*), a covered place (e.g. a tent), hence a stage, hence a scene thereon, hence a scene in general: IE r, *\*skā-*, var *\*skāi-*, as in Skt *chāyá*, brilliance, lustre, (but also, by that 'perversity' which characterizes language) shade, a shadow—cf the cognate Gr *skiá*, shade, a shadow, and, sem, contrast Go *skeirs*, clear, bright.

### Greek-Latin

2. Gr *skēnē* has adj *skēnikos*, whence L *scēnicus* (*scaenicus*), MF-F *scénique*, E *scenic*. L *scēna* develops its own adj, LL *scēnārius*, of the stage, whence It *scenario*, adopted by E (cf the F *scénario*); It *scenario* becomes thoroughly anglicized in the form *scenery*, orig with theatrical denotations and connotations. The Mus *scena* is adopted from It (from L).

3. Gr *skēnē* has the derivative prefix-cpd *proskēnion*, lit a stage at the front (*pro-*), hence the part in front of the curtain, whence L *proscēnium*, adopted by E.

4. Gr *skiá*, shadow, has full cpd *skiouros*, lit the 'shadow-tail'; Gr *oura*, tail, is akin to E *arse*. *Skiouros* becomes L *sciūrus*, with VL metathesis *\*scūrius*, whence the VL dim *\*scūriōlus*, whence OF-MF *escuriuel*, MF *esquireul* (F *écureuil*), whence late ME *squirel*, *squyrel*, E *squirrel*.

5. Prob akin to Gr *skiá* and *skēnē* is L *scintilla*, ? lit 'a little shiner' (*-illa*, dim suffix; *-t-*, perh euphonic), a spark, adopted by SciE. L *scintilla* has the derivative v *scintillāre*, to sparkle, with presp *scintillans*, o/s *scintillant-*, whence E *scintillant*, sparkling, and with pp *scintillātus*, whence 'to *scintillate*'; derivative L *scintillātiō*, o/s *scintillātiōn-*, becomes EF-F and, prob independently, E *scintillation*, whence, anl, *scintillator*. The LL adj *scintillōsus* yields the rare E *scintillose* and *scintillous*.

6. L *scintilla* becomes, by metathesis, the VL *\*stincilla*, whence MF *estencelle*, whence MF *estenceler*, whence E 'to *stencil*', whence the n *stencil*.

7. MF *estencelle* has the L-influenced var *estincelle*, whence the EF-F *étincelle*, whence E *tinsel*, with derivative adj and v.

### Germanic

8. Akin to Gr *skēnē* and L *scēna*, varr *scaena* and *scaina*, is OE *scīnan*, ME *shinen*, later *shinen*, E 'to *shine*': cf OFris *skīna* (with n *skīn*), MD *schinen*, D *schijnen*, OS *scīnan*, OHG *scīnan*, MHG *schīnen*, G *scheinen* (n *Schein*), Go *skeinan*, ON *skīna*. 'To *shine*,' whence the n *shine*, has presp, vn *shining* and agent *shiner*.

9. The OE *scīnan*, to shine, has the OE freq *scimrian* (? a 'thinning' of *\*scīnrian*), to shine fitfully, hence faintly, ME *schimeren*, E 'to *shimmer*': cf OE *scīma*, a shining, brightness, Go *skeima*, torch, lantern, MD-D and LG *schemeren*, G *schimmern*, Sw *skimra*, to shimmer.

10. Prob not deriving from, but app influenced by the cognate OE *scīr*, ME *shire*, clear, bright

(cf Go *skeirs*, OS *skīri*, MHG *schīr*, G *schier*, ON *skīrr*), is E *sheer*, bright, hence pure, hence sole, hence also transparent, perpendicular, ME *schere*, prob from ON *skaerr*.

**scenery, scenic.** See prec, para 2.

**scent.** See SENSE, para 13.

**scepter** (AE), **sceptre.** See SHAFT, para 3.

**schedular, schedule.** See the 2nd SHED, para 5.

**schema, schematic, schematism** (whence, anl, **schematist**), **schematize, scheme** (n, hence v, whence **schemer** and **scheming**); **sketch**, n (whence **sketchy**), hence v (whence **sketcher** and **sketching**)—cf **esquisse** and **schizzo** and G *Sieg*, victory, as in **Siegfried, Sigismund**; sep SCHOOL (of instruction) —sep HECTIC, HECTOR—sep EPOCH.

1. *Scheme* derives from LL *schēma*—adopted by learnèd E: Gr *skhēma*, a form, an outline, from Gr *ekhein*, to have, to hold, future *skhēsō* (var of *hexō*): PGr *\*hekhein*: IE r, *\*segh-*, as in Skt *sáhatē*, he masters or overpowers, and as in Go *sigis*, victory.

2. Gr *skhēma* has o/s *schēmat-*, whence both the rare adj *skhēmatikos*, which prob suggested E *schematic*, and the v *skhēmatizein*, to form, LL *schēmatizāre*, E 'to schematize' (cf F *schématiser*); *skhēmatizein* itself has derivative *skhēmatismos*, ML *schematismus*, E *schematism* (F *schématisme*).

3. Akin to Gr *skhēma* is Gr *skhedios*, extempore, approximate, with derivative n *skhedion*: whence LL *schedius*, extempore, with n *schedium*: It *schizzo*, a sketch, whence both EF *esquiche*, later *esquisse*, and D *schets*, leading to E *sketch*; with derivative 'to *sketch*', cf It *schizzare* (from *schizzo*), EF *esquicher*, F *esquisser*, D *schetsen*. Both It *schizzo* and F *esquisse* have been adopted by E, the former among the Italianates, the latter among the Gallomanes.

4. Deriving from IE *\*segh-* are such forms as OIr *segaim*, I attain, and Go *sigis*, victory, and syn OHG *sigu* (cf OE *sige*), MHG *sige*, G *Sieg*; G *Siegfried* combines victory with peace (OHG *fridu*, MHG *fride*, G *Friede*), and G *Sigismund* calls upon OHG *munt*, protection.

**schism, schismatic.** See the 2nd SHED, para 6.

**schist, schistose.** See the 2nd SHED, para 7.

**schizoid; schizont.** See the 2nd SHED, para 8.

**schizophrenia, -phrenic.** Cf the 2nd SHED, para 8.

**schnapper.** See SNAP (heading).

**schnitzel**, adopted from G, is lit 'a slice': from *schnitzen*, int of *schneiden*, to cut, MHG *snīden*, OHG *snīdan*, akin to Go *sneithan* and ON *snītha*: o.o.o.

**schola.** See the 2nd SCHOOL, para 2.

**scholar**, whence **scholarly** and **scholarship**. See the 2nd SCHOOL, para 3.

**scholastic, scholasticate, scholasticism.** See the 2nd SCHOOL, para 4.

**scholiast; scholium.** See the 2nd SCHOOL, para 5.

**school** (1), of fish. See SKILL, para 2.

**school** (2), of instruction, hence adj and v (whence **schooling**), with numerous and obvious cpds, e.g. **-boy, -girl, -house, -man, -master, -mistress, -teacher; schola, scholar** (whence **scholarly**

and **scholarship**); **scholastic** (whence **scholasticism**), **scholasticate**; **scholiast** (whence **scholiastic**) and **scholium**; cf the sep SCHEMA.

1. *School* derives from ME *scole*, itself partly from OE *scōl* (from LL *scola*) and partly from OF-MF *escole* (EF-F *école*); the OF word derives from L *schola*, a school: Gr *skholē*, orig a halt, hence a rest, leisure, hence employment for leisure, esp such employment for children, hence training or instruction, hence schooling, hence a school: from Gr *ekhein*, to have, to hold, pt *eskhon* and presperf *eskhēka*: f.a.e., SCHEMA, para 1. With E *school* and OE *scōl*, cf OHG *scuola*, MHG *schuole*, G *Schule*, and ON *skōli*.

2. L *schola* survives in academic E and in such a cpd as the Mus *schola cantorum*, a school for singers (cf the *Schola Cantorum* in the Rue St Jacques, Paris).

3. L *schola* (LL *scola*) has the LL adj *scholāris* (*scolāris*), belonging to school, whence the ML n 'schoolchild', whence OF *escoler*, MF *escolier* (F *écolier*), whence ME *scoler*, E reshaped *scholar*: cf OHG *scuolari*, G *Schüler*.

4. Gr *skolē*, a lecture, a school, has derivative v *skholazein*, to keep a school, to give lectures, with derivative adj *skholastikos*, whence L *scholasticus* (cf LL 'a learnèd man'), whence both MF-F *scolastique* and E *scholastic*. F *scolastique* has derivative *scolasticat*, anglicized as *scholasticate*, a Catholic seminary.

5. Gr *skolē* has derivative *skholion*, an annotation (usu marginal), whence ML *scholium*, adopted—mostly in pl *scholia*—by the world of scholarship. From Gr *skholion* comes the LGr *skholiastēs*, whence ML *scholiasta*, whence both EF *scholiaste* (F *scoliaste*) and E *scholiast*.

**schooner** is of D spelling (cf G *Schoner*) but E (Northern) dial and Sc origin: *scoon*, to skin along the water, a var of *scun*, to fly through the air, to skim swiftly along: app from ON *skunda*, to speed. (EDD.)

**schottische.** See SCOT, para 4.

**sciatic** (nerve), **sciatica**; **ischiadic, ischial, ischiatic, ischium.**

1. *Sciatic* derives from MF-F *sciatique*, LL *sciaticus*, aphetic for L *ischiadicus*, Gr *iskhiadikos*, adj of *iskhion*, the hip-joint, whence L *ischium*, adopted by SciE; from LL *sciaticus*, Med has coined *sciatica*. With Gr *iskhion* cf Skt *sákthi*, hip.

2. L *ischiadicus* yields E *ischiadic*, with var *ischiatic* deriving from the inferior LL spelling *ischiaticus*; L *ischium* yields *ischial*.

**scibile.** See para 2 of:

**science, scient, sciential, scientific, scientism, scientist**—**sciolism, sciolist** (whence **sciolistic**), **sciolous** — **scious** — **scibile.** — Compounds: **adscititious**; **conscience, conscient** (whence **inconscient**), **conscientious, conscionable** (whence neg **unconscionable**), **conscious** (whence **consciousness** and **subconcious** and the negg **unconscious, -ness**); **inscience, inscient**; **nescience, nescient**—cf **nice** (whence **niceness**), **nicety**; **omniscience, omniscient**; **plebiscite**, q.v. at PEOPLE, para 8; **prescience,**

**prescient.**—Perh akin to the 2nd SHED (where, e.g. SCISSION).

Simple

1. All these terms spring from L *scīre*, to know; prob orig to cut through, hence to decide: perh cf Skt *chyáti*, he cuts, and Ir *scían*, a knife (E & M). L *scindere* could be a nasalized cognate, *scin-* answering to *sci-*: cf the 2nd SHED.

2. *Scire* has derivative LL adj *scibilis*, knowable, whence the Phil *scibile*, something knowable, prop the neu of the adj, and the L adj *scius*, knowing, whence the rare E *scious*; the L dim *sciolus*, knowing but little, yields the now rare *sciolous*, whence, anl, *sciolism* and *sciolist*.

3. *Scire* has presp *sciens*, o/s *scient-*, whence the rare E *scient*, adj hence n. On L *scient-* arises L *scientia*, knowledge, whence OF-F *science*, adopted by E; the derivative LL adj *\*scientiālis* (deduced from the LL adv *scientiāliter*), occurring in ML, becomes *sciential*. The ML cpd adj *scientificus*, knowledge-making, becomes MF-F *scientifique* and E *scientific*. On L *scient*ia are formed *scientism* and *scientize* and esp *scientist*, which, unrecorded before 1840 (OED), prob owes something to It *scienziato* (Boccaccio; archaic), a learnèd man.

Compound

4. For convenience, the cpds are best treated in alphabetical order. The 1st represents the sole survival of an E word deriving from L *sciscere*, to seek to know, the inch of *scire*. *Sciscere* has the cpd *adsiscere*, to adjoin by decree, pp *adsciots*, whence—after *adventitious*—the E *adscititiuus*, supplemental, additional.

5. L *conscius* (*con-*, together), sharing knowledge, yields *conscious*. On *conscius* arises *conscīre*, to know at the same time, i.e. to be conscious of, with presp *consciens*, o/s *conscient-*, whence the E *conscient*; derivative L *conscientia* becomes OF-F *conscience*, adopted by E, whence the irreg *conscionable*: derivative ML *conscientiōsus* becomes EF-F *consciencieux*, f *-ieuse*, whence E *conscientious*.

6. *Scientia* has neg *inscientia*, whence the rare E *inscience*, ignorance; *sciens* has neg *insciens*, o/s *inscient-*, E *inscient*.

7. *Scire* has neg *nescire*, not (*ne-*) to know, with presp *nesciens*, o/s *nescient-*, whence E *nescient*; derivative LL *nescientia* yields *nescience*. From *nescire* comes the L adj *nescius*, ignorant, whence OF-EF *nice*, ignorant, innocent, whence ME *nice*, foolish, whence shy, hence discriminating ('a *nice* taste in literature'), hence agreeable, pleasant; derivative OF-MF *niceté*, ignorance, folly, gives us the syn *nicety*, with new senses running parallel to those of the adj, esp 'delicacy of feeling or of taste'.

8. Anl with LL *omnipotentia*, omnipotence, ML forms *omniscientia*, whence *omniscience*, whence, anl, *omniscient*—cf the Theol ML *omniscius*.

9. *Scire* has the cpd *praescīre*, to know *prae-* or in advance, presp *praesciens*, o/s *praescient-*,

whence E *prescient*; derivative LL *praescientia*, foreknowledge, becomes OF-MF *prescience* (MF-F *pré-*), adopted by E.

**scind.** See the 2nd SHED, para 3.

**scintilla, scintillant, scintillate, scintillation.** See SCENE, para 5.

**sciolism, sciolist, sciolous.** See SCIENCE, para 2.

**scion,** also (esp in AE) spelt **cion,** ME *syon, sioun,* derives from OF-MF *cion* (F *scion*): Frankish *\*kith* (cf OHG *kīdi*) a (plant's) shoot+ the dim suffix *-on*; the OGmc r of *\*kith, kidi,* is *\*ki-,* to burst forth—cf the Go pp us-*ki*jans, (of seeds) having come forth, OE *cīnan,* to burst, OHG *chīmo,* MHG *kīme,* G *Kei*m, a seed, a germ. (Walshe, at *Keim.*)

**scissile, scission.** See the 2nd SHED, para 3.

**scissors:** ME *sisours*: MF *cisoires,* large scissors (cf *ciseaux,* scissors): LL *cisōria,* pl of *cisōrium,* a cutting instrument: perh via VL from L *caesus,* pp of *caedere,* to cut (cf *caesura*). The *sc-* is f/e: a confusion caused by ML *scissor,* a tailor, from L *scindere.*

**scissure.** See the 2nd SHED, para 3.

**scleriasis,** a morbid induration; **sclerosis,** a hardening of tissues or arteries: SciL (Med) from Gr *sklēriāsis* and *sklērōsis*: Gr *sklēr*os, hard+ suffixes *-iasis* and *-osis.* The corresp adjj are *scleriatic* and *sclerotic,* formed on Gr patterns.

**scoff,** n, hence v, whence **scoffer** and **scoffing.** See SHOVE, para 4.

**scold,** n, hence v, whence **scolding; scald** or **skald.** *Scold,* a person given to ribaldry, hence to abuse or fault-finding, derives from ME *scold* or *scolde,* earlier *scald,* prob from ON *skāld,* a poet— whence E *scald* (*sk-*)—esp as a satirist; cf ON *skāldskapr,* poetry, esp if satirical or libellous. With ON *skāld,* cf OIr *scél,* Ga *sgeul,* narration, narrative.

**sconce** (1), a candlestick. See RECONDITE.

**sconce** (2), a detached defensive work, a redoubt: late MHG-G *schanze* (rather than D *schans*): ? for *\*schranze,* var of MHG-G *schranke,* a barrier, akin to OHG *screnchēn,* to lay crosswise. (Walshe.)

2. *Sconce* acquires the cpd **ensconce,** to shelter (esp oneself) as if in redoubt.

**scone.** See SHEEN, para 2.

**scoop.** See SHOVE, para 5.

**scoot.** See SHOOT.

**scope,** a target, hence an intention, a theme, hence range, opportunity, space in which to move; for *-scope, -scopic, -scopy,* etc., see the element *-scope.*

*Scope* derives, via It *scopo,* from L *scopus,* earlier *scopos,* trln of Gr *skopos,* a watcher, also a visual aim, from *skop*ein, to view, intimately related to the syn *skep*testhai: Gr r, *skep-,* app a metathesis of *spek-,* and therefore id with L *spec*ere, to look, to see: cf SPECTACLE.

**scorbutic,** of or like scurvy: late EF-F *scorbutique,* adj of EF-F *scorbut*: ML *scorbutus*: app from Ru *skrobota,* via a Gmc language.

**scorch** (v, hence n), whence **scorcher** and pa, vn **scorching**: sense and form, app from ME *scorken,*

from ON *skorpna,* to dry up, with form influenced by OF-MF *escorchier,* MF *escorcher* (F *écorcher*), from LL *excorticāre,* to scrape, or strip, the bark off, from L *cortex,* bark. With ON *skorpna,* cf ON *skorpinn,* shrivelled, and perh ON *skarpr* (there- fore E SHARP).

**score.** See SHARE, para 5.

**scoria,** refuse, dross, is adopted from L: Gr *skōria,* an *-ia* derivative of *skōr,* dung: cf the syn Skt ava*skara* and Hit *sakkar* (gen *saknas*), var *zakkar.*—Hence 'to *scorify*', whence, anl, *scorifi- cation.*

**scorn** (n and v), whence **scornful.** *Scorn,* n, derives from ME *scorn,* earlier *scarn,* aphetic from OF-MF *escarn*; 'to *scorn*', from ME *scornen,* earlier *scarnen,* from OF-MF *escarnir,* var of *escharnir,* to mock, to scorn, to humiliate: both of Gmc origin—cf OHG *skern* (*scërn*), MHG *schërn,* mockery, scorn, OHG *skernōn* (*scërnōn*), to mock, scorn. The ME change from *-a-* to *-o-* perh arises from OF-EF *escorner* (F *écorner*), to deprive of horns, hence to despoil, hence to mock, to humiliate, from VL *\*excornāre,* from L *cornu,* a horn; the OHG words perh bear the basic sense —'to cut'.

**Scorpio** (Astr and zodiacal), **scorpion; scorpene** and **sculpin.** L *scorpiō* has gen *scorpiōnis,* o/s *scorpiōn-,* whence, prob via OF-F, the E *scorpion*: and L *scorpiō* derives from Gr *skorpiōn* (gen *skorpiōnos*), var of *skorpios,* a scorpion, also a prickly sea-fish, whence the syn Gr *skorpaina,* L *scorpaena,* F *scorpène* (obs), E *scorpene.* The Gr *skorpios, skorpiōn* has s *skorp-,* extn of IE *\*skor-,* var of *\*sker-,* to cut.

2. App deriving from or at the least cognate with F *scorpène* is that very spiny fish the *sculpin.*

**scot** and **scot-free.** See SHOOT, para 2. (For sl *scot,* ill-temper, see para 5 of the next.)

**Scot; Scotch** (adj, hence n), **Scots** (adj), **Scottish** —cf **schottische; Scotia** (Nova Scotia) and **Scot- land; Scott; Scotticism; Scotty;** sl **scot** and **scotty.**

1. A *Scot* or (obs) a *Scott* (extant as surname) derives from OE *Scott,* pl *Scottas,* the Irish, from LL *Scotti,* the Irish, itself from OIr *Scuit,* the Irish, nom sing *Scot:* ? 'the Wanderers'—cf Ga *sguit,* a wanderer.

2. The OE adj is *Scyttisc,* whence—? influenced by ML *Scotticus*—ME *Scottisc,* E *Scottish*; the EE var *Scottis* becomes, by contr, the E adj *Scots*; ME *Scottisc* yields also *Scotch,* whence *Scotchman.*

3. *Scotland* is the 'land of the Scots', and *Scotia* a ML territorial (*-ia*) derivative of LL *Scoti; Nova Scotia,* 'the New Scotland', is still noted for its *Scots*; ML *Scot(t)icus,* adj of *Scot(t)i,* accounts for *Scotticism,* anl with *Anglicism.*

4. E *Scottish* becomes G *schottisch,* whence the lively round dance known as the *schottische*; cf that older, statelier dance the F have named the *écossaise,* elliptical for *danse écossaise,* Scottish dance, the F adj *écossais* deriving from *l'Ecosse,* Scotland.

5. With sl *scot,* a fit of bad temper, and its adj *scotty,* cf the syn Ir n *irish.* (The dog *Scotty* is coll

for 'Scottish terrier'.) With Scotch for 'Scotch whisky', cf Irish for 'Irish whiskey'.

scotch, to cut superficially, but also to wound, hence n, derives from AF escocher, to notch, from OF-F coche, a notch, from VL *cocca (cf It cocca, a notch), from L coccum, excrescence on a plant. (B & W.)

Scotch. See SCOT, para 2—cf para 5.

scoter. See SHOOT, para 13.

Scotia, Scotland. See SCOT, para 3.

Scots, adj. See SCOT, para 2.

Scott, Scotticism, Scottish. See SCOT, paras 1 and 3.

scotty and Scotty. See SCOT, para 5.

scoundrel, whence scoundrelly, is o.o.o.: ? anl with wastrel and by aphesis from AF escoundre, OF-MF escondre, esp in the reflexive 'to hide oneself away', from L ex, out of+condere, to place, as EW has suggested; note, however, that escondre is also a var of OF-EF escondire, to excuse oneself, from VL *excondicere (dicere, to say).

scour (1), to rub hard, to purge, whence scourings. See CURE, para 3.

scour (2), to run hard, to decamp. See COURSE, para 11.

scourge, n and v. The n derives from ME scourge (var scurge), earlier scorge, from OF-MF escorge, whence MF escorgier, whence ME scorgen, later scourgen, whence 'to scourge': and OF-MF escorge derives from L corrigia, a strap, a whip, orig a shoe-lace, akin to OIr cuimrech, fetters, and conriug, I tie together (E & M); cf also Ga cuibrech or cuidhreach, Cor carhar or carghar (pl cargharow), a fetter: is there a C r com-, con-, cum-, cuim-, akin to L cum, along with, hence, in vv, together?

scout (1), a spy, hence v. 'To scout,' ME scouten, derives from ME scoute, whence 'a scout': and ME scoute is aphetic for OF-MF escoute, a spy, from escouter, earlier escolter, for ascolter: VL *ascultāre, for L auscultāre, to listen to, to hear, attentively: cf auscultate, q.v. at EAR (L auris).

scout (2), to reject contemptuously. See SHOOT, para 14.

scow: D schouw: MD schou, schouwe: o.o.o.: perh akin to MD schoewe (D schoe), a shoe: from shape-resemblance of a scow to a clog.

scowl (v, hence n), whence scowling, pa, vn, ME scoulen: app of Scan origin—cf Da skule.

2. Cf also skulk (whence pa skulking), akin to Da skulke.

scrabble. See SCAMBLE, para 3.

scrag, n (whence scraggy), a lean, tough person or quadruped, hence a scrawny person and the nape of (a sheep's) neck, whence 'to scrag': of Scan origin, as are so many scr- words: cf Sw dial scragg, something haggard or torn, skraka, a tall, very thin man or dry tree, and the cognate Nor skragg (? also skrogg).

scram is short for scramble, q.v. at SCAMBLE, para 3.

scran, broken victuals, hence food (dial and sl) o.o.o.: ? a b/f from scrannel.

scrannel; scranny. See SCRAWNY.

scrap. See SCAMBLE, para 4.

scrape. See SCAMBLE, para 4.

scratch, v (whence scratcher and scratching), hence n (whence scratchy);—grate, to scrape harshly, to rub vigorously, whence pa grating—cf grater; regrate, regrater.—Cf the sep SCRIBE.

1. 'To scratch' blends ME scratten, to scratch, with syn ME cracchen (MD cratsen): cf MHG schratzen (? int s-) and OHG krazzōn, MHG-G kratzen, to scratch, and ON krota, to engrave, and, says Walshe, the nasalized Lith grándau, I scrape.

2. Akin to OHG krazzōn is OF-MF grater (MF-F gratter), to scratch, to scrape: whence 'to grate', whence a grater (cf EF-F grattoir).

3. OF-MF grater has cpd OF-MF regrater (later regratter), to scrape again, hence 'to regrate', both in masons' work and in commerce; the derivative OF-MF agent regratier (F regrattier) becomes E regrater, a middleman.

scrawl, v hence n, o.o.o., is perh a (dial) var of 'to scroll', q.v. at SHRED: from ornate hand-writing's tendency to become illegible.

scrawny and its var scranny derive, as does the orig dim (-el) scrannel, thin, lean and weak, from Scan: cf Nor dial skran, thin, desiccated, and Sw dial skran, weak; perh cf also the Scan words for lumber and trash.

screak. See SCREECH, para 1.

scream. See SCREECH, para 2.

scree is a b/f from the pl screes, itself from ON skrītha, a landslide, from skrītha, to slip, to slide, akin to OE scrīthan, OS scrīdan, OHG scrīdan or scrītan: prob echoic.

screech and screak and shriek; scream: all vv, with derivative id nn, and with agents in -er, paa and vnn in -ing: and all echoic. 'To screech', EE scritch, comes from ME skrichen, and 'to creak' is a var, prob influenced by ON skraekja, to screech, to shriek, whence prob the ME schriken, E 'to shriek': cf the bird shrike, OE scrīc, a thrush, akin to Ice skrīkja, Sw skrika, thrush, lit the shrieker.

2. Prob akin to ON skraekja are ON scraema, to terrify (? orig by screeching), and skraemast, to flee (? from the rushing sound of flight), whence app ME scremen, E 'to scream'.

3. The Scan r is perh echoic *skrī (skree-) with extnn in -ch, -k, and -m; the IE base is perh *krī- (kree-), as in F crier (cf E CRY), with the int prefix s- added in Scan, where initial s so often occurs.

screed. See SHRED, para 3.

screen, n hence v, whence screenage, screener, screening: ME scren, aphetic for: MF escren, var escran (F écran), by metathesis from: MD scherm, scheerm: cf OHG scirm, MHG schirm, protection (cf G Schirm, umbrella), and MHG schirmen, var schermen, to fence: ? akin, as Walshe suggests, to Skt čarma, the skin. From the appearance of a protective screen derives the goldminers' screen or sieve, whence 'to screen' or scrutinize thoroughly before admission; the older sense 'to protect' derives from the very nature of the protective screen itself.

**screeve.** See SCRIBE, para 4.

**screw** (n, hence v), whence **screwy; scrobe.** *Screw*, earlier *scrue*, derives by aphesis from MF-EF *escroue* (EF-F *écrou*): VL *\*scrova*: L *scrōfa*, a sow, influenced by L *scrobis*, *\*scroba*, ditch, hence vulva. With *scrobis*, cf Ru *skrebu*, I scratch: therefore cf SCRIBE.

2. From L *scrobis* comes the Zoo *scrobe*, a groove.

3. L *scrōfa*, a (breeding) sow, is by LL used in the pl *scrōfae* for glandular swellings (esp in the neck), 'perh by a fanciful comparison of the glandular swellings to little pigs' (Webster): whence the syn dim pl *scrōfulae*, whence ML *scrōfula*, the old 'King's evil', adopted by E, with adj *scrofulous*, prob after EF-F *scrofuleux*, f *scrofuleuse*.

**scribble, scribbler.** See para 6 of:

**scribe,** v, hence n (whence **scribal); script,** adj (surviving in cpds) and n (whence **scrip,** a certificate)—**scription,** whence, anl, **scriptive—scriptor, scriptorium** (and **escritoire), scriptory** (adj, whence, anl, **scriptorial)—scripture** (whence **scriptural,** whence **scripturalism, scripturalist), scripturient; scribble,** v (whence **scribbler),** hence n; **screeve,** v (whence **screever),** hence n, and **scrive; scrivener; serif —scarify, scarification** (whence, anl, **scarificator);—shrift, shrive, Shrovetide.**—Cpds from L *scrībere* and its pp *scriptus*: **adscript, adscription, adscriptitious, adscriptive—cf ascribe, ascript, ascription, ascriptitious; circumscribe, circumscript, circumscription** (whence, anl, **circumscriptive); conscribe, conscript** (adj, hence n and v), **conscription** (whence, direct, **conscriptional** and, anl, **conscriptive); describe, description, descriptive—cf descrive; inscribe, inscript, inscription** (whence, anl, **inscriptive); interscribe, interscription; perscribe; postscript, postscriptum; prescribe, prescript, prescriptible, prescription, prescriptive, prescriptorial; proscribe, proscript, proscription** (whence, anl, **proscriptive); rescribe, rescript, rescription** (whence, anl, **rescriptive); subscribe** (whence **subscriber), subscript, subscription, subscriptive—cf subscrive; superscribe, superscript** (adj- and n), **superscription; transcribe, transcript, transcription** (whence, anl, **transcriptive).**

### Indo-European

1. The basic idea is 'to scratch', hence 'to scratch characters upon bark or wax', hence 'to write': sem cf WRITE. For the lit Gmc-Sl 'scratch' group, see SCRATCH. The 'scratch-write' terms occur in Gr, L, Gmc: Gr *skariph*asthai, to scratch, *skariph*os, a stylus: L *scrībere*, to trace characters, to write; ON *hrīfa*, to scratch, OFris *skrīva*, to write, to prescribe a penalty (cf OE *scrīfan*, to prescribe a penalty or a penance, to shrive), OHG *scrīban*, MHG *schrīben*, G *schreiben*, MD *schriven*, D *schrijven*, to write.

### I. Simples: i, Germanic

2. OE *scrīfan*, to prescribe a penance on,

becomes ME *scriven, schriven,* finally *shriven,* whence 'to shrive', pt *shrove,* pp *shriven.* The *shrove* form leads, irreg, to late ME *shroftide, schroftide,* E *Shrovetide,* the *tide* or time of confession before Lent; akin to *scrīf-,* r of *scrīfan,* is OE *scrift,* whence ME *schrift* and, retained by E, *shrift,* a shriving, a confession.

3. *Serif,* a printing term for a cross-stroke at head or foot of a letter, prob derives from D *schreef,* a written stroke, akin to *schrijven,* to write.

4. Three other words that perh come from D are *screeve, scrivener, scrive.* The 1st, cant then sl, for 'to write or draw (on the pavement)', prob comes from It *scrivere* (L *scribere*), to write, but could come from D *schrijven*; the 2nd, from earlier *scrivein,* is usu said to derive from OF-MF *escrivain* (F *écrivain*), from VL *\*scrībānem,* acc of *scrība,* a scribe, but could derive from MD *schrivein,* a scrivener (cf MD *schriver,* D *schrijver,* a writer); the 3rd (*scrive,* to write), usu said to derive from OF-MF *escrivre* (MF *escrire,* F *écrire*), to write, could derive from MD *schriven,* to write.

### Simples: ii, Greek

5. Gr *skariphasthai,* to scratch, becomes L *scarīfāre,* later (influenced by L *sacrificāre*) *scarīficāre,* to scratch or cut the skin of, whence MF-F *scarifier,* whence 'to *scarify';* derivative ML *scarīficātiō,* acc *scarīficātiōnem,* yields MF-F *scarification,* adopted by E.

### Simples: iii, Latin

6. L *scrībere* yields 'to *scribe';* its derivative *scrība,* a penman, a clerk, secretary, yields MF-F *scribe,* adopted by E. *Scrībere* acquires, in ML, the freq *scrībillāre,* to write very (or too) often or much, to write hastily, whence 'to *scribble'.*

7. *Scrībere* has pp *scriptus,* either upon or from which numerous E words form or derive. *Scriptus* becomes the adj *script,* obs except in cpds (e.g., *manuscript,* q.v. at MANUAL); the neu *scriptum,* used as n, becomes—perh via OF-MF *escript*— the E *script,* n.

8. Derivative L *scrīptiō, o/s scrīptiōn-,* becomes E *scription; scriptor* is adopted; *scriptōrius* becomes *scriptory,* and its ML derivative *scriptōrium,* a writing-room, is adopted—as is the OF-MF derivative *escritoire,* but in the sense of F *écritoire,* a writing-desk; *scrīptūra,* (the art of) writing, LL holy scripture, and its pl *scrīptūrae,* the Scriptures, become *scripture, Scripture, the Scriptures,* with adj *scriptural* from LL *scrīptūrālis; scrīptūrīre,* to be eager to write, has presp *scrīptūriens, o/s scrīptūrient-,* whence the adj *scripturient,* whence, anl, *scripturience*—cf *cacoëthes scrībendi,* the itch to write (Gr *kakoëthēs,* a *kakos* or bad *ēthos* or habit).

### II. Compounds of L *scrībere,* pp *script*us

9. L *adscrībere* (*ad,* towards), to add by writing, and its eased var *āscrībere,* with pp and pp-

derivatives *adscriptus, āscriptus—adscriptiō, ās-criptiō*, o/s *-iōnem—a(d)scriptīcius—a(d)scriptiuus*, ML *-ivus—*yield *ascribe, adscript* (adj and n), *a(d)scription, a(d)scriptitious, a(d)scriptive.*

10. L *circumscrībere*, to draw a line about or around (*circum*), pp *circumscriptus*, derivatives *circumscriptiō*, yield *circumscribe, circumscript, circumscription*, all with the connotation of 'narrow limits'.

11. L *conscrībere*, to write *con-* or together, to enrol, pp *conscriptus*, derivative *conscriptiō* (o/s *-iōn-*), yield *conscribe, conscript, conscription.*

12. L *dēscrībere*, to write from (*dē-*) an exemplar or model, to copy, pp *dēscriptus*, derivatives *dēscriptiō* (o/s *-iōn-*), LL *dēscriptiōnālis* and *dēscriptīuus* (ML *-īvus*), yield *describe, description, descriptional, descriptive.* L *dēscrībere* becomes OF-MF *descrivre* (MF *descrire*, F *décrire*), whence the now only Sc *descrive.*

13. L *inscrībere*, to write in(to), pp *inscriptus*, derivatives *inscriptiō* (o/s *-iōn-*) and LL *inscriptura*, yield *inscribe, inscription*, (obs) *inscripture* with pa *inscriptured.*

14. L *interscrībere*, to write *inter-* or between, yields *interscribe*, whence, anl, *interscription.*

15. L *perscrībere*, to write *per-*, in detail, about, derivative *perscriptiō*, give us the rare *perscribe* and *perscription.*

16. L *postscrībere*, to write after (the main part), pp *postscriptus*, neu *postscriptum* used as n, account for *postscribe* (rare) and *postscript*, adj and n.

17. L *praescrībere*, to write at the top, hence state in advance and authoritatively, pp *prae-scriptus*, derivatives *praescrīptiō* (o/s *-iōn-*) and *praescrīptīuus*, ML *-īvus*, yield—the last, in form only—*prescribe, prescript* (adj and n), *prescription, prescriptive.* E *prescriptible* is adopted from MF-F, which formed it, anl, from MF-F *prescription.*

18. L *prōscrībere*, to write publicly, to publish (esp the name of a person condemned to death or exile), pp *prōscriptus*, derivative *prōscriptiō*, o/s *-iōn-*, yield *proscribe, proscript* (adj and n), *proscription.*

19. L *rescrībere*, (of the emperor) to write *re-*, back, i.e. in reply, hence to render a decision, pp *rescrīptūs*, neu *rescrīptum* used as n, LL *rescrīptiō*, o/s *-iōn-*, produce *rescribe, rescript* (n), *rescription.*

20. L *subscrībere*, to put one's signature under (*sub*) an accusation, LL to set apart (esp money) or to appropriate, pp *subscrīptus*, derivatives *subscrīptiō* and LL *subscrīptīuus*, ML *-īvus*, explain *subscribe, subscript* (adj and n), *subscription, subscriptive.* L *subscrībere* becomes MF *subscrire*, EF *soubscrire* (F *souscrire*), with *subscriv-, soub-scriv-* in certain parts: whence Sc *subscrive.*

21. LL *superscrībere*, to write above, make a note above the line, pp *superscriptus*, derivative *superscrīptiō*, o/s *-iōn-*, yield *superscribe, super-script*, adj and (from L neu *-scrīptum*) n, *super-scription.*

22. L *transcrībere*, to write across, i.e. to transfer in writing, to copy, pp *transcrīptus* (neu *-scrīptum*

used as n), derivative LL *transcrīptiō*, o/s *-iōn-*, originate *transcribe, transcript, transcription.*

23. Several of the *-scription* nn, e.g. *prescription* and *transcription*, owe something to F intervention.

**scrimmage.** See SKIRMISH.

**scrimp.** See SCANT, para 4.—Hence, app, the sl *scrimshank*, to scamp one's work, to malinger: to which, perh, is akin the o.o.o. SCRIMSHAW (unless from a PN).

**scrip** (1), wallet. See SCARF, para 2.

**scrip** (2), certificate. A slovening of:

**script.** See SCRIBE, para 7.

**scription, scriptional; scriptorium, scriptory; scriptural, scripture, Scriptures; scripturient.** See SCRIBE, para 8.

**scrive.** See SCRIBE, para 4.

**scrivener.** See SCRIBE, para 4.

**scrobe.** See SCREW, para 2.

**scrofula, scrofulous.** See SCREW, para 3.

**scrolar, scroll.** See SHRED, para 5.

**scrotum**, whence *scrotal.* See SHRED, para 1.

**scrounge.** See SCRUNGE.

**scrub** (1), vegetation. See SHRUB, para 2.

**scrub** (2), to rub (clothes, etc.) hard as one washes, hence n and also *scrubber* and *scrubbing*: MD and LG *schrubben* (D *schrobben*): cf Sw *skrubba*, Da *skrubbe*: prob echoic and perh, via *\*srub-*, an int of the IE r of RUB.

**scruff** (1), dandruff, is a dial metathesis of *scurf*, q.v. at SCARF, para 2. Hence the dial and coll adj *scruffy.*

**scruff** (2), nape of neck, is a var of the syn SCUFF, of Gmc origin: cf Go *skuft* and—*p* for *f*—ON *skopt*, hair.

**scrum** and **scrummage.** Cf *scrimmage*; see SKIRMISH.

**scrunge; scrounge.** The latter is a sl (orig dial) var of the former, a dial word for 'to squeeze'—hence for 'to pilfer': a var, perh a derivative, of dial SCRUNCH, to crunch: echoic.

**scruple** (n, v), **scrupulosity, scrupulous.** See SHRED, para 7.

**scrutable, scrutability—inscrutable, inscruta-bility; scrutate, scrutator; scrutineer, scrutinize, scrutiny.** See SHRED, para 8.

**scud, scuddle.** See the 3rd SCUTTLE.

**scudo.** See SCUTAGE, para 5.

**scuff** (1), nape of neck. See the 2nd SCRUFF.

**scuff** (2), to shuffle. See SHOVE, para 3.

**scuffle.** See SHOVE, para 3.

**scull** (oar), n hence v, occurs in ME—and is o.o.o.: ?, however, a sense-development from the Sc *scull*, a shallow wicker basket, itself from ON *skjōla*, a bucket.

**scullery.** See SCUTAGE, para 4.

**scullion**, ME *sculyon*, represents MF *escouillon*, from OF-MF *escoveillon*, itself a dim of OF *escove*, a broom, from L *scōpa.*

**sculpin.** See SCORPIO, para 2.

**sculptor**, whence anl **sculptress; sculpture**, n (hence v), whence—as in F—*sculptural* and—after *picturesque*—**sculpturesque; sculpsit.**

1. The jocular 'to *sculpt*' derives from F *sculpter*,

from L *sculpt*us, pp of *sculp*ere, to carve; cf *sculpsit*, he has carved. *Sculp*ere is a mdfn of *scalp*ere, to scratch: o.o.o.

2. On the pp *sculpt*us arise *sculptor*, a carver, adopted by E, and *sculptūra*, whence late MF-F, whence E, *sculpture*.

**scum; scumble.** See SKIM, para 1 and heading.

**scunner.** See SHUN, para 2.

**scup,** an A marine fish: short for the syn **scuppaug:** Alg *mishcùppauog* (pl): *mishe*, big (perh cf Gr *megas*, E *much*)+*kuppe*, close-set (ref the scales)+-*uog*, a suffix denoting plurality. (Mathews; Webster.)

**scupper.** See SHOVE, para 6.

**scurf, scurfy.** See the 2nd SCARF, para 2.

**scurril** (or **scurrile**)—**scurrility**—**scurrilous.** The 3rd is an extn of the 1st; the 2nd derives from L *scurrīlitās*, derivative of that L adj which generates E *scurril*, var *scurrile*: *scurrīlis*, an -*īlis* derivative of *scurra*, a buffoon, a parasite, earlier a 'city slicker', orig a townee: o.o.o.: ? Etruscan (E & M); ? from *excurrere*, to run all over the place, esp out of bounds (connoted by *ex*, out of).

**scurry,** to run briskly, blends either *s*camper or, less prob, *s*catter+*hurry*.

**scurvy,** adj and n. See the 2nd SCARF, para 2.

**scut.** See the 3rd SCUTTLE.

**scutage, scutate; escuage; scutcheon** and **escutcheon; scute,** whence **scutal; scutella, Scutellaria, scutellate, scutellum; scutular, scutulate, scutulum; scutum;—scuttle,** a large, shallow dish (obs) or wickerwork basket, hence as in 'coal *scuttle*';—**scudo** and **escudo**—cf **écu;—esquire** and **squire** (n, hence v), **squirearchy, squireen.**—Cf the elements *scutati-, scutelli-, scuti-*.

1. L *scūtum*, a large oblong shield, is perh akin to Gr *skutos*, a hide, hence leather, and therefore perh to Skt *skâuti, skunāti*, he covers, from IE r *\*skeut-*, to cover, prob an *s*- int of *\*keut-*, as in Gr *kutos*, a hide; but it may be of C origin—cf MW *isgaud*, a shield, and MW and Cor *eskit*, a shoe (and *shoe* is itself perh akin to *scūtum*: Walshe), and Ir *sciath*, W *ysgwyd* (? for *\*scuit*), OBr *scoit*, a shield; perh also OIr *scáth* (Ga *sgàth*), shelter. (E & M; Hofmann; Malvezin[1].)

2. L *scūtum* has been adopted by Zoo; its dim *scūtulum* by Med. *Scūtum* is anglicized as *scute*, extant only in Zoo ('a horny plate'); its derivative adj *scūtātus* becomes *scutate*.

3. The dim *scutulum*, whence E *scutular*, has suggested SciL *scūtulātus*, whence *scutulate*. SciL, moreover, has coined the dim *scutella*, whence, anl, *scutellar*; both, however, owe something to L *scutella*, tray or salver, a dim of L *scutra*, a wooden platter, prob akin to *scūtum*; and L *scutella* has originated Bot *Scutellaria* and *scutellate*.

4. L *scutella*, a tray, becomes OE *scutel*, whence E *scuttle* (for coal); but it also becomes OF-MF *escuele* (F *écuelle*), whence MF *escuelerie*, a place (connoted by -*erie*) where dishes are washed, whence, by aphesis, ME *squillerye*, whence E *scullery*.

5. L *scūtum* becomes Sp and Port *escudo*, a

shield, whence the coins so named; it also becomes OF *escut*, OF-MF *escu*, a shield, later a coin, F *écu*.

6. L *scūtum* has the ML derivative *scūtagium*, whence E *scutage*, a fee paid by a knight in lieu of military service: cf para 8; cf also MF *escuage* (from *escu*; F *écuage*), a knight's military service, adopted by E.

7. L *scūtum* becomes VL *\*scūtiō*, acc *scūtiō*nem, whence MF *escuçon* (F *écusson*), with ONF var *escuchon*, whence E *escutcheon*, with aphetic var *scutcheon*.

8. With *escutcheon-scutcheon*, cf *esqurie-squire*; *squire* derives from ME *squier*, aphetic for ME *esquier*, whence *esquire*; and ME *esquier* is adopted from MF *esquier*, a var of OF-MF *escuier* (F *écuyer*), itself from LL *scūtārius*, a guardsman of the Emperor's court, in L a maker of shields, from the adj *scūtārius*, of or belonging to a shield.

9. *Squire* has the Anglo-Ir dim (-*een*) *squireen*, a petty squire, and the E *squirearchy*, lit rule (cf the element -*arch*) by squires, hence the rural gentry.

**scutch,** to loosen and dress cotton or silk, hence the machine for doing so: aphetic, from MF *escouche*, perh of Gmc, esp Scan, origin (cf Nor *skoka*), but, imm from MF *escoucher* (F *écoucher*), more prob deriving from VL *excussāre*, from L *excussus*, pp of *excutere*, to cause, by shaking, to fall. (DAF.)

**scutcheon.** See SCUTAGE, para 7.

**scutella, scutellar, scutellate; scutellum.** See SCUTAGE, para 3.

**scutter.** See the 3rd SCUTTLE, para 2.

**scuttle** (1), for coal. See SCUTAGE, para 4.

**scuttle** (2), a small opening, esp in a ship; as v, hence to sink a ship by perforating its bottom: prob influenced by F in its passage from Sp *escotilla*, dim of *escote*, an opening made in a fabric, perh from Go *skauts*, extremity or 'edge' of a garment—cf OHG *scōzza*, MHG *schōze*, G *Schoss*, a coat-tail—perh an IE int *s*-prefix cognate of L *cauda*, tail. (B & W; Walshe.)

**scuttle** (3), to scurry, hence n;—**scut,** perh a tail, also a v; **scutter;—scud,** to run swiftly as if propelled, hence n; **scuddle;—skid,** to slide noisily.

1. *Scuddle*, a freq (-*le*) of 'to *scud*', suggests that *scuttle* is **a** freq of 'to *scut*'. It would follow that 'to *scut*' (to scurry) perh derives from *scut*, the tail of a hare or a rabbit, esp noticeable when the creature is fleeing; *scut*, a tail, remains o.o.o., and *scud* remains a prob cognate of *scut*.

2. *Scutter*, however, is clearly a freq (-*ter*) presumably—but not certainly—of 'to *scut*'. One cannot safely do more than say that prob all these words are cognates, one of another, and that, orig, they are prob echoic.

3. *Skid*, to slide gratingly or roughly, is a thinning of *scud*.

**scutular, scutulate, scutulum.** See SCUTAGE, paras 2 and 3.

**scutum.** See SCUTAGE, paras 1 and 2.

**Scylla and Charybdis, between,** between two dangers, either of which is difficult to avoid even

if the c her has been avoided: in the straits of
Messina, *Scylla* (L, from Gr *Skulla*) was a rock
named after a female monster, *Charybdis* (L,
from Gr *Kharubdis*), a whirlpool named after
another. The Gr names are o.o.o.

**scythe.** See the 2nd SAW, para 3.

**Scyth, Scythia, Scythian** (adj, hence n). The 3rd
derives from the 2nd, L word from Gr *Skuthia*, a
territorial (*-ia*) derivative of *Skuthēs*, whence E
*Scyth. Skuthēs* perh derives either from or through
Per *akhšaēna-*, of a dull complexion. (Enci It.)

**sea** (n, hence adj), with many obvious cpds, e.g.
**seaman** (OE *sāemann*); **Zeeland** and **New Zealand.**

1. *New Zealand* anglicizes D *Nieuw Zeeland*,
bestowed by its discoverer (1642), Tasman, in
memory of the D maritime province *Zeeland*, 'Sea
Land'.

2. *Sea*, ME *see*, derives from OE *sāe*: cf OFris
*sē*, sea, OS and OHG *sēo*, sea or lake, MHG *sē*,
G *See*, MD *see, se*, D *zee*, ON *sāer*, sea, and Ga
*saiws*, lake.

**seal** (1), a marine mammal: ME *sele*: OE *seolh*:
cf OHG *selah* and ON *selr* (silent *r*).

**seal** (2), on letter, hence v. See SIGN, para 4.

**seam.** See SEW, para 2.

**seaman,** whence **seamanship.** See SEA (heading).

**seamstress.** See SEW, para 3.

**seamy.** See SEW (heading).

**séance.** See SIT, para 9.

**sear** (1), adj, whence v—adj now usu **sere; sear,**
v;—**sorrel** (colour).

1. *Sear*, dried up, withered, reverts to OE *sēar*,
and its var *sere* to the ME form, *seer*: and OE *sēar*
is akin to MD *soor*, MD-ED *zoor*, LG *zoor*; to OE
*sēarian* (whence 'to sear'), OHG *sōrēn*, to wither;
to Lith *sausas*, dry, and Skt *śoṣa*, drying up. The
Gr *auein*, to parch, is prob unrelated, for its basic
sense is 'to drain, to exhaust'.

2. The colour *sorrel* derives from MF *sorel*, dim
of OF *sor*, yellow-brown, from Frankish *\*saur*, ref
leaves of trees, akin to the Gmc words noted
above.

**sear** (2), that catch which, in a firearm, holds the
hammer at cock; **seraglio; serry,** with pt, pp (hence
pa) **serried.**

1. *Sear* derives from OF-F *serre*, from OF-F
*serrer*, to bar, to close, to lock: VL *serrāre*: LL
*serāre*, to bar: L *sera*, bar of a door, hence a bolt,
a lock: o.o.o.

2. OF-F *serrer*, to bar, bolt, later to press or
crowd, has pp *serré*, whence 'to *serry*'—press,
crowd.

3. VL *\*serrāre*, to bar, to close, to lock, has
derivative *serrāculum*, whence It *serraglio*, a palisaded enclosure, later—by confusion with MF-EF
*serrail* (F *sérail*), from Tu *serāī* (cf caravan*serai*)—
a palace, a harem.

**search.** See CIRCLE, para 5.

**season, seasonal, seasonable.** See the 2nd SOW,
para 4.

**seat.** See SIT, para 20.

**sebaceous, sebacic, sebum.** See SOAP, para 3.

**sec.** See DESICCATE.

**secant; secateur(s).** See the 2nd SAW, para 6.

**secede.** See CEDE, para 12.

**secern.** See SECRECY, para 2.

**secession.** See CEDE, para 12

**seclude, seclusion** (whence, anl, **seclusive**).
*Seclusion* derives from ML *sēclūsiōn-*, o/s of
*sēclūsiō*, from *sēclūsus*, pp of *sēclūdere*, to close
off; *sē-*, apart+*-clūdere*, c/f of *claudere*, to close,
to close up: cf CLAUSE.

**second** (adj, n, v), **secondary, seconde; Secundus,
secundine.**

1. L *secundus*, second (next after the first), orig
following, derives from *sequi*, to follow, pp
*secūtus*: f.a.e., SEQUENCE. Hence, the second-
eldest (child). *Secundus* has the LL derivative
*secundinae* (pl), the afterbirth, whence E *secundine*,
usu in pl, perh after MF-F *secondines*.

2. The fencing position *seconde* is adopted from
F, orig the f of the adj *second*. L *secundus* becomes
OF *segonz*, MF-F *second*, adopted by E; the E n
*second* derives from MF-F *seconde*, from L *secunda
minūta*, second minute, a minute being *prima minūta*
(*minūta* being for *pars minūta*), first minute (part
or division of time); the v *second* derives from
late MF-F *seconder* (whence the pron of the military sense), from L *secundāre*, to aid, from *secundus*,
which, moreover, bears the extn *secundārius*, of
the second rank, whence E *secondary*—cf the MF-F
*secondaire*.

**secrecy, secret** (adj, n); **secrete, secretin, secretion** (whence, anl, **secretive**), **secretory; secretary**
(**secretary bird**), whence **secretarial**—cf **secretariat;
secern, secernment.**

1. *Secrecy* is for *secret*, adj+suffix *-cy*; *secret*,
n, is adopted from OF-F *secret*, from L *secrētum*,
a hidden place, prop the neu of the pp-pa *secrētus*,
separated, whence the OF-F, whence E, adj
*secret*.

2. L *secrētus* is the pp of *sēcernere*, to separate:
*sē-*, apart+*cernere*, to pass through a sieve, hence
to decide: cf CRISIS. *Secernere* yields 'to *secern*',
whence the n *secernment* (cf *discernment*).

3. L *secrētus* leads to the E v *secrete*, to conceal,
(in Bio) to separate; derivative *secrētiō*, o/s of
*secrētiōn-*, becomes late MF-F *secrétion*, whence
E *secretion*. The F *secrétoire* (from *secrét*ion)
becomes E *secretory*. Chem *secretin*=*secrete*+
*-in*.

4. L *secrētum*, a secret place, means in LL the
office of state officials, a secretariat, whence the
adj *secrētārius*, attested by the LL n 'secretary',
esp in *secrētārii sacri consistorii*, secretaries in the
emperor's court (Souter): whence OF-F *secrétaire*,
orig a confidant (depository of *secrēta* or secrets),
whence E *secretary*. A *secretary bird* has a crest
resembling 'a bunch of pens stuck behind the ear'
(Webster). Derivative EF-F *secrétariat* becomes E
*secretariat*, var *-iate*.

**secretary, secretariat.** See prec, final para.

**secrete, secretin, secretion, secretory.** See
SECRECY, para 3.

**sect** (1), a cion. See the 2nd SAW, para 7.

**sect** (2), a religious creed or its believers;

sectarian (whence sectarianism), sectary; sept, division of a tribe, a social group.

1. *Sect* derives from MF-F *secte*, L *secta*, a party, a Phil school, LL the Church, from *sequi*, to follow, pp *secūtus*: f.a.e., SEQUENCE. L *secta* has the derivative ML n *sectārius*, whence *sectary*—perh influenced by EF-F *sectaire* (from *secte*); *sectary* has derivative adj, hence n, *sectarian*.

2. E *sect* acquires the irreg var *sept*, app influenced by L *saeptum*, an enclosure, LL a sanctuary.

sectile; section, sectional; sector. See the 2nd SAW, para 8.

secular, secularism, secularity, secularize. See SEED, para 3.

secundine; Secundus. See SECOND, para 1.

secure, security. See CURE, para 6.

sedan, for sedan chair, brought in C17 from Spain to England, owes the idea to the Sp *sillón* (from L *sella*, a chair, cf SADDLE) but clearly not its name. EW has suggested that the E monopolist controlling their use in England coined *sedan* from L *sedēre*, to sit; I'd say that he got it from L *sēdem*, acc of *sēdēs*, a seat, from *sedēre*: f.a.e., SIT.

sedate, sedation, sedative. See SIT, para 4.

sedent. See SIT, para 5.

sedentary. See SIT, para 5.

sedge. See the 2nd SAW, para 4.

sedilia. See SIT, para 3.

sediment, sedimentary. See SIT, para 3.

sedition (whence seditionary, adj hence n), seditious. *Sedition* comes from MF *sedition* (F *sé-*), from L *sēditiōnem*, acc of *sēditiō*, as if from *\*sēdīre*, to go aside, hence to rebel: *sed-* (*sē-*), apart +*īre*, to go: cf ISSUE. L *sēditiō* generates *seditiōsus*, whence MF *seditieux* (F *sé-*), f *seditieuse*, whence E *seditious*.

seduce (whence seducer), seduction, seductive. See DUKE, para 6 (at *sēducere*).

sedulous: L *sēdulus*, zealous, lit guileless: *sē-*, apart, connoting 'without'+*dolus*, guile, trickery, a ruse: cf DOLE, guile.

see (1), n. See SIT, para 3.

see (2), v, pp saw (OE *saeh, seah*, ME *sagh, sah*), pt seen (OE ge*sewen*, ME *sewen*, later *sen* or *sene*), whence unseen; foresee, -saw, -seen, whence unforeseen; far-seeing (*far*+presp *seeing*); seer, from 'to *see*';—sight (n, hence v), whence far-sighted and foresight—auf wiedersehen.—Cf the sep SAY.

1. 'To *see*' derives, via ME *seen*, earlier *seon*, from OE *sēon*: cf OFris *siā*, OS *sehan*, OHG *sehan*, MHG-G *sehen*, Go *saihwan*, MD *sien*, D *zien*, ON *siā* (cf Da, Nor, Sw *se*): Gmc r, *\*sehw-*; IE r, *\*sekw-* (Walshe): cf Hit *sakwa*, the eyes, and perh Hit *sak-* (or *sakk-*), var *sekk-*, to know (if one sees, one knows).

2. OE *sēon* has cpd fore*sēon*, to see beforehand, whence *foresee*.

3. Intimately cognate to OE *sēon*, esp to the pp ge*sewen*, is OE *gesiht*, varr *gesihth* and *gesiehth*: cf MHG *siht*, G *Sicht*, sight, and OHG *gisiht*, MHG *gesiht*, G *Gesicht*, power of sight; cf also MD *gesichte, gesicht*, D *gezicht*.

seed (n, v), whence seedling and seedy; secular (adj and n), whence—perh influenced by F—secularism, secularist, secularize, whence secularization.

1. 'To *seed*' derives from OE *saēdian*, itself from OE *saēd*, whence ME *sed* or *seed*, E *seed*: and OE *saēd* is akin to OFris *sēd*, OS *sād*, OHG-MHG *sāt* G *Saat*, MD *saet, sait, zaet*, D *zaad*, ON *sāth*, *saethi*, and to the sep sow, v.

2. The Go *mana-sēths*, seed of men, i.e. mankind, hence the world, brings us to L *saeculum*, OL *saeclum*, generation (cf Gr *phulon*), as in *saecla hominum*, whence the period of a generation, hence a vaguely longer period, esp a century, finally, in LL, mankind, the world (of human beings): o.o.o., but prob akin to L *satus*, pp of *serere*, to sow.

3. The derivative L adj *saeculāris* takes, in LL, the sense 'worldly, profane', whence OF *seculer* (MF *seculier*, F *séculier*), whence E *secular*. Already in LL is *saeculāris* used as n, whence, ult, the E n; and the ML derivative *saeculāritās* yields *secularity*.

seek, pt and pp sought (OE *sohte*, pp ge*soht*), whence seeker and pa, vn seeking; dial var sick;—beseech (pt, pp besought, var beseeched), whence the pa beseeching;—cf the sep SAKE, where see FORSAKE;—ransack and ramshackle.—Latin: presage (n, v), whence presageful and presagement; sagacity.—Greek: hegemony, hegumen; eisegesis, adj eisegetical, and exegesis, exegete, exegetic (with E extn exegetical).

### Germanic

1. 'To *seek*', ME *secen, sechen*, OE *sēcan*, is akin to OS *sōkian*, OHG *suohhan, suohhēn*, MHG *suochen*, G *suchen*, Go *sōkjan*, ON *soekja*: Gmc r, *\*sōk-*.

2. ME *sechen, seken* has cpd bi*sechen*, -*seken*, with *bi-* for *be-*, vaguely int; whence 'to *beseech*': cf G *besuchen*, to visit.

3. Akin to ON *soekja*, to seek, is ON *rannsaka*, to search a *rann*, or house, for stolen goods, whence ME *ransaken*, E 'to *ransack*', which has freq *ransackle*, pp *ransackled*, whence *ranshackled*, whence the eased *ramshackled*, whence the still further eased *ramshackle*, adj.

4. Cf the sep SAKE.

### Latin

5. With OE *sēcan*, cf sagacious, sagacity: late MF-F *sagace*, EF-F *sagacité*: L *sagācem*, acc of *sagāx* (o/s *sagāc-*), and (derivative of *sagāx*) *sagācitās*: prob deriving from—certainly intimately cognate with—*sāgīre*, to perceive keenly with the senses or acutely with the mind, akin to *sāga*, sorceress: cf SEEK.

6. L *sāgīre*, to trace or track, hence to perceive keenly, has cpd prae*sāgīre*, to perceive beforehand, predict, forbode, whence *praesāgium*, a prediction (augury) or a foreboding, whence EF-F *présage*, E *presage*; 'to *presage*' comes from EF-F *présager* (from *présage*).

## Greek

7. Akin to L *sāgīre* and OE *sēcan*, although with *h-* for *s-*, is Gr *hēgeisthai* (r *hēg-*), to seek, whence *hēgemōn*, a guide (who seeks the way), or a leader (who seeks and enforces it), whence *hēgemonia*, leadership, hence, esp a state's, predominant influence, whence E *hegemony*, with adj *hegemonic*, perh imm from Gr *hēgemonikos*. Gr *hēgeisthai* has presp *hēgoumenos*, which, used as n, leads to LL-ML *hēgūmenus*, an abbot, whence E *hegumen*.

8. Gr *hēgeisthai*, to guide, to lead, has two prefix-cpds affecting E:

*eisēgeisthai* (*eis*, into), to introduce, whence *eisēgēsis*, an introduction (as of extraneous matter), whence E *eisegesis*, faulty interpretation, caused by introducing one's own ideas,—and one who does this is an *eisegete*, Gr *eisēgētēs*;

*exēgeisthai* (*ex*, out of), connoting 'to guide or lead (someone) out of a complexity', denoting 'to explain or interpret' a text, has derivative *exēgēsis*, whence E *exegesis*, with adj *exegetic*, Gr *exēgētikos* and agent *exegete*, Gr *exēgētēs*.

## Indo-European

9. With the Gmc, L, Gr words cited above, cf OIr *sáigim* (s *sáig-*), I seek, and perh the suggestive Cor *hembronk*, to lead or conduct. The IE r is app *\*sāg-*, var *\*sēg-*, to have a keen sense of smell for, to seek: perh cf Hit *sagāis*, an omen.

**seem; seemly.** See SAME, para 18.

**seen.** See the 2nd SEE.

**seep, seepage.** See SUP, para 5.

**seer.** See SEE (heading).

**seersucker,** a light linen—occ cotton—fabric, comes from Hind *šīršakar*, itself from the *shīr u shakar*, milk and sugar (Per *shakar*: cf SUGAR), hence a striped garment.

**seethe,** whence pa **seething; sodden,** origin the pp of *seethe*; **sod** of earth, whence **soddy; sud, suds,** whence **sudsy.**

1. 'To *seethe*' or boil (vt, whence vi) derives, via ME *sethen*, from OE *sēothan*: cf OHG *siodan*, MHG-G *sieden*, MD *sieden*, D *zieden*, ON *siōtha*, cf also Go *sauths*, ON *sauthr* (later a sheep), a burnt offering: app Gmc only.

2. App akin to *seethe* is *sod* of earth, from MD-MLG *sode* (MD-D *sode*, *zode*).

3. Akin to MD *sode*, a sod, is MD *sudde*, a marsh, whence prob E *sud*, *suds*, a marsh, hence soap suds. The MD *sudde* has the revealing var *sodde*.

**segment, segmentate.** See the 2nd SAW, para 9.

**segregate, segregation.** See GREGAL, para 7.

**seidel,** a large, usu hinge-covered, glass for beer: G *Seidel*, a pint: MHG *sīdel*: L *situla*, a bucket: o.o.o.

**seigneur, seignior, seigniory, seignorial.** See SENILE, paras 4 and 5.

**seine,** a large fishing net, comes from OE *segne*, influenced by MF-F *seine*: L *sagēna*: Gr *sagēnē*: o.o.o. The river *Seine* is of very different origin,

for it derives, like It *Senna*, from L *Sequana*, prob not from *sequi*, to follow.

**seisin.** See SEIZE.

**seismic; sistrum.** The former derives from Gr *seismos*, earthquake, from *seiein*, to shake, whence also Gr *seistron*, L *sistrum*, a jingling instrument, adopted by E (cf the F *sistre*). Cf the element *-seism*.

**seize, seizin** (or **seisin**), **seizure.** 'To *seize*'—whence *seizure*—comes from ME *seisen* (*saisen*): OF-MF *seisir*, *saisir* (F id): ML *sacīre*, to take (legal) possession: Frankish *\*sakjan*: cf OS *saca*, OHG *sahha*, a lawsuit. But, beyond OF, the origin is confused.—OF *saisir* has OF-F derivative *saisine*, whence E *seizin*.

**sejunct, sejunction, sejunctive.** See JOIN, para 14.

**seldom:** OE *seldum*, varr *seldon*, *seldan*: cf OFris *selden*, *sielden*, OHG *seltan*, MHG-G *selten*, Go *sildaleiks*, marvellous (lit 'seldom the like'), ON *sialdan*: o.o.o.

**select** (adj, v), **selection, selective, selector.** See LEGEND, para 15.

**Selene** (occ **Selena**), whence **selenian; selenite; selenium,** whence **selenic** (whence, anl, **selenate**); cf the element *seleno-*.

1. *Selenium* = Gr *selēnē*, the moon + Chem *-ium*. *Selenite*, an inhabitant of the moon, derives from Gr *selēnitēs*, n from adj, the adj occurring in *selēnitēs* (*lithos*), the moon stone, whence the Min E n; the Chem n *selenite* = *selen*ium + Chem *-ite*.

2. The moon is, moreover, personified as *Selēnē*, Goddess of the Moon; *selēnē* (Doric *selana*) is an extn of Gr *selas*, light, brilliance: perh cf Skt *svargás*, heaven. (Hofmann.)

**self** (pl **selves**), whence **selfish** (whence **selfishness**) and **selfless; selvedge** (whence **selvage**) = *self-edge*. —*Self* comes straight down from OE *self*, varr *seolf* and *sylf*: cf OFris and OS *self*, OHG *selb*, MHG *selber* (gen *selbes*), G *selber*, *selbst*, MD *self*, *selve*, *zelve*, D *zelb*, Go *silba*, ON *sialfr*—perh also OIr *selb*, Ga *sealbh*, W *helw*, OC *\*selva*, possession.

**sell,** a saddle. See SIT, para 3.

**sell,** v. See SALE.

**sellate.** See SIT, para 3.

**selvage, selvedge.** See SELF (heading).

**semantic,** adj, and **semantics,** n. The former derives from the Gr adj *sēmantikos*, bearing a meaning, from *sēmainein*, to mean; the derivative Gr n 'he *sēmantikē*', science of meanings, whence F 'la *sémantique*', anglicized as *semantics*: cf the element *sema-*, 2nd para.

**semasiology.** See the element *sema-*, 2nd para.

**semblable, semblance, semblant.** See SAFE, para 10.

**semen.** See the 2nd SOW, para 2.

**semester.** See the element *-mester*.

**semi-,** half, a half, is L *sēmi-*, the 'answer' to Gr *hēmi-*: cf Skt *sāmi-* and OHG *sāmi-*, OE *sam-*: prob orig 'one-sided', it is akin to the *sim-* of L *simplex* (q.v. at PLY. para 18), 'one-folded'. (E & M.)

**seminal, seminar, seminary; seminate, semination.** See the 2nd sow, para 2.

**Seminole**: Creek *Simanóle*, a runaway, a separatist. (DAE.)

**Semite** (whence **Semitism**), **Semitic** (whence **Semitics**); **anti-Semite,** n, whence **anti-Semitic** and **anti-Semitism.**

The adj *Semitic* derives from *Semite*, whence *anti-Semite*, with *Semite* narrowed to 'Jew'; the *anti-* terms owe something to F *antisémite* and its derivative *antisémitisme*. A *Semite*—member of a Caucasian race that includes Jews and Arabs and, anciently, Aramaeans, Phoenicians, Assyrians, Babylonians, derives from modern L *Semita*, an *-ita* or descendant of LL *Sem*, Gr *Sēm*, H *Shēm*, lit 'name' or 'renown', E *Shem*, Noah's eldest son.

**semivocal.** See VOCABLE, para 9.

**semolina; simnel.** *Semolina* changes It *semolino*, dim of *semola*, bran, from L *simila*, the finest wheat flour: akin to Gr *semídalis*: both from Ass *samídu* (cf Syrian *semídā*, Georgian *simindoj*), fine meal; for IE, cf also Skt *samitha-*, meal, and Arm *simindr*, fine meal. (Hofmann.) Perh Medit.

2. L *simila* acquires, in OF-MF, the dim *simenel*, adopted by ME: whence, by contr, E *simnel*, a fine-flour bread or biscuit, with new sense in *simnel cake*.

**sempervivium.** See VIVA, para 6.

**sempiternal.** See AGE, para 4.

**sempstress.** See SEW, para 3.

**senary.** See SIX, para 5.

**senate, senator, senatorial.** See SENILE, para 3.

**send,** pt and pp **sent; godsend;** ult cf the sep SENSE. 'To *send*' comes from OE *sendan*, akin to OFris *senda*, OS *sendian*, OHG *sentēn*, MHG-G *senden*, Go *sandjan*, MD *senden*, D *zenden*, ON *senda*, and to many OGmc words for 'a going, a journey, a way': 'to *send*' is a caus of Gmc *\*sinth-*, to go, with a cognate in, e.g., L *sentis*, a path. (Walshe.)

2. *Godsend=God's send*, sending or message, *send* being from OE *sand*, from *sendan*.

**sendal.** See INDIA, para 3.

**Seneca** (1) of Rome. See SENILE, para 2.

**Seneca** (2), an Iroquoian tribe; **senega.** The 2nd stands for *Seneca* (*root*), connected, geog, with the *Seneca* tribe: D *Sennecaas*, the Seneca, the Oneida and two other Iroquoian tribes: Mohegan *A'sinnika*, Oneida: trans of Iroquois *Oněñiute' roñnon'*, Oneida, lit 'people of the standing boulder' (from a great stone in an Oneida village) or 'place of the stone'. *Oneida* itself is an 'Anglicized compressed form of the common Iroquois term *tüoněñ' iote*, "there it it-rock has set up (continuative)", i.e. a rock that something set up and is still standing (Hodge)'. (Webster; Mathews.)

**Senecio.** See SENILE, para 2.

**senectitude.** See SENILE, para 3.

**senescence, senescent.** See SENILE, para 3.

**seneschal,** steward of a large estate: OF-MF *seneschal* (F *sénéchal*): ML *seniscalcus*: OHG *siniscalh*, (lit) the oldest servant: cf Go *sineigs*, older, *sinista*, oldest + *skalks*, a servant. B & W,

however, derive the OF word from Frankish *siniskalk*, oldest servant.

**senile,** whence **senilism** and **senility** (cf F *sénilité*); **Seneca,** Roman author; **Senecio; senectitude; senescence,** from **senescent, senium;**—**senior,** adj (whence **seniority**) and n—cf **seigneur** (and **monseigneur**), **seigneurial** and **seignorial, seigneury**—**seignior** (whence **seignioralty**), **seigniorage, seigniory**—**senhor, senhora**—**señor, señora, señorita**—**signor** (and **monsignor**), **signora, signorina**—cf also **sieur** (and **monsieur,** pl **messieurs**), and **sir, sire, sirrah,** AIr **sor** and **sorry**—also **surly,** whence **surliness;**—**senate, senator, senatorial, senatus consultum;**—cf the sep SENESCHAL.

### Indo-European

1. The word that originates this group is L *senex* (r *sen-*; gen *senis*), old, used also as n 'old man' or 'one of the older men, an elder'. The IE r is *\*sen-*, the etymon *\*senos*, with var *\*henos* in C and in Gr: cf Gr *henos*, Lith *señas*, Arm *hin*, Skt *sánas*, Av *hano*, and, in C, OIr *sen*, Ir and Ga *sean*, Mx *shenn*, Gaul *seno-* (PN only) and, with *h* for *s*, OW *hen*, W *hen*, Cor *henn, hēn, hean, hane*, Br *hen*, old, and cf also OIr *seniu*, Br *hena*, Go *sineigs*, older—the L *senior*; and, again, Go *sinista*, oldest.

### Latin Derivatives from *senex*

2. In OL, *senex* app had an o/s *senec-*, attested by:

*seneca,* (?) old man, preserved in the PN *Seneca*; *seneciō,* old man, hence, from 'the white hairs' of its tuft, the plant groundsel, Bot *Senecio*; *senectūs,* old age, with ML extn *senectitūdō*, whence *senectitude*.

### Latin Derivatives from r *sen-*

3. From r *sen-*, old, comes *senēre*, to be old, whence *senēscere,* to begin to grow old, presp *senēscens*, o/s *senēscent-,* whence E *senescent*; *senium,* (the effects of) old age, adopted by Med; *senīlis,* exhibiting old age, whence late OF-F *sénile,* whence E *senile*; *senātus* (suffix *-ātus*), an assembly of old, or older, men, esp a legislative assembly, whence OF-MF *senat* (EF-F *sénat*), adopted by ME, whence *senate*; derivative *senator* becomes OF-MF *senator*, var *senatour* (EF-F *sénateur*), the latter adopted by ME, whence *senator*; the derivative L adj *senātōrius* becomes EF-F *sénatorial*, whence E *senatorial*.

### Latin Derivatives of *senior*, older

4. *Senex,* old, r *sen-*, has comp *senior*, older, hence an elder, complementary to the adj-n *iunior*, ML *junior*; both adj and n have been adopted by E. The L n *senior*, in LL an Elder of the Church, occ an abbot, takes in R the foll forms preserved by E:

It *signor* (before a name: Mr), *signore*, gentle-

man, whence the f *signora*, married lady (Mrs),
whence *signorina*, unmarried lady (Miss);

Port *senhor*, whence f *senhora*, whence (Miss)
*senhorita*; Sp *señor*, whence f *señora*, whence
*señorita*;

EF-F *seigneur*, a gentleman, a noble, influenced
by L *dominus*, whose F derivatives it has largely
displaced; as address, on levels below the titled,
displaced, in C16, by MF-F *monsieur*, for *mon
sieur*, my lord, with *sieur* a contr of *seigneur*; OF-F
*monseigneur*, now only Eccl, has perh suggested
the It *monsignor*.

5. EF-F *seigneur* derives from OF-MF *seignor*
(L *senior*), whence E *seignior*. Derivative OF-MF
*seignorie* and EF-F *seigneurie* yield resp E *seigniory*
and *seigneury*; derivative OF-MF *seignorage*
becomes E *seigniorage*; whereas E *seignorial* is
adopted from MF, *seigneurial* is adopted from
EF-F.

6. OF-MF *seignor*, later *seigneur*, has OF-F var
*sire*, from VL *\*seior* for LL *senior* spoken rapidly
in address; and OF-MF *sire* had acc *sieur*, preserved in *monsieur*.

7. OF-F *sire* becomes ME-E *sir*, used in ME-EE
for 'gentleman, nobleman', then only in address
with more gen social connotations. *Sir*, in address,
acquires the pej var *sirrah* (long archaic); cf the
AE *sirree*, an int of *sir* in address.

8. E *sir*, in address, becomes AIr semi-literate
*sor*, with dim *sorry*.

9. *Sir*, a lord, has ME-EE adj *sirly*, whence
EE-E *surly*, in EE 'arrogant' (cf 'a *lordly* air'),
hence 'abrupt and rude', hence 'gruffly churlish'.

senhor, senhora, senhorita, See prec, para 4.
senior. See SENILE, para 3.
senium. See SENILE, para 3.
senna: ML *senna*, var of *sena*: Ar *sana*.
sennet. See SIGN, para 7.
señor, señora, señorita. See SENILE, para 4.
sensate, sensation, etc. See para 3 of:
sense (n, hence v), whence senseless and commonsense; nonsense, whence nonsensical; sensate and
insensate, sensation, whence sensational, whence
sensationalism; sensible, sensibility—cf insensible,
insensibility; sensific, sensify; sensile; sension,
whence perh sensism; sensitive (neg insensitive),
whence sensitivity and, anl, sensitize; sensorium,
whence sensorial and, anl, sensory; sensual (whence
sensualism and sensualist and sensualize), sensuality;
sensum, sensuous, whence sensuousness.—Derivatives from L *sentīre*: sentence (n, v), sentential,
sententiary, sententious; sentient, whence sentience
—whence the negg insentience, insentient; sentiment, whence sentimental, whence sentimentalism,
sentimentalist, sentimentality, sentimentalize;—
sentinel (n, hence v) and sentry;—scent, v, hence n,
whence scentless.—Compound derivatives: assent
(n, v), assentaneous, assentation (whence, anl,
assentatious), (from 'to *assent*') assentive and
assentor; consension, (consensual, from) consensus,
consent (n, v), consentaneous (whence consentaneity), consentient (whence consentience), consentive; dissension, dissent (v, hence n—and agent

dissenter), dissentient (whence dissentience), dissentious; presentient, presentiment; resent (v,
hence obs n, whence resentful), resentment.

### Indo-European

1. The E *sens-* words derive either from the L n
*sensus* (gen *-ūs*), formed from the pp, or from
*sensus*, the pp of *sentīre*, to feel, hence to be of an
opinion, hence also to express a sentiment: the
pp *sensus* perh stands for *\*sentsus*; the r of *sentīre*
is *sent-*, app akin to OHG-MHG *sin*, G *Sinn*, sense,
meaning, itself prob imm from OHG *sinnan*, to go,
to journey, to think: cf the relationship of L
*sentīre* to L *sentis*, a path (by which one feels one's
way): cf, therefore, SEND.

### Latin Simples: i, in *sens-*

2. L *sensus*, gen *sensūs*, becomes OF-F *sens*,
whence E *sense*; the cpd *commonsense* owes something to EF-F *sens commun*, from L *commūnis
sensus*, a trans of Gr *hē koinē aisthēsis* (E & M),
as *nonsense* prob does to MF-F *non-sens*, lack of
good sense.

3. The L n *sensus* has the LL derivative *sensātus*,
endowed with intelligence, sensible, whence E
*sensate*. On *sensātus*, LL builds *sensātiō*, (an)
understanding, an idea, ML consciousness of
external stimuli or of bodily feeling, o/s *sensātiōn-*,
whence MF-F *sensation*, adopted by E. The LL
neg *insensātus*, lacking intelligence, lacking feeling
(inanimate), yields *insensate*.

4. On *sens-*, s of the pp *sensus*, arise L *sensilis*,
capable of feeling, E *sensile*, and L *sensibilis*,
perceptive, intelligent, whence MF-F *sensible*,
adopted by E; derivative LL *sensibilitās*, feeling,
perception, becomes MF-F *sensibilité*, whence E
*sensibility*. The LL negg *insensibilis* and *insensi-
bilitās* become, prob via MF-F, the E *insensible* and
*insensibility*. The LL *sensificus*, producing sensibility, and *sensificāre*, to endow with sensibility,
and *sensificātor*, creator of sensibility, account for
*sensific*, *sensify*, (anl) *sensificatory*.

5. The pp-derivative *sensiō*, o/s *sensiōn-*, occurring in L only in cpds, has suggested the SciL
*sensiō*, whence E *sension*, experience of feeling.

6. The ML extn *sensitivus* becomes MF-F *sensitif*,
f *sensitive*, adopted by E; the plant called *sensitive*,
whose leaves fold up when touched, is adopted
from late EF-F.

7. LL *sensōrium* (Boethius, trans of Aristotle),
the brain as the receiving-point of the senses, is
adopted by F and E as a Physio and Psy term.

8. LL *sensuālis*, belonging to or appreciated by
the senses, and its derivative *sensuālitās*, o/s
*sensuālitāt-*, becomes MF-F *sensuel* and OF-F
*sensualité*, with 'pleasures of the senses' predominant from C16, whence E *sensual* and *sensuality*;
with *sensualism*, cf the F *sensualisme*. As a favourable complementary to the increasingly pej *sensual*,
*sensuality*, E has coined *sensuous* (L *sensus*, a feeling + E suffix *-ous*).

9. And as n from the L pp *sensus*, Phil has coined
*sensum*, lit a thing felt.

Latin Simples: ii, in *sent-*

10. L *sentīre*, to feel, hence to discern by the senses, has the extant presp *sentiens*, o/s *sentient-*, whence E *sentient*, and app the lost presp *\*sentens*, o/s *sentent-*, whence *sententia*, an impression (of the mind), an opinion, hence a statement, esp a legal verdict or a gram sentence: whence OF-F *sentence* (orig legal), adopted by E; derivative MF-F *sentencier* yields 'to *sentence*' (to prison). The derivative LL adj *sententiālis*, in the form of a sentence, esp gnomic, becomes E *sentential*; derivative L *sententiōsus* becomes MF-F *sentencieux*, f *-ieuse*, and E *sententious*.

11. From *sentīre*, ML derives *sentimentum*, whence OF *sentement*, MF-F *sentiment*, adopted by E.

12. L *sentīre*, to perceive by the senses, becomes VL *sentināre*, to avoid danger, whence It *sentinella*, EF-F *sentinelle*, EE-E *sentinel*, whence the EE var *centrinel* (or *-onel*), whence, by b/f, *sentry*.

13. L *sentīre*, to feel, to smell, becomes OF-F *sentir*, whence, as 'to smell', the ME *sent*, E *scent*, v.

Prefix-Compound derivatives in *sens-* and in *sent-*

14. L *adsentīre*, eased to *assentīre*, to join one's sentiment or opinion to (*ad*) another's, has the int *assentāri*, to share the opinion of, to approve, whence OF-MF *assenter*, whence 'to *assent*'; *assent*, n, is adopted from MF (from *assenter*). Derivative LL *assentāneus* and L *assentātiō*, o/s *assentātiōn-*, yield *assentaneous* and *assentation*.

15. L *consentīre* (*con-*, with), to be of the same opinion, becomes OF-F *consentir*, whence 'to *consent*'; the n *consent* derives from MF *consente*; *consentment*, from OF-F *consentement*. On the L pp *consens*us are formed *consensiō*, o/s *consensiōn-*, and the n *consensus* (gen *-ūs*), whence E *consension* and *consensus*; the presp *consentiens*, o/s *consentient-*, yields *consentient*. LL *consentāneus* and *consentiuus*, ML *-ivus*, yield *consentaneous* (whence *consentaneity*) and *consentive*.

16. L *dissentīre*, to be of a different feeling or opinion, becomes the late MF-F (archaic) *dissentir*, whence 'to *dissent*'; presp *dissentiens*, o/s *dissentient-*, becomes *dissentient*. From the pp *dissensus*, L *dissensiō*, disagreement, LL schism, acc *dissensiōnem*, becomes OF-F *dissension*, adopted by E, with derivative adj *dissentious*.

17. L *praesentīre*, to perceive or feel in advance, has presp *praesentiens*, o/s *praesentient-*, whence E *presentient*; *praesentīre* becomes EF-F *pressentir*, whence EF-F *pressentiment*, whence, reshaped after L, the E *presentiment*.

18. OF-F *sentir* (L *sentīre*) has the MF-F cpd *ressentir* (for *\*resentir*), to feel back (*re-*) at, whence 'to *resent*'; the MF derivative *ressentement* (EF-F *ressentiment*) becomes E *resentment*.

**sensibility, sensible.** See prec, para 4.
**sensific, sensify, sensile.** See SENSE, para 4.
**sension.** See SENSE, para 5.
**sensitive.** See SENSE, para 6.

**sensorium.** See SENSE, para 7.
**sensual, sensuality; sensuous.** See SENSE, para 8; for derivatives, the heading.
**sensum.** See SENSE, para 9.
**sentence** (n, v), **sentential, sententious.** See SENSE, para 10.
**sentiment.** See SENSE, para 11.
**sentinel; sentry.** See SENSE, para 12.
**separable, separate, separation, separator.** See PARE, para 8.
**sepia**, a cuttlefish, hence the pigment secreted thereby: LL, from Gr, *sēpia*, app from *sēp*ein, to befoul (here, to befoul the sea-water), akin to *sapros*, filthy.
**sepone, sepose.** See POSE, para 20.
**sepoy**: Port *sipaio* (*ci-*): Hi, from Per, *sipāhī*, (adj) of the *sipāh* or army. Cf *spahi*, a contr of Tu, from Per, *sipāhī*, (man) of the army.
**sepsis.** See the element *-sepsis*.
**sept** (1), division of a tribe. See SECT, para 2.
**sept** (2); **septate.** See SEPTUM.
**septan; septave.** See SEVEN, para 6.
**September**, adopted from L, was the seventh (L *septem*, 7) month of the ancient Roman year; for the suffix *-ber*, cf *October, November, December*; for *septem*, see, f.a.e., SEVEN.
**septenary; septennate, septennial.** See SEVEN, para 5; para 4.
**septic.** See the element *-sepsis*.
**septimal, septimanal, Septimus.** See SEVEN, para 5.
**septuagenarian** and **septuagenary** derive from L *septuagēnārius*, adj of *septuagēni*, 70 apiece, from *septuaginta*, 70, whence 'the *Septuagint*' or those 70 scholars who translated the Old Testament into Greek, hence this Gr text. Cf SEVEN.
**septum**, an enclosure, whence the anglicized **sept** and, anl, **septate**, whence **septation; transept.** *Septum*, adopted from L, is a var of *saeptum*, orig the neu of *saeptus*, pp of *saepīre*, to enclose with a hedge, from *saepes*, a hedge, hence an enclosure, perh akin to Gr *haimos*, a thornbush, brushwood, and *haimasia*, a hedge thereof. The ML *transseptum*, whence E *transept*, is a contr of L *transuersum septum*, lit a transverse enclosure.
**septuple.** See SEVEN, para 5, s.f.
**sepulcher** (AE), **sepulchre, sepulchral; sepulture.** L *sepulcrum*, inferior var *sepulchrum*, a burial place, becomes OF-MF *sepulcre* (F *sé-*), var *sepulchre*, adopted by ME; derivative *sepulcrālis*, inferior *sepulchrālis*, becomes late MF-F *sépulcral* and E *sepulchral*. L *sepulcrum* derives from *sepelīre*, to bury, pp *sepultus*, whence *sepultūra*, whence MF *sepulture* (F *sé-*). *Sepelīre*, s and r *sepel-*, is perh akin to Ve *saparyáte* (*r* for *l*), he honours: a proper burial is an honouring of the dead (E & M); improb from L *sē-*, apart+VL *\*pela*, for *pala*, a shovel ('to shovel away').
**sequacious.** See SEQUENCE, para 2.
**sequel.** See para 2 of:
**sequence** (whence **sequential**), **sequent; sequacious, sequacity; sequel; sequitur** and **non sequitur;**
**sue** (whence **suer**), **suit** (n, hence v, whence **suitable**),

and **suite** and **suitor.**—Cpds, i, of *sue*: **ensue;** **(pursuance,** from) **pursuant, pursue** (whence **pursuer), pursuit, pursuivant.**—Cpds, ii, direct from L *sequī*: **consecution, consecutive, consequence** (whence **consequential), consequent,** and the negg **inconsequence** (whence **inconsequential), inconsequent; executant, execute, execution** (whence **executioner), executive** (adj, hence n), **executor, executorial, executory, executrix, exequial, exequy; obsequence, obsequent, obsequious, obsequy** (whence **obsequial); persecute, persecution** (whence, anl, **persecutive** and **persecutory), persecutor; prosecute, prosecution, prosecutor; subsecute** (whence, anl, **subsecutive), subsequence, subsequent.**—Cf the sep EXTRINSIC and SECOND, SEQUESTER, SOCIAL.

## Indo-European

1. The entire group derives, whether directly or via F, from L *sequī*, to follow, presp *sequens*, pp *secūtus*: and *sequī* is akin to Skt *sácatē*, he follows, Ve *sáce*, I follow, Lith *sèkti*, to follow, MIr *sechim, sechur*, I follow, Cor *sewé, sewyé, sywé*, to follow, C etymon *\*sekwo*, I follow, and, with *h* for *s*, and *p* for *q*, Gr *hepomai*, I follow: IE r, *\*seku-, \*sekw-*, to follow.

## Latin Simples

2. L *sequ-* has two notable L derivatives:
*sequāx* (o/s *sequāc-*), tending to follow, whence E *sequacious*, with LL derivative *sequācitās*, o/s *sequācitāt-*, yielding *sequacity*;
*sequēla*, that which follows, consequence, LL a retinue, is adopted by learnèd E and, by MF-F, changed to *séquelle*, whence E *sequel*.
3. The presp *sequens*, o/s *sequent-*, becomes the E adj *sequent*; derivative LL *sequentia* becomes MF *sequence*, EF-F *séquence*, E *sequence*. The pp *secūtus* becomes E *secute*, occurring only in cpds. L *sequitur*, (he, she,) it follows, esp in neg *non sequitur*, it does not follow, have become E nn: 'logical inference' and 'illogical inference'.

## French Simples

4. L *sequī*, to follow, has the VL var *\*sequere*, whence OF *sivre*, MF-F *suivre*, esp OF 'il *siut*', he follows, soon 'il *suit*': whence ME *suen* (*suwen, siuen*, etc.): E 'to *sue*'.
5. The VL *\*sequere* has pp *sequitus*, whence, for *\*sequita pars*, the VL n *\*sequita*, whence OF *siute*, whence MF-F *suite*, whence ME *suite*, whence, with differentiated senses, E *suit* and *suite*, whence *suitor* (? via AF).

## French Compounds

6. 'To *ensue*' derives from OF-MF *enseu*, pp of OF-EF *ensevre, ensivre*: either *en*, L *in+sivre, sevre*, or from VL *\*insequere*, cpd of VL *\*sequere*. —Hence, anl, *ensuant*: cf *pursuant*.
7. 'To *pursue*', ME *pursuen*, derives from MF *poursuir* (EF-F *poursuivre*), from OF *persuir*, from VL *\*prosequere*, var of L *prōsequī* (as in para 13). The E adj *pursuant* derives from MF *poursuiant*, presp of *poursuir*; the E n *pursuivant*, from EF-F

*poursuivant*, orig the presp of *poursuivre*. MF *poursuir* has MF-F derivative *poursuite*, whence ME *pourseut*, E *pursuit*.

## Latin Compounds

8. L *consequī*, to put oneself in the following of (connoted by *con-*, together) or in pursuit of, hence to attain to, to obtain, has pp *consecūtus*, whence both L *consecūtiō*, o/s *consecūtiōn-*, whence E *consecution*, a chain of argument or, in Gram, a series, and, anl, late MF-F *consécutif* (f *-ive*), whence perh E *consecutive* (more prob, anl from the E n). The presp *consequens*, o/s *consequent-*, whence E *consequent*—perh via MF-F *conséquent*. Derivative L *consequentia* yields E *consequence*—perh via MF *consequence* (late MF-F *consé-*). The L negg adj *inconsequens*, o/s *inconsequent-*, and its derivative *inconsequentia* yield E *inconsequent, inconsequence*—cf EF-F *inconséquent, inconséquence*.
9. L *exsequī*, to follow *ex* or out, i.e. to the end, to follow continuously or vigorously, or to the grave, has pp *exsecūtus*, often eased to *execūtus*, whence—perh via the ML *executāre*—the MF-F *exécuter*, whence 'to *execute*'; derivative F *exécutant* becomes E *executant*. The LL derivatives *exsecūtiō, execūtiō* (o/s *execūtiōn-*), judicial prosecution or sentence, and *exsecūtor, execūtor*, attorney, executioner, with f *exsecūtrix, execūtrix*, one who carries out a task, and *exsecūtōrius, execūtōrius*, (adj) carrying out a task, yield resp *execution, executor* (app via AF *executour*), *executrix, executory*, all with some assistance from the corresp OF-MF words. The MF-F *exécutif*, f *-ive*, perh influenced E *executive*, prob anl from E *execution*.
10. L *exsequī*, to follow (a corpse) to the grave, has derivative *exsequiae, exequiae*, a funeral cortege, whence, perh via EF *exeques*, the E *exequies*—cf *obsequies*. Derivative L *exsequiālis, exequiālis*, yields E *exequial*.
11. L *obsequī* (*ob-*, towards), to comply with, has presp *obsequens*, o/s *obsequent-*, whence the E adj *obsequent*; derivative L *obsequentia* becomes *obsequence*. By confusion with *exsequiae*, LL *obsequium*, military service, court of officials, acquires, in ML, the derivative *obsequiae*, funeral service, whence, perh via EF-F *obsèques*, the E *obsequies*, whence E *obsequial*, with form perh patterned by LL *obsequiālis*, complaisant, a mdfn of L *obsequiōsus*, compliant, whence—perh via late MF-F *obséquieux*, f *-ieuse*—E *obsequious*.
12. L *persequī*, to follow *per* or thoroughly, hence persistently, hence to pursue (e.g., in law), hence, in LL, to persecute (Christians), has pp *persecūtus*, whence 'to *persecute*' (cf MF-F *persécuter*); derivative L *persecūtiō* (o/s *-cūtiōn-*), in LL persecution of Christians, becomes OF-MF *persecution* (late MF-F *persé-*), adopted by E; derivative LL *persecūtor*, declared enemy, esp of Christians, becomes OF-MF *persecuteur* (late MF-F *persé-*), whence, via AF *persecutour*, the E *persecutor*.
13. L *prōsequī*, to follow *pro* or forward, to

pursue, has pp *prōsecūtus*, whence 'to *prosecute*'; derivatives L *prōsecūtiō*, o/s *prōsecūtiōn-*, and LL *prōsecūtor*, an official escort, ML in legal sense, become E *prosecution* and *prosecutor*.

14. L *subsequī*, to follow under (*sub*), hence to succeed to, has presp *subsequens*, o/s *subsequent-*, whence the adj *subsequent* (cf MF-F *subséquent*); derivative LL *subsequentia* becomes E *subsequence*; and the pp *subsecūtus* and its derivative *subsecūtiō* (o/s *-secūtiōn-*) yield the rare 'to *subsecute*' and *subsecution*, whence, anl, *subsecutive* (cf the C16 F *subsécutif*).

**sequester** (n, v), **sequestrate, sequestration, sequestrator.** Akin to L *sequī*, to follow, is L *sequester*, a legal depository, orig an adj, from L *secus*, otherwise, IE r *seku-*, *sekw-*, to follow. Derivative *sequestrum* or *sequestre*, object deposited, yields the Med n *sequestrum* and the legal n *sequester*. L *sequester* has LL derivative *sequestrāre*, to deposit, hence to abstract, whence MF-F *séquestrer*, whence 'to *sequester*', to remove for a time; the pp *sequestrātus* yields 'to *sequestrate*', to confiscate; derivative LL *sequestrātiō* (o/s *-atiōn-*) becomes late MF-F *séquestration* and, perh independently, E *sequestration*; LL *sequestrātor* has been adopted.

**sequin:** EF-F *sequin* (cf C16 *chequin*): MF *essequin*: It *zecchino*, orig a Venetian gold coin, from It *zecca*, a mint: Ar *dār as-sikka*, a mint, cpd of Ar *sikka*, a coin. (Prati.)

**sequitur.** See SEQUENCE, para 3.

**sequoia:** SciL *Sequoia*, the giant pine: *Sequoya*, anglicized form of Cherokee *Sikwâyĭ*, that half-breed Cherokee (†1843) who invented the Cherokee syllabary.

**seraglio.** See the 2nd SEAR, para 3.

**seraph**—true pl, *seraphim*—is a b/ from LL *seraphīm* (var *seraphīn*, whence F *séraphin*), trln of L *şĕrāphīm*, pl, from H *saraph*, to burn: 'the radiant ones'. *Seraphic* owes something to the late MF-F *séraphique*.

**Serb, Serbia** (whence **Serbian**, adj hence n), with outmoded varr **Serv, Servia, Servian**; c/f **Serbo-; Sorb**, whence **Sorbian**, adj hence n.

1. *Serbia* derives from Serbo-Croat *Srbija*, itself from Serb *Srb*, a Serb, ? ult akin to LGr *serbos*, a slave: cf SLAV.

2. *Sorb*, a Wend, derives from G *Sorbe*, itself of Sl origin and akin to *Serb*.

**sere.** See the 1st SEAR.

**serenade, serenata.** See SERENE, para 2.

**serendipity**, the gift of felicitous, fortuitous discovery: Horace Walpole's coinage, ref his tale *The Three Princes of Serendip*: *Serendip* is a var of *Serendib*: Ar *Sarandīb*, Ceylon: cf Skt *Siṃhala*, Ceylon+Skt *dvīpa*, an island: cf CEYLON.

**serene, serenity; serenade** (n, hence v), **serenata; —soirée.— elixir.**

1. *Serenity* comes from OF-MF *serenité* (F *sérénité*), from L *serēnitātem*, acc of *serēnitās*, a derivative of *serēnus*, (of the sky, the weather) clear and peaceful, hence fig: prob an extn of L *sērus*, late, esp of the evening, whence the adv

*sērō*, late (cf the LL *sēra*, the evening), whence OF-F *soir*, with extn *soirée*, the duration of the evening, hence also an evening's entertainment, adopted by E; perh akin to Gr *xēros*, dry, therefore to Skt *kṣārás*, burning. IE r, *ksēr-*, dry.

2. L *serēnus* becomes It *sereno*, whence It *serenata*, adopted by E; It *serenata* becomes EF-F *sérénade*, whence E *serenade*.

3. Gr *xēros*, dry, has derivative *xerion*, a powder (Med), whence Ar *al-iksīr*, whence ML *elixir*, adopted by E; the E form, however, may have come from MF *elixir* (F *é-*), earlier *eslissir* (from the Ar).

**serf.** See SERVE, para 5.

**serge, sergedesoy; Seric, seric; silk** (n, hence adj and v), whence **silky—silken—silkworm.**

1. *Serge*, reshaped after EF-F *serge*, derives from ME *sarge*, adopted from OF-EF: VL *sarica*: L *sērica*, prop the f of adj *sēricus*, silken: Gr *sērikos*, adj of *sēr*, a silkworm; b/f from *Sēres*, the Chinese: Ch *se*, silk. The adj *Seric=*L *Sēricus*, Gr *Sērikos*; the adj *seric=*L *sēricus*.

2. The F *serge de soie*, lit 'serge of silk', becomes E *sergedesoy*.

3. L *sērica uestis*, silk garment, generates LL *sēricum*, silk, prob suggested by Gr *sērikon*, prop the neu of *sērikos*: silk reaching N Europe via Sl countries, Gr *sērikon* or LL *sēricum* passes through, e.g., Ru *shelk* and Lith *silkai* to become ON *silki* and OE *seolc* (or *seoloc*), ME *selk*, later *silk*, E *silk*; the *l* for *r* is perh caused by the well-known Ch difficulty with *r*. (See esp P².)

4. OE *seoloc*, *seolc* have adj *seolocen*, *seolcen*, whence *silken*; OE *seolc* occurs in the cpd *seolc-wyrm*, whence *silkworm* (cf WORM).

**sergeant**, legal var **serjeant; sergeanty, serjeanty.** The latter pair, denoting a rather menial feudal tenure, derives from EF-MF *sergentie*, *serjantie*, themselves from OF-F *sergent*, OF-MF *serjant*: ML *servientem*, acc of *serviens*, LL *seruiens*, a public servant, prop the presp of *seruīre*, ML *servīre*: f.a.e., SERVE.

**sergedesoy.** See SERGE, para 2.

**serial, serialize.** See SERIES (heading).

**Seric, seric.** See SERGE, para 1, s.f. For *seri-*cpds, see the element *seri-*.

**series**, with s *seri-*, whence both **serial**, adj, whence n, whence **serialize**, whence **serialization**, and the Sci adj **seriate**, whence, anl, **seriation; Sertularia, sertulum, sertum; sort** (n and v, whence **sorter** and **sorting**), **sortiment, sortition—sorcerer** (whence, anl, **sorceress**), **sorcery**. Compounds: i, of *sort*: **sortilege;—assort, assortment; consort** (n, hence v), **consortion, consortium;** sep resort; ii, of *series*: **assert, assertion** (whence, anl, **assertive**), **assertor; consertal; desert**, wasteland, whence adj and v (to abandon: whence, in part, **deserter**), **desertion; disert—dissert—dissertate, dissertation, dissertator; exert,** whence, anl, **exertion,** whence, anl, **exertive**—cf **exsert,** whence, anl, **exsertion; insert** (v, hence n), **insertion, insertive; intersert, intersertal, intersertion; subsert; transsert.**—Perh cf the sep SERMON.

## Indo-European

1. L *serere*, to attach one after another, tie together, to arrange, has s and r *ser*-: and that r is id with the IE r *\*ser*-, to tie together, to join: cf Gr *eirein* (? for *\*heirein*), to fasten together, *herma*, an ear-pendant, *hormos*, a necklace, *hormathos*, a rank, row, file, Skt *sarat*- and OLith *séris*, a thread, ON *sörvi*, necklace of threaded pearls, perh Go *sarwa*, armour, OIr *sernaid*, he ties, OIr *sreth*, Ga *sreath*, a rank or row, OIr *sáir, sáer*, Ga *saor*, W *saer*, a joiner (carpenter).

### L serere: Simples

2. For E, the most important derivation of L *serere* is L *seriēs*, a file, row, linking, uninterrupted succession: adopted by E—cf F *série*. The pp *sertus* has neu *sertum*, whence SciL *sertum* with its SciL dim *sertulum*; cf the Bot *Sertularia*, as if from *\*sertulārius*, adj of L *serta*, garlands, orig the neu pl of the pp.

### L sors: Simples

3. Akin to L *serere* is L *sors* (s and r *sor*-), a tablet used in casting lots, hence a decision by lot, a share fixed by lot, hence fate, hence, in LL, manner or way, a rank or condition, in short a kind or sort: whence OF-F *sort*, lot, fate, share, MF-F *sorte*, condition, kind, whence E *sort*. 'To *sort*' derives partly from the n *sort*, partly as aphesis of *assort*, partly from late MF-F *assortir* (cf para 6). L *sors* has v *sortīri*, to cast lots, draw by lot, pp *sortītus*,whence *sortītiō*, o/s *sortitiōn*-, E *sortition*; *sortīri* becomes both the It *sortire*, whence *sortimento*, an assorting, whence G *sortimentieren*, to sift tea, whence 'to *sortiment*', and the OF-F *sortir*, whence, finally, the military *sortie* and whence, early, *ressortir*—see the sep *resort*.

4. OF-F *sort*, lot, fate, has pl *sorts*, whence Gallic ML *sorcerius*, OF-F *sorcier*, whence E *sorcerer*, perh influenced by ME *sorcerie* (whence E *sorcery*), adopted from MF *sorcerie* (F *sorcellerie*, for *\*sorcererie*), itself from OF-F *sorcier*; E *sorcery* has derivative adj *sorcerous*, now rare.

### L sors: Compounds

5. L *sors* has, relevant to E, the full cpd *sortilegus*, lit 'fate-reading' (for *-legus*, cf LEGEND), hence, as n, 'fate-reader', i.e. a soothsayer; whence—rather than from the derivative ML *sortilegium*, a casting of lots—comes late MF-F *sortilège*, divination, hence witchery, whence E *sortilege*.

6. L *sors* has two prefix-cpds affecting E, the one arising in F, the other in L:

from MF-F *sorte* comes late MF-F *assortir*, to arrange, dispose, sort into classes or groups or shares, whence 'to *assort*'; derivative EF-F *assortiment* has suggested E *assortment* ('to *assort*'+ *-ment*);

L *consors* (*con*-, with), o/s *consort*-, sharing— hence, a sharer of—a lot, a decision by lot, a fate, hence a partner, a colleague, a companion, whence

MF-F *consort*; derivative L *consortium*, partnership, association, company, a company, not only is adopted by E but also, via MF *consorte*, a company, it becomes syn E *consort* (obs), whence 'to *consort*' or keep company; and anl derivative *consortiō* (o/s *consortiōn*-), an association, yields E *consortion*; from F: *resort*, q.v. sep.

### L serere: Compounds

7. L *adserere*, to attach *ad*, to, oneself, usu *asserere*, hence to vindicate or defend, hence to assert, has pp *assertus*, whence 'to *assert*'; LL derivatives *assertiō*, o/s *assertiōn*-, and *assertor*, become, the former perh via MF-F, the E *assertion* and *assertor*.

8. L *conserere*, to join together, has pp *consertus*, with neu *consertum* used as n: whence the E adj *consertal*.

9. L *dēserere*, to detach oneself *dē*- or from, hence to let go, to relinquish, to abandon, has pp *dēsertus*, whence OF-F *desert* (F *désert*), forsaken, adopted by E, now mostly as the adj derivative from the E n *desert*, a (dry) wasteland, which, adopted from OF-MF *desert*, EF-F *désert*, comes from LL *dēsertum*, var *dēserta* (cf the L *dēserta*, neu pl), orig the neu of the pp-used-as-adj *dēsertus*. 'To *desert*' comes from OF-MF *deserter* (F *dé*-), to abandon, itself either from the OF-MF adj *desert* or from LL *dēsertare* (from L *dēsertus*); E *deserter*=MF *deserteur* (EF-F *dé*-), prob from LL *desertor*, apostate (from *dēsertus*), rather than from OF-MF *deserter*.

10. L *disserere*, to treat fully (*dis*- connoting distribution), to discuss, has pp *dissertus*, whence 'to *dissert*'; the freq *dissertāre* has pp *dissertātus*, whence 'to *dissertate*', and its LL derivatives *dissertātiō*, o/s *dissertātiōn*-, and *dissertātor* become E *dissertation*, *dissertator*.

11. App from the L pp *dissertus* comes the L adj *disertus*, eloquent, whence MF-F *disert*, adopted by E—now only literary and rare.

12. L *exserere*, to pull (from, *ex*, a place of attachment), pull from below, has pp *exsertus*, whence 'to *exsert*' or protrude; whence, anl, the Bot *exsertile* and *exsertion*.

13. L *exsertus* has the 'eased' var *exertus*, whence 'to *exert*', to thrust forth (obs), to put forth, e.g., one's strength, e.g. in pressure.

14. L *inserere*, to set *in*, within, to introduce (into), has pp *insertus*, whence 'to *insert*'; derivative LL *insertiō*, o/s *insertiōn*-, and L *insertiuus*, ML *-ivus*, yield E *insertion* and *insertive*.

15. L *interserere*, to tie between, hence to insert, has pp *intersertus*, whence 'to *intersert*' and, from both, *intersertal*; derivative LL *intersertiō*, o/s *intersertiōn*-, yields *intersertion*.

16. LL *subserere*, to put (secretly) *sub* or under, to subjoin, has pp *subsertus*, whence the learnèd adj and v *subsert*; and L *transsertus* (from *\*transserere*), grafted, yields the Sci adj and v *transsert*.

**serif.** See SCRIBE, para 3.

**seriosity** (rare), **serious** (whence **seriousness**); c/f **serio**-, as in **serio-comic**.

*Seriosity* derives, anl, from *serious*: and *serious* from MF-F *sérieux*, f *sérieuse*, LL *sēriōsus*, extn of L *sērius*, weighty in manner, grave: cf Lith *svarùs*, heavy, *sveriù*, I weigh—OHG *swāri*, MHG *swaere*, G *schwer*, OS *swār*, OFris *swēr*, OE *swāēr*, heavy, Go *swērs*, (much)honoured, lit weighty, ON *svārr*—and prob (*h* for *s*) Gr *herma*, ballast. (Walshe.)

**serjeant.** See SERGEANT.

**sermon, sermonic, sermonize.** See SWEAR, para 3.

**serous.** See SERUM.

**serpent, serpentine.** See REPTILE, para 4.

**serpiginous, serpigo.** See REPTILE, para 5.

**serpolet.** See REPTILE, para 6.

**Serpula.** See REPTILE, para 7.

**serra.** See SERRATE, para 1.

**serradella; serran, serrana, serrano.** See para 3 of:

**serrate and serratus;** whence, anl, **serratic** and—unless from LL *serrātiō*, a sawing—**serration; serrature; serra** and **sierra** (cf **sierra nevada**); **serradella; serran, serrana, serrano, Serranidae; serrulate,** whence, anl, **serrulation.**

1. This group rests firmly upon L *serra*, the cutting instrument known as a saw: o.o.o.: ? echoic. L *serra* has been adopted by Zoo.

2. L *serra* acquires, in ML, the sense 'mountain', from its saw-like ridges. This *serra* becomes Sp *sierra*, a mountain range—c the *Sierra Nevada* or snow-covered range.

3. L *serra* has derivative pcp-type adj *serrātus*, toothed, or jaggèd, like a saw, whence both E *serrate* and Med *serratus*, elliptical for *s. musculus*; on L *serrātus* is formed LL *serratūra*, a sawing, whence E *serrature*, serration.

4. From L *serra* derives Port *serradela*, E *serradella*, a herb. The Cuban Sp *serrano*, a fish, prob owes its form to Sp *serrano*, of the mountains; cf the SciL *serrana*, another fish, and *serran* (yet another fish), an anglicized form of SciL *Serranus*, cf Sci *Serranidae*: all going back to L *serra*, a saw.

5. L *serra* has dim *serrula*, whence, anl, the E adj *serrulate*, delicately or finely serrate.

**serried.** See the 2nd SEAR, para 2.

**serrulate.** See SERRATE, para 5.

**serry.** See the 2nd SEAR, para 2.

**Sertularia, sertulum, sertum.** See SERIES, para 2.

**serum, serous, serosity;** cf the element *sero-*;—**heresy** (and **heresiarch**), **heretic** (adj, with E extn **heretical,** and n); **diaeresis** (AE **die-**), **diaeretic** (AE **die-**);—**horme** (whence **hormic**), **hormone** (whence **hormonal, -nic**).

1. *Serosity* derives from EF-F *sérosité*, itself from EF-F *séreux*, f *séreuse*, whence E *serous*; *séreux* derives from F *sérum*: L *serum*, whey, hence any thinned liquid, esp the watery portion of blood: cf Skt *sárati*, it flows, *sarás* (adj), flowing, *sarít*, a watercourse: IE r, *ser-*, to flow.

2. Akin to the Skt and the L is Gr *oros* (for *horos*), whey, itself akin to Gr *hormē*, an impulse (prob cf Skt *sármas*, a flowing), lit an outflowing of emotion: whence Psy *horme* (dissyllabic). Intimately related to Gr *hormē* is Gr *hormaein* (s

*horma-*, r *horm-*), to excite, with presp *hormōn*, whence the Physio n *hormone*.

3. Prob akin to Gr *hormē* is Gr *hairein*, to seize, to take, with derivative n *hairesis*, a taking, esp for oneself, hence a choosing, hence a sect, esp if aberrant, hence an unorthodox religious creed: LL *haeresis*, often *heresis*: OF *eresie*, OF-MF *heresie* (EF-F *hérésie*), adopted by ME: E *heresy*. The derivative Gr adj *hairetikos* becomes LL *haereticus*, adj hence n, often *hereticus*: MF *heretique* (EF-F *hérétique*): ME *heretike*: E *heretic*.

4. Gr *hairein*, to seize, to take, has cpd *diairein* (*dia*, through), to divide, whence *diairesis*, LL *diaeresis*, adopted by E; the derivative Gr adj *diairetikos* yields *diaeretic*.

**Serv, Servia, Servian.** See SERB.

**servage.** See SERVE, para 5.

**serval,** an Afr wild cat: either Sp 'gato *cerval*' or Port 'lobo *cerval*', lynx: lit, *stag*-like wild cat or wolf: *cerval* deriving from ML *cervus*, L *ceruus*, a stag, lit the horned animal: cf HORN.

**servant.** See para 4 of:

**serve** (whence **server** and **servery**); **servant; service** (n, hence adj and v), **serviceable; servient** (whence **serviential**); **serviette; servile, servility; servitor,** whence **servitorial; servitude**—cf **serf** (whence **serfdom**), **serfage, servage;** cf the sep SERGEANT.—Compounds: **deserve** (whence **pa deserving**)—cf **desert,** merit, now usu in pl, and **dessert; disserve, disservice** (whence **disserviceable**); **subserve, subservient** (whence **subservience**).

Indo-European

1. Behind all these words stand L *seruus*, ML *servus*, slave, adj hence n, and its derivative *seruīre*, ML *servīre*, to be a slave, (vt) to be a slave to, hence to serve. The L s and r *seru-* (ML *serv-*) answers to the IE r *ser-*, which, like *uer-* (*wer-*), is a var of the IE *swer-*, to be in the service of, perh to guard; but the often alleged kinship between L *seruus*, (a) slave, and *seruāre*, ML *servāre*, to guard, to preserve, is far from being proved.

Simples

2. L *seruus* has adj *seruīlis*, ML *servīlis*, slavish, whence MF-F and E *servile*; derivative EF-F *servilité* yields *servility*. L *seruīre* has pp *seruitus*, on which are formed:

*seruitium*, ML *servitium*, slavery, the condition of being a servant, whence OF-early MF *servise*, MF-F *service*, both adopted by ME, the latter surviving; derivative MF *servisable*, *serviçable*, adopted by ME, becomes E *serviceable*;

LL *seruitor*, ML *servitor*, becomes OF-MF *servitor*, ME *servitour*, E *servitor*;

L *seruitūdō*, ML *servitūdō*, becomes MF-F *servitude*, adopted by E.

3. L *seruīre* has presp *seruiens*, o/s *seruient-*, ML *servient-*, whence the E legal adj *servient*.

4. *Seruīre*, ML *servīre*, itself becomes OF-F *servir*, ME *servien* (cf late OE *servian*), *serven*, whence 'to *serve*'. From the OF-F presp *servant*, f

*servante*, both used also as nn (perh after LL *seruiens*, a public servant), orig one who serves, hence, C16 onwards, in modern sense, comes ME *servant* (var *servaunt*), retained by E. OF-F *servir* has MF-F derivative *serviette*, predominantly a towel; adopted by E, it acquires the sense 'table napkin' (a little towel).

5. L *seruus*, ML *servus*, becomes OF-F *serf*, slave, hence, feudally, a bonded servant, adopted by E, as in the OF-F derivative *servage*, usu anglicized as *serfage*.

### Compounds

6. L *seruīre* has two cpds affecting E: *dēseruīre*, to serve well or zealously (*dē-* used int), and *subseruīre*, to serve in a minor way or capacity. *Dēseruīre*, ML *dēservīre*, becomes OF-EF *deservir*, to merit, whence 'to *deserve*'; via VL *\*deservita*, things merited (prop the neu pl of the pp), used as f sing, comes OF-EF *deserte*, merit, whence E *desert*, merit, now mostly in pl.

7. F *servir* acquires the MF-F cpd *desservir* (*des-* for *de-*, L *dē*, from), to remove, esp from the table, what has been served: whence EF-F *dessert*, the removal itself, hence that which comes onto the table after the main courses; adopted by E.

8. MF-F *desservir* gains—from the 'removal of main dishes' sense—the sense 'to render a bad service to'; derivative EF-F *desservice* has suggested the E *disservice*.

9. L *subseruīre*, ML *subservīre*, to serve in a minor way, hence to assist unimportantly, to help promote, whence 'to *subsere*'; the presp *subseruiens*, o/s *subseruient-*, ML *subservient-*, yields *subservient*.

**service, serviceable.** See SERVE, para 2.
**servient.** See SERVE, para 3.
**serviette.** See SERVE, para 4, s.f.
**servile, servility.** See SERVE, para 2.
**servitor; servitude.** See SERVE, para 2.

**sesame, sesamoid, Sesamum.** The 2nd derives from Gr *sēsamoeidēs*, resembling sesame: *sēsamo-*, c/f+*-eidēs*, from *eidos*, form. *Sesame* derives, prob via late MF-F *sésame*, from L *sesama*, *sesamum* (whence the Sci *Sesamum*): Gr *sēsamē*, *sēsamon*: of Sem origin, says Hofmann, who adduces Ass *šamaššanu*, Aram *šūmšemā*, sesame: but perh Medit, for Eg has *shemshem*-t (*t* merely indicating f gender), sesame seed.

**sesquipedalian.** See the element *sesqui-*.
**sessile.** See SIT, para 8.
**session.** See SIT, para 8.
**sestet.** See SIX, para 6.
**sestina.** See SIX, para 4.
**set** (n, v). See SIT, para 21.

**seta, setaceous, setose.** The 3rd derives from L *saetōsus*, *sētosus*, bristly, the 2nd from the syn LL *saetācius*, *sētācius*, adjj of L *saeta*, *sēta*, a bristle, shaggy hair (quadrupeds'); *seta* has been adopted by Bio and Bot. L *sēta*, *saeta*, is o.o.o.

**settee, setter, setting, settle** (n, v), **settlement.** See SIT, para 22; for SETTEE, para 21, s.f.

**seven, seventh; seventeen, seventeenth; seventy,**

**seventieth;**—**septem, septave, septenary** (adj hence n), **septennate, septennial, septet** (or **septette**), **septimal, septimanal, Septimus, septuple** (whence **septuplet** and **septuplicate**)—cf the sep SEPTEMBER, SEPTUAGENARIAN, SEPTUAGINT; — **hebdomad, hebdomadal, hebdomadary** — **heptad, heptagon, heptameter** (after **hexameter**).

### Indo-European

1. This group contains three sub-groups: Gr (*h-* for *s-*), L, Gmc (*f* for *p*): IE r, *\*sept-*, with Gr var *hept-*. Among the chief particularizations of the IE r we find OE *seofon*, E *seven*—Go, OS, OHG *sibun*, MHG *siben*, G *sieben*, MD *seven*, *zeven*, D *zeven*, ON *siau*; OSl *sedmĭ*, Lith *septyni*; OIr *secht*, Ga *seachd*, W *saith*, Cor *seith*, Br *seih*; Tokh A *spät*;—L *septem*; Gr *hepta*; Hit *siptamiya*, 7th; Skt *saptá*, Av *hapta*.

### Greek

2. Gr *hepta* has derivative *heptas*, a set of 7, gen *heptados*: L *heptas*, gen *heptadis*, E *heptad*. Of the many Gr cpds affecting E, note *heptagōnos*, seven-cornered (*gōnia*, a corner, hence an angle), whence the Geom n *heptagon*.

3. Gr *hepta* has ordinal *hebdomos*, 7th, s and r *hebd-* (*b* for *p*, *d* for *t*): whence Gr *hebdomas*, a set of 7, gen *hebdomados*, L *hebdomas*, gen *hebdomadis*, o/s *hebdomad-*, E *hebdomad*; the derivative LL adj *hebdomadārius*, a monk performing a duty for a week, yields the E n *hebdomadary*, the E adj coming from EF-F *hebdomadaire*.

### Latin

4. L *septem*, 7, besides becoming F *sept*, appears in many E cpds, e.g. *septennate* (F *septennat*), a period of 7 years, and *septennial* (L *septennium*: cf ANNUAL), lasting 7, or occurring every 7, years.

5. L *septem* has the foll simple L derivatives relevant to E:

*September*—see the sep SEPTEMBER;
*septēni*, 7 each, whence *septēnārius*, whence *septenary*;
*septimus*, 7th, whence both the PN *Septimus* and the adj *septimal*;
*septimānus* (extn of *septimus*), concerning the number 7, whence LL *septimāna*, a week, whence both the E adj *septimanal*, weekly, and OF-F *semaine*, a week;
*septuaginta*, 70—see the sep SEPTUAGENARIAN;
LL *septuplus*, seven-fold (cf PLY), whence *septuple*.

6. L *septem* accounts also for SciL *septānus*, whence—after *quartan*—E *septan*, esp in *septan fever*, and for the Mus *septave*—after *octave*.

### Germanic

7. E *seven* comes, through ME *seven*, earlier *seoven*, earliest *seofen*, from OE *seofon*; *seventh*, ME *seventhe*, from OE *seofotha*, *siofunda*, from *seofon*;—*seventeen*, ME *seventene*, from OE *seofontiene*, *-tēne*, *-tȳne* (7+10: cf TEN), and *seventeenth*

ME *sevententhe*, from OE *seofontēotha*; *seventy*, from OE *seofontig* (7 × 10), and *seventieth*, ME *seventithe*, from OE *seofontigotha*.

sever. See PARE, para 9.

several, severalty. See PARE, para 10.

severance. See PARE, para 9.

severe, severity; asseverate, asseveration, asseverative—perseverance, perseverant, perseverate, perseveration, persevere.

1. *Severity* derives from OF-MF *severité*, EF-F *sévérité*, from ML *sevēritātem*, acc of *sevēritās*, L *seuēritās*, from L *seuērus* (ML *sevērus*), austere, grave, morally hard: prob (E & M) *sē-*, apart+ *uērus*, true, by a sem development still obscure. L *seuērus* becomes OF *severe*, MF *sevère* (EF-F *sévère*), whence E *severe*.

2. L *seuērus* has cpd *adseuērāre* (*ad-* used int), usu *asseuērāre*, to affirm either vigorously or persistently, with pp *asseuērātus*, ML *assevērātus*, whence 'to *asseverate*'; derivatives L *asseuērātiō*, ML *assevērātiō*, o/s *assevērātiōn-*, and LL *asseuēratiuus*, ML *assevērātivus*, yield *asseveration* and *asseverative*.

3. The L cpd *perseuērāre*, to continue firmly to (do something), whence OF-MF *perseverer* (EF-F *persévérer*), E *persevere*, has presp *perseuērans*, o/s *perseuērant-*, ML acc *perseverantem*, OF-MF *perseverant* (EF-F *persévérant*), E *perseverant*; derivative LL *perseuērantia*, long duration, becomes OF-MF *perseverance* (EF-F *persévérance*), adopted by E. The pp *perseuērātus* has suggested the Psy v *perseverate*; its LL derivative *perseuērātiō*, continuance, persistence, o/s *perseuērātiōn-*, ML *persev-*, yields *perseveration*.

sew, pt sewed, pp sewn, presp and vn sewing; seam, n (whence seamy), hence v—seamstress and sempstress; sutra, suture; accouter (AE), accoutre, accoutrement (AE -ter).

1. 'To *sew*', ME *sewen* (var *sowen*), comes from OE *sīwan*, var *sēowian*, akin to OFris *sīa*, OHG *siuwan*, Go *siujan*, ON *sȳja*: cf also Lith *siúti*, OSl *siti*, L *suere*, to sew, Skt *sīvyati*, he sews, *syūtás*, sewn: IE r, *\*syū-*, var *\*sū-*, to sew.

2. Akin to OE *siwan* is OE *sēam*, akin to OFris *sām*, OHG-MHG *soum*, G *Saum*, ON *saumr*—and Skt *syūman*.

3. OE *sēam* has derivative *sēamestre*, whence ME *seamster*, whence E *seamstress*, var *sempstress*; *sēamestre* and *seamster* are f; *-ess* has been added in order to render the sex unmistakable.

4. L *suere*, to sew, has pp *sūrus*, whence L *sūtor*, lit a sewer, hence a shoemaker, and *sūtūra*, a sewing, esp in surgery, whence EF-F *suture*, adopted by E.

5. Akin to Skt *syūtás*, sewn, is Skt *sūtra*, a thread, hence a string of precepts, a collection of aphorisms, whence E *sutra*, a precept, esp a collection of precepts, with varr in Buddhism and Jainism.

6. Not imm recognizable as related to *sew* is 'to *accoutre*': EF-F *accoutrer*, MF *accostrer*, to dress or equip: VL *\*accōstūrāre*, for *\*acconsūtāre* (ac- for ad-), from LL *consūtūra*, a stitching together,

extn of LL *consūtiō*, a sewing, from L *consuere*, to sew: *con-*, together+*suere*.

sewage, sewer (for sewage). *Sewer*, id in ME, derives from AF *sewere*, aphetic for MF *esseveur*, itself from MF *essever*, to drain: either OF-MF *es-*, L *ex-*, out+OF-MF *ever*, to drench, or from VL *\*exaquāre*, to take water out of, to empty of water: cf AQUA, water. From E *sewer* comes, with change of suffix, *sewage* (*-age* is collective).

sewing; sewn. See SEW (heading).

sex, whence the pa *-sexed* and the coll sexy; sexual, whence sexuality (cf the F *sexualité*) and sexualist, sexualize.—*Sexual* derives from LL *sexuālis*, adj of L *sexus* (gen *-ūs*); the neu var *secus* has suggested kinship with L *secare*, to cut: ? orig, with ref to female sex, a division.

sexagenarian, sexagenary, sexagesimal, sexangle, sexennial. See SIX, para 4.

sext, sextain, sextan; sextant. See SIX, para 4.

sextet; sextic. See SIX, para 6.

sextile; sexto. See SIX, para 4.

sexton. See SACRAMENT, para 7.

sextuple, sextuplicate. See SIX, para 6.

sexual, sexuality. See SEX.

shab. See SCAB, para 2.

shabble. See SABRE, para 2.

shabby. See SCAB, para 2.

shack (1), harvest gleanings, hence refuse: dial var of SHAKE used as n.

shack (2), a hut, a small, primitive sort of house: app a b/f from syn AE (dial) *shackle*: ASp, esp Mexican Sp, *xacal* (later *jacal*), pron *shacal*: Aztec *xacalli*, a wooden hut. (Mathews.)

shackle, n hence v: ME *schakle*, *schakkyl*: OE *sceacul*, *scacul*, a shackle: cf MD-D *schakel*, MD var *schaeckel*, ON *skökull*, a cart-pole: all these Gmc words look like dim forms—could the origin be the OGmc simples corresp to SHAKE?

shad, a deep-bodied, herring-like fish: OE *sceadd*: o.o.o.: prob C—cf EIr *scatán*, Ir *scadán*, G *sgadan*, Mx *skeddan*, a herring, and W *ysgadan*, herrings.

shaddock derives from Captain *Shaddock*, who, in 1696, introduced into Barbados the seed he had brought from the EI.

shade (n, hence v), whence shady; shadow, n, whence shadowy, and v; shed, n.

1. *Shed*, a light structure (a lean-to, an outbuilding), usu open in front, represents a var, prob orig dial, of *shad*, itself a var of the n *shade* in sense 'shelter'.

2. *Shade*, comparative darkness, a space sheltered from the sun, derives, via ME *schade*, from OE *scead*, in its var *sceadu*, oblique cases *sceadwe* becoming ME *schadewe*, later *shadowe*, E *shadow*, but also generating the OE v *sceadwian*, ME *schadewen*, var *schadowen*, later *shadowen*, E 'to *shadow*': and OE *sceadu* is akin to OS *skado*, OHG *scato* (gen *scatawes*), MHG *schate*, G *Schatten*, Go *skadus*, MD *schade*, *schadewe*, *schaduwe*, D *schaduw*, OIr *scáth* (? also the syn MIr *scáil*, Ga *sgàil*), Cor *scōd*, shade, a shadow, and Gr *skotos*,

darkness; and, without *s*-, the Alb *kot*: IE r, app
\**skot*-, shade, shadow, darkness.

**shaft** (n, hence v); **scape**, n, as in Bot and Zoo;
**scepter** (AE) or **sceptre** (n hence v, whence the pa
**sceptered, sceptred**).

1. *Shaft*, ME *schaft*, comes from OE *sceaft*: cf
OFris *skeft*, OHG *scaft* (esp a spear), MHG-G
*schaft*, MD *schaft*, D *schacht*, ON *skapt*, a (long)
handle of, usu, a spear; cf also Lett *škeps*, spear, L
*scāpus*, shaft, stalk, and Doric Gr *skapon*, a staff,
Gr *skēptron*, a staff, esp a sceptre: IE r, \**skap*-,
varr \**skep*- and \**skop*-, all occurring also without
the IE prefix *s*-. (Hofmann.)

2. L *scāpus* yields E *scape*, a Bot peduncle,
loosely any flower-stalk, a Zoo stem, an Arch
shaft.

3. Gr *skēptron* becomes L *sceptrum*, OF-F
*sceptre*, adopted by E.

**shag**, coarse hair or wool (hence a cormorant
and a coarse tobacco), hence also adj and v—and
the adj **shaggy** and the cpd **shagbark** (with shaggy
outer bark); **shaw**, a thicket; **skeg**, afterpart of a
ship's keel.

1. *Shag*, coarse, matted hair, comes from OE
*sceacga*, bushy hair: cf ON *skegg*, beard, and its
modern Scan cognates.

2. With OE *sceacga*, cf OE *scaga*, a thicket,
whence ME *schawe*, E *shaw*, akin to ON *skōgr*, a
wood, and its modern Scan cognates.

3. Akin to all those words is the naut E *skeg*,
from D *scheg*, *schegge*, from Da *skjeg*; cf ON
*skaga*, to shelter or protect.

**shagreen.** See the 2nd CHAGRIN.

**shah.** See CHECK.

**shake** (v, hence n), pt **shook**, pp **shaken**; whence
**shaker, shaking, shaky; Shakespeare** or **-spere**,
whence **Shakespearean.**

*Shakespeare* is simply 'a *shake-spear*': and 'to
*shake*' comes, through ME *shaken*, earlier *schaken*,
from OE *scacan*, *sceacan*: cf ON *skaka*, to shake,
also OS *scacan*, OHG *scachōn*, to flee (cf sem the sl
'*shake* a leg' and 'stir one's pins'), and, without the
*s*- prefix, Skt *khájati*, he churns, and perh OB
*skakati*, to hop; ult also the 2nd SHOCK, basically
'to shake', both being, orig, echoic.

**shako:** F *shako*, var *schako*: Hu *shako*, written
*csakó*, lit 'peaked (cap)': MHG *zacke* (now usu
*Zacken*), a peak, prop a prong: cf MD *tacke*, varr
*tac*, *teck*, D *tak*, a twig: perh (Walshe) cf Gr
*daknein* (s *dakn*-, r *dak*-), to bite.

**shaky.** See SHAKE (heading).

**shale**, in Min, derives from *shale*, a shell (obs),
a fish's scale (now dial): ME *schale*, *schal*: OE
*scealu*, *scalu*, a shell, a drinking-cup, a balance: cf
SHELL.

**shall** and **shilly-shally; should.** *Shall* and *should*:
ME *shal*, earlier *schal*, pt *sholde*, earlier *scholde*:
OE *scal*, *sceal*, I am obliged or bound (to do something), pt *scolde*, *sceolde*, the corresp inf being
*sculan*: cf OS and Go *skulan*, OHG *scolan* (G
*sollen*), to be bound, obliged, OHG *sculd*, obligation, debt (G *Schuld*), ON *skula*, to be bound: 'this
v was orig used in all Gmc languages to express the

future' (Walshe); but it occurs also in Sl—cf Lith
*skeléti*, to be bound to, to owe, and *skolà*, a debt.

2. *Shilly-shally*=*shill-I*, *shall-I?*, *shill-I* being a
thinning of *shall-I*: 'Shall I, *shall* I . . .?'

**shallop.** Cf **sloop**; see SLEEVE, para 2.

**shallot.** See SCALLION, para 2.

**shallow**, adj hence n; **shoal**, adj hence n (sand
bank);—**skeleton**, whence, by b/f, **skeletal** and
**skeletin** (Chem -*in*) and the c/f **skeleto**-.

1. The adj *shallow*, ME *schalowe*, prob derives
from OE *sceald*, shallow: ? by confusion with
HOLLOW. With OE *sceald*, cf Sw *skäll*, G *schal*,
insipid, MHG *schal*, dull.

2. OE *sceald* becomes ME *scheald*, later *schold*,
whence the 'eased' E *shoal*, as in '*shoal* water':
hence that which renders the water *shoal* or
shallow—a sand bar or a sand bank.

3. Akin to OE *sceald*, shallow, is Gr *skeletos*
(s *skelet*-, r *skel*-), parched, desiccated, either deriving from or at least cognate with Gr *skellein* (s
*skell*-, r *skel*-), to parch, to dry up, therefore prob
akin to Gr *sklēros*, dry: IE r, \**skel*-, to dry up (vt),
var (without the IE s-), \**kel*-, as in Lett *kàlss*, thin,
meagre, and *kàlst*, to dry up. (Hofmann.) Gr
*skeletos* has neu *skeleton*, used as n elliptical for
*skeleton sōma*, a dried-up body, a skeleton, prob
suggested by Gr *skeletos*, itself used as n, but
signifying 'mummy' not 'skeleton': whence E
*skeleton* (cf the F *squelette* also, in C16, written
*scelete*).

**sham.** See SHAME, para 3.

**shamble**, v; **shambles.** See SCAMBLE, para 2.

**shame**, n, whence **shameful** and **shameless** (OE
*scamleas*) and v, whence pa, vn **shaming**; **shamefaced; ashamed.**—Perh cf the sep CHEMISE.

1. *Shamefaced* is f/e for *shamefast*, '(held) *fast*,
i.e. firm, by shame'. 'To *shame*' comes from OE
*scamian*, *sceamian*, from OE *scamu*, *sceamu*,
whence, via ME *schame*, the E n *shame*: and the OE
n *scamu*, *sceamu* is akin to OFris *skame*, OS
*skama*, OHG *scama*, MHG *schame*, G *Scham*,
shame, modesty, MD *schame*, *schaem* (adj),
ashamed, *schamen*, to be ashamed (OHG *scamēn*,
Go vr *skaman sik*). These OGmc nn and vv are
perh related to Go ga-*hamōn*, to dress (to cover
oneself), and to OHG *hamo*, clothing, and OHG
*hemidi* (MHG *hemede*, G *Hemd*), OE *hemethe*, a
shirt, a chemise. The IE r is app \**skam*-, var (without
IE prefix *s*-) \**kam*- (Gmc \**kam*-): cf Gaul
*camisia*, whence F *chemise*. (Walshe.)

2. OE *scamian* has cpd *āscamian*, to shame,
whence the rare 'to *ashame*', with pp *ashamed*,
retained as adj.

3. E *shame*, n, has dial var *sham*, whence perh
*sham*, orig a fraudulent trick, hence an imposture:
it causes shame.

**shammy.** See CHAMOIS.

**shampoo**, v hence n: Hind *champo*, a massage
described by European travellers in India since
1616 (B & W): app orig the imperative of Hind
*shampna*, to perform this massage.

**shamrock:** Ir *seamrōg* (cf Ga *seamrag*): MIr
*semrach*: dim of EIr *semar*, Ir *seamar*, clover.

**shandy,** beer and either lemonade or ginger-beer, shortens **shandy gaff:** o.o.o.: ? from low London sl *shant o' gatter*, a pot of beer, with London sl *gaff* (as in 'a penny *gaff*') substituted for *gatter*.

**shanghai** (1), a slingshot, is a f/e—after *Shanghai*—derivative of Sc *shangan*, a cleft stick, from Ga *seangan*.

**shanghai** (2), to render (someone) insensible, esp by drugging his liquor, put him aboard and enlist him as a sailor: from *Shanghai*, where this practice either originated or earliest flourished. Lit, *Shanghai* is 'above'—i.e., at—'the sea'.

**shank** (n hence v), whence *Longshanks*, lit 'long-legs': ME *shanke*, earlier *scanke*: OE *scanca, sceanca*, the shin: cf OFris *skunk, skunka*, thigh, MD *schenke, schinke*, leg, MHG-G *schenkel*, thigh, OHG *scinca*, thigh, MHG *schinke*, thigh, ham, G *Schinken*, ham—cf also ON *skakkr* (for *\*skankr*), bent sideways, and prob Gr *skazein*, OHG *hinchan*, MHG-G *hinken*, ON *hinka*, to limp, Skt *khanjati*, he limps; IE r, app *\*kheng-*, var *\*khong*, with varr *\*skheng-, \*skhong-*, where *s*- is the vaguely int IE prefix.

**shanty** (1), a hut. See GANTRY, para 2.

**shanty** (2), a lively song, is a var of the naut *chanty, chantey*, prob from F *Chantez!* Sing!, from *chanter*, to sing: cf *chant*, q.v. at HEN.

**shape,** n (whence **shapeless** and **shapely**) and v, whence **shaper, shaping;** hence **misshape,** pp-pa **misshapen;** the suffix **-ship** (ME *-schipe*, OE *-scipe*, from OE *sceap*).—'To *shape*', ME *shapen*, earlier *schapen*, comes from the ME n *schap*, a shape, later *shap*, whence E *shape*, n: and ME *schap* comes from OE *-sceap*, as in ge-*sceap*, something shaped or created, a creature, from OE *sceppan, scieppan, scyppan*, to shape, (also) to do or effect: cf OFris *skeppa*, OS *skeppian*, OHG *scaffēn*, MHG-G *schaffen*, to create, to obtain, MD *schepen*, D *scheppen*, to make or form, Go ga-*skapjan*, ON *skapa, skepja*; perh akin to such 'scrape-scratch-dig' words as OHG *scaban* (MHG-G *schaben*), ON *skafa*, L *scabere*, Gr *skaptein*; IE r *\*skap-*, var *\*skabh-*. (Feist; Walshe.)

**shard.** See para 4 of:

**share** of a plough (whence **ploughshare,** AE **plowshare:** ME *plouhschare*) and **share,** a portion, whence 'to **share**', with paa **shared, sharing,** and agent **sharer; shear,** n (now **shears**) and v, with pt **shore** (archaic) and **sheared,** pp **shorn,** occ **sheared,** whence agent **shearer** and vn, pa **shearing;** naut **sheer,** v; **shard** and **sherd; score,** a notch, a tally (esp one of 20), whence 'to **score**' (whence **scorer**) or notch, hence to count; **shore** of the sea; **short** (adj, hence adv and n; and v)—(from *short*, adj) **shortage** and **shorten**—such obvious cpds as **short-arm, -cake, -circuit, -coming, -cut, -hand, -horn, -sighted, -term, -winded,** etc.—**shortly** and **short-ness;—shirt** and **skirt; scabbard,** n hence v.—Cf the sep SHARP and SHRED and prob CARNAL and CURT and such 'leather' words as CORTEX and CUIRASS.

1. Behind all these words lies the idea 'to divide,

or separate, by cutting'. A plough*share* or *-blade*, ME *schar* derives from OE *scear*, akin to OFris *sker*, OHG *-scar* in *plōhscar* (MHG *pfluoschar*, G *Pflugschar*); and *share*, a portion, ME *schare*, derives from OE *scaru* or *scearu*, which, like OE *scear*, either derives from or is intimately related to OE *sceran*, to cut.

2. OE *sceran*, to cut, esp to shear, with varr *scieran* and *scyran*, not only generates OE *scēar*, pl *scēara*, a pair of shears, whence E *shear*, pl *shears*, but becomes ME *scheren*, later *sheren*, whence 'to *shear*'. OE *sceran*, the most funda-mental of all the E words in this group, is akin to OFris *skera*, OHG *sceran*, G *scheren*, MD *scherren*, MD-D *scheren*, ON *skera*, to cut, to spear—Cor *scar*, a separation, *kescar*, to separate, W *ysgar*, Ga *sgar*, OIr *scaraim*, OC *\*skaraō*, I separate—Lith *skirti*, to separate—and, without the IE prefix *s-*, Gr *keirein*, to cut or shear, Hit *karss-*, to cut, esp to cut off, and prob L *carō*, flesh (E CARNAL): IE r, *\*ker-*, var *\*sker-*, to cut.

3. Basically 'to divide by cutting', 'to *shear*' has the naut var 'to *sheer*', (to cause) to deviate from a course.

4. *Shard* and *sherd* derive from ME *shard* and *sherd*, themselves diverging from OE *sceard*, orig a pp from the r of OE *sceran*, to cut, to shear: akin to MD *schard(e)*, D *schaard*, a fragment, MHG-G *scharte*, a dent (cf OHG *scart*, dented), ON *skarth*, a dent.

5. Akin to OE *sceran* is the syn ON *skera*, with derivative—or, at least, very close cognate—ON *skor*, a notch, hence a tally, whence ME *scor*, E *score*.

6. With E *score*, ME *scor*, cf E sea*shore*, ME *schore*, prob from an OE *\*score* derived from OE *scieran*, var of *sceran*, to cut or shear: either 'that which is cut, or shorn, off', hence an edge or border, or 'that which cuts off' (land from sea): MD *schoor*, MD-D *schor*, a mud flat.

7. The 'cut off' idea occurs a so in the E adj *short*, ME *schort*, OE *scort, sceort*: cf OHG *scurz*, short (and OHG-G *kurz*, ON *kortr*, short, L *curtus*), MHG *scherze*, a piece cut off, OFris *skortinge*, a shortening (prob from OE), *skerta*, to shorten, ON *skort*, a lack or deficiency, OSl *oskórd*, a hatchet, Lith *skardus*, steep. (Walshe; Holthausen.) OE *scort* or *sceort* has derivatives OE *sceortian*, whence the obs 'to *short*', make or become short—the modern EI v derives from 'to *short*-circuit'; *sceortlīce*, whence *shortly*; *sceortness*, whence *shortness*.

8. The idea of '(a garment) cut *short*' or '*short* (garment)' is present in E *shirt*, ME *schirte*, earlier *schurte*, from OE *scyrte*, a short garment, a kirtle (cf CURT); cf MHG *schurz*, G *Schurze*, apron, MD *schorte*, D *schort*, apron, petticoat.

9. With those Gmc words, cf ON *skyrta*, a shirt, a kirtle, whence ME *skyrt*, E *skirt*: akin to Sw *skört*, skirt, *skjorta*, shirt, Da *skiorte*, skirt, *skiört*, petticoat.—Hence 'to *skirt*'.

10. OHG *-scar*, a blade (cf para 1), hence a sword, combines with OHG *bergan*, to hide (cf G

*bergen*), to produce OF *\*escarberc*, whence, by dissimilation, OF *escalberc*, whence AF *escauberc* (or *-bert*), whence ME *scauberc*, later *scabbard*, retained by E.

**shark** (n, hence v), the fish, prob derives from **shark**, a parasite, a sharper, with derivative v: the 'sharper' *shark* app derives from G *Schurke*, a rogue (OHG fir-*scurgo*, a rogue), with emphasis upon greed and rapacity. G *Schurke* comes from *schürgen*, to vex or plague, mdfn of *schüren*, to poke, to stir up, MHG *schürn*, either deriving from or akin to OHG *scora*, Go *-skaúrō*, a shovel.

2. App also from G *Schurke* comes—unless it merely 'thins' *shark*—the E *shirk*, a sharper (obs), whence a malingerer: whence 'to *shirk*': whence *shirker* and vn, pa *shirking*.

**sharp**, adj (whence **sharpen**, naut **sharpie, sharpness**), hence adv and n and v (OE *scerpan*), whence the agent **sharper** and the pa, vn **sharping**; from the adj, such self-evident cpds as **cardsharper** and **sharp-set, -shooter, -tailed**; cf the sep SCARP.

The adj *sharp*, ME *scharp*, OE *scearp*, is akin to OFris *skarp*, *skerp*, OS *skarp*, OHG *scarf*, MHG-G *scharf*, MD *scharp*, *schaerp*, MD-D *scherp*, ON *skarpr*—and ult to *shear*, q.v. at SHARE, para 2.

**shatter.** See SCATTER.

**shave, shaven, shaveling.** See SCAB, para 5.

**shaw.** See SHAG, para 2.

**shawl** (n, hence v) comes, via Hind, from Per *shāl*.

**Shawnee**, member of an Alg tribe: Shawnee *shawunogi*, lit 'southerners' (they came from Tennessee): from *shawun*, the south. (Webster.)

**she.** See HE, para 7.

**sheaf**, pl *sheaves*: ME *sheef*, earlier *shef*, earliest *schef*: OE *scēaf*: cf OHG *scoub*, MHG *schoub*, *schoup*, G *Schaub*, OS *skōf*, MD *schov*e, MD-D *schoof*, a sheaf, ON *skauf*, a fox's brush: IE r, perh *\*skei-*, to cut—cf Skt *chyáti*, he cuts.—From the pl *sheaves* comes the v 'to *sheave*' or gather into sheaves.

**shealing.** See SHIELING.

**shear, shearer, shearing, shears.** See SHARE, para 2.—With the bird *shearwater* ('cut-water'), cf the G *Wasserscherer*, 'water-cutter'.

**sheath**, whence, from the sheath over part of the upper mandible, the bird **sheathbill**, and **sheathfish**, now usu **sheatfish**; hence also 'to **sheathe**' (cf OFris *skētha*), whence the vn **sheathing**.—A *sheath*, ME *schethe*, comes from OE *scǣth*, var of *scēath*: cf OFris *skēth*, OS *skēthia*, OHG *skeida*, MHG-G *scheide*, MD *scheide*, *schede*, D *scheede*, ON *skeithir* (pl): perh also cf the 2nd SHED: basic idea 'a separating cover' (Walshe).

**sheave**, a slice, a grooved wheel or pulley. See the 1st SHIVER, s.f.

**sheave**, v. See SHEAF, s.f.

**shebeen**, an illicit grog-shop: Ir *sībīn*, var *sēibīn*, a little (*-īn*) mug, hence inferior ale: cf, sem, the G *Krug*, a pitcher or a pot, hence a pot-house, a tavern, and, phon, perh the Cor *seth*, *seith*, a pot.

**shed** (1), a light structure. See SHADE, para 1.

**shed** (2), to separate (now only dial), hence to pour forth, cast off, whence **shedder** and **shedding**; **watershed**; **shingle** (of a roof), hence a signboard, also a short haircut, n hence v;—**scissile, scission, scissura, scissure; scind - abscind, abscissa, abscission—rescind, rescission, rescissory;—schedule**, n (whence **schedular**), hence v; **schism, schismatic; schist, schistose; schizoid, schizont;** cf the element *-schisis*, where (s.f.) see SCHIZOPHRENIA.—Prob cf the sep SHEATH.

## Indo-European

1. The n *shed*, a separation, as in *watershed* (cf G *Wasserscheide*), derives from OE *scēada*, itself from OE *scēadan* (? contr *scādan*), to separate, whence, via ME *scheden*, *shaeden*, to separate, to pour, the E 'to *shed*': cf OFris *skētha*, OS *skēthan*, OHG *sceidan*, MHG-G *scheiden*, Go *skaidan*; Lith *skiédžiu*, I separate, and *skiesti*, to separate; Gr *skhizein* (? for *\*skhidsein*), to split; nasalized L *scindere*, to split or cleave, pret *scīdī*, and Skt *chinádmi*, I split, and *chinátti*, *chinttē*, he splits; cf also OIr *scīath*, shoulderblade, shield: IE r, *\*skhid-*, to split, hence to separate. The *s*-less Ve *khidáti*, he tears, and L *caedere*, to cut, indicate that the IE r *\*skhid-* is prob a reinforced var of *\*khid-*, to cut.

2. With the Gmc group focussed by 'to shed', cf the partly Gmc-partly L *shingle*, a piece of wood sawn or split small and thin, used esp in roofing: ME *shingle*, for *skindle*: L *scindula*, akin to and prob deriving from L *scindere*, to split.

## Latin: *scindere*, þp *scissus*

3. L *scindere*, to split, hence to tear, whence, from 'splitting or tearing apart', to separate, divide, even—occ—to interrupt, yields 'to *scind*', rare except in cpds. The L pp *sciss*us (cf the supine *sciss*um) has three L derivatives affecting E:

LL *scissilis*, (easily) splittable, whence EF-F *scissile*, adopted by E;

LL *scissiō*, acc *scissiōnem*, MF-F *scission*, adopted by E;

L *scissūra*, whence E *scissure*, a cleft (in Med, the L form).

4. L *scindere* has the foll relevant prefix-cpds:

*abscindere*, to split or tear, hence to cut, *ab-* or off, whence 'to *abscind*'; the pp *abscissus* has f *abscissa*, which, used as Geom n (prob elliptical for *abscissa linea*), is adopted by E (cf the F *abscisse*); it also has derivative *abscissiō*, o/s *abscissiōn-*, whence E *abscission*;

*rescindere*, to split, hence cut, back, hence to cut off, yields 'to *rescind*', now usu to abolish (a law); on the pp *resciss*us are formed LL *rescissiō*, o/s *rescissiōn-*, whence E *rescission*, and LL *rescissōrius*, whence *rescissory*.

## Greek

5. Gr *skhizein* (for *\*skhidsein*), to split, has derivative *skhidē*, a split piece of wood, whence L *scida*, a leaf or sheet of papyrus, var *scheda* or *sceda*, with LL dim *scedula*, *scidola*, predominantly *schedula*, a piece or slip or scrap of paper, whence

—prob via OF-MF *cedule* (extant)—the E *schedule*, orig a written document, esp governmental; the E adj *schedular* was app prompted by F *cédulaire*.

6. Gr *skizein*, s and r *skhiz-*, has the further derivative *skhisma*, whence LL *schisma*, whence, via the LL var *scisma*, the OF *cisme*, MF *scisme*, adopted by ME; whence, resp, the reshaped EF-F *schisme* and the reshaped E *schism*. Derivative Gr *skhismatikos* becomes LL *schismaticus*, MF *cismatique*, later *scismatique*, EF-F *schismatique* and, perh independently, E *schismatic*.

7. Gr *skhizein*, to split, has the pa *skhistos*, split, divided, hence divisible, whence L *schistus* (*lapis*), a stone easily split or cut, whence, via F *schiste*, the E *schist*; the E adj *schistose* is prob indebted to the F adj *schisteux*, f *schisteuse*.

8. On the Gr s *skhiz-*, anglicized as *schiz-*, is formed *schizoid* (suffix *-oid*), lit tending to split, applied esp to *schizophrenia* ('split mind'); from the presp *skizōn*, o/s *skhizont-*, comes the Zoo n *schizont*.

**shee** or, occ, **sidhe**; **banshee.** A *banshee* or female spirit warning of death, derives from Ga *beanshīth*: Ga-Ir *bean* (OIr *ben*), a woman+Ga *sith*, fairy-like, preternatural (cf *sītheach*, a fairy), akin to Ir *sīod*, a fairy abode, whence syn E *sidhe*, usu *shee*, and to Ir *síde*, fairy folk, whence syn E *shee*; cf also Mx *sheeaghan*, a fairy, and, for Ga *bean*, OIr *ben*, a woman, the OC r *\*ben-*, var of *\*gen-*, to engender (E GENERAL).

**sheen**, adj, hence n and v; **scone.** Sheen, radiant, resplendent, comes, through ME *schene*, from OE *scēne*, *scȳne*, *scīene*, splendid: cf OFris *skēne*, var *skōne*, OS *scōni*, OHG *sconi*, MHG *schoene*, G *schön*, Go *skauns*, MD *schone*, MD-D *schoon*, and ult to E SHOW: Gmc etymon, *\*skauniz*.

2. Prob from MD *schoonbrot* (D *-brod*), lit 'clear, or bright, bread', fine bread, comes E *scone*.

**sheep**, whence **sheepish**; **shepherd** (n, hence v), whence **shepherdess** (suffix *-ess*). *Sheep* (sing and pl) derives from ME *shep*, *scheep*, from OE *scēp*, contr of *scēap*: cf OFris *skēp*, OS *skāp*, OHG *scāf*, MHG *schāf*, G *Schaf*, MD *schaep*, D *schaap*: o.o.o.: perh ult Medit—cf Eg *sàu*, *sa*, *sua*, *s-t*.—The fish *sheepshead* has teeth like a sheep's.

2. OE *scēap* has cpd *scēaphyrde*, whence ME *schephirde*, *-herde* (cf MD *schaepherde*), whence E *shepherd*; cf HERD.

**sheer** (1), adj, bright, pure, transparent, perpendicular (whence the naut n). See SCENE, para 10.

**sheer** (2), naut v. See SHARE, para 3.

**sheet**, fabric cover, naut rope. See SHOOT, v, para 4.

**sheik** or **sheikh**, occ **shaik(h)**; **cacique.**

1. *Sheik*(h) anglicizes Ar *shaykh* or *cheikh*, prop an old man, hence an elder, hence a chief. With Ar *shaykh*, *cheikh*, cf the Eg *skhemu*, *kherpa*, a chief.

2. A WI chief, or petty king, is a *cacique*: adopted from Sp, which adopts it either from Carib, as the best all-Sp dictt hold, or from Taino, which adapted it from Arawak *kassequa*, a chief, as Webster proposes; but Arawak could, as Georg

Friederici suggests, have vocalized it, in the course of the slave-traffic, from the Ar r *CHK*; Santamaria, however, derives it from Mayan *cah*, hand, as the symbol of power or authority+*tsic*, or *tsik*, to honour, to obey. An Amerind origin seems preferable to the Ar origin. Provisionally, I accept Santamaria's theory.

**shekel:** H *sheqel*: from *shāqal*, to weigh, prob orig in barter.

**sheldrake**=*sheld*, speckled (now dial), akin to the syn MD *schillede* (cf MIIG *schillen*, G *schillern*, to vary, or fluctuate, in colour)+DRAKE, male of duck.

**shelf**, pl **shelves**, whence prob 'to *shelve*' (orig to put away, out of mind, on a shelf); **scalpel.**

1. *Shelf*, ME *shelfe*, OE *scielfe*, *scylfe*, is akin to MD *schelf* and, with p for f, the L *scalpe*re, to scrape, carve, cut (therefore cf *sculpture*): IE r, perh *\*skel-*, to curve or cause to curve.

2. L *scalpere* has derivative *scalprum*, a cutting tool, with dim *scalpellum*: whence EF *scalpelle*, F *scalpel*, adopted by E.

**shell**, n (whence adj **shelly**), hence v; **shellac**, q.v. at the 2nd lac, para 4; **shelter**, n, hence v; **shield** (n and v), whence **shield-bearer**; **skull**—cf NUMSKULL.

### Indo-European

1. *Shell*, ME *shelle*, OE *scell* (varr *sciell* and *scyll*), is akin to MD *schelle*, D *schel*, OHG *scala*, MHG-G *schale*, ON *skel*, a sea shell—and Go *skalja*, a tile, OB *skolika*, a mussel shell (cf Lith *skala*, a wood-splinter), and Gr *skallein*, to dig, therefore prob ON *skilia*, to split (cf Lith *skeliù*): IE r, *\*skel-* (extn of *\*kel-*), to split, to cut. Therefore cf SCALE (of fish).

2. *Shield*, ME *sheld*, OE *sceld*, *scild*, *scyld*, is akin to OFris *skeld*, *skelde*, OS *scild*, OHG *scilt*, MHG *schilt*, G *Schild*, Go *skildus*, MD *schelt*, *schilt*, D *schild*, ON *skiöldr*, and prob Lith *skiltis*, a slice: o.o.o.: basic sense, perh 'a board' used for protection.

3. OE *scild*, shield, has cpd *scildtruma* (cf TRIM), lit a shield band, i.e. a troop of men carrying shields: whence ME *scheldtrome*, eased to *scheltrome*, whence later ME *scheltrun*, whence E 'a shelter'.

4. With OHG *scala*, ON *skel*, a sea shell, cf Nor *skalla*, Sw *skulle*, ME *skulle*, E *skull*, essentially a hard, bony case.

**shellac.** See the 2nd LAC, para 4.

**shelta**, secret language of Ir (hence also of Sc) tinkers, anglicizes Ir *sheldru*, perh from OIr *bēlre*, speech: ? cf Ir *sceala*, a word, a message.

**shelter.** See SHELL, para 3.

**shelve.** See SHELF (heading).

**shepherd.** See SHEEP, para 2.

**sherbet.** See the 2nd SHRUB, para 2.

**sherd.** See SHARE, para 4.

**sheriff.** See SHIRE, para 2.

**sherry.** See CAESAR, para 5.

**Shetland**—whence **Shetland Pony**—and its var **Zetland** derive from ON *Hjaltland*, perh 'High Land'.

shew, as in shewbread. See SHOW.

shibboleth, a criterion in form of word or saying, a watchword, arises in *Judges*, xiii, where the Gileadites used H *shibbōleth*, ear of corn, to detect the Ephraimites, who, unable to pronounce *sh*, had to say *sibbōleth*.

shice, shicer. See SHOOT, para 5.

shield. See SHELL, para 2.

shieling, shealing, a shepherd's hut during summer, a summer pasturage, is a dim of Sc *shiel*, *sheal*, akin to ON *skjōl*, a shelter. (EDD.)

shift, v, basically to divide, hence to change (the position of), whence the n shift (including 'chemise'); whence shifter and pa, vn shifting, also shiftless and shifty, orig adaptable, resourceful.— 'To *shift*' comes, through ME *shiften*, earlier *schiften*, from OE *sciftan*, to divide: cf the syn OFris *skiƿta* (var *skiffa*) and D-LG *schiften*, as well as ON *skipta*, to arrange; prob akin, ult, to the 2nd SHED.

shilling: ME *shilling*, earlier *schilling*, OE *scilling*, is akin to OFris *skilling*, OHG *scilling*, MHG *schillinc*, G *Schilling*, Go *skilliggs* (pron *skillings*), and the ON *skillingr*, with modern Scan cognates: prob echoic, from Gmc *\*skel-*, to resound—cf OHG *scal*, G *Schall*, resonance, and, sem, E sl *chink*, F sl *clinquaille*, Hu *pengö*, lit 'coin that goes *peng!*'—cf E *ping!* (Walshe.)

shilly-shally. See SHALL, para 2.

shimmer. See SCENE, para 9.

shimmy, coll for a *chemise*, becomes the name of a tremulous dance.

shin (n, hence v), whence shinny, informal hockey, with varr shindy, shinty; chine; skein, in basketwork and metallurgy.

1. *Shin*, the tibia, comes from ME *shine*, earlier *schine*, from OE *scinu*, and shinbone from OE *scinbān*: cf MHG *schinebein*, G *Schienbein*, a cpd of OHG *scina*, MHG *schine*, G *Schiene*, a splint, a rail, the tibia, MD *schene*, D *scheen*, the shin: app an *s*-prefix var of the r in Gr *kíōn* (o/s *kíon-*), a pillar, with which prob cf the syn Arm *siun* and certainly cf MHG *schīe*, a post, and OE *scīa*, shin.

2. D *scheen* has a derivative basketwork sense, whence E skein.

3. OHG *scina*, tibia, has Frankish var *\*skina*, whence OF-MF *eschine* (F *échine*), whence the aphetic E *chine*. 'To *chine*' owes something to OF-MF *eschiner*, F *échiner*.

shindig (sl), a festive occasion, and shindy (sl), an uproar, a fracas, are o.o.o.: prob of C origin—? cf Ga *sìnteag*, a skip or a jump, from Ga *sìn*, to stretch, OIr *sínim*, I stretch.

shindy (1), hockey. See SHIN (heading). Perh influenced by:

shindy (2), uproar. See SHINDIG.

shine, pt and pp *shone*, with modern var (vt) shined; whence n shine, agent shiner, pa, vn shining, adj shiny. See SCENE, para 8.

shingle (1), of roof. See the 2nd SHED, para 2.

shingle (2), of seashore, is app echoic: cf Nor *singl*, pebbles. The earlier form *chingle* suggests a n-from-v *chingle*, freq of 'to *chink*', itself echoic.

shingles (disease). See CINCH, para 7.

shinny, hockey. See SHIN (heading).

Shinto, the J national religion, is J *Shintō*, the *tō* (from Ch *tao*) or way, hence doctrine, of the *shin* or gods. *Shin* is ult related, prob to Ar *jinn*, pl of *jinni*, a demon of the wilderness, and perh to Basque *Jinko*, *Jainko*, God.

shinty, hockey. See SHIN (heading).

shiny. See SHINE (heading).

ship, n—whence shipshape, shipwreck (n, hence v)—and v, whence, in part, shipper (cf OE *scipere*, a sailor)—cf skipper; skiff;—equip, equipage, equipment.

1. 'To *ship*' derives, in part, from the modern n *ship* and, in part, from OE *scipian*, to take ship— cf *gescipian*, to supply with ships. OE *scipian* derives from OE *scip*, whence ME *schip*, later *ship*, retained by E: and OE *scip* is akin to OFris *skip*, OS *scip*, OHG *scif* (var *scef*), MHG *schif* (var *schef*), G *Schiff*, Go *skip*, MD *scheep*, *schep*, *schip* (also D), ON *skip*: o.o.o.: but perh akin to SHAPE.

2. App from OHG *scif*, MHG *schif*, comes It *schifo*, whence late MF-F *esquif*, whence, by aphesis, the E *skiff*.

3. MD *schip* has derivative *schipper*, a ship's captain, whence E *skipper*, n hence v.

4. From a LG form of OHG *scif*, a ship, comes OF-MF *esquiper* (EF-F *équiper*), to fit out, orig a ship, later a body of men, finally an individual: whence E 'to *equip*'. Derivative late MF-F *équipage* and EF-F *équipement* becomes E *equipage*, *equipment*.

shippen, shippon. See SHOP.

shire; sheriff. *Shire* derives from OE *scīr*, official business, administration, hence an administrative division, hence a county: o.o.o.: but akin to OHG *scīra*, an official charge, official business.

2. OE *scīr* has cpd *scīrgerēfa*, whence ME *shereve*, E *sheriff*: cf REEVE. The ME *shereve* becomes, by contr, *shreve*, E *shrieve* (archaic), with derivative *shrievalty*, office of sheriff.

shirk, shirker. See SHARK, para 2.

shirt. See SHARE, para 8.

shit; shite. See SHOOT, para 6.

shive. See:

shiver (1), n and v—a fragment, to break into fragments, whence shivereens (*-een*=the Ir dim *-īn*); skewer, n hence v.

A *skewer* app derives from E dial *skiver*, a skewer, from *shiver*, a fragment, ME *schivere*, *schivre*, *scifre*, akin to OHG *scivaro*, *scivero*, MHG *schiver*, a splinter, G *Schiefer*, a slate, themselves akin to OHG *scība*, MHG *schībe*, G *Scheibe*, ON *skīfa*, ME *schīve*, a slice, whence E *shive*, a slice, a fragment, var *sheave*, both now mostly dial, although the latter has several tech E senses. ME *schivere*, a fragment, has derivative v *schiveren*, whence 'to *shiver*' or break into small pieces.

shiver (2), to tremble with cold or fear, whence n; whence also the pa, vn shivering and the adj shivery. 'To *shiver*' comes from ME *chiveren*, o.o.o.; the var ME *cheveren* suggests a possible connexion—via EE *cheverel*, ME *chevrelle*, leather made of kidskin, from OF-MF *chevrele* (F *chevreau*), a kid, dim of *chevre* (F *chèvre*), a goat, L *capra*—with 'to CAPER'.

**shoad.** See SHODDY.

**shoal** (1), adj 'shallow', hence n. See SHALLOW, para 2.

**shoal** (2) of fish. See SKILL, para 2.

**shock** (1), a heap of grain-sheaves, hence v; dial var, **shook**.

*Shock*, ME *schokke*, is akin to MHG *schoc* (MLG *schok*), a heap, G *Schock*, heap, shock (of grain), MD *schoc, schocke*, a heap: cf, without the IE int prefix *s*-, the G *Hocke*, Lith *kúgis*, haystack, heap of hay.

**shock** (2), v and n, to jolt or shake violently, a violent impact. The n derives, in part from 'to *shock*' and in part from EF-F *choc*, n, from MF-F *choquer*, to shake violently, whence the ME *schokken*, whence 'to *shock*': and MF-F *choquer* is app of Gmc origin—cf ED *schocken*, D *schokken*, to jolt, and ED *schocke*, a swing, D *schok*, a jolt, and esp OHG *scoc*, a swinging movement: perh echoic; perh akin to SHAKE.—Hence the pa *shocking*.

**shod.** See SHOE (heading).

**shoddy**, reclaimed wool, whence the adj, is o.o.o.: cf the Min *shoad* or *shode*, a detached fragment of vein material, also, collectively, a series of such fragments, and N. Country *shade*, a fragment, which are akin to—prob derived from —OE *scādan*, to divide, to separate, and therefore akin to the v SHED.

**shode.** See prec.

**shoe**, archaic and dial pl **shoon**; 'to shoe', pt and pp **shod**; cf the sep OBSCURE.

'To *shoe*' derives from OE *scōian, scēogan*, from OE *scōh, scēoh*, whence ME *scho*, later *sho*, E *shoe*: and OE *scōh*, with var *scēoh*, is akin to OFris *skōch, scōh*, OS *skōh*, OHG *scuoh*, MHG *schuoch*, G *Schuh*, Go *skōhs*, MD *schoech, schoeh, schoewe, schoe* (as in D), later *schoen, schuen*, ON *skōr* (cf Da *sko*); prob to OHG *scūra*, a barn, and L *scūtum*, a shield; perh to Skt *kōśa*-, a container or a case; see also OBSCURE (*ob-+scure*).

**shoneen.** See JOHN, para 1.

**shook** (1), a bundle of sheaves. See the 1st SHOCK (heading).

**shook** (2), pt of shake (heading).

**shoot** (v, hence n), whence **shooter** and pa, vn **shooting**; pt and pp **shot**; **shot**, n—cf scot, a contribution, whence **scot-free**; **shotten**;—**sheet**, covering, naut rope, whence the corresp vv; **shit** (var **shite**), v hence n—cf **shitehawk, shitepoke**—cf also **shice, shicer**, prob **shyster**; **shut**, whence **shutter**; **shuttle**, n hence adj and v, **shuttlecock** (*shuttle*, n+ *cock* bird, from its crest);—**skeet**; **skit**, n (whence **skittish**) and v—cf **skite** (n and v), **blatherskite**; **skitter** and **skittle**, usu in pl, n, whence v;—**scoot**, n and v (whence **scooter**)—cf **scoter**—cf also **scout**, to scoff at, with pa, vn **scouting**; perh **shout**, v, hence n.

1. 'To *shoot*' has basic sense 'to get rid of, throw or propel forcefully, to let fly', e.g. a stone, a dart, an arrow, hence 'to hit thus': and it derives, via ME *shotien*, earlier *scheoten*, from OE *scēotan*, akin to MD-D *schieten*, OFris *skiāta*, OS *sciotan*, OHG *sciozzan, sciozan*, MHG *schiezan*, to hurl, to shoot, G *schiessen*, to shoot, Crimean Go *schieten* (Go *\*skiutan*), ON *skiōta* (*skjōta*)—and the OE var, or secondary, *sceotian*, and its source *scotian*, to shoot (someone) with a missile; cf also Lith *šáuti*, to shoot. (Walshe.) There is reason—cf Boisacq and Holthausen—to think that the OGmc *sk-, sch-* vv represent a reinforcement (the IE int prefix *s*-) of an IE r in *k*- (? orig *\*kh*-): cf OSl *is-kydati*, to cast out, and perh Gr *kuda*zein, to scoff at (cf E *scout* in para 14 below), the basic IE sense being 'to cast or throw'.

2. Intimately akin to—indeed, prob deriving from—OE *scēotan* is OE *sceot*, from basic *scot*, a shooting, and ge*sceot*, a missile. From OE *scot* derives ME *schot*, later *shot*, retained by E, with senses 'a shooting—a missile—and, prob from the casting of lots, a reckoning, a contribution'; with the 3rd sense, cf OFris and ON *skot*, MD-D *schot*, and, of course, E *scot*, a contribution, a tax, which prob comes from ON *skot*.

3. A *shotten* herring has '*shot* forth' its spawn: OE *scoten, sceoten*, pp of *scēotan*.

4. A *sheet* or covering, ME *shete*, earlier *schete*, derives from OE *scēte*, with var *scīete*, a piece of cloth, a sheet, akin to OE *scēat*, a projecting corner, a (fold of) cloth, and *scēata*, a corner, esp the lower corner of a sail, but also a cloth: cf MD *schote*, MD-D *schoot*, sheet, a person's lap, OHG *scōzza*, MHG *schōze*, G *Schoss*, lap, coat-tail, OFris *skot*, Go *skauts*, ON *skaut*. The 'corner of sail' sense of OE *scēata* occurs in the OE cpd *scēatlīne*, whence, prob by abbr, the naut E *sheet*, a rope with which one regulates the angle of a sail.

5. Prob—from uninhibited excretion—akin to OHG *scioz(z)an*, MHG *schiezen*, G *schiessen*, to shoot, is OHG *scīzan*, MHG *schīzen* G *scheissen*, to defecate, whence the agent *Scheisser*, whence the Aus Min *shicer*, an unproductive lode or mine, whence the E sl *shicer*, a worthless person, whence, by b/f, the sl *shice*, worthless, spurious, used also as n, 'base money'. A corruption of G *Scheisser* is the AE, orig sl, *shyster* (? for *\*Scheisster*), a pettifogger, esp a pettifogging lawyer. (Note that some authorities adjudge the G v to be cognate with G *scheiden*, to separate.)

6. Very closely akin to OHG *scīzan* are the syn ON *skīta* and OE *scītan*, whence ME *schīten* (cf the id MLG form), later *schite, schyte, shyte*, whence the E 'to *shit*' and its var 'to *shite*'. The E n *shit*, var *shite*, is, in ME, *schīte*, as also in MLG, the MHG form being *schīze*. Like the simples, the foll cpds are no longer in polite use: *shitehawk* and *shitepoke*, birds, and *shithouse*.

7. OE *scēotan*, to shoot, has agent *scytta*, a form that helps us to understand the, at first sight, obscure connexion of 'to *shoot*' with 'to *shut*': the orig sense of 'to *shut*' a door is revealed by 'to *shoot* a bolt' (or arrow) and 'to *shoot* the bolt' of

a door—in order to fasten the bolt, to fasten with a bolt, hence to close that which the bolt serves to fasten: ME *shutten*, with varr *schutten* and *schetten* or *schitten*: OE *scyttan*, to bolt (a door), to close it, perh a deliberately thinned var of *scēotan*: cf MD *schotten*, MD-D *schutten*. With derivative E *shutter*, cf MD *schutter*, *schotter*.

8. OE *scēotan*, to shoot, has derivative or, at the least, cognate OE *scutel*, *scytel*, a missile (cf OE *gesceot*): EE, now rare, *shittle*: (prob after 'to shut') E *shuttle*. Cf ON *skutill*, a harpoon, MLG *shotel* (=G *Schoss*), and Da, Sw *skyttel*, a shuttle: all these forms prob represent a dim of the n occurring in, e.g., OE ges*ceot*, a missile.

9. The naut *skeet*—hence a form of trap-shooting—usu said to be o.o.o., has an origin easily deducible from its meaning, 'a scoop, fixed to the end of a long pole and used to *throw* water on yacht sails (and thus to tighten the canvas)': it is lit a *shooter* or 'thrower' (of water) and prob it derives from a Scan or perh a D form of the v 'to *shoot*'.

10. Prob of Scan origin is *skit*, to leap aside, jump about: cf ON *skytta*, *skyti* (cf OE *scytta*), a shooter, a marksman, and the vv in para 1 above; hence 'to *skit*' or gibe (at), whence 'a *skit*', a lightly satirical piece, but also an easily frightened horse, a silly flirtatious girl, etc.

11. A var spelling, pron, and sense-change, of 'to *skit*' is 'to *skite*', to dart or dash about, hence to act objectionably, esp to boast, whence 'a *skite*' or boaster, with cpd *blatherskite* (cf BLATHER).

12. 'To *skit*', jump about, caper, has freq *skitter*; moreover, it has prob suggested, or rather, both it and *shuttle*, n, have suggested the n *skittle*, a pin used in the game deriving its name *skittles* therefrom.

13. Akin to *shoot* are *scoot*, a sudden flow of water (Sc), and 'to *scoot*', to shoot, or squirt, water forth, hence, orig dial and coll, to dart away, to decamp; dial 'to *scoot*' or dart (away), has var *scote*, whence, app, the sea duck called the *scoter*.

14. *Scout*, to scoff at, hence to reject contemptuously, has, in its passage from Scan, perh been form-influenced by 'to *shout*'; both its sense and its form are related to *skit* (para 10): cf ON *skūta*, a gibe, *skūti*, a scolding, and *scīota*, to shoot: cf, sem, 'to stand to be *shot* at' or strongly criticized.

15. 'To *shout*', ME *shouten*, is o.o.o., yet prob of Scan origin: cf, phon, *scout*, to scoff at, and sem the possibility that, orig, 'to *shout*' was 'to *shoot* forth words or, rather, interjections or curses'. Hence the pa, vn *shouting*.

**shop**, n (hence v), whence **shopkeeper** (cf KEEP) and **shopworn** (cf WEAR); whence the pa, vn **shopping**, the agent **shopper**, the adj **shoppy**; **shoplifter**, q.v. at the 3rd LIFT.

*Shop*, ME *shoppe*, earlier *schoppe*, OE *sceoppa* (a trans of LL-ML *gāzophylacium*, an Eccl strongbox or treasury, Gr *gazophulákion*), akin to OE *scypen*, a shed, E *shippen* or *-on*, a cowshed, OHG *scopf, scof*, MHG *schuppen*, G *Schuppen*, LG *schup*,

a shed, and perh akin to OHG *scioban*, MHG-G *schieben*, OE *scūfan*: see SHOVE.

**shore** (1), of sea. See SHARE, para 6.

**shore** (2), a support, to support. 'To *shore*', ME *schoren*, derives from the ME n *schore*, whence 'a *shore*' or prop: and ME *schore* is akin to—perh adopted from—MD (and LG) *schore* (D *schoor*), itself akin to ON *skortha*: ? cf E *shear* (q.v. at SHARE, para 2), as being cut off (Webster).

**shore** (3): pt of **shear**.

**short**, **shorten**, **shortly**, **shortness**. See SHARE, para 7.

**shot**, n. See SHOOT, para 2.—Pt and pp: ibid (heading).

**shotten**. See SHOOT, para 3.

**should**. See SHALL.

**shoulder**, n (whence **shoulder blade**, etc.), hence v: ME *shulder*, earlier *schulder*: OE *sculdor*: cf OFris *skolder*, *skulder(e)*, OHG *scultarra*, MHG-G *schulter*, D *schoulder*, Da *shulder*: o.o.o.—? akin to L *scapula*.

**shout**. See SHOOT, para 15.

**shove**, v hence n; **shovel**, n hence v, whence, from its broad bill, the river duck **shovel(l)er**; **shuffle**, v hence n; derivative **shovelboard**, **shuffleboard**; **scoff**, n hence v, whence **scoffer**, **scoffing**; **scuff**, v hence n; **scuffle**, v hence n; **scoop**, n and v; **scupper**, n hence v.

1. 'To *shove*', ME *shoven*, *shouven*, OE *scūfan*, is akin to OFris *skūva*, MD *schuven*, *schuyven*, D *schuiven*, OHG *scioban*, MHG-G *schieben*, to push, to shove, Go af-*skiuban*, to shove, or push, off, ON *skūfa*, and, importantly, Skt *kṣubh*, a push, and, prob, Lith *skùbti*, to hasten: IE r, prob *skeubh-*, to push or shove.

2. Akin to OE *scūfan* is OE *scofl*, ME *schovele*, *schovel*, E *shovel*: cf OHG *scūval*, MHG *schüfel*, G *Schaufel*, MD *schuffel*, D *schoffel*.

3. 'To *shuffle*', a freq (*-le*) from OE *scūfan*, has prob been influenced by *shovel*; cf LG *schuffeln*. With *shuffle*, cf 'to *scuffle*', prob a freq of 'to *scuff*', app a derivative—with widely divergent senses—of OE *scūfan*; cf the Sw *skuffa*, to shove.

4. *A scoff* or gibe, ME *scof*, is akin to the syn OFris *skof*, OHG *scof, scoph*, ON *skop* or *skaup*, OSw *skiup*, and to Da *skuffe*, to deceive, to mock—and prob to OE *scūfan*, to push or shove, one form of mockery being a persistent shoving-about.

5. Also, in part, akin to *shove*, and to *shovel*, is a *scoop* or large ladle: ME *scope*: partly from MD *schoppe* (cf MLG *schuppe*), a shovel, but mainly from MD *schöpe* (id in MLG), a scoop, akin to G *schopfen* (OHG *scepfan*), to draw water, of an entirely different origin (G *schaffen*, E 'to SHAPE').

6. Obscurely yet very prob akin to 'a *scoop*' is the late ME-E *scupper*, an opening that allows water to flow overboard from a ship's deck.

**shovel**. See prec, para 2.

**shovel(l)er**. See SHOVE (heading).

**show** (v, hence n), pt **showed**, pp **shown**—archaic **shew**, **shewed**, **shewn**; whence **shewbread**, **showbread**, the vn **showing**, the adj **showy**.

1. 'To *show*', ME *schowen* or *schewen* (later *shewen*), var *showen*, OE *scēawian*, to look at, is akin to OFris *skāwia*, var *skōwia* (contr *skōia*), with secondary *skūa*, OS *scawōn*, *skauwōn*, OHG *scouwōn*, MHG *schouwen*, G *schauen*, MD *schauwen*, MD-D *schouwen*, Da *skue*, to look: the transition from OE *scēawian*, to look at, to E *show*, cause to be looked at, is explained by the fact that the E v denotes 'the same action from the opposite point of view' (Walshe).—With the OFris secondary *skūa* and perh the Da *skue*, cf OHG *scū-kar*, Go *skuggwa* (for *skuwwa*), a mirror.

2. The r *skeu-*, var *skou-*, is not merely Gmc; it occurs also in Gr thus*skóos*, a watcher of sacrifices, i.e. a sacrificial priest. Moreover, all these *sk-*, *sh-* words represent a reinforcement, by the IE int prefix *s-*, of IE *keu-*, *kou-*, to watch: cf Lith *kavóju*, I watch, L *caueō*, I watch carefully, am on guard against, Gr *koéō*, I notice, perceive, as one does by watching, and Skt *kavís*, adj and n seer, hence sage.—Cf the sep CAUTION and HEAR.

**shower** (n, hence v), whence **showery**, comes from ME *shour*, earlier *schour*, from OE *scūr*, akin to OFris *skūr*, OHG *scūr*, MHG *schūr*, G *Schauer*, a shower, Go *skūra* (*windis*), a gale, ON *skūr*, shower: app a reinforcement, by IE prefix *s-*, of IE *kur-*, *kaur*—cf the L *caurus*, the N.W. wind. (Walshe, who adduces two Sl form-and-sense cognates in *sh-*.)

**showy.** See SHOW (heading).

**shrab.** See the 2nd SHRUB, para 1.

**shrapnel** commemorates its inventor (c1803), General Henry *Shrapnel* (1761–1842).

**shred**, n and v (whence pa **shredded** and agent **shredder**); **screed**, n and v; **scroll**, n (whence the adj **scrolar**), hence v, with cpd **enscroll** or **inscroll**—cf **escrow**; **shroud**, n and v, with cpd **enshroud**; **scrotum**, whence **scrotal**; **scruple**, **scrupulosity**, **scrupulous**—whence neg **unscrupulous**; **scrutable**, whence, anl, **scrutability**—**inscrutable**, whence, anl, **inscrutability**—**scrutate**, **scrutation**, **scrutator**—**scrutiny**, whence **scrutineer** (cf *mutineer* from *mutiny*) and **scrutinize** and **scrutinous**—cf **perscrutate**, whence, anl, **perscrutation**.—Cf, ult, 'to SHEAR'.

1. 'To *shred*', ME *shreden*, earlier *schreden*, OE *scrēadian*, to cut, esp to cut off or into small pieces, derives from the OE n *scrēade*, whence ME *schrede*, later *shrede*, E *shred*: cf the vv OHG *scrōtan*, G *schroten* (cf MHG *verschröten*, to hack to pieces), and MD *schrooden*, *schroden*, and the nn OFris *skrēd* (cf MLG *schrāt*), OHG *scrōt*, a cut, MHG *schrōt*, a sawn-off log, G *Schrot*, a log or block (of wood), MD *schrode*, D *schroode*, a cut-off piece, ON *skrjōthar*, a shred; Lith *skraudùs*, brittle (easily flaked off); L *scrōtum*, adopted by Med, prob a var, both phon and sem, of L *scrautum*, a quiver for arrows; prob, with *o-u* mutation, L *scrūpus*, a sharp pebble; perh L *scrūta* (pl), cast-off or very old clothes; Gr *grútē* (syn with L *scrūta*) and its cognate *grūméā*, (a bag for) old clothes, frippery, trumpery, if *scrūta* does belong to this group, suggest an IE r *krud-*,

*krut-*, with reinforced (IE prefix *s-*) varr *skrud-*, *skrut-*, to cut (perh also tear by cutting).

2. With *shredder*, cf OFris *skrēdere*, a cutter, and LG *Schrader*, a tailor.

3. 'To *screed*', orig to tear, derives from OE *scrēadian*, from the n *scrēade*, a shred, whence (with *sk-* for *sh-* pron) the n *screed*, orig a piece, a strip, torn off, hence a long list, hence a long discourse, whether spoken or, as now usu, written.

4. Akin to OE *scrēade* is OE *scrūd*, clothing (cut off or out), a garment, ME *schrud*, later *shrud*, finally *shroud*, a garment, retained by E, esp as a garment for the dead; whence 'to *shroud*', perh in part from OE *scrȳdan* (*scrūdan*), from *scrūd*.

5. With MD *schroode*, *schrode*, a piece cut off (as in para 1), cf the syn Frankish *skroda*, whence OF-EF *escroue*, orig a piece of fabric or leather, then a piece of parchment (and finally, as *écrou*, an entry in a prison roll): whence ME *scrowe*, whence—after *rowle*, a roll or record—EE *scrowle*, hence E *scroll*, influenced by E *roll*.

6. MF *escroue*, a piece of parchment, hence a roll of written records, becomes the legal E *escrow*, with narrowed sense.

7. L *scrūpus*, a sharp pebble or stone, whence fig, in Cicero, anxiety, a keen uneasiness; the fig sense is usu conveyed by the dim *scrūpulus*, lit a small sharp stone: whence MF-F *scrupule*, whence E *scruple*, whence 'to *scruple*'. Derivative L *scrūpulōsus* becomes MF-F *scrupuleux*, f *scrupuleuse*, whence E *scrupulous*; and the secondary derivative, LL *scrūpulōsitās*, o/s *scrūpulōsitāt-*, passes through EF-F into E *scrupulosity*.

8. L *scrūta* (pl), old clothes, frippery, has derivative *scrūtāri*, *scrūtāre*, to search, to fossick, as an old-clothes man does in a heap of discarded garments, hence to examine (lit and fig), whence LL *scrūtabilis*, searchable, and its LL neg *inscrūtabilis*, unsearchable, i.e. impenetrable: whence E *scrutable* and (late MF-F and) E *inscrutable*. L *scrūtāri*, *-āre*, has pp *scrūtātus*, whence 'to *scrutate*' or investigate closely and in detail; derivatives *scrūtātiō* (o/s *scrūtātiōn-*) and *scrūtātōr* become E *scrutation* and (late MF-F *scrutateur* and) E *scrutator*. L *scrūtāri*, *-āre*, has the further derivative, the LL *scrūtinium*, a minute search, whence E *scrutiny* (cf the EF-F *scrutin*).

9. L *scrūtāri* has the cpd *perscrūtāri*, to examine per- or thoroughly, with pp *perscrūtātus*, whence 'to *perscrutate*'.

**shrew**, n, whence **shrew**, adj (obs), and **shrewish**: as person, first in ME: from ME-E *shrew*, earlier *shrewe*, earliest *schrewe*, OE *scrēawa*, *scrǣwa*, that tiny quadruped the shrew-mouse, supposed, by folklore, to be venomous: o.o.o.: perh 'the squeaker', from the Gmc r present in, e.g., OFris *skrīa*, OHG *scrīan*, MHG *schrīen*, G *schreien*, to cry: IE r *skrei-*, or *skrī-*, to cry, itself a reinforcement, by the IE prefix *s-*, of IE *krei-*, *krī-*, as in Gr *krízō*, I scream. Cf:

**shrewd**: EE *shrewed*, malicious, formed from *shrew*, ME-E (obs) malignant, malicious, from the *shrew*(mouse), much as *crabbed* from *crab*, the crustacean, and *dogged*, from *dog*.

**shrewish.** See SHREW (heading).

**shriek.** See SCREECH, para 1.

**shrievalty.** See SHIRE, para 2.

**shrift.** See SCRIBE, para 2.

**shrike.** See SCREECH, para 1, s.f.

**shrill,** adj and v; **skirl,** v, hence n. The adj *shrill* (cf G *schrill*, LG *schrell*), ME *shrille*, earlier *schrille*, is intimately related to ME *schrillen*, to cry piercingly: ? a 'thinning' of the etymon in OE *scralle*tan, to sound loudly, early G *schrallen*, to bark loudly, with 'thinned' sense in Sw *skrälla*, to shrill: echoic (cf YELL).

2. With Sw *skrälla* and esp with Nor *skrylla*, Nor dial *skrella*, to shrill, cf 'to *skirl*', as the bagpipes do, of Scan origin: cf also the Sc, and N Country dial *shirl*, a metathesis of *shrill*, adj.

**shrimp.** See SCANT, para 5.

**shrine,** n hence v, with cpd **enshrine:** ME *schrin*: OE *scrīn*; like OFris *skrīn* and OF-MF *escrin* (F *écrin*), from L *scrīnium*, a circular portable case or chest: o.o.o.: but Gr *krikos*, a finger-ring, OSl *krivŭ*, Lith *kreivas*, curved, suggest that L *scrī-* is a int (IE prefix *s-*) of IE *\*krī-, krei-*, curved, with metathesis to *kīr-* attested by Gr *kirkos*, finger-ring, and L *circus*, orig a circle.

**shrink, shrinkage.** See SCANT, para 5.

**shrive.** See SCRIBE, para 2.

**shrivel** is app of Scan origin: cf Sw *skryvla*, to wrinkle: OScan r *\*skru-, \*skri-*, to wrinkle, with extnn varying according to the particular Scan language.

**shriven.** See SCRIBE, para 2.

**shroud.** See SHRED, para 4.

**Shrovetide.** See SCRIBE, para 2.

**shrub** (1), a very small tree, a bush, whence **shrubbery** (*shrub*+euphonic *b*+collective suffix *-ery*) and the adj **shrubby; scrub,** a shrubby vegetation, whence **scrub,** undersized, inferior, and the adj **scrubby.**

1. A *shrub*, ME *shrubbe*, earlier *schrubbe*, a shrub, derives from OE *scrybb*, a shrubbery: cf Da *skrub*, brushwood, and Nor *skrubba*, a dwarf cornel tree: ? cf the Scan r *skru-* noted at SHRIVEL.

2. The Da *skrub* leads directly to E *scrub*.

**shrub** (2) and **shrab,** a fruit-acid liquor, laced with spirit; **sherbet** and **sorbet; sirup,** now usu **syrup,** whence **syrupy.**

1. *Shrab* is a contr of Hind, from coll Ar, *sharāb*, from Ar *shurb*, a drink; Ar *shurb* yields, by metathesis, the E *shrub*.

2. Ar *shurb*, coll Ar *sharāb*, derive from Ar *shariba*, to drink, whence also Ar *sharbah*, a drink, whence Per and Tu *sharbāt*, a fruit-juice drink, whence E *sherbet*. Cf *sorbet*, sherbet, adopted from EF-F *sorbet*: It *sorbetto*: Tu *chorbet*, a blend of Tu *sharbāt*+vulgar Ar *chourba, shurba*, from Ar *shurb*.

3. Coll Ar *sharāb* (as above) becomes ML *sirupus, syrupus*, whence OF-F *sirop*, whence ME *sirop, syrop* whence E *sirup, syrup*.

**shrug,** v to draw up and usu to contract the shoulders, EE *shrugge*, late ME *schrugge*, is o.o.o. —but cf Da *skrugge*, to stoop or crouch, Sw dial *skrugge*, to walk with a stoop.

**shrunken.** See SCANT (heading).

**shuck,** a shell, a husk, whence 'to *shuck*' and the interj **shucks!**: app from some Alg word—cf Narragansett *anâwsuck*, shells.

**shudder** (v, hence n): ME *shoderen, shuderen*, earlier *schuderen*: cf LG *schuddern*, to shudder, MD *schudden* (also D), *schodden*, to shake, MHG *schūdern*, G *schaudern*, OS *skuddian*, to shudder, OHG *scutēn, scuttēn*, to shake, and, further off, L *quatere*, to shake: cf, therefore, QUASH. App ME *schuderen* is a freq of a Gmc r *schud-*, to shake.

**shuffle.** See SHOVE, para 3.

**shun; shunt; scunner.**

1. 'To *shun*,' ME *shunien*, earlier *schunien*, OE *scunian*, is o.o.o.; and 'to *shunt*' (imm from dial), ME *shunten*, earlier *schunten*, to avoid, is perh an int derivative from ME *schunien*: ? akin to the 1st SHY.

2. The Sc and North Country *scunner*, an intense dislike, a strong aversion, derives from 'to *scunner*', app a freq derivative from ME *shunien*.

**shut.** See SHOOT, para 7.

**shutter.** See SHOOT, para 7, s.f.

**shuttle.** See SHOOT, para 8.

**shuttlecock.** See SHOOT (heading).

**shy** (1), adj, whence **shyness** and 'to *shy*' or shrink away, to start, ME *schey*, earlier *sceouh*: OE *scēoh*, timid, hence shy, akin to MD *schu*, *schouw*, D *schuw*, MHG *schiech*, G *scheuchen* (v): perh an orig int (IE prefix *s-*) form of an IE r in *\*keu-*, to hide; the Da *sky*, shy (adj), also v, to avoid, points to kinship with SHUN.

**shy** (2), to fling (e.g., a stone), is o.o.o.: perh related to the v in prec.

**shyster.** See SHOOT, para 5.

**sial.** See SILICA, s.f.

**Siam,** whence **Siamese** (adj, hence n, esp of cats and twins); **siamoise.** The 3rd, adopted from late EF-F, is prop the f of adj *siamois*, Siamese: and F and E *Siam* derives from Siamese *Saiam, Sayam*, app a corruption of Burmese *Shan*, a collective name for Burma's eastern neighbours (Enci It).

**sib.** See GOD, para 8.

**Siberia,** whence **Siberian** (adj, hence n), is a European (late C16 onwards) derivative of Ru *Sibir*, a locality near Tobolsk.

**sibilance** derives from **sibilant:** L *sībilant-*, o/s of *sībilans*, presp of *sībilāre*, to hiss, from L *sībilus*, a whistling, a hissing, a hiss: echoic. Perh cf:

**sibyl, sibylline.** The latter derives from L *sibyllinus*, the adj of L *sibylla*, trln of Gr *sibulla*, a prophetess attached to a shrine or temple: *Sibulla*, the sibyl of Cumae: o.o.o.: ? orig 'The Hisser', akin to L *sībilus*.

**siccative.** See DESICCATE.

**Siceliot, Sicilian** (adj, hence n), **Siciliana, sicilienne, Sicily.**

*Sicily* derives from L *Sicilia*, from Gr *Sikelia*, land of the *Sikeloi* (L *Siculi*); a Greek colonist of Sicily is a *Sikeliotēs*, whence E *Siceliot*; the It adj is *siciliano* (cf ML *Siciliani*, the Sicilians), whence *siciliana* (sc *danza*), a rustic dance, E *Siciliana*; the F adj is *sicilien*, whence the rich poplin called *sicilienne*, adopted by E. *Sicilian* derives partly from *Sicily*, partly from F *sicilien*.

**sick** (1), adj, whence the extn **sickly**, the adj **sickish**, the v **sicken** (whence the pa **sickening**), the n **sickness**.

*Sick*, ME *sik*, *sek*, OE *sēoc*, is akin to OS *seoc*, *siok*, OFris *siāk*, OHG *sioh*, MHG-G *siech*, Go *siuks*, MD *siec*, MD-D *ziek*, ON *siūkr*, and, with *h* for *s*, the Arm *hiuc*anim, I am ill.

**sick** (2), to search out, to chase, is a dial var of SEEK.

**sickle.** See the 2nd SAW, para 5.

**sickly, sickness.** See the 1st SICK (heading).

**side** (n, whence adj and v, whence **siding**, vn), whence **sideboard, sideling** now usu **sidelong** (adv hence adj), **sideways**; **alongside**—**beside, besides**—**inside** and **outside**; **sidle**.

1. *Side*, a border, a facing surface (hence of the body), comes from OE *sīde*, akin to OFris *sīde*, OS *sīda*, OHG *sīta*, MHG *sīte*, G *Seite*, MD *side*, *zide*, *sijt*, D *zijde*, ON *sītha*, a side, and to OE *sīd*, spacious, whence the now dial *side*, spacious, long and flowing, hence also to ON *sīthr* (adj), hanging down.

2. From *side*, n, perh influenced by *sideling*, comes 'to *sidle*', prob orig freq.

**sidereal.** See CONSIDERATE, para 3.

**siderite**, orig loadstone: L *sidēritis*, loadstone: Gr *sidēritis* (elliptical for *s. lithos*, lit iron-stone), var of *sidēritēs*, adj of *sidēros*, iron: ? from Asia Minor.

**sideways.** See SIDE (heading).

**sidhe.** See SHEE.

**sidle.** See SIDE, para 2.

**Sieg** (G), victory. See SCHEMA, para 4.

**siege.** See SIT, para 3, s.f.

**sierra**, adopted from Sp, derives from L *serra*: cf SERRATE.

**siesta.** See SIX, para 6.

**sieur.** See SENILE, para 6.

**sieve** (n, hence v) and **sift**, whence **sifter, sifting**. 'To *sift*', OE *siftan*, derives from OE *sife*, whence ME *sive*, E **sieve** (n): cf OHG *sib*, MHG *sip*, G *Sieb*: perh (Walshe) akin to L *dissipāre*, to scatter: from *\*sipāre*, *\*supāre*, to throw—cf Skt *kṣip*áti, he throws (E & M).

**sift.** See prec.

**sigh**, id in ME, derives from ME *sighen*, var *sihen*, from *sihte*, pt of *sihen*, var of *sicken*: OE *sīcan*: echoic—cf MD *versīken* (int *ver-*), *suchten*, *sochten*, D *zuchten*, to sigh, MD *sucht, socht*, OHG-MHG *sūft*, a sigh, OHG *sūfen*, to draw breath, *sufteōn, suftōn*, MHG *siufzen* (earlier *siuftēn*), G *seufzen*, to sigh.

**sight.** See SEE, para 3.

**sigil, sigillary, sigillate.** See SIGN, para 3.

**sigma** (whence **sigmate**), **sigmoid**. *Sigma* is the Gr *s*: capital *Σ*, small final *ς*, small elsewhere *σ*); whence Gr *sigmoeidēs*, *s*-shaped, whence E *sigmoid* (suffix *-oid*). The Gr letter comes from Phoenician.

**sign**, n and v (whence **signer** and pa, **vn signing**)—**signum**; **sain**, to cross oneself; **sigil, sigillary, sigillate**, whence, anl, **sigillation** and (unless imm from MF *sigillatif*, f *-ive*) **sigillative**—cf **seal**, n and v (stamp); **signal**, adj (whence **signalize**) and n (whence **signalman**), whence v (whence **signaller, signalling**)—cf **signalment**; **signary, signate, signation, signatory, signature**; **signet** and **sennet**.—Full cpds: **significance, significant**—whence the negg **insignificance, insignificant** — **significate, signification, significative, significator, significatory, significavit, significs, signify** (whence **signifier**); **tocsin**.—Prefix-Cpds: **adsignification, adsignify, assign**, n and v (whence—perh suggested by the MF-F word—**assignable**), **assignat, assignation, assignee**, whence, anl, **assignor, assignment**; **consign** (whence **consignee, consignment, consignor**), **consignation, consignificant, consignification, consignify**; **design** (n and v, whence **designer**), **designate** (adj and v), **designation, designative, designator**; **ensign**, n and v, and **insigne, insignia**; **obsignate, obsignation**; **presignificant, presignification, presignify**; **resign** (whence pa **resigned** and **resignee**), **resignation**; **subsign, subsignation**.—Cf the sep SEEM and perh the 1st SAW.

1. L *signum*, a distinguishing mark, a sign, a signal, has s *sign-*, r *sig-*: o.o.o.: but prob akin to the *sec-* of L *secāre* (s and r *sec-*), to cut, f.a.e. SAW, a cutting tool, esp if the first distinguishing marks consisted of notches cut in wood, etc.; much less prob akin to the IE r *\*sekw-*, to follow, as in L *sequī*, f.a.e. SEQUENCE.

2. L *signum* survives in learnèd E, but the truly E form is *sign*, from OF-F *signe*, from L *signum*; Eccl *sign of the Cross* is a trans of LL *signum crucis*. 'To *sign*' derives, via MF-F *signer*, from L *signāre* (from *signum*). The MF-EF var *seigner* (or *-ier*) has perh influenced the now archaic 'to *sain*', ME *sainen*, earlier *seynen*, from OE *segnian* (from L *signāre*).

3. L *signum*, r *sig-*, has dim *sigillum*, a statuette, a seal, whence E *sigil*; the derivative LL adj *sigillārius*, of statues or marionettes, has prompted the E adj *sigillary*, of a seal or seals, and originates the LL *sigillārium*, image or idol of a pagan god, and *Sigillāria*, feast of the images (during the Saturnalia), and suggests Sci *Sigillaria*, a genus of fossil trees. Derivative L *sigillātus* yields the E adj and v *sigillate*.

4. L *sigillum* becomes MF *seel* (later *scel*, finally *sceau*), whence ME *seel*, E *seal*, a stamped design; derivative MF *seeler* (later *sceler*, finally *sceller*) becomes ME *seelen, selen*, E 'to *seal*'.

5. L *signum* has LL adj *signālis*, intended as, or to give, a sign, whence, in part, the E adj *signal*; the derivative VL *\*signale*, prop the neu of the adj, used as n 'something intended as a sign', produces the OF *seignal*, whence, after OF-F *signe*, the MF-F *signal*, adopted by E; derivative EF *segnaler*, later *signaler*, to render distinguished (modern sense, C18 onwards), has pp *signalé*, whence, in part, the E adj *signal*. 'To *signal*' derives partly from the E n *signal*, partly from the F v *signaler*

whence, by the way, *signalement*, a systematic, esp if by police, description of a person, whence the E *signalment*.

6. Whereas E *signary* is an E formation (*sign*um +suffix *-ary*), *signate* derives from L *signātus*, pp of *signāre*, to mark, to distinguish. On the pp s *signāt-* are formed the foll L words relevant to E:

LL *signātiō*, a marking sign, o/s *signātiōn-*, whence E *signation*;

LL *signātor*, a marker, adopted by E;

L *signātōrius*, relating to a mark or sign, E *signatory*, adj hence n;

LL *signātūra*, a marking (orig of sheep), hence, in F and E, one's personal mark or signature, EF-F whence E *signature*.

7. MF-F *signer* has MF-F derivative *signet* (first as *sinet*), a ring serving as a seal, adopted by E. MF *sinet* has var *senet*, whence EE-E (archaic) *sennet*, a theatrical signal on a trumpet.

8. L *signum* occurs in two full E cpds: *tocsin* and *signify* (etc.). *Tocsin* is adopted from EF-F *tocsin*, MF *touquesain*, OProv *tocasenh*: *toca*, it touches (*tocar*: E *touch*)+*senh*, a church-bell, from the syn LL *signum*, from the L sense 'signal'.

9. 'To *signify*' derives from OF-F *signifier*, from L *significāre*, to make a distinguishing mark, hence to show by marks or signs, to mean: *signi-*, c/f of *signum*+*-ficāre*, c/f of *facere*, to make. The presp *significans* has o/s *significant-*, whence E *significant*; derivative LL *significantia* yields E *significance*; the negg *insignificance*, *insignificant*, were perh prompted by LL *insignificatiuus* (ML *-ivus*), undefined. The pp *significātus* has neu *significātum*, whence the learnèd E n *significate*. On the pp s *significāt-* arise

L *significātiō*, acc *significātiōn*em, OF-F *significa-tion*, adopted by E;

LL *significātiuus* (ML *-ivus*), indicative, symptomatic, significant, MF-F *significatif*, f *-ive*, whence E *significative*;

LL *significātor*, a signifier, adopted by E astrology;

LL *significātōrius* (syn of *significātiuus*), E *significatory*.

10. L *significāre* has the derivative LL adj *significus*, notable, whence, in part, the E n *significs*, the theory or science (?) of meaning; and L *significauit*, ML *significavit*, he has signified, is now a Eccl E n.

11. Of the prefix-cpds, best taken alphabetically, the 1st is LL *adsignificātiō*, an additional meaning, whence E *adsignification*, whence, by b/f, *adsignify*, to denote additionally (*ad*, towards).

12. L has the v *assignāre* (*as-* for *ad-*), to appoint, whence OF-F *assigner*, whence 'to *assign*'; the F derivatives EF-F *assignat* and MF-F *assignation* are adopted by E; MF *assignement* becomes *assignment*; the pp *assigné*, f *-ée*, yields *assignee*.

13. L *consignāre* (*con-*, together, hence an int prefix), to mark with a seal, to confirm in writing, LL to entrust, becomes MF-F *consigner*, whence 'to *consign*'; derivative L *consignātiō* (from pp

*consignāt*us), o/s *consignātiōn-*, becomes (MF-F and) E *consignation*. The *significāre* cpd *consignificāre* (LL), its pp *consignificātus* and the derivative *consignificātiō* yield 'to *consignify*', *consignificate*, *consignification*.

14. L *dēsignāre* (*dē-* used int), to mark out, LL to name, becomes MF-F *designer*, whence 'to *design*'; pp *dēsignātus* yields the adj and v *designate*, and the derivatives L *dēsignātiō*, o/s *dēsignātiōn-*, LL *dēsignātiuus*, ML *-ivus*, and LL *dēsignātor* yield E *designation* (cf MF-F *désignation*), *designative* (cf EF-F *désignatif*), *designator*.

15. L *insignis*, distinguished by a particular mark, hence distinguished, notable, becomes the late MF-F *insigne*, adopted by E but long obs; the L neu *insigne* is used as n, a distinguishing mark of office, authority, honour, with pl *insignia*, adopted by E. This L pl, taken as f sing, becomes OF-F *enseigne*, a distinguishing mark, then a standard (flag), then, in C16, a standard-bearer: whence, in the 2nd and 3rd senses, the E *ensign*.

16. L *obsignāre*, to close (connoted by *ob-*) with a seal, hence merely to seal, has pp *obsignātus*, whence both the E 'to *obsignate*' and the LL *obsignātiō* (o/s *obsignātiōn-*), the 'seal' of baptism, whence E *obsignation*.

17. L *praesignificāre*, to mark—hence to signify —beforehand, accounts for 'to *presignify*'; derivative *praesignificātiō* (o/s *-ātiōn-*), for *presignification*; presp *praesignificans*, o/s *-ficant-*, for *presignificant*.

18. L *resignāre*, to seal *re-* or back, i.e. to unseal, hence to annul, also to abdicate or resign: MF-F *résigner*: E 'to *resign*'. Derivative ML *resignātiō* (o/s *-ātiōn-*), the act of resigning from a benefice, becomes MF-F *résignation*, whence E *resignation*.

19. L *subsignāre*, lit to undersign, hence, LL, to assign, yields 'to *subsign*'; derivative LL *subsignātiō*, signature, E *subsignation*, likewise rare.

**signal, signalize, signalment.** See prec, para 5.

**signary, signate, signation, signatory.** See SIGN, para 6.

**signature.** See SIGN, para 6, s.f.

**signet.** See SIGN, para 7.

**significance, significant, signification, significative, signify.** See SIGN, para 9.

**signor, signora, signorina.** See SENILE, para 4.

**signum.** See SIGN, para 1.

**Sikh**, whence **Sikhism**, comes from the Hi for a disciple: Skt *śishya*.

**silage.** See SILO.

**silence** (n, hence v, whence **silencer**), **silent, silentiary**;—**site** (n, hence v), **situate, situation, situs.**

1. L *silēre*, to say nothing, keep quiet, has presp *silens*, o/s *silent-*, whence E *silent*; derivative L *silentium* becomes OF-F *silence*, adopted by E; *silentium* acquires, in LL, the derivative *silentiārius*, a law-court usher, whence E *silentiary*, with new sense 'advocate, or devotee, of silence'. The IE r is perh *si-*: cf Gr *sigē*, silence, OHG *swīgan*, MHG *swīgen*, G *schweigen*, OE *swīgian*; the Gmc words suggest a var r *suī-*; yet note Go ana-*silan*, to

fall silent, ON *sil*, standing, or quietly flowing, water, OFris *sil*, a sluice. (Feist.)

2. This IE \**si*- app occurs also in L *sinere*, to allow, esp allow to be in a place, pp *situs*, used as adj 'situated', whence the n *situs* (gen *-ūs*), a position, a situation; whence E *site*. Derivative LL-ML *situāre*, to place, has the pp *situātus*, whence the E adj and v *situate*; ML *situātiō* (*situā*tus+*-iō*, n suffix), o/s *situātiōn-*, becomes, perh via MF-F, the E *situation*.

**silex.** See SILICA.

**silhouette** is a b/f from *à la silhouette*, from the F Comptroller-General, E de *Silhouette*, who, arriving unexpectedly (1759) at high office, proved incompetent, the phrase denoting 'badly made or done, incomplete', whence in 1801 the n *silhouette*. (B & M.) Cf the F surname *Silhol*, from dial *silhol*, var of *selhol*, dim of F *seau*, a pail.

**silica** (whence **silicate** and **silicic** and **silicon**), **siliceous, silex.** *Siliceous* comes from L *siliceus*, adj of *silex* (o.o.o.), any very hard stone, esp flint; on the o/s *silic-*, SciL forms *silica*. From 'silicate of quartz' derives *silicosis* (suffix *-osis*, connoting a disease); and from *silica*+*al*umina comes *sial*.

**silk, silken, silkworm, silky.** See SERGE, paras 3-4.

**sill**, the base of a frame: ME *sille*, var *sylle*: OE *syl* or *syll*: cf OHG *swelli*, MHG *swelle*, G *Schwelle*, ON *syll*, *svill*, a threshold, OFris *bedd*selma, bedstead, E *selma*, a bed, Gr *selma*, a beam, *selis*, a plank, prob Lith *suólas*, a bench, perh L *solum*, ground, soil, orig the flat, lower part of a whole, prob Go *ga-suljan*, to establish: the IE r is perh \**suel-*, flat base.

**sillabub.** See para 2 of:

**silly**, whence **silliness**, derives from ME *seely*, *sely*: OE *sāelig*, good, happy, adj of *sāel*, good fortune, happiness: cf the syn OS *sālig* and OHG *sālīg*, MHG *saelec*, happy, G *selig*, blest, Go *sēls*, good, MD *salich, zalich*, D *zalig*, blest, ON *saell*, good, kind: perh cf L *sōl*āri, to console, and—with *h* for *s*—Gr *hil*aros (for \**hel*aros), cheerful: IE r, \**sel-*, happy.

2. *Silly bub*, simple liquor, becomes *sillabub* (cf dial *sillibank*), cider—or wine—mixed with milk to form a soft curd.

**silo**, whence **silage; ensilage, ensile.** *Ensilage*, adopted from F, derives from F *ensiler*, to put into (*en*) a silo; E from F *silo* is adopted from Sp; Sp *silo* derives, with *l* for *r*, from L *sirus*, trln of Gr *siros*, o.o.o., but perh from Gr *Suria*, Syria, silos having first been used in the Fertile Crescent: Egypt—Palestine, Syria—Mesopotamia.

**silt.** See SALT, para 11.

**Silurian:** L *Silure*s, an ancient people of S. Wales: prob of C origin.

**silva, silvan, Silvanus.** See SAVAGE, para 2.

**silver** (n, hence adj and v), whence **silvern** (OE *sylfren, seolfren*) and **silvery** and numerous cpds, all self-explanatory.

*Silver*, ME *silver* or *selver*, earlier *seolver*, derives from OE *seolfor, siolfor* (*-fur*), *silofr, sylofr*, akin to OFris *selover, selver, silver*, OS *silubar*, OHG

*silabar*, MHG-G *silber*, Go *silubr*, MD *selver, silver*, D *zilver*, ON *silfr*, also to Lith *sidābras* and one or two other Sl words: o.o.o.: perh Medit— ? cf Eg *ḥetch* silver, and Hit \**hattus*, the Hattic (Hittite) metal, silver.

**silvicolous, silvics, silviculture.** See SAVAGE, para 4.

**Simeon.** See SIMONY.

**simian.** See the element *simo-*.

**similar, similarity; simile; similitude.** See SAME, para 5.

**simmer** eases the earlier syn *simper*, itself echoic.

**simnel.** See SEMOLINA, para 2.

**simony:** OF-F *simonie*: Eccl ML *simonia*, whence *simoniacus*, late MF-F *simoniaque*, E *simoniac*: *simonia* refers to *Simon* (the Magician: Magus), who attempted to bribe Saints Peter and Paul (Acts, viii, 9-24): *Simon*, L *Simon*, Gr *Simōn*, var *Seimōn*, H *Shim'ōn*, bearing, the bearer, whence also, via LGr *Sumeōn*, the LL *Simeon*, adopted by E.

**simoon** or **simoom**, a strong, suffocatingly hot, dry wind, represents Ar *samūn, semūn*, poisoning, from *samm*, to poison.

**simper**, to smile affectedly (whence the n), is app of Scan origin: cf the Da dial *simper*, var *semper*, coy, affected.

**simple, simplex, simplicity, simplify.** See PLY, paras 18-19.

**simulacrum.** See SAME, para 8, s.f.

**simulate, simulation.** See SAME, para 8.

**simultaneous.** See SAME, para 7.

**sin**, n and v (whence **sinner** and **sinning**); **sinful, sinless.** The two adjj derive, as OE *synfull, synlēas*, from the OE n *syn, synn*, whence also OE *syngian*, ME *sinegen, singen*, later *sinnen*, whence 'to *sin*': and OE *syn, synn*, is related to OFris *sinne*, OS *sundia*, OHG *suntea*, MHG-G *sünde*, MD *sende, sunde, sonde*, D *zonde*, ON *synd*, and, further off, to L *sōns* (o/s *sont-*), guilty, and 'morbus *sonticus*', a dangerous illness or disease; perh also to ON *sannr*, true, (but also) guilty. The sem and phon history at the Skt stage is obscure.

**since:** C16 *sins*, C15-16 *syns*: contr of ME *sithens*, contr of *sithenes*: ME *sithen*+gen-hence-adv ending *-es*: OE *siththan*, afterwards, (lit) after that: OE *sith*, after (prep and adv)+OE *thon*, instr of OE form of THE.

**sincere, sincerity.** The latter comes, through MF-F *sincérité*, from L *sincēritātem*, acc of *sincēritās*, itself from *sincērus*, pure (unmixed), whence EF-F *sincère*, whence E *sincere*; **insincere**, from LL *insincērus*, impure, with derivative LL *insincēritās*, whence E **insincerity**. L *sincērus* app has ult r *sin-*, id with the *sim-*, single, of L *simplex*. (E & M.)

**sincipital, sinciput.** See CHIEF, para 2, s.f.

**Sind, Sindh, Sindhi.** See INDIA, para 2.

**sindon.** See INDIA, para 3.

**sine and cosine; sinus, sinuate, sinuous, sinuosity; insinuate** (whence **insinuating**), **insinuation, insinuative, insinuator** (whence, anl, **insinuatory**).

1. *Cosine*=*co. sinus*=complementi *sinus*, the sine

of the complement; and Math *sine* comes from L *sinus* (gen *-ūs*), a concave fold, esp of a garment, hence breast, hence shelter, the L word (o.o.o.) being retained by An and Zoo for 'a cavity'.

2. L *sinus* has adj *sinuōsus*, bending in and out, hence serpentine, whence EF-F *sinueux*, f *sinueuse*, with EF-F derivative *sinuosité*: whence E *sinuous* and *sinuosity*.

3. L *sinus* (s *sinu-*) has v *sinuāre*, to wind in and out, with pp *sinuātus*, whence the E adj and v *sinuate*; derivative LL *sinuātiō*, o/s *sinuātiōn-*, yields *sinuation*.

4. L *sinuāre* is app a b/f from L *insinuāre*, esp in *se insinuāre*, to snake one's way into a place, hence into someone's confidence; the pp *insinuātus* yields 'to *insinuate*', and its LL derivatives *insinuātiō*, *insinuātiuus* (ML *-ivus*), *insinuātor*, all with senses mainly different from those of F and E, become E *insinuation*, *insinuative*, *insinuator*.

sinecure is the 'solid' of *sine(-)cura*, n, from Eccl ML *sine cūra*, without (L *sine*) care (L *cūra*: see CURE) of souls.

sinew (n, hence v), whence sinewy (adj *-y*), comes, via ME *sinewe*, *senewe*, from OE *sinu*, *seonu*: cf OHG *senawa*, MHG *senewe*, *sene*, G *Sehne*, MD *senewe*, *senuwe*, *zenuwe*, D *zenuw*, ON *sin* (cf Da *sene*), and Skt *snāvas* (? for *\*senāwas*): IE r, *\*sen-*, var *\*sin-*.

sinful. See SIN.

sing, pt sang (occ sung), pp sung; whence singer and pa, vn singing;—song, songster (whence, anl, songstress);—perh singe, v hence n.

1. *Sing*, OE *singan*, is akin to OHG *singan*, MHG-G *singen*, OS *singan*, MD *singen*, MD-D *zingen*, to sing, Go *siggwan* (pron *sing-wan*), to intone or sing, ON *syngva* (*syngja*), Da *synge*, to sing.

2. *Song*, OE *song*, has OE var *sang*, akin to OHG-MHG *sanc*, G *Sang*, a singing, a song, Go *saggws* (pron *sangws*), MD *sanc*, *zanc*, *sang*, D *zang*, ON *söngr*; cf, remotely, Gr *omphē* (? for *\*songhwā*). Walshe suggests that the OGmc vv derive, by b/f, from the PGmc nn.—*Songster*, orig f, derives, in part from *song*, in part from OE *sangestre*, female singer.

3. Perh akin to OE *singan*, to sing, is OE *sengan*, ME *sengen*, E 'to *singe*': cf OFris *senga*, *sendza* (*sandza*), MHG-G *sengen*, MD *singen*, *sengen*, D *zengen*: both Walshe, firmly, and Webster, tentatively, suggest that OGmc *seng-* is the caus form of OGmc *sing-*, to sing: 'to make (the flames) sing' or 'hiss'.

singe. See prec para.

singer. See SING (heading).

Singhalese, Sinhalese. See CEYLON.

single. See SAME, para 14.

singlet; singleton. See SAME, para 15.

singletree. See SWING (heading).

singular, singularity. See SAME, para 14.

sinister, whence the adjj sinistral, sinistrate (cf LL *sinistrātus*; hence sinistration), sinistrous and the Chem n sinistrin (Chem suffix *-in*); cf the element *sinistr(o)-*.

*Sinister*, app imm from L, prob comes into E via the MF-F *sinistre*: L *sinister*, (placed or situated) on the left, cf the derivative *sinistrum*, the left side, and *sinistra*, the left hand, the complement of *dextra*, the right hand: hence unfavourable, orig in the language of augury; the modern E and F sense arises in C15 F. L *sinister* is o.o.o.; the suffix is *-ter*, as in *dexter*.

sink (v, hence n), pt sank (occ sunk), pp sunk, ppa sunken: ME *sinken*, OE *sincan*: cf OS *sincan*, OHG *sinchan*, MHG-G *sinken*, Go *sigqan* (? pron *singan*), MD *senken*, *sinken*, D *zinken*, ON *sökkva*, to sink, Lith *senkù*, I sink: IE r, prob *\*sengh-* or *\*senkh-*, to collapse.

sinless, sinner. See SIN.

Sinn Fein: Ir *sinn fein*, we ourselves.

Sinologue. See the element *Sinico-*.

sinuate, sinuation. See SINE, para 3.

sinuosity, sinuous. See SINE, para 2.

sinus. See SINE, para 1.

Sion. See ZION.

Siouan is the adj of *Sioux* (pron *see-oó*), adopted from F: a shortening of F Nadowess*ioux*: Chippewa *Nâdowessi*, lit 'little snake, enemy', the Dakota tribe: app a dim of *Nâdowe*, lit 'big snake', the Iroquois. (Mathews; Webster.)

sip. See SUP, para 4.

siphon (n, hence v), siphonium, siphuncle; cf the element *siphoni-* (or *-no-*).

*Siphuncle* derives from L *siphunculus*, dim of *siphō*, tube, siphon, acc *siphōnem*, whence EF-F *siphon*, adopted by E; the L word derives from Gr *siphōn*, with dim *siphōnion*, whence the SciL *siphonium* in Zoo.

sippet. See SUP.

sir. See SENILE, para 7.

sire. See SENILE, para 6.

Siren, siren, syren. The 3rd, esp as 'warning instrument' (or its sound), is prop a misspelling of the 2nd; the 2nd, a dangerously attractive woman, orig luring by song, generalizes the 1st, one of a group of minor female divinities enchanting sailors to their doom, as in The Odyssey: L *Siren*: Gr *Seirēn*: ? 'The Binder, the Spellbinder', as Hofmann implies—cf Gr *seirá*, Ionic *seiré*, a rope, and—for the IE r *\*sei-*, to bind—Skt *syáti*, he binds. The adj *sirenic*, with extn *sirenical*, prob derives from Gr *seirēnikos*, Syren-like.

sirloin. See LOIN, para 2.

sirocco: It *sirocco*, *scirocco*: Ar *sharqī*, eastern, used elliptically for an easterly wind: *sharq*, the east+adj suffix *-ī*.

sirrah, sirree. See SENILE, para 7.

sirup, sirupy. See the 2nd SHRUB, para 3.

sisal stands for *sisal hemp*, hemp from *Sisal*, once a seaport of Yucatan in CA: Mayan *sisal*, cold waters.

siscowet. See CISCO.

sise. See SIX, para 6.

sissy: adj of *sis*, a girl, prop a *sis*ter. Hence n.

sist (v, hence n).—Cpds in *-sist*, v (and its derivatives): assist (v, hence n), assistance, assistant, (from *assist*) assistful and assistless; consist, consistence (with extn consistency), consistent, consistorial, consistorian, consistory; desist, desistance, desistive; exist, existence, existent, existential, existentialism; insist, insistent, insistence; persist, persistence (with extn persistency), persistent; resist (v. hence n)—resistable, resistible and irresistible— resistance, resistant—(from *resist*) resistful and resistless—resistive, whence, anl, resistivity—resistor and resister, both from *resist*; subsist, subsistence, subsistent, subsistential.

1. 'To *sist*', to stay (vt) or cause to stand, comes from L *sistere* (s *sist*-), to cause to stand: *sistere*, then, is the caus of L *stāre*, to stand, *stō*, I stand: cf STATE: f.a.e., STAND. (The STAND constellation is so vast that, in this dictionary, it would be inconvenient to have only one entry: see the groups at STATE and at STAND.)

2. Of the numerous cpds, the first is *assist*, MF-F *assister*, to cause to stand *ad* or by, hence to stand by (someone); the F presp *assistant*, used also as n, is adopted by E, as is its derivative the MF-F *assistance*. L *assistere*, to stand near.

3. L *consistere* (int *con*-), to stand firm, yields— perh via MF-F *consister*—'to *consist*'; the presp *consistens*, o/s *consistent*-, used as adj by LL, becomes *consistent* (cf F *consistant*), whence *inconsistent*; derivative LL *consistentia* yields MF *consistence* (F -*ance*), adopted by E. On the L s *consist*- arises LL *consistōrium*, a place of assembly, hence an assembly, whence ONF *consistorie* (OF-F *consistoire*), whence E *consistory*; derivative ML *consistoriālis*, adj, and LL *consistoriānus*, adj and n, become E *consistorial* (as in MF-F) and E *consistorian*, adj and n.

4. L *dēsistere*, to cease *dē*- or from, to renounce, becomes MF-F (*se*) *désister*, whence 'to *desist*', whence, anl, *desistance* and *desistive*.

5. L *exsistere*, LL *existere*, to stand forth, emerge, to exist, becomes MF-F *exister*, whence 'to *exist*'; presp *exsistens*, *existens*, o/s *ex(s)istent*-, yields *existent*; derivative LL *ex(s)istentia* yields MF-F *existence*, adopted by E. LL *ex(s)istentia* has —prob after *essentialis*—derivative adj *ex(s)istentiālis*, whence E *existential*, whence *existentialism*— cf F *existenciel*, *existencialisme*. The LL neg *inex(s)istens*, unsubstantial, non-existent, becomes E *inexistent* (cf F *inexistant*), whence, unless from EF-F *inexistence*, the E *inexistence*; *non-existent* and *non-existence* prob owe something to F *nonexistant*, *non-existence*.

6. L *insistere*, to stand *in* or upon, to apply oneself diligently to, to insist, becomes MF-F *insister*, whence 'to *insist*'; the L presp *insistens*, o/*sinsistent*-, yields *insistent*, adj, whence *insistence* (cf F *insistance*).

7. L *persistere*, to stand *per*- or firm, becomes MF-F *persister*, whence 'to *persist*'; the L presp *persistens*, o/s *persistent*-, E *persistent*; derivative LL *persistentia*, E *persistence* (cf MF-F *persistance*).

8. L *resistere*, to cause to stand *re*- or back, to stand against, to withstand or oppose, passes through MF-F *résister*, into E 'to *resist*', whence *resistable* and—cf F *résistible*—*resistible*, with neg *irresistible* perh prompted by F *irrésistible*, from ML *irresistibilis*. The F presp *résistant*, used as adj, becomes E *resistant*, and derivative MF-F *résistance*, perh suggested by LL *resistentia*, becomes *resistance*; *resistive*='to *resist*'+adj -*ive*.

9. L *subsistere* (L *sub*, under, connotes endurance—cf *suffer*), to stay still or alive, to endure, LL to exist, to subsist, yields MF-F *subsister* and, perh independently, E *subsist*; the L presp *subsistens*, o/s *subsistent*-, yields *subsistent*; derivative LL *subsistentia*, substance, leads to at least the form of E *subsistence*; the occ var *subsistance* is prob adopted from EF-F. Derivative LL *subsistentiālis*, endowed with existence or life, yields E *subsistential*.

**sister.** See ADDENDA.

**sistrum.** See SEISMIC.

**sit** (v, hence n), whence **sitter** and pa, vn **sitting**— pt **sat**, archaic **sate**—pp **sat**, obs **sitten**; **set** (v, hence n), whence **settee**, **setter** and pa, vn **setting**— cf **settle**, n and v (whence **settlement** and **settler**); sep SADDLE; **seat**, n, hence v, whence pa, vn **seating**; **sedate**, **sedation**, **sedative**—**sedent**, **sedentary**, **sederunt**—**sedilia**, **sediment** (whence **sedimentary**)—**see**, n—**sessile**, **session** (whence **sessional**, **sessionary**); **séance**; **siege**, **besiege** (whence **besieger** and pa, vn **besieging**).—Cpd in -*sede*: **supersede**, **supersedeas**, **supersession** (whence, anl, **supersessive**)—cf **surcease**, v, hence n.—Cpds in -*sid*-, from L -*sidēre*, c/f of *sedēre*, and in -*sess*: **assess**, **assession**, **assessor**—**assident**, **assiduity**, **assiduous**— cf **assize(s)**, whence **assizer**, cf also **sizar** and **size**; **dissidence**, **dissident** (adj, hence n); **insidiate**, **insidious**; **obsidional** (whence, anl, the var **obsidionary**)—**obsess** (whence, anl, **obsessive**), **obsession** (whence **obsessional**), **obsessor**; sep POSSESS, etc.; **preside**, **presidence** and **presidency**, **president** (adj and n), **presidential**, **presidium** (whence **presidial**); **reside**, **residence** (whence the var **residency**), **resident** (adj, hence n; whence **residential**), **residentiary**—cf **residue** (whence, anl, **residual**, **residuary**), **residuum**; **subside**, **subsidence**, **subsident**, **subsidiary** (adj, hence n), **subsidy** (whence, anl, **subsidize**); cf the sep SOOT.—Gr *hedra*, a seat, see the element -*hedral*; **Sanhedrin**; cf CATHEDRAL, q.v. at the sep CHAIR.

### Indo-European

1. With E *sit*, *seat*, *set*, akin to L *sedēre*, to sit, and, with *h*- for *s*-, Gr *hedra*, a seat, cf also Skt *sīdati*, he sits, and *sādas*, a seat, OSl *sēditŭ*, he is seated, Lith *sēdēti*, to sit, OIr *saidi*, thou art seated, W *assedu*, Br *azéza* (for *\*adseda*), to sit: IE r, *\*sed*-.

### Greek

2. As Gr *hedra* stands for *\*sedra*, so the syn *hedos* stands for *\*sedos*.—*Chair* has, with *cathedral*, been treated at the former word; there remains only *Sanhedrin*: LH *sanhedrīn*: Gr *sunédrion*, lit a sitting *sun*- or together, hence an assembly, -(*h*)*edrion* being an end-c/f of *hedra*; cf the LL *synedrium*, a council-chamber.

Latin

3. L *sedēre* (s and r, *sed-*), to sit, has derivative nn:

*sēdēs*, a seat, acc *sēdem*, whence OF-MF *sied*, *sie*, the latter yielding the E *see*, a seat, esp of power or dignity, e.g. of a bishop, hence the seat or focus of a bishopric;

*sedīle*, a seat, pl *sedīlia*, adopted by Eccl E;

*sedimen*, var *sedimentum*, a sitting, a settlement, hence what has settled at the bottom, whence (EF-F *sédiment* and) E *sediment*;

\*sedla, eased to *sella*, a seat, esp on horseback, whence OF-F *selle*, whence E *sell*, a saddle (archaic; obs, a throne); hence the learnèd E adj *sellate*;

VL \*sedica or \*sedicum, a seat, whence OF-MF *siege*, a place where one sits, also where one establishes oneself, EF-F *siège*; the military sense arises either in late OF or in very early MF, and from MF *siege*, var *sege*, comes ME *sege* and E *siege*, whence the rare 'to *siege*', usu expressed by 'to *besiege*', ME *besegen* (*be-*, round about, locally *by*).

4. Before passing to the presp and pp (and their derivatives) of *sedēre*, it is well to note the var *sidēre*, occurring in *possidēre*, to own (see the sep POSSESS), and the caus *sedāre*, to cause to sit, hence to quieten or keep quiet, to allay or calm, with pp *sedātus*, whence the E adj (and obs v) *sedate*; derivatives *sedātiō*, o/s *sedātiōn-*, and ML *sedātivus*, tending to calm, yield E *sedation* and *sedative*, adj hence n.

5. L *sedēre*, to sit, has presp *sedens*, o/s *sedent-*, whence the E adj *sedent*, sitting. On the o/s *sedent-* arises L *sedentārius*, habitually or necessarily sitting, late MF-F *sédentaire*, E *sedentary*. The v-part *sedērunt*, they have sat, has become an E legal n.

6. The cpd *supersedēre*, to sit *super* or above, to be superior to, hence to omit or forbear doing, yields late MF-EF *superseder*, whence 'to *supersede*', the occ var *supercede* deriving from the MF-EF var *superceder*; both L *supersedēre* and *supersedeas*, Mayst thou forbear, have become E legal nn. The pp *supersessus* has derivative ML *supersessiō*, o/s *-sessiōn-*, whence E *supersession*.

7. L *supersedēre*, in its legal sense 'to stay', becomes OF-F *surseoir*, pp *sursis*, whence, influenced by CEASE, the E 'to *surcease*', to desist.

8. L *sedēre* has pp *sessus*, s *sess-*, on which arise L *sessilis*, capable of serving as seat or base, whence E *sessile*;

L *sessiō*, o/s *sessiōn-*, whence E *session*.

9. L *sedēre* becomes OF-F *seoir*, with presp *seant*, later *séant*, whence the EF-F n *séance*, a sitting, a session, esp of spiritualists.

Latin Compounds in *sid-* and *sess-*

10. The predominant c/f of *sedēre* is *-sidēre*, presp *-sidens* (o/s *-sident*), pp *-sessus*. The 1st is *adsidēre*, to sit *ad*, at or by, usu eased to *assidēre* (s *assid-*), with presp *assidens*, o/s *assident-*, whence the Med E adj *assident*. On the s *assid-* is formed

the L adj *assiduus*, constantly sitting near, hence diligent, persistent, whence E *assiduous*; the derivative *assiduitās*, acc *assiduitātem*, yields MF-F *assiduité*, whence E *assiduity*.

11. *Assidēre* has pp *assessus*, whence *assessiō*, o/s *assessiōn-*, E *assession*; whence also the LL *assessāre*, to value or rate for taxing (cf the syn LL sense of *assidēre*), E 'to *assess*', whence *assessment*; whence also *assessor*, a sitter-beside, LL a valuer for taxes, MF-F *assesseur*, E *assessor*.

12. L *assidēre* becomes OF-F *asseoir*, pp *assis*, f *assise* used as OF-F n, session, esp, MF-F, in a lawcourt: whence ME *assise*: E *assize*, esp in the pl, periodical sessions of justice. Aphetic for *assize*, esp in sense 'assessment', is *size*, a standard of conduct, etc., physical extent, hence proportions, at the University of Cambridge an allowance of victuals, whence *sizar*. The OF-F *assise*, settlement, a basic layer (of, e.g., cement), develops the sense 'a setting', hence 'a material that sets', whence E *size*, glue, shellac, etc., with derivative v.

13. L *dissidēre*, to sit *dis-* or apart, hence to sit opposite, to differ in opinion, has presp *dissidens*, o/s *dissident-*, whence E *dissident*; derivative L *dissidentia* yields E *dissidence*.

14. L *insidēre*, to sit in, has derivative *insidiae*, an ambush, with adj *insidiōsus*, late MF-F *insidieux*, f *insidieuse*, E *insidious*, and with v *insidiāri*, to lie in ambush, pp *insidiātus*, whence *insidiātiō*, o/s *insidiātiōn-*, whence the obsol *insidiate*, *insidation*.

15. L *obsidēre*, to sit, hence be established, in front of (a place), to occupy it, has pp *obsessus*, whence 'to *obsess*'; derivative *obsessiō*, o/s *obsessiōn-*, yields (late MF-F and) E *obsession*, and agent *obsessor* is adopted. On the L inf s *obsid-* is formed *obsidiō*, a siege, o/s *obsidiōn-*, with adj *obsidiōnālis*, whence E *obsidional*.

16. L *praesidēre*, to sit in front of, hence in authority over, whence late MF-F *présider*, E 'to *preside*'. The presp *praesidens*, o/s *praesident-*, yields MF *president*, EF-F *pré-*, whence E *president*, n, the adj coming from L *praesident-*; derivative MF-F *présidence* becomes E *presidence*, with var *presidency*; derivative ML *praesidentiālis* yields E *presidential* (cf F *présidentiel*). On the L inf s *praesid-* arises *praesidium*, a presiding over, hence a garrison, a defence, adopted by E, whence the adj *presidial*—? prompted by the LL *praesidiārius*.

17. L *residēre*, to sit back (*re-*), hence to stay behind, hence to remain, hence, in LL, to sojourn, yields, via late MF-F *résider*, the E 'to *reside*'; the presp *residens*, acc *residentem*, becomes MF *resident*, EF-F *résident*, E *resident*, adj; derivative MF *residence*, EF-F *résidence*, leads to E *residence*; the derivative ML adj *residentiārius*, resident, becomes the Eccl *residentiary*.

18. Also on the L inf s *resid-* is formed the L adj *residuus*, with neu *residuum* used as n, both adopted by E and, via MF-F *residu*, anglicized as *residue*.

19. L *subsidēre*, to sit under, hence to sit or be

placed in reserve, affords us 'to *subside*'. Derivative *subsidium*, troops placed in reserve, hence support or assistance, hence a loan, a tax, whence MF-F *subside*, AF *subsidie*, E *subsidy*; the derivative L adj *subsidiārius* becomes (MF-F *subsidiaire* and) E *subsidiary*. The presp *subsidens*, o/s *subsident-*, accounts for E *subsident*; its derivative *subsidentia* for E *subsidence*.

## Germanic

20. 'To *sit*', ME *sitten*, OE *sittan*, is akin to OFris *sitta*, OS *sittian*, OHG *sizzan*, MHG-G *sitzen*, Go *sitan*, MD *sitten*, D *zitten*, ON *sitia* (*sitja*). Akin to ON *sitia*, to sit, is ON *saeti*, a seat, whence ME *saete*, var *sete*, whence E *seat*.

21. The OGmc vv for 'to sit' have a corresp caus 'to seat', the OE being *settan*, ME *setten*, E *set*: cf OFris *setta*, OS *settian*, OHG *sezzēn*, MHG-G *setzen*, MD *setten*, D *zetten*, Go *satjan*.—'To *set*' has derivative *settee*, where one 'sets (oneself or others) down'.

22. Not a freq of OE *settan*, but a derivative of OE *setl*, a seat, is OE *setlan*, ME *setlen*, E 'to *settle*', orig to place in a seat, hence to place oneself there, to establish oneself: and OE *setl*, whence ME *setil* or *setel*, whence E *settle* (n), is akin to OHG *sezzal*, MHG *sezzel*, G *Sessel*, and Go *sitls* —and, further off, L *sella* (for *\*sedla*) and OB *sedlo*, a saddle (cf SADDLE itself).

**site.** See SILENCE, para 2.

**sitter, sitting.** See SIT (heading).

**situate, situation.** See SILENCE, para 2.

**Siva.** See CITY (heading).

**Siwash, siwash** (n, v). Both *siwash*, an Alaskan dog, and 'to *siwash*', to live like a Red Indian, esp to travel very light, derive from *Siwash*, an Indian of the N Pacific coast of America: and *Siwash* itself is a Chinook-jargon word—a corruption of the F *sauvage*, uncivilized, wild (f.a.e., SAVAGE).

**six, sixth—sixteen, sixteenth—sixty, sixtieth;** L **sex, 6—sexagenary, Sexagesima, sexagesimal; sexangle, sexennial—sext—sextain, sextan—sextant— sextet (or sextette)—sextic, sextile—sexto—sextuple** (whence **sextuplet,** whence, anl, **sextuplicate**); **senary; sestet; sestina; siesta; sise; Sistine; sixte.**— Gr **hex:** cf the element **hexa-;** for E cpds, see HEX-; **samite.**

1. E *six*, OE *six*, *siex*, *seox*, is akin to OFris *sex*, OS *sehs*, OHG-MHG *sehs*, G *sechs*, MD *ses*, *sesse*, D *zes*, Go *saihs*; ON *sex*; OIr *sé*, Ga *sè*, W *chwech*, Br *c'houech*, Cor *whēgh*, *whēh*, *hwēh*, Mx *shey*; Tokh *šäk*; OSl *šĕstĭ*, Lith *šešì*; with *h-* for *s-*, Gr *hex* (dial *wex*); Skt *šaš*, Av *khšvaš*; Gmc etymon, *\*sehs*; IE etymon, *\*sueks*, *\*sweks*, perh an *s*-reinforcement of *\*ueks* or *\*weks*—cf Arm *veç* and OP *uschts*. (Hofmann.)

2. OE *six* has derivative *sixta*, whence E *sixth*: cf OFris *\*sexta*, OHG *sehsto*, G *sechste*, Go *saihsta*, OIr *sessed*, Lith *šeštas*, L *sextus*, Gr *hektos*.

3. OE *six* has the further derivatives *sixtēne* or *sixtȳne*, with ordinal *sixtēotha*, and *sixtig* or *siextig*, with ordinal *sixtigotha* or *sixtiogotha*: whence E *sixteen* and, in part, *sixteenth*, and E

*sixty* and *sixtieth*. All four words have numerous IE, esp Gmc, cognates.

4. L *sex*, 6, occurs in the foll derivatives notably relevant to E:

*sexāgēni*, 60 each, with adj *sexāgēnārius*, whence E *sexagenary*, whence the n *sexagenarian*, a person 60 years old;

*sexāgēsimus*, 60th, f *sexāgēsima* used as n in LL *sexāgēsima* (sc *diēs*, day), our *Sexagesima* (Sunday); the ML extn *sexāgēsimālis* becomes E *sexagesimal*;

*sexangulus*, 6-angled, whence E *sexangle*, a hexagon;

*sexennium*, a 6-year (*annus*, c/f *-enn-*) period, adopted by E, which forms the adj *sexennial*;

*sextus*, 6th, f *sexta*, used as n by LL, whence E *sext*, a canonical hour; whence It *sesto*, with derivative *sestina*, a verse-form adopted by E, with var (as in F) *sestine*;

*sextāneus*, belonging to the 6th, whence SciL *sextanus*, whence the Med E adj and n *sextan*; the L and SciL adjj have, influenced by It *sestina*, (obs) F *sestine*, prompted E *sextain*;

*sextans* (from *sextus*), o/s *sextant-*, a 6th part, yields E *sextant*, in Math the 6th part of a circle, hence the naut instrument;

*sextīlis*, 6th, used also as n: whence E *sextile*;

*sexto*, abl of *sextus*, used as E n in the making of books.

5. The L for '6 each' is *sēni* (for *\*sexnoi*), which has adj *sēnārius*, comprising 6 units; whence E *senary*.

6. Less directly from L are:

*sextet*, *sextette*: L *sextus*+n-dim *-et*; cf *sestet*, from It *sestetto*, an *-etto* n from *sesto*, 6th (L *sextus*);

*sextic*, adj hence n: L *sextus*+adj *-ic*;

*sextuple*: L *sextus*+*-uple*, as in *quadruple*, *quintuple*, etc.;

*sise*, a cast of 6 (in dicing): OF *sis* (F *six*): L *sex*;

*sixte*, in fencing: EF-F *sixte*, var of OF-MF *siste*, 6th (L *sextus*);

*siesta:* adopted from Sp for '6th (hour)': suggested by L *sexta hora*;

*Sistine:* It *sistino*, adj for any Pope named *Sixtus* (*sixtus*: a late ML var of L *sextus*, 6th): famous to bookmen and art-lovers.

7. Of the E words derived from Gr *hex*, 6, the least obvious, perh the most interesting, is *samite*, which comes from OF-MF *samit*, from ML *samitum*, an aphetic var of *examitum*, from MGr *hexamiton*, from Gr *hexamitos*, six-thread: *hexa-*, c/f of *hex*+*mitos*, a thread: cf *dimity*.

**sixteen, sixteenth.** See prec, para 3.

**sixth.** See SIX, para 2.

**sixtieth, sixty.** See SIX, para 3.

**sizar.** See SIT, para 12.

**size,** magnitude, glue; hence v (whence **sizable**) corresp to each sense. See SIT, para 12.

**sizzle,** whence pa, vn **sizzling:** a freq of *siss* or *sizz*, a, or to, hiss: echoic.

**sjambok:** SAfr *sjambok*: Mal *cambok*, a nasalized derivative from Per *chābuk*, a whip.

**skald.** See SCOLD.

**skate** (1), the fish: ON *skata*: o.o.o.

**skate** (2), for moving on ice (whence the v), is a b/f from earlier *skates*, a trln of ED (C16) *schaetse* (D *skaats*): OF-MF *eschace* (F *échasse*), orig a stilt (cf OProv *escassa*, a cripple's crutch): Frankish *\*skatja*—cf Fris *skatja*, a stilt, and LG *schake*, a shank, a bone, the earliest skates being quadrupeds' thin bones (Webster).

**skedaddle.** See SCATTER, para 2.

**skeet.** See SHOOT, para 9.

**skeg.** See SHAG, para 3.

**skein** (1), of yarn, silk, wool: ME *skeyne*: MF *escaigne* (F *écagne*): o.o.o.: perh a reinforcement (IE prefix *s*-) of L *canna*, a reed, for (Dauzat) early reelers or winders consisted of reeds.

**skein** (2), in basketwork. See SHIN, para 2.

**skeletal, skeleton.** See SHALLOW, para 3.

**skelp,** n and v: Sc, Ir, E dial for '(to deliver) a smart blow': echoic.

**skep,** a coarse round basket, hence a measure of capacity, with var **skip:** ME *skep*: ON *skeppa*: cf OHG *scaf*, a measure, and OHG *scefil*, MHG-G *scheffel*, a bushel: perh from the Gmc word for 'to make' (e.g. OHG *scaffen*, MHG-G *schaffen*; E 'to shape').

**skeptic, skeptical, skepticism.** See ADDENDA.

**sketch** (n, hence v), whence **sketchy.** See SCHEMA, para 3.

**skew** (1), in architecture: ME *skewe*, earlier *scuwe*: aphetically from OF-MF *escu* (F *écu*): L *scūtum* a shield: f.a.e., SCUTAGE.

**skew** (2), vi and vt, to turn obliquely, to twist, whence the adj and n **skew:** ME *skewen*: ONF *eskiuer, escuer*: OF-MF *eschiuver* (F *esquiver*): cf ESCHEW—SHUN—SHY, adj.—Hence **skewness** and **skewy.**

**skewbald.** See SKY, para 2.

**skewer.** See the 1st SHIVER.

**skewness, skewy.** See the 2nd SKEW, s.f.

**ski,** n hence v (whence **skier**), is adopted from Nor and comes from ON *skīth*, a billet of wood, akin to OE *scīd, scīde*, whence E *shide*, a thin board, and to OHG *scit*, MHG *schīt*, G *Scheit*, a log: f.a.e., the 2nd SHED.

2. From ON *skīth* derives, ult, the E *skid*, a log, or a plank, set under, e.g., a structure or on a roll-way.

**skiagraphy, skiapod.** See the element *scia*-.

**skid** (1), n (hence v), a supporting log, etc. See SKI, para 2.

**skid** (2), v (hence n), to slide noisily. See the 3rd SCUTTLE, para 3.

**skiff.** See SHIP, para 2.

**skill,** n (whence **skilful**) and v (whence the pa **skilled**); a shoal or school of fish.

1. *Skill*, n, discernment or judgement (obs), hence the ability to use one's judgement or knowledge, esp in a particular art or science, derives, through ME *skile* or *skil*, from ON *skil*, discernment, very closely related to ON *skilja*, to part or separate, hence to distinguish, whence ME *skilen*, E 'to skill': cf MD-D ver*schillend*, different, from

MD-D ver*schillen*, to differ (cf MD-D ver*schil*, difference), MLG *schillen*, to differ (*schele*, a difference): there are several OHG-G cognates.

2. A *school* of fish is adopted from MD-D *school*, MD var *schole*, akin to the syn E *shoal*, from OE *scolu, sceolu*, a company or troop, akin to OS *skola*.

**skillagalee,** var of **skilligalee; skilly.** The 3rd is short for the 2nd: dial and s for gruel or a thin broth: o.o.o.: prob of C origin—cf Ga *sgilig*, shelled grain, from Ga *sgil*, a husk, a shell, akin to ON *skilja*, to separate (cf SKILL).

**skillet,** a small cooking pot or kettle, frying-pan, etc.: o.o.o.: perh from MF *escuelette*, dim of OF-MF *escuelle* (F *écuelle*), a pan: L *scutella* (a salver), q.v. at SCUTAGE.

**skilligalee, skilly.** See SKILLAGALEE.

**skim,** v (whence **skimmer**), hence n and—prob for *skimmed*—adj; **scum,** n (whence **scummy**) and v; **scumble,** v (freq of 'to *scum*'), hence n; **meerschaum.**

1. 'To *skim*', late ME-E, is a thinning of ME *scume*, E 'to *scum*', itself from the ME n *scume*, whence the E n *scum*: and ME *scume* comes from MD *schume, schūm, schuum*, akin to OHG *scūm*, MHG *schūm*, G *Schaum*, foam, and perh, ult, to L *scūtum* (see SCUTAGE).

2. G *Schaum* occurs in the cpd *Meerschaum*, lit 'sea-foam'—cf E MERE, a pond, a lake.

**skimp, skimpy.** See SCANT, para 3.

**skin,** n (whence **skinny**), hence v (whence **skinner**); **skinflint** (one who would *skin* a *flint*).— A *skin* or hide came into ME from ON *skinn* (cf Sw *skinn*); literally that which one peels off, it is akin to MD *schinnen*, D *schinden*, OHG *scintan*, MHG-G *schinden*, to flay, MHG *schint*, a peel, and Br *scant* (? for *\*scantos*), a fish-scale, Ir *scáinim*, I tear or burst, Ga *sgáin*, to tear or burst, Cor *cen*, a skin or peel, OC r *\*scan* (var of *\*scal*), to tear (Malvezin).

**skink** (a small lizard): L *scincus*: Gr *skinkos* (σκίγκος), var *skingos* (σκίγγος): o.o.o.: ? Medit —cf Eg *ḥentasu*, *ḥunta*, a lizard.

**skip** (1), a basket. See SKEP.

**skip** (2), to move with light, low leaps (whence **skipper, skipping**), hence n: ME *skippen*: a thinned derivative from the OScan *\*skop*-, to leap, to run, attested by ON *skopa* and OSw *skoppa*, var *skuppa*: cf also Lith *skùbti*, to hasten, MHG *schüft*, a gallop, and perh OE *wīd-scop*, ? running far and wide. (Holthausen.)

**skipper,** captain. See SHIP, para 3.

**skirl.** See SHRILL, para 2.

**skirmish,** n and v; **scrimmage,** n, hence v, and its orig dial var **scrummage** (n, hence v), with shortened form **scrum,** n hence v, whence **scrummer** and **scrumming.**

*Scrimmage*, orig a skirmish, hence a fencing bout, hence a confused struggle, whence the Rugby Football sense, is an alteration, app at first a Sc, and a NE E dial, of *skirmish*, via a dial and illiterate *scrimmish*: and a *skirmish*, ME *scarmishe*, earlier *skarmoch(e)*, derives from late MF-EF *escarmuche* (earlier MF *escharmuches*; F *escarmouche*), prob from It *scaramuccia*, prob of Gmc origin; 'to *skirmish*', ME *skirmishen*, earlier *scarmishen*, prob from OF-EF *escremir*, to fight with the sword, from OGmc (western) *\*skirmjan*— cf MHG *schirmen*, to fence, and OHG *scirm*, MHG-G *schirm*, protection. It is prob, not certain, that the presumed OGmc origin of It *scaramuccia* is id with the Gmc origin of OF *escremir*.

**skirt.** See SHARE, para 9.

**sklt.** See SHOOT, para 10.

**skite.** See SHOOT, para 11.

**skitter.** See SHOOT, para 12.

**skittish.** See SHOOT (heading).

**skittle, skittles.** See SHOOT, para 12.

**skoal!:** Nor, Da *skaal!*, from *skaal*, a cup: ON *skāl*, a bowl.

**skua**, of Scan origin, is akin to ON *skūfr*, OHG *scubil*, Ru *čub*, *čup*, a tuft, a knob.

**skulk.** See SCOWL, para 2.

**skull.** See SHELL, para 4.

**skunk**, a fur-bearing quadruped able to emit a stinking secretion (whence the fig use), is of Alg origin: cf, esp, Abnaki *segonku*, a skunk, and even Massachusett *sagket*, a urinator.

**sky**, n (whence **skyey**), hence v, with cpd **ensky**; many obvious cpds, e.g. **skylark** (cf LARK) and **skyscraper**.—*Sky* comes, by way of ME *skie*, sky, cloud, from ON *skȳ*, a cloud, hence a cloudy sky: cf ON *skuggi*, OE *scua* or *scuwa*, OHG *scūwo*, a shadow, with a Gmc var indicated by the syn OE *scēo* and OS *skio*; therefore of the *-scu-* of L *obscūrus*, dark, shadowy, and Skt *skutás*, covered, and therefore ot L *scūtum*, a shield (cf SCUTAGE): basically, the *sky* is 'the coverer'.

2. The ON *skȳ*, a cloudy sky, becomes ME *skewe* (pl *skewes*), to which, app, is akin the ME *skewed*, (of a horse, etc.) piebald, whence—after pie*bald*—the E *skewbald*.

**slab** (1), n (whence **slabby**), hence v: a thick slice, a plate, of, e.g., bread, meat, timber: ME *slab*, earlier *slabbe*, *sclabbe*, is o.o.o. but perh akin to MF *esclate* (F *éclat*), a fragment, a shred, from OF-MF *esclater* (F *éclater*), perh from Frankish *\*slaitan* (cf OHG *slēzan*, G *schleissen*), to tear or slit. Cf SLAT (1).

**slab** (2), slime, hence (also in part from next term) a dull lout—**slobber**, v, hence n; **slub**, mire—**slubber**, v; cf the obs redup **slibber-slabber**, or derivatively (?) **slibber-sauce**, a sloppy food or medicine or cosmetic.

1. In this group, E and E dial exhaust the gamut of the IE short vowels, for dial fills the gap in the list by offering *sleb*, a large underlip (tending to be wet), and *slebby*, a var of *slabby*, sloppy or greasy; the basic idea is '(a sloppy or slovenly or sickening) wetness, hence mire, ooze, slime'; the languages mostly concerned are app E, D, LG, Ice.

2. The now mainly dial *slab*, mire, slime, comes from Scan, perh direct from the syn, now obs, Da *slab*—cf Sw dial *slabb*.

3. 'To *slabber*', to drool, slobber, gulp, prob comes from LG: cf the syn LG *slabberen*, a freq (denoted by *-er-*) of a Gmc v attested by MD-D *slabben*, var *slebben*; cf also the Ice *slafra*.

4. 'To *slaver*', or drool, is prob of Scan origin: ? ult from the ON origin of Ice *slafra*.

5. The mostly AIr *slob*, mire, ooze, whence the Can *slob*, mushy ice, either derives from or was prompted by the syn Ir *slab*. Akin is 'to *slobber*' or drool: app of D (or LG) origin—cf MD *-slobberen*, *slubberen*, D *slobberen*: cf 'to *slabber*'.

6. *Slub*, slime, slush, comes from MD *slubbe*: cf the related MD *slubberen* and MLG *slubbern*, from either or both of which comes 'to *slubber*' or daub.

7. The D-LG words mentioned in paras 5-6 also denote 'to lap (milk)', as also do D *slabberen* and *slabben*. Ult, all these words are echoic.

**slabber**, to drool. See prec, para 3.

**slack** (adj, n, v), **slacken**, **slackness**, **slacks**. See LANGUID, para 16.

**slag**, dross, whence **slaggy**, derives from MLG *slagge* (whence, via LG *slacke*, the G *Schlacke*): orig, 'scales which fly off when metal is struck' (Walshe)—therefore from OHG *slahan*, MHG *slahen*, G *schlagen*, to strike: cf the E SLAY.

**slain.** See SLAY (heading).

**slake.** See LANGUID, para 17.

**slam** (v, hence n), to strike hard and sharply, is, imm, of Scan origin and, ult, echoic: cf the syn Nor *slemma*, var *slemba*, and *slam*, a sharp slap or blow.

**slander.** See ASCEND, para 3.

**slang**, **slangy**. See SLING, para 2.

**slant**, v (whence the pa **slanting**), hence n, whence adv **aslant** (*a-*, on—sc *the*—*slant*), used also as adj, whence prob the adj **slant**.

'To *slant*' comes from ME *slenten*, to slope, also to slide: cf Nor dial *slenta*, to slope, Sw *slinta*, to slide: nasalized derivatives of the Scan r attested by ON *sletta*, to slide: ? echoic.

**slap**, n, hence adv and v; hence such cpds as **slapdash**, **slapjack**, **slapstick**.

A *slap*, ME *slappe*, like the late MHG *slappe* (G *Schlappe*), a blow in the face, is patently echoic.

**slash** (v, hence n), whence agent **slasher** and pa, vn **slashing**, derives from ME *slaschen*: o.o.o.: perh cf the OF-MF *esclaschier*, var of *esclacier*, to break, itself prob of Gmc origin: ult, echoic.

**slat**, a piece of slate, a lath; **slate**, a flat layer— or a piece—of laminated rock, usu rectangular, hence the rock so called, whence **slaty**.

*Slat*, ME *sclat*, derives, by aphesis, from OF-MF *esclat* (F *éclat*), which, deriving from *esclater* (F *éclater*), means a piece broken off, a fragment or a splinter; *slate*, ME *sclate*, derives similarly from OF-MF *esclate*, f of *esclat*: and OF-MF *esclater* is —via Frankish—app akin to OHG *slīzan*, G *schleissen*, and E SLIT—therefore to the 1st SLAB.

**slat** (2), to throw smartly or violently (now mostly dial); **slattern**.

*Slat*, like *slap*, is echoic: cf ON *sletta*, to slap, to throw. It has the freq *slatter* (? influenced by *scatter*), to spill, or slop, carelessly, vi to be slovenly: clearly akin is *slattern*, a sloven.

**slate.** See the 1st SLAT.

**slatter, slattern.** See 2nd SLAT.

**slaughter.** See SLAY, para 2.

**Slav.** See para 1 of:

**slave** (n, hence v, with cpd **enslave,** whence **enslavement**), whence the agent **slaver, slavery, slavish; Slav, Slavic—Slavonia,** whence **Slavonian** (adj, hence n) and **Slavonic—Slovak** (cf CZECHO-SLOVAK) and **Slovene** (n, hence adj).

1. Both *slave* and *Slav* occur in ME as *sclaue, sclave,* and *Sclaue, Sclave,* both from ML *sclavus, Sclavus*; the ML var *slavus, Slavus* accounts for EE-E *slave, Slav.* The original sense, therefore, is 'a Slav'; that of 'slave' arose mainly from the fact that 'during the eastward expansion of the Germans in the Middle Ages the Slav populations were enslaved or destroyed' (Walshe, who aptly cfs, sem, the OE *wealh*, a Celt, a slave: see WELSH) and, much less, from the raids made by the Venetians upon Slavonia during the Crusades (B & W). Cf MF-F *esclave* and *Slave*, and late MHG *slave* and, as in G, *sklave*, a slave.

2. ML *Slavus* is the nearer to the OSl forms; ML *Sclavus*, to the imm source, LGr *Sklabos*, a Slav, app a contr derivative of LGr *Sklabēnos*, Slavic (cf ByzGr *Sklauēnos*, ML *Sclavenus*); *Slavic* derives, ult, from the LGr adj *Sklabikos.* The OSl *Slověne*, a Slav, lit 'the speaker' (hence 'intelligent person'), derives from OSl *slovo*, a word, opp the Germans, who were called 'the mutes'.

3. The principal modern Sl names for the Slavs are Ru *Slavjane*, Pol *Slowiane*, Cz *Slované*, Serbo-Croat *Slaweni* or *Sloveni*; and the foll names of countries or regions all mean, ult, 'land of the Slavs': *Slavonia* (earlier *Sclavonia*—cf F *Escla-vonie*), Serbo-Croat *Slavonija*, a region of Yugoslavia; *Slovakia*, Slovene *Slovensko*; *Slovenia*, Slovene *Slovenija*, another region of Yugoslavia. With *Slavonia* (*Scl-*), cf the LGr *Sklabinia*, ML *Sclavinia*, a Slavic settlement in Macedonia, and with *Slavonic* cf ML *sclavonicus*, servile; *Slovakia* derives (*-ia*) from *Slovak*, from Cz *slovák*, orig a Slav; *Slovenia*, from *Slovene*, from G *Slowene*, from the Slovene name.

**slaver** (1), a slave-trader or -ship. See prec (heading).

**slaver** (2), to drool. See the 2nd SLAB, para 3.

**slavery.** See SLAVE (heading).

**Slavic.** See SLAVE, para 2.

**slavish.** See SLAVE (heading).

**Slavonia, Slavonian, Slavonic.** See SLAVE, para 3 and heading.

**slaw,** sliced cabbage as salad: D *sla*, contr of *salade*, adopted from F: f.a.e., SALT.

**slay** (whence **slayer**), pt **slew**, pp **slain; slaughter** (n, hence v), whence **slaughterhouse, -man,** etc.— cf **onslaught; sledge**, a large, heavy hammer, whence, taut, **sledgehammer**—cf **sley**; perh **sly**, whence **slyness**, and therefore **sleight** and **sloyd.**

1. 'To *slay*' derives, by a kind of b/f (prob influenced by the pp and by OFris), from ME *slan*, varr *slaen* and *sleen*, from OE *slēan*, to slay, and (for *slan*) ON *slā*: cf OFris *slā*, OS *slahan*, OHG *slahan*, MHG *slahen*, occ *slān*, G *schlagen*, Go *slahan*, MD *slaen*, D *slann*, ON *slā*, to strike, and OIr *slacaim, sligim*, I strike, Ga *slaic*, a heavy or noisy stroke or blow, Ga *slaightire*, a rogue, Ir *slaidhteoir*, MIr *slataile*, a robber.

2. Akin to and prob deriving from OE *slēan* is OE *sleaht*, slaughter, whence ME *slaht, slaught*; the latter form survives in E *onslaught*, a slaughter on, i.e. a fierce or murderous attack. ME *slaht, slaught* has influenced ME *slaghter, slaughter, slauhter*, which comes from ON *slātr*, butcher's meat.

3. The heavy hammer known as a *sledge* derives from OE *slecg*, akin to ON *sleggia* (*sleggja*) and MD-D *slegge*, themselves akin to the OGmc 'strike, hence slay' words. The *sley* of weaving— a batten, a lathe—derives from OE *slege*, akin to OFris *slei* and OS *slegi*, lit a heavy stroke.

4. Prob akin to E *slay*, OE *slēan*, is E *sly*, orig shrewd, clever, skilful, ME *sli*, earliest *sleih*, earliest *slegh*, from the ON *slaegr*: cf, sem, the G *ver-schlagen*, cunning, sly, and *schlagfertig*, ready (*fertig*) to strike (*schlagen*), hence ready-witted (Webster), and also MHG *verslahen*, to cheat.

5. ON *sloegr*, skilful, shrewd, cunning, sly, has derivative *slaegth*, skill, cunning, slyness: whence ME *sleght*, later *sleighte* and *sliht*: whence E *sleight*, skill, cunning, whence *sleight*(-)*of*(-)*hand.*

6. Akin to ON *sloegth* is Sw *slöjd*, skill, dexterity skilled work: whence E *sloyd*, (a system of) manual training.

**sleave.** See SLIVER.

**sled** (n, hence v, whence **sledding**)—**sledge**, vehicular—**sleigh; slide** (v, hence n), pt and pp **slid**—**slidder**—**slither.**

1. The basic idea of the group is 'to slide': and *slide* itself comes from ME *sliden*, OE *slīdan* akin to OE *slidor*, slippery, whence OE *sliderian*, E *slidder* (now dial), to slide, whence the adj *sliddery*: cf *slithery*, from the n *slither*, from 'to *slither*', a var of *slidder.*

2. With OE *slīdan* and OE *slidor*, cf Lith *slidùs*, smooth, slippery, and MHG *slīten*, to slide: akin to all of which is E *sled*, ME *sledde*, adopted from MD *sledde* (as still in D), akin to OHG *slito*, MHG *slite*, G *Schlitten*, a sleigh. Cf the now dial E *slead*, ME *slede*, adopted from D *slede*, akin to MD *sledde.*

3. Akin to MD *slede* is MD *sleedse*, whence E *sledge*, the vehicle; and MD *slede* becomes ED-D *slee*, whence E SLEIGH.

**sledge** (1), a heavy hammer. See SLAY, para 3.

**sledge** (2), a vehicle. See SLED, para 3.

**sleek, sleekness.** See the 1st LIME, para 2.

**sleep** (n, v, with pt, pp **slept**), **sleeper, sleeping** (from 'to *sleep*'), **sleepy.** The last derives from OE *slæpig*, from OE *slæp*, whence the E n *sleep*; *sleeper* derives from OE *slæpere*, from OE *slæpan*, whence ME *slepen*, E 'to *sleep*'. OE *slæp* is akin to OFris *slēp*, OS *slāp*, OHG *slāf*, G *Schlaf*, Go *slēps*, MD *slaep*, D *slaap*; OE *slǣpan* to OFris *slēpa*, OS *slāpan*, OHG *slāffan*, MHG *slāfen*, G *schlafen*, Go *slēpan*, MD-D *slapan*; and all these are akin to OHG-MHG *slaf*, G *schlaff*, flabby, loose, OSl *slabū*, flabby, soft, weak. The Gmc r is \**slāp*- ;the IE r,\**slab*- or *slāb*-,app a reinforcement, with IE prefix *s*-, of an IE r \**lab*- or *lāb*-, as in L *lābī*, to glide, to slip, *labāre*, to totter, and, nasalized, Skt *lámbate*, it hangs down, and, with vowelchange, OIr *lobur*, weak, and those revelatory ON complements, *lūta*, to fall, give way, and *slūta* (var *slota*), to hang down.

**sleet**: ME *sleet*, earlier *slete*: OE \**slēte*: cf MHG *slōze*, G *Schlösse*, hail, sleet, and Nor dial *slute*, Da *slud*, Sw *sludd* or *sludde*.

**sleeve (n, hence v), sleeveless; sloop; slop; slope (n, hence v) and aslope.**

1. *Sleeveless*, OE *slēflēas*, derives from OE *slēf*, varr *slȳf*, *slīef*, whence ME *sleve*, later *sleeve*, retained by E: cf OE *slēfan*, *slīfan*, to slip, to put (clothes) on, *slūpan*, Go *sliupan*, to slip, and ult the L *lūbricus* (E LUBRIC), slippery.

2. OE *slūpan* has the further cognates MLG *slūpen*, MD *slupen*, *sluypen*, D *sluipen*, to slip: app akin to the D words is the D *sloep*, ED *sloepe*, whence E *sloop*; ED *sloepe* becomes F *chaloupe*, whence E *shallop*.

3. Also akin to OE *slūpan*, to slip, is ME *sloppe*, a loose garment, whence E *slop*, whence *slops*, ready-made, usu cheap, clothes: ME *sloppe* comes imm from MD *slop*, akin to MD *slupen*.

4. Again akin to OE *slūpan* is OE *sloppe* in *cūsloppe*, var *cūslyppe*, whence E *cowslip*, cowdroppings; OE *-sloppe* becomes, in ME, the independent *sloppe*, whence E *slop*, slush, liquid food (*slops*), kitchen or bedroom waste (*slops*). Hence, both 'to slop' or spill carelessly, and the adj *sloppy*. Cf *slip*, curds and whey, liquid clay, etc.: ME *slyp*, slime, curds: OE *slypa*, any sticky substance, akin to *slūpan*.

5. OE *slūpan* has cpd *āslūpan*, to slip away, with pp *āslopen*, whence prob, by b/f, the E n *slope*, an incline of land, as in a hillside, whence the adv *aslope* (*a-*, on), used derivatively as adj.

**sleigh.** See SLED, para 3.

**sleight(-of-hand).** See SLAY, para 5.

**slender**, whence **slenderness**, comes from ME *slendre*, *sclendre*: prob aphetic for MF *esclendre*, slender, slim; cf MD-ED *slinder*, thin, slender: o.o.o: ? cf ODa *slente*, to weaken, whence Da *slentre*, to lounge or stroll (cf G *schlendern*, to saunter).

**sleuth**, a trail or track (obs), whence **sleuthhound**, a bloodhound, whence **sleuth**, a detective (orig AE), whence 'to sleuth' or play the detective: ME *sleuth*, a man's or a beast's track: ON *slōth*, whence also the syn OF-EF *esclot*, whence, by aphesis, the E *slot*, a deer's track.

**slew**, pt of slay.

**slew**, to veer. See SLUE.

**sley.** See SLAY, para 3.

**slibber-sauce, -slabber.** See the 2nd SLAB (heading, s.f.).

**slice**, n, hence v (whence **slicer**); **slit**, n and v; cf the sep SLAT (1).

1. A *slice*, orig a sliver or a splinter, comes from ME *slice*, earlier *sclise*, aphetic for OF-MF *esclice*, *esclisse* (F *éclisse*), from OF-MF *esclisser* (*esclicer*), itself from Frankish *slizzan*, to split: cf OHG *slīzan*, MHG *slīzen*, G *schleissen*, to slit: prob echoic.

2. Akin to those OGmc words are ON *slīta*, OS *slītan*, OFris *slīta*, to split, tear, slit, Lith *skleisti*, to separate, and OE *slītan*, to tear, to slit, whence ME *sliten*, later *slitten*, whence 'to slit'; the n *slit* derives from ME *slitte*, from ME *slitten*.

**slick**, adj and v. See the 1st LIME, para 2. Whence **slicker**, agent and instrument.

**slidder.** See SLED, para 1.

**slide.** See SLED, para 1. Whence *slider* and *sliding*.

**slight**, adj (hence v: cf D *slechten*), whence **slightly, slightness.**

*Slight*, ME *slight*, *sleght*, orig smooth, level, prob derives from MD *slicht*, MD-D *slecht*, plain: cf OFris *sliucht*, OHG-MHG *sleht*, level, MHG *slihten*, to smoothe, whence MHG *sliht*, G *schlicht*, smooth, plain, simple, Go *slaihts*, ON *slēttr*, smooth: prob akin to Gr *lissos* (? for \**slikwjos*), smooth, as Walshe suggests.

**slim**, orig worthless (cf the sl sense 'cunning'), whence **slimness**, is adopted from D *slim*, MD *slim*, var *slem*, *slemp*, *slimp*, oblique, crooked, bad: cf G *schlimm*, bad, MHG *slimp*, oblique, crooked, OHG *slimpī*, a slope, and Lith *slīps* (for \**slimpas*), crooked, steep. (Walshe.) Cf, ult, the 1st LIME.

**slime, slimy.** See the 1st LIME, para 1.

**sling**, pt **slang** (archaic; dial) or **slung**, pp **slung**; the n **sling**; **slang**, n, whence **slangy**;—**slink**, pt **slank** (obsol) or **slunk**, pp **slunk**, the adj and n **slink**, the adj **slinky.**

1. A stone-throwing *sling*, ME *sling*, *slinge*, prob derives from ME *sling*, *slyng*, earlier *slynge*, to strike with a missile from a sling, from OE *slingan*, to twist, to wind; the hoisting device known as a *sling* (whence 'to sling' or place, or raise, in one), ME *slyng*, var *sleng*, is prob akin to the weaponname. With OE *slingan*, cf OHG *slingan*, MHG *slingen*, G *schlingen*, to twist, to wind, ON *slyngva*, to throw, and OFris *slinge*, OHG *slinga*, a sling (for stone-throwing); there are Sl cognates.

2. Perh from 'to sling'—prob from the dial pp *slang*—and therefore elliptical for '*slang*, i.e. slung, language', is the n *slang*, orig the language of the underworld, now merely the unconventional (nondial) speech of all classes: cf the sl '*sling* off at', to cheek, to abuse, and Nor *slengja kjeften*, to use slang (lit, to sling the jaw), and *slengjeord*. (See esp P and P[1] at *slang*.)

3. Akin to OE *slingan*, to twist or wind, is OE *slincan*, whence 'to slink': cf Lith *slìnkti*, to creep, Sw *slinka*, to creep, to glide, MD *slenken*, MD-D *slinken*, to dwindle away. As vt, *slink* means to cast (a calf) prematurely—as does dial *sling*; hence the adj and n *slink*, (calf) prematurely cast; the adj *slinky* comes from 'to slink' or glide furtively.

**slink, slinky.** See prec, para 3.

SLIP

632

SLUICE

**slip** (1), n, slime, liquid clay, etc. See SLEEVE, para 4, s.f.

**slip** (2), n, a twig or shoot cut for, e.g., grafting, hence a narrow strip, something or someone long and slender (and young), derives from MD-MLG *slippe*, akin to or deriving from MD-MLG *slippen*, to cut on a slant, hence to take cuttings of or from, whence ME *slippen*, E 'to slip'. The MD-MLG words are perh akin to *slit*, q.v. at SLICE, para 2.

**slip** (3), to leave quietly or secretly (esp with *away* or *out*), to slide (and fall), also vt, as to put or take off (clothes) quickly or easily, to escape (enemies or memory); hence the corresp n, whence, for a few senses, the adj.

1. 'To slip', ME *slippen*, derives from MD-MLG *slippen*, intimately related to syn OHG *slippēn* and to OHG *slūpfēn*, MHG *slüpfen*, G *schlupfen*, to slip, and numerous other Gmc words either syn or cognate; also to, e.g., L *lūbricus* (for *slūbricus*), slippery, and therefore, ult, to E SLEEVE. The interrelationships are complex; several, rather obscure.

2. That which one slips easily onto the foot is a *slipper*; also from 'to slip', as v of motion, comes *slippy*.

**slip** (4), to cut on a slant. See the 2nd SLIP.

**slipper.** See the 3rd SLIP, para 2.

**slippery**: extn of the now dial *slipper*: OE *slipor*: cf *slop* at SLEEVE, para 4.

**slippy.** See the 3rd SLIP, para 2.

**slipslop** is a redup of *slop(s)*, liquid food; hence as adj. See SLEEVE, para 4.

**slit.** See SLICE, para 2.

**slither.** See SLED, para 1.

**slive.** See:

**sliver**, a long thin, usu cut off, piece, a splinter, derives from *slive*, to cut thin, to split, to slice, ME *sliven*, *OE *slīfan*, akin to OE *-slǣfan*, to separate, esp the filaments of a thread, whence the tech E 'to sleave'.

**slob**; **slobber.** See the 2nd SLAB, para 5.

**sloe.** See LIVID, s.f.

**slog** (v, hence n), whence **slogger** and **slogging**; **slug**, n and v (whence **slugger**, **slugging**). 'To slog' and 'to slug', to strike (a person) heavily, are either echoic or derivatives from a MD or MLG form of 'to SLAY', orig to smite: cf D *slag*, a heavy blow, G *schlagen*, MD *slagen*, to smite.

**slogan**: a contr of Ga *sluagh-ghairm*, a battle-cry, lit an army's war-cry: *sluagh*, army+*gairm*, a cry, a call: from OIr *slúag* (*slóg*) and *gairm*.

**sloop.** See SLEEVE, para 2.

**slop** (loose garment; liquid food;—to spill). See SLEEVE, paras 3–4.

**slope.** See SLEEVE, para 5.

**sloppy, slops.** See SLEEVE, para 4.

**slosh, sloshy.** See SLUSH, para 1.

**slot** (1), a deer's track. See SLEUTH.

**slot** (2), a bolt for a door: ME *slot*: MD *slot*, akin to MD *sloten*, varr *sluten* and *sluyten*, D *sluiten*, to close: cf also OFris *slot*, a lock, and OFris *slūta*. OHG *sliozan* (MHG *sliezen*, G *schliessen*), to close, and OHG-MHG *slōz*, G

*Schloss*, a lock (whence a castle): OGmc etymon, prob *skliutan*, to close, shut, lock, with IE r *skleud-*, reinforcement (in *s-*) of *kleud-*: cf L *claud*ere, to shut, and E CLAUSE. (Walshe.)

**slot** (3), a hollow (now only Sc), hence an aperture, esp if long, narrow, shallow, whence the v: ME *slot*: by aphesis from OF-EF *esclot*: therefore perh ult akin to *slot*, a trace or a track, q.v. at SLEUTH.

**sloth, slothful.** See SLOW.

**slouch, slouchy.** See the 1st SLUG, para 1.

**slough** (1), mire, a bog: ME *slough*, earlier *slogh*: OE *slōh*: o.o.o.

**slough** (2), a (serpent's) skin, hence the v: ME *slouh*, *slughe*: cf G *Schlauch*, a leather bag, MHG *slūch*, a skin, esp a snake's, OS *sluk*, a snakeskin.

**Slovak, Slovakia.** See SLAVE, para 3.

**sloven**, a rogue, a loafer (obs), hence a careless, lazy person, whence both 'to sloven' and slovenly: ME *sloveyn*: ME *-ein* (E *-ane*, *-an*) from OF-F *-ain* from L *-ānus* adj-hence-n suffix, tacked to an easing (*v* for *f*) of MD(-D) *slof*, careless: o.o.o.: ? akin to Bavarian *schlauch*, LG *slū*, G *schlau*, sly or cunning, therefore to E *sly*, q.v. at SLAY.

**Slovene, Slovenia.** See SLAVE, para 3.

**slow** (adj hence v—cf OE *slāwian*), whence **slowness**, cf **slowly** (OE *slāwlīce*); **sloth**, whence **slothful**.

*Sloth*, ME *slouthe*, derives from ME *slow*, earlier *slaw*, from OE *slāw*, whence obviously the E *slow*; generic *sloth*, laziness, idleness, becomes specific *sloth*, the slow-moving CA-SAm arboreal quadruped. OE *slāw* is akin to OFris *slēwich*, slow, dull, blunt, OS *slēu*, OHG *slēo*, MD *slee*, *sleu*, *sleeu*, sour, dull, blunt, slow (D *sleeuw*, sour), ON *sliōr* (*sljōr*), Sw *slö*, blunt, dull.

**slowworm.** See the 1st LIME, para 4.

**sloyd.** See SLAY, para 6.

**slub, slubber.** See the 2nd SLAB, para 6.

**sludge.** See SLUSH, para 2.

**slue** or **slew**, to turn about a fixed point (naut), is o.o.o.: perh akin to SLAY in its basic sense 'to smite'.

**slug** (1), a slow, lazy person (whence **sluggish** and **sluggard**: *slug*+euphonic *-g-*+pej suffix *-ard*), now only dial, hence the garden slug and, from the orig shape, a bullet; **slouch**, an awkward, clumsy fellow, a lazy lout, hence his gait, whence 'to slouch', whence **sloucher, slouching, slouchy**.

1. A *slouch*, formerly also *slouk*, is akin to D *sluik*, lax, languid, and esp to Nor dial *slauk*, a languid, or lax, person.

2. *Slouch* is also akin to E *slug*: ME *slugge*, a sluggard, int akin to ME *sluggen*, to be lazy or languid: cf Sw dial *slugga*, to be languid and slow: ? ult akin to the OGmc words for 'slow' and 'dull, blunt'.

**slug** (2), n and v, (to strike) a heavy blow. See SLOG.

**sluggard, sluggish.** See the 1st SLUG (heading).

**sluice**, n, hence v: ME *scluse*: by aphesis from MF *escluse* (F *écluse*): LL *exclūsa*, prob elliptical for *aqua exclūsa*, water shut out: L *exclūsa*, f of *exclūsus*, pp of *exclūdere*, to shut out: *ex*, out+the c/f of *claudere*, to shut: f.a.e., CLOSE.

**slum** (n, hence v), whence **slummy**: o.o.o.: ? a b/f from *slumber*, n, or *slumbrous*, from slums having, orig, been—to the majority—unknown, back streets or alleys, wrongly presumed to be sleepy and quiet.

**slumber**, v, hence n (whence **slumberous**, often contr to **slumbrous**): ME *slumberen*, var of *slumeren*: OE *slumerian*, from OE *slūma*, a sleep (cf ME *slumer*, MHG *slummer*). The ME *slumen*, to sleep, would perh indicate that OE *slumerian* was orig a freq: cf ME *slumi*, sleepy: MD *slumen*, *sluymen*, and *slumeren*, D *sluimeren*; MHG *slummen*, MLG *slomen*, and late MHG *slumern*, *slummern*, G *schlummern*: prob (Walshe) cf Go *slawan*, to be silent.

**slump**, a marked decline, comes from *slump*, to drop suddenly, (earlier) to sink, or fall, suddenly, as into a bog, from *slump*, a bog or a boggy place: app echoic—cf the E, mostly dial, and the Nor dial *slump*, the noise made by falling into bog or water, and Nor dial *slumpa*, to fall into water, but also cf LG *slump*, a bog or a marsh, E dial *slamp*, moist, wet, miry, and perh MHG *slam*, G *Schlamm*, mud.

**slung.** See SLING (heading).—**slunk.** See *slink* at SLING (heading).

**slur**, whether n or v, and whatever the sense, derives ult from the now dial *slur*, thin mud, watery mire, app from ME *sloor*, mire, itself prob from MD: cf MD *sloren*, MD-D *sleuren*, to drag, ? orig in the mud, to do in a slovenly way, and MD *slore*, D *sloor*, a slovenly girl, a slut: o.o.o. Hence 'to *slur*' or sully, to slander or disparage, whence *slur*, a stigma, an aspersion; 'to *slur*' or trick (obs), hence to pass silently over, hence in Mus and Phon, comes, via or influenced by *slur*, to sully, from the n in its primary sense; *slur*, a trick, a glide in dancing (both obs), a silent passing-over or a slovening, in Mus and Phon, comes from the Mus-Phon v.

**slush**, n (hence v), whence **slushy**, adj hence n; **slosh**, n (hence v), whence **sloshy**; **sludge**, n (hence v), whence **sludgy**—cf **slutch**, n (hence v), whence **slutchy**;—? **slut**, whence **sluttery** and **sluttish**.

1. *Slush* and *slosh*, liquid mud, are prob of Scan origin: cf the Sw *slask*, wetness, liquid filth, and *slaska*, to paddle or wallow; dial and sl-coll *slosh*, to strike, follows echoically.

2. Akin to *slush* are *sludge*, mire, ooze, and the syn var *slutch*; the latter is prob the earlier—cf ME *slich*, liquid mud, slime, akin to MHG *slich*, MLG *slik*; note also ME *sluchched*, muddy, ? orig the pp of a v deriving from OE *\*sluch*, *\*slych*, whence ME *slich*. Clearly, therefore, the entire group may be akin to *slick*, q.v. at the 1st LIME (birdlime).

3. *Slut*, ME *slutte*, a dirty, slovenly woman, is prob akin to the syn MD *slode*, G dial *schlutte*, var *schlutz*, Sw *slusk*, with cognates in Da and Nor; but perh it is akin to ME *sluchched*, muddy.

**slut.** See prec para.

**slutch.** See SLUSH, para ?.

**sly.** See SLAY, para 4.

**smack** (1), a kind of sloop: D *smak*, MLG *smacke*: o.o.o.: ? id with next, from the sound of the waves smacking its sides.

**smack** (2), noise of lips, hence a loud kiss, a smart blow: echoic: cf MD *smack*. Hence the corresp v.

**smack** (3), a characteristic flavour: ME *smak*: OE *smaec*: cf OFris *smek*, OHG *smac*, G *Geschmack*, MD *smac*, D *smaak*: o.o.o. OE *smaec* has derivative *smaeccan*, whence ME *smaken*, whence the syn E 'to *smack*', to have a taste (of): cf OHG *smacchēn*.

**small** (adj, hence n—esp **smalls**, perhaps imm from *small clothes*), whence **smallness**: ME *smal*: OE *smael*: cf OFris *smel*, narrow, small, OS *smal*, OHG-MHG *smal*, small, G *schmal*, narrow, Go *smals*, small, MD-D *smael*, *smal*, small, D *smal*, narrow, ON *smār*, small, and *smali*, small beasts, esp sheep or goats; and, without *s*, OSl *malŭ*, small, Gr *mēlon*, a sheep, a goat, and OIr and Cor *mīl*, a beast—and perh L *malus*, evil.

**smallpox.** See POCK, para 1.

**smalt.** See MELT, para 4.

**smarm**, to smear (dial), to gush or flatter (coll), whence **smarmy**, oily, fulsomely flattering: a dial mdfn of *smear*, q.v. at EMERY.

**smart**, adj (whence **smartness**), n, v.

1. The n *smart*, a tingling local pain, derives from ME *smerte*, prob from the ME adj *smerte*, causing such a pain, later *smart*, retained by E: and the ME adj *smerte* derives from OE *smeart*, intimately related to OE *smeortan*, to feel such a pain, whence ME *smerten*, E 'to *smart*'. With OE *smeortan* cf OHG *smerzan*, MHG *smerzen*, G *schmerzen* (and the n OHG *smerzo*, MHG *smerze*, G *Schmerz*), and MD *smerten*, smarten (n: *smerte*, *smarte*, *smart*—this last, also D), and Gr *smerdnos*, terrible, horrible: IE r *\*smer-*, an *s-* reinforcement of IE *\*mer-*, varr *\*mar-*, *\*mor-*, to rub—cf Skt *mardati*, he rubs or destroys, Gr *marainein*, to rub or wear, hence to waste, away, L *mordēre*, to bite.

2. The *\*mar-* var of the IE r *\*mer-* is seen in 'to *mar*', ME *marren*, *merren*, OE *merran*, *mirran*, to hinder or dissipate: cf OFris *mēra*, OS *merrian*, OHG *merran*, *marrjan*, to hinder, Go *marzjan*, to hinder, to offend, and prob ON *meria* (*merja*), OHG *mēren*, to strike, to crush, therefore to Skt *mṛṇắti*, he crushes.

3. The var *\*mor-* occurs in L *mortārium*, the trough in which a building cement mortar is kneaded, hence any such container, hence also the cement itself: via OE *mortere* comes ME *morter*, E *mortar*, the container; and via OF-F *mortier* comes ME *mortier*, whence, after the container, the E *mortar* or building cement.

4. Cf the sep MARBLE, MARS (MARTIAL), MORSEL.

**smash**, v (whence **smasher** and **smashing**), hence n: echoic: ? orig an int (with IE prefix *s-*) of **mash**.

**smatter**, v (whence the vn **smattering**), hence n: to spatter or spot, hence to defile, whence to speak (a language) in a spotty, i.e. superficial, manner:

ME *smateren*, to chatter: prob echoic (cf *natter*)—cf Sw *smattra*, to clatter, and, further off, Da *klapre*, to clatter, to rattle.

**smear.** See EMERY.

**smegma**: L *smegma*, a detergent: Gr *smēgma*, soap, unguent, o/s *smegmat-*, whence the E adj *smegmatic*: from *smēkhein*, to wash off or away: IE r, *\*smē-*, to smear.

**smell**, pt **smelled** (or **smelt**), pp **smelt** (or **smelled**), whence **smeller, smelling**; **smolder** (AE) or **smoulder**.

1. A **smell**, ME *smel*, *smeol*, *smil*, *smol*, derives from ME *smellen*—whence 'to smell'—varr *smillen*, *smullen*: and the ME v is akin to LG *smellen*, *smelen*, *schmelen*, *smölen*, to reek or smoke, and MD *smolen*, D *smeulen*, to smoulder.

2. Akin to MD *smolen* is ME *smolderen*, whence AE 'to smolder' and E 'to smoulder', to choke (obs), hence, vi, to burn smokily and flamelessly: ? orig an int derivative from MD.

**smelt** (1), a small fish: OE *smelt*, with Scan cognates.

**smelt** (2), v. See MELT, para 2.

**smelt** (3), pt and pp. See SMELL (heading).

**smilax** (greenbrier; bindweed): L *smilax*, bindweed: Gr *smilax*, Attic *milax*, holm-oak, yew, kidney-bean, bindweed: o.o.o.: ? akin to Gr *smilē*, a chisel, lancet, billhook.

**smile.** See MIRACLE, paras 1 and 6.

**smirch**, v (hence n), with int cp d **besmirch**, is a thinned derivative of ME *smorchen*: o.o.o.: ? by aphesis from MF-EF *esmorcher*, to torture, to hurt, also (and lit) to cause to bite, a var of MF-F *amorcer*, to bait, from MF-F *amorce*, a bait, from the pp of OF-MF *amordre*, to (cause to) bite: VL *\*admordere*, from L *admordēre*: int *ad-*+*mordēre*, to bite.

**smirk.** See MIRACLE, paras 1 and 6.

**smite**, pt **smit** or **smote**, pp **smitten**, whence the dial **smit**, a heavy stroke or blow; **smithereens**.

1. 'To smite' derives from ME *smiten*, *smyten*, to strike hard, from OE *smītan*, to smear; sense-development, unclear, but perh via 'to throw mud at'. OE *smītan* is akin to OFris *šmīta*, to smite, to fling, OHG *smīzan*, MHG *smīzen*, to rub, to strike, G *schmeissen*, to fling or throw, Go ga*smeitan*, to smear, MD (and LG) *smiten*, to throw, to smite, D *smijten*, to throw or fling: ? a Gmc reinforcement (IE int prefix *s-*) of the r attested by L *mit*tere, to let fly (e.g., an arrow).

2. Akin to the Gmc words is Ir *smiodar*, a fragment, with dim *smidirīn*, whence E *smithereens*, tiny fragments.

**smith**, n (and v), with many cpds, e.g. **blacksmith** and **goldsmith**; **smithy**, a *-y* derivative of *smith*, n, prompted by OE *smiththe* (from OE *smith*).

'To smith' derives from OE *smithian*, from the OE n *smith*, whence E *smith*, one who forges (metal), hence one who makes with his hands: cf OFris and OS *smith*, OHG *smid*, MHG *smit*, G *Schmied*, Go *-smitha*, MD *smet*, *smit*, *smid* (also D), ON *smithr*, Da and Sw *smed*: Gmc *smit-* is an extn of the IE r, *\*smei-*, *smi-*, to cut or hew, cf Gr *smilē*, a knife, billhook, sculptor's chisel, and

*sminyē* (σμινύη), a hoe: and IE r *\*smei-*, *smi-* is itself an int of IE *\*mei-*, *mi-*, with Gmc extn *\*meid-*, *\*meit-*, to cut, as in, e.g., Go *maitan*, to cut, with C cognates.

**smithereens.** See SMITE, para 2.

**smithy.** See SMITH (heading).

**smock** (n, hence v); **smug** (adj, hence n and v), **smuggle** (whence **smuggler** and **smuggling**).

1. A *smock* or long, loose garment, whether outer or inner, derives from OE *smoc*: cf ON *smokkr*, OHG *smocco*, a smock, D *smuk*, finery, adornment, and MHG *smucken*, G *schmücken*, to adorn, the caus of MHG *smiegen*, *schmiegen*, to nestle, in its sense 'to slip into (clothes)', OFris *smuge*, OE *smūgan*, to creep, ON *smiūga*, to creep through a narrow opening. (Walshe.)

2. *Smug*, orig smartly or trimly dressed, derives from the syn LG *smuk*—cf D *smuk* above.

3. Akin to OE *smūgan* and ON *smiūga* (as above) is LG *smuggeln*, whence E 'to smuggle', lit to creep in to land with (a cargo of) contraband goods: cf the syn D *smokkelen*.

**smog** = *sm*oke + f*og*.

**smoke**, n (whence **smoky**) and v (whence **smoker, smoking**).

The n *smoke* comes from OE *smoca*, akin to OE *smocian*, var *smēocan*, whence 'to smoke': cf MHG *smouch*, G *Schmauch*, smoke, and G *schmauchen*, to emit a thick smoke, MD *smooc*, D (and LG) *smook*, n, and MD *smoken*, to emit smoke, and also Gr *smukhein*, to smoulder, and Lith *smaugti*, to suffocate. The IE r *\*smeugh-* or *\*smeukh-* is app a reinforcement (IE prefix *s-*) of IE r *\*meugh-* or *\*meukh-*, attested by Arm *mux*, OIr *much*, W *mwg*, Cor *mōc*, *mōg*, *mōk*, Br *moguet*.

**smolder.** See SMELL, para 2.

**smooth**, adj (whence **smoothness**), hence n; v, with var **smoothe**.

'To smooth(e)' comes from ME *smothen*, from the ME adj *smothe*, whence also the E adj *smooth*; ME *smothe* comes from OE *smōth*. The OE var *smēthe* (*smoēthe*) becomes ME *smethe*, whence the dial E *smeeth*, a mist or a haze. But both OE *smōth* and OE *smēthe* are o.o.o.

**smother**, n and v; **smore**, n, v. 'To smother' comes from ME *smortheren*, from ME *smorther*, whence also the E n *smother*, thick, hence suffocating, smoke: and ME *smorther* comes from OE *smorian*, to suffocate or smother, whence the now dial v, hence n, *smore*: cf MD *smooren*, MD-D and MLG *smoren*, to smother or stifle (G *schmoren*, to fry, to stew).

**smoulder.** See SMELL, para 2.

**smudge**, n and v, derives from ME *smogen*, to smear—and **smutch** is a var; **smut** (whence **smutty**), from LG *smutt*, is perh akin. Cf ME *smoten*, *smotten*, to besmirch, syn MHG *smutzen*, and MHG *smutz* (G *Schmutz*), grease, dirt; cf also in cpds, ME *-smoteren* and MD *-smodderen* (and *-smodden*). Like the interrelationships, the origins of *smudge* and *smut* are obscure; several senses of *smudge* lead one to suspect a connexion with *smoke*

(EW)—perh cf Ga *smùid*, smoke, and EIr *smút*, a cloud.

**smug.** See SMOCK, para 2.

**smuggle.** See SMOCK, para 3.

**smut.** See SMUDGE.

**smutch.** See SMUDGE.

**smutty.** See SMUDGE.

**snack.** See SNATCH, para 2.

**snaffle** (n, hence v) app derives from MD-D *snavel*, beak, snout, nose, akin to OFris *snavel*, the mouth; and MD-D *snavel* is cognate with the syn MD *snabbe*, *snab*, D *snab*; MD *snab(be)*, more-over, represents the IE prefix *s-*+the Gmc r attested by E *neb*, beak, nose (cf NIB).

**snag**, a broken-off or jagged projection (hence as v), whence **snaggled**, eased to **snaggle**, jagged, roughly uneven: ult from ON *snagi*, a sharp point; cf Nor dial *snage*, a projecting point.

**snail**: ME *snaile*: OE *snaegl*, *snaegel*, *snegel*: cf ON *snigill*, MHG *snegel*, snail, and OHG *snecco*, MHG *snecke*, G *Schnecke*, snail, slug; cf also OHG *snachan*, *snahhan*, to creep.

2. A snail being essentially a 'creeper', *snail* is akin to *snake* (n, hence v), from OE *snaca*, akin to ON *snākr*, a snake, and MLG *snake*, G *Schnake*, a water-snake; phon, cf Lith *sñake*, snail, slug.

3. Both *snail* and *snake* therefore suggest 'to sneak' (whence 'a sneak'): ME *sniken* (pron *sneeken*): OE *snīcan*, to creep, with ON and modern Scan cognates.

4. The IE r would appear to be *snā-, varr *snē-*, *snĕ-*, to creep or crawl.

**snake**, n (hence v), whence **snaky**. See prec, para 2.—Hence, from its 'snaky' neck, the *snakebird*, and, from being reputedly a cure for snake-bites, *snakewood*. (Webster.)

**snap** (v, hence n), whence **snapper** (one fish has var *schnapper*): either MD or MLG *snappen*, which, like MHG *snappen* (G *schnappen*), are akin to and perh deriving from ON *snappa*, *snapa*, var *snōpa*, to snatch, to snap: prob echoic.—From the n: **snappy**.

**snare.** See NARROW, para 2.

**snarl** (1), a snare, hence a tangle, whence the v, derives from *snare* but is influenced, phon, by:

**snarl** (2), to growl gnashingly, hence to speak thus, hence the n: app a dim of C16 *snar*: MD-D *snarren* (cf MHG *snarren*, G *schnarren*, to roar, to rattle): echoic.

2. With EE *snar*, cf ME *sneren*, whence 'to sneer' (whence the n): cf Da *snaerre*, to 'grin' like a snarling dog.

3. With both *snar* and *sneer*, cf 'to snore', ME *snoren*, akin to LG *snoren*, *snorken*, *snurken*, MD-D *snorken*, MHG *snarchen*, G *schnarchen*, Sw *snarka*, to snore.

4. ME *snoren*, to snore, has freq *snorten*, whence 'to snort'.

5. With *snarl*, *sneer*, *snore* (and *snort*), cf MHG *snurren*, G *schnurren*, to buzz or drone; all these words are expressive variations of a central phon and sem theme.

**snatch**, v hence n; **snack**, n hence v; **sneck**, n hence v.

1. 'To *snatch*' derives from ME *snacchen* (var *snecchen*): cf MD *snacken*, var *snaken*, to long for (? orig to snatch at), to snap.

2. ME *snacchen* has the dial derivative *snack*, to snap, whence E *snack*, a (dog's) snap or bite (now dial), hence a share or portion, as in *go snacks*, to go shares; hence also a quick bite of food, hence a quick, light meal.

3. ME *snecchen* has derivative *snekke*, the latch of a door, prob from the 'snap' or click it makes; hence *sneck*, now only E dial and Sc.

**sneak.** See SNAIL, para 3.

**sneck.** See SNATCH, para 3.

**sneer.** See SNARL, para 2.

**sneeze**, v hence n: ME *snesen*, an easing of ME *fnesen*: OE *fnēosan*: cf MD *fniesen*, D *fniezen*, to sneeze, and ON *fnŷsa*, to snort; influenced, in its passage from Gr *pnein*, to breathe, by the OGmc forms of the now E dial and Sc *neeze* (*neese*), ME *nesen*, perh from ON *hniōsa*, OHG *niosan*, MHG-G *niesen*, MD *niesen*, D *niezen*, and, more remotely, Lith *skiaudēti*, to sneeze, and Skt *kṣauti*, he sneezes: both words, ult echoic.

**snib** (1), to bolt or fasten a door, hence n, both now Sc: cf MLG *snibbe*, a beak.

**snib** (2), to snub. See SNUB.

**snick** (v, hence n), to cut slightly, to nick, is app a b/f from **snick and snee**, to thrust cuttingly: (by assimilation of *st* to *sn*, from) D *steken*, to stab (cf STICK)+E *and*+D *snijen*, an easing of D *snijden* (MD *sniden*: cf OHG *snīdan*, G *schneiden*).

**snicker** and its var **snigger**—vv, hence nn—are echoic. The former, in its sense 'to whinny', recalls the syn 'to *nicker*', akin to the no less echoic *neigh*.

**sniff; sniffle; sl snifter.** See SNUFF, paras 1 (s.f.) and 2.

**snigger.** See SNICKER.

**snip** (v, hence n), whence **snipper** and **snippet** (dim *-et*): (? MD-)D *snippen*, cf G *schnippen*: perh echoic.

**snipe** (n, hence v, whence **sniper, sniping**): ME *snype*: ON *-snīpe* (cf Nor *snipe* and Da *sneppe*).

**snippet.** See SNIP.

**snivel.** See SNUFF, para 3.

**snob**, cobbler, hence (sl) a townee, a plebeian, hence a toady and a superior person: o.o.o.: EW, who cfs *snip*, a tailor, suggests kinship with SNUB (to cut short).—Hence **snobbery**.

**snood.** See NERVE, para 7.

**snooker**, whence the pa **snookered**, is short for **snooker pool** (cf POOL) and is o.o.o.: perh a 'bit-by-bit' game, from *snook*, a dial var of *snack*, a portion.

**snoop**, whence **snooper**, derives from D *snoepen*: o.o.o.

**snooty.** See SNOUT, para 2.

**snooze**, n and v, is o.o.o.: ? a mutilated blend of *snore*+*doze*.

**snore.** See SNARL, para 3.

**snort.** See SNARL, para 4.

**snot**—whence **snotty**, adj hence n—derives, by aphesis, from OE *gesnot* (cf OFris *snotta*): cf LG and MD *snotte*, MD-D *snot*, nasal mucus, and, f.a.e., see:

**snout**, an elephant's trunk (obsol), a quadruped's long nose: ME *snoute*, earlier *snute*: cf LG *snūte*, MD *snute*, D *snuit*, G *Schnauze*, Sw *snut*; cf also OHG *snūzēn*, MHG *sniuzen*, G *schneuzen*, ON *snȳta*, to blow one's nose.

2. MD *snute*, D *snuit* accounts for E *snoot*, snout, hence face, whence *snooty*, nose-in-the-air, supercilious.

**snow, snowy.** See NEVADA, para 1.

**snub**, v, hence n: syn **snib**, v, hence n. 'To *snub*' comes, via ME *snubben*, from ON *snubba*, to chide or reprove; ME *snubben* has the thinned var *snibben*, whence 'to *snib*', now E dial and Sc; and ON *snubba* is perh akin to ON *snȳta*—cf, sem, SNOUT, para 2.

**snuff**, to put out (a candle), whence **snuffer**, derives from a candle's *snuff* or charred end, which itself derives from *snuff*, an inhalation, a (strong) sniff, whence the pulverized tobacco sniffed up the nostrils: from 'to *snuff*', to inhale strongly: MD *snuffen*, akin to MHG *snūfen*, G *schnaufen*, to draw breath, late MHG *snupfe*, G *Schnupfen*, a cold in the head. 'To *snuff*' has thinned var 'to *sniff*', whence the sl *snifter*.

2. 'To *snuff*' has, moreover, the freq *snuffle*; cf D *snuffelen*, MD *snoffelen*, LG *snüffeln*, G *schnüffeln*. 'To *snuffle* has the thinned var 'to *sniffle*'.

3. Akin to *snuffle* is ME *snivelen*, whence 'to *snivel*'; the ME var' *snuvelen* recalls the MD *snuyfelen*; also akin is OE *snȳflan*.

4. Perh 'behind all these words denoting nasal activity there is a Gmc base *\*frue-* of echoic or gestural origin (Walshe): cf the Gr *pneuma*, breath: and note the reinforcement with the IE int prefix *s-*.

**snuffle.** See prec, para 2.

**snug**, adj, hence n and v, with freq **snuggle**; **snuggery** (*snug*, adj+euphonic *-g-*+*-ery*, connoting 'a place'). The adj *snug*, orig naut, with sense 'trim, well-ordered', perh comes from EDa *snyg*, tidy, cf the syn Da *snög* and Sw *snygg*, prob via D *snugger*, clever, smart, and EFris *snugge*.

**so**, adv, whence the adj, conj (for *so that*), pron, interjection: ME *so*, earlier *sa*, earliest *swa*: OE *swā*, thus: cf OFris *sā* or *sō*, OS *sō*, OHG-MHG *sō*, G *so*, MD *so*, *soo*, *zo*, *zoo* (retained by D), Ga *swa*, so, Go *swē*, as; ON *svā* (pron *sua*, *swa*), with modern Scan cognates; the reflexive L *se* (himself, themselves) corresp to L *suus*, his own, their own; Gr *hōs* (ὥς, ὥς), so, thus, and the var ὥς (*hōs*), as, the former corresp to IE *\*sō* (instr)+suffix *-s*, the latter to PGr *wōs*, IE *\*suō* (Hofmann).

2. OE *swā* combines with *al*, *ael*, *eal*, all, to form OE *alswā*, *aelswā*, *ealswā*, whence ME *al so*, E *also*.

3. Cf SUCH and WHICH.

**soak.** See SUCK, para 1.

**soap**, n (whence **soapy**), hence v; with many cpds, all sufficiently obvious;—**sapo, saponcaceous, saponify** (and **saponification**), **saponin(e), saponite;**

—**sebum, sebaceous** (whence, anl, **sebacic**); **suet,** whence **suety.**

1. *Soap*, ME *sope*, OE *sāpe*, perh akin to OE *sāp*, resin: cf—with *f* for *p*—OHG *seiffa*, MHG-G *seife*, and, retaining *p*, the MD *sepe*, *seep*, *seipe*, *zepe*, D *zeep*, soap; L *sāpō*, o/s *sāpōn-*, soap, and the prob related—with *b* for *p*—L *sēbum*, tallow; prob cf OE *sipian*, MHG *sīfen*, to trickle or seep, 'perh because urine was once used in soap' (Walshe). For L *sāpō*, E & M postulate an origin either Gmc or C—Walshe, a Gmc (*\*saipjō*)—Malvezin, the C etymon *\*sapon*: cf the foll C words, all pointing to a kinship rather with L *sēbum* than with L *sāpō*, *sāpōn-*: Ga *siabunn*, Cor *seban*, W *sebon*, Mx *sheabin*. It is tempting to enlist Hit *sapiya-* (r *sap-*), to cleanse.

2. L *sāpō* is retained by Pharmacy; its SciL adj *sāpōnaceus* yields E *saponaceous*; its LL adj *sāpōnārius* occurs in the Bot *Saponaria*, whence *saponary*, the soapwort. On the o/s *sāpōn-*, F has built *saponifier*, *saponification*, Chem *saponine*, all adopted by E; and Sw has built *saponit*, whence E *saponite*.

3. L *sēbum*, tallow, grease, is retained by An; its LL adj *sēbāceus* yields *sebaceous*. *Sēbum* becomes OF *seu*, *siu*, and, by metathesis, *sui* (whence MF-F *suif*), whence the AF *sue*, with ME dim (*-et*) *suet*.

**soar**, v, hence n, also the pa, vn **soaring**; **aura**, a zephyr (obs), a subtle, usu invisible, exhalation or emanation, whence **aural.**

1. 'To *soar*' derives from ME *soren*, itself by aphesis from OF-MF *essorer*, to expose to the air in order to dry, whence the MF-(archaic)F falconry term *s'essorer*, to raise itself into the air, the imm source of the ME word: VL *\*exaurāre*, to expose to the air: L *ex-*, used int+L *aura*, a light breeze+*-āre*, inf suffix.

2. L *aura*, adopted by E, was itself adopted from Gr (αὔρα): akin to Gr *āēr*, air.

**sob.** See SUP, para 2.

**sober, sobriety.** See EBRIETY, para 4.

**sobriquet**, adopted from EF-F, derives from the late MF syn *soubriquet*, from the MF *soubriquet*, a chuck under the chin: both chuck and nickname are endearments: but MF *soubriquet* is o.o.o.: the C16 F *soubarbade*, a chuck under the *barbe*, beard, hence under the chin, suggests MF *soub-* for *soubs*, *soubz*, under, from VL *subtus*, under (prep), from L *subtus*, under (adv), an extn of *sub*, under+some lost OF-MF derivative, in *ri-* (cf *ricaner*, a blend of *rire*+ONF re*caner*), of Frankish *\*kinni*, the jaw (cf OPicard *kenne*, the cheek)+n-dim *-et*.

2. The occ E var *soubriquet* prob represents MF-F *sobriquet* influenced by *soubrette*.

**soc, socage; soke.** *Socage* is an AF derivative of *soc*, likewise a term of Old and Medieval E Law: and ME-E *soc*, like the syn and commoner ME-E *soke*, derives from ML, esp AL, *soca*, itself from OE *sōcn*, whence, via ME *socne*, later *socen*, the now only hist E *soken*: cf ON *sōkn*, an attack, a complaint, and Go *sōkns*, an investigation, a debate or a controversy; cf also OE *sacan*, to quarrel; therefore cf SAKE.

**soccer.** See SOCIAL, para 5.

**sociability, sociable.** See para 2 of:

**social** (adj, hence n—elliptical for *s. gathering*), whence **socialism, socialist, socialize** (cf the F *socialisme, -iste, -iser*), **socialite, sociality** (perh rather from L *sociālitās*, o/s *sociālitāt-*); **sociation,** whence, anl, **sociative; society,** whence **societal;** cf the element *socio-*, as in **sociology** (*socio-+-logy*), whence **sociological** and **sociologist; socius.**— Prefix-cpds: **associate,** adj (hence n), and v, **association** (whence, anl, **associative** and **soccer**); **consociate,** adj (hence n) and v, **consociation** (whence, anl, **consociative**); **dissociable, dissocial, dissociate** (adj and v), **dissociation; insociable** (whence, anl, **insociality**) and **insocial.**

1. At the base stands L *socius*, a companion, an associate: prob akin to Ve *sákkā*, a companion; perh, at a prehistoric IE stage, akin to L *sequī* (cf SEQUENCE).

2. Retained by learnèd E, L *socius* has adj *sociālis*, whence both F and E *social*, and v *sociāre*, to ally oneself with another, with derivative *sociābilis*, whence EF-F and, perh independently, E *sociable*, whence, anl, *sociability*.

3. L *sociāre* has pp *sociātus*, whence the now rare adj (hence n) and v *sociate*; derivative LL *sociātiō*, o/s *sociātiōn-*, yields the (obsol) *sociation*; both words truly alive only in the cpds.

4. L *socius* has the derivative abstract n *societās*, companionship, association, alliance, society (organized group): whence OF-F *société*, E *society*; *society*, elliptical for *high society*, is modern.

Compounds

5. L *adsociāre*, usu assimilated as *associāre*, to take as a companion or as an ally, *ad*, to, oneself, becomes MF-F *associer*, with derivative *associable*, adopted by E. The pp *associātus* yields both adj and v *associate*. Derivative L *associātiō*, o/s *associātiōn-*, becomes MF *association*, adopted by E. From *Association* Football comes, anl with *rugger* from *Rugby* Football, *soccer*; the phon process involved is 'the Oxford-*er*' (see P).

6. L *consociāre* (*con-*, with, hence together), to associate (vt), has pp *consociātus*, whence the adj and v *consociate*; derivative *consociātiō*, o/s *consociātiōn-*, yields *consociation*.

7. D *dissociāre*, to disjoin oneself from, has derivatives *dissociābilis*, whence *dissociable*, and, anl, LL *dissociālis*, which phon suggests the different-sensed E *dissocial*. The pp *dissociātus* yields the adj and v *dissociate*; derivative *dissociātiō*, o/s *dissociātiōn-*, becomes EF-F and E *dissociation*.

8. Suggested by L *sociābilis* and *sociālis*, the L *insociābilis* and LL *insociālis* yield EF-F and E *insociable* and E *insocial*.

**society.** See prec, para 4.

**sociologist, sociology.** See SOCIAL (heading).

**sock** (1), orig a low shoe, hence a short stocking:

ME *sock*: OE *socc*: L *soccus*, a low-heeled shoe: Gr *sukkhos*: perh from Skt—cf (with *h* for *s*) the Av *haxa*, sole of foot.

**sock** (2), a ploughshare. See the 1st SOW, para 6.

**sock** (3), to throw or hit violently: sl: o.o.o.: prob echoic.

**socket.** See the 1st SOW, para 6.

**Socratic,** L *Sōcraticus*, Gr *Sōkratikos*, is the adj of *Socrates*, Gr *Sōkratēs*: ? for *Zōkratēs*, ruler of *Zōē*, life: Lord of Life.

**sod** (1), adj. See SODDEN.

**sod** (2), turf, a turf, app derives from MD-MLG *sode* (var *zode*, retained by D): OFris *sāda, sātha*: o.o.o.: for one theory, see SEETHE, para 2.

**sod** (3): sl: see SODOM.

**soda,** whence **sodium** (Chem suffix *-ium*), whence **sodic:** ML (and It) *soda*, abbr of ML *sodanum*, lit 'a headache cure', from ML *soda*, headache: Ar *ṣudāʿ*, a splitting headache, from *ṣādaʿ*, to split. (Webster. B & W, however, derive ML-It *soda* from Ar *suwwād*, a plant whose ashes yield an excellent sodium carbonate.)

**sodality:** L *sodālitāt-*, o/s of *sodālitās*, companionship, fellowship: from *sodālis*, member of a brotherhood, college etc.: ? akin to L *socer* (see SOCIAL).

**sodden** was orig a var of *sod*, pp of SEETHE.

**sodium.** See SODA.

**Sodom,** from LL *Sodoma*, comes, via LGr, from H; the Gr word has n *Sodomītēs* (*-itēs*, a descendant), whence LL *Sodomīta*, whence OF-F *sodomite*, adopted by E (whence the sl *sod*, n, hence v); the adj *Sodomite*, of Sodom, comes from LL *Sodomītus*, suggested by the Gr; *sodomy* anglicizes MF-F *sodomie*, itself from OF-F *sodome* (from LL *Sodoma*). Cf *Genesis*, chh. 18 and 19.

**sofa,** orig a divan: adopted from EF-F: prob via Tu *sofa*: from Ar *suffa* (*ṣuffah*), a cushion, hence a raised platform covered with cushions. Cf, sem, *divan*.

**soft** (adj, hence n, whence coll **softie, softy**), whence **soften** (whence **softener, softening**); **softness.**—*Softness* comes from OE *sōftness*, later *sōftnyss*, ease or rest, akin to OE *sēfte*, whence the adv *sōfte*, later also adj—cf ME *softe* (adj and adv), whence E *soft*, adj and adv: cf OFris *sēft* (adj), attested by *sēftichēd*, gentleness, softness, OS *sāfto*, adv, OHG *senfti*, adj, *sanfto*, adv, MHG *senfte*, adj, *sanfte*, adv, G *sanft*, gentle, soft, and (phon, the most revelatory) MD *saeft*, *saft—sochte—saechte, sachte, zachte*, and D *zacht* (cf LG *sacht*). If the nasal (*n*) is basic, cf the Go *samjan*, to please. (Walshe.)

**sog** (mostly dial), to soak, whence n, a bog, whence the adj **soggy:** o.o.o.: perh akin to *soak*, q.v. at SUCK.

**soil** (1), earth. See the 2nd SOLE, para 2.

**soil** (2), a mire, to stain or pollute. See the 1st SOW (pig), para 4.

**soirée.** See SERENE, para 1.

**sojourn.** See DIANA, para 11.

**soke, soken.** See SOC.

**Sol.** See SOLAR.

sola; sola topi. See TOPI.

solace—n and v (whence *solacement*)—and solatium; consolable, consolation, consolatory, console (v)—and inconsolable.

1. *Inconsolable* derives, perh via EF-F *inconsolable*, from L *inconsōlābilis*, the neg of *consōlābilis*, whence, perh via late MF-F, the E *consolable*.

2. L *consōlābilis* derives from *consōlāri*, whence MF-F *consoler*, whence 'to *console*'; on the pp *consōlāt*us are formed both *consōlātiō*, acc *consōlātiōnem*, whence OF-F *consolation*, adopted by E, and *consōlātōrius*, whence E *consolatory*.

3. *Consōlāri*=*con*-, used int+*sōlāri*, to comfort, with pp *sōlāt*us, whence both the n *sōlātium*, LL *sōlācium*, whence OF-EF *solas* (*soḷaz*), adopted by ME, whence late ME-E *solace*, and the LL v *sōlāciāri*, *sōlāciāre*, whence—unless imm from OF *solas*—OF-EF *solacier*, whence 'to *solace*'.

4. L *sōlāri* is perh—with *h* for *s*—akin to Gr *hilaros*, cheerful; if so, then cf SILLY.

solan, a gannet, whence solan goose: ON and Ice *sūla*, gannet+(prob+)ON *önd*, a duck.

solanin, or -*ine*; solanum. See para 2 of:

solar, adj (whence solar plexus, with ganglia radiating like rays from the sun) and n—solarium —solarize (*solar*, adj+-*ize*), whence solarization—solanum, whence solanin(e)—Sol; solstice, solstitial. —Helios, heliacal, helium; cf the element *heli*(*o*)-, where see HELIANTHUS, HELIOTROPE, etc.—L prefix-cpd: insolate, insolation; cf parasol.—Gr prefix-cpds: aphelion and parhelion.—Cf the sep SUN.

### Indo-European

1. L *sōl*, the sun, whence personified *Sōl*, is akin to OE and ON *sōl*, Go *sauil*, Lith *sáule*, Skt *sū́ryas* (*r* for *l*); also to the *h*- for *s* group represented by Gr *hēlios* and, in C, the W *haul*, Cor *haul*, *hoal*, *heuul*, Br *héaul*, *hiaul*—contrast the perh related OIr *sūl*, eye. The IE r is perh *sāuel*-; for the -*n* varr, see SUN.

2. L *sōl* has three adjj: *sōlānus*, with neu *sōlānum* used for the plant nightshade; *sōlāris*, whence E *solar*; and *sōlārius*, with neu *sōlārium* meaning a sundial and a sun-gallery, -porch, -terrace, which, adopted by E, has—via OE *solor*, *soler* (cf the OF-EF syn *solier*)—the anglicized form *solar*.

3. L *sōl* has the full cpd *sōlstitium*: *sōl*, sun+ -*stitium*, a standing still, from *sistere*, to cause to stand (still), to stand still (cf SIST): MF-F *solstice*, adopted by E. The derivative ML *sōlstitiālis* yields (F and) E *solstitial*.

4. Akin to L *sōl* is the syn Gr *hēlios*, s *hēli*-, r *hēl*-; the personified *Hēlios* is the Sun God. The derivative adj *hēliakos* becomes LL *hēliacus*, whence E *heliac*, usu in extn *heliacal*; and from Gr *hēlios*, SciL has coined *helium* (Chem suffix -*ium*).

5. From L *sōl* comes, as if via *solāre*, to sun, the pp *sōlātus*, whence the LL *insōlāre*, to expose to (*in*-) the sun, with pp *insōlātus*, whence 'to *insolate*'; derivative *insōlātiō*, o/s *insōlātiōn*-, yields EF-F and, perh independently, E *insolation*.

Contrast *parasol*: EF-F *parasol*: It *parasole*, something that wards off (*para*, from *parare*) the sun (*sole*).

6. Gr *hēlios* radiates in three E prefix-cpds: *parēlios*, adj, beside (*para*) the sun, is used as n, a mock sun, as also is the neu *parēlion*, whence E *parhelion*; whence, anl, *aphelion* (Gr *apo*, from, away from).

solarium. See prec, para 2.

solarization, solarize. See SOLAR (heading).

sold. See SELL (heading).

soldan. See SULTAN.

solder. See SOLID, para 4.

soldier, soldiery. See SOLID, para 5.

sole (1), adj ('alone')—solo—solus; solitaire, solitary—and solitude;—sullen.—Full cpds: soliloquize, soliloquy; solipsism, whence, anl, solipsist (whence solipsistic).—Prefix-cpds: desolate (adj and v), desolation, desolator.—Perh insula, insular, insulate (whence, anl, insulation and insulator)—cf insulin; isle, islet (and islot); isolate (adj and v), isolation (whence, anl, isolative).

1. *Sole* derives—cf the OF *sol*—from L *sōlus*, alone, solitary: o.o.o.: ? for *sēlos*: *sē*-, privative prefix+suffix -*lo*+nom -*s*, as E & M propose. Perh, however, L *sōlus* is ult akin to Gr *holos*, whole, entire: *s* for *h*, vowel-quantity changed, the one basic idea regarded from a different angle. L *sōlus*, which occurs in E stage-directions (cf *soliloquy*), becomes It *solo*, adj hence n, adopted by E.

2. *Sōlus* has the foll derivatives affecting E: *sōlitās*, a being alone, whence *sōlitārius*, whence E *solitary* and OF-F *solitaire*, the latter, used as n (in jewellery and card-games), being adopted by E;

*sōlitūdō*, whence MF-F *solitude*, adopted by E;

VL *sōlānus*, lonely (cf the LL *sōlitāneus*, private), whence—? via AF from OF *sol*—ME *solain*, *solein*, EE *solen*, later *sollen*, whence *sullen* —but occ *sullen* is derived from the ME forms of SOLEMN.

3. Perhaps the principal E full cpds from L *sōlus* are:

*soliloquy*, from L *sōliloquium*: an 'alone' speaking, with -*loquium* deriving from *loquī*, to speak; hence *soliloquize*;

*solipsism* (in Phil): *sōlus*+*ipse*, (one)self+-*ism*.

4. L *sōlus* has the prefix-cpd *dēsōlāre*, to leave (someone) by himself or alone, hence to depopulate: *de*- used int+*solus*+-*āre*. The pp *dēsōlātus* yields, in E, both the adj and the v *desolate*; the derivative LL *dēsōlātiō*, solitude, a desert, has acc *dēsōlātiōnem*, whence OF-MF *desolation* (EF-F *dé*-), adopted by E, and LL *dēsōlātor*, he who abandons, becomes—perh via EF-F *désolateur*—the E *desolator*.

### L *insula*

5. Perh akin to L *sōlus* is L *īnsula*, an island, explained by f/e as the f (used as n) of adj *insulus*, formed from OL *en salos*, (that is) in the open sea,

and by several modern philologists as formed elliptically from 'terra *in salo*', land in the sea; L *in*, E in(to)+the abl of *salum*, the sea. Perh L *īnsula* stands for L *\*īnsōla*, f of adj *īnsōlus*, an int of *sōlus*, by itself, alone: 'terra *īnsōla*', land by itself (in sea or lake), becomes *īnsula*, to avoid confusion with L *sōl*, sun.

6. From L *īnsula*, retained by learnèd E, Sci derives *insulin*: *insula*+Chem *-in*. More importantly, L derives:

LL *īnsulāris*, of or on an island, whence EF-F *insulaire* and E *insular*, whence *insularity*;

L *īnsulātus* (as if the pp of *\*īnsulāre*), turned into an island, hence shut off, or secluded, as in an island, whence the adj and v *insulate*.

7. L *īnsula* becomes VL *\*isula*, *\*iscla*, whence OF-MF *isle*, adopted by E, as are the MF-EF dim *islet* and the EF-F dim *islot*.

8. L *īnsula*—? rather OL-become-L-LL *īnsōla*—leads to It *isola*, whence the v *isolare*, pp *isolato*, separated as an island is (cf L *īnsulātus*), whence EF-F *isolé*, whence, anl, the E pa *isolated*, whence, by b/f, 'to *isolate*'; the adj *isolate* derives rather from It *isolato*. EF-F *isolé* produces the v *isoler*, whence, anl, *isolation*, adopted by E.

**sole** (2), of foot, and the fish; whence 'to **sole**'; **soil** (earth).

1. L *solum*, the flat, lower part of anything, e.g. the bed of the sea, a floor, hence the base or foundation, and also the ground, or soil that forms it. In its sense 'sole of foot', *solum* gives way to its derivative *solea*, which, prob via VL *\*sola*, yields OE-MF-E *sole*. L *solea* has the secondary sense 'flat fish', whence, via VL *\*sola*, comes the OProv *sola*, whence MF-F *sole*, adopted by E.

2. L *solum*, ground, floor, etc., becomes OF-MF *suel*, MF *soil* (cf late MF-F *seuil*), adopted by ME and retained by E.

**solecism, solecist** (whence **solecistic**), **solecize.** At *Soloi*, in Cilicia (SE Asia Minor), the Athenian colonists ended, in their isolation from the homeland, by speaking Attic Greek corruptly and carelessly: whence Gr *soloikos* (*-ikos*, adj suffix), incorrect of speech, whence *soloikizein*, to speak—hence also to write—incorrectly, whence E 'to *solecize*'; *soloikizein* generates also *soloikismos* and *soloikistēs*, whence, resp, L *soloecismus*, MF *soloecisme*, late MF-F *solécisme*, E *solecism*, and LL *soloecista*, E *solecist*.

**solemn, solemnity, solemnization** and **solemnize.** *Solemnization* comes from MF *solemnisation*, itself from MF *solemniser* (EF-F *solenniser*), whence 'to *solemnize*'; and the MF v comes from the LL *sollemnizāre*, to celebrate (e.g., a mass). *Solemnity* represents OF-MF *solemnité*, from L *solemnitātem*, acc of *solemnitās*, the abstract-n derivative of *solemnis*, var of *sollennis*, performed ritualistically or in dignified detail: app *sollus*, entire, complete, whole+an adj extn. L *sol(l)emnis* became OF-MF *solempne, solemne*, both adopted by ME, whence E *solemn*.

**solenoid.** See the element *soleno-*.

**solferino.** See SULPHATE, para 2.

**solicit, solicitant, solicitation, solicitor, solicitous, solicitude.**

'To *solicit*' derives from MF-F *solliciter*, from L *sollicitāre*, lit to shake violently, from *sollicitus*, violently, lit entirely, moved, hence troubled: *solli-*, c/f of *sollus*, entire (cf *saluus*, SAFE)+*citus*, pp of *ciēre*, to set in movement (cf CITE). The presp *sollicitans*, o/s *sollicitant-*, prompts *solicitant*, adj hence n; on the pp *sollicitātus* is formed *sollicitātiō*, acc *sollicitātiōnem*, whence MF-F *sollicitation*, whence E *solicitation*. L *sollicitus*, whence E *solicitous*, has derivative *sollicitūdō*, whence MF-F *sollicitude*, whence E *solicitude*. MF-F *solliciter* has agent MF-F *solliciteur*, whence E *solicitor*.

**solid** (adj and n), **solidarity, solidary, solidate, solidify, solidity, solidum, solidus** (cf F *sol, sou*, and It *soldo*); **solder**, n, hence v; **soldier** (n, hence v), whence **soldierly** and **soldiery; console**, n; **consolidant, consolidate** (adj and v), **consolidation, consolidative, consolidator**—cf **consols.**

1. The adj *solid* comes from MF-F *solide*: L *solidus*, full, massive, hence firm or resistant; also complete, entire: an altered extn of L *sollus*, entire, itself related to L *saluus* (ML *salvus*), entire, intact (cf SAFE). The n *solid* prob derives from the L *solidum*, in Geom a solid figure, from the neu of *solidus*. *Solidus*, elliptical for *solidus nummus*, has the LL contr *soldus*, whence It *soldo* and OF *solt*,' MF *sol*, later MF-F *sou*.

2. L *solidus* has derivatives *soliditās*, whence MF-F *solidité*, whence E *solidity*, and *solidāre*, to render solid, LL to establish firmly, with pp *solidātus*, whence 'to *solidate*'.

3. F *solide* has the foll derivatives affecting E: EF-F *solidaire*, whence E *solidary*; derivative *solidarité*, whence E *solidarity*; F *solidifier* (cf the obs It *solidificare*) and the anl *solidification* perh suggested 'to *solidify*' and *solidification*.

4. L *solidāre*, to make solid, becomes OF-MF *solder* (F *souder*), to join by melting, whence, via the derivative MF n *soldure* (F *soudure*), the EE *soldure*, whence E *solder*.

5. L *soldus*, contr of the coin *solidus*, becomes OF *sold* (var *soud*), payment, esp a soldier's pay, whence OF-MF *soldier*, adopted by EE, the earlier forms deriving from OF-MF varr of the OF word.

6. LL *solidāre*, to establish firmly (cf para 2), has the int cpd *consolidāre*, with presp *consolidans*, o/s *consolidant-*, whence E *consolidant*, and pp *consolidātus*, whence the adj and v *consolidate*; derivative *consolidātiō*, acc *consolidātiōnem*, becomes MF-F *consolidation*, adopted by E—as is the LL agent *consolidātor*; F *consolidation* has suggested F *consolidatif*, f *-ive*, which perh suggests E *consolidative*. By b/f from 'consolidated annuities' we get *consols*.

7. L *consolidāre* and *solidus*, adj, app produced an adj *\*consolidus*, whence the LL n *consolida*, the plant comfrey, named (in L) from its astringent and curative properties, whence EF-F *consoude*, whence, by f/e after *sound*, healthy, the E *consound*.

—*Comfrey* itself, ME *cumfirie*, earlier *confirie*, is adopted from OF-MF *confirie*: perh from OF-MF *firie*, a mdfn of *fege* (F *foie*), the liver, app ult from L *fīcus*, a fig.

**solidarity, solidary.** See prec, para 3.

**solidification, solidify.** See SOLID, para 3.

**solidity.** See SOLID, para 2.

**solidum, solidus.** See SOLID, para 1.

**soliloquize, soliloquy.** See the 1st SOLE, para 3.

**solipsism.** See 1st SOLE, para 3.

**solitaire** (diamond; patience as card-game). See 1st SOLE, para 2.

**solitary, solitude.** See 1st SOLE, para 2.

**solo,** whence **soloist.** See 1st SOLE, para 1, s.f.

**Solomon,** whence **Solomonic,** is adopted from LL *Solomōn* (var *Salomōn*): LGr *Solomōn*, var *Salōmōn*: H *Shelōmōh*, peaceable, from *shālōm*, peace.

**solstice, solstitial.** See SOLAR, para 3.

**soluble.** See LOSE, para 3.

**solus.** See the 1st SOLE, para 1, s.f.

**solute, solution.** See LOSE, para 4.

**solve** (whence **solvable**), **solvent.** See LOSE, para 4.

**soma** (1), a beverage (Oriental) from the leafless EI vine *soma*, comes from Skt—cf (*h* for *s*) the Av *haoma*.

**soma** (2), as used in An and Zoo, derives from Gr *sōma*, the (usu human) body: o.o.o., Hofmann's alignment with IE *tum-*, to swell (L *tumēre*) being unconvincing. The Gr adj *sōmatikos* yields E *somatic*; E *somite*=Gr *sōma*+n-suffix *-ite*, and its adj is *somitic*. For cpds, cf the element *-soma*.

**somber** (AE) or **sombre; sombrero.** See UMBRA, para 10.

**some.** See SAME, para 1, s.f.—Hence **somebody, someone,** etc.

**somersault.** See SALLY, para 8.

**somite.** See the 2nd SOMA.

**somnambulism,** etc.; **somniferous.** See para 4 of:

**somnolence, somnolent; somnambulate, somnambulism** (whence, anl, **somnambulist,** whence **somnambulistic**); **somnifacient, somniferous, somniloquy** (whence, anl, **somniloquous**); **somnolescent,** whence **somnolescence;**—**insomnia** (whence the adj and n **insomniac**), **insomnious.**—**sopite** (adj and v), **soporiferous, soporific** (ad , hence n), **soporose.**—**Hypnos, hypnosis, hypnotic** (whence, anl, **hypnotism, hypnotist, hypnotize**).

1. L *somnus*, sleep, personified as *Somnus*, God of Sleep, is akin to the syn Gr *hupnos*, personified as *Hupnos*, E *Hypnos*, itself akin to Skt *svapna*, sleep, a dream, *svápati*, he sleeps; cf L *sōpīre*, to send to sleep, *sōpor*, so mething that induces sleep, hence (a heavy) sleep; cf also ON *sofa*, to sleep, and ON *svefn*, OE *swefn*, sleep, a dream, Sl *sŭpati*, to sleep, Lith *sapnas*, a dream, and C cognates. IE r, *\*sup-* (with varr), to sleep.

2. L *somnus* has the foll derivative relevant to E:

LL *somnolentus*, sleepy, whence late MF-F *somnolent*, adopted by E; derivative LL *somno-*

*lentia* yields EF-F and E *somnolence. Somnolescent, somnolescence* are anl formations.

3. The neg L *insomnis* (*in-*, not), sleepless, has derivative *insomnium*, with var *insomnia*, adopted by E; its adj *insomniōsus* yields *insomnious.*

4. The L cpd *somnifer*, sleep-bringing (*ferre*, to bring), not only becomes EF-F *somnifère* and, perh independently, E *somniferous*, but prob suggested such other E cpds as *somnambulate*, to walk in one's sleep (cf *ambulate* at AMBULANCE) and *somnambule*, a sleep-walker, adopted from F, with derivative F *somnambulisme* leading to E *somnambulism; somnifacient*, sleep-causing (adj, hence n), which=*somni-*, c/f of *somnus*+*-facient*, from L *facient-*, o/s of *faciens*, presp of *facere*, to make; *somniloquy* (*somni-*+*-loquy*, as in *soliloquy*).

5. The cognate L *sōpīre*, to send to sleep, has pp *sōpītus*, whence the now rare E adj and v *sopite*, (to render) drowsy. The derivative *sōpor*, adopted by learnèd E, has adj *sōporōsus*, whence E *soporose*; the cpd *sōpōrifer*, (heavy) sleep-inducing, yields *soporiferous; soporific*, however, derives from late EF-F *soporifique*, sleep-making: *sōpori-*, c/f of L *sōpor*+*-fique* (E *-fic*), L *-ficus*, -making, from *facere.*

6. Gr *hupnos* has derivative *hupnoun*, to put to sleep, whence *hupnōtikos*, tending to sleep, LL *hypnōticus*, EF-F *hypnotique*, E *hypnotic*; SciL has, from Gr *hupnos*, coined *hypnosis* (suffix *-osis*), adopted by E (cf the F *hypnose*).

**son:** ME *sone*, earlier *sune*: OE *sunu*: cf OFris and OS *sunu*, OHG *sunu*, MHG *sun*, G *Sohn*, Go *sunus*, MD *sone, soon, zone*, D *zoon*; ON *sunr, sonr* (cf Sw *son*); Lith *sūnùs*, OSl *synŭ*; Skt *sūnúš*: cf also Tokh B *soyä*, son, Skt *sūté*, she gives birth, OIr *suth*, birth, and—with *h* for *s*—Gr *huios* (υἱός), a son: IE etymon, perh *\*su-iús*, birth, to give birth, with r *\*su-.* (Walshe; Hofmann.)

**sonable; sonant,** whence **sonance; sonata** and **sonnet; sonic; sonority, sonorous;**—**sound** (noise, n and v), whence **sounder** and **sounding**—cf **resound,** v .hence n.—L prefix-cpds: **absonant; assonance** (whence, anl, **assonantal**) and **assonant; consonance, consonant** (adj and n, whence **consonantal**), **consonate, consonous; dissonance, dissonant, dissonous; insonic; resonance, resonant, resonate, resonator; supersonant, supersonic** (adj, hence n).

1. L *sonāre*, to make a noise or cause it to be heard, whence to sing, to sound, is akin to—if not the source of—*sonus*, a sound: cf Skt *svanás*, a noise, a sound, and *svánati*, it sounds or resounds, and Ir *-seinn*, it sounds: IE r, *\*suen-*, *\*swen-*, perh with var *\*swer-*, as in L *susurrus.*

2. The corresp E word is *sound*; the n comes, through ME *soun*, from OF-F *son*, from L *sonus*; the v, from ME *sounen*, earlier *sonen* and *sunen*, from OF *soner, suner* (MF-F *sonner*), from L *sonāre.* The cpd 'to resound', ME *resounen*, comes from OF-MF *resoner* (EF-F *résonner*), from L *resonāre* (*re-*, back), to resound.

3. L *sonus* has the doublet *sonor*, with adj *sonōrus*, whence E *sonorous* (cf EF-F *sonore*); derivative LL *sonōritās* becomes late MF-F

*sonorité* and, perh independently, E *sonority*.
*Sonic* is an E formation: L *son*us+adj *-ic*.

4. OF-F *son* acquires in OProv the sense 'poem', with dim *sonet*, whence It *sonnetto*, whence EF-F *sonnet*, adopted by E; cf *sonata*, adopted—in F as in E—from It, perh orig 'musica *sonata*', music played, not sung (*cantata*), f of *sonato*, pp of *sonare*, from L *sonāre*; and L *sonāre* has derivative *sonābilis*, capable of being sound, whence E *sonable*, and presp *sonans*, o/s *sonant-*, whence E *sonant*, adj hence n.

### Latin Prefix-Compounds

5. Of the numerous L prefix-cpds of *sonāre*, the foll affect E:
*absonāre*, to sound discordantly, with presp *absonans*, o/s *absonant-*, whence the E adj *absonant*, discordant;
*adsonāre*, usu assimilated as *assonāre*, to sound *ad* or towards, to echo, hence, in LL (cf LL *assonus*, harmonious), to sound harmoniously, with presp *assonans*, o/s *assonant-*, whence E *assonant*; but E *assonance* is adopted from late EF-F, which forms it, anl, from L *assonāre*—the LL syn is *assonātiō*;
*consonāre*, to sound *con-* or together, to be in harmony, with presp *consonans*, o/s *consonant-*, whence the OF-F, hence E, adj *consonant*; L *consonans*, used as n, becomes the E n *consonant*; the derivative LL *consonantia*, harmony, becomes OF-F, hence E, *consonance*; the pp *consonātus* yields 'to *consonate*'; the cognate L adj *consonus* produces E *consonous*, sounding simultaneously;
*dissonāre*, to be discordant, has presp *dissonans*, o/s *dissonant-*, used by LL as adj, whence the E adj *dissonant*, and the derivative LL *dissonantia* becomes E (and F) *dissonance*; the cognate L adj *dissonus* yields E *dissonous*;
(E *imsonic*, echoic=*im*itation+*sonic*;)
*resonāre*, to resound, to echo, has presp *resonans*, o/s *resonant-*, whence the E adj *resonant*; derivative L *resonantia* yields late MF-F *résonance*, whence E *resonance*; the pp *resonātus* accounts for 'to *resonate*'; SciL coins *resonator*;
(*supersonant*, n, and *supersonic*, adj hence n=L *super*, above+*sonant* and *sonic*).

**sonata.** See SONABLE, para 4.
**song, songster.** See SING, para 2.
**sonic.** See SONABLE, para 3, s.f.
**sonnet**, whence **sonneteer.** See SONABLE, para 4.
**sonority, sonorous.** See SONABLE, para 3.
**soon**, whence comp **sooner** and sup **soonest**, is ME *sone*, OE *sōna*, akin to OFris *sōn*, *sān*, OHG *sān*, OS *sān*, *sāna*, *sāno*, and Go *suns*.

**soot**, whence (in ME) **sooty**: ME *soot*, earlier *sot*: OE *sōt*: cf MD *soet*, *zoet*, ON *sōt*, Lith *súodys*, OSl *sažda*, OIr *súidi*, *súith*, Ir *súitche*, Ga *sùich*, *sùith*, and, with *h* for *s*, W *huddygl*: perh ult akin to SIT.

**sooth**, adj and n, whence the cpd **soothsayer** (*-sayer*, agent of say); **soothe**, whence the pa, vn **soothing;—suttee.**
1. The n *sooth*, truth, comes from OE *sōth*, n

use of the adj *sōth*, whence, via ME *sooth*, the E adj (now archaic) *sooth*: and the OE adj *sōth* is akin to OFris and OS *sōth*, OHG *sand*, ON *sannr*, true, real—therefore cf Skt *sant*, *sat*, real, present, existing, from *as*, to be, akin to L *esse*, to be, and E *is*: cf ESSE.
2. 'To *soothe*', orig to confirm or prove to be true, comes, via ME *sothien*, to verify, from OE *sōthian*, from the adj *sōth*.
3. Akin to the OGmc words cited in para 1 are such words for 'to excuse' or 'to deny' as Go *sunjōn*, to excuse, and ON *synja*, to deny or refuse, whence ML *sunnia*, *sonia*, an excuse, hindrance, whence the ML cpd *exoniāre* (*ex*, out of), later *essoniāre*, whence MF *essonier*, *essoignier*, whence the E legal v *essoin*; the E n derives, via MF, from ML *essonia*, *exonia*.
4. Skt *sat* (*sant*, genuine) has f *satī*, whence the n *satī*, a faithful wife, whence Hi *satī*, later *sattī*, a wife cremating herself on her husband's funeral pyre: whence E *suttee*.

**sooty.** See SOOT.
**sop.** See SUP, para 3.
**sophism, sophist, sophistic, sophisticate** (adj—whence n—and v, whence the pa **sophisticated**), **sophistication, sophistry**; for cpds (except for sep PHILOSOPHER), see the element *-soph.*
1. Gr *sophos*, wise, mentally adroit, originates all these words: o.o.o.: Boisacq and Hofmann approve Brugmann's postulation of IE etymon *tuoghos*, *tuoguhos*. The derivative *sophia*, wisdom, becomes the now rare E *sophy*, so frequent as a 2nd element, as in *philosophy*.
2. Gr *sophos* has the foll simple derivatives affecting E:
*sophizein*, to make wise, and *sophizesthai*, to become wise, whence *sophisma*, a logical argument, esp if subtle or fallacious, whence L *sophisma*, MF-F *sophisme*, OF-early MF *soffime*, ME *sophime*, EE-E *sophism*;
*sophistēs* (from *sophizein*), a teacher of rhetoric, skilful argument, shrewd living, LL *sophista*, MF-F *sophiste*, E *sophist*;
*sophistikos* (from *sophistēs*), L *sophisticus*, E *sophistic*, with extn *sophistical*.
3. At the L stage arises the ML *sophisticāre* (from L *sophisticus*), with pp *sophisticātus*, whence the E adj and v *sophisticate*; on *sophisticātus* is built ML *sophisticātiō*, acc *sophisticātiōnem*, whence MF-F *sophistication*, adopted by E.
4. MF-F *sophiste* has derivative MF *sophistrie* (MF-EF *sophisterie*, superseded by EF-F *sophisti-querie*), adopted by ME, whence E *sophistry*.

**sophomore.** See the element *-soph.*
**sophy.** See SOPHISM, para 1, s.f.
**sopite.** See SOMNOLENCE, para 5.
**sopor, soporiferous, soporific.** See SOMNOLENCE, para 6.
**soppy.** See SUP, para 3.
**soprano.** See SUPER, para 4.
**sor, sir.** See SENILE, para 8.
**Sorb, Sorbian.** See SERB, para 2.
**sorbent**, absorbent. Cf ABSORB.

**sorbet.** See the 2nd SHRUB, para 2.

**sorcerer, sorcerous, sorcery.** See SERIES, para 4.

**sordes; sordid.** See SWART, para 2.

**sordine.** See SURD, para 4.

**sore,** adj (whence **soreness**) and n; **sorry,** adj. The n *sore*, ME *sor*, earlier *sar*, comes from OE *sār*, from the adj *sār*, distressing, grievous, painful, whence the syn ME *sar*, later *sor*, E *sore*: akin to OHG *sēr*, painful (cf OHG *sēro*, MHG *sēre*, painfully, G *sehr*, very), OS *sēr*, MD *seer*, D *zeer*, ON *sārr*, painful, and Go *sáir*, OFris *sēr*, a wound, pain, and perh OIr *sáeth*, disease, wound, hurt.

2. The OE n *sār* has adj *sārig*, sad, ME *sary*, later *sory*, E *sorry*, painful, grievous, grieved, with gradual weakening of sense.

**sorghum** is a SciL derivative (var *sorgum*) of It *sorgo*, used by E for sweet (or sugar) sorghum: o.o.o.: perh from L *syricum*, for *Syricum gramen*, Syrian grass. (Prati postulates *Syricus*.)

**sororal, sorority.** See COUSIN, s.f.

**sorrel** (1), colour. See the 1st SEAR, para 1.

**sorrel** (2), plant. See SOUR, para 2.

**sorrow** (n and v), **sorrowful.** The adj derives, via ME *sorweful*, from OE *sorgful*, from OE *sorg, sorh*, whence both OE *sorgian*, ME *sorwen*, later *sorowen*, E 'to *sorrow*', and ME *sorge, sorwe*, later *sorewe*, E *sorrow*, n: cf OHG *soraga*, MHG-G *sorge*, OS *sorga*, Go *saúrga*, MD *sorge, zorge*, D *zorg*, ON *sorg*, all with the related sense 'care or anxiety': perh cf Lith *sérgiu*, I guard, and even perh Hit *saru*pa, discord, quarrel, but this may rather belong to SORE.

**sorry** (1), adj. See SORE, para 2.

**sorry** (2), n. See SENILE, para 8.

**sort,** n, v. See SERIES, para 3.

**sortie** is adopted from EF-F, from OF-F *sortir*, app from L *sortīri*, to draw by lots: f.a.e., SERIES.

**sortilege.** See SERIES, para 5.

**sortiment, sortition.** See SERIES, para 3, s.f.

**S.O.S.** or SOS, a signal for help, was chosen because, in Morse, it is easy, both to transmit and to receive.

**sostenuto.** See TENABLE, para 8.

**sot,** whence the adj **sottish** and **besotted** (int *be-*); **sottise.** The last, adopted from MF-F, is a derivative of the OF-F *sot*, adj and n, itself from ML *sottus*, stupid: o.o.o.: Du Cange favours, but does not assert, a punning, ironic origin in Johannes *Scotus* or *Scottus*, known as *Duns* (cf DUNCE) *Scotus* or 'the Subtle Doctor'—a famous medieval scholastic philosopher.

**sotto voce,** adopted from It, is lit 'under (the) voice', hence under one's breath, in a low voice.

**sou.** See SOLID, para 1, s.f.

**soubrette.** See SUPER, para 3.

**soubriquet.** See SOBRIQUET, para 2.

**soufflé.** See FLATUS, para 10.

**sough.** See ECHO.

**sought:** pt and pp of SEEK.

**soul,** whence **soulful, soulless,** comes, via ME *soule*, earlier *saule*, from OE *sāl, sāwl*, contr of *sāwel*: cf OFris *sēle*, OS and OHG *sēola, siola*, OHG *sēla, sēula*, MHG *sēle*, G *Seele*, Go *saiwala*,

MD *siele, siel, ziele*, D *ziel*, ON *sāla, sāl*: o.o.o.

**soum.** See SUM, para 4.

**sound** (1), adj (flawless, unharmed): ME *sound*, earlier *sund*: OE *sund, gesund* (*ge-*, an int prefix): cf OFris *sund*, OHG *gisunt* (*gi-* is Gmc *ge-*), MHG *gesunt*, G *gesund*, MD *gesunt, gesont*, D *gezond*: o.o.o.: prob akin to L *sānus* (cf SANE).

**sound** (2), an inlet (Geog): ME *sound*, earlier *sund*: OE *sund*: cf ON *sund*: prob cf SWIM (in water).

**sound** (3), noise. See SONABLE, para 2.

**sounder,** herd of wild boars, wild boar; OE *sundre*, var *sonre*: cf OE *sunor, suner*, herd of wild boars: of Gmc origin.

**soup.** See SUP, para 3.

**soupçon.** See SPECTACLE, para 17.

**souple.** See PLY, para 18.

**sour,** adj (hence n) and v, **sourness** (OE *sūrness*); **sorrel** (plant); **surette.**

1. 'To *sour*' derives from OE *sūrian* (vt, vi), from the adj *sūr*, whence ME *sur*, later *sour*, E *sour*: cf OHG-MHG *sūr*, G *sauer* (whence *Sauerkraut*, 'sour vegetable': OHG-MHG *krūt*), MD *suyr*, *suur, zure*, D *zuur*, ON *sūrr* (Da *suur*), Lith *sūras*, salty, OSl *syrŭ*, raw.

2. From OGmc, the OF-F *sur*, sour, has derivatives MF *surele* (F *surelle*), whence E *sorrel*, a sour-juiced plant, and the dim MF-F *suret*, sourish, whence, as n, *suret*, varr *surète, surette*, the wood sorrel, whence, in AE, *surette*, a tree with edible, although tart, berries.

**source.** See SURGE, para 2.

**sourdough,** a prospector in Canada (or Alaska), orig carried a lump of *sour dough* with which to bake bread.

**souse,** a pickle, a drenching—to pickle or to drench. See SALT, para 10.

**soutane:** F *soutane*: EF *sottane*: It *sottana*, orig an under-garment: It *sotto*, under+n-suffix *-ana*: ult from L *sub*, under.

**south** (n, hence adj and v); **southeast** (adv—OE *sūthēast*—hence adj and n); **southerly,** adj (*south+ -erly*, as in *northerly*), hence n; **southern** (OE *sūtherne*)—whence **southron,** adj (cf *Briton*) and (S-) n; **southward,** adv (OE *sūthweard*), hence adj and n—cf **southwards,** adv (OE *sūthweardes*), **southwest,** adv (OE *sūthwest*), hence adj and n.— Many cpd place-names: e.g., **Suffolk, Surrey, Sussex,** as well as the obvious **Southampton, Southwark,** etc.

1. *South*, ME *south*, earlier *suth*, comes from OE *sūth*: *\*sunth*, land that, to the Old World of the Northern Hemisphere, lies in the sun, or a direction that leads to sunnier parts of the earth: cf OHG *sund*, south wind, and *sundan*, MHG *sunden* (G *Süden*, from MD *sūden*), OFris and OS *sūth*, ON *sunnr, suthr* (with modern Scan cognates): f.a.e., SUN.

2. Of the full cpds, perh most notable are:

*Southampton*, OE *Sūthhamtun*;

*Southwark*, OE *Sūthgeweorc*, soon *Sūthweorc*, orig the southern fortifications;

*Suffolk*, OE *Sūthfolchi, Sūthfolc*, the southern

folk; hence the *Suffolk punch*, a draught horse orig peculiar to the region;

*Surrey*, OE *Sūthrige*, the southern district (orig, kingdom: cf REX); hence the light, four-wheeled carriage popularized in that county;

*Sussex*, OE *Sūth Seaxe*, the South Saxons, hence their homeland; *sussexite* (Min *-ite*) was first found in *Sussex* County, New Jersey.

**Southampton.** See prec, para 2.

**southeast, southerly, southern.** See SOUTH (heading).

**southron, Southron.** See SOUTH (heading).

**southward, southwards.** See SOUTH (heading).

**Southward.** See SOUTH, para 2.

**southwest.** See SOUTH (heading).

**souvenir.** See VENUE.

**sovereign, sovereignty.** See SUPER, para 5.

**soviet:** Ru *sovjet*, a council: prefix *so-*, together (cf E *co-*, L *con-*, from L *cum*, with)+the Ru r for 'to speak', as in Ru *otvjet*, an answer. (EW.)

**sovran, sovranty.** See SUPER, para 5.

**sow** (1), a female pig (adult): ME *sowe*, earlier *suwe*: OE *sugu*, an extn of the syn Gmc etymon *su*, as in OE *sū*, OHG-MHG *sū*, G *Sau*, MD *seuge*, *suege, soge, zoge*, D *zeug, zog*, ON *sȳr* (Sw *sugga*, *so*, Da *so*); EIr *socc* (Ga *soc*), a (pig's) snout, hence a ploughshare, and Cor *hōch, hōgh*, W *hwch*, Br *houch*, a sow, all varr of a C r *su-*, to produce (young), the sow being noted for its numerous progeny; Let *suveñs*, a piglet; Tokh B *suwo*; L *sūs* (gen *suis*); Gr (*sus* and) *hus*; Av *hū* (for *huvō*), a boar, Skt *sūkarás*, a hog; and Hit *šah*, a pig—perh cf Hit *sahar*, dirt. The IE etymon is *sūs*; the IE r is *sū-*, either 'to produce (young)', as Malvezin suggests, or echoic (Hofmann, Webster, *et alii*).

2. Akin to OE *sū*, a sow, is OE *swīn*, a hog, ME *swin*, E *swine*: OFris, OS, OHG-MHG *swīn*, G *Schwein*, Go *swein*, MD *swin* (rare), *swijn*, later —as in D—*zwijn*, ON *svīn*; cf OSl *svinŭ*, LL *suīnus*, Gr *húīnos*, of a pig, hence piggish.—Derivatives: *swineherd, swinish*.

3. The Gr *húīnos* (ὕïνος) is akin to Gr *huaina*, whence L *hyaena*, OF-MF *hyene* (EF-F *hyène*) and, prob independently, E *hyena*. Cf the sep HOG: a hyena resembles one.

4. L *sūs* has derivative adj *suīlis*, attested by the n *suīle*, a pigsty, whence perh OF-MF *soil* (EF-F *souille*), a pig's wallowing place, a mire, with derivative OF-MF *soillier* (EF-F *souiller*), to bemire, to stain (lit and fig), whence ME *soilen*, E 'to *soil*', whence, in return, the E n *soil*, a stain. But more prob 'a *soil*' comes, in all senses, from to '*soil*', ME *soilen*: and OF-F *soillier* more prob derives from VL *suculāre*, from LL *sūculus*, a piglet (from *sūs*, s and r *sū-*), as both Dauzat and B & W propose.

5. OF-MF *soillier* has the MF var *suller*, whence E 'to *sully*', whence E *sullage*.

6. The EIr *socc*, a pig's snout, a ploughshare, cited in para 1, is akin to Gaul *soccus*, a ploughshare, whence OF-F *soc*, whence the syn E, now mainly Sc, *sock*; and OF-F *soc* acquires the

AF dim *soket*, spearhead resembling, in shape, a ploughshare, whence E *socket*, with natural sense-divergences.

**sow** (2), to plant (seeds) by scattering them onto the prepared soil; pt **sowed**, pp **sown**; hence **sower** (OE *sāwere*) and pa, vn **sowing**; **semen, seminal, seminar, seminary**—cf **disseminate, dissemination; season**, n (whence **seasonal**), hence v (whence **seasonable** and **seasoning**); sep SECULAR, SECULARITY, SECULARIZE, qq.v at the sep SEED.—Cf also the sep SATURDAY and SATURN.

1. 'To *sow*', ME *sowen*, var *sawen*, comes from OE *sāwan*: cf OFris *sēa*, OS *sājan*, OHG *sāen*, MHG *saejen*, G *Säen*, Go *saian*, MD *seyen*, *saeyen, zayen, zaeyen*, D *zaaijen*, ON *sā*, also Lith *séti*, OB *sěti*, to sow, and L *sēui* (ML *sēvi*), I have sown (inf *serere*), and, in C, with *ī* for *ē*, OIr *sil*, Ga *sìol*, and, with *h* for *s*, OW *hīl*. The IE r is *sē-* or *sē-*, to sow, with Gmc var *sā-* or *sā-*.

2. L *serere* (s *ser-*, r *se-*), to sow, has derivative *sēmen* (o/s *sēmin-*), a sowing, hence that which is sown; adopted by Bot and Physio. The foll derivatives concern E:

*sēminālis*, whence MF-F *séminal*, whence E *seminal*;

*sēminārium*, a seed-plot, prop the neu of adj *sēminārius*; hence both the G *Seminar*, E *seminar* (at a university), and E *seminary*, orig as in L, hence a secondary school, whence *seminarian* and —after F *séminariste*—*seminarist*;

*sēmināre*, to sow, pp *sēminātus*, whence 'to '*seminate*' (rare), the derivative L *sēminātiō*, o/s *sēminātiōn-*, yielding *semination*.

3. *Sēmināre* has the cpd *dissēmināre* (*dis-*, apart), to scatter seeds, with pp *dissēminātus*, whence 'to *disseminate*'; derivative *dissēminātiō*, o/s *-ātiōn-*, yields *dissemination*.

4. *Serere* has pp *satus*, whence *satiō*, a sowing, acc *satiōn*em, whence OF-F *saison* (cf OProv *sazon*), with OF-MF varr *seison, seson*, whence ME *seson*, whence E *season*; 'to *season*'—basically to render fit for the season—derives from the E n, but perh owes something to the syn MF-F *assaisonner* (*as-*=L *ad*, toward:). *Seasonable* comes imm from AF; with *seasonal*, cf LL *sationālis*, fit for sowing.

**soy; soya.** The Oriental sauce known as *soy* comes through Jap *shōyū* from Ch; it is made from beans, esp the *soybean* (*soy*+*bean*). The E form *soya* (*bean*) derives from D and G *soja*, D var *soya*, F *soya*, from Jap *shōyū*, and has perh been influenced by a word used mainly in India—*soya*, fennel, from Hi *soyā*, itself from Skt *śāleya*.

**spa:** *Spa*, a small Belgian town, famous since C16 for its mineral springs.

**space**, n, hence v (perh influenced by late MF-F *espacer*, from OF-F *espace*)—**spacious**—**spatial** (anl from E *space* after L *spatium*)—**spatiate**, whence, anl, **spatiation**; **expatiate** (adj and v), whence, anl, **expatiation** and **expatiatory**; **interspace**, whence, anl, **interspatial**.

1. E-ME *space* derives, by aphesis, from OF-F *espace*, from L *spatium*, prob an *s-* reinforcement

(IE int prefix *s*-) of a derivative of L *patēre*, to lie open: cf Lith *splečiù* beside *platùs*, wide-open, large. (E & M.) Cf PATENT.

2. L *spatium* has adj *spatiōsus*, whence OF-MF *spacieux*, f *spacieuse*, whence E *spacious*; derivative LL *spatiōsitās*, o/s *spatiōsitāt*-, yields E *spatiosity*, ousted by the E formation *spaciousness*. Derivative *spatiāri*, to take a walk, has pp *spatiātus*, whence 'to *spatiate*' (now rare).

3. *Spatiāri* has cpd *exspatiāri*, with contr *expatiāri*, to walk, or go, far and wide (*ex*-, out of, used int), with pp *exspatiātus*, whence 'to *expatiate*'.

4. *Spatium* has the LL cpd *interspatium*, an interval, whence E *interspace*.

5. Cf the sep SPEED.

**spade.** See SPOON, para 2.

**spaghetti,** adopted from It, is the pl of *spaghetto*, dim of *spago*, a cord: o.o.o.

**spahi.** See SEPOY.

**Spain, Spaniard, Spanish; spaniel; Hispania, Hispanic** (whence **Hispanicism** and, anl, **Hispanist,** a scholar in Spanish).

1. *Spain* derives, by aphesis, from OF-MF *Espaigne* (F *Espagne*): LL *Spānia*: L *Hispānia*: L *Hispān*us, Spanish, a Spaniard+-*ia*, denoting a land, a region. The L city-name *Hispalis*, Seville, suggests that the prehistoric name of Spain was *\*Hispa*, prob of C-Iberian origin.

2. *Spanish* reshapes ME *Spainish*, which= *Spain*+adj -*ish*, but recalls LL *Spānus*; and *Spaniard* derives, by aphesis, from OF-MF *Espaignart* (*Espaigne*+-*art*).

3. A *spaniel* is lit a Spanish dog: MF (chien) *espaignol* (later *espagnel*, finally *épagneul*): Sp *español*, Spanish, from *España* (cf It *Spagna*), from L *Hispānia*.

4. L *Hispānia* has adj *Hispānicus*, whence E *Hispanic* (cf the obs F *hispanique*).

**spale** (dial) and **spall,** a splinter, a chip, whence 'to *spall*', to break into fragments (mining and masonry), derive from ME *spalle*, as dial *spalt*, var *spald*, to chip, derives from ME *spalden*, both perh akin to ON *spölr*, a short piece; ME *spalden* app comes from MD *spalden*, akin to OHG *spaltan*, MHG-G *spalten*, to split, itself akin to Skt *sphuṭáti* (for *\*sphultáti*). Cf SPOIL.

**span** (n and v), **spanner**—cf **inspan** and **outspan; spin,** v (whence **spinnet** and **spinning,** as in **spinning jenny**), hence n—cf **spinster; spindle** (n, hence adj and v), whence **spindly; spider,** whence **spidery.**— **spasm** (whence **spasmic**), **spasmodic, spastic.**

'To *span*' comes imm from 'a *span*', but ult from OE *spannan*, itself from the OE n *spann*, whence the E n *span*: with OE *spannan*, cf OFris *spanna* (var *sponna*), OHG *spannan*, G (and MD-D) *spannen*, whence *Spanner*, whence E *spanner*, the tool; with OE *spann*, cf OFris *spann* (var *sponn*), OHG *spanna*, G *Spanne*, MD-D *span*, and ON *spönn*. Ult all the OGmc words are akin to Gr *spaein*, *spān*, to drag or draw (see para 6).

2. From MD-D *span* comes 'a *span* of oxen'; from MD-D *spannen* comes *span*, to attach

(horses) to a vehicle, whence to *inspan* or harness to, *outspan* to unharness from, a waggon; all, SAfr usages.

3. OE *spannan*, to span, to clasp, to attach, to yoke or harness up, has, app, a thinned derivative *spinnan*, to spin (a web, or web and woof), to twist or writhe (cf para 6)—whence 'to *spin*'; and OE *spinnan* is akin to OFris *spinna*, OHG *spinnan*, MHG-G *spinnen*, Go *spinnan*, ON *spinna*. In ME, 'to *spin*' has agent *spinster* (-*ster*, f agent), a woman that spins, hence an unmarried gentlewoman, hence any unmarried woman.

4. Akin to OE *spinnan*, to spin, is OE *spinel*, a spindle, akin to OHG *spinnala*, *spinnila*, MHG *spinnel*; but *spindle* itself comes, via MD -*spindel* (only in cpds, the MD single being *spille* or *spil*), supported by ED-D and G *spindel*, from OFris *spindel*.

5. OE *spinnan*, to spin, acquires, in ME, the derivative *spithre*, lit a spinner, but in usage a spider, whence the 'eased' E *spider*: cf MHG-G *Spinne* (OHG *spinna*, from *spinnan*, to spin), a spider.

6. Mentioned in para 1, s.f., and compared in para 3, the Gr *spáō*, I draw (a sword), pull or drag, and later, in Med, to cause a convulsion, with inf *spáein*, often contr to *spān*, derives from IE *\*speor *\*spi*-, to stretch.

7. Gr *spān*, pt *espassa*, has derivative n *spasmos*, a convulsion, whence, via L *spasmus* and MF-F *spasme*, the E *spasm*. Whereas Gr *spasmos* has adj *spasmōdēs*, whence, via ML *spasmodicus*, the (F *spasmodique* and) E *spasmodic*, Gr *spān* has adj *spastikos*, whence L *spasticus*, whence E *spastic*, adj hence n.

**spandrel,** o.o.o., perh derives, via AF, by aphesis from OF-MF *espandre* (F *épandre*): L *expandere*, to spread out: *ex*-, out+*pandere*, to spread, perh akin to *patēre*, to lie open (cf PATENT).

**spangle,** a bright dress-ornament, hence v, derives from ME *spangel*, dim of ME *spang*, from OE *spange*, a clasp, a brooch; cf OHG *spanga*, MHG-G *spange*, MD *spaenge*, *spange*, D *spang*, a brooch, ON *spöng*, a spangle: Walshe proposes kinship with Gr *sphēkóō*, I bind tightly; I suggest kinship with E *span*—cf OFris *spann*, *sponn*, both a span and a brooch.

**Spaniard.** See SPAIN, para 2.

**spaniel.** See SPAIN, para 3.

**Spanish.** See SPAIN, para 2.

**spank,** to strike with open hand, hence n and 'a **spanking**'; hence prob the adj **spanking,** moving in a lively manner and at a brisk pace, whence, by b/f, 'to **spank**' or move thus: echoic.

**spanner** (tool). See SPAN, para 1.

**span-new.** See SPIKE, para 4.

**spar** (1), a timber, e.g. a beam, later—naut—a mast, a boom; **spear** (n, hence v), whence, by shape-resemblance, **spearfish, -grass, -mint, -wood, -wort** (OE *sperewyrt*: cf WORT), and, even more obviously, **spearhead, -man,** and the adj **speary.**

1. A *spar*, ME *sparre*, is akin to OHG *sparro*,

G *Sparren*, MD-D *spar*, ON *sparri* (with modern Scan cognates).

2. A *spear*, ME *spere*, OE *spere*, is akin to OFris *sper*, *spere*, *spiri*, OHG-MHG *sper*, G *Speer*, MD *spare*, *spere*, *sper*, *sperre*, D *speer*, ON *spiör* (*spjör*)—and prob to L *sparus* (s and r *spar-*), a hunting-spear. Akin is *spar*, to fasten (a door or a gate): ME *sparren*, aphetically from OE *be-* and *gesparrian*: cf OHG *sperrēn*, MHG-G *sperren*, to protect with spars, hence to barricade.

**spar** (2), a non-metallic mineral. See FELDSPAR.

**spar** (3), as a boxer does. See PARE, para 3.

**spar** (4). See the 1st SPAR, para 2, s.f.

**spare**, adj (hence n) and v (whence **sparing**).

The adj *spare*, not being used, reserved, derives from OE *spaer*, sparing, and 'to *spare*' from the intimately related OE *sparian*, not to use, to forbear: cf OFris *sparia*, OHG *sparōn*, G *sparen*, MD-D *sparen*, ON *spara*, and, for the adj, OHG *spar*, MD *sparich*, ON *sparr*, sparing, OSl *sporŭ*, long-lasting, and Skt *sphāra*, extensive. Cf the sep SPEED.

**sparge.** See SPARSE, para 1.

**sparhawk.** See SPARROW, para 2.

**spark**, n and v; **sparkle**, v and n; **sparklet.** See SPARSE, paras 6–7.

**sparrow** (sparrowgrass; f/e for ASPARAGUS), ME *sparowe*, earlier *sparewe*, earliest *sparwa*, derives from OE *spearwa*: cf OHG *sparo*, MHG *spar* (gen *sparwes*), whence the MHG dim *sperlinc*, G *Sperling*—Go *sparwa*—ON *spörr*; cf also (Walshe) OP *spurglis*, Gr *spergoulos*, a small field-bird —? akin to Gr *sperkhomenos* (prop a presp), speedy, hasty, the sparrow being a notably lively bird.

2. E **sparhawk**, the sparrow hawk, comes from ME *sparhauk*, from OE *spearhafoc*.

**sparse** (whence **sparseness** and—? after *scarcity* —**sparsity**), **sparsile**; **sparge** (v, hence n), whence **sparger**; **spark**, n (whence **sparkish**) and v (whence **sparker** and **sparking**)—**sparkle**, n (whence the dim **sparklet**) and v (whence **sparkler**, **sparkling**); **sprinkle**, v (whence **sprinkler**, **sprinkling**), hence n. —Cpds from L *spargere*: **asperge**, **aspergillum**, **aspergillus** (whence **aspergillin** and **aspergillosis**)— **asperse**, **aspersion** (whence, anl, **aspersive**), **aspersorium**; **disperse** (whence **dispersal**), **dispersion** (whence, anl, **dispersity** and **dispersive**); **intersperse**, whence **interspersal** and, anl, **interspersion.**— **speak**, whence **speaker**, **speaking**, and AE **speakeasy**; pt **spoke**, archaic **spake**, and pp **spoken**; **speech** (whence **speechify**), **speechless** (OE *spāēclēas*) —cf **spokesman.**

1. *Sparse* derives from L *sparsus*, pp of *spargere*, to scatter or strew; on *spars*us is formed the LL *sparsilis*, whence E *sparsile*; from the inf *spargere* comes, via MF, the E 'to *sparge*', to sprinkle.

2. L *spargere* is akin to Gr *spargan*, (vi) to swell, to teem or abound: both vv have s *sparg-*, r *spar-*: cf Skt *sphŭrjati*, it breaks, or bursts, forth, and Av fra-*sparega*, a branch, a twig, and Lith *spùrgas*, a sprout: IE r, *sper-*, var *spar-*, with extn *sphereg-*, var *sphareg-*, to sprout, to strew, to scatter.—

The Gr *speirein*, to sow (seeds), esp by broadcasting them, is a var of *sper-*: cf SPERM, para 1.

## Compounds from L *spargere*

3. The c/f of *spargere* is *-spergere*, with pp *-spersus* and derivative n-*spersiō*(o/s-*spersiōn*). Of the numerous L cpds, only three have affected general E; the others are both erudite and, even so, rare. The first is *adspergere* (int *ad-*), eased to *aspergere*, to scatter, strew, sprinkle, whence— via OF-F *asperger*—'to *asperge*'; derivative Eccl ML *aspergillum*, a sprinkling-brush or perforated globe, is retained by EcclE; the var *aspergillus* is now used mainly by Bot. The pp *aspersus* yields 'to *asperse*', orig to besprinkle, now to bespatter with calumny; derivative *aspersiō*, o/s *aspersiōn-*, yields OF-F *aspersion*, adopted by E, and derivative EcclML *aspersōrium*, basin for holy water, is retained by EcclE.

4. L *dispergere* (*di-* for *dis-*, apart, connoting an extensive scattering), to cause to scatter, has s *disperg-*, whence the Sci *dispergate* (*-ate* as v-suffix). The pp *dispersus* yields the now rare adj *disperse*, via late MF-EF *dispers*, f *disperse*, and 'to *disperse*', via late MF-F *disperser*; derivative LL *dispersiō*, o/s *dispersiōn*, becomes MF-F *dispersion*, adopted by E.

5. L *interspergere*, to scatter *inter* or among, to scatter here and there, has pp *interspersus*, whence 'to *intersperse*'.

## Germanic Cognates of L *spargere*

6. 'To *spark*', or issue in sparks, derives from OE *spearcian*, from OE *spearca*, an ignited particle or tiny fragment, var *spaerca*, whence, resp, ME *sperke* and *sparka*, *sparc*, whence E *spark*; cf the related ON *sparkr*, brisk, lively, whence ult the E *spark*, a gallant (esp in the taut 'a gay, or bright, *spark*'), whence the AE coll v *spark*, play the beau to.

7. 'To *spark*' has the freq 'to *sparkle*', whence— unless it be a dim of the n *spark*—the n *sparkle*; *sparklet* is certainly a dim of the n *spark*.

8. Prob akin to L *spargere* is 'to *sprinkle*', which is clearly a freq and prob a nasalization of a metathetic var of IE *spar-* or *sper-*, to scatter, strew, sprinkle. 'To *sprinkle*', ME *sprenkelen*, is closely akin to D *sprenkelen*, to sprinkle (from MD *sprenkel*, a small spot, etc., var *sprinkel*), and G *sprenkeln*, to spot or fleck (from G *Sprenkel*, MHG *sprinkel*, a speckle, MLG a freckle). This Gmc sub-group is perh, although less prob, related, not to L *spargere* but (Walshe) to Gr *perknos*, variegated, with addition of the IE int prefix *s-*.

## The Scattering or Sowing of Sounds-as-Words

9. The Gmc *sprek-*, *sprik-* r prob attested by 'sprinkle' words occurs in OE *spreccan*, *sprecan*, with eased var *specan*, whence, via ME *speken*, E 'to *speak*': and OE *sprecan* is akin to OFris *spreka*, OS *sprekan*, OHG *sprehhan* (var *spehhan*), MHG-G *sprechen*, MD *spreecken*, MD-D *spreken*: cf also ON *spraka*, to crackle, and Skt *spŭrjati*, it

crackles or roars, and, in C, the W *ffraeth*, eloquent.

10. Most intimately related to OE *sprecan*, *specan*, to speak, is OE *sprāēc*, *sprēc*, with eased varr *spāēc*, *spēc*, a speaking, whether the power of speech, or speech in general, or a particular speaking, whence ME *speche*, E *speech*: cf OFris *sprēke* (var *sprētze*), OHG *sprāhha*, MHG *sprāche*, G *Sprache*, MLG *sprāke*, MD *sprāke*, *spraecke*, *spraec*, D *spraak*, and also cf MD *spraecwort*, a spoken word.

11. 'To *speak*' has the dial derivative *speak*, speech, a saying, which has—prob after the pt *spoke*—the var *spoke*, whence app the otherwise puzzling *spokesman* (a *spoke's man*).

**spart, spartein(e), Spartium.** See the 2nd SPIRE, para 5.

**Spartan,** adj, hence n: L *Spartanus*, adj of *Sparta*: (Doric) Gr *Sparta*, Attic *Spartē*, the capital of Laconia in the ancient Peloponnesus; the inhabitants were noted for hard discipline and for the utmost fortitude and courage. Gr (hē) *Spartē* is elliptical for (hē khōra) *spartē*, the sown place.

**spasm, spasmic, spasmodic, spastic.** See SPAN, para 7.

**spat, spats; spatter.** The base is app *spat*, a var—now only Sc—of SPOT, a small stain, a fleck, a freckle, etc., hence, collectively, some spots of rain; hence 'to *spat*', of which 'to *spatter*' is a freq, with n derivative therefrom. *Spatter* occurs in the cpd *spatterdash*, a legging or gaiter worn against spatters of water or mud; used mostly in pl, it has the b/f *spats*. Moreover, the etym obscure *spat*, a young bivalve (esp a young oyster), perh derives from *spat*, a spot; and *splatter*, n and v, app blends *splash* and *spatter*.

**spatchcock.** See SPIKE, para 3.

**spate,** a freshet, a heavy shower, hence a very large quantity or number (as of words), is o.o.o.: perh, by aphesis, from MF *espoit*, gushing of a spring: *es-*, L *ex*, out of; 2nd element, o.o.o.

**spatha, spathal, spathe.** See SPOON, para 3.

**spatial.** See SPACE (heading).

**spatter, spatterdash.** See SPAT.

**spatula, spatulate.** See SPOON, para 4.

**spavin,** disease of a horse's hock, whence **spavined:** ME *spaveyne*, an aphesis, and an easing, of MF *esparvain*, *esparvin* (F *éparvin*): o.o.o.: perh from Frankish *\*sparwun*, acc of *\*sparo*, a sparrow, either from a shape-resemblance or from a resemblance of the bird's flight to the horse's gait (B & W).

**spawn,** v (whence **spawner** and **spawning**), hence n (whence **spawny**): ME *spawnen*, earlier *spanen*: by aphesis from OF-MF *espandre* (F *épandre*), orig to shed: L *expandere*, to stretch, to spread out: *ex-*, out, used int+*pandere*, to stretch, spread, prob akin to *patēre*, to lie open (cf PATENT).

**spay.** See SPOON, para 5.

**speak,** whence **speaker** and **speaking.** See SPARSE, para 9.

**spear, spearhead, spearmint, spearsman.** See the 1st SPAR, para 2.

**special** (adj, hence n), whence **specialism, specialist** (perh prompted by F *spécialiste*), **specialize** (whence **specialization**)—**speciality** and **specialty; especial; specific** (adj, hence n), **specification, specify; specie, species, speciosity, specious; spice** (n, whence **spicy**, and v), **spicery.**

1. The basis of all these words is provided by the L *speciēs*, a sight, hence the outward form or shape, hence a sort or kind: *speciēs* derives from L *speciō*, I look at, I see: therefore cf and, f.a.e., see SPECTACLE.

2. L *speciēs* is adopted by E, orig in the senses 'mental image' and 'visible form' and later as a term in Bio (*genus* and *species*). From the L phrase *in speciē*, in form, in kind, hence in coin, derives E *specie*, coin in general, esp of gold or silver.

3. L *speciēs* has both the L adj *speciōsus*, whence E *specious*, the LL derivative *speciōsitās* (o/s *speciōsitāt-*) yielding E *speciosity*, and the LL cpd adj *specificus*, species-making (-*ficus* from -*ficere*, c/f of *facere*, to make), whence EF-F *spécifique* and, perh independently, E *specific*; derivative LL *specificāre*, to endow with form (to specify), becomes MF *especifier*, later *spécifier*, whence 'to *specify*'; on the pp *specificātus* is formed the ML *specificātiō*, o/s *specificātiōn-*, whence, prob via MF-F *spécification*, the E *specification*.

4. L *speciēs*, in its sense '(own) form or shape, hence kind or sort', has LL adj *speciālis* (opp *generālis*), whence OF-MF *especial* and *special* (F *spécial*), whence E *especial* and *special*; derivative LL *speciālitās* (o/s *speciālitāt-*), a particular quality, becomes MF *specialité* (F *spé-*), whence E *speciality*; the MF var *especialté* accounts—by aphesis—for the E var *specialty*.

5. L *speciēs* acquires, in LL, the sense 'articles of merchandise, esp aromatics and spices', whence OF-MF *espice* (later *epice*, F *épice*), whence, by aphesis, the ME-E *spice*, with gradually narrowing sense; derivative MF *espicerie* (later *épicerie*) similarly gives us *spicery*. Derivative MF *espicer*, to trade in spices, F to season with spices, yields 'to *spice*'.

**specie.** See prec, para 2.

**species.** See SPECIAL, para 2.

**specific, specification, specify.** See SPECIAL, para 3.

**specimen.** See SPECTACLE, para 3.

**speciosity, specious.** See SPECIAL, para 3.

**speck** (1), n (hence v), a spot, whence **specky; speckle** (n, hence v), whence pa **speckled** and adj **speckly.** A *speckle* is prob the dim of *speck*: cf MD *speckel*. A *speck*, ME *spekke*, derives from OE *specca*: of Gmc origin.

**speck** (2), blubber, bacon, derives, like the now only Sc *spick*, blubber, fat or grease, from OE *spec*, *spic*, akin to OFris *spec*, OHG-MHG *spec*, G *Speck*, MD *spec*, *speck*, D *spek*, bacon, and ON *spik*, blubber: perh cf, without IE *s-*, the Gr *piōn*, fat, and prob cf Skt *sphij* (*sphigī-*), hind-quarters (cf, sem, BACON).

**spectacle** (and **spectacles**), **spectacular, spectator; specter** (AE) or **spectre** (whence **spectral**), **spectrum**

—cf the element *spectro-*; **specular, speculum; speculate, speculation, speculative, speculator, speculatory; specimen.**—Cpds from L *spectāre* and from L *-spicere* (c/f of *specere*), pp *-spectus*, derivative n *-spectiō* and adj *-spectiuus* (ML *-spectivus*) and agent *-spector*: aspect; **circumspect, circumspection;** conspectus, whence, anl, **conspective**—cf **conspicuity, conspicuous; despicable**— cf **despise** (whence, in part, **despisable** and, entirely, **despisal**)—**despite** (whence **despiteful** and **despiteous**), n, v (obs), prep—**spite**, n (whence **spiteful**), hence v; **expect, expectable, expectance (expectancy), expectant, expectation, expectative; inspect, inspection** (whence **inspectional**), **inspective, inspector** (whence **inspectoral** or **-ial, inspectorate,** (anl) **inspectress**); **perspective** (adj and n)—cf **perspicacity, perspicacious,** and **perspicuity, perspicuous; prospect** (n and v), **prospection, prospective** (adj, hence n), **prospector, prospectus; respect** (n, v), **respectable** (whence, anl, **respectability**), **respectant, respective** (whence **irrespective**)—and, from the n, **respectful, respectless,** and, from the v, **respecter; respite,** n and v; **retrospect** (n, v), whence, anl, **retrospection** and **retrospective; suspect** (adj— whence n—and v), cf **suspicion** and **suspicious; transpicuous.**—'Disguised': **espial, espy; espionage; spy,** n (whence **spyglass**) and v (whence **spying**).— Cf the sep AUSPICE, AUSPICIOUS, qq.v. at AVIARY; sep FRONTISPIECE, q.v. at FRONT; SPECIES, SPECIFIC, SPECIFY, SPECIOUS, qq.v. at SPECIAL. —Cf also the sep, more remote SCEPTIC (in ADDENDA) and SCOPE.

Indo-European

1. Behind all these words, lies L *specere* (c/f *-spicere*), to perceive with the eyes, to see, to look at, with s and r *spec-*, answering to IE *\*spek-* (var *\*spak-*), which app has the metathetic mdfn *\*skep-*, as in Gr *skeptomai* (s *skept-*, r *skep-*), I observe, with the normal *e-o* mutation in the n *skopos*; there is also an *s*-less var *\*pek-* or *-pak*, attested in Skt. The corresp Gmc words are rare, with *h* (prob for *kh*) for *k*. Of the numerous cognates of L *specere*, the foll are, in even the most cursory treatment, worth noting: Skt *spāśati, pāśyati*, he sees, *spaṣṭás*, seen, *spaṭ*, a seer; OHG *speha*, close attention, *spehōn*, MHG *spehen*, to examine closely, G *spähen*, to spy out, OHG *spāhi*, wise, shrewd, MHG *spaehe*, skilful, ON *spā*, prophecy.

2. The L s and r *spec-* occurs in the derivative *speculum*, a mirror (that into which one looks), adopted by E, with various erudite, Sci, tech senses; the derivative adj *speculāris* yields E *specular*. L *specere* has the closely related derivative *specula*, a watch-tower or look-out, whence *speculāri*, to watch from one, to spy out, with pp *speculātus*, whence 'to *speculate*', to meditate, hence to theorize, whence the commerical sense; derivatives LL *speculātiō* (o/s *speculātiōn-*), LL *speculatiuus* (ML *-ivus*), L *speculātor*, L *speculā-rōtius*, yield E *speculation* (? imm from MF-F *spéculation*), *speculative* (from MF-F *spéculatif*, f

*-ive*), *speculator* (cf late EF-F *spéculateur*), *speculatory*.

3. The L *spec-* occurs also in L *specimen*, something that indicates (e.g., the quality), adopted by E—cf the F *spécimen*.

4. On the L pp *spec*tus is formed L *spectrum*, an appearance, esp an image, later a ghostly appearance, an apparition, adopted by E and given a new sense, that of Phys; L *spectrum* becomes EF-F *spectre*, adopted by E.

5. L *specere* has the freq *spectāre*, to look at habitually, hence to fix one's eyes upon, with pp *spectā*tus, whence *spectā*tor, whence late MF-F *spectateur* and E *spectator*. *Spect*āre has the derivative *spectāculum*, something often looked at or worth looking at, whence OF-F *spectacle*, adopted by E; the adj *spectacular* is an anl E formation. From *spectāculum* in its LL sense 'the act of seeing' comes the ME-EE *spectacle*, a spyglass, a mirror, whence *spectacles* in the modern sense.

Compounds from L *specere* and *spectāre*

6. L *aspicere*, eased form of *adspicere* (*ad-* used int), to look at, has pp *aspec*tus, whence the n *aspectus* (gen *-ūs*), whence late MF-F and, prob independently, E *aspect*; the astrological 'to *aspect*', however, derives from L *aspectāre*, the int of *aspicere*.

7. L *circumspicere*, to look *circum*, about or around, oneself, has pp *circumspectus*, whence the E adj *circumspect*; derivative LL *circumspectiō* (o/s *circumspectiōn-*), the act of looking around, becomes E *circumspection*, with the new sense 'discretion' or 'caution'. Cf the MF-F *circonspect, circonspection*.

8. L *conspicere* (*con-* used int), to perceive, has pp *conspec*tus, whence the n *conspectus* (gen *-ūs*), a mental survey (LL, the zodiac), adopted by E. *Conspic*ere has derivative adj *conspicuus*, whence E *conspicuous*; the LL off-shoot *conspicuitās*, o/s *conspicuitāt-*, yields *conspicuity*.

9. L *dēspicere*, to look *dē-* or down upon, becomes OF-MF *despire*, with certain forms in *despis-*, whence perh ME *despisen*, whence 'to *despise*'; prob, however, ME *despisen* comes from OF-MF *despiser* (var *-ier*), whence OF-MF *despisable*, adopted by E; this OF-MF *despiser*, *-ier*, would derive from a VL *\*dēspectiāre* (from L *dēspicere*). L *dēspicere* has pp *dēspec*tus, whence the n *dēspectus* (gen *-ūs*), whence both the rare E *despect*, contempt, and OF-MF *despit* (EF-F *dépit*), adopted by ME, whence E *despite*; ME *despit* becomes, by aphesis, E *spite*; OF-MF *despit* has derivative v *despiter*, whence 'to *despite*', to despise (archaic). The phrase *in despite of*—whence by aphesis, *in spite of*—derives from (OF *en despit*, whence) MF *en despit de*, orig in contempt of.

10. L *dēspicere* has the syn mdfn *dēspicāri*, whence LL *dēspicābilis*, contemptible, whence E *despicable*.

11. L *spectāre*, to gaze at, has the important cpd *exspectāre*, usu eased to *expectāre*, to look *ex*, out,

connoting out for, whence 'to *expect*'; derivative LL *expectābilis*, L *expectātiō* (o/s *expectātiōn*-), ML *expectātivus*, the L presp *expectans*, o/s *expectant*-, and its ML derivative *expectantia*, yield resp E *expectable*, MF-EF—whence E—*expectation*, EF-F *expectative*, adopted by E, late MF-F—whence E—*expectant*, E *expectance*, with var *expectancy*.

12. L *inspicere*, to look *in* or into, to examine or study, has pp *inspectus*, whence 'to *inspect*'. Derivatives L *inspectiō* (o/s *inspectiōn*-), LL *inspectiuus* (ML *-ivus*), L *inspector*, yield E *inspection*, E *inspective*, E *inspector* (cf late EF-F *inspecteur*).

13. L *perspicere*, to look *per* or through, has pp *perspectus*, whence the ML derivative *perspectivus*, whence the E adj *perspective*; elliptical ML *perspectiva* (*ars*, art) becomes the OF-F n *perspective*, adopted by E. *Perspicere* has two L adjj:

*perspicāx*, able to see through, hence keen or acute, with o/s *perspicāc*-, whence (late MF-F *perspicace* and) E *perspicacious*, the (LL-)ML derivative *perspicācitās*, o/s *perspicācitāt*-, yielding (late MF-F *perspicacité* and) E *perspicacity*;

*perspicuus*, capable of being looked through, transparent, with derivative *perspicuitās*, whence E *perspicuous* and *perspicuity*.

14. L *prōspicere*, to look *prō* or forward, also to foresee, has pp *prōspectus*, whence the n *prōspectus* (gen *-ūs*), whence E *prospect*; 'to *prospect*', on the other hand, derives from L *prōspectāre*, to look forward, an int of *prōspicere*. On the L pp *prōspectus* are built LL *prōspectiō*, o/s *prōspectiōn*-, LL *prōspectiuus* (ML *-ivus*), suitable for getting a view from, and LL *prōspector*, one who foresees, the n *prōspectus*, whence, resp, E *prospection*, E *prospective*, E *prospector* (only in form, the Min sense deriving from 'to *prospect*'), F and E *prospectus*, lit a forward view.

15. L *respicere*, to turn round (implied by *re*-, back) to look at, hence to feel a regard, or admiration, for, has pp *respectus*, whence 'to *respect*', the n *respect* coming, perh via MF-F, from the L n *respectus* (gen *-ūs*). On the pp *respectus* are formed ML *respectābilis* and ML *respectīvus*, whence (late MF-F and) E *respectable* and (late MF-F *respectif*, f *-ive*, and) E *respective*. The L n *respectus* becomes OF-MF *respit* (F *répit*), whence E *respite*; derivative OF-MF *respiter* produces 'to *respite*'.

16. L *retrospicere*, to look *retro* or backwards, has pp *retrospectus*, whence the E *retrospect*, adj, n, v.

17. L *subspicere*, usu eased to *suspicere*, to raise one's head—*sub*, under, hence from under—in order to look at, hence to admire and, from the opp angle, to look at askance, has pp *suspectus*, whence, via MF-F, the E adj *suspect*; 'to *suspect*' derives, via EF-F *suspecter*, from LL *suspectāri*, int of *suspicere*. Derivative L *suspiciō* (*suspicere*+ abstract-n *-iō*), distrust, has acc *suspiciōnem*, whence OF-F *suspicion*, adopted by E; the F *soupçon*, however, derives, via OF-EF *sospeçon*, from LL *suspectiōnem*, acc of *suspectiō* (pp s

*suspect-*+*-iō*). L *suspicere* has derivative adj— influenced by *suspiciō*—*suspiciōsus*, whence MF *suspicieus*, whence E *suspicious*.

18. L *transpicere*, to see across, hence, loosely, to see through, has suggested *transpicuous*, transparent, clearly understood, anl with *conspicuous*.

'Disguised' Derivatives

19. OHG *spehōn*, to examine closely, to investigate (cf para 1), is id in Frankish: and from Frankish *spehōn* comes OF-MF *espier* (F *épier*), to watch closely, whence E 'to *espy*'; derivative MF *espiaille* yields E *espial*, a spying, a thing espied; derivative OF-MF *espie* (EF-F *épie*, archaic), a spying, hence one who espies or spies, is adopted by ME, which, by aphesis, converts it to *spie*, whence E *spy*. OF-MF *espier* passes into ME as *espien*, later *spien*, whence 'to *spy*'.

20. Id in origin with OF-MF *espie*, (a spying, hence) a spy, is It *spia*, whence the—prop, aug— It *spione*, whence MF-F *espion*, whence late MF-F *espionner*, to act as a spy, whence EF-F *espionnage*, (systematic or governmental) spying, whence E *espionage*.

**spectator.** See prec, para 5.

**specter, spectral, spectre.** See SPECTACLE, para 4.

**spectrum.** See SPECTACLE, para 4.

**specular.** See SPECTACLE, para 2.

**speculate, speculation, speculative, speculator, speculatory.** See SPECTACLE, para 2.

**speculum.** See SPECTACLE, para 2.

**sped:** pt, pp of 'to speed'.

**speech, speechify, speechless.** See SPARSE, para 10 (and heading).

**speed,** n and v (pt sped); **speedy.** 'To *speed*', to go, to fare (lit and fig), esp to fare successfully, but also to hasten ('The early bird . . .'), derives from ME *spēden*, to fare, esp to prosper, to hasten or go fast, from OE *spēdan*, to fare (lit and fig), esp prosperously, prob from the OE n *spēd*, the way one fares, esp prosperity, whence ME *spēde*, prosperity, speed, whence the E *speed*; derivative OE *spēdig*, prosperous, becomes ME *spēdi*, prosperous, swift, whence E *speedy*, swift. Cf OHG *spuot*, success, *spuōn*, to succeed, OS *spōdian*, MD *spoeden*, to succeed, D *spoed*, swiftness, haste, MD *spoedich*, *spuedich*, successful, swift, D *spoedig*, swift; and, further off, Skt *sphāyati*, he increases, and prob SPACE and SPARE.

**speer** or **speir.** See SPUR, para 3.

**spell** (1), a relief, a rest, and to relieve, to rest. The n derives from the v, which derives from OE *spelian*, to stand in, or take, another's place, from OE *spala*, a deputy: o.o.o.: perh akin to **pal**, E Romany *pal*, Continental Romany *plal*, var of *pral*, ult akin to and prob even derived from Skt *bhratr* (cf E BROTHER),

**spell** (2). See the 1st SPILL.

**spell** (3), a spoken word, a (short) story, a charm; to **spell** (pt **spelled**, **spelt**, pp **spelt**), to speak (obs), to name, to write, to name, in order, the letters of a word, whence the pa, vn **spelling**.

'To *spell*', in the last sense, derives from OF-MF

*espelir, espeler* (F *épeler*); the now only dia 'to *spell'* or speak, to relate, derives from OE *spellian*; both the OF and the OE vv are of Gmc origin, the latter prob deriving imm from OE *spell*, a story, a saying, speech or language, whence E *spell*, now only an incantation (esp magical, lit or fig): cf OFris *spel, spil*, OS and OHG *spel*, Go *spill*, ON *spiall* (*spjall*): o.o.o.

spelt (whence speltoid), a variety of wheat: OE *spelt*: LL *spelta*, perh of Gmc (E & M), perh of Pannonian origin (Walshe). With OE *spelt*, cf OHG *spelta, spelza*, MHG *spelte*, G *Spelt*.

spence, spencer. See PEND, para 18.

spend; spendthrift. See PEND, para 18.

sperm (whence spermic), spermaceti (for other cpds, see the element *-sperm*), spermary, spermatic, spermatium; spore (whence the SciL dim sporidium) —cf the element *-spora, sporo-*; sporadic.

1. *Sporadic* (cf F *sporadique*) derives from ML *sporadicus*, trln of Gr *sporadikos*, scattered (like seed), ad of Gr *spora*, a seed, a sowing, whence, prob via SciL *spora*, the E *spore*: and Gr *spora* is akin (Gr *-o-* in nn, *-e-* in vv) to Gr *speirein*, to sow: *speir-* is a var of the IE r *\*sper-*, to strew or scatter: f.a.e., SPARSE, para 2.

2. Gr *speirein* has derivative *sperma* (o/s *spermat-*), semen, hence seed or germ: whence, via LL *sperma* and MF *esperme* (F *sperme*), the ME *sperme*, E *sperm*. The derivative Gr adj *spermatikos* becomes LL *spermaticus* and MF-F *spermatique*, whence E *spermatic*; on the LL s *spermat-* is formed the SciL *spermatium*—cf SciL *spermarium* (formed from LL *sperma*), whence E *spermary*.

3. The ML, whence E, *spermaceti* = LL *sperma* + *cēti*, of a *cētus* or whale.

spet. See the 1st SPIT, para 2.

spew. See the 2nd SPIT, para 3.

sphacel, sphacelus (whence, anl, sphacelate and sphacelous).

*Sphacelus* is the SciL shape of Gr *sphakelos*, a convulsion, a painful spasm, a gangrene, app an *-elos* derivative of Gr *\*sphak-*, a var of IE *\*sphek-*, to draw, pull, tug, itself an extn of *\*sphe-*, to stretch. The Med *sphacel* derives from EF-F *sphacèle* (from Gr).

sphagnum, a peat moss: SciL: Gr *sphagnos*: o.o.o.

sphenoid: Gr *sphēnoeidēs*, wedge-shaped: *sphēno-*, c/f of *sphēn*, a wedge + *-eidēs*, -shaped, from *eidos*, form, shape.

sphere (n, hence v—esp as ensphere), spheric (now usu in extn spherical), spheroid; hemisphere, whence, anl, hemispherical; cf the element *-sphaera*, where also *-sphere, sphaero-, sphero-*.

1. *Spheroid* derives from L *sphaeroeides*, trln of Gr *sphairoeidēs*: *sphairo-*, c/f of *sphaira*, a ball, a sphere + *-eidēs*, -shaped, from *eidos*, a shape or form; *spheric*, adj, derives from LL *sphaericus*, trln of Gr *sphairikos*, adj of *sphaira*. Gr *sphaira*, Ionic *sphairē*, is o.o.o.

2. *Hemisphere* = EF-F *hemisphère* (MF *emispere*): LL *hemisphaerium*: Gr *hēmisphairion*: *hēmi-*, half + an *-ion* derivative of *sphaira*.

sphincter. See para 2 of:

sphinx, whence, anl, the adjj sphingal and sphingine.

1. Orig the *Sphinx* of Thebes, an oracular divinity, hence any such divinity, esp if a poser of difficult riddles, hence any enigmatic person—cf the *Sphinx* of Giza, near Cairo, a Gr naming of an Eg image—*sphinx* has come into both F and E —through L—from Gr *Σφίγξ*, gen *Σφιγγός*, *Sphingos*: from *sphingein*, to bind tightly, to squeeze or throttle: perh cf—without *n*—ON *spīkr*, a nail, and Let *spaiglis, spaigle*, a forked stick for catching crayfish, and—without *p(h)*— MIr *sēn* (? for *\*spig-no-*), a net: IE r, *\*spheig-*, var *sphīg-* to bind. (Hofmann.)

2. Gr *sphingein* has another derivative: *sphinktēr* (*σφιγκτήρ*), whence LL *sphincter*, E *sphincter*, the sphincter-muscle, which is contractile.

sphygmic and sphygmoid. Gr *sphugmos*, the pulse + E adj-suffix *-ic* and *-oid*.

spica, spical, spicant, spicate. See SPIKE, para 8.

spice, spicery. See SPECIAL, para 5.

spicilege. See the element *spici-*.

spick, fat, blubber. See the 2nd SPECK.

spick-and-span. See SPIKE, para 4.

spicose, spicous, spicula, spicular, spiculate, spicule, spiculum. See SPIKE, paras 8 and 9, and cf heading (latter part).

spicy. See SPECIAL (heading, s.f.).

spider. See SPAN, para 5.

spiel (n, v) and spieler. The 2nd, adopted from G and meaning a player, esp at cards, particularly if a gambler, derives from G *spielen*, to play, whence 'to spiel'; the derivative G n *Spiel* becomes AE and Aus E *spiel*, which, like the v, is sl, both with the additional sense of '(to utter) smooth, deceptive speech'. G *spielen*, MHG *spiln*, OHG *spilōn*, is akin to OFris *spilia* (n *spil* or *spel*), OE *spilian*, ON *spila*: o.o.o.

spiffing, spiffy. See SPIV.

spifflicate varies spifflicate, either a blend of *spill* and *suffocate* or a droll mdfn of 'to *suffocate*', with gradual weakening of sense.

Spig, a Spanish American, a Mexican, but orig and prob a Sp-speaking Negro, is short for the syn Spiggoty, which, for some lost reason, shows the influence of spigot on '*speaga* de Engleesh', esp perh in 'No *speaga* de Engleesh', I don't speak English. (Mathews.)

spigot, ME var *speget*, is perh of D or LG origin: cf D *spiegat*, a scupper (hole), and *spie*, a peg, plug, spigot: perh cf Prov *espigou*, a bung; prob cf next.

spike, n (whence spiky), hence v; spikenard; spitchcock and spatchcock; spick-and-span; spire (of grass; of church); prob spile, a peg, and perh the sep spigot; spoke of a wheel.—L cognates: spica (whence spical, spicose, spicous), spicant, spicate; spicula (whence, anl, spicular), spiculate (adj and v), spicule (whence, anl, spiculose, spiculous), spiculum.—Cognates without *s-*: the sep PIE, bird, and PIKE, a sharp point, the weapon. —Perh cf SPINE.

1. E-ME *spike* is akin to and prob it derives from OE *spīcing*, a large nail: cf esp ON *spíkr*, a spike, and *spík*, a splinter, which have cognates in Gmc and in Sl; note also L *spīca*, a sharp point, a spike, an ear of corn. The r *spīk-*, *spīc-*, seems, like L *spīna*, a thorn, r *spīn-*, to be an extn of an IE r *\*spī-*, *\*spei-*, a sharp point.

2. *Spikenard* is a trans of ML *spica nardi*, lit a sharp point of nard, hence the fragrant ointment prepared from a plant: ME *narde*, MF *narde* (F *nard*), L *nardus*, Gr *nardos*, (prob via Sem—cf H *nerd*—from) Skt *nalada*, the spikenard plant of India.

3. *Spitchcock*, an eel split and cooked, derives from ME *\*spiche*, a spike+*coke*, a cook; *spatchcock*, a fowl split and grilled after a hasty killing, is a mdfn of *spitchcock*, influenced by de*spatch*, speed.

4. *Spick and span* is short for *spick and span-new*, a redup (prompted by *spick*, a dial var of *spike*) of ME-E *span-new*, from ON *spänn* (or *spän*) *nȳr*, lit 'chip-new'—as fresh and clean as a chip newly chopped off; cf, sem, 'as *bright* as a new *pin*'. ON *nȳr* is akin to E NEW, and ON *spänn* to syn OHG *span*, to OE *spōn* (E SPOON) and to Gr *sphēn*, a wedge (cf the element *spheno-*).

5. *Spile*, a splinter (now only dial), a wooden peg or pin, a spigot (dial), comes from MLG *spile*, splinter, wooden-peg, akin to syn MD *spile*, MD-D *spijl*, MHG *spīl*, a spear-point, and to ON *spila*, a skewer, Let *spihle*, a wooden pin, Gr *spīlas*, *-os*, a sharp rock, a reef: Gmc *spīl-* is app, like *spic* (\**spik-*) and *spin-*, an extn of IE *\*spī-*, *\*spei-*, a sharp point.

6. Certainly akin to *spike* is the *spoke* of a wheel: ME *spoke*, earlier *spake*: OE *spāca*, akin to OHG *speihha*, MHG-G *Speiche*, MD *speke*, *speec*, D *speek*, MLG *spēke*.

7. E *spire*, a slender stalk or blade of grass, hence a tapering top-end, as in '*spire* of a church', derives from ME *spire*, earlier *spir*, a blade of grass, from OE *spīr*: cf ON *spīra*, MLG *spīr*, a stalk, and MD *spier*, a blade of grass: app yet another extn (*spīr-*) of IE *\*spī-*, *\*spei-*, a sharp point.

## L *spīca* and its derivatives

8. L *spīca*, sharp point (as in a spike), an ear of corn, is adopted by learnèd and SciE. Derivative *spīcāre*, to furnish with ears of corn or with sharp points, or spikes, has presp *spīcans*, o/s *spīcant-*, whence E *spicant* and pp *spīcātus*, whence the E adj *spicate*.

9. L *spīca* has dim *spīculum*, a little sharp point, hence a dart, adopted by learnèd E, with SciL var *spicula* and with E derivative *spicule*, whence, anl, the adj *spicular*; derivative L *spīculāre*, to furnish with sharp points, to sharpen, has pp *spīculātus*, whence the E adj and v *spiculate*.

**spikenard.** See prec, para 2.

**spile,** n. See SPIKE, para 5.

**spill** (1), a splinter, hence a slender piece or roll of anything, whence **spillikin,** var **spilikin,** is partly a var of *spell*, a splinter (ME-OE *speld*, akin to

OHG *spaltan*, MHG-G *spalten*, to split: cf SPALE), and partly from *spile* (q.v. at SPIKE), and, perh, partly from MD *spille* (D *spil*), a spindle.

**spill** (2), to destroy, kill, hence to mar or maim, hence to punish (all obs), hence to cause to fall, to flow out or over, whence the n: ME *spillen*: OE *spillan*, which has syn cognate *spildan*: cf ON *spilla*, to destroy (cf Sw *spilla*, to spill), MD-D and LG *spillen*, MD *spilden*, OHG *spildan*, to squander, and ult OHG *spaltan*, MHG-G *spalten*, to split, and the 1st SPILL.

2. From 'to *spill*' comes *spilth*, a spilling, an effusion, prob after *tilth* from 'to *till*'.

**spin.** See SPAN, para 3.

**spinach** comes, by aphesis, from MF *espinach*, *espinache* (var *espinage* and *espinoche*), thence, with different suffix, MF *espinard(e)*, F *épinard*: ML *spinachia* or *-acia*, *spinachium* or *-acium*: (perh via Sp *espinaca*—cf Andalusian Ar *isbinākh* —from) Ar *isbānakh*, earlier *isfānākh*: Per *isfānākh*, var *isfānāj*. The medieval Sp phase, which introduces *p* for *b*, perh shows the influence of the Ar-Per form *ispānukh*; it was the Arabs who introduced the spinach into Spain, whence it spread to the rest of Europe. (Webster; B & W; Prati.)

**spinal.** See SPINE, para 2.

**spindle.** See SPAN, para 4.

**spine** (whence **spineless** and **spiny**), **spinal,** Min **spinel** or **spinelle,** **spinescent** (whence **spinescence**), **spinet** (Mus), **spinney,** **spinose** (whence, anl, the var **spinous**), **spinosity,** **spinule** (whence, anl, **spinulate** and **spinulose**).—**pinion** (machinery); **pinnacle,** n hence v; sep FIN (whence FINNY).

1. E-ME *spine* derives, via OF-MF *espine*, from L *spīna*, a thornbush (partly superseded by *spīnus*), hence a prickle and, by development of sense, the spine of the back: akin, on the one hand, to such other extnn of IE *\*spī-* (\**spei-*), a sharp point, as *spike*, q.v., and *spile* and *spire*; and, on the other, perh to L *pinna*, a feather, without the IE int prefix *s-* and with shortened vowel.

2. L *spīna* has LL adj *spīnālis*, of the human spine, whence (EF-F and) E *spinal*; the derivative L adj *spīnōsus* yields E *spinose*, and the LL offshoot *spīnōsitās*, o/s *spīnōsitāt-*, yields *spinosity*. The derivative LL *spīnescere*, to be covered with thorns, has presp *spīnescens*, o/s *spīnescent-*, whence E *spinescent*; and the dim *spīnula* yields F and E *spinule*.

3. Derivative L *spīnētum* (*spīna*, *spīn*us, thornbush+*-ētum*, connoting 'plantation', as in *arborētum*) has the VL var *\*spīnēta*, whence OF-MF *espinei* (varr *espinoi*, *espinoie*, cf F *épinaie*), whence, by aphesis, E *spinney* (cf the archaic syn *spinet*, direct from L).

4. L *spīna* is retained by It, which forms two dimm:

*spinella*, var *spinello*, a little thorn, hence— from its 'thorny' crystals—that mineral which F derivatively names *spinelle*, adopted by E, which varies it to *spinel*, now more common;

*spinetta*, a little thorn, hence the Mus *spinetta* (obs var *spinetto*)—from those parts of the

mechanism which are shaped like little thorns—
an instrument that becomes EF *espinette* (F
*épinette*), whence, by aphesis, E *spinet*,—the It
Mus name perh aided by the Venetian musician
Giovanni *Spinetti* ('Little Thorns'), who flourished
in the latter half of C15 (Enci It).

### Cognates without *s-*

5. Perh akin to L *spīna* is L *pinna*, a feather,
whence, by shape-resemblance, certain tech objects,
esp what E calls a *pinion*, imm from MF-F *pignon*,
from VL *\*pinniōnem*, acc of *\*pinniō*, a mdfn of
L *pinna*. Cf E *pinnate*.

6. L *pinna*, also from shape-resemblance, has,
in Arch, the sense 'a gable' (as MF-F *pignon* likewise has), a sense assumed by LL *pinnāculum* (lit
a small wing—influenced by L *penna*), whence
MF-F *pinacle*, whence E *pinnacle*, orig an Arch
term, hence—as for F *pinacle*—a summit in
general.

**spinel, spinelle.** See prec, para 4.

**spinescence, spinescent.** See SPINE, para 2.

**spinet.** See SPINE, para 3, s.f., for 'spinney';
para 4, for Mus instrument.

**Spinifex.** See the element *spini-*, para 2; cf
SPINE.

**spink,** a chaffinch. See FINCH.

**spinnaker,** a large 3-cornered sail, is o.o.o.: said
to derive from a famous yacht of the middle
1860's, The *Sphinx*.

**spinner,** whence **spinneret** (dim *-et*). See SPAN
(heading).

**spinney.** See SPINE, para 3.

**spinose, spinosity.** See SPINE, para 2.—**spinous:**
id (heading).

**spinster.** See SPAN, para 3.

**spinule.** See SPINE, para 2, s.f.

**spiny.** See SPINE (heading).

**spiracle.** See SPIRIT, para 6.

**Spiraea.** See the 2nd SPIRE, para 4.

**spiral.** See the 2nd SPIRE, para 2.

**spirant.** See SPIRIT, para 6.

**spirate, spiration.** See SPIRIT, para 6.

**spire** (1), whether of grass or of a church. See
SPIKE, para 7.

**spire** (2), a twist or a coil, a curl or a whorl;
**spiral,** adj and n; **spirillum; Spiraea;** cf the elements
*spiri-* and *spiro-* (1).—**spart, sparteine, spartium,
esparto.**

1. This *spire*, adopted from EF-F, comes from
L *spīra*, trln of syn Gr *speira*, perh for *\*speria*, s
and r *\*sper-*, from the IE r, *\*sper-* (var *\*spher-*),
to turn, to twist: cf the Gr *sparton*, a rope, and
*spartos*, the broom (shrub), OLith *spartas*, a bond,
a fetter, Lith *springti*, to strangle.

2. L *spīra* has the derivative ML adj *spīrālis*,
whence the (EF-F and) E *spiral*; the E n *spiral*
derives from the EF-F n *spirale* (from the EF adj
*spiral*); hence 'to *spiral*'.

3. L *spīra* has dim *spīrillum*, adopted by SciE.

4. Gr *speira* has—? via an adj *\*speiraios*—the
derivative *speiraia*, a genus of shrubs, whence L
*spiraea*, adopted by Bot.

5. The related Gr *spartos*, the shrub we call
'broom', has, in Aristotle, the var *sparton*, whence
L *spartum*, whence both E *spart*, the Sp broom,
and Sp *esparto*, a tough grass of which cordage and
baskets are made, a term adopted by E. From L
*spartum* comes SciL *Spartium* (Bot), whence Chem
extracts *sparteine* or *spartein* (Chem suffix *-ine, -in*).

**spirillum.** See prec, para 3.

**spirit** (n, hence adj and v—esp in the int
**inspirit**), whence the pa **spirited, spiritism, spiritless,
spiritous, spirits; spirital** and **spiritual** (adj, hence
n), whence **spiritualism** (cf the F *spiritualisme*)—
**spiritualist** (cf F *spiritualiste*), whence, anl,
**spiritualistic—spiritualize** (cf EF-F *spiritualiser*);
**spirituality; spirituel; spirituous,** whence, anl,
**spirituosity; spiritus;—spright** (obs; whence
**sprightly),** var of **sprite** (whence the obs **spritely);
esprit,** esp in **esprit de corps.**—Simple derivatives
of L *spīrāre*, to breathe: **spiracle,** whence, anl,
**spiracular; spirant,** adj and n; **spirate,** adj and n;
**spiration.**—Prefix-Compounds of L *spīrāre*: **aspirant** (adj, n), **aspirata, aspirate** (adj—hence n—and
v), **aspiration, aspirative, aspirator** and **aspiratory**
(both, anl, from 'to *aspirate*'), **aspire** (whence the
pa **aspiring); conspiracy, conspirant, conspiration**
(whence, anl, **conspirative), conspirator** (whence
**conspiratorial), conspire** (whence **conspiring); expirant, expirate, expiration** (whence, anl, **expirator**
and **expiratory), expire** (whence **expiry); inspirable,
inspirant, inspirate** (obs), **inspiration** (whence
**inspirational** and, anl, **inspirative), inspirator**
(whence, anl, **inspiratory), inspire** (whence the pa
**inspired** and the pa, vn **inspiring); perspirable,
perspirant, perspiration** (whence, anl, **perspirative**
and **perspiratory), perspire** (whence **perspiring);
respirable, respiration** (whence **respirational** and,
anl, **respirative), respirator, respiratory, respire;
suspiration** (whence, anl, **suspirative), suspire;
transpiration** (whence, anl, **transpiratory), transpire.**

### Echoic

1. The base is afforded by L *spīrāre*, to breathe,
s and r *spīr-*, as clearly echoic as one could wish:
cf, for echoism, the Gr *anemos*, wind, L *anima*,
breath, life, soul. The L n *spīritus* (gen *-ūs*), a
breathing, a breath, the breath of life, life, the
soul, has s *spīrit-* and r *spīr-*, and therefore (E & M)
stands to *spīrāre* as L *halitus*, an exhalation, does
to *halāre*, to breathe, themselves echoic, with the
effortful *h-* performing much the same office as
the sibilant *s*; cf the effort expressed—and entailed
—by Gr *pneuma*, breath, air, wind.

### L *spīritus*

2. L *spīritus* becomes OF *espirit*, MF-F *esprit*,
whence, by aphesis—unless (as is more prob)
direct from L—the E *spirit*; the Chem sense, which
leads to the liquor sense (usu in pl *spirits*), derives
from the ML of the alchemists.

3. L *spīritus* acquires in LL the sense 'the
Divine spirit' (esp as *spīritus sanctus*); the LL adj
*spīritālis*, breathed, (but esp) of the Holy Spirit,
hence pure, becomes E *spirital*, now only in the

adv *spiritally*, by means of the breath, by breathing. *Spīritālis* is, by ML, modified to *spīrituālis*, whence —perh via MF *espirituel*, EF-F *spirituel*—the E *spiritual*; derivative ML *spīrituālitās* becomes MF *espiritualité*, EF-F *spiritualité*, and, perh independently, E *spirituality*. In C17, F *spirituel* takes— after *esprit*—the senses 'ethereal' and 'witty', partly adopted by E; in C16, F forms, from L *spīritus* in its ML Chem and Med senses, the adj *spiritueux*, f *spiritueuse*, with liquor sense in C18; whence the E *spirituous*. *Spīritus* itself is retained by learnèd E, whether phon or pharmaceutical.

4. F *esprit de corps*, spirit of a body of men, corporate honour, has been adopted by E, esp in the combatant Services.

5. MF-F *esprit* becomes, by aphesis, ME *spryt*, whence E *sprite*, var *spright*, orig the spirit, inspiration, later a ghost, finally an elf.

L *spīrāre*: Simple Derivatives

6. L *spīrāre*, to breathe, has the foll simple derivatives relevant to E:
*spīrāculum*, an air- or breathing-hole, whence E *spiracle*, in Geol a vent, in Zoo a breathing orifice; presp *spīrans*, o/s *spīrant-*, whence the E adj and n *spirant*;
pp *spīrātus*, whence the E adj, hence n, *spirate*; *spīrātiō*, o/s *spīrātiōn-*, whence E *spiration*, mostly in Theo: the Divine breath, the Holy Spirit.

L *spīrāre*: Prefix-Compound Derivatives

7. L *adspīrāre*, to breathe *ad* or towards or upon, usu in eased form *aspīrāre*, has presp *aspīrans*, o/s *aspīrant-*, which yields—prob via F—the E adj and n *aspirant*; and pp *aspīrātus*, whence E *aspirate*, derivative L *aspīrātiō*, o/s *aspīrātiōn-*, and LL *aspīrātiuus*, ML *-ivus*, aspirated (Gram), yield *aspiration*—prob via OF-F *aspiration*—with Gram sense deriving from 'to *aspirate*', and *aspirative*. 'To *aspire*' comes from OF-F *aspirer* (from L *aspīrāre*).

8. L *conspīrāre*, to breathe together, hence to agree, hence to plot together, becomes MF (? OF)-F *conspirer*, whence 'to *conspire*'; derivative L *conspīrātiō*, o/s *conspīrātiōn-*, and *conspīrātor*— both formed on the pp *conspīrāt*us—yield OF-F *conspiration* and MF-F *conspirateur*: whence *conspiration* (rare) and, imm from AF *conspiratour*, E *conspirator*. The presp *conspīrans*, o/s *conspīrant-*, gives us the adj, hence n, *conspirant*. *Conspiracy*, superseding *conspiration*, derives from ME *conspiracie*, adopted from MF *conspiracie*, var of *conspiratie* (? anl from *conspiration*).

9. L *exspīrāre*, to breathe *ex* or out, to exhale, usu in eased form *expīrāre*, becomes OF-MF *espirer*, MF-F *expirer*, whence 'to *expire*'. The presp *expīrans*, o/s *expīrant-*, yields the E n *expirant*; pp *expīrātus* yields the phon adj *expirate*; derivative L *expīrātiō*, o/s *expīrātiōn-*, yields (late MF-F and) E *expiration*.

10. L *inspīrāre*, to breathe in or into, LL to breathe religious or divine feeling into, becomes OF-F *inspirer*, whence 'to *inspire*', whence *inspirable*. The presp *inspīrans*, o/s *inspīrant-*, yields the rare n *inspirant*; on the pp *inspīrātus* (whence obs 'to *inspirate*') are formed LL *inspīrātiō*, o/s *inspīrātiōn-*, and LL *inspīrātor*, whence, via OF-F *inspiration* and late MF-F *inspirateur*, the E *inspiration* and *inspirator*.

11. L *perspīrāre*, to breathe *per*, through or throughout, becomes EF *perspirer*, with the sense 'to sweat', whence E 'to *perspire*' (not in L); EF *perspiration* and *perspirable* (both, anl, from *perspirer*) are adopted by E; E *perspirant*, a sweat gland, derives from 'to *perspire*'—after L *perspīrant-*, o/s of *perspīrans*, presp of *perspīrāre*.

12. L *respīrāre*, to breathe back or again, to inhale and then exhale, becomes OF-F *respirer*, whence 'to *respire*'; derivative LL *respīrābilis* yields late MF-F, whence E, *respirable*; on the pp *respīrātus* are formed L *respīrātiō*, o/s *respīrātiōn-*, and LL *respīratōrius*, whence late MF-F, whence E, *respiration* and E *respiratory*, the latter prompting the anl *respirator*.

13. L *subspīrāre*, to breathe *sub-* or from under, to sigh, mostly in the eased form *suspīrāre*, yields OF-MF *suspirer* (F *soupirer*) and, app independently, E 'to *suspire*'; derivative L *suspīrātiō*, o/s *suspīrātiōn-*, leads to E *suspiration*.

14. ML *transpīrāre*, lit to breathe across or over, hence through, becomes EF-F *transpirer*, with fig sense arising in C18, whence 'to *transpire*'; derivative ML *transpīrātiō*, o/s *transpīrātiōn-*, becomes EF-F *transpiration*, adopted by E.

**spirits** (liquor). See prec, para 2.

**spiritual, spiritualism, spiritualist, spirituality, spiritualize.** See SPIRIT, para 3—and heading.

**spirituel.** See SPIRIT, para 3.

**spirituous.** See SPIRIT, para 3, s.f.

**spiritus.** See SPIRIT, para 3, s.f.

**spirt.** See SPROUT, para 3.

**spit** (1), a spike holding meat over fire, whence **turnspit**, derives from ME *spitte*, var *spite*, from OE *spitu*: cf the syn OHG-MHG *spiz*, G *Spiess*, MD-D *spit*: words akin to OHG *spizzi*, MHG *spitze*, G *Spitz*, sharp, themselves akin to L *spīna*, a thorn, and esp to L *spīca*, a sharp point, an ear of corn, therefore to E SPIKE (f.a.e.).

2. MD *spit* has var *spet*, whence—or from some medieval Gmc cognate—the Sp *espeto* and the It and F dial *spet*, adopted by E; this small barracuda is named 'the spit' because of its sharp nose and long narrow body.

**spit** (2), to eject saliva or phlegm (whence the n **spit**), pt **spat** (occ **spit**), pp **spat** (archaic **spitten**, as in the **spitten image**, turned by f/e into **the spitting image**); presp and vn **spitting**, agent **spitter**; **spitfire**, one who, fig, spits fire;—**spittle**, **spittoon** (*spit*, n+euphonic *-t-+-oon*, It *-one*: cf It *ballone* and *cartone*);—**sputum**, whence **sputative**, tending to spit—prob after *putative*; **spue** (now only dial), var of **spew**, v, hence n; **conspue**;—**spout**, v (whence agent **spouter** and pa, vn **spouting**) and n (whence **waterspout**).

1. 'To *spit*' derives from OE *spittan*, intimately

related to the syn OE *spǣtan*, which has, in part, caused the pt, pp *spat*: cf also ON *spȳta* (Da *spytte*) and G *spützen*: echoic.

2. The n *spit*, that which one spits, has dim *spittle*, saliva.

3. Akin to OE *spittan* and *spǣtan* is L *spūtāre*, to spit, from *spūtum*, saliva, adopted by E, esp for (Med) phlegm; *spūtum* is itself from *sput*us, the pp of *spūere*, to spit.

4. Akin to L *spūere* is OE *spīwan*, *spiwian*, ME *spiwen*, *speowen*, later *spewen*, E 'to *spew*', to spit out, esp to vomit: cf OFris *spīa*, OS *spīwan*, OHG *spīwan*, MHG *spēwen*, *spien*, G *speien*, to spew, to spit, MD *spouwen*, *spuen* and, as in D, *spuwen*, Öo *speiwan*, to spit, ON *spȳja*, to spew.—L *spūere* has the cpd *conspūere* (int *con*-), to spit upon, to reject contemptuously, whence, perh via EF-F *conspuer*, the E 'to *conspue*'.

5. L *conspūere* becomes Port *cuspir*, to spit, whence *cuspideira*, a spittoon, whence E *cuspidor*—a form influenced by Port *cuspidor*, a spitter (from *cuspir*): cf Sp *escupidera*, a spittoon, from *escupir*, to spit (L *ex*, out of + *conspūere*).

6. Akin to *spit* is 'to *spout*', ME *spouten*, to spout, to vomit, akin to D *spuiten*, Sw *sputa*, to spout. Prob cf SPLUTTER.

7. *Spit*, *spew*, *spout* should also be aligned with MHG-G *spucken*, to spit, Lith *spiáuti*, to spit (*spiáuju*, I spit, OB *pljujǫ*), Gr *ptúein*, to spit, Skt *sthīvati*, var *kṣīvati*, he spits. The IE r is *spiēu*- or *spīu*- or *spiŭ*-, var *sphiēu*-, etc.; the Gr *ptúein* has the revelatory mdfn *pūtizein* and, moreover, suggests that IE *spiēu*- (etc.) is a reinforced (IE int prefix *s*-) or more obviously echoic var of a basic *piēu*-, *pīu*-, *piŭ*-.

**spitchcock.** See SPIKE, para 3.

**spite, spiteful.** See SPECTACLE, para 9.

**spitfire.** See the 2nd SPIT (heading).

**spitting image, the.** See 2nd SPIT (heading).

**spittle.** See 2nd SPIT, para 2.

**spiv**, a shady practitioner of 'easy' money, was orig race-course cant, but, by 1950, almost Standard: o.o.o.: perh from dial *spif* (*spiff*), smart, dandified. Hence *spivvery*. (P.)

**splanchnic**, visceral. See the element *splanchno*-.

**splash**, v hence n, with dial var **splosh**, is an *s*-int of the echoic **plash**. Derivative: *splashy*.

**splat** (of chair). See PLANE, para 22.

**splatter.** See SPAT, s.f.

**splay**, adj, n, v. See PLY, para 10.

**spleen**, whence **spleeny** (-y, adj); **splenetic** **splenial, splenic.**

1. E *spleen*, the milt, formerly reputed to be the source or seat of emotions ranging from violent mirth (obs meaning) to ill-temper and anger (cf 'to vent one's *spleen*') derives less prob from OF-MF *esplen* (from LL) than imm from LL *splēn*, itself from Gr *splēn*, akin to Av *spereza*, OSl *slezena*, OIr *selg*—and to the *s*-less L *liēn* and Skt *plīhán*-, o/s of *plīhá*, and, with *b* for *p*, the Lith *blužnis* (? for *lihēn*). The IE r *spelegh*- extn *speleghen*, with varr in *sph*-, has contr *splegh*- and *spleghn*-,

and is app a reinforcement (IE int prefix *s*-) of *plegh*-, *pleghn*. (E & M; Hofmann.)

2. The derivative Gr adj *splēnikos* becomes ML *splēnicus*, whence E *splenic*, of the spleen; the LL mdfn *splēnēticus* (var *splēnīticus*) yields E *splenetic*; the Gr *splēnion* (prop a dim of *splēn*), a bandage, strictly one that covers the spleen, becomes ML *splēnium*, a plaster (Med), a patch, and *splēnium* has prompted the E adj *splenial*, used by An and Zoo.

**splendent, splendescent.** See para 2 of:

**splendid; splendor** (AE) or **splendour**, whence both **splendiferous** (*splendor* + connective -*i*- + -*ferous*, -bearing or -bringing), whence, anl, the sl **splendacious**, and **splendorous; splendent** and **re-splendent, resplendence** or **resplendency, splend-escent.**

1. *Splendid* comes, prob via MF-F *splendiae*, from L *splendidus*, which, like L *splendor*, comes from *splendēre*, to shine; E *splendor* comes from L *splendor*, either directly or via OF-F *splendeur*. L *splendēre*, s and r *splend*-, is akin to Gr *splēndos*, ashes, and to Skt *sphuliṅgas*, a spark: IE r, *splend*-, an *s*- extn of *plend*-, brightness; MIr *lēss*, light, suggests that the ult IE r is *plēd*-, extn *splēd*-. The C languages show the illuminating catena, *lānd*-, *plānd*, *splānd*, often without the *d*; the OC r is app *lān*-, extn *land*-, with varr *plan(d)*- and *splan(d)*-; cf MIr *láinn*, brilliant, shining, Ga *lannair*, brilliance, Mx *loan*, light, brightness, and Cor *splān*, late Cor *splādn*, brilliant, *splānna*, to shine.

2. L *splendēre* has presp *splendens*, o/s *splendent*-, whence the E adj *splendent*; the derivative L inch *splendescere*, to become bright, has presp *splend-escens*, o/s *splendescent*-, whence the E adj *splendescent*.

3. The L cpd *resplendēre* (*re*-, again, used int), to shine brightly, has presp *resplendens*, o/s *re-splendent*-, whence E *resplendent*; derivative LL *resplendentia*, brilliance, yields *resplendence*.

**splenetic, splenial, splenic, splenium.** See SPLEEN, para 2.

**splice.** See FLINT, para 6.

**splint.** See FLINT, para 4.

**splinter.** See FLINT, para 4.

**split.** See FLINT, para 5.

**splosh.** See SPLASH.

**splotch** prob derives from OE *splott*, a spot, much as *blotch* from *blot*.

**splutter** is an echoic (*spl*-) var of *sputter*: cf *splatter*, from *spatter*: and *sputter* itself prob derives from *sput*, as *spatter* does from *spat*, but, from another angle, *sputter* is an *s*- reinforcement of *putter*, v. All these vv (with derivative nn) are echoic.

**spoil**, n and v (whence **spoilage** and **spoiler** and pa, vn **spoiling**); **spoliate, spoliation** (whence, anl, **spoliative**—cf the F *spoliatif*), **spoliator, spolium**;—**despoil, despoliation.**

1. The n *spoil* derives, by aphesis, from OF-MF *espoille*, itself from OF-MF *espoiller* (var -*ier*), whence ME *spoilen*, whence 'to *spoil*': and OF-MF

*espoiller*, *-ier*, derives from L *spoliāre*, to strip (a beast's) hide or skin, from *spolium*, a hide or skin stripped off, hence arms stripped from an enemy, hence booty: cf the syn Gr *spolas*, itself akin to several Gr words in *spal-*; indeed, the IE r is prob *\*spal-*, to strip off; therefore cf SPALE.

2. L *spolium* is retained by Eccl E; *spoliāre* has pp *spoliātus*, whence the obsol *spoliate*, to plunder. Derivatives *spoliātiō*, o/s *spoliātiōn-*, and *spoliātor*, become E *spoliation* (perh via late MF-F) and *spoliator* (cf late MF-F *spoliateur*).

3. The cpd *dēspoliāre* (*dē-*, from, used int) becomes OF-MF *despoiller* (EF-F *dépouiller*), whence 'to *despoil*'; derivative LL *dēspoliātiō*, o/s *dēspoliātiōn-*, yields *despoliation*.

**spoke** (of wheel). See SPIKE, para 6.

**spoke** (pt), **spoken**. See SPARSE, heading and para 9.

**spokesman**. See SPARSE, para 11.

**spoliate, spoliation, spoliator**. See SPOIL, para 2.

**spondaic, spondee**. See DESPOND, para 6.

**spondulicks, -ics, -ix**, sl for 'money', usu stated to be o.o.o., perh comes from Gr *\*spondulika*, mock-learnedly derived from LGr *spondulia*, pl of *spondulion* (Gr *sphondulion*), a vertebra, a mussel or an oyster, a voting pebble: cf, sem, the cowries formerly used in some Asian and, as still, in many African countries for money.

**sponge**, whence **spongy**. See FUNGUS, para 2.

**sponk**. See SPUNK.

**sponsor**. See DESPOND, para 5.—For **sponsal**, cf SPOUSAL.

**spontaneity, spontaneous**. The adj comes from LL *spontāneus*, of one's own free will, from L *sponte*, as in *mea sponte*, of (lit, with) my own will, *sponte*, voluntarily, prop the abl of *\*spons*, itself o.o.o., but perh, as the ancient Romans thought: from L *spondēre*, to promise.—The L adj becomes MF-F *spontané*, whence late EF-F *spontanéité*, whence E *spontaneity*.

**spoof**, n, whence v, derives from *Spoof*, a game invented, with this arbitrary name, by the E comedian Arthur Roberts (1852–1933).

**spook** (whence **spooky**): D *spook*: MD *spooc*, akin to the syn MLG *spōk*, G *Spuk*, cf Sw *spok*, a scarecrow: o.o.o.

**spool**: ME *spole*: MD *spoele* (D *spoel*), akin to G *Spule*, MHG *spuole*, OHG *spuola*: perh cf SPALE.

**spoon** (n, hence v), whence **spoonbill** (a bird having a spoon-shaped bill);—**spade**, whether implement (whence v) or card; **spatha** or **spathe**, whence **spathal, spatula** (whence **spatular**), **spatulate, spatule; spay; espalier; epaulette,** AE **epaulet; épée**.

1. *Spoon*, a chip of wood (obs), hence a spoon (cf the flat little wooden spoons used for eating ice-cream), derives from ME *spon*, spoon, chip, from OE *spōn*, a chip: cf ON *spōnn*, chip, spoon, and OHG-MHG *spān*, G *Span*, a chip, MD *spaen*, D *spaan*, a spoon: perh cf Gr *sphēn*, a wedge.

2. OE *spōn*, OHG *spān*, etc., are prob *-n-* extnn of an IE r *\*spē-*, var *\*spā-*, anything flat (? and wide); this IE r has another extn—one in *-t-* (*-th-, -d-*), as in E *spade*, from OE *spaedu* or *spadu*, akin to OFris *spada*, OS *spado*, *spato*, MHG *spatel* (dim), EG *spatten*, G *Spaten*, MD-D *spade*, ON *spathi*, a spade; also to L *spatha*, Gr *spathē*, a broadsword, a spatula. The card sense derives from Sp *espada* (L *spatha*, *spata*), a sword, from the sword-device on the corresp Sp cards.

3. Gr *spathē* becomes L *spatha*, whence the BotE *spatha* and the BotF, hence BotE, *spathe*.

4. L *spatha* has var *spata*, whence the dim *spatula*, in LL an animal's shoulder, but orig a spatula, hence the E word *spatula*, a flat, spoon-like implement for spreading pastes or paints; the var *spatule* is adopted from MF-F. SciL coins *spatulātus*, spoon-shaped, whence E *spatulate* (cf the F *spatulé*).

5. L *spatha*, a broadsword, yields C10 F *spede*, later—as still in MF—*espee*, whence OF-MF *espeer*, to pierce or cut with a sword, whence AF *espeier*, whence, by aphesis, E 'to *spay*', to cut out the ovaries of ewe, sow, mare, cow, etc.

6. OF-MF *espee* becomes EF-F *épée*, adopted by E, esp in fencing; LL *spatula*, shoulder, becomes OF *espalde*, *\*espadle*, *espalle*, later *espaule*, whence EF-F *épaule*, with EF-F dim *épaulette*, orig a shoulder-piece, later a badge of officer's rank and, as such, becoming E *epaulette*.

7. LL *spatula*, shoulder, becomes It *spalla*, shoulder, whence It *spalliera*, a support, whence EF-F *espalier*, soon acquiring the modern sense, adopted by E.

**spoonerism**: *Spoonerism*: *-ism*, tacked onto the Rev. Dr William *Spooner* (1844–1930), who, for many years Warden of New College, Oxford, is credited with a few genuine and many apocryphal felicities of the '*blushing crow*' for '*crushing blow*' variety.

**spoor**. See SPUR, para 2.

**sporadic**. See SPERM, para 1.

**sporangium**. See the element *sporangi-*.

**spore**. See SPERM, para 1.

**sporo-** words. Cf the element *-spora*.

**sporran**. See PURSE, para 3.

**sport, sportive**. See the 3rd PORT, para 7.

**spot**, n (whence **spotty**) and v (whence the pa **spotted**, the agent **spotter**, the pa, vn **spotting**). 'To *spot*', ME *spotten*, derives from ME *spot*, n, retained by E: and ME *spot* is related to the syn MD *spot*, *spotte*, EFris *spot*, and to ON *spotti*, a (small) bit: perh cf SPAT.

**spousals, spouse**. Cf *espouse*, but see DESPOND, para 4.

**spout**. See the 2nd SPIT, para 5.

**spraddle**. See SPRAWL.

**sprag**. See the 1st SPRAY.

**sprain**. See the 2nd PRESS, para 13.

**sprat**, a small herring, hence—from its small size and value—a sixpence (sl): ME *sprot* or *sprotte*: OE *sprott*: cf MD-D *sprot*: o.o.o.: if regarded as any *young* herring, OE *sprott* is perh akin to OE *sprote*, a sprout.

**sprawl** (v, hence n; whence agent **sprawler and**

pa, vn **sprawling**, and adj **sprawly; spraddle**. 'To *sprawl*', ME *spraulen*, derives from OE *sprēawlian*: cf OHG *spratalōn* and ON *sprökla*. An old Gmc var lies behind the dial *spraddle*—perh influenced by *straddle*, q.v. at STRIDE.

**spray** (1), a young or small shoot, a twig (now Sc), hence, collectively, as in 'a spray of clematis': ME *spray*, akin to the syn Da *sprag*, Sw dial *spragge*, which have, moreover, assisted in the genesis of E *sprag*, a wooden billet or prop, or the brake of a vehicle: intimately related to OE *spraec*, a shoot, cf ON *sprek*, a stick, to which, in its turn, E *sprig*, ME *sprigge*, must be related—cf LG *sprikk*, Fris *sprik* or *sprikke*.

**spray** (2), n and v, (to scatter) small drops of flying water: EE *spray*, to sprinkle: MD *sprayen*, *spraeyen*: cf MHG *spraewen*, to spray, to fly, G *sprühen*, to spray, and OHG-MHG *spriu*, G *Spreu*, chaff (which 'flies about'): ? cf L *spargere*, to scatter (Walshe), q.v. at SPARSE, as MD *spreyen*, to spread, perh suggests.

**spread** (id in pt and pp), v, hence n (whence **spready**); whence **spreader** and pa, vn **spreading**; **spread eagle** and **spread-eagle**, adj and v.

1. 'To *spread*', ME *spreden*, OE *sprǣdan*, is akin to MD *spreden*, *spreeden*, *spreiden*, MLG *spreiden*, D *spreiden*, OHG and G *spreiten*, and several Scan words: OGmc etymon, *spraidjan* (Kluge). The OGmc r *spraid*, var *sprād-* and *sprēd-*, is app an extn of the IE *sprē-*, etc., itself perh a metathesis of that IE *sper-*, to scatter or distribute, which we see in Gr *speirein*, to sow by scattering.

2. The Her *spread eagle* has open, raised wings and extended legs, hence the adj *spread-eagle*, like such an eagle, and the v *spread-eagle*, to stretch (a living creature) out like one, whence the pa *spread-eagled*.

**spree; spreath**. *Spree*, earlier also *spray*, app derives, like the Sc *spreath* (var *spreagh*), booty, esp of cattle, hence a raid, esp on cattle, from Ga *sprēidh*: EIr *spréid*, var *spré*: prob, with reinforcement in *s-* (int), from, or, at the least, akin to, L *praeda*, booty—cf the Cor *prēdhya*, *prēdha*, to prey on, to live by prey, deduced from *prēth*, he preys on. Cf PREY.

**sprig**. See the 1st SPRAY, s.f.

**spright, sprightly**. See SPIRIT, para 5—and heading.

**spring**, whether as a leap or, derivatively, a source of water or a season (a re-beginning), derives from OE *spring*, itself from OE *springan*, to leap, whence, via ME *springen*, E 'to *spring*', with pt *sprang*, occ *sprung*, and with pp, hence pa, *sprung*, and presp and vn *springing*: cf OFris *springa*, OS *springan*, OHG *springan*, MHG-G *springen*, ON *springa*: prob cf, without *n*, the Gr *sperkh*esthai, to hasten, and Skt *spṛah*ayati, he desires, *spárdhatē*, he is emulous, and perh, without the IE int prefix *s-*, the OB *prǫga*, a locust (famed as a leaper): ? akin, ult, to the 2nd SPRAY.

2. The simple derivatives and the cpds are straightforward: e.g., the agent *springer* and the adj *springy*; and *springboard—springbok*, adopted from D, lit 'a leaping buck'—*springtide*. The SAfr *klipspringer*, a small antelope, is adopted from D, lit 'a cliff springer'—cf G *Klippe*, E CLIFF.

3. A *springe* or 'springing' trap for birds and quadrupeds, derives—after 'to *spring*'—from ME *sprenge*, from ME *sprengen*, to cause to leap, from OE *sprengan*, caus of *springan*.

**springbok**. See prec, para 2.

**springe**. See SPRING, para 3.

**sprinkle, sprinkler, sprinkling**. See SPARSE, para 8.

**sprint** (v, hence n), whence **sprinter** and **sprinting**, derives, by *e* to *i*, from ME *sprenten*, to run, to leap, which, prob like MHG *sprenzen*, OHG *sprinzan*, is perh of Scan origin: from the ON *sprenten*, later *spretta*, to leap or run; ME *sprenten*, however, perh derives from OE ge-*sprintan*, to (cause to) burst forth.

**sprit**, whence **spritsail**. See SPROUT, para 2.

**sprite, spritely**. See SPIRIT, para 5—and heading.

**sprocket**, occ **sproket**, is o.o.o.: perh a dim (*-et*), with vowel-change, of *sprag*, q.v. at the 1st SPRAY. (EW.)

**sprout**, v, hence n; **sprit; spirt** or **spurt**, v, hence n.

1. 'To *sprout*', ME *sprouten*, earlier *spruten*, derives from OE *sprūtan*: cf OFris *sprūta*, OS *sprūtan*, MHG *spriezen*, G *spriessen*, and the int MHG *sprützen*, G *spritzen*, MD *spruten*, *spruyten*, D *spruiten*. With the E n *sprout*, cf ME *sprote*, OE *sprota*, OHG *sprozzo*, G *Sprosse*, ON *sproti*. Cf the 2nd SPRAY.

2. Akin to OE *sprota*, a sprout, is OE *sprēot*, a pole, a spear, ME *sprete*, *spret*, E *sprit*, as in *bowsprit* (ME *bouspret*, prob from MLG *bochspret*, cf D *boegspriet*) and *spritsail*.

3. Akin to the naut *sprit* is the dial *sprit*, a sprout, from *sprit*, to sprout, from OE *spryttan*, intimately related to OE *sprūtan*; OE *spryttan* becomes ME *sprutten*, whence, by metathesis, 'to *spurt*' or gush, with var *spirt*.

**spruce**, the tree—'smart'—the v. See PRUSSIA, para 2.

**sprung**. See SPRING, para 1.

**spry**, nimble, lively: E from AE from E dial: prob Scan (cf Sw dial *sprygg*, very lively: EDD): perh from *spright*, q.v. at SPIRIT, para 5.

**spud**, a dagger (obs), a small spade for weed-removal, a digging-knife, hence, in dial (whence coll), a potato, whence '*Spud* Murphy', both the vegetable and the surname being notably Irish; hence, 'to *spud*'. A *spud*, ME *spudde*, a digging-knife, app derives from ON *spjōt*, *spiōt*, a spear (cf ON *spjōti*, a sharp point), akin to OS *spiot*, OHG *spioz*: cf, therefore, the 1st SPIT, and also SPIKE.

**spume** (whence **spumy**), **spumose** or **spumous**. The 3rd derives from EF-F *spumeuse*, f of *spumeux*, from L *spūmōsus* (whence E *spumose*), adj of *spūma*, foam, whence—perh via MF *espume*—the E *spume*: f.a.e., FOAM.

**spun**: pp and pt of 'to *spin*', q.v. at SPAN, para 3.

**spunk** (occ **sponk**), whence the adj **spunky**: coll

for 'courage, dash', Standard for 'kindling' or 'tinder'. See FUNGUS, para 3.

**spur**, of a horse-rider, hence an incitement and in Topo, hence 'to spur'; **speer** and **spoor**; **spurn**, v, hence n.

1. *Spur*, ME *spure* or *spora*, derives from OE *spura* or *spora*: cf OHG *sporo*, MHG *spor*, G *Sporn* (pl *Sporen*), MD *spore*, MD-D *spoor*, ON *spori*.

2. OE *spora*, a spur, is akin to OE *spor*, a footstep, a footprint, akin to the syn MD *spore*, *spor*, MD-D *spoor*, adopted by E: cf OHG-MHG *spor*, MHG-G *spur*, ON *spor*.

3. Akin to OE *spor*, footprint, and OE *spura*, a spur, is OE *spyrian*, to follow the tracks of, to track down, to investigate, ME *spuryen*, *spuren*, later *spire*, E 'to *speir* or *speer*' (now mostly Sc), to inquire: cf MD *sporen*, D *speuren*, OHG *spurēn*, MHG *spürn*, G *spüren*, ON *spyrja*.

4. Akin to OE *spyrian* is OE *spurnan*, to kick, hence to reject violently, ME *spurnen*, E 'to *spurn*': cf OFris *spurna*, OS and OHG *spurnan*, ON *spyrna*—and, further off, L *spernere*, to thrust away (? orig with the foot), to spurn or despise, and still further off and without *n*, the Lith *spìrti*, to kick, Skt *sphuráti*, he kicks, pushes with the foot, tramples on: IE r, *sphur-*, *spher-*, varr *spur-*, *sper-*, to knock or push with the foot.

**spurious**: L *spurius*, illegitimate, hence false, inauthentic: app Etruscan and perh related to L *spurcus*, impure, hence filthy, itself prob Etruscan. (E & M.)

**spurn.** See SPUR, para 4.

**spurt.** See SPROUT, para 3.

**sputative.** See the 2nd SPIT, heading and para 3.

**sputter.** See SPLUTTER.

**sputum.** See the 2nd SPIT, para 3.

**spy.** See SPECTACLE, para 19.

**squab.** See QUAVER, para 2.

**squabble**, is prob echoic: cf Sw dial *skvabbel*, a quarrel: perh cf prec.

**squad; squadron.** *Squad* comes from EF *esquade* (soon *escouade*): Sp *escuadra* (cf It *squadra*), lit a square: VL *exquādra*, from *exquādrāre*, to make square, an *ex-* (vaguely int) extn of L *quādrāre*, to square, from *quādra*, a square, from *quattuor*, 4: f.a.e., QUADRA. It *squadra* has, in its military sense, the aug *squadrone*, whence EF *squadron*, adopted by E.

**squalid; squalor.** The former derives from L *squālidus*, scaly, filthy: like L *squālor*, whence E *squalor*, it derives from *squālēre*, to be scaly, filthy, itself from *squālus*, scaly, hence greasy, filthy, perh akin to L *squāma*, a scale, whence the adj *squāmōsus*, whence E *squamose* and *squamous* (cf the element *squami-*); the Italic r would then be *squā-*, a scale.

**squall** (1), a strong and sudden wind, is of Scan origin: cf Sw *sqval*regn, a violent rain-shower, *sqval*, a violent gushing or running of water, prob echoic and perh akin to:

**squall** (2), to yell or scream discordantly, hence n: app of Scan origin: cf ON *skvala*, to shriek, Sw

*sqvāla*: echoic—cf Ga *sgal*, a howl. 'To *squeal*' is of the same origin, with a closer Scan cognate in Nor *skvella*.

**squalor.** See SQUALID.

**squama** (Bot); **squamose, squamous.** See SQUALID.

**squander** is o.o.o.: perh (EW) akin to G ver*schwenden*, to squander, caus of ver*schwinden*, to disappear: *ver-*, int prefix+*schwinden*, to dwindle, OHG *swintan*, akin to OE *swindan*.

**square**, adj, n, v. The adj *square* derives, by aphesis, from MF *esquarré*, pp of *esquarrer* (EF *équarrer*, F *équarrir*); VL *exquadrāre*: *ex-* used int +L *quadrāre*, to square, from *quadra*, a square, from the adj *quadrus*, from *quattuor*: f.a.e., QUADRA. The MF *esquarrer* yields 'to *square*'; the E n *square* comes, by aphesis, from MF *esquarre* (var *esquerre*, EF-F *équerre*): VL *exquadra*, from the VL v *exquadrāre*.

**squarson.** See PERSON, para 7.

**squash** (1), the NA fruit: of Alg origin: by ellipsis (and aphesis) from Narranganset askúta-*squash* (cf Massachuset *askoot-asquash*), lit 'eaten green' (Webster); Alg *asq* means 'raw'.

**squash** (2), the game, is elliptical for *squash* rackets, from:

**squash** (3), to crush, to beat—or press—into pulp: by aphesis from MF *esquasser*: VL *exquassāre*, int of L *quassāre*: cf QUASH.

**squat**, short and thick, (orig) sitting on one's heels, is the pp (var *squatted*) of 'to *squat*', to sit on one's heels, (orig vt) to strike down, to crush: ME *squatten*, to crush: by aphesis from MF *esquater*, var of *esquatir*: *es-*, L *ex-*+*quatir*, to strike down, to crush, L *quatere*, to shake violently: see QUASH and cf SQUASH.—Derivatives: *squatter*, agent, and *squatting*, pa and vn.

**squaw** comes, by aphesis, from Narraganset *esquaw*, a woman (cf the Massachuset *squas*).

**squawk** is a var of **squeak**: echoic—cf Sw *sqväka*, to croak. The echoic r *squa-*, var *sque-*, occurs also in *squall* and *squeal*.

**squeal** (v, hence n), whence **squealer** and **squealing.** See the 2nd SQUALL.

**squeamish.** See the 1st SWIM, para 3.

**squeegee.** See para 2 of:

**squeeze**, v (hence n), whence **squeezer** and **squeezing**; **squeegee** and **squilgee**; **squelch**, n and v.

1. 'To *squeeze*' derives, with *s-* reinforcement and via ME *queisen*, from OE *cwēsan* (varr *cwīsan*, *cwȳsan*): o.o.o.: perh akin to QUASH; cf the relationship of *squash* to *quash*.

2. *Squeegee* either alters *squeezee* (for *squeezie* or *squeezy*) or derives from *squeege*, a dial var of *squeeze*; the naut *squilgee* is perh a mdfn—? after *squelch*—of *squeegee*.

3. *Squelch* could be independent and echoic, but is prob akin to *squeeze*—perh after *belch*.

**squelch.** See prec, para 3.

**squib** (n, hence v). See SWEEP, para 3.

**squid.** See SQUIRT.

**squilgee.** See SQUEEZE, para 2.

**squill, squilla.** *Squill*, the sea onion, derives from the syn L *scilla* (from Gr *skilla*), by confusion with L *squilla*, a crustacean, adopted by Zoo; yet both L *scilla* and L *squilla* are prob akin to Gr *skilla* (o.o.o.).

**squint** (dial var **squinny**), v, hence n; prob from the ME-E adv *squint*, obliquely, whence also—unless, by aphesis, from the adv-adj *asquint*—the adj *squint*: the adv *squint* derives from the earlier-recorded adv, hence adj, *asquint*, obliquely, squintingly, which, like the C15–16 syn *askoyne*, is o.o.o.: perh akin to the D *schuin*, oblique, and *schuinte*, a slope, a slant, the *a*- being 'on', but both of the D words are recorded much later than *asquint*; more prob, as EW suggests, from a lost OF-MF adv formed from L *ex*, out of + *cuneus*, a wedge.

**squire, squireen.** See SCUTAGE, paras 8 and 9.

**squirm** (v, hence n), whence **squirmy**, is o.o.o.: ? imitative; ? rather from MHG *schirmen*, to fence, ref the slight deflections of the fencer's body.

**squirrel.** See SCENE, para 4.

**squirt** (v hence n), dial var **squit**; syn dial **swirt**;—**squid**.

*Squid* is a thickening of dial *squit*, an easing of *squirt*, itself prob a var of dial *swirt*, which is app of LG origin: cf LG *swirtjen*, to squirt: prob echoic.

**stab** (v, hence n) is a var of 'to *stob*', from *stob*, a stake, a nail, a var of *stub*, q.v. at TYPE, para 7.

**stability, stabilize.** See para 1 of:

**stable**, adj and n; **stabile**; **stability**, whence, anl, **stabilize**, whence **stabilizer** and, anl, **stabilization**; **instability**; **constable, constabulary**; **establish, establishment**—whence **disestablish, disestablishment.**—Cf the sep STAND and STATE.

1. The n *stable* (for horses) derives, by aphesis, from OF-MF *estable* (EF-F *étable*): VL *stabula*: from the neu pl, taken as f sing, of L *stabulum*, a dwelling, from the *sta*- of *stāre*, to stand, *stat*, he stands; the adj *stable* derives similarly from OF-MF *estable* (EF-F *stable*): L *stabilis*, standing firm, hence firmly placed, from *stāre*. *Stabilis* has derivative *stabilitās*, acc *stabilitātem*, whence MF-F *stabilité*, whence E *stability*; *instability* comes from late MF-F *instabilité*, from L *instabilitātem*, acc of *instabilitās*, from *instabilis* (neg of *stabilis*), whence MF-F *instable*, adopted by E but fast giving way to the E mdfn *unstable*.

2. L *stabulum* occurs in the LL virtual cpd *comes stabuli*, master (cf COUNT, n) of the stable, whence OF *cunestables*, MF *conestable*, adopted by E, whence E *constable*; the derivative ML adj *constabulārius* yields the E adj, whence n, *constabulary*, with widely yet naturally diverging modern sense.

3. L *stabilis* has derivative *stabilīre*, to make firm, to place firmly, whence OF-MF *establir* (F *établir*), whence, from parts in *establiss*-, the ME *establissen*, whence 'to *establish*'; derivative OF-MF *establissement* (F *étab*-) contributes towards *establishment*.

4. Cf STAND (f.a.e.) and cf STATE.

**staccato.** See TACH, para 5.

**stack.** See STAKE, para 2.

**staddle.** See STALWART.

**stadium**: L *stadium*, trln of Gr *stadion*, a measure

of about 200 yards: a mdfn—after *stadion*, neu of the Gr adj *stadios*, stable, established—of the older *spadion*, from *span*, to stretch.

**staff** (n, hence v), pl **staves** or **staffs**; **stave**, a b/f from *staves*—whence 'to stave', with pt, pp **stove**; **distaff**—cf dizen, with int bedizen, whence **bedizenment**;—**stem**, n, whence v.

1. *Staff*, a pole, a rod, a stick for support, comes, through ME *staf*, from OE *staef*: cf OS *staf*, MD-D *staf*, Go *stafs*, OFris *stef*, OHG-MHG *stap*, G *Stab* (cf OHG *stabēn*, to be stiff), ON *stafr* (cf Sw *staf* and Da *stav*); also Let *stabs*, a pillar, Lith *stēbas*, a staff, and prob OSl *stoborŭ*, a pillar; and Skt *stabnāti*, he supports. The IE s is *\*stab*-, var *\*stabh*-; the IE r, *\*stā*-, to stand upright: f.a.e., STAND.

2. OE *staef* has the cpd *distaef*, a contr of *\*disestaef* (cf the ME *dysestafe*); whence ME *distaf*, E *distaff*, the staff for holding the flax, or the wool, used in spinning, the 1st element being akin to MLG *dise* (LG *diesse*), the bunch of flax (hence of wool) placed on a distaff.

3. MLG *dise* yields MD *disen*, to dress (a distaff) with flax ready for spinning: whence the syn EE *dizen*, whence the late EE-E sense 'to deck out, to overdress'.

4. Akin to OE *staef* is OE *staefn*, stem of a tree, hence of a ship, with var *stefn*, whence *stemn*, still further eased to *stemm*, whence E *stem*: cf OHG-MHG *stam*, G *Stamm*, MD *stamme*, MD-D *stam*, a tree-trunk, a stem, and MD *stemme*, *stevene*, MD-D *steven*, stern of ship, ON *stafn, stamn*, stem of ship, and OIr *tamon* (for *\*stamon*), a tree-trunk, hence a pedigree (cf G *Stamm*, a tribe), and Gr *stamnos*, a jar. (Walshe.)

**stag**, ME *stag*, prob derives from OE *\*stagga*, var *\*stacga*, an adult male quadruped or bird, hence esp an adult male deer (mostly the red deer): cf ON *steggi*, male bird, in Ice also a male cat; cf further, the OE *stician*, E STICK, to pierce, OHG *stehhan*, MHG-G *stechen*, to prick, to sting, and, with *n*, OE *stingan*, E *sting*.

**stage.** See STAND, para 6.

**stagger.** See STAKE, para 3.

**stagnant**, whence **stagnancy**; **stagnate, stagnation**; **stagnum**;—? **stanch** (a pool) and **tank** (whence **tanker**)—perh **tankard**.

1. L *stāgnum*, a pool of standing water, a pond, is o.o.o.: prob akin to Gr *stagōn*, a drip, *stages* (pl), drips or drops, *stazein*, to drip, and *staktos*, a dripping, an oozing, with IE r *\*stag*-, to flow—present, moreover, in C, as, e.g., in OBr *staer*, a stream.

2. L *stāgnum* has derivative *stāgnāre*, (of water) to be standing still, vt to cause to stand still or to stagnate, with presp *stāgnans*, o/s *stāgnant*-, whence EF-F and E *stagnant*, and with pp *stāgnātus*, whence 'to *stagnate*'; *stagnation* is adopted from F, which coins it from L *stāgnāt*us.

3. L *stāgnum* perh becomes VL *\*stancum*, whence OF *estanc* (MF *estang*, F *étang*), whence ME *stang* or *stanc*, whence E—now mostly E dial and Sc—*stank*, pond, reservoir, weir. B & W,

however, relate OF *estanc* to OF *estancher*—see para 6.

4. L *stagnum* app becomes Sp *estanque*, whence perh, by aphesis, the Port *tanque*, whence the E *tank*, in India a pool or a reservoir, elsewhere usu a cistern or other large receptacle for storage of water. B & W, however, relate Sp *estanque* to OF *estancher*—see para 6.

5. Improbably related to *tank* is *tankard*, app from EF *tanquart* (and ED *tanckaert*), app from ML *tancardus*, perh from the PN *Tancard*—cf, sem, *toby* (jug)—as EW proposes.

6. Perh from L *stagnum* comes a VL *stagnicāre*, contr to *stancāre*, whence OF-MF *estancher* (F *étancher*), to stop the flow of, hence also to quench (thirst): whence, by aphesis, the ME *stanchen*, whence 'to stanch' (preferred by AE), and its var *staunchen*, whence 'to *staunch*' (preferred by E), esp 'to stop the flow of blood from' (a wound). The adj *stanch* or *staunch*, (orig) watertight, (hence) firmly loyal, comes either from the OF *estanc*, f *estanche*, or from MF-EF *estanche* in both genders (F *étanche*, watertight). B & W derive OF-MF *estancher*—whence the OF-EF adj *estanc*, later *estanche*—from a VL *stanticāre*, to cause to stand, to check, from L *stāre*, to stand. Note that OF-MF *estancher* means variously 'to stop or check, to exhaust, to dry up, to weary', cf the OProv *estancar*, to stop or check, the Sp *estancar*, to stop the flow of, It *stancare*, to fatigue or weary; and the adj *estanc*, *estanche*, means 'exhausted, feeble', as do the OProv *estanc* and the It *stanco*. (B & W are perh wrong.)

**staid.** See STAND, para 19, s.f.

**stain** (v, hence n, whence **stainless**), is short for **distain**: ME *disteinen*: MF *desteindre* (F *déteindre*), to remove the colour (of): *des*, L *dis*-, apart+OF-F *teindre*, L *tingere*, to colour. L *tingere* (pp *tinctus*), to steep in a liquid, e.g. coloured water, hence to dye, has s and r *ting*-, akin to the TENG- of Gr *tengō* (τέγγω), I moisten; IE r *teng*-, perh nasalized mdfn of *teg*-.

2. L *tingere* yields 'to *tinge*', whence 'a *tinge*'.

3. The L pp *tinctus*, coloured, yields both the adj and the v *tinct*; the derivative L n *tinctus* (gen -*ūs*), a dipping, a dyeing, yields the E n *tinct*, whence the now more general *tint*, whence 'to *tint*'. On the L pp *tinct*us are formed L *tinctūra*, a dyeing, whence E *tincture*, whence 'to *tincture*', and LL *tinctiō* (o/s *tinctiōn*-), a dipping, whence E *tinction*.

4. L *tinctus*, pp, becomes Port *tinto*, with f *tinta*, used as n for a red wine—and adopted by E; it also becomes Sp *tinto*, used as n for a sweet red wine, whence the obsol E *tent*.

5. L *tinctūra* becomes the OF-F *teinture*, a dyeing, whence the obs E *tainture*, recorded here because it links with 'to *taint*', which, in sense 'to corrupt', derives partly from 'to ATTAINT' and partly from *taint*, to tinge or dye (obs), which clearly derives from OF-F *teint*, pp of *teindre*, which comes from L *tingere*; the n *taint*, a stain, corruption, derives partly from *attaint* and partly from the obs E sense 'a tincture, a colour', which

clearly derives from the OF-F n *teint*, reinforced by the MF-F n *teinte*, both of which come from the OF-F pp *teint*.

**stair**—whence **staircase** and **stairway**—derives, via ME *steir*, earlier *steyer*, from OE *staēger*, lit 'the riser': cf OE *stīgan*, to rise, to climb; cf also OFris *stīga*, OHG *stīgan*, MHG *stīgen*, G *steigen*, Go *steigan*, ON *stīga*, to climb, and MD *steger*, a ladder, D *steiger*, a scaffolding: Gmc r, *stīg*-; IE r, *steigh*-: prob cf Gr *steikhō*, I go. (Walshe.)

**stake**, n, whence v; **stack**, n, whence v, whence **stacker**; **stagger**, v, whence n; **estacade** and **stockade**;—**stock**, n (whence 'stocks and shares', whence **stockbroker**), whence 'to stock' and **stocking** (cf *legging* from *leg*), **stocky**; **stoke**, v (basically, to thrust or stick), whence **stoker**, whence both 'to stoke' and **stokehold**, **stokehole**; **stucco**.

1. *Stake*, basically a slim, pointed length of wood to be set in the ground as a support, hence as a mark (cf 'to *stake* a claim'), whence the gambling sense, comes from OE *staca*: cf MD *stake*, *staec*, D *staak*, MLG *stake*, G *Staken*, OSw *staki*, Sw *stake*, a stake, and Lett *stēge*, a stick, and Lith *stag*aras, a dry stalk: therefore, presumably, STICK (f.a.e.).

2. E-ME *stack* derives from ON *stakkr*, akin to OE *staca*.

3. 'To *stagger*' comes, through ME *stakeren*, from ON *stakra*, to stagger, to push or thrust, akin to ON *stakkr*.

4. From one or other of the OGmc 'stake' words noted above comes Prov *estaca*, a stake, whence Prov *estacado*, whence perh EF-F *estacade*, adopted by E for a defensive dike of stakes; but the EF var *steccade* indicates rather the It *steccata*, a boom, a stockade, from It *stecca*, a stake, of Gmc origin (Dauzat; B & W).

5. EF-F *estacade* has the EF v ar *estocade*, a f/e var prompted by EF-F *estocade*, a blow with an *estoc* or rapier; whence the E *s ockade*.

6. *Stock*, a tree-stump, a log, a (thick) wooden post, derives from the approx ˢʸⁿ OE *stocc*: cf OFris *stokk*, OHG-MHG *stock*, G *Stock* (whence the *Alpenstock*, E *a*-, used by mountaineers: 'stick of the Alps'), MD *stoc*, *stock*, D *stok*, ON *stokkr* (cf ON *stakkr* in para 2)—and also OE *stycce*, OFris *stekk*, G *Stück*, a piece.

7. Intimately related to OE *stocc*, E *stock*, is 'to stoke', ME *stoken*, to thrust or stab: MF-EF *estoquier* (*estochier*), to stab with a rapier, hence to thrust or strike, from OF-F *estoc*, a rapier, of Gmc origin (as in prec para).

8. Akin to OE *stycce*, G *Stück*, a piece, is the It *stucco*, any plastic material stuck on in 'pieces'; indeed, It *stucco* prob derives, via a Longobardic *stukki*, from the OHG form of G *Stück*, i.e. *stucchi* (MHG *stücke*), a piece, a crust, plaster; EF-F *stuc* and G *Stuck*, stucco, comes from the It word.

**stalactite** (downward), and **stalagmite** (upward): SciL *stalactites*, SciL *stalagmites*: Gr *stalaktos* (adj), dripping, Gr *stalagmos*, a dripping: Gr *stalassein*, to drip: cf the 4th STALE.

**stale** (1), adj, whence both 'to *stale*', or render stale, and **staleness**: ME *stale*, cf MD *stel* and E *stall* (f.a.e.).

**stale** (2), a handle: ME *stale*: OE *stalu*: cf OE *stela*, ME *stele*, E dial *steal*, a stalk, later a rung, MD *stael, stale,* MLG *stale*, a post, chair leg, and the 1st STALK.

**stale** (3), a lure, a decoy. See STALL, para 2.

**stale** (4), v, (of horses and cattle) to urinate, whence the corresp n: ME *stalen*: cf MD *stal*, horse's urine, and esp MD-D and MGH-G *stallen*, (of horses) to urinate, and Gr *stalassein* (s *stalass*, r *stal*-), to drip: IE r *\*stel*-, var *\*stal*-, to drip, to urinate. (Cf STALACTITE.)

**stalemate.** See STALL, para 2.

**stalk** (1), of a plant: ME *stalke*, akin to the 2nd STALE and to:

**stalk** (2), to walk quietly or cautiously, also vt: ME *stalken*: OE be*stealcian* (int *be-*), to walk cautiously or furtively: cf Da *stalke*, to walk cautiously (obs), to strut, OE *stealc*, steep, Lith *stalgus*, stiff, rigid, defiant, and the 1st STALK.

**stall**, a standing place, fixed position, a place— a compartment—for horses or oxen, and many subsidiary and derivative senses, hence 'to **stall**', with corresp senses; **stale**, a lure, a decoy (now only dial), whence—after SE *stall*—the underworld n and v *stall*; **stalemate**, n, whence v; **forestall** and **install, installation, installment** (or **instalment**)—and the sep PEDESTAL; **stallion;** sep STALE (1) and STALK (1)—and STOUT; **still,** adj; **stilt; stool**—and **faldstool** and **fauteuil; stoop,** a post.—Gr: **stele, systaltic, systole, diastole, stole** and **apostle, apostolate, apostolic.**—L: sep **epistle, epistolary** and (perh) **local, locate, location,** etc., with cpds (incl **couch**), and **stolid, stolidity,** and **stultify.**

### Indo-European

1. *Stall*, a stand, a station, a fixed position, whence naturally all the other senses, derives, via ME *stal*, from OE *stall* or *steall*, stand, station, place, esp a seat or a stable: cf OFris *stall*, OHG-MHG *stal*, a place, G *Stall*, a stable, a sty (very closely linked to G *Stelle*, a place, itself to OHG *stellēn*, MHG-G *stellen*, to place, or set, upright), MD *stalle, stall*, MD-D *stal*, a stand or station, a place, ON *stallr*, a support, a pedestal; cf also Gr *stellō*, I place or set, I send, and Skt *sthalati*, he stands, and possibly L *locus*, a place. Cf para 7.

### Germanic

2. Of Gmc origin (prob Frankish *\*stall*, a place, a position) is OF-MF *estal*, a place or something placed, whence AF *estale*, a lure, a decoy, whence prob ME *stale*, an ambush, hence, in chess, a stalemate, whence the taut *stalemate, mate* being a checkmate.

3. The E *stall*, n, has derivative 'to *stall*'; cpds: *forestall*, ME *forstallen*, from ME *forestal*, interception, OE *forsteal*, var of *foresteall*, lit a *steall* or *stall*, a placing (of oneself) *fore*, in front of (another person);

*install* (occ *instal*), from MF-F *installer*, from ML *installāre*, to set *in* a *stallum* or place in a choir, to establish possession of an eccl office, ML *stallum* deriving from OHG-MHG *stal* (cf para 1), a place, a stall; derivative ML *installātiō*, o/s *installātiōn*-, becomes MF-F *installation*, adopted by E;

*instal(l)ment*, however, blends 'to *install*' with earlier *estallment*, from *estall*, to agree to pay at regular intervals, from OF-MF *estaler* (F *étaler*), to stop, later to place or fix or arrange, from OF-MF *estal* (F *étal*), a stop, a position, from OHG-MHG *stal*.

4. With OHG-MHG *stal*, a place, a position, cf the syn Frankish *\*stall* (as in para 2), whence ML *stallum*, a stable, whence ML *stalliō*, a stallion, with acc *stalliōnem*, whence MF *estalon* (F *étalon*), var *estalion*, whence, by aphesis, the E *stallion*.

5. Akin to OE *stall, steall* (as in para 1) is—a thinned form—OE *stille*, motionless, quiet, ME *stille*, E *still*: cf OFris *stille*, OS *stilli*, OHG *stilli*, MHG *stille*, G *still*, MD *stille*, MD-D *stil*—and— without *s*—the Lith *tìlti*, to become silent. (Walshe.)

6. This *stil-* thinning occurs also in E *stilt*, ME *stilte*: cf Da *stylte*, OHG *stelza*, MHG-G *stelze* and, ult, the 1st STALK. The derivative *stilt*, to raise on stilts, has pp *stilted*, used as adj—esp of style.

7. Also akin to OE *stall*, place, position, seat, is OE *stōl*, a seat, which gradually narrows its meaning: cf OFris (and OS) *stōl*, OHG-MHG *stuol*, G *Stuhl*, MD *stole*, D *stoel*, seat, stool, Go *stōls*, a throne (cf the obs syn E *stall*), ON *stōll*: Gmc r, *\*stōl-*; IE r, *\*stāl-*, varr *\*stēl-*, *\*stel-*: cf Gr *stēlē*, a pillar, Lith pa-*stólas*, a stand, OB *stolŭ*, a seat, a throne. (Walshe.)

8. OHG *stuol* has cpd *faldstuol* (cf E FOLD), whence ML *faldistolium*, whence E *faldstool*; the var ML *faldistorium* (with *r* for *l*) yields the his, E *faldistory*; both of the E words mean 'a folding stool', esp one used by a bishop.

9. From OHG *faldstuol*, prob via Frankish *\*faldistōl*, comes OF *faldestoel*, MF *faldestueil*, eased to MF-EF *faudeteuil*, whence the EF-F contr *fauteuil*, adopted by E.

10. Akin to ON *stōll*, seat, stool, is ON *stolpi*, whence ME *stolpe*, var *stulpe*, whence the eased, now mainly dial, E *stoop*, a post, a support, esp a prop (in a mine); there are OSl cognates.

### Greek

11. Gr *stēlē*, an upright gravestone, hence a pillar, has been adopted by E and, by Bot, sense-adapted; akin to Gr *stellein*—cf paras 1 and 7.

12. Gr *stellein*, s *stell-*, r *stel-*, has a corresp n in *stol-*: *stolē*, a long, loose garment, whence L *stola*, whence OE-E *stole*, esp in the Eccl sense 'a long, narrow, usu silken band, falling from the shoulders', whence the feminine adornment.

13. With Gr *stolē*, cf the *-stole* occurring in E *systole* and *diastole*, the contraction and the dilatation of the heart: SciL *systole*, Gr *sustolē*, a

syllable-shortening, from *sustellein*, to contract, from *sun-*, with+*stellein*, to send, place, set; SciL *diastole*, Gr *diastolē*, a syllable-lengthening, from *diastellein*, to put apart or asunder, from *dia*, through+*stellein*. The Physio sense has been added by Sci; the LL *diastolē* and *systolē* are gram or rhetorical terms.

14. From Gr *sustellein*, to contract, derives also the adj *sustaltikos*, whence LL *systalticus*, whence E *systaltic* and F *systaltique*, contractile.

15. Gr *stellein* has another prefix-cpd relevant to E: *apostellein*, to send *apo-* or away, whence *apostolos*, one who is sent away, esp (in NT) forth into the world to preach: LL *apostolus*: OF-MF *apostle* (var *apostre*, whence F *apôtre*): adopted by ME. The derivative LL *apostolātus* (gen -*ūs*) yields EF-F *apostolat* and, perh independently, E *apostolate*. Gr *apostolos* has adj *apostolikos*, whence LL *apostolicus*, MF-F *apostolique*, E *apostolic*.

Latin

16. The L cognates *epistola* (-*ula*), *stolidus*, *stultus*, and perh *locus* are here treated sep at EPISTLE, STOLID, STULTIFY and LOCAL.

**stallion.** See prec, para 4.

**stalwart** (adj, hence n) and archaic **stalworth**; **staddle**, n, hence v.

*stalwart* derives from ME *stalworth*: OE *staēl-wyrthe* (-*wierthe*), for earlier *statholwierthe*, firmly based, lit 'worthy in its base or foundation': OE *stathol* (-*ul*), a (firm) seat or base, whence ME *stathel*, E *staddle*, a support (obs), a small tree, the base of a hayrick+*wierthe*, worthy (cf WORTH). The OE *stathol* or *stathul* is akin to OFris *stathul*, base, foundation, and ON *stöthull*, a milk-stand, a milking-place, and OHG *stadal*, a barn—and ult to STAND.

**stamen**, L and Sci pl **stamina**; **stamina**, whence **staminal**; **staminate**, **stamineous** (anglicized var **stamineal**); **stamin** and **stammel**.

1. L *stāmen*, the warp (filaments forming an upright thread), a thread, a fibre, derives from the *stā-* of L *stāre*, to stand, *stat*, he stands: cf Gr *stēmon*, the warp, from *histanai*, to stand: f.a.e., STAND.—Hence the Bot *stamen*.

2. L *stāmen* has o/s *stāmin-*, whence the pl *stāmina*, which, regarded as nerves, hence sinews, leads to the E *stamina*, essential parts (obs), hence physical and mental vigour, esp the power of endurance.

3. Prob from L *stāmen* comes L *stāminātus*, consisting of threads, whence E *staminate*; certainly from *stāmen* comes the adj *stāmineus*, made of, or covered with, threads, whence E *stamineous*.

4. From L *stāmineus* comes the VL n *\*stāminea*, whence OF-MF *estamine* (EF-F *étamine*), a coarse woollen fabric, whence E *stamin*; from the EF-F *étamine* derives the syn, but obs, *tamine* or *tamin*, whence, app, the woollen (wool-and-cotton) fabric called *tammy*.

5. L *stāmina*, neu pl taken as f sing, yields MF-EF *estame*, woollen thread, prop a southern var of MF *estaim* (F *étaim*); *estame* has dimm *estamel*

and *estamet*, the former accounting, by aphesis, for E *stammel*, a woollen fabric usu dyed red, syn of *stamin*, hence the colour and also an undergarment made of this material.

**stammer**, v, hence n; (wine-making) **stum**, n, hence v (cf the D *stommen*); dial **stummer**; **stumble**, v (whence **stumbling-block**), hence n.

1. 'To *stammer*' has come, through ME *stameren*, from OE *stamerian*: cf the OE adj *stamer* (also -*or* and -*ur*), stammering, and, syn adjj, the Go *stamms*, OHG *stamal*, ON *stamr*; cf these vv—OHG *stammalōn*, MHG *stameln*, G *stammeln*, LG and D *stameren*, MD *stameren*, *stamelen*, app the freqq of vv in *stam-*, e.g. OHG *stammēn*, MD *stamen*, ON *stama* (cf Sw *stamma*).

2. The OGmc r *\*stam-*, to stammer, also (adj) stammering, has var *\*stum-*, dumb, as in OHG-MHG *stum*, G *stumm*, MD *stum*, MD-D *stom*; from D *stom*, MD *stum*, used as n 'must' (the dumb or silent 'worker'), comes the E *stum*, (partly) fermented grape-juice.

3. The OGmc r *\*stum-*, dumb, influenced by the OGmc r *\*stam-*, to stammer, occurs in the ON *stumra*, to stumble, whence ME *stumren*, soon eased to *stumlen*, whence—for the *b*, prob cf *tumble*—the E 'to *stumble*': cf the syn MD *stommelen* and EFris *stummeln*. The ON *stumra* and ME *stumren* retain the *r* in the syn E dial *stummer*.

**stamp**, v (whence **stamper** and **stamping**), hence n; **stampede**, n, hence v; **step**, n, hence v, whence **stepper** and **stepping**, whence **stepping-stone**; **stoop**, a porch; **stump**, n (whence **stumpy**), hence v (whence **stumper** and **stumping**); sep STAPLE.

1. 'To *stamp*', to beat or pound (now dial), to strike heavily with sole of foot, derives from ME *stampen*, which, in its passage from OE *stempan*, has app been influenced by MD *stampen* (var *stempen*), also a typically LG form: cf OHG *stamfōr*, *stampfōn*, MHG-G *stampfen*, to pound or stamp; OFris *stamp*, OHG *stampf*, a cudgel (G, a pestle); (without *n*) ON *stappa*; (with *e*, and with *b* for *p*) Gr *stembein*, to pound or stamp, to handle very roughly; perh (without *s-*) L *temnere*, to spurn. The IE r is app *\*stemb-*.

2. Of Gmc origin is Prov *estampir*, to pound or stamp, whence *estampida*, a pounding or a stamping, adopted by Sp, whence the ASp sense 'a violent, impetuous running, esp of cattle', whence, by aphesis, AE, whence E, *stampede*. With the Prov *estampir*, cf Sp *estampar*, to imprint by stamping.

3. With ON *stappa*, to pound or stamp, cf OFris *stapa*, *steppa*, OHG *stepfen*, MD *steppen*, MD-D *stappen*, and esp OE *staepan*, *steppan*, to step; cf also these nn ('a step')—OE *staepe*, *stepe*, E *step*, OFris *stap*, *stepe*, MD *step*, MD-D *stap*, OHG *stapfo*, G *Stapfe*, a footstep.

4. Akin to MD-D *stap*, a footstep, is MD *stoop* (*stoup*), *stoope*, *stope*, *stoepe*, later—as still—*stoep*, a small porch, having seats at the front door of a house: a D custom introduced both into SAfr, as *stoep*, and into New Amsterdam, renamed New York, as *stoop*.—With MD *stoop(e)*, *stoup*, *stope*,

*stoep(e)*, cf—with *f* for *p*—OHG *stuofa*, MHG *stuofe*, G *Stufe*, a (stair, etc.) step, a degree, and esp the syn OS *stōpo*.

5. With the OGmc (and MD) words cited above, cf the E *stump*, that part of a felled tree which remains after the trunk has been cut off: ME *stumpe* or *stompe*: cf MD *stump*, MD-D *stomp*, MLG *stump*, OHG-MHG-G *stumpf*, ON *stumpr*, and the intimately related OHG *stumbal*, MHG *stumbel*, G *Stummel*, a piece (e.g. of a limb) cut off, but also a stump, and late MHG ver*stümbelen* (*ver-*, an int prefix), G *verstümmeln*, to mutilate.

**stampede.** See prec, para 2.

**stance.** Cf *stanza*, but see STAND, para 9.

**stanch,** adj and v. See STAGNANT, para 6.

**stanchion.** Cf *stanza*, but see STAND, para 9.

**stand** represents so large a group of words that one could hardly, in such a work as this, treat all of them under the one heading; the various sub-groups and the isolated terms are, however, at least mentioned; the principal developments are shown, and the argument is set forth clearly and, so far as possible, systematically. The numerous cross-references should enable even the unwariest of readers to fill in the gaps.

### Indo-European

1. 'To *stand*' (cf para 41), OE *standan*, is akin to OHG *stantan*: OE *stand-*, OHG *stant-*, are extnn of *stan-*, which, like the *stat-* of L and Gr, is itself an extn of IE *\*sta-*, to hold oneself upright (to stand), which has var *\*stath-*, seen both in Skt and in Go and ON. The IE r *\*sta-*, *\*stha-*, shows the vowel-changes *\*ste-*, *\*sti-*, *\*sto-*, *\*stu-* (and *\*sthe-*, etc.).

2. Of the very numerous cognates of 'to *stand*', OE *standan*, the foll are perh among the most important and suggestive: OFris, OS, OHG *stān*, OHG *stēn*, OFris *standa*, *stonda*, OS *standan*, ON *standa*, OB *stati*, OSl *stojati*, Lith *stóti*; L *stāre*, presp *stans*, o/s *stant-*, pp *status*; Gr *stēnai*, to stand, *histanai*, to cause to stand—perh cf Hit *istanta-*, to tarry (or stand awhile), *istantanu-*, to cause to tarry; Av *hištaiti*, Skt *tíṣṭhati*, he stands upright, he remains standing, these forms constituting redupp in—resp—*s* (here *h*) and *t*. Note also such C forms as EIr and Ga *stad*, a pause (cf ON *statha*, a standing), Ga *stad*, to pause, and, corresp to L *sistere* (the freq of *stāre*: see the sep SIST group), the OIr *sessim*, I stand, Ga *seas*, and Ga *seasamh*, an upright posture, EIr *sessam* or *-om*, a standing.

3. The corresp nn, indeed, exhibit no irreg deviations: they conform, in the main, to the *stand-* and *stat-* extnn of IE *\*sta-*, to stand.

4. Prob the simplest treatment is to arrange the many E 'stand' words in the historical order of the originating languages—Gr; L, with the R off-shoots; C; Gmc—and, at the end of each language-group, to list the chief words accorded a sep entry.

### Greek

5. Whereas Gr *histanai*, to cause to stand (hence, to weigh), has derivatives *histos*, a loom, and dim *histion* (see Elements at *histio-*), Gr *stēnai*, to stand, has derivative *stasis*, a standing, a standing still, hence a pause, a stop, a stoppage, adopted by Physio: cf the learnèd terms listed at *-stasis* in Elements. The corresp Gr adj is *statikos*, causing a stand or a pause, hence, skilled in weighing: whence SciL *staticus*, whence E *static* (cf F *statique*), whence, in Phys, the neg *astatic* (Gr *a-*, not); Gr 'he *statikē* tekhnē', the *weighing* art, leads to the E n *statics*. Cf the element *stato-*.

6. Gr *statikos* may have generated a VL *\*staticus* (perh rather *status*, pp of *stāre*+*-icus*, anl with other adjj); whatever its origin, VL *\*staticus* has neu *\*staticum*, whence OF-MF *estage* (EF-F *étage*), situation or condition, a dwelling, hence the storey of a building or the stage of a theatre, whence, by aphesis, the ME *stage*, retaining the var F senses.

7. Several Gr prefix-cpds affect E:
*existanai*, to put (*histanai*) out of (*ex-*) place, to derange, whence *ekstasis*, LL *ecstasis*, a trance, MF *extasie* (F *extase*), E *extasy*, now usu—after LL—*ecstasy*; the derivative Gr *extatikos* becomes EF-F *extatique*, whence E *extatic*, now usu *ecstatic*;
*proïstanai*, to stand, hence to place or set (*histanai*), before or forward (*pro-*), whence *pro-statēs*, a stander before, whence the E adj *prostate* (gland)—perh adopted from EF-F *prostate*;
*sunistanai*, to stand, hence to place or set together (*sun-*, from *sun*, with), whence *sustēma*, a placing together, hence a number of things placed together, whence LL *systēma*, whence (EF-F *système* and) E *system*; derivative Gr *sustēmatikos* becomes LL *systēmaticus*, whence (EF-F *systématique* and) E *systematic*; on LL *systemat*icus is built 'to *systematize*' (cf F *systématiser*).

8. Sep treated Gr derivatives-in-E include *apostle*, q.v. at STALL, para 15—*stele*—*stole* (the garment)—and at STALL, paras 13 and 14, *systole* (and *diastole*) and *systaltic*.

### Latin: A, Simples

9. L *stāre*, to stand, has presp *stans*, o/s *stant-*, whence VL *\*stantia*, a standing, whence these four words:
Sp *estancia*, a standing, hence, in ASp, a standing of livestock, esp cattle, hence a cattle ranch;
It *stanza*, a dwelling, but also a 'dwelling' or stop in versification, hence the paragraphic unit of a poem, adopted by E;
OF-MF *estance* (F *étance*), the act or posture of standing, whence, by aphesis, the E *stance*; whence, via the derivative sense, 'a stay, a support';
OF-MF *estançon* (F *étançon*), with the MF, mostly Picard, var *estanchon*, whence, by aphesis, the ME *stanchon*, whence E *stanchion*.

10. Two L forms of the v *stāre* occur in learnèd E: *stet*, Let him (or her or it) stand, adopted by printers, hence by scholars and authors; and *locus standi*, a place of standing, hence, in Law, the

right to appear in a court, hence, in general, the right to be heard.

11. L *stāre* has pp *status*, s *stat-*, used also as adj 'upright, fixed, secure', whence:

L *statārius*, remaining upright, immobile, whence E *statary*, fixed, stationary; perh anl is the origin of Her *statant*, standing, upright, as if from an adj *\*statans*, o/s *\*statant-*;

L *statiō*, o/s *statiōn-*, a standing immobile, hence a residence or station, a military post, (LL) a religious assemblage: whence OF *estacion*, soon reduced to *stacion* (F *station*), adopted by ME, whence—reshaped after the *L*—E *station*, whence 'to *station*'—cf EF-F *stationner*; the derivative L *stationālis* yields E *stational*, and LL *stationārius* yields E *stationary*; the ML n use of *stationārius* for a bookseller, from his *statiō* in the market place, accounts for ME *stacyonere*, whence E *stationer*, orig a bookseller or a publisher, hence a vendor of writing materials, whence *stationery*, at first spelt *stationary*.

12. On L *stat-* arise both LL *statiuus*, ML *stativus*, immobile, whence the military and gram E *stative*, and the L agent *stator*, adopted by E, for Sci and Tech, with new senses.

13. Then there is the statuary group, also from *stat-*:

*statua*, a statue, whence OF-F *statue*, with F dim *statuette*, both adopted by E; the derivative L adj *statuārius* yields (late MF-F *statuaire* and) E *statuary*; the derivative nn *statuārius*, a sculptor, and *statuāria*, elliptical for *statuāria ars*, the statuary art, become E *statuary*, archaic in the former sense; the E formation *statuesque*=*statue* +suffix *-esque*—prob after *picturesque*.

14. With L *statua*, cf L *statūra*, an upright position, hence bodily height: whence OF-MF *estature*, whence late MF-F *stature*, adopted by E.

15. But by far the most important L derivative of pp *status* is the n *status* (gen *-ūs*), the way one stands, attitude, hence condition, position (esp political, hence also social: adopted by E): whence MF *estat* (EF-F *état*), whence E *estate*, orig with the L senses. MF *estat* becomes, by aphesis, the ME *stat*, whence—prob after *estate*—the E *state*, retaining most of the L senses and all the F senses, esp that of a political, and of a national, unit or power, whence *stateless*; *stately* derives from the earlier senses. The derivative v 'to *state*'—unrecorded before late C16—orig meant 'to fix or establish, e.g. in a condition', hence 'to fix the particulars of, to express, in detail, hence definitely'; in usage, the int of 'to say'. Hence *statement*.

16. 'To *state*' has cpd 'to *instate*' or establish in rank or office, whence 'to *reinstate*', whence, anl, *reinstatement*.

17. The L n *status* becomes It *stato*, with derivative *statista*, a statesman, whence the rare E *statist*. But the adj *statistic*, now usu *statistical*, derives from the n *statistic*, now *statistics* (after *mathematics*, *politics*, etc.), from the F n *statistique* (1771), itself from the G *Statistik* (1749), prompted by the academic L *collegium statisticum*, a college occupying itself with this subject, either from the assumed ML adj *statisticus* or from L *status*+the suffix *-isticum* present in *phlogisticun*, likewise a modern academic L neologism. (B & W.) *Statistician*=the n *statistic*+suffix *-ian*; cf the F *statisticien*.

18. L *status*, n, has the further derivative *statuere*, to cause to stand erect, hence to establish, to ordain, with pp *statūtus*, whence the LL n *statūtum*, an ordinance or a decree: whence MF *estatut*, soon reduced to *statut*, which, adopted by ME, becomes E *statute*. Derivative EF-F *statutaire* becomes E *statutory*.

19. Not imm recognizable as a derivative from a L simple, is 'to *stay*', to stand or depend upon (obsol), hence to wait or tarry, hence to remain or dwell, hence to endure (vi), with derivative corresp n: late ME-E, 'to *stay*' derives, by aphesis, from OF-MF *ester*, to stand, to dwell or remain, from L *stāre*. From the pp *staid* (for *stayed*) comes the adj *staid*, settled, sedate.

20. More difficult is *standard*: whereas the 'banner' and derivative senses come, by aphesis, from OF-MF *estendard* (F *étendard*), prob from OF-MF *estendre* (F *étendre*), from L *extendere* (*ex-*, out+*tendere*, to stretch: cf TEND), the 'recognized authority, accepted criterion or measure' senses app derive, in late ME, from 'to *stand*' in its senses 'to be upright, to remain, to endure'; nevertheless, these latter senses could well derive from that of 'banner'. *Standard*, authority, measure, criterion, is used derivatively as adj and as a tech v; *standard*, n, has the further derivative 'to *standardize*', to regularize, whence *standardization*.

21. The principal sep-treated singles are *stable* and *stamen*.

### Latin: *B*, Prefix-Compounds

22. Except for the cpds in *-sist* (*assist*, *consist*, *desist*, etc.)—to be found at SIST (L *sistere*, freq of *stāre*)—the foll are the chief prefix-cpds of L *stāre*, to stand:

*circumstāre*, to stand *circum* or around, presp *circumstans*, o/s *circumstant-*, whence the n *circumstantia*, whence MF *circumstance* (F *circonstance*), adopted by E; from the L word E coins *circumstantial*;

*constāre* (int *con-*), to stand firm, presp *constans*, acc *constantem*, whence MF-F *constant*, adopted by E; derivative L *constantia* becomes MF-F *constance*, whence the PN *Constance*, both adopted by E—*constance* is superseded by *constancy* (direct from L *constantia*); Law L *constat*, it is evident, is preserved by Law E, and it generates the F *constater*, whence 'to *constate*';

*constāre*, to stand firm, has the secondary sense 'to be put up for sale at (such and such a price)', whence OF-MF *coster* (var *couster*, whence EF-F *coûter*), with derivative OF-MF n *cost* (var *coust*, whence EF-F *coût*): whence the E 'to *cost*' and 'the *cost*', whence *costly*;

*constituere* (*con-*, together+*-stituere*, c/f of *statuere*—see para 18), to establish, with presp *constituens*, o/s *constituent-*, whence the E adj, hence n, *constituent*, whence *constituency* (for *\*constituentcy*), and with pp *constitūtus*, whence both E 'to *constitute*' and L *constitūtiō*, acc *constitutiōnem*, whence OF-F *constitution*, adopted by E, whence *constitutional* (adj, hence n), whence *constitutionalism* and *-ist*; derivative late MF-F *constitutif*, f *-ive*, prob suggested the E adj *constitutive*.

23. With L *constituere*, cf L *dēstituere*, to establish (*dē-* used int), LL to leave alone, to abandon (*dē-*, down from, away from), with pp *dēstitūtus*, whence, in E, the obs v and the extant adj *destitute*, and, in L, the subsidiary n *dēstitūtiō*, acc *dēstitūtiōnem*, whence MF-F, hence E, *destitution*.

24. L *stāre* has numerous other prefix-cpds, e.g. *distāre*, to stand *di-*, for *dis-*, apart, hence away, with presp *distans*, acc *distantem*, whence MF-F *distant*, adopted by E; derivative L *distantia* becomes MF-F *distance*, likewise adopted by E, with off-shoot v 'to *distance*'. E *distant* has the irreg An mdfn *distal*, remote.

25. L *exstāre*, often eased to *extāre*, to stand *ex* or out of, hence high, prominent, hence to survive, has presp *exstans*, usu *extans*, o/s *extant-*, whence the E adj *extant*, whence *extancy*.

26. L *instāre*, to stand *in* or over against, hence to be menacing or urgent or imminent, has presp *instans*, acc *instantem*, whence the MF-F adj, hence n (of time), *instant*, adopted by E. The derivative L *instantia* yields both the E *instancy*, urgency, and the MF-F *instance*, adopted by E; the sense 'example' is modern—and E. On the L presp s *instant-* is formed the EF-F *instantané*, whence—? after *simultaneous*—the E *instantaneous*; derivative F *instantanéité* yields *instantaneity*.

27. L *instituere*, to place (*-stituere*, from *statuere*) *in* or upon, to establish or initiate has pp *institūtus*, whence 'to *institute*'; the pa-become-n *institūtum*, pl *institūta*, yields late MF-F *institut*, whence the E *institute*. *Institūtus*, pa, has derivative *institūtiō*, acc *institūtiōnem*, whence OF-F *institution*, adopted by E, with adjj *institutionary* and *institutional*, whence *institutionalism*, *-ist*, etc. Whereas E *institutor* is adopted from L, *institutive* is coined, anl, from *institution*.

28. LL *interstāre*, to stand *inter* or between, has derivative adj *interstēs*, intermediate, whence the n *interstitium*, becoming MF-F *interstice*, adopted by E; *interstitial*=*interstitium*+adj suffix *-al*.

29. L *obstāre*, to stand *ob* or over against, hence (LL) to oppose, has derivative *obstāculum*, whence MF-F *obstacle*, adopted by E; Eccl ML forms the phrase *Nihil obstat*, Nothing stands in the way. Related L *obstināre*, to attempt firmly, to persist in doing, has the s *-stin-* found in *dēstināre* (E *destine*); it is, in fact, a c/f of *\*stanāre*, a nasal var of *stāre*. The pp *obstinātus* yields E *obstinate*, whence *\*obstinatecy*, whence *obstinacy*. Also related to *obstāre* is *obstetrix*, with *-stetrix* the f of agent *stator*; a stander-by, as, indeed, a midwife is. Derivative adjj L *obstetrīcius*, LL *obstetrīcalis*,

yield E *obstetric*, *obstetrical*, the former leading into agent *obstetrician* and science *obstetrics*.

30. LL *obstāre*, to oppose, becomes OF-MF *oster*, which develops the sense 'to dipossess, to eject' (F *ôter*); whence AF *ouster*: whence 'to *oust*'.

31. L *prōstituere*, to place *prō* or forward, to expose, hence to expose oneself for sexual sale, has pp *prōstitūtus*, whence 'to *prostitute*'; the f *prōstitūta*, used as n, becomes E *prostitute*; derivative LL *prōstitūtiō* has acc *prōstitūtiōnem*, whence MF-F and—perh independently—E *prostitution*; the derivative LL agent *prōstitūtor* is adopted by E.

32. L *restāre*, to stand *re-* or back, to remain behind, to remain, becomes OF-F *rester*, to remain, be left over, whence the MF-F n *reste*, a remainder, whence the syn E n *rest*. ('To *rest*' or get repose is of entirely different origin.) Either from OF-MF *rester* or from VL *\*restivus* (from L *restāre*) comes the OF-MF adj *restif* (F *rétif*), f *restive*, whence the E *restive*, with gradually weakening senses.

33. L *restituere*, to place back, to restore, has pp *restitūtus*, whence both 'to *restitute*' and L *restitūtiō*, acc *restitūtiōnem*, whence MF-F, hence E, *restitution*; derivative agent *restitūtor* is adopted by E and derivative adj *restitūtorius* becomes *restitutory*.

34. L *substāre*, to stand under, hence to resist, to persist, to subsist, has pp *substans*, o/s *substant-*, whence the rare E adj *substant*, firm. Derivative L *substantia*, that which 'stands under', or underlies, appearance, yields OF-F *substance*, adopted by E; its LL adj *substantiālis* yields MF-F *substantiel*, whence the reshaped E *substantial*, and the resulting LL n *substantiālitās*, o/s *-itāt-*, yields E *substantiality*. The other LL adj, *substantiuus*, ML *-ivus*, becomes MF-F *substantif*, f *-ive*, whence E *substantive*, confirmed, solid, hence n, with adj *substantival*, perh from LL *substantiuālis*, ML *-ivālis*. LL *substantiātus* (from *\*substantiāre*, to endow with substance) yields 'to *substantiate*', whence *substantiation*.

35. LL *substantiālis* has the LL cpd *consubstantiālis*, whence E *consubstantial*; derivative LL *consubstantiālitās* accounts for *consubstantiality*. ML forms the v *transsubstantiāre*, to transform, with pp *transsubstantiātus*, whence 'to *transubstantiate*'; derivative ML *transsubstantiō*, o/s *transsubstantiōn-*, yields, perh via late MF-F *transsubstantiation*, the E *transubstantiation*.

36. L *substituere*, to place under, to put in the place (of something else), has pp *substitūtus*, whence both the n (imm from the L *substitūtum*) and the v *substitute*; derivative LL *substitūtiō* has acc *substitūtiōnem*, whence MF-F *substitution*, adopted by E; the derivative LL adj *substitūtiuus*, ML *-ivus*, explains at least the form of E *substitutive*.

37. L *superstāre*, to stand over, to dominate, has derivative adj *superstes*, remaining above or on top, hence surviving, whence, by an obscure sem development (? excrescence, superfluity), the n *superstitiō*, a soothsaying or, in a wider sense, the

opp of religion, with acc *superstitiōnem*, whence
MF-F *superstition*, adopted by E; the derivative L
adj *superstitiōsus* becomes MF-F *superstitieux*,
whence E *superstitious*.

38. Cf also the sep *contrast—destination* (*destiny*)
—*solstice* (at SOLAR).

### Celtic

39. *Varlet* is an OF-F var of OF *vaslet*, whence
MF *vallet*, MF-F *valet*. In F, the former retains its
orig sense 'young nobleman, esp a squire in the
service of a knight', hence 'a well-born young man
attendant at a court', hence, as *valet*, 'an attendant', hence 'a servant'; the modern sense of *valet*
was firmly established by C17, and since adopted
by E, which, moreover, has degraded *varlet* to
'knave' or 'low fellow' (archaic)—cf, sem, *knave*
itself. OF *vaslet*, a dim (-*et*), derives from a LL-ML
dim of LL *\*uassus*, ML *\*vassus*, an attendant,
whence ML *vassallus*, whence OF-F *vassal*, one
who vows loyalty to a lord and is protected by
him, hence a well-born man doing so—adopted by
E. LL *\*uassus* has the derivative *uassus uassorum*,
ML *vassus vassorum*, vassal of vassals, hence a
feudal lord next below a knight; whence OF-MF
*vavassor*, var *vavassour*, whence ME *vavasour*,
retained by hist E, with var *vavasor*. OF *vassal* has
the OF-F derivative *vasselage*, whence E *vassalage*.

40. The LL *\*uassus*, ML *\*vassus*, derives from
OC *\*vassos*, a man, esp a householder, akin to
*\*vastis*, a house, from *\*vas*, to dwell, live in a
house (Malvezin): cf the W and Cor *gwās*, a youth,
a servant, Br *gwaz*, a man (a male), and OIr *foss*,
a servant, and therefore the distant Skt *upasthāna*,
a standing by or near (someone), hence attendance.

### Germanic

41. In addition to *stand* (para 1), deriving from a
nasal (*stan*-) extn of IE *sta*- (varr *\*ste*-, *\*stu*-, etc.),
to hold oneself upright, Gmc affords a trio of
words, all lacking *n*, all ending in *d*, and all, therefore, representing *\*stad*-, a var of *\*stat*- or *\*stath*-,
the other common extn of IE *\*sta*-: and these
three E words are *stead*, *steed*, *stud* (horse).

42. *Stead*, a place, esp a farm, derives from ME,
from OE *stede* (OE var *stedi*), a place: cf OFris
*sted*, *stede*, *stedi*, OS *stedi*, var *stad*, OHG-MHG
*stat*, G *Statt* (cf *Stadt*, a town), Go *staths*, ON
*tathr*, cf MD-D *stad*, a town. From OE *stede*
come ME *steden*, E 'to *stead*' or place, and OE
*tedefaest*, fast—i.e., firm—in place, hence un-
changing, E *steadfast*, and, thereby influenced,
*steady*, and the Sc *steading*, a farmhouse; cf
*homestead*, from OE *hāmstede*—cf OFris *hēm-
sted(e)*.

43. *Steed*, a horse (archaic), and *stud*, a herd of
(breeding) horses, hence the place where they are
kept, are doublets: *steed*, ME *stede*, OE *stēda*, a
male horse, esp for war or for breeding, the latter
being also known as OE *stodhors*, E *studhorse*,
from OE *stōd*, whence ME *stod* or *stode*, whence E
*stud*: with OE *stēda* and *stōd*, cf ON *stōth*, a stud
and OHG *stuot*, a drove of horses, MHG *stuot*,

a breeding mare, G *Stute*, any mare: cf also Lith
*stodas*, a drove of horses, and OB *stado*, a herd,
esp of horses. (Walshe.)

44. Sep treated Gmc cognates include *stall*,
*stallion*, *stalwart*, the naut *stay*, *stithy*, *stool*.

**standard.** See prec, para 20.

**stank**, a pond. See STAGNANT, para 3.

**stannary, stannic, stannous, stannum; tin** (n,
hence adj and v), whence TINNY.

1. E from OE *tin* is related to ON *tin* (with
modern Scan cognates), OHG-MHG *zin*, G *Zinn*:
usu said to be o.o.o.: but are not the OGmc words
the *s*-less cognates of L *stannum* (var *stagnum*), tin,
stated by Pliny to be a Gaul invention? A C origin
of *stannum*, therefore, is far from impossible; nor,
Cornwall being famous in antiquity (even among
the Phoenicians) for its tin-mines, is it irrelevant,
or even misleading, to note the foll C words for
tin: Cor *stēn* or *stean*, Ga *stàn* or *staoin*, Ir *stán*,
Mx *stainney*, W *ystaen*, *ystain*, of which the Cor
forms are prob prototypic.

2. From L *stannum* (s *stann*-, r *stan*-) come ML
*stannāria*, a tin-mine, whence E *stannary—stannic*
(*stann*um + Chem -*ic*)—*stannous* (suffix -*ous*)—and
the element *stanno*-.

**stannel.** See YELL, para 4.

**stanza.** See STAND, para 9.

**staple**, a post or pillar (obs), a pointed loop of
iron or wire for driving into wood, etc.; cognately,
a settled market, hence a, or the, principal commodity of a market; hence adj and v, whence
**stapler.**

2. The 'mart' and the 'commodity' *staple* derives
from MF *estaple*, a mart, from syn MD *stapel*,
*stappel*, *stapele*; and this MD word, meaning also
the looped attaching-device, is akin to OE *stapol*,
a post, a pillar, a step: cf ON *stöpull*, a post, and
therefore E *step* (q.v. at STAMP, para 3). The sem
link between pillar, post, step, and market is perh
afforded by the exhibition of merchandise upon
pillars, posts, steps.

**star** (n, hence adj and v), whence **starry** and
numerous cpds, all obvious; **sterling**, n, hence adj;
**stella, stellar, stellate** (whence **stellation**)—con-
**stellate** (adj and v), **constellation** (whence, anl,
**constellatory**); **aster, asterisk, asterism, asteroid**
(adj, hence n), **astral, astrology** and **astronomy**—
cf **disaster, disastrous.**

1. *Star*, ME *sterre*, OE *steorra*, is akin to OFris
*stēra*, OS *sterro*, OHG *sterro*, *sterno*, MHG *sterne*,
G *Stern*, Go *stairnō*, MD *sterne*, *sterre*, D *ster*, ON
*stjarna*—Cor *steren*, *sterran*—Ir *sterenn*—L *stēlla*—
Gr *astēr*, a star, *astron*, a constellation—Skt *stár*—
Hit *astiras*—and such forms as Tokh A *śre-n* (pl)
and Arm *astl*. The IE r is prob *\*ster*-, with var
*\*stel*-.

2. *Sterling*, the legal and standard money of
Great Britain, derives from ME *sterling*, a silver
penny: app a dim of ME *sterre*, a star—a device
found on certain medieval pennies.

### Latin

3. L *stēlla* derives, ult, from the IE *\*stel*-; it

survives in E as the PN *Stella*. L *stēlla* has, relevant to E, these derivatives:

LL *stellāris*, whence *stellar*;

L *stellātus*, whence *stellate*.

4. *Stellātus* has the LL cpd *constellātus*, whence the adj and v *constellate*; derivative LL *constellātiō*, acc *constellātiōnem*, yields MF-F, whence E, *constellation*.

### Greek

5. Gr *astēr*, a star, is adopted by L, whence E *aster*, a star (obs), hence a star-shaped flower. Derivatives *asteriskos*, a little star—*asterismos*, a constellation—*asteroeidēs*, star-like, become, resp, L *asteriscus*, E *asterisk*—E *asterism*—E *asteroid*.

6. Gr *astron*, a constellation, also a single star, becomes L *astrum*, with adj *astrālis*, whence E *astral*.

7. Gr *astron* has c/f *astro-*, occurring notably in the cpds:

*astrolabon*, lit a star-taker (*labein, lambanein*, to take), whence ML *astrolabium*, OF *astrelabe*, MF-F *astrolabe*, adopted by E;

*astrologos*, an astronomer (lit, star-discourser; *logos*, from *legein*, to speak), whence *astrologia*, adopted by L, whence MF-F *astrologie*, whence E *astrology* whence, anl, *astrologer*;

*astronomos*, astronomer (lit, star-arranger, from *nemein*, to distribute or arrange), whence *astronomia*, adopted by L, whence OF-F *astronomie*, whence E *astronomy*, whence, anl, *astronomer*.

8. Gr *astron* or, rather, L *astrum* becomes It *astro*, with cpd *disastro* (*dis-*, L *dis-*, connoting deviation), an event not favourable to one's stars, with adj *disastroso* (cf the L adj *astrōsus*, born under an unlucky star): whence EF-F *désastre* and *désastreux*, f *désastreuse*: whence E *disaster* and *disastrous*.

**starboard.** See the 2nd STEER, para 2.

**starch** (n, hence v), whence **starchy**: ME *starche*, var of ME *sterche*, from ME *sterchen*, OE *stercan*, to stiffen: OE *stearc*, stiff, whence, in its turn, ME-E *stark*, stiff, rigid, hence harsh, unadorned: and OE *stearc* is akin to OFris *sterk*, OS *starc*, OHG-MHG *starc*, G *stark*, MD *starc, sterc*, D *sterk*, ON *sterkr*; ult to:

**stare** (v, hence n) derives from OE *starian*: cf OHG *starēn*, G *starren*, MD *starren*, MD-D *staren*, LG *staren*, ON *stara*: cf G *starr*, stiff, ON *störr*, big, proud, Lith *stóras*, thick, Gr *stereos*, hard, Skt *sthirā́ś*, strong: cf also STARCH. The IE r is app \**star-*, var \**ster-*, \**stor-*, etc., stiff, strong. Cf STERILE, STERN (adj), STORK.

**stark**, adj, hence adv. See STARCH.

**stark-naked.** See the 1st START.

**starling.** See the 1st TERN.

**start** (1), an animal's tail; whence **redstart**, a small, red-tailed bird, and, by f/e, **stark-naked**, ME *start-* or *stert-naked*, (lit) tail-naked. *Start*, ME *stert* (later *start*), OE *steort*, is akin to OFris *stert*, OHG-G *sterz*, MLG-MD *stert, start*, D *staart*, ON *stertr*, and to:

**start** (2), to move suddenly and jumpily, vi,

hence vt, to cause to do so, hence to begin, whence **starter** and pa, vn **starting**; **startle** (v, hence n), whence the pa, vn **startling**.

'To *startle*' comes from ME *stertlen*, OE *steartlian*, to stumble: akin to OE *styrtan*, to jump up, itself akin to—perh the source of—ME *sterten*, whence 'to *start*': cf OFris *sterta*, OHG *sturzēn*, MHG-G *stürzen*, to hurl or plunge, MD *sterten*, *sturten*, MD-D *storten*, to rush, to fall: o.o.o.; prob echoic.

**startle, startling.** See prec.

**starvation, starve.** See TORPID.

**stasis.** See STAND, para 5.

**statant; statary.** See STAND, para 11.

**state** (n and v), **statement**. See STAND, para 15.

**static, statics.** See STAND, para 5.

**station, stationary, stationer, stationery.** See STAND, para 11.

**statist, statistic(al), statistician, statistics.** See STAND, para 17.

**stative.** See STAND, para 12.

**stator.** See STAND, para 12.

**statuary, statue, statuesque, statuette.** See STAND, para 13.

**stature.** See STAND, para 14.

**status.** See STAND, para 15.

**statute, statutory.** See STAND, para 18.

**staunch**, adj and v. See STAGNANT, para 6.

**stauro-** words. See Elements and, f.a.e., cf the 2nd STEER.

**stave.** See STAFF (heading).

**stay** (1), a strong rope supporting a mast, hence as naut v; 'to *stay*' or hold up, prop, support, whence the n in sense 'a prop, a support', whence a woman's **stays**.

1. The naut rope derives from OE *staeg*, akin to ON, D, G *stag*, MD *staeye*, MLG *stach*: cf the Skt *stákati*, he withstands: IE r, perh \**stag-*.

2. With that n *stay*, cf MF *estaie* (F *étai*), a prop, whence MF *estaier* (F *étayer*), to prop up, to support, whence the syn E 'to *stay*': the MF n *estaie* derives from MD *staeye* (as above).

3. Cf, ult, STAND.

**stay** (2), to remain or tarry. See STAND, para 19.

**stays** (women's). See the 1st STAY (heading).

**stead, steadfast, steading, steady** (adj, hence n and v). See STAND, para 42.

**steak.** See STICK, para 14.

**steal** (1), a stalk, a rung—dial. See the 2nd STALE.

**steal** (2), to take unlawfully, pt **stole**, pp **stolen**; hence the agent **stealer** and the pa, vn **stealing**; **stealth**, whence **stealthy**.

*Stealth*, ME *stelthe*, comes from ME *stelen*, whence 'to *steal*': and ME *stelen* comes from OE *stelan*; cf OFris *stela*, OS and OHG *stelan*, MHG *steln*, G *stehlen*, Go *stilan*, MD-D *stelen*, ON *stela*: perh akin to Gr *sterein*, to take away, to rob, with s and r *ster-*: IE r, ? \**ster-*, with OGmc \**steran* becoming OGmc *stelan*, *stela*, etc. (Boisacq.)

**steam**, n (whence **steamy**) and v (whence **steamer** and **steaming**). 'To *steam*' derives from OE *stēman*, var *stȳman*, to emit vapour, from OE *stēam*, vapour, smoke, whence, via ME *stēam*, *stēm*, *steem*, the E n *steam*: cf MD-D *stoom*, steam: ? echoic, from the hissing of steam.

**stearic, stearin(e).** See STONE, para 3.

**steatite.** See STONE, para 4.

**steed.** See STAND, para 43.

**steel,** n (whence steely) and v. 'To *steel*' derives, via ME *stēlen*, from OE *stȳlan*, itself from OE *stȳle*, var of *stēli* (*staeli*), later *stēl*, whence E *steel*: cf OS *stehli*, MD *stael*, D *staal*, OHG *stahal*, MHG *stahel*, *stāl*, G *Stahl*, and ON *stāl*: ? orig 'something very firm and strong'—cf Av *staxra*, firm, strong. (Walshe.)

**steenbok.** See STONE, para 2.

**steep,** adj and v. See the 3rd STOOP, para 2.

**steeple, steeplejack.** See the 3rd STOOP, para 4.

**steer** (1), a potential bull castrated before maturity; **tauric, taurine, Taurus** and **Taurid**—cf **toreador, torero,** and the elements *tauri-*, *tauro-*.

1. E-ME *steer* comes from OE *stēor*, akin to OHG *stior*, OHG-G and D *stier*, Go *stiur*, ON *stjörr* and, without *s*, *thjörr*; also without the IE int prefix *s-*: OIr *tarb*, Ga *tarbh*, Mx *tarroo*, Cor *tarow*, Br *tarv*, W *tarw*, OC *\*tarvos*; Lith *tauras*, OSl *turŭ*, an aurochs, OP *tauris*, a buffalo; L *taurus*, Umbrian *toru*; Gr *tauros*; but Av *staora*, heavy beasts (both bovine and equine). The IE etymon is app *\*tauros*, but the word is prob Medit: cf Aram *tōr* and H *šor* (Hofmann)—perh Sumerian *tūr*, a cattle-yard—and perh even Eg *àatru*, stud bulls.

2. L *taurus* has adj *taurīnus*, whence E *taurine*; E *tauric*, however, represents *taurus+*adj suffix *-ic*. In Astr, *Taurus* is the Bull, whence the *Taurids* or meteors app radiating from Taurus: *Taurus+-id*, descendant, off-shoot.

3. L *taurus* becomes Sp *toro*, whence both *torero* (*toro+*agent *-ero*) and *torear*, to fight bulls, with derivative *toreador*; both adopted by E.

**steer** (2), to guide (a ship) with a rudder, whence **steerage,** agent **steerer,** pa, vn **steering; steersman;** —**starboard;** stern, n.—Cf the sep STORE.

1. 'To *steer*,' ME *steeren*, OE *stȳran*, a contr of *stiēran*, var of *stēoran*, is akin to OFris *stiōra*, *stiūra*, OHG *stiuren*, to direct, G *steuern*, to steer, Go *stiurjan*, to guide, to establish, MD *stieren*, *stuyren*, MD-D *sturen*, to steer, ON *stȳra*, to steer, to govern: cf these nn, OE *stēor*, OFris *stiūre*, OHG *stiura*, MHG *stiure*, G *Steuer*, ON *stȳri*, a rudder, which prob precede the vv: cf the ON *staurr*, Gr *stauros*, a stake: ? ult from the IE r *\*sta-*, to stand.

2. OE *stēor*, rudder, has the cpds *stēoresmann*, man of the rudder, whence *steersman*, and *stēorbord*, the steering side, whence ME *sterbord*, E *starboard*.

3. Akin to OFris *stiūre* and ON *stȳri*, rudder, are the syn OFris *stiärne* and ON *stiörn*, the latter prob originating ME *steorne*, almost imm contr to *stern*, orig a rudder, hence the after part of a ship.— Whence *astern*: *a-*, in+*stern*.

**steeve.** See STIFF, para 2.

**stegano-** and **stego-** words. See the element *stegano-*.

**stein.** See STONE, para 2.

**stele,** whence the adj **stelar.** See STALL, para 11.

**Stella, stellar, stellate.** See STAR, para 3.

**stem** (1), of plant. See STAFF, para 4.

**stem** (2), to stop, dam, check: ME *stemmen*: ON *stemma*, akin to syn OS *stemmian* and to MHG *stemmen*, to stiffen, G *stemmen*, to prop: ult to the n *stem*, q.v. at STAFF.

**stench.** See STINK, para 2.

**stencil.** See SCENE, para 6.

**stenographer, stenography.** See the element *steno-*.

**stentorian.** See the element *stentoro-*.

**step,** n and v. See STAMP, para 3.

**step-,** as in *stepmother, stepchild*, etc.: OE *stēop-*, which has Gmc cognates, related to such vv as OE *āstēpan*, *āstȳpan*, and OHG ar*stiufan*, to bereave; the simple form occurs in the ON *stiūpr*, stepson, and *stiūpa*, stepmother. The chief extant cpds are: *stepchild*, OE *stēopcild*; *stepdaughter*, OE *stēopdohtor*; *stepfather*, OE *stēopfaeder*; *stepmother*, OE *stēopmōdor*; *stepson*, OE *stēopsunu*: mostly with cognate forms in the other OGmc tongues. Perh (Holthausen) related to OHG-MHG *stampf*, blunt, OHG-G *stumpf*, a stump.

**steppe:** Ru *step*', a waste place, wasteland.

**stereoscope; stereotype,** whence 'to **stereotype**' and the pa **stereotyped.** See the element *stereo-* and cf:

**sterile, sterility, sterilize, sterilization.** *Sterile*, barren, comes—perh via MF-F *stérile*—from L *sterilis*, s *steril-*, ult r *\*ster-*: cf Gr *steira*, (woman or cow that is) unfruitful, Skt *starís*, unfruitful cow, and also Go *stairō* (fem), unfruitful, OHG *stero*, a widow: themselves akin to Gr *stereos*, solid, hard: IE *\*ster-*, unfruitful, and the id *\*ster-*, stiff, hard, solid. (Hofmann.) L *sterilis* has derivative *sterilitās*, whence MF-F *stérilité* and E *sterility*; MF-F *stérile* has the late MF-F derivative *stériliser*, whence *stérilisation*: whence E 'to *sterilize*' and *sterilization*. Cf STARCH.

**sterling.** See STAR, para 2.

**stern** (1), adj, whence **sternness**: ME *sterne* (var *sturne*): OE *stierne* (var *styrne*): app an *-n* extn of r *stier-* or *styr-*, akin to the *stor-* of G *storrig*, obstinate, OHG *storro*, MHG *storre*, a tree-stump, OHG *storrēn*, to project strongly or stiffly, themselves akin to MHG *sterre*, G *starr*, rigid; cf, therefore, STARE and STERILE.

**stern** (2), of ship. See the 2nd STEER, para 3.

**sterna.** See the 1st TERN.

**sternal,** from SciL *sternalis*, is the adj of SciL, hence E, *sternum*, the breastbone, from Gr *sternon*, the chest, ? 'the broad part': IE r, *\*ster-*, to be wide—cf OHG *stirna*, MHG *stirne*, G *Stirn*, the forehead, OE *steornede*, having a broad forehead, and perh L *sternere*, to spread out, and Skt *stirnás*, strewn. (Hofmann; Walshe.) Zoo *sternite*= *sternum+-ite*, n-suffix.

**sternutation.** See:

**stertor, stertorous.** The latter—cf the F *stertoreux*

—derives from the former; the former, from L *stertere*, s *stert-*, to snore, a *t* extn, as L *sternuere*, to sneeze, is an *n* extn, of an echoic IE r *\*ster-*, to make a noise through the nose. L *sternuere* has the int *sternūtāre*, whence *sternūtātiō*, o/s *sternūta-tiōn-*, whence E *sternutation*; the corresp adj *sternutatory* comes from EF-F *sternutatoire*, from L *sternūtāre*.

**stet.** See STAND, para 10.

**stethoscope.** See the element *stetho-*.

**stevedore.** See STIFF, para 2.

**stew,** n and v. The n *stew*, ME *stue, stuwe*, prob comes rather from the ME *stuwen*, to bathe in hot water, than from the OF-MF n *estuve* (F *étuve*), which derives from OF-MF *estuver*, whence, by aphesis, the ME *stuwen*: and OF-MF *estuver* comes from VL *extūfāre*: *ex-*, out+*\*tūfus*, trln of Gr *stuphos*, vapour, smoke. Cf FUME and THYME.

**steward.** See the 1st STY, para 2.

**sthenia, sthenic; neurasthenia, neurasthenic.** Gr *sthenos*, strength, power, perh akin to Skt *saghnóti*, it is full-grown, has SciL derivative *sthenia*, with adj *sthenicus*, whence Med and Psy *sthenic*. The Gr *astheneia*, weakness (*a-*, privative prefix), combines with *neuron*, a nerve, to form SciL *neurasthenia*, whence, anl, *neurasthenic*; cf NERVE.

**stich, stichic.** See the 3rd STY, para 2.

**stick,** n and v (pt **stuck**)—whence **sticker, sticking, sticky** (whence **stickiness**); **stickleback; steak; stitch,** n, hence v;—**stigma, stigmatic** (whence, anl, **stigmatism**), **stigmatize**—cf the derivative (Gr *a-*, not) **astigmatic, astigmatism;**—**distinguish** (whence **distinguishable** and pa **distinguished**), **distinct** (whence **distinctness**), **distinction,** whence, anl, **distinctive**—cf the LL *distinctiuus* implied by the LL adv *distinctiue*, ML *distinctive*, in a characteristic manner; **instigant, instigate, instigation** (whence, anl, **instigative**), **instigator, instigatory**—and **instinct,** adj, and **instinct,** n, whence, anl, both **instinctive** and **instinctual;—style** (n, hence v), whence **stylish, stylist** (whence, anl, **stylistic,** whence, in turn, **stylistics**), **stylize** (whence **stylization**)—cf the element *-stylar* (*stylo-*)—**stylus, stylet, stiletto; stimulant** (adj, hence n), **stimulate, stimulation** (whence, anl, **stimulative**), **stimulator** (whence, anl, **stimulatory**).—Without *s-*: **ticket** (n, hence v) and **etiquette; tiger** (whence **tigerish**), **tigress, tigrine; Tigris.**

### Indo-European

1. The E n *stick*, OE *sticca*, and the closely related 'to *stick*', to pierce, OE *stician*, *\*stecan*, have numerous cognates in Gmc, both old and modern, as well as in other IE languages, esp L (*stimulus*, a goad, *stilus*, a pointed instrument, *-stinguere*, to prick, etc.)—Gr (*stigma*, the mark made by a pointed instrument)—OPer (*tigra*, pointed) and Skt (*tigmás*, pointed). The IE r is *\*tei-*, var *\*ti-*, to pierce, usu in the reinforced *\*stei-* (*s-*, int prefix) or *\*sti-*, with extnn *\*teig-*, *\*steig-*, or *\*tig-*, *\*stig-*, and *\*stil-* and *\*stim-* (both attested by L).

### Iranian

2. From Iranian, E gets two words belonging to this constellation: *tiger* and *Tigris*. *Tiger* derives from ME *tigre*, adopted from OF-F *tigre*, from L *tigris*, itself adopted from Gr (τίγρις), which adapted some old Iranian word related—like L-from-Gr *Tigris*, the river, from OPer *Tigra*—to Av *tighra-*, pointed, and *tighri-*, an arrow (notably pointed): the tiger is arrow-swift; the river in its upper reaches, very rapid. The F fem *tigresse* at least prompted the E *tigress*; the L adj *tigrīnus* yields E *tigrine*.

### Greek

3. Gr *stigma*, a pricked mark, hence a brand, was adopted by L, whence by E, with Sci and tech pl *stigmata*, as in L and Gr; and the ML derivative *stigmāticus* becomes E *stigmatic*. On the L-from-Gr o/s *stigmat-*, ML formed also *stigmatizāre*, to brand (cf the syn LL *stigmāre*), whence 'to *stigmatize*'. Gr *stigma* derives from Gr *stizein* (? for *\*stigiein*), to prick or pierce: r *stig-*: cf the *stig-* of L *instigāre* and the *stich-*, var *stech-*, of the Gmc words.

### Latin

4. The L words *-stīgāre* (and the nasalized *-stinguere*), *stilus*, *stimulus*, neatly exhibit the principal extnn (*stig-*, *stil-*, *stim-*) of the IE r *\*sti-*, var of *\*stei-*. L *-stīgāre* occurs in *instīgāre*, to goad (someone) on (to do something), to excite or incite. The presp *instīgans*, o/s *instīgant-*, yields the E n *instigant*; the pp *instīgātus* yields 'to *instigate*'. On the pps *instīgāt-*, L forms *instīgātiō* (o/s *instīgātiōn-*), *instīgātor*, LL *instīgatōrius*, whence the E words, resp *instigation* (perh adopted from MF-F)—*instigator* (cf the MF-F *instigateur*)—*instigatory*.

5. L *-stīgāre*, to goad, has the corresp nasal form, *-stinguere*, *\*-stingere*, to goad—not to be confused with the self-contained, entirely distinct *stinguere*, to quench. L *-stinguere*, to goad, has two cpds relevant to E: *distinguere* and *instinguere*.

6. L *distinguere*, var *distingere* (*dis-*, apart), to separate by means of pricked marks, becomes MF-F *distinguer*, whence, irreg (after the *-iss-* forms of F vv in *-ir*, as *languir*, presp *languissant*), 'to *distinguish*', whence *distinguished* and *distinguishing*. The L pp *distinctus* becomes MF-F *distinct*, adopted by E; and the derivative L *distinctiō*, acc *distinctiōnem*, becomes OF-F *distinction*, adopted by E.

7. L *instinguere*, var *instingere* (*in-* prob int), to goad, to incite or instigate, has pp *instinctus*, whence the E adj *instinct*, impelled or animated (obsol), hence imbued; but the E n *instinct* derives—perh via late MF-F *instinct*—from L *instinctus* (gen *-ūs*), itself from the L pp.

8. The IE r *\*sti-*, in its L extn *stil-*, occurs in L *stilus*, a sharp-pointed instrument, esp for writing on wax, hence, in LL, one's manner of writing, whence MF *stile*, procedure (legal or military), whence, with form influenced by incorrect L *stylus*

(after Gr *stulos*, pillar, column), the EF-F *style*, in modern sense, borrowed by E. The derivative F *styliste, stylistique, styliser* have perh aided the formation of E *stylist, stylistic, stylize*.

9. L *stilus* becomes It *stilo*, with new sense 'dagger', whence the dim *stiletto*, adopted by E; from It *stiletto*, F derives *stylet* (*-y-* from L *stylus*), adopted by E, now mainly as in F, for a surgical probe.

10. The IE r *\*sti-*, in its L extn *stim-*, occurs in *stimulus*, a goad (lit and fig), adopted by E; prob orig a little goad (dim *-ulus*). The derivative *stimulāre*, to goad, hence to incite, to arouse, has presp *stimulans*, o/s *stimulant-*, whence the E adj, hence n, *stimulant*; the pp *stimulātus* and its derivatives *stimulātiō* (o/s *stimulātiōn-*) and *stimulātor* result, resp, in 'to *stimulate*', *stimulation*, *stimulator*.

### Germanic

11. A *stick* or (dry) piece of wood, e.g. a small branch, a twig, comes from ME *sticke*, from OE *sticca*, akin to OFris *stekk*, OHG *stec(c)ho*, G *Stechen*, ON *stik*, and to OE *stician*, to pierce.

12. 'To *stick*,' to pierce, to fix by piercing, hence by other means, comes from ME *stikien*, aided by ME *steken* (whence the pt, pp *stuck*): OE *stician* and OE *\*stecan*: cf OFris *steka*, OS *stekan*, OHG *stehhan*, MHG-G *stechen*; cf the L and Gr words cited above.

13. Akin to OE *stician*, to pierce or prick, is OE *sticel*, a prickle or thorn, whence dial E *stickle*, a bristle, whence the small bristle-backed fish named *stickleback*.

14. The ON *stik*, a stick, has derivative *stika*, to impale, from which, or at least akin to which, is ON *steik*, a slice of meat roasted on a spit, whence the E *steak*.

15. Akin to, or deriving from, OE *stician*, to prick, is OE *stice*, a pricking, a puncture, whence ME *stiche*, E *stitch*, a pricking pain, hence a single pass of a needle, hence a single turn of the thread: cf OFris *stek, steke*, and OHG *stih*, MHG-G *stich* (akin to OHG *stehhan*, G *stechen*), and esp OHG *sticchan*, MHG *sticken*, to embroider—a thinned derivative of *stehhan, stechen*.

16. Very closely related to MHG-MG *stechen* is MD-D *steken*, var *sticken* or *stikken*, to impale (also to embroider), whence MF *estiquer* (*-quier*), whence MF *estiquet, estiquette*, whence EF-F *étiquette*, a label, a ticket, hence certain labels implying a certain order, a certain rank, hence, EF-F, court ceremonial, hence formal good manners, adopted by E. The 'label' sense of MF *estiquet, estiquette*, EF-F *étiquette*, leads, by aphesis, to E *ticket*; 'to *ticket*' prob owes something to EF-F *étiqueter*, to put a label on.

**stickle**, to intervene between opponents (obs), hence to contend, or hold out, on small points, whence a **stickler** and **stickling**: perh from ME *stihtlen*, to arrange, control, govern, the freq of the syn ME *stihten*, OE *stihtan* (*-ian*), akin to ON *stētta*, to aid: o.o.o.

**stickleback.** See STICK, para 13.
**sticky.** See STICK (heading).
**stiff** (adj, hence sl n), whence stif̃ness and stiffen, whence stiffener, stiffening; steeve, stevedore; stipe, stipulate, stipulation, stipulator (whence, anl, stipulatory), stipule (whence, anl, stipular); sep CONSTIPATE, CONSTIPATION—and COSTIVE.

1. E-ME *stiff* derives from OE *stīf*: cf OFris *stēf*, OHG-MHG *stif*, G *steif*, MD *stief*, MD-D *stijf*, ON *stīfr*, Lith *stiprùs*, firm, L *stīpes*, a post, *stīpāre*, to compress, Gr *stiphros*, compressed, compact, and, with *b* for *p*, the syn *stibaros* (cf *steibein*, to compress by trampling): IE r, *\*steip-* or *\*stip-*, compact, stiff.

2. L *stīpāre*, to compress, becomes It *stivare*, to stow cargo, load a ship, whence *stiva*, a ship's hold, whence EF-F *estive*, the loading of a ship, whence F *estiver*, to stow goods, whence, by aphesis, E 'to *steeve*' or stow; cf E *stevedore*, from Sp *estivador*, a loader or stower, from *estivar*, to stow, from L *stīpāre*.

3. L *stīpes*, a round stake fixed in the ground, a stock, a post, later a plant's stem, is retained by Bot, which has also adopted F *stipe* (L *stīpes*). L *stīpes* has dim *stipula*, a (little) stem or stalk, whence E *stipule*, adopted by E.

4. Akin to L *stīpes* and *stipula* is (? L-)LL *stipulus*, firm, from or akin to which is L *stipulāri*, LL *stipulāre*, to formally engage another or oneself to do something, with pp *stipulātus*, whence 'to *stipulate*'; derivative *stipulātiō*, acc *stipulātiōnem*, becomes MF-F and, perh independently, E *stipulation*.

**stifle**: ME *stuflen* or *stufflen*: app, by aphesis, from MF *estouffer* (E *étouffer*), var *estofer* (C13): o.o.o.: perh cf OHG *stopfōn*, MHG-G *stopfen*, to stuff (cf E 'to *stop*'); after all, the commonest way to stifle someone is to stuff material into mouth and nostrils.

**stigma, stigmatic, stigmatize.** See STICK, para 3.

**stile** (1), ME *stile*, OE *stigel*, a ladder, a step, is akin to OHG *stigila*, a stile, and OE *stīgan*, OFris *stīga*, OHG *stīgan*, MHG *stīgen*, G *steigen*, Go *steigan*, ON *stīga*, to climb: Gmc r *stīg-*, IE r *\*steigh-*, to climb.

**stile** (2), an upright piece in frame or panel. See STOIC, para 2.

**stiletto.** See STICK, para 9.

**still** (1), motionless, tranquil. See STALL, para 5. The adv, whence the conj, comes from the OE *stille*, which is the OE adj *stille* used as adv.

**still** (2), silence, calm, derives from the adj.

**still** (3), a vessel used in distilling liquids, derives from the obsol *still*, to (cause to) drip, from the syn L *stillāre*, which has cpd *distillāre* (? for *dēstillāre*), to fall drop by drop, whence MF-F *distiller*, whence 'to *distill*,' var *distil*', whence *distiller*; derivative *distillātiō*, acc *distillātiōnem*, yields, prob via the MF-F word, the E *distillation*; derivative EF-F *distillatoire* becomes E *distillatory*; derivative F *distillerie* (*distiller*+*-erie*) perh intervenes for *distillery*.—L *stillāre*, by the way, comes from L *stilla*, a drop of water, itself akin to the syn Gr *stilē*.

2. L *stillāre* has the further cpd *instillāre*, to put (a liquid) in, drop by drop, whence, perh via EF-F *instiller*, the E 'to *instill*' (or *instil*); derivative L *instillātiō*, o/s *instillātiōn-*, yields, perh via EF-F, *instillation*.

**still** (4), (vt) to stop, to quieten, to calm, hence vi: OE *stillan*, akin to the OE adj *stille* (see 1st STILL): cf the G *stillen* and ON *stilla*.

**stillborn**=born *still* or motionless.

**stillness**: from the 1st STILL: cf OFris *stillnisse*.

**stilt, stilted.** See STALL, para 6.

**stimulant, stimulate, stimulation; stimulus.** See STICK, para 10.

**sting**, n (whence **stingray**) and v (whence **stinger** and **stinging**), pt **stang** (obsol) or **stung**, pp **stung**; **stingo**; **stingy**, miserly.

1. 'A *sting*' comes straight down from OE *sting*, itself from OE *stingan*, akin to the syn ON *stinga* and to ON *stanga*, to prick: prob a nasal mdfn of OGmc *\*stag-*, to pierce, a var of IE *\*stigh-*, to prick (see STICK).

2. *Stingo* (sl), a sharp, strong liquor, merely adds *-o* (a typical Cockney suffix) to *sting*, ref its 'bite'.

3. *Stingy*, close-fisted, derives from *stinge*, a dial var of *sting*; *stinge*, pron *stindge*, accounts for the pron *stindgy*. Cf the sl '*sting*', to rob or charge exorbitantly.

**stink**, v (whence **stinker** and **stinking**, pa and vn), hence n; numerous—and entirely obvious—cpds; —**stench**.

1. 'To *stink*,' OE *stincan*, to emit a (whether good or bad) smell, is akin to OHG *stinchan* (good or bad), MHG *stinken* (usu bad), G *stinken* (bad), MD *stenken, stincken*, MD-D *stinken*: o.o.o.: ? an *s-* reinforcement of an IE r *\*tang-*: cf Gr *tangos*, rancid. (Walshe.)

2. With MD *stenken*, cf MD *stanc, stanck*, MD-D *stank*, and OE *stenc*, E **stench**, a strong, esp a bad, smell.

**stint** (v, hence n), to cause to cease, to bound or confine, to restrict: ME *stinten*, earlier *stenten*, earliest *stunten*, to cause to cease: OE *styntan*, to dull or blunten: app a nasal mdfn of an OGmc r *\*stut-*, to stop or cut short—cf ON *stuttr*, short, *stytta*, to shorten, and perh G *stutzen*, to cut back, to be taken aback, from MHG *stutz*, a push, and OHG *stōzan*, MHG *stōzen*, G *stossen*, to push.

**stipe.** See STIFF, para 3.

**stipend, stipendiary.** See PEND, para 26.

**stipple** (v, hence n), like so many other Art terms, comes from D: D *stippelen*, to make dots or points, freq of MD-D *stippen*, to prick, to dot, from MD-D *stip*, a point, a dot: o.o.o.: the r *stip-* is, however, prob a var of the OGmc words exemplfied by E STICK, to prick.

**stipulate, stipulation.** See STIFF, para 4.

**stipule**, with adj **stipular.** See STIFF, para 3.

**stir** (v hence n), whence **stirless** and **stirring**: ME *stiren*, varr *steren* and *sturen*: OE *styrian*: cf OFris *stêra*, OHG *stōrēn*, MHG *stoeren*, to scatter, to destroy, G *stören*, to disturb, MD *stueren, stoeren, stooren*, MD-D *storen*, to disturb, and ON *styrr*, a disturbance: OGmc r *\*stur-*, varr

*\*ster-* and *\*stor-*: ? an *s-* reinforcement (IE int prefix *s-*) of an IE r *\*tur-*: cf L *turbāre* (s *turb-*, OL r *\*tur-*), to disturb.

2. Akin to OE *styrian* is OE-ME-E *storm* (whence *stormy*), a violent disturbance of the atmosphere: cf ON *stormr*, a storm, OHG *sturm*, storm, battle, G *Storm*, storm, attack (whence E '*storm* troops'), MD *storem* (showing clearly the intimate relationship of the n to the v), *stoorm*, MD-D *storm*. 'To *storm*' perh owes something to MD *stuermen, stoormen*, MD-D *stormen*, (of the weather) to storm.

**stirrup, stirrup-cup.** See ROPE, para 2.

**stitch.** See STICK, para 15.

**stithy**, an anvil: ON *stethi*: ? by thinning of form and by narrowing of sense, from ON *stathr*, a place, akin to E *stead*, q.v. at STAND, para 42.

**stoat; stot.** These words are doublets: both derive from ME *stot* (pron wavering from *stōt* to *stŏt*), a horse, a bullock, a stoat; the latter, meaning a young horse (obs) or a steer, is now only dial. ME *stot* derives from OE *stott, stotte*, an inferior horse, akin to MD *stute*, a mare, and ON *stūtr*, a bull, cf Nor and Sw *stut*, Da *stud*, a bullock.

**stob.** See STAB.

**stock.** See STAKE, para 6.

**stockade.** See STAKE, para 5.

**stocking.** See STAKE, heading and para 6.

**stodge**, v, hence n, whence **stodgy**, is o.o.o.: prob a dial var of 'to STUFF'.

**stoep.** See STAMP, para 4.

**Stoic, stoic** (adj, with extn **stoical**; n), whence **Stoicism, stoicism** (cf the F *stoïcisme*). The adj *stoic* and 'a *stoic*' (courageously and quietly bearing pain or grief) come from the adj and n *Stoic*: perh via late MF-F *Stoïque*: L *Stoïcus*, adj and n, (of) a Stoic philosopher: Gr *Stōïkos*, a Stoic, adj *stōïkos*, from *stōïkos*, of or in a colonnade, the adj of *stoá*, a roofed colonnade, a porch—notably that in which, at Athens, Zeno and his successors taught, in C4 B.C., a noble, resigned philosophy. Gr *stoá* is akin to Gr *stulos*, a column or pillar, itself akin to Skt *sthū́nā*, a pillar: IE r *\*sthou-* or *\*sthau-*, contr *\*sthu-*, a post, a pillar. Cf the element *-stylar*.

2. From Gr *stulos*, a column, come the *-style* of, e.g., *peristyle* (see the element *-stylar*), the Arch adj *stylar*, and prob *stile*, an upright piece in a frame or a panel.

**stoke, stoker.** See STAKE, para 7 (cf the heading).

**stole** (1), garment. See STALL, para 12.

**stole** (2), v, and **stolen.** See STEAL (heading).

**stolid, stolidity.** The latter derives from L *stoliditās*, o/s *stoliditāt-*, from *stolidus*, foolish, stupid, whence E *stolid*: o.o.o.: ? akin, ult, to STALL.

**stoma, stomatic; stomach** (n, hence v), whence **stomacher—stomachal** and **stomachic**; cf the element *stoma-*, where, e.g., STOMATOLOGY.

1. The Gr *stoma* (o/s *stomat-*), the mouth, is retained by An and Zoo; whence the adjj *stomatal* and *stomatic*. Gr *stoma* is akin to Av *staman-*, a quadruped's, esp a dog's, mouth, and Hit *štamar*,

mouth; there are also C and OGmc cognates. (Hofmann.)

2. Very closely related to, perh deriving from, Gr *stoma* is Gr *stomakhos*, gullet, 'neck' of bladder or uterus or (later) stomach, hence the stomach itself: whence L *stomachus*, OF *estomach*, MF-F *estomac*, by aphesis the E *stomach*. The adjj *stomachal* and *stomachic* owe much to late MF-F *stomacal* and EF-F *stomachique*, the former from from L *stomachus*, the latter from L *stomachicus*, from Gr *stomakhikos*, adj of *stomakhos*.

stone (n, hence v—cf OE *stǽnan*); stony; numerous cpds, e.g., stonechat, a bird whose alarm-note resembles the jarring of pebble on pebble—stonecrop (OE *stāncropp*), a plant growing on rocks and stones—stonegall (see YELL, para 4) —Stonehenge—stonemason—stonewall, adj, 'as resistant as a wall' (*Stonewall* Jackson), hence as a cricketing v—stonework (OE *stānweorc*)—as in such picturesque cpd adjj as stone-build, -cold, -deaf.—steenbok; stein.—stearate, stearic, stearin; steatite.

1. *Stone* comes from ME *ston*, var *stan*, from OE *stān*: cf OFris and OS *stēn*, OHG-MHG-G *stein*, Go *stains*, MD *stein*, *stien*, MD-D *steen*, ON *steinn* (with modern Scan cognates); OB *stēna*, a wall; Gr *stion*, var *stiā*, a pebble: IE r, *stai-*, varr *stei-*, *sti-*, a stone; perh ult akin to *sta-*, to stand. OE *stān* has adj *stānig*, whence E *stony*; the notable PlN cpd *Stonehenge* derives from ME *Stonheng*, earlier *Stanhenge*, earliest (C12) *Stanenges*, lit 'hanging stone', hence 'hanging monument' (cf 'to HANG'): Ekwall.

2. Whereas *steenbok*, which has irreg var *steinbok*, is adopted from D and is lit 'a stone, or rock, buck', *stein* is adopted from the derivative sense 'earthenware mug for beer' of G *Stein*, a stone.

3. Gr *stion*, var *stiā*, a pebble, is related to Gr *steār*, fat, tallow, whence F *stéarique* and *stéarine*: whence E *stearic* and *stearine* (or *-in*): whence, anl, E *stearate* (Chem suffix *-ate*).

4. Gr *steār* has gen *steātos*, whence L *steatitis*, whence E *steatite* (Min suffix *-ite*).

stood: pt and pp of STAND.

stooge. See STUDENT, para 3.

stook, a shock of corn (AE) or of grains, beans, etc., prob derives from D *stuk* (MD *stuc*), cf MLG *stuke* and G *Stauche*: cf ult the n STICK.

stool (n, hence v). See STALL, para 7; cf STAND.

stoop (1), a porch. See STAMP, para 4.

stoop (2), a post or a prop. See STALL, para 10.

stoop (3), (of persons) to bend downward and forward, whence pa, vn stooping and also the n stoop, such a bending; steep, adj and v; steeple (n, hence v), whence steeplechase (? from the goal being orig a church steeple—conspicuous landmark) and *steeplejack* (*jack*=*Jack*, generic for a man); stoup.

1. 'To *stoop*' derives from ME *stoupen*, *stupen*, from OE *stūpian*, s and r *stūp-*: cf MD *stupen*, *stuypen*, to stoop, to bow, Sw *stupa*, to tilt or fall,

ON *stūpa*, to stand upright, to stick up (the position from which one bows or stoops).

2. Akin to OE *stūpian*, to stoop, is OE *stēap*, lofty, whence ME *stēp*, later *steep*, steep, E *steep*: cf MHG *stief* (*f* for *p*), steep. To stand something—orig, to stand it upright—in liquid and let it soak is 'to *steep*' it: ME *stepen*, perh from ON *steypa*, which has modern Scan cognates.

3. With ON *steypa*, to steep, and OE *stēap*, lofty, cf OE *stēap*, a drinking vessel, akin to ON *staup* and MD-D *stoop*, which combine to give us the E *stoup*. Cf also the OHG *stouf*, G *Stauf*.

4. Also akin to OE *stēap*, lofty, is OE *stēpel* (var *sty̆pel*), whence ME *stepel* and E *steeple*.

stop (v, hence n), whence stoppage, stopper, pa and vn stopping; stopple; estop (v, hence n), whence estoppage—cf estoppel.—stuff, n (whence stuffy) and v (whence stuffer and stuffing)—cf stuff and nonsense !; Med stupe.

1. 'To *stop*,' ME *stoppen*, derives from OE *-stoppian*, to close a gap or an aperture, esp in *forstoppian*, to plug up: cf MD-D *stoppen*, MD *stuppen*, to close up, MHG-G *stopfen*, OHG *stopfōn*, to stuff, MLG-G *stoppen* and OFris *stoppia*, to stop up: app all from VL-ML *\*stuppāre*, to stop with tow, from L *stuppa*, tow, ML a stopper, a cork, itself from Gr *stuppē* (occ *stupē*), akin to Skt *stūpas*, *stupás*, a tuft of hair: IE r, *\*stup-*, to become compact, form into a round mass, esp spherical, extn of syn *\*stu-*, perh akin to IE *\*sta-*, to stand. (Walshe; Hofmann.)

Note, sem, that what stops up, checks; and that what is stopped up, ceases.

2. Certain stoppers or plugs are called *stopple*, ME *stoppel*, from *stoppen*, to stop up.

3. Cf the legal *estoppel*, from MF *estopail* (or *-aille*), a bung, a stopper, from OF-MF *estoper* (F *étouper*), to stop up, from OF-MF *estope*, a bung, a stopper, from the syn ML *stuppa*. The OF-MF *estoper* becomes AF *estopper*, whence 'to *estop*' or stop up, hence, in Law, to impede.

4. From L *stuppa*, var *stupa*, comes *stupe*, soaked tow or cloth applied to an injury.

5. OHG *stopfōn* (MHG-G *stopfen*), to stuff, as noted above, app becomes MF *estoffer* (F *étoffer*), whence, by aphesis, ME *stoffen*, later *stuffen*, whence 'to *stuff*'; either from MF *estoffer* or from L *stuppa* comes the MF *estoffe* (F *étoffe*), any kind of material or, indeed, matter, whence, by aphesis, ME *stoffe*, later—as still—*stuff*. 'Inferior *stuff*' leads to the senses 'refuse, trash, rubbish' and 'nonsense': whence *Stuff and nonsense*.

stopple. See prec, para 2.

stopper. See STOP (heading).

storage. See:

store (n and v), whence storage, storehouse, storekeeper, storeroom; instauration, instaurator; restaur, restaurant, restaurateur, restauration—cf restoration (whence, anl, restorative), restore.—Cf the 2nd STEER.

1. *Store*, orig something, e.g. food, kept for future use (cf *stores*, supplies, provisions), derives, via ME *stor* and by aphesis, from OF-MF *estor*,

supplies, provisions, from OF-EF *estorer*, to establish or construct, to supply, e.g. with provisions, whence, by aphesis, ME *storen*, E 'to *store*': and OF-EF *estorer* derives from L *instaurāre*, to renew, esp the forces or supplies of, whence L *instaurātiō*, o/s *instaurātiōn-*, and *instaurātor*: whence learnèd E *instauration* and *instaurator*.

2. Cf L *restaurāre*, to give back (something either lost or removed), whence late MF-F *restaurer*, whence the legal n *restaur*, adopted by E, and the general late MF-EF *restaurateur*, a restorer, whence, in C18, a restaurant-keeper, adopted by E; *restaurant* itself is adopted from F, where orig (C17) it had denoted 'restorative food'. Derivative LL *restaurātiō*, acc *restaurātiōn*em, becomes MF-F *restauration*, adopted by E.

3. Late MF-F *restaurer* derives imm from OF-MF *restorer* (from L *restaurāre*), whence ME *restoren*, whence 'to *restore*'; and MF-F, hence E, *restauration* leads, anl, to E *restoration*.

**storey.** See HISTORY, para 5.

**stork,** OE *storc*, is related to ON *storkr* (cf Da, Nor, Sw *stork*) and OHG *storah*, MHG-G *storch*: prob, by vowel-mutation, from the r of *stark*, q.v. at STARCH, and so named, either 'from its rigid legs' (Webster) or 'from its stiff posture' (Walshe).

**storm, stormy.** See STIR, para 2.

**storting.** See THING, para 1.

**story.** See HISTORY, para 4.

**stot.** See STOAT.

**stoup.** See the 3rd STOOP, para 3.

**stout,** whence **stoutness;** ? **stultify,** whence, anl, **stultification.**

1. E-ME *stout*, orig strong and firm, derives, by aphesis, from MF *estout*, var of OF-MF *estolt*, foolish, stupid, senseless, extremely rash, arrogant: prob either, via the Normans, from ON *stoltr*, proud, arrogant, or from OHG-MHG *stolz*, arrogant, foolish, MD *stolt*, later *stoud*, MD-D *stout*: perh ult akin to L *stultus* (s and r *stult-*), foolish, stupid, akin to L *stolidus* (E *stolid*) and therefore prob to E *stall*.

2. L *stultus* has the LL derivative cpd *stultificāre*, to render foolish or stupid; whence 'to *stultify*', now mostly in a weakened sense.

**stove,** comes from OE *stofa* (cf the syn ON *stofa*), a heatable room, esp for a bath, but has, in transit, been strongly influenced by MD *stove* (MD-D *stoof*), a heated room, thence a foot-stove: cf OHG *stuba*, MHG *stube*, a bathroom, G *Stube*, a room. In G, the sense has expanded; in E, contracted.

**stow,** to place conveniently or (esp of freight) arrange compactly, whence **stowage:** ME *stowen*: ME *stowe*, from OE *stōw*, a place, as still in PlN n (cf *Stowe, Godstow*): cf the syn OFris *stō*: ? ult akin to STALL.

**strabismus.** See the element *strabismo-*.

**straddle.** See STRIDE (heading).

**strafe,** to punish, hence to bombard, to castigate, comes from MHG-G *strafen*, to punish, prob from the syn OFris *straffia*: ? echoic.

**straggle** (v, hence n), whence **straggler** and the pa, vn **straggling:** prob from dial *strackle*, the freq of dial *strake* (ME *straken*), to roam: f.a.e., STRETCH. Perh, however, akin to L *strāgulus* (adj), stretching, being stretched, from *sternere*, to spread.

**straight, straighten, straightness.** See STRETCH, para 2.

**strain** (1), orig a getting, a gain, hence a begetting, hence descent or stock, hence an inherited characteristic, hence a sustained note (in music; influenced by the 2nd **strain**), general tenor, mood: ME *strēn, streen*, earliest *streon*: OE *strēon*, var *striōn*, a getting, a begetting: cf OE *strēonan, striēnan, strȳnan*, to get, to gain, to beget, and OHG *striunan*, to get or gain: o.o.o.

**strain** (2) (v, hence n), whence **strainer** and **straining; strangle,** whence **strangler; strait**—cf **strict, striction, stricture; strigil,** whence **strigilate; string** and **stringent;**—**strong, strength** (whence **strengthen,** whence **strengthener** and **strengthening**). —Cpds: **astrict, astriction**—**astringe, astringent,** whence **astringency; constrain, constraint**—**constrict, constriction, constrictive, constrictor**—**constringe, constringent; distrain, distraint**—**distress** (n and v), whence **distressful, distressing,** and, by contr, **stress**—**district; obstriction; perstringe; prestige; restrain, restraint**—**restrict, restriction, restrictive** —**restringent.**

## Indo-European

1. 'To *strain*' or draw (e.g., a rope) tight, but also to stretch effortfully, both with their naturally derivative senses, comes, through ME *stranen* or *streynen*, from OF-MF *estraindre* or *estreindre* (F *étreindre*): L *stringere*, to draw tight or clasp tightly, to press or contract, hence, naut, to graze or scrape: cf—without the nasal—L *strigilis*, a body-scraper: cf also Gr *strangalē*, a halter, *strangos* (στραγγός), twisted, and *stranx* (στράγξ), a drop squeezed out; perh Lett *stringu, stringt*, to wither (? lit to become contracted); certainly MIr *srengim*, I draw (tight) or drag, and Mx *strigg*, a squeezing, *striggey*, to squeeze: IE r, prob \**streg-* (or \**streig-*), with varr \**strag-* and \**strig-*, with nasal varr \**streng-*, \**strang-*, \**string-*, to draw close, press tight, contract.

## Greek

2. Gr *strangalē* (στραγγάλη), a rope or cord, a halter, s *strangal-*, r *strang-*, has derivative *strangalan*, to put a halter on, to strangle, with var *strangaleuein*, whence L *strangulāre*, whence OF-MF *estrangler* (F *étrangler*), whence 'to *strangle*'; *strangler* perh owes something to the derivative MF *estrangleur*; *strangulation* comes, prob via EF-F, from L *strangulātiō* (o/s -*ātiōn-*), from the L pp *strangulātus*.

## Latin: A, Simples

3. L *stringere*, to draw tight, to contract, has

presp *stringens*, o/s *stringent-*, whence E *stringent*, whence *stringency*; the pp *strictus*, whence both E *strict* (whence *strictness*) and OF-MF *estreit* (var *estroit*, F *étroit*), used as adj, hence also as n, whence the ME *streit*, *streyt*, later *strait*, adj and n. The L pp *strict*us has derivatives *strictiō*, o/s *strictiōn-*, a constricting, and *strictūra*, a constriction: whence E *striction* and *stricture*.

4. The cognate L *strigilis*, s *strigil-* (r *strig-*), a scraper, for use after a bath or after exercise, becomes—perh via EF-F *strigile*—the E *strigil*, with derivative sense in Zoo.

### Latin: *B*, Compounds

5. L *stringere* has many cpds that, either directly or through F, have got into E. Alphabetically, the first is *astringere* (for *adstringere*: *ad*, to, towards), to draw tight, with presp *astringens*, o/s *astringent-*, whence, perh via EF-F, the E *astringent*, and with pp *astrictus*, whence 'to *astrict*'; derivative L *astrictiō*, o/s *astrictiōn-*, yields *astriction*.

6. L *constringere*, to draw *con-* or together, yields 'to *constringe*'; presp *constringens*, o/s *constringent-*, E *constringent*; pp *constrictus*, and its derivatives *constrictiō* (o/s *constrictiōn-*), LL *constrictiuus* (ML *-ivus*), SciL *constrictor*, whence, resp, 'to *constrict*', *constriction* (perh via MF-F), *constrictive*, *constrictor* (esp in 'boa *constrictor*').

7. L *constringere*, moreover, becomes OF-MF *constreindre* or *constraindre* (F *contraindre*), whence 'to *constrain*'; derivative OF-MF *constreinte*, *-strainte*, accounts for the E *constraint*.

8. L *distringere*, to draw or pull *dis-* or asunder, becomes OF-MF *destreindre*, *destraindre*, whence ME *destreinen*, whence the reshaped E 'to *distrain*'; the derivative OF-MF *destreinte*, *destrainte*, explains *distraint*.

9. L *distringere* has pp *districtus*, LL adj 'separate', ML n 'a district', whence, via late MF-F, the E *district*. Also from the L pp *districtus* comes VL \**districtia*, a being torn asunder, whence OF-MF *destrece* (F *détresse*), ME *destresse*, *distresse*, E *distress*; derivative OF-MF *destrecier* produces 'to *distress*'; by aphesis, *distress* becomes *stress*.

10. L *obstringere*, to legally oblige (someone to do something), has pp *obstrictus*, whence LL *obstrictiō*, o/s *obstrictiōn-*, E *obstriction*; and L *perstringere*, to bind thoroughly, gives us 'to *perstringe*', to censure.

11. L *praestringere*, to bind beforehand—cf *praestringere oculos*, to bind up the eyes of, hence to dazzle—has derivative \**praestrigiae* (pl), eased to *praestigiae*, a juggler's or a conjuror's passes, hence tricks, whence LL *praestīgium*, conjuring tricks collectively, hence (an) illusion or a delusion, whence EF-F *prestige* (modern sense: C18), adopted by E; the adj *prestigious* derives from EF-F *prestigieux*, f *prestigieuse*, from LL *praestigiōsus*, dazzling (from the n in *-ium*).

12. L *restringere*, to bind back or strongly, to hold in check, whence OF-EF *restraindre* (OF-F *restreindre*), ME *restreinen*, E 'to *restrain*'; deriva-

tive OF-EF *restrainte* becomes E *restraint*. The L presp *restringens*, o/s *restringent-*, leads to E *restringent*, and the pp *restrictus* to 'to *restrict*'; derivative LL *restrictiō*, o/s *restrictiōn-*, late MF-F, hence prob E, *restriction*; derivative MF-F *restrictif*, f *restrictive*, E *restrictive*.

### Germanic

13. Akin to L *string*ere, to draw tight, is OE *streng*, ME *streng* and—? influenced by MD—later *string*, E *string*, a slender cord, whence 'to *string*' and *stringy*: cf MD *stringe*, *strenc*, *strenge*, D *streng*, OHG *strang*, MHG *stranc*, G *Strang*, ON *strengr*.

14. 'To *string*' has pt *strung* and pp, occ *stringed* (imm from the n), usu *strung*, used as adj, esp in *high-strung*.

15. Closely akin to OE *streng* is OE-E *strong*, OE var *strang*: cf OHG *strengi*, MHG *strenge*, strong (G *streng*, strict), MD *strenc*, *strenge*, MD-D *streng*, strong, ON *strangr*, strong, harsh. Akin to, prob deriving from, OE *strange*, *strong*, is OE *strengthu*, ME *strengthe*, E *strength*: cf *long*—*length*: cf also OHG *strengida*, strength, and OFris *strenza*, ON *strengja*, to strengthen.

**strait**, adj and n (usu **straits**). See prec, para 3.

**strake**. See STRETCH, para 3.

**stramineous**. See STRATUM, para 7.

**strand** (1), a beach, a shore, hence 'to **strand**', orig to run (a ship) ashore, to abandon on a lonely or desert shore: ME-OE *strand* (ME var *strond*): cf MD *strant*, *strande*, D *strand*, MLG-MHG *strant*, G *Strand*, ON *strönd* (with modern Scan cognates), cf ON *strind*, land: o.o.o.; but, as Walshe suggests, perh a reinforcement (IE int prefix *s-*) of the OGmc *rand*, var *rant*, edge, rim —cf OE and G *rand*, OHG-MHG *rant*, ON *rönd*.

**strand** (2), a fibre or thread of a plaited string, cord, rope, hence several or many fibres, etc., plaited together, as in '*strand* of hair', whence 'to *strand*': app influenced, in form, by the prec: MF-AF *estran*, var *estren*: either from OHG *streno*, MHG-MD *strene* (D *streen*, G *Strähne*), a plait, a skein, or, less prob, from OHG *strang*, MHG *stranc* (G *Strang*), a rope, a string, or perh from both of the OHG-MHG (MD) words sensefused or confused. (EW.)

**strange** (whence **strangeness**) and **stranger**; 'to **estrange**', whence **estrangement**; **extraneous**, whence, anl, **extraneity**.

1. A **stranger** comes, by aphesis, from MF *estranger* (F *étranger*), a derivative of OF-MF *estrange* (F *étrange*), external, foreign, hence extraordinary, whence, by aphesis, the E *strange*. OF-MF *estrange* has the derivative OF-EF *estranger* (or *-gier*), to put outside, to expel, hence to alienate, whence 'to *estrange*'.

2. OF-MF *estrange* derives from L *extrāneus*, external, hence foreign, LL irrelevant, from *extra*, on the outside, itself from *ex*, out of: whence the E *extraneous*.

**strangle**, **strangler**, **strangulation**. See the 2nd STRAIN, para 2.

strap, n, hence v, whence **strapper** and **strapping**; **strop** (n, hence v); **strophe, strophic**; cf the cpds **antistrophe, antistrophic**—**apostrophe**, in rhetoric and in grammar—**catastrophe**, whence **catastrophic** and **catastrophism**—**espistrophe**; **strobic, strobile**; **stromb, Strombus**; cf the elements *strepho-* or *strepto-* (where, e.g., *streptococcus*) and *strabismo-*.

1. *Strap* is a var, orig dial, of *strop*, a thong—usu of leather—for tying or holding things together: ME *stroppe, strope*: mainly from OE *stropp*, partly from MF *estrop* (F *étrope*), itself prob from OE: L *stroppus*: Gr *strophos*, a cord, a band, from *strephein*, to turn, to twist, to plait: IE r, *\*strebh-* (ult *\*streb-*), to turn.

2. Also from *strephein* comes Gr *strophē*, a turning, hence the movement of the Gr chorus in turning from one side of the orchestra to the other, hence the first stanza of a choral ode: LL *strophē*: EF-F, whence E, *strophe*. The derivative Gr adj *strophikos* (rather of *strophos* than of *strophē*) prob suggested the E *strophic*.

3. Gr *strephein* has cpds affecting E:

*antistrophē*, the returning of the chorus in, hence the corresp part of, a choral dance, from *antistrephe n*, to turn *anti* or to the opposite side: whence, via LL *antistrophē*, the E *antistrophe*; derivative Gr *antistrophikos* yields *antistrophic*;

*apostrophē*, in rhetoric a feigned turning away from one's audience to address someone (usu dead), from *apostrephein*, to turn *apo* or away from, becomes LL *apostropha* (var *apostrophē*), EF-F and E *apostrophe*, whence 'to *apostrophize*';

*apostrophos*, the 'turning away' or omission of a letter, likewise from *apostrephein*, to turn away, becomes LL *apostrophus* (var *apostrophos*), whence EF-F and E *apostrophe*;

*katastrophē*, a lit overturning (*kata,* down), hence a fig upsetting, hence a conclusion, esp in drama, of a tragedy, hence ruin, a great misfortune: whence L *catastropha*, whence EF-F and E *catastrophe*; whence, anl, *catastrophic*—perh cf LGr *katas'rophikōs*, in the manner of a tragedy's conclusion;

*epistrophē*, (in rhetoric) a turning *epi* or towards, from *epistrephein*, to turn towards, is adopted by LL, hence by E.

4. The ult IE r *\*streb-*, to turn, is seen in Gr *strobos*, a whirling, whence the E adj *strobic*, spinning like a top; the Gr dim *strobilos*, anything twisted, esp a pine-cone, becomes LL *strobīlus*, a pine-cone, F and E *strobile*, in Bot a cone or a cone-like aggregation; Gr *strobilos* has derivative *strobilē*, a lint-plug cone-shaped, whence SciL *strobila* (Zoo).

5. Corresp to Gr *strobos*, a whirling, is the nasalized *strombos*, a cone-like mollusc, whence L *strombus*, adopted by Zoo, and the anglicized *stromb*.

**stratagem, strategic, strategist, strategy.** The Gr *stratos*, an army, was orig an encamped army and lit a 'spread' army: cf STRATUM, but, f.a.e., see STREW. Combined with Gr *agein*, to drive, to lead

(f.a.e., AGENT), *stratos* forms *stratēgos*, leader of an army, a general, whence:

*stratēgein*, to lead an army, be a general, whence *stratēgēma*, a general's trick to deceive the enemy: L *strategema*: It *stratagemma*; late MF *strattegeme*: EF-F *stratagème*: E *stratagem*;

*stratēgeia*, generalship: F *stratégie*, E *strategy*;

*stratēgikos*, of, for, by a general: F *stratégique*: E *strategic*.

F *stratégie* has derivative *stratégiste*, whence E *strategist*.

**strath; strathspey.** See STRATUM, para 2.

**stratification, stratify.** See para 5 of STRATUM.

**stratigraphy.** See the element *strati-*.

**stratosphere,** the upper 'stratum' of the atmosphere: F *stratosphère*: strato-, irreg c/f (*strati-* would be correct) of L *stratum*, a covering, a layer +*sphere*, F *sphère*: f.a.e., STRATUM and SPHERE.

**stratum** (pl **strata**) and **stratus**; **stratal** and **stratic**; **stratification, stratify;—consternate, consternation**; **prostrate** (adj, hence v), **prostration**; **substratum;—street; strath** and **strathspey; estrade; stray**, adj, n, v; **astray** (adv, hence adj) and **estray** (n, hence adj); **stramineous.**—Cf the sep STRATAGEM and the sep group gathered at STREW.

1. Both *stratal* and *stratic*, adjj, are E formations from *stratum*, itself adopted from L *strātum* (s *strāt-*), an artificial layer, coat, bed, orig the neu of *strātus*, pp of *sternere*, to spread; on the pps *strāt-* is formed L *strātus* (gen *-ūs*), a spreading out or a being spread out, whence the cloud-form we call *stratus*. L *sternere* has s *stern-* and r *ster-*, akin to Gr *stornunai* (s *storn-*, r, *stor-*), to spread or strew, and Skt *strtás*, (re-)strewn, covered: f.a.e., STREW.

2. The L pp *strātus*, with f *strāta* and neu *strātum*, has, in C, the cognate *strath*, (the flat part of) a (widc) valley, imm from Ga *srath*, itself from OIr *srath*. Hence the Sc district *Strath Spey*, whence the dance, hence the music called *strathspey*.

3. Elliptical for L *uia* (ML *via*) *strāta* is LL *strāta*, a paved road, a street, whence OE *strǣt*, ME *strete*, E *street*.

4. L *strātum*, layer, bed, LL platform, becomes Sp *estrado*, whence the F *estrade*, platform, dais, adopted by E.

5. L *sternere*, pp *strātus*, possesses a full cpd relevant to E; ML *strātificāre*, to form (*-ficāre*, c/f of *facere*, to make) a *strātum* or layer, with derivative n *strātificātiō*, o/s *strātificātiōn-*: whence, prob via EF-F *stratifier* and *stratification*, the E 'to *stratify*' and *stratification*.

6. L *sternere* has three prefix-cpds relevant to E:

*consternere* (*con-* used int), to deject, with mdfn *consternāre*, to cast down, perplex, pp *consternātus*, whence 'to *consternate*'; derivative L *consternātiō*, o/s *consternātiōn-*, yields EF-F and, perh independently, E *consternation*;

*prōsternere*, to spread, hence throw, *prō* or forward, pp *prōstrātus*, whence the E adj and v *prostrate*; derivative L *prōstrātiō*, o/s *prōstrātiōn-*, yields EF-F *prostration*, adopted by E;

*substernere*, to spread, or strew, *sub* or under, has pp *substrātus*, neu *substrātum*, used as n and adopted by E.

7. The L r *ster-* exhibits the metathesis *\*stre-*, var *\*strā-*, attested by the L pp *strāt-* (an extn); *\*strā-* occurs in L *strāmen*, straw, with adj *strāmineus*, whence E *stramineous*: cf E *straw* at STREW.

8. LL *strāta*, a street, has a VL adj *\*strātarius*, roving—or ownerless in—the streets, whence the OF-EF *estraier*, roving, abandoned, ownerless, with closely linked OF-MF *estraier*, to wander, to be lost: whence the E adj and v *stray*; the E n *stray* is adopted from AF *stray*, var *strai*, aphetic for *estrai*, from the OF-MF v *estraier*. The AF *estrai* has var *estray*, retained by legal E; and AF *estray* has, in E, the var *astray*, adv and adj (cf 'to go *astray*').

**stratus.** See prec, para 1.

**stravage.** See VAGABOND, para 4.

**straw; strawberry.** See STREW, para 2.

**stray,** adj, n, v. See STRATUM, para 8.

**streak, streaky.** See STRIKE, para 4.

**stream** (n, hence v, whence **streamer** and **streaming**), whence **streamlet** (dim *-let*)—**streamline**—**streamy.**

*Stream,* OE *strēam,* is akin to OFris *strām,* OHG-MHG *stroum, strom,* G *Strom,* D *stroom* and, with slightly different sense, MD *strume, strum, struum,* ON *straumr* (modern Scan cognates); Ga *sramh,* (a jet of) milk flowing from a cow's udder, Ga and OIr *sruth,* OIr *srūaim,* Cor *strēth,* OC *\*srutu-,* a stream; OSl *struja,* Lith *strove* or *srove,* a flowing, a stream; Skt *srávati,* it flows; and, without *s,* Gr *rhusis,* a flowing—cf the sep RHYME.

**streek.** See STRETCH.

**street.** See STRATUM, para 3.

**strength,** whence **strengthen.** See the 2nd STRAIN, para 15.

**strenuous:** L *strēnuus,* active, lively, courageous: from L *strēna,* a good augury, hence a gift either accompanying or celebrating a favourable augury or occasion (cf the OF-EF *estreine,* F *étrenne*): prob of Sabine origin; perh akin to Gr *strēnēs,* rough, harsh, strong.

**strepent, streperous, strepitant, strepitous, strepor; obstreperous,** whence the dial **obstropolous** or **obstropulous.**

*Obstreperous* derives from ML *obstreperus,* from L *obstrepere,* to make a noise (cf LL *obstrepitāre,* to interrupt with noise): *ob-,* towards, opposed to +*strepere,* to make a noise, esp if dull and violent: echoic, as are, e.g., *stertere* and *crepere.* (E & M.) *Strepere* has presp *strepens,* o/s *strepent-,* whence the E adj *strepent*; the LL adj *streperus,* noisy, becomes *streperous*; LL forms *strepor* (*strepere+ -or,* as in L *rumor*), adopted by Sci. L *strepere* acquires the freq *strepitāre,* with pp *strepitans,* o/s *strepitant-,* whence E *strepitant*; also on the supine *strepit*um is formed the L n *strepitus* (gen *-ūs*), whence the E adj *strepitous.*

**streptococcus.** See the element *strepho-.*

**stress.** See the 2nd STRAIN, para 9, s.f.

**stretch,** v (hence n), whence **stretcher** and **stretching**; sep **straggle, straggler; straight** (adj, hence adv and n), whence **straighten** and **straightness; strake; streek.**

1. 'To *stretch*', ME *strecchen* (var *streken,* whence the Sc, and E dial, *streek,* to extend, lay out), OE *streccan,* is related to OFris *strekka,* OHG *strecchēn,* MHG-G *strecken,* MD *stricken, strecken,* D *strekken*: o.o.o.: but it is prob either a metathesis of the IE r *\*ster-,* stiff, strong, q.v. at STARCH and esp at STARE, s.f., as certain authorities (e.g., Webster) suggest, or ult akin to REACH.

2. OE *streccan* has pp *streht*; ME *strecchen,* pp *streght,* later *streight,* both employed also as adj, whence the E adj *straight.*

3. Akin to ME *streken* (var of *strecchen*) is ME-E *strake,* a plank used in shipbuilding.

**strew,** archaic **strow**; pt **strewed,** archaic **strowed**; pp **strewn** (archaic **strown**), now often **strewed**;— **straw.—stroma.**

1. 'To *strew*', ME *strewen* (var *strawen*), OE *streāwian,* var *streōwian,* is akin to OFris *strēwa,* OS *strōian,* OHG *strewēn,* MHG *ströuwen,* G *streuen,* Go *straujan,* MD *struwen, strouwen, stroyen, strooyen,* D *strooijen,* ON *strā*; also to L *sternere,* pp *strātus* (see STRATUM), spread, and *struere* (s and r *stru-*), to pile up (see STRUCTURE); to Gr *strōnnunai,* perh a metathesis of the var *stornunai*; and to Skt *stṛṇóti,* var *stṛṇáti,* he strews or scatters: IE r, app *\*ster-,* to stretch, to strew, to scatter: cf STRETCH, para 1.

2. Akin to OE *streāwian, streōwian,* to strew, is OE *strēaw,* whence ME *stree, stre,* later *straw,* E *straw*: cf the ON *strā,* OS and OHG-MHG *strō* (gen *strāwes*), G *Stroh,* MD-D *stroo,* and the L *strāmen,* straw strewn about. OE *strēaw,* straw, hay, has cpd *strēawberige,* a *berige* or berry prob either 'from being found under mown grass' (Webster) or 'from the tiny strawlike particles which cover the fruit' (EW).

3. Gr *strōnnunai,* to strew, has derivative *strōma,* a strawing, a bed-covering, a mattress, which is adopted by LL and then, with sense-adaptations, by An and Bot; whence the adj *stromal.* Cf the element *-stroma.*

**stria, striate, striation.** See STRIKE, para 6.

**stricken.** See STRIKE (heading).

**strickle.** See STRIKE, para 2.

**strict, striction, stricture.** See the 2nd STRAIN, para 3.

**stride** (v, hence n)—pt **strode**—pp **stridden; straddle** (v, hence n)—akin to the now dial **striddle,** a freq of 'to *stride*';—**strive,** pt **strove,** pp **striven; strife.**

1. 'To *stride*,' OE *strīdan,* to stride (i.e. to walk purposefully), also to straddle, is akin to MD *striden, strieden,* D *strijden,* MLG *striden,* to stride.

2. Those Gmc words are closely related to the group represented by 'to *strive*', ME *striven,* deriving from OF-EF *estriver,* to try hard, (MF-

EF) to quarrel, itself from OF-EF *estrif*, a var of OF *estrit*, app from OHG *strīt*, a quarrel, id in MHG, *Streit* in G: cf OFris *strīda*, OS *strīdian*, OHG *strītan*, ON *strītha*, to quarrel, MLG and MD *streven*, ED *strijven*, to strive, MHG *streben*, to try hard, G *streben*, to strive.

3. The E *strife* comes, by aphesis, from OF-EF *estrif*, a quarrel, contest, effort: cf OFris and OS *strīd*, OHG-MHG *strīt*, ON *strīth*. These OGmc words are o.o.o.; prob, however, the OGmc \**strīt-*, a, or to, quarrel, is either echoic or (Walshe) akin to L *līs*, o/s *līt-*, a quarrel, a lawsuit: OL *stlīs*, o/s *stlīt-*: *stl-* easily becomes *str-*, for the *l-r* (and *r-l*) transition forms a pillar of IE phonology. The IE \**stlīt-*, \**strīt-*, is perh echoic.

**strident** (whence **stridence** or **stridency**), **stridor**; **stridulous**, whence, anl (as in the R languages), **stridulant**, **stridulate**, **stridulation**.

*Stridulous* comes from L *strīdulus*, gratingly shrill, from *strīd-*, the s and r of *strīdere*, to make a gratingly shrill, or harsh, noise: echoic: cf L *strepere* (E **STREPENT**). L *strīdere* has presp *strīdens*, o/s *strīdent-*, whence E **strident**; derivative L *strīdor* is adopted by erudite, esp Med, E.

**strife.** See STRIDE, para 3.

**strigil.** See the 2nd STRAIN, para 4.

**strike** (v, hence n), pt **struck**, pp **struck** or—now, except as adj, archaic—**stricken**; hence the agent **striker** and the pa, vn **striking**; **strickle**; **stroke**, n and v; **streak**, n (whence **streaky**), hence v; **stripe**, n (whence **stripy**), hence v (whence **striper**); **stria**, **striate** (adj and v, whence **striated** and **striation**), **striature**;—? **trickle**, v, hence n.

1. 'To *strike*,' ME *strīken*, to strike, rub, stroke, move, go, OE *strīcan*, to rub, stroke, move, go (a sense preserved in 'Let's *strike* across country'): cf OFris *strīka*, OHG *strīhhan*, MHG *strīchen*, G *streichen*, to rub, to stroke, MLG *strīken*, to stroke or strike, MD *striken*, later *strijcken*, to stroke or strike, to move or go, D *strijken*, to strike, and ON *strȳkja*, to rub, to stroke; cf also L *stringere* in its derivative sense 'to rub, to graze', L *stria*, a furrow; Gr *strinx*, a line or row; and, ult, STRAIN (see, esp, para 1).

2. Akin to OE *strīcan*, to stroke, is OE *stricel*, whence E **strickle**, (in farming) a striking or whetting or dressing instrument: cf the syn MD *strekel*, *streeckel*.

3. Also akin to OE *strīcan* is OE *strācian*, ME *straken*, var *stroken*, whence 'to *stroke*', to rub gently; from the ME v comes the ME n *strak* or *strok*, whence *stroke*.

4. Very closely akin to OE *strīcan* is OE *strica*, stroke (of a pen), a streak, ME *stric*, *strike*, with varr *strek*, *streke*, E *streak*: cf OFris *strike*, OHG *strih*, MHG-G *strich*, Go *striks*, MD *streke*, *streec*, D *streek*.

5. Akin to MD *streec*, *streke*, is MD *stripe* (as also in LG), adopted by E: cf MHG *strīfe*, G *Streifen*, a strip.

6. Akin to the OGmc words noted above is L *stria*, a furrow, a channel, a threadlike line (cf the virtually syn *striga*), whence E *stria*, a minute

channel, furrow, channel, hence, in Med, a line, or a stripe, on the skin. Derivative L *striātus*, channelled, grooved, furrowed, yields the E adj and v *striate*; *striātus*, in turn, has derivative *striātura*, marked with tiny, parallel furrows or lines, whence E *striature*.

7. OE *strīcan*, to rub, stroke, go, has also the sense 'to flow', ME *stricken*, freq *stricklen*, whence, prob, the ME *triklen*, E 'to *trickle*'.

**string.** See the 2nd STRAIN, para 13.

**stringency**, **stringent**. See the 2nd STRAIN, para 3.

**stringy.** See the 2nd STRAIN, para 13.

**strip**, v (hence n—'a longish, narrow piece'—influenced by *stripe*, n, q.v. at STRIKE, para 5), whence **stripper** and **stripping** and also **stripling** (dim *-ling*).

'To *strip*' or deprive, esp of a covering (skin, roof, clothes, etc.), comes through ME *stripen*, earlier *strupen*, from OE *-strȳpan*, in *bestrȳpan* or *-strīpan* (int *be-*), to plunder: cf MD *struppen*, *stroppen*, *stropen*, D *stroopen*, MHG *stroufen*, and MHG *strīfe*, *Streifen*, a strip; with cognates in Frisian.

**stripe.** See STRIKE, para 5.

**stripling.** See STRIP (heading); cf, sem, 'a *chip* off the old block'.

**strive.** See STRIDE, para 2; **striven:** ib (heading).

**strobic**, **strobile**. See STRAP, para 4.

**stroke.** See STRIKE, para 3.

**stroll** (v, hence n)—whence **stroller** and **strolling** —prob comes from G *strollen*, a dial cognate of *strolchen*, to tramp or wander, from *Strolch*, a tramp or vagabond, itself from Swiss *strolche*, var *strolle*, to wander; 'to *stroll*' might, however, derive from G *strol*chen. (Walshe.)

**stroma.** See STREW, para 3.

**stromb**, **Strombus.** See STRAP, para 5.

**strong.** See the 2nd STRAIN, para 15.

**strontianite** and, anl, **strontium** (whence, anl, **strontic**) come from *Strontian*, a village in Argyllshire, Scotland, where this Chem element was discovered.

**strop.** See STRAP, para 1.

**strophe**, **strophic.** See STRAP, para 2.

**strow**, **strowed**, **strown.** See STREW (heading).

**struck.** See STRIKE (heading).

**structure**, whence **structural**; **construct** (adj—whence n—and v), **construction**, **constructive**, **constructor**—cf **construe** (v, hence n); **destroy**, **destroyer**—cf **destructible**, **destruction**, **destructive**, **destructor**; **instruct**, **instruction** (whence **instructional**), **instructive**, **instructor**—cf **instrument**, **instrumental** (whence, anl, **instrumentalism**, **instrumentalist**, **instrumentality**), **instrumentation**—cf also **industry**, **industrial** (whence **industrialism** and **industrialist**), **industrious**; **obstruct**, **obstruction** (whence, anl, **obstructive** and **obstructor**); **reconstruct**, **reconstruction**; **substruct**, **substruction**, **substructure**; **superstruct**, **superstruction**, **superstructure**.

1. This group rests firmly upon L *struere* (s and r, *stru-*), to arrange in piles, to pile up, hence to

build or construct; most of the E words come from the pp *structus* (s *struct-*), whence L *structūra*, a construction, that which is constructed, whence MF-F *structure*, adopted by E. L *stru*ere is ult akin to E STREW.

2. *Struere* has many cpds. The first that affects modern E is *construere*, to pile up *con-* or together, to construct, LL to build up (a sentence), whence 'to *construe*' (cf the MF *construer*). The pp *constructus* yields both adj and v *construct*. On *construct*us, L forms *constructiō*, acc *constructiōnem*, whence OF-F *construction*, adopted by E—LL *constructiuus*, ML *-ivus*, whence *constructive*—LL *constructor*, a builder, adopted by E.

3. LL forms the cpd *reconstruere*, to rebuild, pp *reconstructus*, whence 'to *reconstruct*'; on EF-F *reconstruire* and OF-F *construction*, F forms *reconstruction*, perh adopted by E.

4. L *dēstruere*, to 'build down (*dē-*)', to demolish, acquires the VL extn *destrūgere*, whence OF-MF *destruire* (F *détruire*), ME *destruien*, later *destroyen*, E 'to *destroy*'; derivative OF-MF *destruiëor* becomes E *destroyer*. L *dēstruere* has pp *dēstructus*, whence LL *dēstructibilis*, whence E *destructible*—*dēstructiō*, acc *dēstructiōnem*, whence OF-F *destruction*, adopted by E—LL *dēstructiuus*, ML *-ivus*, MF-F *destructif* (f *-ive*), E *destructive*—LL *dēstructor*, whence (late MF-F *destructeur* and) E *destructor*.

5. L *instruere*, to build *in-* or into, onto, hence to equip or furnish, hence, LL, to furnish someone with knowledge, to teach, has pp *instructus* (used also as adj, whence the obs E adj *instruct* and F *instruit*), whence 'to *instruct*'. On the pp *instructus*, L forms *instructiō*, LL education, with acc *instructiōnem*, whence MF-F *instruction*, adopted by E—and *instructor*, a builder-up, a preparer, ML a teacher, adopted by E (cf MF-F *instructeur*). The derivative MF-F *instructif*, f *-ive*, becomes E *instructive*.

6. Also from L *instruere*, s *instru-*, is formed the L *instrūmentum*, something that serves to equip or furnish, a tool, whence OF-F *instrument*, adopted by E; derivative MF-F *instrumental* and F *instrumentation* have been adopted by E, and F *instrumentiste* has perh suggested E *instrumentalist*.

7. Perh akin to L *instruere* is L *industria*, zeal, activity, purposeful effort, whence OF-F *industrie*, (orig) activity, (C18 onwards) the ensemble of trades dealing with raw materials and primary products, whence E *industry*; derivative L *industriuus*, zealous, active, has the LL extn *industriōsus*, whence late MF-F *industrieux*, f *industrieuse*, whence prob, rather than from L *industriōsus*, the E *industrious*; the ML mdfn *industriālis* becomes F *industriel*, whence the reshaped E *industrial*.

8. L *obstruere*, to pile, hence build, *ob* or up against, hence to block up, has pp *obstructus*, whence 'to *obstruct*'; derivative L *obstructiō*, o/s *obstructiōn-*, yields—perh via EF-F—the E *obstruction*.

9. L *substruere*, to build *sub* or beneath, has pp *substructus*, whence 'to *substruct*'; derivative L *substructiō*, o/s *substructiōn-*, yields (EF-F and) E *substruction*, whence—after *structure*—*substructure*.

10. L *superstruere*, to build *super*, above, hence upon, has pp *superstructus*, whence 'to *superstruct*', whence, anl, the rare *superstruction*; *superstructure* = *super*+*structure*.

**struggle**, v, hence n, derives from ME *struglen*, var *strogelen*: o.o.o.: perh, in part, echoic; perh a blend of *strife* and *tuggle*, freq of 'to *tug*'.

**strum** and the syn **thrum**, to play rudimentarily or roughly or monotonously on, e.g., a piano, are echoic: cf HUM.

**struma, strumose, strumous.** See the element *strumi-*.

**strumpet** (n, hence v), ME var *strompet*, is o.o.o.: perh akin to MD *strompen* (s *stromp-*), to stride, to stalk (vi): ? 'a stalker' of men.

**strung.** See the 2nd STRAIN, para 14.

**strut**, to swell (now only dial), hence to walk pompously or swaggeringly, derives from ME *strūten*, var *strouten*, to strut, to swell, from OE *strūtian*, to stand out either stiffly or projectingly, to swell: cf Da *strutte*, to project, MHG-G *strotzen*, to swell, MHG *striuzen*, to contend, to resist, and *strūz* (G *Strauss*), a fight: o.o.o. Hence the n *strut*, a swaggering or pompous walk (ME *strūt*, *strout*, contention, strife), and app also, from its stiff, resistant nature (cf LG *strutt*, rigid), the *strut* of architects and engineers.

**struthious.** See OSTRICH, para 2.

**strychnine** (occ **strychnin**), whence, anl, **strychnic**: F *strychnine*: L *strychnos*: Gr *strukhnos*, the deadly nightshade: o.o.o.

**stub.** See TYPE, para 7.

**stubble**: ME *stobil* or *stoble*: (by aphesis from) OF-MF *estuble*: ML *stupula*: L *stipula*, stalk, stubble: f.a.e., STIFF, esp para 3 (*stipule*).

**stubborn.** See TYPE, para 8.

**stucco.** See STAKE, para 8.

**stuck.** See STICK, para 12.

**stud** (of horses). See STAND, para 43.

**stud** (2), a trunk or a post (both obs), a projecting knob, a large-headed nail, a knobbed fastener (e.g., of a collar): OE *studu*, a post: cf MHG-G *stutze*, D *stut*, a prop, OHG *-stutzen*, MHG-G *stützen*, to prop or support, ON *stoth*, a post, *stythia*, to prop, and Lett *stute*, a support: IE r, *\*stu-*, to prop—cf Gr *stulos*, a pillar.

**student, studio, studious, study; 'stooge'.**

L *studēre*, to be zealous or eager, hence to apply oneself (esp mentally) to, to study, LL to practise: s and r, *stud-*, prob akin to L *tundere*, to strike, a nasalized form of r *\*tud-*; the *s-* of *studēre* is app the IE int prefix.

2. *Studēre* has presp *studens*, o/s *student-*, whence E *student*; *studēre* itself becomes OF-MF *estudier* (F *étudier*), whence, by aphesis, ME *studien*, E 'to *study*'; the n *study* comes from ME *studie*, aphetic for MF *estudie* (OF *estudie*), from L *studium*, zeal, application (to learning), from *studēre*. L *studium* has derivative adj *studiōsus*, whence OF-F *studieux*, f *studieuse*, and—app independently—E *studious*.

3. L *studium* acquires in LL the sense 'a place of study', whence It *studio*, esp of painters, and F *étude* (OF *estuide*), esp in Mus: both adopted by E.

4. App from *student* (influenced by *studious* pron *stoo-djus*) comes the orig AE sl (vaudeville) *stooge*, one who 'feeds' the comedian, hence anyone serving as an assistant, whence 'to *stooge*'.

**stuff, stuffing, stuffy.** See STOP, para 5.

**stultify.** See STOUT, para 2.

**stum.** See STAMMER, para 2.

**stumble.** See STAMMER, para 3.

**stump, stumper, stumpy.** See STAMP, para 5.

**stun.** See THUNDER, para 8.

**stung.** See STING (heading).

**stunt**, orig a feat in athletics (and AE coll), is either a dial var of E *stint*, a task, or a derivative of G *Stunde*, an hour, MHG-OHG *stunt*, a point of time, cf the syn MD *stont*, D *stond*, themselves akin to **stand**.

**stunt** (2), to check, or to hinder, the normal growth of, whence the pa **stunted**, derives from the now only dial adj **stunt**, undersized, OE *stunt*, dull, stupid, sense-influenced by ON *stuttr*, Nor *stutt*, short: f.a.e., STINT.

**stupe** (Med). See STOP, para 4.

**stupefaction, stupefy; stupendous; stupid, stupidity; stupor.** See TYPE, para 5.

**stuprate, stupration, struprum.** See TYPE, para 6.

**sturdy.** See ADDENDA TO DICTIONARY.

**sturgeon** comes, by aphesis, from MF-F *esturgeon*, of Frankish origin: cf OHG *sturio* (MHG *stüre*, G *Stör*) and ON *styria*, prob akin to ON *störr*, big, 'as the largest river-fish' (Walshe).

**stutter.** See PIERCE, para 4.

**sty** (1), a pen or enclosure, esp in **pigsty; steward,** whence **stewardess; Stewart, Stuart.**

1. *Sty*, OE *stī*, is akin to ON *stī*, a stall, *stīa*, a sty, a kennel, OHG *stīga*, MHG *stīge*, a (small-) cattle pen.

2. OE *stī*, var *stīg*, has cpd *stīweard* (*stigweard*), lit 'warden of the sty', ME *stiward*, E *steward*, with rapidly elevated status. E *steward* has the mainly Sc var *stewart*, which, used as PN, is anglicized as *Stuart*.

**sty** (2), an inflamed swelling on eyelid, is app a b/f from the now dial *styany*—f/e apprehended as *sty on eye*—from ME-EE *styan*, itself from OE *stīgend*, from OE *stīgan*, to rise, (hence) to swell: cf:

**sty** (3), to ascend (obs), ME *styen, stien*, OE *stīgan* (cf prec), akin to the syn OHG *stīgan* (G *steigen*), OFris *stīga*, Go *steigan*, ON *stīga*, themselves akin to Gr *steikhein*, to go, to walk, and Skt *stighnōti*, he walks, he climbs: IE r, *\*steig-*, to step, to walk.

2. Very closely related to Gr *steikhein*, to walk (make a long line of steps), is Gr *stikhos*, a line, a row, whence, prob via LL *stichus*, a line of writing, the E *stich*, a line of verse: cf both *distich*, a two-line group, esp the couplet, L *distichon*, Gr *distikhon*, prop the neu of the adj *distikhos* (*di-*, two-), having two lines, and *acrostic* (for *\*acrostich*), EF-F *acrostiche*, L *acrostichis*, Gr

*akrostikhis*, var of *akrostikhion*, being *akro-*, c/f of *akros*, extreme (esp at the top) + a derivative of *stikhos*, a line.

**Stygian.** See STYX.

**-style**, as in *peristyle*. See the element *-stylar*.

**style, stylish, stylist, stylistic, stylize.** See STICK, para 8.

**stylet.** See STICK, para 9.

**stylus.** See STICK, para 8.

**stymie** (n, hence v), orig Sc, app comes from earlier Sc *stymie*, a dim-sighted, hence awkward-moving, person, from *styme*, a (mere) glimpse, a glimmer (but no more): o.o.o.

**styptic**: L *stypticus*, astringent, Gr *stuptikos*, from *stuptos*, the pp of *stuphein*, to contract: cf Gr *stuptikon*, LL *stypticum*, an astringent, LL *stypsis*, from Gr *stupsis* (στῦψις), astringency, adopted by Med.

**Styx**, a river to be crossed by the dead, comes from L *Styx*, trln of Gr *Stux* (gen *Stugos*), akin to Gr *stugein*, to hate, and *stux*, frost, cold (lit 'the *hated*'): IE r, *\*stu-*, to be stiff. The adj of *Stux* is *Stugios*, whence L *Stygius*, whence E *Stygian*.

**suasible, suasion, suasive.** See para 3 of:

**suave, suavity**—cf sweet (adj, hence n and obsol v), whence **sweeten, sweetness** (OE *swētness*), and many cpds, e.g. **sweetbread, sweetheart, sweetmeat, sweet pea, sweetsop; suade, suasible, suasion, suasive—assuage, assuagement, assuasive—dissuade, dissuasion, dissuasive—persuade** (whence **persuadable** and **persuader**), **persuasible, persuasion, persuasive;—hedonic, hedonism, hedonist.**

1. Adopted from EF-F, *suave* comes from ML *suāvis*, neu *suāve*, L *suāuis, suāue*; and *suavity* adapts OF-F *suavité*, from ML *suāvitatem*, acc of *suāvitās*, L *suāuitās*, from *suāuis*, sweet to taste and smell, gentle or soft to the touch, agreeable to the eye.

2. Akin to L *suāuis* is E **sweet**, ME *swete*, var *swote*, from OE *swēte*, adv *swōte*: cf OFris *swēte*, OS *swōti*, OHG *swuozi, suozi*, MHG *süeze*, G *süss*, Go *sūts*, MD *suete, soete, soet, zoete*, D *zoet*, ON *soetr*.

3. L *suāuis* stands for *\*suāduis*. The r *suād*- occurs also in L *suādēre*, to counsel or advise, whence the now dial 'to *suade*'; derivatives L *suāsibilis*, L *suāsio* (o/s *suāsiōn-*), L *suāsōrius* yield **suasible, suasion, suasory; suasive** is an anl E formation.

4. L *suādēre* has two cpds affecting E:

*dissuādēre*, to counsel from (*dis-*, apart), i.e. against, becomes—perh via MF-F *dissuader*—the E 'to *dissuade*', and its derivative *dissuāsiō*, o/s *dissuāsiōn-*, yields **dissuasion**, whence, anl, *dissuasive* (after *persuasive*);

*persuādēre*, to counsel thoroughly (int *per-*), becomes MF-F *persuader*, whence 'to *persuade*'; derivatives *persuāsibilis* and *persuāsiō*, o/s *persuāsiōn-*, become **persuasible** and MF-F *persuasion*, adopted by E; derivative late MF-F *persuasif*, f *persuasive*, becomes E *persuasive*.

5. L *suāuis*, ML *suāvis*, has the ML derivative *suāviāre* (*suāviāri*), to give pleasure to: and it

occurs in OF-MF *assuagier*, var *assoagier*, formed as if from ML *\*assuāviāre* (*-āri*): *ad*, to, towards+ *suāviāre* (*-āri*). OF-MF *assuagier* becomes ME *asuagie* ᵢ or *aswagen* (a phon var), whence 'to assuage'; derivative OF-MF *assuagement* (*asso-, asu-*) becomes *assuagement*. E *assuasive* derives, irreg, from *assuage*, as if from L *\*assuāsus*, pp of *\*assuādēre* (*ad*+*suādere*).

6. L *suāuis*, sweet, is akin to Gr *hēdus*, sweet, whence *hēdonē*, pleasure, with adj *hēdonikos*, whence E *hedonic*, extn *hedonical*; whence, anl, *hedonism* and *hedonist* (whence *hedonistic*).

7. Akin to L *suāuis* (for *\*suāduis*), sweet, is L *suādus*, persuasive, so illuminatingly related to Gr *hēdus*, sweet: akin to all these is Skt *svādús*, var *svādvi̇́*, sweet: cf Skt *svādatē*, he takes pleasure in or is pleased to, and *svādma*, sweetness. The Gmc r is *\*swōt-*; the IE r, *\*swād-* (*\*suād-*), sweet.

**sub.** L *sub*, the prep 'under'—see Prefixes— occurs in a vast number of E words, sometimes in its lit sense, sometimes fig—whether 'subordinately' or 'partially' or 'secretly'. For the majority of words not listed below, one needs only to consult what is obviously the main word, as e.g. in 'sub*conscious*'.

**subaltern,** adj, hence n: late MF-F *subalterne*: LL *subalternus*, subordinate: L *sub*, under+ *alternus*, alternate, from *alter*, other (cf E *altruism*).

**subconscious(ness).** See SCIENCE (heading).

**subdivide, -division.** A *sub-* derivative of DIVIDE.

**subdual.** See DUKE, heading, s.f.

**subduce, subduction.** See DUKE, para 6 (at *sub-ducere*).

**subdue.** See DUKE, para 9, s.f.

**subfusc.** See OBFUSCATE, s.f.

**subjacent:** ML *subjacent-*, o/s of ML *subjacens*, L *subiacens*, presp of *subiacēre*, to lie (*iacēre*) under (*sub*): cf *adjacent* and:

**subject,** adj, n, v; **subjection, subjective** (adj, hence n). In E, as for F *sujet*, the adj precedes the n; both of the E uses come from F; the F (MF *suget*, OF *sugez*) comes from ML *subjectus*, pp of *subjicere*, L *subiicere* (*subicere*), to throw, hence to bring or place under: *sub*, under+*-i(i)cere*, c/f of *iacere*, to throw, the active aspect of *iacēre*, to lie down: f.a.e., JET.—'To *subject*' derives from MF *subjecter*, ML *subjectāre*, L *subiectāre*, freq of *subiicere*; *subjection* and *subjective* derive from OF-MF *subjection* (ML *subjectiōnem*, acc of *subjectiō*, L *subiectiō*, from the pp *subiectus*) and late MF-F *subjectif*, f *-ive* (ML *subjectivus*).

**subjoin, subjoinder.** See JOIN, para 17, s.f.

**subjugate, subjugation.** See JOIN, para 13, s.f.

**subjunct, subjunction, subjunctive.** See JOIN, para 14, s.f.

**sublate, sublation.** See the 1st TOLL, para 6.

**sublimate, sublimation.** See LIMIT, para 9.

**sublime, sublimity.** See LIMIT, para 9.

**subliminal.** See LIMIT, para 9.

**sublunary.** See the 3rd LIGHT, para 12.

**submarine.** See the 2nd MERE, para 3, s.f.

**submerge, submerse, submersion.** See MERGE, para 5.

**submission, submissive, submit.** See MISSION, para 21.

**submotive.** See MOVE (heading, s.f.).

**subnormal**=L *sub*, under+*normal*, the adj of norm.

**subordinate, subordination.** See ORDER, para 14.

**suborn, subornation:** MF-F *suborner* and its derivative MF-F *subornation:* L *subornāre*, lit to equip (*ornāre*: cf ORNAMENT) secretly (*sub-*), and ML *subornātiō*, o/s *subornātiōn*.

**subpoena.** See PAIN, para 1.

**subrogate, subrogation.** See ROGATION, para 12.

**subscribe, subscript, subscription.** See SCRIBE, para 20.

**subscrive.** See SCRIBE, para 20, s.f.

**subsection.** See the 2nd SAW, para 14.

**subsecute, subsecution; subsequence, subsequent.** See SEQUENCE, para 14.

**subsert.** See SERIES, para 16.

**subserve, subservience, subservient.** See SERVE, para 9.

**subside, subsidence, subsident; subsidiary, subsidy.** See SIT, para 19.

**subsign.** See SIGN, para 19.

**subsist, subsistence, subsistent, subsistential.** See SIST, para 9.

**substance, substantial, substantiate, substantive.** See STAND, para 34.

**substitute, substitution, substitutive.** See STAND, para 36.

**substratum.** See STRATUM, para 6, s.f.

**substruct, substruction, substructure.** See STRUCTURE, para 9.

**subsume, subsumption, subsumptive.** See SUMPTION, para 6.

**subtend, subtense.** See TEND, para 20.

**subterfuge.** See FUGITIVE, para 7.

**subterranean, subterrene.** See TERRA, para 6.

**subtile,** whence—cf the F *subtiliser*—**subtilize; subtle, subtlety.** *Subtile*, now only literary, derives from MF-F *subtil*: L *subtīlis*, fine-woven, hence delicate, ingenious: *sub*, under+*tēla*, a (weaver's) web, from *texere*, to weave. L *subtīlis* also becomes OF-MF *soutil*, ME *sotill*, E *subtle*; L *subtīlitās* becomes OF-MF *soutilté*, ME *sotelte*, *sotilte*, *sutilte*, E *subtlety*.

**subtract, subtraction.** See TRACT, para 22.

**subtropical.** Cf TROPE, para 3.

**suburb, suburban.** See URBAN, para 2.

**subvene, subvention.** See VENUE, para 22.

**subversion, subversive, subvert.** See VERSE, para 15.

**succeed.** See CEDE, para 13.

**success, successful, succession, successive, successor.** See CEDE, para 14.

**succinct.** See CINCH, para 5.

**succor.** See SUCCOUR.

**succory.** See CHICORY, para 2.

**succour,** AE **succor.** See COURSE, para 10 (at *succurrere*).

**succubus.** See HIVE, para 5, s.f.

**succulent.** See SUCK, para 3.

**succumb.** See HIVE, para 8, s.f.

**succursal.** See COURSE, para 10 (at *succurrere*).

**such,** whence **suchlike** (cf LIKE) and **suchness:** late ME *such*, earlier *swich*, still earlier *swilc* or *swulc*, OE *swelc, swilc, swylc:* cf OFris *sālik, salk, sēlik, selk, sullik, sulk, suk,* OS *sulīh,* OHG *sulīh, solīh,* MHG *sulich,* MHG-G *solch,* and ON *slīkr,* with modern Scan cognates: whereas the MD forms leading to D *zulk* exhibit both the extreme vocalic uncertainty and the hesitation between two syllables and one, (thus:) *selc, solc, swelc, swilc, suelc, suilc, sulec, sulic, sullich, sulch, sulc, zulc,* the Go syn *swaleiks* indicates that the basic meaning is 'so-bodied, having such a body' (hence 'so, i.e. thus, shaped'): *swa,* so, q.v. at so+*leik,* a body, q.v. at LIKE.

**suck** (v, hence n), whence **sucker** and the pa, vn **sucking**—whence also the freq (*-le*) 'to suckle', whence **suckler** and the pa, vn **suckling**—cf **honeysuckle; soak** (v, hence n), whence **soakage, soaker,** pa and vn **soaking;—succulent,** whence **succulence,** with var **succulency; suction,** whence, imm, **suctional** and, anl, the Zoo **Suctoria.**

1. 'To *soak*,' ME *soken,* OE *socian,* to lie in, e.g., water and thus become saturated, is akin to 'to *suck*', ME *suken* (*souken*) OE *sūcan:* cf OE *sūgan* (the *g* exhibits the common O Gmc trend), OHG *sūgan,* MHG *sūgen,* G *saugen,* MD *sugen, zugen, suken, suygen, suyken,* D *zuigen,* ON *sūga;* OIr *sūgim,* I suck, Ga *sūghadh,* a soaking, OIr *sūg-,* Ga *sūgh,* juice; Lith *sùkt,* to suck; L *sūgere,* to suck. The IE r is prob *\*suk-* (*\*seuk-*), to suck, an extn of the *\*sū-* or *\*seu-,* which, occurring in SUP (cf Skt *sūpas,* broth), perh means 'moisture'.

2. The freq 'to *suckle*' has the force of a caus: cf the syn OHG *sougēn,* G *säugen,* clearly the caus of *saugen,* to suck. (Walshe.) *Suckle* has influenced the passage of *honeysuckle,* ME *hunisuccle* (*honysocle*), from OE *hunigsūce,* privet—a plant suckable for honey. (Cf HONEY.)

3. L *sūgere,* to suck, has pp *sūctus,* s *sūct-,* whence LL *sūctiō,* o/s *sūctiōn-,* whence MF *suction* (F *succion*), adopted by E. Akin to L *sūgere,* pp *sūctus,* is L *sūcus,* var *succus,* juice, whence LL *sūculentus,* var *succulentus,* juicy (esp if agreeably so), full of sap (lit and fig), whence late MF-F and, perh independently, E *succulent.*

**suckle.** See prec, heading and para 2.

**sucrose.** See SUGAR, para 2.

**suction.** See SUCK, para 3.

**sudamen, sudation, sudatory.** See SWEAT, para 2.

**sudden** (whence **suddenness**), **suddenty.** The Sc *suddenty* derives, by contr, from MF *sodeineté* (F *soudaineté*), from MF *sodein, sodain, sudain* (F *soudain*), whence ME *sodain, sodein,* E *sudden:* and MF *sodein, sodain* derives from VL *\*subitānus,* mdfn of L *subitāneus,* an extn of syn *subitus,* itself from *subitum,* the supine of *subīre* (lit, to go, *īre,* under, *sub*), to come or steal upon: f.a.e., ISSUE.

**sudor, sudorific.** See SWEAT, para 2.

**suds.** See SEETHE, para 2.

**sue.** See SEQUENCE, para 4.

**suède.** See SWEDEN, para 2.

**suet.** See SOAP, para 3.

**suffer** (whence **sufferer** and pa, vn **suffering,** as in long-suffering), **sufferable, sufferance, insufferable.**

*Insufferable,* the neg of *sufferable,* was perh suggested by F *insouffrable,* neg of *souffrable,* OF-MF *soufrable* (whence E *sufferable*), from MF *soufrir* (F *souffrir*), OF-MF *sofrir, sufrir,* whence ME *soffren, suffren,* whence 'to *suffer*'; E *sufferance* reshapes ME *suffrance,* adopted from OF-MF *sufrance* (F *souffrance*), from *sufrir.* OF-MF *sufrir* derives from VL *sufferīre,* mdfn of L *sufferre,* to bear (*ferre*), under (*sub*), hence to support (lit and fig): f.a.e., FERTILE.

**suffice, sufficiency, sufficient; insufficiency, insufficient.** The negg derive from LL *insufficientia* (from the L adj) and LL *insufficiens,* o/s *insufficient-:* corresp to LL *sufficientia,* whence E *sufficiency,* and L *sufficiens,* o/s *sufficient-,* prop the presp of *sufficere,* to make, hence put, under (*suf-* for *sub-*), hence to substitute, hence to be a substitute for: f.a.e., FACT. L *sufficere* becomes OF-MF *soufire,* late MF-F *suffire,* whence, via the pres s *suffis-* (as in *suffis*ant, presp, and 'ils *suffis*ent'), the ME *suffisen,* later *sufficen,* whence 'to *suffice*'.

**suffix.** See FIX, para 3.

**sufflate, sufflation.** See FLATUS, para 9.

**suffocate, suffocation** (whence, anl, **suffocative**); **fauces, faucal.**

1. *Suffocation* is adopted from MF-F, which derives it from L *suffocātiōnem,* acc of *suffocātiō,* itself from *suffocātus,* pp of *suffocāre,* to choke (someone): lit, to put one's hands 'under' (*sub*) the *fauces,* neck or throat, of.

2. L *fauces,* throat, gullet, (exterior part of the) neck, is prop the pl of the syn *faux,* gen *faucis,* o/s *fauc-:* o.o.o. Adopted by An, Zoo, Bot, *fauces* has the adj *faucal* (*fauc-*+*-al*).

**Suffolk.** See NORFOLK.

**suffragan.** See FRACTION, para 11.

**suffrage,** whence **suffragette.** See FRACTION, para 11.

**suffuse, suffusion.** See the 2nd FOUND, para 14.

**sugar,** n (whence **sugary**), hence v (cf the F *sucrer*); **sucrose; saccharin,** n, and derivatively **saccharine** (adj and var n, whence **saccharinic**), whence, anl, **saccharate** (Chem *-ate*), **saccharic, saccharose**—cf the element *sacchar-*; **jaggery.**

1. *Sugar,* ME *suger,* earlier *sugre,* earliest *sucre,* derives from MF-F *sucre,* OF-MF *sukere:* It *zucchero:* Ar *sukkar* (*soukkar*): Perh *shakar:* Prakrit *sakkara:* Skt *śārkarā,* sugar, orig grit or gravel—cf Gr *krokalai,* gravel, pl of *krokalē,* a pebble. Note that the *-ar* form prob shows the influence of ML *succarum* (var *zugurum*), app an extn of LL *zuecar* (cf the Sp *azucar,* where *a*- represents Ar *al,* the), itself from the Ar word; note also that the Per intervention illustrates the fact that sugar was first refined in Persia. (Webster; E & M; Hofmann.)

2. From F *sucre,* Chem derives *sucrose*—prob after *saccharose*—by adding the suffix *-ose* (cf *dextrose, glucose,* etc.).

3. In *saccharose, -ose* is tacked onto *sacchar-,* the base of *saccharin,* which tacks the Chem suffix *-in*

to L *sacchar*um, a kind of sugar made from bamboo shoots: Gr *sákkharon*, var of *sákkhari*, itself a var of *sákkhar* (σάκχαρ): Pali *sakkharā*, this sort of sugar: Skt *śárkarā* (as above).

4. Skt *śárkarā* becomes Hi *jāgrī*, crude sugar, whence E *jaggery*.

**suggest, suggestible, suggestion, suggestive.** See GERUND, para 14.

**suicide** (n, hence v), whence **suicidal**, is adopted from F: in F, *suicide* the person derives from *suicide* the act: and the latter, both in form and in senses, imitates the F *homicide*: L *sui*, of oneself+ L *-cidium*, a slaying, and *-cida*, a slayer, c/ff of *caedere*, to slay.

**suit, suitable, suite, suitor.** See SEQUENCE, para 5.

**sulfur.** See SULPHATE.

**sulk** (v, hence n), **sulky** (adj and n). 'To *sulk*' comes, by b/f, from *sulky*, sullen, whence the carriage *sulky*, built for use by only one person: and the adj *sulky* app comes, with the suffix -*y* for the ending -*en*, from ME *sulken*, OE -*solcen*, slothful, as in *āsolcen*, orig the pp of -*seolcan*, as in *aseolcan*, to be slothful, to be weak: cf MHG *selken*, to drop, to droop. (Webster.)

**sullage.** See the 1st SOW, para 5.

**sullen.** See the 1st SOLE, para 2, s.f.

**sully.** See the 1st SOW, para 5.

**sulphate, sulphide, sulphite; sulphuric, sulphurous; sulphur,** var **sulfur.** The first three come from *sulph-*, r of *sulphur*, whence *sulphuric* (cf the F *sulfurique*); *sulphureous* comes from L *sulphureus*, and *sulphurous*, like F *sulfureux*, comes from LL *sulphurōsus*, adj of *sulphur*, var *sulfur*, both being varr of *sulpur*, o.o.o.

2. From *sulf-*, r of L *sulfur*, comes the syn It *solfo* (*zolfo*(, whence the adj *solferino*, dark-red, whence the PlN *Solferino*, scene (1859) of a battle, which, by the way, gave its name to a dye called also *magenta*.

**sultan, sultana, sultanate; soldan; Soudan or Sudan.**

1. *Soldan* is reshaped from ME *soudan*, adopted from late MF-EF *soudan*, a sultan—a form preserved in 'the *Soudan* (or *Sudan*)', formerly ruled by the Sultan of Egypt, lit '(the Land of) the Sultan'. Like MF-F *soudan*, the EF-F *sultan*, adopted by E, derives, via Tu-Ar *soltān*, from Ar *sultān*, a ruler, (orig) power, dominion, itself from Syriac.

2. A sultan's wife is a *sultana*, adopted from It (the f of *sultano*); his dominion is a *sultanate* (-*ate*, connoting 'possession')—perh from F *sultanat*. The *sultana grape*, hence the *sultana* (*raisin*), is grown near Smyrna in Turkey; but the dictionaries omit to explain why these particular grapes and raisins are called *sultanas*; yet the explanation is simple—these grapes are seedless.

**sultry.** See SWELTER (heading).

**sum** (n and v) and **soum; summa, summary** (adj, n), whence **summarize,** whence **summarization; summit;—consummate** (adj, v), **consummation** (whence, anl, **consummative**), **consummator**—cf **consommé.**

1. 'To *sum*' derives from OF-MF *summer* (MF-F *sommer*), ML *summāre*, to calculate the total of, LL to bring to the culminating point, from L *summa*, elliptical for *res summa*, the highest thing, hence the aggregate or total of the parts, esp—from *summa linea*, the highest line—the total of a set of figures (esp monetary), 'from the Romans', like the Greeks', habit of counting upwards from the foot' of a column of figures (E & M), hence a sum of money, also the essential or most important part or point, in ML a comprehensive treatise, notably Thomas Aquinas's *Summa Theologica*.—The L n *summa* becomes OF-MF *summe* (MF-F *somme*), adopted by ME (var *somme*), whence 'a *sum*'.

2. L *summa* has a derivative that concerns E: **summārius*, containing a summing-up, whence LL *summārius*, an accountant, and L *summārium*, an abstract or an abridgement, whence the E n *summary*, whence, in part, the adj *summary*.

3. From LL-ML *summāre*, pp *summātus* (s *summāt-*), comes the Modern L *summātiō*, o/s *summātiōn-*, whence E *summation*, which, however, prob owes something to MF-F *sommation* (from *sommer*); and from the adj *summus*, highest, comes the LL *summitās*, the top part or highest point, whence E *summit*, owing perh something to OF *summet* (MF-F *sommet*), dim of OF *sum, som*, varr of OF-MF *summe*, MF-F *somme*.

4. The odd-looking *soum* (mostly Sc), a fixed area of pastureland, is merely a var of E *sum*.

5. The L *summa*, a total, a sum, has the derivative prefix-cpd *consummāre* (*con-* used int), to sum up, hence to finish or complete, to achieve, with pp *consummātus*, whence both the E adj and the E v *consummate*. Derivatives LL *consummātiō* (o/s *consummātiōn-*), a completion, LL *consummātor*, a completer or achiever, LL *consummatōrius*, yield OF-MF *consummation* (MF-F *consommation*), adopted by E—(EF-F *consommateur* and) E *consum(m)ator*—E *consummatory*.

6. L *consummāre* becomes OF-MF *consumer*, MF-F *consommer*, with pp *consommé* used as adj and then, in EF-F, as n—as n influenced by OF-F *consumer*, to consume, a confusion existing already in LL between *consummāre* and *consūmere*. The culinary *consommé* was adopted by E.

**sumac,** var **sumach:** MF-F *sumac*: ML (Med or apothecaries') *sumach*: Ar *summāq*.

**summa.** See SUM, para 1.

**summary.** See SUM, para 2.—SUMMATION: ibid, para 3.

**summer** (n, hence v); whence **summery; gossamer, gosmore.**

1. *Summer*, ME *sumer* (var *somer*), OE *sumer, sumor*, is akin to OFris *sumur*, OS *sumar*, OHG *sumar*, MHG *sumer*, G *Sommer*, MD *sommer, somer*, MD-D *zomer*, ON *sumar* (with modern Scan cognates); OIr *sam* and, with abstract suffix -*rad, samrad* (Ga *sàmhradh*), OC *samo-*, there being the normal *h*-for-*s* variation in W and Cor *hâf*, Cor and Br *hân*; Arm *amaṙn*; Av *hama*,

summer, and Skt *sámā*, a year, a half-year, a season. The IE r is app *\*sam-*, var *\*sem-*, summer.

2. ME *sumer* or *somer* occurs in the cpd *gosesomer*, often contr to *gossomer* or *gossum(m)er*, lit 'goose summer'—? warm November weather, suitable for the eating of geese—hence, cobwebs floating in calm, esp calm autumnal, weather, hence *gossamer*, applied also to a cobweb-like fabric: cf, sem, the G *fliegender Sommer*, lit 'flying summer', hence gossamer. In dial E, *gossamer* is applied to plant-down, whence, prob, *gosmore*, a herb with feather-like leaves and feathery tufts.

**summerset.** See SALLY, para 8.

**summit.** See SUM, para 3.

**summon, summons.** The latter comes, through ME *somouns*, from OF-MF *somons, sumons, sumuns*, a vn from OF-MF *somondre, sumondre, sumundre* (var *semondre*), to convoke, to bid come, esp to a meeting: VL *\*summonere*, assimilation of VL *\*submonere*: L *summonēre*, for *submonēre*, to warn (*monēre*) secretly (connoted by *sub*, under): cf ad*monish* and *monition, monitor*, qq.v. at MIND. —The OF-MF *summundre, sumondre, somondre* becomes ME *sumonen* (*somonen*), whence 'to *summon*'.

**summum bonum:** L 'the highest good': cf SUM, para 1, and BONNY.

**sump.** See SWAMP.

**sumption; sumptuary, sumptuous.**—Cpds: assume assumpsit, assumption, assumptive; consume (whence consumer), consumptible, consumption (whence, anl, consumptive, adj hence n); presume (whence presumable), presumption, presumptive, presumptuous; resume, résumé, resumption, resumptive; subsume (whence, anl, subsumption).

1. *Sumption*, a taking, e.g. for granted—*sumptuary—sumptuosity, sumptuous*, derive from L *sumptiō* (o/s *sumptiōn-*)—L *sumptuārius*—L *sumptuōsitās*, from *sumptuōsus*: cf EF-F *somptuaire*, MF-F *somptueux*, f *somptueuse*, late MF-F *somptuosité*. All the L words are formed upon *sumptus*, pp of *sūmere*, to take (upon oneself), to take charge of, hence to undertake, to take by choice, also to spend: o.o.o.: perh *sus*- (for *sub*-), eased to *sū-*+*emere*, to take (cf EMPTION).

2. L *assūmere*, for *adsūmere*, to take *ad*, to oneself, to borrow, yields (late MF-F *assumer* and) 'to *assume*'; derivative from the pp *assumpt*us are *assumptiō* (o/s *assumptiōn-*) and *assumptiuus*, ML *assumptivus*, whence—cf the OF-F *assomption—assumption* (Eccl senses from LL) and *assumptive*. The legal *assumpsit* is sense-adapted from L *assumpsit*, he has undertaken.

3. L *consūmere*, to take *con-* or completely, to devour or destroy (e.g., by fire), yields OF-F *consumer*, whence 'to *consume*'. On the pp *consumptus* are formed LL *consumptībilis*, whence E *consumptible*; *consumptiō*, o/s *consumptiōn-*, whence *consumption* (cf MF-F *consomption*).

4. L *praesūmere*, to take *prae-* or in advance, hence, for granted, hence, in LL, to be arrogant or think arrogantly, whence OF-MF *presumer*

(F *pré*), whence 'to *presume*'. On the pp *praesumptus* are formed *praesumptiō*, o/s *praesumptiōn-*, whence OF-MF *praesumpcion*, MF *presomption* (F *pré*-), whence E *presumption*; LL *praesumptiuus*, ML *-ivus*, OF-MF *presumptif*, MF *presomptif* (F *pré*-), whence E *presumptive*; LL *praesumptuōsus*, OF *presumptueux*, MF-F *presomptueux* (F *pré*-), E *presumptuous*. The inferior E *presumptious* goes back to LL *praesumptiōsus*, arrogant, conceited.

5. L *resumere*, to take, or to take up, again, becomes MF-F *résumer*, whence 'to *resume*'; used as n, the F pp *résumé* is adopted by E. On the L pp *resumptus* are formed LL *resumptiō*, o/s *resumptiōn-*, whence, perh via F, the E *resumption*, and LL *resumptiuus*, ML *-ivus*, whence E *resumptive*.

6. Formed anl with the prec E vv in *-sume* is 'to *subsume*', lit to take, hence to put or include, under.

**sun** (n, hence v), whence sunny; Sunday; many other cpds, all self-explanatory; cf the sep SOLAR and the sep SOUTH.

1. *Sun*, ME *sunne* (var *sonne*), OE *sunne*, is related to OFris *sunne*, OS *sunna*, OHG *sunna*, MHG-G *sonne*, Go *sunnō*, MD *sunne, sonne, zonne*, D *zon*, ON *sunna*; perh the OIr, Ga, Mx *grian*, W *greian*; Av *khvēng*, of the sun (for *\*soan-s*), and *xvan*vant (? *khvan*vant), sunny. If the IE r be *\*swon-*, and if that of L *sōl* be *\*swol-*, the ult base is *\*swo-*, to shine. Cf para 3.

2. OE *sunne* has cpd *sunnandaeg*, whence E *Sunday*, lit 'the day of the sun', prompted by L *dies solis*: cf OFris *sunnan-dei*, OHG *sunnuntag*, G *Sonntag*, ON *sunnudagr*.

3. Akin to L *sōl* (q.v. at *solar*) is Gr *hēlios*, s *hēli-*, r *hēl-*; the Sun God, therefore, is *Hēlios*. The derivative Gr adj is *hēliakos*, whence Astron *heliac*, extn *heliacal*. The c/f of *hēlios* is *hēlio-*, occurring in such cpds as *helianthus* and *heliotrope*, qq.v. at the element *helio-*.

**sundae**, as Mencken and Mathews admit, is, like the obs spelling *sundi* (or *S*—), a derivative of *Sunday*, a common spelling c1900–1908; both of those authorities, like Webster, think the term o.o.o. Whitehall suggests 'from being orig sold only on this day'. Perh rather because, whereas an ordinary ice-cream was good enough for a weekday, only this special kind was good enough for a Sunday.

**Sunday.** See SUN, para 2.

**sunder** and **asunder; sundry.** 'To *sunder*', ME *sundren*, OE *-sundrian, -syndrian*, occurring in cpds: perh from OE *sundor*, separately, asunder: cf OHG *suntarōn*, ON *sundra*, to sunder, and OFris *sunder*, OS *sundar*, OHG *suntar*, MHG *sunder*, G *sonder*, MD *sunder, sonder*, MD-D *zonder*, without, Go *sundrō*, separately, alone, ON *sundr*, asunder: cf also Skt *sanútar*, far away, *sanitúr*, separately—therefore cf L *sine*, without, and Ir *sain*, Cor *kēn*, different. The IE r is app *\*sen-*, separately; Gr has an *s-*less var in *aneu*, without. IE *\*sen-* is perh an extn of a basic *\*se-*, as in the L privative prefix *se-* (as in *separate*).

2. *Sundry*, ME var *sondry*, derives from OE

*syndrig*, akin to OE *sundor*, apart, separately: cf the syn OHG *sundric*.

**sunk, sunken.** See SINK (heading).

**sup**, to sip (whence **sup**, a mouthful, a sip) and to take supper—cf **supper**; **seep** (v, hence n), whence **seepage**; **sip** (v, hence n), whence **sipper** and **sipping**; **sop** (n and v), whence **sopping** and **soppy**; **soup**, whence **soupy;—sob**.

1. *Sup*, take supper, comes partly from ME *soupen*, *supen*, to drink in sips, and partly from OF-MF *soper*, *super* (F *souper*), to take one's evening meal (F to take supper); *supper*, the evening meal, comes from ME *super*, var *soper*, from OF-MF *super* (*soper*), the v used as n; 'to *sup*' or sip has been influenced by *supper*, but comes, in form, from ME *soupen*, *supen*, from OE *sūpan*, akin to MD *supen* (var *zupen*), D *zuipen*, OFris *sūpa*, to sip, OHG *sūfan*, MHG *sūfen*, G *saufen*, ON *sūpa* (with modern Scan cognates): ult echoic.

2. With the ON *sūpa*, cf the syn Da *söbe*: cf also 'to *sob*' or weep convulsively (as if in sips), ME *sobben*, akin to OE *sēofian*, *sīofian*, to wail or complain: cf OHG *sūfan*, MHG *sūfen*, to sip, used also for 'to draw breath' (whence OHG-MHG *sūft*, a sigh), and MHG *siufzen*, G *seufzen*, to sigh: all clearly echoic.

3. OF-MF *soper*, *super*, to take one's evening meal, derives from (doubtless OF-)MF *supe*, *sope*, later *soupe*, a piece of bread steeped in broth or soup, hence, in EF, bread soup, hence soup: whence E *soup*. OF-MF *supe*, MF-F *soupe*, comes from LL *suppa*, a slice of bread dipped in gravy, a sop (Souter), itself prob of Gmc origin: cf E *sop*, from OE *sopp* (cf ON *soppa*), whence OE *soppian*, to steep or dip in a liquid, whence 'to *sop*'.

4. Akin to—and prob a thinned derivative from —OE *sūpan*, to sip, is ME *sippen*, E 'to *sip*': cf OE *sypian*, *sipian*, and LG *sippen*, to sip. Hence, sense-influenced by 'a *sop*', comes *sippet*.

5. Akin, phon, to OE *sypian*, *sipian*, to sip, is 'to *seep*', to leak slowly through pores or very small interstices: but prob imm, both phon and sem, from MD *sipen*, to drip.

**super**, above, over, occurring in so many prefix-cpds, is the syn L adv and prep *super*, akin to Gr *huper* (*h* for *s*); also to L *sub*, under, up under. Clearly, then, L *sub* and *super* represent a *b-p* alternation (sense-imposed), *super* being *sup-*+ suffix *-er*: and they answer to an IE *\*sup-* (var *\*sub-*), very prob an extn of *\*su-*, applied to the 'above-and-below' relationship: cf OVER, Skt *úpari*, Go *ufar*, above; cf also Gr *hupo*, Skt *úpa*, under.

2. Most of the *super-* cpds not listed below are explained by the main word it prefixes. But L *super* has a few direct, simple derivatives that are best treated here.

3. L *super* has derivative *superāre*, to overcome, whence *superābilis*, neg *insuperābilis*, whence E *superable* and *insuperable*; *superāre* becomes Prov *soubra*, to be (fig) above, whence *soubret*, coy, f *soubreto*, whence the EF-F theatrical *soubrette*, a coquettish lady's-maid, adopted by E; L *super*

acquires the adj *supernus*, being above, hence on high, hence sublime, heavenly, whence MF-EF *supernal* (F *-nel*), adopted by E.

4. L *super* also acquires the VL adj *\*superānus*, whence It *soprano*, adj, hence n, adopted by Mus, as is the It cpd *mezzo-soprano*, a 'medium soprano', half-way between soprano and contralto.

5. Also from VL *\*superānus* comes the OF-MF adj *sovrain*, whence the archaic adj, hence n, *sovran*, with *sovranty* deriving from OF-MF *sovraineté*. The OF-MF adj *sovrain* has varr *souvrain* and esp *soverain* (cf F *souverain*), whence ME *soverain* (*-ein*), *soverayn* (*-eyn*), E *sovereign*. The OF-MF *soverain* (*sovrain*), F *souverain*, is used also as n, whence the E n 'a king'; the sense 'gold coin' derives from the royal heads effigied on coins. OF *soverain*, *sovrain* has the abstract OF-MF derivative *soveraineté* (*sovraineté*; F *souveraineté*), whence ME *soverainetee* (etc.), whence E *sovereignty*. (Cf the complementary SUZERAIN.)

**superabound; superabundance, superabundant.** See UNDA, para 4.

**superadd**: L *superaddere*.—**superaddition**: LL *superadditiō*, o/s *superadditiōn-*. Cf SUPER and ADD.

**superannuate, superannuation**. See ANNUAL, para 4.

**superb**: F *superbe*, magnificent, EF-F imposingly beautiful, OF-EF haughty: L *superbus*, (arrogantly) proud, (orig) lofty: *super*, above+ suffix *-bus*—cf L *prōbus* from *prō* (E & M).

**supercargo.** See CARGO.

**superciliary, supercilious.** See CILIARY, para 2.

**supererogate, supererogation, supererogatory.** See ROGATION, para 14.

**superfetate, superfetation.** See FETUS, para 2.

**superficial, superficiality, superficies.** See FACE, para 7.

**superfine**: late EF-F *superfin*, f *-fine*, whence, in the 1890's, the abbr *super*, which has influenced the E sl word.

**superfluity, superfluous.** See FLUENT, para 10.

**superhuman.** See HOMO, para 9.

**superimpose, superimposition.** See POSE, para 11, s.f.

**superintend, superintendence, superintendent.** See TEND, para 21.

**superior** (adj, hence n), **superiority; supreme, supremacy.** L *super* (cf SUPER) has adj *superus*, being, or placed, above, with comp *superior*, adopted by OF-MF (F *supérieur*) and, in turn, by E, the derivative *superiority* coming, via late MF-F *superiorité*, from ML *superioritās*; and with sup *suprēmus*, whence, perh via late MF-F *suprême*, the E *supreme*, the derivative *supremacy* being *supreme*+*-acy*.

**superlative.** See the 1st TOLL, para 6.

**superman.** See MAN, para 3.

**supernaculum**, adv. (to drink) to the last drop: mock-L cpd of *super*, above+*\*naculum*, a fingernail: G 'auf den *Nagel* trinken', to drink to the nail—no drop falling onto one's thumb-nail from an upturned glass.

supernal. See SUPER, para 3.
supernatural. See NATIVE, para 10.
supernumerary. See NIMBLE, para 5, s.f.
superpose, superposition. See POSE, para 21.
superscribe, superscription. See SCRIBE, para 21.
supersede, supersession. See SIT, para 6.
supersonant, supersonic. See SONABLE, para 5, s.f.
superstition, superstitious. See STAND, para 37.
superstruct, superstruction, superstructure. See STRUCTURE, para 10.
supervene, supervenient, supervention. See VENUE, para 23.
supervise, supervision, supervisor, supervisory. See VIDE, para 14.
supervolute. See VOLUBLE, para 4, s.f.
supinate (whence, anl, supinator), supination, supine (adj and n). *Supination* derives, phon, from LL *supīnātiōn-*, o/s of *supīnātiō*, regurgitation, formed from *supīnātus*—whence 'to *supinate*'—the pp of L *supīnāre*, to turn or bend or lay backwards, from *supīnus*, overturned backwards, lying on one's back, hence, in LL, listless, whence E *supine*, the derivative *supinity* coming from LL *supīnitās*; the *supine* of Gram goes back to LL *supīnum*, sc *uerbum*, a word. L *supīnus* perh stands for *\*subinus*, an *-inus* adj from *sub*, under.
supper. See SUP, para 1.
supplant, supplantation, supplanter. See the 1st PLANT, para 2.
supple, supplejack. See PLY, para 28.
supplement, supplementary, suppletory. See PLENARY, para 16.
suppliant. See PLY, para 17, s.f.
supplicant, supplicate, supplication. See PLY, para 17.
supply. See PLENARY, para 16, s.f.
support, supportable, supporter. See the 3rd PORT, para 13.
suppose, supposition, supposititious, suppository. See POSE, para 22.
suppress, suppression, suppressor. See the 2nd PRESS, para 14.
suppurant, suppurate, suppuration, suppurative: L *suppurant-*, o/s of *suppurans*, presp—*suppurātus*, pp—*suppurātiō* (o/s *suppurātiōn*), from *suppurātus*—F *suppuratif*, f *-ive*, from F *suppuration*: the L words from *suppurāre*, to yield pus: f.a.e., PUS.
supra-, L *supra*, above (mostly adv), occurring in many cpds, is intimately related to SUPER: in L, it contracts *supera*, abl of *supera*, f of *superus* (q.v. at SUPERIOR). These cpds tend to be Sci and, in general speech, rare.
suprahuman. See HOMO, para 9.
supramundane. See MUNDANE, para 2.
supremacy, supreme. See SUPERIOR.
surcease. See SIT, para 7.
surcharge. See CAR, para 4, s.f.
surcingle. See CINCH, para 6.
surd, surdity—cf absurd, absurdity; sordine;—swarm, n, hence v.

1. *Surdity*, deafness, comes—perh via EF-F

surdité—from L *surditās*, itself from *surdus*, deaf: o.o.o.: kinship with L *sonāre*, to sound, is both phon and sem improb; but L *surdus* is perh akin to such C words as OIr-Ir *bodar*, Ga *bodhar* (id in Cor).

2. L *surdus* has the secondary meaning 'indistinct (to hearing, also to smell, etc.)', whence the E adj *surd*, esp in Math for 'inexpressible in rational numbers', hence as n.

3. L *surdus* has the prefix-cpd *absurdus*, discordant, hence incongruous, hence making no sense; derivative LL *absurditās*: whence MF-F *absurde* (OF-MF *absorde*) and MF-F *absurdité*: E *absurd*, *absurdity*.

4. L *surdus* becomes It *sordo*, with cxtn *sordino*, f *sordina*, which, employed as Mus n, yields EF-F *sourdine*, whence the reshaped E *sordine*, which, inserted in a trumpet's mouth, dulls the sound.

5. There are those who, not very convincingly, relate L *surdus* to the echoic L *susurrus*, a humming, a murmuring, a rustling, a whispering, adopted by E. L *susurrus* has derivative LL *susurrāre*, to whisper, presp *susurrans*, o/s *susurrant-*, E *susurrant*, adj, and pp *susurrātus*, whence 'to *susurrate*'.

6. Perh akin to at least one of these words is E *swarm*, a vast number of bees emigrating or settling, from OE *swearm*: cf OHG-G *swarm* (of bees), G *Schwarm*, any swarm, MD *swarm*, D *zwerm*, a swarm of bees, ON *svarmr* (pron thus), a tumult: perh cf Skt *svárati*, it resounds, and *svara*, a sound, a noise.

sure. See CURE, para 7.
surette. See SOUR, para 2, s.f.
surety. See CURE, para 7.
surf. See FLATUS, final para.
surface. See FACE, para 8.
surfeit (n, hence v): ME *surfet*: MF *surfait*, OF-MF *sorfait*, (an) excess, prop the pp of OF-MF *sorfaire* (MF-F *surfaire*), to overdo: *sur*, over (L *super*)+*faire*, to do (cf FACT).
surge (v, whence, mainly, n—partly from L *surgere*), surgent, surrection; source—resource, whence resourceful and resourceless.—Cpds: insurge, insurgent (whence insurgence and insurgency), insurrection (whence insurrectionary, adj, hence n); resurge, resurgent (whence resurgence, -cy), resurrect, resurrection (whence resurrectionary, resurrectionism, etc.); sep RUCTION.

1. The adj *surgent* derives from L *surgent-*, o/s of *surgens*, presp of *surgere*, to rise, whence, via EF-F *surgir* (late MF *sourgir*), 'to *surge*'; the L pp *surrectus* leads to LL *surrectiō*, a rising, o/s *surrectiōn-*, whence the rare E *surrection*. L *surgere* is a contr of *surregere*, vi, itself an assimilation of *subregere*, vt, to direct (*regere*) from under (*sub*): f.a.e., REX.

2. L *surgere* becomes OF-F *sourdre* (OF-MF var *sordre*), whence the OF-MF *sourse* (EF-F *source*), orig the f of the pp: ME *sours*, whence, influenced by EF-F, the E *source*. For *resource*, see para 5.

3. The L cpd *insurgere*, to rise in, hence up into, hence up, yields—perh via EF-F (*s'*)*insurger*—'to

*insurge*'. The presp *insurgens*, o/s *insurgent*-, accounts for the E adj-hence-n *insurgent*; the pp *insurrectus* for 'to *insurrect*'; derivative LL *insurrectiō*, o/s *insurrectiōn*-, for MF-F *insurrection*, adopted by E.

4. L *resurgere*, to rise *re*- or again, yields 'to *resurge*'; its presp *resurgens*, o/s *resurgent*-, E *resurgent*; its pp *resurrectus*, E 'to *resurrect*'; derivative LL *resurrectiō*, o/s *resurrectiōn*-, OF-F *resurrection*, adopted by E.

5. L *resurgere* becomes OF-F *ressourdre*, whence the OF-MF n *ressourse* (prop the f of the pp), EF-F *ressource*, E *resource*.

**surgeon, surgery, surgical.** *Surgeon* derives from ME *surgien*, adopted from AF *surgien*, contr of MF *serurgien*, var of OF-MF *cirurgien* (F *chirurgien*): from OF-MF *cirurgie*, MF var *serurgie* (EF-F *chirurgie*)—whence, via the MF contr *surgerie*, the ME *surgerie*, E *surgery*. OF-MF *cirurgie* derives from L *chīrurgia*, trln of Gr *kheirourgia*, lit 'a working (*ourgia*) with the hands' (*kheir*, hand). The adj *surgical* comes, anl, from *surg*ery; prompted by the archaic *chirurgical*, extn of *chirurgic*, from L *chirurgicus* (Gr *kheirourgikos*)—cf the archaic *chirurgeon* (EF-F *chirurgien*).

**surly.** See SENILE, para 9.

**surmise** (n, hence v): MF-EF *surmise* (var *sormise*), an accusation: orig the f of the pp of *surmettre* (*sormettre*), lit to put (*mettre*, L *mittere*) *sur* (L *super*) upon, to impose, to accuse: f.a.e., MISSION. An accusation implies a supposition or guilt; hence, any supposition or conjecture.

**surmount.** See MINATORY, para 10, s.f.

**surmullet.** See MELANCHOLY, para 6.

**surname.** See NAME, para 7.

**surpass.** See PACE, para 5.

**surplice:** OF-MF *surpliz* (later, *surplis*): ML *superpellicium*: *super*, over+LL *pellicia*, a fur robe, prob the f of the adj *pellīcius*, made of skin, esp of fur, from *pellis*, skin.

**surplus** (whence **surplusage**), n, hence adj: OF-F *surplus*: OF-F *sur*, over (L *super*)+*plus*, more (L *plus*).

**surprise, surprising.** See PREHEND, para 14.

**surrealism, surrealist.** See the 1st REAL, para 1.

**surrender.** See RENDER, para 6.

**surreption.** See REPTILE, para 2.

**surreptitious.** See RAPT, para 12.

**surrey,** a horse-drawn four-wheeled, double-seated carriage, derives from the E county *Surrey*: OE *Suthrige*, partly from the pl *Suthrige*, the inhabitants of the region, partly from the OE name of the region itself: *Sūthergē*: *sūth*, south+*gē*, district.

**surrogate, surrogation.** See ROGATION, para 13.

**surround, surroundings.** See UNDA, para 4, s.f.

**surtax.** See TACT, para 7, s.f.

**surveillance, surveillant.** See VIGOR, para 6, s.f.

**survey, surveyor.** See VIDE, para 14, s.f.

**survival, survive, survivor.** See VIVA, para 6, s.f.

**susceptibility, susceptible.** See CAPABILITY, para 7, s.f.

**suscitate, suscitation.** See CITE, para 6.

**suspect.** See SPECTACLE, para 17.

**suspend, suspender; suspense, suspension, suspensive.** See PEND, para 27.

**suspicion, suspicious.** See SPECTACLE, para 17.

**suspiration, suspire.** See SPIRIT, para 13.

**Sussex** (whence—from the New Jersey county—**sussexite**): OE *Sūth Seaxe*, the land of the *Suth Seaxe* or South Saxons: f.a.e., SOUTH and SAXON.

**sustain, sustenance, sustentation, sustention.** See TENABLE, para 8.

**susurrant, susurrate, susurrus.** See SURD, para 5.

**sutler:** ED *soeteler* (D *zoetelaar*), agential derivative of ED *soetelen* (D *zoetelen*), to do the dirty work: cf the syn MHG *sudelen* (G *sudeln*), to dirty, cf MHG *sudel*, a dirty cook: akin to OHG *siodan*, MHG-G *sieden*, to boil—therefore cf SEETHE.

**sutra.** See SEW, para 5.

**suttee.** See SOOTH, para 4.

**suture.** See SEW, para 4.

**suzerain, suzerainty:** MF-F *suzerain*, *suzeraineté*, earliest as *suserenete*: OF-F *sus*, above (VL *sūsum*, L *sūrsum*, on high, above: *subs*, for *sub*+*uorsum*, *uersum*, neu of *uorsus*, *uersus*, pp of *uertere*, to turn)+, or anl with, EF-F *souverain* (OF-MF *sovrain*—cf SUPER, para 5).

**svelte.** See VELLICATE, para 2.

**swab,** n, comes from the v, itself a b/f from **swabber**, a sailor employed in washing (*swabbing*) the decks: D *zwabber*, akin to D *zwabberen*, to *swab* (a deck), perh a freq from MLG *swabben*, to splash—cf the syn LG *schwabbeln*, G *schwappeln*, app from the interj *schwabb!*, slap!, splash!: echoic.

**swaddle, swaddling-clothes.** See SWATH, para 3.

**swag,** orig a bag crammed full, hence a swaying motion, a wooden or metal wreath or festoon used in decoration, (Aus) a tramp's bundle (whence the coll *swaggie*, a tramp): from EE-E (now dial) *swag*, to sway, akin to Nor *svaga*, to sway, from ON *sveigja*, to sway, swing, bend; also from ON *sveigja* comes Nor *svagga*, to walk unsteadily, which has perh influenced E 'to *swagger*', to strut, prop the freq of 'to *swag*' or sway.

2. Also from ON *sveigja*, to sway, comes ME *sweiyen*, later *sweyen*, then *swayen*, whence 'to *sway*' (whence the n): perh cf the D *zwaaijen*, to swing (vi). The ON *sveigja* is prob akin (a cognate without *n*) to OE-OHG *swingan* (f.a.e.: SWING).

**swage,** a moulding in Arch: MF *souage* (F *suage*), an *-age* derivative of OF *soue*, a cord: LL *sōca*, of C origin (Dauzat): cf Br *sūg* (for *\*sōg*), a cord, and perh Ga *sùgan*, a straw-rope.

**swagger,** v, hence n. See SWAG, para 1, s.f.

**swaggie.** See SWAG, para 1.

**Swahili,** a Bantu people with an admixture of Ar blood, hence their language: Ar *sawāḥil*, coasts (they occupy the Afr coasts off Zanzibar), the pl of *sāḥil*+the adj suffix *-i*. In Swahili, *Mswahili* is a Swahili; and *Kiswahili*, the Swahili language.

**swain; boatswain** (coll **bo'sun**) and **coxswain** (abbr **cox**). Orig a male, esp a knight's, servant, *swain* (ME *swein*) derives from ON *sveinn*, a boy, esp if a servant, akin to OE *swān*, a (swine)herd, and OS *swēn*, OHG *swein*, a boy, a male servant—cf also Sw *swen*, Da *svend*, a lad, a journeyman.

2. E *swain* has two modern cpds: *boatswain* (cf BOAT) and *coxswain* (a *cock*'s or cockboat's *swain* or 'servant').

**swale**, a depression, or a shallow valley, esp in a moor or a plain, was orig a cool or shaded place; app it derives from ON *svalr*, cool—cf the syn Nor and Sw *sval*.

**swallow** (1), the bird: ME *swalowe*: OE *swalewe* (contr *swalwe*), predominantly *swealwe*, akin to OFris *swale*, OS *swala*, OHG *swalowa*, MHG *swalwe*, G *Schwalbe*, MD *swaluwe* (*zwaluwe*), *swalewe*, *swaluē*, D *zwaluw*, and ON *svala*—perh (Walshe) to Lett *svalstīt*, to move hither and thither; 'the darter'. But cf para 4 of:

**swallow** (2), to take, through the mouth and gullet, into the stomach: ME *swolewen*, *swolwen*, *swelwen*, *swelghen*: OE *swelgan*: cf OHG *swelahan*, *swelgan*, MHG *swelhen*, *swelgen*, G *schwelgen*, and ON *svelgia*, *svelja*.

2. Akin to 'to *swallow*' is 'to *swill*', ME *swilen*, to wash, OE *swilian*, occ *swillan*, to wash, but also to gargle. Hence the n *swill*, as in *swill-tub*, a tub of semi-liquid food for pigs. Both of these vv are clearly echoic.

3. OE *swelgan*, to swallow, perh occurs in OE *gundeswelge*, a medicinal herb, ? lit 'pus (*gunde*) swallower', later, by f/e, *grundeswelge* (as if lit 'ground-swallower (hence absorber)'), with var *grundeswylige*, whence ME *grundswilie*, E *groundsel*.

4. All the best philological opinion is opposed to what it calls the f/e derivation of *swallow* the bird from *swallow* the verb; phon, the orthodox position is—or, at an easy glance, appears to be—unassailable. 'A partridge is always game': and I suggest that the bird-name does, in fact, derive from the v, for the foll reasons: the swallow darts here and there, its mouth ever agape, seeking to swallow the insects it encounters (cf *fly-catcher*)—cf the prob origin of the bird *duck* in 'to *duck*' or dive; the predominant first-vowel *a* of the bird-name and the predominant first-vowel *e* of the v do rather suggest a deliberate differentiation; the discrepancy of the 2nd (or 3rd) syllable perh merely exemplifies the fact that such consonant-shifts (here, as in *yard*-*ward*) do sometimes occur within a group (here, the Gmc) forming one of the IE languages, and not only in the transition from one group to another.

**swam.** See SWIM (heading).

**swamp** (n, hence v), whence **swampy; sump.**

*Sump* has been adopted from MLG *sump*, a morass; prob also of LG origin is *swamp*, for cf the MHG-MLG *swamp* (OHG *schwamb*), var *swam*, G *Schwamm*, Go *swamms*, a sponge, OE *swamm*, Da and Sw *svamp*, sponge, fungus—cf also MHG-G *sumpf*, a swamp. OGmc, therefore, exhibits four varr—with or without *w*, with or without *b* (*p*); and should prob be related to Gr *somphos*, loose, porous, spongy (Walshe). The IE etymon is perh *\*suombhos*, *\*swombhos* (Hofmann), app with var

*\*sombhos*. But the ON *suöppr*, *svöppr*, a sponge, suggests a non-nasal IE r *\*suob*, *\*swob* (? cf E *swab*), which, without *w*, is *\*sob* (? cf E *sob*, *sop*, *sup*), with basic idea 'wetness, dampness'.

**swan**, whence the AE euphem for 'to swear' ('I *swan!*'); whence **swannery** (cf MD *swanerie*), **swan's-down, swan song** (folklore tale of swans 'singing' before they die), **swan-upping** (the marking of young swans on the *upper* mandible)

*Swan*, id in OE, var *swon*, is akin to OHG-G *swan*, G *Schwan*, MD *swan*, *swane*, *swaen*, *zwane*, D *zwaan*, ON *svanr* (with modern Scan cognates): perh—for the *w*, cf It *suòno*, a sound (L *sonus*)—cf L *sonāre*, to sound, and Skt *svánati*, it resounds, ? from the singing swan: cf, sem and phon, HEN (Walshe) and, phon, SOUND.

**swank**, n (whence **swanky**), adj, v: o.o.o.: perh cf MHG *swanc*, G *Schwank*, a jest.

**swap** (pron and often written **swop**), v, hence n: orig to strike, hence to strike a bargain, hence to exchange: ME *swappen*, to strike: o.o.o.: prob echoic, perh cf SWEEP.

**sward**, orig a skin: OE *sweard*, a skin, a covering: cf OFris *swarde*, skin, MHG *swarte*, hairy scalp, G *Schwarte*, (thick) skin, MD *swarde*, *swaerde*, hairy scalp, thick hair, ON *svörthr*, skin, sward. 'The development of the meaning in E is Scan: Da *grönsvaerd*, "greensward" ' (Walshe).

**swarm.** See SURD, para 6.

**swart**, var **swarth**, whence the extn **swarthy; sordes, sordid.**

1. *Swart*, blackish, dark-complexioned, ME *swart*, OE *sweart*, black, is akin to the syn OFris *swart*, *swert*, OS *swart*, LG *swart*, MD *swert*, *swart*, MD-D *zwart*, OHG-MHG *swarz*, G *schwarz*, Go *swarts*, ON *svartr* (Sw *svart*)—and, without *w*, the ON *sorta*, black colour, and Da *sort*, black, blackish, and, with *d* for *t*, L *sordidus*, filthy. OE *sweart* has derivative *sweartness*, E *swartness*.

2. L *sordidus*, filthy, becomes late MF-F *sordide*, whence E *sordid*; it derives from L *sordēs*, filth (lit and fig), adopted by SciE; *sordēs* is perh akin to L *suāsum*, brown colour (? for *\*swart-tum*). The IE r is app *\*sword-*, filthy, black, with Gmc var *\*sward-*, and with *w*-less varr.

**swash** (v, hence n)—whence **swashbuckler** (cf BUCKLER, a shield)—and its thinned var **swish** (v, hence n) are echoic. Cf the many other words in *-ash*.

**swastika**: Skt *svastika*: *svasti*, well-being, welfare, from *su*, well+*asti*, lit 'is', hence 'being' (n).

**swat** (v, hence n) is echoic. Var: *swot*.

**swath**, a track or truce, hence the sweep of a scythe; var **swathe; swathe**, to bind or wrap with a band of cloth, to swaddle, hence (?) n, with var **swath**, a bandage, (pl) swaddling clothes; **swaddle**, a swaddling band, occ a bandage, hence (?) the v, whence **swaddling clothes.**

1. *Swath*, a track, comes from the syn OE *swaeth*, *swathu*; cf OFris *swethe*, a boundary (made with a scythe), MD *swade*, *swat*, *zwat*, MD-D

*zward, zwade*, MLG *swade, swat*, MHG *swade*, G *Schwad*, and prob E *swathe*.

2. *Swathe* derives from OE *swath-* (only in cpds), itself akin to—? deriving from—the OE v *swathian*, whence 'to *swathe*' or bandage or swaddle.

3. 'To *swaddle*,' ME *swathlen*, to bind, to swaddle, app derives from ME *swathel-* (cpds only), itself from OE *swaethil* (var *swethel*), a band, intimately related to OE *swathian*, to bind, to swaddle, which is prob related to OE *swaeth* (as in para 1): cf also ME *swathel*, tightly bound, and MD *swadel*, OHG *swedil*, a swaddling cloth.

**swathe**, to bind with a cloth band; and the corresp n. See prec, para 2.

**sway.** See SWAG, para 2.

**swear** (pt **sware**, archaic, and **swore**, pp **sworn**), whence the agent **swearer** and the pa, vn **swearing; answer**, n and v; **sermon** (n, hence v), whence **sermonic** and **sermonize.**

1. 'To *swear*' comes from ME *sweren*, earlier *swerien*, from OE *swerian*: cf OFris *swera*, OS *swerian*, OHG *swerian*, MHG *swern*, G *schwören*, Go *swaran*, MD *swaren, sweren*, MD-D *zweren*, ON *sveria (-ja)*.

2. Akin to ON *sveria*, to swear an oath, is ON *svara*, to answer: cf OE *andswaru*, lit a swearing *and-*, against (cf L *anti*), whence ME *andsware*, eased in E to *answer*; the v *answer* derives, via ME *andswerien*, from OE *andswerian, andswarian*, from the n *andswaru*.

3. The OGmc *swer-*, to swear (an oath), is perh akin to L *sermō*, conversation, if *serm-* be an extn of *ser-* and *ser-* a *w-*less cognate of *swer-*; the ancients (and E & M), however, think *sermō* an extn of the *ser-* in L *series*, E *series*: 'a series of words'. L *sermō* has acc *sermōn*em, whence OF-F *sermon*, whence ME *sermoun* or *sermun*, whence E *sermon*. 'To *sermon*' (archaic) derives from OF-F *sermonner* (from *sermon*).

**sweat**, n (whence **sweaty**) and v. 'To *sweat*,' ME *sweten*, OE *swaētan*, derives from the OE n *swāt*, whence ME *swot*, whence, after the v *sweat*, the E *sweat*. The OE n *swāt* is akin to OFris and OS *swēt*, OHG-MHG *sweiz*, G *Schweiss*, MD *swete*, *sweit*, *sweet*, MD-D *zweet*, ON *sveiti* (cf Sw *svett*): cf L *sūdor*, n, *sūdāre*, v; cf also Skt *svēdas* and, with *h-* for *s-*, Gr *hidrōs*. The OGmc r is *\*swait-*, varr *\*swīt-* and *\*swit-*; the IE r, *\*sweid-, \*swoid-* (as in L), *\*swīd-* or *\*swid-*. (Walshe.)

2. L *sūdāre*, to sweat, has pp *sūdātus*, whence *sūdātiō*, o/s *sūdātiōn-*, and *sūdātōrius*, adj, with neu *sūdātōrium* used as n: whence E *sudation* and *sudatory*, adj and n. *Sūdāre*, s and r *sūd-*, has derivative adj *sūdārius*, with neu *sūdārium* used as n: whence E *sudarium* and n *sudary*. L *sūdor*, adopted by Sci, has adjj *sudoral, sudoric*, and the SciL cpd *sūdorificus*, whence E *sudorific*, lit 'sweat-making, hence -causing', perh imm from EF-F *sudorifique*. Cf the SciL *sūdamen* (*sūdāre+* suffix *-men*) of Med.

3. L *sūdāre* has cpd *exsūdāre*, to sweat *ex* or out, often eased to *exūdāre*, whence 'to *exude*'; on the pp *ex(s)ūdāt*us is formed the LL *ex(s)ūdātiō*, o/s *ex(s)ūdātiōn-*, whence E *exudation*, whence, anl, the adj *exudatory*.

4. From L *sūdāre*, erudite F has formed *transsuder* (*trans*, across, hence through) with derivative *transsudation*: whence the eased E 'to *transude*' and *transudation*.

**Swede**, hence **swede** (turnip); **Sweden; Swedenborgian; Swedish**, adj, hence n; **suède.**

1. *Swede* has been adopted from MD-MLG *Swede* (cf G *Schwede*), var *Zwede*; *Sweden*, from MD *Sweden* (cf D *Zweden*); *Swedish*=*Swede*+adj *-ish* (cf G *Schwedisch*). The r *Swed-* is app an extn of *Swe-, Sue-*: cf OE *Swēon*, L *Suiones*, the Swedes; cf also Sw *Sverige*, OSw *Svearicke*, OE *Swiorice*, the kingdom of the Swedes. *Swedenborgian* is the adj of Emanuel *Swedenborg* (1688–1772), a Sw philosopher and writer about religion, who changed his name from *Swedberg* because his family's homestead was called *Sveden*.

2. From F *Suède*, Sweden, comes a leather we call *suède*, either from a process first practised there or (EW) from *gants de Suède*, Swedish gloves.

**sweep**, v (pt and pp **swept**), hence n, hence also **sweeper** and pa, vn **sweeping**, and **chimney-sweep** and **sweepstakes** (winner 'sweeping away' all the stakes); **swipe**, v, hence n, a mere var of **sweep; swoop**, v, hence n; **swift**, adj hence n (esp the bird), **swiftly, swiftness; squib**, n, hence v.

1. 'To *sweep*,' ME *swepen*, is akin to ME *swopen*, whence 'to *swoop*'; ME *swopen* comes from OE *swāpan*, to rush, to sweep along, akin to OFris *swēpene*, a sweeping, ON *sveipa*, to swoop, to sweep, to wrap, OHG *sweifan*, MHG *sweifen*, to swing, G *schweifen*, to roam, to sweep, and OHG *sweban*, MHG *sweben*, to float, to soar, G *schweben*, to soar or hover.

2. OE *swiftlīce*, E *swiftly*, and OE-E *swiftness* derive from the OE-E adj *swift*, akin to ON *svīfa*, to rove, move swiftly, OHG *sweibōn*, to soar, OE *swipu* and MD *swiep, swiepe, sweep, swepe, swepe*, D *zweep*, a whip, and OE *swāpan*, to sweep.

3. Prob deriving from ON *svīfa*, to move swiftly, to swoop, to dart, is ME *swippen*, to move swiftly, with var *squippen*, whence, app, the E *squib*, a fire-cracker, hence, a brief, witty speech or writing.

**sweet, sweeten, sweetheart, sweetness.** See SUAVE, para 2 and heading.

**swell**, v (pt **swelled**, pp **swelled** or **swollen**), hence n, whence the adj; hence also the pa, vn **swelling**. 'To *swell*' comes from OE *swellan*, akin to MD *swellen, zwellen*, to cause to swell, D *zwellen*, to swell, OFris *swella*, OS and OHG *swellan*, MHG *swellen*, G *Schwellen*, Go uf*swalleins*, pride, lit a swelling-up, ON *svella*—perh also (E & M) to L *insolescere*, to swell, to increase: *in-*, used int+ *sol-* (? a *w-*less var of *\*swol-*)+*-esc*, the characteristic inch formative+*-ere*, inf ending.

**swelter**, v (hence n), whence the pa **sweltering** and the adj **sweltry**; dial **swelt; sultry**, a var of **sweltry.**

1. The now dial *swelt*, to succumb to heat, derives from ME *swelten*, to faint, to die, from OE *sweltan*, to die, akin to ON *svelta*, to die, to hunger,

OS *sweltan* and Go *swiltan*, to die, MD *swilten*, *swelten*, to thirst, to hunger, to pine away—and Lith *svilti* (vi), to parch, to burn slowly.

2. From ME *swelten*, to faint, to die, comes the freq-int 'to *swelter*', orig to faint, to feel faint, from heat, hence to sweat, (of the weather) to be oppressively hot.

3. With OE *sweltan*, cf OE *swelan*, to waste away, esp to melt away, akin to MLG *swelen*, G *schwelen*, to burn slowly or smokily, and OE *swōl*, heat.

**swerve**, v, hence n: ME *swerven*: OE *sweorfan*, to rub off, to scour, to file: cf OFris *swerva*, to rove, OS *swerbhan*, to wipe off, OHG *swerban*, to wipe off, MHG *swerben* (vi), to whirl, Go af*swairban*, to wipe off, MD *swerven*, MD-D *zwerven*, to rove, to swerve, ON *sverfa*, to file; cf also Go *hwairban*, to rove or wander. The IE r is perh *\*kwerbh-*, with the s-for-h var *\*skwerbh-*, (?) to move crookedly or obliquely or waveringly. (Feist.)

**swift**. See SWEEP, para 2.

**swifter** (naut n). See SWIVEL, para 2.

**swiftly, swiftness**. See SWEEP, para 2.

**swig**, n, hence v, to drink (dial and coll): o.o.o.: perh from dial *swig*, to sway (cf *sway*, at SWAG, para 2)—from the motions of one's head, and the wavings of one's glass, as one drinks.

**swill**. See the 2nd SWALLOW, para 2.

**swim** (1), dizziness, esp if temporary, hence the v (to be, or feel, dizzy): ME *swime*: OE *swīma*: cf OFris *swīma*, MD *swijm*, D *zwijm*, OHG *swintan*, MHG *swinden*, G *schwinden*, to dwindle, ON *svīmi* (and the v *svīma*, to dwindle), OE *swindan*, to dwindle.

2. OHG *swintan*, to dwindle, has the freq *swintilōn*, MHG *swindeln*, G *schwindeln*, to feel dizzy, to cheat, whence G *Schwindler*, a cheat, a rogue, whence E *swindler*, whence, by b/f, 'to *swindle*', whence 'a *swindle*'.

3. OE *swīma* becomes ME *swime*, var *swem*, *sweem*, whence, app, the ME *sweymous*, var *squaymous*, whence E *squeamish*.

**swim** (2), v (pt **swam**, pp **swum**), hence n and the agent **swimmer** (cf MD *swimmer*), and the pa, vn **swimming**. 'To *swim*,' OE *swimman*, is cognate with OHG *swimman*, MHG *swimmen*, G *schwimmen*, MD *swimmen*, *swemmen*, MD-D *zwemmen*, ON *svimma* (var *symja*): perh akin to SWEEP.

**swindle, swindler**. See prec, para 2.

**swine**. See the 1st SOW, para 2.

**swing**, v (pt **swang**, now usu **swung**, pp **swung**), hence n; **swinge**, v (hence n), with pa **swingeing**; **swingle**, whence **swingletree**, with f/e var **singletree**; **swink**, n and v; **switch**, n (hence v), whence **switchback, -board, -yard**, etc.

1. 'To *swing*,' ME *swingen*, to beat, swing, vibrate, OE *swingan*, to scourge or beat, to beat the wings, i.e. to flutter, is akin to OFris *swinga*, OS and OLG-OHG *swingan*, MHG *swingen*, G *schwingen*, to oscillate, to swing.

2. OE *swingan* has caus *swengan*, to cause to flutter or swing, to shake, whence ME *swengen*,

whence—with *i* from *swing*— E 'to *swinge*', to beat.

3. Akin to OE *swingan* is OE *swingele, swingel*, a scourging, a heavy blow, a whip or a scourge, whence E *swingle*: cf MD *swinghel*, a flax-beater's implement, varr *swingel, swengel*. Hence, 'to *swingle*' flax: cf MD *swinghelen, swingelen*.

4. Also akin to OE *swingan* is OE *swincan*, to toil, whence 'to *swink*' (archaic) or 'punish' oneself; derivative OE *swinc* or *geswinc* yields the n *swink*.

5. Akin to MD *swing(h)el* is MD *swick*, a whip, whence, app, EE *swits*, E *switch*, which, if not of MD, is prob cognate LG, origin. The modern sense comes from the smart tap or stroke with which one depresses a lever.

**swinge, swingeing**. See prec, para 2.

**swingle** and **swingletree**. See SWING, para 3 and heading.

**swinish**. See the 1st SOW, para 2.

**swink**. See SWING, para 4.

**swipe**. See SWEEP (heading).

**swirl**, to move eddyingly, hence n, is Scan: cf Nor *svirla* (freq of the syn *sverra*), Da *svirre*, to whirl, and therefore perh MHG *swirren*, to swarm, G *schwirren*, to whir.

2. With *swirl*, cf *whirl*, to turn rapidly (vi, hence vt): ME *whirlen*, from ON *hvirfla* (pron hw-), the freq of ON *hverfa* (pron hw-), to turn: cf the G *wirbeln*, freq of *werben*, to solicit, MHG *werben*, to be active, OHG *hwerban*, to turn; cf also MD-D *wervelen*, to turn rapidly, freq of MD *werven*. Here we have a good example of the IE h-s alternation, with extn *hw-sw, hw-* becoming (as, e.g., in *who*) *wh-*.

3. With G *schwirren*, to whir, as adduced in para 1, cf E 'to *whir*', whence the n: cf Da *hvirre* (pron hw-), to whir.

**swish**. See SWASH.

**Swiss**, adj and n, comes from F *suisse*, adj and n: MHG *Suīz, Swīz*—cf MD *Switse*, a Swiss. With *Switzerland*, cf MD *Switserland*.

**switch**. See SWING, para 5.

**swivel**, n, hence v; **swifter**, n. E-ME *swivel*, a mechanical part that turns on a bolt or a pin, comes app from ON *sveifla* (pron sw-), to turn, a freq of *svifa*, to turn or rove—cf OE *swīfan*, to move.

2. EE *swifter*, a naut rope (retaining the capstan-bars in their sockets while the capstan is being turned), derives, as instr (-er), from the late ME-E naut v *swift*, to tauten or make fast with a rope: perh akin to *swivel*; perh to ON *svipta*, to reef (itself prob cognate).

**swizzle**, a compounded intoxicant, whence the **swizzlestick** used in mixing one, is o.o.o.: ? a sl or coll alteration of *swindle* (cf the archaic school-sl *swizzle*, a swindle): so pleasant to drink—and so treacherous.

**swollen**. See SWELL (heading).

**swoon**, v, hence n: ME *swōnen, swounen, swōynen*, app a b/f from ME *swowening, swōyning*, a swooning: from OE ge*swogen*, having fainted, in a faint (cf ge*swōgung*, a swooning), the pp of *swōgan, to faint, improb from OE swōgan, to make a (loud) noise, to move noisily or violently.

**swoop.** See SWEEP, para 1.

**swop.** See SWAP.

**sword** (n, hence v), whence many cpds, all phon and sem self-explanatory: EE-late ME sworde; ME swerd: OE sweord: cf OFris and OS swerd, OHG-MHG swert, G Schwert, MD swert, swaert, swart, swaerd, sward, D zwaard, ON sverth (with modern Scan cognates): OGmc r *swerd-: ? a var of hwerd-, extn of r *kwer-, to cut, as in Hit kwer-, to cut or cut off; the Hit var kur- suggests kinship with the richly attested syn IE r *ker- (cf Gr keirō, I cut).

**swore, sworn.** See SWEAR (heading).

**swot:** var of SWAT.

**sybarite** and **sybaritic,** a voluptuary and voluptuous, luxurious: Sybarite, Sybaritic: L Sybarita, Sybariticus: Gr Subaritēs, whence Subaritikos: Gr Subaris, an ancient Gr city that, situated in southeastern Italy, was famous for the luxurious, pleasure-seeking habits of many of its inhabitants. The E sybarite was perh adopted from EF-F.

**sybil, sybilline.** See SIBYL.

**sycamore.** See MULBERRY, para 3.

**sycophancy, sycophant, sycophantic.** The 1st derives from L sȳcophantia, trln of Gr sukophantia; the 3rd, anl, from Gr sukophantikos; both of the Gr words come from sukophant-, s of sukophantēs, an accuser (esp if false), a rogue, whence L sȳcophanta, whence, perh via late MF-EF sicophante, EF-F sycophante, the E sycophant, orig an informer, hence a parasite, a flatterer. Gr sukophantēs=suko-, c/f of sukon, a fig+-phantēs, a show-er, an agential derivative of phainein, to show: sukon is prob an Aegean or Asia Minor word; for phainein, see FANCY. Sukophantēs is lit 'a fig-shower' for any of three or four reasons: orig such an informer as denounced those who sold contraband figs or who stole fruit from the sacred fig-trees, as the ancients explained it; a rogue, because, as Boisacq proposes, he was addicted to the indecent gesture indicated by the MF-F faire la figue (à quelqu'un), trans of It far la fica (later, le fiche), 'to make the fig'—cf Shakespeare's fig and fico—a phrase based upon It fica in its low and trivial sense pudendum nuliebre, a sense attached already to the Gr sukon.

**Sydney,** whence **Sydneyite,** was named after the 1st Viscount of Sydney, who happened to be Secretary for the Colonies when, in 1788, Port Jackson was discovered and settled.

**syenite,** whence **syenitic,** derives from L Syenites (lapis), stone of Syene, Gr Suēnē: this sort of granite was first quarried at Syene in Upper Egypt.

**syllabary, syllabic, syllabication** (whence, anl, the v **syllabicate**), **syllable** (n, hence v); **monosyllabic, monosyllable—dissyllabic, dissyllable—trisyllabic, trisyllable—tetrasyllabic, tetrasyllable—polysyllabic, polysyllable.**

1. All these words derive from Gr sullabē, whence L syllaba, whence OF-MF sillabe (MF-F syllabe), whence, by assimilation (l to ll), ME

sillable, E syllable. Lit 'what has been taken—hence, is held—together' (letters taken together to form a sound), Gr sullabē=sul- (for sun-, together, from sun, with)+labē, a taking, what has been taken, from lab-, the pt s of lambanein, to take (lamb-, nasal form of IE *lab-, to take+infixed formative -an-+inf suffix -ein).

2. Gr. sullabē has adj sullabikos, whence LL syllabicos, ML syllabicus, EF-F syllabique, E syllabic, whence, anl, syllabication; syllabary, a table of syllables, derives from modern L syllabarium, form-suggested by LL syllabārius, a boy in a spelling class; syllaba+adj-n suffix -ārius.

3. The chief E cpds are these:

monosyllable, whence, anl, -syllabic: EF-F monosyllabe, adj and n: LL monosyllabus, -syllabos, adj: Gr monosullabos, adj, with rare var monosullabikos, of one syllable;

dissyllable, whence, anl, dissyllabic: EF-F dissyllabe, adj and n: L dissyllabus, inferior var of disyllabus, adj: Gr disullabos, of two syllables;

trisyllable, whence, anl, trisyllabic: F trissyllabique, adj, trissyllabe, adj and n: L trisyllabus, adj, cf LL trisyllaba, trisyllabic words: Gr trisullabos, of three syllables;

tetrasyllable, whence, anl, tetrasyllabic: LL tetrasyllabus, adj: Gr tetrasullabos, of four syllables;

polysyllable, polysyllabic: late MF-F polysyllabe, adj and n: ML polysyllabus, LL polusyllabus, adj: Gr polusullabos, many-syllabled.

**syllabus** is adopted from EcclL syllabus, a list: alteration—? after syllabas, acc pl of syllaba (see prec)—of L sillybus, from Gr sillubos, a strip of parchment: o.o.o.

**syllogism, syllogistic.** See LEGEND, para 30.

**sylph,** a (young) slender and graceful woman, whence **sylphic:** EF-F sylphe (first written sylfe): Paracelsus's sylphus, a mortal but soulless, tiny elemental being of the air: L sylphus, a genius of air and woods: o.o.o. EF-F sylphe has derivative sylphide, whence E sylphid.

**sylva, sylvan, Sylvanus.** See SAVAGE, paras 2 and 3; **Sylvester, Sylvia:** ib, paras 4 and 5.

**symbiosis, symbiotic.** Symbiosis is the SciL trln of Gr sumbiōsis, a living (-biōsis) together (sun), from sumbioun, to live together: cf the element bio- and such E words as biology.

**symbol, symbolic, symbolism, symbolist** (whence **symbolistic**), **symbolize** (whence **symbolization**). A symbol derives from late MF-F symbole, LL symbolum, var symbolus, the baptismal creed, L symbolum, -lus, a mark or sign as a means of recognition, Gr sumbolon, from sumballein, to throw, hence put, together, to compare; derivative Gr sumbolikos becomes LL symbolicus, whence (cf EF-F symbolique) the E symbolic, with extn symbolical. Derivative ML symbolizāre becomes MF-F symboliser, whence 'to symbolize'; and the anl F symbolisme and symboliste yield E symbolism and symbolist.

**symmetric(al), symmetry.** See MEASURE, para 4, s.f.

sympathetic, sympathize, sympathy. See PATHIC, s.f.

symphony, whence, anl, the adjj symphonic and symphonious, derives—perh via OF-MF simphonie, EF-F symphonie—from L symphonia, trln of Gr sumphōnia: sum- for sun-, together (sun, with)+ an -ia derivative of phōnē, a sound (cf PHONE).

symphysis, symphytic. SciL symphysis and *symphyticus: Gr sumphusis and its derivative sumphutikos: from sumphuein, to cause to grow (phuein) together (sun-): f.a.e., PHYSIC.

symposium, adopted from L, is a trln of Gr sumposion, a convivial party, dining together and then either talking or listening to music: sum-, together (sun, with)+posis, a drinking (cf POTABLE).

symptom, symptomatic: EF-F symptôme, symptomatique: LL symptōma (gen symptomatis), in Med sense: Gr sumptōma (gen sumptomatos), orig a coincidence, whence the adj sumptōmatikos (whence the F adj): sumpiptein, to fall (piptein) together (sun-), to coincide. Cf the element symptomato-.

synagogue, whence synagogal and synagogical, has been adopted from MF-F synagogue, OF-MF sinagoge: LL synagōga, (the place of) a Jewish religious meeting: syn LGr sunagōga: Gr sunagōga, an assembly, lit a bringing together: sunagein, to bring (agein, to lead: f.a.e., ACT) together (sun-, from sun, with).

synchronic, synchronize, synchronous. See CHRONIC, para 2.

synclinal, syncline. See CLIME, para 6.

syncopate, syncopation. See the element -copate.

syndetic. See ASYNDETON.

synergetic, synergism, synergy. See ENERGETIC, para 3.

synod, synodic. See ODOGRAPH, para 7.

synonym, synonymous, synonymy. See NAME, para 3, and cf the element -onym.

synopsis, synoptic. See OPTIC, para 3.

synovitis is a SciL tacking of -itis, connoting 'disease', to synovia, that An term for a transparent lubricating fluid ('oiling' the articulations, etc.) which SciL has adopted from Paracelsus (1493–1541)—who coined synovia from we know not what.

syntactic(al), syntax. Syntactical is an extn of syntactic, from Gr suntaktikos, adj of suntaxis, a putting together, hence in order, whence, via L syntaxis, much used in the Gram sense, the EF-F syntaxe, whence E syntax. Gr suntaxis derives from suntassein, to arrange together in an orderly way: sun-, together (sun, with)+tassein, to put in order (cf TACTIC).

synthesis, synthesize, synthetic. See THESIS, para 16.

syphilis, syphilitic. The latter derives, via F syphilitique, from SciL syphiliticus, adj of SciL syphilis, the venereal disease: Syphilis, a Latin poem that, published in 1530, was written by the It humanist Fracastoro, who coined it from the shepherd hero of the poem: Syphilus, var of Siphylus, itself a var of Sypilus, Niobe's elder son, born near the Lydian Mt Sipylus in Asia Minor. (B & W.)

syren. See SIREN.

Syria, Syriac, Syrian; Assyria, Assyrian. Gr Suria becomes L Syria, adopted by E; derivative Gr Suriakos becomes L Syriacus, whence F syriaque and E Syriac, adj, hence n; Syrian, however, comes from F syrien (OF-MF sirien), from L Syrius (from Syria).

2. Although perh influenced by Gr Suria (L Syria), the Gr Assuria, L Assyria, adopted by E, is of different origin: Gr Assuria is elliptical for Assuria gē, the Assyrian land, from the adj Assurios, itself a b/f from Assuroi, the Assyrians: Assuroi derives, like their capital city Assur, from their god Assur, better Aššur, i.e. Ashshur (loosely Ashur), with very ancient var Ašir, i.e. Ashir: o.o.o.; but, if of Sem origin (as were the Assyrians), Ashshur perh means 'The Benign' (Enci It); cf Hit assus, kind, good. L Assyria becomes F Assyrie, whence the adj assyrien, whence—unless independently from E Assyria—the E adj, hence n, Assyrian, with c/f Assyrio-, as in Assyriology.

syringa; syringe (n, hence v); syrinx; seringa. Seringa is the Port, whence the Sp and F, form of the syringa shrub; hence the F seringue, a syringe, the hollowed-out stems being used for pipes, flutes, syringes. The shrub syringa is a SciL sense-derivative from ML-LL syringa, syringia, a fistula, an injection, whence the E syringe, injections being expelled from tubes: and LL syringa, -gia, derives from Gr suring- (L syring-), the o/s of surinx, a tube, a pipe, itself from Skt surungā, a tube. Gr surinx (σῦριγξ) is personified as Surinx, a nymph changed by Pan into a clump of reeds, from which he fashioned his pipes; whence L Syrinx, whence SciL syrinx, a bird's vocal organ.

syrup. See the 2nd SHRUB, para 3.

systaltic. See STALL, para 14.

system, systematic, systematize. See STAND, para 7, s.f.

systole. See STALL, para 13.

syzygy. See JOIN, para 9.

# T

tab, n, hence v, is o.o.o.: ? akin to TAG.

tabard: ME *tabart*: o.o.o.: prob of Gmc origin and perh akin to prec.

tabby, a striped taffeta, whence the cat (whence a gossiping woman): EF-F *tabis*, aphetic for MF *atabis*: Ar '*Attābī*, (fabric) of *Attāb*, that quarter of Baghdad where it was orig manufactured: '*Attāb*, a member of the Ommiad family (fl 661–750).

tabella. See TABLE, para 3.

tabellion. See TABLE, para 3.

tabernacle. See TAVERN, para 2, s.f.

tabes, tabid, tabific. See THAW.

tablature. See para 4 of:

table (n, hence v), tabella, tabellion, tablature, tableau, tablet, tabloid, tabula, tabular, tabulate (adj and v), tabulation (whence, anl, tabulator); entablature, entablement; retable; taffrail.

1. *Table* is adopted from OF-F *table*: L *tabula*, a plank, OL var *tabola* (cf It *tavola*, a table), hence in VL, a table: o.o.o.: the basic sense of L *tabula* being 'a plank', hence a small flat board for writing, one may perh relate the Hit *tapulli*, a plate, a dish.

2. L *tabula* has the derivative adjj *tabulāris*, shaped like a plank, hence like a table, whence E *tabular*, and *tabulātus*, made of planks, whence the adj (rare) and v *tabulate*, which, however, could derive from LL *tabulātus*, pp of *tabulāre*, to fit with planks. Derivative *tabulātiō*, o/s *tabulātiōn-*, yields *tabulation*.

3. L *tabula* has dim *tabella*, adopted, like *tabula*, by SciE; the pl *tabellae* was used esp for 'writing tablets'. L *tabella* has the LL derivative *tabelliō* (o/s *tabelliōn-*), a notary, a scrivener, whence MF-F *tabellion*, adopted by E.

4. OF-F *table* has the foll derivatives affecting E: EF-F *tablature* (from ML *tablatūra*, for *tabulatūra*), adopted by E: cf MF-F *entablature* (prompted by It *intavolatura*, a wainscot), likewise adopted by E, as also is the OF-F *entablement*; MF-F *tableau* (sense-development unclear), adopted by E; MF-F *tablette*, orig a small flat board, whence E *tablet*; EF-F *retable* (from Sp *retablo*: *re-*, back, to the rear + *tabla*, a plank, from L *tabula*), adopted by E.

5. E *table* + suffix *-oid* yields the proprietary name *Tabloid*, a concentrated drug (etc.), whence a small, compact newspaper.

6. L *tabula* becomes MD *tavele, taefle, taeffel, tafle*, MD-D *tafel*, whence MD *tavereel, taeffereel,*

*tafreel*, MD-ED *taffereel*, a panel, whence EE *tafferel*, a panel, whence, by f/e (both phon and sem) after E *rail*, the E *taffrail*.

tableau. See prec, para 4.

tablet. See TABLE, para 4.

tabloid. See TABLE, para 5.

taboo anglicizes tabu, orig the Tongan word for 'sacred', akin to the syn Tahitian, Samoan, Maori *tapu*; hence the n.

tabor, taboret—tabour, tabouret. See TAMBOUR, para 1.

tabu. See TABOO.

tabula, tabular, tabulate, tabulation, tabulator. See TABLE, para 2.

tach or tache, a buckle, a clasp, and v; tack, n, hence v.—Cpds of *tach*: attach, attaché, attachment; detach, detachment; attack; staccato.

1. The now dial *tach, tache*, to attach, derives from the now archaic *tach* or *tache*, a nail, buckle, clasp, itself from OF-MF *tache*, a fastening, a nail; this *tache* has the ONF var *taque*, whence E *tack*. The OF-F *tache* is app aphetic for OF-MF *estache*, a stake, from Frankish *\*stakka* (cf E STAKE).

2. OF-MF *estache* has the OF-MF derivative v *estachier*, with mdfn OF *atachier*, OF-MF *attachier*, MF-F *attacher*, whence ME *attachen*, whence 'to *attach*'; derivative MF-F *attachement* becomes E *attachment*; the n *attaché* is prop the pp of *attacher*.

3. Of the same OGmc origin as OF *atachier, attachier*, is It *attaccare*, to attach, to join, hence to join battle with, whence EF-F *attaquer*, whence E 'to *attack*', whence *attacker* and *attacking*; the derivative EF-F n *attaque* yields the E n *attack*.

4. OF-MF *tache*, a fastening, has derivative OF-MF *destachier*, MF *destacher*, EF-F *détacher*, whence 'to *detach*'; derivative EF-F *détachement* yields E *detachment*.

5. Corresp to It *attacare* is It *distaccare*, to detach, with 'lopped' var *staccare*, pp *staccato*, used as Mus adj 'with every note sharply detached from the prec and foll notes'.

tache (1). See prec, para 1.

tache (2), a spot, a blemish, is adopted from MF-F *tache*, orig a distinctive mark, EF-F a spot, stain, blemish: OF-MF *teche*: of Gmc origin— cf *token*; f.a.e., TEACH. From OF-MF *teche* comes ME *tecche*, a bad habit, whence E *techy*, var *tetchy*, peevish, irascible.

tachygraphy; tachymeter. See the element *tacheo-*.

tacit—Tacitean, Tacitus—taciturn, taciturnity; reticence, reticent.

1. L *tacēre*, to be silent, to silence, has s and r *tac-* and is akin to Go *thahan*, to be silent, and W *gosteg*, Ga *tosd*, EIr *tost*, silence. The L pp is *tacitus*, used as adj 'silent', whence both the PN *Tacitus*, whence the E adj *Tacitean*, and late MF-F *tacite*, whence E *tacit*. The L extn *taciturnus* becomes the late MF-F *taciturne*, whence E *taciturn*; the L derivative *taciturnitās*, acc *taciturnitātem*, yields MF-F *taciturnité*, whence E *taciturnity*.

2. L *tacēre* has c/f *-ticēre*, as in *reticēre* (revaguely int), to keep silent, presp *reticens*, o/s *reticent-*, whence E *reticent*; derivative L *reticentia* yields (EF-F *réticence* and) E *reticence*.

tack (1), a fastening device, e.g. a small nail. See TACH, para 1.

tack (2), substance, esp food, app shortens:

tackle, instrument, gear, equipment, whence 'to tackle', orig to equip with tackle (D and LG cognates): ME *takel*, adopted from MD-D, MLG *takel*: o.o.o.: ? ult akin to Gr *taxis*, an arrangement.

tact, whence tactful and tactless; tactile and tactual; taction; tangent, whence both tangency, var tangence, and tangential; tangible (whence tangibility) and intangible (whence intangibility); tango, n, hence v; taste, n (whence tasteful, tasteless, tasty) and v (whence taster, tasting)—distaste; tax, v, hence n—taxable, taxation (whence taxational), taxer, task, n, hence v.—Cpds: attain, whence attainment—attainder—attaint, n and v—attinge, attingent; contact (n, whence adj and v, whence contactor), contactual—contagion, contagious—perh contaminable, contaminate, contamination (whence, anl, contaminative)—contango—contiguity contiguous—contingence, contingency, contingent; entire, entirety; intact, intactile; integer, integral (adj, hence n), integrant, integrate (whence integrator), integration (whence, anl, integrative), integrity; redintegrate, redintegration (whence, anl, redintegrative).

1. The base of the group is app *tag-* (var *teg-*) or *tak-* (var *tek-*: cf Go *tēkan*, to touch), which we see in the pp *tactus* (? *taktus*, *tagtus*) and perh in L con*tāg*io, with c/f *-tig-* in L at*tig*uus and con*tig*uus. L *tang*ere (pp *tactus*) is a nasal var of *tag-*, to touch, with c/f *-ting*ere. In short, this group seems to be no older than L.

## Simples

2. L *tangere* has presp *tangens*, o/s *tangent-*, whence the E adj *tangent*, whence the n *tangent*, prob influenced by the EF-F n *tangente*. The E *tangence*, with extn *tangency*, is perh indebted to F *tangence* (from adj *tangent*), whence the F adj *tangentiel*, whence perh the E *tangential*.

3. From L *tangere* comes the LL *tangibilis*, whence MF-F *tangible*, adopted by E; derivative F *tangibilité* perh prompted *tangibility*. The ML neg

*intangibilis* yields late MF-F *intangible*, adopted by E.

4. L *tangere* becomes Sp *tangir*, with subsidiary sense (already in L) 'to pluck the strings of, to play' a musical instrument, whence *tango*, music, a dance, a festival, whence Argentine Sp *tango*, a fiesta, a specific kind of dance, adopted by E, F, etc.

5. On the L pp *tactus* are formed the foll words relevant to E:

*tactiō*, a touching, o/s *tāctiōn-*, whence *taction*; syn *tāctus* (gen *-ūs*), whence MF-F *tact*, adopted by E;

(partly from the n *tāctus*) *tāctilis*, with neg *intāctilis*, whence EF-F *tactile*, adopted by E, and E *intactile*.

6. The E adj *tactual* derives—after *visual*—from E *tact*; cf the F *tactuel*, after *visuel*.

7. L *tangere* has the int *taxāre*, to touch hard or sharply, to handle, to estimate or value: whence MF-F *taxer*, whence 'to *tax*', whence the n—cf ML *taxa* and MF-F *taxe*. The ML *taxa* becomes OF-MF *tasche* (EF-F *tâche*), ONF *tasque*, ME *taske*, E *task*, whence *taskmaster*. *Taxāre* also means 'to blame, to point out or mention', senses extant in E. Derivative L *taxātiō*, a valuing, LL blame, acc *taxātiōnem*, becomes MF-F *taxation*, adopted by E. MF-F *taxer* has AF derivative *taxable*, retained by E, which gets *taxer* from AF *taxour*, from ML *taxātor* (from *taxātus*, pp of *taxāre*). *Surtax* comes from EF-F *surtaxe*.

8. L *taxāre* has freq *taxitāre*, whence VL *tastāre*, whence OF-MF *taster* (F *tâter*), to feel, to taste, whence the syn ME *tasten*, whence 'to *taste*'. The derivative OF-MF n *tast* leads to the E n *taste*.

9. 'To *distaste*'—whence the n, whence *distasteful*—merely prefixes *dis-*, implying negation, to 'to *taste*'.

## Compounds

10. L *tangere* has prefix-cpds in *-tingere*; esp *attingere* and *contingere*. *Attingere*, to touch upon (*ad*, towards), yields the obsol 'to *attinge*'; presp *attingens*, o/s *attingent-*, yields the adj *attingent*, in contact.

11. L *attingere* has the VL var *attangere*, whence OF-MF *attaindre* (var *ataindre*; MF-F *atteindre*), whence ME *at(t)ainen*, *atteinen*, whence 'to *attain*'; in E, as in F, the senses ramify; one is 'to accuse, hence to convict', and OF-MF *at(t)aindre*, used as n, explains the E n *attainder*. Moreover, OF-MF *at(t)aindre* has pp *at(t)aint*, which has f *at(t)ainte*, later *atteinte*, which, used as n, becomes ME *atteynt*, an accusation, a conviction, E *attaint*; the ME n acquires the derivative v *atteynten*, whence 'to *attaint*'. Both *attainder* and *attaint* have f/e influenced by *taint*.

12. L *contingere* (*con-* vaguely int), to touch upon, hence to arrive at, hence to happen, has presp *contingens*, o/s *contingent-*, whence the MF-F adj and EF-F n *contingent*, adopted by E. Derivative LL *contingentia* becomes MF-F

*contingence*, adopted by E, with var *contingency*. The Stock Exchange term *contango* is perh a mock-L derivative of *contingent*.

13. L *contingere* has pp *contactus*, whence the L n *contactus* (gen *-ūs*), whence EF-F and, perh independently, E *contact*, whence anl—after *tactual—contactual*.

14. Akin to *conting*ere and esp to *contact*us, pp and n, is L *contāgiō*, a touching, contact, acc *contāgiōnem*, whence MF-F *contagion*, adopted by E; the derivative LL adj *contāgiōsus* becomes MF-F *contagieux*, f *contagieuse*, whence E *contagious*. The r *tag-* prob lies behind L *contāmināre* (? for *contagmināre*: cf the formation of *examināre* or rather of its imm source *examen*), to get into touch with, hence to soil by contact, whence the LL *contāminābilis*, with neg *incontāminābilis*, whence E *contaminable, incontaminable*. From the pp *contāminātus* derive both the adj and the v *contaminate*; its LL derivative *contāminātiō*, o/s *contāminātiōn-*, yields *contamination*.

15. Also, though without n, akin to *conting*ere is the L adj *contig*uus, whence E *contiguous* (cf MF-F *contigu*); derivative LL *contiguitās*, acc *contiguitātem*, yields late MF-F *contiguité* and perh independently E *contiguity*.

16. The var r *teg-* noted in para 1 occurs in L *integer*, untouched, whole, adopted by learnèd E, which uses it mainly as n. The LL-ML mdfn *integrālis* (*integr-*, o/s of *integer*+adj suffix *-ālis*) becomes MF-F *intégral*, whence E *integral*. L *integer*, o/s *integr-*, has derivative v *integrāre* (in-vaguely int), to re-establish as before, to renew, with presp *integrans*, o/s *integrant-*, whence E *integrant*—cf E *integrand*, from L *integrandus*, gerundive of *integrāre*. The L pp *integrātus* yields the E adj and v *integrate*; derivative L *integrātiō*, o/s *integrātiōn-*, yields *integration*. L *integer*, o/s *integr-*, has the further derivative *integritās*, acc *integritātem*, whence late MF-F *intégrité*, whence E *integrity*.

17. L *integrāre* has cpd *redintegrāre*, to restore, pp *redintegrātus*, whence the E adj and v *redintegrate*; derivative *redintegrātiō*, o/s *-ātiōn-*, yields *redintegration*.

18. With L *integer*, cf L *intactus*: *in-*, not+ *tactus*, touched: hence unbroken, entire: whence (EF-F and) E *intact*. The derivative L *intāctilis*— after *tactilis*—gives us *intactile*.

19. L *integer* becomes OF-F *entier*, whence ME *enter* and E *entire*; derivative MF-EF *entiereté* accounts for *entirety*.

**tactic, tactical, tactics—tactician; taxis; sep** SYNTAX, SYNTACTICAL.

1. *Tactical* is an E extn of the now obsol adj *tactic*, from Gr *taktikos*, adj formed from *tassein*, Attic *tattein*, to put in its right place, to arrange: IE r, *tag-*, to place fittingly. The Gr adj has f *taktikē*, as in *taktikē tekhnē*, the science or art of arrangement, esp in war, whence the F *la tactique*, whence—cf *ethics* from *ethic*—E *tactics*, and also F *tacticien*, whence E *tactician*.

2. Gr *tassein* has derivative *taxis*, arrangement,

adopted by learnèd E; whence *taxonomy*, the law (*nomos*), hence art, of arrangement.

**tactile.** See TACT, para 5.

**taction.** See TACT, para 5.

**tactual.** See TACT, para 6.

**tadpole.** See the 1st POLL, para 3.

**tael.** See the 1st TOLL, para 7.

**taeni-words.** See that element.

**taffeta**: MF-F *taffetas*: It *taffetà*, ML *taffeta*: Per *tāfta*(*h*), lit twisted, spun, woven, from *tāftan*, to twist, spin, weave.

**taffrail.** See TABLE, para 6.

**taffy** or **toffy, toffee; taffia, tafia.** *Toffee* or *toffy* is app an E phon and sem var of AE *taffy*, 'a kind of pulled candy made usually of molasses or brown sugar' (Webster)—itself perh from *taffia* (or *tafia*), a WI spirit distilled from sugar-cane juice; a Creole word o.o.o.: but perh (B & W) short for the syn Creole *ratafia* or (Mathews) the syn Mal word.

**tag**, a loose fabric-end or fragment, a rag, hence a tab, whence 'to **tag**'; whence—after **rag**—the redup **tagrag**, with the extn **tagrag and bobtail**. *Tag* is prob of Scan origin—cf Sw *tagg*, a point, a prickle, and Nor *tag*, a jagged point or piece: OGmc \**tagga* (Torp).

**tail** (1) of an animal's body, whence v ('*tail* off, *tail* along', etc.); with such cpds as **tailband, -board, -end, -piece**, etc.—all obvious.

*Tail*, ME *tail*, earlier *tayl*, derives from OE *taegl*, var *taegel*: cf ON *tagl*, Go *tagl* (hair), OHG *zagal*, MHG *zagel*, MLG *tagel* (a rope-end)—and prob OIr *dūal*, a lock of hair, a fringe: OGmc r, \**tagl-*; IE r, *dokl-* (Walshe)—or is it merely the OC r? Cf Ga *dual*, a ply of rope, and prob Cor *gols*, a lock of hair.

**tail** (2), adj, n, v, (something) cut to size, to cut thus, hence to limit; **entail**, n, v—**detail**, n, v— **retail**, n, v; **tailor**, n, hence v; **tallage; tally**, n, hence v.

1. This group goes back to L *tālea*, var *tālia*, a twig, a stake, a sharp point: o.o.o. *Tālia* has derivative LL-VL *tāliāre*, to cut, to split, whence OF-MF *taillier* (MF-F *tailler*) whence, 'to *tail*' or cut to size (obs), to limit, esp with an entail; from the derivative OF-MF pp *taillié* and OF-F n *taille* come the E adj and E n *tail*, extant only as legal terms.

2. The E legal n *entail* app derives from the E legal v *entail*, itself from OF-MF *entaillier*, MF-F *entailler*, with derivative OF-F n *entaille*, which perh influenced the E n.

3. OF-MF *taillier*, MF-F *tailler*, has derivative agent *tailleor* (later *tailleur*), already used in C12 in the modern sense; whence the E *tailor*. Cf the MF-F derivative *taillage*, a toll, adopted by ME, with extant var *tallage*.

4. LL-VL-ML *tālia* is adopted by AL, whence AF *tallie* (perh influenced by the OF-F n *taille*), whence E *tally*, orig a stick or wooden tablet on which notches were cut to record numbers.

5. OF-MF *taillier*, MF-F *tailler*, has two prefix-cpds relevant to E: OF-MF *detaillier* and OF-MF

*retaillier*. The former (whence MF-F *détailler*), to cut off, esp into pieces, yields 'to *detail*'; the derivative OF-MF n *detail* (later *détail*) yields the E n *detail*.

6. OF-MF *retaillier* (MF-F *retailler*), to cut back, hence off, hence into pieces, has derivative OF-MF n *retaille* (EF-F *ré-*), var *retail*, adopted by AF, whence E *retail*, whence the E v (prob influenced by the F v), whence *retailer*.

**tailor.** See prec, para 3.

**taint.** See STAIN, para 5.

**take,** v (hence n), pt **took,** pp **taken,** whence agent **taker** and pa, vn **taking; intake**—**partake, partaker, partaking**—**retake,** v, hence n.

1. 'To *take*,' ME *taken*, late OE *tacan*, derives from ON *taka* (pt *tōk*, pp *tekinn*)—cf OSw *taka*, Sw *taga*, Go *tēkan*, MD *tāken* (and prob MLG *tacken*, to touch): IE r, perh *dag-*, *dak-*, with OGmc offshoot *tag-*, *tak-*.

2. 'To *take in*' results in an *intake*; 'to *take again*' becomes 'to *retake*'. 'To *partake*' is a b/f from *partaking* and *partaker*, which sloven *part-taking* and *part-taker*, which translate the L *particeps*, adj, hence also n, from *partem cap*ere, to take a part: cf *participate*.

**talc, talcum:** EF-F *talc*: ML *talcum* (s *talc-*): Ar *ṭalq*: Per *talk*. The F *talc* perh comes direct from Ar.

**tale, talesman.** See the 2nd TELL, para 2.

**talent,** whence **talented,** is ME *talent*, the sum of money, desire, (late) ability: syn MF *talent*: OF *talent*, the sum of money: L *talentum*, from Gr *talanton*, the sum of money, (from) a definite weight, (from) a thing weighed, (from) a balance: cf Skt *tulá*, a balance, a weight, *tulayáti*, he weighs, and the *tol-* of L *tolerāre*, (lit) to support, app an extn of *tollere*, to raise (a weight), with cognates in Gr, C, Gmc: cf the 1st TOLL.

**taligrade.** See the element *tali-*.

**talion.** See RETALIATE, para 1.

**talisman** is adopted from EF-F *talismán*, which, like Sp *talismán* and It *talismano*, comes from coll Ar *ṭilsamān*, pl of *ṭilsam*, a metathesis of Ar *ṭilasm*, itself from MGr *telesma*, a sanctified object (as, orig, was a talisman), LGr an initiatory religious rite, Gr a payment, (lit) a completion, from Gr *telein*, to complete—cf TELEOLOGY.—Hence, perh after F *talismanique*, the adj *talismanic*.

**talk, talkative, talker.** See the 2nd TELL, para 3.

**tall.** See the 2nd TELL, para 4.

**tallage.** See the 2nd TAIL, para 3.

**tallboy.** See the 2nd TELL (heading).

**tallow,** whence **tallowy** and such obvious cpds as **tallow-face, -weed, -wood.** *Tallow*, ME *talgh*, prob comes from MD-MLG *talch* (ED *talgh*, D *talk*, cf G *Talg*): akin to ON *tólgr* and perh to Go *tulgus*, firm: IE r, *dalg-*, varr *delg-*, *dolg-*, *dulg-*. (Feist.)

**tally.** See the 2nd TAIL, para 4.

**Talmud,** the corpus of ancient Jewish canonical and civil law, derives from H *talmūdh*, doctrine, lit instruction or study, from *lāmadh*, to learn.

**talon; talus; tassel.** E-ME *talon* is adopted from OF-F, which takes it from VL *tālōn*em, acc of *tālō*, heel, a bird's spur, a mdfn of L *tālus*, the ankle (Med E *talus*, ankle-bone), hence the heel, s and r *tāl-*, akin to OIr *sál*, Ga *sàil*, W *sawdl*, heel.

2. L *tālus* has dim *taxillus* (? for *talsillus*, contr of *talusillus*), a small die (in gambling), whence VL *tassellus*: OF-MF *tassel* (F *tasseau*, a bracket), the small plaque of a buckle or clasp, hence an ornamental small square of fabric or a small mending-piece: ME *tassel*, as in 1st OF-MF sense: E *tassel*.

**tamale,** a Mexican seasoned dish of minced meat and crushed maize: ASp *tamales*, pl of the syn *tamal*: Nahuatl *tamalli*. (DAE.)

**tamarack,** a NA larch, is of Alg origin.

**tamarin,** a SAm marmoset, is adopted from F (EF *tamary*), which adopts it from Galibi—the language of the Caribs of F Guiana.

**tamarind.** See INDIA, para 5.—Whence, at the It stage, the It condiment *tamara*.

**tamarisk:** LL *tamariscus*, extn of L *tamarīx*, var *tamarīcē*: o.o.o.: perh (B & W) ult akin to Ar *tamār* (as in *tamarind*).

**tambour, tambourin, tambourine; tabor (tabour), taboret (tabouret), taborin (or -ine); timbal, timbale.**

1. *Tambourine* anglicizes the late MF-F *tambourin*, dim of MF-F *tambour*, OF *tambor*, a drum, hence an embroidery-frame shaped like the frame of a drum: cf Port *atambor*. Earlier is OF-EF *tabour, tabor*, likewise adopted by E: cf Per *tabīr*. The *n* (F *m*) infix exists already in coll Ar *ṭanbūr* (Ar *ṭunbūr*), a drum, from Per *ṭanbūr*, a Mus instrument; but OF-EF *tabor, tabour*, must have derived from an *n*-less Ar or Per form. The old F word has two dimm: *tabo(u)ret* (late MF-F) and *tabo(u)rin* (late MF-EF), both adopted by E.

2. *Timbal* anglicizes F *timbale*, a kettledrum; the Mus senses of both words are modern. Late MF-F *timbale* is a f/e mdfn—after *cymbale*—of MF *tamballe*, itself a f/e mdfn—after *tambour*—of Sp *atabal*: Ar *aṭṭabal*, a coll assimilation of Ar *al-ṭabl*, the (*al*) drum (*ṭabl*).

**tame,** adj (whence **tameness**) and v (whence **tamer**); **domitable** and **indomitable.**—Cf the sep ADAMANT (where DIAMOND)—DOE—DOMESTIC (where DAME).

1. 'To *tame*' derives from ME *tamen* (cf MD *tamen*), from the ME—whence E—adj *tame*: OE *tam*, akin to ON *tamr*, MD *tem, taem*, MD-D *tam*, OHG-MHG *zam*, G *zahm*; also to the vv ON *temja*, OHG *zemmen*, G *zähmen*, Go *gatamjan*, L *domāre*, Gr *daman*, to subdue or tame, Skt *dāmayáti*, he tames, he is tame, OIr *domnaim*, I bind fast, and Hit *damass-, tamass-*, to oppress. The IE r is perh *dam-*, with var *dem-* and *dom-*, to subdue, to tame.

2. L *domāre*, to tame, has the app freq, yet syn, derivative *domitāre*, whence *domitābilis* and LL *indomitābilis*, untamable: whence E *domitable* and *indomitable*.

**Tamil,** the oldest, richest, best known of the

Dravidian (non-IE) languages: Dravidian *Tamiḷ*, var *Tamiṟ* (cf Skt *Dramiḷa* and Prakrit and Pali *Damiḷa*): o.o.o.

**Tammany**, corruption in municipal government, derives from *Tammany* Hall (orig occupied by the *Tammany* Benevolent Society), occupied by a political club controlling the Democratic party of New York City: from the wise and friendly Delaware chieftain *Tamanen* or *Tamanend*, usu *Tammany*, lit 'the affable', who flourished c1700.

**tammy.** See STAMEN, para 4.

**tam-o'-shanter**, a Sc flat-topped, top-tasselled cap, commemorates Robert Burns's drunken eponymous farmer *Tam o' Shanter*, Tom of Shanter.

**tamp**, whence agent **tamper** and pa, vn **tamping** —cf **tampion** and **tampon; tompion; tap**, faucet, slap.

1. The 1st prob derives from F *tamponner*, to stop up, bung, plug, from F *tampon; tompion* is a var of *tampion*, which anglicizes *tampon*, itself adopted from EF-F *tampon*, a nasalized var of MF *tapon*, aug of MF-EF *tape*, a cork, bung, plug, from OF-EF *taper*, to cork, bung, plug, from the syn Frankish \**tappōn*: cf OHG *zapho*, MHG *zapfe*, G *Zapfen*, a bung, a tap, and OE *taeppa*, ME *tappe*, E *tap*, a faucet (whence the v), akin to ON *tappi*, MD *tappe*, MD-D *tap*, a bung. *Tap* has derivative *tappet* (*tap*+euphonic *t*+dim *-et*): cf the formation of *tippet*.

2. OF-EF *taper*, to stop up, to bung or cork, is perh akin to OF-F *taper*, to strike with the flat of the hand, which could be a sem development from 'to stop up'—cf the sem development of E *plug*. More prob, however, OF-F *taper*, to slap, to tap—whence E 'to *tap*', whence the n (perh suggested by the MF-F derivative n *tape*)—is echoic.

**tamper** (1), n. See prec (heading).

**tamper** (2), v. See TEMPER, para 2.

**tampion.** See TAMP, para 1.

**tampon.** See TAMP, para 1.

**tam-tam.** See TOM-TOM.

**tan**, n and v, whence **tanner** (cf MF-F *tanneur*), cf **tannery** (perh from MF-F *tannerie*), **tanning; tannic** and **tannin; tawny** and **tenné**.

1. The E n *tan* is adopted from MF-F *tan*: ML *tanum* (s and r *tan-*): perh from OHG *tanna*, an oak, tan being made from oak-bark. 'To *tan*' comes from MF-F *tanner*, either from the F n or from ML *tannāre* (from *tanum*).

2. MF-F *tan* has the derivative *tanin* (Chem *-in*), whence E *tannin*; E *tan*, n, has derivative *tannic* (*tan*+euphonic *n*+adj *-ic*).

3. MF-F *tanner* has pp *tanné*, with var *tenné*, which, used as Her n, denotes a bright-brown colour; in MF, *tanner* has also the pp *tané* (var of *tanné*), whence E *tawny*.

**tandem**, two horses (hence cyclists) one behind the other: L *tandem*, by a jocose extn of sense from 'at last' to 'lengthwise'.

**tang**, prong, fang, sharp flavour. See LANGUAGE, para 6.—For the seaweed, see TANGLE, para 3.

**tangency, tangent, tangential.** See TACT, para 2.

**tangerine**: *Tangerine*, adj and n, 'native of *Tangier*': Sp (and F) *Tanger*: L *Tingē* or *Tingi*: prob Hamitic.

**tangibility, tangible.** See TACT, para 3.

**tangle**, v, hence n: a contr of ME *tangil, tangel*, nasal var of *tagil, tagel, tagle*, app of Scan origin: cf the syn Sw dial *taggla* (Webster). Perh, however, ME *tagel(-il)* derives, by aphesis, from AF *entagler*, from ME *takel* (see TACKLE), as EW proposes.

2. 'To *tangle*' has the EE-E prefix cpd 'to *entangle*', whence *entanglement*.

3. *Tangle*, large seaweed, much too late to supply the origin of the v, comes from ON *thöngull*, extn of *thang*, whence E *tang*, a large, coarse seaweed.

**tango.** See TACT, para 4.

**tank, tanker.** See STAGNANT, para 4.

**tankard.** See STAGNANT, para 5.

**tanner, tannery.** See TAN (heading).

**tannic, tannin.** See TAN, para 2.

**tansy**: MF *tanesie* (F *tanaisie*): VL \**tanacēta*: L *tanacētum*: o.o.o.

**tantalic**=*tantal*um+adj *-ic*; **tantalum**, a metallic element difficult to isolate=*Tantal*us+Chem *-um*; **Tantalus**, whence both **tantalus**, a locked liquor-cabinet, and 'to **tantalize**', was that myth Gr *Tantalos* who, as punishment, stood in a lake without being able to quench his thirst or to reach the fruit-laden branches suspended over him. *Tantalos*=*tan-tal*-os, dissimilation of \**tal-tal*, redup of the IE r \**tel-* or \**tal-*, to drag or carry, with var *tol-*, as in L *tollere*. (Hofmann.) 'To *tantalize*' was perh form-suggested by Gr *tantalizein*, to wave about.

**tantamount**, adj: *tantamount*, n (obs): AF *tant amunter*, to amount to as much: OF-F *tant*, L *tant*um, so much+OF-MF *amonter*, to ascend, raise, increase, from OF-F *amont*, upward, L *ad montem*, towards the mountain (cf AMOUNT).

**tap.** See TAMP, paras 1 (faucet) and 2 (slap).

**tape**, n (hence v), whence **red tape** (used on legal documents) and **tapeworm; tapestry**—cf **tapet, tapetum**, 'on the **tapis**'.

1. *Tape*, ME *tape*, earlier *tappe*, comes from OE *taeppe*, akin to Gr *tapēs*, a rug or a carpet, with dim *tapētion*, which, pron *tapition* in Byz Gr, becomes OF-F *tapis*, a carpet, whence 'on the *tapis*' or carpet—standing before 'the boss' in his office.

2. Whereas Gr *tapēs*, o/s *tapēt-* (gen *tapētos*), becomes L *tapēte*, LL *tapētum, tapētium*, whence both the different-sensed Bot *tapetum* and the ME-E *tapet*, OF-F *tapis* has MF-F derivative *tapisserie* (cf the late MF-F v *tapisser*), whence E *tapestry*, with *-t-* perh from ME-E *tapet*; *tapestry* is, as it were, a wall-carpet.

3. Gr *tapēs*, with Attic varr *tapis* and *dapis*, is prob of Iranian origin: cf Per *tāftan*, to turn, spin, weave: IE r \**tap-*, to turn, to spin, ult akin to IE r \**ten-*, to stretch (as in L *tendere*, s *tend-*, r *ten-*): perh Medit, for cf Eg *qen*, rug, carpet.

**taper.** See PAPER, para 2.

**tapestry.** See TAPE, para 2.

**tapet, tapetum.** See TAPE, para 2.

**tapeworm.** See TAPE (heading).

**tapioca:** Port (whence Sp and F) *tapioca*: Brazilian natives' Tupi and Guarani *tipyóca*, *typyóca*: *ty*, juice+*pȳa*, heart+*ocō*, to be removed. (Webster.)

**tapir,** adopted from Sp, comes from Tupi *tapira, tapyra*, any large quadruped.

**tapis.** See TAPE, para 1.

**tappet.** See TAMP, para 1, s.f.

**tar** (n, hence v), whence the adj **tarry; tarpaulin,** derivatively a sailor, hence **tar,** a sailor.

*Tarpaulin* app=*tar*+*paulin*, for *palling*, a covering, from *pall*, a cloth. *Tar*, ME *tarre*, earlier *terre*, derives from OE *teru, teora*, tar, and the var *tierwa, tyrwa*, tar, resin, gum: cf ON *tiara (tjara)*, MD *tarre, tar, ter*, MD-D *teer*, LG *tēr*, G *Teer*, and, with *d* for *t*, Lett *darva*, tar, and Lith *dervà*, pine-wood: ult, therefore, cf TREE. (Walshe.)

**tarantella.** See para 2 of:

**tarantula**—cf **tarantulite; tarantism**—cf **Taranto, Tarentum, Tarentine; tarantella.**

1. About 700 B.C., the Greeks settled in southern Italy and founded the city of *Taras*, gen *Tarantos*, o/s *Tarant-*, whence L *Tarentum*, with adj *Tarentīnus*, E *Tarentine*. *Tarentum* becomes It *Tarento*, later *Taranto*, whence It *tarantismo*, whence SciL *tarantismus* and Med E *tarantism*, with var *tarentism* adapting F *tarantisme* (from *Tarente*, from It *Tarento*), a nervous complaint f/l attributed to the bite of the *tarantula*, a large spider common to the country around Taranto. *Tarantula* is adopted from ML, which thus adapts It *taràntola*, from *Taranto*; cf the F *tarentule*, from the It var *tarentola*, from *Tarento*. At *Tarantula Spring*, in Nevada, was discovered that variety of rock which we call *tarantulite* (Min *-ite*).

2. The It people f/l supposed the tarantula's bite to be curable by lively dancing, whence the *tarantella*, a var of *taràntola* (the spider); the F *tarentelle* derives from the It var *tarentèlla*.

**tardy,** whence **tardiness;** cf the element *tardi-*; **retard, retardance, retardant, retardation, retardative, retardment.**

L *tardus*, slow, is o.o.o.; from the adv *tardē* comes the VL-LL-ML extn *\*tardīvus*, whence OF-F *tardif* (OF-early MF nom *tardis*), f *tardive*, whence both E *tardive* and E *tardy*. *Tardus* has derivative v *tardāre*, with cpd *retardāre*, to cause to slow down so as to be *re-* or behind, whence MF-F *retarder*, whence 'to *retard*'; the presp *retardans*, o/s *retardant-*, and pp *retardātus*, with derivative *retardātiō*, o/s *retardātiōn-*, yield E *retardant* and *retardate*, v, adj, n, and MF-F, hence E, *retardation*, whence, anl, *retardative* (cf F *retardatif*) and *retardatory* (cf F *retardataire*).

**tare** (1), (seed of) a vetch—like dial *tarefitch*, the wild vetch—app comes into ME from MD *teeru*, varr *terwe, taruwe* (MD-D *tarwe*), wheat: o.o.o. The wild vetch tends to grow in grain, esp wheat, fields.

**tare** (2), a reduction, an allowance; MF-F *tare*: It *tara*: Ar *ṭarḥa*, a deduction, lit what one throws away (rejects), from *ṭaraḥa*, to throw (away), hence to reject, to deduct.

**target** comes from MF-F *targette*, dim of OF-F *targe*, a small, usu circular, shield; the latter, adopted by E, is now archaic. OF-F *targe*, from Frankish *\*targa*, is akin to OE *targe*, OE and ON *targa*, a buckler, OHG *zarga* (G *Zarge*), a frame or a case.

**Targum:** H *Targūm*: Aram *targūm*, (an) interpretation.

**tariff,** like F *tariffe*, later *tarif*, comes from It *tariffa*: Ar *ta'rif*, notification, from *'arifa*, to notify, to explain.

**tarmac.** See MACADAM.

**tarn:** ME *terne*: ult from ON *tjarn (tiarn)*, var *tjörn*.

**tarnish,** v, whence n, derives from such parts of the MF-F *ternir*, to dull or dim, as presp *ternissant* and nous *ternissons*, we tarnish: of Gmc origin— cf OHG *tarnjan*, to hide, to obscure, and OE *dearn, derne*, OFris *dern*, OS *derni*, OHG *tarni*, hidden, obscure.

**taro** is a Maori and Tahitian word: cf Samoan *talo* and prob Hawaiian *kalo*. (Tregear.)

**tarot** is adopted from EF-F *tarot*, which has the C16 var *tarau*: prob via It *tarocco*, pl *tarocchi*: Eg *Tar*, a specific god of the nether world, *taru*, the gods of that world. These cards, used in fortune-telling, bear 'pictures' of supernatural or divine powers, mostly inimical to man.

2. L *Tartarus*, trln of Gr *Tartaros*, the nether world (the infernal regions) of Gr myth, is ignored by the etymologists of Gr: but does not *Tartaros*= *tar-tar*+formative *-o-*+nom suffix *-s*, with *tar-tar* a redup of *tar*, a god of the underworld, adopted from the Eg *tar* of para 1? The adj *Tartarean, -ian*, substitutes *-ean, -ian*, for the *-eus* of L *Tartareus*, trln of Gr *Tartareios*.

3. Gr *Tartaros*, L *Tartarus*, has influenced the spellings *Tartar, Tartary*, qq.v. at TATAR.

4. Perh *tar-* is a Medit r: ? cf the Hit *tarrh-*, to be powerful, to control: '(the) powerful (one)'.

**tarpaulin.** See TAR.

**tarpon,** a large A marine fish, is o.o.o.: as Webster points out, the D *tarpoen* and the Guiana native *trapoeng* perh both derive from E.

**tarragon.** See DRAGON, para 4.

**tarry** (1), adj. See TAR (heading).

**tarry** (2), v, to vex or irritate (obs), to fatigue, to wait for, whence the vi, to wait, to delay: ME *tarien*, to vex, hinder, delay: OE *tergan, tirgan, tyrgan*, to vex or irritate: cf MD-D *tergen*, G *zergen*: OGmc (Western) *\*targjan*: IE r, *\*dergh-* (Kluge). The change from *e* to *a* was app caused by the syn OF-MF *tarĬer*, of the same origin; cf, however, Hit *tarkumma-*, to announce, to explain.

**tarsal,** adj (*-al*) of **tarsus; tarsier; metatarsus.** The last is a SciL cpd of *meta-*, between+*tarsus*; the 3rd, adopted from F, is an agential *-ier* derivative of EF-F *tarse*, from L *tarsus*; and *tarsus* itself is a trln of Gr *tarsos*, a hurdle for drying things on, a flat object, hence the flat of the foot. With the Attic var *tarros*, cf OHG *darra*, G *Darre*, a kiln. The IE r is perh *\*ters-*, to dry (vt), as Hofmann proposes.

**tart** (1), adj, whence **tartness**, comes from OE *teart*, sharp, severe: perh cf 'to TEAR'.

**tart** (2), n, ME *tarte*, is adopted from MF-F *tarte*, perh orig a var of OF-F *tourte*, from LL *torta* (*panis*), a round (loaf of) bread, a cake, o.o.o. The sl *tart*, a prostitute, is short for *jam tart*, a sweet 'dish'.

**tartan** is o.o.o.: perh either a contr of MF-F *tiretaine*, itself o.o.o., or a contr of ME *tartarin*, lit a cloth or fabric 'of Tartary'. (B & W.)

**tartar** (1). See TARTAR, para 2.

**tartar** (2), wine-sediment, hence a re-crystallized substance: ME *tartre*: EF-F *tartre*: MF *tartaire*: ML (presumably also LL, to judge by the LL adj *tartarālis*) *tartarum*: MGr *tartaron*: o.o.o.—Hence *tartaric*.

**Tartar**, a kind of Mongol, derives from ML *Tartarus*, a f/e reshaping—after L *Tartarus*, the nether world—of Per *Tātār*, whence the more correct form *Tatar*; Per *Tātār*, of Tatar origin, affords the Oriental parallel to Gr *barbaros* (*bar-bar-os*), q.v. at BARBARIAN.

2. Fierce and ruthless soldiers, the Tatars occasioned the generic *Tartar*, usu written *tartar*. From *Tatar*, *Tartar*, derives *Tatary*, *Tartary*.

**tartaric**. See the 2nd TARTAR, s.f.

**Tartarean (-ian)**, **Tartarus**. See TAROT, para 2.

**task, taskmaster**. See TACT, para 7.

**Tasmania**, whence **Tasmanian** (adj, hence n) and **tasmanite** (Min -*ite*), was, in 1853, named after the D navigator Abel *Tasman* (1602–59), who discovered it in 1642 and called it Van Diemen's Land.

**tassel**. See TALON, para 2.

**taste, tasteful, tasteless, tasty**. See TACT, para 8 and heading.

**Tatar, Tatary**. See TARTAR.

**tat**. See TATTING.

**tatler**. See TATTLE.

**tatter**, n, hence v, whence the pa **tattered**; **tatterdemalion**. *Tatter*, a part either torn and hanging, or torn off (a rag), is of Scan origin, with several modern cognates. A *tatterdemalion* or *ragamuffin* is perh a somewhat arbitrary cpd of *tattered*+*mal*, evil+agential -*ion*, or *tattered*+ euphonic -*e*-+*mal*, bad+*one*.

**tatting**, the process of making a knotted lace, derives, as does the v **tat**, from dial *tat*, a tuft of wool, of Scan origin: cf Ice *taeta*, to tease wool.

**tattle** (v, hence n)—whence **tattler**, (formerly) occ spelt **tatler**—derives from MD *tatelen*, to babble (var *tateren*), to stammer: echoic: cf BABBLE.

**tattoo** (1), a military call, hence an evening entertainment, is an easing of earlier *taptoo*: D *taptoe*, lit a tap(house)-shut: D *tap*, a faucet+*toe* (adj), shut, akin to TO.

**tattoo** (2), picture(s), etc., pricked indelibly into the skin, hence the v: Tahitian *tatu*, a puncturing —cf Maori *ta*, to paint, to tattoo. (Tregear.)

**taught**. See TEACH.

**taunt** (1), adj. See TAUT, para 2.

**taunt** (2), v, hence n. See TEMPT, para 5.

**tauric, Taurid, taurine, Taurus**. See the 1st STEER, para 2.

**taut**, whence **tauten**; **taunt**, adj.

1. *Taut* derives from EE *taught*, from ME *toght*, var *toht*, tough, firm, binding, tight: ? akin to OE *togian*, *tēon*, to pull—or rather (OED) to TIGHT.

2. Perh related to *taut* is the naut *taunt*, very tall or high: o.o.o.: doubtfully from OF-MF *autant*, to the full (EF-F so much).

**tautochronous**; **tautology**, whence **tautological**. See the element *tauto-*.

**tavern, taverner**; **tabernacle**, whence, anl, **tabernacular**; **trabeated, trabecula**—cf **trave, architrave**; **thorp**; **troop** (n, hence v), whence **trooper** (cf F *troupier*)—cf **troupe**, whence **trouper**.

1. *Tavern* is ME *taverne*, adopted from MF-F, which takes it from L *taberna*, perh orig any wooden habitation, but in practice a shop, esp a wine-shop: o.o.o.: perh either Etruscan (E & M) or a metathesis for *\*traberna*, from L *trabs*, a wooden beam (Webster *et alii*).—L *taberna* has derivative *tabernārius*, a tavern-frequenter or -keeper, whence MF-F *tavernier*, adapted by E as *taverner*, archaic except as PN *Taverner*. Another derivative is the dim *tabernāculum*, a tent, LL the Jewish tabernacle: OF-F *tabernacle*, adopted by E.

2. L *trabs* (gen *trabis*), a beam, has Oscan and Umbrian cognates: cf also Lith *trobà*, a house, OBr, OW, EIr *treb*, a house, a homestead, EIr *trebaim*, I inhabit, and ON *thorp*, a small enclosure.

3. L *trabs* has dim *trabecula*, a little beam, adopted by Sci, with various specialized senses and with derivative adj *trabecular*. The adj *trabal* represents L *trabālis* (*trab*-, s and r of *trabs*+adj suffix -*ālis*); *trabeated* is an E formation.

4. L *trabs*, a beam, becomes OF-MF *tref*, MF *trave*, whence MF-F *travée*, the space between beams, whence ME-E *trave*, used in Arch; cf *architrave*, adopted from EF-F, from It, *architrave*: *archi*-, principal+*trave*, from L *trabs*.

5. With ON *thorp*, a small enclosure (as in para 2), cf OHG-G *dorf*, a village, OS and OFris *thorp*, a hamlet, Go *thaurp*, a field, a farm, a landed estate, and OE *thorp*, a hamlet, retained by E— var *thorpe*—esp in PlNn.

6. OE *thorp* has the metathetic var *throp*, which perh helps to explain the OGmc origin of LL-ML *tropus*, a herd, whence OF-F *troupe*, derivative agent F *troupier*, the former adopted, the latter adapted, by E, in their theatrical senses. OF-F *troupe*, orig a herd, whence a company of people, hence in military sense, becomes E *troop*.

7. Note that the OGmc forms adduced in paras 2, 5, and 6, go back to the OGmc r *\*thurp*-; the IE r is *\*turb*-, as in L *turba*, Gr *turbē*, a crowd, a mob. (Walshe.)

**taw** (1), a 'shooter' in the game of marbles. Like

the *tee* in certain ball-games, *taw* prob derives from the letter T used as a mark; the Gr name of that letter is *tau*. (EW.)

**taw** (2), to dress (hemp), obs—to prepare (hides and skins) with alum—comes, through ME *tawen*, from OE *tāwian*, to dress (hemp), hence to beat: cf OFris *tāwa*, OS *tōian*, Go *taujan*, MD *tauwen*, MD-D *touwen*, to make, to do. Cf TOOL, f.a.e.

**tawdry**, whence **tawdriness**, comes from *tawdry laces*, a contr of *St Audrey's laces*, necklets sold at *St Audrey's* fair medievally held at Ely: *St Audrey* ult derives from OE *Aethelthrȳth*, latinized as *Etheldreda*.

**tawny.** See TAN, para 3.

**tax, taxable, taxation.** See TACT, para 7.

**taxis; taxonomy.** See TACTIC, para 2.—For **taxidermy**, cf the element *taxeo-* (*taxi-*).

**tea; 'char'; theine** or **thein.** The 3rd derives from F *théine* (Chem suffix *-ine*), from F *thé* (1664); and *thé*, like the E *tea*, prob derives from Mal *tēh* (whence the early pron *tay*—perh influenced by the id F pron).

2. Mal *tēh* is an adaptation of Ch *chia* or *tcha*, whence E *cha*, a specified rolled tea, and sl *char*, any tea.

**teach**, pt **taught** (ME *taughte*, earlier *tahte*: OE *tāēhte*, *tāhte*), pp **taught** (OE *getāēht*, *getāht*); hence **teacher** and pa **teaching** (the vn comes from OE *tāēcing*, var *tāēcung*);—**teen**, n and v; **token**, n and v—whence **betoken.**—insurance **policy.**

1. 'To *teach*' or show, guide (obs senses), hence to guide educationally, to show to (someone) by way oi instruction, derives, via ME *techen*, from OE *tāēcan*, akin to OE *tācen*, *tācn*, a token, whence, indeed, ME *taken*, later *token*—as still in E. With OE *tāēcnian*, cf OFris *tēknia* and OHG *zeihhinēn*, MHG *zeichenen*, G *zeichnen*, to provide wth means of recognition or knowing, and OHG *zeigōn*, MHG-G *zeigen*, to show; with OE *tācen*, *tācn*, cf OFris *tēken*, OS *tēcan*, OHG *zeihhan*, MHG-G *zeichen*, Go *taikns*, ON *teikn*. With both, cf—further off—L *dīcere*, to show, hence to say, and Gr *deiknumi*, I show: f.a.e., DICT.

2. Akin to the OGmc words cited above are the now mainly dial *teen*, injury, grief, vexation, and 'to *teen*' or harm, distress, vex: ME *tene*, from OE *tēona*, injury, reproach, and OE *tȳnan*, *tēonian*, to vex, to slander, to accuse: cf the ON *tiōn* (*tjōn*), n, and OE *tēon*, OFris *tiōna*, *tiūna*, OS *tiohan*, OHG *zīhan*, MHG *zīhen*, G *zeihen*, to accuse, Go *gateihan*, to proclaim.

3. Gr *deiknunai*, to show, has cpd *apodeiknunai* (*apo-*, off), to show forth, whence *apodeixis*, a proof, ByzGr a receipt, whence ML *apodixa*, a receipt, whence It *pólizza*, MF-F *police*, orig a certificate, then, C16 onwards, a contract, whence the E *policy* of insurance.

**teak:** Port *teca*: *tēkka*, *tēkku*, in Malayalam, a Dravidic language, spoken on India's Malabar coast. Cf the F *teck*, orig *teka*.

**teal** comes from ME *tele*: cf—perh a b/f from—D *teling*, var *taling*, MD *taling*, var *talinc*: o.o.o.

**team**, whence **teamster** and **teamwork**, is ME

*tem, team*, from OE *tēam*, offspring, a line of harnessed animals: cf LG *toom*, offspring, team, bridle, MD *tome*, MD-D *toom*, a bridle, OHG-MHG *zoum*, G *Zaum*, ON *taumr*, a bridle: akin to OHG *ziohan*, MHG-G *ziehen*, to draw or pull: therefore cf the E 'to TOW'.

**tear** (1) in the eye, whence **tearful** and **tearless**; **lachryma, lachyrmal, lachrymatory, lachrymose**; cf the element *dacryo-*.

1. *Tear*, ME *ter*, *tere*, OE *tēar*, *taeher*, *tēagor*, is akin to OFris *tār*, OHG *zahar*, MHG *zaker*, G *Zähre*, Go *tagr*, ON *tār*; OIr *der*, Ga *deur*, W *dagr*, Cor *dagar*, *dager*, OC *\*dakrū*; Gr *dakru*, extn *dakruma*, whence OL *dacruma*, whence—cf *lingua* for *dingua*—*lacruma*, usu in var *lacrima*; IE etymon *\*dakru*.

2. L *lacrima* has the inferior spelling *lachryma*, which has shaped all the E derivatives:

*lachrymal*, from ML *lachrymālis*, *lacrimālis*;
*lachrymatory*, LL *lacrimatōrius*;
*lachrymose*, L *lacrimōsus*.

**tear** (2), to rend, whence the n; pt **tore** (archaic **tare**); pp **torn.**

'To *tear*,' ME *teren*, OE *teran*, is related to OFris *tera*, to consume, OS far*terian* (*far-*, akin to G *ver-*, int prefix), to consume, OHG *firzeran*, to destroy, MHG ver*zern*, G *zehren*, to consume, use up, Go ga*tairan*, to destroy, MD *eeren*, MD-D *teren*, to consume, ON *taera*, to use, to use up—also to OHG *zerrēn*, MHG-G *zerren*, to pull about, to tear; OB *derö*, I tear, and Lith *dirti*, to flay; Arm *terem*, I flay; Gr *derō*, I flay; Skt *dar-*, to burst, *darnáti*, he bursts; IE r, *\*der-*, to rend, esp to flay.

**tease**, v (whence **teaser** and **teasing**), whence n; **teasel; touse**, whence **touser** or **towser**, a large, boisterous dog; **tousle** and **tussle.**

1. 'To *tease*', ME *tesen*, OE *tāēsan*, to pluck, to disentangle, to comb, were orig applied to flax and wool: cf MD *tēsen*, *teesen*, D *teezen*, OHG *zeisan*, MHG-G *zeisen*: perh echoic.

2. Akin to OE *tāēsan* is OE *tāēsel*, ME *tesel*, E *teasel*: cf OHG *zeisila*. The teasel has a flowered head, with very stiff, hooked bracts; dried, the head was formerly used to produce a nap on woollen fabrics.

3. Akin to ME *tesen* is ME *-tousen*, *-tusen*, akin to OFris *tūsen*, to pull about, to rend, and OHG *zizūsōn*, MHG *zizūsen*, G *zausen*, to tousle: 'perh' (as Walshe suggests) 'related to L *-dumus* "bramble" (for *\*dusmos*)'.

4. ME *-tusen* acquires the freq 'to *tussle*'—a sense-differentiated doublet of *tousle*.

**teasel.** See para 2 of prec.

**teat:** ME, from OF-MF, *tete* (F *tette*): OGmc (western) *\*titta*: cf MHG-G *zitze*, MLG and MD *titte*, and OE *tit*, *titt*, whence, via ME *titte*, this particular pron, now held to be vulgar: cf Arm*-tit*, breast, and Gr *titthē* (τίτθη), *nipple*: IE r, *\*dhei-*, to suck (Hofmann). Cf TITILLATE.

**technic**, adj (with extn **technical**, whence **technicality**) and n (cf **technics**)—**technician**—**technique**; cf the element *techni-*, var *techno-*, where see, e.g.

technology; tectonic, adj and n (usu in pl), architectonic, adj and n (cf architectonics)—architect, architecture (whence architectural); test (a shell, a cupel, a trial), testaceous, testudo—cf tester, testy, tête-à-tête; text, textile (adj, hence n), textual, texture (whence textural)—context (whence, anl, contextual), contexture—pretext, n, hence v; tissue, whence tissual; toga; toil, a snare, usu in pl —toilet, toilette; telary (with derivative syn telarian)—cf tiller of a boat; cf the sep subtle; tectum, tegula, tegument, tile (n, hence v)—thatch, n and v (whence thatcher)—cpds detect, detection, detective, detector, and protect, protection, protective, protector (whence protectorate).

1. The interrelationships of Gr *tekhnē*, a manual skill, and Gr *tektōn*, a carpenter, with L *tegere*, to cover, and L *texere*, to weave, are not entirely clear: but that the two L words are related to each other, and the Gr to the L, can hardly be doubted. Sem, building (lit and fig) is either stated or implied in all three groups; phon, the relationship is abundantly clear.

## Gr tekhnē

2. Gr *tekhnē* (s and r *tekhn-*, extn of *tekh-*), a working with the hands, a craft, manual skill, an art, art, is akin to Gr *tektōn*, Skt *tákṣan*, a carpenter, a builder, and Skt *tákṣati*, he forms, constructs, carpenters; phon id with *tákṣ*ati is L *texere*, to weave, hence, fig, to construct, with pp *textus*. Cf also the Hit *takkss-* (*taks-*), to join, build. Prob akin to those Skt, Gr, L words is L *tegere*, to cover, hence to put a roof onto, with s *teg-* and pp *tectus*. At first sight distinct from all these words, the L *tēla*, a weaving, a web, represents the IE etymon *\*teksala*, whence *\*tesla*, whence *tēla* (Hofmann). The IE r is *\*tekh-*, to put in hand, work on, build, carpenter, which app has the transitional form *\*tekh-*.

3. The adj of Gr *tekhnē* is *tekhnikos*, whence the F *technique* and the E *technic*, with the *-al* extn *technical*. The F adj *technique* soon became also n, adopted—finally—by E; the derivative F *technicien* produces E *technician*.

## Gr tektōn

4. Gr *tektōn*, a carpenter, a builder, perh for *\*tekhtōn* (*\*tekht-* an extn of *tekh-*), has adj *tektonikos*, whence LL *tectonicus*, whence E *tectonic*, whence the n *tectonics*.

5. A Gr master-builder, an architect, is an *arkhitektōn*, with *arkhi-* connoting 'chief, principal'; the adj *arkhitektonikos* becomes LL *architectonicus*, MF-F *architectonique*, E *architectonic*, used also as n, mostly in pl. *Arkhitektōn*, moreover, becomes L *architecton*, latinized still further to *architectus*, whence EF-F *architecte*, whence E *architect*; L *architectus* has derivative *architectūra*, whence EF-F *architecture*, adopted by E.

## L tegere

6. L *tegere*, to cover, s and r *teg-*, has pp *tectus*, whence *tectum*, a roof, adopted by An, with adj

*tectal*; the L c/f *tecti-* occurs in E: see the element *tecti-*.

7. From *teg*ere derives L *tegumen*, a covering, var *tegumentum*, with contrr *tegmen*, *tegmentum*, both adopted by SciE; *tegumentum* becomes (F *tégument* and) E *tegument*. Also from *tegere*, but with vowel-change, comes L *toga*, a covering, hence a garment, esp a Roman citizen's (formal) outer garment, a sense preserved in E. L *toga* becomes MF-EF *togue*, EF-F *toge*, adopted by EE, whence the underworld *togeman* (*-man*, a suffix), a cloak, a coat, whence, by b/f, the underworld, later sl, *tog*, a coat, pl *togs*, outer garments, clothes.

8. Also from *teg*ere derives L *tegula*, a tile, adopted by An, with adj *tegular*. *Tegula* becomes OE *tigule*, anglicized further as *tigele*, contr to *tigle*, whence ME *tigel*, contr to *tile*, retained by E. Akin to L *tegula*, a tile, and *tectum*, a roof, is OE *thaec*, a roof, with numerous cognates in Gmc, both old and modern; *thaec* yields ME *thak* and *thacche*, the latter giving us *thatch*; the cognate OE *theccan*, *theccean*, becomes ME *thecchen*, whence, after the n, 'to *thatch*'.

9. L *tegere* has prefix-cpds; two affect E; *dētegere* and *prōtegere*. *Dētegere*, to uncover, to expose, has pp *dētectus*, whence the E adj and v *detect*; the LL derivatives *dētectiō*, o/s *dētectiōn-*, and *dētector* account for E *detection* (whence, anl, *detective*, adj, hence n) and *detector*.

10. L *prōtegere*, to cover *prō-* or in front, hence to shelter or guard, has pp *prōtectus*, whence 'to protect'. The LL derivatives *prōtectiō*, o/s *prōtectiōn-*, and *prōtector* become E *protection* (via OF-F) and *protector* (cf the MF-F *protecteur*). *Protective* derives anl from *protection*; *protégé* is prop the pp of MF-F *protéger*, to protect.

## L texere

11. L *texere*, to weave, prob stands for *\*tegsere* a weakening of *\*teghsere*, var of *\*tekhsere* (r *\*tekh-*+extn s-+inf suffix *-ere*). Its pp *text*us has the derivative n *textus* (gen *-ūs*), something woven, hence the 'woven' structure of a narrative, hence tenor, narrative, whence the modern sense 'text': whence OF-F *texte*, with modern sense from C13 onwards (B & W): whence E *text*. Derivative late MF-F *textuel* yields E *textual*. L *textūra*, tissue, becomes late MF-F *texture*, adopted by E; and L *textilis*, woven, becomes F and E *textile*.

12. L *texere* becomes OF-EF *tistre* (reshaped, by F, to *tisser*), with pp *tissu*, used in MF-F as n, whence E *tissue*.

13. L *texere* has two prefix-cpds affecting E: *contexere* and *praetexere*. *Contexere*, to weave *con-* or together, hence to join, has pp *context*us, whence the n *contextus* (gen *-ūs*), whence EF-F *contexte* and, perh independently, E *context*; from the L pp, EF-F has, after L *textūra*, coined *contexture*, adopted by E. *Praetexere*, to weave *prae-* or in front, hence to allege in excuse, has pp *praetextus*, neu *praetextum*, used as n, whence EF-F *prétexte*, whence E *pretext*.

14. Prob akin to the L pp and n *textus* are L *testa*, an earthen vessel of baked clay, hence a shell, a potsherd, and L *testū* or *testum*, an earthen vessel. From *testa* comes the Zoo *test*, a hard outer shell. L *testa* has the derivative L *testāceus*, *lit* '(made) of baked earth', whence *testaceous*; the L neu *testāceum* is used as n for a shell-covered creature, whence the Zoo *Testacea*, the order of such creatures, whence the E adj, hence n, *testacean*. Cf the L *testūdō*, a tortoise, its shell, hence a protective cover, a word very closely related to *testū*, an earthen vessel; from the o/s *testūdin-* come the E formation *testudinal* and the L *testūdinātus*, whence E *testudinate*.

15. L *testum*, the var of *testū*, an earthen vessel, becomes OF-MF *test* (F *têt*), potsherd, shell, that refining vessel the cupel, whence ME-E *teste*, EE-E *test*, orig a cupel, hence a means of refining, therefore of testing, hence—from examination, or trial, by cupel—any critical examination or trial; whence 'to *test*', whence the agent *tester* and the pa, vn *testing*.

16. As early as in L, the senses—esp the derivative senses—of *testa* and *testum* became confused; both of the L words came to mean 'the skull'; in VL, *testa* went further, for it came to designate 'the head', in which sense it occurs in OF-MF *teste* (F *tête*), whence MF *testiere* (F *têtière*), a headpiece, a helmet, whence the syn ME *testere*, whence E *tester*, a bed-canopy frame, the canopy itself; whence also MF *testu* (F *têtu*), obstinate, headstrong, perh suggesting the AF *testif*, E *testy*, petulant, irascible, irritable.

17. OF-MF *teste*, head, becomes EF-F *tête*, whence the adv phrase *tête à tête*, head to head, intimately, whence the n *tête-à-tête*, an intimate conversation; both adopted by E.

18. Cognate with L *texere*, to weave, is L *tēla*, a weaving, a web: cf para 2, s.f. From *tēla* derives the E *telary* (adj suffix -*ary*), web-spinning, prob influenced by ML *tēlarium*, a weaver's beam, whence MF *telier*, var *tellier*, whence E *tiller*, now only—except in dial—a boat's 'lever' for steering.

19. L *tēla* becomes OF-MF *teile*, later *toile*, a cloth, cloth, a spider's web, whence *toiles* (pl), nets; whence E *toil*, a net, *toils*, snares. OF-MF *teile* has dim MF *tellette*, later *toilette*, a little cloth, then, in EF-F, a cloth for keeping toilet accessories clean, hence the table on which they are placed, then, C17, the act of dressing or adorning oneself, finally, in C18, clothes and adornments, whence, naturally, the current senses, all adopted by E and anglicized in form *toilet*, whence *toiletry*.

**techy.** See the 2nd TACHE.

**tectal.** See TECHNIC, para 6.

**tectonic(s).** See TECHNIC, para 4.

**tectum.** See TECHNIC, para 6.

**ted,** to spread (grass) for drying, whence **tedder,** prob derives from ON *tethja* (s *teth-*), to dung (a field)—which entails spreading: cf ON *tath*, dung, and OHG *zettēn*, to spread out: perh cf Gr *dat*eomai, I share out—which entails spreading—

and Skt *ditás* (adj), shared, distributed: IE r, *det-*, to spread, distribute, share.

**teddy bear:** *Teddy* (pet-form of *Theodore*) Roosevelt (1858–1919), ref his fondness for big-game hunting.

**Teddy boy** is a would-be 'tough', dressed in a parody of the outer garments characteristic of a smart young fellow in the reign of Edward (*Teddy*) VII: 1901–10.

**tedious, tedium.** The latter represents L *taedium*, disgust, LL sadness, grief, whence LL *taediōsus*, sad, irksome, the latter sense predominating in MF *tedieus* (MF-EF *tedieux*), whence E *tedious*: and L *taedium* derives from *taedet*, it is disgusting, LL it irks: o.o.o.

**tee** in certain ball-games. See the 1st TAW.

**teem** (1), to be pregnant, to produce fruit, hence to be prolific; whence the pa, vn **teeming:** ME *temen*: OE *tēman*, occ *tȳman* and *tīeman*: cf OE *tēam*, offspring, therefore cf TEAM.

**teem** (2), to pour out, to empty (now only dial), hence, vi, to rain (very) heavily: ME *temen*: ON *toema*: cf OFris *tēma*, OS *tōmian*, to empty, and ON *tōmr*, OE *tōm*, OS *tōmig*, OHG *zuomig*, empty. 2. From OE *tōm*, ME *tom*, comes the mainly dial *toom*, empty.

**teen.** See TEACH, para 2.

**teenage, teenager, teens.** See TEN, para 4.

**teeter.** See TITTER.

**teeth; teethe.** See TOOTH.

**teetotal; teetotum.** See TOTAL, para 4.

**tegula, tegular.** See TECHNIC, para 8.

**tegument.** See TECHNIC, para 7.

**teind.** See TEN, para 5.

**tel** in Ar PlNn; **tell,** a mound, a hill. The former is a var of the latter: and the latter, used by archaeologists to denote an ancient and artificial mound containing relics of a past civilization, is the Ar *tall*.

**telary.** See TECHNIC, para 18.

**tele-.** See Prefixes.

**telegram.** See GRAMMAR, para 6.

**telegraph.** See GRAMMAR, para 9.

**teleology.** See the element *teleo-*.

**telepathic** comes, anl, from **telepathy,** coined by the E author and psychologist F. W. H. Myers (1843–1901) in 1882: *tele-*, from afar+-*pathy*, a feeling (f.a.e., PATHIC).

**telephone, telephonic, telephonist, telephony.** See PHONE, para 3.

**telescope** (n, hence v), whence **telescopic:** EF-F *télescope*: SciL *telescopium*, from Gr *tēleskopos*, far-seeing or -viewing (f.a.e., SCOPE).

**television:** *tele-*, from after+*vision* (q.v. at VIDE).

**tell** (1), a mound. See TEL.

**tell** (2), to relate—pt (OE *tealde*) and pp **told** (OE *geteald*), whence **teller** and pa, vn **telling; tale** (whence **telltale,** n, hence adj);—**talk** (v, hence n), whence **talkative** (suffix -*ative*), **talker, talking;**—**tall,** whence **tallboy.**

1. 'To *tell*,' OE *tellan*, to state, narrate, count, is akin to OFris *tella*, OS *tellian*, OHG *zellēn*, MD

*telen*, MD-D *tellen*, to count, and ON *telja*, to count, to say.

2. Akin to OE *tellan* is OE *talu*, a narrative, (a) speech, whence E *tale*: cf ON *tal, tala*, speech, a number, with modern Scan cognates—OS *tala*, speech, a number, OFris *tale, tele*, OHG *zala*, MHG *zal*, G *Zahl*, MD-D *tal*, number, MD *tale*, D *taal*, speech: ? ult akin to *tally*, q.v. at the 2nd TAIL, para 4.

3. 'To *talk*,' ME *talken*, is akin to EFris *talken*; the ME *talken* is app an int, from OE *tellan*, to say, to tell.

4. Prob akin to the OE-ME words noted above is *tall*, orig docile, quick to learn: ME *tal*, docile, seemly, tall: OE ge*tael* (pl ge*tale*), quick (whether physically or mentally), ready (e.g., to learn): cf Go un*tals*, indocile, slow to learn, OHG gi*zal*, quick.

**telluric, tellurium, tellurous.** See the element *telluri-*.

**temerarious; temerity.** See TENEBROUS, para 2.

**temper**, v, hence n; **temperament**, whence **temperamental; temperance, temperate**—**intemperance, intemperate; temperative; temperature; tempera; tamper**, to meddle; **distemper**, n and v.— **tempest, tempestuous**—cf **intempestive;**—**tempo, temporal** (both senses), **temporality; temporary; temporize, temporization; contemporaneous, contemporary**, adj, hence n; **extemporal, extemporaneous, extemporary, extempore.**—**temple**, whether Eccl or An—**Templar; template** or **templet.**—**tense** (grammatical).—**contemplate, contemplation, contemplative, contemplator, contemplatory.**

1. The interconnexions of the *temper-tempest, temporal-temple* groups are not at all points clear; there is some doubt whether these groups are indeed connected. The degree and the validity of the doubt will emerge.

### L *temperāre*

2. First of all, 'to *tamper* with', deriving from F *tempérer* (L *temperāre*), is a doublet of 'to *temper*'—cf the latter in its tech sense 'to mix (clay) with water', perh influenced by F *tremper*, earlier *temprer*.

3. The n *temper*, orig the state of a compound having ingredients proportionately mixed, comes straight from 'to *temper*', to mix proportionately, hence to regulate or determine by mixing, hence esp by moderating: OE *temprian*, to mix proportionately, to regulate, to moderate: cf the syn ON *tempra*, OHG *temprōn* (*temparōn*), MLG *temperen*: all from L *temperāre*; the E word was influenced by OF-MF *temprer* (F *tempérer*), likewise from the syn L *temperāre*, s *temper-*, prob a vocalization of \**tempr-*, extn of r *temp-*: o.o.o.: perh, as many hold, akin to L *tempus* (s and r *temp-*), time.

4. L *temperāre* has presp *temperans*, o/s *temperant-* (cf the obs E adj *temperant*), whence *temperantia*, whence MF *temperance* (F *tempérance*) and, perh independently, E *temperance*; the L neg *intemperantia* becomes MF-F *intempérance*, E *intemperance*. The pp *temperātus*, used as adj, and the neg *intemperātus* yield the E adjj *temperate* and

*intemperate*. On the pps *temperāt-* are formed LL *temperātiuus*, ML *-ivus*, whence E *temperative*, and L *temperatūra*, due measure or proportion, temperament, temperature, whence EF-F *tempéra-ture* and prob independently E *temperature*. From the pres s *temper-* comes L *temperamentum*, due measure or proportion, hence a man's physical 'balance', hence the modern sense: EF-F *tempéra-ment* and prob independently E *temperament*. Finally, L *temperāre* remains It *temperare*, with derivative n *tempera*, adopted by painters throughout the civilized world.

5. L *temperāre* has the LL prefix-cpd *distemper-āre*, to mix badly, hence to disorder (cf the Med LL-ML *distemperantia*, unhealthy air conditions); whence MF *destemprer*, whence E 'to *distemper*' or disorder, derange, whence the n *distemper*, malady, esp of a particular kind among dogs. But LL *distemperāre* also means 'to mix', the *dis*-being, here, vaguely int: MF *destemprer* (var *destremper*, F *détremprer*), to soak, to steep, later to mix colours, in a certain way, whence the painters' v, whence n, *distemper*.

### L *tempus*

6. Perh akin to L *temperāre*, which may orig have borne the connotation 'to do things at the right time—at the suitable season', is L *tempus*, time, esp in its fractional aspect, hence a season; s and r *temp-*; ult IE r, as for *temperāre* and also for *templum*, perh *tem-*, to cut, hence to divide (cf TOME).

7. L *tempus* becomes OF *tens*, reshaped, in C14, to *temps*; whence the E *tense*, time-indication in Grammar. It also—from being misapprehended as m instead of neu—becomes It *tempo*, whence the European Mus term *tempo*.

8. L *tempus* has o/s *tempor-*, whence several L derivatives germane to E:

*temporālis*, of or in time, LL worldly (not of eternity, not spiritual); whence E *temporal* and F *temporel*, in OF-MF sometimes *temporal*; derivative LL *temporālitās* yields *temporality*;

LL *temporāneus*, E *temporaneous* (now rare);

L *temporārius*, E *temporary* and EF-F *temporaire*;

ML *temporizāre*, to pass the time, MF-F *temporiser*, whence EF-F *temporisation*; whence E 'to *temporize*' and *temporization*.

9. From L *tempus* comes the OL *tempestus* (adj suffix *-estus*), timely, superseded by *tempestīuus*, ML *-īvus*, with neg *intempestīuus*, ML *-īvus*; whence E *tempestive* and *intempestive*, both now rare.

10. From the L adj *tempestus* derive the nn \**tempesta* and *tempestus*, the latter superseded by *tempestās*, whence the LL adj *tempestuōsus*, whence MF *tempestueus* (M *tempêtueux*), f *tempestueuse*, whence E *tempestuous*; E *tempest*, however, comes from OF-MF *tempeste* (F *tempête*), itself from VL \**tempesta*, time, a period of time, a season good or bad, esp the latter, hence a storm.

11. LL *temporāneus* and L *temporārius*, as in para 8, have—either in or anl with L—prefix-cpds

in *con-*, with, here connoting synchrony, and *ex-*, out of, here connoting unexpectedness:

L *contemporāneus*, living or happening, hence originating, in the same period, whence E *contemporaneous*, whence, anl, *contemporaneity*: cf EF-F *contemporain* and, perh the imm source of the E word, F *contemporanéité*;

L *contemporāneus* and LL *contemporālis* contribute to the formation of E *contemporary*;

LL *extemporāneus*, extempore, yields E *extemporaneous*; but the E *extemporary* derives—after *temporary*—from E *extempore*, adj from adv, spoken at the time, without preparation, from L *ex tempore*, out of time, therefore immediately, at the very time the occasion arises, precise time, the very moment.

### L *templum* (1), a place of religious worship

12. The L *templum*, s *templ-*, r *temp-*, was orig that space 'cut off' or demarcated, by the augur, in the heavens and on earth, in which he collected and interpreted omens, hence a space consecrated to the gods, a precinct, hence the edifice in which they were worshipped (E & M): whence OF-F *temple*, adopted by E. Situated near the Jewish *temple* in Jerusalem was the headquarters building of the military order, created in C12, of MF-F 'les *Templiers*' (B & W), whence 'the *Templars*'.

### L *templum* (2), a transverse beam

13. Either from the transverse lines traced by the augur in the *templum* or sacred space or from the figure traced by the transverse beams determining the orig simple *templum* or sacred edifice comes L *templum*, a transverse beam (E & M): whence MF-F *temple*, whence the E weaving term *temple*; MF-F *temple* has the (obs) dim *templet*, adopted by E, which, by f/e after *plate*, anglicizes it as *template*.

### E *temple* of the head

14. Influenced by L *templum*, E *temple*—as in para 12 (and perh as in para 13)—becomes also 'the space that, on either side of the head, lies behind the eye and adjoins the forehead'. This E *temple* is adopted from OF-EF *temple* (EF-F *tempe*): VL *\*tempula*, a dim formed from L *tempora*, pl of *tempus* (o/s *tempor-*), the An temple, used mostly in the pl, with LL adj *temporālis*, whence EF-F *temporal*, adopted by E. Despite the contrary opinion of numerous Classical and other scholars, L *tempus*, the An temple, is prob id with the earlier-recorded, far more widely used, L *tempus*, time: in the temples one can see the beat of that Physio chronometer the pulse.

### L *contemplāre*

15. From L *templum*, a precinct, a sacred edifice, derives L *contemplāre*, var *-āri*, to view *con-* or intensely or long: either because, from a temple precinct or a temple edifice, the augur can see all around him or because the temple itself can be seen from all sides, as Varro indicated in C1 B.C. *Contemplāre* has presp *contemplans*, o/s *contemplant-*, whence the E *contemplant*, adj and n, and pp *contemplātus*, whence 'to *contemplate*'. On the pps *contemplāt-* are formed these words relevant to E:

*contemplātiō*, acc *contemplātiōnem*, OF-F *contemplation*, adopted by E;

*contemplātīuus*, ML *-īvus*, OF-F *contemplatif*, f *-ive*, adopted by E;

*contemplātor*, whence—perh via MF-F *contemplateur*—E *contemplator*;

LL *contemplātōrius*, whence E *contemplatory*. From the pres s *contempl-* derives LL *contemplābilis*, visible, whence E *contemplable*, able to be contemplated.

### Indo-European

16. One does not need to be a profound philosopher nor even an acute philologist to be able to perceive that in L *temperāre*, to mix judiciously (as strong liquor with water: cf, sem, the F *couper le vin*), to regulate, to modify—in L *tempus*, time finite or divided into seasons or periods, hence in L *tempestās*—in L *tempus*, the An temple—and in L *templum*, a delimited space, a transverse beam, the idea 'to cut, to cut out, to cut off', hence of 'division, whether spatial or temporal' (the notorious space-time continuum, as valid in language as in science), is either clearly denoted or potently connoted.

17. That, phon, the IE r is *\*tem-*, var *\*ten-*, and that, sem, *\*tem-* or *\*ten-* signifies 'to cut, to cut off or out'-is, one would suppose, incontrovertible; the only L word perh foreign to the group is *temperāre*. Cf the TOME group.

18. Without cluttering the ground with a mass of IE cognates, one should adduce as esp significant such words as Gr *temnein*, to cut (pret *etemon* and *etamon*), pres s *temn-*, r *tem-*, and the cognate *temenos* (? for *\*temnos*), syn, in all important aspects, with religious *templum*.

**tempera.** See prec, para 4, s.f.

**temperament; temperance, temperant; temperate, temperative; temperature.** See TEMPER, para 4.

**tempest, tempestive, tempestuous.** See TEMPER, paras 9 and 10.

**Templar.** See TEMPER, para 12.

**template.** See TEMPER, para 13.

**temple** (1), anatomical. See TEMPER, para 14.

**temple** (2), religious. See TEMPER, para 12.

**temple** (3), transverse beam; in weaving. See TEMPLE, para 13.

**templet.** See TEMPER, para 13.

**tempo.** See TEMPER, para 7.

**temporal** (1), anatomical. See TEMPER, para 14.

**temporal** (2), of time; **temporality; temporaneous; temporary; temporize.** See TEMPER, para 8.

**tempt** (whence **tempter** and pa, vn **tempting**), **temptation; tent**, a probe, a roll of lint, and **tent**, to probe; **taunt**, v, hence n; **tentacle**, whence, anl, the adj **tentacular** (cf *spectacle—spectacular*)—cf **tentative; attempt**, v, hence n.

1. 'To *tempt*' comes, through ME *tempten*, *tenten*, and OF-MF *tempter*, MF-F *tenter*, from L *temptāre*, to touch, to feel experimentally, to try or test, to undertake, to attack: in form a freq, *temptāre* is o.o.o.—and distinct from *tentāre*, to agitate, a freq-int of *tendere*, to stretch; *tentāre* has influenced the VL form of L *temptāre*, the MF-F form *tenter*, the ME *tenten*, E 'to *tent*'.

2. *Temptāre* has pp *temptātus*, whence *temptātiō*, o/s *temptātiōn-*, whence OF-MF *temptation* (later *tentation*), adopted by E.

3. *Temptāre* has the cpd *attemptāre*, to feel *ad* or towards, whence MF-EF *atempter*, *attempter* (EF-F *attenter*), whence 'to *attempt*'.

4. MF-F *tenter* leads to the surgical E 'to *tent*'; the MF-F derivative n *tente* becomes the E n *tent*, orig a probe, hence lint used in surgical dressing.

5. MF-F *tenter* has MF-EF var *tanter*, whence E 'to *taunt*'—which exhibits a specialized sem development.

6. L *temptāre*, often eased to *tentāre*, has the SciL derivative *tentāculum*, whence E *tentacle*, with adj *tentacular* (cf the F *tentaculaire*, from *tentacule*, from *tentāculum*); it also has the derivative ML adj *tentātivus*, whence E *tentative*; the E n *tentative* was prob suggested by the EF-F n *tentative*, from the scholastic ML *tentātiva* (prop the f of the adj), a university test or examination.

**ten, tenth**—cf **-teen, -teenth**, and **teenage, teenager**, and **-ty** (as in *twenty, thirty*, etc.); **teind**; **tithe** and **tithing**; cf the sep DECEM group.

1. *Ten*, OE *tēn* or *tȳn*, contrr of *tīen*, is akin to OFris *tiān* (contrr *tēne, tīne*), OS *tehan*, OHG *zehan*, MHG *zehen*, G *zehn*, Go *taihun*, MD-D *tien*, ON *tiu*, and Arm *tasn*; the other IE *cognates* are of the Gr *dek*a, L *dec*em, OIr *deich*, Skt *daśa* types—see DECEM.

2. In the numbers *thirteen–nineteen*, **-teen**, whence **-teenth**, derives from OE **-tēne, -tȳne**, contrr of *-tīene*, with cognates in the other Gmc languages; and in the numbers *twenty–ninety*, **-ty** (whence **-tieth**) derives from OE *-tig*, with OGmc cognates.

3. E *tenth*=*ten*+*-th*, the *-th* deriving from ME *tethe*, from OE *tēotha*, tenth: cf, e.g., MD *tende*, *tinde*, MD-D *tiende*, and OFris *tiānda*.

4. *Teenage*—whence *teenager*—is for *\*teensage*: one's *teens* (13–19), from *-teen* (para 2)+*age*.

5. OE *tīen, tēn*, becomes ME *tyen, teon, tēne*, 10, whence ME *teind, teinde* (and *tend, tende*), 10th, which, used as n, accounts for the Sc *teind*, a tithe.

6. *Tithe* itself derives from the ME n use of *tithe*, var of *tethe*, from OE *tēotha, tēogetha*, 10th (as in para 3). OE *tēotha* has derivative v *tēothian*, whence both 'to *tithe*' and OE *tēothung*, whence *tithing*.

**tenable; tenace, tenacious, tenacity, tenaculum, tenaille**—**tenancy, tenant** (n, hence v; hence also **tenantry**) — **tenement** — **tenet** — **tenon** — **tenor** and **tenure**. Cpds: **abstain, abstention, abstinence, abstinent**; sep CONTAIN, CONTENT, CONTINENCE, CONTINENT—INCONTINENCE, INCONTINENT—CONTINUAL, CONTINUE, CONTINUANCE; sep DETAIN, DETENTION; sep ENTERTAIN, ENTERTAINMENT; sep MAINTAIN, MAINTENANCE; **obtain, obtention**; sep PERTAIN, PERTINENCE, PERTINENT—IMPERTINENCE, IMPERTINENT—APPERTAIN; **retain** (whence the agential **retainer**), **retainer** (legal), **retent, retention, retentive, retentor**—**retinue; sustain** (whence, anl, **sustention**, whence **sustentive**), **sustenance, sustenant, sustentation** (whence, anl, **sustentative**), **sustentator**).

1. All these words derive from L *tenēre*, to hold, (vi) to hold firm, to endure; presp *tenens*, o/s *tenent-*; pp *tentus* (for *\*tenetus*); c/f *-tinēre*, presp *-tinens*, o/s *-tinent-*, pp *-tentus*; derivative abstract nn, *-tinentia* and *-tentiō*, o/s *-tentiōn-*: derivative parts and forms that recur throughout the group with a notable regularity, as does *-tain* (indicating passage through F). L *tenēre* is intimately related to L *tendere* (s *tend-*, r *ten-*), to stretch: f.a.e., TEND.

### Simples

2. L *tenēre* becomes OF-F *tenir*, whence OF-F *tenable*, adopted by E; the OF-F presp *tenant*, used as n by MF-F, has also been adopted. *Tenancy*, however, prob=*tenant*+*-cy*, although it has perh been influenced by ML *tenentia* (presp o/s *tenent-*+*-ia*)—cf also the OF-MF *tenance*. OF-F *tenir* has other derivatives affecting E: OF-EF *tenement* (perh imm from ML *tenementum*), adopted by E; OF-F *tenure*, adopted by E. *Tenor*, coming straight from L, perh owes something to OF-MF *teneor*, AF *tenour*, a holder (F *teneur*); but *tenon*, in carpentry, is adopted from MF-F, which forms it from OF-F *tenir*.

3. L *tenet*, he holds, becomes the E *tenet*, a belief held to be true; L *tenāx*, acc *tenācem* (o/s *tenāc-*), and its derivative *tenācitās*, acc *tenācitātem*, becomes EF-F *tenace* (which, as n, is adopted by E), influencing E *tenacious* (L *tenāc-*+E *ious*), and late MF-F *ténacité*, whence E *tenacity*. LL *tenāculum* (*ten-*+*-āculum*), adopted by SciE, has pl *tenācula*, used by VL as a sing f n, whence OF-F *tenaille*, a pair of pincers, hence (MF-F) a term used in fortification and adopted by E, as is the derivative MF-F *tenaillon*.

### Compounds

4. L *tenēre* has the foll prefix-cpd vv relevant to E: *abstinēre, continēre, dētinēre, obtinēre, pertinēre* (corresp adj *pertināx*—E *pertinacious*), *retinēre, sustinēre*. See the sep entries at CONTAIN, DETAIN, ENTERTAIN, MAINTAIN, PERTAIN.

5. *Abstinēre*, to hold (oneself) *ab* or from, to withhold (vt and vi), becomes MF-F *abstenir* (mostly as vr), ME *abstenen, absteynen*, E 'to *abstain*'; the presp *abstinens*, o/s *abstinent-*, and its derivative n *abstinentia* become OF-F *abstinent* and *abstinence*, both adopted by E; the pp *abstentus* has derivative LL *abstentiō*, o/s *abstentiōn-*, whence E *abstention*.

6. L *obtinēre* (*ob*, towards, against), to get hold

of, either with effort or purposely, becomes MF-F *obtenir* (s *obten-*), whence 'to *obtain*'; derivative LL *obtentiō* (pps *obtent-+-iō*), acc *obtentiōn*em, yields EF-F *obtention*, adopted by E.

7. L *retinēre*, to hold *-re* or back, to keep possession of, becomes VL *\*retenere*, whence OF-F *retenir* (s *reten-*), whence ME *reteynen*, *retaynen*, E 'to *retain*'; used as n, OF-F *retenir* yields the legal *retainer*; derivative OF-F *retenue* (cf the pp *retenu*) is adopted by ME and becomes E *retinue*. L *retinēre* has pp *retentus*, neu *retentum*, which, used as n, yields the Psy *retent*; on the pp s *retent-* are formed L *retentiō*, acc *retentiōn*em, whence MF-F *retention*, adopted by E, and *retentor*, adopted by E, and ML *retentīvus*, whence MF-EF *retentif*, E *retentive*.

8. L *sustinēre*, to hold *sus-*, for *subs-*, for *sub*, from under, to uphold, yields VL *\*sustinīre*, OF-MF *sustenir* (var *sostenir*; EF-F *soutenir*), ME *sustenen*, *sustinen*, E 'to *sustain*'. The L presp *sustinens*, o/s *sustinent-*, yields MF-EF *sustenant* (*sostenant*; F *soutenant*), E *sustenant* (archaic adj), and the derivative LL *sustinentia*, endurance, at least prompted MF-EF *sustenance* (EF-F *soutenance*), adopted by E. L *sustinēre* has the int *sustentāre*, to maintain, with pp *sustentāt*us, whence both the LL *sustentātiō*, acc *sustentātiōn*em, MF-F *sustentation*, adopted by E, and LL *sustentātor*, likewise adopted.

tenace (in card-games). See prec, para 3.
tenacious, tenacity. See TENABLE, para 3.
tenaculum; tenaille. See TENABLE, para 3.
tenancy, tenant. See TENABLE, para 2.

tench: MF-EF *tenche* (F *tanche*): LL *tinca:* prob of C (Gaul) origin, 'from a nasalization of *tic*, to dye, with the sense of spotting with little dots' (Malvezin[1]): cf the Poitou dial *tinche* (Malvezin).

tend, to attend. See next, para 7, s.f.

tend, tendance, tendency, tendent, tendential and tendentious; tender, agent—legal n—v; tendon, tendinous; tense (adj, hence v), tensile, tension (obs tention), tensive, tenson, tensor; tent, a portable cloth shelter, tenter, a frame for stretching cloth, whence tenterhook, whence 'be on tenterhooks'; tentorium, whence, anl, tentorial.—Cpds: attend, attendance, attendant (adj, hence n)—attensity.—attent, attention, attentive, whence the negg inattention (but perh adoption from F) and inattentive (cf the F *inattentif*); contend, contention, contentious; detent, détente; distend, distention; extend, extense, extensible, extension, extensive, extensor, extent; intend, intendment, intense (whence intensify, whence, anl, intensification), intensity, intensive, intent (adj and n), intention, intentional, intentive—cf 'double *entendre*' and '*entente* cordiale'; ostend, ostensible, ostension, ostensive, ostensory, ostent, ostentation, ostentatious; portend, portent, portentous; pretend (whence pretender), pretendant, pretense (pretence), pretension (pretention), pretentious; protend, protension (whence, anl, protensive), protensity; subtend, subtense (adj and n); superintend, superintendence, superintendent—cf intendance, intendant.—The

allied group: thin, adj (whence thinness) and v (whence the pa, vn thinning); tenuity, tenuous—attenuate (adj and v, whence attenuator), attenuation—extenuate (whence extenuator), extenuation, extenuatory; tender, adj, whence tenderfoot, tenderloin, tenderness; tendril and tendron; tetanus (whence, anl, tetanism, tetanize, tetanoid) and tetanic; hypotenuse; tone, tonal, tonality, tonic (adj and n)—whence, resp, the negg atonic, atonal, atonality—intonation, intone—cf the element *tono-*.
—Cf the sep DANCE and esp the sep TENABLE.

### Indo-European

1. All these words spring from the IE r *\*ten-* (varr *\*tan-*, *\*tein-*, *\*ton-*, *\*tun-*, occ with *d* for *t*-), to stretch (? also to span): cf Ve *tanóti*, *tan*uté (cf Homeric *tán*utai), he stretches, Gr *tein*ō (for *\*tenio*), I stretch, *ten*ō, I shall stretch, L *ten*eō, I hold (? orig 'I keep at a stretch'), with such extnn as L *tendo*, Lith *temp*iù, I stretch. The IE r occurs also in C and Gmc—cf para 26 (*thin*).

### L *tendere*, to stretch: Simples

2. L *tend*ere, to stretch (vt), to be stretched to (tend to), becomes OF-F *tendre*, whence, by easement, the ME-E 'to *tend*', orig, and always mainly, vi; whence *tendance*. The L v has presp *tendens*, o/s *tendent-*, whence, rather than from the F presp *tendant*, the erudite E adj *tendent*; L *tendent-* issues in the ML n *tendentia*, whence *tendency*, whence, anl, *tendentious* (cf the F *tendancieux*, from MF-F *tendance*) and *tendential*. OF-F *tendre*, in its senses 'to extend, to offer', yields E 'to *tender*', whence the Law term *tender*, as in 'legal *tender*' or exchange.

3. L *tendere*, to stretch, s *tend-*, has the ML derivative *tendō*, acc *tendōn*em (perh cf the syn LL *tenōn*, from Gr *tenōn*), whence MF-F *tendon*—adopted by E—with derivative EF-F adj *tendineux*, f *tendineuse*, whence E *tendinous*.

4. L *tendere* has pp *tensus*, var *tentus*, both fruitful for E. *Tensus* yields the E adj *tense* and the SciL *tensilis*, whence E *tensile*. Built on the pp *tens*us are the LL *tensiō*, acc *tensiōn*em, whence late MF-F and—prob independently—E *tension*, and LL *tensībilis*, whence E *tensible*, stretchable, and ML *tensitās*, E *tensity* (perh anl from *tense*), and ML *tensor*, adopted by E. F, moreover, accounts for *tensive* (F *tensif*) and *tenson*, a lyric-debate: OF-F *tenson*, from OF *tencier* (F *tancer*), to reprimand, orig to make an effort, from VL *\*tentiāre*, from L *tentus*, pp of *tendere*.

5. The L var pp *tent*us has f *tenta*, whence the ML n *tenta* and MF-F *tente*, whence E *tent*: cf L *tendere pelles*, to stretch skins, whence L *tendere*, to put up tents; cf also LL *tentōrius*, of or for tents, whence the n *tentōrium*, a tent, adopted by An and Zoo.

6. From OF-F *tendre*, but after MF-F *tente*, is formed EF-F *tenture*, the re-shaping of OF-F *tendeure*: cf LL *praetentūra*, an ententment that is *prae-* or in advance, a frontier garrison (Souter),

which perh contributed towards ME *tenture*, lit a stretching, a frame for stretching cloth, whence E *tenter*.

### L *tendere*, to stretch: Compounds

7. L *attendere*, to stretch (esp the mind) *ad* or towards, to pay attention to, becomes OF-MF *atendre*, MF-F *attendre*, ME *atenden*, later *attenden*, E 'to *attend*'. Derivative OF-MF *atendance* and the OF-MF presp *atendant*, later *attendant*, yield the ME *attendaunce*, E *attendance*, and E *attendant*. The derivative OF-MF *atente*, MF-F *attente*, an awaiting, expectation, whence the obs E *attent*, has the adj *attentif*, f *attentive* (cf the ML *attentīvus*), whence E *attentive*. Whereas the *attensity* of Psy=attributive sensory clarity+ the *-tensity* of Psy cpds, *attention* is adopted from EF-F, which derives it from L *attentiōnem*, acc of *attentiō*, from *attentus*, pp of *attendere*.—'To *tend*,' as a syn of 'to attend', is, in fact, aphetic for 'to *attend*'.

8. L *contendere* (int *con*-), to stretch, esp oneself, with all one's strength, to strive, esp in competition, yields OF-EF *contendre*, to strive, dispute, compete, whence E 'to *contend*'; derivative L *contentiō*, acc *contentiōnem*, and *contentiōsus* yield OF-F *contention* and MF-F *contentieux*, f *-ieuse*, whence E *contention* and *contentious*.

9. L *dētendere*, to unstretch, to lessen the tension of, becomes OF-F *détendre*, whence the MF-F *détente*, adopted by European diplomacy and, as a tech, anglicized to *detent*.

10. L *distendere*, to stretch *dis-* or apart, yields 'to *distend*'; from the L pp *distentus* comes L *distentiō* (var *distensiō*), o/s *distention*-, whence— perh prompted by MF-F *distension*—E *distention*.

11. L *extendere*, to stretch out, to stretch to the full, becomes ME *extenden*, E 'to *extend*'. On the L pp *extensus* are formed LL *extensiō*, o/s *extension*-, whence MF-F and, prob independently, E *extension*, and LL *extensiuus*, ML *-ivus*, whence (MF-F *extensif* and) E *extensive*, and LL *extensor*, adopted—in form—by An. *Extensible* is adopted from MF-F, which forms it, anl, from *extension*; and *extent* derives from AF *extente*, var of *estente*, adoption of OF-EF *estente*, itself from the f of OF *estent*, lost pp of OF-EF *estendre* (F *étendre*), from L *extendere*.

12. L *intendere*, to stretch into (*in-*) or towards, be directed at, to have the purpose or pretension of, to plan, leads to E 'to *intend*', a reshaping of ME *entenden*, from OF-F *entendre* (L *intendere*), which, used as n, is part-adopted in the cpd *double entendre* (var of *double entente*), a deliberate, often an indelicate, ambiguity: cf '*entente* cordiale', a friendly understanding, OF-F *entente*, from OF *entent*, lost pp of *entendre*, and ME-E *entendement* (anglicized as *intendment*), adopted from OF-F (from *entendre*).

13. L *intendere* has pp *intensus*, var *intentus*; both important to E. L *intensus*, used by LL as adj 'forcible' and 'eager', yields MF-F *intense*, adopted by E, whence *intensity* (cf F *intensité*); derivative

MF-F *intensif* accounts for E *intensive*; derivative LL *intensiō*, o/s *intension*-, yields E *intension*.

14. L *intentus*, used as adj 'attentive', explains the E adj *intent*; the n *intent* derives, via ME and OF-MF *entent*, from L *intentum*, prop the neu of *intentus*. On the L pp *intentus* are formed L *intentiō*, acc *intentiōnem*, whence OF-F *intention*, adopted by E, the derivative ML adj *intentiōnālis* yielding E *intentional* (cf the late MF-F *intentionnel*); and LL *intentīuus*, ML *-īvus*, whence— perh via MF *ententif*—the E *intentive*.

15. L *ostendere* (for *\*obs-tendere*, for *obtendere*, which does exist), to stretch *ob-* or in front of, towards, to expose, to exhibit or show, results in the archaic 'to *ostend*'. On the pp *ostensus*, var *ostentus*, are formed LL *ostensiō*, var *ostentiō*, o/ss in *-iōn-*, whence *ostension*, *ostention*, and ML *ostensōrium*, adopted by EcclE and anglicized as *ostensory*, and ML *ostensīvus*, whence MF-EF *ostensif*, f *-ive*, whence E *ostensive*; but learnèd F has superseded *ostensif* with *ostensible*, adopted by E. The var pp *ostentus* occasions the n *ostentum*, whence the learnèd and literary E *ostent*.

16. L *ostendere* acquires the int-freq *ostentāre*, to show affectedly or blatantly or pridefully, with pp *ostentātus*, whence the obsol 'to *ostentate*'. On that L pp are formed L *ostentātiō*, acc *ostentā-tiōnem*, whence MF-F *ostentation*, duly adopted by E, and LL *ostentātīcius*, which has helped towards E *ostentatious* (anl from *ostentation*).

17. L *portendere* (*por*-, an ancient var of *prō*-), to stretch before or into the future, to presage or predict, becomes 'to *portend*'; from the pp *portentus* comes *portentum*, a presage, whence a marvel, whence a monster—hence the E *portent*; derivative L *portentōsus* gives us *portentous*.

18. L *praetendere*, to stretch *prae-* or forward-hence to assert and to simulate, yields (MFF, *prétendre* and) 'to *pretend*'; late MF-F *prétendant* becomes E *pretendant*. The ML pp *praetensus* (L *praetentus*) is, in the f *praetensa*, used as n—a thing asserted, whence AF *pretensse*, whence E *pretense*, var *pretence*; derivative EF-F *prétention* and its F adj *prétentieux* have at least prompted E *pretension* and *pretentious*.

19. L *prōtendere*, to stretch *prō-* or forth, becomes 'to *protend*' (obsol); from the pp *prō-tensus* come L *prōtensiō*, o/s *prōtension*-, whence *protension* (obsol) and the Psy *protensity* (after *intensity*).

20. L *subtendere*, to stretch *sub* or under, and its pp *subtensus*, yield the Math 'to *subtend*' and *subtense*.

21. LL *superintendere* (*super*, over+*intendere*), to supervise, with presp *superintendens*, o/s *super-intendent*-, whence ML *superintendentia*, yield 'to *superintend*' and *superintendent* (id in MF; F *sur-intendant*) and *superintendence*. From (? OF-) MF *superintendent* comes OF-F *intendant*, with EF-F derivative *intendance*, both adopted by E.

### L *tener* and L *tenuis*

22. L *tener*, tender, both physically (esp of

young, growing things) and morally, in LL occ
slender or thin, becomes OF *tenre (attested by
tenrement and tenreté), whence the eased tendre,
adopted by ME, whence E tender, whence—prob
suggested by MF-F tendresse—tenderness.

23. From OF-F tendre comes tendron, (OF) a
cartilage, (MF) a tender shoot, a sprout, adopted
by E; tendron has the MF-F (obs) dim tendrille, a
tender little sprig or branch, whence E tendril.

24. Very prob akin to L tener (s and r ten-) is
L tenuis (s tenu-, the u- often consonantal; r,
ten-), thin, fine-drawn, hence tender, weak: whence
—cf the EF-F tenu—the E tenuous. Derivative L
tenuitās, acc tenuitātem, yields late MF-F ténuité
and E tenuity.

25. L tenuis has two derivative prefix-cpd vv
that affect E:

attenuāre (at- for ad-, vaguely int), to make thin,
presp attenuans, o/s attenuant-, whence the Med E
adj, hence n, attenuant; pp attenuātus, whence the
adj and v attenuate; derivative LL attenuātiō, acc
attenuātiōnem, whence EF-F atténuation, whence
E attenuation;

extenuāre, to thin out, hence to loosen, to
weaken, with presp extenuans, o/s extenuant-,
whence the rare E extenuant, and pp extenuātus,
whence 'to extenuate'; derivative LL extenuātiō,
acc extenuātiōnem, MF-F exténuation, E extenuation; and LL extenuātōrius, weakening, whence E
extenuatory.

### E thin

26. With L tenuis, cf the Skt tanús and Lith
ténvas, and such C forms as Br teneù, Cor tanow,
W teneu, Ga and OIr tana, Mx thanney, with OC
r *ten-, var *tan-, to stretch. With all these, as
with the L and Gr words, cf the Gmc group: OE
thynne, ME thunne, thenne, thinne, E thin, with
OE derivative thynnyss, ME thinnesse, E thinness;
OFris thenne, OHG dunni, MHG dünne, G dünn;
ON thunnr: OGmc r, *thun-.

### Greek

27. The Gr r is ten-, with var tan-: cf tanaos,
stretched (out), hence long. Gr teinein, to stretch,
has cpd hupoteinein, to stretch hupo- or under, with
presp hupoteinōn, f hupoteinousa, as in hupoteinousa pleura, a side subtending, whence the
n hupoteinousa, whence LL hypotēnūsa, EF-F
hypoténuse, E hypotenuse; the E adj hypotenusal
derives from LL hypotēnūsalis (from hypotēnūsa).

28. Gr teinein has pp tetanos (te+tan+o+s),
used as Med n for a disease characterized by
muscular spasms, whence L tetanus, adopted by E.

29. By the usual e-o mutation, Gr teinein (for
*teniein) has the cognate n tonos (s and r ton-), a
stretching, hence a raising of the voice, a pitch or
an accent, a measure or a metre: L tonus: OF-F
ton: E tone. The derivative ML adj tonālis yields
tonal, whence tonality: cf F tonal and tonalité. The
Gr adj is tonikos, whence tonic (cf F tonique). E
tonal, tonality, tonic have the negg (Gr a-, not)
atonal, atonality, atonic (cf F atonique): cf Gr

atonos, toneless, whence the MedGr atonia, slackness, whence LL atonia, debility, whence Med
MF-F atonie and, prob independently, E atony.

30. L tonus acquires the LL-ML cpd intonāre
(in- vaguely int?), whence OF-F entonner and,
independently, E 'to intone'; from the pp intonātus
come both 'to intonate', has, to intone, (phon) to voice,
and MF-F, whence E, intonation. Note that this
intonāre has been confused with—and prob caused
by—L intonāre, to thunder, an int of the syn
tonāre, which (cf THUNDER) has nothing whatever
to do with L tonus.

tendency, tendential, tendentious. See prec, para 2.
tender, adj. See TEND, para 22.
tender, legal n. See TEND, para 2, s.f.
tendon. See TEND, para 3.
tendril; tendron. See TEND, para 23.
tenebrous; temerarious, temerity. Tenebrous,
dusky, gloomy, comes from OF-MF tenebrus (F
ténébreux): L tenebrōsus, adj of tenebrae (pl; no
sing), shades, darkness, conserved in the Eccl
Tenebrae: akin to the syn Skt támas, gen támasas,
and to Ve támisrās, a dark night, and also to the
L adv temere.

2. L temere, blindly, hence carelessly, unthink-
ingly, chancily, riskily, has, with corresp senses,
the derivatives temeritās (as if from an adj *temerus,
from the adv) and temerārius: whence MF-F
témérité, whence E temerity, and MF-F téméraire
and, independently, E temerarious.

tenement. See TENABLE, para 2.
tenet. See TENABLE, para 3.
tenné. See TAN, para 3.
tennis: ME tenys, teneys, tenetz, tennes: prob
via F: either from F Tenez!, Hold (it), i.e. Receive
(it—the ball), uttered by the server, or from Ar
Tinnīs, that Lower-Egyptian medieval city which
was famous for its fabrics: 'the early balls were
made of light cloth' (Webster): cf the Ar origin
of the tennis racket. Orig applied to Royal Tennis
(early played esp by royalty), it was modified, in
1874, as lawn tennis, now usu tennis.

Tennysonian: Alfred, Lord Tennyson (1809–92)
+adj -ian: Tennyson, a var of Tennison (var
Tenneson) or Tenison: Denison: Denis' son.

tenon. See TENABLE, para 2, s.f.
tenor. See TENABLE, para 2. The tenor voice
(hence the singer), late MF-F ténor, It tenore (L
tenor), was so named because it took up and held
the dominant part.

tense (1), adj, hence v. See TEND, para 4.
tense (2), n (Gram). See TEMPER, para 7.
tensible, tensile, tension, tensity, tensive, tensor.
See TEND, para 4.
tent (1), a portable skin or canvas or cloth
shelter. See TEND, para 5.
tent (2), a wine. See STAIN, para 4.
tent (3), to probe—and corresp surgical n. See
TEMPT, para 4.
tentacle. See TEMPT, para 6.
tentative. See TEMPT, para 6.
tenter, a frame; tenterhook(s). See TEND, para 6
and heading.

tenth. See TEN, para 3.

tentorium. See TEND, para 5.

tenuis, tenuity, tenuous. See TEND, para 24.

tenure. See TENABLE, para 2.

teocalli, a CAm or a Mexican temple, is the Sp adoption (var *teucalé*) of Nahuatl *teocalli*, (the) god's house: *teotl*, a god (? cf L *deus*, Gr *theos* and *Zeus*)+*calli*, a house.

tepee, a Plains Indians' tent, represents Siouan, esp Dakotan, *tipi*: *ti*, to live (somewhere), to dwell +*pi*, used for: '(a place) used for living'.

tepefy: tepid, tepidity. The 3rd comes from LL *tepiditās*, lukewarmness, from L *tepidus*, lukewarm, whence E *tepid*: and *tepidus* comes from *tepēre* (s and r *tep*-), to be warm: IE r, **tep*-, to be warm. The LL cpd *tepefacere*, to cause (*facere*, to make, hence to render) to be tepid, has become E 'to *tepefy*'.

tequila, a Mexican plant, hence the liquor made from its juice, is a Sp name: from the Mexican district of *Tequila*, famed for the manufacture of this liquor: Nahuatl *Tequilan* or 'Place of the Divide'. (Webster.)

teratology. See the element *terato*-.

terbium. See YTTERBIUM.

terce, tercel. See THREE, para 7.

tercentenary. See THREE, para 5.

tercet. See THREE, para 7.

terebellum. See THROW, para 3.

terebinth, terebinthine. See TURPENTINE, para 1.

terebra, terebrate, terebration. See THROW, para 3.

teredo. See THROW, para 9.

terete. See the element *tereti*-.

tergiversate, tergiversation. See the element *tergi*-.

term (n hence v), whence termless and termly; terminable (interminable), terminal, terminate (adj and v), termination (whence, anl, terminative), terminator, terminer, terminer, terminology (cf the element *termino*-), terminus; determinant, determinate (adj, hence n), determination, determinative (adj, hence n), determine (whence the pa determined and—cf the F *déterminisme*—the Phil determinism)—cf predeterminant, predeterminate (adj), predetermination, predetermine (whence predeterminism); exterminable, exterminate, extermination (whence, anl, exterminative and exterminatory), exterminator; indeterminable, indeterminate;— thrum (in weaving); tram (a bar, a shaft, a shafted vehicle), with cpds tramline and tramway.

1. *Term* derives from MF-F *terme*, a word, or an expression: ML *terminus*, a definition, a expression: L *terminus*, a boundary, an end (cf LL 'a pause or a stop in reading or in writing'): *termin*-, o/s of syn OL *termen*: cf Gr *terma*, *termōn*, an end, a limit; perh cf L *trans*.

2. L *terminus*, adopted by E with gradually narrowing sense, has adj *terminālis*, whence E terminal, adj, hence n. The derivative v *termināre* has the derivative LL adj *terminābilis*, whence E terminable, and neg *interminābilis*, whence E interminable. From the pp *terminātus*, whence the

E v and adj *terminate* (neg adj *interminate*), are formed both L *terminātiō*, acc *terminātiō*nem, whence OF-MF *termination* (MF-F *terminaison*), adopted by E, and LL *terminātor*, adopted by E. L *termināre* becomes OF-F *terminer*, adopted by E as a legal term in *oyer and terminer*; and from L *terminus*, erudite F coined—after thé*ologie*, etc.— *terminologie*, whence E *terminology*, with anl adj *terminological*.

3. Ult akin to L *terminus* (s *termin*-, r *term*-) is E *thrum*, a weaver's warp thread, a row of such threads, with several derivative senses, as in the naut pl *thrums*, short pieces of yarn: ME *thrum*, var *throm*: OE *thrum*, an end-piece: cf ON *thrömr*, an edge or brim, and OHG *trum*, *drum*, an end, a fragment, G *Trümmer* (pl), ruins.

4. Akin to those Gmc words is E *tram*, orig dial and prob deriving imm from LG *traam*, a beam, bar, handle.

### Prefix-Compounds

5. LL *dētermināre*, to mark out, to distinguish, to indicate, to decide (a Law case) or bring (a Med case) to a crisis, becomes OF-MF *determiner* (EF-F *dé*-), whence 'to *determine*'. The LL derivatives *dēterminābilis* and—from the pp *dēterminātus*—*dēterminātiō* (acc *dēterminātiō*nem), Med *dēterminātiuus* (ML *-ivus*), yield resp OF-MF *determinable* (F *dé*-), adopted by E—from the pp, the adj *determinate*—MF-F *détermination*, E *determination*—F *déterminatif*, E *determinative*. The LL negg *indēterminābilis*, *indēterminātiō*, *indēterminātus* produce E *indeterminable*, *indetermination*, *indeterminate*. The presp *dēterminans*, o/s *dēterminant*, produces the E adj, hence n, *determinant*.

6. LL *dētermināre* has its own cpd: *praedētermināre*, to settle *prae*- or beforehand, esp as an Eccl word, whence EF-F *prédéterminer*, with EF-F derivative *prédétermination*: hence E 'to *predetermine*' and *predetermination*. The LL presp *praedēterminans*, o/s *-ant*, and pp *praedēterminātus* yield the adjj *predeterminant* and *predeterminate*.

7. L *extermināre*, to put *ex*, outside, the *termini* or boundaries, to banish, LL to destroy utterly, has the foll derivatives affecting E:

LL *exterminābilis*, whence *exterminable*;

pp *exterminātus*, whence 'to *exterminate*';

*exterminātiō* (LL destruction), acc *exterminātiō*nem, OF-F *extermination*, adopted by E;

LL *exterminātor*, a destroyer, adopted by E— cf the MF-F *exterminateur*;

LL *exterminātōrius*, destructive, whence *exterminatory*;

LL *inexterminābilis*, imperishable, whence *inexterminable*.

termagant: ME *Termagant*, a rough, vociferous Mohammedan deity in the morality plays, with ME var *Tervagant*: the *-m-* form is prob a scribal error, for the source is OF-MF *Tervagant* (var *-an*), itself app a var of *Trivigant* (var *-an*): cf the It *Trivigante*, prob the intermediary of an Ar word.

**terminable, terminal.** See TERM, para 2.
**terminate, termination, terminator, terminology, terminus.** See TERM, para 2.
**termite, Termes.** See THROW, para 4.
**termly.** See TERM (heading).
**tern** (1); **starling, sterna.** The 1st, prob coming from ON *therna* (cf Da *terne* and Sw *türne*), app has r *ter-* and represents an *s*-less var of the r *star-* attested by OE *staer*, E dial *stare*, a starling, OE *staerlinc*, ME *sterlyng*, E *starling* being, in form, a dim, and by the OE var *stearn* or *stern* (Shetlands dial *starn*), with SciL derivative *Sterna*. Cf OHG *stara*, MHG-G *star*, ON *stari*—and L *sturnus* (s *sturn-*, r *stur-*)—and prob Gr *psar* (Ionic *psēr*) or *psaros*.
**tern** (2), a set of three. See THREE, para 8.
**ternary, ternate; ternion.** See THREE, para 8.
**terpene, terpine, terpineol, terpinol.** See TURPENTINE, para 2.
**Terpsichore, terpsichorean.** See CHOIR, para 1.
**terra**—terra cotta—terra firma; **terrace,** n, hence v—cf trass; **terrain** and **terrane** and **terrene; terraqueous; terrestrial; terrier; terrigenous; terrine** and **tureen; territorial** (whence **territorialism**), **territory;**—F: **terre**—terre à terre—terreplein—terre-verte—parterre;—**inter, interment,** cf **disinter, disinterment; mediterranean** (whence **Mediterranean**); **subterrane, subterranean, subterrene; turmeric.**—Cf the sep THIRST.

### Indo-European

1. L *terra*, dry land (opp the sea), the earth hence a part of the earth, a region or a country: cf W, Ga, OIr *tēr*, Cor *tȳr* (voc *tir*), land, earth, country, OC etymon *\*tērsos* (cf PL *\*tersa* or *\*tērsa*, ? for *\*ter-es-a*): o.o.o.: connexion with L *torrēre* (*tor-r-ēre*), to parch, is improb. Tentatively I propose that L *terra* consonantizes *\*taia*, extn of *\*ta*; that *taia, ta,* answer to Gr *gaia* (cf *Gaia*, the Earth God), Doric *ga*, Attic *gē*; and that here we have a Medit r *\*ta-*, var *\*ga-*—cf Eg *ta*, land, a land, earth, the earth, the world, *Ta*, the primeval Earth-God, *taia*, lands, the world.

2. Whereas *terra firma* is L (firm or solid land), *terra cotta* is It (cooked earth: It *terra+cotta*, f of *cotto*, L *coctus*, cooked).

3. The foll L derivatives of *terra* affect E:
VL *\*terrāceus*, earthy, f *\*terrācea*, used as n, becomes OProv *terrassa*, late MF-F *terrasse*, E *terrace*, 'to *terrace*' perh owing something to the EF *terrasser*; OProv *terrassa*, however, perh derives from OProv *terra* (from L); cf It *terrazzo* (from It *terra*), whence ED *terras*, contr to ED-D *tras*, whence G *Trass*, whence E *trass*, used in hydraulic cement;
ML *terra merita*, lit 'deserving earth', becomes F *terre-mérite*, EE *turmerick*, E *turmeric*;
L *terrēnus*, earthy, E *terrene*, the n *terrene* coming from derivative L *terrēnum*, whence also the OF-F *terrain*, adopted by E, with the Geol mdfn *terrane*;
ML *terrāqueus*, of land and *aqua*, water, whence *terraqueous*;

L *terrestris*, neu *terrestre*, whence, perh via OF-F *terrestre*, the E *terrestrial* (adj suffix -*ial*);
LL *terrārius*, earthly, ML earthy, of land, esp in *terrārius liber*, a book dealing with landed estates, whence EF-F, whence E, *terrier*, now an inventory of property; cf OF-F *terrier*, a quadruped's den or burrow, which, from ML *terrārium*, prob contributed towards F *chien terrier*, abbr to *terrier*, adopted by E;
LL *terrigenus*, earth-born, E *terrigenous*;
VL *\*terrīnus* (from L *terrēnus*), earthy, whence the OF-MF adj *terrin*, whence MF-F *terrine*, orig an earthenware dish, adopted by E, which anglicizes it, in special sense, as *tureen*;
L *territōrium* (*terri-*, c/f of *terra+-tōrium*, as in *dormitōrium*), whence both MF-F *territoire* and E *territory*; derivative LL *territōriālis* becomes (F and) E *territorial*, with cpd *extraterritorial*, as in 'e. waters', outside (*extra*) the territorial limits.

4. From OF-F *terre* (L *terra*) have come several cpds:
*terre-à-terre*, lit 'earth to earth', orig (EF) applied to a horse that takes short steps and keeps close to the ground;
*terre-plein* (EF-F) adapts It *terrapieno*, from It *terrapienare*, to fill with earth: whence Eng E *terreplein*;
*terre-verte*, lit 'green (*vert*, ML *veridis*) earth', glauconite, adopted by E;
and *parterre* (EF-F), from *par terre*, by—hence on—(the) earth.

5. OF-F *terre* has the derivative OF-F *enterrer*, to put into (*en*) the earth, to bury, whence OF-F *enterrement*: whence ME *enteren, enterment,* whence the reshaped E 'to *inter*' and *interment*. The late MF-F (obsol) derivative *désenterrer* produces 'to *disinter*', whence *disinterment*.

6. L *terrēnus* has, in cpds, the var -*terrāneus*, as in
*mediterrāneus* (*medi-*, c/f of *medius*, situated in the middle), whence the obs E *mediterrane*, displaced by *mediterranean* (adj suffix -*ean*), whence, elliptically, 'the *Mediterranean*' (sea)—as already in LL *Mediterrāneus*;
*subterrāneus* (*sub*, under), whence *subterranean*; cf the learnèd E *subterrene*, from L *subterrēnus*.
**terrace.** See prec, para 3.
**terra cotta.** See TERRA, para 2.
**terrain.** See TERRA, para 3.
**terrane.** See TERRA, para 3.
**terrapin,** an edible NA turtle, is of Alg orig, with new suffix: cf the Lenape *turupe*, a little turtle.
**terraqueous.** See TERRA, para 3.
**terrene.** See TERRA, para 3.
**terreplein.** See TERRA, para 4.
**terrestrial.** See TERRA, para 3.
**terre-verte.** See TERRA, para 4.
**terrible.** See TERROR, para 3.
**terrier,** a landed-estate document, a dog. See TERRA, para 3.
**terrific, terrify.** See TERROR, para 3.
**terrigenous.** See TERRA, para 3.

terrine. See TERRA, para 3.

territorial, territory. See TERRA, para 3, s.f.

terror, terrorism, terrorist, terrorize; terrible and terrific, terrify;—deter, deterrent (whence, anl, deterrence), adj hence n.

1. *Deterrent* comes from L *dēterrent-*, o/s of *dēterrens*, presp of *dēterrēre*, to frighten from, hence away: *dē*, down from+*terrēre*, to frighten badly.

2. L *terrēre*, to cause to tremble, has s *terr-* and r *ter-*: cf the cognate *tremere*, to tremble, s *trem-*, r *tre-* (of which, app, *ter-* is, in *terrēre*, a metathesis): cf TREMBLE.

3. L *terrēre*, s *terr-*, has three simple derivatives affecting E:

*terror* (cf L *horror* and *tremor*), MF-F *terreur*, E *terror*;

*terrĭbilis*, OF-F *terrible*, adopted by E;

*terrificus*, E *terrific*, and *terrificāre*, MF-F *terrifier*, E *terrify*.

4. E *terrorism, terrorist, terrorize*, owe much to three words coined by F in the mid-1790's: *terrorisme, terroriste, terroriser*.

terry (cloth): o.o.o.: perh F *tiré*, drawn, pp of *tirer*, to draw or pull.

terse (whence terseness) and tersion; absterge, abstergent, abstersion, abstersive; deterge, detergent, detersion.

1. *Terse* derives from L *tersus*, adj from the pp of *tergere*, to rub off or away: o.o.o.: ? an *s-less* var of the *sterg-* of Gr *stergis*, var of *stlengis*, a scraper. From *tersus* comes, anl, *tersion*.

2. L *tergere* has two cpds relevant to E:

*abstergere* (*abs-* for *ab-*, from, away from), to rub or wipe away, whence 'to *absterge*'; presp *abstergens*, o/s *abstergent-*, EF-F n *abstergent*, adopted by E; from the L pp *abstersus*, both the erudite EF-F *abstersion*, adopted by E, and the erudite EF-F adj *abstersif*, f *-ive*, whence E *abstersive*, adj hence n;

*dētergere*, to rub or wipe *dē*, from, hence away, whence 'to *deterge*' (cf EF-F *déterger*); presp *dētergens*, o/s *dētergent-*, (EF-F *détergent* and) E *detergent*, adj hence n; pp *dētersus*, whence LL *dētersiō*, acc *dētersiōn*em, EF-F *détersion*, E *detersion*; anl EF-F *détersif*, f *-ive*, becomes E *detersive*, adj hence n.

tertial, tertian, tertiary; tertius, tertium quid. See THREE, para 6.

terza rima; terzet, terzetto. See THREE, para 7.

tessellate, tessellation. See FOUR, para 8.

test, a shell: see TECHNIC, para 14.—A trial (whence 'to *test*'): ib, para 15.

testacean. See TECHNIC, para 14.

testacy. See heading of:

testament (and Testament), testamental, testamentary; testamur; testate (whence testacy, for *testatecy*), testation, testator, testatrix, testatum; testicle, testicular, testiculate; testificate, testification (whence, anl, testifactory), testify; testimonial (adj and n), testimony; testis, pl testes.—Cpds: attest, attestation (whence, anl, attestative); contest (v, hence n), contestant, contestation; detest, detestable, detestation; incontestable; intestable, intestate (whence intestacy); obtest, obtestation; protest (n and v, whence protester), protestant (and Protestant), protestation.—Ult akin to the sep THREE constellation.

1. All these words originate in L *testis* (s and r *test-*), a witness. *Testis* app stands for *\*terstis*, metathetic for *\*trestis*, var of *\*tristis*; *tri-* (cf THREE) 3+the *st-* of *stō*, I stand, *stāre*, to stand+formative *-i-*+nom *-s*. In short, *\*tristis* is substituted for *\*tristans* (*tri*, 3+*stans*, presp of *stāre*), with agential *-is* for presp *-ans*: he who stands in the third part, he who stands by, a third party, as it were an intermediary between accuser and accused. (Developed from E & M.)

### Simples

2. L *testis* has the derivative sense 'testicle', adopted by SciE, with pl *testes*: a witness to virility. The dim but syn *testiculus* and its derivatives *testiculāris* and *testiculātus* yield resp *testicle*, *testicular*, *testiculate*.

3. L *testis*, a witness, has the foll simple derivatives affecting E:

*testificāre*, to make a legal declaration (*-ficāre*, c/f of *facere*, to make), pp *testificātus*, derivative *testificātiō*, o/s *testificātiōn-*, whence, resp, 'to *testify*', *testificate*, *testification*;

*testimōnium*, the bearing of witness, a solemn declaration (esp by a witness), whence OF-MF *testimoigne, testemoine, testemonie*, ONF *testemonie*, whence E *testimony*; derivative LL *testimōniālis* becomes MF-F *testimonial*, adopted by E; the n *testimonial* is indebted to LL *testimōniāles* (sc *literae*), a certificate;

*testor*, vt and vi, I bear witness (to), pp *testātus*, whence E *testate*; the neu *testātum* becomes a legal E n—cf *testāmur*, we testify, adopted by universities.

4. *Testāri*, to bear witness (to), hence to take for witness, hence to make a will, has derivative *testāmentum*, a taking for witness, hence a will, whence MF-F *testament*, adopted by E; derivative *testāmentārius* becomes (EF-F *testamentaire* and) E *testamentary*. Already in LL does *testāmentum* become *nouum* (ML *novum*) and *uetus* (ML *vetus*) *testāmentum*, The New and The Old Testament: whence the OF-F *Testament*, adopted by E. The ML *testāmentālis*, relating to the Testament, yields E *testamental*.

5. On L *testātus*, pp of *testāri*, are formed *testātiō*, o/s *testātiōn-*, whence E *testation*— *testātor*, adopted by E (cf the MF-F *testateur*)— *testātrix*, likewise adopted.

### Prefix-Compounds

6. L *testātus*, used both actively and passively, has neg *intestātus*, not having witnessed, not having been witnessed: from the sense 'not having made a will' comes E *intestate*. From *testāri* comes— anl after *intestātus*—L *intestābilis*, whence legal *intestable*.

7. *Testāri* gathers a number of prefix-cpds, most of them relevant to E. The first is *adtestāri*, usu

eased to *attestāri*, to certify, pp *attestāt*us, whence
*attestātiō*, acc *attestātiō*nem, whence MF-F *attester*,
E 'to *attest*', and MF-F *attestation*, adopted by E.

8. L *contestāri* (*con-* vaguely int), to bring
together the witnesses for both parties, whence
*contestāri lītem*, to call witness in order to begin
a lawsuit, presp *contestans*, o/s *contestant-*, pp
*contestāt*us, whence *contestātiō*, acc *contestātiō*nem,
result in, resp, MF-F *contester*, F 'to *contest*'—
E *contestant*, adj and, perh after F, n—MF-F
*contestation*, adopted by E. Derivative EF-F
*contestable* and its EF-F neg *incontestable* are both
adopted by E.

9. L *dētestāri* (int *dē-*), to reject the testimony of,
hence to curse, to detest, the derivative *dētestābilis*
(whence LL *dētestabilitās*, o/s *-itāt-*, whence E
*detestability*), the pp *dētestāt*us, whence *dētestātiō*,
acc *dētestātiō*nem, become MF-F *détester*, *dé-
testable*, *détestation*, whence E *detest*, *detestable*,
*detestation*.

10. L *obtestāri*, to bear witness *ob-* or towards,
and—from the pp *obtestātus*—*obtestātiō*, o/s
*obtestātiōn-*, yield 'to *obtest*' and *obtestation*.

11. L *prōtestāri*, to declare *prō-*, forward, hence
publicly, presp *prōtestans*, o/s *prōtestant-*, pp
*prōtestāt*us, whence LL *prōtestātiō*, a solemn
declaration, acc *protestātiō*nem, become MF-F
*protester*, EF-F *protestant*, MF-F *protestation*: E
'to *protest*', *protestant* (adj and n), *protestation*.
Derivative late MF-EF *protest* (F *protêt*) and EF-F
*protestantisme* become the E n *protest* and *Pro-
testantism*. Eccl EF-F *protestant*, n, was adopted
from G *Protestant*, a name given to Luther's
partisans.

**testate, testation, testator, testatum.** See prec,
paras 3 and 5.

**tester**, a canopy. See TECHNIC, para 16.

**testicle, testicular, testiculate.** See TESTAMENT,
para 2.

**testificate, testification, testify.** See TESTAMENT,
para 3.

**testimonial, testimony.** See TESTAMENT, para 3.

**testis.** See TESTAMENT, para 2.

**testitudinal, testudinate, testudo.** See TECHNIC,
para 14.

**testy.** See TECHNIC, para 16, s.f.

**tetanic, tetanus.** See TEND, para 28.

**tetchy.** See the 2nd TACHE.

**tête à tête.** See TECHNIC, para 17.

**tether** (n, hence v): ME *tether*, var of *tethir*,
earlier *tedir*: prob from ON *tjothr* (cf Sw *tjuder*),
influenced by OFris *tiäder*—cf OHG *zeotar*, a
waggon-pole, and MLG *tüder*, a tether.

**tetra-** words. See the element *tetra-*, where, e.g.,
*tetragon* and *tetrameter*. For *tetralogy*, see
LEGEND, para 32; for *tetrasyllabic*, see SYLLABLE,
para 3.

**Teuton, Teutonic.** See DUTCH, para 2.

**Texan**, adj, hence n=*Tex*as+adj suffix *-an*;
**Texas**, adopted from ASp, comes from Caddoan
(SW U.S.A.) *techas*, friends, allies, ref a group
of East Texan Amerindians allied against the
Apache.

**text.** See TECHNIC, para 11.

**textile.** See TECHNIC, para 11.

**textual.** See TECHNIC, para 11.

**texture.** See TECHNIC, para 11, s.f.

**thalami-** (**thalamo-**); **thalasso-** (**thalatto-**); **thalli-**
(**thallo-**). For E words—all learnèd, the 1st and
3rd groups also Sci—corresp to those c/ff, see the
elements thus indicated.

**Thames**: OE *Temes*: early ML *Tamisa*: L
*Tamesa* (Tacitus) and *Tamesis* (Caesar), the imm
source of the OE word: akin to Skt *Tamasa*, a
tributary of The Ganges, from *tamasás*, dark:
The Dark River. (Ekwall.)

**than.** See THE, para 7.

**thane**, whence *thanage*, is a Sc shape of ME
*thein*, earlier *thegn*: OE *thegn*, with var *thegen*: cf
OFris *thiäner*, a servant, OS *thegan*, a boy, a
follower, a warrior, OHG *degan*, MHG-G *degen*,
a warrior, a thane, ON *thegn*, a freeman, a thane,
and, further off, the Gr *teknon*, a child (*etekon*,
I gave birth), and Skt *takman-*, a child.

**thank, thankful, thankless, thanks, thanksgiving.**
See THINK, para 3.

**that.** See THE, para 2.

**thatch.** See TECHNIC, para 8, s.f.

**thaumaturge, thaumaturgy.** See the element
*thaumato-*.

**thaw**, v, hence n; **tabes, tabid, tabific.** 'To *thaw*'
derives from OE *thāwian*, akin to OHG *douwēn*,
MHG *töuwen*, G *tauen*, MD *douwen*, D *dooiyen*,
ON *theyja*—OB *tajati*, to melt, to thaw—L *tābēre*,
to melt, hence to perish, and its derivative n
*tābēs*, a thawing, LL corruption of the flesh, a
wasting away, and adj *tābidus*, E *tabid*, and the
cpd adj *tābificus*, causing tabes—Doric Gr *tākō*,
Attic *tēkō*, I melt—OIr *tām*, tabes, Ir *toineadh*, a
thaw, Ga *aiteamh* (n and v), Cor *tedha*, to thaw
(*teth*, he thaws), W *tawdd*, a state of fusion, (adj)
melted, *toddi*, to melt or dissolve—Ossetic (Indo-
Iranian) *tain*, *tajun*, (of snow) to melt. The IE r is
therefore *tā-*, varr *tēi-*, *tei-*, *tī-* or *tl-*, to melt.
(Cf Walshe; E & M; Hofmann.)

**the**; **then, thence**—**than**; **there**, cf **thereat, thereby,
therefor, therefore, therefrom, therein, thereof,
thereon, thereupon, therewith**; **thither**; **that** and
**those**—**this** and **these**; **they, them, their, theirs**;
**thus**; cf the sep BOTH and the sep SINCE.

1. The definite article *the* comes from late OE
*thē*, which had displaced the earlier *sē* (cf Skt *sā*),
the: cf OFris and OS *the*, the, OHG-MHG *der*
(m), *diu* (f ), *daz* (neu), (orig) that, (later) the, G *der*,
*die*, *das*: f.a.e., para 12.

2. E *that*, pron and adj, comes from OE *thaet*,
the neu of the demonstrative adj and pron (also
a relative pron): cf ON *that* (neu), Go *thata* (neu),
MD *datte*, MD-D *dat*, OHG-MHG *daz*, G *das*,
OFris *thet*: f.a.e., para 12. The pl is *those*, ME
*thos*, earlier *thas*, OE *thās*, orig the pl of OE
*thēs*, this. The conj *that* derives from the demonstrative pron (in the acc), used in apposition before
the governed clause.

3. *These*, OE *thās*, ME *thas*, with varr *thaes*,
*thes*, *these*, is the pl of E *this*, ME *this*, *thes*, OE

*thēs* (m), *thēos* or *thīos* (f), *this* (neu): cf ON *thesse, thessi,* OFris *this* (f *thius,* neu *thit*), MD *dese,* D *deze,* OS *these,* OHG *deser* (f *desiu,* neu *diz*), MHG *diser* (f *disiu,* neu *ditz*), G *dieser*: from the s of OE *thē,* that+*sē,* that: in short, an int by sem redup.

4. *They,* ME *thei (thai),* comes from ON *their,* they, orig the m nom pl of ON *sā* (m), *sū* (f), *that* (neu), that; the acc *them* comes from OE *thǣm,* dat pl of OE *thē,* that, the, but shows the influence of the corresp ON *theim,* used for 'they'.

5. E *their,* possessive adj, derives from *their,* possessive pron ('of them'): ME *thair*: ON *theira,* var of *theirra,* of them—but orig the gen pl of ON *that* (neu; f *sū,* m *sā*), that, the: ON *their(r)a* is very closely related to OE *thāra,* var *thǣra,* gen pl of *thē. Theirs=their's.*

6. E-ME-OE *thus,* in this way, is akin to OFris and OS *thus,* MD-D *dus* (MD var *dos*), OHG *sus.*

7. E *then* is a doublet of—indeed, id with—*than*; dial E still employs *then* for 'than'. E *than,* prob at first 'from that (place or point), from there', derives from ME *than (thanne),* varr *then (thenne)* and *thon (thonne),* than, then: OE *thanne, thaenne, thonne,* at that time, (but also) than: cf OFris and OS *than,* OHG-MHG *danne, denne,* G *dann,* then, and OHG-MHG *denne* (var *danne*), G *denn,* than (in G, *denn* and *dann* did not become clearly distinguished until C18), Go *than,* MD *danne,* MD-D *dan,* then.

8. E *thence,* ME *thens,* earlier *thennes* (var *thannes*), where *-s* is an adv, orig the possessive suffix, still earlier *thenne,* var of *thanne,* derives from OE *thanon, thanan* (var *thonan*): akin to OS *thanan* (cf OFris *thana*) and OHG *danān, danana,* MHG-G *dannen.*

9. E *there,* at that place or point, ME *ther* or *thar,* OE *thēr, thǣr, thār,* is akin to OFris *thēr* (or *thēr*), OS *thar,* OHG *dār* (MHG *da,* G *da*), Go *thar,* MD *daer, dare, dar,* D *daar,* ON *thar*: IE r, *\*tar-.*

10. OE *thǣr*—the predominant form—has many cpds extant in E, the principal being these: OE *thāēr abūtan* (cf ABOUT): *thereabout,* the *-s* var exhibiting the adv *-s*;

OE *thāēr aet* (cf AT): *thereat*;
OE *thāērbig* (cf BY): *thereby*;
ME *therfore* (cf FOR), for that (now *therefor*); later, for that reason: *therefore*;
OE *thāērin* (cf IN): *therein*:
OE *thāērof* (cf OF): *thereof*:
OE *thāēron* (cf ON): *thereon*;
OE *thāērŭt* (or *-ūte*: cf OUT): *thereout* (archaic);
OE *thāērtō* (cf TO): *thereto*;
OE *thāērunder* (cf UNDER): *thereunder*;
OE *thāēr uppan* (cf *upon*: UP+ON): *thereupon*;
OE *thāērwith* (cf WITH): *therewith,* whence—after *withal,* q.v. at WITH—*therewithal,* adv, hence n ('means').

11. E *thither,* to that point, ME-from-OE *thider,* var of *thaeder,* comes from the s of OE *thaet*: for

the suffix, cf ON *thāthra,* there, and Go *thathrō,* thence.

### Indo-European

12. Besides all the OGmc cognates listed above, there are many other IE cognates: but we need concern ourselves only with those which mean 'the', orig 'that', and answer to *the* and *that.* The principal non-Gmc cognates are perh: L *iste* (m), *ista* (f), *istud* (neu), pron and adj 'that', *is-* being merely a formative particle and the r *\*te-* occurring also in, e.g., *tum,* then, and *tot,* so many; Gr *to* (neu), the; Skt *tat,* for *tad* (neu)—note that, as in OGmc, the m and f are in *s-,* not *t-,* thus Skt *sa* and *sā,* Gr *ho* (for *\*so*) and *hē* (for *\*sē*), OE *sē* and *sēo,* Go *sa* and *sō,* ON *sā* and *sū*; Lith *tàs* (m), *tà* (f), Ru *tŭ* (m), *ta* (f), OB *tŭ, ta,* neu *to* (perh after Gr); Tokh B *te* (neu; m *se,* f *sāu*); Alb ke-*ta,* this, *te,* when, *tē,* whither; Hit *tā* (neu pl; m sing *tas* or *sas*—an illuminating alternation); note also the Gr acc *ton* (m), *tēn* (f), *to* (neu), and the Skt acc *tám,* f *tǎm,* neu *tád.*

13. The IE etymons, therefore, were app *\*so,* f *\*sā,* neu *\*tod,* of which only the 3rd is strictly relevant; the IE r is *\*t-,* vocalized *\*ta-, \*te-, \*to-, \*tu-.* In certain IE languages, *t-* gives way to *d-,* as, e.g., in Arm *da,* this, *doyn,* the (or that) same, and, occupying the final position, in Ga *ud* (but OIr *út*), that, and Ga *iad,* they, and Ga *sud* (but EIr *sūt, siut*) that.

14. The word is perh Medit: cf Eg *then,* this, and *thui,* that, and *ti,* there: forms that well accord with a Medit r *\*t-,* vocalized *\*ta-, \*te-, \*ti-, \*to-, \*tu-,* with varr in *\*th-* and *\*d-* and, in C, *\*-d* (or *\*-t*).

**theater** (AE) or **theatre; theatral, theatric (theatrical)**—whence **theatricize** (cf the LL *theātrizāre*).—**theorem; theoretic** (now usu **theoretical**), **theory** (whence, anl, **theorist**).—Cf the sep THAUMATURGE, q.v. at the element *thaumato-.*

1. *Theater* is the AE spelling of E *theatre,* adopted from MF-EF (F *théâtre*), which takes it from L *theātrum,* trln of Gr *theatron,* akin to Gr *thea,* a sight, and esp to Gr *theasthai,* to view, itself akin to Gr *thauma,* a thing compelling the gaze, a wonder, and Gr *theōrein,* to look at: IE r, *\*dheu-,* var *\*dhau-,* to look at.

2. Gr *theatron* has adj *theatrikos,* whence LL *theātricus,* E *theatric,* with *-al* extn *theatrical*; L *theātrum* has its native adj *theatrālis,* whence EF-F *théâtral,* which prob suggested E *theatral.*

3. Gr *theōrein,* to look at, has derivative *theōrēma,* a seeing, a sight, an object of study, hence a speculation, hence a theorem: L *theōrēma,* EF-F *théorème* and, perh independently, E *theorem.*

4. Gr *theōrein* has another derivative n: *theōria,* a looking, a seeing, an observing or a contemplation, hence a speculation: LL *theōria*: late MF-F *théorie*: E *theory.* The Gr adj *theōrikos* becomes LL *theōricus,* (MF-F *théorique* and) E *theoric* (obsol): the current E adj *theoretical* is an *-al* extn of E *theoretic,* which, like F *théorétique,* derives from

LL *theōrēticus*, trln of Gr *theōrētikos*, adj corresp to *theōrēma*. Whereas the obsol E *theorician* derives from EF-F *théoricien* (*théorie*+mathematicien), *theorist* is a native E formation (*theory*+agential *-ist*).

theca. See THESIS, para 2.
thee. See THOU, para 2.
theft. See THIEF.
thegn. A var of THANE.
thein(e). See TEA.
their, theirs. See THE, para 5.

theism, theist (whence theistic). *Theist* (cf F *théiste*) derives, anl, from *theism*, which=Gr *theos*, a god+*-ism*. Gr *theos* represents IE *\*dhesos*: cf Skt *dhíṣnyas*, pious, devout, and Arm *dikh*, gods.

2. The prefix-cpds *atheism, atheist—monotheism, monotheist—pantheism, pantheist*, all with adjj *-theistic*, derive, resp, from F *athéisme, athéiste* (Gr *a-*, not)—Gr *mono-*, sole+*theism, theist*—Gr *pan-*, all+*theism, theist*.

them. See THE, para 4.
thema, thematic, theme. See THESIS, para 3.
then. See THE, para 7.
thence. See THE, para 8.
theocracy, theodicy, theogony. See the element *theo-*.

theologian, theologic, theological, theology. The last derives from MF-EF *theologie* (later *théo-*): LL *theologia*, adopted from Gr: from Gr *theologos*, a theologian: *theo-*, c/f of *theos*, a god (cf THEISM) +*-logos*, a discourser, from *logos*, reason, word, esp, in LGr, the Word of God. Derivative MF-EF *theologien* (later *théo-*) leads to E *theologian*. Derivative Gr *theologikos* becomes LL *theologicus*, whence MF-EF *theologique* (F *théo-*), whence E *theologic*, superseded by *theological*, from ML *theologicālis* (extn of LL *theologicus*).

theophany. See FANCY, para 7. Cf THEISM.
theorem. See THEATRE, para 3.
theoretical, theorist, theory. See THEATRE, para 4.

theosophy—whence, anl, theosophical and theosophist—derives from ML, from LGr, *theosophia*, a knowledge of the divine, from *theosophos*, one who is wise in divine matters: *theo-*, c/f of *theos*, a god (L Gr *Theos*, God)+*sophos*, wise (cf SOPHISM).

therapeutic (whence therapeutics), therapy. *Therapeutic* derives, perh via EF-F *thérapeutique*, from Gr *therapeutikos*, adj of *therapeutēs*, an attendant (esp a Med attendant), agent of *therapeuein*, to take care of, from *theraps*, an attendant, whence Gr *therapeia* (medical) attendance, whence E *therapy*. Gr *theraps*, acc *therapa*,s *therap-*,has r *ther-*: IE *\*dher-*, to hold (up), to support.

there. See THE, para 9.
thereabout(s), thereat, thereby, therefor, therefore, therein, thereof, thereon, thereout, thereto, thereunder, thereupon, therewith, therewithal. See THE, para 10.

theriac, theriaca. See FIERCE, para 4.

therm, whence thermal and thermic and thermion (whence thermionic); cf the element *-therm-*, where see, e.g., thermatology, thermometer, thermostat. The heat-unit *therm* derives from Gr *thermē*, heat, from *thermos*, warm: f.a.e., WARM.

therology. See the element *-there*.
thesaurus. See THESIS, para 4.
these. See THE, para 3.

thesis (pl theses), thetic; theca, thecium, cf the element *theco-*; thema, thematic, theme; thesaurus—cf treasure (n, hence v), treasurer, treasury; tick, a cover.—Prefix-cpds: antithesis, antithetic; apothecary; diathesis; epithesis, epithet, epithetic; hypothec, hypothecary, hypothecate, hypothecation—hypothesis, hypothetic(al); metathesis, metathetic(al); parenthesis, parenthetic(al); prosthesis, prosthetic; prothesis, prothetic; synthesis, synthetic(al), synthesize.

1. *Thesis*, via L from Gr *thesis*, a thing placed, hence laid down, hence a statement, and the adj *thetic*, via LL *theticus* from Gr *thetikos*, fit for placing, from *thetos*, placed,—these two words establish the pattern. Gr *thetos* is the pp of *tithenai*, to place or set: *ti-*, redup+*then-*+inf *-ai*: *then-*, extn of r *the-*, corresp to the IE r *\*dhe-*, to place, set, lay down: cognates in Skt (and Ve), Hit, L, Sl, Tokh (A and B), OGmc. The *-e-* of both *the-* and *dhe-* may be either long or short, but basically it was prob long. Ult cf DO.

2. Akin to Gr *tithenai* is Gr *thēkē*, a small container, whence L *thēca*, adopted by Bot for a capsule and by Zoo and An for a case, with SciL derivative *thecium*; ult from L *hēca* comes, prob via MD *tike* (D *tijk*), the E *tick*, a strong cover or case, esp for bolster or mattress; whence the n *ticking*.

3. From Gr *tithenai*, to place, lay (down), comes Gr *thema*, what one lays down or states or poses, hence the subject proposed (for discussion or discourse): adopted by L, it is then adopted by learnèd E (and G), with adj *thematic*, from Gr *thematikos*; the predominant E form, however, is *theme*, from EF-F *thème* (MF *teme*, whence ME *teme*).

4. Akin to Gr *thesis*, but with long *e*, is Gr *thēsauros* (with 2nd element o.o.o.), a store of objects laid up or by, hence treasure: L *thēsaurus* (in LL, often *thensaurus*): E *thesaurus*, a store, a storehouse, a literary, or a lexicographical, repository.

5. L *thēsaurus* becomes OF-MF *tresor* (EF-F *tré-*), adopted by ME, with var *tresour*, whence E *treasure*. *Treasurer* owes much to OF-MF *tresorier* (EF-F *tré-*), itself indebted to LL *thēsaurārius*, a treasurer; *treasury* is a reshaping—after *treasure*—of ME *tresorie*, a contr of MF *tresorerie* (EF-F *tré-*), from OF-MF *tresor*.

### Prefix-Compounds

6. Gr *antitithenai*, to set *anti-* or against, to oppose, has n *antithesis*, adopted—via L—by E, with adj *antithetic*, from LL *antitheticus* (Gr *antithetikos*).

7. Gr *apotithenai*, to put *apo-* or away, has derivative *apothēkē*, whence L *apothēca*, whence

LL *apothēcārius*, a shopkeeper, OF-MF *apothe-caire* (F *apothécaire*), varr *apoticaire*, *apotecaire*, ME *apotecary*, reshaped E *apothecary*.

8. Gr *diatithenai*, to place *dia-*, asunder, hence separately, to arrange, has n *diathesis*, adopted by SciL and employed in Med, with anl adj *diathetic*.

9. Gr *epitithenai*, to place or put *epi-*, upon, hence to add, has n *epithesis*, with adj *epithetikos*: whence LL *epithesis*, adopted by E, with adj *epithetic*. The Gr pp *epithetos* has neu *epitheton*, used as n for 'an added word', i.e. an adj: L *epitheton*: EF-F *epithète*, an adj, hence a significant name: E *epithet*.

10. Gr *hupotithenai*, to put *hupo-* or under, to pledge, with n *hupothēkē*, something pledged or legally involved, whence L *hypothēca*, MF-F *hypothèque*, E *hypothec*. Derivative ML *hypothē-sārius* becomes MF-F *hypothécaire*, E *hypothecary*. L *hypothēca* has derivative ML *hypothēcāre*, to pledge, pp *hypothēcātus*, whence 'to *hypothecate*'; derivative ML *hypothēcātiō*, o/s *hypothēcātiōn-*, yields *hypothecation*.

11. Gr *hupotithenai* has also the n *hupothesis*, a supposition, a foundation for argument, with adj *hupothetikos*: LL *hypothesis*, *hypotheticus*: perh via EF-F *hypothèse* and MF-F *hypothétique*: E *hypo-thesis*, *hypothetic*—often in extn *hypothetical*.

12. Gr *metatithenai*, to place *meta*, beyond or after, hence to transpose, has n *metathesis*, adopted by LL, hence by E, with anl adj *metathetic*.

13. Gr *parentithenai* (*para*, beside+*en*, in), to put (something) in beside something else, to insert, has n *parenthesis*, adopted by LL, hence by E; *paren-thetic* (extn *parenthetical*) derives from anl formed ML *parentheticus*.

14. Gr *prostithenai*, to put *pros*, to or towards, has n *prosthesis*, an addition, with adj *prosthetikos*: LL *prosthesis*, adopted by E, with adj *prosthetic*.

15. Gr *protithenai*, to place or set *pro-* or before, has n *prothesis*, adopted—prob via ML—by E, with adj *prothetic* (Gr *prothetikos*).

16. Gr *suntithenai*, to place *sun-* or together, has n *sunthesis*, whence, via Med LL *synthesis*, the E *synthesis*, whence, anl, 'to *synthesize*'. Gr *sunthe-tikos* becomes E *synthetic* (cf EF-F *synthétique*). 'To *synthetize*' derives from F *synthétiser*, itself prob suggested by Go *sunthetizesthai*.

**thetic.** See THESIS, para 1.

**thew**, a custom or habit (obs), a virtue or strength (obs), hence a muscle: ME *thew*, earlier *theau*, manner, custom, strength: OE *thēaw*, manner, habit: cf OFris *thāw*, OS *thau*, OHG *dau*, custom, habit: o.o.o.

**they.** See THE, para 4.

**thick**, whence **thicken** and **thickness**; **thicket**. The last, a thick growth of trees, comes from OE *thiccet*, from the OE adj *thicce*, whence ME *thicke* and E *thick*: cf OFris *thikke*, OS *thikki*, OHG *dicchi*, MHG *dicke*, G *dick*, MD *dicke*, *dic*, D *dik*, ON *thykkr*—cf also OIr *tiug*, Ir and Ga *tiugh*, W *tew*, Cor *teu* (*tew*), Br *teù*, *tiù*, Mx *chiu*. The OGmc r is *\*thik-*; the IE r, *\*tig-*.

**thief** (pl **thieves**), **thieve**, **thievish** (from *thief* after *thieves*); **theft**. 'To *thieve*' derives from OE *thēofian*, from OE *thēof*, var *thīof*, whence ME *theef* or *thef*, whence *thief*. Also from OE *thēof*, *thīof*, comes OE *thēofth* (var *thīefth*), dissimilated var *thēoft*: ME *theofthe*, *thiefthe*, slovened *thefte*: E *theft*. OE *thēof* (*thīof*) is akin to OFris *thiāf*, OS *theof*, *thiof*, Go *thiufs*, ON *thiōfr*, OHG *diob*, MHG *diep*, G *Dieb*, MD-D *dief*: o.o.o.: ? (Webster) cf Lith *tupèti*, to crouch.

**thigh**; **thumb** and **thimble**;—**tomb**; **tumefacient**, **tumefaction**, **tumefy**, **tumescent**, **tumid**, **tumidity**, **tumor** (AE) or **tumour**; **tumulose**, **tumulus**; **tumult**, **tumultuary**, **tumultuous**;—**tuber**, **tuberose** (adj, n), **tuberosity**, **tuberous** and **tubercle**, **tubercular**, **tuber-culin**, **tuberculosis**, **tuberculous**, cf **protuberant** (whence **protuberance**), **protuberate**; **truffle**—cf **trifle**, n and v (whence agent **trifler** and pa, vn **trifling**); perh **turgent**, **turgescent** (whence **turges-cence**), **turgid** (whence, anl, **turgidity**), **turgor**.

### Indo-European and Germanic

1, *Thigh*, ME *thi* or *thih*, var *theh*, derives from OE *thīoh*, var *thēoh*, contr *thēh*: cf OFris *thiāch*, OHG *dioh*, MD *die*, D *dij*, *dije*, thigh, and ON *thjō*, thigh, rump—Lith *tukti*, to become fat, and *taukas*, animal-fat—OIr *tōn*, rump, and MIr *tomm*, Ga and W *tom*, a large mound, a knoll—L *tumēre*, to swell—Gr *tumbos*, a (burial) mound—perh Skt *tumbas*, a large cucumber. The IE r is prob *\*tubh-*, to be fat or thick, to swell, with nasalized var *\*tumbh-*; but *\*tubh-* itself prob amplifies a syn IE *\*tu-*.

2. The 'fat' or 'swollen' basic idea recurs in E *thumb* ('the fattest—hence strongest—finger'): ME *thombe* or *thoumbe*, earlier *thume*: OE *thūma*: cf OFris *thūma*, OS *thūmo*, MD *dume*, *duum*, *duym*, D *duim*, OHG *dūmo*, MHG *dūme*, G *Daumen*, thumb, ON *thumall*, a glove's thumb.

3. OE *thūma*, a thumb, has derivative *thȳmel*, whence E *thimble*; the intrusive *b* arrives—under the influence of ME *tho(u)mbe*—in C15.

### Latin and Romance

4. L *tūber*, a swelling, a knot (in a tree), a plant that is prob the truffle, is adopted by Bot for a fleshy (underground) shoot or stem, as of the potato; its adj *tūberōsus* becomes the adjj *tuberose* and *tuberous*, the latter prob via EF-F *tubéreux*, f *tubéreuse*, whence EF-F *tubérosité*, E *tuberosity*; the derivative EF-F n *tubéreuse* (for *plante tubér-euse*) prob suggested the E *tuberose*, the bulbous flowering herb.

5. L *tūber* has the dim *tūberculum*, whence E *tubercle* (cf EF-F *tubercule*, MF *tubercle*), a small excrescence on a plant, adopted by An, Med, Bot, with naturally deviating senses. The Med *tubercle*, F *tubercule*, a small, rounded, morbid growth, leads to:

*tubercular*, formed anl from *tubercle*;

*tuberculous*, via F *tuberculeux*, f *tuberculeuse*;

*tuberculosis* (*-osis*, disease), suggested by F *tuberculose*;

*tuberculin, -ine*: L *tubercul*um+Chem *-in, -ine*.

6. L *tūber*, a swelling, a knob, has the LL derivative cpd v *prōtūberāre*, to swell or bulge *prō-*, forwards, hence out, with presp *prōtūberans*, o/s *protuberant-*, whence (EF-F *protubérant* and) E *protuberant*; and with pp *prōtūberātus*, whence 'to *protuberate*'.

7. L *tūber* (the plant) has the Osco-Umbrian var *\*tūfer*, whence VL *tūfera*, whence, by metathesis, the OProv *trufa* (cf the It *truffa*), whence MF-F *truffe*, whence E *truffle*; the *l* has perh come from MF-EF *trufle*, a var of MF-EF *trufe*, mockery, cheating.

8. MF-EF *trufle*, deception, mockery, and its derivative v *trufler* (var of *trufer*) become the ME n *trufle*, the ME v *truflen*: thinned to *trifle* and *triflen* or *trifelen*: whence the E n and v *trifle*, with sense gradually weakened from 'mockery' to 'jest' to 'something of small importance' and 'to act frivolously'; already in MF there existed *truferie* (from *trufer*), mockery, a jest, jesting. MF-EF *trufe*, var *trufle*, is o.o.o., but not impossibly akin to MF-F *truffe*.

9. Akin to L *tūber* is L *tumēre*, to be swollen, to swell, whence both the n *tumor*, whence—perh via MF *tumour* (F *tumeur*)—the AE *tumor*, E *tumour*, and the adj *tumidus*, whence E *tumid*, and derivative LL *tumiditās*, whence *tumidity*. L *tumēre* has the inch *tumescere*, to begin to swell, to swell up, with presp *tumescens*, o/s *tumescent-*, whence E *tumescent*, whence *tumescence*; it also has the cpd *tumefacere*, to cause to swell, whence EF-F *tuméfier*, whence 'to *tumefy*'; and the presp *tumefaciens*, o/s *tumefacient-*, and the pp *tumefactus*, whence the learnèd EF-F *tuméfaction*, become the E *tumefacient* and *tumefaction*.

10. Akin to L *tumēre* is L *tumulus*, a hillock, a (large) mound, esp one that covers a corpse; orig, indeed, *tumulus* was prob a dim of *tumor*. L *tumulus* has the adj *tumulōsus*, whence E *tumulose*; the var E adj *tumular* comes from F *tumulaire* (L *tumul-*+adj *-aire*).

11. Also akin to L *tumēre*, to swell, hence to be vain or conceited, is L *tumultus* (gen *-ūs*), the 'swelling' or agitation, commotion, uprising, of a mob, whence MF-F *tumulte*, whence E *tumult*. The derivative L adjj *tumultuārius* and *tumultuōsus* become MF-F *tumultuaire, tumultueux* (f *-euse*), whence E *tumultuary, tumultuous*.—L *tumultus* is perh linked, phon, with L *tumulus* by the Skt n and adj *tumulas*, tumult, noisy.

12. Unless akin to L *tumēre*, L *turgēre*, to be swollen and hard, is o.o.o.: but surely both *tum-* and *turg-* are extenn of IE *\*tu-*, to be swollen? *Turgēre* has derivative adj *turgidus*, whence E *turgid*, and derivative n *turgor*, adopted by E. Its inch *turgescere*, to become hard and swollen, yields 'to *turgesce*' ; its presp *turgescens*, o/s *turgescent-*, yields *turgescent*, whence, anl, *turgescence*.

### Greek

13. Akin to L *tumulus*, a mound covering the dead, is the syn Gr *tumbos*, whence the LL *tumba*, a mound-grave, hence any grave: OF-F *tombe*, with AF var *tumbe*: ME *tumb, toumb(e), tombe*, later *tomb*: E *tomb*, with adj *tombal* perh adopted from F.

**thill.** See the 2nd DEAL.

**thimble.** See THIGH, para 3.

**thin.** See TEND, para 26.

**thine.** See THOU, para 2.

**thing,** whence the coll **thingummy** and the adj **thingy**; whence also the cpds **anything, everything, nothing, something; storting**—cf the sep HUSTING, q.v. at HOUSE, para 4.

1. The *Storting*, Norway's parliament, derives from ON *stōrthing*, the great (*stōrr*) assembly (*thing*).

2. The E *thing*, OE *thing*, a thing (single object, whether material or immaterial), a thing of value, a circumstance, a cause, a means, a meeting convened, a court or an assembly: intimately related to OE *thingan*, to negotiate (about *things*) and *thingian*, to intercede, to reconcile: related also to ON *thing*, a thing, an assembly (whether political or judicial), syn OS and virtually syn OFris *thing*, OHG-MHG *dinc*, an assembly, a court, G *Ding*, a thing, MD *dinc* (*dync*), *dinge*, MD-D *ding*, Go *theihs* (from *\*thinhs*), time, prob the Langobardic *thinx*: with the OE *thingan* and *thingian*, cf OFris *thingia*, OS *thingōn*, OHG *dingōn*, MHG *dingen*, to negotiate, G *dingen*, to bargain, to hire. The OGmc r is *\*thinh-* or *\*thingh-*, and the IE r *\*tenkw-*; perh ult akin to the TEMPER group, esp to L *tempus*, time.

**think** (pt and pp **thought**), whence **thinkable, thinker, thinking; thought,** n, whence **thoughtful and thoughtless; thank,** n, whence **thankful** (OE *thancfull*), and **thankless—thanks** (pl of the n *thank*), whence **thanksgiving,** whence **Thanksgiving Day.**

1. 'To *think*' owes the *-i-* to the *think* of *methinks*, it seems to me, ME *thinken*, var of *thinchen*, var *thunchen*, from OE *thyncan* or *thyncean*, to seem or appear, akin to OFris *thinza*, OS *thunkian*, OHG *dunchen*, G *dünken*, to seem (impersonal), Go *thugkjan* (pron *thunkyan*), ult related to 'to *think*' or form in the mind, ME *thenken*, var of *thenchen*, from OS *thencan* or *thencean*, pt *thōhte*: cf OFris *thenka, thanka, thenza*, OS *thenkian*, OHG *denchen*, MHG-G *denken*, Go *thagkjan* (pron *thankyan*), to think, ON *thekkia*, to know: OGmc r, *\*thank-*, IE r perh *\*tong-* (cf L-of-non-L-origin *tongēre*, to know). (Walshe.)

2. From OE *thenc(e)an*, to think, pt *thōhte*, derives OE *gethōht*, also shortened as *thōht*, whence ME *thoght* or *thouht*, whence the E 'a *thought*': cf MHG (ge)*dāht*.

3. Akin to OE *thenc(e)an*, to think, is *thancian*, whence 'to *thank*': cf OFris *thankia, thonkia*, OS *thankōn*, ON *thakka*. The OE n perh comes straight from OE *thanc, thonc*, a thought, hence a grateful thought, hence the expression of such a thought: whence the n *thank*, now usu in the pl: cf OFris and OS *thank, thonk*, OHG-MHG *danc*, G *Dank*, MD *danc*, thought, meaning, thanks, **D**

THIO- 714 THORP

dank, Go *thagks* (pron *thanks*), thought, thanks, ON *thŏkk*.

thio- words. See that element.

third, whence thirdly. See THREE, para 2.

thirl. See THOROUGH, para 2.

thirst (n, v), thirsty, athirst; toast, v, hence n; torrent, whence torrential; torrid (whence torridity) —cf torrefaction, torrefy.

1. *Athirst*, ME *ofthurst*, is a b/f from OE *ofthyrsted*, pp of *ofthyrstan*: *of-*, here vaguely int+ *thyrstan*, whence 'to thirst'. OE *thyrstan* derives from OE *thurst*, whence ME *thurst*, later *thirst*, retained by E: and OE *thurst* is akin to OS *thurst*, Go *thaúrstei* (cf *thaúrsus*, dry), ON *thorsti* (cf Da *törst*), OHG-G *durst*, MD *durst*, MD-D *dorst*— Homeric Gr *tersesthai*, to become dry, Gr *tersainein*, to dry up (vt), and Skt *tarsáyati*, he dries up (vt), *trsyati*, he thirsts, *torsús*, thirsty—and also L *torrēre*, (vt) to dry, dry up. The IE r is *ters-*, to dry (vt).

2. OE *thurst* has adj *thurstig*, *thyrstig*—cf OFris *thorstich* and OS *thurstig*—whence E *thirsty*.

3. L *torrēre*, to cause to become dry, esp to burn, to consume with fire, with presp *torrens*, o/s *torrent-*, used as adj 'burning', hence 'roaring' (as a fire does) or 'boiling', whence the E adj *torrent* (obsol) and the OF-F n *torrent*, adopted by E, a violent stream (? orig of lava).

4. From L *torrēre* comes the L adj *torridus*, whence—perh via late MF-F *torride*—the E *torrid*.

5. *Torrēre* has pp *tostus*, whence the LL *tostāre*, to roast, to grill, whence OF-MF *toster*, whence the MF *tostée*, a grilled slice of bread: whence, resp, the E v and the E n *toast*. From such a slice having formerly been dipped in the wine in which one drinks to another's health, comes *toast*, the person to whom one drinks and the action itself.

6. *Torrēre* has the cpd *torrefacere*, to roast, or dry, with fire, with pp *torrefactus*, whence EF-F *torréfier*, E *torrefy*, and EF-F *torréfaction*, E *torrefaction*.

thirteen, thirteenth; thirtieth, thirty. See THREE, para 4.

this. See THE, para 3.

thistle, whence thistly, comes from ME *thistil*, OE *thistel*: cf ON *thistill*, OHG *distil*, *distila*, *distula*, MHG-G *distel*, MD *destel*, *diestel*, MD-D *distel*: OGmc etymon, *thistilo*.

thither. See THE, para 11.

thole (1), a wooden (later, a metal) pin serving as fulcrum for a rowing-boat's oar: OE *thol*, *tholl*: cf OFris *tholl*, ON *thollr*, a (young) fir, hence a thole, MD *dolle*, MD-D *dol*, and perh the syn Gr *tulos*: ? cf, ult, THIGH.

thole (2), v. See the 1st TOLL, para 2.

Thomas, whence the pet-form Tom; Thomism, Thomist (whence Thomistic); tomboy, tomcat.

1. *Thomas*, adopted from LL *Thomas* ('doubting Thomas' the Apostle): LGr *Thōmas*: Aram *Tĕ'ōma*, (lit), a twin. From *Thomas* Aquinas (C13), greatest of medieval philosophers, comes the philosophical and religious system we call *Thomism*,

its adherents *Thomists*, imm from F *thomisme* and *thomiste*: *Thomas*+*-isme*, *-iste*.

2. The pet-form *Tom* gets rid of an entirely unnecessary *h*. From the widespread use of *Tom*— cf that of *Jack*—comes the sense 'male', as in *tomboy* and *tomcat*, orig *Tom boy* and *Tom cat*.

thong; twinge; whang.

1. *Thong*, ME *thong*, earlier *thwong* or *thwang*, derives from OE *thwong*, var of *thwang*, akin to ON *thvengr*, a thong.

2. Akin to *thong* is *twinge*, n from v: ME *twengen*: OE *twengan*, to squeeze: cf OFris and OS *thwinga*, to constrain, OFris *thwang* or *thwong*, constraint, compulsion, OHG *thwingan*, *dwingan*, MHG *dwingen*, *twingen*, G *zwingen*, to compel, to oppress, and OHG *dwang*, MHG *twanc*, G *Zwang*, compulsion, oppression, ON *thvinga*, to constrain, to oppress: prob (Walshe) akin to Skt *tvanákti*, he pulls together, pulls close.

3. From OE *thwang*, a thong, comes—at least, in part, for the v is perh, in part, echoic—'to *whang*' or thrash (dial), to hurl (dial and Sc), whence the n.

Thor. See THUNDER, paras 1 and 3.

thoracic, thorax. See the element *thoraci-*.

thorite, thorium. See THUNDER, para 3.

thorn, thorny; turbot.

1. *Thorn*, coming unchanged from OE, is akin to OFris (and OS) *thorn*, Go *thaúrnus*, ON *thorn*, OHG-G *dorn*, MD *doren*, *dorn*, D *doorn*: cf also OB *trǐnŭ*, thorn, Skt *t[o]rnam*, blade of grass, Gr *ternax*, stem of thistle, and such C words as Ir *trāinīn*, a little (-*īn*) blade of grass, Cor *drain*, *draen*, *drēn*, Br *dren*, *drein*, W *drain*, thorn: IE r, *torn-*. (Holthausen.)

2. OE *thorn* has adj *thornig*, whence *thorny*.

3. IE *torn-* appears in OSw *törn*, thorn, with cpd *törnbut*, lit—from its prickles—'thorny flatfish' (cf BUTT, end): whence OF *tourbout*, MF-F *turbot*, adopted by E.

thorough, adj (whence thoroughness, and such cpds as thorough-going and -paced) and adv (whence, e.g., thoroughbred) and prep (whence, prob, thoroughfare)—var through (whence throughout); thirl; thrill (v, hence n), whence the pa thrilling and agent-instr thriller.

1. The adj—like the adv—*thorough* derives, by contr, from the now archaic prep *thorough*, ME *thoru*, *thoruh*, *thuruh*, varr of ME *thurgh*, *thurh*: OE *thurh*, akin to OFris *thruch*, OS *thurh*, Go *thaírh* (cf Go *thairkō*, a hole), OHG *duruh*, MHG *durh*, G *durch*, MD *dure*, *duere*, *doer*, *dore*, *doorch*, *dorch*, D *door*; with cognates in L (*trāns*), C, Skt.

2. OE *thurh* has derivative *thyrel*, holed, perforated, hence a hole, whence *thyrelian*, contr *thyrlian*, to pierce, ME *thurlen*, thinned to *thirlen*, whence 'to *thirl*', whence *thirl*, a perforation; both v and n are now mainly dial.

3. ME *thirlen* has the metathetic var *thrillen*, to pierce, whence 'to *thrill*', to pierce (obs), hence esp with horror or delight, whence the modern n 'sensation of delight'.

thorp or thorpe. See TAVERN, para 5.

**those.** See THE, para 2.

**thou, thee; thy, thine.**

1. *Thou*, ME *thou*, earlier *thu*, derives from OE *thū, thu*: cf OFris (and OS) *thū*, Go *thu*, ON *thū*, OHG-G *du*, OHG-MHG var *dū*; cf also Ir and Ga *tu*, W and Cor *ti* (Cor var *to*), L *tū*, Doric Gr *tú* (Attic *sú*), OB *ty*, Lith *tu*, Skt *tvam*. The OGmc etymon is *\*thu*, with *u* long or short; the IE, *tu*, with *u* long or short. (Walshe.)

2. *Thee*, acc of *thou*, derives from OE *thē*, acc and dat of *thū*; *thy* derives from ME *thy*, earlier *thī*, a shortened—? rather a worn-down—form of ME *thin*, whence E *thine*: from OE *thīn*, orig the gen of *thū, thu*: cf ON *thinn*, possessive pron, from *thīn*, of thee, and OHG-MHG *dīn*, G *dein*, thy, Go *theins*, possessive pron: OGmc etymon, *thīnaz*; IE, *\*tīnos*. (Walshe.)

**though:** ME *thogh, thoh, thouh*: ON *thō*: cf OS *thōh*, OHG *doh*, Go *thau*, and OE *thēah, thāeh*, all 'though' and also at least tending to mean 'yet': OGmc etymon, *\*thau*; IE, *\*kwe*. (Walshe.)

**thought,** n: **thoughtful, thoughtless.** See THINK, para 2 and heading.

**thousand,** whence **thousandth,** comes, via ME *thousend*, earlier *thusend*, from OE *thūsend*: cf OFris *thūsend, thusind, thusindig*, MD *dusent* and *dusant* (with *-ich* varr), D *duizend*, Go *thūsindi*, OHG *thūsunt, dūsunt, tūsund*, MHG *tūsent*, G *tausend*, ON *thūsund*; Lith *túkstantis*, Ru *tysyacha*, OB *tysęšta*; prob cf Skt *tavás*, strong. The 2nd element is app the *hund-* of E *hundred*, G *hundert*: and therefore 1,000=strong 100. (Walshe.)

**thrall,** n, hence v—now usu **enthral** (int *en-*); whence **thraldom** (cf the suffix *-dom* and the n DOOM). A *thrall*, orig a bondman, virtually a slave, derives from ME *thral*; OE *thrǣl*: ON *thraell*: cf OHG *dregil* or *drigil*, a servant, and perh OE *thraegan*, Go *thragjan*, to run, and OFris *thralle*, quick.

**thrash** (whence vn **thrashing**), **thrasher** (bird); **thresh** (whence **thresher**) and **threshold.**

1. 'To *thrash*' is a dial var of 'to *thresh*', whence the dial bird-name *thresher*, whence E *thrasher*: 'to *thresh*', to beat grain, comes, through ME *threschen*, from OE *threscan*, var *therscan*, to tread, hence to thresh: cf OHG *dreskan*, MHG-G *dreschen*, MD *derschen*, D *dorschen*, Go *thriskan*, ON *threskja*—also Lith *trašketi*, to break—and L *terere*, to rub, to beat (grain)—cf TERSE.

2. *Threshold*, ME *threshwold* or *threswold*, comes from OE *therscwold* or *therscold* (cf ON *threskjöldr*): *therscan+*a doubtful 2nd element (? 'to *hold*').

**thrawn.** See THROW.

**thread, threadbare.** See THREAD, para 2.

**threat** (n, v), **threaten** (whence the pa **threatening**).

'To *threaten*' derives from OE *thrēatnian*, to compel, itself—as also OE *thrēatian*, to press, to threaten, whence the archaic 'to *threat*'—from OE *thrēat*, a crowd, a throng, hence a crowding, esp an overcrowding, whence compulsion or oppression: ME *thrēat*, a crowd, oppression, a threat: E

*threat*. OE *thrēat* is akin to OE *thrēotan*, Go us*thriutan*, to vex, to weary, OHG er*driozan*, MHG ver*driezen*, G ver*driessen*, to vex, to grieve, ON *thriōta*, to fail, to lack—OSl *trudite*, to vex, to weary—L *trūdere*, to push. Cf THRUST.

**three** and **third—thirteen** and **thirteenth—thirty** and **thirtieth—and thrice; tertius** and **tertium quid —tertial, tertian, tertiary—tercel—tercet, terzetto —terce** and **tierce—tercentenary; tern, ternary, ternate, ternion; trinity, Trinity; trey and trio, triolet; triad;** the *tri-* cpds—e.g., **triangle, tripod** and **tripos,** etc.; **trammel** and the sep DRILL (a fabric); cf the sep TESTAMENT.

### Indo-European

1. E *three*, OE *thrī* or *thrīe*, f and neu *thrēo*, is akin to OFris *thrē*, m, *thriā*, f, and *thriū*, neu, OS *thria* (var *threa*), Go *threis*, neu *thrija*, MD *dre*, *dri* (*dry*), MD-D *drie*, OHG-MHG *drē, drīe*, m, OHG *drio*, f, OHG *driu*, neu, G *drei*, ON *thrīr*, m, *thrīar*, f, *thrīu*, neu; Lith *trys*, Ru *tri*, OSl *trije*; OC *\*treis*—Br, W (f *teir*), OIr-Ir (f *teoir*), Ga *trī*—Cor *trȳ* (in cpds, occ *tre-*), Mx *troor*; L *trēs*, neu *tria*; Gr *treis*, neu *tria*; Skt *tráyas*, Ve *trī* (cf the OSl *tri*); Hit *tri-*. The IE etymon was app *\*trey-es*; the IE r, *trey-*, var *\*trī-*, whence the predominant IE c/f *tri-*, which, in L, has —? by metathesis—the rare var *ter-*, which occurs also in *tertius*, third.

### Germanic

2. OE *thrī(e)*, f and neu *thrēo*, become ME *thrī*, *thrēo*, *thrē*, with the 1st predominating and the 2nd increasingly rare; whence E *three*. The OE cardinal *thrī* acquires the ordinal *thridda*, whence ME *thridde*, whence, by metathesis, the E *third*, adj, hence also n. With OE *thridda*, cf OFris *thredda*, OS *thriddio*, Go *thridja*, OHG *dritto*, MHG-G *dritte*, ON *thrithe* or *thrithi*, Gr *tritos*.

3. OE *thrī* has adv *thriga*, predominantly *thriwa*, three times, whence ME *thrie*, later *thries* (adv suffix *-s*, orig the suffix *-s, -es*, of the gen), whence E *thrice*. With OE *thriwa*, cf OS *thriwo* and OFris *thria*—and Hit *triyanna*.

4. OE *thrī, thrēo*, has both the cpd *thrēotēne* or *-tȳne* (lit 3+10), whence ME *threttene* and—? after *third*—E *thirteen*, whence *thirteenth* (cf the OE *thrēotēotha*); and the cpd *thrētig* (lit 3×10), var *thrittig*, whence ME *thritty*, whence, by metathesis, E *thirty*, whence *thirtieth* (cf the OE *thrītigōtha*).

### Latin

5. The var L r *ter-* occurs in, e.g., *tercentenary*—an E formation, after *bicentenary*: LL *centenārium*, a hundred pieces.

6. It occurs also in L *tertius*, third (*ter+-tius*, adj suffix), adopted by E, as in 'Smith *Tertius*'. The scholastic L *tertium quid*, a third somewhat, something that falls beyond a supposedly exhaustive 'either-or', has been adopted and jocosely sense-adapted by E. E *tertial*=L *terti*us+the E adj suffix *-al*; but *tertian* derives from L *tertiānus*, an *-ānus* extn of *terti*us, and *tertiary* derives from L

*tertiārius*, containing or constituting a third part or share.

7. Also from L *tertius* come:

*terce*, a Sc (from F) var of *tierce*, adopted from OF-F *tierce* (OF-MF var *terce*), orig the f of the OF-F *tiers*, from L *tertius*;

*tercel*, a male goshawk or peregrine falcon, adopted from OF-MF *tercel*, var *terçuel*, from ML *tertiolus*, VL *\*tertiolus*, dim of *tertius*, the bird being named 'a third part' for any of several f/e reasons, of which the best is that the male is one-third smaller than the female;

*tercet*, three successive verse-lines with but a single rhyme, from It *terzetto*, dim of *terzo*, third (L *tertius*);

It *terza rima*, lit 'third rhyme', hence 'triple rhyme', adopted as a literary term;

It *terzetto*, adopted as a Mus term for a vocal trio.

8. The var L r *ter-* occurs yet again in *terni*, three by three, three each, triple, whence E *tern*, threefold. L *terni* has the foll derivatives relevant to E:

L *ternārius*, triple, (of a verse-line) having three feet, whence E *ternary*;

Sci L *ternātus*, consisting of—or arranged in—threes, E *ternate*;

L *terniō*, o/s *terniōn-*, the number 3, whence E *ternion*, esp a set of 3;

and, though more prob from *trīni*,

LL *trīnitās*, the number 3, esp *Trīnitās*, the Trinity, whence OF-F *Trinité*, whence E *Trinity*; the EF-F derivative *trinitarien* becomes E *Trinitarian*.

9. L *terni* has the var *trīni* (prob from *tria*), three each, whence *trīnus*, triple, whence OF-MF *trin*, f *trine*, the latter being adopted by E.

10. L *trēs*, 3, becomes OF-MF *treis* (EF-F *trois*), with var *treie*, imm from the L neu *tria*; as a dicing term, *treie* becomes E *trey*. Also from L *tria* comes It *trio*, collective 3, adopted by EF-F, whence the E word; EF *trio* app has the dim *triolet*, adopted by E.

### Greek

11. Gr *treis*, neu *tria*, has derivative *trias*, a set of three (gen *triados*), whence LL *trias* (gen *triadis*), acc *triadem*, whence EF-F *triade* and, perh independently, E *triad*, with derivative adj *triadic*. LL *trias* is adopted by European Geol, the system having in Germany a threefold division; whence the adj *Triassic*.

12. Gr *treis*, *tria*, and L *trēs*, *tria*, have the c/f *tri-*, the L being prob imitative of the Gr. Of the numerous E *tri-* cpds coming straight from either Gr or L, or imitating Gr and L cpds, the chief are perhaps these:

*triangle*, adopted from MF-F: L *triangulus* (cf the n ANGLE); *triangular*, late MF-F *triangulaire*, LL *triangulāris* (from *triangulus*); *triangulation*, ML *triangulātiōn-*, o/s of *triangulātiō* (anl from *triangulus*);

*tribasic* = *tri-* + E *basic*, adj of BASE, n;

*tribrach*, LL *tribrachus*, L *tribrachys*, Gr *tribrakhus*, having 3 short (*brakhus*) syllables;

*triceps*, a SciL sense-adaptation of L *triceps*, having three heads (L *caput*, a head);

*trichord*, Gr *trikhordos*, 3-stringed (*khordē*, a string);

*trichotomy*, a division into three: after *dichotomy*: Gr *trikha*, threefold+*-tomy*, a cutting, hence a division (Gr *tomē*: cf TOME);

*tricolor*, F *tricolore* (the flag), EF *tricolor*, 3-coloured;

*tricycle*: see CYCLE, para 1;

*trident*: see DENTAL, para 2;

*triennial*: see ANNUAL, para 3;

*trifid*, L *trifidus*, 3-cleft;

*Trifolium*, adopted from L for 'the 3-leaved'—cf *trefoil*;

*triglyph*, L *triglyphus*, Gr *trigluphos* (*gluphē*, a carving: E *glyph*);

*trigononometry*: see the element *trigono-*;

*trilingual*, after *bilingual*: L *trilinguis*, 3-tongued; *trillon* = *tri-* + *million*;

*trilogy*: see LEGEND, para 32;

*trimester*: see the element *-mester*;

*trimeter*, L *trimetrus*, Gr *trimetros*, 3-measured (cf *meter* at MEASURE);

*trimorphous*, Gr *trimorphos*, 3-shaped or -formed (cf MORPHEUS); whence, anl, *trimorphism*;

*trinomial*, after *binomial* (q.v.);

*tripartite*: see PART, para 4;

*triphthong* = *tri-* + *diphthong*;

*triplane* = *tri-* + *plane*: cf *biplane*;

*triple*, *triplex*, *triplicate*, *triplication*: see PLY, para 24;

*tripod*, *tripos*: see FOOT, para 27;

*triptych*, Gr *triptukhos*;

*trireme*, L *trirēmis*, (a boat having) 3 banks of *rēmi* or oars—cf late MF-F *trirème*;

*trisyllabic*, *trisyllable*: see SYLLABLE, para 3;

*tritone*, Gr *tritonos*, 3-toned;

*triumvirate*: see the element *-vir*;

*trivial*, *trivium*: see TRIVIA.

12. A 'disguised' cpd—cf the fabric DRILL—is the n-whence-v *trammel*: OF-MF(-F) *tramail* (F *trémail*): LL *trēmaculum*, a 3-meshed net for catching fish: *trē-* (from *trēs*) + *macula*, a mesh + suffix *-um*.

**threne, threnody.** See ODE, para 10.

**threpsology.** See the element *threpso-*.

**thresh, threshold.** See THRASH.

**thrice.** See THREE, para 3.

**thrift, thrifty.** See THRIVE, para 2.

**thrill, thrilling.** See THOROUGH, para 3.

**thring.** See THRONG.

**thrips**, a wood worm, is adopted from L *thrips* from Gr θρίψ, perh 'the borer' and akin to Go *dreiban*, OHG *trīban*, to push. (Hofmann.)

**thrive**, pt throve, pp thriven; hence the pa **thriving; thrift**, whence thrifty, whence **thriftiness**.

1. 'To *thrive*,' ME *thriven*, comes from ON *thrīfast*, to grasp for oneself: vr of ON *thrīfa*, var *threifa*, to grasp, with modern Scan cognates: o.o.o.

2. From ON *threifa*, *thrīfa*, comes ON *thrif*, *thrift*, whence ME-E *thrift*, lit '(the result of) grasping for oneself', hence a thriving condition, hence good management, hence frugality.

**throat**, whence the c/f **-throated** and the adj **throaty**; **thropple**, n, whence v, and **throttle**, n, whence v.

1. *Throat*, ME *throte*, derives from OE *throte* or *throtu*: cf OHG *drozza*, OS *strota*, OFris *strot-*, MD *stroot*, *strodt*, *strote*, D *strot*: o.o.o.

2. The mainly dial *thropple*, throat, windpipe, prob derives from OE *throtbolla*, gullet, windpipe, Adam's apple.

3. The n *throttle* is almost certainly a shortening of *\*throatle*, dim of *throat*: for the form, perh cf OHG *drōscala*, MHG *droschel*, G *Drossel*, a thrush and E *throstle*.

**throb** (v, hence n; whence the pa, vn **throbbing**): ME *throbben*: app echoic.

**throe**, n, now usu in the pl **throes**: ME *throwe*, earlier *thrawe*: OE *thrāwu*, a var of OE *thrēa*, a threatening, a compulsion or oppression, hence suffering: ? influenced by ON *thrā*, a throe or extreme pang or pain: cf G *drohen*, to threaten, MHG *drōn*, a b/f from MHG *drō*, a threat—cf OHG *drewen*, to threaten: o.o.o. (Walshe.)

**thrombosis.** See the element *thrombo-*.

**throne**, n (whence the adj **thronal**) and v, now usu in the derivative cpd **enthrone**, whence **enthronement**; **dethrone**, whence **dethronement**, prob owes something to EF-F *détrôner*.

'To *throne*,' reshaped after the n *throne*, derives from ME *tronen*, from ME *trone*, whence—by reshaping after the L word—E *throne*; ME *trone* was adopted from OF-MF *trone* (F *trône*): L *thronus*: Gr *thronos*: akin to the sep FIRM.

**throng**, n, whence both the E v and the Sc (and E dial) adj, derives from ME *throng*, a var of *thrang*: OE *thrang* or *gethrang*: cf ON *thröng*, OHG-MHG *dranc*, G *Drang*, a throng, a thrusting or an urging: cf also OE *thringan* (whence the now only dial 'to *thring*'), to crowd, OFris ur-*thringa*, to oppress, OS *thringan*, to crowd, OHG *dringan*, G *dringen*, to thrust, MHG *dringen*, to crowd a prince at court, Go *threihan* (for *\*thrinhan*), MD *drengen*, MD-D *dringen*, ON *thryngva*: cf also Lith *treñkti*, to push, to jolt, and esp Skt *thrakhta-*, pressed together (Walshe): either echoic or, at the least, expressive.

**thropple.** See THROAT, para 2.

**throstle.** See the 1st THRUSH, para 2.

**throttle.** See THROAT, para 3.

**through.** See THOROUGH, para 1.

**throve**: pt of THRIVE.

**throw**, pt **threw**, pp **thrown** (with Sc var **thrawn**, crooked, perverse); whence the n **throw** and numerous cpds—**throwback**, **throw-in**, **throw-out**, etc.; **thread**, n, whence both the v and **threadbare.** —L cognates: terebella, terebra; Termes, termite; tribulate, tribulation; triturate, trituration, triturator; attrite, attrition, attritus—contrite, contrition—detriment (whence detrimental), detrition, detritus. —Gr cognates teredo; tribade, diatribe; trema;

trepan (n, v), trepanation; trephine, n, hence v.—Cf the sep THRASH and TURN.

### Indo-European

1. 'To *throw*,' ME *throwen*, earlier *thrawen*, to throw, to twist, OE *thrāwan*, to twist, to cause to turn, is akin to OHG *drāen* and *drājan*, MHG *draejen*, G *drehen*, MD *dreyen*, *drayen*, *draeyen*, D *draaien* (*draaijen*), to turn, to twist; L *terere*, to rub, to rub away, to thrash, pp *trītus*, and *terebra*, an auger; Gr *tribeīn*, to rub, *tetralneīn*, to pierce, *trēma*, a hole (made by, e.g., piercing), *teireīn* (for *\*teriein*), to pierce or bore, to turn; OB *trўti*, to rub, *tēro*, I rub, and Lith *tìrti*, to pry into, to investigate; Skt *turás*, wounded, injured; perh Hit *teripp-*, to plough (pierce the soil). The IE r is *\*ter-*, to rub, to turn or twist, to pierce or bore. (E & M; Hofmann.)

### Germanic

2. Akin to OE *thrāwan*, to twist or turn, is OE *thrāēd*, ME *threed* or *thred*, E *thread*: cf OFris *thrēd*, ON *thrāthr*, a thread, OHG-MHG *drāt*, thread, wire, G *Draht*, wire, MD *draet*, D *draad*, thread.

### Latin

3. L *terere*, to rub, to rub away, to wear away, to waste, to beat grain, has s and r *ter-*, extn *tere-*, as in *terebra*, a drill, an auger, with dim *terebellus*, with SciL mdfn *terebellum*; *terebra* and *terebellum* appear in learnèd E. L *terebra* has the LL derivative *terebrāre*, to pierce, pp *terebrātus*, whence both E *terebrate* (adj and v) and ML *terebrātiō*, o/s *terebrātiōn-*, whence E *terebration*.

4. Prob from the L r *ter-* comes LL *termes* (s and r *term-*, an extn), a wood worm, o/s *termit-*, whence the Zoo *Termes* and the E *termite*.

5. L *ter-* has the metathesis *\*tre-*, var *\*trē-*, with mdfn *trī-*, occurring not only in the pp *trītus* and supine *trītum* but also in *trībulum* (occ *tribula*), a threshing-sledge, a wooden platform studded, underneath, with nails or sharp flints, whence *trībulāre*, to beat grain with one, hence to harass, to afflict, pp *trībulātus*, whence both 'to *tribulate*' (rare) and LL *trībulātiō*, acc *trībulātiōn*em, whence MF-F *tribulation*, adopted by E.

6. On the L pp *trītus* is formed *trītūra*, a beating of grain, a rubbing away, whence the LL *trītūrāre*, to thresh, pp *trītūrātus*, whence the E adj and v *triturate*; the LL derivatives *trītūrātiō*, acc *trītūrātiōn*em, and *trītūrātor* become E *trituration* (perh via MF-F) and *triturator*.

7. Straight from the L pp *trītus*, used as adj, comes E *trite*, whence *triteness*.

8. L *terere*, to rub, to rub away, has prefix-cpds; the foll concern E:

*atterere*, to rub *ad* or against, to wear out by rubbing, pp *attrītus*, whence the Theo adj *attrite*; whereas the derivative LL *attrītiō*, o/s *attrītiōn-*, yields *attrition*, the derivative L n *attrītus* (gen *-ūs*) is adopted by Geol;

*conterere* (*con-*, vaguely int), to wear away by

rubbing, to grind, hence to abase, pp *contrītus*, used also as adj, whence OF-F *contrit*, f *contrite*, whence E *contrite*; derivative LL *contrītiō*, acc *contrītiōn*em, yields OF-F *contrition*, adopted by E;

*dēterere* (*dē-*, away from, *dē*, down from), to remove by rubbing, hence diminish, to destroy, pp *dētrītus*, whence the n *dētrītus* (gen *-ūs*), a rubbing away, hence that which is rubbed away, adopted by Geol; derivative ML *dētrītiō*, o/s *dētrītiōn-*, yields *detrition*. On the r *dētrī-* (cf para 5 above) was formed *dētrīmentum*, a rubbing—hence a wearing —away, hence a diminution, a loss, whence MF *detriment*, EF-F *détriment*, whence E *detriment*.

### Greek

9. Gr *teirein* (IE r *ter-*), to rub, has derivative *terēdōn*, lit 'a wearer-away', a worm that gnaws either wood (cf *termes* in para 4 above) or clothes; whence—as if the Gr word had been *terēdō*, gen *terēdonos*—the L *terēdō*, adopted by Zoo.

10. Akin to Gr *teirein*, to rub, is the syn Gr *tribein* (s and r *trib-*, extn of the IE var *tri-*); whence Gr *tribas*, gen *tribados*—L *tribas*, gen *tribadis*—EF-F *tribade*, adopted by E (a Lesbian), whence *tribadism*.

11. Gr *tribein*, to rub, has the cpd *diatribein*, to rub *dia* or through, to rub away, hence to spend time (cf L *terere tempus*, to spend time uselessly); whence *diatribē*, an erudite discussion, L *diatriba*, EF-F *diatribe*, with modern sense conferred by Voltaire in 1734 (B & W)—adopted by E.

12. The IE var r *trē-* occurs in Gr *trēma*, a perforation, a hole; whence Bot *Trema*, a genus of shrubs, with a fruit that has holes.

13. Akin to Gr *trēma* is the syn Gr *trupa*, whence *trupan*, to pierce or bore, whence *trupanon* (c/f *trupano-*, E *trypano-*), a piercing or boring instrument, whence ML *trepanum*, a surgical instrument, late MF *trépane*, EF-F *trépan*, and its derivatives, late MF-F *trépaner* and MF-F *trépanation*: whence, resp, the E words *trepan*, n, and 'to *trepan*' and *trepanation*.

14. E *trepan*, n, has the mdfn *trephine*, an improvement on the trepan.

**thrum** (1), usu in pl **thrums**. See TERM, para 3.

**thrum** (2), to strum. See STRUM.

**thrush** (1), the bird; **throstle**. *Thrush*, ME *thrusche*, OE *thrysce*, var *thraesce*, is akin to OHG *drōscala*, MHG *drōschel*, G *Drossel*: perh cf L *turdus*, a thrush, and, with the IE int prefix *s-*, Gr *strouthos*, a bird, esp a sparrow and then predominantly an ostrich ('*the* bird').

2. Also akin to OE *thrysce*, *thraēsce*, is OE *throstle*, ME *throstel*, E *throstle*.

**thrush** (2), an affection of the infantile mouth and throat, has, in its passage from Scan, been influenced by THRUSH (1): o.o.o.

**thrust**, v (hence n), whence the agent **thruster** and the pa **thrusting**, derives from ME *thrusten*, varr *thristen* and *thresten*—from ON *thrўsta*, to thrust, to compel: o.o.o.: perh cf THREAT and prob cf L *trūdere*, to push, to thrust, pp *trūsus*.

2. L *trūdere* has several prefix-cpds relevant to E, the first being *abstrūdere*, to push or thrust away, pp *abstrūsus*, used also as adj 'thrust out of sight, secret, hence very difficult to understand': whence, prob via MF-F *abstrus*, f *abstruse*, the E *abstruse*.

3. L *dētrūdere*, to thrust *dē*, down, hence away, yields 'to *detrude*'; from the LL *dētrūsiō* (from the pp *dētrūsus*), o/s *dētrūsiōn-*, comes *detrusion*.

4. L *extrūdere*, to thrust *ex* or out, yields 'to *extrude*'; the pp *extrūsus* has suggested E *extrusile*, *extrusion*, *extrusive*.

5. L *intrūdere*, to thrust (something) into, hence upon, yields 'to *intrude*', now usu for 'to *intrude* oneself', whence *intruder*; from the pp *intrūsus*, MF-F has formed *intrusion*, adopted by E, whence, anl, *intrusive*.

6. L *obtrūdere*, to thrust towards or upon, yields 'to *obtrude*', to thrust forward, esp unasked; derivative LL *obtrūsiō*, o/s *obtrūsiōn-*, gives us *obtrusion*, whence, anl, *obtrusive*.

7. L *prōtrūdere*, to thrust *prō-* or forward, becomes 'to *protrude*' (vt and vi), whence, anl, *protrusion* and *protrusive*.

8. L *retrūdere*, to thrust back, becomes 'to *retrude*', whence, anl, *retrusible* and *retrusion*.

**thud**, v and n, is prob echoic; for the form, however, cf ME *thuden* (OE *thyddan*), to push or press.

**thug**, **thuggee**. The latter derives from Hi *ṭhagī*, prop the adj of Hi (and Mahratti) *ṭhag*: Prakrit *thaga*, an easing of Skt *sthaga*, a rogue, a cheat, (also adj) dishonest: Skt *sthagati*, he hides: cf *thatch* at TECHNIC, para 8. A *thug*, or rough, derives from *Thug*, a member of that religious fraternity in which murder had been regarded as a profession and which, by 1840, was suppressed by British soldiers in India. Cf, sem, ASSASSIN.

**thumb**. See THIGH, para 2.

**thump**. See BUMP.

**thunder**, n (whence **thunderous** and **thundery**) and v (whence **thunderer** and the pa, vn **thundering**); hence numerous cpds, mostly self-explanatory— e.g., **thunderbird, -bolt, -clap, -cloud, -fish** (supposed to foretell thunderstorms: Webster), **-head, -stone, -strike** (esp as pa **thunderstruck**), **-worm** (leaving its burrows after a thundershower: Webster);—**Thor, thorite, thorium; Thursday; blunderbuss.**—L: **tonant, tonite, tonitruous; astonish, astonishment**— **astonied**—**astound**, whence pa **astounding** and **astoundment; detonate, detonation** (whence, anl, **detonator**); **tornado.**—**stun**, whence **stunner** and **stunning.**

### Indo-European

1. 'To *thunder*' derives from ME *thunderen*, earlier *thuneren*, from OE *thunrian*, itself app from OE *thunor*, whence ME *thuner*, *thoner*, later *thonder*, *thunder*, the latter retained by E: and OE *thunor* is akin to OFris *thuner* and, with *d-* for *th-*, OHG *donar*, MHG *doner*, G *Donner*, MD *dunder*, *donre*, *dondere*, MD-D *donder*, and, without nasalization, ON *Thōrr*, the Thunder God (E *Thor*); likewise akin, but with *t-* for Gmc *th-* or *d-*,

are L *tonāre*, to thunder, and *tonitrus*, *tonitru*, thunder, and Ve *tányati*, it thunders, *tanyatús*, a thundering; akin also, but bearing the IE int prefix *s-*, are Skt *stanati*, *stanayati*, it thunders, and Gr *stenein*, to groan, to moan, and, in Sl, such words as Lith *stenèti*, OSl *stenati*, Ru *stonàt*, to groan.

### Germanic

2. From MD-D *donder* comes D *donderbus*, lit a thunder-box, hence a musket, whence, by f/e, the E *blunderbuss*.

3. From ON *Thōrr*, the Thunder-God, comes E *Thor*, whence both *thorite* (Min *-ite*) and *thorium* (Chem *-ium*), discovered in *thorite*. ON *Thōrr* has cpd *Thōrsdagr* (whence, anl, OE *Thurresdaeg*), whence ME *Thoresday*, later *Thuresdai*, then *Thursdaye*, whence E *Thursday*: cf OFris *thunresdei* and OHG *donarestag*, G *Donnerstag*.

### Latin

4. L *tonāre*, to thunder, has presp *tonans*, whence both the adj *tonant* (from the L o/s *tonant-*) and *Jupiter Tonans*, Jupiter the Thunderer, whence *The Thunderer*, a C19 name for *The Times*. From *tonāre* come E *tonite* (Min *-ite*) and *tonitrus*, var *tonitru*, thunder, with LL adj *tonitruālis*, which has suggested E *tonitruous*, and with derivative LL *tonitruāre*, to thunder, presp *tonitruans*, o/s *tonitruant-*, whence the E adj *tonitruant*.

5. L *tonāre* has at least two cpds that affect E: L *dētonāre* and VL *\*extonāre* (for L *attonāre*). *Dētonāre* (int *dē-*) has pp *dētonātus*, whence 'to detonate'; the anl late EF-F derivative *détonation* leads to *detonation*; with *detonator*, cf the F *détonateur*.

6. VL *\*extonāre*, to affect violently (int *ex-*)—to stupefy—with noise, becomes OF-MF *estoner*, whence ME *astonen*, *astonien* (*astunien*), whence, on the anl of E derivatives from OF-F vv in *-ir*, E 'to *astonish*', whence *astonishment*—prompted by the syn MF *estonement* (F *étonnement*).

7. ME *astonen* has pp *astoned*, with var *astouned*, contr to *astound*, whence the now archaic adj *astound*, whence 'to *astound*'. Also from ME *astonen* comes the now archaic 'to *astony*', pp *astonied*.

8. OF-MF *estoner*, to resound, hence to stun, becomes, as we have seen, *astonien* or *astunien*, whence, by aphesis, ME *stonien*, *stunien*, E 'to *stun*'.

9. That E *tornado* comes from Sp, all are agreed, but whereas certain authorities assert that *tornado* is an adoption of Sp *tornado*, others assert that it is a f/e adaptation of Sp *tronada*, a thunderstorm, from *tronar*, to thunder, an assimilation from L *tonāre*. Despite the OED, *tornado* is a Sp word, the substantival use of *tornado*, the pp of *tornar*, to turn.

**Thunderer, The.** See prec, para 4.
**thurible.** See THYME, para 3.
**thurifer.** See the element *thuri-*.
**Thursday.** See THUNDER, para 3.
**thus.** See THE, para 6.

**thwack**, v, hence n: echoic: cf WHACK.
**thwaite.** See WHITTLE, para 2.
**thwart.** See QUEER, para 2.
**thwittle.** See WHITTLE, para 1.
**thy.** See THOU, para 2.
**thyine.** See THYME, para 2.
**thylacine.** See the element *thylaco-*.
**thyme** (whence **thymy**)—whence **thymol** (*-ol*); **thyine; thurible.**

1. *Thyme*, reshaped after EF-F *thym*, comes from ME *tyme*: MF *tym*: L *thymus*. Gr *thumos* (var *thumon*, whence L *thymum*): akin to Gr *thūmos*, courage (cf THYMUS), and to Gr *thúon*, a tree with sweetly odorous wood, whence Gr *thumiama*, incense—and ult to L *fumus*, therefore to E FUME.

2. Akin to Gr *thúon*, is Gr *thúa*, var *thuía*, a fragrant African tree, whence the adj *thuinos*, LL *thyinus*, E *thyine*.

3. Akin to Gr *thúon* and *thúa* is Gr *thúos*, incense, hence sacrificial incense, hence sacrifice, whence L *thus* (*tus*), o/s *thur-* (*tur-*), whence L *thuribulum* (*tur-*), whence E *thurible*, a censer.

**thymic, thymine.** See THYMUS.
**thymol.** See THYME (heading).
**thymus**, in An a gland, is the SciL form of Gr *thūmos*, courage, akin to Skt *dhūmás*, smoke; f.a.e., FUME. (Cf THYME, para 1.) Hence the adj *thymic* and the Chem *thymin* or *thymine* (Chem suffix *-in*, *-ine*).
**thyreo-** words. See the element *thyreo-*.
**thyroid; parathyroid.** The latter merely prefixes Gr *para*, beside, alongside, to *thyroid*, which derives from EF-F *thyroïde*: MGr *thuroïdes*, doorshaped, a false reading of LGr *thureoeidēs*, shieldor buckler-shaped: *thureos*, a long shield + *eidos*, form. Gr *thureos* derives from *thura*, a door; in shape, it resembles a door.
**thyro-** words. See *thyro-* at the element *thyreo-*.
**thyrsus**, a Bacchic wand, is adopted from L; it derives from Gr *thursos*: o.o.o.: ? Thracian or Phrygian.

2. L *thyrsus*, such a wand, hence, in Bot, a stalk, a stem, becomes VL *\*tursus*, whence It *torso*, a stalk, hence, orig jocularly, the An sense 'trunk', whence EF-F *torse* and E *torso*.
**tiara**, whence the dim **tiarella**, is adopted from L, from Gr, *tiārā*, var *tiārās*: o.o.o.: prob Oriental —cf OPer *tara*.
**Tibet**—whence **Tibetan**, adj, hence n—'seems to have passed to us through the Ar name (*Tibat*, *Tobbat*), drawn from the ancient Ch name (*Tu-pat*, *Tu-fan*)': Enci It.
**tibia** (whence *tibial*): L *tībia*, a flute, hence—cf the sem development of Gr *aulos*, a flute, hence the blow-hole of cetaceans or the funnel of a cuttlefish—the bone: o.o.o. (E & M; L & S.)
**tick** (1), a small arachnid: ME *tike*, var of *teke*: either borrowed from MD *teke*, var *tieke* (cf D *teek*, *tiek*), or surviving from a slightly dubious OE *ticia*: cf MHG *zeche*, MHG-G *zecke*: perh (Kluge) OGmc *\*tikan*, from IE *\*deigh-*, a nipping insect: cf Arm *tiz* (Walshe).

**tick** (2), a cover. See THESIS, para 2.

**tick** (3), to pat or tap lightly or gently, hence both as in 'the clock *ticks*' and 'to *tick*—hence *tick off*—the answers'; hence n: cf MD *teeckenen, teekenen, teikenen, teken*, D *tikken*: app echoic.— Hence the agent-instrument *ticker* and the pa, vn *ticking*.

**ticket**. See STICK, para 16.

**ticking** (1), of a mattress. See THESIS, para 2.— (2). See the 3rd TICK.

**tickle**, whence **tickler** and **ticklish**. See KITTLE, s.f.

**tick-tack** and **tick-tock** are echoic redupp of the 3rd TICK.

**tidal**. See TIDE.

**tidbit**. See TITBIT.

**tiddley**. See TIDE, para 4.

**tiddlywinks**. See para 4 of:

**tide**, whence **tidal**; **tidings**; **tidy** (whence **tidiness**) —'tiddl(e)y'—tiddlywinks—titivate or tittivate, whence tit(t)ivation; betide.—time, n, whence both 'to time' (whence the vn timing) and timeless and timely (whence untimely), and such obvious cpds as timekeeper, -piece, -serving, -table; betimes.—Perh cf the sep DEMOCRACY.

1. The *tides* of the sea were so named, in C14, from their occurrence at regular *times*: the basic sense of *tide* (ME *tide*, earlier *tid*: OE *tīd*) was 'time', hence a definite time, hence an opportune time, as in '*Time and tide* wait for no man' (C16): cf OFris and OS *tīd*, MD *tide-*, D *tijd*, ON *tīth*, OHG-MHG *zīt*, G *Zeit*.

2. *Time*, ME *time*, OE *tima*, is akin to ON *tīmi* (with modern Scan cognates). It is therefore clear that, already in ON and OE, *time* and *tide* were doublets: they have the same r, but different suffixes: the OGmc r, then, is *tī-*, corresp to an IE r *dī-*: cf Arm *ti*, time, and the Skt goddess *Aditiš* (*a-*, not+*ditiš*), 'the timeless, hence eternal, one': perh cf also Skt *dáyatē*, he divides, he apportions, and Gr *daiomai*, I divide or apportion —and therefore cf Gr *dēmos*, the people, which has C cognates. (Walshe.)

3. Whereas the only non-obvious derivative of *time* is *betimes* (*be-*, for *by*+*times*, with adv suffix *-s*), *tide* has:

*betide*, to happen, to happen to, ME *bitiden*: *bi-* (E *be-*)+*tiden*, to happen, OE *tīdan*;

*tiding*, an occurrence, a happening (archaic), an account, now mostly in pl *tidings*: ME *tidinge, tithinge, tidinde*: app influenced, in its passage from OE *tīdung*, by ON *tīdende, tīthindi* (pl);

*tidy*, ME *tidy, tidi*, from *tid*, time or season: orig, seasonable or opportune: cf MD *tidich*, D *tijdig*, timely.

4. App from *tidy*, neat, comes—via the dial (S.W. England) *tidivate* (*tiddi-*)—'to *titivate*' (or *titti-*), perh after such L-derivative vv as *captivate*; certainly from *tidy* comes the Nav sl *tiddly* or *tiddley*. In general sl, *tiddley* means 'very small' (? after *tiny*), whence prob the game of *tiddly-winks*: *tiddly*, from the smallness of the disks,

*winks* because of their 'winking' movement when they are struck.

**tiding(s)**. See prec, para 3.

**tidy**. See TIDE, para 3.

**tie**, n and v. See TOW (3), para 4.

**tier**, layer, rank, row, esp in a series: OF-EF *tire*, var of OF *tiere*, a row or rank: o.o.o.: dubiously related to OHG *ziarī*, MHG *ziere*, G *Zier*, an ornament (E *tire*, for *attire*, adornment, dress; cf ARTILLERY).

**tierce**. See THREE, para 7.

**tiff**, a slight quarrel, prob eases the Sc, and Northern E dial, *tift*, a puff of wind, itself app echoic.

**tiffany**. See FANCY, para 7, s.f.

**tiffin** slovens **tiffing**, a drinking, vn of *tiff*, to drink, from *tiff*, a small drink or draught: ? orig a sniff: cf ON *thefa*, to lsniff, and *thefr*, a sniff, a smell, a taste. (Webster.)

**tiger**. See STICK, para 2.

**tight** (adj, hence adv), whence **tighten** (v suffix *-en*) and **tightness**: ME *tight*, earlier *tigt*, still earlier *thight* or *thyht*: either deriving from or, at the least, related to ON *thēttr*: cf MHG *dhīte*, G *dicht*, tight, thick, MD *dichte*, MD-D *dicht*: prob akin either (Webster) to Lith *tánkus*, tight, and Skt *tanakti*, it draws together, or (Walshe) to L *tectus*, covered, hence impenetrable (cf TECHNIC, para 6).

**tigress; tigrine**. See STICK, para 2.

**Tigris**. See STICK, para 2.

**tike**. See TYKE.

**tilbury**, a two-wheeled horse-drawn carriage, was designed by one *Tilbury*, a London coach-builder: from the PlN *Tilbury*, OE *Tilaburg*, Tila's burg (or fort).

**tilde**. See TITLE.

**tile**. See TECHNIC, para 8.

**till** (1), orig a tray or drawer in a chest or a trunk: EE *tille, tylle*: ME *tillen, tyllen*, to pull or draw: OE *-tyllan*, as in *fortyllan*, to draw away: cf OFris *tilia* and OS *tilōn*: o.o.o.: ? akin to OE *tēon*, to pull or draw (cf the v TOW).—Cf the 3rd TOLL.

**till** (2), orig to work hard for, to strive for, to gain (obs), to cultivate (land): ME *tilen*, earlier *tilien*: OE *tilian* (var *teolian*), to work hard for, to cultivate: cf, sem, LABOR (LABOUR): cf, phon, OS *tilian*, to earn or get, MD *teilen, teelen*, to get, plough, propagate, D *telen*, to propagate, G *zielen*, to aim, OHG-MHG *zil*, G *Ziel*, aim, goal, Go *til*, opportunity, and *tils*, opportune, suitable, and, in C, the OIr *dil*, agreeable, pleasant, Ga *dil*, zealous, OC *dilis*, agreeable. Cf also the next entry.

2. 'To *till*' has the derivatives *tillage* and, already in OE, *tilth*.

**till** (3), prep, whence conj; **until**. E *till*, to (a place of arrival, whether in space or in time), hence throughout a period, or, termination implied, with interval, from one point of time to another, derives, via ME *till*, earlier *til*, from OE *til*, itself perhaps deriving from, certainly related intimately to, ON *til*: cf also OFris *til*. Those

OGmc prepp are closely akin to these OGmc adjj: OE and OFris *til*, good, and Go *tils*, opportune— cf prec. The basic idea of till (2) and (3) is app: a striving for the good and the agreeable.

2. ME *til* has cpd until, var ontil (*un-* as in UNTO, q.v.): whence E *until*. Perh it would be more sensible to pose (with EW) the substitution of *until* (or *ontil*) for *unto*.

**tillage.** See the 2nd TILL, para 2.

**tiller** of a boat. See TECHNIC, para 18.—(2) a cultivator: from the 2nd TILL.

**tilt** (1), a covering, a tent (both obs), an awning, (in Newfoundland) a log hut: ME *telt*, var of *teld*: OE *teld* or *geteld*: cf OHG *zelt* or *gizelt*, MHG *zelt* or *gezelt*, G *Zelt*, MD *telt*, *telde*, ON *tiald* (*tjald*)—and ON *tjalda*, OE *bcteldan*, to cover; the *ge-* and *be-* are int prefixes.

**tilt** (2); **tilt at windmills.** *Tilt*, to cause to totter or overturn (obs), hence vi (obs), whence to (cause to) slope or shift, derives from ME *tilten*, var *tulten*, to totter, to totter and fall, ult from OE *tealt*, unsteady: cf OE *tealtian*, to be unsteady, *tealtrian*, to totter, akin to ON *tyllast*, to cause to fall (cf Sw *tulta*, Nor *tylta*), and MD-D *touteren* (? for *\*toulteren*), to tremble.

2. To '*tilt* at windmills' or fight an imaginary enemy or evil, derives from an exploit of Don Quixote's: cf QUIXOTIC.

**tilth.** See the 2nd TILL, para 2.

**timbal, timbale.** See TAMBOUR, para 2.

**timber,** n and v (whence the pa -timbered); cf the sep DOMESTIC.

'To *timber*' derives from OE *timbran* (*-ian*), akin to OFris *timbria* (occ eased to *timmeria*), Go *timrjan*, ON *timbra*: and OE *timbran* (*-ian*) derives from OE-E *timber*, wood, a building, akin to OFris *timber*, OS *timber*, a building, a room, Go *timrja*, a builder, OHG *zimbar*, MHG *zimber*, timber, a wooden dwelling (or room), G *Zimmer*, a room, MD *timber*, *timmer*, wood, a building, D *timmer*, a room, ON *timbr*, timber: OGmc words with Sl, L, Gr, Skt cognates in *d*- (see DOMESTIC).

**timbre.** See TYMP, para 2.

**timbrel.** See TYMP, para 3.

**time, timeless, timely.** See TIDE, para 2.

**timid, timidity**—cf **intimidate, intimidation** (whence, anl, **intimidatory); timor** and **timorous.**

*Intimidation* is adopted from EF-F, which forms it, anl, from EF-F *intimider*, from ML *intimidāre*, to strike fear into, pp *intimidātus*, whence 'to intimidate'; ML *intimidāre* (cf LL *intimorātus*, full of fear) derives from L *timidus*, which, like *timor* (adopted by E, but rare), derives from *timēre*, to fear, to be afraid, akin to Gr *déos* (? for *\*deios*, for *\*dweios*), fear, and perh Gr *deinos*, terrible: IE r, *\*duei*, *\*dwei-*, to fear.

2. Whereas L *timor* has derivative LL adj *timorōsus*, whence, via MF *timoreus*, the E *timorous*, L *timidus*—whence late MF-F *timide*, whence E *timid*—has derivative *timiditās*, acc *itmiditātem*, whence late MF-F *timidité*, whence E *timidity*.

---

**timocracy.** See the element *timo-*.

**timorous.** See TIMID, para 2.

**Timothy, timothy.** The latter, elliptical for '*Timothy* grass', derives from *Timothy* Hanson, who, c1720, carried the seed from New York to Carolina (Webster): and *Timothy* derives from MF-F *Timothée*, L *Timotheus*, Gr *Timotheos*, 'God-honouring': Gr *timos*, honour+*theos*, a god, LGr *Theos*, God.

**tin.** See STANNARY, para 1.

**tinct, tinction, tincture.** See STAIN, para 3.

**tinder** (whence **tinderbox** and **tinder fungus**): ME *tinder*: OE *tynder*, var *tyndre*: cf ON *tundr*, OHG *zuntra*, *zuntara*, G *Zunder*: OGmc words that prob derive from the corresp vv—OE *-tendan*, ON *tendra*, Go *tundnan* (vi), *tandjan* (vt), OHG *zundēn*, MHG-G *zünden*, to kindle, MHG *zinden*, to glow.

**tine** (1), a slender, pointed projection, as of a fork or an antler, esp if one of a set, eases ME, from OE, *tind*, akin to the syn ON *tindr* (Sw *tinne*) and MHG *zint*, and prob to OHG *zinna*, MHG-G *zinne*, a pinnacle, a battlement, and to OHG *zinko*, MHG-G *zinke*, a spike: perh (Walshe) related to OHG *zand*, MHG *zant*, later *zan*, G *Zahn*, a tooth (cf TOOTH).

**tine** (2). See TOWN, para 1.

**ting.** See TINK.

**tingle.** See para 1 of:

**tink,** whence the freq **tinkle** (v, hence n), of which **tingle** (v, hence n) is a doublet (imm from 'to *ting*'), with gradual sense-differentiation; hence also **tinker** (from the noise he makes, whence 'to **tinker**'), with var **tinkler** (now E dial and Sc); **ting,** a var of **tink**; **tingtang,** an E dial, and Sc, redup of *ting*: whence prob the E **dingdong**. All these words are echoic; 'to *tink*' derives imm from ME *tinken*.

2. They are related to L *tintinnābulum*, a bell, adopted by E, with anl E adj **tintinnabular**; L *tintinnābulum* (cf the syn LL *tintinnus*) derives from L *tintinnāre*, itself a redup of L *tinnīre*, to jingle, itself clearly echoic. *Tintinnābulum* has derivative *tintinnābulātus*, whence 'to **tintinnabulate**', whence, anl, **tintinnabulation**.

**tinker,** n, hence v. See prec, para 1.

**tinkle,** v, hence n. See TINK, para 1.

**tinny:** adj of *tin*, q.v. at STANNARY, para 1.

**tinsel.** See SCENE, para 7.

**tint.** See STAIN, para 3.

**tintinnabular, tintinnabulation, tintinnabulum.** See TINK, para 2.

**tiny:** ME *tine*: o.o.o.: prob either (OED) C15-early 17 *tine*, little, also, as n, a very little+adj suffix *-y*, or (EW) a shortening of late MF-F tan*tinet*, a little: perh (E.P.) from *tine*, a slender pointed projection that, relatively to that to which it is attached, is small.

**tip** (1), n (point at summit), hence v; **tip,** to tap, hence n; **tip-toe; tip-top; tippet; tipple,** to drink, hence n; **tipster;—top,** summit, hence v (whence **topper** and pa **topping); topsy-turvy; tope,** v; **toupee, toupet; toff**—cf **tuft** (n, hence v), whence **tufted.**

## A *tip* or pointed end

1. *Tip*, a pointed extremity, ME *tip*, is akin to MD-D *tip*, MD var *tep*, MLG *tip*, Da *tip*, Sw *tipp*, and also to MHG-G *zipfel*, dim of *zipf*, itself perh akin to OHG *zapho*, MHG *zapfe*, G *Zapfen*, a tap or bung (Walshe). Cf para 6.

2. *Tiptoe*, esp 'walk on *tiptoe*', is—obviously— the tip of one's toe, esp of all one's toes; *tiptop* is the tip of the top, hence an adj (cf the AE coll *tops*, first-rate).

3. *Tippet*, ME *tipet*, was orig, it seems, a dim of ME *tip*, var *tippe*, a point: cf MHG-G *zipfel* (as in para 1).

4. Akin to *tip*, a point, is 'to *tip*' or strike lightly (prob orig on the *tip*), itself akin to G *tippen*, to tap; hence the cricketing phrase *tip-and-run*, n, whence adj ('*tip-and-run*' raids'); hence also, but much earlier, the sl sense 'to give', whence 'to give (someone) a warning or information', now SE, hence as n (a hint), whence the racing *tipster* (agential *-ster*).

5. Also akin to *tip*, a point, and *tip*, to tap, is 'to *tipple*', perh imm from Nor *tipla*, to tipple: cf dial G *zipfeln*, to eat and drink little but often, from the MHG-G n *zipfel* (as in para 1).

## A *top* or summit

6. ME-E *tip*, a pointed end, is app a thinned derivative of OE-ME-E *top* (predominant OE: *topp*), a summit: cf MD-D *top* (MD var *tob*), top, OFris *topp*, top of a tree, a tuft, OHG-G *zopf*, orig a pointed end, top of a tree, hence a tuft, ON *toppr*, top, tuft (cf Da *top*, Sw *topp*, top, pinnacle).

7. Prob from *top* comes *topsy-turvy*, earlier *topsy-tervy*; app for \**top so tervy*, top so overturned—cf ME *terven*, to roll, and the syn OE *tearflian*.

8. Akin to OE *topp*, OE-E *top*, is OF-MF *top*, tip, summit, of Gmc origin, whence Sp *tope*, tip, summit, whence Sp *topar*, (of a quadruped) to butt with the horns, to strike against, to meet (cf the syn OF *toper*), *topo*, I strike or encounter, whence EF-F *toper*, to cover a stake, esp *tope!* (for *Je tope*, I agree), 'Agreed!': whence E 'to *tope*', prob orig of drinking as acceptance of a bargain or a wager, hence to drink habitually or excessively, whence *toper*.

9. OF *top*, summit, has var *toup*, with OF-F dim *toupet*, a tip, whence a head of hair, esp if false, adopted by E and anglicized as *toupee*.

10. Prob from OHG-G *zopf*, top of tree, a tuft, comes MF *toffe*, *tofe*, *tufe* (EF-F *touffe*): whence ME-E *tuft*, whence the Oxford and Cambridge Universities' sense 'a gold tassel worn by titled students', whence the University sl 'a wearer thereof', with dial var *toft*, whence the eased *toff*, a dandy, hence a fine fellow.

**tip** (2), to overturn, to cause to slant or slope, to tilt, hence also vi, hence also n; whence the freq **tipple** and—influenced by *tipple*—the adj **tipsy** (for \**tippy*); **topple**, to tumble over, pitch head first, to tilt, with sense from the approx syn *tipple* and with form from both *top*, summit, and *tipple*.

'To *tip*' or overturn, incline, tilt, derives from late ME *type*: o.o.o.: prob, however, from ME *tip*, a pointed extremity, from causing either end of an object to become visible.

**tip-and-run.** See the 1st TIP, para 4.

**tippet.** See the 1st TIP, para 3.

**tipple** (1), to drink frequently. See the 1st TIP, para 5.

**tipple** (2), to topple. See the 2nd TIP (heading).

**tipster.** See the 1st TIP, para 4, s.f.

**tipsy.** See the 2nd TIP (heading).

**tiptoe; tiptop.** See the 1st TIP, para 2.

**tirade; tire,** to pull; **retire** (whence **retiral),** **retirement.**

1. *Retirement* is adopted from late MF-F, which forms it from MF-F *retirer*, to draw or pull back, whence E 'to *retire*'.

2. MF-F *retirer* derives from OF-F *tirer*, to pull or draw, whence the obs EE-E 'to *tire*', (esp of a hawk) to pull, tear, seize; cf *tirade*, adopted from EF-F, where the orig sense was 'action of drawing or pulling', from It *tirata*, from It *tirare*, to pull or draw. It *tirare* is, of course, akin to and prob derived from OF-F *tirer*, or perh imm from OProv *tirar*, itself prob from OF *tirer*: and OF *tirer* is perh a shortened derivative from OF-EF *martirer* (OF-MF var *martirier*), to martyrize, hence to torture, ref 'the *drawing* and quartering' of medieval torture, from OF-MF *martire* (E *martyr*), as B & W propose; Dauzat, however, prefers a VL \**tirāre*, to rend, from the OGmc origin of, e.g., E 'to TEAR'; perhaps—a mere guess—OF-F *tirer* is a doublet of OF-F *traire*, in that, ult, it could, via some provincial mutilation, derive from L *trahere*, to pull, to draw.

**tire** (1), apparel (obs), headdress (archaic), esp, with var **tyre**, 'covering' of a vehicular wheel. See ATTIRE, s.f.

**tire** (2), to dress (archaic). See ATTIRE.

**tire** (3), to weary or fatigue, whence the pa **tired** and the pa, vn **tiring**, and the adjj **tireless** and **tiresome**: OE *-tȳrian* or *-tīerian*, *tīoran* or *tēorian*: o.o.o.

**tiro,** or **tyro,** is adopted from ML *tīrō*, *tyrō*, LL *tīrō*, a novice (Eccl): L *tīrō*, a military recruit: o.o.o.: ? ult from, or akin to, *trahere*—'one *drawn* into military service'.

**tisane.** See PESTLE, para 5.

**tissue.** See TECHNIC, para 12.

**tit** (1). See TEAT.

**tit** (2), basically any small quadruped or bird or thing; **titbit; titlark; titmouse; tomtit.**

1. This *tit* is prob, as Webster suggests, orig— among the Scan languages—'a child's word for small animal or thing; cf OW *titlingr* small bird [cf the dial E *titling*], Ice *tittr* titmouse, small plug or pin, Nor dial *tīta* small object': perh the small object was orig *tit*, var pron of TEAT.

2. *Titbit* is a sem duplication: *tit*, something small+*bit*, a small piece; hence, because 'All good things come in small packets' (an E proverb seldom recorded), a small delicacy.

3. *Titlark*, a pipit, merely prefixes *tit* to *lark*.

*Titmouse*, now usu *tit*, is another duplication: ME *titemose, titmase*: *tit*+OE *māse*, a titmouse, akin to OHG *meisa*, MHG-G *meise*, MD *meise, meese, mese*, D *mees*, ON *meisingr*. The f/e *-mouse* prob arises from the bird's nesting in holes.

4. *Tomtit=Tom*, used generically+*tit*; cf *tomcat*.

**Titan, Titanic** (whence **titanic**). The adj *Titanic* derives from Gr *Titanikos*, from Gr *Tītắn*, whence, via L, the E *Titan*. The *Titans* were the primeval deities (whence Zeus and the Olympians) of Ancient Greece; the word derives from Gr *tītŏ́*, sun—a word coming prob from Asia Minor. (Hofmann.) Hence the Chem *titanium* (suffix *-ium*), whence the Min *titanite* (suffix *-ite*).

**titbit.** See the 2nd TIT, para 2.

**tit for tat** is perh a f/c alteration, after the 2nd TIT, of *tip for tap*. (EW.)

**tithe.** See TEN, para 6.

**titillant, titillate, titillation** (whence, anl, **titillative** and **titillator**).

L *titillāre*, to tickle (lit, hence fig), is app a redup of L *titta*, a nipple (cf TEAT). The L presp *titillans*, o/s *titillant-*, yields the E adj, hence n, *titillant*; the pp *titillātus* yields both E 'to *titillate*' (cf OF-F *titiller*) and L *titillātiō*, acc *titillātiōn*em, whence MF-F *titillation*, adopted by E.

**titivate, titivation.** See TIDE, para 4.

**titlark.** See the 2nd TIT, para 3.

**title,** n and v; **titular,** with extn **titulary,** adj, hence n; **titulus; entitle,** whence **entitlement**—cf **intitule; titrate,** whence, anl, **titration; tilde; tittle.**

1. L *titulus*, a written notification, esp one borne, in a triumph, at the end of a staff, or at a funeral, also a notice of sale, whence an inscription, the name of a book, whence, further, renown, glory, and, in LL, official authority or power,—this word is app a redup, perh of a term meaning 'staff' or 'plank': cf OE *thel*, a plank, as E & M suggest; add ON *thil, thili*, OS *thili*, OHG *dil, dili*, a plank.

2. L *titulus* becomes OF-early MF *title* (whence, with *r* for *l*, MF-F *titre*), adopted by E; derivative MF *titler* (whence—after *titre—titrer*) accounts for 'to *title*'. An erudite EF-F derivative from L *titulus* is *titulaire*, whence both E *titular* and, in part, E *titulary*. L *titulus* is retained by erudite E.

3. Perh influenced by OF-MF *title* is ME *titel*, var *titil*, from L *titulus*; whence E *tittle*, a point or other small mark used to indicate pron or emphasis, hence a jot, anything tiny. With the Gram sense of *tittle*, cf *tilde*, the diacritic in Sp *ñ*, for this adoption from Sp likewise comes from L *titulus*.

4. The F *titrer*+the v suffix *-ate* combine to give us the Chem E *titrate*, suggested by the syn meaning of the F v; whence *titration*.

5. L *titulus* has derivative LL *titŭlāre*, to title (a book), with int *intitŭlāre*, whence both 'to *intitule*' (esp a legislative act) and MF *entituler* (F *in-*), whence, influenced by OF-MF *title*, the AF *entitler*, whence 'to *entitle*'.

**titmouse.** See the 2nd TIT, para 3.

**titrate, titration.** See TITLE, para 4.

**titter** (v, hence n): prob from ON *titra*, to

tremble, to shake, cf Nor dial *titra*, to shake with laughter; perh, however, independent and echoic. ON *titra* certainly becomes ME *titeren*, whence both E 'to *teeter*' and the syn dial E *titter*. With ON *titra*, cf OHG *zitarōn*, MHG *zitern*, G *zittern*, to tremble. The redup present in the three OGmc words is 'picturesque': cf the redup in the prob related L *titubāre*, to totter, hence to waver, to hesitate, pp *titubātus*, whence 'to *titubate*'; *titubation* derives from L *titubātiō* (o/s *titubātiōn-*), from *titubāt*us.

**tittle.** See TITLE, para 3.

**tittle-tattle** is a redup of TATTLE.

**titubate, titubation.** See TITTER, s.f.

**titular, titulary.** See TITLE, para 2.

**tmema, tmesis.** See TOME, para 3.

**to; too.** The latter is a doublet of the former: *too* derives from *to* used as adv, esp in sense 'besides'. The prep *to*, OE *tō*, is akin to OFris *tō*, adv, and *to* (varr *te, ti*), prep; OS *tō*, prep; MD-D *te*, prep, and *toe*, adv (*to-* in c/ff); OHG *zō, zuo, zua*, MHG *zuo* (stressed), *ze* (unstressed), G *zu*; and, with *d* instead of *t*, Go *du*, Lith *da*, OB *do*—cf the enclitic Av *-da*, Gr *-de* (*oikade*, homewards), L *-do* (*quando*, when), OL *-du* (*indu*, an int of *in*, in, into). The IE base is app *\*do*, towards, to.

Cf *indigenous* and tat*to*.

**toad,** whence the adj **toady,** whence—prompted by earlier **toadeater**—the n **toady,** a sycophant, whence 'to **toady**'; such obvious cpds as **toadfish** (appearance) and **toadstool** (ditto).—Cf TADPOLE, q.v. at the 1st POLL.

A *toad*, ME *tode*, earlier *tade*, derives from OE *tādie*, var *tādige*: o.o.o.

**toast.** See THIRST, para 5.

**tobacco:** Sp *tabaco* (whence also EF-F *tabac*; C17 var, *tobac*): Taino (Caribbean) *tabaco*, a small roll of tobacco leaves, also a pipe the Antilles Indians used for the inhalation of smoke: perh ult (Webster) from Tupi *tabóca*, a reed. The E form of the word prob owes something to *Tobago*, a West Indian island.—*Tobacconist=tobacco+* euphonic or learnèd f/e *n*+agential *-ist*.

**toboggan:** Can F *tobagan*: of Alg origin—cf Micmac *tobāgun*, a hand-sled made of skins. (Webster.)

**toby** (1), is elliptical for '*Toby* jug': dim of *Tobias*: LL *Tobias*: LGr *Tŏbias* (or *-eias*): H *Tobhīyāh*, whence the var *Tobiah*: 'the Lord, my good'. Why the jug—or, for that matter, the dog *Toby* of Punch-and-Judy shows—was named after the OT son of Tobit, is not precisely known; but, for the jug, cf *jeroboam* and *rehoboam*, and for the dog—well, Tobias did have a favourite dog.

**toby** (2), as in the underworld 'the high *toby*', robbery by highwaymen (mounted), and 'the low *toby*', robbery by footpads, derives from Shelta *tobar*, a road, a metathesis of the syn EIr-Ir *bóthar*, a road: cf Ga *bothar*, a lane. (See esp P¹.)

**toccata.** See TOUCH, para 3.

**Tocharian.** See TOKHARIAN.

**tocsin.** See SIGN, para 8.

**today:** OE *to daege*, at—hence on—(the) day.

toddle. See TOTTER.

toddy slovens Hi *tāṛī*, juice of the palmyra, from *tāṛī*, adj of *tāṛ*, from Skt *tāla*, the palmyra tree.

to-do. See DO, para 2.

toe (n, hence v): ME *too*, var *taa*: OE *tā*, perh short for the var *tahe*: cf OHG *zēha*, MHG *zēhe*, G *Zah*, *Zehe*, OFris *tāne*, MLG *tēn*, *tēne*, and *tē*, *tēwe*, MD-D *teen*, ON *tā*: cf, further off, L *digitus*, finger, toe (E DIGIT); therefore, perh, cf Gr *deiknumi*, I show (E DICT).—Hence such cpds as *toe-hold* and *toenail*.

toff. See the 1st TIP, para 10.

toffee. See TAFFY.

toga. See TECHNIC, para 7.

together. See GATHER, para 2.

toggle, occ toggel, is app a dim from *tog*, obs var of TUG.

togs. See TECHNIC, para 7, s.f.

toil (1), a snare, a net. See TECHNIC, para 19.

toil (2), hard work, and 'to toil', whence toiler and pa, vn toiling. The n *toil* is adopted from AF *toil*, a struggling, a struggle, turmoil, which comes from OF-EF *tooil*, *toeil*, itself from OF-EF *tooillier*, *toeillier*, to stir, to stir up (cf F *touiller*), to roll in the dirt, to struggle, whence the syn ME *toilen* (also to toil), whence 'to *toil*': and OF-EF *tooillier*, *toeillier*, derives from L *tudiculāre*, to pound or crush, from *tudicula*, a small mill for pounding olives, from *tudes*, a mallet, a hammer, a denasalized derivative of *tundere*, to strike, beat, pound.

toilet, toilette. See TECHNIC, para 19.

toils, in the. See TECHNIC, para 19.

Tokay comes from the vineyards of *Tokay* in Hungary.

token. See TEACH, para 1.

Tokharian, often Tocharian, blends the form of Gr Strabo's (B.C.–A.D.) *Tokharoi* (pl), an Asiatic people or tribe, and the sense of Uigur (East Turkic) *Tokhri* or *Tukhri*, the language of the *Tokharians*.

Tokio or Tokyo: Jap *Tōkyō*, Eastern Capital.

tolbooth. See the 1st TOLL (heading).

told: pt of TELL.

Toledo is a (sword-)blade manufactured a *Toledo*, Spain: L *Tolētum*.

tolerable, tolerance, tolerant, tolerate, toleration, tolerator. See para 5 of:

toll (1), a tax, a paid due, whence tollbar, tollbooth, var tolbooth (ME *tolbothe*)—-gate, -house, -keeper, etc.; toll, to take away; thole, to endure; tael and the sep TALENT and ATLAS; extol, whence extolment.—tolerable (whence, anl, tolerability), tolerance or occ tolerancy, tolerant, tolerate, toleration (whence, anl, tolerative), tolerator—cf intolerable (occ intolerancy), intolerant.—Cpds in -*late*: ablation, ablative (adj, hence n), collate, collation, collative, collator; delate, delation, delator; dilatory; sep ELATE, ELATION, etc.; illation, illative; sep LEGISLATIVE, LEGISLATION, etc. (see LEGAL); sep OBLATE, OBLATION, etc.; prelacy, prelate (whence prelatic), prelation; prolate, prolation, prolative; sep RELATE, RELATION,

etc.; sublate, sublation; superlative, adj, hence n; translate, translation, translative, translator.

## Indo-European

1. Whereas the now only hist *toll*, to take away, derives from L *tollere*, to raise, to remove, a *toll* or tax, ME *tol*, derives from OE *tol*, *toll*, var *tolne*: cf OFris *tolen*, *tolene*, *tolne*, OS *tolna*, OHG-MHG *zol*, G *Zoll*, ON *tollr*: and all these OGmc words derive from ML *tolōnēum*, -*īum*, from LL *tolōnēum*, -*īum*, from Gr *tolōneion*, a toll-house or customhouse, from *telōnēs*, a tax-collector, from *telos*, a tax, akin to *tlēnai*, to hold up, to support, to bear, pp *tlētos*, Doric *tlātos*, both 'enduring' and 'having to be endured', whence, in part at least, the OL *tlātus*, L *lātus*, pp of the related L *tollere* and used as the pp of *ferre*, to carry, to bear, to bring, precisely as *tulī* (OL *tatulī*), pret of *tollere*, is used as the pret of *ferre*. With L *tollere* and Gr *tlēnai* (OGr varr *talássai*, *telássai*), cf Skt *tulayāti*, he raises, he weighs, and *tulá̄*, a balance (pair of scales)—Ir *tlenaid*, he removes, W *tlawd*, needy, wretched (having much to endure), and perh Ga *giulain*, to carry, support, endure—Go *thulan*, OS *tholōn*, OHG *dolēn*, MHG *doln*, to endure, the closely related OHG-MHG *dult*, tolerance (G *Geduld*), whence OHG-MHG *dulten*, G *dulden*, to endure, to tolerate, ON *thola*, OE *tholian*, to endure. There are cognates also in Arm and Sl. The IE r is \**tel*-, with var \**tl*-, to raise, to remove, to carry, to support, to endure. (E & M; Hofmann; Walshe.)

2. OE *tholian*, to endure, becomes ME *tholen*, whence 'to *thole*', now archaic when not dial.

3. L *tollere* has the cpd *extollere*, to lift out, to raise high, hence to exalt, whence 'to *extol*'.

4. Before passing to the E -*late*, -*lation*, -*lative* derivatives of L *lātus*, it is as well to dispose of the derivatives of L *tolerāre*, orig (though rarely) to support a weight, hence to endure: app for \**tollerāre*: toll*ere*+-*erāre*; such formations are not unknown—and this one was sem aided by *onerāre*, to load, from *onus*, a load, which prop=*oner*-, o/s of *onus*+-*āre*, not *onus*+-*erāre*. (E & M.)

5. L *tolerāre* has derivative *tolerābilis*, whence MF-F *tolérable*, whence E *tolerable*; the neg L *intolerābilis* becomes MF-F *intolérable*, whence E *intolerable*. The L presp *tolerans*, also adj, with acc *tolerantem*, yields late MF-F *tolérant*, whence E *tolerant*; derivative L *tolerantia* yields late MF-F *tolérance*, whence E *tolerance*. The negg L *intolerans*, o/s *intolerant*-, and *intolerantia* become EF-F *intolérant*, *intolérance*, whence E *intolerant*, *intolerance*. The L pp *tolerātus* generates both 'to tolerate' and L *tolerātiō*, o/s *tolerātiōn*-, whence perh via EF *tolération*, the E *toleration*, and the LL agent *tolerātor*, adopted by E.

## Prefix-Compounds in -late

6. L *tollere*, to raise, to remove, has pp *lātus*, used as the pp of *ferre*, to carry or bear. The cpds of *ferre* have pp in -*lātus*: and here it is convenient to list the E derivatives in -*late* (abstract n -*lation*,

adj *-lative*, agent *-lator*). The sep *-fer* cpds are, of course, to be found elsewhere. The following *-latus* prefix-cpds affect E:

*ablātus*, serving as pp of *auferre* (for \**abferre*), to carry away, with derivatives *ablātiō*, o/s *ablātiōn-*, and *ablatiuus*, ML *-ivus*, whence E *ablation* and *ablative*, lit 'relative to removal';

*collātus*, serving as pp of *conferre*, to bring together, with derivatives *collātiō* (acc *collātiōn*em), LL *collātiuus*, ML *-ivus*, LL *collātor*, whence, resp, 'to *collate*', *collation* (via MF-F *collation*), *collative*, *collator*;

*dēlātus*, serving as pp of *dēferre*, to carry, hence bring, down, with derivatives *dēlātiō*, an accusation, *dēlator*, whence 'to *delate*', *delation* (perh via EF-F *délation*), *delator* (cf EF-F *délateur*);

*dilātus*, serving as pp of *differre*, to delay, with derivative LL *dilātōrius* (prop dilat*us*+adj *-ōrius*), tending to delay, delaying, whence MF-F *dilatoire*, whence E *dilatory*;

*ēlātus*, serving as pp of *efferre*, to carry out: see sep entry at ELATE;

*illātus*, serving as pp of *inferre*, to carry, hence bring, in, with derivatives LL *illātiō*, o/s *illātiōn-*, and LL *illātiuus*, ML *-ivus*, whence E *illation* and *illative*;

see the sep LEGISLATE;

*oblātus*, serving as pp of *offerre*, to bring *ob* or forward, hence to offer:see the sep entry at OBLATE;

*praelātus*, serving as pp of *praeferre*, to carry in front, hence to prefer: see PRELACY;

*prōlātus*, serving as pp of *prōferre*, to bring *prō* or forth, with derivatives *prōlātiō* (o/s *prōlātiōn-*), LL 'pronunciation', and LL *prōlātiuus*, ML *-ivus*, whence E *prolation* and *prolative*;

*relātus*, serving as pp of *referre*, to carry back: see sep RELATE;

*sublātus*, serving as pp of *sufferre* (for \**subferre*), to support, but, in 'to *sublate*' and *sublation* (L *sublātiō*, o/s *sublātiōn-*), taking its sense from *tollere*, to remove;

*superlātus*, both serving as pp of *superferre*, to place over, hence beyond and above, and used also as adj 'excessive', with LL derivative *superlātiuus*, ML *-ivus*, adj and n 'superlative' in Gram, whence, via MF-F (Gram: C16 onwards) *superlatif*, f *superlative*, the E *superlative*;

*translātus*, serving as pp of *transferre*, to carry across, to transfer, with derivatives *translātiō* (acc *translātiōn*em), a transferring, in LL removal to heaven (Eccl) and a version (Grammarians'), LL *translātiuus*, ML *-ivus*, deduced from LL *translātiuue*, figuratively, and LL *translātor*, copyist, translator, whence, resp, 'to *translate*' (both senses), *translation* (perh via late MF-F), *translative*, *translator* (prob via MF *translatour*).

### Non-Latin

7. Besides the sep Gr ATLAS and TALENT, there is *tael*, an Eastern Asiatic weight, a Ch coin: Port and Sp *tael*: Mal *tail*, *tahil*, a measure of weight: prob from Hi *tolā*, a weight, from Skt *tulā*, a weight, a balance (cf para 1 above).

**toll** (2), to remove. See prec, para 1.

**toll** (3), to pull or draw, hence to entice (game), hence also to pull a bell (whence vi): ME *tollen*, var of ME *tullen*, *tillen*, *tyllen*: f.a.e., the 1st TILL.

**tollbar, -booth, -gate, -house**, etc. See the 1st TOLL (heading).

**tolu, toluene, toluic, toluol**. The 1st is adopted from Sp *tolu*, 'balsam of *Tolú*': exported from Santiago de *Tolú*, seaport of Colombia. The others =*tolu*+benzene; *tolu*+adj *-ic*; *tolu*+benz*ol*.

**Tom.** See THOMAS.

**tomahawk** (n, hence *v*)—formerly also *tomhawk* or *tomhog*—is of very widespread Alg origin, with varr, always recognizable, among the tribes.

**tomato, tomatillo**. The latter, adopted from ASp, is the dim of ASp, hence Sp, *tomate*, whence, with the famous Sp suffix *-o*, the E *tomato*; *tomate* eases the Nahuatl *tomatl*.

**tomb, tombal**. See THIGH, para 13.

**tombola**, adopted from It, derives from *tombolare*, to fall head downwards, from the obs. *tombare*, to fall: cf OF-F *tomber* (OF-MF *tumber*): VL \**tumbāre*, to fall: ? echoic. (Dauzat.) Perh cf TUMBLE.

**tomboy; tomcat.** See THOMAS, para 2.

**tome, -tome, -tomy** and **-ectomy** (as in *appendectomy*); **tmema** and **tmesis; anatomical, anatomist, anatomize** (whence **anatomization**), **anatomy; atom** (whence **atomism, atomize**), **atomic** (whence **atomicity**), **atomy; diatom, diatomous; entomic, entomology** (whence **entomological** and **entomologist**); **epitome.**—L: **tonsorial, tonsurate, tonsure;** sep CONTEMPT, where also CONTEMN.—Cf, ult, the TEMPER group.

1. *Tome* comes, via EF-F *tome* and LL *tomus*, from Gr *tomos*, a piece cut out or off, hence part of a book, a volume, with c/f *-tomon*: corresp to Gr *temn*ein, to cut, akin to L *temn*ere, to despise) superseded by the int cpd *contemnere* (E *contemn*, and to MIr *tamnaim*, I hew off, and Lith *timì*, *tinti*, to sharpen by hammering: IE r, \**ten-*, to cut, (Hofmann.)

2. The c/ff *-tome* (dissyllabic) or *-tomy*, a cutting, a section, and *-ectomy* (cf Gr *ektomē*, an excision), occur esp in surgical terms, e.g. *pharyngotomy*, *arteriotomy*, *gastrectomy*. Cf *-tome*, etc., in Elements.

3. Akin to Gr *temn*ein, to cut, are Gr *tmēma* (app for \**temnēma*: suffix *-ēma*), a section, adopted by Bot, and *tmēsis* (app for \**temnēsis*: suffix *-ēsis*), in Gram a cutting by interpolation, as in 'what place soever' (Webster), adopted—via LL—by Gram.

4. Gr exhibits several prefix-cpds that have impinged upon E, as, e.g., *anatemnein*, to cut *ana-* or up, whence *anatomē*, later *anatomia*, adopted by LL, whence MF-F *anatomie*, whence *anatomy*. The derivative Gr adj *anatomikos* becomes LL *anatomicus*, EF-F *anatomique*, E *anatomic*, now usu in extn *anatomical*. Derivative EF-F *anatomiste* and *anatomiser* and F *anatomisme* account for E *anatomist*, *anatomize*, *anatomism*.

5. Gr *atomos* (*a-*, not), uncut, hence undivided,

hence indivisible, hence also n, becomes L *atomus*, MF-F *atome*, E *atom*. The derivative EF-F *atomique* and F *atomisme* and *atomiste* yield E *atomic* (whence *atomical*), *atomism*, *atomist*; *atomize* imitates *anatomize*; and *atomy* results from the f/e false division *an atomy*.

6. Gr *diatemnein*, to cut *dia-* or through, has adj *diatomos* whence both the Bot n *diatom* and the Min adj *diatomous*.

7. Gr *entomos*, cut *en-* or in, hence nearly cut in two, has neu *entomon* used also as n, an insect (sem cf L *insectum*, E *insect*): whence the E *entomic*, of, for, like an insect or insects, and the F *ento-mologie* (*entomo-*, c/f of *entomon*+*-logie*, E *-logy*: cf the element *-loger*), whence E *entomology*.

8. Gr *epitemnein*, to cut *epi-* or upon, hence into, hence to cut short, has derivative *epitomē*, lit a superficial incision and fig an abridgement: whence LL *epitomē*, a summary exposition, EF-F *epitome* (now *épitomé*), adopted by E.

9. Prob akin to Gr *temnein*, to cut, is Gr *tendein*, to gnaw (cut with one's teeth): certainly akin to Gr *tend*ein is L *tond*ēre, LL *tondere*, to shear, hence to shave, pp *tōns*us, whence both *tōnsūra*, a shearing, a shaving, whence MF-F *tonsure*, adopted by E, and *tōnsor*, a shearer, hence a barber, with adj *tōnsōrius*, whence E *tonsorial*.

**tomfoolery** derives, anl, from *tomfool*, orig *Tom Fool*: cf THOMAS, para 2.

**tommy**, a loaf, or a ration, of bread, hence provisions, prob derives from bread distributed on St. *Thomas*'s day. (See esp P.)

**tommyrot**, nonsense, app combines *tommy*, for *Tommy*, dim of *Tom*, pet-form of **Thomas**+*rot* in its sense 'dry rot'.

**tomorrow**. See MORN, para 2.

**tompion**. See TAMP, para 1.

**tomtit**. See the 2nd TIT, para 4.

**tom-tom** is a var of, and now more usual than, *tam-tam*, adopted from Hi: meaning a Chinese gong or similar percussion-instrument, it is clearly echoic.

**ton** (1), the weight 2,240 pounds, whence **tonnage; tonneau; tun; tunnel**, n, hence v.

1. A *ton* comes from ME *tonne*, var of *tunne*, a large cask, whence E *tun*; the modern sense, arising late in C15, derives naturally from the capacity of a very large tun. ME *tunne* comes from OE *tunne*, akin to OFris *tonne*, var of *tunne*, OHG *tunna*, MHG *tunne*, G *Tonne*, MD *tonne*, D *ton*, ON *tunna*: all, either via ML *tunna*, *tonna* (whence OF-F *tonne*), from C, or all, incl C, from ML that is itself o.o.o.; EIr (whence Ga) has *tunna*, a tun, later a ton; the Cor and W *tonnel* or *tonel* are prob loans, via Br, from F.

2. OF-F *tonne* has the OF-F derivative *tonneau*, a cask, whence, in late C19–20, the afterbody of an automobile: adopted by E.

3. OF-F *tonne* has the further derivative *tonnelle*, orig (C14) a cask, hence, very soon, from the shape of a long cask, a longish arbour covered, top and sides, with interlacing branches: whence, via the MF var *tonel*, the late ME *tonel*, EE *tonnel*, whence

E *tunnel*, with the modern sense arising late in C18. (DAF; OED.)

**ton** (2), as in *le bon ton*, often simply *le ton*, the prevailing fashion, answers E *tone* (q.v. at TEND).

**tonal, tonality**. See TEND, para 29.

**tonant**. See THUNDER, para 4.

**tone**. See TEND, para 29.

**tong** (1). See LANGUAGE, para 7.

**tong** (2), an association, a secret society, of Chinese, is the Cantonese *t'ong* (Pekinese *t'ang*), a hall—meetings being held in halls.

**tongs**. See LANGUAGE, para 7.

**tongue**. See LANGUAGE, para 1, s.f.

**tonic**. See TEND, para 29.

**tonite**. See THUNDER, para 4.

**tonitruant, tonitruous**. See THUNDER, para 4.

**tonnage**. See the 1st TON (heading).

**tonneau**. See the 1st TON, para 2.

**tonology**. See the element *-tone* and cf *tone* at TEND, para 29.

**tonsil** is a b/f from *tonsils* (c1600), which comes, via EF *tonsilles*, from L *tōnsillae*, the tonsils, app a dim of *tōlēs* (pl) a goitre: o.o.o.: ? Gaul.—Hence the SciL *tonsillitis*, whence, anl, *tonsillitic*.

**tonsorial, tonsure**. See TOME, para 9.

**tontine**, a collective and eliminatory form of life-insurance, is adopted from F *tontine* (1663): It *tontina* (*la tontina reale*, 1653), elliptical for *pólizza Tontina*: Lorenzo *Tonti*+suffix *-ina*. This Tonti (1630–95) was a Neapolitan banker.

**too**. See TO.

**took**. See TAKE (heading).

**tool** (n, hence v): ME *tool*, earlier *tol*: OE *tōl*: cf ON *tōl* (pl) and OFris *tāwa*, OS *tōian*, Go *taujan*, to make with the hands, to do: OGmc r, **tōu-*, IE r, **dou-*, to make. (Feist.)

**toom**, empty. See the 2nd TEEM, para 2.

**toot** (a horn), v hence n, is echoic: cf MD *tuten*, MD-D *toeten*, G *tuten*, Sw *tuta*: cf also the equally echoic E *hoot*. 'To *toot*' has freq **tootle**.

**toot** (2), to peep. See TOUT.

**tooth** (pl **teeth**), whence **toothsome** (adj *-some*) and **toothy** (adj *-y*) and such cpds as **toothache**, 'fight (with) **tooth and nail**' or grimly, **toothpick**, **toothwort** (from the tooth-like scales on the stem of its root); **tusk** and its var **tush**.—L cognates: **dancetté**—**dent** (a tooth-like notch), **dental, dentary**, **dentate, dentelated, dentelle, denticle** (whence, anl, **denticular**), **denticulate, dentil, dentin** or **dentine**, **dentist** (whence **dentistry**), **dentition, denture**.— Prefix-cpds: **edentate; indent** (n, hence v), **indenta-tion, indention, indenture** (n, hence v); **redan**.—Full cpds: **dandelion; dentifrice; bident** and **trident** (whence **tridental**), **tridentate**.—Gr cognates: **odontic, odontoid**; for **mastodon**, see the element *-odon*.

### Indo-European

1. *Tooth*, ME *tooth*, earlier *toth*, comes from OE *tōth*: cf OFris *tōth*, OS *tand* (id in D), OHG *zand*, MHG *zant* or *zan*, G *Zahn*, MD *tant*, MD-D *tand*, Go *tunthus*, ON *tönn*. The OGmc r is **tanth-*; the

IE *dent-* or *dont-*, perh extnn of *den-*, *don-*, themselves perh for *eden(t)-*, *edon(t)-*, suggesting that teeth are 'eaters', cf L *dēns* (o/s *dent-*); Arm *atamn*: Gr *odōn* (o/s *odont-*), Aeolic pl *edontes*; Lith and OP *dantès*; Cor *dans*, Br and W *dant*, OIr *dét* (denasalized), OC etymon *\*dants*; Skt *dán*, acc *dántam*, gen *datás*.—With the OE pl *tēth*, cf the ON pl *tethr*.

### Germanic

2. Akin to the OGmc words noted above, esp to Go *tunthus*, is OE *tusc*, ME *tusch*, E *tush*, a long tooth, a tusk; OE *tusc* has the var *tux*, ME *tux*, later *tusk*, retained by E. With OE *tusc*, *tux*, cf the OFris *tusch* or *tusk*.

### Latin

3. L *dēns*, acc *dent*em, becomes OF-F *dent*, adopted by E for a tooth-like notch, hence, esp in pl, the projections separating such notches.

4. The foll F derivatives of OF-F *dent* have been either adopted or adapted by E: EF-F, whence E, *dental*; MF *dentele*, little tooth, whence both the EF-F pa *dentelé*, whence, anl, the E *dentel(l)ated*, and the EF-F *dentelle*, lace, adopted by E, and also EF-F *dentelure*, likewise adopted; MF *dentille*, E *dentil*; F *dentiste*, E *dentist*; MF-F *denture*, adopted; the Her F *danché*, whence perh, by suggestion, the Her E *dancetté*.

5. Not from F, but from L (although two via F), come:

*dentary*, F *dentaire*, L *dentārius* (o/s *dent-*+-*ārius*);

*dentate*, L *dentātus*;

*denticle*, L *denticulus*, dim of *dēns*;

*denticulate*, L *denticulātus*, from *denticulus*;

*dentition*, F *dentition*, L *dentitiō*nem, acc of *dentitiō*.

6. Formed from L *dēns*, o/s *dent-*, but not from L derivatives, are:

*dentin*, a notch—imm from E *dent*, a tooth-like notch;

*dentin*, *dentine*, an An term, the 'ivory' of a tooth.

### Latin (and French) Prefix-Compounds

7. L *ēdentāre*, to break (someone's) teeth, to render toothless, has pp *ēdentātus*, whence the E adj *edentate* (cf the OF-F v *édenter*).

8. ML *indentāre*, to make tooth-like notches in, becomes OF-MF *endenter*, ME *endenten*, whence 'to *indent*', hence to sever a document in such a way that the contractual halves will fit together, whence to bind by indenture, etc. The derivative MF *endenteüre*, later *endenture*, is adopted by ME, whence E *indenture*. The ML pp *indentātus* has suggested *indentation*, with contr *indention* (partly from 'to *indent*').

9. From OF-F *dent* comes the EF *redent*, a double—lit an 'again'—notching, hence a term in fortification, later *redan*, adopted by E.

### Latin (and French) Full Compounds

10. OF-F *dent* occurs in the EF-F phrasal n *dent de lion*, lit a lion's tooth, hence a plant with tooth-like taproots: E *dandelion*. But EF-F *dentrifrice*, adopted by E, comes from L *dentifricium*; c/f *denti-*+-*fricium*, (something for) rubbing, from *fricāre*, to rub.

11. L *bidēns*, having two teeth, two-pronged, hence n, o/s *bident-*, yields E *bident*; and L *tridēns*, having three teeth or prongs, hence n, o/s *trident-*, yields MF-F *trident*, adopted by E.

### Greek

12. Gr *odōn*, a tooth, has o/s *odont-*, whence the E adj *odontic*; derivative Gr *odontoeidēs*, tooth-shaped (*eidos*, form, shape) suggests E *odontoid*, tooth-like.

13. Cf the element -*odon*, *odonto-*.

**tootle.** See TOOT.

**top** (1), a summit. See the 1st TIP, para 6.

**top** (2), a child's toy, is id in ME and OE: cf OHG-MHG-dial G *topf*, a top (and prob, from the shape-resemblance, MHG-G *topf*, a pot), and MD *top*, *dop*, a top, and prob MLG *dop*, a hollow, a dish; OProv *topin*, a pot, and OF-MF *topoie*, MF-F *toupie*, a top, derive from OGmc. Walshe relates MHG-G *topf*, a pot, to OHG *tiof*, *tiuf*, MHG-G *tief*, deep: therefore cf DEEP.

**topaz:** ME *topace*: OF-MF *topace*, var of *topase* (F *topaze*): L *topazus*: Gr *topazos* (var *topazion*): *Topazos*, the Gr name of that island in the Red Sea where chrysolites—not unlike topaz—were discovered.

**tope, toper.** See the 1st TIP, para 8.

**topi**, var **topee**, a pith helmet: Hi *ṭopī*, a hat, itself perh (EW) from Port *tope* (var *topo*), summit. Often called a *sola topi*, from Hi *solā*, a shrub with pithy stems used in the making of sun-helmets.

**topia, topiary.** See para 3 of:

**topic**, adj (now always in the extn **topical**, whence **topicality**) and n; **topia, topiary** (whence **topiarist**); cf the element -*tope*, *topo-*, where, e.g., **topography** and **toponomy**.

1. The base is Gr *topos*, a place; IE *\*top-*, the spot one comes from or goes to or strives to reach: perh akin to certain OGmc and Sl words meaning 'to arrive at, attain', and 'to become'. (Hofmann.)

2. Gr *topos* has adj *topikos*, of, in, for a place, whence LL *topicus*, whence E *topic*, whence *topical*. The E n *topic* derives from L *Topica*, trln of Aristotle's *Ta Topika* (neu pl), 'The Common-places': *topikos*, concerning commonplaces: *topoi*, commonplaces, pl of *topos*, a place.

3. Gr *topos*, a place, has the LGr dim *topion*, a small place, pl *topia*, adopted by LL in sense 'ornamental gardens', whence ML *topiārius*, concerning such gardens or landscape-gardening, whence E *topiary*.

**topknot, topless, topman, topmast** (and **top-gallant**), **top-notch:** derivatives of *top*, summit, q.v. at the 1st TIP, para 6.

**topography** (whence **topographical**) and **topo-nomy** (whence **toponymic**). See the element *-tope*.

**topper, topping.** See the 1st TIP (heading).

**topple.** See the 2nd TIP (heading).

**topsy-turvy.** See the 1st TIP, para 7.

**toque; tuque.** The former, adopted from late MF-F, is akin to Sp *toca* and the It *tocca*, var *tocco*: o.o.o. The latter is a Can F form-and-sense adaptation of F *toque*.

**tor.** See TOWER, para 1.

**torch.** See TORT, para 3.

**tore,** n. See TORUS.

**tore,** v. See the 2nd TEAR (heading).

**toreador, torero.** See the 1st STEER, para 3.

**toreutics.** See the element *toreumato-*.

**toric.** See TORUS.

**torment, tormentil, tormentor.** See TORT, para 4.

**torn.** See the 2nd TEAR (heading).

**tornado.** See THUNDER, para 9.

**torose.** See TORUS.

**torpedo.** See para 2 of:

**torpid** (whence **Torpids** and **torpidity**), **torpor** (whence **torporific**), **torpedo; starve, starvation.**

1. *Torpid*, sluggish, numb, derives from L *torpidus*, itself from *torpēre*, to be numb or sluggish: cf the syn Lith *tirpti*, Ru *terpnut*, to become numb, OSl u-*trŭposta*, they became numb. (E & M.)

2. Also from L *torpēre* derive both *torpor*, numbness, sluggishness, whence—perh aided by late MF-F *torpeur*—the E *torpor*, and *torpēdō* (suffix *-ēdō*), numbness, hence the fish known as the crampfish or the electric ray, adopted by Zoo and sense-adapted, from its 'cramping' effects, by E for a weapon that orig, as invented and named, c1806, by Robert Fulton, consisted of a towed or floating mine. (OED.)

3. Perh akin to *torpid* is 'to *starve*' (whence, anl, *starvation*): ME *sterven*, to die, hence, in E, to die from hunger: OE *steorfan*: cf OFris *sterva*, OHG *sterban*, G *sterben*, to die, ON *starf*, labour or toil, Gr *sterphnios*, stiff: sem cf E dial *starve with cold* and sl *stiff*, a corpse. (Walshe.)

**torque.** See TORT, para 3.

**torrefaction, torrefy.** See THIRST, para 6.

**torrent, torrential.** See THIRST, para 3.

**torrid.** See THIRST, para 4.

**torsion.** See TORT, para 2, s.f.

**torso.** See THYRSUS, para 2.

**tort, tortious, tortuous, tortuosity; torment, tormentil, tormentor; torque** and **torch; torsion,** whence, anl, **torsive; tortile; torture** (n, hence v), **turturous;—turd.**—Prefix-cpds: **contort, contortion** (whence, anl, **contortive** and, agentially, **contortionist**); **detorsion; distort, distortion** (whence, anl, **distortive**); **extort, extortion** (whence, anl, **extortionate** and **extortive** and, agentially, **extortionist**); **intorsion, intort; retort** (Chem n), 'to **retort**' (whence the rejoinder **retort**), **retortion.**

1. A *tort* or wrongful act derives from ML-*VL *tortum*, prop the neu of *tortus*, pp of *torquēre* (VL *torquere*), to cause to turn, to twist, hence to torture (physically); the s *torq-* derives, by metathesis, from an IE *trokw-*.

2. Whereas *tortious* derives, anl, from E *tort*, *tortuous* derives, via OF-F *tortueux*, f *tortueuse*, from L *tortuōsus*, from *tortus* (gen *tortūs*), a twisting, from the pp *tortus*, whence also the LL *tortūra*, whence MF-F *torture*, adopted by E; derivative late MF-F *torturer* perh suggested 'to *torture*', and derivative MF *tortureus* became AF *torturous*, adopted by E; *tortuosity* comes from LL *tortuōsitās* (from *tortuōsus*). The L pp *tortus* has two further simple derivatives affecting E: *tortilis*, twisted, twistable, whence E *tortile*, and LL *tortiō*, with var *torsiō*, o/s *torsiōn-*, whence E *torsion*.

3. Akin to L *torquēre* is L *torquēs*, a twisted collar or necklace or chain, whence E *torque*. L *torquēs* has var *torquis*, whence VL *torqua*, var *torca*, whence OF-F *torche*, orig syn with L, hence MF-F *torche*, a flaming light, whence E *torch*. (See esp B & W.)

4. Also akin to L *torquēre* is L *tormentum* (? an easing of *torqmentum* or a contr of *tortimentum*), an instrument of torture (hence torture itself), a missile-throwing engine: whence OF-MF *torment*, OF-F *tourment*, ME *tourment, torment*, E *torment*. Derivative OF-F *to(u)rmenter* yields 'to *torment*'. L *tormentum*, torture, severe pain, has the ML dim derivative *tormentilla*, a plant supposed to allay toothache, MF-F *tormentille*, E *tormentil*. Derivative OF-MF *tormenteor, tormentere*, an official torturer, prob contributed to E *tormentor*.

5. A less easily recognizable simple E derivative from L *torquēre* is the now vulgar *turd*, which, deriving from OE *tord*, is related to OF-F *tordre*, to twist, which comes, via VL *torcere*, from L *torquēre*.

### Prefix-Compounds from Latin

6. Of the numerous L prefix-cpds of *torquēre*, refoll affect extant E: *con-, dē-, dis-, ex-, in-,* the *torquēre*.

7. L *contorquēre*, to twist together or strongly, has pp *contortus*, whence 'to *contort*'; derivative L *contortiō*, o/s *contortiōn-*, yields *contortion* (cf MF-F *contorsion*).

8. Whereas *dētorquēre*, to twist aside, has suggested the Med *detorsion*, L *distorquēre*, pp *distortus*, has yielded 'to *distort*'; derivative LL *distortiō*, o/s *distortiōn-*, accounts for *distortion* (cf EF-F *distorsion*).

9. L *extorquēre*, to twist out of or from, has pp *extortus*, whence 'to *extort*'; derivative LL *extortiō*, o/s *extortiōn-*, yields *extortion* (cf MF-F *extorsion*).

10. L *intorquēre*, to twist in or into, has pp *intortus* and derivative *intortiō*, o/s *intortiōn-*, whence 'to *intort*' and *intortion*.

11. L *retorquēre*, to twist (or bend) back or backwards, has pp *retortus*, whence 'to *retort*'; the sense 'to return (an argument)' exists already in L. The Chem n *retort* comes, via EF-F *retorte*, from ML *retorta*, prop the f of pp *retortus*. From ML *retortiō*, o/s *retortiōn-*, derives *retortion* (cf F *rétorsion*).

**tortile.** See prec, para 2.

**tortious.** See TORT, para 2.

**tortoise; turtle.** The latter is naut f/e—after *turtle*dove—for F *tortue*, itself from OProv *tortuga*, alteration—after *tort*, something twisted (a wrong), the tortoise having 'twisted' feet—of OProv *tartuga* (cf It and Port *tartaruga*): LL *tartarūca*, beast of Tartarus: corruption of LL *tartarūchus*, of Tartarus: LGr *tartaroukhos*, irreg formed from *Tartaros*, the lower world (cf TAROT, para 2). The tortoise 'was taken to symbolize heretics' (B & W).

**tortuosity, tortuous.** See TORT, para 2.

**torture, torturous.** See TORT, para 2.

**torus, tore, toric, torose; torulus,** whence SciL **torula,** whence **torulosis.** The L *torus*, a swelling, protuberance, elevation, knot, in Arch a convex moulding, the fat or brawny part of an animal body, is o.o.o.: ? akin to Gr *tornos*, a circle, anything round. The L *torus* becomes EF-F *tore* (Arch), adopted by E; whence the adjj *toric* and *toroid*. The adj *torose*, however, derives from L *torōsus*, from *torus*, whence also the dim *torulus*, whence, in turn, the Sci adj *torulose*.

**Tory,** orig an evicted Irishman turned highwayman (the political sense arising only in the late 1670's), derives from the Ir *tōruidhe*, lit a pursuer but used for a robber, a 'wanted' man: cf OIr *toracht*, pursuit. In those two Ir words, the base is *tōr-*: cf EIr *tōir*, pursuit, a body of troops, and Ga *tōir*, pursuit, a band of pursuers.

**tosh,** nonsense, is o.o.o.: ? a *t*-for-*b* alteration of BOSH.

**toss** (v, hence n): o.o.o.: cf Nor dial *tossa*, to scatter: perh an *s*-less var of the *stoss*- in G *stossen*, MHG *stōzen*, OHG *stōzan*, Go *stautan*, to push.

**tot** (1), a small thing (e.g., drink) or a little child: o.o.o.: prob cf Da *tommeltot*, Sw *tutte*, a little child, ON *tuttr*, a dwarf, OHG *tutta, tuta*, a nipple, and Gr *tutthos* (τυτθός), small, still very young. (Holthausen; Hofmann.)

**tot** (2). See heading of:

**total** (adj, hence n, whence v), whence, by shortening, **tot**, a total, (coll) an exercise in totalling, whence the coll 'to tot up'; **totality,** whence **totalitarian; totalize,** whence **totalizator,** whence the coll **to•te; teetotal,** whence **teetotaller** and **teetotalism; teetotum** and **factotum.**

1. The adj *total* is adopted from MF-F, which derives it from ML *tōtālis*, an *-ālis* extn of L *tōt*us, whole, all (no part omitted): o.o.o.: perh (E & M) akin to the r *tot*- of Umbrian *tota* (acc), Oscan *toute* (nom), a city, a city-state, OIr *tūath*, Go *thiuda*, a people, a nation.

2. ML *tōtāl*is has derivative *tōtālitās*, acc *tōtālitā*tem, whence MF-F *totalité*, whence E *totality*.

3. MF-F *total* has derivatives *totaliser, totalisation, totalisateur*: cf the earlier E 'to *totalize*' and *totalization* and the from-F-derivative *totalizator* (or *-isator*).

4. E *teetotal*=*t-total*, with redup-int *t*-; adj, hence n, esp one who entirely abstains from strong drink. And *teetotum*=*t-totum*, where *t*- represents *T*, for L *totum*, all, the all, prop the neu

of the adj *tōtus* and implying, orig (in games of chance), 'Take *all* the stakes'; the sem transition to *teetotum*, a child's top, finger twirled, is not entirely clear.

5. With *teetotum*, cf *factotum*, adopted from ML: from L *fac tōtum*, Do everything! Hence *Johannes factotum*, an eruditely punning 'translation' of *Jack*-of-*all*-trades.

**tote** (1), a totalizator. See prec (heading).

**tote** (2), to carry, esp on one's person: coll (AE), very general: o.o.o.: app of West Afr origin—cf *tota, tuta*, to pick up, to carry, in the native diall of Angola and the Belgian Congo. (Mathews.)

**totem** is an Alg word—cf the Cree *ototema* and the Ojibway and Chippeway *ototeman*, his relations; the s is *ote*-. (Mathews.)

**tother**=*t'other*=*the other*: cf OTHER.

**totter; tottle; totty.** 'To *totter*' derives from ME *toteren*, o.o.o.: perh akin to TITTER; perh to OE *tealtrian*, E dial *tolter*, to hobble. 'To *tottle*' is app a freq of 'to *totter*'; and *totty*, ME *toty*, shaky, app derives from 'to *totter*'.

**toucan,** adopted from EF-F, comes—through Sp *tucan* or perh rather Port *tucano*—from Tupi *tucano, tucan*. (Tupi is a Brazilian native language.)

**touch,** n (whence **touchy**) and v (whence the pa **touching**), and **retouch** (whence the vn **retouching**); whence many cpds, all sufficiently obvious;—**toccata**—**tuck,** to beat (a drum), whence n 'fanfare' and **tucket;** sep TOCSIN, q.v. at SIGN, para 8.

1. The n *touch* derives from MF-F *touche*, itself from the OF-MF v *tochier*, var *tuchier*, MF *touchier* (EF-F *toucher*), whence 'to *touch*': and OF *tochier* derives from VL *toccāre*, to strike (a gong, a bell, etc.), from *toc*, a purely echoic word (cf a clock's tick-*tock*).

2. OF *tochier* or *tuchier* has the MF derivative *retochier, retuchier*, to touch *re*- or again, EF-F *retoucher*, whence 'to *retouch*'.

3. VL *toccāre* becomes It *toccare*, with pp *toccato*, whence the n *toccata*, adopted as a Mus term.

4. OF *tochier* has the ONF form *toquer*, whence the now mostly Sc *tuck*, to beat, to sound (a drum); *tucket*, a fanfare of trumpets, app blends 'to *tuck*' and *toccata*.

**tough** (adj, hence n), whence **toughen** and **toughness,** derives from ME *tough*: OE *tōh*: cf MD *taye, tay, taey* (D *taai*), Eastern MD *tege*—cf LG *tage, tau, taa*—and OHG *zāhi*, MHG *zaehe*, G *Zäh*: cf also OE *getenge* (nasalized form), oppressive, and OHG *zangar*, sharp, biting. (Walshe.)

With the n *tough*, sem cf the syn n *rough*.

**toupee** and **toupet.** See the 1st TIP, para 9.

**tour.** See TURN, para 7.

**tourbillion, tourbillon.** See TURBID, para 2, s.f.

**tourist.** See TURN, para 7.

**tourmaline** (var **tur-**) is adopted from F (early var *tourmalin*), which thus adapts the Singhalese *tormalli*, carnelian.

**tournament** and **tourney.** See TURN, para 8

tourniquet. See TURN, para 9.

touse, touser, tousle. See TEASE, paras 3 and 4 and heading.

tout, to peer, hence, orig in the underworld, to keep watch, comes from ME *tuten*, to peep or peer, from OE *tȳtan*, to peep out, itself prob akin to OE *tōtian*, to project, (? also) to peep out, whence the now dial *toot*, to sprout, to spy: cf MD *tote*, *toot*, D *tuit*, a spout, a nozzle, a snout. An obscure group.

2. Hence the n *tout*, orig one who keeps watch, hence a spy, now esp for a bookmaker.

tow (1), the coarse part of flax or hemp: ME *tow*; OE *tow* (in cpds), a spinning or a weaving: cf the 2nd TAW, ON *tō*, a tuft of wool (in spinning), MD *tou*, *touw*, *touwe*, tow.

tow (2), a rope: OE *tohlīne*, with cognates in OGmc: akin to next.

tow (3), to pull along: ME *towen*: OE *togian*, to drag or pull: cf OFris *togia*, to pull about, ON *toga*, OHG *zogōn*, to pull or drag, and the intimately related group formed by OE *tēon*, OHG *ziohan*, MHG-G *ziehen*, Go *tiuhan*, to pull or draw: cf, further off, L *dūcere*, to lead (q.v. at DUKE).—Hence the n, as in 'a ship *in tow*'.

2. *Tug*, n, derives from 'to *tug*' or pull hard at: ME *tuggen*, var of *toggen*, an int derivative from OE *togian*, to pull.

3. Akin to the vv *tug* and *tow* is 'to *tuck*', to tug away or off, to pluck, hence to pull up in a fold: ME *tuken*, to tug, also to reprimand: OE *tūcian*, to harass, to ill-treat, akin to OHG *zucchēn*, MHG-G *zucken*, to jerk or shake or tug, int of OHG *ziohan*, MHG-G *ziehen*, and MD *tucken*, *tocken*, to tug. (Walshe.)

4. A *tie*, band, bond—cf OE *tēh*, contr of *tēah*, var *tēag*—derives from 'to *tie*': ME *tien*, var *teyen*: OE *tigan*, itself from *tēah*, *tēag*, a rope: cf ON *taug*, a rope, and the OGmc words noted in para 1. The n *tie* has var *tye*, obs except as a nau*t* and mining term.

5. Akin to all those Gmc words is E *toy*, perh adopted from MD *toy*, *tooy*, D *tuig*, gear, a gadget —cf esp D speel*tuig*, playthings (lit 'play-gear'); cf OHG-MHG *geziuc*, G *Zeug*, an instrument, a gadget, and the syn ON *tȳge* and OE ge*tēoh*. (Walshe.)

6. The adj *wanton*—whence both n and v— ill-bred, badly educated, untrained, hence undisciplined, hence very—whence excessively—gay, derives from ME *wanton*, var of *wantoun*, a slovening of *wantowen*: wan- (cf WANE), wanting in, (hence) not+the pa *towen*, brought up, educated, from OE *togen*, pp of *tēon* (cf para 1): cf the archaic *wanhope*.

7. Cf the sep TAUT and the sep TEAM.

toward, towards. See VERSE, para 3.

towel: ME *towele*, earlier *towaille*: OF-MF *toaille* (archaic F *touaille*), a cloth used for wiping or drying: Western Gmc *\*thwahlja*, deduced from OHG *dwahila*, MHG *twehele*, G *Zwehle*, MD *dwale*, *dwael*, *dwele*, a towel (D *dwaal*, an altarcloth), OE *thwēal*, a washing, and the OGmc

words for 'to wash (oneself)'—cf OP *twaxtan*, a bathing-apron. (B & W; Walshe.)

tower, n, hence v (whence the pa towering); tor; turret.—Tyrrhenian; Tuscan, Tuscany; Etruscan, Etruria.

1. Whereas *tor* comes from OE *torr*, either akin to or more prob deriving from L *turris*, a lofty palace or fortified place, esp a tower, *turret* comes, via ME *turet*, varr *toret* and *touret*, from MF *turet*, *touret*, *toret*, dim of OF *tor*, *tour* (extant), varr of OF-MF *tur*, from L *turris*; *tower*, as shown by the ME varr *towr*, *tour*, *tor*, represents OE *tor* as influenced by MF-F *tour*.

2. L *turris* is akin to—prob derived from—Gr *turrhis*, var *tursis*, which itself app comes, perh via the Etruscans, from either the Aegean or Asia Minor: and is therefore related to L *Tyrrhēni*, Gr *Turrhēnoi*, var *Tursēnoi*, the Etruscans (? 'The Tower-Builders'), and to the derivative adj Gr *Turrhēnos*, L *Tyrrhēnus*, whence E *Tyrrhenian*, as in 'the *Tyrrhenian* Sea'.

3. Related to Gr *Turrhēnoi*, L *Tyrrhēni*, the Etruscans, is the Gr *Etrouria*, L *Etrūria*, land of the Etruscans, with adj *Etruscus*, whence E *Etruscan* (adj, hence n: cf F *Etrusque*); and very closely linked to L *Etruscus* is L *Tuscus*, an Etruscan, with adj *Tuscānus*, whence E *Tuscan* (adj, hence n); derivative L *Tuscānia* yields E *Tuscany*.

4. The entire ancient history of all these words, esp of their interconnexions, is obscure. It does, however, seem probable that the r is \**tur*-, with s *turrh*- or *turs*- (*rh-s* is a frequent IE alternation); and that there were the metatheses \**trur(rh)*- and \**trus*- (with eased var \**tuskh*-), which underwent vocalic extnn \**etrur*- and \**etrusc*-.

town (whence townee, townish, towny)—township—townsman; tine, to enclose; dun, a fort.

1. The now dial *tine*, to shut or enclose, derives from OE *tȳnan*, from *tūn*, an enclosure, a hedge or a fence, a manor, a settlement, a village, a town, whence, via ME *tun*, later *toun*, the E *town*: and OE *tūn* is akin to OFris and OS *tūn*, a hedge, a courtyard, OHG-MHG *zūn*, G *Zaun*, a fence, ON *tūn*, an enclosure, a homestead, a manor; also to OIr *dūn*, a citadel, whence E *dun* or *doon*, a fortified homestead—cf Ga *dūn*, W *dīn*, Cor *dīn* and *tīn*, and the Celticized L *-dūnum* in PlNn (e.g., *Lugdūnum*, Lyons); perh also to the *dun-*, *tun-*, of Hit *tunak(k)essar*, holy place in a temple.

2. OE *tūn* has two cpds extant in E: *tūnscipe*, orig the inhabitants of a *tūn*, whence *township*, and *tūnesmann*, a single inhabitant, whence *townsman*.

towser. See TEASE (heading; cf para 3).

toxic, whence toxicity and, anl, toxin, var toxine (Chem suffix *-in*, *-ine*); toxicant, toxication; cf the element *toxi-*, *toxo-*, where, in para 2, find toxicology, toxiphobia, toxophilite (-phily); intoxicant (adj, hence n), intoxicate (adj and v), intoxication (whence, anl, intoxicative).

1. *Toxic*, adj hence n, derives—perh via OF-F *toxique*—from ML *toxicus*, adj, from L *toxicum*, a poison, trln of Gr *toxikon* (*pharmakon*), lit

arrow-poison, from *toxikos*, adj of *toxon*, a bow (weapon), an arrow, from Scythian *\*takhsha-*, a bow (Hofmann): ? akin to Sumerian *tuk*ul, a weapon.

2. L *toxicum*, a poison, has the LL derivative *toxicāre*, to smear with poison, presp *toxicans*, o/s *toxicant-*, whence E *toxicant*, poisonous, and pp *toxicātus*, whence ML *toxicātiō*, a poisoning, o/s *toxicātiōn-*, whence E *toxication*.

3. LL *toxicāre* acquires, in ML, the prefix-cpd *intoxicāre* (int *in-*), to poison, hence to drug, with presp *intoxicans*, o/s *intoxicant-*, whence E *intoxicant*, causing drunkenness, and pp *intoxicātus*, whence the late ME adj and v *intoxicate*, poisoned, drugged, to poison or drug, whence, in EE, the modern sense. ML *intoxicāre* becomes late MF-F *intoxiquer*, whence, anl (after ML *toxicātiō*), the late MF-F *intoxication*, adopted by EE, orig a poisoning, then (C17) in modern senses.

**toxicology.** See the element *toxi-*, para 2.

**toxophilite, toxophily.** See the element *toxi-*, *toxo-*, para 2.

**toy.** See the 3rd TOW, para 5.

**trabal, trabeated, trabecular.** See TAVERN, para 3.

**trace** (n and v), **tracery, traces.** See TRACT, para 2.

**trachea, tracheotomy, trachyte.** See the element *tracheo-*.

**track,** n (whence **tracklayer, trackless, trackway**) and v (whence **tracker** and **tracking**); '**to track**' or **tow**—cf **trek** (n, v) and **trigger.**

1. 'To *track*', or follow the traces of, derives from the n *track*, a mark left by a moving person or animal: MF *trac*, trace of a quadruped: prob of OGmc origin and akin to DRAW (f.a.e.).

2. E *track*, a trace, a path, has influenced the form of E *track*, to draw (e.g., a ship) along, which derives from MD *trecken*, D *trekken*, to draw (along), whence 'to *trek*' (occ *treck*); the derivative D n *trek* is adopted by E.

3. MD *trecken* has derivative agent-instrument *trecker*, var *treker* (D *trekker*): whence EE *tricker*, E *trigger*.

**tract, tractability, tractable, tractate, a** treatise (whence **tract**, a religious pamphlet, whence **tractarian**), **tractator, tractile, traction, tractor, tractrix; trait**—cf **trace**, n and v (whence **traceable, tracer, tracery**)—cf **traces** (in harness) and **retrace; trail** (v, hence n), whence **trailer** and **trailing**—cf **trawl**, v (hence n), whence **trawler** and **trawling; train,** n and v (whence **trained band**, now **trainband**— **trainer**—pa, vn **training**)—cf **entrain; treat** (v, hence n), **treatable, treatise, treatment, treaty; maltreat**, whence **maltreatment.**—Prefix-cpds in *-tract*, *-traction*, *-tractive*, *-tractor*, and in such F derivatives as *-trait*, *-tray*, *-treat*: **abstract** (adj, n, v), **abstraction** (whence, anl, **abstractive**); **attract, attraction, attractive; contract** (n, v), **contractile, contractility, contraction, contractor, contractual, contracture** cf **contrectation; detract, detraction, detractive, detractor, detractory; distract** (adj, v), **distraction** (whence, anl, **distractive**); **extract** (n, v),

**extraction, extractive, extractor**—cf **estreat,** n, hence v; **intractable, intractile**—cf **entreat**, whence **entreatment** and **entreaty; protract** (whence **protractile** and **protractor**) and **protraction**—cf **portrait** (whence **portraitist**), **portraiture, portray** (whence **portrayal**); **retract, retractation, retractile, retraction** (whence, anl, **retractive**), **retractor**—cf **retreat** (n, hence v), whence, anl, **retreative; subtract, subtraction** (whence, anl, **subtractive**).

1. All these words are either simples or prefix-cpds of either L *trahere*, to draw (along), pp *tractus*, or of its freq-int *tractāre*, to draw violently or long or effortfully, hence, prob from the tracing of furrows, to work, to work hard at, hence to handle (a person) or treat (a subject), pp *tractātus*. L *trahere* is o.o.o.: but prob akin to DRAW.

### Simples from L *trahere*

2. The pp *tractus* has, directly and indirectly, a number of derivatives. The derivative n *tractus* (gen *-ūs*), the action of drawing (along), hence a continuous march, a drawn stroke, hence a delimitation by marches or by strokes, hence the area delimited, a region, district, quarter: whence E *tract* of land. But L *tractus* also becomes OF-F *trait*, an act of drawing (various senses), a stroke in the delineation of character, hence a personal characteristic, adopted by E. The OF-MF pl *traiz* or *trais* becomes ME *trays*, pl, whence E *traces* in harness, whence the b/f sing *trace*. But a *trace* or path, whence, via the pl, a track, comes into ME from MF-EF *trace*, var *trac*, itself from OF-MF *tracier* (EF-F *tracer*), whence ME *tracen*, E 'to *trace*': and OF-MF *tracier* derives, via VL *\*tractiāre*, from the L n *tractus*. Derivative MF *retracier*, EF-F *retracer*, produces 'to *retrace*'.

3. From the r *trah-* (? *\*tragh-*) of *trahere* comes L *tragula*, a dragnet, also a kind of sledge, whence VL *\*tragulāre*, to drag or draw along, to tow, whence MF *trailler*, ME *trailen*, E 'to *trail*', orig to drag, whence, prob (by dial var), 'to *trawl*'.

4. Also from *trah-*, *\*tragh-*, comes VL *\*tragināre*, to draw or drag along, whence OF-MF *trahiner, traïner* (F *traîner*), whence ME *traynen, trainen*, whence 'to *train*', with var senses developing as in—and mostly in imitation of—F. The derivative OF-MF *trahin, traïn* (F *train*), and the gradually differentiated OF-MF *traïne* (F *traine*), yield—sometimes by confusion—the E n *train*. The derivative OF-MF *entraïner* (EF-F *entraîner*) leads to E *entrain*.

5. The L pp *tractus* has the ML derivative *tractiō*, the action of drawing, or state of being drawn, along, acc *tractiōn*em, whence EF-F *traction*, adopted by E, whence, anl, the SciL *tractor* (cf the F *tracteur*), become general, and the anl SciL *tractrix* (Geom). E *tractile*=L *tract*us (pp)+*-ile*, anl with so many other such adjj.

### Simples from L *tractāre*

6. The int-freq *tractāre*—see para 1—has derivative adj *tractābilis*, manageable, whence *tractābilitās* o/s *tractābilitāt-*, with eng *intractābilis*:

whence, resp, E *tractable, tractability*, and *intractable*, whence, anl, *intractability*; OF-MF *tractable* and MF-EF *intractable* perh intervened.

7. L *tractāre* has pp *tractāt*us, whence the n *tractātus* (gen *-ūs*), a handling, hence a treatise, whence E *tractate*, whence, with sense rapidly narrowing, the shortened *tract* or pamphlet; whence, anl, *tractarian*, whence *Tractarian*, one of the authors of the famous *Tracts for the Times* (1833–41). From the pp *tractāt*us comes also *tractātor*, a masseur, LL a commentator, a homilist, adopted by erudite E.

8. L *tractāre* becomes OF-MF *traitier* (MF-F *traiter*), var *tretier*, whence ME *treten*, whence 'to *treat*'; derivative MF-F *traitement* prob suggested E *treatment*. *Treatable* derives, via ME *tretable*, from OF-F *traitable*; *treatise*, ME *tretis*, from AF *tretis*, itself either from a lost derivative of OF-MF *tretier* or from OF-MF *traitis* (or *-iz*), well made, from the syn VL *tractīcius* (cf LL *Tractīcius*, nickname of Heliogabalus, whose corpse was *dragged* through the streets: Souter), from *tractus*, pp of *trahere*; *treaty*, a treatise, ME *tretee*, from MF-F *traité*, a treatise, from the L n *tractātus*, but *treaty*, a negotiation, a pact, from MF-F *traité*, an agreement, from OF-MF *traitier*.

9. OF-MF *traitier*, MF-F *traiter*, has the EF-F cpd *maltraiter*, whence 'to *maltreat*'.

Prefix-Compounds from L *trahere* and *tractāre*

10. L *abstrahere*, to remove—*abs*, for *ab*, away from—by pulling, has pp *abstractus*, used also as LL adj 'incorporeal', whence both the adj (hence n) and the v *abstract*; derivative L *abstractiō*, a removal, LL an abduction, acc *abstractiō*nem, becomes MF-F *abstraction*, adopted by E; and derivative L *abstractor* is also adopted, with mdfn *abstracter*.

11. L *attrahere*, to draw *ad* or towards, has pp *attractus*, whence 'to *attract*'; the LL derivatives *attractiō* (acc *attractiō*nem) and *attractiuus* (ML *-ivus*) become MF-F *attraction*, adopted by E, and MF-F *attractif*, f *-ive*, whence E *attractive*.

12. L *contrahere*, to draw *con-* or together, has pp *contractus*, whence—cf the syn F *contracter*—'to *contract*' or reduce the volume of; 'to *contract*' or enter into an agreement with (someone) or about or for (something) derives from the syn MF-F *contracter*, itself from L *contractus* (gen *-ūs*), from the pp. A *contract* or agreement likewise comes from L n *contractus*—via MF *contract* (EF-F *contrat*). The L pp *contractus* has derivative *contractiō*, acc *contractiō*nem, whence MF-F *contraction*, adopted by E; the learnèd F derivative *contractile*, whence *contractilité*—whence E *contractile* and *contractility*; the LL derivative LL *contractor*, one who undertakes an obligation, is adopted by E, and L *contractūra* becomes EF-F *contracture*, adopted by E. *Contractual* adapts EF-F *contractuel*, formed from the L n *contractus*, an agreement. With *contraction*, cf *contrectation*, from *contrectātiō*n-, o/s of LL *contrectātiō*, a handling, from *contrectāt*us, pp of *contrectāre*, var

of *contractāre*, to enter into contact with: *con-*, with+*tractāre*, to handle.

13. L *dētrahere*, to draw or pull *dē-* or down, to take away, to take away from, has pp *dētractus*, whence 'to *detract*'; derivative L *dētractiō* (acc *dētractiō*nem), LL a slandering, and L *dētractor* yield OF-EF *detraction* and MF *detracteur* (EF-F *dé-*), whence E *detraction* and—prob via AF *detractour*—E *detractor*; derivative LL *dētractōrius* accounts for *detractory*, and MF *detractif* (anl from *detraction*) for *detractive*.

14. L *distrahere*, to draw or pull *dis-* or apart, hence fig, has pp *distractus*, whence the E adj (obsol) and v *distract*; derivative L *distractiō*, acc *distractiō*nem, yields MF-F *distraction*, adopted by E.

15. L *extrahere*, to draw or pull *ex* or out, has pp *extractus*, whence the adj (hence n) and v *extract*; derivative LL *extractiō*, acc *extractiō*nem, yields OF-MF *estration*, MF-F *extraction*, adopted by E, whence—perh aided by EF-F *extractif*—*extractive* and, again anl, *extractor*.

16. L *extrahere* has the VL var *\*extragere*, whence OF-MF *estraire* (whence, by reshaping, the late MF-F *extraire*), with pp *estrait*, whence the MF n *estraite*, whence E *estreat*.

17. Whereas E *intractile*=L *in-*, not+*tractile*, *intreat* is the anglicized var of 'to *entreat*', which derives, through ME *entreten*, to treat, to request rather than to beg, from MF *entraiter*; *en-*, L *in-*, used int+*traiter*: ult suggested by L *intrahere*. Hence, anl, *entreatment* (archaic) and *entreaty* (var *in-*).

18. L *prōtrahere*, to draw or pull *prō*, forward or forth, has pp *prōtractus*, whence 'to *protract*'; derivative LL *prōtractiō*, o/s *prōtractiō*n-, yields *protraction*.

19. L *prōtrahere* becomes, by metathesis of *prō-*, OF-EF *portraire*, var *pourtraire*, to design or draw, whence ME *portraien* and *pourtraien*, whence 'to *portray*' and the obsol 'to *pourtray*'; derivative OF-F *portrait* and late OF-EF *portraiture* are adopted by E.

20. L *retrahere*, to draw or pull *re-* or back, to take back, has pp *retractus*, whence 'to *retract*' in its orig lit sense; 'to *retract*' or withdraw (an accusation), however, derives from MF-F *rétracter*, itself from L *retractāre*, to handle (*tractāre*) again, hence, in LL, to reconsider, hence to withdraw an accusation. Whereas E *retraction* derives, like EF-F *rétraction*, from L *retractiō* (o/s *retractiō*n-), from the pp *retractus*, E *retractation* derives from MF-F *rétractation*, from L *retractātiō*nem, acc of *retractātiō*, from *retractāt*us, pp of *retractāre*; and whereas E *retractile* is prob adopted from F (an erudite formation: from the L pp *retractus*), E *retractor* adopts the sense of SciL *retractor* and the form of LL *retractor*, one who takes away.

21. L *retrahere* becomes OF-MF *retraire*, pp *retrait*, var *retret*, both used also as n, with doublet *retraite*, whence the E n *retreat*, an act of retiring, a place whither to retire (whence the religious sense); hence 'to *retreat*'.

22. L *subtrahere*, to draw or pull *sub-*, from under, has pp *subtractus*, whence 'to *subtract*'; derivative LL *subtractiō* (o/s *subtractiōn-*), a withdrawal, esp in arithmetic, yields *subtraction*; cf the Math *subtrahend*, from LL *subtrahendus*, that is to be subtracted.

tractability, tractable. See prec, para 6.

tractarian—Tractarian. See TRACT, para 7.

tractate, tractator. See TRACT, para 7.

tractile, traction, tractor, tractrix. See TRACT, para 5.

trade, trader, tradesman; -union, -wind. See TREAD, para 3.

tradition, traditional (whence traditionalism and traditionalist and, anl, traditionary); traditor—cf traitor, whence traitorous—treason, whence treasonable and treasonous—extradite, extradition; betray, whence betrayal and betrayer.

1. Behind this sense-various group stands L *trādere*, to hand over, to hand on, to deliver, hence to betray: *trā-*, a c/f of *trans*, beyond, hence, by weakening, across+-*dere*, a c/f of *dare*, orig to place, hence to place in the hands of, to give: cf DATA (DATE).

2. L *trādere* has pp *trāditu*s, whence both *trāditiō* and *trāditor*. The former, acc *trāditiō*nem, yields MF-F *tradition*, adopted by E, with derivative *traditional* perh owing something to ML *trāditiōnalis* (cf the F *traditionnel*); MF-F *tradition* occurs in Voltaire's *extradition*, a handing-over (L *trāditiō*) from (*ex*) one country to another: adopted by E, it yields, by b/f, 'to *extradite*'. The latter, *trāditor*, a hander-over, a traitor, is adopted by Eccl historians; and from *trāditor* comes VL *\*trādītor*, whence OF-EF *traître*, acc *traïtor* (or -*ur*), whence ME *traitour*, whence E *traitor*.

3. L *traditiōnem*, acc of *trāditiō*, a handing-over, becomes OF-MF *traïson* (or -*un*), whence ME *traisoun*, *treisun*, *tresun*, whence E *treason*.

4. L *trādere* becomes OF-MF *traïr* (EF-F *trahir*), whence ME *traien*, EE 'to *tray*'; 'to *betray*' derives from ME *betraien* (int *be-*+*traien*).

traditor. See prec, para 2, s.f.

traduce, traduction. See DUKE, para 6, s.f.

traffic: F *trafic*: It *traffico*, from *trafficare*, to trade; 'to *traffic*' comes from late MF-F *trafiquer* (It *trafficare*). The It v is o.o.o.: ? from ML *trāvehere*, L *trāuehere*, var of *transuehere*, to carry across (from country to country), via some It dial mdfn, including the common alternation of *v-f*.

tragedian, tragedy, tragic, tragicomedy. See ODE, para 11.

tragopan. See ODE, para 11.

trail, trailer. See TRACT, para 2 and heading.

train, trainer, training. See TRACT, para 4 and heading.

train oil is taut for earlier *train*, var of *trayne*, var of *trane*: MLG *trān*—cf MHG *trān*, a drop of, e.g., oil, OHG *trahan*; MHG *trān* had pl *trēne*, whence, by b/f, the late MHG *trēne*, whence G *Träne*, a tear: perh by metathesis *\*trah-* from OGmc *\*tahr-*, as in OHG *zahar*, MHG *aher*, G

*Zahre*, a tear, akin to Go *tagr*, ON *tar*, hence to E TEAR of the eye. (Walshe.)

With MLG *trān*, cf MD *trane*, *traen*, D *traan*, a tear, and D *traan*, train oil—oil from (usu the right) whale.

trait. See TRACT, para 2.

traitor, whence traitorous. See TRADITION, para 2, s.f.

traject (n and v), trajectile, trajection, trajectory (adj, hence n).

L *trālīcere*, often contr to *trāicere*, to throw across, represents *trā-*, a c/f of *trans*, across+ -*iicere*, -*icere*, c/f of *iacere*, ML *jacere*, to throw (f.a.e.: JET). The pp *trāiectus*, ML *trājectus*, yields the E v and n *traject*, whence, anl, *trajectile*, adj, hence n; derivative ML *trajectōrius* (prob already in LL) yields E *trajectory*, perh imm from EF-F *trajectoire*, and derivative L *trāiectiō*, o/s *trāiec-tiōn-*, ML *trājectiōn-*, yields E *trajection*.

tram. See TERM, para 4.

trammel. See THREE, para 12.

tramontane. See MINATORY, para 8.

tramp, v, hence n; trample, v, hence n; trap (n and v), snare, whence trapper and trapping—cf entrap; trap, a kind of rock; trip, v (whence tripper), hence n.

1. 'To *tramp*' or walk heavily, hence to travel on foot, derives from ME *trampen*: cf MLG *trampen* and Go -*trimpan* and, without *m*, the MLG and MD-D *trappen*, to stamp, to tread: ult cf TREAD.

2. ME *trampen* has freq *trampelen*, whence 'to *trample*': cf the syn MHG-G *trampeln*, akin to MHG-G *treppe*, a staircase.

3. 'To *trap*' or snare, ME *trappen*, derives from OE -*traeppan*, -*treppan*, itself from OE *traeppe*, *treppe*, a snare, whence ME *trappe*, E *trap*: cf MD *trap*, *trappe*, and OHG *trapo*: cf also, both phon and sem, TREAD, a trap being that which is unwittingly trodden upon. Cf OF-F *trappe* (from Frankish *\*trappa*), whence MF *entrapper* or *entraper*, whence 'to *entrap*'.

4. The Geol *trap*, a dark igneous rock, esp basalt, derives from Sw *trapp*, which has cognates in Da, G, D: such rock occurs in masses rising much as *steps* do.

5. To *trip* or move quickly and lightly, ME *trippen*, var *trepen*, comes from OF *triper* (or *tripper*), var *treper*, of Gmc origin: cf the syn MD *trippen*, D *trippelen*, G *trippeln*, and OE *treppan*, to tread: words that, phon and sem, represent 'thinnings' of those noted in para 1. The senses 'to (cause to) stumble' and 'to make an excursion for pleasure' (now rare, but the imm source of 'a *trip*' or short journey), follow easily from the orig sense.

trample. See prec, para 2.

trance. See TRANSIENT, para 2.

tranquil, tranquillity, tranquillize. See QUIET, para 9.

transact, transaction (whence transactional). The latter derives, prob via MF-F from L *transactiōn-*, o/s of *transactiō*, formed from *transactus*, pp of *transigere*, to drive across: *trans*, across+-*igere*, c/f of *agere*, to drive (cf ACT and AGENT). Also from pp *transactus* comes 'to *transact*'.

**transalpine**: L *transalpīnus*, across the Alps: cf ALPINE.

**transatlantic**: *trans*, across+*Atlantic*: cf ATLAS.

**transcend, transcendence, transcendent(al)**. See ASCEND, final para.

**transcribe, transcript, transcription**. See SCRIBE, para 22.

**transcurrent**. See COURSE, para 10, s.f.

**transect, transection**. See the 2nd SAW, para 14.

**transept**. See SEPTUM, s.f.

**transfer** (v, hence n), whence **transferable**; **transferent**, whence, anl, **transference**. *Transferent* derives from L *transferent-*, o/s of *transferens*, presp of *transferre*, to bear or carry across (*trans*, across+*ferre*, to bear: f.a.e. FERTILE, whence, perh via F, 'to *transfer*').

**transfiguration, transfigure**. See FIGURE, para 8.

**transfix, transfixion**. See FIX, para 3, s.f.

**transform, transformation**. See FORM, para 8.

**transfuse, transfusion**. See the 2nd FOUND, para 15.

**transgress, transgression, transgressive, transgressor**. See GRADE, para 18.

**transient** (whence **transience** and **transiency**), **transire, transit, transition** (whence **transitional**), **transitive, transitory**; **trance**, n hence v, whence the int **entrance**; **trounce**.

1. L *transīre*, to go across, hence over,—whence the E Customs n *transire*, papers of clearance and entry,—merely prefixes *trans*, across, to *īre*, to go (f.a.e.: ISSUE). The presp *transiens*, o/s *transeunt-*, VL *transient-*, becomes the E adj *transient*; from the pp *transit*us derive L *transitiō*, acc *transitiōn*em, EF-F *transition*, adopted by E—LL *transitiuus*, ML *-ivus*, EF-F *transitif*, f *transitive*, E *transitive* —LL *transitōrius*, MF-F *transitoire*, E *transitory*— L *transitus*, n (gen *-ūs*), passage (a passing), It *transito*, EF-F *transit*, adopted by E.

2. L *transīre* becomes OF-F *transir*, OF-EF to pass from life to death, whence the OF-F n *transe*, OF-MF death, late MF-F excessive fear, hence a swoon, ME *traunce* or *trance*, the latter extant, with naturally divergent senses.

3. Orig 'to terrify', *trounce* app derives from latish ME *traunce*, v from the ME n *traunce*.

**translate, translation, translator**. See the 1st TOLL, para 6, s.f.

**transliterate, transliteration**. See LETTER, para 9.

**translucent**, whence **translucence** and **translucency**, represents L *translūcent-*, o/s of *translūcens*, presp of *translūcēre*, to shine across, hence through: *trans*, across+*lūcēre*, to shine (cf the 3rd LIGHT, f.a.e.).

**transmarine**: L *transmarīnus*: *trans*, across, beyond+*marīnus*, adj of *māre*, the sea: cf the n MERE.

**transmigrant, transmigrate, transmigration**. See MIGRANT, para 6.

**transmissible, transmission, transmit**. See MISSION, para 23.

**transmogrify** (whence **transmogrification**) is a

jocose blend of *transmigrate*, for the form, and of *transmute*, for the sense.

**transmutable, transmutation, transmute**. See MUTABLE, para 8.

**transom, trestle**. The former prob eases L *transtrum*, a cross-bar; *trans*, across+suffix *-strum*; from the LL dim *transtellum* comes VL *\*transtillum*, var *\*trāstillum*, whence OF-MF *trestel* (EF-F *tréteau*): whence E *trestle*, a bar or beam leg-supported.

**transparence, transparency, transparent**. The 3rd, adopted from MF-F, derives from ML *transparent-*, o/s of *transparens*, presp of *transparēre*, to show or appear (L *parēre*) through (*trans*, across, beyond). Derivative ML *transparentia* yields MF-F *transparence*, adopted by E, which modifies it to *transparency*.—Cf the v PEER.

**transpicuous**. See SPECTACLE, para 18.

**transpiration, transpire**. See SPIRIT, para 14.

**transplant, transplantation**. See the 2nd PLANT, para 5.

**transpontine**. See PONS, para 7.

**transport, transportation**. See the 3rd PORT, final para.

**transpose, transposition**. See POSE, para 23.

**tranship**=**transship**, to ship *trans* or over the sea.

**transsert**. See SERIES, para 16.

**transubstantiate, transubstantiation**. See STAND, para 35.

**transudation, transude**. See SWEAT, para 4.

**Transvaal**. See VALE, para 1.

**transvection**. See VIA, para 12.

**transversal, transverse, transversion, transvert**. See VERSE, para 15.

**trap** (1), snare, and (2), a kind of rock: see TRAMP, paras 3 and 4.

**trap** (3). Cf TRAPS, but see DRAB, para 3, s.f.

**trapeze, trapezium, trapezius, trapezoid**. See FOOT, para 26.

**trapper**. See TRAMP, para 3.

**trappings**. See DRAB, para 3.

**traps**, personal belongings. See DRAB, para 3, s.f.

**trash**, refuse, rubbish, whence **trashy**: Scan: cf ON *tros*, fallen twigs and leaves, rubbish, Nor dial *tras*, twigs, and *trask*, rubbish, but also cf OE *trūs*, fallen branches, twigs, leaves. (Holthausen.)

**trass** comes, perh via G *Trass*, from D *tras* (o.o.o.).

**trauma, traumatic**. See the element *traumato-*.

**travail** (1), n and v (labour); **travel**, v (whence **traveller** and **travelling**), hence n.

'To *travel*', orig to labour, is id with 'to *travail*', ME *travellen*, earlier *travailen*: OF-MF *traveillier*, *travaillier* (EF-F *travailler*): VL *\*tripāliāre*, to torture with the (VL) *tripālium*, a three(*tri*-)-staked instrument of torture (cf LL *trepalium*), from L *tripalis*, three-staked, from L *pālus*, a stake: f.a.e., the n PALE.—From the OF v derives the OF-F n *travail*, adopted by ME. Cf:

**travail** (2), a mechanical device—a frame—for confining and taming cattle and horses; **travois**, var **travoy**.

The Can F *travois*, var *travoy*, a primitive, two-poled, horse- or dog-drawn vehicle, is a mdfn of F *travail*, the frame described above, from VL *tripālium* (as in the 1st TRAVAIL).

**trave.** See TAVERN, para 4.

**travel, traveller, travelling.** See the 1st TRAVAIL.

**traversary, traverse** (adj, n, v). See VERSE, para 15, s.f.

**travesty.** See VEST, para 3, s.f.

**travois, travoy.** See the 2nd TRAVAIL.

**trawl, trawler.** See TRACT, para 3 and heading.

**tray:** ME *tray*, earlier *trey*: OE *trēg, trīg, trīeg*: akin to TREE (f.a.e.).

**treacherous, treachery.** See TRICK, para 1.

**treacle.** See FIERCE, para 5.

**tread** (whence the n), pt **trod**, pp **trodden; treadle,** n, hence v; **trade** (n, hence v), whence **trader** (cf OFris *-tradere*), **tradesman** (*trade's man*), and such cpds as **trade-mark, -name, -union, -wind** (blowing, from the east, in a regular *trade* or course towards the equator); **trot,** n, v.

1. 'To *tread*'—walk on or over (hence vi)—comes, via ME *treden*, from OE *tredan*: cf OFris *treda*, OS *tredan*, OHG *tretan*, MHG-G *treten*, and, differently vowelled, Go *trudan*, ON *troda, trodha*, OSw *trodha*, cf MD *troden*, var *traden*, but usu *treden*, as in D and in LG: cf, further off, Gr *dromos*, a running, a course, Skt *dramati*, he runs, and *dravati*, it runs, flows, melts: therefore cf DROME and TRAMP.

2. From or akin to OE *tredan* is the n *-tredd*, a treading, a tread, as in *wīntredd*, a place where grapes are trodden out, hence a wine-press. This OE n has dim *tredel*, whence ME *tredil, tredyl*, E *treadle*.

3. Akin to *tread*, v and n, is *trade*, app adopted, in ME, from the MD-MLG *trade*, a course, a track, a path: cf OS *trada* and OHG *trata*—and the OGmc vv in para 1.

4. Akin to—indeed, prob a freq-int of—OHG *tretan* is OHG *trottōn*, to tread (esp to tread often), whence both MHG-G *trotten*, to trot, and the syn OF-MF *troter*, MF-F *trotter*, whence, in turn, ME *trotten*, E 'to *trot*'; then *trot* is adopted from OF-F. A *trotter*, agent of 'to *trot*', perh owes something to EF-F *trotteur* (from *trotter*).

**treadle.** See prec, para 2.

**treadmill** and **treadwheel** = *tread*, v + the nn *mill* and *wheel*.

**treason, treasonable, treasonous.** See TRADITION, para 3.

**treasure, treasurer, treasury.** See THESIS, para 5.

**treat, treatable, treatise, treatment, treaty.** See TRACT, para 8.

**treble:** ME, from OF-MF, *treble*, a popular form of *triple*: L *triplus*: cf E *triple* at PLY, para 24.

**tree.**—Sep: TAR—TRAY—TRIG, adj—TRIM—TROUGH—TRUE (TRUTH)—TRUG.—**dryad, dryas** —**hamadryad;** sep DURABLE; sep LARCH.

1. *Tree*: ME *tree*, earlier *tre*, earliest *treo*: OE *trēo* (var *trēow*), a tree, hence wood: cf OFris *trē*, OS *treo* or *trio*, Go *triu*, ON *trē*; OIr *daur* (? for *\*daru*), gen *darach*, EIr *dair*, Ir *darach, darog*, Ga

*darach*, Cor *dār*, pl *deri* (*dery*), *deru, derow*, W *dār*, pl *deri, derw*, Br *derō*, all meaning an oak or oak-timber; Lith *dervà*, pine-wood; Alb *dru*, a tree, an oak; Gr *doru*, a wooden beam or shaft or spear, and *drus*, a tree, *the* tree—i.e., the oak; Skt *dấru-, dru-*, an oak, *drumá-*, a tree: IE r, *\*der-*, esp in extn *\*dereu-* (cf the Gr *doru*): a tree, esp the oak.

2. Gr *drus*, a tree, has the derivative *druas* (suffix *-as*), a wood nymph, form-adopted and sense-adapted by Bot. Gr *druas*, pl *druades*, becomes L *dryas*, pl *dryades*, acc sing *dryadem*, whence MF-F *dryade*, whence E *dryad*; the Gr cpd *Hamadruas*, usu in pl *Hamadruades*, special wood nymphs with lives depending upon (connoted by Gr *hama*, along with, together with) the trees to which they are attached, becomes L *Hamadryas*, acc *Hamadryadem*, whence late MF-F *hamadryade*, whence E *hamadryad*.

**trefoil:** C15–16 *trefeuil* (F *trèfle*): VL *\*trifolum*: L *trifolium*, the three-leaved (plant), the clover.

**trek.** See TRACK, para 2.

**trellis:** OF-early MF *treliz* (early MF *tresliz*; MF-F *treillis*), a woven fabric, orig an adj: VL *\*trilīcius*: L *trilīcis*, gen of *trilēx*, three-threaded; as early as C13, not only was the OF-MF word form- and esp sense-influenced by OF-F *treille*, a vine-arbour (L *trichila*), but it took the senses 'lattice' and 'trellis'. (B & W.)

**trema.** See THROW, para 12.

**tremble** (v, hence n), whence **trembler** and **trembling; (delirium) tremens, tremendous, tremolant, tremolo, tremor, tremulant, tremulate, tremulous; turmoil,** v (now rare), whence the n.

1. All these words derive from L *tremere*, to tremble, hence to tremble before, be afraid of, whence both *tremendus*, that is to be feared, whence E *tremendous*, and *tremulus*, trembling, esp in fear, whence E *tremulous*, and *tremor*, a trembling, both lit and fig, adopted by E (cf the OF-MF *tremor*, MF *tremour*, EF-F *trémeur*).— L *tremere* is app an *-m* extn of that r *tre-* which prob occurs in L *trepidus*, alarmed, perturbed, s *trepid-*, r prob *trep-*; cf the *tres-* of Skt *trásati*, he trembles, and Gr *tressai*, to tremble. This *tre-* seems to be a metathesis of the IE r *\*ter-*, to tremble: cf Skt *taralás*, palpitant. (E & M.)

2. From L *tremulus* come both It *tremolo*, adopted as a Mus term, and ML *tremulāre*, with pp *tremulātus*, whence 'to *tremulate*', whence, anl, *tremulation*, and with presp *tremulans*, o/s *tremulant-*, whence both E *tremulant* and It *tremolante*, whence E *tremolant*.

3. L *tremere* has presp *tremens*, occurring, for E, in the adopted phrasal n *delirium tremens*, trembling delirium.

4. Perh from L *tremere* comes *turmoil*, which, o.o.o., could well be a f/e alteration (after *turn* and *moil*) of MF-EF *tremouille*, the hopper of a mill, as Webster proposes, but is more prob from a lost MF *tremouiller*, an *-ouiller* derivative from L *tremere*.

**tremendous.** See prec, para 1.

**tremolo, tremolant, tremor, tremulant, tremulate, tremulous.** See TREMBLE, para 2.

**trench** (n and v), **trenchant** (whence **trenchancy**), **trencher; entrench, entrenchment,** and **retrench, retrenchment; trinket; truncate** (adj and v), **truncation.**

1. The base is supplied by L *truncus*, (of a tree) lopped of branches, hence mutilated: o.o.o.: perh (E & M) a nasalized phon and sem var of *trux* (o/s *truc-*), ferocious, cruel.

2. *Truncus* has derivative *truncāre*, to lop off branches, to shorten or reduce by cutting, to mutilate, pp *truncātus*, whence both E *truncate*, adj and v, and LL *truncātiō*, a lopping, mutilation, o/s *truncātiōn-*, whence E *truncation*.

3. L *truncāre* becomes OF-MF *trenchier* (MF-F *trancher*), to cut, whence 'to *trench*', with 'dig a trench' senses perh from the n *trench*, which derives from MF *trenche* (later *tranche*), from *trenchier*. OF-MF *trenchier* has derivative agent MF *trencheoir* (F *tranchoir*) or *trencheor*, whence E *trencher*, orig a knife, hence a board, a platter, on which to carve meat; and the OF-MF presp *trenchant* (F *tranchant*) explains the E adj *trenchant*.

4. Whereas 'to *entrench*', prop to cut into, whence anl *entrenchment*, represents *en*, in, into+ to *trench*, 'to *retrench*', prop to cut back (*re-*), comes from OF-MF *retrenchier*, var *-er* (cf F *retrancher*), whence the OF-MF *retrenchement* (later *retranchement*), whence, in part, E *retrenchment*, formed in part from the E v.

5. OF-MF *trenchier* has the MF-EF derivative *trenchet* (MF-F var *tranchet*), a (shoemaker's) knife, which, passing through ONF *trenquet*, becomes ME *trenket*, with prob derivative sense 'a toy knife worn by medieval women as an ornament', whence E *trinket*, a small ornament. (EW.)

**trencher, whence trencherman.** See prec, para 3.

**trend,** v, hence n; **trendle, trindle, trundle.**

1. 'To *trend*' or skirt (obs), to turn in a certain direction, derives from ME *trenden*, from OE *trendan*, to roll, to turn about (vi): cf OE *trendel*, a circle, OFris *trind* or *trund*, round, circular, MHG *trendel*, a ball, MLG *trendel*, a disk.

2. From the r of the OGmc words derives OF-EF *trondeler*, to roll, which has influenced the passage of the syn *trendle* (obs) and *trindle* (now dial) from OE *trendel*; 'to *trundle*', a phon var of those two E vv, perh owes its form partly to the n *trundle*, a small wheel, a hoop, a round tub, etc., phon var of *trendle* (OE *trendel*). (EW.)

**trepan.** See THROW, para 13.

**trepang.** Mal *tĕripani*.

**trephine.** See THROW, para 14.

**trepid, trepidant** (whence **trepidancy**), **trepidation; intrepid, intrepidity.**

1. L *trepidus*, restless, pawing the ground, app has s *trepid-*, r *\*trep-*, extn of *\*tre-*, metathesis of IE *\*ter-*, to tremble: cf TREMBLE.

2. *Trepidus* yields E *trepid*, whence, anl, *trepidity*; derivative L *trepidāre*, to paw and stamp the ground, to be restless, to tremble, has presp *trepidans*, o/s *trepidant-*, E *trepidant* (cf the F *trépidant*),

and pp *trepidātus*, whence 'to *trepidate*' or feel anxious; derivative L *trepidātiō*, acc *trepidātiōn*em, becomes MF-F *trépidation*, E *trepidation*.

3. The L neg *intrepidus* becomes late MF-F *intrépide*, whence, anl, the EF-F *intrépidité*: whence E *intrepid* and *intrepidity*.

**trespass.** See PACE, para 5.

**tress,** n and v: OF-MF *trece* (EF-F *tresse*) and OF-MF *trecer* (EF-F *tresser*): It *treccia* and *trecciare*: o.o.o.: perh from L *tricae* (pl), trifles, as in E *extricate* and *intricate*.

**trestle.** See TRANSOM.

**trews.** See TROUSERS.

**trey.** See THREE, para 10.

**tri-,** connoting 'three' or 'thrice' or 'by, or in, threes'. Cf THREE.

**triad, triadic.** See THREE, para 11.

**trial.** See TRY.

**triangle, triangular, triangulation.** See THREE, para 11.

**Trias, Triassic.** See THREE, para 11.

**tribade, tribadism.** See THROW, para 10.

**tribal, tribe.** See TRIBUTE, para 2.

**tribasic.** See THREE, para 11.

**tribrach.** See THREE, para 11.

**tribulation.** See THROW, para 5.

**tribunal, tribune.** See TRIBUTE, para 3.

**tributary.** See para 4 of:

**tribute** (n and v), **tributary; tribune, tribunal; tribe, tribal.**—Cpds: **attribute** (n, v), **attribution, attributive, attributor; contribute, contribution, contributor, contributory** (occ *-ary*); **distribute** (whence **distributary**), **distribution, distributive, distributor; retribute, retribution** (whence, anl, **retributive**), **retributor.**

1. This group derives from L *tribus* (gen *-ūs*), a division of the Roman peop le, a tribe, LL one of the twelve Jewish tribes: o.o.o.: perh from a division into three (L *tri-*) tribes. But, more prob, of C origin: cf OIr and OBr *treb*, OC *\*treba*, a dwelling, a habitation, and W *trew*, a village. (Malvezin¹.)

2. L *tribus*, becomes MF-F *tribu*, whence, prob, the E *tribe*, whence, anl, *tribal*.

3. L *tribus* has derivative *tribūnus*, orig an adj 'of the tribe(s)', hence the magistrate of the tribe, hence a local-governmental official: MF-F *tribun*: E *tribune*. The Arch *tribune* is adopted from MF-F, which takes it from It *tribuna*, itself from L *tribūnāl*. L *tribūnus* has adj *tribūnālis*, with neu *tribūnāle* used as n, usu in shortened form *tribūnal*, 'place where the tribunes sit', hence 'a raised seat, a platform': OF-F *tribunal*, adopted by E.

4. L *tribus* has the derivative v *tribuere*, to divide (esp a tax) among the tribes, hence to allot, to distribute or share, to grant, hence to bestow, to attribute. The pp *tribūtus* has neu *tribūtum*, used as n, unless *tribūtum* be the neu of an adj *tribūtus*, concerning the tribes, hence a tax paid by the tribes: whence, prob via MF-F *tribut*, the E *tribute*. L *tribūtum* has adj *tribūtārius*, hence, in LL, the n *tribūtārius*, a tribe, a people, that pays tribute: whence, prob via OF-F *tributaire*, the E

adj and n *tributary*, not used in the Geog sense until c1830.

5. L *tribuere* has four cpds relevant to E, the first being *attribuere*, to bestow *ad* or upon, pp *attribūtus*, whence 'to attribute'; the neu *attribūtum* used as n, yields MF-F *attribut*, whence E *attribute*; derivatives L *attribūtiō* (acc *attribūtiōnem*) and LL *attribūtor* become MF-F *attribution*, adopted by E, and E *attributor*; *attributive* derives from EF-F *attributif*, f *-ive*, itself formed anl from MF-F *attribution*.

6. L *contribuere*, to pay, hence to grant or give, *con-* or in common with others, has pp *contribūtus*, whence 'to contribute'. Derivative LL *contribūtiō* (acc *contribūtiōnem*) and LL *contribūtārius*, jointly taxed, yield MF-F *contribution*, adopted by E, and E *contributary*, superseded by *contributory*; *contributor* derives from AF *contributour*, itself formed anl from MF *contribution*.

7. L *distribuere*, to allot *dis-* or collectively, has pp *distribūtus*, whence 'to distribute'. Derivative L *distribūtiō* (acc *distribūtiōnem*), LL *distribūtīuus* (ML *-īvus*), LL *distribūtor* yield MF-F *distribution*, MF-F *distributif*, MF-F *distributeur*, whence E *distribution*, *distributive*, *distributor*.

8. L *retribuere*, to grant or give in return, to pay back, has pp *retribūtus*, whence the obsol 'to retribute'. Derivative L *retribūtiō* (acc *retribūtiōnem*), a paying back, LL recompense, punishment for sin, and LL *retribūtor* become MF-F *retribution*, adopted by E, and E *retributor*.

**trice, in a**: late ME-EE *at a trice*, at or with one tug or pull: from 'to *trice*' or pull suddenly (obs), to haul up: ME *tricen*, *trycen*, *trisen*: MD *trīsen*, *triesen* (D *trijsen*), to hoist, from *trīse*, *trijs*, *trijsse*, a windlass, a pulley: cf MLG *trīsse*, a pulley, a rope: o.o.o.

**triceps.** See THREE, para 11.

**trichiasis; trichina**, whence **trichinosis** (suffix *-osis*) and **trichinous** (unless imm from Gr *tri-khinos*); **trichite**, whence **trichitic**; **trichoma**; cf the element *-tricha*, *tricho-*, where, e.g., *trichology*.

1. The 1st is a SciL derivative of Gr *trikhiasis*, which tacks the Med suffix *-iasis* (cf E *iatric*) to *trikho-*, a c/f based on *trikhos*, gen of *thrix*, hair: cf Ir gairb- *driuch*, a bristle, and perh Mx *friogan*, a bristle: IE etymon, *\*drigu*, a hair, a bristle (Hofmann).

2. Derivative Gr *trikhinos*, hairy, has suggested the SciL *trichina*, a small, slender, hair-like worm.

3. From the Gr c/f *trikh(o)-* comes the Bot, Geol, Zoo *trichite* (suffix *-ite*), a small hair-like, hence needle-like, formation, and the Bot and Zoo *trichoma* (suffix *-oma*).

**trichord.** See THREE, para 11.

**trichotomy.** See THREE, para 11.

**trick**, v (whence **trickster**), hence n (whence **trickery** and **tricky**), with pl **tricks**, whence **tricksy**; **treacherous, treachery.**

1. Whereas *treacherous* derives from OF-MF *trecheros* (*-ous*), *treachery* derives, via ME, from OF-MF *trecherie* (MF-F *tricherie*), deceit; both of these old F words, from OF-MF *trechier* (MF

*trichier*, later *tricher*), to cheat: o.o.o.: ? from a dial derivative of a VL form (? *\*trectiāre* for *\*tractiāre*) of L *tractāre*, to handle.

2. MF *trichier* (late MF-F *tricher*) becomes ONF *trikier*, whence the ONF n *trike*, *trique*, whence E *trick*; the E v app derives partly from the E n and partly from the OF-ONF v.

**trickle.** See STRIKE, para 7.

**trickster, tricksy, tricky.** See TRICK (heading).

**tricolor.** See THREE, para 11.

**tricycle.** See CYCLE, para 1.

**trident.** See TOOTH, para 11.

**triennial.** See ANNUAL, para 3.

**trier.** See TRY (heading).

**trifid.** See THREE, para 11.

**trifle**, n, v (whence **trifler** and **trifling**). See THIGH, para 8.

**Trifolium.** See THREE, para 11.

**trig**, adj. See TRUE, para 8.

**trigger.** See TRACK, para 3.

**triglyph.** See THREE, para 11.

**trigonometry**, whence **trigonometric(al)**. See the element *trigono-*.

**trilby**, a soft felt hat, and sl **trilbies**, feet: from a kind of hat worn by the chief male characters, and from heroine Trilby's shapely feet, in George du Maurier's novel of artistic-bohemian Paris: *Trilby*, 1894, illustrated with his own line-drawings. The name *Trilby* is artificial, but, since she sang divinely, it perh puns on F *triller* (to *trill*) and, because she sang 'instinctively' and only under hypnosis, perh, though still less likely, *bébé* (baby): *triller+bébé*.

**trilingual.** See THREE, para 11.

**trill** (1), Mus v, hence n: It *trillare*: echoic.

**trill** (2), to whirl or twirl (obs), to trickle (obsol). See the 3rd DRILL.

**trillion.** See THREE, para 11.

**trilogy.** See LEGEND, para 32.

**trim**, v (hence n, whence adj), whence **trimmer** and **trimming**: ME *trimen*, var *trumen*: OE *trym-man*, *trymian*, to render strong, to set in order, from OE *trum*, strong, firm: cf TRUE and TREE.

**trimester.** See the element *-mester*.

**trimeter.** See THREE, para 11.

**trimorphous.** See THREE, para 11.

**trindle.** See TREND, para 2.

**trine.** See THREE, para 9.

**Trinitarian, Trinity.** See THREE, para 8.

**trinket.** See TRENCH, para 5.

**trinomial.** See THREE, para 11, and cf BINOMIAL.

**trio; triolet.** See THREE, para 10.

**trip.** See TRAMP, para 5.

**tripartite.** See PART, para 4.

**tripe**: MF-F *tripe* (cf Sp *tripa*): 'perh borrowed, via one of the south-European languages, from Ar *therb*, the fold of a piece of cloth' (B & W).

**triphthong.** See THREE, para 11.

**triplane.** See THREE, para 11.

**triple, triplet, triplex, triplicate.** See PLY, para 24.

**tripod, tripos.** See FOOT, para 27.

**tripper, tripping.** See *trip* at TRAMP, para 5 (and heading).

triptych. See THREE, para 11.

trireme. See THREE, para 11.

trisyllabic, trisyllable. See SYLLABLE, para 3.

trite. See THROW, para 7.

Triton among the minnows: L *Triton*: Gr *Tritōn*, son of Poseidon, the God of the Sea: perh of C origin: cf OIr *triath* (gen *trethan*), the sea: OC etymon *Triaton. (Hofmann.)

tritone. See THREE, para 11.

triturate, trituration, triturator. See THROW, para 6.

triumph (n, v), triumphal, triumphant; trump (in cards), n, hence v; ruff, a card game.

1. 'To *triumph*' derives from MF *triumpher* (later *triompher*), from L *triumphāre*, itself from L *triumphus*, whence OF-MF *triumphe* (later *triomphe*), whence the E n *triumph*; the adj *triumphal* is adopted from OF-MF, which derives it from L *triumphālis* (from *triumphus*). L *triumphus*, OL *triumpus*, app comes—perh via Etruscan—from Gr *thriambos*, a Bacchic procession. (E & M.) Gr *thriambos* is perh (Hofmann) a mdfn of *triambos, a triple-time, as music or as march-step. *Triumphant* derives from MF *triumphant* (later *triomphant*), prop the presp of *triumpher*.

2. From E *triumph* comes, by slovening, *trump*, one of a suit of cards rating higher than any card in any other suit: prob sense-influenced by late MF-EF *triomphe*, name of a card game, hence, in F, a trump card, and perh form-influenced by *trumpāre, the VL shape of *triumphāre*.

3. App a jocose mdfn of the card-game *triomphe* is EF *ronfle*, eased to *roffle*, whence E *ruff*, the predecessor of whist: cf the syn C16-17 It *ronfa*, from *trionfo*. (EW.)

triumvir, triumvirate. See the element -*vir* and cf THREE and VIRILE.

trivet, a three-legged support: OE *trefet*: *triped*-, o/s of LL *tripēs*, a tripod, from L *tripēs*, three-footed: cf *tripod*, see FOOT.

trivia, trivial, triviality; trivium. See VIA, para 15, s.f.

Troad, Troadic. See TROJAN, para 1.

trochaic, trochee; trochanter; troche, whence trochal; trochilic, trochilics, trochilus; trochlea, whence trochlear; trochoid; ? troco; truck, a (small, strong) vehicular wheel, hence a hand-conveyance, hence an open, railroad goods-waggon or (AE) a strong, motor-driven wagon; truckle (a small wheel), truckle bed, 'to truckle'.—Cf the element -*troch*.

1. Despite their superficial variety, all these words spring, by an entirely natural phon and sem development, from Gr *trokhós*, a wheel, itself from *trekhein*, to run (hence to revolve): with *trokhós*, a wheel, cf Gr *trókhos*, a running, a course, and *trókhis*, a runner, a messenger, and OC *drogon, a wheel (OIr *droch*): IE r, *dregh-, var *drekh-, to run. (Hofmann.)

2. Direct from Gr *trokhós*, a wheel, come E *troche*, a (circular) medicinal tablet, and E *trochoid* (suffix -*oid*), wheel-shaped, hence as n; Gr *trókhos*, a running, has the adj *trokhaios*, whence, elliptical

for *trokhaios pous*, 'running foot' in versification, the n *trokhaios*, whence L *trochaeus*, whence, perh via EF-F *trochée*, the E *trochee*. The Gr n *trokhaios* acquires its own adj: *trokhaiikos*, contr to *trokhaïkos*, whence L *trochaïcus*, whence (F *trochaïque* and) E *trochaic*.

3. From Gr *trekhein*, to run, but prob after *trókhos*, a running, comes Gr *trokhantēr*, a runner, whence the SciL (An and Zoo) *trochanter*.

4. Also from Gr *trekhein* comes Gr *trokhileia*, later *trokhilia*, perh orig 'a little something that runs, hence rolls or turns', hence a block-and-tackle equipment, a pulley-sheaf or a windlass-roller, whence the E adj *trochilic* and n *trochilics*. Cf the Gr *trokhilos* (likewise from *trekhein*), an Egyptian, or a spur-winged, plover, hence, fancifully, an Arch term, but also a syn of *trokhileia*: whence L *trochilus*, adopted by E, both in Zoo and in Arch.

5. Gr *trokhileia*, later *trokhilia*, becomes, by contr, L *trochlea*, whence the An *trochlea*, a pulley-like structure, whence the adj *trochlear*; with the form of L *trochlea*, cf that of LL *trocleatim*, by means of a pulley (Souter).

6. The game of *troco*, a predecessor of billiards, app derives—? after Gr *trokhós*—either from Sp *truco* or from It *trucco*, both slightly resembling billiards.

7. Gr *trokhós*, a wheel, becomes L *trochus*, a metal hoop, whence perh the E *truck*, a wheel, a wheeled conveyance (as in heading), whence 'to *truck*' or convey in one; *truck* has dim *truckle* (perh, however, from L *trochlea*, as in para 5), a small wheel, whence *truckle bed*, a small wheeled bed that, orig, could be pushed under a large bed, as a young pupil's under a master's—whence 'to *truckle*' or sleep in a truckle bed (obs), whence to act subserviently to another person. (EW.)

trochanter. See prec, para 3.

troche. See TROCHAIC, para 2.

trochilic, trochilics, trochilus. See TROCHAIC, para 4.

trochlea, trochlear. See TROCHAIC, para 5.

trochoid. See TROCHAIC, para 2.

troco. See TROCHAIC, para 6.

troglodyte, troglodytic. See the element *troglo-*. Akin to:

trogon is SciL for Gr *trōgōn*, presp of *trōgein*, to gnaw: IE r, *trog-, var of *treg-, to gnaw: perh cf the (?) metathetic L *terg*ere, to rub away. (Hofmann.) Cf TROUT.

Troic, Troilus. See para 1 of:

Trojan, adj, hence n; Troad, whence Troadic; Troic; Troilus (butterfly); Troy—? troy (weight).

1. All these words, except perh the last, derive from Gr *Trōs* or *Trōos*, the founder of Troy. The Gr adj *Trōikos* becomes L *Trōicus*, whence E *Troic*; the region *Trōas* (capital, Troy) has gen *Trōados*, whence, via L, the E *Troad*; Gr *Trōilos*, lit 'descendant of Tros' (Priam's son), becomes L *Trōilus*, adopted by E (as in Shakespeare's *Troilus and Cressida*), whence, fancifully, the *Troilus*—now usu *troilus*—butterfly.

2. The city of founder *Trōs* was named *Troia* (var *Troíē*), dissyllabic, or *Troïa*, trisyllabic, whence L *Troia*, ML *Troja*, whence E *Troy*, with derivative L adj *Troianus*, ML *Trojanus*, whence E *Trojan*, the phrase '(work or fight) *like a Trojan*' commemorating the courage and tenacity of the defenders of Troy against the Greeks.

3. App influenced by L *Troia*, Troy—OF-MF *Troye*, MF-F *Troie*—was the F city of *Troyes* (hardly deriving from its L name *Augustobona*), where, during the Middle Ages, the great fairs established, for all Europe, the weight-standard *Troyes*, whence E *Troy*, whence *troy* (*weight*).

**troll** (1), n; **trull.** The *troll*, fabled in OGmc Myth to inhabit caves and hills, derives from ON *troll* (cf the Da *trold*, an elf), a giant, a demon, whence, perh, the MHG *trolle*, G *Trulle*, a strumpet, a slut, whence, prob, the E *trull*, a strumpet (obsol).

**troll** (2), v (hence n)—**trolley**, var **trolly**—**trollop**, n, hence v.

1. *Troll*, vt, to turn or revolve (obs), to trundle or roll (whence the fishing sense), hence to circulate (e.g., drinks), hence to sing the successive parts of a drinking song, with corresp vi senses: ME *trollen* (vi), to roll, to wander: OF-EF *troller*, in OF-MF a vt, to walk about, hence, in late MF-EF, to run here and there (whence later EF-F *trôler*, to drag about, but also to ramble): MHG (? also OHG) *trollen*, to run with short steps (G to toddle, to loll): prob (Walshe) akin—though without the IE int prefix *s*—to G *Strolch*, a vagabond.

2. App from *troll*, (vi, vt) to roll or trundle, comes *trolley* or *trolly*, perh assisted by a lost EF-F \**trollée*, \**trolée*—cf the EF *trollerie*, (of dogs) an aimless ranging.

3. Also from *troll*, to ramble, to stroll, comes *trollop*, a slattern (obsol)—hence a loose woman, a prostitute. The suffix *-op* was perh suggested by the *-ope* of the doubly syn EF-F *salope*, obscurely formed from MF-F *sale*, dirty.

**trolley.** See prec, para 2.

**trollop.** See the 2nd TROLL, para 3.

**trolly.** See the 2nd TROLL, para 2.

**trombone.** See the 2nd TRUMP, para 3.

**trona.** See NITER, para 5.

**troop, trooper.** See TAVERN, para 6.

**trope**—cf the element *-trope* (*-tropal, tropo-*, etc.); **tropic**, adj (now often in extn **tropical**, whence **subtropical**), hence n, now usu in pl; **tropism**; **trophy**; **entropy**; ? **turpitude**; prob cf the sep TROUBADOUR group.

1. *Trope*, lit a turning, a turn, esp of language, hence a figure of speech, is adopted from EF-F, which takes it from Grammarians' L *tropus* (occ *tropos*), trln of Gr *tropos*, a turn(ing), akin—with the normal n *-o-* and v *-e-* alternation—to Gr *trepein* (s and r *trep-*), to turn: cf the Doric and Ionic Gr var *trapein*, Skt *trápatē*, he is ashamed (lit, he turns away), *trapā*, shame, and the Hit *teripp-*, to plough (lit to turn the soil): IE r \**terp-* (Hit *teripp-* a vocalized mdfn ?), to turn. (Hofmann.)

2. From E *trope*, a turning, derives the Bio

*tropism* (*-ism*); and Gr *tropos*, a trope, has LGr cpd *tropologia*, a figurative way of speaking or writing, whence, via LL, the E *tropology*.

3. Gr *tropos* has adj *tropikos*, turning, whence, via *tropikos kuklos* (a turning circle), the n *tropikos*, the solstice whether vernal or autumnal: whence resp the E adj (via L *tropicus*) and the E n *tropic* —cf EF-F *tropique*.

4. Gr *tropos* has the var or doublet *tropē*, with special sense 'a turning about the enemy, a routing of the enemy, a victory': whence the adj *tropaios*, with neu *tropaion* used as n (monument to victory), whence L *tropaeum*, with incorrect LL varr *trophaeum, tropheum*, whence late MF-F *trophée*, whence E *trophy*.

5. Of the *-tropy* prefix-cpd derivatives, *entropy* forms a good example: a Sci blend of E *energy*+ Gr *tropē*, a turning, hence a change.

### Questionable

6. E *turpitude*, adopted from MF-F, comes from L *turpitūdinem*, acc of *turpitūdō*, vileness, from *turpis*, shameful, s and r *turp-*: orig applied to physical defect, *turpis* is o.o.o., unless it be akin to Gr *trepein*: *turp-* for \**terp-*, metathesis of *trep-*: ? prop 'twisted', hence 'malformed'.

**trophic; atrophy**, n, hence v. The adj *trophic*, relating to nourishment, derives from Gr *trophikos*, the adj of *trophē*, a nourishing, nourishment, akin to *trephein*, to nourish, to nurse: IE r \**drebh-*, (?) to flow. For *trophology*, see the element *-trophia*.

2. Gr *trophē*, nourishment, has neg (*a-*) *atrophia*, adopted by LL, whence EF-F *atrophie*, whence E *atrophy*.

**trophy.** See TROPE, para 4.

**tropic, tropical.** See TROPE, para 3.

**tropology.** See TROPE, para 2.

**trot.** See TREAD, para 4.

**troth.** See TRUE, para 6.

**trotters**, a pig's feet: pl of *trotter*, agent and instr of 'to *trot*', q.v. at TREAD.

**troubadour, trovatore, trouvere; (treasure-)trove; trover;—contrive**, whence **contrivance** and **contriver; retrieve**, v (hence n), whence **retrieval** (n suffix *-al*) and agent **retriever.**

1. Both the It *trovatore* and the EF-F *troubadour* come from OProv *trobador*, a poet-musician, a lyric poet, from OProv *trobar*, to compose a song, hence a poem: VL \**tropāre*—attested by LL *attropāre*, to compare, and *contropāre*, to apply metaphorically—which, orig meaning 'to compose an air, hence a poem', came to mean 'to invent, to discover' and hence 'to find' (as also OProv *trobar*). From VL \**tropāre* app derive also OF-MF *trover* (MF-F *trouver*), which, orig syn with OProv *trobar*, soon came to mean 'to find'; derivative OF-MF *trovere*, EF-F *trouvère*, is adopted by E for a specifically F troubadour. MF *trover*, to find, was, by AF, used as n, whence, with sense-change, the legal *trover*; and the pp *trové* becomes E *trove*, a thing found or discovered, obs except in *treasure-trove*, itself orig a legal term.

2. VL \**tropāre* prob derives from L *tropus*, a

figure of rhetoric, a figure of speech (cf TROPE, para 1), as the LL cpds *attropāre* and *contropāre* have led B & W, and others, to propose.

3. OF-MF *trover* (EF-F *trouver*) has two prefix-cpds affecting E:

OF-MF *controver* (EF-F *controuver*), to imagine, to invent—the *con-* is vaguely int, and the cpd was perh suggested by LL *contropāre*—has such forms as 'il *contrueve*' and 'ils *contruevent*', with varr in *-treuv-*, which help to explain the passing of the derivative ME *controven* into *contrueven*, later *contreven*, later *contreve*, whence, perh influenced by OF-MF *trovaille* (EF-F *trouvaille*), a lucky find, the EE-E 'to *contrive*', whence EE-E *contrivance*.

OF-MF *retrover* (EF-F *retrouver*), to find *re-* or again, to recover, with such forms as 'il *retrueve*', var *retreuve*, whence late ME *retreve*, whence 'to *retrieve*'.

**trouble, troublesome, troublous.** See TURBID, para 3.

**trough**: ME *trough*, earlier *trogh*: OE *trog* or *troh*, with cognates in the other OGmc languages, as, e.g., ON *trog* and OHG-MHG *troc* (G *Trog*): f.a.e., TREE.

**trounce.** See TRANSIENT, para 3.

**troupe, trouper.** See TAVERN, para 6.

**trousers**: anl with *drawer(s)*, but sing **trouser**: anl with *drawer(s)*, but from archaic *trouse*, Ga var *trews*: Ga and Ir *triubhas*: perh from MF *trebus*, LL *tubraci* (var *tibraci*); perh of Gmc origin and meaning 'thigh breeches' (EW).

**trousseau.** See TRUSS, para 2.

**trout**: OE *trūht*: LL *tructa, tructus*, phon and sem varr of LL *trocta*, (prob) a shark: Gr *trōktēs*, a sharp-toothed marine fish: Gr *trōgein*, to gnaw: f.a.e., TROGON.

**trouvère** and **trovatore.** See TROUBADOUR, para 1.

**trove; trover.** See TROUBADOUR, para 1.

**trow.** See TRUE, para 7.

**trowel.** See TWIRL, para 2.

**Troy; troy** (weight). See TROJAN, para 3.

**truant**, orig a vagrant (whence **truancy**), whence v (obsol) and adj: OF-MF *truant*, a vagabond, var of *truand* (extant): Gaul *\*trugant-*: cf OIr *trōg*, Ir *truag*, miserable, poor, with the importantly relevant dim *trōgán*—Ga *truagh*, miserable, and *truaghan*, a poor, miserable creature, a vagabond— W *trū* (for *\*trug*), *trūan*, miserable, poor and distressed—Br *truant*—Cor *trū, trūan, trōc* (var *trōt*): C etymon, *\*trug*, poor, miserable, wretched, distressed. (Malvezin.)

**truce.** See TRUE, para 3.

**trucidation.** See TRUCULENT, para 2.

**truck** (1), a conveyance. See TROCHAIC, para 7.

**truck** (2), to barter, to exchange, and n. The E n *truck*, exchange, barter, hence commercial, whence social, intercourse, derives from EF *troque*, EF-F *troc*, itself from MF-F *troquer*, whence E 'to *truck*' or exchange, to barter: o.o.o., but prob, as Malvezin has proposed, from C *\*troc* (var of *\*trac*, to run), to come and go, to exchange goods,

attested by numerous extant C synonyms and approximations.

**truckle**, n and v; **truckle bed.** See TROCHAIC, para 7.

**truculent, truculency** or **truculence; trucidation.**

1. *Truculence* derives from L *truculentia*, from L *truculentus* (cf the LL var *truculens*, o/s *truculent-*), ferocious, cruel, whence, via EF-F, the E *truculent*: and *truculentus* derives, by extn, from L *truc-*, o/s of *trux*, ferocious, cruel, prob akin to Ir *trū* (gen *troich*), fated to die, with cognates in Skt and Hit, and perh akin to L *truncus*, mutilated (E & M).

2. Also from *trux*, o/s *truc-*, comes *trucidāre*, to slay ferociously or cruelly, pp *trucidātus*, whence *trucidātiō*, (ferocious) slaughter, whence the rare E *trucidation*.

**trudge.** See TRUSS, para 3.

**true**, adj (whence **truism** and 'to **true**'), **truly**, **truth** (whence **truthful**)—cf **untrue, untruth** (whence **untruthful**); **truce**, whence **trucial; trust**, n (whence **trustful** and **trusty**, adj hence n, and **trustworthy**) and v (whence **trustee**)—cf **distrust** (v, hence n) and **entrust; tryst**, n, hence v; **troth**, n, hence v, and **betroth**, whence pa **betrothed** and **betrothal; trow**, v; **trig**, adj, hence v.

### Indo-European

1. The adj *true*, ME *trewe*, comes from OE *trēowe*, loyal, trusty, akin to and perh deriving from OE *trēow*, loyalty, fidelity, and perh—even prob—related to OE *trēow, trēo*, E TREE: ? 'as firm and as straight as a tree': phon and sem cf OFris *triōwe, triūwe*, (both forms) adj and n, OS *triuwi*, adj, and *treuwa*, n, OHG *gi-triuwi*, late MHG *triuwe*, G *treu*, adj, Go *triggws*, adj, *triggwa*, n, MD *truw, truwe, trauwe, trowe, trou, trouwe*, D *trouw* (all adj and n), and ON *trū*, n, *tryggr*, adj; OP *drawis*, belief, faith; W *derw*, true, OIr *derb*, certain.

### Germanic

2. OE *trēowe*, faithful, has derivatives *trēowlīce*, whence *truly*, and *trēowth* (*trīewth*), whence ME *treowthe, treuthe, trouthe*, later *truthe*, finally *truth*, as still. The OE neg adj *untrēowe* and the corresp n *untrēowth* become E *untrue* and *untruth*.

3. The OE n *trēow*, fidelity, loyalty, becomes ME *trewe*, fidelity, hence a pledge of fidelity, pl *trewes*, whence, by b/f, E *truce*.

4. Akin to the OE *trēow*, fidelity, and OE *trēow*, faithful, and ON *trū*, faith, is ON *traust*, (a feeling of) security, akin to which is ME *trost, trust*, E *trust*; 'to *trust*' comes from ME *trusten, trosten*, varr *tresten, tristen*, app from ON *treysta* (vr), to trust, from or akin to ON *traust*. The E 'to *trust*' has prefix-cpds *distrust* (*dis-*, apart, connoting negation) and *entrust* (*en-*, in, into, hence to).

5. E *tryst*, an appointment to meet, an appointed meeting, was orig (ME *triste, tryste, tristre*), a station to which game was driven: OF-MF *triste* (var *tristre*): like ML *trista*, prob from Scan. (EW.)

6. E *troth*, ME *trowthe*, comes from OE *trēowth*

(as in para 2) and is therefore a doublet of *truth*: *troth* is a pledging of, a pledged, fidelity.

7. E *trow*, to believe (obs), hence to suppose (archaic), comes, via ME *trowen*, from OE *trēowan*, var *-ian*, lit to have *trēow* or faith in, hence to believe: cf the syn OFris *triūwa*.

8. *Trig*, now dial, is basically 'trusty, loyal', hence 'neat' or 'trim': ME *trigg*: ON *tryggr*, loyal (cf para 1).

**truffle.** See THIGH, para 7.

**truism.** See TRUE (heading).

**trull.** See the 1st TROLL.

**truly.** See TRUE, para 2.

**trump** (1), in cards. See TRIUMPH, para 2.

**trump** (2), a trumpet; **trumpet**, n, hence v, whence **trumpeter**; **trombone**; **trunk**, proboscis;—**drum**, n, hence v (whence **drummer** and **drumming**).

1. *Trump*, the Mus instrument, derives, via ME *trumpe*, earlier *trompe*, from OF-F *trompe*, of Gmc origin: cf OHG *trumpa*, var of *trumba*, and ON *trumba*: echoic.

2. OF-F *trompe* has the MF-F dim *trompette*, whence E *trumpet*.

3. Also of Gmc origin is It *tromba*, with aug *trombone*, adopted by E.

4. OF-F *trompe*, trumpet, acquires, in F, the sense 'an elephant's proboscis', by shape-resemblance, whence, by confusion with *trunk* of a tree, the E 'elephant's *trunk*'.

5. Prob from OHG *trumba* and prob via MD-D *trommel*, MD *tromp(e)*, D *trom*, MHG *trumbel* (G *Trommel*), comes the E *drum*.

**truncate, truncation.** See TRENCH, para 1.

**truncheon.** See the 1st TRUNK, para 2.

**trundle.** See TREND, para 2.

**trunk** (1) of tree, whence a leather or cloth chest or box: OF-F *tronc*: L *truncus*, trunk of tree or of the human body, akin to and perh deriving from the adj *truncus*, lopped (of a branch): cf *truncate* at TRENCH, para 1.

2. L *truncus* has the VL derivative *truncĭō*, acc *truncĭōn*em, whence OF-F *tronçon*, with OF-MF var *tronchon*, whence ME *tronchoun*, the shaft of a broken ('lopped') spear, whence E *truncheon*, with divergent senses.

**trunk** (2), elephant's. See the 1st TRUMP, para 4.

**trunnion:** MF-F *trognon*, app from *tronc*: cf the 1st TRUNK.

**truss; trudge; trousseau.** The n *truss*, ME *trusse*, derives from MF-F *trousse* (OF *torse*), from MF-F *trousser*, var *trusser*: metathesis of OF *torser*: o.o.o., but perh from VL *torcĭāre*, from VL *torca*, a bundle, a *torch*: f.a.e., TORT. MF *trusser* becomes ME *trussen*, whence 'to *truss*', orig to pack into a bundle.

2. A *trousseau* is adopted from F: dim of MF-F *trousse*.

3. Orig to pack (one's clothes), hence to pack off, to be off, to depart, *trudge* perh derives from MF *trusser*: cf the passage of 'to *forge*' from 'to *force*'. (EW.)

**trust, trustful, trustworthy, trusty.** See TRUE, para 4 and heading.

**truth, truthful.** See TRUE, para 2 and heading.

**try** (v, hence n), whence the agent **trier** and the pa, vn **trying**; **trial**; **trysail** (*try*, n+*sail*)—used instead of another sail. *Trial*, adopted from AF, derives from OF-F *trier*, to sift, hence to pick out, to select: cf the syn OProv *triar*: o.o.o.: perh (despite B & W) from VL *trītāre*, to grind (corn): cf THROW, para 7. OF-F *trier* becomes ME *trien*, to pick out, to select, whence 'to *try*', orig as in ME, with naturally developing senses—several from MF-F.

**trypano-** words. See the element *trypan(o)-*.

**trysail.** See TRY (heading).

**tryst.** See TRUE, para 5.

**Tsar.** See CAESAR, para 4.

**tsetse** comes, via Afrikaans, from the Bantu languages—cf esp Sesuto *ntsintsi*, a fly: prob echoic.

**tub** (n, hence v), whence the adj **tubby**: ME *tubbe*, var *tobbe*: MD *tubbe*, var *tobbe* (as still): cf MLG *tubbe*, prob related to OHG *zwibar*, *zubar*, MHG-G *zuber*: kinship with L *tubus*, a tube, seems likely (Walshe): therefore cf NEXT.

**tuba, tubage, tubal, tubate; tube, tubular, tubulate** (adj, v), **tubulation, tubule, tubulous, tubulus;** cf the element *tubi-* (*tubo-*; *tubuli-*, *tubulo-*).

1. L *tuba*, a straight trumpet, is akin to and prob derived from L *tubus* (o.o.o.), a tube, a pipe; whereas the former is form-adopted, sense-adapted by E (cf LL 'sonorous eloquence': Souter), the latter becomes late MF-F *tube*, adopted by E; and partly from L *tuba*, partly from E *tube*, come *tubage* (collective suffix *-age*), *tubal* (adj suffix *-al*), *tubate* (as if from L *tubātus*).

2. L *tuba* and *tubus* have dim *tubula* and dim *tubulus*; only the latter has affected E, and this it does in:

*tubule*, with derivative anl adjj *tubular* (cf the F *tubulaire*) and *tubulous*;

*tubulate*, from L *tubulātus* (from *tubulus*);

*tubulation*, from L *tubulātiōn-*, o/s of *tubulātiō*, from *tubulātus*.

**tubby.** See TUB.

**tube.** See TUBA, para 1.

**tuber.** See THIGH, para 4.

**tubercle.** See THIGH, para 5.

**tubercular, tuberculin, tuberculosis, tuberculous.** See THIGH, para 5.

**tuberose, tuberous.** See THIGH, para 4.

**tubular, tubulate, tubulation, tubulous, tubulus.** See TUBA, para 2.

**tuck** (1), to draw up in a fold, hence n **tuck** and **tucker.** See the 3rd TOW, para 3.

**tuck** (2), to strike, to sound; hence n. See TOUCH, para 4.

**tucket,** a fanfare. See TOUCH, para 4.

**Tudor,** n, hence adj: an English dynasty (1485–1603) sprung from Owen *Tudor*, who, a Welshman, married Henry V's widow, Catherine: prob a W form of *Theodore*, L *Theodorus*, G *Theodōros*, lit 'God's gift'.

**Tuesday.** See DIANA, para 3, s.f.

**tufa; tuff.** The latter represents late MF-F *tuf*,

the former an irreg E reshaping: from It *tufo*, a soft, sandy stone, the volcanic detritus of the Neapolitan region: L *tofus*, varr *tophus* and *tufus*: o.o.o. Derivative L *tŏfāceus*, *-ius*, becomes It *tufaceo* and E *tufaceous*.

**tuft**, whence **tufty.** See the 1st TIP, para 10.

**tug.** See the 3rd TOW, para 2.

**tuition,** whence, anl, **tuitive; tutelage, tutelary; tutor** (n, hence v), **tutorial** (adj, hence n);—**intuent, intuit, intuition, intuitive.**

1. *Tuition* is adopted from MF-F (sense 'protection'), which derives it from L *tuitiōnem*, acc of *tuitiō*, a guarding, a protecting, from *tuit*us, var of *tūtus*, pp of *tuērī*, to guard, hence to look at, observe: o.o.o., but perh akin to certain Skt (and allied) words meaning 'strong' or 'much'.

2. From *tūt-*, s of the pp *tūtus*, comes the agent *tūtor*, a protector, (in law) a guardian, adopted by E, with scholastic sense deriving from the legal; the derivative adj *tūtōrius* leads to E *tutorial*.

3. Also from *tūt-* comes LL *tūtēlāris*, whence E *tutelar*, largely superseded by *tutelary*, which derives rather from EF-F *tutélaire*; EF *tutelage*, adopted by E, irreg attaches the suffix *-age* to L *tūtēla*, protection, defence.

4. L *tuērī* has the prefix-cpd *intuērī*, to look *in-* or upon, with presp *intuens*, o/s *intuent-*, whence the E adj *intuent*, and with pp *intuitus*, whence 'to *intuit*'—unless a b/f from E *intuition*. On the L pp *intuitus* are formed both LL*intuitiō*, acc *intuitiōnem*, whence late MF-F *intuition*, adopted by E, and ML *intuitivus*, whence late MF-F *intuitif*, f *-ive*, whence E *intuitive*.

**tulip; turban.** *Tulip* comes from ED *tulipa* (D *tulp*): EF *tulipan* (F *tulipe*): coll Tu *tülbend* (läle), the white tulip, a poetical sense-development from *tulbend*, a turban, ref both the shape (primarily) and the colour of the turban.

2. Coll Tu *tülbend* is a var of Tu *dülbend*, a turban, from Per *dülband*, a sash, hence a sash worn as a turban, hence a turban; and coll Tu *tülbend* becomes late MF-EF *tolliban*, contr in EF *tulban*, with EF var—retained by F—*turban* (*r* for *l*), duly adopted by E: yet another example of the numerous Oriental words that have come into E via F.

**tumble,** v (whence **tumbler**), hence n; **tumbrel,** var **tumbril.**

1. 'To *tumble*' derives from ME *tumblen*, freq of *tumben* (var *tomben*, influenced by F): OE *tumbian*, to do a cartwheel, also to dance vigorously: cf ON *tumba*, OF-MF *tumber*, MF-F *tomber*, to fall, and OF-MF *tumer*, to gambol, to dance, MD *tumen*, freq *tumelen* (D *tuimelen*): prob echoic (cf RUMBLE).—Cf TOMBOLA.

2. From MF-F *tomber*, to fall, derives MF-EF *tomberel* (EF-F *tombereau*): late ME *tomberel*, *tombrel*: EE-E *tumbrel*, var *tumbril*.

**tumefacient, tumefaction; tumescence, tumescent; tumid, tumidity; tumor, tumorous, tumour.** See THIGH, para 9.

**tump-line,** now usu **tumpline**: *tump*+*line*: *tump*,

of Alg origin—cf esp Massachusett *tămpăn*, a pack-strap worn across the forehead. (Mathews.)

**tumular, tumulous.** See THIGH, para 10.

**tumult, tumultuary, tumultuous.** See THIGH. para 11.

**tumulus.** See THIGH, para 10.

**tun.** See the 1st TON, para 1.

**tuna:** Sp: Taino (Caribbean) *tuna*.

**tundra,** adopted from Ru, is a Lapp word, orig the cpd *tun-tur*, lit 'marsh-plain' (EW).

**tune,** n (whence **tuneful** and **tuneless**)—hence v (whence **tunable, tuner, tuning**): ME *tune*, *tun*, var of ME *ton*, *tone*: cf TONE. Hence 'to *attune*' for *\*adtune*, to bring into harmony (L *ad*, towards); whence **attunement.**

**tungsten:** a Sw cpd—*tung*, heavy+*sten*, a stone: a metallic element as heavy as gold.

**tunic, tunicate.** The latter derives from L *tunicātus*, clothed with a tunic: as L *togātus*, from L *toga*, so L *tunicātus* from L *tunica*. L *tunica*, which becomes OF-F *tunique*, whence E *tunic*, is id with Gr *khitōn*: and both are of Sem origin, the intermediaries being prob the Phoenicians and perh—later—the Etruscans: cf H *kethōnet*, a tunic, and Ar *kattán*, linen: ? orig 'linen (garment)'. The Eg *ketn* (? from Gr) and *shenṭit* suggest that this is a Medit word. The derivative dim *tuniculus* explains E *tunicle*.

**tunnel.** See the 1st TUN, para 3.

**tunny** is an E dim formation (*tun*+euphonic *n*+ dim *-y*) from MF-F *thon* (pron *ton*; rapidly, almost *tun*): OProv *ton*: coll L *thunnus*, L *thynnus*: Gr *thunnos*: o.o.o.: of Aegean origin, as also is H *tannīn*. (Hofmann.)

**tup,** a ram, hence 'to **tup**' or copulate with, but also to butt, hence to beat: ME *tuppe* or *tupe*: o.o.o.: ? ult akin to the IE r *\*tud-*, to knock, to strike, as in Skt *tudáti*, he knocks, and enlarged in Gr *tuptein* (*p* for *d*), to strike, and nasalized in L *tund*ere, to strike: *\*tud-*, extn of basic *\*tu-* or *\*teu-*, to knock.

**Tupi,** a Tupian Indian or his language, belonging to the valley of the Amazon, hence the adj **Tupian:** a native Tupi word.

**tuque.** See TOQUE.

**turban.** See TULIP, para 2.

**turbary.** See TURF, para 2.

**turbid,** whence **turbidity; turbulence, turbulent**— cf **trouble** (whence **troublesome**), **troublous; turbine** (whence **turbinal**), **tourbillon, turbo; turbit.**— Prefix-cpds: **conturbation; disturb, disturbance, disturber; perturb, perturbable (and imperturbable), perturbation;** full cpd, **masturbate, masturbation, masturbator.**

1. As the obs E *turb*, a crowd, indicates, the imm originating word is L *turba*, agitation, disorder (of a crowd), hence a crowd either in motion or in disorder, hence a crowd, esp of the populace: prob from Gr *turbē*, confusion, disorder, tumult: IE *\*tur-*, var *\*tuer-*, to turn, to whirl, to be in a state of agitation or disturbance (Hofmann).

2. L *turba* has several derivatives and intimate cognates relevant to E; such as:

*turbidus*, (of water) cloudy and troubled, hence confused: E *turbid*;

*turbulentus* (suffix *-ulentus*), OF-F *turbulent*, adopted by E, with *turbulence* either adopted from EF-F or coming direct from LL *turbulentia*;

*turbare*, to render cloudy and troubled, to confuse, presp *turbans*, o/s *turbant-*, and pp *turbātus*, whence both *turbātiō*, o/s *turbātiōn-*, and agent *turbātor*, all occurring in E prefix-cpds (see para 5) but, as simples, no longer in current E;

*turbō* (gen *turbinis*, o/s *turbin-*), any object animated with a rapid, circular movement, e.g. a whirlwind, a waterspout, a cyclone, but also a spinning top, the revolution of a star, etc.: adopted by Zoo, it also figures in ordinary E in the form *turbine*, adopted from F (from L *turbinem*, acc of *turbō*); *turbinate* (cf the EF-F *turbiné*) comes from L *turbinātus* (from *turbin-*)—*turbit*, a fancy pigeon, prob from L *turbo*, a top+n suffix *-it*—*tourbillion*, anglicized var of *tourbillon*, adopted from F (dating from C12 *torbeillon*).

3. VL blends—? confuses—L *turbidus* and *turbulentus* to produce \**turbulus*, whence \**turbulāre* (cf the syn LL *turbidāre*, to render cloudy, to confuse), whence OF *trubler*, OF-F *troubler*, whence ME *trublen*, E 'to *trouble*'; the E n *trouble* is adopted from MF-F *trouble*, var *truble*, from the v; the adj *troublous* comes from MF *troubleus*, from the n.

4. L *turbāre*, to render (water or sky) cloudy, to agitate confusedly, to confuse, has one full cpd affecting E: *masturbāri* (occ *-āre*), perh (E & M) a f/e adaptation of Gr *mastropeuein*, to seduce as a pandar does (app a cpd derivative of Homeric *maiomai*, I desire ardently, pursue amorously+ *trop-*, from *trepein*, to turn), after L *mas*, male, a male (? VL male element). Whereas *masturbator* is adopted from LL *masturbātor*, from the pp *masturbātus*, whence 'to *masturbate*', *masturbation* is adopted from EF-F, which derives it from LL *masturbātiōnem*, acc of *masturbātiō*, itself from the L pp.

5. L *turbāre* has the foll prefix-cpds affecting E:

*conturbāre* (*con-* used int), to disturb, perturb, very much, pp *conturbātus*, whence *conturbātiō*, o/s *conturbātiōn-*, whence E *conturbation* (perh influenced by EF);

*disturbāre*, to confuse by disruption (connoted by *dis-*, apart), whence OF-EF *destorber*, EF *disturber*, whence ME *destourben*, *-turben*, whence, influenced by EF *disturber*, 'to *disturb*'; the derivative OF-EF *destorbance* and OF-MF *destorbeor* become E *disturbance* and *disturber* (of, e.g., the peace);

*perturbāre*, to confuse thoroughly, pp *perturbātus*, whence 'to *perturbate*', virtually displaced by 'to *perturb*', ME *perturben*, *-tourben*, from MF *pertourber*, MF-EF *perturber* (from L *perturbāre*); derivative LL *perturbātor* and L *perturbātiō*, acc *berturbātiōnem*, become, in turn, MF-F *perturpateur*, *perturbation*, and E *perturbator*, *perturbation*.

**turbinate; turbine.** See prec, para 2.

**turbit; turbo.** See TURBID, para 2.

**turbot.** See THORN, para 3.

**turbulence, turbulent.** See TURBID, para 2.

**turd.** See TORT, para 5.

**tureen.** See TERRA, para 3 (at *terrīnus*).

**turf**, n (hence v), whence **turfy**; **turbary**.

1. Coming right down from OE *turf*, the word is akin to OFris and OLG *turf*, OHG *zurba*, turf, G *Torf*, MD *torf*, MD-D *turf*, peat, ON *torf*, *torfa*, turf, peat, and ult to Skt *darbhás*, a tuft of grass.

2. Also of OGmc origin is OF-F *tourbe*, peat, imm from Frankish \**turba*; derivative MF *turbière*, MF-F *tourbière*, MF var *turberie*, *tourberie*, a peat bog, have, along with ML *turbāria* (from ML *turba*, peat, from OGmc), led to E *turbary*, the right to dig turf or peat, a place where one digs it.

**turgescence, turgescent, turgid, turgidity, turgor.** See THIGH, para 12.

**Turk; Turkey, turkey; Turkestan; Turki, Turkic, Turkish** (adj, hence n); **Turkoman** or **Turcoman; turquoise.**

1. A *Turk* derives from MF-F *turc*, which comes either from Tu(-Ar)-Per *Turk*, *Tourk*, or from ML *Turcus*, b/f from *Turci* (pl), itself from Byz Gr *Tourkoi* (pl), an adaptation of Ch *T'u-küe*; the Tu-Per *Turk*, *Tourk*, comes—prob via Byz Gr *Tourkoi*—from the Ch. In Tu, *turk* means 'strength': ? therefore 'The Strong (People)'.

2. MF-F *Turc* has derivative (la) *Turquie*, whence E *Turkey*, whence *Turkey cock*, whence *turkey cock*, whence *turkey*: the bird came into Europe from Africa, but by way of *Turkey*.

3. MF *Turc* had MF adj *turqueis*, *turquois* (*turcois*), whence *la pierre turquoise* (*-queise*, etc.), whence the MF-F *turquoise* (MF var *-queise*), adopted by E: either because this precious stone was first found in Asia Minor or because it reached Europe through Turkey.

4. Per *Turk* has adj *Turkī*, used derivatively as n and adopted by E, which from it forms, anl, the adj (hence n) *Turkic*; E *Turkish*, however, comes from MF *turqueis*, adj of *Turc*. *Turcoman* derives from Per *Turkmān*, like (*-man*) a (Per) *Turk*. *Turkestan*, var *-istan*, app=Per *Turkī*, adj (*-ī*) of *Turk*+*-stān*, a country, as in Per *Hindūstān*, India.

**turmeric.** See TERRA, para 3.

**turmoil.** See TREMBLE, para 4.

**turn**, v (whence **turner**: cf OF-MF *iorneur*, MF-F *tourneur*), hence n; numerous cpds, all easily explicable by the 2nd element—note esp **turncoat, -key, -pike** (either *pike*, a sharp point, or the weapon), **-sole** (treated in para 2), **-stile; turnip;**— **return**, n and v; **attorn, attorney, attornment.**— **tour** (n, hence v, whence **touring**), whence **tourist; tournament—tourney—tourniquet; contour; detour** n, hence v.

### Indo-European

1. 'To *turn*'—basically 'to move circularly' (vt, hence also vi)—comes from ME *turnen*, var *tournen*, from OE *turnian*, var of *tyrnan*, with ME interception of OF-MF *torner*, MF *turner*, MF-F

*tourner*: both OE and OF from L *tornāre*, to fashion in a lathe, to round off, hence to turn: from L *tornus*, a lathe: G *tornos*, a turner's (cf LL *tornātor*) or a carpenter's tool for rounding off this or that object, hence a circuit, hence a circle: ? a nasal mdfn of IE n *\*tor-*, corresp to IE v *\*ter-*, to rub, e.g. to shape by rubbing away. (Boisacq.)

### Full Compounds

2. Not imm recognizable are the two full cpds *turnip* and *turnsole*. The former, EE-E (obs) *turnep*, EE *turnepe*, seems to blend the n *turn* (ref its round shape)+ME-EE *nepe*, a turnip, OE *nāep*, L *nāpus*: o.o.o.—prob (E & M) Medit. The latter anglicizes MF-F *tournesol*, from It *tornasole* (or Sp *tornasol*): It *tornar*e, Sp *tornar*, to turn+It *sole*, Sp *sol*, the sun: the flower, otherwise named *heliotrope* (a sem doublet), turns to the sun.

### Prefix-Compounds

3. The most obvious prefix-cpd is 'to *return*', ME *returnen*, var *retournen*, earlier *retornen*, from OF-MF *retorner*, MF *returner* (cf the C9 L-Gallic *returnar*): *re-*, back+*torner*, *turner* (as in para 1), to turn. The n *return* derives from ME *retorn*, prob from MF *retorne* (from *retorner*).

4. Less easy is the legal v *attorn*: OF-MF *atorner*, varr *atourner*, *aturner*, to arrange, to dispose or distribute: *a* (F *à*), L *ad*, to+*torner*, *tourner*, *turner*: cf the ML *atturnāre*, *attornāre*. *Atorner* has pp *atorné*, which, used as n, becomes the ME *atorne*, *aturne*, EE *atorneye*, *aturneye*, E *attorney*.

5. *Contour*, adopted from EF-F, derives—anl with *tour*, a turn—from It *contorno*, itself from It *contornare*, VL *\*contornāre*: L *con-*, together, collectively+L *tornāre* (as in para 1).

6. *Detour* comes from EF-F *détour* (MF *detour*), which derives—anl with *tour*, a turn—from OF-MF *detorner*, MF *detourner* (EF-F *dé-*): *de-*, away from+*torner*, *tourner*.

### French-derived Simples

7. L *tornus* (as in para 1) became OF *torn*, which very soon eased to *tor*, which, influenced by MF-F *tourner*, became *tour*, which, in EF, acquired the further sense 'a voyage, a trip': and this sense and that form passed, late in C17, into E; the orig F sense ('a turn') is conserved in *tour de force*. EF-F *tour*, a voyage, was adopted by E: whence 'to *tour*': whence *tourist*.

8. OF-MF *torner* (MF-F *tourner*) has the derivative—a mdfn—*torneier*, *tornoier*, MF *tournoier*, whence ME *turnaien*, E 'to *tourney*'; whereas the derivative OF-MF n *tornei*, *tornoi* (MF-F *tournoi*) yields ME *torneie*, *tourneie*, *turnay*, whence E *tourney*, the derivative OF-MF *torneiment*, *tornoiement*, yields ME *tornement*, *turnement*, whence E *tournament*, orig syn with the n *tourney*, a jousting, hence certain other competitive, knock-out sports and games.

9. E *tourniquet*, a device to stop bleeding, is adopted from EF-F, and is often treated as a derivative of MF-F *tourner*, but prob that EF-F word derives from MF *tourniquet*, a coat of arms, from MF *turniquet*, a sort of tunic, var of *turniquel*, a derivative of MF *turnicle*, a f/e alteration (after MF *turner*, *tourner*) of *tunicle*, from L *tunicula*, dim of *tunica*, a tunic. (B & W.)

**turner.** See prec (heading).

**turnip.** See TURN, para 2.

**turnpike.** See TURN (heading).

**turnsole.** See TURN, para 2.

**turnspit.** See the 1st SPIT (heading).

**turpentine; terpene, terpineol, terpinol; terebinth, terebinthine.**

1. *Turpentine* is a *p-*for-*b* derivative—via EF *terpentin*—of late ME-EE *terbentyne* (*-tine*): MF *turbentine*, MF-OF *terbentine*, from L *terebenthinus* (whence, directly, E *terebinthine*), adj of *terebinthus* (whence, prob via MF *terebinthe*, F *térébinthe*, the E *terebinth*), the turpentine tree: Gr *terebinthos*, the tree, cf *terebinthinē* (*rhētinē*), terebinthine resin, i.e. turpentine. The Gr *terebinthos* was orig *terminthos*, o.o.o., but prob pre-Gr; in short, Aegean (Hofmann).

2. The EE *terp*entin has been used by Chem to form *terpene* (Chem suffix *-ene*), with var *terpine* or *terpin*, whence, in turn, the Chem *terpineol* and *terpinol* (*-ol*, var of *-ole*, from L *oleum*, oil).

**turpitude.** See TROPE, para 6.

**turquoise.** See TURK, para 3.

**turret.** See TOWER, para 1.

**turtle** (1), whence the taut **turtledove.** *Turtle*, a turtledove, comes from OE *turtle* (f), *turtla* (m): a dissimilation of L *turtur*, echoic of the bird's cooing—cf 'coo like a turtledove'.

**turtle** (2). See TORTOISE.

**Tuscan, Tuscany.** See TOWER, para 3.

**tush,** a tusk. See TOOTH, para 2.

**tushery,** an archaically literary style: *tush!*+collective suffix- *ery*.

**tusk.** See TOOTH, para 2.

**tussah,** var **tusseh,** loosely **tusser,** whence the anglicized **tussore.** The *tussah*, a silkworm producing a brownish silk, hence the silk itself, derives from the syn Hi *tasar*: from Skt *tasara*, perh an easing of the var *trasara*, a shuttle.

**tussle.** See TEASE, para 4.

**tussock** is an *-ock* (dim suffix) derivative of a Scan word attested by Da *tusse*, Sw *tuss*, a wad, a ball of wool, and Sw dial *tuss*, a handful, a wisp, of hay.

**tussore.** See TUSSAH.

**tutelage, tutelary.** See TUITION, para 3.

**tutor, tutorial.** See TUITION, para 2.

**tutti frutti,** adopted from It, is lit 'all fruits': cf E *total* and *fruit*.

**tuxedo:** *Tuxedo*: *Tuxedo jacket*, for a man's evening wear: *Tuxedo Park*, a fashionable resort and club near *Tuxedo Lake*, New York State: Lenape (of the Delaware group of the Alg languages) *p'tuksit*, a wolf, lit 'he has a round foot', used as the name of a sub-tribe of Alg Indians. (P²; Mathews; Webster.)

**twaddle** is a thickening of the syn **twattle**, an echoic v, hence n, prob with *-attle* as in *tattle*.

**twain.** See TWO, para 1.

**twang**, v, hence n: echoic.

**twattle.** See TWADDLE.

**tweak.** See TWITCH, para 2.

**tweed.** See *twill* at TWO, para 6.

**tweedledum** and **tweedledee.** See TWIDDLE, para 1.

**tweezers** is an instr-agent formed in *-er* from *twees, tweese*, aphetic for *etweese*, pl of EE *etwee*: EF-F *étui*, OF-MF *estui*, a (small) case: from OF-EF *estuier, estoier*, to put into a case, to enclose: o.o.o.

**twelfth, twelve.** See TWO, para 2.

**twentieth, twenty.** See TWO, para 3.

**twibil(l).** See TWO, para 4.

**twice.** See TWO, para 5.

**twiddle** (v, hence n), whence **twiddler** and pa, vn **twiddling; tweedle**—cf **tweedledum** and **tweedledee.**

1. 'To *tweedle*' is a dial var of *twiddle*: and prob from the pa-vn *tweedling*, (something) insignificant or trifling, comes *tweedledum* and *tweedledee*, two things virtually identical or, at the least, alike, the phrase being coined by the C18 E satirist John Byrom.

2. 'To *twiddle*,' to twirl, to touch lightly and fussily, is app echoic and of Scan origin; perh cf TWITCH.

**twifold.** See TWO, para 4.

**twig** (1), a small branch, a shoot, comes from OE *twīg*, var *twigge*, akin tò OHG *zwīg*, MHG *zwīc*, G *Zweig*, MD *twijch*, D *twijg*: orig '(something) forked' or divided in two: cf Skt *dvikás*, double, and therefore ult TWO.

**twig** (2), to understand, to detect: coll: either Ga *tuig* or, less prob, the syn Ir *twuigim* (OIr *tuiccim, tuccim*), I understand.

**twilight.** See TWO, para 4.

**twill.** See TWO, para 6.

**twin.** See TWO, para 7.

**twine.** See TWO, para 8.

**twinge.** See THONG, para 2.

**twinkle** (v, hence n), whence **twinkler** and pa, vn **twinkling**: ME *twinklen*: OE *twinclian*, freq of OE *\*twincian* (*\*twincan*) as attested by ME *twinken* to wink or to blink: cf MHG *zwinken*, G *zwinkern*, to wink, to twinkle: app a picturesque or imitative word.

**twirl; trowel.** 'To *twirl*'—whence the n *twirl*, whence the adj *twirly*—has app been sense-influenced by *whirl* but seems to come from or, at the least, be akin to OE *thwiril*, a flail, a stirrer (as for a churn), intimately related to OE *thweran*, to twirl: cf Nor dial *tvirla*, to twirl, and OHG *dwiril*, MHG *twirl*, G *Quirl*, a whisk, and ON *thvara*, to twirl; perh cf, further off, the L *trua* and the Gr *torune*, a ladle, a stirring-spoon (Walshe), and the L dim *trulla*, a small ladle or stirring-spoon, hence also a trowel.

2. L *trulla*, trowel, has the LL var *truella*, whence OF-MF (N dial) *trouele, troele* (MF *truele*,

MF-F *truelle*): ME *trowelle, trouell, trowylle, truel*: E *trowel*, n, hence v.

**twist, twister, twisting, twisty.** See TWO, para 9.

**twit.** See VIDE, para 10.

**twitch**, v (whence **twitcher, twitchet, twitching**), hence n; **tweak**, v (whence **tweaker** and **tweaking**), hence n.

1. 'To *twitch*' derives from ME *twicchen*, akin to OE *twiccian* and MHG-G *zwicken*, to pinch; cf also LG *twikken*, to tweak.

2. ME *twicchen* has var *twikken*, whence 'to *tweak*'.

**twitter**, v (whence **twitterer** and pa, vn **twittering**), hence n: ME *twiteren*: echoic—cf OHG *zwizzirōn*, MHG *zwitzern*, G *zwitschern*—and Sw *kvittra*, Da *kvidre*. (Walshe.)

**twixt** and **betwixt.** See para 10 of:

**two** (adj, hence n), whence **twofold, -handed, -pence** (coll **tuppence**), **-some; twain; twelfth, twelve** (adj, hence n); **twentieth, twenty** (adj, hence n); **twibill, twifold, twilight; twice; tweed** and **twill;** sep TWIG; **twin**, n hence adj and v (whence **twinning**); **twine, twist**, v (hence n), whence **twister** and pa, vn **twisting; twixt** and **betwixt.**—Cf the DUAL (L *duo*) group, and such words as DOUBLE, DOUBT, DOZEN, all sep treated.

1. *Two*, ME *two*, var *twa*, f and neu, and *twei, twein* (earlier *tweien*), m—the imm source of E *twain*. The ME forms derive from OE *twā* (f and neu), *twēgen* (m), *tū* (neu): cf OFris *twā* (f, neu) and *twēne* (m)—OS *twā* (f), *twēne* (m), *twē* (neu)—OHG-MHG *zwō* (f), *zwēne* (m), *zwei* (neu)—G *zwei* (all genders)—Go *twai, twōs, twu*—MD *twe, twee, twene, tween, twa*, D *twee*—ON *tveir, tvaer, tvau* (*tv-* pron thus), with modern Scan cognates; between these *t-* forms and the *d-* forms of L, Gr, Skt, the C forms (in *d-*) perh form a link; the IE etymon perh veered between *\*duwo* and *\*dwi*. Cf the DUO group.

2. *Twelve*, ME *twelve*, earlier *twelf*, comes from OE *twelf*: cf OFris *twelef, twelif, twelf, tolef*—OS *twelif*—Go *twalif*—OHG-MHG *zwelif*, G *zwölf*—ON *tōlf*: lit, (10+) 2 leave, i.e. left over: for the formation, cf Lith *dvý-lika*—and E ELEVEN. *Twelfth*, ME *twelfthe*, earlier *twelfte*, comes from OE *twelfta* (from *twelf*): cf OFris *twelefta, twilifta, tol(e)fta*.

3. *Twenty*, ME *twenty*, earlier *twenti*, comes from OE *twēntig* or *twentig*: cf OFris *tweintich* or *twintich*—OS *twēntig*—OHG *zweinzug*, MHG *zweinzec, zwēnzec*, G *zwanzig*; the Go *twai tigjus*, two tens, gives the clue to the formation of all these OGmc words, *-ty* denoting (as in *thirty, forty*, etc.) 'tens' or perh rather 'times ten'. *Twentieth*, ME *twentithe*, comes from OE *twenti-gotha*: cf OFris *twintig(o)sta*, var *twintigesta*.

4. OE *twā, tū*, has the c/f *twi-*, preserved intact by ME and E: cf OFris *twi-*, ON *tvi-*, Skt *dvi-*. *Twi-* occurs in OE-E *twibill* (*bill* or *bil*, a cutting instrument) and *twifold* (OE *twifeald*), superseded by *twofold*, and *twilight*, ME *twilight* (ME *twi-*+*light*, OE *lēoht*)—cf G *Zwielicht*.

5. *Twice*, ME *twies*, tacks the adv-orig-gen

ending -s to ME twie, twice, from OE twigea, twiga, twiwa, extnn of the c/f twi-: with the OE forms, cf OFris twīa and OS twīo.

6. The fabric twill, ME twile, comes from OE twili, another extn of twi-: cf the G Zwillich: sem, it is 'the two-thread (fabric)'—cf drill, 'the three-thread (fabric)'. The Sc form of twill is tweel, whence, by f/e association with the Tweed River of a manufacturing region of Scotland, the E tweed.

7. The E-ME adj-hence-n twin derives from OE twinn, two, a pair of numbers intimately related: cf OFris twīne, Go twaihnai, ON tvinnr, tvennr, pron twin, twen; cf also OSw twinlinger and OHG zwinling, MHG zwinelinc, G Zwilling, twin, and Lith dvynù, twins. (Walshe.)

8. 'To twine' or twist together, ME twynen, perhaps comes rather from ON tvinna than from the OE n twīn, whence E twine; lit a double or twisted thread, OE twīn is related to ON tvinni and MHG-G zwirn (cf OHG zwirnēn, to twine).

9. 'To twist,' ME twisten, comes from OE -twist (whence, in part, the E n twist), occurring in cpds, and meaning lit 'made of two strands', esp of two strands twined together: cf OE twist, a branch, and ON tvistra, to separate, and OFris twist, MHG-G zwist, a dissension, and Skt dvěsti, he hates. (Walshe.)

10. The prep 'twixt shortens betwixt, ME be-twixt but usu betwix or bitwix, from OE betweox, orig a scribal var of betweohs, an -s extn of betweoh, var betwih: be-, bi-, by+-tweoh, -twih, from OE twā, twēgen, tū, two (as in para 1).

tycoon, orig written also taikun: Jap taikun, a great lord, from Ch taikun, a great prince.

tye. See tie at the 3rd TOW, para 4.

tyke, a country bumpkin, a rural lout, not pej in 'Yorkshire tyke', now rarely tike: ME-EE tike, tyke, a dog, esp a mongrel: ON tīk, a bitch. The 'rustic or bumpkin' sense, however, as OED points out, is perh of C origin—cf OW taiawc, Cor tioc, tyoc, tyac, a husbandman, a rustic.

tymp, in mining, is a b/f from tympan, a door-panel: and tympan is adopted from EF-F tympan (EF tympane) as an Arch term, but occurring in OF as 'kettledrum': L tympanum a (square) door-panel, a kettledrum: syn Gr tumpanon, s tumpan-, r tump-, a nasal var of the r tup- (s tupt-) of tuptein, to beat, to strike: cf TYPE. L tympanum has been adopted by E, esp—apart from Arch and Zoo—in the sense 'ear-drum', which prob comes from C17-20 F tympan (occ Sci tympanum); hence the adj tympanic. But tympany, inflation (lit and fig), derives from ML tympanias, from Gr tumpanias, distention, inflation, from tumpanon, whence also Gr tumpanitēs, a dropsical distention of the abdomen, whence LL tympanitēs, whence MedE tympanites, with adj tympanitic, from LL tympanīticus (from the LL n).

2. Gr tumpanon becomes ByzGr tumbanon, whence OF *timbene, whence, by contr, *timbne, whence OF-F timbre, orig a kettledrum, hence a church-bell that one strikes with a hammer, hence a table-bell, hence, in C17, the Mus sense, duly adopted by ME-E. (B & W.)

3. ME timbre, kettledrum, acquires the dim (-el) timbrel, a small kettledrum or hand-drum, a tambourine.

type, a mark or impression caused by beating or striking, hence a symbol, hence either the general character or a particular form, an example, a model, a particular sort, order, class, in, e.g., Bio or Chem, with the printing deriving from the orig sense; whence the adj typal and 'to type' (with var senses corresp to those of the n).

2. The genesis of E type is this: late MF-F type: LL typus (occ tipus), a fig rather than lit 'pattern, type, prototype, model, symbol' (Souter), a recurring pattern in maladies: syn LGr tupos: Gr tupos, a mark, an impression, caused by a blow or sharp stroke: from tup-, the r of tuptein (s tupt-), to beat or strike: cf Skt tupati, he strikes or knocks, and OSl tŭpŭtati, to trample, to stamp on.

3. E type has certain self-explanatory cpds, e.g., typesetting and typewriter, the latter suggesting typist (type+agential -ist). Rather from LL typus, however, comes typify (c/f typi-+-fy, to make). Typical derives from ML typicālis, an -ālis extn of LL typicus, symbolical, characteristic, from syn LGr tupikos, from Gr tupikos, impressional, from Gr tupos in its orig, i.e. lit, sense. The Gr c/f tupo- becomes F and E typo-: see the element -type, where, e.g., archetype and typology.

### An IE Variant

4. But IE *tup-, to beat or strike, has the var *stup-, with the IE prefix s-, orig an int: cf Skt prastumpati, he knocks (pra-, a prefix: stump-, a nasal mdfn); but also cf such L words as stupēre and stuprum, treated forthwith.

5. L stupēre, to be knocked stupid or insensible, to remain so, has s and r stup-, extn of IE *stu-. The foll L derivatives affect E:

stupendus, (that is) to be feared, astounding, whence E stupendous;

stupidus, whence—perh via EF-F stupide—E stupid, the derivative L stupiditās, acc stupiditātem, yielding EF-F stupidité and E stupidity;

stupor, adopted by E (cf MF-F stupeur);

cpd stupefacere, to render (facere, to make) stupid, whence EF-F stupéfier, whence 'to stupefy', the presp stupefaciens, o/s stupefacient-, yielding stupefacient, adj hence n, and the pp stupefactus yielding LL stupefactiō, acc stupefactiōnem, whence EF-F stupéfaction, whence E stupefaction.

6. The cognate L stuprum, shame, dishonour, hence dishonour resulting from debauch or rape (adopted as a Law term), represents r stup-+ extn -r-+-um (neu n); the derivative n stuprāre has pp stuprātus, which yields 'to stuprate', whence, anl, stupration.

### A Germanic Cognate

7. Akin to Gr tuptein, to beat or strike, is Gr stupos, a tree-stump: related thereto are the ON syn doublets stūfr (f for p) and stubbr or stubbi

(*b* for *p*): related to ON *stubbr, stubbi*, is OE *stubb, stybb*, whence—cf MD *stubbe, stobbe*—E *stub*, a tree-stump, with naturally derivative senses, ending (?) in cigarette *stub*, cheque-book *stubs*, etc.; whence 'to *stub*' and *stubby*.

8. Prob from OE *stubb, stybb*, comes ME *stoburn* or *stiborn*, whence E *stubborn*, whence *stubbornness*.

**typhoid**, adj, hence n; **typhus**. The former=*typh*us+*-oid*: (a) typhus-like (disease). The latter is a SciL phon and sem adaptation of Gr *tuphos*, vapour, smoke, fumes, hence, Med, a stupor caused by fever: cf Skt *dhūmás*, vapour, smoke: therefore cf FUME.

**typhoon**: Cantonese *tai-fung*, a great wind: f/e influenced by EE *tuphon, tuphan, tufon*, from Ar *tūfān*, from Gr *tuphōn*, a hurricane, from *Tuphōn*, God of Winds, akin to Gr *tuphos*, q.v. at TYPHOID.

**typhus**. See TYPHOID.

**typical, typify, typist**. See TYPE, para 3.

**typography**—whence, anl, **typographer** (cf EF-F *typographe*) and **typographic** (cf EF-F *typographique*), with extn **typographical**—derives from EF-F *typographie*, itself from late ML *typographia*: L *typo-*, from Gr *tupo-*, c/f of *tupos*, q.v. at TYPE, para 2+ML *graphia*, from Gr *-grapheia* (cf *graph* at GRAMMAR).

**typtology**. See the element *typto-*.

**tyrannic**, usu in extn **tyrannical; tyrannicide; tyrannize; tyrannous** (*-ous* substituted for the *-ic* of *tyrannic*); **tyranny; tyrant**.

1. These words come into E via OF-F and L from Gr *turannos*, a lord, a master, a prince, a king, esp an absolute master or ruler, a despot, and its Gr derivatives; *turannos* itself is prob a native

of either the Aegean or Asia Minor (? Phrygia or Lydia); cf Etruscan *Turan*, the Ruler, a by-name of Venus. If, however, the r be *\*tur-*, not *\*turan-*, the word is perh related to Skt *tŭrvati*, he subjugates or conquers: cf, I think, the *tar* of Hit *tarhh-*, to 'be powerful; control, conquer' (Sturtevant)—note esp *tarruhhanzi*, they are powerful, they conquer.

2. Gr *turannos* (τύραννος) becomes L *tyrannus*, OF-MF *tiran* (EF-F *tyran*), with faulty var *tirant*, later *tyrant*, by f/e association with *-ant*, the presp of vv in *-er*: ME *tirant, tyran*: E *tyrant*. Gr *turannos* has the foll derivatives relevant to E:

*turannikos*, L *tyrannicus*, MF-F *tyrannique* and, perh independently, E *tyrannic*;

*turannizein*, LL *tyrannizāre*, MF-F *tyranniser*, E 'to *tyrannize*';

*turannia* (abstract suffix *-ia*), LL *tyrannia*, MF *tirannie* (EF-F *tyrannie*), ME *tirannye*, E *tyranny*;

L *tyrannicīda*, the agent, and *tyrannicīdium*, the deed, has 2nd element in *-cid-*, a c/f of *caedere*, to slay: whence E *tyrannicide*, perh suggested by late MF-F *tyrannicide* (deed).

**tyre**. See the 1st TIRE.

**Tyrian**, elliptical for **Tyrian blue** or **Tyrian purple** (also called **Tyrian dye**), derives from L *Tyrius*, adj of *Tyrus*; trlnn of Gr *Turios*, adj, and *Turos*, the ancient Phoenician city of Tyre. Gr *Turos* is an IE reshaping of Sem *\*Sūr*: cf H *Zōr* and Ar *Es Sūr*, 'The Rock', from its partly insular situation.

**tyro**. See TIRO.

**tyro-** words, e.g., **tyromancy**: see the element *tyro-*.

**Tyrrhenian**. See TOWER, para 2.

**Tzar**. See *Czar* at CAESAR.

# U

---

**uberous, uberty.** See UDDER, para 2.

**ubiety, ubiquitarian, ubiquitary, ubiquitous, ubiquity.**

1. These words derive from L *ubi*, where, akin to Ve *kŭ*, IE *\*kū*: cf the extnn Ve *kúva-, kva-*, Skt *kúha*, Hit *kuwapi, kuwapit*, OSl *kŭde*: cf L *ibi*, there, for *ibi* exhibits both the locative *-i* and the medial *b*. The *u-* of *ubi* is app that of *unde*, whence, *umquam*, ever, and also of *quī*, who, *quis*, who?: an IE indication of the relative. (E & M.)

2. From L *ubi*, Sci and Phil L has coined *ubietas*, whereness, whence *ubiety*.

3. L *ubi* has derivative *ubique*, everywhere; the L *-que* connotes 'ever' or 'any': cf *quisque*, whosoever. From L *ubique* derives the learnèd, orig Phil and Theo, EF-F *ubiquité*, whence *ubiquity*, whence, anl, both *ubiquitary* (perh imm from Bossuet's *ubiquitaire*) and *ubiquitous*; from *ubiquitary* come the adj *ubiquitarian* and the Theol n *Ubiquitarian*.

**udder,** whence **udderless; uberous, uberty; exuberance, exuberant, exuberate.**

1. *Udder*, ME *udder*, earlier *uder*, OE *ūder*, is akin to OFris *ūder*, var *jāder* (*iāder*), OHG *ūtar*, *ūtiro*, MHG *iuter*, G *Euter*, MD *uder*, later *uyer*, D *uier*, ON *iūgr* (*jūgr*), Sw *jufver*—Lith *ūdróju*—L *ūber* (for *\*ūder*)—Gr *outhar* (gen *outhatos*)—Skt *ū́dhar* (gen *ū́dhnas*)—IE r, *\*udh-*, var *\*oudh-*, mdfn *\*ēudh-*. (Hofmann; Walshe.)

2. L *ūber*, udder, has adj *ūberōsus*, whence *uberous*, and n *ūbertās* (o/s *ūbertāt-*), whence *uberty*, and v *ūberāre*, to be fruitful, LL to fertilize.

3. L *ūberāre* has prefix-cpd *exūberāre*, to be very (connoted by int *ex-*) fruitful, hence to be abundant, with presp *exūberans*, acc *exūberant*em, whence late MF-F *exubérant*, whence E *exuberant*; derivative L *exūberantia* becomes EF-F *exubérance*, whence E *exuberance*. From the L pp *exūberātus* come both 'to *exuberate*' and the LL *exūberātiō*, o/s *exūberātiōn-*, an overflow, hence excess, whence *exuberation*.

**udometer.** See the element *udo-*.

**ug, ugly** (whence **ugliness**). The now dial *ug*, to feel, to cause to feel, disgust, ME *uggen*, comes from ON *ugga*, to fear. Akin to ON *ugga* is ON *uggr*, (a) fear, whence *uggligr*, causing fear, dreadful, whence ME *uglike*, later *ugly*, retained by E, orig 'dreadul, terrible'. The ON *ugga*, to fear, and *uggr*, fear, dread, are o.o.o.: prob cf

Cor *hager* (*-or*) and *uthek*, ugly, ferocious threatening.

**uhlan,** a firearm-bearing lancer: G *Uhlan, Ulan*: Pol *ulan*, soldier in Tatar costume: via Tu: Tatar *ulan*, a youth.

**Ugrian, Ugric.** See OGRE, para 2.

**ukase:** Ru *ukaz*, lit a command, hence an edict: cf Ru *ukasati*, to publish, ? lit, to give *out* (Skt *ud*).

**ukulele,** adopted from Hawaiian, is, in that language, orig and prop a flea: Hawaiian *uku*, an insect+*lele*, to fly or leap: 'from the movement of the fingers' (Webster). With *lele*, cf the syn Tahitian *rere* (*r* for *l*).

**ulcer, ulcerate, ulceration** (whence, anl, **ulcerative**), **ulcerous.**

*Ulcer* comes from the MF-F *ulcère*, from L *ulcer-*, o/s of *ulcus*, a live wound, an ulcer, hence fig: akin to Gr *helkos*, a wound, an ulcer, Skt *árśas*, haemorrhoids: IE r, perh *\*elk-*, a (running) wound.

2. L *ulcus*, o/s *ulcer-*, has adj *ulcerōsus*, whence late MF-F *ulcéreux*, f *-euse*, and, perh independently, E *ulcerous*; *ulcus* also has derivative v *ulcerāre*, with pp *ulcerātus*, whence both 'to *ulcerate*' and L *ulcerātiō*, acc *ulcerātiōn*em, whence MF-F *ulcération*, whence E *ulceration*.

**uletic; ulitis.** The former learnedly adds the adj suffix *-etic*, the latter—a SciL word—tacks *-itis*, connoting 'disease', to SciL (? also VL-ML) *\*ūlum*, trln of Gr *oulon*, gum of mouth. Cf the element *ulo-*.

**ullage:** MF *eullage* (EF-F *ouillage*), from MF *aouillier*, later *-er* (EF-F *ouiller*): OF-MF *aoeillier* (var *aoillier*), to fill a cask up to the *oeil* or 'eye' or bung: OF *a* (F *à*), L *ad*, to+OF-MF *ueil*, OF-F *oeil*, eye, L *oculus*+euphonic *-l-*+OF-MF inf *-ier* (F *-er*).

**ulna,** whence, anl, the E adj *ulnar*, and the SciL n *ulnare*: adopted from L *ulna*, the forearm: cf Gr *ōlénē*, elbow, OIr *uilenn*, an angle, OHG *elina*, MHG *elene*, G *Elle*, an ell: cf ELL.

**ulster,** a long, loose overcoat: *Ulster*, that Ir province in which, at Belfast, the fabric was orig made: via AF and slightly earlier AL, from ON *Ulfastir*, var of *Ulaztir* or *Ulathstir* (OED): app of C origin: cf OIr *Ulaidh* (gen *Uladh*), men of Ulster+OIr *tēr*, land, represented also in Ga, W, Cor (L *terra*).

**ulterior; ultima** (cf **ultima Thule**), **ultimate** (whence **ultimacy**), **ultimatum, ultimo; penultimate;**

**ultra** (whence **ultraism**), as in **ultra vires**—**ultra-crepidarian**—**ultramarine**—**ultramontane** (see MINATORY, para 8)—**ultramundane**—and the straight-forward cpd **ultra-violet; ultroneous;—outrage** (n, v), **outrageous.**

1. *Ultra*, in E an adv and a prep, hence an adj (whence n), is L *ultrā*, adv, hence prep: for *\*ulterā*, the abl (used as adv) of *\*ulter*, f *\*ultera*, neu *\*ulterum*, adj 'situated beyond': OL and archaic L prep *uls* (? for *\*ults*), beyond: for the final *s*, cf that of L *cis*, on this side of, *uls* and *cis* being complementaries; *uls* is akin to L *alius*, other, hence also to L *ille*, that (adj), that one. (E & M.)

2. Corresp to the adv and prep *ultrā* is the adv *ultrō*, whence the adj *ultrōneus*, going beyond (the demanded), hence voluntary or spontaneous, whence E *ultroneous*.

3. L *ultrā*, beyond, occurs in Law L *ultrā vīrēs*, beyond the force or strength (pl of ML *vīs*, L *uīs*, strength), hence beyond legal power, i.e. exceeding one's authority. *Ultrā* occurs in the foll E full cpds:

*ultracrepidarian* (adj, hence n), a jocularly erudite formation, in *-arian* (L *-ārius*), from the L *ultra crepid*am, beyond one's sandal, ref the L proverb *Ne sutor ultra crepidam iudicaret*, Let not the cobbler judge (in matters) above his sandal, Let the cobbler stick to his last;

*ultramarine*, n, Sp *ultramarino*, n, elliptical for *azul* (azure) *ultramarino*, from *ultramar*, a country beyond the sea (*mar*, L *mare*), the pigment *ultramarine* having orig been made from crushed lapis lazuli, brought from beyond the sea;

*ultramontane*: see MINATORY, para 8;

*ultramundane*: L *ultrāmundānus*, situated or operating beyond the world—*ultrā*+*mundānus*, mundane.

4. L *\*ulter*, situated beyond, has comp *ulterior*, situated further off, whence, as also the EF-F *ultérieur*, the E *ulterior*. It also has the sup *ultimus*, f *ultima*, neu *ultimum*, the most distant, with m and neu abl *ultimō*, as in *ultimō mensē*, in the last month, whence commercial E *ult(imo)*; the f *ultima*—used in Phon for the final syllable of a word—occurs in L *ultima Thule*, the land furthest north so far as the ancient Romans knew (perh Mainland in the Shetlands), hence any far-distant, vaguely-known country, or a very remote goal— L *Thulē, Thylē*, Gr *Thulē, Thoulē*.

5. L *ultimus* has derivative LL *ultimāre*, to come to an end, pp *ultimātus*, whence the E adj, hence n, *ultimate*; the neu *ultimātum* was, by diplomats, employed—cf the formation, use, sense of *imperātum*—as n, 'the final notification or warning', hence its general currency.

6. L *ultimus* has the cpd *paenultimus*, the last but one, lit 'almost (*paene*) the last', whence *paenultima*, elliptical for *p. syllaba*, last syllable but one; whence, after E *ultimate*, the E *penultimate*.

7. L *ultrā* becomes OF-MF *ultre* (MF-EF *oultre*, EF-F *outre*), whence OF-MF *ultrage*, MF *oultrage*, later *outrage*, orig excess, hence intemperance,

hence disgraceful excess or intemperance, adopted by E, whence 'to *outrage*', perh suggested by EF-F *outrager*; derivative OF-MF *ultrageus*, MF *oultrageus*, EF-F *outrageux*, f *outrageuse*, accounts for E *outrageous*.

**ultima** and **ultima Thule.** See prec, para 4.
**ultimacy, ultimate, ultimatum.** See ULTERIOR, para 5.
**ultra.** See ULTERIOR, para 1 (and heading).
**ultracrepidarian, ultramarine.** See ULTERIOR, para 3.
**ultramontane.** See MINATORY, para 8.
**ultramundane.** See ULTERIOR, para 3, s. f.
**ultra vires.** See ULTERIOR, para 3.
**ultroneous.** See ULTERIOR, para 2.
**ululant; ululate, ululation.**—**howl** (v, hence n), whence 'howler' and **howling**, pa and vn; **howlet.**

1. L *ululāre*, s *ulul-*, a redup of IE *\*ul-*, var *\*hul-*, to howl (beasts or men): echoic: cf Gr *hulān* (s and r *hul-*), to bark, Lith *ulóti* and redup *ulūlóti*, to utter the cry *ulo-*, Skt *úlūkas*, an owl.

2. L *ululāre* has presp *ululans*, o/s *ululant-*, whence the E adj *ululant*, and pp *ululātus*, whence both 'to *ululate*' and LL *ululātiō*, o/s *ululātiōn-*, whence *ululation*.

3. Akin to the words noted in para 1 are OHG *hwilōn*, to rejoice (howl with joy), MHG *hiuweln, hiulen*, to howl, G *heulen*, to howl, OHG *hūwila*, owl, MD *ulen, hulen*, later *huylen*, D *huilen*, to howl; perh imm from, but prob merely akin to, the MD words is ME *houlen*, whence 'to *howl*'.

4. *Howlet*, a small or young owl (owlet), is not a var of *owlet* (q.v. at OWL), but app a derivative from EF-F *hulotte*, the common wood-owl, but in dial a howlet: and EF-F *hulotte* perh comes from MHG *hiulen, hiuweln*, to howl, but prob (B & W) comes from MF-F *huler*, to howl, itself from L *ululāre*.

**Ulysses.** See ODIUM, para 9.
**umbel, umbellate, umbelliferous, umbellule.** See UMBRA, para 5.
**umber** (1); **Umbria**, whence **Umbrian**, adj, hence n.

1. The brown-earth pigment *umber* derives from F *ombre*, elliptical for *terre d'ombre*, from It *terra d'ombra*, app a f/e corruption of *terra d'Umbria*, with It *ombra* (L *umbra*) intervening, earth of *Umbria*: cf, sem, *sienna*, from It *terra di Siena*, earth of Siena.

2. It-from-L *Umbria* derives, with 'region' suffix *-ia*, from L *Umbri*, an ancient people of central Italy: by shortening from Gr *Ombrikoi* (o.o.o.).

**umber** (2), shadow, grayling. See UMBRA, para 3.
**umbilical, umbilicus.** See OMPHALIC.
**umbles.** See LOIN, para 4.
**umbo** (whence **umbonal**). See OMPHALIC.
**umbra**, whence **umbral** (cf LL *umbrālis*, retired, private: Souter); **umbrage, umbrageous**— **umbratile; umbrella; umber**, shade—cf **umbrette; umbriferous; umbrose, umbrous; umbel, umbellate, umbelliferous.**—Cpds: **adumbrant, adumbrate, adumbration** (whence, anl, **adumbrative** and **adumbratory**); **inumbrate, inumbration; obumbrant,**

obumbrate (adj and v), obumbration; penumbra, whence, anl, penumbral and penumbrous; sombre, AE somber—cf sombrero.

1. Behind all these words there looms L *umbra*, a shadow, shade or a shade, hence various fig uses (e.g., ghost): o.o.o.: but (E & M) cf Skt *andhás*, Av *andō*, blind, Ve *ándhas*, obscurity; for the suffix, cf the *-bra* of L *\*tenebra*, sing of L *tenebrae*, obscurity, shadows. L *umbra* is adopted by E and invested with several Sci and tech meanings.

2. L *umbra* has four adjj that affect E: *umbrātilis*, whence E *umbratile*; *umbrōsus*, whence *umbrose* and *umbrous* (cf the OF-MF *ombreux*); *umbrāticus*, whence perh the OF-F *ombrage*, shade, shadow, more prob deriving, by suffix *-age*, from OF-F *ombre* (L *umbra*); OF-F *ombre* had the OF-MF var *umbre*, whence OF-MF *umbrage* (var of *ombrage*), whence late ME-E *umbrage*; the modern sense of *umbrage* arose as early as in C14 F. Derivative MF-EF *umbrageux*, f *-euse*, yields E *umbrageous*; *umbrifer*, shade-bringing, whence *umbriferous*.

3. OF-MF *umbre* has become E *umber*, esp in the sense 'a grayling' (fish)—already in L *umbra*. From the OF-MF form, SciL has coined *umbretta*, whence *umbrette*, an African wading bird.

4. L *umbra* has dim *umbella*, a sunshade, with LL f/e var (after *umbra*) *umbrella*, whence—via the It *ombrello* or its EF-F derivative *ombrelle*—the E *umbrella*.

5. The L dim *umbella* yields the Bot *umbel*—perh via EF-F *ombelle*. From L *umbella*, SciL has coined both *umbellātus*, whence *umbellate*, and—after L *umbrifer*—*umbellifer*, whence, anl, *umbelliferous*.

6. L *umbra* has further affected E by its cpds, of which the first is the painters' *adumbrāre*, to sketch (lit, to shadow *ad* or towards), hence, fig, to foreshadow. Whereas the presp *adumbrans*, o/s *adumbrant-*, leads to the E adj-hence-n *adumbrant*, the pp *adumbrātus* leads both to 'to *adumbrate*' and to L *adumbrātiō*, o/s *adumbrātiōn-*, whence E *adumbration*.

7. L *inumbrāre*, to shade *in*, hence to shade, has pp *inumbrātus*, whence both 'to *inumbrate*' and the LL *inumbrātiō*, o/s *inumbrātiōn-*, whence *inumbration*.

8. L *obumbrāre*, to overshadow ('over' connoted by L *ob-*), has presp *obumbrans*, o/s *obumbrant-*, whence the Sci adj *obumbrant*, overshadowing, hence overhanging, as certain feathers overhang; the pp *obumbrātus* yields the E adj and v *obumbrate* and the LL n *obumbrātiō*, o/s *obumbrātiōn-*, whence *obumbration*.

9. From L *paene*, almost, and *umbra*, a shadow, EF-F has formed *pénombre*, whence, anl, the E *penumbra*.

10. LL *subumbrāre*, to overshadow (lit), to put lit into the shade, yields Sp *sombrar*, to produce shade, whence the n *sombra*, shade, whence prob —by a course not yet charted—the late MF-F *sombre*, shaded, hence, in EF-F, the modern sense,

whence E *sombre*, AE *somber*. From Sp *sombra*, shade, comes the instr *sombrero* (suffix *-ero*), a broad-brimmed hat, whence, via ASp, the A and E word.

**umbrage, umbrageous.** See prec, para 2.
**umbratile.** See UMBRA, para 2.
**umbrella.** See UMBRA, para 4.
**umbrette.** See UMBRA, para 3.
**Umbrian.** See the 1st UMBER, para 2.
**umbrose, umbrous.** See UMBRA, para 2.
**umlaut.** See LOUD, para 3.
**umpire.** See PAIR, para 8.

**un-** (1), not, comes straight down from OE *un-*, akin to OFris, OS, OHG-G, Go *un-*; to Gr and Skt *an-* (or *a-*); to L *in-*; C *an-*, with such varr as Ga *chan*, Cor *nan*, OIr *nicon*. Hence *un-* is akin also to L *non*, *ne*, not, E *no*, *not*, etc.

In this dictionary, only a few '*un-* not' words are included; those, for some particular reason. Most of the 'neg *un-*' words are imm deducible from the r word that follows the neg.

**un-** (2), forming, when it precedes a v, a v that expresses the contrary or a reversal (as in *unbend*) and, when it precedes a n, a v that expresses a privation of, a release from, or a removal of whatever the n element denotes or connotes (as in *unman* and *unyoke*): ME *un-*: OE *un-* or *on-*, unaccented forms of *and-*, against: cf OFris and Go *and-*, OFris var *end-* or *enda-*, OS *ande* or *endi-*, OHG *anti* or *enti*, G *ent-*, C *\*and-*, *\*ande-*, L *ante*, Gr and Skt *anti*. Therefore cf the prefixes *ante* and *anti*, which express two aspects of the one basic idea.

Only a few of the '*un-*, reversal or privation' vv are treated sep in the foll pages; those few, for some good reason.

**Una.** See ONE, para 2.
**unable** anglicizes L *inhabilis*.
**unanimity, unanimous.** See ANIMAL, para 6, and cf ONE, para 6.
**unaware.** See WARY (heading).
**unbelief, unbelievable.** The latter is merely the neg of *believable* (from *believe*, q.v. at LEAVE, n); the former was perh suggested by OE *ungelēafa*.
**unbind:** OE *unbindan*.
**uncanny:** *un-*, not+*canny* (cf *ken*, q.v. at CAN, v).
**uncertain, uncertainty.** See CERTAIN, para 4.
**unchristian:** cf OE *uncristen*.
**uncia, uncial.** See ONE, para 5.
**uncle, 'nunks' and 'nunky'; avuncular.**

1. Both *nunks* and *nunky* are coll derivatives of the now dial *nuncle*, itself from '*an uncle*', and '*mine uncle*', 'thine *uncle*': and E-ME *uncle* comes from OF-MF *uncle* (MF-F *oncle*): L *aunclus*, contr of *auunculus*, a maternal uncle: *auus*, an ancestor, esp a grandfather+dim *-unculus*. L *auus* is akin to Arm *haw*, grandfather, OE *ēam*, uncle, OHG-MHG *ōheim*, maternal uncle, G *Ohm*, uncle, MD *ohem*, *ome*, MD-D *oom*, uncle, Cor *ounter*, maternal uncle: IE r, *\*au-*, *\*aw-*, ancestor, esp grandfather.

2. L *auunculus*, becomes ML *avunculus*, whence, anl, the E adj *avuncular* (cf F *avunculaire*.)

**unco**, adv from adj, is a Sc reduction of ME-E *uncouth*, OE *uncūth*, unknown.

**unconscionable**, **unconscious(ness)**. See CON-SCIENCE (heading).

**uncouth** (cf UNCO). See the v CAN, para 3.

**unction**, **unctuosity**, **unctuous**; **unguent**, **unguentarium**, **unguentary**; **ointment**; **anoint**, whence **anointment**.

1. *Unction* derives from L *unctiōn-*, o/s of *unctiō*, an oiling, a being oiled, in LL with the sign of the Cross, *unctuous* from ML *unctuōsus*, mdfn of LL *unctōsus*, oily, and *unctuosity* from MF *unctuosité* (later *onctuosité*) from ML *unctuōsitā-tem*, acc of *unctuōsitās* (from *unctuōsus*). All three are, in L, formed from L *unct-*, s of *unctus*, pp of *unguere*, to apply a perfumed oil to, to oil, LL to anoint with the sign of the Cross. L *unguere* has s *ungu-*, r *ung-*, perh a nasalization of an IE *\*agh-* or *\*akh-*, oil or grease, to oil or to grease; cf Skt *anákti*, he anoints.

2. L *unguere* has derivative *unguen*, superseded by the extn *unguentum*, whence E *unguent* (cf MF-F *onguent*), a lubricant, a salve, an ointment; the derivative L adj *unguentārius* yields *unguentary*, and the subsidiary *unguentārium*, prop the neu of the adj, is retained by erudite E.

3. L *unguentum* becomes VL *\*unguimentum*, whence OF-EF *oignement*, unguent, an anointing, whence ME *oinement*, whence the reshaped E *ointment*.

4. L *unguere* has the cpd *inunguere*, to oil into, hence to smear on, to anoint, whence OF-MF *enoindre*, with pp *enoint*, f *enointe*, whence late ME-E 'to *anoint*'.

**unda**, **undine**, **ondine**; **undulant**, **undulate**, **undulation** (whence, anl, **undulative**, **undulatory**);—**inundant**, **inundate**, **inundation** (whence, anl, **inundatory**);—**abound**, **abundance**, **abundant**; **redound**, **redundance**, **redundant**; **superabound**, **superabundance**, **superabundant**; **surround** (v, hence n), whence the pa **surrounding** and the vn **surroundings**.

1. L *unda*, water in motion, a wave, is akin to Skt *undáti*, the waters spread or stretch out (sing *unátti*); *und-* is a var of IE *\*ud-*, water, as in Skt *udnás* and, aspirated, Gr *húdōr* (gen *húdatos*); ult akin to WATER.

2. L *unda* has the SciL derivative *undina*, either coined by Paracelsus or popularized by him: hence G *Undine*, whence the E *undine*; adopted also is the EF-F *ondine*, prob from Paracelsus.

3. L *unda* has the VL dim *undula*, whence the adj *undulātus*, wavy, whence the E adj, hence v, *undulate*; whence also the learnèd EF-F *ondulation*, which prob suggested E *undulation*, as F *ondulatoire* perh suggested *undulatory*.

4. L *unda* itself acquires the v *undāre*, (of the sea) to be agitated, hence to flow or move in waves, with pp *undātus* and presp *undans*, o/s *undant-*. *Undāre* has the foll cpds affecting E:

*abundāre* (*ab-* used int), to overflow, hence to abound, presp *abundans*, o/s *abundant-*, with derivative *abundantia*; whence OF-MF *abundant* (MF-F *abondant*) and OF-MF *abundance* (later *abondance*), both adopted by ME-E; 'to *abound*' comes from ME *abounden*, MF-F *abonder*, OF-MF *abunder*, from L *abundāre*;

*inundāre*, to flow (over) into, presp *inundans*, o/s *inundant-*, E adj *inundant*, and pp *inundātus*, whence both 'to *inundate*' and L *inundātiō*, acc *inundātiōnem*, whence MF *inundacion*, MF-EF *inundation* (later *inondation*), adopted by E;

*redundāre* (*re-* vaguely int), to overflow, hence to be very or too abundant, whence OF-MF *redunder*, MF-F *redonder*, whence 'to *redound*' with senses developing as in EF-F; the L presp *redundans*, o/s *redundant-*, and its derivative n *redundantia*, yield E *redundant* and *redundance*, with the MF derivatives perh intervening;

LL *superabundāre*, to overflow, hence to be in excess, whence—cf MF *superabonder*—'to *superabound*', after *abound*; the LL presp *superabundans* (o/s *superabundant-*), used as adj, and its LL derivative *superabundantia* yield *superabundant* and *superabundance*;

LL *superundāre*, to overflow, becomes OF-MF *surunder*, *suronder*, *surounder*, whence 'to *surround*', with the current sense arising early in C17 by f/e association with *round*.

**undeniable**. See NEGATE, para 3, s.f.

**under**, with numerous cpds, mostly obvious—note esp **underclothes** (whence the coll **undies**), **undergo** (cf OE *undergān*, to undermine), **underlay** (OE *underlecgan*), **underlie** (OE *underlicgan*), **underneath** (see NETHER, para 2), sep **understand**, **undertone** (under, hence subdued), **underworld** (world *under* the earth), **underwrite** (OE *underwrītan*, to sign, sense-influenced by L *subscribere*, to subscribe).

*Under*, prep and adv (whence adj), descends from OE *under*, prep and adv, akin to OFris *under*, OS *undar*, *under*, OHG *untar*, MHG-G *unter*, Go *undar*, MD *under-* (in cpds), MD-D *onder*: Gmc etymon, *\*under*; IE etymon, *\*andhér*, *\*ondhér*, *\*undhér*, prob *\*indhér*. (Walshe.)

**undergo**, pt **underwent**, pp **undergone**. See prec (heading).

**underlay**; **underlie**. See UNDER (heading).

**underling**; late OE *underling*; cf the 2nd suffix *-ling*.

**underneath**. See NETHER, para 2.

**understand**, pt and pp **understood**: ME *understanden*: OE *understandan*, to understand, lit and orig 'to stand under': f.a.e., STAND. The derivative n *understanding* is id in OE.

**undertaker** of funerals: late EE-E agent of **undertake**, to take upon oneself, whence, late ME-E, the vn **undertaking**: f.a.e., TAKE.

**undertone**. See UNDER (heading).

**underwrite**, whence **underwriter**. See UNDER (heading, s.f.).

**undies**. See UNDER (heading).

**undine**. See UNDA, para 2.

**undo**, **undoing**, **undone**. See DO, para 1.

**undulant**, **undulate**, **undulation**, **undulatory**. See UNDA, para 3.

**uneven**: OE *unefen*, *unefn*: f.a.e., EVEN.

**unfair,** orig unseemly or unlovely, comes from OE *unfa ger*: f.a.e., FAIR.

**unfold:** OE *unfealdan*: f.a.e., FOLD.

**ungainly.** See GAINLY.

**unguent, unguentarium, unguentary.** See UNCTION, para 2.

**unguis, ungula, ungulate.** See NAIL, para 2.

**unholy:** OE *unhālig*: f.a.e., HOLY.

**unicity.** See ONE, para 3.

**unicorn.** See HORN, para 5, and cf ONE, para 6.

**uniform** (adj, n), **uniformity.** See FORM, para 9, and cf ONE, para 6.

**unify,** whence, anl, **unification,** derives—perh via late MF-F *unifier*—from LL *ūnificāre*: L *unus* (cf ONE)+-*ficāre*, c/f of *facere*, to make.

**unilateral,** one-sided: like F *unilatéral*, either from SciL *unilateralis* or from L *ūnī-*, c/f of *ūnus*, 1+E *lateral* (q.v.).

**unintelligent, unintelligible.** See LEGEND, para 11, s.f.

**union.** See ONE, para 3.

**unique.** See ONE, para 3.

**unison, unisonous.** The latter comes from LL *ūnisonus*, having only one sound, monotonous: whence the MF-F n *unsison*, whence E *unison*; *in unison* was prob suggested by EF-F *à l'unisson* (lit and fig).

**unit.** See ONE, para 3, s.f.

**unite, unity.** See ONE, para 3, s.f.

**univalent.** See the element *uni-*.

**universal, universality, universe; university.** See ONE, para 7.

**univocal.** See VOCABLE, para 9, s.f.

**unjust**=*un-*, not+*just*, q.v. at JURY, para 5.

**unkind,** rather cruel, has sense-developed from OE *uncynde*, unnatural (not what one would expect from a member of one's family): cf KIN.

**unless:** C15–16 *onlesse, onles,* also *onlesse (onles) that,* lit 'in less' and 'in less (case) that': C16–17 *unlesse* (C16 onwards: *unless*): cf ON and LESS.

**unlike, unlikelihood, unlikely.** See LIKE, para 4.

**unlock:** cf the syn OE *unlūcan*.

**unman; unmanly.** See MAN, para 3.

**unmeet:** OE *unmǣte*, not meet: for the adj *meet*, cf *mete*, to measure, q.v. at MEASURE.

**unreal, unreality.** See the 1st REAL, para 1.

**unstable.** See STABLE, para 1, s.f.

**until.** See the 3rd TILL, para 2.

**unto** (ME-E): that *un-*, as far as, which we see also in *until* (q.v. at the 3rd TILL, para 2): cf the syn OS *unto*, OHG *unzi*, and the OS conj *und*, until.

**untrue, untruth** (whence **untruthful**). See TRUE, para 2, s.f.

**unwieldy.** See VALUE, para 2—and heading.

**unwisdom, unwise, unwisely:** OE *unwīsdōm*, OE *unwīs*, OE *unwīslīce*: f.a.e., VIDE (esp para 8).

**unwitting,** adj, derives from the presp *unwitting*, not knowing: OE *unwitende*; **unwitty** from OE *unwittig*, devoid of understanding: both of the OE words have cognates in the other OGmc languages: f.a.e., VIDE.

**unwonted.** See VENERABLE, heading; cf para 11.

**unwritten:** OE *unwriten*: cf WRITE.

**unyoke:** OE *ungeocian*: cf *yoke*, q.v. at JOIN, para 20.

**up, upper** (hence n, esp in pl); **upmost, uppermost; 'uppity' and uppish; upon; upward, upwards;** —numerous cpds, easily deducible from the r word, but note esp **upbraid—upholster, upholsterer, upholstery — upland(s) — uplift — upright — uproar,** whence **uproarious—upset—upshot—upstart—uptake.**

1. *Up,* adv, hence prep, later also adj, derives from OE *up,* var *upp,* cf OE *uppe,* on high: akin to OFris *up,* var *op,* MD *uppe, up-* (in cpds), *oppe,* MD-D *op,* OS *uppa, upp, up,* OHG-MHG *ūf,* G *auf,* Go *iuf,* ON *upp, uppi* (with modern Scan cognates)—and E OVER—and perh Hit *up-,* (of the sun) to rise.

2. *Up* used as adj has comp *upper,* whence *uppermost; upmost=*'the most *up*' (adj). Also from *up,* adj, come *uppish* (adj suffix *-ish*) and AE (coll and dial) *uppity* and E dial *uppy,* tetchy.

3. Adv (and adv) and prep cpds of *up* are the prep *upon,* ME *upon,* var *uppon,* i.e. *up on,* and the adv, hence adj, *upward,* OE *upweard,* whence OE *upweardes* (gen, used as adv), whence *upwards.*

4. The adv *up* occurs in many nn and v, the foll being perh the best worth recording:

*upbraid,* q.v. at BRAID, para 2;

*upholsterer,* a taut-agential extn of late ME-EE *upholster,* an easing of *upholdster* (suffix *-ster*), mdfn of ME-EE *upholder,* in ME a tradesman (who holds up or exhibits his goods); from the n *upholster* derive, by b/f, the v *upholster* and, by adding suffix *-y,* the n *upholstery;*

*upright,* whence *uprightly* and *uprightness*: see REX, para 3, s.f.;

*uproar,* either from MD *uproer* (MD-D *oproer*) or from MLG *uprōr* (cf G *Aufruhr*): the Gmc *up,* etc.+the Gmc forms of 'to *roar*';

*upshot,* orig (C16-early C17), the final shot in an archery contest: *up,* adv+*shot,* n, q.v. at the v *shoot.*

**upas:** elliptical for Mal *pohon upas* (cf the E var *bohun upas*), tree of poison.

**upbraid.** See BRAID, para 2.

**upholster, upholsterer, upholstery.** See UP, para 4.

**upon.** See UP, para 3.

**upper, uppers.** See UP (heading).

**uppish, 'uppity'.** See UP, para 2.

**upright.** See REX, para 3, s.f.

**uproar.** See UP, para 4.

**upshot.** See UP, para 4, s.f.

**upward, upwards.** See UP, para 3.

**Urals, Ural-Altaic**—cf Altai; **uralite.** The Min *uralite* tacks the Min n-suffix *-ite* to *Ural* Mountains (commonly called the *Urals*), where it was discovered: and whereas *Ural* is prob a native Ru word, *Altai* (whence *Altaic*) is perh Mongol—? the Mongol *alta,* var *altan,* gold. (Enci It.)

**Urania, Uranus; uranite, uranium** (whence, anl, **uranic** and **diuranate:** *di-,* Gr *dis,* twice+*uranium*

+Chem n-suffix -*ate*); cf the element *urano*-, where see *uranology* and *uranoscopy*;—**Varuna**.

1. *Urania*, the Muse of Astronomy, is the L trln of Gr *Ourania*, from *ourania*, the f of *ouranios*, the adj of *ouranos*, the heavens, the sky, personified as *Ouranos*, the Lord of Heaven, the husband of Gaia (Earth) and the father of the Titans, whence LL *Uranus*, whence the planet *Uranus* discovered by Herschel in 1781. In 1789 the G chemist Klaproth discovered an element he named *Uran*, in honour of Herschel; from the F form *urane* the F chemist Péligot named, in 1841, the element he, in turn, discovered—*uranium* (Chem element suffix -*ium*), adopted by E. Derivative from G *Uran* is G *Uranit*, whence the F *uranite*, adopted by E. (B & W.)

2. App cognate with Gr *Ouranos*, the god of the sky, is Skt *Váruṇas*, in Hinduism the guardian—after having been the creator—of cosmic order, whence E *Varuna*.

3. Gr *ouranos*, the heavens (heaven), the sky, is the Attic form, the Lesbian being *oranos*, *orranos*, and the Doric and Boeotian *ōranos*. Whereas Boisacq supports Kretschmer in proposing an IE etymon *\*oworanos*, prob earlier *\*oworwanos* and *\*worwanos*, Hofmann proposes *\*worsanos* and suggests that, as 'the moistener' or 'the drencher', hence 'the fertilizer', *ouranos*, the sky, is perh akin to *ouron*, urine (cf URINE). But are Gr *ouranos*, s and r *ouran*-, and prob Skt *Váruṇas*, s and r *Varuṇ*- (? orig *\*Uaruṇ*-), perh rather akin to Hit *wara*-, to burn (vi), which has such forms as the presp *waranza* and the imp *warānu*, var *uranu*, with an IE basic idea 'the burner, the giver of heat'?

**urazin.** See URINE, para 5.

**urban, urbane, urbanity** (whence, anl, **urbanize**, whence **urbanization**); **conurbation; suburb, suburban** (whence **suburbanite**).

1. *Conurbation*, an aggregation of urban communities about a great city (e.g., London), is a bureaucratic invention: *con*-, together+*urb*(an)+ -*ation*.

2. *Suburban* derives from late MF-F *suburbain*, from L *suburbānus*, the adj of *suburbium*, but formed after L *urbānus* (see next para). L *suburbium* =*sub*-, under, hence towards or up against, very near+*urbi*-, c/f (from the s and r *urb*-) of *urbs*, a city+n-suffix -*um*. L *suburbium* becomes MF (and prob EF) *suburbe*, whence E *suburb*.

3. *Urban* comes, perh via MF-F *urbain*, f *urbaine*, from L *urbānus*, adj of *urbs*; already in L, *urbānus* meant, derivatively, 'civilized, polished, refined, witty', a sense it retained, along with 'of a, or the, city', in MF-F *urbain*, whence E *urbane*, orig (C16) a mere var of *urban*, then (C17) in the 'civilized' sense: cf the phon and sem differentiation of *human* and *humane*. L *urbānus* has derivative *urbānitās*, whence MF-F *urbanité*, whence E *urbanity*.

4. *Urbs* (gen *urbis*) is o.o.o.: Webster proposes kinship with L *uerber* (ML *verber*: cf VERVAIN), a rod; a city having orig been an aggregation of

persons living within a palisaded enclosure. Very tentatively I suggest that the L r *urb*- is a contr of *\*uerb*-, extn of *uer*- (ML *ver*-), the r of L *uer*tere, to turn, pp *uer*sus, a city being that point to which the inhabitants of the entire neighbourhood naturally turn in order to do business or to get news. If, however, the L r *urb*- be an extn of *\*ur*-, then L *urbs* is prob akin to Hit *uru*, town, city.

**urceolar, urceolate, urceole, urceolus, urceus.** See URN, para 2.

**urchin.** See HEARSE, para 4, s.f.

**Urdu.** See HORDE.

**ure**, obs n and v; **inure**, whence, anl, **inurement**. The now only hist n *ure* (whence the v), use or custom, came into ME from OF-MF *ueuvre*, *euvre*, work (F *oeuvre*)—from L *opera*: f.a.e., OPERA. ME-E *ure* has the late ME-E derivative cpd *inure*, to accustom, to habituate, hence, in E, to harden: cf the LL *inoperāri*, to 'work (in), to produce, manifest' (Souter).

**urea, ureal.** See URINE, para 4.

**ureter.** See URINE, para 6.

**urethan.** See URINE, para 5.

**urethra, urethral.** See URINE, para 6.

**uretic.** See URINE, para 6.

**urge, urgency, urgent.** See WREAK, para 6.

**uric.** See URINE, para 4.

**urinal; urinary; urinate.** See para 3 and (for *urinate*) para 2 of:

**urine; urinal, urinary, urinate** (whence urination —cf the obs F *urination*—and urinative), **urinous; urea**, whence **ureal; ureter; urethan; urethra**, whence **urethral; uretic; uric; urazin(e)**;—**diuretic**, whence, anl, **diuresis; enuresis, enuretic**.

1. E-ME *urine* is adopted from OF-F *urine*, a reshaping of OF-EF *orine*, from VL *\*aurīna*, a f/e alteration—from the colour of L *aurum*, gold—of L *ūrīna*, whence OF-F *urine*: and L *ūrīna* is ult akin to Gr *ouron*, urine, and *ourein*, to urinate, *ouria*, a waterfowl, themselves (r *our*-) akin to Skt *vār*, *vāri*, water, *varṣám*, rain, *varṣati*, it rains— Tokh A *wär*, water—OE *waer*, ON *ver*, the sea, ON *ūr*, fine rain, a drizzle—Lith *júreis*, *júrios* (pl), the sea, OP *wurs*, a pond—and such C words as MIr *fáraim*, I pour (Ir, I gush, etc.), W *gweren*, dampness, and perh Cor *dour*, *dowr*, *dūr*, *dōr*, water, urine. The IE r is app *\*wer*-, to water, to besprinkle; but 'water' (n) was prob the primary sense. (E & M, Boisacq, Hofmann, Holthausen.)

2. This basic sense appears in L *ūrīnāri*, to plunge into water, to dive, pp *ūrīnātus*, whence, but with sense from *ūrīna*, the E 'to urinate'.

3. L *ūrīna* has two L adjj: LL *ūrīnālis*, of or for urine, whence the ML n *ūrīnal*, a place for urinating, whence OF-MF *orinal*, whence the reshaped EF-F *urinal*, adopted by E; and SciL *ūrīnōsus*, whence E *urinous*, which might, however, derive from EF-F *urineux* (*urine*+-*eux*). The adj *urinary* derives from EF-F *urinaire* (*urine*+-*aire*).

4. Whereas *uric* derives from F *urique* (*urine*+ adj suffix -*ique*), *urea* (the solid part of urine) derives from F *urée* (*urine*+f n-suffix -*ée*), coined, late in C18, by the F chemist Fourcroy.

5. From *urée*, F forms *uréthane* (*-éthane* from *éther*, ether), whence E *urethan*; from G *Urin*, G forms *Urazin* (*-azin* from Hydr*azin*, E *hydrazine*), whence E *urazine* or *urazin*.

6. From *ouron*, Gr forms *ourētēr* (agential-instr suffix *-ētēr*), the duct carrying urine from kidney to bladder: whence SciL, hence SciE, *ureter*; cf that other Gr derivative *ourēthra*, the duct or canal carrying off urine from the bladder, whence LL *ūrēthra*, adopted by SciE. Gr *ouron*, moreover, has adj *ourētikos*, whence LL *ūrēticus*, whence E *uretic*.

7. Gr *ourein* has two prefix-cpds affecting E: *diourein* (*dia*, through, used int), to pass water, whence the adj *diourētikos*, LL *diūrēticus*, E *diuretic*, whence, anl, *diuresis*; and the syn *enourein* (*en*, in, used int), whence—after *diuretic* and *diuresis*—E *enuretic* and *enuresis*.

**urinology.** See the element *urini-*. f.a.e., URINE.

**urn** (n, hence v, esp in the int form **inurn**), **urnal**, **urceolar, urceolate, urceole, urceolus, urceus.**

1. *Urnal* derives from L *urnālis*, the adj of *urna*, an urn, akin to L *urceus*, a two-handled vase or pot, which, like L *orca*, a big-bellied vase or pot, a tun, is akin to Gr *hurkhē*, Aeolic Gr *urkhē*, an earthenware jar: perh all three are of common Medit origin. L *urna* becomes EF-F and ME *urne*, E *urn*.

2. L *urceus* is preserved by Classical erudition. The dim *urceolus*, a little vase, pot, jar, is retained, with slightly modified senses, by Bot and Zoo, the truly E form being *urceole* (cf F *urcéole*: Bot); the L adj of *urceolus* is *urceolāris*, whence E *urceolar*, whence prob, by anl, the erudite adj *urceolate*, shaped like a small urn.

**uro-** words, all Sci: see the two elements *uro-*.

**ursine.** See the element *ursi-*.

**Urtica, urticant, urticaria** (whence **urticarial** and **urticarious**), **urticate, urtication, urticose.**

The Bot *Urtica*, the genus of nettles, represents L *urtīca*, a nettle: o.o.o.; associated by L f/e with *ūrere* (s and r *ur-*), to burn, from the 'burning' sensation caused by nettle-stings. The derivative ML *urticāre*, to sting as with nettles, has presp *urtīcans*, o/s *urtīcant-*, whence the E adj *urticant*, and pp *urtīcātus*, whence the adj and v *urticate*, whence, anl, *urtication*. Derivative SciL *urtīcosus* yields *urticose*; also from L *urtīca* derives, as if from an adj *urtīcārius*, SciL *urtīcāria*, an inflammatory disease.

**us; use, ours; nosism** and **nostrum.**

1. E-ME *us* comes from OE *ūs*, us, to us: cf OFris, OS *ūs*, Go and OHG-G *uns*, MD *us* (var *uus*), MD-D *ons*, ON *oss*; cf also L *nōs*, we, us— Gr *hēmās* (pl), us, and *nō*, Homeric *nōi* (dual), we two, us two—Skt *nas*, us, *nāu*, our two, Hit *anzās* us, to us (*anzel*, our).

2. Very closely akin to OE *ūs* is OE *ūre*, our: cf Go *unsar*, G *unser*, and, without *n*, the OFris *ūse*, OS *ūsa*, *ūse*. *Ours*, possessive pronoun, ME *ures*, was orig the gen of ME *ure*, OE *ūre*, ours, and therefore doubly a possessive.

3. From L *nōs*, we, us, comes E *nosism* (suffix

*-ism*); from L *nōstrum*, the neu sing of *nōster*, our, itself from *nōs*, comes the E *nostrum*, 'our medicine', hence an infallible, a quack, medicine.

**usage; usance.** See para 5 of:

**use**, n (whence **useful** and **useless**) and v (whence **usable** and the pa **used**); **usage; usance; usitate, usitation, usitative; usual** (adj, hence n), whence **usualism** and **usually; usurer, usurious, usury;** for both **usucapient, usucapion, usucapt,** and **usufruct, usufructuary** (adj, n), see the element *usu-*;— **utensil; utile, utility** (whence **utilitarian**, adj hence n—cf **humanity, humanitarian**), **utilize, utilization; inutile, inutility.**—Prefix-cpds: **abuse** (n, v), **abusive**, and **disabuse—disuse** (v, hence n), **disutility** (anl from *utility*)—**misuse**, v, hence n.;— **usurp, usurpation, usurpatory.**

1. All these words stand firmly upon L *ūtī* (s and r *ūt-*), to use, make use of, hence to have relationships with; the pp *ūsus* is prob for *\*ūtsus*. The OL forms are *oetī*, to use, *oetile*, useful, *oesus*, pp. The word has a very long history, but only in the Italic languages, e.g. Oscan (*úittiuf*, acc pl: L *ūsūs*) and Pelignian *oisa* (f sing of the pp: L *ūsa*). Perh Medit: ? *oet-*, var *oit-*.

2. L *ūtī* has adj *ūtilis*, whence OF-F *utile*, adopted by E; derivative *ūtilitās*, acc *ūtilitāt*em, yields OF-F *utilité*, whence *utility*; from F *utile* comes F *utiliser*, whence *utilisation*, whence E *utilize*, *utilization*. The L negg *inutilis*, *inutilitās*, yield OF-F *inutile*, MF-F *inutilité*, whence E *inutile*, *inutility*.

3. Also from the s *ūt-* comes *ūtēnsilis*, usable, whence the neu pl, used as n, *ūtēnsilia*, implements, whence, by b/f, the MF *utensile*, whence (after *user*) the late MF-F *ustensile*, whence E *utensil*.

4. The pp *ūsus* generates VL *ūsāre*, to use, whence OF-F *user*, ME *usen*, E 'to use'; the E n *use* comes from OF-MF *us*, use (itself from L *ūsus*, gen *ūsūs*, from the pp), adopted by ME, the longer form prevailing. OF-F *user* has derivatives OF-F (obs) *usable* and MF-EF *usance*, both adopted by E; with the F neg *inusable* contrast the E *unusable*.

5. Whereas both B & W and Dauzat derive OF-F, hence ME-E, *usage* from OF *us* (*use*), both OED and Webster derive OF-F, hence ME-E, *usage* from ML *ūsāticum*, prop the neu of the ML (? from VL) adj *ūsāticus*.

6. From the L pp *ūsus* comes the LL freq *ūsitāre*, to use often, with pp *ūsitātus*, whence both the rare 'to *usitate*' and LL *ūsitātiō*, o/s *ūsitātiōn-*, whence E *usitation*, whence, anl, the Gram adj *usitative*.

7. The L n *ūsus* (gen *ūsūs*) has LL adj *ūsuālis*, whence MF *usual* (MF-F *usuel*), adopted by latish ME.

8. The L pp *ūsus* has derivative n *ūsūra*, use, esp, in Law, usury, whence OF-F *usure*, whence— prob influenced by ML *ūsūria* (mdfn pf L *ūsūra*)— the ME *usurie*, E *usury*, whence *usurious*; E-ME *usurer* adapts MF *usureor*, MF-F *usurier*.

9. The foll L and F-imitative-of-L prefix-cpds have affected E:

L *abūtī*, to consume by use, hence to use up, hence to turn away from (*ab*) its proper use, with pp *abūsus*, whence MF-F *abuser*, whence 'to abuse'; the derivative L n *abūsus* (gen -*ūs*) becomes MF-F *abus*, whence the E n *abuse*; that L n has the LL derivative adj *abūsiuus*, misused, whence MF-F *abusif*, f *abusive*, whence E *abusive*;

EF-F *désabuser* (*dés-*+*abuser*) yields 'to disabuse';

MF-EF *desuser* (*des-*, L *dis-*+*user*) yields 'to disuse', whence *disuse*, n; but *disutility* merely prefixes *dis-* to *utility*;

MF *mesuser*, EF-F *mésuser*, has at least suggested 'to *misuse*', whence the n *misuse*; *misusage* owes something to the EF *mésusage* (from *mésuser*).

10. L *ūtī* or, rather, its pp *ūsus*, has a full cpd not imm recognizable: *ūsurpāre*, to take possession of by use, esp by use and custom—explained thus by E & M: 'A law term, which was perh employed at first, of one who took a woman (*rapere*) without benefit of legal rites of marriage. . . . It was then applied to every sort of object in the sense "to appropriate to oneself, take possession or cognizance of" and then in that of "to usurp" '; in short, they imply, for they do not exhibit, nor even state, the catena: \**ūsū rapere* becomes \**ūsūrapere*, whence, by contr, \**ūsurpere*, whence *ūsurpāre*. From L *ūsurpāre* derives MF-F *usurper*, whence 'to *usurp*'. Derivative L *ūsurpātiō*, acc *ūsurpātiōnem*, explains MF-F *usurpation*, adopted by E; LL *ūsurpātor*, a usurper, suggested the LL *ūsurpātōrius*, whence E *usurpatory*.

usher. See ORAL, para 5.

usitate, usitation, usitative. See USE, para 6.

usquebaugh. See WHISKEY.

usual. See USE, para 7.

usucapion; usufruct. See the element *usu-*.

usurer, usurious. See USE, para 8.

usurp (whence usurper), usurpation (whence, anl, usurpative), usurpatory. See USE, para 10.

usury. See USE, para 8.

utensil. See USE, para 3.

uterus. See HYSTERIA, para 1, s.f. The adj *uterine* derives from late MF-F *utérin*, f *utérine*, from LL *uterīnus*, adj of *uterus*.

utile, utilitarian, utility, utilize. See USE, para 2 and, for the 2nd, the heading.

utmost. See OUT, para 3.

Utopia, whence Utopian (adj, hence n), originates in Sir Thomas More's *Utopia*, 1516; *Utopia*, an imaginary paradisal island: SciL, as if from LGr \**Outopia*: *ou*, not+*topos*, a place+-*ia*, suffix connoting 'region'.

utricle. See the element *utri-*.

utter (1), adj. See OUT, para 3. Cf:

utter (2), v: ME *uttren*, *outren*, lit 'to put out or forth' (cf the sl 'to get *off* one's chest'): ME adv *utter* (*uttere*), outside+inf suffix -*en*: OE *ūtter*, *ūtor*, comp of *ūt*, out: f.a.e., OUT. Hence utterance.

uttermost: UTTER, adj+MOST.

uvula (whence, anl, uvular), uvulitis. The third tacks -*itis*, denoting 'disease', to ML *ūvula*, LL *ūuula* (Galen and Hippocrates), the uvula, orig a little grape: dim of L *ūua* (ML *ūva*), a grape: perh cf Lith *ūga*, a berry, OSl vin-*jaga*, a grape, and Gr *oā*, Ionic *oē*, *oiē*, a service-tree, and *oön*, its fruit: ? cf E YEW.

uxorial is an occ var (-*ial* for -*ious*) of uxorious, from L *uxōrius*, relating to a wife or, for the man, to marriage, adj of *uxor*, a wife: cf Oscan *usurs* (corresp to L *uxōrēs*, wives) and Pelignian *usur* (corresp to L *uxor*): o.o.o.: perh for \**iuxor*, i.e. \**iugsor*—cf -*iux*, for \*-*iugs*, in *coniux*, wife: f.a.e., JOIN.

# V

vacancy, vacant, vacate, vacation (whence vacational and vacationist); vacuate, vacuation—cf evacuant, evacuate, evacuation (whence, anl, evacuator, whence, anl, evacuee); vacuity, vacuolar, vacuole, vacuous; vacuum;—void, adj (hence n) and v (whence voidable), voidance, voider; avoid, whence avoidable and avoidance; devoid, adj and v. —vain, vanity; vanish (whence pa, vn vanishing) and evanish, evanesce; vaunt, v, hence n; inane (adj, hence ⁊n), inanition, inanity.—wane, n and v; want, n and v—cf wanton, adj, hence n and v.—vast, adj (whence vastly and vastness), vastitude, vastity, vasty—vastate, vastation, cf devastate, devastation (whence, anl, devastative), devastator, devastavit—waste, adj, n (whence wasteful), v (whence wastage and the pa, vn wasting), waster, wastrel.

1. Here we have three L words, uacāre, to be empty, hence vacant or unoccupied, uānus, empty, emptied (of what was there), hence hollow, without substance, hence vain, and uastus, ravaged, desolated (also ravaging, desolating, devastating), hence uncultivated, desert, hence—deserts tending to be very large—vast, immense: all with IE cognates, esp in Gmc; the Gr cognates, remote in form, have scarcely influenced E; the C cognates, phon close, are likewise unproductive for E.

2. It is wrong to say, with E & M, that the only common denominator is u-, for prob there is *ua- and perh there is *uas-, with extnn *uasc-, as in L uascus, empty, hence trifling—*uasn-, as in L uānus, for *uasnus—and *uast-, as in L uastus. The difficulty presented by L uacāre is perh explicable by postulating that word to be a worn-down form of *uascāre, from or akin to uascus, empty, from *uasc-, extn of *uas-, IE r for 'empty'. (E & M, by the way, postulate the scribal var *was- for uascus, uastus, uānus.) Unexpected confirmation occurs in Hit: wakkar-, r wak-, to be lacking. The foll C words—not quite certainly of L origin—appear to support an IE trinity of extnn, either from *ua- or prob from the more precise *uas-.

Cor guāg, gwāg, gwāk, vacant, empty, vain (as n, a vacuum), with gu- (gw-) corresp to w-, a frequent IE alternation, and with -g or -k for -c;

MIr fáen, weak, Ga faóin, idle, trifling, silly, and Mx feayn, empty;

OIr fás, fáas, Ga fàs, empty, vacant, and Mx faasagh (adj), waste, desert—and Cor guastia, to waste; corresp to the uas- of L.

Other IE cognates will be cited in the foll paras.

3. L uacāre, to be empty, hence unoccupied, has presp uacans, o/s uacant-, ML vacant-, OF-F vacant (from the ML acc vacantem), adopted by E; the L neu pl adj uacantia becomes the ML f sing n vacantia, whence E vacancy. The pp uacātus, ML v-, yields 'to vacate'; derivative L uacātiō, ML vacātiō, acc vacātiōnem, becomes MF vacation, a holiday (but the other F senses come from MF-F vaguer, from ML vacāre)—adopted by E.

4. L uacāre has derivative adj uacuus, ML vacuus, whence E vacuous; the ML neu vacuum, used as n, is adopted by E; the derivative n uacuitās, ML v-, becomes E vacuity—perh imm from MF-F vacuité (from the ML acc vacuitātem); adopted from F is vacuole, derived, as a dim, from F vacuum, and adapted as E vacuolar is the F adj vacuolaire.

5. L uacuus has the LL derivative v uacuāre, ML vacuāre, to rid (somebody) of (something), to annul, with pp uacuātus and derivative n uacuātiō, an emptying, whence, via the ML v-, the E 'to vacuate' and vacuation, both obsol. The LL cpd ēuacuāre, ML ēvacuāre, to empty, has presp ēuacuans (o/s -uant-) and pp ēuacuātus, whence ēuacuātiō, an emptying: whence, resp, the E adj, hence n, evacuant—'to evacuate'—evacuation, prob imm from MF-F évacuation (ML acc ēvacuātiōnem). The irreg evacuee derives, anl, from 'to evacuate'.

6. L uacuāre has the OL var uocuāre, whence the freq uocitāre, to empty often, used as int, to empty completely, whence the spoken (VL) adj uocitus, ML *vocitus, whence OF-MF vuit, f vuide, with dial var voit, f voide, whence ME void or voide, the former prevailing into E. OF-MF vuit, vuide, has the OF-MF derivative v vuidier, vuider, with dial varr voidier, voider, whence 'to void'; the OF-MF derivatives vuideor, vuidance, dial voideor, voidance, become E voider (partly from the E v) and voidance.

7. OF-MF vuid(i)er, dial void(i)er, has the OF-MF cpd esvuid(i)er (es- being L ex-, out of), dial esvoid(i)er, a vaguely int 'to make empty': whence ME avoiden, whence 'to avoid'.

8. OF-MF vuid(i)er, void(i)er, has another cpd: desvuid(i)er, desvoid(i)er, to empty out (connoted by des- for de, down from), whence the now obs 'to devoid', whence imm the E adj devoid, prompted no doubt by the OF-MF pp desvoid(i)é used as adj.

756

## Vanity

9. L *uānus*, empty or emptied, hence without substance, hence vain, has IE cognates not hitherto mentioned, e.g. Skt *ūnás* (Av *ūna-*), defective, incomplete (lacking in something), Gr *eunis* (εὖνις), deprived, Arm *unain, unayn*, empty, Go *wans* and ON *vanr*, defective, ME *wan-* (as in E *wanton*), ON *vanta*, to lack.

10. L *uānus* becomes OF-F *vain* (OF-MF var *vein*): ME *vaine* (*vein*): E *vain*. The phrase *in vain* derives from OF-F *en vain* (cf It *in vano*), from ML *in vānum*, LL *in uānum*, imitative of Gr *eis kenon*; LL affords the synn *in uāne* and *in uānō*. *Vanity* comes from OF-F *vanité*, from ML *vanitāt*em, acc of *vānitās*, L *uānitās*, from *uānus*.

11. L *uānus* has derivative *uānescere*, to disappear, with int *ēuānescere*, whence VL \**exvanire*, OF-MF *esvanir* (var *esvanuir*: EF-F *évanouir*), whence (from, e.g., the presp *esvaniss*ant) 'to *evanish*' and, by aphesis, ME *vanissen, vanisshen* (or *-ysshen*), 'to *vanish*'. L *ēuānescere* (*ē-*, out of), ML *ēvānescere*, yields 'to *evanesce*'; its presp *ēuānescens*, o/s *ēuānescent-*, yields the E adj *evanescent*, whence, anl, *evanescence*.

12. L *uānus* has another derivative v: the LL \**uānitāre*, to be vain (attested by LL *uānitantes*, vain or foolish people: pl of presp used as n: Souter): whence OF-F *vanter*, orig to be vain or boastful, whence E 'to *vaunt*', whence the n *vaunt*.

13. Closely related to L *uānus* is L *inānis*, which was perh, orig, an int of *uānus*: int \**in-+uānus*: \**inuānus*, whence *inānis*, empty. L *inānis* yields E *inane*; its derivative *inānitās*, E *inanity*; its LL derivative *inānitiō*, acc *inānitiōn*em, MF-F *inanition*, adopted by E.

14. Akin to ON *vanr*, Go *wans*, defective (para 9 above), are OHG *wan-, wana-*, (in cpds) lacking in, and OE *wanian* (*wonian*), to be lacking, to be diminished: the latter becomes ME *wanien*, E 'to *wane*', the intimately cognate OE n *wana* becoming the ME-E n *wane*; the former occurs in ME *wantowen*, ME *wantoun*, ME-E *wanton*, the ME *-towen* representing OE *togen*, pp of *tēon*, to draw or pull, hence to train, bring up, educate, the lit sense being 'deficient in training, hence in discipline'.

15. ON *vanr*, defective, lacking, has neu *vant*, whence, partly, the E n *want*, itself partly from 'to *want*', which derives from ME *wanten*, from ON *vanta*, to lack, intimately akin to and prob derived from ON *vant*.

## Vastness

16. L *uastus*, ML *vastus*, ravaged or desolated, hence uncultivated, hence desert, hence very extensive, immense, yields (late MF-F *vaste* and) E *vast*; Shakespeare's adj *vasty* is either *vast*, adj, with extn *-y*, or, more prob, *vast*, n+adj suffix *-y*. The L derivative nn *uastitās*, o/s *uastitāt-*, ML *vastitāt-*, and *uastitūdō*, ML *vastitūdō*, yield E *vastity* (obsol) and *vastitude*.

17. L *uastus* has derivative v *uastāre*, to render desolate, to lay waste, pp *uastātus*, ML *vastātus*, whence both 'to *vastate*' and L *uastātiō*, o/s *uastātiōn-*, ML *vastātiōn-*, whence E *vastation*. Much commoner in E is the prefix-cpd *devastate*, with subsidiaries *devastation* and *devastator*: ML *dēvastātus*, L *dēuastātus*, pp of *dēuastāre* (*dē-* used int), to lay utterly waste—ML *dēvastātiōn-*, o/s of *dēvastātiō*, LL *dēuastātiō* (from the pp)—ML *dēvastātor*, LL *dēuastātor* (from the pp). The legal n *devastavit* derives from the ML form of L *dēuastauit*, he has laid waste.

18. Akin to L *uastus* are OHG *wuosti*, MHG *wüeste*, G *wüst*, OFris *wost*, OS *wosti*, OE *wēste*, which, esp the last, have strongly influenced the passage of the E adj *waste*, ME *wast*, from ONF *wast*, itself a var (*w-* for *gu-*) of OF-MF *guast*, var *gast*, which comes from ML *vastus*, L *uastus*. The E n *waste*, ME *waste*, var *wast*, derives from the ONF n *waste*, *wast*, var of OF-MF *guast, gast*, prop the adj used as n; cf the syn OE *wēsten*, OFris *wēstene* (var *wōstene*), OS *wōstunnia*, OHG *wuostī*, MHG *wüeste*, G *Wüste*. The E v 'to *waste*' (orig, to lay waste), ME *wasten*, derives from ONF *waster*, var of OF-MF *guaster, gaster* (F *gâter*, to spoil), itself from ML *vastāre*, L *uastāre*, to lay waste. The agent *waster* comes from AF *wastour*, from the ONF v *waster*. *Wastrel* comes from 'to *waste*', with suffix *-rel* perh suggested by *scoundrel*; the sense 'good-for-nothing person', orig dial, is modern (c1840), the orig sense being 'waste land' (Cornwall: EE); hence 'a rejected imperfect article of manufacture' (late C18). Dates: O.E.D.

**vaccenic, vaccinate** (whence, anl, **vaccination, vaccinator, vaccinatory**), **vaccine** (whence **vaccinal**); **vaquero**, whence—f/e influenced by *buck*, a dashing fellow—the A, hence also Can, **buckaroo**.

1. The south-western AE *vaquero*, cowboy, herdsman, is adopted from Sp, which derives it, by agential *-ero*, from Sp *vaca*, a cow, from the syn ML *vacca*, L *uacca*.

2. L *uacca*, a cow, is akin to Skt *vaça* (*vasá*), a heifer that has calved for the first time. *Uacca* has adj *uaccīnus*, f *-īna*, neu *īnum*, whence the E adj *vaccine* (cf the F *vaccin*), of, for, from a cow or cows; hence the E n *vaccine* (cf F *vaccin*); the Chem adj *vaccenic* is a mdfn of the adj *vaccine*. The E n *vaccine* generates, anl, the v 'to *vaccinate*'—cf the F *vacciner*, from the n *vaccin*.

**vacillant, vacillate** (whence the pa **vacillating** and the agent **vacillator**), **vacillation** (whence, anl, **vacillatory**).—**variable** (whence **invariable**, unless from MF-F **invariable**), **variability** (and **invariability**), **variance, variant** (cf the derivative Math **invariance, invariant**), **variate, variation** (whence, anl, **variative** and **variator**), **variety** (whence **varietal**), **variorum, various, vary** (whence pa **varied**, pa **varying**—with negg **unvaried, unvarying**); **variegate**, whence **variegation; variola** (whence, anl, the adj **variolar**) and **variolate** (adj, hence v, whence **variolation**), **variole, variolite** (whence **variolitic**); **vair** and **miniver.—varica** (whence **varical**), **varicate** (whence the Med **varication**), **varicose** (whence **varicosity**), **varicosis, varix** (Sci pl **varices**).—**varus**

(adj and n)—cf **vara**; **divaricate**, adj and v (whence, prob after the *pre-* subsidiaries, **divarication** and **divaricator**); **prevaricate**, **prevarication**, **prevaricator**, **prevaricatory**.

## General

1. We are dealing with the E resultants of four L words: *uacillāre*, to waver (lit and fig), to totter; *uarius*, (esp of human and animal skin) speckled, spotted, hence diverse; *uarix* (o/s *uaric-*), a swollen vein, esp in the leg; and *uārus*, knock-kneed, (of the legs) crooked, bent apart, hence—prob influenced by *uarius*—turned crookedly, hence diverse. E & M treat these four words as having each a distinct origin; but that the 2nd, 3rd, 4th are inter-related seems at least possible; the relationship of the 1st to the others presents app the greatest difficulty. Sem, the relationship between 'to waver' and 'crooked' is scarcely abstruse; phon, the relationship between *uacillāre* and *uāricāre* (from *uāricus*, extn of *uārus*), to stand with legs apart, to cause (one's steps) to straddle, hence, fig, to stray, to wander from one's path, is perh this: *uāricāre* becomes \**uālicāre* (*l* for *r*), whence, by metathesis, \**uācilāre*, whence, by expressive gemination, L *uācillāre*. That *uacillāre* is recorded earlier than *uāricāre* is not necessarily preclusive, for *uacillāre* is prob not earlier than *uāricus*, certainly not earlier than *uārus*. Nevertheless, *uacillāre* could well be an imitative word, independent of the others.

2. L *uarius*, *uarix*, *uārus* have, or app have, in common the r *uar-*, which connotes, or app connotes, the basic meaning 'deviating, or a deviation, from the normal or usual': *uarius*, deviating from a clear hue, hence spotted; *uarix*, a deviation from a normal vein, hence a dilated vein—? elliptical for \**uēna uarix*; *uārus*, deviating from the straight, hence crooked. (This idea could also be postulated for *uacillāre*.) The r *uar-* is perh worn down from an IE \**kuar-* (contr *kar-*), crooked, bent, curved; that is, *uārus* perh represents \**kuārus*. If that be so, then these L *uar-* (*uār-*) words are perh akin, either to the Skt *kakras*, a wheel, or to E QUEER.

## Particular

3. L *uacillāre*, to waver (lit, hence fig), has presp *uacillans*, o/s *uacillant-*, ML *v-*, whence the E adj *vacillant*; pp *uacillātus* yields both 'to *vacillate*' and L *uacillātiō*, o/s *uacillātiōn-*, whence EF-F and, perh independently, E *vacillation*.

4. L *uarius*, ML *varius*, spotted, speckled, hence diverse, yields E *various*; the L derivative n *uarietās*, acc *uarietātem*, yields OF-F *variété*, whence E *variety*. The L derivative v *uariāre* has the foll parts and subsidiaries affecting E:

LL *uariābilis*, MF-F *variable*, adopted by E; MF-F *variabilité* becomes E *variability*, and EF-F *invariabilité* becomes *invariability*;

presp *uarians*, o/s *uariant-*, and derivative *uariantia*, OF-MF *variant*, *variance*, whence—unless direct from the ML forms—the E words;

*uariāre* itself becomes EF-F *varier*, whence ME *varien*, whence 'to *vary*';

pp *uariātus*, whence 'to *variate*'; derivative *uariātiō*, acc *uariātiōn*em, MF-F *variation*, adopted by E;

*uariegāre* (*uari-*, c/f of *uarius*+-*egāre*, c/f of *agere*, to drive, hence to make or do), to make diverse—in short, a syn of *uariāre*—has pp *uariegātus*, whence 'to *variegate*';

LL *uariola*, a pustule, ML *variola*, smallpox, is, in form, a dim of *uarius*—perh the f of an adj \**uariolus*; adopted, along with MF-F *variole*, by Sci; derivative LL *uariolātus*, having pustules, yields the Med adj *variolate*; the adj *variolous* derives from ML *variolōsus* from ML *variola*;

*uariorum*, m and neu pl of *uarius*, whence, via the scholiasts' phrase *cum notis uariorum*, with notes of (i.e., by) various persons, the European n and adj *variorum*.

5. L *uarius*, various, variegated, ML *varius*, becomes OF-MF *vair*, used also as OF-F for a grey, or greyish, squirrel-fur, hence a term in H: adopted by E. Derivative MF *menu vair* (*menu*, little, from L *minūtus*, lit 'diminished'), such fur as part of a costume, becomes E *miniver*.

6. L *uarix* (gen *uaricis*) and its LL derivative syn *uarica*, a dilated vein, are both adopted by Med E. The L adj *uaricōsus* (*uaric-*, o/s of *uarix*+adj suffix -*ōsus*) yields E *varicose* (cf the EF-F *variqueux*). The Med adj *varicate*, var *varicated*, and the Med n *varicosis*, merely tack adj -*ate* and n ('disease') -*osis* to *varic-*, o/s of ML *varix*, L *uarix*.

7. L *uārus*, knock-kneed, hence (of legs) crooked, passes into MedE as both adj and, derivatively, n. L *uārus* has f *uāra*, used as n 'a forked stick supporting a net', whence Sp and Port *vara*, a staff, a stick, a wand, hence a measure of length, hence (*square vara*) of area.

8. L *uārus* has extn *uāricus*, whence LL *uāricāre*, to straddle, (later) to stray or wander, with two cpds relevant to E:

*diuāricāre* (*di-* for *dis-*, apart), to stretch apart, pp *diuāricātus*, ML *divāricātus*, whence 'to *divaricate*', with derivatives formed after those of—

*praeuāricāri*, to pass in front (*prae-*), or over, by straddling, to walk crookedly, hence, in the lawcourts, (of an advocate) to enter into collusion with the adversary, hence, in LL, to transgress, pp *praeuāricātus*, whence 'to *prevaricate*', with senses gradually weakening; derivatives *praeuāricātiō* (o/s -*cātiōn-*), *praeuāricātor*, LL *praeuāricātōrius*, yield OF-F *prévarication*, E *prevarication*—MF-F *prévaricateur*, E *prevaricator*—E *prevaricatory*.

**vacuate, vacuation.** See VACANT, para 5.

**vacuity, vacuole, vacuous, vacuum.** See VACANT, para 4.

**vade** and **vade-mecum**; **vadose**; **'vamoose'** and **'mosey'**.—Prefix-cpds of L *uādere*, pp *uāsus*: **evade**, **evasion**, **evasive**; **invade** (whence **invader**), **invasion**, **invasive**; **pervade**, **pervasion** (whence, anl. **pervasive**).—Gmc cognates: **wade**, whence agent-instr **wader(s)** and pa, vn **wading**; **waddle**, v, hence n.

1. L *uādere* (ML *vādere*), to go, to advance, yields 'to *vade*' or go away; the imp *uade*, ML *vade*, occurs in *vade-mecum*, L *uade-mecum*, Go with (*cum*) me!, a handbook. Akin to L *uādere* is L *uādum*, a ford, i.e. a place where one can advance across a river, a shallow, with adj *uādōsus*, ML *vādōsus*, whence the Geol *vadose*. The IE r is app *\*wad-*, to go (forward), hence to ford a river, with Gmc cognates (cf paras 7 and 8 below).

2. L *uādere* has three prefix-cpds that affect E: *ēuādere*, to go *ē*- or out of, to escape; *inuādere*, to go *in*- or into, to attack (esp a country); *peruādere*, to go *per*- or throughout, to penetrate.

3. L *ēuādere*, ML *ēvādere*, becomes MF-F *évader*, whence 'to *evade*'; derivative from the pp *ēuāsus* is LL *ēuāsiō*, ML *ēvāsiō*, acc *ēvāsiōn*em, whence MF-F *évasion*, whence F *évasif*, f *évasive*: whence E *evasion* and *evasive*.

4. L *inuādere*, ML *invādere*, yields 'to *invade*'; LL *inuāsiō* (from the L pp *inuāsus*), ML *invāsiō*, acc *invāsiōnem*, yields OF-F *invasion*, whence F *invasif*, f *invasive*: whence E *invasion, invasive*.

5. L *peruādere*, ML *pervādere*, and its pp-derivative the LL *peruāsiō*, ML *pervāsio*, o/s *pervasiōn-*, yield 'to *pervade*' and *pervasion*.

6. L *uādere*, ML *vādere*, in addition to supplying je *vais*, tu *vas*, il *va*, supplies Sp *vamos*, let us go, whence the south-western; then general, A sl, then coll, *vamoose*, occ *vamose*, to decamp, whence, by shortening, the sl 'to *mosey*'.

## Germanic Cognates

7. Akin to L *uādere* and *uādum*, with its LL derivative *uādāre*, to ford (a river), is OE *wadan*, to go, to advance, esp across a river—ME *waden*—E 'to *wade*': cf OFris *wada*, OHG *watan*, MHG-G *waten*, MD-D *waden*, ON *vatha* (with modern Scan cognates); cf OHG *wat*, a ford.

8. 'To *wade*' has freq 'to *waddle*' (*wade*+euphonic or here a merely formative *d*+freq *-le*): cf MHG *wadelen* and the syn echoic G development *watscheln*. (Walshe.)

**vae victis.** See WOE, para 1.

**vagabond** (adj, hence n), **vagabondage**; **vagary**, whence **vagarious** (whence, anl, **vagarity**); **vagrant** (adj and n), whence **vagrancy**; **vague** (whence **vagueness**), **vagus** (nerve).—Cpds: **divagate**, **divagation**; **evagation**; **extravagance**, **extravagant**, **extravaganza**, **extravagate**—cf **stravage**; **pervagate**, **pervagation**.

1. L *uagus*, ML *vagus*, wandering, errant, going as whim or chance suggests, is o.o.o.: perh cf the nasalized Skt *vángati*, he limps, and OHG *wanchan*, MHG-G *wanken*, to waver, and, without *n*, the syn ON *vakka*—therefore cf WINK.

2. L *uagus*, ML *vagus*—cf its dim *uagulus*, ML *v-*, whence E *vagulous*—becomes OF-F *vague*, wandering, vagabond, EF-F indeterminate, imprecise: whence E *vague* (L sense obs). ML *vagus* survives in MedE for 'the *vagus* nerve' (cranial).

3. L *uagus* has the foll simple derivatives affecting E:

*uagābundus* (adj), wandering about, from *uagāri*, to stroll or wander about (from *uagus*)+adj suffix *-bundus*: whence MF-F *vagabond*, adopted by E, as is the F derivative *vagabondage*;

*uagāri*, ML *v-*, becomes It *vagare*, whence the EE-E n (and EE v) *vagary*;

L *vagāri* has presp *vagans*, whence MF-F *vagant*, which has influenced the passage, into E, of EF-MF *wacrant* (*waucrant*), presp of OF-MF *wacrer* (*waucrer*), var of *walcrer*, of Gmc origin (cf WALK); OF-MF *wacrant* app becomes E *vagrant*.

4. L *uagāri*, ML *vagāri*, has the foll prefix-cpds relevant to E:

*diuagāri* (*di-* for *dis-*, apart), to wander about, to stray from the right path, pp *diuagātus*, ML *divagātus*, whence 'to *divagate*'; derivative LL *diuagātiō*, ML *divagātiō*, acc *divagātiōn*em, yields EF-F *divagation*, adopted by E;

*ēuagāri*, to wander *ē*-, out, forth, has pp *ēuāgātus*, whence LL *ēuagātio*, a digression, acc *ēuagātiōn*em, ML *-v-*, whence EF-F *évagation*, whence E *evagation*;

ML *extravagāri*, to wander outside (*extra-*) the bounds, presp *extravagans*, o/s *extravagant-*, whence MF-F, hence E, *extravagant*; derivative EF-F *extravagance* is likewise adopted; *extravaganza* comes from It; the It var *stravaganza* affords a clue to the origin of the Sc, and Northern E dial, 'to *stravage*', imm, by aphesis, from EF-F *extravaguer*;

*peruagāri*, to wander *per-*, all through, to wander extensively, pp *peruagātus*, ML *pervagātus*, whence 'to *pervagate*'; derivative LL *peruagātiō*, o/s *peruagātiōn-*, ML *pervagātiōn-*, yields *pervagation*.

**vagary.** See prec, para 3.

**vagina.** See VANILLA.

**vagrancy, vagrant.** See VAGABOND, para 3.

**vague**, whence **vagueness**. See VAGABOND, para 2.

**vagulous, vagus.** See VAGABOND, para 2.

**vail**, to lower or doff. See VALE, valley, para 2.—

**vail**, aphetic for *avail*. See VALUE, para 12.

**vain; in vain.** See VACANT, para 10.

**vair.** See VACILLANT, para 5.

**valance; valenciennes.** See VALUE, para 4.

**valbellite.** See para 1, s.f., of:

**vale, valley; Transvaal** and **valbellite; avale**—cf **vail**, to doff, and **avalanche; vaudeville.**

1. *Vale* derives from OF-F *val*: ML *vallis, vallēs*, L *uallis, -ēs*, r *ual-*: perh akin to L *uoluere* (s *uolu-*, r *uol-*), to roll. OF-F *val* has OF-F derivative *vallée*, ME *valeie*, later *vale* (dyssyllabic): E *valley*. Whereas *Transvaal*=L *trans*, across+D *vaal*, a valley, *valbellite*=It *Val Bello* ('beautiful valley')+Min *-ite*, *Val Bello* being in Piedmont, Italy.

2. OF-F *val* has the derivative *a val*, (down) to (the) valley, hence downwards, whence OF-F *avaler*, to lower, whence the obsol 'to *avale*', whence, by aphesis, 'to *vail*' or to lower, to doff.

3. Prob influenced by OF-F *aval*, downwards, is EF-F *avalanche*, adopted by E: Swiss *avalantse*, earlier *lavantse*: OProv *lavanca*, ? from VL: LL *labīna*, from *labī*, to slide.

4. F *Vau* (for *val*) *de Vire*, a district in Calvados, France, becomes MF *vaudevire*, a topical song of the region, whence EF-F *vaudeville* (after *ville*, city), with developing senses: adopted by E.

**valediction, valedictory.** See VALUE, para 21.

**valence, valency, valent, valentine.** See VALUE, para 3.

**valerian,** whence, anl, **valeric.** See VALUE, para 5.

**valet.** See STAND, para 39.

**valetudinarian.** See VALUE, para 6.

**Valhalla.** See VALKYRIE.

**valiance, valiancy, valiant.** See VALUE, para 7.

**valid, validate, validation, validity.** See VALUE, para 8.

**valise:** EF-F *valise*: It *valigia*: prob ML *valisia*: perh Ar *walīha*: o.o.o. (B & W.)

**Valkyrie—Valhalla:** ON *valhöll*, hall (*höll*, a kingly hall: cf E *hall*) of the slain—ON *valkyrja*, *Valkyria*, chooser (from *kjōsa*, to choose: cf *choose*) of the slain: ON *val-*, c/f of *valr*, the slain, akin to OE *wael*, OHG-MHG *wal*, battlefield, defeat, and OE *wōl*, a plague, OHG *wuol*, slaughter, defeat. (Walshe.)

**valley.** See VALE, para 1.

**valor** (AE) or **valour; valorize; valorous.** See VALUE, para 9.

**valse.** See VOLUBLE, para 9.

**valuable; valuate, valuation.** See heading (*valuable*) and para 10 of:

**value,** n (whence **valueless**), and v, whence **valuable** (adj, hence n) and **valuer; valance** and **valenciennes; valence, valency, valent, valentine; valerian; valeric; valetudinarian; valiance, valiancy, valiant; valid, validate, validation, validity; valor** (AE), **valour, valorous, valorization, valorize;** Gmc cognates: **wield,** v (whence **wielder**) and obs n (whence **wieldy,** whence **unwieldy**); sep HERALD.—Full cpds and prefix cpds in *val-, -val*, and *-valesc-*, and *-vail*: **ambivalence, ambivalent; avail; convalesce, convalescence, convalescent; countervail; devaluate, devaluation, devalue; equivalence, equivalent** (adj, hence n); **evaluate, evaluation; invalid** (adj, n), **invalidate, invalidation, invalidism; invaluable; prevail** (whence the pa **prevailing**), **prevalence, prevalent; revalescence, revalescent; revalidate,** whence **revalidation; revalorize,** whence **revalorization;— Vale!; valediction, valedictory.**

## Indo-European

1. L *ualēre*, to be strong, hence well, has s and r *ual-*, from an IE r *wal-*, varr *wel-* and *wol-*: cf OHG *waltan*, MHG-G *walten* (s *walt-*: t for *d*), OFris *walda*, OS and Go *waldan*, ON *valda*, to govern, (vi) to have power—Tokh A *wäl*, Tokh B *walo*, a (great) chief, a prince—OP *wāldnikans* (acc pl), kings—several other OSl and Sl forms, perh from OGmc—OIr *flaith*, dominion (exercised power), sovereignty, a chief, a prince, Ga *flath*, chief, prince, Cor *gallos* or *-us*, power, and *gulād*, region, country (cf the syn W *gwlād*), OC etymon (power, he who exercises it) *vlatos*, r *vlat-*.

## Germanic

2. Akin to OFris *walda*, OS and Go *waldan*, OHG *waltan*, as above, is the syn OE *wealdan*, caus *wieldan*, whence ME *welden*, have power over, E 'to *wield*'; akin to the OE v is the OE n *weald, geweald, gewield*, whence the long obs E n *wield*.

## Latin—and French—Simples

3. L *ualēre*, ML *valēre*, r *ual-, val-*, have presp *ualens, valens*, o/s *ualent-, valent-*, whence the E adj *valent*, now only in Chem and in cpds; derivative LL *ualentia*, ML *v-*, power, competence, yields Chem and Phys *valence* (perh imm from F) and *valency*.

4. From L *ualens*, o/s *ualent-*, derives the PlN *Ualentia*, ML *Valentia*, MF-F *Valence*, whence—because this drapery was first made there—the E *valance*. The derivative L PN *Ualentius* (imm from *Ualens*), ML *V-*, has dim *Ualentiniānus*, whence, from a late C7 Merovingian treasurer bearing a Gmc name thus latinized, the ML *Valentiniana* urbs (city) whence OF-F *Valenciennes*, whence F, hence E, *valenciennes*, lace made there. The PN *Ualens*, ML *Valens*, has another relevant derivative: *Ualentīnus*, ML *V-*, whence F *Valentin* and E *Valentine*. From the F 'St *Valentin*' comes EF-F *valentin*, var *valentine*, the latter form being adopted by E: on St Valentine's Day (February 14) girls chose a sweetheart (*valentin*); hence a missive (*valentine*) sent to one; the custom travelled to England.

5. App from L *ualēre*, ML *v-*, comes ML *valeriāna*, elliptical for *herba valeriāna*, prob because some medieval physician *Valerius* discovered the Med virtues of the herb. Hence the Chem adj *valerianic*, now usu contr to *valeric*.

6. L *ualēre*, s *ual-*, has derivative *ualētūdō*, good health, then good or ill health, finally bad health, with o/s *ualētūdin-*, whence the adj *ualētūdinārius* (also used as n), whence the MF-F *valétudinaire*, whence E *valetudinary*, largely displaced by *valetudinarian* (*-ian* substituted for *-y*).

7. L *ualēre*, ML *valēre*, becomes OF-F *valoir*, with presp *valant*, varr *vaillant, vailant*, used also as adj: whence ME-E *valiant*. Derivative OF-MF *valiance* (varr *vaillance, vaillance*) was adopted by ME, with the var *valiancy* naturally and anl resulting.

8. L *ualēre* has derivative adj *ualidus*, ML *validus*, whence EF-F *valide*, whence E *valid*; derivative LL *ualiditās*, ML *v-*, acc *validitātem*, yields EF-F *validité*, whence E *validity*; and derivative LL *ualidāre*, to strengthen, has pp *ualidātus*, whence both 'to *validate*' and ML *validātiō*, acc *validātiōnem*, whence EF-F *validation*, adopted by E.

9. L *ualēre* has derivative n *ualor*, whence OF *valor, -ur, -our*, the last being adopted by ME and retained by E; AE has reshaped the E word. Derivative ML *valorōsus* becomes OF-F *valeureux*, f *valeureuse*, whence E *valorous*. The erudite F

*valorisation* becomes E *valorization*, whence, by b/f, 'to *valorize*'.

10. OF-F *valoir* has pp *valu*, f *value*, whence, prob elliptical for *chose* (thing) *value*, the OF-F n *value*, whence ME *valu*, *valeu*, ME-E *value*, whence 'to *value*'—prob assisted by OF-F *valuer*, much as *valuable* has prob been assisted by MF-F *valuable*. OF-F *valuer* has the MF-EF derivative *valuation*, whence prob the E word: cf *evaluation* in para 17.

### Latin—and French—Compounds

11. Prob suggested by *equivalent* (see para 16) is *ambivalent* (*ambi-*, c/f of L *ambō*, both), whence, anl, *ambivalence*.

12. 'To *avail*,' whence the n, derives from ME *availen*: prob via AF, from OF-MF *a* (F *à*, L *ad*), to+*valoir*. Hence *available*.

13. 'To *convalesce*' derives from L *conualescere*, to begin to grow strong (after illness): *con-* used int +*ualescere*, inch of *ualēre*; the L presp *conual-escens*, o/s *conualescent-*, becomes MF-F *conval-escent*, adopted by E; derivative LL *conualescentia* becomes MF-F *convalescence*, likewise adopted.

14. 'To *countervail*' derives from MF-EF *contre-valoir*: OF-F *contre*, L *contra*, against+*valoir*.

15. 'To *devaluate*,' whence *devaluation*, and 'to *devalue*', are formed anl with the E words in para 17.

16. *Equivalence* and *equivalent* come from MF-F *équivalence* and *équivalent*, themselves from ML *aequivalentia* and *aequivalent*em, acc of *aequivalens*, presp of *aequivalēre*, to have equal power, hence value: *aequi-*, c/f of *aequus*, equal+*valēre*, L *ualēre*.

17. 'To *evaluate*' derives, by b/f, from *evalua-tion*, from MF-F *évaluation*, formed anl from MF-F *évaluer*, from OF-F *valuer*.

18. L *ualidus* has neg *inualidus*, ML *invalidus*, whence the EF-F *invalide* and the E *invalid* (adj); the differentiated E n *invalid*—whence *invalidism*—owes its pron to the F adj (hence n). The late MF-F v *invalider*, to render not-valid, has derivative EF-F *invalidation*, adopted by E, which therefrom, by b/f, derives 'to *invalidate*'. *Invaluable*=*in-*, not +*valuable*.

19. 'To *prevail*' derives from late MF-F *pré-valoir*, from ML *praevalēre* (L *-ualēre*), to gain power, esp superior power: *prae-*, in front. The presp *praeualens*, o/s *praeualent-*, ML *-valent-*, yields the E adj *prevalent*; the LL derivative *praeualentia*, superior power, yields E *prevalence*, which perh owes something to EF *prévalence*.

20. *Revalescence* derives from *revalescent*, from ML *revalescent-*, o/s of *revalescens*, presp of *revalescere*, L *reualescere*, to begin to grow strong again. *Revalidate* and *revalorize* merely prefix *re-*, again, anew, to *validate* and *valorize* (see para 9).

21. From L *Ualē*, ML *Valē*, Be strong, Be well, used in saying goodbye, comes L *ualedīcere*, to say goodbye; from the pp *ualedictus*, comes, after E *diction*, the E *valediction*, whence, anl, *valedictory*.

**valval, valvate, valve, valvular.** The 1st derives from the 3rd; the 3rd is adopted from EF-F, which derives it from modern L *valva*, itself from L *ualua*, the leaf of a folding door, akin to L *uoluere*, ML *volvere*, to roll. L *ualua* has dim *ualuula*, ML *valvula*, whence E *valvular*, and v *ualuāre*, pp *ualuātus*, whence the E adj *valvate*: f.a.e., VOLUBLE.

**vambrace.** See the 1st VAN, para 4.

**vamoose.** See VADE, para 6.

**vamp** (1), of shoe. See the 1st VAN, para 4.

**vamp** (2). See:

**vampire** (whence **vampiric** and **vampirism**). *Vampire*, a blood-sucking ghost or reanimated person, hence a blackmailer, a *femme fatale* (whence the sl *vamp*, n, hence v), derives from F *vampire*: G *Vampir*: Serbian *vampir*, nasalized mdfn of a Sl word occurring elsewhere as, e.g., Bulg *vapir* (var *vepir*), Pol, Cz, Ukrainian *upiór* (*upyr*), *uper*; cf also, but with *b* for *p*, the dial Tu *uber*, a witch.

**van** (1), the front of, e.g., an army, the **vanguard**; **vantage** and **advantage** (v, hence n), **advantageous**; **vamp** (of a shoe) and **vambrace**; **advance** (n, v), **advancement**; **En avant!** and **avant-garde**.

1. This *van* is short for *vanguard*, an easing of *vantguard*, aphetic for *avant-guard*: OF-F *avant-garde*: *avant* (LL *abante*: L *ab*+*ante*), before+*garde* (cf GUARD). F *en avant*, to(wards) the front is known in E.

2. OF-F *avant* has derivative (*-age*) OF-F *avantage*, adopted by ME, whence—cf next para—both E *advantage* and, by aphesis, *vantage*; deriva-tive MF-F *avantager* and late MF-F *avantageux* (f *-geuse*) yield 'to *advantage*' and *advantageous*.

3. LL *abante*, from in front of, has derivative VL *\*abantiare*, to put in front, whence OF-F *avancer* (whence the MF-F n *avance*, perh prompting the E n), whence ME *avancen*, whence—with intrusive *-d-*, as if from L *ad*, towards—'to *advance*'; derivative OF-F *avancement* becomes E *advance-ment*.

4. OF-F *avant* has derivative cpds MF *avantpié* (F *avant-pied*), lit 'fore-foot', and MF *avanbras* (F *avant-bras*), lit 'fore-arm': whence ME *vampe*, E *vamp*, orig a sock, and E *vambrace*.

**van** (2), a vehicle. See CARAVAN, s.f.

**van** (3), a winnowing fan. See the 1st WIND, para 8.

**vanadic** derives, anl, from the Chem element **vanadium**, SciL (suffix *-ium*) alteration of ON *Vanad*is, the goddess Freya: ? 'The Guardian (Goddess)'.

**Vandal, vandal, vandalism.** The 3rd derives from F *vandalisme*, from Voltaire's *vandale*, whence E *vandal*: from OF-F *Vandale*, one of the Vandals, a Gmc tribe that, at the beginning of C5 A.D., ravaged Gaul and Spain (B & W): ML *Vandali*, L *Uandali*, L var *Uandili*, of Gmc origin (o.o.o.).

**vandyke.** See DIG, s.f.

**vane; paravane.** The latter combines *para-*, against+*vane*, a weathercock: ME *vane*, a dial var (*v* for *f*) of ME *fane*, weathercock, lit a banner: OE *fana*, a banner: cf OFris and Go *fana*, OHG *fano*, ON *fani*: cf, with *p* for *f*, the L *pannus*, a rag, a cloth: cf PAN.

**vanguard.** See the 1st VAN, para 1.

**vanilla** is a SciL reshaping of Sp *vainilla*, a little sheath, dim of *vaina*, a sheath, a pod: ML *vāgīna*, L *uāgīna*, a sheath, whence the Med sense: o.o.o.

**vanish.** See VACANT, para 11.

**vanity.** See VACANT, para 10.

**vanquish.** See VICTOR, para 1.

**vantage.** See the 1st VAN, para 2.

**vapid** (whence **vapidity**): ML *vapidus*, L *uapidus*: from L *uappa*, wine that has lost its 'life' and savour: o.o.o., but perh akin to L *uapor* (see next).

2. Perh related to L *uapidus*, insipid, is L *fatuus*, foolish, whence E *fatuous*, with derivative L *fatuitās*, acc *fatuitātem*, yielding, via MF-F *fatuité*, the E *fatuity*. The otherwise o.o.o. L *fatuus* could result from L *uapidus* becoming VL *\*fapidus*, then *\*fatidus*, then, by contr, *\*fatdus*, then, by easing, *fatuus*.

3. L *fatuus*, foolish, has the LL derivative *infatuāre*, pp *infatuātus*, whence *infatuātiō*, o/s *infatuātiōn-*, whence resp 'to *infatuate*' and, perh via EF-F, *infatuation*.

**vapor** (AE) or **vapour; vaporization, vaporize; vaporose, vaporous; evaporate, evaporation** (whence anl, **evaporator**).

1. *Vapor* is a L-reshaping of ME-E *vapour*, adopted from MF *vapour*, varr *vapor, vapeur* (extant): ML *vapor*: L *uapor*: OL *uapos* (o/s *uapor-*): prob akin to Gr *kapnos*, smoke, vapour, *kapuein*, to exhale, and to OSl *kypēti*, to boil, and Lith *kvāpas*, smoke, vapour, *kvēpia*, a vapour that is spreading, *kvepéti*, emit an odour. Hofmann derives Gr *kapnos* from PGr *\*kwapnos*, with IE r *\*kwap-*, var of *\*kwep-*, (vi) to scatter, to stray.

2. Derivative L *uaporōsus*, ML *v-*, becomes MF-F *vaporeux*, f *-euse*, and, perh independently, E *vaporous*; E *vaporose* comes straight from ML.

3. From MF-F *vapeur*, but after the ML *vapor*, F derives *vaporiser*, whence *vaporisation*: hence E 'to *vaporize*' and *vaporization*.

4. L *uapor* has derivative v *uaporāre*, with prefix-cpd *ēuaporāre*, ML *ēvaporāre*, pp *ēvaporātus*, whence 'to *evaporate*'; derivative L *ēuaporātiō* and LL *ēuaporātiuus*, ML forms in *ēvap-*, yield MF-F *évaporation*, whence E *evaporation*, and E *evaporative*.

**vaquero.** See VACCENIC, para 1.

**vara.** See VACILLATE, para 7.

**varec** or **varech.** See WREAK, para 4.

**variability, variable; variance, variant; variate, variation.** See VACILLANT, para 4.

**varicose, varicosis.** See VACILLANT, para 6.

**variegate, variegation.** See VACILLANT, para 4.

**variety.** See VACILLANT, para 4.

**variola, variolate, variole, variolous.** See VACILLANT, para 4.

**variorum.** See VACILLANT, para 4.

**various.** See VACILLANT, para 4.

**varix.** See VACILLANT, para 6.

**varlet.** See STAND, para 39.

**varnish.** 'To *varnish*,' ME *varneschen*, earlier *vernysshen*, derives from OF-F *vernisser* (cf the slightly later *vernir*) from OF *verniz*, OF-F *vernis*,

whence, via ME *vernisch*, the E n *varnish*: (prob via It *vernice*), from ML *veronix, veronice*, an odoriferous resin: LGr *verenikē*, prob from Gr *Berenikē* (a city in Cyrenaica, North Africa), whence perh the first varnishes were exported to Greece and Italy; some kind of resin served as the earliest varnish. (Dauzat; Prati.)

**Varuna.** See URANIA, para 2.

**varus.** See VACILLANT, para 7.

**vary.** See VACILLANT, para 4, s.f.

**vascular.** See para 2 of:

**vase; vasculum, vascular, vasculose, vasculous;** cf the element *vasi-* (*vaso-*); **extravasate, extravasation; vessel.**

1. 'To *extravasate*,' whence *extravasation*, is formed anl from SciF *extravaser*, itself formed anl after OF-F *transvaser* (L *trans*, across+ML *vas*+ inf *-er*) with base resting on ML *vās*, L *uās*.

2. L *uās*, a recipient, more tall than wide, for liquids, has var *uāsum*: o.o.o. L *uās*, ML *vās*, becomes EF-F *vase*, adopted by E. The L dim *uāsculum*, adopted by learnèd E, has suggested the F adjj *vasculaire* and *vasculeux*, f *-euse*: whence E *vascular* and *vasculous*, the var *vasculose* implying VL *\*uasculōsus*, ML *\*v-*.

3. L *uās* has another dim: *uāscellum*, with pl *uāscella*, apprehended by VL as f sing: VL *uāscella*, ML *vāscella*, yields OF-MF *vessele, vesselle* (F *vaisselle*), with var *vessel* adopted by ME; the sense 'ship' derives from the fact that an empty vase made of light material will float,—a sense that arose in F as early as C12.

**vaseline:** proprietary name *Vaseline*, formed irresponsibly (as so many trade-names are formed): G *Wasser* (pron *v-*)+Gr *elaion*, olive-oil+Chem suffix *-ine*.

**vassal, vassalage.** See STAND, para 39.

**vast, vastitude, vastitity, vastness, vasty.** See VACANT, para 16 and, for *vastness*, the heading.

**vat**, a large tub or cistern, is a south-western dial var (*v* for *f*) of ME-(obsol)E *fat*: OE *faet*: cf OS *fat*, OHG *faz*, MHG *vaz*, G *Fass*, D *vat*, ON *fat*, themselves akin to OE *fatian*, OFris *fatia*, OHG *fazzōn*, MHG *vazzen*, G *fassen*, to contain: *vat*, therefore, is simply 'container'. (Walshe.)

**vatic.** See the element *vati-* and, f.a.e., WEDNESDAY, para 3.

**Vatican:** F *Vatican*: It *Vaticano*: ML *Vātīcānus*: L *Uātīcānus*, elliptical for *Uātīcānus mons* (or perh *collis*), the Vatican hill. From the Pope's palace having long been situated here, comes the sense '(the seat of) papal government and power'. L *Uātīcānus* is o.o.o.—but perh orig from a temple or shrine affected to the use of *uātēs* or soothsayers and prophets (cf the element *vati-*).

**vaticinate.** See the element *vati-*.

**vaudeville.** See VALE, para 4.

**vault** (1), arched roof. See VOLUBLE, para 3.

**vault** (2), to leap, hence a leap. See VOLUBLE, para 3.

**vaunt.** See VACANT, para 12.

**vavasor (-our).** See STAND, para 39.

**veal.** See WETHER, para 3.

**vection.** See VIA, para 10.

**vectis.** See VEX, para 2.

**vector.** See WAY, para 10.

**Veda, Vedanta.** See VIDE, para 5.

**vedette.** See VIGOR, para 5, s.f.

**veer** and (of ships) **wear; environ,** v (whence **environment,** whence **environmental**), and **environs,** n.

1. 'To *wear*' or cause (a ship) to go about, is a f/e corruption of 'to *veer*' (vt, vi): OF-F *virer*: VL *virāre, uirāre*: app an alteration—perh after LL *gyrāre*, to turn (anything) around—of L *uibrāre*, to shake, brandish. (B & W.)

2. OF-F *virer* has the OF-EF derivative *viron*, a circle, a round, the country around, whence OF-F *environ* (*en*, in), around (prep; then, in C16, adv), whence MF-EF *à l'environ*, in the neighbourhood or vicinity, whence, in C17, the pl n *environs*, adopted by E. Also from the OF prep *environ* comes the OF-F v *environner*, whence 'to environ'; the late MF-EF *environnement* prob suggested the rare EE *environment*, but the C19-20 use of the word app derives rather from 'to *environ*'.

**vegetable; vegetal; vegetarian; vegetate, vegetation; vegete.** See VIGOR, para 2.

**vehemence, vehement.** See VIA, para 11.

**vehicle, vehicular.** See VIA, para 11.

**veil,** n and v, with neg **unveil**—hence pa, vn (un)**veiling; velar** (adj, hence, in Phon, n)—**velarium**—**velation**—**velum; reveal, revelation** (**Revelation**), **revelatory.**—**voile**—**wick** (of lamp).

1. 'To *veil*' comes from ME *veilen*, from the ME n *veile*, whence the E n *veil*: and ME *veile* is adopted from ONF *veile*, which, like OF-F *voile*, derives from ML-VL *vēla*, f sing, from L *uēla*, pl of *uēlum*, a sail, but also (a piece of) drapery, an awning: IE etymon, *wegslom*, from *weg-*, to weave. (E & M.)

2. L *uēlum* has adj *uēlāris*, of a sail or drapery, ML *v-*, whence E *velar*, and v *uēlāre*, to cover with a drapery or an awning, pp *uēlātus*, ML *v-*, whence both the E adj *velate* and the LL n *uēlatio*, ML *v-*, o/s *vēlātiōn-*, whence E *velation*, a veiling. L *uēlum* has extn *uēlārium*, ML *v-*, a covering drapery, adopted by Sci.

3. L *uēlāre* has prefix-cpd *reuēlāre*, to pull back the curtain, or covering, from, hence to disclose: whence OF-MF *reveler* (EF-F *ré-*), whence 'to *reveal*'. Derivative LL *reuēlātiō* (from the pp *reuēlāt*us), an uncovering, hence of a secret, acc *reuēlātiōnem*, ML *revē-*, becomes OF-MF *revelation* (EF-F *ré-*), adopted by E. The misuse *Revelations* is a f/e pl of (The) *Revelation* (of St John): LL *Reuēlātiō*: cf sem the Gr-derived syn *Apocalypse*. Also from L *reuēlāt-*, the s of the pp, comes the LL adj *reuēlātōrius*, (of dreams) revealing, whence the E *revelatory*.

4. VL *uēla, vēla*, drapery, OF-F *voile*, orig a sail, drapery, acquires, in F, the sense 'a thin dress-material'—and, in that sense, has been adopted by E.

5. Akin to L *uēlum* are OHG *wichili*, a thing rolled, or wound up, and *wiocha*, G *Wieche*, dial G *wicke*, wick, MD *wicke, wieche, wieke*, D *wiek*, lamp-wick, roll of lint: and akin to these is OE *wēoce, wēoc*, a wick, ME *weke*, later *wike*, finally *wicke*, whence E *wick*.

**vein,** n, hence v; **venation, venous** (whence Med **intravenous**—L *intra*, within); **venule.**

*Vein*, ME-from-OF-F *veine*, derives from ML *vēna*, L *uēna*, any conduit, esp a vein or, usu in pl, a 'vein' in marble, wood, etc.: o.o.o.: perh akin to VIA. Derivatives *uēnōsus* and dim *uēnula* yield E *venous* (var *venose*) and *venule*; *venation* is a learnèd formation: ML *vēna+-ation*, anl with all such nn formed as if from a pp.

**velar, velate, velation.** See VEIL, para 2.

**veld, veldt; veldschoen.** See FIELD, para 3.

**velleity.** See VOLITION, para 5.

**vellicate, vellication** (whence, anl, **vellicative**);—**lanugo; svelte.**—**avulse, avulsion; convulsant** (adj, hence n), **convulse, convulsion, convulsionary, convulsive; divulse, divulsion** (whence, anl, **divulsive**); **evulse, evulsion; revulsant,** (obsol) **revulse, revulsion, revulsive.**

1. *Vellication* derives from ML *vellicātiōn-*, o/s of *vellicātiō*, L *uel-*, from *uellicātus*—whence 'to *vellicate*', to (cause to) twitch—the pp of *uellicāre*, a freq of *uellere*, to tug violently, to pluck (e.g., hairs): r *uel-*: perh from an IE r *wel-*: cf Arm *gelmn*, a fleece (plucked by hand before shears were invented), which answers to the syn L *uellus*: perh cf also L *lāna*, wool, whence *lānūgō*, thick down, whence SciE *lanugo*; there are also prob cognates in Gr and Go—if that be so, cf WOOL. Certainly cf VELVET.

2. Prob related is *svelte*, adopted from EF-F, which thus adapts It *svelto*, adj use of the pp of *svèllere*, to pluck out, hence to lengthen, to set free: app from L *ēuellere*, ML *ēvellere*, to pluck out. (Prati.) Cf para 6 below.

3. L *uellere* has certain prefix-cpds relevant to E; they are all formed with the pp *uulsus*, ML *vulsus*, s *vuls-*.

4. L *auellere*, to pluck or tear a- or away from, off, has pp *auulsus*, ML *avulsus*, whence 'to *avulse*'; derivative *auulsiō*, o/s *auulsiōn-*, ML *avulsiōn-*, yields *avulsion*.

5. L *conuellere* (*con-* used int), to pluck violently, to shake, has pp *conuulsus*, ML *convulsus*, whence both 'to *convulse*' and EF-F *convulser*, presp *convulsant*, adopted by E as an adj; derivative *conuulsiō*, acc *conuulsiōnem* (ML *-vul-*), becomes EF-F *convulsion*, adopted by E; EF-F *convulsion* has derivatives EF-F *convulsif* and F *convulsionnaire* (adj and n), whence E *convulsive* and *convulsionary*.

6. L *diuellere*, to pluck apart, and *ēuellere*, to pluck out, pp *di-* and *ē-uulsus*, derivatives *di-* and *ē-uulsio*, ML o/s in *-vulsiōn-*, yield *divulse, evulse*, and *divulsion, evulsion*.

7. L *reuellere*, to pluck or pull back or away, has pp *reuulsus*, whence *reuulsiō*, acc *reuulsiōnem*: whence 'to *revulse*' and EF-F *révulsion*, with anl adj *révulsif*: whence E *revulsion* and *revulsive*, both with Med and general senses.

**vellum.** See WETHER, para 3.

velocity (cf the element *veloci-*, e.g. for **veloc-ipede**): MF-F *vélocité*: ML *vēlocitāt*em, acc of *vēlocitās*, L *uēlocitās*, from *uēlox*, rapid, agile: perh cf L *uēles*, a lightly armed foot-soldier: o.o.o.: perh akin to the r of *vegetable*, q.v. at VIGOR.

**velours.** See VELVET, para 2.

**velum**, as used by Sci: cf VEIL, para 1.

**velure.** See VELVET, para 2.

**velutinous.** See para 2, s.f., of:

**velvet**, whence **velvety** (cf the F *velouté*) and **velveteen** (*-een* vaguely dim: cf *sateen* and *satin*); **velours** and **velure**; **velutinous.**—**villose, villosity, villous**—and **villus.**—Cf the sep WOOL.

1. Perh akin to L *uellus*, a fleece—see VELLICATE, para 1—is L *uillus*, a tuft of hair, pl *uilli*, hairs, down: otherwise, *uillus* is o.o.o. The ML form *villus* has been adopted by An and Zoo; the adj *uillōsus*, ML *v-*, covered with soft hairs or down, yields *villose* and *villous* (cf the F *villeux*), whence, anl, *villosity* (cf F *villosité*).

2. ML *villōsus* becomes OProv *velos*, adj used as n, whence OF-EF *velous*, whence EF-F *velours*, which E both adopts and, as *velure*, adapts. OF-EF *velous* acquires a late MF-F adj *velouté*, velvety, whence that 'smooth' sauce known as *velouté*; the corresp OProv adj *velut* has app influenced It *velluto*, velvet, whence, ult, the E adj *velutinous*.

3. L *uillus* has the LL-VL adj *uillūtus*, whence OF-F *velu*, whence the AF n *veluet* (dim *-et*), whence, *-u-* being misapprehended as *-v-*, the ME-E *velvet*.

**venal, venality; vend, vendible, vendition, vendor.**

1. *Venal*, capable of being sold or bought, and *venality*, willingness to be sold or bought, derive from OF-F *vénal* and EF-F *vénalité*: ML *vēnālis* and *vēnalitāt*em, acc of *vēnalitās*: L *uēnālis* and its derivative LL *uēnalitās*: L *\*uēnus* or *\*uēnum*, attested by the acc *uēnum*, a sale: cf Skt *vasnám*, a price, and Gr *ōnē* (for *\*wōnē*), a purchase, the price of purchase: IE r, *\*wes-*, varr *\*was-* (as in Hit *was-*, to buy) and *\*wos-* (as in Gr).

2. From the L *uēnum dare*, to put up for sale, comes *uēnundare*, whence *uendere*, to sell, whence, via OF-F *vendre*, 'to vend'. The L derivatives *uendibilis*, *uenditiō* (o/s *uenditiōn-*), *uenditor*, yield E *vendible*, *vendition*, *vendor* (adopted from AF: var of OF-MF *vendeor*, EF-F *vendeur*, from *vendre*).

**venatic.** See VENERABLE, para 5.

**venation.** See VEIN.

**vend.** See VENAL, para 2.

**vendetta.** See DICT, para 22.

**vendible, vendition, vendor.** See VENAL, para 2.

**veneer**, n and v, comes from G *furnier* and *furnieren*, varr in *four-*: OF-F *fournir*, to furnish—cf FURNISH.

**veneniferous, venenific.** See para 6 of:

**venerable** (**venerability**), **venerate, veneration, venerative; venereal, venery** (both senses), **Venus; venial** (whence **veniality**); **venison**—cf **venatic; venom, venomous**—**veneniferous, venenific.**—Gmc cognates: **win** (v, hence n), whence **winner, winning,**

pa and vn (often in pl), pa, pt, **won**—**winsome; ween**, whence pa, vn, **weening**, esp in over-**weening; wont** (adj, n, v), whence pa **wonted** (neg **unwonted**) —cf **wean; wish**, v (hence n, whence **wishful**), pa, vn **wishing**—cf **wistful.**

1. *Venerable* comes from OF-F *vénérable* (orig accentless): ML *venerābilis*, L *uenerābilis*, from *uenerāri* (early, also *-āre*), to address (to a god) a request or supplication for a favour or a forgiveness, hence to pay the utmost respect to; derivative LL *uenerabilitās* yields *venerability*. From the pp *uenerātus* and its derivatives L *uenerātiō*, LL *uenerātiuus*, L *uenerātor*, come, via the ML forms in *v-*, 'to *venerate*'—*veneration*, prob imm from OF-MF *veneration* (EF-F *véné-*)—*venerative*—*venerator*.

2. L *uenerāre*, *-āri*, perh basically 'to express a (strong) wish or desire to', has s *uener-*, an extn of the *uen-* we see in L *uenia* and L *Uenus* (ML *Venus*): this *uen-*, app meaning 'to desire, to love', occurs, with varr *\*wan-*, *\*win-*, *\*won-*, *\*wun-*, in such words as Skt *vắnchati*, he desires, Ve *vánas-*, loving, esp in cpds, e.g., *gīr-vaṇas*, hymn-loving (adj)—OHG *wunskan*, G *wünschen*, to desire, to wish, OHG *wunna*, great joy—E *wish* and *win*. Perh cf also Hit *wen-*, to desire (a woman) violently, 'sleep' with her, violate her—the precise meanings are obscure.

### Latin Cognates

3. L *Uenus*, ML *Venus*, orig a goddess of beauty, later identified with Gr Aphrodite, goddess of physical love (opp Psyche, goddess of spiritual love), becomes in the European languages the goddess of both physical beauty and physical love —cf the G *Venusberg* (Venus's Mountain). *Uenus* is a personification of *uenus*, at once physical love, the act of love, the person loved, and such qualities as arouse love, esp charm, grace, seductiveness. The adj of *uenus* is *uenustus*, whence the obsol E *venust*, charming, graceful, seductive; that of *Uenus* is *uenereus* (*-ius*), pertaining to Venus—cf the LL *ueneria* (neu pl n, from the neu pl adj), sexual intercourse—whence the obs E *venereous*, displaced by *venereal* (*-eal* for *-eous*). *Venery*, love-making, represents *Venus*+*-ery*. (For *venery*, hunting, see para 5, s.f.)

4. The r *uen-* occurs in L *uenia*, favour or forgiveness accorded by the gods, hence, in LL and usu in pl, God's forgiveness or pardon to men; the derivative LL adj *ueniālis*, ML *v-*, pardonable, yields MF *venial* (soon becoming *véniel*), adopted by E.

5. The r *uen-* occurs also in *uenāri*, to hunt (game), prob orig to desire and to pursue (cf *win*, para 8 below): perh this v with the long vowel *ē* represents an int or a freq, or a freq-int, of a v, with short vowel *ĕ* and with r *uen-*, attested by *uenerāri* (cf para 1): cf Skt *vanóti*, Av *vanaiti*, he gains, overcomes. On the pp *uenātus* are formed the LL adjj *uenāticus*, *uenātōrius*, whence the now rare E *venatic*, *venatory*, and the n *uenātiō*, hunting, that which is hunted, that which is obtained by hunting,

ML acc *vēnātiōnem*, whence OF-MF *veneison* (later *venaison*), adopted by ME, with varr *veneson* and *venison*, the latter surviving—with sense gradually restricted. The agent *uēnātor*, ML *vēnātor*, a hunter, becomes OF-F *veneur*, whence, anl, the MF-F *vénerie*, hunting, the chase, whence the syn E *venery*.

6. Akin to L *Uenus* is L *uenēnum* (s *uenēn-*, r *uen-*), a love-philtre, hence any philtre, hence a poison, whence *uenēnifer* (*-fer*, -bearing) and *uenēnificus* (*-ficus*, making): E *veneniferous* and *venenific*. L *uenēnum*, poison, has the VL mdfn *\*uenimen*, *\*venimen*, whence OF-MF *venim* (EF-F *venin*, adopted by Biochem): ME *venim*: E *venom*; *venomous* derives from ME *venimous*, from OF-F *venimeux*, from OF-MF *venim*.

## Germanic Cognates

7. Logically, it is preferable to begin with 'to wish': ME *wischen*, var of *wuschen*: OE *wyscan*: cf OHG *wynskan*, G *wünschen*, to wish, and OE *wusc*, OHG *wunsc*, MHG-G *wunsch*, (without the digamma) ON *ōskr*, Skt *vāñchā*, a wish: all originating in 'desire' and tending to weaken to 'wish'. From the derivative *wishful* comes, by f/e association with the interj *whist*, *wistful*.

8. Then one may consider 'to *win*', to endeavour desirously, to struggle, hence to contend, hence, vt, to obtain by strenuous endeavour, hence by contest or battle: ME *winnen*: OE *winnan*, to strive, struggle, fight: cf OFris *winna*, OS and OHG *winnan*, to strive, to toil, OHG *gewinnan* (*ge-* is int), MHG *gewinnen*, to gain by effort, G to gain or win, ON *vinna*, to toil, to gain by toil, to gain—cf Go *winnan*, to torment oneself, and Skt *vanóti*, he conquers. Here, the OGmc r *\*win-* is app a thinning of the *wun-* attested by OHG *wunskan*, to desire. (Walshe.)

9. OGmc *wun-* recurs in OE *wynsum*, E *winsome* (suffix *-sum*, E *-some*): cf OHG *wunnisam*, causing joy or pleasure, and Go un*wun*ands, not agreeable, sad.

10. 'To *ween*,' to expect, to hope (obs senses), to think, to suppose, derives from ME *wenen*, OE *wēnan*: cf OFris *wēna*, OS *wānian*, Go *wēnjan*, G *wähnen* (from the n), MD *wenen*, *waenen*, *wanen*, ON *vāna*, and such corresp nn as OE *wēn*, OFris *wēn*, OS *wān*, Go *wāns*, ON *vān*, expectation, hope, OHG *wān*, hope, MHG *wān*, belief, G *Wahn*, illusion, delusion. The OGmc *wēn-* is app phon differentiated from OGmc *wun-* to reinforce a sem differentiation (either a weakening or merely another aspect).

11. Yet another aspect and another phon differentiation occur in the adj *wont*, accustomed, whence both the n *wont*, custom, and the v *wont*, to be accustomed, (vt) to accustom: ME *wunt*, a contr of *woned*, pp of *wonen*, for *wonien*, varr of *wunen*, *wunien*, to be accustomed, to dwell, from OE *wunian*, to dwell, hence to remain, hence to be accustomed, but prob influenced by the intimately related ME adj *wone*, accustomed, from OE *gewun*, usu *gewuna*: cf OFris *wunia*, *wonia*, OS *wunōn*,

OHG *wonēn*, MHG *wonen*, G *wohnen*, MD-D *wonen*, to dwell, ON *una*, to dwell, to be content. Cf the prob related OE *wynn*, OHG *wunna*, *wünni*, G *Wonne*, OS *wunnia*, OIr *fonn*, joy, Cor *wonys*, to dwell, and *vaner*, a custom. As Walshe remarks, the basic meaning of the OGmc words for 'to dwell' is prob 'to rejoice somewhere'.

12. Related to the OE adj *gewun*(*a*), accustomed (and to *wunian*, to dwell, hence to be accustomed), is the vowel-thinned, sense-narrowed OE *wenian*, to accustom a child, or a young quadruped, to do without its mother's milk: ME *wenen*: E 'to *wean*': cf the syn OE *āwenian*, G *entwöhnen* (a specialization of 'sich *entwohnen*', to disaccustom oneself), and certain OGmc words formed in *wen-* and meaning 'to accustom'.

## Conclusion

13. Starting from IE *\*wen-*, to desire, take pleasure, love, we have ranged, phon, through *\*wan-* (Skt, Gmc, C) and *\*wĕn-* (Hit, L, Gmc), and *\*win-* (Gmc) and *\*won-* (Gmc, C), to *\*wun-* (Gmc), and, sem, from 'to desire' to the strengthened 'to poison (with a love-philtre)'—and 'to pursue', whether in love or in the chase—'to obtain, esp by purposive desire', and to the weakened 'to wish'— 'to hope, suppose, think'—'to take pleasure in being somewhere', 'to dwell'—'to become accustomed, to accustom'. In short, four IE languages or language-groups—Hit (prob), Skt, C, Gmc—have run a complete phon and a nearly completely sem gamut. (If the denasalized Lith *výti*, to hunt, be truly akin, as E & M assume, we must add S1.)

**venereal**. See prec, para 3.

**venery**, love-making; hunting, the chase. See VENERABLE, paras 3, s.f., and 5, s.f.

**Venetian, Venice**. The former (adj, hence n) derives—perh via MF-F *vénitien*—from ML *Venētiānus*, the adj of ML *Venētia*, the city and region (LL-L *Uenētia*: *-ia* connoting 'district' or 'region') inhabited by an ancient tribe or people named the *Uenēti* (ML *V-*), a name that, like the people, was prob of Illyrian origin. ML *Venētia* became It *Venezia* and F *Vénice*, whence E *Venice*. The highly civilized medieval and modern Venetians have furnished many European languages with the names of social and domestic amenities (balls, blinds, glass, windows, etc.) and of artists' colours (blue, green, white, etc.).

**venge, vengeable, vengeance, vengeful, venger, vengress**. See DICT, para 21.

**venial**. See VENERABLE, para 4.

**Venice**. See VENETIAN.

**venin**. See VENERABLE, para 6.

**venison**. See VENERABLE, para 5.

**venom, venomous**. See VENERABLE, para 6.

**venous**. See VEIN.

**vent** (1), a (small) opening, for the escape or discharge of air, gas, fluid, hence 'to vent': orig a f/e var (after OF-F *vent*, wind) of *fent*, earlier *fente*, adopted from MF-F *fente*, orig the f of obs *fent*, pp of OF-F *fendre*, L *findere*, to split: cf FISSURE.

**vent** (2), in hunting. See the 1st WIND, para 5.

**ventilate, ventilation, ventilator.** See the 1st WIND, para 6.

**ventose, ventosity.** See the 1st WIND, para 7.

**ventral, ventricle** (whence, anl, **ventricular**); **ventriloquism, ventriloquist, ventriloquy.**

*Ventral* derives from ML *ventrālis*, L *uentrālis*, adj of *uenter* (o/s *uentr-*), the belly: prob akin to L *uterus*, the womb, with ending *-er* reminiscent of that of Gr *gastēr*, belly, stomach. The dim *uentriculus*, ML *v-*, orig 'little belly', hence 'stomach', means also 'ventricle': whence E *ventricle*. The LL cpd *uentriloquus* (prop an adj), one speaking from the stomach, becomes EF-F *ventriloque*, whence, with taut agential *-ist*, the E *ventriloquist*, whence anl *ventriloquism*, largely superseding *ventriloquy* (F *ventriloquie*, from *ventriloque*).—Cf VESICA.

**venture, venturer, venturesome, venturous.** See para 5 of:

**venue,** adopted from OF-F, was orig the f of *venu*, pp of *venir*, ML *venīre*, L *uenīre*, to come, ult akin to COME itself. The IE r is app *\*gwen-*, var *\*gwem-*, perh extnn of *\*gwe-*, var *\*gwa-*, occ with worn-down forms (the *-w* lost): cf such diversities as OE *cuman*, Go *qiman*, to come—Gr *bainō* (s *bain-*), I come—Skt *gámati*, he comes, Ve *jagama*, I have come—Tokh B ke*kamu* (pp), come. (E & M.) But Hit *we-*, to come, *wenzi*, they come, suggests an ult r *we-* and an ult kinship with VIA, q.v. at para 16.

2. Apart from *venue* and *venīre* (in legal phrases), the L *uenīre*—presp *ueniens*, o/s *uenient-* (derivative nn in *-tia*), and supine *uentum*, pp *-uentus*, whence nn in *-uentiō* and *-uentus* (gen *-ūs*)—affects E only in cpds; but in a vast number of cpds, all reflecting the ML forms in *v-*, whether the *-vene* of, e.g., *convene*, or the *-venant* (F) or *-venient* (L) of, e.g., *covenant* and *revenant*, or *convenient*, or the *-vent*, *vent-*, of, e.g., *advent* and *venture*, or several L or F derivatives or cognates or varr of those basic forms. Unless one takes these cpds in the alphabetical order of their L (or ML) originals, the most appalling confusion is likely to ensue.

3. L *aduenīre*, ML *advenīre*, to come towards or to, to arrive, hence (of events) to happen, yields 'to *advene*'; the presp *adueniens*, o/s *aduenient-*, E adj *advenient*, whence *advenience*; pp *aduentus*, whence both the n *aduentus*, E *advent*, whence *Advent*, whence *Adventism* and *Adventist*, and the adj *aduentitius* (prop *-īcius*), E *adventitious*; *adventive* app derives from EF-F *adventif*.

4. Also from the L pp *aduentus*, ML *adventus*, comes VL *\*aduentūra*, ML *adventūra*, whence OF-F *aventure*, with derivatives OF-F *aventurer* and OF-MF *aventuros* (EF-F *aventureux*): whence, resp, ME *aventure*, E *adventure*—ME *aventuren*, E 'to *adventure*', whence *adventurer*—ME *aventurous*, E *adventurous*—the *-d-* reintroduced from L.

5. ME *aventure* becomes, by aphesis, *venture*, whence both *venturesome* and 'to *venture*,' whence *venturer*; ME *aventurous* likewise becomes *venturous*.

6. *Avenue,* however, is adopted from OF-F, which derives it from *avenu*, pp of *avenir*, the

OF-MF form of EF-F *advenir*, ML *advenīre*: app it was orig the path or road by which one arrived at a great house.

7. L *anteuenīre*, to come before, presp *anteueniens*, o/s *-uenient-*, accounts for the E adj *antevenient*.

8. L *circumuenīre*, to come around, to encompass, hence to forestall or baffle, has pp *circumuentus*, whence 'to *circumvent*'; derivative LL *circumuentiō*, o/s *-uentiōn-*, explains *circumvention*.

9. L *conuenīre*, to come together, to assemble, hence to agree together, becomes OF-F *convenir*, whence 'to *convene*'. The L presp *conueniens*, o/s *conuenient-*, yields *convenient*; derivative L *conuenientia*, agreement or harmony, appositeness or fitness, yields *convenience*. But the OF-F *convenir* affords us several doublets: *convenance*, *convenant* (*convenable*).

10. On the L pp *conuentus* are formed *conuentiō* (acc *conuentiōn*em) and *conuentus* (gen *-ūs*): whence, via MF-F, *convention*, with *conventional* deriving—perh via late MF-F *conventionnel*—from derivative LL *conuentiōnālis*; and, from the ML sense 'nunnery', the E *convent*, with *conventual* deriving, via MF *conventual*, EF-F *conventuel*, from ML *conventuālis*. *Conventicle* derives from L *conuenticulum*, dim of the L n *conuentus*.

11. OF-F *convenir* has the contr OF-F var *covenir*, presp *covenant*, which, used as MF n, is adopted by E; hence 'to *covenant*', whence *covenanter*.

12. LL *contrauenīre*, to come against, hence contrary to, yields MF-F *contrevenir* and, prob independently, 'to *contravene*'; *contravention*, however, is app adopted from the MF-F word, formed as if from ML *\*contrauentiō*, acc *contrauentiōnem*.

13. L *ēuenīre*, to come, hence issue, from, hence to result, has pp *ēuentus*, whence the n *ēuentus* (gen *-ūs*), a result, a happening, whence late MF-EF *évent*, whence E *event*, whence *eventful*; *eventual* owes something to F *éventuel* (from L *ēuentus*).

14. L *inconueniens* (from *conueniens*, as in para 9), o/s *inconuenient-*, becomes MF-F *inconvénient*, whence E *inconvenient*; derivative LL *inconuientia* (disagreement) becomes MF-EF *inconvénience*, whence E *inconvenience*.

15. L *interuenīre*, to come between, and its LL derivative *interuentiō* (acc *interuentiōnem*), mediation, pass, through MF-F *intervenir* and *intervention*, into 'to *intervene*' and *intervention*.

16. L *inuenīre*, to come upon, hence to meet with, hence to find, to discover, has pp *inuentus*, whence *inuentiō* (acc *inuentiōnem*), *inuentor*, LL *inuentārium*, ML *inuentōrium*: whence E *invention*, *inventor*, *inventory*, all perh via the late MF-F corresp words. *Inventive* prob derives from late MF-F *inventif*; 'to *invent*'—cf EF-F *inventer*—comes from the L pp *inuentus*.

17. L *obuenīre*, to come up against, hence to befall, has pp *obuentus*, whence LL *obuentiō* (o/s *obuentiōn-*), revenue, whence the sense-changed E *obvention*.

18. L *peruenīre*, to come through, hence to succeed, yields OF-F *parvenir*, pp *parvenu*, used in F as n, adopted by E; 'one who has "won through" ' soon became a pej term.

19. L *praeuenīre*, to come in front or before, LL to anticipate, to prejudice, to overcome, yields the now rare 'to *prevene*'. On its pp *praeuentus*—whence 'to *prevent*'—are formed LL *praeuentiō* (acc *praeuentiōnem*) and LL *praeuentor*, whence *prevention* (via MF-F) and *preventor*; *preventive* (cf F *préventif*) is formed anl from *prevention*. The rare *prevenient*, whence *prevenience*, derives from ML *praevenient-*, o/s of the presp: cf the EF-F *prévenant*.

20. L *prōuenīre*, to come forward or forth, hence to come to light, hence (LL) to succeed, has presp *prōueniens*, o/s *prōuenient-*, whence E *provenient*, whence *provenience*, a source, an origin. The MF-F derivative *provenir* has subsidiary F *provenance*, adopted by E.

21. L *reuenīre*, to come back or again, to return, becomes OF-F *revenir*, presp *revenant*, used, in F, as n 'ghost', adopted by E; the pp *revenu* has a derivative n, the MF *revenue* and EF-F *revenu*, whence E *revenue*.

22. L *subuenīre*, to come under, hence to the help of, has pp *subuentus*, whence LL *subuentiō*, acc *subuentiōnem*, MF-F *subvention*, adopted by E. Derivative MF-F *souvenir*, to remember—hence n, duly adopted by E—was adumbrated in LL-ML.

23. L *superuenīre*, to come over, hence upon, accounts for 'to *supervene*'; presp *superueniens*, o/s *-uenient-*, for the adj *supervenient*.

**Venus; venust.** See VENERABLE, para 3.

**veracious, veracity; verdict** (see DICT, para 11, s.f.); **veridic** (see DICT, para 11); **verifiable, verification, verificative** (whence, anl, **verificatory**), **verify; verisimilitude** (see DICT, para 11); **verism; veritable, verity; very**, adj (whence **verily**), hence adv (cf, sem, *true* and *truly*.—**aver, averment.**

1. *Veracious* comes from ML *vērāc(is)*, L *uērāc(is)*, gen of *uērāx*, truthful, an extn of *uērus*, true, veritable; *veracity*, like F *véracité*, from ML *vērācitas*, from *vērāx*. L *uērus*, s and r *uēr-*, derives from IE *wēr-*, true: cf OFris *wēr*, OHG-MHG *wār*, G *wahr*, Go *wērs*, true, and Go tuz-*wērjan*, to doubt—OIr *fīr*, Ga *fìor*, W and Br *gwīr*, Cor *guir, wyr*, Mx *feer*, OC etymon, *\*vēros*, true—Sl *vēra*, belief—Pahlavi *vāvar*, authentic.

2. The foll L derivatives of *uērus* concern E: *uēritās*, acc *uēritātem*, OF *veritet*, MF *verite*, EF-F *vérité*, E *verity*; derivative OF-MF *veritable* (EF-F *vé-*) is adopted by E;

ML *verificāre*, MF *verifier*, EF-F *vé-*, E 'to *verify*'; derivatives late MF-F *vérifiable*, MF *verification* (EF-F *vé-*) and EF-F *vérificatif* yield E *verifiable, verification, verificative*.

3. Learnedly from ML *vērus* comes the F *vérisme*, E *verism*. From L *uērus* comes VL *\*uēraius*, later *\*vēraius*, whence OF-early MF *verai* (later *vrai*): whence ME *verai*, varr *veray, verray*: E *very*, true, now only literary and archaic, as in '*very* God'.

4. ML *vērus* became OF-MF *voir*, whence OF-MF *averer* (OF-EF var *averir*), F *avérer*, whence 'to *aver*', with *averment* perh suggested by MF-EF *averement* (from the v).

**veranda, verandah**: the shorter form influenced by Port *varanda*: Hi *baraṇḍā* or Bengali *bārāṇḍā*, a portico, and Hi *barāmdā*, a veranda: Per *barāmda*, portico.

**verb, verbal** (whence **verbalism, -ist, -ize**: cf EF-F *verbaliser*), **verbatim** (adv, hence adj), **verbiage, verbile, verbose, verbosity, verby** (from *verb*); **verve.**—**adverb, adverbial; proverb, proverbial.**—Gmc: **word,** n, v (whence **wordage,** vn **wording, wordless**), **wordy;**—**byword.**—Gr: sep RHETOR, RHETORIC, RHETORICAL.

1. *Wordy* derives from OE *wordig* (suffix *-ig*), the adj of OE *word*, which has come straight down to E: and OE *word* is akin to OS and OFris *word*, OFris varr *werd* and *wird*, MD *waert, waerd, woort, wort, word,* D *woord,* Go *waúrd*—and to OP *wīrds*, a word, Lith *var̃das*, a name—as well as to L *uerbum*. OE *word* has cpd *bīword* (*bī*, by), whence *byword*.

2. L *uerbum*, ML *verbum*, a word, LL the divine Logos (the active Word of God), becomes F *verbe*, Theo in OF, a word in MF-EF, and a verb from C12 onwards, whence E *verb*: and L *uerbum* app derives from IE *\*werdh-*, a word, from IE *\*wer-*, to speak, a word being, primarily, that which is spoken: cf Gr *eirō* (for *\*weirō*), I say, and esp *eréō* (Attic *erō*), I shall say, for *\*weréō, werō*, akin to—prob the origin of—Gr *rhētōr* (for *\*wrhētōr*), a speaker, esp an orator, and *rhēma* (for *\*wrhēma*), a word, and Skt *vrátam*, a vow, and prob OSl *rota*, a sworn oath. *Word* is perh, as one might expect of so fundamental a concept, Medit: ? cf Eg *tcheṭ-t*, something spoken, a word.—For the Gr-derived *rhetor, rhetoric, rhetorical, rhetorician,* see the sep entry at RHETOR.

3. L *uerbum* has LL adj *uerbālis*, ML *verbālis*, whence MF-F *verbal*, adopted by E. In ML, *verbum* acquires the derivative adv *verbatim*, word by word (cf the formation of ML *seriātim*, in a series), adopted by E.

4. The L adj of L *uerbum* is *uerbōsus*, whence LL *uerbōsitās*, acc *uerbōsitātem*: E *verbose* (cf MF-F *verbeux*, f *verbeuse*) and EF-F *verbosité*, E *verbosity*. The erudite E *verbile* (L *uerbum*+adj *-ile*) is formed anl with *tactile* and *audile*.

5. L *uerbōsus* has LL derivative *uerbosāre*, to talk for the sake of talking (Souter): this LL v perh prompted the formation, from OF-F *verbe*, of the late MF-EF *verbier, verbeier, verboier*, to gossip, whence late EF-F *verbiage*, the use of needless or foolish words, adopted by E.

6. L *uerbum*, word, has pl *uerba*, VL-ML *verba*, whence the f sing *\*verba*, whence OF-F *verve*, fantasy, hence (C17) a marked aptitude for or ability in, hence a lively imagination, mental or artistic 'dash': adopted by E.

7. L *uerbum* has two Gram prefix-cpds: *aduerbium*, LL adj *aduerbiālis*; *prōuerbium*, LL adj *prōuerbiālis*: OF *averbe*, late MF-F *adverbe*, E

*adverb*, the adj direct from ML *adverbiālis*; OF-F *proverbe*, EF-F *proverbial*, E *proverb* and *proverbial*.

**verbatim.** See prec, para 3.

**verbena.** See VERVAIN, para 1; VERBENATE: ib, para 2.

**verberate, verberation.** See VERVAIN, para 2.

**verbiage.** See VERB, para 5.

**verbile.** See VERB, para 4, s.f.

**verbose, verbosity.** See VERB, para 4.

**verdant** (whence **verdancy**), **verderer, verdigris, verditer, verdoy, verdure** (whence **verdurous**); **verjuice** (see JUICE, s.f.); **vireo; virescent** (whence **virescence**); **virid, viridescent** (whence **viridescence**), **viridian, viridine, viridity; vert.**

1. The base is L *uirēre*, ML *virēre*, (of plants) to be green: o.o.o. It has the derivative inch *uirescere*, to begin to become green, presp *uirescens*, o/s *uirescent-*, ML *v-*, whence the E adj *virescent*. On *uir-*, the s and r of *uirēre*, is formed *uireō*, a small bird with olive-green feathers (cf F *verdet*), whence E *vireo*.

2. *Uirēre*, r *uir-*, has derivative adj *uiridus*, ML *v-*, whence the E adj *virid*, now often in extn *viridian*—cf the Chem *viridine* (or *-in*): ML *viridu*s +Chem *-ine* or *-in*. Derivative L *uiriditās* yields *viridity*. Derivative LL *uiridescere*, to begin to grow green, has presp *uiridescens*, o/s *uiridescent-*, ML *v-*, whence the E adj *viridescent*.

3. L *uiridis* is, in VL, contr to *virdis*, whence OF-F *vert* (f *verte*), used also as n, whence the F forestry term *vert*, every growing thing that is green-leaved, esp—in hunting—coverts. In OF-MF, the f adj *verte* has var *verde*, whence OF-EF *verdure* (EF-F *verdeur*), adopted by E, whence, on the r *verd-*, the E *verdant*, presumably suggested by OF-EF *verdoiant* (EF-F *verdoyant*), presp of OF-EF *verdoier* (EF-F *-oyer*), from *verde*; the pp *verdoié, verdoyé*, becomes Her *verdoy*, (of a border) charged with greenery. MF-F *verdier* (*verd*e+ agential *-ier*) becomes the E *verder*, whence, taut, *verderer* (*-or*).

4. The F-derived cpds are:

*verdigris*, ME *verdegrees*, earlier *verdegrece*, earliest *vertegrece*, MF *verdegris* (later *vert-de-gris*), a f/e alteration—after *gris*, grey—of MF *vert-de-Grice*, lit, although one doesn't know precisely why, 'green of Greece';

*verditer*, F *vert-de-terre*, lit 'green of earth' (cf TERRA);

*verjuice*—see JUICE, s.f.

**verdict.** See DICT, para 11, s.f.

**verdigris.** See VERDANT, para 4.

**verditer.** See VERDANT, para 4.

**verdure, verdurous.** See VERDANT, para 3.

**verge** (1), a rod, a staff; **verger.—whisk**, n, hence v.

1. E-ME *verge* is adopted from OF-F, which takes it from ML *virga* (L *uirga*), a supple branch or twig, hence a wand, rod, staff: o.o.o.: perh akin to ON *visk*—cf OHG *wisc*, MHG-G *wisch*—whence prob the ME *wisk*, E *whisk*, whence 'to *whisk*', whence *whisker*, usu in pl *whiskers*, whence the pa *whiskered*; perh the OGmc *wisk* was orig

a quick, light, sweeping or brushing stroke made with a leafy twig.

2. Whereas ME *verge*, a rod, has derivative *verger* (? from AF), lit a rod-bearer, L *uirga* has derivatives *uirgātus*, provided with rods, whence ML *virgāta*, the land contained by a *virga terrae* or rod of land (cf, sem, the E *rod*), whence E *virgate*, and dim *uirgula*, ML *virgula*, whence EF-F *virgule*, a comma—from its shape.

3. The King's marshal of the household, in medieval England, carried a *verge* or staff of office: hence, the area comprised by a circle with radius of 12 miles from the King's court, wherever he might be, and within which the King's peace obtained, was *within the verge*: hence *verge*, a boundary, a limit, a margin, an edge, esp in *on the verge*; hence 'to *verge*' or be on the verge or border, to be on the point of.

**verge** (2), a boundary or limit, to border (on). See prec, para 3.

**verge** (3), to lean towards, to incline, **vergent** (whence **vergence, -cy**); **converge, convergent** (whence **convergence**)—**diverge, divergence** (var **divergency**), **divergent.**—Cf the sep WRENCH.

1. *Vergent* derives from ML *vergent-*, o/s of *vergens*, L *uergens*, presp of *uergere*, to incline, lean towards, vi and vt: o.o.o.: perh cf Skt *varjati*, he bends or inclines. L *uergere*, ML *vergere*, yields syn 'to *verge*'.

2. LL *conuergere*, to meet together, ML *conv-*, gives us 'to *converge*'; the presp *conuergens*, ML *convergens*, o/s *convergent-*, E *convergent* (id in EF-F).

3. L *diuergere* (*di-* for *dis-*, apart, to one side) yields 'to *diverge*'; its presp *diuergens*, o/s *diuergent-*, ML *divergent-*, the adj *divergent*, whence—cf late EF-F *divergence*—the n *divergence*.

**vergence, vergency, vergent.** See prec, para 1.

**verger.** See the 1st VERGE, para 2.

**veridic.** See DICT, para 11.

**verifiable, verification, verificative, verify.** See VERACIOUS, para 2.

**verily.** See VERACIOUS (heading).

**verisimilitude.** See the element *veri-*.

**verism.** See VERACIOUS, para 3.

**veritable, verity.** See VERACIOUS, para 2.

**verjuice.** See JUICE, s.f.

**vermeil** and **vermilion**; **Vermes** (whence **vermian**, worm-like) and **vermis**—**vermicelli**—**vermicular**—**vermiculate, vermiculation, vermicule, vermiculose**—**vermiform**; **varment** (**-int**) and **vermin, verminate, vermination, verminous.**—**worm** n, hence v), whence **worm-eaten, wormer, wormy**; **wormwood**—cf **vermouth**, occ **vermuth.**

1. *Vermeil*, n, hence adj, is adopted from OF-F *vermeil*, adj, hence n; ML *vermiculus*, LL *uermiculus*, adj from LL n, the colour scarlet, earlier the cochineal insect, in L a little worm, dim of L *uermis*, a worm. The OF-F derivative *vermillon*, the cochineal insect, hence the colour, is anglicized as *vermilion*.

2. L *uermis*, a worm, has s and r *uerm-*: cf OS and OHG-MHG-G *wurm*, Go *waurms*, OE *wyrm*

or *wurm*, and, without digamma, the ON *ormr* (modern Scan *orm*); cf also the Gr *rhomos* (or *\*wromos*), a wood-worm, and, further off, the IE r from which *kermes* and *crimson* are derived.

3. L *uermiculus*, ML *v-*, becomes E *vermicule*; EF-F *vermiculaire* (ML *vermicul*us+adj *-aire*) becomes E *vermicular*. The foll L derivatives of *uermiculus* have, in their ML (*v-*) forms, affected E:

*uermiculāri*, to be full of worms, to be worm-eaten, pp *uermiculātus*, used as adj for a 'wormy' mosaic floor, whence the E adj and v *vermiculate*; derivative L *uermiculātiō*, a being, or the result of being, worm-eaten, o/s *uermiculātiōn-*, whence *vermiculation*;

LL *uermiculōsus*, wormy, E *vermiculose* and *vermiculous*;

VL *\*vermicellus*, a little worm, It *vermicello*, pl *vermicelli*, used for a corded paste smaller than spaghetti; adopted by E.

4. L *uermis* has c/f *uermi-*, ML *vermi-*: for cpds, cf, in general, the element *vermi-*, but note esp *vermiform*, from EF-F *vermiforme*: c/f *vermi-*+ *-forme*, as in *multiforme*. (B & W.) The ML sing *vermis* and pl *vermes* are employed by Sci.

5. L *uermis*, r *uerm-*, has the doublet *vermen*, o/s *vermin-*, whence both the adj *uerminōsus*, ML *v-*, whence, in part, E *verminous*, and the v *uermināri*, to have worms, pp *uerminātus*, whence the E adj and v *verminate*; the derivative L *uerminātiō*, the disease 'worms', o/s *uerminātiōn-*, yields *vermination*.

6. This L o/s *uermin-*, ML *vermin-*, has app influenced the formation of OF-F *vermine* from OF-MF *verm* (later *ver*), itself from ML *vermis*, L *uermis*; the OF-EF var *vermin* was adopted by E, and the derivative OF-F *vermineux* has contributed towards E *verminous*. The sense-change from 'worm' to 'small, noxious animal' arises from disgust; in this, too, the E word imitates the F word.

### Germanic

7. OE *wyrm*, *wurm*, becomes ME *wirm* (*werm*), *wurm*, finally *worm*, retained by E. *Wormwood* derives—after *worm*—from OE *wermōd*: cf OHG *werimuota*, MHG *wermuot*, G *Wermut*, whence F *vermout*. The OGmc words app combine *wer*, man +*mut*, courage (E *mood*), 'perh because used as an aphrodisiac'; but the false division *werm-* led to a very potent f/e association with *wurm*, *wyrm*. (Walshe.)

**vermicelli**. See prec, para 3, s.f.

**vermicular, vermiculate, vermiculation, vermicule.** See VERMEIL, para 3.

**vermicide; vermiform; vermigerous.** See the element *vermi-* and, for the 2nd, VERMEIL, para 4.

**vermilion.** See VERMEIL, para 1, s.f.

**vermin.** See VERMEIL, para 6.—**verminous**: ib, paras 5 and 6.

**vermouth**, Gallic *vermout* and hybrid **vermuth.** See VERMEIL, para 7.

**vernacular** (adj, hence n): ML *vernācula*, f, and *vernāculus*, m, born in one's master's house, L

*uer-*; from *uerna*, a slave born there: o.o.o.—? Etruscan.

**vernal** comes, like OF-F *vernal*, from ML *vernālis*, L *uernālis*, extn of *uernus*, of the Spring, from *uēr* (ML *vēr*), the Spring: cf the syn ON *vār*, Gr *éar* (for *\*wéar*), and perh OSl *vesna*, Skt *vasantás*: IE etymon, *\*uesr* (*wesr*)—perh cf OIr *errech*, Ga *eàrrach*. (Hofmann.)

**verruca, verrucose.** See WART, s.f.

**versant, versate.** See para 12 of VERSE.

**versatile, versatility; versation.** See para 12, s.f., of:

**verse**, n—cf **vers libre**, and **versicle, versification, versify** (whence **versifier**); **verse**, v—cf **versable, versant, versate, versatile** (and **versatility**), **versation, versative**—**versed**; **version, versor, versus; vert**, to turn, and coll n; **vertebra** (whence, anl, **vertebral**), **vertebrate** (adj, hence n; whence, anl, **vertebration**)—with neg **invertebrate** (*in-*, not); **vertex** (pl **vertices**), **vertical, verticil, verticity; vertible; vertiginous, vertigo; vortex** (pl **vortices**), **vorticose**—cf **vortical** and **vorticity**, anl after **vertical, verticity**.—Cpds of *-versant, -versate, -versation*—of *-verse, -version, -versity, -versor*—and of *-vert* (v, hence n), *-vertible, -vertor*, etc., with the L prefixes (or their R derivatives): *a-, ad-, ante-, con-, contra-, di-, ē-, extro-, in-, intra- (intro-), ob-, per-, pro-, re-, retro-, sub-, tra-* or *-trans-*.—For **animadvert**, see sep ANIMADVERSION; for **universe** (**university**, etc.), see ONE, para 7; for **tergiversate** (**tergiversation**), see the element *tergi-*; for **divorce**, see that entry.—Gmc cognates: **-ward, -wards**, as in *backward, forward, toward*, etc., and **worth**, to become, and **weird**, destiny, whence the adj.—Sl cognate: **verst**.—Cf the sep VERVAIN.

### Indo-European

1. The IE r is *\*wert-* (L and Sl), to turn, with varr *\*wart-* (Skt) and *\*wort-* (the *e-o* alternation is commoner in Gr than in L); in Gmc, the final *t* tends to become *th, dh, d*, the OGmc r being *\*werth-*. Besides L *uert-*, ML *vert-*, note such forms as Skt *vártate*, he turns; OL *uortere*, to turn; Lith *veřsti*, to return (something), and OB *vrŭtéti*, to turn; Go *wairtha*, I become. But the IE *\*wert-*, *uert-*, is an extn of IE *\*wer-*, *\*uer-*, to turn: cf VERVAIN, para 5, s.f.

### Germanic

2. Akin to Go *wairthan*, to become, are OHG *werdan*, MHG-G *werden*, OS *werthan*, OFris *wertha*, ON *vertha*—and OE *weorthan*, ME *wurthen, worthen*, E *worth*, obs except in such archaic phrases as 'Woe *worth* the day', lit 'Woe become to the day', hence 'Woe betide the day' or, e.g., the man.

3. Closely related to those Gmc words are OHG *-wert, -wart*, G *-wärts*, OS *-werd, -ward*, OFris *-ward*, Go *-wairths*, ON *-verthr*—and OE *-weard* and, with the orig gen ending *-es, -weardes*, whence E *-ward* and *-wards*. These endings connote a turning, a being turned, in the direction denoted by the prec element (*back-, down-, for-* and *fro-, in-, to-,*

*up-*, etc.), hence a tendency in that direction. The forms in *-wards* are primarily and still usu advv; those in *-ward* primarily adjj, but often, esp in AE, used as advv. Of the numerous cpds, perh the best worth noting are:

*backward* (ME-E) and *backwards* (EE-E): cf BACK;

*downward* (ME-E) and *downwards* (EE-E): aphetic for obs *adownward* (OE *adūnweard*): cf DOWN;

*forward* (OE-E) and *forwards* (late ME-E): cf FORE, forward(s);

*froward* (ME-E adj, long archaic): *fro*, as in *to and fro*: cf FROM;

*homeward*(*s*): see HOME;

*inward* (OE-E) and *inwards* (EE-E); from adj *inward* comes the late ME-E adv *inwardly*; cf IN;

*rearward*, adj and adv (EE-E), and *rearwards* (not before C19); cf REAR;

*toward* (OE-E adj and prep) and *towards* (OE-E adv): cf TO;

*upward* (OE-E) and *upwards* (OE-E): cf UP;

*way ward* (ME-E): cf WAY.

4. Akin to OE *weorthan*, to become, and to its other OGmc shapes, is OE *wyrd*, fate, destiny, fortune (esp if ill): ME *werde* or *wirde*: E *weird*. Cf the OFris *werd*, *werde*, death, and OS *wurth* and OHG *wurt*, fate, destiny.—Hence the archaizing adj *weird* (sisters), concerned with fate, hence magical, hence merely very strange.—The n is obsol, except in Sc *dree one's weird*, to endure (OE *drēogan*) one's fate.

### Slavic

5. Akin to the IE words noted in para 1 is Ru *verst*, whence G *Werst*, F *verste*, E *verst*; approx a kilometre: Ru *versta*, a verst, orig a line or row (hence age of life)—cf Ru *vrŭsta*, age of life, and L *uersus*, ML *versus*, a furrow, lit a turning.

### Latin: Simples

6. L *uertere*, to turn, s and r *uert-*, ML *vert-* yields 'to *vert*' or turn, bend, in a given direction. The presp *uertens*, o/s *uertent-*, and gerundive *uertendus* occur only in E cpds: the pp *uersus*, ML *versus*, s *vers-*, and its derivatives, incl the int *uersāre*, ML *v-*, occur in both simples and cpds.

7. From the L inf s *uert-* derive four L nn well represented in E: *uertebra* and *uertex* and its var *uortex* and *uertigo*. *Uertebra*, ML *v-*, an articulation or joint, esp of the spinal column, is adopted by An and Zoo. Derivative *uertebrātus*, provided with *vertebrae*, gives us *vertebrate*, whence the neg *invertebrate*: cf F *invertébré*.

8. L *uertex*, ML *v-*, a whirl, e.g. a whirlpool, hence, app from a supposed whirling centre, the pole of the heavens, hence a summit (e.g. the crown of the head), the top or crest: adopted by Astr, Math, An, Zoo, with the ML pl *vertices*. The derivative LL adj *uerticālis* yields EF-F and, prob independently, E *vertical*; its dim *uerticillus* yields *verticil*; the SciL *verticitās* (*uertic-*, o/s of *uertex*+ *-itās*), E *verticity*. Very closely related to L *uertex*,

in its senses 'a whirl, a whirlpool', is L *uertigō*, ML *v-*, a whirlpool, but also dizziness: adopted by E; the L o/s is *uertigin-*. Derivative L *uertiginōsus*, ML *v-*, becomes EF-F *vertigineux* and, perh independently, E *vertiginous*.

9. L *uertex* has the (orig, and long, syn) var *uortex*, ML *v-*, adopted by E in the sense '(heart of) a whirlpool', hence any whirling centre, with the ML pl *vortices*. From the o/s *uortic-*, ML *v-*, come L *uorticōsus*, whence E *vorticose*—and F *vorticelle*, whence E *vorticel*—and E *vorticism*.

10. The pp *uersus*, ML *versus*, has derivative n *uersus* (gen *-ūs*), a turning (active and passive), hence a furrow and, anl, a line of writing, hence, in poetry, a verse: whence OF-F *vers*, orig a stanza, and OE *fers*, ME *fers* and, under F influence, *vers*, whence E *verse*. Derivative L *uersiculus*, whence— cf EF *versicule*—the E *versicle*. Both F *vers libre*, free verse, and the MF-F dim *verset* (*vers*+*-et*) have been adopted by E. The L cpd *uersificāre* (*-ficāre*, c/f of *facere*, to make) and its derivative *uersificātiō*, o/s *uersificātiōn-*, yield MF-F *versifier* and EF-F *versification*, whence ME *versifien*, E 'to *versify*', and *versification*.—Note that 'to *verse*' or familiarize comes from EF *verser*, from L *versāri*; esp the EF-F *versé*, E *versed* (pa).

11. L *uersus* (gen *-ūs*) has the ML mdfn *versiō*, acc *versiōn*em, whence EF-F *version*, a (manner of) translating, a translation, adopted by E. From the L pp *uers*us, ML *versus*, comes the SciL *versor*. The L pp *uersus*, ML *v-*, is also used as adv, hence prep, 'turned towards, facing, hence opposed', whence the E prep *versus*—cf the syn OF-F *vers*; cf E *verso* (opp *recto*), deriving from L *uerso*, the abl of the pp.

12. From the L pp *uers*us is formed the L int *uersāre*, vt, with passive *uersāri* employed to mean 'to be turned often', hence to be situated, to dwell, hence to be engaged in or occupied with, with pp *uersātus* meaning 'familiar with, versed in'. The presp *uersans*, o/s *uersant-*, ML *versant-*, yields the E adj *versant*, (mentally) engaged, skilled (in)— cf *conversant*, in para 13 below; the pp *uersātus* yields the rare 'to *versate*'. From *uersātus*, pp of *uersāre*, are formed:

*uersātilis*, capable of being turned, whence, perh via EF-F, the E *versatile*, whence—cf F *versatilité* —*versatility*;

*uersātiō*, a turning or a being turned, o/s *uersātiōn-*, E *versation*, whence, anl, *versative*.

### Latin: Prefix-Compounds

13. L *uersāri*, to be situated or occupied, has cpd *conuersāri*, ML *conv-*, to associate with, whence OF-F *converser*, whence 'to *converse*'. Derivatives ML *conversābilis*—L presp *conuersans* o/s *conuersant-* (ML *conversant-*)—(from pp *conuersātus*) LL *conuersātiō*, a mode of life, esp conversation, ML acc *conversātiōn*em, these yield E *conversable*, *conversant*, *conversation* (adopted from OF-F), whence *conversational* and, anl, *conversative*. From the ML o/s *conversātiōn-* comes It *conversazione*, adopted, in its latest sense, by E.

14. L *uertere*, to turn, has numerous prefix-cpds, which follow so regular a pattern that, except for F interventions, the L originals can be tersely listed thus, with ML *v* instead of L *u*: -*vertere*; gerundive -*vertendus*; adj -*vertibilis*, with derivative n in -*vertibilitās*; presp -*vertens*, o/s *vertent*-, derivative n (usu LL) -*vertentia*; pp -*versus*, with derivative nn in -*us* (gen -*ūs*) and in -*iō*, o/s -*iōn*-, and in -*itās*, and derivative adjj in -*versārius* and -*versībilis*. The religious and ethical senses come mostly from LL-ML.

15. With that general pattern in mind, one has only to exhibit the L prefix-cpds and their meanings, and then note the principal E derivatives, with an indication of F intervention.

*advertere*, to turn *ad* or to, towards: *advert*, *advertent*, *advertence* (imm from F), neg *inadvertence* from ML *inadvertentia*; *adversary* (as in L, adj hence n; via MF-F *adversaire*), *adverse*, *adversity* (MF-F *adversité*);—*advertise* (whence *advertiser*), *advertisement*, re-shapings of F forms in *av*-, MF also *adv*-, and orig 'notice, notify (notification)';

*antevertere*, to turn *ante*, before, in front: *antevert*, *anteversion*;

*avertere*, to turn *a*-, away: *avert*; *averse*, *aversion* (cf EF-F);

*controvertere*, to turn against, to turn in the opposite direction: *controvert*; *controversial*, *controversion*, *controversy*;

*convertere*, to turn *con*-, thoroughly: *convert* (OF-F *convertir*), hence n (cf *pervert*); *converse*, adj, v (OF-F *converser*), hence n; *conversion* (OF-F), whence, anl, *conversive*;

*divertere*, to turn *di*- for *dis*-, aside: *divert* (MF-F *divertir*); *divers*, *diverse*, from OF-F *divers*, f *diverse*; *diversion* (MF-F); *divertisement* (late MF-F *divertissement*);

*ēvertere*, to turn out, hence over, to overthrow: *evert*, *eversion*;

anl E *extravert*, *extrovert*, *extroversion*: L *extrō*, outside (adv)+*vertere*; in Psy and Psychi, opp *introvert*, *introversion*, themselves formed anl: L *intrō*, within;

*invertere*, to turn in, to turn opposite: *invert* (cf EF-F *invertir*); *inversion* (as also in EF-F);

*obvertere*, to turn *ob*, towards or against: *obvert*; *obverse* (adj, hence n); *obversion*;

*pervertere*, to turn *per*- or thoroughly, hence to cause to turn out badly: *pervert* (OF-F *pervertir*), v hence n; *perverse* (OF-F *pervers*, f *perverse*) and *perversion* (as also in EF-F) and *perversity* (OF-F *perversité*);

*prōvertere*, to turn forward, pp *prōversus*, whence the contr *prōrsus*, eased to *prōsus*, which, used as adj, occurs in *prōsa ōrātiō*, speech going straight ahead without turns (*versūs*), whence the syn *prōsa*, whence MF-F *prose*, adopted by E; derivative LL *prōsaïcus* leads to late MF-F *prosaïque*, whence E *prosaic*;

anl E *retrovert*, *retroversion*: L *retrō*, backwards; *revertere*, to turn back (vi, vt): *revert* (OF-EF *revertir*); *reverse* (OF-F *revers*, f *reverse*), whence

n; the v 'to *reverse*', however, app derives from OF-EF *reverser*, from LL *reuersāre*, to turn around, cf *uersāre*, the active of *uersāri* (para 13); *reversal*, from 'to *reverse*'; *reversible* (EF-F *réversible*); *reversion* (MF-F), whence *reversionary*;

*subvertere*, to turn, hence overturn, from under, hence from the foundations: *subvert* (MF-F *subvertir*); *subversion* (OF-F), whence, anl, the F *subversif*, f -*ive*, whence E *subversive*.

*transvertere*, to turn beyond: *transvert* (obs); *transversal* (late MF-F), *transverse* (adj hence n); *transversion*;

anl with prec is 'to *traverse*', which, however, comes imm from OF-F *traverser*: VL-LL *trāversāre*, LL *transuersāre*, to cross (cf para 13); the E n *traverse* is adopted from OF-F (from VL *trāversa*, prop the f of *trāversus*, for L *transversus*): cf *transverse*.

**verset.** See prec, para 10.
**versicle.** See VERSE, para 10.
**versification, versify.** See VERSE, para 10.
**version.** See VERSE, para 11.
**verso.** See VERSE, para 11.
**verst.** See VERSE, para 5.
**versus**, against. See VERSE, para 11.
**vert**, greenery. See VERDANT, para 3.
**vert**, to turn or bend. See VERSE, para 6.
**vertebra, vertebrate.** See VERSE, para 7.
**vertex, vertical, verticil.** See VERSE, para 8.
**vertiginous, vertigo.** See VERSE, para 8, s.f.
**vertu.** See VIRILE, para 3, s.f.
**vervain** and **verbena**—cf **verbenate**; **verberate**, **verberation**—**reverberant**, **reverberate**, **reverberation.**—**rhabdite**—cf the element *rhabdo*-; **rhamnus**; **rhombus.**—**warp**, n and v (whence pa **warped** and pa, vn **warping**). These words form a sister constellation of the VERSE group.

1. *Vervain* derives from OF-F *verveine*, VL *vervāna*, L *uerbēna* (ML *verbēna*), whence E *verbena*: and L *uerbēna*, s *uerbēn*-, r *uerb*-, is intimately linked with L *uerbera* (pl), blows or lashes with a whip, s *uerber*-, r *uerb*-: with both, cf Lith *virbas*, a young branch, a rod or staff, OSl *vrūba*, a willow (Serb *vŕba*), and, further off, the Gr *rhabdos*, a wand, a rod, *rhapis*, a wand, a staff, and, nasalized, *rhamnos*, a (prickly) shrub, and *rhombos*, a spinning top (cf *rhembein*, to whirl around, to turn). Also related is the *warp* group—see para 5 below.

2. L *uerbēna* has derivative *uerbēnātus*, crowned with boughs: whence 'to *verbenate*'. Cf 'to *verberate*': ML *verberātus*, L *uerberātus*, pp of *uerberāre*, to flog, hence to strike, maltreat, from *uerbera*. Derivative L *uerberātiō*, o/s *uerberātiōn*-, yields *verberation*.

3. L *uerberāre* has prefix-cpd *reuerberāre*, to strike in return, to repel, presp *reuerberans*, o/s *reuerberant*-, ML *rev*-, whence E *reverberant*, and pp *reuerberātus*, whence both 'to *reverberate*', now mostly of sound, and LL *reuerberātiō*, acc *reuerberātiōnem*, whence MF-F *réverbération*, whence E *reverberation*.

4. From Gr *rhabdos* come the element *rhabdo*-

q.v., and Zoo *rhabdite*; from Gr *rhamnos*, the LL *rhamnus*, adopted by Bot; from Gr *rhombos*, the LL *rhombus*, adopted by Geom, and anglicized as *rhomb*, and sense-adapted, by Chem.

5. Akin to those Gr and esp those L words are these Gmc words for 'to throw or cast': Go *waírpan*; OHG *werpfan*, eased to *werfan*, whence MHG-G *werfen*; OS *werpan*, MD *weorpen, worpen, waerpen, warpen*, MD-D *werpen*; ON *verpa*—and OE *weorpan*, ME *werpen, warpen*, E 'to *warp*', to throw or expel (both obs), hence to twist violently or out of shape. Closely akin to OE *weorpan* is OE *wearp*, (in weaving) a warp, E *warp*, with later senses influenced by the v. The OGmc vv derive from an OGmc r *werp-, perh (Walshe) from *werkw-, corresp to IE r *wergw-: ? rather from OGmc *werbh-, extn of IE *werb-, *uerb-, a form that returns us to the L r *uerb-. The ult IE r, therefore, is app *uer-, to turn, to bend: cf VERSE, para 1.

**verve.** See VERB, para 6.

**very.** See VERACIOUS, para 3.

**vesica, vesical, vesicant, vesicatory, vesicle, vesicula**; element *vesico-*.

The L *uēsīca*, ML *vēsīca*, a bladder, is prob related to L *uenter*, ML *venter*, the belly, q.v. at VENTRAL: cf Skt *vastás*, a bladder. Both ML *vēsīca* and its dim *vēsīcula* have been adopted by An, Med, Zoo, the latter more common in the form *vesicle* (perh imm from EF-F *vésicule*, whence certainly E *vesicule*); derivative LL *uēsīcālis* becomes EF-F *vésical*, whence E *vesical*, and derivative LL *uēsīcāre*, to form bladders, hence blisters, has presp *uēsīcans*, o/s *uēsīcant-*, and pp *uēsīcātus*, whence, via the ML forms in *v-* and then via EF-F, the E *vesicant* and *vesicatory*.

**vesper (vespers), vesperal.** See WEST, para 3.

**vespine (and vespal).** See WEAVE, para 10.

**vessel.** See VASE, para 3.

**vest,** n and v (whence pa **vested** and **vestee;**) **vestiary;** ? **vestibule,** whence, anl, **vestibular; vestiture; vestment; vestry; vesture,** n hence v.— Prefix-cpds: **devest; divest,** whence, anl, **divestitive, divestiture, divestment; invest** (whence **investment, investor,** and, anl, **investitive), investiture; revest**— cf **revet, revetment; transvest, transvestite**—cf **travesty.**—Gmc: **wear** (v, hence n), whence **wearable, wearer,** pa and vn **wearing,** pt **wore** and pp **worn.**

1. 'To *vest*' or clothe, dress, comes, via OF-MF *vestir* (F *vêtir*), from ML *vestīre*, L *uestīre*, itself from *uestis*, a garment, whence, via It *vesta* and F *veste*, the E *vest*, orig any garment (esp a robe), with modern senses narrowing and also diverging and, as between one European language and another, even contradicting. For IE cognates, see paras 4 and esp 5.

2. L *uestis* (ML *vestis*) has the foll simple derivatives relevant to E:

*uestiārium*, wardrobe, a robing-room: OF-F *vestiaire*: E *vestiary* and, through the OF-MF var *vestiarie*, the ME *vestrye*, E *vestry*;

*uestimentum*, a garment, OF-MF *vestement* (F *vêtement*), E *vestment*;

ML *vestītūra*, E *vestiture* and, via OF-MF *vesteüre, vesture* (F *vêture*), E *vesture*;

perh L *uestibulum* (? *uesti-*, c/f of *uestis*+ *-bulum*, as in *stabulum*), a forecourt, entrance hall (between outer door and hall proper): but prob o.o.o., the orig sense having nothing to do with clothes.

3. The relevant L prefix-cpds, with others imitating them, are:

*dēuestīre* and dial var *disuestīre*: OF-MF *desvestir*, MF *devester*: E 'to *devest*', now only legal ('to deprive');

ML *disvestīre, divestīre*, influencing E 'to *devest* to become *divest*;

*inuestīre*, to put clothes on, to surround (a sense retained by E—imm from late MF-EF): whence It *investire*, E 'to *invest*' money; the orig L sense recurs in ML *investītūra*, an enrobing, whence E *investiture*;

*reuestīre* (*re-* vaguely int), to clothe in an honorific fashion: OF-MF *revestir* (F *revêtir*): E 'to *revest*'; derivative MF *revestement* (sense as in v) becomes EF-F *revêtement* in military sense, whence E *revetment*; 'to *revet*' from military EF-F *revêtir*;

*trans*, across+*uestīre*, to clothe, yield 'to *transvest*' or wear the clothes of the opp sex, whence a *transvestite* (*-ite*=L *-ita*=Gr *-ités*, agential); they yield also It *travestire*, to disguise, whence EF-F *travestir*, with pp *travesti*, whence the E adj *travesty* (obs), whence 'a *travesty*,' whence, in turn, 'to *travesty*'; the connotation of absurdity is already present in the F v.

4. Akin to L *uestīre*, to clothe, is Go *wasjan*, to clothe, and, phon more distant, the syn ON *verja*, OHG *werēn, werien*, (prob) OFris *weria*, and OE *werian*, ME *werien*, later *weren*, E 'to *wear*', the sense 'to impair' deriving from much-worn, becoming worn-away, clothes.

5. The *-s-* of L *uestīre* and *uestis*, and of Go *wasjan*, to wear, *wasti*, clothing, garment, is seen also in Skt *váste*, he dons, he wears, clothes, *vástram*, clothing, and in Hit *wass-, wēss-*, to put on or wear (clothes), to clothe, to cover, and Tokh B *yässītar*, he is clothed, *wasttsī*, clothing; cf also Cor *gwesca* (or *-ga*), to clothe, Br *gwish*, a garment, and Doric Gr *westra*, late Gr *gestra*, a garment, Gr *hennunai* (for *wesnunnai*), to clothe. The IE r, then, is *wes-*, to clothe.

**vestal,** virginal, derives from *vestal virgin*: ML *Vestālis* (*virgō*): L *Uestālis* (*uirgō*), adj of *Uesta*, goddess of the hearth: perh cf Gr *Hestia*, goddess of hearth and home, and, if that be correct, then prob Skt *vásati*, he dwells: ? also Go *was*, I was, and Ir *feiss*, a sojourn, Cor *vēth*, a dwelling place. But the entire subject is vexed and obscure.

**vestiary.** See VEST, para 2.

**vestibule.** See VEST, para 2, s.f.

**vestige,** whence **vestigial; investigable, investigate, investigation** (whence, anl, **investigative), investigator** (whence, anl, **investigatory).**

1. *Vestige*, late MF-F *vestige*, comes from ML

*vestīgium*, L *uestīgium*, a footprint, hence a trace in general: from *uestīgāre*, to follow the footprints of, to track, hence to go in search of: o.o.o.: perh cf Hit *aus-*, to see for oneself, to observe.

2. L *uestīgare* has cpd *inuestīgāre* (*in-* used int), to carefully look into, s *inuestīg-*, whence LL *inuestīgabilis*, traceable, whence E *investigable*. The pp *inuestīgātus* yields both 'to *investigate*' and L *inuestīgātiō*, acc *inuestīgātiōn*em, MF-F *investigation*, adopted by E, and L *inuestīgātor*, whence—perh via late MF-F *investigateur*—the E *investigator*.

**vestiture**; **vestment**. See VEST, para 2.

**vestry.** See VEST, para 2.

**vesture.** See VEST, para 2.

**vet.** See WETHER (heading).

**vetch.** See the 1st PERIWINKLE, para 3.

**veteran.** See WETHER, para 4.

**veterinarian, veterinary.** See WETHER, para 5.

**veto:** ML *vetō*, L *uetō*, I forbid (*uetāre*, s and r *uet-*): o.o.o.: perh (E & M) of C origin—cf OW *guet*id, he says, and W *gwed* (obs), a saying or utterance, and dy-*wed*af, I say: sem, the link offers no serious difficulty, for if one says, e.g., that another must do something, one implicitly forbids him to do something else (usu the contrary).

**vetust.** See WETHER, para 3.

**vex, vexation** (whence, anl, **vexatious**). L *uexāre* (ML *vexāre*), to agitate, hence to torment, to harass, is prob akin to—indeed, it may be a freq, or a freq-int, of—*uehere*, to transport, whether on horse or by a vehicle or on a ship: f.a.e., VIA. ML *vexāre* becomes MF-F *vexer*, whence 'to *vex*'; on the L pp *uexātus* is formed L *uexātiō*, ML *vexātiō*, acc *vexātiōn*em, MF-F *vexation*, adopted by E.

2. App more closely related to *uexāre* (? for *\*uecsāre*, s *\*uecs-*, r *\*uec-*) than to *uehere* is L *uectis* (s *uect-*, ? r *uec-*), a lever, a pole or bar, whence the obstetrical tech E *vectis*.

**via, Via Dolorosa, via media, viable, viability; viaduct; viaticum; viator,** whence **viatorial; voyage** (n, v), **voyager** and **voyageur.**—**vehemence, vehement**—**vehicle, vehicular**—**vection, vector** (whence **vectorial**).—Prefix-cpds of L *uia*, ML *via*, away: **convey** (whence **conveyer** (**-or**) and **conveyance**)—**convoy; deviate, deviation** (whence, anl, **deviative**), **deviator** (whence, anl, **deviatory**), **devious; envoy; invoice; obviate, obviation, obvious; pervious** and **impervious; previous; renvoy; trivia, trivial, triviality, trivium.**—Prefix-cpds of L *uehere*, ML *vehere*, to transport: **advection, advectitious, advehent; convection** (whence, by b/f 'to **convect**' and, imm, **convectional** and, anl, **convective** and **convector**)—**convex** (adj, hence n and v), **convexity; evection; invection**—**invective** (adj and n)—**inveigh; provect, provection; revehent; transvection,** whence, anl, **transvectant.**

Gmc cognates: **wag** (v, hence n), **waggery, waggish**—cf **waggle** (v, hence n); **waggon** or **wagon** (mostly AE), whence **wag(g)onage, wag(g)oner, wag(g)onette** (dim *-ette*)—cf **wagon-lit; wain,** whence **wainwright** (*wright*, a builder).—**way, wayfare** (whence **wayfarer, wayfaring**), **waylay, way-** ward—cf **ways** and **means.**—**away**—**always.**—**weigh** (whence **weigher** and pa, vn **weighing**) and **weight,** n (whence **weighty**), hence v; **wey.**

Cf the sep VEX and perh the sep VEIN.

### Germanic

1. 'To **waggle**' is the freq of 'to **wag**', to swing from side to side, ME *waggen*, akin to OE *wagian*, to move, to wag, and therefore also to OHG *wegan*, int *bewëgan*, MHG *bewëgen*, G *bewegen*, MD *wegen*, var *weggen*, D *bewegen*, MHG *wacken* (int of *wagen*, related to *bewëgen*), Go *wagjan*, to move, ON *vagga*, a cradle, and OE *wegan*, to move, to transport, therefore to L *uehere*, to convey: see 'Indo-European' below.—The n *wag*, in sense 'joker', perh comes imm from the obs *wag-halter*, a rogue, a humorous fellow; hence *waggery* and *waggish*.

2. A **waggon** or **wagon** derives from MD-D *wagen*, MD var *waghen*: cf OHG *wagan*, MHG-G *wagen*, and Crimean Go *waghen*. Very closely related to OHG *wagan* are OS *wagan*, ON *vagn* and OE *waegen*, varr *waegn* and *wāen*; OE *wāēn* becomes ME-E *wain*, now mainly rural and always horse-drawn—for the form, cf esp OFris *wain*, *wein*. See 'Indo-European' for the pre-Gmc cognates.

3. The F **wagon-lit** or sleeping-car on a railway train, adopted by several European languages, represents F-from-E *wagon* + *lit*, a bed (cf LIE, to be recumbent).

4. **Way,** ME *way*, earlier *wey*, derives from OE *weg*: cf OFris *wei*, contr *wī*, OS *weg*, OHG *weg*, MHG *wec*, G *Wёg*, Go *wigs*, ON *vegr*, and cf OE *wegan*, OHG *wёgan*, L *uehere*, etc., as well as the L *uia*: see 'Indo-European'.

5. The foll full cpds of *way* are either very old or etym notable:

'to **wayfare**', a b/f from ME *weifarende*, OE *wegfarende*, wayfaring (adj), var *wegfёrende*: from *weg* + *farende*, presp of *faran*, to go (cf FARE);

'to **waylay**': after *way* and *lay*, but imitative of MLG-MHG *wegelagen*, to lie waiting (for someone) on the way or road, to ambush, from *wegelage*, an ambush;

**wayward:** ME *weiward*, aphetic for *aweiward*, turned away: cf para 3 of VERSE.

6. Note also *away*, ME *awey*, *awei*, OE *aweg*, worn-down form of *anweg* (*onweg*), on (the) way, i.e. on one's way, esp in departure, and *always*, late ME-EE *alwayes*, C14 *alleweyes*, C13 *alles weis*, gen of *alle wei*, every way, hence every time, on every occasion. (OED.)

7. OE *wegan* (cf paras 1 and 4 above), to move, to bear or carry, hence to weigh, becomes ME *weghen*, varr *weyen* and *weien*, whence E 'to *weigh*': cf OFris *wega*, MHG *wegen* (G *wiegen*: akin to OHG *wegan*, to move, to carry), MD-D *wegen*, ON *vega*, to move, carry, weigh: cf the L, Skt, other cognates adduced in 'Indo-European'.

8. Intimately related to OE *wegan*, to weigh, is OE *gewiht*, abr *wiht*, ME *wight*, var *weght*, E

*weight*: cf ON *vaett*, a weighing-device, a weight:
cf OFris *wicht*, MHG *gewiht*, G *Gewicht*, MD
*wechte*, *wecht*, *wichte*, MD-D *wicht*, D *gewicht*. The
late ME-E *weighty* was perh prompted by the syn
MD *wichtich*, MHG *wihtec* (sold by weight), OFris
*wichtich*.

9. The Ir, Sc, E, mostly rural, weight called the
*wey* derives from ME *weye*, OE *wǣge*, *wǣg*, and is
likewise intimately related to OE *wegan*, to weigh.
*Wey* is a doublet of the (except in dial) obs n
*weigh*.

Latin: *uehere*, ML *vehere*, to carry, transport

10. With OE (and OHG) *wegan*, to move, to
transport, cf L *uehere* (for *\*weghere*), to carry or
bear, whether on a horse or in a vehicle or on (in)
a ship, i.e. to transport, itself akin also to Skt
*váhati*, he transports in car or carriage: cf also
'Indo-European'. L *uehere*, ML *vehere*, has presp
*uehens*, o/s *uehent-* (occurring in several learnèd E
adjj), and pp *uectus* (IE *\*weghtos*), ML *vectus*, s
*uect-*, whence the abstract n *uectiō* and agent
*uector*, with ML forms in *v-*. ML *vectio*, o/s
*vectiōn-*, becomes E *vection*; ML *vector* is adopted
by E—cf the F *vecteur*.

11. From *uehere* perh derives *uehemēns*, hot-
tempered, furious, violent, acc *uehement*em, ML
*v-*, whence OF-MF *vehement* (EF-F *véhé-*), whence
E *vehement*; derivative L *uehementia* yields late
MF-F *véhémence*, whence E *vehement*; from *uehere*
certainly derives *uehiculum*, whence EF-F *véhicule*,
whence E *vehicle*, with *vehicular* coming from
derivative LL *uehiculāris*.

12. L *uehere* has the foll prefix-cpds affecting E:
*aduehere*, to carry to, presp *aduehens*, o/s
*aduehent-*, whence the E adj *advehent*, to which
*revehent* (from L *revehere*, to carry back) is complementary, and pp *aduectus*, whence both *aduectiō*,
o/s *aduectiōn-*, whence *advection*, and *aduectīcius*,
whence *advectitious*;

*conuehere*, to bring together, pp *conuectus*,
whence LL *conuectiō*, o/s *conuectiōn-*, whence E
*convection*; derivative L *conuexus* and its own
derivative *conuexitās*, acc *conuexitātem*, yield
MF-F *convexe* and late MF-F *convexité*, whence E
*convex* and *convexity*;

*ēuehere*, to carry out or forth, pp *ēvectus*,
whence *ēuectiō*, o/s *ēuectiōn-*, whence E *evection*;

*inuehere*, to carry into, hence against, hence, esp
as *inuehi*, to attack with words, yields 'to *inveigh*';
from the pp *inuectus* come both the LL adj
*invectīuus*, whence the E adj *invective*, the E n
being adopted from MF-F *invective*, itself from LL
*inuectīua* (*orātiō*), violent speech, and the L n
*inuectiō*, o/s *inuectiōn-*, whence E *invection*;

*prōuehere*, to carry forward, pp *prōuectus*,
whence both the E adj (obs) and v *provect*, and the
LL *prōuectiō*, o/s *prōuectiōn-*, E *provection*;

*reuehere*—see *aduehere* above;

*transuehere*, to carry across or over, pp *transu-
ectus*, whence *transuectiō*, o/s *-uectiōn-*, E *transvection*.

Latin *uia*, ML *via*, way

13. L *uia* (OL *ueha*, from IE *\*weghya*), a way
(other than a mere path), a road, a street, hence a
route (a way habitually travelled), also a march, a
journey, hence also a way of life, even a method, is
of Italic origin—cognate with the words noted in
'Indo-European'. Hence E *via*, by way of, from L
*uiā*, abl of *uia*. L phrases common to most European languages are LL *Uia* (ML *Via*) *Dolorosa*,
the Christians' name for that road by which, in
Jerusalem, Christ went from judgement-hall to
Golgotha; and *uia* (ML *via*) *media*, a, or the middle,
way.

14. L *uia* has the foll simple derivatives relevant
to E:

LL *uiabilis*, (of a road) passable, whence E
*viable* (not from F *vie*, life, as sometimes stated);
*viability* was perh suggested by F *viabilité*, a
learnèd formation from ML *viabilis*;

(E *viaduct*, anl with E *aqueduct*, from L *aquae
ductus*, lit 'a water-conduit';)

L *uiāticus*, of the way or journey, whence E
*viatic*; the L neu *uiāticum* is used as n, money or
provisions for journey, and is adopted by E, now
mostly in Eccl sense (already in LL); from the LL
later and secondary sense 'a journey' comes OF
*veiage*, MF *veage*, *viage*, *voiage*, EF-F *voyage*,
whence ME *veage*, *viage*, E *voyage*, 'to *voyage*'
coming from MF-F *voyager*, with Can *voyageur*
and E *voyager* coming from MF-F *voyageur* (from
*voyager*).

15. L *uia*, ML *via*, exhibits the foll prefix-cpds
relevant to E.

VL *\*conuiāre*, *conviāre*, to travel with, whence
OF-MF *conveier*, to accompany, to escort, later
OF-MF-EF *convoier*, EF-F *convoyer*: whence E 'to
*convey*' and E 'to *convoy*', with the E n deriving
from OF-F *convoi* (from the v);

L *dēuius* (from *dē uiā*, down from the way, hence
off the highroad), whence E *devious*; derivative LL
*dēuiāre*, to turn off into another road, pp *dēuiātus*,
whence both 'to *deviate*' and LL *dēuiātiō*, acc
*dēuiātiōn*em, ML *dēvi-*, whence late MF-F *dévia-
tion*, whence E *deviation*, and ML *dēviātor*, whence
E *deviator*;

VL *\*inuiāre*, *inviāre*, to begin a journey or undertake one, hence to set on a journey, hence to send:
OF-EF *envoier*, EF-F *envoyer*, pp *envoyé*, hence n
(one who has been sent), whence E *envoy*, an
emissary; derivative OF-F *envoi* (MF-EF *envoy*),
something sent, esp a literary 'postscript', yields
E *envoi*, anglicized as *envoy*; from F *envois* (pl of
*envoi*), goods sent or forwarded, comes—prob via
commercial F *lettre d'envoi*, letter of advice, and
app via EE *invoys*, pl of *invoy*, an early form of
*envoy*—the E *invoice*;

L *obuius* (ML *obv-*), placed or coming in the way
(*ob uiam*), yields E *obvious*; derivative LL *obuiāre*,
to meet or encounter, hence to remedy, pp *obuiātus*,
whence 'to *obviate*', and subsidiary LL *obuiātiō*, an
encountering, o/s *obuiātiōn-*, whence E *obviation*;

L *peruius*, with a way through, hence penetrable,

yields E *pervious*, the neg *impervious* deriving from L *imperuius*;

L *praeuius*, in the way before, leading the way, E *previous*;

(*renvoy*, MF-F *renvoi*, early var *renvoy*—from OF-F *renvoier*, *renvoyer*: *re-*, back+*envoier*, *envoyer*; cf *envoy* above;)

L *triuius*, divided into, or shared by, three ways, whence the n *triuium*, a three-roaded or -streeted crossways, hence ML *trivium*, the three liberal arts (cf *quadrivium*): hence also L *triuiālis*, of, esp characteristic of, a cross-roads, hence common to all, banal: whence EF-F *trivial*, adopted by E, with *triviality* deriving from EF-F *trivialité*; thè L neu pl *triuia*, ML *trivia*, is adopted by learnèd E for 'trifles'.

### Indo-European

16. Most of the notable IE cognates have been adduced in paras 1, 2, 4, 7, 8, 10, 13, but the foll should also be noted: Go *wigs*, a road; Lith *veže*, a wheel-rut, and OSl *vesti*, to move, to go; Pamphylian Gr *wekheto*, let him transport, and Gr *\*wokhos*, hence *okhos*, a chariot; OIr *fén*, cf *wain* in para 2. The OGmc r is app *\*wagh-*; the IE r, *\*wegh-*, to go in, to transport by, a vehicle, a special application of IE *\*wegh-*, to move, set moving. This *\*wegh-* is, I surmise, itself an extn of an ult *\*we-*, to move (vi), to walk, to go, hence to go away, to come to. This would mean that the *\*wen-* of L *uenīre*, to come, is also an extn of IE *\*we-*, (of human being or any other animal) to move from one place or point to another; this, again, implies that, as *\*wen-* is the 'to come' extn, so the *īr-*, *it-*, of L *īre*, to go, supine *itum*, represents *\*wir-*, *\*wit-*, an extn in *-r-* or *-t-* of *\*wī-*, *wi-*, with vowel differentiated in order to mark the differentiated sense 'to go away'. The Hit *we-*, s *wen-*, q.v. at VENUE, is relevant.

**viability, viable.** See prec, para 14.

**Via Dolorosa.** See VIA, para 13.

**viaduct.** See VIA, para 14.

**vial.** See PHIAL, para 2.

**via media.** See VIA, para 13.

**viand.** See VIVA, para 4.

**viatic, viaticum.** See VIA, para 14.

**vibraculum.** See VIBRATE, para 1.

**vibrancy, vibrant.** See para 1 of:

**vibrate** (whence **vibrator**), **vibratile**, **vibration**, **vibrato**, **vibratory**; **vibraculum**; **vibrant**, whence **vibrancy**; **Vibrio** (whence, anl, **vibrioid**), **vibrion**; **vibrissa**;—**waif**; **waive**, **waiver**; **wave**, v, hence n (whence **wavy**)—cf **waver**, whence **wavering**; **wife**, **wifehood**, **wifely**, **wive**; **woman**, whence—after the *wife* derivatives—**womanish**, **womanize**, **womanhood**, **womanly**;—**wipe** (v, hence n), whence **wiper**; —**viper** (whence **viperous**), **viperine**; **weever** and **wivern**.—**whip** (n, v), whence **whipcord**, **whiplash**—and other cpds, esp **whippoorwill**; whence also **whipper** (note **whippersnapper**) and **whipping**—note **whippet**;—**guipure**.

### Latin

1. L *uibrāre*, vt and vi, ML *vibrāre*, to shake rapidly, to brandish, to dart, has presp *uibrans*, o/s *uibrant-*, whence the E adj *vibrant*, and pp *uibrātus*, whence 'to *vibrate*'. Derivative LL *uibrātiō*, acc *uibrātiōn*em, o/s *uibrātiōn-*, yields EF-F and perh independently E *vibration*; F and E *vibratile* has been formed anl, as also F *vibratoire*, E *vibratory*; *vibrator* comes straight from 'to *vibrate*'. L *uibrāre*, ML *v-*, becomes It *vibrare*, pp *vibrato*, used elliptically for *movimento vibrato* and adopted by Music everywhere. From the L s *uibr-*, L has formed *uibrissa*, usu in pl (*-ae*), those stiff hairs which grow in the nostrils, adopted by An and Zoo; SciL, *vibraculum* and *Vibrio*; learnèd F, *vibrion*, adopted by SciE.

2. Perh akin to L *uibrāre* (? for *\*uiberāre*) is L *uīpera*, ML *vīpera*, a viper, f/e derived by the ancient Romans from *\*uiuipera*: *uīui-* (ML *vīvi-*), c/f of *uīuus* (ML *vīvus*), alive+a c/f of *parere*, to produce young, but nowadays usu associated with *uibrāre*. The L adj *uīperīnus* becomes EF-F *vipérin* and, perh independently, E *viperine*; the L n becomes MF *vipere* (occ contr to *vipre*; EF-F *vipère*), whence, rather than direct from ML *vīpera*, the E *viper*.

3. ML *vīpera* becomes OF-F *guivre*, with ONF var *wivre*, whence E *weever*, a fish with venomous spines; ONF *wivre* also yields AF *wivre*, whence ME *wivere*, whence E *wivern*, a fabulous creature, the *n* perh suggested by that of EF-F *vipérin*—cf the excrescent *-n* of *bittern*. (EW.) Var: *wyvern*.

### Germanic

4. The n *whip*, ME *whippe* or *wippe*, prob derives from ME *whippen*, *wippen*, whence, of course, 'to *whip*': and the ME v is akin to MD-D *wippen*, to brandish (cf MD *wippe*, *wip*, a whip)—to MHG *wipfen*, *wippen*, G *wippen*, to rock, and MHG *wifen*, to twist—and to L *uibrāre* as well as to *wipe* (next para). 'To *whip*' has such derivative senses as 'to move smartly or nimbly' (vt and vi), whence that swift and lively dog the *whippet*. Note also both *whippersnapper*, one who snaps at the whip, presumption implying insignificance, and that nocturnal Am bird the *whippoorwill* from its call 'Whip poor Will!'

5. Closely related to the v *whip* is the v *wipe*, ME *wipen*, OE *wīpian*: phon cf Go *weipan* and MD *wīpen*, to wreathe, and MHG *wifen*, to cause to swing, to twist or wind. Cf also *guipure*, a heavy, large-patterned silk, adopted from MF-F, which derives it (suffix *-ure*) from MF-F *guiper*, to cover with silk: Frankish *\*wipan*, (in weaving) to envelop in silk—akin to MHG *wifen*, Go *weipan*.

6. With *wipe* and *guipure*, cf 'to *waive*': ME *waiven* or *weiven*, to set aside, discard, abandon: AF *waiver*, *weiver*, *weyver*, adopted (or slightly adapted) from ONF, which, characteristically, exhibits *w-* where OF exhibits *gu-*: OF *gaiver*, var *guever*: prob of Scan, certainly of Gmc, origin: cf ON *veifa*, to vibrate, OE *wǣfan*, to envelop or

wrap up, and next para. The legal n *waiver* derives from AF *weyver* used as n.

7. Intimately related to ON *-veifa*, to vibrate, is ON *veif*, anything that is vibrating or flapping or waving: and from ON *veif* or its group derives, prob, the MF *guaif*, *gaif*, an abandoned or unclaimed animal, an estray, the adj *g(u)aif* being derivative; OE *guaif* becomes ONF *waif*, whence AF, whence ME-E, *waif*, orig a legal term. (EW derives MF *gaif* from L *uacuus*, empty, and OF *gaiver* from L *uacāre*, to empty; but a Scan origin seems, on all counts, the most likely.)

8. More intimately related to ON *-veifa*, to vibrate, is the syn ON *-vāfa*, itself akin to OE *wāfian*, to wave (vi), esp with the hands, ME *waven*, E 'to *wave*', whence the n *wave*, a billow. ME *waven* acquires—?ˈanl with ON *vafra*, to be restless, to hover about (cf OE *waefre*, restless)— the freq *waveren*, whence 'to *waver*': cf MHG-G *wabern*, to be in agitated motion (Walshe).

9. Thus we come, primarily to *wife* and secondarily to *woman*. *Wife* derives, via ME *wif*, a wife, a woman, from OE *wīf*, orig a woman, hence also a wife: cf OFris (and OS) *wīf*, OHG *wīb*, MHG *wīp*, G *Weib*, MD *wief*, *wif*, *wiif*, MD-D *wijf*, and ON *vīf*, all orig and predominantly a woman. OE *wīf* has the foll derivatives extant in E: *wīfhād*, E *wifehood*; *wīfian*, to take as wife, E 'to *wive*' (obsol), influenced by *wives*, pl of *wife*; *wīflīc*, E *wifely*—cf MD *wifelic*; and *housewife* (ME *hūsewif*, contr *huswif*, whence *hussy*)—cf HOUSE. Sem, the Gmc word for a woman app means either 'the vibrator' (IE) or 'the veiled one' (OGmc)—cf ON *vīfinn*, veiled (adj), akin to ON *veifa*, to vibrate, to wave (as a veil does in the wind); the former notion is the more basic and, hist, the more prob.

10. OE *wīf*, woman, wife, has the important cpd *wīfmann* (orig m), lit a 'woman, hence female, human being', the generic OE *mann*, E *man*, as opp the particular *mann*, *man*, male human being: OE var, the eased *wīmmann*: ME *wifmon* and *wimman* (cf the pron of E *women*), then *wumman* (cf the pron of E *woman*) or *womman*, finally *woman*: E *woman*.

## Indo-European

11. L *uibrāre* has s *uibr-*, but r *uib-*, from a syn IE \**weib-*; and \**weib-* is a var of \**weip-*, to tremble, to vibrate, attested by L *uīpera*, also the Skt *vépate*, he is agitated, he trembles. (Perh E *gimp* and *wimple* represent nasalizations.)

**viburnum**: ML form of L *uīburnum*, the wayfaring tree: perh not entirely f/e is the derivation L *uia*, a way or road + L la*burnum*.

**vicar** (whence **vicarage**), **vicarial**, **vicariate**, **vicarious**; **vice-**, as in **vice versa** and **viceroy**; **vicissitude**, whence, anl, **vicissitudinous**; **viscount**, **viscountess**, **viscounty**.—Prob **week**, whence **week-end** (whence **week-ender**) and **weekly**; perh **weak** (**weaken**, etc.).

1. All the *vic-* (and *vis-*) words derive from ML *vicis*, abl *vice*, L *uicis*, abl *uice*; L *uicis* was orig the gen of L \**uix* (acc *uicem*) or perh rather of L

\**uicis*, LL *uices*—cf LL *prima*, *secunda*, *tertia*, etc., *uices*, the 1st, 2nd, 3rd, etc., time, and LL *multis uicibus*, many times, as well as LL *uices agens* (acc *uices agentem*), a deputy, and the LL pl *uices*, public offices. (Souter.) L \**uix* (for \**vics*) or \**uicis* has r *uic-*, prob akin to Gr *eikein*, \**weikein*, OS *wīkan*, OFris *wīka* (*wiāka*), to yield, OHG *wehsal*, MHG *wehsel*, G *Wechsel*, a change, ON *vīxl*, an exchange: therefore prob to E *week* and *weak* (as below) and their OE forms and OGmc cognates, which are supported by, e.g., Lett *wīkt*, to bend, and Skt *vijátē*, *véjatē*, he (it) rebounds or goes loose or trembles. (Hofmann; Walshe.)

## Latin

2. The L abl *uice* occurs in *uice uersa*, ML *vice versa*, lit 'the occasion having been turned, i.e. changed', reciprocally, conversely, and in such cpds as *vice-chancellor* (from MF-F), *-consul* (from EF-F), *-president*, *vicereine* (adopted from F) and *viceroy* (from EF-F *vice-roi*); for *vicegerent*, see GERUND, para 2, s.f.

3. On the s and r *uic-*, L forms the adj *uicārius*, ML *v-*, whence E *vicarious*; used as n, L *uicārius*, a deputy (LL, a bishop's deputy), becomes OF-F *vicaire*, whence ME *vicair*, later *viker*, *vicar*, the last being retained by E. OF-F *vicaire* forms the EF-F adj *vicarial*, adopted by E, and the late MF-F n *vicariat* (perh rather from the ML n *vicāriātus*, gen *-ūs*), whence E *vicariate*.

4. Also from the L s *uic-* comes L *uicissitūdō*, whence MF-F *vicissitude*, adopted by E.

5. But from the abl *uice* (cf para 2 above) comes —cf LL *uicedominus*, administrator of a royal domain (Souter)—the ML *vicecomes*, a count, whence—after F *comte* and its OF forms—OF *vezcuntes*, promptly reshaped to *vizcomte*, *viscomte*, later *vicomte*: hence ME *vicounte*, reshaped, after OF-MF *vis-*, to E *viscount* (s silent); the derivative OF *viscomtesse*, later *vicomtesse*, and MF *viscomté*, later *vicomté*, yield E *viscountess* and *viscounty* (s silent in both).

## Germanic

6. Very prob akin to OHG *wehsal* (cf para 1 above) are OHG *wehha*, a week, var *wohha* ('*o* from *e* by influence of *w*: cf *wohl*': Walshe), MHG-G *woche*, OS *wica*, OFris *wike*, MD *weec*, *weeck*, *wek*, *weke*, D *week*, Go *wikō*, ON *vika* (cf Sw *vecka*)— and OE *wucu* or *wice* or, predominantly, *wicu*, whence ME *wike*, later *weke*, whence E *week*: a week represents a turn-about, a change marked by the rest-day (Christian Sunday, Jewish Sabbath) —an artificial, man-ordained change or succession, opp the lunar month and the solar year.

7. Walshe, Webster and others relate—the 1st confidently, the 2nd tentatively—OHG *wehsal*, G *Wechsel*, and OHG *wehha* (G *Woche*), to OHG *wīchan*, MHG *wīchen*, G *weichen*, OFris *wīka*, OS *wīcan*, to yield or give way, fall back, ON *vīkia* (*vīkja*)—also to OHG *weih*, MHG-G *weich*, OE *wāc*, weak, and esp to the syn ON *veikr*, whence imm the ME *weik*, whence E *weak*, whence 'to

*weaken*', whence the pa, vn *weakening—weakling* (*-ling*)—*weakly—weakness*, etc.

8. All three words app go back to an IE *\*weik-* (ult *\*wei-*), to bend, weaken, change, with var *\*weig-* (as in Skt *vijátē*), as Hofmann proposes.

**vice** (1), **vicious, vitiosity; vitiable, vitiate** (obs adj, v), **vitiation, vitiator; vituperable, vituperate, vituperation, vituperative.**

1. *Vice*, moral failing or fault, is adopted from OF-F *vice*, from ML *vicium*, L *uitium*, with s *uiti-* and r *uit-*, perh from an IE *\*wi-*, whence, e.g., Sl *vina* (cf Lett *vaina*), a fault. Derivative L *uitiōsus*, ML *viciōsus*, yields OF-MF *vicious* (F *vicieux*, f *vicieuse*), adopted by E. L *uitiōsus* has derivative *uitiōsitās*, whence E *vitiosity* (obsol).

2. Also from L *uitium* derives L *uitiāre*, to render faulty, to corrupt, whence LL *uitiābilis*, whence E *vitiable*; the pp *uitiātus* yields 'to *vitiate*' (cf MF-F *vicier*), and its derivatives L *uitiātiō*, o/s *uitiātiōn-*, and *uitiātor*, become E *vitiation* and *vitiator*.

3. L *uitium* acquires the cpd *uituperāre*, to find fault with, or faults in, hence to blame, to slander; the 2nd element (*-perāre*) is o.o.o.,—but could it derive, irreg, from *parere*, to bring forth?

4. *Uituperāre* has derivative *uituperābilis*, whence E *vituperable*; from the pp *uituperātus* comes 'to *vituperate*'; from derivative L *uituperātiō*, o/s *uituperātiōn-*, E *vituperation*; from LL *uituperā-tiuus*, censorious, ML *vituperātivus*, E *vituperative*.

**vice** (2). See VISE.

**vice-**, as in **vice-chancellor, -gerent, -roy,** etc. See VICAR, para 2.

**vicinage, vicinal, vicinity; vill, villa, village** (whence **villager**)—**ville, -ville; villein, ville(i)nage** —cf **villain, villainous, villainy.**—**wick,** a village— cf **viking.**

1. L *uīcus* (s and r, *uīc-*), a cluster of houses, a city quarter, a city, but also a village, is akin to Skt *veçás* (*vesás*), a house, *viś-*, a settlement, OSl *vīsĭ*, a village, Go *weihs*, village, and to Gr *oikos* (for *\*woikos*), a house (cf E *economy*). The IE r is *weik-*, the social unit—a family in its home.

2. L *uīcus* has adj *uīcīnus*, of the same city quarter or of the same village, hence neighbouring, whence the rare E *vicine*; *uīcīnus* has derivative *uīcīnitās*, neighbourhood (whether particular or generic), whence E *vicinity*; *vicinage*, however, comes into ME from MF *visenage* (EF-F *voisin-age*), from VL *\*vīcīnātus* (gen *-ūs*), itself from L *uīcīnus*.

3. Akin to L *uīcus* is L *uīlla*, a farmstead, a country house, hence, in LL, a village: whence the It, hence the E, *villa*, a country property, hence a country (thence a seaside) house. From LL *uīlla*, ML *v-*, comes OF-F *ville*, in medieval times a (large) village, a small township, whence the hist E *vill*. OF-F *ville*, a large town, a city, occurs in modern E and A PlNn. L *uīlla* has the adj *uīllāticus*, of a rural domain (rare E *villatic*), whence ML *vīllāgium*, an assemblage of farms belonging to a (great) country house, MF-F *village*, adopted by ME-E.

4. L *uīlla*, a country house, LL *uīlla*, a village attached thereto, possesses its own LL adj, *uīllānus*, used also as n, whence OF-F *vilain*, a peasant, whence AF *vilein*, whence E *villein*, a free peasant, preserved as a feudal term, of which *villain*, orig syn with AF *vilein*, is a doublet, taken straight from MF, the pej sense of EF-F passing likewise into E. OF-F *vilain* has derivatives OF-MF *vilenage*, *villenage*, the latter adopted by E, with var *villeinage*—OF-MF *vileneus*, whence, influenced by *vilain*, the E *villainous*—and OF *vilanie*, MF-F *vilenie*, orig a feudal term, rendered pej by f/e association with OF-F *vil*, cheap, hence vulgar, despicable, whence ME *vilenie*, *vilanie*, whence E *villainy*.

5. Akin to Go *weihs*, a village (para 1 above), are the syn OFris *wīk* and esp OE *wīc*, whence E *wick*, extant only in PlNn, some being prob influenced by ON *vīk*, a creek, a small bay, whence the syn E *wick*. Prob from ON *vīk* is ON *vīkingr*, ? 'an *-ingr* or man of the creeks and small bays' (cf OE *wīcing*): the Norse *vikings* of C8-10 raided the coastline of Europe by landing in any suitable *vīk* and thence plundering the neighbourhood.

**vicious.** See the 1st VICE, para 1.

**vicissitude.** See VICAR, para 4.

**victim,** whence **victimize,** whence **victimization.** —**wile,** whence **wily**—cf **guile,** n (whence **guileful**) and v (archaic), whence 'to **beguile**', whence **beguilement** and **beguiler.**—**witch,** n and v (pa **witching**), **witchcraft, witchery** (*witch*, n+suffix *-ery*); **bewitch** (int *be-*+*witch*, v), pa **bewitching.**

1. *Victim*, late MF-F *victime*, ML *victima*, L *uictima*, a sacrificial victim, is akin to Go *weihs*, consecrated, holy, and *weihan*, to consecrate, OHG *wīhēn*, MHG *wīhen*, G *weihen*, to consecrate, and OHG *wīh*, MHG *wīch*, holy. L *uictima*, suffix *-ima* (cf L *sacrima* from *sacr-*, o/s of *sacer*, conse-crated), has s, app *uict-* and r, app *uic-*: IE r, ? *\*weik-*, ? to sacrifice.

2. Prob akin to L *uictima* is OE *wicca* (m), *wicce* (f), whence ME *wicche*, E *witch*; derivative OE *wiccian*, to be a witch, to practise the craft, leads us to 'to *witch*' and to OE *wiccecraeft*, witchcraft. Cf MG *wicken*, syn with OE *wiccian*.

3. Akin to OE *wicca*, *wicce*, s *wic-*, is OE *wigle*, witchcraft, sorcery, whence OF-MF *guile*, ONF var *\*wile*, whence late OE *wil*, ME *wile*, retained by E, with gradually weakening sense; and OF-MF *guile*, var *guille*, becomes ME *gile*, *guile*, the latter retained by E; derivative MF *guiler* yields 'to *guile*'. Perh, however, the OF-MF n comes rather from OHG, or OFris, *wigila*.

**victor, Victoria** (**victoria**), **Victorian** (whence **Victoriana**), **victorine, victorious; victor ludorum**— see ludicrous, para 2; **victress; vincent** (**Vincent**), **vincible** and **invincible** (whence, anl, **invincibility**), **Invictus.**—Other L prefix-cpds: **convict** (adj, n, v), **conviction, convictive**—and **convince,** whence **con-vincement** and, anl, **convincible; evict, eviction**— and **evince,** whence **evincible.**—R derivative: **vanquish.**—Gmc cognate: **wight,** brave.

1. The archaic *wight*, brave, ME *wight*, earlier

*wiht*, derives from ON *vīgt*, neu of *vīgr*, fighting-fit, akin to ON *vīg*, war, a battle, and to the L *uic-* of *uictor*, ML *victor*; *vanquish*, ME *venquishen*, *venquissen*, derives from the *vainquiss-* (*vanquiss-*) parts of OF-MF *vainquir*, var of OF-MF *veintre* (EF-F *vaincre*), from ML *vincere*, L *uincere*, to overcome in battle.

2. L *uincere*, s *uinc-*, has presp *uincens*, o/s *uincent-*, whence the rare adj *vincent* and the PN *Vincent*; derivative *uincibilis* (*uinc-*+suffix *-ibilis*) yields *vincible*, and the neg *inuincibilis* yields, via MF-F, *invincible*. On the pp *uict*us, neg *inuictus* (used in mottoes and in W. E. Henley's title), are formed *uictor*, ML *v-*, adopted by E, and L *uictoria*, ML *v-*, OF-MF *victorie* (later *victoire*), adopted by ME, whence E *victory*; derivative L *uictoriōsus* becomes OF-MF *victorious*, MF-F *victorieux* (f *victorieuse*), whence E *victorious*. L *uictoria*, ML *v-*, was adopted as a PN, and Queen *Victoria* is commemorated in the carriage known as a *victoria* (E use from F). The dim F *Victorine* leads to *victorine*, a long-ended fur tippet—perh imm from a famous modiste or from a furrier's trade-name for the article.

3. L *uictor* has f *uictrix*, which has suggested E *victress*, formed—cf *actor*, *actress*—to complement *victor*.

4. L *uincere* nasalizes the L s and r *uic-*, from an IE *\*wig-*, var *\*wik-*, to fight: cf OIr *fich*im, I fight; OE *wīgan*, Go *weihan*, to fight, OFris and OS *wīgand*, OHG *wīgant*, OE *wīgend*, a warrior.

5. L *uincere* has two prefix-cpds relevant, in their ML *v-* shapes, to E:

*conuincere*, to convince, to prove, to refute, whence 'to *convince*'; pp *conuictus* yields both the adj, hence n, and the v *convict*; derivative LL *conuictiō*, o/s *conuictiōn-*, E (and F) *conviction*, and LL *conuictīuus*, E *convictive*;

*ēuincere* (*ē-* used int), to overcome completely, to succeed in proving, LL to claim for oneself, yields 'to *evince*', orig as in L; pp *ēuictus* yields 'to *evict*', and from the derivative LL *ēuictiō*, acc *ēuictiōn*em, comes MF-F *éviction*, whence E *eviction*.

**victual, victualler, victuals.** See VIVA, para 4.

**vicuña**, a SAm ruminant, is adopted from Sp, which thus adapts Quechuan *huik' uña*; the var *vigonia* derives from F *vigogne*, EF *vicugne*, from the Sp word.

**vide**, See!—cf *vide infra* and *supra*, see herein (esp below) and see above; **videlicet** (contr **viz.**); **view**, n, hence v; **visa** (n, hence v) and **visé**—**visage** (n, hence v), cf **envisage**—**vis-à-vis**—**visibility**, **visible**, and **invisibility**, **invisible**—**visile**—**vision** (n, hence v, with int **envision**), **visionary** (adj, hence n) —**visit** (n, v), **visitant**, **visitation**, **visitatorial**, **visitor** —**visor**, var **vizor**—**vista**—**visual**, whence **visuality** and **visualize**, whence **visualization.**—**Veda**, **Vedanta.**—Prefix-cpds of L *uidēre*, ML *vidēre*, and of the pp *uīsus*, ML *vīsus*, incl the R, esp F, interventions and formations; and of the L int *uisāre*, ML *v-*, with its freq *uīsitāre*, ML *v-*: **advice, advise** (whence **advisable**)—cf **aviso**; **evidence** (n, hence

v), **evident, evidential**; **invidious** and **envious, envy** (n, v); **interview**, n, hence v, whence **interviewer**; **previse, prevision** (n, hence v); **provide, providence, provident** (with negg **improvidence, improvident**)—**providore, provedore**—**provision** (n, hence v), whence **provisional**—**proviso, prudence, prudent**; **purvey, purveyance, purveyor**—cf **purview**; **review**, n, hence v, whence **reviewal** and **reviewer**—cf **revue**; **revise** (v, whence **revisal** and the n **revise** and **reviser**), **revision** (whence **revisionism, revisionist**); **revisit**; **supervise, supervision, supervisor**; **survey** (v, whence n and pa, vn **surveying**), **surveyor.**—For **clairvoyance, clairvoyant**, see CLEAR.—Gmc cognates: **wit**—n (whence **witless**) and v—**witty**, whence **wittiness**; **twit**; **wise**, adj, n, v—cf **wiseacre, wisecrack, wisenheimer**—**wisdom**; **wizard**, whence **wizardry**; **guidance, guide**; for **righteous**, see REX, para 2; for the Gr cognates, see the sep HISTORY and IDEA; for C, DRUID.

### Latin

1. The direction *vide* is the imp sing of ML *vidēre*, L *uidēre*, s *uid-*, to see; *videlicet* = *vidēre licet*, it is permissible to see, hence namely, contr *viz*.

2. The presp is *uidens*, o/s *uident-*; the pp *uīsus*, s *uīs-*, and on this s are formed E *visile*, anl with *audile* and *tactile*; L *uīsibilis*, whence OF-F *visible*, adopted by E, the derivative LL *uīsibilitās*, acc *uīsibilitāt*em, yielding EF-F *visibilité*, whence E *visibility*, the negg *inuīsibilis*, LL *inuīsibilitās*, acc *-itātem*, yielding MF-F *invisible*, adopted by E, and EF-F *invisibilité*, whence E *iuvisibility*; L *uīsiō*, acc *uīsiōn*em, becomes OF-F *vision*, adopted by E, the F derivative *visionnaire* leading to E *visionary*; the n *uīsus* (gen *-ūs*), whence both LL *uīsuālis*, (EF-F *visuel* and) E *visual*, and OF-MF *vis*, a face, whence OF-F *visage*, adopted by E, the derivative EF-F *envisager*, to confront, yielding 'to *envisage*', and MF *visiere* (EF-F *visière*), AF *viser*, adopted by ME, whence E *visor*, occ *vizor*, and late MF-F *vis-à-vis* (adv), face to face, adopted by E, and—neu pl of pp *uīsus*—L *uīsa*, things seen, hence an endorsement, adopted by EF-F, with var *visé*, both F forms being in turn adopted by E.

3. L *uidēre* becomes OF-MF *veoir* (late MF-F *voir*), pp *veü* (F *vu*), f *veüe* used as n, F *vue*, whence E *view*, whence 'to *view*'; it also becomes It *vedere*, with pp *veduto* and *visto*, f *vista*, which, used as n, is adopted by E.

4. L *uidēre*, pp *uīsus*, has int *uīsere*, vt and vi, to seek to see, go to see, visit, examine, whence E 'to *\*vise*'; *uīsere* has freq *uīsitāre*, to go often to see, to see often, with presp *uīsitans*, o/s *uīsitant-*, whence E *visitant*, and with pp *uīsitātus*, whence LL *uīsitātiō*, acc *uīsitātiōn*em, and LL *uīsitātor*: whence OF-F *visiter*, OF-F *visitation*, and, imm from *visiter*, MF-F *visiteur*: whence 'to *visit*', *visitation*, AF *visitour*, E *visitor*, with *visitatorial* suggested by LL *uīsitātor*.

### Sanskrit

5. With L *uidēre*, ML *vidēre* (s *vid-*), to see, cf

Skt *veda*, I know (? orig, I see), from—or intimately related to—which is Skt *veda*, knowledge, (esp) sacred knowledge, hence a book containing it, whence E *Veda*, a collection of early Skt sacred works; derivative Skt *Vedānta*=*Ved*a+*ant*a, end.

## Germanic

6. Akin to both the Skt and the L words cited above are the Gmc *wit* and *wise*, with, of course, their cognates. The n *wit*, descending unchanged from OE, is akin to OFris *witt*, OS *giwitt*, (*ge-*, int prefix), OHG *wizzē*, MHG *witze*, knowledge, wisdom, G *Witz*, (good) sense, (modern-sensed) wit, Go *witi*, ON *vit* (cf Da *vid* and Sw *vett*)—cf Skt *vidyā*, knowledge. Derivative OE *witig*, var *wittig*, becomes E *witty*, orig wise, with sem change accompanying that of the n.

7. OE *wit* prob derives from OE *witan*, to know, *wāt*, (I) know, ME *wot*, whence the archaic *wot*—ME *witen*—E 'to *wit*', obs except in 'to *wit*', namely: cf OFris *wita*, OS *witan*, OHG *wizzan*, MHG *wizzen*, G *wissen*, Go *wait*, I know (lit, I have seen), pres perfect inf *witan*, MD *weiten*, *wieten*, *wetten*, MD-D *weten*, ON *vita*.

8. Akin to OE *wit* and *witan* is OE *wīs*, knowledgeable, esp if very much so, hence sagacious, ME *wīs*, ? *wus*, *wise*, E *wise*: cf OFris and OS *wīs*, shrewd, discerning, OHG *wīsi*, MHG *wīse*, knowledgeable, learnèd, experienced, G *weise*, sagacious, Go *unweis*, unwise—cf OFris *unwiss*, OE *unwīs*, E *unwise*; cf also MD *wies*, *wis*, *wise*, *wiis*, MD-D *wijs*, and ON *vīss*. Derivative OE *wīsdōm* (cf the id OFris) becomes *wisdom*; derivative ME *wisard* (? cf MF *guischart*) becomes *wizard*, orig a very shrewd (int -*ard*), a wise, man, hence esp in magic, whence the adj (debased in World War II).

9. Intimately related to OE *wīs*, knowledgeable, is the OE n *wīse*, knowledge, hence a knowing how to do, thence a manner of doing, things, E *wise*, obsol except in such phrases as *in any*, *in no*, *wise*, in any, no, way or manner; also intimately related is the OE v *wīsian*, to render knowledgeable or shrewd, hence to guide or advise, E 'to *wise*', obs except in dial, the A sl '*wise* up' deriving from the adj, as do *wisecrack*, a wittily funny remark (*crack*, a witticism), and A sl *wisenheimer* (occ contr to *wiseheimer*), ref the G PN ending -*heimer*, esp in *Guggenheimer*. *Wiseacre*, however, comes from MD *wijssegger*, a soothsayer (cf MD *wijsseggen*, to say true), from OHG *wīssago*, f/e for *wīzago*, a prophet (cf OE *wītega*)—cf OHG *wīzagōn*, with f/e var *wīssāgon*. Note that both OE *wīse* and OE *wīsian* have numerous OGmc cognates.

10. For *righteous* ('right-wise'), see REX, para 2. 'To *twit*' is aphetic for ME *atwiten*, from OE *aetwītan*, to reproach (*aet-* being E *at*), the orig sense being to take cognizance of. The even less imm recognizable 'to *guide*' (whence *guidance*) derives from MF-F *guider*, itself from the source of the E n *guide*: MF-F *guide*, from OProv (? and It) *guida*, app from the OProv v *guidar*, itself from Frankish *wītan*, to show the direction to, clearly akin to OHG *wīsēn* (MHG *wīsen*, G *weisen*),

to show, point out, therefore to OE *wīsian* (as in para 9).

## Indo-European

11. Besides the Skt, L, OGmc words, already noted, there exist Gr *idein*, for *widein*, to see, *oida*, for *woida*, (I have seen, hence) I know, OSl *vědě*, I know, OP *waidimai*, we know, OIr ro-*fess*, it is known, W *gwidd* (*g-widd*), knowledge. (For the Gr cognates, see the sep HISTORY and IDEA.) The IE r is *weid-*, to see (truly), therefore to know. (E & M.)

## Latin Prefix-Compounds

12. L prefix-cpds are of *uīsitāre* (cf para 4) — *uīsere* (ib)—*uidēre*. *Uīsitāre* has only one, and that at the F stage: *revisiter* (*re*, again+ *visiter*), whence 'to *revisit*'.

13. *Uīsere* has two that affect E:

VL *aduīsāre* (for *aduīsere*), to give one's opinion to, whence MF-F *aviser* (perh, however, a F cpd of *viser*, from L *uīsāre*), whence ME *avisen*, whence (after L *ad*) the reshaped E 'to *advise*', whence *adviser*, with *advisement* reshaping the MF-EF *avisement* (from *aviser*); but VL *aduīsāre* derives from VL *aduīsum*, a view, hence an opinion, from L *uīsum*, prop the neu sing of *uīsus*, seen (cf para 2), whence MF-F *avis*, adopted by ME, whence the reshaped E *advice*,—but MF-F *avis* derives rather from OF-MF Ce m'est *avis*, from OF Ce m'est *a vis*, lit 'this, to me, is for (an) opinion', itself from OF Ce m'est *vis*, as B & W propose, the *vis* being OF-MF *vis*, from L *uīsus* (gen -*ūs*), prop 'sight, vision', hence 'appearance, aspect', hence 'face'. Cf F, hence E, *aviso*, a dispatch boat, adopted from Sp, where it is elliptical for *barca de aviso*, a vessel of—i.e., employed in carrying—(letters of) advice.

L *reuīsere*, to go again (*re-*) to see, ML *revīsere*, whence MF-EF *reviser* (EF-F *ré-*), whence 'to *revise*'; derivative L *reuīsiō*, acc *reuīsiōn*em, becomes MF-EF *revision* (EF-F *ré-*), adopted by E, with E *reviser* perh indebted to EF-F *réviseur*.

14. L *uidēre*, ML *v-*, has, in the prefix-cpds, presp -*uidens*, o/s -*uident-*, ML -*vident-*, derivative n -*uidentia*, ML -*videntia*, app a derivative n -*uīsus*, ML -*vīsus*, derivative n -*uīsiō*, ML -*vīsiō*, acc -*visionem*. Add F -*voir*, c/f of *voir*, to see, and -*vue*, c/f of *vue*, vision, sight, hence a sight, and you can easily follow the genesis of the foll L prefix-cpds, notes being added, where necessary, for R interventions:

L *ēuidēns*, acc *ēuident*em, and *ēuidentia*, as if from *ēuidēre* but, in the fact, Ciceronian transs of Gr Phil terms: MF *evident*, *evidence*, EF-F *é-*: E *evident*, *evidence*;

OF-F *entrevoir*, to see imperfectly (connoted by *entre*, L *inter*, between), pp *entreveü*, later *entrevu*, whence the late MF-F *entrevue*, whence the reshaped E *interview*;

L *inuidēre*, to see intensively, hence to envy, whence *inuidia* and its adj *inuidiōsus*, the latter affording E *invidious*, the former, via VL *inveia* the OF-F *envie*, E *envy*; derivative OF-F *envier*, whence late MF-F *enviable*, and MF *envieus*, later *envieux* (f *envieuse*), yield E 'to *envy*'—*enviable*—*envious*;

L *praeuidēre*, to foresee, pp *praeuīsus*, whence both 'to *previse*' and LL *praeuīsiō*, o/s *praeuīsiōn-*, E *prevision*;

L *prōuidēre*, to foresee, hence to provide for or against, whence 'to *provide*'; presp *prōuidens*, o/s *prōuident-*, E *provident*, and its LL derivative *prōuidentia*, OF-F *providence*, adopted by E, whence, anl, *providential*; *providore* is f/e for *provedor*, from Sp *proveedor* (from *proveer*, L *prōuidēre*); the L pp *prōuīsus*, ML *prōvīsus*, abl *prōvīso*, (it) having been provided, gives us *proviso*; L *prōuīsio* (from pp *prōuīsus*), acc *prōuīsiōn*em, becomes MF-F *provision*, adopted by E;

L *prōuidens* has, via *\*proudens*, the derivative adj *prūdens*, foreseeing, acc *prūdent*em, whence OF-F *prudent*, adopted by E; derivative L *prūdentia* becomes MF-F, whence E, *prudence*; E *prudential*=L *prudentia*+E adj suffix *-al*; the L neg *imprūdens*, *imprūdentia*, yield MF-F, whence E, *imprudent*, *imprudence*;—these words, therefore, are doublets of *providence*, *provident*, *providential*, *improvident*, etc;

L *prōuidēre*, ML *prōv-*, becomes OF-MF *porveoir* (later *pourvoir*), var *porveier* (ils *porveient*, they foresee or provide), ME *porveien*, *purveien*, E 'to *purvey*'; the derivative MF *porveance* and *porveor*, varr in *pour-*, yield, via ME, the E *purveyance* and *purveyor*; from the OF-MF pp *porveü*, MF *pourveü* (EF-F *pourvu*), comes the E n *purview*;

L *reuidēre*, to see again, ML *rev-*, becomes OF-MF *reveoir* (MF-F *revoir*), pp *reveü*, whence MF *reveüe*, EF-F *revue*, whence the E nn *review* and, with sense arising in C19 F, *revue*;

L. *superuidēre*, to see over (*super*), to oversee, pp *superuīsus*, whence both 'to *supervise*' and ML *supervisor*, adopted by E, whence, anl, *supervision*;

suggested by ML *supervidēre*, but formed from *sor*, later *sur*, over+*veoir*, later *voir*, to see, is OF-MF *sorveeir*, *sorveoir*, MF *surveeir*, *surveoir*, whence 'to *survey*'; derivative MF *surveor*, *surveour*, yields, via AF *surveiour*, the E *surveyor*.

**videlicet.** See prec, para 1.

**vidual, viduate, viduous.** See WIDOW, para 2.

**vie**, presp and vn **vying**; **envy**, to vie; **invitation, invitatory** (adj, n), **invite** (pa **inviting**).

1. 'To *vie*' derives from ME *vien*, short for *envien*, whence the archaic *envy*, to strive: and ME *envien* derives from OF-EF *envier*, to challenge (in gambling), itself from ML *invītāre*, to invite, L *inuītāre*, o.o.o., perh related to L *inuītus*, unwilling, itself o.o.o. (? from an adj *\*uītus*—cf Skt *vītás*, agreeable, pleasant: E & M).

2. L *inuītāre*, ML *inv-*, becomes MF-F *inviter*, whence 'to *invite*'. On the pp *inuītāt*us are formed *inuītātiō*, acc *inuītātiōn*em, and the LL adj *inuītātōrius*, whence the ML n *invītātorium*: whence MF-F *invitation*, adopted by E, and the E adj and n *invitatory*.

**vielle.** See FIDDLE, para 3.

**Vienna**, like its G name *Wien*, comes from ML *Vindobona*, L *Uindobona*, o.o.o.: perh of C origin —? either 'White (*uind*) City' or 'Vindo's City'. Some of the derivatives—e.g., *Vienna bread*—are apposite; others—e.g., *Vienna steak*—merely fanciful.

**view**, whence **viewy** (cf the F *voyant*). See VIDE, para 3.

**vigil, vigilance, vigilant, vigilante, vigilate, vigilation.** See VIGOR, para 5.

**vigneron, vignette.** See VINE, para 3.

**vigonia.** See VICUÑA.

**vigor** (AE) or **vigour**—**vigoroso** and **vigorous**; **invigorant** and **invigorate**, whence, anl, **invigoration, invigorative, invigorator**—whence **reinvigorate, reinvigoration**—cf **revigorate,** **revigoration**.—**vigil, vigilance, vigilant, vigilante, vigilate, vigilation**—cf **vedette; invigilate**, whence, anl, **invigilation** and **invigilator; pervigilate, pervigilation, pervigilium; reveille; surveillance, surveillant.**—**vegete, vegetable** (adj and n), **vegetal, vegetant, vegetarian, vegetate, vegetation, vegetative.**—Gmc cognates: **waft**, v (hence n), whence **waftage; wait** (n, v), **waiter** (whence, anl, **waitress**)—cf **await; wake** (v, whence **waking**; hence n, whence **wakeful**)—**waken** (whence pa, vn **wakening**), cf **awake** (adj, v), **awaken** (whence pa, vn **awakening**); **watch,** v (whence **watcher** and pa, vn **watching**) and n (whence **watchdog, watchful, watchkeeper, watchless, watchmaker, watchman, watchtower, watchword**).—**bivouac**, n, hence v.

### Indo-European

1. In order to provide a vantage-point from which to inspect the seemingly disparate senses, the less contradictory forms, of the words and ideas listed or implied above, it is well to remember that there does exist a well-attested IE r *\*weg-*, from which all the forms have, or at the least could have, derived or diverged, and that the basic idea 'good health' implying 'vigour', or perh 'vigour' implying 'good health', is borne out with a quite astonishing uniformity. This r *\*weg-*, with var *\*wēg-* and with the 'thinning' *\*wig-*, is confirmed by the foll representative, but not exhaustive, list: Skt *vāgas*, *vájas*, strength, vigour, and *vājáyati*, he incited (? orig 'invigorated'); L *uegēre* (s and r *ueg-*), to impart strength (occ also movement) or 'life' to, to excite, and L *uigēre* (s and r *uig-*), to be strong or vigorous, to be in good health—a clear example of 'thinned' sense marked by 'thinned' sound; the L adj *uigil*, in excellent health, wide-awake—here we begin to perceive the relationship of the L to the Gmc words; OHG *wahhēn*, MHG-G *wachen* (s and r *wach-*, ? for *\*wagh-*), OE *wacian* (r *wac-*), to be awake, to watch—cf OHG *wecchēn*, MHG-G *wecken*, OE *weccean*, to waken (vt), both with r *wech-*, ? for *\*wegh-*.

### Latin: *uegēre*

2. L *uegēre*, ML *v-*, to animate or enliven, to

invigorate, to arouse, s *ueg-*, has pp *uegetus*, used as adj 'lively, vigorous', whence E *vegete*. L *uegetus* has derivative *uegetāre*, to animate, in LL to be animated, esp (of plants) to grow, pp *uegetātus*, whence 'to *vegetate*'; derivative LL adj *uegetābilis*, refreshing, vivifying, becomes the EF adj, hence also n, *végétable*, whence the E adj and n *vegetable*; derivative ML *vegetātiō*, acc *vegetātiōn*em, and ML *vegetātivus* yield EF-F *végétation* and MF-F *végétatif*, f *-ive*, whence E *vegetation* and *vegetative*. The E adj *vegetant* comes from ML *vegetant-*, o/s of *vegetans*, LL *u-*, presp of LL *uegetāre*, (vi) to grow. From ML *veget*āre comes the ML adj *vegetālis*, whence EF-F *végétal*, whence E *vegetal*; EF-F *végétal* has derivative *végétarien*, whence *végétarianisme*: whence E *vegetarian, vegetarianism*.

### Latin: *uigēre*

3. L *uigēre*, to be in good health or vigorous, has derivative *uigor*, ML *vigor*, whence OF-MF *vigor*, MF var *vigour* (EF-F *vigueur*), whence ME *vigor, vigour*, the latter becoming E, and the former, AE; derivative ML *vigorōsus* suggested OF-EF *vigorous* (EF-F *vigoureux*), adopted by E, and certainly produced It *vigoroso*, adopted by Mus.

4. L *uigor* engenders LL *uigorāre*, to be strong, which perh prompted the EF *envigorer* (*en*, L *in+* OF-EF *vigor+*inf *-er*), whence, anl, the E 'to *invigorate*', whence, anl, *invigorant* and *invigoration*; cf ML *revigorāre* (*re-+vigorāre*, L *u-*), to recharge with health or vigour, pp *revigorātus*, whence 'to *revigorate*', whence *revigoration*.

### Latin: *uigil*

5. L *uigil*, ML *vigil*, wide-awake, alert, has var *uigilis*, neu pl *uigilia*, whence the f sing *uigilia*, a period of wakefulness, a keeping watch, whence OF *vigilie*, MF-F *vigile*, E *vigil*. Derivative *uigil-āre*, to remain awake, to keep watch, has presp *uigilans*, o/s *uigilant-*, whence *uigilantia*, and pp *uigilātus*, whence LL *uigilātiō*, o/s *uigilātiōn-*: late MF-F *vigilant, vigilance*, both adopted by E; 'to *vigilate*' and *vigilation*. ML *vigilāre* becomes Sp *velar*, whence the n *vela*, a watching, a keeping guard, hence a guard or sentinel, with dim *veleta*, whence, by f/e influence of It *ved*ere, to see, the It military *vedetta*, whence EF-F *vedette*, adopted by E, orig as a military and then also as a naval term.

6. *Uigilāre* has three prefix-cpds affecting E: *ēuigilāre* (*ē-* used int) becomes VL-ML *exvigil-āre*, whence OF-MF *esveillier* (MF-EF *esveiller*, EF-F *éveiller*), to awaken, to rouse, whence (*re-*, again) MF *resveillier*, MF-EF *resveiller*, EF-F *réveiller*, vr *se r.*, whence *Reveillez-vous*, Wake up!, whence E *reveille* (contrast F *réveil*);

*inuigilāre*, to keep watch *in-* or over, pp *inuigilātus*, whence 'to *invigilate*';

*peruigilāre* (*per-* used int), to keep long and faithful watch, pp *peruigilātus*, whence the literary 'to *pervigilate*'; derivative *peruigilium* survives esp in the title *Pervigilium Veneris*, an exquisite anonymous LL poem lovingly translated by Arthur Quiller-Couch.

From ML *vigilāre* comes OF-F *veiller*, to watch, whence the EF-F *surveiller*, to watch *sur-* (L *super*) or over, presp *surveillant* used as adj, hence also as n, whence EF-F *surveillance*, supervision, both adopted by E.

### Germanic: *waft*

7. 'To *waft*' is very much a subsidiary of *watch* (para 10), for it derives, in C16 and by b/f, from the late ME-EE *wafter*, a convoy of ships, itself app from MD-D (and MLG-LG) *wachter*, prob from a late MD-ED var *wahter*, from late MD-ED *wahten* (the *h* heavily aspirated), a var of MD-D (and MLG-LG) *wachten*, to watch, to guard.

### Germanic *wait*

8. 'To *wait*,' ME *waiten*, comes from *waitier*, the ONF form of OF-MF *gaitier* (*guaitier*; EF-F *guetter*), to watch, from Frankish *wāhtōn*: cf OHG *wahhēn*, to be wide-awake, to watch, and, in general, the vv adduced in the next two paras. From ME *waiten* comes ME *waitere*, E *waiter*, orig a watchman: cf ONF *waitiere*. The E n *wait*, orig a watchman, a guard, comes from ME *waite*, adopted from ONF *waite*, orig a watching, a being on guard, itself either from the syn OHG *wahta* or from the ONF v.

### Germanic *wake*

9. 'To *wake*', orig to watch, to keep vigil, derives from ME *waken*—pt *wok*, whence E *woke*, and pp *waken*, whence E *woken* (now less common than *waked*)—OE *wacan* (vi), to wake, prob influenced by the cognate ME *wakien*—pt and pp *waked*—from OE *wacian*, var of OE *waeccan*, to be awake, to watch: cf OFris *wakia*, OS *wakōn*, OHG *wahhēn*, MHG-G *wachen*, Go *wakan*, ON *vaka*. 'To *wake*' is a doublet of 'to *watch*'.

### Germanic *watch*

10. 'To *watch*,' ME *wacchen*, OE *waeccan*, *wacian*, is intimately related to OE *wacan*: therefore cf the prec para. Very closely akin to OE *waeccan*, if not, indeed, derived therefrom, is the OE n *waecce*, ME *wacche*, E *watch*, orig a being awake, a vigil, a guarding, hence a sentinel, hence also a division of the night, hence any allotted division of time, hence that which measures division of time, esp a small chronometer.

### Germanic *await* and *awake, awaken*

11. Whereas ONF *waitier* has prefix-cpd *await-ier*, to wait (*a*, F *à*, L *ad*) for, whence ME *awaiten*, whence 'to *await*', OE *wacian* has prefix-cpd *āwacian* (pt *āwacode*, E *awoke*), whence 'to *awake*'; and OE *waeccan* has caus *āwaecnan* (pt *āwōc*, E *awoke*), whence 'to *awaken*'; the latter OE v has influenced the passage of the former. The adj *awake* is a worn-down form of *awaken*, obs pp of *awake*. Also relevant to 'to *wake*' and G *wachen*, is *bivouac*, adopted from F, where it

occurs earliest as *biwacht*: Swiss *bīwaeht*, corresp to G *Beiwacht*, var of *Beiwache*, a watching, or a guarding, *bei-*, near to: orig a supplementary night-guard by the entire force.

**viking.** See VICINAGE, para 5.

**vile,** whence **vileness; revile,** whence **revilement;** for **vilify** and **vilipend,** see the element *vili-*.

'To *revile*' comes from OF-MF *reviler*, to cheapen, to despise (*re-*, used int+*vil*+-*er*): and OF-F *vil*, whence E *vile*, comes from ML *vīlis*, L *uīlis*, cheap, hence very, hence too, cheap, hence of little moral value, hence base, evil: o.o.o.

**vill; villa; village.** See VICINAGE, para 3.

**villain, villainous, villainy.** See VICINAGE, para 4. Cf:

**villanelle,** adopted from EF-F, derives from It *villanella*, a village song (or dance), from *villano*, of a village: cf VILLAIN.

**villatic.** See VICINAGE, para 3.

**ville.** See VICINAGE, para 3.

**villein, villeinage.** See VICINAGE, para 4.

**villose, villosity, villous, villus.** See VELVET, para 1.

**vim.** See VIS, para 1.

**vinaceous, vinage.** See VINE, para 5.

**vinaigrette, vinaigrous.** See VINE, para 5.

**vinal.** See VINE, para 5.

**vinasse.** See VINE, para 5.

**vincent, Vincent.** See VICTOR, para 2.

**vinculum.** See the 1st PERIWINKLE, para 2.

**vindemial, vindemiate.** See VINE, para 7.

**vindicate, vindication, vindicative, vindicator.** See DICT, para 20.

**vindictive.** See DICT, para 20.

**vine** (whence **viny**), **vinery, vineyard; vineal, vineatic; vinic; vino; vinose, vinosity, vinous; vinolent, vinaceous, vinage, vinasse; vinaigre, vinaigrette, vinaigrous; vinegar; vigne, vigneron, vignette; vintage; vintner.—wine** (n, hence v), whence **winy; wineberry** and **whinberry; winer** and **winery.—oenin, oenology;** cf the element *oeno-*.

### Indo-European

1. All these words are from either L or Gr, but neither the L nor the Gr sources are of IE origin: the IE words and their Sem and Ham cognates come, or app come, from Medit, not the IE from Sem or Ham, nor vice versa. The Medit base is attested, in IE, by Gr *oinos*, for \**woinos*, wine, and *oinē* for \**woinē*, vine, by the corresp L *uīnum* and *uīnea*, by the Alb *vēne*, by the Arm *gini*, and by Etruscan *vinu*; in Sem by H *jajin* and, in part, by Abyssinian *wain*; in Ham, by—in part—Abyssinian *wain*, and perh by Eg *kam*, wine, and *hemi*, a kind of wine. The initial-consonant varr *w* (*u*) and *v*, *g* and *j*, *h* and *k*, are regular enough; the final-consonant var from *n* to *m* (Eg only) is expectable; the vowel-range—*oi*, *ī*, *ai*, *ē*, *ĕ*, *ă*—is narrower than might have been postulated.—The C words (*f-* in Ir and Ga, *gu-* or *gw-* in Br, Cor, W) are irrelevant, for, like the Gmc, they derive from L. Whereas Hofmann proposes origin in Asia Minor or in Caucasia, Webster prefers

the Aegean, and Boisacq hesitates between the Aegean and Caucasia (cf Georgian *qvino*); the EnciIt suggests Armenia, but an Armenia perh deriving it from the Orient; Walshe says 'prob of Caucasian origin'.

### Greek

2. Gr *oinos*, for \**woinos*, wine, and *oinē*, for \**woinē*, vine, have not entered everyday E; they produce such erudite or such Sci terms as *oenology* (cf the element *-logy*, q.v. at *-loger*), wine-lore, and Chem *oenin* (suffix *-in*), and *oinomancy*, divination (cf the element *-mancy*) by means of wine, esp its colour. But Gr (*w*)*oinos* and (*w*)*oinē* are important for their parallelism to L *uīnum* and *uīnea*.

### Latin: *uīnea*, the vine

3. L *uīnea* (ML *vīnea*), prop the f of *uīneus*, rare adj of *uīnum*, becomes OF-MF *vine*, adopted by E; but OF-MF *vine* promptly acquires the var *vigne*, whence both MF-F *vigneron*, wine-grower, adopted by E, and MF-F *vignette*, orig an ornament in the form of vine-leaves and twigs and tendrils, likewise adopted by E.

4. L *uīnea* has two adjj, *uīneālis* and *uīneāticus*, whence E *vineal* and *vineatic*; and E *vine* two extant derivatives, *vinery* and *vineyard*, f/e for *vineyard* (OE *wīngeard*).

### Latin: *uīnum*, wine

5. L *uīnum* becomes OF-F *vin*, as in *vin ordinaire* and *vin rosé*. *Uīnum* has—besides *uīneus*—the adjj *uīnāceus*, *uīnālis*, *uīnōlentus* (wine-loving, drunken), *uīnōsus*: whence E *vinaceous*, *vinal*, *vinolent*, *vinose* and, prob via OF-F *vineus* (f *-euse*), *vinous*; derivative LL *uīnōsitās*, o/s *uīnōsitāt-*, yields *vinosity* (cf F *vinosité*). F *vin* has the simple derivatives *vinage* and *vinasse*, both adopted by E, and the cpd *vinaigre*, dim *vinaigrette* (adopted by E), whence both E *vinaigrous* and E *vinegar* (cf EAGER, para 2); for such cpds as *viniculture* and *vinology*, see the element *vini-*. E *vinic*=ML *vīnum*+adj suffix *-ic*.

6. Two notable E words remain: *vintage* and *vintner*. The latter is a contr of ME *vintener*, mdfn of *viniter*, from MF-EF *vinetier* (*vinotier*), ML *vinētārius* or *-ōrius*, a vintner, itself perh suggested either by L *uīnētum*, a vineyard, or by L *uīnitor*, a wine-grower.

7. *Vintner* has f/e intervened in the formation of E *vintage* from ME *vindage*, var of *vendage*, for *vendange*: EF-F *vendange*, MF-EF *vendenge*: ML *vindēmia*: L *uindēmia*, a season's 'harvest' from the grape-vines: *uīnum*+*dēmere*, to take off or from (cf the *-deem* of *redeem*)+suffix *-ia*. *Uindēmia* has LL adj *uindēmiālis*, whence E *vindemial*, and *uindēmiāre*, pp *uindēmiātus*, whence 'to *vindemiate*', both E words being rare and literary.

### English *wine* from Latin *uīnum*

8. L *uīnum* becomes—cf F *vin* in para 5—OE *wīn*, ME *win*, E *wine*: cf Go *wein*, OHG(-MHG)-OS-OFris *wīn*, ON *vīn*. From *wine* come *winery* (cf para 4)—*winer*, orig a vintner—*winebibber*—

and *wineberry*, f/e alteration of OE *wīnberige*, a grape, whence, direct, the obs *winberry*, whence, by f/e equation of *win* to WHIN, the current *whinberry*.

**vineal, vineatic.** See prec, para 4.

**vinegar.** See EAGER, para 2, and cf VINE, para 5.

**vinery; vineyard.** See VINE, para 4.

**vinolent; vinose, vinosity, vinous.** See VINE, para 5.

**vintage.** See VINE, para 7.

**vintner.** See VINE, para 6.

**viol, viola.** Sec FIDDLE, para 3.

**violaceous.** See IODINE, para 2.

**violate, violation, violator.** See VIS, para 2.

**violence, violent.** See VIS, para 3.

**violet.** See IODINE, para 2.

**violin, violinist; violoncello, violoncellist.** See FIDDLE, paras 3 and 4.

**viper, viperine.** See VIBRATE, para 2.

**virago.** See VIRILE, para 2.

**vireo.** See VERDANT, para 1, s.f.

**virescent.** See VERDANT, para 1.

**virgate.** See the 1st VERGE, para 2.

**virgin** (n, hence adj), **virginal**, the name **Virginia, virginity, Virgo; devirginate**, whence, anl, **devirgination**.

1. E & M have declared that, like the syn Gr *parthenos*, L *uirgō* (ML *virgō*), a human female not yet 'known' by a man, is o.o.o. Perh *uirgō* is a contr of *\*uirigō*, itself a contr of *\*uiriigō*: *uiri-*, c/f of *uir*, a man+*ig-*, c/f of *eg-*, r of *egēre*, to lack+ nom ending -*ō*: a girl or a woman that has lacked a man. (Again *ex castris ignorantiae*: Could *parthenos* be an 'easing' of *\*parsthenos*, contr of *\*parasthenos*, with n-suffix -*os* substituted for adj-suffix -*ēs*, *\*parasthenēs* (cf *asthenēs*, weak: *a-*, not, without) meaning 'short of (complete) strength': *para*, beside, just missing+*sthenos*, strength, prowess: a human female lacking that fulfilment, that better health and strength, which ensue upon marriage?) Webster, however, suggests that *uirgō* is akin to L *uirga*, a supple and flexible branch: 'the supple one'?

2. L *uirgō*, whence the zodiacal *Virgo*, has acc *uirgin*em (o/s uir*gin*-), ML *v-*, whence OF *virgine*, OF-MF *virgene* (MF *virge*, late MF-F *vierge*), ME *virgine*, E *virgin*. The derivative adj *uirginālis* becomes OF-F *virginal*, adopted by E, and the derivative n *uirginitās*, acc *uirginitat*em, becomes OF-F *virginité*, whence E *virginity*; the derivative PN *Uirginius* has f *Virginia*, adopted by E, whence, after 'the *Virgin* Queen', the E province, then A state, of *Virginia*.

3. From the o/s *uirgin*-, ML *virgin*-, ML formed *dēvirgināre*, to deflower, pp *dēvirginātus*, whence 'to *devirginate*'.

**virgule.** See the 1st VERGE, para 2.

**virial.** See VIS, para 1.

**virid, viridian, viridine.** See VERDANT, para 2.

**virile, virility; virago.**—virtual, virtue, virtuosity, virtuoso, virtuous.—Gmc: obs wer; werewolf.

1. *Virile* and *virility* derive from late MF-F *viril, virilité*: ML *virīlis, virīlitās*: L *uirīlis*, whence

*uirīlitās*, acc *uirīlitātem*: L *uir*, a man (opp woman): akin to Skt *vīrás*, Lith *výras*; Go *wair*, OFris, OS, OHG, OE *wer*, with OE var *were*, as in *werewulf*, lit 'man-wolf', whence E *werewolf* (cf WOLF); ON *verr*; OIr *fer*, W *gwr*, OC etymon *\*viros*. The IE r alternates between *\*wir-* and *\*wīr-*. Perh ult akin to L *uīs*, strength, pl *uīres*.

2. Irreg from L *uir* comes L *uirāgō*, a woman as strong and brave as a man: whence late MF-F *virago* (pej), adopted by E.

3. Formed from L *uir* is *uirtus*, much as *iuventus*, youth, from *iuven*is, young; orig '(male) strength', it soon comes to mean both 'courage' and 'moral worth' (in women, narrowed to 'chastity'): OF-F *vertu*, adopted by ME: hence, reshaped after L, the E *virtue*. Derivative ML *virtuālis* yields EF-F *virtuel* and E *virtual*, and derivative LL *uirtuōsus* becomes OF-MF *vertuos*, with var *vertuous* (cf EF-F *vertueux*, f -*ueuse*)—ME *vertuous*—reshaped E *virtuous*. The It derivative *virtuoso* (imm from *virtú*), used as n, acquires sense 'man of exceptional merit or talent' and, as such, is adopted by E (cf EF-F *virtuose*); F *vertu* occurs in *objets de vertú*, adopted by E, and It *virtù* in the collective E syn *virtu*; F *virtuosité* (imm from F *virtuose*) becomes E *virtuosity*.

**virose, virosis.** See VIRULENCE, para 1.

**virtual, virtue, virtuosity, virtuoso, virtuous.** See VIRILE, para 3.

**virulence, virulent; virose, virosis; viruliferous**— cf **virific.**—**ooze**, whence **oozy**; contrast **ooze, sap,** juice, whence 'to **ooze**' or **percolate.**—**weasel,** whence the adj **weaselly** and the phrase (Theodore Roosevelt's) **weasel words,** from a weasel's sucking out the contents of an egg.

1. L *uīrus*, ML *vīrus*, the sap or juice of plants, slime, whence, from poisonous plants, poison: adopted by F and E, which add several nuances. L *uīrus* is akin to Skt *viṣa*, Av *vīša-* or *vīša-*, and, phon more remote, MIr *fī*; cf also paras 2 and 3. There are two derivative L adjj: *uīrulentus*, whence LL *uīrulentia*, and *uīrōsus*, whence, resp, late MF-F *virulent*, EF-F *virulence*, both adopted by E, and E *virose*, which has perh prompted SciL *virosis*. Whereas E *virific*=ML *virus*+forma-tive -*i-*+-*fic*, making, *viruliferous*=E virulent+ formative -*i-*+-*ferous*, bringing, hence causing.

2. Prob akin to L *uīrus* are ON *veisa*, slime, and OE *wāse*, slimy mud, whence ME *wose*, whence E *ooze*. *Ooze*, mire, has app been influenced by *ooze*, sap or juice, from OE *wōs*, akin to the syn MLG *wōs* and Lett *vasa*. In both E words, there has been a wearing-down, comparable to that of Gr *īós* (for *\*wīsós*).

3. Perh akin to L *uīrus* and esp to the *uīrus*-related Skt *visra*, musty-smelling, is OE *wesole, wesle*, ME *wesele*, E *weasel*, certainly akin to OHG *wisala*, MHG *wisele*, G *Wiesel*, MD *wesele, wesel, wessel*, D *wezel*, and ON *vīsla*—perh cf OHG *wisa*, MHG *wise*, G *Wiese*, a meadow, ON *veisa*, a puddle, OE *wās*, mire, dampness. (Walshe.)

4. The IE r is prob *\*weis-*.

**vis,** as in **vis comica; vim; virial.**—**violable** (neg inviolable), violate, violation, violator.—violence, violent.

1. *Vim*, energy, is adopted from the acc of ML *vīs*, L *uīs*, strength, esp as exercised against someone, hence violence; the ML *vīs* occurs in *vis comica*, the comic spirit. The L pl is *uīrēs*, with s *uīr-*, whence G *Virial*, the E *virial* of Phys. L *uīs* is akin to the approx syn Homeric Gr *īs*, for *\*wīs*, and Skt *váyas*. The IE r is *\*wī-*, strength, vigour.

2. The IE r *\*wī-*, L *uī-*, occurs in L *uiolāre*, to force, to do violence to, hence esp to rape (a woman). Derivative *uiolābilis* and its LL neg *inuiolābilis* yield E *violable* and *inviolable*, with *inviolability* deriving from LL *inuiolābilitās*. From the pp *uiolātus* come E 'to *violate*' and the archaic adj *violate* (neg *inviolate*), and also L *uiolātiō* (acc *uiolātiōnem*) and L *uiolātor*, whence MF-F *violation*, adopted by E, and MF-F *violateur*, whence—unless straight from L—the E *violator*.

3. Also from the L r *uī-* comes L *uiolentus* (adj suffix *-olentus*), whence *uiolentia*: thence, via MF-F, the E *violent* and *violence*.

**visa.** See VIDE, para 2, s.f.

**visage.** See VIDE, para 2.

**vis-à-vis.** See VIDE, para 2.

**viscera, visceral, viscerous;** cf the element *viscero-*; **eviscerate, evisceration.**

1. L *uīscus* (o/s *uīscer-*), usu in pl *uīscera*, entrails, ML *v-*, adopted by E: and L *uīscus* is prob related to the syn ML *vistilia*, and also to Skt *veṣka*, a noose, ON *visp*, a wisp, and therefore to E *whisk*, with 'basic idea: to turn, wind' (Webster).

2. Derivative LL *uīscerālis* yields *visceral*, with mdfn *viscerous*—perh suggested by LL *uīscereus*.

3. Derivative *ēuīscerāre*, to disembowel, has pp *ēuīscerātus*, whence both 'to *eviscerate*' and LL *ēuīscerātiō*, o/s *ēuīscerātiōn-*, whence *evisceration*.

**viscid** (whence **viscidity**), **viscose, viscosity, viscous, Viscum** (whence Chem *viscin*, suffix *-in*).

1. L *uiscum*, mistletoe (Bot *Viscum*), hence the birdlime extracted from its berries, is akin to Gr *ixos* (for *\*wixos*), glue, and perh to OHG *wīhsela*, G *Weichsel*, OSl *višnja*, a cherry. (Hofmann.)

2. L *uiscum*, s *uisc-*, has LL adjj *uiscidus* and *uiscōsus*, whence ML *viscōsitās*; whence E *viscid* and E *viscose* and, perh through MF-F *visqueux*, f *-ueuse*, E *viscous*; ML *viscōsitās*, acc *viscōsitātem*, becomes MF-F *viscosité*, whence E *viscosity*.

**viscount, viscountess, viscounty.** See the 1st COUNT, para 3, and cf VICAR, para 5.

**viscous.** See VISCID, para 2.

**vise,** often **vice,** a screw (obs), hence a firm-holding tool, a clamp, whence 'to *vise* or *vice*': ME *vis*, *vice* (or *vyce*), a spiral stair: OF-F *vis*, OF-MF var *viz*, a spiral stair, a screw: ML *vītis*, L *uītis*, a vine-tendril (VL a screw), a vine, perh akin to *uiēre*, to braid, to interweave; cf the element *viti-*, where, e.g., *viticulture*, grape-growing.

**visé.** See VIDE, para 2, s.f.

**visibility, visible.** See VIDE, para 2.

**Visigoth.** See GOTH, para 2.

**visile.** See VIDE, para 2.

**vision, visionary.** See VIDE, para 2.

**visit, visitant, visitation, visitatorial, visitor.** See VIDE, para 4.

**visor.** See VIDE, para 2.

**vista.** See VIDE, para 3.

**visual, visualize.** See VIDE, para 2.

**vita; vital, vitality, vitalize; vitamin (-ine).** See VIVA, para 3.

**vitellin (or -ine), vitellus.** See WETHER, para 2.

**vitiable, vitiate, vitiation, vitiosity.** See the 1st VICE, para 1.

**vitrage, vitrail, vitrain, vitreous** (whence, anl, **vitreosity** and, with *-eal* for *-eous*, **vitreal**), **vitrescent** (*vitr*eous+*escent*), **vitric** (whence **vitrics**), **vitrine; vitriol** (whence the v **vitriolate**) **vitriolic;** cf the element *vitri-*, var *vitro-*.—**woad.,**

1. L *uitrum* (ML *vitrum*), glass—orig defectively transparent and of a greenish hue—hence, from that greenish-glassy hue, the plant woad: app not a native Italic word, but borrowed, and adapted, from OGmc: cf OFris *wēd*, OHG-MHG *weit*, G *Waid*, Go *wizdila*, OE *wād*, this last becoming ME *wod*, E *woad* (var *wad* or *wade*); prob also (Walshe) Gr *isátis*, for *\*wisátis*. The IE r is perh *\*wīd-*.

2. L *uitrum* has adj *uitreus*, whence E *vitreous*; *vitric*, however, represents ML *vitr*um+adj suffix *-ic*. L *uitrum*, ML *v-*, has the further relevant derivative *vitriolum* (*vitri-*, c/f+dim *-olum*), so named from the glassy sheen of this sulphate: whence MF-F *vitriol*, adopted by E, the F adj *vitriolique* accounting for E *vitriolic*.

3. L *uitrum*, ML *vitrum*, becomes MF-F *vitre*, with the foll derivatives adopted by E: EF-F *vitrage*, EF-F *vitrail* (late MF *vitral*), EF-F *vitrine* (1836 in sense 'glass showcase'). B & W.

**vitular, vituline.** See WETHER, para 2.

**vituperable, vituperate, vituperation, vituperative.** See the 1st VICE, paras 3 and 4.

**viva, viva!, viva-voce, qui-vive, vive le roi!, viveur, bon-vivant, modus vivendi; vivacious, vivacity; vivarium; vivid,** whence **vividness.**—For the full cpds **vivification, vivify—viviparous—vivisection,** see the element *vivi-*.—**vital, vitality, vitalize.**—**victual(s)** and **viand.**—L prefix-cpds: **convivial, convivium; redivivus; revival, revive; sempervivum; survival, survive, survivor**—Gmc cognates: **quick** (adj, hence adv and n), whence **quicken** and **quickness; quickly; quicksand** and **quicksilver;**—**quitch grass.**—**whitlow.**—C: **whiskey,** q.v. at AQUA, para 6.—Gr cognates: **zodiac, zodiacal; Zoe, zoic, zoism, zooid, zoon**—**zoology,** whence **zoological** (note **zoological gardens,** whence, by abbr and by ellipsis, **zoo**) and, anl, **zoologist** and **zoologize; zoophyte, zoospore,** and, anl, many other cpds—cf the element *zoo-*. Sep BION.

### Latin: Simples

1. L *uīuus*, ML *vīvus*, alive, comes from *uīuere*, ML *vīvere*, to be alive, to live, s *uīu-*: for the IE cognates, see para 14. The words and phrases adopted from L or from a R derivative include:

*vīva!* (Long) live . . .!: It: ML *vivat*, Let him live, from ML *vivere*; cf *vive le roi!*, (Long) live the king (L *rex*): F;

*viva-voce*, an oral examination, coll shortened to *viva*, is L *uīua uoce*, lit 'with live voice', i.e. by word of mouth;

*modus vivendi*, a way of life: ML: L *modus uīuendi*, a way, or mode, of living;

*viveur*, lit 'one who lives', esp 'one who lives well' (materialistic), syn with *bon-vivant*, '(a) good-living' (man): F;

*qui-vive, on the*, on the alert: from the late MF-F n *qui-vive*, itself from *Qui vive* (subj), Who lives? Who goes there?

2. Those simple L derivatives of *uīvere* (s *uīu-*, ML *vīv-*), to live, which concern E, include:

*uīuāx*, ML *vīvāx*, full of life, lively, whence LL *uīuācitās*, ML *vīvācitās* (acc *vīvācitāt*em): whence It *vivace*, adopted by Mus, and E *vivacious* (perh imm from a VL-ML *\*vīvācius*); late MF-F *vivacité*, whence E *vivacity*;

*uīuidus*, ML *vīvidus*, animated, very lively, hence brilliant, whence E *vivid*;

*uīuārius*, pertaining to living creatures, whence *uīuārium*, ML *vīvārium*, a fish-pond or -preserve, whence E *vivarium*, further anglicized as *vivary*.

3. L *uīuere*, s *uīu-*, has r *uī-* (ML *vī-*), present also in *uīta* (s *uīt-*, r *uī-*), life, the opp of death, hence also, either a means or a way of life: cf erudite E *vita*, a biography, from ML *vīta*. The derivative L adj *uītālis* and its own derivative *uītālitās* yield MF-F *vital*, adopted by E, and EF-F *vitalité*, whence E *vitality*; derivative F *vitaliser* and *vitalisme* account for 'to *vitalize*' and *vitalism*.

4. L *uīuere* has gerundive *uīuendus*, neu pl *uiuenda*, whence VL *vīvanda*, taken as sing n: whence OF-F *viande*, orig 'food', hence, from C15, 'flesh as food', whence E *viand*, esp in pl for 'provisions, fare'. *Victual*, now usu pl, is reshaped (but with the mute-*c* pron retained), perh imm after EF-F *victuailles* and certainly, ult, after L, from ME *vitaille*, adopted from MF (the OF-early MF form is *vituaille*): ML *vīctuālia*, LL *uīctuālia*, orig the neu pl of LL adj *uīctuālis*, itself from L *uīctus* (gen *-ūs*), a means of living, a diet, from *uī-*, the r of *uīuere*. 'To *victual*' derives partly from the E n and partly from the OF-EF *avitailler* and its derivative, the late MF-F *ravitailler*, which has prompted 'to *revictual*'. *Victualler* derives partly from 'to *victual*' and partly from MF *vitaillier* (EF-F *victuailleur*).

## Latin Compounds

5. For the full cpds *vivification* (*vivify*)—*viviparous*—*vivisection*, see the element *vivi-*.

6. The foll L prefix-cpds have affected E:

*conuīua*, a fellow-banqueter, whence L *conuīuium*, a banquet, whence LL *conuīuiālis*, whence E *convivial*, whence *conviviality*;

L *rediuīuus*, ML *redivīvus*, living *re-* or again, hence revived, adopted by literary E;

L *reuiuere*, to live again, ML *revīvere*: OF-F *revivre*, whence, after ML *vīvus*, the E 'to *revive*'; LL *reuiuificāre*, to bring to life again (*re-* +

*uīuificāre*), pp *reuīuificātus*, whence LL *reuīuificatiō*, o/s *-ficātiōn-*: whence 'to *revivify*' and *revivification*;

L *semperuīuus*, ML *-vīvus*, whence L *semperuīuum*, LL *semperuīua*, ML *semperviva*, whence E *semperive*, the everlasting (plant, flower), displaced by Bot (SciL) *Sempervivium*;

L *superuīuere*, ML *-vīvere*, to live on, go on living, whence OF-F *survivre* (OF-MF var *sor-*), whence 'to *survive*', whence both *survival* and *survivor*; the obsol *survivance* is adopted from EF-F.

## Germanic

7. Akin to L *uīuus* (perh for *\*qūiuus*, ? ult for *\*guiguus* or *\*gwiguus*), is OE *cwic*, *cwicu*, alive, living ('the *quick* and the dead'), ME *cwic*, later *quic*, latest *quick*, E *quick*: cf OFris and OS *quik*, OHG *queck*. OE *cwic* has derivative *cwician*, to restore to, or to endow with, life, whence 'to *quick*', superseded by ME-E 'to *quicken*'.

8. Intimately related to and prob derived from OE *cwic*, alive, is OE *cwice*, whence *quitch*, so named from its 'persistence' in living; *couch grass* is a f/e mdfn of *quitch grass*, which does somewhat resemble a thick, springy mat.

9. The derivative *quick*, sensitive flesh, esp under a finger- or a toe-nail, perh helps to explain the mysterious *whitlow*, a painful inflammation of the last phalanx of a toe or finger, for app it derives from dial *whickflaw*, for dial *quickflaw*, a flaw, esp an inflammation, at or very near the quick: cf ON *kvika* (from the adj *kvikr*), the quick. The element *whick-* becomes *white*, as in the dial var *whiteflaw*, then *whit-*, as in the var *whitflaw*, by f/e: in a fully developed whitlow, the surface is white.

## Greek

10. Akin to L *uīuus* is Gr *bios*, life, mode or life, prob for *\*biwos* (IE *\*guiuos*): cf para 14. For the simple *bion* and for the cpds *biography* and *biology*, see the sep entries.

11. Akin to Gr *bios* and L *uīuere* are Gr *zēn*, to live, and—with the normal '*e* in vv, *o* in nn' alternation—*zōos*, alive, living, neu *zōon*, perh adopted by Zoo as *zoon*, which, however, is more prob an adaptation of Gr *zōion*, a living creature, itself prob from *zōos*; cf Gr *zōē*, life, whence the PN *Zoe* and the n *zoism*; *zooid*, prompted by Gr *zōieidēs*, like (*-eidēs*) a *zōion* or animal. Note both that the *zē-* of *zēn* answers to IE *\*gui-* (cf para 14) and that *bios* has extn *biotos*, life, whence the adj *biotikos*, whence E *biotic*, whence *anti-biotic*, adj hence n.

12. Gr *zōion* has c/f *zōo-*, contr *zō-*; whence E *zoo-*, as in *zoology*, the science (cf *-logy* at element *-loger*) of animal life—*zoophyte*, ult from Gr *zōophuton* (cf the element *-phyte*, a plant)—*zoospore* (cf SPORE and the element *-spora*).

13. From Gr *zōion* derives the dim *zōidion* (LL *zōdion*), with adj *zōidiakos*, as in *zōidiakos kuklos*, an animal circle, hence the elliptical n *zōidiakos*, whence, partly by contr, the L *zōdiacus* (Cicero),

whence MF-F *zodiaque*, whence E *zodiac*; derivative late MF-F *zodiacal* is adopted by E.

## Indo-European

14. Besides L *uīuus* and *uīta*, OE *cwic*, Gr *bios* and *zēn*, the foll IE cognates are to be noted: Go *qius*, gen *qiwis*—W *byw*, OIr *bīu*, *bīo*—OSl *žive* and Lith *gyvas*—Skt *jīvás*, all 'alive, living', with connotation 'lively'. There are corresp vv—cf Skt *jívati*, OSl *živetŭ*, OP *giwa*, he lives, Arm *keam*, I live, and OSl *žiti*, Hit *hwes*, to live (*hwiszi*, he lives, and *hwesas*, *hwesus*, *hwisas*, alive, esp—of meat—raw).

15. The IE r is app \**guei-* or \**guī-*, to live, with extnn in *-o* and *-u*; the \**gu-* is occ represented as \**gw-*; of OE *cwic*, the IE original would perh be \**gwig-*.

**vivacious, vivacity.** See prec, para 2.

**vivarium, vivary.** See VIVA, para 2.

**vivid.** See VIVA, para 2.

**vivification, vivify; viviparous; vivisection; vivisepulture.** See the element *vivi-*.

**vixen.** See FOX, para 2.

**viz.** See VIDE, para 1.

**vizier** or **vizir**: late MF-F *vizir*, Tu *vezīr*, *vizīr*: Per *vizīr*: OPer *vitchira*: cf Ar *wazīr*, lit a porter, from *wazara*, to carry a burden, itself from Per.

**vizor.** See VIDE, para 2.

**vocable, vocabulary, vocabulum; vocal, vocalism, vocalist, vocality, vocalize** (whence **vocalization**); **vocation** (whence **vocational**), **vocative** (adj, hence n); **vociferant, vociferate, vociferation, vociferous; vocule; voice** (n, hence v), whence **voiceless; vouch, voucher, vouchsafe; vowel; vox humana** and **vox populi**—cf **voix céleste.**—Gr: **epic, epos.**—L cpds, incl R derivatives: **advocacy, advocate** (n, v), **advocation, advocatory; advowson: avocation,** whence, **anl, avocative; avouch,** whence **avouchment; avow,** whence **avowal; convocant, convocate, convocation—convoke; equivocal, equivocate, equivocation, equivoque; evocable, evocation, evocative, evocatory—evoke; invocable, invocation—invoke; plurivocal; provocable, provocation, provocative—provoke; revocable** (and **irrevocable), revocation—revoke; semivocal; univocal.**

## European

1. Behind all these words stands L *uōx* (ML *vōx*), o/s *uōc-*: cf Skt *vāk*, Av *vāxš* (acc *vāčem*), the voice, and *váčas*, a word—Tokh A *wak*, B *wek*, voice—MIr *fūaimm*, a noise (Ga *fuaim*), OC etymon \**vokmen*, and syn Cor *guith* or *gyc* (*gyk*) —OP *wackis*, a war-cry—Homeric *opon* (acc), Attic *épos* (nom), a word, for \**wopon* and \**wepos*— OHG *giwahe*, fame: for vv, cf Skt *vakti*, Ve *vivakti* (*vi-* redup), he speaks, *vavǎca*, he has spoken, Skt *vocá-*, he spoke—OP *wackī*twei, to entice (speak fair words to)—OHG gi-*wah*annēn (*gi-* int), MHG gew*äh*enen (pt gew*uoc*), Gerw*äh*nen. The OGmc r is \**wah-*; the IE, \**wek-* alternating with \**wok-*, the voice, to speak. (E & M; Hofmann; Walshe.) Perh cf also the Hit *wek-*, to ask, *wekun*, I asked.

## Greek

2. Gr *epos*, speech, a word, hence a story (in verse), a song (esp of war or adventure), is adopted by E for epic, whether general or particular; the derivative adj *epikos* becomes L *epicus*, whence both EF-F *épique* and, prob independently, E *epic*, adj, hence also n.

## Latin: Simples

3. L *uōx*, the voice, hence *uōces*, sounds made by the voice, esp words, hence also in sing, has the ML form *vōx*, as in *vōx Dei*, the voice of God, and *vōx populi*, that of the people, as well as in the organ-stops *vōx angelica* (F *voix céleste*) and *vōx humana*.

4. L *uōx*, ML *vōx*, acc *vōcem*, yields OF *voiz*, MF *vois* (EF-F *voix*, reshaped after L): ME *vois* or *voys*, later *voice*: E *voice*, whence 'to *voice*'; whence *voiceful* and *voiceless*.

5. On the L o/s *uōc-* (ML *vōc-*) are formed the foll L simples relevant to E:

*uōcālis*, endowed with voice or speech, whence (EF-F and) E *vocal*, with extn *vocalic*, of or like the vowel sounds; derivative LL *uōcālitās*, euphony, gives us *vocality*; derivative F *vocaliser* (prob after It *vocalizzare*) and its own derivative *vocalisation* lead to E 'to *vocalize*' and *vocalization*, and derivative F *vocaliste* to E *vocalist*;

*uōcālis littera*, a fully voiced letter, is used elliptically as n *uōcālis*, whence MF *voiel* (EF-F *voyelle*), whence E *vowel*;

*uōcula*, a feeble voice-sound, whence Phon *vocule*;

and esp the v *uocāre*, to name (apply a sound to), to address, to call, hence also to invoke, with presp *uocans*, o/s *uocant*, whence E *-vocant* in cpds, and pp *uocātus* (ML *v-*), whence 'to *vocate*', rare outside cpds; on the pp s *uocāt-* are formed *uocātiō*, a calling, a summons, acc *uocātiōn*em (ML *v-*), the adjj *uocātiuus* and *uocātōrius*, and the LL agent *uocātor*: whence, resp, OF-F *vocation*, adopted by E—E *vocatīve* (prob imm from MF-F *vocatif*)— E *-vocatory*—E *-vocator*.

6. Also from L *uocāre* derives *uocābulum*, a manner, or a means, of summoning, hence a name, hence a noun (opp *uerbum*, ML *verbum*): MF-F *vocable*, adop'ed by E for a word (esp in its phon aspect). The derivative ML adj *vocabulārius* has neu *vocabulārium*, a receptacle (implied by *-ārium*) of words, hence an orderly assemblage of words: late MF-F *vocabulaire*: E *vocabulary*.

7. On L *uōci-*, cf of *uōx*, is—perh as if for *uōciferre*—formed *uōciferāri* (LL *-āre*), to cry out: presp *uōciferans*, o/s *uōciferant-*, E *vociferant*; pp *uōciferātus*, whence both 'to *vociferate*' and L *uōciferātiō*, acc *uōciferātiōn*em, MF-F *vocifération*, E. *vociferation*; *vociferous*, anl from F *vocifère*.

## Romance: Simples

8. L *uocāre* becomes OF-MF *vochier*, MF *voucher*, whence 'to *vouch*'—partly aphetic for 'to *avouch*', which came into ME from MF *avochier*,

later *avoucher*, from ML *advocāre* (LL *aduocāre*): cf para 10.

### Latin: Full Compounds

9. L *uōcālis* has cpd *semiuōcālis*, whence E *semivocal*; and L *uōc-*, o/s of *uōx*, has three cpd adjj in -*uōcus*:

LL *aequiuocus*, of id sound (or form), but not of id meaning, whence not only MF-EF adj, EF-F n, *équivoque*, whence E *equivoque*, occ anglicized as *equivoke*, both slightly obsol, but also, after E *vocal*, E *equivocal*; derivative LL *aequiuocāre*, to be equal in name, but not in meaning, to, pp *aequiuocātus*, whence both 'to *equivocate*' and LL *aequiuocātiō*, o/s -*uocātiōn-*, whence E *equivocation*;

ML *pluriuocus*, of more than two meanings, whence, anl, E *plurivocal*;

LL *uniuocus*, of only one name or meaning, whence, anl, E *univocal*, opp *equivocal*.

### Latin: Prefix-Compounds

10. The foll L prefix-cpds, either of *uocāre* or of its pp *uocātus*, have affected E:

*aduocātus*, he who assists a man summoned *ad*, to, justice, OF-EF *advocat* (EF-F *avocat*), E *advocate*; derivative ML *advocātia* yields—prob via MF—the E *advocacy*; derivative L *aduocātiō*, o/s *aduocātiōn-*, yields *advocation*, and from the ML acc *advocātiōn*em derives OF-MF *avoaison*, *avoeison*, whence ME *avoueisoun*, *avoweisoun*, whence E *advowson*, a legal term; LL *aduocātor* perh suggested, anl, the E *advocatory*;

*aduocāre* becomes OF-F *avouer*, orig to recognize as one's overlord, hence as valid, hence (late MF-F) to acknowledge (a fault), whence ME *avowen*, E 'to *avow*';

*auocāre*, to call away, pp *auocātus*, whence *auocātiō*, o/s *auocātiōn-*, whence E *avocation*, orig a subsidiary occupation;

*conuocāre*, to call together, pp *conuocātus*, whence both *conuocātiō* and LL *conuocātor*: MF-F *convoquer*, E 'to *convoke*'—MF-F *convocation*, adopted by E—E *convocator*; the E n *convocant* derives from ML *convocant-*, o/s of *convocans*, L *conuocans*, presp of *conuocāre*;

*ēuocāre*, to call ē-, out, to summon forth, becomes MF-F *évoquer*, whence 'to *evoke*', and derivative F *évocable*, E *evocable*; derivative *ēuocātiō*, o/s *ēuocātiōn-*, becomes E *evocation*, whence, anl, *evocative*; LL *ēuocātor* becomes *evocator*, perh imm suggested by F *évocateur*;

*inuocāre*, to call *in-*, upon, EF-F *invoquer*, E 'to *invoke*', whence, anl, *invocable*; derivative (from pp *inuocātus*) *inuocātiō*, ML acc *invocātiōn*em, OF-F *invocation*, adopted by E;

*prōuocāre*, to call *prō-* or forth, OF-F *provoquer*, E 'to *provoke*'; LL *prōuocābilis*, E *provocable*; derivative (from pp *prōuocātus*) *prōuocātiō*, ML acc *prōvocātiōn*em, MF-F *provocation*, adopted by E, and LL *prōuocātiuus*, ML *prōvocātivus*, E *provocative*;

*reuocāre*, to call *re-* or back, MF-F *révoquer*, E

'to *revoke*'; derivative *reuocābilis*, neg *irreuocābilis*, late MF-F *révocable*, *irrévocable*, E *revocable*, *irrevocable*; (from pp *reuocātus*) *reuocātiō*, ML acc *revocātiōn*em, MF-F *révocation*, E *revocation*, and LL *reuocatōrius*, E *revocatory*.

**vocabulary.** See prec, para 6.

**vocal, vocalist, vocality, vocalize.** See VOCABLE, para 5.

**vocation, vocative** (Gram n, already in LL). See VOCABLE, par 5, s.f.

**vociferant, vociferate, vociferation, vociferous.** See VOCABLE, para 7.

**vocule.** See VOCABLE, para 5.

**vodka.** See WATER, para 5.

**vogue,** adopted from late MF-F, derives from MF-F *voguer*, to row (a boat): cf, sem, the coll 'be in the *swim*': either from OProv *vogar* or from It *vogare*, both of the one origin, but that origin, o.o.o.—unless OGmc; perh an -*o-* mdfn of OHG *wēgan* (var be*wēgan*), MHG be*wēgen*, G be*wēgen*, to cause to move (cf VIA).

**voice, voiceless.** See VOCABLE, para 4.

**void, voidance, voider.** See VACANT, para 6.

**voile.** See VEIL, paras 1 and 4.

**voix céleste.** See VOCABLE, para 3.

**vol, volador, volage, volant, volar, volatile, volatility, volatilize, vol-au-vent, vole, volery, volet, volitant, volitation, volitorial; volley** (n, hence v); **volplane,** q.v. at PLANE, para 3, s.f.

1. The Her term *vol*, adopted from OF-F, is lit 'flight'; it derives from OF-F *voler*, to fly, from ML *volāre*, L *uolāre*: o.o.o.: perh (E & M) akin to Skt *garuḍás* (adj), flying (cf L *uolucer*).

2. OF-F *vol*, flight, occurs also in the F-hence-E cookery term *vol-au-vent*, so named—'flight in the wind'—because it is so light. From *voler* come:

*volant*, presp used as adj, hence also as n; both adj and n, adopted by E;

the EF-F card-game term, *vole*, a 'grand slam'—a full flight;

late OF-F *volée*, a flight, hence that of a ball, whence E *volley*;

MF-F *volerie*, a flying, and MF-F *volière*, a (large) birdcage, whence—phon from the former, sem from the latter—E *volery*;

MF-F *volet*, a 'flying' veil (women's), hence an art term, both adopted by E.

3. Irreg from ML *vol*āre, to fly, comes the adj *volar*, of, in, for, by flight—not to be confused with *volar*, of, on, for (etc.) sole of foot or palm of hand, from ML *vola*, L *uola*, sole, palm.

4. ML *volāre* becomes Sp *volar*, whence Sp *volador*, applied, in AE, to several species of flying fish.

5. L *uolāre* has the foll L derivatives affecting E: *uolāticus*, flying, hence flighty, whence OF-F *volage*, flighty, partly adopted by E;

*uolātilis*, MF-EF *volatil*, E *volatile*; derivative EF-F *volatilité*, EF-F *volatiliser*, its F derivative *volatilisation*, become E *volatility*, 'to *volatilize*', *volatilization*.

6. *uolāre* has the freq, used also as int, *uolitāre* to flit about, to flutter, presp *uolitans*, o/s *uolitant-*

ML *v-*, whence E *volitant*, and pp *uolitātus*, ML *v-* whence both 'to *volitate*' and LL *uolitātiō*, a fl ttering (esp of leaves), o/s *uolitātiōn-*, ML *v-*, whence E *volitation*—cf the OF-F v *voleter*. From ML *volit*āre SciL has formed *volitores*, birds that fly, whence the E adj *volitorial*.

**volatility, volatile.** See prec, para 5, s.f.

**volcanic, volcano; Vulcan, Vulcanian, vulcanite, vulcanize.**

*Volcanic* comes from F *volcanique*, itself influenced by the var *vo-* of the F and It n in its passage from It *vulcanico*, the adj of *vulcano*, var *volcano*, from It *Vulcano*, *Volcano*, from ML *Vulcānus*, *Volcānus*, L *Uu-*, whence E *Vulcan*, that god who, in L, has adj *Uulcānius*, ML *Vu-*, whence E *Vulcanian*; E *Vulcan* has derivatives *vulcanite* and *vulcanize*, whence *vulcanization*. L *Uulcānus* or *Uolcānus* app derives, phon, from Cretan *Welkhanos* and owes its sense 'the god of (destructive) fire' to the Etruscans, who perh brought the Cretan name to Italy and there changed it.

**vole** (1), the mouse-like rodent, is elliptical for dial *volemouse*, of Scan origin: cf Nor dial *voll*, a field, from the syn ON *völlr*, itself akin to E *wold*, a forest (obs), hence a low wooded hill (obsol), hence an upland plain, even one that lacks a wood: ME *wold*, *wāld*, woodland, a weald, from OE *weald*, a wood, a forest, wooded high land, whence the E doublet *weald*. OE *weald* is akin to OFris and OS *wald*, OHG-MHG *walt*, G *Wald*, a forest: o.o.o.: perh (Walshe) cf WILD.

**vole** (2), in card-games. See VOL, para 2.

**volency, volent.** See VOLITION, para 2.

**volery; volet.** See VOL, para 2.

**volitant, volitate, volitation.** See VOL, para 6.

**volition,** whence **volitional** and, anl, both **volitient** and **volitive; voluntary** (adj, hence n), whence, direct, **voluntaryism** and, anl, **voluntarism**—**involuntary; voluntative; volunteer,** adj and n (whence v); **volence, volency,** and **volent,** esp in **benevolence, benevolent,** and **malevolence, malevolent; voluptuary, voluptuous; velleity;—nolle** (prosequi), **noli me tangere, nolition.**—Gmc cognates: **will,** n, whence **willful** (cf FULL), now usu **wilful; will,** v, (1) to wish strongly, to enjoin, whence the pa, vn **willing,** and (2), auxiliary; **willy-nilly; wilt** (2 person sing); **won't; would** and **would-be;—William,** whence the flower-name **sweet william**—**Will** and **will-o'-the-wisp**—**Willy:** cf **Bill, Billy, billy; guillemot;—well,** adv, hence adj—**welcome**—**welfare** and **farewell; weal, wealth,** and **commonweal, commonwealth;—wale,** n (a choice) and v (to choose).—Cf the sep GALA (where also GALLANT).

1. L *uelle* (ML *v-*), to wish, to wish strongly, is prob for *\*uolle* for *\*uolere*, s and r *uol-* (ML *vol-*): cf L *uolō*, I wish, OL *uolt* (L *uult*), he wishes: akin to Lith pa-*velt*, OSI *veléti*, to command, Go *wili*, he wishes (cf *will* below), and prob—with *r* for *l*—the Ve *vurīta*, may he wish, and Skt *váram*, a wish; also to Gr *elpomai*, I hope, *elpis*, a hope, both for *\*welp-*, an extn of *\*wel-*. The IE r is prob *\*wel-*, with varr *\*wal-*, *\*wil-*, *\*wol-*, *\*wul-*, to wish, to

wish strongly, hence to hope, to command. For the *e-o* mutation, cf OHG *wellēn*, MHG *wellen*, later *wollen*, G *wollen*, to wish; for the *a* var, cf *wale* below.

### Latin

2. L *uelle* has presp *uolens*, used also as adj 'well-wishing, favourable', o/s *uolent-*, ML *v-*, whence E *volent*; derivative LL *uolentia* yields *\*volence*, *volency*. The L adj *uolens* has cpds *beneuolens*, whence *beneuolentia*, and *maleuolens*, whence *maleuolentia*: MF-EF *benevolence*, adopted by E; E *benevolent*: E *malevolence*, *malevolent*.

3. The L *uol-*, ML *vol-*, of *uolō* and *uolens*, occurs in the foll simple derivatives relevant to E:

ML *volitiō*, acc *volitiōn*em, EF-F *volition*, adopted by E;

L *uoluntās*, ML *v-*, orig goodwill, hence strong wish, intention, hence, in Phil, will (a wish that lasts, and gets things done), whence the adj *uoluntārius*, whence—cf MF-F *volontaire*—the E *voluntary*; the LL neg *inuoluntārius* gives us *involuntary* (cf MF-F *involontaire*); from the MF-F *volontaire* (also n already in EF) in its MF-EF var *voluntaire* comes the E adj and n *volunteer*.

4. Akin to L *uolō* and *uolens* is L *uolup*, neu of *\*uolupis*, agreeable (that which one wishes for oneself or for another), app a vocalization of *\*uolpis*, s *\*uolp-*: cf the *\*welp-* of PGr *\*welpis*, a hope. Hence L *uoluptās* (-*tās* perh for -*itās*), pleasure as opp pain, hence a physical, esp sexual, pleasure, with adjj *uoluptuārius* (for orig *uoluptārius*) also as n, and *uoluptuōsus*, whence, via the ML forms in *v-*, the E n *voluptuary* and MF-F *voluptueux*, f -*ueuse*, E *voluptuous*.

5. Straight from L *uelle* or rather from ML *velle* comes the ML *velleitās* (in Phil): EF-F *velléité*, E *velleity*.

6. L *uelle* has neg *nolle*, to not wish, to be unwilling, prob as a b/f from and contr of *ne*, not+*uolō*, I wish; *nōlī* (imp) and *nolle* and *nōlō*, I do not wish, occur in such legal phrases as *noli me tangere*, Do not touch me, *nolle prosequi* (to be unwilling to prosecute) and *nolo contendere* (I do not wish to assert innocence). As opp *volition*, arises *nolition*—coined by F and adopted by E.

### Germanic

7. The E n *will*, a wish, a firm intention, the power of choosing, hence 'a last will and testament', derives, via ME *will*, varr *wille*, *wile*, from OE *willa* (var *will*): cf OFris *willa*, Go *wilja*, OS *willio*, OHG *willo*, MHG-G *wille*, MD *wille*, MD-D *wil*, ON *vili* (with modern Scan cognates): all very intimately related to the OE and other OGmc vv mentioned in the next two paras.

8. Corresp exactly to *will*, n, is 'to *will*' or wish for, hence to desire, to command, to determine to do, to influence by one's will, and finally to bequeath by will: archaic 'thou *willest*' and 'God *willeth*'; pt and pp *willed*: OE *willian*: cf OFris *willa* (*wella*), Go *wiljan*, ON *vilja*.

9. Closely related to OE *willian* is OE *willan* (pt

*wolde*), ME *willen* (pt *wolde*), E *will*, without inf or imp (pt *would*); now only auxiliary, except perh in the jocose 'What *wilt* thou' and the Prayer Book '*Wilt* thou take this man—or this woman—to be . . .?' Cf OSl *voliti*, to wish. The coll adj *would-be*, as in 'a *would-be* gentleman', derives from 'one who *would be*'—wishes to be—something; the contr *won't* (cf *sha'n't*) derives from *woll not*, *woll* being an obs form of *will*; *willy-nilly* is 'will he—won't he' (perh after L *nolens uolens*, unwilling (or) willing), *nilly* deriving from the obs *nill*, to be not willing, to refuse, from OE *nyllan*: *ne*, not+*willan*.

10. From OHG *willo*, will, firm intention (cf para 7), comes the PN *Willehelm* (var *Willi-*), lit 'Helmet of Strong Purpose' (G *Wilhelm*), whence ONF *Willame*, var *-aume*, E *William*, shortened to *Will*, whence folklore *Will o' the wisp*, whence *will-o'-the-wisp*; the pet-form *Bill* has dim *Billy*, whence, by personification of the object, *billy*, a policeman's truncheon.

11. The OF-F name corresp to ONF *Willa(u)me* is *Guillaume*, which has dim *Guillemot*, whence, by personification, the EF-F bird *guillemot*, adopted by E.

12. Akin to OE *willa*, strong wish (cf para 7), is ON *val*, a choice, whence ME *wale*, whence *walen*, E *wale* and 'to *wale*', both obs except in dial; with ON *val*, cf the syn OHG *wale*, MHG *wal*, G *Wahl*.

13. Also akin to OE *willa* is OE *wel*, ME *wel*, late ME *well*, E *well*, adv, whence—via such phrases as 'to feel *well*'—the adj *well*: OE *wel* is akin to OFris *wel*, *wal*, *wol*, OS *wela*, *wala*, *wola*, OHG *wela*, *wola*, MHG *wol*, G *wohl*, MD *wael*, *wail*, *wal*, *wale*, *wole*, *wele*, *weel*, MD-D *wel*, Go *waila*, ON *vel*; basic meaning, 'according to one's will or wish' (Webster).

14. OE *willa* has c/f *wil-*, as in *wilcuma*, a comer (or guest) after one's own wish or will, whence the ME adj *wilcume*, later *welcume*, finally *welcome*, extant in E, whence the n *welcome*, hospitable greeting or treatment; 'to *welcome*' derives from OE *wilcumian* (from *wilcuma*).

15. The adv *wel* occurs in *welfare*, from ME *wel fare*, a well-faring (*fare*, to go, OE *faran*); cf the parting good-wish *Fare well!*, Travel safely, whence the n, *farewell*.

16. Akin to OE *wel* is the OE n *weola*, contr *wela*, whence ME *wele*, E *weal* (cf OS *welo*), wealth (obs), prosperity (obsol), the state (influenced by *commonweal*); ME *wele* has derivative *welthe*, whence E *wealth*, with derivative adj *wealthy*.

17. E *weal* acquires, late in ME, the cpd *common weal*, later *commonweal*, general or public welfare; E *wealth* acquires, in EE, the cpd *commonwealth*, general welfare (obs), the body politic, the state, hence a group of states united for the common weal.

**volitorial.** See VOL, para 6, s.f.

**volley.** See VOL, para 2.

**volplane.** See PLANE, para 3, s.f.

**volt** (1), in horsemanship. Cf VAULT (leap), q.v. at VOLUBLE, para 3.

**volt** (2), in El, whence **voltage**; **voltaic**. The 3rd represents *Voltaic*, adj of Alessandro *Volta* (1745–1827), who devised a machine to measure el currents: whence E *volt*. The PN *Volta* is akin to *vault*, leap.

**Voltaire**, whence **Voltairean** or **Voltairian**: François-Marie Arouet de *Voltaire* (1694–1778), who himself, as a young man, added the 'de Voltaire' from *Voltaire*, his mother's small country-estate.

**volte-face.** See para 3 of:

**voluble**, **volubility**; **volume**, **voluminous**; **volutate**, whence **volutation**; **volute** (adj and n), **volution**; **volva** and **vulva**; **volve** (obs), **volvelle**, **volvent**, **Volvox**, **volvulus**; sep **valve**; **volt** (leap), **volte-face** —cf **vault**, a or to leap, and **vault**, an arched structure.—L prefix-cpds: **advolution**; **circumvolute**, **circumvolution**—**circumvolve**; **convolute**, **convolution**—**convolve**, **convolvulus**; **devolution**, **devolve**; **evolve**, **evolution** (whence **evolutionary**, **evolutionist**, etc.); **interval**; **involucre**—**involute**, **involution**—**involve**, whence **involvement**; **revolt** (n, v), whence the pa **revolting**—**revoluble**—**revolute** (adj), **revolution** (whence **revolutionist**), **revolutionary**—**revolve**, whence **revolver** and pa **revolving**; **supervolute**.—Gr cognates: **elytron**; **helix**, **helical**.—Gmc cognates: **wale**, a stripe—cf **weal**, **wheal**; **walk** (v, hence n), whence **walker** and pa, vn **walking**; **wall** (n, hence v)—cf **interval**; **wallow**, v, hence n; **waltz**; **well** of water, and 'to **well**'—cf **weld**, v (hence n), whence **welder** and **welding**; **welt**, n and dial v—**welter**, v, hence n (whence **welterweight**); **whelk**, a marine snail; **willow**, whence **willowy**—cf **willy**, a large basket.

### Indo-European

1. The key to all the L derivatives, and a cognate of the Gr and Gmc words, is L *uoluere* (ML *volvere*), s and r *uolu-*, to roll or cause to roll, hence to turn over in one's mind; the presp is *uoluens*, o/s *uoluent-* (ML *volvent-*), and the pp *uolūtus* (ML *volūtus*), whence the n *uolūtiō*, o/s *uolūtiōn-* (ML *volūtiōn-*). The r *uolu-* represents an IE *\*wolw-*, a var of *\*welw-*, to roll, occurring without *-w-* in certain IE words. The principal cognates of L *uoluere* are perh Gr *helix* (for *\*welix*), spiral, *elutron*, an envelope (container, case), *eluein* (for *\*weluein*), to roll, and *eiluein* (for *\*weiluein*), to enfold or enwrap—OSl *valiti*, to roll—Skt *válāte*, he turns (round)—EIr *fillim*, I turn, Ga *fill*, to fold or plait, Cor *vaylé*, to wrap, OC *\*yelvo-*, to roll or fold—OHG *wellan*, to roll, and *wallan*, to bubble well, MHG-G *wallen*, and syn OFris *walla*, OS and OE *wallan* (cf E *well* below), Go *afwalwjan*, to roll out, ON *vella*, to boil, and the Gmc causatives noted in para 10 below.

### Latin: Simples

2. L *uoluere*, to roll, whence the obs 'to *volve*', has the foll simple derivatives affecting E: *uolūbilis* (ML *v-*), rolling, turning rapidly, hence

rapid, whence *uolūbilitās*, mobility, also facility of speech, o/s *uolūbilitāt-* (ML *v-*): hence E *voluble* and late MF-F *volubilité*, whence E *volubility*;

*uoluens* (presp), ML o/s *volvent-*, E adj *volvent*; *uolūmen*, a roll, a fold, esp a roll or fold of writing, hence a book: MF-F *volume*, adopted by E; derivative LL *uolūminōsus*, having many coils or folds, whence (F *volumineux* and) E *voluminous*; the senses 'compass, capacity, amplitude' arise in late MF and are taken over by E, with the adj following suit;

*uolūta* (from the pp), a spiral conformation, a scroll-like form: It *voluta*: EF-F *volute*, adopted by E; the E adj *volute* derives from the ML pp *volūtus*;

LL *uolūtiō*, a rolling, a twisting, ML an arch or a vault, o/s *uolūtion-*, whence E *volution*;

*uolūtāre*, to roll often (a freq, hence also an int, of *uoluere*), pp *uolūtātus*, whence 'to *volutate*' or roll about, wallow; derivative *uolūtātiō*, o/s *-ātiōn-*, yields E *volutation*;

*uolua* (ML *volva*), var *uulua* (ML *vulva*), a covering or wrapping, an integument, hence womb and, in Physio sense, vulva; *volva* is adopted by Bot (a membranous sac), *vulva* by Physio and Med (external genital organs of the female): cf Skt *ulva*, var *ulba*, womb, vulva;

ML *volvella* (in form, a dim of *volva*), var *volvellum*, whence E *volvelle*, a device known also as a *lunary*;

SciL *Volvox* (Bio)=ML *volv*(ere)+L suffix *-ox*;

L *uoluola*, var *uoluulus* (in form, a dim), is another name for the *conuoluulus*, ML *convolvulus*, the bindweed, adopted by Bot, hence by ordinary E; *uoluulus*, ML *volvulus*, is form-adopted, sense-adapted, by Med.

3. L *uoluere*, VL-ML *volvere*, has the VL derivative *\*volvita*, whence the ML contr *volta*, a turn, hence a turn in the air: It *volta*: EF-F *volte*, E *volt*, a tech in riding; cf It *volta-faccia*, a turn-face, a turning back to front, hence any complete reversal: EF-F *volte-face*, adopted by E. Also from It *volta*, a leap, EF-F *volte*, comes the E n *vault*, a leap, esp upon or over something; It *volta*, a leap, has derivative *voltare*, to leap, whence late MF-F *volter*, whence 'to *vault*'. VL *\*volvita*, a turn, acquires the further sense 'an arched structure, esp as forming a roof or a ceiling', whence OF-MF *volte*, var *vaulte*, MF *voüte*, *vaüte*, ME *voute*, *vawte*, whence, with *l* restored either from OF-MF or from ML, the E *vault*; derivative MF *voüter*, *vaüter*, var *vaulter*, yields ME *vouten*, *vauten*, whence, after the n, E 'to *vault*' or form, or cover with, a vault.

### Latin: Prefix-Compounds

4. Of the numerous L prefix-cpds of *uoluere*, ML *volvere*, the foll have entered into E:

*aduoluere*, to roll *ad* or towards, pp *aduolūtus*, ML *advolūtus*, whence, anl, the E *advolution*, a rolling towards;

*circumuoluere*, to roll *circum*, around or about, whence 'to *circumvolve*'; from the pp *circumuo-*

*lūtus* derives the E adj *circumvolute*, whence, anl, *circumvolution*;

*conuoluere*, ML *convolvere*, to roll or wrap thoroughly (int *con-*), to enwrap, whence 'to *convolve*'; from the pp *conuolūtus*, ML *-volūtus*, derives the adj and v *convolute*, whence, anl, *convolution*; for the cognate *convolvulus*, see para 2 (above), s.f.;

*dēuoluere*, ML *dēvolvere*, to roll *dē-* or down, whence 'to *devolve*', orig vt, whence the modern sense, to be handed over, to fall, to, as an obligation; pp *dēuolūtus* yields both the rare adj (and obs v) *devolute* and the LL n *dēuolūtiō*, corruption, ML as in the E derivative *devolution*;

*ēuoluere*, ML *ēvolvere*, to roll *ē-* or out, forth, to unroll, whence 'to *evolve*'; the pp *ēuolūtus*, ML *ēvolūtus*, becomes the Geom n, Bot adj, *evolute*; derivative *ēuolūtiō*, ML o/s *ēvolūtiōn-*, yields EF-F *évolution*, whence E *evolution*;

*inuoluere*, ML *involvere*, to envelop, roll up, wrap up, whence 'to *involve*'; pp *inuolūtus*, ML *involūtus*, yields both the tech adj, Geom n, *involute* and the L *inuolūtiō*, ML o/s *involūtiōn-*, whence E *involution*; from L *inuoluere* derives L *inuolucrum*, a wrapping, a wrapper, an envelope or covering, whence EF-F *involucre*, adopted by E;

*reuoluere*, ML *revolvere*, to roll back, hence to turn around, whence late MF-EF *revolver*, whence —though perh imm from ML—'to *revolve*'; pp *reuolūtus*, ML *rev-*, yields both the E adj *revolute* and the LL n *reuolūtiō*, ML acc *revolūtiōnem*, OF-MF *revolution* (EF-F *ré-*), whence E *revolution*; derivative F *révolutionnaire* (1789) becomes E *revolutionary*, adj hence n; as it were blending L *uolubīlis* (see para 2 above) and *reuoluere* is L *reuolūbilis*, whence E *revoluble*, revolvable; from the It derivative *rivoltare*, to turn back (vt), comes late MF-F *révolter*, whence EF-F *révolte*: whence 'to *revolt*' and 'a *revolt*';

*superuoluere*, ML *-volvere*, to roll *super* or over, pp *superuolūtus*, ML *-volūtus*, accounts for the E Bot adj *supervolute*.

### Greek

5. For *helix*, see HELICAL. The Zoo *elytron* is a SciL coinage from Gr *elutron*, an envelope or case, from *eluein*, to roll around (cf para 1); anl from E *elytron* derives the E adj *elytroid*.

### Germanic

6. Some of the OGmc cognates of L *uoluere*, to roll, have been noted in para 1. It is, therefore, convenient to list the Gmc E cognates in alphabetical order. *Wale*, a long or longish mark resulting from lash of whip or blow of rod, hence a ridge, ME *wale*, derives from OE *walu*, akin to Go *walus*, a rod or staff (cf OFris *walu-bera*, a staff-bearer), ON *völr*, a stick with a circular section, and L *uallus*, a stake (cf *uallum*, a palisade): IE base, either *\*waslo-* or *\*walso-* (E & M), a stake, a staff, a rod. E *weal* is merely a var of E *wale*; syn E *wheal* is, in turn, a var of *weal*, a wale, by

VOLUBLE 791 VORACIOUS

f/e confusion with *wheal* (ME *whele*), a pustule, itself related to *whelk* (para 15 below).

7. 'To *walk*,' ME *walken* and *walkien* (pt *walkede*), to walk, OE *wealcan* and *wealcian*, to roll, hence to turn or revolve, is akin to various OGmc vv (esp ON *valka*) meaning 'to full (cloth)' or 'to beat, to work (felt, etc.) by beating' or simply 'to roll'; perh also to L *ualgus*, bow-legged, and certainly to L *uoluere*, to roll, and Skt *válgati*, he skips. As Walshe has suggested, the ME sense 'to walk' has perh derived from the OE senses—from the idea 'to walk with a rolling motion' (as a sailor does).

8. *Wall*, OE *weall*, comes from L *uallum*, a palisaded defensive structure, hence gradually a more solid defence, prob from *uallus*, a stake (cf para 6 above). The derivative L *interuallum*, ML *intervallum*, a space between (*inter*) ramparts, hence a separating space (finally of time): MF-F *intervalle*: E *interval*.

9. 'To *wallow*,' ME *walwen*, OE *wealwian*, to roll oneself about in, e.g., mud or mire, as a pig does, is very closely akin to OE *wielwan* (vt), to roll, itself akin to Go -*walwjan*, to roll: cf para 1 above.

10. 'To *waltz*'—cf the F *valser*—derives from G *walzen*, MHG *walzen*, OHG *walzan*, to roll (vi), which has caus *wälzen*, to roll (vt), MHG *welzen*, OHG *walzēn* (cf Go us-*waltjan*, to roll about); G *walzen*, to roll (vi), has derivative (Austrian) *walzer*, the action of rolling, hence of turning around, hence a dance, whence—prob via F *valse* (1800)—the E n *waltz*; E *waltzer* is prob indebted to F *valseur* (1801).

11. A *well* of water, ME *welle*, OE *wella*, *wiella* (*wylla*), and 'to *well*' or issue, to spring, to flow, as water does, syn ME *wellen*, OE (vt, i.e. caus) *wellan* (*waellan*), *wyllan*, *wiellan*, are very closely akin to OE *weallan* (vi), to well, to bubble forth, to boil: cf also OFris *walla*, OS *wallan*, OHG *wallan*, MHG-G *wallen*, Go *waljan*, to well up, to undulate, and ON *vella*, to boil; and OE *wiell*, a well, OFris *walla*, a well, a spring of water, and OHG *wella*, MHG-G *welle*, a wave, ON *vell*, a bubbling, and several Sl and Skt words for 'a wave', as well as, ult, L *uoluere*, Gr *eluein* (for *weluein*), to roll: cf para 1.

12. 'To *well*' has pp *welled*, whence, by b/f, 'to *weld*', orig by a process of heating metal to a fluid or, at the least, to a plastic state.

13. The dial 'to *welt*' or roll or turn, esp to overturn (vi, vt), comes from ME *welten*, from ON *velta*, to roll (vi); app from ME *welten* comes the ME n *welte*, whence E *welt*, a ridge, a raised stripe, etc.

14. With ME *welten*, to roll, hence to turn, cf ME *weltren*, vi, to roll or tumble about, to wallow; ME *weltren* app derives imm from MD *welteren*, akin to MLG *weltern*, *waltern*; cf the syn ME *walteren*. The ending -*eren* or -*ern* denotes a freq: here of ME *walten*, OE *wealtan*, OHG *walzan* (vi), *walzēn* (vt), ON *velta*: cf paras 9 and 10 above.

15. A *whelk* or large marine snail, ME *welke* or *wilke*, OE *weoloc* or *wioloc*, is akin to MD-D

*welc* or *wilc*, MD *wulc*, D *wulk*, and also to Go -*walwjan*, to roll—'named from its spiral shell' (Webster). The -*h*- has been f/e added by confusion with E *whelk*, a pustule, ME *whelke*, OE *hwylca* (from *hwelian*, to suppurate): cf para 6, s.f., above.

16. *Willow* (tree), ME *wilowe*, vocalization of ME *wilwe*, from OE *welig*, is akin to MD *wilge* (D *wilg*), *willige* (or -*ege*), *willich*, *wulge*—Gr *helikē* (for *welikē*), a willow, and the adj *helix*, spiral, twisted, and therefore to L *uoluere*, to roll, hence to turn.

17. Very closely akin to OE *welig*, willow, is OE *wilige*, a large wicker-basket, made orig of willow twigs: hence the now dial *willy*.

volume, voluminous. See prec, para 2.
voluntary, volunteer. See VOLITION, para 3.
voluptuary, voluptuous. See VOLITION, para 4.
volute, volution. See VOLUBLE, para 2.
volva. See VOLUBLE, para 2.
volvelle. See VOLUBLE, para 2.
volvent. See VOLUBLE, para 2.
Volvox. See VOLUBLE, para 2.
volvulus. See VOLUBLE, para 2.
vomer. See WEDGE, para 3.
vomica. See para 1 of:
vomit (n, v), vomitive, vomitory (adj, hence n); emesis, emetic, emetine.

1. L *uomere*, ML *v*-, to discharge (pus), vomit, has s *uom*-, whence L *uomica*, a vomit, an abscess, adopted by Med, and pp *uomitus*, whence 'to *vomit*'; the E n *vomit* derives from the L n *uomitus* (gen -*ūs*), from the s of the pp, whence also the adj *uomitōrius*, whence *vomitory*, adj, hence n; *vomitive* derives from F *vomitif* (f -*ive*), itself an -*itif* formation from OF-F *vomir* (VL *vomīre* for L *uomere*).

2. L *uomere*, s and r *uom*-, is akin to the syn Gr *emein* (for *wemein*), whence the n *emesis* and the anl adj *emetikos*, whence the Med *emesis* and L *emeticus*, E *emetic* (adj, hence n).

3. With L *uomere* and Gr *emein*, *wemein*, cf the syn Lith *vémti* and Skt *vámiti*, *vamati*, he vomits, and *vāṃtás*, vomited (pp); cf also the ON *vaema*, *vāma*, sea-sickness. The IE r is app *wem*-, to vomit.

voodoo and hoodoo. The latter is an AE var of the former, which comes from Creole F *voudou*, from the Gulf of Guinea Negro word *vodu*, occurring both in Jeji (Dahomey) and in Ewe (Togoland and Dahomey) and meaning 'a good, or a bad, spirit or demon', hence 'a fetish'. (Mathews.)

voracious, voracity; devour; -vorous (from ML -*vorus*, L -*uorus*), as in *carnivorous*, flesh-eating (cf CARNAL)—herbivorous, grass-eating (cf HERB)—insectivorous (cf section)—omnivorous (cf the element *omni*-); sep GORGE.

1. L *uorāre*, to eat greedily, has s and r *uor*- (ML *vor*-), whence the adj *uorāx*, o/s *uorāc*-, whence—cf EF-F *vorace*—the E *voracious*; derivative L *uorācitās*, ML acc *vorācitāt*em, yields MF-F *voracité*, whence E *voracity*.

2. L *uorāre* has the int *dēuorāre*, to eat or swallow

greedily and completely, whence OF-MF *devourer*, whence 'to *devour*'.

3. L *uorāre*, r *uor-*, is akin to Gr *bora*, food, and *-boros*, corresp to L *-uorus* and Skt *garas*; cf Skt *girāti*, he swallows, Arm *keri*, I eat, and *ker*, meat, food, and Lith *gérti*, to swallow. The IE r is app *\*gwer-*, to swallow.

**vortex, vorticose.** See VERSE, para 9.

**votal, votary** (whence, anl, **votaress**), **vote** (n, hence v, whence **voter**), **votive**; **vow** (n, v); **devote**, **devotion**—cf devout.—**woo** (whence **wooable** and the pa, vn **wooing**), **wooer**.

1. L *uouēre*, ML *vovēre*, to make a vow, to vow, has s and r *uou-*, with var *uō-* in the pp *uōtus*, whence the n *uōtum*, whence E *vote*, orig a vow, hence a prayer or an ardent wish (all obs), whence the modern sense; hence, anl, *votal*, the L adj being *uōtīuus*, ML *vōtīvus*, whence—perh via MF-F *votif*, f *votive*—the E *votive*; the E adj and n *votary* derives imm from E *vote* but as if from ML *\*vōtārius*. Note that E *votal* was perh influenced by ML *vōtālis*; 'to *vote*', imm from the n, was perh influenced by LL *uōtāre*, ML *vōtāre*.

2. L *uouēre* is prob akin to Ve *vāghát-*, making a vow (presp), hence a supplicant, and perh akin to Gr *eukhomai* (for *\*weukhomai*, r *\*weukh-*), I pray, and *eukhē* (for *\*weukhē*), a vow; the IE r, therefore, is perh *\*wogh-* or *\*wogwh-*.

3. Whereas 'to *vow*' comes from OF-F *vouer*, itself either from OF-MF *vou* (EF-F *voeu*), from ML *vōtum*, L *uōtūm*, as above, or perh from ML *vōtāre*, LL *uōtāre*, the n *vow* comes from that OF-MF n *vou*.

4. Prob akin to L-LL *uouēre* is OE *wōgian*, ME *wowen*, E 'to *woo*', to court, esp if for marriage; derivative OE *wōgere* leads, anl, to **wooer**.

5. L *uouēre* has int *dēuouēre*, ML *dēvovēre*, to vow firmly or without reservation, hence to consecrate, with pp *dēuōtus*, ML *dēvōtus*, whence both E 'to *devote*' and L *dēuōtiō*, ML acc *devōtiōn*em, whence OF-MF *devotion* (EF-F *dé*), adopted by E; ML *dēvōtus* yields OF-MF *devot* (EF-F *dévot*), with OF-MF var *devout*, adopted by E. The Christian senses of *devotion* and, of course, *devout* had arisen as early as in LL, whence pp *dēuōtus* became also an adj.

**vouch, voucher.** See VOCABLE, para 8 (and heading).

**vouchsafe** = *vouch* (cf VOCABLE, para 8), guarantee, (to be) *safe* (cf SAFE).

**vow.** See VOTAL, para 3.

**vowel.** See VOCABLE, para 5.

**vox angelica, — Dei, — humana, — populi.** See VOCABLE, para 3.

**voyage, voyager, voyageur.** See VIA, para 14.

**Vulcan, vulcanite, vulcanize.** See VOLCANIC.

**vulgar, vulgarism, vulgarity, vulgarize; Vulgate, vulgus; divulgation, divulge; promulgate, promulgation, promulge.**

1. L *uulgus*, ML *vulgus*, the common people, OL *uolgus*, is o.o.o., but perh, as Webster proposes, akin to Skt *vargas*, a (large) body of men, Br *gwalc'h*, satiety (an over-sufficiency), W *gwala*,

sufficiency (cf the syn Cor *gwalgh*). The adj is *uolgāris*, *uulgāris*, ML *vulgāris*, whence both E *vulgar* (cf MF-F *vulgaire*) and LL *uolgāritās*, *uulgāritās*, the multitude, hence the multitude's behaviour, ML acc *vulgāritāt*em, whence late MF-F *vulgarité*, whence E *vulgarity*. The formations EF-F *vulgariser* (prob from ML *vulgarizāre*) and F *vulgarisme* become E 'to *vulgarize*' (whence *vulgarization*: cf F *vulgarisation*) and *vulgarism*. Derivative L *uolgāre*, *uulgāre*, ML *vulgāre*, has pp *uolgātus* (*uul-*), ML *volgatus* (*vul-*), whence the LL adj *uulgātus*, in general circulation, esp in *uulgāta editio*, the Septuagint, or L trans thereof, whence ML *Vulgāta*, St Jerome's L trans of the Bible as a whole: E 'the *Vulgate*'.

2. L *uolgus*, *uulgus*, ML *vulgus*, has two cpds affecting E:

*dīuolgāre*, *dīuulgāre*, ML *dīvulgāre*, to make widely (*dī*=*dis-*) known to the people, pp *dīuolgātus* (ML *dīvulgātus*), whence the LL *dīuulgātiō*, ML acc *dīvulgātiōn*em: whence 'to *divulge*' and, perh via EF-F, *divulgation*;

*prōuolgāre*, *prōuulgāre*, whence the altered *prōmulgāre*, to declare publicly, by open proclamation (*prō*, forth, connotes 'out in the open'), whence 'to *promulge*' (cf the MF-F *promulguer*); the L pp *prōmulgātus* yields 'to *promulgate*'; the from-the-pp derivatives LL *prōmulgātiō*, acc *prōmulgātiōn*em, and LL *prōmulgātor*, become MF-F *promulgation*, adopted by E, and *promulgator*.

**vuln; vulnerable** (whence, anl, **vulnerability**) and **invulnerable** (whence **invulnerability**); **vulnerary**; **vulnific.**—**vulture, vulturine.**

1. The Her *vuln* derives from ML *vulnerāre*, to wound, LL *uulnerāre*, var of *uolnerāre*, itself from L *uolnus*, *uulnus*, a wound (whether physical or, derivatively, psychological). The s is *uoln-*, *uuln-*; the r, *uol-*, *uul-*: cf the syn Gr *oulē* (? for *\*wolna*)— Hit *walh-*, *walhanna-*, to strike, to attack, *walhūn*, I strike or attack, *walhanzi*, they attack—OP *ūlint* (? for *wālint*), to fight against—W *gweli*, Br *gouli*, Cor *guli*, *goly*, a wound, OIr *fuil*, blood, *fuili*, bloody wounds, Ga *fuil* and Mx *fuill*, blood; perh cf *uellere* (r *uel-*), to tear or rend, and prob cf OS *wolian*, to defeat, OHG *wuol*, a defeat, ON *valr*, those who have died on the battlefield. If the relationship of L *uolnus* to L *uellere* be valid, the IE r is prob *\*wel-*, to tear or rend, as Hofmann has proposed.

2. L *uolnerāre*, *uul-*, has derivative LL *uolnerābilis*, neg *inuolnerābilis*, ML *vulnerābilis* and *invulnerābilis*, E *vulnerable*, *invulnerable* (cf EF-F *vulnérable*, F *vulnérabilité*, and late MF-F *invulnérable*, F *invulnérabilité*); the adj *uolnerārius*, *uul-*, ML *vul-*, whence—cf EF-F *vulnéraire*—E *vulnerary*; the LL adj *uulnerōsus*, ML *vul-*, E *vulnerose*. L *uolnus*, *uulnus*, ML *vulnus*, c/f *uulni-*, *vulni-*, has the cpd adj *uolnificus*, *uulnificus*, VL *vulnificus*, wound-causing, E *vulnific*.

3. Perh akin to *uolnus*, *uulnus*, a wound, and prob akin to L *uellere*, to tear or rend, is, with r *uol-*, *uul-*, and s *uolt-*, *uult-*, the L *uoltur*, var *uultur*, ML *voltur*, *vultur*, acc *volturem*, *vulturem*, that

bird of prey which rends its victims: OF-early MF *voltor*, MF *voltour*, late MF *voutour* (EF-F *vautour*): ME-E *vulture*. Derivative *uolturīnus* (*uul-*), ML *vulturīnus*, yields *vulturine*.

Vulpes is the ML *vulpēs*, L *uulpēs*, var of *uolpēs*, a fox; the derivative L adj *uolpīnus*, *uulpīnus*, ML *vulpīnus*, yields E *vulpine*. The E coinage *vulpicide*=ML *vulpi-*, c/f of *vulpēs*+*-cida*, a slayer, or *-cidium*, a slaying.

With L *uolpēs*, *uulpēs*, perh (E & M) cf Lith *vilpišy̆s*, a wild cat. But Lith *vilpišy̆s* is perh related to Lith *vilk*as, a wolf, which is very prob related to OE *wulf* (E *wolf*, q.v.): tentatively I suggest that both L *uulpēs* and E *wolf* derive, ult, from an IE *\*wulkw-* denoting any carnivorous, swift, sly or treacherous quadruped resembling either a wolf or a fox or a large wild cat; the obscurity of L *lupus*, a wolf—by common consent, although less easily, equated to E *wolf*—tends to support this suggestion.

vulture, vulturine. See VULN, para 3.

vulva (whence vulvitis: suffix *-itis*). See VOLUBLE, para 2.

vying. See VIE (heading).

# W

w perh owes its existence to the initial L-LL *u* before a vowel, as in *uacāre* (to be empty), pron *wacāre*; L-LL *uu-*, as in *uulnus*, becomes VL-ML *vulnus*; late ML adopts *w-* for AL words latinized from OE and ME. The OE *w* is adopted from the Runic alphabet; *w-*, moreover, is well attested by the equivalent digamma of PGr and in Hittite. But the not yet fully disentangled relationships of *u–v–w* hardly belong here; see, e.g., David Diringer, *The Alphabet*, revised ed., 1949.

wabble. See WOBBLE.

wad, n, hence v, whence wadding: F *ouate* (1674), a kind of cotton growing around an Oriental fruit and coming from Alexandria, to Marseilles, hence a soft plug: o.o.o., say B & W; prob (Webster) from Ar *ḫujātus*, anything that surrounds. The tree came into Egypt from Syria.

waddle. See VADE, para 8.

wade (1), n. A var of WOAD.

wade (2), v. See VADE, para 7.

wadge. See WEDGE, para 2.

wadi: Ar *wādi*: ? ult akin to WATER.

wafer. See WEAVE, para 4.

waffle. See WEAVE, para 5.

waft, waftage. See VIGOR, para 7.

wag (n, v). See VIA, para 1.

wage, wager, wages. See the 2nd GAGE, para 3.

waggery, waggish. See VIA (heading).

waggle. See VIA, para 1.

waggon, wagon. See VIA, para 2.

wagon-lit. See VIA, para 3.

wagtail: constantly wags (VIA, para 1) its tail (cf TAILOR).

waif. See VIBRATE, para 7.

wail. See WOE, para 2.

wain. See VIA, para 2.

wainscot shows the f/e influence of E *wain* but comes from MLG *wagenschot*, var *wagenscot*, itself app *wagen*, waggon+*schot*, a board (cf 'to *shoot* a door-bolt), the orig sense of the cpd being lost. (EW.)

waist, waistcoat. See the 2nd WAX, para 2.

wait (n, v), waiter. See VIGOR, para 8.

waive, waiver. See VIBRATE, para 6.

wake (1), a wet open space in an extent of ice (now only dial), hence a passage cut through ice (obs) and the track a ship leaves in water: ult from ON *vök*, syn with earliest E meaning, itself very closely akin to ON *vökr*, damp, rather wet: ult cf HUMOR.

wake (2), to be (alertly) awake, hence n. See VIGOR, para 9.

wale (1), a choice, to choose. See VOLITION, para 12.

wale (2), a stripe. See VOLUBLE, para 6.

Wales. See FLANDERS, para 5.

walk, walker, walking. See VOLUBLE, para 7.

wall. See VOLUBLE, para 8.

wallaby. See KANGAROO.

Wallachian. See FLANDERS, para 4.

wallah, a servant, a worker, hence coll a fellow, is the Hind suffix *-vālā*, connoting 'doer': sem, cf L *-ārius* in nn.

wallaroo. See KANGAROO.

wallet; wattle.

*Wallet*, orig a pack, a knapsack, comes from ME *walet*: o.o.o., unless a metathesis of ME *watel*, a bag, itself perh id with *wattle*, (a framework of) plaited twigs, esp as used in fences, hence, in Aus, the *wattle* tree: OE *watel*, *watol*, *watul* (o.o.o.), whence app, though far from certainly, the *wattles* of a bird or a reptile.

wall-eyed—whence, by b/f, wall-eye—comes, by f/e, from ME *wawileyid*: ON *vagleygr*: *vagl*, a beam, esp in the eye+*eygr*, -eyed, from *auga*, an eye.

Walloon. See FLANDERS, para 4.

wallop. See GALLOP.

wallow. See VOLUBLE, para 9.

walnut. See FLANDERS, para 7.

walrus. See HORSE, para 1.

waltz (n, v), waltzer. See VOLUBLE, para 10.

wamble, to feel nausea: ME *wamblen*: of Scan origin; app a freq from ON *vāma*, nausea: cf VOMIT. Hence dial and coll 'the *wambles*' and *wambly*.

wame. See WOMB.

wampum, a string of shell-beads worn ornamentally or pledged ceremonially or used as money: Alg *wampom*peag, *wampum*peage, white wampum: *wab*, white+*umpe*, a string+*-ag*, a suffix denoting the pl. AE *wampum* was very early shortened, by the settlers in NA, from *wampum peag*, the Alg single word being apprehended as two words. (Mathews.)

wan, E-ME, pale, colourless, derives from OE *wan* or *wann* (predominant form), var *won* or *wonn*, lead-coloured, lurid, greyly dark: o.o.o.: perh (EW) akin to OE *wan*, deficient—cf *wane*, *want*, at paras 14 and 15 of VACANT.

**wand.** See the 2nd WIND, para 3.

**wander, wanderer, wanderlust.** See the 2nd WIND, para 4.

**wane.** See VACANT, para 14.

**wangle** is app a nasalization of *waggle*, q.v. at VIA, para 1.

**want.** See VACANT, para 15. Hence *wanting*.

**wanton.** See the 3rd TOW, para 6; cf VACANT, para 14.

**wapentake,** a regional division, hence its lawcourt, hence the bailiff: OE *wǣpentac*: ON *vǎpnatac*, a taking of weapons, hence a touching of weapons in assent.

**wapiti,** a large NA deer, comes from Shawnee (an Alg language) *wapiti*, lit 'white rump', to distinguish it from the much darker moose: cf Cree *wǎpitiu, wǎpitayoo*, it is pale. (Mathews.)

**war** (n, hence v), whence **warfare** (lit a *fare* or going to war) and **warlike; warrior.**—'C'est la *guerre*'; **guerrilla, guerrillero.**

1. *Warrior*, ME *werriour* or *werraiour*, derives from ONF *werreior* (corresp to OF-MF *guerrëor*, MF-EF *guerroïeor*: EF-F *guerrier*), from ONF *werreier, werier* (cf OF-F *guerroyer*, early *-oier*), to make war, from ONF *werre*, war (cf OF-F *guerre*): OHG *werra*, confusion, a quarrel, strife, akin to OHG *werran*, MHG *werren*, verwerren, G verwirren, to confuse: perh akin to E WORSE. (Walshe.) E *war* comes from late OE-ME, from ONF, *werre*.

2. OF-F *guerre*, war, is known to many Britons and Americans from the phrase 'C'est la *guerre*', It's the war (1914–1918)—cf E 'There's a war on' (1939–1945), to excuse any and every lapse or inefficiency or deficiency.

3. Corresp to OF-F *guerre* is Sp *guerra* (from OHG *werra*), whence *guerrilla*, lit 'little war'; one who fights in a guerrilla (loosely *guerilla*) band is, in Sp, a *guerrillero*, but, in E and AE, a *guerrilla*, whence, by f/e, the orig underworld *gorilla* (perh, however, from the huge ape, f/e influenced by the individual *guerrilla*).

**warble, warbler.** See WHARF, para 2.

**-ward.** See VERSE, para 3.

**ward** (n, v), **warden** (whence **wardency** and obsol **wardenry), warder** (whence, anl, **wardress), wardrobe, wardroom; wraith; award** (n, v) and **reward** (n, v); **Edward** (whence **Edwardian**), pet-forms **Ned** (whence **neddy**) and **Ted,** whence **Teddy,** whence **Teddy boy**—cf **Teddy bear.**—**guard** (n, v), **guardant** or **gardant, guardian** (whence **guardianship), guardroom** (*guard*, n+*room*), **guardsman** (a *guard's man*); **rearguard** and **safeguard; regard,** n (whence **regardful** and **regardless,** adj hence adv), **regardant** (whence **regardance, -ancy**)—and **disregard** (v, hence n, whence **disregardful**), itself merely the prefix *dis-*+'to *regard*'.

1. *Ward* and *guard* are doublets, as, largely, are their derivatives: whereas the *w*- forms represent OGmc and ONF (from OGmc) origins and intermediaries, the *g*- forms represent OF-MF (from OGmc) origins; *guardian, guarder, guardroom,* correspond to *warden, warder, wardroom.*

2. Etym, the key-word is *ward*, whether the n,

from OE *weard* (f), a watching or guarding, a body of men keeping watch or guard, or the v, from ME *wardien*, OE *weardian*, to keep, esp to keep safe, to protect: both have numerous OGmc, incl ON, syn cognates—perh cf esp the OFris v *wardia* and the OHG *warta*, n: cf also G *wahren*, to preserve, Go *wars*, cautious, and perh Gr *ouros* (? for *wouros*), a watchman, and Skt *varūta*, a protector: IE r, *wer-*, to keep, keep safe, guard, protect. Perh cf WARN, WARREN, WARY.—The 'to parry' sense follows naturally from the basic senses.

3. *Warden* comes from ME *wardein*, adopted from ONF; the ONF var *wardien* 'answers' MF-F *gardien*, OF *gardenc. Warder* comes from AF *wardere*, var *wardour*, prob from ONF and corresp to OF-MF *gardeor* (EF-F *gardeur*).

4. Whereas *wardroom* (1801: OED) merely combines *ward*, a keeping or guarding, with *room*, *wardrobe* derives from ME *warderobe*, adopted from ONF and corresp to MF-F *garde-robe*, lit (a place for) the keeping of robes or garments in general.

5. Akin to OE *weard* (m), one who watches or guards, is the syn ON *vörthr*, whence, in C16, the Sc *warth*, whence, by metathesis, the Sc *wraith*, a guardian angel, hence a person's ghost seen—as a warning, a means of protection—shortly or imm before his death, hence any apparition: introduced into England by Burns and Scott.

6. OE *weardian*, ME *wardien*, E 'to *ward*', has two prefix-cpds: *award* and *reward*. 'To *award*' derives from AF *awarder*, from ONF *eswarder*, corresp to OF-MF *esgarder*—*es-*, L *ex-*, out of, used int+ONF *warder* (OF-F *garder*); 'an *award*', ME from AF *award*, from ONF *esward, eswart*, corresp to OF-MF *esgard, esgart* (EF-F *égard*), and derived from or intimately related to the ONF v.

7. 'To *reward*,' ME *rewarden*, to reward, orig to regard, comes from ONF *rewarder*, to regard, corresp to OF-MF *reguarder*, MF-F *regarder*: OF-F from L *re-*, back, again+ONF *warder*. The ME-E n *reward* is adopted from ONF *reward*, corresp to OF-MF *reguard*, MF-F *regard*.

8. OE *weard* (m), a watchman, a guard, occurs in the PN *Ēadweard*, derived from *Ēadward*, whence *Edward*: '(the) property-defender': *ēad*, property. The adj *Edwardian* is applied esp to the reign of King Edward VII: 1901–1910. During that reign, smart young men tended to wear 'stovepipe' trousers. And when there arose, c1950, a cult of Edwardiana, the gangs of young toughs and hooligans aped their dress, esp the trousers, and came to be known as *Teddy boys*. (For *Teddy bear*, from *Theodore*, see THEISM.)

### The *g*- Words

9. Corresp to *ward*, n, is EF-F *garde*, OF-MF *guarde* (from *guarder*), orig the action of guarding, hence E *guard*; 'to *guard*' comes from OF-MF *guarder* (EF-F *garder*): of OGmc origin—cf the syn OHG *wartēn*, MHG-G *warten*, and the related ON *vartha*. OF *guardenc* (*guarder*+OGmc suffix

*-enc*, Gmc *-ing*), *gardenc*, MF *guardien* (EF-F *gardien*), yields E *guardian*. The Her *guardant*, var *gardant*, is prop the OF-MF presp of *guarder*, later *garder*.

10. For *rearguard*, see REAR; for *safeguard* (a *safe guard* or guarding), cf its prompter the MF-F *sauvegarde*, a safe guarding or keeping—cf SAFE. Hence 'to *safeguard*'—cf F *sauvegarder*.

11. 'A *regard*' is adopted from OF-F, from OF-MF *reguarder*, MF-F *regarder* (whence, via AF, the E adj *regardant*—prop the F presp), lit *re-*, back, again (hence continually or even continuously)+*guarder*, later *garder*: perh orig 'to keep (someone) in view', whether for his safety or for one's own, whence the idea of solicitude, hence of respect and affection.

**wardrobe; wardroom.** See WARD, para 3; cf ROBE, para 2, s.f.

**-wards.** See VERSE, para 3.

**ware** (1), adj. See WARY.

**ware** (2), n, (collectively) articles for sale: ME *ware*: OE *waru*: cf OFris *ware*, *were*, MHG-G *ware*, MD *were*, *waer*, *ware*, D *waar*, ON *vara*, with modern Scan cognates: perh ult akin, as 'property which is carefully guarded' (Walshe), to *ward*, and prob akin to MHG *ware*, a (watchful) attention.—Hence **warehouse.**

**ware** (3), v, to take careful heed (vt, of), now dial, except in the imp ('*Ware* fences!'): OE *warian*, be on one's guard, (vt) to warn, guard, ward off: cf the syn or approx syn OFris *waria*, OS *warōn*, OHG bi*warōn*, ON *vara*. Cf *ware*, adj, q.v. at WARY.

**warfare.** See WAR (heading).

**warlock**: ME *warloghe*, a deceiver (esp the Devil): OE *wǣrloga*: OE *wǣr*, a covenant+ *-loga*, a liar, akin to—prob deriving from—OE *lēogan*, to tell lies.

**warm,** adj (hence n) and v (whence **warmer** and **warming**); **warmth** (*warm*, adj+abstract suffix *-th*). —Cf the sep *therm* and the element *-therm, thermo-*, as well as the sep FURNACE.

'To *warm*' derives from OE *wearmian*, itself from the OE adj *wearm*, whence the E adj *warm*: and OE *wearm* is akin to OFris, OS, OHG-MHG-G, MD-D *warm* (MD varr: *werm*, *waerm*, *warme*), ON *varmr*. With OE *wearman*, cf Go *warmjan*; with the OGmc adjj, cf Skt *gharmás*, a glowing heat, L *formus*, warm, Gr *thermos*. The OGmc r is app *\*warm-* for (*\*gwarm-*); the IE r, *\*ghwerm-*, varr *\*ghwarm-* and esp *\*ghworm-*, warm.

**warn, warning** (n), **warnish, warnison—warison; warrandice, warrantise—warrant** (n; hence v, whence **warrantable**—neg **unwarrantable**), **warrantor, warranty;—weir.**—Cognates in *gu-* and *g-*: **garment** (n, hence v); **garnish** (v, hence n, hence, also, **garnishment**); **garniture; garret, garrison** (n, hence v); **guarantee** (n, hence v), **guarantor, guaranty.**—Perh cf the sep WARREN.

1. 'A *warning*' derives from OE *warnung* (vocalized as *warenung*), with var *wearnung*, vn from OE *wearnian*, contr *warnian* (vocalized *warenian*), whence *warnien*, later *warnen*, whence

'to *warn*': and OE *wearnian, warnian*, is very closely related to OE *wearn*, a hindrance or obstacle, (? hence) a denial or a refusal, and related also to OFris *warna, werna*, OS *warnian, wernien*, ON *varna*, to refuse, and OHG *warnōn*, MHG-G *warnen*, to warn—therefore prob, further off, MHG *warn*, to observe, G *wahren*, to preserve, ON *vara*, to warn, and therefore perh ult the E WARD. But the interrelationships of all these words are still imprecise.

2. From the common OGmc *\*warnōn*, app in form *\*warnjan*, with related sense 'to supply, to provide or provide with, to prepare (e.g., by warning)', comes ONF *warnir*, whence, from the pres *warniss*-forms, both *warnish*, to provision (obs), to warn (now only Sc), and *warnison* (obs), provision, a garrison. Cf *warison*, property, a reward (both obs), and the giving of an alarm (military and archaic): adopted from ONF, from ONF *warir*, to defend, to heal, corresp to OF *guarir*, MF *garir* (EF-F *guérir*), orig to defend, whence, almost imm, to heal or cure, whence, via the ONF pres forms in *wariss-*, the obs 'to *warish*'. ONF *warir* comes from the OGmc *\*war-*, of which *\*warn-* is an extn.

3. ONF *warir* has presp *warant*, whence—perh aided by OHG *werénto*, a defender, a defence, a protection, orig the presp of *werén*, to defend, to guarantee (cf OFris *wera, wara*, OS *werian*, MHG *wern*, G *wehren*, Go *warjan*)—ME *warant*, soon also *warrant*, a defender, a safeguard (both obs), hence an authorization, a certificate, an official, or a legal, certificate, a guarantee. ONF *warant* has derivative v *warantir* (cf OF-F *garantir*), whence ME *waranten* (or *-enten*), soon also *warranten*, whence 'to *warrant*', whence both *warrantable* and *warrantor*. Also from ONF *warant* comes ONF *warantie* (cf OF *guarantie*, MF-F *garantie*,) whence late ME *war(r)antie*, EE-E *warranty*. ONF *warantir* has derivative *warantise* (cf OF *guarantise*, MF *garantise*), adopted by ME, but now archaic except in the Sc var *warrandice*.

4. Akin to OFris *wera*, OS *wearian*, is the syn OE *werian*, to defend or protect, hence to check or hinder others: and OE *werian* has derivative or very close cognate *wer*, a weir or a dam (cf OFris *were*, OHG *weri*, G *Wehr*, a defence, a dam, and ON *ver*): ME *wer*: E *weir*.

### Cognates in *gu-, g-*

5. Corresp to ONF-from-OGmc *w-* is OF-MF *gu-*, MF-F *g-*, as implied in paras 2–4 above, and as attested in numerous other doublets (esp *ward*—*guard*). Corresp to ONF *warnir* is OF-MF *guarnir*, MF-F *garnir*, orig to supply (with), to provide, hence to prepare, hence to furnish, hence to adorn, with pres forms in *garniss-*, whence ME *garnissen*, soon also *garnisshen*, whence 'to *garnish*'. OF-MF *guarnir*, MF-F *garnir* has the foll derivatives either adapted or even adopted by E:

OF-MF *guarnement*, MF-F *garnement*, protector, protection, hence clothing, garments, a garment, whence ME *garnement*, a garment, whence, by contr, late ME-E *garment*;

MF *garneture*, late MF-F *garniture*, a furnishing, a garnishing, adopted by E;

MF-F *garnison*, a means of defence, hence, in C17, a body of troops defending a castle or a city, whence ME *garnisoun*, which f/e influenced the imm source of E *garrison*—i.e., ME *garisoun*, equipment, provisions, protection, occ a deliverance, itself from OF-MF *garison* (var *guarison*: cf EF-F *guérison*), from *garir, guarir*, as in para 2 above.

6. Closely linked with E *garrison*, and with *weir*, is E *garret*: ME *garette*, earlier *garite*, a watchtower or a look-out, adopted from syn MF *garite* (EF-F *guérite*), also a shelter, a (place of) refuge, prob from OProv *garida*, from the same source as MF-F *garir*, OF-MF *guarir*, as in para 2 above.

7. Corresp to *warrant, warrantor, warranty* (para 3 above) are *guarantee, guarantor, guaranty*; it is *guaranty* which forms the new base, for it comes from OF-MF *guarantie* (MF-F *garantie*), from OF-MF *guarantir* (MF-F *garantir*), from OF-MF *guarant* (MF-F *garant*): cf para 3. From *guaranty* derive—anl with *warrantor—guarantor*, and—anl with such words as *advisee, assignee, donee, grantee, lessee*, and prompted by the active *guarantor, donor, lessor*, etc.—the n *guarantee*, orig the agent, hence also the act, hence, again, the deed of security.

**warnish, warnison.** See prec, para 2.

**warp.** See VERVAIN, para 5.

**warrant, warrantable, warrantor, warranty.** See WARN, para 3.

**warren, warrener.**

The latter, imm from the former, owes something to ONF *warenier* (cf the MF *garennier*); *warren*, orig a game-preserve (now a rabbits' breeding place), an area reserved by the feudal lord for hunting or fishing, ME *wareyne*, comes from ONF *warenne*, corresp to MF-F *garenne*, a doublet of MF *varenne*, waste land, but also a game-preserve: *varenne* app from ML *warenna*, a game-preserve (CC11–15), itself either from ONF *warir*, to defend, keep safe (cf WARN, para 2), as B & W suggest, or of C origin, as suggested by 'Webster', where MIr *farr*, a post, is not very satisfactorily adduced; clearly there has been confusion—but precisely when and how, and of exactly what with what?

**warrior.** See WAR, para 1.

**wart** (whence **warty** and **warthog**): ME *wart*, var *wert*: OE *wearte*: cf OFris *warte*, MHG-G *warze*, ON *varta*—and perh the syn ML *verrūca*, L *uerrūca*, orig an eminence, and, if that relationship be genuine, then also Skt *várṣman-*, Lith *viršùs*, a summit, and OSl *vrŭxu* (adv), on high. ML *verrūca* has been adopted by Med, with adj *verrucose*, from ML *verrūcōsus* (L *uerrūcōsus*).

**wary**, whence **wariness**—cf **ware**, adj; **aware**, whence **awareness**, whence the neg **unaware**, whence at **unawares** (archaic) and **unawareness**; **beware.**

1. *Wary* derives from the dissyllabic ME *ware*, var of *war*, from OE *waer*, var of *gewaer* (*ge-* is int); the archaic adj *ware* derives from ME *war*.

OE *waer, gewaer*, is akin to OHG *giwar*, MHG *gewar*, G *gewahr*, Go *wars*, ON *varr* (cf Da *var*); to OHG *wara*, attention, esp in OHG (and OS) *wara neman*, MHG *war nemen*, to take note, pay heed, G *wahrnehmen*, to perceive, and *wahren*, to preserve—and therefore prob ult to WARREN, WARN, and perh WARD.

2. OE *gewaer* becomes ME *iwar*, whence E *aware*; and E *ware*, wary, naturally occurs in '*Be ware!*', whence, by b/f, *beware*, to be on one's guard, to be cautious.

**was** derives from OE *waes*, **were** from OE *wǣre*, resp the 1st and 3rd person, and the 2nd person, singular; **were** in the pl derives from OE *wǣron*, they were: and all three OE forms derive from OE *wesan* to be: these are completely normal strong past tenses.

2. OE *wesan* is akin to OFris *wesa*, OS *wesan*, OHG *wesan* (pt *was*), MHG *wesen* (whence the G n *Wesen*, being, existence), Go *wisan* (pt *was*), MD *weisen*, usu *wesen*, D *wezen*, to be: cf also, with v- for w-: Skt *vásati*, he remains or dwells (lit, continues to be), and ML *Vesta*, LL-L *Uesta*, the ancient It goddess of *dwellings*, and Mx *va*, (I) was, and *ve*, (it) was; moreover, with *b* for *v*: Cor *bās*, usu *bôs*, to be. The IE r is prob *wes-*, to dwell, for, among the Gmc languages, not only in E does this v serve as the pt or impf of 'to be'.

3. Cf WASSAIL.

**wash** (v, hence n), whence **washer, washing, washy** (whence redup **wishy-washy**), as well as such self-explanatory cpds as **washboard, -house, washerwoman.**

'To *wash*' comes from ME *waschen*: OE *waescan* (var *wascan*): cf OHG *wascan*, MHG-G *waschen*, MD *wassen*, late MD-D *wasschen*, late ON and Sw *vaska*. 'Prob Gmc *waskan-* for *wat-skan-* (cf *Wasser*). Cf OIr *uisce* (for *udskio-*) "water" ' (Walshe): if that kinship be valid, as prob it is—'to *wash*' is 'to apply *water* to'—then cf WATER.

**Washington**, the capital of the US, and the 1st President, prob derives from *Washington* in County Durham, England: early forms *Wassyngtona, Wassinton*: app 'the village (*tūn*) of *Wassa*'s people'. (Ekwall.) Hence the Bot *Washingtonia*.

**washy.** See WASH (heading).

**wasp, waspish.** See WEAVE, para 9.

**wastage, waste, wasteful, waster, wastrel.** See VACANT, para 18 and heading.

**wassail**, a carousing, from the spiced liquor accompanying *Wassail!*, an expression of festive benevolence: ME *Waes haeil!*, Be well!: ON *Ves heill!* (whence OE *wes hāl!*). Cf WAS and HAIL, to greet or salute.

**wast**, thou, you were: cf WAS.

**watch** (n, v), **watcher, watchful, watching, watchman, watchword.** See VIGOR, para 10 and heading.

**water** (n, v), whence pa, vn **watering** and **waterish** (*-ish*, adj); **waterless** and **watery**; very numerous cpds, mostly self-explanatory—perh note esp **waterbuck** (anglicizing D *waterbok*)—**waterchat** (SA bird—cf CHAT, light conversation) —**watercourse** and **watercress**—**waterfall** (cf the

OE *waetergefeall*)—waterfowl—waterlily, water-line—waterlogged, from waterlog, to render as heavy or unmanageable as a log (esp a log saturated with water) by letting water in—waterman, a boatman—watermark—watermelon—waterproof (proof against water)—watersnake—waterspout—watertight (cf *waterproof*)—waterway (OE *waeter-weg*)—waterwork (defence against water), whence waterworks.—wet (n, v), whence pa, vn wetting and wetness.—winter (n, hence v), wintry.—vodka.—Cf the sep WASH and WHISK(E)Y—UNDA, UNDULATE—OTTER and HYDRA (and HYDRANT)—DROPSY.

1. 'To *water*' derives from OE *waeterian*, itself from OE *waeter*, whence ME *waeter*, *weter*, finally *water*, retained by E: and OE *waeter* is akin to OFris *water*, *weter*, OS *watar*, Go *watō*, OHG *wazzar*, MHG *wazzer*, G *Wasser*, MD *wetere*, *watere*, *watre*, MD-D *water*—and Hit *wātar*, *wetār*, dat *weteni*, *witeni*; cf, with *v-*: OSl *voda*; with *u-*: Skt *udán* (gen *udnás*) and L *unda*, the *-n-* infix occurring also in ON *vatn* and Lith *vanduō*; with *h-*: Gr *hudōr*, gen *hudatos*. There are also cognates in Alb, Arm, C (e.g., OIr *uisce*), Phrygian (perh), Umbrian. Cf *wet*, in para 3.

2. OE *waeter* has adj *waeterig*, whence *watery*, and *waeterlēas*, whence *waterless*.

3. Akin to OE *waeter*, water, is OE *wāēt*, wet, whence *wāētan*, E 'to *wet*'; partly from OE *wāēt* and partly from ME *wette*, *wete*, pp used as adj (varr *wett*, hence *wet*), comes the E adj *wet*. The OE adj *wāēt* is akin to OFris *wet* and ON *vāthr*, *vātr*.

4. Akin to OE *waeter* and *wāēt*, but with the occ IE *-n-* infix, is OE-ME-E *winter*, whence OE *wintrig*, E *wintry*, and 'to *winter*' (cf MD *winteren*): cf OFris *winter*, OS *wintar*, OHG *wintar*, MHG-G *winter*, MD *wenter*, MD-D *winter*, Go *wintrus*, and, without *-n-*, the ON *vetr*: 'the rainy or wet season' (Webster); perh 'the white season' (cf OIr *find*, white), because, in the OGmc period, 'time was measured by nights and winters' (Walshe).

5. OSl and Ru *voda*, water (cf para 1), has derivative *vodka*, in form a dim and in sense 'little water', so named, prob, because it is a distillation.

6. The IE r is app *wed-*, water, itself prob, ult, Medit—cf Ar *oued*, a river, and Eg *ḥua*, water, the latter suggesting kinship with L *aqua*, which (if for *waqua*) is not impossibly related to E *water*. The Medit r is perh *wa-*.

**Waterloo**, meet one's, to be defeated, as Napoleon Bonaparte was, in 1815, by Wellington near *Waterloo*, a town situated nine miles from Brussels: perh '(The) Place of Water (Meadows)', *loo* corresp to OF-MF *leu* (EF-F *lieu*), L *locus*, a place.

**watt** comes from that Sc inventor James *Watt* (1736–1819) who discovered the steam engine. Hence *wattage*, electrical power expressed in these units.

**wattle.** See WALLET.

**wave** (n, v), **wavy.** See VIBRATE, para 8.

**waver**, v. See VIBRATE, para 8.

**wax** (1), beeswax, etc., whence the adjj **waxen**, **waxy**, and the cpd **waxwork(s)**: OE *weax*: cf OFris *wax*, OS *wahs*, OHG-MHG *wahs*, G *Wachs*, MD *wasch*, *wass* (occ *wasse*), MD-D *was*, ON *vax* (Sw *vax*, Da *vox*), Lith *váškas*, OSl *voskŭ*.

**wax** (2), to grow, whether in size or in numbers, in strength (or intensity) or in prosperity; **waist**; sep EKE, v, and sep AUGMENT.

1. 'To *wax*' comes from OE *weaxan*: cf OFris *waxa*, OS *wahsan*, OHG *wahsan*, MHG *wahsen*, G *wachsen*, Go *wahsjan*, MD *wasschen*, MD-D *wassen*, ON *vaxa-* and, further off, L *auxī*, I caused to grow (pt of *augēre*), Gr *auxein* (perh for *awxein*), extn *auxanein*, to increase (vt), Skt *vahšanam*, growth, and (a redup) *vavakṣa*, he has grown, Lith *áuskštas*, high, lit (full-)grown. The IE r is perh *weg-*, var *wag-*, to grow (vi and vt).

2. *Waist*, whence *waistcoat* (a coat not descending below the waist), comes from ME *wast*, the waist, orig stature, from ME *waxen*, to increase in size (OE *weaxan*): cf OHG *wahst*, Go *wahstus*, ON *vöxtr*, stature, orig growth. The *waist* is so named because here the body begins, whether up or down, to grow thicker.

**waxen.** See the 1st WAX.

**way.** See VIA, para 4.

**wayfare—waylay—wayward.** See VIA, para 5.

**wayzgoose**, a printers' annual picnic or other entertainment, is an extn of *waygoose* (late C17–19, then mostly dial): usu said to be o.o.o., but prob (EW) a f/e mdfn of *wakegoose*, a goose served at a wake.

**we**, OE *wē*, is akin to OS *wē*, OFris (and OS) *wī*, MD and LG *wi*, MD *wie*, *wii*, late MD-D *wij*, Go *weis*, OHG-MHG-G *wir*, OHG var *wer*, ON *vēr* (but Da and Sw *vi*), OSl *vě* (we two), Tokh *was*—and, away back, Skt *vayám* and Hit *wēs*, *wěs*.

**weak, weaken, weakly, weakness.** See VICAR, para 7.

**weal** (1), a long mark left by lash of whip or stroke of cane or rod. See VOLUBLE, para 6.

**weal** (2), prosperity. See VOLITION, para 16. Cf WEALTH.

**weald.** See the 1st VOLE, s.f.

**wealth, wealthy.** See VOLITION, para 16.

**wean.** See VENERABLE, para 12.

**weapon** (n, hence v), whence **weaponry** (collective suffix *-ery*, *-ry*): ME *wepen*: OE *wāēpen*: cf OFris *wāpen*, *wēpen*, *wēpern*, OS *wāpan*, Go *wēpna* (pl), ON *vāpn*, and, with *f* for *p*, OHG *waffan*, MHG *wafen*, G *Waffe*, but cf MHG *wāpen*, G *Wappen*, a coat-of-arms, and its source, the MD *wāpen* (var *wāpene*), D *wapen*, coat-of-arms, weapon. Walshe suggests—not asserts—kinship with Gr *hoplon* (? for *woplon*), a weapon.

**wear** (1), of clothes. See VEST, para 4.

**wear** (2), of a ship. See VEER, para 1.

**weary, weariness.**

The latter derives from OE *wērigness*, from OE *wērig*, whence ME *weri*, whence, perh after *wear*, the E *weary*; and OE *wērig* is akin to the syn OS *wōrig*, OHG *wuorag*, and also to ON *ōrr*, bewildered, OE *wōrian*, to wander, ON *ōrar* (? for *wŏrar*), attacks of insanity, and Gr *hŏrakian*, to feel faint, to faint: IE r, *\*wŏr-*, dizziness. OE *wērig* has derivative v *wērigian*, whence ME *werien*, E 'to *weary*'.

**weasel**. See VIRULENCE, para 3.

**weather** (n, hence v), whence **weatherbeaten, weathercock**, a vane orig shaped like a cock; **wither**, whence the pa, vn **withering**.

1. *Weather* derives from ME-from-OE *weder*, akin to OFris *weder*, OS *wedar*, OHG *wetar*, MHG *weter*, G *Wetter*, MD-D *weder*, MD *wedere*, *widdere*, *widder*, ON *vethr*, OSl *vedro*, good weather, *vetrŭ*, (the state of the) air, esp wind, Lith *vētra*, bad weather, esp a storm; cf the corresp collectives or intt (connoted by *ge-, gi-*): OE *geweder*, weather, temperature (of the air), and OHG *giwitiri*, MHG *gewitere*, bad weather, G *Gewitter*, a thunderstorm; and perh *wind*. The ult IE r is perh *\*we-*, with extnn *\*wedh-*, as here, and *\*wen-*, as in WIND (1).

2. OE *weder* has derivative v *wederian*, to be (some sort of) weather, ME *wederen*, E 'to *weather*'; the OE vn *wederung* finally becomes E *weathering*.

3. ME *wederen* has the var *wideren*, whence—prob after *weather*—E 'to *wither*': cf G ver*wittern*, to be weatherworn, hence to deteriorate, esp to decay, and G *verwettert*, weather-beaten.

**weathering**, n. See prec, para 2.

**weave** (whence **weaver**—whence **weaverbird**—and **weaving**), pt **wove**, pp **woven** (hence adj—cf the cpd adj **interwoven**); **web**, n (whence **webby**) and v (whence **webbing**)—cf **webster**; **weft** and **woof**; **wafer** and **waffle**, a battercake—contrast **waffle**, to flap; **gauffer** (**gaufre**) or **goffer**, cf **gopher**; —**wasp**, whence the adjj **waspish, waspy**—cf **vespal, vespiary, vespine**.

1. 'To *weave*'—whence *weave*, a woven fabric or a pattern of weaving—derives from ME *weven*, from OE *wefan* (pt *waef*, ME *wof*; pp *wefen*, ge*wefen*, ME *wofyn*, -*woven*): cf OHG *weban*, MHG-G *weben*, MD-D *weven*, ON *vefa, vefja*—and OFris *weber*, a weaver; cf also Gr *huph*ainein, to weave, *huphē, huphos*, a web, webbing, and Skt *ubhnáti*, he weaves together, and *ūrṇa-vábhis*, a spider, prob, lit, a wool-weaver. The IE r is *\*webh-*, to plait, to weave.

2. Akin to OE *wefan* are OE *webbian*, whence 'to *web*', and the OE n *webb*, ME-E *web*: cf the syn MD *webbe*, D *web*, OHG *weppi*, G *gewebe*, ON *vefr*—and prob OHG *waba*, MHG-G *wabe*, a honeycomb, which looks almost as if the framework has been woven. From OE *webbian* comes OE *webbestre*, a female—later, any—weaver, E *webster* (archaic), whence *Webster*.

3. Akin to—? from—OE *wefan*, to weave, is OE *wefta* or *weft*, the threads crossing the warp, whence E *weft*: corresp to ON *veptr*. Cf *woof*, the threads that, in a woven fabric, cross the warp: f/e (after 'to *weave*') from ME *oof*: OE *ōwef*, lit a weaving on (*ō-* for *on*)—i.e., on the warp.

4. Akin prob to the OGmc words for 'to weave' and certainly to OHG *waba*, MHG-G *wabe*, honeycomb, is the ONF *waufre* (corresp to OF-F

*gaufre*), a thin, crisp biscuit or small cake, app imm from Frankish *\*wafel*: whence ME *wafre*, whence—prob influenced by MD *wafer*—E *wafer*.

5. Perh imm from Frankish *\*wafel* comes MD-D *wafel*, MD-ED var *waffel*: whence E *waffle*, a battercake, not to be confused with the dial and coll *waffle*, to flutter, a freq of dial *waff*, to wave, akin to *wave*, q.v. at VIBRATE.

6. OF-F *gaufre*, a wafer, has, like its EF-F dim *gaufrette*, been adopted by culinary E.

7. OF-F *gaufre*, meaning also a honeycomb, has derivative EF-F v *gaufrer*, to work a honeycomb effect into such fabrics as velvet or cloth: whence E 'to *gauffer*', now rare for the more thoroughly anglicized 'to *goffer*', whence 'a *goffer*', occ short for '*goffering* iron'.

8. From OF-F *gaufre*, a honeycomb, and prob influenced by E 'to *goffer*', comes that NA rodent the *gopher*, addicted to 'honeycombing' the ground where it lives. But AE *gopher*, a hard-shelled land tortoise, shortens *megopher* (the earliest spelling), in which -*gopher* is prob f/e, for the accepted form is *magofer*, app of Amerind origin. (Mathews.)

### The Wasp

9. A notable weaver is the *wasp*: ME *waspe*: OE *waesp*, a metathesis of the basic *waeps* (cf the dial and nursery *wops*), var *waefs*: cf OHG *wafsa, wefsa*, MHG *wefse*, late MHG-G *wespe*, MD *wespe*, D *wesp*; cf also OP *wobse*, OSl *vosa* (Ru *osa*), Lith *vapsa*. In short, the OGmc and OSl forms are, sem, closely related and phon, app and prob, related to the ancient words for 'to weave'; cf also the L *uespa*, ML *vespa*, a wasp, forms that have app influenced one or two of the Gmc and Sl words: cf, further (*gu-* for *w-*), the OBr *guohi* (acc pl) wood-wasps, hornets, and Cor *gūhien* (or *gūhyen*), a wasp. By adducing the syn Av *vanžaka-*, Baluchi *gvalz*, E & M render an IE *\*wops-*, varr *\*waps-* and *\*weps-*, virtually certain.

10. From ML *vespa*, learnèd E has formed the learned adjj *vespal* and *vespine*; *vespiary*, a wasps' nest or colony, blends ML *vespa*+*api*ary, a nest or colony of bees.

**weazen, weazened**. See WIZEN.

**web** (n, v), **webbing, webby, webster, Webster**. See WEAVE, para 2.

**wed, wedding**. See the 2nd GAGE, para 4.

**wedge** (n, hence v)—**wadge** or **wodge**; **wig**, seed-cake or currant bun.—**vomer**.

1. A *wedge*, ME *wegge*, OE *wecg*, is akin to ON *veggr*, a wedge, and OHG *weggi, wecki*, MHG *wecke*, a wedge-shaped pastry, G *Weck*, a bread-roll, MD *wegghe, wegge, wigge*, a wedge, a wedge-shaped pastry. From MD (and MLG) *wigge*, in latter sense, D *wig*, comes the E, now only dial, *wig* or *wigg*, a kind of cake or bun.

2. App a dial var of *wedge* is *wadge* or *wodge*, a bulky object, (coll) a bundle of papers, etc.; hence the adj *wadgy* or *wodgy*.

3. Akin to the OGmc words adduced in para 1 are OHG *waganso*, a ploughshare, and OP *wagnis*, a colter (knife forward of the ploughshare): and

all of these words are ult akin to L *uōmis*, var *uōmer*, ML *vōmer*, a ploughshare, a term adopted by An and Zoo: perh cf also the syn Gr *hunnis* (*hunnē*) and Hesiod's *ophnis*. The IE r is perh *wegh-*, to sting or prick (Hofmann).

**wedlock.** See the 2nd GAGE, para 4, s.f.

**Wednesday; Woden** and **Odin,** occ **Othin; wood,** adj, and **odinite.**

1. *Wednesday* comes from ME *wednesdai*, slovenly for earlier *wodnesdai*, itself from OE *wōdnes daeg*, Woden's day—sem, a trans of LL *diēs Mercurii* (Mercury's day—the corresp day of the old Roman week): cf D *woensdag*, MD *woensdach*, earlier *wudensdach*, MLG *wōdensdach*, ON *ōthinsdagr* (Othinn's day): cf DAY and, for the 1st element *Woden*, principal divinity of the OGmc peoples, the OE *Wōden*, OS *Wōdan*, OHG *Wuotan*, G *Wotan*, ON *Ōthinn*.

2. ON *Ōthinn* becomes E *Othin*, usu—from the alternative trln *Odhinn*—*Odin*, whence Geol *odinite*, topo from *Odin*, familiar form of *Odenwald* (Odin's wood) in Germany.

3. The ON *Ōthinn* is perh analysable as 'friendly, i.e. gracious, god' or, less prob, 'friend of the gods', but he was primarily a storm-god; *Ōth-* would seem to be a *w*-less (or perh unaspirated) form of *Wōd-* (*Wōt, Wuot-*). OHG *Wuotan*, G *Wotan*, E *Woden*, OE *Wōden*, however, is related to OHG *wuot*, Go *wōds*, OE *wōd*, archaic E *wood*, mad, ON *ōthr*, possessed, inspired, divinely mad, and OHG-MHG *wuot*, G *Wut*, madness, to which, moreover, the syn ON *ōēthi* is related. The relationship of ON *ōēthi* and *Ōthinn* to ON *ōthr*, poetry, OE *wōd*, song, merely accords with the ancient and modern conception of poetry as the literary expression of a divine madness: cf the related L *uātēs* (*uātis*), ML *vātēs* (*vātis*), a prophet, an inspired singer, a poet.

**wee** and coll **weeny** (whence—after *teeny* for *tiny* —the coll redup **teeny-weeny**).

The ad *wee*, very small, comes, by a sort of b/f, from the ME *we* or *wei*, a little bit; *we* or *wei* is prob the *wey* (a measure of weight) mentioned at VIA, para 9. *Weeny* imitates *teeny*.

**weed** (1), a garment, usu in pl: ME *wede*, OE *wāēde*, var *wāēd*: cf OFris *wēde* or *wēd*, OS *wādi*, OHG-MHG *wāt*, a garment, ON *vāth*, texture, Skt *otave*, to weave, Lith *áudžiu*, I weave. The OGmc r is app *wāēth-*; the IE r, *wēdh-*.

**weed** (2), a rank grass or undergrowth (hence 'to *w2ed*'), whence **weedy**: ME *weed*, earlier *weod*: OE *w?od*: cf OS *wiod* and the vv 'to weed', OS *wiodōn* and MD-D *wieden*: o.o.o.

**week, weekly.** See VICAR, para 6.

**ween.** See VENERABLE, para 10.

**weep,** whence **weeper, weeping,** coll **weepy** (adj, hence n), pt and pp **wept**: ME *wepen*: OE *wēpan* (pt *wēop*): cf OFris *wēpa*, OS *wōpian*, OHG *wuoffan, wuoffēn*, MHG *wuofen*, OLG *wōpian* (pt *weop*), Go *wōpjan*, ON *ōēpa* (pt *ōēpta*), to lament, and the nn OE and OS *wōp*, OHG *wuof*, ON *ōp*; cf, further off, OSl *vabiti*, to summon (orig with a loud cry), to decoy. The OGmc r is prob *wōp-*;

the IE r, either *wōb-* or *wāb-*, varr *uōb-, *uāb-*. (Walshe.)

**weeping willow:** from its straight-drooping branches.

**weever.** See VIBRATE, para 3.

**weft.** See WEAVE, para 3.

**weigh, weight, weighty.** See VIA, paras 7 and 8.

**weir.** See WARN, para 4.

**weird,** fate, whence the adj. See DRUDGE, para 2, and cf WORTH, to become, q.v. at VERSE, para 2; cf also VERSE, para 4.

**weka,** N.Z. bird: Maori: akin to Tongan *veka*, Samoan *ve'a*, names for birds neither id nor yet widely dissimilar: prob from a similarity of note or cry.

**welcome.** See VOLITION, para 14.

**weld, welder, welding.** See VOLUBLE, para 12.

**welfare.** See VOLITION, para 15.

**welkin.** See the 2nd WILT.

**well** (1), adv, hence adj. See VOLITION, para 13.

**well** (2), n (of water). See VOLUBLE, para 11.

**well** (3), v, to issue as water does. See VOLUBLE, para 11.

**wellington** (boot). See BLUCHER.

**Welsh; to welsh.** See FLANDERS, paras 5 and 6.

**welt.** See VOLUBLE, para 13.

**welter.** See VOLUBLE, para 14.

**Weltpolitik, Weltschmerz.** See WORLD, para 2.

**wen** (tumour, cyst): OE *wenn*: cf D *wen*, MLG *wene*, dial G *wenne*: o.o.o.: ? akin to WOUND.

**wench,** n, hence v, whence **wencher** and **wenching; winch** (n, hence v)—cf **wince; wink** (v, hence n) —cf **lapwing.**

1. *Wench*, late ME *wenche*, a child (either sex), a girl, is short for ME *wenchel*, child, girl, from OE *wencel*, var *wincel*, a child: cf *winch, wink*, as below, and perh ON *vākr*, a child.

2. A *winch*, ME *wynch*, OE *wince*, a reel, a winch, is akin to *wince*, to shrink, ME *wincen*, var *winchen* (occ *wenchen*), which comes, prob via AF, from an ONF *w-* form of OF-MF *guencer* (or *-ier*), *guenchir* (or *-ier*), to totter, vacillate, be evasive, from OHG *wanchan*, MHG-G *wanken*, to waver, to totter—cf the syn ON *vakka*.

3. Closely related to *winch* and *wince* is 'to *wink*', ME *winken*, OE *wincian*: cf OHG *winchan*, MHG *winken*, to beckon, to wink, G *winken*, MD *winken*, MD-D *wenken*, to beckon, to signal; cf also Lith *vengti*, to avoid, and perh, ult, L *uagāri*, to wander (cf, phon, ON *vakka*).

4. With OE *wincian*, cf OE *hlēapewince*, lit a 'leap-beckoning' (cf LEAP), whence ME *leepwynke*, later *lapwynke*, whence, f/e (after *wing*), E *lapwing* a bird that, by its app wounded flight, lures enemies away from its young.

**Wend, Wendic** or **Wendish.** See the 2nd WIND para 6.

**wend,** pt **wended, went.** See the 2nd WIND, para 5

**wept.** See WEEP.

**were,** v. See WAS, para 1.

**werewolf.** See VIRILE, para 1.

**wergild.** See YIELD, para 2.

**Wesleyan,** whence **Wesleyanism,** derives from

John *Wesley* (1703–91), the founder of Methodism (occ Wesleyanism): 'he of *Wesley*', an easing of *Westley*, the western glade or meadow, OE *lēah*. (Ekwall.)

west, adj, adv, n; hence the Sc adj **wester**, whence, in part, **wester**, to move to the west, whence the vn **westering**; **westerly** (adj, hence n), **western**, adj (hence n), whence the nn **westerner**, **westernism**, and the v **westernize**; **Westminster**; **westward** (adv, hence adj), whence **westwardly**.— **vesper** (**Vesper**), **vesperal** (adj, hence n), **vesperian** (from *vesper*)—cf **vespers**, **Vespertilio**, **vespertine**; **Hesper**, **Hesperia**, **Hesperian**, **Hesperides** (whence, by b/f, **Hesperid** and, anl, the adj **Hesperidean** or **-ian**) ,**hesperidium**, **Hesperis**, **Hesperus**.

1. The n and adj *west* derive from the OE-E adv *west*, akin to OFris *west* (n), OHG *westan*, MHG *westen*, (both) from the west, G *Westen*, the west; MD *weest*, *west* (as D), adj and n; ON *vestr* (cf Da and Sw *vest*), adj and n. Cf also L *uesper* (ML *v-*), Gr *hespera*, OSl *večerŭ*, Lith *vākaras*, evening— the meaning also of the C words OIr *fescor*, Ga *feasgar*, Mx *fastyr*, and W *ucher*, Cor gorth*uher*, garth*uher*, both with var *-uer*. The west is the region, the place, the line, the direction of the setting sun; the basic idea is 'evening', with that of 'west' naturally ensuing; and the IE r is *\*wes-*, with extnn *\*wesp-*, as in Gr (*h-* for *w-*) and L, and *\*west-*, as in Gmc.

2. OE *west*, from or to or in the west (orig the region of the sun as it sets), has derivative adj *westerne*, E *western*; to it the adj *westerly*— although prop an adj *-ly* extn of the ME-E adj *wester*—perh owes something. OE *west* has the derivative extn (perh orig a cpd) *westweard* (adv), towards the west: cf the G *westwärts*. *Westminster* is simply the vicinity of the *minster* in the *west* of Tudor (and earlier) and Jacobean London, when the City (in the east) and Parliament (in the west) were connected by Whitehall; the building of the Abbey began c1250 on a site already venerable. *Westminster*, moreover, has become syn with 'the seat of government in Great Britain': cf *Washington*.

### Latin

3. Corresp to OGmc *west-* is L *uesp-*, as in the adj *uesper*, of the evening, used also as n, the evening, the Evening Star (*Uesper*), hence the west, and, in its ML form *vesper*, adopted by E, now mostly in the pl *vespers*, evensong, a sense current already in Eccl LL. The LL *uesperālis* and L *uespertīnus*, of the evening, become E *vesperal* and *vespertine*; with L *uespertīnus*, cf L *uespertīliō*, a bat (issuing at dusk): whence Zoo *Vespertilio*, whence the adj *vespertilian*—cf the syn LL *uespertīlioneus*.

### Greek

4. Corresp to L *uesper* is Gr *hesperos*, adj and n, (of) the evening, whence *hesperos* (*astēr*), the Evening Star, whence L *Hesperus*, adopted by E, which occ shortens it to *Hesper*. The f *hesperā* is used for both 'evening' and, derivatively, the west,

with its own adj *hesperios* (whence L *hesperius*, whence, in part, E *Hesperian*), f *hesperis*, which, used as n, accounts for L *hesperis*, the damewort, Bot E *Hesperis*. Gr *hesperā* has derivative *Hesperides* (adopted by L, then by E), the nymphs guarding the golden apples bestowed by Gaea upon Hera and that garden, situated at the extreme *west* of the known world, in which they grew, hence the Fortunate Isles; hence, from the colour, the Bot *hesperidium*.

**Westminster.** See prec, para 2.

**wet.** See WATER, para 3.

**wether — veal — vellum; vitellin(e), vitellus — vitular, vituline.**—veteran (adj, hence n); **veterinary**, whence **vet** (n, hence v); **veterate** (obs)—**inveterate**, whence **inveteracy** (for *\*inveteratecy*), **vetust**.— **etesian**.

1. *Wether*, a castrated ram, ME OE *wether*, is akin to OS *wethar*, *withar*, OHG *widar*, MHG *wider*, G *Widder*, MD-D *weder*, ON *vethr*, a ram, Go *withrus*, a lamb, a sheep. Cf also L *uitulus*, a calf, Doric Gr *etelon*, Aeolic Gr *etalon*, a yearling, Skt *vatsás*, a calf, a yearling, and such varying forms and senses as OIr *feis*, Cor *guis*, *guiz*, *gwis*, Br *guéz*, *guiz*, a sow, and Mx *oasht*, a wether. In OGmc, the basic sense is app 'a one-year old male sheep'; in L and Skt 'a one-year old (male) calf'; in both, 'a yearling': and the sem and phon connexion with 'age' is manifested by: L *uetus*, *uetustus*, old—Alb *vjet*, Gr *etos* (Doric *wetos*), Skt *vatsarás*, a year—OLith *vetušas*, OSl *vetŭchŭ*, old— Hit *wet-* or *wett-*, varr *wit(t)-* and *wid-*, a year, as in *wettanza*, a year, *wettantatar* or *widandanne*, a period of a year, and *wetti*, in a year. Note also the link supplied by L *ueternus*, old, and L *ueternīus*, (of a domestic quadruped) old enough, fit, to carry burdens, hence relating to a domestic quadruped, esp if a beast of burden. The IE r is therefore *\*wet-* (*\*uet-*), a year.

### Latin

2. L *uitulus*, ML *vitulus*, a calf, has adj *uitulīnus*, whence E *vituline*, var *vitular* (ML *vitul*us+suffix *-ar*); the dim *uitellus*, a little calf, hence the yolk of an egg, is, in its ML form, adopted by Sci: whence the Sci n *vitellin* and adj *vitelline* (perh imm from the L adj *uitellīnus*).

3. ML *vitellus* becomes OF-MF *veel* (EF-F *veau*), *vel*, adopted by ME, later *vele*, E *veal*; from OF-MF *veel*, *vel*, derives MF *veeslin*, later *veelin*, EF-F *vélin*, orig calf-gut, later calf-skin, treated like parchment, whence E *vellum*.

4. L *uetus*, old, has the syn extn *uetustus*, ML *v-*, whence the literary *vetust*, ancient, antique.

5. L *uetus* has gen *ueteris*, o/s *ueter-*, whence the extn *ueterānus*, old, aged, LL (orig of a soldier) much-experienced, also, as n, a retired official: whence the E adj and—perh imm from EF-F *vétéran*—n.

6. Also on L *ueter-*, o/s of *uetus*, old, is formed the adj *ueterīnus*, (of beasts) old enough to carry a burden, hence relating to a beast of burden, whence

*ïueterīnae*, beasts of burden, whence the adj *ueter-nārius*, whence *ueterināria* ars, whence elliptical LL *ueterināria*, the veterinary art; L *ueterīnārius* becomes EF-F *vétérinaire*, whence—unless direct from L—the E *veterinary*; from *veterinary surgeon* derives the coll *vet*.

7. Also from L *ueter-*, o/s of *uetus*, derives *ueterascere*, to (begin to) grow old, whence the adj *ueterātus*, aged, long-established, whence the obs E *veterate*. Int L *inueterātus*: E *inveterate*.

### Greek

8. Gr *etos*, a year, has adj *etēsios*, returning each year, whence *etēsiai* (for *e. anemoi*), annual winds, L *etēsiae*, EF *etesies*, EF-F *étésiens*, whence E *etesians*, whence, by b/f, the adj *etesian*.

**wey**, a weight. See VIA, para 9.

**whack**, v, hence n; **thwack**, v, hence n; (now dial) **thack**, v, hence n.

The 1st and the 2nd are int varr of the 3rd, which derives from OE *thaccian*, to pat, pat firmly: app echoic. For the echoic element *-ack*, cf *clack*, *crack*, *smack*, etc.

**whale**, n, hence v; **narwhal**; for **walrus**, cf HORSE, para 1.

1. *Whale*, ME *whal*, derives from OE *hwael*: cf OS *hwal*, OHG-MHG *wal*, OHG *walvisc*, MHG *walvisch*, G *Walfisch*, MD *wal*, *wael*, both also with *-visch* attached, ON *hvalr*—and prob MHG-G *wels*, the shad—and perh L *squalus*, a dogfish—OP *kalis*, a shad—Skt *chāla-*, a freshwater fish, *kara-*, a (large) fish. (The OIr *hualr*, a large fish, perh comes from ON.)

2. ON *hvalr* has cpd *nāhvalr* (app for *\*nārhvalr*: *nār*, a corpse, the allusion being to its 'deathly' or whitish colour), whence modern Scan *narhval*, whence E *narwhal* or *narwal*.

**whang**. See THONG, para 3.

**whap** (v, hence n), var **whop**; weak var **wap**; to strike: echoic. Hence **whopper** and **whopping**.

**wharf**, whence **wharfage**, whence **\*wharfager**, whence—after *passenger*—**wharfinger**; **warble**, v (whence **warbler** and **warbling**), hence n (whence **warbly**); **whirl** (v, hence n), whence **whirligig**, a whirly toy (esp a top or a top-like toy)—**whirlpool** —suggested by the syn ON *hvirfilvindr*—**whirlwind**; **whorl** (n, hence v), whence **whorly**. Cf the sep CARPUS (and the element *carpo-*).

1. *Wharf*, ME *wharf*, *wharfe*, *wherf*, *hwerf*, comes from OE *hwerf*, *hwearf*, a turning, a turn, hence a busy place, e.g. a river-bank, a sea-shore, hence a wharf: cf MD *warf*, *waerf*, MD-MLG-D *werf*, Sw *varf*, and the foll OGmc vv: OE *hweorfan*, to turn, turn about, be active, and syn OHG *hwerfan*, *hwerban*, MHG *hwerben* (G, to solicit), and Go *hwaírban*, to wander, ON *hverfa*, to turn: perh also Gr *karpos*, the wrist, the swivel or turning-point of the hand, for *\*kwarpos*, and Skt *śŭrpam*, *çŭrpam*, a winnowing-fan: IE r, *\*kwerp-*, var *\*kwerb-*, to keep turning, to be active: ? orig from the IE r *\*wer-*, to turn.

2. 'To *warble*,' ME *werbelen*, derives from ONF *werbler* (corresp to OF-MF *guerbler*), of Gmc

origin—cf OHG *wirbil*, MHG *wirbel*, lit that which goes round and round.

3. 'To *whirl*,' ME *whirlen*, derives from ON *hvirfla*, a freq of *hverfa*: cf G *wirbeln*—from the MHG n *wirbel* (OHG *wirbil*, a weakened var of *hwirbil*)—and MD-D *wervelen*, MD var *worvelen*. The E n *whirl*, although imm from the v, does owe something to the OE *hwierfel*, itself akin to OFris *hwarvel*.

4. *Whorl*, occ (mostly dial) var *wharl*, comes from ME *wharle*, *whorlwyl*, varr *wharwyl*, *whorwyl* (*-wil*), a spindle-whorl or flywheel: cf the syn MD-ED *worvel* (D *wervel*), which perh supplies the imm origin—certainly not supplied by the syn OE *hweorfa*.

**what, whatever, whatnot**. See WHO, para 1 and heading.

**wheal**. See VOLUBLE, para 15.

**wheat, wheatear, wheaten**. See WHITE, paras 5 and 6.

**wheedle**, whence **wheedler** and pa, vn **wheedling**: o.o.o: perh from OE *wǣdlian*, to beg (be a beggar), be in want, from *wǣdl*, want, poverty, akin to OHG *wātalī*, poverty, and *wādalōn*, to be a vagrant; rather (with EW) from the G *wedeln*, (of a dog) to wag the tail, whence *anwedeln*, to wag the tail on, to fawn on, to wheedle. G *wedeln* comes from MHG *wadelen*, from OHG *wadal*, *wedil* (cf G *Wedel*), a fan, a tail.

**wheel** (n, hence adj and v), whence **wheeler** and pa, vn **wheeling**, and such self-explanatory cpds as **wheelbarrow** (for the 2nd element, cf the v BEAR) and **wheelwright** (for the 2nd element, cf WORK).— Cf the sep POLE (Geog) and the element *tele-*.

*Wheel*, ME *wheel*, derives from earlier ME *hweol*, from OE *hwēol*, app a contr of OE *hweowol* (var *hweogul*): cf the syn OFris *hwēl*, MD *wiele*, *wyel*, MD-D *wiel*, MLG *wēl*, ON *hjōl*, Ga *cuibhle*, OSl *kolo*, Gr *kuklos*, Skt *cakrás*—and also L *colere*, to bestir oneself, be busy, to live in, to cultivate—Skt *cárati*, he moves (vi)—Gr *pelomai*, I move (vi), and *polos*, an axis, and *telos*, an end (to which one moves). The IE r is prob *\*kwel-*, to move around (vi).

**wheeple** and **wheetle**. See WHINE, para 3, s.f.

**wheeze, wheezy**. See QUERY, para 1.

**whelk** (1), marine snail, (2) pustule. See voluble, para 15.

**whelm**—whence **overwhelm**, whence the pa **over-whelming**—derives from ME *hwelmen*, to turn upside down: app a f/e blend of OE *helmian*, to cover (cf E *helm*, *helmet*), and OE *-hwelfan* in *āhwelfan*, to cover over, hence to overcome completely, *-hwelfan* being related to OHG *-welfan*, MHG *welben* (G *wölben*), to (over)arch, and ON *hvelfa*, to overturn, and, distantly, the Gr *kolpos*, bosom.

**whelp**, n, hence v; **Guelph**.

*Whelp* derives from OE *hwelp*, a puppy, young dog, akin to OS *hwelp*, MD-D *welp*, MD *welpe*, *wolpe*, *wulpe*, OHG *hwelf*, OHG-MHG *welf*, ON *hvelpr*: all perh from the corresp OGmc vv for 'to howl'—e.g., OE *hwelan*.

2. OHG-MHG *welf* becomes the ML family-name *Guelphus*, whence—prob via It *Guelfo*—the E *Guelph*.

**when, whence, whenever.** See WHO, para 2.

**where, whereas, whereat, whereby, wherefore, wherefrom, wherein, whereof, whereon, whereto, whereupon, wherever, wherewith, wherewithal.** See WHO, para 2.

**wherry**, o.o.o., is perh akin to the naut *wear*, q.v. at VEER, para 1.

**whet**, to sharpen, derives from OE *hwettan*, whence OE *hwetstān*, whence *whetstone*: and OE *hwettan* is akin to OHG *hwezzēn* (*wezzēn*), MHG-G *wetzen*, MD-D *wetten*, ON *hvetja*, to sharpen, and Go ga-*hwatjan*, to incite (*ga-* is int): all prob from the corresp OGmc adjj, as, e.g., OHG *hwaz*, OS *hwat*, OE *hwaet*.

**whether.** See WHO, para 2.

**whetstone.** See WHET.

**whey**: ME *whey*, earlier *hwey*: OE *hwāeig*, *hwāēg*, *hwēg*: cf MD *weye*, *wey*, D *wei*, MLG *hoie*, whey, and Go *hwatho*, foam—and perh, as a link between the prec and the foll terms, OSl *kvasŭ*, leaven, Skt *kvathati*, it seethes—Prakrit *chāsī*, buttermilk, L *cāseus*, cheese; therefore cf CHEESE.

**which, whichever.** See WHO, para 2.

**whicker**, to neigh, is echoic: cf WHINNY, q.v. at WHINE.

**whidah bird** exemplifies erudite f/e: prob *widow bird* (black, with long tail feathers resembling a widow's veil), it was altered to conform with an erroneous belief that it should be *Whydah bird* after *Whydah*, now *Ouidah*, in Dahomey.

**whiff**, n and v, is echoic: cf ME *weffe*, steam, vapour, a whiff. 'To *whiff*' has freq *whiffle*.

**Whig**, approx a Liberal, shortens *Whiggamore*, a C18 opponent of the Sc Conservatives: earlier *Whiggamaire*, app one who *whigs*—drives or urges on—a *mare* or horse. 'To *whig*' is prob echoic.

**while**, whence **whiles** (*-s*, orig the gen ending, indicates an adv), whence, in turn, **whilst**; **whilom**; **awhile** (*a-* for *an*, E *on*+the article *a* understood+the n *while*).

The conj *while* is short for (*the*) *while that* or (*the*) *while as*, with *for* understood before the phrase; 'You do that *while* I do this'='You do that for, i.e. during, the time that I do this'; and *whilom* derives from OE *hwīlum*, lit '(for the) times', *hwīlum* being the dat pl of *hwīl*, a space of time, an occasion, whence the E n *while*, as in 'every once in a while'; cf OFris *hwīle*, OS *hwīl*, OHG *hwīla*, MHG *wīle*, G *Weile*, a space of time, cf ON *hvīla*, a breathing-space, a rest: also, further off, cf L *quiēs*, a rest, quiet, and *tranquillus*, restful, and, with *č-* for *tch-*, and r for *l*, Skt *čirás*, lasting. Therefore cf QUIET.

'To *while* away' the time blends, prob by f/e, *while*, a time, and *wile*, to beguile.

**whim**, whence **whimsy** (pl *whims*+adj *-y*), whence **whimsical**, seems to be of Scan origin, prob traceable, ult, to ON *hvima*, to let one's eyes wander.

**whimbrel**, a curlew, and **whimper** (v, hence n), are extnn of the echoic \**whim*, a whining.

**whimsical, whimsy.** See WHIM.

**whin**, with cognates in modern Scan, is app related to ON *hvein*, a marshy field, attested in PlNn.

**whinberry.** See VINE, para 8, s.f.

**whinchat**, a *chatt*ering bird that frequents whin, is, in dial, a *furze-* or *gorse-chat*.

**whine** (v, hence n); **whinny**, whence **Houyhnhnm** (pron *whinnim*); **hinny**, n and v; **whisper**, v, hence n; **whistle** (n and v), **whistler** (OE *hwistlere*); **wheeple** and **wheetle**; cf the sep WHICKER.

1. 'To *whine*,' ME *whinen*, derives from OE *hwīnan*, to utter a *whiz* sound—cf the syn ON *hvīna*; and *whinny* is a shortening of *whine*—cf Swift's *Houyhnhnms*, a noble race of horses, in *Gulliver's Travels*.

2. 'To *whinny*' is clearly related to L *hinnīre*, to whinny, to neigh; *hinnīre* has f/e influenced L *hinnus*, a hybrid of stallion and ass, prop \**innus* from Gr *innos*, a mule, thought to be of Caucasian origin.

3. Akin to *whine* and *whinny* are 'to *whisper*', OE *hwisprian*, and 'to *whistle*', OE *hwistlian* (to hiss): both of the OE vv have OGmc, incl ON, cognates: all, obviously, are ult echoic. Cf the purely echoic, mostly dial *wheeple* (esp of a curlew) and *wheetle*.

**whinny.** See prec, para 1.

**whip, whippersnapper, whippet, whippoorwill.** See VIBRATE, para 4.

**whir.** See SWIRL, para 3.

**whirl.** See SWIRL, para 2; cf WHARF, para 3.

**whirligig.** See GIG, s.f.—cf WHARF (heading).

**whirlwind.** See WHARF (heading).

**whisk**, n, v; **whisker(s)**. See the 1st VERGE, para 1.

**whiskey** (Irish) or **whisky** (Scotch). See AQUA, para 6.

**whisper.** See WHINE, para 3.

**whist**, adj and n; **whist!** See HUSH, para 2.

**whistle, whistler.** See WHINE, para 3—and heading.

**whit; wight.**—Cf the sep AUGHT and NAUGHT (NOUGHT).

*Whit*, esp in *not a whit*, stands for *wit*: ME *wiht*: OE *wiht*, a thing, a creature; and *wight* (archaic), a creature, a man, comes from the ME var *wight*. OE *wiht* is akin to OS *wiht*, OHG-MHG *wiht*, G *Wicht*, MD *wecht*, creature, thing, MD-D *wicht*, a child, Go *waihts*, thing, ON *vītr*, creature, thing—and OSl *veštĭ*, a thing.

**white** (adj, whence **whitish** and **whity**; hence adv, n, v), **whiten, whiteness; whiting**; numerous cpds, mostly explicable by the 2nd element—but note esp **Whitsunday, Whitsuntide**.—**wheat** (whence **wheaty**), **wheatear, wheaten**.—**edelweiss**.

1. *White*, ME *whit*, OE *hwīt*, is akin to OFris *hwīt* (var *hwitt*), OS *hwīt*, OHG *hwīz*, later *wīz*, MHG *wīz*, G *weiss*, Go *hweits*, MD *witte*, MD-D *wit*, ON *hvītr*; cf also Skt *śvētás* and such Sl forms as OSl *svētŭ*, light (n), the dawn, *svitati*, to become bright, to dawn, Lith *šveisti*, to cause to be light or

bright, and *švidùs*, white-gleaming. The IE r is app *\*kweit-*, with var *\*kweid-*, gleaming, white.

2. OE *hwīt* has the derivative *hwītness*, whence *whiteness*, and ME *whit* the derivative *whitenen* (perh influenced by ON *hvītna*), whence 'to *whiten*'. Akin to *white*, but imm deriving from MD *wijting*—itself MD *wijt* (var of *wit*)+suffix *-ing*—is the fish *whiting*.

3. OE *hwīt* has the notable virtual cpd *hwīta sunnandaeg*, lit 'white Sunday'—prob from the white vestments worn at, e.g., baptism; hence *Whitsunday*; whence, anl and f/e by a false division of the prec, the ME virtual cpd *white sune tide*, whence *Whitsuntide*.

4. Akin to OE *hwīt*, white, is OE *hwǣte*, ME *whete*, E *wheat*, with its whitish grain and esp its white flour: cf OFris *hwēte*, OS *hwēti*, OHG *hweizi*, MHG *weize*, G *Weizen*, Go *hwaiteis*, MD *weet, weite, weiten*, MD-D *weit*, ON *hveiti*.

5. That white-rumped small bird we call the *wheatear* app contains a double f/e alteration: prob it represents *white-ear*, with *white* becoming *wheat* and with *ear* influenced by the *ear* of cereals and the *ear* of hearing, and also with *ear* representing *\*er*, a false sing of ME *ers*, rump (cf ARSE), apprehended as a pl.

6. OE *hwǣt*, wheat, has adj *hwǣten*, whence *wheaten*.

7. G *weiss* occurs in the G cpd *Edelweiss*, lit 'a white nobleman', fanciful name for an Alpine plant and its white bloom—the Swiss floral emblem; adopted by numerous European languages, incl E.

**whither.** See WHO, para 2, s.f.
**whiting.** See WHITE, para 2, s.f.
**whitlow.** See VIVA, para 9.
**Whitsunday, Whitsuntide.** See WHITE, para 3.
**whittle, thwittle, thwaite; doit.**

1. *Whittle*, to cut, or pare, away with a knife, derives from *whittle*, a (large) knife, e.g. a butcher's: ME *thwitel*, whence the now dial 'to *thwittle*': from OE *thwītan*, ,o cut (cf the dial *thwīte*, to cut, to carve): akin to ON *thveita*, to hew.

2. Akin to ON *thveita* is ON *thveit*, a piece of land (as it were, cut out from its vicinity): whence E *thwaite*, woodland with the trees cut down, also a meadow.

3. Also very intimately related to ON *thveita*, to hew, is ON *thveiti*, var *thveit*, lit a 'cut-out' piece of metal, a small copper coin, whence prob the MD *deyt, dueyt, duit* (as still), *doyt*, the last adopted by E and altered to *doit*, esp in *not worth a doit*, not worth a farthing.

**whiz** or **whizz** (v, hence n)—whence **whizzer** and **whizzing** and such cpds as **whizz-bang** and **whizgig** (*gig*, a whirling toy)—is obviously echoic.

**who,** acc **whom** and gen **whose,** whence **whoever, whomever, whosoever; what,** whence **whatever** and **whatnot; when** (whence **whenever), whence; where** (hence **wherever),** with cpds in *-as, -at, -for, -fore* (adv, hence n), *-in, -of, -on, -through, -to, -upon, -with* (with extn *-withal*, now used as n); **whether;**

which (hence **whichever); whither; why;**—sep HOW.
—Also sep: KICKSHAW; QUALIFY, QUALITY, etc., treated at QUALE—QUANTITY, etc., at QUANTIC—QUORUM—QUOTE (QUOTA, QUOTIENT).

1. All these E *wh-* words derive from OE *hw-*; all the other corresp Gmc words in *w-* likewise derive from OGmc *hw-*: and OGmc *hw-* answers to IE *kw-*, predominantly vocalized *\*kwi-*, with varr *\*kwa-, \*kwe-*, esp *\*kwo-*. Cf the L *qui*, f *quae*, neu *quod*, the relative 'who-which', and the corresp interrogative *quis*, f *quae* (OL *quā*), *quid*, 'who?—which?—what?'; but cognates are afforded also by C, Sl, Gr, Skt, Hit, Tokh, Arm, not only for these primary relative and interrogative pronouns, but also for the subsidiary 'when'—'whence'—'where' —'whether'—'whither'—'why'. The basic pronoun is the interrogative; the relative follows naturally from it; and the relative-interrogative is perh an expressive extn of IE *\*i-*, he, that one. Medit? Perh cf Eg *aut* (? for *\*waut* for *\*kwaut*), who, which, and *ausu* (? for *\*wausu* for *\*kwausu*), what?

2. In the following summary, only the ME and OE forms and the phon closest Gmc cognates are noted:

*who*, ME *who*, var *wha*, OE *hwā* (cf OFris *hwā*);

*whom*, ME *whom*, var *wham*, OE (dat) *hwām*, *hwǣm*;

*whose*, ME *whos*, var *whas*, OE *hwaes*;—

*what*, OE *hwaet* (neu of *hwā*); cf OFris *hwet* and OS *hwat*;—

*which*, ME *which*, var *whilk*, OE *hwilc* (*hwylc*), var *hwelc*; cf OS *hwilik*, OFris *hwelik* or *hwelk*, OHG *hwelīh*, Go *hwileiks*;—

*when* (adv, hence conj), ME *when* or *whan*, var *whenne* or *whanne*, OE *hwaenne, hwanne*, occ *hwonne*—cf OS *hwan*, OFris *hwan* or *hwen*, OHG *hwanne*, Go *hwan*;

*whence*, ME *whens, whennes* (adv *-s* is prop the gen), var *whenne, whanene*, OE *hwanan, hwanon* (or *-one*), occ *hwonan*, from the OE forms for 'when'—cf the OS *hwanan* and the OFris *hwana, hwona*;—

*where*, ME *wher* or *whar*, OE *hwǣr*—cf OFris *hwēr*, OS *hwār*, Go *hwar*, ON *hvar*;—

*whether*, orig 'which. (of two)', ME id, OE *hwether* or *hwaether*—cf OFris *hwedder, hweder*, OS *hwethar*, OHG *hwedar*;—

*whither*, ME *whider*, OE *hwider*—cf Go *hwadrē* (and *hwathrō*, whence);—

*why*, ME *why* and *whi*, corresp to OE *hwȳ* and *hwī*, prop the instr of *hwā*, neu *hwaet*: cf ON *hv* and Go *hwē*, the latter germane also to OE *hū*, ME *hu, hou*, finally—as in E—*how* (q.v. sep).

**whole,** whence **wholly**—cf **whole cloth (out of), wholemeal, wholesale, wholesome; hail,** v, and **hale,** adj; **heal** (whence **healer** and pa, vn **healing**)— **health,** whence **healthful, healthless** (obsol), **healthy** (whence **healthiness**).

1. The n *whole* derives from the adj *whole*, ME *hole* (*hoole*), var *hale*, OE *hāl*, sound (complete), healthy: cf OFris *hēl*, OS *hēl*, OHG-MHG-G *heil*, Go *hails*, MD *hiel*, MD-D *heel*, ON *heill*, syn OSl

*cēlŭ*, OP *kailūstiskan*, health, Gr *koilu*, the beautiful (prop, neu adj). The OGmc etym is *\*hailaz*; the IE, *\*koilos*; the IE r, *\*kail-*, *\*koil-*.

2. From *whole cloth*, a (large) uncut piece of cloth, derives (of a story, a lie) 'made *out of whole cloth*'—a sheer fabrication; *whole meal=meal* (grain coarsely ground) of *entire*-wheat; *wholesale*, goods sold in large quantities, hence the corresp adj, whence the sense 'both extensive and undiscriminating or indiscriminate'. *Wholesome* is much older; it derives from ME *holsum*, itself perh from ON *heilsamr*—cf MD *heilsam*, D *heilzaam*, G *heilsam*.

3. From ON *heill*, sound, healthy, comes ME *heil*, *hail*, used in greeting (cf *wassail*), whence ME *heilen*, *hailen*, to greet, whence 'to *hail*' or greet. With *Hail!*, cf G *Heil!* and Go *Hails!*: for 'Be *hail*' or well, 'Long Life!' But from E *hāl*, sound, healthy, comes ME *hal*, later *hale*, retained by E.

4. Akin to OE *hāl*, healthy, is OE *hāelan*, ME *haelen*, *helen*, E 'to *heal*': cf the syn OFris *hēla* and OS *hēlian*, and OHG *heilēn*, to become, also to make, well, MHG-G *heilen*, to cure, Go *hailjan*, MD *heilen*, *hielen*, *helen*, MD-D *heelen*.

5. OE *hāl*, well, has derivative *hāelth* (abstract suffix *-th*)—ME *helthe*—E *health*.

**whom.** See WHO, para 2.

**whoop** (v, hence n), whence **whooping cough** and **AE whoopee!** (whence the sl 'to make whoopee'): ME *whopen*, *whoupen*, loose varr of *hopen*, *houpen*: OF-MF *hoper*, *houper*, *huper*: from the echoic interj *hop*, *houp*, *hup*—cf F *hoop-la!*, whence the carnival game *hoopla*.

**whop, whopper, whopping.** See WHAP.

**whore, whoredom, whorish.** See CHARITABLE, para 2.

**whorl.** See WHARF, para 4.

**whortleberry.** See at BLACKBERRY.

**whose.** See WHO, para 2.

**why.** See WHO, para 2, s.f.

**wick** (1), of lamp. See VEIL, para 5.

**wick** (2), a village, a small bay. See VICINAGE, para 5.

**wicked** (whence **wickedness**): ME *wicked*: f/e formed from ME *wicke*, wicked, from ME *wiken*, from OE *wīcan*, to be weak, to give way, and therefore cf E *weak*, q.v. at VICAR, para 7. Cf:

**wicker** (whence **wickerwork**—cf WORK): ME *wyker*, *wekir*, osier: cf the dial Sw *vikker*, willow, and ON *vīkja*, OE *wīcan*, to be weak, to be pliable, to bend easily: therefore cf prec and prob:

**wicket**, a small gate, a small door set in a large one, hence the wicket (orig of two stumps) in cricket, whence **wicket-keeper**: ME *wiket*, adopted from ONF: corresp to OF-F *guichet*, orig also a nook, a small hiding-place: perh a dim (*-et*) from ON *vik*, nook (cf ON *vīkja*, to turn).

**wickiup.** See WIGWAM.

**wide**, adv, derives from OE *wīde*, itself from the OE adj *wīd*, whence the E adj *wide*, whence both *widen* and *width*—cf *breadth* from *broad*, *length* from *long*, etc. The OE *wīd* is akin to OFris (and OS) *wīd*, MD *wide*, *wijdde*, *wijt*, D *wijd*, OHG-

MHG *wīt*, G *weit*, ON *vīthr* (cf Da and Sw *vit*)—and perh Skt *vītás*, straight, prob to Skt *vi*, asunder. Cf WITH.

**widgeon**, occ **wigeon**, a species of duck, app comes from an (ONF and) AF var of F *vigeon* (obs varr *vingeon*, *gingeon*): ML *vipiōn*em, acc of *vipiō*, a small crane: phon cf *pigeon* from L *pipiō*, acc *pipiōn*em: both *vipiō* and *pipiō* are echoic of the cries, notes, calls.

**widow** (n, hence v), whence **widower**—cf **widow's mite** (*Mark*, xii, 42); **vidual, viduate** (adj and n), **viduity, viduous;** sep DIVIDE, DIVISION; sep DEVICE and DEVISE; sep INDIVIDUAL.

1. *Widow*, ME *widewe* (contr *widwe*), OE *widuwe*, *weoduwe*, *wuduwe*, is akin to OFris *widwe* (occ *wide*), OS *widuwa*, MD *wedewe* (*-wi*), *weduwi*, MD-D *weduwe*, OHG *wituwa*, MHG *witewe*, G *Witwe*, Go *widuwō*: cf Skt *vidhāv*a, OP *widdewŭ*, OSl *vĭdova*, *vŭdova*, ML *vidua*, L *uidua*, prop the f of the adj *uiduus*, bereft, widowed; cf also Gr *ēitheos* (int *ē-*+*\*withewos*, corresp to L *uiduus*), unmarried, hence an unmarried young man, and, with *f* for *u* (*v*), the OIr *fedb*—for the *-b*, perh cf early modern HG *Wittib*, var of *Witwe*. With OHG *wituwa*, G *Witwe*, prob cf OHG *weiso*, MHG *weise*, G *Waise*, an orphan, and perh OHG *wīsan*, to avoid; and with Skt *vidhāvā*, a widow, cf Skt *vídhyati*, he bores through, divides or separates by boring or piercing, and the nasalized Skt *vindhátē*, (it) becomes empty. The IE r, therefore, is *\*widh-*, to sunder, part, separate.

2. From L *uiduus*, ML *viduus*, and its derivative *uiduitās*, comes E *viduous* and E *viduity*; from the LL extn *uiduālis*, ML *v-*, comes E *vidual*; from the derivative L v *uiduāre*, pp *uiduātus*, comes the adj *viduate*, and from the derivative LL n *uiduātus* (gen *-ūs*), widowhood, comes the Eccl *viduate* or order of widows.

**width.** See WIDE.

**wield.** See VALUE, para 2.

**wienerwurst.** See WURST, para 2.

**wife, wifehood, wifely.** See VIBRATE, para 9.

**wig** (1), a cake, a bun. See WEDGE, para 1, s.f.

**wig** (2), of hair. See *periwig* at PETER, para 12.

**wiggle** is a thinning of *waggle*, q.v. at VIA, para 1.

**wight** (1), adj. See VICTOR, para 1.

**wight** (2), n. See WHIT.

**wigwam** and **wickiup**, the anglicized form of **wikiup**: the 'Red Indian' hut, resp of the Great Lakes (and points East) and of the arid W and SW USA: the Amerind r is *wik-*, var *wig-*, app 'to dwell': *wigwam* is lit 'their dwelling', and *wikiup* 'a dwelling': cf Menominee *wíkiop*, Sauk (or Sac) *kickapoo*, Fox *wikiyap*, *wĭkiyapi*; Ojibway *wigiwam*, Lenape *wikwam*, Abnaki *wigouam*, *wigwam*. (Webster; Mathews.)

**wild** (adj, hence adv and—cf MD *wilde*—n)—whence the n **wildling** (*-ling*, a person, animal, thing, that belongs to); **wildebeest** and **wild-goose chase** (occ **race**); **wilderness**—cf 'to **wilder**' and its derivative 'to **bewilder**' (int *be-*), whence **bewildering** and **bewilderment**.

1. *Wild*, untamed, uncultivated, hence savage, ME *wild*, earlier *wilde*, OE *wilde*, is related to OFris *wilde*, OS *wildi*, MD *welde*, *welt*, *wilt*, *wilde*, MD-D *wild*, OHG *wildi*, MHG *wilde*, G *wild*, Go *wiltheis*, ON *villr* (but Da and Sw *vild*), W *gwyllt* (as n, wilderness), Cor *gwyls*, *guyls*, and perh Ga *allaidh*, OIr *allaid*: prob akin to G *Wald*, a forest —cf, sem, the origin of SAVAGE.

2. The *wild* cpds are mostly self-explanatory, but note esp the adj *wildcat* (mine, well, etc.) from 'the *wild cat*'—*wild-goose chase* (or *race*), a pursuit as futile as that after a wild goose—*wildebeest*, adopted from SAfr, lit 'wild beast', in fact a gnu.

3. OE *wilde* has derivative *wildor*, *wilder*, a wild beast, whence OE-ME *wilderne*, wild, savage, deserted, ME *wilderne*, wilderness, whence—with abstract suffix *-ness* substituted for *-ne*—*wilderness*: cf MD *weldernesse*, *wildernesse*, *wildernisse*, D *wildernis*. Note that OE *wilder*, *wildor*, wild beast, is a contr of OE *wildeor*, itself an easing of OE *wild-dēor*, wild beast, OE *dēor* being both generic and particular.

4. 'To *wilder*' (EE-E) or lead astray—virtually superseded by its int, *bewilder*—derives either by b/f from *wilderness* or, more prob, from MD ver-*wilderen*, freq of *verwilden*, akin to G *wildern*, Da for*vilde*, ON *villa*, to lead astray, to perplex (utterly), or, less prob, from ME *wilderne*, a wilderness.

**wildebeest.** See prec, para 2.
**wilder,** v. See WILD, para 4.
**wilderness.** See WILD, para 3.
**wile.** See VICTIM, para 3.
**wilful.** See VOLITION, heading and para 7.
**will** (1), n. See VOLITION, para 7.
**will** (2), full v. See VOLITION, para 8.
**will** (3), auxiliary v. See VOLITION, para 9.
**William.** See VOLITION, para 10.
**will-o'-the-wisp.** See VOLITION, para 10.
**willow,** whence **willowy.** See VOLUBLE, para 16.
**willy,** a basket. See VOLUBLE, para 17.
**willy-nilly.** See VOLITION, para 9.
**wilt** (thou). See VOLITION, para 9.

**wilt,** to droop, to become flaccid, whence n: dial var **welt**: EE *welk*: ME *welken*: MD *welken*, to wither (D *verwelken*): cf OHG-MHG *welc*, G *welk*, (orig) damp, (soon) faded; cf also OB *vlaga*, dampness, therefore OHG *wolkan*, MHG *wolken*, G *Wolke*, a cloud, therefore cf OE *wolcen*, a cloud, ME *wolcne*, *weolcne*, *welcne*, *welkne*, *welkene*, a cloud, the sky, E *welkin*, the sky, loosely the atmosphere.

**wily.** See VICTIM, para 3.
**wimble.** See GIMLET.
**wimple; gimp, guimpe.**

1. *Wimple*, a woman's head-, neck-, chin-covering of silk or linen: ME-from-OE *wimpel*: cf OFris *wimpel*, OHG *wimpal*, MHG-G *wimpel*, MD *wimpel*, *wempel*, *wumpel*, ON *vimpill* (Da, Sw *vimpel*): o.o.o.: but app a dim of OGmc *\*wimp*.

2. Frankish *\*wimpil* becomes OF *guimple*, whence MF-F *guimpe*, a chemisette: whence E

*gimp*, a narrow piece of ornamental fabric, used for trimming of dresses or for upholstery.

**win.** See VENERABLE, para 8.
**wince.** See WENCH, para 2.
**winch.** See WENCH, para 2.

**wind** (1), n; **windy; window; wing** (n, hence v); **winnow.**—**van; fan** (n, hence v).—**vent** (in hunting); **ventail; ventilate, ventilation, ventilator; ventose, ventosity.**—cf the sep AIR, ASTHMA—and WEATHER.

1. *Wind*, fast-moving air, OE *wind*, is akin to OFris (and OS) *wind*, OHG-MHG *wint*, G *Wind*, Go *winds*, MD *went*, *wint*, D *wind*, ON *vindr*, wind—to W *gwynt*, Cor *guenz*, *guins*, *gwens*, *gwins*, wind, and Br *guenteréz*, a winnowing-van—to L *uentus*, ML *ventus*, Tokh A *wänt*, Tokh B *yente*—perh Hit hu*wantes*, winds—and to the *n*-less Skt *vāta*, wind, *vāti*, it blows, Gr *aētēs* (? for *\*waētēs*), a very strong wind, OHG *wājan*, MHG *waejen*, G *wehen*, Go *waian*, OE *wāwan*, OFris *wāia*, (of the wind) to blow. The IE r is app *\*we-*, nasal extn *\*wen-*, to blow.

### Germanic

2. OE *wind* has derivative adj *windig*, E *windy*; and ON *vindr* has the cpd *vindauga*, an eye (cf EYE) of the wind, i.e. an opening for the air to enter, whence ME *windoge*, later *windowe*, E *window*. Such cpds as *windflower* (after Gr *anemonē*, from *anemos*, wind), *-gauge*, *-hover* (the kestrel), *-jammer*, *-mill*, *-pipe*, *-rose*, *-row*, are self-explanatory.

3. OE *wind* has derivative v *windwian*, to blow (chaff) away (from grain) by means of air-currents: whence ME *windewen*, later *winewen*, whence 'to *winnow*'.

4. Akin to the OGmc words for 'to blow' adduced in para 1, is the syn D *waaien*, which means also 'to fly'; akin also is ON *vāengr* (cf Da, Sw *vinge*), a wing, whence ME *wenge*, later *winge*, E *wing*.

### Latin and French

5. L *uentus* (gen *uenti*), ML *ventus*, wind, becomes OF-F *vent*, whence OF-F *venter*, to blow, MF-F to track by scent: whence the syn E 'to *vent*', used also as n, both obs except as hunting techh. OF-F *vent* has OF-F derivative *ventail* (suffix *-ail*), the air-admitting lower half of a helmet, adopted by E, now only hist.

6. L *uentus* has—perh suggested by the dim *uentulus*, a slight wind—the derivative v *uentilāre*, ML *v-*, to expose to the air, hence also to winnow, with pp *uentilātus*, whence *uentilātiō* and *uentilātor* (winnowing-van): E 'to *ventilate*'—*ventilation* (perh imm from MF-F)—*ventilator*.

7. L *uentus* has adj *uentōsus*, windy, whence *uentōsitās*, windiness, LL flatulence: E *ventose, ventosity*.

8. Perh akin to L *uentus* is L *uannus*, ML *v-*, a winnowing-van or *-fan*: whence both OF-F *van*, adopted by E, and OE *fann* (*f* for ML *v-*), a basket —or a capacious shovel—for tossing grain into the

air and thus throwing out the chaff (obs), whence—
cf the EF-F *éventail* (from MF-F *éventer*, prefix-
cpd of *venter*)—the hand-manipulated *fan*, whence
the birds named *fantail*, having a fan-shaped tail.

wind (2), to turn repeatedly (pt, pp **wound**), hence
**wind**, a winding-device; **windas** (obs) and **windlass**.
—**wand; wander**, whence **wanderer** and pa, vn
**wandering**—cf **wanderlust**.—**wend** (and **Wend**,
whence **Wendic, Wendish**), pt **went**—now serving
as pt of 'to *go*', hence the need for the modern pt
**wended**.

1. 'To *wind*' comes from ME *winden*, from OE
*windan*: cf OFris *winda*, OS *windan*, OHG *wintan*,
MHG-G *winden*, Go *-windan*, MD *wenden*, *wijn-
den*, MD-D *winden*, ON *vinda*: cf also the OGmc
words in the ensuing paras.

2. With the obs *windas*, ME *wyndas*, from ON
*vindāss*, lit a winding-pole (*āss*), cf Ice *vindilāss*,
whence E *windlass*.

3. Akin to ON *vinda*, to wind, is ON *vöndr*, a
slender, supple stick cut from a tree: ME *wond*,
later *wand*, retained by E: cf Go *wandus*.

4. Akin to OE *windan*, to wind, is—? influenced
by *wand*—OE *wandrian*, (vi) to move about aim-
lessly: ME *wandrien*, later *wandren*, whence 'to
*wander*': cf MD *wanderen*, var of *wandelen*, and
MHG-G *wandern*, to wander—and OHG *wantalōn*,
MHG-G *wandeln*, to change (vi), G to wander,
itself akin to G *winden*: 'to *wander*' is 'to take a
*winding* course'. G *wandern*, to wander, has cpd
*wanderlust*, a longing (cf E *lust*) to wander,
adopted by E.

5. With OHG *wantalōn*, MHG-G *wandeln*, to
change (vi), cf OHG *wentēn*, MHG-G *wenden*, to
turn (vt)—the caus of OHG *wintan*, MHG-G
*winden*, and the syn OFris *wenda*, OS *wendian*, Go
*wandjan*, ON *venda* (Sw *vända*) and esp OE
*wendan* (vi), to turn, to go, ME *wenden*, E 'to
*wend*'. Note that *went* first occurs c1200 and was
orig also a pp.

6. Perh from MHG-G *wenden*, to turn, comes G
*Wende*, E *Wend*, the name of a Slavic people in
East Germany: remnants or 'pockets' of an early
medieval migration that was repelled.

**windflower, windhover**. See the 1st WIND, para 2.
**windlass**. See the 2nd WIND, para 2.
**window**. See the 1st WIND, para 2.
**windy**. See the 1st WIND, para 2.
**wine, wine-bibber, winer, winery**. See VINE,
para 8.
**wing**. See the 1st WIND, para 4.
**wink**. See WENCH, para 3.
**winkle** (shell-fish). See the 2nd PERIWINKLE, s.f.
**winnow**. See the 1st WIND, para 3.
**winsome**. See VENERABLE, para 9.
**winter, wintry**. See WATER, para 4.
**wipe**, See VIBRATE, para 5.
**wire**, whence **wireless** (adj, hence n—short for
**wireless telegraphy**), **wiring** (vn), **wiry; withe** and
**withy; gyve; ferrule**.

1. *Wire*, ME *wyre*, earlier *wir*, OE *wīr*, is related
to OHG *wiara*, fine gold work, MLG *wīre*, wire,
ON *-vīrr* (wire) in *vīravirki*, wirework or filigree,

L *uiriae* (pl), LL *uiria* (sing), armlet, bracelet—said
by Pliny, to be of C origin—cf OIr and Ga *fiar*,
twisted, crooked, W *gwyro*, to slant, be crooked,
OC *veiro-*, (to be) oblique or crooked—an origin
perh more prob than that in L *uiēre* (ML *v-*), to
plait, but cf para 3, s.f.

2. Akin to OE *wīr* is OE *withthe*, ME *wyth* or
*withe*, E *withe*, a flexible thin branch, or long twig,
used for binding. From ME *withe*, in sense 'band'
or 'halter', perh derives, by AF mdfn (*gu-, g-*, for
*v-, w-*), the ME *give*, E *gyve*, mostly in pl.

3. Very closely akin to OE *withthe* is OE *wīthig*
(? for *withthig*, orig the adj, connoted by *-ig*, of
*withthe*), a willow-twig, a willow tree (obsol), hence
ME *withi*, E *withy*: cf ON *vith, vithja*, a slender,
flexible twig, and *vīthir*, a willow—OHG *wīda*,
MHG *wīde*, G *Weide*, a willow—perh also cf Gr
*eitea, itea* (for *witea*), willow, Lith *žilvytis*, a grey
willow, *vytìs*, willow-twig, OSl *vyti*, to plait, L
*uītis*, a vine, a vine-tendril, and *uiēre*, to plait.

4. L *uiriae*, LL *uiria*, armlet or bracelet, has dim
L *uiriolae*, LL *uiriola*, ML *viriola*, a small bracelet,
whence OF *virol*, MF-F *virole*, whence late ME
*verelle*, EE *verrel(l)*, *verril(l)*, EE *ferrel* or *ferril*, E
*ferrule*: the *f-* forms are f/e, as if the word derived
from a dim of L *ferrum*, iron.

**Wisconsin** State derives from W. river, itself lit
'(the) place, hence region, of the beaver's or musk-
rat's hole' (Ojibway *Wishkonsing*).

**wisdom**. See VIDE, para 8.
**wise** (1), adj. See VIDE, para 8.
**wise** (2), n. See VIDE, para 9.
**wiseacre**. See VIDE, para 9, s.f.
**wisecrack**. See VIDE, para 9.
**wisenheimer**. See VIDE, para 9.
**wish, wishful**. See VENERABLE, para 7.
**wishy-washy**. See WASH (heading).
**wisp** (n, hence v), whence **wispy**: ME *wisp*, of
Scan origin, ult the ON *visk*: therefore cf E *whisk*,
q.v. at the 1st VERGE, para 1.
**Wistaria** (**wistaria**), erroneously **Wisteria** (**wisteria**), is named after the A scientist Caspar *Wistar*
(1761–1818).
**wistful**. See VENERABLE, para 7, s.f.
**wit**, n. See VIDE, para 6.
**wit**, v. See VIDE, para 7.
**witch, witchcraft, witchery, witching**. See VICTIM,
para 2—and the heading.
**witch hazel**. See WYCH.
**witenagemot** or **witenagemote** is the meeting
(OE *gemōt*: cf E *moot* at MEET) of the *witan* or
royal, or national, council in AS times (OE *witan*,
pl of *wita*, a councillor or counsellor, lit a wise
man: cf *wit* and *wise* at VIDE, paras 8 and 9).
**with**, whence **withal** (for *with-all*)—**withdraw,
withdrawal, withdrawn**, qq.v. at DRAW, para 2—
**withhold** (to hold against, hence back)—**within** (ME
*withinne*, earlier *withinnen*, OE *withinnan*: cf IN)—
**without** (ME *withoute*, earlier *withouten*, OE
*withūtan*: cf OUT)—**withstand** (OE *withstandan*, to
stand *with*, i.e. against); **withernam** and **withershins,
Sc widdershins; withers**.—Cf the element *iso-* and
the sep GUERDON.

1. *With*, ME *with*, (along) with, against, OE *with*, against, over against, opposite, hence, positionally, very close to, hence with, is akin to OFris *with*, *withe*, OS *with*, ON *vith*, against, and the intimately—almost inseparably—related extnn: OE *wither*, OFris *wither*, OS *withar*, OHG *widar*, MHG-G *wider*, Go *withra*, MD-D *weder*, against, and notably Skt *vitarám*, further (the comp of *vi-*, apart), and Av *vithra*, separate. If, as seems prob, the IE r be *wi-*, private, particular, withdrawn, separate, then Gr *idios* (if for *widios*), private, is cognate—therefore cf *idiom*, *idiot*, etc.

2. OE *wither*, against, has two cpds worth particularization: *withernam*, a seizure (*nām*, from *niman*, to take—cf OHG *neman*, G *nehmen*) against, i.e. as a reprisal, a term in early E Law; and *withershins*, contrariwise, from OE *withersȳnes*, backwards, with E dial and Sc f/e var *widdershins*, OE *withersȳnes*, var *-sines*, with 2nd element (adv *-s*) coming from ON *sinni*, a way or direction (cf SEND).

3. OE *wither*, against, is used also as n 'opposition', ME *wither*, resistance, whence a horse's *withers* (ridge between the shoulder-blades): lit 'the parts taking the strain—resisting the pull—in pulling a load'.

**withal.** See prec (heading).

**withdraw, withdrawal, withdrawn.** See DRAW, para 2.

**withe.** See WIRE, para 2.

**wither.** See WEATHER, para 3.

**withernam.** See WITH, para 2.

**withers.** See WITH, para 3.

**withhold; within; without; withstand.** See WITH (heading).

**withy.** See WIRE, para 3.

**witless; witling:** *wit*, n (see VIDE, para 6)+ suffix *-less*; *wit*, n+dim suffix *-ling*.

**witness** (n, hence v): OE *witness*, *gewitness* (*ge-*, prop int, is here merely formative), knowledge (*-ness*, abstract suffix, tacked on to *wit*, n, q.v. at VIDE, para 6), esp testimony, hence one who testifies.

**witticism, witty.** See VIDE, para 6, s.f.

**wive**, to marry (a woman); **wives**, pl n. See VIBRATE, para 9.

**wivern.** See VIBRATE, para 3.

**wizard.** See VIDE, para 8, s.f.

**wizen**, to shrivel, var **weazen**, now usu in pa **wizened** (occ **weazened**): ME *wisenen*: OE *wisnian* (var *weosnian*): cf ON *visna*, to wither, OHG *wesanōn*, to become dry, Lith *vystì*, ML *viescere*, L *u-*, to fade or wither. The IE r is app *wes-*, to fade or wither.

**woad.** See VITRAGE, para 1.

**wobble** (occ written **wabble**), v, hence n, whence also the adj **wobbly:** echoic or, at the least, 'picturesque': cf the syn LG *wabbeln* and esp MHG *wabeln*, var of MHG-G *wabern*, to be in agitated motion; cf (*f* for *b*) the ON *vafra*. (Walshe.)

**Woden.** See WEDNESDAY, para 3.

**wodge.** See WEDGE, para 2.

**woe** (whence **woeful**) and **woebegone** (ME *wo begon*, encompassed—pp *begon*, from OE *begān*, *bigān*, to go *bi-* or about, around); **wail** (v, hence n —whence the obsol **wailful**); *vae victis!*

1. *Woe*, grief, derives from ME *wo* or *woo*, var of *wa*, itself from the OE interj *wā*: cf OFris (and OS) *wē*, OHG-MHG *wē* (gen *wēwes*), Go *wai*, ON *vei* (with modern Scan varr), all orig interjj: cf ML *vae*, L *uae*, esp in *uae uictis*, ML *vae victis* (woe to the vanquished: dat pl of pp *uictus*, conquered) —Gr *oi* and its cpds *ouai*, ah woe, and *oimoi*, woe (is to) me, parallel to L *oiei*—Skt *uvé*—and, in C, OIr *fé* and Cor *gew*, *gu*, and, in cpds, *go-*. But such a word is, in its interj origin, world-wide, and the derivative n is prob at least Medit in its range: cf Eg *ah*, woe.

2. Akin to OE *wā* is ON *vāla*, *vāela*, whence ME *wailen*, *weilen*, E 'to wail'—lit, to 'cry *woe!*'

**wold.** See the 1st VOLE.

**wolf** (n, hence v), whence **wolfish; wolverine; wolfram, wolframite.**—**lupus, lupin, lupine; lobo;** cf the element *lupi-*.

1. *Wolf*, ME-OE *wulf*, is akin to OS *wulf*, OFris *wolf*, Go *wulfs*, OHG-MHG-G *wolf*, ON *ūlfr* (for *wulfr*), the OGmc etymon being *wulfaz* for *wulhwaz*. The IE etymon is *wulqos* (Walshe): cf L *lupus* (? for *wulpus*, itself for *wulqus*)—Gr *lukos*—Lith *vilkas*—Skt *vṛkas* (*virkas*)—and cognates in OSl, Alb, Arm. Perh 'the tearer or render' and therefore akin to IE *wel-*, to tear, as in L *uellere* (Hofmann). Perh cf VULPINE.

2. Irreg from E *wolf* comes E *wolverine*, var *-ene*: this A carnivore has many wolfish features and qualities. *Wolframite* comes from G *Wolframit*, an extn of *Wolfram*, adopted (*wolfram*) by E—in Chem, tungsten, and in Min, wolframite. G *Wolfram* is a f/e substitution of the PN *Wolfram* ('Wolf Raven'—OHG *hraban*, MHG *raben*) for early modern HG *wolfrumb*, lit 'wolf-turnip': the metal is 'found in turnip-like lumps' (Walshe).

3. L *lupus*, a wolf, acquires in ML the Med sense 'ulcer', whence the modern Med *lupus*; the derivative L adj *lupīnus* becomes E *lupine*; the E n *lupine* (plant and its flower), var *lupin*, comes, via MF-F *lupin*, from L *lupīnus* used as n, lit 'wolf-pea, -pease'.

4. L *lupus* becomes Sp *lobo*, whence the timber-wolf of the south-western United States—where Sp influence is so strong.

**wolfram, wolframite.** See prec, para 2.

**wolverene, usu wolverine.** See WOLF, para 2.

**woman, womanhood, womanish, womanize, womanly.** See VIBRATE, para 10 and heading.

**womb** and **wame.** The latter is an E dial, and a Sc, var of the former: and the former derives from ME *wombe*, *wambe*, from OE *wamb*, occ *womb*: cf OFris *wamme*, *womme*, OS and Go *wamba*, OHG *wamba*, MHG *wambe*, MHG-G *wamme*, ON *vömb*, words tending to mean, primarily, 'belly' or 'paunch'; perh (Walshe) cf also W *gumbe*lanc, womb; if so, perh cf the OC r *gamb-*, to curve, as in OIr *camb*, *camm*, Ga *cam*, curving, bent, W *cam*, crooked, Cor *camma*, *gamma*, to curve.

**won:** pt, pp of **win.**

**wonder** (n and v), **wonderful, wonderment** (from the v), **wonderwork, wondrous** (adj and adv).

'To *wonder*' derives from OE *wundrian*, to be affected with astonishment, from the OE n *wundor*, whence ME *wunder*, later *wonder*, retained by E. OE *wundor* is akin to OFris *wunder*, OS *wundar*, OHG *wuntar*, MHG-G *wunder*, MD *wunder*, MD-D *wonder*, ON *undr*: o.o.o.: perh (Walshe) akin to OHG *wunna*, MHG *wunne*, G *Wonne*, joy, delight. OE *wundor* has the derivatives *wundorfull*, E *wonderful*, and *wundorweorc*, E *wonderwork*; and ME *wonder* has gen *wonders*, used as adj and adv, whence, f/e as if a contr of *\*wonderous*, the adj and adv *wondrous*.

**wont**, adj, n, v. See VENERABLE, para 11.

**won't**, will not. See VOLITION, para 9.

**wonted**, accustomed. See VENERABLE, para 11.

**woo.** See VOTAL, para 4.

**wood** (1), adj 'mad'. See WEDNESDAY, para 3.

**wood** (2), n, a large, dense growth of trees, hence the material 'wood': ME *wode, wude*: OE *wudu, wiodu, widu*, the last being app the basic form—cf OS *widu*, OHG *witu*, ON *vithr* (Sw, Da *ved*), a wood, timber, *vitha*, timber, and, in C, OIr *fid*, a tree, Ga and Ir *fiodh*, a wood, timber, OW *guid*, a tree, W *gwȳdd*, Br *guida*, Cor *gwydh, guit*, trees, shrubs, the OC etymon being *\*vidus*, the r *\*vid-*. The IE r is prob *\*wid-*, valid (in modern times, at least) only for Europe.

2. OE *wudu, wiodu, widu* has derivatives and cpds:

OE *wudubind*, whence E *woodbind*, with var—orig dial—*woodbine* (cf BINE);

OE *wuducock*, E *woodcock*;

OE *wuduland*, E *woodland*;

OE *wudurofe* (2nd element, o.o.o.), E *woodruff*;

OE *wudig*, E *woody*—cf the coll AE *woodsy*, coined after *folksy*.

3. EE-E *wood* has derivative adj *wooden* and very numerous cpds, mostly self-explanatory. Note, however, esp:

*woodchuck*, a woodpecker, from *chuck*, to tap;

*woodchuck*, a ground hog: perh a f/e alteration of some northern Alg word for the wejack, an A and Can bird called also a pekan or a fisher; or cf *wejack* itself. Cf, phon, the Cree *otchek* (and Chippewa *otchig*), the wejack or pekan or fisher, and, sem, the prob transference by white traders of an Amerind name for a bird to a marmot. (Mathews.)

**wooer, wooing.** See VOTAL, para 4.

**woof.** See WEAVE, para 3.

**wool** (whence **woolly,** adj, hence n)—**woollen,** AE **woolen; Woolsack.—flannel,** n, hence adj and v.—Cf the sep VELVET, where also VELOURS.

1. *Wool(l)en* derives from ME *wollen*, OE *wullen* (cf MD *wullen*, MD-D *wollen*), from OE *wull*, whence ME *wulle, wolle*, E *wool*: cf OFris *wulle, wolle*, OHG *wolla*, MHG-G *wolle*, Go *wulla*, MD *wulle, wolle*, MD-D *wol*, ON *ull*—Lith *vilna*, OB *vlena*—Skt *ū́rṇā*—L *lāna* (cf *vellus*, a fleece), Gr *lēnos*, Doric *lānos*—MIr and Ga *olann*, Mx *ollan*, W *gwlān*, Cor *gulān, glān*, Br *gulān*, OC *\*vlana* (MacLennan): cf VELVET.

2. 'The *Woolsack*' or office of Lord Chancellor derives from the divan-shaped sack of wool upon which he sits in the House of Lords.

3. The W *gwlān*, wool, has derivative *gwlanen*, flannel, whence, with *f* for *gw-* and with suffix *-el* for suffix *-en*, the E word *flannel* itself.

**Woolsack, the.** See prec, para 2.

**word, wordy.** See VERB, para 1.

**wore:** pt of **wear.**

**work** (n and v), whence **workable, worker,** pa and vn **working, workless, workshop** (cf SHOP); cpds from OE: **workaday, workday, workhouse, workman** (whence **workmanship**).—**wrought** and **wright.** —Cf the sep ENERGY, ERG, ORGAN, and such sep cpds as BULWARK and SURGEON.

1. 'To *work*', ME *werken, wurchen*, derives from OE *wyrcan, wyrcean, wircan*: cf the n in next para: cf also OFris *werka, werkia, -wirka, -wirkia, wirza*, O Swerkon, *wirkian*, OHG *wurchēn*, MHG *würken*, MHG-G *wirken*, Go *waúrkjan*, MD *warken, wirken, wierken, weerken*, MD-D *werken*, ON *verka, yrkja* (*yrkia*).

2. The n *work*, ME *work, werk, weork* or *weorc*, derives from OE *worc, werc, weorc*, akin to OFris (and OS) *werk*, OHG *werah, werc*, MHG *werch, werc*, G *Werk*, MD *warc, weorc, werc*, D *werk*, Go *gawaúrki*, ON *verkr*: cf also Gr *ergon* (for *\*wergon*, dial var *\*wargon*), whence the sep ENERGY and ERG, and Gr *organon*, something used in working, whence the sep ORGAN, and Av *vareza-*, activity (lit 'works'), and *verezyeiti*, he is active (lit 'works'). The IE r is *\*werg-*, to work, var *\*worg-*: cf, with *g-* for *w-*, the Arm *gorc*, work. (Hofmann.)

3. OE *worc, werc, weorc*, or their ME forms, have the foll notable cpds extant in E:

ME *werkeday*, whence E *workaday*, characteristic of work, hence, occ, humdrum; cf

OE *weorcdaeg*, E *workday* (opp Sunday);

OE *weorchūs*, E *workhouse*;

OE *weorcmann*, E *workman*.

4. The OE v *wyrcan* (or *-ean*), *wircan*, has pt *worhte*, with metathetic var *wrohte* (cf OFris *-wrocht*), and pp *geworht*: whence the E pt and pp *wrought*, the pp being used also as adj, usu implying 'well or finely, delicately, worked or made'. Very closely related to those OE words and forms is OE *wyrhta*, with metathetic var *wryhta*, a worker, esp in wood, whence the E *wright*: cf OFris *wrichta* and OHG *wurhto*, a hired workman. E *wright* is now obsol, except in such cpds as *cartwright, millwright, playwright, shipwright, wainwright, wheelwright*.

**workaday** and **workday, workhouse; workman.** See prec, para 3.

**world, worldly** (whence **worldliness** and the negg **unworldly, unworldliness**); **Weltpolitik, Weltschmerz.** —Cf the sep OLD and the sep WEREWOLF.

1. *Worldly* comes, through ME *worldlích*, from OE *woroldlīc*, the adj (*-līc*, -like) of *worold*, contr of *weorold*, whence, through ME *weoreld, weorld, werld* or *world*, the E *world*: and OE *weorold*,

*worold*, is related to OFris *warld*, OHG *weralt*, MHG *werelt*, *werlt*, MHG-G *welt*, OS *werold*, MD *warelt*, *werelt*, *werlt*, *welt*, D *wereld*, ON *veröld*: the *wer*, man, that occurs in *werewolf*+the OGmc forms of *old*, e.g. OHG-MHG-G *alt*, Go *altheis*, OE *ald*, cf Go *alds*, age: lit, therefore, '(the) man-old' or 'man-age', i.e. mankind's age, the age of the earth inhabited by mankind.

2. The G *Welt* occurs in such cpds as *Weltpolitik*, world policy, international politics, esp Germany's pre-1939 imperialism, and *Weltschmerz*, world-pain, a romantic pessimism about the world's present and future state.

**worm, wormer, wormy.** See VERMEIL, paras 2 and esp 7—cf the heading.

**worn**: pp of 'to wear'.

**worry.** See WRENCH, para 6.

**worse**, adv and adj (whence the obs v 'to worse', whence **worsement**—anl with *betterment*—and **worsen**); **worst**, adj, hence also adv, n, v (anl with obs 'to worse').

1. *Worse* and *worst* are the comp and the sup of an adj lacking a positive: they serve as comp and sup to BAD. The adv *worse* derives from OE *wyrs*, *wiers* (cognates in the other OGmc languages), very intimately related to the adj: OE *wyrsa*, *wiersa*, ME *wurse*, *werse*, late ME-E *worse*: cf OS *wirsa*, OHG *wirsiro*, Go *wairsiza*—and, app with *-sr-* become *-rr-*—OFris *werra*, var *wirra*, and ON *verri*.

2. With E 'to *worsen*', cf OHG *wirsōn*, to corrupt, and OFris *wersia*, to differ, demur, be in opposition: perh, therefore, these words are related to WAR.

3. *Worst*, ME *wurst*, *werst*, later *worst*, derives from OE *wurresta*, *wyrst*, *wersta*, akin to OFris *wersta*, OHG *wirsisto*, ON *verstr*: all corresp to the comps adduced in para 1.

**worship, worshipful.** See the 1st WORTH, para 4.

**worst.** See WORSE, para 3.

**worsted** was orig a fine woollen fabric made at *Worsted* (now *Worstead*) in Norfolk, England: lit, the place (*stead*) of the *worth* or enclosure (Ekwall).

**wort.** See RADICAL, para 10.

**worth** (1), adj and n, **worthful, worthless, worthy,** adj (whence **worthiness**), hence n; **worship** (n, hence v), whence **worshipful**; sep STALWART.

1. The n *worth*, value, ME *worth*, *wurth*, comes from OE *weorth*, *wurth*, *wyrthu*: cf OFris (and OS) *werth*, OHG *werd*, MHG-G *wert*, Go *wairth*, MD *wert*, *weert*, *waert*, *waerd*, D *waard*, ON *verth*; cf also W *gwerth*, price, perh Cor *vry*, value, and Av *averetā-*, possession.

2. Derivatives of the n include *worthful*, OE *weorthfull*—*worthless*, OE *weorthlēas*—*worthy*, ME *worthi* or *wurthi* (from the ME n), akin to OFris *werthich*.

3. The adj *worth*, valuable, desirable, worthy (all obs), hence, meriting, as in '*worth* consideration', (having property, etc.) equal in value to, as in 'He's *worth* a million', pregnant or elliptical constructions, derives from ME *worth*, *wurth*, *werth*,

approx corresp to OE *weorth*, *wurth*, *wierthe*, akin to OFris (and OS) *werth*, Go *wairths*, OHG *werd*, G *wert* or *werth*, ON *verthr*—and almost inextricably associated with the nn cited in para 1. The IE r is perh *\*wert*, worth, value, price, itself perh an extn of that IE *\*wer-*, to turn, which lies behind the v *worth*.

4. The OE adj and the OE n *weorth* prob combine to form the 1st element of the OE n *weorthscipe* (suffix *-scipe*, state, condition, quality, etc.): ME *wurthscipe*, later *wurscipe*, *worscipe*: E *worship*. From the ME n comes the ME v *wurthscipen*, later *wurscipen*, *worscipen*, whence 'to *worship*'; from the ME v comes ME *worschipere*, whence *worshipper*.

**worth** (2), v, to become. See VERSE, para 2.

**worthless.** See the 1st WORTH, para 2.

**worthy.** See the 1st WORTH, para 2.

**would.** See VOLITION, para 9.

**wound** (n and v), whence **woundless** and the archaic **woundy**, adj, hence adv; **zounds!**; sep WEN.

1. 'To *wound*' derives from OE *wundian* (cf OFris *wundia*), itself from the n *wund*—whence ME *wunde*, later *wounde*, E *wound*: cf OFris *wunde*, OS *wunda*, OHG *wunta*, MHG-G *wunde*, MD *wunde*, MD-D *wonde*, D *wond*, ON *und*; cf also the corresp adjj for 'wounded' or '(very) sore'— OE (and OS) *wund*, OHG-MHG *wunt*, G *wund*, Go *wunds*, ON *und*.

2. With the archaic *woundy*, lit 'producing, or characterized by, wounds', hence 'excessive', whence 'excessively', cf sem the archaic *plaguy*, a pej int adj, hence adv—esp as L *plāga* means a severe blow, hence a wound, LL a plague.

3. From *wound*, n, comes the oath *God's wounds!*, whence, via '*'s wounds!*', the contr *zounds!*

**wove**, pt and occ as tech adj; **woven**, pp of WEAVE.

**wowser**, a person censorious of minor vices or even of such entertainments as Sunday sports or the music-hall: Aus coll, so widely used as now to rank as familiar SE: o.o.o.: perh an 'easing'— after *booser*, *boozer*, drunkard, public-house—of *\*wower*, one who barks—cries *wow!*—at anything he condemns, from a dog's *wow-wow*, or *bow-wow*. The dog's *wow(-wow)* explains the A sl *wow*, a success.

**wrack.** See WREAK, paras 3 and 4.

**wraith.** See WARD, para 5.

**wrangle, wrangler.** See WRENCH, para 4.

**wrap** (v, hence n), whence **wrappage** (cf *package*) —**wrapper**—pa, vn **wrapping.**—**rhapsodic** (and its extn **rhapsodical**)—**rhapsodist** and **rhapsodize**, both anl from **rhapsody.**

1. 'To *wrap*—ME *wrappen*—is app of imm Scan origin: cf Lith *verptì*, to spin, *varpste*, a spool, a spindle, Lett *verpata*, a parting (e.g., of the hair), and Gr *rhaptein*, to sew together.

2. Gr *rhaptein* has s *rhapt-*, r *rhap-*, and is perh akin to Skt *várpas-*, cunning; the IE r is app *\*wrep-* (var *\*werp-*), to spin. (Hofmann.) Akin to Gr *rhaptein* (pt *errapsa*) is Gr *rhapsōidos*, a weaver of songs (cf ODE): whence EF-F *rapsode*, whence the

reshaped learnèd E *rhapsode*. Gr *rhapsōidos* has two derivatives relevant to E:

*rhapsōidia*, a rhapsode's (recitation of a) song or part of an epic, whence EF-F *rapsodie*, E *rhapsody*; *rhapsōidikos*, whence E *rhapsodic*.

**wrasse**: Cor *wrāch, guerāch, gurāgh*, orig a hag— cf the syn W *gwrach*.

**wrath**, whence **wrathful** and the A coll **wrathy**; **wroth** (deeply angry).

1. *Wrath*, violent or resentful anger, ME *wrathe*, earlier *wraththe*, earliest *wraeththe*, OE *wrǣ́ththu* or *wrǣ́ththo*, derives from the OE adj *wrāth*, whence ME *wrath*, later *wroth*, E *wroth*. The basic sense of OE *wrāth* is 'crooked', lit, hence fig, whence 'bad, cruel': cf OE *wrīthan*, to twist, to bind or bind up, OFris (and OS) *wrēth*, evil, cunning, OHG *reid*, twisted, MD *wret, wreat, wrede*, D *wreed*, cruel, ON *reithr*, angry, evil.

2. OE *wrīthan*, to twist, bind (up)—pt *wrāth*— becomes ME *wrīthen*, E 'to *writhe*', to twist into coils, now usu vi, esp to twist and turn, esp in torment or shame: cf OHG *rīdan*, ON *rītha*, to twist about, to wind, to roll (up); cf also the syn Lith *reistì*.

3. Intimately related to OE *wrīthan* is OE *writha*, something twisted, hence plaited or inter-twined: ME *wrethe*: E *wreath*. Partly from ME *wrethe* and partly from ME *wrethen*, var *writhen*, pp of *writhen*, to writhe (OE *wrīthan*), com E 'to *wreathe*'.

4. Also akin to OE *wrīthan*, to twist, is OE *wrīgian*, (vi) to turn, to turn as one moves or goes, whence ME *wrⁱen*, E 'to *wry*' or twist (vi, vt), now archaic. Partly direct from 'to *wry*', and partly as an 'easing' of its pp *wried*, comes the adj *wry*. With OE *wrīgian*, cf OFris *wrīgia*, to bend or stoop, MLG *wrīch*, twisted, bent, hence cranky, MD *wrīgen, wrijgen*, to wind, to twist—and perh Gr *rhoikos*, bent, crooked.—Hence *awry*: *a-*, on (+ the)+*wry*, on the oblique, hence oblique.

5. Yet another cognate of OE *wrīthan*, to twist, is OE *wrǣstan*, to twist violently—esp away, to wrench: ME *wresten*, E 'to *wrest*', whence the n *wrest*: cf ON *reista*, to wrest. Note the sep WRIST.

6. OE *wrǣstan* has the presumed freq *wrǣst-lian*, whence ME *wrastlen, wrestlen*, E dial 'to *wrastle*' (A dial *wrassle*) and E 'to *wrestle*', whence 'a *wrestle*'; the OE *wrǣstlian* has agent *wrǣstlere*, whence E *wrestler*.

**wray** and **bewray**. The archaic *wray*, to denounce, to betray, derives from OE *wrēgan*, to accuse: cf OFris *wrōgia* (and *wrēia*), OS *wrōgian*, OHG *ruogēn* (G *rugen*, to censure), Go *wrōhjan*, to accuse, and Go *wrōhs*, an accusation, and ON *roegja*, to accuse. From OE *wrēgan* derives the ME int *bewreyen, bewraien*, E 'to *bewray*' or accuse, malign, hence to expose, to reveal.

**wreak** (v and n), whence **wreaker** (ME *wrēkere*), **wreakful** and **wreakless**, all archaic; **wreck** (n, hence v—whence **wreckage, wrecker** and **wrecking**) —cf **wrack** (n, hence v); **varec**; **wretch, wretched** (whence **wretchedness**).—**urge** (v, hence n), **urgent** (whence **urgency**).

1. 'To *wreak*', to drive out, to banish (both obs), to avenge, to punish, to inflict, ME *wreken*, OE *wrecan*, is akin to OFris *wreka*, OS *wrekan* (*wrecan*) OHG *rechan*, OLG *wrecan*, Go *wrikan*, ON *reka*— also to Lith *vargtì*, to suffer hardship or distress, and L *urgēre*, to press close or hard, hence to pursue, and perh Skt *vrájati*, (vi) he presses for-ward. The IE r is perh *wrēg-*, metathetic var *wērg-*, with short *e* var of each form: to press, to urge, to drive.

2. Akin to OE *wrecan* is OE *wrek, wrec*, some-thing driven ashore from the sea, a wreck, whence, in fact, *wreck*: cf the syn ON *rek*, intimately related to *reka*, to drive.

3. Akin to OE *wrek, wrec*, is OE *wraec*, that which is driven, whence E *wrack*, a wreck, a ruin, archaic except in *wrack and ruin*, now usu spelt *rack and ruin*; the EE-E *wrack* has perh been influenced by MD *wrac, wracke* (MLG *wrak*), a shipwreck, and *wrac, wraec* (MLG *wrak*), broken, damaged, unsound.

4. With E *wrack* in its derivative sense 'seaweed' (perh from its resemblance to wreckage), cf *varec*, seaweed, adopted from MF-F *varec* (OF *warec*) or *varech*, orig 'wreckage', 'seaweed' occurring in Norman F as early as C14; itself from OE *wraec*. (B & W.)

5. OE *wrecan*, to drive out, to punish, has derivative *wraecca, wrecca*, ME *wrecche*, E *wretch*, a fugitive or an exile (obs), hence a (very) miserable person, hence an unfortunate, hence a contemp-tible person: cf OHG *recchio*, MHG *recke*, a banished warrior (whence G *Recke*, a warrior, a hero), and OS *wrekkio*, an outlaw—cf also the OHG adj *wreh*, exiled. E *wretch* has derivative adj *wretched* (pp *-ed* used adj).

6. L *urgēre*, to press hard, to pursue, yields 'to *urge*'; its presp *urgens*, LL-ML also adj, acc *urgentem*, yields MF-F *urgent*, adopted by E; *urgency*—for *urgentcy*—is perh slightly indebted to the EF-F derivative *urgence*.

**wreath** and **wreathe**. See WRATH, para 3.

**wreck**, whence **shipwreck**. See WREAK, para 2.

**wren**: ME *wrenne*: OE *wrenna, wraenna* (with metathetic varr *werna, waerna*): cf OHG *wrendo* (dim var *rendilo*) and ON *rindill*: o.o.o.

**wrench**, n and v; **wring**; **wrangle**, whence **wrangler**; **wrinkle** (n, hence v); **wrong**, adj (hence adv), n (whence the v, and **wrongful**); **worry**.

1. A *wrench*, in ME 'deceit', OE *wrenc*, deceit, lit a twisting, is akin to MHG *ranc*, a rapid twist-ing, G *Rank*, deceit, G *Ranke*, a tendril, and esp to OHG *renkēn*, MHG-G *renken*, to wrench, the caus of *ringen, wringen*, to wring, id with OHG *ringan*, MHG-G *ringen*, to wrestle or strive. Cf OE *wrencan*, to twist, hence to deceive, ME *wrenchen*, to twist or wrench, E 'to *wrench*'.

2. Cf, therefore, 'to *wring*' (pt, pp *wrung*): ME *wringen*, OE *wringan*: cf, besides the OGmc vv in para 1, MD *wrengen, vringen*, MD-D *wringen*.

3. Thus we arrive at *wrong*: the adj and n *wrong* are retained from the ME adj and n *wrong*, var of the ME adj and n *wrang*, themselves from the

OE n *wrang*; the ME adj *wrang* has been influenced
—perh suggested—by the ON adj *rangr*, twisted,
awry, wrong: cf MD *wranc, wrange*, D *wrang*,
bitter, and therefore the sep *rancid*. The ME n
*wrang* has adj *wrangwis*, whence the now mainly
Sc *wrongous*.

4. Also cognate with 'to *wring*' is 'to *wrangle*',
ME *wrangelen*, clearly a freq of ME *\*wrangen*, to
contend, to strive: cf the syn MLG *wrangen* and
the OGmc vv in para 1. From the basic sense 'to
dispute' comes the University of Cambridge
*wrangler*.

5. Yet another cognate of 'to *wring*' is 'a *wrinkle*',
OE *wrincle*: cf the syn ED *wrinckel* and the MD
*wrinckelen*, to wrinkle; the OHG *runzala*, MHG
*runzele*, G *Runzel*, dimm of the syn OHG *runza*,
MHG *runke*, and the *n*-less ON *hrukka*, perh
represent a distinct r.

6. Prob akin to 'to *wring*' is 'to *worry*' (whence
the n *worry*, whence the adj *worrisome*): ME
*worowen*, earlier *wirien*: OE *wyrgan*: cf OHG
*wurgēn*, MHG-G *würgen*, to throttle or choke,
with MHG var er*wergen*, (vi) to choke; cf also
Lith *veržiù*, I bind tightly.

**wrest.** See WRATH, para 5.

**wrestle, wrestler.** See WRATH, para 6.

**wretch, wretched.** See WREAK, para 5.

**wrick:** var of the 2nd RICK.

**wriggle.** See the 2nd RICK, s.f.

**wright.** See WORK, para 4.

**wring.** See WRENCH, para 2.

**wrinkle.** See WRENCH, para 5.

**wrist,** whence the dim **wristlet** and the adj
**wristy;** cf the sep WREST, q.v. at WRATH, para 5.

*Wrist*, id in ME (var *wriste*) and in OE, is akin
to OFris *wrist*, ankle, MHG *riste*, G *Rist*, ankle,
MD *wrist*, wrist, ankle, ON *rist*, *vrist*, ankle (cf
Da *vrist*, instep): the point, or bodily part, at
which the hand or the foot twists: therefore cf
*wrest* and *writhe*, qq.v. at WRATH.

**writ,** n. See para 2 of WRITE.

**writ,** pt and pp. See heading and para 1 of:

**write,** pt **wrote** (archaic **writ**), pp **written** (archaic
**writ**); **writer**; **writing,** n.

1. 'To *write*' comes, via ME *writen*, from OE
*wrītan* (var *wrītian*), pt *wrāt*, pp *writen*, orig to
scratch, carve, incise, hence to scratch or incise

runes or symbols, hence letters on wood, bark,
etc., hence to write as we know writing: cf OFris
*wrīta*, OS *wrītan* (orig, to tear), ON *rīta*, *vrīta*,
to write, *vrit*, a letter, Go *writs*, a stroke or a dash,
hence a letter; cf also MD *riten*, D *rijten*, OHG
*wrīzan* or *rīzan*, MHG *rīzen*, G *reissen*, to tear or
rend: sem, cf GRAMMAR and GRAPH: IE r, perh
*\*wreid-*, to tear or scratch, hence to write.

2. OE *wrītan* has derivative *wrītere*, E *writer*,
and vn *wrīting*, E *writing*, and the intimate, prob
derivative, cognate OE-ME-E n *writ*, a writing,
hence a legal (orig, written) document: cf ON *vrit*
or *rit*.

**writhe.** See WRATH, para 2.

**writing,** n. See WRITE, para 2.

**wrong,** whence **wrongful; wrongous.** See WRENCH,
para 3.

**wrote.** See WRITE, para 1.

**wroth.** See WRATH, para 1.

**wrought.** See WORK, para 4.

**wry.** See WRATH, para 4.—Hence the bird
*wryneck*.

**wurst,** a sausage, is mostly AE: adopted from
OHG-MHG-G *wurst*, MLG var *worst*: perh akin
to G *wirr*, MHG *wirre*. confused, and OHG
*wirren*, MHG ver*wirren*, G ver*wirren*, to confuse,
therefore perh to WORSE.

2. In AE, *wurst* occurs esp in *liverwurst*, from
G *Liberwurst*, a liver-sausage, and *wienerwurst*
G *W-*), a Vienna sausage.

**wych,** as in *wych-elm* and *wych-hazel*, is an EE-E
var (? a purposive differentiation) of *witch*, ME
*wiche* or *wyche*, OE *wice* or *wic*: o.o.o.: but perh
(OED) from OGmc *\*wik-*, to bend, to be pliable,
as in OE *wīcan* (E *weaken*), OFris *wīka*, OS *wīcan*,
OHG *wīchan*, to give way: cf LG *wieke*, a wych-
elm.

**Wyandot** or **-otte,** an orig A breed of domestic
fowls, derives from the *Wyandot(te)* tribe of 'Red
Indians': Huron *Wendat*, app 'Islanders' or
'Peninsula-Dwellers' (Mathews).

**Wyoming** (whence **Wyomingite**) comes from the
Lenape—ult an Alg language—PIN *M'chetuwó-
mink*, lit 'upon the great plain' (Webster)—or,
according to another trans, 'large plains'.

**wyvern.** See VIBRATE, para 3, s.f.

# X

X, an unknown quantity, orig stood, as an abbr of *xei*, for Ar *shei*, a thing, anything, something, hence, in Medieval Math, the unknown.— As 'Christ', *X* represents the Gr capital letter khi (*kh: X*), initial of *Khristos*, whence L *Christus*, E *Christ*.

xanthic, xanthous. See HARE, para 3. Such Chem terms as *xanthin(e)* and *xanthone*, and the element *xantho-*, likewise derive from Gr *xanthos*, yellow.

xenia (Bot), xenogamy, xenomania, xenophobia (hatred of foreigners). See the element *-xene*. *Xenophobe*, hater of foreigners, is prob adapted from F *xénophobe*.

xerophagy, xerophilous, xerophyte. See the element *xero-*.

xiphias, a swordfish (obsol), and Xiphias, a genus of fishes, also the constellation Dorado: L-from-Gr *xiphias*, a swordfish, a comet shaped like a sword: from Gr *xiphos*, a sword: o.o.o.: ? Medit—cf Aram *sajefa*, Ar *saifun*, Eg *sefĕt*, a sword (Boisacq). The derivative Gr adj *xiphoeidēs*, sword-shaped, yields *xiphoid*.

xylan (Chem suffix *-an*)—xylem (adopted from G)—xyloid, wood-like, all derive from post-Classical L *xylon*, trln of Gr *xulon* (s and r *xul-*), wood. Cf the element *xylo-*.

For xylophone, cf that element.

# Y

yacht (n, hence v—whence yachting), whence yachtsman; yegg.

1. *Yacht* anglicizes D *jacht*, MD *jacht, jaecht, jachte*, var *jaget*, cf MD *jachtschip* or *jaghtschip*, a ship built for pursuing pirates, from *jacht* (etc.), pursuit, the chase, from MD-D *jagen*, to pursue, to hunt: cf the syn OFris *jagia*, OHG *jagōn*, MHG-G *jagen*, and ON *iaga* (*jaga*), to drive—perh (Walshe) akin to Skt *yahúś*, restless.

2. The orig underworld term *yegg*, an itinerant safe-breaker, is said—app f/e—to derive from one John *Yegg*, safe-breaker; prob, however, it derives from G *jäger*, a hunter, from *jagen*.

yahoo, E a degraded man or youth, a vicious hooligan, AE a lout, a poor white, common-nouns *Yahoo*, one of Swift's *Yahoos*, creatures having the form and all the vices, none of the virtues, of man: perh (Webster) 'after the Cariban tribe the *Yahos*, or *Yaos*, on the coast near the borderland of Brazil and French Guiana', but more prob the 'name of a degraded E African tribe often mentioned by early travellers' (EW); perh from the contemptuous call *yah-hoo!*, extn of *yah!*, expressive of disgust, contempt, derision; possibly an erudite Swiftian pun on Gr *iauō* (*ίαύω*), I sleep or rest or lodge, and therefore sem equivalent to 'The *Dopes*'.

Yahveh or -weh, whence Yahvism (or -wism), Yahvist (or -wist)—whence, in turn, Yahvistic (or -wistic); varr in Jah-; Jehovah, whence Jehovist, whence Jehovistic.

*Yahweh* or *-veh* is a modern, and prob the correct, trln of the H name occurring in The Bible as *Jehovah*; *Jahveh* (*-weh*), a half-way form. The predominant H form is *Yĕhōwāh*, the vowel points (diacritics) being adopted from *adōnāi*, 'my Lord'. The H r *HVH* seems to imply H *hayah* (or *hawah*), to be: *Yahveh* (*Yahweh*) would then be 'The Eternal'.

yak, a large ox of central Asia, esp of Tibet, anglicizes the Tibetan *gyak*.

yam: perh via F *iame*: certainly from Port *inhame*, a yam: Senegal (part of the Guinea region of W Africa) *nyami*, to eat.

yammer, to lament (obsol), hence to chatter (coll and dial): OE *geōmrian* (occ *geōmerian*), to sigh, groan, mourn, lament, bewail, imm from OE *geōmor*, sorrowful: indebted also to MD *jamer*, MD-D *jammer*, distress, misery—cf OHG *jāmar*, MHG *jāmer*, G *Jammer*, sorrow, and OS *jāmar*,

OFris *jōmerlik*, sorrowful: OGmc r, perh *jāēmur-*; IE r, *jēmur-*: cf Gr *hēmeros*, gentle. (Walshe.)

yank, n and v: a sharp blow or pull, to pull or tug sharply: o.o.o.: ? akin to the now only dial *yerk*, var of JERK.

Yankee, prop a native or a citizen of the New England states of the U.S.A., hence loosely a British coll for any American: both of the theories —an Amerind corruption (orig *Yengees*, b/f *Yengee*) of *English*, and a corruption of F *Anglais*, an Englishman—are very prob f/e fancies: the most likely explanation is that *Yankee* represents D *Janke*, dim of D *Jan*, John, as applied by the New York (orig New Amsterdam) Dutch to the English settlers in Connecticut. (Webster strongly, Mathews less strongly, DAE lukewarmly, support the *Janke* origin.)

yap, dial var yaup, is echoic.

yard (1), an enclosure, esp a small one in front /of or behind a building, esp a house or a castle: ME *yard*, earlier *yerd*: OE *geard*: cf OFris *garda*, a garden, OS *gardo*, garden, but *gard*, a yard, MD *gaerde, garde, gaert, gairde, gerde, geerde*, a yard, a court, OHG *garto*, MHG *garte*, G *Garten*, garden, OHG *gart*, an enclosure, Go *garda*, a stable, a sheepfold, and *gards*, a house, ON *garthr* (whence E *garth*), yard, court; cf also OIr *gort*, a field—L *hortus*, a garden, Gr *khortos*, an enclosure. The OGmc etymon would be *garthaz*; the IE, *ghortos*. (Walshe.)

Cf the sep COURT and GARDEN.

yard (2), a measure, whence yardage, yardarm (retaining the orig sense) and yardstick: ME *yerde*: OE *gierd, gyrd, gerd*, a stick, a rod, hence a measure, esp that of three feet: cf MD *gaerde, gaert, gerd, geerde*, MD-D *garde*, rod, the measure, OHG *gerto*, MHG-G *gerte*, a rod, a staff, OS *gerde*, rod, the measure: cf also OHG *gart*, ON *gaddr*, Go *gazds*, a goad—cf, therefore, the E GAD, a goad; prob cf L *hasta*, a spear, a comparison supported by the Go *gazds*.

With *yard* in its archaic sense 'penis', cf the F *verge*.

yare (now dial), adj and adv: ME *yare*, adj, adv: OE *gearu, gearo*, ready, made ready, complete, and *geare, gearwe*, completely, perfectly: with numerous OGmc cognates: app int *ga-, ge-+*aro*, ready (cf OS *aru*, ON *örr*, ready)—note esp the Gr *arariskō*, I fit together. (Walshe.)

yarn (n, hence v); hernia; cf the sep CORD.

*Yarn*, spun flax, wool, cotton, etc., hence any spun filament, esp as used in rope-making, hence —cf 'He spins a good *yarn*'—the orig coll, now familiar SE, usu fictional story of adventure, arising from the sailors' and deep-sea fishers' practice of reminiscing and story-telling while they are sedentarily engaged, e.g. in yarn-twisting: OE *gearn*: cf OHG-MHG-G *garn*, MD *gaern*, *garn*, MD-D *garen*, ON *garn*: orig 'thread made from gut'—cf ON *garner* (pl), entrails, Lith *žarnà*, gut, entrails, L *hernia*, a rupture, and *hīra*, an intestine, and *haru-* in *haruspex* (lit 'inspector of entrails'), Gr *khordē*, an intestine, Skt *hira*, a vein: OGmc r, *\*garna-*; IE r, *\*ghar-*, occ *\*gher-* (+formative *-no-*), an intestine.

**yarrow**: ME *yarowe*, earlier *yarwe*: OE *gearwe*: cf MD *garwe*, *gerwe*, D *gerw*, OHG *garawa*, *garwa*, G *Garbe*, yarrow.

**yaw**, naut v (hence n), to go off course, steer wildly: o.o.o.: perh ult akin to ON *jaga*, to move to and fro, itself o.o.o.

**yawl.** See the 2nd JOLLY.

**yawn** (v, hence n).—hiatus; dehisce, dehiscent (whence **dehiscence**).

1. 'To *yawn*': ME *gānien*, var *gōnien*: OE *gānian*: intervention by ME *yonen*, var *yenen*, from OE *geonian*, *ginian*, (in cpds) *-gīnan*, to be wide-open, to yawn: cf OHG *ginēn*, MHG *ginen*, *genen*, G *gähnen*, ON *gīna*, to yawn. The OHG *gin-* is an extn of *\*gi-* or *\*gī-*, a var of IE *\*ghī-*, to be wide-open, to yawn: cf OB *zijati*, Lith *žioti*, Gr *khainein*, L *hiāre*, to be gaping, to yawn.

2. L *hiāre*, pp *hiātus*, has derivative n *hiātus* (gen *-ūs*), a mouth-opening, a gap, adopted— ? via EF-F—by E.

3. L *hiāre* has inch *hiscere* (vi), to open, (os person) to open one's mouth, with int *dēhiscere*, whence 'to *dehisce*'; from the presp *dēhiscens*, o/s *dēhiscent-*, comes the adj *dehiscent*.

**yawp.** See YELP.

**ye.** See YOU, para 1.

**yea**—cf yea and nay; yes, whence yes-man.

1. *Yea*, archaic for *yes*, comes, through ME *ye* or *ya*, from OE *gēa*, *gē* (pron approx as *yea* is): cf OFris *gē*, *yē*, *dzē*, OS *jā*, OHG *jā*, MHG *jā*, *ja*, G *ja*, Go *ja* (cf *jai*, indeed), MD *jae*, MD-D *ja*, ON *jā*—Lith, *ja*, *je*—Cor *īa*, *ya*, Br *ia*, W *ie*: OGmc *\*jā*; IE, perh (Walshe) *\*je*—cf Gr *ē* (ἦ), indeed.

2. The adj *yea-and-nay*, vacillating, derives from vacillant *yea and nay*: cf the modern 'Yes—and no'.

3. *Yes*, ME *yes* or *yis*, derives from OE *gēse* (var *gīse*), contr of *gēase*, an 'easing' of *gēa swā*, yea, (it is) so: cf so. A '*yes*-man' is one who says *yes* to—agrees with—everything said to him: cf the OHG *jā-herre* (Walshe).

**year**, yearling, yearly. See HORA, para 4.

**yearn** (whence the pa, vn **yearning**), yearnful; eucharist; sep EXHORT.

1. 'To *yearn*,' ME *yernen*, OE *giernan*, *gyrnan*, *geornian*, is intimately related to OE *georn*, eager, (very) desirous: cf OHG *gerno*, MHG *gerne*, G *gern*, adv, and OHG *gern*, adj, OS *gern*, adj, and *gernean*, *(-ian)*, to desire, Go *faíhu-gairns*, avari-

cious (lit 'property-eager'), MD *gaerne*, *gerne*, D *gaarne*, adv, ON *gjarn*, adj, and *girna*, to desire; cf also perh L *hortāri*, to urge, and certainly OIr *gor*, glad, Ir *togairim*, I desire, Ga to*garrach*, desirable, Gr *khairein* (for *\*khariein*), to rejoice, and Skt *háryati*, (he) is fond of—forms corresp to OHG *girī*, G *Gier*, greed, and OHG *ger*, desirous. The IE r, therefore, is *\*gher-*, var *ghar-*, to desire, and the E v exemplifies an extn in *-u*.

2. Gr *khairein*, to be glad, has derivative *kharizesthai*, to show favour to, whence, with the adv *eu*, well, the cpd adj *eukharistos*, grateful, whence *eukharistia*, a thanks-giving, whence, via Eccl LGr, the LL *eucharistia*, the holy sacrament, whence OF-F *eucharistie*, whence E *Eucharist*; the adj *eucharistic* comes from EF-F *eucharistique*, ML *eucharisticus*, Eccl LGr *eukharistikos* (adj of the corresp n).

**yeast**, whence yeasty; sep ECZEMA.

*Yeast*, ME *yeest*, *yest*, OE *gist*, *gyst*, is akin to MD *gest*, MD-D *gist*, yeast, MHG *gist*, *gis*, G *Gischt*, yeast, foam, OHG *jesan*, MHG *jesen*, (vi) to ferment, ON *jöstr*, *jastr*, yeast—and to Gr *zestos*, boiled, and Skt *yásati*, it boils or seethes. The IE r is app *\*jes-* (*yes-*), to seethe.

**yegg.** See YACHT, para 2.

**yell** (v, hence n); gale—cf NIGHTINGALE, q.v. at NIGHT; celandine; stannel.

1. 'To *yell*', ME *yellen*, OE *giellan*, varr *gillan* and *gyllan*, is related to OHG *gellan*, MHG-G *gellen*, MD *gellen*, D *gillen*.

2. Also cognate—and imm relevant to *gale*—are OS (and OHG) *galan*, ON *gala*, OE *galan*, to sing, which last yields the obs 'to *gale*' or sing and the *-gale* of *nightingale* ('night singer') and prob *gale*, a stiff breeze. Clearly the origin is echoic: IE *\*ghel-*, to cry out.

3. This IE r occurs also in Gr *khelīdōn*, the swallow, whence, by folklore, the Gr plant-name *khelidonia* (prop the f of the derivative adj *khelidonios*), L *chelidonia* (sc *herba*), MF *celidonia* (EF-F *chélidoine*), ME *celidoine*, whence—with intrusive *-n-* perh after such words as *almandine* (obs) or *amandine*, and *olivine*—the E *celandine*.

4. With OE *nihtegale*, the nightingale, cf OE *stāngella*, lit 'stone-yeller' (crying from the rocks), whence E *stonegall*; the OE var *stāngilla* becomes, by attrition and negligence, the now mostly dial *stannel*, the kestrel.

5. Cf YELP.

**yellow.** See GOLD, para 1.

**yelp** (v, hence n), whence **yelper**: ME *yelpen*, to boast (noisily): OE *gielpan*, varr *gilpan* and *gylpan*, to boast, to exult: cf OHG *gelpf*, *gelf*, arrogant, MHG *gel(p)f*, arrogance, ON *gjálpa*, to yelp (hence, prob, the EE-E sense), whence, in part, 'to *yaup* or *yawp*'. The OGmc r *\*gelp-*, IE *\*ghelb-*, is merely an extn of IE *\*ghel-*, q.v. at YELL, para 2, s.f.

**yen**, Japan's monetary unit, is, in Jap, a mdfn of Ch *yüan*, a circle, a round (object), hence a coin. Oddly enough, the sl *yen*, an intense craving, also comes from Ch: Pekinese *yen*, opium (lit, smoke).

**yeoman**, whence **yeomanry** (-*ry* for -*ery*, collective suffix): ME *yoman*, *yuman*, *yeman*, *yiman*: o.o.o.: but prob worn-down forms of ME *yong-man*, *yungman*, etc., an attendant or servant (app, orig youthful): cf YOUNG and MAN. (OED.) EW aptly cfs the sem development of the phon cognate G *Junker*. Webster, however, suggests that the ME forms tend to exhibit both a phon and a sem relationship to OFris *gāman*, a villager, lit 'man of the *gā* or rural district'—cf OS *gō*, Go *gawi*, OHG *gawi* or *gewi*, MHG *gou*, G *Gau*, and perh Alb *gavar*, a region (Walshe).

**yerk.** See JERK; cf YANK.

**yes.** See YEA, para 3.

**yester**, adj—as in **yestereve**, the contr **yestreen**, **yesteryear**—is a b/f from the *yester* of **yesterday** and **yesternight**: OE *geostran daeg* (ME *yisterdai*) and OE *gystran niht*. OE *geostran daeg* is taut for *geostran*, varr *geostra*, *giestran*, *gystran* (and metathetic *gyrstan*), yesterday: cf OHG *gestarōn*, *gesteron*, MHG *gesteren*, G *gestern*, MD *gister*, *gistere*, MD-D *gisteren*, the sense 'tomorrow' occurring in Go, OHG, ON; cf also L *herī* (for \**hesī*), yesterday, and its derivative adj *hesternus* (cf *hodiernus*, adj of *hodie*, today), whence, with another suffix, the E *hesternal*—Gr *khthes*—Skt *hyás*—Alb *dje*. The IE r is perh \**ghjes-* or \**ghthjes*, with var \**ghes-*, yesterday.

**yet**, orig an adv 'hitherto' or 'still' ('Is there *yet* time?'), hence a conj: ME *yet*, *yete*, *yit*: OE *gīt* or *gȳt*, *gīet*, *gīeta* or *gēta*: cf OFris *jēta* (*iēta*), *ēta*, *īta*: ? akin, ult, to Go *ju*, now, hence to L *iam* (ML *jam*), henceforth, soon.

**yew; uvula**, whence, anl, the adj **uvular**.

1. A *yew*, ME *ew* or *ewe*, OE *ēow*, *īow*, *īw*, is akin to OHG *īga*, *īwa*, MHG *īwe*, G *Eibe*, OS *īch*, and to such C forms as W *yw*, Cor *hivin*, *hiuin*, Br *ivin*, and MIr *eo*, OIr *ibar*, Ga *iubhar*; with the Br and Cor forms, cf OSl *iva*, the willow, and Gaul *ivos*, yew, whence OF-F *if*; the ON *ȳr*, yew, exhibits a var. If, as Hofmann proposes, the IE etymon be \**oiua* (\**oiwa*), then cf Gr *oā*, Ionic Gr *oē*, LGr *oiē*, the service (or sorb) tree, with fruit known as 'sorb apple'.

2. Prob akin to Gr *oiē*, *oā*, is L *ūua*, ML *ūva*, a grape, hence a berry, LL (Med) *uvula*, with LL (Med) dim *ūuula*, ML *ūvula*, whence the MedE *uvula*, whence *uvulitis* (suffix -*itis*).

**Yiddish.** See JEW, para 5.

**yield**, v, hence, imm in its modern sense, the n (cf OE *gield*, from the OE v)—whence **yielder** and pa, vn **yielding**; **gild** or **guild**; **geld**, a Crown tax; **gelt**.

1. 'To *yield*' comes, via ME *yelden*, *yilden*, from OE *geldan*, var *gieldan*, to offer (in money), to pay or pay back, to give, cf OFris *jelda*, OS *geldan*, MHG *gelten*, to be worth, to compensate, G *gelten*, to count as, Go *us-gildan*, to recompense or requite, MD *gilden*, MD-D *gelden*, to cost, ON *gjalda*, *gialda*, to pay, esp to pay up. The OGmc r is perh \**geldh-*; the IE r, perh \**gelt-*. (Walshe.)

2. Intimately related to OE *geldan*, *gieldan*, to pay, is OE *gield*, *gild*, *geld*, a payment, hence a tribute, a tax, whence E *geld*, a Crown tax; cf OE-E *wergild*, the value set on the life of a *wer* or human being.

3. Intimately related to OE *gield*, *geld*, *gild*, derivatively a company self-supporting by subscriptions, is the syn ON *gildi*, whence ME *gilde*, whence E *gild* or *guild*.

4. Also akin to OE *gield*, *geld*, is OHG-MHG *gelt*, payment, interest, G *Geld*, money: the old form, the modern sense, characterize the now jocular and obsol E *gelt*, money.

**yip**, v (hence n), is both echoic and a 'thinning' of YAP.

**yodel.** See JUBILANCE, para 2.

**yoga**, **yogi.** See JOIN, para 5.

**yoghourt**, **yoghurt**, **jogurt**: Tu *yoghurt*, via Bulgarian *jugurt*. F *yaourt* comes from the Bulg var *jaurt*.

**yoke.** See JOIN, para 20.

**yokel.** See JOIN, para 20, s.f.

**yolk.** See GOLD, para 2.

**Yom Kippur**, the Jewish 'Day of Atonement', is the syn H *yōm kippūr*.

**yon** (adj, hence adv), **yond** (adv, hence adj), **yonder** (adv, hence adj); **beyond**.

1. E-ME adj *yon* derives from the rare OE *geon*, that (person or thing over there), yonder: cf OFris *jen*, *jena*, OHG *jenēr*, MHG-G *jener*, Go *jains*; cf also ON *enn*, *inn*, OSl *onŭ*, Lith *ans*, Hit *eni*, *enin*; and perh Gr *hon* (*ŏv*), the acc of the relative pronoun 'who' (and therefore Skt *yas*), hence also L *is*, that one, he. The group *geon*—*jen*—*jenēr*—*enn*—etc., prob exhibits an -*n* extn of IE *ei*-, that (adj), that one.

2. Very closely akin to the OE adj *geon* is the OE *geond*, both prep 'through, throughout' and adv 'over there, yonder': whence ME *yeond*, later *yond*, retained by E. Cf OFris *jonda* (prep), near, and Go *jaind*, thither.

3. OE *geond* has the int *begeondan*, adv 'further off, yonder' and prep 'besides': ME *biyeonde*, later *biyonde*: E *beyond*.

4. The ME adv *yond* (as in para 2), over there, has the approx syn ME-E extn *yonder*, adv (indicated by -*er*, corresp to an earlier -*re*), 'at that point, or in that (visible) place, over there at some distance': cf Go *jaindre*, MD *gender*, *gonder*, *gunder*, MD-D *ginder*, MLG *ginder*, (over) there.

**yore, of.** See HORA, para 4.

**York**, whence **Yorkish** and **Yorkist**; **New York**; **Yorkshire**, whence **Yorkshire pudding**, a traditional delicacy of Yorkshire; **'yorker'**.

1. *Yorkshire* derives from late OE-ME *Eoforwīcscīr*, the *shire* of *Eoforwīc* (York), the OE-ME alteration—f/e after OE *eofor*, a boar—of ML *Eboracum* (var *Eburacum*—cf Domesday Book's *Euruic*): a trln of LGr *Ebórakon* (Ptolemy), York: perh from the Gaul PN *Eburos*, itself prob a personification of Gaul *eburos*, a yew tree (cf YEW): hence 'Region of Yew Trees'. (Ekwall.)

2. *New York* was named—in honour of the

Duke of *York*, King Charles II's brother—by the British troops capturing the place in 1664 from the Dutch, who had called it *New Amsterdam*. The Dukes of York take the name from the city of *York*, ME *York*, earlier *Yeork*, from *Eoforwīc*.

3. Prob from *Yorkshire* comes the puzzling *yorker* of cricket: that is, if it was the Yorkshire County Cricket Club's players who first specialized in bowling in this particular way (a ball that lands at that point of the batting crease at which the batsman holds his bat to the ground, tech the block-hole); ? influenced by *yerker*, dial var of *jerker*, that which jerks (the batsman out).

**you, your, yours; ye.**

1. *You*, orig pl only, comes from ME *you*, earlier *eou*, earliest *eow*, acc and dat, the ME nom being *ye* (the now archaic E *ye*)—from OE *gē* (occ *ge*): ME *eow* represents OE *ēow*, acc and dat of *gē*. The OE acc-dat *ēow* has many cognates in OGmc (and elsewhere), but we need cite only the cognates, or at least some of the cognates, of the OE nom *gē* (*ge*): OFris *gī* (occ *ī*), OS *gī* or *ge*, OHG-MHG *ir*, G *ihr*, ON *ēr*, MD *gi*, *ge*, D *gij*; cf Alb *ju*, Go *jus*, Lith *jūs*, Gr *humeis* (Dor *hūmes*), Skt *yūyám* (*yūjám*), a *y*- var of *vas*—therefore cf also L *uōs* (ML *vōs*) and OB *vy*. The IE r is app *iu*- (*ju*-), prob pron *yoo*. (Hofmann; Walshe.)

2. OE *gē*, ye, has gen *ēower*, of you, whence ME *eower*, later *eowr*, finally *your*, orig pronoun, then adj: cf OFris *iuwer*, OHG *iuwēr*, MHG *iuwer*, G *euer*, OS *iuwar*, Go *izwar*, ON *ythuarr*. It is from the pronoun *your*, of you, that *yours* derives, the possessive -*s* being orig a taut usage.

**young, youngster; younker.** See JUVENILE, paras 4 and 5.

**your** and yours. See YOU, para 2.

**youth, youthful.** See JUVENILE, para 4.

**yowl.** See JUBILANCE, para 3.

**ypsiliform,** See the element *ypsili*-.

**ytterbium:** *Ytterby* (in Sweden)+Chem -*ium*: cf the element *yttri*-.

**yuca** and its SciL derivative **yucca** come from Sp *yuca*, itself adopted from Taino (an extinct WI language), var *iucca*.

**Yuga** (occ *Yug*). See JOIN, para 6.

**Jugoslav,** orig *Jugo-Slav*, sets before *Slav* the Serbo-Croat element *jugo*-, c/f of *jug*, the south, the south wind, itself from the syn OSl *jugŭ* (o.o.o.): the Jugoslavs are lit 'the southern Slavs' (Serbs, Croats, Slovenes).

**Yule,** Christmas Day, whence **Yuletide,** Christmastide, comes from ME *yol*, OE *gēol*, var *geohhol*: cf ON *jōl*, OSw *jūl* (pl), Sw *jul*, Christmas, and ON *ȳler*, *ȳlir*, Go *jiuleis*, esp OE *gēola*, *iūla*, *giuli*, *gȳle* (Bede), all meaning 'the *Yule* month', December: o.o.o. (see esp Feist), most of the theories postulating either '(the time of) the year's *change*' or 'season of *play* and rejoicing'. Very tentatively indeed I suggest that OE *gēol* derives from an OE *gēul*, metathetic cognate of L *gelŭ* (n), cold (cf E *gelid*, q.v. at COLD): that, in short, OE *gēola*, December, is, in the Northern Hemisphere, a month notoriously cold, with *gēol*, Yule, falling in what is usu its coldest period; 'the *cold* month' and 'the festival—the most important day —of the *cold* season'.

# Z

zaffer or zaffre. See SAFFRON, para 2.
zany. See JOHN, para 1.
Zarathustra. See ZOROASTER.
zareba, occ zareeba: Ar *zarība, zarībah*, a cattle-pen or sheepfold, perh orig one improvised with thorn-bushes, hence a camp, prob orig an improvised camp: cf the much less vocalized Ar *zarb*, a sheepfold (OED): Ar r *zrb*.

Zea (Bot), whence zea (Pharm): L *zea*, a kind of grain: Gr *zéa*, earlier *zeiá*, earliest *zeiai*, wheat, barley: cf Skt *yávas*, grain (and Lith *javaĩ*, pl), Per *jav*, barley, Cor *yees, ys, yz, īs, īz, eys* (etc.), barley, and prob EIr and Ga *eórna*, barley. The IE r is perh *\*ieu-ia* (*yeu-ya*); but the word could well be Medit—cf Eg *su-t*, grain, wheat, *buţ*, barley (? also *beţ-t*, barley, wheat, millet).

zeal, zealot (whence zealotic and zealotry), zealous; jealous, jealousy—cf jalouse, jalousie.

1. *Zeal* derives—perh via MF *zel*, late MF-EF *zele*, EF-F *zèle*—from LL *zēlus*, fervour, zeal, trln of Gr *zēlos* (Dor c *zālos*), zeal, spirit of emulation, hence jealousy: o.o.o.: perh cf Gr *zēmia*, punishment: i.e., *-l* and *-m* extnn of an IE r *\*dia-, \*dja-, \*za-*, to strive.

2. Gr *zēlos* has derivative *zēloō*, I am emulous for, whence the agent *zēlōtēs*, an emulous person, LL *zēlōtēs*, E zealot; and LL *zēlus* has the ML derivative adj *zēlōsus*, whence E zealous.

3. ML *zēlōsus* becomes OF-MF *gelos, gelous, jelos, jelous* (late MF-F *jaloux*, f *jalouse*): ME *gelus, jealous*, the latter surviving; derivative OF-MF *gelosie, gelousie, jelosie, jelousie*, yields E jealousy.

4. OF-MF *gelo(u)s, jelo(u)s*, has the MF derivative v *jelo(u)ser*, whence late MF-F *jalouser*, to be jealous or suspicious about, to suspect, whence E —now mostly E dial and Sc—'to jalouse'. The OF-MF *jelousie* becomes late MF-F *jalousie*, jealousy, used—C17 onwards, and at first jokingly —of a such a trellis or shutter or blind as permits one to see without being seen, a sense prob borrowed from the cognate It *gelosia*, itself used thus as early as the late C15 (Prati). 'Trellis' *jalousie* has been adopted by E.

zebra (whence zebraic, zebrine, zebroid): Port *zebra*, f, and *zebro*, m, this Afr cross between horse and ass, from C16 onward: Sp and Port *zebro*, f *zebra*, the wild ass, until C16, when the wild ass disappeared from the Iberian peninsula: *zebro* perh from the wind-god *Zephyrus*, because of the swiftness of zebras (B & W); but prob—via Por and Sp—from Amharic (official Abyssinian) *zebrā*, the zebra (Webster). The hybrids *zebrinny* and *zebrula* or *zebrule* perh blend *zebra* with *hinny* (q.v. at WHINNY) and *mule*.

zebu, from F *zébu*, supposed by Buffon to be of Afr origin, is app a blend of—perh rather a mere confusion between—Tibetan *mdzopo*, a zebu, and Tibetan *zeu* or *zeba*, a zebu's hump.

zeitgeist: G *Zeitgeist*, lit 'time-spirit', *Zeit*, time, being akin to E *tide* and *time*, and *-geist* to E *ghost*.

Zend-Avesta is lit the *Avesta*, the sacred Zoroastrian books, and their interpretation (Per *zend*, from Pahlavi *zand*); *Avesta* is the Per shape of Pahlavi *apastāk*, that which is postulated, that which has been established, hence a fundamental text or a book.

zenith, whence zenithal (unless from EF-F *zénithal*): ME *cenith* (*senyth*) or *cenit*: MF *cenith, cenit* (F *zénith*): from the medieval scribes' false reading *senit* for Ar *samt*, zenith, esp in *samt ar-rās*, way or road or path (above) the head, as opp the nadir: Ar *samt*, lit 'road or route', derives from L *sēmita*, path, itself o.o.o.—unless, as some hold, it be a cpd of *sē*, aside + *\*mita*, from *meāre* (r *me-*), to go, to pass.

2. Ar *samt* in the form *as-samt*, the way (*as-* for *al*, the, by assimilation), becomes, via its pl *assumūt*, EF-F *azimut*, whence E azimuth.

zenocentric, zenography. See the element *zeno-*.
zeolite. See the element *zeo-*.

zephyr comes, perh via EF-F *zéphyr*, from L *zephyrus*, trln of Gr *zephuros*, the west wind, hence a gentle breeze or a soft wind; the personified sylvan god *Zephuros*, L *Zephyrus*, is a literary E adoption—with or without the capital. Gr *zephuros* is o.o.o.: but prob (Hofmann) it is akin to Gr *zophos*, the dark, esp the dark side, i.e. the west; or perh it is simply echoic.

zero. See CIPHER.

zest, orig a piece of lemon-peel added for piquancy (whence zestful), derives from EF *zest* (later, as still, *zeste*): o.o.o.: but perh an alteration of the syn earlier EF *zec* (o.o.o.)—either, as B & W propose, after EF-F *baste*, 'Enough!' (It *basta*, it is enough) or, as Dauzat prefers and B & W mention, after the echoic *zest*, 'Nonsense!', as in 'être entre le zist et le *zest*', to be neither one thing nor the other. At a wild guess, I submit the possibility that *zest* comes from It *gusto*, lemon-peel added for piquancy, or from some other European derivative (cf late ME *gusto*, E *gust*, OF *gost*, MF *gust*, *goust*, Sp *gusto*) of L *gustus* (see GUST)—via a dial var.

**zeugma.** See JOIN, para 7.

**Zeus.** See DIANA, para 3.

**zibeline.** See SABLE.

**zibet** or **zibeth.** See CIVET.

**zigzag** (n, hence adj and v): EF-F *zigzag*: G *Zickzack*, orig the adv *zickzack*, in such a line or fashion: echoic, perh with elements G *Zacke*, a jaggèd or serrated edge, and *Zicke*, as in *Zicke machen*, to dodge about.

**zinc** comes, like F *zinc*, from G *Zink*, zinc: early modern HG *zincken*: 'prob id with [G] *Zinke* [, *Zinken*, a spike], because when melted it forms spikes' (Walshe). G-MHG *zinke*, OHG *zinko*, a spike, is perh akin to G *Zahn*, MHG *zant*, OHG *zand*, a tooth (f.a.e., TOOTH).

**zinnia** was thus named by Linnaeus in honour of that brilliant G anatomist J. G. *Zinn* (1727–59), who, a professor at Göttingen, was also something of a botanist.

**Zion**, whence **Zionism** and, anl, **Zionist**: H *Tsīyōn*, orig the Jebusite fortified place situated on the eastern hill: o.o.o.

**zip**, n, hence v (whence **zipper**), is neatly echoic.

**zircon**, whence **zirconium**; (Min) **jargon**, occ spelt **jargoon**.

*Zircon*, adopted from F, is an irreg early C19 mdfn of the syn F—whence E—*jargon*, yellow diamond, itself either (via Sp and Port) from Ar *zarqūn*, this gem, from Per *zarqūn*, golden-hued, or from It *giargone*, itself either of that Ar-Per origin or (Dauzat) less prob akin to OF-MF *jagonce*, *jargonce*, from L *hyacinthus* in its 'precious stone' sense.

**zither.** See GUITAR.

**zodiac, zodiacal.** See VIVA, para 13.

**Zoe, zoism.** See VIVA, para 11.

**zombi**, now usu **zombie**, 'a dead body . . . made to walk and act and move as if it were alive' (W. B. Seabrook), hence, coll, a person only half alive: Kongo (a Bu language) *zumbi*, a fetish (python as deity).

**zone** and **zonal**, whence, anl, the adjj **zonary** and **zonate.**

*Zonal* comes from the LL *zōnalis*, adj of L *zōna*, trln of Gr *zōnē*, a girdle, a belt, hence anything resembling one, esp a zone of the earth's sphere; L *zōna* becomes OF-F *zone*, adopted by E. Gr *zōnē* is intimately related to Gr *zōnnunai* (r *zōn-*), to gird, pp *zōstos*, s *zōst-*, r *zōs-*: IE r, prob *zōs-* (*djōs-*) or *iōs-* (*yōs-*), to gird, attested by the Av pp *yāsta-*, girded, by Alb, by OSl and Lith.

**zoo**, orig coll, is short for '*zoo*logical garden(s)'; **zoological** (cf F *zoologique*) derives—as, anl, does **zoologist**—from **zoology** (cf the later F *zoologie*), formed as if from SciL *\*zoologia*, but strictly a cpd of the elements *zoo-*, life+*-logy*, science. The c/f *zoo-* derives from Gr *zōion*, an animal, SciE *zoon*: cf Gr *zōē*, life: f.a.e., VIVA.

2. Most of the *zoo-* cpds are explained by the 2nd element; note esp *zoophyte*, coined by Rabelais in 1546; cf the element *-phyte*.

**zooid.** See VIVA, para 11.

**zoom**, v hence n, is echoic of the noise made by aircraft.

**zoon.** See ZOO, para 1.

**zoophyte.** See ZOO, para 2.

**zoril**, a SAfr polecat, represents F *zorille* (from Sp), **zorilla** and **zorillo** the Sp *zorrilla*, f, and *zorrillo*, m, dimm of *zorra*, vixen, and *zorro*, fox. In some parts of CA and SA, *zorro* denotes a grey fox, *zorrillo* a skunk. Occurring also in Port, *zorra* (-*o*) is o.o.o.

**Zoroaster**, whence **Zoroastrian**, whence, in turn, **Zoroastrianism**; **Zarathustra**.

*Zoroaster* derives, prob via F *Zoroastre* (cf It *Zoroastro*), from L *Zoroastres*, from Gr *Zōroastrēs*: an approximation to the correct *Zarathushtra* (*Zarathuštra*), whence Nietzsche's *Also sprach Zarathustra*, Thus spake Zarathustra, published in 1883–84 and, incidentally, popularizing the form *Zarathustra*. The Av *Zarathuštra* is lit 'he whose camels are old—he of the old camels'; Av *uštra*, a camel+Av *zarant-* (Skt *járant-*), old. (Enci It.)

**zorrillo** and **zorro.** See ZORIL.

**Zouave**, adopted from F (1831), designates an infantry corps raised in Algeria and consisting, orig, of Algerians, and derives from *Zouaoua*, a gallicized form of Ar *Zwāwà*, corresp to the native Berber name for this Kabyle tribe, one of the Berber group: *Igawāwen*. (Enci It.)

**zounds!** See WOUND, para 3.

**Zulu** (n, hence adj), whence, app from the Zulu's colourful headdress, the artificial fly called **zulu**: Zulu (Bu-speaking) *Zulu*, the Zulu nation: from the eponymous chieftain *aZulu*.

**zwieback**, (AE) a kind of rusk: G *Zwieback*, '(something) twice-baked': *zwie-*, twice, from OHG-G *zwei*, 2+*-back*, from MHG-G *backen*, to bake (cf BAKE): cf *biscuit*, '(something) twice-cooked'.

**zygoma** (whence, anl, **zygomatic**), **zygon**, **zygosis**, **zygote.**

See JOIN, para 8; cf the element *zygo-*. The 1st perh comes imm from EF-F *zygoma*, and its adj perh from EF-F *zygomatique*.

**zymase**; **zyme** (whence **zymic** and **zymoid**); cf the element *-zyme*; cf the element *zymo-*, where, e.g., **zymology**; **zymosis, zymotic**; **zymurgy.**

*Zymase* derives, with Chem suffix *-ase*, from *zyme*, a ferment, Gr *zūmē*, ferment, leaven: cf Gr *zuthos*, barley-beer, and Gr *zōmos*, broth: IE r, perh *\*ieu-* or *yeu-*, (in cookery) to mix—cf Skt *yáúti*, he mixes, and several C words for 'broth' (cf JUICE).

Gr *zūmē* has derivatives *zūmōsis*, fermentation, whence the SciL *zymosis*, and *zūmoun*, to ferment, whence the adj *zūmōtikos*, causing fermentation, whence E *zymotic* and F *zymotique*.

*Zymurgy*, the chemistry of fermentation, esp in brewing, is lit 'a ferment-working' (*-urgy*, Gr *-ourgia*, -work: cf E *erg*).

# COMMENTARY

**am** (p. 14). Professor John W. Clark, of the University of Minnesota, writes: 'You might reconsider your association of *are* and *art* with *am* and *is*. You agree with the OED, Wyld, Sievers, but disagree with Holthausen and Prokosch (A Comparative Germanic Grammar, p. 221), who, I cannot help feeling, have the best of it; their opponents would seem necessarily to assume the *r* to be Vernerian, or at least a case of rhotacism of some kind, and I don't see how it can be.'

**boy** (p. 56). In *Medium Ævum*, October 1940 (IX, 121–54), 'The Etymology and Meaning of *Boy*' and again in 1943 (XII, 71–76), 'Middle English and Middle Dutch *Boye*'—Dr E. J. Dobson has scrupulously and lengthily surveyed the problem, yet arrived at no firm solution.

**burden** (2), on p. 64. In *Anglia*, 1956, Professor H. M. Flasdieck writes instructively and eruditely upon Elizabethan *faburden* (F *faux-bourdon*) and E *burden*, as well as upon a number of related words.

**capital** (p. 78, l. 4). The noun *capital* mentioned is the monetary capital; the EF-F n *capital* prob stands for EF-F 'fond *capital*'. As elliptical for '*capital* city', it was app prompted by late EF-F *capitale*, for EF-F 'ville *capitale*'; as elliptical for '*capital* letter', by F *capitale*, for F 'lettre *capitale*'. But ME-E *capital*, the 'head' or top part of a column, derives from OF-MF *capitel* (cf the OF-MF *chapitel*, var of OF-F *chapiteau*): LL *capitellum* (cf L *capitulum*)—dim of L *caput*, head.

**cart** (p. 81) comes, more prob, from the syn ON *kartr*.

**cotton** (p. 123). The OF-F *coton* perhaps derives rather from It *cotóne*, itself from the Ar word: Sp *cotón* is printed cotton, the word for cotton being *algodón*, with the Ar article *al* retained.

**dream** (p. 166). For a closely argued and philologically buttressed treatment, see Professor Simeon Potter's 'On the Etymology of Dream' in *Archivum Linguisticum*, Vol. IV, pp. 148–54, published in 1952.

**elephant** (p. 179). For a more comprehensive treatment, see 'Elephantine' in my book, *A Charm of Words*, 1960.

**feud** (2), on p. 209. In *The Review of English Studies*, 1956, Dr E. J. Dobson derives the word from an early northern ME *fae-hude*, 'foehood' or enmity. If that etymology be correct, as well it may, then cf FOE (p. 244) and the suffix *-hood* at **-head**.

**filch** (p. 212). In *Modern Language Notes*, 1955, Professor Kemp Malone proposes derivation from OE *gefylce* (ge-*fylce*), a large body of people, an army, an army division or troop, and traces a possible semantic development.

**flamenco** (p. 218)—treated at FLANDERS, para 3 (p. 218). But Professor Dr Don Francisco Sánchez-Castañer, of the University of Valencia, holds that the Sp word *flamenco* is, in fact, two homonyms with disparate—almost contrasted—meanings: (1) from Gmc *Vlaming*, Fleming, with the secondary meaning: stout, strong, fair-haired, ruddy-cheeked (as the Spanish King's Flemish guardsmen); (2) from Ar *fellah mengo*, Moorish troubadours, predecessors of the Catalan and Provençal troubadours, hence Gipsy musicians, singers and dancers, esp of Sevilla and Andalusia, hence romantic, dreaming, languid, sentimental. For a general discussion, which, however, implicatively disagrees with Sánchez-Castañer's twofold etymology, see J. Corominas, *Diccionario Crítico Etimológico de la Lengua Castellana* (vol. II, 1954) at heading 'Flamenco'.

**ginger** (p. 254). In his book, *Etymology: with Especial Reference to English*, 1958 (and therefore much too late for me to be able to consult it), Professor Ross brilliantly summarizes the evidence. That book contains a section of 'Selected English etymologies' meriting the attention of even the most erudite, and including notably *ale, cross, jade* (horse), *last, snow, walrus, yolk, yule*.

**haggis**, treated at **hack** (2), para 4, s.f., on p. 274. In *Romance Philology*, 1958, Professor C. H. Livingston, article 'Etymology of English "haggis"', derives it from ONF *haguier*, to chop or hash. (Admittedly the derivation from ON *höggva* presents certain difficulties.)

**keelson** (p. 327). In *Notes and Queries*, 1955, Mr D. B. Sands in his article 'A New Approach to the Etymology of English "Keelson"' points out that Continental cognates pretty clearly indicate a compound of *keel* and *swine* and suggests the sort of symbolism involved.

**macabre** (p. 370). In *Studia Philologica et Litteraria in Honorem H. Spitzer*, 1959, Professor H. Sperber deals with the semantic difficulty and suggests that the author of some early dance of death felt that it would be an excellent idea to revitalize the stereotyped character of the preacher by identifying him with the 'notorious' Judas Maccabaeus.

**market** (p. 382). In *The Modern Language Review*, April 1952 (XLVIII, No. 2, pp. 152–4), Professor Norman Davis discusses 'the route by which the word *market*, which obviously goes back ultimately to Latin *mercatus*, came into the language'. He suggests that *market* 'came into English from a Germanic language rather than from French'—esp OHG and OS—and adduces some convincing evidence.

**mayonnaise** (p. 388). In her *Madame de Pompadour*, 1957, Miss Nancy Mitford suggests that the name celebrated the capture of Fort St Philippe at *Mahon* by the Maréchal de Richelieu. There being no butter or cream on the island, the Marshal's *chef* devised a sauce made only of eggs and oil—and honorifically called it *sauce Mahonnaise*.

**Pall Mall** (p. 466—but treated at MALL, para 1, on p. 374). In *Anglia*, 1954, Professor H. M. Flasdieck's article 'Pall Mall' occupied an entire issue and dealt with certain associated words.

**physic**, para 6 (p. 493). But J. H. Randall, *Aristotle*, New York, 1960, points out, at p. 108, that the name *metaphysics* did not, after all, originate with Aristotle, who usually called it 'first philosophy'. The lectures or notebooks were first assembled, 250 years later, by Andronikos of Rhodes, who called them *Ta Meta ta Phusika*, 'the Writings that come after those on Physics'—in the Andronikos edition. (With thanks to David A. Kuhn).

**plow** (p. 504) has, by Professor Simeon Potter in 'On the Etymology of *Plough*' in *Nadbitkaz Prac Filologicnych* (tom xviii cz. 2), Warsaw, 1964, been shown to be, not of Germanic but of Celtic origin: Gaulish *\*plo-*, as in Pliny's *plau*morati. Professor Potter convincingly suggests that the plough was invented by the Rhaetian Gauls (cf Walshe's guess) and says that the word passed to the Germans, hence to the Scandinavians, finally to the English.

**pyramid** (p. 538) was conclusively shown by Professor Doctor Karl Lang in his article 'Die Etymologie des Wortes Pyramide' in *Anthropos*, XVIII–XIX (1923-1924), pp. 551-3, to be an Egyptian word: *pi*, the masculine article+*mr*, a pyramid.

**rack** (7)—on p. 546—has, by Klas Bernhard Johannes Karlgren in *Philology and Ancient China*, 1926, been derived, not from Ar, but from other and earlier sources; it exists, as *arakke*, in Ainu, 'a language that entered the Japanese islands in pre-historic times'. Dr Karlgren summarizes thus: 'In the stem *arak-*, *rak-*, we have a Central and North Asiatic word which already in pre-Christian times reached all the races of the extreme Orient,

was incorporated in Chinese, and conquered the whole world via Arabian'.

**racket** (1), in its underworld sense, may have (as Dr Nicola Cerri, Jr, proposes) been influenced by It *ricatto*, blackmail, kidnapping, or even derived from it and then f/e reshaped after *racket*, din.

**rash** (2)—a rash on the skin—and **rasher** (both on p. 551). Professor C. H. Livingston—'Old French *essüer*, *ressüer* in English' (*Romance Philology*, 1957-58, Vol. XI, pp. 254-67)—derives dial *rash*, adj and v ('dry'), from *ressüer*, a compound form of OF *essüer*, and from dial *rash*, v, he derives *rasher*, from which, in turn, he derives the obsolete *rash*, to cut or slash.

**skein—travel—trawl—troll**—and **reel**. See Professor C. H. Livingston's important monograph, *Skein-Winding Reels* (University of Michigan, 1957): dealing mainly with French terms, yet valuable for these five English words.

**these** and **those** (treated at THE, paras 2 and 3 on pp. 709-10). John W. Clark writes: 'I suspect, strongly, that NE [i.e., Modern English] *those* is not a reflex (with *e* added in accordance with modern spelling conventions) of ME *thos*, OE *thās*, with the mysteriously transferred meaning from pl of *this* to pl of *that*, but rather a reflex of ME *tho*, OE *thā*, plus an *-se* from *these*, which in turn I should take to be an ME pl formation from the masc sing n *thes* (OE *thēs*)—plus the levelled and generalized ME pl ending (adj) *-e*. This displaced, I take it, *thas*, *thos*, in the sense of the pl of *this*, and they have no reflex in NE at all. *Those* would, according to this view, be formed analogically from *these*, with a misapprehension of the composition of *these* as *the-se* rather than as *thes-e*. Otherwise OE *thās* seems to have undergone a most puzzling—and unlikely—change from th sense of L *illi* to the sense of L *hi*.'

**vain**, treated—on p. 757—at VACANCY, para 9. See 'Aspects of Emptiness' in *A Charm of Words*, where, admittedly, I deal with only the L members of the group. Nevertheless, I think that, despite the difference in quantity of the r vowels, L *uānus* is ult akin to the synonymous Gr *kenos*, touched on at CENOTAPH and, in ELEMENTS, at the 2nd CENO-.

**water** (p. 797). See esp my article in *A Charm of Words*. The distribution of the word is even wider than I had thought; for instance, it occurs, in a clearly recognizable form, in several North American Indian languages or, at least, dialects. I hope that some day I shall be able to write a monograph on this word.

**yule** (p. 817). For the theoretical IE origins, see esp Alan S. C. Ross, *Etymology*, pp. 163-4.

# A LIST OF PREFIXES

W EBSTER'S definition is clear and serviceable: 'One or more letters or syllables combined or united with the beginning of a word to modify its signification, as *pre-* in *pre*fix, *con-* in *con*jure. Prefixes are abstract and have merely formative function, as in *un*necessary, *fore*ordain, *post*pone.'

Strictly, a prefix should consist of either a preposition or an adverb. The original preposition or adverb is often hardly recognizable, except by the student of language.

The following list omits the false prefixes of science, e.g. *ab*(*s*)- for 'absolute' and *ac-* for 'alicyclic': they are not prefixes at all; they are abbreviations. A word that exists, in its own right, as an entry in the Dictionary—for example, *after*, *through*—is either ignored or referred to its place in the Dictionary. On the other hand, such prefixes as (English) *a-*, *be-*, *for-*, (English) *mis-*, *un-*, are included in a list predominantly Greek and Latin and Latin-derived French.

For the few abbreviations employed, see Abbreviations. Whereas a cross-reference to an italicized word (e.g., '*cor-*. See *co-*') applies to that word as recorded in this list, a cross-reference to a word in small capitals (e.g., '*mis-* (1): cf MINUS', or '*mis-*(1): cf *minus* at MINOR') sends you to an entry in the Dictionary.

**a-** (1). The pre-consonantal form of Gr *an-*, without (noun), not (adjective, adverb). This 'privative alpha', as it is sometimes called, is akin to Skt *an-*, *a-*, L *in-*, Germanic *un-* (not). Occurring in, e.g., *anarchy*, lawlessness (*an*-archy)—the hybrid *amoral*, lacking morals (*a*-moral)—*agnostic*, not knowing (*a*-gnostic)—and *anhydrous*, waterless (*an*-hydrous, *h*- being an exception to the rule '*a-* before consonants').

**a-** (2). The Gr *a-*, with (cf Skt *sa-*), together, as in *acolyte* and *Adelphi*.

**a-** (3). A variant of L *ab*, from, away, away from, separated or departed from; akin to Indo-Iranian *apa-*, Gr *ap*(*o*)-, Go *ap-* and E *of* and *off*. Examples: *avert* (*a*-vert), to turn away, ward off—*abrupt*, broken off or away (L *abruptus*=*ab*-ruptus)—*abhorrent* (*ab*-horrent), shuddering away from, (hence) causing someone to shudder away. Cf also *abs-* and *av-* and, in *advance*, even *adv-*.

**a-** (4). A variant or, rather, a reduced form of L *ad*, to, towards, akin to Celtic *ad-* and Go *at*. The form *ad-* occurs in, e.g., *advent*, from ML *adventus* (L *aduentus*); the reduced form, in *ascend*, L *ascendere*, to climb to, *aspect*, etc., and also in words adopted from French, as *avenue*, or derived from French, as *achieve*. The prefix *ad-* normally

experiences assimilation before *b*, *c*, *f*, *g*, *l*, *n*, *p*, *r*, *s*, *t*: see *ab-*, *ac-*, *af-*, *ag-*, *al-*, *an-*, *ap-*, *ar-*, *as-*, *at-*.

**a-** (5). A reduced form of OE *an*, *on*, having the basic sense 'in contact with esp something beneath' and being akin to OGmc *an*(*a*), Gr *ana*, Av *ana*. (See ON.) Examples, showing the nuances 'on', 'in', 'at': *ashore*, on (the) shore; *afire*, on fire; *nowadays*; *aloud*; He is *a*-dying, he who so recently was *a*-laughing, though *a*-begging. Cf *ac*-(2).

**a-** (6). A much-reduced form of OE *of*, off, (hence) from—cf, therefore, OF and OFF—as in *adown*, from OE *of dūne*, off the hill, and *anew*, of new (cf *of late*, recently).

**a-** (7). A development, through ME *i-*, from OE *ge-*, together, (hence) strongly, (hence) completely; as in *aware*, ME *iwar*, OE *gewaer*. Cf, therefore, *ge-* and *i-*, variant of *y-*.

**a-** (8). This short-*a* prefix has been 'thinned' from OE *ā-*, akin to Go *ur-* (G *er-*) or *us-*, with basic meaning 'out' but now vaguely intensive (cf 'an *out*-and-*out* liar'), as in dial *abear*, to endure, *arise*, to rise out of, e.g., bed, and *ago*, from *agon*, pp of ME *agon*, from OE *āgān*, to pass away, lit 'to go (*gān*) out (*ā-*)': cf to 'pass *away*' and 'to pass *out*' (faint). Cf *or-* (1).

**a-** (9), with variants *ad-* and *as-*. Vague in

822

meaning, it appears usually to connote 'to' and
therefore to approximate to (3), L *ad*, and therefore to be akin to the Fr *à*: cf Spenser's *addoom*, to
'deem' or adjudicate (*a-*, to+euphonic *-d-*+*doom*),
and the archaic *amate* (*a-*+*mate*, to checkmate,
overcome)—from OF *amater* or *amatir* (*a*, i.e.
*à*+*mater*), to subdue, dishearten.

Then there are several minor varieties, e.g.:

**a-** (10). A reduction of *at*, as in *ado*, to do, from
ME *at do*, Northern for *to do*. See ADO.

**a-** (11). A violent reduction of OE *and-*, against
(cf Gr *anti*, as well as *anti-* below), as in '*along* the
coast'.

**a-** (12). The interjection *ah*, as in *alas*, from OF
*alas*( F *hélas*), where *a-* represents L *ah*.

**a-** (13). An at first careless rendering of L *ē-*, as
in *amend*, ME *amenden*, OF *amender*, from L
*ēmendāre*. Cf *e-*.

**a-** (14). In the mysterious *avast* (to cease),
occurring only as naut term, e.g. '*Avast* heaving'
or '*Avast* there!', the *a-* may be that of (12).

**a-** (15). The Ar *al*, the, as in *apricot*, F *abricot*
(Ar *al-burqūq*).

**a-** (16). For *af-*, as in *afraid* for *affrayed*. See *af-*
(2).

**a-** (17). For the indefinite article *a*, as in *apace*
(formerly *a-pace*) for *a pace* and as in *apiece*
(formerly often *a-piece*) for *a piece*.

**ab-** (1) is an assimilated c/f of *ad-* before *b*, as in
*abbreviate*, from *abbreviātus*, ML pp of L *abbreuiāre* for *ad-breuiāre*.

**ab-** (2), **abs-**. See *a-* (3), variant of L *ab*, from,
away from. The form *abs-*, which occurs in *abstain*,
from L *abstinēre* (*abs-*+*-tinēre*, combining-form of
*tenēre*, to hold), is to *ab-* what Gr ἄψ (*aps*) is to ἀπό
(*apo*).

**ac-** (1) is the form taken by *ad-* before *c*, as in L
*accidere*, to befall, presp *accidens*, o/s *accident-*,
whence E *accident*, and before *q*, as in L *acquirere*,
whence 'to *acquire*'.

**ac-** (2), as in *acknowledge*, comes from ME *a-*,
from OE *on*. A variation, therefore, of *a-* (5).

**ac-** (3), as in *accursed*, pp of 'to *accurse*', ME
*acursien*. The ME *a-* here=OE *ā-*, lit 'out' but
mostly an intensive. Cf *a-* (8).

**ad-**. L *ad*, to, towards: see *a-* (4).

**ad**(v)-=*a*(v)-, where *a-*=*ab-*, from, away—cf
*a-* (3) above. Only in ADVANCE, where *a*(*b*) has
been confused with *ad-*.

**af-** (1). The form taken by *ad-* before *f*, as in
L *affirmāre*, whence 'to *affirm*'. In *affair*, *af-* stands
for F *à-* (OF *a*, F *à*, to) from L *ad-*.

**af-** (2), as in *affright*, derives from ME *a-*, OE
*ā-*: cf *a-* (16).

**af-** (3), as in *afford*, derives from ME *a-* (*aforthen*), for *i-* or *y-*, from OE *ge-* (*geforthian*). Cf,
therefore, *a-* (7) and *y-*.

**af-** (4), as in *affray*, comes from OF *ef-*, from L
*ex*, out of: cf *ef-*.

**ag-**. For *ad-* before *g*, as in L *aggressus*, whence
'to *aggress*'. Cf:

**al-** (1). For *ad-* before *l*, as in L *allegātiō*, o/s
*allegātiōn-*, whence E *allegation*. The change may

happen at a later stage, as in *allegiance*, where *al-*
represents the ME *a-* (from L *ad-*) of *alegeaunce*
(*a-*+OF *ligeance*).

**al-** (2), in nn from Ar (often through Sp), is
etymologically the Ar *al*, the, as in *alchemy* and
*algebra*. See esp 'Articled Nouns' in P⁴.

**al-** (3), as in *alligator*, is the Sp *el*, the, *alligator*
being 'Hobson-Jobson' for Sp *el lagarto*, the lizard.

**al-** (4), as in *almighty*, is simply *all*: *almighty* for
*all-mighty* (all-powerful).

**am-** (1), Gr. As in *ambrosia*, adopted from Gr,
this *am-* is a softening of privative *an-*, q.v. at *a-*
(1), *ambrosia* (food of the Olympian gods) combining and deriving from *an-*, not+*brotos*, mortal.

**am-** (2), L. As in *amputate*, this *am-* is a shortened
form, existing already in L, of *ambi-*.

**am-** (3), L via F. In *ambush*, ME *enbussen* or
*enbuschen*, from OF *embussier* or *embuschier*, *am-*
represents F *en*, in(to), from L *in*, in(to)+a stem
we see in BUSH.

**ama-**: see *hama-*.

**ambi-**—before a vowel, *amb-* (perhaps cf AMBASSADOR)—comes direct from L *amb*(*i*)-, around,
about, as in 'ambition' (L *ambitiō*, lit 'a going (*itiō*,
o/s *itiōn-*) about') and '*ambi*dextrous', from ML
*ambidexter*, right-handed on both sides. *Ambi* is
akin to Gr *amphi*: and as *amphi* derives from
*amphō*, both, so *ambi* derives from *ambo*, both.
For *ambo-* and *ampho-*, see Elements. Cf:

**amphi-**—before a vowel, *amph-*—comes direct
from Greek *amphi*, on both sides, (hence) around,
as in '*amphi*bious' and '*amph*anthium'. Cf prec.

**an-** (1). See *a-* (1).

**an-** (2). See *ana-*.

**an-** (3). The form taken by *ad-* before *n-*, as in
L *annotāre*, pp *annotātus*, whence 'to *annotate*'.

**an-** (4) is a rare variant, directly of *am-* (2), q.v.,
and therefore indirectly of *ambi-*.

**an-** (5), as in *anoint*, represents F *en-*, in(to), from
L *in-* (prep *in*, in, into): cf *en-* (1).

**an-** (6), in *answer*, is short for OE *and-*, against,
akin to *anti-*.

**an-** (7), as in *ancestor*, descends from L *ante*,
before (L *antecessor*, one who goes before).

**an-** (8), in *anent*, *anon*, derives from ME *an-*,
from the OE prep *on*: OE *onefen*, lit 'on even' (on
an even with); ME *anan*, lit 'in one' (moment).

**an-** (9), in *another*, is simply the article (*a*), *an*:
an other.

**ana-**; before vowels, *an-*. From *an*(*a*)-, c/f of Gr
*ana*, on, up, upwards, above, back, backwards,
again, throughout, (hence) very much, excessively;
Gr *ana* is akin to E *on*; IE *ano*, on high. Examples:
'*anachronism*', from Gr *anakhronismos*, and
*anagoge*, from Gr *anagōgē*, a leading (*agōgē*) up.
[*anci-*. See ANCIENT and cf *ante-*.]

**ann-** (1), in *anneal*, derives from ME *an-* for OE
*on*: cf, therefore, *an-* (8).

**ann-** (2), in *annoy*, derives from ME *an-*, AF *an-*
(OF *an*), from L *in*, in. See ANNOY itself and cf *an-*
(5).

**ant-**. See *anti-*.

**ante-**, which remains *ante-* before a vowel, is the

L *ante*, before (preposition and adverb). Examples: *ante-Christian*, *ante-room*. In *anticipate*, *ante-* becomes *anti-*, by confusion with *anti-* below.

**anth-**, in *anthem* (q.v. in Dict), is a rare variant of:

**anti-**—before a vowel, often *ant-*—represents Gr *ant(i)-*, c/f of *anti*, against, whether physically or morally, as in Gr *antarktikos*, whence E '*antarctic*', and '*anti-* Darwinism'. The Gr *anti* is akin to L *ante*, before (whether in space or in time) and Skt *anti*, opposite (adv): that which is physically *before* or in front of something is *over against* it, hence *against* it.

**ap-** (1). See *apo-*.

**ap-** (2). The form taken by L *ad*, to, towards, before *p*, as in L *appendere*, whence, via French, 'to *append*', to hang (something) to. In *appal(l)*, *ap*=F *a-*, derived from F *a*=L *ad*.

**ap-** (3), in *aperient*, is perhaps a variant of L *ab*, q.v. at *a-* (3).

**ap-** (4). Like *Fitz* in *Fitzgibbon* and *Mac* in *Macbeth*, *ap-* signifies 'son of'. From OW *map* (W *mab*), son, itself akin to Scots and Irish *Mac*. Functionally, therefore, a compound-forming element, yet hardly to be included in Elements.

**aph-**. See:

**apo-**; *aph-* before aspirated vowel; before ordinary vowel, *ap-*; meaning 'from, away, away from; off, off from', as in Gr *apokrupha*, L hence E *apocrypha*, '(things) hidden away'—cf *cryptic* from Gr *kruptikos*—or *apostle*, Gr *apostolos*, a person sent *apo* or away—or *apagoge*, from Gr *apagōgē* (*ap-*+*agōgē*, a leading)—or *apheresis*, L *aphaeresis*, Gr *aphairesis*, compounded of *apo*, away+*hairein*, to take. Akin to L *ab*, OHG *aba*, Skt *ápa*, OPer *apa*, E *off*.

**ar-** (1). L *ad-* before *r*, as in 'to *arrive*', ultimately from L *ad riuam*, to come *to* the *shore*, and as in *arrogate*. In *arraign*, *ar-*=OF *a-*, c/f of *a*=L *ad*.

**ar-** (2), in *artichoke* represents the Ar article *al*, the; via It *articiocco*.

[**arch-**, **arche-**, **archi-**. Being neither prepositional nor adverbial, these intimately interconnected 'prefixes' are strictly compound-formers and are therefore treated in their right place: Elements.]

**as-** (1) is merely *ad-* before *s*, as in L *ascribere* (for *adscribere*), whence 'to *ascribe*', or in L *assistere*, whence 'to *assist*'. Cf *at-* (1).

**as-** (2), in *astonish*, *astound*, derives from ME *as-*, from OF *es-*, from L *ex-*: cf *ex-* (1).

**as-** (3), in *assagai*, is the Ar article *al*, the.

**at-** (1)=*ad-* before *t*, as in L *attentāre*, whence, through French, 'to *attempt*'. See ATTEMPT.

**at-** (2), in *atone* (q.v. in Dict), is simply the E prep *at*.

**av-** occurs, e.g., in *avaunt* (cf *avant*), where F *av-* = L *ab*, from, away.

**avant-**, meaning 'before', occurs only in such a gallicism as *avant-garde*; it represents L *ab ante*, from in front.

**ba-**, in *balance* (OF *balance*), represents L *bi-*, from *bis*, twice. Cf, therefore, *bi-* (1).

**be-**, akin to OFris *be* or *bī*, OHG *bī*, Goth *bi*, by, near (cf, therefore, *by-* and BY), but also to Gr *amphi*, about, around, occurs only in verbs, mostly transitive, falling into two notable groups, the intensive (from verbs only) and the causative (usu from adjectives) or approximately causative, and into such others as privative and denominative. See the following nine entries.

**be-** (1). Intensive, connoting 'about, around, over', as in *bedeck*. Cf:

**be-** (2). Intensive, connoting 'on both or all sides, all around, all over', as in *beclasp*, *becloud*, *bedim*.

**be-** (3). Intensive, connoting 'thoroughly' or 'repeatedly' or 'violently', as in *bedrowse* (render thoroughly drowsy), *bechase* (to chase repeatedly), *belabour* (to beat violently).

**be-** (4). Intensive, connoting 'overmuch, excessively', as in *befringe*, *belaud*, *bediamond*; *bediamond*, like *berobe*, suggests ostentation.

**be-** (5). Causative (from adjectives or from nouns), as in *becalm* and *bedunce*.

**be-** (6). Approximately causative or predominantly causative, with connotation 'to affect with, treat or provide with, cover with' (and analogous nuances); always deriving from nouns and often exemplified in (mostly past) participial adjectives rather than in 'straight' verbs. Thus: *befrock(ed)*, *befurbelowed*, *bemusk*, *beplumed*. Frequently jocose or ironic or sarcastic.

**be-** (7). Privative, connoting removal or departure and deriving either from verbs or from nouns, thus: *bereave*, *beglide*, *behead*.

**be-** (8). Denominative (from nouns, occasionally from adjectives), to name, call, style, as in *belady*, *bewhore*, *belord*, *berogue*; *bestupid*, *befunny*.

**be-** (9). Transitives (from verbs), connoting a prepositional relationship between verb and object, the preposition understood being usually *against*, *at*, *by*, *for*, *on*, *over*, *to*, *with*, as in *beshout* (shout against, at, but also for), *beshine* (shine on, upon), *besigh* (sigh for or over), *becross* (decorate with a cross, make the sign of the cross over), *bemire* (cover with mire), *betide* (happen to).

**bene-**. The L adv *bene*, well, used as a c/f, as in *benediction* and *benvolence*. Contrast *male-*.

**bi-** (1), indicating either 'two' or 'twice' (or 'doubly'), comes from Latin and should therefore be compared with *bin-* and *bis-*. The L *bi-*, *bin-*, *bis-* are akin to E *twi-* (q.v. below), Gr *di-*, Skt *dvi-*, themselves consequently related intimately to E *two*, L *duo*, Gr *duo* (Homeric *duō*). Exx: *bipedal*, having two feet; *bipinnate*, twice pinnate; connotative of combination: *biracial*; lasting two, occurring every two, e.g. years, as *biennial*, *bimonthly*, (ambiguously) twice in, as *biweekly*, appearing twice a week, and therefore confusable with *biweekly*, appearing every two weeks. (To this 'twice (in)' *bi*, *semi-* is preferable.) Connoting 'consisting of two parts', as *bicycle*, or 'divide into two', as *bisect*; anatomically: *bi-auricular*, having two auricles—or pertaining to them; chemically: *bicarbonate*, *bisulphate*.

'*Bi-* and *di-* are [in chemistry] sometimes interchangeable, but *di-* is now usually preferred in most senses' (Webster).

**bi-** (2), in *bishop*, derives from OE *bi-*, for Gr *epi-*: cf *epi-* below.

**bin-**, divided into, or consisting of, two parts as in *binoculars*, comes from L *bīni*, two by two, itself from *bis*, twice: cf *terni* from *ter*, thrice.

**bis-**, twice, as in *bisaxillary*, *biscuit*, twice cooked, and *bissextile*, is used, notably in Anatomy and Medicine, where a vowel or *c* or *s* follows. The L *bis* derives from *duis*, itself from the stem of *duo*, two. Cf *bi-* (1).

**by-**, as in *bystander*, has the basic sense of the preposition and its derivatives, *by* adv and *by* adj: 'near'. The derivative sense 'beyond' occurs in *by-pass*. See BY and cf BYE.

**cat-**. See:

**cata-**; before an unaspirated vowel, *cat-*; before an aspirated vowel, hence before *h*, *cath-*; and *cato-*, variant of *cata-*. These come from Greek: *cata-* from *kata-*, c/f of prep *kata*, 'down', hence adv 'downwards'; *kat-*; *kath-*; *katō*, a distinct form of adv *kata*. In combination, the principal senses are: down, downwards; hence, according to —but also, against, contrary to; back, back again; and often as a mere intensive. In English it is sometimes difficult to assess the value of the prefix: witness, e.g., *catalogue*. The variants *kat(a)-*, *kath-*, as in *katabatic*, *katharsis*, are, in English, to be discouraged: what's wrong with *catabatic* and *catharsis*? Examples that do reveal the sense of the preposition or the adverb include *catachresis*, (something that is) contrary to usage—*cataclastic*, broken down, thoroughly broken—*catholic*— *catocathartic*, a remedial purgative.

**cato-**. See prec.

**circu-**, as in *circuitous*, is a rare 'weakening' of:

**circum-** is the c/f of the adv *circum* (originally the acc of L *circus*), meaning 'round about', hence 'around', as in 'To *circum*navigate the globe', but used also with nouns (*circum*gyration) and esp with adjectives (*circum*central, *circum*oral, *circum*-Saturnian). For ulterior etymology, see CIRCUS.

**cis-** represents the L prep *cis*, on this side of, (hence) on the near side of, as in *cis-Alpine*. Occ transferred to time, as in *cis-Augustan*. Perhaps akin to OS *sĭ*, Lith *šis*, and Hit *kās*, hither, *kēz*, on this side.

**citra-** represents the L adv and prep *citrā*, on this side (of), as in *citramontane*. Strictly, L *citrā* is the f abl of the adj *citer*, hither. The stem is *ci-* (ki-), answering to PGr *\*ki-* (or *\*ky-*): cf also Go *hi-*. For both *cis* and *citra*, see esp E & M.

**co-**, with, together, jointly. The form taken by *com-* (c/f of *cum*) before a vowel and often before *h* (*cohabit*) and *w* (*co-worker*).

**coi-**, in *coil* (q.v. in Dict), is for *col-*, q.v. at *cum-*.

**col-**, with, etc. See *cum-*: *col-* is an assimilated form of *com-* before *l*.

**com-**, with, etc. See *cum-*, of which it constitutes the basic c/f in v cpds. Cf *co-* and:

**con-**, with, etc. The form taken by *com-* before any consonant except *b*, *h*, *l*, *m*, *p*, *r*, *w*, and often (as in *connect*) before *n*. See *cum*.

**contra-**. The L adv and prep *contrā*, against, over against, facing, (adv) on the contrary. *Contrā=con* (see *cum*)+*-trā*, adv suffix, occurring already in Skt *átra*, here, and *tátra*, there. In E cpds, *contra* signifies 'against' or 'contrary, in opposition', as in *contradict*, *contradistinction*. Cf the adj *contrary* and the adv *counter*, and also *contro-* (q.v. below).

**contre-**, seen only in such gallicisms as *contredanse* and *contretemps*, is simply the F form of L *contra-*.

**contro-**. The L adv *contrō*, doublet of *contrā*; as in *controversy*.

**cor-**. As in *corrupt*, *cor-* is an assimilated form of *com-* before *r*. Therefore see *cum*.

**cou-**, as in *couch* and *cousin*, stands for *com-*, q.v. at *cum*. (Skeat.)

**coun-**, in *council* (and *counsel*), in *count* and *countenance*, stands for *com-*, q.v. at *cum-*. (Skeat.)

**counter-** is the c/f of the E adv *counter*, from F *contre* (adv), from the L prep *contrā*, against. Exx: *counterfeit*, *countermand*, *counterpane*, *counterpoise*, *countersign*.

**cu-**, as in *custom*, stands for *com-* or *con-*, qq.v. at:

**cum**, as in *cum laude*, (on diplomas) with praise, i.e. honourably, 'caravan-*cum*-house' and *Chorlton-cum-Hardy*, represents the L prep *cum*, with, along with.

As a preverb (prefix serving to build cpds), it has two main forms: *com-* (or *con-*) and *co-*; and, as assimilated forms of *com-*, the varieties *col-* and *cor-*. See, above, *co-*, *com-*, *con-*. The nasal (*m* or *n*) is not essential: cf L *cohors*, gen *cohortis*, o/s *cohort-*, E *cohort*, and Celtic *co-* alongside *com-*, *con-*; cf also OS *kŭ* alongside Vedic *kám*. Prob IE r: *\*co-* or *ko-*, with variant *\*ca-* or *ka-*.

In cpds *co-*, *com-*, *con-*, etc., connote, usu, 'together', often '(in) reunion', occ 'very'.

**cur-**, in 'to *curry* (a horse)', comes, via OF *cor-*, from L *com-*, q.v. at *cum*.

**de-** (1). The L prep *dē*, from, down from, away from; (hence) coming from, originating in, as a result of; sometimes merely intensive. There are kindred forms in the early Italic dialects Oscan and Umbrian, and also in Celtic. Exx: *depend*, *descend*; *delegate*; (intensively) *denude*, *derelict*; (reversal, deprivation) *declassify*, *decapitate*.

**de-** (2). When, however, E *de-* represents the OF *des-*, it comes from L *dis-* (see below): as perhaps in *destroy* and certainly in *defeat*. Cf *deluge*, adopted from OF-MF, from L *dīluuium*, where *dī-* stands for *dis-*: cf *di-* (2).

**de-** (3), in *devil* (OE *dēofol*, *-ful*, LL *diabolus*, Gr *diabolos*), represents *dia-*.

**dea-**, in *deacon*, like *de-* in *devil*, comes from Gr *dia-*, q.v. below.

**demi-**. The F *demi*, half, a half, c/f *demi-*, comes as adj from the L adj *dīmidius*, half, itself a compound of *dī-* (i.e. *dis-*)+adj *medius*, middle, and as n from L *dīmidium* (cf MEDIUM). Lit in *demicanton, demigroat, demilune*; 'curtailed' in *demirobe*; 'inferior' or 'informal' in *demilustre, demitoilet.* (Examples from Webster.)

**des-.** A Romance—usu F, occ Sp—shape of L *dis-*, as in *descant* and *despatch*. Cf esp *dis-*. (2) Chemistry uses it, for *de-* (free from, deprive of), before vowels, as in *desoxymorphine.*

[**dh-** is not a true prefix. Its use serves to indicate a Hindi, occ Marathi, word, usu of Skt origin; as in *dharma, dhobi, dhow.*]

**di-** (1). Short for *dia-*, q.v.; before vowels, as in *·diactinic.*

**di-** (2). For L *dī-*, for *dis-* (q.v.), connoting separation or reversal; as in *didromy* and *diminish.*

**di-** (3). For Gr *dis*, twice (see 2nd *dis-*), as in *dilemma, diploma*, the Gr coin *distater.*

**di-** (4). For L *dē-*, as in *distil*: cf *de-* (1).

**dia-** represents the Gr prep *dia*, through, throughout, as in *diachronic*; occ an intensive; often, from the idea of (e.g., cutting) 'through', in nuances 'asunder'—'apart'—'across', as in *diapositive*. Before a vowel, often *di-*, as in *diactinic*. This prefix 'seems to be a transformation of IE *\*dis* (L *dis-*, OHG *zir*, Alb *tš-*) "in two, separately" (*\*di*[*s*]*a*, after *meta*, etc.), cf *diaskhizō*, L *discindo*. "I cut in two, split" ' (Boisacq).

**dif-.** See *dis-* (1).

**dir-.** See:

**dis-** is the L *dis-*, apart, asunder, in two. In Mod E, *dis-* is the only form, as in *disassociate*, but in words coming entirely from Latin, the following variations are noticeable: occ *dir-* before vowels, *dis-* being very much commoner; *dif-* before *f*, as in *differ*; *di-* before *b, d, g, l, m, n, r, v*, occ *j*, as in *direct, direption* (lit, a tearing asunder, hence away). The general meaning is 'separation', as in *dismiss*; hence, deprivation, reversal, negation, as in *disable, disqualify*. For the etymology cf *dia-*.

(2) Gr *dis*, twice, doubly, double, as in *disdiapason, disdiazo-*. Rare.

**do-**, in *dozen*, and *dou-*, in *double*, come, through F, from L *duo*, two. Cf:

**du-** may be called the c/f of L *duo*, two, and occurs, e.g., in *duel, duet, duplex*. See DUO and cf *dual* (L *duālis*: *du-+-ālis*). Cf the prec entry.

**dys-** is the L form of Gr *dus-*, badly, ill (adv), severely, akin to Skt *dus-*; *dus-* seems, indeed, to have been the IE stem; cf also Go *tuz-*, OHG *zur-*, OIr *du-* or *do-*, OE *to-*, ON *tor-*, and the Skt variant *dur-*. Exx: *dyslogia*, difficulty in expressing ideas in speech; *dysphemistic*—the opp of *euphemistic*; *dysphoria*, a general malaise.

**e-** (1), as in *eject, emit, erupt*. See *ex-*. In words from F from L (e.g., *eloign*) *e-* derives from OF *es-* for L *ex-*.

**e-** (2), in *enough*, derives from ME *i-*, from OE *ge-* (*genōh*): cf, therefore (*i-* at) *y-* near end of this list.

**e-** (3), in *escalade, escarpment, escutcheon,*

*especial, espouse, espy, esquire, estate*, and in a few less familiar words, has been adopted from F, which prefixes it to words in *sc-, sp-, sq-, st-* ('impure *s*', as some call it) because of the difficulty in pronouncing those four combinations. (Skeat.) This purely phonetic addition occurs also n It.

**é-**, in such gallicisms as *élite* and *émigré*, is F *é*, from OF *es*, from L *ex-*. Cf *e-* (1).

**ec-**, out (of), represents the Gr *ek*, as in *ecbatic*, the adj of *ecbasis* (Gr *ekbasis*), a going out, (hence) a digression, and as in *ecstasy* (Gr *ekstasis*). Cf *ex-* (1).

**ecto-** or, before a vowel, *ect-* comes from *ekto-*, c/f of the Gr adv and prep *ektos*, outside, externally, as in *ectoplasm*. *Ektos*, outside, is to *ek*, out of, as *entos*, within, is to *en*, in: cf, therefore, *ek-* and *ex-* (1).

**ef-** is the form taken by L *ē* or *ex* before *f*, as in *effect*, from L *effectus*, itself from *efficere*.

**eis-** comes straight from Gr *eis*, into, and occurs only in words adopted or slightly adapted from Greek, as *eisegesis*, from Gr *eisēgēsis*: *eis*+(n from) *hēgeisthai*, to lead.

**el-** (1) is an assimilated form, already in Gr, of *en-* (see the 2nd *en-*), as in *ellipse*.

**el-** (2), in *elixir* (q.v. in Dict) and *elemi* (a kind of resin), is the Ar *al*, the. Cf *al-* (2).

**em-** (1) is the form taken by 1st *en-* (from L *in*, in, into) before *b*, as in *embellish*—before *m*, as in *emmarvel*—and before *p*, as in *employ*: all from F words; all, therefore, from the F prefix *en-* (for L *in-*).

**em-** (2). But *em-* occ represents Gr *en* (in), which itself, in certain combinations (before *m, p, ph*), becomes *em-*, as in *emmetros*, proportional, proportioned (*en+metron*, a measure), whence the cpd *emmetropia*, and as in *emphasis*. Cf the 2nd form of *en-*.

**emb-** in at least one word (*embassy*) seems to vary *amb-*, variant of *ambi-*, q.v.

**en-** (1) represents F *en*, in, into, from L *in*, in, into, in words coming from French or formed on the analogy of such borrowings from French, as in *enchant, enchase, engulf, engloom*. The force of *en-* is often merely intensive.

**en-** (2). But cf *em-* (2) above, for *en-* may also represent Gr *en*, in, as in *encaustic, endemic, energy, enthusiasm*: in short, this *en* occurs only in words taken from Greek or in words formed on the analogy of such E words.

**en-** (3), in *enemy*, derives, through F, from L *in-*, not. Cf the 1st *en-* and the 2nd *in-*.

**endo-**; before a vowel, usu *end-*. Adopted from Gr, where it constitutes the c/f of the adv and prep *endon*, (on the) inside; *endon=en*, in+a suffix. Exx: *endogamy*, inbreeding, and *endogenous*, produced or originating from within. Cf *ento-*.

**enter-** (1). The E shape of F *entre-*, c/f of the prep *entre* (L *inter*), between, among—occurring in F *entrechat, entremets*—from L *inter*; as in *entertain* (F *entretenir*) and *enterprise* (F *entreprise*). Cf *inter-*.

enter- (2) is merely the prevocalic form of *entero-*, q.v. at *enter(o)-* in Elements.

ento-; before a vowel, usu *ent-*. Within, (hence) inner. Adopted from Greek, where *ent(o)-* constitutes the c/f of the adv *entos* (cf L *intus*), inside, within, the opp of *ektos* (q.v. at *ecto-*); *entos=en*, in+-*tos*, suffix indicating origin. Exx: *entogastric*, *entozoic*.

entre- is the F original of 1st *enter-*, q.v., and therefore comes from L *inter*, between, among.

cp-. See *cpi-*.

eph-. See *epi-*.

epi-; before an ordinary vowel, *ep-*; before an aspirated vowel, *eph-*. The Gr prep *epi* means 'on, upon, onto', hence 'towards, to', and is akin to Skt *api*, near to, beside, beyond, and Lith *apie*, about, around, near, at. Exx: *epact*, from Gr *epaktos* (*ep-*+*aktos*, from *agein*, to lead or bring); *ephemeral*, adj of *ephemera*, from Gr *ephēmeros* (*epi* becoming *eph* before *hēmera*, a day); *epigram*, from Gr *epigramma* (*epi*+*gramma*, something written).

es- is the form taken by *ex-* in a few E words of Romance origin, esp It and F; e.g., *escambio*, *escape*, *escheat*, *escort*, *estreat*.

eso-, within, (hence) internal; hence, in Organic Chem, directly attached, direct attachment, to a ring, as in *esoneural*. Opp *exo-*, q.v. Adapted from the Gr adv *esō*, which, as the Ionic variant *eisō* shows, is intimately related to *eis*, q.v. at *eis-*.

eu-, well, comes straight from Gr *eu*, well, itself orig the neu of the adj *eus*, good, strong, valiant, answering to IE *\*esus* (*esu-*+*s*), root *\*es*, akin to E *is*: '\**esu-s*, \*existent, \*alive, hence valiant' (Boisacq). Exx: *eugenic*, *eupeptic*, *euphemism*, *eutropic*. Cf:

ev-. The form assumed by Gr *eu* in ML, as in *Evadne*, *evangel*, the exhilarated outcry *evoe*, *Evonymus*. Cf *eu-*.

ex- (1); *ef-* before *f*, as in *effusion*; *e-* before *b* (*ebriety*)—*d* (*educe*)—*g* (*egestion*)—and *l* (*elapse*) —*m* (*emerge*)—*n* (*enarration*)—*r* (*erase*)—and *v* (*evade*). In F words, it often occurs as *es-* (*escape*), aphetically *s-* (*scape*), or as *é-* (*élan*). L *ex* corresponds to Gr *ek* or, before an aspirated vowel, *ex*; and is akin to OS *iz-*, Lett *iz*, Lith *is*, OIr *ess-*, Gaulish *eks-*. The IE etymon was presumably *\*eks*, with variant *\*egs* or *\*egz*.

In E words, the principal denotations and connotations are these: out, out of, as in *exhale*; out from, off from, off, from, as in *exeunt*; coming out of, and ascending, as in *efferent* and *extol*, and even in *exalt*; beyond, as in *exceed*; away from, as in *expatriate*; (derivatively) separated from, lacking, without, as in *exanimate*; in inchoative vv, change of state, as in *effervesce*; completion, as in *effect* and *exhaust*; an intensive (cf intensive *de-*), as in *excruciate*; adopted from a LL usage, *ex*+n connotes a person *out of* a rank, position, office held formerly, as in *ex-king*, *ex-president*.

ex- (2), in *excise* (q.v. in Dict), prob comes from L *ad-*, to.

ex- (3). See:

exo-; before a vowel, usu *ex-*. The Gr *exō-* repre-

sents the prep *exō*, out of, outside, a derivative from *ex*, out of, from: see *ex-* (1), 1st para. Its general English meaning is 'out of' or 'external', as in *exoneural*; in Chem it often connotes 'outward'.

[extero- appears more fittingly in the Compound-Forming Elements list.]

extra- represents the L adv and prep *extrā*, on the outside (opp *intus*)—outside of (opp *intrā*), beyond—hence, without, except, except for. Exx: *extravert*, one who lives externally; *extracostal*, outside of the ribs; *extramundane*, beyond the (physical) world; *extraordinary*, beyond the ordinary, (hence) most unusual. The connotation 'beyond' leads to the idea of intensification, as in *extra-special*, very special indeed.

Etymologically *extrā* is the f abl of the adj *exter*, (placed) on the outside—cf *citrā*; *exter* clearly derives from *ex* (see 1st *ex-*).

Cf *stra-*.

extro-, as in *extrovert*, variant of *extravert*, has been formed from *extra-* on the analogy, and as the opp, of *intro-*, q.v. The L *extrō* occurs only in L *extrorsum*.

for- (1) is akin not only to prep *for* (q.v. for etymology) but also to such OGmc prefixes as ON *for-*, OHG *fir-*, Go *fra-*. Although no longer used to form words, it survives in *forfend*, to prohibit or avert; *forget*, *forgo*, to omit or fail to get, to go without; *forswear*, to reject, or renounce, formally; *fordo*, to slay; *forspent*, utterly spent (exhausted); *forlorn*, utterly lost. The connotations there implied are 'prohibition, destruction; failure, omission; thoroughly'; certain obsolete words exhibit one or two additional connotations or functions.

for- (2), in *forfeit* (q.v. in Dict), comes from F *for-*, from L *foris*, out of doors, itself from *foris*, door, with cognates in Skt, OSl, OHG.

for- (3), in *forever*, *forasmuch*, is obviously the prep *for* (q.v. in Dict): cf *for ever* and *for as much as*.

for- (4), in *forward* and in the slovenly *forbear* for *forebear* (ancestor), is identical, in origin and sense, with:

fore- (1), as in *foregoing* (preceding, earlier) and *forebears* (ancestors). For etymology, see FORE.

fore- (2), in (to) *forebear* for (to) *forbear*, is slovenly for *for-* (1).

forth-, only in *forthcoming* and *forthwith*, has come straight down from OE. (Skeat.) See the adv FORTH in the Dictionary.

fro-, in *froward*, comes from ON *frā*, from. See adv *fro* at FROM in Dict.

gain-, in *gainsay* and dial *gainstand*, to withstand, and archaic *gainbuy*, to redeem, derives from OE *gēan*: see AGAINST in Dict.

ger-, like *ker-*, is an echoic prefix occurring only in sl and coll words. It may, in its weaker form, *ge-*, owe something to the G prefix *ge-*, esp where it appears in Yiddish. Both *ger-* and *ge-* are occ interchangeable with *ker-* and *ke-* resp, as in *ger-*

or *ker-doing* (or *-doink*), an AF exclamation apropos, and indicative, of a crash.

**hama-**, as in *hamacratic* (of, by, for government based on mutual action), comes from the Gr adv *hama*, together. Occ, loosely, *ama-*, as in the photographic *amacratic*.

**hemi-**, half-, as in *hemisphere*, merely adapts Gr *hēmi-*, akin to L *sēmi-* (q.v.), OHG *sāmi-*, OE *sām-*. The IE stem may therefore have been either \**hsēm-* or *hsām-*. Cf the formation of Gr *huper-*, q.v. at *hyper-*. Cf also *me-* below.

**hyp-**. See *hypo-*.

**hyper-**, over, above, beyond, beyond the ordinary or normal, transcending, excessively, as in *hyperbole* and *hypercritical*, represents Gr *huper-*, c/f of the prep *huper*, over or above, beyond or exceeding. As Gr *hēmi-* is akin to L *semi*, so is *huper* akin to L *super*: the IE stem may therefore have been \**hsuper*, the *s* dropping out in Gr, the *h* in L. Cf OHG *ubir* and Skt *upári* and see *hypo-*.

**hyph-**. See:

**hypo-**; before an unaspirated vowel, often *hyp-*; before an aspirated vowel, *hyph-*. The E meanings 'below, beneath, less than the ordinary or the normal'—the opp, therefore, of *hyper*—correspond to those of Gr *hupo-*, c/f of the prep *hupo*, below, beneath. *Hupo* is akin to OPer (and Av) *upa*, towards, and also to L *sub*, under: as *huper* to *super*, so *hupo* to *sub* (? orig *sup*). The IE \**hupo-* or \**hsupo-*, whence Gr *hupo*, prob forms the origin of *huper*. Exx: *hypocrite, hypodermic, hypothesis*; *hypallage, hyparterial*; *hyphen*.

**i-**. See *y-*. (2) See the 2nd *in-*.

**il-** is the form taken by *in-*, not, before *l*, as in *illegal*, and also by *in-*, in, into, as in *illumine*. Cf *im-* and esp *in-*.

**im-**=*in-*, not, before *m*, as in *immense*, and before *p*, as in *improper*; before *b*, as in *imbue*; (2), not, before *m*, as in *imminent*; and before *p*, as in *impend*.

**in-** (1), in, within, into, towards, comes either from the E prep and adv *in*, as in *inborn, income, inside*, or from L *in* (same senses), as in *indebted, invade*. Except in such softenings as *immesh, impark*, the E *in-* remains *in-*, but the L *in-* experiences these changes: *il-* before *l*, as above; *im-* before *b, m, p*, as above; *ir-* before *r*, as under. In the L derivatives, *in-* (*il-, im-, ir-*) has often a merely intensive force, as in *imprison*. Cf *em-* and 1st *en-*.

**in-** (2). Again from L, where it forms an inseparable prefix with no originating adv or prep, this *in-*, akin to the synonymous E prefix *un-*, means 'not' and experiences, in L, the same assimilations as we have noticed in *in-* (1), with an additional one—before *gn* it becomes *i*, as in *ignobilis*, whence *ignoble*, and in *ignōrāre*, whence E *ignore*. Exx: *inadvertent, incapable, illicit, immature, improper, irregular*.

**indi-** or, before a vowel, *ind-*, as in *indigenous* and *indigent* (*ind-+-igent*), represents PL *indu*, within,

cognate with Gr *endon*, within. (Skeat.) Cf *endo-* above.

**infra-**, below or beneath in position, situation, series, status, as in *infracostal, infrahuman*, (hence) inferior, as in *infranatural*, but also (as in *infraterritorial*) within, represents the L adv and prep *infrā*, beneath, lower, physically and morally—opp *suprā*—and akin to L *inferus*, with cognates in Skt.

**intel-**. See:

**inter-**, between, among, as in *interfere, interlace*; (hence) mutual or reciprocal, as in *intercourse*; (occ) at intervals, as in *intermittent*; rarely privative, as in *interdict*: comes from the L prep *inter*, between or among. *Inter-* appears in the assimilated form *intel-* in *intellect, intelligent*, etc. The L prep consists of basic *in*, in, and the loc suffix *-ter*: cf *subter* (from *sub*, under) and Skt *antar*, between, and:

**intra-**, within, situated within, as in *intramural, intravenous*, (hence) into, as in *intrasusception, intravert*, comes from the L prep *intrā*, within, on the inside of, within the limits of (opp *extrā*): and *intrā* derives from *in*, very much as *extrā* derives from *ex*, *-trā* being a loc suffix with Skt cognates. Cf:

**intro-**, to or towards a place within, inwards, is, in effect, the L adv *intrō*, on the inside, in the interior; *intrō*, adv (only in LL does it derivatively become a prep), answers to *intrā*, prep. Exx: *introduce, introvert, introsusception*. Cf also:

**intus-**, on the inside, (but predominantly) to the inside, within, into, comes from the L adv *intus*, from within, (but mostly) on or to the inside; *intus* answers to Gr *entos* (*en*, in, into+-*tos*), with a suffix—L *-tus*, Gr *-tos*, Skt *-tas*—that, like *-trā*, is fundamentally a loc suffix. Rare in English, it is exemplified by *intussusception* (cf *intra-* and *intro-susception*).

**ir-**, as in *irruption* and *irrational*, is the assimilated form of *in-* (q.v.) before *r*: both of *in-*, in(to), and of *in-*, not.

**iss-**, occurring only in *issue* (*issuance, issuant*, etc.), derives from OF *iss-*, from L *ex-*: cf, therefore, *es-*.

**juxta-**, situated or put beside or very close to, as in *juxtaposition*, comes from the ML adv and prep *juxta*, i.e. L and LL *iuxta*, which, meaning 'so as to touch'; very close, very close to', derives from *iugum* (ML *jugum*), a yoke, and is therefore akin to *iungere* (ML *jungere*), to join or unite. For further etymology, cf YOKE.

**k-** is an intensive prefix in, e.g., *knut*—or *k-nut*, for often the *k* is pronounced almost as a separate syllable—a very smart, usu young, man about town, as in the popular Edwardian song, 'Gilbert, the filbert, Colonel of the Knuts'. Perhaps cf *ker-* below.

**kata-**, as in *katabasis*, a going down, is the Gr form of *cata-*, q.v.

**ker-** or, in weaker, less usu form, *ke-*. An echoic

prefix, connoting the impact or sound of a heavy blow, fall, collision, etc., as in *kerflop*, *kerwallop*. Cf *ger-* (q.v.), with which it is occ interchangeable. The prefix *ke(r)-* prob preceded *ge(r)-*, for it seems to be intimately related to the echoic *kr-* of such words as *crash, crump, crush*, and also, more obscurely, to the *khr-* of, e.g., *Christmas*, which, as an exclamation, tends to become, often does become, *Ker-ristmas!* Perhaps cf *k-* above and the *ter-* of the jocularly emphatic *terwenty*, twenty.

**l-** (1), in *lone*, is simply a c/f of the adj ALL.

**l-** (2), in *limbeck* and *lute*, is the Ar *al*, the. Cf *al-* (2).

**l-** (3), in *loriot* (the golden oriole), is the F article *l'*, the: *loriot* represents F *l'oriot*.

**la-** represents the It f singular *la*, the, in the E-from-It *lavolta*; the Sp f sing *la*, the, in E *lariat*, from Sp *la reata*; the F f sing *la*, the, in AE *lavalier*, AE and E *laval(l)iere*, from F *lavallière*, from *La Vallière*, Louis XIV's favourite. See esp 'Articled Nouns' in P[4].

**M-**, in the Bantu languages, indicates 'a person, esp a member of a tribe', as in *M-Swahili*; pl, *Wa-*, as in *Wa-Swahili*, the Swahili tribesmen.

**mal-, male-**, represent, the former the F *mal* (from L), the latter the L *male*, badly, ill (adv), the adv of *malus*, bad, with cognates in Gr and Skt. Exx: *malapert* (OF *mal apert*); *malcontent*, straight from F; *malpractice*; *maltreat*;—*malefactor*, straight from L; *malediction* (from the o/s of L *maledictiō*); *malevolent* (o/s of ML *malevolens*, L *maleuolens*, lit 'ill-wishing').

**me-**, in *megrim*, stands for *hemi-* (half-), q.v.; *megrim*, ME *migrym* or *mygrene*, from OF *migraine*, from LL *hēmicrania*, from Gr *hēmikrania*.

**meta-**; *met-* before an unaspirated vowel; *meth-* before an aspirated vowel. The predominant senses, in both Gr and E words, are 'along with; after', which branch off into 'in succession to, posterity, after', as in *metachronism* and *method*; 'change' (something that happens afterwards) or 'transfer, trans-', as in *metamorphosis* and *metempsychosis*; 'beyond', as in *metaphysics*—hence 'higher', as in *metapsychosis*. The Gr *meta* is akin to Go *mith*, OHG *mit* or *miti*, OE *mid*, ON *meth*, with; to the *med(i)-* of L *medius*, in the middle; and to IE *\*medh(i)-* (root *\*me-*), in the middle—cf Gr *mesos* (from IE *\*medhios*), in the middle.

**meth-**. See prec.

**mis-** (1), from L *minus*, less, but through OF *mes-* (F *més-* or *mé-*): as in *mischance*, ME *meschance*, OF *mescheance*, and *mischief*, ME *meschef*, OF *meschief*. Connotation: bad, badly—ill (adj and adv)—wrong, wrongly.

**mis-** (2), from OE *mis-*, akin to ON *mis-*, Go *missa-*, OHG *missa-* or *missi-*; orig, pp from the stem present in OE *mīthan*, Go *maidjan*, OHG *mīdan*, to change, perhaps with emphasis on 'change for the worse'. Exx: *misbehave, mislead, misspend*, and *misdeed, misgiving*. It becomes merely negative in *mislike*, merely intensive in *misdoubt*.

Usage has long—indeed, since c1650—tended to confuse *mis-* (1) and *mis-* (2). The confusion is entirely natural, for psychologically and semantically the fundamental ideas of 'less' and 'change, change for the worse' are very closely akin, one to the other. *Mislike* orig signified 'to be displeasing to', as in 'It *mislikes* me much' (OE *mislīcian*), but the predominant sense has, since 1900 at the latest, been 'to dislike', as in 'I *mislike* that man'.

**n-** (1)=*ne*, not, as in *never*, not ever, from OE *nǣfre*, consisting of OE *ne*, not+OE *ǣfre*, ever. As an active prefix, *n-* (and *ne-*) ceased to exist soon after ME became EE. The OE-ME *ne* is akin to L *ne*, not, which we see in *neuter* (*ne+uter*) and *nefarious* and *null*.

**n-** (2), as in *newt* and *nickname*, is the *-n* of the E article *an*, the: *an ewt, an ekename* resp become *a newt, a nickname*. See 'Articled Nouns' in P[4].

**ne-**. See *n-* (1). In L c/ff, *ne-* before *o* and *l* often took the stronger form *neg-*, prob developed from *nec-*, c/f of *nec*, an emphatic form of the adv *ne: negō*, I deny (cf E *negation*); *negōtium* (*neg-+ōtium*), whence, ult, E *negotiate*; *neglegere* (variant *neclegere*), whence, ult, *neglect*.

**neg-**. See prec.

**non-**, not, merely makes a c/f of the L adv *non*, not, which derived from PL *noenum*, i.e. *neoenum*, not one (thing), *oenum* being the PL form of L *ūnum*. Occ *non-* merges with a noun, as in *nonconformist* and *nonsense*; usu it precedes an adj, as in *non-Christian* and *non-religious*. *Non-*, it is clear, is less emphatic than *in-* or *un-*; usu, so far from denoting an opposite, it merely connotes a negation.

**o'-** is a shortening of *of* or *on*, as in Shakespeare's 'turning o' the tide'; therefore cf *a-* (5) and *a-* (6).

**o-** (2) represents L *ob-* (q.v.), as in *omit* (L *omittere*).

**ob-**, towards or facing, as in *obverse*—against, as in *object*—upon, over, as in *obfuscate*, but also down, as in *oblige*—completely, thoroughly, (very) much, as in *obdurate*; in modern scientific and technical words, reversely, as in *obovate*.

The following assimilations are common: *ob-* before *c* becomes *oc-*, as in *occur*; before *f*, becomes *of-*, as in *offend* and *offer*; before *g*, becomes *og-*, as in the obsolete *oggannition*, a snarl, from L *oggannīre* (*ob+gannīre*), to snarl at; before *p*, becomes *op-*, as in *opponent*.

L *ob* is akin to Gr *epi*, upon, towards (cf *epi-* above).

**oc-**. See *ob-*, 2nd para.

**of-** (1). See *ob-*, 2nd para.

**of-** (2), in *offal*, does duty for *off-*: *offal=off-fall*: but *offfal(l)* would have been phonetically absurd. (Skeat.)

**off-**, as in *offset*, is the adv *off*, q.v. in Dict. Cf prec.

**og-**. See *ob-*, 2nd para.

on-, as in *oncoming*, is the adv and prep *on*, q.v. in Dict.

op-. See *ob-*, 2nd para.

opiso-: from Gr *opisō*, backwards, as in *opisometer*, an instrument for the measurement of curves. Cf:

opisth(o)-: Gr *opisth(o)-*, c/f of *opisthen*, at the back (cf *opiso-*), as in *opisthognathous* (cf *-gnatha*), having jaws that retreat; *opisthograph*; *opisthosomal* (cf *-some*).

opsi-: Gr *opsi-*, c/f of adv *opse*, late, too late; prob IE s and r, *op-*, var of the *ap-* of Gr *apo*, (away) from—cf L *abs* and *ab*. Exx: *opsigamy*, late marriage, from Gr *opsigamia* (cf *-gam*).

or- (1), in *ordeal* and *ort(s)*, has a prefix that, occurring in OE as *or-*, OFris as *or-*, MD as *oor-*, G as *ur-* or *er-*, Go as *us-*, has basic meaning 'out' and is therefore akin to *a-* (8), q.v.

or- (2), in *orlop*, contracts D *over*(loop), over.

os-, in *ostensible*, which consists of *os-*+*tensible*, is either a worn-down or merely a phonetically convenient form of *obs-*, a variant of *ob-*, q.v.

out-. See adv OUT in the Dict. Cf also *ut-*, *utt-*, near end of this list.

outr-, in *outrage*, represents F *outre* (as in *outremer*, beyond the sea, (hence) foreign lands), from L *ultrā*, beyond: see *ultra-*.

over-. See OVER in the Dict.

pa-, in *palsy*, shortens *para-* (1), q.v.: ME *palesie*, earlier *parlesie* (or *-sey*): OF *paralysie*, LL *paralysis*, Gr *paralusis*.

palin-, as in *palindrome*, *palingenesis*, *palinode*, but *palim-* in *palimpsest*, means 'back again': Gr *palin*, back, again; app from an IE stem that means 'to turn'. (Boisacq.)

par- (1), as in *parboil*, *pardie!*, is Fr *par-*, thoroughly (as also in *parget*), by: i.e., the F prep *par*, by, thoroughly, from L *per*: see *per-* below.

par- (2). In *parget*, F *par-* may rather derive, via OF *por-*, from L *prō-*, forward(s).

par- (3). See *para-* (3).

par- (4). See:

para-; before a vowel, *par-*. The basic sense of Gr *para* is 'beside' or 'alongside', hence 'aside from' or 'beyond', hence (?) 'amiss': and these recur in E words, e.g. *paragraph*, *paraphrase*, *parody*, with the additional nuances 'abnormal' (to the side of, but at some distance), as in *paranoia*, and 'closely resembling', as in *paraselene*, a mock moon, and *paratyphoid*.

The Gr *para* is akin to L *por-*, as in *portendere* (E *portend*)—an alternation of *prō-*; *para*, therefore, is akin also to L *prae*. There are several early IE cognates. Cf *pro-* below.

para- (2). In *parachute*, *parapet*, *parasol*, *para-* connotes 'defence against'. Although these words come imm from French, the prefix *para-* here represents *para!*, the imperative of It *parare*, to defend (itself from L *parāre*, to prepare).

para- (3), in *paradise*; shortened to *par-* in *parvis*; is Av *pairi*, around, akin to Gr *peri*: cf, therefore, *peri-*.

pel- is the assimilated form of *per-* (q.v.) before *l*, as in *pellucid*.

pene- or, before a vowel, *pen-*, signifying 'almost', stands for the L adv *paene*, almost, of obscure ulterior origin, as in *peneplain* (or *-plane*) and *peninsula* (*pen*+*insula*, island). The L word is app of non-Italic origin.

per-, through, (hence) by means of, and, in combination, throughout, hence thoroughly, hence as an intensive, represents L *per*, c/f of the L prep *per*, through, hence, in combination, thoroughly, with assimilation *pel-* before *l*. The L *per* is akin to the Gr prep *peri*, around, round about, (hence) concerning, and to Skt *pari*: see *peri-* below. Exx: *perambulate*, *perception*, *persecute*, *pervert*, *perturb*.

In French, L *per* becomes *par*, by, and, in combination, thoroughly: the former occurs in the oath *pardie!*, the latter in *parboil*. But in E words, F *par* may become *per*, as in *perchance*—and, by analogy, *perhaps*.

Cf *pel-*. There is a variant *pil-*, seen in PILGRIM.

peri-, adopted from Gr *peri-*, comes from the adv and prep *peri*, all round, round about, (hence) concerning, and, in combination, occ a mere intensive: as in *perimeter*, *periphery*, *periscope*, *pericranium*, *period*. The Gr word is akin to Skt *pári*, adv (all round) and prep (around), OPer *pariy*, Alb *per*, L *per*, also OHG *fir-* or *far-*, OS *firi-*, OE *fyr-*. Boisacq postulates an IE r *per*, 'expressing the execution of a movement forward or of an effort directed to a precise end'. That IE stem *per* has, in combination, a shortened form *pr-* as in Gr *pro-* or *prō-*, and L *prō-*, forward, to the fore.

pil-. See *per-*, at end.

po-, in *position*, *positive*, is aphetic for L *apo*, close kin to *ap*, the PL form of *ab*—cf *a-* (3) and *apo-*.

pol-. See:

por- (1), in *portend*, represents L *por-* (as in *portendere*), an allied form of L *prō-*, q.v. at the 2nd *pro-*. 'It appears as *pol-* in *pollute*' and perhaps as *pos-* in *possess*. (Skeat.)

por- (2). In E words from F, *por-*, like *pur-* (q.v. below), represents an early form of *pour-*, the F re-shaping of the 2nd *pro-*. Example: *portrait*.

pos-. See *por-* (1), at end.

post-, after (in time), as in *postdate*, *postpone*, *post-Shakespearean*, after (in place, position, point, etc.), as in *postfrontal*, behind the forehead, and, in medicine, occurring as a result of, as in *post(-) neuralgic*, comes from the L *post*, after, behind (prep, adv, prefix)—opp *ante*, before; and L *post* is akin to Skt *paśca*, Av *pāskat*, OPers *pasā*, after, and to TokhB *post*, OSl *pozde*. The IE r appears to be *pos*, with variant *pas*.

pour-, as in the gallicisms *pourboire*, *pourparler*, *pourpoint*, *poursuivant*, is a c/f of the F prep *pour*, for, OF *por*, VL *por*, L *prō*: see the 2nd *pro-*.

pr-, in *prison* and *prize*, is ult identical with L *pre-*, which=*prae-*. (Skeat.) See:

prae-, surviving in legal terms (e.g., *praemunire*) and in Roman-historical terms (*praenomen*, *praetor*, etc.); otherwise *pre-*, as in *preamble, prefect, pretext*; sometimes through F *pré-*; ML *pre-* or *prae-*; L *prae-*, in c/ff often *pre-*, from the L prep and adv *prae*, PL *prai*, before, akin to *prō*, q.v. at 2nd *pro-*: cf Oscan *prai*, Umbrian *pre*, and, with varying shades of meaning, OP *prei*, OSl *pri*. Cf also:

**praeter-**, only in 'Roman' survivals and in archaistic spellings; elsewhere *preter-*, as in *preterit(e), pretermit, preternatural*: L *praeter*, in front of, (hence) beyond, (hence) not counting, except. *Praeter* was orig either a comp of *prae* or a *prae-* derivative analogous to *subter* from *sub*, or *inter* from *in*.

**pre-**. See *prae-*.

**preter-**. See *praeter-*.

**pri-**, as in *prior* and *prime, private* and *deprive*, occurs only in words coming from L and is a variant of or, at the least, closely akin to *prae-* (*pre-*) and L *pro*.

**pro-** (1). The Gr *pro-* or *prō-*, before, whether in space or in time, comes from IE *\*pro* or *prō*, to the fore or front: cf Skt *prá-*, Av *fra-* or *frā-*, OPer *fra-*, L *pro-* or *prō-*, OSl *pro-* or *pra-*, OHG *fir-*. Exx: *problem, proboscis, proscenium; prologue*; in SciE, primitive or rudimentary, as in *progamete*.

**pro-** (2). The L *pro-*, forward, forth, is akin to and was much influenced by Gr *pro* or *prō*, before. The basic sense of the L adv and prep *pro*, forward, in front (of), occurs in such words as *proceed, progress, project*.

These basic senses of L *prŏ* imply that somebody or something is behind one, therefore shielded or sheltered or protected by one: thus have arisen the nuances 'in defence of, for the sake of, in behalf of' and so forth, as in *procure* and *prolocutor* and, with the accentuated nuance 'in favour of', in such modern terms as *pro-American, pro-British, pro-Joyce*.

The basic senses of L *prŏ* also imply 'in the place of, instead of': hence, substituted for', as in *proconsul*.

For etymology, cf 1st *pro-*. For variations showing F influence, see *por-, pour-, pur-*.

**pro-** (3) is, in *provost*, an odd deviation from *prae-, pre-*. (Skeat.)

**prod-**, in *prodelision* (lit a 'forward', i.e. 'before', elision),=2nd *pro-*, q.v. Cf L *prodesse* (*prod+esse*).

**pros-**, as in *proselyte* and *prosody*, connotes 'towards', hence 'concerning'; in *prosenchyma*, 'near'; in *prosencephalon*, 'fore-'. A Gr preverb, it comes from *pros*, a Gr adv (at the side; besides) and prep (towards, beside, near to). The dial variant *proti* helps us to see the kinship of *pros* to Skt *práti*, towards, and OSl *protivŭ*, face to face with, and Lett *prett'*, over against. The IE etymon is presumably *\*proti*, against, over against, facing, perhaps having an ult form *\*prati*. Cf the compound-forming element *prot(o)-*, and also:

**proso-** is a c/f deriving from Gr *prosō*, forwards, onwards—an extension of *pros*; c/f Gr *exō* from *ex*. The E prefix occurs only in Sci and tech words, with the general meanings 'in front', as in *prosobranchia, prosodetic, prosopyle*—'passing to, or into, another', as in *prosodemic*—'developing progressively' or 'progressive development', as in *prosoplasia*.

**pu-**, in *puny*; **puis-** in *puisne*; these two prefixes represent F forms of L *postea*, afterwards, F *puisné* meaning 'later-born'.

**pur-**, as in *purchase* (OF *porchacier*), to pursue—hence to seek—and obtain, hence to obtain by seeking with a price (to purchase, as we now understand *purchase*), in *purfle* (OF *porfiler*), in *purloin, purport* (and *purpose*), *pursue-, purvey, purview*: this *pur-* comes from OF *pur*, variant *por* (EF-F *pour*), ML *por*, L *pro*: cf the 2nd *pro-*.

**r-**, in *rally* (F *rallier*),=*re-*, q.v.; it would be better to say that, in F, *re-allier* became *rallier*.

**re-**, back (to an original place or state), backwards, or merely connoting '(to hold oneself) back from advancing or from doing something definite', as in *return* or *revert—recline—*(third nuance) *refrain. Re-* comes, sometimes via F *re-* or *ré-*, from L *re-*, answering to no recorded adv or prep and akin to nothing more remote, whether in space or in time, than the syn Umbrian *re-*.

A spatial deviation—a very natural deviation—is that constituted by the connotation of 'such a movement in a contrary direction as destroys what has been done' (E & M), as in *recluse, renounce, resign, reveal*.

Deriving from the sense 'back in space or in time or in state' is that of 'again', as in *recant, rejoin, renew, repeat*.

The L variant *red-* may have been the orig form, but in Classical L appears only before a vowel, as in *redarguere* (E *redargue*), *redimere* (E *redeem*), *redīre* (whence *reditiō*, whence the obs *redition*), *redundāre* (E *redound*).

**rear-**, as in *rearguard*, derives from AF *rere-*. See *rere-*.

**red-**, as in *redaction* and *redeem*. See *re-*, last para.

**rere-**, in *rerebrace, rerecount, reredos, reresupper, rereward*, is an AF form that more usu became *rear-*. *Rere-* existed in OF as a variant of *riere*, from L *rētrō*.

**retro-**, backwards, (hence, in E) back, comes from the L adv *retrō*, formed from *re-*, back, as *intrō* from *in* or as *extrō* from *ex*. Exx: *retrograde, retrospect*; (An) 'situated behind', as in *retronasal*, behind the nose.

**rip-**, as in *rip-roaring, rip-roarious, rip-snorting*, is an intensive in humorous, usu sl, words: cf *ripping*, very good. Clearly echoic in origin. Cf *ker-*.

**s-** (1), in *spend, spite, stain*, is a lopped form of L *dis-* (see 1st *dis-*); it occurs mostly in words that, like *spite, splay, sport, stain*, have come from or through F.

**s-** (2), in *sample*, derives from OF *es-*, from L *ex-*. Cf *ex-*.

**s-** (3), in *sure*, represents, ult, the L priv *sē-*. Therefore cf *se-* (1).

**s-** (4), in *sombre*; ult represents L *sub-*, q.v. below.

**s-** (5), an IE int, occ intrusive, and occurring esp in Gr but also in Gmc. Mentioned frequently in the Dict.

**sans-**, which is, in effect, the F prep *sans*, without, from L *sine* (cf *sine-* below), occurs only in such gallicisms as *sans-culotte* (and *-culottism*) and *sansgêne*, casual behaviour, *sans-serif* and *Sans Souci*, Frederick the Great's palace at Potsdam.

**satis-**, as in *satisfy* and *satispassion* (a suffering that is theologically acceptable),=L *satis*, enough, akin to Go *saths*, Ir *sathech*, sated, OP *satuinei*, thou satest, Ionic Gr *asaō*, I sate. The IE r is prob *sat-*.

**sē-** (1) or, before a vowel, *sed-*. This L prefix indicates separation, parting, privation, and it derives from a PL prep, meaning 'without'—superseded by *sine* (cf *sine-* below). *Sē-*, *sed-* perhaps forms the origin of the L conj *sed*, but; certainly it is akin to Umbrian *sei*, to Arm *k'ec*, detached or separated, and Sl *sveni*, outside (prep). Exx: *secede*, to move away; *secern*, *secret*, *secrete*; *secure*, free from *cura* or anxiety; *sedition* (a going aside or away); *seduce* (to lead aside, hence astray); *select* (lit, to gather aside); *separate* (lit, to make ready—on the side, at a distance); obs *sepose*, to set aside or apart; and perhaps *sober*.

**se-** (2), in *semester*, is L *sex*, 6.

**semi-**, adopted from L *sēmi-*, half-, akin to Gr *hēmi-*, half (see *hemi-* above) and more obviously Skt *sāmi*, and OE *sām-*. Exx: *semi-acid*, *semidetached*, *semi-Gothic*, *semi-liquid*; in AE, such words are written solid.

**sin-** is the form taken by L *sēmi-* in L *sinciput*, (lit) half a head, sense-adapted by An, with adj *sincipital*.

**sine-**, as notably in only one word, *sinecure*, from ML *sine cūra*, without cure—i.e., without cure (care) of souls. The L prep *sine*, without, occurs in several L phrases, e.g. *sine qua non*. Cf *sans-*.

**so-** (1), in *sober* (*sobriety*), is L *sō-*, variation of privative *sē-*: cf, therefore, *se-* above.

**so-** (2), in *sojourn*, comes, via OF, from L *sub-* (VL *\*subdiurnāre*): cf *sub-* below.

**sopr-**, as in *soprano*, is short for It *sopra-*, from L *sūprā-* (q.v.).

**sover-**, in *sovereign*, comes from OF, where *sover-* derives from L *super*: cf *super-* below.

**su-**. See *sub-*, at end of 3rd para.

**sub-**, predominantly 'under' or, derivatively, 'less than, inferior to', is, in effect, the L *sub*, predominantly 'under' (opp *super*), hence 'in the vicinity of, or within reach of', hence 'very soon after'; nor is the connotation 'inferior (to)' absent in certain L words.

L *sub* is akin to Gr *hupo*, Skt *úpa*, under, Arm *hup*, near, and to synn or near-synn in OGmc and OC. The *s-* may represent a much-worn-down form of *ex*, for the basic sense was app 'from under' or 'from under up to'. (See esp E & M, OED, Webster.)

Whereas all modern E words not of L origin—

E words after (say) the late C18—are coined with prefix *sub-*, words coming direct, or as if direct, from L preserve the L assimilations: *suc-* before *c*, as in *succeed*; *suf-* before *f*, as in *suffer*; *sug-* before *g*, as in *suggest*; *sup-* before *p*, as in *supply*; before *m*, *sub-* usu becomes *sum-*, as in *summon*, and before *r*, *sub-* usu becomes *sur-*, as in *surreptitious*; moreover, 'before *c*, *p*, and *t* it sometimes takes the form *sus-* by the dropping of *b* from a collateral form, *subs-*' (Webster)—cf *abs* (beside *ab*). Exx include *susceptible*, *suspire*, *sustain*. In *sudden* and *suspect*, the prefix has been worn down to *su-*.

The chief senses of E *sub-* words are: 'under', as in *submarine*, *subterranean*; 'down', as in *submerge*; 'in an inferior degree or state'—'somewhat' or 'slightly'—'subnormally' or 'almost' as in *subacid*; 'next lower than'—'subordinate or inferior to', as in *sublieutenant* (cf *subaltern*) and *sub-species*; 'repetition' or 'division', as in *subclassify*, *subdivision*, *sub-science*; 'immediately after', as in *subapostolic*.

Note also the following specialties:

An, Bot, Zoo: 'situated under', as in *subcutaneous*;

Chem: 'with only small quantities or proportion of the constituent named', as in *suboxide*;

Geo, Geol: 'near (the base of); bordering or verging upon', as in *subalpine*, *subarctic*;

Med: 'less than usually', as in *subacute*.

**subter-**, below or beneath, as in *subterfuge*, *subter(-)surface*, (hence) less than, as in *subter(-)human*, is the L adv and prep *subter*, under, beneath; as *inter* from *in*, so *subter* from *sub* (see *sub-*), of which it was orig the comp.

**suc-**. See *sub-*, 3rd para.

**suf-**. See *sub-*, 3rd para.

**sug-**. See *sub-*, 3rd para.

**sum-**. See *sub-*, 3rd para.

**sup-**. See *sub-*, 3rd para.

**super-** derives from the L adv, prep, preverb *super*, which, akin to Gr *huper* (q.v.), is opp *sub*, under, but also very intimately related to it: cf the 2nd para of *sub-* and note E & M's verdict, 'The *sub*, *super* group is manifestly related to Skt *úpa* and *úpari*, Go *uf* and *ufar*, etc.' The predominant senses of L *super* are 'on, above, over (the top of)', hence 'beyond, more than'. Exx: (physical situation) *superintend*, *supersoil* (opp *subsoil*), *superstructure*; (degree, class) *supernatural*, *superman*; (excess) *super-refined*, perhaps *supererogation*; (later) *superannuate*. The orig sense tends to be obscured in such words as *supercilious*, *superficies*, *superfluous*, *superlative*, *supersede*, *superstition*, *supervene*. In certain words that reach us via F, *super-* has become *sur-*, as in *surcharge*, *surface*, *surfeit*, *survive*.

**supra-**, above, higher than, (in An) on the dorsal side of, represents the L adv and prep *suprā*, orig the f abl *superā* (hence *suprā*) of an adj *\*super*, *supērus*, (in physical position) superior. *Suprā* has the same meanings as the L adv and prep *super* (q.v. at *super-* above) and is opp *infrā* (q.v. at *infra-*). For the form, cf L *infrā* and *intrā*; for the anterior etymology, cf *sub* (q.v. at *sub-*). English exx: *supracaudal* (above the tail), *supranasal, supra-normal, supravital*.

**sur-** (1). See *sub-*, 3rd para.

**sur-** (2). See *super-*, last sentence.

**sus-**. See *sub-*, 3rd para.

**sy-**, as in *system* and *systole*, is a shortened form of E *syn-*, as the Gr orig *su-* is of *sun-*.

**syl-**. The assimilated form taken by *syn-* before *l*, as in *syllable, syllapsis, syllogism*. Cf:

**sym-**. The assimilated form of *syn-* before *b, m, p*, as in *symbiosis, symmetry, sympathy*.

**syn-**: *syl-* before *l, sym-* before, *b, m, p*. In E words, it means '(along or together) with', whether spatially or temporally, as in *synagogue* and *synthesis*; occ there is a connotation of association or concurrence, as in *synergism, synonym, syntax. Syn-* represents the L form of Gr *sun-*, the c/f of the prep *sun*, (along) with, in space or in time, i.e. together or simultaneously. The Gr *sun* was orig *xun*. Existing in PGr *xun* (with variant *xu*), it has no 'assured cognates outside Greek', as Boisacq remarks; he does, however, compare OSl *sŭ*, with, and, reservedly, Lit *sù*, with. And is not *xun* or *sun* akin to L *cum*, with? The IE root accounting for *xun, sun, cum* would prob be either *\*ksun*, perh with variant *\*ksum*, or *\*kum*, perh with variant *\*kun*; the *\*ks-*, *\*k-* forms being alternatives.

**t-** (1), in *tautology*, represents *to*, neu s of the Gr definite article 'the'. (Skeat.)

**t-** (2), in *tawdry*, is the final letter of *saint*; (*Sain*)*t Awdry* has become *tawdry*. (Skeat.)

**t-** (3), in *twit*, is aphetic for ME *at-*, from OE *aet-*: OE *aetwītan* yields *twit*. (Skeat.)

**ter-**, thrice or threefold, as in *tercentenary*, is merely the L adv *ter*, thrice. Cf *tri-* below and see THREE.

**thorough-**, in *thoroughfare*, is simply a variant of prep THROUGH; in *thorough-going*, of the adj *through*.

**to-** (1), an intensive, connoting 'asunder, (all) to pieces', as in *all to-brake* (*Judges*, ix, 53) and *to-break*, or 'away', as in *to-go*, or 'completely, entirely, (or no more than) severely', as in *to-beat*, occurs only in a few archaic and dial words. It derives from OE *to-*, asunder, and is therefore akin to OFris *to-*, *te-*, *ti-* and OS *te-* or *ti-*, OHG *zar-* or *zer-*, Go *dis-*, L *dis-*; notably cf TWO.

**to-** (2), in *today, tomorrow, tonight*, derives from OE *tō-*, c/f of the prep *to*, q.v. in Dict.

**tra-; tran-**. See:

**trans-**: before a word beginning in *s*, it usu drops the *s*, as in *transcend, transcribe* and *transude*, to 'sweat' through (F *transsuder*; *-suder* from L *sudāre*); in a few other words, *trans-* softens to *tra-* (L *trā-*), as in *tradition, traduce, trajectory*, the obs *tralation* (a metaphor), the obs *tralucent* (displaced by *translucent*), the v and n *traverse* (cf the adj *transverse*).

The chief senses of *trans-* in E words are: '(over) across', hence 'beyond', 'on the other side of'; as in *transalpine*; *transmit* and *transfer*, where the connotation of 'exchange' occurs; *translate*.

The L *trans* is akin to W *tra*, beyond, and perhaps to Skt *tiráh*, Av *tarō*, across, beyond, Skt *tárati*, he crosses, traverses, and to the second part of L *intrāre*; almost certainly to OE *thurh*, through (cf, therefore, THROUGH).

**tre-** (1), in *treason*, is a shape taken in ME (and continued in EE-E) by OF-from-L *tra-*, q.v. at *trans-*.

**tre-** (2), in *treble*, represents L *tri-*, thrice (cf *tri-* below), akin to *tres*, three. With *treble* cf *triple*.

**tres-** is a form occ taken in OF by *trans*; as in the E *trespass*.

**tri-**, having or divided into three parts, occurring thrice or in three ways, as in *tricycle, trifarious* (cf *multifarious*), *trigonometry, tripod, trisect, triennial*. It comes either from L *tri-* or from Gr *tri-*, often through F *tri-*, and is therefore akin to E THREE, L *tres*, three, Skt *tris*, thrice.

**tris-**: Gr *tris-*, c/f of *tris*, thrice, from *treis*, three. Ex: *Trisagion*, the hymn known as 'The Thrice Holy' (Gr *hagios*, holy). The rare var *triakis-*, from Gr *triakis*, thrice, occurs in Geom terms.

**twi-**, 'two-' or 'twice', 'double' or 'doubly'—as in *twibill, twi-faced, twilight*, has descended from OE *twi-*, akin to OFris and OLG *twi-*, OHG *zwi-*, ON *tvī-*, and to Skt *dvi-*: cf, therefore, (*twice* at) TWO.

**u-**. See UTOPIA.

**ultra-**, beyond, as in *ultramarine, ultramundane*— on the other side (*ultramontane*)—transcending (*ultramicroscopic*)—hence, beyond the usual or the normal, i.e. excessively, as in *ultramodern*, is, in effect, the L prefix *ultra-*, from the adv and prep *ultrā*, beyond, on the other side (of), further than— opp *citrā*. Now, *ultrā* was orig the f abl of an adj *\*ulter*, being or lying beyond (cf *citer*, q.v. at *citra-* above); itself from the PL prep *uls*, beyond, opp *cis* (see *cis-* above).

**um-**, in *umpire* (for *numpire*), derives from F *non*, not (cf *non-*). Therefore cf *n-* (2).

**umbe-**, archaic for 'about' or 'around', as in *umbecast* and *umbethink*, comes from OE *ymbe* (influenced by ON *umb*), akin to OFris *umb* or *umbe*, OHG and OS *umbi* (Mod *um*) and L *ambi*, on both sides (of): cf *ambi-*, q.v.

**umu-**. In Bantu, it indicates 'human being'. Cf *M-* above.

**un-** (1), before adjj and advv, occ before nn, means 'not', as in *unable, unruly, uncomfortably, unbelief*, and is usu neutral (merely 'not') rather than 'contrary', as in *unmoral* opp *immoral*. It occurs more often with stems of Gmc origin than with those of Gr or L origin.

This *un-* descends unchanged from the OE *un-*, which is akin to OFris, OHG (and G), OS *un-*, ON *ū-* or *ō*——to OIr *an-* (or *in-*), Ga, W, Cor, Br *an-*; to L *in-*; to Gr *an-* (before vowels); to Skt *an-* (or *a-*). Cf, therefore, *a-* (1) and *in-* (2) above.

**un-** (2), before a v and occ before a pa there-from, connotes 'reversal' or 'the contrary', as in *unbend, untie, undone*; often it goes with nn to form vv connoting either the deprivation of the thing designated by the n, as in *unman* and *unyoke*, or the removal of someone, something, from the thing designated by the n, as in *unearth*; sometimes *un-* merely intensifies, as in *unloose*.

This *un-*, ME *un-*, descends from OE *un-* or *on-*, akin to the *and-* of, e.g., *andswerian* (EE-E *answer*), lit 'to swear against'—to Go *and-*—and to Gr *anti*, against: cf, therefore, *anti-* above.

**un-** (3), in *until* and *unto*. *Until* is 'a substituted form of *unto*' (Skeat): and *unto*=*undto*, where *-to* is the prep *to* and *und-* is akin to, prob adopted from, OFris *und*, unto, akin to OS *und*, unto.

**un-** (4). See *uni-* in the Elements list.

**ut-**, in *utmost*, answers to the adv *out*, q.v. in the Dict.

**utter-** (1), in *uttermost*, answers to *outer*, q.v. at *out* in Dict.

**utter** (2), in *utterance*, is a distortion of the *outre-* (cf *outr-* above) shortened to *outr-* in F *outrance*, which, though a gallicism, occurs in E.

**v-**, in *van* (of an army) and *vanguard*, stands ult for L *ab-*, q.v. at *a-* (3).

**ve-**, as prob in *vestibule* and perh in *vestige*, resp from (L *uestibulum*) ML *vestibulum* and from (L *uestigium*) ML *vestigium*, means—perh it only appears to mean—apart (from); *ue-*, ML *ve-*, might therefore be akin to *se-*, q.v. above.

**Wa-.** See *M-*.

**wan-**, no longer an active prefix, occurs notably in *wanton* and in such archaisms as *wanchance*, *wangrace*, *wanhope*, and in such Scotticisms as *wanhap*, *wanrest*, *wanruly*, *wanthrift*, *wanworth*. This privative, connoting 'lack of, lacking', or 'deficiency of, deficient in', comes from OE *wan-* (variant *won-*), akin to OHG *wan-* or *wana-*, ON *vanr*, Skt *ūna*, lacking, and Go *wans*, Gr *eunis* (stem *eun-*), bereaved: cf, therefore, WANE.

**wel-**, in *welcome* and *welfare*, is merely the survival of the OE form of the adv WELL.

**[wh-** is not a prefix: where it does not stand for the mod form of OE *hw-*, as in *who* for OE *hwā*, it commonly indicates an echoic word, as *whack*, *wham*, *whang*, *whap* or *whop*.]

**with-**, as in *withdraw* and *withhold*, bearing the sense 'back' or 'away', and as in *withstand* (and *withstay*) and *withsay*, sense 'against', is merely a c/f of the prep WITH, q.v.

**y-** or **i-**, from ME *y-* or *i-*, from OE *ge-*, akin to Go *ga-* and OHG *gi-* or *ga-*, has either a vague, yet strong, associative connotation, as in *y-fere*, in company, together, *y-lome*, continually, or a perfective connotation, as in *y-clept*, *y-dought* (thriving), *y-wrought*, and other pp archaisms of Edmund Spenser and his disciples; cf the intensive connotation of *y-leave* (OE *gelāēfan*), to leave utterly, to abandon.

**za-**, 'very': Aeolic Gr form of *dia-* used intensively; in E, it occurs only in Zoo, e.g. in *Zalambdodonta*: *za-*, very+*lambda*, as $\Lambda$, capital of Gr $\lambda$+ *-odonta*, pl of *-odon*, tooth: insectivores having molars with V crowns—V being, roughly, $\Lambda$ upside down.

## ADDENDUM

**tele-** (or, before a vowel, **tel-**) as in *telegraph*, *telepathy*, *telescope*, *television* (all recorded on p. 699), means 'operating at or from a distance', represents Gr *tēle-* or *tēl-*, from the adv *tēle*, far off, far away, from afar, and is akin to Gr *telos*, end; see, therefore, the element *telo-*.

# A LIST OF SUFFIXES

$S$UFFIXES that, like *-craft* (*handicraft*) and *-fold* (*manifold*), are in fact ordinary words forming what were originally compounds and are therefore proper words (**craft, fold**) have been omitted. But such borderline cases as *-dom* (cf DOOM) are noted here: their inclusion is demanded by common sense.

For the sake of convenience the two most important connective elements *-i-* and *-o*, as in *curv-i- form* and *the-o-logy*, are included.

**-a** (1), disguised interjection of extremely vague expletive or intensive force, as in Shakespeare's 'A merry heart goes all the day, Your sad tires in a mile-a' (Webster). Cf the *-o* in *all-aliv(e)o*: see *-o*, disguised interjection.

**-a** (2), illiterate for *of*, as in 'A *coupla* days' or '*kinda* cute', mostly American, and as in *cuppa*, elliptical for '*cup of* tea', orig Australian.

**-a** (3), a jocular convention for representing, often quite inaccurately, the speech of an uneducated Italian speaking English. Such an Italian does tend to say 'You like*a* drink*a*?'

**-a** (4), indicating the adoption of a L f singular n, as in *Minerva* and *formula*, or of a Gr f sing n, as in *Ida* (Mount) and *idea*.

**-a** (5), indicating a R f sing, as in *stanza* (It) and *sierra* (Sp).

**-a** (6), in f personal names, as *Anna, Augusta, Clara, Rosa, Tessa*.

**-a** (7), in names of continents, as *Africa, America, Asia, Australia, Antarctica*. Cf *-ia* below.

**-a** (8), in pl nn of Gr and L origin, whether from a neu n or from a neu adj used as a n: as in Gr *automata* and *phenomena*; or in L *impedimenta* or *realia* (in L an adj used as a n).

**-a** (9), in L m nn, connoting agent and corresp to Gr *-ēs*, as in *Agricola*.

**-ability.** See *-bility*.

**-able.** See 1st *-ble*.

**-ac**, adj—hence in nn. Sometimes direct from Gr *-akos*, more often via L *-acus*, occ via F *-aque* (usu from L); quite often the L adj has merely been formed anl with Gr. Exx: *demoniac*, from LL *daemoniacus*; *elegiac*, from LL *elegiacus*, from Gr *elegeiakos*; *hypochondriac*, F *hypochondriaque*, ML *hypochondriacus*, Gr *hupokhondriakos*; *iliac*, (? via F *iliaque*) from L *iliacus*; *maniac*, from ML *maniacus*; *Syriac*, L *Syriakos*, Gr *Suriakos*.

It is, however, permissible and philologically more sensible to regard all such words as words bearing suffix *-iac*, not *-ac*, for the stems are respectively *demon-* (LL *daemon-*), *eleg-*, *hypo-*

*chond(r)-* (Gr *hupokhond(r)-*), *il-*, *man-*, *Syr-* (Gr *Sur-*): it is the combining-forms, not the stems, which end in *i*, thus *demoni-* (LL *daemoni-*), *elegi-* (Gr *elegei-*), *hypochondri-* (Gr *hupokhondri-*), *ili-*, *mani-*, *Syri-*. With *maniac*, orig an adj only, cf *manic*, adj only, which derives from Gr *manikos*. (There is no such Gr word as *maniakos* until we reach modern times.)

Note that, as with *-ic* (q.v. below), the suffix *-al* is often added, as in *demoniacal, hypochondriacal, maniacal*.

**-acal** is simply *-ac* with *-al* (q.v.) added, as in *maniacal, demoniacal, hypochondriacal*, for all of which the shorter form has, since the late C19, been the more usual.

**-ace**, from L nouns in *-ātiō, -ātium, -ācea, -ācem* (acc of *-āx*), *-ācia*; often through OF *-ais* or *-aise* or *-ace*, occ *-asse*. Exx: *furnace*, from OF *fornais(e)*, L *fornāx*; *menace*, adopted from OF, from L *minācia*; *palace*, OF *palais*, L *palātium*; *pinnace*, F *pinasse* or *pinace*, It *pinaccia* (suffix *-accia*), VL *\*pinācea*; *populace*, adopted from F, from It *popolaccio* (suffix *-accio*); *preface*, adopted from OF, from L *praefātiō*; *space*, OF *espace*, L *spātium*; *terrace*, adopted from OF, from VL *\*terrācea*.

**-acea**, as in *Crustacea* (cf *crustacean* at *-acean* below), is the neupl of L *-āceus*; it occurs in names of Zoo orders and classes. Therefore cf the prec entry. Cf also *-ace* and:

**-aceae**, as in *Rosaceae* (cf *rosaceous*), is the fpl of L *-āceus*; it means 'of the (e.g. rose) kind' or 'of the nature of' (e.g., the rose). Cf prec.

**-acean**, as in *crustacean* and *rosacean*, is the adj answering to nn in *-ācea, -āceae* resp. Therefore it should be related to *-an*, and to *-n* for *-an*. Cf:

**-aceous** is the predominant E 'answer' to L *-āceus*, connoting either 'belonging to' or 'of the nature of', hence 'resembling'; as in *cretaceous, farinaceous, herbaceous, rosaceous, saponaceous*. Cf prec.

**-acious** answers to L *-āx*, gen *-ācis*, as in *tenāx*

835

gen *tenācis*, o/s *tenāc-*. In E, *-ious* (q.v. below) has been added to the o/s; thus *fallacious, sagacious, tenacious, veracious*, etc. Cf:

-acity indicates quality, as in *tenacity* and *veracity*, and derives, usu via F *-acité*, from L *-ācitās* or rather, if via F, from the acc *-ācitātem*, as most philologists hold, although possibly from the o/s *-ācitāt-*: perh F *ténacité* and certainly *véracité*: L *tenācitās*, o/s *tenācitāt-*, acc *tenācitātem*, and ML *verācitās, verācitāt-, verācitātem*. Therefore *-acity* is the n suffix corresponding to the adj suffix *-acious*.

-acle, n; -acular, adj; -aculum, n—this L form or, rather, original being often retained in E, though usu with a specialized sense, alongside the E derivative form *-acle*; the adjj, usu answering to no such adjj in L, have been formed on the analogy of such words as *regular* and, later, *molecular* (cf *-ular* below). The resemblance of L *-aculum* to the L dim *-ulum* is superficial and accidental. Exx:

*receptacle*, from L *receptăculum* (also in E); no adj.

*spectacle*, adopted from OF, from L *spectaculum*; adj *spectacular*.

*spiracle*, from L *spirāculum* (also in E); adj *spiracular*.

*tentacle*, from ML *tentāculum* (also in E); adj *tentacular*.

All the L nouns, it will be noticed, derive from the inf s of first-conjugational vv: *recept(āre)—spect(āre)—spir(āre)—tent(āre)*. The suffix therefore connotes either 'that which does' (whatever the action or process of the v may be), as in *receptacle* and *tentacle*, or 'that which receives' (the action or process), as in *spectacle* and *spiracle*.

-acy has been so neatly summarized by Webster that it were fatuous to refrain from the flattery of quotation: '. . . denoting *quality, state, office*, etc. It is derived from various sources, esp from Latin *-acia* (cf *-acious, -y*), as in effic*acy*; or after Latin *-atia* corresponding to nouns in *-atus* (cf French *-atie* . . .), as in prim*acy*; or from Greek *-ateia*, as in pir*acy*; or after analogous English nouns, and even adjectives, in *-ate*, as in accur*acy*, priv*acy*.' Cf *-cy*.

-ad (1), adv, signifies 'towards, in the direction of', as in *dorsad*, towards the back (L *dorsum*), and *ventrad*, towards the ventral (or belly, L acc *uentrem*, ML *ventrem*) side, and represents the L prep *ad*, towards: cf L *ad dorsum, ad uentrem*.

-ad (2), n, derives from Gr *-ad-* (gen *-ados*, from nom *-as*), often through L *-ad-* (gen *-adis*, nom *-as*), and bears at least three different meanings:

(*a*) An aggregate of (so many) parts, as in *monad*, LL *monas*, o/s *monad-* (gen *monadis*), Gr *monas*, gen *monados*, from *monos*, alone (cf *mono-* in Combining Elements list), and in *myriad*, via LL *myrias*, o/s *myriad-* (gen *myriadis*), from Gr *murias*, o/s *muriad-*, gen *muriados*; also in, e.g., *chiliad, decad* (better known in the F form *decade*), *dyad, hebdomad, pentad, tetrad, triad*. In Chem, *-ad* indicates valence, as in *monad, pentad*, etc.

(*b*) A f patronymic, as in *dryad*, a nymph born of and intimately associated with a tree, from L *dryad-*, o/s of *dryas*, from Gr *druas*, o/s *druad-* and in *naiad*, a nymph born of and associated with water, L *naiad-*, o/s of *naias*, adopted from Gr. In Bot, *-ad* indicates the member of a group, as in *cycad* (from Gr *kukas*).

(*c*) In epic or burlesque epic poems, it refers to the titular subject, as in *Iliad*, the story of Ilion (Troy), and *Columbiad* (Columbia, the U.S.A.), or analogously to the titular 'hero', as in *Adoniad* (Adonis) and *Dunciad* (the generic dunce). Cf, therefore, the *-id* of *Aeneid* and *Thebaid*.

-ad (3). See the 2nd *-ade*, para (*b*).

-ada, as in *armada* (see ARMS, para 5), comes from Sp; f, it corresponds to m *-ado*.

-ade (1). See the 2nd *-ad*, para (*a*).

-ade (2) comes from F *-ade*, itself either from Prov or Sp or Port *-ada* or from It *-ata*, both *-ada* and *-ata* deriving from LL *-āta*. The three chief significations are:

(*a*) Act, action, as in *cannonade*, from F *canonnade*, from It *cannonata*, itself an *-ata* formation from It (from L) *canna*, a cane or reed.

(*b*) Result, consequence, product of an action, hence a thing made by a certain process. Occ spelt *-ad*. Exx: *arcade*, F from Prov *arcada*, from VL *\*arca*, arch; *orangeade*, on analogy of *lemonade* (F *limonade*); *ballad*, OF *balade*, Prov *balada* from *balar*, from LL *ballāre*, to dance; *salad*, OF *salade*, Prov *salada* from *salar*, to salt, from L *sal*, salt.

(*c*) A person, a group, engaging in an activity, as in *cavalcade*, adopted from F, which adapted it from It *cavalcata* (L *caballus*, a nag).

-ado, in words adopted or adapted from Sp or rarely from Port, corresponds to F *-ade* (q.v. at the 2nd *-ade*) and derives from L *-ātus* (n): *bastinado*, from Sp *bastonada*; *bravado*, for Sp *bravada*; *desperado*, adopted from Old Sp; *renegado* (superseded by its derivative *renegade*), adopted from Sp; *tornado*, adopted from Sp.

-ae is a L fpl, preserved only in erudite words, esp in Sci: for instance, *formulae* and *algae*.

-age either derives from, or is formed anl with other words derived from, OF-F *-age*, itself usu straight from, but occ anl with other F nn from, LL *-āticum*, which would seem to be a cpd suffix: *-at-+-icum*, n from neu of adj *-icus* (cf *-ic* below). The chief senses of the numerous words in *-age*, of which more than a few are hybrids, may, provided that we do not insist on the distinctions, be summarized thus:

(*a*) Collective or quasi-collective, as in *luggage* and *baggage*; *foliage* and *herbage* and *pasturage*; *mileage* and *acreage*; *cordage* and *plumage*; *average* and *assemblage*; *tonnage*; *cellarage* (passive; 'charge' sense belongs to (*f*) below); *peerage*.

(*b*) Place of action or abode, as in *passage* and *anchorage*; *parsonage, orphanage, hermitage*. Cf:

(*c*) Agent: *hostage* and *savage*.

(*d*) Act or process: *marriage; carnage, outrage, pillage, plunderage, ravage; pilgrimage* (linking with (*a*) above), *passage* (in its active sense); *salvage, tillage*.

(*e*) Result of action or process: *cleavage*,

stoppage; wastage; breakage and damage; shrinkage; message and voyage; heritage and mortgage; ensilage and vintage; mirage and visage; badinage and persiflage and language; coinage and advantage.

(f) Cost of action, fee or charge for a specific service: cartage, carriage, freightage, porterage; poundage and postage; brokerage and demurrage; pilotage; towage and wharfage; scutage and tallage.

(g) Miscellaneously abstract, esp in nn adopted or adapted from F: courage and umbrage; bondage, vassalage, pupilage; espionage and brigandage; dotage and homage; verbiage. Several of these might go into groups (d) and (e).

-ago occurs only in a very few words adopted from L—e.g., lumbago, plantago, plumbago, virago —and it bears, often in L and occ in E, an unfavourable connotation; but L -āgō sometimes appears to connote 'a kind of' or 'a species of', as in the 2nd and 3rd examples.

-ai is a Gr fpl, usu found in E in the L transliteration -ae: cf hetairai, usu in the L form hetaerae, courtesans.

-ails. See -als.

-ain is the Gallic shape of L -ānus (cf -an below), orig adj, hence often n, as in certain; captain (ME capitain, OF capitaine); chieftain; villain.

-air, -aire, as in corsair, doctrinaire, millionaire, derives from F -aire, itself from L -ārius, denoting either an agent or, at the least, a person. Cf -ar, -ary, -eer, below.

-al, adj, comes from L -ālis, belonging or appropriate to, resembling, the n implied in the adj. The E adj comes either directly from L or through F -al (occ -el); also it may occur in native formations anl with other adjj in -al. Direct: normal, L normālis, and regal, L regālis; from F, as in mural, F mural, L murālis, in royal, adopted from F, from L regālis, and as in mutual, F mutuel, but L mutuus; native formation: oral, spoken, from or-, o/s of L ōs (gen oris), the mouth. This suffix is often added to adjj in -ic, usu with a slight consequent change of sense, as in politic— political.

-al, n (1). A suffix occurring in nn orig adjj, as oval, n from adj from F oval (f ovale) from ov-, stem of ML ovum, L ouum, egg.

-al, n (2). This -al, which serves to form nn of action from vv, comes either from intermediary F -aille (occ -al) or direct from the L -ālia, being the neupl of adj -ālis (cf, therefore, -al, adj) but often used as a pl n—a pl n that occ became apprehended as a f sing. Exx: acquittal, perh from E 'to acquit' but perh from OF aquital (cf F acquitter); arrival, AF arrivaille—cf OF arival, bank of stream (therefore see ARRIVE); battle, ME batail, OF bataille, L battālia.

-al, n (3), as in portal, adopted from OF (cf F portail) from ML portāle, strictly neu adj (of *portālis) from porta, gate. Here, then, the L adj used as n is sing, not pl; contrast -al, n (2).

-al, n (4), in several animal-names, e.g. caracal and jackal, is of Tu origin; in caracal certainly, in

jackal perh, it means 'ear'. In serval, from Port, it represents L -ālis: cf, therefore, -al, adj.

-alia comes straight from L, where it represents a neupl, usu of an adj in -ālis; thus regalia, from L regālis, and the Phil realia, realities (lit, real things), from ML reālis, from rēs (s rē-), a thing.

-ality is a cpd suffix: -al, adj+-ity, n (q.v. below). It comes either through F -alité or direct from L -ālitās, o/s -ālitāt-; occ it occurs first in E—but anl with other -ity words.

-als, var -ails, is simply the pl of -al, n (2). Exx: entrails, OF entrailles, LL intrālia; victuals, ME vitaille, OF vitaille, ML victuālis (LL uictuālia), on which the modern spelling has been refashioned— cf vitals, pl of vital adj used as n, from OF vital, from ML vītālis, L uītālis.

-ama: Gr -ama, occ via L: conn, '(a thing) heard or seen or whatever else the implied v denotes'. Thus, acroama, via L from Gr akroama (s akro-), from akroasthai (s akro-), to hear; cyclorama, panorama, etc., the 2nd element being horama, a thing seen—hor-+-ama. The corresponding adj suffix is -atic, from Gr -atikos; as in acroamatic, from Gr akroamatikos.

-an (1), adj—hence an, n—derives from L -ānus, either directly or through F -ain, occ its variant -en; or it is analogously formed first in E. The predominant sense is 'belonging to', hence often 'characteristic of'. Exx: human, OF humain, L humānus; silvan, late OF silvain, from ML silva (L silua), a forest. In Zoo, -an frequently serves as the sing of pl group-names in -a, -ae, etc., as crustacean (n), pl Crustacea. Cf -ana below.

-an (2), n. In Chem it indicates certain substances, e.g. pentosan and tolan. This -an derives from -an (1), q.v.

-ana, as in Americana, pieces of information about America, or Meredithiana (with connective -i), gossip about Meredith, is simply the L npl, used as n, of adj -ānus. Hence ana used independently, as in 'The ana concerning Whitman are almost as numerous as the ana of Dr Johnson (Johnsoniana)'. The L orig of both -ana and ana rests in such a phrase as ML dicta Vergiliāna, the sayings of Vergilius (Virgil). Cf ANA.

-ance, -ancy; -ence, -ency. Note, first, that the comparatively modern -ancy, -ency (formed perh anl with -cy, q.v. below) indicate state or condition, quality or degree, as the originals do in L; secondly, that mod E formations in -ance and -ence, e.g. continuance, forbearance, riddance, and emergence, connote action or an act, a process, function, as do such adoptions (e.g., assistance, parlance) from OF as have been formed from the F presp in -ant but anl with the next group; thirdly, that this next group consists of OF nn deriving from L nn in -antia (VL, occ ML, -ancia), -entia (VL-ML -encia), abstracts built upon the L presp c/ff -ant- and -ent-, E exx being elegance and endurance; fourthly, that the OF and F action-nn and process- nn in -ance (as at 'secondly' above) may represent either L -antia or L -entia, but that in some E words in -ance deriving from OF -ance from L

-entia, the L e has been restored, with the result that we find such inconsistencies as 'resistance', OF resistence (Mod résistance), LL resistentia, but 'subsistence', LL subsistentia; 'attendance', OF atendance, from OF atendre, from L attendere, but 'superintendence', ML superintendentia.

Most of these words are ult of L origin or have been formed as if from L; most -ence words are imm of F origin or, at the least, formation.

Cf -ant and -ent.

**-and (1); -end (1).** Most nn that, of more than one syllable, end in -and, -end, derive from the L gerundives in -and-, -end-, i.e. from one of the nom sing forms: -andus, -anda, -andum, or -endus, -enda, -endum, resp m, f, neu; or from one of the pl forms: -andi, -andae, -anda, or -endi, -endae, -enda: resp m, f, neu. Exx:

deodand, ML deodandum (neu sing), lit something dandum, to be given, Deo, to God;

multiplicand, L (numerus) multiplicandus (m sing), (number) to be multiplied;

dividend, (via EF-F dividende from) ML dividendum, L diuidendum (neu sing), lit something to be divided;

reverend, ML reverendus, L reuerendus (m sing), to be revered, hence used as n.

Less regular are:

lavender, from ML lavanda, L lauanda (f sing)—this intrusive r occurs also in provender;

viand(s), ML vivenda, L uiuenda (neupl).

Cf -andum (-endum) below.

**-and (2); -end (2);** often shortened to **-nd.** In errand, fiend, friend, husband, wind, and a few other native words, -(a)nd and -(e)nde and -inde represent the old suffix of the presp, -and being Scots and N, -ende being Midland, -inde Southern, and are to be compared with L -ant(em) and -ent(em). Errand, for example, derives from OE ǣrende, lit 'a sending', a message; and fiend from OE fēond, orig presp of fēon, to hate. See also -nd.

**-and (3).** See -ant, n.

**-andum, -endum.** The L neu sing form adopted by E and comparable to -and (1), -end (1) above. Thus: memorandum, pl memoranda, and notandum, pl notanda; addendum, pl addenda, and corrigendum, pl corrigenda.

**-ane (1),** adj, as in mundane (via F, from L mundānus), is a rare variant of -an, 1 (q.v. above); it therefore means 'belonging to, (hence) characteristic of'. In humane we have a doublet of human, a doublet arising perh because the latter reaches E through OF-F humain, the former direct from L humānus, but perh because, in early Mod E, such words were written indifferently -an or -ane.

**-ane (2),** n, is a Chem suffix, as in octane. (Contrast the rare Med adj octan, occurring on the eighth day.) This -ane, arbitrarily formed, parallels Chem -ene, -ine, -one.

**-ane (3),** n, is a variant of, and regarded as less correct than, -an (2), n, q.v. above.

**-aneity.** See next, s.f.

**-aneous,** in contemporaneous, instantaneous, momentaneous, simultaneous, answers to a little-used L adj suffix -āneus, as in contemporāneus and LL mōmentāneus (stems contempor-, moment-), whence the E words; simultaneous imitates momentaneous, as app instantaneous also does. The F form is -ané, as in instantané, momentané, simultané. The rare abstract-n suffix -aneity, as in instantaneity, may have been influenced by the F -anéité, as in instantanéité; cf -eity below.

**-ant (1) and -ent,** adjj, answer to -ance and -ence, qq.v. at -ance above; nn in -ant, -ent, either derive straight from adjj or have been formed anl with other adjj in -ant, -ent.—Cf the adjj and nn in -ient, -ience.

Whereas E -ent must come either direct from -ent-, the c/f of the L presp -ens (whether 2nd or 3rd conjugation), as in regent, or through F -ent, or have been formed anl with L -ent, the E -ant comes, whether through F or direct, from L -ant, as in clamant (direct) or claimant (via F), or has been formed anl with L -ant-, c/f of presp -ans (1st conjunction)—or, in the ME period, from OF -ant representing not L -ant but L ent, for, in OF, -ant stood for either L -ant- or L -ent-. In CC16–17, F restored the -e- where the L had -ent-. Hence such confusions as pendant, pendent—ascendant, ascendent—assistant but persistent. The practice of reserving -ant for nn, -ent for adjj, is modern.

The nn in -ant (or -ent) connote agency or instrumentality, as in defendant, inhabitant, suppliant, errant; agent, regent, student, torrent.

**-ant (2),** n through OF-F from L from Gr, as in adamant, elephant, sycophant, derives from the Gr o/s: thus, adamant, OF adamant, L adamant- (nom adamas, gen adamantis), Gr adamant- (nom adamas, gen adamantos); elephant, via OF from Gr elephant- (nom elephas, gen elephantos); sycophant, L sycophanta, Gr sukophantēs (o/s sukophant-); cf gigantic and giant, from Gr gigas, o/s gigant-.

**-ar (1),** adj, as in consular and regular, connotes 'belonging to or characteristic of' and comes either direct from L -āris (cf -ālis, exemplified at -al, adj) or through ME -er from OF -er or -ier. Exx: consular, from L consulāris (consul+-āris); insular, from L insulāris (insul(a)+(-ā)ris); popular, from L populāris (popul(us)+-āris); regular, ME reguler, OF reguler, L regulāris.

**-ar (2),** adj, now only in dial words, comp -er, as in hear for higher. (Webster.)

**-ar (3),** n, a rare variant of agential -er or -or, qq.v, occurs in such words as beggar (cf 'a noted question-begger'), from ME begger or beggar, from MF-F begard (perhaps cf -ard); liar, ME liere; pedlar (and peddler), ME pedlere.

**-ar (4),** n, as in bursar and justiciar, derives from L -ārius (m) or -ārium (neu), either direct as in bursar, from ML bursārius, from bursa, a purse, or in justiciar, ML justiciārius, from L iustitia, justice, or through F -ier, usu via VL -erius for L -ārius, as in mortar, from ME morter (from OE mortere from L mortārium) influenced by OF mortier, or in Templar, ME templere, OF templier,

ML *templārius*, or in *vicar*, ME *viker* or *vicair*, from OF *vicaire*, from ML *vicārius* (L *uicārius*).
Cf *-ary* for the corresponding adj; cf also agential *-er*.

**-ard, -art**, as in *braggart, coward, drunkard*, is, except in Proper Names, unfavourable, connoting either excess or discredit or both. It comes from OF or MF (occ EF), which took it from OHG or MHG *-hart*, akin to the E adj HARD, q.v. Exx: *braggart*, EF *bragard* (cf BRAG)—*coward*, OF *couard*—*drunkard*, from E adj *drunk*+*-ard*—*dullard*, similarly formed—*Leonard*, adopted from OF, from G *Leonhard* (lion-hard, i.e. lion-brave)—*niggard* from ME *nig*, a niggard, with depreciatory *-ard* for good measure—*Richard*, from OF (of OHG origin)—*sluggard*, consisting of *slug*, n+euphonic *-g-*+*-ard*.

In *Spaniard* (cf *Lombard* and *Savoyard*) the *-ard* was prob depreciatory at first, as indeed it may have been in such bird-names as *bustard, canard, haggard, mallard*. In such thing-names as *billiards, mustard, petard, placard, poniard, standard, tankard*, the etym sense 'hard' survives; perh also in the mod *blizzard*.

**-aria**, a SciL plural suffix adopted from L *-āria*, neupl of adjj in *-ārius*, is used in Bot and Zoo for 'group' names, as e.g. in *Utricularia* and *Madreporaria*.

**-arian**, adj, answers to nn ending in *-aria* or in *-ary*: Thus: *madreporarian* and *dromedarian*; cf such analogous formations as *utilitarian*, consisting of *utilit*(y)+*-arian*, and *agrarian*, from L *agrārius* (*agr-*, c/f of *ager*, a field+*-ārius*). It is a compound of *ari-*, for *-ari(a)* or *-ary*,+adj *-an*.

**-arian**, n, either comes from L *-āriānus* or has been formed analogously with such derivatives: and, as *-āriānus* combines *-āri-* and *-ānus*, so the analogously formed E words attach *-arian* to the E stem. Exx: *antiquarian*, n from adj *antiquarian*, itself either from *antiquary* (L *antiquārius*) by adding *-an* to *antiquari-* (for *antiquary*) or, although prompted by *antiquary*, from s *antiqu-*+*-arian*; *grammarian*, OF *gramarien* (later *grammairien*) from *gramaire*; *librarian*, formed similarly (cf the L *librārius*, adj henc n: therefore *librarian* prob=*librari-*+*an*); *latitudinarian*, combining *latitūdin-* (c/f of L *latitūdō*)+*-arian*; in *octogenarian*, *-arian* supersedes the *-ārius* (properly yielding *-ary*, as in the obs *octogenary*); *vegetarian* combines the *veget-* of 'vegetables' with *-arian*.

**-arious**, as in *gregarious* and *precarious*, either answers directly to the L adj suffix *-ārius*, as I tend to believe, or compounds the *-ari-* of (L *-ārius* and) E *-arian*, E *-ary*, with E *-ous*; cf *-ary* (adj), q.v. below; although E *-ary* answers to F *-aire* or to its L orig *-ārius*, E *-arious* certainly does not answer to F *-aire*: but that modification could work in either direction. Exx: *gregarious*, from L *gregārius*, *greg-* (o/s of *grex*, a herd or flock)+*-ārius*; *precarious*, L *precārius*, *prec-* (o/s of *prex*, prayer)+*-ārius*. But in *bifarious* and *multifarious*, *-farious* is an indivisible element, q.v. in the list of compound-forming elements;

and in *nefarious*, *nefar-* is an o/s—of different origin.

**-arity** answers to adj *-ar*, as in *insularity*—*insular*, *regularity*—*regular*, *vulgarity*—*vulgar*, and is therefore a cpd suffix, *-ar*, adj+*-ity*, abstract n, corresponding to though seldom formed from L *-āritāt-*, o/s of *-āritās*, consisting of *-ār(i)-*+*-itās*. Exx: *insularity*=*insular* (*insul-*+*-ar*)+*-ity*; *regularity*=F *régularité*, formed, analogously with other F nn in *-arité*, from L *regulāris*; *vulgarity*, from *vulgāritāt-*, o/s of ML *vulgāritās*, L *uulgāritās* (*uulg-*+*-ār(i)-*+*-(i)tās*. Cf *-ari-* in the entries at *-arian* and *-arious*, and likewise the important *-ity* below.

**-arium**, as in *aquarium, honorarium, vivarium*, indicates either '(a thing) belonging to or, at the least, connected with' or 'a place for' the n or v implied by the s of the word; it occurs in words adopted or, at most, adapted from L. Thus: *honorarium*, elliptical already in L for *honorārium donum*, therefore strictly the neus of the adj *honorārius*, the true E derivative being *honorary*; *vivarium*, ML form of the neus of *uiuārius*, concerned with living, or belonging to living creatures—cf *aquarium*, properly the neus of *aquārius*, watery. Cf, therefore, the next entry and also *-orium*.

**-arius** occurs only in words adopted from L, as *Aquarius*, that constellation which is represented by a man emptying a vase of *aqua* or water. Cf *-aria*, *-arian*, *-arious*, *-arium* above.

**-art.** See *-ard*.

**-ary** (1), adj, is a variant of *-ar* (1), for it derives, or has been formed anl with derivations, from L *-āris* and therefore indicates 'belonging to, or characteristic of', as in *exemplary*, from L *exemplāris*, consisting of *exempl*(um)+*-āris*, and in *military*, from F *militaire*, from L *militāris*, consisting of *milit-*, o/s of *miles*, a soldier+*-āris*.

**-ary** (2), adj, from L *-ārius* (m) or *-āria* (f) or *-ārium* (neu), either direct, as in *mercenary* from *mercenārius*, or via OF *-ier* (as in *pannier*) or Mod F *-aire* (as in *sedentary*). General sense: as for *-ary* (1). Cf:

**-ary** (3), n, connotes 'person belonging to, or working at or in', as *actuary*, from L *actuārius*, and *notary*, from L *notārius*, or (cf *-arium*) 'thing belonging to, esp a place for', as in *vocabulary*, from ML *vocabulārium*, a place for vocables. Cf, therefore *-ary* (2).

**-as** indicates a Greek Proper Name or Proper adj, often adopted or adapted by L, as in Gr *Aineias*, L *Aeneas*, and Gr and L *Ilias* (orig an adj). The o/s is *-ad-*, as in *Iliad-*, the gen being Gr *Iliados*, L *Iliadis*. The Gr suffix *-as* would therefore seem to connote family or racial descent: cf Gr *-is*, o/s *-id-*.

**-asia**, as in *euthanasia* (*eu*+*than*+*-asia*), is a Gr suffix, which has, in Med, been made equivalent to *-asis*, q.v. below. It has an occ variant—an 'Englishing'—*-asy*, as in the rare *euthanasy*. The answering adj form, though rare, is *-asian*, as in *euthanasian*.

**-asian.** See prec, s.f.

**-asis,** as in *metasomasis,* is, according to the angle from which one regards it, either a Med suffix or a Med c/f: strictly, it is a suffix, for it constitutes an extension of the important *-sis,* q.v. below, and is therefore also to be compared to *-iasis,* q.v. It was orig Gr, but in mod terms it is a SciL formation.

**-asm,** as in *chasm, enthusiasm, orgasm, phantasm, pleonasm, sarcasm, spasm,* comes from Gr *-asma* (preserved in *miasma* and obsol *phantasma*) or *-asmos,* occ via L *-asma, -asmus* and F *-asme.* It occurs chiefly in abstract words, yet it at least appears to connote a greater activity than does the parallel and more widely used *-ism,* q.v. below. Exx: *chasm,* L *chasma,* Gr *khasma* (a 'materialization' of *khaos,* chaos); *enthusiasm,* LL *enthūsiasmos,* Gr *enthousiasmos; orgasm,* F *orgasme,* Gr *orgasmos* —cf *orgiasmos,* whence the rare *orgiasm; phantasm,* ME *fantasme,* adopted from MF, from L *phantasma,* adopted from Gr, cf *phantasy* (and *phantom*) at FANCY; *pleonasm,* LL *pleonasmus,* Gr *pleonasmos; sarcasm,* (perh via F *sarcasme,* from) LL *sarcasmos,* Gr *sarkasmos; spasm,* MF-F *spasme,* ML *spasma,* L *spasmus,* Gr *spasmos.* Adj either in *-ic,* as *chasmic, miasmic, orgasmic,* or *-astic,* as in *orgiastic,* from the Gr adj corresponding to the Gr n.

**-asma.** See prec.

**-ass, -asse,** are 'disguises' of L *-ācea,* the f of adj suffix *-āceus* (cf *-aceous* above), thus: *cuirass,* F *cuirasse* (a *leather* breastplate), It *corazza,* VL *\*coracea,* adj become n, from L *coriāceus,* (made) of leather; *crevasse,* adopted from F, from OF *crevace,* which could, just possibly, come from VL *\*crepacea,* but rather comes from OF *crever,* to break, both deriving, the former obscurely, the latter clearly, from L *crepāre,* my own proposal being, however, that the effective origin lies either in LL *creptūra,* or in ML *crepātura,* a crevice.

**-ast,** as in *scholiast,* derives from Gr *-astēs* and is equivalent to *-ist,* q.v. below. Exx: *enthusiast,* Gr *enthousiastēs,* and *scholiast,* ML *scholiasta,* from late Gr *skholiastēs,* from *skholion,* a marginal note. Cf *-asm* and *-astic.*

**-aster** in E connotes inferiority (*criticaster, poetaster*) or even worthlessness (*oleaster*), senses derivative from those denoting smallness or a partial, or a slight, resemblance. Exx: *oleaster,* wild olive (tree), from L *oleaster,* olive (*tree*); *poetaster,* Mod L formation=*poet+-aster.*

**-astic,** adj, is a cpd suffix, usu answering to *-ast;* it consists of *-ast-+-ic,* q.v.; its predecessors are L *-asticus,* occ via F *-astique,* and Gr *-astikos.* Exx: *scholastic,* L *scholasticus,* Gr *skholastikos; paraphrastic,* ML *paraphrasticus,* Gr *paraphrastikos; encomiastic,* Gr *enkōmiastikos.*

**-asy.** See *-asia.*

**-at** (1), n, as in *diplomat,* from F *diplomate,* and as in *quadrat* (cf *quadrate*), from L *quadrātus,* squared, are rare variants of *-ate* (1), q.v.

**-at** (2), n from L v, as in *habitat,* from L *habitat,* he or it dwells. Cf the subj parallel *-eat* below.

**-ata.** See *-ato.*

**-ate** (1), adj, whether pa or, derivatively, 'straight' adj, either derives from, or has been formed by analogy with adjj formed from, the L *-ātus* (rarely from the f *-āta*), the pp suffix of 1st-conj vv (inf *-āre*). Exx: *desolate,* L *dēsolātus,* pp of *dēsolāre; emasculate,* now only literary for 'emasculated', from L *ēmasculātus,* pp of *ēmasculāre.* An ex of adj formed from n—such words occur mostly in Bot and Zoo—is *chordate,* from L *chorda,* cord.

**-ate** (2), n from the L n-suffix *-ātus* (4th declension; gen in *-ātūs*), denoting either office (or function) or occ a person holding that office or serving in that function. Exx: *episcopate,* LL *episcopātus* (gen *-atūs*); *magistrate,* L *magistrātus* (gen *-atūs*); *tribunate,* (perhaps via F *tribunat,* from) L *tribunātus* (gen *-atūs*).

**-ate** (3), n from L *-ātus,* 1st-conj pp, as in *legate,* via OF *legat* from L *legātus,* pp of *legāre.*

**-ate** (4), n from L *-ātum,* neu of pp *-ātus,* is a Chem suffix, as in *nitrate* from *nitr*(ic acid), *sulphate* from *sulph*(uric acid), and also *alcoholate* from *alcohol, methylate* from *methyl* on the analogy of *alcoholate.*

**-ate** (5), v, as in *concentrate* and *venerate,* is formed by converting the L pp *-ātus* to *-ate:* cf the 1st *-ate* above. Thus *fascinate* comes from L *fascinātus,* pp of *fascināre,* and *venerate* from L *uenerāri.* There are also many anl formations, as, e.g., *concentrate,* from prefix *con-*+L *centr*(um: centre)+*-ate,* and *incapacitate,* from *in-,* not+ *capacit*(y)+*-ate.*

**-atic** is a cpd suffix (*-at-+-ic,* q.v.) of Gr origin in *-atikos* or, when not from Gr, of L origin in *-aticus;* occ via the F *-atique.* Exx: *asthmatic,* consisting of *asthm*(a)+(a)*tic,* from L *asthmaticus,* from Gr *asthmatikos; Adriatic,* L *Adriaticus; lymphatic,* L *lymphaticus.* General sense: of the nature of.

**-atile** is another cpd suffix (*-at-+-ile,* q.v.), as in *versatile* (*vers-+-at-+-ile*), perhaps via F *versatile,* certainly from ML *versātilis,* L *uersātilis.* General sense: able, or tending, to (e.g., turn).

**-atim** is a L adv suffix, added to the o/s of a n, as in *seriatim;* it connotes either 'in' or esp 'in the manner of'. Cf *verbatim* (L *uerbatim,* from *uerbum,* a word), app formed after *seriatim.*

**-ation** is yet another cpd suffix (*-at-+-ion,* q.v.), as in *consideration.* It derives from L *-ātiōn-,* c/f of *-ātiō,* either direct, as (prob) in *reconciliation, reconciliātiōn-,* c/f of *reconciliātiō,* or through F *-ation* (for the acc *-ātiōnem*), as (perh) in *reconciliation,* adopted from OF *reconciliation,* itself from *reconciliātiōnem,* acc of *reconcilitātiō.* In general sense, *-ation* corresponds to the verbal n in *-ing* (*osculation*=kiss*ing*).

It will be noted that many, prob most, of these nn in *-ation* answer to a v in *-ate,* as *relation— relate;* a special class is that of *-isation* or *-ization,* answering to vv in *-ize:* see the separate entries at (1) *-isation, -ization,* and (2) *-ise, -ize.*

The principal senses indicated by -ation may be summarily arranged thus:

(1) abstractness (state or condition, quality or degree): as in *estimation*, the quality of being esteemed, and *occupation*, the condition of being occupied; occ with an implication of process or continuance or manner, as in *alteration*, a nuance linked very closely with:

(2) action, as in *continuation* and *visitation*;

(3) result of an action, product of a process, as in *proclamation* and *discoloration*.

**-atious** is an adj answering to—though it occurs much less often than— -*ation*, as in *flirtatious*— *flirtation* and *vexatious*—*vexation*. Like the other -*at*- suffixes, it is or can be regarded as a cpd (-*at*-+ -*ious*); in one aspect, -*atious* represents an extension of -*ious*, q.v. Cf:

**-ative** (1), with connotation 'tending to (whatever the v denotes)', comes from ML -*ātīvus*, from L -*ātīuus*, either direct or through F -*atif*, f -*ative*, or anl with such adjj. Exx: *amative*, either *am*-, s of *amāre*, to love+-*ative*, or *amāt*-, s of *amātus*, pp of *amāre*+-*ive*, q.v.; *creative*, a similar formation; *demonstrative*, F *démonstratif*, ML *demonstrātīvus* (L -*īuus*); *productive*, ML *productīvus*, perh via F *productif*. Occ it is attached to native words, as in *talkative*.

**-ative** (2), 'having the quality, or being of the state or condition, of' (the noun implied), answers to nn in -*ity*, the -*y* being discarded; thus *quantitative*, *qualitative* derive from *quantity*, *quality*. This -*ative* was prompted by -*ative* (1), which, in a sense, it imitates.

**-ato**, m, and **-ata**, f, represents It pp adjj; thus *appassionata* as in the so-called *Sonata Appassionata*, and *appassionato*, a musical direction ('impassioned'), derive from It *appassionare* (s *appassion*-), to render passionate.

**-ator**, an extended form of agential -*or*, answers to L vv in -*āre*, as in *amator* (*am*-, s of *amāre*, to love+-*ātor*). Some authorities, however, regard *amator* and all other such formations as consisting of the pp s (e.g., *amāt*-)+agential -*or*. Cf:

**-atorius, -atory**, may likewise be regarded as -*at*- (belonging to the pps)+-*ōrius, -ory*, qq.v. below, or as -*atōrious, -atory*, attached to the simple inf s, as in the rare *amatorious*, the usu *amatory*, from L *amatōrius*. In a few words, the formation would appear to be agent -*ātor*+adj -*y*, as perh in *clamatory*, from L *clamatōrius*. (In short, suffixes are far more complex and complicated than prefixes.) Cf:

**-ature** is either a cpd suffix (-*at*-+-*ure*, q.v.) or a mere ghost of one, the true suffix being -*ure*, as below. Exx: *armature*, L *armātūra*, from *armāre* (s *arm*-), pp *armātus* (pps *armāt*-); *creature*, adopted from OF, which took it from LL *creatūra*, from *creāre* (s *cre*-), pp *creātus* (pp s *creāt*-). Here, I think, the true suffix is -*ure*, q.v.

**-bility**, n; **-ble**, adj. The latter, short for -*bile*, has n -*bility* (-*bile* become -*bili*-+*ty*; or -*bil*- (for -*bile*)+-*ity*). They derive, sometimes via F -*ble*,

-*bilité*, from L -*bilis*, m and f, -*bile*, neu, and -*bilāt*-, c/f of -*bilitās*, or, for F words, -*bilitātem*, acc; many adjj and nn have been formed analogously. The nn are abstract, their originating adjj are qualitative. Exx: *horrible*, adopted from OF, from L *horribilis*, from *horrēre*, to tremble or shiver with cold or dread—obsol *horribility*, OF *horribilité*, as though from L *\*horribilitās* and perh influenced by ML *horriditās*; *vulnerable*, ML *vulnerābilis*, LL *uulnerābilis*, hence *vulnerability*; *able*, OF (*h*)*able*, L *habilis*—rare *hability*, OF *habilité*, L *habilitātem*, acc of *habilitās*, lit 'ability to hold'.

Although -*ability, -able* are by far the commonest forms and although they tend, in new formations, to oust the others, there do exist certain variations, either deriving from or formed anl upon the orig L suffixes. Exx of all forms:

-*ability, -able*: *arability*, from *arable*, from L *arābilis*, neu *arābile*; *rectifiable* (whence *rectifiability*), from 'to *rectify*'; *receivable* (whence *receivability*), from 'to *receive*', but prob influenced by F *recevable*; *get-at-ability*, from *get-at-able*, from 'to *get at*'. This group is swollen by all derivatives from F -*able*, which tends to embrace L -*ēbilis* and -*ibilis* as well as -*ābilis*.

-*ebility, -eble*, very rare and fast being displaced by -*ibility, -ible*: *delebility*, from *deleble* (now usu *delibility*, from *delible*), from L *dēlēbilis*, neu *dēlēbile*, from *dēlēre*, to wipe out; disguised in *feeble*, OF *feble*, *fleble*, L *flēbilis*, from *flēre*, to weep;

-*ibility, -ible*: *perceptibility*, from LL *perceptibilitās*, from LL *perceptibilis, -ibile*, from *percipere*, to *perceive*;

-*ubility, -uble*: *solubility*, from *soluble*, adopted from MF-F, from LL *solūbilis*, neu *solūbile*, from *soluere*, to loosen, (hence) to dissolve.

**-ble** (1). See prec.

**-ble** (2). A variant of -*ple*, q.v. Of F origin, this -*ble*, denoting 'fold' (as in *manifold*), occurs in *double*, adopted from OF *double*, from L *duplus*, and *treble*, through OF from L *triplus*.

**-bond**. See:

**-bund, -bon d; -cund**. Whereas -*bund* derives from L -*bundus*, f -*bunda*, and -*bond* from the same but through F -*bond*, f -*bonde*, -*cund* derives from L -*cundus*, f -*cunda*. The general connotation is 'tending to' (do whatever the v denotes). Exx: *facund*, perh via F *facond*, certainly from L *facundus*, (lit) tending to *fāri* or speak, (hence) eloquent; *jocund*, OF *jocond*, ML *jocundus*, L *iucundus*, from *iuuāre*, to help; *moribund*, L *moribundus*, from *morī*, to die; *pudibund*, bashful, L *pudibundus*, from *pudēre*, to be bashful, to feel ashamed; *rubicund*, (perh v F *rubicond*) from L *rubicundus*, from *rubēre*, to be red; *vagabond*, adopted from OF *vagabond*, ML *vagabundus*, L *uagabundus*, from ML *vagāri*, L *uagāri*, to wander. Cf -*und* (as in *rotund*), q.v. below.

**-by**, in place-names, e.g. *Rugby*, descends from OE *by*, a dwelling-place, esp a farmhouse, (hence? a village (cf Danish and Swedish *by*, a village, a town): and OE *by* either comes from, or at the least is intimately akin to, ON *byr*, a farm, a village (cf E *byre*), from ON *bua*, to dwell.

**-c.** See *-ic*.

**-cade** is not a true suffix, for it has merely been borrowed from *cavalcade*—and perh been influenced by the *-ade* of *parade*—to form such monstrosities as *motorcade*, an automobile procession.

[**-caster.** See the list of learnèd compound-forming elements. The same remark holds good for *-cester* and *-chester*.]

**-ce**, adv, as in *once, twice, thrice*, and in *hence, thence, whence*, represents the OE gen suffix *-es*, as in *dayes*, by day—cf the mod dial '*of* a night', at night, and '*of* a morning', in the morning.

**-cel**, as in Her *lioncel*, a small lion, is an OF dim suffix; cf the *-el* of OF *lionnel*, lit a lion, whence *Lionel*, and more pertinently the It dim *-cello*, as in *monticello*, from L *-cellus*, as in LL *monticellus*, a small mountain: cf also L *-ellus* (and L *-ulus*), of which L *-cellus*, F and E *-cel*, would seem to be extensions.

**-ch** (1), adj, is 'a syncopated form of *-ish*, as in French, Scotch' (Webster). See, therefore, *-ish*, adj.

**-ch** (2), n: ME *-che*: OE *-ce*. Exx: *birch* and *church*. Its connotation is 'of or belonging to'. It may also answer to G *-che*, as in *larch*, and to Sp *-cha*, as in *cinch*.

**-ch** (3), v, as in *reach, search, teach*, occurs in transitive vv and seems to connote a purposive effort, a striving.

**-chre**, as in *sepluchre*. Var of *-cre*, q.v.

[**-city** answers to adj *-cious*. But these are not true suffixes, for the *-c-* belongs to an o/s ending in *-c*: cf *ferocity* (adj *ferocious*), from L *ferōcitās*, itself from the adj *ferōx*, o/s *ferōc-*. Cf *-ious* and *-ity*.]

**-cle** (1), dim n. Most words in *-cle* have passed through F; the originating L form is *-culus* (m), *-cula* (f), *-culum* (neu), qq.v. at *-cule*. Exx: *article*, via MF-F, from L *articulus*, dim of *artus*, a joint; *clavicle*, F *clavicule*, ML *clavicula*, dim from L *clauis*, a key; *corpuscle*, like *corpuscule*, from L *corpusculum*; *cuticle*, L *cuticula*; *particle*, L *particula*. Perhaps a cpd suffix: *-(i)c+-le*.

**-cle** (2), n. In a few *-cle* nn, the force of *-cle* can only with difficulty be described as diminutive. They are words ending in *-acle*, from L *-āculum*, and deriving, not, as in *-cle* (1), from nn, but from vv. Exx: *miracle*, via OF, from L *mirāculum*, from *mirāri*, to wonder or wonder at (s *mir-*); *oracle*, via OF, from L *orāculum*, from *orāre* (s *or-*), to speak, esp to pray; *receptacle*, L *receptāculum*, from *receptāre* (s *recept-*); *spectacle*, via OF, from L *spectāculum*, from *spectāre* (s *spect-*), to look at. The connotation, clearly, is 'object at which the action of the implied verb is directed'. Perhaps a cpd suffix: *-ac+-le*. Cf prec.

**-cose.** See *-icose*.

[**-craft.** See CRAFT.]

**-cre** or **-chre**, as in *fulcre, lucre*, (?) *massacre*,

*sepulchre*, derives from L *-crum*, thus: *fulcre*, an Englishing of L *fulcrum*; *lucre*, L *lucrum*; *massacre*, adopted from F of doubtful origin but with suffix on analogy of other F nn in *-cre*; *sepulchre*, ME *sepulchre* (adopted from OF), from L *sepulcrum* or, rather, its var *sepulchrum*. The L nn derive from vv—or, at the least, from the ss of vv; *-crum* therefore connotes action—lifting, gain, killing, burying, etc.

**-cula, -culum, -culus; -cule.** The last is the E, often after F, form of L *-cula*, f, *-culum*, neu, or *-culus*, m, dim suffix, with pl *-culae*, f, or *-cula*, neu, or *-culi*, m. Exx: *animalcule*, L *animalculum* (also in E), dim of *animal*; *auricula*, adopted from L f dim of *auris* (s *aur-*), ear; *homuncule* (or *homuncle*), from L *homunculus* (also in E), dim of *homo*, man; *minuscule*, adopted from F, from L *minusculus*, rather small, dim of *minor*, neu *minus* (s *min-*), lesser. See also *-ula*.

**-cund.** See *-bund*.

**-cy** represents Gr *-keia* or *-kia*, *-teia* or *-tia*, whether direct or via VL-ML *-c a* or L *-tia* or then via F *-tie*; the L word may have been formed analogously with other L words, the F with other F words, the E with other E words. It indicates state or condition or quality—cf, therefore, the native *-hood* and *-ship*—and its connotation is therefore of abstractness. 'A special use of these suffixes [*-cy, -sy*] is to denote rank and office: *curacy, episcopacy, magistracy, papacy, cornetcy, ensigncy; minstrelsy*. Some of the above have also a collective sense; *legacy* has a concrete meaning' (Sweet). Exx: *bankrupt*=*bankrupt*+*-cy*; *infancy*, from L *infantia*; *secrecy*=*secret*+*-cy*. The L and Gr forms appear best in such cpd suffixes as *-acy* (*aristocracy*, MF *aristocracie*, L *aristocratia*, Gr *aristokratia*) and *-ancy* (*constancy*, L *constantia*, and *chiromancy*—cf, in the Elements list, *-mancy*, from Gr *manteia*) and *-ency* (*clemency*, L *clementia*). Cf esp *-ce*, but also *-acy, -ancy, -ency* above. A parallel var is *-sy*, q.v. below.

**-d** (1), adj of Gmc origin, with vaguely concrete connotation. Exx: *bald*, ME *balled*, cf Da *baeldet*; *cold*, OE *cald* or *ceald*, cf OS *kald* and ON *kaldr*; *dead*, OE *dead*; *loud*, OE *hlūd*, cf OS *hlūd*; *wild*, OE *wilde*, cf OFris *wilde*, OS and OHG *wildi*.

**-d** (2) or **-de**, in nn. 'Nouns formed with this suffix usually denote the result of some action, and can generally be traced to some verbal stem': Nesfield, who instances *blood*, OE *blōd*—cf *bleed*, OE *blēdan*; *brand*, ON *brandr*—cf ON *brenna*, to burn; *bread*, OE *brēad*—cf OE *brēowan*, EE-E *brew*, v; *deed*, OE *dǣd*—cf OE *dōn*, EE-E *do*; *flood, glede, need, seed, shard* or *sherd, speed, thread, suds*—words that prove his contention.

**-der** (1). Of Gmc origin, it indicates 'result of' (implied v), with an abstract connotation, as in *murder*, OE *morthor*, akin to *myrthian* (s *myrth-*), to murder. Cf *-ter* (4).

**-der** (2): Gmc: 'instrument'. Ex: *bladder*, OE *blǣddre*.

[**-dle.** See *-le*, n, and *-le*, v.]

-dom, OE -*dōm* (cf G -*tum*), is of the same root as DOOM, q.v. It indicates office or dignity or jurisdiction, hence region; exx: *earldom, kingdom, heathendom*: such words being derived from nn. When -*dom* is suffixed to adjj, it connotes state or condition, as in *freedom* and *wisdom*. A modern connotation, that of collectivity (cf *heathendom*), occurs in, e.g., *officialdom*.

-e (1). In most words, -*e* is a mute final, doing duty either for such Gr suffixes as -*a* and -*ē* and -*os* or for such L suffixes as -*a* and -*us*; exx: *tome, tone, trope, type*. When pronounced (*ee*), as in *epitome* and *hyperbole*, it stands for the Gr η (*ē*).
-e (2). In adjj adopted from F, it normally represents the f sing, as in *petite*; that is, whenever the F adj has not the sole form -*e*, as in *drôle*, anglicized as *droll*, and in *svelte*.
-e (3). In words adopted from It, it usu represents the pl of f adjj and nn in -*a*.
-é, as in *employé, habitué, outré, protégé, roué, soigné*, occurs only in words adopted from F; all the nn except *roué* have f counterparts in -*ée*, q.v.
[-ea is the pl of Gr words in -*eon* or of L words in -*eum*. Strictly, the -*e*- either belongs to the s or is a connective; the same is true of -*eae*, the suffix being -*ae*.]
-ean, often through F -*éen*, means the same as -*an* or -*ane* and 'is a lengthened form of L -*aeus*, -*eus*, the lengthened -*aeanus* occurring in L itself in some words' (Sweet). Exx: *cerulean*, L *caeruleus*; *European*, F *Européen*, L *europaeus*, Gr *eurōpaios*; *herculean*, L *herculeus*; *Mediterranean* (cf *mediterrane*), L *mediterrāneus*.
-eat, as in *caveat, exeat*, and -iat, as in *fiat*, indicates a 3rd person sing of the pres subj of L vv.
-ed (1), in adjj, as 'foliat*ed*', 'pig-head*ed*', derives analogously from -*ed* (2); whereas such words as *foliated* come from vv, those of the *calyxed* and *pig-headed* types come from nn whether simple or cpd. The connotation is 'possessed of' (a calyx, a pig-head—i.e., an obstinate one). Cf -*t*.
-ed (2), in pp, as in 'He had hasten*ed*', derives from OE -*ede* or -*ode* or -*ade*. Cf -*t*.
-ed (3), in pt, as in 'He hasten*ed*', derives from OE -*ed* or -*od* or -*ad*.
-ee, as in *assignee, grantee, lessee*, derives either from or as if from -*é*, the m suffix of the F pp. Occurring mostly in legal terms, it forms the correlative of the agential -*or* (as in *assignor, lessor*, etc.); it connotes the person to or for whom something is done. Cf -*ey*, below, and:
-ée is the f pp of F vv, as in *divorcée* (a divorced woman) and Pierre Loti's *Les Désenchantées*. This form undoubtedly reinforced the influence of F -*é* (as in *divorcé*, a divorced man) in the genesis of the prec suffix. The F -*é* comes from L -*ātus*, m; -*ée* from L -*āta*, f.
-eel, as in *genteel*, is a var of -*ile* (1), q.v.
-een (1), in *birdeen, colleen, girleen, squireen*, is an Anglo-Ir dim prob akin to L -*inus*, f -*ina*, of

vaguely dim conn in Classical L and LL, but definitely dim in mod formations (e.g., Angel*ina*) —cf. -*ina*, q.v. The Ir dim is -*īn*, pron -*een*, as in *cailín*, whence *colleen*.
-een (2), in *sateen*, occ written *satine* (pron *sateen*), from *satin*, and in *velveteen*, from *velvet*, connotes inferiority, *sateen* being a cotton fabric with a satin-like surface, and *velveteen* being velvet made entirely from cotton. The general conn, therefore, is 'inferior dim', not, as in (1), 'dear dim'; nevertheless, -*een* (2) prob derives from -*een* (1).
-eer (1), n, like -*ar* and -*er* and esp like -*ier*, usu comes from VL -*erius* (L -*ārius*), through OF -*ier*; on all other occasions, -*eer* nn have been formed analogously. Exx: *gazetteer*, orig a newspaper editor, from F *gazettier*; *muleteer*, from F *muletier*; *pamphleteer*=*pamphlet*+-*eer*; *pioneer*, EE *pioner*, from F *pionnier*; *privateer*=*privat*(*e*)+(*e*)*er*; *volunteer* EF *voluntaire* (Mod *volontaire*).
-eer (2), v, as in *domineer*, represents the F 1st-conj inf suffix -*er* (*dominer*); *volunteer*, v, derives, however, from the n.
-eet (1), adj of L origin, as in *discreet*, is a rare var of -*ete*, q.v. below.
-eet (2), adj of Gmc origin. Exx: *fleet*, prob from ON; *sweet*, OE *swēte*. Cf -*t* (2), adj of Gmc origin.
-ei represents the gen sing of the L 5th declension, as in 'Fid*ei* Defensor', the Defender of the Faith. But it may also represent the dat sing of the same declension, as in the latinism *fideicommissum*, lit '(a thing) committed—i.e., entrusted—to faith'.
-eign, as in *foreign*, 'disguises' -*an* or esp -*ain*: ME *foreine* or *forene*, OF *forain* (f *foraine*), LL *forānus* (*for*-+-*ānus*), from the L adv -*foras* (var of *foris*), out of doors.
-ein, -eine, merely vary the chem suffixes -*in*,- *ine*, qq.v.: -*eine* is usu reserved for bases, -*ein* for non-bases. (Webster.)
-eity, as in *homogeneity*, is an extension of -*ity*, q.v. The -*e*- is that which occurs also in -*eous*.
-el (1), adj, as in *cruel*, usu answers to L -*ēlis* (var of -*ilis*, q.v. at -*il* and -*ile*)—as in L *crudēlis*, which, through OF *cruel*, yields E *cruel*, cf the obs *fidel* or *fidell* or *fidele*, faithful, via F *fidèle*, from L *fidēlis*. Occ, however, as in *scrannel*, it is formed on the analogy of OE -*el*: cf -*le*, adj (q.v.)
-el (2), n, is dim, as in *chapel*, OF *chapele*, LL *cappella*, f dim from L *cappa*, and in *citadel*, F *citadelle*, It *cittadella*, dim of *cittade*, a city. It comes, often via OF-F and occ via It, from the L dim -*ellus* (m) or -*ella* (f) or -*ellum*. But in a few words, e.g. *navel, runnel*, it appears to be a native dim. Cf -*le* (and -*l*) and -*elle*.
-el, (3), n, as in *cautel, quarrel* and *sequel*, represents the L suffix -*ēla*: thus, *cautel*, OF *cautele*, L *cautēla*, from *cauēre*, to be wary; *quarrel*, OF *querele*, L *querēla*, from *querī*, to complain; *sequel*, F *séquelle*, L *sequēla*, from *sequī*, to follow. This suffix, quite distinct from -*el* (2), seems merely to indicate '(n of) action corresponding to v'. Cf -*ele*.
-el (4), n. In *hovel*, of unknown origin, the suffix

*-el* is likewise of unknown conn. But, as Skeat has proposed, *hovel* is perh the dim of OE *hof,* a house, and *-el* therefore identical with *-el* (2).

*-el* (5), v, as in *drivel* and *snivel,* is a var of *-le,* v (q.v. below) in its freq conn: ME *-elen,* OE *-lian.*

*-ela,* as in *cautela* and *sequela,* is an adoption from L: cf *-el* (3) above.

*-ele,* as in *clientele,* represents OF *-ele* (F *-èle*), from L *-ēla*: cf prec and *-el* (3).

*-ella* is an adoption of, or a formation anl with, L *-ella,* f dim suffix, answering to m *-ellus* (and neu *-ellum*). Exx: *Cinderella* (*cinder*+*-ella*; suggested by F *Cendrillon*); *Libella,* old Sci name for a dragonfly; *umbrella,* adapted from It *ombrella.* Cf:

*-elle* is an adoption of F *-elle,* f dim corresponding to L *-ella*; as in *bagatelle.* Cf prec and:

*-elli,* pl of L *-ellus,* It *-ello,* m dim suffix, as in *vermicelli,* pl of It *vermicello,* lit a small worm.

*-ello.* It m dim suffix, as in *niello* and *violoncello.* In the latter, as in *vermicelli* (see prec), the *-c-* is itself a suffix, presumably dim.

*-ellum* is the L neu dim answering to the m dim *-ellus.* Both *-ellum* and *-ellus* occur in only a few latinisms, e.g. *flagellum.* Cf the prec four entries and *-el* (2).

*-ellus.* See prec.

*-em,* as in *diadem, emblem, system, theorem,* represents the Gr *-ēma,* n suffix for a formation from a v, often through L *-ēma* and OF-MF *-eme* or F *-ème*; the Gr n connotes result from the action of the v, as in *diadēma,* from *diadein,* to bind round. Cf *-m* (3), *-ma, -me* (2) and *-eme.*

*-ema,* as in *enema,* represents Gr *-ema* (short *e*), app a var of Gr *-ēma.* Cf prec and:

*-eme* (adj in *-emic*), as in *phoneme* and, imitatively, in *morpheme,* represents Gr *-ēma* and therefore forms a var of *-em.*

*-en* (1), adj of L origin, as in *alien,* adopted from OF, itself from L *aliēnus*; *mizzen,* F *misaine,* It *mezzana* (elliptical for *mezzana vela*), f of *mezzano,* middle, from LL *mediānus,* and in *sullen,* ME *solein,* via OF from VL *\*solānus,* solitary, from *solus,* alone. A variant of *-an* (1), q.v.—from L *-ānus* or *-ēnus.*

*-en* (2), adj of OE origin and connoting 'made, or consisting, of', as in *ashen, golden, leaden, oaken, oaten, wheaten, wooden,* thus: *ashen,* whether relating to the ash tree or to *ash*es; *golden,* ME *golden*—cf OE *gylden*; *leaden,* OE *lēaden*; *oaken* = *oak* + *-en*; *oaten* = *oat* + *-en*; *wheaten,* OE *hwǣten*; *wooden* = *wood*+*-en.* The OE *-en* is akin to Go *-eins,* L *-inus,* Gr *-inos*: cf, therefore, *-in, -ine,* adjj; cf also:

*-en* (3), n, is to be compared very closely with prec. 'The similarity of meaning between material nouns and adjectives has in some cases led to the conversion of adjectives in *-en* into nouns, as in *linen* = OE *linen* "flaxen" from *lin* "flax", and the tree names *aspen* = OE *aespe, linden* = OE *lind* fem.': Sweet.

*-en* (4), n. In pl, as *ashen, brethren, children, eyen, hosen, oxen*: cf the *-ne* of *kine* and the *-n*

of *shoon.* Thus *brethren* derives from ME *bretheren.* ME *-en* derives from OE *-an.*

*-en* (5), n dim, as in *chicken,* OE *cicen,* and *maiden,* OE *maegden* (cf OE *maegth* for the stem), derives from OE *-en*; with *maegden,* cf G *mädchen.*

*-en* (6), n in f suffixes, as in *vixen,* dial for *fixen,* OE *fyxen,* f of OE *fox*: cf the obs *wylfen,* f of OE *wulf,* wolf, with its MHG syn *wulfinne* (suffix *-inne*).

*-en* (7), agential n, as in *haven,* OE *haefen* (or *-ene*)—cf ON *höfn*—and as in *token,* OE *tācen*— cf OFris *tēken,* OS *tēkan,* OHG *zeihhan*; lit the have-er or holder and the show-er or indicator. Cf, therefore, agential *-n* and *-on.* But agential *-en* sometimes originates in L: e.g., *citizen,* influenced by *denizen* (ult from L *dē intus,* from within), and *scrivener,* with superfluous *-er.*

*-en* (8), as in *burden* (OE *byrthen*), has a passive conn: lit, that which is borne—cf *bairn,* that which is born, and also, for the suffix, *loan,* that which is lent. Cf the corresponding *-n,* n, and esp the pp *-en,* q.v. at *-en* (11) below.

*-en* (9). In *heaven*—cf the shortened *-n* of *main,* strength (OE *maegen*—cf OHG *magan*) and *thegn* (Mod E *thane*)—the suffix *-en* is of vague connotation; the OE *heofon* is akin to OS *hevan.* This Mod E *-en,* therefore, is akin to PG *\*-an* or *\*-on.*

*-en* (10), v, as in *frighten, lengthen, shorten, strengthen, weaken,* usu from adjj but also, as in *frighten,* from nn; its conn is 'to render' whatever the adj indicates or 'to induce' (in someone or something) whatever state or condition or quality the n denotes. Exx: *frighten* = *fright,* n+*-en*; *lengthen* = *length* + *-en*; *shorten* = *short,* adj+*-en*; *strengthen* = *strength* + *-en*; *weaken* = *weak,* adj+ *-en.* This suffix hardly antedates 1500—in written records; it has been formed on the analogy of OE vv in *-nian,* of which the initial *-n-* has been lost and the *-i-* discarded, to accord with ME vv in *-en.* But it might be argued that E *-en* owes something to Scan vv in *-na.*

*-en* (11), the pp ending of most strong vv, as in *broken,* OE *brocen*; *drunken,* OE *druncen*; *fallen,* OE *feallen*; *ridden,* ME *iriden,* later *riden.* The OE *-en* has a cognate in Skt *-na.* From these pp forms derive the answering pp adjj, as in 'the *drunken* fellow'. Cf *-en* (8) above.

*-ence, -ency.* See *-ance, -ancy* above.

*-end.* See *-and.*

*-endum.* See *-andum.*

*-ene,* as in *benzene* and *toluene,* is a Chem suffix indicating a hydrocarbon; cf the *-ane* of *octane.* Prob suggested by the L adj suffix *-ēnus,* the Gr *-ēnos,* connoting nature or quality. Hence the commercial use of *-ene* to denote almost any kind of substance.

*-engro,* connoting 'man' or 'fellow', as in *Lavengro* (lit Man of Words), represents the Romany cpd suffix *-engero,* which = *-en,* denoting a pl+*-kera,* an adj suffix+*-o,* a common m n-suffix.

*-ent,* adj and n. See *-ant* (1) above.

*-eny.* See *-iny* below.

*-eous,* as in *aqueous, igneous, vitreous,* derives

from L -*eus*, composed of or resembling the implied n, thus: *aqueous*, from L *\*aqueus*, assumed on the analogy of other L adjj in -*eus*; *igneous*, L *igneus*, from *ignis*, fire; *vitreous*, from ML *vitreus*, L *uitreus*, glassy, from *uitrum*, glass. Cf -*ous*. (In *righteous* we see the -*wise* of ME *rightwise* discarded for -(*e*)*ous*; in *gorgeous* we see OF *gorgias*, which= stem *gorg*-+connective -*i*-+-*as*, adj and n suffix, becoming *gorg*-+-*e*- for -*i*-+-*ous*.)

-er (1), adj of comp degree, as in *faster*, *slower*, *better*, *finer* (i.e. *fin*(e)+-*er*), derives from OE -*ra*, as in *better*, OE *betera*: cf ON *betri*, OHG *bezziro*, Go *batiza*, L *melior*, Gr *beltiōn*, and perh Skt *bhadra* (good).

The -*er* of comp advv derives from OE -*or*, akin to OHG and OS -*ōr* and Go -*ōs*, -*ōz*. The adv *better*, deriving from OE *bet*, has been influenced by analogy: cf the L *melius* and the Gr *beltion*. (See esp O.E.D.)

-er (2), adj, as in *eager*, AE *meager* (E *meagre*), derives from L -*er*; an -*re* spelling indicates passage via F. Thus: *eager*, ME *egre*, OF *aigre*, L *ácer*; *meager* or *meagre*, ME *megre*, OF *megre* or *maigre*, L *macer*—cf the eccl *maigre*. This -*er*, very common in L and having conn 'quality', has occ been taken direct by E from L, as in *dexter* and *sinister*—contrast F *dextre* and *sinistre*.

-er (3), adv. For some advv, see -*er* (1), second para. For the -*er* of *ever*, hence of *never*, see -*re* (2), the adv -*re* of *here* and *there*.

-er (4), n, agential (orig m) or instrumental straight from v, as in *murderer* from *murder* and *player* from *play*; where the v ends in -*e*, as in *hate*, *poke*, that -*e* is dropped, as in *hater*, *poker*. Although most of the exx are modern, this -*er* derives from OE -*ere*, which, like Go -*areis* and OHG -*ari* (G -*er*), came orig from L -*ārius* (m) or -*ārium* (neu). Cf:

-er (5), n denoting 'person or thing connected with', as in *carpenter*, *garner*, *grocer*, comes—usu via AF -*er*, OF -*ier*—from L -*ārius* (m) or -*ārium* (neu), from another n. Exx: *carpenter*, ONF *carpentier* (cf the surnames *Carpentier*, *Carpenter*), LL *carpentārius*, from *carpentum*; *garner*, a granary from OF *gernier*, metathesis of *grenier*, from L *grānārium*, from *grānum*; *grocer*, ME *grosser*, OF *grossier*, ML *grossārius*, from *grossus*. Cf prec.

-er (6), n, links very closely with prec. This group consists of nn from E nn, thus *hatter* from *hat*, *philologer* from *philolog*(*y*), *purser* from *purse*, and the general conn is 'one concerned with'. Both -*er* (5) and -*er* (6) are neutral, whereas -*er* (4) is active. Note the variants bow*yer*, law*yer*, saw*yer*, and coll*ier*, glaz*ier*, haul*ier*.

-er (7), agent of L origin (via OF-F) in -*ātor*, which represents the predominant L agential suffix -*or* attached to the pp s. Exx: *commander*, OF *comandeor* (F *commandeur*), analogously from *comander*, from a VL var of *commendāre*; *compiler*, OF *compileor*, L *compīlātor*, from *compīlāre*, to gather together; *diviner*, OF *divineor*, ML *divinātor*, LL *diuinātor*, from *diuināre*, to foresee; *interpreter*,

OF *interpreteur*, LL *interpretātor*, from *interpretāri*.

-er (8), n, denoting 'a resident in, a native of', as in *Londoner*, *Northerner*, *foreigner* and *villager*; deriving from n or adj, this -*er* may be compared to the -*er* of G *Engländer*, Englishman.

-er (9), n, person or thing attaining to a certain size, height, weight, strength, etc.: as in sixty-pound*er*, six-foot*er*, half-mil*er*, Forty-Nin*er*. Perh cf prec and prob cf:

-er (10), n, a person, an object, an action connected with or related to the idea implicit in the stem. Exx: back-hand*er*, fac*er*, head*er*, newcom*er*, old-tim*er*. With -*er* (4) and, less, (5)–(10) cf the agential -*or* below.

-er (11). Alternative for -*or*, as in *carburetter*.

-er (12), n, denoting or, at the vaguest, connoting 'action or process of' whatever the v indicates, as in *dinner* and *supper* and, exemplifying certain legal terms, *demurrer* and *waiver*; all of which derive from, or are adoptions of, OF-MF or AF pres-infs, thus: *demurrer*, OF *demorer*; *dinner*, ME *diner*, OF *disner*; *disclaimer*, AF *desclamer*; *supper*, ME *soper* or *super*, adopted from OF; *waiver*, AF *weyver*.

-er (13), n. The suffix in *udder*, from OE *ūder* (akin to OHG *ūtar*, L *über*, Gr *outhar*, Skt *ūdhar*), has a meaning difficult to determine. It is perh the same as that in *finger*, OE *finger*, akin to OHG *fingar*, ON *fingr*; *hammer*, OE *hamer* or *hamor*, akin to ON *hamarr*; *hunger*, OE *hungor*, akin to OFris *hunger*, OHG *hungar*, ON *hungr*; *silver*, OE *seolfor*, akin to OFris *selover*, ON *silfr*; *summer*, OF *sumor* or *sumer*, akin to OFris *sumur*, OHG *sumar*, ON *sumar*.

-er (14), n, as in *counter*, via OF from ML *computatōrium*—*dormer*, OF *dormeor*, L *dormitōrium*—*laver*, via OF from ML *lavatōrium*, LL *lauatōrium*—*manger*, via OF from VL *\*manducatōria*, from L *manducāre*, obviously comes from the L suffix -*ōrium* or its occ var -*ōria*, with conn 'a place' for the action denoted by the v stem (to calculate—sleep—wash—eat). Cf, therefore, -*ory* below.

-er (15), in freq vv, as *batter* (?) and *clatter* and *patter* and *shatter*—*quaver* and *quiver* and *shiver*—*flitter* and *glitter*—*mutter*, *sputter*, *stutter*. The origin, therefore, is vaguely echoic; all the stems are echoic.

-er (16). See -*re* (4).

-er (17), v, in *sever*, corresponds approximately to L -*āre*, 1st-conj pres-inf suffix; and in *batter*, ult from L, to L -*ere* (*battuere*, LL *battere*)—cf *render*, OF *rendre*, VL *\*rendere* (after *prendere*), from *reddere*.

-erel is a dim, often pej. Exx: *cockerel*=*cock*+ -*erel*; ? *doggerel*, ME *dogerel*; *dotterel*, app from obs *dote*, a stupid fellow, 'to dote' in its obs sense 'to act foolishly'; *gangrel*, a vagabond, app= Scots *gang*, to go+(*e*)*rel*; *hoggerel*, a hogget, app =*hog*, an unshorn sheep not more than a year old +euphonic *g*+-*erel*; ? *mackerel*, MF *maquerel*— but here the dim suffix is very prob -*el*, for the

**-er-** is almost certainly part of the stem; *mongrel* is app for *mongerel*=dial *mong*, to mix+*-erel*; *pickerel*, a young pike, for *pikerel*, i.e. *pik(e)*+ *(e)rel*. But *-rel* may fairly be said to exist in its own right, alongside *-erel*. Cf *-rel* below.

**-erion**, as in *criterion*, is a cpd: *-er*+*-ion*, or rather Gr *-ēr*+connective *-i-*+*-on*; *-ēr* is agential or instrumental, *-on* corresponds to L *-um*. The L shape of Gr *-ērion* is *-ērium*.

**-erly**, adj, connoting 'direction whence', is a mod suffix, thus: *easterly*=*east*, adv+*-erly*; the same process applies to *northerly*, *southerly*, *westerly*. Prob *-erly* is a cpd: an adj *-er*, connoting direction+adj *-ly*.

**-ern** (1), adj, connotes direction and derives from OE *-erne*, as in *eastern* (OE *ēasterne*) and *western* (OE *westerne*), *northern* (OE *northerne*) and *southern* (OE *sūtherne*). Cf prec.

**-ern** (2), n, as in *cavern*, *cistern*, *lantern*, *tavern*, answers to L *-erna* and, derivatively, F *-erne*. Thus: *cavern*, OF *caverne*, ML *caverna*, L *cauerna*, from *cauus* (s *cau-*), hollow; *cistern*, ME *cisterne*, adopted from OF, from L *cisterna*, from *cista*, a box or chest; *lantern*, OF *lanterne*, L *lanterna* (s *lant-*), from Gr *lamptēr* (s *lamp-*), a light; *tavern*, ME *taverne*, adopted from OF, from L *taberna* for *traberna*, from *trabes* or *trabis*, a beam (timber). L *-erna* seems to be of Etruscan origin.

**-ero**, a Sp agential and instrumental suffix, corresponding to *-ier*, q.v. Exx: *bolero*, a very lively Sp dance, from Sp *bola*, a ball+*-ero*; *sombrero*, Sp *sombra*, shade, shadow+*-ero*; *torero*, Sp *toro*, a bull+*-ero*; *vaquero*, a cowboy, for *vachero*, from *vaca*, a cow+*-ero*.

**-ery** (1): ME *-erie*: OF-MF *-erie*, app from *-ier* (q.v. below) or *-er*, themselves from L *-ārius*, with abstract *-ie* (? L *-ia*) added; *-ery* often becomes *-ry*, as in *chivalry*, from OF *chevalerie* or *chivalerie*. In Mod E 'this suffix is mainly used in derivatives from nouns, and occasionally from adjectives, expressing (*a*) actions or qualities, as in *bigotry*, *devilry*, *drudgery*, *pedantry*, *revelry*, *peasantry*; (*b*) condition, as in *outlawry*, *slavery*; (*c*) occupation, trade, art, etc., as in *casuistry*, *palmistry*, *chemistry*, *heraldry*; (*d*) the place of actions, occupations etc., as in *nunnery*, *nursery*, *vestry* . . .; (*e*) the result or product of action etc., as in *poetry*, *tapestry*; (*f*) collectivity, as in *infantry* . . ., *peasantry*, *yeomanry*', as Sweet has so concisely determined.

**-ery** (2), as in *mystery*: L *-ērium*, Gr *-ērion*. Conn: 'state of' (the person indicated by the stem).

**-es** (1), adv, in *whiles* (s *whil-*: cf *whilom*), is a survival of OE *-es*, suffix of gen sing of nn; cf *-wards* in relation to *-ward*.

**-es** (2), n. Suffix indicating the plural of nn ending in *s* or *sh* or *f* (*e*) or in *y* preceded by a cons. Exx: iris*es*, blush*es*, leav*es*, kniv*es*, ladi*es*.

**-es** (3), n. Adopted from L, as in the latinism *aciēs*, keenness of sight.

**-es** (4), n, in *riches*=ME *richesse*, adopted from OF-F and, as a doublet, preserved in E. See also *-esse*.

**-es** (5), v. Indicates 3rd person sing, pres Indicative, as in 'he blush*es*'—'he qualifi*es*'. Cf, therefore, *-s*, v.

**-esce**, v; **-escence**, n, with var **-escency**; **-escent**, adj; **-escible**, adj: resp from L *-ēscere*, pres inf of inch vv; *-ēscentia*, abstract n from such a v, =*-ēscent-*, o/s of presp+abstract suffix *-ia*; *-ēscent-*, o/s presp of inch vv; *-ēscibilis*, an *-ibilis* (cf *-ible* at *-ble* above) type of adj for inch vv. Exx: *effervesce*, ML *effervescere*, L *efferuēscere*; *effervescence*, *-ncy*=*efferv-*+*-escence*, *-escency*; *effervescent*, ML *effervēscent-*, o/s of ML pres p *effervēscens*; *effervescible*=*efferv-*+*-escible*.

**-ese** (1), adj and derivative n: L *-ensis*, m and f (neu *-ense*), often via OF *-eis*; but, in most E words (e.g., *Chinese*, *Japanese*, *Maltese*), by analogy. Belonging to, originating in, native to a country, hence a native of or a resident in or the language of a country. Hence, n only, a style peculiar to a certain person, as *Carlylese*, or class, as *journalese*.

**-ese** (2), n. Chem *-ese* is an alteration of chem *-ase*, q.v.

**-esis**, as in *energesis*, *exergesis*, denotes action— or a process of action; it derives from Gr *-ēsis*, often through L *-ēsis*, or from Gr *-esis* (cf *-etic*).

**-esque**: adopted from F, which adapted it from It *-esco*, f *-esca*, L *-iscus*, f *-isca*, perh of Gmc origin; many E words have been formed by analogy. Exx: *arabesque*, orig an adj from It *arabesco*; *picturesque*, F *pittoresque*, It *pittoresco*; *statuesque* =*statu(e)*+*-esque*. A doublet of *-ish*, adj.

**-ess** (1), as in *poetess*, *shepherdess*, and as in *actress* and *songstress*, indicates the f of the main n: in many E words, by analogy; occ, however, from OF *-esse*, from LL *-issa* from Gr *-issa* or from a word formed anl at the L or esp only the F stage. Exx: *authoress*=*author*+*-ess*, *shepherdess* =*shepherd*+*-ess*; *actress*=*act(o)r*+*-ess*, rather than deriving from F *actrice*—cf *seamstress*, which=*seamst(e)r*+*-ess*, and *songstress*, which= *songst(e)r*+*-ess*; *countess*, OF *contesse* (EF-F *comtesse*).

**-ess** (2), orig adj, but in ModE only n—m not f. Exx: *burgess*, ME *burgeis*, adopted from OF, from *burc* or *burg*, fort, fortified place, fortified city, from LL *burgus*, of Gmc origin, although OF *burgeis* may represent a LL adj *\*burgensis*; *marquess*, MF *marquis*, OF *markis*, from ML *markensis*, from *marca*, frontier or march.

**-ess** (3). See:

**-esse**, as in *largesse*, AE *largess*, and as in *noblesse oblige*, has been adopted from OF. The OF *largesse* derives from VL *\*largitia*; OF *-esse* therefore=VL or LL or even L *-itia*, abstract-n suffix. Cf *duress*, from L *dūritia*, and *fortress*, from OF *forteresse*.

**-est** (1), adj and adv, denoting the superlative degree: OE *-est* or *-ost*, akin to ON *-(a)str*, Go *-ists* or *-osts*, Gr *-istos*, Skt *-istha*. Exx: sweet*est*; earli*est*; soon*est*; *best*, OE *best*, short for *betst*, itself short for *betest*.

**-est** (2), n—as in *earnest*, ME *ernes*, OF *erres*, and, clearly of different origin, in *harvest*, OE *haerfest*, akin to OHG *herbist*—is worth noting only because these words may, in their EE-E forms, reflect the influence of (1).

**-est** (3), v. Archaic suffix of the 2nd person singular, as in 'thou livest'; in mod usage, mostly *-st*, as in *canst, didst, mayst*. It comes down from OE *-est*.

**-et** (1), adj, as in *dulcet*, a refashioning, after L *dulcis*, of *doucet*, F dim of *doux*, f *douce*, from L *dulcis*, sweet; and as in *russet*, F *rousset*, dim of *roux*, f *rousse*. In short, a gallicism.

**-et** (2) occurs in E nn from F dim nn in *-et*, as in *billet-doux*; *crotchet* (ME *crochet*, adopted from the OF dim of *croc*, a hook); *fillet*, OF *filet*, dim of *fil*, a thread; *fleuret, floret*, both from F—cf *floweret* (*flower*+*-et*). The originating F word sometimes ends, not in the m *-et* but in the f *-ette* (cf *-ette* below), as in *islet* from OF *islette*, dim of *isle* (ModF *île*); sometimes ModE has reshaped *-ette* gallicisms into *-et* false-gallicisms, as, e.g., in *octet* for *octette, quintet* for *quintette, sextet* for *sextette*.

**-et** (3): a rare var of *-th* (1), q.v. below. Ex: *thicket*, OE *thiccet*, prob from *thicce*, thick.

**-ete** (1), adj, as in *complete, discrete*: of same origin as (3) below.

**-ete** (2), n, as in *gamete*, L *gameta* (var *gametis*), (a grecism for:) wife, Gr *gametē*, wife (cf *gametēs*, husband), from *gamein* (s *gam*-), to marry. The F form is *-ète*. Conn: 'agent', corresponding to the implied v.

**-ete** (3), v, as in *deplete* and *secrete*, derives from *-ētus*, the pp suffix of L vv in *-ēre*. Cf, in short, the much commoner vv in *-ate*, q.v. above.

**-eth** (1), adj, as in twenti*eth*. See numerical *-th* (the 1st *-th*).

**-eth** (2), v, as in *dieth, doeth* (*doth*), *knoweth, singeth, thinketh*: archaic: from the OE suffix *-eth* or *-ath* or, shortened, *-th*.

**-etic**, adj, corresponds to *-esis*, n, as in *genesis*, adj *genetic*. It comes, often through L *-ēticus*, from Gr *-ētikos*, as in *pathetic* (cf F *pathétique*), LL *pathēticus*, Gr *pathētikos*, from *pathētos*, undergoing, or subject to, suffering, from *pathein*, to suffer. It may be argued that the true suffix is *-ic* and that *-et-* belongs to stems ending in *-et*; but those stems are subsidiary or derivative, as in *gen*(esis, -etic) and in *path*(etic). Cf:

**-etin**, in Chem, is a cpd suffix: *-et*(um)+chem *-in*. Thus *quercetin* corresponds to *quercin*.

**-etion**, as in *completion*, is simply the form taken by derivatives from the L 2nd conj, as compared with *-ation* from the 1st conj. A cpd. Base: *-ion*, q.v.

**-etive** corresponds, for the L 2nd conj (pres inf *-ēre*), to the *-ative*, q.v., deriving from the L 1st conj (*-āre*). Ex: *completive*, ML *complētīvus*, L *-īuus*.

**-etta** is the It 'answer' to F *-ette*, as *-etto* is the It 'answer' to F *-et*. It occurs in, e.g., *burletta*, dim of *burla*, jest, mockery, and *operetta*, dim of Mus *opera*.

**-ette**, n, is the f counterpart of the m *-et* (2)

above. In E words, esp those formed by analogy, the dim force is often lost, as in *etiquette*. Exx: *cigarette*, lit a little cigar, adopted from F; *serviette*, form-adopted but sense-adapted from F, which derives it from *servir*, v used as n; *undergraduette*, *-ette* being substituted for *-ate*.

**-etto**—cf *-etta* above—occurs only in a few italianisms, e.g. *falsetto*, dim of *falso*, and *stiletto*, dim of *stilo*, a dagger.

**-etum**, as in *arboretum*, a plantation, *pinetum*, a pine grove, *rosetum*, a rosery, denotes 'plantation, grove, clump'; all three words come straight from L, as does the less-used *quercetum*, a plantation of oak-trees. The L basic words are resp *arbor, pinus* (s *pin*), *rosa* (s *ros*-), *quercus* (s *querc*-). The basic sense of L *-ētum* seems to be: 'group, collection' (of plants, esp shrubs and trees) or even 'collectivity' (of plants).

**-ety** displaces *-ity* in certain nn derived from L adjj and advv having stem in *-i*; e.g. *ebriety*, from *ēbrietās*, from *ēbrius*; *dubiety*, from *dubietās* from *dubius*; *propriety*, from *proprietās* from *proprius*; *satiety*, from *satietās* from *satis*. The Romans avoided the ending *-iitas*.

**-eur** (1), as in *grandeur* and *hauteur*, both gallicisms, is the F form of L *-or*, abstract suffix, connoting state or quality. But F *liqueur* answers to L *liquor*, where *-or* connotes agency or materiality.

**-eur** (2), agential: adopted from F *-eur*, itself from L *-or*. Exx: *amateur*, L *amātor*; *connoisseur*, OF *conoisseor*, from *conoistre*, to know, from L *cognōscere*; *littérateur* (accent usu omitted), LL *litterātor*.

**-ey** (1), adj, as in *clayey* and *skyey*—that is, for nn ending in *-y*—takes the place of *-y*, adj, q.v. below.

**-ey** (2), n, as in *attorney*, from OF *atorné*, has been described as the weak form of *-ee* (*lessee, patentee, refugee*), q.v. above. (Sweet.) Ex: *journey*, OF *journee*, a day's duration. The OF-F *-ée* and OF-F *-é* may derive from L *-āta*, f, or *-ātus*, m.

**-ey** (3), n, as in *Turkey*, is a variant of *-y*, n (q.v. below), as it occurs in names of countries; it comes, usu via ME and OF *-ie*, from L *-ia*. *Turkey*=ME *Turkie*, from OF, from *Turc*, a Turk.

**-ey** (4), n dim, a rare var of *-y* (9), q.v. Exx: *donkey, monkey*.

**-ey** (5), n: OE *-ig*. Ex: *honey*, OE *hunig*, akin to OS *honeg* and OHG *honag*. A suffix of obscure meaning.

**-ezza**. An It abstract-n suffix.

[**-fare**. See Dict at FARE.]

[**-fex**; **-fic**. See Compound-forming Elements—at *fac*-.]

[**-fold**. See Dict at FOLD.]

[**-ful**. See Dict at FULL.]

[**-fy**. See Elements at *fac*-.]

**-gle** (1), in nn, is, I think, only an app suffix. In such words as *beagle, bugle, eagle, shingle*, the *-g-* would appear to belong to the stem.

-gle (2), v, is an extension of echoic (and freq) -le, q.v.; as in *straggle, wriggle*.

-go hardly occurs outside of -*ago* and -*igo*, qq.v.

[-ham, in place-names: see Dict at HOME.]

-head, as in *godhead* and *maidenhead*, is now rare for the var -*hood*, as in *boyhood, childhood, girlhood, knighthood, manhood, womanhood*, from nn, and in *hardihood*, from adj, the conn being 'state, quality; rank'. Webster notes the resultant secondary senses, 'concrete instance'—as in *falsehood*, and (from the nuance 'rank') 'collectivity', as in *brotherhood* and *sisterhood*. Whereas -*head* originates in OE -*hed*, -*hood* originates in OE -*hōd* or -*hād*, from the since-disappeared independent words *hōd* or *hād* (var *hed*), state, condition, quality, (?) hence rank, order. Exx: *brotherhood*= *brother*+-*hood*; *childhood*, from OE *cildhād*; *falsehood*=*false*+-*hood*; *girlhood*=*girl*+-*hood*; *godhead*, from ME *godhed*; *hardihood*=*hardy*+ -*hood*; *knighthood*, from OE *cnihthād*, collective *youth*; *maidenhead* app=var of *maidenhood*, from OE *maegdenhād*; *manhood*=*man*+-*hood*; *sisterhood*=*sister*+-*hood*; *womanhood*=*woman*+-*hood*. OE -*hād*, -*hed*, or their orig independents, have cognates in OS *hēd* and OHG *heit* (whence the very common G suffix -*heit*) and, with different meanings, Go *haidus*, manner, and ON *heither*, honour; prob also Skt *ketu*, brightness (cf *citra*, bright); and perh E HOT. For the native history of this suffix, see esp Sweet's *English Grammar*, I, 461-2.

-hood. See prec.

-i (1), adj. *Iraki*, of Irak, hence a native of Irak; *Punjabi*, of the Punjab, hence a native of the Punjab—Hindi *Panjābī*, from *Panjāb*. An Indo-Iranian adj suffix.

-i (2), n, indicates the pl of L 2nd-dec nn in -*us*, as in *radii* from *radius*; cf *foci*, pl of *focus*. But also of L 2nd-dec nn in -*er*, as *pueri* from *puer*, a boy, and *agri* from *ager*, a field.

-i (3), n, occurs also in the pl of It nn in -*o*, as *banditti* for It pl *banditi*, from *bandito*, and *stiletti* from *stiletto*, or in -*e*, as in *dilettanti* from *dilettante*.

-i-, connective, has been adopted from L, where it occurs in true cpds, as ML *omnivorus* (*omn*-+ -*i*-+-*vorus*), whence E *omnivorous*, and in cpds with second element a terminal, as *aurifer* (*aur*-+ -*i*-+-*fer*), whence E *auriferous*. Its basic conn, where it does not merely signify 'and' or 'connected with', is 'of' or 'for' or 'like'. As -*o*- is the specifically Gr connective, so -*i*- is the characteristically L connective.

Sometimes a thematic -*i*-, i.e. an -*i*- belonging to the stem, resembles a connective -*i*-; occ it is difficult to distinguish them, esp in words derived from L nn in -*ius* or -*ium* or -*ia*. Thus *fluvial* comes from ML *fluviālis*, L *fluuiālis*, from L *fluuis* (ML *fluvius*), which has s *fluui*- (ML *fluvi*-); the adj suffix is therefore -*ālis*, E -*al*. In *clavichord*, ML *clavichordium* the first element is *clav*- (L

*clau*-), the -*i*- is connective, the second element is -*chordium*, from *chorda*, because L *clauis*, ML *clavis*, has s *clau*-, ML *clav*-, not *claui*-, *clavi*-. Whereas *fluuius* is declined fluui-*um*, -*i*, -*o*, pl -*i*, -*os*, -*orum*, -*is*, with s obviously *fluui*-, *clauis* is declined clau-*em*, -*is*, -*i*, -*e*, pl -*es*, -*ium*, -*ibus*, with s obviously *clau*-.

-ia, in words adopted from L, represents either a f sing, of abstract conn, or a neu pl of nn in -*ium*, of concrete or objective conn; in words from Gr, whether direct or via L, -*ia* likewise represents either a f sing, abstract, of nn in -*ia* or a neu pl, concrete, of nn in -*ion*. Strictly the -*a* is identical with -*a* (4) above, for the -*i*- is the connective listed above as -*i*-. There are also many mod words, not deriving from either Gr or L, but formed anl with Gr or L sing nn in -*ia* or with Gr or L neu pl nn in -*ia*.

Exx: (countries) *Mauretania*, L *Mauretania* or *Mauritania*, from *Mauri*, the Moors, from Gr *Mauroi*—*Media*, L *Media*, Gr *Mēdia*—*Rhodesia*= (Cecil) *Rhodes*+-*ia*; (diseases) *neuralgia*, a Mod L coinage—*aphasia*, revived by Med from Gr *aphasia*; (Chem) *morphia*, a Med coinage from *Morpheus*; (miscellaneous from Gr or L) *magnesia*, *phantasmagoria*, *sepia*, and, pll, *bacteria* (Gr) *memorabilia* (L), *Bacchanalia* and other Classical festivals; (generic sing names of plants) *dahlia*, *wistaria*; (Zoo pl names, from or on L, of orders, etc.) *Reptilia*.

-iac. See -*ac*, 2nd para.

-ial+a thematic or a connective -*i*-+-*al*, adj, q.v. above; cf L -*iālis*, m and f, and -*iāle*, neu. Exx: *fluvial*=*fluvi*- (L *fluui*-)+-*al*, adj (L -*ālis*), with thematic -*i*-; *clavial*=*clav*- (L *clau*-)+-*i*-+ -*al*, where, clearly, the -*i*- is connective. In short, -*ial* is a cpd suffix.

-ian, adj—hence n; when n without originating adj, the n has been formed anl with other -*ian* nn. This suffix usu comes either direct from L -*iānus* (f -*iāna*, neu -*iānum*) or through F -*ien*, f -*ienne*; occ it comes from F adjj or nn formed anl; in ModE formations it is mostly analogous with other E words. In many words from L or F, and indeed in the few L words deriving from Gr -*ianos*, where, by the way, the n may precede the adj, the -*i*- is connective, as it is in most ModE words. A cpd suffix: cf -*ial* above.

Exx: *Christian* (adj, very early, from n): L *christiānus*, n and adj: Gr *khristianos*, n, from *Khristos*, the Christ, where, the s being *khrist*-, the -*i*- must be connective; *barbarian*, adj and n: F *barbarien*, on L *\*barbariānus*, s *barbar*-; *Kantian*, adj and n=*Kant*+-*ian* (-*i*- connective +-*an*). Sweet has remarked that its conn is the same as that of -*an* and that it is 'especially frequent in adjectives and nouns expressing occupation, rank, etc.: *historian, librarian, musician, physician, tragedian; patrician, plebeian*'.

-iana (1) represents the L f sing or neu pl of, or corresponding to, adjj and nn in -*iānus*; 'from use of -*ana* after stems ending in *i*' (Webster).

-iana (2). See -*ana*.

**-iat.** See *-eat* above.

**-ible.** See (*-ble* at) *-bility* above.

**-ic** (1), adj, general conn 'of', hence 'belonging to', whence also 'for' and 'with', hence 'connected with'; hence, further, 'characteristic of, like' or 'characterized by'.

Now, *-ic* adjj may be native words, formed anl with other E adjj in *-ic*; the ME form, if there be one, may be *-ike*, but is more prob *-yke*; and *-yke* or *-ike* or EE *-ick* can derive either from F *-ique* or from L *-icus* (the usu origin of F *-ique*), whether directly or via F, or from Gr *-ikos* (often the origin of L *-icus*), whether directly or, as usu, via L *-icus* (and perh F *-ique*). Although generically the L suffix *-icus* owes much to Gr *-ikos*, an *-icus* adj need not come from an *-ikos* adj; it freq derives from a L n, and that n need not be of Gr origin. This suffix, whether *-ikos* or *-icus* or *-ique* or *-ick* or *-ic*, is so common at every historical and linguistic stage that, at all stages after the Gr (and perhaps there too), it was virtually autonomous.

Exx: *angelic=angelick, angelyke*: F *angélique*: L *angelicus*: Gr *angelikos* (ἀγγελικός), from *angelos* (s *angel*-), ἄγγελος, an angel; *bucolic*, L *bucolicus*, Gr *boukolikos*; *pudic*, F *pudique*, L *pudicus*; *volcanic*, F *volcanique*, It *vulcanico*, an *-ico*, i.e. It, reshaping of ML *vulcānius*, L *uulcānius*, Vulcanian; *vitriolic*; F *vitriolique*; *Byronic= Byron*+*-ic*, prob after *Miltonic*.

Whereas OED and Webster regard *-ic* (*-ique*, *-icus*, *-ikos*) as a genuine suffix, app consisting in L of *-ic*-+*-us* and in Gr of *-ik*-+*-os*, Skeat asserts that the *i* is thematic and that the true suffix is *-c* (L *-cus*, Gr *-kos*); his examples, *civic* and *logic*, are particularly unfortunate, for, of L *ciuis* (ML *civis*), the s is *ciu*- (ML *civ*-) and of Gr *logikos* the s is *log*-, as it is of *logos*.

**-ic** (2), n. Simply the *-ic* adj, as prec, used as a n, as in *classic* and *magic*. The n may have been one as early as in Gr, although even that Gr n began as an adj, as in *music*; sometimes it is a L adj become L n and then taken over by E, as in *public*, (prob via F) from L *pūblicus*. Cf *-ics* below.

**-ical**, adj, is a cpd of *-ic*, adj+*-al*, adj, both as above. In general, it is an elaboration of *-ic*; never an intensification of *-al*. Where the two forms *-ic* and *-ical* co-exist and there is no need to differentiate, the longer form dies out, e.g. *generical* has given way to *generic*. But where there is a need to differentiate, either the two forms are retained, with one form acquiring a different nuance, or, if there is only one form, the other form (whether *-ic* or *-ical*) is created. Where a word in *-ic* or *-ics* is used solely as a n, the corresponding adj is *-ical*: thus, *music*—*musical*, *politics*—*political*. The distinction between *politic* and *political*, *ethic* and *ethical*, *comic* and *comical*, and so forth, is a matter of usage, not merely of suffixes.

**-ice** (1), n: ME *-ice* or *-ise*: OF *-ice* or *-ise*: LL *-icius* (etc.): L *-itius*, f *-itia*, neu *-itium*, but esp *-itia*, for that suffix occurs freq in abstract nn, and, not much less, *-itium*, connoting 'act or period of' whatever the adj or v indicates. Exx:

*justice*, OF *justice* (or *-ise*), ML *jūstitia*, L *iūstitia*, from *iūstus* (s *iūst*-, ML *jūst*-), just, equitable, fairminded; *novice*, adopted from OF, from ML *novicius* or *novitius*, L *nouicius*, *-itius*, from *nouus*, new; *service*, through OF from ML *servitium*, L *seruitium*, from *seruīre*, to serve.

**-ice** (2), v: from OF *-iser*, from L *-icāre*, as in AE 'to prac*tice*'.

**-icel**, as in *radicel* (cf F *radicelle*), a dim of *radix*, a root, is a cpd: *-ic*+*-el*, dim suffix. Cf *-icle* and *-icule* below.

**-ician**, conn 'an exponent of, an expert in' (a field indicated by the n), as in *magician, musician*: F *-icien*, a cpd of *-ic*, q.v.+F *-ien*, q.v. at *-ian* above. Among mod formations, devised anl, are such horrors as *mortician* (*mort*-, o/s of L *mors*, death+the *-ician* of *physician*) and *beautician* (*beaut*(*y*)+the *-ician* of *magician*).

**-icism**, strictly a cpd (*-ic*, as above+*-ism*, as below), derives from Gr *-ikismos*, often via L *-icismus*; in some E words, *-icism* is added, not as the cpd it is, but as a simple suffix, with conn 'an example of the basic idea' implied by the s. Exx: *Atticism*, from Gr *attikismos*; *witticism=wit*+ euphonic *t*+*-icism*, prob after *criticism*. Cf:

**-icist**, as in *publicist* (F *publiciste*, G *Publizist*), has been modelled upon Gr agential nn in *-ikistēs*, itself a cpd—*-ik*-, which becomes *-ic*, and *-istēs*, which becomes *-ist*. Cf *simplicist*: *simpl*(ism)+ *-icist*.

**-icity**: F *icité*: L *-ıcitāt*-, o/s of the cpd suffix *-icitās* (*-ic*+*-itās*, q.v. at *-ity* below), with conn 'abstractness', esp 'quality of' (the adj involved). Exx: *felicity*, OF *felicité* (F *félicité*), L *fēlicitās*, o/s *fēlicitāt*-, from *fēlix*, happy; *rapacity*, L *rapācitās*, o/s *rapācitāt*-, from *rapāx*, addicted to seizing.

**-icle** derives from L *-icula*, f of the dim suffix *-iculus*, and is clearly a cpd of *-ic*, q.v. above, and *-ula*, f of the dim *-ulus*, q.v. at *-ule* below; cf also *-le*. Exx: *particle*, L *particula*, dim of *pars* (o/s *part*-), a part; *radicle*, L *rādicula*, dim of *rādix*, a root. Cf *-icel* and *-icule*.

**-icon** occurs in a few grecisms, such as *ono-masticon*, through ML from Gr *onomastikon*, elliptical for *o. biblion*, a book concerned with names (*onoma*, a name), and Ranulphus Higden's *Polycronycon* or *Polychronicon*, and the obs *chronicon*, a chronicle. Clearly *-icon=*Gr *-ikon*, neu of *-ikos*: *-ik*-+*-on*, neu n suffix.

**-icose**, as in *bellicose* (L *bellicōsus*, either an extension of *bellicus*, of war, itself from *bellum*, war, or direct from *bellum*), would appear to be a cpd: *-ic*-, q.v. above+*-ose*, q.v. below.

**-ics**, indicating, as in *ethics, metaphysics, politics*, a science or a system and connoting 'matters concerned with' the n implied in the s, imitates Gr *-ika* (L *-ica*), neu pl of the adj *-ikos*, as in *ta ēthika*, τὰ ἠθικά, (lit) the ethical matters, hence ethics; the sing, predominant—in, e.g., *logic, magic, music*—until c1590, has, e.g. in *ethic* and *metaphysic*, been revived in late C19-20, prob after F and, less, G practice: cf F *l'éthique* (f) and *la* *métaphysique* and G *Ethik* (f) and *Metaphysik* (f). Sweet has, of *mathematics* (Gr *ta mathēmatika*), well said that it is an imitation of the Gr usage, 'aided by the English habit of making adjectives into nouns by adding the plur *-s*, as in *greens*, *news* and the vulgar *rheumatics=rheumatism*'. See *-ic* (1) and (2) above.

**-icular.** The adj answering to:

**-icule** derives from the cpd L suffix *-iculus* (m), *-icula* (f), *-iculum* (neu): *-ic*, q.v. above+*-ulus* (*-a*, *-um*), q.v. below at *-ule*; it is, therefore, an extended dim. Exx: *reticule*, F *réticule*, L *rēticulum* (itself adopted by E as a term in An and Bot and Zoo), dim of *rēte*, a net: *monticule*, adopted from F, from LL *monticulus*, a little *mons* (o/s *mont-*) or mountain.

**-iculum** occurs in a few Sci and tech words. See prec, and cf *-icular*.

**-id** (1), adj, as in *acid, candid, liquid, morbid, placid, rabid, solid, splendid, turbid, vapid*, derives, sometimes via F *-ide*, from L *-idus*, f *-ida*, neu *-idum*; several of these words—esp *acid, liquid* and *solid*—are used derivatively as nn. Thus: *acid*, perh via F *acide*, from L *acidus*, from *acēre*, to be sour; *candid*, perh via F *candide*, from L *candidus*, from *candēre*, to be snow-white; *rabid*, L *rabidus*, from *rabere*, to rave.

**-id** (2), n. See prec.

**-id** (3), n. Prob suggested by *acid* in *-id* (1): *-id* in Chem=chem *-ide*, q.v. below.

**-id** (4), n, occurs in words from Gr *-is*, gen *-idos*, often via L *-is*, gen *-idis* (occ existing independently of Gr) and then via F *-ide* (which may come from L only or, indeed, be formed anl in F itself); a few E words exist autonomously— i.e., by anl formation. Exx: *chrysalid*, via L from Gr *khrusalis*, gen *khrusalidos*; *pyramid*, L *pyramis*, gen *pyramidis*, from Gr *puramis*, gen *puramidos*. In Bot it denotes 'member of' (a family denoted by the s), as in *amaryllid* (Gr *Amarullis*, gen *-idos*); therefore cf:

**-id** (5), n, either derives from and is used for *-ida*, q.v. below, as in *acarid*, or denotes a member of a Zoo family (*idae*, q.v. below), as in *clupeid*, one of the *Clupeidae* or herrings. Cf both *-id* (4) and esp:

**-id** (6), n, patronymic, as in *Nereid* (via L from Gr *Nēreis*, gen *Nēreidos*), daughter of *Nēreus*, derives from L *-is*, gen *-idis*, nom pl *-ides*, from Gr *-is*, gen *-idos*, nom pl *-ides*. E uses it esp in Astr—e.g., *Leonid*, one of the shooting stars associated with the constellation *Leo* (L *leō*, gen *leōnis*)—and in the names of epic or mock-epic poems, e.g. *Aeneid*, from the o/s *Aenēid-* of L *Aenēis*, Virgil's epic about Aeneas. Cf *-ad* (2, *c*) and *-id* (4) and (5) and also *-idae* and:

**-ida** is a Mod L suffix, prompted by *-id* (6) and, in Zoo, indicating groups, classes, orders, as in *Arachnida*, from Gr *arakhnē*, a spider, via LL *arachne*, and *Scorpionida*, from L *scorpiō* (o/s *scorpiōn-*), a scorpion. The adj and derivative n are formed in *-idan*.

**-idae**, used in patronymic group-names, e.g.

*Seleucidae* (from *Seleucus* Nicator), represents the pl of L *-ides*, indicating 'descendant of', from Gr *-ides*: cf, therefore, *-id* (5). The adj is formed in *-idan*, e.g. *Seleucidan*. In Zoo it denotes a family of animals and there it takes the place of the gen suffix in the name of the most important or best-known genus, thus: Equ*idae*, from *equi*, the gen sing of *equus*, a horse.

**-idan**, adj. See *-ida* and *-idae*.

**-ide**, in Chem, indicates a cpd, as in *chloride* (from *chlor*ine). All such nn have been formed anl with *oxide*.

**-idin, -idine**, are chem cpd suffixes, consisting of chem *-id* (for *-ide*)+chem *-in* or *-ine*: cf, therefore, *-ide* and *-ine*, n.

**-idinous**, adj of nn in *-ido*: L *-īdinōsus*, adj from *-īdō*, n: general conn 'emotional state or condition'. Best ex: *libidinous*, perh via *libidineuse*, f of F *libidineux*, from L *libīdinōsus*, formed by attaching the common adj suffix *-ōsus* (conn 'of the quality implied by the n') to *libīdin-*, o/s of *libīdō*, pleasure, esp sexual pleasure, desire, lust, itself formed by attaching to *lib-*, the s of the impersonal v *libet*, it pleases, the rare suffix *-īdō*, with vague conn 'n of (emotional) state or condition'.

**-idity**, abstract n, attaches *-ity*, q.v., to *-id*, adj, q.v. at *-id* (1). Thus: *timidity*, from L *timiditās* (r *tim-*)—gen *timiditātis*—from the adj *timidus*.

**-ie**, formerly a spelling of *-y*, n, as in *beautie*, is, in ModE, restricted to use as a dim, notably in pet-names and other endearments, thus: *birdie*, from *bird*; *dearie*, from *dear* (n); *Johnnie*, though still often *Johnny*, from *John*. Cf *-y* (6).

**-ience, -iency**, n; **-ient**, adj. Cpds of connective, sometimes of thematic *-i-*, q.v.+*-ence, -ency*, qq.v. at *-ance*, and *-ent*, q.v. at *-ant* (1).

**-ier** (1): F *-ier*: L *-ārius* or, occ, the VL *-erius*. See *-eer* (1). Exx: *cavalier*, adopted from F, from It *cavaliere* from LL *caballārius*, from *caballus*, a horse; *chevalier*, adopted from OF, from *caballārius*; *grenadier*, adopted from F, from F *grenade*, from ML (pomum) *grānātum*, a much-grained, i.e. seeded, apple.

**-ier** (2), n suffix occurring in words of ME origin of various sources, general conn 'doer':
(a) from OF-MF *-ier*, as in *cottier*, OF *cotier*, from *cote*, a cote, as in *dovecote, sheepcote*;
(b) as in *collier*: see *-er* (6);
(c) *i* for final *y* of a v+agential *-er*: see *-er* (4). Ex: *carrier*.

**-ies** occurs only in a few nn adopted from L, as *aciēs*, acuity of vision (with stem *ac-* as in L *ācer* and E *acerate*), and as *rabiēs*, madness. Its general conn is 'an example of the adj implied'.

**-iff**, adj hence n, as esp in *caitiff*, derives from ONF or OF *-if*, itself from ML *-īvus* (*captīvus*) from L *-īuus*. Ex: *plaintiff* (adj become n), OF *plaintif* (adj). Cf *-ive* below.

[**-ify.** See Elements at *fac-*.]

**-ige**, as in *Félibrige*, the brotherhood of *Félibres* or Provençal writers, seems to come from L *-igium*, an objective n-suffix. (*Félibre*, from Prov *Felibre*, prob from ML *felibris*, a nursling.)

**-iginous**, adj of L nn in *-īgō*, which has conn 'physical weakness or deterioration'; the adj is based upon *-īgin-*, the o/s of *-īgō*; the n itself is built upon the pres inf s of vv in *-ere*. Exx: *impetiginous*, ML *impetīginōsus*, adj of L *impetīgō*, from *impetere*, to assail; *vertiginous*, ML *vertiginōsus* (L *uert-*), from ML *vertigō* (L *uertīgō*), from L *uertere*, ML *vertere*, to turn.

**-ikin** is an extended form of *-kin*, q.v. Ex: *manikin*, prob from D *manneken*, but reshaped thus: *man*+connective *-i-*+*kin*.

**-il** (1), adj. See *-ile* (1), adj.

**-il** (2), n=chem *-ile*, q.v.

**-ile** (1), adj; **-il**, adj. The former comes usu direct from L *-ilis*, neu *-ile*; the latter through F *-il*, F *-ile*, or OF *-ile*. General conn: 'tending to' do or be whatever the implied v or n denotes. Thus: *fragile*, (perh via F) from L *fragilis*, from *frangere*, to break, but *frail* via OF *fraile*; *mobile*, L *mōbilis*, neu *mōbile*; *fossil*, F *fossile*; *civil*, F *civil*, ML *cīvīlis*, L *cīuīlis*; *gentile*, L *gentīlis*.

**-ile** (2), n; **-il**: chem suffixes. The *-ile* nn are formed as—some of them, on—*nitrile*, *nitr-*+*-ile* adj used as n; *-il* is a var, as in *nitril*, *anisil*.

**-ility**, abstract n, is a cpd of *-il(e)*, adj+*-ity*, q.v. below. Exx: *civility*, OF *civilité*, ML *cīvīlitās*, o/s *cīvīlitāt-* (L *cīuīlitāt-*); *fragility*, L *fragilité*, L *fragilitās*, o/s *fragilitāt-*.

**-im**, as in *cherubim* (sing *cherub*, H *kerūbh*) and *seraphim* (H *ṣerāphīm*), is a n suffix indicating the pl and belonging to H; the var *-in* (*cherubin*, *seraphin*) is incorrect.

**-in** (1). See prec.

**-in** (2), as in *cousin*, *dolphin*, *goblin*, *vermin*, and (things) *bulletin*, *resin*, represents adj (see the var *-ine*) become n and derives, often through F *-in*, f *-ine*, always ult from L *-inus*, f *-ina*, L *-inum*. Exx: *bulletin*, adopted from F, from It *bullettino*, dim of *bulla*, taken over from L; *cousin*, OF *cousin*, earlier *cosin*, ML *cosīnus*, L *consobrīnus*; *goblin*, F *gobelin*, ML *gobelīnus*, perh Gr *kobalos*; *resin*, F *résine*, L *rēsīna*, Gr *rhētinē*; *vermin*, OF *vermin(e)*, perh from ML *vermen*, o/s *vermin-*, rather than from ML *vermis* (L *uermis*).

**-in** (3): *-inem*, acc of L nn in *-ō*. Exx: *margin*, ME *margine*, L *marginem* (o/s *margin-*), acc of *margō*; *origin*, F *origine*, L *originem*; *virgin*, OF *virgine*, L *uirginem*. (Nesfield.)

**-in** (4). In Pharm, *-in* occurs in 'names of remedial preparations, often corresponding to adjectives in *-ic*, as in antipyrin' (Webster): a usage closely akin to that of chem *-in*, q.v. at *-ine*, chem n.

**-ina** (1), f suffix in L (? on archetypal *fēmina*), reappearing in It and Sp and in mod imitations, esp in Proper Names; when it is a queen's or other royal name, the influence of *regina* is perceptible. Exx: *Wilhelmina* and Sp *Guillelmina*; *czarina*, *tsarina*. It corresponds to m *-inus*, q.v. esp at *-ine* (2). Cf *-ine* (4) and:

**-ina** (2), neupl suffix of L adj *-inus*. Zoo uses it, with *animalia* understood, in names of orders and sub-orders, thus: *Acarina*, from Mod L *Acarus*, from Gr *akari*, a cheese mite. Cf:

**-inae**, fpl suffix of L adj *-inus*. Zoo uses it, with *bēstiae* (beasts) understood, in names of sub-families, thus: *Felinae*, from *fel-*, s of *Felidae*, the cat family, a Mod L term coined from L *fēlis*, a cat. Cf *-ina* (2).

**-ine** (1), adj of—or imitative of—Gr origin: Gr *-inos*, often via L *-inus*: conn 'made of, of the nature of, like' (e.g., a material specified by the n implied). Exx: *adamantine*, L *adamantinus*, Gr *adamantinos*, from *adamant-*, o/s of *adamas*; *amethystine*, L *amethystinus*, Gr *amethustinos*; *ivorine*, OF *ivorin*, f *ivorine* (Mod *ivoirin*, *-e*); *opaline*, from *opal*, after *amethystine*, *crystalline*, etc. Cf:

**-ine** (2), adj, of L origin *-īnus*, f *-īna*, neu *-īnum*—often via F *-in*, f *-ine*: conn 'of' or 'belonging to', hence 'like'. Thus: *canine*, L *canīnus*, from *canis* (s *can-*), a dog; *feminine*, OF *feminin*, f *feminine* (Mod F *féminin*, *-e*), L *fēminīnus*, from *fēmina*, a woman. Etym, this suffix is identical with *-ine* (1); it belongs, however, to indigenous L words, not to learnèd L words of Gr origin.

**-ine** (3), abstract n, as in *discipline* and *medicine*; L *-īna*, usu via F *-ine*. Thus: *discipline*, adopted from OF, from L *disciplīna*, from *discipulus*, a learner; *medicine*, adopted from OF (cf Mod F *médecine*), L *medicīna*, from *medicus*, a physician; *rapine*, (perh through F *rapine*) from L *rapīna*, from *rapere*, to seize.

**-ine** (4), n: a f suffix, usu from F *-ine*, but answering to L *-ina* (see *-ina* (1) above). Exx: *heroine*, (perh via F *héroïne*) from L *hēroina*, from Gr *hēroinē*, the f of *hērōs*; *landgravine*, prob either from D *landgravin* or from G *Landgräfin*, the f of *Landgraf*, but perh adopted from F *landgravine*; *Albertine*, adopted from F; *Caroline*, adopted from F, prob from It *Carolina*, ? dim of *Carola*, f of ML *Carolus*.

**-ine** (5), n. In Chem, *-ine* or *-in* denotes, as in *chlorine*, an element or, as in *arsine*, a cpd. In Organic Chem, it is (a) a var of *-yne*, q.v.; (b) a basic cpd, as *quinine*. Organic bases: *-ine*; neutral substances: *-in*, as in *gelatin* (but also *gelatine*, cf F *gélatine*, from L *gelāta*). In Chem, *-in* is gradually displacing *-ine*. In Min, *-ine* (now rare)=*-ite*, q.v. (Based upon Webster.)

**-ineae**, fpl of L *-ineus* (roughly 'of the nature of', hence 'like'), occurs in Bot names of tribes or sub-families; Webster adduces *Abietineae*, from L *abiēs* (o/s *abiet-*), a fir tree.

**-ing** (1), adj, derives from *-ing*, suffix of the presp: 'Birds that are habitually *singing* become known as "*singing birds*" '. This *-ing* derives, by confusion with the vbl n suffix *-inge* (later *-ing*), from *-inde*, a late form of OE *-ende*; naturally enough, presp *-ing* ended by becoming identical in form with vbl n *-ing*. The OE *-ende* is akin to Go *-and-* and to L *-ant-*, *-ent-* (o/ss of *-ans*, *-ens*) and, far back, to Skt *-ant-*; cf also the Gr *-ont-* (o/s of *-ōn*). Cf:

**-ing** (2), vbl n: ME *-ing*: OE *-ing*, but also *-ung*,

akin to D -*ing* and G -*ung*: deriving, therefore, from vv but later, analogously, from nn, advv, etc.: gen conn, 'action abstractly regarded' (action, not act). 'A *shouting* was heard, a *killing* was suspected.' The association is often merely causal, actively in 'The *making* of a bed isn't as simple as it sounds', passively in 'the *writing* on the wall'—or collective, as in 'There's not enough material for *bedding*'. Cf -*ings* below.

-**ing** (3), in nn denoting 'a belonging to, (hence) a descent from', esp, therefore, in patronymics, as *atheling*, OE *aetheling*, a noble, from *aethelo*, nobility or high lineage, and in dimm, as *wilding*, an uncultivated plant, and *shilling*, OE *scilling*, identical with the OHG and OS forms. Here, prob, are to be included such fish-names as *herring* and *whiting*.

-**ing** (4), n, in place-names, sometimes=*ing*, a meadow (ON *eng*), but sometimes a patronymic, as in *Reading*. But, as Ekwall has shown, geog and topo -*ing* is very obscure indeed; app he thinks the patronymic conn to be preponderant. In the cpd suffixes -*ingham* and -*ington*, -*ing* is almost certainly patronymic, as in *Buckingham* and *Wellington*.

-**ings**, n, is the pl of vbl n -*ing* (see 2nd -*ing* above), with conn 'something casually associated with the act, often esp in the pl; as, sweep*ings*, earn*ings*, etc.' (Webster.)

? -**iny**; -**eny**: as in *ignominy*, *larceny*, resp from F *ignominie*, L *ignōminia*, disgrace, and, via F, from L *latrōcinium*. These are Nesfield's suffixes; I'd say that *ignōminia*=*ig* (=*in*, not)+*nōmin*-, o/s of *nōmen*, name+abstract -*ia*, and that the suffix in *larceny* is -*ceny* for -*ciny*, as in the obs syn *latrociny*, *latrōcinium* being *latrō*, a thief+-*cinium*.

-**ion**, abstract n: either from F -*ion*, which derives from—or has been formed anl with—L -*iōn*-, part of the o/s of abstract nn in -*iō*. The conn is either 'action' or 'process' (or a result thereof) or 'state' or 'condition' or 'a thing so conditioned'. Exx: *action*, through MF from L *actiō*, o/s *actiōn*-, from *act*-, s of *actus*, pp of *agere*, to do; *condition*, OF *condicion*, L *conditiōn*- (better *con-diciōn*-), o/s of *conditiō*, better *condiciō*; *dominion*, adopted from OF, from *dominiōn*-, o/s of ML *dominiō*, from L *dominium* (as in *condominium*); *solution*, OF *solucion*, L *solūtiōn*-, o/s of *solūtiō*, from *soluere*, to loosen.

Cf -*ation*, -*etion* above, and -*ition*, -*ution* below: these are simply extensions of -*ion*. Cf also the merely apparent suffixes -*sion*, -*tion*, qq.v. at the former.

-**ior**=the L comp adj suffix -*ior*, sometimes via the F derivative -*ieur*. Thus: *exterior*, adopted from L, the comp of *exterus*, outward, and *interior*, adopted from L; *inferior*, adopted from L, as, through OF, was *superior*. Cf -*er* (1), the E cognate, and -*or*, a L var.

-**ious**, conn 'of the nature of', in E adds -*ous* (q.v. below) to thematic *i* and, in L, adds -*iōsus* to thematic *i*, as in *invidious*, ML *invidiōsus*, L *inuidiōsus*, from *inuidia*. Adjj in -*ious* often answer

to nn in -*ion*, as *ambitious*, L *ambitiōsus*, perh via F *ambitieuse*, f of *ambitieux*.

-**ique** (1), adj, is the F form of the suffix -*ic* (see -*ic* (1) above), for which, in EE, it often occurs; it survives in *antique*, adopted from F, from L *antiquus*. Note also *oblique* and *unique*. Cf:

-**ique** (2), n, as in *critique* (a criticism), adopted from F, which probably took it from Gr (*hē*)*kritikē* (*tekhnē*), (the) critical (art); as in *physique*, adopted from F, from L *physica*, from Gr *phusikē* (f adj used as n); and as in *technique*, adopted from F, which derived *la techique* from the adj *technique*, from Gr *tekhnikos*: this -*ique* corresponds to -*ic*, n (q.v. at -*ic* (2) above). Cf also -*ics*.

-**is** (1), adj: a Scots and N dial form of -*ish*, connoting 'like'.

-**is** (2), n, occurs, as a recognizable suffix, only in words adopted or, at most, slightly adapted from Gr or L -*is*, as in *Artemis* and bot *Arabis*. In Proper Names, -*is* conr*ɔ*tes 'descent'; in plant- and animal-life names, 'origin in, (hence) of the nature of'.

-**isation**. See -*ization* below.

-**ise** (1), n, is a survival of ME -*ise*, var of -*ice*, q.v. above. Ex: *franchise*, adopted from OF-F, from *franchir*, to free. Such modern words as *expertise* come straight from F.

-**ise** (2), v: a var of -*ize*, q.v.

-**ish** (1), adj: OE -*isc*, akin to OHG -*isc*, Go -*isks*, ON -*iskr*, Gr -*iskos*; cf It -*esco* and ML -*iscus* (as in *Franciscus*, Frankish), app of Gmc origin, but akin to Gr -*iskos*. General conn: 'of'— 'belonging to', hence 'resembling'. Formed from: (1) National or tribal names, as in *English*, OE *Englisc*, from *Engle*, the Angles; *Frankish*, of the Franks, hence, as n, their language. (2) From Common Nouns, as in *boyish* (*boy*+-*ish*), *childish* (OE *cildisc*), *selfish* (*self*+-*ish*), *womanish* (*woman* +-*ish*); such adjj as *childish*, *womanish* and esp *selfish* have contributed to the unfavourable tinge so often attaching to adj -*ish*. (3) From adjj, and tending to mean 'somewhat', as *coldish* and *warmish*, *tallish* and *shortish*, and esp in colour-adjj, as *bluish*, *greenish*, *whitish*. These link with such adjj from nn as *bookish* and *feverish*, with their conn 'verging upon' or 'tending to resemble'.

-**ish** (2), n. From the adj, esp in languages, as *English*, *Gaulish*, *Swedish*, *Turkish*; or from the v, as in *polish*. But in several words it represents L -*ix* (gen -*icis*), as in *radish*, It *radice*, L *rādix* (o/s *rādic*-).

-**ish** (3), v: ME -*issen* or -*isshen*, OF-F -*iss*-, occurring in the presp, the ind pres pl, the pres subj; -*iss*- app derives from or is modelled upon VL -*isc*-, pres inf -*iscere*; in (at least orig) inch vv —cf -*esce* (L-*ēscere*) above. Exx: *finish*, OF *fenir*, or, as very soon, *finir*, or rather from such forms as *finissant*, *finisse*, *finissent*, *finissons*, *finessez*, (perhaps via VL *\*finiscere*) from L *finīre*; *flourish*, ME *florisshen* or *flurisshen*, OF *florir* or *flurir*, from VL *\*florīre* for L *florēre*; cf *abolish*, *establish*, *nourish*, *perish*, *polish*, *punish*. Hence, anl, in certain vv of E origin, as in *famish* from *famine*.

**-isk**, n: Gr *-iskos*, usu via L *-iscus*; basic conn: 'little'. Exx: *asterisk*, (lit) a little star, L *asteriscus*, Gr *asteriskos*, dim of *astēr*, a star; *basilisk*, L *basiliscus*, Gr *basiliskos*, (lit) a little king, transferred to a kind of serpent, from *basileus* (s *basil-*), a king; *disc*, L *discus*, Gr *diskos*; *obelisk*, L *obeliscus*, Gr *obeliskos*, from *obelos*, a pillar. In *tamarisk*, from LL *tamariscus*, the ulterior origin is unknown. As perh in *discus*, the *-isk* need not always be dim; the form is Gr, the very few L potentials being prob anl.

**-ism**=Gr *-ismos*, often via L *-ismus* or F *-isme*—or both; its conn is abstract; in general, it answers to vv in *-ize* and esp to agents in *-ist*, with their adjj in *-istic*. Its principal manifestations are these: whereas, formed from vv, it indicates action, as in *baptism*, OF *baptesme*, LL from Gr *baptismos*, from *baptizein*, to baptize, formed from nn it indicates the manner of action, as in *despotism*, or the conduct to be expected of the person implied, as in *heroism* or *Micawberism*. Very common too is the conn 'state, condition' (or the fact of being such-and-such), as in *hypnotism* or *barbarism*. Flowing from the general 'action' and 'state' connotations is that of 'doctrine' or 'mental or moral practice or habit', as in *materialism*, or 'adherence to' (a doctrine, a theory), as in *Catholicsm*. Hence, 'characteristic, esp a peculiarity', as in *Briticism*. In Med it denotes an abnormal state or condition, consequent upon excess in (the thing denoted by the n implied), as in *alcoholism*.

The adj is usu *-istic*; the agential n, *-ist*. Cf F *-isme*, *-istique*, *-iste*.

(Based upon Webster.)

**-ison**: an OF equivalent (varr *-isoun*, *-aisun*, etc.) to F *-aison*, usu *-ation* (cf *-ation* above), from L *-ātiōnem*, acc of nn in *-ātiō*. Ex: *comparison*, OF *comparisun*, L *comparātiōnem*, acc of *comparātiō*, a comparing.

**-issimus** occurs only in nn taken direct from the m sup of L adjj, as *Simplicissimus*.

**-ist**. (Cf *-ast*.) It comes from Gr *-istēs*, often through L *-ista* and occ through F *-iste* as well; an astonishing number of such words have been coined at the F stage. Answering to abstract n *-ism* and having adj *-istic*, *-ist* ult derives, I suspect, from Gr *histanai*, to stand, but it is usu associated with *-ize*, Gr *-izein*. Conn: one who does or practises, hence one who operates on or plays, and one who professes or, at the least, adheres to a doctrine or a theory. Exx: *theorist*, app *theor*(y)+ *-ist*; *atheist*, F *athéiste*.

**-istan**. See *-stan* below.

**-istic**: F *-istique*, L *-isticus*, Gr *-istikos*: but an *-istic* adj may have been coined at any of these four stages. The Gr *-istikos* corresponds to agent *-ist* or abstract *-ism*, hence to v *-ize*; itself it=*-ist-*+ *-ikos*, therefore cf both *-ist* and esp *-ic*, adj. Conn: of, of the nature of, belonging to. Exx: *characteristic*, Gr *kharaktēristikos*; *idealistic*=*ideal*+ *-istic*; *sophistic*, L *sophisticus*, Gr *sophistikos*.

**-istical** merely=*-istic*+*-al*, adj (q.v.).

**-it** (1), adj, derives from L *-itus*, pp suffix of 3rd-conj vv, as in *preterit*, adopted from MF, from L *praeteritus*, from *praeterīre*, to go by, pass beyond. Such adjj tend to become nn, as in *preterit*.

**-it** (2), n. See prec. But usu it represents the *-itus* indicating the 4th dec, as in *obit*, adopted from OF, from L *obitus* (gen *obitūs*); but it may also represent L *-itum*, consisting of thematic *-it-*+neu *-um*, as in *cubit*, from L *cubitum*. In such words as *adit*, the *-it* is the suffix of the 3rd person of the pres ind of L 3rd-conj vv. Then, too, it may descend from L *-ita* or Gr *-itēs*, as in *hermit*, OF (*h*)*ermite*, L *erēmīta*, Gr *erēmitēs*, and *Jesuit*, ML *Jesuita*, from *Jesus*. Cf *-ite*, n.

**-it** (3), v, as in *permit*, derives from the latter part of the s of a L v (*permit-t-ere*)—so with *admit*, *commit*, *demit*, *intermit*, *pretermit*, *remit*, *submit*, *transmit*.

**-ita** is a Sp f dim, adopted in a few Hispanicisms, as *Margarita* and *margarita*. Cf *-ito*.

**-ite** (1), adj, as in *exquisite* and *polite*, stands for L *-ītus* (f *-īta*, neu *-ītum*), pp suffix. Exx: *exquisite*, L *exquisītus*, pp of *exquirere*, to seek out—cf *requisite*; *favo*(u)*rite*, OF *favorit*, from It *favorito*, from *favorire*, to favour, from L *fauēre* (ML *favēre*); *polite*, L *polītus*, pp of *polīre*.

**-ite** (2), n: Gr *-itēs*, f *-itis*, often through L *-ita* and F *-ite*. Such words can, anl, be formed at any level. Conn: one who, or that which, is of a country or a material origin indicated by the implied basic n. Exx: *Canaanite*=*Canaan*+*-ite*; *Jacobite*, ML *Jacobita*; *lyddite*, from *Lydd*. But sometimes it has the same origin as (1) above, as in *granite*, It *granito*, adj become n.; this is common in Min and—e.g., *ammonite*—in Pal; also in Zoo, for a part of the body, as in *somite* (*sōm-*, the s of Gr *sōma*, body+*-ite*).

**-ite** (3), n. In Chem it is an arbitrary var of *-ate*.

**-ite** (4), v, as in *expedite*, usu derives from L *-itus*, pp of vv in *-ĕre* or in *-īre*. Exx: *expedite*, from L *expedītus*, from *expedīre*; *unite*, from *unītus*, from *unīre*.

**-itic**: Gr *-itikos*, often through L *-iticus* and F *-itique*. Conn: of, of the nature of, (hence) resembling or characterized by. It corresponds to nn in *-ite*, as *sybarite* and *Sybaritic*: L *Sybarita*, Gr *Subaritēs*, and L *Sybariticus*, Gr *Subaritikos*; and also to nn in *-itis*, as *arthritis* and *arthritic* (Gr *arthritikos*, via L *arthriticus* and F *arthritique*).

**-ition**. (Cf *-ation*, esp, but also *-etion* and *-ution*.) This suffix derives from L *-itiōn-*, the o/s (gen *-itiōnis*) of abstract nn in *-itiō*, themselves from vv with pp in *-itus*. It is therefore a cpd. Exx: *abolition*, adopted from F, from *abolitiōn-*, o/s of *abolitiō*, from *abolēre*; *condition*, OF *condicion*, L *conditiō* (inferior for *condiciō*), o/s *condiciōn-*. The basic conn is that of action viewed abstractly. Cf:

**-itious**, as in *fictitious*, connotes 'of, of the nature of; characterized by'. It derives from L *-icius*, formed either from a n or from a pp. Exx: *adventitious*, ML *adventicius*, L *aduentīcius*, from the n *aduentus*; *fictitious*, L *fictīcius*, from *fictiō*—cf *factitious*.

**-itis**, designating a disease, esp if inflammatory, of the part designated by the n forming the base of the word, as in *arthritis*, adopted, via L, from Gr: an *-itis* of an *arthron* or joint; orig, *-itis* was the f sing of the adj suffix *-itēs*, the n understood being the f *nosos*, disease; *arthritis*, therefore, is (*hē*) *arthritis* (nosos), the disease of the joints. Hence, jocularly, with conn 'mania', as in *electionitis*.

**-itish** is a cpd: *ite*, adj and n+-*ish* adj; it answers to nn in *-ite* (see the 2nd *-ite*). Ex: *Moabitish*: Moabite (i.e., *Moab*+-*ite*) itself derives from LL *Moabites*, from Gr *Mōabitēs*, from the Heb adj *Mō'ābī*. Clearly, then, *-itish* may be related to *-itic*, L *-iticus*, Gr *-itikos*: cf the var *Moabitic*.

**-itive**, strictly, is only app a suffix: the *-it-* is thematic, as in *punitive*, ML *punītivus*, built upon the pp *punītus* (s *punīt-*); at best it is a cpd. If, however, one admits *-ative*, *-etive*, *-utive*, one must admit *-itive*. (I regard all these forms as thematic extensions of *-ive*.)

**-ito** is a Sp dim (m), both of adjj and of nn: adopted in such words as *bonito* (adj—and perh the n), from *bueno* (L *bonus*), good—*mosquito*, from *mosca*, a fly (L *musca*)—*negrito*, from *negro*, black (L *niger*). Cf *-ita*.

**-itol** is a chem cpd suffix: chem *-ite*+chem *-ol*: as in *mannitol*. (Webster.) Strictly, *-ol* (oil) is an element.

**-itous**=L *-itōsus*, often via F *-iteux*, f *-iteuse*. Of this cpd, only *-ous* is truly a suffix, for *-it-* belongs to the s of the n in *-ity*. Conn: of, of the nature of, characterized by. Exx: *calamitous*, F *calamiteux*, f *-euse*, L *calamitōsus*, from *calamitās*; *necessitous* either=*necessit*(y)+-*ous* or derives from F *nécessiteuse*, f of *nécessiteux*—cf ML *necestuōsus*.

**'-itude** from L *-itūdō* forms abstract nouns from adjectives: *beatitude*, *fortitude*, *lassitude*, *solicitude*. In *multitude* it has developed a concrete meaning' (Sweet). The adj is *-itudinous*, as in *multitudinous*, which=*multitud*(e)+-*inous*, or even *multitudin-*(o/s of L *multitūdō*)+-*ous*. Strictly the *-it-* is thematic both in *beatitude*, *fortitude*, and in *multitudinous*, etc. The n suffix, therefore, is properly *-ude*, the adj suffix either *-inous* or *-ous*.

**-iture**, as in *garniture*, adopted from F, from *garnir*, to garnish, and as in the rare *nouriture*, from F *nourriture*, from *nourrir*, to nourish, appears to be a cpd of *-it-*+-*ure*, for the F nn are either based upon or formed on the analogy of L nn *-itūra*, where *-it-* derives from a pp in *-itus*. See, therefore, *-ure*.

**-ity** represents L *-itās*, often via F *-ité*. In L, the *-i-* is usu thematic, only occ connective: the true suffix, therefore, is *-ty*, q.v. Formed from adjj, nn in *-ity* are abstract, connoting 'nature or condition or state, quality or degree'. Exx: *calamity*, F *calamité*, L *calamitāt-*, o/s of *calamitās*; *ubiquity*, which=L *ubiqu*(e), everywhere+-*ity*—cf F *ubiquité*.

**-ium** is the L form (neu n of 2nd dec) corresponding to and often derived from Gr *-ion*. Sci usu prefers the L to the Gr form. Ex: *geranium*, adopted from L, which thus adapted Gr *geranion*.

Hence the use of *-ium* to indicate the chem elements, as *helium*, from Gr *hēlios*, the sun.

**-ius**, as in *radius*, occurs only in nn adopted from L; since the *-i-* is thematic, the true suffix is *-us*, q.v.

**-ive**, adj—hence often n: ML *-īvus*, f *-īva*, neu *-īvum*, L *-īuus*, etc.: often via F *-ive*, f of *-if*. Primary conn: having the nature or quality of a thing (implied by a v); hence, secondary conn: tending to the action indicated (by a v). Exx: *active*, (perh via F *actif*, *-ive*) from ML *actīvus* (L *actīuus*), from *act-*, the s of the pp *actus* of *agere*, to drive, do actively, practise; *conclusive*, ML *conclusīvus*, LL *conclusīuus*, from *concludere*; adj become n: *abrasive*, prob *abras*(ion)+-*ive*.

**-ivious**, as in *oblivious*, is only app a suffix, for the *-iv-* (L *-iu*) is thematic, the suffix being *-ous*, q.v.—The same stricture applies to *-ivity*, as in *declivity*, though not to the *-ivity* of *activity*, where it is a cpd suffix, answering to the *-ivitās* of ML *activitās*.

**-ivity.** See prec.

**-ix**, which has been adopted from L (itself deriving from or analogous with Gr *-ix*), occurs only in a very few learnèd words. Exx: *calix*, *radix*, *spadix*.

**-ization**, abstract n, is a cpd of *iz-*, as in *-ize*, q.v., and *-ation*; var: *-isation*—cf *civilisation*, *civilization*.

**-ize**; var *-ise*: Gr *-izein*, LL (hence It) *-izare*, F *-iser*: the last stage accounts for the formerly very frequent, now rapidly diminishing, forms in *-ise* (advertise, devise, surprise). In a vt, the conn is either 'to subject (someone, -thing) to something', 'as in *baptize*, or 'render (someone, -thing) like or conformable with', as in *sterilize*, the s indicating, in both classes, the direction taken or attempted; hence, in Chem, to treat something in a specific manner, as in *oxidize*. In a vi, the conn is 'to act in a certain way; to practise or profess something' (indicated by the s), as in *bo anize*. Exx: *advertise*, perh a back-formation from *advertisement*; *botanize*, perh *botan*(y)+-*ize* but prob from F *botaniser*; *catechize*, LL *catechizāre*, Gr *katēkhizein*; *cauterize*, LL *cauterizāre*, Gr *kautēriazein*; *solecize*, Gr *soloikizein*. Except in vv from Proper Adjj and Nn, Gr *-izein* has always an intensive force, often with a freq conn. Some *-izein* vv derive from a simple v, as we see in *catechize*. Basically, therefore, *-izein* is a cpd: intensive (? orig echoic) *-iz-*+ordinary inf *-ein*.

**-ized**, pp adj from *-ize*, as in *civilized*.

**-izing** (1), presp adj from *-ize*, as in 'a *cauterizing* agent'.

**-izing** (2), vn from *-ize*, as in 'His greatest weakness lies in his habit of *philosophizing* instead of acting'.

**-k** (1), adj, as in *quick*, *slack*, *slick*, and as in *weak*, derives from OE *-c*, which occurs in not a single native ModE adj. In the first three examples, the suffix is perh *-ck* rather than *-k*.

**-k** (2), n, occurs mainly in words formed from adjj or vv—and from OE *-c* or ME *-c*. Esq a dim, as in *stirk*, a young bullock: OE *stirc* or *styric*, dim of *stēor*, a steer.

**-k** (3), v. Many native vv in *-k* are echoic. A few are either freq or intensive or both, as *hark* (*heark*, *heark-en*), *lurk*, *skulk*, *smirk*, *stalk*, (?) *talk*, *walk*. Usu from ME *-ken*, OE *-cian*, *-ccian*, or *-cnian*, themselves either from OE *-can* or *-cian* or *-cnian* or from ON *-ka*.

**-kin, -kins**; F **-quin**. The dim suffix *-kin*, the same in ME, derives from MD *-kin* or *-kijn* akin to OHG *-kīn* or *-chīn*, G *-chen*. Exx: *firkin*, late ME *ferdekyn*, on MD *\*vierdekijn*; *lambkin* = *lamb* + *-kin*; *kilderkin*, from MD *kilderkijn*; *manikin*, from D *manneken*, represents, in its E form, *man* + connective *-i-* + *-kin*. *Mannequin* also derives from the D word. The *-kins* form, as in *sonnikins*, has been influenced by such personal names as *Jenkins*, *Sim(p)kins*, *Tom(p)kins*, *Wilkins*, which mean 'son of *Jenkin*, *Sim(p)kin*, etc.'; the latter are themselves dimm for *John*, *Tom*, *Will*(iam), etc.

**-l** (1), adj: OE *-l*, app for *-el*, as in *foul*, OE *fūl*. Cf *-el* and *-le*, adjj.

**-l** (2), n: OE *-el*. It is either agential or instrumental or, occ, indicative of the result of action. Exx: (agential, etc) *awl*, OE *awel*, (lit) that which pierces—*fowl*, OE *fugol*, that which flies—*hail*—*pail*—*sail*—*tail*—*stool*; (dim) ? *girl*, ME *girle*, *gerle*, *gurle*—*snail*, OE *snaeg(e)l* or *snegel*, (lit) the little creeper. Cf *-le*, n.

**-l** (3), v: usu freq, though occ merely continuative. Many such vv are also echoic. (Cf *-le*, much commoner and with a wider conn.) Exx: *drawl*, app from *draw*; ? *hurl*, ME *hurlen*; *kneel*, OE *cnēowlian*, prob from *cnēow*, the knee; *mewl*, akin to *mew*; *snarl*, from obs syn *snar*; *wail*, ME *wailen* or *weilen*, from ON *vǣla* or *vāla*; *whirl*, ME *whirlen*, from ON.

**-le** (1), adj. When part of *-able*, *-eble*, *-ible*, *-uble*, qq.v., it usu = L *-ilis*. Cf:

**-le** (2), adj, as in *humble* and *gentle*, derives from L *-ilis* through F *-le*, as in *humble*, adopted from OF, from L *humilis*, or through F *-il*, f *-ille*, as in *gentle*, OF *gentil*, L *gentīlis*. Conn: of (the nature of) the nn indicated by the s. Cf *-el* (1).

**-le** (3), adj. More important than (2) is the native group of adjj from ME *-el* (or *-il*) or OE *-ol*, 'indicating a tendency to the action expressed by the verb from which the adjective is derived, as in *brickle* [ME *brekil*, *brokel*, from OE *brecan*, to break], *brittle* [ME *britel*, from OE *brēotan*, to break], *fickle* [ME *fikel*, OE *ficol*]': Webster.

**-le** (4), n: OE *-el*, dim, sometimes corresponding to L *-illa* or *-illus*. Exx: *axle*, ME *axel*, akin to L *axilla*, dim of *axis*; *freckle*, app *frek-* (s of ME *freken* from ON *freknuo*) + *-le*; ? *icicle*; *kettle*, ult from L *catillus*, dim of *catinus*, a deep vessel.

**-le** (5), n: OE *-el*, agent or instrument. Exx: *beadle*, OE *bydel*; *girdle*, OE *gyrdel*, akin to—if not indeed derived from—*gyrdan*, to encircle.

**-le** (6), n. Echoic nn in *-le* usu derive from the vv. Cf:

**-le** (7), n. Of various L, through F, origins, as in the exx: *battle*, OF *bataille*, L *battālia*, from *battuere*, to strike; *bottle*, ME *botel*, OF *bouteille*, LL *buticula*; *cattle*, ONF *catel*, L *capitāle*; *couple*, adopted from OF from L *copula*; *mantle*, through OF from L *mantellum*, of obscure origin, but prob dim; *pestle*, OF *pestel*, L *pistillum* (or *-illus*), another dim; *trestle*, from L of *-illum* suffix.

**-le** (8), v: orig, always either freq or dim, and often echoic, as in *crumble* and *crumple*—*joggle* and *jostle*—*sparkle* and *twinkle*. Usu of Gmc origin; occ F, with E *-le* added, as in *gobble* (*gob* + euphonic *b* + *-le*), from F *gober*, to swallow. Cf:

**-le** (9), v: causal: a special application of prec. Exx: *startle* and *stifle*.

**-ledge**, in *knowledge*, is obscure. ME exhibits such various forms as *-lage*, *-lege*, *-leche*; nor does the word precede ME. I suggest that ME *knowlage* = *knowage*, where *-age* is collective (see *-age* (a) above) and that the intrusive *-l-* has arisen by false analogy with the *-lege* of such words as *privilege* and *sacrilege*. Sweet derives the n *knowledge* from the v *knowledge*, as others have done; he also explains *-ledge* as deriving from *-laecan*, as in *genēalaecan*, to approach, and *-laecan* as deriving from *lāc*, gift, (earlier) action in general.

**-lent**, adj, as in *corpulent*: L *-lentus* (f *-lenta*, neu *-lentum*) or *-lent-*, o/s of *-lens*; conn: 'showing a tendency towards' something indicated by a n; or towards action denoted by a v. Exx: *corpulent*, via F from L *corpulentus*, from *corpus*, the body; *esculent*, L *esculentus*, from *ēsca*, food; *opulent*, either L *opulentus* or, its originator, *opulent-*, o/s of *opulens*, from *ops*, riches; *pestilent*, L *pestilent-*, o/s of *pestilens*, from *pestis*, a grave epidemic disease.

[**-less.** See Elements.]

**-let**, adj: a cpd, formed from F *-el* (L *-ellus*, *-ella*, *-ellum*) and F *-et*, both dim: see *-el*, n, and *-et*, n, above. Purely and basically dim in, e.g., *bracelet*, orig an OF *-et* dim of *bracel*, (lit) a little arm, from L *brachiāle*, and *ringlet*, which = *ring* + *-let*, *-let* derivatively denotes 'something worn on or around' (the n designated by the s), as in *armlet*, which = *arm* + *-let*, and partly in *bracelet*.

[**-like**, adj. and adv. See Elements. The true suffix is *-ly*, adj and adv, qq.v.]

**-ling** (1), adj, derives either, as in *darkling*, from *-ling*, adv, or, as in *darling*, from *-ling*, n.

**-ling** (2); **-lings**, adv The latter, occurring only in advv, arises in the gen of an OE n (cf the adv *of a day*); it forms a var of *-ling*, adv, which, deriving from OE *-ling*, is 'prob akin to Lith *-link*, *linkti*, to bend, incline' (Webster). The basic conn is 'direction', as in the Scots and E dial *backlin(g)s*, but the derivative conn 'state, condition' (? hence) 'manner', predominates, although, even here, 'direction' is felt. Exx: *darkling*, in the dark (? orig, towards the dark, into the dark); *grovel(l)ing* or *grovel(l)ings*, prostrately, app from an old adv *groof*, approximately syn, itself from ON.

**-ling** (3), n: OE *-ling*, akin to OHG *-ling* and Go *-liggs*: conn, 'A person or other living creature belonging to or possessing the qualities of' whatever is indicated by the s, as in *darling*, OE *dēorling*, (lit) a dear one, and *worldling*, *world*+*-ling*; hence, dim—often a pej dim—as in *gosling*, ME *gos*, a goose+*-ling*, and *princeling*, *prince*+*-ling*. Cf *-long* below.—Skeat regards OE *-ling*, at least in its use, as a cpd of dim *-el* and of *-ing* (3)—a suffix he postulates to be orig dim.

**-lings.** See *-ling* (2).

**-lock,** in *wedlock*: ME *-lok*, OE *-lāc*, with conn 'action', as in the OE *rēaflāc*, robbery, from *rēafian* (s *rēaf-*), to plunder.

**-long,** adv: conn 'direction': very closely akin to 2nd *-ling*, q.v. Exx: *sidelong* (*side*+*-long*), perh a var of *sideling* (*side*+adv *-ling*), sideways; *headlong*, ME *hedling*.

**-ly** (1), adj. ME *-lich*: OE *-lic*, usu *-līc*, from *līc*, body (as in *lich gate*: see LIKE in Dict): conn, 'resembling'—hence 'characteristic of'. Exx: *fatherly*, OE *faederlīc*, father-like; *manly*=*man*+*-ly*. Attached to nn of time, it means '(happening) every', as in *nightly*, OE *nihtlīc*.

**-ly** (2), adv: ME *-liche*=OE *-līce* or *-lice*; or, very commonly, anl. Conn: 'in the manner of' the adj or rarely the n forming the base. Exx: *badly*=*bad*+*-ly*; *quickly*, OE *cwiculīce*; *slowly*, OE *slāwlīce*; (from n) *partly*=*part*+*-ly*. By far the most frequent of E adv suffixes.

**-m** (1). See *-asm* and *-ism*, also *-em*, *-im*, *-om*, *-um*.

**-m** (2). In *doom* (OE *dōm*), *-m* app connotes 'result of the v' (*deem*); it is akin to the *-m* of Gr *themis* (s *them-*), law; in *foam* (OE *fām*), to that of L *spūma*, s *spūm-*; in *haulm* (OE *healm*), to that of L *culmus* (s *culm-*), a stalk, and Gr *kalamos* (s *kalam-*), a reed, and *kalamē*, a stalk. 'The A.S. [i.e., OE] suffix is *-m*, answering to Goth *-ma*, L *-ma-s*, Gr *-μο-σ* [*mo-s*] (*-μη*[*-mē*])': Skeat, who, to *haulm*, compares also Ru *soloma*, straw. The basic conn is app 'a (striking) manifestation of' whatever the s denotes; this conn is also present, I think, in *bream*, *dream*, *scream*, *stream*—in *gleam*—and in *beam*, *ream*, *seam*, *team*, even though these words lack cognates in L and Gr and even though the *-m* is, in several, thematic; several are akin to Skt words. The influence of this *-m* suffix may have affected also *cream*, from Gr *khrisma*. Cf *-me* (2) below.

**-m** (3) is a 'shortened' var of *-me* and is to be related to *-ma*, for it comes from the Gr suffix *-ma*. Exx: *axiom*, *phlegm*, *problem*. See *ma-*.

**-m** (4): L *-men*, through F *-me*. Exx: *charm*, OF *charme*, L *carmen*, song, perhaps from and almost certainly akin to *canere*, to sing; *realm*, OF *realme*, VL *\*regālimen*, L *regālis*, akin to *regere*, to rule. Whereas *carmen* is a singing, *\*regālimen* is a ruling —hence, a region, a country, ruled: the conn would therefore seem to be 'result or product of' the implied v. Cf the L *-me* below.

**-ma,** as in *aroma*, *asthma*, *diploma*, *dogma*, *drama*, *enema*, *enigma*, *panorama*, *stigma*, comes straight from Gr; these words, in fact, have been adopted from Gr. Anglicized forms occur either as *-m* (see prec) or as *-me* (2), q.v. below, or as *-em*, q.v. above. App *-ma* connotes 'the product, or the result, of' (the implied v).

[**-man.** See MAN in Dict. In WOMAN it is perh less obviously 'man'.]

**-mans,** occurring only in the language of the underworld, appears at its most obvious in *darkmans*, darkness, the dark, and *lightmans*, the (full) light of day. It corresponds to the *-ment* of F advv and, of Skt origin, is therefore a form taken by the IE s of L *mens*, E MIND.

[**-mas.** See Elements and cf (the religious) MASS.]

**-mat.** See:

**-mate,** as in *climate*, and *-mat-*, as in *climatic*, *dramatic*, *emblematic*, *prismatic*, etc., represents IE *mn-to*, seen esp in Gr *-ma-to*. 'The suffix *-το* [*-to*] is added to oblique cases of sbs [substantives= nouns] ending in *-μα* [*ma*] ... This suffix *-ματο* [*-mato*] answers to L *-mentum*' (Skeat): cf, therefore, *-mans* above and the L *mens*, E MIND.

**-me** (1), adj, as in *extreme*, *prime*, *supreme*, derives from the L sup *-mus*: *extrēmus*, *prīmus*, *suprēmus*.

**-me** (2), n, from Gr *-ma* (cf, however, *anagram*), occ via L *-ma* and occ also via F *-me* or *-mme*. Usu the conn is 'result or product of' the implied v. Exx: *gram*(*me*), F *gramme*, LL *gramma*, Gr *gramma*; *clime*, L *clima*, Gr *klima*, from *klinein*, to slope; *programme*, F *programme*, LL *programma*, Gr *programma*, from *prographein*; *scheme*, LL *schēma*, Gr *skhēma*, akin to—perh from—*skhein*, to have, hold, check.

**-me** (3), n, from L *-men*, occ via F *-me*. Exx: *crime*, adopted from OF, from L *crīmen*, from *cernere*, to decide in a court of law; *legume*, F *légume*, L *legūmen*, prob from *legere*, to gather; *volume*, adopted from OF, from ML *volumen*, L *uolūmen*, from *uoluere*, to roll. The conn, evidently, is 'the result or product of' the v implied.

**-me** (4), n, as in *dime*, adopted from OF, from L *decima* (pars), the tenth part, and in *prime*, the first hour of the day, OE *prim*, L *prīma* (hora), represents L *-ma*, f of the adj suffix *-mus*. Cf (1).

**-me** (5), as in *name*, OE *nama* (akin to L *nōmen* and Gr *onoma*), is a rare suffix, akin to, yet distinct from, *-me* (3). Cf also *-ma* and *-men*.

**-meal,** as in *piecemeal*, has conn 'the portion taken at one time'. Formerly used more freely (as in the obsol *inchmeal*) in the formation of quantitative advv, it derives, through ME *-mele*, from OE *-maelum*, orig the dat pl of *mael*, a measure—the orig form of MEAL. Strictly, therefore, *-meal* is rather an element than a suffix.

**-men** is an adoption of the L *-men*, occurring only and very properly in words taken over bodily from L, as *acumen*, from *acuere*, to sharpen; *bitumen*; *gravamen*, the ML form of LL *grauāmen*, from L *grauāre*, to burden; *omen*; *regimen*, from *regere*, to guide; *specimen*, from *specere*, to look. Conn: result or product of the action implied by the originating v: cf, therefore, *-me* (3).

**-mena** and **-menon** come straight from Gr and

are rare and erudite. They represent the neu pl and the neu sing respectively of the presp of the middle, or of the passive, voice of Gr vv. Exx: *prolegomena*, pl construed as sing and much commoner than the sing *prolegomenon*, a preliminary discourse or introductory treatise, from *prolegomenos*, the passive pres of *prolegein*, to say or state beforehand, the adj being *prolegomenary* or *prolegomenous*; *hapax legomenon* (pl *hapax legomena*), lit something said only once, hence a word, or occ a form, recorded only once, the Gr being ἅπαξ λεγόμενον; *phenomenon*, LL *phaenomenon*, Gr *phainomenon*, neu presp of *phainesthai*, to appear or seem, from *phainein*, to show, the pl being *phenomena*, Gr *phainomena*.

**-ment** (cf *-mente*) is strictly an element, but, as *-mentum*, it occurs so often in L that it there became a suffix with the orig meaning (L *mens*, E *mind*) darkened or lost; often it comes into E through OF or F *-ment*. This n suffix occurs in nn formed mostly from vv. The L *-mentum* consists of *-men-* (cf *-men* above) and *-tum* and corresponds to Gr *-ma-to-*. Its conn is fundamentally 'result or product of' the action of the implied v and may be divided into:

concrete result or product, as in *increment*, L *incrēmentum*, from *incrēscere*, to increase; *attachment*, F *attachement*, from *attacher*, to attach; *entanglement*, which=*entangle*+*-ment*; or a physical means or instrument, as in *ornament*, OF *ornement*, L *ornāmentum*, from *ornāre* (s *orn-*), and *nutriment*, L *nūtrīmentum*, from *nūtrīre*—cf *nourishment*, OF *norrisse-ment* (influenced by F *nourrir*), from OF *norrir*, from L *nūtrīre*;

action: as in *abridgement*, OF *abregement*, from *abregier*, from ML *abbreviāre*, L *abbreuiāre*; *government*, OF *governement*, from OF *governer*, from L *gubernāre*; *statement*=*state* (v)+ *-ment*;

state, quality, condition: *amazement*=(to) *amaze* +*-ment*; (hence) manner, as in *arrangement*, adopted from F, from the v *arranger*.

**-menta.** See *-mentum*.

**-mental**, adj, answers to *-ment* and *-mentum*. In E words, the formation is usu: the *-ment* n+*-al*, adj suffix, as in *excremental* and *incremental*. *Instrumental* comes direct from F, where it=F *instrument*+F *-al*. Cf:

**-mentality** (cf *-ity* and *-ty*), as in *instrumentality*, derives from prec and answers to *-ment*.

**-mente** occurs only in Mus and as an Italicism; e.g., *rapidamente*, adv of *rapido*, and *subitamente*, from *subito*. It *-mente*=F *-ment*, a suffix denoting manner: cf *-ment* above. The adv force arises from the fact that the It *-mente* derives from L *-mente*, (lit) with a mind, (hence) with or in an attitude of mind, (hence) in a manner indicated by the adj forming the s; as in the mus *appassionatamente*, with a mind, hence with a heart, impassioned; cf *-mans* above.

**-mentum** (cf *prec*) is the L source of *-ment*, q.v., and is preserved, occ alongside an E form, in a few

erudite, esp if Med, terms. Exx: *argumentum* (ad hominem), pl *argumenta* (esp in Logic); *excrē-mentum*, usu the pl *excrēmenta*. The L *-mentum* comes from *-mento*, a cpd of the IE suffixes *-men* (cf *-men* above)+*-to*; cf Gr *-mato* (*-ma*+*-to*), as at *-mate* above.

**-mme**, as in *programme* and in (other) F words, e.g. *telegramme*, is merely the F form of E *-me* (2); cf *-m* (3).

**-mo**, as in the Americanism *sixteenmo* for E *sextodecimo* (cf *duodecimo*), is a bookbinding suffix, indicating 'the number of leaves made by folding a sheet of paper' (Webster); theoretically it can apply only to *decimo* (10), practically to *duodecimo* (12), upwards, and it represents the abl of L ordinals (m in *-imus*).

[**-monger.** See Elements.]

**-monious**, adj, from *-mony*, n, the latter, often via F *-monie* or *-moine*, from L *-mōnia* or *-mōnium*, the former sometimes deriving from L adj in *-mōniōsus*, occ via F *-monieux* or the f *-monieuse*. The L n-suffix denotes a resultant, whether concrete or abstract. Exx: *acrimony*, (perh via F *acrimonie*, from) L *ācrimōnia*, from *ācer*, sharp, the adj *acrimonious* passing through F from ML *ācrimōniōsus*; *alimony*, L *alimōnia*, from *alere*, to nourish; *matrimony*, OF *matrimoine*, L *matrimōn-ium*, from *māter*, mother.

[**-most.** See Elements.]

**-mus** occurs in a few nn adopted from L, as *Decimus* and *primus*. In L, of course, it is an adj suffix.

**-n** (1), adj, as in *leathern* and *silvern*, is short for the *-en* of e.g. *golden*. See *-en* (2). Cf:

**-n** (2), adj, as in *fain*, derives from OE *-en*, akin to OS *-an* and ON *-inn*.

**-n** (3), in the pp of certain strong vv, mostly used as adjj and also as nn, as *blown*, *flown*, *known*, *sown*: cf *-en* (11), q.v.

**-n** (4), adv, as in *then* and *when* (and basically in *hence*, *thence*, *whence*), derives from OE *-nne*, perh, as Nesfield suggests, akin to the acc m, as in OE *hwone*, acc m of *hwā*, who. But a comparison with the *n* in OE *siththan*, Scots *syne*, since; with that of G *dann*, then, *wann*, when, and numerous other Gmc forms in *-n* or *-n-* for 'then' and 'when'; with that of L *nunc*, now, *dein*, *deinde*, then, *quando*, when?, with that of Gr *nun*, now, *epan*, *epen*, after that; with forms in Sl and esp in Skt: such a comparison leads us to suppose that *-n* or *-n-* is an IE formative element indicative of time expressed in advv.

**-n** (5), n, as in *thegn* (thane), OE *thegen* or *thegn*, is of OE (and Common Gmc) origin and only the vaguest meaning; in this particular word, it perh=*-en* (7), the agential *-en*, as also in *main*, that which can: cf *rain*, that which dampens or wets — *sun*, that which shines (?) *thorn*, that which pierces—*wain*, that which carries (Nesfield). Sweet notes that it interchanges with *-en* and (native) *-on*.

**-n** (6), v, is short for *-en* (10), q.v.—the *-en* of

*lengthen* and *shorten*—and derives from OE *-an* or usu *-ian* or ME *-en*. Exx: *fawn*, OE *fagnian* or *fahnian*; *drown*, ME *drunen* or *drounen*; *learn*, OE *leornian*; *own*, OE *āgnian*; *turn*, OE *turnian* or *tyrnan*; *win*, OE *winnan*.

**-nce, -ncy.** See *-ance, -ancy*, an entry including *-ence, -ency* and, of course, *-ience, -iency*.

**-nd,** n, is 'short' for *-and* (Northern), *-ende* (Midland), *-inde* (Southern), varr of the old presp suffix of vv. See *-and* (2) above. Of the predominant Midland *-end* (or *-nd*), Sweet remarks that '*-end* "-er" is the noun-form of the present participle ending *-ende*, and forms nouns denoting agents from verbs, such as *hāēland* "healer" . . . It became extinct in ME, its place being supplied by the ending *-ere*. But it still survives disguised in *friend* =OE *frēond*, literally "lover", and *fiend*=OE *fēond* "enemy", literally "hater".'

**-ness:** OE *-ness* or *-nes*, or *-nis*, or *-nys(s)*, akin to OHG *-nissa* (G *-nis* or *-niss*), OS *-nissi*, Go *-inassus* (cf the OHG var *-nassi*); orig the *-n* (occ *-in*) was thematic and therefore did not beong to the suffix proper. Fundamentally abstract and indicative of state or condition, quality or degree, as in *greatness, goodness, illness*, it yet forms a few nn (as *wilderness* and *witness*) that clearly retain the idea of abstractness. Orig it went only with native, but fairly soon it came to be added to, adjj of L derivation also, for which, nevertheless, *-ity* is still preferred, as in *spirituality* for *spiritualness*. Exx: *goodness*, OE *gōdnes*; *illness*=*ill*+*-ness*; *witness*, OE *witness* or *gewitness*—cf OE *gelīcnis*, whence *likeness*; jocosely in 'the *whyness* of life'. (Webster.)

**-o** (1) occurs in words adopted from the L abl of 2nd-declension nn in *-us* or *-um*, as in *quarto* and *octavo* (for *in quarto, in octavo*; cf *folio* for *in folio*)—*in loco parentis*—*pro bono publico*.

**-o** (2) occurs in nn or, occ, adjj adopted or slightly adapted from It or Port or Sp. It and Sp *-o* mostly derives from, or has been formed as if from, L 2nd-declension *-us* or *-um*. Exx: *cameo*, It *cammeo*; *cargo*, Sp word; *casino*, dim of It *casa*, a house; *flamingo*, adopted from Port, itself from Sp *flamenco*; *fresco*, It; *gusto*, It; Sp *junta*, whence E *junto*; *manifesto*, It; *mulatto*, Port and Sp; *negro*, Sp; *oratorio*, It; *scenario*, It; *seraglio*, from It *serraglio*; *studio*, It; *torso*, It; *virtuoso*, It; *volcano*, It.

**-o** (3), as in 'All alive*o*', very closely resembles the disguised interjection noted at *-a* (1) above, q.v.

**-o** (4) might be described as 'the slangy or, at best, coll *-o*', as in AIr *boyo*, one of 'the boys', and as in several Aus slang terms, e.g. *afto*, afternoon, and *goodo*, good.

**-o-,** connective, occ represents the L abl *-o*, rarely a L adv ending in *o*; exx: *dorso-*, as in *dorso-caudal*—*proximo-*, as in *proximo(-)lingual*—*retro-*, as in *retroflex*; undoubtedly, even here, the use of *-o-* with words of L origin has been in-

fluenced by the heavily preponderant Gr *-o-*. (The true L connective is *-i-*, q.v. above.)

The connective *-o-* is essentially and notably Gr. In Gr cpds, this *-o-* is usu 'the stem vowel' of the 1st element. In, e.g., *logos*, word, discourse, thought, the s is *log-*, the s vowel is *-o*, as we see from *logo-s, logo-n, logo-i*, etc.: hence, *log-o-graphy, log-o-metric*. Occ *o*—so powerful in its connective influence—takes the place of another s vowel; and sometimes it is added, for euphony, to a s ending in a consonant. When the 2nd element begins with a vowel, connective *o* is usu omitted, as in *aristarchy* (*aristo-*+*-archy*), from Gr *aristarkhia*, where the 2nd element is *arkhia*. When used with adjj, it constitutes an adv modification, as in *dolichocephalic*, or it expresses mutuality, as in '*Anglo-*French relations' and 'the *Franco-*Prussian War'. Very often *-o-* connotes (rather than denotes) some prep relationship, as in *osteopathy, pathology, Russophobia*.

**-ock,** dim of OE origin. Exx: *bullock*, OE *bulluc*, a young bull; *buttock*=*butt*, n+*-ock*; ? *cassock*, by analogy with other E nn in *-ock* (F *casaque*, It *casacca*, prob on s (*cas-*) of LL *casubla*); ? *haddock*, ME *had(d)ok*, perh from F *hadot* (s *had-*); *hillock*= *hill*+*-ock*; ? *hummock*, perh=*hump*+*-ock*, the *p* being assimilated to *m*; ? *paddock*, a deviation from the now Scots, and E dial, *parrock*, OE *pearruc* or *-oc*; *paddock*, a frog, a toad, ME *paddok*, dim of *padde*, a toad; *tussock*, perh from Swed dial *tuss*, a handful of hay. The *-ock* of *shamrock* derives from the cognate Ir suffix *-og*: Ir *seamróg* (cf Ga *seamrag*) is a dim of *seamur*.

**-ode** is either adj, conn 'like', or—more usu—n, conn 'a thing that resembles' (the n implied by the s), as in *cladode* (cf *clad(o)-* in Elements) and *geode*, a nodule of stone. In Bot and Zoo, the pl *-odes* indicates a generic name, as *Acanthodes*. The sing *-ode* derives from Gr *-ōdēs*, neu *-ōdes*: connective *-o-*+*-eidēs*, like, from *eidos*, a form. Cf *-oid* and *-oidea* below, and also:

**-ody:** Gr *-ōdia*, from *-ōdēs* (as in prec); *-ōdia* is therefore a cpd, the 2nd suffix being *-ia*, q.v. In Bot it signifies 'a becoming like, (hence) a metamorphosis into', as in *petalody*, suggested by Gr *petalōdēs*, leaf-like.

**-oic,** used in Chem for naming acids and related cpds, as in *naphthoic*, derives from *benzoic*. (Webster.)

**-oid,** adj—hence often n: Gr *-oeidēs*, which= connective *-o-*+*-eidēs*, q.v. at *-ode* above: occ through L *-oīdes* and then F *-oīde*. Exx: *adenoid*, Gr *adenoidēs*, glandular; *haemorrhoid*, m—adj *haemorrhoidal*; *spheroid*, n, from L *sphaeroides*, (lit) ball-like, (hence) spherical, Gr *sphairoeidēs*, from *sphaira*, a sphere—adj *spheroidal*. The adj suffix *-oidal*=*-oid*+adj *-al*, q.v. See also *-oidea*.

**-oidal.** See prec.

**-oidea,** SciL suffix, based on *-oid*. This Zoo suffix designates a class or, in Ent, a superfamily. 'Nouns denoting individual members are formed in *-oid*, derivative adjectives in *-oidean*' (Webster);

*-oidean=-oid+-ean.* Ex: *Muscoidea*, from L *nusca*, a fly.

**-oidean.** See prec.

**-oideus,** denoting muscles, as *rhomboideus*, is a SciL suffix=*-oid+*L *-eus*, q.v. at *-eous* above. (Webster.)

**-oin,** in Chem terms, e.g. *acetoin*, derives from *benz*oin.

[**-ol** and **-ole,** so common in Chem, are Elements.]

[**-ology.** See Elements.]

**-om** (1), adv, as in *seldom*, derives from OE *-um*, suffix of the dat pl. Exx: *seldom*, OE *seldum*, but also *seldan* and *selden*—cf OFris *sielden*, OHG *seltan*; *whilom*, OE *hwīlum*, (lit) at times, akin to OHG *hwilōm*.

**-om** (2), n, as in *bosom, bottom, fathom*, corresponds to *-m* (2) q.v. above. 'The *o* of this final *-om* was formerly not written; cf A.S. *bōsm, botm, faethm*. And, in fact, the final *-m* is here vocalic' (Skeat). With OE *bōsm* cf OFris *bōsm* and OHG *buosam*; with OE *botm*, OHG *bodam* and OS *bodom*; with OE *faethm*, OHG *fadam* or *fadum*. Ult, all three are akin to vv; indeed, they seem to denote the result of the action of the implied v.

**-oma,** n; **-omatous,** derivative adj. The n *-oma* has been either adopted or, at the lowest, formed anl with the Gr *-ōma*, o/s *-ōmat-* (e.g., gen *-ōmatos*). In Med, *-oma* indicates a morbid affection of the part designated by the basic n, as in *sarcoma*, from Gr *sarkōma*, from *sarx*, flesh, o/s *sark-*; the adj *sarcomatous=sark+-omatous.* Cf:

**-ome,** in Bot, indicates a group, a mass, a stem, and merely anglicizes Gr *-ōma*, q.v. in prec. All these words owe much to the exemplar *rhizome*. Exx: *caulome=caul-* (q.v. in Elements)+*-ome*; *rhizome*, Gr *rhizōma*, the mass of a tree's roots, a stem, (hence) a clan, a race.

**-on** (1), of Gr origin, represents either *-ōn*, whether n or presp m, as in *archon*, via L *archon* from Gr *arkhōn—dragon*, adopted from F, from Gr *drakōn—horizon*, via L *horizon*, from Gr *horizōn—phaeton*, via L from Gr *Phaithōn*, or *-on*, neu n or, occ, neu adj, as in *automaton*, from the neu s of Gr *automatos*, self-acting, and *criterion*, from Gr *kritērion*. In Phys it designates an ult particle, as in *proton*, from Gr *prōton*, neu of *prōtos*, first; in Chem, an inert gas, as in *argon*, adopted from Gr *argon*, neu of *argos*, sluggish.

**-on** (2), of L origin: *-ōnem*, acc of nn in *-ō*, o/s *-ōn-*. Exx: *capon*, OE *capūn*, from L *capōnem*, acc of *capō*; *carbon*, via F *carbone*, from *carbōnem*, acc of L *carbō*; *glutton*, via OF from *glutōnem*, acc of L *glūtō* or *gluttō*; *sermon*, via OF from *sermōnem*, acc of L *sermō*. The conn seems to be 'result or product of' the implied or kindred v.

**-on** (3), of L origin: *-ōnus*, m, or *-ōna*, f, or *-ōnum*, neu. Exx: *matron*, via OF *matrone*, from L *mātrōna*, which=*matr-*, o/s of *mater*, mother | *-ōna*; *patron*, via OF, from L *patrōnus*, which= *patr-*, o/s of *pater*, father+*-ōnus*. Clearly, *-ōnus*, *-ōna* are here aug (big father, big mother): here, therefore, we have the origin of *-on*, (4)-(6).

**-on** (4), of It origin (*-one*), is aug; occ it passes through F *-on*. Exx: *gabion*, adopted from F, from It *gabbione*, a large cage, from *gabbia*, cage, L *cauea*, ML *cavea*; *medallion*, via F *médaillon*, from It *medaglione*, aug of *medaglia*; *million*, early F *millione*, aug of *mille*, 1000; *squadron*, It *squadrone*. Cf prec and *-one* (2) and:

**-on** (5), of Sp origin (*-on*), is likewise aug; it is closely akin to It *-one*, q.v. in prec. Ex: *galleon*, Sp *galeón*, from *galea*, adopted from ML. Cf prec.

**-on** (6), of independent F origin (*-on*), an aug that is akin to *-on* (3)-(5), qq.v. Exx: *caparison*, F *caparaçon*, from Prov *caparassoun*, from *capa*, a cape (for wearing); *flagon*, OF *flacon*, lit a large flask.

**-on** (7), from F *-ain* (L *-ānus*, denoting either 'agent' or, at vaguest, 'person': cf *-an* (1) above). Ex (sole ex ?): *sexton*, a doublet of *sacristan*, from OF *secrestein*, ML *sacristānus*.

**-on** (8), a suffix of native origin, in words of Gmc stock; a var of agential *-en*, q.v. at *-en* (7). Ex: *wag(g)on*, either from OE *waegen* (or *waegn*) or from MD *waghen*.

**-one** (1), of Gr origin (*-ōn*). Exx: *cyclone*, either from Gr *kuklōn*, (presp) moving in circles, or irregularly from *kuklos*, a circle, perh from the gen pl *kuklōn*; *ozone*, from Gr *ozōn*, presp of *ozein*, to smell.

**-one** (2): Gr *-ōnē*; conn 'female descendant'. It occurs in Chem, e.g. *acetone*.

**-one** (3): It *-one*, aug suffix. Exx: *trombone*, It *trombone*, aug of *tromba*, a trumpet; *violone*, It *violone*, aug of *viola*, a viol. Cf *-on* (3)-(6), esp *-on* (4); also *-oon* (1).

**-ont,** n: Gr *-ont-*, o/s of presp *-ōn*. Prototype: *schizont*, a Zoo cell, from *skhizont-*, o/s of *skhizōn*, presp of *skhizein*, to cleave (cf *schism* in Dict). Ex, likewise in Zoo: *sporont*, analogously from *spor(e)* +*-ont*. Cf the *-ont-* in *horizontal*.

**-oon** (1), aug: It *-one* (prob L *-ōna*, f of *-ōnus*: see 3rd *-on*) or Sp *-ón*; usu through F *-on*. For this aug, cf *-on* (3)-(6). Exx: *balloon*, prob through F *ballon* and certainly from It *ballone*, aug of *balla*, a ball; *bassoon*, via F *basson*, from It *bassone*, aug of *basso*, low, deep: *cartoon*, F *carton*, It *cartone*, from *carta*, paper; *musketoon*, F *mousqueton*, It *moschettone*, from *moschetto*, a kind of hawk.

**-oon** (2), non-augmentative: It *-one* or Sp *-ón*; occ via F *-on*; rarely from independent F. Exx: *buffoon*, F *bouffon*, It *buffone*, from *buffare*, to play tricks, make jests; *dragoon*, F *dragon*, L *dracōnem*, acc of *dracō*—cf *dragon*; *macaroon*, F *macaron*, It *maccherone*; *maroon*, F *marron*, Sp *cimarrón*; *poltroon*, F *poltron*, It *poltrone*, from *poltro*, bed; *quadroon*, Sp *cuarterón*. Conn: one who notably does or notably is. Analogous formation: *spittoon*, which=*spit*+euphonic *t*+*-oon*.

**-or** (1), adj, in *major* and *minor*, is a var of *-ior* as in *inferior* and *superior*. Adopted from L. See **-ior.**

**-or** (2), abstract n, either adopted from L *-or* or passing through OF-MF *-or* or *-our* or *-ur*; or, of course, formed analogously at either the F or the E stage. At the ME level, the form is *-or* or *-our* or *-ur*. Exx: *error*, L from *errāre* (s *err-*), to wander; *pallor*, L from *pallēre*, to be pale. Words that have passed through OF *-our* or *-ur* tend, in E, to be spelt *-our*; AE prefers the L *-or*. Exx: *fervour*, OF *fervour* or *fervor*, ML *fervor*, L *feruor*, from ML *fervēre*, L *feruēre*, and *honour*, ME *honor*, *honour*, *onur*, OF *honor*, *honur*, *onur*, *enour*, L *honor*.

**-or** (3), agential n, either adopted from L *-or*, often via OF-MF *-or*, *-ur*, *-our*, or F *-eur*, or deriving ult from L *-ātor* but imm from OF *-eör* or *-eür* (F *-eur*). Exx: *actor*, L from *act-*, pp s of *agere*, to drive, ply, do; *creditor*, F *créditeur*, L *crēditor*, from *crēdere* (s *crēd-*), to believe; *donor*; OF *donëor*, L *donātor*, from *donāre* (s *don-*), to give. An agent may become an instrument, as in *ejector*, which=*eject*+*-or*; there are many such analogous agents and instruments; e.g., *sailor*. Strictly *-or* goes with words of L origin, *-er* (see *-er* (4) above) with words of Gmc origin; but *bachelor* comes from OF *bacheler*, *-er* being OF var agential suffix. The correlative is *-ee*, q.v., as in *lessor—lessee*.

**-or** (4), n, from OF-F *-oir* or OF-MF *-our* or *-eor*. Exx: *manor*, OF *manoir*, from *manoir*, to stay, dwell, from L *manēre*; *mirror*, OF *mirour*, *mireor*, from VL *miratōrium*, from L *mirāri*, to gaze at; *parlor*, British E *parlour*, OF *parleor*, ML *parlatōrium*, a place for talking. The conn is 'a thing for, a place for'.

**-ora**: either Gr *-ορα*, *-ora*, or Gr *-ωρα*, *-ōra*. Exx: *agora*, Gr *agora*, an assembly (hence, place of assembly), from *agein* (s *ag-*), to lead or drive—cf AGENT; *plethora*, LL *plethora*, Gr *plēthōra*, from *plēthein* (s *plēth-*), to be, to become, full. Conn: 'result of the action or process' of the v concerned.

**-ore.** Exx: *commodore*, earlier *commandore*, F *commandeur*, from *commander*; *stevedore*, Sp *estivador*, a packer, from *estivar*, from L *stipāre*. Conn: agent. Cf, therefore, *-or* (3).

**-orious** is a cpd adj suffix, formed of the *ōri*- of L *-ōrius* (see *-ory*, adj)+*-ous*, q.v. Exx: *censorious*, L *censōrius*, from *censor*; *gubernatorious*, LL *gubernatōrius*, from L *gubernator*; *notorious*, ML *notōrius*, from L *notus*, (well) known; *victirious*, ML *victōriōsus*, L *uictōriōsus*. Sometimes, as we see, the origin seems to be simply L *-ōrius* via OF *-orios*.

**-orium**, n suffix, with conn 'something belonging to', esp 'a place for' or 'a thing used for'. Adopted from L, it was, there, orig the neu of adj in *-ōrius*. Exx: *auditorium*, L from *auditōrius* (for hearing), from *audīre* (s *aud-*), to hear; *crematōrium*, Mod L, by analogy—cf ML *laboratōrium*. Cf *-arium* above and the 2nd *-ory* below.

**-ory** (1), adj: L *-ōrius*, f *-ōria*, neu *-ōrium*; occ through ONF *-ori*, f *-orie*, or OF *-oir*, f *-oire*. Conn: belonging to, (hence) serving for, used for: cf prec. Exx: *auditory*, L *auditōrius*, pp s *audit-* (from *audīre*, to hear)+*-ōrius*; *sensory*, from the LL n *sensōrium*, itself from an unrecorded adj *sensorius*, from *sens-*, the pp s of *sentīre*, to feel. Cf:

**-ory** (2), n: L *-ōrium*, occ through ONF *-orie* or F *-oire*. Merely the E shape of *-orium*, q.v. above.

Exx: *conservatory*, ML *conservatōrium*, from ML *conservāre*, L *conseruāre*; *consistory*, ONF *consistorie*, L *consistōrium*, a place for sitting together (*consistere*); *offertory*, LL *offertōrium*.

**-os**, n: Gr *-os*, n and adj, or *ōs*: corresponding to L *-us*, n and adj. Exx: *Dolichos*, a bot genus, from Gr *dolikhos*, long or narrow; *Helios*, the Gr sun-god *Hēlios*; *rhinoceros*, through L from Gr *rhinokerōs*. (Webster.)

**-ose** (1), adj: from L *-ōsus* and therefore a 'doublet' of *-ous*, q.v. Conn: intimately, esp if excessively, associated with the implied n. Exx: *morose*, L *morōsus*, from *mor-*, the o/s of *mos*, custom, habit (of life); *verbose*, ML *verbōsus*, L *uerbōsus*, from *uerbum*, a word. (Cf *-ous*.) The corresponding nn have *-osity*, from—or on the analogy of words from—L nn in *-ōsitāt-*, o/s of *-ōsitās*, as *verbosity*, ML *verbōsitās*, LL *uerbōsitās*; *porosity*, perh via F *porosité*, certainly from ML *porōsitās*.

**-ose** (2), n. This chem suffix has been borrowed from F, which based it on F *glucose*, itself from Gr *gleukos*, sweet wine. Exx: *albumose*, *cellulose*, *fructose*.

**-osis**: Gr *-ōsis*, often via L *-osis*: conn, 'condition' or 'state', esp if excessive or diseased, hence 'process', hence 'physiological formation or increase'. Exx: *hypnosis*, SciL, perh prompted by L *hypnoticus*; *narcosis*, SciL from Gr *narkōsis*; *varicosis*=*varic*(ose)+*-osis*. The adj is *-otic*, as below.

**-osity.** See *-ose* (1), last sentence.

**-ot** (1): Gr *-ōtēs*, often through L *-ōta*. Exx: *pilot* and *zealot* (Gr *zēlōtēs*), where the conn is 'doer, user'. Usu, however, *-ot* is a mere var of *-ote* (q.v.), 'native or inhabitant of'.

**-ot** (2): occurring in words adopted or adapted from F, where *-ot* is a dim, as it is in words adapted from It (*-otta*). Exx: *ballot*, It *ballotta*, a little ball, from *balla*, a ball; *parrot*, F *Perrot*, dim of *Pierre* —cf *Pierrot*, another dim of *Pierre*.

**-ote**: Gr *-ōtēs*, often through L *-ōta* and occ through F *-ot*: conn 'native or inhabitant of', as in *Cypriote*, now usu *Cypriot*, F *Cypriot*, post-Class Gr *Kupriōtēs*. Gr *-ōtēs* is app a cpd of *-ot*+'agent' or 'inhabitant' *-ēs*.

**-otic**: adj suffix, of Gr origin (*-ōtikos*), answering to nn in *-ōsis*, q.v. above. Ex: *narcotic*, imm from either F *narcotique* or ML *narcoticus*, from Gr *narkōtikos* (s *nark-*), from *narkoun* (s *nark-*), to benumb or stupefy; *neurotic*, *neur*(osis)+*-otic*, from *neuron*, a nerve.

**-our.** See *-or* (2), the abstract *-or*. In late ME and also in EE, the agential instrumental *-or* was also spelt *-our*, which, indeed, predominated during that period, owing to the influence of OF-MF *-our* in such nn. Very rarely *-our* represents the L *-(āt)ōrium*, as in *parlour*, OF *parleor* for *parleoir*, from ML *parlātōrium*, a place for talking.

**-ous**: L *-ōsus*, f *-ōsa*, neu *-ōsum*: often via OF *-ous* or *-os*, *-us* or *-eus*, occ via Mod F *-eux*, f *-euse*. (Cf *-ose* above.) Sometimes *-ous* represents Gr *-os*, usu via L *-ōsus*. Conn: (richly) possessing, of the nature of, like (the n implied). Exx: *gracious*, OF *gracious*, L *grātiōsus*, from *grātia*; *joyous*, OF *joyous*, ML *gaudiōsus*, from *gaudia*; *polygamous*, Gr *polugamos*, in a state of *polygamy*. Cf also *-eous*.

**-ow** (1), adj: OE *-u* or *-we*. Exx: *callow*, ME *calewe* or *calu*, OE *calu*; *mellow*, ME *melwe*, OE *melu*, meal (flour); *yellow*, ME *yelow*, *yelwe*, OE *geolu*. Conn: of the nature or quality of. Cf *-w* (1).

**-ow** (2), n: OE *-we* or *-wa*. Exx: *barrow*, ME *barow*, *barewe*, from OE *beran*, to bear—therefore, lit, the bearer or carrier; *meadow*, OE *māēdwe*, nom *māēd*—? that which is mown; *shadow*, ME *shadowe* or *schadewe*, from an oblique form of OE *sceadu*—? that which shades. Cf *-w* (2).

**-ple**, as in *duple*, *triple*, *quadruple*, *simple*: either from L *-plex*, as seen from the naturalized words *duplex*, *triplex*, *complex*, or from the cognate *-plus*, as seen from *duple*. Exx: *duple*, L *duplus*; *quadruple*, F *quadruple*, L *quadruplus*; *quintuple*, F *quintuple*, LL *quintuplex*; *sextuple*, from L *sex*, six, by analogy with *quadruple*; *simple*, OF *simple*, L *simplex*; *triple*, perh via F *triple*, certainly from L *triplex*. The conn is 'fold', as in *manifold*, which is syn with *multiple* (F *multiple*, L *multiplex*). See, therefore, *-plex* in the Elements list.

**-quin**. See *-kin*.

**-r** (1), adj, as in *fair*, ME *fayer* or *faiger*, OE *faeger*—cf ON *fagr* and OHG *fagar*. It derives from OE *-er*. Cf *-er* (2), non-comp adj.

**-r** (2), n, as in *lair*: OE *-cr* or *-er*: conn, either 'instrument' or 'action' or 'result of action': cf, therefore, agential *-er*, q.v. at *-er* (4) above. Exx: *lair*, ME *leir*, OE *leger* (cf OHG *legar*), act of lying, a place for lying; *stair*, ME *steir* or *steyer*, OE *staēger*; both of which clearly derive from vv—OE *licgan*, to lie (down), and OE *stīgan*, to ascend.

**-ra**, as in *Hydra* (s *Hyd-*, which=Gr *Hud-*). *Hydra*, the monster living in the marshy lake of Lerna, is, through L *Hydra*, the Gr *Hudra*, from *hudōr* (s *hud-*), water; *-ra* is a f suffix, the m suffix being *-ro*. Cf the *-ra* of L *lutra*, an otter, and the corresponding Skt *-rás* and Zend *-ra*.

**-re** (1), adj. See *-er* (2), the adj suffix of *eager* and AE *meager*.

**-re** (2) and *-er*, adv: OE *-re* or *-r*: predominant conn, 'time'—hence 'place (in time, hence in space)'. Exx: *ever*, ME *ever* or, earlier, *aefre*, OE *aēfre*—hence *never*, OE *naēfre*; *here*, ME *her*, OE *hēr*, a form common in the Old Gmc languages; *there*, ME *ther* or *thar*, OE *thāēr*, *thār*, *thēr*, cf Go and ON *thar*; *where*, ME *wher* or *whar*, OE *hwāēr*, cf Go *hwar* and OHG *hwār*.

**-re** (3), n. A rare var of agential-instrumental *-er*. Ex: *squire*, aphetic for *esquire*, OF *esquier* or *escuier*, L *scūtārius* (s *scut-*), a shicld-bcarcr, from *scūtum*, a shield: here, *-re* ult=*-ārius*.

**-re** (4), n, as in *calibre*: F *-re*. Exx: *calibre* (AE *caliber*), F *calibre*, It *calibro*; *fibre* (AE *fiber*), F *fibre*, L *fibra*. The conn is very vague, although it

does seem to connote 'a concrete result, or a concrete form, of some action or process'.

**-red** (1): ME *-rede*: OE *-rāēden*, from *rāēden*, rule, stipulation, direction, condition, state. Same conn as *-head*, q.v. Exx: *hatred*, ME *hatred*, earlier *hatreden*, with *-reden*=OE *-rāēden*; *kindred*, which consists of *kin*+intrusive *d*+*-red*, from ME *kinrede* or *kynrede*, earlier *kynreden* or *kunreden*.

**-red** (2), in *hundred*, OE *hundred*, which=*hund*, 100+*-red*, akin to OFris *rethe*, Go *rathjo*, a number, a reckoning, hence ult to REASON.

**-rel**, dim: a reduced form of *-erel*, q.v. above. See esp OED at *-rel*.

**-ress**. See *-tress*.

**-ric** or archaic **-rick**. Sole (?) ex: *bishopric*, OE *bisceoprīce*, where *-rīce*=*rīce*, dominion, kingdom; *rīce* is akin to L *regnum*. Strictly, a c/f, an Element.

**-rix**. See *-trix*.

**-ry**. A reduced form of *-ery* (1), q.v. above. Exx: *chivalry*, *jewelry* (cf *jewellery*), *revelry*, *rivalry*, *yeomanry* (an analogous formation).

**-s** (1), adv: short for *-es* (1) above, i.e. for OE *-es*, gen of neu and strong m nn. Exx: *always*, which=*all*+*way*+adv *-s*; *besides*, an *-s* var (cf ME *bisides*) of adv *beside*; *days*, by day, during the day, as in 'He lay awake *nights* and moped *days*'; *eftsoons*, ME *eftsones*, a var of *eftsone*; *needs*, necessarily, OE *nēdes*; *unawares*, an analogous var of adv *unaware*.

**-s** (2), n, is very common in words adopted from Gr and L, where *-s* is the most freq suffix for the nom case: notably in Gr words ending in *-as*, *-is*, and esp *-os*, and in L words ending in *-as*, *es*, *-is* and esp *-us*. Exx: Greek, *Lycidas* (Gr *Lukidas*), *aphesis* (Gr *aphēsis*), *pathos*; Latin, *adamas*, *animus*, etc. See also the separate Gr and L endings.

**-s** (3), n. The usual pl of native nn, as *boy*—*boys*: ME *-s*, *-es*, from OE *-as*.

**-s** (4), v. The usual suffix for the 3rd person sing of the pres ind, as 'He *hits*'. From MSc *-s*, *-es*, a Northern form supplanting Midland *-eth*. Cf *-es* (5) above.

**-se** (1), adj, as in *diverse* and *sparse*: L *-tus*, pp, changed into *-sus* in certain combb, esp in predominantly adj forms or in adjj presumably pps at first. Exx: *dense*, F *dense*, L *densus*; *diverse*, OF *divers*, ML *diversus*, pp of ML *divertere*, L *diuertere*, to turn in various directions; *sparse*, L *sparsus*, pp of *spargere*, to strew or scatter. (Sweet.)

**-se** (2), adv. A var of adv *-es*, q.v. at *-es* (1) above; cf prec. Ex: *else*, OE *elles*, gen of a lost adj *elle*, 'other', akin to OHG *elles*, otherwise.

**-se** (3), n: Gr *-sis*. Exx: *apocalypse*, LL *apocalypsis*, Gr *apokalupsis*; *base*, F *base*, L *basis*, Gr *basis*; *phase*, Gr *phasis*. Conn: result of a v. Cf *-sis*.

**-se** (4), v: OE *-sian*. Ex: *cleanse*, OE *claēnsian*, from *claēne*, clean; *glimpse*, earlier *glimse*, cf MHG *glimpsen* and E *gleam* and *glim*. A var is presented by *bless*, ME *bletsen*, OE *bletsian* or *bledsian* or *bloedsian*, from OE *blōd*, blood, 'the original meaning being "to sprinkle (the altar) with blood" ' (Sweet). Clearly *-se* is a freq suffix.

**-sh** (1), adj, as in *fresh* and *rash*, is perh a var of the dim *-ish* (see 1st *-ish*). Exx: *fresh*, OE *fersc*, influenced by *fresche*, the f of OF *fres* or *freis*; *rash*, MLG *rasch*. But in *Welsh*—cf *Irish*, *Turkish* —the suffix *-sh*, so far from being dim, merely connotes 'characteristic of, belonging to' (esp the country or the people designated by the n): *Welsh*, OE *waelisc* or *welisc*, from *wealh*, a stranger, a foreigner. Cf also *-ch* (1): the *-ch* of *French* and *Scotch*.

**-sh** (2), n. In *dish*, *-sh*=Gr *-skos*, via L *-scus*. a var of Gr *-sk*, q.v. below.

**-sh** (3), v. Except for vv in *-ish*, q.v. at *-ish* (3) above, *-sh* tends to be echoic, as in *clash*, *dash*, *flash*, *gash*, *smash*, *splash*—*swish*—*splosh*—*gush*.

**-ship**: ME *-schipe*: OE *-scipe*, akin to OFris *-skipe*, OHG *-scaf*, G *-schaft*. Orig with adjj, as in *hardship*, but now only with nn, mostly with nn designating persons. The chief senses of *-ship* are (1) state, condition, quality, as in *hardship* (*hard*+ *-ship*), *friendship* (OE *frēondscipe*), *kinship* (*kin*+ *-ship*); (2) something exhibiting or involving a state or a quality, as in *fellowship* ( *fellow*+*-ship*) and *township* (OE *tūnscipe*); (3) a dignity, an office, a profession, as in *lordship* (OE *hlāfordscipe*), *clerkship* (*clerk*+*-ship*); (4) one entitled to the rank denoted by the basic n, as in 'His *Lordship*'; (5) a special ability, esp a skill or an art, as in *statesmanship*, *seamanship*, *batsmanship*. As those exx show, the fundamental conn is 'a shaping (to an end), a creating': *-ship*, OE *-scipe*, is akin to OE *scieppan*, to shape, to create: cf, therefore, SHAPE.

**-sion.** See *-tion*. Note the co-existence of *torsion*, *distortion*.

**-sis:** Gr *-sis*, often through L *-sis*; conn: 'state, condition', esp as the result of a clearly discernible v. Exx: *analysis*, ML *analysis*, Gr *analusis*, from *analuein*, to unloose, (hence) to resolve into its elements; *catalysis*, Gr *katalusis*. But mostly in the extended forms *-asis*, *-esis*, *-osis*, qq.v.

**-sk** (1), Gr. But the true suffix is *-isk*, q.v. above.

**-sk** (2), Scan. Conn: 'self', such vv being orig reflexive. Exx: *bask*, from ON *bathask*, to bathe oneself, from *batha*, to bathe; *busk*, ME *busken*, from ON *būask*, to prepare oneself, from *būa*, to prepare. Ult *-sk* is a reduction of ON *sik*, self, akin to Go *sik*, OHG *sih*, L *se*.

**-some** (1), adj, as in *winsome*: OE *-sum*, akin to OHG (and G) *-sam*, ON *-samr*, Go *-sams*: ult id with SAME, Lit 'like' or 'same as', it connotes possession, to a marked degree, of the quality denoted by the base of the adj: that base is usu n, sometimes v. Exx: *awesome*=*awe*, n+*-some*; *fearsome*=*fear*, n or v+*-some*; *loathsome*=*loath*, n+*-some*, the late ME form being *lothsom*; *winsome*, OE *wynsum* (*wynn*, joy+*-sum*)—cf OHG *wunnisam*.

**-some** (2), n: OE *sum*, q.v. at SOME: conn 'in all' or '(working or playing) together'. Exx: *twosome*, *threesome*, *foursome*, all mod words.

**-ss.** See *-se* (3).

**-st** (1), adj and adv=sup *-est*. See *-est* (1) above.

**-st** (2), n: OE *-st*: cf *-est* (2). Conn: 'an instance

of the vn, e.g. *trusting*' or 'the vn, e.g. *trusting*, regarded as an entity'; app it derives orig from the corresponding v. Exx: *blast*, OE *blǣst*, akin to— ? from—*blawan*, to blow; *grist*, OE *grīst*, from *grindan*, to grind; *mist*, OE *mist*—cf late ME *miselen*, to drizzle; *trust*, either from ON *traust* or from OE *trauwan*, to trust; *tryst*, doublet of *trust*.

**-st** (3), prep, as *amidst*. Exx: *amidst*, ME *amiddes*, from OE *on middan*, in the middle. 'The *s* is an adverbial genitive ending [see *-s* (1) above]; the *t* is excrescent, as in *whilst*' (Webster); *amongst*, ME *amongist*, *amonges*; *whilst*, by analogy with *amidst*, *amongst*, from *while*—an explanation fitting the adv, the conj, the prep *whilst*.

**-ster; -stress.** Orig f, but later m or common, *-ster* derives from OE *-estre* or *-istre*, akin to MD *-ster*. In *songster* and *seamster* and *spinster*, it is f; the change from f to m or common has caused *seamster* to become *seamstress* and the f of *songster* to become *songstress*; *-stress* is a double suffix (and, strictly, a double f)=*-ster*+*-ess* (q.v. above), *-steress* becoming *-stress*. The conn is 'agent', esp one who works at the activity, occupation, profession, trade, skill denoted by the base of the word, usu a n but sometimes a v and occ, as in *youngster*, an adj. In the mod period, *-ster* is occ depreciatory, as in *rhymester*: a usage influenced by *-aster* (as in *poetaster*), q.v. above. Exx: *roadster*=*road*+*-ster*; *seamster* (OE *sēamestre*), later *sempster*, both now m; *seamstress*, *sempstress*=the former+*-ess*; *songster*, OE *sangestre*; *songstress*=*songster*+*-ess*, *songsteress* becoming *songstress*; *spinster*, ME *spinster* (*spin*, v+*-ster*), akin to MD *spinster*; *Webster*, surname from *webster*, a weaver (orig f), OE *webbestre*; *youngster*=*young*+*-ster*.

**-stress.** See prec.

**-sy** (1), as in *minstrelsy*, is a rare var of *-cy* (as in *fallacy*), q.v. above, from VL-ML *-cia* or L *-tia*, or from Gr *-keia* (*-kia*) or *-teia* (*-tia*).

**-sy** (2), as in *ecstasy*: Gr *-sis*. Thus: *ecstasy* or occ *extasy*, MF *extasie*, LL *ecstasis*, Gr *ekstasis*, from *existanai*, to derange; *palsy*, ME *palesie* for *parlesie* (or *-sy*), OF *paralysie*, Gr *paralusis*. Cf, therefore, *-sis* above.

**-t** (1), adj of L origin in *-tus*, f *-ta*, neu *-tum*: from the pp of L vv. Exx: *abrupt*, L *abruptus*, pp of *abrumpere*, to break off; *content*, via OF from L *contentus*, pp of *continēre*, to hold together; *extinct*, L *extinctus*, pp of *extinguere*, to put out (e.g., a fire). Cf, therefore, the adjj in *-ate*, *-ete*, *-ite*, *-ute*, qq.v. separately.

**-t** (2), adj of Gmc origin, as in *right*: OE *-t*. Exx: *bright*, ME *briht*, OE *bryht*, app for the more usu *beorht*, with cognates in the old Gmc languages; *right*, ME *right*, earlier *riht*, OE *riht*, with old Gmc cognates; *slight*, ME *slight*, *sleht*, with old Gmc cognates. Very old Gmc adjj of quality, and of independent origin.

**-t** (3), n of Gr origin: occ via L. Sometimes from Gr *-tē* (*-τη*), via L *-ta*, as in *crypt*, L *crypta*, Gr *kruptē*, from pp *kruptos*, hidden, and *cist*, L *cista*, Gr *kistē*; rarely from Gr *-ta*, as in *diet*, OF *diet*, L *diaeta*, Gr *diaita*, more often from the Gr agential *-tēs* (-της), as in *poet*, OF *poëte*, L *poēta*, Gr *poiëtēs*, and *prophet*, OF *prophete*, L *prophēta*, Gr *prophētēs*.

**-t** (4), n of L origin, as in *act*. Exx: *act*, L *actus*, a doing, and *actum*, a thing done, from *agere*, to ply, to do; *fact*, L *factum*, a deed, from *facere*, to make or do. Such words ult represent the L pp in *-tus*: cf: *-t* (1): therefore they derive from pp adjj. As in *counterfeit* (imm from F), the *t* is strictly thematic.

**-t** (5), n, as in *drought*, is a var of *-th*, with an abstract conn (=*-ness*, q.v.). Exx: *drought* (with var *drouth*), ME *droght*, earlier *drougth*, OE *drūgath*, from *drugian*, to dry; *height* (rare var *highth*), ME *heighte*, *heighthe*, OE *hīehthu*, *hēahthu* —cf *hēah*, high; *sleight*, ME *sleight*, *sleighte*, *sleght*, from ON *slǣgth*. Perh also *night*, ME *niht*, OE *niht*, usu *neaht*, with many IE cognates: Gmc, Celtic, Slavic, L (*noct-*, o/s of *nox*), Gr (*nukt-*, o/s of *nux*), Skt *nakta*, *nakti*.

**-t** (6), n of action, derived from v. Exx: *fight*, ME *fight*, earlier *feht*, OE *feoht*, from *feohtan*, to fight; *flight*, ME *fliht* or *fluht*, akin to OE *flēon*, to flee; *fright*, ME *frigt* or *freght*, OE *fryhto*, app for var *fyrhto*, prob from *fyrhtan*, to frighten; *gift*, ME *gift*, app from ON *gift*, akin to OE *gifan*, *giefan*; *thrift*, ME *thrift*, adopted from ON, from *thrīfast*, to thrive.

**-t** (7), n: var of *-est* (2) and *-st* (2), qq.v. above: of OE origin. Exx: *rust*, OE *rūst* (prob also *rust*), akin to obs *rud*, red, from OE *rudu*; *wrist*, OE *wrist*, akin to *wrīthan*, to twist.

**-t** (8), preterite of certain weak (i.e., regular) vv, as alternative of *-ed*: see *-ed* (3) above. Exx: *burnt* for *burned*, *stript* for *stripped*.

**-t** (9), pp—hence pp adj—for, and usu deriving from, *-ed*. Ex: *bought* (ME *boht*), *dwelt*, *spent*.

**-te** (1), adj and derivative n. See *-ate*, *-ete*, *-ite*, *-ute*, all of L origin. Cf also *-t* (1) and (4).

**-te** (2), n: Gr origin in *-tēs* (-της), an agential suffix. Ex: *apostate*, OF *apostate*, L *apostata*, Gr *apostatēs*. Cf *-t* (3), s.f.

[**-teen**. See Elements.]

**-ter** (1), n of Gr origin. Ex: *presbyter*, LL *presbyter*, Gr *presbuteros*, where the suffix *-teros* indicates the m comp of adjj (cf *proteros*, former); *-ter* is a very ancient comp suffix in IE.

[**-ter** (2), n of Gr origin in *-tron*, often through L *-trum* and occ through F *-tre*. Also in form *-tre*, predominantly E, *-ter* being mostly AE. Exx: *diameter*, OF *diametre*, L *diametrus*, Gr *diametros*; *meter* and *metre*, OF *metre* (F *mètre*), L *metrum*, Gr *metron*; *scepter* or *sceptre*, OF *sceptre*, L *sceptrum*, Gr *skēptron*. The conn is: agent or instrument. But this is only an app suffix, for the *t* of *-ter* is thematic, as it also is in *-ter* words deriving from L *-trum* independently of Gr *-tron*, as in *filter*, F *filtre*, ML *filtrum*.]

**-ter** (3): Gmc; conn: ? 'agent'. Exx: *daughter*, OE *dohtor* or *dohter*; *sister*, perh ON *systir*, akin to OE *sweostor* (or *-er*).

**-ter** (4), n of Gmc origin; conn 'result of' (implied v), with an abstract tinge. Exx: *laughter*, OE *hleahtor*, akin to *hlehhan*, to laugh; *slaughter*, ME *slauhter*, from ON *slātr*, akin to OE *slēan*. Virtually the same OE or other Gmc suffixes as in (3). In *murder* and *slaughter*, the *d/t* is prob thematic; in *laughter*, prob not.

**-teria**. Arbitrary from *cafeteria*, as in AE *radioteria*.

**-tery**, as in *artery*, *cemetery*, *mystery*: of Gr origin. Exx: *artery*, L *artēria*, Gr *artēria*; *cautery*, L *cautērium*; *cemetery*, LL *coemetērium*, Gr *koimētērion*; *mystery*, L *mystērium*, Gr *mustērion*; *phylactery*, LL *phylactērium*, Gr *phulaktērion*; *psaltery*, OF *psalterie*, LL *psaltērium*, Gr *psaltērion*. Gr *-ēria*, *-ērion*, hence L *-ēria*, *-ērium*, denotes a result of the action of a v (always discernible). But the *t* of *-tery* might fairly be adjudged thematic: see, therefore, *-ery* (2).

**-th** (1), ordinal adj: after a vowel, *-eth*; OE *-(o)tha*. Exx: *fourth*—cf OE *fēortha*, from *fēower*, 4; *fifth*, OE *fīfta*; *twentieth*, OE *twentigotha*.

**-th** (2), n abstract from adj or v: imm Gmc, ult of ancient IE stock. Exx: *birth*, ME from or akin to ON *byrth* (var of *burthr*), akin to Go (ga)*baurths* and to the OE v *beran*; *health*, OE *hǣlth*, from *hāl*, hale; *truth*, OE *trēowth*—cf *trēowe*, faithful. Skeat equates *-th* to Gmc *-thi* and IE *-ti*, very common, esp in L.

**-th** (3), v: a var of *-eth* (2), q.v.—the suffix of the press ind, 3rd person sing, as in *doth* and *hath*.

**-ther** (1), adj and pronoun, as in *either* and *other*. Exx: *either*, ME *aither*, OE *ǣgther*; *other*; OE *ōther*; pronoun *whether*, OE *hwether*, *hwaether*. The Gmc suffix alternates between *-ther* and *-thar*, and *-der* and *-dar*; and *-er* occurs in L, as in *uter*, and in Gr, as in *poteros*.

**-ther** (2), adv, as in *hither*: OE *-der*: conn, 'towards'. Exx: *hither*, OE *hider*; *thither*, OE *thider*; *whither*, OE *hwider*. All three with several IE cognates, esp Gmc. Cf the 2nd *-re*.

**-ther** (3), n: Gmc: concrete. Exx: *heather*, ME *hudder* or *hathir*, perh ON *heithr*; *leather*, OE *lether*, akin to ON *lethr*, OHG *ledar*.

**-ther** (4): Gmc: agent or instrument. Exx: *brother*, OE *brōther*, akin to OS *brothar*, ON *brōthir*, OHG *bruodar*, Skt *brǎtar-*; *father*, OE *faeder*, akin to OS *fadar*, ON *fathir*—also to L *pater*, Gr *patēr*; *mother*, OE *mōdor*, akin to OS *mōdar*, ON *mōthir*—also to L *māter*, Gr *mētēr*, Skt *matr*;—*lather*, OE *lēathor*; *weather* (? 'that which withers', v.t.), OE *weder*, akin to OS *wedar*, OHG *wetar*; *wether*, OE *wether*, with many cognates, Gmc and other. The OE forms of the suffix are, therefore, *-thor*, *-dor*, *-der*.

**-tic**, adj. See *-atic*, *-etic*, *itic*, *-otic*, *-utic*.

**-tion**, a cpd abstract-n suffix, deriving from L *-tiōn-*, o/s of nn in *-tiō*, often via OF *-cion* or F *-tion*; formed from vv; and denoting action, hence both the corresponding abstraction and the concrete result or a concrete instance. Commoner than the var *-sion* (as in *tension*) and much commoner than the var *-xion* (*connexion*, *reflexion*). Ex: *caution*, adopted from OF, from *cautiōnem* (o/s *cautiōn-*), the acc of *cautiō*, from *cauēre* (s *cau-*), to be on guard. The answering adj form is *-tious*, as in *cautious*, from L *cautus*.—Cf *-ion*. Prop, the *-t-* is thematic and belongs to the s of the L pp.

**-tious.** See prec.

[**-to,** in *hereto*, *thereto*, and *into*, *onto*, is the prep TO.]

[**-ton,** in place-names, e.g. *Boston*, is identical with TOWN. See Elements.]

**-tor** (1), as in *polyhistor* (Gr *poluistōr*, erudite), a person of many-sided learning, represents Gr *-tōr*, akin to *-tēr*, of general agential conn. Thus, *polyhistor*, 'a much-knower', πολυίστωρ=πολύ, much+ίστωρ, one who knows.

**-tor** (2). Cf *-ator* and see *-or* (3).

**-tre,** no f Gr origin *-tron*, often via L *-trum* (or from some L n formed analogously) and occ via F *-tre* (whether from the Gr or the L suffix). See the 2nd *-ter*.

**-tress,** f agential suffix answering to m *-ter* or *-tor*, where the *-t-* is thematic; strictly, the suffix is *-ress*, not *-tress*, and this *-ress* is clearly short, at least in principle, for *-eress* or *-oress*, as we see from *actor*, *actress*—*hunter*, *huntress*—*seamster*, *seamstress*.

**-trice,** in e.g. *executrice*, is obs for *-trix*, q.v., sometimes via It or F *-trice*: cf It *esecutrice*, F *exécutrice*. It survives, however, for It (occ via F) *-trice* in e.g. *cantatrice*.

**-trix,** as in *aviatrix*, *executrix*, *testatrix*, is a f agential, corresponding to m *-tor*: L *-trix*, as in *bellatrix*, a female warrior (m *bellator*). Clearly a cpd, prob short for *-torix*; the true f 'answer' to L *-or* is L *-rix*.

**-tude,** n; **-tudinous,** adj. See *-itude*.

**-ty** (1), abstract n of L origin in *-tās*, o/s *-tāt-* (gen *-tātis*), often via OF *-te* or *té*, or F *-té*. (Cf, therefore, *-ity*.) Exx: *beauty*, OF *beaute* or *beute*, VL *bellitās* (acc *bellitātem*), from *bellus*, pretty; *liberty*, OF *liberté*, L *libertās*, o/s *libertāt-*, from *liber*, free; *vanity*, OF *vanité*, ML *vānitās*, o/s *vānitāt-*, from ML *vānus* (L *uānus*), empty.

**-ty** (2): OE *-tig*, akin to OFris *-tich*, ON *-tigr*, Go *-tigus*, G *-zig*: in numerals, denoting 'tens', as *twenty*, two tens, OE *twēntig*, OFris *twintich*; *thirty*, by metathesis from OE *thrītig*.

[**-ual,** as in *gradual* (ML *graduālis*, from *gradus*, a step) and *punctual* (ML *punctuālis*, from *punctus*, a point), is only an app suffix, for the *u* is thematic. See *-al*, adj.]

**-ubility,** n; **-uble,** adj. See *-bility*.

**-ude,** n; **-udinous,** adj. See *-itude*.

**-ula,** f; **-ulum,** neu; **-ulus,** m; pl, resp **-ulae, -ula, -uli.** These are L forms of dim nn, and the anglicized *-ule* often comes through F. The E adj corresponding to all forms is *-ular*, occ through F *-ulaire*, from L *-ulāris*, m and f, and *-ulāre*, neu; *-ular*, however, sometimes derives from such L nn

in *-ulus*, *-ula*, *-ulum* as are not, at first sight, dim or as, rarely, are not dim at all.

Exx: *cellule*, analogously from *cell*—adj, *cellular*; *homuncule*, L *homunculus*, pl *homunculi* (both adopted by SciE), dim of *homo*, a man; *molecule*, F *molécule*, analogously from L *mōles*, mass—adj, *molecular*, analogously from *molecule*; *regula*, adopted by Arch from the L for a ruler (for measuring), the f dim, as *regulus*, a petty ruler, is the m dim, of *rex*, a king, a ruler—adj, *regular*, L *regulāris*, from *regula*; *secular*, L *saeculāris*, from *saeculum*, a generation, a race, (hence the races of) the world, *saeculum* being prob dim in neu *-ulum* from *saec-* for ? *ser-*, the s of *serere*, to sow (seeds). Cf *-cule*.

**-ulae.** See prec.

**-ular,** adj. See *-ula*.

**-ulent,** adj: L *-ulentus*, often via F *-ulent*: conn, 'rich in' or 'having many or much'. Exx: *corpulent*, adopted from F, from L *corpulentus*, from *corpus* (s *corp-*), body; *fraudulent*, via OF, from L *fraudulentus*, from *fraud-*, o/s of *fraus*, trickery.

**-uli.** See *-ula*.

**-ulose:** L *-ulōsus*, a cpd of *-ul*(us)+*-ōsus*, occ via F *-uleux*, f *-uleuse*: conn, 'rich in' or 'characterized by' (cf, therefore, *-ulent*). Exx: *cellulose*, an analogous formation, consisting of *cell*+ *-ulose*; *fabulose* (a rare var of *fabulous*), L *fābulōsus*; *granulose*, likewise analogous. Cf:

**-ulous:** (*a*) L *-ulōsus*, occ via F *-uleux*, f *-uleuse*: conn as prec. Ex: *fabulous*, L *fābulōsus*, from *fābula*, a fable, itself from *fāri*, to say.

(*b*) L *-ulus*: conn, 'tending to' (do what the implied v denotes). Ex: L *crēdulus*, from *crēdere* (s *crēd-*), to believe.

**-ulum, -ulus.** See *-ula*.

**-um:** L *-um*, neu n of 2nd dec: conn, 'concrete object' or 'physical aspect of one'. The E words come either directly or imitatively from L. Exx: *forum*, adopted from L; *medium*, L n from adj *medius*, middle; *platinum*, SciL from earlier *platina*.

**-und** (1), adj: L *-undus*. conn, 'of the nature of' (the n implied). Exx: *jocund*, via OF from ML *jocundus*, LL *iocundus*, from L *iūcundus*, pleasant, but influenced by *iocus*, a joke: *rotund*, L *rotundus*, from *rota*, a wheel.

**-und** (2), n. In *gerund*, *-und*=L *-undium* (LL *gerundium*, n from *gerere*, to bear).

**-uous:** sometimes L *-uus* (connective *-u-*+adj *-us*) and sometimes L *-uōsus* (connective *-u-*+ *-ōsus*), occ via OF *-uous* or F *-ueux*, f *-ueuse*: conn, 'of the nature of' or 'belonging to' or, if from a v, 'tending to'. Exx: *ambiguous*, L *ambiguus*, from *ambigere*, to wander about; *fatuous*, L *fatuus*; *impetuous*, F *impétueuse*, f of *impétueux*, from L *impetuōsus*, from the n *impetus*.

**-ure** (1), n. L *-ūra*—often via F *-ure*—app from the implied v, with consequent conn 'act or process, or being', as in *censure*, adopted from F, from L *censūra*, from *censēre*, to value, (hence) to tax; *culture*, F *culture*, L *cultūra*, from *colere*, to cultivate; 'result' of the v's action, as in *picture*, L *pictūra*, from *pict-*, pp s of *pingere*, to paint; 'personal state or condition, rank or office', as in *judicature*, F *judicature*, ML *jūdicatūra*, from ML *jūdicāre*, L *iūdicāre*, to (ad)judge; 'instrument or means of action', as in *ligature*, F *ligature*, LL *ligatūra*; from *ligāre*, L, to tie or bind. (Webster.)

-ure (2), n: OF n in *-ir*, occ from OF inf in *-ir*; rarely an OF n in *-or*: abstract conn. Exx: *leisure*, ME *leiser(e)*, OF *leisir* (F *loisir*), from L *licere*, to be permissible; *pleasure*, ME *plesure*, earlier *plesir*, OF *plesir*, orig an inf from L *placēre*, to please; *treasure*, ME *treso(u)r*, OF *tresor*, L *thesaurus*.

-uret, -uretum: chem suffixes, the former (earlier *-ure*) from the latter; *-urētum* is strictly L for the *-ure* we find in F *sulfure* (from L *sulphur*, of obscure origin) and also in *curbure* and *phosphure*.

-urient, as in *esurient*: L *-urient-*, o/s of presp *-uriens*, characteristic of desiderative vv: conn, therefore, 'desirous' (of doing what the implied v denotes). Exx: *esurient*, L *esurient-*, o/s of *esuriens*, presp of *esurīre*, to desire to eat, from *edere*, to eat; *parturient*, L *parturient-*, o/s of *parturiens*, presp of *parturīre*, to desire to bring forth, from *parere*, to bring forth (e.g., children).

-urn: L *-urnus*: conn, 'of the nature or quality of; resembling'. Exx: *nocturn* (adj), L *nocturnus*, of night, from *noct-*, o/s of *nox*, night; *taciturn*, perh via F *taciturne*, from L *taciturnus*, from *tacitus*, pp of *tacēre*, to be silent.

[-urous, as in the rare *pleasurous* and in *adventurous*, OF *aventuros*, is merely *-ous* added to nn in *-ure*, esp *-ure* (2).]

-ury, in *usury*, is a 'disguise' of *-ure* (1): OF *usure*, L *ūsūra* (ᴦ *us-*), from *ūsus*, pp of *ūtī*, to use: cf ML *ūsūria*.

-us: L *-us* (2nd declension m, or 3rd declension neu)—or imitative thereof; conn, 'concrete' (whether animate or inanimate). The L *-us* occ derives from Gr *-os* (see *-os* above). Exx: *acanthus*, adopted from L, itself from Gr *akanthos*; *genus*, pl *genera*, both adopted from L; *focus*, from L; *radius*, pl *radii*, from L; *syllabus*, a SciL misreading of Cicero's *sittybas* (acc pl).

-ute, as in *absolute* and *destitute*: adj from L *-ūtus*, pp of certain 3rd-conj vv: cf, therefore, the adj suffixes *-ate*, *-ete*, *-ite*. Exx: *absolute*, L *absolūtus*, pp of *absoluere*, to set free; *destitute*, L *dēstitūtus*, pp of *dēstituere*, to forsake; *minute* (adj), L *minūtus*, pp of *minuere*, to lessen. Cf:

-utive, adj (hence n): ML *-ūtīvus* (L *-ūtiuus*): conn, 'achieving' what the implied v denotes. Exx: *diminutive*, F *diminutive*, f of *diminutif*, ML *dīminūtīvus*, LL *dīminūtīuus*, pp of *dīminuere*, (vt) to diminish; obs *solutive*, ML *solūtīvus*. Strictly, an *-īuus*, ML *-īvus*, addition to pps in *-ūtus*; analogously in E, an *-ive* addition to adjj in *-ute* (q.v.): therefore cf *-ative*, *-etive*, *-itive*.

-w (1), adj: OE *-w* or *-we*, of vague conn. Exx: *few*, OE *feawe*; *raw*, OE *hrǣw* or *hrēaw*; *slow*, OE *slāw*. Cf *-ow* (1), q.v.

-w (2), n: OE *-w* or *-wa* or *-we* or *-wu*, of vague conn. Exx: *claw*, OE *clawu* (or *clēa*); *dew*, OE *dēaw*; *snow*, OE *snāw*; *stow* (a place, as in *Stow-market*), OE *stōw*; *straw*, OE *strēawe*. The OE suffix has close kin in the old Gmc languages. Cf *-ow* (2).

-ward, -wards. See WARD in the Dict. The OE *-weard*, from an obs adj connected with *weorthan*= L *uertere*, ML *vertere*, to turn, 'forms adjectives from nouns, adjectives, and adverbs: *hāmweard* [E *homeward*] . . . *inneweard* [*inward*] from *hām* "home" . . . *inne* "within" ' (Sweet).

[-wart, as in *stalwart*. See WORTH, adj, in Dict.]

[-wise, adv, as in *likewise*, derives from the n *wise*, way, manner; thus, *likewise* comes from *in like wise*, *nowise* from *in no wise*. See WISE, n, in Dict.]

-x (1). See *-trix*.

-x (2), as in *calyx*, *climax*, *helix*, *thorax*: Gr ξ (*x*), n suffix with conn 'concrete object'. Exx: *calyx*, L *calyx*, Gr *kalux*; *climax*, L *clīmax*, Gr *klīmax* (s *klīm-*), a staircase, from *klīnein* (s *klīn-*); *helix*, L from Gr *helix*; *thorax*, L *thorax*, Gr *thōrax*.

-x (3), of L origin: *calix*, a chalice, adopted from L *calix*, a cup; *vortex*, adopted from ML, where, meaning 'whirlpool', it is a var of *vertex*, L *uertex*, from *uertere*, to turn. The conn is 'concrete'.

-xion is, in origin and meaning, similar to *-tion*, q.v. Exx: *connexion*, L *connexiōn-*, o/s of *connexiō*, (lit) a binding together; *reflexion* (var of *reflection*), OF *reflexion*, from *reflexiōnem* (o/s *reflexiōn-*), acc of *reflexiō*. Strictly, the *-x* is thematic.

-y (1), adj, perh of ML origin in *-īvus*, prob via AF *-if*: conn 'tending to', usu 'achieving'. Exx: ? *jolly*; ? *massy*; *testy*, AF *testif*; ? *tetchy*. The connexion with L *-īuus*, ML *-īvus* is extremely doubtful; and AF *-if* applies in only a few exx.

-y (2), adj: OE *-ig*, akin to OHG *-īg* or *ig*, occ *-ag*, ON *-igr*, and ult to Skt *-ka*: conn, 'of'—'full of'—'having'—'characterized by'—the implied n, as in *icy*, OE *īsig*, from *īs*, ice, and in *stony*, OE *stānig*, from *stān*; 'tending to' do what the implied v denotes, as in *sleepy*, OE *slǣpig*, from *slǣpan*, to sleep: a mod development—'rather' the adj implied, as in *chilly*, which=*chill*, cold (adj)+*-y*; a mod coll development—'rather like' or 'suggesting' the n implied, as in *bumpy* (*bump*, n+*-y*). The prob similar monosyllabic adjj in *-y*, e.g. *dry*, *sly*, *spry*, are ult of Gmc origin: OE *dryge*—ON *slaegr*—? Sw.

-y (3), n of Gr origin in *-ia* or *-eia*, often via L *-ia* and then occ via OF or F *-ie*: abstract conn. (Anl formations have arisen at the L—the F—the E stage.) Exx: *poesy*, OF *poësie*, L *poēsis*, Gr *poēsis*, *poiēsis*, from *poiein*, to make; *story*, OF *estoire*, L *historia*, Gr *historia*, from *histōr*, an erudite person.

-y (4), n occurring in 1st element of cpds of Gr origin (adj in *-us*, neu *-u*). Exx: *barytone*, It *baritono*, Gr *barutonos*, deep-toned, from *barus*, heavy; *pachyderm*, Gr *pachydermos*, thick-skinned, from *pakhus*, thick.

**-y** (5), n of L origin in *-ium*, occ through OF-F *-ie*: conn, 'result of action'. Exx: *augury*, OF *augurie*, L *augurium*, from *augurāri* (s *augur-*), to augur; *colloquy*, L *colloquium*, from *colloqui*, to speak together; *perjury*, OF *parjurie*, ML *perurium*, L *periūrium*, from *periūrāre*, to swear (a person) over.

**-y** (6), n of L origin in *-ia*, often via AF or OF or F *-ie*: conn, 'result of action'. Ex: *injury*, AF *injurie*, ML *injūria*, L *iniūria*, abstract n from *iniūrius*, unjust; and such country names as *Germany* (*Germania*) and *Italy* (*Italia*).

**-y** (7), n, ult of L origin in *-āta*, *-ātus* or *-ātum*, whether n or a pp base or the f and m and neu of the pp of vv in *-āre*, but imm from OF or F *-é*, m (L m and neu), and *ée*, f (L f), and issuing in E, either as n, e.g. *army*, F *armée*, L *armāta*, f of *armātus*, pp of *armāre*, to arm, and *treaty*, OF *traité* or *traitie*, from L *tractātus* (gen *-ūs*), from *tractāre*, to handle; or as heraldic adj, as in *bendy*, OF *bendé* (F *bandé*).

**-y** (8), n of L origin in *-iēs*. Exx: *effigy*, (perh via F *effigie*, from) L *effigiēs*, from *effingere*, to fashion, shape, form; *progeny*, OF *progenie*, L *prōgeniēs*, from *prōgignere*, to bring forth (children). Conn is clearly 'result of the implied v's action or process'.

**-y** (9), n dim of Gmc, esp D, origin; perh suggested by *baby*. Exx: *doggy* or *doggie*, lit a small dog, hence a pet-name address to a dog; *kitty*, a small cat, a kitten. Cf *-ie*.

**-y** (10), n of Gmc origin: OE *-e*, place of action. Exx: *smith*, OE *smiththe*, cf ON *smithja*; cf *stithy*, ON *stethi*, an anvil.

**-y** (11), n of Gmc origin: OE *-ig*, conn, 'concrete object'. Exx: *body*, OE *bodig*; *ivy*, OE *ifig*.

**-y** (12), v: ME *-ien* or OE *-ian*, inf suffix. Exx: *bury*, ME *berien*, OE *byrgan*; *ferry*, ME *ferien*, OE *ferian*;

**-y** (13), v: ONF *-ier* or OF *-(e)er*, influenced if ME by *-ien* (cf prec). Ex: *carry*, ONF *carier*, from *car*, a car; *curry* (a horse), ME *curraien* or *curreien*, from OF *correer*.

**-yer**: agential *-ier*, q.v. at *-ier* (2). It occurs after a *w* or a vowel. Exx: *bowyer=bow+-yer*; *lawyer=law+-yer*; *sawyer=saw+-yer*. In short, these are mod formations. See also agential *-er* and cf the var *-eer*.

[**-yl**, F *-yle*, occurring in chem terms, is strictly an element: see Elements.]

**-yne**. An arbitrary var of chem *-ine*, q.v. at *-ine* (5), in the special sense: 'acetylene hydrocarbon'.

**-ys**: Gr *-us*, through LL *-ys*. Only in a few erudite words, as *drys*, an oak, a germander, from Gr δρῦς.

**-ysm**: Gr *-usmos*, usu through LL *-ysmus* and occ through F *-ysme*: app a var of Gr *-ismos*, L *-ismus*, E *-ism* (q.v.). Exx: *cataclysm*, F *cataclysme*, L *cataclysmus*, Gr *kataklusmos*, from *katakluzein*, to inundate; *paroxysm*, F *paroxysme*, Gr *paroxusmos*, from *paroxunein*, to sharpen. Adjj add *-ic*, q.v.

**-yte**. A var of geological, mineralogical, petrographical *-ite*: see *ite* (2).

**-ze** (1), n, with derivative adj *-zy*; such *-ze* nn as are echoic, usu come from vv, themselves echoic; the n corresponds either to F *-se*, as in *breeze*, n (adj *breezy*), F *brise*, and *prize*, OF *prise*, or to OE *-s*, as in *furze*, OE *fyrs*.

**-ze** (2), v: echoic. Exx: *sneeze*, OE *snēosan*; *wheeze*, of echoic Gmc origin. Adjj n *-y*.

**-ze** (3), v: non-echoic, from OE *-san*. Ex: *freeze*, OE *frēosan*. Cf (to) *prize*, from F *priser*.

*N.B.* Strictly, the *-z-* of (1)–(3) is thematic.

# ELEMENTS

I N Science and Technology and in the other specialist vocabularies of scholarship and learning, many elements occur in words so little used in everyday speech and writing, and a few elements have become so much changed or have been so thoroughly incorporated, that the ordinary person does not know or does not recognize them. The elements themselves or the words they form, or go towards forming, are nevertheless important, even though the words cannot appear in the body of a well-planned, rigorously selective etymological dictionary of English.

Yet, with their help, an averagely intelligent person can ascertain, at least approximately, the meaning of a vast number of erudite terms. What, for instance, can the average person make of such a group as *acroasphyxia, acroblast, acrocarpous, acrocephaly, acrochordon, acrocyst* and not less than forty other *acro*-compounds, especially when he would hardly find them in a short general dictionary? He knows one word in the group: *acrobat*: but he has forgotten its etymology, even if he ever knew it, and probably doesn't think of relating it to *acrophobia* and the *Acropolis*. But with the help of the ensuing list of elements, he will be able to deduce the meaning of most of the terms in a group predominantly erudite.

English elements are, in the main, excluded. One doesn't need to be either scholarly or particularly intelligent to realize that the *fold* of *twofold, manifold*, is in origin the same word as a *fold* in gown or ground, or that the *wel* of *welcome* is identical with the *well* of *well-behaved*, or to recognize the *like* of *suchlike* for what it is. I have, however, made an exception of (say) the *-ty* of *twenty, thirty*, etc.

Strictly, an element consists of an adjective or a noun or a verb. A preposition or an adverb derived from a preposition does not form an element: it forms either a prefix, and is then to be found in the list of prefixes, or occasionally a suffix, and is then to be found in the list of suffixes; if, like *to* in *thereto*, it is manifestly an independent word, it will appear in its right place in the Dictionary proper.

'See (*a word in italics*)' means: See the italicized word at its alphabetical place in this list. 'See Dict at (a word in SMALL CAPITALS)' or 'See (THAT WORD)' means: Consult the Dictionary at that word. If the reference is obvious, 'See Dict' suffices. The same holds good for 'Cf . . .'

Some elements occur in only one position—the first or the second; or, if the word (e.g. *trinitrotoluene*) consists of more than two elements, the first or the last. Many occur, although occasionally in different forms, in either the first or the second or last, or indeed medially. If in doubt, consult Prefixes. The two most important connective vowels are *-i-* and especially *-o-*. If the element following either the first or the medial element begins with a vowel, the *-i-* or the *-o-* is usually

867

omitted, although numerous scientific and technical words flout this euphonious tendency.

**abdomino-**, 'of, in, for the abdomen': *abdōmin-* (o/s of L *abdōmen*)+connective *-o-*. Cf ABDOMEN.

**aberro-**: for *aberration*, as in *aberrometer* and *aberroscope*, instruments used in Optics. Cf ERR.

**abio-**: a cpd c/f, as in *abiogenesis*: prefix *a-*, not+*bio-*, life. Cf *bio-*.

**aborti-**, as in *aborticide* (cf *-cide*) and *abortifacient* (cf *-facient*): from L *abortus*, an abortion.

**abro-**. A var of *habro-*, as in *Abrocoma* (cf *-coma*).

**abysso-**, '(in) the depths of the sea', as in *abyssopelagic* (cf *archipelago*): *abyss-*, s of L *abyssus*, from Gr *abussos*, abyss+the connective *-o-*.

**ac-**, 'a point' (Gr *akē*, s and r *ak-*), occurs in *acantho-*, *aceto-*, *acido-*, *acou(-o)-*, *acro-*, qq.v. below, and also, as r, in such words as *acerb*, *acies*, *acrid*, *acuity* and *acute*. This r is general IE *ak-*.

**acantho-** or, before a vowel, **acanth-**, 'thorn(y), spine, spiny': *acanth(o)-*, L *acanth(o)-*, adapted from *akanth(o)-*, c/f of Gr *akanthos*, L and E *acanthus*, a prickly herb: lit 'spiny flower' (cf the *ac-* of ACME, and *anth(o)-* below). Exx: *acanthology*, the science of spines; *acanthopod*, spiny-footed (cf *-pod* below). Adj: *acanthoid* (suffix *-oid*).

**acari-**, **acaro-**, 'an or the itch; mites'—as in *acaricide* (cf *-cide*) and *acarophobia*, a morbid fear of the itch; *acaro-* attaches the connective *-o-* to *acar-*, adaptation of *akar-*, s of Gr *akari*, a mite: o.o.o.: ? something not cut off or away, i.e. indivisible—cf ATOM. Adj: *acaroid* (cf suffix *-oid*).

**accelero-**: for *accelerate* or *acceleration*, as in *accelerograph* and *accelerometer*.

**-ace**, 'a summit having (*x*) faces', as in *tessarace*, a tetrahedral summit: cf *tessara-* below: *-ace*=Gr *akē*, a point, s *ak-*, as in *acerb*, *acme*, etc. Cf *ac-* above and *aceto-* below.

**acephalo-**, 'headless': Gr *akephalos*, consisting of privative *a-* (prefix)+an adj form of *kephalē*, the head: Ex: *acephalocyst*. Adj: *acephalous*.

**aceto-** or, before a vowel, **acet-**: from L *acētum* (s *acēt-*), acid, a derivative of the IE *ak-*, a point, hence sharpness: cf *ac-* and *-ace* above and esp ACID. Exx: *acetolysis* (cf *-lysis* at *-lyse* below); *acetometer*; *aceturic*. Cf:

**achill(o)-**: for *Achilles' (tendon)*, as in *achillodynia* (cf *-odynia*).

**acido-**, a c/f of ACID. Ex: *acidophile*—cf *-phile* below. Do not confuse with the *acido-* of *acidology*, the science, a knowledge, of surgical appliances: this *acido-* adapts *akido*, c/f of Gr *akis*, o/s *akid-*, a splinter, skin to *akē*, a point, q.v. at *-ace* above and *acro-* below.

**acini-**: from L *acinus*, a grape or grape-stone, o.o.o. Ex: *aciniform*. Adj: *acinose* (L *acinōsus*).

**acou-**, short form, and **acouo-**, long form, conn 'hearing': from Gr *akouein* (s *akou-*) to hear. Ex: *acoumeter*, an instrument for measuring the acuteness of hearing. Also *-acousia*, *-acousis*. 'degree or quality of hearing': Gr *akousis*, ability to hear: ex, *dysacousia* or *-acousis*, defective hearing. Cf ACOUSTIC.

**acro-**; before a vowel, **acr-**: Gr *akros*, at the furthest point, esp vertically, from *akē*, a point. Exx: ACROBAT; *acrocarpous*, bearing fruit (cf *-carpous* at *carpo-* below) at the top; *acrodrome*, running (cf *-drome* below) to a point; *acrophobia*, a dread of heights; *Acropolis*, the high-set citadel (cf *-polis*) of Athens; *acrostic* (cf *-stich* below).

**-actine**; **actinio-**, **actino-** or, before a vowel, **actin-**: resp 'rayed' (adj)—c/f of *Actinia*, a genus of sea anemones, formed of *actin-*+suffix *-ia*—'ray(s), radiated structure': cf *actinium*, a radioactive element (*actin-*+-chem suffix *-ium*). These c/ff come from Gr *aktis*, a ray, gen *aktinos*, o/s *aktin-*, akin to Skt *aktus*, light, (basically) radiance. Exx: *pentactine* (cf *penta-* below), 5-rayed; *actiniochrome* (cf *chromo-*); *actinodrome* (cf *-drome*), *actinometer*, *actinospere*, *actinosome*, *actinotherapy*.

**acu-**: from L *acus*, a needle, as in *aculosure*. Cf:

**acuti-**, **acuto-**: from L *acūtus*, sharp(-pointed): cf ACUTE. Exx: *acutifoliate*, *acutograve*.

**-adelphia**; **adelpho-**: 'brotherhood', as in *Philadelphia* (cf *phil-*); 'brother', as in *adelpholite* (cf—*-lite*): from Gr *adelphos*, a brother, (lit) of one womb. (See esp Boisacq.)

**-aden**; **adeno-** or, before a vowel, **aden-**: resp 'type of gland' and 'gland' or 'glandular': Gr *adēn*, a gland, gen *adenos*, o/s *aden-*, akin to L *inguen*. Exx: *thyraden* (cf *thyroid* and, below, *thyro-*); *adenoneural* (cf *neuro-*): cf *adenoid*, Gr *adenoeidēs*, like, of the form of, a gland. Cf *-oid* in Suffixes.

**adipo-** or, before a vowel, **adip-**: 'fat(s)' or 'fatty tissue': L *adeps*, fat (n), gen *adipis*, o/s *adip-*, akin to—indeed, perh from—Gr *aleipha*, fat. Ex: *adipometer*. Cf the adj *adipose* (from SciL *adiposus*) and its derivative n *adiposity*.

**adreno-**: for *adrenal*; as in Biochem *adrenotropic*.

**adversi-**: from ML *adversus* (L *aduersus*), opposite, as in *adversifoliate* (cf *-foliate*). Cf *adverse*; f.a.e., VERSE.

**aegi-**; **aego-** or, before a vowel, **aeg-**: 'goat' or 'goat-like': Gr *aix*, a goat, gen *aigos*, o/s *aig-*; perh cf Skt *ajā*, female, and *ajás*, male goat; cf Arm *aic*, she-goat. Exx: *Aigipan*, (the goat-like) Pan; *Aegopodium*, a 'goat-footed' herb.

**aeluro-** or, before a vowel, **aelur-**: 'cat' or 'cat-like': Gr *ailouros* (s *ailour-*), a cat, perh lit 'tailwagger'. Ex: *aelurophobia*, a dread of cats.

**-aemia**. See *haema-*.

**aeoli-**, **aeolo-**: from L *Aeolus*, god of winds. Exx: *aeolipile* (or *-pyle*), a primitive ancient steamengine: *Aeoli*, of Aeolus, *pila*, a ball, or Gr *pulē*, a doorway, in its ML form *pylum* or esp *pilum*; *aeolomelodicon*, a wind instrument.

**aequi-**. An obs form of *equi-*, equal.

**aero-** or **aëro-** or, before a vowel, **aer-** or **aër-**:

'air' or 'aerial'; hence, 'gas' (or 'gases') or 'gaseous': Gr *aero-*, c/f of *aēr*, air, gen *aeros*, akin to Gr, hence L, *aura* and to Lith *oras*, air: cf AIR. Exx: *aerobatics*, which=*aero-*+the *-batics* of *acrobatics*; *aeromarine*; *aeronaut*, lit 'sailor of the air'; *aeroplane*; *aerostat*. The L form *aeri-* occurs in, e.g., *aerify*, to aerate.

**aesthesi-; aesthesio-**. See *asthesi-, esthesio-*.

**aetheo-**: from Gr *aēthēs*, unusual (*a-* not+*ēthos*, custom); as in Bot *aetheogamous* (cf *-gam*). Cf ETHIC.

**aethio-; aetho-: aethrio-**: resp from Gr *\*aithios*, bright; Gr *aithos*, light, fire (whence *\*aithios*); Gr *aithrios*, light, clear: all akin to *aithein* (s *aith-*), to burn. Exx: Bot *Aethionema* (cf *-nema*); *aethogen* (cf *-gen*); *aethrioscope* (cf *-scope*).

**aetio-**. See *etio-*.

**aët(o)-; -aëtus** or **-aetus**: from Gr *aetos* (s *aet-*), an eagle. Exx: *Aëtosaurus*; *Circaëtus*.

**-aeval**. See *-eval*.

**Afro-**, occ **Afr-**: 'African' or, as in *Afro-Asiatic*, 'African and': from L *Afer*, African (adj). Cf AFRICA.

**agamo-** or, before a vowel, **agam-**: 'asexual': from *agamous*, Gr *agamos*, unmarried: a cpd c/f: *a-*, not+*gamo-* (see *-gam*). Ex: *agamogenesis*.

**agarici-**: from L *agaricum*, a fungus, from Gr *agarikon*, whence E *agaric*. Ex: *agariciform*, mushroom-shaped.

**agath(o)**: Gr *agatho-*, c/f of *agathos*, good, perh akin to Go *gōths*, OHG *guot*, Mod G *gut*, E *good*: if the *a-* is merely formative, the division of the Gr word is *a-*+*gath-*+*-os*. Exx: *agathod(a)emon*, one's good angel (or genius), Gr *agathodaimōn* (cf DEMON); *agathology*, the doctrine (cf *-logy* at *-loger*) of good.

**agati-**: for *agate*, as in *agatiferous*, (of rocks) *agate*-producing, lit -bearing (*-ferous* at *-fer*).

**aglao-**: from Gr *aglaos*, bright; as in Bot *Aglaonema* (cf *-nema*) and *aglaozonia* (*zōnē*, a girdle).

**agnoio-**: from Gr *agnoia*, ignorance: cf AGNOSTIC. Ex: *agnoiology*, doctrine of ignorance.

**-agogue; -agogy**: 'leading' (adj) or 'leader', hence 'guiding, inducing'; the corresponding vn: Gr *agōgos*, (adj) leading, guiding; Gr *agōgia*, leading (n): from *agein*, to lead, to guide: cf ACT. Ex: *pedagogue*, L *paedagōgus*, Gr *paidagōgos*, child-guiding (adj), hence a teacher—cf *paedo-*; *pedagogy*, via late MF-F *pédagogie*, from Gr *paidagōgia*.

**-agonist**, adj **-agonistic**: from Gr *agōnistēs* (adj *agōnistikos*), one who contends for a prize in the games, hence of an actor; from *agōn*, a contest, from *agein*, to drive, lead, celebrate: cf AGONY. Exx: *protagonist* (cf *proto-*), Gr *prōtagōnistēs*, the first, hence most important, actor in a Gr drama, hence any notable leader or spokesman; *deuteragonist* (cf *deutero-*), the second actor, Gr *deuteragōnistēs*; *tritagonist*—see *trito-*.

**agora-**, as in *agoraphobia* (cf *-phobia*): Gr *agora*, a place of assembly (s *agor-*), hence a marketplace, from *ageirein* (s *ageir-*), to assemble (e.g., the people): f.a.e., ACT.

**-agra**: Gr *-agra*, denoting gout, hence (loosely)

an access of pain; from *agra*, a seizing, a hunting. Exx: *melagra* and *podagra* (cf *-pod*).

**agri-**, L c/f, and **agro-**, Gr c/f: L *ager*, a field, gen *agri*, s *agr-*, akin to Gr *agros*, a field: 'of or pertaining to a field, hence of, in, by, for agriculture'. Exx: *agriculture*, L *agricultūra*, cultivation of a field; *agronomy*, field-crop production, from Gr *agronomos*, rural (cf *-nomy*). Cf:

**agrio-**: 'savage' (adj and n): c/f of Gr *agrios*, (lit) of the field, (hence) uncultivated, (hence) wild, savage, itself from *agros*, a field—cf prec. Ex: *agriology*, a study—esp of the customs—of uncivilized peoples.

**agro-**. See *agri-*.

**aitho-**: from Gr *aithos*, burnt (dark) brown— cf *aetheo-*. Ex: *aithochroi* (cf *-chroia*), peoples coloured a reddish brown.

**aitio-**. See *etio-*.

**akro-**. An old spelling of *acro-*.

**albi-; alb(o)-** or, before a vowel, **alb-**: 'white': L *albus*, q.v. at ALB. Exx: *albiflorous*, white-flowered; *albocracy*, government (cf *-cracy*) by white men. Cf:

**albumini-; albumin(o)-**; occ shortened to **albumo-**; 'albumen' or 'albumin': L *albūmen*, white of egg, from *albus*, white (cf prec)+suffix *-men* (q.v. in Suffixes); L *albūmen* has o/s *albūmin-*. Exx: *albuminimeter* (cf *-meter*); *albuminoscope* (cf *-scope*) and *albumoscope*.

**alco-**: for *alcohol*, as in *alcogel(-atin)* and *alcovinometer* (cf *vino-*).—Also *alcoholo-*, as in *alcoholomania*.

**aldo-**: for *aldehyde*, as in *aldomin* and *aldohexose*.

**alectoro-; alectryo-**: from Gr *alektōr*, var *alektruōn*, a cock (bird). Exx: *Alectorpodes* (*-podes*, pl of *-pous*, c/f of *pous*, a foot); *alectryomachy*, cock-fighting, a cock fight (*-machy*).

**aletho-**: 'true': Gr *alētho-*, c/f of *alēthēs*, true, which consists of privative *a-* (Prefixes)+*lēth-*, derived from *lanthanō*, I forgot: cf LETHE. Exx: *alethoscope*, an instrument that, for viewing pictures, has a lens that makes objects seem natural; *alethiology*, the science of truth, esp of evidence, from the derivative abstract n, *alētheia*, truth.

**aleuro-**: 'flour': Gr *aleuro-*, c/f of *aleuron*, flour. Exx: *aleuromancy*, divination (cf *-mancy*) by flour; *aleurometer*, an instrument for assessing the quality of flour.

**alexi-**: 'counteracting' or 'counteraction; antidote': adopted from Gr, where it is a c/f of *alexein* (s *alex-*), to ward off: cf Skt *rákṣati*, he protects. Exx: *alexipharmic*, adj and n, '(serving as) an antidote to poison', from Gr *alexipharmakos* (cf PHARMACIST); *alexipyretic*, a febrifuge; cf *alexin* (chem suffix *-in*), a defensive or protective substance.

**alg-**, short for **algo-**; **-algia** (obs *-algy*), **-algic**; **algio-**: 'pain': Gr *algos*, pain. Both *-algia* and *alg(o)-* come direct from Gr; *algio-* derives from *-algia*; adj *-algic*=*alg-*+*-ic*, q.v. in Suffixes. IE r: *\*aleg-*, which becomes Gr *alg-*; cognates in L. Exx: *neuralgia*, nerve-pain—cf *neuri-*, *neuro-* below;

*neuralgic*; *algiomuscular*; *algogenic*, pain-producing (cf *-genic* at *-gen*); *algometry*, the measurement of pain.

**ali-**: 'wing': L *ala*, armpit, shoulder, (predominantly) wing, akin to *axis* and therefore possessing numerous IE cognates. (The adj is *alar*, L *alāris*.) Exx: *aliferous*, *aligerous*, winged—cf *-ferous* at *-fer*, and *-gerous* at *-ger*; *aliform*, wing-shaped; *alinasal* (cf NOSE); *aliped*, wing-footed, as the bat; *alitrunk* (cf TRUNK).

**-alia**: 'a realm (of animal life)': Gr *halia*, an assembly. Ex: *Bassalia*, the abyssal zone, from L *bassus*, deep.

**alieni-**: L *aliēni-*, c/f of *aliēnus*, belonging to another (cf ALIEN). Ex: *alienigenate*, L *aliēnigenus*, foreign by birth.

**allago-**: from Gr *allagē*, a change, an exchange, from *allassein*, to (ex)change. Exx: *allagophyllous* (cf *-phyllous* at *-phyll*), alternate-leaved. Cf the rare syn *allasso-*, as in *allassotonic*.

**allant(o)-**, a very learned c/f occurring only in Chem and An, in ref to *allantoic*, the adj of *allantois*, an organ in embryos: Gr *allas*, a sausage, o/s *allant-*.

**allasso-**. See *allago-*.

**allelo-**: Gr *allēlo-*, c/f of *allēlōn*, one another, from *allos* (cf *allo-*); in E 'reciprocal(ly)'. Ex: Bio *allelomorph* (cf *-morph*).

**all(o)-**: 'difference, differentiation' or 'extraneousness' or 'reversal': adoption of Gr *all(o)-*, c/f of *allos*, other, (hence) different, akin to L *alius*; IE s *al-*. Exx: *allochromatic*, accidentally pigmented; *allomorph* (cf *-morph*); *allopathy*, opp *homeopathy*—cf *-pathy* at *path(o)-*; *allotropy* (cf *-tropic*).

**alni-**: from L *alnus*, an alder tree: s *aln-*, extn of IE r *al-*. Ex: *alniresinol*.

**alpha-**. See Dict at ALPHABET.

**alphito-**: from Gr *alphiton*, barley meal: cf Alb *el'p*, barley. Ex: *alphitomancy*, divination (*-mancy*) thereby; *alphitomorphous* (cf *-morph*).

**alpi-**: from L *Alpes*, the Alps: cf ALPINE. Ex: *alpigene* (cf *-gene* at *-gen*), growing on mountains.

**alterni-**, 'alternate(ly)': from L *alternus*, alternate. Ex: *alternipetalous*. Cf ALTER and:

**altero-**: from L *alter*, another (cf *alter ego*, one's other I or self); as in *alterocentric*, opp *egocentric*.

**alti-**, 'high': adopted from L *alti-*, c/f of *altus*, high, orig the pp of *alere*, to nourish, cf OE *alan*, ON *ala*. Exx: *altigraph*; *altiloquent* (cf *eloquent*); *altimeter*; *altisonant*.—Also *alto-*, as in *altocumulus* (clouds).

**alumini-**; **alumin(o)-**: the former, 'alum' or 'alumin(i)um'; the latter, 'alumin(i)um' only. See ALUMIN(I)UM. Exx: *aluminiferous*, containing either alum or alumin(i)um; *aluminiform*, having the form of an alum; *aluminothermy*, a heating (cf *-therm*) process in metallurgy. The shorter form *alumo-* is rare.

**alveoli-**; **alveol(o)-**: An and Zoo 'alveolus' or 'alveolus and' or the adj 'alveolar' (*alveol-*+ adj suffix *-ar*): ML *alveolus* (s *alveol-*), L *alueolus*, a small cavity, dim of *alueus*, a cavity, akin to

*aluus*, ML *alvus*, belly, itself akin to Gr *aulos*, a flute. Exx: *alveoliform*; *alveolectomy*; *alveololabial*, *-lingual*, *-nasal*.

[**amb(i)-** (1), 'about' or 'around'. See Prefixes.]

**ambi-** (2), 'both': a c/f adopted from L, from the pronoun *ambō*, both. Exx: AMBIDEXTROUS, *ambivalent*, *ambivert* (midway between extrovert and introvert). Cf *amph(i)-*, *ampho-*.

**ambly(o)-**: 'dull' or 'dulled'; hence 'obtuse (-angled)': Gr *amblu-*, c/f of *amblus*, blunt, dull, for *\*amlus*, from *amalos*, weak, soft, akin to *malakos*, soft, weak. Exx: *amblyopia*, weak sight (cf *-opia* at *-ope*); *amblyoscope*, a remedial instrument for weak sight.

**ambo-** (1): 'both', as in *ambosexual* and *amboceptor*. Cf *ambi-* (2).

**ambo-** (2): in ref to Gr *ambōn*, an edge, a rim, hence a pulpit: as in *Ambocoelia*. (Very rare; as also is *ambo-* for Med *ambos*, G *Amboss*.)

**ambulo-**, as in *ambulomancy*, divination (*-mancy*) by walking, comes from L *ambulāre*, to walk. Cf AMBLE.

**amenti-**: from L *amentum*, a catkin (or, in Bot, *ament*): o.o.o. Exx: *amentiferous* (cf *-ferous* at *-fer*), catkin-bearing.

**ametr(o)-**: from Gr *ametros* (privative *a-*+ *metron*, a measure), irregular. Exx: *ametrometer*, an instrument for determining *ametropia* (cf *-opia* at *-ope*), irregular refraction of the eyes. F.a.e., MEASURE.

**amid(o)-**: c/f of the chem cpd *amide* (ammonia+ the chem suffix *-ide*). Ex: *amidophosphoric*. Cf:

**-amin(e)**; **amino-**: c/ff of the chem cpd *amine* (ammonia+the chem suffix *-ine*). Ex: *aminophenol*. Cf prec.

**ammino-**: for *ammine* (ammonia+chem *-ine*).

**amm(o)-**: 'sand': Gr *amm(o)-*, from *ammos*, sand, a var of *amathos*, ? for *\*samathos* (cf SAND). Ex: *ammophilous*, (of plants) sand-loving.

**ammoni(o)-**: **ammon(o)-**: c/ff, the former of *ammonia* or *ammonium*; the latter of *ammonia* only.

**ammoniti-**: for *ammonite*, a fossil shell, as in *ammonitiferous* (cf *-ferous* at *-fer*).

**amni-**: L *amni-*, c/f of *amnis*, a stream; app of C origin. Ex: *amnicolous* (cf *-colous*).

**amnio-**: '(of) the amnion', a Gr word for a caul: akin to Gr *amē*, a pail. Ex: *amniomancy* (cf *-mancy*).

**amoebi-**; **amoebo-**: 'amoeba' (SciL, from Gr *amoibē*, a change). Exx: *amoebicide*—cf *-cide* at *-cidal*; *amoebiform*; *amoebocyte*, cf *-cyte*.

**ampel(o)-**: Gr *ampel(o)-*, c/f of *ampelos*, a vine (app pre-Gr), as in *ampelotherapy*, the grape cure.

**amph(i)-**, **ampho-**: 'both': from Gr *amphō*, both, *amph(i)-* being a c/f already in Gr: cf *ambi-* (2). Exx: *amphanthium* (cf *antho-*); *amphitheatre*, *amphophilic*.

**amplexi-**: from L *amplexus*, an encircling (hence, an embrace), prop a cpd of *am(bi)-*+*plectere*, to twine, enlace; as in *amplexicaul*, (of a leaf) clasping a stem (cf *cauli-*).

**amygdal(o)-**: '(of) the tonsil(s)': L *amygdala*, an

almond, hence a tonsil: a word prob from Asia Minor. Ex: *amygdalectomy*, cf *-ectomy* at *-tome*.

**amyli-; amyl(o)-**: '(of) starch': L *amylum*, better *amilum*, from Gr *amulon*. Exx: *amyliferous*, cf *-ferous* at *-fer*; *amylodextrin, amylogenesis, amylolysis*, and other chem terms.

**amyo-**, as in *amyotrophy*: cpd of privative *a-* + *myo-*.

**analytico:-** for *analytic* (and).

**anarcho-**: either for *anarchy*, as in *anarchosyndicalism*, or for *anarchic*, as in *anarcho-individualist(ic)*.

**anatomico-**: 'anatomic' or 'anatomic and', as in *anatomicobiological*: L *anatomicus*. See ANATOMY.

**ancylo-**: from Gr *ankulos*, curved, akin to E (Geom) ANGLE. Ex: *Ancylokeras* (Gr *keras*, horn). Also *ankylo-*, q.v.

**andr(o)-; -andria, -androus, -andry**: 'mankind' or 'man the male': base, *andr-*, the o/s of Gr *anēr*, gen *andros*, a man, cf Arm *air*. The bot n-comb *-andria* corresponds to the adj *-androus*, as does the general *-andry*, from Gr *-andria*. The comb *andro-* or, before a vowel, *andr-* is an adoption from Gr. Exx: *androcentric*, with the male predominant; *androgynous*, Gr *androgunos*, (lit) man-woman-ish, of both sexes; *androphagous*, man-eating, cf *-phaga*; *polyandria* or *polyandry*, Gr *poluandria*, itself from *poluandros*, several-husbanded, whence *polyandrous*.

**anem(o)-**: 'wind', occ 'current of air' or even 'inhalation': Gr *anem(o)-*, from *anemos*, wind, akin to L *animus* and Skt *anilas*, breath, wind, of echoic origin. Exx: *anemometer*, an instrument measuring wind-force; bot *anemophilous*. Cf *anemone*, Gr *anemōnē*, derivative from *anemos*.

**angelo-**: c/f, adopted from Gr, of ANGEL. Exx: *angelocracy, angelology*.

**angi(o)-**: '(of) a seed or blood or lymph vessel', as in *angiocarpous* (cf *-carpous* at *carpo-*)—*angiology*—*angioneurosis*—*angiotomy* (cf *-tome*): Gr c/f *angeio-*, from *angeion*, a vessel, perh akin to L *angulus*. Cf *-angium* (from *angeion*), denoting 'type of vessel', as in *gonangium* (cf the 2nd *-gon*).

**Anglo-**: 'English' or 'English and': LL *Angli*, the English. Cf ENGLISH. Ex: *Anglo-French*.

**angui-**, 'snake' or 'snake-like': L *anguis*, a snake, s *angu-*, with cognates, none very close, in many other IE languages. Exx: *anguiform*; *anguiped*, L *anguiped-*, o/s of *anguipes*, snake-footed. The L dim *anguilla*, an eel, has c/f *anguilli-*, as in *anguilliform*.

**angulato-; anguli-, angulo-**: resp 'angulate(ly)' or 'angulate and', and 'angle': from L *angulātus*, angled, itself from *angulus*, an angle, whence, obviously, *anguli-* and *angulo-*: see ANGLE. Exx: *angulometer, anguliferous, angulatosinuous*.

**angusti-**; 'narrow': L *angustus* (s *angust-*), narrow: cf ANGUISH. Exx: *angustifoliate*, narrow-leaved; *angustisellate*, (lit) narrow-saddled (L *sella*, a saddle).

**anhydr(o)-**: 'deficiency of water': Gr *anudros*, waterless, which = *an-* (for privative *a-*) + *hudōr*, water + adj suffix *-os*. Ex: *anhydremia* (cf *-emia*).

**anilido-**, for *anilide*; **anilino-**, for *aniline*; **anilo-**, for *anil*. Only in Chem.

**anis(o)-**: 'unequal' or 'dissimilar': adopted from Gr *anis(o)-*, from *anisos*, unequal, which consists of *an-* (antevocalic form of privative prefix *a-*) + *isos*, equal: cf *iso-*. Exx: *anisogamous* (cf *-gamous* at *-gam*); *anisogeny; anisometric; anisotropic*.

**ankyl(o)-**: 'bent, crooked' or 'crookedness': Gr *ankulos*, curved (see ANGLE). Exx: *ankylenteron* (cf *-enteron* at *entero-*); *ankylosaurus* (cf *-saurus* at *-saur*). Also *ancylo-*, q.v.

**anni-**: L *anni-*: see ANNIVERSARY.

[**ano-** (1): 'upper': Gr *anō*, up, upward. Strictly a prefix. Ex: *anocarpous*, cf *-carpous* at *carpo-*.]

**ano-** (2): 'anus' or 'anal' (or 'anal and'): L *ānus* (s *ān-*), a ring, hence the fundament, akin to OIr *ānne* or *āinne*, ring. Ex: *anoscopy*, cf *-scopy* at *-scope*.

**anomal(o)-**: 'irregular': from Gr *anōmalos* (s *anōmal-*), uneven, irregular, anomalous; *anomalous* itself = L *anomalus*, from Gr *anōmalos*, which consists of *an-*, not (var of privative *a-*) + *homalos*, even, an extension of *homos*, same; *anomaly* = L *anomalia*, from Gr *anōmalia*, itself from *anōmalos*. Exx: *anomaloflorous*, having irregular flowers; *anomaloscope* (cf *-scope*), an instrument that tests faulty colour-vision.

**anom(o)-**: from Gr *anomos*, lawless (*a-*, not + *nomos*, law); in E, 'irregular' or 'abnormal', as in *anomophyllous* (cf *-phyllous* at *-phyll*).

**anopl(o)-**: 'unarmed' or 'unprotected' (in Zoo): Gr *anoplos*, unarmed (*an-*, not + *hoplon*, a weapon). Ex: *anoplocephalic*, unprotected, or unarmed, of head.

**antenni-**, as in *antenniferous* (*-ferous*, q.v. at *-fer*) and *antenniform*: c/f of *antenna*, an insect's or crustacean's feeler, sense-adapted from L *antenna*, a sail-yard; *antenna* (pl *antennae*), better *antemna*, is of obscure, app non-L, origin, but perh a conflation of *\*ante-tangentia*, fore-touchers, apprehended as sing: cf the etym of ANTLERS. E *antenna* yields the adjj *antennal* (*-al*) and *antennary* (*-ary*).

**anter(o)-**: 'in front' or 'anterior' (before, in place —hence in time) or 'anterior and' or 'from front to': as if from L *\*anterus*, imagined positive of comp *anterior* (from *ante*, before: cf *ante-* in Prefixes). Exx: *anterocclusion; anterodorsal, anterospinal; anteroventral*. Mostly in An terms.

**anth-** before a vowel, otherwise **antho-**; **-anthema** and **-anthemum**; **-anthera, -antherous, -anthery**; **-anthes**; **-anthous**; **-anthus**. The base is Gr *anthos* (s *anth-*), a flower, and *anth(o)-* denotes 'flower' or 'flowery, flowerlike': cf Skt *ándhas-*, a herb. Exx: *anthobiology; anthology*, (lit) a flower-gathering— Gr *anthologia*, from *anthologos*, (adj) flower-gathering, *-logos* deriving from *legein*, to gather. Through L comes *-anthus*, n, as in *polyanthus*, SciL from Gr *poluanthos*, rich in flowers; adj *-anthous*, deriving from the Gr adj *-anthos*, is exemplified in *monanthous*, bearing a single bloom —cf *mon(o)-*. Gr *anthos* (n) yields also the element *-anthēs* or, in E, *-anthes*, as *Zephyranthes* (a genus name). The derivative Gr *antherōs*, flowery, accounts for the adj -*antherous* and the n -*anthera* and, answering to -*antherous*, the n -*anthery*. The element -*anthemum*, as in *chrysanthemum* (Gr *khrusanthemon*, the golden flower), is a SciL form of Gr -*anthemon*; and -*anthema* derives, through L, from Gr -*anthēma*, lit a flowering, hence an eruptive skin-disease, as in *exanthema*, Gr *exanthēma*, from *exanthein*, to come out in flower.

**anthrac(o)-**: 'coal' or 'carbuncle': Gr *anthrak(o)-*, c/f of *anthrax* (o/s *anthrak-*), coal, (hence) a carbuncle. Cf ANTHRACITE. Exx: *anthraciferous*, where *anthraci-* is a var ('of coal'); *anthracomancy*, divination (-*mancy*) by live coals. The chem *anthr(a)-* is an arbitrary element.

**anthrop(o)-**: 'man; human being': Gr *anthrōp(o)-*, c/f of *anthrōpos*, (generic) man, s *anthrōp-*, akin to *anēr*, o/s *andr-* (see *andro-* above). Exx: *anthropogenesis* or -*geny*; *anthropology*, *anthropologist*, etc; *anthroposophy* (cf PHILOSOPHY). The element -*anthropy*, as in *misanthropy* (cf *miso-*), answers to Gr -*anthrōpia*, as in *misanthrōpia*: cf MISANTHROPE.

**-anthus.** See *anth-*.

**antr(o)-**: 'cavern' or, esp in Med, 'cavity': L *antrum*, from Gr *antron* (s *antr-*), prob akin either to Gr *anemos*, wind (cavern=blow-hole) or to L *ancra*, a depression. Ex: *antroscope* (cf SCOPE). Adj: *antral*.

**aort(o)-**: c/f of *aorta*, a SciL reshaping of Gr *aortē*, from *airein* (s *air-*), to heave or lift. Exx: *aortolith*, a calculus (cf -*lith* at *litho-*) in the aorta; *aortotomy* (cf -*tomy* at -*tome*). The adj *aortic* has c/f *aortico-*, 'aortic and'.

**aperto-**: from L *apertus*, open(ed), but used for E *aperture*, as in *apertometer*.

**aphan(o)-**: from Gr *aphanēs* (*a-*, not+-*phanēs*, visible: cf -*phane* and PHENOMENON); as in *aphanophyre* (cf -*phyre*). There is a var *apheno-*, as in *aphenoscope* (cf -*scope*).

**-aphia**: a SciL c/f, from Gr *haphē*, touch or a touching, from *haptein* (s *hapt-*), to touch, akin to Skt *yabh-*. Ex: *oxyaphia*, acuteness (cf *oxy-*) of touch.

**aphidi-**: for *aphid* (a plant-sucking insect), as in *aphidivorous* (cf -*vorous* at -*vora*). *Aphid* derives from *Aphid-*, o/s of SciL *Aphis*, a genus of plant lice, perh (Webster) from Gr *apheidēs*, lavish.

**aphno-**: from Gr *aphnos*, wealth, as in *aphnology*, the doctrine or science (cf -*logy* at -*loger*) of wealth.

**aphoto-**: from Gr *aphōs* (gen *aphōtos*), lightless (*a-*, not+*phōs*, light), as in *aphototropic* (adj), avoiding light by turning away from it (cf -*tropic* at -*tropal*). Cf PHOTOGRAPH.

**aphr(o)-**: Gr, from *aphros*, foam, with possible Skt cognates. Exx: *Aphrodite*, The Foam-Born (cf -*ite* in Suffixes); *aphrolite* (cf -*lite*).

**api-**: c/f of L *apis* (s *ap-*), a bee, perh akin to BEE itself. Exx: *apiculture*, bee-keeping, and *apiphobia*, a dread of bees. *Apiary*=L *apiarium*.

**apico-**: c/f of L (hence E) *apex*, summit, o/s *apic-*: cf APFX. Ex: *apicectomy*, the excision (cf -*ectomy* at -*tome*) thereof.

**aplano-**: c/f from Gr *aplanēs*, fixed (esp of stars), which consists of privative *a-*+*planos*, errant (c) Nor *flana*, to wander here and there: Hofmann). Exx: *aplanobacter* (cf -*bacter*) and *aplanospore* (cf -*spore*).

**aplo-**. A var of *haplo-*, as in *aplobasalt*.

**appendic(o)-**: for Med *appendix*, as in *appendicostomy*.

**-apsis**: c/f of Gr *hapsis*, union, fusion, as in *mitapsis* (cf *mito-*), from *haptein*, to touch. Cf -*aphia*.

**aqueo-; aqui-, aquo-**: resp 'of water' and 'presence or action of, or resemblance to, water': *aqueo-*, from L *aqueus*, adj; *aqui-* and *aquo-*, from L *aqua* (s *aqu-*), water, akin to Go *ahwa*; cf AQUA. Exx: *aqueoglacial*; *aquiform*; *aquo-*, only in chem terms, e.g., *aquocellulitis* (cf *cellule* at CELL and, in Suffixes, -*itis*).

**Arabo-**: 'Arabian—or Arabic and' c/f of ARAB, but based upon L *Arabus*.

**arachn(o)-**: c/f of Gr *arakhnē*, a spider, akin to L *arāneus*, whence the c/ff *aranei-*, *araneo-*; perh 'the web creature', hence 'web-maker', from Gr *arkus*, a net. Ex: *arachnology*, the science of spiders —cf the Zoo *Arachnida*, a class including spiders.

**arbori-**: 'of a tree, of trees': L *arbor* (gen *arboris*), a tree, adj *arboreus*, whence E *arboreal* (cf -*al*, adj, in Suffixes). Exx: *arboriculture* and *arboricole*, (adj), tree-dwelling.

**-arch, -archic, -archy.—arch-; archae(o)-** or mod **arche(o)-; arche-; archi-**. Resp (1) 'ruler'—(2) 'of rule or a ruler'—(3) 'rule' (government); (4) 'first in time or rank', hence 'chief, principal' and 'primitive'—(5) 'ancient, primitive'—(6) 'in the beginning, primary'—(7) 'chief' or 'primitive, original'. The Gr originals, with E exx, are these: (1) -*arkhēs* or -*arkhos*, ruler, occ via LL -*archa*—as in MONARCH; (2) -*arkhikos*, of a ruler—as in *monarchic*; (3) -*arkhia*, rule, occ via LL -*archia*—as in *monarchy*.—(4) *arkh-*, short for *arkhi-*, from the s of *arkhein*, to be first, cf -*arkhos* or -*arkhēs*, as in (1), and of *arkhē*, a beginning or origin—exx, *archbishop* and anl *archduke*, *archpiece*; (5) *arkhai(o)-*, from *arkhaios*, ancient or primitive, from *arkhē*—as in *arch(a)eology*; (6) *arkhē*, beginning, origin—as in *archetype*; (7) *arkhi-*, occ via LL *archi-*, strictly the complete form of (4)—as in *archiepiscopal* and *architect*.

Note that (1), -*arch*, has a Bot var, as in *pentarch*, having five strands, from Gr *arkhē*, a beginning.

That all seven (eight) forms have a common origin is clear from the fact that 'the first in time' tends to be 'the first in rank or importance' and that it also tends to be 'primitive'.

**archo-**: 'rectal': from Gr *arkhos*, rectum, of obscure origin—perhaps the *ar-* is akin to the *ar-* of E *arse*, the *or-* of syn Gr *orros*, the *or-* of L *ōr-*, o/s of *ōs*, mouth. Only in med terms.

**arci-, arco-**: '(of) a bow', hence '(of) an arc': from L *arcus*, a bow; cf OE *earh*, arrow. Exx: *arciform*, *arcograph* (-*graph*), *arcosolium*, an arched cell in a Roman catacomb.

**-arctia**: SciL element from L *arctāre* (s *arct-*), to press together; as in *aortarctia*—cf *aort(o)-* above.

**arcto-**: Gr *arkt(o)*-, c/f of *arktos*, a bear, as in *Arcturus* (Gr *ouros*, a guard), or the North, as in *Arctogaea* (Gr *gaia*, land). Cf ARCTIC.

**areni-**: '(of) sand': L *arēna* or *harēna*, sand, o.o.o. Ex: *arenicolous*, dwelling—or burrowing—in sand.

**areo-** (1): 'Mars' or, in Astr, 'Martian': Gr *Arēs* (gen *Areos*), the god of war. Exx: *areography*, *Areopagus* (the hill of Ares or Mars).

**areo-** (2): Gr *araios*, thin, (hence) rare, o.o.o. Ex: *areometer*.

**areto-**: c/f from Gr *aretē*, virtue, akin to *areiōn*, better, and *aristos*, best. Exx: the obs *aretology*, ethics; the rare *aretalics*, the science of virtue.

**-arge**. See *argyro-*.

**argenti-, argent(o)**: resp 'silver' and 'containing silver and': L *argentum* (s *argent*-); cf the poetical *argent* (n and adj), silver. Exx: *argentiferous*; *argentometry* (*-metry*, q.v. at *-meter*). Cf the next and *argyro-*.

**argillaceo-**, c/f of *argillaceous*, clayey (L *argillāceus*, s *argill*-); **argillo-**, c/f of *argillous* (L *argillōsus*) and denoting 'containing clay and'. The basic L word is *argilla* (clay), adopted from Gr, which forms it from *argos*, white, akin to L *argentum*, silver, and to:

**argyr(o)-**, adopted from Gr *argur(o)*-, the c/f of *arguros*, silver, from *argos*, white. Only in SciL words. The end c/f *-arge* has the same origin, as in *litharge* (cf *-lith* at *-lice*). Cf *argenti-*.

**arist(o)-**, adopted from Gr: c/f of *aristos*, best, akin to *areiōn*, better; of very ancient IE descent, with cognates in Skt and OPer. Ex: *aristocracy* (*-crat, -cratic*, qq.v. at *-crat*).

Do not confuse with the rare *aristology*, the art and science of dining—from Gr *ariston*, breakfast or lunch.

**arithmetico-**, c/f of L *arithmeticus* or of E *arithmetical*; **-arithm**, c/f from—**arithm(o)-**, c/f of —Gr *arithmos*, number, itself from IE r *\*ar*-. Exx: *logarithm*—cf *logarithmo-*; *arithmomania*, obsession with—esp the counting of—numbers; *arithmometer*, a calculating machine. Cf ARITHMETIC.

**armi-**; 'of or in or by weapons': L c/f of *arma*, weapons (cf ARMY). Exx: *armigerous*, bearing, or entitled to bear (cf *-ger*), heraldic arms; *armipotent*, potent in weapons, mighty in battle.

**arsenico-**, c/f of *arsenic*, as in *arsenicophagy*, arsenic-eating (habit); **arsen(o)-**, another c/f of *arsenic*, as in *arsenotherapy*. Cf ARSENIC.

**arteri(o)-**, adopted from the Gr c/f of *artēria*, artery: 'artery' or 'arterial (and)'. Ex: *arteriosclerosis*, hardening (cf *sclero-*) of the arteries. Cf ARTERY.

**arthr(o)-**, adopted from Gr c/f of *arthron*, a joint—cf Gr *artios*, complete, L *artūs*, joints, all of ancient IE origin. Ex: *arthrology*, the science of (the body's) joints; cf *arthritis*, direct from Gr, with adj *arthritic* (Gr *arthritikos*). Cf *artio-*.

**arti-** (1), as in *artifact*: c/f of L *ars*, art, o/s *art-* (see ART).

**arti-** (2), as in *artiphyllous* (cf *-phyllous* at *-phyll*): cf of L *artūs*, joints. Cf *arthro-*.

**artio-**: c/f of Gr *artios*, even (s *art-*): IE *\*ar-*, to join. Ex: *artiodactyl*, (an) even-toed (mammal).

**arto-**: adopted from the Gr c/f of *artos*, bread: o.o.o. Ex: *artophagy*, the practice or habit of eating bread.

**arundi-**: L *arundi-*, c/f of *arundō*, a reed; as in *arundiferous*, reed-bearing.

**arvi-**: from ML *arvum*, L *aruum*, cultivated land, a (cultivated) field, from *arāre* (s *ar-*), to plough. Exx: *arvicoline* (or *-colous*, q.v.), field-dwelling; *arviculture*, the growing of field crops.

**Aryo-**: c/f of *Aryan*, from Skt *ārya*, noble (cf Gr *aristos*, best): denotes 'Aryan and', as in *Aryo-Indian*.

**aryteno-**: c/f of *aryenoid*, lit 'ladle-shaped', Gr *arutainoeidēs*, from *arutaina*, a ladle.

**asci-** or **asco-**; **ascidi(o)-**: resp 'bag, bladder' and '(of or like a) bladder-shaped plant organ': SciL *ascus* (s *asc-*) from Gr *askos* (s *ask-*), a wine-skin, bag, bladder; SciL *ascidium*, from Gr *askidion*, dim of *askos*. Exx: *asciferous* or *ascigerous*, bearing asci (fungus sacs); *ascogenous*; *ascidiferous*, *ascidiform*. Gr *askos* is o.o o.; perh akin to *sakkos* (L *saccus*), from Sem *saq*.

**ascidi(o)-**. See prec.

**asperi-**, as in *asperifolious*, rough-leaved: from L *asper*, rough. Cf ASPERITY.

**aspid(o)-**; **-aspis**: 'shield' or 'shield-like': borrowed from Gr, where they are c/ff of *aspis*, a shield, o/s *aspid-*, perh from *spidios*, wide. Exx: *aspidomancy* (cf *-mancy*) and *Odontaspis*, a nametype found only in a few erudite terms.

**Assyrio-, Assyro-**: c/ff of L *Assyria* and *Assyrius*, from resp Gr *Assuria* or *Assuriē* (*gē*, land) and Gr *Assurios*, adj from *Assurioi*, the Assyrians. Exx: *Assyriology* and *Assyro-Babylonian*.

**-aster**; **aster(o)-**; **astri-** or **astr(o)-**: resp 'star', 'star'; 'of the stars; astral': resp Gr *astēr*, a star; Gr *aster-*, *astero-*, from *astēr*; from L *astrum* (Gr *astron*); Gr *astr-*, *astro-*, from Gr *astron*, a star, var of *astēr*: for all, cf STAR. Exx: such Bot, Bio and Zoo names as *clypeaster*, *disaster*; (Pal) *Asterolepis*; *astriferous*, star-bearing, ASTRONOMY, *astrophysics*.

**-asthenia**; **asthen(o)-**: 'debility'; '(of) debility': Gr *astheneia*, debility, from *asthenēs*, weak, whence *astheno-*. Lit, *asthenēs*=privative *a-*, not+*sthenos*, strong. Exx: *neurasthenia*, nerve-weakness (cf *neuro-*); *asthenology*, the scientific study (cf *-logy* at *-loger*) of debility, and *asthenosophere*, a 'zone of weakness' far below the earth's surface.

**astragal(o)-**: 'relation to or connexion with the *astragalus*', a tarsal bone: L *astragalus*, from Gr *astragalos*, a vertebra, akin to Gr *ostrakon*, a hard shell. Exx: *astragalotibial*; *astragalomancy*, divination (*-mancy*) by small bones—or by dice.

**astri-, astro-**. See *-aster*.

**ataxo-**: for *ataxia* (Gr, 'lack of arrangement, disorder'), as in *ataxo-phemia*, imperfect speech: privative *a+taxia*, akin to *taxis*, arrangement—cf TAX.

**atel(o)-**: 'defect of development or structure' (esp in An and Med): from Gr *atelēs*, imperfect, *a-*, not+*telos*, end, purpose (cf *tele-*). Ex: *atelocephalous* (cf *cephalo-*).

**athero-**, as in Bot *Atherosperma* (cf *-sperm*), comes from Gr *athēr* (gen *atheros*), a beard of corn; in Med, it=*atheroma*, itself ult of same origin.

**athro-**: from Gr *athroos* (adj), collected, as in *athrogenic* (cf *-genic* at *-gen*).

**Atlanto-, Atlo-; atloido-.** Whereas *Atlanto-* denotes either 'Atlantal (of Atlas) and' or 'Atlantic (and)', *Atlo-* denotes only 'Atlantal and'; *Atloido* denotes 'Atlantal and'. The base is *Atlas*, the mountain (see ATLAS), whence *Atlo-*; from the c/f *Atlant-* comes *Atlanto-*. Exx: *Atlanto-Mediterranean*, *Atlantosaurus* (cf *-saur*), *atloido-occipital* (*atlas* in its derivative An sense).

**atmid(o)-**: from *atmid-*, o/s of Gr *atmis*, smoke or vapour, akin to *atmos*, q.v. in next entry. Ex: *atmidometer*, an atmometer or evaporation-measurer.

**atm(o)-**, adopted from Gr, *atm(o)-* being the c/f of *atmos*, vapour—cf ATMOSPHERE. Ex: *atmograph*, *atmology*.

**atomi- or atomo-; atomico-**: 'atoms'; 'atomic': from *atomic*, from ATOM. Exx: *atomiferous*, atom-bearing (cf *-ferous* at *-fer*); *atomology*.

**atra-.** See *atro-*.

**atrio-**: 'atrium' or, in An, 'atrial and': from L *ātrium*, the principal room in an Ancient Roman house; hence a term in An and Zoo; *ātrium*, either Etruscan or from L *āter* (see *atro-*). Ex: *atriopore* (cf PORE).

**atro-**: 'black and': from L *āter*, black, o/s *ātr-*, app orig 'blackened by fire'—cf Av *atars*, fire. Ex: *atrosanguineous*, black-blooded (cf SANGUINE). The var *atra-* occurs in *atrabiliar*, F *atrabiliaire*, from L *ātra bīlis*, black bile.

**-atrophia**: 'a (specified) type of atrophy': SciL formation from Gr *atrophia*, lack of food (privative *a-*+*-trophia*, q.v.). Ex: *splenatrophia* (cf SPLEEN).

**au-.** See *avi-*.

**audio-**: 'hearing' or 'of hearing; audible': a Sci c/f from L *audīre* (s *aud-*), to hear, perhaps suggested by *audiō*, I hear; *audi-* also occurs; cf AUDIBLE. Exx: *audiogram*, *audiometer*; *audiphone*.

**aulac(o)**: Gr *aulak(o)-*, c/f of *aulax*, var of *alox*, a furrow. Ex: *aulacocarpous* (cf *-carpous* at *carpo-*).

**aulo-**: 'a tubular object or structure': Gr *aulo-*, c/f of *aulos* (s *aul-*), a flute—cf L *aulu(u)s*, flute, and Lit *aulys*, a beanstalk. Ex: *aulophyte* (cf *-phyte*).

**aureo-; aur(i)-, auro-**: 'golden'; 'gold' or 'of gold': L *aureus*, golden, from L *aurum* or LGr *auron*, gold, s *aur-*, var of IE *aus-*, as in OP *ausis* and Tokh A *väs*, gold. Exx: *Aureobasidium* (cf *basidio-*); *auriferous*, gold-bearing; *aurophobia*. Cf AUREATE.

**auri-** (1). See prec.

**auri-** (2): 'the ear' or, in An and Physio, 'aural and': L *auris*, the ear, s *aur-*, an extension of IE *au-*, itself with a var *ou-*. Exx: *auriform*, *aurinasal*. The adj is *aural*. Cf:

**auriculo-**: 'auricular and': L *auricula*, auricle (external ear; a chamber of the heart), lit the dim of *auris*, ear. Ex: *auriculocranial*.

**auro-** (1). See *aureo-*.

**auro-** (2); 'wind': Gr *aura*, wind, akin to Gr *aēr*, air. Ex: *aurophore* (cf *-phora*).

**Austro-**: 'Austria and', as in *Austro-Hungary*. But also, as in *Austro-Malayan*, 'Australian and'. Cf AUSTRIA and:

**austro-**: 'the south wind', as in *austromancy* (cf *-mancy*), or 'south (and)', as in *Austro-Asiatic*, South-Asiatic::from L *auster*, the south wind: cf AUSTRALIA. Cf prec.

**auth-.** See:

**aut(o)-; auth- or authi-**, only before aspirated words: 'of or by or for or in oneself': Gr *aut(o)-*, *aut(h)-*, c/f of *autos*, self or, as adj, same, perh akin to Gr *au* (αὐ). Exx: *autocrat(ic)*; *autodidact*, a self-taught person: cf DIDACTIC; AUTOGRAPH; AUTOMATON; AUTOMOBILE; *authigenic* (Gr *authigenēs*, born on the spot).

Hence, short for *automobile*, as in *autocar*.

**automat(o)-**: adopted from Gr: c/f of *automatos*, self-acting: cf AUTOMATIC. Ex: *automatograph*.

**-auxe; auxo-**: 'enlargement of a part' (specified); 'concerned with or due to increase or growth': Gr *auxē*, increase; Gr c/f *auxo-*, from *auxein* (s *aux-*), to increase, cf IE *\*aug-* or *\*augs-* and L *augēre* (s *aug-*), to increase. Exx: *enterauxe* (cf *entero-*); *auxograph*, *auxotonic*.

**aveno-**: from ML *avēna*, L *auēna*, oats (cf F *avoine*)—cf OSl *ovĭsŭ* and OPr *wise*; prob non-IE. Ex: *avenolith* (cf *-lith* at *-lite*).

**avi-**: 'bird': ML *avis*, L *auis* (s *au-*), a bird, akin to Vedic *vés*. Exx: *avicolous* (cf *-colous*), *aviculture*. The s *au-* yields also *auspice*, whence *auspicious*: F *auspice*, L *auspicium*, from *auspex*, a bird-inspector, i.e. an augur, from *auis*+*specere* or *spicere*, to see.

**axi-; axio-; ax(o)-; axono-**: L c/f *axi-*, from *axis* (s *ax-*), axle, axis; mod c/f; Gr *ax(o)-*, from *axōn* (s *ax-*), axis; *axon-*, o/s of *axōn*+connective *o*: all denote 'axis'. L *axis* is intimately akin to Gr *axōn*. See AXIS. Exx: *axilemma*; *axiolite*; *axostyle*; *axonometry*.

**axino-**: from Gr *axinē*, an axe, as in *axinomancy* (cf *-mancy*).

**axio-** (1). See *axi-*.

**axio-** (2), as in *axiology*, the science of values: Gr *axios*, of like value, worthy—cf AXIOM.

**axo-, axono-.** See *axi-*.

**az(o)-**: chem c/f of *azote*, nitrogen, 'so named by Lavoisier because it is incapable of supporting life' (Webster). It occurs only in chem terms. Another c/f of *azote* is *azot(o)-*, similarly restricted: cf *azoxy-*, which=*az-*+*oxy-*.

**azygo-**: c/f of *azygous*, odd (not one of a pair): lit 'unyoked'—Gr *a-*, not+*zug(on)*, a yoke—cf YOKE. Ex: *azygospore*.

**bacci-**: 'berry': L *bacca* or *bāca*, a berry: a word either of Medit stock or akin to the wine-god *Bacchus*, from Gr βάγχος, imperfectly apprehended. Exx: *bacciferous*, from L *bac(c)ifer*; *bacciform*; *baccivorous* (cf *-vora*).

**bacilli-; bacill(o)-**: '(of) a *bacillus*', SciL from LL *bacillus*, var of L *bacillum*, dim of *baculum*, a staff or a stick, akin to Gr *baktron*, a form indicating that the IE s is *bak-*. Exx: *bacilliform*, *bacilligenic*; *bacillophobia*. Cf *baculi-* and:

**-bacter; bacteri(o)-**: 'a bacterial organism'; 'bacteria' or 'bacterial': *bacteria* is the pl of *bacterium*, SciL for Gr *baktērion*, dim of *baktron*, a staff, akin to L *baculum* (cf *baculi-*): bacteria are tiny rod-shaped organisms. Exx: *nitrobacter* (cf *nitro-*); *bactericide* (cf *-cide* at *-cidal*); *bacteriology*, the science of bacteria; *bacterioscopy* (cf *-scopy* at *-scope*). Cf prec.

**baculi-**: 'rod' or 'staff', as in *baculiform*, or 'cane' or 'reed', as in *baculiferous*: L *baculum*, rod, staff. Cf *bacilli-* and *-bacter*.

**balaeni-, balaeno-**: 'whale': L *balaena*, from Gr *phallaina*, itself prob akin to *phallos* (L *phallus*); IE s *bhel-*, to swell.

**balani-, balan(o)-**: 'acorn' and, in Med, 'gland': *balani-*, from L *balanus*, acorn; *balano-* from its Gr original, *balanos* (s *balan-*), akin to L *glans*. Exx: *balaniferous*; *balanophore* (cf *-phore*).

**balneo-**: irreg from L *balneum*, a bath, app for the var *balineum*, itself from Gr *balaneion*, neu n from adj *balaneios* (s *balan-*), wet, dripping—cf Skt *galanas*, dripping (drop by drop). Ex: *balneology*, the science of (therapeutic) bathing.

**balsami-**: for *balsam*, as in *balsamiferous*, balsam-producing (cf *-ferous* at *-fer*).

**-bar,** adj **-baric; bari-, bar(o)-, bary-**: 'weight'; 'heavy': Gr *baros*, weight, and *barus* (s *bar-*), heavy, themselves akin to L *grauis* (ML *gravis*) and Go *kaurus*. The truly Gr c/f is *bar(o)-*; *bary-* is LL, and *bari-* a var thereof. Exx: *isobar* (cf *iso-*), from *baros*; *centrobaric*; *baritone*, *barytone*, It *baritono*, Gr *barutonos*, from *barus*; *barograph*, *barometer* (*barometrical*), *baroscope*, all from the n *baros*.

**basi-, baso-**: 'the base' or 'forming a base'; (An) 'relating to the basion'—*basi-* only; 'walking' (n): L *basis*, from Gr *basis*, from *bainō*, I go or walk: see BASE, n. Exx: *basicranial* (cf *cranio-*); *basipetal* (*-petal*); *basophobia*, a dread of walking. Cf:

**basidio-**: 'basidial' (of a basidium, a fungus form): c/f of *basidium*, SciL dim from Gr *basis*, base. Ex: *basidiospore*. Cf prec.

**-bat** (n); **-batic** (adj): Gr *-batos*, -walking (adj); *-bat+*suffix *-ic*. Cf ACROBAT.

**batho-; bathy-**: 'depth'; 'the ocean depths' or, in An and Med, 'the body's inner parts': c/f from Gr *bathos*, depth (whence the E *bathos*); c/f from Gr *bathus*, deep, prob akin to Gr *bēssa*, Doric *bassa*, a glen. Exx: *bathophobia*, a dread of depths —opp *acrophobia*, q.v. at *acro-*; *bathysphere*.

**bato-** (1): from Gr *batos*, a bramble (o.o.o.); as in *Batodendron* (Gr *dendron*, a tree).

**bato-** (2): from Gr *batos*, passable, from *bainein*, to walk, to step, to go. Prob in *batophobia* (cf *-phobia* at *-phobe*), a dread of passing close to high buildings.

**bato-** (3): from Gr *batos*, a skate or a ray (fish); as in *Batocrinus* (cf *-crinus*).

**batrach(o)-**: adapted from Gr *batrakh(o)-*, c/f of *batrakhos*, a frog, of echoic origin. Ex: *batrachophagous*, frog-eating (cf *-phaga*).

**-bdella; bdell(o)-**: 'leech': Gr *bdella*, a leech, akin to *bdallein*, to milk, to suck: 'the sucker'. Ex: *bdellotomy* (cf *-tomy* at *-tome*).

**Belgo-**: for *Belgium* and *Belgian*. Ex: *Belgophile* (cf *-phil*).

**belli-**: 'war': c/f of L *bellum*, war, o.o.o. Exx: *belliferous*, bringing war; *belligerent*, waging war, hence n; *bellipotent*, powerful (cf POTENT) in war, all three words having L forebears: cf the adj *bellicose* (L *bellicōsus*, from *bellicus*, of war) and the war goddess *Bellona*.

**belo-; belono-**: resp from Gr *belos* (s *bel-*), an arrow, and from its extension (? dim) *belonē* (? *bel-*+formative element *-on-*+*ē*, f sing), a needle. Exx: *belomancy*, divination (*-mancy*) with arrows; *belonosphaerite* (cf *-sphaera*; Min suffix *-ite*).

[**bene-**: 'well': the L adv *bene*. See Prefixes.]

**benz(o)-**: a chem c/f of *benzene*. Ex: *benzoperoxide*.

**-bet.** See ALPHABET.

**beta,** only in Chem: Gr *bēta*, the letter *b*. Exx: *beta-glucose*, *beta ray*.

**betaino-** for Chem *betaine*, itself=L *bēta*, beet+chem *-ine*. Ex: *betainogen*.

**bi-** or, before vowels, **bin-**: 'two', hence 'twice' (cf prefix *bis-*): L *bi-*, for *dwi-*, from *duo*, two, akin to E TWO. Exx: *bicycle*, (a device with) two wheels (cf *cyclo-*); *bifurcate* (cf FORK); *bilateral*.

**-bia,** pl, and **-bia,** f sing, **-bium,** neu s, **-bius,** m sing; adj **-bious; bi(o)-**: 'life', 'living organisms': Gr *bios* (Gr c/f *bio-*), s *bi-*: see BIOGRAPHY. Exx: *aerobia*, pl of *aerobium*, an aerobe—an organism that can live only where oxygen is present; *Zenobia* (cf *zeno-*); AMPHIBIOUS (Gr *amphibios*); BIOGRAPHY, BIOLOGY. Cf *-by*.

**Biblico-**: c/f of *Biblic(al)*. See BIBLE. Cf:

**biblio-**: Gr *biblio-*, c/f of *biblion*, a book: cf BIBLE. Exx: *bibliography* (cf *-graphy* at *-graph*), *bibliolatry* (cf *-latry* at *-later*), *bibliomania* (cf *-mania* at *-measure*), *bibliophile* (cf *-phil*).

**bicro-,** 'one billionth', as in *bicrofarad*: anl with *micro-*.

**bili-**: 'bile' or, in Biochemistry, 'derived from bile': L *bīlis* (s *bīl-*), cf E BILE. Ex: *biliverdin*, a green pigment found in bile.

**bin-**. See *bi-*.

**bio-; -bious**. See *-bia*.

[**bis-**, twice. See Prefixes.]

**bismuto-, bismutho**: chem c/ff of *bismuth*, G *Bismuth*.

**-blast; -blastic; -blasty;—blast(o)-**: 'a formative cell'; 'formative, germinating'; 'germinal formation';—'a budding'; budding', '(of) the early embryo': all four relative to Bio: Gr *blastos*, a sprout or shoot; E adj in *-ic*, used only as a 2nd element; Gr c/f *-blastia*; Gr c/f *blast(o)-*. Exx:

*odontoblast* (cf *odonto-*); *epiblastic* (*epi-* in Prefixes); *heteroblasty* (*hetero-*); *blastoderm* (*-derm*), *blastospore* (cf *-spora*).

**blenni-; blenn(o)-**: 'of mucus'; 'presence of, or connected with, mucus: Gr *blenna*, cf OIr *blinn*, slaver, pus. Exx: *blenniform*; *blennogenous*.

**blephar(o)-; -blepharon**: 'eyelid'; '(specified) disease of the eyelid': *blephar(o)-*, direct from the Gr c/f of *blepharon*, an eyelid, akin to—? from *blepein* (s *blep-*), to glance or see. Exx: *blepharotomy*; *varicoblepharon*.

**-bola, -bole, -bolic, -bolism, -bolist; bolo-**: generically, '(a) stroke, stroking': resp LL *-bola*; Gr *-bolē*; Gr *-bolikos*; Gr *-bolismos*; Gr *-bolistēs*; c/f of Gr *bolē*, (lit) a throw(ing) or cast(ing), (hence) a stroke, from *ballein* (s *bal-*), to throw or cast. Exx: geometrical *parabola*, (perh via LL *parabola*) from Gr *parabolē*, (lit) a cast to the side; ME *parabole*, a parable; *parabolic*, LL *parabolicus*, LGr *parabolikos*; *bolograph*, *bolometer*.

**boni-**, c/f of L *bonus*, good, as in *boniform*, partaking of, or resembling, good; *Boniface*. Cf BOON.

**bor(o)-**: a chem c/f of *boron*, itself from *borax* (via F from Ar from Per *būrah*). Ex: *borocarbide*.

**botan(o)-**, a c/f adopted from Gr, from *botanē*, a plant: see BOTANY. Ex *botanophile*.

**bothri(o)-; bothr(o)-**: 'sucker', as on a tapeworm, c/f of *bothrium*, from Gr *bothrion*, dim of *bothros*, 'trench' or 'trough'—perh akin to Gr *bathus*, deep—whence the c/f *bothro-*, as in *bothrodendron*.

**botry(o)-**: 'cluster of grapes': perh via L *botru(u)s*; certainly from Gr *botrus*, c/f *botru(o)-*, o.o.o. Ex: *botryogen* (*-gen*), *botryolite* (*-lite*).

**botuli-**, as in *botuliform*, sausage-shaped: L *botulus*, prob of Oscan origin: cf *botulism*, (lit) sausage-poisoning.

**bovi-**, a c/f adopted from ML *bōv-*, L *bōu-*, o/s of *bōs*, an ox, akin to Gr *boós* or *bous*—cf BOVINE. With denotation 'cattle', it occurs in, e.g., *boviculture*, *boviform*. The c/f *bovo-*, as in *bovovaccine*, answers to the adj *bovine*.

**-brach; brachisto-; brachy-**: 'short'; 'shortest'; 'short': *brachisto-*, as in *brachistocephalic*, (lit) shortest-headed, represents Gr *brakhistos*, sup of *brakhus*, short, whence both the end-element *-brach*, as in *amphibrach*, a trisyllabic metric foot (◡–◡) that is short at both ends, and the front element *brachy-*, as in *brachycephalic*, short-headed, and *brachypterous*, short-winged (*-pterous* at *-ptera*). Gr *brakhus*, s *brakh-*, is akin to L *breuis*, s *breu-*, and also to Gr *brakhiōn*, forearm, arm; therefore cf:

**brachi(o)-**: 'the arm' and, in An, 'connexion with the arm; of the arm and': L *brachium* or *bracchium*, from Gr *brakhiōn*, forearm or arm. Exx: *Brachiopod* (cf *-pod*), one of the molluscs, lit 'arm-footed'; *Brachiosaurus*, a huge dinosaurus with forelegs longer than its hind legs. Cf prec.

**brady-** represents Gr *bradu-*, c/f of *bradus* (s *brad-*), slow, sluggish, perh akin to L *gurdus*, heavy, stupid. Exx: *bradycardia* (*-cardia*), sluggish

(action of the) heart; *bradycrotic*, slow-pulsed (*-crotic*).

**-branch; -branchia**, adj **-branchiate; branchi-, branchi(o)-**: 'a branchiate creature', as in *cirribranch* (*cirri-*); 'gills', as in *podobranchia* (*podo-*, q.v. at *-pod*); 'gills', as in *branchicolous*, 'living (*-colous*) parasitically upon gills'; 'relation to, or connexion with gills', as in *branchiocardiac* and *branchiosaur*. The L *branchia* transliterates Gr *brankhia*, gills, pl of *brankhion* (βράγχιον), a fin, cognate with *bronkhos* (βρόγχος), windpipe, throat —therefore cf *bronchi-*.

**brevi-**, adopted from ML *brevi* (L *breui-*), c/f of *brevis* (L *breuis*), short, brief: cf BRIEF. Exx: *breviloquence*, ML *breviloquentia*, a brief manner of speaking; *breviped* (*-ped*), short-legged; *brevipennate*, short-winged.

**Brito-**: 'British': from *Briton*—cf BRITAIN. Ex: *Brito-Icelandic*.

**brom(o)-**: Gr *bromo-*, *brom-*, c/ff of *bromos* (s *brom-*), var *brōmos*, a stink: in Chem, 'bromine', a blend of F *brome*, bromine+E chlor*ine*. Ex: *bromomania*.

**bronchi-; bronchi(o)-; bronch(o)-**: 'a bronchus, or the bronchi', c/f from Gr *bronkhos*, windpipe; 'bronchial', c/f of *bronchium*, the sing of *bronchia*, the bronchial tubes; 'bronchial' or 'bronchial and', adapted from Gr *bronkho-*, *bronkh-*, c/ff of *bronkhos* (whence *bronchus*, a subdivision of the windpipe). Exx: *bronchiloquy*, ? wheezy speech; *bronchiospasm*; *bronchotomy* (*-tomy*, q.v. at *-tome*).

**bronte-, bront(o)-**: 'thunder': Gr *brontē*, c/f *bronto-*, *bront-*, akin to Etrusco-Latin *frontesia* (Hofmann); orig echoic (?). Exx *brontephobia*, var of *brontophobia*, dread of thunder.

**broto-**, as in *brotocrystal*: from Gr *brōtos*, gnawed, to be eaten, prob the pp of *bibrōskein* (r *brōsk-*), to eat up.

**bry(o)-**: adapted from Gr *bru(o)-*, c/f of *bruon* (s *bru-*), moss, app akin to *bruein*, to gush forth. Ex: *bryology*, the science of mosses.

**bu-**, as in *bucentaur* (cf CENTAUR), *Bucephalus* (the 'ox-headed' horse of Alexander the Great), *Buceros* (cf *-ceros*): Gr *bou-*, c/f of *bous*, ox: cf BOVINE.

**bucco-**: 'of the cheek and': L *bucca*, cheek, perh of C origin (r *\*buc-*, to swell). Ex: *buccolingual*, of cheeks and tongue.

**bulbi-, bulbo-**: 'bulb' and 'of (or like) a bulb and': the former, regularly from L *bulbus*, the latter a SciL c/f from *bulbus*, itself a derivative of Gr *bolbos*. Exx: *bulbiferous*, *bulbifrom*; *bulbospinal*.

**-bulia**: 'a (specified) state of the will', Gr *boulē*, s *boul-* (Hofmann compares *ballein*, to cast). Ex: *hyperbulia*, excessive (cf *hyper-* in Prefixes) desire for action.

**bulli-**: from L *bulla*, a bubble, akin—sem, at the least—to L *bulbus* (cf *bulbi-*). Ex: *bulliform*, puckered.

**buno-**: from Gr *bounos*, mound, hill, akin to *boubōn*, (a swelling in) the groin. Ex: *bunodon*, (adj, hence n), having tubercles on the molar teeth, pl *Bunodonta*.

**Burmo-**, for 'Burma' or 'Burmese and', as in *Burmo-Chinese*.

**bursi-**, as in *bursiform*, purse-shaped: from L *bursa*, a purse: cf PURSE.

**but-; butyr(o)-**: the former, only in Chem, e.g. *butane, butene, butyl*, and pragmatically short for *butyro-*, the c/f of *butyric*, of or from butter: see BUTTER for L *būtyrum*, Gr *bouturon*.

**-by**: perh via L *-bium*, from Gr *-bion*, as in *cenoby*, usu *coenoby*, perh via LL *coenobium*, a convent, from Gr *koinobion*, community life. See *-bia*.

**byssi-, bysso-**: from L *byssus*, fine flax, (hence) fine linen, from Gr *bussos*, with cognates in Ham and Sem. Exx: *byssiferous* (cf *-ferous* at *-fer*) and *byssogenous* (cf *-genous* at *gen*), both with E sense 'tuft'.

**-cace; cach-; cac(o)-**: adaptation of the Gr c/f *-kakē*, for *kakē*, badness—in E, vitiated condition, as in *arthrocace* (cf *arthro-*); *cach-* (Gr *kakh-*), the aspirated form of *cac-* (Gr *kak-*), the prevocalic shortening of *caco-* (Gr *kako-*), from *kakos*, bad, perh from *kakkē*, human excrement, cf L *cacāre* (s *cac-*), to *cack* or defecate; *kakkē* and *cacāre* are nursery words. Exx: *cachexia*, from Gr *kakhexia* (cf *hexi-*); *cacophony*, dissonance, discord.

**cacti-**: for *cactus*, as in *cactiform*, cactus-like.

**cadmi-, cadm(o)-**: for *cadmium* (cf the Chem suffix *-ium*), a ductile metal, from *cadmia*, itself from Gr *kadmeia*, from the Gr myth character *Kadmos* (*Cadmus*). Exx: *cadmiferous* (cf *-ferous* at *-fer*); *cadmopone* (after 'lithopone').

**caduci-**: (lit) 'falling', (hence) 'deciduous': L *cadūcus*, falling (adj), failing, from *cadere* (s *cad-*), to fall; see CADENCE. Ex: *caducicorn* (cf *-corn*), having deciduous antlers.

**caeci-; caec(o)-**, mod ceco-: 'of the caecum' (the blind gut); 'the caecum' (adj *caecal*) or 'caecal and': base, L *caecus* (s *caec-*, ModE *cec-*), blind, akin to OIr *caech* and Go *haihs*, one-eyed; *caecum* is n from the neu of the adj. Exx: *caeciform*, shaped like the *caecum*; *caecotomy*; *cecograph*.

**cael(o)-**. See *coel(i)-*.

**caen(o)-**. See *ceno-*.

**Caesaro-; caesaro-**: for *Caesarian*; from CAESAR. Exx: *Caesarotomy* (cf *-tomy* at *-tome*); *caesaro-papism* or *-papacy*, the exercise, by secular rulers, of power over the Papacy.

**cain(o)-**. See *ceno-*.

**calami-, calam(o)-**: 'a reed' or 'reeds': resp L *calamus* and, origin of the L word, Gr *kalamos*, a reed. Exx: *calamiferous, Calamospermae* (cf *-sperm*).

**calathi-**: from L *calathus*, from Gr *kalathos*, a basket narrow at the base, (perh) a cup, as in *calathiform*, cup-shaped; cf Skt *kathina-*, a saucepan.

**calcaneo-**: In An and Zoo, 'of the calcaneum (a bone) and': LL *calcāneum*, the heel, from *calx*, o/s *calc-*, the heel. Ex: *calcaneotibial*. Cf *calcari-*.

**calcareo-; calci-; calcio-; calc(o)-**: resp 'calcareous'; 'lime' or 'calcium'; 'presence of calcium';

'lime' or chalk: resp L *calcārius*, of or with lime, calcareous; L *calx*, gen *calcis*, o/s *calc-*, lime; c/f of *calcium*; (*calco-*) irreg from L *calx*, *calc-*, lime, akin to and perh from Gr *khalix*, a pebble, limestone, of ancient IE stock. Exx: *calcareo-sulphurous*; *calciferous, calcimeter*; *calcography*, art of drawing with chalks. *Calcium* is a SciL formation from *calx*, lime.

**calcari-**: 'spur' (of cock bird): L *calcar*, a cock's spur, from *calc-* o/s of *calx* heel (cf *calcaneo-*). Ex: *calcariferous*.

**calcei-**: 'shoe, slipper': L *calceus*, shoe, from *calx*, o/s *calc-*, heel. Ex: *calceiform*, (in Bot) slipper-shaped. Cf *calcaneo-* and *calcari-*.

**calci-; calcio-; calco-**. See *calcareo-*.

**calculi-**: 'pebble': L *calculus*, either a dim or a reduplication of *calx* lime(stone). Ex: *calculiform*, pebble-shaped.

**cal(e)-; cali-; calori-**: 'warm': from L *calēre* (s *cal-*), to be warm; *calidus*, warm; *calor*, warmth, heat; words with an IE s *\*kal*. Exx: *calefactory*, adj (L *calefactōrius*) and n (ML *calefactōrium*), and *calelectricity*; *caliduct*; *calorigenic, calorimeter*.

**cali-** (1). See prec.

**cali-** (2). See *calli-*.

**cali-** (3): irreg for *calidi-* (L *calidus*, very warm), as in *caliduct*.

**calici-**: 'cup', hence 'bell': L *calix* (o/s *calic-*), a cup, a goblet, akin to Gr *kalux*, a flower's calyx, which is cup-shaped. Ex: *caliciform*, bell-shaped. Cf *calyci-*.

**calio-**: from Gr *kalia* (s *kal-*: cf *calypto-*), a hut, a nest. Ex: *caliology*, a study—the science—of birds' nests.

**calli-**, occ **callo-; calo-**: resp Gr *kalli-*, c/f of *kallos*, beauty, as in *calligraphy* (Gr *kalligraphia*), *callipygous* (Gr *kallipugos*); as in *Callorhynchus*, 'fair-snouted' (fish); Gr *kalo-*, c/f of *kalos*, beautiful, as in *calotype*. The c/f *cali-*, as in *calisthenics* (*callisthenics*), is a var of *calli-*. With Gr *kalos* and *kallos*, cf Skt *kalyas*, healthy.

**calori-**. See *cale-*.

**caly-**. A shortened—and rare—var (as in *calyphyomy*) of:

**calyci-; calyc(o)-**: 'calyx': *calyci-*, from L *calyc-*, o/s of *calyx*; *calyco-* or, before a vowel, *calyc-*, from Gr *kaluko-, kaluk-*, from *kalux* (o/s *kaluk-*), calyx of flower. Exx: *calyciflorous*; *Calycophora* (cf *-phora*). Cf *calici-*.

**calypt(o)-**: 'covered': Gr *kaluptos*, covered, hidden, as in *calyptoblastic*. Cf *calyptri-, calyptro-*, c/ff of Gr *kaluptra*, a covering, as in *calyptriform* and *calyptrogen*. Gr *kaluptein*, to hide, has s *kalupt-*, an extension of IE *\*kal-* or *\*kel-*, to cover, shelter, hide, as in L *celāre*, to hide, and E *cell*.

**cambi-, cambio-**: c/ff of the SciL sense-adaptation (in Bot) of LL *cambium*, exchange—cf ML *cambiāre*, to exchange; a word of app C origin: r *\*camb-*, to turn. Ex: *cambiform, cambiogenetic*.

**Cambro-**: c/f of *Cambrian*, adj of ML *Cambria*, Wales, from W *Cymru*, itself prob from *Cymry*, the Welsh (people), pl of *Cymro*: cf CYMRIC. Ex: *Cambro-Briton*.

**camelo-.** See *camelopard* at CAMEL.

**-campa; campo-:** from Gr *kampē*, a caterpillar. Only in Zoo techh.

**campani-, campano-:** c/ff of LL *campāna*, a bell, of echoic origin. Exx: *campaniform*, bell-shaped, and *campanology*, science (cf *-logy* at *-loger*) of bells, art of ringing bells.

**camph(o)-, camphor(o)-:** c/ff of *camphor* (perh via MF *camphore*): ML *camphora*; Ar *kāfūr*, Mal *kāpūr*. Exx: *camphocarboxylic*; *camphoroyl* (cf *-yl*).

**campi-:** c/f of L *campus*, a field—cf *campto-* and esp CAMP. Ex: *campimeter*, a term in Psy.

**campo-.** See *-campa*.

**campto-** (in Bot and Zoo): Gr *kamptos*, flexible, akin to *kamptein*, to bend or curve, and *kampē*, a bend (in a river); akin also to *cambio-* and perh to L *campus*, a field (cf prec entry). Ex: *camptodrome*, (Bot adj) having a bent course (cf *-drome*). Cf:

**campyl(o)-:** Gr c/f *kampulo-, kampul-*, from *kampulos*, curved; akin to *campto-, cambio-*, prob *campi-*. Exx: *campylodrome, campylotropous* (cf *-tropic*).

**canali-,** 'canal': from L *canālis*, a canal or a channel: cf CANAL. Ex: *canaliform*, canal-like.

**canceri-, cancero-; cancri-:** the first two, c/ff of E CANCER; the third, of L *cancer*, a crab. Exx: *cancerigenic* (*-genic* at *-gen*)—*cancerophobia*; *cancriform, cancrivorous*. Cf *carcino-*.

**cannabi-:** for L *cannabis*, hemp, as in *cannabinol* (cf *-ol*).

**canth(o)-:** c/f of SciL *canthus*, eye-corner, from Gr *kanthos*, prob of C origin, with IE s *\*kanth-*: cf *campto-*. Ex: *canthotomy* (*-tomy* at *-tome*).

**capilli-:** c/f of L *capillus*, hair, perh related to *caput* (head), o/s *capit-*, and to *pilus*, a hair. Exx: *capilliculture, capilliform*. Cf the adj *capillary* (L *capillāris*).

**capno-:** c/f of Gr *kapnos*, smoke, of ancient IE stock. Ex: *capnomancy*, divination (cf *-mancy*) by smoke.

**capri-,** adopted from L, c/f of *caper*, o/s *capr-*, a goat, perh of C origin; cf 'to *caper*'. Exx: *Capricorn*, the Goat-Horned; *capripede*, goat-footed. Cf:

**capro-:** chem c/f of *caproic*, ult of same origin as prec.

**capsuli-, capsulo-:** c/ff of *capsule* (L *capsula*, a small box: cf CASE, a box). Exx: *capsuliferous, capsulotomy*.

**carb(o)-:** c/f of E CARBON; loosely for *carbonic*. Ex: *carbohydrate*. But *carboni-* represents the c/f of L *carbō*, o/s *carbōn-*; as in *carboniferous* and *carbonimeter*.

**carboni-.** See prec.

**carburo-:** for *carburet*; as in *carburometer*.

**carcin(o)-,** adopted from Gr *karkino-, karkin-*, c/ff of *karkinos*, a crab, (hence) cancer—akin to Skt *karkaṭas* and also L *cancer*; cf *canceri-* above. Exx: (crab) *carcinology*; (cancer) *carcinosarcoma* (cf *sarco-* below).

**-cardia, -cardium; cardia-, cardi(o)-:** resp a (specified) kind of heart-trouble or oddity, as in *stenocardia* (cf *steno-*), or, in Zoo, animals having a specified kind of heart, as in *Isocardia* (*iso-*), from Gr *kardia*, the heart—a membrane connected with the heart, as in *endocardium* (*endo-*), from the Gr c/f *-kardion*, from *kardia*—*cardia-* and *cardi(o)-*, cardiac (of or belonging to the heart), as in *cardiatomy, cardiology, cardi(o)-* deriving from the Gr c/f *kardio-, kardi-*, from *kardia*. F.a.e., HEART.

**cardo-:** c/f of Gr *kardos* (s *kard-*), a thistle, as in *cardophagous*, thistle-eating. Cf:

**carico-:** c/f of L *carex*, o/s *caric-*, sedge; the s *car-* may be akin to the *car-* of L *cardu(u)s*, Gr *kardos*, thistle. Ex: *carcilogy*.

**carini-:** for L *carīna*, a ship's keel; esp in An, Bot, Zoo; e.g., *cariniform*, keel-shaped Cf CAREEN.

**-caris,** in generic names of crustacea, represents the Gr *karis*, a shrimp, a prawn, perh from *kara*, the head.

**carni-:** c/f of L *carō*, flesh, gen *carnis*, o/s *carn-*: cf CARNAL. Exx: *carniferous, carniform*, E formations; *carnivore*, via F from ML *carnivorus* (whence E *carnivorous*), L *carniuorus*—cf DEVOUR.

**-carp, -carpous, -carpus, -carpy; carp(o)-:** resp 'fruit'—'having (specified) fruit' or 'having (so many) fruits'—a Latinized form of *karpos*, in Bot generic names—'a (named) manner of fruiting'; 'fruit-': Gr *karpo-, karp-*, c/ff of *karpos*, fruit (s *karp-*), akin to L *carpere* (s *carp-*), to gather, and Gr *keirein* (s *keir-*), to cut, to gather, to harvest; the IE s *\*ker-* or *\*kar-* means 'to cut, to gather (fruit)'; fundamentally, therefore, *karpos* means 'that which is cut or plucked or gathered'. Exx: *endocarp* (*endo-*), *schizocarp* (*schizo-*)—*oligocarpous*, bearing few (*oligo-*) fruits, and *monocarpous*, single-fruited—*syncarpy* (cf *syn-* in Prefixes), 'collective' fruiting; *carpogam* (*-gam*), *carpogenous, carpology, carpophagous* (fruit-eating), *carpospore* (cf *-spore* at *-spora*).

**carpho-;** from Gr *karphos*, a (rice) straw. Exx: *carpholite* (*-lite*) and *Carphophis* (*-ophis*).

**carpo-** (1). See *-carp-*.

**carpo-** (2) or, before a vowel, **carp-:** in An, 'the carpus', or 'carpal' (of the carpus) or 'carpal and': Gr *karpo-, karp-*, c/ff of *karpos*, the carpus or wrist, with fewer IE cognates than has *karpos*, fruit; IE s *\*kerp-* (or *\*kerb-*) or *\*karp-* (or *\*karb-*), to turn, to be mobile. Ex: *carpopedal* (cf *ped-*, foot).

**-carpous; -carpy.** See *carp-*.

**carto-; charto-:** 'map' or 'chart' or both: L *carta* or *charta*, from Gr *khartēs*, orig a sheet of papyrus, hence of paper: cf CARD. Exx: *cartograph, -er, -y*, and *cartomancy*; *chartology* (cartography or art of map-drawing) and *chartometer*.

**cary(o)- or kary(o)-:** Gr *karu(o)-*, c/f of *karuon*, nut or kernel, via L *caryon* (s *cary-*): in Bio, nucleus of a cell, perh akin to Gr *kara*, the head, or to the IE s *\*kar-*, to be hard. Exx: *caryopsis* (cf *-opsis*); *karyochrome, karyplasm, karyosome*.

**case(o)-:** c/f of *casein* (milk protein), itself consisting of *case-*, the s of L *cāseus*, cheese, and chem *-in* (see Suffixes). Ex: *caseolysis* (*-lysis*, q.v. at *-lyse*).

castano-: from Gr *kastanos*, chestnut tree: cf CHESTNUT. Ex: *Castanopsis* (cf *-opsis* at *-opsia*).

-caster, -cester, -chester; castra-: 'fortified place, esp fortified town': L *castra*, a camp: cf CASTLE. The first three occur only in place-names, *-chester* being the most, *-caster* the least anglicized. Exx: *Doncaster, Worcester, Manchester*; *castrametation*, camp-measuring, hence camp-making, the 2nd element deriving from L *metari*, to measure off (a camp-site): cf *-meter*.

cathodo-: for *cathode*, as in *cathodograph* (cf *-graph*).

Catholici-: for *Catholic*.

catoptro-: from Gr *katoptron*, a mirror (*kat-* for prefix *kata-*, see *cata-*+the Gr root for 'to see'—cf OPTIC). Ex: *catoptromancy*, divination (*-mancy*) with a mirror.

caudi-; caud(o)-: 'of the tail'; 'caudal (of the tail)' or 'caudal and': L *cauda* (s *caud-*), the tail, o.o.o. Exx: *caudiform*; *caudodorsal*.

cauli-, as in *caulicolous, cauliflory, cauliflorous* (but not *cauliflower*), *cauliform*, and caulo-, as in *caulomer, caulotaxy*: the former from L *caulis*, a stalk, itself akin to, perh from, Gr *kaulos*, whence *caul(o)-*; with cognates in OC and OSl.

causi-: L *causi-*, c/f of *causa*, a law-case: cf CAUSE. Ex: *causidical*, of, for, by pleading (*dicere*, to say) a case.

cav-; cavo-: c/f of ML *cavus* (L *cauus*), hollow —see CAVE. Exx: *cavicorn*, hollow-horned, and *cavo-relievo*, for It *cavo-rilievo*, hollow relief. Cf *caverni-*, from ML *caverna*, a cavern, from *cavus* (L *cauus*), as in *cavernicolous* (cf *-colous*), cave-dwelling.

cecidio-, cecido-, as in *cecidiology, cecidogenous*: c/ff of Gr *kēkis*, gall-nut, o/s *kēkid-*, perh akin to *kēkis*, a gushing forth.

ceco-: c/f of L *caecus*, blind (see *caeci-* above), as in *cecograph*, a device that helps the blind to write.

-cele. See *-coele*.

celi(o)-. See *coeli(o)-*

celli-: c/f of E CELL. Exx: *celliferous, celliform, cellifugal, cellipetal*. Cf:

cello-: c/f of *cellulose* (see CELL). Ex: *cellobiose*. Cf:

celluli-; cellul(o)-: 'cell' or 'cellulle'; 'cellular and' or '(nerve) cell': c/ff of *cellule* (see CELL). Exx: *celluliferous*; *cellulofibrous*.

celo-. See *coel-*.

celti-, as in *celtiform*, shaped like a celt: from LL *celtis*, a chisel—perh cf MIr *celtair*, a spear.

Celt(o)-, as in *Celto-Iberian* and *Celtomaniac, Celtophil*: c/f of *Celt* or *Celtic*. See CELT.

cemento-: c/f of *cementum* (of a tooth: cf CEMENT). Ex: *cementoblast*.

-cene; ceno-: 'recent, new': Gr *kainos* (s *gain-*), fresh, new, cf Skt *kaínas*, young; prob IE s, *ken-*. Exx: *Eocene, Miocene*, geol periods; *cenogenesis, Cenozoic*.

ceno- (1). See prec.

ceno- (2): from Gr *kenos* (s *ken-*), empty: perh ult akin to L *uānus* (E VAIN). Ex: *cenotaph*, an empty tomb, via EF-F *cénotaphe* from L *cenotaphium*, itself from Gr *kenotaphion* (cf the *-taph* of *epitaph*).

ceno- (3). A rare var of *coen(o)-*, as in *cenoby*.

-cenosis: (Med) 'discharge', (Surg) 'removal': Gr *kenōsis*, an emptying (cf *-osis* in Suffixes). Ex: *lithocenosis* (*litho-*). Cf the 2nd *ceno-*.

centauro-, as in *centauromachy*, a fight in which centaurs participate: from Gr *Kentauros*, a Centaur (a Thessalian half-man, half-horse), perh 'he who spurs horses' (Boisacq, 'Conjectural')—cf Gr *kentron*, a spur.

centi-; before a vowel, cent-. L c/f of *centum* (s *cent-*), a hundred; cf Skt *sata-*. Either 'a hundred', as *centigrade, centenary* (LL *centenārium*: cf *-enary*), *centipede*, or, on the F pattern, 'a hundredth part', as in *centigram, centimetre*.

centri-, centr(o)-; -centric; resp 'centre', c/f of L *centrum* (s *centr-*); 'centre', c/f *kentro-* of Gr *kentron* (s *kentr-*); 'centering on', 'tending towards, or turning round, a centre', from ML *-centricus*. L *centrum* comes straight from Gr *kentron*; see CENTER. Exx: *centrifugal* (*-fugal*) and *centripetal* (*-petal*); *centrobaric* (cf *-bar*) and *centrosphere*.

cephal(o)-; -cephalic or -cephalous; -cephalus, -cephaly: *cephal(o)-* adapts Gr *kephalo-, kephal-*, c/f of *kephalē*, the head; IE s *khebh-* or *ghebh-*: cf Macedonian Gr *kebalē* and Go *gibla*, top, summit. Exx: *cephalograph* (cf *-graph*) and *cephalomancy* (cf *-mancy*); *brachycephalic* or *brachycephalous*, short-headed (cf *brachy-*)—cf the Gr *brakhukephalos*; *Bucephalus* (cf *bu-*), Gr *Boukephalos*; *brachycephaly, -cephaly* being prompted by Gr *kephalē*.

-cera, -ceras, -cerous; cerat(o)-, occ kerat(o)-, shortened form, kera-: resp Zoo 'horn', as in *Rhopalocera* (cf *rhopalo-*); Bot and Zoo genera, as *Tinoceras* (cf *tino-*); corresponding E adj; Gr *kerat(o)-*, c/f of *keras*, horn, o/s *kerat-*, as in *ceratoglossal*; *keralite*, hornstone. Gr *keras* has r *ker-*; cf IE r *ker-* or *kar-*, and L *cornu* (E CORN).

cerauno-: Gr *keruano-*, c/f of *keraunos* (s *keraun-*), thunderbolt, ult echoic. Exx: *ceraunograph, ceraunomancy, ceraunoscopy*.

-cercal; -cercy; cerc(o)-: resp '-tailed'; 'a (specified type of) tail formation'; 'tail'; *cerc(o)-*=Gr *kerko-, kerk-*, c/f of *kerkos* (s *kerk-*), a tail: o.o.o. Exx: *homocercal* (Gr *homo-*); *heterocercy* (*hetero-*); *cercopithecus*, Gr *kerkopithēkos*, a (long-) tailed monkey.

cerebelli-, as in *cerebellifugal* (cf *-fugal*), and cerebello-, as in *cerebellocortex*: c/ff of L *cerebellum*, dim of *cerebrum*, brain. Cf:

cerebri-; cerebr(o)-: 'the brain'; 'the brain' or 'of the brain (and)': L *cerebrum*, the brain, s *cerebr-*: cf CEREBRAL. Exx: *cerebriform, cerebrifugal*; *cerebrology, cerebrospinal*.

ceri-; cer(o)-: c/f of L *cēra* (s *cēr-*), wax, as in *cerigerous*, wax-bearing; (*cero-*) adapted from *kēr(o)-*, c/f of Gr *kēros*, wax (s *kēr-*), akin to—perh the origin of—the L word. Exx: *cerography*, Gr *kērographia*, writing or designing upon wax;

*ceroplastics,* Gr *kēroplastikē* (*tekhnē*), lit the wax-modelling art. Cf:

**cerio-,** as in *Ceriomyces* (cf *-myces*), a genus of fungi: from Gr *kērion,* a honeycomb. Cf prec.

**-ceros:** Gr *-kerōs,* c/f of *keras,* horn (of animal), akin to L *cornu* (cf *-corn*). Exx: RHINOCEROS; *Stephanoceros* (cf *stephano-*).

**certi-.** See *certify* at CERTAIN.

**ceruleo-:** from L *caeruleus,* sky-blue, akin to L *caelum,* the sky; as in *ceruleolactite.*

**cerumini-:** for *cerumen,* ear-wax, from L *cēra,* wax. Ex: *ceruminiferous* (cf *-ferous* at *-fer*).

**-cerus,** as in *Tetracerus* (cf *tetra-,* four): from Gr *-kerōs,* horned, from *keras,* horn: cf *-cera.*

**cervi-,** as in *cervicorn,* horned (i.e., antlered) like a stag or ML *cervus,* L *ceruus* (r *cer-*), perh 'the horned (animal)'—cf L *cornu,* horn.

**cervici-,** more often **cervic(o)-:** 'of the neck (and)' ML *cervix,* o/s *cervic-* (L *ceruic-*), the neck, prob (lit) 'the head-biinding (part)'. Exx: *cervicispinal, cervicofacial.*

**-cester.** See *-caster.*

**cet(o)-:** Gr *kēto-,* c/f of *kētos* (s *ket-*), a cetacean (itself=the dervative L *cēt*(us)+*-acean,* q.v. in Suffixes) or whale; Gr *kētos* is o.o.o. Ex: *cetology.* The var *ceti-,* as in *ceticide* (cf *-cide,* killer or a killing), comes from the L *cētus.*

**chada-:** from *chad-,* aorist s of Gr *chandanein* (s *chandan-*). to grasp, hold, contain; IE r, *\*ghend-,* to grasp, c ɪ L *prehendere* (*pre-*+*hend-*+*-ere*). Ex: *chadacryst* (cf *-cryst*), a crystal enclosed within a crystal.

**chaen(o)-:** from Gr *khainein* (s *khain-*), to gape; IE r, *\*ghan-,* an extension of *\*gha-* or *\*ghai-* or *\*ghe-* or *\*ghei-.* Exx: Bot *Chaenactis* (Gr *aktis,* a ray: cf *-actine*) and *Chaenolobus* (Gr *lobos,* a lobe: cf LOBE).

**-chaeta, -chaetes, -chaetus** (adj of all three: *-chaetous*); **chaeti-; chaet(o)-** or **cheto-:** 'spine' or 'bristle': first three, Gr *-khaitēs* (*-χαιτης*), -haired; *chaeti-,* c/f of SciL *chaeta,* from *khaitē; chaet(o)-,* c/f of Gr *khaitē,* (lock of) hair, mane, IE *\*ghaita*— cf Av *gaēsa,* lock of hair. Exx: Zoo *Spirochaeta* (cf *spiro-*); *Connochaetes* (Gr *konnos,* a beard); *chaetiferous; chaetophorous,* bristle-bearing (cf *-phora*).

**chalazi-, chalazo-:** c/ff of Gr *khalaza,* hail-stone, hence a pimple, IE r *\*gheled-.* Mostly in Bot and Embryology, as *chalazogam* (cf *-gam*).

**chalced(o)-:** for *chalcedony,* from L *chalcēdonius* (adj as n), prob from Gr *Khalkēdōn,* Chalcedon, a town in Asia Minor. Ex: *chalcedonyx.*

**-chalcite; chalco-** or **chalko-:** Gr *khalkos,* copper, c/f *khalko-*; IE r *\*ghel*(e)*gh-.* Exx: *leucochalcite,* which=*leuco-*+*chalc-*+Min *-ite* (Suffixes): *chalco-lithic* (cf *-lith*), *chalcotript,* a rubber (Gr *triptēs*) of monumental brasses; *chalkography.*

**Chaldaeo-:** from L *Chaldaeus,* a Chaldean.

**chalico-:** from Gr *khalix* (gen *khalikos*), a pebble —akin to L *calx,* chalkstone. Ex: *chalicothere* (cf *-there*).

**chalko-.** See *-chalcite.*

**chamae-** or **chame-:** 'low': Gr *khamai* (s *kham-*),

on the ground, akin to L *humi,* with many IE cognates, the IE root being prob *\*ghem-:* cf HOMO. Exx: *chamae-,* in Bot and Zoo; *chameleon,* L *chamaeleon,* Gr *khamaileōn,* the earth-lion (cf LION).

**chancri-:** for *chancre,* as in *chancriform.* Cf CANCER.

**charto-.** See *carto-.*

**chasmo-:** from Gr *khasma,* an opening, a gap (cf CHASM). Exx: the Bot *chasmogamy* (cf *-gam*) and *chasmophyte* (cf *-phyte*).

**chavi-, chavic-:** only in Chem, e.g. *chavicol* (cf *-ol,* oil): from *Chavica* (betel), ? named after a botanist.

**-cheiria** or **-chiria; cheir(o)-** or **chir(o)-:** 'type of hand-formation'; '(the) hand': Gr *kheir,* c/f *kheiro-*; IE r *\*gher,* to grasp, cf Tokh A *tsar.* Exx: *macrochiria,* long-handedness; *ch(e)irography,* handwriting; *ch(e)irology* and *ch(e)iromancy,* palmistry; *chiropractic,* manipulation (of joints, esp of spine)—cf *-practic.*

**cheilo-.** See *chilo-* at *-chilia.*

**chel(i)-; chel(o)-:** c/ff of Gr *khēlē* (s *khēl-*), a claw: IE *\*ghā-* or *\*ghei-*—cf CLAW. Exx: *chelicera* (cf *-cera*), *cheliferous, cheliform; chelophore* (cf *-phora*), *Chelura* (cf *-ura*).

**chelid(o)-:** c/f from Gr *khelīdon,* the swallow, IE r *\*khel-* or *\*ghel-.* Ex: *Chelidosaurus* (cf *-saur*).

**chelo-** (1). See *cheli-.*

**chelo-** (2); **chel(y)-:** Gr *khelus,* a tortoise, cf the syn OSl *žely;* IE r, prob *\*ghelea-,* an extension of *\*ghel-.* Exx: *Chelodina* (Gr *deinos,* terrible), a genus of Aus fresh-water turtles; *Chelydra,* genus of common turtles, from Gr *kheludros,* a tortoise, orig an amphibious serpent: Gr *-udros,* end c/f of *hudōr,* water—cf *-hydrous.*

**chemi-; chemico-; chem(o)-,** with var **chemio-:** c/ff of resp *chemical-chemic,* denoting 'relation to chemistry'—*chemical,* denoting 'relation to chemical action'. See CHEMICAL. Exx: *chemiatry* (cf *-iatry* at *-iatric*), *chemigraphy; chemicocautery; chemokinesis, chemotherapy; chemiotropic.*

**chen(o)-:** adaptation of Gr *khēno-, khēn-,* c/f of *khēn* (gen *khēnos,* s *khēn-*), a goose, with cognates in Skt and other IE languages. Ex: *chenopod,* lit 'goose-footed'.

**cherso-:** Gr *kherso-,* c/f of *khersos,* land, as in *khersonēsos,* a peninsula, whence, via L, the E *chersonese* (cf *-nese,* island).

**-chester.** See *-caster.*

**cheto-.** See *chaeto-* at *-chaeta.*

**chiasmo-; chiasto-:** resp from Gr *khiasma,* two lines crossed as in Gr *χ* (khi), whence the ModL *chiasmus*—*khiasma* deriving from *khiazein,* itself from *khi;* and from *khiastos,* marked with a khi (*χ*), the pp of *khiazein.* Exx: *Chiasmodon* (cf *-odon*) and *chiastolite* (cf *-lite*).

**chili-, chilia-:** 'a thousand': Gr *khilioi,* 1,000: IE *\*ghesllo-,* cf L *mille.* Exx: *chiliarch,* leader (cf *-arch*) of 1,000 men; *chiliahedron,* a 1,000-faceted polyhedron (cf *-hedron*).

**-chilia; -chilus; chil(o)-** or **cheil(o)-:** 1st, 'lip

formation'; the others, 'lip': Gr *kheilo-, khil-*, c/ff of *kheilos*, s *kheil-*: cf GILL (fish's). Ex: *chilotomy*.

chin(o)-: c/f of SciL *chinium*, quinine, as in *chinotoxin, chinol*.

Chino-: c/f of *China* or of *Chinese* (*and*). Ex: *Chino-Japanese*. Cf *sino-*.

chio-; chion(o)-: c/ff from Gr *khiōn*, snow, o/s *khion-*, akin to Gr *kheima*, L *hiems*, winter. Exx: *chiolite* (cf -*lite*): *Chionodoxa*, (lit) the glory of the snow—a genus of lilies.

-chiria; chir(o)-: See -*cheiria*.

-chirurgia: from Gr *kheirourgia* (lit, hand-work), surgery: cf SURGERY. Ex: *pneumochirurgia* (cf *pneumo-*).

chitino-: c/f of *chitinous*; chito-, c/f of *chitin*, a Biochem term, derived from Gr *khitōn*, coat of shell (hence of mail, etc.).

chlamyd(o)-: Gr *khlamud(o)-*, c/f of *khlamus*, o/s *klamud-*, a mantle. Ex: *chlamydospore* (cf -*spora*). A secondary c/f appears in *chlamyphore*, as if from a Gr c/f *khlamu-*.

chlo-: from Gr *khloē*, verdure (cf the next). Ex: *chloanthite* (cf -*anth*).

chlor o)-: c/f of Gr *khlōros*, light-green, s *khlōr-*; cf the IE r \**ghlo(r)-* or \**khlo(r)-*: a word with numerous cognates. In Chem, this c/f denotes the presence of chlorine, as in *chloroform*, the 2nd element representing *formyl*; in Med, chloroma or chlorosis. Next to *chloroform*, the most notable cpd is perh *chlorophyl(l)*, the light-green colouring matter of plants (-*phyll*). Cf prec.

-choanite, adj -choanitic; choano-: c/ff of Gr *khoanē*, a funnel, s *khoan-*, akin to Skt *hóman-*, libation, and esp to Gr *kheō* (s *khe-*), I pour out. Exx: *Holochoanites*, pl (cf *holo-*); *cloiochoanitic* (cf *cloio-*); *choanocyte* (-*cyte*); *choanosome* (cf -*soma*).

-choerus: SciL from Gr *khoiros* (s *khoir-*), a pig—cf Gr dial *khurra*, a sow, and perh L *sūs* (gen *suis*, \**sueris*), pig, sow. Ex: *Hydrochoerus* (cf *hydro-*), a Zoo genus.

chole-, chol(o)-; -cholia, -choly: c/f (*chole-*) of Gr *kholē* and (*cholo-*) of its var *kholos*, bile or gall, the Gr c/f being *khole-* or *khol-*; Gr -*kholia*; its anglicism -*choly*. The Gr word is akin to L *fel*, E *gall*; IE r is prob \**ghel-*, yellow (cf YELLOW itself). Exx: *cholecyst*; *cholochrome*; *melancholy*, from *melancholia*, itself adopted from Gr (cf *melano-*). The c/f *chole-* has a compound: *choledoch(o)-*, c/f of Gr *kholedokhos*, bile-containing. Semantically cf -*chondri-*.

choledoch(o)-. See prec, s.f.

cholero-: for *cholera*, as in *cholerophobia*. Cf CHOLER.

chondri-, chondri(o)-, chondr(o)-; -chondria, -chondry: *chondri-* is a var of *chondro-* and a short form of *chondrio-*; *chondrio-* is the c/f of Gr *khondrion*, dim of *khondros*, (lit) grit or grain, (hence) cartilage, whence obviously *chondro-*, itself a Gr c/f; -*chondry* merely anglicizes -*chondria*, from Gr -*khondria*, an abstract c/f from *khondros*. Exx: *chondrigen, chondriome*; *chondriosome*; *chondrocostal, chondrophore*; *hypochondry, -dria*, through L from Gr *hupokhondria*, orig the neu pl

of *hupokhondrios*, adj formed of *hupo* (cf *hypo-*), under + *khondros*, cartilage, the derivative adj being *hupokhondriakos*, whence, via ML and EF-F, the E *hypochondriac*, adj hence n.

-chord, -chordal; chord(o)-: 'string' or 'stringed instrument', from Gr -*khordon* (neu of adj -*khordos*), as in *clavichord* (cf the 2nd *clavi-*); 'relating to the notochord' (q.v. at *noto-*), as in *epichordal*; *chord(o)-*=Gr c/f *khordo-, khord-*, from *khordē* (whence ult -*khordon*), and denotes cither 'the vocal cords', as in *chordotonal*, or 'the notochord', as in *chordotomy*. The Gr *khordē* derives from IE \**gher-*, to fasten. Cf *chorio-*.

-chore: 'a plant distributed by (a specified) agency', as in *zoochore*: from Gr *khōrein* (s *khōr-*), to spread. Adj: -*chorous*.

chore-: c/f of Gr *khoreia*, a dance, as in *choreography*, now usu *choreography*, (the art of) stage, esp ballet, dancing. Cf CHORUS, the 2nd *choro-*, and:

chorei-: c/f of *chorea*, St Vitus's dance: c/f of Gr *khoreia*, a dance.

choreo-. See *chore-*.

chori-. See next. (Also see *chori-* in Prefixes.)

chori(o)-: c/f of *chorion*, a membrane, from Gr *khorion*. IE r, prob \**gher*, to grasp, contain, envelop. Ex: *choriocarcinoma*. Cf -*chord*.

chorist(o)-: c/f from Gr *khōristos*, separated, pp of *khōrizein*, to separate, divide, from *khōris*, separately. Ex: *choristoblastoma*.

chor(o)- (1): Gr *khōro-, khōr-*, c/f of *khōros*, a place (s *khōr-*). Exx: *chorography*, Gr *khōrographia*; *chorology*.

choro- (2): c/f from Gr *khoros*, (a) dance, s *khor-*, perh by reduction from *khortos*, grass, feeding place, enclosure, court: cf COURT. Ex: *choromania*. Cf:

chorto-: Gr *khorto-*, from *khortos*, grass—cf COURT. Ex: *chortosterol*.

chreo-; -chresis, -chrestic; chresto-: resp c/f of Gr *khreios*, useful, as in *chreotechnics*; Gr *khrēsis*, use, as in *catachresis*, misuse (*cata-* in Prefixes); adj from Gr *khrēstos*, useful, as in *catachrestic*; c/f of *khrēstos*, as in *chrestomathy*, Gr *khrēstomatheia* (cf -*math*); all these Gr words derive from *khrēsthai* (s *khrē-*), to use, with many IE cognates.

Christi-; Christo-: c/f of L *Christus*; c/f of Gr *Khristos*, the Christ. Exx: *Christicide* (cf -*cide*); *Christocentric*. See CHRISTIAN.

I:-chroia, -chroic, -chroid, -chroöus, -chromasia, -chrome, -chromia, -chromy; II: chromat(o)-, chromi-, chromidio-, chrom(o)-. The origins are separately these: I: Gr *khroia*, colour, E -*chroia* denoting discoloration, as in *cacochroia* (cf *caco-*), with adjj -*chroic, -chroid, -chroöus*, as in *erythrochroic* (cf *erythro-*), *xanthochroid* (*xantho-*), *isochroous* (*iso-*); -*chromasia*, 'condition of pigmentation', a cpd of Gr *khrōma*, colour + suffix -*asia*; -*chromia* (*chrom-* + *-ia*), anglicized as -*chromy*, comes from *khrōma*, whence also -*chrome* and *chrome* (cf the adj *chromatic*, via L from Gr *khrōmatikos*); II: *chromat(o)-*, from Gr *khrōmato-* *khrōmat-*, c/f of *khrōma*, colour, o/s *khrōmat-*, denotes 'colour' or 'pigment(ation)', as in *chromatophore*; *chromi-*, c/f of *chromium* (a SciL formation from *chrome*); *chromidio-*, c/f of *chromidium*; *chrom(o)-*, c/f from Gr *khrōma*, denotes 'colour' or 'pigment' or 'pigmentation', as in *chromogen* (*-gen*), *chromolithograph*, *chromometer*, *chromophore* (of *-phora*), *chromosome* (cf *-soma*).

The Gr *khrōma*, s *khrōm-*, has few and only very ancient parallels; *khrōm-* appears to be an *-m* extension of IE \**khro-* or \**ghro-*.

**-chromis:** a Zoo c/f, in fish names: from Gr *khromis*, some kind of marine fish.

**chromo-; -chromy.** See *-chroia*.

**-chrone, -chronous; chron(o)-:** resp Math c/f from Gr *khronos*; general adj from *-khronos*; *chron(o)-*, adaptation of Gr *khrono-*, *khron-*, c/f of *khronos*, time, s *khron-*; cf CHRONIC. Exx: *synchrone*, *synchronous*; *chronology*, *chronometer*. See CHRONIC.

**chrys(o)-:** Gr *khruso-*, *khrus-*, c/f of *khrusos* (s *khrus-*), gold—cf CHRYSALIS. Exx: *chrysanthemum* (cf *anth-*), Gr *khrusanthemon*, and *chrysolite*, *chrysoprase*.

**chrysto-,** as in Geol *chrystocrene* (cf *-crene*): app for *crystal*.

**-chylia; chyli-, chyl(o)-:** 'condition of the chyle'; *chyli-*, a var of *chyl(o)-* from Gr *khulo-*, *khul-*, from *khulos* (s *khul-*), (lit) juice, (hence) chyle—a modification of lymph; *khulos* derives from *kheein* (s *khe-*), to pour, akin to JUICE. Exx: *hypochylia*; *chyliferous*; *chylocyst*. Cf:

**-chyme; chymi-:** end c/f of E *chyme* (Physio); ordinary c/f of *chyme*, ult from Gr *khumos*, juice, from *kheeein*, to pour: cf prec. Ex: *chymiferous* (cf *-ferous* at *-fer*).

**ciconi-:** from L *cicōnia*, a stork, perh a redup of *canere* (s can-), to sing. Ex: *ciconiform*, stork-like.

**[-cid-:** c/f of L *cadere*, to fall, as in *accident*, *deciduous*, *incident*. Cf CADENCE.]

**-cidal; -cide:** L *-cīda+-al*, adj; (*-cide*) L *-cīda*, -slayer, and *-cīdium*, a slaying, from *caedere*, to slay, kill. With the s *caed-*, basically 'to cut (down)', e.g. trees, perh cf Skt *khidáti*, he tears. Exx: *homicidal*, adj of HOMICIDE, man-slayer, now usu a man-slaying; anl *bactericidal*, *bactericide*, and *insecticidal*, *insecticide*; *matricide*, *parricide* (for *patricide*).

**-cil; cili- or cilii-; cili(o)-:** c/ff of L *cilium*, eyelid s *cil-*: cf F *cil*, eyelash)—cf Gr *kalia*, a hut, a nest, and the root of L *celāre* (s *cel-*), to hide. Exx: *palpocil*; *ciliform* or *ciliiform*; *ciliectomy*; *ciliotomy*.

**cimi-, cimici-,** c/ff of L *cīmex* (s *cīm-*), o/s *cīmic-*, a (bed) bug, o.o.o. Exx: *cimicide*, *cimicifugin*.

**cincho-** (Chem only): for *cinchonine* (a Chem *-ine* derivative of *cinchona* (see P² and P⁴). Ex: *cincholoipon* (Gr *to loipon*, the remainder: cf the 2nd *lipo-*). The related *cinchono-* stands for *cinchona*, as in *cinchonclogy*, the pharmaceutics of *cinchona*.

**cine-** (1); **cinemato-, cinemo-; cinet(o)-.** The base is *cin-* or *kin-*, the latter being the s of Gr *kinein*, to move; other relevant Gr forms are *kinēma*, a moving, a motion (s *kinēm-*), with o/s *kinēmat-*;

*kinēsis*, motion; *kinētos* (adj), moving. The E derivatives in *cin-* were orig *kin-*, which is still preferred in a few, esp if non-cinematic, terms: cf *kinesi-*. Exx: *cinecamera*, with *cine-* deriving from CINEMA, itself from *cinematograph*; *cineplasty*, see *kine-*; *cinemograph*: *cinetographic*, *-scopic*, see *kine-*.

**cine-** (2): ML *cine-*, from L *cinis* (gen *cineris*), ashes: cf *incinerator*. Ex: *cinefaction*, a turning into ashes—cf FACTION.

**cinque-:** F *cinq*, or It *cinque*, five, from L *quinque*. Exx: It *cinquecento*, the 16th century; *cinque* for F *cinq* occurs in *cinquefoil*, *cinquepace*, *cinquepoint*, *Cinque Ports*; cf *cinquain*, adopted from F (*cinq*+ *-ain*, as in *quatrain*).

**cion(o)-:** adapted from Gr *kiono-*, *kion-*, c/f of *kiōn*, column, uvula, s *kion-*: cf Arm *siun*, column, pillar. Exx: *cionectomy*, *cionotomy*.

**cirrho-.** A var of *cirro-* in:

**cirri-; cirro-:** c/ff from L *cirrus*, curl, ringlet, hence cirrus cloud and, in Zoo, a small, flexible appendage or 'arm': o.o.o. Exx: *cirriform*, *cirrigerous*, *cirriped*; *cirro-cumulus* and *-stratus*.

**cirro-** (1). See prec.

**cirro-** (2): adapted from Gr *kirrho-*, c/f of *kirrhos*, tawny, as in *cirrolite*.

**cirs(o)-:** Gr *kirso-*, *kirs-*, c/f of *kirsos* (s *kirs-*), a dilated or varicose vein, perh akin to *kissos* (s *kis-* or *kiss-*), ivy, from which it may, by the resemblance of ivy stems to large varicose veins, have derived. Ex: *cirsotomy*.

**cisto-:** Gr *kisto-*, c/f of *kistē*, a box: cf *cysto-* at *-cyst*. Ex: *cistophorus*, a coin bearing (cf *-phora*) the mystic cyst.

**citi-:** from L *citus* (s *cit-*: cf ex*cite*), swift, as in *citigrade*, applied to spiders that 'walk quickly', i.e. run: cf *-grade*.

**-citri; citro-:** c/f of L *citrus*, citron tree (cf CITRON); c/f of *citron*, its fruit. Exx: *citri-culture*; *citrometer*.

**clad(o)-; -cladous:** 'sprout, slip'; 'having branches of a specified type': Gr *klados* (s *klad-*), sprout: cf GLADIATOR. Exx: *cladanthous* (cf *antho-*); *cladophyll* (cf *-phyll*); *acanthocladous* (*acantho-*).

**-clase; -clasia; -clast, -clastic:** resp c/f of Gr *klasis*, a fracture; SciL c/f of the same; (*-clast*) c/f from Gr *-klastēs*, -breaker, hence the adj *-clastic*, from Gr *klastos*, broken: all, therefore, from Gr *klān*, to break, *klaō*, I break (s *kla-*)—cf the not entirely accidental kinship of E *clash*. Exx: *clinoclase* (cf *clino-*), *hemoclasia* (cf *hemo-*); ICONOCLAST, idol-breaker; and, in Surg, *cranioclast* (an instrument).

**classi-.** See *classify* at CLASS. The derivative *classico-* (L *classicus*: cf CLASSIC) means either 'the classics', as in *classicolatry* (*-latry*, worship: see *-later*), or 'classical and', as in *classico-mathematical*.

**clathr-:** L *clathri*, lattice, from Gr *klēthra*: cf *clathrate*, latticed.

**claustro-:** from L *claustrum*, an enclosure, cf *claustra*, bars, locks, etc., from *claudere*, to close, shut, confine, pp *clausus*. Ex: *claustrophobia*, a dread (cf *-phobia* at *-phobe*) of being in an enclosed space, esp a building or a room. Cf CLOISTER.

**clavi-** (1): ML *clāva* (L *clāua*), a club, perh ult of same origin as (2). Ex: *claviform*, club-shaped, and *Claviceps*, lit the club-headed.

**clavi-** (2): ML *clāvis* (L *clāuis*), a key; s, as in (1), *clāu-*; akin to *claudere*, to shut: cf CLOSE. Ex: *clavichord*, ML *clavicordium*, a keyboard instrument.

**claviculo-**: c/f of ML *clāvicula*, dim of *clāvis* (see prec): used in ref to the clavicle and meaning 'clavicular and', as in *claviculo-humeral*. (Webster.)

**cleid(o)-; cleist(o)-; -cleisis** or **-clisis**: Gr *kleido-*, *kleid-*, c/f of *kleis* (o/s *kleid-*), a key, and, in E, denoting either 'key', as in *cleidomancy*, or 'the clavicle', as in *cleidotomy*, or 'of the clavicle and', as in *cleidocranial*; (*cleisto-*) from Gr *kleistos*, closed, as in *cleistogamy* (cf *-gam*); (*-cl(e)isis*) from Gr *kleisis*, closure, as in *enterocleisis* (*entero-* in Prefixes). Both Gr *kleistos* and Gr *kleisis* come from Gr *kleiein*, to close or shut (s *klei-*), akin to L *claudere*; *kleiein* and *kleis* (s *klei-*) are intimately akin.

**-clema**: from Gr *klēma* (s *klēm-*), a twig, prob from *klaō*, I break (s *kla-*), it denotes 'branched thus or thus'. Cf *clematis*, Gr *klēmatis*.

**clepto-**. See *klepto-*.

**clerico-**: c/f of *clerical*, prob via LL *clēricus*: denoting 'clerical (and)', as in *clerico-historical*. Cf CLERIC.

**clero-**: adaptation of Gr *klēro-*, c/f of *klēros* (s *klēr-*), a lot, as in *cleromancy* (divination by the casting of lots), hence an inheritance, as in *cleronomy* (cf *-nomy* at *nomo-*).

**climato-**, c/f of *climate*; *climo-*, a shortened c/f (*climate*+connective *-o-*): L *clīmāt-*, o/s of *clīma*, itself from Gr *klīma* (s *klīm-*), o/s *klīmat-*, from *klīnein* (s *klīn-*), to incline, to slope. Exx: *climatography*, *climatology*; *climograph*.

**-clinic** or **-clinous**, 'tending, inclined, leaning (towards)': the former from Gr *klīnikos*, from *klīnē*, bed, from *klīnein*, to lean; the latter by influence of suffix *-ous*. Ex: *matroclinic* or *-clinous*, cf *matri-*. Cf:

**clin(o)-**: cf Gr *klīno-*, *klīn-*, c/f of *klīnē*, a bed or a couch, as in *Clinopodium* (cf PEW), or of *klīnein* (s *klīn-*), to incline—whence, of course, *klīnē*; the place where one reclines—as in *clinograph*, *clinometer*; occ with sense 'to decline' (v.i.), as in *clinology*. Cf INCLINE and LEAN (v).

**-clinous**. See *-clinic*.

**cloio-**: from Gr *kloios*, a collar, prob akin to *kleiein* (s *klei-*), to shut or close, to confine. Ex: *cloiochoanitic*.

**clonico-**: for 'clonic (and)', as in *clonicotonic*; *clonic*, irregularly convulsive, is the adj of Med *clonus*, a SciL term for Gr *klonos* (s *klon-*), a movement both confused and violent, perh akin to *kellein* (s *kell-*), to drive on, and *kelēs*, a swift-sailing vessel, a riding-horse.

**clon(o)-**: from Gr *klōn*, a branch, prob akin to *klados*, a twig. Ex: *clonothrix* (cf *-thrix*, hair), a genus of bacteria.

**clup(e)-**: from L *clupea*, a small river-fish. Ex: the Chem *clupanodonic*—2nd element, from Gr *anodōn*, toothless (cf *-odon*).

**clypei-, clypeo-**: c/ff of L *clypeus* (s *clyp-*, perh for *clup-*), a shield, of obscure origin (Etruscan ?). Ex: *clypeiform*, shaped like a shield; *clypeofrontal*.

**-cnema, -cnemia, -cnemus; adj -cnemic**: from Gr *knēmē*, the lower leg, the shinbone; cf the OIr *cnaim*, a bone. Ex: *platycnemic* (cf *platy-*).

**cnid(o)-**: c/f of Zoo *cnida*, itself SciL for Gr *knidē*, (sea) nettle. Exx: *cnidoblast* (cf *-blast*) and *cnidophore* (cf *-phora*).

**coagulo-**: for *coagulate*, as in *coagulometer*, instrument for measuring coagulation.

**cobalti-, cobalto-**: c/ff of *cobalt*; the former= *cobalt*+connective *-i-*, the latter *cobalt*+connective *-o-*. *Cobalt* adapts G *Kobalt*, modified from *Kobold*, a goblin, MHG *kobolt*, app akin to G *koben*, a hut, OE *cofa*, a room; *-olt*, *-old* may represent *walt*, *wald*, power (cf WIELD), and MHG *kobolt* may therefore represent OHG *\*kobwalto*: *kobolt*, *-old*, would mean 'house spirit', 'the metal being so called by miners, because it was troublesome' (Webster). Exx: *cobaltrinitrite*, *cobaltocyanic*.

**cobri-**, as in *cobriform*: for *cobra*.

**-coccal, -coccic**, etc., derive from Gr *kokkos*, grain, seed, pip; *-coccal*, *-ic*, *-oid*, adjj answering to *-coccus*, end-element of *coccus*, as in *streptococcus* (cf *strepto-*); *coccidi(o)-*, *coccido-*, c/ff of *coccidium* (s *coccid-*), a SciL dim of *kokkos*, as in *Coccidioides*, *Coccidiomorpha*, *coccidology*. Exx of *cocc(o)-*: *coccobacillus*, *coccolith*, *coccosphere*.

SciL *coccus* has a SciL dim: *cocculus*, with c/f *cocculi-*, as in *cocculiferous*.

**coccygeo-; coccyg(o)-**: c/f of *coccygeal* (adj of *coccyx*) and denoting 'coccygeal and', as in *coccygeo(-)anal*; c/f of *coccyx*, Gr *kokkux* (o/s *kokkug-*), the coccyx, or end of the spine in man; cognates in Skt. Exx: *coccygectomy*, *coccygotomy*, *coccygomorphic*.

**cochlei-; cochli(o)-, cochlo-**: c/f of *cochlea*, adopted from L, adapted from Gr *kokhlias*, a snail, from *kokhlos*, a 'spiralled' shellfish, akin to *konkhē*, a mussel; *cochlio-* and *cochlo-*, c/ff of *kokhlos*. Exx: *Cochliodontidae* (cf *odont(o)-*+ suffix *-idea*); *Cochlospermum*. Cf *cochleari-*, from L *cochleāre*, a spoon for snail-eating, hence any spoon; as in *cochlearifoliate*, having spoon-shaped leaves.

Cf COCKLE and CONCH.

**cocto-**: from L *coctus*, cooked, pp of *coquere*; cf COOK. Ex: *cocto(-)precipitin*.

**-coele**, occ **-cele; -coelus**; 'cavity, ventricle'; 'a (specified) type of cavity', c/f of *coelia*, (in An) a cavity, from Gr *koilia*, a bodily cavity (s *koil-*: therefore cf CELL), adj *coeliac* or *celiac*. Exx: *neurocoele* (cf *neuro-*); *heterocoelus* (cf *hetero-*). Cf next three.

**coeli-** or **caeli-; coelo-** or **caelo-**: c/ff of L *coelum*, better *caelum*, the sky, s *cael-*, o.o.o., perh cf Gr *koilos*, hollow. Exx: *Coelicolist*, heaven-worshipper, and *coeligenous* (cf *-genous* at *-gen*); *caelometer*, an Astr instrument.

**coeli(o)-**: adaptation of Gr *koilio-*, *koili-*, c/f of *koilia*, belly (cf prec). Exx: *coelialgia* (cf *-algia* at *alg-*) and *coeliotomy* (cf *-tomy* at *-tome*). A mod var is *celi-*, as in *celialgia*. Cf:

**coel(o)-**: from Gr *koilo-*, *koil-*, c/f of *koilos*, hollow: cf prec. Ex: *coeloblastic* (cf *-blastic* at *-blast*).

**coelomo-**: c/f of An *coelom* or *-ome*, as in *coelomopore* (cf PORE).

**-coelus.** See *-coele.*

**coen(o)-**: from Gr *koino-*, *koin-*, c/f of *koinos*, common, shared in common, s *koin-*, akin to L *cum*, earlier *com*, with. Exx: *coenobium* (anglicized as *cenoby*), from Gr *koinobion*, community life (*bio-*), hence a term in Bio and Bot; *coenocyte* (*-cyte*); *coenotype.*

**col-.** See 1st *colo-.*

**-cole.** See *-colous.*

**cole(o)-**: from Gr *koleo-*, *kole-*, c/f of *koleos*, a sheath, s *kole-*, akin to L *culleus*, a leather bag, s *culle-*, both perh from a word of general Medit stock (E & M). Exx: *Coleoptera*, a Zoo order of insects, from Gr *koleopteros*, sheath-winged (cf *-ptera*); *coleorhiza* (cf *-rhiza*).

**coli-** (1). See the 1st *colo-.* Cf:

**coli-** (2): c/f of *coli*, a bacterial species (from the An *colon*). Ex: *colibacterin.*

**coli-** (3): from L *cōlum*, a strainer (cf E *colander*); as in *coliform* (cf *-form*).

**-coline.** See *-colous.*

**-coll**, as in *glycocoll* (cf *glyco-* at *glu-*); **colla-**, as in *collagen*; **coll(o)-**, as in *colloblast* (*-blast*), *collotype*: c/ff of Gr *kolla* (s *koll-*), glue. *Coll(o)-* serves also, e.g. in *collochemistry*, as the c/f of *colloid*, itself=*coll-*, for Gr *koll*(a), glue+*-oid*, 'like', q.v. in Suffixes. Cf *collodio-.*

**colli-**: from L *collum*, s *col*(*l*)-, the neck; basic sense, either 'that which is aloft' or 'that which turns' (see E & M). Ex: *colliform*, neck-shaped.

**collodio-**: c/f of *collodion*, from Gr *kollōdēs*, glue-like, from *kolla*, glue. Ex: *collodiotype*. Cf:

**colloido-**: for *colloid*, of glue, or (n) a glue-like substance: cf *-coll*. Ex: *colloido-chemical.*

**col(o)-** (1): 'the colon' or 'of the colon and': c/f of L *colon*, from Gr *kolon*, the An colon—cf An COLON. Exx: *colectomy*, *colotomy* (cf *-ectomy* and *-tomy* at *-tome*); *colopuncture*. Cf *colono-.*

**colo-** (2): c/f from Gr *kōlon*, limb, s *kōl-*. Ex: *colometry*, measurement (cf *-metry* at *-meter*) of verses or manuscripts by cola—cf literary COLON.

**colon(o)-**: c/f of the An *colon*—cf *colo-* (1). Ex: *colonoscopy* (cf *-scopy* at *-scope*).

**colori-**: c/f of L *color*, hence of AE *color*, E *colour*—see COLOR. Exx: *colorific* (*-fic*) and *colorimeter* (*-meter*).

**-colous** and **-coline** and **-cole**: 'living or growing in': all from L *-cola*, adj and esp n—'inhabiting', 'inhabitant': cf COLONY and CULTURE. Exx: *saxicolous*, *-coline*, *-cole*, rock-inhabiting; *arenicolous*, sand-inhabiting; *agricole* (cf *agri-*), a farmer—*agricolous*, agricultural.

**colp(o)-**; **-colpos**: the former, c/f adapted from Gr *kolpo-*, *kolp-*, c/f of *kolpos*, the womb, s *kolp-*, which is perh the IE s also. Exx: *colposcopy*, *aerocolpos.*

**colubri-**: from L *coluber*, f *colubra*, a serpent; as in *colubriform*, snaky.

**columbo-**: c/f of *columbium*, a chem element.

**columelli-**; **columni-**: the former, from L *columella*, a small column, the dim of *columna*, a column, whence *columni-*. Exx: *columelliform* and *columniferous* (cf *-ferous* at *-fer*).

**-coma; come-** and **comi-**: c/f (only in Bot and Zoo) of Gr *komē* (s *kom-*), hair; (*comi-*) c/f of its L derivative *coma* (s *com-*); see COMET. Exx: *Abrocoma*, rodents with soft, fine hair (cf *habro-*); *comephorous* (cf *-phorous* at *-phora*), bearing—i.e., having—hair. *Comiferous* (*-ferous*, q.v. at *-fer*).

**comburi-**: from L *combūrere* (s *combūr-*), to burn up, burn entirely (*com-*, with+intrusive *b* (as in *ambūrere*)+*ūrere*, to burn): cf COMBUSTION. Exx: *comburimeter* and *comburivorous* (cf *-vorous* at *-vora*).

**cometo-**: for *comet*, as in *cometology*, the lore and science of comets.

**comi-** (1). See *coma.*

**comi-** (2). See next.

**comico-**: 'comic': c/f from L *comicus*—see COMEDY. Ex: *comico-tragic*. Occ shortened to *comi-*, as in *comitragedy.*

**commi-**: from Gr *kommi*, gum: cf GUM. Ex: *Commiphora* (cf *-phora*), a genus of balsam-yielding trees.

**comparo-**: for *compare*, as in *comparograph*, a device for fingerprint-comparison.

**compresso-**: for *compression*, as in *compresso-meter*, a compression-measurer.

**concavo-**: for *concave*, as in *concavo-convex.*

**condyl(o)-**: c/f from Gr *kondulos* (s *kondul-*), a knuckle, hence (?) a knob, with cognates in Skt. Ex: the Zoo *Condylopoda* (cf *-pod*, foot).

**-cone; coni-; conico-; con(o)-**: 1st, from Gr *konos*; *coni-*=L *cōni-*, c/f of *cōnus*, a cone; (*conico-*) 'conical and' or 'conically', cf the Gr c/f *-kōnikos*, *kōnikos* being 'cone-shaped', the adj of *kōnos* (whence the L word), a cone; (*cono-*), 'a cone', Gr *kōno-* *kōn-*, c/f of *kōnos*. See CONE. Exx: *longicone*; *conifer* (cf *-fer*), *coniform*; *conico-elongate*; *conoplain.*

**coni-.** See prec and next.

**conidi(o)-**; **coni(o)-**: c/f of *conidium* (SciL from Gr *konis*, dust), an asexual spore; c/f, meaning 'dust', adapted from Gr *konio-*, *koni-*, from *konis*, perh a vocalization of *\*knis* and therefore deriving, ult, from an IE s *\*knid-* (Hofmann); cf L *cinis*, ashes, and Skt *kiknasas*, ground grain. The c/f *-conite*, 'type of dust', is an *-ite* (q.v. in Suffixes) modification of Gr *konis.*

Exx: *conidiferous* (*-ferous*, q.v. at *-fer*) and *conidiophore* (cf *-phora*); *conichalcite* (cf *-chalcite*) and *Coniophora* (*-phora*); *xanthoconite* (cf *xantho-*). The rare var *koni(o)-* occurs in *koniology*, the science of (atmospheric) dust.

**conjugato-**: from ML *conjugātus* (L *coniugātus*),

yoked together (cf YOKE), hence 'conjugate (and)' or 'conjugately', as in *conjugato-pinnate* (cf *-pinnate*).

**cono-.** See *coni-*.

**conoido-**, 'as or like a *conoid*' or cone-shaped solid. Ex: *conoidospherical*.

**convexo-**: for *convex*, as in *convexo-concave*.

**-copate, -cope**: from Gr *koptein*, to cut, s *kopt-*, an extension of *kop-*, cf OF *coper*, EF-F *couper*, to cut, IE *\*kap-, \*kep-, \*kop-, \*kup-*. Exx: *apocope*, Gr *apokopē*, a cutting off; *apocopate*, Mod L *apocopātus*, pp of *apocopāre*, to cut off, a reshaping of Gr *apokoptein*; *syncope*, LL *syncope* or *-copa*, Gr *sunkopē*, a cutting up; *syncopate*, ppa and v, from L *syncopātus*, pp of *syncopāre*, a reshaping of Gr *sunkoptein*. Cf *copro-*.

**cope(o)-**: from Gr *kōpē* (s *kōp-*), an oar, akin to Gr *kaptein*, to grasp, and L *capere*, to grasp, take. Exx: *Copeognatha* (*-gnatha*), *Copepoda* (cf *-pod*).

**copr(o)-**: Gr *kopro-*, c/f of *kopros*, dung, s *kopr-*, app an extension of *\*kop-*, to cut (cf *-copate*): which is sem probable; cf the different sem origin of *turd* (L *tord-ere*). Cf also, however, Skt *sákṛt*, dung-heap, with a likely IE r *\*kok-* or *\*kak-* (L *cacāre*).

Exx: *copraemia* or *-emia* (cf *-haemia*); *coprolalia* (cf *-lalia*), disgusting speech; *coprolite* (*-lite*), fossil dung; *coprology*, a study of faeces, (hence) disgusting literature, adj *coprological*—cf *coprophilia*, love of filth; *coprophagy*, the habit, esp among insects and birds, of dung-eating, adj *coprophagous* (cf *-phaga*).

**cor-.** See *coro-*.

**coraco-**: c/f of *coracoid*, (lit) resembling a crow's beak, as in *coracopectoral* (cf *pectori-*); from Gr *korax*, a raven—obviously echoic. Cf *-corax*, raven, crow, in such generic names as *Phalacrocorax* (cormorants).

**coralli-**: 'coral': L *corallum*, from Gr *korallion* (see CORAL). Ex: *coralliform*.

**-corax-.** See *coraco-*.

**cordi-**: from *cord-*, o/s of L *cor* (gen *cordis*), heart: see *-cardia* and, ult, HEART. Exx: *cordidcole*, heart-worshipper; CORDIFORM.

**cordyl(o)-**: Gr *kordulē*, a club, *kordul-* being an extension of *kord-*, from IE r *\*kerad-*, a modification of *\*ker-*, to whirl (Hofmann). Ex: *Cordylanthus* (cf *antho-*).

**core-.** See *coro-* and cf:

**-coria**: 'a (specified) condition of the pupil' (of the eye): Gr *-koria*, c/f of *korē*, pupil, from *korē*, a girl, via the derivative sense 'little image', from 'doll', from 'girl'; *korē-koros* is akin to L *creāre*, to create. Ex: *isocoria* (cf *iso-*). Cf *coro-* below.

**-coris**, occurring only in Bot generic names: Gr *koris*, an insect, a bug.

**cormo-**: c/f of Bot and Zoo *cormus*, from Gr *kormos*, a (tree-)trunk, from *keirō*, I cut.

**-corn; corneo-; corni-, cornu-**: resp '-horn'; 'horny and'; 'horn': L *-cornis*, as in *ūnicornis*, (the) one-horned (beast); L *corneus*, horny; L *cornū*, (animal's) horn. Exx: *longicorn*, long-horned;

*corneocalcareous*; *corniferous*, *corniform*; *cornucopia*, horn of plenty (cf COPIOUS); *cornulite* (horn-shaped stone). Cf *corn* (on one's foot) and HORN itself.

**cor(o)-; core-**: 'pupil' (of eye): see *-coria*. Exx: *corotomy*; *coreplasty*.

**coroni-; corono-**: 'of a crown', as in *coroniform*; 'coronal', as in *coronofacial*: both from L *corōna*, itself from Gr *korōnē*, a crown—see CROWN itself.

**corpori-**, as in *corporify* (cf *-fy*): from L *corpus*, body, gen *corporis*.

**cortici-; cortico-**: 'bark' or 'of bark'; in An, 'cortex' or 'cortical and': L *cortex*, o/s *cortic-*, s *cort-*, an extension of *kor-* (cf Sl *kora*, bark), akin to IE *\*ker*, to cut. Exx: *corticiferous*, *corticiform*; *corticospinal*.

**corvi-**, as in *corviform*, like a crow: from ML *corvus*, L *coruus*, a raven.

**cory-.** See *corypho-*.

**corymbi-**: 'a flat-topped cluster of flowers', as in L *corymbus*, from Gr *korumbos*, and in the E *corymbiform*. Basic sense: 'head'. Cf *corypha*.

**-corynus**, only in Zoo generic names (entomology): Gr *korunē*, a club: cf *cordylo-*.

**coryph(o)-; cory-**, a shortened form: 'head' or 'summit' or 'point': Gr *koruphē*, akin to *korumbos*, q.v. at *corymbi-*. Exx: *Coryphodon* (cf *-odon*), *coryphylly* (cf *-phyll*). Cf L and E *coryphaeus*, Gr *koruphaios*, EF-F *coryphée*, E *coryphee*, chorusleader, ballet-leader.

**coscino-**: from Gr *koskinon*, a sieve; as in *coscinomancy*, divination (cf *-mancy*) with a sieve.

**cosmeto-; cosmico-; cosm(o)-**: resp 'cosmetics', from Gr *kosmētos*, well-ordered; c/f of *cosmic*, and denoting 'cosmical', from *kosmikos*, of the cosmos or world; 'world', Gr *kosmo-*, c/f of *kosmos*, order, (hence) the world, see COSMOS. Exx: *cosmetology*, the art and science of cosmetics; *cosmico-natural*; *cosmocracy* (cf *-cracy*)—*cosmogony* (cf *-gonia*)—*cosmology*—*cosmopolis*, a world city (cf *-polis*), *cosmopolite* (Gr *kosmopolitēs*), a citizen of the world, with adj *cosmopolitan*.

**-costal** and **-costate; costi-** and **costo-**: resp 'of the ribs', as in *intercostal*; 'having ribs', as in *quadricostate* (four-ribbed); 'rib(s)' or 'of the ribs', as in *costiform* and *costotomy*, *costo-abdominal*: all from L *costa*, a rib, s *cost-*, prob akin to OSl *hosti*, a bone, L *os*, Skt *ásthi*; *k-* would therefore be a prefix (E & M).

**-cotyl, -cotylous, -cotyly; cotyli-** and **cotylo-**: resp c/f of Bot and Embryological *cotyledon*, with adj *-cotylous* and with 'condition' n *-cotyly*; c/f from Gr *kotulē*; c/f of *cotyloid*, cup-shaped: the common sense-origin is Gr *kotulēdōn*, a cup-shaped hollow; the form-origin, via L *cotyla*, is Gr *kotulē*, a cup, whence, obviously, *kotulēdōn*; the r *kot-* renders attractive the occ-proposed kinship with the Gr *kot-* words for 'head'. Exx: *dicotyl, dicotylous, dicotyly; Cotylophora* (cf *-phora*).

**coulo-**: for *coulomb* (Phys), as in *coulometer*.

**cox(o)-**: c/f of L *coxa*, hip; IE s *\*kaks-* or *\*koks-*, an articulation or joint: cf Ir *coss*, foot, and Skt *kakṣa*: perh akin to AXIS. Exx: *coxalgia* (cf *-algia*, as in *neuralgia*); *coxo-femoral*.

-cracy, -crat, -cratic; crato-: resp abstract n—agent n—adj of either—c/f='power-' (not from a Gr c/f): Gr *-kratia* (cf the abstract suffix *-ia*)—via F *-crate*, from Gr *-kratēs*—Gr *-kratikos*, often via L *-craticus*, occ via F *-cratique*: the etym base is Gr *kratos*, strength, might, power, hence esp political power: IE r *\*krat-* or *\*kret-*, with numerous IE *derivatives*. Exx:ARISTOCRACY (etc.); DEMOCRAT; *plutocracy*, Gr *ploutokratia*, rule by wealth (Gr *ploutos*)—whence, by b/f, *plutocrat*, with adj *plutocratic*; *cratometer*, a (physical) power-measurer.

-crania, -cranial; cranio-: resp Gr *-krania*, c/f of *kranion*, the skull, r *kran-*, perh for *\*karan-* or *\*keran-*, cf Gr *kara*, head; c/f of *cranial*, adj of E from ML *cranium*; adapted from Gr *kranio-*, c/f of *kranion*. Exx: *amphicrania*, *brachycranial*, *craniometry* (head-measurement).

-crase, -crasis, -crasy: 1st two, from Gr *krasis*, a mixing; *-crasy*, either from Gr *-krasia*, c/f of *krasis* (from *kerannumi*, I mix: cf Skt *srīṇáti*, he mixes), or from *krasis* itself. Exx: *idocrase* (cf *ido-*); *idiosyncrasy*, Gr *idiosunkrasia*, 'a private mixing or mixture', with adj *idiosyncratic*; *syncrasy*, a blending, Gr *sunkrasis* (*sun*, with).

craspedo-: from Gr *kraspedon*, a border, perh a cpd of *\*kras-* for the *kran-* of *kranion*, skull (apprehended as 'head')+*pedon*, ground, as Hofmann proposes. Ex: *craspedodromous* (cf *-dromous* at *-drome*), running to border, (in Bot) running to the margin.

crassi-, as in *crassilingual*, thick-tongued: from L *crassus*, thick, fat: cf CRASS.

-crat, -cratic; crato-. See *-cracy*.

cremno-, as in *cremnophobia*, dread of precipices and high cliffs: from Gr *kremnos*, a cliff. Akin to:

cremo-, as in Bot *cremocarp* (cf *-carp*): from Gr *kremannunai* (s *kreman-*; r *krem-*), to hang, the origin also of prec.

-crenate: for Bot *crenate*, 'having the margin cut into rounded scallops', from L *crena*, a notch.

-crene, as in *Hippocrene*, *chrystocrene*: Gr *-krēnē*, end c/f of *krēnē*, a fountain. Cf *creno-* (Gr *krēno-*), as in *crenology*, the science of (mineral) springs.

creo-: from Gr *kreas*, flesh, gen *kreōs*, akin to Skt *kravís-*. Ex: *creophagy*, adj *creophagous*, flesh-eating. Cf:

creos(o)-: c/f of *creosote*, as in *creosol*, which=*creos*(o)-+*-ol*, oil. The 2nd element comes from Gr *sōzein* (s *sōz-*), to preserve; for the 1st, see prec.

-crete, as in *calcrete*, a type of limestone, represents the *-crete* of CONCRETE (n).

Creto-: c/f of *Cretan*.

cribri-: 'a sieve': L *crībrum* (s *crībr-*, ? for *crīber-*). Ex: *cribriform*.

crico-: 'the cricoid cartilage' or, in adjj, 'cricoid and': Gr *krikos* (s *krik-*), a ring: a var of *kikros* and therefore akin to CIRCLE. Exx: *cricotomy*; *cricothyroid*.

crimino-: 'crime' or 'of crime': *crīmin-*, o/s of

L *crīmen*, (an accusation of) crime—see CRIME and cf the adj *criminal*. Exx: *criminogenesis*, the origin of crime; *criminology*, the (scientific) study of crime.

crini-: 'hair': L *crīnis* (s *crīn-*), akin to *crista*, a (bird's crest). Exx: *criniculture*, *crinigerous* (L *criniger*, long-haired).

-crinus: a SciL c/f of *crinoid*, itself from Gr *krinoeidēs*, lily-like, from *krinon* (s *krin-*), a lily. Ex: *Actinocrinus*.

crio-: 'a ram' (animal): Gr *krios*, lit 'the horned' —cf *keraos*, horned. Exx: *crioboly*, ram-sacrifice (cf *-bole* at *-bola*); *criophore*; *criosphinx*.

cristi- '(bird's) crest': L *crista*, a cock's comb—cf *crinis*, q.v. at *crini-*. Ex: *cristiform*.

criterio-, as in *criteriology*, the logic of criteria: for *criterion*.

critho-, as in *crithomancy*, divination (*-mancy*) with barley cakes: from Gr *krithai* (pl), barley, Homeric *krî*: IE r, prob *kri-*.

critico-: from L *criticus* (see CRITIC) and denoting either 'critic', *criticophobia*, a dread of critics, or 'critical and', as in *critico-philosophical*.

croceo-: Chem c/f of *croceous*, saffron-coloured: from L *croceus*, adj of *crocus*, saffron, from Gr *krokos*, of Sem origin—cf H *karkom*, saffron. Ex: *croceo-cobaltic*. Cf the 2nd *croco-*.

croco- (1). See CROCODILE.

croco- (2): from Gr *krokos*, saffron: see *croceo-*. Ex: *crocosmia* (cf *-osma*).

crom-: (via F *crom-*) from G *krumm*, crooked, akin to OHG *kramph*, crooked, and, one may suspect, Gr *kampulos*; IE r, perh *\*kam-*, with var *\*kram-*. Ex: *cromorna*, F *cromorne*, G *Krummhorn* (lit 'crooked horn'), a reed stop in an organ.

crotali-; -crotic: 'of a *Crotalus* or rattlesnake', as in *crotaliform*; in, e.g., *dicrotic*, 'pulse-beat' of a specified kind: SciL *crotalus*, from Gr *krotalon*, a rattle; *krotalon* derives from *krotos* (whence *-crotic*), the beat, marked by hands and feet, of dancing, s *krot-*, IE s *\*kret-*.

croto-: Gr *krotōn*, a tick, whence *Croton* (adj *crotonic*), a genus of herbs and shrubs with seeds that resemble ticks. Ex: *Crotophaga* (cf *-phaga*).

crouno-: '(mineral-water) spring': Gr *krounos*, a spring, a stream—cf *krēnē*, a spring, as in *Hippocrene*. Ex: *crounotherapy*.

cruci-: 'a cross' or 'of a cross': L and E c/f of L *crux*, o/s *cruc-*: see CROSS. Exx: *crucifix*, L *crucifixus*—for the 2nd element, see FIX; *cruciferous* (cf *-ferous* at *-fer*); *cruciform*.

cruro-: '(of) the thigh': irreg from L *crūr-*, o/s of *crūs*, thigh, (usu) leg, whence the E adj *crural*. Ex: *crurotarsal*.

crymo-: from Gr *krumos*, frost, s *krum-* (cf E *rime*). Ex: *crymotherapy*. Cf:

cry(o)-: Gr *kruo-*, c/f of *kruos*, icy-cold, s *kru-*: perh cf the *cru-* of L *crusta*. Exx: *cryogen* (cf *-gen*), a refrigerant; *cryoscope*. Cf *-cryst*.

crypt(o)-: Gr *kruptos*, covered or hidden, (hence) secret, pp of *kruptein*, to hide, s *krupt-*: cf E CRYPT, CRYPTIC. Exx: *cryptogam* (*-gam*), *cryptogram*, *cryptology*, *cryptoscopy*.

-cryst; crystalli-, crystall(o)-: c/f of CRYSTAL; c/ff, prompted either by L *crystallum* or usu by its Gr original *krustallos*, ice, (hence) crystal: cf, therefore, *crymo*- and *cryo*-. Exx: *phenocryst*; *crystalliferous*; *crystallogenic, crystallography*.

A secondary c/f is *crysto*-, which=*cryst*al+the *-o-* of *crystallo*-. Ex: *crystograph*.

cten(o)-: Gr *kteno*-, c/f of *kten*-, o/s of *kteis*, a comb, akin to L pe*cten*, gen *pectinis*. Ex: *ctenocyst, ctenodactyl.*

cteto-: from Gr *ktetos*, acquirable, adj use of the pp of *ktaomai* (s *kta*-), I procure for myself, cf Skt *kṣáyati*, he possesses or controls. Ex: *ctetology*, the Bio of acquired characteristics.

-ctonus: Gr *-ktonos*, -slayer, from *ktinein* (s *ktin*-), to slay. Mostly in Ent, e.g. *dendroctonus* (cf *dendro*-), a bark beetle.

cubi-; cubo-: 'cube', from L *cubus*, as in *cubiform*; 'cube' or 'cubital (and)', from Gr *kubos*, a cube, a cubical die, s *kub*- (see CUBE), as in *cubomancy*, divination (*-mancy*) with dice.

cubito-: 'cubital (and)', of the forearm, as in *cubitodigital*: L *cubitus*, forearm, elbow, from Gr *kubiton*, elbow.

cubo-. See *cubi*-.

cuculi-: from the obviously echoic L *cuculus* (cf CUCKOO). Ex: *cuculiform.*

cucumi-: from L *cucumis*, a cucumber. Ex: *cucumiform.*

culici-: from *culic*-, o/s of L *culex*, a gnat, a mosquito, s *cul*-; cf the (?) insect-suffix in *cīmex*, a (bed) bug, and *pulex*, a flea (E & M); cf also the rhyming resemblance of *cul*- to *pul*-. Exx: *culiciform, culicifugal* (cf *-fugal*, as in *centrifugal*).

culmi-: L *culmus*, a stalk, a stem, s *culm*-, akin to the *kal(a)m*- of Gr *kalamos*, a reed, and E *haulm*. Ex: *culmicolous*, stalk-living.

culti-, rare, in two different senses: in *cultigen* it=*culti*vate or *culti*vation; in *cultirostral* it=L *culter*, the c(o)ulter of a plow.

cuma-, as in *cumaphyte* (cf *-phyte*): from Gr *kuma*, a wave, perh akin to L *cumulus*.

[-cumb-, as in *recumbent*, lying back: L *cumbere*, an extension of *cubāre*, to lie down, be lying down.]

cumo-: for *cumic* (from *cumin*: Gr *kuminon*, of Sem origin). Only in Chem.

cumuli-; cumulo-: 'heap or mass', esp a cumulus cloud; 'of a cumulus': L *cumulus*, a heap, which, otherwise difficult to explain, might be a blend of *culmen*+*tumulus*. Exx: *cumuliform*; *cumulo-cirrus.*

cuncti-, as in *cunctipotent*, all-powerful: from L *cunctus*, whole, entire, pl *cuncti*, all, perh, as the ancients said, *co-iuncti*, joined together.

cunei-, cuneo-: c/ff of L *cuneus*, a wedge, s *cune*- with the r *cun*-. Exx: *cuneiform*, wedge-shaped; *cuneo-cuboid.*

cupri-, cupr(o)-: c/ff of L *cuprum*, copper: see COPPER. Exx: *cupriferous*, copper-bearing; *cupromanganese*, a copper alloy with manganese.

cupuli-, as in *cupuliform*: c/f of L *cūpula*, a little cup, dim of *cūpa*, a tub, (LL) a cup; s, therefore, *cup*-, cf CUP.

[-cur. See CURRENT and cf *occur, recur.*]

curie-, as in *curiescopy* (cf *-scopy* at *-scope*) and *curietherapy*, implies 'radioactive': from Mme Marie *Curie* (1867–1934).

curio-, 'literal, directly pictorial': from Gr *kurios*, lordly, authoritative, proper, from *kuros*, power, might; akin to Skt *sáras*, strong, powerful. Ex: *curiologic(al)*, from Gr *kuriologikos*, speaking properly or literally.

curvi-; curvo-: c/f of ML *curvus* (L *curuus*), curved, as in *curviform*; c/f of E CURVE, as in *curvometer*, which=*curv*(e)+*-o-*+*-meter.*

[-cuss, as in the obs *incuss* and in *concuss*: see CONCUSS.]

cuti-, cuto-: L *cuti*-, c/f of *cutis*, skin, s *cut*-; *cuto*-, irreg; IE *\*kut-*. Exx: *cuticolo(u)r*, skin-coloured, and *cutocellulose.*

-cyan, adj and n -cyanic; cyan(o)-: 'a bluish colouring-matter', as in *leucocyan* (cf *leuco*-); 'dark-blue', as in *cyanide* (Chem suffix *-ide*) and *cyanogen* (*-gen*): Gr *kuano*-, c/f of *kuanos* (s *kuan*-), lapis-lazuli, hence the colour dark-blue: o.o.o.

cyathi-; cyath(o)-: 'cup', as in *cyathiform*, from L *cyathus*; 'cup-shaped', as in *cyatholith, cyathozooid*, from the Gr original *kuathos* (s *kuath*-), akin to *kuein*, to be big with child; IE r *\*ku*- or *\*keu*-.

cycadi- and cycad(o)-: from Gr *kukas* (gen *kukados*), incorrect for *koikas*, acc pl of *koix*, a doum palm; cf E *Cycas*, a genus of tropical palm-like trees. Ex: *Cycadophyta* (cf *-phyta*).

cycl(o)-: basically 'circle' or 'circular', the context usu clarifying: often via the LL derivative *cyclus*: Gr *kuklo*-, *kukl*-, c/f of *kuklos*, a circle, hence also a cycle; the word is app a reduplication: see CIRCLE. Exx: *cyclograph, cyclomania, cyclorama, cyclotron*. The answering adj is *-cyclic*, as in *hexacyclic* (cf *hexa*-).

cyclono-: c/f of CYCLONE. Ex: *cyclonology.*

cylindri-; cylindr(o)-: '(of) a cylinder', as in *cylindriform*; 'cylindrical' or 'cylindrical and', as in *cylindrocephalic*, with a cylinder-shaped head. *Cylindro-*=Gr *kulindro*-, c/f of *kulindros*: see CYLINDER.

cymato-, rarely kymato-: from *kumat*-, o/s of Gr *kuma* (see *cymi*-). Ex: *kymatology*, now usu *cymatology*. Cf *cymi*-.

cymbi-; cymbo-: c/f of L *cymba*, a boat, from Gr *kumbē*, whence the c/f *cymbo*-. Exx: *cymbiform*, boat-shaped; *cymbocephaly.*

cymi-; cymo-: c/f of *cyme*, an inflorescence; from Gr *kumo*-, c/f of *kuma*, a wave, a sprout, from *kuein*, to be pregnant, cf *cyatho*-. Exx: *cymiferous*; *cymograph, cymometer, cymoscope*. The gen *kuamatos* yields *cymato*-, as in *cymatology*, the science of waves.

cymo- (1). See *cymi*-.

cymo- (2): c/f of *cymene*, from Gr *kuminon*, whence E *cumin*; *kuminon*, s *kumin*-, is of Sem origin—cf H *kammōn*. Ex: *cymogene* (*-gene*, q.v. at *-gen*).

cyn(o)-: Gr *kuno*-, *kun*-, c/f of *kuōn*, o/s *kun*- (gen *kunos*), a dog: cf L *canis*, s *can*-, and see

CYNIC. Exx: *cynocephalous*, dog-headed; *cyno-phobia*; CYNOSURE.

**cyph(o)-**: from Gr *kuphos* (s *kuph-*), bent, stooping, hump-backed, IE r *\*kubh-*. Ex: *cypho-nautes*, a Zoo term, but lit 'the hunchback sailor'.

**Cypri-; Cypro-**: the former SciL from Gr; the latter from Gr *Kupro-*, c/f of *Kupris*, Venus. Exx: *Cypripedium*, lady's-slipper, (lit) Venus's little foot (Gr *podion*); *Cypro-Phoenician*.

**cyprin(o)-**: c/f from Gr *kuprinos*, a carp: prob cf prec. Ex: *Cyprinodontidae*, which=*cyprin(o)-*+ *-odont*+suffix *-idae*, pl of *-ida*.

**Cypro-**. See *Cypri-*.

**cypselo-**: from Gr *kupselos*, a swift, akin to *kuphos*, bent forward. Ex: *Cypselomorphae* (cf *-morph*).

**cyrt(o)-**: Gr *kurto-*, c/f of *kurtos*, bent, curved, as in *cyrtometer*; *kurtos* is akin to Gr *korōnē*, anything curved, esp a CROWN.

**-cyst, -cystis; cysti-, cyst(o)-**: 'pouch, cyst', as in *macrocyst* (cf *macro-*); 'bladder' or 'cyst', in generic names, as *Macrocystis*; 'bladder, cyst', as in *cystiform*; (*cysto-*) 'connexion with, or likeness to, a bladder or a cyst', as in *cystocyte* (cf *-cyte*), *cystophore* (cf *-phora*), *cystoscope*. From Gr *kustis*, a bladder, akin to *kistē*, a box, cf *cisto-*.

**-cyte**, a cell; **cytio-**, cell, as in *cytioderm* (cf *-derm*); **cyt(o)-**, likeness to, or connexion with, a cell or cells, Gr *kuto-*, c/f of *kutos* (s *kut-*), a hollow vessel—as in *cytochrome* (cf *-chroia*) and *cytology*, the science of Zoo cells.

**Czecho-**: for *Czech*, as in *Czechoslovakia*.

**Daco-**: for *Dacia* or *Dacian*, as in *Daco-Roman*.

**dacry(o)-**: 'in relation to, connected with, tears or the tear-ducts': Gr *dakruo-*, c/f of *dakru* or *dakruon*, a tear, akin to L *lacrima*, Go *tagr*; IE *\*dakr-*. Exx: *dacryocyst*, the tear sac, hence the secondary *dacrycyst(o)-*.

1. **dactylio-**; 2, **dactyl(o)-**; 3, **-dactylous**, Gr *-daktulos*, -fingered, hence digitated; 1, Gr *daktulio-*, from *daktulios*, finger-ring, from *daktulos*, finger; 2, Gr *daktulo-*, *daktul-*, c/f of *daktulos*, whence, by the way, E *dactyl*, the metrical foot (-◡◡) of the pointing finger; ulterior etymology obscure. Exx: *dactylioglyph* (cf *-glyph*), *dactylio-graphy*, *dactyliomancy*; *dactylogram*, a fingerprint —*dactylography*—*dactyloscopy*.

**dad(o)-**: from *dāid-*, o/s of Gr *dāis*, a torch. Exx: *Dadoxylon* (cf *xylo-*, wood) and *daduchus*, a orch-bearer (*ekhein*, s *ekh-*, to have, to hold).

**daemon(o)-**. See *demono-*.

**damni-**: LL *damni-*, c/f of L *damnum*, damage, a fine (for damages). Ex: *damnify*. Cf DAMN.

**Dano-**: 'Danish (and)', as in *Dano-Norwegian*: *Dane*, b/f from Da *Daner*, Danes—LL *Danni*, ? cf *dannus*, headman of a village, app a Gaulish word (E & M).

**Danto-**: for *Dante*, as in *Dantology*, Dante lore, the study of Dante.

**dapi-**: from L *daps* (gen *dapis*), a feast, perh akin to Gr *deipnon*, dinner. Ex: *dapifer* (cf *-fer*), a steward or a butler.

**dasi-**, a SciL irregularity for **dasy-**, Gr *dasu-* c/f of *dasus*, dense, (? hence) shaggy, rough, s *das-*, akin to L *densus*, E DENSE. Exx: *Dasiphora* (cf *-phora*); *dasymeter*, a meter for gaseous density; *dasyure*, a thick-tailed animal, cf *-ure*.

**dativo-**: 'in or for the dative': ML *datīvus* (L *datīuus*), suitable for giving; cf DATE (chrono-logical). Ex: *dativo-gerundial*.

**dec(a)-**: 'ten', Gr *deka*, 10, as in *decalogue*, *decathlon*; hence, in the metric system, 'ten times', as in *decalitre* (*-liter*). Gr *deka* is akin to L *decem*, Skt *dása*, ult E TEN. Cf *deci-*, *decu-* and:

**decem-**: 'ten': adopted from L (cf prec). Ex: *decemfoliate*, ten-leaved. Cf:

**deci-**: 'a tenth of': F *déci-*, from L *decimus*, tenth: cf DECIMAL.

**declino-**, as in *declinometer* (for measuring declinations: cf DECLINE): from L *dēclīnāre*, to decline.

**decre-**: for *decrement*; as in *decremeter*.

**-dectes**, only in Zoo generic names: from Gr *dēktēs*, a biter, from *dēdek-*, the s of an imperfect v; IE r: *\*dek-*.

**decu-**: L c/f of *decem*, 10, as in *decuplus*, whence the E *decuple*, tenfold; cf *decury* (L *decuria*), a section or group of ten persons, and *decuman* (L *decumānus*), every tenth, as in 'a decuman wave' (Webster). Cf *deca-*, *decem-*, *deci-*.

**deflecto-**: for *deflect*; as in *deflectometer*.

**dehydr(o)-**: for *dehydrated* or *dehydrogenated*. In Chem only.

**dei-; deo-**: 'of a god'; 'to God': L *deus*, a god, and *Deus*, God, cf DEISM. Exx: *deicide*, *deific*, *deiparous*; *deodand*, something to be given to God, hence forfeit to the Crown.

**deino-**. See *dino-*.

**deipno-**: Gr *deipno-*, c/f of *deipnon*, dinner. Exx: *deipnophobia*, a dread of dinner or of (formal) meals; *deipnosophist*, a wise or skilful table-talker, from Gr *deipnosophistēs*—cf SOPHIST.

**deka-**: var, now rare, of *deca-*.

**deliri-**: for *delirium*, as in *delirifacient*, delirium-causing, -causer.

**delo-**: Gr *dēlo-*, c/f of *dēlos*, evident or visible, s *dēl-*. Exx: *delomorphous*, definite in form (cf *-morph*).

**-delphis; delphin-, delpho-**: c/ff of Gr *delphis*, a dolphin, gen *delphinos*, o/s *delphin-*. Exx: *Delphin-apterus*, *-apterus* being SciL for Gr *apteros*, wingless (cf *-ptera*); *delphocurarine*, *delpho-* being an abbr form of *delphinio-*, from *delphinion*, lark-spur, from *delphis*, a dolphin, the larkspur being 'so named from the shape of the nectary' (Webster).

**delta-, delto-**: c/ff of DELTA; as in *deltohedron*.

**-dema**: from Gr *demas*, body. Only in Zoo.

**demi-**: 'a half', adj 'half': OF-F *demi*, VL *dīmedius*, for L *dīmidius*, which=*dī-* (for *dis*)+ *medius*, middle. Exx: *demicannon*, *demilune*, *demisong*, *demiwolf*.

**dem(o)-**: Gr *dēmo-*, *dēm-*, c/f of *dēmos*, a town-ship, (hence) populace, s *dēm-*: cf DEMOCRACY. Exx: *demagogue* (cf *-agogue*); *democrat* (*-crat* at

-*cracy*); *demography*, the statistical study of populations—cf *demotics*, sociology.

**demon(o)-**: from Gr *daimōn*, o/s *daimon*-, via LL *daemon*-: cf DEMON. Exx: *demonolatry* (cf -*latry* at -*later*), *demonology*. Occ *daemon(o)*-, as in *daemonurgy*. The var *demoni*- is rare and stands for E *demon*.

**dendr(o)-; -dendron**: Gr *dendro*-, *dendr*-, c/f of *dendron*, a tree, s *dendr*-. Exx: *dendrology*, treelore; *Liriodendron*.

1, **dentato**-; 2 **denti**-, 3 **dento**-; 4 **dentino**-; 5 -**dent**, -toothed: 1, from L *dentātus*, toothed; 2, 3, 5, L *dent*-, o/s of *dens*, a tooth, gen *dentis*; 4, c/f of *dentine*, the 'ivory' of a tooth: cf DENTAL. Exx: *dentatoserrate*; *dentifrice* (L *fricāre*, to rub)—*dentosurgical*; *dentinoblast* (-*blast*); *soricident*, having teeth like those of a shrew.

**deo**-. See *dei*-.

**deonto**-: from *deont*-, o/s of Gr (*to*) *deon* (gen *deontos*), necessity—cf *dei*, it is necessary. Ex: *deontology*, the ethics of duty.

1 -**derm**, 2 -**derma**, 3 -**dermatous**, 4 -**dermia**, 5 -**dermis**, 6 -**dermy**;—7, **dermat(o)**-; 8, **derm(o)**-: 1, anglicized form of 2, Gr *derma*, skin, hide; 3, *dermat(o)*+suffix -*ous*; 4, Gr c/f -*dermia* (cf Med -*ia*), denoting type or condition of skin; 5, Gr -*dermis*, denoting layer of skin; 6, E shape of 4; 7, Gr *dermato*-, *dermat*-, c/f of *derma*, o/s *dermat*- (gen *dermatos*); 8, Gr *dermo*-, *derm*-, a shortened c/f of *derma*. Gr *derma* has s *derm*-; IE r *der*-, there being many IE cognates. Cf the 2nd *dero*-.

Exx: *ectoderm* (cf the prefix *ecto*-, external); *leucoderma* (cf *leuco*-), *scleroderma* (cf *sclero*-); *sclerodermatous*; *leucodermia*, *pachydermia*; *epidermis* (cf prefix *epi*-), *taxidermy* (*taxi*-); *dermatography*, *dermatology*; *dermographic*, *dermophobe*, a person habitually fearful of even minor skin injuries.

**der(o)**- (1): c/f from Gr *derē*, the neck, s *der*-, IE s app *guer*-. Ex: *derodidymus*, a two-necked monster.

**dero**- (2): Gr *deros*, skin, a var of *derma*: cf *derm*. Ex: *Derotremata*, a tailed amphibian that retains gill-slits (Gr *trema*, o/s *tremat*-, a hole or slit).

**deserti**-: for *desert*, as in *deserticolous*, desert-inhabiting (cf -*colous*).

**desiodo**-: Chem 'removal of iodine': *de*- blended with *dis*-, prefacing *iodo*-. Ex: *desiodothyroxine* (*thyroxine*=*thyr*-+*ox*-+-*ine*).

**desmidi(o)-; desm(o)**-, occ **desma**-: the alga *desmid*, from Gr *desmidion*, dim of *desmis* (o/s *desmid*-), a var of *desmos*, a bond, a ligature, whence the Gr c/f *desmo*-, adopted by E, and the irreg *desma*-. *Desmos*, s *desm*-, from *deō*, I bind, s *de*-, IE r *de*-, to bind. Exx: *desmidiology*; *desmogen*, *Desmognathae*, *desmoplasm*, *desmopathy*; *desmachyme* (cf -*chyme*). Cf *desmoid*, of a ligament.

**deuter(o)**-, occ abbr **deut(o)**-: Gr *deutero*-, *deuter*-, c/f of *deuteros*, second, (hence) secondary, perh from *duō*, s *du*-, two; for the suffix, cf *proteros*, from *pro*, forwards. Exx: *deuterogamy*, second

marriage—*Deuteronomy*, 'the second law' (cf -*nomy* at -*nome*)—*deuteroscopy*; *deutobromide*, *deutonymph*.—Cf *deuterio*-, for *deuterium*, hydrogen of atomic weight 2.

**dexio-; dextro**-: '(on) the right hand; dextral': Gr *dexios*, as in *dexiotropism* (*dexio*+*trop*(e)+ -*ism*); *dextro*-, L *dexter*, o/s *dextr*-, as in *dextrocardial*, *dextro-rotatory*, *dextroversion*. Cf DEXTROUS.

**diabol(o)**-: from Gr *diabolos*, devil: for ult etym, see DEVIL itself. Ex: *diabolology*.

**diadocho**-: from Gr *diadochos*, adj and n, succeeding, successor, from *diadekhomai* (s *diadekh*-), I take over (from another). Ex: *diadochokinesia* (cf *kinesia* at *kinesi*-).

**diago**-: from Gr *diagein*, to transmit (prefix *dia*+*agein*, q.v. at ACT). Ex: *diagometer* (cf -*meter*).

**dialecto**-: for *dialect*, as in *dialectology*, a study of dialect(s).

**diamido-; diamino**-: for *diamide* and *diamine*. Only in Chem.

**diaphano**-: from Gr *diaphanēs*, transparent; as in *diaphanoscopy* (cf -*scopy* at -*scope*).

**diazo**-: Chem cpd of prefix *di*-+element *azo*-; as in *diazobenzene*.

**dibenzo**-, 'presence of two benzene rings'; **dibromo**-, 'presence of two bromine atoms': only in Chem. Cf *benzo*- and *bromo*-. (Webster.)

**dicaeo**-: Gr *dikaio*-, c/f of *dikaios*, just, from *dikē*, justice. Ex: *dicaeology* (Gr *dikaiologia*), defence by justification.

**dichlor(o)**-, 'presence of two chlorine atoms': cf prefix *di*- and element *chloro*-.

**dich(o)**-: Gr *dikho*-, *dikh*-, c/f of *dikha*, in two, (hence) asunder, akin to *duō*, two. Exx: *dichoptic*, *dichotomy* (-*tomy*, q.v. at -*tome*).

**dichroo**-: from Gr *dikhroos*, two-coloured. Occ shortened to *dichro*-. Ex: *dichro(o)scope*.

**dicrano**-: from Gr *dikranos*, two-headed: cf -*crania*.

**dicty(o)-; rarely diktyo- or dikyton**-: Gr *diktuo*-, c/f of *diktuon*, a net—'that which is cast', akin to *dikein* (s *dik*-), to cast. Exx: *dictyogen*, *dictyosome*, *dictyostele*; var *diktyon*-, in *diktyonite* (Min suffix -*ite*).

**didym(o)-; -didymus**: Gr *didumo*-, c/f of *didumos* (whence -*didymus*), twin, perh a reduplication of *du*-, the s of *duō*, two. Exx: *didymolite* (cf -*lite*); *gastrodidymus* (cf *gastro*- at -*gaster*).

**dieto**-: c/f of *diet*, as in *dietotherapy*. Cf DIET.

**diffusio**-: for *diffusion*, as in *diffusiometer*.

**digi**-: c/f of *digitalis*. Ex: *digitoxin*.

**digitato**-: c/f of *digitate*, -fingered. Cf:

**digiti-; digito**-: c/f of L *digitus*, finger or toe, as in *digitigrade*, walking (mostly) on the toes; (*digito*-) c/f of E *digit*, as in *digitoplantar*.

**dihalo-; diketo-; diodo**-: 'presence of two halogen atoms; two ketone groups; two iodine atoms'. (Webster.)

**diktyo**-. See *dictyo*-.

**dilato**-: for *dilatation* or *dilate*; as in *dilatometer*.

**dimethyl-; dinaphtha- or dinaphth(o)**-: 'presence

of two methyl groups; two naphthalene rings'. (Webster.)

**dinitro-**, only in Chem: 'the presence of *two nitro* groups', as in *dinitrotuluene*.

**din(o)-**: from Gr *deinos*, terrible: applied to extinct creatures, e.g. *Dinornis* (Gr *ornis*, bird)— *dinosaur* (cf SAURIAN)—*Dinotherium* (Gr *thēr*, wild beast).

**dioecio-**: for Bio *dioecious*, as in *dioeciopolygamous*.

**diol-**: *di-*, two+*-ol*, oil; **-dione**; *di-*, two+Chem suffix *-one*.

**diphthero-**: c/f of *diphtheria*.

**diphy-**: from Gr *diphuēs*, of double nature or form, (hence) twofold, as in *diphygenic* (cf *-genic* at *-gen*); for the 2nd element, cf PHYSIC.

**dipl(o)-**: Gr *diplo-*, *dipl-*, c/f of *diploos*, twofold (cf L *duplex*). Exx: *diplocardiac*, *diplogenesis*, DIPLOMA, *Diplozoon*.

**dips(o)-**: from Gr *dipsos*, var of *dipsa* (δίψα), thirst. Ex: *dipsomania*, *Dipsosaurus*.

**diptero-**: c/f of *dipterous* (Gr *dipteros*, two-winged), as in *dipterocarp*.

**disci-** and **disc(o)-**: 'disk' or 'disk-like': the former, as in *disciform*, from L *discus*; the latter, as in *discomycete*, from its original, the Gr *diskos*, a quoit, a disk. The end c/f *-discus* occurs in Zoo. Cf DISK.

**disso-**, **ditto-**: from Gr *dissos*, Attic *dittos*, double, doubled, ult akin to *duō*, two. Exx: *dissogeny* (*-geny*, q.v. at *-gen*); *dittology*, a double reading—a term of textual criticism.

**dist(o)-**: c/f of *distal*, remote from the point of attachment. Ex: *distocclusion*.

**disulpho-**, only in Chem. *di-*, two+*sulpho-*. Cf *dithi*(o-)-: *di-*, two+*thio-*.

**ditto-**. See *disso-*.

**diversi-**: from ML *dīversus* (L *dīuersus*), different, diverse. Ex: *diversicolo(u)red*.

**docimo-**: from Gr *dokimē*, a test, intimately akin to *dokeuein* (s *dokeu-*; r, ? *dok-*), to observe closely. Ex: *docimology*, a treatise on, a study of, assaying.

**doco-**: from Gr *dokos* (s *dok-*), a beam; as in the Zoo *Docoglossa* (cf *-glossa*).

**dodec(a)-**: from Gr *dōdeka*, twelve (*duō*, 2+*deka*, 10). Ex: *dodecahedron* (cf *-hedron*).

**dolich(o)-**: Gr *dolikho-*, *dolikh-*, c/f of *dolikhos*, long, long and narrow, akin to Skt *dīrghás*, Hit *daluga-*; IE r *delegh-*, cf *dlonghos*, as in L *longus*. (Hofmann.) Exx: *dolichocephalic*, long-headed, and *dolichofacial*, long-faced.

**dolio-**: from L *dolium*, a large jar. (E & M for a precarious etym.) Ex: *dolioform*, barrel-shaped.

**-dolops**, only in Ent generic names: from Gr *dolops*, one who, that which, lies in ambush, for *dolos*, wile, guile, treachery.

**dolori-**: from L *dolor*, pain, grief, from *dolēre*, to be pained or grieved—cf DOLOROUS. Exx: *dolorific*, pain-causing; *dolorifuge*, pain-banisher.

**domi-**: from L *domus*, a house: cf DOMESTIC. Ex: *domify* (cf *-fy*).

**dora-**; 'hide', hence (as in *doraphobia*) 'fur':

from Gr *dora* (s *dor-*), hide (skin), from *derō* (s *der-*), I flay or skin (an animal).

**dorsi-**; **dorso-**: the back, of or on the back: *dorsi-* is the true L c/f of *dorsum*, app a contraction of the adv *dēorsum*, itself for *dēuorsum*, neu of *dēuorsus*, pp of *dēuortere*, ancient form of *dēuertere* (*dē*, down from+*uertere*, to turn); *dorso-* is analogous with the very numerous Gr c/ff in *-o-*. Exx: *dorsispinal*, *dorsiventral*; *dorsocaudal*, *dorsoventral*.

**dory-**: from Gr *doru*, a shaft, a spear, akin to Skt *dấru*, timber, and Hit *taru-*, tree, timber; IE r, *dor-*, tree. Ex: *doryphorus*, (image, statue, of) a spear-bearer, Gr *doruphoros*.

**dosi-**; **doso-**, occ **dosio-**: c/f of LL *dosis*, a dose; (*doso-*) c/f of E DOSE. Exx: *dosimetry*, the measurement of doses; *dosology*, occ *dosiology*, the science of doses.

**dothi-**, **dothien-**, **dothio-**: c/ff of Gr *dothiēn*, var *dothiōn*, an abscess or a boil, s *dothi-*. Ex: *dothienenteritis*.

**-dox**, **-doxy**; **doxo-**: *-dox*, 'of (a specified) opinion'; *-doxy*, 'opinion'—'a body of opinion'; *doxo-*, 'opinion': the rest from the 1st, from Gr *-doxos*, holding an opinion: from Gr *doxa*, opinion; *doxa*=*dok-s-a*, cf *dokein* (s *dok-*), to think, esp to suppose. Exx: *orthodox*, *paradox*; *orthodoxy*; *doxographer* and, embodying the praise' sense of *doxa*, *doxology*.

**draco-**; **dracont(o)-**: the former, L *dracō*, from Gr *drakōn*, gen *drakontos*, whence *dracont*(o)-: see DRAGON. Exx: Bot *Dracocephalum* (Gr *kephalē*, head); *dracontiasis* (cf *-iasis*).

**dramatico-**: for 'dramatic and', as in *dramaticomusical*.

**drapeto-**, adopted from the Gr c/f of *drapetēs*, a runaway, akin to *dramein*, to run (cf *-drome*). Ex: *drapetomania*.

**drepani-**: from Gr *drepanon*, a sickle, from *drepein* (s *drep-*), to gather. Ex: *drepaniform*, sickle-shaped.

**-drome**, adj **-dromous**; **drom(o)-**: resp Gr *dromos*, a running, a course; Gr *-dromos* (adj), running; Gr *drom*(o)-, c/f of *dromos*, a course, e.g. a race-course: from *dramein* (s *dram-*), to run: *dram-*, var *drom-*, is an extension of the basic IE r *dra-*. Exx: *hippodrome*, (lit) a horse-race course, and *aerodrome* (cf *aero-*); *prodomous*, running forward; *dromomania*. Cf *dromedary*, orig a particularly speedy camel: LL *dromedārius* (*camēlus*), from L *dromas*, a dromedary, from Gr *dromas* (adj), running, genitive *dromados*, from *dramein*, to run; cf Skt *dramati*, he runs.

**droso-**: from Gr *drosos* (s *dros-*), dew. Exx: *drosograph*, a self-registering *drosometer*, a dew-measuring instrument.

**drupi-**: for E *drupe* (L *drup(p)a*, Gr *druppa*, an over-ripe olive); as in *drupiferous* (cf *-ferous* at *-fer*).

**-drymium**: SciL, from Gr *drumos*, a coppice: denoting a (specified) type of coppice. Cf:

**dry(o)-**: Gr *druo-*, *dru-*, c/f of *drus* (gen *druos*), the oak (lit, 'the tree': cf TREE). Only in Bot; e.g., *Dryophyllum, Dryopteris*.

**-duct**: for *duct*; as in *aqueduct*.

**dulci-**: from L *dulcis*, sweet, perh akin to Gr *glukos* (cf *glyco-* at *glu-*). Exx: *dulcifluous* (cf *-fluence*); *dulcigenic* (*-genic* at *-gen*).

**duo-**: L *duo* or, incorrectly, for E *dyo-*, the Gr *duō*, two. Exx: *duoliteral, duologue*.

**duodecim-**: L *duodecim* (*duo+decem*), twelve. Ex: *duodecimfid* (cf *-fid*).

**duoden(o)-**: from *duodenum* (adopted from ML *duodēnum*, so named from its length of 12 fingers' breadth; from L *duodēni*, twelve apiece): denoting 'relation to, or connexion with, the *duodenum*'. Ex: *duodenotomy* (cf *-tomy* at *-tome*) and the adj *duodenal*.

**duplo-**: a Chem suffix, which means 'doubling': L *duplus*, double.

**duro-**: from L *dūrus*, hard; as in *durometer* (cf *-meter*).

**dy-**: Gr *du-*, from *duō*, two; as in *dyphone* (cf *dyophone* at *dyo-*); also short for *dyo-*, as in *dyaster* (cf *-aster*). Cf TWO.

**-dymus**: 'a (specified) kind of mingled monstrosity', the corresponding 'condition' nn taking the form *-dymia*: SciL end-elements, from the Gr end-element *-dumos*, a fold, ? akin to *enduma* (base, *-duma*), a garment.

**dyn(a)-**: a very E c/f from Gr *duna-*, the base of *dunamis*, power—see next entry. Exx: *dynagraph, dynameter, dynamotor*.

**dynami-, dynamo-; -dynamia, -dynamous**: the first is rare, the true c/f being *dynamo-*, from Gr *dunamis*, power; *-dynamia* is SciL for *dunamis*, s *dunam-*, base prob *dun-*; *-dynamous*, having power = Gr *-dunamos*. Exx: *dynamogenesis, dynanometer*. Cf:

**-dyne**: c/f of *dyne*, a unit of force, adopted from F, which adapted it from *dun-*, the base of Gr *dunamis*, power: cf DYNAMIC. Ex: *heterodyne*.

**dy(o)-**: from Gr *duō*, two; as in *dyophone* (cf *-phone*).

**[dys-**. See Prefixes.**]**

**dysmorpho-**: from Gr *dusmorphos*, misshapen; as in *dysmorphophobia*, a dread of being misshapen.

**-dytes**, occ **-dyta**: from Gr *dutēs*, a diver, from *duō*, I dive. A Zoo, esp an Orn, generic name, as in *Pelodytes*.

**eccentro-**: from Gr *ekkentros*, off from centre: mechanically *eccentric*: for etym, see CENTRE. Ex: *eccentrometer* (cf *-meter*).

**ecclesiastico-; ecclesi(o)-**: c/f of ECCLESIASTIC, via L *ecclēsiasticus*; c/f of L *ecclēsia* (Gr *ekklēsia*), the church, as in *ecclesiarch* (cf *-arch*) and *ecclesiology*.

**eccrino-**: from Gr *ekkrinein* (prefix *ek-*, out+ *krinein*, to separate: cf CRITIC), as in *eccrinology*, the physiology of secretions (and excretions).

**echin(o)-**: Gr *ekhin(o)-*, c/f of *ekhinos*, hedgehog (cf *echinus*, sea urchin), s *ekhin-*, base *ekh-*, IE r *gher-* or *kher-*. Exx: *echinocactus*, a very

spiny cactus; *echinochrome* (cf *-chrome* at *-chroia*); *echinology*. Dim: *echinuli-*, as in *echinuliform*.

**echo-**: for E *echo*; as in *echolalia* (cf *-lalia*).

**-eclexis**: 'sexual selection' (Bio): Gr *eklexis*, selection, lit 'a choosing out'. Ex: *ampheclexis*.

**eco-, oeco-, oiko-**: the E, the L, the Gr form of Gr *oiko-*, c/f of *oikos*, house, (hence) household management: denoting 'habitat or environment; domestic relations': for ult etym, see ECONOMY. Exx: *ecology*, economic, *ecophobia* (a dread of home). Cf *-oeca*.

**-ectasia, -ectasis**: c/ff of Med *ectasia, ectasis*, dilatation: Gr *ektasis*: *ek*, out, cf Prefix *ec-*, and *-tasis*, a stretching, from *teinein* to stretch; cf TEND. Ex: *neurectasis*.

**-ectome, -ectomy**. See *-tome*, last para.

**[ect(o)-**. See Prefixes.**]**

**ectro-**: 'congenital lack or absence': from Gr *ektrōsis*, miscarriage, *ek*, out+*trōsis*, a wound, an injury or damage, from *trōein* (s *trō-*), to wound, injure, damage. Exx: *ectrogeny* (cf *-geny* at *-gen*) and *ectromelus*, a limbless monster (cf *-melus* at *-melia*).

**ede(o)-**: from Gr *aidoia*, genitals, lit 'the modest parts': neupl of *aidoios*, bashful, from *aidomai* (s *aid-*), I am ashamed. Exx: *edeology, edeotomy*.

**edri(o)-**: c/f of Gr *hedrion*, a little seat, dim of Gr *hedra*, a seat: cf *-hedral*. Ex: *Edriophthalma*.

**effluvio-**: from ML *effluvium* (L *effluuium*), a flowing out. Ex: *effluviography* (cf *-graphy* at *-graph*).

**effusio-**: for *effusion*, as in Phys *effusiometer*.

**egil(o)-**: from Gr *aigilos*, a herb that goats enjoy, from *aig-*, o/s of *aix* (gen *aigos*), a goat. Ex: *egilops* (Gr *aigilōps*: *ōps*, eye), an ulcer in the corner of the eye. Cf:

**ego-** (1): from Gr *aigo-*, c/f of *aix* (gen *aigos*), a goat: cf prec. Ex: Med *egophony* (cf *-phony* at *-phone*), 'bleating voice'.

**ego-** (2), as in *egocentric, egomania*: see EGO.

**Egypto-**: Gr *Aigupto-*, c/f of *Aiguptos*, Egypt. Ex: *Egypto-Greek*.

**eid(o)-**: 'image' or 'figure': Gr *eido-*, c/f of *eidos* (s *eid-*), form (cf suffix *-oid*). Exx: *eidograph*, *eidoptometry* (*eid-+opto-+-metry*), *kaleidoscope* (*kal-* for *cal*(o)-+*eido-+-scope*). Cf *eidolo-*, from Gr *eidolon*, image, dim of *eidos*; as in *eidolology*, the science of mental imagery; cf IDOL.

**eikono-**: from Gr *eikon-*, c/f of *eikōn*, image, s *eik-*, perh for IE *weik-*. Exx: *eikonology*. See the more general *icon(o)-*.

**eka-**, only in Chem, as *ekaboron, eka-iodine*: Skt *eka*, one.

**elaeo-; elaio-**: *elaeo-*, L form of Gr *elaio-*, c/f of *elaion*, oil, esp olive oil, r *el-*: cf the *ol-* of L *oleum*. Exx: *elaeoblast, elaioplast, elaiosome*. Cf *eleo-*.

**elaph(o)-**: from Gr *elaphos* (s *elaph-*), a stag. Exx: *Elaphoglossum* (cf *-glossa*) and *elaphure* (cf *-ure*, tail).

**elasm(o)-**: from Gr *elasmos*, a metal plate: cf ELASTIC. Exx: *elasmobranch* (cf *-branch*), *elasmosaur*.

elasto-, as in *elastometer*: for *elasticity*.

elatro-: from Gr *elatēr*, one who, that which, drives, from *elaunein*, to drive: cf ELASTIC. Ex: *elatrometer*, an instrument for measuring gas-pressures.

electro-: Gr *ēlektro-*, c/f of *ēlektron*, amber: cf ELECTRIC. Exx: *electroballistics, electrochemical, electrograph, electromotive*.

eleo-: a mod var of *elaeo-*, q.v. above. Ex: *eleoblast*.

eleuther(o)-: Gr *eleuthro-*, c/f of *eleutheros*, free, perh an extension of *\*leutheros* (cf L *līber*, free), IE *\*leudheros*, base *leud-*. Exx: *eleutheropetalous, eleutheromania*.

ellipso-: for *ellipse*, as in *ellipsograph*.

elo-: from Gr *helos*, a marsh; perh for *\*selos*—cf Skt *sáras-*, a pool. Ex: Pal *Elotherium* (cf *-therium* at *-there*).

elytr(o)-: from Gr *elutro-, elutr-*, c/f of *elutron*, a sheath, from *eluein* (s *elu-*), to roll or wind round, perh orig *weluein*, akin to L *uoluere* (ML *volvere*). Exx: *elytriform, elytrotomy*. The var *elytri-* comes from SciL *elytrum*, as in *elytriferous* (cf *-ferous* at *-fer*).

-ematoma: from *hematoma*, a swelling that contains blood (cf *haemo-*). Only in Med.

embio-: from the Gr adj *embios*, in life (cf *-bia*). Ex: *Embiotocidae* (*tokos*, offspring; suffix *-idae*).

emblemato-, as in *emblematology*: from Gr *emblēma*, gen *emblēmatos*: cf EMBLEM and:

embol(o)-: Gr *embolo-, embol-*, c/f of *embolos*, a wedge, from *emballein*, to throw or cast in: cf EMBLEM. Exx: *embolomerous* (cf *-merous* at *-mer*). The subsidiary *emboli-*, as in *emboliform*, comes from *embolus* (L, from Gr *embolos*), foreign matter in the blood.

embry(o)-: Gr *embruo-, embru-*, c/f of *embruon*, fetus, lit '(something) swelling within': *en*, in+ neu of presp *bruōn*, from *bruein*, to swell. Exx: *embryogenesis, embryology, embryoscope*.

emet(o)-: from Gr *emetos*, a vomiting, cf EMETIC, ult akin to VOMIT itself. Ex: *emetology*.

-emia. See *haem-*.

empid(o)-: from Gr *empis* (gen *empidos*), a mosquito. Ex: Zoo *Empidonax* (*anax*, a king), a genus of flycatchers.

empyo-: from Gr *empuos*, suppurating (cf PUS). Only in Med.

empyro-, as in *empyromancy*, divination (*-mancy*) by fire: from Gr *empuros*, in fire: cf *pyro-*.

enali(o)-: from Gr *enalios*, of the sea (*en*, in+ *hals*, the sea, cf *halo-*). Ex: *Enaliornis* (*ornis*, a bird) and *enaliosaur* (cf *-saur*).

enantio-: adopted from Gr, the c/f of *enantios*, opposite (*en+anti+*adj suffix *-os*). Exx: *enantiomorph, enantiopathy, enantiotropy*.

-enary. See *-ennial*.

encephal(o)-: -encephalia (condition of brain); -encephalus (type of brain disease): from Gr *enkephalos*, the brain, and from two SciL derivatives of SciL *encephalon* (for Gr *enkephalos*): *enkephalos* combines *en*, in+*kephalē*, the head (cf *cephalo-*).

Exx: *encephalograph*, an X-ray photograph of the brain; *encephalotomy; sclerencephalia* (cf *sclero-*).

encho-: from Gr *enkhos* (s *enkh-*), a spear (ἔγχος); as in *Enchodus* (cf *-odus* at *-odon*).

-enchyma, -enchysis: from the *-enchyma* of *parenchyma*, a Bot tissue; Gr *enkhusis*, a pouring-in, as in *dermenchysis* (cf *-derm*); *enkhusis=en*, in+ *khusis*, a pouring, from *khéein* (s *khe-*), to pour.

engy-: from Gr *engus* (ἔγγυς), near; as in *engyscope*, a reflecting microscope.

enigmato-: from Gr *ainigmat-*, o/s of *ainigma*, an enigma. Ex: *enigmatography*. Cf ENIGMA.

enne(a)-: Gr *ennea*, nine—cf NINE. Exx: *enneagon, enneastyle* (cf *-style*).

-ennial, adj of -ennium, L c/f of *annus*, a year, as in Mod L *millennium*, a thousand years; *-enary*, as in *centenary*, answers to L *-enārium* (*centenārium*, a hundred years). Exx: *biennial, triennial*.

enstato-: for Min *enstatite* (from Gr *enstatēs*, an adversary). Ex: *enstatolite* (cf *-lite*).

enter(o)-: Gr *entero-, enter-*, c/f of *enteron*, an intestine, lit 'an inner part'. Exx: *enterocyst, enterotomy*. Cf the prefix *ento-* and the derivative *enteritis*.

entom(o)-: from Gr *entomon*, insect, strictly the neu of the adj *entomos*, cut in two—*en*, in+the n root of *temnein*, to cut: 'so called because nearly cut in two' (Webster). Exx: *entomology*, the science (cf *-logy* at *-loger*) of insects; *entomophagous*, insectivorous or insect-eating (cf *-phaga*); *entomotomy*, the dissection (*-tomy*, q.v. at *-tome*) of insects.

entozoo-: for Zoo *entozoa* (SciL: prefix *ento-*+ *-zoa*); as in *entozoology*.

eo-: 'connected, or connexion, with a very early period of time': Gr *ēō-*, c/f of *ēōs*, dawn, hence the dawn of time; cf IE *\*āusōs*. Exx: *Eocene* (*-cene*), *eolith* (*-lith*), *eosaurus* (*-saur*). Cf:

eosino-: c/f of *eosin* (from *ēōs*, dawn—rosy dawn): as in *eosinophile*. Cf prec.

epeiro-: from Gr *ēpeiros*, the mainland (cf the *Epirus* of Greece), prob akin to OE *ōfer*, bank, shore. Ex: Geol *epeirogeny* (cf *-geny* at *-gen*).

ephemero-, as in Zoo *ephemeromorph* (cf *-morph*): from Gr *ephēmeros*—cf EPHEMERAL.

epidemio-: either from EF-F *épidémie* or from the obsol E *epidemy* (itself from F), an epidemic: cf EPIDEMIC. Ex: *epidemiology*, the medical treatment of epidemics.

epidermo: c/f of *epidermis* (prefix *epi-*+*-dermis*, q.v. at *-derm*). Ex: *epidermolysis* (cf *-lysis*).

epididymo-: c/f of *epididymis* (Gr *epididumis*). Med only.

epiplo-: from Gr *epiploon* (in An: the great omentum). Ex: *epiplopexy* (cf *-pexy*).

episcopi-; episcopo-: from L *episcopus* and (*episcopo-*) Gr *episkopos*, an overseer (later, a bishop): cf BISHOP. Exx: *episcopicide*, the slaying of a bishop; *episcopolatry*, bishop-worship.

episio-: from Gr *episeion*, region of the pubes. Med only.

epistemo-: from Gr *epistēmē*, knowledge (*epi-*, upon+*histēmi*, I place), 'a placing of oneself in

the position required for'—hence 'comprehension':
cf, sem, *understanding*. Ex: *epistemology*, the philosophy (cf *-logy* at *-loger*) of knowledge.

**epistolo-**: from Gr *epistolē*, a letter—cf EPISTLE.
Ex: *epistolography*, letter-writing.

**epitheli(o)-**: c/f of *epithelium*, a SciL term: Gr
*epi*, upon+*thēlē*, nipple. Ex: *Epitheliolytic* (cf
*-lysis*).

**epizootio-**: for *epizootic*, common to many
quadrupeds at one time (cf *epidemic* for mankind).
Ex: *epizootiology*.

**-ēpy**, as in *cacoëpy*, (a) bad pronunciation, and
*orthoëpy*, (a) good pronunciation: from Gr *epos*
(s *ep-*), a word, akin to Skt *vácas-*, speech, a word.

**equi-**: L *aequi-*, c/f of *aequus*, equal—cf EQUAL.
Exx: *equiangular, equidistant, equilateral, equilibrium, equiliteral, equinox, equipoise, equivalent*.

**er-**: from Gr *ēr*, the spring; as in *Eranthis* (cf
*-anthis* at *-anth*, flower).

**erem(o)-**: Gr *erēmo-, erēm-*, c/f of *erēmos*,
lonely—cf HERMIT. Ex: *eremology*, the science of
deserts.

**-ergate, ergat(o)-; erg(o)-; -ergy**: resp Gr *ergatēs*
(s *erg-*), a worker; from *ergatēs; ergon* (s *erg-*),
work; Gr *-ergia*, end-c/f of *ergon*, prob for
*wergon*—hence akin to WORK. Exx: *ergatocracy*,
government by the manual workers; *ergolatry*, an
idolatrous devotion to work; *ergophobia*, dread of
work; *synergy* (cf prefix *syn-*, with, together).

**erico-**: from L *erica* or *ericē*, a heath, from Gr
*ereikē* or *erikē*; as in *ericophyte* (*-phyte*).

**erio-**: Gr *erio-*, c/f of *erion*, wool, akin to L
*ariēs*, a ram. Exx: *eriometer, eriophyllous*.

**ero-, eroto-**: resp from Gr *erōs*, physical love,
and Gr *erōto-*, its c/f, based upon the o/s *erōt-*:
from *eramai*, I love, s *er-*: cf EROTIC. Exx: *ero-
genous; erotomania* (Gr *erōtomania*), *erotopathy*.

**-erpeton**: from Gr *herpeton*, a creeping thing: cf
*herpeto-*.

**eruci-**: from L *ērūca*, a caterpillar; as in *eruci-
vorous* (cf *-vorous* at *-vora*).

**erysipelo-**: for *erisypelas*, from Gr *erusipelas*,
akin to Gr *eruthros*, red, and *pella*, L *pellis*, skin,
hide. Ex: *Erysipelothrix* (cf *-thrix*, hair).

**erythro-** (1): Gr *eruthro-, eruthr-*, c/f of *eruthros*,
red, akin to L *ruber* and E RED. Ex: *erythrocyte*
(*-cyte*), a red blood-corpuscle; *erythrogenic;
erythrophobia*, a fear of the colour red.

**erythro-** (2): short for *erythrocyto-*, the c/f of
*erythrocyte* (see prec), as in *erythroblast*.

**eschato-**: from Gr *eschatos*, the further, the
ultimate, akin to *ex*, out of. Ex: *eschatology*, the
doctrine or philosophy of ultimates (e.g., death):
cf *-logy* at *-loger*.

**esophag(o)-**: from *esophagus*, the mod spelling of
SciL *oesophagus*, Gr *oisophagos* (cf *-phaga*). Ex:
*esophagotomy*.

**esteri-**: c/f of the Chem cpd *ester*. Ex: *ester-
iferous*.

**-estes**: Gr *-estēs*, -eater, from *esthiein*, to eat:
only in Orn terms.

**-esthes**: from Gr *esthēs*, clothing, dress: mostly
in Ent.

**esthesio-**, mod form of *aesthesio-*: from Gr
*aisthēsis*, sensation, active sense-perception: cf
ESTHETIC. Exx: *esthesiogen, esthesiology*.

**estheto-**: from Gr *aisthētos*, perceived, or perceptible, by the senses. Ex: *esthetology*. See prec.

**estivo-**: from ML *aestīvus* (L *aestīuus*), of the
summer ('estival': L *aestīuālis*), from *aestas*, summer. Ex: *estivo-autumnal*.

**estra-, estri-, estro-**: from L *oestrus*, from Gr
*oistros* (s *oistr-*, r *oist-*), a gadfly, hence a sting,
hence fury, frenzy. Exx: *estradiol; estriol* (cf 2nd
*-ol*); *estrogen* (cf *-gen*).

**eteo-**. See *etymo-*.

**etheri-, ethero-**: c/ff of ETHER, as in *etheriform*.

**ethico-**: 'of ethics and': Gr *ēthiko-*, c/f of
*ēthikos*: cf ETHICAL. Ex: *ethicopolitical*.

**ethmo-**: Gr *ēthmo-*, c/f of *ēthmos*, a sieve, r
*ēth-*, from *ēthein* (s *ēth-*), to filter, with many IE
cognates. Exx, with meaning 'ethmoid' (Gr
*ēthmoeidēs*, sieve-like), referring to the nasal
capsule: *ethmofrontal, ethmonasal*, (with lit sense
'sieve') *ethmolith*.

**ethn(o)-**: from Gr *ethnos*, race, nation, prob akin
to *ethos, ēthos*, custom, with s *ethn-* an extension
of *eth-*, the s of *ethos* Exx: *ethno-botany, ethno-
centric, ethnogeny, eth·nography, ethnology, ethno-
zoology*.

**etio-**, the E form of L *aetio-*, transliteration of
Gr *aitio-*, c/f of *aitia*, cause, s *ait-*. Exx: *aetiogenic*,
now usu *etiogenic; aitiotropic*, now usu *etiotropic;
etiology*, via LL from Gr *aitiologia*, the science (cf
*-logy* at *-loger*) of causes.

**Etrusco-**: from L *Etruscus*, Etruscan, the adj of
*Etruria*; as in *Etruscology*.

**etymo-**: Gr *etumo-*, c/f of *etumos*, true, akin to
*eteos*, true, both akin to *etazein*, to establish with
proof: cf ETYMOLOGY. Ex: *etymography* (cf
*-graphy* at *-graph*), historically precise spelling. Cf
the rare *eteo-* (as in *Eteocretan*, of the original
Cretans): from *eteos*.

**eucho-**: from Gr *eukhē*, a vow, a prayer, s *eukh-*
(*eukhomai*, I pray). Ex: *euchologion*, anglicized as
*euchology*, from LGr *eukhologion*, a prayer book
—cf *-logy* at *-loger*.

**eudio-**: from Gr *eudia*, fine, clear weather, from
*eudios*, (of air or weather) fine and clear: *eu*, well
(adv)+the r of DIANA. Ex: *eudiometer*, an instrument formerly used for determining the purity of
the air, now for gases.

**Eur(o)-**, short for **Europe(o)-**, the mod form of
*Europae(o)-*, c/f of *European*, via L *Europaeus;
Europo-*, however,=Europe. Exx: *Eurasia, Eura-
sian; Europeo-American; Europocentric*.

**eury-**: Gr *euru-*, c/f of *eurus*, broad, wide, s
*eur-*, akin to Skt *uru* (*urús*), s *ur-*. Exx: *eury-
cephalic*, broad-headed; *eurygnathic*, wide-jawed;
*eurypygous* (or *-pygal*), broad-rumped. Cf:

**-eurysis**: Surg c/f, 'a dilatory operation on
a specified part', from *eurunein*, to widen, to
stretch. Ex: *colpeurysis* (cf *colpo-*). Cf prec.

**euthy-**: Gr *euthu-*, c/f of *euthus* (s *euth-*),
straight, as in *euthycomic* (or *-comous*), straight-
haired. Perh *euthus=eu*, well+a lost pp *thus*,

placed, from *tithēmi*, I place—cf the future *thēsō*, s *thēs-*.

**-eval**, mod form of **-aeval**, as in *medieval*, formerly *mediaeval*: ML *aevālis*, L *aeuālis*, adj of *aeuum*, ML *aevum*, age, life. Cf AGE.

**excito-**, as in *excitoglandular, excitomuscular*, denotes 'stimulating' and derives from *excit-*, the s of L *excitāre*, to excite.

**exoto-**: from Gr *exōtikos*, from without, foreign (cf EXOTIC), or from E *exotic*. Ex: *exotospore*.

**extenso-**, as in *extensometer*, an instrument for measuring extension, derives from L *extensus*, extended. Cf EXTEND.

**externo-**, as in *externomedian*, derives from L *externus*, external.

**extero-**: from L *exter*, external, exterior, from *ex*, outside of, out from. Ex: *exteroceptive* (cf *receptive*).

**fabi-**, as in *fabiform*, bean-shaped: from L *faba* (cf F *fève*), a bean—cf OP *babo*.

**-facient**: 'making or causing': L *facient-*, o/s of presp *faciens*, from *facere*, to make: see *-fic*. Ex: *somnifacient*, sleep-causing, cf *somni-*. Cf the *fac-* of *facsimile* ('Do the like!') and *factotum* ('Do everything!').

**facio-**: 'facial (and)': from L *faciēs* (s *faci-*), face: cf FACE. Ex: *faciolingual*.

**-fact**, as in *artifact*,=L *factus*, made, pp of *facere*, to make. (Cf *-facient, -faction, -fact, -fic*.)

**-faction; -factive; -factory**: from L *-factiō* (gen *-factiōnis*), from *factiō*, a making, from *facere*, to make; *-factive*, cf F *factive*, the f of *factif*, -making; *-factory* (adj), from LL and ML *-factōrius*, -making. See SATISFACTION and *-facient, -fact, -fect*.

**fagi-, fago-**: from L *fāgus*, beech (tree): cf Gr *phagos*.

**falci-**: from *falc-*, the o/s of L *falx* (gen *falcis*), a sickle, perh from Ligurian. Ex: *falciform*.

**fall(o)-**: a short-cutting c/f for *Fallopian tube* (the oviduct in all mammals). Exx: *fallectomy, fallotomy*.

**falsi-**. L *falsi-*, c/f of *falsus*; cf FALSE. Exx: *falsidical*, false-speaking, L *falsidicus* (*dicere*, to say); *falsify*, q.v. at FALSE.

**farado-**: c/f of *faradic* (ex physicist *Faraday*), as in *farado(-)muscular*.

**-farious**: L *-fārius* (adj), -fold, an 'adjective back-formed from *bifāriam* [in two parts; on both sides] and serving to form a whole series of multiplicative adjectives or adverbs: *bi-, tri-, quadri-, multi-fārius*, and [adverbs in] *-āriam*. The Latin word *bifāriam* recalls the Sanskrit type: *dvi-dhā*, "double" ' (E & M). Exx: *bifarious, trifarious, multifarious, omnifarious*.

**fascio-**: an An c/f of *fascia* (condensed connective tissue), as in *fasciotomy*.

**fati-**: L *fāti-*, c/f of *fātum*, fate: see FATE. Exx: *fatidic(al)*, prophetic, lit 'fate-telling', from L *fātidīcus*; *fatiferous*; *fatiloquent*.

**faun(o)-**: for *fauna*, as in *faunology*.

**favi-**: from ML *favus*, L *fauus* (s *fau-*), honeycomb, perh, as E & M suggest, akin to *fauēre* (ML *favēre*), to favour, s *fau-*. Ex: *faviform*.

**febri-**: L *febri-*, c/f of *febris*, fever (cf FEVER). Exx: *febricide*, a fever-'killer'; *febrific*, fever-producing; *febrifuge*, an antidote (cf *-fuge*) to fever.

**feca-**: for *fecal* (*faecal*), as in *fecalith*.

**-fect**, as in *confect, infect, refect*, derives from *-fectus*, pp of vv in *-ficere*, cpds of *facere*, to make: nn in *-fection*, adjj in *-fective*. Cf *-facient, -fact, -faction*; and:

**-feit**: a gallicized form of the prec, as in *counterfeit*.

**feli-**: from L *fēlis* (s *fēl-*), a cat; the L adj *fēlinus*, E *feline*, yields the c/f *felino-*, as in *felinophobia*, a dread of cats.

**felici-**, as in *felicify*, to render happy: from L *fēlix* (gen *fēlīcis*), happy. Cf FELICITY.

**felino-**. See *feli-*.

**felso-**: from G *Fels*, a rock. Ex: *felsophyre* (*-phyre*).

**femino-**: from L *fēmina*, woman: cf FEMALE. Exx: *feminology, feminophobe* (woman-hater).

**femoro-**: from *femor-*, o/s of L *femur* (o.o.o.), thigh: 'femoral (and)'. Ex: *femorocaudal*. Adj: *femoral*, from LL *femorālis*.

**-fer, -ference, -ferent, -ferous**: L *-fer*, mainly agential; L *-ferentia*, itself from L *ferent-* (whence E *-ferent*), o/s of *ferens*, presp of *ferre*, to bear, carry; *-ferous*=L *-fer*+E *-ous* (Suffixes): hence, 'producer (of)'—'production (of)'—'producing' (adj)—'productive (of)'. Exx: *conifer*, cone-bearer, whence *coniferous*; *-ferent*, mostly in derivatives from cpd vv, as in *deferent, different, efferent*; *cruciferous*, cross-bearing. Cf the cognate E *bear*, to carry.

**fermento-**: for *ferment(ation)*, as in *fermentology*.

**-ferous**. See *-fer*.

**ferri-, ferro-**: L *ferri-*, Mod E *ferro-*, c/ff of L *ferrum*, iron, s *fer(r)-*, o.o.o.; adjj, *ferrous* (general) and *ferric* (Chem). Exx: *ferricyanide, ferriferous; ferro-alloy, ferro(-)cyanide, ferromagnetic*. The E *ferrous* suggested SciL *ferrosus*, whence the o/f *ferroso-*.

**ferroso-**. See prec.

**festi-, festo-**: from L *festa*, a festival: cf FEAST. Exx: *festilogy* or *festology*, a treatise on festivals.

**feti-**, now rarely **foeti-**; **feto-**, now rarely **foeto-**: c/ff of L *fētus*, inferior form *foetus*, a birth, the embryo, the young, hence, in E, denoting 'the young in the womb': the L n *fētus* is akin to L *fētus*, filled with young, fructified. Exx: *fetiferous*, bearing young; *fetography*.

**-fex**, as in *artifex, pontifex, spinifex*,='maker' (of objects requiring art or skill—of bridges—of spines or thorns): a n, adopted from L and answering to the E adj *-fic* (or *-ficial*).

**fibrilli-; fibrino-; fibri-, fibr(o)-**: c/f of *fibril*, from SciL *fibrilla*, dim of *fibra*, whence the c/ff *fibri-* (L form) and *fibro-* (Gr form) and whence also the biochemical term *fibrin*, whence the c/f *fibrino-*; *fibroso-* comes from SciL *fibrosus*, fibrous.

Cf FIBER (FIBRE). Exx: *fibrilliform, fibriform, fibrocartilage; fibrinocellular.*

1, -fic; 2, -fical and 3, -ficial; 4 -ficate, 5 -fication, 6 -ficative, 7 -ficator, 8 -ficatory; 9, -fice; 10, -ficence; 11, -ficent and 12, -ficient; 13, -ficiary. Basically *-fic-* is the c/f of *fac-,* the s of *facere,* to make; it occurs only in cpd vv and in their derivatives or cognates: cf *-facient, -fact, -fect,* and therefore FACT.

1, -fic: (occ via F *-fique*) from L *-ficus,* 'making' (adj), as in *beneficus, somnificus,* E *benefic, somnific;* always after either connective or thematic *-i-,* cf *malefic, morbific.*

2, -fical, as in *pontifical:* L *-ficālis,* as in * pontificālis: -fic,* adj *-alis.*

3, -ficial, as in *pontificial,* var of *pontifical,* and *beneficial,* from L *beneficiālis, -ficiālis* being a var of *-fical.* Cf (9), *-fice.*

4, -ficate, as in *certificate* (ML *certificātus,* pp of *certificāre,* to make certain), represents L *-ficātus,* pp of LL and ML cpd vv in *-ficāre.* The var *-ficiate* indicates direct derivation from nn in *-ficium;* as in *maleficiate,* from ML *maleficiātus,* bewitched.

5, -fication, as in *certification:* (occ via F *-fication*) from *-ficātiōn-* (acc *-ficātiōnem*), o/s of *-ficātiō,* from vv in *-ficāre,* LL and ML var of *-ficere.*

6, -ficative, 'tending to make'—as in *certificative,* represents *-ficate* (as in (4) above)+suffix *-ive.*

7, -ficator, 'maker': as in *certificator:* LL and ML *-ficātor.* Cf:

8, -ficatory, 'serving to make': as in *certificatory* (ML *certificātōrius*): LL, ML *-ficātōrius.*

9, -fice, as in *benefice* (L *beneficium*) and obs *malefice* (L *maleficium*), derives, usu via OF *-fice,* from L *-ficium,* more objective than *-ficātiō* (see (5) above). Cf the next four paragraphs.

10, -ficence, as in *beneficence, maleficence,* derives, occ via OF *-ficence,* from L *-ficentia,* as *beneficentia, maleficentia.* Cf:

11, -ficent, as in *beneficent* and *maleficent,* derives from L *-ficent,* o/s of *-ficens,* presp of cpd vv in *-ficere.* Cf prec and:

12, -ficient, as in *deficient,* represents *-ficient-,* o/s of *-ficiens,* presp of several vv in *-ficere,* as in *dēficere,* to be lacking. The corresponding abstract n ends in E *-ficience,* now usu *-ficiency,* and derives from L *-ficientia,* as LL *dēficientia.* Cf (9)–(11) above.

13, -ficiary (the n comes straight from the adj): L *-ficiārius,* as in *beneficiārius,* whence the adj *beneficiary.*

Cf *-fier* and *-fy.*

fici-: from L *fīcus,* a fig: cf FIG. Ex: *ficiform,* (shaped) like a fig.

-ficial, -ficiary, -ficient. See *-fic.*

-fid: 'divided into (e.g. seven) parts'; in Bot, 'lobed' or 'cleft': L *-fidus,* a c/f deriving from the s of *findere,* to split, of which only the present tenses are nasalized; Skt and the Gmc languages possess cognates. Exx: *bifid* (L *bifidus*), *trifid* (L *trifidus*), *septemfid,* etc; *pinnatifid* (*pinnati-*).

fide-, fidei-: resp the abl and the dat of L *fidēs,* faith. Exx: *fideicommissary; fidejussion* (*iubēre,* to order).

-fier, the agent corresponding to vv in *-fy,* F *-fier,* L *-ficare,* itself from adj *-ficus,* itself from *-ficere,* the cpd-v form of *facere,* to make: see *-fic* above and FACT in the Dict. Exx: *justifier; justify,* OF *justifier,* ML *jūstificāre,* LL *iūstificāre,* to make just or right.

-filar; filari-. See the 2nd *fili-.*

fili- (1): 'son' (L *fīlius*) or 'daughter' (L *fīlia*): rare except in *filicide* (cf *-cide*). The more usual c/f of *fīlius* is *filio-,* q.v.

fili- (2): 'thread', from L *fīlum,* a thread, s *fīl-,* perh akin to *hīlum.* Exx: *filiferous, filiform, filigrane* (and *filigree*), *filipendulous.*

The E adj from L *fīlum* is *filar* (cf the adj suffix *-ar*), with c/f *-filar,* as in *interfilar* (prefix *inter-*); and Bot and Med exhibit a derivative *Filaria,* a genus of thread-like worms, with c/f *filari-,* as in *filaricidal* (cf *-cidal*), deadly to Filaria.

filici-: L *filic-,* o/s of *filix,* fern, prob akin to *filum,* thread. Ex *filiciform* (cf *-form*).

filio-: from L *fīlius,* son: cf FILIAL. Exx: *filionymic* (cf *-onym*), *filiopietistic.* Cf *fili-* (1).

fimbri-, fimbrio-: from L *fimbria,* a fringe, whence also *fimbriated,* fringed. Exx: *Fimbristylus,* a genus of sedges; *fimbriodentate.*

fimi-: from L *fimus* (s *fim-*), dung, perhaps a thinned form of L *fumus,* smoke, from the exhalations of fresh dung. Ex: *fimicolous* (cf *-colous*), applied to beetles inhabiting dung.

fini-: from L *fīnis,* end: cf FINAL. Ex: *finific* (n from adj), a limiting element; *finifugal* (cf *-fugal*), tending to avoid decisions, escapist.

Finno-: c/f of *Finn* or *Finnish.* Esp in *Finno-Ugric.*

-fique: the F form of L *-ficus* and therefore parallel to *-fic,* q.v.

fissi-: 'cleft' or 'divided': from L *fissus,* pp of *findere,* to split: cf FISSURE. Exx: *fissi-costate, fissiparous* (cf *-parous*).

fistuli-, as in *fistuliform,* fistular (L *fistulāris*), lit 'of a *fistula*', orig a pipe, perh akin to ON *blistra,* to blow, to pipe.

flabelli-: 'fan-shaped': from L *flabellum,* a fan, dim of *flabrum,* a breath of wind, from *flāre,* to blow (*flō,* I blow), clearly echoic—cf BLOW (v). Exx: *flabellifoliate, flabelliform.*

flagelli-: from L *flagellum,* a whip, dim of *flagrum,* a (large) whip: for the formation, cf *flabellum* from *flabrum.* Ex: *flagelliform.*

flammi-: from L *flamma,* a flame, prob echoic. Exx: *flammiferous* (L *flammifer*), *flammivomous* (ML *flammivomus,* L *-uomus*), flame-vomiting.

[-flate, as in *deflate, inflate, insufflate:* see INFLATE.]

flavi-; flavo-: from ML *flāvus,* L *flāuus* (s *flāu-*), yellow. Exx: *flavicomous,* yellow-haired; *flavopurpurin.*

[-flect, -flection or flexion; -flex, adj and n: as a cpd, only in *genuflect,* L *genuflectere,* to bend the knee (see *genu-*), and its derivatives. The vv go back to L *flectere* (s *flect-*), to bend; the n *-flection*, a mod spelling, and *-flexion* to LL *-flexiō*, gen *-flexiōnis*; the n *-flex* to L *flexus* (gen *flexūs*), the adj *-flex* to L *flexus*, pp of *flectere*. See FLEX.]

**flocci-**, app only in *floccipend*, from L *flocci pendere*, lit 'to weigh as a FLOCK of wool', hence to rate as of small account.

**flori-**; **-floral**, **-florous**: from *flōr-*, o/s of L *flōs* (gen *flōris*), flower—cf FLOWER. Exx: *floriculture*; *florigraphy* (the 'language' of flowers); *floriscope*; *florisugent*, flower-sucking;— *thalamifloral* (cf *thalami-*); *uniflorous*, *multiflorous*.

**-fluence**, **-fluent**, **-fluous**, **-flux**. Exx: *influence*, *refluent*, *mellifluous*, *efflux*, all from L *fluere*, to flow. See FLOW and cf *fluo-*. The c/f *fluidi-*, in *fluidify*, to render liquid, comes from E FLUID.

**fluo-**: from L *fluor*, a flowing, but indicating its derivative *fluorine* (cf Chem suffix *-ine*). Exx: *fluoboric*, *fluophosphate*. Cf prec and:

**fluoro-**: c/f of *fluorine* or *fluorescence*. Exx: *fluorobenzene*, *fluoroscope*. Cf *-fluence* and *fluo-*.

**fluvi-**, **fluvio-**: from ML *fluvius*, L *fluuius*, a river, from *fluere*, to flow: cf FLOW. Exx: *fluvicoline* (cf *-coline* at *-colous*); *fluvioglacial*, *fluviograph*, *fluviology*, *fluviomarine*, *fluvioterrestrial*. Cf FLOW and:

[**-flux**, as in *efflux*, *influx*, *reflux*, from L *fluere*, to flow. See FLOW.]

**foci-**, **foco-**: c/ff of FOCUS (n), q.v. Exx: *focimeter*, *focometer*.

**foli-**, **folio-**; **-foliate**, **-folious**: c/ff of L *folium* (s *fol-*), a leaf, whence the E *folio*; *-foliate*, c/f of E *foliate*; (*-folious*) L *foliōsus*, -leaved, leafy. Exx: *folicolous*, *foliferous*; *foliobranch*. The subsidiary *foliolo-* comes from SciL *foliolum*, dim of *folium*.

**foramini-**: from *foramin-*, o/s of L *forāmen* (r *for-*), from *forāre* (s *for-*), to pierce or bore); the adopted E *foramen*=a small opening or aperture or orifice. Ex: *foraminiferous*, having foramina.

**forci-**, irregular form; **forcipi-**, regular: from *forcip-*, o/s of L *forceps*, forceps, pincers, perh akin to L *formus*, hot. Exx: *forcipressure*, for *forcipipressure*; *forcipiform*, shaped like forceps. Prob cf:

**forfici-**, as in *forficiform*, shaped like scissors: L *forfex* (gen *forficis*), shears.

**-form**, adj: '-shaped': (occ via F *-forme*, from) L *-formis*, c/f of *forma*, form, shape: see FORM. Like *-fer(ous)* and *-fic* (etc), *-form* occurs very often indeed. Exx: *multiform*, *uniform*; *oviform* (cf *ovi-*), egg-shaped.

**-form**, n: c/f of *formyl*, as in *iodoform*. Cf *formo-*.

**formi-**, irregular for **formici-**, regular E c/f from L *formīca* (var *furmīca*), an ant, prob akin to syn Gr *murmēx*. Exx: *formicide*, an ant-killer; *formicivorous*, ant-eating. Cf:

**form(o)-**: a Chem c/f for either *formic* or *formyl*, both, by the way, from L *formīca*, an ant (see prec). Ex: *formaldehyde*.

**forti-**. See FORTIFY.

**fossi-**, as in *fossiform*, like a fossa (An cavity), L *fossa*, a ditch. Cf:

**fossili-**: c/f of FOSSIL. Exx: *fossiliferous*, *fossilify*.

**fovei-**, as in *foveiform*, like a ML *fovea* (L *fouea*) or small pit, prob from *fodere*, to dig (out), to hollow.

**fracto-**: 'ragged cloud-mass': from L *fractus*, broken—cf FRACTION. Ex: *fracto-nimbus*. Occ *fracti-*; in Zoo.

**-frage**, n; **-fragous**, adj: as in *saxifrage*, L *saxifraga*, lit 'rock-breaker', and *saxifragous*, L *saxifragus* (cf *saxi-*).

**Franco-**: ML c/f of *Francus*, a Frank—cf FRANK. It denotes 'French (and)', as in 'the Franco-German War'.

**fratri-**: L *frātri*, c/f of *frāter*, brother, o/s *frātr-*; cf FRATERNAL. Ex: *fratricide*.

**frigo-**, irregular E, and **frigori-**, regular L c/f of *frigor* (n), cold; cf FRIGID. Exx: *frigotherapy*; *frigorific* (L *frigorificus*); *frigorimeter* (cf *-meter*).

**frondi-**: from *frond-*, o/s of L *frons* (gen *frondis*), a leafy branch, foliage: cf FROND. Exx: *frondiform*; *frondiferous* and *frondigerous*; *frondivorous*.

**fronti-**, **fronto-**: from *front-*, o/s of L *frons* (gen *frontis*), forehead: cf FRONT. Exx: *frontispiece* (ML *frontispicium*); *frontonasal*, *frontopontine*.

**fructi-**: L *frūcti-*, c/f of *frūctus*, fruit: see FRUIT. Exx: *fructiculture*, *fructify*, *fructivorous*. Cf:

**frugi-**: from *frūg-*, o/s of L *frūx* (gen *frūgis*), fruit, akin to *frūctus* (see prec); indeed, both *frūctus* and *frūx* derive from L *fruī* (s *fru-*), to have the use of, hence to enjoy. Exx: *frugiferous*, *frugivorous*.

**fuci-**: from L *fucus* (s *fuc-*), rock lichen, seaweed, from Gr *phukos* (s *phuk-*), a loan-word from Sem. Exx: *fuciphagous* and its syn, *fucivorous*. The irreg *fuco-* represents either E *fucus* or E *fucose*.

**-fugal**, adj; **-fuge**, n: the former derives, in E, from the latter; the latter from F *-fuge*, a c/f from L *fugāre* (s *fug-*), to put to flight: cf FUGITIVE. Exx: *centrifugal*; *febrifuge*, from EF-F *fébrifuge*, LL *febrifug(i)a*, and *vermifuge*, adopted from F, adjj *febrifugal*, *vermifugal*.

**fulci-**, as in *fulciform*, like a prop: from L *fulcīre* (s *fulc-*), to prop.

**fumar(o)-**, as in *fumaryl* (Chem suffix *-yl*): for *fumaric* (acid), from L *fūmus*—see next.

**fumi-**: L *fūmi-*, c/f of *fūmus* (s *fūm-*), smoke: cf FUME. Exx: *fumiduct*, *fumiferous*.

**fundi-**, as in *fundiform*, sling- or loop-shaped: from L *funda*, a sling.

**fungi-**, **fungo-**: c/ff of E *fungus*, adopted from L, perh from Gr *sphongos*, a sponge. Exx: *fungiform*, *fungivorous*; *fungology*. The SciL dim *fungillus* has c/f *fungilli-*, as in *fungilliform*.

**fun(i)-**: from L *fūnis* (s *fūn-*), a rope: o.o.o. Exx: *funambulist*, a rope-walker, cf L *ambulāre* (s *ambul-*), to walk, and agential suffix *-ist*; *funipendulous*.

**furci-**; L *furci-*, c/f of *furca*, a fork: cf FORK. Exx: *furciferous* from L *furcifer*; *furciform*.

**furo-**, 'relation to *furan*', itself=L*fur*fur, bran+ Chem suffix *-an* or *-ane*. Ex: *furodiazole*.

**fusco-**: from L *fuscus*, tawny, dark-coloured (s

*fusc-*: cf E *subfusc*, dim), akin to L *furuus* (ML *furvus*), sombre, dark and to OE *dosk*, ModE *dusk*. Exx: *fusco-ferruginous, fusco-hyaline*.

**fusi-**: from L *fūsus* (s *fūs-*), a spindle; as in *fusiform*—cf the adj *fusoid* (suffix *-oid*).

**-fy**: see *-fier*. Exx: *amplify*, F *amplifier*, L *amplificāre*; *rectify*, F *rectifier*, LL *rectificāre*. Also used with non-L words, as in *dandify*, from *dandy*, and in *uglify*, from *ugly*. Cf *-fic*.

**-galactia; galact(o)-**: a Med c/f, *galakt* , o/s of Gr *gala* (s *gal-*), milk+Med *-ia*; Gr *galakto-*, c/f of the same: cf GALAXY. Exx: *cacogalactia*, a bad (*caco-*) milk-secretion; *galactocele* (*-cele*), *galactometer, galactophore* (cf *-phora*), *galacto-poiesis* (formation—cf POET—of milk), *galacto-scope*.

**galei-**, as in *galeiform*, shaped like a helmet: L *galea*, a helmet. Cf *galeo-*.

**galeno-**: from L *galena*, lead ore, lead dross, perh from Gr *galēnē*, a type of lead ore. Ex: *galeno-bismutite*; cf the adj *galenoid*.

**galeo-**: from Gr *galeē* (γαλέη), a weasel, whence perh L *galea*, a helmet: cf Skt *giris, girikā*, a mouse. Exx: *Galeopithecus, Galeorchis, Galeorhinus*.

**galli-** (1); **gallo-**: c/ff of L *galla* (s *gal-*), gall, gall-nut. Exx: *gallicolous* (cf *-colous*), inhabiting galls or excrescences; *gallification*;—*galloflavine, gallotannate*.

**galli-** (2), as in *Galliformes*, fowls, including the domestic fowl: L *gallus*, a cock, perh lit 'the Gaulish (bird)'.

**galli-** (3): c/f of *gallium*, a metallic element, from L *Gallia*, Gaul. Cf:

**Gallo-**: 'Gaulish (and)' or, predominantly, 'French (and)': from L *Gallus*, a Gaul. Exx: *Gallo-Roman*; *Gallo-Britain, Gallomania*.

**gallo-**: c/f of *gallic* (acid): see *galli-* (1).

**galvano-**: 'galvanic' or 'galvanism', from *Galvani*, discoverer of dynamic element. Exx: *galvanograph, galvanotherapy*.

**1 -gam, 2 -gamae, 3 -gamist, 4 -gamous, 5 -gamy; 6 -gamete, 7 gameto-; 8 gamo-**: 6, 7 come from Gr *gametēs*, husband, or *gametē*, wife, themselves from *gamein* (s *gam-*), to marry, intimately akin to *gamos* (s *gam-*), marriage, whence all the other c/ff, and akin to *gambros* (*gambr-*, extension of *gam-*), son-in-law, brother-in-law, fiancé. Exx: *cryptogam*; *-gamae*, pl n answering to adj *-gamous*, as in *monogamous*; *bigamist*; *monogamy*;—*gametogenesis*; *gamogenesis*. See MONOGAMY.

**gamma-**, as in *gammacism*, difficulty in pronouncing the gutturals (e.g., *g* and *k*), in *gamma function*, in *g. moth*, in *g. ray*, is the Gr letter γ, gamma, corresponding to the E hard *g*. The letter is of Sem origin.

**gamo-** ; *-gamous, -gamy*. See *-gam*.

**gangli-, ganglio-**: the former, short for the latter; Gr *ganglio-* (γάγγλιο-), c/f of *ganglion*, an excrescence, swelling, tumour; hence, in Med, a nerve centre, as in *gangliocyte, ganglioform, ganglio-neural*.

**gano-**: from Gr *ganos* (s *gan-*), brightness; *gan-*

appears to be an extension of the IE r *\*ga*, bright, brightness. Exx: *Ganocephala, Ganodonta, ganophyllite*; *ganomalite* (cf *-lite*) comes from the Gr derivative n, *ganōma*, brightness.

**gasi-, gaso-**: c/ff of *gas*. Exx: *gasify*; *gasogenic, gasometer*.

**-gaster, -gastria, -gastric; gaster(o)-; gastri-, gastr-(o)-**: all from Gr *gastēr* (s *gast-*), belly, gen *gastros*, hence o/s *gastr-*: akin to Gr *gemein* (s *gem-*), to be full (of), and *gemos*, the intestines contained by the belly. Exx: *peptogaster* (cf *pepto-*); *Microgastria* (*micro-*); *pneumogastric* (*pneumo-*); *gasteralgia* (*-algia*) and *gasteropod* (*-pod*); *gastriloquist*, a ventriloquist; *gastro-centrous, gastronomy, gastrotomy* (cf *-tome*).

**ge-**, as in *geode*. See *geo-*.

**gelati-**, short form of **gelatini-** or **gelatino-**, c/ff of *gelatin* (cf JELLY). Exx: *gelatification*; *gelatinigerous, gelatinotype*.

**gelo-; geloto-**: the former from the nom, the latter from the o/s of Gr *gelōs*, gen *gelōtos*, laughter, s *gel-*, from *gelaō* (s *gel-*), I laugh, IE s *\*gel-* (cf Arm *calr*, laughter). Exx: *gelogenic, gelotometer, gelototherapy*.

**gemini-**: L *gemini*, twins, from *geminus*, double (orig, one of twins), of IE s *gem-*, cf Skt *yamás*, matched, twin. Ex: *geminiflorous*, flowering in pairs.

**gemmi-**; loosely **gemmo-**: from L *gemma*, a precious stone, orig a bud, the transition arising from the shapes and colours of buds: see GEM. Exx: *gemmiferous, gemmiform, gemmiparous*, where 'bud' determines the sense; *gemmology*, the science of precious stones.

**1, -gen or 2, its occ var, -gene; 3, -genesia or 4, -genesis; 5, -genetic; 6, -genic; 7, -genin; 8, -genous; 9, -geny;—10, gen(o)-**. The pattern of the E words has been determined both by *-gen*, from F *-gène*, from Gr *-genēs*, born, (hence) of a certain kind, and by *gen-* (short for *geno-*), from Gr *genos* (s *gen-*), race, kind, sex: see GENERAL. Exx: (1, 2) *oxygen*, *Eugene* (cf *eugenics*); (3, 4) *paragenesia* or *paragenesis*, the formation of minerals in contact (side by side: cf *para-* in Prefixes); 5, c/f of *genetic*, as in *pangenetic*; 6, (syn of *-genetic* and *-genous*)— c/f of *genic*, the adj corresponding to nn in *-gen* and *-geny*, as in *acrogenic*; 7, *-gen*+chem *-in*, denoting a substance formed from another, as in *digitonin*; 8, adj answering to nn in *-gen* and *-geny*, and referring, like *-gen*, either to a substance producing or yielding or to a substance produced or yielded by, as in *alkaligenous* (active) and *neurogenous* (passive); 9, from Gr *-geneia*, denoting origin, creation—in *cosmogeny*, it is syn with *-genesis*, and in *biogeny, ontogeny*, etc, it denotes (science of) the origin or production of something specified; 10, see above—exx, *genoblast* (cf *-blast*) and *genotype*.

**genio-**: Gr *geneio-*, c/f of *geneion*, chin, from *genus*, jaw: cf CHIN. Exx: *genioplasty*; *genioglossal*. Cf *genyo-* and *-gnatha*.

**genito-**: 'genital' or 'genital and': F *génito-*, a shortening of ML *\*genitivo-* (L *\*genitiuo-*), from *gignere*, to beget. Ex: *genito(-)crural*.

**-genous.** See *-gen*.

**genu-:** L *genu*, c/f of *genū* (s *gen*-), knee, akin to Gr *gonu* (s *gon*-) and Skt *jǎnu* (s *jan*-) and, less obviously, Go *kniu*, E KNEE. Ex: *genuflect*, to bend the knee, from ML *genuflectere*, whence *genuflexiō*, o/s *genuflexiōn*-, whence E *genuflection*. Cf *-gon* (1).

**-geny.** See *-gen*.

**genyo-:** c/f of Gr *genus* (s *gen*-), the under jaw. Ex: *genyoplasty*. Cf *genio*-.

**ge(o)-:** Gr *geō*-, c/f of *gaia*, esp in var *gē*, the earth. Exx: *geocentric*, *geode* (cf 1st *-ode*), *geodesy* (Gr *geōdaisia*; 2nd element, from *daiein*, s *dai*-, to divide), GEOGRAPHY, GEOLOGY, GEOMETRY, *George*, *geotropy*. See the *ge-* complex.

**gephyr(o)-:** from Gr *gephura*, a bridge, as in *gephyrocercal* (cf *-cercal*). Gr γέφυρα (Boeotian βέφυρα, Cretan δέφυρα) app consists of a prefix γε-, *ge*-, of vague origin (perh akin to Gmc *ge*-, q.v. in Prefixes), and *φυρά*, *phura*, s *phur*-, for φορά, *phora*, from *pherein* (s *pher*-), to bear or carry —cf the *fer*- of L *fero*, I bear. Contrast and cf:

**-ger; -gerence** and **-gerent;** **-gerous:** resp 'bearer', as in *armiger* (adopted from L), arms-bearer; 'bearing, carrying' (n), as in *belligerence*—'bearing' (adj), as in *belligerent*, L *belligerant*-, o/s of *belligerans*, presp of *belligerāre*, from *belliger*, warwaging, from *bellum*, war+*gerere*, to wage, (orig) to bear or carry, presp *gerens*, o/s *gerent*-; *-gerous*, as in *armigerous*, answers either to L *-gerus* or to L *-ger*+E *-ous*. *Gerere*, of ancient L stock, has no irrefutable IE cognates: see JEST.

**gerato-,** as in *geratology*, a study of decadence: from *gerat*-, o/s of Gr *geras* (gen *geratos*), old age. Cf *gero*-.

**geri-.** See *gero*-.

**Germano-:** for *Germany*, as in *Germanocentric*, or for *German*, as in *Germanophile* and *Germanophobia*.

**germi-:** c/f of E GERM. Exx: *germicide* (*-cide*), *germifuge* (cf *-fugal*), *germiparity* (L *parere*, to produce young).

**ger(o)-** or **geri-;** 2, **geront(o)-:** from Gr *geras* or *gēras* (s *ger*-), old age, as in *geriatrics* (cf *-iatric*), medicine as applied to the old, and *gerocomy* (Gr *gerokomia*, 2nd element from *komein*, s *kom*-, to take care of), medical science as affecting the old; 2, *geront*-, o/s of Gr *gerōn* (gen *gerontos*), an old man—cf Skt *járant*-, old—as in *gerontocracy*, rule by the old, and *gerontology*, the scientific study of (the phenomena of) old age. Cf *gerato*-.

**-gerous.** See *-ger*.

**-geton:** Gr *geitōn*, a neighbour: s *geit*-, o.o.o. Ex: *Zyzzogeton*, q.v. at *zyzzo*-.

**-geusia:** a Med c/f, denoting 'condition of the sense of taste' and deriving from Gr *geusis*, taste, akin to *geuomai* (s *geu*-), I taste, akin to Skt *jōsati*, he tastes. Ex: *cacogeusia* (cf *caco*-, bad).

**giganti-** and **giganto-:** resp from *gigant*-, o/s of L *gigas* (gen *gigantis*), a giant, and from *giganto*-, c/f of the archetypal Gr *gigas*, gen *gigantos*: see GIANT. Exx: *giganticide* (cf *-cide*) and *gigantology*, *gigantomachy* (a battle between giants).

**gingiv(o)-:** 'the gums' or 'gingival—of the gums': from ML *gingīva*, L *gingīua*, a gum (of the mouth) --? a redup of *gena*, the cheek. Ex: *gingivolabial*.

**ginglymo-,** with shortening *gingly*-, as in *ginglyform*: from SciL *ginglymus*, from Gr *ginglumos* (γίγγλυμος), a hinge-like join—? a redup of IE *\*glu*-, to bend. Ex: *ginglymostoma* (cf *-stoma*).

**glaci-;** **glacio-:** resp from L *glaciēs* (s *glaci*-), ice, as in *glacification*, and from E *glacier*, as in *glaciology*, *glaciometer*, *glacionatant*.

**glandi-;** **glanduli-:** L *glandi*-, c/f of *glans*, o/s *gland*-, acorn; c/f of E *glandule*, from L *glandula*, dim of *glans*. Cf GLAND. Exx: *glandiferous*, from L *glandifer*; *glanduliform*.

**glauco-:** Gr *glauko*-, c/f of *glaukos*, silvery; silvery or bluish grey; grey: perh IE s *\*glau*-+ extension *k*- (or *ko*-)+*-os*, adj suffix. Exx: *glauco*(-) *chroite* (cf *-chroia*) and *glaucophane* (cf *-phane*).

**gleno-,** as in *glenohumeral*, of the glenoid cavity and the humerus: from Gr *glēnē*, socket of a joint, akin to *glēnos*, brilliant object; IE r, *\*gle*- or *\*gel*-.

**-glia:** from Gr *glia*, glue, cf *gluco*- below: in E, denoting 'fine glue-like tissue', as in *neuroglia* (*neuro*-). Cf also *-gloea*.

**gliri-,** as in Zoo *gliriform*: from L *glīs* (gen *glīris*), a dormouse, perh akin to Skt *giris*, a mouse.

**globi-;** **globo-:** from E *globe* or L *globus*; (*globo*-) from L *globus* (s *glob*-), a round body or object: see GLOBE. Exx: *globiferous*; *globo-cumulus*, *globosphaerite*. The L dim *globulus* (whence *globule*) yields the c/f *globuli*-, as in *globulimeter*.

**-gloea;** *gloeo*- or Grecized *gloio*-: c/ff of SciL *gloea*, from Gr *gloia*, glue. Exx: *zoogloea*; *gloeosporiose*, *Gloiopeltis*.

**glomero-;** **glomerulo-:** from *glomer*-, the inf s of L *glomerāre* (r *glom*-), to aggregate, to compact; (*glomerulo*-) from *glomerule*, a small compact or convoluted mass, from SciL *glomerulus*, dim of L *glomus*, a ball, akin to *glomerāre*: cf CONGLOMERATION. Exx: Geol *glomeroporphyritic* and Med *glomerulonephritis*.

**glori-.** See *glorify* at GLORY.

**-glossa, -glossia, -glot; gloss(o)-; glotti-; glotto-:** all, except *glotti*- (from *glottis*, Gr *glōttis*, itself from *glōtta*), ult from Gr *glōssa* or *glōtta*, tongue, akin to Gr *glōkhis* (γλωχίς), a projecting point, IE r *\*glō*-, extension *\*glōkh*-: see GLOSS. Exx: *Eriglossa*; (Gr *-glōssia*) *baryglossia*; *polyglot*, q.v. at *poly*-; (*glosso*-, mostly Med) *glossograph*, *glossology*, *glossotomy*; *glottiscope*; *glottogenic*, concerning the genesis of language, *glottology*.

**gluc(o)-** (1) or **glyc(o)-;** **glycer(o)-:** resp the c/f of Gr *glukus*, sweet, ? from IE *\*dlukos* (cf L *dulcis*, s *dulc*-), as in *glucofrangulin* and *glycogen*; and the c/f of *glyceric* or *glycerol*, as in *glycerogel*, *glycerophosphoric*. Cf:

**gluco-** (2): c/f of *glucose*: only in Chem. *Glucose* comes from Gr *gleukos*, sweet wine, intimately akin to *glukos*, q.v. in prec.

**glumi-:** for Bot *glume*, a chaffy bract, from L *glūma*, a husk. Ex: *glumiferous* (cf *-ferous* at *-fer*).

**gluteo-:** from SciL *gluteus*, a certain back

muscle, from Gr *gloutos*, rump, s *glout*-, with several IE cognates. Ex: *gluteo-femoral*.

**glycero-; glyco-.** See *gluco-* (1).

**gly(o)-**, only in Chem: for *glycol*, as in *glyoxal*.

**-glyph; glypho-;—glypt(o)-**: resp Gr *gluphē*, a carving, as in *triglyph* (Gr *trigluphos*), from *gluphein* (s *gluph*-), to carve, (hence) to engrave—whence *glypho*-, as in *glyphography*; (*glypto*-) Gr *gluptos*, carven, pp of *gluphein*—as in *glyptology*. Of *gluphein* the IE r seems to be \**gleubh*-, to cut, whittle, chip.

**-gnatha, pl -gnathae; -gnathia, -gnathism; -gnathus, pl -gnathi; adj -gnathic, -gnathous;— gnath(o)-**: all from Gr *gnathos* (s *gnath*-), jaw, perh akin to L *nāsus*, nose, prob akin to Skt *hánus*, jaw, and certainly to Gr *genus*, lower jaw: cf *genio-* above. Whereas *-gnatha*, *-gnathae* occur in Zoo class-names and *-gnathus*, *-gnathi* in Zoo generic names and *-gnathia* and *-gnathism* denote jaw-conditions, *gnath(o)-* is a general Sci c/f, with general adj *-gnathous*, answering to Gr *-gnathos* (-jawed), and with Sci adj *-gnathic* (*gnath*-+adj suffix *-ic*). Exx: *Desmognathae* (cf *desmo*-); *brachygnathia* or *-gnathism* (*brachy*-); *eurygnathous* (*-eury*-) and *prognathous* (prefix *pro*-, forward); *gnathometer*, *gnathopod* (*-pod*).

**gnomo-; -gnomy**: Gr *gnōmo*-, as in *gnōmologia*, whence *gnomology*: *gnōmē*, a judgement, hence a maxim or an aphorism+*-logia*, c/f of *logos*, a discourse; (*-gnomy*), from Gr *-gnōmia* (from *gnōmē*), art or science of judging, as in *physiognomy*. Cf:

**gnomono-**: for *gnomon*, from Gr *gnōmōn*, one who knows, a sundial's pointer or index: cf prec and next. Ex: *gnomonology*.

**-gnosia, -gnosis, -gnostic, -gnosy; gnosio-**: *-gnosia*=*-gnosis* (Gr *gnōsis*), as also does *-gnosy*, anglicized form of Gr *-gnōsia*; *-gnostic*, adj of *-gnosis*, comes from Gr *gnōstikos*; *gnosio*-, c/f of *gnōsis*, γνῶσις, which derives from *gignōskein* (*gi-gnōsk-ein*), to know. (Cf prec two entries.) See AGNOSTIC.

Exx: *barognosis* (cf *baro*-) and *diagnosis* and *prognosis*; *diagnostic*; *nephelognosy* (*nephelo*-); *gnosiology*, the theory of knowledge.

**gompho-**: from Gr *gomphos* (s *gomph*-), bolt or nail, IE \**gombh*-. Exx: *Gomphocarpus*, *gomphodent*.

**-gon** (1), **gonio-; gon-, gony(o)-**: resp Gr *-gōnon*, c/f of *gōnia*, angle (s *gōn*-); Gr *gōnio*-, c/f of *gōnia*, angle, akin to *gonu* (s *gon*-), knee, whence *gon-* and *gony(o)-*; cognate are Skt *jánu*, L *genu*, Go *kniu*, E KNEE. Exx: *pentagon*; *goniocraniometry*, measurement of head-angles (cf *cranio*- and *-meter*); *gonalgia*, *gonarthritis*; *gonyalgia*, *gonyocele* (cf *-cele*).

**-gon** (2), 2, **-gone**; 3, **gona-**; 4, **goneo-**; 5, **gonidio-**; 6, **-gonidium**; 7, **gonimo-**; 8, **-gonium**; 9, **gon(o)-**; 10, **-gony**: *-gon*, Bio var of *-gone*,=*gonium*, a SciL c/f derived from Gr *-gonos*, (adj) begetting or producing, and denoting 'mother cell or structure'; *-gone*, hence *-gon* and *-gonium*, derives from Gr *gonē* (s *gon*-), offspring; *gona*-, as in *gonapod*, is a c/f of *gonad*, a sexual gland; *goneo-* derives from Gr *goneus*, a begetter, as in *goneoclinic*, 'favouring'

one parent; *gonidio*-, c/f of *gonidium* (itself used as an end-element), an asexual reproductive cell; *gonimo*-, from Gr *gonimos* (itself from *gonē*, offspring), reproductive, as in *gonimoblast* (cf *-blast*); *gon(o)*- comes from Gr *gono*- or *gon*-, c/f of *gonos* or *gonē*, procreation, hence offspring, as in *gonoblast*, *gonococcus*, *gonophore*, *gonosome*, *gonotome*; *-gony*, via L, from Gr *-gonia*, from *gignesthai*, to be born. See KIN. Additional exx: *archegonium*; *gonaduct*; *goneopoiesis*; *androgonidium*; *cosmogony*, *theogony*.

**gona-; -gone; goneo-; -gonidium; -gonimo-.** See prec.

**gonio-.** See the 1st *-gon*.

**-gonium, -gony.** See the 2nd *-gon*.

**-gono.** See the 2nd *-gon*.

**gonyo-.** See the 1st *-gon*.

**Goti-**, as in Geol *Gotiglacial*: for *Got*land, which =southern Sweden. *Got*=Goth.

**-grad**, as in *Petrograd* (*Leningrad*), *Stalingrad*, represents 'city' of the person named. *Grad* is common Slavonic for 'town' or 'city'.

**-grade; gradio-** or **grado-**: all from L *gradus* (s *grad*-), a step, stepping, walking, from *gradi*, to step, to walk; the first coming via F *-grade*, 'pertaining to (manner of) walking', as in *plantigrade*, walking on the soles (and touching with heels). *Gradio*-, as in *gradiometer*, merely varies *grado*-, as in *gradometer*.

**Graeco-.** See *Greco*-.

**-gram** (1) or **-gramme**: c/f of *gram* (unit of weight), as in *centigram*, *kilogram*; *-gramme* is the F form.

**-gram** (2); **gramo-**: from Gr *-gramma* or occ, as in *tetragram*, *-grammon*, c/ff of *gramma*, a letter of the alphabet, from the root of *graphein*, to write (cf *-graph* and *grapho*-). See GRAMMAR. Exx: *anagram*, *telegram*; *gramophone*.

**gramini-, gramino-**: c/ff, the former truly L, of *grāmen* (gen *grāminis*), grass, o.o.o., but perh from an IE s meaning 'to eat', as E & M suggest, or from an IE r for 'to grow' and therefore akin to *grow* and *green*. Exx: *graminivorous* (cf *-vora*); *graminology*, the science of grasses.

**-gramme.** See the 1st *-gram*.

**gramo-.** See the 2nd *-gram*.

**grandi-**: c/f of L *grandis* (s *grand*-), grand, o.o.o. Exx: *grandiloquent* (cf ELOQUENCE) and *grandisonant* or *-sonous*.

**grani-**, the true L c/f, or **grano-**, by analogy with other *-o-* c/ff; **granuli-** and **granulo-**: resp from *grānum* (s *grān*-), a grain, and from its LL dim *grānulum*: see GRAIN. Exx: *graniform*, *granolite* (cf *-lite*); *granuliferous* (cf *-fer*), *granulocyte* (cf *-cyte*). Cf:

**graniti-**: c/f of *granite*, q.v. at GRAIN. Ex: *granitiform*.

**granuli-, granulo-.** See *grani*-.

**-graph, -grapher, -graphia, -graphic, -graphy; graphi-, grapho-.** For the IE r and cognates, see GRAMMAR. The effective origin of the c/ff lies in Gr *graphein* (s *graph*-), to write. In detail: *-graph*, cf F *-graphe*, derives from Gr *-graphos*, occ via L

*-graphus*; the agential (*-er*) n answering to *-graphy*, the anglicized form (cf F *-graphie*) of *-graphia*, itself adopted from Gr *-graphia*, '-writing', as in *biographer*, *biography*; *-graphic*, cf *graphic* at GRAMMAR; *graphi-*, as in *graphiology*, is irregular for *grapho-*, itself from Gr *graphē*, writing, as in *graphology*, *graphomania*, *graphometry* (F *graphométrie*), *graphoscope*, *graphospasm* (writer's cramp), *graphostatic*. Cf:

**grapto-**: c/f from Gr *graptos*, written, engraved, pp of *graphein*, to write (see prec and cf GRAPHIC). Exx: *graptolite* (*-lite*) and *graptomancy* (*-mancy*).

**grati-**. See GRATIFY.

**gravi-**, c/f from ML *gravis* (L *grauis*), heavy, q.v. at GRAVE, adj; and *gravito-*, c/f of E *gravity*. Exx: *gravific* (*-fic* at *fac-*), *gravimeter*; *gravitometer*.

**Greco-**, the mod form of *Graeco-*, from L *Graecus*, a Greek, (adj) Greek—see GREEK. Exx: *Graeco-Roman* (art), *Greco-Roman* (wrestling).

**greffo-**, in *greffotome* (cf *-tome*), a knife used in skin-grafting: F *greffe*, a grafting: cf 'to GRAFT (plants)'.

**[-gress**, as in *aggress*, *congress*, *digress*, *egress*, *progress*, *regress*, *transgress*: the nn from L *-gressus* (gen *-gressūs*), a going; the vv from L *-gressus*, gone, the pp of *gradi*, to step, to go: cf GRADE.]

**grossi-**: for *gross*; as in *grossify*, to render—or to become—gross.

**gryllo-**: for Gr *grullos* (s *grul-*), via L *gryllus*, a cricket: prob echoic; cf IE r *\*gru-*, to grunt or grumble. Ex: *Gryllotalpa* (L *talpa*—cf F *taupe*—a mole), a genus of crickets.

**guani-** or **guano-**: for *guano* (birds' dung, rich in phosphates: adopted from Sp, from Quechuan *huanu*, dung), whence *guanine*, whence *guanidine*, which has c/f *guanido-*. Exx: *guaniferous* (cf *-fer*); *guanophore* (cf *-phora*).

**gummi-**: for *gum* (q.v. in Dict); as in *gummiferous*, gum-bearing.

**guno-**, as in *gunocracy*: a var of *gyno-*, q.v. at *-gyn*.

**gutti-** (1): c/f from L *gutta*, a drop (cf GUTTER), as in *guttiform*, drop-shaped.

**gutti-** (2): c/f of GUTTA-PERCHA as in *guttiferous*, gum-yielding.

**gutturo-**: c/f from L *guttur*, throat (cf GUTTURAL), as in *gutturo-nasal*.

**gymn(o)-**: Gr *gumn(o)-*, c/f of *gumnos* (s *gumn-*), uncovered, naked: Cf *gymnasium* at NAKED. Exx: *gymnanthous* (cf *anth-*); *gymnoblastic* (cf *-blast*), *gymnocarpous* (cf *-carp*), *gymnosophist* (cf SOPHIST), *gymnospore* (*-spora*).

**-gyn** (or **-gyne**), **-gynous**; **-gynist**;—**gynae-**, mod **gyne-**; **gynaeo-**, mod **gyneo-**; **gyn(o)-**; **gynaeco-**, mod **gyneco-**; **gynandro-**. The element *-gyn* denotes, as in *hexagyn*, a plant having six pistils, the n corresponding to the adj *-gynous*, from Gr *-gunos* (woman; (adj) female), from *gunē*, a woman, s *gun-*; *-gynist*=*gyn-* (for *gyno-*)+agential *-ist*, as in *misogynist*, woman-hater; *gynae-*, mod *gyne-*, represents the L form of Gr *gunē*, woman; *gynaeo-*, mod *gyneo-*, latinizes *gunaio-*, c/f of Gr *gunaios*,

of or for (a) woman, and likewise *gyneco-* modernizes *gynaeco-*, L for *gunaiko-*, c/f of Gr *gunaikos*, womanish, female; *gyn(o)-*, Gr *gun(o)-*, c/f of *gunē*, woman; *gynandro-*=*gyn-*+*andro-*, q.v. For cognates, cf QUEAN.

Exx: *androgyne*, *androgynous*, hermaphroditic (L *androgynus*, from Gr *androgunos*); *gynephobia*, a dread of women; *gynecocracy* (Gr *gunaikokratia*), petticoat government; *gyneolatry*, woman-worship; *gynocracy*, *gynogenesis*, *gynophore*; *gynandromorphism* (Zoo), *gynandrosporous* (Bot).

**gypsi-**, **gypso-** (1): c/f of *gypsum* (hydrous calcium sulphate), adopted from L, from Gr *gupsos* (chalk), of Sem origin. Exx: *gypsiferous*, gypsum-bearing, and *gypsography*, (the art of) engraving on gypsum.

**gypso-** (2): for *gypsy*, *gipsy*, as in *gypsology*. Occ *gypsio-*, as in *gypsiologist*.

**gyro-**: Gr *guro-*, c/f of *guros*, a circle, a circular motion, latinized as *gyrus*: cf GYRATE. Exx: *gyrometer*, *gyromancy*, *gyroscope*.

**habro-**: from Gr *habros* (s *habr-*), graceful, delicate, dainty, tender, as in *Habronema* (cf *-nema*): perh of Sem origin.

**hadr(o)-**: Gr c/f of *hadros*, abundant, thick, ripe, perh akin to Skt *sándras*, thick, and prob akin to Gr *hadēn*, enough. Exx: *hadromycosis* (cf *myco-*) and *Hadrosaurus*, a heavy dinosaur.

**haema-** or **hema-**, **haem(o)-** or **hem(o)-**, **haemat(o)-** or **hemat(o)-**; **-haemia** or **-hemia**, or **-aemia** or **-emia**. The *-ae-* spellings represent L, the *-e-* forms represent general ModE, forms of Gr *-ai-*, the Gr c/ff being *haim(o)-* and *haimat(o)-*; *ha ema-* or *hema-* is irregular, being neither Gr nor even L; in E, *haema-* and *haem(o)-* and *haemat(o)-* are retained for most of the strictly Sci references. The origin is Gr *haima* (gen *haimatos*), blood: o.o.o.

Exx: *haematherm* (or *hema-*), a warm-blooded animal, cf *-therm*; *Haemanthus* (*-anth*); *haemoglobin*, a Biochem term, cf GLOBE; *haemophilia* (or *hemo-*), a tendency (cf *-philia* at *-phil*) to profuse bleeding or *haemorrhage*, EF-F *hémorrhagie*, L *haemorrhagia*, Gr *haimorrhagia*, *-rrhagia* deriving from *rhēgnunai*, to break or burst; *haemorrhoid*, usu in pl, from MF-F *hémorroïdes*, L *haemorrhoidae*, Gr *haimorrhoides* (sc *phlebes*, veins) tending to discharge (cf Gr *rhein*, to flow) blood-*haematothermal*, warm-blooded; *septicaemia* or *septicemia*, a morbid blood-condition—from Gr *sēptikos*, rotting, septic, and Gr *-aimia*, end-c/f of *haima*, blood (gen *haimatos*).

**hagi(o)-**: Gr *hagio-*, c/f of *hagios*, holy, sacred, perh akin to Skt *yáyati*, he sacrifices, and *yájyas*, venerable. Exx: *hagiarchy* (cf *-arch*); *hagiocracy* (cf *-cracy*); *hagiography* and *hagiology*, a writing about, hence a book of, saints; *hagiolatry*, saint-worship (cf *idolatry*); *hagiophobia*, a dread of holy persons or things; *hagioscope*, a church squint.

**hali-** or **halo-**: both adopted from Gr: c/ff of *hals* (gen *halos*; s *hal-*); m, salt—cf L *sal*—f, the sea: cf *halmē*, sea-water, and several Gmc and Sl cognates. Exx: *halibios*, sea-life, and *haliplankton*;

*halogen*, any chlorine element (cf *-gen*); *halomancy*, divination (*-mancy*) by means of salt; *halophilous*, growing in salt water; *halophyte*, a plant (cf *-phyte*) flourishing in salt water, or growing naturally in salt-impregnated soil.

**halio-**. A var of the prec, as in *haliography*, a description (cf *-graph*) of the sea.

**halo-**. See *hali-*.

**hamamelid(o)-**: from Gr *hamamēlis* (gen *-mēlidos*), either a medlar or a service tree: *hama-*, together + *mēlon*, a fruit. Ex: *Hamamelidanthemum*.

**hamartio-**: from Gr *hamartia*, failure, esp sin, akin to *hamartanein*, to fail, to sin. Ex: *hamartiology*, the theology of sin.

**hami-**, as in *hamiform*, resembling a hook, and *hamirostrate*, hook-beaked: from L *hāmus*, a hook, akin to the syn OHG *hamo*.

**Hamito-**: c/f of *Hamite*, as in *Hamito-Negro*, or of *Hamitic*, as in *Hamito-Semitic. Hamite* (whence *Hamitic*)=descendant, E *-ite*, L *-ita*, Gr *-itēs*, of *Ham*, L *Cham*, Gr *Kham.* Cf *Khem*, Egypt, and *Ammon. Ham* is perh 'the dark-skinned (one)'.

**hapl(o)-**: Gr *hapl(o)-*, c/f of *haploos*, single—lit, of one (*heis*, one) fold, contrast Gr *diploos*, of two folds; cf, therefore, E *ply*, n. Exx: (Bot) *haplocaulescent*, having a simple axis (cf *-cauli-* above); *haplology*, the (unconscious) running of two syllables into one; *haploscope*, a simple form of stereoscope. Cf the adj *haploid*, single in appearance, as if from Gr *\*haploeidēs*, single-like (suffix *-oid*)

**hapt(o)-**: from L *haptein* (s *hapt-*), to fasten, akin to *hapē*, a fastening: IE r, prob *\*iabh-*; cf Vedic *āpa*, he has reached. Ex: *haptometer*, an instrument recording acuteness of touch.

**harmoni-, harmono-**: from Gr *harmonia*, proportion, concord, HARMONY. Exx: *harmoniphon* (cf *-phon*); *harmonograph.* Cf:

**harmo-**: from Gr *harmos*, a joint (cf prec), s *harm-*, app akin to L *armentum*, a herd of e.g. cattle; IE r, *\*ar-*. Ex: Min *harmotome* (cf *-tome*).

**harpsi-**. See *harpsichord* at CHORD.

**hastato-**: from L *hastātus*, spear-shaped, from *hasta*, a spear, perh akin to E *gad*, a spike. Ex: *hastalo-sagittate*, of or like a spear and an arrow. Cf the rare *hasti-*, ML c/f of *hasta*, as in *hastiludium* (L *ludus*, play, a sport), E *hastilude*, spear-play.

**hauyno-**: for Min *hauynite*, itself from the F mineralogist *Hauy*. Ex: *hauynophyre* (cf *-phyre*).

**hebe-**: from Gr *hēbē* (ἥβη), youth, puberty—cf *Hebe*, the Goddess of Youth: of IE stock, with Sl cognates. In Med, *hebe-* denotes either puberty, as in *hebephrenia*, or the pubes, as in *hebetomy*; in Bot, pubescent, downy, as in *hebeanthous*, bearing downy flowers.

**hecato-, hecatom-, hecaton-**: Gr *hekaton*, 100— cf HUNDRED. Exx: *hecatophyllous*, 100-leafed; *hecatomb*, Gr *hekatombē* (2nd element, from *bous*, ox)—*hecatomped*, (adj) measuring 100 feet; *hecatonstylon*, a 100-columned building. Cf:

**hect(o)-**: Fr *hect(o)-*, from Gr *hekaton*, 100—cf HUNDRED. Exx: *hectare, hectolitre, hectowatt.*

**hederi-**: L *hederi-*, c/f of *hedera* (o.o.o.), ivy; as in *hederigerent*, ivy-bearing, cf L *hederiger* (cf *-ger*).

**hedono-**. See *hedy-*.

**-hedral**, adj answering to n *-hedron*, from Gr *-edron*, c/f of *hedra*, a seat, a base (cf syn *hedranon*) akin to syn *hedos* (s *hed-*), for primitive *\*sedos*, akin to Skt *sádas-*, seat; IE r *\*sed-*, var *\*sad-*. Exx: *octahedral, octahedron*, an 8-faced solid; *polyhedral, polyhedron* (cf *poly-*).

**hedy-**: Gr *hēdu-*, c/f of *hēdus* (s *hēd-*), sweet, (hence) pleasant, whence *hēdonē* (s *hēdon-*, c/f *hēdono-*), pleasure, whence *hēdonikos*, pleasurable (s *hēdon-* + adj *-ikos*). Exx: *hedyphane, hedysarum*; *hedonology.* Gr *hēdus* is akin to L *suāuis* (E *suave*) and E SWEET.

**helc(o)-**: from Gr *helkos* (s *helk-*), a festering wound, an ulcer, akin to L *ulcus* (s *ulc-*), gen *ulceris*, and to Skt *árśas-*, haemorrhoids. Ex: *helcology*, the Med science of ulcers.

**heli-; helic(o)-**: *heli-*, c/f of Gr *helissein*, to roll; *helic(o)-*, from Gr *helik(o)-*, c/f of *helix* (gen *helikos*), a roll, a spiral, a helix, akin to *helissein*, prob for *\*welissein*, r *\*wel-* or *\*uel-*, q.v. in L *uoluere*, to turn. Exx: *Heliamphora*, a pitcher plant; *helicograph, helicogyre, helicometry, helicopter* (F *hélicoptère*, 2nd element Gr *pteron*, a wing: its propellers revolve on a vertical axis).

**heli-** (2). See *helio-*.

**helic(o)-**. See the 1st *heli-*.

**heli(o)-; -helion**: Gr *hēli(o)-*, c/f of *hēlios*, the sun, akin to W *haul*, sun, OIr *súl*, eye, Lith *sáule*, L *sol*, sun, E SUN; IE r, *\*sāuel-*. (Hofmann.) Exx: *helianthus*, sunflower—cf *helichrysum* (L term for the marigold), a yellow-flowering plant; *heliocentric; heliogram, heliograph; heliotherapy; heliotrope* (Gr *hēliotropion* (via L *heliotropium* and F *héliotrope*), a plant turning (*tropein*, s *trope-*, see TROPIC) to the sun.

The element *-helion* occurs in the Astr terms *aphelion* and *parhelion* (Gr *parēlion*).

**Helleno-**, 'a Hellene'—'Hellenic and': Gr *Hellēno-*, c/f of *Hellēn*, a Hellene, a Greek—cf *Hellas*, Greece. Exx: *Hellenocentric; Helleno-Italic.*

**helminth(o)**: Gr *helminth(o)-*, c/f from *helminthos*, the gen of *helmins*, a worm, with ult r *hel-* for *\*uel-* (*\*wel-*), to turn: *helmins* or *helmis* is therefore 'the turner' (Even a worm . . .). Exx: *helminthagogue*, a vermifuge or worm-dispeller; *helminthology*, worm-lore.

**helo-** (1): Gr *helo-*, c/f of *helos* (s *hel-*), a marsh; perh for *\*selos*, akin to Skt *sáras-*, sea. Ex: *helobious*, (adj) marsh-living (cf *-bia*).

**helo-** (2): Gr *hēlo-*, c/f of *hēlos*, a nail, perh akin to L *uallus*, a stake, a paling. Ex: *helotomy*, cutting of corns.

**hema-, hemato-**. See *haema-*.

**hemer(o)-**: from Gr *hēmer(o)-*, c/f of *hēmera*, a day; most of the non-Attic forms are of the *ēmar* or *amer* pattern, ? from an IE *\*amar* or *\*amer* or *\*amor.* Exx: *hemerobious*, living for only a day; *hemerology* (Gr *hēmerologion*), a calendar.

**hemi-**, half: Gr *hēmi-*, half, akin to L *sēmi-*, OHG *sāmi-*, Skt *sāmi-*. Exx: *hemicycle*, via L and

F, from Gr *hēmikuklon*; *hemiplegia*, paralysis (cf
*-plegia*) of a lateral half of the body; *hemisphere*,
via MF-F from Gr *hemisphairion*; *hemistich*, half
a poetic verse-line, Gr *hēmistikhion*. With Gr *hēmi*,
cf L *sēmi* and Skt *sā mi-*.

**hemo-.** See *haema-*.

**hen-.** See *heno-*.

**hendec(a)-:** Gr *hendeka-*, c/f of *hendeka*, 11
(*hen*, 1+*deka*, 10). Exx: *hendecagon* (cf *-gon*), a
polygon of 11 angles, therefore sides; *hendeca-
syllabic*, 11-syllabled, from *hendecasyllable* (Gr
*hendekasullabos*, 11-syllabled).

**heno-:** Gr *heno-*, c/f of *heis* (neu *hen*), one, gen
*henos*. Exx: *henotheism*, belief in one god; cf
*hendiadys*, LL word formed from Gr *hen dia
duoin*, lit 'one by two'.

**heorto-:** Gr *heorto-*, c/f of *heortē*, a feast, a
religious festival, perh with IE r *\*uer-*, to turn. Ex:
*heortology*, the history and system of the liturgical
year.

**hepatico-:** c/f of *hepatic*: see next.

**hepat(o)-:** from Gr *hēpat(o)-*, c/f of *hēpar* (gen
*hēpatos*), the liver, with cognates in Sl, L, Skt.
Exx: (1) 'the liver', as in *hepatectomy* (cf *-ectomy*
at *-tome*), *hepatopancreas*, and *hepatology*; (2)
'hepatic (L *hēpaticus*, Gr *hēpatikos*) and', as in
*hepatocolic*.

**hept(a)-:** Gr *hept(a)-*, c/f of *hepta*, seven, akin to
L *septem*, Skt *saptá*, E SEVEN. Exx: *heptagon*, a
7-angled, -sided, polygon; *Heptameron*, a collection of stories, covering 7 days (cf *hemero-*);
*heptometer*, a verse-line of 7 feet; *heptarchy*, (a)
government by 7 persons.

**Heracleo-,** 'of *Herakles* (Hercules)', as in *Hera-
cleopolite* (cf *cosmopolite*), a citizen of Heracleop-
olis—cf *-polis*—in Middle Egypt.

**herbi-:** L *herbi-*, c/f of *herba*, (a) grass, a herb:
cf HERB. Exx: *herbiferous*, herb-bearing, L *herbifer*
(cf *-fer*); *herbivorous*, grass- and herb-eating (cf
*-vora*).

**herco-:** from Gr *herkos* (s *herk-*), a fence, a
(secondarily) a barrier, perh akin to L *sarcina*, a
bundle. Ex: Bot *hercogamy* (cf *-gamy* at *-gam*).

**heredi-, heredo-:** from L *hērēs* (gen *hērēdis*), an
heir: cf HEIR. Exx: *heredipety* (L *peterė*, s *pet-*, to
seek), legacy-seeking; *heredo(-)tuberculosis*.

**heresi(o)-:** an Englishing of Gr *hairesi-*, c/f of
*hairesis*, heresy, from *hairein* (s *hair-*), to seize, to
take: cf HERESY. Exx: *heresiarch*, L *haeresiarcha*,
Gr *hairesiarkhēs*, a heresy-leader; *heresiography*
and *heresiology*.

**hermo-, Hermo-:** Gr *hermo-*=*Hermo-*, c/f of
*Hermēs*, the god Hermes. Exx: *hermodactyl*, lit
'Hermes's finger'; *hermoglyphic*, a statuary, from
the Gr adj *hermogluphikos* (cf *-glyph*).

**hernio-:** as in *herniology*; c/f from *hernia*, L
word akin to YARN.

**heroi-; hero-; heroo-:** *heroi-*, c/f of *heroic*—
denoting 'heroic and', as in *heroicomic*; as in
*Herophile*, Gr *hēro-*, c/f of *Hērō*; *heroo-*, Gr
*hērōo-*, c/f of *hērōs*, a hero, as in *heroögony* (cf the
2nd *-gon*): cf HERO.

**1, herpeti-; 2, herpeto-:** 1, c/f from Gr *herpēs*

(gen *herpētōs*), the skin disease herpes, and of the
cognate *herpeton*, a reptile; *herpeto-*, true Gr c/f of
*herpeton*. The common origin lies in Gr *herpein* (s
*herp-*: cf L *serp-*, as in *scrpere*, to glide or
creep), to creep: cf SERPENT. Exx: *herpetiform*,
herpeslike and (2) reptilian; *herpetology*, *herpeto-
phobia*.

**hesper(o)-:** from Gr *hesperos*, western—cf
*Hesperus*, the Evening Star: cf VESPERS. Ex:
*Hesperornis* (Gr *ornis*, a bird: cf *-ornis*).

**hetaero-:** from Gr *hetaira*, (a female companion,
hence) a superior mistress, a concubine; of ancient
IE stock. Exx: *hetaerocracy*, a government by
mistresses; *hetaerolite*, a specific mineral, found in
*companionship* with another.

**heter(o)-:** Gr *hetero-*, c/f of *heteros*, other—
strictly a comp ('the other of two')—akin to Gr
*heis*, neu *hen*, one, and E SIMPLE. Exx: *heteraxial*,
HETERDOX (Gr *heterodoxos*), *heterodyne* (cf *-dyne*),
*heterogamous* (cf *-gam*) *heterogeneous* (ML *hetero-
geneus*, Gr *heterogenēs*: Gr *genos*, race, kind) and
*heterogeneity* (ML *heterogeneitās*), *heterogony* (cf
*-gony* at 2nd *-gon*), *heterology* (lack of correspondence), *heteromorphic* (cf *-morph*), *heteronomy* (cf
*-nome*), *heteronym* (cf *-onym* at *onom-*), *heterophyllous* (cf *-phyll*), *heterosexual*, *heterotrophic* (cf
*-trophia*).

**hex(a)-:** Gr *hex(a)-*, c/f of *hex*, 6—cf L *sex*, 6,
and see SIX. Exx: *hexagon*, *hexagram*, *hexameter*
(Gr *hexametros* (*stikhos*), a verse-line of 6 feet),
*hexapod* (Gr *hexapodos*, gen of *hexapous*, 6-footed),
*hexarchy* (a group of 6 states).

**hexico-:** from *hexikos*, gen of Gr *hexis*, habit;
with the s *hex-*, cf *ekh-*, the s of *ekhein*, to have or
possess: semantically cf *behaviour*, q.v. at BEHAVE.
Ex: *hexicology*, ecology, bionomics.

**Hiberno-:** as in *Hibernology*, the study of Irish
history, and as in *Hiberno-Celtic*, (adj and n)
Irish-Celtic: from *Hibernia* (whence *Hibernian*, adj
and n), the L name for Ireland. *Hibernia* is perh a
re-shaping of Ptolemy's Ἰονεϱνία, *Ionernia*, itself
o.o.o.

**hidro- (1):** from Gr *hidrōs*, sweat (akin to *hudōr*,
water: cf the 2nd *hydro-*). Exx: *hidromancy*, divination (*-mancy*) by sweat; *hidropoietic*, sweat-causing
(*-poietic*).

**hidro- (2).** See *hydro-* (2).

**hieraco-:** from Gr *hierax* (gen *hierakos*), a hawk
(? lit 'the swift one'); as in *hieracosphinx* (cf
SPHINX), a hawk-headed sphinx.

**hieratico-:** for *hieratic*, sacerdotal, priestly, via
LL *hierāticus* from Gr *hieratikos*, an elaboration of
*hieros*, sacred, holy; cf *hiero-* and *hieratic*. Ex:
*hieratico-domestic*.

**-hieric:** from Gr *hieron*, the sacrum (*os sacrum*,
the lowest bone of the spine), as in *brachyhieric* (cf
*-brach*) and *platyhieric* (cf *platy-*). A special application of the Gr *hieros*, holy, therefore cf:

**hier(o)-:** Gr *hiero-*, c/f of *hieros*, holy, sacred:
cf HIERARCHY. Exx: *hierocracy*, government by
ecclesiastics; *hieroglyphic* (adj, hence n), via LL
*hieroglyphicus*, from Gr *hierogluphikos*, pertaining
to sacred writing; *hierology*; *hieromancy*; *hiero-*

*phant*, Gr *hierophantēs*, a priest, lit 'one who shows sacred things'.

**hilaro-**: from L *hilaris* (*-rus*), cheerful: cf HILARIOUS. Ex: *hilaro-tragedy*, tragicomedy.

**hili-**: for Bot *hilum*, pl *hila*, sense-adapted from L *hilum* (s *hīl-*), a trifle, prob orig a var of *fīlum* (s *īl-*), a thread: IE r *phil*- perh yields both *fil-* and *hilf* and also *pil-*, as in *pilus* (s *pil-*), hair, so closely re-s-embling threads. Ex: *hiliferous* (cf *-ferous* at *-fer*), hilum (or hila)-bearing.

**himanto-**: Gr *himanto-*, c/f of *himas* (gen *himantos*), a thong; perh, obscurely, from an IE r *si-* or *sei-*, to bind: cf Skt *syáti* or *sináti*, he binds. Ex: *Himantopus*, a genus of waders (birds), from Gr *himantopous*, *pous* being a foot.

**hipp(o)-**: Gr *hipp(o)-*, c/f of *hippos*, a horse, akin to L *equus*. Exx: *hipparch*, a commander of cavalry; *hippodrome*, a horse(-race) course; HIPPO-POTAMUS. Cf:

**-hippus**: a SciL end-element, esp in Palaeontology, from Gr *hippos*, q.v. in prec.

**hirco-**: from L *hircus* (s *hirc-*, r *hir-*), a he-goat, perh akin to Samnite L *hirpus*, a wolf. Ex: *hirco-cervus* (F *hircocerf*), adopted from ML; a fabulous creature, half-goat, half stag (cf *cervi-*).

**hirmo-**: MGr (*h*)*eirmo-*, c/f of MGr (*h*)*eirmos* (Gr *heirmos*), a series, from *eirein* (s *eir-*), to fasten together, to join, cf SERIES, as in Eccl *hirmologion*, a book of *hirmoi* or hymns with fixed melody and rhythm.

**hirsuto-**: from L *hirsūtus*, whence *hirsute*; prob akin to *horrēre*, to bristle. Ex: *hirsuto-rufous*, red-haired.

**hirudini-**: from *hirūdin-*, o/s of L *hirūdō*, a leech, s *hirūd-*, r prob *hir-* (*-ūdō*—cf the E suffix *-ude*—being a suffix, cf *testudo*, a tortoise). Ex: *hirudini-culture*, the rearing of leeches.

**Hispano-**, 'Spanish and' or 'Spain': from L *Hispānus*, Spanish, a b/f from *Hispāni*, the Spaniards: cf SPANISH. Exx: *Hispano-American*, *Hispanophile*.

**histi(o)-, hist(o)-**: *histio-*, from Gr *histion*, sail, web, itself from Gr *histos* (cf *histo-*), loom, web, akin to L *stāmen*, q.v. at STAMEN. In the derivative sense, Med 'tissue', *histo-* has virtually displaced *histio-*. Exx: *histiology*, now *histology*, the science (cf *-logy* at *-loger*) of animal tissue; *histolysis* (cf *-lysis* at *-lyse*); *histozoic* (cf *-zoic* at *zo-*).

**historico-**, 'historic and'; **historio-**, 'history': c/f, resp of *historic*, and adopted from Gr *historio-*, c/f of *historia*: see HISTORY. Exx: *historico-ethical*; *historiographer* (via F and L, from Gr *historio-graphos*), *historiometry*, a statistical treatment of history.

**histrio-**: L *histriō* (gen *histriōnis*; LL adj *his-triōnicus*, whence E *histrionic*), an actor; of Etruscan origin. Exx: Zoo *Histriobdella* (cf *-bdella*), a genus of invertebrates; *Histriomastix*, ML *histrio-mastix*, scourge of actors, cf *-mastix* at *mastigo-*.

**Hittito-**, often shortened to **Hitto-**: for *Hittite* (H *Ḥittim*, Hittites, s *Ḥitt-*), n and adj. Ex: *Hittitology* or *Hittology*, the study or science of Hittite language or history.

**hodo-**: Gr *hodo-*, c/f of *hodos* (ὁδός), path, way —cf the 2nd *odo-*. Exx: Math *hodograph* and Nav *hodometrical*.

**holc(o)-**: from Gr *holkos* (s *holk-*), a furrow, cf the syn L *sulcus* (s *sulc-*, r *sul-*). Exx: *holcodont* (cf *-odont*), with teeth set furrow-wise; *Holconoti* (cf the 1st *noto-*), an order of fishes.

**hol(o)-**: Gr *hol(o)-*, c/f of *holos*, entire, whole, from *olwos*, itself from IE *soluos*—cf Skt *sárvas*, intact, entire, and L *saluus* (ML *salvus*), safe, and E SAFE. Exx: *holarctic*, referring to all the arctic regions; *holocaust*, a burnt offering (sacrifice), via OF-F and L from Gr *holokauston*, neu of *holo-kaustos*, burnt (cf CAUSTIC) whole; *holograph*, a document (cf *-graph*), esp a letter, written entirely by its signatory; *holomorphic* (cf *-morph*); *holotype*. The r *hol-*+suffix *-ism*=*holism*, a philosophy emphasizing wholes, with adj *holistic* (suffix *-istic*).

**homal(o)-**, adopted from Gr, c/f of *homalos*, even, smooth, a derivative of *homos*: cf *homeo-* and *homo-*. Exx: *homalogonatous*, lit 'even-kneed'; *Homalonotus*.

**homeo-**, mod for *homoeo-*, which, orig, was L for the now rare *homoio-*, the Gr c/f of *homoios*, like, similar, akin to and prob derived from *homos*, q.v. at *homo-*. Exx: *hom(o)eopathy*, cure of disease (cf *-pathy* at *-path*) by 'resemblances'; *hom(o)eotypic* or *-ical*; *homoeomery*, the likeness of the ultimate substances—cf *-mery* at *-mer*; *homoiothermic* (cf *-therm*); *homoiousia*, for *homoia ousia*, similar being or essence, hence essential likeness.

**homi-; homini-**; 'man': from L *homō* (man), s *hom-*; gen *hominis*, o/s *homin-*, whence the c/f *homini-*. See HOMO for cognates, etc. Exx: *homicide*, agent, from L *homicīda*; the crime from L *homi-cīdium* (cf *-cide* at *-cidal*); *hominiform*, man-shaped, in human form, and *hominivorous*, man-eating.

**homo-**; before a vowel, **hom-**: Gr *hom(o)-*, c/f of *homos* (s *hom-*), the same, one and the same—common or joint—like, whence both *homoios*, similar (see *homeo-*) and *homalos*, even, smooth (see *homalo-*): akin to E SAME. Exx: *homodromous* (cf *-drome*); *homogamy*, interbreeding; *homogeneous*, ML *homogeneus*, Gr *homogenēs*, of the same race or kind, and *homogeny*, Gr *homogeneia*; *homograph*; *homologous*, Gr *homologos*, assentient, lit 'of the same speech or thought', and n *homologue* from EF-F adj *homologue*, from Gr *ho-mologos* (or ML *homologus*); *homonym*, EF-F *homonyme*, L adj *homonymus*, Gr *homōnumos*, of the same name; *homophone*; *homorganic*; *homo-type*.

**homoeo-; homoio-**. See *homeo-*.

**honori-**. See *honorific* at HONOR.

**hopl(o)-**: Gr *hopl(o)-*, c/f of *hoplon*, a weapon, of uncertain kinship. In E words it denotes either 'arms' (or 'arms and armour') or 'heavily armed'. Exx: *Hoplocephalus*; *hoplomachy*, a (mock) battle under arms.

**horismo-**: from Gr *horismos*, a marking-out with boundaries, a delimitation, from *horos*, a boundary. cf the 2nd *horo-*. Ex: Zoo *horismology*.

**horizo-**: for HORIZON, as in *horizometer*.

**hormo-**: from Gr *hormos* (s *horm-*), a chain, prob akin to *heirmos*, q.v. at *hirmo-*. Ex: Bot *hormogon(e)* or *hormogonium* (*goneia*, generation—cf the 2nd *-gon*).

**hormono-**: c/f of *hormone* (Gr *hormōn*, presp of *hormein*, to excite), as in *hormonology*.

**horo-** (1): Gr *hōro-*, c/f of *hōra*, hour—see HOUR. Exx: *horography*; *horologe*, a timepiece, via OF and L from Gr *hōrologion*; *horology*; *horoscope* (cf *-scope*).

**horo-** (2): Gr *horo-*, c/f of *horos*, a boundary, a limit, a term, app from PGr \**woroos*, a furrow—cf the L *uruus* (ML *urvus*), a furrow, hence the circuit of a town. Ex: *horograph* (Math). Cf *horismo-*.

**horri-**: c/f of L *horrēre* (s *horr-*), to bristle (of hairs), hence to shiver, shudder, to feel fear: cf HEARSE. Exx: *horrific*, L *horrificus*; *horripilant*, *horripilātion*.

**horti-**: L *horti-*, from *hortus*, a garden, esp in *horticulture*, L *horti cultura*, lit 'a garden's cultivation'; cf Gr *khortos*, an enclosure, and E COURT and YARD.

**hosio-**: LGr *hosio-*, c/f of *hosios*, holy, akin to SOOTH. Ex: *hosiomartyr*, LGr-MGr *hosiomartur*.

**humani-**, 'human': from L *humānus*; as in *humaniform*, anthropomorphic, and in *humanify*, to render human, to incarnate. Cf HUMAN.

**humero-**, 'humeral and': c/f of E from L *humerus* (better *umerus*), the shoulder, akin to Go *ams*, Gr *ōmos*, Skt *aṁsa*. Ex: *humero-dorsal*. *Humerus*, the bone of the upper arm, explains—via *humorous*—'the *funny* bone'.

**humi-** (1): c/f, perh prompted by the loc *humi*, on the ground—from L *humus*, earth, soil: cf HUMAN. Exx: *humbicubation* (*cubāre*, to lie down); *humifuse*, spread (L *fusus*, pp of *fundere*, to spread) over the ground; *humify*, to convert (lit 'make': cf *-fy*) into humus.

**humi-** (2); **humidi-**: 'humid, moist, damp': resp from L *humēre* (s *hum-*), to be damp, and from its derivative *humidus*, damp, or from its E shape *humid*. Exx: *humify*, from LL *humificāre*, to render moist; *humidify*, from *humid*.

**humori-**, **humoro-**: for *humo(u)r*, as in *humorific* (cf *-fic*) and *humorology*.

**hungri-**: for *hunger*, as in *hungrify*, to make (someone) hungry.

**hy-**. See *hyo-*.

**hyaen(o)-**: from L *hyaena*, a hyena: cf HYENA. Exx: *Hyaenarctos*, a Pal bear of the Arctic; *Hyaenodon* (cf *-odon*), another Pal creature. The var *hyeni-* (for *hyena*) occurs in *hyeniform*.

**hyalin(o)**: c/f of E *hyaline* (see next).

**hyal(o)-**, 'glass or glassy': Gr *hual(o)-*, c/f of *hualos*, any transparent stone, (later) glass, whence the adjj *hualeos* or *hualinos* (whence E *hyaline*), of glass, and *hualoeis*, *hualōdēs*, glass-like; IE s, prob \**sualo-*. Exx: *hyalescent* (cf the suffix *-escent*); *hyalogen* (*-gen*); *hyalograph*; *hyalophane*; *hyaloplasm*; *hyalotype*. Cf prec.

**hyb(o)-**: from Gr *hubos* (s *hub-*), hump-backed, perh akin to Lith *subinė* (? r *sub-*), hinder part. Exx: *Hybanthus* (cf *-anthus* at *-anth*, flower)—

'referring to the dorsa swelling' (Webster); Pal *Hybodus*, extinct sharks with 'hump-backed' teeth (cf *-odus* at *-odon*).

**hydat-**. See *hydato-*.

**hydati-**; **hydatidi-**: from *hudatis* (s *hudat-*), a watery vesicle; (*hydatidi-*) from its o/s *hudatid-*, the gen being *hudatidos*: from *hudōr* (gen *hudatos*), water: cf next entry and the 2nd *hydro-*. Exx: *hydatiform*, *hydatigenous*; *hydatidiform*.

**hydat(o)-**: Gr *hudat(o)-*, c/f of *hudōr* (gen *hudatos*), water: cf prec and the 2nd *hydro-*. Exx: *hydathode*, a waterpore, from *hudat(o)-*+Gr *hodos*, way—cf *cathode*; *hydatogenesis*, *hydatomorphic*.

**hydno-**: from Gr *hudnon* (s *hudn-*, r *hud-*), an edible fungus (? truffle), perh akin to *hudōr*, water. Ex: Bot *Hydnocarpus* (cf *-carp*).

**hydr-**. See *hydro-*.

**hydrazi-**, **hydrazo-**; **hydrazino-**: c/f, resp *hydr-*+*azi-*; *hydr-*+*azo-*; (*hydrazino-*) of hydrazine. Only in Chem.

**hydri-**: from L *Hydra*, Gr *Hudra* (itself from *hudōr*, water). Ex: *hydriform*.

**hydrio-**: from Gr *hudria*, a water (*hudōr*) jar, an urn. Ex: *Hydriotaphia*, Sir Thomas Browne's Urn Burial (cf epi*taph*).

**hydro-** (1). Incorrect for the 1st *hidro-*.

**hydro-** (2); before vowel, **hydr-**: Gr *hudr(o)-*, c/f of *hudōr*, water: for origin and cognates, see WATER. The context will determine whether *hydr(o)-* means 'water' (or 'of water') or, derivatively, 'hydrophyte' (in Bot) or 'hydrogen' (in Chem) or 'presence of (excessive or morbid) water' (in Med) or 'a hydrous compound' (in Min) or 'hydroid' (in Zoo). Exx: HYDRAULIC; *hydrocarbon*; *hydrocephalus*; *hydrochloric*; HYDROGEN; *hydromancy*; *hydropathic*; *hydroplane*; HYDROPHOBIA; *hydrosphere*; *hydrostatic*; *hydrosulphate* and *-sulphide*; *Hydrozoa*.

**-hydrous**: adj end-element, corresponding to *hydro-*, esp in orig sense 'water'. Ex: *anhydrous*, waterless (Gr *anudros*).

**hyeni-**. See *hyaeno-*.

**hyet(o)-**: Gr *huet(o)-*, c/f of *huetos* (s *huet-*), rain, akin to *hudōr*, water. Exx: *hyetography*, *hyetology*; *hyetometer*, a rain-gauge.

**hygei-**, **hygi-**, rarely **hyge-**: from Gr *hugieia*, health: cf HYGIENE. Exx: *hygeiolatry*, excessive care of one's health; *hygiology*, rarely *hygeology*, the science of hygiene.

**hygr(o)-**: Gr *hugr(o)-*, c/f of *hugros*, moisture, wet(ness), akin to *hudōr*, water: in E, denoting 'humidity'. Exx: *hygrology*, *hygrometer*, *hygrophanous*, *hygrophobia* (cf HYDROPHOBIA), *hygroscope*, *hygrostatics*.

**hyl(o)-**: Gr *hul(o)-*, c/f of *hūlē*, wood, (hence) material, matter, akin to Gr *xulon* (cf *-xylon* at *xylo-*). Exx: *hylogeny*, *hylomorphism*, *hylotheism*, *hylozoism*.

**hymeni-**, **hymenio-**: c/ff of SciL *hymenium* (from Gr *humēn*: see next), as used in Bot. Exx: *hymenicolar*, *hymeniferous*; *hymeniophore*.

**hymen(o)-**: Gr *humen(o)-*, c/f of *humēn*, mmebrane, hence, in Physio, the hymen: see HYMEN.

Exx: *hymenogeny* (cf *-geny* at *-gen*); *hymenophore* (cf *-phora*); *Hymenoptera*, Gr *humenopteros*, membrane-winged; *hymenotomy* (cf TOME).

**hymn(o)-**: Gr *humn(o)-*, c/f of *humnos*, a hymn: cf HYMN. Exx: *hymnody* (cf the 3rd *-ode*); *hymnology*.

**hyo-** (1): Gr *huo-*, c/f of *hus* (s *hu-*), a wild pig, a sow, gen *huos*, akin to Av *hu-*, a boar, Tokh *Bsuwo*, a sow, L *sūs*, E sow (n). Ex: *Hyoscyamus*, with the 2nd element=Gr *kuamos*, a bean.

**hyo-** (2); before vowel, **hy-**: Gr *hu(o)-*, c/f of Gr *Y*, upsilon (*u*). Hence, by shape-resemblance (the bone named *hyoid*, 'U-like', is shaped like the capital U), it denotes, in E cpds, 'connected, or connexion, with the hyoid bone or arch' or 'hyoid and'. Exx: *hyoglossal*; *hyomental* (L *mentum*, the chin); *hyostylic*.

**hypho-**: from Gr *huphē*, web, tissue, akin to WEB. Ex: *hyphodrome* (adj), running through the leaf-tissues—cf *-drome*.

**hypn(o)-**: Gr *hupno-*, *hupn-*, c/f of *hupnos*, sleep, akin to L *somnus* (cf INSOMNIA); IE s, *supnos* (r *sup-*+extension or modification *-n-*+ *-os*). Exx: *hypnagogic*, sleep-inducing; HYPNOSIS, adj HYPNOTIC.

**hyps(i)-; hypso-**: resp Gr *hups(i)-*, c/f of *hupsi*, on high, aloft, elevated, and Gr *hupso-*, c/f of *hupsos*, height, s *hups-*, akin to the adv and prep *huper*, over: cf OVER. Exx: *hypsicephalic*, having a lofty skull; *hypsodont*, having high-crowned teeth; *hypsography*, (description of) topographic relief; *hypsometer*; *hypsophobia*, a dread of high places— cf the syn *acrophobia*.

**hyrac(o)-**: from *hurak-*, o/s of Gr *hurax*, a shrewmouse, akin to the syn L *sōrex* (F *souris*). Exx: *Hyracodon* (cf *-odon*) and *Hyracotherium* (cf *-therium* at *-there*).

**hysteri-**: c/f of *hysteria*, as in *hysteriform*; cf:

**hyster(o)-** (1), '(connexion with) the womb'— 'hysteria'—'hysterical and': from Gr *hustera*, the womb, perh akin to the syn L *uterus* and to Skt *udáram*, belly, a hollow. Exx: *hysterocele* (*-cele*); *hystero-epilepsy*; *hysterogenic* (cf next entry); *hysterology*, the (medical) science of the womb; *hysteroscope*.

**hystero-** (2): c/f of Gr *husteros*, later, akin to Skt *uttáras*, the higher. Ex: *hysterogen(ic)*, produced later.

**hystrico-**: from *hustrik-*, c/f of Gr *hustrix* (gen *hustrikos*), a porcupine. Ex: *Hystricomorpha* (cf *-morpha* at *-morph*), a division of rodents.

**iamato-**: from *iamat-*, o/s of Gr *iama* (gen *iamatos*), medicine: cf *-iatric*. Ex: *iamatology* (cf *-logy* at *-loger*), the therapeutics of remedies.

**iambo-**: Gr *iambo-*, c/f of *iambos*, an iambus. Ex: *iambographer*, Gr *iambographos*, a writer (cf *-grapher* at *-graph*) of iambic verse.

**-iasis**: Gr *-iasis*, a process, perh from *eimi*, I go, but influenced by Gr *iāsis*, a cure; hence, in Med, a morbid process or condition, as in *elephantiasis* (adopted from Gr), the enormous enlargement of a limb, surfaced with skin hard, rough, fissured like an *elephant's* hide; *hoppychondriasis*, the patho-

logical aspect of HYPOCHONDRIA; *satyriasis* (Gr *saturiasis*: cf SATYR), constant and excessive sexual desire in the male.

**-iatric**, adj, whence the n **-iatrics**; **-iatrist**, agent; **-iatria** or **-iatry**, generic and abstract n;—**iatr(o)-**: resp Gr *iatrikos* (from *iatros*), curative, tending to heal, of healing; s *iatr-*+agential *-ist* (Suffixes); Gr *iatreia* (whence the SciL *-iatria*), medical treatment, a healing or curing;—Gr *iatro-*, c/f of *iatros*, a physician. The Gr *iatros*, whence *iatreia*, derives from *iasthai* (s *iasth-*), to heal—a modification of *iainein* (s *iain-*) to (re)animate, to warm (again), to refresh, from PGr *isaniō*, IE *isnio*, I set moving: cf Skt *işaņyáti*, he sets moving, he excites, and *işaņat*, be set moving, be excited. IE r, prob *ĭs-* or *eis-*, to stir (v.t.). (Boisacq.)

Exx: *psychiatric(al)*—cf PSYCHE; *pediatrics*, the medical care and treatment of children—cf PEDA-GOGUE; *psychiatrist*; *nestiatria* (cf *nesti-*); *psychiatry*, from SciL *psychiatria*;—*iatrochemistry*, *iatrology*, *iatrophysics*.

**Ibero-**: from L *Iberus*, Iberian, an Iberian, b/f from *Hiberes* or *Iberes*, the Iberians (Gr *Ibēres*): denotes 'Iberian (and)', as in *Ibero-Celtic*.

**ichneumoni-**, as in *ichneumoniform*, resembling an ichneumon fly, and **ichneumono-**, as in *ichneumonology*: from Gr *ikhneumōn*, 'the tracker' (see next), a mongoose, a weasel.

**ichno-**: Gr *ikhno-*, c/f of *ikhnos*, a trace or track, a footprint, a footstep: s *ikhn-*, extension of r *ikh-*, IE r *ik(h)-* or *igh-* or *eigh-*, to go. Exx: *ichnology*, the study or knowledge (cf *-logy* at *loger*) of fossil footprints; *ichnomancy*, divination (cf *-mancy*) by footprints.

**ichthy(o)-**: from Gr *ikhthus*, gen *ikhthuos*, akin to Lith *žuvis*; prob IE r, *ikhu-*. Exx: *ichthyography* and *ichthyology*, a description (cf *-graph*), the study (*-logy*), of fishes; *ichthyolatry*, fish-worship; *ichthyophagous* (cf *-phaga*), fish-eating; *ichthyosaurus*, an extinct fish-like SAURIAN. The end-element is *-ichthys*, as in *Nemichthys* (cf *-nema*).

**-icide**. As *-i-* is a mere connective, see *-cide* at *-cidal*.

**icon(o)-**: Gr *eikon(o)-*, c/f of *eikōn* (gen *eikonos*; r *eik-*), an image, app from a PGr *eik-*, to seem (cf Homeric *eike*, it seemed good), for *weik-*, as several Sl parallels indicate. Exx: *iconoclast* (cf *-clast* at *-clase*), from MGr *eikonoklastēs*, an image-breaker, hence a revolutionary, with adj *iconoclastic* and abstract n *iconoclasm*; *iconography* (Gr *eikonographia*, via ML); *iconolatry*, image-worship (cf the element *-later*); *iconometer*, a Mod Phys, Mod Surveying, Mod Photographic coinage, lit 'image-measurer'.

**icosa-; icos(i)-**: Gr *eikosa-*, *eikos(i)-*, c/ff of *eikosi*, 20, app for *weikosi*—cf L *uiginti* (ML *viginti*) and Skt *vimśatis*. Exx: *icosahedron* (Gr *eikosaedron*: cf *-hedron* at *-hedral*), a 20-sided polyhedron; *icositetrahedron*, a 24-sided polyhedron.

**ictero-**: from Gr *ikteros*, whence SciL *icterus*, jaundice, o.o.o. Exx: *icterogenetic* or *-genic*, (adj) jaundice-producing; *icteroh(a)ematuria* (*ictero-*+ *haemat-*+*-uria*). Cf:

-ictis: from Gr *iktis*, the yellow-breasted marten: Cf prec. Ex: Zoo *Galictis*, a grison (SAm mammal).

idea-. See:

ideo-: F *idéo-*, from Gr *idea*, idea: cf IDEA. Exx: *ideogeny*, (science of) the origin (cf *-geny* at *-gen*) of ideas; *ideogram*, a pictorial symbol in writing with adj *ideographic*; *ideology*, F *idéologie*; *ideophone*, an idea-conveying sound. In *ideagenous*, idea-producing (cf *-genous* at *-gen*), we have the E IDEA.

idio-: Gr *idio-*, c/f of *idios*, one's own, private, proper, peculiar: cf IDIOM. Exx: *idiocrasy* (Gr *idiokrasia*), now usu *idiosyncrasy* (Gr *idiosunkrasia*: *idio-*+*sunkrasia*, a mixing together); *idiograph*, a mark—hence a signature—peculiar to one person; *idiopathy*; *idioplasm*; *idiothermous*, where the Biochem and Med sense 'warm-blooded' occurs.

ido-: F *ido-*, from Gr *eidos*, form. Ex: *idocrase* (cf *-crase*), vesuvianite. Cf the next.—In Chem, however, *ido-*, as in *idosaccharic*, is short for *idonic(acid)*, itself=L *ī*dem, the same+gul*onic*.

idolo-: Gr *eidōl(o)-*, c/f of *eidōlon*, an image, an idol (cf IDOL), from *eidos*, form, shape. Exx: *idoloclast*, an iconoclast (cf *icono-*); *idolomania*.

-idrosis: Gr *-idrōsis*, end-c/f of *hidrōs*, sweat (cf the 1st *hidro-*). Ex: *chromidrosis*, (secretion of) morbidly coloured perspiration.

-ific, -ify. The initial *i* being merely connective, see *-fic* and *-fy*.

igneo-; igni-: resp from L *igneus*, of fire, fiery, and from its origin, *ignis*, fire: cf IGNITE. Exx: *igneo(-)aqueous*; *igniferous*, *igniform*, *ignipotent* (having power over, or mastery of, fire).

ile(o)-, ili(o)-, 'iliac and': resp c/f of *ileum* and c/f of *ilium*, varr of L *īle*, the groin, the flank (of the body), itself refashioned from the pl *īlia*, perhaps—despite the sense—akin to Gr *ilia*; IE s, ? *il-*. Exx: *ileocolic* (of the ileum and the colon); *iliocaudal*, *iliolumbar*.

illumino-, as in *illuminometer*, stands for *illumination*.

ilmeno-, in Min *ilmenorutile*=*ilmenite*.

imido-: c/f of *imide*, a Chem cpd, as in *imidogen*. Cf:

imino-: c/f of *imine*, another Chem cpd, as in *iminohydrin*.

immuno-: for *immune*, as in *immunology*, the science of medical immunity.

impari-, 'unequal': from L *impar* (*in-*, not+*par*, equal), unequal, (of numbers) odd. Exx: *imparidigitate*; *imparisyllabic*.

impedo-: for *impedance*, as in *impedometer*.

inclino-: for *incline*, as in *inclinometer*.

incud(o)-: from *incūd-*, the o/s of L *incūs* (gen *incūdis*), an anvil, applied, in An and Zoo, to bone-structure. Ex: *incudectomy*, excision of the incus.

indi-, indico-; Ind(o)-: *indi-*, short for *indico-*, c/f from L *indicum*, indigo, a product of India; *Ind(o)-*, Gr c/f of the adj *Indos*, Indian (East-Indian): cf INDIA. Exx: *indi-*, in names of pigments; *indicolite* (*indico-*+*-lite*); *Indo-Chinese*.

indolo-, in Chem only: for *indole* (*indigo*+*-ol*).

inducto-, as in *inductoscope*: for *induction*.

industro-: for *industrial*, as in *industro-chemical*.

inequi-: from L *in-*, not+*equi-*, equal. Ex: *inequipotential*. (The L negative is *iniquus*, not *inequus* or *inaequus*.)

infanti-: LL *infanti-*, c/f of L *infans* (gen *infantis*): cf INFANT. Ex: *infanticide*, LL *infanticīdium*, child-murder (cf *-cide* at *-cidal*).

infero-, 'on the under side', as in *inferobranchiate* (cf *-branch*), or 'below and', as in *inferofrontal*: a SciL c/f from L *inferus*, lower. (Webster).

infinito-: for *infinite*; as in *infinito-absolute*.

inguin(o)-: from L *inguen*, the groin, gen *inguinis*: for 'groin', as in *inguinodynia* (cf *-odynia*, pain); and for 'inguinal (L *inguinālis*) and', as in *inguinocrural*.

ino-: from Gr *is* (gen *inos*), muscle, akin to L *uīs*, ML *vīs*, force, strength. Ex: *inogenous*.

insecti-, insecto-: from L *insectum*, an insect: cf SECTION. Exx: *insecticide* (cf *-cidal*) and *insectivorous*, insect-eating; *insectology*, entomology.

inspiro-, as in *inspirometer*: for *inspire*, to inhale.

integri-, integro-: c/ff of and from L *integer*, untouched, intact—cf TACT. Exx: *integrifolious*, *integro-differential*.

intermedio-: from L *intermedius*, set in the middle: cf INTERMEDIARY. Ex: *intermedio(-)lateral*.

interno-: from L *internus*, internal: cf INTERN. Ex: *internobasal*.

intestini-, intestino-: the former, from L *intestīnum*, an intestine, the latter from E *intestine* and='intestinal and'. Exx: *intestiniform*; *intestinovesical*.

io- (1): Gr *io-*, c/f of *ion*, a violet, app from a PGr *\*wion*—cf the L *uiola* (ML *viola*). Ex: *iolite* (cf *-lite*).

io- (2), iodo-: resp c/f of *iodine* and c/f of SciL *iodum* (iodine), as in *iodoform*.

iono-: c/f of *ion* (an electrified particle: Gr *ion*. neu of *iōn*, presp of *ienai*, to go)—as in *ionogen*. Cf *ionto-*, as in *iontophoresis*, from the o/s *iont-* of *iōn*,

ipsi-, as in *ipsilateral*, on or affecting the same side (of the body): from L *ipse*, (he) himself; hence, in cpds, the same.

Irano-: for 'Iranian and', as in *Irano-Arabic*.

iri-: for *iris*, as in *iriscope*.

iridico-, c/f of *iridic*; irido- (as in *iridioplatinum*), c/f of the metallic element *iridium*; *irid(o)-*, c/f of Gr *iris* (gen *iridos*), a rainbow, hence the iris of the eye, as in *iridophore* and *iridotomy*. Cf IRIS.

irrito-: for *irritate* or *irritation*, as in the nervous state known to Physio as *irritomotility* (from *motile*, excessively mobile).

is-. See *iso-*.

isallo-=*is(o)-*+*allo-*, qq.v., as in *isallotherm* (cf *-therm*).

isat(o)-: from Gr *isatis*, woad, perh for PGr *\*wisatis*, akin to L *uitrum*, woad—cf WOAD; used as a c/f of E *isatin*, as in *isatogen*.

ischi(o)-: Gr *iskhi(o)-*, c/f of *iskhion*, hip, s *iskhi-*, where, in the light of Skt *sákthi*, the thighbone, *i-* is app prosthetic. Exx: *ischialgia*, *ischiocaudal*, *ischiovertebral*.

**isch(o)-**, 'suppression—stoppage—lack': Gr *iskh(o)-*, c/f from *iskhein* (s *iskh-*), to check or restrain, a freq of *ekhein* (s *ekh-*), to have, to hold. Exx: *ischury* (cf *-uria*), retention of urine; *ischocholia*, deficiency in the bile (cf *chole-*).

**ischy(o)-**: from Gr *iskhus* (gen *iskhuos*), strength, prob akin to *ekhein* (s *ekh-*), to have, to hold (cf prec). Ex: *Ischyodus* (cf *-odus* at *-odon*).

**isidi-**: c/f of *isidium* (from *Isis*), as in *isidiferous* or *-phorous*.

**is(o)-**: Gr *iso-*, c/f of *isos* (s *is-*), equal, prob from PGr *\*wisos* and akin to Skt *visu-*, equally. Exx: *isagon* (Gr *isogōnios*); *isandrous* (cf *andro-*); *isobar* (cf *-bar*); *isochronal* or *-chronous*; *isomeric, isomerous* (cf *-mer*); *isomorphic* (cf *-morph*); *isosceles*, lit 'equal-legged', Gr *isoskelēs* (*skelos, leg*); *isotherm* (cf THERM); *isotope* (Gr *topos*, a place).

**istio-**: irreg from Gr *histion*, a sail (cf *histio-*); as in *Istiophorous* (cf *-phorus* at *-phora*), the genus of sailfishes and marlins.

**Ital(o)-**, 'Italian and': from L *Italus*, Italian—cf ITALIAN. Ex: *Italo-Greek, Italomania*.

**itho-; ithy-**: both (the former irreg, the latter= Gr *ithu-*) from Gr *īthus*, straight, perh akin to Skt *sādhus*, even, upright; as in Zoo *ithomiinae* (2nd element, ? Gr *ōmos*, the shoulder) and in *ithyphallic*.

**ja-.** See *jateo-*.

**jaculi-**: from ML *jaculum*, L *iaculum*, a dart, from *iacere*, to throw. Ex: *jaculiferous* (cf *-ferous* at *-fer*).

**jani-, Jani-**: as in *janiceps*, a monster with two fused heads (L *caput*, head), opposite-facing, and *Janiform*, two-faced, as was ML *Jānus*, L *Iānus*, the spirit or quasi-god of *iānuae* or gates and doors —cf JANITOR.

**Japano-**: c/f of *Japan*, as in *Japanology, Japanophile, Japanophobe*.

**jaspi-; jaspo-**: the former from E *jasper*, the latter from Gr *iasp(o)-*, c/f of *iaspis* (Sem in origin), whence, via L *iaspis*, ML *jaspis*, and OF *jaspe, jaspre*, and ME *jaspe* and *jaspre*, the Mod E word. Exx: *jaspilite* (cf *-lite*) and *jasponyx* (Gr *iasponux*: cf *-onyx* at *-onycha*).

**jateo-**, occ **jato-**: from Gr *iatēs* (usu *iatēr*), a physician, cf *-iatric*. Exx: *Jateorhiza*, a genus of woody vines, and *jat(e)orhizine*, an alkaloid derivative—cf *-rhiza*, -root.
There is a shortened form: *ja-*, as in *Jatropha* (adj *jatrophic*), an Am genus of herbs yielding medicinal oils: cf *-trophia*, from Gr *trophē*, nourishment.

**[-ject**, as in *abject, conjecture, dejected, eject, inject, object, project, reject, subject, trajectory*: ML *-jectus*, L *-iectus*, pp of *-icere*, the c/f of *iacere*, ML *jacere*, to throw or cast.]

**jejun(o)-**: c/f of 'the *jejunum*' or middle division of the small intestine, from ML *jējūnus*, L *iēiūnus*, empty or dry, whence the E adj *jejune*, akin to *iēientāre*, to break one's fast. Ex: *jejunotomy*.

**Jesuito-**: for *Jesuit*, as in *Jesuitocracy*, rule by Jesuits. (Cf JESUS.)

**joco-**, as in *joco-serious*, stands for E *jocose*.

**jolli-.** See *jollification* at JOLLY.

**jovi-**, 'the planet Jupiter': from ML *Jovis*, L *Iovis*, the gen of *Jupiter*: cf JOVE. Ex: Astr *jovilabe*, cf *-labe*.

**Judaeo-**, mod **Judeo-**: from Gr *Ioudaios*, Judaean, and ML *Judaei*, the Jews. Denoting either 'the Jews' (or 'Judaism'), as in *Jud(a)eophile*, or 'Jewish and', as in *Jud(a)eo-Arabic*. Cf JEW. Occ, the irreg *Judo-*, as in *Judophobism*, a dread of (the) Jews—loosely, anti-Semitism.

**Jugo-** or **Yugo-**: Serbo-Croatian *jugo-*, c/f of *jug*, the south wind, from OSl *jugŭ*. Ex: *Jugoslavia*, from *Jugoslav* (cf *Slav* at SLAVE).

**junci-**, as in *junciform*, rush-like: from ML *juncus*, L *iuncus*, a rush (plant), perh akin to *iungere*, to join.

**juris-**: ML *jūris* (L *iūris*), gen of *jūs* (L *iūs*), law—cf JUST. Exx: *jurisconsult*, L *iūrisconsultus*, a man skilled in the law (cf CONSULT); *jurisdiction*, L *iūrisdictiōn-*, o/s of *iūrisdictiō* (cf DICTION); *jurisprudence*, L *iūrisprūdentia* (cf PRUDENCE).

**justi-.** See *justify* at JUST.

**kak(o)-.** A rare var of *caco-*, bad; as in *kakidrosis*, which=*kak(o)-*+Gr *hidr(ōs)*, sweat+suffix *-osis*. Cf:

**kakisto-**: from Gr *kakistos*, worst, sup of *kakos* (cf prec). Ex: *kakistocracy* (cf *-cracy*), rule, control, government, by the worst people.

**kali-**, as in *kaliform, kaligenous* (cf *-genous* at *gen*): *kali* (Ar *qili*), short for ALKALI.

**kal(o)-.** See *calo-* at *calli-*. Ex: *kaleidoscope* (adj *-scopic*), which=*kal(o)-*+Gr *eido(s)*, form+*-scope*.

**karyo-.** See *caryo-*. Ex: *karyogenesis* (cf GENESIS).

**katharo-**: from Gr *katharos*, pure, akin to *katharsis*, E *catharsis*, purification, from *kathairein*, to cleanse: *kath-*, q.v. at prefix *cata-*+*hairein*, to take (away). Ex: *katharometer* (cf *-meter*), used in determining the composition of a gas.

**kel-.** A rare frontal form, answering to *-cele*. Ex: *kelectomy* (cf *-ectomy* at *-tome*).

**ken(o)-.** See the 2nd *ceno-*.

**kentro-**: from Gr *kentron*, a point—cf *centri-*. Ex: *kentrolite* (cf *-lite*).

**kera-, kerato.** See *-cera*.

**kerauno-.** See *cerauno-*. Ex: *keraunograph*.

**kero-**: from Gr *kēros* (s *kēr-*), wax, akin to L *cēra*. Exx: *kerogen* (cf *-gen*) and *kerosene* (cf the Chem suffix *-ene*).

**keto-**: c/f of *ketone* (G *Keton*, aphetic for F *acétone*: cf ACID+Chem suffix *-one*). Ex: *ketogenesis*.

**kilo-**: adopted from F, from Gr *khilioi*, 1000, akin to L *mille*. Exx: *kilocycle, kilogram(me), kilometre* (or *-meter*), *kilowatt*.

**kinesi-**; 2, **-kinesia**; 3, **-kinesis**; 4, **-kinetic**; 5, **kineto-**; 6, **kin(o)-**: resp Gr *kinēsi-*, c/f of *kinēsis*, movement; 2, Gr-*kinēsia*, end-element from *kinēsis*; 3, Gr *kinēsis*; 4, *-kinetic*, c/f of *kinetic*, from Gr *kinētikos*, of or by movement; 5, from Gr *kinētos*, moving (lit, moved), *kinētos* being the pp of *kinein*, s *kin-*, to move; 6, *kino-* derives from *kinein*.
The s *kin-* is an extension of *ki-*, s of *kiein*, to go;

IE r, *ki or *qi, cf the -ci- of L accītus, a summons, cf acciēre, to summon (ad+cīre or ciēre). (Hofmann.)

Exx: kinesimeter, a movement-measuring instrument; hyperkinesia or -kinesis, an unduly or abnormally increased movement (of the muscles); chemokinesis, an activity, increased by a chemical agent, of free-moving organisms, with adj chemokinetic; kinetogenic, tending to originate, or in fact originating, movement—cf kinetogenesis, dynamic(al) evolution; kinology, kinoplasm (cf -plasm), kinospore (cf -spora).
Cf the entry at cine-.

-klept; klepto-: Gr kleptēs, a thief; Gr klepto-, c/f of kleptēs, denoting, in E, either 'thief' or usu 'theft': either deriving from or intimately akin to kleptein (s klept-), to steal, akin to L clepere, to steal, and Go hlifan and E lift. Exx: biblioklept, a book-thief; kleptomania, a mania for, and kleptophobia, a dread of, theft.

kono-. See coni(o)- at conidio-.

-kont, denoting in Bot 'flagellum' (a cell's whip-like process): Gr kontos (s kont-), a pole or staff, from or akin to kenteō (s kent-), I prick; cognates in Celtic and elsewhere; IE r, *kent-, to prick.

krato-. A var, now rare, of crato-, q.v. at -crat.

krit(o)-: from Gr kritēs, a discerner, critic, judge: cf CRITIC. Ex: kritarchy (cf -archy), the Judges' government of Israel.

kryo-. A var of cryo-.

krypto-. A rare var of crypto-.

kymo-. See, at cymi-, the now much-preferred cymo-.

kypho-. See cypho-.

kyto-. Now rare for -cyto, q.v. at -cyte.


-labe, 'implement or instrument': Gr -labon, '(anything) that handles', c/f of labon, neu of labōn, presp of lambanein, to grasp, to take: lamb- (nasalized lab-)+-an-, extension or modification+ -ein, inf suffix: IE r, *lab(h)-. Ex: astrolabe, (lit) a star-grasper—it determines the positions of stars (cf astro- at -aster); hence jovilabe, q.v. at jovi-. Cf labido-.

labe-: L labe-, c/f of labāre, to totter, freq(?) of lābī, to slip, to fall. Ex: labefy, to weaken (v.t.), from L labefacere, pp labefactus, whence the rare adj labefact, weakened, and the rare v labefact, to labefy. Cf LAPSE.

labid(o)-: from labid-, o/s of Gr labis (gen labidos), a pair of forceps (cf -labe). Exx: labidophorous (cf -phorous at -phora), bearing—hence, possessing—organs resembling forceps; Labidura (cf -ura), a genus of earwigs.

labio-: from L labium, usu in pl; akin to L labra, lips, and to E LIP. It denotes either 'lips', as in labiograph and labiomancy (lip-reading), labioplasty, or 'labial (ML labiālis, of the lip or lips) and', as in labiodental, labionasal, labiovelar.

labro-: from Gr labros, fierce, perh akin to lab-, the aorist s of lambanein: cf -labe; as in Labrosaurus, a ferocious dinosaur.

labyrinthi-, labyrintho-: the former from L labyrinthus, the latter from its source, the Gr laburinthos: cf LABYRINTH.

lacerti-, as in lacertiform: from L lacerta, a lizard: cf LIZARD.

lachn(o)-: from Gr lakhnē (or lakhnos), soft fine hair, down. Exx: Bot Lachnanthes (cf -anth, flower); Zoo Lachnosterna (cf sterno-).

lachrymi-, lachrymo-: from L lacrima, earlier lacruma for dacruma, akin to Hellenistic Gr dakruma, with cognates in several IE languages; IE r, *dakru-. The spelling lachryma is faulty, but at one time common, as in Lachryma Christi, from ML. Exx: lachrymiform, tear-shaped; lachrymogenic (-genic, q.v. at -gen), lachrymonasal. Cf lachrymatory (suffix -atory) and lachrymose (L lacrimōsus).

lacini-, as in laciniform: from L lacīnia, a lappet, app akin to L lacer, torn, lacerated.

laco-: from Gr lakkos, a pond or a tank: cf LAKE. Ex: Lacosomatidae, which=laco-+somat(o), q.v. at -soma+suffix -idae.

lacti-; lact(o)-: LL lacti-, c/f of L lac (gen lactis), milk, akin to Gr gala, gen galaktos, cf GALAXY; lacto-, by analogy with other -o- c/ff. Exx: lactiferous, milk-yielding, and lactific, milk-producing; lactoscope, lactovegetarian.

laemo-. See the 1st lemo-.

laeo-, '(to) the left': from Gr laios (s lai-), left on the left, akin to L laeuus (ML laevus). Ex: laeotropic, sinistral.

laevo-. See levo-.

-lagnia, only in Med and Psy: from Gr lagneia, coïtion, lust, from lagnos, lustful, akin to Gr lagaros, relaxed, languorous, and L languēre, to be languorous, emotionally relaxed. Ex: osmolagnia (cf osmo- at -osma).

lag(o)-: Gr lag(o)-, c/f of lagōs, a hare, lit 'the slack-eared'—cf lagaros, slack, flabby, and ous, ear. Exx: lagophthalmos (or -mus), inability of eye(s) to fully close—'from the notion that a hare sleeps with his eyes open' (Webster); lagopodous, hare-footed (cf -pod); lagostoma, hare-lip (cf -stoma).

laimo-. See the 1st lemo-.

-lalia; lalo-: both adopted from Gr: from Gr lalia, talk, chatter, prattle, and lalos, babbling, prattle, akin to L lallāre, to prattle, and deriving, ult, from exclamatory la-la—cf lullaby at LULL. Exx: Eulalia, (she of the) fair speech; in Med, denoting a (specified kind of) speech-disorder, as in bradylalia, excessively slow or sluggish (cf brady-) speech; laloneurosis, a speech-neurosis; laloplegia, loss (-plegia)—through paralysis—of the power to speak.

lamelli-, 'lamellate' (consisting of thin layers, sheets, leaves, plates): from L lamella, dim of lamina, sheet, leaf—cf next. Exx: lamellicorn, a beetle with plated antennae; lamelliferous; lamelliform.

lamin(i)-: from L lāmina, sheet or thin layer (usu of metal), hence a flake, a plate; perh akin to ON lamar, a hinge. Exx: laminiferous, laminiform, laminiplantar (-plantar). Cf prec.

lampade-: Gr *lampadē-*, c/f of *lampas* (gen *lampados*), a torch: cf next. Ex: *lampadephore* (Gr *lampadēphoros*), torch-bearer (cf *-phora*).

lampr(o)-: Gr *lampr(o)-*, c/f of *lampros*, shining, bright, clear—cf LAMP. Exx: *lamprophony*, clear ringing speech; *lamprophyre* (*-phyre*), basalt containing bright flakes. Cf prec.

lanci-: for *lance*; as in *lanciform*, lance-shaped.

lani-; lan(o)-: L *lani-*, E *lano-* on Gr model: c/ff of L *lāna*, wool, akin to Doric Gr *lanos*, Attic *lēnos*—to Av *varna-* (Skt *ū́rṇā*)—and to OSl *vlŭna*. Exx: *laniferous*, from L *lānifer*, and *lanific*, from L *lānificus*; *lanoceric* (cf *ceri-*) and *lanolin* (*lan-+-ol-* +Chem suffix *-in*, *-ine*). Cf *delaine*, from F *de laine*, of wool.

lanthan(o)-; lantho-: from Gr *lanthanein* (s *lanthan-*, r *lanth-*, IE r *lat-*), to lie hidden: cf LATENT. Ex: *Lanthanotus*; *lanthopine*.

lapar(o)-, 'the flank, (loosely) the abdominal wall' (Med and Surg): from Gr *lapara*, the flank (a hollow part of the body), akin to Gr *lapathos*, a hollow, a cavity. Exx: *laparoscopy*, *laparotomy* and *laparectomy*.

lapidi-: from *lapid-*, o/s of L *lapis* (gen *lapidis*), a stone; *lapis* is o.o.o. Exx: *lapidicolous*, living (cf *-colous*) under stones; *lapidiferous*, from L *lapidifer*, stone-bearing; *lapidific* (cf *-fic*). Cf di*lapid*ate.

lapilli-, as in *lapilliform*: from L *lapillus*, dim of *lapis*—cf prec.

largi-, as in *largifical*, generous (cf *-fical* at *-fic*): L *largi-*, c/f of *largus*, abundant: cf LARGE.

laryng(o)-: adopted from Gr, c/f of *larunx* (gen *larungos*), the larynx, orig echoic. Exx: *laryngo-graph*, *laryngology*, *laryngoscope*.

-later; -latria or -latry; -latrous: resp Gr *-latrēs*, worship, via L *-latria* and then, for E *-latry*, via F *-latrie*; *latr-+*E adj suffix *-ous*. Exx: *bibliolater*, *bibliolatry*, *bibliolatrous*, cf *biblio-*; *idolater*, *idolatry*, *idolatrous*, cf IDOL.

lateri-, latero-: c/ff, the latter in Sci only, of L *latus* (gen *lateris*), side, perh akin to L *lātus*, wide, broad. Exx: *latericumbent*, lying on one's or its side; *laterifloral*, having lateral flowers; *laterigrade*, sideways-running, as do crabs and certain spiders; —*latero-abdominal*, *lateroposition*, *laterotorsion*.

lati-: L *lāti-*, c/f of *lātus*, wide, broad: cf LATI-TUDE. Exx: *laticlave* (LL *lāticlāuus*, ML *-clāvus*), a broad stripe; *laticostate*, broad-ribbed; *lātifundium* (L), a large country estate.

latici-: from L *latex*, a fluid, gen *laticis*, perh akin to Gr *latax*. Ex: *laticiferous*, bearing latex in its Bot sense.

-latrous; -latry. See *-later*.

lauri-, 'laurel'; laur(o)-, 'lauric acid' (derived from laurel berries): from L *laurus* (s *laur-*), laurel: cf LAUREL. Ex: *laurotetanine* (cf TETANUS).

laxi-, 'loose', hence 'scattered', as in *laxiflorous*: from L *laxus*, loose—cf LAX.

lecan(o)-: from Gr *lekanē* (later, *lak-*), akin to syn L *lanx* (gen *lancis*): IE r, perh *lek-*, to bend or bow, to curve or be curved. Ex: *lecanomancy*, divination (*-mancy*) by basin-water, and *lecano-scopy*, a fixed gazing at basin-water.

lechri(o)-: from Gr *lekhrios*, oblique; IE r *(e)lek-*. Ex: *Lechriodonta*, a genus of salamanders with teeth (cf *-odon*) set obliquely.

-lecithal; lecith(o)-: c/f of *lecithal*, having a yolk; and of *lecithin*, which=*lecith(al)*+the Chem suffix *-in*; *lecithal* comes from Gr *lekithos*, a yolk—app a term imported into Gr. Exx: *homolecithal*, having a uniformly (cf *homo-*) distributed yolk; *lecitho-protein*.

leco-: from Gr *lekos*, a dish, akin to L *lanx*, a plate. Ex: *lecotropal* (cf *-tropal*), shaped like a horseshoe.

lecto-, as in *lectotype*: from Gr *lektos*, chosen, pp of *legein*, to pick, to select: cf the *-lect* in *collect*, *elect*, *select*, and the c/ff *-lege* (2) and *-lexia*.

-lege (1), as in *privilege*, comes from L *lex*, a law, gen *legis*, o/s *leg-*; cf LEGAL.

-lege (2), as in *florilege* and *sacrilege*, comes from L *legere* (s *leg-*), to gather—cf LEGEND for cognates. Thus, *florilegium* or (cf F *florilège*) *florilege*, from L *florilegus*, (lit) flower-culling, (hence) an anthology, the L term being, indeed, prompted by Gr *anthologia*; and *sacrilege*, adopted from OF, from L *sacrilegium*, from *sacrilegus*, a gatherer—hence, a stealer—of sacred things.

legi-, lego-: from L *lēx* (gen *lēgis*), law: cf LEGAL. Exx: *legific* (cf *-fic*), law-making; *lego-literary*.

leio-, occ lio-: from Gr *leios* (s *lei-*), smooth, IE s *lei-*, smooth. Exx: *leiodermatous*, smooth-skinned (cf *-derm*); *Leiotrichi*, the smooth-haired peoples (cf *-trichia*).

-lemma; lemmo-: c/ff from Gr *lemma*, rind, husk, app for *lep+-ma*, n-suffix: IE r *lep-*, to remove the rind or husk from, occurs in Gr *lepein* (s *lep-*), to peel, to husk. Exx: as 'sheath' in An *axilemma* (cf *axi-*); as 'neurilemma' (outer sheath of a nerve-fibre) in *lemmocyte* (cf *-cyte*). Cf *lepido-*.

lemo- (1); earlier laemo-, L form; earliest, laimo-, Gr form: Gr *laimo-*, c/f of *laimos*, the gullet (esophagus), s *laim-*, perh an extension of IE r *lei-*. Ex: *laemo(-)paralysis*.

lemo- (2). A var of *loimo-*, q.v.

lemuri-, as in *lemuriform*, lemur-like: cf LEMUR.

leni-: L *lēni-*, c/f of *lēnis*, soft, mild, s *lēn-*, cf LENIENT. Exx: *lenify*, to soften; in Pharm it denotes 'lenitive'.

lenti-: from L *lens* (gen *lentis*), a lentil; hence, in E, it denotes either 'lentil', as in *lentiform*, or derivatively 'lens' (cf LENS), as in *lentigerous*.

leon-, leont(o)-: c/ff of Gr *leōn* (gen *leontos*), a lion—cf LION. Exx: *Leonotis*, a SciL term from *leōn+ous* (gen *ōtos*), ear; *leontiasis*, leprosy rendering the face leonine in appearance and size—cf *-iasis* above; *leontocephalous*, lion-headed.

lepid(o)-: Gr *lepid(o)-*, c/f of *lepis*, a scale, gen *lepidos*; IE r, *lep-*, to peel or husk: cf *-lemma*. Exx: *lepidolite*, a scaly mica (cf *-lite*); *Lepidoptera* (cf *-ptera*), butterflies and moths, usu scaly-winged— hence *lepidopterology*. Cf:

lepo-: from Gr *lepos*, a rind or husk or scale: cf prec and *-lemma*. Exx: *lepocyte* (*-cyte*)—*lepospon-dylous* (Gr *spondulos*, a vertebra)—*lepothrix* (cf *-thrix*).

**lepori-**: from *lepor-*, the o/s of L *lepus*, a hare. Ex: *leporiform*.

**lepr(o)-**: c/f of Gr *lepra*, leprosy—cf LEPER. Ex: *leprology*.

**-lepsia, -lepsis, -lepsy; -lept; -leptic**: -*lepsia* is the SciL (from Gr *-lepsia*), *-lepsis* a Grecized form (the Gr being *-lēpsis*), *-lepsy* (via F *-lepsie*) the E form, denoting 'a seizure'; *-lept*, n from Gr pa *-lēptos*; *-leptic*, adj,=*-lept*+suffix *-ic*. From or akin to Gr *lambanein* (cf *-labe*). Exx: *catalepsis* (prefix *cata-*), now *catalepsy*, from Gr *katalēpsis*—*catalept*, from Gr *katalēptos*, seized—*cataleptic*, LL *catalēpticus*, Gr *katalēptikos*; *nympholepsia*, *nympholepsy* = *nympho-*+ *-lepsy*—*nympholept*, n from Gr *numpholēptos*, caught or seized by nymphs —hence, *nympholeptic*.

**lept(o)-**: Gr *lept(o)-*, c/f of *leptos* in senses 'small, weak, delicate, thin, fine': s *lept-*, perh an extension or modification of IE *lep-*: ? cf L *lepidus*, graceful; but cf *lepo-*. Exx: *leptocephalus*, one who has an exceptionally narrow skull (cf *cephalo-*); *leptodermous*, thin-skinned (*-derm*); *leptometer*, used in oil-testing; *leptotene* (*-tene*).

**-less** stands midway between suffix and element. Here the *less* it represents is the adj LESS: OE *-lēas*, from independent *lēas*, akin to E LOSE. Exx: from nn, *childless*, *witless*—*countless*: from vv, *ceaseless*, *dauntless*, *tireless*.

**-lestes; lesto-**: from Gr *leistēs*, a robber, akin to *leia*, booty, L *lucrum*, profit, and Skt *lótram*, booty. Exx: Zoo, Pal *Caenolestes* (cf *caeno-* at *ceno-*), a genus of carnivorous marsupials; *lestobiosis* (*lesto-*+ *bi(o)-*+ suffix *-osis*), emphasizing theft of food.

**lethi-**, as in *lethiferous* (L *lēthifer*, for *lētifer*), death-bringing: from L *lētum*, death: o.o.o.

**letho-**: Gr *lētho-*, c/f of *lēthē*, forgetfulness—cf LETHE. In E cpds it denotes 'forgetting', as in *lethologica*, a strong tendency to forget words.

**Letto-**, 'Lettish and': for *Lett*, as in *Letto-Slavic*.

**leuc(o)-**: Gr *leuk(o)-*, c/f of *leukos*, white, s *leuk-*, akin to L *lūc-*, o/s of *lūx*, light, and s of *lūcet*, it is light: cf LUCID. Exx: *leucanthous*, white-flowered (cf *-anth*); *leucocyte* (*-cyte*), a white blood-corpuscle; *leucophanite* (cf *-phane*), a mineral having glass-like crystals; *leucorrh(o)ea*.

**leur(o)-**: from Gr *leuros*, smooth, s *leur-*. Only in Zoo generic names.

**levo-**, mod form of **laevo-**: from ML *laevus*, L *laeuus*, akin to Gr *laios* (cf *laeo-*), situated on the left. Denoting 'on or to the left' (in Chem, 'levorotatory'), it occurs in, e.g., *l(a)evoduction*—*l(a)evo-rotation* (adj, *-rotatory*), rotation to the left (anti-clockwise); *l(a)evoversion*.

**-lexia; lexi-**: from Gr *lexis*, speech, from *legein*, to speak (s *leg-*). The former occurs only in Med and Psy, as in *bradylexia*; the latter in e.g. *lexigraphy*, the art of defining words, and *lexiphanic* (cf *-phane*), bombastic. Cf:

**lexico-**: Gr *lexiko-*, c/f of *lexikon*, a vocabulary, elliptical for *lexikon biblion*, a word-book; *lexikon*, is the neu of *lexikos*, the adj of *lexis*—therefore cf prec.

**libero-; liberti-**: c/f of *liberating*, adj, and of *liberty*; cf LIBERAL. Exx: *libero-motor*, adj; *liberticide*.

**libo-**: irreg for *libano-*, from Gr *libanos*, a frankincense tree. Ex: *Libocedrus* (Gr *kedros*, cedar).

**libri-**: from L *liber* (gen *libri*), a book, (orig) inner bark, hence bast. Ex: *libriform*. Cf LIBEL.

**libro-**: from L *līber* (gen *līberi*), free. Ex: *liberoplast* (cf *-plast* at *-plasm*).

**Libyo-**: from *Libya*, itself from Gr *Libuē*, it denotes 'Libyan and'. Ex: *Libyo-Phoenician*.

**licheni-, lichn(o)-**: c/ff of *lichen*, as in *lichenivorous*, lichen-eating, and *lichenology*.

**lichno-**: from Gr *likhnos*, greedy, akin to Skt *lédhi*, to lick, and nasalized L *lingere*; IE r, *ligh-* or *lig-*. Ex: Zoo *Lichnophora* (cf *-phora*).

**lien(o)-**: from L *liēn*, the spleen, akin (? by psilosis) to L *splēn*, from Gr *splēn*: cf SPLEEN. Ex: *lienogastric*, of the spleen and stomach.

**ligni-, lign(o)-**: from L *lignum*, wood, s, *lign*-modification of *lig-*, from IE *leg-*, to gather: cf LEGEND. Exx: *ligniferous*, *lignivorous*; *lignography*, wood-engraving.

**liguli-**, 'ligulate' (strap-shaped): c/f of *ligule*, a strap, L *ligula*, ? confused with *lingula*, a little *lingua* or tongue, e.g. of leather. Ex: *liguliflorous*.

**-like** (cf *-less*) stands midway between element and suffix: ult of the same origin as the adj LIKE. Cf *-ful* (here treated as a suffix) for FULL.

**lili-**: c/f of LILY; cf the *lili-* of L *līliētum*, a lily-garden. Ex: *liliform*.

**limaci-**: from L *limāx* (gen *limācis*), a slug. Ex: *limaciform*. Perh cf:

**limbi-**: from L *limbus*, hem or border: cf LIMBO. Ex: *limbiferous*.

**limi- (1); limo-**: L *līmi-*, c/f of *līmus*, mud, s *līm-*, IE r *lei-* (cf Gr *leimōn*, a wet field, a water meadow); *limo-*, app from Gr *limo-* for *leimo-*, from *leimōn*. Exx: *limicolous* (cf *-colous*), living in mud, and *limnivorous*, mud-eating; Bot *Limodorum*, Gr *l(e)imodoron*, 'gift of the water meadow'.

**limi- (2)**, loose for *limito-*, LL *līmito-*, *līmi-*, c/ff of L *līmes*, as in *limitrophe*, adopted from F, from LL *līmitrophus*, from regular *līmitotrophus*, a hybrid of L *līmes*, a boundary, gen *līmitis* (cf LIMIT) and Gr *-trophos*, from *trephein*, to nourish.

**limn(i)-**, loose for **limn(o)-**: Gr *limn(o)-*, c/f of *limnē*, pool, marshy lake, marsh—perh cf *limi-* (1). Exx: *limnobiology*, the science of freshwater life; *limnimeter*, better *limnometer*, an instrument measuring lake-levels; *limnology*; *limnophilous*.

**limo-**. See the 1st *limi-*.

**linei-, lineo-**, 'line'—as in *lineiform*, *lineograph*, and 'linear and'—as in *lineocircular*: from L *līnea*, line: cf LINE.

**lingui-; linguli-; linguo-**: c/f from L *lingua*, the tongue; (*linguli-*) c/f from *lingula*, its dim; (*linguo-*) irreg E c/f of *lingua*, used to denote either 'the tongue' or 'lingual and' or 'lingually': cf LINGUAL. Exx: *linguipotence*, mastery of languages; *linguiform*; *linguopalatal*.

**lino- (1)**: c/f of E *line*, as in *linometer* and *linotype*.

**lino-** (2): c/f from L *līnum* (s *līn*-: cf LINEN), flax, as in *Linanthus* (cf *-anth*, -flower) and *linoleum*.

**lio-.** See *leio-*.

**lipar(o)-**: Gr *lipar(o)-*, c/f of *liparos*, oily, fatty, from *lipos*, fat, s *lip-*, perh from an IE r *\*leip-*, to smear. Ex: *liparocele*. Cf:

**lip(o)-** (1): Gr *lip(o)-*, c/f of *lipos*, fat: see prec. Exx: *lipocardiac*, *lipogenetic*.

**lipo-** (2): Gr *lipo-*, c/f of *leipesthai* (s *leip-*), to be lacking, cf *leipein*, to leave, abandon, to fail (v.t.); aorist s, *-lip-*; IE r, perh *\*leik-* or *\*lik-*, nasalized in L *linquere* (s *linq-*). Exx: *lipogram*, a writing, a word, not possessing a certain letter, cf *lipography*, writing or word from which a letter or a syllable has been unwittingly omitted; *lipotype*, a plant, an animal, of a type always absent from a region; *lipoxenous* (in Bot), host-deserting (cf *xeno-*).

**lipsano-**: from Gr *leipsanon*, a relic (something left behind: cf the 2nd *lipo-*). Exx: *lipsanographer*, *lipsanotheca* (cf *-theca*).

**lique-; liqui-**: c/f from L *liquēre*, to be liquid, as in *liquefy* (cf *-fy*); (*liqui-*) rare and irregular, as in *liquiform*, for E *liquid* or L *liquidus*: cf LIQUID. The rare *liquido-* merely represents E *liquid*, as in *liquidogenous*, liquid-forming.

**lirelli-**: from *lirella*, a SciL dim from L *līra*, a furrow—cf DELIRIUM. Ex: Bot *lirelliform*.

**lirio-**: from Gr *leirion*, a lily: cf LILY. Ex: *Liriodendron* (cf *dendra*).

**liro-**: from Gr *leiros* (s *leir-*), pale: IE r, perh *\*lei-*. Ex: the Min *liroconite* (cf *conio-* at *conidio-*).

**liss(o)-**: from Gr *lissos*, smooth, cf syn *lispos*, *lisphos*: IE r, ? *\*lis-*. Exx: Bio *Lissencephala* (*liss-* + Gr *enkephalos*, the brain); *lissotrichous*, straight-haired (cf *tricho-*).

**-lite,** n, and its adj **-litic; -lith,** n, and adj **-lithic; lith(o)-**: F *-lite*, for *-lithe*, from Gr *lithos*, a stone, whence, occ via F *-lithe*, the E *-lith*, whence (prompted by Gr *lithikos*, stony) *-lithic*; *lith(o)-*, adopted from Gr; IE s, prob *\*lith-*. Exx: *dendrolite*, a fossil plant (cf *dendro-*); *monolith* (*mono-*), *monolithic; litharge*, via OF from L *lithargyrus*, from Gr *litharguros* (Gr *arguros*, silver); *lithogenesis; lithography*, the art of writing or designing on stone; *lithology; lithophagous* (cf *-phaga*); *lithotomy; lithotype*.

**lithio-**: for *lithium* (from *lithos*): see prec.

**litho-.** See *-lite*.

**liti-**: SciL c/f from Gr *litos*, smooth, plain, straightforward, akin to Gr *leios*, smooth, even, L *leuis*; IE r, *\*lei-*. Ex: Zoo *Litiopa* (Gr *opē*, an opening). Also *lito-*, from *litos*; as in Pal *Litopterna* (Gr *pterna*, heel).

**-litic.** See *-lite*.

**lito-.** See *liti-*.

**litui-**: from L *lituus*, a curved staff, and for Math *lituus*. Ex: *lituiform*.

**liturgio-**: for E *liturgy* or LL *līturgia*; esp *liturgiology*.

**-lobate(d), lobato-; lobi-, lobo-, -lobus**: c/ff of *lobate*, having or resembling lobes; (*lobi-*) c/f of SciL *lobus* (whence obviously *-lobus*), from Gr

*lobos*, whence *lobo-*: cf LOBE. Exx: *equilobate*; *lobato-digitate; lobiped; lobotomy; Gonolobus.*

**lochio-**: c/f of *lochia* (Med), from Gr *lokhia*, n from neu pl of *lokhios*, of or in childbirth: akin to LIE, to be prostrate. Ex: *lochiorrh(o)ea*.

**loco-**: from L *locus*, a place, cf LOCAL. Exx: *locodescriptive; locomotive*, (something) that moves from place to place.

**-log.** An Am var of *-logue*, q.v. at *-loger*.

**logarithmo-**: c/f of *logarithm* (cf *arithmetic*), lit 'an account', hence 'an indicator' of number. Cf: 1, **-loger;** 2, **-logia;** 3, **-logian;** 4, **-logic(al);** 5, **-logist;** 6, **-logue;** 7, **-logy;** 8, **log(o)-:** 1, L *-logus* (or *-logia*)+agential suffix *-er*, as in *chronologer* (cf *chrono-* at *-chrone*) and *philologer*; 2, L *-logia*, from or after Gr *-logia*, from *legein*, to speak (cf LOGIC), as in *apologia*; 3, E suffix *-an* added to L or Gr *-logia*, as in *philologian* and *theologian*; 4, Gr *-logikos* (often via L *-logicus*), the adj corresponding to *-logia* (but itself paralleling Gr *logikos*), as in *astrological*, *geologic(al)*, *philological*, *theological*; 5, *-log(y)*+agential suffix *-ist*, as in *geologist* and *philologist*; 6, via F from L *-logus* or direct from Gr *-logos*, as in *dialogue*, but now esp as in *travelogue*; 7, F *-logie*, from or after L *-logia*, itself from or after Gr *-logia*—cf (2) above—as in *astrology, geology, philology, theology*, although in, e.g., *martyrology* (ML *martyrologium*), the origin is L *-logium*, from or after Gr *-logion*, as in *seismologion*, whence, ult, *seismology*; 8, *logo-* or, before a vowel, *log-*: Gr *log(o)-*, c/f of *logos*, word, speech or a discourse, thought, from *legein*, to say, as in *logodaedaly* (Gr *logodaidalia*), verbal trick, 'jeu de mots'—*logograph*, a riddle (Gr *griphos*, fishing-net, hence—through difficulty of freeing oneself from one—a riddle)—*logorrh(o)ea*, a flow of words—*logotype*.

**loimo-**: Gr *loimo-*, c/f of *loimos* (s *loim-*), a plague, hence (in E) a pestilence, prob akin to Gr *limos*, hunger. Ex: *loimology*.

**lonch(o)-**: Gr *lonkh(o)-*, c/f of *lonkhē*, a lance ('the *long* [weapon]'). Ex: *Lonchocarpus*. Cf:

**longi-; longo-**: resp L *longi-*, c/f of *longus*, long, and *longo-*, app only in LL *Longobardi*. Exx: *longicorn* (L *cornu*, horn), long-horned, or -antenna'd; *longiloquence*, long-windedness; *longirostrine*, long-jawed (cf *rostri-*). Cf LONG.

**lophi(o)-** and **loph(o)-; -lophus**: Gr *lophi(o)-*, c/f of *lophion*, a small crest, the dim of *lophos* (a crest), whence *loph(o)-* and *-lophus*. Exx: *Lophiomys* (Gr *mus*, mouse); *lophodont*, having teeth (cf *-odon*) with ridges ('crests') on grinding surfaces; *lophophore* (cf *-phora*); *Conolophus* (cf *cono-* at *-cone*).

**lopo-**: from Gr *lopos*, husk, shell (cf LEPO-, q.v.). Ex: *lopolith*, a stone with a basin-shaped base.

**-loquence; -loquent; -loquy**: L *-loquentia*; *-loquent*, the c/f of presp *loquens*, speaking; *-loquium*: all from *loquī* (s *loq-*), to speak. See esp ELOQUENCE. Exx: *grandiloquence* (cf *grandi-*), *-loquent*; SOLILOQUY.

**loti-; loto-**: the former from L *lōtus*, the latter from its source, the Gr *lōtos*, from H *lōt*. Exx:

*lotiform* and *Lotophagi*, the Lotos-eaters (cf *-phaga*).

**lox(o)-**: Gr *lox(o)-*, c/f of *loxos*, oblique, perh answering to an IE s *loks-*, extension of r *lok-*; prob cf Gr *lekhrios*, crooked. Exx: *loxocosm* (cf COSMIC); *loxodromic* (cf *-drome*); *loxotomy* (in Surg).

**lubri-**, as in the rare *lubrify* (F *lubrifier*), cf *-fy*: from L *lūbricus*, slippery, lecherous. Cf LUBRICITY.

**luci-**: L *lūci-*, c/f of *lūx* (gen *lucis*), light: cf LUCID, Exx: *Lucifer*, the light-bringer, cf *lucific*, light-making; *lucifugous*, light-fleeing or -avoiding; *lucimeter*.

**lucri-**: L *lucri-*, c/f of *lucrum*, monetary gain— cf LUCRE. Ex: *lucrific*, profitable.

**lucti-**: L *lucti-*, c/f of *luctus*, sorrow: cf LUGU-BRIOUS. Ex: *luctiferous*, sorrow-bringing (cf *-ferous* at *fer*).

**ludi-**: L *ludi-*, c/f of *ludus*, sport, a game: cf *-lude*, in *allude*, *delude*, etc. Ex: *ludification*, from L *ludificātiō*.

**ludicro-**: c/f of *ludicrous*, as in *ludicro-pathetic*.

**lumb(o)-**, 'the loin' or 'of the loin and': from L *lumbus* (s *lumb-*), the loins. Exx: *lumbo-abdominal*, *lumbodynia* (cf *-odynia*).

**lumbrici-**, as in *lumbriciform*, worm-like: from L *lumbricus*, an earthworm.

**lumini-**, **lumino-**: the former the true, the latter an analogous c/f of L *lūmen*, light, s *lūm-*, cf L *lūx* and E LUMINOUS. Exx: *luminiferous*, yielding (cf *-fer*) or producing light; *luminologist*, a student of *luminescence*.

**luni-**: from L *lūna*, the moon: cf LUNACY. Exx: *luniform*, moon-shaped; 'lunar and': *lunisolar*, *lunitidal*.

**lupi-**: from L *lupus*, a wolf, hence the skin-disease lupus; akin to Gr *lukos* (cf *lyco-*). Exx: *lupicide*, *lupiform*.

**luteo-**: from L *luteus*, brownish or orange-yellow, prob akin to *lūridus* (cf LURID). Exx: (Bot) *luteo-fulvous*, orange-tawny; (Chem) *luteo-cobaltic*, a yellow cobaltic (salt).

**lychno-**: Gr *lukhno-*, c/f of *lukhnos*, a lamp, *lukhn-* being an extension of *lukh-*, akin to Gr *leukos* (s *leuk-*), shining, bright: cf LUCID. Exx: *lychnomancy* (Gr *lukhnomant(e)ia*); *lychnoscope*, a side window placed low down.

**lyco-**: before a vowel, **lyc-**: Gr *luk(o)-*, c/f of *lukos* (s *luk-*), a wolf, akin to L *lupus* (s *lup-*: cf *lupi-* above); IE *luk(u)os*, var *ulquos* (cf the E WOLF). Exx: *lycanthropy* (Gr *lukanthrōpia*), in witchcraft the assumption of a wolf's form and characteristics, but in Med that kind of insanity in which the person (cf *anthropo-*) thinks he is a wolf; *lycopod*, a wolf's-foot (*-pod*) or club moss.

**lygo-**: from Gr *lugos*, a willow twig. Ex: *Lygosoma* (cf *-soma*), a slender lizard.

**lymphangi(o)-**: c/f of *lymphangial*, of the lymphatic vessels (*lymph-*+*angi(o)*, q.v. above). Ex: *lymphangiotomy* (cf *-tomy* at *-tome*). Cf:

**lymphato-**; **lymph(o)-**: resp the c/f of *lymphatic*, as in *lynphatolysis*, and the c/f of *lymph*, from L *lympha*, from Gr *numphē* (cf NYMPH), as in

*lymphagogue* (*-agogue*), a substance increasing the flow of lymph, and *lymphology*, the study or science of the lymphatic system.

**ly(o)-**: from Gr *luein* (s *lu-*), to loose or free, to dissolve: cf, therefore, *-lyse*. Exx: *lyencephalous*, adj of Zoo *Lyencephala* (Gr *enkephalos*, the brain: *en*, in+*kephalē*, the head); *lyophile* and *lyophobe*, in Colloid Chem. Cf *-lyse*.

**lypo-**: from Gr *lupē*, grief, with cognates in Ru, Lith, Skt, and prob IE r *leup-* or *lup-*. Ex: *lypothymia* (cf *-thymia*).

**lyri-**: c/f of *lyre*, as in *lyriform*: cf LYRIC, of which the c/f is *lyrico-*.

1, **-lyse** or 2, **-lyze**; 3, **-lysis**; 4, **-lyst**; 5, **-lyte**; 6, **-lytic**;—7, **lys(i)-**: 1, from F *-lyser* (from L); 2, from L *-lizāre*, from Gr *-lusis*, from *lusis*, a loosing, freeing, dissolving, from *luein* (s *lu-*), to free, IE r *lu-*; 3, L *-lysis*, Gr *-lusis*; 4, F *-lyste* (from *-lyse*, for L *-lysis*); 5, either from Gr *-lutēs*, denoting 'agent' (a looser, freer, dissolver) as in *litholyte*, or from Gr *-lutos*, denoting '(something) freed, dissolved', as in *electrolyte*; 6, L *-lyticus*, Gr *-luti-kos*, from *lutikos*, tending to loose, to free, to dissolve;—7, L *lys(i)-* or its Gr original, *lus(i)-*, c/f of *lusis* (SciL *lysis*).

Exx: *analyse* or *-lyze*, F *analyser* (from *analyse*, analysis); *analysis*, ML *analysis*, Gr *analusis*, from *analuein*, to unloose (prefix *ana*+*luein*, to loose); *analyst* (F *analyste*) and, by analogy, *catalyst*; *catalyte*; *analytic*, ML *analyticus*, Gr *analutikos*, and *catalytic*; *lysigenic* or *-genous* (cf *-genic*, *-genous* at *-gen*) and *lysimeter*.

Cf LOSE.

**lyso-**: for Biochem *lysin*, as in *lysogenesis*. Cf prec.

**lysso-**: from Gr *lussa* (Attic *lutta*, whence L *lytta*, adopted by SciE), madness, whence E *lyssa*, rabies, whence *lyssophobia*, a morbid fear of hydro-phobia. The Gr *lussa* may derive from an IE r *leu-* or *lu-*, to be agitated (Boisacq).

**lyxo-**: c/f of *lyxose* (anagram of *xylose*), an artificial sugar.

**-lyze.** See *-lyse.*

**machairo-**: from Gr *makhaira*, dagger, cutlass, akin to Gr *makhomai* (s *makh-*), I fight; perh akin to Sp, hence E, *machete*; IE r, prob *magh-*. Ex: Pal *Machairodus* (cf *-odus* at *-odon*, -tooth).

**-machia**, **-machy**; **macho-**: resp the L and the E (occ via F *-machie*) form of Gr *-makhia*, c/f of *makhē*, a battle (whence the c/f *macho-*), hence also contest or warfare; cf *makhomai* (s *makh-*), I fight; perh akin to Gr *megas* (s *meg-*) and L *magnus*, great, cf Skt *majmán* (s *maj-*), greatness. Exx: *logomachy* (Gr *logomakhia*), a battle (or war) of words (cf *-loger*); *tauromachy* (Gr *tauromakhia*), a bullfight, or bullfighting, cf *tauro-*; *machopolyp*, a defensive zooid.

**machino-**: for *machine*, as in *machinofacture*, an article made by machine—opp *manufacture*.

**macho-.** See *-machia.*

**macr(o)-**: Gr *makr(o)-*, c/f of *makros* (s *makr-*), long in space or in time, akin to L *macer* (s *mac-*), lean, and Hit *makhanza* (s *mak-*), lean. Exx: (Bot, Zoo) 'elongated', as in *macrocarpous* (cf *-carpous* at *-carp*) and *macrosepalous*, with very long sepals; (An, Med) 'excessive development (of)', as in *macrocephalous*, having an unusually large head; (mostly in Bio) 'larger-sized unit (within a specified type)', as in *macrocyte* (cf *-cyte*).

**maculi-, maculo-**: from L *macula*, a spot, a small stain or discoloration. Cf IMMACULATE. Exx: *maculiferous*, spotted; *maculo(-)cerebral*.

**madre-**, as in *madrepore* (cf *-pore*), whence the subsidiary c/f *madrepori-*: It *madre*, mother, from L *māter* (cf *mātri-*), as in It *madrepora*, F *madrépore*, E *madrepore*.

**magico-**, 'magical and': for *magic*, as in *magicoreligious*.

**magiro-**: from Gr *mageiros* (s *mageir-*), a cook; prob basic idea, 'to knead'; as in *magirology*= *magirics* (Gr *ta mageirika*, cooks' matters), the art of cooking.

**magna-**. See *magni-*.

**magn(e)-**. See *magneto-*.

**magnesio-**; for *magnesium*, as in *magnesioferrite*.

**magneto-**: c/f of *magnetic* and denoting 'magnetic force', as in *magnetometer*, or 'magnetic', as in *magneto-electric*, or 'magneto-electric', as in *magneto(-)telephone*. Cf MAGNET. Less common is Faraday's *magn(e)-*, as in *magnecrystallic* and *magnelectric*.

**magn(i)-**; (?) only in cinematics, **magna-**; (?) only in Min, **magno-**: L *magn(i)-*, c/f of *magnus*, great: cf MAGNITUDE. Exx: *magnanimous*, L *magnanimus*, lit 'of a great *animus* or mind'; *magnification*, *magnificent*; *magniloquence* (L *magniloquentia*), grandiloquence;—*magnascope*;—*magnochromite*.

**maha-**, as in *Mahabharata* ('The Great Story')— *Mahadeva* ('the great god')—*maharaja* ('the great ruler or king'), f *maharani*—*mahatna* ('the great soul', hence 'the great-soul'd', 'the wise')— *Mahavamsa* ('The Great Chronicle')—*Mahayana* ('the great vehicle'), the theistic form of Buddhism: Skt *mahā*, great, akin to L *magnus*.

**makro-**. A rare var of *macro-*.

**mal-**, evilly: F *mal*: cf *male-*.

**-malacia; malac(o)-**: from Gr *malakia*, softness, from *malakos*, soft, whence Gr *malak(o)-*, whence E *malac(o)-*, which, however, occ derives from Gr *malakia* (neupl), molluscs; IE s, *malak-* or *melak-*, perh an extension of IE r *mel-*; ? cf L *mollis*, soft. Exx: *osteomalacia*, a bone-softening disease, cf *osteo-*; *malacodermous*, soft-skinned (cf *-derm*); *malacology*, the science of molluscs.

**malario-**: for *malaria*, as in *malariology*.

**Malayo-**, 'Malayan and': c/f from *Malay*.

**male-**, evil(ly): L *male*, evilly: cf *malign* at MALICE.

**mallei-, malleo-**: c/ff of L *malleus*, a mallet, a hammer, perh 'a popular adaptation of Gr μάλις' (E & M), apple-tree, but prob rather a native Italic word. Exx: *malleiform*; *malleo-incudal*.

**mallo-** (1): from Gr *mallon*, more, the comp of *mala*, very, akin to L *multus*, n *multum*, much.

Ex: *malloseismic*, more (than is customary) subject to earthquakes—cf *-seismic*.

**mallo-** (2): from Gr *mallos*, a flock of wool, perh akin to Lith *mèlas*, cloth. Ex: *mallophagous*, wool-eating (cf *-phaga*).

**mal(o)-**: Chem c/f of *malic* (acid).

**mamm(i)-**, 'breast', and **mammilli-**, 'nipple': resp L *mamma* and *mam(m)illa*: cf MAMMA. Exx: *mammalgia* (cf *-algia*), *mammiferous*, *mammiform*; *mammilliform*.

**mammono-**: for *mammon*, as in *mammonolatry*.

**-mancy**, abstract n; **-mancer**, agential n; **-mantic**, adj; **manto-**: often via OF *-mancie*, from LL *-mantia*, itself from Gr *-manteia*, c/f of *manteia*, divination; (*-mancer*) either *-manc(y)*+agential *-er*, or from OF *-manceur*; (*-mantic*) prob suggested by LL *-manticus* or its orig, the Gr *mantikos*, prophetic; (*manto-*), from Gr *mantis*, a prophet. Exx: *chiromancy*, *-mancer*, *-mantic*; *necromancy*, via OF-F and L from Gr *nekromanteia*, divination by communication with the dead—*necromancer*, from OF *nigromanceur*—*necromantic*, perh from LL *necromanticus*; *mantology*, divination, prophecy. Cf MANIA and MIND.

**mandel(o)-**: Chem c/f of *mandelic* (from G *Mandel*, an almond).

**mandibulo-**, 'mandibular and': from LL *mandibula*, the mandible, from *mandere*, to chew; *mand-* is perh echoic. Ex: *mandibulo-suspensorial*.

**mandri-**, as in *mandriarch*, head (cf *-arch*) of a monkish order: from Gr *mandra*, a monastery, akin to Skt *mandurá*, a stable.

1 **-mane**, 2 **-mania**, 3 **-maniac**; 4 **manic-**: 1, F *-mane*, as in *Anglomane*, the E form being *-maniac*, adj used derivatively as n, as in *Anglomaniac*; 2, 'madness'—hence 'a craze (for)', from Gr *-mania*, c/f of *mania*, madness; 3, c/f of *maniac*, like F *maniaque* from LL *maniacus*, from L *mania*, from Gr; *manic-*, esp in *manic-depressive*, comes from Gr *manikos*, the adj of *mania*, which is akin to MIND. Ex: *erotomania*, from Gr *erōtomania*.

**mangani-, mangano-**: c/ff of *manganese*, as in *manganiferous*, *mangano-calcite*; *mangano-*, also a Chem c/f of *manganous*. Akin to MAGNESIA.

**mani-** (1): via F *mani-* (influenced by next) from Gr *mono-*, c/f of *monos*, sole, single, alone, as in *manichord*, clavichord (orig one-stringed), via F *manichordion*, *manicorde*, via LL *monochordon*, from Gr *monokhordon*.

**mani-** (2): L *mani-*, c/f of *manus*, the hand: cf MANUAL. Exx: *manicure* (cf CURE) and *maniform*, hand-shaped; cf MANIFEST.

**mani-** (3): for *many*, as in *manifold*, *maniform*.

**-mania, -maniac; -manic**. See *-mane*.

**manni-** (1): for *manna*, as in *manniferous*; (2) for *man*, as in *mannify* (cf *-fy*).

**manno-**: c/f of *mannose* (*mannitol*+*-ose*), as in *mannoheptose*.

**mano-**: Gr *mano-*, c/f of *manos* (s *man-*), thin, rare, rarefied; applied esp to gases. Exx: *manograph* and *manometer*. Akin to *mono-*.

**-mantic; manto-**. See *-mancy*.

**manu-**: L *manu-*, c/f of *manus*, the hand: cf

**mani-** (2). Exx: *manucaption*, from ML *manucaptiō* (gen *-captiōnis*), a taking by the hand; *manuduction* (cf DUCT); MANUFACTURE; *manumit* (cf MISSION).

**margariti-, margarito-; margaro-:** c/ff (the first, L) of L *margarīta*, a pearl; *margaro-*, from Gr *margaros*, a pearl oyster, or *margaron*, a pearl (cf MARGARINE). Exx: *margaritiferous*, pearl-bearing; *margaritomancy*, divination (cf *-mancy*) by pearls.

**margini-,** as in *marginirostral* (cf *-rostral*), and *margino-*, as in *marginoplasty* (cf *-plasia*): for *margin*.

**mari-:** L *mari-*, c/f of *mare* (s *mar-*), the sea: cf MARINE. Exx: *maricolous* (cf *-colous*), living in the sea; *marigraph*, a tide-gauge. The c/f *marin(o)-*, from L *marīnus*, of the sea, is rare; ex, *marinorama* (cf *-orama*).

**Mari-:** c/f of LL *Maria* (esp the Virgin Mary), as in *Mariolatry*, worship (cf *-later*) of the Virgin Mary, and *Mariology* (cf *Christology*).

**marin(o)-.** See *mari-*.

**mariti-,** as in *mariticide*, a murder, by wife, of husband, or such a murderess: from L *maritus*, a husband: cf MARRY.

**martyro-:** ML *martyro-*, c/f of LL *martyr* (see MARTYR). Ex: *martyrology*, from ML *martyrologium*.

**-mas:** c/f of *Mass* in its sense 'feast day', as in *Candlemas, Christmas, Martinmas, Michaelmas*.

**masculo-,** 'masculine' or 'masculine and': from L *masculus*, male: cf MASCULINE. Ex: *masculofeminine*.

**-mastia; mast(o)-:** c/ff of Gr *mastos*, the (usu female) breast, prob akin to *madan* (s *mad-*), μαδᾶν, to be damp, to flow, IE s *mad*.Exx: ('mammary condition') *macromastia*; ('the, esp female, breast') *mastology*—('mastoid and') *masto-occipital*.

**mastig(o)-; -mastix:** Gr *mastig(o)-* and *-mastix*, c/ff of *mastix* (gen *mastigos*), a whip; IE r, prob *mas-*. Exx: *Mastigophora* (cf *-phora*); *mastigure* (cf *-ure*, Gr *oura*, tail); *Homeromastix* (Gr Ὁμηρομάστιξ), a critic scourging Homer, and such analogous terms as *Satiromastix*.

**masto-.** See *-mastia*.

**materno-,** as in *maternology*: for *maternity*.

**-math.** See *-mathy*, s.f.

**mathematico-:** c/f of *mathematic*(al); denoting 'mathematical and', as in *mathematico-philosophical*.

**-mathy:** Gr *-matheia*, -learning, from *mathein*, to learn: cf MATHEMATIC. Exx: *chrestomathy* (Gr *khrēstomatheia*, perh via F *chrestomathie*), cf *chresto-* at *chreo-*; *polymathy* (cf *poly-*), vast and various learning. Note also *-math*, learner, hence student, scholar, as in *polymath* (cf *-poly*), an extremely erudite person, from Gr *polumathēs*.

**matri-;** rarely **matro-:** L *mātri-*, c/f of *māter* (gen *mātris*, o/s *mātr-*), mother; *matro-*, by Gr influence: cf MOTHER. Exx: *matriarch*=*matri-*+the *-arch* (cf *-arch* above) of E *patriarch*; *matricide* (cf *-cide* at *-cidal*); *matrilineal;—matroclinous* (or *-clinic*), being more like mother than father—cf INCLINE; *matronymic*, cf *patronymic*.

**mavro-:** from L Gr *mauros*, black, very dark (cf

MOOR). Exx: (? *Mavrogordato*), *mavrodaphne* (Gr *daphnē*, laurel)—a Mod Gr wine.

**maxilli-, maxillo-:** from L *maxilla*, (lower) jawbone, perh orig a dim of *mala*, (upper) jawbone. Exx: *maxilliform, maxillo(-)labial*.

**Mayo-:** for *Mayan*, as in *Mayologist*.

**maz(o)-** (1): from Gr *mazos*, a breast, akin to *mastos*, q.v. at *-mastia* above. Exx: *mazolysis* (cf *-lysis* at *-lyse*) and *mazopathy*.

**mazo-** (2). Gr *mazo-*, c/f of *maza*, a barley cake (prob 'something *kneaded*'), but, in Med, denoting 'placenta'. Ex: *mazopathy* (cf *-path*).

**meato-:** a Surg c/f of L *meātus*, a passage, from *meāre* (s *me-*), to go. Exx: *meatoscope, meatotomy*.

**mechanico-; mechano-:** the former, for *mechanic(al)*; the latter, from Gr *mēkhano-*, from *mēkhanē*, a machine: cf MECHANIC. Exx: 'mechanics', as in *mechanology*; 'mechanism', as in *mechanomorphism*; 'mechanical means', as in *mechanolatry* and *mechanotherapy*.

**mec(o)-:** Gr *mēko-*, c/f of Gr *mēkos*, length, akin to *makros*, long (q.v. at *macro-*). Ex: *mecometer*, *mekometer*, a length-measuring instrument.

**mecono-:** from Gr *mēkonion*, opium, from *mēkōn*, poppy, s *mēk-*, prob an exoticism. Ex: MECONOLOGY.

**medi-.** See *medio-*.

**mediastino-:** from An *mediastinum*, from ML *mediastīnus*, medial, from L *medius*, middle. Ex: *mediastino-pericarditis*.

**medico-:** from L *medicus*, medical. Exx: 'medical', as in *medicopsychology*; 'medical and', as in *medico(-)legal*.

**medi(o)-:** from L *medius*, middle, akin to MIDDLE: E senses, 'medially'—'intermediately'—'in the middle'. Exx: *Mediterranean; medio-perforate; medio-palatal; medio-silicic*.

**Medo-:** Gr *Mēdo-*, c/f of *Mēdos*, a Mede, Median: ('Median and') *Medo-Persian*.

**medulli-:** from L (and An and Bot) *medulla*, narrow, pith, perh a var of Italic *merulla*, influenced by *medius*, middle. Ex: *medulli-spinal*.

**medusi-:** for the Zoo *medusa*, a jellyfish, from L *Medūsa*, Gr *Medousa*, orig the f presp of *medein* (s *med-*), to rule over. Ex: *medusiform*.

**meg(a)-; megal(o)-; -megaly:** Gr *meg(a)-*; Gr *megal(o)-*; SciL *-megalia*, from Gr *megalē*, f of *megas*, great, gen *megalou*: cf MUCH and MICKLE. Exx: *megascope, megalith, megaphone, megapod, megatherium; megalomania, megalosaur; gastromegaly*, an abnormal enlargement of the belly.

**meio-:** from Gr *meiōn*, neu *meion*, lesser, smaller; IE s *mei-*, to diminish (L *minuere*: cf MINUS). Exx: *meiobar* (cf *-bar*), *meiophylly* (cf *-phyll*).

**meizo-:** from Gr *meizōn*, neu *meizon*, greater, comp of *megas* (q.v. at *mega-*). Ex: *meizoseismic*.

**meko-.** See *meco-*.

**mel-** (1). See *mela-*.

**mel-** (2): from Gr *mēla*, cheeks, from *mēlon*, apple (L *mālum*). Ex: *meloncus* (cf *-oncus*). Also *melo-*, as in *meloplasty*, the plastic restoration of a cheek.

**mel-** (3): from Gr *melos*, a limb; IE s, *\*mel-*. Exx: *melagra* (cf *-agra*) and *melalgia* (cf *-algia* at *alg-*).

**mel(a)-; -melane; melano-, Melano-:** resp from Gr *melas*, black; either from the neu *melan* or from the o/s *melan-* thereof; from the Gr c/f *melan(o)-*; and from E *Melanesian*. The adj *melas*, f *melaina*, is prob for *\*melanos*: cf Skt *malinás*. The IE r is app *\*mel-* or perhaps *\*mal-*, with varr *\*mol-* and *\*mul-*. Exx: *melaconite* (*mela-* + *kon-*, from *konis*, dust + the Min suffix *-ite*)—*melagranite*—*Melanesian* (cf *-nese*); *sideromelane* (cf 1st *sidero-*); *melanophore* (cf *-phora*)—*melanopathy* (SciL *melanopathia*)—*melanoscope*—*melanotrichous* (cf *-trichia*), dark-haired; *Melano-Papuan*. Cf MELANCHOLY.

**melassi-:** from *melasses*, var of *molasses*; e.g., *melassigenic* (cf *-genic* at *-gen*).

**meli-, melli-; melitto-:** *meli-*, from Gr *meli*, honey; *melli-*, L *melli-*, c/f of *mel* (gen *mellis*), honey, akin to and perh derived from the Gr word, with IE r *\*mel-*; *melitto-* comes from Gr *melitta*, var *melissa*, a honey-bee, itself clearly derivative from *meli*, honey. Exx: *Melianthus* (cf *anth-*)—*meliceris*, Gr *melikēris* (from *kēros*, wax)—*melilite*, a mineral coloured honey-yellow—*melilot*, Gr *melilōtos* (cf LOTUS), a kind of clover—*meliphagous*, honey-eating: *melliferous* (cf *-fer*)—*mellifluous*, LL *mellifluus*—*mellivorous*, honey-eating; *melittology*, such entomology as treats of bees.

**-melia**, a condition of the limbs; **-melus**, a monster thus affected: c/ff from Gr *melos*, a limb; IE r, *\*mel-* or *\*mal-*. Exx: *schistomelia* (cf *schisto-*, cleft) and *anisomelus* (*aniso-*, unequal).

**melitto-; melli-.** See *meli-*.

**melo-** (1). See the 2nd *mel-*.

**melo-** (2): Gr *melo-*, c/f of *melos*, song, a sense derivative from *melos*, limb: cf, therefore, *-melia*. Exx: MELODRAMA, MELODY, *melograph* (F *mélographe*: cf *-graph*), *melomania*, *melophone* (a sort of concertina).

**-melus.** See *-melia*.

**membrani-**, 'membrane'—as in *membraniferous*; **membrano-**, 'membrane'—as in *membranology*; or 'membranous and'—as in *membrano-nervous*. *Membrane* comes from L *membrāna*, skin covering the *membra* or limbs: cf MEMBER.

**meni-:** from Gr *mēnē*, the moon: cf MOON. Ex: *menisperm*. Cf the 1st *meno-* and:

**-menia:** a SciL c/f from Gr *mēniaia* (neupl), menses, as in *catamenia* and *xeromenia*. Cf prec.

**mening(o)-:** Gr *mēning(o)-*, c/f of *mēninx*, gen *mēningos*, membrane, app akin to Gr *mēros*, thigh. Med uses *mening(o)* to denote 'meninges' (the membranes enveloping the brain), as in *meningitis* and *meningo-cephalitis*, and 'meningeal and', as in *meningo(-)cortical*.

**menisci-; menisco-:** c/ff from SciL *meniscus*, from Gr *mēniskos*, a (small) crescent, dim of *mēnē*, the moon: cf *meni-* and *-menia* and MOON. Exx: *menisciform*, crescent-shaped; *Meniscotheridae* (Gr *thērion*, a wild beast: cf *therio-*), prehistoric beasts, 'in allusion to the crescents of the molars' (Webster).

**meno-** (1): Gr *mēno-*, c/f of *mēn*, month, akin to *mēnē*, moon: cf MOON. Exx: *menology* and *menopause* (menstrual period: cf PAUSE). Cf *meni-*.

**meno-** (2): from Gr *menein* (s *men-*), to remain, akin to L *manēre* (s *man-*): cf MANOR. Exx: *menognathous* (cf *-gnatha*) and *Menorhyncha* (Gr *rhunkhos*, snout).

**menth(o)-:** c/f of *menthol*. Only in Chem.

**menti-** (1): from L *mens* (gen *mentis*), mind: cf MIND. Ex: *menticultural* and *mentiferous*, telepathic.

**menti-** (2); **mento-:** from L *mentum* (s *ment-*), the chin, app composed of IE *\*men-*, to jut out (or up: cf L *mons*) + extension *t* + *-um*, neu-n suffix (E & M). Exx: *mentigerous*; having a chin; *mentolabial*, of chin and lips.

**mer-** (1): c/f of E *mere*, the sea, akin to ⌐ *mare*: Ex: *mermaid*.

**mer-** (2) and **-mer.** See the 1st *mero-*.

**mercapto-:** for Chem *mercaptan* (ML *mercurium captans*).

**mercuri-**, 'mercuric', and **mercur(o)-**, 'mercury': both from E MERCURY. Only in Chem.

**merdi-:** from L *merda*, excrement, dung, perh (? by psilosis) akin to Lith *smirdeit*, OSI *smrudeti*, to stink. Ex: *merdivorous*, the L syn of Gr *coprophagous*.

**meri-.** See the 1st *mero-*.

**-meric**, adj, and **-merism**, n of condition: from *isomeric*. Exx: *polymeric*, *polymerism*.

**-meris.** See:

**meristo-:** from Gr *meristos*, divided, from *meris*, a part or share—therefore cf the 1st *mero-*. Ex: Bot *meristogenous* (cf *-genous* at *-gen*).

**mermith(o)-**, 'mermithized' (infested with slender parasitic worms): from *mermith-*, the o/s of Gr *mermis* (gen *mermithos*), a cord, a stout thread. Ex: *mermithogyne* (cf *-gyn*).

**mer(o)-;** 2, **meri-;** 3, **-mer;** 4, **-mere;** 5, **-meric** (cf *-meric* above); 6, **-meris;** 7, **-merous;** 8, **-mery:** Gr *meros* (s *mer-*), a fraction, a part, a share—cf MERIT; 2, from the var *meris*, part, share; 3, deriving from Gr *-merēs*, c/f of *meros*, and, in E, denoting 'member of a class' as in Chem *isomer*; 4, from *meros*, and corresponding in Bot and Zoo to Chem *-mer*; 5, the adj of *-mer* and *-mere* (cf *-meric*, separate entry above); 6, from *meris*, used in Bot and Zoo generic names; 7, Gr *-merēs* (from *meros*: cf sense 3), '-partite', but denoting, in E, 'of so many or suchlike parts'; 8, n answering to (7) and deriving from Gr *-mereia*.

Exx: *merogenesis*, *meroplankton*; *mericarp*; *isomer*, *metamer*, *polymer*; *arthromere*; *isomeric*, *polymeric*; *Piptomeris*; *hexamerous*, *homomerous*; *isomery*.

**mero-** (2): Gr *mēro-*, c/f of *mēros* (s *mēr-*), thigh; akin to L *membrum*, a limb; IE r, perh *\*mesro-*. Ex: *mero-algia*. Cf:

**-merus**, only in Ent generic names: answers to prec.

**meryc(o)-;-meryx:** from Gr *mērux* (gen *merukos*), a ruminating animal, prob of echoic origin. Exx: *Merychippus* (Gr *hippos*, a horse) and

*Merycopotamus*(Gr *potamos*, river: cf *hippopotamus*); *-meryx* in Pal generic names.

**mes-.** See *meso-*.

**mesati-:** from Gr *mesatos*, midmost, from *mesos*, middle (cf *meso-*), as in *mesaticephalic*. Cf:

**mesio-,** 'of the mesion or meson' (in dentistry): from *mesion*, from *meson*, neu of *mesos*, middle. Ex: *mesiolingual*. Cf:

**mes(o)-:** Gr *mes(o)-*, c/f of *mesos*, middle, akin to L *medius* and E MIDDLE. Exx: ('intermediate; in the middle') *mesentery* (ML *mesenterium*, Gr *mesenterion*: cf *entero-*)—*Mesopotamia*, the land (Geog suffix *-ia*) intermediate between the rivers (cf *potamo-*)—*mesobar*—*mesocephalic*—*mesotherm*; ('intermediate in type') *mesolite*; special senses in An and Chem.

**-mester,** adj *-mestral* or *-mestrial*: *semester*, G *Semester*, a period or term of six months, from L *sēmestris* (*sē-* for *sex*, 6+*-mestris*, from *mensis*, a month), six-monthly, adj *semestral*, *-mestrial* (suffixes *-al*, *-ial*); *trimester*, F *trimestre*, from L *trimestris* (*tri-*, 3), three-monthly, with adj *trimestrial* or *trimestral* (*-ial*, *-al*). Cf MENSES.

**metalli-; metall(o):** L *metalli-*, c/f of *metallum*; Gr *metall(o)-*, c/f of *metallon* (whence the L word), metal (cf METAL). Exx: *metalliferous*; *metallography*, *metallurgy* (SciL *metallurgia*, from Gr *metallourgos*, metal-worker—cf *-ergy* at *-ergate*).

**meteor(o)-:** c/f of E METEOR, q.v. Exx: *meteorograph*, *meteorology*, *meteoroscope*.

**-meter.** See *-metre*.

**meth(o)-:** c/f of *methyl* (from *methylene*, F *méthylène*, 'wood spirit': Gr *methu*, wine+Gr *hulē*, wood+Chem suffix *-ene*), as in *methoxyl*.

**methodo-:** from Gr *methodos*, esp in *methodology* (cf *-logy* at *-loger*). Cf METHOD.

**metopo-:** from Gr *metōpon*, the forehead—*met(a)*, after+*ōps* (pl *ōpes* or *ōpa*), *metōpon* being the part after, hence imm above, the eyes. Exx: *metopomancy*, divination (*-mancy*) with forehead or the entire face; *metoscopy* (cf *-scopy* at *-scope*), character-reading from the lines of the forehead.

**-metra; -metrium:** both from Gr *mētra*, the womb: denoting 'condition of' and 'part of' the womb. Exx: *hydrometra*, dropsy of the womb; *myometrium*, muscular part of womb. Cf the 3rd *metro-*.

**-metre** or 2, **-meter;** 3, **metr(o)-;** 4, **-metry:** E and Am c/f of *metre*, *meter*, the length-measure; 2 only, c/f of the *meter* of e.g. *gas meter*; 3, from Gr *metron*, a measure—cf METER; 4, from Gr *-metria* (from *metron*) and denoting 'art of measuring'. Exx: *kilometre* or *-meter*; *gasometer*; *metrology*, *metronome*; GEOMETRY.

**-metrium.** See *-metra*.

**metro-** (1). See *-metre*.

**metro-** (2): Gr *mētro-*, c/f of *mētēr*, mother, akin to L *māter* and E MOTHER. Ex: METROPOLIS. Cf:

**metro-** (3): Gr *mētr(o)-*, c/f of *mētra*, womb, akin to *mētēr*, mother. Ex: *metroscope*.

**-metry.** See *-metre*.

**mezzo-:** It *mezzo*, middle, from L *medius* (cf *medio-*). Exx: *mezzograph*; *mezzorilievo*; *mezzosoprano*; *mezzotint* (It *mezzotinto*).

**mi-.** See *mio-*.

**miasmato-** and **miasmo-:** the latter, from E *miasma*; the former from *miasmat-*, the o/s of Gr *miasma*, defilement: cf MIASMA. Exx: *miasmatology*, *miasmology*.

**micr(o)-:** Gr *mīkr(o)-*, c/f of *mīkros*, small, an Attic and Ionic var of *smīkros*; IE r, *smīk-* or *smeik* or *smēk-*. In E the element denotes primarily 'small', as in *microcosm* (LL *microcosmus*, from Gr *mikros kosmos*, 'the little world', i.e. man) and *micrology*; hence 'the enlargement of small objects', as in MICROSCOPE—cf *microphone*; and many special Sci nuances. Further exx: *microbarograph*; *microfilm* (used in cinemas); *microphysics*; and several hundred others.

**milio-:** from SciL *Miliola*, dim of L *milium* (s *mili-*), millet: cf MILLET. Ex: *miliolite* (cf *-lite*).

**mille-; milli-:** L *mille-*; from L *mille*, a thousand: cf MILE. Exx: *millepede* (cf *centipede*); *millimetre* (*-meter*)—*milligram*(*me*)—*millimicron*.

**mimeo-; mim(o)-:** the former is rare (notably occurring in 'to *mimeograph*') for the latter, which comes from Gr *mim(o)-*, c/f of *mimos*, a mimic, a MIME (q.v.). Exx: *mimodrama*, *mimography*, *mimotype* (in Zoo). The end c/f *-mimus* occurs esp in Ent generic names.

**mini-:** from L *minor*, lesser, smaller: cf MINOR. Exx: *minibus*, a small, light bus; *minify* (cf *-fy*, to make or render). In *minicamera*, however, *mini-* is short for *miniature*; and in *minimetric*, for *minim*.

**mi(o)-:** from Gr *meio-*, c/f of *meiōn*, lesser, smaller: cf prec. Exx: *miargyrite* (*mi-*+*argyrite*, argentite); *Miocene* (cf *-cene*), succeeding to the *Eocene* (geol period).

**misce-:** from L *miscēre* (s *misc-*: cf MIX), to mingle. Ex: *miscegenation* (L *genus*, animal stock, human race, cf *-gen*), interbreeding—esp of one colour with another.

**-mise, -miss, -mit,** as in *promise*—*dismiss*—*omit*: from *missum*, the supine—*missus*, the pp—*mittere*, the inf of L *mittō*, I send: cf MISSION. Ex: *manumit*.

**miseri-:** from L *miserēri*, to feel pity; esp in *misericord*, via F from L *misericordia* (cf *cordi-*).

**mis(o)-:** Gr *mis(o)-*, c/f of *misos* (s *mis-*), hatred, and *misein* (a *mis-*), to hate. Exx: *misandry*, hatred of men; *misanthropy*, hatred of mankind; *misogamy*, hatred of marriage; *misogyny*, hatred of women; *misology*, hatred of argument; *misosophy*, hatred of wisdom. Cf MISANTHROPY.

**-miss; mit.** See *-mise*.

**mit(o)-:** Gr *mit(o)-*, c/f of *mitos*, a thread, s *mit-*; perh cf Hit *mitis*, thread, string. Exx: *mitogenetic*, *mitosome* (cf *-soma*).

**-mixis; mixo-:** resp Gr *mixis*, a mingling (hence, in E, 'mixed'), and its Gr c/f *mixo-*: cf MIX. Exx: *apomixis*, (in Bio) asexual reproduction; *mixobarbaric*, semi-barbaric (Gr *mixobarbaros*), *mixotrophic*. Cf:

**mixti-:** from L *mixtus*, mingled, mixed: cf MIX. Ex: *mixtilineal*.

**mnemi-, mnemo-:** *-mnesia* (adj *-mnesiac*), **-mnesis**

(adj -mnetic): first two, c/ff from *mnēmē*, memory, ult akin to MIND; for E *amnesia*; from Gr *mnēsis*, a remembering. Exx: *Mnemiopsis* (cf -*ops*); *mnemotechny*, the art of remembering, (hence) mnemonics; *cryptomnesia*; *hypermnesis*.

-**mobile**, as in AUTOMOBILE; from the E adj *mobile*.

**modi-**. See MODIFY.

**mogi-**: Gr *mogi-*, c/f of *mogis*, with difficulty, akin to—from—*mogos*, labour, difficulty, akin to Lith *smagus*, Lett *smags*, heavy; IE r, prob \**smog-*. Ex: *mogitocia* (q.v. at -*tocia*).

**molari-**: from L *molāris*, a millstone, from *mola*, a mill. Ex: *molarimeter*. But in *molariform*, shaped like a molar, it stands for *molar* (tooth).

**molli-**, as in *mollify*: L *molli-*, c/f of *mollis*, soft; IE r, perh \**mel-*.

**mollusci-**: for SciL *mollusca*, a mollusc, as in *molluscivorous*.

**molybd(o)-**: Gr *molubd(o)-*, c/f of *molubdos*, lead (metal), ? of Iberian origin. Ex: *molybdomenite*, selenite: *molybdo-*+*men-* (Gr *mēnē*, moon) | Min suffix -*ite*.

**momio-**, as in *momiology*, the love and science of mummies: from F *momie*, a mummy: cf MUMMY.

**mon-**. See *mono-*.

**monadi-**, **monado-**: c/ff of *monad*, as in *monadigerous*, *monadology*. Cf *mono-*.

**monarchico-**, for E *monarchic*; *monarcho-*, from Gr *monarkhia*, monarchy, as in *monarchomachic*, opposed to monarchy, cf -*machia*.

-**monas**, 'unit' in Zoo generic names: LL *monas*, gen *monadis*, from Gr *monas* (gen *monados*), s *mon-*, from *monos* (s *mon-*), alone: cf MONASTERY.

**Mongolo-**, 'Mongolian and': for *Mongol*: e.g., *Mongolo-Tatar*.

**monili-**: from L *monīle*, a necklace: cf OIr *muinel*, neck, and Skt *mányā*, nape of neck. Ex: *moniliform*.

**monimo-**: from Gr *monimos*, a stable, either from or akin to *menein* (L *manēre*), to remain. Ex: *monimostylic* (Gr *stulos*, a pillar).

**mon(o)-**: Gr *mon(o)-*, c/f of *monos* (s *mon-*), alone: cf MONASTERY. E nuances range from 'alone' to 'only' or 'only one', esp 'of or for or by only one'. Exx: *monocellular*; *monochromatic* and *monochrome*; *monocrat* (cf -*crat*); *monocyclic*; *monodrama*, acted by one person; *monody* (via LL *monōdia* from Gr *monōidia*, from *monōidos*, singing alone): an ode sung by one voice in a tragedy, hence a dirge; MONOGAMY; *monogenesis*; MONOGRAM; MONOGRAPH; *monolith* (cf -*lith* at -*lite*); MONOLOGUE; *monomania*; *monomorphic* (cf -*morph*); *monophonous*; MONOPOLY; MONOSYLLABLE; MONOTONY; *monotype*; *monovalent*.

**monstri-**: L *mōnstri-*, c/f of *mōnstrum*, a divine omen (or warning) of disaster, hence a monster. Exx: *monstricide* (cf -*cidal*)—*monstriferous*, producing or tending to produce monsters—*monstrify* (cf -*fy*).

**monti-**: L *monti-*, c/f of *mons* (gen *montis*), a MOUNTAIN. Exx: *monticoline*, mountain-haunting (cf -*colous*) and *montiform*.

**morbi-**: from L *morbus* (s *morb-*), disease: cf MORBID. Ex: *morbiferous*, disease-carrying or -producing; *morbific*, disease-causing. The ML dim *morbilli*, measles, explains the c/f *morbilli-*, as in *morbilliform*, (of a disease) resembling measles.

**mor(i)-**: either from L *morus* or from its source, perh rather its cognate, the Gr *moron* (s *mor-*), mulberry, of common Medit origin. Ex: *moriform*, mulberry-shaped.

**moro-**: Gr *mōro-*, c/f of *mōros*, stupid, foolish, akin to Skt *mūras*, stupid. Exx: *morology* (Gr *mōrologia*, foolish talk), nonsense, *sophomore*, and *morosoph* (Gr *mōrosophos*), an erudite fool. Cf *moron*, from Gr *mōron*, the neu of *mōros*: 'silly thing'.

-**morph**; 2, -**morpha**, pl -**morphae**; 3, -**morphic**; 4, -**morphism**; 5, -**morphosis**, adj -**morphotic**; 6, -**morphous**; 7, -**morphy**;—8, **morph(o)-**; cf *morphino-*, *morphio-* (next entry): -*morph*, from Gr *morphē*, form, denotes 'one distinguished by a (named) form', with corresponding adj in -*morphic* or -*morphous*; 2, SciL, from Gr *morphē*, with adjj -*morphic*; 3, -*ic* adj from *morphē*, with abstract nn ('state, condition') in -*morphism* or -*morphy*; 5, from Gr *morphōsis*, a forming or shaping, the E c/f denoting 'development'; the adj -*morphotic* was suggested by Gr *morphōtikos*, fit for forming, able to form; 6, Gr adj -*morphos*, from *morphē*, the E c/f denoting 'of a particular form'; 7, see (3) and cf abstract-n suffix -*y*; and, of course, Gr *morpho-*, true c/f of *morphē*. The IE r was prob \**morgh-* (perh \**mergh*): cf L *forma*, s *form-*, which, if in fact related to Gr *morphē* (s *morph-*), was clearly a transposition.

Exx: *holomorph* (in Math—cf *holo-*); in Zoo, *Cetomorpha* (cf *ceto-*) and *Alectomorphae*; *anthropomorphic* (anthropo-), *anthropomorphism*; *heteromorphosis* (hetero-); *amorphous*, formless, shapeless, from Gr *amorphos*, the *a-* being a privative prefix; *amorphy*, rare for *amorphism*; *morphology* (cf -*logy* at -*loger*), the study of forms—*morphometry* (cf -*metry* at -*metre*)—*morphoplasm* (-*plasm*).

**morphino-**; **morphio-**: c/f of *morphine*; c/f of *morphia*: two words deriving from *Morpheus*, the Shaper (*morph-*+Gr -*eus*, agent), the God of Dreams. Exx: *morphinomania*, *morphiomania*.

-**morphite**, as in *pyromorphite*, adds Min suffix -*ite* to -*morph*.

**morpho-**; -**morphosis**, -**morphous**; -**morphy**. See -*morph*.

**morti-**. See MORTIFY.

**Mosa-**, as in Pal *Mosasaurus* (cf -*saur*): from L *Mosa*, the river Meuse.

**moschi-**, as in *moschiferous*, musk-producing: ML *moschus*: cf MUSK.

**moti-**, **moto-**; -**motive**: c/f from L *mōtus* (gen *motūs*), motion; c/f for *motion*—or for *motor*; c/f of adj, hence n, *motive*. See MOTION. Exx: *motific*; *motograph*, *motophone*; *automotive*, *locomotive*.

**muci-**, **muc(o)-**; -**mucoso-**: from L *mūcus*, slime, mucus; (*mucoso-*) from the L adj *mūcōsus*, slimy, mucous. Exx: *mucific, mucivorous; mucofibrous; mucosogranular.* L *mūcus* (s *mūc-*) is akin to Gr *muxa* (? *muk-s-a*); IE r, prob \**muk-* or \**mug-*. The subsidiary *mucino-,* as in *mucinogen* (cf *-gen*), stands for Biochem *mucin* (Chem suffix -in), itself from *mucus.*

**mucroni-**: from L *mūcrō,* a sharp point, gen *mūcrōnis,* o/s *mūcrōn-,* perh akin to Gr a*mussō* (? for a*muksō*), I tear. Exx: *mucroniferous,* sharp-pointed, and *mucroniform.*

**mult(i)-**: L *multi-,* c/f of the adj *multus,* much, *multi,* many: cf MULTITUDE. Exx: *multangular,* many-angled; *multifarious,* lit 'speaking [L *fāri,* to speak] in many ways', of many kinds; *multiform; multilateral,* many-sided; *multimillionaire;* MULTI-PLY, *multiplicity; multipotent; multisonous.*

**mummi-**: for *mummy* (preserved corpse), as in *mummiform* and *mummify.* Cf *momi-.*

**mundi-** (1): from L *mundus* (s *mund-*), the world, perh akin to MOVE: cf MUNDANE. Ex: *mundivagant,* world-wandering.

**mundi-** (2): LL *mundi-,* c/f of L *mundus,* clean. Ex: *mundificant,* from *mundificans* (gen *-ficantis*), presp of *mundificāre,* to make clean.

**muri-** (1): from L *mūrus* (s *mūr-*), a wall: cf MURAL. Ex: *muriform,* like a wall made of bricks.

**muri-** (2): from L *mūs,* a mouse, gen *mūris,* s *mūr-*; IE r, app \**mur-.* Ex: *muriform,* mouse-like.

**muscari-**, as in *muscariform,* brush-shaped: from L *muscārium,* a fly-whisk, ex *musca:* see next.

**musci-** (1): from L *musca,* a fly, as in *muscicide* and *musciform.* The IE r would seem to be \**mu-.*

**musci-** (2); **musco-**: from L *muscus,* moss: cf MOSS. Exx: *muscicole,* living (cf *-colous*) in moss; *muscology.*

**muscul(o)-**: from *musculus,* a muscle: cf MUSCLE. Exx: *musculo-cutaneous* and *musculo-spiral.*

**museo-**: for *museum,* as in *museology,* the systematic collecting (Gr *legein,* to gather) and assemblage of objects for a museum.

**musico-**: for *music,* as in *musicologist,* or for *musical* (and), as in *musico-poetic.*

**Muso-**: from L *Mūsa* (cf MUSE). Ex: Zoo *Musophagi.*

**muta-, muto-; -mute**: from L *mūtāre* (s *mūt-*), to change (v.t.): cf MUTABLE. Exx: *muta-rotation, mutoscope; commute, permute.*

**my-.** See *myo-.*

**-mya**: from Gr *mus,* muscle, gen *muos.* Only in Conchology. Cf *myo-.*

**1 -myces; 2 -mycete, -mycetes; 3 mycet(o)-; 4 myc(o)-; 5 -mycosis.** 1, from Gr *mukēs,* fungus; 2, *-mycetes* (whence the sing *mycete*), from Gr *mukētes,* pl of *mukēs;* 3, from *mukētos,* gen of *mukēs;* 4, for *muko-,* from *mukēs;* 5, for *mycosis,* infestation of a bodily part by fungi. Exx: *Actinomyces; Schizomycetes; Myceto-phagous;—mycology, mycoplasm.*

**-myelia, myelino-, -myelitis; myel(o)-**: resp from Gr *-muelos,* c/f of *muelos,* marrow; from E *myelin* (Gr *muel*(os)+Chem suffix *-in*); for E *myelitis,* nflammation of the spinal cord; from Gr *muel*(o)-, c/f of Gr *muelos,* itself akin to *mus* (gen *muos*),

muscle. Exx: *micromyelia, myelinogenesis, osteo-myelitis; myelalgia, myelopathy.*

**-myia; myi(o)-**: from Gr *muia,* a fly, c/f *muio-*: akin to L *musca.* Ex: *Myiarchus.*

**myl(o)-**: Gr *mul*(o)-, c/f of *mulē,* a mill or a millstone, ult akin to MILL, denotes, in E, 'molar', as in *mylohyoid.*

**my(o)-**: Gr *mu*(o)-, c/f of *mus* (gen *muos;* s *mu-*), a mouse, hence a muscle. Exx: 'mouse', as in *Myomorpha* and *myomancy;* usu 'muscle', as in *myocardium,* muscular portion of heart-wall— *myodynamics — myogen — myograph — myology— myophore—myothermic.* Cf:

**myom(o)-**: for *myoma* (*my-*+suffix *-oma*), as in *myomotomy.*

**myri(a)-; myri(o)-**: resp Gr *mūria*s, a literal myriad (10,000), and the Gr c/f *mūri*(o)-, vaguely yet decidedly very numerous—countless. Cf MYRIAD. Exx: *myriagram*(me), *myrialitre, myria-metre; myriorama, myrioscope.*

**myringo-**: for *myringa,* the tympanic membrane (ML *myringa,* LL *mēninga,* Gr *mēninx*: cf *meningo-*above), as in *myringotomy.*

**myrio-.** See *myria-.*

**myristici-**, as in *myristicivorous,* (of birds) feeding on nutmegs—SciL *Myristica,* from Gr *muris-tikos,* good as a salve (*murizein,* to anoint).

**myrmeco-, myrmo-, -myrmex**: Gr *murmēko-,* c/f of *murmēx* (whence *-myrmex*), ant, gen *murmēkos,* akin to Skt *vamrás* and L *formīca.* Exx: *myrmeco-logy,* ant-lore, and *myrmecophagous,* ant-eating. The var *myrmo-* comes from the Gr var *murmox;* ex, *myrmotherine,* feeding on ants—cf Gr *thēran,* to hunt.

**myro-**: Gr *muro-,* c/f of *muron,* a sweet juice oozing from a plant, (hence) an unguent, app akin (with IE prefix *s-*) to Gr *smuris,* emery-powder, hence to E SMEAR. Exx: obs *myropolist* (Gr *muropolēs*), a perfumier; *Myrothamnus* (a shrub, Gr *thamnos*).

**myrrho-**, as in *myrrhophore* (cf *-phora*), simply stands for *myrrh.*

**myrti-**: from L *myrtus* (Gr *murtos*): cf MYRTLE. Exx: *myrtiform, myrtol* (cf *-ol-* below).

**-mys**: from Gr *mus,* a mouse, as in *Cynomys* (cf *cyno-*).

**mys(o)-**: from Gr *musos,* a soiling or staining, defilement, akin to Gr *mudos,* mildew. Ex: *myso-phobia,* a dread of dirt.

**myst-; mysteri(o)-; mystico-**: from, resp, Gr *mustēs* (s *must-*), an initiate of the religious mysteries; Gr *mustērion,* a religious mystery; Gr *mustikos,* of, by or for a religious mystery or a sacred rite. Cf MYSTERY. Exx: *mystagogue,* an initiator into, or an interpreter of, mysteries—Gr *mustagōgos,* cf *-agogue; mysteriosophy* (Gr *sophia,* wisdom); *mystico-religious.* In *mystify, mysti-* app represents *mystic.*

**mythico-; mytho-**: c/f of E *mythic,* as in *mythico-historical;* via LL *mȳtho-,* from Gr *mutho-,* as in *mythogenesis,* MYTHOLOGY, *mytho-poetic.* In *mythify, mythi-* represents *myth.*

**mytili-; mytilo-**: the former from L *mytilus,* a

sea mussel, from Gr *mutilos*, whence *mytilo-*. Exx: *mytiliform*, resembling a mussel; *mytilotoxine*, poisonous matter available in mussels.

**myxa-**: from Gr *muxa*, slime, mucus: cf *muci-* and MUCUS. Only in Zoo generic names. Cf:

**myx(o)-**: Gr *mux(o)-*, c/f of *muxa*, slime, mucus: cf *muci-*. Exx: 'mucous gland'—*myxadenitis*; 'mucous tissue'—*myxocyte* (cf *-cyte*); 'myxoma (a jelly-like tumour) combined with another (duly specified)'—*myxomycetes* (cf *-mycetes*), *myxorrhoea*.

**-myza**, pl, and **-myzon**, sing; **myzo-**: Zoo c/ff, from Gr *muzein* (s *muz-*), to suck; (*myzo-*) Bot c/f, of same origin. Exx: *Myzostoma* (cf *-stoma*).

**naemor-**: a SciL c/f from *nemoris*, gen of L *nemus*, a grove: cf the 2nd *nemo-*. Ex: Zoo *Naemorhedus*, a genus of goat, 2nd element L *haedus*, a goat.

**nann(o)-**, loosely; correctly **nan(o)-**: Gr *nan(o)-*, c/f of *nanos*, a dwarf, perh orig a nursery word. Exx: *nannander*, (in Bot) a dwarf male; *nannoplankton*, the smallest plankton;—*nanocephalic*; *nanomelus*, a short-limbed (cf *-melia*) monstrosity.

**nao-**: from Gr *naos*, a temple, akin to *naiō* (s *nai-*), I dwell. Ex: *naology*, a study of sacred buildings.

**naphth(o)-**: c/f for E *naphtha*, itself adopted from Gr; Gr νάφθα is akin to Per *naft* and Av *napta*, moist, IE r prob *nebh-*. Ex: *naphtho(-)quinone*.

**napi-**: from L *năpus* (s *năp-*), a turnip—prob a Medit word. Ex: *napiform*, (in Bot: of roots) turnip-shaped.

**narco-**: from Gr *narkē*, numbness, torpor, *stupor*: cf NARCOTIC. Exx: *narcohypnia*, numbness imm after sleep (cf *hypno-*); *narcolepsy* (cf *-lepsia*). Cf:

**narcotico-**, 'narcotic and': from E *narcotic*: cf prec. Ex: *narcotico-somniferous*.

**nari-**: from L *năris*, nostril, akin to *năsus*, nose: cf next. Ex: *nariform*, nostril-shaped.

**nasi-, naso-; nasuti-**: c/ff from L *năsus*, nose—cf *nari-* and E NOSE; c/f from L *năsūtus*, '(long-)nosed'. Exx: *nasilabial*, of nose and lips; *nasology*; *nasutiform*, nose-like.

**-nastic**, adj, and **-nasty**, n, only in Plant Physiology: from Gr *nastos*, close-pressed, from *nassein* (s *nass-*), to press close, to squeeze, prob of echoic origin. Exx: *thermonastic*, *thermonasty* (cf *thermo-*).

**nasuti-**. See *nasi-*.

**nati-** (1): from L *nates*, the buttocks, akin to Gr *nōton*, the back (cf *noto-*): as in *natiform*, buttock-shaped.

**nati-** (2): from L *nātus* (gen *nātūs*, s *nāt-*), birth, from *născi*, to be born, *nātus*, born. Ex: *natimortality*, rate of still births.

**natro-**: c/f of E *natron*: cf NITRE. Ex: *natrolite* (cf *-lite*).

**naturo-**: a rare c/f from L *nātūra*: cf NATURE. Ex: *naturopathy*, treatment by 'natural' methods.

**nau-; nauti-**: Gr *nau-*, c/f of *naus*, ship; (the rare *nauti-*) from derivative Gr *nautēs*, via L *nauta*, a sailor: cf E NAVAL. Exx: *naufragous*, causing or

caused by shipwreck (L *naufragus*, on analogy of Gr *nauagia*); *naupathia*, sea-sickness; *nauscopy*, the seeing (cf *-scope*) of very distant ships;—*nautiform*, resembling a ship. Cf:

**nav(i)-**: from ML *năvis*, L *năuis* (s *nău-*: cf prec), a ship. Exx: *navarch*, L *năuarchus*, an admiral; *naviform*; *navigerous*, capable of bearing or floating ships. In *navicert*, *navi-* stands for *naval* (*cert*ificate)

**ne-**. See *neo-*.

**nebuli-**: from L *nebula*, mist, a cloud: see NEBULA. Ex: *nebuliferous*, having cloud-like spots.

**necr(o)-**: Gr *nekr(o)-*, c/f of *nekros*, a corpse: cf NOXIOUS. Exx: *necrology* (cf *-logy* at *-loge*), a register or roll of the dead; *necromancy*, divination by communication with the dead, from Gr *nekromanteia* (cf *-mancy*), via L and F; *necropolis*, city (*-polis*) of the dead, i.e. a cemetery; *necrotomy* (cf *-tomy* at *-tome*), dissection of corpses.

**-nectae; nect(o)-**: resp a SciL pl c/f from Gr *nēktēs*, a swimmer, with corresponding adj *-nectous* (prompted by Gr *nektos*), and a Sci c/f from Gr *nektos* (adj), swimming, from *neō*, I swim, akin to L *nō*, I swim. Exx: *Physonectae*, *physonectous*, in Zoo; in Zoo: *nectocalyx*, a swimming bell—*nectopod*, a limb for swimming—*Necturus* (cf *-ure*), a large-tailed salamander.

**nectari-, nectaro-**: c/ff resp of L *nectar* and of the derivative E *nectar*: cf NECTAR. Exx: *nectariferous* and *nectarivorous*, nectar-secreting and -eating; *nectaro-*, only in Bot.

**negro-**: for *Negro*, as *negrophobia*, a morbid fear of Negroes.

**-nema; nema-, nemato-, nemo-**: c/ff from Gr *nēma*, a thread, a Gr word with many IE cognates. Exx: *Scytonema* (cf *scyto-*); *Nemalion* (SciL; Gr *leōn*, a lion); (*nemato-*: Gr *nēmat-*, o/s of *nēma*) *nematocyst* (cf *-cyst*) and *nematology*; *Nemopanthus* (*nemo-*+Gr *pous*, foot+*-anthus* for Gr *anthos*, a flower).

**nemo-** (1). See prec.

**nemo-** (2): from Gr *nemos* (s *nem-*), a wood, wooded pasture, glade, akin to syn L *nemus* (gen *nemoris*). Ex: *nemophily*, a love of woods and glades.

**ne(o)-**: Gr *ne(o)-*, c/f of *neos*, new, recent, akin to L *nouus* (ML *novus*): cf NEW. Exx: 'new' or 'recent'—*neo-Attic*, *neologism*, new-word-ism; 'a new and different form or period' of a faith, religious or philosophical, or a language—*Neo-Catholic*, *Neo-Darwinism*; 'neozoic'—*neolithic*; in Bot and Zoo, 'recent' or 'extant'—*neobotany*; in Bio, 'an immature, or a recently developed, form or part'—*neofetus* and *neomorph* (*-morph*); 'the New World'—*Nearctic*. (Based on Webster.)

**nepheli-; nephel(o)-**: the former, loose for Gr *nephel(o)-*, c/f of *nephelē*, a cloud, akin to L *nebula* and *nubes*. Exx: *nepheligenous*; *nephelometer* (nuance: 'cloudiness') and *nepheloscope*. Cf:

**nepho-**: Gr *nepho-*, c/f of *nephos*, a cloud, cf *nephelē* in prec; *nephograph*, a camera for cloud-effects; *nephology*, the meteorology of clouds.

**nephr(o)-**; secondarily, **-nephritis** and **-nephrosis**: Gr *nephr(o)-*, c/f of *nephros* (s *nephr-*), kidney, as in the Gr derivative (hence LL and Med E) *nephritis* (cf Med suffix *-itis*) and the SciL derivative *nephrosis* (cf suffix *-osis*); of IE stock, the r being perh *\*negh(u)r-*. Exx: *gastronephritis* (cf *gastro-*); *nephralgia*, kidney trouble—*nephrocyte* (*-cyte*)— *nephrolith* — *nephrology* — *nephropathy* — *nephrotomy—nephrotoxic*.

Neptuni-: for *Neptune* (L *Neptūnus*), as in *Neptunicentric*.

nereidi-; nereo-: both for the Zoo *Nereid*, from Gr *Nēreis* (gen *Nēreidos*), a daughter of *Nēreus*, a sea god, akin to *naein* (s *na-*), to flow. Exx: *nereidiform* and Bot *Nereocystis* (cf *-cyst*).

nertero-: from Gr *nerteros*, lower, and pl *nerteroi*, those of the Classic underworld, the dead, perh for *enerteroi*—cf *eneroi*, those below. Ex: *nerterology*, the lore concerning the dead.

nervi-, nervo-: E c/ff of ML *nervus*, L *neruus*, tendon, muscle, (hence) nerve, akin to Gr *neuron* (cf *neuro-* below). Exx: *nerviduct, nervimotor*; *nervomuscular, nervosanguineous*.

-nese; -nesia (adj -nesian); -nesus;—neso-: *-nese* is the E form of L *-nēsus* from Gr *-nēsos*, c/f— as is *nēso-* (whence *neso-*)—of *nēsos*, island, hence, in some cpds, region; *-nesia* (cf the Geog suffix *-ia*) is a SciL derivative from Gr *nēsos* (s *nēs-*), perh from an IE r meaning 'to swim': ? '(the) land that swims in the sea'. Exx: *Peloponnese*, usu *Peloponnesus*, from Gr *Peloponnēsos* (the land of Pelops) and *Chersonese* (Gr *Khersonēsos*); *Indonesia*, adj *Indonesian*, and *Micronesia* and *Polynesia*; *Nesonetta*, a flightless duck (Gr *nētta*) of the Auckland Islands.

nest(i)-: from Gr *nēstis*, (a) fasting, from *ne-*, not+*edein*, to eat. Exx: *nestiatria* (cf *-iatric*)= *nestitherapy*, a fasting cure.

-neura, 2 -neural, 3 -neure, 4 -neuria, 5 -neuric; 6 neuri-, 7 neur(o)-: 1, the pl of Gr *neuron*, nerve, denoting, in E, Zoo class-names, as *Schizoneura* (cf *schizo-*); 2, c/f of E adj *neural*, of, for, by a nerve or the nerves, as in *cardioneural* (cf *cardio-* at *-cardia*: heart); 3, *-neure* ('nerve cell'), from Gr *neuron*, as in *axoneure* (cf *axo-*: axis); 4, SciL term —'state of the nervous system'—from Gr *neur*(on) +Med suffix *-ia*, as in *dysneuria* (prefix *dys-*: bad); 5, 'having (thus many) neurons' or nerve cells, *neur-*+adj suffix *-ic*, as in *polyneuric* (*poly-*); 6, SciL c/f from Gr *neuron*, as in *neurilemma* (cf *-lemma*); 7, Gr *neur(o)-*, c/f of *neuron*, denoting in E 'nerve' or 'nervous tissue' or 'nervous system', as in *neuralgia* (cf *-algia*, pain)—*neurasthenia* (adj *neurasthenic*), 2nd element Gr *asthenia*, weakness— *neurocardiac* — *neurology* — *neurophagia* — *neuropathology* — *neuropsychosis* — *neurotomy* — *neurovaccine*.

neutro-: c/f for E *neutral*, as in *neutroceptor* and *neutrophile*.

nidi-, true L c/f, and nido-, analogous c/f, from L *nīdus* (IE r *\*nī-*), a nest. Exx: *nidicolous*, reared (cf *-colous*) in the nest—*nidificate*, to build nest(s), L *nīdificāre*, pp *nidificātus—nidifugous*, tending to flee the nest; *nidology*, bird's-nest lore.

nigri-: LL *nigri-*, c/f of L *niger* (gen *nigri*), black:

cf NEGRO. Ex: *nigrify*, LL *nigrificāre*, to make or render black.

nimbi-: L *nimbi-*, c/f of *nimbus* (s *nimb-*), rainstorm, rain-cloud, cloud, mist: cf NIMBUS. Exx: *nimbiferous*, rain-bearing, (hence) rain-producing; *nimbification*, a rain-making, (hence) the forming of clouds.

nitramino-: for *nitramine* (*nitr(o)-*+*amine*). Only in Chem. Cf:

nitrato-: c/f for *nitrate*; only in Chem.

nitri-; nitr(o)-: resp from L *nitrum*, and from its original, the Gr *nitron* (c/f *nitro-*), nitre: see NITRE. Exx: *nitrification, nitriferous*; *nitrobacteria*, NITROGEN, *nitroglycerin(e)*. Cf:

nitrilo-: c/f for NITRILE; in Chem only.

nitrito-: c/f for NITRITE; in Chem only.

nitro-. See *nitri-*.

nitroso-: from L *nitrōsus*, nitrous. Ex: *nitrosochloride*. Cf *nitri-*.

nivi-: from L *nix*, snow, ML gen *nivis* (L *niuis*): akin to the syn Homeric *niphas* (s *niph-*) and W *nyf*; all—cf Ir *snigid*, it snows—are akin to SNOW. Ex: *nivicolous* (cf *-colous*), living either in or amid snow; cf *niveous* (ML *niveus*, L *niueus*), snowy, and *nivosity*, degree-or state of snow (from ML *nivōsus*, L *niuōsus*, snowy).

noci-: from L *nocēre* (s *noc-*), to harm or hurt: cf NOXIOUS. Ex: *nociperception*, (in Med) perception of painful stimuli.

noct(i)-, nocto-: the true L c/f and an analogous c/f of L *nox* (gen *noctis*), night; akin to NIGHT. Exx: *noctambulant*, sleep-walking, adj and n; *noctiluca* (adopted from L), a shiner by night, i.e. phosphorus, a luminous marine organism; *noctivagant, noctivagous* (ML *noctivāgus*, L *-uāgus*), night-wandering;—*noc ograph, noctovision*.

nodi-: from L *nōdus* (s *nōd-*), a knot, akin ult to E NET (n). Exx: *nodicorn*, having knot-like antennae (cf *-corn*); *nodiferous*, node-producing; *nodiflorous*, flowering at the nodes or stem-joints.

noema-: Gr *noēma*, the understanding, from *noein*, to think, know by thinking, cf *nous*, mind. Exx: *noematachograph, noematachometer*: *noema*+ *tacho-* (from Gr *takhos*, swiftness)+*-graph, -meter*. Cf *noo-*.

-nomen; nomen-: L *-nōmen, nomen-*, c/ff of *nōmen*, a name, akin to NAME. Exx: L *agnōmen* (*ad*, to+*nōmen*), an additional cognomen; L *cognōmen* (*co-*, with+*nōmen*), family name; L *praenōmen* (*prae*, before+*nomēn*), equivalent to a Christian name;—*nomenclature* (L *nōmenclatūra*), a naming-system, akin to *nōmenclātor* (L), a caller (L *calāre*, to call) or recounter of names.

nom(o)-; -nomy: Gr *nomo-*, c/f of *nómos* (νόμος), usage, law, occ of *nomós* (νομός), a district—in effect, the same word, both (s *nom-*) deriving from *nemein* (s *nem-*), to divide—cf NOMAD; *-nomy*, Gr *-nomia*, from *nomos*, law. Exx: *nomarch* (cf *-arch*), the chief magistrate of a mod Gr district; *nomocracy* (cf *-cracy*), government by law; *nomography*, the art of law-drafting; *nomology*, the science of law; *nomothetic*(al), legislative; *-nomy*, 'a system of laws' or 'a field of knowledge', as in ASTRONOMY and *bionomy*.

**-nomy.** See *nomo-*.

**-non(a)-**: from L *nōnus* (s *nōn-*), ninth; mostly in Chem, e.g. *nonacosane* and *nonadecane*, and, less, in Math, e.g. *nonagon*, a 9-sided figure.

**noo-**: Gr *noo-*, from Gr *nóos*, Attic *nous*, the mind—cf *noema-*. Exx: *noology*, the science of intuitive reason; *nooscopic* (cf *-scope*), of or for or by an inspection of the mind.

**normo-**: c/f for *normal* (q.v. at NORM.)

**nos(o)-; -nosus**: resp Gr *nos(o)-*, c/f of *nosos*, disease, and (*-nosus*) a Latinizing of *nosos*, s *nos-*, of obscure origin. Exx: *nosography*, a description—hence, a classification—of diseases; *nosology*, the description, hence the treatment of disease; *nosomania*, a suffering from an imaginary disease;— *myonosus*.

**nost(o)-**: from Gr *nostos*, a return to one's home, from *neomai*, I go or come, I return, app for PGr *\*nesomai*, from an IE r *nes-*, to go, or come, esp home. Exx: *nostalgia* (whence *nostalgic*), pain for a return home, homesickness, cf *-algia*; *nostology*, in Bio the study of the senile stages of organisms.

**nostri-**: L *nostri*, gen sing of *noster*, our. Ex: *nostrificate* (cf *-ficate* at *-fic*), to accept as (equal to) one's own (esp, degrees).

**-nosus.** See *noso-*.

**notho-**: Gr *notho-*, c/f of *nothos*, illegitimate, spurious, whence, via L *nothus*, the rare adj *nothous*. Ex: *Nothofagus*, a 'spurious' beech (L *fagus*); *Nothosaurus* (cf *-saur*).

**noti-.** See *notify* at NOTE.

**notio-**: from L *notius*, southern, from Gr *notios*, damp, rainy, southern, from *notos*, south wind. Ex: Zoo *Notiosorex* (cf *sorici-*).

**not(o)-; -notus**: from Gr *nōt(o)-*, c/f of *nōton*, the back, akin to L *nates*, the buttocks; (*-notus*) from the L *notus*, from the Gr var *nōtos*, the back. Exx: *notochord*; *nototribe*, back-touching (from Gr *tribein*, to rub); *Camponotus* (from Gr *kampē*, a bending). Contrast:

**noto-** (2): from Gr *notos*, the south wind, the south. Exx: *Notogaea*, a Biogeographical realm in the Southern Hemisphere; *Notornis*, a New Zealand flightless bird—'a bird of the South'; *Notoryctes*, a marsupial mole—'a digger (Gr *oruktēs*) of the South'.

**-notus.** See the 1st *noto-*.

**novem-, noven-**: from ML *nōvem* (L *nōuem*), nine: cf NOVEMBER. Exx: *novemcostate* (cf *-costal*), nine-ribbed, and *novemfid*, cut into nine segments; *novendial* (ML *nōvendiālis*, L *nōuen-*), lasting nine days (L *diēs*, a day), and *novennial* (ML *nōvennis*, L *nōu-*), coming every ninth year (cf *-ennial*).

**novi-, nov(o)-**: from ML *novus* (L *nouus*), new— cf NEW. Exx: *novilunar*, of or at the new moon (cf *lunar*, of the L *lūna* or moon); *Novanglian*, (a person) of New England, and *Novo-Zelanian*, of or in or for or by New Zealand.

**nubi-**: L *nūbi-*, c/f of *nūbes* (s *nūb-*), a cloud, prob akin to *nebula*. Exx: *nubiferous* and *nubi-* *genous*, cloud-producing, and *nubiform*, cloud-shaped.

**nuch(i)-**: from ML *nucha* (cf MF-F *nuque*), the nape, from Ar *nukhā'*, spinal marrow. Ex: *nuchalgia* (cf *-algia*).

**nuci-**: L *nuci-*, c/f of *nux* (gen *nucis*), a nut: akin to NUT. Exx: *nuciculture*, nut-growing; *nucivorous*, nut-eating. Cf:

**nuclei-, nucle(o)-**: c/ff for E *nucleus*, as in *nucleiform* and *nucleofugal*, tending to flee the nucleus. Cf:

**nucleolo-**: cf for (L and E) *nucleolus*, as in Bio *nucleolocentrosome*: *nucleolo-*+*centro-*+*-some*, q.v. at *-soma*.

**nudi-**: L *nūdi-*, c/f of *nūdus* (s *nūd-*), naked: cf NUDE. Exx: *nudicaudate*, hairlessly tailed, and *nudiflorous*, having bare-surfaced flowers.

**nugi-**: L *nūgi-*, c/f of *nūgae*, trifles, whence LL *nūgacitās* (gen *-citātis*), triviality, E *nugacity*, and, via *nūgāri*, to trifle, L *nūgātōrius*, trifling, *-Enugatory*. Exx: *nugify* (cf *-fy*) and *nugilogue* (cf *logue* at *-loger*).

**nulli-**: L *nūlli-*, c/f of *nūllus*, null, non-existent (*ne*, not+*ūllus*, any). Exx: *nullifidian*, a sceptic (cf *fide-*); *nullify* (LL *nūllificāre*, to render null); in Bot, *nulliplex* and *nullipore*.

**numero-**: from L *numerus*, number, as in *numerology*, the (pseudo) science of numbers. Cf NUMBER.

**numismato-**: for *numismatic*, of or relating to coins, itself via F from L *numisma*, a coin, from Gr *nomisma*, the current coin(age), from *nomos*, law (cf the 1st *nomo-*). Ex: *numismatology*, now usu *numismatics* (cf *ethics* from adj *ethic*).

**nummi-**: from L *nummus*, a coin, perh from Gr *nomimos*, lawful (from *nomos*—cf *nomo-*), but perh rather a conflation of L *numerus*, number. Ex: *nummiform*, coin-shaped.

**nutri-**: from L *nūtrīre* (s *nūtr-*), to nourish; as in *nutrify* (cf *-fy*).

**nycteri-; -nycteris**: from Gr *nukteris*, a bat, from *nukt-*, o/s of *nux*, night. It occurs only in Zoo generic names. Cf:

**nyct(i)-, nyct(o)-**: from Gr *nukt(i)-*, *nukt(o)-*, c/ff of *nux* (gen *nuktos*), night, akin to L *nox* (cf *nocti-* above) and E NIGHT. Exx: *nyctalopia* (adopted from LL), from L *nyctalops*, from Gr *nuktalōps*, a person suffering from either night- or day-blindness, but perh a direct adaptation of LGr *nuktalōpia* (*nukt-*+*al*(aos), blind+*opia*, vision, from *ōps*, eye); *nyctitropism*, the tendency of e.g. clover leaflets to assume special nocturnal positions; *nyctophobia* (cf *-phobe*).

**-nym.** See *-onym*.

**nympho-**: from Gr *numpho-*, c/f of *numphē*, a nymph: cf NYMPH. Exx: *nympholepsy*, a being ecstatically enchanted by a nymph; *nymphomania*, an habitual excess of eroticism in a woman.

**-nyxis**: from Gr *nuxis*, a pricking or a stabbing, from *nussein*, Attic *nuttein*, to prod or prick or stab. In Surg it denotes a puncture, as in *scleronyxis* (cf *sclero-*).

**oari(o)-**: from Gr *ōiarion*, a small egg, from *ōion*,

an egg; syn with *ovario-*, q.v. Exx: *oarialgia* and *oariotomy*.

**objecti-.** See *objectify* at OBJECT.

**obtusi-:** from L *obtūsus*, obtuse, lit blunted, from *obtundere*, to blunt. Ex: *obtusipennate*, blunt-feathered. Cf *contusion*.

**occipito-:** for E *occiput*, adopted from L *occiput* (*ob*, towards+*caput*, the head—cf CAPITAL), gen *occipitis*, o/s *occipit-*, whence the ML adj *occipitālis*, whence *occipital*: 'occipital and', as in *occipitofrontal*.

**occluso-:** from L *occlūsus*, closed (from *claudere*, to shut, close). Ex: *occlusometer*. Cf CLOSE.

**oceano-:** c/f for OCEAN. Exx: *oceanography* (cf *-graphy* at *-graph*), the geography of the ocean.

**ocelli-:** from L *ocellus*, a little eye, hence an eye-like spot; dim of *oculus*, q.v. at *oculi-*. Exx: *ocelliferous, ocelliform*. Cf EYE.

**ochlo-:** Gr *okhlo-*, c/f of *okhlos*, a crowd, a mob, the populace; basic idea perh 'a stirring, a moving'—? cf WAGGON. Exx: *ochlocracy*, via F *ochlocratie* from Gr *okhlokratia*, mob-rule (cf *-cracy*); *ochlophobia*, a morbid fear of crowds.

**ochro-:** Gr *ōkhro-*, c/f of *ōkhros*, pale-yellow, the n being *ōkhra*, whence *ochre*. Ex: *ochrolite* (cf *-lite*, stone).

**oct(a)-, oct(o)-, octu-:** 1st, 2nd, from Gr *okta-, okt(ō)-*, c/ff of *oktō*, eight; *octo-* occ from derivative L *octo; octu-*, L *octu-*, c/f of *octo*; cf EIGHT. Exx: *octachord*, an eight-stringed instrument, from Gr *oktakhordos*, having eight strings; *octagon*, via L from Gr *oktagōnos*, eight-cornered; *octahedron*, Gr *oktaedron*, from *oktaedros*, eight-sided; *octameter*, n from LL adj *octameter*, from Gr *oktametros*, having eight (metrical) feet; *octangular*, from L *octangulus*, eight-cornered; *octarchy* (cf *-archy*, rule, at *-arch*), a state ruled by, or government by, eight persons; OCTOPUS; *octuplication*, LL *octuplicatio* (gen *-plicationis*).

**oculi-, ocul(o)-:** from L *oculus*, an eye: cf EYE. Exx: *oculiform*, eye-shaped; *oculomotor* (adj), eyeball-moving; *oculo-nasal*, of the eye and nose.

**ocy-:** Gr *ōku-*, c/f of *ōkus*, swift, akin to L *ocior*, swifter, and Skt *āçús*, swift. Exx: the Zoo *Ocydromus, Ocypode, Ocroë*, all from Gr originals.

**-od; -odic-:** c/f of *od* (adj *odic*), Reisenbach's supposed natural force or power, arbitrarily named, yet perhaps from Gr *hodos*, the way: cf the 2nd *-ode*. Exx: *crystallod, magnetod, pantod*; adjj in *-odic*.

**-ode** (1), 'thing that resembles' as in *geode* (cf *geo-*); pl *-odes*, esp for generic names in Bot and Zoo, as in *Acanthodes* (cf *acantho-*). From Gr *-ōdēs* (pl *-ōdes*), c/f formed from connective *-o-* and *-eidēs*, like, similar, from *eidos*, form. Cf *-ody*, from Gr *-ōdia*, a resembling, hence a transformation into, as in *petalody*.

**-ode** (2), as in *cathode* (cf prefix *cata-*) and *electrode*: from Gr *hodos*, path or way: cf and see the 2nd *odo-*.

**-ode** (3) or obs *-ody*; adj *-odic*; agent *-odist*: first two, from Gr *-ōidia*, c/f of *ōidē*, a song; *-odic*, from Gr *-ōidikos*; *-odist=od(e)*+suffix *-ist*. Exx:

*palinode*, obs *-ody*, Gr *palinōidia* (παλινῳδία), a singing-again or *-back*, a recantation; *palinodic*, Gr *palinōidikos*. Cf ODE.

**-odic.** See *-od* and *-ode* (3).

**odio-:** from L *odor*, smell, but shape-influenced by L *odium*. Ex: *odiometer*, for the detection of odorous vapours.

**odo-** (1), 'tooth': irregular c/f from Gr *odōn*, a tooth, and occurring only in such Zoo techh as *Odobenus* and *Odocoileus*. Cf *-odon*.

**odo-** (2), 'way': from Gr *hodo-*, c/f of *hodos* (ὁδός), 'path, road, route, way', s *hod-*, app akin to the *ced-* of L *cēdere*, to go; IE s, perh *khed-* or *khod-* Ex: *odograph*, an instrument measuring either distance or, for a walker, length and pace of stride—cf *odometer*. Cf *hodo-*.

**odo-** (3): irreg from E *odo(u)r*, as in *odophone*. Cf *odori-*.

**1 -odon; 2 -odont, 3 -odonta, 4 -odontes, 5 -odontia, 6 -odonty; 7 -odus;—8 odont(o)-:** 1, Gr *-odōn*, c/f of *odōn* (gen *odontos*), a tooth, with E denotation '-toothed', as in *mastodon* (cf *masto-* at *-mastia*), 'so called from the conical [lit, breast-shaped] projections upon its molar teeth' (Webster); 2, from *odont-*, o/s of *odōn*, with pll *-odonta*, occ *-odontes*, as in *lophodont* (cf *lopho-*) and *Bunodonta* (cf *buno-*); 5 (*-odontia*) 'form or condition or treatment of teeth', from *odont-*, o/s of *odōn*+Med suffix *-ia*, as in *macrodontia* (cf *macro-*); 6 (*-odonty*) 'type of formation of the teeth', from *odont-*+*-y* (n suffix), as in *selenodonty* (cf *seleno-*, from Gr *selēnē*, the moon); 7 (*-odus*), Gr *-odous*, c/f of *odous* (better *odōn*), tooth, with E denotation '-toothed', as in *Chiasmodus*, from Gr *khiasma*, two lines set crosswise; 8 (*odonto-*), Gr o/s *odont-*+connective *-o-* (usu omitted before a vowel), as in *odontology*, tooth-lore, and *odontotomy* (cf *-tomy* at *-tome*).

**odori-; odoro-:** the former=L *odori-*, c/f of *odor*, odour; the latter, by Gr *influence*, from L *odor*: cf ODOR. Exx: *odoriferous*, smell-yielding, now usu sweet-scented, perfumed, from L *odorifer* (cf *-fer*); *odorometer*.

**-ody.** See the 1st and 3rd *-ode*.

**-odyne; -odynia:** resp from Gr *odunē*, pain, as is adj *anodyne*, L *anodynus*, Gr *anodunos*, free from —hence, assuaging—pain; and from Gr *-odunia*, c/f of *odunē* (s *odun-*), perh from IE r *ed-*, to eat (into); hence, in E, morbid pain, as in *neurodynia* (cf *neuro-* at *-neura*). Adjj in *-odynic*, as in *anodynic, neurodynic*.

**-oeca, -oecia; oeco-:** first two, from Gr *oikos*, a house, the former in Zoo, the latter in Bot; *oeco-*, a now rare var of *eco-*, q.v. Exx: *Bioeca; Monoecia; oecodomic* (Gr *oikodomikos*, skilled in building), architectural, and *oecumenic* (Gr *oikomenikos*, adj of *oikoumenē* (*gē*: the inhabited world), world-wide, general—cf ECONOMIC.

**oede-, oedi-:** from Gr *oidein* (s *oid-*), to swell. Only in Zoo; exx, *Oedemeridae* and *Oedicnemus*. The var *oedo-*, as in *Oedogonium*, occurs only in Bot.

**oen(o)-:** the L form of Gr *oin(o)-*, c/f of *oinos*,

wine, akin to L *uīnum*, ML *vīnum*: cf WINE. Exx: *oenocyte* (cf *-cyte*)—*oenology*, a study (*-logy*) of wines—*oenomancy*, divination (*-mancy*) by wine—*oenophilist*, a wine-lover—*oenopoetic*, concerned with wine-making (cf POET). The subsidiary *oenanth(o)-*, occurring in Chem, derives from Gr *oinanthē* (*oinē*, vine+*anthē*, bloom).

**oesophag(o)-**. See *esophago-*.

**oestr(i)-**: from L *oestrus*, Gr *oistros*, a gadfly, (hence) fury, frenzy: cf IRE. Ex: *oestriasis* (cf *-iasis*).

**oïdio-**: from SciL *oïdium*, fungus, lit a dim from Gr *ōion* (cf L *ouum*, ML *ovum*), an egg. Ex: *oïdiomycosis* (cf *-mycosis* at *-myces*).

**oiko-**: a now very rare var of *eco-*, q.v. Ex: *oikology*, ecology; also, household management.

**oino-**: a now rare var of *oeno-*, q.v. Exx: *oinology*, *oinomancy*.

**-ol** (1), as in *cresol* and *glycerol*, derives from alcoho*l* and represents either 'alcohol' or 'phenol'.

**-ol** (2), as in *benzol*, is a var of *-ole*, and derives from L *oleum*, olive oil (from *olea*, an olive or an olive tree)—cf OIL.

**-ole**. See prec.

**ole-**. Short, before a vowel, for *oleo-*, q.v. in:

**olei-; oleo-**: resp from L *oleum* and from L *oleo-*, c/f of *oleum*, olive—hence, any—oil: cf the 2nd *-ol*. Exx: *oleiferous*, oil-producing; *oleograph*, *oleometer*, *oleoresin*, *oleothorax*. In Chem, *oleo-* is the c/f for *oleic* and *olein*, as in *oleomargarine*.

**olfacto-**: for *olfactory*, of, by, for the sense of smell, from L *olfacere*, to smell, from *odefacere*, to cause to smell. Exx: *olfactology*, *olfactometer*.

**-olic; -olid(e)**: in Chem terms only.

**olig(o)-**: Gr *olig(o)-*, c/f of *oligos*, small, and the pl *oligoi*, the few, s *olig-*, akin to Gr *loigos* (s *loig-*), ruin, death. Exx: *oligarchy*, rule by the few; *oligodontous*, scant-toothed; *oligophrenia*, feeble-mindedness.

**olivi-**: ML *olīvi-*, L *olīui-*, c/f of *olīva*, *olīua*, olive(-tree): cf OLIVE. Ex: *oliviferous*, ML *olīvifer*, L *olīuifer*, olive-bearing, hence -producing.

[**-ology** is not an element: it represents the dominant Gr, hence the predominant E, connective *-o-*+*-logy*, q.v. at *-loger*. But the frequency of its occurrence accounts for the individual *ology* of 'the *ologies* and *isms*'.]

**olpidi-**: irreg from Gr *olpis* (gen *olpidos*), a leather flask. Ex: Bot *Olpidiaster*.

**ombri-; ombro-**: the former, anl with the L connective *-i-*, the latter true to Gr *ombro-*, c/f of *ombros*, a shower, rain, akin to Skt *ámbhas*, water, and perh to L *imber*, a (heavy) shower, rain. Exx: *ombrifuge* (cf *-fuge*), a protection from rain; *ombrograph*, *ombrometer*, forms of rain-gauge; *ombrophilous* and *-phobous*, (in Bot) capable—incapable—of withstanding much rain.

**oment(o)-**: for L and E (in An) *omentum*, a kind of caul, prob from root of L *induere*, to cover, and *exuere*, to pull off, to shed. Ex: *omentotomy* (cf *-tomy* at *-tome*).

**omma-, ommato-**: from Gr *omma*, the eye, gen *ommatos*: perh (Hofmann) for *\*opma*: cf *-ope*.

Exx: *Ommastrephes*, lit 'the eye-turners'; *ommatophore* (cf *-phore* at *-phora*).

**omni-**: L *omni-*, c/f of *omnis*, neu *omne*, all (quantity), and *omnes*, neu *omnia* (number): cf OMNIBUS. Exx: *omnifarious*, of all shapes or sizes, L *omnifārius* (cf *-farious*); *omnipotence*, unlimited power (cf POTENT) in everything, from LL *omnipotentia*, from L *omnipotens* (gen *-potentis*), whence *omnipotent*; *omnipresent*, ML *omnipraesens* (gen *-praesentis*: cf PRESENT); *omniscience*, all-knowledge, ML *omniscientia*; *omnivorous* (cf *-vora*), all-devouring, anything-eating, from ML *omnivorus*, L *omniuorus*.

**om(o)-** (1): Gr *ōmo-*, c/f of *ōmos*, the shoulder, akin to L *humerus*, cf *humero-*. Exx: *omodynia*, pain (cf *-odyne*) in the shoulder; *omoplate*, the scapula or shoulder-blade, from Gr *ōmoplatē*, a *platē* being a FLAT surface.

**omo-** (2): Gr *ōmo-*, c/f of *ōmos*, raw, akin to syn Skt *amas*, OIr *om*; IE s, prob *ōmo-*, alternating with *ŏmo-* and having var *ăma-*; r, *\*om-*, *\*am-*. Ex: *omophagous*, habitually eating (cf *-phagous* at *-phaga*) raw flesh, Gr *ōmophagos*.

**omphal(o)-; -omphalus**: Gr *omphal(o)-*, c/f of *omphalos* (s *omphal-*), the navel—indeed, see NAVEL; *omphalus*, the SciL form of Gr *omphalos*. Exx: *omphaloskepsis*, (a) navel-gazing—a practice of the *omphalopsychites* (cf *psycho-*) or Hesychasts (from Gr *hēsukhos*, calm, still, still and calm) or contemplatives.

**oncho-**, as in *onchocerciasis* (*oncho-*+*cerc-* for Gr *kerk*(os), a tail+*-iasis*), is a var of:

**onco-** (1): from Gr *onkos*, weight, (a) mass, bulk, largeness, as in *oncometer*, but in Mod Gr and E Med a tumour, as in *oncology* and *oncotomy*. The Gr *óγκος*, *onkos*, seems to be an altered metathesis of the *enenk-* of *ἐνεγκεῖν*, *enenkein* (an aorist inf), to carry; the IE s was perh *\*enek-* to reach, (but also) to carry, as Boisacq proposes. Cf the derivative SciL *-oncus*, a tumour in a (specified) part, as in *nephroncus* (cf *nephr-*, for *nephro-*, 'kidney-').

**onco-** (2): from Gr *onkos* (*óγκος*), a hook or a barb, s *onk-*, akin to the *unc-* of L *uncus*, hooked, hence, n, a hook, and to Gr *ankōn* (*ἀγκών*), angle or hook of the arm, i.e. the elbow. Ex: *Oncorhynchus* (cf *-rhynchus* at *rhyncho-*, 'snout').

**-oncus**. See the 1st *onco-*, at end.

**ondo-**: from OF-F *onde* (L *unda*), a wave: cf *undi-*. Exx: *ondometer*, *ondoscope*.

**oneir(o)-; oneiro-; onir(o)-**: Gr *oneir(o)-*, c/f of *oneiros* (s *oneir-*), a dream; cf the syn Aeolic *onoiros* and Cretan *anairos*—and Arm *anurj*; IE r, *\*onar-* or *\*oner-* or *\*onir-* or *\*onor-*, with varr *\*anar-*, *aner-*, etc. Exx: *oneirocritic(al)*, Gr *oneirokritikos*, skilled in—or relating to—the interpretation of dreams; *oneiromancy*, divination (*-mancy*) by dream.

**onisci-**: from SciL *Oniscus*, a genus of wood lice, from the syn Gr *oniskos*, orig 'the little ass', dim of *onos*, ass.

**-onium**: Chem c/f for *ammonium*, as in *sulphonium*.

**ono-** (1): Gr *ono-*, c/f of *onos*, an ass, akin to L *asinus*, akin to Sumerian *anšu*, *anše*: cf ASS. Exx: *Onobrychis*, Gr *onobrukhis*, lit 'ass-fodder', from *brukhein*, to eat greedily; *onocentaur*, Gr *onokentauros*; *onolatry*, ass-worship. Cf *onisco-*.

**ono-** (2): a faulty c/f from Gr *onoma*, a name: cf next. Ex: *onomancy* (cf *-mancy*), divination by names.

**onomato-**: Gr *onomato-*, c/f of *onoma*, a name, gen *onomatos*, o/s *onomat-*; akin to L *nōmen*, E NAME. Exx: *onomatology*, terminology; *onomatomania*, a senseless repetition of certain words or phrases; *onomatopoeia*, lit 'name-making', the LL form of Gr *onomatopoiia*, 2nd element from *poiein*, to make (cf POET). Cf *-onym*.

**onto-**: either from Gr *ont-*, o/s of *-ōn* (gen *ontos*), existing, being, or from Gr 'ta *onta*', the existents, the things that are, the realities, reality, *onta* being the neupl of *ōn*, existing. Exx: *ontogeny* (cf *-geny* at *-gen*); *ontography*; *ontology*, the philosophy (cf *-logy* at *-loger*) of reality, from Eccl L *ontologia* (cf *-logia*).

1 **-onycha**, 2 **-onyches**, 3 **-onychia**, 4 **-onychus**, 5 **-onyx**; 6 **onycho-**: (1)-(3), pll of (4), *-onychus*, SciL from Gr *-onukhos*, from *onux* (whence 5, *-onyx*), nail or claw, or rather from its o/s *onukh-* (gen *onukhos*), cf NAIL; 6, *onycho-*, from Gr *onukh(o)-*, c/f of *onux*, gen *onukhos*. Exx: *scleronychia* (cf *sclero-*); *acronyx*; *onychopathy*, *onychophagy* (nail-eating, i.e. -biting).

**-onym**, **-onyma**, **-onymic**, **-onymous**, **-onymy**: *-onyma* comes from the f sing or the neupl of Gr *-ōnumos* (adj), 'named'; *-onym*, name, comes from Gr *-ōnumon*, c/f of *onuma*, var of *onoma* (cf *onomato-* above), a name; *-onymic*, from LL *-onymicus*, from Gr *-ōnumikos*, from *onuma*—in E, adj and derivative n; *-onymous*, adj, from Gr *-ōnumos*, from *onuma*; *-onymy*, (occ via F *-onymie*) from Gr *-ōnumia*. Cf L *nōmen* and E NAME.

Exx: *pseudonym*, F *pseudonyme*, from Gr *pseudōnumos* (adj), bearing a false name (cf *pseudo-*), whence directly the adj *pseudonymous*; *Anonyma*, fanciful female name, and *anonyma*, the innominate artery, but also, as pl, anonymous works; *patronymic*, n from adj, LL *patrōnymicus*, Gr *patrōnumikos*, from *patēr*, father, and *onuma*; *anonymous*, Gr *anōnumos*, nameless (privative *a-*); *synonymy*, LL *synōnymia*, Gr *suncnumia*, from *sunōnumos*, named together, whence LL *synōnymus*, whence *synonymous*—cf *synonym*, like F *synonyme* from LL *synōnyma*, pl of *synōnymum*, L attempt at Gr *sunōnumon*, orig the neu s of *sunōnumos* synonymous.

**-onyx.** See *-onycha*.

**oö-**; **oöphor(o)-** and **oöthec(o)-**: resp Gr *ōo-*, c/f of *ōion*, an egg, akin to L *ōuum* (ML *ōvum*); from SciL *oöphoron*, an ovary, *oö-*+the neu of Gr *-phoros*, bearing, from *pherein*, to bear; from SciL *oötheca*, an egg-case, *oö-*+L *thēca*, from Gr *thēkē*, a case (container). Exx: *oöcyst*, *-cyte*, *-gamete*, *-gonium*, *-lite*, *-logy*, *-mancy*, *-meter*, *-phyte*, *-plasm*, *-spore*; *oöphoromania*, insanity caused by disease of ovaries.

**opaci-**: from L *opācus*—cf OPAQUE. Ex: *opacify* (cf *-fy*).

1 **-ope**, 2 **-opia**, 3 **-opic**, 4 **-opis**, 5 **-ops**, 6 **-opy**: 1, from Gr *-ōps*, c/f of *ōps*, eye; 2, from L *-opia*, from Gr *-ōpia*, from *ōps*, gen *ōpos*, *-opy* being, occ via F *-opie*, the E shape; 3, from or anl with Gr *-ōpikos*, occ via L *-opicus* and F *-opique*; 4, Gr *-ōpis*, *-eyed*, like (4) from *ōp-*, the o/s of *ōps*, whence the *-ops* of *Cyclops* and many Sci terms.

Exx: *myope*, a short-sighted person, adopted from EF-F, from LL *myops*, from Gr *muōps* (gen *muōpos*), i.e. *mu-*, s of *muein*, to close+*-ops*; *myopia*, SciL, and *myopy*, from F *myopie*; *Cyclopic*, of or like a Cyclops, from Gr *kuklōpikos*, adj of Gr *kuklōps*, L and E *Cyclops*, (the) round-eyed (one), from *kuklos* (c/f *kukl(o)-*), a circle+*-ōps*.

**opera-**, as in *operameter* (an instrument for counting rotations): L *opera*, pl of *opus* (gen *operis*), work; but in *operalogue* it=E *opera*.

**operculi-**: for E, from L, *operculum*, a cover or lid, (hence, in Zoo) a lid-like part or process; from *operīre*, to cover. Ex: *operculiferous*.

**ophi(o)-**; **-ophis**: Gr *ophi(o)-*, c/f of *ophis* (whence *-ophis*), a serpent, s *oph-*, akin to L *anguis* (cf *angui-* above); IE etymon *\*oghis* or *\*eghis*, r *\*ogh-* or *\*egh-*. Exx: *Ophioglossum* or adder's-tongue (Bot), *ophiolatry* or serpent-worship, *ophiolite* or serpentine, *ophiomorphic*, *Ophisaurus*; *Hydrophis*. The Gr dim *ophidion*, a little snake, yields the c/f *ophidio-*, as in *ophidiophobia*, a dread of snakes.

**ophthalm(o)-**: Gr *ophthalm(o)-*, c/f of *ophthalmos*, eye, app akin to *ōps* (q.v. at *-ope*) and *opsis*, sight (q.v. at *-opsia*). Exx: *ophthalmology*, the science of the eyes; *ophthalmoscope*, an instrument for looking (cf *-scope*) inside the eye. For end-c/ff we have *-ophthalma*, as in *Edriophthalma* (from Gr *hedra*, a seat: cf *-hedral*), and, ? loosely, *-ophthalmia*, as in *Podophthalmia* (cf *-pod*), both being neupl forms; *-ophthalmia*, Gr *-ophthalmia* (f sing), for *ophthalmia*, inflammation of the eye, as in *cirsophthalmia* (cf *cirso-*); *-ophthalmus*, a SciL c/f, as in *megalophthalmus* (cf *megalo-* at *mega-*).

**-opia**, **-opic.** See *-ope*.

**opio-**: for L *opium* or adopted E OPIUM, as in *opiomania*. Cf *opo-*.

**-opis.** See *-ope*.

**opo-**: Gr *opo-*, c/f of *opos* (s *op-*), juice, perh of non-IE origin. Ex: *opobalsam(um)*, L *opobalsamum*, Gr *opobalsamon* (*opo-*+*balsamon*, balsam); *opopanax*, adopted from Gr, 2nd element *panax*, pl *panakes*, some sort of herb, from *panakēs*, all-curing; *opotherapy*.

**oppositi-**: from L *oppositus*, (placed or situated) opposite, cf OPPOSITE. Ex: *oppositiflorous*.

**-ops.** See *-ope*.

**-opsia**, Gr and derivative L form, and **-opsy**, its E shape; **-opsis;**—**opsio-**: resp Gr *-opsia*; Gr *-opsis*; (*opsio-*) from Gr *opsis*, sight, whence obviously *-opsis* and almost as obviously *-opsia*; *opsis* is akin to Homeric *osse*, the two eyes, and both to *ōps*, eye (cf *-ope* above): cf OPTIC. Exx: *anopsia*, blindness (cf prefix *an-*, not); *Amblyopsis*, a blindfish (cf *ambly-*); *opsiometer*, an optometer (for measuring sight).

**opsoni-, opsono-**: c/ff for *opsonin*, a blood-serum constituent, from Gr *opsōnein*, to purchase victuals. Exx: *opsoniferous* and *opsonotherapy*.

**1 opti-, 2 optico-, 3 opto-; 4 -optic, 5 -opticon**: 1–3 are all c/ff of the E adj *optic*, but 1 and 3 denote 'vision' or 'the eye' and 2 denotes 'optic and'; 4, another c/f of *optic*, denotes 'of the eye, optic'; 5 stands for *stereopticon* (cf *stereo-*), a highly developed magic lantern; for all, cf OPTIC. Exx: *optigraph*, an instrument that copies (cf *-graph*) landscapes; *optico(-)chemical*; 'vision', as in *optology* and *optometer*, and '(of the) eye', as in *optotype*; *magneto-optic* and *synoptic*, Gr *sunoptikos*, from *sunopsis*, a general view; *panopticon*.

**or-**: F *or-*, irreg for L *auri*, of gold: cf the 1st *ori-*. Ex: *orpiment*, yellow arsenic, adopted from OF, from L *auripigmentum*, pigment of gold.

**-orama**: from Gr *horama*, a sight or view or spectacle, from *horan*, to see. Exx: *cyclorama* (cf *cyclo-*); *diorama* (prefix *di-* for *dia-*, through); *panorama*, an all-inclusive view, cf *pan-*.

**orbi-**: from L *orbis*: cf ORB. Ex: *orbific* (cf *-fic*), world-creating.

**orbito-**: a Med c/f from L *orbita*, orbit, esp the orbit of the eye: cf *orbit* at ORB. Exx: ('the orbit') *orbitotomy* (cf *-tomy* at *-tome*); ('of the orbit and') *orbitonasal*.

**orcheso-**: from Gr *orkhēsis*, (art of) dancing: cf ORCHESTRA. Ex: *orchesography*, a treatise on dancing.

**orchid(o)-; orchi(o)-**: c/f from *orkhidos* (via L *orchidis*), an imaginary gen of *orkhis*, and c/f for ORCHID; (*orchio-*) c/f from Gr *orkhis*, gen *orkhios*, testicle (see ORCHID). Exx: ('testicle') *orchidotomy*; ('orchid') *orchidomania*; *orchiotomy*. Cf the Med *-orchism*, denoting a (specified) testicular condition or form, as in *cryptorchism* (cf *cryto-*), and:

**orcho-**: Gr *orkho-*, a c/f of *orkhis*, testicle, as in *orkhotomia*, whence E *orchotomy*. Cf prec.

**ore(o)-**: Gr *ore(o)-*, c/f of *oros* (gen *oreos*), a mountain: cf the An *oro-*. Ex: *oreortyx*, a mountain quail (Gr *ortux*, a quail).

**-orexia**: Med L, from Gr *orexis* (s *orex-*), appetite, strong desire, akin to *oregein* (s *oreg-*), to stretch; IE r, *reg-* or *rek-*. Ex: *parorexia*, perverted appetite (cf prefix *para-*).

**organi-; organo-**: c/f for E *organ*, as in *organific*; Gr *organo-*, c/f of *organon*, an organ: see ORGAN. Ex: *organogen* (cf *-gen*) — *organography* — *organology*.

**ori-** (1), 'boundary' or 'limit': either from Gr *horos* (ὅρος) or from its prob cognate, L *ōra*, edge, seashore; both words are o.o.o. Ex: *oriconic*, *oricyclic*. Cf the 3rd *oro-*.

**ori-** (2), 'mountain' or 'of the mountain(s)': Gr *orei-* or *ori-*, c/f of *oros*, a mountain: cf the 1st *oro-*. Exx: *orichalch*, an ancient precious substance, yellow-hued, via L from Gr *oreikhalkos* (cf *chalco-*); *origan*, an aromatic mint, perh via F, from L *origanum*, from Gr *or(e)iganon*, prob from

*oros+ganos* (cf *gano-*), brightness, bright beauty, beauty.

**ori-** (3), 'mouth' or 'of the mouth': L *ōri-*, c/f of *ōs* (gen *ōris*), mouth: cf ORAL. Exx: *orifacial* and *orifice* (L *ōrificium*, (lit) a mouth-making); *oriform*, *orinasal*.

**ori-** (4), 'gold' or 'of gold' (golden): via OF *ori-* or *orie-*, from L *aure-* or *aurea(-)*, ult from *aurum* (s *aur-*). Exx: *oriflamme*, adopted from F, from OF *orieflambe*, from L *aurea flamma* (golden flame), by folk-etymology for *labari flamma* (LL *labarum*, from LGr *labaron*, imperial standard); *oriole*, from OF *oriol*, L *aureolus*, rather golden, from *aureus*, golden, from *aurum*.

**orismo-**: from Gr *horismos*, a delimitation (cf the 1st *ori-*), a definition, as in *orismology*, the defining of technical terms.

**-ornis, -ornithes; ornis-; ornithi-, ornitho-** (before vowel, ornith-): resp from Gr *ornis* (s *orn-*), a bird, whence *ornis-*, pl *ornithes*, whence *-ornithes*; Gr *ornith(o)-*, c/f of *ornis*, o/s *ornith-*, akin to OHG *arn*, eagle, pl *erni-*, and Hit *haras*, gen *haranas*, eagle; IE r, perh *ar-*, varr *er-* and *or-*, with extensions in *-n*. Exx: *Dinornis*, a prehistoric bird (cf *dino-*, terrible), pl *Dinornithes*; *orniscopy*, for *ornis-scopy*, ornithomancy; *ornithivorous*, bird-eating; *ornithobiography*—*ornithology* (cf *-logy* at *-logia*) bird-lore, whence *ornithologist* —*ornithomancy*, Gr *ornithomanteia*, divination (cf *-mancy*) by birds—*ornithophilous*, (of plants) bird-loving—*ornithoscopy*, Gr *ornithoskopia*, ornithomancy—*ornithotomy*, dissection of birds.

**oro-** (1), 'mountain' or 'of the mountain(s)': Gr *oro-*, c/f of *oros*, mountain; IE s, prob *or-*, with var *er-*, an elevation. Exx: *orocratic* (cf *-cratic* at *-cracy*); *orogeny*, mountain-making (n), cf *-geny* at *-gen*; *orography* and *orology*; *orometer*.

**oro-** (2), 'whey', hence 'serum': from Gr *oros* (s *or-*), whey, akin to L *serum* (see SERUM). Ex: *orotherapy*. Cf *orrho-*.

**oro-** (3), 'mouth' or 'of the mouth': from *ōr-*, o/s of L *ōs* (gen *ōris*), mouth—cf the 3rd *ori-*. Exx: *orolingual*; *oropharynx*; *orotund*, lit 'round-mouthed', hence 'clear and loud', from Horace's *ore rotundo*, with round mouth.

**orrho-**: Gr *orrho-*, c/f of *orrhos*, serum, akin to Gr *oros*, whey—cf the 2nd *oro-*. Ex: *orrhology*, the science (*-logy*) of serums.

**orth(o)-**: Gr *orth(o)-*, c/f of *orthos*, straight, s *orth-*, akin to Skt *ūrdvás*, high, and perh to L *arduus*, steep. Exx: *orthobiosis*, right living; ORTHODOX; *orthoëpy*, correct pronunciation (Gr *epos*, a word); *orthography*, correct spelling (lit, correct writing); *orthop(a)edics*, the prevention— or the correction—of deformity, esp in children (*pais*, a child, gen *paidos*: cf the 1st *ped-*); *orthoptic*, of, for, by correct vision; *orthoscope*; *orthotectic* (cf *-tect*).

**orycto-**: from Gr *oruktos*, dug (up), quarried, from *orukhein* (s *orukh-*), earlier *orussein*, to dig; IE r, prob *(e)reu(k)-*, the *e-* being perh a prefix. Ex: *oryctology*, either palaeontology or mineralogy.

**oryzi-, oryz(o)-**: from L *oryza*, from Gr *oruza*,

rice: cf RICE. Exx: *oryzivorous*, rice-eating, and *Oryzorictes*, 'rice-diggers' (cf *orycto-*), small moles of Madagascar.

**osche(o)-:** from Gr *oskheon*, the scrotum. Ex: *oscheolith*.

**oscillo-:** from L *ōscillāre*, to swing or oscillate: cf OSCILLATE. Exx: *oscillogram*, *oscillograph*; *oscillometer*, *oscilloscope*.

**Osco-:** for *Oscan*, as in *Osco-Umbrian* (languages).

**osculi-,** as in *osculiferous* (cf *-fer*): from L *ōsculum*, a little mouth, hence, in Zoo, an orifice in a sponge or a tapeworm's sucker; dim of *ōs*, mouth.

**1 -osma;—2 osma-, 3 osmio-, 4 osm(o)-:** 1, '-smelling' (n), as in *Coprosma*, from Gr *-osmos*, an end-c/f of *osmē*, a smell; 2, rare (*osmazome*, 2nd element being Gr *zōmos*, juice, broth); 3, for SciL *osmium*; 4, Gr *osmo-*, c/f of *osmē*, a smell, as in *Osmanthus*, *osmology*, but in Chem a c/f for *osmious*, the adj of *osmium*. Gr *osmē* is akin to Gr *odmē*, dust, smoke, and to L *odor*, *osmē* being for *\*odsmē*; IE r, *od-*.

**osmo-** (1). See prec.

**osmo-** (2): c/f for E *osmosis*, itself=*osmo-*, from *ōsmos*, an impulse (from *ōthein*, to push or impel) +suffix *-osis*. Ex: *osmometer*.

**-osmosis,** with its adj **-osmotic:** c/f of *osmosis* (see prec). Ex: *chemosmosis*, chemical action through a membrane.

**-osphresia; osphresio-:** Med c/ff from Gr *osphrēsis*, sense of smell (cf *-osma*), with adj *-osphretic* (Gr *osphrētikos*), as in *oxyosphresia*, *oxyosphretic*; *osphresiology*.

**osphy(o)-:** from Gr *osphus*, the hip or loin, gen *osphuos*. Ex: *osphyalgia* (cf *-algia*, pain).

**osseo-; ossi-:** resp c/f from L *osseus*, osseous or bony, from *os* (gen *ossis*), a bone, and L *ossi-*, c/f of *os*, akin to Gr *osteon* (cf *osteo-*) and Skt *asthi*; IE r, prob *\*ast-*, with var *\*ost-*. Exx: *osseo(-)neurotic*, of bone and nerve; *ossiferous*, bone-producing; *ossification*, from 'to *ossify*', itself perh from F *ossifier*, to convert or be turned into bone.

**ost-,** short for **osteo-**, as also is **oste-; -osteon, -osteus, -ostosis:** Gr *oste(o)-*, c/f of *osteon*, a bone, akin to L *os* (gen *ossis*), var *ossum*—cf prec; (*-osteus*) from Gr *-osteos*, -boned, from *osteon*, whence *-osteon*; for *ostosis*, bone-formation (*osteon*+suffix *-osis*). Exx: *ostalgia* or *ostealgia*; *osteology*, the science of bones; *osteometry*, bone-measurement; *osteopathy*, treatment of bone-diseases (cf *-pathy* at *-path*); *osteophone*; *osteotomy*; *—otosteon*, a bone in the ear; *Gasterosteus*; *sarcostosis*, ossification of muscle (cf *sarco-*).

**-ostraca; ostraco-:** Gr *ostraka*, pl of *ostrakon*, a tile, a shell, and denoting, in E *-ostraca*, crustaceans' orders, divisions, etc., as in *Arthostraca* (cf *arthro-*), with adjj *-ostracan* or *-ostracous*; Gr *ostrako-*, c/f of *ostrakon*, as in *ostracology*, conchology. Cf OSTRACIZE.

**ostrei-, ostre(o)-:** the former from L *ostreum*, var *ostrea*, oyster, and the latter from its Gr original, *ostreon*, pl *ostrea*, akin to *ostrakon* (see prec). Exx: *ostreiculture*, oyster-culture, and *ostreophagous*, oyster-eating (cf *-phaga*).

**-otic; ot(o)-:** c/f of the adj *otic* (Gr *ōtikos*), of the ear; Gr *ōt(o)-*, c/f of *ous* (gen *ōtos*), the ear, akin to Av and OSl *uši*, the two ears, and OSl *ucho*, OIr *āu*, *ō*, L *auris*, an ear; with the *-r-* form, cf OHG *ōra*, *ōri-*, and ON *eyra*—therefore E EAR; IE etymon, app *\*ous* or *\*aus*. Exx: *binotic*, of or for both ears: *otolith* (cf *-lite*), a 'stone' in the ear of vertebrates, and *otology*, science of the ear. The Gr dim *ōtion* has c/f *otio-*, as in *Otiorhynchidae*. Cf:

**otico-:** from Gr *ōtikos*, of the *ous* (gen *ōtos*) or ear: cf prec. Ex: *oticodinia* (Gr *dinē*, a whirling), vertigo arising from ear trouble. Cf *otio-*.

**otidi-:** from Gr *ōtis* (gen *ōtidos*), a bustard. Ex: *Otidiphaps* (Gr *phaps*, a wild pigeon).

**otio-,** as in the Zoo *Otiorhynchidea* (cf *rhyncho-*): from Gr *ōtion*, a little ear, dim of *ous*: cf *-otic*.

**oto-.** See *-otic*.

**ovali-:** for *oval*, as in *ovaliform*.

**ovari(o)-, ovato-; ovi-, ov(o)-:** resp c/f of SciL *ovarium*, an ovary, as in *ovariotomy* (cf *-tomy* at *-tome*); from ML *ovātus* (L *ouātus*), ovate (egg-shaped), as in *ovatoconical*; ML *ōvi-* (L *ōui-*), c/f of ML *ōvum* (L *ōuum*), an egg—cf OVAL—as in *oviduct*, a duct for the passage of eggs, and *oviparous*, producing young from eggs, from ML *ōviparus* (L *ōui-*), cf *-parous* at *-para*; (*ovo-*) by Gr example (see *oo-*) from ML *ōvum*, L *ōuum*, as in *ovology*, the embryology of eggs. The subsidiary *ovuli-*, as in *ovuliferous*, stands for *ovule*, F dim of ML *ovum*.

**ox-** (1): short for *oxalo-*. Ex: *oxamide*.

**ox-** (2): 'presence of *oxygen*', as in *oxazole*, and therefore the pre-vocalic form of the syn *oxa-*, as in *oxadiazole*.

**oxa-.** See prec.

**oxalato-:** for *oxalate*. Cf:

**oxal(o)-:** for OXALIC.

**oxidi-, oxido-:** like the prec five terms, in Chem only: 'oxide' or 'oxidation', as in *oxidimetry* (cf *-metry* at *-meter*) and *oxido(-)reduction*.

**oxo-,** 'presence of *oxygen*': from the 2nd *oxy-*, as in *oxozone*.

**oxy-** (1): Gr *oxu-*, c/f of *oxùs*, sharp, keen, (hence) acid, as in *oxymoron*, something sharply foolish (cf the E *moron*), hence the figure of speech in *toilsome idleness* or *busy holiday*: cf OXYGEN.

**oxy-** (2): 'presence of *oxygen*', as in *oxyacetylene*.

**ozo-; ozoni-; ozono-:** the 2nd and 3rd, for *ozone*, as in *ozoniferous* and *ozonometry*; the 1st, from Gr *ozo-*, c/f from *ozein* (s *oz-*), to smell, and denoting '(bad) smell', as in *ozocerite*. The r *oz-* is akin to the r *od-* of L *odor*.

**pachno-,** as in Min *pachnolite* (*-lite*, *-stone*): from Gr *pakhnē*, hoar frost, akin to *pagos*, ice; IE r, *\*pag-*. Cf *pago-*.

**pachy-:** Gr *pakhu-*, c/f of *pakhus*, thick, s *pakh-*, akin to Skt *bahús*, much (or great), many, and the nasalized Hit *pankus*, widespread, great. (Hofmann.) Exx: *pachyderm*, from F *pachyderme*, and *pachydermous*, both from Gr *pakhudermos*, thick-skinned (cf *-derm*); also SciL *Pachydermata* and its adj *pachydermatous*.

**paci-**, c/f of L *pāx* (gen *pācis*), peace. Notably, only in PACIFIC, *pacify*, etc.

**-paedes**: from Gr *paides*, children, from *pais*, a child. Only in Zoo.

**paedo-**. A now rare and typically L var of the 1st *pedo-*. Cf *paido-*.

**pagano-**: from LL *pāgānus*, a pagan: cf PAGAN. Ex: *pagano-Christian*.

**pagio-**: from Gr *pagios*, firm, app akin to *pagos*, ice; cf *pachno-*. Ex: Zoo *Pagiopoda* (cf *-pod*). Cf the next two.

**pago-**, as in *pagoscope*, an instrument for determining, immediately, whether the dew-point is below freezing: from Gr *pagos*, frost, a freezing, hence a fixation, s *pag-*; IE s, *pāg-* or *pag-*. Cf:

**-pagus**: a SciL, esp Med, c/f from Gr *pagos*, a being fixed, a fixing or fixation: cf prec. Ex: *thoracopagus*, 'a twin monster united at the thorax' (Webster).

**paido-**. A now very rare, typically Gr, var of the 1st *pedo-*. Cf *paedo-*.

**palai(o)-**, Gr form; **palae(o)-**, L form; **pale(o)-**, predominant Am and increasingly common E form: Gr *palai(o)-*, whence L *palae(o)-*, c/ff of Gr *palaios*, whence L *palaeus*, ancient, (very) old; prob akin to Skt *caramás*, last, extreme, and W *pell*, distant, *pellaf*, outermost, and Cor *pell*, Br *pèl*, far, distantly. Exx: *palaiotype*; *Palaeomastodon*, *Palaeornis* (cf *-ornis*); *paleobotany*, *paleolithic*, belonging to the Stone Age (cf *-lith* at *-lite*); *paleology*, a study of (prehistoric) antiquities; *pal(a)eontology*, the science (*-logy*) of ancient (*palaeo-*) things (*onto-*), i.e. periods; *Pal(a)eozoic* (cf *-zoic* at *zo-*).

**palato-**, either 'the palate', as in *palatogram* (cf the 2nd *-gram*) and *palatometer*, or, in adjj, 'of the palate and', as in *palatoglossal*, of the palate and tongue (cf *-glossa*).

**pale(o)-**. See *palai(o)-*.

**pali-, palim-, palin-**: Gr *pali-, palim-, palin-*, c/ff of *palin* (Pontic Gr *pali*), backwards, in opposition, again, s *pal-*; IE r, prob *pal-*, with varr *pel-* and, ? less frequent, *pol-*. Exx: *palikinesia, palilalia*, both indicating a quite pathological repetition, the former of movement, the latter of speech: *palilogy*, from LL *palilogia*, from Gr *palilogia*, rhetorical, esp if emphatic, repetition of a word;—*palimpsest*, a parchment or tablet written on, several times, with first writing erased, from L *palimpsēstus*, Gr *palimpsēstos*, again scratched or scraped or rubbed, 2nd element being the pp of Gr *psēn*, to rub (away);—*palindrome*, a word reading the same, either way, from Gr *palindromos*, (adj) running back (cf *-drome*); *palingenesis*; *palinode*, LL *palinōdia*, Gr *palinōidia*, a song or an ode, that retracts something already sung, hence a recantation—cf ODE.

**palladio-** and **pallado-**: in Chem, c/ff for *palladium*, a rare metallic element.

**pallidi-**: from L *pallidus*, pale (cf PALE, adj), as in *pallidiflorous*, pale-flowered.

**pallio-**: c/f for Met *pallium*, a mantle of cloud (L *pallium*, a cloak), as in *palliostratus*, and for An *pallium*, the cerebral cortex, as in *palliocardiac*.

**pallo-**, as in *pallograph* and *pallometric*, comes from the Gr *pallein* (s *pall-*), to shake or quake or quiver. Cf *palmo-*.

**palmati-**; **palmi-**: from L *palmātus*, hand-shaped, as in *palmati(-)lobate*; from L *palma*, the palm of the hand, hence, prob by folk-etymology, a palm-tree, as in *palmiform*, shaped like the palm of the hand, and *palmiped*, broad-footed. See PALM.

**palmo-**: from Gr *palmos*, (a) pulsation, prob akin to PULSE (a regular beat, esp of the heart); IE r, prob *pel-*, with extension *pelm-*. Exx: *palmoscopy*, observation (cf *-scope*) of the heart-beat; via the SciL *palmus*: *palmospasmus*. Cf *pallo-*.

**palpi-**, rarely **palpo-**: L *palpus*, the (soft) palm of the hand, hence SciL *palpus*, a feeler: cf PALPITATE. Exx: *palpifer* (Zoo), *palpiform*; *palpocil* (cf *-cil*), a hairlike feeler.

**paludi-**: L *palūdi-*, c/f of *palūs* (gen *palūdis*), a marsh, as in *paludicole*, a creature living in a marsh or the marshes, and *paludiferous*, marsh-producing. L *palūs* is prob akin to Gr *plados*, dampness, app by metathesis, and to Skt *palva am*, a pond, a marsh.

**pam-** is the form taken, before *p*, by *pan-*; as in *pampharmacon* and the obs *pamphagous*, omnivorous.

**pampini-, pampino-**: c/ff from L *pampinus*, a tendril, app from Medit stock. Exx: *pampiniform*, *pampinocele* (*-cele*).

**pan-**, before *p*, usu *pam-*, q.v.: Gr *pan-*, c/f of *pan*, neus of *pas* (gen *pantos*), every, all (quantitative sing; distributive pl, *pantes*, neu *panta*); IE r, prob *kuān-*, o/s *kuānt-*; cf the Cretan and Thessalian *pansa* and the Hit *pankus*.

Exx: *panacea*, a cure-all, Gr *panakeia*, from *panakēs*, all-healing, 2nd element from *akeisthai*, to heal; *pancreas* (cf next entry), via SciL from Gr *pankreas*, (lit) all flesh, with adj *pancreatic*; *pandemic*, LL *pandēmus*, Gr *pandēmos* (or *-dēmios*), of, by, for all the people, from *dēmos* (cf *demo-*), the people; *pandemonium*, from Mod L *Pandemonium*, 'the place, abode of' all the demons (Gr *daimōn*, a spirit, a demon); *Pandora*, 'All the Gifts' —Gr *dōra*, pl of *dōron*, a gift; *panegyric*, n from adj, from EF-F *panégyrique*, L *panēgyricus*, Gr *panēgurikos*, adj of *panēguris*, a gathering of the people, from *aguris*, an assembly, var of *agora*, from *agein*, s *ag-*, to lead—cf L *agere*, to drive; *panoply*, full (suit of) armour, Gr *panoplia*, from *hopla*, armour, the pl of *hoplon*, an implement; *panoptic*, Gr *panoptēs*, all-regarding, i.e. containing everything in one view—cf OPTIC; *panorama=pan +-orama* (q.v.),), lit an all-inclusive view; *pansophy*, universal wisdom, from Gr *pansophos*, all-wise—cf SOPHIST; *pantechnicon*, a bazaar for all kinds of artistic work, hence a storehouse, hence an all-holding furniture van; *pantheism*, God in everything and everywhere (cf *theo-*); *pantheon*, via L from Gr *pantheion*, the place for all the gods, orig the neu of *pantheios*, of all the gods, from *theos*, a god; PANTOMIME. Cf *panto-*.

**pancreat(o)-**: from *pankreat-*, the o/s of Gr *pankreas* (*kreas*, flesh); as in *pancreatalgia*, *pancreatotomy*. The subsidiary *pancreatico-*, as in *pancreaticosplenic*, stands for '*pancreatic* (and)'. Cf *pan-*.

**panduri-**, as in *panduriform:* from LL *pandura*, a pandura, a bandore.

**pani-**: from L *pānis* (s *pān-*), bread: cf PANTRY. Ex: *panivorous* (cf *-vorous* at *-vora*).

**panta-**. Incorrect for *panto-*. Ex: *pantagraph*.

**panto-**: Gr *panto-*, c/f of *pas*, neu *pan*, gen *pantos*: cf *pan-*. Exx: *pantalgia* (cf *-algia*), *pantisocracy* (*panto-*+*iso-*+*cracy*), *pantograph*, an instrument for copying (cf *-graph*) maps or plans on any agreed scale; PANTOMIME; *pantomnesia* (cf *-mnesia* at *mnemi-*), a memory retaining something of everything ever known.

**papi-**. See *papo-*.

**papilli-, papillo-**: c/ff of L *papilla*, nipple of the breast. Exx: *papilliform*, nipple-shaped; *papillosarcoma*.

**papo-**; rarely *papi-*: from L *papa*, in its ML sense 'the Pope, or a pope'. Ex: *papolatry*, popeworship; *papicolist*, a papist. (Cf PAPA.)

**pappi-**: c/f of Bot *pappus*, a sense adapted from that ('an old man') of L *pappus*, from Gr *pappos*—cf PAPA. Ex: *pappiferous*.

**papuli-, papulo-**: c/ff for *papule*, from L *papula*, a pimple, akin to L *papilla* (see *papilli-*). Exx: *papuliferous* and *papulopustule*.

**papyro-**: from L *papyrus*, from Gr *papuros*—see PAPER. Ex: *papyrology*, the study of papyri.

**-para**, n; **-parous**, adj: L *-parus*, f *-para*, -bearing (young), (hence) producing, from *parere* (s *par-*), to give birth to: cf PARENT. Exx: *floriparous*, LL *flōriparus*, flower-producing; *oviparous* (cf *ovi-*) and *viviparous* (cf *vivi-*);—L *prīmipara*, a woman bearing her first baby, adopted by Med.

**paralleli-; parallel(o)-**: resp for *parallel*, as in *parallelinervate*, and from Gr *parallēlo-*, c/f of *parallēlos*, parallel (see PARALLEL), as in *parallelogram*, via F and L from Gr *parallēlogrammon*, the 2nd element deriving from *grammē*, a line.

**paramio-**: irreg from Gr *paroimia*, a proverb (*par(a)-*, prefix+*oimē*, a saying). Cf *paroemio-*.

**parasiti-; parasito-**: the former for L *parasītus*; the latter for PARASITE; as in *parasiticide* (cf *-cidal*) and *parasitology*, the study of parasites.

**parci-**: L *parci-*, c/f of *parcus*, sparing, niggardly, from *parcēre*, to spare. Exx: *parcidentate*, (in Zoo) possessed of few teeth—cf DENTAL; *parciloquy*, niggardliness of speech, L *parciloquium*—cf *-loquy*.

**parei(a)-**: from Gr *pareia*, cheek: '(the part) by the ear' (cf L *auris*, ear). Ex: Pal *Pareiasauria*.

**parenti-**: from L *parens* (gen *parentis*), a parent, from *parere*, to bear (a child). Ex: *parenticide*.

**pari-**: from L *pār* (gen *paris*), equal: see *par-*. Mostly in Bot and Zoo, as in *paridigitate*, equaltoed.

**parieto-**: in An, for *parietal* (n from adj), itself

from LL *parietālis*, adj of *pariēs*, a wall. Ex: *parietofrontal*.

**paroemio-**: from Gr *paroimia*, a proverb: cf *paramio-*. Ex: *paroemiology*, the study of proverbs.

**-parous**. See *-para*.

**parri-**, in *parricide*, stands for *patri-*, c/f of L *pater*, father. Cf *patri-*.

**parsono-**: for *parson*, as in *parsonolatry* (cf *-latry* at *-later*).

**partheno-**: Gr *partheno-*, c/f of *parthenos*, a maiden: denoting 'virgin' or 'asexual', as in *parthenogenesis*, virgin birth, but mostly in Zoo and Bot; *parthenology*, the medical study of virginity. The *Parthenon* (Gr *Parthenōn*) is dedicated to Athena, the virgin goddess.

**parti-**, as in *parti-coloured*, and its anglicized form **party-**, as in *party-wall*, represents the F *parti*, divided (from *partir*, to divide, ult from L *pars*, a PART), hence, occ, dividing. In *participate*, however, *parti-* is the L c/f.

**parturi-**, as in *parturifacient* (cf *-facient*), derives from L *parturīre*, to desire to give birth, whence LL *parturitiō* (gen *-iōnis*), whence E *parturition*, childbirth.

**parvi-**: ML *parvi-* (L *parui-*), c/f of ML *parvus* (L *paruus*), little, small, akin to *pauci*, few. Ex: *parviflorous*, small-flowered.

**pasi-**: from Gr *pasi* (dat pl of *pas*, q.v. at *pan-*), for all persons or things. Ex: *pasigraphy*, a universal language.

**passeri-**: from L *passer*, a sparrow, as in *passeriform*, like a sparrow.

**passi-**, as in Bot *Passiflora* and *Passiflorales* (cf *flori-*): from L *passio*, suffering, the Passion.

**passiono-**: for E *passion*; as in *passionometer*.

**passo-**, in *passometer*, an instrument (cf *-meter*) for recording a person's steps, represents L *passus* (gen *passūs*), a step—akin to PACE.

**pasto-**: from Gr *pastos*, a shrine, perh akin to *passō*, I sprinkle. Ex: *pastophor(us)*, 'shrinebearer' (cf *-phora*), an inferior priest.

**patelli-, patello-**: from L *patella*, a small pan (dim of *patina*, a pan or dish), esp the knee-pan. Exx: *patelliform*, *patello(-)femoral*.

**-path**, 2 **-pathia**, 3 **-pathic**, 4 **-pathy**; 5 **path(o)-**: resp Gr *-pathēs*, one suffering from, as in *neuropath* (cf *neuro-* at *-neura*), a nervous case, and *psychopath* (cf *psycho-*), one mentally and spiritually ill, hence, occ, one skilled in a special treatment, as in *psychopath-*, from *pathos*, a suffering; 2, the L (from Gr) *-pathia*, anglicized as *-pathy*, with corresponding adj *-pathic*, often after Gr *-pathikos*, from *pathikos*, the adj of *pathos* (akin to *pathein*, to suffer: see PATHOS), 2-4 being exemplified by *psychopathia* and *psychopathy*, adj *psychopathic*, and *telepathy*, *telepathic*, cf *tele-*; 5, Gr *path(o)-*, c/f of *pathos*, (a) suffering, as in *pathology*, the science (*-logy*) of disease(s), via F *pathologie* from Mod L *pathologia*.

**patr(i)-; patro-**: resp L *patri-*, c/f of *pater* (gen *patris*), and Gr *patro-*, c/f of *patēr* (gen *patros*), father: cf FATHER. Exx: *patricide*, an E form of *parricide*, q.v. at *parri-*; *patrimony*; *Patripassian*, from LL *Patripassiani*;—*patrology*, the teachings of the Church Fathers; *patronymic* (adj, hence n), LL *patrōnymicus*, Gr *patrōnumikos*, 2nd element *onuma*, *onoma*, a name (cf *onomato-*).

But *patri-* may represent Gr *patri-*, c/f of *patria* (from *patēr*), lineage, as in *patriarchy*, Gr *patriarkhia*, and *patriarch*, OF-F *patriarche*, LL *patriarcha*, Gr *patriarkhēs*, *-arkhēs* deriving from *arkhos*, a chief (cf *-arch*). Cf:

patrio-: c/f of L *patria*, one's own country, from *pater*, father. Ex: *patriolatry*, worship (cf *-latry* at *-later*) of one's country. Cf *patri-* and, f.a.e., FATHER.

pauci-: L *pauci-*, c/f of *pauci*, few (sing *paucus* is rare), s *pau-*; cf *paul(l)us*, little. Ex: *paucifolious*, having few leaves, and *pauciloquy*, a little-speaking, i.e. brevity of speech, from Plautus's *pauciloquium* (cf *-loquy* at *-loquence*). Cf the derivative *paucity*, fewness, from L *paucitās* (gen *paucitātis*): *pau*+ extension *-c-*+*-itas* (E suffix *-ity*). Cf:

paulo-: from Gr *paula*, a rest, akin to (? from) *pauomai* (s *pau-*), I pause: cf PAUSE. Ex: Bot *paulospore* (cf *-spora*).

pauro-, as in Zoo *paurometabolism* and *Pauropoda*, comes from Gr *pauros*, small, *pau-*+extension *r-*+*-os*; akin to L *paucus* and *parvus*, qq.v. at *parvi-* and *pauci-*.

pectinato-, from L *pectinātus* (combed), pp of *pectināre*, to comb, but in E denoting 'comb-shaped'; and *pectini-*, c/f of *pecten* (whence *pectināre*), gen *pectinis*, akin to *pectere* (s *pect-*), to comb, to card (wool), akin to—prob from —Gr *pekein* (s *perk-*), to comb. Exx: *pectinato-pinnate* (cf *pennati-*); *pectiniferous*, *pectiniform*.

pecto-: from Gr *pēktos*, compacted, from *pēgnunai*, to render stiff, as in *pectolith* (cf *-lite*); or for the adj (*pectic*) of the derivative *pectin* (Chem suffix *-in*), as in *pectocellulose*, where *pecto-* derives from a secondary sense of *pēktos*: 'coagulated' or 'curdled'.

pectori-: from L *pectus* (gen *pectoris*), the breast, external chest, perh akin to L *pexus*, woolly (the matted chests of some males): Ex: *pectoriloquy* (from F *pectoriloquie*—for 2nd element, cf *-loquy* at *-loquence*), 'distinct sound of a patient's voice heard in ausculation' (Webster). The adj *pectoral*, of the breast or chest (hence, n, something—*pectorale*—worn there), comes from L *pectorālis* (n, *pectorāle*): *pector-*, o/s=adj suffix *-alis*.

-ped. A var of *-pede*, as in *biped*.

ped-. Prevocalic *pedo-*; occ prevocalic *pedi-*.

pedati-: from L *pedātus*, having feet or a foot, from *pēs* (gen *pedis*), a foot. Ex: *pedatiform*, (in Bot) with ribs arranged like toes. Cf:

-pede: from *ped-*, o/s of L *pēs* (gen *pedis*), a foot, often via F *-pède*. Exx: *centipede* and *millipede*; *velocipede*. See:

pedi- (1) or, before vowel, ped-: L *pedi-*, c/f of *pēs*, a foot, gen *pedis*, o/s *ped-*, akin to E FOOT. Exx: *pedicure* (L *cūra*, care); *pedigerous*, possessing (cf *-ger*) feet; PEDIGREE; *pedomancy*, divination (*-mancy*) by the soles of the feet; *pedometer* (F *pédomètre*). Cf *-pede*.

pedi- (2). See *pedio-*.

pediculi-: a var of the 1st *pediculo-*. Ex: *pediculicide*, anything that kills lice.

pediculo- (1): from L *pediculus*, a louse, as in *pediculophobia*, a dread of being lousy.

pediculo- (2): from L *pediculus*, dim of *pēs* (gen *pedis*), a foot; denoting in An and Bot a slender stalk. Ex: *pediculofrontal*.

pedio- or, before a vowel, pedi: Gr *pedio-*, c/f of *pedion*, a plain, the sole of the foot, as in *pedialgia*, pain in the sole of the foot; Zoo *Pedioecetes*, the sharp-tailed grouse, lit 'plains-dwellers' (Gr *oiketēs*, a dweller); *pedionomite*, a plains-dweller, from Gr *pedionomos*+n suffix *-ite*; Gr *pedion* is akin to Gr *pedon* (ground), q.v. at the 2nd *pedo-*.

pedo- (1); before a vowel, ped-: 'child': Gr *paid(o)-*, c/f of *pais*, a child a boy, gen *paidos*, o/s *paid-*, often via L *paed(o)-*; akin to L *puer*, a boy, and E FOAL. Exx: *pedagogue* (see PEDANT); *pediatric*, of, by, for child-care (cf *-iatric*); *pedodontia*, the care of children's teeth (cf *-odon*); *pedology* (or *paed-*), the study of children; *pedomorphism*; *pedotrophy*, Gr *paidotrophia*, child-nourishment (hence, the proper rearing of children) —cf *-trophia*.

pedo- (2): 'ground': from Gr *pedon* (s *ped-*), ground, akin to Skt *padam* and Hit *pedan* (dative *pedi*), a place; IE *pedom*, s *ped-*. Exx: *pedograph*, an instrument for recording ground covered on a journey; *pedology*, the science of soils.

pedo- (3): 'foot': a non-L c/f from *pēs* (o/s *ped-*), a foot: cf the 1st *pedi-*. Exx: *pedometer*, which records steps taken, hence the approximate distance walked: *pedomotive*, moved by foot-power.

pegmato-: c/f for *pegmatite*, (two varieties of) granite, itself from Gr *pēgma* (gen *pēgmatos*), something fastened (together), 'in allusion to the quartz and feldspar in graphic granite' (Webster). Ex: *pegmatophyre* (cf *-phyre*), (cf *-pexy*).

pego-: from Gr *pēgē*, a fountain; IE s, prob *pag-* or *peg-*. Ex: *pegomancy*, divination (cf *-mancy*) by springs.

peira-: Gr *peira*, a trial or attempt, akin to *peirō*, I try. Ex: *peirameter*.

pelag(o)- (and -pelago): Gr *pelag(o)-*, c/f of *pelagos*, the sea; IE r, prob *pelag-* or *plag-*. Exx: *archipelago*, lit 'chief sea'; in Zoo, *Pelagothuria*.

pelargo-: from Gr *pelargos*, a stork, perh lit '(the bird) with grey-and-white plumage' (Gr *argos*, white). The derivative *Pelargonium*, a variety of geranium, has adj *pelargonic*, with c/f *pelargono-*.

pelecy-: from Gr *pelekus*, a hatchet. Ex: Zoo *Pelecypoda* (cf *-pod*).

-pellic: Med c/f, 'having a (specified) type of pelvis': from Gr *pella*, a (wooden) bowl. Ex: *platypellic* (cf *platy-*, flat).

pelmat-; -pelmous: both from Gr *pelma*, the sole of the foot, the former from the o/s *pelmat-*, IE r perh *pel-*, 'high'. Exx: *pelmatogram*, a recorded footprint; *nomopelmous* (in Zoo; cf *nomo-*).

**pel(o)-**: Gr *pēl(o)-*, c/f of *pēlos* (s *pēl-*), mud or clay, prob akin to L *palūs*, a marsh. Ex: *Pelodytes*, a genus of frogs ('mud divers': cf *-dytes*).

**pelti-, pelto-**: from L *pelta* (Gr *peltē*), a buckler, a small shield, as in *peltigerous*, shield-bearing; *peltogaster* (cf *-gaster*). The L adj *peltātus*, provided or protected with a shield, yields E *peltate*, with c/ff *peltati-, peltato-*, as in *peltatodigitate*.

**pelvi-**, occ extended to **pelvio-**: ML *pelvi-* (L *pelui-*), c/f of ML *pelvis* (L *peluis*), akin to Skt *pālūvī*, some kind of vessel. Exx: *pelvimeter*; *pelviotomy* (cf *-tome*). Cf:

**pelyco-**: from *peluk-*, o/s of Gr *pelux*, a wooden bowl, (hence) the pelvis (cf prec); IE r, prob *\*pel-*. Ex: *pelycology*, the (Med) science of the pelvis.

**pen-**. See *pente-*, five.

**pencilli-**, as in *pencilliform*: for *pencil*.

**penetro-**, 'radiant energy': for 'to *penetrate*', as in *penetrometer*.

**penia-**: from Gr *penia* (s *pen-*), dearth, poverty, akin to *penomai* (s *pen-*), I work painfully, and *ponos* (s *pon-*), fatigue, physical or moral suffering; IE r, prob *\*pen-*, var *\*pon-*. Hence, in E, deficiency, as in *thrombopenia* (cf *thrombo-*).

**penicilli-**: for L *pēnicillus*, a pencil: cf PENI-CILLIN. Ex: *penicilliform*, pencil-shaped. Cf *pencilli-*.

**pennati-**. A var of *pinnati-*, as in *pennatisect*.

**penni-**, irreg **penno-**; **-pennine**: L *penni-*, c/f of *penna* (s *pen-*: cf PEN for writing), a feather; (*-pennine*) a var of E *pennate*, feather-shaped. Exx: *pennipotent*, strong on the wing; *pennoplume*; *longipennine*, long-feathered.

**peno-**: from L *poena*, or Gr *poinē*, punishment: cf PAIN. Ex: *penology*, the study (*-logy*) of punishment, esp of criminals.

**penta-** or, before a vowel, **pent-** or, before an aspirated vowel, **penth-**; occ in shorter form, **pen-**: Gr *pent(a)-*, *penth-*, c/ff of *pente*, five, akin to L *quinque* and E FIVE. Exx: *pendecagon*; *pentagon*, LL *pentagōnum*, Gr *pentagōnon*—cf *-gon*; *penta-gram*, Gr *pentagrammon*, from *pentagrammos*, five-lined; *pentameter*, adopted from L: from Gr *pentametros*, five-measured, i.e. -footed; *pentarchy*, government by five—Gr *pentarkhia*; *Pentateuch*, the first five books (Gr *teukhos*, a tool, a book) of The Old Testament; *penthemimer*, LL *penthē-mimeris* (or *-es*), Gr *penthēmimerēs*, 2nd element *hēmimerēs*, halved.

**-pepsia**, adj **-peptic**: Gr *-pepsia*, a type of digestion, from *pepsis*, digestion, whence, through G, *pepsin* (Chem suffix *-in*); *-peptic* (and independent *peptic*), from Gr *peptikos*, from *pepsis*; akin to *peptein*, to cook, akin to Skt *paktás*, cooked, and L *coquere*, to cook; IE r, prob *\*pek(u)-*; assimilated in L, thus: *\*queq-*, var *\*quoq-*. (Hofmann.) Exx: *dyspepsia*, adopted from L, from Gr *duspepsĭa* (Gr *dus*, badly: cf prefix *dys-*)—adj *dyspeptic*; *eupepsia*, adopted from Gr (cf the prefix *eu-*, well)—adj, *eupeptic*, Gr *eupept(os)* +suffix *-ic*; cf *autopepsia*, *-peptic*.

**-pepsinia**; **pepsino-**: from and for *pepsin*. Cf prec and:

**pepto-, pepton-**: from and for *peptone* (from Gr *pepton*, a thing cooked), as in *peptogenic*, easily digestible, and *pepton(a)emia*. Cf *-pepsia*.

**perci-**: from L *perca*, a perch (fish), as in *perciform*, perch-like.

**percno-**: from Gr *perknos*, dusky; IE r, either *\*perk-* or *\*prek-*. Ex: Bot *percnosome* (cf *-soma*).

**perco-**: from L *perca*, a perch: cf *perci-* and PERCH (fish). Ex: Zoo *Percomorphi* (cf *-morph*).

**pereio-**: irreg from Gr *peraioun*, to transport; as in *pereiopod* (cf *-pod*).

**perenni-**: for *perennial*, as in Zoo *perenni-branchiate* (cf *-branch*).

**pericardi(o)-**: a Med and Surg c/f for *peri-cardium*, '(the thing) about the heart', as in *pericardiotomy*. Cf *-cardia*.

**peridi-**, as in *peridiform*: for *peridium*, outer envelope, from Gr *pēridion*, dim of *pēra*, a wallet.

**perineo-**: Med c/f for the An *perineum* (prefix *peri-*+*inaō*, I evacuate); as in *perineocele* (cf *-cele*).

**periodo-**: for *period*, as in *periodology*, a study, the science, of periodicity.

**periosteo-**: for *periosteum*, LL *periosteon*, from Gr adj *periosteos*, around the bones. Ex: *peri-osteotomy*. Cf *osteo-*.

**peripher(o)-**, as in *peripheroneural*: for *peri-pheral*, the adj of *periphery*, the line bounding a surface, esp a circle, (prob via EF-F *périphérie*) from LL *peripheria*, from Gr *periphereia*, itself= prefix *peri-*, around+*phereia*, a carrying, from *pherein* (s *pher-*), to carry, akin to L *ferre* (s *fer-*), to carry.

**perisso-**: from Gr *perissos*, (of numbers) odd. Exx: *perissodactyl*; *perissology*, an excess of words, Gr *perissologia*.

**peritone(o)-**: from, and for, *peritoneum* (a tech of An and Zoo), as in *peritonealgia* and *peritoneo-scope*.

**perli-**: via F from ML *perla*: cf PEARL. Ex: *perligenous*, pearl-producing.

**permea-**, as in *permeameter*: for 'to *permeate*'.

**Permo-**, as in Geol *Permo(-)carboniferous*: for 'Permian (and)'.

**pero-** (1): Gr *pēro-*, c/f of *pēros* (s *pēr-*), maimed, akin to Gr *pērna*, evil, misfortune, injury. Only in Med and Zoo; e.g., *peromelous*, maimed of limb (cf *-melia*).

**pero-** (2): from Gr *pēra* (o.o.o.), a pouch or wallet. Only in Zoo—e.g., *Perognathus*.

**peroneo-** and **perono-**: for *peroneus*, a muscle of the lower leg, SciL name from Gr *peronē*, (pin, hence) fibula, whence *perono-*. Exx: *peroneotarsal* and *Peronospora* (cf *-spora*).

**personi-**: as in *personify*, q.v. at PERSON.

**perspecto-**, as in *perspectograph*: from L *perspectus*, pp of *perspicere*, to look through: cf PERSPECTIVE.

**pesti-**; **pesto-**: L *pesti-*, c/f of *pestis*, a plague; and (*pesto-*) a c/f analogous with Gr c/ff: cf PEST. Exx: *pestiferous*, L *pestifer(us)*, plague-bearing, and *pestifugous*, plague-dispelling (L *fugāre*, to cause to flee); *pestology*, the science (*-logy*) of (chiefly insect) pests.

**-petal,** esp in *centripetal,* seeking the centre; Mod L *-petus,* seeking, from *petere,* to seek.

**petali-,** from L *petalum;* **petal(o)-,** Gr *petal(o)-,* c/f of *petalon* (s *petal-*), a leaf, cf PETAL; adj *-petalous,* from SciL *-petalus.* Exx: *petaliferous, petalomania, platypetalous* (flat-petalled: cf *platy-*).

**petri-, petro-:** the former from L *petra,* a rock; the latter from Gr *petra,* rock, or *petros,* stone. Exx: *petricolous,* living (cf *-colous*) in a rock or among the rocks; *petrogenesis,* the genesis or origin of rocks; *petrography,* description of rocks, and *petrology,* the entire science of rocks; PETROLEUM.

**petroli-:** for *petroleum,* as in *petrolific* (cf *-fic*).

**-pexy,** E; **-pexia,** SciL; **-pexis,** Grecized: from Gr *pēxis,* a fastening, from *pēgnunai,* to fasten. Cf *pegmato-*.

**pezo-,** as in *pezograph,* comes from Gr *peza,* a foot; in *Pezaphaps,* from Gr *pezos,* on foot, akin to L *pēs,* gen *pedis:* cf the 1st *pedi-*.

**phac(o)-:** Gr *phak(o)-,* c/f of *phakos* (s *phak-*), a lentil, hence a wart, a lens, etc., akin to L *faba,* a bean; from the E adj *phacoid* comes the c/f *phacoido-.* Exx: *phacolith* (cf *-lith* at *-lite*), *phacometer* (for measuring the refraction of lenses); *phacoidoscope.*

**phaen(o)-,** now rarely **phaino-:** Gr *phain(o)-,* c/f from *phainein* (s *phain-*), to show, whence, incidentally, the E *phantasy* (FANCY) and *phantom.* Exx: *phaenantherous* (cf *-antherous* at *anth-*) and, also in Bot, *phaenogam.* For mod form, see esp PHENOMENON.

**phaeo-:** from Gr *phaios,* dun-coloured, dusky; with Baltic cognates. Occ in Bot, e.g., *phaeophyll* (cf *-phyll*).

**-phaga,** 2 **-phage,** 3 **-phagous,** 4 **-phagus,** 5 **-phagy;** 6 **phago-:** resp a SciL pl, 'eaters of (a specified sort) of food'—cf 4; 2, a F-type derivative of L *-phagus* (see 4) and denoting 'an eater of (something specified)', hence, in Bio, 'a cell destructive of'; 3, from or on the Gr adj *-phagos,* -eating; 4, *-phagus,* L n from Gr adj *-phagos,* -eating, as in *sarcophagus* (see next para); 5 *-phagy,* E form of L *-phagia,* from Gr *-phagia,* c/f from *phagein* (s *phag-*), to eat, akin to Skt *bhájati,* he shares (out), apportions, and *bhágas,* one who apportions, and to several terms in Zend and Old Persian (cf *baksheesh*); 6, Gr *phago-,* c/f from *phagein.*

Exx: *Entomophaga,* insect-eaters, with adj *entomophagous,* insectivorous; *ostreophage,* an oyster-eater; *anthropophagous,* man-eating; *sarcophagus* (cf *sarco-*), L word from Gr *sarkophagos,* orig an adj, 'flesh-eating', then, via *lithos sarkophagos,* a flesh-eating stone, i.e. a tomb, a n—cf the E adj *sarcophagous,* flesh-eating, straight from the Gr adj; *anthropophagy* (Gr *anthrōpophagia*), with typical 'addiction' n *anthropophagism; phagocyte,* a cell (cf *-cyte*) that destroys bacteria, etc., and *phagomania,* insatiable hunger as a symptom or aspect of insanity.

**phagocyto-:** for *phagocyte,* as in *phagocytolytic* cf *-lyse*). See prec.

**phaino-.** See *phaeno-*.

**phalacro-:** from Gr *phalakros,* bald; as in *Phalacrocorax* (*korax,* a crow: cf *coraco-*).

**phalaen(o)-:** from Gr *phalaina,* a moth. Ex: Bot *Phalainopsis* (*opsis,* appearance).

**-phalangia; phalangi-:** 'a condition (cf suffix *-ia*) of the *phalanges*' (digital bones of hand or foot), as in *brachyphalangia* (cf *brachy-*); c/f of *phalanx,* pl *phalanges,* as in *phalangigrade,* (of a quadruped) walking (cf *-grade*) on the phalanxes. The An and Zoo sense of *phalanx* existed already in the Gr φάλαγξ, *phalanx,* better known to most of us as the typical Ancient Gr line of battle—a close-set formation of ranks and files: the fingers and toes of most vertebrates are close-set, this being the basic idea also of *phalanger* (*phalang-,* o/s+ agential suffix *-er*).

**phall(o)-:** Gr *phall(o)-,* c/f of *phallos* (whence L *phallus*), the penis; IE r, prob *bhal-* or *bhel-*. Only in An and Med.

**-phane,** 2 **-phanous,** 3 **-phant,** 4 **-phany;** 5 **phaner(o)-,** 6 **phantasmo-,** 7 **phanto-,** loosely **phanta-:** all ult from Gr *phainein,* (v.t.) to show, (v.i.) to appear—see FANCY: 1, Gr *-phanes,* neus of *-phanēs,*-appearing, hence 'a substance appearing like'; 2, perh from ML *-phanus=*Gr *-phanēs,* -appearing; 3, LL *-phanta,* earlier *-phantes,* from Gr *-phantēs,* one who shows; 4, from LL *-phania,* from Gr *-phaneia,* c/f from *phainein,* to show; 5, Gr *phaner(o)-,* c/f of *phaneros,* visible, (hence) manifest; 6, E c/f for E *phantasm* (Gr *phantasma*), the *phan-* of 4–6 representing a var of the *phain-* in *phainein,* which, in certain tenses, has *phan-;* 7, *phanto-,* from Gr *phantos,* visible.

Exx: *cellophane,* adj of trade-name *Cellophane; diaphanous,* ML *diaphanus,* Gr *diaphanēs,* showing through, from *diaphainein,* to show through (prefix *dia-*); *hierophant,* LL *hierophanta* (earlier *-phantes*), Gr *hierophantēs,* one who shows holy things, a priest; *Epiphany,* via OF from LL *epiphania,* Gr *epiphaneia,* from *epiphainein,* to manifest (cf prefix *epi-*); *phanerogenic,* of straightforward or obvious origin, and *phaneroscope; phantasmology; phantoscope,* loosely *phantascope.*

**pharmaco-:** Gr *pharmako-,* c/f of *pharmakon,* a drug, a medicine, prob from a PGr *pharma.* Exx: *pharmacology,* the science of medicines; *pharmacopoeia,* Gr *pharmakopoiïa,* the making (from *poiein,* to make) of medicines, hence a standard list and description of medicines; cf *pharmacy* (whence *pharmacist*), via MF and ML from Gr *pharmakeia,* the use of drugs, and *pharmaceutic* (EF-F *pharmaceutique*), now usu *pharmaceutical,* from LL *pharmaceuticus,* from Gr *pharmakeutikos,* from *pharmakeuein,* to use or administer medicine(s).

**pharo-** (1): from Gr *pharos,* a lighthouse, from the isle of *Pharos* in Egyptian harbour of Alexandria, the locality of a very famous lighthouse. Ex: *pharology,* the lore and science of lighthouses.

**pharo-** (2): from Gr *pharos,* a mantle; IE r, perh *bher-.* Ex: Zoo *Pharomacrus* (cf *macro-*).

**pharyng(o)-:** Gr *pharung(o)-,* c/f of *pharunx* (gen

*pharungos*), the pharynx, akin to the syn L *frūmen* (? from *\*frug(s)men*). Ex: *pharyngology* and *pharyngoscope*.

**phascol(o)-**: loosely **phasco-**: from Gr *phaskōlos*, a pouch. Exx: *Phascogale* (Gr *galē*, a weasel), a small rat-like marsupial; *Phascolarctos* (Gr *arktos*, a bear), the 'native bear' or koala of Australia; *Phascolomys* (Gr *mus*, a mouse), a wombat.

**phaseo-**: for *Phaseolus*, a Bot genus (beans), as in *phaseolunatin*; from L *phasēlus* (Gr *phasēlos*), perh akin to L *faba*.

**-phasia.** See *-phemia*.

**phaso-**, as in Chem *phasotropy*: for *phase*.

**phell(o)-**: Gr *phell(o)-*, c/f of *phellos*, cork; IE r, prob *bhel-*, to swell. Exx: *phelloderm* (cf *-derm*); *phellogen* (*-gen*).

**-phemia; -phemism**, adj **-phemistic; -phasia**: resp Gr *-phēmia*, c/f of *phēmē*, speech, akin to *phēmi*, I say, akin to the syn IE *\*bhami*; Gr *-phēmismos*; Gr *-phasia*, from *phanai*, to speak. Exx: *dysphemia*, *dysphemism, dysphemistic*, opp *euphemia, euphemism* (Gr *euphēmismos*), *euphemistic*; *dysphasia* (prefix *dys-*) and *tachyphasia*, very rapid (cf *tachy-*) speech.

**-phen, -phene; phen(o)-**: for *phene*, benzene; (*pheno-*) for *phenyl*. Only in Chem.

**phenakisto-**: from Gr *phenakistēs*, a deceiver, an elaboration of *phenax*, gen *phenakos*; as in *phenakistoscope*.

**-phene.** See *-phen*.

**phenio-.** See *phoenico-*.

**pheno-** (1). See *-phen*.

**pheno-** (2). A var of *phaeno-*, as esp in PHENOMENON, but also via F *phéno-*, as in *phenocryst* (F *phénocryste*).

**pheno-** (3). Short for *phenomeno-*, as in Bio *phenology* for Phil *phenomenology*.

**pheo-.** A var of *phaeo-*.

**-pher**, either from or on Gr *-pheros* (whence certainly *-pherous*) or from its source, *pherein* (s *pher-*), to bear or carry, corresponds to (E from) L *-fer*. Exx: *Christopher*, from LGr *Khristophoros*, (adj) Christ-bearing; *chronopher*, a time-carrying (hence, -signalling) instrument; *sceptropherous*.

**-phil** or **-phile**, 2 **-phila**, pl **-philae**, 3 **-philia** and 4 **-phily**, 5 **-philous**, 6 **-philism**, 7 **-philist**, 8 **-philus**; 9 **phil(o)-**: all, ult, from Gr *philos*, loving, fond, akin to *philein*, to love, be fond of or addicted to, s and r *phil-*, IE r prob either *\*phil-* or *\*bhil-*, to be fond of: resp Gr *-philos*, (adj) -loving, or Gr *philēs*, -lover; 2 and 8, *-phila* and *-philae*, both pl, and *-philus*, sing, from Gr *-philos*, but as if via L *-phila*, neupl, *-philae*, fpl, and *-philus*, m sing; 3, 4, E *-phily*, perh influenced by F *-philie*, for SciL, from Gr, *-philia*; 5 (*-philous*), from Gr *-philos*; 6, 7, (*-philism*) the suffixes *-ism* attached to *phil*(e, *-ia, -ous*), and *-ist* attached to *-phil*(*ism*); 9 (*philo-*) Gr *phil(o)-*, c/f of *philos*, loving, fond or well-disposed.

Exx: *Americanophil, Anglophil*(e), *bibliophile* (cf *biblio-*); *Anthophila*, esp bees, and *Spermophilus*, a genus of seed-lovers; *spasmophilia, alcoholo-*

*philia*, and *toxophily*, the (study and) love of archery—cf *toxo-*; *dendrophilous*, tree-loving—cf *dendro-*; *xenophilism*, an addiction to foreigners (*xenoi*); *zoophilist*, an animal lover;—PHILANTHROPY and PHILOLOGY and PHILOSOPHY.

**philosophico-**: for *philosophic*; denoting 'philosophical and'.

**phleb(o)-**: Gr *phleb(o)-*, c/f of *phleps* (φλέψ), a vein; IE r, perh *\*bhel-*, to swell. Exx: *phlebology*, the An, and Med, knowledge of the veins; *phlebitis*, inflammation of vein—cf the suffix *-itis*; *phlebotomy* (cf *-tome*).

**phlo-**: from Gr *phloos* (s *phlo-*), bark of tree, as in *phlobaphene*: *phlo-*+Gr *baph*(e), a dyeing+Chem *-ene*. Cf:

**phloeo-**: from Gr *phloios*, bark (of trees), akin to *phlein, phluein*, to flow; basic idea, the juice in bark. Ex: *phloeophagous*, bark-eating.

**phlogo-**: Gr *phlogo-*, c/f of *phlox* (gen *phlogos*), fire, from *phlegein*, to burn, perh from IE *\*bhel-*, to swell. Exx: Med *phlogogenetic*, causing inflammation; *phlogopite*, a flame-coloured mica (Min suffix *-ite*)—from Gr *phlogōpos*, fire-like (*ōps*, a face, gen *ōpos*).

**phlor(o)-**: for *phlorizin* and *phloroglucinol*: only in Chem.

**-phlysis**, as in *emphlysis*, comes from Gr *phlusis*, an eruption.

**-phobe**, 2 **-phobia**, 3 **-phobiac**, 4 **-phobic**, 5 **-phobous**; 6 **phob(o)-**: all, ult, from Gr *phobos* (s *phob-*), fear, flight, akin to *phebesthai* (s *pheb-*), to flee; IE r, perh *\*pheb-*, but prob *\*bheg-* (Hofmann).

Exx: 1, from Gr *-phobos*, -fearing, (hence) excessively fearing, as in *Anglophobe*; 2, Gr *-phobia* (whence the SciL, hence the E, n *phobia*), like 1 from Gr *phobos*, as in *hydrophobia* (cf the 2nd *hydro-*), adopted from L, from Gr *hudrophobia*; 3 (*-phobiac*)=*phobi*(a)+suffix *-ac*, on analogy of *maniac*; 4 (*-phobic*), from Gr *-phobikos*, as in *hudrophobikos*, whence, via L *hydrophobicus*, the E *hydrophobic*; 5 (*-phobous*), Gr *-phobos*, -fearing, as in *heliophobous* (cf *helio-*), sun-fearing; 6, Gr *phob(o)-*, c/f of *phobos*, fear, as in *phobophobia*, an excessive fear of being afraid or of one's own fears.

**phoc(o)-**: from Gr *phōkē*, a seal, as in *Phocodontia* (cf *-odontia* at *-odon*).

**phoenic(o)-** or **phenico-**: the former, a L shape (occ shortened, via F *phéni-*, to *pheni-*) of Gr *phoiniko-*, c/f of *phoinix*, purple-red, akin to *phoinios*, blood-red. Exx: *Phoenicopterus* (cf *-ptera*), genus of flamingos; *phoenicurous*, red-tailed, from Gr *phoinikouros*, the redstart or redtail (Gr *oura*, tail).

**pholid(o)-**: Gr *pholid(o)-*, c/f of *pholis*, a scale, perh akin to *phellos* (cork), q.v. at *phello-*. Ex: *pholidolite*, a kind of silica (cf *-lite*).

**-phon** or **-phone, -phonia** or, more often **-phony; phon(o)-**: resp Gr *-phōnon*, c/f from *phōnē*, a sound or a voice; Gr *-phōnia*, from *phōnē*; Gr *phōn(o)-*, c/f of *phōnē*: f.a.e., PHONETIC. Exx: *-phone* for musical instruments: *sousaphone*

(*Sousa*) and *xylophone* (*xylo-*); -*phone*, for sound-transmitting instruments: *dictaphone* (*dictate*) and GRAMOPHONE ('written sound') and TELEPHONE ('speech from afar');—-*phonia*, -*phony*, for type of sound: *acrophony* (*acro-*) and *baryphony* (*bary-*), *dysphonia* (Gr *dusphōnia*), difficulty in pronouncing, and *euphony* (Gr *euphōnia*), ease in pronouncing, (but primarily) pleasing sound;—*phonogram*, *phonograph*, *phonology*, *phonophore* (cf next).

-**phora**, 2 -**phore**, 3 -**phoresis**, 4 -**phoria**, 5 -**phorous**, 6 -**phorus**; 7 **phor**(o)-: all from Gr *phor-*, the s of the nn deriving from *pherein* (s *pher-*, akin to the *fer* of syn L *ferre*), to carry, IE s, *bher-*, resp SciL from Gr -*phoros*, -bearing; 2, Gr -*phoros*, neu -*phoron*, -bearing; 3, Gr *phorēsis*, a being borne; 4, Gr -*phoria*, a bearing; 5, Gr *phoros-*, -*bearing*; 6, Gr -*phoros*, bearing, (used as n) a bearer; 7, Gr *phoro-*, c/f of *phora*, motion, (esp) rapid motion.

Exx: (mostly in Bot and Zoo, with adj -*phoran*) *Cladophora* (cf *clado-*); 2, *semaphore*, a sign-bearer, a signal-conveyer (cf *sema-*); 3, *pathophoresis* (cf *patho-* at -*path*); 4 (with adj -*phoric*), *heterophoria* (cf *hetero-*); 5, *phosphorous* and 6, *phosphorus*, L from Gr *phōsphoros*, a light-bringer (cf *phos-*); 7, *phorometer*, *phoronomy*, *phoroscope*.

**phos-**; **photo-**: from Gr *phōs*, light, and *phōt*(o)-, c/f of *phōs*, gen *phōtos*, IE r prob **bhos-** (cf Skt *bhás-*, light) or **bhot-**. Exx: *phosgene* (cf -*gene* at -*gen*) and *phosphorus* (cf prec); *photogenic* (cf -*genic* at -*gen*), generating light, (but also) appearing to advantage in a photograph; PHOTOGRAPH and *photometer*.

**phosphato-**: c/f of *phosphate*.

**phospho-**. A shortened c/f of *phosphorus*. Cf:

**phosphor**(o)-: c/f of *phosphorus* and of *phosphoric* and of *phosphorescence*.

**phot**(o)-. See *phos-*. It also stands for *photoelectric*, as in *photo-emission*.

**phragmo-**: from Gr *phragma* or *phragmos* (s *phrag-*), a fence, perh akin to L *farcīre* (s *farc-*), to stuff. Ex: *phragmocone* (cf CONE).

**phraseo-**: Mod Gr *phraseo-*, from Gr *phrasis*, speech; in E, denoting 'phrase': cf PHRASE. Exx: *phraseogram* and *phraseology* (q.v. at PHRASE). Cf:

-**phrasia**; -**phrasis**: Med c/f from Gr *phrasis* (see prec), denoting 'a (disordered) way of speech', as in *bradyphrasia* (cf *brady-*); Gr -*phrasis*, as in *paraphrasis*, and *periphrasis*, adopted, via L, from Gr.

-**phrasy**: ML or LL -*phrasia*, from Gr, from *phrēn*, heart or mind; as in *euphrasy*, from *euphrainein* (*eu*, well+*phrain-* for *phrēn*+inf suffix -*ein*), to delight. Cf -*phrenia*.

**phreato-**: for *phreatic*, of or for or like a well, from Gr *phreat-*, o/s of *phrear*, a well. Ex: *phreatophyte* (cf -*phyte*).

-**phrenia**, adj -**phrenic**; **phrenico-**; **phren**(o)-: resp SciL c/f from Gr *phrēn*, the mind, the heart—cf the independent adj *phrenic*, F *phrénique*; (*phrenico-*) c/f of E *phrenic*; Gr *phren*(o)-, c/f of *phrēn*: cf FRENZY. Exx: *bradyphrenia* (cf -*brady*), adj *bradyphrenic*; *phrenicotomy*, cutting of a

phrenic nerve; *phrenocardia* (cf -*cardia*) and *phrenology*, the study (cf -*logy* at -*loger*) of a person's heart and mind by his 'bumps'—cf the F *phrénologie*.

**phryn**(o)-: from Gr *phrunē*, a toad; only in Zoo, as in *Phrynosoma* (cf -*soma*); 'the brown creature'—cf BROWN.

**phthal**(o)-: c/f for *phthalic* (Chem).

**phthio-**: for *phthisis*; a shortened form of the next.

**phthisio-**: for and from *phthisis* (adopted from Gr, from *phthiein*, s *phthi-*, to waste away)—as in *phthisiology*, the science of pulmonary consumption.

**phthongo-**: from Gr *phthongos*, voice, akin to *phōnē*, sound. Ex: *phthongometer*.

**phyco-**: from Gr *phukos* (whence L *fucus*), seaweed, as in *phycology*, the science of algae or seaweed. Bot has -*phyceae*, denoting a class or an order of seaweed (algae), with adj -*phyceous*.

**phygo-**: from Gr *phugein* or *pheugein*, to avoid, s *phug-*, *pheug-*, cf L *fugere* (s *fug-*) and E FUGITIVE. Ex: *phygogalactic*, tending to check the secretion of milk.

**phyl-**. See *phylo-*.

**phylaco-**; **phylacto-**: from Gr *phulax* (gen *phulakos*), a guard, akin to *phulassein* (to guard), whence *phylacto-*. Exx: *phylacobiosis* and *phylacto-carp*, techh of Zoo.

-**phyll**, 2 -**phyllous**, 3 -**phyllum**, 4 -**phylly**; 5 **phyll**(o)-, occ 6 **phylli-**: all from Gr *phullon* (s *phull-*), a leaf, akin to L *folium*, a leaf, and E BLOOM: resp Gr *phullon*, via L *phyllum* (whence 3); 2, Gr -*phullos*, -leaved; 4, Gr -*phullia*—via L -*phyllia*—from *phullon*; 5, Gr *phull*(o)-, c/f of *phullon*; 6, a latinized var.

Exx: *chlorophyll* (cf *chloro-*), the green colouring-matter of plants, esp of their leaves; *heterophyllous*, having leaves of more than one shape, cf *hetero-*; *Chrysophyllum* (cf *chryso-*, of gold); *sclerophylly* (cf *sclero-*); *phyllophorous*, leaf-bearing or -producing (cf -*phorous* at -*phora*) and *phyllotaxy* (Gr *taxis*, arrangement); *phylliform*, leaf-shaped.

**phyl**(o)-; -**phyly**: Gr *phul*(o)-, c/f of *phulon*, a tribe, a racial stock, a race (IE r, *bhul-*, with numerous descendants)—in E, denotes also SciL *phylum*, one of the primary divisions of animal and vegetable life; (-*phyly*) from the var *phulē*, a clan. Exx: *phylology*; *phylogeny*, the genesis (cf -*geny* at *gen*) and evolution of a phylum;—*organophyly* (cf *organo-*).

-**phyma**, as in *arthrophyma*, inflamed swelling of a joint (*arthro-*) or of joints, represents L *phyma*, from Gr *phuma* (cf PHYSIC); the o/s *phumat-* yields the c/f *phymat*(o)-, as in *phymatorhysin* (Gr *rhusis*, a flowing, cf *rheo-*).

-**phyre**: F -*phyre*, from *porphyre*, porphyry; adj -**phyric**. Ex: *leucophyre* (*leuco-*).

**physa-**; **physallo-**: Gr *phusa*, a bellows, and its derivative *phusallis*, a bladder; of echoic origin. Exx: *physagogue*, a flatulence-leader, hence -dispeller; *physalite* (cf -*lite*); *Physallospora* (cf -*spora*). Cf *physo-*.

**physico-**; **physi(o)-**; occ an independent **physi-**: from Gr *phusikos*, natural, physical, from *phusis*, nature, whence, via the Gr c/f *phusio-*, the E *physi(o)-*; independent *physi-* comes from *phusis*: cf PHYSIC. Exx: *physico(-)mental*; *physianthropy*; *physiognomy*, art of reading (cf *-gnomy* at *gnomo-*) the nature, or character, from physical, esp facial, traits, hence the face itself; *physiography*, physical geography; PHYSIOLOGY; *physitheism*, the attribution of corporeality to the gods or to God.

**physo-**: Gr *phuso-*, c/f of *phusa*, a bellows (cf *physa-*): denoting, in Med, the presence of gas, as in *physocele* (cf *-cele*) and, in Bot and Zoo, an air bladder, as in *physostomous* (cf *-stomous* at *-stoma*).

**-phyte** and 2, **-phytum** and 3, 4, pll **-phytes** and **-phyta**; 5, **-phytic**; 6, **phyti-** and 7, **phyt(o)-**: 2, the Latinized form of E *-phyte*, from Gr *-phuton*, from *phuton*, a plant; 4, *-phyta*=Gr *-phuta*, neupl, and 3 a Latinized and fpl; 5, *-phytic*=Gr *phutikos*, of plants, vegetative; 6, a Latinized var of the Gr *phuto-* (via L *phyto-*), from *phuton*, akin to *phuein* (s *phu-*), to produce, and *phunai* (s *phu-*), to be born or produced; IE r, prob *bhu-*. (The element *-phytia* occurs only in Biochem.) Exx: *zoophyte* (Gr *zōophuton*), an 'animal (Gr *zōion*) plant', formerly a plant that somehow resembles an animal, now an animal that resembles a plant; 2, 3, 4 occur in names of classifications in Bot and Zoo; *sporophytic* (cf *-spora*); *phytiform*, plant-like; *phytography*, descriptive botany; *phytophagous*, plant-eating (cf *herbivorous*).

**pi-**. See *pio-*.

**pia(r)-**; **piaro-**: the former, as in *piarh(a)emia* (cf *-haemia* at *haema-*), represents the Gr n *piar*, fat; the latter, as in *piaropus* (cf *-pus* at *-pod*), the Gr adj *piaros*, fat, akin to the syn *piōn*, itself akin to the equivalent Skt *pivan-*. Cf *pio-*.

**pici-**: from L *pīcus*, a woodpecker—prob echoic. Ex: *piciform*, like a woodpecker.

**-picrin(e)**; **picr(o)-**: the former (only in Chem) from—the latter=*pikr(o)-*, the Gr c/f of—Gr *pikros*, bitter; IE r, perh *pik- or *peik-*. Exx: *picrolite* (cf *-lite*), *picrotoxin*.

**picto-**: from L *pictus* (painted), the pp of *pingere*, to paint: cf PICTURE. Ex: *pictograph*, a picture—writing, an idea indicated by picture.

**piezo-**, 'pressure': from Gr *piezein* (s *piez-*), to press, akin to Skt *pīḍa*, pressure, and various other IE words. Exx: *piezo(-)chemistry*; *piezometer*, a pressure-register.

**pigmento-**: for *pigment*, as in *pigmentophage* (cf *-phaga*).

**pilei-**, **pileo-**: from L *pileus*, a fur cap, akin to *pilus*, hair. Exx: *pileiform*, cap-shaped, and *pileorhiza* (Gr *rhiza*, a root). Cf the 2nd *pilo-*.

**pili-**; **pilo-** (1): from L *pilus*, hair, akin to Gr *pilos*, felt. Exx: *piliferous*, hair-bearing or producing, and *piliform*, hairlike; *pilocystic* (cf *-cyst*). The s *pil-* occurs also in, e.g., 'depilatory', a hair-remover, and 'horripilation' (see *horri-*).

**pilo-** (1). See prec.

**pilo-** (2): Gr *pilo-*, c/f of *pilos*, felt (the fabric),

akin to L *pilus*, hair, IE s *pil-*. Ex: *Pilocarpus* (cf *-carpus* at *-carp*).

**pilo-** (3): from Gr *pilos* (s *pil-*), a ball, akin to the syn L *pila* and E PILL. Ex: *Pilobolus*, a genus of *fungi* that forcibly expel their ripe spore cases or sacs, the 2nd element being from Gr *bolos*, a throwing (cf *-bola*).

**pina-**, in names of dyes: from Gr *pinax* (s *pin-*), a plank, a tablet, a picture, akin to Skt *pínākam*, a stick, a club, OSl *pĭnĭ*, a tree-trunk; from the Gr o/s *pinak-* comes the c/f *pinak(o)-*, occurring in E as *pinako-* or *pinaco-*; the Gr dim *pinakion* yields the rare E c/f *pinakio-*. Exx: *pinachrome*, in photography (cf *-chrome* at *-chroia*); *pinacocyte* (*-cyte*); *pinakotheke*—cf the G *Pinakothek*—from Gr *pinakothēkē*, a *thēkē* (cf *-theca*) or repository, e.g. a gallery, of pictures; *pinakiolite* (cf *-lite*).

**pingue-**, **pingui-**: L *pingue-*, *pingui-*, c/f of the adj *pinguis*, fat. Exx: *pinguefaction*, from *pinguefy*, to render fat, from L *pinguefacere*; *pinguinitescent*, (of hair) greasily shining, the 2nd element being *nitescent-*, o/s of *nitescens*, presp of L *nitescere*, to glitter, freq of *nitēre*, to shine.

**pini-**: L *pīni-*, c/f of *pīnus*: see PINE. Ex: *pinivorous*, pine-eating (cf *-vora*).

**-pinnate**; **pinnati-** and **pinnato-**; **pinni-**: resp an end c/f of *pinnate*, feathered, feather-like; and c/ff of L *pinnātus*, feathered, from *pinna*, a feather, whence the L, hence E, c/f *pinni-*, feather, (hence also) fin; akin to FIN. Exx: *digitato-pinnate*; *pinnatiped*, feather-footed, and *pinnatodentate*; *pinniform*.

**pinno-**: Gr *pinno-*, c/f of Gr, hence L, *pinna*, a bivalve, as in *Pinnotheres*, SciL from Gr *pinnotēres*, bivalve-guarders, from *tērein* (s *tēr-*, to guard).

**pi(o)-**: from the Gr n *piōn*, fat, of the same r *pi-* as the syn *piar*, perh akin to L *pinguis*. Ex: *pioscope*, a lactoscope or cream-determiner.

**piperi-**, **pipero(n)-**, only in Chem: from L *piper*—cf PEPPER.

**pipto-**: from Gr *piptein*, to fall. Only in Bot and Pharm.

**piri-**, **piro-**: from L *pirum*—cf PEAR. Ex: *piroplasma* (cf *-plasm*).

**pisci-**: L *pisci-*, c/f of *piscis*, a fish: cf FISH. Exx: *pisciculture*, fish-breeding and rearing; PISCIFORM, fish-shaped or -like; *piscivorous*, fish-eating.

**pisi-**: from L *pisum*, a pea: cf PEA. Ex: *pisiform*, pea-shaped.

**pistilli-**: from Sci L *pistillum*, a pistil, akin to PESTLE. Ex: *pistilliferous*.

**pistio-** or **pisto-**: from Gr *pistis*, faith, akin to L *fides*. Exx: *pistiology*, the doctrine of (religious) faith; *pistology*, the theology of faith.

**pithano-**: Gr *pithano-*, c/f of *pithanos*, persuasive (s *pithan-*, r *pith-*), akin to *peithō*, I persuade. Ex: *pithanology*, rhetorical persuasiveness.

**pithec(o)-**; **-pithecus**: c/ff, the latter Latinized, from Gr *pithēkos*, an ape; IE r *b(h)iah-*, with basic idea 'half', an ape being a half-man. Exx: *Pithecanthropus*, ape man; *pithecological*, concerning the study of apes; *Sivapithecus*.

**pitto-**, as in *pittospore*, a plant of the genus

*Pittosporum* (cf *-spora*): from Gr *pitta*, pitch (viscous)—cf PITCH. n.

**pityo-**, as in *pityocampa*, from Gr *pituokampē*, the larva (Gr *kampē*, a caterpillar) of a moth that frequents pine trees (Gr *pitus*, a pine tree, gen *pituos*).

**pityro-**: Gr *pitur(o)*-, c/f of *pituron*, bran. Exx: *pityriasis*, Gr *pituriasis* (cf *-iasis*), and Bot *Pityrogramma*.

**plac(o)-**: Gr *plak(o)*-, c/f of *plax* (gen *plakos*, s *plak-*), a tablet, a plate; IE s, *\*plak-*. Exx: *placoderm* (cf *-derm*) and *placoplast* (cf *-plast* at *-plasm*).

Gr *plax* has derivative *plakous*, a flat cake, acc *plakounta*, whence the L *placenta*, a cake, whence its An, Med, Zoo special senses, with c/f *placenti-*, as in *placentiferous* or *placentigerous*, placenta-bearing: cf *-fer* and *-ger*.

**plagi(o)-**: Gr *plagi(o)*-, c/f of *plagios*, oblique, on the slant, akin to *pelagos*, the open sea, and L *plānus*. Exx: *plagiocephalism* (cf *cephalo-*); *plagioclase* (G *Plagioklas*; cf *-clase*); *plagiograph*.

**plani-**: L *plāni-*, c/f of *plānus*, evel, plane: cf PLAIN. Exx: *planigraph*, *planimeter* (F *planimètre*), *planiscope*. Cf *plano-* (2).

**planeto-**: for *planet*, as in *planetology*.

**-plania**: Gr *-plania*, c/f of *planē*, a wandering (course), akin to *plax*, q.v. at *plagio-*. Ex: *uroplania*. Cf:

**plan(o)-** (1): Gr *plan(o)*-, c/f of *planos*, roaming, wandering (cf prec), as in *planoblast* (cf *-blast*) and *planogamete* (cf *-gam*).

**plano-** (2): irreg from L *plānus*, level, plane: cf *plani-*. Exx: ('flatly') *planorotund*; ('flat, or plane, and') *planoconvex*.

**planti-** (1): from L *planta*—cf PLANT. Ex: *plantivorous*, (of insects, worms) plant-eating (cf *-vora*).

**planti-** (2): from L *planta*, sole of foot, either from the IE s *\*plat-*, as in Gr *platūs*, level, flat, with an *-n-* infix (cf L *iungere—iugum*), or, by 'telescoping', from the (pars) *plānāta*, levelled, (hence) flat, of the foot. Ex: *plantigrade* (cf *-grade*), walking on the soles.

**planto-**: for *planter*, as in *plantocracy*, rule by planters.

**-plasia** or **-plasy**; 3 **-plasis**; 4 **-plasm** or **-plasma**, with adjj **-plasmic**; 7 **-plasmia**; 8 **-plast**; 9 **-plastic**; 10 **-plasty**; 11 **plasmato-**, 12 **plasm(o)-**: all ult from or intimately akin to Gr *plassein* (s *plass-*), to form or mould, cf E PLASTER: resp, 1, SciL, Englished as *-plasy*, from 3, Gr *-plasis*, c/f of *plasis*, a forming or moulding, from *plassein*; 4 is the E form (cf F *-plasme*) of LL from Gr *-plasma*, c/f of *plasma*, anything formed, anything moulded; (7) a SciL c/f from E, from LL, from Gr *plasma*; 8 (*-plast*), from the Gr adj c/f *-plastos*, -formed, orig the pp of *plassein*; 9 (*-plastic*) from Gr *plastikos* (whence, via L *plasticus*, the adj *plastic*), formable, fit for moulding, plastic; 10 (*-plasty*), Gr *-plastia*, a moulding, prob from *plastos*, moulded;—11, *plasmato-*, Gr *plasmato-*, c/f of *plasma*, o/s *plasmat-*; 12, *plasmo-*, from E *plasm*.

Exx: *macroplasia* (cf *macro-*); *heteroplasy* (*hetero-*); *paraplasis* (prefix *para-*); *mythoplasm*, *protoplasm*(a); *protoplasmic*; *oligoplasmia* (*oligo-*); *gypsoplast* (*gypso-*); *bioplastic* (*bio-*); *osteoplasty* (cf *osteo-*); *plasmatoparous* (cf *-parous* at *-para*); *plasmolysis* (cf *-lysis* at *-lyse*).

**platalei-**: from L *platalea*, the spoonbill, perh akin to *platy-*. Ex: *plataleiform*, spoon-billed.

**platini-**, **platin(o)-**; **platinoso-**, **platos(o)-**: the first two are c/ff of E *platinum* (cf PLATE), as in *platiniferous* (cf *-ferous* at *-fer*); *platoso-* is short for *platinoso-*, c/f of *platinous*.

**plat(y)-**: Gr *plat(u)*-, c/f of *platus* (s *plat-*), broad (or wide), flat: cf PLATE. Exx: *platycephalous*, having a flat-crowned head; PLATYPUS.

**plazo-**: from Gr *plazein* (s *plaz-*), to bewilder. Ex: *plazolite* (cf *-lite*).

**plebi-**: L *plēbi-*, c/f of *plēbs* (gen *plēbis*), the people—exclusive of the noble families: cf PLEBEIAN. Exx: *plebicolar*, *-colous* (cf *-colous*), courting the favour of the common people, from L *plēbicola*, one who does this; *plebiscite*, prob via F *plébiscite*, certainly from L *plēbiscītum*, a decision of the people, the 2nd element (*scītum*, a decree) deriving from *sciscere*, freq of *scīre*, to know—cf SCIENCE.

**plec(o)-**; **plect(o)-**: via SciL from Gr *plekein* (s *plek-*), to twist or twine; (*plecto-*) from Gr *plektos* (twisted), pp of *plekein*; IE s, prob *\*plek-*. Exx: *Plecotus*, a genus of long-eared bats—from Gr *ous*, ear, gen *ōtos* (cf the element *-otic*); *Plectognathi*, an order of fishes, lit 'the twisted-jaws' (Gr *gnathos*, jaw, cf *-gnatha*).

**-plegia** or **-plegy**; **plego-**, occ **plega-**: Gr *-plēgia* (Englished as *-plegy*), c/f of *plēgē*, a stroke, whence the E c/f *plego-*, with irregular var *plega-*; akin to Gr *plēssein* (Attic *plēttein*), to strike; IE r, prob *\*plag-* or *\*plak-*, varr *\*pleg-* or *\*plek-*. Exx: *hemiplegia* (or *-plegy*), partial (cf *hemi-*, half) paralysis; Med *plegaphonia*; *plegometer*, an instrument measuring the force of blows.

**pleio-**, **pleo-**, **plio-**: from Gr *pleiōn*, Homeric *pleōn*, more, neu *pleion*, *pleon*, akin to L *plūres*, more (persons); IE r, prob *\*plei-* or *plē-*. Exx: *Pleiocene*, occ *Pliocene* (cf *-cene*); *pleomorphism* (Gr *morphē*, form: cf *-morph*). Cf:

**pleisto-**: from Gr *pleistos*, most (cf prec), as in *Pleistocene*, the most recent (cf *-cene*). Geol epoch next below the present.

**plemyra-**: from Gr *plēmura*, the high tide, prob akin to *plērēs*, full. Ex: *plemyrameter*. Cf:

**pleni-**: L *plēni-*, c/f of *plēnus*, full, akin to *plēre*, to fill (s *plē-*). Exx: *plenilune*, full moon (L *plēnilūnium*); *plenipotent*, from *plēnipotent-*, o/s of L *plēnipotens*, fully powerful (L *potens*—cf POTENT), whence ML *plēnipotentiārius* (cf the E suffix *-ary* from L *-ārius*), whence the E *plenipotentiary*. Cf *plero-*.

**pleo-**. See *pleio-*.

**plero-**: from Gr *plēro-*, c/f of *plērēs* (s *plēr-*), full, as in *plerocercoid* (cf *cerco-* at *-cercal*)— *pleromorph* (cf *-morph*)—*plerophory* (Gr *plērō-phoria*), cf *-phoria* at *-phora*. Cf *pleni-*.

plesi(o)-: Gr *plēsi(o)*-, c/f of the adj *plēsios*, close, near, akin to—perh from—*pelas*, (prep) near; IE r, prob *pel*-. Exx: *plesiomorphous* (cf -*morphous* at -*morph*) and *Plesiosaurus* (cf -*saur*).

plessi-; plexi-: from Gr *plēssein* (s *plēss*-, app echoic), to strike, as in *plessigraph*, a form of *pleximeter*; *plexi*-, from Gr *plēxis*, a stroke, from *plēssein*.

plethysmo-: from Gr *plēthusmos*, an enlargement, akin to *pimplēmi*, I fill. Ex: Physio *plethysmograph*.

-pleura; pleuri-, pleur(o)-: all from Gr *pleura*, a rib, the side, with *pleuro*- a genuine Gr c/f: cf PLEURISY. Exx: *endopleura* (prefix *endo*-); *pleuriseptate* (cf -*septate*); *pleurocarpous* (cf -*carp*). The adj is -*pleurous*.

-plex and plexi- (2); -plicate and plicato-: L -*plex*, -fold, from *plicāre* (s *plic*-), to fold; (*plexi*-) from L *plexus*, a twining, from *plectere* (s *plect*-), to twine; last two, from L *plicātus*, pp of *plicāre*, to fold. Cf PLY.

Exx: *multiplex* and *plexiform*; *duplicate* and *plicato-contorted*.

plexi- (1). See *plessi*-.

plexi- (2). See -*plex*.

-plexia, a var of -*plegia*, q.v.: from Gr -*plēxia*, from *plēxis*, a stroke.

-plicate; plicato-: both from *plicate*, folded. Exx: *triplicate*; *plicatolobate* (cf -*lobate*). Cf -*plex* and:

plici-: from ML *plica*, a fold, from L *plicāre* (s *plic*-), to fold: cf prec. Ex: *pliciform* (cf -*form*).

plinthi-: for *plinth* (Gr *plinthos*, a brick, a plinth), as in *plinthiform*.

plio-. See *pleio*-.

-ploid=Gr -*ploos*, folded+suffix -*oid*. Ex: *polyploid*, manifold.

plu-: from L *plūs*, more; in E, denotes 'more than', as in *pluperfect*. Cf *pluri*-.

plumbi-, plumbo-: from L *plumbum* (s *plumb*-), lead (Min): cf PLUMB. Exx: *plumbiferous*, lead-producing (cf -*ferous* at -*fer*); *plumbo(-)solvent*.

plumi-: L *plūmi*-, cf of L *plūma*, a feather: cf PLUME. Ex: *plumiped(e)*, feather-footed. The L dim *plūmula* yields c/f *plumuli*-, as in *plumuliform*.

pluri-: L *plūri*-, deriving from *plūs*, more, gen *plūris*, and, in E, denoting 'several' or even 'many': cf PLURAL. Exx: *pluri-axial*, *plurilateral*, *plurivalent*. The shortened *plur*- occurs in *plurennial*, (a plant) lasting for some years (cf -*ennial*).

plut(o): Gr *plout(o)*-, c/f of *ploutos*, wealth. Exx: PLUTOCRACY; *plutology*, the economic study of wealth, and *plutonomy*, political economy.

plutono-: for E *plutonic*, igneous.

pluvio-: from ML *pluvia* (L *pluuia*), rain, from the adj *pluuius*, rainy, itself from *pluere* (s *plu*-), to rain. Exx: *pluviometer*, a rain-gauge, and *pluviograph*, a self-registering rain-gauge.

-ply (cf -*plex* and PLY, n): see MULTIPLY.

-pnea or -pnoea; 3 pneo-; 4 pneum(a)-, 5 pneumato-; 6 pneumo-; 7 pneumon(o)-; 8 -pneusta: resp Gr -*pnoia* (L -*pnoea*, E -*pnea*), c/f of *pnoē*, a breathing, akin to *pneō*, I breathe—see PNEUMATIC;

3, from *pneō* (s *pne*-), I breathe; 4, from Gr *pneuma*, air, wind; 5, Gr *pneumat(o)*-, c/f of *pneuma*, gen *pneumatos*; 6, from Gr *pneumōn*, lung ('the breather'); 7, from Gr *pneumōn*, gen *pneumonos*; 8, from Gr -*pneustos*, breathed, pp of *pneō*.

Exx: *bromopn(o)ea*, bad breath—cf *dyspn(o)ea*, difficult breathing; *pneometer*; *pneumarthrosis*= *pneum*(a)+*arthr*(o)-+suffix -*osis*; *pneumatograph*, *pneumatology*, *pneumatophore* (cf -*phora*); *pneumococcus* (cf *cocci*-); *pneumonography*, X-ray photography of the lungs; (a Zoo division breathing in a specified way; adj -*pneustal*) *Pharynopneusta*.

pocilli-, as in *pocilliform*, cup-shaped: from L *pocillum*, a small cup, dim of *poculum* (akin to *pōtus*, 'who has drunk'), whence *poculi*-, as in *poculiform*.

-pod or -pode; 2 -podal; 3 -poda; 4 -podia; 5 -podium; 6 -podous, 7 -pus; 8 pod(o)-: all ult from Gr *pous*, a foot, gen *podos* (s *pod*-), akin to L *pēs* (gen *pedis*, s *ped*-), a foot: resp Gr -*podos*, neu -*podon*, end c/f of *pous*; 2, adj of (1)—cf suffix -*al*; 3, Gr -*poda*, end c/f of *pous*; 4, Gr -*podia*, end c/f (-*pod*+Med -*ia*) of *pous*; 5, L -*podium*, from Gr -*podion*, c/f of *podion*, dim ('a small foot') of *pous*; 6, Gr -*podos*, -footed, from *pous*—*podous* answering to nn in -*poda*; 7, SciL -*pus*, from Gr -*pous*, -footed, from *pous*; 8, Gr *pod(o)*-, c/f of *pous*.

Exx: *hexapod*, a six-footed animal, Gr *hexapous* —gen *hexapodos*; ANTIPODES; 2, *antipodal*; 3, *Decapoda* (cf *deca*-), ten-footed crustaceans; 4, *platypodia*, flat (cf *platy*-) -footedness; 5, *mesopodium*, middle (*meso*-) portion of foot or of foot-like part; 6, *hexapodous*, six footed, cf *hexa*-; 7, OCTOPUS and PLATYPUS; 9, *podology*, the science of the (human) feet—in Bot, a stalk, as in *Podocarpus* (cf -*carp*), and in Zoo, a stalk or peduncle, as in *Podophthalmia*, the stalk-eyed crustaceans, cf *ophthalmo*-.

poë-: Gr *poē*-, c/f of *poa*, grass. Ex: *poëphagous*, grass-eating.

poecil(o)-, occ poikilo-: Gr *poikil(o)*-, c/f of *poikilos*, variegated, various, from a PGr *poikos*, s *poik*-; IE r, *peik*-, cf L *pingere* and esp E PAINT. Exx: *poecilonomy* (cf -*onym*), 'the use of several names for one thing' (Webster); *poikilothermic* (cf -*therm*), having a variable bodily temperature.

-poeia, 2 -poësis or -poiesis, 3 -poietic; 4 poetico-, 5 poeto-: all ult from Gr *poiein* (s *poi*-), to make (see POET): resp from Gr -*poiia*, a making, from *poiein*; 2, Gr -*poiēsis*, terminal c/f of *poiēsis* (*poēsis*), a thing being made, poetry, from *poiein*; 3, from Gr -*poiētikos*, c/f of *poiētikos*, adj answering to *poiēsis*; 4, for E *poetic*, aided by Gr *poiētikos*; 5, Gr *poiēto*-, c/f of *poiētēs* (a poet).

Exx: *onomatopoeia*, adopted from LL, from Gr *onomatopoiia* (cf *onomato*-); *onomatopoësis*, from Gr *onomatopoiēsis*, and *hematopoiesis*, blood-formation; *hematopoietic* and *cosmopoietic*, from Gr *kosmopoiētikos*, world-making; *poetico-philosophic*; *poetomachy*, a 'war' between poets (cf -*machia*).

-pogon; pogon(o)-: from Gr *pōgōn* (gen *pōgonos*) a beard. Exx: *Calopogon* (cf *calo*- at *calli*-); *pogo-*

*niasis* (cf *-iasis*) and *pogonology*, the study of, a treatise on, beards.

**-poiesis; -poietic.** See *-poeia*.

**poikilo-.** See *poecilo-*.

**-pointic**=point, n+adj suffix *-ic*, as in *three-pointic*.

**polari-,** 'polar': from ML *polāris*, adj of L *polus*: cf POLE. (of earth). Exx: *polarimeter*, in Optics, where also *polariscope*.

**-pole, -polis; -polite,** whence **-politan:** from Gr *polis*, a city (cf POLICE). Exx: *metropole*, archaic for *metropolis*, but denoting also a metropolitan see—from *metropolis*, via LL from Gr *mētropolis*, (lit) mother city, hence a country's chief city; *metropolite*, LL *mētropolita*, Gr *mētropolitēs*, from *mētropolis*; *metropolitan*, adj (hence n), LL *mētropolitānus*, from *mētropolita*. Cf *cosmopolite*, Gr *kosmopolitēs*, a citizen of the cosmos or world, hence the adj *cosmopolitan*; *cosmopolis*, after *metropolis*. Cf *politico-*.

**polemo-,** as in *polemoscope*, lit 'a war glass': from Gr *polemos*, war: cf POLEMIC.

**poli(o)-:** Gr *poli(o)-*, c/f of *polios* (s *poli-*), grey, akin to FALLOW, pale. In E, *polio-* usu denotes 'relation to the *grey* matter of the brain—or of the spinal cord', as in *poliencephalitis* (for *encephalitis*, a disease of the brain, cf *encephalo-*); *poliomyelitis* (abbr *polio*), inflammation of the spinal cord's grey matter—cf *-myelitis* at *-myelia*.

**-polis, -politan, -polite.** See *-pole*.

**politico-:** from Gr *politikos*, civic, political. Exx: 'politics'—*politicomania*; 'political': *politico-commercial*.

**pollin(i)-:** from L *pollen*, gen *pollinis*: cf POLLEN. Exx: *polliniferous*, pollen-producing (cf *-ferous* at *-fer*); *pollinivorous*, pollen-eating (*-vorous* at *-vore*). Loosely *polleni-*.

**polto-:** from Gr *poltos*, porridge, akin to *palē*, fine meal. Ex: *poltophagous*, porridge-eating; *poltophagic*, given to eating food until it resembles porridge: cf *-phaga*.

**poly-:** via LL *poly-*, from Gr *polu-*, c/f of *polus* (neu *polu*), much, *polloi*, many: akin to E FULL. In E it denotes 'many' (not 'much'), with such variations as 'plurality' and 'diversity'. Exx: *polyandry*, q.v. at *andro-*; *polyanthus*, lit 'the many-flowered' (cf *anth-*); *polychromatic*, *-chrome* (Gr *polukhrōmos*), many-coloured; *polygamous* (cf *-gam*), having several marriages, hence several wives or husbands, Gr *polugamos*, whence *polugamia*, whence E *polygamy*; *polyglot* (n from adj), Gr *poluglōttos*, many-tongued (cf *-glossa*); *polygon* (cf the 1st *gon-*); *polygraph*, Gr *polugraphos* (adj), writing much; *polyhedron* (cf *-hedral*); *polymath*, q.v. at *-mathy*; *polymorphous*, having many forms or characteristics (cf *-morph*); *Polynesia*, SciL from F *Polynésie*, 'the many-islanded' (cf *-nesia* at *-nese*); *polyp*, F *polype*, L *polypus*, Gr *polupous*, many-footed, hence (now obs in E) an octopus; *polyphonic*, from Gr *poluphōnos*, having many sounds; *polysemant* (adj) and *polysemia*, (having) a multiplicity of meanings—Gr *polusēmantos* and SciL, with the 2nd element from *sēmeia*, pl of Gr *sēm-*

*eion*, a sign or signification, from *sēma*, a sign (cf SEMANTIC); *polysyllabic*, ML *polysyllabus*, Gr *polusullabos*, from *sullabē*, a SYLLABLE; *polytechnic*, F *polytechnique*, Gr *polutekhnos*, from *tekhnē*, an art, a craft; *polytheism*, F *polythéisme*, from Gr *polutheos*, of many gods (cf *theo-*); *polytrophic*, Gr *polutrophos*, nutritious (sense obs in E); *polyvalent*, many-valued, cf *-valent*.

**polypi-:** for *polypus*, a polyp, as in *polypiferous* (cf *-ferous* at *-fer*).

**-pomatous,** 'hinged': from Gr *pōma* (gen *pōmatos*), a lid; IE r *pō-*, to protect (Boisacq). Ex: *arthropomatous* (cf *arthro-*), applied to molluscs having hinged shells.

**pomi-, pomo-:** the latter ('fruit'), influenced by Gr; the former ('apple' or 'fruit'), L *pōmi-*, c/f of *pōmum*, (a) fruit, esp the apple. Exx: *pomiculture*, fruit-growing, and *pomiferous* (L *pōmifer*), apple-bearing; *pomology*, fruit-growing considered scientifically; cf the Bot *pome*, from OF-MF *pome* (EF-F *pomme*), apple, from VL *\*poma*, from L *pōmum*.

**pondero-:** from *ponder-*, o/s of L *pondus*, weight: cf PONDER. Ex: *ponderomotive*.

**ponero-:** from Gr *ponēros*, wicked, akin to *ponos*, fatigue, suffering, pain. Ex: *ponerology*, the theological treatment of evil.

**ponti-, ponto-:** from L *pons* (gen *pontis*), a bridge: *pontify*, via F from ML *pontificāre*, from L *pontifex* (q.v. at PONTIFF); *pontocerebellar*, (in An) of the pons and the cerebellum.

**popo-, Popo-:** for 'a *pope*, the *Pope*, popes': as in *popolatry* and *popomastix* (cf *-mastix*).

**populi-:** from L *populus*, the people: cf PEOPLE. Ex: *populicide*, a massacre of the people.

**-pora, -pore; pori-, poro-:** all from Gr *poros* (s *por-*), an opening, a PORE: resp, SciL pl, used in Zoo generic names, as *Millepora*; (*-pore*) from Gr *poros*, as in *blastopore* (cf *-blast*); (*pori-*) from L *porus*, from Gr *poros*, as in *poriform*; (*poro-*) from Gr *poros*, as in Bot *porogamy* and *poroscope*.

**porn(o)-:** from L *pornē*, a prostitute. Exx: *pornocracy* (cf *-cracy*), rule by licentious women; *pornography* (whence the adj *pornographic*), a description of prostitution, hence of licentitiousness in general, cf *pornographer* (cf *-grapher* at *-graph*), from Gr *pornographos*, a writer on prostitution, hence a licentious writer.

**poro-.** See *-pora*.

**porphyr(o)-:** Gr *porphuro-*, c/f of *porphura* (n), purple, and of *porphuros* (adj), purple: akin to PURPLE. Exx: *porphyroblast* (cf *-blast*); *porphyrogene*, royal-born, b/f from *porphyrogenite*, itself, via ML, from LGr *porphurogennētos*, begotten in, hence born to, the purple; *porphyrophore* (cf *-phora*). The rock *porphyry* comes from Gr *porphura* (n) and *porphuros*, as above, via ML *porphyreus* and then It *porfiro* and finally OF *porfire* (Mod F *porphyre*).

**poso-:** from Gr *posos*, how much, how great, akin to L *quot*, how many (cf QUOTA). Ex: *posology*, (Med) dosology, (Math) the doctrine and science (cf -*logy* at -*loger*) of pure quantity (and quantities).

**postero-**: from L *posterus*, placed behind, hinder; denoting either 'at the back' or 'posterior and': cf POSTERIOR. Ex: *postero*(-)*lateral*. Cf *postremo-*.

**posth-**, short for **postho-**; **posthe-**; **posthio-**: from Gr *posthē*, penis, prepuce; *posthia*, prepuce; *posthion*, little or small penis. Rare outside Med.

**postremo-**, as in *postremogeniture*, ultimogeniture: from L *postrēmus*, last. Cf *postero-*.

**potam(o)-**; **-potamia**, **-potamus**: Gr *potamo-*, c/f of *potamos*, a river, akin to Gr *petomai*, I fly, and *piptō*, I fall down, and Skt *patati*, he falls or flies, and E FEATHER. Exx: HIPPOPOTAMUS; *Mesopotamia*, q.v. at *meso-*; *Potamogeton*, a genus of aquatic herbs, adapted from L *potamogeton*, pondweed, from Gr *potamogeitōn*—*geitōn*, a neighbour; *potamology*, river-lore; *potamophilous*, river-loving.

**potassi-**, **potassio-**: c/ff of E *potassium*.

**potentio-**, as in EI *potentiometer*: for *potential*.

**poticho-**: app only in *potichomania* (victim: -*manist*), 'the craze for . . . imitating painted porcelain ware by coating the inside of glass vessels' (Webster), from F *potichomanie*, from *potiche*, a porcelain vase (from *pot*)+-*manie*, mania.

**-practic**. See -*praxia*.

**praseo-**; **praso-**: the former, from Gr *prasios* (s *prasi-*), leek-coloured (leek-green), from *prason* (s *pras-*), a leek, whence the c/f *praso-*; *prason* is akin to the syn L *porrum*, both—independently—of Medit stock. Exx: *praseolite* (-*lite*) and *prasophagous*, n *prasophagy*, leek-eating, cf *phaga*.

**prat(i)-**: from L *prātum*, a meadow, perh (*r* for *l*) akin to Gr *platus*, flat. Ex: *pratincole*, lit a meadow-inhabiter (*incola*).

1 **-praxia**, 2 **-praxis**; 3 adj **-practic**: 1, 'performance of movement(s)', Gr -*praxia*, a c/f from *praxis*, a doing, action, from *prassein*, to do, perform, practise; 2, Gr -*praxis*, from *praxis*; 3, from Gr *praktikos*, fit for doing, effective—cf *practical* at PRACTICE. The forward c/ff are *praxino-* (from the o/s *praxin-*), as in *praxinoscope*, and *praxio-*, as in *praxiology*.

Exx: *echopraxia*, an as-it-were echoic repetition of others' actions; *chiropraxis* or *chiropractic* (n from adj), a manual adjustment of the (esp spinal) joints; *chiropractic*, adj.

**presby-**, **presbyo-**: Gr *presbu-*, c/f of *presbus*, old, (hence) an old man, akin to Skt *purás*, in front of, before (place; hence, time): cf PRESBYTERIAN. Exx: *presbyophrenia*, senile dementia (cf -*phrenia*) and *presbyopia* (cf -*opia* at -*ope*), defective vision caused by old age, whence *presbyopic*.

**pressi-**: from L *pressus*, pressed, pp of *premere* (s *prem-*). Ex: Zoo *Pressirostres*.

**presti-**. See PRESTIDIGITATION.

**pri-**. See *prio-*.

**primi-**; **primo-**: L *prīmi-*, c/f of *prīmus*, first; LL and ML *prīmo-*, from *prīmus*. Cf PRIME. Exx: *primigenial* (L *prīmigeni*(us)+suffix -*al*), first generated, hence primal or primary; Med *primi-*

*gravida*, pregnant for the first time, from ML *gravidus* (L *grauidus*), from ML *gravis*, L *grauis*, heavy; *primogenitor* (an ancestor), adopted from ML—cf *primogeniture*, ML *prīmogenitūra*, from L *genitūra*, a begetting, from *gignere*, to beget; *primordial*, LL *prīmordiālis*, adj of L *prīmordium*, the beginning, from *ordīri*, to begin a web (cf *exordium*), to begin.

**pri(o)-**; **-prion**; **prion(o)-**: all from Gr *priōn* (gen *prionos*), a saw for cutting, akin to *priō* (s *pri-*), I saw or saw through, itself akin to *peirō* (s *peir-*), I pierce; IE r, perh \**peir-* or \**per*, to penetrate. Exx: Zoo adj *priodont*, small-mandibled (*pri-* for *prio-* for *priono-*+*odont-*, o/s of Gr *odōn*, a tooth); -*prion*, only in generic names in Ichthyology; *prionodont*, having a serrate row of teeth; *Prionops*, a genus of birds, 'saw-face' (Gr *ōps*, face). Cf:

**priso-**: from Gr *prisis*, a sawing (cf prec), as in *prisometer*. Cf:

**prist(o)-**: from Gr *pristis*, (?) a sawfish. Ex: Pal *Pristodus* (cf -*odus* at -*odon*). Cf *pris-*.

**privi-**; **-privic**: ML *prīvi-*, L *prīui-*, from *prīuus*, private, as in PRIVILEGE; (-*privic*) from ML *prīvus*, L *prīuus*, in its secondary sense 'deprived (of), deficient (in)', as in *calciprivic*, deficient in calcium. Cf PRIVATE.

**proboscidi-**, occ shortened to **probosci-**: From L *proboscis* (gen *proboscidis*), from Gr *proboskis*, (gen *proboskidos*), elephant's trunk, snout; *pro*, forwards+*boskein* (s *bosk-*), to pasture (v.t.): ? orig 'a means of providing food' (Boisacq). Ex: *probosci(di)form*.

**proct(o)-**: Gr *prōkt(o)-*, c/f of *prōktos*, anus; in E, denotes 'rectum'. Ex: *proctology*, the medical science of anus and rectum. The end c/f -*proctous* is the adj corresponding to Zoo classes -*procta*, -*proctus*, and 'condition' n -*proctia*.

**proli-**: L *prōli-*, c/f of *prōles* (s *prōl-*), offspring. Exx: *proliferate*, perh from *proliferation*, itself suggested by *proliferous* (cf -*ferous* at -*fer*), reproducing freely; PROLIFIC.

**prono-**: from L *prōnus*, leaning *prō* or forward. Ex: *pronograde*, walking as human beings do, with the body slightly forward of horizontal.

**prophetico-**: from Gr *prophētikos*, prophetic, as in *prophetico-Messianic*.

**propion(o)-**: for *propionic* (*proto-*+Gr *piōn*, fat+ suffix -*ic*). Only in Chem.

**prosi-**, in *prosify*. See PROSE.

**prosop(o)-**: Gr *prosōp(o)-*, c/f of *prosōpon*, face, lit, (the part) at the side of or towards the eyes, *ōps*, an eye, pl *ōpes*, *ōpa*. Exx: *prosopography*, description (-*graphy*, Gr -*graphia*: cf -*graph*) of the face; *prosopopoeia*, the rhetorical figure of an absent person speaking or of a dead person alive and present, from Gr *prosōpopoiia*, where *prosōpon*, face, is by extension a person—cf -*poeia*, -making.

The adj is -*prosopous*, from Gr -*prosōpos*, -faced, as in *megaprosopous*, large-faced, with corresp nn ('condition') in -*prosopia*.

**prostat(o)-**: for *prostate*.

**prosth(o)-**: for *prosthesis* in, e.g., Surg.

**protei-**: for *Proteus*; as in *proteiform*, protean.

**prote(o)-**: from Gr *prōteion*, neu of *prōteios*, primary. In Chem and Biochem, it denotes either 'protein' or 'proteid', as in *proteolysis* (cf *-lysis* at *-lyse*); or, in Zoo, 'protean'.

**proter(o)-**: from Gr *proteros*, earlier, former (from *pro*, forward). Exx: *proteranthous* (cf *-anthous* at *anth-*), flowering before it has leaves; *Proterozoic* (cf *-zoic* at *zo-*). Cf the next two.

**protisto-**: from Gr *prōtistos*, first; as in *protistology*, the biology of the Protista.

**prot(o)-**: Gr *prōt(o)-*, c/f of *prōtos*, first (in time, status, type), a sup adj (cf prec) formed from *pro*, forward. Exx: *protocol*, via F and ML from Gr *prōtokollon*, the *first* leaf *glued* (*kolla*, glue: cf *-coll*) to papyrus rolls and having on it a description of the contents, hence, unit (in E), a set of official, e.g. diplomatic, formulas; *protoplasm*, G *Protoplasma*, lit the first form or mould (cf *-plasm*); *prototype*, via F and Mod L from Gr *prōtotupon*, orig the neu of *prōtotupos*, primitive, of the earliest *tupos* or type; *Protoza* (cf *-zoa* at *zo-*).

**proximo-**: from L *proximus*, nearest; cf PROXIMATE. Ex: *proximo(-)lingual*.

**pruni-**: from L *prūnum*, a plum: cf PRUNE. Ex: *pruniferous*, plum-bearing (cf *-fer*).

**Prussi-**: for *Prussian*, as in *Prussify*, now usu Prussianize.

**psalm(o)-**: from Gr *psalmos*, a psalm: cf PSALM. Exx: *psalmody*, via LL from Gr *psalmōidia*, a psalm-singing, hence a collection of psalms, cf ODE; *psalmograph*, a psalm-writer, via LL from Gr *psalmographos*.

**psamm(o)-**: Gr *psamm(o)-*, c/f of *psammos*, s *psam(m)-*, sand, and perh akin to SAND itself. Exx: *Psammophis*, lit 'sand snake' (cf *-ophis* at *ophio-*); *psammophyte* (cf *-phyte*), a plant living in sand.

**pseph(o)-**: from Gr *psēphos* (ψῆφος), a pebble, perh akin to prec. Exx: *psephomancy*, divination (cf *-mancy*) by pebbles; *Psephurus* (cf *-ure*: Gr *oura*, tail).

**pseud(o)-**: Gr *pseud(o)-*, c/f of *pseudēs*, false, influenced by *pseudos*, falsehood; s *pseud-*, perh akin to Arm *sut*, false. Exx: *pseudaphia* (Gr *haphē*, touch) or *pseudesthesia*, defective or imaginary (sense of) feeling; *pseudepigraphous*, falsely signed or wrongly attributed, from Gr *pseudepigraphos* (cf *epigraph*), whence also *pseudepigrapha*, writings incorrectly attributed to Biblical characters; *pseudomorph* (cf *-morph*); *pseudonym* and *pseudonymous*, both (the n, via F) from Gr *pseudōnumos*, using a false *onuma* or name.

**psil(o)-**: Gr *psilo-*, c/f of *psilos*, bare, (hence) mere, s *psil-*; IE r prob *bhes-* or *bhis-*. Exx: *psilology*, mere or empty talk, and *psilosophy*, empty or superficial philosophy.

The neu *psilon* occurs in the Gr letter-names *epsilon* (ἒ ψιλόν, bare, written simply) and *upsilon* (ὒ ψιλόν or ῒο ὒψιλόν, the bare *v* (*u*) written simply).

**psittac(i)-**: from L *psittacus*, from Gr *psittakos*, a parrot, perh—whatever its linguistic origin—echoic. Exx: *Psittaciformes*, birds that are parrot-

like (FORM); *psittacosis*, parrot disease (cf suffix *-osis*).

**psomo-**, as in *psomophagy* (cf *-phaga*), eating without properly chewing: from Gr *psōmos*, a morsel, app, like the next, from or akin to *psō*, I scratch, reduce to dust.

**psoro-**: from Gr *psōros*, an itching, as in *psorosperm* (cf *-sperm*), or from the syn *psōra*, as in *Psorophora* (cf *-phora*); the derivative Gr *psōriasis*, E Med *psoriasis*, yields c/f *psoriasi-*, as in *psoriasiform*. Cf prec.

**-psyche**; **psych(o)-**: the former from Gr *psukhē*, the latter from Gr *psukh(o)-*, c/f of *psukhē* (ψυχή), the breath of life, the soul: see PSYCHE. In E cpds, it denotes 'mental life', as in PSYCHIATRY and PSYCHOLOGY; a (formless) spirit, a ghost, as in *psychogram* (cf the 2nd *-gram*); 'psychology, or its methods', as in *psycho(-)analysis* (ANALYSIS) and *psychotherapy* (THERAPY); 'psychic (i.e., of the soul or spirit) and', as in *psychosomatic*, of, by, for mind and body (cf *-soma*). Cf:

**psychro-**: from Gr *psukhros*, cold, which (*psukh-*+infix *-r-+-os*, adj suffix) is clearly akin to *psukhē* (s *psukh*,), soul, (lit) breath: cf prec. Exx: *psychrometer*; *psychrophobia*, a dread of cold or of anything cold.

**-ptene**; **pteno-**: from Gr *ptēnos*, winged, volatile, whence the c/f *ptēno-*, whence E *pteno-*, -winged, -feathered; akin to Gr *pteron*, a wing (see next). Exx: only in Zoo, esp Orn, as, e.g., *eloptene* and *Ptenoglossa*.

1 **-ptera**, 2 **-pteris**, 3 **-pterous**, 4 **-pterus**, 5 **-pteryx**; 6 **pterido-**, 7 **pter(o)-**, 8 **pterygo-**, 9 **pterylo-**: all ult from Gr *pteron* (pl *ptera*), a feather, (hence, collectively) a wing, akin to Skt *pattra*, feather, wing, (from the 'ribbing') leaf—to Hittite *pettar* or *pittar*, a wing—to L *penna*—and to E FEATHER: resp, Gr *-ptera* (from *ptera*, feathers, wings), denoting, in Zoo, 'creatures with so many, or such, wings or winglike parts', as in *Hemiptera*, an order of insects; 2, Gr *-pteris*, from *pteris*, a fern—*pter(is)* from *pter*(on), in Bot genera, e.g. *Ornithopteris* (ornitho-); 3, Gr *-pteros*, -winged, from *pteron*—denoting, in Bot and Zoo, 'with so many, or such, wings, etc.', e.g. *trichopterous* (*tricho-*), of the Trichoptera or caddis flies; 4, 'wing', SciL from Gr *pteron*, as in Zoo *Trachypterus* (cf *trachy-*, rough); 5, Sci L *-pteryx*, from Gr *-pterux*, c/f of *pterux* (s *pter-*), a wing, a fin—cf *pter*(on)—denoting, in Bot, Pal, Zoo, '-winged' or '-finned', as in *Dipteryx*; in Ich, usu *-pterygii*, from Gr *pterugion* (dim of *pteron*), as in *Pleuropterygii* (pleuro-); 6, Gr *pterido-*, c/f of *pteris* (gen *pteridos*), a fern, as in *pteridology*, the science of ferns; 7, Gr *pter(o)-*, c/f of *pteron*, feather, wing, as in *pterocarpous*, bearing wingèd fruit—*pterodactyl*, an extinct flying reptile (Gr *daktulos*, finger, toe), also known as a *pterosaur* (cf *-saur*); 8, Gr *pterugo-*, c/f of *pterux*, (wing,) fin, gen *pterugos*—esp in An and Zoo, e.g. *pterygo(-)palatal*; *pterylo-*, for SciL *pteryla*, as if a dim from Gr *pteron*, as in *pterylography*. Cf:

**-ptile**; **ptil(o)-**; **-ptilus**; from Gr *ptilon*, a (soft) feather, down (of birds), akin to *pteron*, a feather, a wing (see prec); Gr *ptil(o)*-, c/f of *ptilon*; Gr *-ptilos*, -feathered, from *ptilon*. Exx: *teleoptile* (cf *teleo-*), a mature feather; *ptilopaedes*, birds with young (Gr *pais*, pl *paides*, children) that, hatching, are down-covered; *heptoptilus* (cf *lepto-*).

**ptocho-**, 'indigent, (n) the poor': from Gr *ptōkhos*, one who cringes (*ptōssein*, to shrink, to cringe), hence a beggar; perh akin to Gr *piptein*, to fall; IE r, perh \**pta-*, s \**pet-*, to fly, to fall. Ex: *ptochocracy*, 'If wishes were horses . . .'. Cf:

**-ptoma; -ptosis**: from Gr *ptōma*, a falling; Gr *-ptōsis*, c/f of *ptōsis*, a falling, akin to *ptōssein*, to cringe (see prec); both denoting, in E, a prolapse (falling forward). Exx: *archoptoma*; *gastroptosis* (cf *gastro-*).

**ptyal(o)-**: from Gr *ptualon* (s *ptual-*), spittle, akin to *ptuein*, to spit, and perh to E SPIT; e.g., *ptyalogenic*, tending to produce spittle. Cf *-ptysis*.

**ptych(o)-**: from Gr *ptukhē* (s *ptukh-*) or from the o/s of \**ptux* (gen *ptukhos*), a fold, a layer, perh akin to Gr *epi* (IE \**epi* or \**pi*), upon. Ex: *Ptychosperma* (cf *-sperm*).

**-ptysis**: (Gr *ptusis*, a spitting, from *ptuein*, to spit—cf *ptyalo-*. Ex: *plasmoptysis* (cf *-plasm*).

**pubi-; pubio-; pubo-**: c/ff (2nd and 3rd, irregular) from L *pūbes*, the pubic hair: cf PUBERTY. Exx: *pubigerous*, pubic-hairy (cf *-gerous* at *-ger*); *pubiotomy* (cf *-tomy* at *-tome*); ('pubic and') *pubo(-)vesical*.

**pulchri-**, as in *pulchrify*, to render (cf *-fy*), beautiful: from the o.o.o. L *pulcher*, f *pulchra* beautiful, whence *pulchritūdō*, beauty, whence E *pulchritude* (adj *-udinous*).

**puli-** (? for *pulici-*): from L *pulex* (gen *pulicis*), a flea; *pulex* is perh akin to E FLEA—cf the Gr *phulla*. Ex: *pulicide* (cf *-cide* at *-cidal*).

**pulmo-; pulmoni-**: c/ff from L *pulmō* (gen *pulmōnis*), a lung; the o/s *pulmōn-* suggests a metathesis of the syn Gr *pleumōn* (gen *pleumonos*). Exx: *pulmogastric*, of lungs and belly; *Pulmonifera*, a SciL neu pl (cf *-fer*) for 'snails having a pulmonary sac instead of a gill'. Shortened form occurs in the blend trade-name *Pulmotor*.

**pulpe-, pulpi-, pulpo-**: the 1st, from L *pulpa*, pith or pulp of fruit (cf PULP); the other two, from E *pulp*. Exx: *pulpefaction* (cf *-faction*); *pulpify* (cf *-fy*); *pulpotomy* (cf *-tomy* at *-tome*), a cutting into the pulp of a tooth.

**pulsi-, pulso-**: for E PULSE (of heart), as in, *pulsific, pulsometer*.

**pulvilli-, pulvini-**: from ML *pulvillus* (L *puluillus*), a little cushion, the dim of ML *pulvīnus* (L *puluīnus*) a cushion. Exx: *pulvilliform, pulviniform*.

**pumici-**: for E *pumice*, from L *pūmex*, gen *pūmicis*, whence also, via OF-F *ponce* (from doublet \**pomex*), the E *pounce*, a fine powder: akin to E FOAM.

**punctato-; puncti-, puncto-**: resp for *punctate*; the 2nd and 3rd, both, the latter irregularly, from L *punctum*, q.v. at POINT. Exx: *punctato(-)striate*; *punctiform*, resembling a point; *punctographic*, of or by the raised points of Braille.

**pupi-**: for *pupa* (in Zoo), as in *pupiferous* (c *-ferous* at *-fer*) and *pupiform*. Cf PUPPET.

**puri-** (1): L *pūri-*, c/f of *pūrus*, pure: cf PURE, where see *purify*.

**puri-** (2): from L *pūr-*, o/s of *pūs*, q.v. at PUS. Ex: Med *puriform*, pus-like. Cf:

**puro-**: irregularly from L *pūr-*, o/s of *pūs* (see prec). Ex: *puro(-)lymph*.

**purpureo-; purpuri-, purpuro-**: from L *purpureus*, (adj) purple, from *purpura*, (n) purple, whence *purpuri-* and *purpuro-*: cf PURPLE. Exx: *purpureocobaltic*; *purpuriferous*, *purpuriform*; *purpurogenous*, occasioning a purple colour.

**-pus.** See *-pod*.

**pusill(i)-**: LL *pusilli-*, c/f of L *pusillus*, rather or very little, akin to *pūsus*, a boy (cf the more usual *puer*). Notably in LL *pusillanimis* (hence E *pusillanimous*, little-couraged), whence *pusillanimitās*, E *pusillanimity*: cf *animus* at ANIMAL.

**pustuli-**, as in *pustuliform*: for L *pustula*, whence E *pustule*: akin to Gr *phusa*, bellows.

**putre-; putri**: the former, from L *putrēre*, to be rotten (cf PUTRID); the latter, from L *putris*, rotten, itself from *putēre*, to be rotten, to stink. Exx: *putrefacient*, causing *putrefaction*, both from *putrefacere*, to cause to go rotten; *putriform*, of putrid appearance.

**py-.** See *pyo-*.

**pycnidio-; pycnio-**: for *pycnidium* and for *pycnium*, both in Bot. Cf:

**pycn(o)-**: Gr *pukn(o)-*, c/f of *puknos*, compact or dense, r *puk-*, IE r \**puk-*. Ex: *pycnometer*, an instrument for measuring the density of liquids. Occ *pykn(o)-*, as in *pyknatom*.

**pyel(o)-**: from Gr *puelos*, a vat, a trough, hence in E Med the pelvis; s *puel-*, perh from \**pluel-*—cf Gr *plunein* (s *plun-*), to wash. Ex: *pyeloscopy*, inspection (cf *-scope*) of the pelvis.

**-pygal, -pygian, -pygous**; in Zoo: **-pyge, -pygia, -pygus; pyg(o)-**: the last=Gr *pug(o)-*, c/f of *pugē* (s *pug-*), the rump, whence all the other forms, whether adj, as in the first three, or n, as in the second three; IE r, app \**pu-*. Exx: (*pygal*); *callipygian, -pygous*, from Gr *kallipugos*, fair-buttocked (Callipygian Venus); *Megalopyge* (cf *megalo-*), of American moths; *pygalgia*, pain in the rump—*Pygopus*, an Australian snake-like lizard, devoid of fore, and having only rudimentary hind limbs (cf *-pus*, foot, at *-pod*).

**pykno-.** See *pycno-*.

**pyl(e)-**: Gr *pul(ē)-*, c/f of *pulē*, a city gate, s *pul-*, perh akin to Skt *gopuram*. (Hofmann.) Exx: *pylethrombosis* (cf *thrombo-*); (terminal *-pyle*) *micropyle* (*micro-*). Cf:

**pylor(o)-**: from Gr *pulōros*, (lit) gate-keeper, hence the lower orifice of the stomach: cf prec; 2nd element, from *horan*, to see. Ex: *pyloroscopy*.

**py(o)-**: Gr *pu(o)-*, c/f of *puon*, pus (cf, therefore, the 2nd *puri-*), akin to L *putēre*, to be rotten, to stink—cf PUTRID. Exx: *pyemia*, blood-poisoning; *pyorrh(o)ea* (cf *-rrhoea*, a flowing), a discharge of pus, esp from or at the sockets of one's teeth.

**-pyra.** See *pyro-*.

**pyramido-:** for *pyramid*, as in *pyramido-tenuate*.

**pyren(o)-:** Gr *purēn(o)*-, c/f of *purēn* (gen *purēnos*), a fruit-stone, with c/f adj *purēnos*, whence E *-pyrenous*. Exx: *pyrenocarp* (cf *-carp*); *tetrapyrenous*, four-stoned (cf *tetra*-).

**pyreto-:** Gr *pureto-*, c/f of *puretos*, fever, from *pūr*, fire, cf *pyro-*. Ex: *pyretology*, the medical treatment of fevers.

**pyrgo-:** Gr *purgo-*, c/f of *purgos*, a tower, perh akin to G *Berg*, a mountain. Ex: *pyrgocephalic*, with a skull high of vertex.

**pyri-:** from ML *pyrum*, for L *pirum* (s *pir*-), a PEAR. Ex: *pyriform*, pear-shaped. Cf *piri*-.

**pyr(o)-; pyriti-; -pyra:** Gr *pur(o)*-, c/f of *pūr* (gen *puros*), fire (cf FIRE); from Gr *puritēs*, of fire, hence a pyrite; (*-pyra*) from Gr *pur*. Exx: *traumatopyra* (cf *traumato-*); *pyritology*; *pyro-*, in nn, 'fire' or 'heat', as in *pyromancy*, divination (*-mancy*) by fire, via OF and ML from Gr *puromanteia*; *pyromania* (hence *-maniac*), a morbid impulse to incendiarism, cf *pyrophobia*, a morbid dread of fire; *pyrometer*, a thermometer for heats beyond the range of mercury; *pyrophorous* (cf *-phorous* at *-phora*); *pyrotechnics*, from adj *pyrotechnic(al)*, of, for, by fireworks;—in adjj, 'pyrogenous', producing –or produced by—heat (cf the Gr *purogenēs*, born of fire), as in *pyromagnetic*; in Chem, 'derivative by heat', as in *pyro-acid* and *pyro-arsenic*; in Geol and Min, 'caused by fire or heat', as in *pyrometamorphism*. (Webster.) Cf:

**pyrrho-:** Gr *purrho-*, c/f of *purrhos*, fire-coloured (cf prec), red or tawny. Ex: *Pyrrhocoridae*, a family of brightly coloured insects—Gr *koris*, an insect.

**pyrro-.** An occ var of prec. Ex: *pyrroporphyrin*.

**pytho-:** from Gr *puthein*, to rot; cf *putre-* and *pyo-*. Ex: *pythogenic*, producing—or being produced by—decomposition or by filth.

**pyxid(o)-:** from *puxid-*, c/f of *puxis*, a box (orig of boxwood), prob akin to L *buxus*, the box tree. Ex: *Pyxidanthera* (cf *-anthera* at *anth-*).

**quadr-**, prevocalic form of **quadri-; quadru-; quadrato-:** the third, for E *quadrate*; the second, L *quadri-*, c/f of *quattuor*, akin to syn Gr *tetra*; *quadru-*, a var of *quadri-*. Exx: *quadrangular*, LL *quadrangulāris*—cf QUADRANGLE; *quadriform*, LL *quadriformis*; *quadrilateral*, four-sided, from L *quadrilater(us)*+adj suffix *-al*, cf LATERAL; *quadriparite*, L *quadripartītus*, divided (from *partīri*, to divide, share out) into four parts; *quadrisyllabic*, four-syllabled; *quadrīvium*, adopted from ML, from L *quadrīuium*, a crossroads (ML *via*, L *uia*, a way, a road)—cf TRIVIAL; *quadrumanous* (L *manus*, a hand); QUADRUPED; *quadruple*, L *quadruplus* (*-plex*, a fold, from *plicāre*, to fold); *quadrato(-)jugal*. Cf *quarti-*.

**quali-**, as in *qualimeter* (in Phys): from L *quālis*, of what sort of nature. Ex: *qualify*, q.v. at QUALITY. Cf:

**quanti-**, as in *quantimeter* and *quantivalence*: from L *quantus*, how large, neu *quantum*, how much. See QUANTITY. Cf prec.

**quart(i)-;** rarely **quarto-:** from L *quārtus*, fourth —the ordinal adj corresp to *quattuor*, four: cf QUART. Ex: *quartiparous*, bearing (cf *-parous* at *-para*) four children or other offspring; *quarto-centenary*. Cf *quadri-*.

**quasi-:** c/f of E from L *quasi*, as if, as it were, apparently, as in *quasihistorical*, apparently or ostensibly historical. The L word prob=*quam si*, as if.

**quater-:** L *quater*, four times (from *quattuor*, four), as in *quatercentenary*.

**quega** (only in EI): based upon *mega-*.

**querci-:** from L *quercus*, an oak, akin to E FIR. Ex: *quercivorous*, oak-eating (cf *-vorous* at *-vore*).

**quin(o)-:** for *quina*, cinchona bark, hence quinine—as in *quinology*, all the scientific lore of the cinchona tree and its product; also for *quinine* —as in *quinolin(e)*, which=*quin(o)-*+*-ol* (L *oleum*, oil)+Chem suffix *-in(e)*.

**quinqu(e)-:** L *quīnqu(e)-*, c/f of *quīnqu(e)*, five: cf next. Ex: *quinquennial* (cf *-ennial*, from L *annus*, a year), from L *quīnquennis*, influenced by L *quīnquennālis*.

**quint(i)-:** L *quīnt(i)*-, c/f of *quīntus* (s *quīnt-*), fifth —the ordinal of *quīnque* (s *quīn-*), five: cf prec and see QUINTET. Ex: *quintessence* (whence *quint-essential*), adopted from F, from ML *quīnta essentia*, the fifth and highest essence, or power, of a physical body or manifestation.

**quot-:** OL *quot-*, c/f of the adv *quot*, how many. Exx: *quotennial*, annual, from L *quotennis*, every year, annually, the E word being influenced both by L *quotennis*, of how many years, how many years old, and by *biennial*, *triennial*, etc.; *quotidian*, prob via OF, from L *quotidiānus*, (adj) daily, from *quotidie*, (adv) daily, from the derivative adj *quotus*, in what number, how many a+*dies*, day. Cf *quali-* and *quanti-*.

**rabi-:** for E RABIES, q.v. Exx: *rabific* (cf *-fic*), causing rabies; *rabiform*, resembling rabies; *rabigenic* (cf *-genic* at *-gen*), rabific.

**racemi-, racemo-:** L *racēmi-*, as in *rācemifer*, cluster-bearing, whence E *racemiferous* (cf *-ferous* at *-fer*), bearing *racemes* (in Bot, a *raceme* is a simple inflorescence), itself from L *racēmus* (s *racēm-*), a cluster of grapes or berries: cf RAISIN. But *racemo-* is a c/f for the E Chem adj *racemic*, as in *racemo(-)carbonic*.

**rachi-**, prevocalic form of **rachio-:** from Gr *rhakhis*, the spine, akin to Gr *rhakhos*, a thorn-bush; IE r, prob *oragh-* or *oregh-*. Exx: *rachialgia*, pain (cf *-algia*) in the spine; *rachiometer*, *rachitomy*. Cf RICKETS.)

The end c/f *-rachidia* is a SciL formation, from the o/s *rhakhid-*; and *rachito-* is for E *rachitis*, as in *rachitogenic*, tending to produce rickets: and either *rachitis* or, more prob, its Gr original, *rhakhitis* (cf suffix *-itis*), leads to *rickets*, influenced by (w)*rick*, a wrench.

Cf *rachy-*, irreg for *rhachy-*, from Gr *rhakhis*, the back or the spine; as in Zoo *Rachycentron* (Gr *kentron*, a sharp point), cf CENTER.

**radi-** (1). See *radici-*.

**radi-** (2): for E *radium*, as in *radiferous*, radium-bearing.

**radiato-**, as in *radiatoporous*, is for E *radiate* (adj), Cf *radio-*.

**radici-**: from L *rādix* (gen *rādicis*), root: cf RADICAL. Exx: *radiciferous*, *radiciform*, *radicivorous* (root-eating). A shortened form, *radi-*, occurs in *radectomy* and *radicolous* (cf *-colous*). The L dim *rādicula* yields the c/f *radiculi-*, as in *radiculectomy* (cf *-ectomy* at *-tome*).

**radio-**: for and from L and E *radius*, as in *radiosymmetrical* and *radio-ulnar*; in Chem and Phys, it denotes either 'radiant energy', as in *radio(-)active*, or 'radioactive', as in *radio(-)chemistry*; in Med, 'by means of radium', as in *radio(-)surgery*; in general, *radio-* can denote 'radio', as in *radiotelegraphy*. Cf the 2nd *radi-*.

**ralli-**: from *Rallus*, a Zoo generic name for the various *rails* (birds), from OF *ralle*, of echoic origin. Ex: *ralliform*.

**ramenti-**: from L *rāmentum*, a scraping (hence its Bot sense), from *rādere*, to scrape, to scratch. Ex: *ramentiferous*, ramenta-bearing.

**rami-**; **ramoso-**, cf *-ramose*; **ramuli-**: resp ML *rāmi-*, c/f of L *rāmus* (s *rām-*), a branch; from L *rāmōsus*, branchy; whence E *ramose*; (*-ramose*) from *ramose*, branched, branchy; from *rāmulus* (dim of *rāmus*), a small branch. Exx: RAMIFY, *ramiferous* (cf *-ferous* at *-fer*); *ramoso(-)pinnate*; *multiramose*, having many branches; *ramuliferous*.

**rani-**: from L *rāna*, a frog—prob echoic. Ex: *ranivorous*, frog-eating (cf *-vora*).

**raphi-**; **raphidi-**: from Gr *rhaphis* (gen *rhaphidos*), a needle, from *rhaptein*, to sew (or stitch) together. Exx: Bot *raphides*, needle-like crystals (in plant cells); *raphidiferous*, containing or producing raphides.

**rare-**, as in *rarefy*, q.v. at RARE, and *rari-*, as in *rari(-)constant*: from L *rārus*.

**rati-**: L *rati-*, c/f of *ratus*, established by calculation, valid: cf RATE. Exx: *ratify*, q.v. at RATE; *ratihibition*, ratification, from LL *ratihibitiō* (gen *-hibitiōnis*), the 2nd element coming from L *-hibitus*, the pp of cpds of *habēre*, to have, to hold.

**reacto-**: for *reaction*, as in *reactology*, (roughly) psychology.

**recipio-**, as in *recipiomotor*, of, by, for the reception of impulses of motion: from L *recipere*, to receive, prompted by *recipiō*, I receive.

**rect(i)-**: LL *recti-*, c/f of L *rectus*, ruled straight, (hence) straight, from *regere*, to direct in a straight line: cf REGENT. Exx: *rectangle*, via F from LL *rectiangulum*, *rectangulum*, 2nd element from *angulus*, an angle; RECTIFY; *rectilinear*, in a straight line, bounded by straight lines, cf LINE; *rectirostral*, straight-beaked (cf *rostri-*). Cf:

**recto-**: for (the) *rectum*, SciL for *rectum intestinum*, lit 'the straight intestine', where *rectum*, therefore, is strictly the neu of *rectus* (see prec). Exx: ('the rectum') *rectoscope* (cf *-scope*); ('rectal and') *recto-abdominal*.

**recurvi-**, **recurvo-**: from ML *recurvus* (L *re-*

*curuus*), curved back. Exx: *recurvirostral*, *recurvopatent*.

**reflecto-**: for *reflection*; e.g., *reflectometer*.

**reflexo-**: for *reflex*, as in *reflexology*.

**refracto-**: for *refraction*, as in *refractometer*.

**regi-**: L *regi-*, c/f of *rex*, a king: cf REGENT. Exx: *regicide*, the slayer, or the slaying (cf *-cide* at *-cidal*), of a king; *regifuge*, the flight (L *fuga*) of kings.

**rego-**: irreg from Gr *rhegos*, a blanket. Ex: *regolith* (cf *-lite*).

**rei-**: from L *rēs*, a thing, a property, gen *rei*. Ex: *reify* (*rei+-fy*, q.v. at *-fier*), to convert (the abstract) into the concrete.

**religio-**, 'religious and': for E *religion*, as in *religio-scientific*.

**remi-**: from L *rēmus*, an oar, from *rāmus*, a branch; as in *remiform*, oar-shaped.

**reni-**, **reno-**: c/ff from L *rēn* (gen *rēnis*), kidney, whence, via the adj *rēnālis*, the E adj *renal*. Exx: *reniform* and *renography*; ('renal and') *reno(-)gastric*.

**reptili-**: for *reptile*, as in *reptilivorous*, reptile-eating.

**resilio-**: for *resilience*, as in *resiliometer*.

**resini-**, **resino-**: the former denoting 'resin', the latter 'resinous and'; both from E *resin*. Exx: *resinify* (F *résinifier*: cf *-fy* at *-fier*), to convert into, or to become, resin; *resino(-)vitreous*, resinous and glassy.

**respiro-**: from L *respirāre* (s *respir-*: *re+spir-*, to breathe), as in *respirometer*.

**resti-**: from L *restis*, a rope: perh cf Skt *rájjus*, cordage. Ex: *restiform*, rope-like.

**reti-**: from L *rēte*, a net, as in *retiform*, net-like. Cf *retino-* and:

**reticul(o)-**: from L, for E, *reticulum* (cf RETICULE), a little net, dim of *rēte* (cf prec): only in Sci terms, e.g. *reticulocyte* (cf *-cyte*) and *reticulo(-)venose*. Cf *reticulato-*, (adj, adv) like a net, as in *reticulato-venose*.

**-retin**; **retin(o)-**: from Gr *rhētinē*, resin, akin to RESIN. Exx: *quiniretin* (*quinine+-retin*); *retinalite* (*retina-+-lite*), a serpentine of resinous lustre, and *retinasphalt* (cf ASPHALT).

**retino-**: from ML *rētina* (of the eye), from L *rēte*, a net (cf *rēti-*): cf RETICULE. Ex: *retinoscopy*, inspection (cf *-scope*) of the eye.

**rhabd(o)-**: Gr *rhabd(o)-*, c/f of *rhabdos*, a rod, a stick, a wand; IE s, prob, *\*uerb-*, an extension of r *\*uer-*, to turn. Exx: *rhabdolith* (*-lith*, q.v. at *-lite*); *rhabdomancy*, divination (*-mancy*) with wands; *rhabdosphere*.

**rhaco-**: from Gr *rhakos*, a tattered garment; as in Bot *Rhacomitrium* (Gr *mitrion*, dim of *mitra*, a kilt).

**Rhaeto-**: for *Rhaetic*, as in *Rhaeto-Romanic*, the Romance dialects of S.E. Switzerland: L *Rhaeticus*, adj of *Rhaetia*, roughly the Tirol and the Grisons.

**rhagadi-**: for L and Med *rhagades*, from Gr *rhagades*, pl of *rhagas*, a fissure. Cf *-rrhage*.

**-rhage.** See *-rrhage*.

**rhamno-**: for *rhamnose*, a crystalline sugar

derived from blackthorn berries: from L, from Gr, *rhamnos*, a prickly shrub. Ex: *rhamnohexose*.

**rhamph(o)-: -rhamphus:** from Gr *rhamphos*, a crooked beak, prob akin to *rhabdos*, q.v. at *rhabdo-*; (*-rhamphus*) SciL c/f from *rhamphos*. Exx: (Zoo) *rhamphotheca* (cf *-theca*); *Sarcorhamphus* (cf *sarco-*).

**-rhaphy.** See *-rrhaphy*.

**rhapido-:** from *rhapid-*, o/s of Gr *rhapis*, a rod, akin to *rhabdos*, q.v. at *rhabdo-*. Ex: *Rhapidophyllum* (cf *-phyllum* at *-phyll*).

**rhegma-,** as in Bio *rhegmatypy*; **rhegno-,** as in Zoo *Rhegnopteri* (cf *-ptera*): Gr *rhēgma*, a fracture, from *rhēgnunai*, to break loose (whence *rhegno-*).

**rhemato-,** as in *rhematology*, the study of the semantic aspect of speech-elements: from Gr *rhēmat-*, the o/s of *rhēma* (whence E *rheme*), a word, from *eirō*, I speak: cf RHETORIC.

**rheo-:** from Gr *rheos* (s *rhe-*), a current, akin to *rheō* (s *rhe-*), I flow. Mostly in Electricity, e.g. *rheostat* (Gr *statos*, static); *rheology*, the science treating of the flow of matter.

**-rheuma.** See *-rrheuma*.

**-rhexis.** See *-rrhexis*.

**rhigo-:** from Gr *rhigos*, frost, the cold, akin to L *frigus*. Ex: *rhigolene* = *rhigo-* + L *ol*eum, oil + chem suffix *-ene*.

**-rhina** and **-rhinus; -rhine** and **-rhinous:** all from *rhīn-*, the o/s of *rhīs*, a nose (see next): the first two occur in Zoo generic names, e.g. *Gymnorhina* (cf *gymno-*) and *Megarhinus* (cf *mega-*); *-rhinous* is an ordinary, *-rhine* (occ *-rhinal*) a SciE, adj for 'having a (specified) kind or type of nose', as in *monorhine* or *monorhinal* (cf *mono-*), and *platyrhine*, flat-nosed (*platy-*).

**rhin(o)-:** Gr *rhīn(o)-*, c/f of *rhīs* (gen *rhīnos*), a nose or snout, lit 'the flow-er or (of liquid) runner'—cf Gr *rheō*, I flow, and element *-rrheuma*. Exx: Med *rhinolith* (cf *-lith* at *-lite*)—*rhinophore* (cf *-phora*)—*rhinoscopy* (cf *-scope*)—and esp *rhinoceros*, L *rhīnocerōs*, Gr *rhīnokerōs*, 'the horn-nose' (from the horn on its nose): *rhino-* + terminal c/f of *keras*, a horn. *Rhinocerotic* comes, via LL *rhīnocerōticus*, from Gr *rhīnokerōtikos*, of or like a rhinoceros.

**rhipid(o)-:** from Gr *rhipis* (gen *rhipidos*), a fan, akin to *rhiptein* (s *rhipt-*, base *rhip-*), to cast or throw. Ex: *Rhipidoglossa*. Cf:

**rhipto-:** from Gr *rhiptos*, thrown out, from *rhiptein*, to throw (cf prec). Ex: *Rhiptoglossa* (cf *glossa*).

**-rhiza, -rhizous; rhiz(o)-:** resp from Gr *rhiza*, a root, akin to L *rādix* and perh to L *radius*; from Gr *-rhizos*, -rooted, from *rhiza*; Gr *rhiz(o)-*, c/f of *rhiza*. Exx: *hydrorhiza* (cf *hydro-*); *oligorhizous* (*oligo-*); *rhizogenic*, root-producing.

**-rhodin; rhod(o)-:** from Gr *rhodon*, a rose, and denoting, in E, a type of red pigment, as in *phytorhodin* (cy *phyto-* at *-phyte*); Gr *rhod(o)-*, c/f of *rhodon* (prob of OPer origin), as in *rhododendron* (cf *-dendron*), adopted from Gr *rhododendron*, rose-laurel (lit tree).

**rhombi-, rhombo-:** the former from L *rhombus*,

the latter being Gr *rhomb(o)-*, the c/f of *rhombos* (whence *rhombus*), a spinning top, (later) a rhombus, with s *rhomb-*, akin to *rhemb-*, the s of Gr *rhembein*, to whirl, to turn around. Exx: *rhombiform*, rhombic, rhomboid, (shaped) like a rhomb or a rhombus; ('a rhomb') *rhombohedron* (cf *-hedron* at *-hedral*) and ('rhombic and') *rhombo*(-) *quadrate* or *-quadratic*.

**rhopal(o)-:** Gr *rhopal(o)-*, c/f of *rhopalon*, a club (heavy stick), s *rhopal-*, extension of *rhop-*, akin to *rhap-*, s of *rhapis*, a root. Ex: *Rhopalura* (cf *-ura*, from Gr *oura*, a tail).

**rhyaco-:** from Gr *rhuak-*, o/s of *rhuax*, a stream (cf *rheo-*) of lava. Ex: *rhyacolite* (cf *-lite*). Cf *rhyo-*.

**rhynch(o)-; -rhynchus:** Gr *rhunkh(o)-*, c/f of *rhunkhos* (whence *-rhynchus*), a snout, a beak, akin to Gr *rhīn* (orig *rhīs*, gen *rhīnos*), a nose, cf *rhino-*. Exx: *rhynchophorous*, beaked (cf *-phora*), cf *Rhynchophora*, the snout beetles; *Harporhynchus* (1st element, from Gr *harpē*, a sickle).

**rhyn(o)-:** irreg for *rhino(o)-*. Ex: *Rhynocheti* (Gr *okhetos*, a channel, a duct).

**rhyo-:** for *rhyolite* (cf *-lite*), a volcanic rock; *rhyo-*, from Gr *rhein*, to flow: cf *rheo-* and *rhyaco-*. Ex: *rhyobasalt*.

**rhyparo-, rhypo-,** as in the synn *rhyparography*, *rhypography*, the *-graphy* (q.v. at *-graph*) or printing (literal or literary) of common, or even of sordid, objects; cf Gr *rhuparographos* (adj), painting foul or sordid objects, from *rhuparos*, filthy, the adj of *rhupos*, filth, prob akin to Skt *sravas*, suppuration.

**rhysi-:** from Gr *rhusis*, a flow(ing); as in *rhysimeter*. Cf *rheo-*, *rhyo-*, *rhyparo-*, and:

**rhythmo-:** LL *rhythmo-*, from Gr *rhuthmo-*, c/f of *rhuthmos* (see RHYTHM). Exx: *rhythmometer* and *rhythmopoeia* (LL, from Gr *rhuthmopoiia*—cf *-poeia*, a making).

**ricini-,** only as ricin-: for Bot *Ricinus*, L *ricinus*, the castor-oil plant. Ex: *ricinoleic*, *ricin-* + chem *oleic*, of or from L *oleum* or oil.

**rigidi-,** as in *rigidify*: for *rigid*.

**rimi-,** as in *rimiform*, shaped like a crack, a fissure, a narrow furrow: from L *rīma*, a crack, a crevasse.

**ripi-:** from L *rīpa*, bank (of a stream), perh akin to Gr *eripnē*, a slope. Ex: *ripicolous* (cf *-colous*), living on the banks of a stream, riparian or riparious (L *rīpārius*).

**rizi-:** from F *riz*, rice, as in *riziform*, like a grain of rice. Cf RICE.

**Romani-; Romano-:** from L *Rōmānus*, Roman (of *Rōma*, Rome): 'Roman', as in *Romaniform*; 'Roman and', as in *Romano-Germanic*. Cf the rare *Romi-*, 'Rome': as in *Romipetal*, Rome-seeking (cf *-petal*).

**röntgeno-:** for *Röntgen*, as in *röntgenotherapy*.

**rori-:** L *rōri-*, c/f of *rōs* (gen *rōris*), dew, akin to Ve *rasá*. Ex: *roriferous*, dew-producing, L *rōrifer*, cf *-ferous* at *-fer*.

**roseo-; rosi-, roso-:** the 1st, from L *roseus*, rosy; the 2nd, from its n, *rosa*, as in *Rosicrucian*; the 3rd, by Gr analogy, from *rosa*, as in *rosolite* (cf *-lite*). Cf ROSE.

**rostri-, rostro-; -rostral:** 1st and 2nd from L *rostrum*, a beak, from *rōdere*, to gnaw; 3rd from LL adj *rostrālis*. Exx: *rostriform*, beak-shaped; ('rostral and') *rostro-caudate*; *unguirostral* (cf *ungui-*).

**rota-.** See *roti-*.

**rotato-:** for E *rotate*, shaped like a (L) *rota* or wheel: 'rotate and', as in *rotato(-)plane*. Cf:

**roti-, roto-;** occ **rota-:** c/ff from L *rota*, a wheel—cf ROTARY. Exx: *rotameter*; *rotiferous* (cf *-ferous* at *-fer*); *rotograph, rotogravure*. The L dim *rotula* yields c/f *rotuli-*, as in *rotuliform*, shaped like a small wheel or, in An, like a knee-pan. Cf prec and:

**rotundi-, rotundo-:** from L *rotundus*, round (like a *rota* or wheel: cf prec). Exx: *rotundifoliate*; *rotundo-oval*.

**-rrhachidian; -rrhachis,** var **-rhachis:** the former, for *rachidian*, of a rachis; the latter, from Gr *rhakhis*, the spine (cf *rachi-*). Only in An and Med.

**-rrhage, -rrhagia, -rrhagy;** adj **-rrhagic:** 1st and 3rd, from 2nd, which=Gr *-rrhagia*, from *rhēgnunai*, to burst. Exx: *h(a)emorrhage*, via F and L from Gr *haimorrhagia*, a bursting-forth of blood (Gr *haima*: cf *haema-*)—with adj *h(a)emorrhagic*.

**-rrhaphy:** Gr *-rrhaphia*, c/f of *rhaphē*, a sewing or stitching: cf *raphi-*. Only in Surg—e.g., *laparorrhaphy* (cf *laparo-*).

**-rrhea.** See -RRHOEA.

**-rrheuma,** occ **-rheuma,** as in *acrorrheuma* (cf *acro-*): cf RHEUM.

**-rrhexis,** occ **-rhexis:** Gr *-rrhēxis*, c/f of *rhēxis*, a fracture, hence, in E Med, a rupture, as in *hepatorrhexis* (cf *hepato-*); from *rhēgnunai*, to burst. Cf *-rrhagia*.

**-rrhinia,** occ **-rhinia:** from *rhin-*, the o/s of Gr *rhīs*, the nose: cf *rhino-*. Ex: ('a certain nasal condition') *cacorrhinia* (cf *caco-*).

**-rrhiza.** Now usu *-rhiza*, q.v.

**-rrhoea;** now often **-rrhea:** via L (*-rrhoea*) from Gr *-rrhoia*, a flow(-ing), from *rhein*, to flow: cf *rheo-*. Exx: *diarrhoea*, Am *diarrhea* (cf the prefix *dia-*, through); *gonorrhoea* (cf *gono*); *logorrhoea*, a ceaseless flow of words (cf *logo-* at *-loger*).

**rube-, rubi-:** L *rube-*, from *rubeus* (s *rub-*), red; L *rubi-*, from *rubēre* (s *rub-*), to be red: cf RED. Exx: *rubefacient*, (something) that causes redness, esp of the skin, L *rubefacient-*, o/s of *rubefaciens*, pp of *rubefacere*, to make *rubeus* or red (cf *-facient*); *rubific*, causing (*-fic*) to be red (*rubēre*). Cf:

**rubri-, rubro-:** from L *ruber* (gen *rubri*), red—cf prec. Exx: *rubrific* (cf *-fic*) and, in An, *rubro(-)spinal*. Cf:

**rufi-, rufo-:** from L *rūfus*, red: cf RED. Exx: *ruficaudate*, red-tailed, and *rufo(-)ferruginous*. Cf *rube-* and *rubri-*.

**rumeno-:** for E *rumen*, from L *rūmen*, the first stomach, the gullet: cf RUMINATE. Ex: *rumenotomy* (cf *-tomy* at *-tome*).

**runi-:** for *rune*, as in *runiform*.

**rupi-:** from L *rūpes* (s *rūp-*), a rock, akin to L

*rumpere* (s *rump-*). to break. Exx: *Rupicapra*, lit 'the she-goat of the rocks'—the genus of the chamois; *rupicolous*, living among, or growing on, rocks—cf *-colous*.

**ruri-:** L *rūri*, c/f of *rūs* (gen *rūris*), the country: cf RURAL. Exx: *ruridecanal*, of or for a rural dean; *rurigenous* (*rurigen-*+adj suffix *-ous*), from L *rūrigena*, born (cf *-gen*) in the country.

**Russi-; Russo-:** for *Russian*; (*Russo-*) for *Russia* or *Russians*, as in *Russolatry*, idolatry of Russia and the Russians; or for *Russian* (*and*), as in *Russo-Japanese* (War); *Russify* (cf *-fy*).

**ruthenio-, rutheno-:** for *ruthenious*, the adj of the rare chem element *ruthenium* (from ML *Ruthenia*, Russia).

**ruti-, rutid(o)-:** from Gr *rhutis* (gen *rhutidos*), a wrinkle. Exx: *rutidosis*, from Gr *rhutidosis*; *Rutiodon* (cf *-odon*).

**rynco-,** as in *ryncosporous*, with a beak-like seed or fruit: a rare var of *rhyncho-*, q.v.

**-saccate.** See *sacco-*.

**sacchari-; sacchar(o)-:** resp from ML *saccharum* and from its Gr original, *sakkhar* (gen *sakkharos*), *sakkharon*, sugar: cf SACCHARIN(E). Ex: *saccharobacillus*.

**sacci-, sacco-; -saccate:** 1st from L *saccus*, 2nd from its source, the Gr *sakkos*—both meaning 'bag' and both, in E, usu denoting the Sci 'sac' (cf SACK, bag); 3rd, for E *saccate*, resembling a pouch or sac. Exx: *sacciferous* (cf *-ferous* at *-fer*); *saccoderm* (*-derm*).

**sacer-.** See SACERDOTAL and cf:

**sacri-; sacro-:** L *sacri-*, c/f of *sacer* (gen *sacri*), sacred; *sacro-*, by Gr influence: cf SACRED. Exx: SACRIFICE and SACRILEGE; SACROSANCT and *sacro-pictorial*.

**sacro-** (1). See prec.

**sacro-** (2): for the An *sacrum*, elliptical for *os sacrum*, the 'sacred bone' (lowest of the spine)—cf prec. Exx: ('the sacrum') *sacrotomy* (cf *-tomy*, a cutting, at *-tome*); ('sacral—of the sacrum—and') *sacro(-)vertebral*.

**safrano-:** for *saffron*, as in *safrano pink*, or for chem *safranine*, as in *safranophile*, susceptible to sufranine. Cf SAFFRON.

**sagitti-, sagitto-:** L *sagitti-*, c/f of *sagitta*, an arrow, perh of Etruscan origin; *sagitto-*, by Gr influence. Exx: *sagittiferous*, arrow-bearing (or -producing), cf *-ferous* at *-fer*; *sagittocyst* (cf *-cyst*).

**salamandri-:** for *salamander*, as in *salamandriform*.

**sali-:** F *sali-*, from L *sāl* (gen *salis*), salt: cf SALT. Exx: *salicyclic*; *saliferous*, salt-bearing; *salify*, from F *salifier* (cf *-fy* at *-fier*).

**salicyl(o)-:** for *salicyclic* (acid). See prec.

**salini-, salino-:** for *saline* (salty), L *salīnus*, from *sal*, salt: cf prec. Exx: *saliniform*, like a salt; *salinometer*, an instrument determining the amount of salt in a solution. Cf:

**sal(o)-:** for *salicylic* (acid), as in *Salol* (*-ol*, oil); or for *salino-*, as in *salometer*.

**salpi-:** for Zoo *Salpa* (SciL, from L *salpa*, a

stock-fish, from Gr *salpē*), as in *salpiform*; or for the next, as in Bot *Salpiglossis* (cf *-glossa*).

salping(o)-; -salpinx: Gr *salping*(o)-, c/f of *salpinx* (gen *salpingos*), a trumpet—whence obviously the end-c/f *-salpinx*; prob echoic. Exx: ('tube, Eustachian or Fallopian') *salpingo*(-) *palatine, salpingoscope*; *hydrosalpinx*.

saluti-, as in *salutiferous* (L *salūtifer*: cf *-fer*): from *salūs* (gen *salūtis*), health.

salvi-, as in *salvific* (rendering safe): ML *salvi-*, LL *salui-*, c/f of *saluus*, safe. Cf SALVATION.

samari-, as in *samariform*: from L *samara*, elm-seed.

Samo-: Gr *Samo-*, c/f of *Samos*, an Aegean island. Exx: Pal *Samotherium* (cf *-there*) and *Samothracian* (Gr *Samothrakios*).

sancti-; sancto-: L *sancti-*, c/f of *sanctus*, holy: cf SAINT; (*sancto-*) app from LL *sancto*(*rum*), of the saints. Exx: *sanctify*, (perh via OF) from LL *santificāre*, to render (cf *-fy* at *-fier*) holy; *sanctilogy*, a history of saints;—*sanctology*, a catalogue, or a history, of saints.

sandi-, as in *sandiferous* (cf *-fer*): for *sand*.

sangui-; sanguineo-; sanguino-: resp L *sangui-*, c/f of *sanguis* (*sang-*+extension *-u-*+n-suffix *-is*), blood—cf SANGUINE; a Med c/f from L *sanguineus*, blood-red; (*sanguino-*) for E *sanguine*. Exx: *sanguiferous*, blood-producing; *sanguineo*(-) *vascular*; *sanguino-choleric*.

sani-: LL *sāni-*, c/f of L *sānus*, healthy—cf SANE. Ex: ('health') *sanipractic* (cf *-practic* at *-praxia*).

sano-: a Med c/f ('of sanies and') from L *saniēs*, pus and blood exuding from ulcers, etc.: perh akin to L *sanguis*, blood. Ex: *sano*(-)*purulent*.

sap(o)-; saponi-: from L *sāpō* (gen *sāpōnis*, o/s *sāpōn-*), soap: cf SOAP. Exx: *sapo-* in Pharmacy; *saponi-* in, e.g., *saponify* (F *saponifier*), to convert into soap, to render (cf *-fy* at *-fier*) *saponaceous* (ML *sāpōnāceus*) or soapy.

sapori-: from L *sapor*, taste, as in *saporific* (cf *-fic*). Cf SAVO(U)R.

sapr(o)-: Gr *sapr*(o)-, c/f of *sapros* (*sap-*+*-r-*+*-os*), putrid, rotten, prob akin to Gr *sēpia*, a cuttlefish, and *sēpein* (s *sēp-*), to render putrid. Exx: *sapr*(*a*)*emia*, gangrenic blood (cf *haema-*); *saprogenic*; *saprophyte* (*-phyte*).

-sarc; sarc(o)-: from Gr *sarx* (gen *sarkos*), flesh —cf SARCASM; Gr *sark*(o)-, c/f of *sarx*. Exx: ('flesh'—'tissue like flesh') *caulosarc* (cf *cauli-*); *sarcology*, the An of the fleshy parts; *sarcophagus*, q.v. in the exx at *-phaga*; *Sarcura* (*-ura*, Gr *oura*, a tail), the thick-tailed rays (fish).

sarruso-, as in *sarrusophone* (cf *sousaphone*): from *Sarrus*, Parisian bandmaster, who devised it in 1856.

Satano-: for and from SATAN, as in *Satanology*.

satyr(o)-: from L *satyrus*, from Gr *saturos*, a satyr (cf SATYR); as in *satyriasis* (cf *-iasis*), from Gr *saturiasis*; *satyromaniac*.

-saur, 2 -saura, 3 -sauria, 4 -saurian, 5 -saurus; 6 saur(o)-: all ult from Gr *saura* (f), *sauros* (m), a lizard, s *saur-* (app, base *sau-*+extension *-r-*), prob akin to Gr *saulos* (? *sau-*+*-l-*+*-os*), *saukros*

(? *sau-*+*-k-*+*-r-*+*-os*), graceful. 1, the c/f of the E form *saur* of L *saurus* (whence, obviously, 5, *-saurus*), from Gr *sauros*; 2, from Gr *-saura*, c/f of *saura*; 3, c/f of SciL *Sauria* (*saur-*+suffix *-ia*), the lizards and, orig, crocodiles; 4, from *saurian* (*Sauria*+adj suffix *-an*), of or for or like a lizard; 6, Gr *saur*(o)-, c/f of *sauros*. The elements *-saurid*, *-sauridae*, are cpds: *saur-*+*-idae* and *-id*, 'descendant(s)'.

Exx: *dinosaur* (cf *dino-*), one of the *Dinosauria*, adj *dinosaurian*; *Brontosaurus* (cf *bronte-*) and *Ichthyosaurus* (cf *ichthyo-*); *saurognathous* (cf *-gnathous* at *-gnatha*).

saxi-: L *saxi-*, c/f of *saxum* (s *sax-*), a rock. Exx: *saxicolous*, rock-inhabiting (cf *-colous*), growing among rocks; *saxifrage* (*-frage*), via OF from L *saxifraga* (? sc *herba*), the rock-breaking (plant), from *saxifragus* (adj), rock-breaking (*saxifragous*).

sax(o)-: from Antoine Joseph *Sax* (1819–94), the inventor, as in *saxhorn, saxophone saxotromba, saxtuba*.

scalari-, as in *scalariform*, ladder-like: from L *scālāria*, a flight of steps: cf SCALE.

scaleno-, as in *scalenohedron* (cf *-hedral*), comes from Gr *skalēnos*, uneven.

-scaph; scaph(o)-: from Gr *skaphē*, a trough, a boat (lit, a dug-out), c/f *skaph*(o)-; akin to *skaptein* (s *skapt-*), to dig. Ex: *scaphocephalic*, having a boat-shaped skull.

scapi-: for *scape*, a peduncle, a stem, a shaft, from L *scapus*, a shaft, from Gr *skapos*, a shaft, a staff: cf SHAFT. Ex: *scapigerous* (cf *-gerous* at *-ger*). Cf:

scapo-: from Gr *skapos*, a staff (cf prec); as in *scapolite* (*-lite*).

scapuli-, scapul(o)-: for *scapula*, the shoulder-blade, and denoting either 'the scapula' or (o-) 'scapular and'. Exx: *scapulimancy* (cf *-mancy*); *scapulo*(-)*vertebral*.

scat(o)-: Gr *skat*(o)-, c/f of *skōr*, ordure (gen *skatos*), akin to Skt *sairya-* and Hit *sakkar*, dung. Exx: *scatology*, the study of excrement, hence the study of or an interest in (literary) filth; *scatomancy* (cf *-mancy*).

-sceles, scel(o)-: Gr *-skelēs*, end-c/f of *skelos* (s *skel-*), leg, whence the c/f *skel*(o)-, whence E *scel*(o)-; IE r, perh *skel-*, to bend or bow. Exx: *isosceles* (triangle), via L from Gr *isoskelēs*—cf *iso-*, equal; *scelotyrbe*, via L from Gr *skeleturbē*, uncertainty (*turbē*, disturbance: cf DISTURB) in stepping, spastic paralysis of legs.

scelido-: from Gr *skelis* (gen *skelidos*), rib, side, but in E Pal apprehended as leg (Gr *skelos*: see prec). Ex: *Scelidosaurus* (cf *-saurus* at *-saur*).

scelo-. See *-sceles*.

sceno-: via L *scaeno-* from Gr *skēno-*, c/f of *skēnē*, a stage, a scene thereon: cf SCENE. Ex: *scenography*, via F and L from Gr *skēnographia* (cf *-graph*).

sceptro-: from Gr *skēptron*, a staff (see SCEPTRE); as in *sceptropherous*, staff (or stick)-carrying, cf *-pherous* at *-pher*.

sceuo-: LGr *skeuo-*, c/f of Gr *skeuos*, a vessel

(container). Exx: *sceuophorion*, a pyx, lit '(sacred) vessel-bearer'.

**schemato-**: from Gr *skhēma* (gen *skhēmatos*), a shape or form, a figure, cf SCHEME; occ shortened to *schema-*. Exx: *schematograph*; *schematomancy*, divination (-*mancy*) by a man's shape; *schematonics*, gestural expression (Gr *tonos*, tone).

**-schesis, -schetic**: from Gr *skhesis*, a checking, hence, in E cpds, suppression, with adj *-schetic*, from Gr *skhetikos*, retentive: from *ekhein* (s *ekh-*), to have, to hold. Exx: *menoschesis, menoschetic* (cf *meno-*).

**-schisis, -schist; schisto-; schiz(o)-**: 1st from Gr *-skhisis*, c/f of *skhisis*, a cleavage (see 2nd); 2nd and 3rd, from Gr *skhistos*, split, cleft (cloven), divided, pp of *skhizein*, to split or cleave; Gk *skhizo-*, c/f of *skhizein*; cf *schism* at SHED. Exx: *-schist*, only in Bio and Bot; ('fissure'—of a specified part) *schistocyte* (-*cyte*) and *schistoscope*; *schizogenous* (-*genous* at *-gen*)—*schizognathous*, split-nosed—*schizophrenic*, adj (hence n) from *schizophrenia*, (the condition of) a split mind (cf *-phrenia*), 'split personality'.

**scia-**: Gr *skia-*, var of *skio-*, c/f of *skia*, a shadow; IE s, prob *skei-* or *ski-*. Exx: *scialytic* (cf *-lytic* at *-lyse*), shadow-dispelling; *sciamachy*, a battle (-*machy*) of, or with, shadows—a mock contest; *sciapodous*, immense-footed, from Gr *Skiapodes*, a fabulous people with feet (cf *-pod*) large enough to be used as sunshades.

The form *scio-* (Gr *skio-*) occurs in, e.g., *sciomancy*, divination (*mancy*) by consulting the shades of the dead, and *sciotheism*, a belief in ghosts as influences on the living.

**scienti-**, see SCIENTIFIC; **scientifico-**, for '*scientific* and', as in *scientifico-religious*.

**scilli-**: for L *scilla*, the squill (bulbous herb): cf SQUILL. Ex: *scillitoxin*, a poison derived from squill.

**scinci-, scinco-**: from L *scincus*, itself from Gr *skinkos*, a skink (a kind of lizard). Ex: Zoo *Scincomorpha* (cf *-morph*).

**scintillo-**: for L (and E) *scintilla*, a spark: cf SCINTILLATE. Exx: *scintillometer* and *scintilloscope*.

**scio-**. See *scia*.

**scirrh(o)-; -scirrhus**: c/ff for SciL *scirrhus*, an indurated gland or tumour, from L *scirros*, from Gr *skirrhos* or *skiros* (s *skir-*), hard, or, as n, an indurated tumour, etc. Exx: *scirrhogastria* (cf *-gaster*) and *mastoscirrhus* (*masto-* at *-mastia*).

**scirto-**: from Gr *skirtan*, to leap; as in Zoo *Scirtopoda*, an order of rotifers (cf *-pod*).

**sciuro-**: from Gr *skiouros*, a squirrel—cf SQUIRREL. Ex: *sciuromorph* (cf *-morph*), a member of the Zoo division *Sciuromorpha*, beavers, squirrels, etc.

**scler(o)-**: Gr *sklēr(o)-*, c/f of *sklēros*, dry, hard (whence the An *sclera*, the hard coat of the eyeball), akin to *skellein* (s *skel-*)—v.t. and v.i.—to dry; IE r, *skel-*. Exx: ('fibrous') *scleroderma* (cf *-derm*); ('of the sclera') *sclero(-)iritis*; cf Med *sclerosis* (*scler-*+suffix *-osis*), induration, from Gr

*sklērōsis*. The rare *scleri-* occurs in Bot *sclerify* (cf *-fy*).

Subsidiaries are *-sclerosis*, as in *arteriosclerosis*, hardening of the arteries, and *sclerotico-*, for *sclerotica* (a SciL var of SciL *sclera*, the hard coat of the eyeball), as in *scleroticotomy* (cf *-tomy* at *-tome*).

**scobi-**, as in *scobiform*, sawdust-like: from L *scobs* (gen *scobis*), sawdust, akin to *scabiēs*, roughness, (hence) the disease scabies, from *scabere* (s *scab-*), to scratch.

**scoleci-, scolec(o)-; -scolex**: 1st, from SciL *scolex*, from Gr *skōlēx*, c/f *skōlēk(o)-*, whence *scolec(o)-*; 3rd, an E c/f from Gr *skōlēx*, a worm, s *skōl-*, perh from IE r *\*skel-*, to bend or curve. Exx: *scoleciform*, shaped like a tapeworm's head; Med *scoleciasis*, from Gr *skōlēkiasis* (cf *-iasis*); *scolekophagous*, worm-eating (cf *-phaga*), from Gr *skōlēkophagos*. Cf:

**scolio-**: Gr *skolio-*, c/f of *skolios*, bent, crooked (cf prec). Ex: *scoliometer*.

**scolo-**: from Gr *skolops* (gen *skolopos*), a pointed instrument, var of *skalops*, prob akin to L *scalpere* (s *scalp-*), to scratch. Ex: *scolophore* (cf *-phora*).

**scombri-**, as in *scombriform*, like a mackerel: from L *scomber*, gen *scombri*, from Gr *skombros*.

**-scope, 2 -scopic, 3 -scopus, 4 -scopy**: all, ult, from Gr *skopein* (s *skop-*), to regard or view (cf SCOPE): resp SciL *-scopium*, from Gr *-skopion*, as in *hudroskopion*, a hydroscope—denoting, in E, a means (usu an instrument) for viewing or inspecting or observing, as in *gyroscope*, adopted from F (from L *gyrus*, Gr *guros*, a circular motion; on analogy of *telescope*)—*kaleidoscope* (Gr *kalos*, beautiful+*eidos*, form+connective *-o-*+*scope*)—MICROSCOPE—and the prototype, TELESCOPE; 2 (-*scopic*), adj of nn in *-scope* and *-scopy*, as, e.g., *stethoscopic* (*stethoscop(e)*+adj *-ic*; cf *stetho-*) and *telescopic*, but also, independently, a c/f derived from Gr *skop(ein)*, to view, and, in E, denoting 'looking in a certain direction', as in *basiscopic*, looking at or towards the base (cf *basi-*); 3 (-*scopus*) SciL (from Gr *skopos*, a watcher), only in Zoo—e.g., *Phylloscopus* (cf *-phyll*); 4 (-*scopy*), Gr *-skopia*, a viewing or inspection or observation, as in *akroskopia*, E *acroscopy*, whence *acroscopic*, looking at or towards the crest, and in *microscopy*, q.v. at MICROSCOPE.

**scopi-**: from L *scōpa*, a broom, by b/f from *scōpae*, a broom, prob akin to L *scapus*, shaft of a column. Exx: *scopiform*, *scopiped* (cf *-ped*, -foot). Cf *scopuli-*.

**-scopic**. See *-scope*.

**scopuli-**: from SciL *scopula*, from L *scōpulae*, a small broom (cf *scopi-*). Exx: *scopuliform*; *Scopulipedes*, bees 'having a brush of hairs on the hind legs for collecting pollen' (Webster).

**-scopus, -scopy**. See *-scope*.

**scori-**, dross, slag: for E from L *scōria*, from Gr *skōria*, from *skōr*, dung. Exx: *scoriform*; *scorify*=*scori(a)*+*-fy*, q.v. at *-fier*.

**scorpi-**, as in *Scorpiūrus*, from LL, from Gr

*skorpiouros*, lit 'the scorpion-tailed (plant)'—cf *-ure*.

**scoto-**: Gr *skoto-*, c/f of *skotos*, darkness, s *skot-*, akin to Go *skadus*, darkness, s *skad-*; IE r, prob *\*skot-*, with var *\*skat-*. Exx: *scotograph*, an instrument for writing without seeing; *scotophobia*, a dread of darkness.

**Scoto-**: from LL *Scotus*, a Scot; denoting 'Scottish (and)', as in *Scoto-Norman*.

**scribbleo-**: for *scribble*, as in *scribbleomania*.

**scroful(o)-**: for E *scrofula*, as in ML—from LL *scrōfulae*, dim (pl) from L *scrōfa*, a breeding sow: 'perh by a fanciful comparison of the glandular swellings to little pigs' (Webster); 'imitation of the Gr χοιράδες' (E & M), *khoirades*, pl (adj as n), of *khoiras* (gen *khoirados*), pig-like, from *khoiros*, a young pig. Ex: *scrofuloderm* (cf *-derm*).

**scroti-, scrot(o)-**: for *scrōtum* (L, also *scrautum*), as in *scrotiform* and *scrotocele* (cf *-cele*).

**sculpto-**: from L *sculptus*, pp of *sculpere*, to carve, from *scalpere*, to scratch. Ex: *sculptograph*. Cf SCULPTOR.

**scutati-; scutelli-; scuti-**: the 2nd, from L *scūtella*, a dish, dim of *scūtum*, a shield, whence, obviously, the c/f *scūti-* (cf SQUIRE); the derivative L *scūtātus*, (lit) shielded, whence E *scutate*, yields *scutati-*, syn with *scuti-*. Exx: *scutelliform*, dish-shaped; *scutiferous*, shield-bearing (cf *-fer*), and *scutiped*. Cf *scyto-*.

**scyllio-**, as in Zoo *Scylliorhinidae* (*rhinē*, a kind of shark): from SciL *Scyllium*, from Gr *skulion*, a dogfish.

**scyphi-, scypho-**: for L *scyphus*, a cup, from Gr *skuphos* (s *skuph-*), c/f *skupho-*, whence the E *scypho-*; perh akin to *skaptein* (s *skapt-*), to dig. Exx: *scyphiphorous* (cf *-phora*) and *Scyphophori*.

**Scytho-**: from L *Scytha*, a Scyth; denotes 'Scythian and', as in *Scytho-Greek*.

**scyt(o)-**: Gr *skut(o)-*, c/f of *skutos*, leather, hence (in E cpds), skin, as in *scytodepsic*, of, by, for tanning, Gr *skutodepsikos*, which=*skuto-*+*deps*(ein), to knead+adj suffix *-ikos* (cf E *-ic*).

**sebasto-**: from Gr *sebastos* (s *sebast-*), august, venerable, from *sebein* (s *seb-*), to fear, honour, revere. Exx: *Sebastichthys*, lit 'sacred fish' (cf *ichthyo-*); *Sebastopol* (cf *-pole*, city).

**sebi-, sebo-**: resp from L *sēbum* (s *sēb-*), tallow, grease, suet, and for derivative Med *sebum*, fatty matter secreted by certain glands (*sebaceous* g., from L *sēbāceus*, adj of *sēbum*); *sēbum* akin to L *sāpō*, E SOAP. Exx: *sebific*, fat-producing (*-fic*); *seborrh(o)ea*, cf *-rrhoea*.

**sec(o)-**, as in Zoo *secodont* (cf *-odon*), having teeth suitable for cutting: from L *secāre* (s *sec-*), to cut. Cf *-sect*.

**secreto-**: for E *secretion*, as in *secretomotor*.

**-sect, -sected**: from L *sectus*, cut (up), divided, pp (for *secātus*) of *secāre*, to cut; syn (*-sected*) from vv in *-sect*. Exx: *multisect*, cut into many parts; *bisected*, divided—by cutting—into two parts. In E, *-sect* is also the inf of vv derived from L cpds of *sēcare*, as in *bisect* and *vivisect*. Cf SECTION.

**secundi-**: L *secundi-*, c/f of *secundus*, second (lit, following): as in *secundigravida*, (Med L) pregnant for the second time.—The var *secundo-* occurs in *secundogeniture* (cf *primogeniture* at *primi-*).

**securi-**: L *secūri-*, c/f of *secūris* (s *secūr-*), an axe or a hatchet, perh akin to *secāre* (s *sec-*), to cut. Exx: the Bot *Securigera* (cf *-ger*).

**-seism**, adj **-seismic**, occ **-seismal**; **seismo-**: all from Gr *seismos* (c/f *seismo-*), an earthquake, from *seiein* (s *sei-*), to shake; IE s, perh *\*sei-*. Exx: *tachyseism* (cf *tachy-*, swift-passing), *-seismic*; *seismology*, the science of earthquakes; *seismometer*; *seismotherapy*, medical treatment by vibratory massage.

**selacho-**: from Gr *selakhos*, a fish with cartilages in place of bones; from *selas*, gleam, light, and therefore akin to *selēnē*, moon (cf *seleno-*). Exx: *Selachostomi* (adj *selachostomous*), an order of fishes, cf *-stoma*.

**seleni(o)-**: for *selenium*, a (lit 'moonlike') non-metallic element, as in *seleniferous*, productive of selenium. Cf:

**selen(o)-**; rarely **seleni-**: Gr *selēn(o)-*, c/f of *selēnē*, the moon, (lit) the glitterer—cf *selas*, a brilliant light or gleam. Exx: the Bot *Selenipedium* (cf *pedio-*); *selenocentric*, with moon as centre; *selenography* (cf *-graph*) and *selenology*.

**selli-**: from L *sella*, a saddle, itself from *sedēre*, to sit. Ex: *selliform*, saddle-shaped.

**sema-, 2 semant(o)-, 3 semasi(o)-, 4 semato-, 5 -seme, 6 semeio-** (rarely **semio-**), **7 semo-**: all, ult, from Gr *sēma* (s *sēm-*), a sign: resp, 1 *sēma*;, perh from Gr *sēmanta*, neupl of *sēmantos*, marked, signified, from *semainein*, to signify, to mean; 3, from Gr *sēmasia*, signification, an extension of *sēma*; 4, from the o/s *sēmat-* of *sēma* (gen *sēmatos*); 5, from Gr *sēma*; 6, from Gr *sēmeion*, a sign, from *sēma*, with which it is syn: 7 (rare), from *sēma*.

Exx: *semaphore* (see *-phora*, 2nd para); *semantology*, semantics—cf *semantic*, from Gr *sēmantikos* (adj, from *sēmainein*), signifying, significant, whence, via the f *semantikē*, F (la) *sémantique*, whence E *semantics*; *semasiology* (cf *-logy* at *-loger*), semantics; *sematology*, semantics—cf the Bio adj *sematic*, vitally significant; *megaseme* (cf *mega-*); *semeiography* and *semeiology*, esp, in Med, of symptoms; *semology* (rare), semantics; Pal *Semionotus*.

[**semi-**. See Prefixes.]

**semini-; seminuli-**: from L *sēmen* (L *ēminis*), seed—cf SEMEN; SciL dim, *seminula*. Exx: *seminific*; *seminuliform*.

**semio-**. See *sema-*.

**Semitico-; Semito-**: both for 'Semitic (and)'; the 2nd, also for 'a *Semite*': cf SEMITE. Ex: *Semitico-* or *Semito-Hamitic*.

**semno-**, as in Zoo *Semnopithecus* (cf *-pithecus*): from Gr *semnos*, revered, holy.

**seni-**: from L *senex* (gen *senis*), old, (n) old man: cf SENIOR. Ex: *senicide*, (the tribal custom of) exterminating the old men.

**sensi-**: L *sensi-*, c/f of *sensus*, a feeling, a sensation, from *sentīre*, to feel, to perceive. Ex: *sensific* (LL *sensificus*), causing perception or sensation.

**senso-:** for 'sensory and', as in *sensoparalysis*. Cf:

**sensori-:** for *sensorium* (LL); also for 'sensorial and', as in *sensorimotor*.

**-sepalous,** as in *gamosepalous* (cf *gamo-* at *-gam*) =SEPAL+adj *-ous*.

**sepi-,** as in Bot *sepicolous* (cf *-colous*), hedge-haunting, comes from L *saepes* (gen *saepis*), a hedge. Cf *-septate*.

**-sepsis, adj -septic:** from Gr *sēpsis*, putrefaction of or in a bodily part, from *sēpein* (s *sēp-*), to render putrid, whence also *sēptikos*, which, via L *sēpticus*, yields *septic*, whence *-septic*. Exx: *antisepsis, antiseptic; sarcosepsis, sarcoseptic*.

**-septate; septato-:** for and from *septate*, having —or divided by—an An or Bot or Phys or Zoo *septum*, from L *septum*, for *saeptum*, a hedge, a fence, an enclosure, from *s(a)epīre*, to hedge (in) or enclose. Exx: *biseptate* (prefix *bi-*) and *septato-articulate*. Cf the 2nd *septo-*.

**septem-:** L *septem-*, from *septem*, seven (cf SEVEN). Exx: SEPTEMBER; *septemfoliate*, seven-leaved. Also *septen-*, as in *septendecimal*, of seventeen (L *septendecim*). Cf the 3rd *septi-*.

**septi-.** See the 1st *septo-*.

**septi-** (2). See the 2nd *septo-*.

**septi-** (3). A var of *septem-*, seven, as in *septifolious*, seven-leaved; *septinsular*, seven-islanded (cf INSULAR); *septivalent*.

**-septic.** See *-sepsis*.

**septico-:** for *septic*, but from L *sēpticus*, q.v. at *-sepsis*.

**septo-** (1) or **septi-:** fromi Gr *sēptos*, putrefied (cf *-sepsis*); as in *septiform* and *septogerm*.

**septo-** (2) or **septi-:** for Sc *septum* (cf *-septate*), a partition, as in *septiferous, septo(-)marginal, septotomy*.

**sequestr(o)-:** for Med *sequestrum*, as in *sequestrotomy* (cf *-tomy* at *-tome*). Cf SEQUESTRATE.

**Serbo-:** for SERBIAN, as in *Serbo-Croat*. Cf *Servo-*.

**seri-; sericeo-; serici-; serico-:** 1st, short for 3rd, *serici-*, from F *serici-*, from LL *sēricum*, silk; 2nd, for 'sericeous (and)', itself from LL *sēriceus*, from *sēricus*, silken, from *sēricum*; *serico-*, from Gr *sērikos*, silken, from *Sēres*, an East Asian people, manufacturers of silk: cf SILK. Exx: *sericulture; sericeo-mentose; sericiculture; Sericocarpus* (cf *-carp*), herbs with silky 'fruit'.

**serio-:** for *serious*, as in *seriocomic*.

**sermono-:** for *sermon*, as in *sermonology*.

**ser(o)-:** in nn, 'relation to *serum*'; in adjj, 'serous and': cf SERUM. Exx: *seralbumin, serogelatinous*.

**serpenti-:** L *serpenti-*, c/f of *serpens* (gen *serpentis*); ex: *serpentivorous*. Cf:

**serpu-,** as in *serpulite* (cf *-lite*, stone): irreg for *serpi-*, from L *\*serpes*, var of *serpens*, a serpent: cf SERPENT.

**serrati-; serrato-:** for *serrate*, as in *serrati(-)rostral*, saw-beaked; (*serrato-*) from L *serrātus*, saw-edged (*serrate*), from *serra*, a saw—denoting 'serrate and', as in *serrato(-)dentate*, saw-toothed. Cf:

**serri-:** SciL and F *serri-*, from L *serra*, a saw, prob of echoic origin. Exx: the Zoo *Serricornia* (cf *-corn*) and *Serrifera*, saw-flies and their like; *serriform*, saw-shaped. Cf prec.

**Servo.** Until c1919, the usual form of *Serbo-*.

**sesqui-:** L *sēsqui-*, one-and-a-half, from *\*sēmisque* —half, akin to *sēmi*+*que*, and. Exx: *sesquicentennial*, of 150 years, hence n (150th anniversary); *sesquipedalian*, L *sēsquipdālis*, of one and a half metrical feet (cf *-pede*), hence, esp of words or of those who use them, very long.

**seti-:** L *sēti-*, c/f of *sēta* (s *sēt-*), usu *saeta*, a bristle: o.o.o. Ex: *setigerous* (cf *-ger*).

**seto-,** as in *Setophaga*, the genus of fly-catching warblers, lit 'moth-eaters' (cf *-phaga*): Gr *sēs* (gen *sētos*), a moth, perh akin to Syrian *sāsā*, a moth (Hofmann).

**setuli-,** as in *setuliform*, of or like a *sētula* or small bristle; dim of *sēta*, q.v. at *seti-*.

**sex-;** irreg, **sexa-; sexi-,** an E var of *sex-:* L *sex-*, c/f of *sex*, six. Exx: *sexangle*, a hexagon, from L *sexangulus*, six-angled; *sex-annulate*, six-ringed; *sex-digital*, six-fingered or -toed; *sexennial* (adj, hence n), lasting, or happening every, six years, from L *sexennium*, a six-year period, from *sexennis*, of or in six years;—*sexadecimal*;—*sexiped* (cf *-ped*), six-footed; *sexivalent*. Cf *sexti-*.

**sexo-:** for *sex*, as in *sexology*. Cf *sexu-*.

**sexti-:** from L *sextus*, sixth, from *sex*, six: an occ var of *sex-*, six-, as in *sextipartition*, division into sixths, and *sextipolar*, having six poles.

**sexu-:** SciL *sexu-*, from L *sexus*, sex; as in *sexupara* (cf *-para*).

**shapo-:** for *shape*, as in *shapometer* (to determine the shapes of pebbles).

**sial(o)-:** Gr *sial(o)-*, c/f of *sialon*, saliva. Exx: *sialagogue* (cf *-agogue*), a medicine that promotes the flow of saliva; *sialology*.

**sicci-,** as in *siccimeter* (for measuring evaporation): from L *siccus*, dry. Cf DESICCATE.

**Sicilo-; Siculo-:** the former for *Sicilian*, the latter for L *Siculus*, Sicilian, and both denoting 'Sicilian and', as in *Sicilo-* (or *Siculo-*) *Norman*.

**-siderite; sider(o)-** (1): c/f for *siderite*, native ferrous carbonate, orig loadstone, as was L *sidēritis*, from Gr *sidēritēs* or *-itis*, of iron, from *sidēros*, iron, whence the c/f *sidēr(o)-*, whence E *sider(o)-*. Exx: *oligosiderite* (cf *oligo-*); *siderography*, (the art of) steel engraving; *sideroscope; siderurgy* (cf *-urgy*), from Gr *sidērourgia*, (a) working in iron.

**sidero-** (2): from *sider-*, o/s of L *sīdus* (gen *sideris*), a star. Exx: *sideromancy*, divination (*-mancy*) by means of the stars; *siderostat* (cf *-stat*), an Astr instrument.

**sigillo-:** for L *sigillum*, a seal—cf SEAL. Ex: *sigillography*, a knowledge and description of seals (*sigilla*).

**sigmo-; sigmoid(o)-:** from Gr *sigma*, the Gr *s*; for *sigmoid* (flexure or artery), *s*-shaped. Exx: *Sigmodontes* (*sigma*+*odontes*, teeth), a Zoo group of rodents, *sigmoidoscope* (cf *-scope*).

**signi-,** as in *signifer* (cf *-fer*), a standard-bearer, and *signify*, q.v. at SIGN, is the L and E c/f of and from *signum*, a sign (distinctive mark) or a signal. Cf the E end-c/f *-sign* in consign and resign, qq.v. at SIGN.

**siliceo-; silici-; silico-**: 1st, for *siliceous*, from L *siliceus*, adj of *silex* (gen *silicis*), a flint, whence *silici-; silic(o)-*, for *silicon*, which, like *silica*, is SciL based upon L *silic-*, the o/s of *silex*. Exx: *siliceocalcareous*; *silicicolous* (cf *-colous*), growing (well) in flinty soil; *silicofluoride* and—'silicic acid' —*silico-alkaline*.

**siliqui-**, as in *siliquiform*: for Bot *siliqua*, adopted from L ('a pod, a husk').

**sillo-** (1): Gr *sillo-*, as in *sillographos*, E *sillographer*, a writer (cf *-grapher* at *-graph*) of satirical poems (Gr *silloi*, pl of *sillos*).

**sillo-** (2): F *sillo-*, from MF-F *siller*, to go, or pass, through the water, akin to MF-F *sillon*, a furrow, Ex: *sillometer* (F *sillomètre*), a ship's speed-measurer.

**Siluro-**, 'Silurian and': from L *Silūres*, an ancient Celtic people of Britain, with adj *Silurian*, applied esp to a Geol period. Ex: *Siluro-Cambrian*.

**silvi-**: from ML *silva*, L *silua*, a wood or forest: cf SILVAN. Exx: *silvicolous* (cf *-colous*), ML *silvicola* (L *silui-*), a woods-dweller; *silviculture*, the growing and care of woods—cf L *siluicultrix*.

**simo-**: Gr *simo-*, c/f of *simos* (s *sim-*), snub-nosed, whence the syn L *simus*, whence *simia*, an ape, whence the E adj *simian* (suffix *-an*). Ex: *Simosaurus* (cf *-saur*).

**simpli-; simplici-**: ML *simpli-*, c/f of L *simplex*, simple; ML *simplici-*, c/f based upon the o/s *simplic-*; cf SIMPLE. Exx: SIMPLIFY; Zoo *Simplicidentata*, rodents having a single pair of upper incisors (cf *dentato-*).

**sin-**: from L *sinapi* or *sinapis*, mustard, from Hell Gr *sinapi* (or *sinapu*), akin to Gr *napu*; perh cf Skt *sarṣapa-*, itself perh of Mal origin. (Hofmann.) Ex: *sinalbin*, a glucoside in white-mustard seeds—cf L *albus*, white.

**Sinico-; Sino-**: 1st, for *Sinic*, which, like the 2nd, comes from LL *Sinae* or from its source, Gr *Sinai*, the Chinese, itself from a Chinese name: cf CHINESE. Exx: *Sinologue*, a scholar in Chinese (language, art, etc.)—cf F *sinologue* (cf *-logue* at *-loger*)—and *Sinology* (*-logy* at *-loger*); *Sinophile* (cf *-phil*). Rarely *Sini-*, as in *Sinify*.

**sinistr(o)-**: L *sinistro-*, c/f of *sinister*, on the left hand: cf SINISTER. Exx: *sinistro(-)cerebral*; Bot *sinistrorse*, twining leftwards, L *sinistrorsus*, short for *sinistrouersus* (ML *-versus*), turned to the left (side).

**Sino-**. See *Sinico-*.

**sinu-; sinuato-**: from L *sinus*, a concave or semicircular fold, a bent or curved surface, e.g. a bay, s *sin-*, o.o.o.; hence L *sinuāre*, to curve, to bend or curve back, with pp *sinuātus*; cf SINUOUS. Exx: *sinu(-)auricular*; *sinuato(-)dentate*.

**siphoni-; siphon(o)-**: 1st, for E *siphon*; 2nd, from Gr *siphōno-*, c/f of *siphōn*, a tube or a pipe: cf SIPHON. Exx: *siphoniferous* (cf *-ferous* at *-fer*); Bot *siphonogamous* (cf *-gamous* at *-gam*), fertilizing

with a pollen tube, and Zoo *Siphonophora* (cf *-phora*).

**siri(o)-**: from L *Sīrius*, from Gr *Seirios*, 'the scorcher'. Exx: *siriasis* (cf *-iasis*), sunstroke; *siriometer* (an Astr measure).

**sismo-**. An occ var of *seismo-*.

**sisto-**, 'stopper, checker, retarder', as in Biochem *sistomensin*: from L *sistere*, freq of *stāre*, to stand: cf the *-sist* of *assist*, *consist*, *desist*, *exist*, *insist*, *persist*, *resist*, *subsist*.

**-site**: from *parasite*; as in Zoo *coenosite* (cf *coeno-*), a free (or, at the least, separable) semi-parasite.

**sitio-; sito-**: from Gr *sition*, app a modification of the syn *sitos* (s *sit-*), grain, food, with c/f *sito-*, whence E *sito-*. Exx: *sitiology*, *sitology*, the study of food, dietetics; *sitiomania*.

**Siva-**: E *Siva*, the great Hindu destructive deity. Only in Pal: e.g., *Sivatherium* (cf *-there*).

**skeleto-**: for E *skeleton*; as in *skeletogenous*, (adj) bone-developing, and *skeletology*.

**skia-, skio-**, as in *skiagraph*, *skiograph*. See *scia-*.

**Slavo-**, 'the Slavs', as in *Slavophobe* (cf *-phobe*); 'Slavic and', as in *Slavo-Germanic*. Cf the *Slavi-* of *Slavify* (cf *-fy*), to render Slavic. Cf:

**slavo-**: for *slave*, as in *slavocracy*.

**smintho-**: from Gr *sminthos*, a mouse, perh of Etruscan origin. Ex: Zoo *Sminthurus* (Gr *oura*, tail, cf *-urus* at *-ura*).

**snob(o)-**: (not always jocose) for *snob*, as in *snobocracy* (cf *-cracy*) and *snobography*.

**soboli-**: from L *soboles* (? for *sorboles*, from *sorbēre*, s *sorb-*), a sucker or shoot, as in Bot *soboliferous*, sucker-producing (cf *-ferous* at *-fer*).

**societo-**, as in *societology* (*society*+connective *-o-*+*-logy*, q.v. at *-loger*); **socio-**, F *socio-*, from L *socius*, a companion (s *soc-*: cf SOCIAL), as in *sociocracy* (cf *-cracy*) and SOCIOLOGY.

**sodio-**: for *sodium* (adj *sodic*), itself an *-ium* derivative from SODA: as in *sodiohydric*.

**solaro-**: for *solar* (latitude, etc.), as in *solarometer*, an instrument to determine (cf *-meter*) a ship's position.

**solemni-**, as in *solemnify*, q.v. at SOLEMN.

**solen(o)-**: Gr *sōlēn(o)-*, c/f of *sōlēn*, a pipe, a channel, gen *sōlēnos*. Exx: *solenocyte* (*-cyte*), *Solenodon* (cf *-odon*), *Solenopsis* (cf *-opsis* at *opsia*); cf the El term *solenoid* (*solen-*+suffix *-oid*), a tubular coil.

**soli-** (1), 'alone'—'solely': L *sōli-*, c/f of the adj *sōlus*, alone: cf SOLE, adj. Exx: *soliloquy* (whence *soliloquist* and *soliloquize*: cf the suffixes *-ist*, *-ize*), from LL *sōliloquium*, a speaking alone—cf *-loquy* at *-loquence*, from L *loquī*, to speak; *soliped* (cf *-ped*); *solipsism*, which=*sol*(us)+*ips*(e), self+suffix *-ism*.

**soli-** (2), 'sun': L *sōli-*, c/f of *sōl*, the sun: cf SOLAR. Exx: *solilunar*, *soliterraneous*, *solitidal*.

**soli-** (3): from L *solum*, soil, ground: cf SOIL. Ex: *solifluction*, the creeping ('flowing': L *fluctiō*, gen *fluctiōnis*: cf FLUENT) of wet soil down a slope.

**solidi-**: for *solid*. Exx: *solidiform*, *solidify* (cf *-fy*).

**solvo-**: for Chem *solvent*, as in *solvolysis* (cf *-lysis* at *-lyse*).

**-soma, 2 -somatous, 3 -some, 4 -somia, 5 -somic, 6 -somus; 7 somatico-, 8 somat(o)-, 9 somo-, 10 -somous**: all, ult, from Gr *sōma* (s *sōm-*), the body of human being or of quadruped, perh akin to Gr *sōros*, a heap, with PGr r *sō-*, a swelling; IE r, perh *su-* or *tu-*, to swell. Resp: 1, from *sōma*, the pl *somata* (Gr *sōmata*) occurring in Zoo classifications; 2, from Gr *-sōmatos* (from *sōmat-*, the o/s of *sōma*); 3, from *sōma*, with adj *-somic*; 5, SciL, from *sōma*; 6, SciL, from *sōma*; 7, for E *somatic* (*somat-+-ic*); 8, Gr *sōmat(o)-*, c/f of *sōma*, gen *sōmatos*; 9 (=*somato-*), a very E and somewhat irreg c/f from *sōma*, with adj *-somous*, both rare.

Exx: *phyllosoma* (cf *-phyll*); *Heterosomata*, a group of fishes 'so named from their unsymmetrical form' (Webster), cf *hetero-*; *heterosomatous*; *acrosome* (cf *acro-*); *nanosomia* (cf *nano-*, dwarf-), adj *nanosomic*; *nanosomus*, the fetus corresponding to *nanosomia* (type of body); *somatico(-)visceral*; ('body') *somatology*, the comp study of the structure of the human body.

**somni-**: L *somni*, c/f of *somnus*, sleep, akin to the syn Gr *hupnos*. Exx: *somniferous* (cf *-ferous* at *-fer*), from L *somnifer*, soporific, and *somnific*, from L *somnificus* (cf *-fic*); *somnipathy*, hypnotic sleep. The irreg *somno-* is rare outside of *somnopathy*, *-pathist*.

**somo-; -somous; -somus.** See *-soma*.

**-sonance, -sonant, -sonous; soni-**: from L *-son-antia*, itself from *-sonant-* (whence E *-sonant*), the o/s of *-sonans*, c/f of *sonans* (gen *sonantis*), presp of *sonāre* (s *son-*), to sound; *-sonic*, from *sonic*, of sound (waves); *-sonous* from L *-sonus*, adj; *soni-* from L *sonus* (s *son-*), a sound: cf SOUND (n). Exx: *dissonance*, LL *dissonantia*, cf prefix *dis-*; *dissonant* —opp *assonant* (whence *assonance*), via F from L *assonant-*, o/s of *assonans*, pp of *assonāre*, to correspond in sound—from L *dissonant-*, o/s of *dissonans*, pp of *dissonāre*, to differ in sound; *clarisonous*, L *clārisonus*, clear-sounding; *super-sonic* (prefix *super*, above, beyond); *soniferous*, sound-producing or -carrying (cf *-ferous* at *-fer*).

**sonori-, sonoro-**: from L *sonōrus*, the adj of *sonor*, a sound, akin to the syn *sonus*—cf prec. Exx: *sonoriferous*; *sonorophone*.

**-soph, 2 -sopher, 3 -sophic, 4 -sophist, 5 -sophy; 6 sophi(o)-, 7 soph(o)-**: ult, all from Gr *sophos* (s *soph-*), wise, cf SOPHIST: resp, Gr *-sophos*, end-c/f of *sophos*, as in *gymnosoph*, rare for *gymnosophist*, b/f from L *gymnosophistae*, Gr *gumnosophistai*, pl n from *gumnos*, naked+*sophistēs*, a philosopher, and in *morosoph*, a foolish wise man (cf *sophomore*), from Gr *mōrosophos*, with E derivatives *morosophist* and *morosophy*; 2, *-sopher*, from PHILO-SOPHER, where the *-er* is an unnecessary E agential *-er*; 3, *-sophic*, for *sophic*, of wisdom, intellectual, Gr *sophikos*; 4—cf 1; 5, *-sophy*, Gr *-sophia*, c/f of *sophia* (s *soph-+*abstract suffix *-ia*), wisdom; 6, *sophio-*, from *sophia*; 7, from *sophos*.

Exx: *gastrosoph*, *gastrosopher*, a gastronomer (cf *gastro-*); *philosophic*; *philosophy*, q.v. at PHILO-SOPHER; *sophiology*, the study and knowledge of ideas; *sophomore* (adj *-moric*), (lit) a wise fool, (hence) a second-year student in American universities.

**sorbe-**, as in *sorbefacient* (cf *-facient*), causing or assisting absorption: from L *sorbēre*, to absorb.

**soredi-**: for Bot *soredium* (SciL, from Gr *sōros*, a heap); as in *sorediform*. Cf:

**sori-.** See *soro-*.

**sorici-**: from *sōric-*, o/s of L *sōrex* (gen *sōricis*), a mouse, akin to the syn Gr *hurax*. In E, denoting 'shrew' (a small rodent, mouse-like in appearance, but mole-like in essentials)—as in *soricident* (cf *-dent* at *dentato-*).

**soro-**, as in Bot *Sorosporium* (cf *-sporium* at *-spora*); comes from Gr *sōros* (s *sor-*), a heap—perh akin to *sōma* (q.v. at *-soma*); *sōros*, via the derivative SciL *sorus*, pl *sori*, yields also *-sorus*, pl *-sori*, as in Bot *soriferous* (cf *-ferous* at *-fer*), sori-bearing, and *uredosorus* (L *ūrēdō*, blight).

**sorori-**: L *sorōri-*, c/f of *soror* (gen *sorōris*), sister: cf SISTER. Ex: *sororicide* (cf *-cide*), a sister-killer, from L *sorōricīda*, and a sister-killing, from LL *sorōricīdium*.

**sorti-**; L *sorti-*, c/f of *sors* (gen *sortis*), a lot— in divination. Cf SORT. Ex: *sortilege*, the art of divination, (hence) sorcery, via OF from ML *sortilegium*, n from L adj *sortilegus*, divinatory, 2nd element from L *legere*, to gather, to select.

**-sorus.** See *soro-*.

**soterio-**, as in *soteriology*, the doctrine of salvation: from Gr *sōtēria*, safety, from *sōterios*, the adj of *sōtēr* (s *sōt-*, extension of *sō-*), a saviour, akin to *sōzein* (s *sōz-*, extension of *sō-*), to save. JE r, perh *sō-*. Cf *sozo-*.

**sousa-**, as in *sousaphone*: for John Philip *Sousa* (1854–1932), Am bandmaster and composer. Cf *saxo-*.

**soz(o)-**: from Gr *sōzein* (s *sōz-*), to save: cf *soterio-*. Ex: *sozolic*, which=*soz(o)*+(phen)*ol*+adj suffix *-ic*.

**spacio-**: an occ, irreg var of *spatio-*.

**spadici-**, as in *spadicifloral*, having flowers on a Bot *spadix*, a spike with fleshy axis: L, from Gr, *spadix*, a broken-off palm-branch, with its fruit.

**spani-, span(o)-**: the former irreg for the latter, from Gr *spanos*, scarce, perh akin to *span*, to draw (apart), to separate. Exx: *spanipelagic*, rarely coming to the surface of the sea (cf *pelago-*); *spanopnoea*, very slow breathing (cf *-pnoea*).

**sparasso-**: from Gr *sparassein*, to tear. Ex: Pal *Sparassodonta* (cf *-odon*, tooth).

**-spasm; spasmato-, spasmo-**: 1st, from Gr *spasmos*, a spasm or convulsion; 2nd, from *spas-mat-*, o/s of Gr *spasma* (gen *spasmastos*), a spasm; 3rd, either from Gr *spasmos* (or E *spasm*) or from E *spasmodic*. Cf SPASM. Exx: *neurospasm* (cf *neuro-*); *spasmatomancy* (cf *-mancy*, divination); *spasmotoxin*, a poison causing violent convulsions.

**-spath**, as in *blepharospath* (cf *blepharo-*): from Gr *spathē*, a blade; in E, forceps. Cf *spatula-*.

**spatilo-**: from Gr *spatilē*, excrement, akin to

*tilan*, to have diarrhoea. Ex: *spatilomancy*, divination (-*mancy*) with excrement.

**spatio-**, 'spatial (and)': from L *spatium*, space; as in *spatio temporal*. Cf SPACE.

**spatula-**, as in *spatulamancy* (cf -*mancy*), and *spatuli-*, as in *spatuliform*, spatula- or spoon-shaped: from L *spatula*, a shoulder, an artist's spatula, dim of *spatha*, from Gr *spathē*, any broad, flat blade (orig of wood), akin to SPADE.

**specio-**: for *species*, as in *speciology* (cf -*logy* at -*loger*). For *speci-*, cf SPECIFY.

**spectro-** (1): for E *spectrum*, as used in Physics—form-adopted, sense-adapted from L *spectrum*, an appearance, esp a SPECTRE (cf next). Exx: *spectrometer*, *spectroscope*.

**spectro-** (2): for Am *specter*, E *spectre* (cf prec); as in *spectrophobia*, a morbid fear of ghosts.

**speedo-**, only in *speedometer*: *speed*+connective -*o*-.

**speleo-**, as in *speleology*, cave-lore, the science of caves: via L *spelaeum* from Gr *spelaion*, a cave.

**-sperm**, 2 -*sperma*, pl -*spermae*; 3 -*spermum*; adjj 4 -*spermal* or 5 -*spermic* or 6 -*spermous* or 7 -*spermatous*; 8 -*spermia* or 9 -*spermy*;—10 *sperma*-; 11 **spermati-** or 12 **spermatio-**; 13 **spermat(o)-**; 14 **spermi-**; 15 **spermio-**; 16 **spermo-**: ult, all from Gr *sperma*, semen, (hence) seed: cf SPERM.

Resp: 1, from Gr *sperma*, mostly Bot and denoting 'seed', as in *angiosperm* (cf *angio*-); 2, a SciL var (pl -*spermae*) of -*sperm*, as in *Lepidosperma* (cf *lepido*-) and *Gymnospermae* (*gymno*-); 3, a SciL (neu, instead of f -*sperma*) var of -*sperm*, and, like 2, denoting 'plant(s) with a specified spermal feature', as in *Anthospermum* (cf *antho*- at -*anth*); 4 (-*spermal*)=E *sperm*+adj -*al*, as in *perispermal* 5 (-*spermic*)=E *sperm*+adj -*ic*, as in *gymnospermic*; 6 (-*spermous*) from Gr -*spermos*, from Gr *sperma*, as in *monospermous* (cf *mono*-), one-seeded; 7 (-*spermatous*) Gr -*spermatos*, from *spermat*-, the o/s of *sperma*, syn with 6, as in *monospermatous*; 8 (-*spermia*) a SciL term deriving from Gr *sperma*; 9, the E shape of -*spermia*, as in *polyspermia* and *polyspermy* (cf *poly*-), many-seededness;— 10 (*sperma*-) a rare var, as in *spermatheca* (cf -*theca*), of *sperma*-; 11–12=c/ff of *spermatium*, a male gamete, a SciL derivative, in Bot, from Gr *sperma*, as in *spermatiferous* and *spermatiogenous*; 13, *spermat(o)*-, a true Gr c/f of Gr *sperma*, gen *spermatos*, as in *spermatogenesis* and *spermatozoon*, pl -*zoa* (cf *zo*-); but 14, *spermi*-, comes from SciL *sperma*, as in *spermi ïduct* and *spermigerous* (cf -*gerous* at -*ger*), and 15, *spermio*-, blends *spermi*- and *spermo*-, as in *spermiogenesis*; 16, *sperm(o)*-, Gr *sperm(o)*-, from *sperma* (cf 13), as in *spermology*, *spermophile*, *spermophore*.

**sphacelo-**: from Gr *sphakelos*, gangrene; IE r, perh *sphak*- or *sphek*-. Exx: *sphaceloderma* (cf -*derm*) and *sphacelotoxin*.

**-sphaera** or 2 -**sphere**; 3 -**spheric(al)**;—4 **sphaer(o)-** or 5 **spher(o)-**:

1, from Gr *sphaira*, via L *sphaera*, whence, via F, the E SPHERE; 2, via L -*sphaerium* from Gr *sphairion*, from *sphaira*; 3 from *spheric(al)*, q.v. at

SPHERE; 5, *sphero*-, is the more E form of 4, *sphaero*-, via LL *sphaero*-, from Gr *sphair(o)*-, c/f of *sphaira*. Exx: (mostly in Bot and Zoo: -*sphaera*) *Microsphaera* (cf *micro*-); *astrosphere* (cf *astro*- at -*aster*); ATMOSPHERE; *cosmosphere* (cf *cosmo*- at *cosmeto*-); HEMISPHERE; *planisphere* (cf *plani*-); *stratosphere*, from F *stratosphère*, 1st element from *stratum*; *hemispheric(al)*, cf *hemi*-, half; *Sphaerocarpus* (cf -*carp*); *spherograph* (cf -*graph*).

**sphagni-**, **sphagno-**: c/ff of SciL *Sphagnum*, a genus of mosses, from Gr *sphagnos*, a kind of moss. Exx: *sphagnicolous*, living (cf -*colous*) in peat or bog mosses; *sphagnology*, the science of peat mosses.

**Sphenisci-**, **Sphenisco-**, only in Zoo: from SciL *Spheniscus*, the genus of the jackass penguins: 'from the shortness of the bird's wings' (Webster), Gr *sphēniskos* meaning 'a little wedge', from *sphēn*, a wedge. Cf:

**sphen(o)-**: Gr *sphēn(o)*-, c/f of *sphēn*, a wedge, perh akin to Gr *spathē*, q.v. at *spatula*-. Exx: *sphenography*, the writing—hence also the deciphering—of cuneiform (wedge-shaped) characters; in adjj, 'wedge-like or -shaped' (*sphenoid*): *sphenolith* (cf -*lith* at -*lite*) and *spheno(-)palatine*.

**sphere**, -**spheric(al)**; **sphero-**. See -*sphaera*.

**sphincter(o)-**: from Gr *sphinktēr* (σφιγκτήρ), a band, hence a muscular ring (e.g., the *sphincter ani*), from *sphingein*, to bind tightly: cf SPHINX. Ex: *sphincterotomy* (cf -*tomy* at -*tome*). Cf:

**sphingo-**, with rare Latinized var, *sphingi*-; -**sphinx**: 1st, from Gr *sphingein* (s *sphing*-), to bind tightly, from *sphinx* (cf SPHINX); 2nd Gr -*sphinx* (-σφιγξ), denoting, in E, a sphinx with a specified kind of head. Exx: *sphingiform*; *sphingometer*; *criosphinx*, a ram-headed sphinx, cf *crio*-.

**sphygmo-**: Gr *sphugmo*-, c/f of *sphugmos*, pulse (of the heart), akin to *sphuzein*, (of the heart) to beat; IE r, prob *sphug*-. Exx: *sphygmograph*, an instrument recording heart-beats; *sphygmology*, a study of the pulse.

**sphyra-**: from *sphura*, a mallet, as in *Sphyrapicus* (L *pīcus*, a woodpecker), a sap-sucking woodpecker.

**spici-**; **spiculi-**, **spiculo-**: L *spīci*-, c/f of *spīca*, ear (of grain, esp corn: cf SPIKE, ear); its dim, *spīculum*, or rather the E derivative, *spicule*, has c/ff *spiculi*-, *spiculo*-. Exx: *spicilege*, an anthology, from L *spīcilegium*, a harvest gleaning (cf the 2nd -*lege*); *spiculiferous* (cf -*ferous* at -*fer*) and *spiculo(-)fibre*.

**spil(o)-**: from Gr *spilos* (s *spil*-), a spot, e.g. a stain, perh akin to L *squalus*, dirty (cf SQUALID). Ex: *Spilogale*, a skunk: 2nd element, Gr *galē*, a weasel.

**spini-**, 2 **spino-**, 3 **spinoso-**, 4 **spinuli-**; 5 **spinuloso-**, 6 -**spinose**: 1, L *spīni*-, c/f of *spīna*, a thorn: cf SPINE; 2, a SciL var of *spini*-; 3, from L *spīnōsus*, the adj of *spīna*; 4, from L *spīnula* (a spinule), the dim of *spīna*; 5, for *spinulose*, covered with tiny thorns or spines; 6, for *spinose*, spiny, full of thorns, from L *spīnōsus*.

Exx: *Spinifex*, SciL, *spini*-+-*fex* (q.v. above).

from *facere*, to make; *spino-muscular*; *spinoso(-)dentate*; *spinuliferous*, bearing (cf *-ferous* at *-fer*) very small spines; *spinuloso(-)serrate*; *bispinose*, two-spined.

**spiraculi-**; **spiro-**: for L *spīrāculum*, an air-hole, from *spīrāre* (s *spīr-*), to breathe; (*spiro-*) from *spīrāre*—denoting, in E, 'respiration'. Cf 'to INSPIRE'. Exx: *spiraculiform*; *spirometer*, an instrument measuring either the capacity of the lungs or the volume of air expelled.

**spiri-**: from L *spīra* (s *spīr-*), a coil (of, e.g., rope), from Gr *speira*: cf SPIRAL, which itself has c/f *spirali-*, whence *spiraliform*. Ex: *spirivalve*, having a spiral shell. Cf:

**spirillo-**: from *spirillum*, a SciL dim of *spira*, a coil (cf prec). Ex: *spirillotropism*—cf *tropism* at TROPE. Cf:

**spir(o)-** (1): from Gr *speir(o)-*, c/f *speira*, a coil— cf *spiri-*. Ex: ('coiled'; spiral') *Spirochaeta*, *spiro-*, *chete* (cf *-chaeta*). Adj, *-spirous*, as in *bispirous*, two-coiled.

**spiro-** (2). See *spiraculi-*.

**splanchn(o)-**: Gr *splankhn(o)-*, c/f of *splankhnon* mostly in pl *splankhna* (σπλάγχνα), entrails, akin to *splēn*, spleen. Exx: *splanchnolith* (cf *-lith* at *-lite*); *splanchnodynia* (cf *-odynia* at *-odyne*).

**spleni-** and **splen(o)-**; **-splenia**: from L *splēn* (gen *splēnis*), the spleen, and (*spleno-*) from *splen* (gen *splēnos*), the Gr source of L *splēn*—akin to the syn Skt *plīhán-*, cf also prec; (*-splenia*) a SciL derivative (suffix *-ia*, in its Med applications) from Gr *splēn*. Exx: *spleniform*; ('spleen') *splenocyte* (*-cyte*) and ('splenic—of the spleen—and') *splenotyphoid*; *hypersplenia* (cf the prefix *hyper-*).

**spodo-**: Gr *spodo-*, c/f of *spodos*, (wood) ashes, s *spod-*, cf the syn Gr *splēdos* (s *splēd-*) and perh even the L *splendēre*, q.v. at SPLENDID. Ex: *spodomancy*, divination (cf *-mancy*) by ashes.

**-spondyli**, **-spondylus**; **spondyl(o)-**: 1st, pl, and 2nd. sing, come from L *spondylus*, itself from Gr *spondulos*, Attic *sphondulos*, a vertebra, akin to *sphadazein* (s *sphadaz-*, ? an extension of r *\*sphad-*), to quiver, and to Skt *spandas*, a quivering; IE r, perh *\*sphad-* or *\*sphed-* or *\*sphod-*, varr *\*spad-*, *\*sped-*, *\*spod-*, nasalized *\*spand-*, etc., or *\*sphand-*, etc. Exx: *Isospondyli* (cf *iso-*) and *Palaeospondylus* (*palaeo-*); *spondylopathy* and *spondylotherapy*. Prob from the 'mussel- or oyster-shell' sense of *spondulos*, pl *sponduloi*, L *spondyli*, comes the slang *spondulic(k)s*, *-ix*, funds, money, cash: cf the monetary use of cowrie shells.

**spongi-** or 2, **spongo-**, cf 3, **spongio-**; 4, **-spongia** or 5, **-spongiae**, with 6, common adj **-spongian**; 7, **-spongium**: all, ult, from Gr *spongos* or *spongia*, a sponge: cf SPONGE. Resp: 1, from E *sponge*; 2, from Gr *spongos*, cf 3, from Gr *spongion*, dim of *spongos*; 4 and 5, SciL c/ff from Gr *spongia*; 6= *spongi-*+adj *-an*; 7, SciL from *spongia*. Exx: *spongiculture*; *spongology* and *spongophore* (cf *-phore* at *-phora*); *spongiocyte* (*-cyte*); *Hyalospongia* (*hyalo-*) and *Silicispongiae* (*silici-*); *hyalospongian*: *neurospongium* (*neuro-*).

**spooko-**: humorous for *spook*, a ghost. Ex: *spookology*.

**-spora**, 2 **-spore**, 3 **-sporic**, 4 **-sporidia**, 5 **-sporium**, 6 **-sporous**; 7 **-spory**; 8 **spori-**, 9 **sporidi-**, 10 **sporo-**, 11 **sporuli-**: all, ult, from Gr *spora* (s *spor-*), a sowing, a seed, either derived from or intimately akin to *speirein* (s *speir-*), to sow: cf SPORE. Resp: 1, from Gr *spora*; 2, from E *spore*; 3, from E *spore*+adj *-ic*; 4, from SciL *sporidium*, dim of SciL *spora* (from Gr *spora*); 5, SciL c/f from Gr *spora*; 6, from Gr *-sporos*, c/f of *spora*, or simply for E *spore* (*spore*+adj *-ous*); 7 (*-spory*), the E form of *\*sporia*, state of seed(s); 8 (*spori-*), a SciL var of 10 (*sporo-*), the true Gr c/f of *spora*; 9 (*sporidi-*) for *sporidium*; 10 (*sporo-*), occurring in many Sci cpds, e.g. *sporophore*, seed- or spore-bearing (cf *-phora*); 11 (*sporuli-*) either from SciL *sporula*, dim of SciL *spora*, or for E *sporule*.

Exx: *Diaspora*, 'the Dispersion' of Jews after the exile in Babylon, cf the prefix *dia-*; *diaspore* (in Min) and *macrospore* (*macro-*), *microspore* (*micro-*) *diasporic*; *Sarcosporidia* (*sarco-*); *Helminthosporium* (*helmintho-*); *homosporous* (*homo-*); *homospory*; *sporicide* (*-cide*, q.v. at *-cidal*); *sporidiferous* (cf *-ferous* at *-fer*); *sporocarp* (*-carp*) and *sporogenesis* and *sporosac*; *sporuliferous*.

**sporangi-**, **sporangio-**; **-sporangiate**, adj of **-sporangium**, occ **-sporange**: for and from SciL *sporaŋgium*, in Bio a tiny primitive reproductive body: Gr *spor*(os), a seed+*angeion*, a receptacle, *ἀγγείον*, akin to *ἀγκών*, *ankōn*, a bend (of, e.g., the arm). Exx: *zoosporange* (cf *zoo-* at *zo-*) and *androsporangium* (*andro-*); *leptosporangiate* (*lepto-*), *sporangiferous* (*-ferous*, q.v. at *-fer*); *sporangiophore* (*-phore*, q.v. at *-phora*).

Cf prec.

**-spore**, **-sporic**, **-sporous**, etc. See -SPORA.

**spumi-**: for *spume* (cf FOAM); as in *spumification* (cf *-fication* at *-fic*).

**squali-**, **squalo-**: for Zoo *Squalus*, from L *squalus*, a large marine fish. Exx: *squaliform*, *Squalodon* (cf *-odon*).

**squami-**, 2 **squamo-**; 3 **squamato-**; 4 **squamoso-**; 5 **squamelli-**; 6 **squamuli-**: all, ult, from L *squāma*, a fish's scale, perh akin to L *squalus*, filthy—cf SQUALID. Resp: 1, L *squāmi-*, c/f of *squāma*; 2, irreg from *squāma*; 3, for E *squamate* (LL *squāmātus*), scaly; 4, from L *squāmōsus* (whence E *squamous*), scaly; 5, for SciL *squamella* (dim of *squāma*), a tiny scale; 6, for L *squāmula*, dim of *squāma*.

Exx: *squamiferous* (cf *-ferous* at *-fer*); *squamo(-)cellular*; *squamato(-)granulous* (cf *granuli-* at *grani-*); *squamoso(-)dentate* (cf *dentato-*); *squamelliform*; *squamuliform*.

**stachy(o)-**: Gr *stakhu(o)-*, c/f of *stakhus*, ear of corn, akin to STING; IE r, *\*stagh-* or *\*stegh-*, nasalized as *\*stengh-*, etc. Ex: *Stachyurus* (cf *-urus* at *-ure*).

**stacto-**: from the Gr adj *staktos*, oozing drop by drop, from *stazein*, to drip: cf STAGNATE, *stagno-*, *stalacti-*.

stadi- or stadio-: for *stadium*; as in *stadimeter* and *stadiometer*.

stagmo-: from Gr *stagma* (s *stag-*), a drop, esp of water, akin to L *stagnum*, a pond; e.g., *stagmometer*.

stagni-, as in *stagnicolous* (cf *-colous*), pond-haunting or -inhabiting: from L *stagnum*, standing water: cf STAGNANT.

stagono-: from Gr *stagōn* (gen *stagonos*), a drop (of water, blood), from *stazein* (s *staz-*), to drop or drip. Ex: *Stagonospora* (cf *-spora*), imperfect fungi.

stalacti- and stalactiti-; stalagmo-: the 1st, irreg for the 2nd as c/f of *stalactite*; the 3rd, from Gr *stalagmos*, a dripping. Exx: *stalacti(ti)form*; *stalagmometer*. Cf stacto- and stagmo-.

stamin(i)-: from *stāmin-*, o/s of L *stāmen* (gen *stāminis*), a thread, (hence) a stamen: cf STAMEN. Ex: *staminigerous* (cf *-gerous* at *-ger*). Cf *-stemonous*.

-stan, as in *Afghanistan, Baluchistan, Hindustan, Pakistan, Turkistan*, means 'country'; it often occurs in the Indic and Iranian languages.

stanni-, stanno-: from L *stannum*, better *stagnum*, a silver-lead alloy, (later) tin; cf L *stagnum*, a pond; perh the superficial similarity of molten tin to a sheet of water caused the former to be named after the latter. (E & M.)

staped(i)-, stapedio-: (the 2nd irreg) from L *stapes* (gen *stapedis*), a stirrup, hence, in E An and Zoo, the stirrup bone (in the ear). Exx: *stapedectomy* (cf *-ectomy* at *-tome*); *stapediform*, stirrup-shaped; An *stapediovestibular*.

staphyl(o)-: Gr *staphul(o)-*, c/f of *staphulē*, a bunch of grapes; IE r, perh *stab(h)-* or *steb(h)-*. In E, it denotes either 'uvula', as in *Staphylococcus*, or 'staphylococcic', as in *staphylo-angina*.

stasi-; -stasia, -stasis: resp from Gr *stasis*, a standing still, a stoppage, akin to *histanai*, to cause to stand: cf STATIC and, here, *-stat*; Gr *-stasia*, end-c/f from *stasis*, and syn with *-stasis*, Gr *-stasis*, for Gr *stasis*. Exx: *stasiphobia*, dread of standing up, and *stasimetric* (adj), measuring position; *menostasia* (cf *meno-*); *thrombostasis* (cf *thrombo-*).

-stat, 2 -static, 3 -statics; 4 stat-, 5 stato-: ult, all from Gr *histanai*, to cause to stand: resp, Gr *-statēs*, something that renders stationary; from the Gr adj *statikos*, causing to stand, but also the c/f of E *static*; c/f of E *statics*; c/f of *static*; from the Gr p adj *statos*, brought to a stand, standing, stationary, fixed. Cf STATIC. Exx: *hydrostat*, from Gr *hudrostatēs*, a hydrostatic balance; *rheostatic* (cf *rheo-*) and *dynamostatic* (cf *dynamo-*); *rheostatics*; *statvolt=stat(ic)+volt*; *statocyst* (*-cyst*) and *statometer*.

statisto-: for *statistics*, as in *statistology*.

stato- (1). See *-stat*.

stato- (2): for E *state* (n), as in *statolatry*, an excessive respect (cf *-latry* at *-later*) for the state.

staur(o)-: Gr *staur(o)-*, c/f of *stauros* (s *staur-*), a cross, akin to the *-staur-* of L *instaurare*, (v.t.) to stand up again, to restore, and to Gr *histanai*, to

cause to stand. Exx: Zoo *stauraxonia* (Gr *axōn*, axis); *staurolatry*, worship of the Cross.

-stearin; steari-, stear(o)-: resp for E *stearin(e)* (adj *stearic*), from F *stéarine*, from Gr *stear*, tallow, whence the E c/f *stear(o)-*; *stear* (στέαρ) is akin to Skt *stīyā*, standing water, and perh to Gr *histanai*, to cause to stand. Exx: *steariform*; *petrostearin* (cf *petro-*); Med *stearrh(o)ea* (cf *-rrhoea*). Cf:

steat(o)-: Gr *steat(o)-*, c/f of *stear*, tallow, gen *steatos*: cf prec. Exx: *steatogenous*, fat-producing (cf *-genous* at *-gen*); *steatopygia*, excessive fat on the buttocks (cf *-pygal*).

stegano-, steg(o)-; -stege, -stegite: resp Gr *stegano-*, c/f of *steganos* (adj of *stegē*), covered, roofed; G *steg(o)-*, c/f of *stegē*, var *stegos*, a covering, a roof, (hence) a house; from Gr *stegē*, a roof; Gr *steg(ē)+*Sci n suffix *-ite*: *stegē* and *stegos* are akin to Gr *stegein* (s *steg-*), to cover; IE r, either *steg-* or *stag-* (cf Skt *sthagati*. he shields, protects), or, without IE prefix *s-*, *teg-* (cf L *tegere*, to cover, protect).

Exx: *steganopod* (cf *-pod*), *steganography* (cryptography); *stegocarpous* (cf *-carpous* at *-carp*); *gastrostege*, a protective scale on a snake's belly (cf *-gaster*); *omostegite* (cf *omo-*).

steiro-: from Gr *steiros*, barren: cf STERILE. Ex Bot *Steironema* (cf *-nema*).

-stele; stelo-: from Gr *stēlē*, an upright stone, a stone pillar, akin to Gr *stellein* (s *stell-*: cf STALL), to set or place; Gr *stēlo-*, c/f of *stēlē*. Exx: *monostele* (cf *mono-*); *stelography*, Gr *stēlographia*, a writing on a stele.

stelli-: L *stēlli-*, c/f of *stēlla*, a star: cf STAR. Exx: *stelliferous* (cf *-ferous* at *-fer*), L *stellifer*, abounding in stars; *stelliscript*, that which the stars write.

stelo-. See *-stele*.

stemmati-: from *stemmat-*, the o/s of Gr *stemma* (pl *stemmata*), a garland, hence, in Zoo, an insect's ocellus or simple eye; akin to Gr *stephein* (s *steph-*), to put round. Ex: *stemmatiform*, resembling a stemma.

-stemonous, 'having such a stamen or so many stamens': Gr *stēmon-*, o/s of *stēmōn*, a thread: cf STAMEN)+adj suffix *-ous*. Ex: Bot *isostemonous*, having as many stamens as perianth divisions.

steno-; -stenosis: from Gr *stenos* (s *sten-*), narrow, close, (hence) little, IE r, prob *sten-*. Exx: *stenogastric*, narrow-abdomened; *stenographer*, from *stenography*, shorthand (whence also *stenographic*, cf F *sténographique*), itself= *steno-+-graphy*, writing, q.v. at *-graph*; *stenometer*; *stenopetalous* and *stenosepalous*, narrow-petaled and -sepaled.

stentoro-: from Gr *stentōr*, a very loud-voiced man (as the herald Stentor in the Iliad), akin to Skt *stānati*, he thunders or roars. The adj *stentorian* is an E *-an* or *-ian* derivative from LL *stentoreus*, from Gr *stentoreios*, adj of *stentōr*. Ex: *stentorophone* (cf *-phon*).

stephan(o)-: from Gr *stephanos* (whence E *Stephen*), a garland or circlet or crown from, *stephein* (s *steph-*), to put (e.g., flowers) round (e.g., one's head); prob IE r, *\*ste-*: cf the *ste-* of Gr *stellein* (s *stel-*), to set, put, place. Ex: *Stephanoceros* (cf *-ceros*).

**sterco-; stercor(i)-**: irreg from L *stercus*, dung, and reg (*stercori-*) from *stercor-*, the o/s (gen *stercoris*) of *stercus*, ? orig echoic. Exx: *stercovorous*, dung-eating (cf *-vorous* at *-vora*); *stercor(a)emia* (cf *haema-*); *stercoricolous*, dung-inhabiting, as certain insects.

**stere(o)-**: Gr *stere(o)-*, c/f of *stereos*, hard, solid, akin to ON *storr*, proud, Skt *sthiráš*, strong, and E STARE. Exx: *stereagnosis*=*stere(o)*+Gr privative prefix *a-*, not+*gnōsis*, knowledge; *stereochemistry*, the chemistry of (the arrangement of) atoms in space; *stereography*, the delineation, on a plane, of solid bodies; *stereoscope* (cf *-scope*), after TELESCOPE; *stereotype* (n, hence v), from the F adj *stéréotype*.

**-steresis**: from Gr *sterēsis*, deprivation, from *stereō* (s *ster-*), I deprive, akin to E STEAL. Ex: *glossosteresis* (cf *glosso-* at *-glossa*).

**sterno-**: from SciL *sternum*, from Gr *sternon*, the breast, chest; IE r, *\*ster-* to stretch: cf L *sternere* (s *stern-*), to stretch, and E STREET. Exx: ('breast') *sternomancy*, divination (*-mancy*) by marks on the breast; ('sternal and') *sternothyroid* (cf *thyro-*). Cf *stetho-*.

**sterro-**: from Gr *sterros*, firm, perh akin to STARK. Ex: *sterrometal*.

**stheno-**: from Gr *stenthos*, strength; as in *sthenochire*, an instrument for strengthening the fingers (Gr *kheir*, hand) for piano-playing.

**steth(o)-**: Gr *stēth(o)-*, c/f of *stēthos* (s *stēth-*: cf *sterno-*), the breast or chest. Exx: *stethometer*, *stethophone*, *stethoscope*—cf *-meter*, *-phore*, *-scope*.

**stibio-**: from L *stibium*, antimony, from Gr *stibi*. Ex: *stibiokonite* (Gr *konis*, dust).

**-stich, -stichous; sticho-**: resp Gr *-stikhon*, end-c/f of *stikhos* (s *stikh-*), a line or row; Gr *-stikhos*, adj c/f of *stikhos*; Gr *stikho-*, front c/f of *stikhos*, akin to E STY (ocular). Exx: *distich*, a couplet, L *distichon*, Gr *distikhon*, n from neus of adj *distikhos*, of two (prefix *di-*) lines; *distichous* (L *distichus*, Gr *distikhos*); *polystichous*, arranged in many (or several) lines or rows, from Gr *polustikhos*.

**stigmati-; stigmeo-** (rare) and **stigmo-**: from L *stigma*, gen *stigmatis*, from Gr *stigma* (gen *stigmatos*); (*stigmeo-*) from Gr *stigmē*, a prick, a point; (*stigmo-*) from the syn Gr *stigmos*: cf STIGMA. Exx: *stigmeology*, art of punctuation; *stigmonose*, a plant disease (cf *noso-*) characterized by dots caused by punctures insect-made. Cf-*stixis* and:

**stigono-**: from Gr *stigōn* (gen *stigōnos*), one who marks, (hence also) one who is marked, akin to *stizein*, to prick. Ex: *stigonomancy*, divination (*-mancy*) by writing on the bark of a tree. Cf prec.

**stilli-**: from L *stilla*, a drop (of water): cf DISTIL. Exx: *stillicide*, a continual dripping (L *cadere*, to fall); *stilliform*, drop-shaped.

**stilo-**, as in Bot *Stilophora* (threadlike seaweed): rom L *stilus*, q.v. at STYLE.

**stilpno-**: from Gr *stilpnos*, shining, radiant, akin to *stilbein*, to shimmer. Ex: *stilpnosiderite*.

**stipi-, 2 stipit(i)-, 3 stipuli-; 4 -stipular, 5 -stipulate**: resp from L *stīpes* (s *stip-*), a stock or branch or post, whence, incidentally, the Bot *stipe*; 2, from *stīpit-*, the o/s of L *stīpes*, gen *stīpitis*; 3, from E *stipule*, via F from L *stipula* (a dim of *stipes*), a stalk or stem; 4, end-c/f of E *stipular*, the adj of *stipule*; 5, c/f of the E adj *stipulate*—cf (the v) STIPULATE. Cf next.

Exx: *stipiform*, *stipitiform*, stalk-like: *stipuliferous* (cf *-ferous* at *-fer*); *bistipular*, *bistipulate*, having two stipules.

**stirpi-**: from L *stirps* (gen *stirpis*), stem, stock: cf EXTIRPATE. Ex: *stirpiculture*, the breeding of special stocks.

**-stixis**: from Gr *stixis*, a puncture, as in *osteostixis* (cf *osteo-*). Cf *stigmeo-* and *stigono-*.

**stoichio-**: from Gr *stoikheion* (s *stoikh-*), a step, (hence) a first principle, a first element, akin to *steikhein* (s *steikh-*), to go, to walk, to advance; IE r, prob *\*stegh-* or *\*steigh-*. Exx: *stoichiology*, the science of the elements composing animal tissues; Chem *stoichiometry* (cf *-metry* at *-meter*).

**-stole**: Gr *-stolē*, an end-c/f from *stellein*, to set or put: cf STALL. Exx: *diastole* and *systole*, from Gr *diastolē* (prefix *dia-*) and *sustolē* (prefix *su-* for *sun*, with).

**stoloni-**, as in Bot *stoloniferous* (cf *-fer*): from L *stolō* (gen *stolōnis*), a shoot, a sucker, akin to Gr *stelekhos*.

**-stoma, 2 -stomata, 3 -stomate, 4 -stomatous, 5 -stome, 6 -stomi, 7 -stomia, 8 -stomous, 9 -stomum, 10 -stomus, 11 -stomy; 12 stoma-, 13 stomati-, 14 stomato-, 15 stom(o)-**: all, ult, from Gr *stoma* (s *stom-*) mouth, akin to Skt *staman-*, muzzle or large mouth, and Hit *stamar*, mouth. Resp: from Gr *stoma* (whence Sci *stoma*, mouth or mouth-like opening); 2, from Gr *stomata*, pl of *stoma*; 3, prob from *stomat-*, o/s of *stoma*; 4=*stomat-*+ suffix *-ous* (—3 and 4 are varr of syn 8); 5 (*-stome*), from ScL, from G, *stoma*; 6, pl of 10 (*-stonus*); 7, Gr *-stomia*, an abstract derivative of *stoma* or perh of *-stomos* (see next); 8 (*-stomous*), from Gr *-stomos*, mouthed, from *stoma*; 9 and 10, *-stomum* and *-stomus* are SciL derivatives of Gr *stoma*, prob influenced by *-stomos*; 11 (*-stomy*), from Gr *-stomia*, cf 7; 12 (*stoma-*), short for *stomato-*; 13 (*stomati-*) irreg for 14, *stomat(o)-*, from Gr *stomat(o)-*, the c/f of *stoma*, gen *stomatos*; 15, *stom(o)-*, from Gr *stom(o)-*, c/f of *stoma*.

Exx: *cryptostoma*, a concealed (*crypto-*) mouth; *Cryptostomata*, a Pal order of creatures with such mouths; *cyclostomate*, round-mouthed, cf *cyclo-*; *cyclostomatous*; *siphonostome* (cf *siphono-*); *Plagiostomi* (*plagio-*); *stenostomia* (*steno-*); *gnathostomous* (*gnatho-*); *Solenostomus* (*soleno-*) and *Amphistomum* (prefix *amphi-*); *lipostomy* (*lipo-*); *stomatiferous* (*-ferous* at *-fer*); *stomatology*, science of the mouth; *stomod(a)eum*, the mouth, section of the alimentary canal: *stom(o)-*+Gr *hodaios*, on the way (*hodos*: ὁδός).

**storio-**: for *story* (tale), as in *storiology*. The var *stori-* occurs in *storify* (cf *-fy*).

**strabismo-**; **strabo-**: for SciL *strabismus*, from Gr *strabismos*, from *strabizein*, to squint, from ad *strabo* (squinting, distorted), whence obviously *strabo-*; *strabos* is akin to *streblos*, crooked, twisted (s *streb-*+extension *-l-*+*-os*); IE r, *\*streb-*, with var *\*strebh-*, to turn or twist. Exx: *strabismometry*, measurement (cf *-meter*) of the extent of *strabismus* —the instrument being a *strabismometer* or a *strabometer*. Cf *strepho-*.

**strati-**: L *strāti-*, c/f of *strātum*, a covering, n from the neus of *strātus*, pp of *sternere*, to spread: cf STRATUM. Exx: *stratiform*, resembling a stratum; *stratify* (cf *-fy*), from ML *strātificāre*; *stratigraphy*, the geology of strata. Cf the 2nd *strato-*.

**strato-** (1): Gr *strato-*, c/f of *stratos* (s *strat-*), an army: cf STRATEGY. Exx: *stratocracy*, government (cf *-cracy*) by an army; *stratography*, a treatise on the handling of an army.

**strato-** (2): for *stratus*, a cloud resembling a vast coverlet: see *strati-*. It denotes 'stratus and', as in *strato-cumulus*.

**stremmato-**, as in *stremmatograph* (for determining stresses in fibres): from Gr *stremma* (gen *stremmatos*), a twist. Cf:

**strepho-**, **strept(o)-**; **strepsi-**: from, resp, Gr *strephein* (s *streph-*), to turn, to twist; Gr *strept(o)-*, c/f of *streptos*, twisted, pp of *strephein*; Gr *strepsis*, a turning, a twisting, akin to *strepsein*, to twist; Gr s, *strep-*; IE r, *\*streb(h)-*, to turn, to twist (cf *strobo-*). Exx: Med *strephosymbolia*, which= *strepho-*+SYMBOL+Med suffix *-ia*; *streptococcus*, bacteria (cf *-coccus*) occurring in chain-formations; *Strepsiceros* (cf *-ceros*) and *Strepsiptera* (cf *-ptera*, from Gr *p eron*, a wing).

**strigi-**: from L *strix* (gen *strigis*), a screech owl: echoic: Ex: *Strigiformes*.

**strobili-**: from LL *strobilus*, a pine cone, from Gr *strobilos*: cf next. Ex: Bot *strobiliferous*, bearing strobiles (from *strobilus*).

**strobo-**: from Gr *strobos*, a whirling, akin to *strephein*, to turn, to twist: cf *strepho-*. Ex: *stroboscope*, an instrument (cf TELESCOPE) for studying motion either variable or periodic.

**-stroma**; **stromati-** or **stromato-**: c/ff of Gr *strōma*, o/s *strōmat-* (gen *strōmatos*), a couch or bed, akin to *strōnnunai*, for *stornunai* (s *storn-*) and L *sternere* (s *stern-*), to strew or spread: cf, therefore, STREET. Exx: *xylostroma* (cf *xylo-*); *stromatiform* and *stromatology*, the science and history of stratified rocks.

**strombi-**; **strombuli-**: from L *strombus*, a spiral snail, and SciL *Strombus*; and from SciL dim *strombulus*. The L *strombus* transliterates Gr *strombos* (s *stromb-*), a nasalized cognate of *strobos* (see *strobo-*); basic idea—'to turn or twist'. Exx: *strombiform*, resembling a member of the Zoo genus Strombus; *strombuliform*, top-shaped.

**stroph(o)-**: Gr *stroph(o)-*, c/f of *strophos* (s *stroph-*), a twisting, a turning, akin to *strephein* (s *streph-*), to turn or twist: cf *strepho-*, *strobo-*, *strombi-*, esp STROPHE. Ex: *Strophanthus*, a genus

of trees having flowers (cf *-anth*) with twisted lobes.

**strumi-**: for L and Med E *strūma* (o.o.o.), an enlargement or swelling (now esp a goitre), as in *strumiferous*, goitre-producing; adjj *strumose*, *strumous*, from the derivative L adj *strumōsus*.

**struthi-**, **struthio-**, **struthioni-**: all for and from L *strūthiō* (gen *strūthiōnis*, o/s *strūthiōn-*), an ostrich, from Gr *strouthiōn*, itself a modification of *strouthos*, a bird: cf OSTRICH. Exx: *struthiform* and *Struthioniformes*; *Struthiomimus* (*-mimus*), *Struthiopteris* (*-ptera*).

**stulti-**: L *stulti-*, c/f of *stultus*, foolish. Exx: STULTIFY; *stultiloquence*, silly chatter (cf *-loquence*).

**stupe-**. See *stupefy*, at STUPID. Cf *stupori-*, for E *stupor*, as in *stuporific*.

**-stylar**, 2 **-style**, 3 **-stylic**, 4 **-stylous**, 5 **-styly**; 6 **styli-**, 7 **styl(o)-**: all, ult, from Gr *stulos*, a pillar, s *stul-*, akin to *staur-*, s of *stauros*, a stake; IE r, prob *\*stu-*, to be firm—or upright—or firmly upright. Resp: 1, adj of *-style*; 2, from Gr *-stulos* (neu *-stulon*), having a specified number of pillars, hence, in Sci, denoting a stylar process; 3, adj c/f from Gr *stulos*; 4, from Gr *-stulos*, having such or so-many pillars; 5, abstract-n formation from, or, at the least, answering to, *-stylous*; 6, for E *style*, a pillar; 7, Gr *stul(o)-*, c/f of *stulos*, a pillar.

Exx: *blastostylar*, adj of *blastostyle* (cf *blasto-*); *peristyle*, via F and L from Gr *peristulon*, a colonnade *peri* or around a courtyard or a building; Zoo *hyostylic* (*hyo-*); *monostylous* and *monostyly* (*mono-*); *styliferous*, bearing (cf *-ferous* at *-fer*) Bot or Zoo styles; *styloglossal* (cf *-glossa*)— *stylolite* (cf *-lite*)—*stylometer*.

**suavi-**: ML *suāvi-*, L *suāui-*, c/f of *suāuis*, ML *suāvis*, sweet: cf SUAVE. Ex: *suaviloquence*, agreeable speech (cf *-loquence*), L *suāuiloquentia*.

**suberi-**: from L *sūber*, cork-tree, whence Bot *suber* (adj *suberic*), cork-tissue, outer bark of cork-tree, perh akin to Gr *suphar*, wrinkled skin. Ex: *suberiferous* (cf *-ferous* at *-fer*).

**succini-**; **succin(o)-**: for E *succin* (amber), ? b/f from the adj *succinic* (F *succinique*), from L *suc(c)inum* (amber), which itself has c/f *succin(o)-*. Prob *suc(c)inum*, akin to Lith *sakas*, resin, has been influenced by L *sūcus* (s *sūc-*), juice; perh, however, *sūcinum* (amber regarded as a solidified distillation) does, after all, derive from *sūcus*. Exx: *succiniferous*, amber-yielding; *succino(-)sulphuric*.

**sucr(o)-**: from F *sucre*, sugar (cf SUGAR); as in *sucro-acid*.

**sudi-**, as in *sudiform*, resembling a stake: from L *sudis*, a stake: o.o.o.

**sudori-**: for L *sūdor*, sweat (cf SWEAT). Ex: *sudorific* (cf *-fic*).

**sui-** (1): L *suī*, of oneself, or, adj, of one's own, the gen of *sē*, oneself, and of *suus*, one's own. Exx: SUICIDE; *suigeneric(al)*, from L *sui generis*, of one's, or its, own kind.

**sui-** (2): from L *sūs* (gen *suis*), a hog, a boar, akin to Gr *hus* (gen *huos*) and Skt *sū-karas*, pig. Ex: *suiform*, porcine, piglike.

**sulci-**, **sulco-**; **sulcato-**: from L *sulcus*, a furrow, whence *sulcāre*, to furrow, with pp *sulcātus*, whence *sulcato-*, furrowed, grooved; *sulcus* is akin to Gr *holkos*, traction, *helkein*, to draw or pull, and perh to Lit *velkù*, I draw or pull. Exx: *sulciform*; An *sulco-marginal*; *sulcato-costate*.

**sulf(o)-**, 2 **sulph(o)-**; 3 **sulfato-**, 4 **sulphato-**; 5 **sulphino-**, 6 **sulphito-**, 7 **sulphon-** or 8 **sulfon-**, 9 **sulphureo-**: all, ult, from L *sulpur, sulphur, sulfur*, o.o.o.: resp, 1, for *sulpho-*, which (2) is app short for the non-existent *sulphuro-*; 3, 4 stand for *sulphate*, as *sulphino-* (5) stands for *sulphinic* and 6 *sulphito-* for *sulphite*; 7, 8 (*sulphon-, sulfon-*) for *sulphonic, sulfonic*; 9 (*sulphureo-*) for *sulphureous*. Exx: *sulfo(-)acid*, *sulpho(-)chloride*; *sulphato* (or *sulfato*)-*carbonic*; *sulphon(-)amine*; *suphureo(-) nitrous*.

**Sumero-**: for *Sumerian*, as in *Sumerology*, a or the study of the ancient Sumerian civilization.

**supero-**: from L *superus*, upper, higher. Ex: ('situated above and'): *superodorsal*. Cf the prefix *super-*.

**surculi-**: from L *surculus*, a sucker, dim of *surus*, a stake, akin to Skt *svárus*, a long stake planted in the earth, and OHG *swir*, a stake. Ex: *surculigerous*, surculose (sucker-producing: cf *-gerous* at *-ger*).

**surdi-**, irreg **surdo-**: from L *surdus* (s *surd-*), deaf: cf ABSURD. Exx: *surdimutism*, the being deaf and dumb (MUTE); *surdo(-)mute*, a deaf-mute.

**sychno-**: from Gr *sukhnos*, much, abounding, frequent perh akin to *sēkos*, an enclosed place. Ex: *sychnocarpous* (cf *-carp*), bearing several successive crops.

**syco-**: Gr *suko-*, c/f of *sukon* (s *suk-*), a fig, as in *sycomancy*, divination by fig leaves, and in SYCOPHANT, q.v.

**syeno-**: for E *syenite*, a granite anciently quarried at *Syene* (L *Syēnē*, Gr *Suēnē*) in Upper Egypt. Exx: *syenodiorite* and *syenogabbro*.

**syllabi-**: L *syllabi-* (only in simple derivatives— not in cpds), from *syllaba* (Gr *sullabē*): see SYLLABLE. Ex: *syllabification* (cf *-fication* at *-fic*).

**sylvi-**. See *silvi-*.

**symbolo-**: Gr *sumbolo-*, c/f of *sumbolon*, a sign: cf SYMBOL. Exx: *symbololatry* (cf *-latry* at *-later*), excessive respect for, or use of, symbols; *symbolology*, rare for *symbology*, which=*symbo(l)*+*-logy*, q.v. at *-loger*. The rare *symbolaeo-* or *symboleo-*, as in *symbol(a)eography*, the art of drawing-up legal documents, comes from the derivative Gr *sumbolaion*, a sign or token, hence a contract.

**symmetro-**: for *symmetry*, as in *symmetrophobia*, an acute dislike of symmetry.

**sympathetico-**, **sympatheto-**, **sympathico-**: resp for *sympathetic*, for the same, and for *sympathic*: cf SYMPATHY. Exx: *sympatheticotonia* (cf *-tonia*); *sympathetoblast* (cf *-blast*); *sympathicotonia*; *sympathomimetic* (cf MIME).

**sympho-**: irreg from Gr *sumphōnos*, harmonious, as in Bot *symphogenous* (cf *-genous* at *-gen*).

**symphori-**: from Gr *sumphoros*, accompanying (cf *-phora*); as in Bot *Symphoricarpos* (Gt *karpos*, fruit, c/f *-carp*).

**symphy-**, **symphyo-**: from Gr *sumphuesthai*, to grow together, or rather from *sumphuēs*, growing together; as in Bot *symphycarpous* (cf *-carpous* at *-carp*).

**sympieso-**, **sympiezo-**: from Gr *sumpiesis*, compression (*piezein*, to press); as in *sympiesometer*.

**symposi-**, as in *symposiarch*, chairman (jocosely toastmaster) of a banquet, from Gr *sumposiarkhēs*, cf *-arch*.

**symptomato-**: from Gr *sumptōma* (a symptom), gen *sumptōmatos*: cf SYMPTOM. Ex: *symptomatology*, the study of Med symptoms.

**synapto-**: from Gr *sunaptos*, fastened together; as in *Synaptosaurus* (cf *-saur*).

**synchro-**; **synchrono-**: resp for E *synchronism*, as in *synchroscope* (cf *-scope*), and for Gr *sunkhronos*, simultaneous, as in *synchronograph* and *synchronology*.

**syndesm(o)-**: from Gr *sundesmos* (*sun-*, with+ *desmos*, a bond); as in *syndesmology*, the anatomy of bodily ligaments, and *syndesmotomy* (cf *-tomy*, a cutting, at *-tome*).

**synechio-**, as in *synechiology*, a doctrine of continuity: from Gr *sunekheia*, (lit) a holding together, (hence) continuity; Surg var *synecho-*, as in *synechotomy* (cf *-tomy* at *-tome*).

**synovi-**: for An *synovia* (cf *synovitis*), as in *synoviparous* (cf *-para*), secreting synovia.

**syphil(o)-**: for E *syphilis*. Exx: *syphilogenesis*, the development (cf *-genesis* at *-gen*); *syphilopsychosis*, a psychosis resulting from syphilis.

**syring(o)-**: Gr *suring(o)-*, c/f of *surinx* (gen *suringos*), a pipe, (hence) a fistula: cf SYRINGE. Ex: *syringotomy* (cf *-tomy* at *-tome*).

**Syrio-**: **Syro-**:- for *Syrian*, as in *Syriology*; Gr *Suro-*, c/f of *Suros*, Syrian, as in *Syro-Roman*.

**tabe-**, **tabi-**, **tabo-**: L *tābe-*, *tābi-*, c/ff of *tābēs* (s *tab-*), a wasting; *tabo-*, irreg from E *tabes*; cf THAW. Exx: *tabefy* (cf *-fy*), to waste away, via F from LL *tābefacere*, to melt; *tabific*, causing (cf *-fic*) waste; *taboparalysis*. The Sci c/f *tabeti-*, as in *tabetiform*, resembling *tabes*, progressive emaciation, comes from a misapprehension: the L gen is *tābis*, not *tābetis*.

**tac-**: a Sci c/f from L *tactus*, (sense of) touch; as in *tacnode* (cf NODE).

**tacheo-**, **tacho-**, **tachy-**; **tachisto-**: 1st, from *takheos*, gen of Gr *takhos*, speed; 2nd from *takhos*; 3rd represents *takhu-*, c/f of Gr *takhus* (s *takh-*), swift, quick, a word o.o.o.; *tachisto-*, from Gr *takhistos* (s *takh-*), swiftest, the sup of *takhus*. Exx: *tacheometer*=*tachometer*, a speed-reckoner; *tachymeter*, a theodolite for quickly determining distances and bearings; *tachygraphy*, shorthand, as if from Gr *takhugraphia*, from *takhugraphos*, a shorthand writer; *tachistoscope* (cf *-scope*)— one of the exceedingly numerous offspring of *telescope*.

**-tactic**: Gr *-taktikos*, c/f of *taktikos*, arrangeable; adj answering to nn in *-taxis*, q.v. at *taxeo-*. Ex: *phyllotactic* (cf *phyllo-*.

**tacto-**: from L *tactus* (s *tact-*), touch (cf TACT)

as in *tactometer*, an instrument testing acuteness of touch.

**taeni-, taenia-; taenio-**: first two, c/ff of L, hence E, *taenia*, a ribbon or fillet, (hence) a tapeworm, from Gr *tainia*, whence the c/f *tainio-*, whence the E c/f *taenio-*; s *taen-*, Gr *tain-*; IE r, \**tan-* or \**ten-* (? akin to the *ten-* of L *tenuis*). Exx: *taeniacide* or *taenicide*, a remedy that destroys (cf *-cide* at *-cidal*) tapeworms; *Taenisomi*, a sub-order of elongate fishes—cf Gr *sōma*, body. Cf *-tene*.

**talco-**: for *talcum*, as in *talcochlorite*.

**tali-, tal(o)-**: from L *tālus* (s *tāl-*), ankle, heel; perh of Celtic origin, certainly of Celtic relationship. Exx: *taligrade* (cf *-grade*), walking mostly on the heels; *talotibial*. The L derivative *tālipēs*, clubfoot, yields c/f *talipo-*, as in Surg *talipomanus*.

**tango-**, 'touch': from L *tangere* (s *tang-*), to. touch: cf TANGENT. Ex: *tangoreceptor*.

**tanni-; tanno-**: the former, for *tannin*; the latter for either *tannin* or *tannic*: cf TAN. Exx: *tanniferous*, tannin-producing (cf *-ferous* at *-fer*); *tannogen* (*-gen*) and *tannometer*.

**tantali-, tantalo-**: for the metallic element *tantalum* (cf TANTALIZE). Exx: *tantali-* or *tantalofluoride*.

**tany-**, 'outstretched': Gr *tanu-*, c/f from *tanuein* (s *tanu-*, r \**tan-*: cf *taeni-* above), to stretch. Ex: *tanystomatous*, with outstretched mouth (cf *-stoma*).

**tapin(o)-**: Gr *tapeino-*, c/f of *tapeinos*, (lit) depressed, low, (hence) base; s *tapein-*, extension of \**tap-*, IE r *tap-*, to press or squeeze. Ex: *tapinocephalic*, having a low, flattened skull (cf *cephalo-*).

**tardi-**: L *tardi-*, c/f of *tardus* (s *tard-*), slow: cf TARDY. Exx: *tardigrade*, slow-paced (cf *-grade* and GRADE); *tardiloquence*, slow speech (cf *-loquence*).

**tarsi-, tars(o)-**: for SciL *tarsus*, the ankle, from Gr *tarsos*, the flat of the foot, esp of the heel; IE r, prob \**tar-* or \**ter-*, with extension \**tars-*, \**ters-*. Exx: Zoo *Tarsipes* (L *pes*, foot); *tarsoplasty* (cf *-plasty* at *-plasia*).

**Tartaro-**: for Gr *Tartaros*, L (and E) *Tartarus*, (loosely) hell, as in *Tartarology*, doctrine about hell.

**tartrato-; tartr(o)-**: for *tartrate*, a salt of TARTAR, which itself has c/f *tartr(o)-*, as in *tartronic* (*tartro-*+*malonic*, from L *malum*, apple).

**tasi-**: from Gr *tasis* (s *tas-*), a stretching, from *teinein* (s *tein-*), to stretch; as in *tasimeter*, an instrument for measuring slight extensions or movements.

**tauri-, taur(o)-**: L *tauri-*, c/f of *taurus*; Gr *tauro-*, c/f of *tauros* (s *taur-*), bull, with various IE cognates and no irrefutable origin. Exx: *tauricide*, bull-killing; *tauromachy*, a bull-fight, bull-fighting (cf *-machy*), from Gr *tauromakhia*; *taurmorphic* (cf *-morph*), an adj applied to ancient Mediterranean bull-shaped vases.

**tauto-**: Gr *tauto-*, c/f of *tauto* (for *to auto*), the same. Exx: *tautochronous*, occupying the same time (cf *-chronous*); *tautology* (cf *-loger*), from Gr *tautologia*, verbal repetition.

**taxeo-, tax(i)-, taxo-; -taxis, -taxy**, with adj **-tactic**: all from Gr *taxis* (s *tax-*), arrangement, from *tassein* (s *tass-*), to arrange; PGr \**tags-é*; IE r, \**tag-*. Exx: *taxeopod* (cf *-pod*, -foot), *taxeo-* representing Gr *taxeōs*, the gen of *taxis*; *taxidermy*, whence *taxidermist*, a preparer and mounter of animal skins: cf *-dermy* at *-derm*; *taxonomy* (cf *-nomy* at *nomo-*), classification; (from Gr *-taxis*, an end-c/f of *taxis*) *syntaxis*, 'modernized' as SYNTAX; *heterotaxy* (cf *hetero-*), abnormal or eccentric arrangement; see *-tactic*.

**techni-, 2 technico-, 3 techno-; 4 -technics, 5 -techny**: all, ult, from Gr *tekhnē*, craft, skill, art: cf TECHNICAL. Resp: 1, irreg for *techno-*; 2, for *technic*(al); 3, Gr *tekhno-*, c/f of *tekhnē*; 4, from Gr *tekhnika*, matters of art or craft; 5, Gr *-tekhnia*, an abstract-n derivative (suffix *-ia*) of *tekhnē*.

Exx: *techniphone* (cf *-phone*), a dumb clavier for the musical exercise of one's fingers; *technicology*, now rare for *technology* (Gr *tekhnologia*, an artfull or systematic treatment); *pyrotechnics* (cf *pyro-*), fireworks; *theotechny* (*theo-*), an imaginary world or society of gods participating in human affairs. Cf the 1st *tecto-*.

**tecno-**: Gr *tekno-*, c/f of *teknon*, a child (s *tekn-*, r *tek-*); as in *tecnology*, child-study.

**-tect**, as in *architect*: from Gr *-tektōn*, end-c/f of *tektōn*, a carpenter, a builder. Cf the 1st *tecto-*.

**tecti-**: either from L *tectus*, covered, pp of *tegere* (s *teg-*), to cover, (hence) to roof (cf PROTECT), as in Zoo *Tectibranchia* (Gr *brankhion*, a gill: cf *-branch*), or from L *tectum*, a roof (n from the neus of *tectus*, covered), as in *tectiform*, resembling a roof or a lid, serving as a lid.

**tecto- (1)**: Gr *tekto-*, c/f of *tektōn* (whence the adj *tektonikos*, E *tectonic*), a carpenter, a builder, akin to *tekhnē*: cf TECHNICAL and ARCHITECT. Exx: *tectosphere* (cf *-sphaera*), the asthenosphere, a hypothetical zone that, 30 miles below the earth's surface, is supposed to yield easily to stresses; *Tectospondyli* (cf *-spondyli*).

**tecto- (2)**: from L *tectum* (s *tect-*), a roof: cf *tecti-*. Ex: *tectocephalic* (cf *cephalo-*), with a roof-shaped head.

**[-teen**, as in *thirteen*, *fourteen* . . . *nineteen*: ME *-tene*, OE *-tyne*, *-tēne*, *-tiene*, akin to G *zehn*, MHG *zehen*, OHG *zehan*, ten: cf TEN.]

**tekno-**: var of *tecno-*, as in *teknonymy* (cf *-onym*, name), the naming, as in certain savage races, of the parent after the child.

**[tele-**, afar off, from afar: see Prefixes.]

**tele(o)-**; occ shortened to **tel-**: from Gr *teleos* (s *tele-*, r *tel-*), complete, perfect, akin to *telos* (s *tele-*, r *tel-*), complete, perfect, akin to *telos* (s *tel-*), end, q.v. at *telo-*. Exx: *Telanthera* (*tel-*=*teleo-*; cf *-anth*, flower); *teleorganic*, vital.—Occ for *telo-*, as in *teleology*, q.v. at *telo-*.

**teleuto-**: from Gr *teleutē*, completion, from *teleos* (cf *teleo-*), complete. Ex: *teleutospore* (cf *-spora*).

**teli-**: from L *tēlum*, a missile, a dart, (later) a

dagger, perh akin to the *tēl-* of Gr *tēlothen*, from afar (from *tēle*, far off). Ex: *teliferous*, dart-bearing or -carrying (cf *-ferous* at *-fer*).

**telio-**: for SciL *telium*, (Bot) spore fruit of the *teliostage* or final stage; from Gr *telos* (gen *teleos*), end: cf *telo-*, Ex: *teliospore* (cf *-spora*).

**telluri-**: for E *telluric*, of or from the earth (L *tellūs*, gen *tellūris*); but also for the non-metallic element *tellurium* (*tellur*(i)+Sci suffix *-ium*), as in *telluriferous* (cf *-fer*). Cf: *telluro-*, for E *tellurous*, of tellurium.

**telmat(o)-**: Gr *telmat(o)-*, c/f of *telma* (gen *telmatos*), stagnant water, slime, mud, akin to *stalassein*, to let drip or run, and E *stale*, (of, e.g., a horse) to urinate; IE r, *\*tel-* or *\*stel*, to drip, with varr *\*(s)tal-*. Ex: *telmatology*, the physiography of swamps, peat bogs, bogs.

**tel(o)-**: Gr *tel(o)-*, c/f of *telos*, end; IE r, *\*tel-*, var *\*pel-*. Ex: *telophase*, the final phase or stage. The gen *teleos* yields the c/f *teleo-*, as in *teleology*, the philosophical study (cf *-logy* at *-loger*) of ends or purposes. Cf:

**telotero-**: from Gr *tēloteros*, adj, and *tēloterō*, adv, farther away—the comp of *tēle*, far off. Ex: *teloteropathy*, telepathy (cf *-path*).

**temno-**: from Gr *temnein* (s *temn-*, r *tem-*), to sever, esp by cutting; IE r, *\*tem-*, var *\*ten-*. Ex: *temnospondylous* (cf *-spondyli*). Cf *-tmema*.

**temporo-**, 'temporal (of the temples) and': irreg from L *tempora*, the temples of the human head; as in *temporo-mandibular* (cf *mandibulo-*).

**tendo-**: for E *tendon*: cf TENDON. Ex: *tendotomy*, the incision or the excision of a tendon. Cf *teno-*.

**-tene**: from Gr *tainia*, a ribbon: cf *taeni-*. Ex: *diplotene* (cf *diplo-*).

**tenebri-**: from L *tenebrae*, shadows, darkness, whence *tenebrōsus*, shadowy, dark, E *tenebrous*; akin to Skt *tamisrās* (pl), dark night. Ex: *tenebrific* (cf *-fic*).

**ten(o)-**; **tenont(o)-**: from Gr *tenōn* (s *ten-*), a tendon, gen *tenontos*, Gr c/f *tenont(o)-*, whence E *tenonto-*; akin to *teinein* (s *tein-*), to stretch; IE r, *\*ten-*. Exx: *tenotomy*, (the act of) dividing a tendon —cf *-tomy* at *-tome*; *tenontology*, the science of tendons. Cf:

**tensi-**; **tensio-**: both for E *tension*—cf TEND and *teno-*. Exx: *tensimeter* and *tensiometer*, instruments for measuring tension.

**tentaculi-**, **tentaculo-**: from L, and for E, *tentaculum*: see TENTACLE and cf TEMPT. Exx: *tentaculiferous*, tentacle-bearing (*-ferous*, q.v. at *-fer*); *tentaculocyst* (*-cyst*).

**tenti-**: for *tent*, as in *tentiform*, tent-shaped.

**tenui-**: L *tenui-*, c/f of *tenuis*, thin, slender; s *tenu-*, r *\*ten-*; from the root of L *tendere*, to stretch: cf *teno-*. Ex: *tenuicostate*, slender-ribbed (cf *-costal*).

**tepe-**: L *tepe-*, as in *tepefacere*, to make, become, tepid: cf TEPID.

**tephra-**, **tephro-**: Gr *tephra*, ashes, c/f *tephro-*, adopted by E, akin to Tokh A *tsak-*, to burn, and Lith *dagas*, summer (=burning) heat; IE r, *\*dhegh-*, to burn. Exx: *tephramancy*, divination

(*-mancy*) by ashes, esp from an altar-fire; (Med, 'grey matter'—from colour of ashes) *tephromyelitic* (cf *-myelia*).

**terat(o)-**: Gr *terat(o)-*, c/f of *teras* (gen *teratos*, s *ter-*), a wonder, e.g. a monster, as in *teratology*, myth-making about monstrous animals, hence (in Med) the study of monstrosities and other horrible abnormalities. Prob akin to Lith *keras*, OSl *čara*, sorcery; IE r, *\*ker-* or *\*kar-*.

**tereti-**: for E *terete*, cylindrical, from L *teres* (gen *teretis*) rounded off—prob orig by rubbing (*terere*, s *ter-*, to rub). Ex: *teretifolious* (cf *foli-*, leaf).

**tergi-**, **tergo-**: L *tergi-*, c/f of *tergum*, the back; *tergo-*, from *tergum* but influenced by the Gr connective *-o-*, as in *tergolateral*, of the back and side. Ex: *tergiversate*, from ML *tergiversātus*, pp of *tergiversāri*, L *-uersāri*, (lit) to turn the back (*terga uertere*), hence to be evasive—for the 2nd element, cf VERSE.

**termino-**: irreg from L *terminus*, a boundary, a terminus, a TERM. Esp in *terminology*, technical terms, jargon, nomenclature.

**termito-**: for E *termite*, an ant: L *termes*, a wood-worm, gen *termitis*, akin to L *terere*, to rub (cf *tereti-*). Ex: *termitophagous*, ant-eating (cf *-phaga*).

**-ternate**; **ternati-** or **ternato-**: c/ff of *ternate* (from L *ternī*, three apiece), consisting of threes, as in *biternate* and *ternati-*(or *ternato-*)*pinnate* (cf *-pinnate*).

**terp(i)-**; **terpsi-**: SciL from Gr *terpein* (s *terp-*), to gladden, as in *terpodion* (Gr *ōidē*, a song), a type of musical keyboard; Gr *terpsi-*, from *terpsis*, enjoyment (from *terpein*), as in *Terpsichorē* (Gr *khoros*, a dancing: cf CHOIR), whence *Terpsichore*, the muse of choral song and dance, whence *Terpsichorean*, of dancing.

**terra-**, **terre-**, **terr(i)-**: c/ff from, only the 3rd of, L *terra*, the earth (dry land)—cf TERRACE. Exx: *terraqueous* (*terra*+*aqueous*, from L *aquā*, water); *terremotive*, seismic, from L *terrae mōtus*, a movement of the earth, an earthquake; *terrigenous* (cf *-genous* at *-gen*), earth-born, from L *terrigena*.

**terri-** (1). See prec.

**terri-** (2); **terrori-**: from L *terrēre*, to frighten, as in TERRIFIC; from the derivative *terror*, as in *terrorific* (cf *-fic*).

**tessara-**: Gr *tessara-*, c/f of *tessares*, neu *tessara*, four: cf *tetra-*. Ex: *tessaraglot*, written, or versed in, four languages (cf *-glossa*).

**testaceo-**: for *Testaceo* (adj *testacean*), from L *testāceum*, a shelled animal, from *testa*, a shard, a shell. Ex: *testaceology*, rare for 'conchology'.

**testi-** (1): from L *testis*, a testicle, as in the Zoo adj *testicond*, having concealed testicles; for *-cond*, cf 'abs*cond*' and 're*cond*ite'—L *condere* (s *cond-*), to conceal.

**testi-** (2): L *testi-*, c/f of *testis*, a witness: cf TESTIFY.

**tetani-**; **tetane-**: the latter from Gr *tetanos*, L hence E *tetanus* (c/f *tetani-*; adj *tetanic*, L *tetanicus*,

Gr *tetanikos*), akin to Gr *teinein* (s *tein-*), to stretch. Ex: *tetanomotor*; *tetaniform*.

**tetart(o)-**, 'one fourth': Gr *tetarto-*, c/f of *tetartos*, fourth, the ordinal of *tessares*, Attic *tettares*, four. Ex: *tetartohedral*, having a quarter of the planes needed for symmetry. Cf *tessara-* and:

**tetr(a)-:** Gr *tetra-*. c/f of Attic *tettares*, *tettara*, four: cf FOUR. Exx: *tetragon* (adj *tetragonal*), a four-angled plane figure, LL *tetragōnum*, Gr *to tetragōnon*, the four-angled, usu the square, orig the neus of *tetragōnos*, four-angled, (usu) square, cf the 1st -*gon*; *tetrahedron*, a four-faced polyhedron, strictly the neus of LGr *tetraedros*, four-sided (cf -*hedral*); *tetralogy* (cf -*logy* at -*loger*), a group of four plays, novels, etc.—cf *trilogy*, a set of three; *tetrameter*, a verse-line of four feet (-*meter*, a measure); *tetrarch*, a governor (cf -*arch*) of one-fourth of a province; *tetrasyllabic*, four-syllabled, cf SYLLABLE; *tetrevangelium*, the four Gospels regarded as a unity: cf EVANGEL.

The subsidiary Gr c/f *tetrakis-*, from *tetrakis*, four times, occurs only in complex Chem terms (e.g., *tetrakisazo*, cf *azo-*).

**-teuthis,** only in Pal and Zoo: from Gr *teuthis* (s *teuth-*), a cuttlefish.

**Teuto-:** for E *Teuton*, as in *Teutolatry*, a worship of things German; or, instead of *Teutonico-*, for *Teutonic* (and), as *Teuto-Celtic*. Also, occ, *Teutono-*, as in *Teutonophobia*. Cf TEUTON.

**thalami-; thalam(o)-:** for L *thalamus*, an inner room, from Gr *thalamos*, with c/f *thalam(o)-*, perh akin to Gr *tholos* (s *thol-*), a circular tomb deep in the side of a hill: with special senses in An and Bot, as in *thalamifloral* (cf *flori-*).

**thalassi(o)-; thalass(o)-** or **thalatto-:** Gr *thalassi-* (*thalassio-* not in Gr), c/f of adj *thalassios*, marine, from *thalassa*, sea, whence the E -*ic* adj *thalassic*; *thalatto-*, Gr c/f of Attic *thalatta*, sea, as *thalasso-* is the Gr c/f of non-Attic Gr *thalassa*, o.o.o. Exx: *thalassiarch*, an admiral (cf -*arch*) and *thalassiophyte* (cf -*phyte*); *thalassocracy*, Gr *thalassokratia*, supremacy (cf -*cracy*) at sea, and *thalassophobia*, a dread of the sea; *thalattology*, sea-lore.

**thalli-; thall(o)-:** *thalli-* for *thallium* (*thall-* + Chem -*ium*), a metallic element, as in *thalliferous*, producing (cf -*ferous* at -*fer*) thallium, but also, irreg, as in *thalliform*, for SciL *thallus*, a Bot term from Gr *thallos* (s *thall-*), a young shoot or branch or frond, akin to *thallein* (s *thall-*), to be green, to blossom; *thall(o)-*, adopted from the Gr c/f of *thallos*, as in *thallophyte* (cf -*phyte*).

**thamn(o)-:** Gr *thamn(o)-*, c/f of *thamnos*, a bush, a shrub, s *thamn-*, r *tham-*; IE r, perh *dham-*, var *dhem-*. Ex: *thamnophile* (cf -*phil*), lit a bush-lover, i.e. an ant shrike.

**-thanasia; thanat(o)-:** from Gr—adopted by E— *euthanasia*, an easy (Gr *eu*, well) death; Gr *thanat(o)-*, c/f of *thanatos*, death, s *thanat-*, r prob *than-*; IE r, perh *dhan-* or *dhen-*, to die. Exx: *electrothanasia*, electrocution; *thanatology*, death-lore, the doctrine of death. The rare adj c/f -*thanatous*, death-producing, comes from *thanatos*.

**thaumat(o)-; thauma-; thaumo-,** non-Gr: Gr *thaumat(o)-*, c/f of *thauma* (gen *thaumatos*), a wonderful thing, a wonder, a miracle; IE r, perh *dhau-* or *dheu-*. Exx: *thaumatology*, a study of, erudition in, wonders and miracles; EF-F, hence E, *thaumaturge* (adj *thaumaturgic*), a wonder-worker, a miracle-worker, via ML *thaumaturgus* from Gr *thaumatourgos* (*thaumato-*+*ergos*, -worker), *thaumaturgy* deriving from Gr *thaumatourgia*, wonder-working; *thaumotrope* (cf -*trope*), an optical instrument; *thaumoscopic* (cf -*scope*).

**the-.** See *theo-*.

**theatro-:** Gr *theatro-*. c/f of *theatron*, a theatre: cf THEATER (-TRE). Exx: *theatromania*, *theatrophobia*.

**-theca,** 2 -**thecium**; 3 **theca-**, 4 **theci-**, 5 **thec(o)-:** all, via L *thēca* (adopted by Sci), from Gr *thēkē*, a box or case, akin to *tithenai*, to put or place (cf THESIS); IE r, *dhe-*. Resp: L -*thēca*, from Gr -*thēkē*, from *thēkē*; 2, SciL from Gr -*thēkē*; 3, E *theca*, a case, a sheath; 4, for L and E *theca*; 5, c/f of Gr *thēkē*.

Exx: *myxotheca* (cf *myxo-*); *Zoothecium* (cf *zoo-* at *zo-*); *thecaphore* (cf -*phora*) and *thecaspore* (cf -*spora*); *theciform*, sheath-like; *thecoglossate*, (of lizards) with a tongue (cf GLOSS) retractable into a sheath.

Cf -*thèque* in Fr *bibliothèque*, a library.

**thei-:** for SciL *Thea*, the tea plant, from the Ch source of TEA. Ex: *theiform*.

**thel(o)-:** Gr *thēl(o)-*, c/f of *thēlē*, a nipple, s *thēl-*, akin to L *fīlia*, *fīlius* (s *fīl-*), daughter, son; IE r, prob *dhēl-* or *dhil-*. Ex: *thelorrhagia*, bleeding at the nipple(s); cf *thelitis*, inflammation (cf suffix -*itis*) of the nipple(s). Cf:

**thely-,** as in *thelyplasty* (cf -*plasty* at -*plasia*), represents Gr *thelu-*, c/f of *thelus* (s *ihel-*), feminine, akin to *thēlē*, as in prec.

**the(o)-:** Gr *the(o)-*, c/f of *theos*, a god, akin to L *deus*: cf THEISM. Exx: *theocracy* (-*cracy*), government by God, or by the gods, (hence) by the Church; *theodicy*, (doctrine of) the justice (Gr *dikē*, justice) of God; *theogony*, the genealogy of the gods—cf the 2nd -GON; THEOLOGY; *theomachy* (-*machy*), a battle against, or among, gods; *theophany*, an appearance or manifestation (cf -*phane*) of God to man, LL *theophania*, Gr *theophaneia*; THEOSOPHY.

**-thèque.** See -*theca*, last para.

**-therapy.** End c/f of THERAPY.

**-there,** 2 -**theria,** 3 -**therium**; 4 **thera-,** 5 **theri(o)-,** 6 **ther(o)-:** 1–3, from Gr *thēr* (gen *thēros*) a beast; 4, from Gr *thēran* (s *thēr-*), to hunt for; 5, Gr *thēri(o)-*, c/f of *thērion*, a beast—an elaboration, or a modification, of *thēr*; 6, Gr *thēr(o)-*, c/f of *thēr*, akin to L *ferus*, wild, savage, untamed.

Exx: *megathere*, *megatherium* (cf *mega-*); *theralite* (cf -*lite*), because, anticipate, it was searched (hunted) for; *theriomancy*, divination (-*mancy*) by observation of wild animals; *therolatry*, worship (-*latry*, q.v. at -*later*) of wild animals, and *therology*, the study of wild animals, the study of mammals.

**-therm; -thermy; thermato-, therm(o)-:** first two, from Gr *thermē* (s *therm-*), heat—cf THERM; (*thermato-*) from *thermat-*, the o/s of the var *therma*, pl *thermata*; (*thermo-*) Gr *therm(o)-*, c/f of *thermē*. Exx: *megatherm* (*mega-*) and *colpotherm* (*colpo-*); *hyperthermy* (prefix *hyper-*); *thermatology*, the science of heat, esp (Med) of the use of hot baths or springs; *thermometer*, a heat-measurer (cf *-meter*)—*thermophile* (*-phile*), an organism thriving in heat—*thermostat* (*-stat*), a device for regulating the heat used.

**thero-.** See *-there.*

**-thesis;** agent, **-thete;** adj, **-thetic:** resp from Gr *thesis*, a having been placed or set, a position; from *-thetēs*, c/f of *thetēs*, one who sets or establishes, and from Gr *thetikos*, fit for placing, from *thetos* (placed), the pp of *tithenai*, to place, set, lay down: cf THESIS. Exx: *cacothesis* (cf *caco-*, bad, at *-cace*), adj *cacothetic*; *thesmothete* (see next). Cf *theso-.*

**thesmo-:** Gr *thesmo-*, c/f of *thesmos*, a law, from the root of *tithenai* (s *tithen-*, r *then-*), to set, to establish. Ex: *thesmothete*, a legislator (cf *-thete* at *-thesis*). Cf prec.

**-thete.** See *-thesis.*

**theso-:** from Gr *thesis* (see *-thesis*), a placing, a deposit; as in *thesocyte* (cf *-cyte*).

**thigmo-:** from Gr *thigma*, touch, contact (s *thigm-*, r *thig-*), akin to *thinganein* (s *thingan-*, r *thing-*, nasalization of *thig-*), to touch with the hand; akin to L *fingere*, to shape, hence create, with the hand; IE r, *\*dheig-* or *\*dheigh-*; cf FEIGN. Ex: *thigmotropism* (cf *-trope*). Cf *thixo-.*

**thin(o)-:** from *thin-*, the o/s of Gr *this* (gen *thinos*), a beach, perh akin to DUNE. Ex: *thinolite* (*-lite*, stone).

**thi(o)-** (occ **thia-**), 2 **thiono-**; 3 **-thial**, 4 **-thionic:** all from Gr *theion* (s *thei-*), brimstone, sulphur, perh from *\*theon* (or *\*theos*), smoke, vapour, and prob from an IE r *\*dheues-* (Hofmann). Resp: *thia-*, as in *thiadiazole*, is a Chem var of *thio-*, a natural c/f from *theion*, as in *Thiobacillus* and *thiocresol*; 2=*thi*(o)-+Chem n suffix *-one*+ connective *-o-*, as in *thionobenzoic*; 3 (*-thial*)= *thi*(o)-+Chem n-suffix *-al*; 4, the c/f of *thionic*, of or containing sulphur, as in *polythionic*.

**thixo-:** from Gr *thixis*, a touch: cf *thigmo-*, q.v. Ex: *thixotropy* (cf *-tropy*, at *-trope*), the property —possessed by some gels—of becoming fluid when shaken.

**thomo-:** from Gr *thōmos*, a heap, akin to OHG *tuom*, a share. Ex: *Thomomys* (cf *-mys*, mouse), a genus of gophers.

**thoraci-, thorac(o)-:** the former, from L *thōrax*, the chest, gen *thōrācis*; the latter, from Gr *thōrak(o)-*, c/f of *thōrax*, perh akin to Skt *dhārakas*, holding, a holder, with IE r *\*dhar-*, varr *\*dher-*, *\*dhor-*. Exx: *thoracispinal*; *thoracalgia* (cf *-algia*, pain) and *thoracoscope*, an instrument for inspecting (cf *-scope*) the cavity of the chest. E *thorax* has adj *thoracic*, with c/f *thoracico-.*

**thori-** and **thoro-:** for *thorium*, which, like *thorite*, derives from *Thor* (ON *Thōrr*), the

Scandinavian God of thunder, the suffixes being the Chem *-ite* and *-ium*. Exx: *thoriferous* (cf *-ferous* at *-fer*), thorium-bearing; *thorogummite=* *thoro-*+E *gum*+euphonic *-m-*+Min suffix *-ite*.

**Thraco-,** 'Thracian and': for *Thracian*; as in *Thraco-Phrygian.*

**thremmato-:** from *thremmat-*, o/s of Gr *thremma*, a nursling; as in *thremmatology*, the Bio science of breeding under domestication.

**thren(o)-:** *thrēn(o)-*, c/f of Gr *thrēnos*, a dirge, whence the literary E *threne*; akin to *threomai* (s *thre-*), I cry aloud, prob orig echoic. Ex: *threnody*, Gr *thrēnōidia* (*ōidē*, a song).

**threo-:** for *threose*, an artificial sugar. Only in Chem.

**threpso-:** from Gr *threpsis* (θρέψις), nourishment, adj *threptikos* (E *threptic*), akin to *thremma* (see *thremmato-*). Ex: *threpsology*, the study, or the science, of nutrition.

**threski-:** from Gr *thrēskia*, worship, from *thrēskos*, religion, akin to *therapōn*, a server, IE r *\*dher(e)-*. Ex: *Threskiornithae*, ibises, the sacred birds of Egypt, cf *-ornis.*

**thrio-:** from Gr *thrios*, a pebble. Ex: *thrioboly*, divination with pebbles: cf Gr *thrioboloos*, a caster (cf *-bole*) of pebbles into the urn.

**-thripsis,** a breaking into small pieces, as in *amygdalothripsis* (cf *amygdalo-*): from Gr *thripsis.*

**-thrix:** Gr *thrix*, hair; as in *lepothrix*, hair in brittle state. See *tricho-.*

**thromb(o)-:** Gr *thromb(o)-*, c/f of *thrombos*, a lump, a clot, akin to Gr *trephein* (s *treph-*), to curdle, (lit) to turn: cf *trepho-*. Exx: *thrombogen* (cf *-gen*); *thromboplastic* (cf *-plastic* at *-plasia*); cf *thrombosis* (which=*thromb(o)-*+Med suffix *-osis*), a clot in the blood-stream.

**thryono-:** from Gr *thruon*, a rush (plant). Ex: *Thryonomys* (cf *-mys*).

**thuri-:** L *thūri-*, c/f of *thūs* (gen *thūris*), incense, from Gr *thuos*; IE r, *\*thu-*. Ex: *thurifer* (E from L), incense-bearer (cf *-fer*)—an acolyte, or an altar boy, carrying a thurible (L *thūribulum*).

**thylac(o)-:** from Gr *thulax* (gen *thulakos*), var *thulakos*, a sack, a pouch, whence *thylacine*, a marsupial (or Tasmanian) wolf. Ex: *Thylacoleo* (Gr *leōn*, L *leō*, a lion).

**-thymia; thym(o)-:** Gr *-thumia*, from *thumos* (s *thum-*), spirit, emotion, courage; Gr *thumo-*, c/f of *thumos*, Gr r *\*thu-*; IE r, prob *\*dheu-* or *\*dhu*: *\*dhu-m-os* becomes *thu-m-os*. Exx: *lypothymia*, excessive or profound mental prostration (Gr *lupē*, grief); *thymogenic* (cf *-genic* at *-gen*), caused by emotion.

**thymo-** (1). See prec.

**thymo-** (2): from Gr *thumon*, thyme, but denoting 'thymol' (*thymo*+*-ol*, oil), as in *thymoquinone.*

**thymo-** (3): from Gr *thumos*, the thymus (gland), as in *thymocyte* (cf *-cyte*). Perh the Gr word is *thūmos*, to distinguish it from the *thumos* of the 1st *thymo-.*

**thyre(o)-, thyro-; -thyris:** from Gr *thureos*, a stone put against a *thura* or door to keep it open, hence an oblong (lit, door-shaped) shield, or perh from its cpd, *thureoeidēs* (from *eidos*, form), shaped like an oblong shield; *thyro-* stands for *thyroid* (Gr *thureoeidēs*); *-thyris*, from Gr *thuris* (dim of *thura*), a small door, a window, (hence) a valve. With the s *thur-*, c/f the *for-* of L *foris*, out of doors, and E DOOR. Exx: *thyreoprotein*; *thyroglossal* (cf *-glossa*, -tongue) and *thyrotherapy*; *-thyris*, only in Zoo generic names.

thyrsi-: L *thyrsi-*, c/f of *thyrsus*, borrowed from Gr *thursos*, Bacchus's ivy- or vine-encircled, (pine) cone-topped staff of office; perh of Thraco-Phrygian origin. Exx: *thyrsiferous*, thyrsus-bearing, and *thyrsigerous*, thyrsus-wielding (L *thyrsiger*: cf *-ger*).

thysan(o)-: Gr *thusan(o)-*, c/f of *thusanos* (s *thusan-*, r *thus-*), a tassel: perh cf TASSEL. Ex: *Thysanocarpus* (cf *-carpus* at *-carp*), a genus of herbs that have pods resembling tassels.

Tibeto-, 'Tibetan and': from *Tibet*; as in *Tibeto-Chinese*.

tibio-: for *tibia*, Med E from L *tībia*, a flute, hence from the shape-resemblance, the An *tibia* (bone from knee to ankle). Ex: ('of the tibia and') *tibiofemoral*.

ticho-: from Gr *teikhos*, a wall, akin to Skt *dēhí*, a wall; IE r, *\*d(h)eigh-*. Ex: *tichodrome*, a wall creeper (cf *-drome*).

tigro-: from *tigroid*, striped as a tiger, but denoting 'tigroid granules', as in *tigrolysis* (cf *-lysis* at *-lyse*).

timbro-: F *timbro-*, from *timbre*, a postage stamp, as in *timbromaniac*, one who is 'mad' on postage stamps. See TIMBRE.

timo-, as in *timocracy* (cf *-cracy*), a state governed by men of honour, ML *timocratia*, Gr *timokratia*: Gr *timo-*, c/f of *timē*, honour, value, intimately akin to *timaō*, I value or honour, and akin to the syn *tiō*, s *ti-*; r of the group, *ti-*.

tino-: from Gr *teinein* (s *tein-*), to stretch; as in Pal *Tinoceras* (cf *-ceras* at *-cera*).

tinto-: for *tint*, as in *tintometer*.

titani- and titano-, for the metallic element *titanium*, itself (Chem suffix *-ium*) from L *Titāni* (or *Titānes*), from Gr *Titānes*, the Titans or Sons of Earth, sing *Titan* (Τιτάν), akin to *titō* (τιτώ), day, sun—cf TITANIC; *Titano-*=Gr *Titāno-*, c/f of *Titan*. Exx: *titaniferous*, yielding titanium; *titanocyanide*; *Titanosaurus* (cf *-saur*).

tithono-: for *tithonic* (from L *Tithōnus*, Gr *Tithōnos*). Ex: *tithonometer*.

-tmema; -tmesis: from Gr *tmēma*, a piece cut off, a segment, hence in Bot a cell; from Gr *tmēsis*, a cutting: both akin to *temnein* (s *temn-*, r *tem-*), to cut: cf *temno-*. Ex: *dolichotmema*, a slender cell: cf *dolicho-*.

-tocia or -tokia, -tocous or -tokous; toco- or toko-: the 3rd and 4th are the adjj answering to the 1st and 2nd (SciL formations); *toco-*, *toko-*=Gr *toko-*, c/f of *tokos* (s *tok-*), childbirth, offspring, akin to *teknon* (s *tek-*), a child, and *tiktein* (r *tik-*, s *tikt-*+inf suffix *-ein*), to give birth to; cf Skt *takman-* (r *tak-*), a child. Exx: *mogitocia* (cf *mogi-*), difficult labour; *tocology*, midwifery.

tol(u)-, 'relation to *toluene*' (*tolu*+benzene) or

'relation to toluic acid': for *tolu*, balsam of Tolu (in Colombia). Ex: *tolualdehyde*. Chem affords also *toluido-* (for *toluide*) and *toluino-* (for *toluidine*).

-toma, 2 -tome, 3 -tomic, 4 -tomous, 5 -tomy; 6 tomo-: all from Gr *tomē* (s *tom-*), a cutting, a section, akin to *temnein* (s *temn-*, r *tem-*), to cut: cf ANATOMY. Resp: 'insects with a specified type of segmentation', from Gr *entoma*, insects; 2, Gr *-tomon*, from *tomos*, (the agent, or the result, of) cutting, with adjj *-tomic* (Gr *-tomikos*) and *-tomous* (Gr *-tomos*, cutting, cut, divided), the former answering also to 5, *-tomy*, from Gr *-tomia*, from *tomē*; 6, from Gr *tomos*, a cut.

Exx: *Neotoma* (cf *neo-*); *gonotome* (cf *gono-*) and *microtome*, an instrument with which to cut sections for microscopic examination; *gastrotomic* (cf *gastro-*); *isotomous* (cf *iso-*); *arteriotomy*, an incision in, an operation on, an artery, from Gr *artēriotomia*; *Tomopteris* (cf *-pteris* at *-ptera*).

Note *-tomize*, the v answering to *-tomy*, as in *laparotomize*, to make an incision in the abdominal wall, n *laparotomy* (cf *laparo-*).

Note also the cpd *-ectome* ('an instrument in ectomy'), from *-ectomy*, a cutting-out, a surgical removal, from Gr *-ektomia*, c/f of *ektomē* (prefix *ek-*+*tomē*); v, *ectomize*.

-tone, 2 -tonia, 3 -tonic, 4 -tonous, 5 -tonus, -tony; 7 tono-, 8 tonico-: all from L *tonus*, a tone, a sound, (orig) a stretching, from Gr *tonos*, tension, hence pitch or accent of the voice: cf TONE. Resp: from E *tone*, or from Gr *-tonos* (end-c/f of *tonos*), occ via LL *-tonus*; 2, Gr *-tonia*, from *tonos*; 3, either from Gr *tonikos* or simply for E *tonic*; 4, var of 3, but deriving from Gr *-tonos*, adj c/f of *tonos*; 5, SciLc/f from L *tonus*; 6, a Med, yet truly E, var of 2 (*-tonia*); 7, Gr *tono-*, c/f of *tonos*; 8, for E *tonic*.

Exx: *barytone*, from the Gr adj *barutonos*, deep-sounding (cf *bary-*), and *demitone*; *isotonia* (*iso-*); *isotonic*=Gr *isotono*s+adj suffix *-ic*; *isotonous*= Gr *isotonos*, having equal tension of unvarying pitch; *geotonus*, Plant Physio 'the normal state of an organ with reference to gravity' (Webster); *isotony*=*isotonia*; *tonology*, the history, or the science (cf *-logy* at *-loger*), of tones or of in tonation—*tonogram* (cf *-gram*)—*tonoscope* (c *-scope*).

tonsill(o)-: for E *tonsil*(s): cf TONSIL. Exx: *tonsillectomy*, surgical excision (cf *-ectomy*) of the tonsils, syn with *tonsillotomy* (cf *-tomy* in prec).

-tope, -topy; top(o)-: from Gr *topos* (s *top-*), place, *topo-* being the Gr c/f: cf TOPIC. Exx: *isotope* (cf *iso-*), in Chem an element occupying the same position in the periodic table; *isotopy*, the fact, or the phenomenon, of isotopes; *topography*, local geography, from Gr *topographia*—*toponarcosis*, a local anaesthetic—*toponymy* (cf *-onymy* at *-onym*), place-name lore, or, in An, the names in regional An—*topophobia*, a dread of certain particular places.

toreumato-: from *toreumat-*, o/s of Gr *toreuma*, embossed work, from *toreuein* (s *toreu-*), to work in relief, (lit) to bore through, akin to *tornos*, a tool for circle-drawing: Ex: *toreumatology*, the art of toreutics (from the Gr adj *toreutikos*).

**tormo-**, as in *tormodont* (cf *-odon*), having socketed teeth: from Gr *tormos*, a socket.

**toro-**, as in *Torosaurus* (cf *-saur*): from L *torus*, a protuberance.

**torpi-**; **torpori-**: from L *torpēre*, to be stiff, whence *torpor* (cf *torpor* at TORPID), whence *torpori-*. Exx: *torpify*; *torporific* (*-fic*).

**torre-**: from L *torrēre*, to cause to dry, to parch: cf TORRID. Ex: *torrefy*, to parch or scorch or subject to (great) heat, L *torrefacere*; n *torrefaction*, F *torréfaction*.

**torsi-**, **torti-**; **torso-**: resp from E *torsion*; from L *tortus*, pp of *torquēre* (s *torq-*, r *tor-*), to twist; and (*torso-*) from ML *torsus*, pp of *torquēre*: cf TORT. Exx: *torsigraph*, a torsion meter; Med *torticollis*, wryneck or stiffneck (L *collum*, neck). The subsidiary *torsio-*, as in *torsiogram*, represents E *torsion*.

**toti-**, **toto-**: from L *tōtus* (adj), whole, s *tōt-*: cf TOTAL. Exx: *totipalmate*, (of certain birds) having webbed feet, cf *palmati*; *toto(-)congenital*, entirely congenital.

**toxi-**; **tox(o)-**; **toxic(o)-**: all, ult, from Gr *toxon* (s *tox-*), a bow (weapon), an arrow, perh a loanword from Scythian (Hofmann), with a cognate in late Skt. Whereas *tox(o)-*, when not short for *toxic(o)-*, is the Gr *tox(o)-*, c/f of *toxon*, *toxi-* stands for E *toxic* or E *toxin*, and *toxic(o)-* comes from Gr *toxikon*, arrow poison (sc *pharmakon*), orig the neus of the adj *toxikos*, of or for a bow or an arrow: cf TOXIC. The end-c/f *-toxin* stands for *toxin*, a poison.

Exx: *toxiferous*, poison-bearing (cf *-ferous* at *-fer*); *toxiphobia*, a dread (cf *-phobe*) of being poisoned;—*toxophily*, the study of, a love for, archery, with adj *toxophilous* and agent *toxophilite*, cf *-phil*; *toxophil* (*toxo-=toxico-*), having an affinity for poisons;—*toxicology*, the science of poisons, with agent *toxicologist*; *toxicophagy* (cf *-phagy* at *-phaga*), the practice of eating poisons.

**trachel(o)-**: Gr *trakhēl(o)-*, c/f of *trakhēlos*, neck, s *trakhēl-*; IE r, perh *trakh-*. Exx: *tracheloclavicular*, of the neck and clavicle; *trachelodynia* (cf *-odynia* at *-odyne*). Cf:

**trache(o)-**, **tracho-**, **trachy-**: 1st, for E from ML *trachea*, from LL *trachia*, from Gr *trakheia* (*artēria*), windpipe, f of adj *trakhus* (s *trakh-*), rough, rocky, akin to Gr *thrassein*, to trouble or disturb, s *thrass-*, IE r *dragh-*; 2nd, a SciL var of Gr *trakhu-*, c/f of *trakhus* and therefore the origin of E *trachy-*. Exx: *trachealgia*, pain (cf *-algia* at *alg-*) in the windpipe; *tracheotomy*, an incision (cf *-tomy* at *-toma*) in the windpipe;—*Trachodon* (cf *-odon*);—*trachycarpous* (cf *-carpous* at *-carp*), bearing rough fruit.

Cf *trachyte*, a rough volcanic rock: *trachy-* + Min suffix *-ite*; adj, *trachytic*.

**tracti-**: for E (printed) *tract*, as in *tractiferous*, tract-carrying.

**tragi-**, **trag(o)-**; **tragico-**: 1st, LL *tragi-*, short for L *tragico-*, c/f of *tragicus*, from Gr *tragikos*, the adj of *tragos*, a he-goat, with c/f *trago-*: cf TRAGIC. Exx: *tragicomedy*, EF-F *tragicomédie*, LL *tragicomoedia*, L *tragicocomoedia*; *tragopan*, a brilliant Asiatic pheasant, from L from Gr *tragopan*, a fabulous bird, lit 'goat-Pan'; *Tragopogon*, Gr *tragopōgōn* (cf *-pogon*), the plant goat's-beard, lit 'goat's beard'); *tragico(-)romantic*.

**trapezi-**, **trapezo-**; **trapezio-**: all for LL *trapezium*: cf TRAPEZE. Exx: *trapeziform*, trapezium-shaped; *trapezohedron* (cf *-hedral*); An *trapeziometacarpal*.

**traumat(o)-**: Gr *traumat(o)-*, c/f of *trauma* (gen *traumatos*), a wound, hence in Psychi a mental shock; akin to *titrōskein* (s *titrōsk-*), to wound, app a redup (*ti-*) of *trōsk-*, akin to *trōein* (s *trō-*), to pierce, to wound. Exx: *traumatology*, the science of wounds; *traumatotropism*, (Bio) an organ's, e.g. a plant root's, modification by wounding. The adj *traumatic* comes through LL *traumaticus* from Gr *traumatikos*, of, for, by a wound.

**trecho-**, occ **treko-**: from Gr *trekhein* (s *trekh-*), to run. Ex: *trechometer* (*trek-*), for measuring distances run by vehicles.

**treg(a)-**, only in El, 'one million millions': trillion+megohm. Ex: *tregerg* (cf ERG).

**treko-**. See *trecho-*.

**-trema**, pl **-tremata**; **tremato-**: from Gr *trēma* (gen *trēmatos*; pl *trēmata*), a hole or orifice, akin to Gr *teirein* (s *teir-*), to rub, L *terere* (s *ter-*); IE r, *ter-* or *teir-*. Exx: *helicotrema* (cf *helico-* at 1st *heli-*); *Derotremata* (cf 2nd *dero-*); *Trematosaurus* (cf *-saur*).

**tremelli-**, as in *tremelliform*: for Bot *Tremella*, a genus of fungi: from L *tremere*, to tremble; cf L *tremulus*, tremulous.

**trepo-**: from Gr *trepein* (s *trep-*), to turn. Ex: *Treponema* (cf *-nema*).

**-tresia**: from Gr *trēsis* (s *trēs-*), a perforation, akin to *tetrainein*, to pierce, s *tetrain-* (redup *te-* on r *train-*). Ex: *sphenotresia* (cf *spheno-*, wedge-).

**triamino-**; **triammino-**. Only in Chem: *tri-* + *amino-* and *ammino-*. Cf *triazolo-*, *tribromino-*, etc.

**-tribe**, **-tripsis**: **tribo-**: 1st, from Gr *tribein* (s *trib-*), to rub, akin to the syn L *terere* (s *ter-*); 2nd, from Gr *tripsis*, a rubbing, from *tribein*; 3rd, from *tribein*. Exx: *nototribe* (Bot adj), touching the back; *xerotripsis* (cf *xero-*), dry friction; *tribometer*, lit 'friction-measurer'.

**-tricha**, **-trichi**, **-trichia**, **-trichous**, **-trichy**; **trich(o)-**, **trichino-**: all from the o/s *trikh-* of Gr *thrix*, hair; IE r, perh *drig(h)-*. Resp, *-tricha*, a SciL pl from Gr *-trikhos* (see *-trichous* below), used for Zoo divisions, as in *Holotricha*, an order of protozoans with little hairs almost entirely (cf *holo-*) covering the body; *-trichi*, a SciL m pl from Gr *-trikhos*, as in *Leiotrichi*, the smooth-haired races; *trikh-* + Med suffix *-ia*, as in *schizotrichia* (cf *schizo-*), an excessive splitting of the hair; (*-trichous*) from Gr *-trikhos*, -haired, from *thrix*, as in *leiotrichous* (cf *leio-*), smooth-haired; *-trichy*, abstract-n for *-trichi*, as in *ulotrichy* (cf 2nd *ulo-*); *trich(o)-*, Gr *trikh(o)-*, c/f of *thrix*, as in *trichogenous* (cf *-genous* at *-gen*), hair-producing, and *trichology*, the science—or the barber's art—of treating the hair; *trichino-*, for *trichina*, a slender worm, from Gr *trikhinos* (f *-ina*), hairy, hair-like, from *thrix*, as in *trichinoscope*, a microscope for detecting trichinae.

**trigon(o)-:** Gr *trigōn(o)-*, c/f of *trigōnos*, triangular (cf the 1st *-gon*). Ex: *trigonometry* (cf *-metry* at *-meter*), adj *-metrical*, the Math of triangles.

**trinitr(o)-,** as in *trinitrocresol*: *tri-+nitro-*, qq.v. above, and *trinitrotoluene* (TNT).

**tripli-; tripl(o)-:** the former, from L *triplex*, triple; the latter, from Gr *triploos*, triple: cf TRIPLE. Exx: *triplicostate* (cf *-costal*); *triplopia*, triple vision (cf *-opia* at *-ope*).

**-tripsis.** See *-tribe*.

**-tripsy:** for *-thrypsy* (cf *-thripsis* above), from Gr *thrupsis*, a breaking-small. Ex: *neutrotripsy* (cf *neuro-*).

**tristi-:** from L *trīstis*, sad (OF-F *triste*). Exx: *tristiloquy* (cf *-loquy* at *-loquence*) and *tristisonous*, sad-sounding.

**tritico-:** from L *trīticum*, wheat, dim (?) of *trītum*, neus of *trītus*, pp of *terere*, to rub, (hence) to beat (grain). Ex: *tritico-nucleic*.

**trit(o)-:** Gr *trit(o)-*, c/f of *tritos*, third: cf THIRD. Exx: *tritagonist*, in Gr drama the actor playing the third most important part, Gr *tritagōnistēs* (cf *-agonist*); Zoo *tritocerebrum*, the third section of an insect's brain.

**-troch, 2 -trocha, 3 -trochal, 4 -trochous, 5 -trochus; 6 trochi-, 7 troch(o)-, 8 trochlei-:** all, ult, and, 1, 2, 5 imm, from Gr *trokhos* (lit, a runner), anything round or circular, esp a wheel, from *trekhein*, to run (s *trekh-*); IE r, *-trekh-* or *-tregh-*, varr of *-trakh-* or *-tragh-*, to run.

Exx: *-troch* ('a ciliated or hairlike band'), as in *mesotroch* (cf *meso-*); 2, 'creatures, or 5, genera, with one or more such bands'; the answering adjj being 3, *-trochal* (as in *prototrochal*) and 4, *-trochous*, as in *mesotrochous*; 6, *trochi-* (as in *trochiferous*, cf *-fer*), from SciL *trochus*, from Gr *trokhos*, which has c/f *trokh(o)-*, whence, 7, *troch(o)*, as in *trochophore* (cf *-phora*); 8, from *trochlea*, a case containing pulleys (hence, in Med, the trochlea of the eye), from Gr *trokhilia*, the sheaf of a pulley, from *trekhein*, to run,—as in *trochleiform*.

Directly, Gr *trokhos* yields *troche*, a medicinal tablet (orig and strictly round); *trochee* comes, via L *trochaeus*, from Gr *trokhaios* (*pous*, foot), running ('a *running* metrical foot'), from *trekhein*, to run.

**troglo-:** Gr *trōglo-*, c/f of *trōglē*, a hole, from *trōgein* (s *trōg-*), to gnaw. Ex: *troglodyte*, a cave-dweller (Gr *duein*, to enter), with adj *troglodytic* (Gr *trōglodutikos*).

**tromo-:** from Gr *tromos*, from *tromein* (s *trom-*), var of *tremein* (s *trem-*), to tremble: cf L *tremere* (s *trem-*) and E TREMBLE. Ex: *tromometer*, an instrument for detecting and measuring earth-tremors however slight.

**tropa-:** for *atropine*, as in *tropacocaine*.

**-tropal, 2 -trope, 3 -tropic, or -tropical, 4 -tropous,** adjj; 5 **-trope,** 6 **-tropia,** 7 **-tropism,** 8 **-tropy,** nn;—9 **tropo-;** 10 **tropido-:** all, ult, from *trop-*, the n-s answering to Gr *trepein* (s *trep-*), to turn: cf TROPE. Resp: 1, *-trop*, from Gr *-tropos* (adj), turning+adj suffix *-al*; 2, occ via F *-trope*, from *-tropos*; 3 *-tropical=-tropic+-al*, but *-tropic* =Gr *-trop(os)+E -ic*, influenced by the adj TROPIC; 4, from *-tropos*, E suffix *-ous*; 5, from Gr *-tropos* (n), end-c/f of *tropos*, a turning, or its var *tropē* (E *trope*, q.v. at TROPIC); 6, *-tropia*, Gr *-tropia*, abstract-n c/f of *tropē*, a turning; 7, *-tropism*, Gr *trop(e)+*suffix *-ism*; 8, *-tropy*, Gr *-tropia* or *-tropē*, c/ff of *tropē*; 9, *tropo-*, Gr *tropo-*, c/f of *tropos*, a turning, a turn; 10, *tropido-*, from Gr *tropis* (gen *tropidos*), a ship's keel—akin to *tropos* and answering to *trepein*, to turn, the keel being that upon which a ship turns.

Exx: *hemitrope* (adj) and *bacteriotropic*; *sematrope* (cf *-sema*), a signalling instrument reflecting the sun's rays, and *thaumatotrope* (cf *thaumato-*), an optical instrument; *hypertropia* (prefix *hyper-*); *neurotropism*, an attraction, towards the central nervous system (cf *neuro-*), of cells or minute organisms; *heliotropy=heliotropism*, the principle behind the turning, towards the sun, of the sunflower or *heliotrope* (whence the colour and its adj)—via F and L from Gr *hēliotropion* (cf *helio-*, c/f of *hēlios*, the sun); *tropology*, figurative speech, LL from Gr *tropologia*—cf *-logia* at *-loger*—with adj *tropologikos*, LL *tropologicus*, E *tropologic*, now usu *tropological*; *tropophilous*, (of plants) thriving in a variable climate or adapted to seasonal variations, cf *-phil*; *Tropidoleptus* (cf *lepto-*, small).

**-trophia** or 2 **-trophy;** 3 **-trophic;** 4 **troph(o)-:** 2 is the E form of *-trophia*, Gr c/f from *trephein* (s *trep-*), to nourish; 3, occ from Gr *trophikos*, nourishing or nursing, nutritive, but usu merely a 'suitable' adj for 1 and 2; 4, *troph(o)-*, Gr *troph(o)-*, c/f from *trephein*; IE r, perh *-trebh-* or *-d(h)rebh-*.

Exx: *cacotrophia* (cf *caco-*, bad) and *pedotrophy*, the (correct) rearing of children (cf 1st *pedo-*), adj *pedotrophic*; *trophoblast* (cf *-blast*)—*trophology*, the science of nutrition—*trophopathy*, any illness or weakness in or of nutrition—*trophospongia* (cf *spongi-*).

**-tropia, -tropic, tropido-, tropo-, tropous, -tropy.** See *-tropal*.

**truncato-:** from L *truncātus*, lopped off: cf TRUNCATE. Ex: *truncato-rotund*.

**trypan(o)-:** Gr *trupan(o)-*, c/f of *trupanon*, an instrument for boring or trepanning, from, or akin to, *trupan*, to bore or pierce; IE r, *-trup-*, an extension of *-tru-* or *-treu-*. Ex: *Trypanosoma* (cf *-soma*, body), a genus of parasites given to entering the human body. Gr *trupan* yields *trypo-*, as in *trypograph*.

**trypsino-,** for *trypsin*; **trypto-,** for *tryptic*. Only in Biochem.

**tuberculi-, tuberculo-; tuberi-:** first two, for L *tūberculum*, a tubercle, dim of *tūber* (whence *tuberi-*), a swelling, hump, truffle, s *tūb-*; akin to

L *tumēre*, to swell; cf TUBER. Exx: *tuberculiferous* (cf *-ferous* at *-fer*); *tuberculotherapy*; *tuberiform*.

**tubi-, 2 tubo-; 3 tubuli-, 4 tubulo-:** 3 and 4, for L *tubulus*, a little tube or pipe, dim of *tubus*, a tube or pipe, s *tub-*, c/ff *tubi-* and, irreg, *tubo-*; akin to L *tuba*, a trumpet: cf TUBE. Exx: *tubicorn*, hollow-horned (cf *-corn*); *tubo(-)abdominal*; *tubuliferous*, bearing tubules, and *tubuliflorous* (cf *flori-*), bearing flowers with tubular corollas; *tubulodermoid* (cf *-derm*).

**tulipi-, tulipo-:** for E *tulip*, as in *tulipiferous*, tulip-bearing, and *tulipomania*, a mania for tulip-growing or -acquiring. Cf TULIP.

**tume-:** L *tume-*, from *tumēre*, to be swollen. Ex: *tumefacient*, from L *tumefaciens*, presp of *tumefacere*, to make swell.

[**-tund,** as in the rare vv *contund* (L *contundere*), *extund* (L *extundere*), *obtund* (L *obtundere*), *retund* (L *retundere*), is worth recording chiefly because *tundere*, to strike repeatedly, to crush, has pp *tūsus*; *contūsus* yields 'to *contuse*', (now) to bruise, and the abstract n *contūsiō* (gen *contūsiōnis*) yields *contusion*, a (severe) bruise.]

**tungsto-:** for *tungsten* (Sw: lit, heavy stone), as in *tungstosilicic*.

**turbidi-,** as in *turbidimeter*, from ML *turbiditās*, turbidity.

**turbinato-; turbini-; turbin(o)-:** 1st, from L *turbinātus*, cone-shaped, from *turbō*, anything that whirls or spins, o/s *turbin-*, whence the 2nd, *turbini-*; the 3rd, *turbin(o)-*, stands for E *turbinal*, scroll-like, cone- or top-shaped. *Turbō* is akin to L *turbāre* (s *turb-*), to disturb—cf DISTURB. Exx: *turbinato(-)concave*; *turbiniform*; *turbinectomy*, a cutting-out (cf *-ectomy* at *-tome*) of turbinated bone(s), and *turbinotomy*, a cutting into such bone(s).

**turbo-:** for E TURBINE, as in *turbo(-)motor*. Cf prec.

**Turco-, Turko-:** from ML *Turco-*, c/f of *Turcus*, a Turk: cf TURK. Exx: *Turkophil*, *Turkophobe*, cf *-phil* and *-phobe*.

**turdi-,** as in *turdiform*, thrush-like: from L *turdus*, a thrush.

**Turko-.** See *Turco-*.

**turri-:** L *turri-*, c/f of *turris* (s *turr-*, r *tur-*), a tower: cf TOWER. Exx: *turrigerous* (cf *-gerous* at *-ger*) or *turriferous* (cf *-ferous* at *-fer*), bearing towers, as a castle would—the former from L *turriger*; *turrilite* (cf *-lite*), molluscs with turreted shells.

[**twi-,** c/f of E TWO, as in *twibill*, has been treated under Prefixes.]

**-ty,** as in *twenty*, *thirty*, etc., denotes 'ten' and derives from OE *-tig*, Go *-tigus*, ON *-tigr*: cf TEN.

**tych(o)-:** Gr *tukhē*, chance, akin to *tunkhanein*, to happen. Ex: *tychoparthenogenesis*.

**tyl(o)-:** Gr *tul(o)-*, c/f of *tulē*, a knob; perh *tu-l-ē*, with the IE *tu-* one sees in, e.g., L *tumēre* (*tu+-m-+-ēre*), to be swollen, and perh in *tūber* (*tū+-b-+-er*), a tumour, an excrescence, a knot in wood. Exx: *Tylosaurus* (cf *-saur*) and *tylostyle* (cf *-style* at *-stylar*).

The derivative Gr *tulōtos*, knobbed, knobby, yields *tylot(o)-*, as in *tylotoxea* (whence *tylotoxeate*), where *-oxea* comes from *oxus*, sharp.

**tympan(o)-:** from L *tympanum* (E *tympan*), a kettledrum, whence, in An and Zoo, the E sense 'eardrum'; from Gr *tumpanon*; IE r, clearly echoic, *\*tump-*. Ex: *tympanotomy* (cf *-tomy* at *-tome*).

The rare var *tympani-* occurs in *tympanichord* and *tympaniform*.

**-type, 2 -typal, 3 -typic, 4 -typy; 5 typi-, 6 typ(o)-:** all, ult, from Gr *tupos* (s *tup-*), an impression (physical): resp, Gr *-tupon*, end-c/f of *tupos*; 2, 3, adjj for 1 and 4, *-typic* predominating in tech words and deriving from Gr *tupikos*, the adj of *tupos*; 4, *-typy*, from Gr *-tupia*, abstract-n derivative (cf suffix *-ia*) from *tupos*; 5, *typi-*, from L *typus*, from *tupos*; 6, *typ(o)-*, Gr *tup(o)-*, c/f of *tupos*. (See TYPE.)

Exx: *archetype*, L *archetypum*, Gr *arkhetupon*, from *arkhetupos*, stamped first—esp as a model (hence, as an exemplar), cf *arche-* at *-arch*; *archetypal*, *archetypic(al)*; *lithotypy* (cf *litho-* at *-lite*); *typify*, q.v. at TYPE; *typography*, the art—as opp the craft—of printing (cf *-graphy* at *-graph*); *typology*, the study of human types.

**typhl(o)-:** from Gr *tuphlon*, the caecum or blind gut, strictly the neus of *tuphlos* (s *tuphl-*, r *tuph-*), blind, akin to OHG *toub*, Mod G *taub*, deaf; IE r, prob *\*d(h)eub(h)-*. Exx: *typhlocele* (cf *-cele*) and *typhlology*, the Sci study of blindness.

**typh(o)-,** 'typhus' or 'typhoid': Gr *tuph(o)-*, c/f of *tuphos* (s *tuph-*) vapour, a fevered stupor: cf TYPHUS. Exx: *typhomalaria*; *typhomania*, delirium caused by typhus or by typhoid; *typhosepsis* (cf *-sepsis*).

**typto-:** from Gr *tuptein* (s *tupt-*, r *tup-*), to strike; as in *typtology*, the lore or study or theory of spirit rappings.

**tyranni-, tyrann(o)-:** the former, L *tyranni-*, c/f of *tyrannus*, from Gr *turannos* (a tyrant), c/f *turanno-*, whence E *tyrann(o)-*. Exx: *tyrannicide* (cf *-cide* at *-cidal*), tyrant-slayer, L *tyrannicīda*, and tyrant-slaying, L *tyrannicīdium*; *tyrannophobia* (cf *-phobe*), a dread of tyrants. See TYRANT.

**tyr(o)-:** Gr *tur(o)-*, c/f of *turos* (s *tur-*), cheese, akin to Skt *tūras*, milk become cheesy; perh from IE r *\*tu-* or *\*teu-*, to swell—cf Gr *tulē* (a knob), q.v. at *tylo-*, and L *tumēre*, to be swollen. Ex: *tyromancy*, divination (cf *-mancy*) by means of cheese.

**udo-,** as in *udometer*, a rain gauge: from L *ūdus*, moist, wet. Cf EXUDE and the 2nd *hydro-*.

**Ugro-:** for E *Ugric*, as in *Ugro-Finnic*. Cf HUNGARIAN.

**ulcero-:** for E *ulcer*, as in *ulcero-membranous*. Cf ULCER.

**ulemo-;** as in *ulemorrhagia*, gum-bleeding: cf the 1st *ulo-*.

**ulno-:** from L *ulna*, elbow: cf ELL. Ex: *ulno(-) radical*.

**ulo- (1):** from Gr *oula* (neupl) the gums, s *oul-*, perh akin to Gr *oulos* (s *oul-*), thick, woolly; IE r, perh *ul- or *uel-, to turn. Exx: *ulotrophia*, atrophy of the gums; *ulorrhagia* (cf *-rrhage*). Cf: **ulo-** (2): from Gr *oulos* (οὖλος), thick or woolly, s *oul-*, cf prec. Ex: *ulotrichy*, the having woolly hair, and *Ulotrichi*, the woolly-haired races.

**ultimo-**, as in *ultimogeniture*, opp *primogeniture*: from L *ultimus*, last—cf ULTIMATE.

**umbell(i)-**: deriving from L *umbella* (dim of *umbra*, shade), a parasol, but, in E, representing its Bot derivative *umbel*, as in *umbelliferous*, umbel-producing (cf *-ferous* at *-fer*). Cf *umbri-*.

**umbilici-** and **umbili-**: for L (hence Med E) *umbilicus*, the navel, from *umbō*, a round or conical projection. Exx: *umbiliciform*, *umbiliform*, resembling a navel.

**umbo-**, as in *umbo-lateral*: L *umbō*, a boss or conical projection. Cf prec.

**umbri-**: L *umbri-*, c/f of *umbra*, a shade or a shadow: cf UMBRAGE. Ex: *umbriferous*, shady, from L *umbrifer* (cf *-fer*). Cf *umbelli-*.

**Umbro-**: from L *Umber*, an Umbrian; as in *Umbro-Oscan*.

**unci-**: from L *uncus*, a hook, akin to Gr *onkos* (cf the 2nd *onco-*). Ex: *unciform*, hook-shaped.

**undec(a)-**: from L *ūndecim* (*ūnus*, 1+*decem*, 10), eleven; as in *undecagon*, an 11-angled figure.

**undi-**: from L *unda*, a wave—cf UNDULATE. Ex: *undigenous*, water-born, generated (cf *-genous* at *-gen*) by water.

**ungui-**: from L *unguis*, nail (of finger), claw, akin to NAIL. Exx: *unguiferous* (cf *-ferous* at *-fer*), nail-producing, and *unguirostral*, horny-billed (as ducks)—cf *rostri-*. Cf:

**unguli-**: from L *ungula*, a hoof—cf prec. Ex: *unguligrade*, walking (cf *-grade*) on hooves.

**uni-**: L *ūni-*, c/f of *ūnus*, one, single: cf numerical ONE. Exx: UNICORN; UNIFORM; *unisonous*, having one sound (cf *-sonous* at *-sonance*) or pitch, (hence) concordant; *univalent*, having one value, single—cf *-valent* at *vale-*.

**universo-**: for *universe*, as in *universology*, the science of the universe.

**Uralo-**, 'Ural and': for *Ural*, as in *Uralo-Altaic*.

**urani-**: for *uranium*, from the planet *Uranus*, Gr *Ouranos*, deification of *ouranos* (s *ouran-*), the sky, the heavens, perh akin to L *ūrīna*, urine: rain comes from the skies. Ex: *uraniferous*, bearing (or containing) uranium. Cf:

**uran(o)-**; **uranoso-**: former, Gr *ouran(o)-*, c/f of *ouranos*, the sky—see prec; latter, for E *uranous*, of, for, with uranium. Exx: *uranography*, the description (cf *-graphy* at *-graph*)—or the science—of the heavens; *uranology*, the science (cf *-logy*, at *-loger*), of—or a treatise on—the heavens; *uranoscopy*, observation (cf *-scopy* at *-scope*) of the heavens;—Chem *uranoso-uranic*.

**urbi-**: from L *urbs* (gen *urbis*), a city: cf URBAN. Ex: *urbicolous* (cf *-colous*), city-inhabiting.

**urcei-**: from L *urceus*, a jar, as in *urceiform*, jar-shaped.

**-ure, -ura, -urous, -urus; ur(o)-**: from Gr *oura* (s *our-*), a tail. The terminal c/ff are thus neatly summarized by Webster at *-urous*: **'-urous.** A combining form, Gr *-ouros*, from *oura*, tail, meaning -tailed, as in brachy*urous* [short-tailed: cf *brachy-*] . . . In *Zool* (and rarely in *Bot*) corresponding nouns denoting genera are formed in -*urus*, and nouns denoting individuals in the genus, in **-ure**, as in Brachy*urus*, brachy*ure* . . . The New Latin *pl.* **-ura** is used for larger classifications, as in Brachy*ura*.' The c/f *ur(o)-* represents Gr *our(o)-*, c/f of *oura*, as in *urohyal* (*uro-*+*hy*oid+ adj suffix *-al*).

**urcdo-**: for L *ūrēdō* (a blast, a blight: from *ūrere*, to burn), esp, in Bot, a rust; cf *uredino-*, from *ūrēdin-*, the o/s of *ūrēdō*. Exx: *uredinology*; *uredospore* (cf *-spora*).

**ure(o)-**: for *urea*, as in *ureosecretory*, of, for, by the secretion of urea. Cf:

**ureter(o)-**: from Gr *ourētēr* (whence SciL *ureter*); as in *ureterotomy* (cf *-tomy* at *-tome*). Cf:

**urethr(o)-**: from Gr *ourēthra*, urethra, as in *urethrometer*. As in *uretero-*, the Gr origin is a derivative of Gr *ouron*, urine: see the 2nd *uro-* and also URINE.

**-urge, -urgic, -urgy** are best exemplified by *demiurge*, Gr *dēmiourgos*, (lit) a worker for the people, (hence) the maker of the world, the Creator, God—but in Plato a subordinate god: *dēmio*(s), of or for the people (cf *demo-*)+*-ergos*, end-c/f from *ergon*, work (cf *-ergate*). The adj *demiurgic*, creative, derives from Gr *dēmiourgikos*; the n *demiurgy* is rare—but cf *thaumaturgy*, wonder-working, Gr *thaumatourgia*, with EF-F, hence E, agent *thaumaturge*, ML *thaumaturgus*, Gr *thaumatourgos* (cf *thaumato-*).

**-uria, -uric; uric(o)-**: resp from Gr *-ouria*, from *ouron*, urine, and denoting 'condition of urine'; from E *uric*, of urine; (*urico-*) for *uric*. Exx: *polyuria* (cf *poly-*), excessive secretion of urine; *polyuric*; *uricolysis* (cf *-lysis* at *-lyse*).

**urini-, urin(o)-**: both from L *ūrīna*, urine, cf esp *urethro-*. Exx: *uriniferous*, urine-producing (cf *-ferous* at *-fer*); *urinology*, the study or science of urine; *urinomancy*, divination (cf *-mancy*) by urine.

**uro-** (1). See *-ura*.

**uro-** (2); before a vowel, **ur-**: Gr *our(o)-*, c/f of *ouron*, urine: cf URINE. Exx: *uromancy*=*urino-mancy*, q.v. at *urini-*; *urology*, the Med Sci of urine.

**-urous.** See *-ura*.

**ursi-**: from L *ursus*, f *ursa*, a bear—cf *Ursa Major*, Dr Johnson, and the adj *ursine* (L *ursīnus*), bearish; *ursus* (*-sa*) is akin to Gr *arktos* and to several words in Av, Skt, Arm. Ex: *ursiform*, bear-shaped.

**-urus.** See *-ura*.

**usu-**: L *ūsū-*, based on *ūsū*, the abl of the n *ūsus*, use: see USE. Exx: *usucapion*, from L *ūsū-capiō* (gen *ūsūcapiōnis*), from *ūsūcapere*, to acquire (*capere*, to take) by use (*ūsū*), esp by long use; *usufruct*, from LL *ūsūfructus*, from L *ūsus frūctus* (enjoyment, or fruit, of use), perh from *ūsus et frūctus*, use and enjoyment (thereof), *frūctus* (see FRUIT) deriving from *fruī*, to enjoy.

**uter(o)-**: for An and Zoo *uterus*, womb, adopted

from L *uterus*, womb, but also abdomen or belly, akin to Skt *udara*. Exx: ('the womb') *uterolith* (cf *-lith* at *-lite*) and *uterotomy* (cf *-tomy* at *-tome*).

**utopo-**: for *Utopia*, as in *utopographer*, one who describes (cf *-grapher* at *-graph*) a UTOPIA.

**utri-**: from L *uter* (gen *utris*), a leather bottle or, occ, bag, perh akin to Gr *hudria*, a water-jar (cf *hydro-*). Ex: *utriform*, shaped like a leather bottle. Cf *utricle*, a little sac, a vesicle, from L *utriculus*, dim of *uter*. Cf:

**utriculi-, utriculo-**: from L *utriculus* (see prec) and, *utriculo-*, for E *utricle*. Exx: *utriculiferous*, bearing—or producing—utricles; *utriculoplasty* (cf *-plasty* at *-plasia*).

**uvi-; uvulo-**: from ML *ūva*, L *ūua* (s *ūu-*), a grape, perh akin to Gr *oiē* or *oa*, a service tree, and therefore to YEW; (*uvulo-*) from *ūvula* (the ML dim of *ūua*, ML *ūva*), the An uvula. Exx: *uvitonic* (acid); *uvulotomy*, the removal (cf *-tomy* at *-tome*) of the uvula.

**vacci-; vaccini-, vaccino-**: all three for E *vaccine*; the 1st, however, properly denotes 'a cow' or 'cows' and comes from ML *vacca*, a cow: cf VAC-CINATE. Exx: *vaccicide*, the killing of a cow (or of cows), but *vaccigenous*, vaccine-producing; *vaccinifer* (cf *-fer*), a person—or an animal—that constitutes a source of vaccine; *vaccinophobia*, a dread of vaccine or of vaccination.

**vacuo-**: for E *vacuum*, as in *vacuometer*. Cf VACANT. The rare *vacue-* occurs only in *vacuefy* (cf *-fy*), to create a vacuum; the word owes its form to ML *vacuefacere*, L *uacuefacere*, to empty.

**vagi-**; for E *vague*, as in *vagiform*, vague of form.

**vagini-, vagin(o)-**: for 'the *vagina*', as in *vagino(-)fixation*, or for '*vaginal* and', as in *vaginicolous* (cf *-colous*), exemplifying 'sheath', the lit meaning of ML *vāgīna*, L *uāgīna*, and in *vagino(-)abdominal* (An sense).

**vago-**: for Med 'the *vagus* nerve', from ML *vagus* (L *uagus*), wandering, errant, s *uag-*, as in *uagāri* to wander: cf VAGRANT. Ex: *vagatomy* (cf *-tomy* at *-tome*).

**vale-**: *-valence*, *-valent*: resp the imperative, 'Be well!' of ML *valēre*, L *ualēre* (s *ual-*), to be strong or well; *-valence*, end-c/f of *valence*, from L *ualens* (ML *valens*), being strong, well, of the value of, whence, via the o/s *ualent-*, ML *valent-*, comes the adj *valent*, whence *-valent* Exx: *valediction* and *valedictory* (adj), suggested by ML *valedictum* (L *uale-*), the supine of *valedicere*, to say farewell, lit 'to say "Be well"'; *equivalence*, ML *aequivalentia* (cf *equi-*) and *univalence* (*uni-+-valence*); *equivalent*, LL *aequiualens* (o/s *-ualent-*), pp of *aequiualēre*, to have equal power, and *ambivalence*, *ambivalent* (*ambi-+-valence*, *-valent*), (the) having complementary and opposite characteristics. Cf VALUE.

**valer(o)-**: for E *valerian* (adj *valeric*), a plant and the calmative drug therefrom: ML *valeriāna*, from ML *valēre* (L *ual-*), to be strong: cf prec. Ex: Chem *valerolactone*.

**valvi-, valvo-; valvul(o)-**: 1st, 2nd, for E *valve*; 3rd, for E *valvula*, a little valve, ML *valvula*, L *ualuula*, dim of *ualua*, ML *valva*, leaf or fold of door. Exx: *valviferous*, having (cf *-ferous* at *-fer*) valves or a valve; *valvotomy* (cf *-tomy* at *-tome*); *valvulotomy*.

**vanadi-, vanad(o)-**: for the Chem element *vanadium*, itself from *Vanad*(is), another name for the Norse goddess Freya+suffix *-ium*. Exx: *vanidiferous* (cf *-fer*); *vanadosilicate*.

**vapo-; vapori-; vaporo-**: resp for E *vapo(u)r*, as in *vapography* (in photography); ML *vapori-*, L *uapori-*, c/f of *uapor*, vapo(u)r, as in *vaporific* (cf *-fic*), vapo(u)r-producing; for E *vapo(u)r*, as in *vaporograph* (in photography: cf *-graph*).

**vari-; vario-**: both from ML *varius*, L *uarius* (s *uar-*), diverse: cf VARIETY. Exx: *varicolo(u)red* and *variometer*.

**varic(o)-**: for Med *varix*, from L *uarix* (s *uar-*), a dilated vein, perh akin to L *uarus* (s *uar-*), a blotch on the skin: cf VARICOSE. Ex: *varicotomy* (cf *-tomy* at *-tome*).

**varioli-, variolo-**: for Med *variola*, smallpox: ML term, from ML *varius*, L *uarius*, in nuance 'spotted'. Exx: *varioliform*, like smallpox; *variolo(-)vaccine*.

**vario-**. See *vari-*

**vasculi-, vascul(o)**: for ML *vāsculum*, L *uāsculum*, dim of *uās*, a vessel, a VASE. Ex: *vasculiform* and *vasculo(-)genesis*. Cf:

**vasi-, vas(o)-**: for Med *vas*, a vessel, a duct, L *uās*, a vessel, a vase: cf VASE. Exx: *vasiferous* (cf *-ferous* at *-fer*) and *vasomotor*.

**vati-**: from ML *vātes*, L *uātes* (gen *uātis*; s *uāt-*), a soothsayer, a prophet, adj *uāticus*, E *vatic*; cf Gaulish pl *ouateis* (s *ouat-*). Ex: *vaticide* (cf *-cide* at *-cidal*), a prophet-slayer or a prophet-slaying. Cf *vaticinate*, to prophesy, from ML *vāticinātus* (L *uāti-*), pp of *vāticināri*, to prophesy; L *uāticināri* may be a cpd of *uāti-* (for *uātes*)+*-cināri*, from *canere*, to sing or to chant.

**vegeti-, vegeto-**: for '*vegetable* (and)', as in *vegetivorous*, vegetable- or vegetation-eating, and *vegeto(-)mineral*.

**veli-**: from ML *vēlum*, L *uēlum*, a veil, a sail: cf REVEAL. Exx: *veliferous*, *veligerous*.

**veloci-; velo-**: both from ML *vēlōx*, L *uēlōx*, rapid; the former from the o/s *uēlōc-*, the latter irreg from *uēlo*(x): cf VELOCITY. Exx: *velocipede*, an early bicycle (or tricycle), cf *-pede* at *-ped*; *velodrome*, F *vélodrome* (cf *-drome*, a course).

**veneni-; veneno-**: from ML *venēnum*, L *uenēnum*, poison: cf VENOM. Exx: *venenific* (cf *-fic*), poison-producing; *veneno(-)salivary*.

**venereo-**: for *venereal* (disease), as in *venereology*. Cf VENUS, whence the c/f *veneri-*, as in Bot *veneriform*.

**veni-, veno-**: from ML *vēna*, L *uēna*, a vein: cf VEIN. Exx: *venipuncture* and *venotomy* (cf *-tomy* at *-tome*). Cf *-venose*, *-venous*, end-c/ff of *venose*, *venous*, veiny, as in *reticulatovenose*, having net-like veins, and 'an *intravenous* injection'.

**venti-, vento-**: from ML *ventus*, L *uentus*, wind:

cf WIND. Ex: *ventifact*, a stone shaped or polished by wind-driven sand, cf *-fact*; *ventometer*, a wind-gauge.

**ventri-**; **ventro-**: ML *ventri-*, L *uentri-*, c/f of *uenter* (gen *uentris*), the belly; *ventro-*, an An and Med c/f from ML *venter*, adj *ventrālis* (L *u-*), whence E *ventral*; perh akin to L *uterus*, belly, womb. Exx: VENTRILOQUIST (a speaker from the stomach), *ventripotent* (large-bellied; gluttonous); *ventrotomy*; ('ventral and') *ventrodorsal*, of or for belly and back.

**ventricoso-**: for *ventricose*, having a (large) belly. Cf prec.

**ventriculo-**: for L, and E An and Zoo, *ventriculus*, dim of *venter* (L *uenter*: see *ventri-*). Ex: *ventriculoscopy* (cf *-scopy* at *-scope*).

**ventro-**. See *ventri-*.

**vera-**. See *veri-*.

**verbi-**; **verbo-**: ML *verbi-*, L *uerbi-*, c/f of *uerbum*, word; *verbo-*, irreg for *verbi-*: cf WORD. Exx: *verbigerate*, (Med) senselessly to repeat a word, from L *uerbigeratum*, supine of *uerbigerāre*, to chatter; *verbomania*.

**vergi-**: for E *verge*, a rod, as in *vergiform*, rod-like.

**veri-**: ML *vēri-*, L *uēri-*, c/f of *uērus* (s *uēr-*), true: cf VERY. Exx: *veridic*, truthful, L *uēridicus* (*dīcere*, to say); VERIFY; *verisimilitude* (adj *-udinous*), from L *uērisimilitūdō*, from *similis*—cf SIMILAR. The rare and irreg *vera-* occurs in *verascope*.

**vermi-**: ML *vermi-*, L *uermi-*, c/f of *uermis*, a worm: cf WORM. Exx: *vermicide*, a worm-killer (cf *-cidal*); *vermiform*; *vermigerous* (cf *-gerous* at *-ger*), infested with, or merely having, worms. The dim *uermiculus* yields the c/f *vermiculi-*; the subsidiary *vermini-* stands for VERMIN.

**verruci-**: for E *verrūca*, a wart (adj *verrucose*, L *uerrūcōsus*), from L *uerrūca*, perh akin to Skt *várṣman-*, summit. Ex: *verruciferous*, wart-producing.

**versi-**: ML *versi-*, L *uersi-*, c/f of *uersus*, a verse (cf VERSE), but occ from L *uersāre* freq of *uertere* (pp *uersus*), to turn. Exx: *versicolo(u)r*, colour-changing, colour-changed or variegated, L *uersicolor* (*uersare+color*); *versify*, to make (cf *-fy*) verses; *versiform*, LL *uersiformis*, varying—or varied—in shape; *versipel*, a form-changing creature, e.g. the werewolf, from L *uersipellis*, skin-changer (L *pellis*, s *pel(l)-*, skin).

**vertebri-**, **vertebr(o)-**: for Med E and ML *vertebra*, L *uertebra*, a segment of the spinal column, from *uertere*, to turn: cf VERTEBRATE. Exx: *vertebriform*; *vertebrectomy* (cf *-ectomy*) and *vertebrocostal* (cf *-costal*).

**verti-**: ML *verti-* (L *uerti-*), c/f of *vertere*, L *uertere* (s *uert-*), to turn, as in *verticordious*, heart-turning or-changing; but also for *vertical*, as in *vertimeter*. Cf VERTICAL and:

**vertico-**: for An *vertex*, the top of the head, L *uertex* (q.v. at VERTICAL). Ex: *vertico-mental* (L *mentum*, the chin).

**vesico-**: from ML (and An) *vēsīca*, L *uēsīca*, a bladder, the bladder, akin to Skt *vastás*, the bladder; IE r, *uās-* or *uēs-*. Exx: ('vesica') *vesicotomy*; ('vesical and') *vesico(-)spinal*. The dim *vesicula* yields c/f *vesicul(o)-*, as in *vesiculectomy* (cf *-ectomy* at *-tome*).

**vestibulo-**: for An *vestibule* (L *uestibulum*); as in *vestibulo(-)spinal*.

**vestri-**: for *vestry*, as in *vestrify*, to make (cf *-fy*) a vestry of.

**vi-**. See *vice-*.

**via-**: ML *via*, L *uia*, a way, a road: cf VIA. Exx: *viaduct*, after *aqueduct*; *viagraph*; *viameter*.

**vibro-**: from L *uibrāre*, ML *vibrāre* (s *vibr-*), to vibrate: cf VIBRATE. Ex: *vibroscope*, an instrument for tracing or observing (*-scope*) vibrations.

**vice-**, 'in the place of', hence 'subordinate to': L *uice* (ML *vice*), abl of *uicis*, a turn, a change: cf VICARIOUS. Exx: *vice-admiral*, *-chancellor*.

**viginti-**: ML *vīgintī-*, L *uīgintī-*, c/f of *uīgintī*, twenty, akin to Skt *vīsaiti*. Ex: *viginti(-)angular*, from LL *uīgintiangulus*, 20-angled.

**vili-**: ML *vīli-*, L *uīli-*, c/f of *uīlis*, cheap: cf VILE. Exx: *vilify*, to cheapen, to debase, to defame, from LL *uīlificāre* (cf *-fy* and *-fic*), the n being *vilification*; *vilipend*, to hold cheap, to speak slightingly of, from MF-F *vilipender*, from L *uīlipendere* (? for *ni(hi)li pendere*, to weigh as nothing), the adj being *vilipendio y*.

**villi-**: from ML *villus*, L *uillus*, shaggy hair, a tuft of hair: cf VELVET. Ex: *villiform*.

**vini-**, **vino-**: ML *vīni-*, L *uīni-*, c/f of *uīnum* (s *uīn-*), wine; *vino-*, from ML *vīnum*, L *uīnum*. See WINE. Exx: *viniculture*, *vinometer* (for determining the purity and strength of wine); *vinology*, a study of the grapevine (secondary sense of L *uīnum*: cf VINE).

**viperi-**: for *viper*, as in *viperiform*, viper-like.

**-vir**, **-virate**; **viri-**: resp from L *-uir*, ML *-vir*, terminal c/f of *uir*, a man, as in E *decemvir*, from L *decemuiri*, the ten magistrates (lit men); from L *-uirātus*, ML *-virātus*, as in *triumvirātus*, government by three men (the *triumviri*); and (*uiri-*) from L *uiri-* (ML *viri-*), c/f of *uir* (gen *uiris*), as in LL *uiripotens* (gen *-potentis*), whence E *viripotent*, (of a girl) fit for marriage.

**virid(i)-**: from ML *viridis*, L *uiridis*, green; cf VERDANT. Ex: *viridigenous*, green(ness)-producing.

**viru-**: for Med *virus*, poison characterizing a disease, from ML *vīrus*, L *uīrus*, slimy liquid: cf VIRUS. Ex: *virucide*, something that destroys virus.

**visceri-**, **viscer(o)-**: for *vīscera*, pl of ML *vīscus* (gen *vīsceris*), L *uīscus* (pl *uīscera*), an internal organ. (See VISCERA.) Exx: *visceri-pericardial*; *visceromotor* (adj), causing activity in the viscera.

**visco-** or **viscosi-**: for E *viscosity*, a slimy stickiness (ML *viscositas*, from LL *uiscōsus*): cf VISCID. Exx: *viscometer* or *viscosimeter*.

**visuo-**: from ML *vīsus*, L *uīsus* (gen *uīsūs*), vision: cf *visual* at VISIBLE. Ex: *visuometer*, an instrument for the measurement of vision; ('visual and') *visuo(-)auditory*, of sight and hearing.

**vita-**: from ML *vīta*, L *uīta* (s *vīt-*, r *vī-*), life akin to *uiuere*, ML *vīvere*, to live: cf VITAL. Exx: *vitascope*, a motion-picture projector. Cf *vito-*.

**vitamino-:** for *vitamin(s)*, as in *vitaminology*.

**vitelli-; vitello-:** from ML *vitellus*, L *uitellus*, the yolk of an egg, prob akin to L *uīta*, life; *vit*(a)+dim *-ellus*, *-a*, *-um*. Exx: *vitelligenous*, yolk-producing (cf *-genous* at -gen); *vitellogene* (cf *-gene* at *-gen*).

**viti-:** ML *vīti-*, L *uīti-*, c/f of *uītis*, ML *vītis*, a vine, esp the grapevine, perh akin to *uiēre* (s *ui-*), to curve, bend, weave. Exx: *viticulture*, grape-growing—cf *viniculture* at *vini-* above; *vitiferous*, L *uitifer*, cf *-ferous* at *-fer*.

**vit(o)-:** irreg from ML *vīta*, L *uīta*, life; denoting 'vital, organic', as in *vitochemic(al)*. Cf *vita-*.

**vitreo-; vitri-; vitro-:** 1st, for E *vitreous*, ML *vitreus* (L *uitreus*), glassy, from ML *vitrum* (L *uitrum*), glass; 2nd, 3rd, the latter irreg, from *vitrum*. Exx: *vitreo(-)electric*; *vitrify* (cf *-fy*), to render, or to become, glass or like glass; *vitrophyre* (cf *-phyre*), a glassy rock that resembles porphyry. Cf VITRIOL.

**vivi-:** ML *vīvi-*, c/f of *vīvus* (s *vīv-*), alive, L *uīuus*, c/f *uīui-*; cf *uiuere* (ML *vīvere*), to be alive, and *vita-* above. See VIVID. Exx: *vivify* (cf *-fy*), from LL *uīuificāre*, whence the n *uīuificātiō* (gen *uīuificātiōnis*), E *vivification*; *viviparous*, ML *vīviparus*, L *uīuiparus*, bringing forth (cf *-parous* at *-para*) living young; *vivisection*, adopted from F: *vivi-+section*, a cutting; *vivisepulture*, the practice of burying people alive.

**voci-:** ML *vōci-*, L *uōci-*, c/f of *uōx* (ML *vōx*), voice: cf VOICE. Exx: *vociculture*, training of the *voice*; *vociferate*, ML *vociferātus*, L *uōcificerātus*, pp of *uōciferāri*, to cry out loudly, lit 'to carry the voice', to make it carry, *-ferāri* coming from *ferre*, to bear, to carry; L n, *uōciferātiō*, ML *v-* (gen *vōciferātiōnis*), E *vociferation*; *vociferous*, F *vocifère*+E suffix *-ous*.

**volcano-.** See *vulcano-*.

**volta-:** for *voltaic* (adj of VOLT), as in *voltameter*, *voltammeter*, *voltaplast* (cf *-plast* at *-plasia*).

**volumeno-; volu-; volumo-:** 1st, irreg for ML *volūmen* (L *uolūmen*); 2nd, 3rd, very irreg for E *volume*: cf VOLUME. Exx: *volumenometer*, *volumeter*, *volumometer*, all in Phys.

**voluti-:** for *volute*, a spiral, as in *volutiform*.

**vomero-:** for E *vomer*, the ploughshare bone in the skull of most vertebrates, from ML *vōmer*, L *uōmer* (refashioned from *uōmer-*, o/s of *uōmis*, gen *uōmeris*), a ploughshare, r *uōm-*, perh akin to the syn Gr *unnis*. Ex: *vomero(-)nasal*.

**-vora, -vore, -vorous:** the ML *-vorus*, c/f of *vorāre*, L *uorāre* (s *uor-*), to devour (cf DEVOUR), yields *-vorous*, which denotes '-eating'; the L neupl *carniuora* yields SciE *carnivora*, the orders and genera of the *carnivores* or flesh-eating animals (cf *carni-*, 'flesh-'), which owes something to F *carnivore*, adj and, derivatively, n.

Exx: *herbivora*, *herbivore*, *herbivorous*: cf *herbi-*.

**vortici-:** for E *vortex*; cf VORTEX. Ex: *vorticiform*, shaped like a vortex.

**voto-:** for n *vote*, as in *votometer*.

**vulcano-; volcano-:** the latter, from E *volcano*, It *volcano*, earlier *vulcano*, from *Vulcano*, Vulcan, whence *vulcano-*: cf VOLCANO. Exx: *volcanology*, *vulcanology*, the science of volcanoes.

**vulni-:** ML *vulni-* (L *uulni-*), c/f of *vulnus* (L *uulnus*), a wound; cf VULNERABLE. Ex: *vulnific* (cf *-fic*), ML *vulnificus*, L *uulnificus*, wound-causing.

**vulpi-:** c/f of ML *vulpes* (L *uulpes*, s *uulp-*), a fox: cf WOLF. Ex: *vulpicide* (cf *-cide* at *-cidal*), a fox-killer, a fox-killing.

**vulvi-, vulvo-:** from ML *vulva*, L *uulua*, the external female genitals, akin to L *uoluere* (ML *volvere*), to wind, turn, roll, the resp ss being *uulu-* and *uolu-*: cf INVOLVE. Exx: *vulviform*, shaped as a cleft oval with projecting lips; *vulvo(-)crural*.

**[-ward, -wards.** See the suffix *-ward(s)*, and esp WARD.]

**[-wise.** See the suffix *-wise*, and esp WISE, n.]

**xanthin(o)-; xanth(o)-:** the latter=Gr *xanth(o)-*, c/f of *xanthos*, yellow, fair, s *xanth-*, prob akin to L *cānus* (s *cān-*), grey-haired, and to OHG *hasan*, grey, hence to E HARE; *xanthin(o)-* stands for Chem *xanthin* and *xanthine*, both, via Chem suffixes *-in*, *-ine*, from *xanthos*. Exx: *xanthinuria*, (Med) the (excessive) presence of xanthine in urine; *xanthochroid* (cf *-chroid* at *-chroia*), of persons having very fair, or yellow, hair and fair complexion; *xanthogenic* (cf *-genic* at *-gen*), producing yellow; *Xanthorrhoea*, a genus of Australian plants, resembling aloes, 'so named from the yellow gum which it exudes' (Webster)—cf *-rrhoea*.

**-xene, -xenous, -xeny; xeno-:** resp from Gr *xenos*, (s *xen-*), a stranger, a guest, a foreigner; from Gr *-xenos*, adj c/f of *xenos*; from Gr *-xenia*, c/f of *xenia*, hospitality, from *xen*(os)+abstract suffix *-ia*; Gr *xen(o)-*, c/f of *xenos*, perh akin to L *hostis*, a stranger, an enemy. Exx: *pyroxene* (cf *pyro-*), a mineral *not native* to igneous rocks, with adj *pyroxenous*; *lipoxeny* (cf *lipo-*), i.e. the abandoning, by a parasitic fungus, of its host; *xenogamy* (cf *-gamy* at *-gam*), in Bot, cross-fertilization; *xenomania*, a craze for foreigners or for foreign art, literature, goods—cf *philoxeny*, hospitality, esp to strangers, Gr *philoxenia*, and *xenophobia*, hatred and fear of foreigners.

**xer(o)-:** Gr *xer(o)-*, c/f of *xeros* (or *xēros*), dry, parched; IE r, perh *kse-* or *ksa-*, cf Skt *kṣáyati*, he or it burns, and *ksarás*, burning. Exx: LL—hence E—*xeromyron*, Gr *xēromuron*, a dry ointment (*muron*, ointment); *xerophagy* (cf *-phagy* at *-phaga*), LL *xērophagia* (adopted from Gr *xērophagia*), dry-eating, i.e. of food other than juicy (meat); Bot *xerophilous* (cf *-philous* at *-phil*), drought-resisting (lit, *-loving*).

**xiphi-, xiph(o)-:** the former, from L *xiphias*, a swordfish, from Gr *xiphias*, from *xiphos* (s *xiph-*), a sword, with c/f *xiph(o)-*, adopted by E: cf XIPHIAS. Exx: *xiphiform*, resembling a swordfish; (*xipho-*, 'sword') *Xiphodon* (cf *-odon*, -tooth), and *xiphophyllous*, (of plants) with sword-shaped leaves; (*xipho-*, 'xiphoid', Gr *xiphoeidēs*, sword-shaped: *eidos*, shape, form) An *xiphocostal*, of the xiphoid process and the ribs (*-costal*).

xylo-; -xylon or -xylum: resp Gr *xul(o)-*, c/f of *xulon*, wood, s *xul-*, with IE r perh *\*x(e)u-* or *\*ks(e)u-*; Gr *-xulon*, terminal c/f, rendered by SciL as *-xylum*. Exx: *Haematoxylon* (cf *haemato-* at *haema-*); *Erythroxylum* (cf *erythro-*); *xylobalsamum*, L transliteration of Gr *xulobalsamon* (cf BALSAM)—*xylography*, wood-engraving—*xylophone*, a wood instrument in music (cf *-phone*, Gr *phōnē*, a sound). The rare *xyle-* occurs in Zoo *Xyleborus*, wood-eating beetles, from Gr *xulēboros*.

xyr(o)-: from Gr *xuron* (s *xur-*), a razor, cf *xureō* (s *xur-*), I shave: prob echoic of the scraping noise. Ex: *xyrichthys*, a razor fish (Ir *ichthus*, a fish).

-ydatis: Gr *-hudatis*, c/f of *hudatis*, a watery vesicle, from *hudōr* (gen *hudatos*), water: cf HYDRANT. Ex: *blepharydatis* (cf *blepharo-*), a vesicle that affects the eyelid.

-yl: F *-yle*, from Gr *hulē* (s *hul-*), wood, (hence) material: cf *hyl(o)-*. Used only for Chem, esp univalent radicals, as in *carbonyl* (cf CARBON) and *ethyl* (cf ETHER). Cf *-ylene*: *-yl*+Chem suffix *-ene*.

-ymenitis=*hymen(o)-*, q.v. above+suffix *-itis*.

ypsili-: irreg for Gr *hupsilon* (s *hupsil-*) as a capital letter—*Y*. Ex: *ypsiliform* (cf *-form*), shaped like capital hupsilon.

yttri-; yttro-: for *yttrium*, a metallic element, from *Ytterby*, in Sweden+Chem suffix *-ium*. Exx: *yttriferous* (cf *-ferous* at *-fer*), *yttrium*-producing; Min *yttrocrasite* (*yttro-*+Gr *krasis*+Min suffix *-ite*).

Yugo-. See *Jugo-*.

zanclo- : from Sicilian Gr *zanklon* (ζάγχλον) a sickle; as in *Zanclodon* (cf *-odon*)—a Pal genus of dinosaurs.

zanth(o)-: incorrect for *xanth(o)-*; as in *Zanthorrhiza* (*zantho-*+Gr *rhiza*, a root).

zelo-, as in *zelotypia*, a morbid zeal, Gr *zēlotupia*, rivalry: cf ZEAL.

-zemia: from Gr *zēmia* (s *zēm-*), loss; as in *sialozemia* (cf *sialo-*), loss or lack of saliva.

zeno-: from Gr *Zēnos*, gen of Ζεύς, Zeus, Jupiter; in E it denotes the planet Jupiter, as in *zenocentric* (cf *-centric* at *centri-*) and in *zenography* (*-graphy* at *-graph*), a description of the planet Jupiter; cf *Zenobia*, which=*Zeno-*+*-bia*, f of *-bios*, c/f of *bios*, life.

zeo-: from Gr *zeō*, I boil, s *ze-*, akin to OHG *iesan*, MHG *jesen* (Mod G *gären*), to ferment, and Skt *yásyati*, he boils. Ex: *zeolite* (cf *-lite*), a hydrous silicate.

zeucto-; zeuglo-: from Gr *zeuktos*, joined, pp of *zeugnumi*, I yoke or join, cf *zygo-*; (*zeuglo-*) from Gr *zeuglē*, loop or strap of a *zeugos* or yoke. Exx: *Zeuctocoelomata* (*zeucto-*+*koilōmata*, pl of *koilōma*, a hollow); *zeuglodont* (cf *-odont* at *-odon*,

-tooth), one of the *Zeuglodonta*—extinct toothed whales.

zinci-; zinco-: both, for E *zinc*; see ZINC. Exx: *zinciferous*, zinc-yielding (cf *-ferous* at *-fer*) and *zincify* (cf *-fy*, to render); *zincography*, printing (cf *-graphy* at *-graph*) on zinc plates.

zirconi-, zircono-; zirco-: the 3rd, a shortened form (as in *zircofluoride*: *zirco*(no)-+*fluor*(o)-+Chem *-ide*) of *zircono-*, of which, as in *zirconiferous* (cf *-ferous* at *-fer*), *zirconi-* is a var; *zircono-*, as in *zirconofluoride*, stands for *zirconium* (*zircon*+Chem *-ium*), a metallic element occurring in *zircon*, F var of F *jargon*, jargoon, app via Port and Ar from Per *zargūn*, gold-coloured.

zo-, also as the prevocalic form of 2 zoo-; 3 zoe-, 4 zoidio- or zoido-; 5 zoologico-;—6 -zoa, 7 -zoic, 8 -zoon: all ult from or intimately akin to *zēn* (ζῆν), to live—cf Skt *jívati*, he lives: resp, 1, *zo-*, from Gr *zōē* (s *zō-*), life; 2, *zoo-*, Gr *zōo-* (prevocalic: *zō-*), c/f of *zōion*, an animal, lit a non-human 'living thing' (*zō-*+neu suffix *-ion*); 3, *zoe-*, Gr *zōē*; 4, *zoidio-* or *zoido-*, for *zoid* (end c/f *-zoid*) or, in full, *zooid* (end c/f *-zooid*), cpd of *zo(o)-*+suffix *-oid*; 5, for *zoologic(al)*; 6, *-zoa*, pl, from Gr *zōia*, pl of *zōion*, an animal; 7, *-zoic*, adj (*-ic*), c/f from *zōion*, animal, or from *zōē*, life; 8, *-zoon*, from *zōion*—cf 6.

Exx: *zoösmosis* (*zo-*, from *zōē*+*-osmosis*); *zoanthropy* (*zo(o)-*+*-anthropy*, q.v. at *anthropo-*), lit 'man-as-animalness', that delusion in which a person believes himself to be an animal and acts like one; *zoehemera*, lit 'the day of a life', a Pal animal's life-period (Gr *hēmera*, a day: cf *hemero-*); *zoophilous* (cf *-philous* at *-phil*) and *zoidogamous* (cf *-gamous* at *-gam*); *zoologico(-)botanical*; *Protozoa*, which. a Zoo phylum of animals (the *protozoans*), is strictly the pl of *protozoon* (cf *proto-*, first, earliest), with adj *protozoic*.

Cf ZOOLOGY.

zoni-; zon(o)-: former, from L *zōna*, a zone, itself from Gr *zōnē*, a girdle, a belt worn around one's middle, with c/f *zōn(o)-*, whence E *zon(o)-*. See ZONE. Exx: *zoniferous* (cf *-ferous* at *-fer*), with a zone or zones; *zono(-)skeleton*. Cf *zosteri-*.

zoo-; -zoon. See *zo-*.

zosteri-; zostero-: the former, from E *zoster*, the disease shingles (herpes zoster), from L *zōster*, shingles, from Gr *zōstēr*, a girdle, (hence) shingles, akin to Gr *zōnē*, a girdle (cf *zoni-*); the latter, from Gr *zōstēr*. Exx: *zosteriform*, resembling herpes zoster (shingles); *Zosterops*, lit 'girdle-eye' (Gr *ōps*), the bird genus 'white-eyes'.

zyg(o)-; 2 zygoto-; 3, -zygomatic, 4 -zygosis, 5 -zygote, 6 -zygous: all, ult, from Gr *zugon* (E *zygon*), a yoke or a crossbar, akin to L *iugum* (ML *jugum*) and E YOKE: resp, 1, Gr *zug(o)-*, c/f of *zugon*; 2, zygoto-, for E *zygote* (Gr *zugōtē*, f of *zugōtos*, yoked, pp of *zugoun*, to yoke), a Bot cell formed by two gametes (Gr *gamos*, marriage) uniting, whence the end c/f *-zygote*; 3, *-zygomatic*, c/f of *zygomatic*, adj of *zygoma* (Gr *zugōma*, a yoke, a crossbar, a bolt or bar, from *zugon*), as used in An; 4, *-zygosis*, c/f of *zygosis* (Gr *zugōsis*, a balancing, from *zugon*), Bot conjugation; 6, *-zygous*, Gr adj c/f *-zugos*, yoked.

Exx: *zygodactyl* (cf *dactylio-*), yoke-toed; *zygotoblast* (cf *-blast*); *sphenozygomatic* (cf *spheno-*); *heterozygosis* (cf *hetero-*) and *heterozygote* and *heterozygous*.

**-zyme**; **zym(o)-**: the former, for *enzyme* (MGr *enzumos*, leavened), a Biochem ferment; the latter, from Gr *zumē*, leaven, and, in Sci, denoting '(of or by or with) ferment'; *zumē* is perh akin to JUICE. Exx: *cacozyme* (cf *caco-*, bad); *zymogen* (F

*zymogène*: cf *-gen*); *zymology*, the study of— or a treatise on—fermentation; *zymoscope* (cf *-scope*); *zymurgy* (cf *-urgy* at *-urge*), the practical chemistry of fermentation.

**zyzzo-**, in Zoo *Zyzzogeton*, a genus of leaf-hopping insects (cf *-geton*): extn of earlier *Zyzza*, perh from E, F, Sp *zigzag*, or the syn G *Zickzack*; prob, however, from Sp *zis, zas*! (*zis-zas*!), a var of *zas, zas*!, echoic of the impact of a blow, the ref being to the noise of these insects, which are allied to the cicadas.

## ADDENDA

**-amat.** See *-omat*, below.

**-ard.** For this element-become-suffix, see Suffixes.

**-burger**, as in so many Am formations, derives from *hamburger* (p. 277) and rests upon the false division (hence upon a false analogy) *ham-burger*. This new element—rather than suffix— *-burger* is to be taken 'as meaning "sandwich with a round bun", and the base to which it is added may refer to its contents, to someone famous, or to whatever strikes the creator's whim', Stuart Robertson and Fredric G. Cassidy, *The Development of Modern English*, 2nd edition, 1954. Exx: *cheeseburger, steakburger, Ikeburger* (after President Eisenhower).

**-omat**, usu debased to *-amat*, derives, via the n *automat*, from *automatic*. Exx: *laundromat*, usu *laundramat*, an automatic laundry, and *chinamat*, for *Chinomat*, a penny-in-the-slot, chop-suey kind of restaurant.

**-teria.** 'From *cafeteria* we derive *-teria* and with cheerful indiscrimination *serveteria, gasateria*, and so on' (Robertson and Cassidy, as above).

**-torium.** 'From *auditorium* we detach *-torium* and make *lubritorium*' (Robertson and Cassidy, as above).

# ADDENDA TO DICTIONARY

**abacus**, an ancient (and, in some parts, current) Near Eastern calculating device, consisting orig of a board on which sand or dust was strewn for writing, hence for counting, then of a frame with sliding balls: L *abacus*, Gr *abax*, gen *abakos*: prob H or Phoenician *abaq* (*abak*), sand, dust.

**abbreviate, abbreviation.** The former comes from ML *abbreviātus*, ex *abbreviāre* (L *abbreuiāre*), from *breuis*; the latter was adopted ex F (itself, of course, from L). Cf BRIEF.

**anent**, about, concerning: ME *anent*, an easing of *anenst*: ME *anen* (cf *again—against*), OE *on emn*, from *on efen*, on even (ground with=beside; hence, touching)—cf dial *anent*, in line with, even with. See, f.a.e., the adj EVEN.

**bairn**, child, is the Sc form of ME-OE *bearn*, akin to ON, Go, OS *barn* and to OE *beran*, to bear: f.a.e., the 2nd BEAR.

**baize**: C17 *bayze*, C16–18 *bayes*, C16–17 *baies*, pl of *bay*: OF *baie* (? for *etoffe baie*): OF-F *bai*, bay-coloured: f.a.e., the adj BAY.

**barnacle**, shell-fish and wild goose: EF *barnacle*, the goose, ? influenced by F *bernicle* in its passage from EF *bernaque* (cf ME *bernake*): ML *bernaca*: o.o.o., but perh from Ir (and Ga) *bairneach*, a

limpet, OC *\*barennīkā*: cf Cor *brennygen*, limpet, perh a dim of Cor *bron*, an udder, a breast.

'The connection of the two senses is due to the ancient superstition that the goose was hatched from shell-fish adhering to trees hanging over the water' (W).

**berserk**, to go; a **berserker** or **berserk** rage. A *berserk* or *berserker* is properly a Norse soldier fighting with a fury called 'the *berserker* rage'; hence, usually *berserk*, an adj: ON (Icelandic) *berserkr*, acc *berserk*: lit, prob 'bear-skin or -coat'. But *baresark*, adv.—'fighting in shirt only, i.e. armourless'—is precisely what it appears to be: in *bare sark*, i.e. with nothing over one's shirt.

**blanket**: AF *blanquete*: from F. *blanc*, white (f.a.e., BLANK)—prob influenced by MF *blanquet*, a white woollen material, F *blanchet*.

**bloomer**, orig. a complete suit for women, then (*bloomers*) a pair of loose trousers gathered at the knees, now often a loose, knee-length undergarment; *bloomer* named after Mrs Amelia Bloomer (1814–94), who did not invent it and who protested against the use of her name. It was, however, in her magazine, *The Lily*, that, at Seneca Falls, New York State, the new costume seems to have been first mentioned (DAE).

**booth,** orig. a shed or small house built of, boughs or boards: ME *bothe*: prob ex ODa *bōth* akin to ON *būth*, a hut, a dwelling, and *būa*, to dwell: f.a.e., the 2nd BOWER.

**bridge** (2), the card-game: earlier *biritch*, 'app. changed to *bridge* from the dealer's *bridging*, or passing, the declaration of trumps to his partner' (Webster): o.o.o.: 'prob. of Levantine origin, since some form of the game appears to have been long known in the Near East' (OED).

**brimstone:** late ME *brimstan(e)* or *brimston(e)*, *brynstan(e)* or *-ston(e)*: late OE *brynstān*: cf ON *brennistein*, sulphur, and MD-MLG *bernsteen*, amber. In short, 'burn-stone'; f.a.e., BURN and STONE.

**bubonic** plague—characterized by *buboes* (ML *būbo*, a swelling in the groin) or large inflamed swellings, esp. in the groin—derives from F *bubonique*, adj of MF-F *bubon*, perh prompted by the MGr adj *boubōnikos*: Gr *boubōn*, swelling in groin: if we cf Gr *bounos*, a hill, we perh arrive at an IE r *bou-, *bū-*, a swelling, a large swelling, a mound, a large mound. Cf:

**bunion:** o.o.o.: perh cf dial E *bunny*, a (small) swelling, esp. one caused by a blow—OF *bugne*, a swelling—and the edible E *bun*. If the comparison be correct, then compare *bubonic*.

**enough, enow:** the former from OE *genōh*, the latter from OE *genōg*; co-existent OE forms of what was orig an adj, itself from OE *genēah*, it is enough: cf Du *genoeg* and G *genug*, OHG adj *ginuog(i)*, adv *ginuog*, and Go *ganōhs*: f.a.e., NEAR.

**exotic:** EF-F *exotique*: L *exōticus*: Gr *exōtikos*, coming from without, i.e. foreign: *exō*, outside: *ex*, out of. Cf *exoteric*, q.v. at ESOTERIC; f.a.e., *ex-* (1) in Prefixes.

**fad,** whence the hybrid n **faddist** and the adjj **faddish, faddy; faddle.** *Fad*, a passing hobby or fashion, has been adopted from an English Midland dial: perh akin to the *fat-* of *fatuous*, q.v. at VAPID, para 1. Webster suggests that the n *fad* may derive from EF-F *fadaise*, from Prov *fadeza*, a folly, ult from L *fatuus*. The freq 'to *faddle*' or trifle comes from 'to *fad*', the v corresponding to n *fad*—although, to be frank, the n may come from the v. 'To *fad*' has the redup 'to *fiddle-faddle*', which Whitehall prefers to regard as 'to *fiddle*'+ 'to *faddle*'. In short, the nexus is as uncertain as the origin of *fad* itself.

**fairy,** adj, comes from the n, the individual from the collective (fairy folk, land of fairies, power of fairies, enchantment): late ME *fairie, faierie*, a fairy, in earlier ME fairy folk: OF-MF *faerie*, then *feerie* (EF-F *féerie*), fairy folk, enchantment: OF-MF *fee* (EF-F *fée*): VL *fāta*, f sing from the neu pl of L *fātum*, destiny: f.a.e., FATE.

**farthingale.** This EE-E, now archaic, word represents EF *vertugale* (or *-galle*), a var of EF *verdugale*: alteration of Sp *verdugado*, so named from the hoops of this hooped skirt: Sp *verdugo*, a young, green shoot: Sp *verde*, green: ML *viridis*: L *uiridis*: f.a.e., VERD.

**fester,** v from n: ME *festre*, a fistula: OF-MF *festre*: L *fistula*, a pipe, a flute (cf Gr *surinx*): o.o.o.

**flagon:** ME *flakon*: MF-F *flacon*: MF *flascon*: LL *flasco*, o/s *flascōn-*: Gmc *flaska*, whence also— perh as adaptation of It *fiasca*, of the same Gmc origin—EF-F *flasque*, whence E *flask*: f.a.e., perh PLY (pp. 505–507). Cf the ML *flasca*, whence the OE *flasce* (Dauzat; Whitehall). But the exact relationship of the It, F, OE-ME words is uncertain.

**flask.** See prec.

**fluff,** whence the adj *fluffy*, is app a mdfn of the syn *flue*, itself prob akin to VELVET.

**former,** adj: ME *former*, var of *forme*: OE *forma*, first. Cf the OE-ME *formest*, foremost: f.a.e., FORE, on p. 228, where cf FOREMOST.

**gin** (1), the drink. Unrecorded before 1714, it represents both a shortening and an alteration of *geneva*, which, first occurring in 1706, is a spirit that, made from grain, is flavoured with juniper berries, adapts Du *genever* but has been influenced by the place-name *Geneva*. Du *genever* comes from OF *genevre*, itself from L *iūniperus*, juniper. (For JUNIPER, see p. 324.)

**guise.** For the phrase 'in this (*or* that) *guise*', cf 'in this (*or* that) *wise*': see VIDE, para 9 on p. 779. Our *guise* has been adopted from OF-F *guise*, itself from Gmc *wisa*, whence It *guisa*, whence, via OF *desguisier*, MF *desguiser*, the E 'to *disguise*', whence the n *disguise*.

**inkling,** a hint, hence a vague idea: vn from archaic E *inkle*, ME *incle*, to hint: perh a freq from OE *inca*, a suspicion.

**ketchup** (f/e *catsup*): Mal *kĕchap*.

**leisure:** ME *leysir*: OF-MF *leisir* (n from v): L *licēre*: cf LICENCE. 'For formation from infinitive and change of suffix in E, of *pleasure*' (W).

**lunch, luncheon.** *Lunch*, as a (usu fairly light) midday meal, shortens *luncheon*. But both words, first recorded in C16, were orig. dial; and dial *luncheon* (or *-ion*), a large lump, esp of food, is an aug—prob influenced by the earlier, now dial, almost syn *nuncheon*—of *lunch*, a lump, itself app a dial var of *lump*: f.a.e., LUMP. The OED pertinently cfs *bunch* from *bump* and *hunch* from *hump*.

This E origin seems preferable to derivation from Sp *lonja*, a slice of meat.

**midriff**: OE *midhrif* (cf OFris *midref* ): lit 'mid-belly'—OE *midd*, middle + *hrif*, belly.

**pad** (4), a road horse, an easy-paced horse for safe road-work, is derived by OED from PAD (1), a path or a road. OED may well be right. Yet I think that the origin lies in ED-D *paard*, a horse thus: *paard* becomes *pard* becomes, in pron, *pahd*, flattened, esp. in N and Midland E, to *pad*. C, PALFREY, and see my *Adventuring among Words*.f

**phoney**, meaning 'counterfeit, spurious, pre-tended', was little known, outside of North America, before American journalists, late in 1939, began to speak of 'the phoney war'. The word does not come from '*funny* business', nor from *tele-phone*, nor yet from one *Forney*, an American jeweller specializing in imitation ware, but, via American *phoney man*, a pedlar of imitation jewellery, from its original, the English *fawney man*, itself an adaptation of the British *fawney cove*, one who practises 'the *fawney rig*' or ring-dropping trick, involving a gilt ring passed off as gold and first described by George Parker in *A View of Society*, 1781. The key-word is the British under-world *fawney*, a finger-ring, a word brought to England by Irish confidence tricksters and deriving from the synonymous Irish *fáinne*. It was probably the Irish who introduced the word into the United States. (See *Adventuring among Words*.)

The variant *phony* was suggested by the variant *fawny*.

**scalp**, orig 'crown of head; skull': ME *scalp* prob of Scan origin (cf ON *skalpr*, a sheath) an; perhaps, as EW proposed, a contraction ofd SCALLOP.

**sceptic**, whence **sceptical; scepticism** (cf the F *scepticisme*); Am spellings, *sk-*.

The n *sceptic*, like the discarded adj *sceptic*, derives imm from EF-F *sceptique*, adj, whence also n, from L *scepticus*, Gr *skeptikos*, akin to *skepsis*, a considering, hence a doubt, itself akin to *skeptesthai*, to look carefully at, to consider: the r is clearly *skep-*, akin to the *skop-* of Gr *skopein*, to view: for the IE framework, therefore, see SCOPE (p. 595).

**scimitar.** The EE *cimitarie* (or *-erie*) or *semiterie* or *cimiter* (or *-ar*) comes from the late MF-F *cimeterre* (EF var *cimi-*): medieval It *cimitara* (It *scimitarra*), which, like the Sp *cimitarra*, presum-ably derives, sem, from Turkey, and prob—despite the phon difficulties, for there may have been f/e 'interference'—does derive, as B & W hold, from Tu (and Per) *šimšir* or *šemšir*, pron *shim-sheer* or *shem-sheer*.

**sister** prob derives, not from OE *sweostor* but, as ME *sister*, from ON *systir*. The predominant OGmc forms have *sw-*; cf OS and OHG *swestar*, MHG *swester* (G *Schwester*), OFris *swester*, Go *swistar*. The OGmc r *\*swestr-* is an extn of IE *\*swesr-* or *\*suesr-*· cf OSl (and Ru) *sestra*, L *soror* for *\*suesor* or perh *\*sosor*, the OL var *seror*, Skt *svásā*, s *svásar-*; the C forms, e.g. OIr *siur*, gen *sethar*—W *chwaer*—Br and Cor *choar*; Arm *khoyr*; Gr voc *eor*, for *\*heor*, nom *\*heōr*, with the char-acteristic IE alternation of *h* and *s*.

The IE etymon is perh *\*swesor* (*\*swes*, one's own + *\*sor*, female); with epenthetic *-t-*, this becomes *\*swestor*.

But IE *\*swesor* is more prob *swes-*, one's own + the agential *-or* or *-er* (cf the 3rd *-or*: Suffixes): in short, not a cpd but a simple, in line with all other family-relationship words (*father, mother, son, daughter, brother*): as it were, 'one's own agent': mother's help, father's joy, brother's ally, sister's companion. See *Adventuring among Words* for a development of this argument.

**sturdy**: late ME *stourdi, sturdi*: OF-MF *estourdi, esturdi*, stunned, dazed, hence (?) reckless, violent, pp of *estourdir*, to stun or daze: o.o.o., but cf It *stordito*, from *stordire*, derived by Prati from *tordo*, a foolish fellow.

**syllabub** is a var of *sillabub*, q.v. at SILLY, para 2.

**syndic**, hence (via F) **syndical**, whence (via F *syndicalisme*) **syndicalism; syndicate**, n and v. *Syndic*: EF-F *syndic* (MF *sindiz*): L *syndicus*, a town's delegate or advocate : Gr *sundikos*, a de-fendant's advocate: *sun*, with + *dikē*, a judgement. The n *syndicate* (EE): late MF-F *syndicat*, a syndic's function, hence (mid C19) a group of workers united to defend their own interests, finally the sense and nuances in which, now, we mostly use it. The v 'to *syndicate*' app comes into EE, not from the n but from ML *syndicātus*, pp of *syndicāre*.

**taxi; taxicab; taximeter.** *Taxi*, the conveyance, shortens *taxicab* (still used in formal contexts): *taxicab* shortens *taximeter cab*, a cab fitted with a 'clock' or meter: *taximeter cab*, or *taximeter motor cab*, was prompted by F *taximètre* (a correction, made c 1906, by the F scholar Th. Reinach, of the barbarous earlier *taxamètre*, itself from G *Taxa-meter*: cf the E *taxameter*, used for some years before *taximeter* displaced it)—which orig desig-nated the meter, then almost immediately the cab itself. (Dauzat.) The word *taximeter* is a cpd of Gr *taxis*, a tax + F *mètre*, meter or 'measurer'.

**wombat**, a burrowing Aus marsupial: Sydney-hinterland Aboriginal *wombach* or *-back* or *-bat*, with occ varr *woomback* and (? aberrant) *womat*.